Concise Oxford American Dictionary

Concise Oxford
American Dictionary

OXFORD
UNIVERSITY PRESS

OXFORD UNIVERSITY PRESS

Oxford University Press, Inc., publishes works that further
Oxford University's objective of excellence
in research, scholarship, and education.

Oxford New York
Auckland   Cape Town   Dar es Salaam   Hong Kong   Karachi
Kuala Lumpur   Madrid   Melbourne   Mexico City   Nairobi
New Delhi   Shanghai   Taipei   Toronto

With offices in
Argentina   Austria   Brazil   Chile   Czech Republic   France   Greece
Guatemala   Hungary   Italy   Japan   Poland   Portugal   Singapore
South Korea   Switzerland   Thailand   Turkey   Ukraine   Vietnam

Published by Oxford University Press, Inc.
198 Madison Avenue, New York, New York, 10016
www.oup.com/us
www.askoxford.com

Oxford is a registered trademark of Oxford University Press

Library of Congress Cataloging-in-Publication Data

Concise Oxford American dictionary.
   p. cm.
  Includes bibliographical references.
  ISBN-13: 978-0-19-530484-8

  1. English language—United States—Dictionaries.   2. Americanisms—
Dictionaries.
  PE1628.C676 2006
  423'.1—dc22

                                    2006001264

10 9 8 7 6 5 4 3

Printed in the United States of America on acid-free paper

Contents

Staff

Erin McKean, *Editor in Chief*

Constance Baboukis, *Managing Editor*

Carol Braham, Alan Hartley, Christine A. Lindberg, *Senior Editors*

Johanna Baboukis, Orin Hargraves, Archie Hobson, Marina Padakis, *Editors*

Grant Barrett, *Assistant Editor*

Sandra Ban, Carol-June Cassidy, Sarah Hilliard, *Keyboarders and Proofreaders*

Elizabeth Jerabek, *Editorial Assistant*

Stephen Perkins, dataformat.com, LLC; Paul Hayslett,
   Programming, Design, and Composition

Preface

The *Concise Oxford American Dictionary*, with more than 180,000 entries and definitions, is intended to be a convenient and complete dictionary for school, work, and home. The Oxford-exclusive core sense/subsense arrangement of definitions is geared to helping you find just the right meaning quickly and efficiently. Sample sentences or phrases for virtually every sense show words in illuminating contexts, and over a thousand fascinating word histories provide useful background on both common and unusual words. More than three hundred illustrations are included, carefully chosen to provide maximum information in places where only a picture will do. The back of the book contains a handy and useful ready reference guide, with information about weights and measures, chemical elements, states and presidents, frequently misspelled words, punctuation, gentle guidance about problematic words, and more.

A dictionary should be a tool for daily use, not a dreaded last resort. We have tried to create not just a book that will satisfy your desire for clear, accurate, and helpful information about words and meanings, but one that is pleasant, easy to use, and a genial companion in your work and leisure.

Erin McKean
Editor in Chief
U.S. Dictionaries
Oxford University Press

Introduction

The *Concise Oxford American Dictionary* is designed to be easy to use and largely self-explanatory. Specialized dictionary symbols and conventions have been avoided wherever possible. These notes are provided as extra help for the user, and as a guide to the structure and principles behind this dictionary.

Structure: Core Sense and Subsense

The first part of speech is the primary one for that word: thus, for **bag** and **balloon** the senses of the noun are given before those for the verb, while for **babble** and **bake** the senses of the verb are given before those of the noun. Within each part of speech, the first definition given is the **core sense**. The core sense is the typical, central, or 'core' meaning of the word in modern American English. The core sense is the one that represents the most literal sense that the word has in ordinary modern American usage. This is not necessarily the same as the oldest meaning, because word meanings change over time. Nor is it necessarily the most frequent meaning, because figurative senses are sometimes the most frequent. It is the meaning accepted by native speakers as the one that is most established as literal and central.

Each word has at least one core sense, which can act as a gateway to other, related subsenses. These subsenses are grouped under the core sense, each one being introduced by a solid square symbol.

co·coon /kəˈko͞on/ ▸*n.* a silky case spun by the larvae of many insects for protection as pupae. ■ a similar structure made by other animals. ■ a covering that prevents the corrosion of metal equipment. ■ something that envelops or surrounds, esp. in a protective or comforting way: *the **cocoon** of her kimono* | *fig. a warm **cocoon** of love.*

There is a logical relationship between each subsense and the core sense under which it appears. The organization of senses according to this logical relationship is designed to help the user, not only in being able to navigate the entry more easily and find relevant senses more readily, but also in building up an understanding of how senses in the language relate to one another.

Many entries have just one core sense. However some entries are more complex and have different strands of meaning, each constituting a core sense. In this case, each core sense is introduced by a bold sense number, and each potentially has its own block of subsenses relating to it.

Labels

Unless otherwise stated, the words and senses recorded in this dictionary are all part of standard English; that is, they are in normal use in both speech and writing everywhere in the world, at many different levels of formality, ranging from official documents to casual conversation. Some words, however, are appropriate only in particular contexts, and these are labeled accordingly.

The *Concise Oxford American Dictionary* uses the following labels:

archaic: very old-fashioned language, not in ordinary use at all today, but sometimes used to give a deliberately old-fashioned effect, or found in works of the past that are still widely read.

dated: no longer used by the majority of English speakers, but still encountered occasionally, especially among the older generation.

derog.: derogatory: language intended to convey a low opinion or cause personal offense.

dial.: dialect: not used in standard American English, but still widely used in certain local regions of the United States.

fig.: figurative: normally used only in nonliteral contexts, or metaphorically

formal: normally used only in writing, in contexts such as official documents.

hist.: historical: still used today, but only to refer to some practice or artifact that is no longer part of the modern world.

humorous: used with the intention of sounding funny, ironic, or playful.

inf: informal: normally used only in contexts such as conversations or letters between friends.

offens: offensive: language that is likely to cause offense, particularly racial offense, whether the speaker intends it or not.

poetic/lit.: found only or mainly in poetry or in literature written in an "elevated" style.

rare: not in normal use.

technical: normally used only in technical and specialist language, though not necessarily restricted to any specific subject field.

vulgar slang: informal language that may cause offense, often because it refers to the bodily functions of sexual activity or excretion, which are still widely regarded as taboo.

Labels are also used to indicate a word is used in a particular region or area (Brit., Austral./NZ) or that it is associated with a subject field or specialist activity (Zool., Philately).

Grammar

The *Concise Oxford American Dictionary* is based on a rigorous examination of the grammatical structures of American English. This information is used to organize entries and define words, but, for the most part, is not made explicit in the definitions. Grammatical information is provided when particular usages are controversial, confusing, or ambiguous.

Patterns that are very frequent or nearly obligatory are presented in bold text, either before the definition or in the example:

push … (**push for**) demand persistently.

sound … question (someone), typically in a cautious or discreet way, as to their opinions or feelings on a subject: *we'll **sound out** our representatives first.*

gouge … (**gouge something out**) cut or force something out roughly or brutally: *one of his eyes had been gouged out.*

When a verb or noun is often used as an adjective, or an adjective is used as a noun, this is indicated either before the definition or in the example.

ac·cor·di·on … [as *adj.*] folding like the bellows of an accordion: *an accordion pleat.*

re·state … state (something) again or differently, esp. in order to correct or to make more clear or convincing: *he restated his opposition to abortion* | [as *adj.*] *restated earnings.*

ab·surd … *adj.* (of an idea or suggestion) wildly unreasonable, illogical, or inappropriate: *it would be absurd to blame contemporary Germans for Nazi crimes* | [as *n.*] (**the absurd**) *he had a keen eye for the absurd.*

A few other explicit labels are used:

[treated as *sing.*]: used to mark a noun that is plural in form but is used with a singular verb, e.g., **mumps** in *mumps is one of the major childhood diseases* or **genetics** in *genetics has played a major role in this work.*

[treated as *sing.* or *pl.*]: used to mark a noun that can be used with either a singular or a plural verb without any change in meaning or in the form of the headword (often called *collective nouns*, because they typically denote groups of people considered collectively), e.g., *the staff are committed to this policy* or *the staff is trying to gag its critics.*

[*tr.*]: used to mark a verb that is transitive, i.e., takes a direct object (the type of direct object often being shown in parentheses in the definition), e.g.,

es·cort … [*tr.*] accompany (someone or something) somewhere, esp. for protection or security, or as a mark of rank: *Shiona escorted Janice to the door.*

[*intr.*]: used to mark a verb that is intransitive, i.e., takes no direct object, e.g.,

a·bound … *v.* [*intr.*] exist in large numbers or amounts: *rumors of a further scandal abound.*

[*attrib.*]: used to mark an adjective that is normally used attributively, i.e., comes before the noun that it modifies, e.g., **leading** in *a leading politician* (not *the politician is leading*, which has a different meaning). Note that attributive use is standard for many adjectives, especially in specialist fields: the [*attrib.*] label is used only to mark those cases in which predicative use would be less usual.

Spelling

The *Concise Oxford American Dictionary* gives advice and information on spelling, particularly those cases that are irregular or that otherwise cause difficulty for native speakers. The main categories are summarized in the following.

Variant spellings

The main form of each word given in the *Concise Oxford American Dictionary* is always the standard American spelling. If there is a standard variant, e.g., a standard British spelling variant, this is indicated at the top of the entry and is cross-referred if its alphabetical position is more than ten entries distant from the main entry.

> **col·or** (*Brit.* **colour**)
>
> **mock·u·men·ta·ry** (also **moc·u·men·ta·ry**)
>
> **foet·id** variant spelling of FETID.

Other variants, such as archaic, old-fashioned, or informal spellings, are cross-referred to the main entry, but are not themselves listed at the parent entry.

> **scollop** archaic spelling of SCALLOP.

Hyphenation

Although standard spelling in English is fixed, the use of hyphenation is not. In standard American English, a few general rules are followed, and these are outlined below.

Hyphenation of noun compounds: There is no hard-and-fast rule to determine whether, for example, **airstream**, **air stream**, or **air-stream** is correct. All forms are found in use: all are recorded in the Oxford databank and other standard texts. However, there is a broad tendency to avoid hyphenation for noun compounds in modern English (except when used to show grammatical function: see below). Thus there is, for example, a preference for **airstream** rather than **air-stream,** and for **air raid** rather than **air-raid**. Although this is a tendency in both American and British English, there is an additional preference in American English for the form to be one word and in British English for the form to be two words; e.g., **airfare** tends to be the most common form in American English, while **air fare** tends to be the most common form in British English. To save space and avoid confusion, only one of the three potential forms of each noun compound (the standard American one) is generally used as the headword form in the *Concise Oxford American Dictionary*. This does not, however, imply that other forms are incorrect or not used.

Grammatical function: Hyphens are also used to perform certain grammatical functions. When a noun compound made up of two separate words (e.g., **credit card**) is placed before another noun and used to modify it, the general rule is that the noun compound becomes hyphenated, e.g., *I have overused my credit card and am now in credit-card debt.* This sort of regular alternation is seen in example sentences in the *Concise Oxford American Dictionary* but is not otherwise explicitly mentioned in the dictionary entries.

A similar alternation is found in compound adjectives such as **well intentioned**. When used predicatively (i.e., after the verb), such adjectives are unhyphenated, but when used attributively (i.e., before the noun), they are hyphenated: *his remarks were well intentioned*; *a well-intentioned remark.*

A general rule governing verb compounds means that, where a noun compound is two words (e.g., **beta test**), any verb derived from it is normally hyphenated (*the system was beta-tested*). Similarly, verbal nouns and adjectives are more often hyphenated than ordinary noun or adjective compounds (e.g., **epoch-making**, **nation-building**).

Inflection

Compared with other languages, English has comparatively few inflections, and those that exist are remarkably regular. We add an *s* to most nouns to make a plural; we add *ed* to most verbs to make a past tense or a past participle, and *ing* to make a present participle.

Occasionally, a difficulty arises: for example, a single consonant after a short stressed vowel is doubled before adding *ed* or *ing* (**hum, hums, humming, hummed**). In addition, words borrowed from other languages generally bring their foreign inflections with them, causing problems for English speakers who are not proficient in those languages.

In all such cases, guidance is given in the *Concise Oxford American Dictionary*. The main areas covered are outlined below.

Verbs

The following forms are regarded as regular and are therefore not shown in the dictionary:

- third person singular present forms adding *s* to the stem (or *es* to stems ending in *s, x, z, sh,* or soft *ch*), e.g., **find → finds**; **crush → crushes**
- past tenses and past participles dropping a final silent *e* and adding *ed* to the stem, e.g., **change → changed**; **dance → danced**
- present participles dropping a final silent *e* and adding *ing* to the stem, e.g., **change → changing**; **dance → dancing**

Other forms are given in the dictionary, notably for:

- verbs that inflect by doubling a consonant, e.g., **bat → batted, batting**
- verbs ending in *y* that inflect by changing *y* to *i*, e.g., **try → tries, tried**
- verbs in which past tense and past participle do not follow the regular *ed* pattern, e.g., **feel →** past **felt**; **awake →** past **awoke**; **→** past part. **awoken**
- present participles that add *ing* but retain a final *e* (in order to make clear that the pronunciation of *g* remains soft), e.g., **singe → singeing**

Nouns

Plurals formed by adding *s* (or *es* when they end in *s, x, z, sh,* or soft *ch*) are regarded as regular and are not shown, e.g., **dog → dogs**; **lunch → lunches.**

Other plural forms are given in the dictionary, notably for:

- nouns ending in *i* or *o*, e.g., **agouti → agoutis**; **albino → albinos**
- nouns ending in *a, um,* or *us* that are or appear to be Latinate forms, e.g., **alumna → alumnae**; **spectrum → spectra**; **alveolus → alveoli**
- nouns ending in *y*, e.g., **fly → flies**; **party → parties**
- nouns with more than one plural form, e.g., **crux → cruxes** or **cruces**; **money → moneys** or **monies**

- nouns with plurals showing a change in the stem, e.g., **foot** → **feet**; **louse** → **lice**
- nouns with plurals unchanged from the singular form are indicated by (pl. same).
- for polysyllabic words, only the changed syllables are shown.

Adjectives

The following forms for comparative and superlative are regarded as regular and are not shown in the dictionary:

- words of one syllable adding *er* and *est*, e.g., **great** → **greater**, **greatest**
- words of one syllable ending in silent e, which drop the *e* and add *er* and *est*, e.g., **brave** → **braver**, **bravest**
- words that form the comparative and superlative by adding "more" and "most"; e.g., **beautiful** → **more beautiful, most beautiful**

Other forms are given in the dictionary, notably for:

- adjectives that form the comparative and superlative by doubling a final consonant, e.g., **hot** → **hotter**, **hottest**
- two-syllable adjectives that form the comparative and superlative with *er* and *est* (typically adjectives ending in *y* and their negative forms), e.g., **happy** → **happier, happiest**; **unhappy** → **unhappier, unhappiest**
- only the changed final syllables are shown.

Syllabification

In the *Concise Oxford American Dictionary*, syllable breaks are shown for main entries and derivatives. Although all possible breaks are shown, there are some conventions that govern how writers break words at the ends of lines. Guidelines include:

- Avoid a break that will leave one letter and a hyphen at the end of the line or one letter (or one letter and a punctuation mark such as a period) at the beginning of a line.
- Avoid breaking a word that is already hyphenated except at that hyphen (e.g., *self-affirmation*; *leather-bound*).
- Never break proper names.
- Avoid breaking abbreviations.

How to Use This Dictionary

Part of speech

Each new part of speech (introduced by ▶)

bag /bag/ ▶ *n.* **1** a container of flexible material with an opening at the top, used for carrying things: *brown paper bags.* ■ an amount held by such a container: *a bag of apples.* ■ a thing resembling a bag in shape. ■ a woman's handbag or purse. ■ a piece of luggage: *she began to unpack her bags.* ■ Baseball a base. **2** the amount of game shot by a hunter. **3** (usu. **bags**) a loose fold of skin under a person's eye: *the bags under his eyes gave him a sad appearance.* **4** *inf., derog.* a woman, esp. an older one, perceived as unpleasant, bad-tempered, or unattractive: *an interfering old bag.* **5** (**one's bag**) *inf.* one's particular interest or taste: *if religion and politics are your bag, you'll find something to interest you here.*

Subsenses (introduced by ■)

Subject label

Verb inflections

▶ *v.* (**bagged, bag·ging**) [*tr.*] **1** put (something) in a bag: *customers bagged their own groceries.* **2** (of a hunter) succeed in killing or catching an animal: *in 1979, handgun hunters bagged 677 deer.* ■ *fig.* succeed in securing (something): *we've bagged three awards for excellence.* ■ *inf.* take, occupy, or reserve (something) before someone else can do so: *get there early to bag a seat in the front row.* **3** [*intr.*] (of clothes, esp. pants) hang loosely or lose shape: *these trousers never bag at the knee.* **4** quit; give up on: *it was a drag to be in the ninth grade at 17, so he bagged it.* —**bag·ful** /-ˌfo͝ol/ *n.* (*pl.* **-fuls**) .

Label (showing level of formality)

Grammatical information (in square brackets)

Phrases (introduced by □)

▶ □ **bag and baggage** with all one's belongings: *he threw her out bag and baggage.* □ **in the bag** *inf.* **1** (of something desirable) as good as secured: *the election is in the bag.* **2** drunk: *I don't think my parents even suspected that I was half in the bag.*

bag·a·telle /ˌbagəˈtel/ ▶ *n.* **1** a thing of little importance; a very easy task: *dealing with these boats was a mere bagatelle for the world's oldest yacht club.* **2** a short, light piece of music, esp. one for the piano.

ba·gel /ˈbāgəl/ ▶ *n.* a dense bread roll in the shape of a ring, made by boiling dough and then baking it.

bag·gage /ˈbagij/ ▶ *n.* personal belongings packed in suitcases for traveling; luggage. ■ *fig.* past experiences or long-held ideas regarded as burdens and impediments: *the emotional baggage I'm hauling around.*

bag·gy /ˈbagē/ ▶ *adj.* (**-gi·er, -gi·est**) (of clothing) loose and hanging in folds: *baggy pants.* ■ (of eyes) with folds of puffy skin below them. —**bag·gi·ly** /ˈbagəlē/ *adv.* —**bag·gi·ness** *n.*

bag la·dy ▶ *n. inf.* a homeless woman who carries her possessions in shopping bags.

Plural form

Typical form (in bold)

bag·man /ˈbagˌman; -mən/ ▶ *n.* (*pl.* **-men**) *inf.* an agent who collects or distributes the proceeds of illicit activities: *one million dollars cash paid to the general's bagman.*

bag·pipe /ˈbagˌpīp/ ▶ *n.* (usu. bagpipes) a musical instrument with reed pipes that are sounded by the pressure of wind emitted from a bag squeezed by the player's arm. Bagpipes are associated esp. with Scotland, but are also used in folk music in Ireland, Northumberland, and France. —**bag·pip·er** /ˈbagˌpīpər/ *n.*

Derivatives (introduced by —)

ba·guette /baˈget/ ▶ *n.* **1** a long, narrow loaf of French bread. **2** a gem, esp. a diamond, cut in a long rectangular shape: *a baguette diamond.*

bagpipes

bah /bä/ ▶ *interj.* an expression of contempt or disagreement: *You think it was an accident? Bah!*

Variant spelling

Ba·ha·'i /bəˈhī/ (also **Ba·ha·i**) ▶ *n.* (*pl.* **-ha·'is**) a monotheistic religion founded in the 19th century as a development of Babism, emphasizing the essential oneness of humankind and of all religions and seeking world peace. The Baha'i faith was founded by the Persian Baha'ullah (1817–92) and his son Abdul Baha (1844–1921). ■ an adherent of the Baha'i faith. —**Ba·ha·'ism** /-ˌizəm/ *n.*

Pronunciation

bail[1] /bāl/ ▶ *n.* the temporary release of an accused person awaiting trial, sometimes on condition that a sum of money is lodged to guarantee their appearance in court: *he has been released on bail.* ■ money paid by or for such a person as security.

▶ *v.* [*tr.*] (usu. **be bailed**) release or secure the release of (a prisoner) on payment of bail: *his son called home to get bailed out of jail.* —**bail·a·ble** *adj.*

▶ □ **jump bail** *inf.* fail to appear for trial after being released on bail: *he jumped bail and was on the run until his arrest.* □ **post bail** pay a sum of money as bail: *I posted bail for him.*

Common collocation (highlighted within the example)

Homograph number (indicates different word with the same spelling)

bail[2] ▶ *n.* **1** a bar that holds something in place, in particular: ■ *Fishing* a bar that guides fishing line on a reel. ■ a bar on a typewriter or

Key to the Pronunciations

This dictionary uses a simple respelling system to show how entries are pronounced, using the symbols listed below. Generally, only the first of two or more identical headwords will have a pronunciation respelling. Where a derivative simply adds a common suffix such as **-ment**, **-ness**, or **-ly** to the headword, the derivative may not have a pronunciation respelling unless some other element of the pronunciation also changes.

a	*as in* **hat** /hat/, **fashion** /ˈfasHən/		ô	*as in* **law** /lô/, **thought** /THôt/, **lore** /lôr/
ā	*as in* **day** /dā/, **rate** /rāt/		oi	*as in* **boy** /boi/, **noisy** /ˈnoizē/
ä	*as in* **lot** /lät/, **father** /ˈfäTHər/, **barn** /bärn/		o͝o	*as in* **wood** /wo͝od/, **sure** /SHo͝or/
			o͞o	*as in* **food** /fo͞od/, **music** /ˈmyo͞ozik/
b	*as in* **big** /big/		ou	*as in* **mouse** /mous/, **coward** /ˈkou-ərd/
CH	*as in* **church** /CHərCH/, **picture** /ˈpikCHər/		p	*as in* **put** /po͝ot/, **cap** /kap/
d	*as in* **dog** /dôg/, **bed** /bed/		r	*as in* **run** /rən/, **fur** /fər/, **spirit** /ˈspirit/
e	*as in* **men** /men/, **bet** /bet/, **ferry** /ˈferē/		s	*as in* **sit** /sit/, **lesson** /ˈlesən/, **face** /fās/
ē	*as in* **feet** /fēt/, **receive** /riˈsēv/		SH	*as in* **shut** /SHət/, **social** /ˈsōSHəl/
e(ə)r	*as in* **air** /e(ə)r/, **care** /ke(ə)r/		t	*as in* **top** /täp/, **seat** /sēt/, **forty** /ˈfôrte/
ə	*as in* **soda** /ˈsōdə/, **mother** /ˈməTHər/, **her** /hər/		TH	*as in* **thin** /THin/, **truth** /tro͞oTH/
			TH	*as in* **then** /THen/, **father** /ˈfäTHər/
f	*as in* **free** /frē/, **graph** /graf/, **tough** /təf/		v	*as in* **very** /ˈverē/, **never** /ˈnevər/
g	*as in* **get** /get/, **exist** /igˈzist/		w	*as in* **wait** /wāt/, **quit** /kwit/
h	*as in* **her** /hər/, **behave** /biˈhāv/		(h)w	*as in* **when** /(h)wen/, **which** /(h)wiCH/
i	*as in* **fit** /fit/, **women** /ˈwimin/		y	*as in* **yet** /yet/, **accuse** /əˈkyo͞oz/
ī	*as in* **time** /tīm/, **hire** /hī(ə)r/, **sky** /skī/		z	*as in* **zipper** /ˈzipər/, **musician** /myo͞oˈziSHən/
i(ə)r	*as in* **ear** /i(ə)r/, **pierce** /pi(ə)rs/		ZH	*as in* **measure** /ˈmeZHər/, **vision** /ˈviZHən/
j	*as in* **judge** /jəj/, **carriage** /ˈkarij/			
k	*as in* **kettle** /ˈketl/, **cut** /kət/, **quick** /kwik/			
l	*as in* **lap** /lap/, **cellar** /ˈselər/, **cradle** /ˈkrādl/			
m	*as in* **main** /mān/, **dam** /dam/			*Foreign Sounds*
n	*as in* **need** /nēd/, **honor** /ˈänər/, **maiden** /ˈmādn/		KH	*as in* **loch** /läKH/, **Hanukkah** /ˈKHänəkə/
			N	*as in* **en route** /än ˈro͞ot/, **bon mot** /ˌbôn ˈmō/
NG	*as in* **sing** /siNG/, **anger** /ˈaNGgər/		œ	*as in* **hors d'oeuvre** /ôr ˈdœvrə/, **adieu** /äˈdyœ/
ō	*as in* **go** /gō/, **promote** /prəˈmōt/		Y	*as in* **couture** /ko͞oˈtYr/

Stress Marks

Stress (or accent) is represented by marks placed before the affected syllable. The primary stress mark is a short, raised vertical line /ˈ/ which signifies that the heaviest emphasis should be placed on the syllable that follows. The secondary stress mark is a short, lowered vertical line /ˌ/ which signifies a somewhat weaker emphasis than on the syllable with primary stress.

Variant Pronunciations

There are several ways in which variant pronunciations are indicated in the respellings.

Some respellings show a pronunciation symbol within parentheses to indicate a possible variation in pronunciation; for example, in **sandwich** /ˈsan(d)wiCH/.

Variant pronunciations may be respelled in full, separated by semicolons. The more common pronunciation is listed first, if this can be determined, but many variants are of equal status.

Variant pronunciations may be indicated by respelling only the part of the word that changes. A hyphen will replace the part of the pronunciation that has remained the same.

Note: A hyphen sometimes serves to separate syllables where the respelling might otherwise look confusing, as at **reinforce** /ˌrē-inˈfôrs/.

Key to the Abbreviations

abbr.; Abbr.	abbreviation	*e.g.*	for example (*exempli gratia*)
adj.	adjective	*Electr.*	Electronics
adv.	adverb	*Entomol.*	Entomology
Aeron.	Aeronautics	*esp.*	especially
Afr.	African	*etc.*	et cetera (and the rest)
Anat.	Anatomy	*F.*	Fahrenheit
Anthropol.	Anthropology	*fem.*	feminine
approx.	approximately	*fig.*	figurative
Archaeol.	Archaeology	*fl. oz.*	fluid ounce, fluid ounces
Archit.	Architecture	*ft.*	foot, feet
Astrol.	Astrology	*Geog.*	Geography
Astron.	Astronomy	*Geol.*	Geology
attrib.	attributive	*Geom.*	Geometry
Austral.	Australian	*Gram.*	Grammar
aux.	auxiliary	*Hist.*	History
Biochem.	Biochemistry	*hist.*	historical
Biol.	Biology	*i.e.*	that is (*id est*)
Bot.	Botany	*in.*	inch, inches
Brit.	British	*inf.*	informal
C	Celsius	*infin.*	infinitive
c.	century; circa (about)	*interj.*	interjection
Can.	Canadian	*interrog.*	interrogative
Chem.	Chemistry	*intr.*	intransitive
cm	centimeter, centimeters	*kg*	kilogram, kilograms
comb.	combination; combining	*km*	kilometer, kilometers
Comput.	Computing	*l*	liter, liters
conj.	conjunction	*lb.*	pound, pounds
contr.	contraction	*lit.*	literary
Crystallog.	Crystallography	*m*	meter, meters
cu.	cubic	*masc.*	masculine
derog.	derogatory	*Math.*	Mathematics
dial.	dialect	*Med.*	Medicine
E.	East	*Meteorol.*	Meteorology
Ecol.	Ecology	*mi.*	mile, miles
Econ.	Economics	*Mil.*	Military

ml	milliliter, milliliters	*pron.*	pronoun
mm	millimeter, millimeters	*pronunc.*	pronunciation
Mus.	Music	*Psychol.*	Psychology
Mythol.	Mythology	*refl.*	reflexive
N.	North	*rel.*	relative
n.	noun	*S.*	South
Naut.	Nautical	*Scot.*	Scottish
offens.	offensive	*sing.*	singular
orig.	originally	*sq.*	square
Ornithol.	Ornithology	*symb.*	symbol
oz.	ounce, ounces	*Theol.*	Theology
part.	participle	*tr.*	transitive
Philos.	Philosophy	*UK*	United Kingdom
Phonet.	Phonetics	*U.S.*	United States
Photog.	Photography	*usu.*	usually
Physiol.	Physiology	*v.*	verb
pl.	plural	*var.*	variant
poss.	possessive	*W.*	West
prep.	preposition	*yd.*	yard, yards
pres.	present	*Zool.*	Zoology

Aa

A¹ /ā/ (also **a**) ▶ *n.* (*pl.* **As** or **A's**) **1** the first letter of the alphabet. ■ denoting the first in a set of items, categories, sizes, etc. ■ denoting the first of two or more hypothetical people or things: *suppose A had killed B.* ■ the highest class of academic mark. ■ (usu. *a*) the first fixed quantity in an algebraic expression. ■ (**A**) the human blood type (in the ABO system) containing the A antigen and lacking the B. **2** a shape like that of a capital A: [in *comb.*] *an A-shape.* **3** *Mus.* the sixth note of the diatonic scale of C major. ■ a key based on a scale with A as its keynote.

A² ▶ *abbr.* ■ ace (used in describing play in bridge and other card games). ■ ampere(s). ■ (**Å**) ångstrom(s). ■ answer. ■ (in personal ads) Asian. ■ a dry cell battery size.

a /ā; ə/ (**an** before a vowel sound) [called the *indefinite article*] ▶ *adj.* **1** used when referring to someone or something for the first time in a text or conversation: *a man came out of the room.* Compare with **THE**. ■ used with units of measurement to mean one such unit: *a hundred.* ■ one single; any: *I simply haven't a thing to wear.* ■ used when mentioning the name of someone not known to the speaker: *a Mr. Smith telephoned.* ■ someone like (the name specified): *you're no better than a Hitler.* **2** used to indicate membership of a class of people or things: *he is a lawyer.* **3** used when expressing rates or ratios; in, to, or for each; per: *typing 60 words a minute.*

AA ▶ *abbr.* ■ Alcoholics Anonymous. ■ antiaircraft. ■ administrative assistant. ■ Associate of Arts. ■ a 1.5-volt dry cell battery size.

aa /ˈä,ä/ ▶ *n. Geol.* basaltic lava forming very rough jagged masses with a light frothy texture.

AAA /ˌtripəl ˈā/ ▶ *abbr.* American Automobile Association. ■ a 1.5-volt dry cell battery size.

aard·vark /ˈärd,värk/ ▶ *n.* a nocturnal burrowing African mammal (*Orycteropus afer,* family Orycteropidae) with long ears, a tubular snout, and a long extensible tongue, feeding on ants and termites. ▷late 18th cent.: from South African Dutch, from *aarde* 'earth' + *vark* 'pig.'

aard·wolf /ˈärd,wŏŏlf/ ▶ *n.* (*pl.* **aard·wolves** /-,wŏŏlvz/) a nocturnal black-striped African mammal (*Proteles cristatus*) of the hyena family, feeding mainly on termites.

AAU ▶ *abbr.* Amateur Athletic Union.

AB¹ ▶ *n.* a human blood type (in the ABO system) containing both the A and B antigens.

AB² ▶ *abbr.* ■ able seaman; able-bodied seaman. ■ Bachelor of Arts. ■ airman basic. ■ *Baseball* at bat.

Ab /äb; äv/ (also **Av**) ▶ *n.* (in the Jewish calendar) the eleventh month of the civil year and the fifth month of the religious year, usually coinciding with parts of July and August.

a·back /əˈbak/ ▶ *adv.* **1** *archaic* toward or situated to the rear: *the little strip of pasture aback of the house.* **2** *Sailing* with the sail pressed backward against the mast by a headwind.
▶ □ **take someone aback** shock or surprise someone.

ab·a·cus /ˈabəkəs/ ▶ *n.* (*pl.* **-cus·es**) **1** an oblong frame with rows of wires or grooves along which beads are slid, used for calculating. **2** *Archit.* the flat slab on top of a capital, supporting the architrave.

a·baft /əˈbaft/ *Naut.* ▶ *adv.* in or behind the stern of a ship.
▶ *prep.* nearer the stern than; behind.

ab·a·lo·ne /ˌabəˈlōnē; ˈabəˌlōnē/ ▶ *n.* an edible

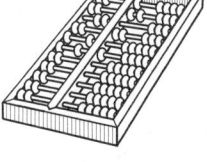
abacus

mollusk (genus *Haliotis,* family Haliotidae) of warm seas that has a shallow ear-shaped shell lined with mother-of-pearl and pierced with respiratory holes. ▷mid 19th cent.: via Latin American Spanish from *aulun,* from an American Indian language of Monterey Bay, California.

a·ban·don /əˈbandən/ ▶ *v.* [*tr.*] **1** give up completely (a course of action, a practice, or a way of thinking): *he had abandoned all pretense of trying to succeed.* ■ discontinue (a scheduled event) before completion. **2** cease to support or look after (someone); desert. ■ leave (a place, typically a building) empty or uninhabited, without intending to return. ■ leave (something, typically a vehicle or a vessel) decisively, esp. as an act of survival. ■ (**abandon someone/something to**) condemn someone or something to (a specified fate) by ceasing to take an interest in or look after them: *an attempt to persuade businesses not to abandon the area to inner-city deprivation.* **3** (**abandon oneself to**) allow oneself to indulge in (a desire or impulse): *abandoning herself to moony fantasies.*
▶ *n.* complete lack of inhibition or restraint: *she sings and sways with total abandon.* —**a·ban·don·ment** *n.*

a·ban·doned /əˈbandənd/ ▶ *adj.* **1** (of a person) having been deserted or cast off: *a home for orphan and abandoned boys.* **2** (of a building or vehicle) remaining empty or unused; having been left for good. **3** unrestrained; uninhibited: *a wild, abandoned dance.*

a·base /əˈbās/ ▶ *v.* [*tr.*] behave in a way so as to belittle or degrade (someone): *I watched my colleagues abasing themselves before the board of trustees.* —**a·base·ment** *n.*

a·bash /əˈbasн/ ▶ *v.* [*tr.*] [usu. as *adj.*] (**abashed**) cause to feel embarrassed, disconcerted, or ashamed: *she was not abashed at being caught.*

a·bate /əˈbāt/ ▶ *v.* [*intr.*] (of something perceived as hostile, threatening, or negative) become less intense or widespread: *the storm suddenly abated.* ■ [*tr.*] cause to become smaller or less intense: *nothing abated his crusading zeal.* ■ [*tr.*] *Law* lessen, reduce, or remove (esp. a nuisance). —**a·bate·ment** *n.*

ab·at·toir /ˈabə,twär/ ▶ *n.* a slaughterhouse. ▷early 19th cent.: from French, from *abattre* 'to fell.'

ab·bess /ˈabis/ ▶ *n.* a woman who is the head of an abbey of nuns.

ab·bey /ˈabē/ ▶ *n.* (*pl.* **-beys**) the building or buildings occupied by a community of monks or nuns.

ab·bot /ˈabət/ ▶ *n.* a man who is the head of an abbey of monks.

ab·bre·vi·ate /əˈbrēvē,āt/ ▶ *v.* [*tr.*] shorten (a word, phrase, or text): *the business of artists and repertory, commonly abbreviated to A&R.*

ab·bre·vi·a·tion /ə,brēvēˈāsнən/ (abbr.: **abbr.**) ▶ *n.* a shortened form of a word or phrase. ■ the process or result of abbreviating.

ABC¹ ▶ *n.* the alphabet. ■ (also **ABCs**) the rudiments of a subject: *the ABCs of emergency heart-lung resuscitation.*

ABC² ▶ *abbr.* American Broadcasting Company.

ab·di·cate /ˈabdi,kāt/ ▶ *v.* [*intr.*] (of a monarch) renounce one's throne: *in 1918 Kaiser Wilhelm abdicated as German emperor* | [*tr.*] *Ferdinand abdicated the throne in favor of the emperor's brother.* ■ [*tr.*] fail to fulfill or undertake (a responsibility or duty): *the government was accused of abdicating its responsibility* | [*intr.*] *the secretary of state should not abdicate from leadership on educational issues.* —**ab·di·ca·tion** /-ˈkāsнən/ *n.*

ab·do·men /ˈabdəmən; abˈdōmən/ ▶ *n.* the part of the body of a vertebrate containing the digestive organs; the belly. In humans and other mammals, it is contained between the diaphragm and the pelvis. ■ *Zool.* the posterior part of the body of an arthropod. —**ab·dom·i·nal** /abˈdämənl/ *adj.*

ab·duct /abˈdəkt/ ▶ *v.* [*tr.*] **1** take (someone) away illegally by force or

A

deception; kidnap. **2** *Physiol.* (of a muscle) move (a limb or part) |away from the midline of the body or from another part. —**ab·duc·tor** *n.*

a·beam /əˈbēm/ ▶*adv.* on a line at right angles to a ship's or an aircraft's length.

a·bed /əˈbed/ ▶*adv. archaic* in bed.

A·be·na·ki /ˌabəˈnakē; ˌäbəˈnä-/ ▶*n.* variant spelling of **ABNAKI**.

ab·er·rant /ˈabərənt; əˈber-/ ▶*adj.* departing from an accepted standard. ■ *chiefly Biol.* diverging from the normal type: *aberrant chromosomes.* —**ab·er·rance** *n.* —**ab·er·ran·cy** *n.* —**ab·er·rant·ly** *adv.*

ab·er·ra·tion /ˌabəˈrāSHən/ ▶*n.* a departure from what is normal, usual, or expected, typically one that is unwelcome. ■ a person whose beliefs or behavior are unusual or unacceptable. ■ a departure from someone's usual moral character or mental ability, typically for the worse. ■ *Biol.* a characteristic that deviates from the normal type: *color aberrations.* ■ *Optics* the failure of rays to converge at one focus because of limitations or defects in a lens or mirror. ■ *Astron.* the apparent displacement of a celestial object from its true position, caused by the relative motion of the observer and the object. —**ab·er·ra·tion·al** /-SHənl/ *adj.*

a·bet /əˈbet/ ▶*v.* (**a·bet·ted, a·bet·ting**) [*tr.*] encourage or assist (someone) to do something wrong, in particular, to commit a crime: *he was guilty of aiding and abetting the murderer.* ■ encourage or assist someone to commit (a crime): *we are aiding and abetting this illegal traffic.* ▷late Middle English (in the sense 'urge to do something good or bad'): from Old French *abeter,* from *a-* (from Latin *ad* 'to, at') + *beter* 'hound, urge on.' —**a·bet·ment** *n.* —**a·bet·tor** /əˈbetər/ (also **a·bet·ter**) *n.*

a·bey·ance /əˈbāəns/ ▶*n.* a state of temporary disuse or suspension: *matters were held in abeyance pending further inquiries.*

ab·hor /abˈhôr/ ▶*v.* (**-horred, -hor·ring**) [*tr.*] *formal* regard with disgust and hatred. —**ab·hor·rer** *n.*

ab·hor·rent /abˈhôrənt; -ˈhär-/ ▶*adj.* inspiring disgust and loathing; repugnant: *racial discrimination was abhorrent to us all.* —**ab·hor·rence** *n.*

a·bide /əˈbīd/ ▶*v.* **1** [*intr.*] (**abide by**) accept or act in accordance with (a rule, decision, or recommendation): *I said I would abide by their decision.* **2** [*tr.*] *inf.* tolerate (someone or something): *if there is one thing I cannot abide it is a lack of discipline.* **3** [*intr.*] (of a feeling or a memory) continue without fading or being lost. ■ *archaic* live; dwell.

a·bid·ing /əˈbīdiNG/ ▶*adj.* (of a feeling or a memory) lasting a long time; enduring: *he had an abiding respect for her.* —**a·bid·ing·ly** *adv.*

a·bil·i·ty /əˈbilitē/ ▶*n.* (pl. **-ties**) **1** the capacity to do something: *the manager had lost his ability to motivate the players.* **2** talent that enables someone to achieve a great deal: *a man of exceptional ability.* ■ (in the context of education) a level of mental power: *a student of average ability.* ■ a special talent or skill: *much depends on the person's abilities and aptitudes.*

a·bi·o·gen·e·sis /ˌābī-ōˈjenəsis/ ▶*n.* technical term for **SPONTANEOUS GENERATION**.

ab·ject /ˈabˌjekt; abˈjekt/ ▶*adj.* **1** (of a situation or condition) extremely bad, unpleasant, and degrading: *abject poverty.* ■ (of an unhappy state of mind) experienced to the maximum degree: *abject misery.* ■ (of a failure) absolute and humiliating. **2** (of a person or their behavior) completely without pride or dignity: *an abject apology.* —**ab·jec·tion** /abˈjekSHən/ *n.* —**ab·ject·ly** *adv.* —**ab·ject·ness** *n.*

ab·jure /abˈjo͝or/ ▶*v.* [*tr.*] *formal* solemnly renounce (a belief, cause, or claim). —**ab·ju·ra·tion** /ˌabjəˈrāSHən/ *n.*

ab·la·tion /əˈblāSHən/ ▶*n.* **1** the surgical removal of body tissue. **2** the removal of snow and ice by melting or evaporation, typically from a glacier or iceberg. ■ the loss of surface material from a spacecraft or meteorite through evaporation or melting caused by friction with the atmosphere. —**ab·late** /əˈblāt/ *v.*

ab·la·tive /ˈablətiv/ ▶*adj. Gram.* relating to or denoting a case (esp. in Latin) of nouns and pronouns (and words in grammatical agreement with them) indicating separation or an agent, instrument, or location. ▶*n. Gram.* a word in the ablative case. ■ (**the ablative**) the ablative case.

ab·laut /ˈabˌlout/ ▶*n.* a change of vowel in related words or forms, e.g., in Germanic strong verbs (e.g., in *sing, sang, sung*).

a·blaze /əˈblāz/ ▶*adj.* burning fiercely. ■ very brightly colored or lighted: *New England is ablaze with color in autumn.* ■ made bright by a strong emotion: *his eyes were ablaze with anger.*

a·ble /ˈābəl/ ▶*adj.* (**a·bler, a·blest**) **1** having the power, skill, means, or opportunity to do something: *he was able to read Greek.* **2** having considerable skill, proficiency, or intelligence: *the dancers were very able.*

a·ble-bod·ied ▶*adj.* fit, strong, and healthy; not physically disabled: *he was the only able-bodied man on the farm.*

a·bloom /əˈblo͞om/ ▶*adj.* covered in flowers.

ab·lu·tion /əˈblo͞oSHən/ ▶*n.* (usu. **ablutions**) the act of washing oneself (often used for humorously formal effect): *the women performed their ablutions.* —**ab·lu·tion·ar·y** *adj.*

a·bly /ˈāblē/ ▶*adv.* skillfully; competently.

ABM ▶*abbr.* antiballistic missile.

Ab·na·ki /abˈnakē; äbˈnä-/ (also **Ab·e·na·ki** /ˌabəˈnakē; ˌäbəˈnä-/) ▶*n.* (pl. same or **-kis**) **1** a member of a North American Indian people of Maine on the Atlantic coast to southern Quebec. **2** either or both of two Algonquian languages, **Eastern Abnaki** and **Western Abnaki**, now nearly extinct.
▶*adj.* of or relating to this people or their language.

ab·ne·gate /ˈabniˌgāt/ ▶*v.* [*tr.*] renounce or reject (something desired or valuable). —**ab·ne·ga·tor** /-ˌgātər/ *n.*

ab·ne·ga·tion /ˌabniˈgāSHən/ ▶*n.* the act of renouncing or rejecting something: *abnegation of political law-making power.* ■ self-denial.

ab·nor·mal /abˈnôrməl/ ▶*adj.* deviating from what is normal or usual, typically in a way that is undesirable or worrying. —**ab·nor·mal·ly** *adv.*

ab·nor·mal·i·ty /ˌabnôrˈmalitē/ ▶*n.* (pl. **-ties**) an abnormal feature, characteristic, or occurrence, typically in a medical context: *a chromosome abnormality.* ■ the quality or state of being abnormal.

a·board /əˈbôrd/ ▶*adv. & prep.* on or into (a ship, aircraft, train, or other vehicle): [as *adv.*] *welcome aboard, sir* | [as *prep.*] *climbing aboard the yacht.* ■ *fig.* into an organization or team as a new member: [as *adv.*] *coming aboard as IBM's new chairman.* ■ *Baseball* on base as a runner: *putting their first batter aboard.*

a·bode¹ /əˈbōd/ ▶*n. formal* or *poetic/lit.* a place of residence; a house or home: *her current abode* | *humorous my humble abode.* ■ *archaic* a stay; a sojourn.

a·bode² ▶*v.* archaic past of **ABIDE**.

a·bol·ish /əˈbäliSH/ ▶*v.* [*tr.*] formally put an end to (a system, practice, or institution). —**a·bol·ish·er** *n.* —**a·bol·ish·ment** *n.*

ab·o·li·tion /ˌabəˈliSHən/ ▶*n.* the action or an act of abolishing a system, practice, or institution: *the abolition of child labor.*

ab·o·li·tion·ist /ˌabəˈliSHənist/ ▶*n.* a person who favors the abolition of a practice or institution, esp. capital punishment or (formerly) slavery. —**ab·o·li·tion·ism** *n.*

A-bomb ▶*n.* short for **ATOM BOMB**.

a·bom·i·na·ble /əˈbäm(ə)nəbəl/ ▶*adj.* causing moral revulsion: *abominable cruelty.* ■ *inf.* very unpleasant. —**a·bom·i·na·bly** /-blē/ *adv.*

a·bom·i·nate /əˈbäməˌnāt/ ▶*v.* [*tr.*] *formal* detest; loathe: *they abominated the very idea of monarchy.* —**a·bom·i·na·tor** /-ˌnātər/ *n.*

a·bom·i·na·tion /əˌbäməˈnāSHən/ ▶*n.* a thing that causes disgust or hatred. ■ a feeling of hatred: *their abomination of indulgence.*

ab·o·rig·i·nal /ˌabəˈrijənl/ ▶*adj.* (of human races, animals, and plants) inhabiting or existing in a land from the earliest times or from before the arrival of colonists; indigenous. ■ (**Aboriginal**) of or relating to the Australian Aboriginals or their languages.
▶*n.* an aboriginal inhabitant of a place. ■ (**Aboriginal**) a person belonging to one of the indigenous peoples of Australia.

ab·o·rig·i·ne /ˌabəˈrijənē/ ▶*n.* a person, animal, or plant that has been in a country or region from earliest times. ■ (**Aborigine**) an aboriginal inhabitant of Australia. ▷mid 19th cent.: back-formation from the 16th-cent. plural *aborigines* 'original inhabitants' (in classical times referring to those of Italy and Greece), from the Latin phrase *ab origine* 'from the beginning.'

a·bort /əˈbôrt/ ▶*v.* [*tr.*] **1** carry out or undergo the abortion of (a fetus). ■ [*intr.*] (of a pregnant woman or female animal) have a miscarriage, with loss of the fetus. ■ [*intr.*] *Biol.* (of an embryonic organ or organism) remain undeveloped; fail to mature. **2** bring to a premature end because of a problem or fault: *the pilot aborted his landing.*
▶*n.* an act of aborting a flight, space mission, or other enterprise.

a·bor·ti·fa·cient /əˌbôrtəˈfāSHənt/ *Med.* ▶*adj.* (chiefly of a drug) causing abortion.
▶*n.* an abortifacient drug.

a·bor·tion /əˈbôrSHən/ ▶*n.* the deliberate termination of a human pregnancy, most often performed during the first 28 weeks of pregnancy. ■ the expulsion of a fetus from the uterus by natural causes before it is able to survive independently. ■ *Biol.* the arrest of the development of an organ, typically a seed or fruit.

a·bor·tion·ist /əˈbôrSHənist/ ▶*n.* a person who carries out abortions (typically applied to someone not working in a hospital, or used to convey disapproval of abortion).

a·bor·tive /əˈbôrtiv/ ▶*adj.* failing to produce the intended result: *her two abortive attempts at suicide.* —**a·bor·tive·ly** *adv.*

ABO system ▶*n.* a system of four basic types (A, AB, B, and O) into

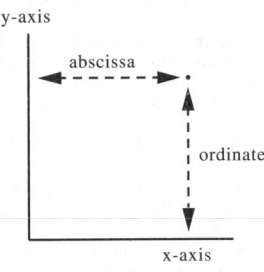

which human blood may be classified, based on the presence or absence of certain inherited antigens.

a·bound /əˈbound/ ▶v. [intr.] exist in large numbers or amounts: *rumors of a further scandal abound.* ■ (**abound in/with**) have in large numbers or amounts: *this land abounds with wildlife.*

a·bout /əˈbout/ ▶prep. **1** on the subject of; concerning: *I was thinking about you.* ■ so as to affect: *there's nothing we can do about it.* ■ (**be about**) be involved or to do with; have the intention of: *it's all about having fun.* **2** used to indicate movement within a particular area: *she looked about the room.* **3** used to express location in a particular place: *rugs strewn about the hall.* ■ used to describe a quality apparent in a person: *there was a look about her that said everything.*
▶adv. **1** used to indicate movement in an area: *men were floundering about.* **2** used to express location in a particular place: *there was a lot of flu about.* **3** (used with a number or quantity) approximately: *he looks about 35.*
▶ □ **about to do something** intending to do something or close to doing something very soon: *the ceremony was about to begin.* □ **be not about to do something** be unwilling to do something: *he is not about to step down.*

a·bout-face ▶n. (chiefly in military contexts) a turn made so as to face the opposite direction: *he did an about-face and marched out.* ■ inf. a complete change of opinion or policy.
▶v. [intr.] turn so as to face the opposite direction.
▶interj. (**about face!**) (in military contexts) a command to make an about-face.

a·bove /əˈbəv/ ▶prep. **1** in extended space over and not touching: *a display of fireworks above the town.* ■ extending upward over: *her arms above her head.* ■ higher than and to one side of; overlooking: *on the wall above the altar.* **2** at a higher level or layer than: *bruises above both eyes.* ■ higher in grade or rank than: *at a level above the common people.* ■ considered of higher status or worth than; too good for: *she married above her.* ■ in preference to: *they chose profit above car safety.* ■ at a higher volume or pitch than: *above a whisper.* **3** higher than (a specified amount, rate, or norm): *above sea level.*
▶adv. at a higher level or layer. ■ higher in grade or rank: *the rank of superintendent or above.* ■ higher than a specified amount, rate, or norm: *boats of 31 ft. or above.* ■ (in printed text) mentioned earlier or further up on the same page: *the two cases described above* | [as *adj.*] *at the above address* | [as *n.*] *since writing the above, I have reconsidered.*
▶ □ **from above** from a position of higher rank or authority. □ **not be above** be capable of stooping to (an unworthy act): *he was not above practical jokes.*

a·bove-board /əˈbəvˌbôrd/ ▶adj. legitimate, honest, and open.
▶adv. legitimately, honestly, and openly.

ab·ra·ca·dab·ra /ˌabrəkəˈdabrə/ ▶interj. a word said by magicians when performing a magic trick.
▶n. inf. an implausibly easy effort to achieve a seemingly difficult feat: *a little abracadabra, and you've got chocolate mousse.* ■ language, typically in the form of gibberish, used to give the impression of arcane knowledge or power.

a·brade /əˈbrād/ ▶v. [tr.] scrape or wear away by friction or erosion: *a landscape slowly abraded by a fine, stinging dust.* —**a·brad·er** n.

a·bra·sion /əˈbrāzhən/ ▶n. the process of scraping or wearing away: *the metal is resistant to abrasion.* ■ an area damaged by scraping or wearing away: *there were cuts and abrasions to the lips and jaw.*

a·bra·sive /əˈbrāsiv; -ziv/ ▶adj. (of a substance or material) capable of polishing or cleaning a hard surface by rubbing or grinding. ■ tending to rub or graze the skin: *the trees were abrasive to the touch.* ■ fig. (of sounds or music) rough to the ear; harsh. ■ fig. (of a person or manner) showing little concern for the feelings of others. —**a·bra·sive·ly** adv.
▶n. a substance used for grinding, polishing, or cleaning a hard surface.

ab·re·ac·tion /ˌabrēˈakshən/ ▶n. Psychol. the expression and consequent release of a repressed emotion, achieved through reliving the experience that caused it. —**ab·re·ac·tive** /-tiv/ adj.

a·breast /əˈbrest/ ▶adv. **1** side by side and facing the same way: *they were riding three abreast.* **2** alongside or even with something: *the cart came abreast of the Americans in their ricksha.* ■ fig. up to date with the latest news, ideas, or information: *keeping abreast of developments.*

a·bridge /əˈbrij/ ▶v. [tr.] (usu. **be abridged**) **1** shorten (a book, movie, speech, or other text) without losing the sense: [as *adj.*] (**abridged**) *an abridged text.* **2** Law curtail (rights or privileges). —**a·bridg·er** n.

a·bridg·ment /əˈbrijmənt/ (also **a·bridge·ment**) ▶n. **1** a shortened version of a larger work. **2** Law a curtailment of rights.

a·broad /əˈbrôd/ ▶adv. **1** in or to a foreign country or countries: *we usually go abroad for a week in May.* **2** in different directions; over a wide area: *seeds scattered abroad.* ■ (of a feeling or rumor) widely current:

there is a new optimistic spirit abroad. ■ freely moving about: *con artists abroad on the streets of the town.*
▶n. foreign countries considered collectively: *servicemen returning from abroad.*

ab·ro·gate /ˈabrəˌgāt/ ▶v. [tr.] formal repeal or do away with (a law, right, or formal agreement). —**ab·ro·ga·tion** /ˌabrəˈgāshən/ n.

ab·rupt /əˈbrəpt/ ▶adj. **1** sudden and unexpected: *the abrupt change of subject.* **2** brief to the point of rudeness; curt. ■ (of a style of speech or writing) not flowing smoothly; disjointed. **3** steep; precipitous: *the abrupt double peak of the mountain.* —**ab·rupt·ly** adv. —**ab·rupt·ness** n.

ABS ▶abbr. ■ acrylonitrile-butadiene-styrene, a composite plastic used to make car bodies and cases for computers and other appliances. ■ anti-lock braking system (for motor vehicles).

abs /abz/ inf. ▶n. the abdominal muscles.

ab·scess /ˈabˌses/ ▶n. a swollen area within body tissue, containing an accumulation of pus.

ab·scis·sa /abˈsisə/ ▶n. (pl. **-scis·sae** /-ˈsisē/ or **-scis·sas**) Math. (in a system of coordinates) the x-coordinate, the distance from a point to the vertical or y-axis measured parallel to the horizontal or x-axis.

abscissa

ab·scis·sion /abˈsizhən/ ▶n. Bot. the natural detachment of parts of a plant, typically dead leaves and ripe fruit. ■ any act of cutting off.

ab·scond /abˈskänd/ ▶v. [intr.] leave hurriedly and secretly, typically to avoid detection or arrest for an unlawful action such as theft: *she absconded with the remaining thousand dollars.* ■ (of someone on bail) fail to surrender oneself for custody at the appointed time. ■ (of a person kept in detention or under supervision) escape. —**ab·scond·er** n.

ab·sence /ˈabsəns/ ▶n. the state of being away from a place or person. ■ an occasion or period of being away from a place or person: *absences from school.* ■ (**absence of**) the nonexistence or lack of: *she found his total absence of facial expression disconcerting.*

ab·sent ▶adj. /ˈabsənt/ **1** not present in a place or at an occasion: *absent from school* | *absent colleagues.* ■ (of a part or feature of the body) not forming part of a creature in which it might be expected: *wings are absent in certain flies.* **2** (of an expression or manner) showing that someone is not paying attention to what is being said or done: *she looked up with an absent smile.*
▶v. /abˈsent/ (**absent oneself**) stay or go away: *people absented themselves because of his presence* | *absented himself from the table.*
▶prep. /abˈsent/ formal without: *employees could not be fired absent other evidence.* —**ab·sent·ly** adv.

ab·sen·tee /ˌabsənˈtē/ ▶n. a person who is expected or required to be present at a place or event but is not.

ab·sen·tee·ism /ˌabsənˈtēˌizəm/ ▶n. the practice of regularly staying away from work or school without good reason.

ab·sent-mind·ed /ˈabsəntˌmīndid/ ▶adj. (of a person or a person's behavior or manner) having or showing a habitually forgetful or inattentive disposition: *an absentminded smile.* —**ab·sent-mind·ed·ly** adv. —**ab·sent-mind·ed·ness** n.

ab·sinthe /ˈabˌsinth/ (also **ab·sinth**) ▶n. **1** the shrub wormwood. **2** a potent green aniseed-flavored liqueur. Prepared from wormwood, it is now largely banned because of its toxicity.

ab·so·lute /ˈabsəˌlo͞ot; ˌabsəˈlo͞ot/ ▶adj. **1** not qualified or diminished in any way; total: *absolute secrecy.* ■ used for general emphasis when expressing an opinion: *the policy is absolute folly.* ■ (of powers or rights) not subject to any limitation: *her absolute authority* | *human right to life is absolute.* ■ (of a ruler) having unrestricted power: *he proclaimed himself absolute monarch.* ■ Law (of a decree) final. **2** viewed or existing

A

independently and not in relation to other things: *absolute moral standards.* ■ *Gram.* (of a construction) syntactically independent of the rest of the sentence, as in *dinner being over, we left the table.* ■ *Gram.* (of a transitive verb) used without an expressed object (e.g., *guns kill*). ■ *Gram.* (of an adjective) used without an expressed noun (e.g., *the brave*).

▶ *n. Philos.* a value or principle that is regarded as universally valid or that may be viewed without relation to other things: *good and evil are presented as absolutes.* ■ (**the absolute**) *Philos.* that which exists without being dependent on anything else. ■ (**the absolute**) *Theol.* ultimate reality; God. —**ab·so·lute·ness** *n.*

ab·so·lute·ly /ˌabsəˈlo͞otlē/ ▶ *adv.* **1** with no qualification, restriction, or limitation; totally.. ■ used to emphasize the truth or appropriateness of a very strong or exaggerated statement: *he absolutely adores that car.* ■ none whatsoever: *she had absolutely no idea what he was talking about.* ■ used to emphasize a statement or opinion: *it's absolutely pouring out there | it's absolutely ages since I went to a party.* ■ [as *interj.*] *inf.* used to express and emphasize one's assent or agreement: *"Did they give you a free hand when you joined the band?" "Absolutely!"* **2** independently; not viewed in relation to other things or factors: *these crimes increased both absolutely and in comparison with other crimes.* ■ *Gram.* (of a verb) without a stated object.

ab·so·lute val·ue ▶ *n.* **1** *Math.* the magnitude of a real number without regard to its sign. The absolute value of a complex number $a^2 + ib$ is the positive square root of $a^2 + b^2$. Also called **MODULUS**. **2** *technical* the actual magnitude of a numerical value, irrespective of its relation to other values.

ab·so·lu·tion /ˌabsəˈlo͞oSHən/ ▶ *n.* formal release from guilt, obligation, or punishment.

ab·so·lut·ism /ˈabsəlo͞oˌtizəm/ ▶ *n.* the acceptance of or belief in absolute principles in political, philosophical, ethical, or theological matters. —**ab·so·lut·ist** *n. & adj.*

ab·solve /əbˈzälv; -ˈsälv/ ▶ *v.* [tr.] set or declare (someone) free from blame, guilt, or responsibility: *the pardon absolved them of any crimes.* ■ *Christian Theol.* give absolution for (a sin).

ab·sorb /əbˈzôrb; -ˈsôrb/ ▶ *v.* [tr.] **1** take in or soak up (energy, or a liquid or other substance) by chemical or physical action, typically gradually: *buildings designed to absorb and retain heat | steroids are absorbed into the bloodstream.* ■ take in and assimilate (information, ideas, or experience). ■ take control of (a smaller or less powerful entity), making it a part of oneself by assimilation: *the family firm was absorbed into a larger group.* ■ use or take up (time or resources) ■ take up and reduce the effect or intensity of (sound or an impact). **2** engross the attention of (someone). —**ab·sorb·a·ble** *adj.* —**ab·sorb·er** *n.*

ab·sorbed /əbˈzôrbd; -ˈsôrbd/ ▶ *adj.* intensely engaged; engrossed: *she sat in an armchair, absorbed in a book.* —**ab·sorb·ed·ly** /-bidlē/ *adv.*

ab·sorb·ent /əbˈzôrbənt; -ˈsôr-/ ▶ *adj.* (of a material) able to soak up liquid easily: *drain on absorbent paper towels.*

▶ *n.* a substance or item that soaks up liquid easily. —**ab·sorb·en·cy** *n.*

ab·sorp·tion /əbˈzôrpSHən; -ˈsôrp-/ ▶ *n.* **1** the process or action by which one thing absorbs or is absorbed by another. **2** the fact or state of being engrossed in something. —**ab·sorp·tive** /-tiv/ *adj.*

ab·stain /abˈstān/ ▶ *v.* [*intr.*] **1** restrain oneself from doing or enjoying something. ■ refrain from drinking alcohol: *most pregnant women abstain or drink very little.* **2** formally decline to vote either for or against a proposal or motion. —**ab·stain·er** *n.*

ab·ste·mi·ous /abˈstēmēəs/ ▶ *adj.* not self-indulgent, esp. when eating and drinking. —**ab·ste·mi·ous·ly** *adv.* —**ab·ste·mi·ous·ness** *n.*

ab·sten·tion /abˈstenSHən/ ▶ *n.* **1** an instance of declining to vote for or against a proposal or motion. **2** the fact or practice of restraining oneself from indulging in something; abstinence. —**ab·sten·tion·ism** /-ˌnizəm/ *n.*

ab·sti·nence /ˈabstənəns/ ▶ *n.* the fact or practice of restraining oneself from indulging in something, typically alcohol. —**ab·sti·nent** *adj.* —**ab·sti·nent·ly** *adv.*

ab·stract ▶ *adj.* /ˈabˌstrakt; ˈabˌstrakt/ existing in thought or as an idea but not having a physical or concrete existence: *abstract concepts such as love or beauty.* ■ dealing with ideas rather than events: *the novel was too abstract to sustain much attention.* ■ not based on a particular instance; theoretical: *we have been discussing the problem in a very abstract manner.* ■ (of a word, esp. a noun) denoting an idea, quality, or state rather than a concrete object. ■ of or relating to art that uses shapes, forms, colors, and textures to create suggestive effects rather than realistic images.

▶ *v.* /abˈstrakt/ [tr.] **1** consider (something) theoretically or separately from something else: *abstracting religion from its historical context.* ■ [*intr.*] form a general idea in this way: *he cannot form a general notion by*

abstracting from particulars. **2** extract or remove (something). **3** make a written summary of (an article or book): *he abstracts material for an online database.*

▶ *n.* /ˈabˌstrakt/ **1** a summary or statement of the contents of a book, article, or formal speech. **2** an abstract work of art. **3** (**the abstract**) that which is abstract; the theoretical consideration of something. —**ab·stract·ly** *adv.* —**ab·strac·tor** /-tər/ *n.*

ab·strac·tion /abˈstrakSHən/ ▶ *n.* **1** the quality of dealing with ideas rather than events. ■ something that exists only as an idea. **2** freedom from representational qualities in art. **3** a state of preoccupation: *his momentary abstraction.* **4** the process of considering something independently of its associations, attributes, or concrete accompaniments: *they tend to interpret Jesus's words in abstraction from any historical context.* **5** the process of removing something, esp. water from a river or other source.

ab·struse /abˈstro͞os/ ▶ *adj.* difficult to understand; obscure. —**ab·struse·ly** *adv.* —**ab·struse·ness** *n.*

ab·surd /əbˈsərd; -ˈzərd/ ▶ *adj.* (of an idea or suggestion) wildly unreasonable, illogical, or inappropriate: *it would be absurd to blame contemporary Germans for Nazi crimes* | [as *n.*] (**the absurd**) *he had a keen eye for the absurd.* ■ (of a person or a person's behavior or actions) foolish; unreasonable. ■ (of an object or situation) arousing amusement or derision; ridiculous. —**ab·surd·ly** *adv.*

ab·surd·i·ty /əbˈsərditē; -ˈzərd-/ ▶ *n.* (*pl.* **-ties**) the quality or state of being ridiculous or wildly unreasonable.

a·bun·dance /əˈbəndəns/ ▶ *n.* a very large quantity of something: *an abundance of wildlife.* ■ the quantity or amount of something, e.g., a chemical element or an animal or plant species, present in a particular area, volume, sample, etc.: *the relative abundances of carbon and nitrogen.* ■ the state or condition of having a copious quantity of something; plentifulness: *vines and figs grew in abundance.* ■ plentifulness of the good things of life; prosperity: *the growth of industry promised wealth and abundance.*

a·bun·dant /əˈbəndənt/ ▶ *adj.* existing or available in large quantities; plentiful. ■ (**abundant in**) having plenty of something: *the riverbanks were abundant in wild plants.* —**a·bun·dant·ly** *adv.*

a·buse ▶ *v.* /əˈbyo͞oz/ [tr.] **1** use (something) to bad effect or for a bad purpose; misuse: *the judge abused his power.* ■ make excessive and habitual use of (alcohol or drugs, esp. illegal ones). **2** treat (a person or an animal) with cruelty or violence, esp. regularly or repeatedly:. ■ assault (someone, esp. a woman or child) sexually. ■ use or treat in such a way as to cause damage or harm: *he had been abusing his body for years.* ■ speak in an insulting and offensive way to or about (someone).

▶ *n.* /əˈbyo͞os/ **1** the improper use of something: *alcohol abuse.* ■ unjust or corrupt practice: *human rights abuses.* **2** cruel and violent treatment of a person or animal: *signs of physical abuse.* ■ violent treatment involving sexual assault, esp. on a repeated basis. ■ insulting and offensive language. —**a·bus·er** *n.*

a·bu·sive /əˈbyo͞osiv; -ziv/ ▶ *adj.* **1** extremely offensive and insulting: *abusive language.* **2** engaging in or characterized by habitual violence and cruelty. **3** involving injustice or illegality: *an abusive manipulation of the system.* —**a·bu·sive·ly** *adv.* —**a·bu·sive·ness** *n.*

a·but /əˈbət/ ▶ *v.* (**a·but·ted, a·but·ting**) [tr.] (of an area of land or a building) be next to or have a common boundary with: *gardens abutting Great Prescott Street* | [*intr.*] *a park abutting on an area of wasteland.* ■ touch or lean upon: *masonry may crumble where a roof abuts it.*

a·but·ment /əˈbətmənt/ ▶ *n.* a structure built to support the lateral pressure of an arch or span, e.g., at the ends of a bridge. ■ the process of supporting something with such a structure. ■ a point at which something abuts against something else.

a·buzz /əˈbəz/ ▶ *adj.* filled with a continuous humming sound: *the room was abuzz with mosquitoes* | *fig. the city was abuzz with rumors.*

a·bys·mal /əˈbizməl/ ▶ *adj.* **1** extremely bad; appalling: *the quality of her work is abysmal.* **2** *poetic/lit.* very deep. —**a·bys·mal·ly** *adv.*

a·byss /əˈbis/ ▶ *n.* a deep or seemingly bottomless chasm: *a rope led down into the dark abyss..* ■ *fig.* a wide or profound difference between people: *the abyss between the two nations.* ■ *fig.* the regions of hell conceived of as a bottomless pit.

a·byss·al /əˈbisəl/ ▶ *adj. chiefly technical* relating to or denoting the depths or bed of the ocean, esp. between about 10,000 and 20,000 feet (3,000 and 6,000 m) down.

AC ▶ *abbr.* ■ (also **ac**) alternating current: ■ (also **ac**) air conditioning. ■ before Christ. ■ athletic club. ■ (**ac.**) acre.

Ac ▶ *symb.* the chemical element actinium.

a/c ▶ *abbr.* ■ account. ■ (also **A/C**) air conditioning.

a·ca·cia /əˈkāSHə/ (also **acacia tree**) ▶ *n.* a tree or shrub (genus *Acacia*) of the pea family that bears spikes or clusters of yellow or white flowers and is frequently thorny.

ac·a·deme /ˌakəˈdēm; ˈakəˌdēm/ ▶ *n.* the academic environment or community; academia.

ac·a·de·mi·a /ˌakəˈdēmēə/ ▶ *n.* the environment or community concerned with the pursuit of research, education, and scholarship.

ac·a·dem·ic /ˌakəˈdemik/ ▶ *adj.* **1** of or relating to education and scholarship. ■ of or relating to an educational or scholarly institution or environment: *students resplendent in academic dress.* ■ (of an institution or a course of study) placing a greater emphasis on reading and study than on technical or practical work. ■ (of a person) interested in or excelling at scholarly pursuits and activities. ■ (of an art form) conventional, esp. in an idealized or excessively formal way. **2** not of practical relevance; of only theoretical interest: *the debate has been largely academic.*
▶ *n.* a teacher or scholar in a college or institute of higher education. —**ac·a·dem·i·cal·ly** *adv.*

a·cad·e·my /əˈkadəmē/ ▶ *n.* (*pl.* **-mies**) **1** a place of study or training in a special field: *a police academy.* ■ *hist.* a place of study. ■ a secondary school, typically a private one. ■ (**the Academy**) the teaching school founded by Plato. **2** a society or institution of distinguished scholars, artists, or scientists, that aims to promote and maintain standards in its particular field: *the National Academy of Sciences.* ■ the community of scholars; academe. ▷late Middle English (denoting the garden where Plato taught): from French *académie* or Latin *academia*, from Greek *akadēmeia*, from *Akadēmos*, the hero after whom Plato's garden was named.

A·ca·di·an /əˈkādēən/ *chiefly hist.* ▶ *adj.* of or relating to Acadia or its people.
▶ *n.* a native or inhabitant of Acadia. ■ *chiefly Can.* a French-speaking descendant of the early French settlers in Acadia. ■ a descendant of the Acadians deported to Louisiana in the 18th century; a Cajun.

a·can·thus /əˈkanTHəs/ ▶ *n.* **1** a herbaceous plant or shrub (genus *Acanthus*, family Acanthaceae) with bold flower spikes and spiny leaves, native to Mediterranean regions. **2** *Archit.* a representation of an acanthus leaf, used as a decoration for Corinthian column capitals.

a cap·pel·la /ˌä kəˈpelə/ ▶ *adj.* & *adv.* (with reference to choral music) without instrumental accompaniment: [as *adj.*] *an a cappella Mass* | [as *adv.*] *the trio usually performs a cappella.*

ac·cede /akˈsēd/ ▶ *v.* [*intr.*] *formal* **1** assent or agree to a demand, request, or treaty: *the authorities did not accede to the strikers' demands.* **2** assume an office or position: *he acceded to the post of director.* ■ become a member of a community or organization: *Albania acceded to the IMF in 1990.*

ac·cel·er·an·do /äkˌseləˈrändō; ak-; äˌCHelə-/ *Mus.* ▶ *adj.* & *adv.* with a gradual increase of speed (used chiefly as a direction).
▶ *n.* (*pl.* **-dos** or **-di** /-dē/) a passage to be performed with such an acceleration.

ac·cel·er·ate /akˈseləˌrāt/ ▶ *v.* [*intr.*] (of a vehicle or other physical object) increase in speed. ■ increase in amount or extent: *inflation started to accelerate.* ■ *Physics* undergo a change in velocity. ■ [*tr.*] cause to go faster: *the question is whether stress accelerates aging.* —**ac·cel·er·a·tive** /-ərətiv; -ˌrātiv/ *adj.*

ac·cel·er·a·tion /akˌseləˈrāSHən/ ▶ *n.* increase in the rate or speed of something. ■ *Physics* the rate of change of velocity per unit of time. ■ a vehicle's capacity to gain speed within a short time.

ac·cel·er·a·tor /akˈseləˌrātər/ ▶ *n.* something that brings about acceleration, in particular: ■ the device, typically a pedal, that controls the speed of a vehicle's engine. ■ *Physics* an apparatus for accelerating charged particles to high velocities. ■ a substance that speeds up a chemical process

ac·cel·er·om·e·ter /akˌseləˈrämitər/ ▶ *n.* an instrument for measuring acceleration.

ac·cent ▶ *n.* /ˈakˌsent/ **1** a distinctive mode of pronunciation of a language, esp. one associated with a particular nation, locality, or social class: *a German accent.* ■ the mode of pronunciation used by native speakers of a language: *she mastered the French accent.* **2** a distinct emphasis given to a syllable or word in speech by stress or pitch. ■ a mark on a letter or word to indicate pitch, stress, or vowel quality. ■ *Mus.* an emphasis on a particular note or chord. **3** a special or particular

emphasis: *the accent is on participation.* ■ a feature that gives a distinctive visual emphasis to something: *blue woodwork and accents of red.*
▶ *v.* /ˈakˌsent; akˈsent/ emphasize (a particular feature): *fabrics that accent the background colors in the room.* ■ *Mus.* play (a note, a beat of the bar, etc.) with an accent. —**ac·cen·tu·al** /akˈsenCHŌŌəl/ *adj.*

ac·cen·tu·ate /akˈsenCHŌŌˌāt/ ▶ *v.* [*tr.*] make more noticeable or prominent: *his jacket unfortunately accentuated his paunch.* —**ac·cen·tu·a·tion** /akˌsenCHŌŌˈāSHən/ *n.*

ac·cept /akˈsept/ ▶ *v.* [*tr.*] **1** consent to receive (a thing offered). ■ agree to undertake (an offered position or responsibility). ■ give an affirmative answer to (an offer or proposal); say yes to: *he would accept their offer* | [*intr.*] *Tim offered Brian a lift home and he accepted.* ■ receive as adequate, valid, or suitable: *the college accepted her* | *credit cards are widely accepted.* ■ regard favorably or with approval; welcome. ■ agree to meet (a draft or bill of exchange) by signing it. ■ (of a thing) be designed to allow (something) to be inserted or applied: *vending machines that accepted 100-yen coins.* **2** believe or come to recognize (an opinion, explanation, etc.) as valid or correct. ■ be prepared to subscribe to (a belief or philosophy): *accept the tenets of the Episcopalian faith.* ■ take upon oneself (a responsibility or liability); acknowledge. ■ tolerate or submit to (something unpleasant or undesired): *they accepted the need to cut expenses.*

ac·cept·a·ble /akˈseptəbəl/ ▶ *adj.* **1** able to be agreed on; suitable: *a solution acceptable to everyone.* ■ adequate; satisfactory: *an acceptable substitute.* ■ pleasing; welcome: *coffee would be most acceptable.* **2** able to be tolerated or allowed: *acceptable levels of lead.* —**ac·cept·a·bil·i·ty** /-ˌseptə-ˈbilitē/ *n.* —**ac·cept·a·ble·ness** *n.* —**ac·cept·a·bly** /-blē/ *adv.*

ac·cept·ance /akˈseptəns/ ▶ *n.* **1** the action of consenting to receive or undertake something offered. ■ agreement to meet a draft or bill of exchange, effected by signing it. ■ a draft or bill so accepted. **2** the action or process of being received as adequate or suitable, typically to be admitted into a group. **3** agreement with or belief in an idea, opinion, or explanation. ■ approval or favorable regard. ■ willingness to tolerate a difficult or unpleasant situation.

ac·cep·tor /akˈseptər/ ▶ *n.* a person or thing that accepts something, in particular: ■ a person or bank that accepts a draft or bill of exchange. ■ *Chem.* an atom or molecule that is able to bind to or accept an electron or other species.

ac·cess /ˈakˌses/ ▶ *n.* **1** a means of approaching or entering a place: *the staircase gives access to the top floor.* ■ the right or opportunity to use or benefit from something: *do you have access to a computer?* ■ the right or opportunity to approach or see someone: *we were denied access to our grandson.* ■ the action or process of obtaining or retrieving information stored in a computer's memory. ■ the condition of being able to be reached or obtained: *improving road access.* **2** an attack or outburst of an emotion: *an access of rage.*
▶ *v.* [*tr.*] (usu. **be accessed**) **1** *Comput.* obtain, examine, or retrieve (data or a file). **2** approach or enter (a place): *private baths accessed via the balcony.* **3** gain the right or opportunity to use or benefit from (something).

ac·ces·si·ble /akˈsesəbəl/ ▶ *adj.* **1** (of a place) able to be reached or entered: *the town is accessible by bus.* ■ (of an object, service, or facility) able to be easily obtained or used: *more accessible to children.* ■ easily understood: *accessible directions.* ■ able to be reached or entered by people in wheelchairs. **2** (of a person, typically one in a position of authority or importance) friendly and easy to talk to; approachable. —**ac·ces·si·bil·i·ty** /-ˌsesəˈbilitē/ *n.* —**ac·ces·si·bly** /-blē/ *adv.*

ac·ces·sion /akˈseSHən/ ▶ *n.* **1** the attainment or acquisition of a position of rank or power, typically that of monarch or president: *the queen's accession to the throne.* ■ the action or process of formally joining or being accepted by an association, institution, or group: *the accession of Spain into the European Community.* **2** a new item added to an existing collection of books, paintings, or artifacts. ■ an amount added to an existing quantity of something. **3** the formal acceptance of a treaty or agreement.
▶ *v.* [*tr.*] (usu. **be accessioned**) record the addition of (a new item) to a library, museum, or other collection.

ac·ces·so·rize /akˈsesəˌrīz/ ▶ *v.* [*tr.*] provide or complement (a garment) with fashion accessories. ■ serve as a fashion accessory to (a garment).

ac·ces·so·ry /akˈses(ə)rē/ ▶ *n.* (*pl.* **-ries**) **1** a thing that can be added to something else in order to make it more useful, versatile, or attractive: *bathroom accessories.* ■ a small article or item of clothing carried or worn to complement a garment or outfit: *hair accessories such as*

acanthus

---

rhinestone-studded barrettes. **2** *Law* someone who gives assistance to the perpetrator of a crime, without directly committing it, sometimes without being present: *an accessory to murder.*
▶*adj. chiefly technical* contributing to or aiding an activity or process in a minor way: *functionally the maxillae are a pair of accessory jaws.*

ac·cess pro·vid·er ▶*n.* another term for **SERVICE PROVIDER**.

ac·cess time ▶*n. Comput.* the time taken to retrieve data from storage.

ac·ciac·ca·tu·ra /ä,CHäkə'tŏŏrə/ ▶*n.* (*pl.* **-tu·ras** or **-tu·re** /-'tŏŏrā; -'tŏŏrē/) *Mus.* a grace note performed as quickly as possible before an essential note of a melody, and falling before the beat.

ac·ci·dent /'aksidənt/ ▶*n.* **1** an unfortunate incident that happens unexpectedly and unintentionally, typically resulting in damage or injury. ■ a crash involving road or other vehicles, typically one that causes serious damage or injury. ■ *inf.* used euphemistically to refer to an incidence of incontinence, typically by a child or an animal. **2** an event that happens by chance or that is without apparent or deliberate cause: *the pregnancy was an accident.* ■ the working of fortune; chance: *he came to Harvard largely through accident.*

ac·ci·den·tal /,aksi'dentl/ ▶*adj.* **1** happening by chance, unintentionally, or unexpectedly. **2** incidental; subsidiary.
▶*n.* **1** *Mus.* a sign raising or lowering a note. **2** *Ornithol.* another term for **VAGRANT**. —**ac·ci·den·tal·ly** *adv.*

ac·ci·dent-prone ▶*adj.* tending to be involved in a greater than average number of accidents.

ac·claim /ə'klām/ ▶*v.* praise enthusiastically and publicly: *the conference was acclaimed as a considerable success.*
▶*n.* enthusiastic and public praise: *she has won acclaim for her commitment to democracy.*

ac·cla·ma·tion /,aklə'māsHən/ ▶*n.* loud and enthusiastic approval, typically to welcome or honor someone or something:
▶ □ **by acclamation** (of election, agreement, etc.) by overwhelming vocal approval and without ballot.

ac·cli·mate /'aklə,māt; ə'klīmit/ ▶*v.* [*intr.*] (usu. **be acclimated**) become accustomed to a new climate or to new conditions: *getting acclimated to the altitude.* ■ *Biol.* respond physiologically or behaviorally to a change in a single environmental factor: *trees may acclimate to high CO$_2$ levels by reducing the number of stomata.* —**ac·cli·ma·tion** /,aklə'māsHən/ *n.*

ac·cli·ma·tize /ə'klīmə,tīz/ ▶*v.* [*intr.*] acclimate: *they acclimatized themselves before ascending Everest.* ■ *Biol.* respond physiologically or behaviorally to changes in a complex of environmental factors. —**ac·cli·ma·ti·za·tion** /ə,klīmətə'zāsHən/ *n.*

ac·cliv·i·ty /ə'klivitē/ ▶*n.* (*pl.* **-ties**) an upward slope. —**ac·cliv·i·tous** /-itəs/ *adj.*

ac·co·lade /'akə,lād; -,läd/ ▶*n.* **1** an award or privilege granted as a special honor or as an acknowledgment of merit. ■ an expression of praise or admiration. **2** a touch on a person's shoulders with a sword at the bestowing of a knighthood.

ac·com·mo·date /ə'kämə,dāt/ ▶*v.* [*tr.*] **1** (of physical space, esp. a building) provide lodging or sufficient space for: *the cabins accommodate up to 6 people.* **2** fit in with the wishes or needs of: *any language must accommodate new concepts.* ■ [*intr.*] (**accommodate to**) adapt to: *making consumers accommodate to the realities of today's marketplace.* —**ac·com·mo·da·tive** /-,dātiv/ *adj.*

ac·com·mo·dat·ing /ə'kämə,dātiNG/ ▶*adj.* fitting in with someone's wishes or demands in a helpful way. —**ac·com·mo·dat·ing·ly** *adv.*

ac·com·mo·da·tion /ə,kämə'dāsHən/ ▶*n.* **1** an action of accommodating or the process of being accommodated. ■ (usu. **accommodations**) a room, group of rooms, or building in which someone may live or stay. ■ (**accommodations**) lodging; room and board: *a number of guesthouse accommodations in Cape Cod.* ■ the available space for occupants in a building, vehicle, or vessel: *there was lifeboat accommodation for 1,178 people.* ■ the provision of a room or lodging: *the building is used exclusively for the accommodation of guests.* **2** a convenient arrangement; a settlement or compromise. ■ the process of adapting or adjusting to someone or something.

ac·com·pa·ni·ment /ə'kəmp(ə)nimənt/ ▶*n.* **1** a musical part that supports or partners a solo instrument, voice, or group: *she sang to a guitar accompaniment.* ■ music played to complement or as background to an activity: *lush string accompaniments to romantic scenes.* **2** something that is supplementary to or complements something else, typically food.

ac·com·pa·nist /ə'kəmpənist/ ▶*n.* a person who provides a musical accompaniment to another musician or to a singer.

ac·com·pa·ny /ə'kəmp(ə)nē/ ▶*v.* (**-nies, -nied**) [*tr.*] **1** go somewhere with (someone) as a companion or escort. **2** (usu. **be accompanied**) be present or occur at the same time as (something else): *the illness is often*

accompanied by nausea. ■ provide (something) as a complement or addition to something else: *ham accompanied by brown bread.* **3** play a musical accompaniment for.

ac·com·plice /ə'kämplis/ ▶*n.* a person who helps another commit a crime. ▷mid 16th cent.: alteration (probably by association with *accompany*) of Middle English *complice* 'an associate,' via Old French from late Latin *complex, complic-* 'allied,' from *com-* 'together' + the root of *plicare* 'to fold.'

ac·com·plish /ə'kämplisH/ ▶*v.* [*tr.*] achieve or complete successfully.

ac·com·plished /ə'kämplisHt/ ▶*adj.* highly trained or skilled: *an accomplished pianist.*

ac·com·plish·ment /ə'kämplisHmənt/ ▶*n.* something that has been achieved successfully. ■ the successful achievement of a task. ■ an activity that a person can do well, typically as a result of study or practice. ■ skill or ability in an activity: *a poet of considerable accomplishment.*

ac·cord /ə'kôrd/ ▶*v.* **1** [*tr.*] give or grant someone (power, status, or recognition): *the powers accorded to ahead of state.* **2** [*intr.*] (**accord with**) (of a concept or fact) be harmonious or consistent with.
▶*n.* an official agreement or treaty. ■ agreement or harmony: *the government and the rebels are in accord on one point.*
▶ □ **of its own accord** without outside intervention: *the rash may go away of its own accord.* □ **of one's own accord** voluntarily.

ac·cord·ance /ə'kôrdns/ ▶*n.* (in phrase **in accordance with**) in a manner conforming with: *the product is disposed of in accordance with federal regulations.*

ac·cord·ing /ə'kôrdiNG/ ▶*adv.* (**according to**) as stated by or in: *the outlook according to financial experts.* ■ in a manner corresponding or conforming to: *according to the directions.* ■ in proportion or relation to: *salary will be fixed according to experience.*

ac·cord·ing·ly /ə'kôrdiNGlē/ ▶*adv.* **1** in a way that is appropriate to the particular circumstances: *we'll read the plans and act accordingly.* **2** consequently; therefore.

ac·cor·di·on /ə'kôrdēən/ ▶*n.* a portable musical instrument with metal reeds blown by bellows, played by means of keys and buttons. ■ [as *adj.*] folding like the bellows of an accordion: *an accordion pleat.* —**ac·cor·di·on·ist** *n.*

accordion

ac·cor·di·on sched·ul·ing ▶*n.* the practice of continually adjusting the work schedule of part-time or temporary workers to accommodate a company's changing labor requirements.

ac·cost /ə'kôst; ə'käst/ ▶*v.* [*tr.*] approach and address (someone) boldly or aggressively. ■ approach (someone) with hostility or harmful intent. ■ approach and address (someone) with sexual intent.

ac·count /ə'kount/ ▶*n.* **1** a report or description of an event or experience. ■ an interpretation or rendering of a piece of music. **2** a record or statement of financial expenditure or receipts relating to a particular period or purpose. ■ the department of a company that deals with such records. **3** an arrangement by which a body holds funds on behalf of a client or supplies goods or services to the client on credit: *a bank account* | *buying things on account.* ■ the balance of funds held under such an arrangement: *I wanted to get some money from the ATM and check my account.* ■ a client having such an arrangement with a supplier: *selling bibles to established accounts in the North.* ■ a contract to do work periodically for a client. **4** importance: *money was of no account to her.*
▶*v.* [*tr.*] consider or regard in a specified way: *her visit could not be accounted a success.*
▶*phrasal v.* **account for 1** give a satisfactory record of (something, typically money, that one is responsible for). ■ provide or serve as a satisfactory explanation or reason for. ■ (usu. **be accounted for**) know the fate or whereabouts of (someone or something), esp. after an accident: *everyone was accounted for after the floods.* **2** supply or make up a specified amount or proportion of: *social security accounts for about a third of total public spending.*
▶ □ **on someone's account** for a specified person's benefit: *don't bother on my account.* □ **on account of** because of. □ **take something into**

account (or **take account of**) consider a specified thing along with other factors before reaching a decision or taking action.

ac·count·a·ble /əˈkountəbəl/ ▶*adj.* **1** (of a person, organization, or institution) required or expected to justify actions or decisions; responsible: *a government accountable to its citizens* | *parents held accountable for their children's actions.* **2** explicable; understandable: *the wry dialogue is not accountable until the third chapter.* —**ac·count·a·bil·i·ty** /ə,kountəˈbilitē/ *n.* —**ac·count·a·bly** /-blē/ *adv.*

ac·count·an·cy /əˈkount(ə)nsē/ ▶*n.* the profession or duties of an accountant.

ac·count·ant /əˈkount(ə)nt/ (abbr.: **acct.**) ▶*n.* a person whose job is to keep or inspect financial accounts. ▷Middle English: from legal French, present participle of Old French *aconter* 'to count,' based on *conter* 'to count' (from Latin *computare* 'to calculate'). The original use was as an adjective meaning 'liable to give an account,' hence denoting a person who must do so.

ac·count·ing /əˈkountiNG/ ▶*n.* the action or process of keeping financial accounts.

ac·cou·tre·ment /əˈkŌŌtərmənt; -trə-/ (also **ac·cou·ter·ment**) ▶*n.* (usu. **accoutrements**) additional items of dress or equipment, or other items carried or worn by a person or used for a particular activity: *the accoutrements of religious ritual.* ■ a soldier's outfit other than weapons and garments.

ac·cred·it /əˈkredit/ ▶*v.* (**-it·ed, -it·ing**) **1** give credit (to someone) for: *accredited with being our leading citizen.* ■ attribute (an action, saying, or quality) to: *the discovery of distillation is usually accredited to the Arabs.* **2** (of an official body) give authority or sanction to (someone or something) when recognized standards have been met: *institutions that do not meet the standards will not be accredited for teacher training.* **3** give official authorization for (someone, typically a diplomat or journalist) to be in a particular place or to hold a particular post: *ambassadors accredited to Baghdad.* —**ac·cred·i·ta·tion** /ə,krediˈtāSHən/ *n.*

ac·cred·it·ed /əˈkreditid/ ▶*adj.* (of a person, organization, or course of study) officially recognized or authorized.

ac·crete /əˈkrēt/ ▶*v.* [*intr.*] grow by accumulation or coalescence: *the ice had accreted into stalactites.* ■ [*tr.*] form (a composite whole or a collection of things) by gradual accumulation.

ac·cre·tion /əˈkrēSHən/ ▶*n.* the process of growth or increase, typically by the gradual accumulation of additional layers or matter. ■ a thing formed or added by such growth or increase. —**ac·cre·tive** /əˈkrētiv/ *adj.*

ac·crue /əˈkrŌŌ/ ▶*v.* (**-crues, -crued, -cru·ing**) [*intr.*] (of sums of money or benefits) be received by someone in regular or increasing amounts over time: *savings will accrue from restructuring* | [as *adj.*] (**accrued**) *accrued interest.* ■ [*tr.*] accumulate or receive (such payments or benefits). ■ [*tr.*] make provision for (a charge) at the end of a financial period for work that has been done but not yet invoiced. —**ac·cru·al** /əˈkrŌŌəl/ *n.*

ac·cul·tur·ate /əˈkəlCHə,rāt/ ▶*v.* assimilate or cause to assimilate a different culture, typically the dominant one: [*intr.*] *he has acculturated to the U.S.* [*tr.*] *the weeks spent acculturating the staff.* —**ac·cul·tur·a·tion** /ə,kəlCHəˈrāSHən/ *n.* —**ac·cul·tur·a·tive** /-ərativ/ *adj.*

ac·cu·mu·late /əˈkyŌŌmyə,lāt/ ▶*v.* [*tr.*] gather together or acquire an increasing number or quantity of: *accumulating evidence.* ■ gradually gather or acquire (a resulting whole): *accumulate a fortune.* ■ [*intr.*] gather or build up: *the toxins accumulate in the brain.*

ac·cu·mu·la·tion /ə,kyŌŌmyəˈlāSHən/ ▶*n.* the acquisition or gradual gathering of something: *the accumulation of wealth.* ■ a mass or quantity of something that has gradually gathered or been acquired. ■ the growth of a sum of money by the regular addition of interest.

ac·cu·mu·la·tive /əˈkyŌŌmyələtiv; -,lātiv/ ▶*adj.* gathering or growing by gradual increases: *the accumulative effects of pollution.*

ac·cu·mu·la·tor /əˈkyŌŌmyə,lātər/ ▶*n.* a person or thing that accumulates things: *accumulator of capital.* ■ *Comput.* a register used to contain the results of an arithmetical or logical operation.

ac·cu·ra·cy /ˈakyərəsē/ ▶*n.* (*pl.* **-cies**) the quality or state of being correct or precise. ■ the ability to perform a task with precision. ■ *technical* the degree to which the result of a measurement, calculation, or specification conforms to the correct value or a standard: *the accuracy of radiocarbon dating.*

ac·cu·rate /ˈakyərit/ ▶*adj.* **1** (of information, measurements, statistics, etc.) correct in all details; exact. ■ (of an instrument or method) capable of giving such information. ■ (of a piece of work) meticulously careful and free from errors. ■ faithfully or fairly representing the truth about someone or something: *an accurate likeness of Mozart.* **2** (of a weapon or the person using it) capable of reaching the intended target. ■ (of a shot or throw, or the person making it) successful in reaching a target. —**ac·cu·rate·ly** *adv.*

ac·curs·ed /əˈkərst; əˈkərsid/ ▶*adj.* **1** *poetic/lit.* under a curse. **2** *inf., dated* used to express strong dislike of or anger toward someone or something: *those accursed books!*

ac·cu·sa·tion /,akyəˈzāSHən; ,akyŌŌ-/ ▶*n.* a charge or claim that someone has done something illegal or wrong. ■ the action or process of making such a charge or claim.

ac·cu·sa·tive /əˈkyŌŌzətiv/ *Gram.* ▶*adj.* relating to or denoting a case of nouns, pronouns, and adjectives that expresses the object of an action or the goal of motion.

▶*n.* a word in the accusative case. ■ (**the accusative**) the accusative case.

ac·cu·sa·to·ri·al /ə,kyŌŌzəˈtôrēəl/ ▶*adj.* *Law* (esp. of a trial or legal procedure) involving accusation by a prosecutor and a verdict reached by an impartial judge or jury.

ac·cu·sa·to·ry /əˈkyŌŌzə,tôrē/ ▶*adj.* indicating or suggesting that one believes a person has done something wrong: *pointing an accusatory finger.*

ac·cuse /əˈkyŌŌz/ ▶*v.* charge (someone) with an offense or crime: *accused of murder.* ■ claim that (someone) has done something wrong. —**ac·cus·er** *n.*

ac·cus·tom /əˈkəstəm/ ▶*v.* [*tr.*] make (someone or something) accept something as normal or usual: *tried to accustom him to their ways.* ■ (**be accustomed to**) be used to: *my eyes became accustomed to the darkness.*

ac·cus·tomed /əˈkəstəmd/ ▶*adj.* customary or usual: *his accustomed route.*

ACE ▶*abbr.* Army Corps of Engineers.

ace /ās/ ▶*n.* **1** a playing card with a single spot on it, ranked as the highest card in its suit in most card games: *the ace of diamonds.* ■ *informal Golf* a hole in one. **2** *inf.* a person who excels at a particular sport or other activity: *a motorcycle ace.* ■ a pilot who has shot down many enemy aircraft, esp. in World War I or World War II. **3** (in tennis and similar games) a service that an opponent is unable to return and thus wins a point.

▶*adj. inf.* very good: *an ace swimmer.*

▶*v.* [*tr.*] *inf.* (in tennis and similar games) serve an ace against (an opponent). ■ *Golf* score an ace on (a hole) or with (a shot). ■ get an A or its equivalent in (a test or exam): *I aced my grammar test.* ■ (**ace someone out**) outdo someone in a competitive situation.

▶ □ **an ace up one's sleeve** (or **in the hole**) a plan or piece of information kept secret until it becomes necessary to use it. □ **hold all the aces** have all the advantages. □ **play one's ace** use one's best, often secret, resource.

a·ce·di·a /əˈsēdēə/ ▶*n.* spiritual or mental sloth; apathy.

a·cel·lu·lar /āˈselyələr/ ▶*adj.* *Biol.* not consisting of, divided into, or containing cells. ■ (esp. of protozoa) consisting of one cell only.

a·ceph·a·lous /āˈsefələs/ ▶*adj.* *Zool.* not having a head. ■ having no leader or chief: *an acephalous society.*

a·cer·bic /əˈsərbik/ ▶*adj.* **1** (esp. of a comment or style of speaking) sharp and forthright: *his acerbic wit.* **2** *archaic* or *technical* tasting sour or bitter. —**a·cer·bi·cal·ly** *adv.* —**a·cer·bi·ty** /-bitē/ *n.*

ac·e·tab·u·lum /,asiˈtabyələm/ ▶*n.* (*pl.* **-la** /-lə/) *Anat.* the socket of the hipbone, into which the head of the femur fits.

a·ce·ta·min·o·phen /ə,sētəˈminəfən/ ▶*n.* an analgesic drug, $C_8H_9NO_2$, used to treat headaches, arthritis, etc., and also to reduce fever.

ac·e·tate /ˈasi,tāt/ ▶*n.* **1** *Chem.* a salt or ester of acetic acid. **2** cellulose acetate, esp. as used to make textile fibers or plastic. ■ a transparency made of cellulose acetate film. ■ a recording disk coated with cellulose acetate.

a·ce·tic /əˈsētik/ ▶*adj.* of or like vinegar or acetic acid.

ac·e·tone /ˈasi,tōn/ ▶*n.* *Chem.* a colorless volatile liquid ketone used as an organic solvent and synthetic reagent.

a·ce·tous /əˈsētəs; ˈasitəs/ ▶*adj.* producing or resembling vinegar: *acetous fermentation.*

a·ce·tyl·cho·line /ə,sētlˈkō,lēn; ,asitl-/ ▶*n.* *Biochem.* a compound that occurs throughout the nervous system, in which it functions as a neurotransmitter.

a·cet·y·lene /əˈsetlən; -,ēn/ ▶*n.* *Chem.* a colorless pungent-smelling hydrocarbon gas (C_2H_2), which burns with a bright flame, used in welding and formerly in lighting.

ACH ▶*abbr.* Automated Clearinghouse.

A·chae·an /əˈkēən/ ▶*adj.* of or relating to Achaea in ancient Greece. ■ (esp. in Homeric contexts) Greek.

▶*n.* an inhabitant of Achaea. ■ (esp. in Homeric contexts) a Greek.

Pronunciation Key ə *ago, up;* ər *over, fur;* a *hat;* ā *ate;* ä *car;* CH *chin;* e *let;* ē *see;* e(ə)r *air;* i *fit;* ī *by;* i(ə)r *ear;* NG *sing;* ō *go;* ô *law, for;* oi *toy;* ŌŌ *good;* ŌŌ *goo;* ou *out;* SH *she;* TH *thin;* <u>TH</u> *then;* (h)w *why;* ZH *vision*

ache /āk/ ▸*n.* a continuous or prolonged dull pain in a part of one's body. ▪ *fig.* an emotion experienced with painful or bittersweet intensity: *an ache in her heart.*
▸*v.* [*intr.*] **1** (of a person) suffer from a continuous dull pain: *I'm aching all over.* ▪ (of a part of one's body) be the source of such a pain. ▪ *fig.* feel intense sadness or compassion: *she looked so tired that my heart ached for her.* **2** feel an intense desire for: *she ached for his touch.* ▹Old English *æce* (noun), *acan* (verb). The modern spelling is largely due to Dr. Johnson, who mistakenly assumed its derivation to be from Greek *akhos* 'pain.' **—ach·ing·ly** *adv.*

a·chene /ā'kēn/ ▸*n. Bot.* a small, dry, one-seeded fruit that does not open to release the seed.

a·chieve /ə'CHēv/ ▸*v.* [*tr.*] reach or attain (a desired objective, level, or result) by effort, skill, or courage: *he achieved his ambition to become a journalist* | [*intr.*] *people striving to achieve.* ▪ accomplish or bring about: *the communist system achieved a basic economic modernization.* **—a·chiev·a·ble** *adj.* **—a·chiev·er** *n.*

a·chieve·ment /ə'CHēvmənt/ ▸*n.* **1** a thing done successfully, typically by effort, courage, or skill: *to reach this stage is a great achievement.* **2** the process or fact of achieving something. ▪ a child's or student's progress in a course of learning, typically as measured by standardized tests or objectives.

ach·y /'ākē/ ▸*adj.* suffering from continuous dull pain.

ac·id /'asid/ ▸*n.* a chemical substance that neutralizes alkalis, dissolves some metals, and turns litmus red; typically, a corrosive or sour-tasting liquid of this kind. Often contrasted with **ALKALI** or **BASE**[1]. ▪ *fig.* bitter or cutting remarks or tone of voice. ▪ *inf.* the drug LSD. ▪ *Chem.* a molecule or other entity that can donate a proton or accept an electron pair in reactions.
▸*adj.* **1** containing acid or having the properties of an acid; in particular, having a pH of less than 7: *poor, acid soils.* **2** sharp-tasting or sour: *acid fruit.* ▪ (of a person's remarks or tone) bitter or cutting. ▪ (of a color) intense or bright: *an acid green.* **—ac·id·ly** *adv.* **—ac·id·y** *adj.*

ac·id·head /'asid,hed/ ▸*n. inf.* a habitual user of the drug LSD.

a·cid·i·fy /ə'sidə,fī/ ▸*v.* (**-fies, -fied**) make or become acid: [*tr.*] *pollutants can acidify surface water* | [*intr.*] *the paper was acidifying.* **—a·cid·i·fi·ca·tion** /ə,sidəfi'kāSHən/ *n.*

a·cid·i·ty /ə'siditē/ ▸*n.* **1** the level of acid in substances such as soil or wine. ▪ such a level in the gastric juices, typically when excessive. **2** the bitterness or sharpness of a person's remarks or tone. **—a·cid·ic** *adj.*

ac·id rain ▸*n.* rainfall made sufficiently acidic by atmospheric pollution that it causes environmental harm, typically to forests and lakes.

ac·id re·flux ▸*n.* a condition in which gastric acid is regurgitated.

ac·id test ▸*n.* a conclusive test of the success or value of something: *the pact with the rebels is an acid test of the government's sincerity.*

a·cid·u·late /ə'sijə,lāt/ ▸*v.* [*tr.*] [usu. as *adj.*] (**acidulated**) make slightly acidic: *acidulated water.* **—a·cid·u·la·tion** /ə,sijə'lāSHən/ *n.*

a·cid·u·lous /ə'sijələs/ ▸*adj.* sharp-tasting or sour. ▪ (of a person's remarks or tone) bitter or cutting.

ac·i·nus /'asənəs/ ▸*n.* (*pl.* **-ni** /-,nī/) *Anat.* **1** a small saclike cavity in a gland, surrounded by secretory cells. **2** a region of the lung supplied with air from one of the terminal bronchioles.

ack-ack /'ak ,ak/ *informal* ▸*n.* an antiaircraft gun. ▪ antiaircraft gunfire.

ac·knowl·edge /ak'nälij/ ▸*v.* [*tr.*] **1** accept or admit the existence or truth of: *the plight of the refugees was acknowledged by the authorities.* **2** (of a body of opinion) recognize the fact or importance or quality of: *the art world has begun to acknowledge his genius.* ▪ express or display gratitude for or appreciation of: *he received a letter acknowledging his services.* ▪ accept the validity or legitimacy of: *Henry acknowledged Richard as his heir.* **3** show that one has noticed or recognized (someone) by making a gesture or greeting: *she refused to acknowledge my presence.* ▪ confirm (receipt of something).

ac·knowl·edg·ment /ak'nälijmənt/ (also **ac·knowl·edge·ment**) ▸*n.* **1** acceptance of the truth or existence of something. **2** the action of expressing or displaying gratitude or appreciation for something: *an award in acknowledgment of his work.* ▪ the action of showing that one has noticed someone or something: *he touched his hat in acknowledgment of the salute.* ▪ a letter confirming receipt of something. **3** (usu. **acknowledgments**) an author's or publisher's statement of indebtedness to others, typically one printed at the beginning of a book.

ACLU ▸*abbr.* American Civil Liberties Union.

ac·me /'akmē/ ▸*n.* the point at which someone or something is best, perfect, or most successful: *physics is the acme of scientific knowledge.*

ac·ne /'aknē/ ▸*n.* the occurrence of inflamed or infected sebaceous glands in the skin; in particular, a condition characterized by red pimples on the face, prevalent chiefly among teenagers. **—ac·ned** *adj.*

ac·o·lyte /'akə,līt/ ▸*n.* a person assisting the celebrant in a religious service or procession. ▪ an assistant or follower.

ac·o·nite /'akə,nīt/ ▸*n.* a poisonous plant (genus *Aconitum*) of the buttercup family, including monkshood. Native to temperate regions of the northern hemisphere, it bears hooded pink or purple flowers. ▪ an extract of such a plant, used as a poison or in medicinal preparations.

a·corn /'ā,kôrn/ ▸*n.* the fruit of the oak, a smooth oval nut in a rough cuplike base.

a·cot·y·le·don /,äkätl'ēdn/ ▸*n.* a plant with no distinct seed-leaves, esp. a fern or moss. **—a·cot·y·le·don·ous** *adj.*

a·cous·tic /ə'ko͞ostik/ ▸*adj.* **1** relating to sound or the sense of hearing: *dogs have a much greater acoustic range than humans.* ▪ (of building materials) used for soundproofing or modifying sound: *acoustic tiles.* ▪ (of an explosive mine or other weapon) able to be set off by sound waves. **2** (of music or musical instruments) not having electrical amplification: *acoustic guitar.*
▸*n.* **1** (usu. **acoustics**) the properties or qualities of a room or building that determine how sound is transmitted in it. ▪ (**acoustic**) the acoustic properties or ambience of a sound recording or of a recording studio. **2** (**acoustics**) [treated as *sing.*] the branch of physics concerned with the properties of sound. **—a·cous·ti·cal** *adj.* **—a·cous·ti·cal·ly** /-ik(ə)lē/ *adv.*

ac·quaint /ə'kwānt/ ▸*v.* [*tr.*] (**acquaint someone with**) make someone aware of or familiar with: *you need to acquaint yourself with the house style.* ▪ (**be acquainted**) be an acquaintance: *I am not acquainted with any young lady of that name* | *I'll leave you two to get acquainted.*

ac·quaint·ance /ə'kwāntns/ ▸*n.* **1** a person's knowledge or experience of something: *acquaintance with the language.* ▪ one's slight knowledge of or friendship with someone: *my acquaintance with Herbert* | *the men of her acquaintance.* **2** a person one knows slightly, but who is not a close friend. ▪ such people considered collectively: *his extensive acquaintance included Oscar Wilde and Yeats.*

ac·qui·esce /,akwē'es/ ▸*v.* [*intr.*] accept something reluctantly but without protest. **—ac·qui·es·cence** /-'esəns/ *n.* **—ac·qui·es·cent** /,akwē-'esənt/ *adj.*

ac·quire /ə'kwī(ə)r/ ▸*v.* [*tr.*] buy or obtain (an object or asset) for oneself. ▪ learn or develop (a skill, habit, or quality). ▪ achieve (a particular reputation) as a result of one's behavior or activities. **—ac·quir·a·ble** *adj.* **—ac·quire·ment** *n.* **—ac·quir·er** *n.*

ac·qui·si·tion /,akwə'ziSHən/ ▸*n.* **1** an asset or object bought or obtained, typically by a library or museum. ▪ an act of purchase of one company by another. ▪ buying or obtaining an asset or object: *Western culture places a high value on material acquisition.* **2** the learning or developing of a skill, habit, or quality: *the acquisition of management skills.*

ac·quis·i·tive /ə'kwizitiv/ ▸*adj.* excessively interested in acquiring money or material things. **—ac·quis·i·tive·ly** *adv.* **—ac·quis·i·tive·ness** *n.*

ac·quit /ə'kwit/ ▸*v.* (**-quit·ted, -quit·ting**) **1** [*tr.*] (usu. **be acquitted**) free (someone) from a criminal charge by a verdict of not guilty: *she was acquitted on all counts.* **2** (**acquit oneself**) conduct oneself or perform in a specified way. ▪ (**acquit oneself of**) *archaic* discharge (a duty or responsibility): *they acquitted themselves of their charge with vigilance.*

ac·quit·tal /ə'kwitl/ ▸*n.* a judgment that a person is not guilty of the crime with which the person has been charged.

a·cre /'ākər/ ▸*n.* a unit of land area equal to 4,840 square yards (0.405 hectare). ▪ (**acres of**) *inf.* a large extent or amount of something.

a·cre·age /'āk(ə)rij/ ▸*n.* an area of land, typically when used for agricultural purposes, but not necessarily measured in acres.

ac·rid /'akrid/ ▸*adj.* having an irritatingly strong and unpleasant taste or smell: *acrid fumes.* ▪ angry and bitter: *an acrid farewell.* **—a·crid·i·ty** /ə-'kriditē/ *n.* **—ac·rid·ly** *adv.*

ac·ri·mo·ni·ous /,akrə'mōnēəs/ ▸*adj.* (typically of speech or a debate) angry and bitter. **—ac·ri·mo·ni·ous·ly** *adv.*

ac·ri·mo·ny /'akrə,mōnē/ ▸*n.* bitterness or ill feeling.

ac·ro·bat /'akrə,bat/ ▸*n.* **1** an entertainer who performs gymnastic feats. **2** a person noted for constant change of mind, allegiance, etc.

ac·ro·bat·ic /,akrə'batik/ ▸*adj.* performing, involving, or adept at spectacular gymnastic feats: *an acrobatic dive.* **—ac·ro·bat·i·cal·ly** /-ik(ə)lē/ *adv.*

ac·ro·bat·ics /,akrə'batiks/ ▸*pl. n.* [usu. treated as *sing.*] *fig.* gymnastic feats: *goes through financial acrobatics to make the monthly payments.*

ac·ro·nym /ˈakrəˌnim/ ▸*n.* a word formed from the initial letters of other words (e.g., *radar, laser*).

ac·ro·pho·bi·a /ˌakrəˈfōbēə/ ▸*n.* extreme or irrational fear of heights. —**ac·ro·pho·bic** /-ˈfōbik/ *adj.* & *n.*

a·crop·o·lis /əˈkräpəlis/ ▸*n.* a citadel or fortified part of an ancient Greek city, typically built on a hill. ▪ (**the Acropolis**) the ancient citadel at Athens, containing the Parthenon and other notable buildings.

a·cross /əˈkrôs; əˈkräs/ ▸*prep.* & *adv.* from one side to the other of (something): ▪ expressing movement over a place or region: *I ran across the street* | [as *adv.*] *he had swum across.* ▪ expressing position or orientation: *the bridge across the river* | [as *adv.*] *he looked across at me.* ▪ [as *adv.*] used with an expression of measurement: *can grow to 4 feet across.* ▪ [as *adv.*] with reference to a crossword puzzle answer that reads horizontally: *19 across.*
▸ □ **across the board** applying to all: *the cutbacks might be across the board.*

a·cros·tic /əˈkrôstik; əˈkräs-/ ▸*n.* a poem, word puzzle, or other composition in which certain letters in each line form a word or words.

a·cryl·ic /əˈkrilik/ ▸*adj.* (of synthetic resins and textile fibers) made from polymers of acrylic acid. ▪ of, relating to, or denoting paints based on acrylic resin as a medium.
▸*n.* **1** an acrylic textile fiber. **2** (often **acrylics**) an acrylic paint.

ACT ▸*abbr.* ▪ American College Test. ▪ Australian Capital Territory.

act /akt/ ▸*v.* [*intr.*] **1** take action; do something: *they urged Washington to act.* ▪ (**act on**) take action according to or in the light of: *I shall certainly act on his suggestion.* ▪ (**act for**) take action in order to bring about: *one's ability to act for community change.* ▪ (**act for/on behalf of**) represent (someone) on a contractual, legal, or paid basis: *he chose an attorney to act for him.* ▪ (**act from/out of**) be motivated by: *you acted from greed.* **2** behave in the way specified: *the man who was acting suspiciously.* ▪ (**act as/like**) behave in the manner of: *try to act like civilized adults.* **3** (**act as**) fulfill the function or serve the purpose of: *they need volunteers to act as foster parents.* ▪ have the effect of: *a five-year sentence will act as a deterrent.* **4** take effect; have a particular effect: *bacteria* **act on** *proteins and sugar.* **5** perform a fictional role in a play, movie, or television production: *she acted in her first professional role at the age of six.* ▪ [*tr.*] perform (a part or role). ▪ behave so as to appear to be; pretend to be: *I acted dumb at first.* ▪ [*tr.*] (**act something out**) perform a narrative as if it were a play: *encouraging students to act out the stories.* ▪ [*tr.*] (**act something out**) *Psychoanalysis* express repressed or unconscious feelings in overt behavior.
▸*phrasal v.* □ **act out** misbehave, esp. when unhappy or stressed. □ **act up** (of a thing) fail to function properly. ▪ (of a person) misbehave.
▸*n.* **1** a thing done; a deed: *a criminal act.* **2** a pretense: *she was* **putting on an act** *and laughing a lot.* ▪ a particular type of behavior or routine: *he did his Sir Galahad act.* **3** *Law* a written ordinance of Congress, or another legislative body; a statute: *the act to abolish slavery.* ▪ a document attesting a legal transaction. ▪ (often **acts**) *dated* the recorded decisions or proceedings of a committee or an academic body. **4** a main division of a play, ballet, or opera. ▪ a set performance: *her one-woman poetry act.* ▪ a performing group: *a sisters act.*
▸ □ **act of God** an instance of uncontrollable natural forces in operation (often used in insurance claims).

act·ing /ˈakting/ ▸*n.* the art or occupation of performing in plays, movies, or television productions: *she studied acting in New York.*
▸*adj.* temporarily doing the duties of another person: *acting director.*

ac·ti·nide /ˈaktəˌnīd/ ▸*n. Chem.* any of the series of fifteen metallic elements from actinium (atomic number 89) to lawrencium (atomic number 103) in the periodic table. They are all radioactive, the heavier members being extremely unstable and not of natural occurrence.

ac·tin·i·um /akˈtinēəm/ ▸*n.* the chemical element of atomic number 89, a radioactive metallic element of the actinide series. It is rare in nature, occurring as an impurity in uranium ores. (Symbol: **Ac**)

ac·ti·nom·e·ter /ˌaktəˈnämitər/ ▸*n. Physics* an instrument for measuring the intensity of radiation, typically ultraviolet radiation.

ac·tin·o·mor·phic /ˌaktənōˈmôrfik/ ▸*adj. Biol.* characterized by radial symmetry, such as a starfish or the flower of a daisy. —**ac·tin·o·mor·phy** /akˈtinəˌmôrfē/ *n.*

ac·tion /ˈakshən/ ▸*n.* **1** the fact or process of doing something, typically to achieve an aim: *demanding tougher action against terrorism* | *if there is a breach of regulations, we will* **take action**. ▪ the way in which something such as a chemical has an effect or influence: *the seeds require the catalytic action of water to release hotness.* ▪ armed conflict: *servicemen listed as* **missing in action** *during the war.* ▪ a military engagement: *a rearguard action.* ▪ the events represented in a story or play: *the action is set in the country.* ▪ *inf.* exciting or notable activity: *people in the media want to be where the action is.* ▪ *inf.* betting. ▪ [as *interj.*] used by a movie director as a command to begin: *lights, camera, action!* **2** a thing done; an act: *she frequently questioned his actions.* ▪ a legal process; a lawsuit. ▪ a gesture or movement: *his actions emphasized his words.* **3** a manner or style of doing something, typically the way in which a mechanism works or a person moves: *a high paddle action in canoeing.* ▪ the mechanism that makes a machine or instrument work: *a piano with an escapement action.*

ac·tion·a·ble /ˈakshənəbəl/ ▸*adj. Law* giving sufficient reason to take legal action: *slanderous remarks are actionable.*

ac·ti·vate /ˈaktəˌvāt/ ▸*v.* [*tr.*] make (something) active or operative. ▪ convert (a substance, molecule, etc.) into a reactive form. —**ac·ti·va·tion** /ˌaktəˈvāshən/ *n.* —**ac·ti·va·tor** /-ˌvātər/ *n.*

ac·tive /ˈaktiv/ ▸*adj.* **1** (of a person) engaging or ready to engage in physically energetic pursuits. ▪ moving or tending to move about vigorously or frequently: *active fish need a larger tank.* ▪ characterized by energetic activity: *they enjoyed an active social life.* ▪ (of a person's mind or imagination) alert and lively. **2** doing things for an organization, cause, or campaign, rather than simply giving it one's support: *she was* **active in** *the affairs of the institute.* ▪ (of a person) participating or engaged in a particular sphere or activity: *a politically active student body.* ▪ (of a person or animal) pursuing their usual occupation or activity, typically at a particular place or time: *tigers are active mainly at night.* **3** working; operative: *the mill was active until 1960.* ▪ (of a bank account) in continuous use. ▪ (of an electrical circuit) capable of modifying its state or characteristics automatically in response to input or feedback. ▪ (of a volcano) currently erupting, or that has erupted within historical times. ▪ (of a disease) in which the symptoms are manifest; not in remission or latent. ▪ having a chemical or biological effect on something: *350 active ingredients have been banned from pesticides.* **4** *Gram.* relating to or denoting the voice that attributes the action of a verb to the person or thing from which it logically proceeds (e.g., of the verbs in *guns kill* and *we saw him*). The opposite of **PASSIVE**.
▸*n. Gram.* an active form of a verb. ▪ (**the active**) the active voice. —**ac·tive·ly** *adv.*

active barrier ▸*n.* a barrier that allows passage of defined agents while preventing or impeding others, in particular: ▪ a security barrier that responds to attempted entries with sensors or personnel. ▪ a physical or chemical barrier that intercepts contaminants or other unwanted substances.

ac·tiv·ism /ˈaktəˌvizəm/ ▸*n.* the policy or action of using vigorous campaigning to bring about political or social change. —**ac·tiv·ist** *n.*

ac·tiv·i·ty /akˈtivitē/ ▸*n.* (*pl.* **-ties**) **1** the condition in which things are happening or being done: *a sustained level of activity in the economy* ▪ busy or vigorous action or movement: *the room was a* **hive of activity**. **2** (usu. **activities**) a thing that a person or group does or has done. ▪ a recreational pursuit or pastime: *a range of sports activities.* ▪ (**activities**) actions taken by a group in order to achieve their aims: *investigating anarchist activities.* **3** the degree to which something displays its characteristic property or behavior: *abnormal liver enzyme activities.* ▪ *Chem.* a thermodynamic quantity representing the effective concentration of a particular component in a solution or other system, equal to its concentration multiplied by an **activity coefficient**.

ac·tor /ˈaktər/ ▸*n.* a person whose profession is acting on the stage, in movies, or on television. ▪ a person who behaves in a way that is not genuine: *in war one must be a good actor.* ▪ a participant in an action or process. ▷late Middle English (originally denoting an agent or administrator): from Latin, 'doer, actor,' from *agere* 'do, act.' The theater sense dates from the 16th cent.

ac·tress /ˈaktris/ ▸*n.* a female actor.

ac·tu·al /ˈakchōōəl/ ▸*adj.* **1** existing in fact; typically as contrasted with what was intended, expected, or believed: *the estimate was less than the actual cost.* ▪ used to emphasize the important aspect of something: *the book could be condensed into half the space, but what of the actual content?* **2** existing now; current: *using actual income to measure expected income.*

ac·tu·al·i·ty /ˌakchōōˈalitē/ ▸*n.* (*pl.* **-ties**) actual existence, typically as contrasted with what was intended, expected, or believed: *the building looked as impressive* **in actuality** *as it did in magazines.* ▪ (**actualities**) existing conditions or facts: *the grim actualities of prison life.*

ac·tu·al·ly /ˈakchōōəlē/ ▸*adv.* **1** as the truth or facts of a situation; really: *the time actually worked on a job.* **2** used to emphasize that something someone has said or done is surprising: *he actually expected me to be* *pleased about it!* ■ used when expressing an opinion, typically one that is not expected: *"Actually," she said icily, "I don't care who you go out with."* ■ used when expressing a contradictory opinion or correcting someone: *"Tom seems to be happy." "He isn't, actually, not any more."* ■ used to introduce a new topic or to add information to a previous statement: *he had a Brooklyn accent—he sounded like my grandfather actually.*

ac·tu·ar·y /ˈakchoō,erē/ ▶ *n.* (*pl.* **-ar·ies**) a person who compiles and analyzes statistics and uses them to calculate insurance risks and premiums. —**ac·tu·ar·i·al** /ˌakchoō'e(ə)rēəl/ *adj.* —**ac·tu·ar·i·al·ly** *adv.*

ac·tu·ate /ˈakchoō,āt/ ▶ *v.* **1** [*tr.*] cause (a machine or device) to operate: *the pendulum actuates an electrical switch.* **2** (usu. **be actuated**) cause (someone) to act in a particular way; motivate: *the defendants were actuated by malice.* —**ac·tu·a·tion** /ˌakchoō'āshən/ *n.* —**ac·tu·a·tor** /-ˈātər/ *n.*

a·cu·i·ty /ə'kyoōitē/ ▶ *n.* sharpness or keenness of thought, vision, or hearing: *intellectual acuity | visual acuity.*

a·cu·men /ə'kyoōmən; 'akyə-/ ▶ *n.* the ability to make good judgments and quick decisions, typically in a particular domain: *business acumen.*

a·cu·mi·nate /ə'kyoōmənit; -,nāt/ ▶ *adj. Biol.* (of a plant or animal structure, e.g., a leaf) tapering to a point.

ac·u·pres·sure /ˈakyə,preshər/ ▶ *n.* another term for SHIATSU.

ac·u·punc·ture /ˈakyə,pəNGkchər/ ▶ *n.* a system of complementary medicine that involves pricking the skin or tissues with needles, used to alleviate pain and to treat various conditions. —**ac·u·punc·tur·ist** /-ist/ *n.*

a·cute /ə'kyoōt/ ▶ *adj.* **1** (of a bad, difficult, or unwelcome situation or phenomenon) present or experienced to a severe or intense degree: *an acute housing shortage.* ■ (of a disease or its symptoms) of short duration but typically severe: *acute appendicitis.* ■ denoting or designed for patients with such conditions: *acute hospital services.* **2** having or showing a perceptive understanding or insight; shrewd: *an acute awareness of changing fashions.* ■ (of a physical sense or faculty) highly developed; keen: *an acute sense of smell.* **3** (of an angle) less than 90°. ■ having a sharp end; pointed. ■ (of a sound) high; shrill.

▶ *n.* short for ACUTE ACCENT. —**a·cute·ly** *adv.* —**a·cute·ness** *n.*

a·cute ac·cent ▶ *n.* a mark (´) placed over certain letters in some languages to indicate an alteration of a sound, as of quality, quantity, or pitch, e.g., in *risqué*).

AD ▶ *abbr.* ■ *Mil.* active duty. ■ armored division. ■ (usu. AD) Anno Domini (used to indicate that a date comes the specified number of years after the accepted date of Christ's birth). ■ athletic director.

ad¹ /ad/ ▶ *n. inf.* an advertisement.

ad² ▶ *n. inf. Tennis* short for ADVANTAGE.

ad·age /ˈadij/ ▶ *n.* a proverb or saying expressing a general truth.

a·da·gio /ə'däjō; ə'däzhē,ō/ *Mus.* ▶ *adj. & adv.* (esp. as a direction) in slow tempo.

Ad·am /ˈadəm/ ▶ (in the biblical and Koranic traditions) the first man. According to the Book of Genesis, Adam was created by God as the progenitor of the human race and lived with Eve in the Garden of Eden.

ad·a·mant /ˈadəmənt/ ▶ *adj.* refusing to be persuaded or to change one's mind: *he is adamant that he is not going to resign.*

▶ *n. archaic* a legendary rock or mineral to which many, often contradictory, properties were attributed. —**ad·a·mance** *n.* —**ad·a·man·cy** /-mənsē/ *n.* —**ad·a·mant·ly** *adv.*

Ad·am's ap·ple ▶ *n.* the projection at the front of the neck formed by the thyroid cartilage of the larynx, often prominent in men.

a·dapt /ə'dapt/ ▶ *v.* [*tr.*] make (something) suitable for a new use or purpose; modify: *hospitals have to be adapted for modern medical practice.* ■ [*intr.*] become adjusted to new conditions: *slow to adapt to change* ■ alter (a text) to make it suitable for filming, broadcasting, or the stage: *the miniseries was adapted from Wouk's novel.* —**a·dap·tive** /-tiv/ *adj.*

a·dapt·a·ble /ə'daptəbəl/ ▶ *adj.* able to adjust to new conditions. ■ able to be modified for a new use or purpose. —**a·dapt·a·bil·i·ty** /ə,daptə-'bilitē/ *n.* —**a·dapt·a·bly** /-blē/ *adv.*

ad·ap·ta·tion /ˌadap'tāshən; ,adəp-/ ▶ *n.* the action or process of adapting or being adapted. ■ a movie, television drama, or stage play that has been adapted from a written work, typically a novel. ■ *Biol.* a change by which an organism or species becomes better suited to its environment: *living in groups is an adaptation that increases the efficiency of hunting.* ■ the process of making such changes: *biochemical adaptation in parasites.*

a·dapt·er /ə'daptər/ (also **a·dap·tor**) ▶ *n.* **1** a device for connecting pieces of equipment that cannot be connected directly. **2** a person who adapts a text for filming, broadcasting, or the stage.

ad·bot /ˈad,bät/ ▶ *n.* a computer program that caches advertising on

personal computers from an Internet-connected server and then displays the advertising when certain linked programs are being used.

ADD ▶ *abbr.* ■ analog digital digital, indicating that a music recording was made in analog format before being mastered and stored digitally. ■ attention deficit disorder.

add /ad/ ▶ *v.* [*tr.*] **1** join (something) to something else so as to increase the size, number, or amount: *a new wing was added to the building* | [*intr.*] *this development added to the problems facing the staff.* ■ [*intr.*] (**add up**) increase in amount, number, or degree: *watch those air miles add up!* ■ put or mix (an ingredient) together with another as one of the stages in the preparation of a dish: *add the flour to the eggs.* ■ put (something) in or on something else so as to improve or alter its quality or nature: *chlorine is added to the water to kill bacteria.* ■ contribute (an enhancing quality) to something. **2** put together (two or more numbers or amounts) to calculate their total value: *they added all the figures up* | [*intr.*] *children learned to add and subtract.* ■ [*intr.*] (**add up to**) amount to: *this adds up to a total of 400 calories* | *fig. these isolated incidents don't add up to a true picture of the situation.* ■ [*intr.*] (**add up**) *inf.* seem reasonable or consistent; make sense: *many things in her story didn't add up.* **3** say as a further remark: *we would like to add our congratulations.* —**add·er** *n.*

ad·den·dum /ə'dendəm/ ▶ *n.* (*pl.* **-da** /-də/, **-dums**) an item of additional material, typically omissions, added at the end of a book or other publication.

ad·der /ˈadər/ ▶ *n.* a small Eurasian viper (*Vipera berus*) that has a dark zigzag pattern on its back and bears live young. ■ used in names of similar or related snakes, e.g., puff adder.

ad·dict /ˈadikt/ ▶ *n.* a person who is addicted to a particular substance, typically an illegal drug. ■ *inf.* an enthusiastic devotee of a specified thing or activity: *a crossword-puzzle addict.*

ad·dict·ed /ə'diktid/ ▶ *adj.* physically and mentally dependent on a particular substance, and unable to stop taking it without incurring adverse effects: *she became addicted to alcohol and diet pills.* ■ enthusiastically devoted to a particular thing or activity: *he's addicted to computers.*

ad·dic·tion /ə'dikshən/ ▶ *n.* the fact or condition of being addicted to a particular substance, thing, or activity.

ad·dic·tive /ə'diktiv/ ▶ *adj.* (of a substance, thing, or activity) causing or likely to cause someone to become addicted to it. ■ of, relating to, or susceptible to the fact of being or becoming addicted to something.

ad·di·tion /ə'dishən/ (abbr.: **addn.**) ▶ *n.* **1** the action or process of adding something to something else: *the hotel has been extended with the addition of more rooms.* ■ a person or thing added or joined, typically in order to improve something: *you will find the coat a useful addition to your wardrobe.* **2** (abbr.: **addn.**) the process or skill of calculating the total of two or more numbers or amounts. ■ *Math.* the process of combining matrices, vectors, or other quantities under specific rules to obtain their sum.

ad·di·tion·al /ə'dishənl/ ▶ *adj.* added, extra, or supplementary to what is already present or available: *we require additional information.* —**ad·di·tion·al·ly** *adv.*

ad·di·tive /ˈaditiv/ ▶ *n.* a substance added to something in small quantities, typically to improve or preserve it: *chemical additives.*

▶ *adj.* characterized by, relating to, or produced by addition: *the combination of these factors has an additive effect.*

ad·dle /ˈadl/ ▶ *v.* [*tr.*] *chiefly humorous* make unable to think clearly; confuse: *being in love must have addled your brain.*

▶ *adj. archaic* (of an egg) rotten.

ad·dress /ə'dres; 'a,dres/ ▶ *n.* **1** the particulars of the place where someone lives or an organization is situated: *they exchanged addresses and agreed to keep in touch.* ■ the place itself: *our officers went to the address.* ■ *Comput.* a binary number that identifies a particular location in a data storage system or computer memory. **2** a formal speech delivered to an audience. ■ *archaic* a person's manner of speaking to someone else.

▶ *v.* [*tr.*] **1** write the name and address of the intended recipient on (an envelope, letter, or package). **2** speak to (a person or an assembly), typically in a formal way: *they addressed themselves to my father.* ■ (**address someone as**) name someone in a specified way when talking or writing: *she addressed my father as "Mr. Stevens."* ■ (**address something to**) say or write remarks or a protest to (someone): *address your complaints to the Board of Review.* **3** think about and begin to deal with (an issue or problem). **4** *Golf* take up one's stance and prepare to hit (the ball). —**ad·dress·er** *n.*

▶ □ **form of address** a name or title used in speaking or writing to a person of a specified rank or function.

ad·dress·ee /ˌadre'sē; ə,dre'sē/ ▶ *n.* the person to whom something, typically a letter, is addressed.

ad·duce /əˈd(y)o͞os/ ▶v. [tr.] cite as evidence: *a number of factors are adduced to explain the situation.* —**ad·duc·i·ble** *adj.*

ad·dy /ˈadē/ ▶n. (pl. **-dies**) *inf.* an address, especially an e-mail address: *I just sent you a note from my other addy.*

ad·e·nine /ˈadnˌēn; -ˌīn/ ▶n. *Biochem.* a purine derivative that is one of the four constituent bases of nucleic acids.

ad·e·noids /ˈadnˌoidz/ ▶pl. n. a mass of enlarged lymphatic tissue between the back of the nose and the throat, often hindering speaking and breathing in young children. —**ad·e·noi·dal** /ˌadnˈoidl/ *adj.*

ad·e·no·ma /ˌadnˈōmə/ ▶n. (pl. **-mas** or **-ma·ta** /-mətə/) *Med.* a benign tumor formed from glandular structures in epithelial tissue.

a·den·o·sine /əˈdenəˌsēn; -sin/ ▶n. *Biochem.* a compound consisting of adenine combined with ribose, one of four nucleoside units in RNA.

a·dept ▶*adj.* /əˈdept/ very skilled or proficient at something: *he is adept at cutting through red tape* | *an adept negotiator.*
▶n. /ˈadept; əˈdept/ a person who is skilled or proficient at something: *they are adepts at kung fu and karate.* —**a·dept·ly** *adv.* —**a·dept·ness** *n.*

ad·e·quate /ˈadikwit/ ▶*adj.* satisfactory or acceptable in quality or quantity: *this office is perfectly adequate for my needs.* —**ad·e·qua·cy** /-kwəsē/ *n.* —**ad·e·quate·ly** *adv.*

ADHD ▶*abbr.* attention deficit hyperactivity disorder.

ad·here /adˈhi(ə)r/ ▶v. [intr.] (**adhere to**) stick fast to (a surface or substance): *paint won't adhere well to a greasy surface.* ■ believe in and follow the practices of: *the people adhere to the Muslim religion.* ■ represent truthfully and in detail: *the account adhered firmly to fact.*

ad·her·ent /adˈhi(ə)rənt; -ˈher-/ ▶n. someone who supports a particular party, person, or set of ideas: *he was a strong adherent of monetarism.*
▶*adj.* sticking fast to an object or surface. —**ad·her·ence** *n.*

ad·he·sion /adˈhēZHən/ ▶n. **1** the action or process of adhering to or gripping a surface or object: *the adhesion of the Scotch tape to the paper.* **2** *Med.* an abnormal union of membranous surfaces due to inflammation or injury.

ad·he·sive /adˈhēsiv; -ziv/ ▶*adj.* able to stick fast to a surface or object; sticky: *an adhesive label.*
▶n. a substance used for sticking objects or materials together; glue. —**ad·he·sive·ly** *adv.* —**ad·he·sive·ness** *n.*

ad hoc /ˈad ˈhäk; ˈhōk/ ▶*adj. & adv.* formed, arranged, or done for a particular purpose only: [as *adj.*] *an ad hoc committee.* | [as *adv.*] *a group constituted ad hoc.*

a·dieu /əˈd(y)o͞o; äˈdyœ/ *chiefly poetic/lit.* ▶*interj.* another term for GOOD-BYE.
▶n. (pl. **a·dieus** or **a·dieux**) a goodbye: *he whispered a fond adieu.*

ad·i·os /ˌädēˈōs; ˌadē-/ ▶*interj. & n.* Spanish term for GOODBYE.

ad·i·pose /ˈadəˌpōs/ ▶*adj.* technical (esp. of body tissue) used for the storage of fat. —**ad·i·pos·i·ty** /ˌadəˈpäsitē/ *n.*

ad·ja·cent /əˈjāsənt/ ▶*adj.* **1** next to or adjoining something else: *adjacent rooms* | *the area adjacent to the fire station.* **2** *Geom.* (of angles) having a common vertex and a common side. —**ad·ja·cen·cy** *n.*

ad·jec·tive /ˈajiktiv/ ▶n. *Gram.* a word or phrase naming an attribute, added to or grammatically related to a noun to modify or describe it. —**ad·jec·ti·val** /ˌajikˈtīvəl/ *adj.* —**ad·jec·ti·val·ly** /ˌajikˈtīvəlē/ *adv.*

ad·join /əˈjoin/ ▶v. [tr.] be next to and joined with (a building, room, or piece of land): *the dining room adjoins a small library.*

ad·journ /əˈjərn/ ▶v. [tr.] (usu. **be adjourned**) break off (a meeting, legal case, or game) with the intention of resuming it later: *the meeting was adjourned until December 4* [intr.] *let's adjourn and reconvene at 2 o'clock.* ■ [intr.] (of people who are together) go somewhere else, typically for refreshment: *they adjourned to a local bar.* ■ put off or postpone (a resolution or sentence). ▷Middle English (in the sense 'summon someone to appear on a particular day'): from Old French *ajorner*, from the phrase *a jorn (nome)* 'to an (appointed) day.' —**ad·journ·ment** *n.*

ad·judge /əˈjəj/ ▶v. [tr.] (usu. **be adjudged**) consider or declare to be true or the case: *she was adjudged guilty.* ■ (**adjudge something to**) (in legal use) award something judicially to (someone): *the court adjudged legal damages to her.* ■ (in legal use) condemn (someone) to pay a penalty. —**ad·judg·ment** (also **ad·judge·ment**) *n.*

ad·ju·di·cate /əˈjo͞odiˌkāt/ ▶v. [intr.] make a formal judgment or decision about a problem or disputed matter: *the committee adjudicates on all betting disputes* | [tr.] *the case was adjudicated in the Supreme Court.* ■ act as a judge in a competition. ■ [tr.] pronounce or declare judicially: *he was adjudicated bankrupt.* —**ad·ju·di·ca·tion** /əˌjo͞odiˈkāSHən/ *n.* —**ad·ju·di·ca·tive** /-ˌkātiv/ *adj.* —**ad·ju·di·ca·tor** /-ˌkātər/ *n.*

ad·junct /ˈajəNGkt/ ▶n. **1** a thing added to something else as a supplementary rather than an essential part: *computer technology is an adjunct to learning.* ■ a person who is another's assistant or subordinate.

2 *Gram.* a word or phrase used to amplify or modify the meaning of another word or words in a sentence.
▶*adj.* connected or added to something, typically in an auxiliary way: *other adjunct therapies include immunotherapy.* ■ (of an academic post) attached to the staff of a college in a temporary or assistant capacity: *an adjunct professor.* [as *n.*] *both adjuncts and tenured professors.* —**ad·junc·tive** /əˈjəNG(k)tiv/ *adj.*

ad·jure /əˈjo͝or/ ▶v. [tr.] *formal* urge or request (someone) solemnly or earnestly to do something: *I adjure you to tell me the truth.* —**ad·ju·ra·tion** /ˌajəˈrāSHən/ *n.* —**ad·jur·a·to·ry** /-ə,tôrē/ *adj.*

ad·just /əˈjəst/ ▶v. **1** [tr.] alter or move (something) slightly in order to achieve the desired fit, appearance, or result: *he smoothed his hair and adjusted his tie.* ■ [intr.] permit small alterations or movements so as to allow a desired fit, appearance, or result to be achieved: *a harness that adjusts to the correct fit.* ■ [intr.] adapt or become used to a new situation: *she must be allowed to grieve and to adjust in her own way* | *his eyes had adjusted to semidarkness.* **2** [tr.] assess (loss or damages) when settling an insurance claim. —**ad·just·a·bil·i·ty** /ə,jəstəˈbilitē/ *n.* —**ad·just·a·ble** *adj.* —**ad·just·er** *n.* —**ad·just·ment** *n.*

ad·just·a·ble rate mort·gage (abbr.: **ARM**) ▶n. a mortgage whose rate of interest is adjusted periodically to reflect market conditions. Also called VARIABLE RATE MORTGAGE.

ad·ju·tant /ˈajətənt/ ▶n. **1** a military officer who acts as an administrative assistant to a senior officer. ■ a person's assistant or deputy. **2** (also **adjutant stork** or **adjutant bird**) a large black-and-white stork (genus *Leptoptilos*) with a massive bill and a bare head and neck, found in India and Southeast Asia. —**ad·ju·tan·cy** *n.*

ad lib /ˈad ˈlib/ ▶v. (**ad libbed, ad lib·bing**) [intr.] speak or perform in public without previously preparing one's words: *Charles had to ad lib because he'd forgotten his script* | [tr.] *she ad libbed half the speech.*
▶n. something spoken or performed in such a way.
▶*adv. & adj.* **1** spoken or performed without previous preparation: *an ad lib commentary* | [as *adv.*] *speaking ad lib.* **2** as much and as often as desired: [as *adv.*] *the price includes meals and drinks ad lib* | [as *adj.*] *the pigs are fed on an ad lib system.*

ad·man /ˈadˌman/ ▶n. (pl. **-men**) *inf.* a person who works in advertising.

ad·min·is·ter /ədˈminəstər/ ▶v. [tr.] **1** manage and be responsible for the running of (a business, organization, etc.). ■ be responsible for the implementation or use of (law or resources). **2** dispense or apply (a remedy or drug). ■ deal out or inflict (punishment): *retribution was administered to those found guilty.* ■ (of a priest) perform the rites of (a sacrament, typically the Eucharist). ■ *archaic* or *Law* direct the taking of (an oath): *the chief justice will administer the oath of office.* **3** [intr.] give help or service: *we must selflessly administer to his needs.* —**ad·min·is·tra·ble** /-strəbəl/ *adj.*

ad·min·is·trate /ədˈminəˌstrāt/ ▶v. [tr.] less common term for ADMINISTER (sense 1).

ad·min·is·tra·tion /ədˌminəˈstrāSHən/ (abbr.: **admin.**) ▶n. **1** the process or activity of running a business, organization, etc.: *the day-to-day administration of the company.* ■ (**the administration**) the people responsible for this, regarded collectively: *the university administration took their demands seriously.* ■ the management of public affairs; government: *the inhabitants voted to remain under French administration.* ■ *Law* the management and disposal of the property of an intestate, deceased person, debtor, or other individual, or of an insolvent company, by a legally appointed administrator: *the company went into administration.* **2** the officials in the executive branch of government under a particular chief executive: *the Bush Administration's demand.* ■ the term of office of a political leader or government: *the early years of the Reagan Administration.* ■ a government agency: *the U.S. Food and Drug Administration.* **3** the action of dispensing, giving, or applying something. *the administration of justice.*

ad·min·is·tra·tive /ədˈminiˌstrātiv; -strətiv/ ▶*adj.* of or relating to the running of a business, organization, etc. —**ad·min·is·tra·tive·ly** *adv.*

ad·min·is·tra·tor /ədˈminəˌstrātər/ ▶n. a person responsible for running a business, organization, etc. ■ *Law* a person legally appointed to manage and dispose of the estate of an intestate, deceased person, debtor, or other individual, or of an insolvent company. ■ a person who performs official duties in some sphere: *administrators of justice.*

ad·mi·ra·ble /ˈadmərəbəl/ ▶*adj.* arousing or deserving respect and approval: *he has one admirable quality—he is totally honest* | *what is admirable in one sex is disdained in the other.* —**ad·mi·ra·bly** /-blē/ *adv.*

ad·mi·ral /ˈadmərəl/ ▸n. **1** a commander of a fleet or naval squadron, or a naval officer of very high rank. ■ a commissioned officer of very high rank in the U.S. Navy or Coast Guard, ranking above a vice admiral. **2** a butterfly (family Nymphalidae) that has dark wings with bold colorful markings. —**ad·mi·ral·ship** /-ˌSHip/ n.

ad·mi·ral·ty /ˈadmərəltē/ ▸n. (pl. **-ties**) **1** the rank or office of an admiral. **2** Law the jurisdiction of courts of law over cases concerning ships or the sea and other navigable waters (maritime law). **3** (**Admiralty**) the department of the British government that once administered the Royal Navy.

ad·mi·ra·tion /ˌadməˈrāSHən/ ▸n. respect and warm approval: *their admiration for each other was genuine.* ■ (**the admiration of**) the object of such feelings: *her house was the admiration of everyone.* ■ pleasurable contemplation: *they were lost in admiration of the scenery.*

ad·mire /ədˈmī(ə)r/ ▸v. [tr.] regard (an object, quality, or person) with respect or warm approval: *I admire your courage.* ■ look at with pleasure: *we were just admiring your garden.* —**ad·mir·ing·ly** adv.

ad·mir·er /ədˈmī(ə)rər/ ▸n. someone who has a particular regard for someone or something: *he was a great admirer of Mark Twain.* ■ a man who is attracted to a particular woman or a woman who is attracted to a particular man: *she's got a secret admirer.*

ad·mis·si·ble /ədˈmisəbəl/ ▸adj. **1** acceptable or valid, esp. as evidence in a court of law: *legally admissible evidence.* **2** having the right to be admitted to a place. —**ad·mis·si·bil·i·ty** /-ˌmisəˈbilitē/ n.

ad·mis·sion /ədˈmiSHən/ ▸n. **1** a statement acknowledging the truth of something: *an admission of guilt.* **2** the process or fact of entering or being allowed to enter a place, organization, or institution: *her condition required frequent hospital admissions* | [as adj.] (**admissions**) *the university admissions office.* ■ the money charged for allowing someone to enter a public place: *admission is $1 for adults and 50 cents for children.* ■ (**admissions**) the number of people entering a place.

ad·mit /ədˈmit/ ▸v. (**-mit·ted, -mit·ting**) **1** [tr.] confess to be true or to be the case, typically with reluctance: *the office admitted that several prisoners had been injured.* ■ [tr.] confess to a (crime or fault, or one's responsibility for it): *he was sentenced to prison after admitting 47 charges of burglary* | [intr.] *he had admitted to a history of sexual misconduct.* ■ acknowledge (a failure or fault): *after searching for an hour, she finally had to admit defeat* | [intr.] *he admits to having failed.* **2** [tr.] allow (someone) to enter a place: *senior citizens are admitted free.* ■ (of a ticket) give (someone) the right to enter a place: *the voucher admits up to four people to the park.* ■ carry out the procedures necessary for (someone) to be received into a hospital for treatment: *she was admitted to the hospital suffering from a chest infection.* ■ allow (a person, country, or organization) to join an organization or group. ■ allow (someone) to share in a privilege: *only a chosen few were admitted to the covenant.* ■ [tr.] accept as valid: *the courts can refuse to admit police evidence which has been illegally obtained.* **3** [intr.] (**admit of**) allow the possibility of: *the need to inform him was too urgent to admit of further delay.*

ad·mit·tance /ədˈmitns/ ▸n. the process or fact of entering or being allowed to enter a place or institution: *people were unable to gain admittance to the hall.*

ad·mit·ted·ly /ədˈmitidlē/ ▸adv. used to introduce a concession or recognition that something is true or is the case: *admittedly, the salary was not wonderful.*

ad·mix·ture /adˈmiksCHər/ ▸n. a mixture. ■ something mixed with something else, typically as a minor ingredient. ■ the action of adding such an ingredient.

ad·mon·ish /ədˈmäniSH/ ▸v. [tr.] warn or reprimand someone firmly: *she admonished me for appearing at breakfast unshaven.* ■ advise or urge (someone) earnestly: *she admonished him to drink no more than one glass of wine.* ■ archaic warn (someone) of something to be avoided: *he admonished the people against the evil of such practices.* —**ad·mon·ish·ment** n. —**ad·mo·ni·tion** /ˌadməˈniSHən/ n. —**ad·mon·i·to·ry** /adˈmäniˌtôrē/ adj.

a·do /əˈdo͞o/ ▸n. trouble or difficulty: *she had much ado to keep up with him.* ■ fuss, esp. about something that is unimportant: *on the face of it, this is much ado about almost nothing.*
▸ □ **without further ado** without any fuss or delay; immediately.

a·do·be /əˈdōbē/ ▸n. a kind of clay used as a building material, typically in the form of sun-dried bricks: [as adj.] *adobe houses.* ■ a brick of such a type. ■ a building constructed from such material.

ad·o·les·cent /ˌadlˈesənt/ ▸adj. (of a young person) in the process of developing from a child into an adult. ■ relating to or characteristic of this process: *his adolescent years* | *adolescent problems.*
▸n. an adolescent boy or girl. —**ad·o·les·cence** n.

A·don·is /əˈdänis/ ▸n. an extremely handsome young man.

a·dopt /əˈdäpt/ ▸v. [tr.] legally take another's child and bring it up as one's own: *there are many people eager to adopt a baby.* ■ take up or start to use or follow (an idea, method, or course of action): *this approach has been adopted by many big banks.* ■ take on or assume (an attitude or position): *adopt a slightly knees-bent position.* ■ formally approve or accept (a report or suggestion): *the committee voted 5–1 to adopt the proposal.* ■ choose (a textbook) as standard or required for a course of study. ■ choose (an animal) to become a house pet: *the best way to know a dog's traits is to adopt a mature dog.* —**a·dopt·a·ble** adj. —**a·dopt·ee** /-ˈtē/ n. —**a·dopt·er** n. —**a·dop·tion** n.

a·dop·tive /əˈdäptiv/ ▸adj. as a result of the adoption of another's child: *adoptive parents.* ■ denoting a country or city to which a person has moved and in which they have chosen to make their permanent place of residence. —**a·dop·tive·ly** adv.

a·dor·a·ble /əˈdôrəbəl/ ▸adj. inspiring great affection; delightful; charming: *she looked just adorable* | *I have four adorable Siamese cats.* —**a·dor·a·bil·i·ty** /ə,dôrəˈbilitē/ n. —**a·dor·a·ble·ness** n. —**a·dor·a·bly** /-blē/ adv.

a·dore /əˈdôr/ ▸v. [tr.] love and respect (someone) deeply. ■ worship; venerate: *he adored the Sacred Host.* ■ inf. like (something or someone) very much: *she adores Mexican cuisine.* ▷late Middle English: via Old French from Latin *adorare* 'to worship,' from *ad-* 'to' + *orare* 'speak, pray.' —**ad·o·ra·tion** /ˌadəˈrāSHən/ n. —**a·dor·er** n. —**a·dor·ing·ly** adv.

a·dorn /əˈdôrn/ ▸v. [tr.] make more beautiful or attractive: *pictures and prints adorned his walls.* —**a·dorn·er** n. —**a·dorn·ment** n.

ADP ▸abbr. ■ Biochem. adenosine diphosphate. ■ automatic data processing.

ad rem /ˈad ˈrem/ ▸adv. & adj. formal relevant to what is being done or discussed at the time.

ad·re·nal /əˈdrēnl/ ▸adj. of, relating to, or denoting a pair of ductless glands situated above the kidneys. Each consists of a core region (**adrenal medulla**) secreting epinephrine and norepinephrine, and an outer region (**adrenal cortex**) secreting corticosteroids.
▸n. (usu. **adrenals**) an adrenal gland.

a·dren·a·line /əˈdrenl-in/ (also **a·dren·a·lin**) ▸n. another term for EPINEPHRINE. ■ (**Adrenalin**) trademark the hormone epinephrine extracted from animals or prepared synthetically for medicinal purposes.

a·drift /əˈdrift/ ▸adj. & adv. (of a boat or its passengers) floating without being either moored or steered: [as adv.] *a cargo ship went adrift* | [as adj.] *the seamen are adrift in lifeboats.* ■ fig. (of a person) without purpose or guidance; lost and confused: [as adj.] *he was adrift in a strange country* | [as adv.] *they were cast adrift in a sea of events.*

a·droit /əˈdroit/ ▸adj. clever or skillful in using the hands or mind: *he was adroit at tax avoidance.* —**a·droit·ly** adv. —**a·droit·ness** n.

ADSL ▸abbr. Telecomm. asynchronous (or asymmetric) digital subscriber line, a method of routing digital data on copper telephone wires, allowing high-speed Internet access and simultaneous use of the line for voice transmission.

ad·sorb /adˈzôrb; -ˈsôrb/ ▸v. [tr.] (of a solid) hold (molecules of a gas or liquid or solute) as a thin film on the outside surface or on internal surfaces within the material: *charcoal will not adsorb nitrates.* —**ad·sorb·a·ble** adj. —**ad·sorb·ent** adj. —**ad·sorp·tion** n. —**ad·sorp·tive** adj.

ad·sorb·ate /adˈzôrbit; -ˈsôr-; -ˌbāt/ ▸n. a substance adsorbed.

ad·u·late /ˈajəˌlāt/ ▸v. [tr.] praise (someone) excessively or obsequiously. —**ad·u·la·tion** /ˌajə-ˈlāSHən/ n. —**ad·u·la·tor** /-ˌlātər/ n. —**ad·u·la·to·ry** /-lə,tôrē/ adj.

a·dult /əˈdəlt; ˈad,əlt/ ▸n. a person who is fully grown or developed. ■ a fully developed animal. ■ Law a person who has reached the age of majority. See MAJORITY (sense 2).
▸adj. (of a person or animal) fully grown or developed. ■ of or for adult people: *adult education.* ■ emotionally and mentally mature. ■ sexually explicit or pornographic (used euphemistically to refer to a movie, book, or magazine). —**a·dult·hood** /-,ho͝od/ n.

a·dul·ter·ate /əˈdəltəˌrāt/ ▸v. [tr.] render (something) poorer in quality by adding another substance, typically an inferior one: *the meat was ground fine and adulterated with potato flour.* —**a·dul·ter·a·tion** /ə,dəltə-ˈrāSHən/ n. —**a·dul·ter·a·tor** /-ˌrātər/ n.

a·dul·ter·er /əˈdəltərər/ ▸n. a person who commits adultery.

a·dul·ter·y /əˈdəlt(ə)rē/ ▸n. voluntary sexual intercourse between a married person and a person who is not his or her spouse. —**a·dul·ter·ous** /-rəs/ adj.

ad·um·brate /ˈadəmˌbrāt; əˈdəm-/ ▸v. [tr.] formal report or represent in outline: *James Madison adumbrated the necessity that the Senate be somewhat insulated from public passions.* ■ indicate faintly: *the walls were not more than adumbrated by the meager light.* ■ foreshadow or symbolize. ■ overshadow or obscure. —**ad·um·bra·tion** /ˌadəmˈbrāSHən/ n. —**ad·um·bra·tive** /əˈdəmbrətiv; ˈadəm,brā-/ adj.

ad·vance /ədˈvans/ ▶v. **1** [intr.] move forward, typically in a purposeful way: *the troops* **advanced** *on the capital* | *she advanced toward him.* ■ make progress: *our knowledge is advancing all the time.* ■ [tr.] cause (an event) to occur at an earlier date than planned: *I advanced the date of the meeting by several weeks.* ■ [tr.] promote or help the progress of (a person, cause, or plan). ■ [tr.] put forward (a theory or suggestion): *the hypothesis I wish to advance in this article.* ■ (esp. of shares of stock) increase in price. **2** lend (money) to (someone): *the bank advanced them a loan.* ■ pay (money) to (someone) before it is due: *he advanced me a month's salary.* ▶n. **1** a forward movement: *the rebels' advance on Madrid was well under way* | *fig. the advance of civilization.* ■ a development or improvement: *genuine* **advances in** *engineering techniques* | *decades of great scientific advance.* ■ an increase or rise in amount, value, or price. **2** an amount of money paid before it is due or for work only partly completed: *the author was paid a $250,000 advance.* ■ a loan. **3** (usu. **advances**) an approach made to someone, typically with the aim of initiating a sexual encounter: *women accused him of* **making** *improper* **advances.** ▶adj. done, sent, or supplied beforehand: *advance notice.* ▶ □ **in advance** ahead in time: *you need to book weeks in advance.* □ **in advance of** before: *we went on in advance of the main group.*

ad·vance·ment /ədˈvansmənt/ ▶n. the process of promoting a cause or plan: *their lives were devoted to the advancement of science.* ■ the promotion of a person in rank or status: *opportunities for career advancement.* ■ development or improvement: *technological advancements.*

ad·van·tage /ədˈvantij/ ▶n. a condition or circumstance that puts one in a favorable or superior position: *she had an* **advantage over** *her mother's generation.* ■ the opportunity to gain something; benefit or profit: *he saw some advantage in the proposal.* ■ a favorable or desirable circumstance or feature; a benefit: *the village's proximity to the town is an advantage.* ■ *Tennis* a player's score in a game when they have won the first point after deuce (and will win the game if they win the next point). ▶v. [tr.] put in a favorable or more favorable position. —**ad·van·ta·geous** /ˌadvənˈtājəs; -van-/ adj. —**ad·van·ta·geous·ly** adv. ▶ □ **take advantage of** **1** make unfair demands on (someone) who cannot or will not resist; exploit or make unfair use of for one's own benefit: *people tend to take advantage of a placid nature.* ■ *dated* (used euphemistically) seduce. **2** make good use of the opportunities offered by (something): *take full advantage of the facilities available.*

ad·vec·tion /adˈvekSHən/ ▶n. the transfer of heat or matter by the flow of a fluid, esp. horizontally in the atmosphere or the sea. —**ad·vect** /-ˈvekt/ v. —**ad·vec·tive** /-tiv/ adj.

ad·vent /ˈadˌvent/ ▶n. the arrival of a notable person, thing, or event. ■ (**Advent**) the first season of the church year, leading up to Christmas and including the four preceding Sundays. ■ (**Advent**) *Christian Theol.* the coming or second coming of Christ.

Ad·vent·ist /ˈadˌventist/ ▶n. a member of any of various Christian sects emphasizing belief in the imminent second coming of Christ. See also Seventh-Day Adventist. —**Ad·vent·ism** /-ˌtizəm/ n.

ad·ven·ti·tious /ˌadvenˈtiSHəs/ ▶adj. happening or carried on according to chance rather than design or inherent nature. ■ coming from outside; not native: *the adventitious population.* ■ *Biol.* formed accidentally or in an unusual anatomical position: *propagation of sour cherries by adventitious shoots.* ■ *Bot.* (of a root) growing directly from the stem or other upper part of a plant. —**ad·ven·ti·tious·ly** adv.

ad·ven·ture /adˈvenCHər; əd-/ ▶n. an unusual and exciting, typically hazardous, experience or activity: *her recent adventures in Italy.* ■ daring and exciting activity calling for enterprise and enthusiasm: *she traveled the world in search of adventure.* ■ *archaic* a commercial speculation. ▶v. [intr.] *dated* engage in hazardous and exciting activity, esp. the exploration of unknown territory. ■ [tr.] *dated* put (something, esp. money or one's life) at risk: *he adventured $3,000 in the purchase of land.* —**ad·ven·ture·some** adj.

ad·ven·tur·er /adˈvenCHərər; əd-/ ▶n. a person who enjoys or seeks adventure. ■ a person willing to take risks or use dishonest methods for personal gain: *a political adventurer.* ■ *archaic* a financial speculator. ■ *archaic* a mercenary soldier.

ad·ven·tur·ism /adˈvenCHəˌrizəm; əd-/ ▶n. the willingness to take risks in business or politics (esp. in the context of foreign policy); actions, or attitudes regarded as daring or reckless. —**ad·ven·tur·ist** n. & adj.

ad·ven·tur·ous /adˈvenCHərəs; əd-/ ▶adj. willing to take risks or to try out new methods, ideas, or experiences. ■ involving new ideas or methods: *they wanted more adventurous meals.* ■ full of excitement: —**ad·ven·tur·ous·ly** adv. —**ad·ven·tur·ous·ness** n.

ad·verb /ˈadˌvərb/ ▶n. *Gram.* a word or phrase that modifies or qualifies an adjective, verb, or other adverb or a word-group, expressing a relation of place, time, circumstance, manner, cause, degree, etc. (e.g., *gently, quite, then, there*).

ad·ver·bi·al /adˈvərbēəl/ *Gram.* ▶adj. like or relating to an adverb. ▶n. a word or phrase functioning like an adverb. —**ad·ver·bi·al·ly** adv.

ad·ver·sar·i·al /ˌadvərˈse(ə)rēəl/ ▶adj. involving or characterized by conflict or opposition: *industry and government had an adversarial relationship.* ■ opposed; hostile. ■ *Law* (of a trial or legal procedure) in which the parties in a dispute have the responsibility for finding and presenting evidence: *an adversarial system of justice.* —**ad·ver·sar·i·al·ly** adv.

ad·ver·sar·y /ˈadvərˌserē/ ▶n. (pl. **-sar·ies**) one's opponent in a contest, conflict, or dispute: *Davis beat his old adversary in the quarterfinals.* ▶adj. another term for **adversarial**: *the confrontations of adversary politics.*

ad·verse /adˈvərs; ˈadvərs/ ▶adj. preventing success or development; harmful; unfavorable: *adverse weather* **conditions.** —**ad·verse·ly** adv.

ad·ver·si·ty /adˈvərsitē/ ▶n. (pl. **-ties**) difficulties; misfortune: *resilience in the face of adversity* | *she overcame many adversities.*

ad·vert /adˈvərt/ ▶v. [intr.] (**advert to**) *formal* refer to in speaking or writing: *he had failed to advert to the consequences of his conduct.*

ad·ver·tise /ˈadvərˌtīz/ ▶v. [tr.] describe or draw attention to (a product, service, or event) in a public medium in order to promote sales or attendance: *a billboard advertising beer* | [intr.] *we had a chance to advertise on television.* ■ seek to fill (a vacancy) by putting a notice in a newspaper or other medium: *for every job we advertise we get a hundred applicants* | [intr.] *he advertised for dancers in the trade papers.* ■ make (a quality or fact) known: *Meryl coughed briefly to advertise her presence.* —**ad·ver·tis·er** n.

ad·ver·tise·ment /ˈadvərˌtīzmənt; ədˈvərtiz-/ ▶n. a notice or announcement in a public medium promoting a product, service, or event or publicizing a job vacancy. ■ (**advertisement for**) *inf.* a person or thing regarded as a means of recommending something: *unhappy clients are not a good advertisement for the company.* ■ *archaic* a notice to readers in a book.

ad·vice /ədˈvīs/ ▶n. guidance or recommendations concerning prudent future action, typically given by someone regarded as knowledgeable or authoritative: *she visited the island on her doctor's advice.* ■ a formal notice of a financial transaction: *remittance advices.* ■ *archaic* information; news: *fresh advices from Europe.*

ad·vis·a·ble /ədˈvīzəbəl/ ▶adj. (of a course of action) to be recommended; sensible: *it is advisable to carry one of the major credit cards* | *early booking is advisable.* —**ad·vis·a·bil·i·ty** /-ˌvīzəˈbilitē/ n. —**ad·vis·a·bly** /-blē/ adv.

ad·vise /ədˈvīz/ ▶v. [tr.] offer suggestions about the best course of action to someone: *I advised him to go home* | [intr.] *we* **advise against** *sending cash by mail.* ■ [tr.] recommend (something): *sleeping pills are not advised.* ■ [tr.] inform (someone) about a fact or situation, typically in a formal or official way: *you will be advised of the requirements* | [tr.] *the lawyer advised the court that his client wished to give evidence.*

ad·vised /ədˈvīzd/ ▶adj. behaving as someone, esp. the speaker, would recommend; sensible; wise: *you* **would be advised to** *do some research.* —**ad·vis·ed·ly** /-ˈvīzid,lē/ adv.

ad·vis·er /ədˈvīzər/ (also **ad·vi·sor**) ▶n. a person who gives advice, typically someone who is expert in a particular field: *the military* **adviser to** *the President.* ■ in a school, college, or university, a teacher or staff counselor who helps a student plan a course of study.

ad·vi·so·ry /ədˈvīzərē/ ▶adj. having or consisting in the power to make recommendations but not to take action enforcing them: *an independent advisory committee* | *the Commission acts in an advisory capacity to the government.* ■ recommended but not compulsory. ▶n. (pl. **-ries**) an official announcement, typically a warning about bad weather conditions: *a frost advisory.*

ad·vo·ca·cy /ˈadvəkəsē/ ▶n. public support for or recommendation of a particular cause or policy. ■ the profession or work of a legal advocate.

ad·vo·cate ▶n. /ˈadvəkit/ a person who publicly supports or recommends a particular cause or policy: *he was an untiring* **advocate of** *economic reform.* ■ a person who pleads on someone else's behalf. ■ a pleader in a court of law; a lawyer. ▶v. /-ˌkāt/ [tr.] publicly recommend or support: *they advocated adherence to Islam.* —**ad·vo·ca·tion** /ˌadvəˈkāSHən/ n. —**ad·vo·ca·tor** /-ˌkātər/ n.

adze /adz/ (**adz**) ▶n. a tool similar to an ax with an arched blade at right angles to the handle, used for cutting or shaping large pieces of wood.

ad·zu·ki /adˈzōōkē/ (also **adzuki bean**) ▶n. **1** a small, round, dark-red edible bean. **2** the bushy leguminous Asian plant (*Vigna angularis*) that produces this bean.

Pronunciation Key ə *ago*, *up*; ər *over*, *fur*; a *hat*; ā *ate*; ä *car*; CH *chin*; e *let*; ē *see*; e(ə)r *air*; i *fit*; ī *by*; i(ə)r *ear*; NG *sing*; ō *go*; ô *law*, *for*; oi *toy*; ŏŏ *good*; ōō *goo*; ou *out*; SH *she*; TH *thin*; TH *then*; (h)w *why*; ZH *vision*

A

ae·gis /ˈējis/ ▶n. the protection, backing, or support of a particular person or organization: *negotiations conducted* **under the aegis of** *the UN.* ■ (in classical art and mythology) an attribute of Zeus (Jupiter) and Athena (Minerva) usually represented as a goatskin shield.

ae·on ▶n. *Brit.* variant spelling of EON.

aer·ate /ˈe(ə)rāt/ ▶v. [tr.] introduce air into (a material): *she would aerate the lawn with high heels.* —**aer·a·tion** /e(ə)rˈāsHən/ n. —**aer·a·tor** /-ātər/ n.

aer·i·al /ˈe(ə)rēəl/ ▶adj. existing, happening, or operating in the air: *an aerial battle.* ■ coming or carried out from the air, esp. using aircraft: *aerial photography.* ■ (of part of a plant) growing above ground: *knobby sections of aerial roots.* ■ (of a bird) spending much of its time in flight. ■ of or in the atmosphere; atmospheric. ■ insubstantial and hard to grasp or define: *fine and aerial distinctions.*
▶n. **1** another term for ANTENNA (sense 2): *jiggle the aerial on the radio.* **2** (**aerials**) a type of maneuver in gymnastics, skiing, or surfing involving freestyle jumps or somersaults. —**aer·i·al·ly** adv.

aer·i·al·ist /ˈe(ə)rēəlist/ ▶n. a person who performs acrobatics high above the ground on a tightrope or trapezes.

aer·ie /ˈe(ə)rē; ˈi(ə)rē/ (also **eyr·ie**) ▶n. a large nest of a bird of prey, esp. an eagle, typically built high in a tree or on a cliff.

aer·o·bat·ics /ˌe(ə)rəˈbatiks/ ▶pl. n. [usu. treated as sing.] feats of spectacular flying performed in one or more aircraft to entertain an audience on the ground. —**aer·o·bat·ic** adj.

aer·obe /ˈe(ə)r,ōb/ ▶n. a microorganism that grows in the presence of air or requires oxygen for growth.

aer·o·bic /eˈrōbik; e(ə)ˈrō-/ ▶adj. *Biol.* relating to, involving, or requiring free oxygen: *simple aerobic bacteria.* ■ relating to or denoting exercise that improves or is intended to improve the efficiency of the body's cardiovascular system in absorbing and transporting oxygen. —**aer·o·bi·cal·ly** adv.

aer·o·bics /eˈrōbiks; e(ə)ˈrō-/ ▶pl. n. [often treated as sing.] vigorous exercises, such as swimming or walking, designed to strengthen the heart and lungs.

aer·o·bi·ol·o·gy /ˌe(ə)rōbīˈäləjē/ ▶n. the study of airborne microorganisms, pollen, spores, and seeds, esp. as agents of infection.

aer·o·dy·nam·ic /ˌe(ə)rōdīˈnamik/ ▶adj. of or relating to aerodynamics: *aerodynamic forces.* ■ of or having a shape that reduces the drag from air moving past: *the plane has a more aerodynamic shape.* —**aer·o·dy·nam·i·cal·ly** adv.

aer·o·dy·nam·ics /ˌe(ə)rōdīˈnamiks/ ▶pl. n. [treated as sing.] the study of the properties of moving air, and esp. of the interaction between the air and solid bodies moving through it. ■ the properties of a solid object regarding the manner in which air flows around it. ■ [treated as pl.] these properties insofar as they result in maximum efficiency of motion. —**aer·o·dy·nam·i·cist** /-ˈnaməsist/ n.

aer·o·nau·tics /ˌe(ə)rəˈnôtiks/ ▶pl. n. [treated as sing.] the science or practice of travel through the air. —**aer·o·nau·tic** adj. (rare) —**aer·o·nau·ti·cal** adj.

aer·o·plane /ˈe(ə)rə,plān/ ▶n. British term for AIRPLANE.

aer·o·sol /ˈerə,sôl; -,säl/ ▶n. a substance enclosed under pressure and able to be released as a fine spray, typically by means of a propellant gas. ■ a container holding such a substance. ■ *Chem.* a colloidal suspension of particles dispersed in air or gas.

aer·o·space /ˈe(ə)rō,spās/ ▶n. the branch of technology and industry concerned with both aviation and space flight.

aes·thete /ˈes,THēt/ (also **es·thete**) ▶n. a person who has or affects to have a special appreciation of art and beauty.

aes·thet·ic /esˈTHetik/ (also **es·thet·ic**) ▶adj. concerned with beauty or the appreciation of beauty: *the pictures give aesthetic pleasure.* ■ giving or designed to give pleasure through beauty; of pleasing appearance.
▶n. a set of principles underlying and guiding the work of a particular artist or artistic movement: *the Cubist aesthetic.* ▷late 18th cent. (in the sense 'relating to perception by the senses'): from Greek *aisthētikos,* from *aisthēta* 'perceptible things,' from *aisthesthai* 'perceive.' The sense 'concerned with beauty' was coined in German in the mid 18th cent. and adopted into English in the early 19th cent., but its use was controversial until late in the century. —**aes·thet·i·cal·ly** /-ik(ə)lē/ adv. *an aesthetically pleasing color combination.*

A·far /ˈä,fär/ ▶n. **1** (pl. same or **A·fars**) a member of a people living in Djibouti, Eritrea, and Ethiopia. **2** the Cushitic language of this people.
▶adj. of or relating to this people or their language.

a·far /əˈfär/ ▶adv. chiefly poetic/lit. at or to a distance: *traveled afar.*

AFB ▶abbr. Air Force Base.

AFC ▶abbr. ■ American Football Conference. ■ automatic frequency control, a system in radios and television that keeps them tuned to an incoming signal.

af·fa·ble /ˈafəbəl/ ▶adj. friendly, good-natured, or easy to talk to. —**af·fa·bil·i·ty** /,afəˈbilitē/ n. —**af·fa·bly** /-blē/ adv.

af·fair /əˈfe(ə)r/ ▶n. **1** an event or sequence of events of a specified kind or that has previously been referred to: *the board admitted responsibility for the affair.* ■ a matter that is a particular person's concern or responsibility: *what you do in your spare time is your affair.* ■ (**affairs**) matters of public interest and importance: *commissions were created to advise on foreign affairs.* ■ (**affairs**) business and financial dealings: *his time was spent in winding up his affairs.* ■ inf. an object of a particular type: *her dress was a black low-cut affair.* **2** a love affair: *his wife is having an affair.*

af·fect¹ /əˈfekt/ ▶v. [tr.] have an effect on; make a difference to: *the dampness began to affect my health.* ■ touch the feelings of (someone); move emotionally: [as adj.] (**affecting**) *a highly affecting account of her experiences.* ■ (of an illness) attack or infect: *people who are affected by AIDS.* —**af·fect·ing·ly** adv.

af·fect² /əˈfekt/ ▶v. [tr.] pretend to have or feel (something): *as usual I affected a supreme unconcern.* ■ use, wear, or assume (something) pretentiously or so as to make an impression on others: *an American who had affected a British accent.*

af·fect³ /ˈafekt; əˈfekt/ ▶n. *Psychol.* emotion or desire, esp. as influencing behavior or action. —**af·fect·less** adj. —**af·fect·less·ness** n.

af·fec·ta·tion /,afekˈtāsHən/ ▶n. behavior, speech, or writing that is artificial and designed to impress: *she called the room her boudoir, which he thought an affectation.* ■ a studied display of real or pretended feeling: *an affectation of calm.*

af·fect·ed /əˈfektid/ ▶adj. **1** influenced or touched by an external factor: *apply moist heat to the affected area.* **2** artificial, pretentious, and designed to impress: *the gesture appeared both affected and stagy.* —**af·fect·ed·ly** adv.

af·fec·tion /əˈfeksHən/ ▶n. **1** a gentle feeling of fondness or liking: *she felt* **affection for** *the wise old lady | he won a place in her affections.* ■ physical expressions of these feelings: *the prisoners crave affection and hence participate in sexual relationships.* **2** archaic the act or process of affecting or being affected. ■ a mental state; an emotion. —**af·fec·tion·al** /-sHənl/ adj.

af·fec·tion·ate /əˈfeksHənit/ ▶adj. readily feeling or showing fondness or tenderness. ■ expressing fondness. —**af·fec·tion·ate·ly** adv.

af·fec·tive /əˈfektiv/ ▶adj. *chiefly Psychol.* relating to moods, feelings, and attitudes: *affective disorders.* —**af·fec·tive·ly** adv. —**af·fec·tiv·i·ty** /,afekˈtivitē/ n.

af·fi·ance /əˈfiəns/ ▶v. (**be affianced**) poetic/lit. be engaged to marry: *Ann Elliott was* **affianced to** *Col. Lewis Morris.*

af·fi·da·vit /,afiˈdāvit/ ▶n. *Law* a written statement confirmed by oath or affirmation, for use as evidence in court.

af·fil·i·ate ▶v. /əˈfilē,āt/ [tr.] (usu. **be affiliated with**) officially attach or connect (a subsidiary group or a person) to an organization: *the college is* **affiliated with** *the University of Wisconsin.* ■ [intr.] officially join or become attached to an organization: *the membership of the National Writers Union voted to* **affiliate with** *the United Auto Workers.*
▶n. /-it/ a person or organization officially attached to a larger body. —**af·fil·i·a·tive** /-ətiv; -,ātiv/ adj.

af·fil·i·a·tion /ə,filēˈāsHən/ ▶n. the state or process of affiliating or being affiliated.

af·fined /əˈfīnd/ ▶adj. archaic related or connected.

af·fin·i·ty /əˈfinitē/ ▶n. (pl. **-ties**) (often **affinity between/for/with**) a spontaneous or natural liking or sympathy for someone or something: *he has an* **affinity for** *the music of Berlioz.* ■ a similarity of characteristics suggesting a relationship, esp. a resemblance in structure between animals, plants, or languages: *a building with no* **affinity to** *contemporary architectural styles.* ■ relationship, esp. by marriage as opposed to blood ties. ■ *chiefly Biochem.* the degree to which a substance tends to combine with another: *the affinity of hemoglobin for oxygen.*

af·firm /əˈfərm/ ▶v. [tr.] state as a fact; assert strongly and publicly: *he affirmed the country's commitment to peace.* ■ declare one's support for; uphold or defend: *the referendum affirmed the republic's right to secede.* ■ *Law* accept or confirm the validity of (a judgment or agreement); ratify. ■ *Law* (of a court) uphold (a decision) on appeal. ■ [intr.] *Law* make a formal declaration rather than taking an oath (e.g., to testify truthfully). —**af·firm·er** n.

af·firm·a·tion /,afərˈmāsHən/ ▶n. the action or process of affirming or being affirmed: *an affirmation of basic human values | he nodded in affirmation.* ■ *Law* a formal declaration by a person who declines to take an oath for reasons of conscience.

af·firm·a·tive /əˈfərmətiv/ ▶*adj.* agreeing with a statement or to a request: *an affirmative answer.* ■ (of a vote) expressing approval or agreement. ■ supportive, hopeful, or encouraging: *the music's natural buoyancy and affirmative character.* ■ active or obligatory: *an affirmative duty to stop crime* ■ *Gram. & Logic* stating that a fact is so; making an assertion.
▶*n.* a statement of agreement with an assertion or request: *he accepted her reply as an affirmative.* ■ (**the affirmative**) a position of agreement or confirmation: *his answer veered toward the affirmative.* ■ *Gram.* a word or particle used in making assertions.
▶*interj.* expressing agreement with a statement or request; yes. —**af·firm·a·tive·ly** *adv.*

af·fix ▶*v.* /əˈfiks/ [*tr.*] stick, attach, or fasten (something) to something else: *he licked the stamp and affixed it to the envelope.*
▶*n.* /ˈaˌfiks/ *Gram.* an additional element placed at the beginning or end of a root, stem, or word, or in the body of a word, to modify its meaning. See also INFIX, PREFIX, SUFFIX. —**af·fix·a·tion** /ˌafikˈsāSHən/ *n.*

af·flict /əˈflikt/ ▶*v.* [*tr.*] (of a problem or illness) cause pain or suffering to; affect or trouble: *serious ills afflict the industry* | [as *pl. n.*] (**the afflicted**) *he comforted the afflicted.* —**af·flic·tive** /-tiv/ *adj.* (*archaic*).

af·flic·tion /əˈflikSHən/ ▶*n.* something that causes pain or suffering: *an affliction of the nervous system.* ■ pain or suffering: *poor people in great affliction.*

af·flu·ent /ˈaflōōənt; əˈflōō-/ ▶*adj.* (esp. of a group or area) having a great deal of money; wealthy: *the affluent societies of the western world* | [as *pl. n.*] (**the affluent**) *only the affluent could afford to travel abroad.* —**af·flu·ence** *n.* —**af·flu·ent·ly** *adv.*

af·flu·en·tial /ˌaflōōˈenCHəl/ *inf.* ▶*adj.* rich and socially influential.
▶*n.* a rich and socially influential person.

af·ford /əˈfôrd/ ▶*v.* [*tr.*] **1** have enough money to pay for: *we could never have afforded to heat the place.* ■ have (a certain amount of something, esp. money or time) available or to spare: *it was taking up more time than he could afford.* ■ be able to do something without risk of adverse consequences: *kings could afford to be wrathful.* **2** provide or supply (an opportunity or facility): *the rooftop terrace affords beautiful views.* —**af·ford·a·ble** *adj.*

af·for·es·ta·tion /əˌfôrəˈstāSHən; əˌfär-/ ▶*v.* [*tr.*] the conversion (of land) into forest, esp. for commercial use. —**af·for·est** /əˈfôrist; əˈfär-/ *v.*

af·fray /əˈfrā/ ▶*n.* *Law, dated* an instance of group fighting in a public place that disturbs the peace: *Lowe was charged with causing an affray.*

af·fri·cate /ˈafrikit/ ▶*n.* *Phonet.* a phoneme that combines a plosive with an immediately following fricative or spirant sharing the same place of articulation, e.g., *ch* as in *chair* and *j* as in *jar.*

af·front /əˈfrənt/ ▶*n.* an action or remark that causes outrage or offense: *he took his son's desertion as a personal affront.*
▶*v.* [*tr.*] (usu. **be affronted**) offend the modesty or values of: *she was affronted by his familiarity.*

Af·ghan /ˈafˌgan/ ▶*n.* **1** a native or national of Afghanistan, or a person of Afghan descent. **2** another term for PASHTO. **3** (**afghan**) a blanket or shawl, typically one knitted or crocheted in strips or squares. **4** short for AFGHAN HOUND.
▶*adj.* of or relating to Afghanistan, its people, or their language.

Af·ghan hound ▶*n.* a tall hunting dog of a breed with long silky hair.

a·fi·ci·o·na·do /əˌfiSH(ē)əˈnädō; əˌfisyə-/ ▶*n.* (*pl.* -**dos**) a person who is very knowledgeable and enthusiastic about an activity, subject, or pastime: *aficionados of the finest wines.* ▷*mid 19th cent.* (denoting a devotee of bullfighting): from Spanish, 'amateur,' past participle of *aficionar* 'become fond of' used as a noun, based on Latin *affectio(n)-* '(favorable) disposition toward,' from *afficere* 'to influence,' from *ad-* 'at, to' + *facere* 'do.'

a·field /əˈfēld/ ▶*adv.* **1** to or at a distance: *competitors from as far afield as Hong Kong.* **2** in the field (usually in reference to hunting).

a·fire /əˈfī(ə)r/ ▶*adv. & adj. chiefly poetic/lit.* on fire; burning: *the whole mill was afire.*

a·flame /əˈflām/ ▶*adv. & adj.* in flames; burning: [as *adv.*] *pour brandy over the steaks and then set aflame.*

a·float /əˈflōt/ ▶*adj. & adv.* floating in water; not sinking: [as *adv.*] *they trod water to keep afloat* | [as *adj.*] *the canoes were still afloat.* ■ on board a ship or boat: *flotilla sailing is a sociable way to explore while living afloat.* ■ *fig.* out of debt or difficulty: [as *adj.*] *I contrived to stay afloat in honest self-employment.* ■ in general circulation; current: [as *adj.*] *the rumor has been afloat that I am far advanced in years.*

a·foot /əˈfŏŏt/ ▶*adv. & adj.* **1** in preparation or progress; happening or beginning to happen: [as *adj.*] *plans are afoot for a festival.* **2** on foot: [as *adv.*] *they were forced to go afoot.*

a·fore /əˈfôr/ ▶*prep. archaic* or *dial.* before.

afore- ▶*prefix* before; previously.

a·fore·thought /əˈfôrˌTHôt/ ▶*adj.* see MALICE AFORETHOUGHT.

a·foul /əˈfoul/ ▶*adv.* into conflict or difficulty with.

a·fraid /əˈfrād/ ▶*adj.* feeling fear or anxiety; frightened: *I'm afraid of dogs.* ■ worried that something undesirable will occur or be done; *she was afraid of antagonizing him.* ■ unwilling or reluctant to do something for fear of the consequences: *I'm afraid to go out on the streets.* ■ (**afraid for**) anxious about the well-being or safety of someone or something: *William was suddenly afraid for her.*
▶ □ **I'm afraid** used to express polite or formal apology or regret: *I'm afraid I don't understand.*

a·fresh /əˈfreSH/ ▶*adv.* in a new or different way: *she left the job to start afresh.*

Af·ri·can /ˈafrikən/ ▶*n.* a person from Africa, esp. a black person. ■ a person of black African descent.
▶*adj.* of or relating to Africa or people of African descent.

Af·ri·ca·na /ˌafriˈkanə; -ˈkänə/ ▶*pl. n.* books, artifacts, and other collectors' items connected with Africa, in particular southern Africa.

Af·ri·can A·mer·i·can ▶*n.* a black American.
▶*adj.* (**African-American**) of or relating to black Americans.

Af·ri·can·ize /ˈafrikəˌnīz/ ▶*v.* [*trans.*] **1** make African in character. ■ (in Africa) restructure (an organization) by replacing white employees with black Africans. **2** [usu. as *adj.*] (**Africanized**) hybridize (honeybees of European stock) with bees of African stock, producing an aggressive strain. In recent years hybrids have spread from Brazil to the U.S., where they have become known colloquially as "killer bees." —**Af·ri·can·i·za·tion** /ˌafrikəniˈzāSHən/ *n.*

Af·ri·kaans /ˌafriˈkänz/ ▶*n.* a language of southern Africa, derived from the form of Dutch brought to the Cape by Protestant settlers in the 17th century, and an official language of South Africa.
▶*adj.* relating to the Afrikaner people or their language.

Af·ri·ka·ner /ˌafriˈkänər/ ▶*n.* an Afrikaans-speaking person in South Africa, esp. one descended from the Dutch and Huguenot settlers of the 17th century. —**Af·ri·ka·ner·dom** /-dəm/ *n.*

Af·ro /ˈafrō/ ▶*n.* a thick hairstyle with very tight curls that sticks out all around the head, like the natural hair of some black people.

Af·ro-A·mer·i·can ▶*adj. & n.* another term for AFRICAN AMERICAN.

aft /aft/ ▶*adv. & adj.* at, near, or toward the stern of a ship or tail of an aircraft: [as *adv.*] *Travis made his way aft* | [as *adj.*] *the aft compartment.*

af·ter /ˈaftər/ ▶*prep.* **1** during the period of time following (an event): *shortly after Christmas* | [as *conj.*] *bathtime ended in a flood after the faucets were left running* | [as *adv.*] *Duke Frederick died soon after.* ■ with a period of time rather than an event: *after a while.* ■ in phrases indicating something happening continuously or repeatedly: *day after day we kept studying.* ■ (used in specifying a time) past: *about ten minutes after two.* ■ during the time following the departure of (someone): *she cleans up after him.* **2** behind: *she went out, shutting the door after her.* ■ (with reference to looking or speaking) in the direction of someone who is moving further away: *she stared after him.* **3** in pursuit or quest of: *chasing after something you can't have.* **4** next to and following in order or importance: *in their order of priorities health comes after housing.* **5** in allusion to (someone or something with the same or a related name): *they named her Pauline, after Barbara's mother.* ■ in imitation of: *a drawing after Millet's The Reapers.* **6** concerning or about: *she has asked after Iris's mother.*
▶*adj.* **1** *archaic* later: *in after years.* **2** *Naut.* nearer the stern: *the after cabin.*
▶ □ **after all** in spite of any indications or expectations to the contrary: *I couldn't come after all.* □ **after hours** after normal working or opening hours: [as *adv.*] *working after hours* | [as *adj.*] *an after-hours jazz club.*

af·ter·birth /ˈaftərˌbərTH/ ▶*n.* the placenta and fetal membranes discharged from the uterus after the birth of offspring.

af·ter·burn·er /ˈaftərˌbərnər/ ▶*n.* an auxiliary burner fitted to the exhaust system of a turbojet engine to increase thrust.

af·ter·care /ˈaftərˌke(ə)r/ ▶*n.* subsequent care or maintenance, in particular: ■ care of a patient after a stay in the hospital or of a person on release from prison.

af·ter·ef·fect /ˈaftəriˌfekt/ ▶*n.* an effect that follows after the primary action of something: *he was suffering the aftereffects of the drug.*

af·ter·glow /ˈaftərˌglō/ ▶*n.* light or radiance remaining in the sky after the sun has set. ■ good feelings remaining after a pleasurable or successful experience: *basking in the afterglow of victory.*

Pronunciation Key ə *ago, up*; ər *over, fur*; a *hat*; ā *ate*; ä *car*; CH *chin*; e *let*; ē *see*; e(ə)r *air*; i *fit*; ī *by*; i(ə)r *ear*; NG *sing*; ō *go*; ô *law, for*; oi *toy*; ŏŏ *good*; ōō *goo*; ou *out*; SH *she*; TH *thin*; TH *then*; (h)w *why*; ZH *vision*

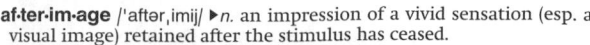

af·ter·im·age /'aftər,imij/ ▸ *n.* an impression of a vivid sensation (esp. a visual image) retained after the stimulus has ceased.

af·ter·life /'aftər,līf/ ▸ *n.* **1** (in some religions) life after death. **2** later life: *they spent much of their afterlife trying to forget the fire.*

af·ter·math /'aftər,maTH/ ▸ *n.* the consequences or aftereffects of an event, esp. when unpleasant: *food prices soared in the aftermath of the drought.*

af·ter·most /'aftər,mōst/ ▸ *adj.* nearest the stern of a ship or tail of an aircraft.

af·ter·noon /,aftər'nōōn/ ▸ *n.* the time from noon or lunchtime to evening: *I telephoned this afternoon | I'll be back at three in the afternoon | she worked on Tuesday afternoons | [as adj.] the afternoon sunshine.* ■ this time on a particular day, characterized by a specified type of activity or particular weather conditions: *an afternoon of drama.*
▸ *adv.* (**afternoons**) *inf.* in the afternoon; every afternoon.

af·ter·shave /'aftər,SHāv/ ▸ *n.* an astringent, typically scented lotion for applying to the skin after shaving.

af·ter·shock /'aftər,SHäk/ ▸ *n.* a smaller earthquake following the main shock of a large earthquake.

af·ter·taste /'aftər,tāst/ ▸ *n.* a taste, typically an unpleasant one, remaining in the mouth after eating or drinking something.

af·ter·tax ▸ *adj.* relating to income that remains after the deduction of taxes due.

af·ter·thought /'aftər,THôt/ ▸ *n.* an item or thing that is thought of or added later: *as an afterthought she said "Thank you."*

af·ter·ward /'aftərwərd/ (also **af·ter·wards** /-wərdz/) ▸ *adv.* at a later or future time; subsequently: *the offender was arrested shortly afterward.*

af·ter·word /'aftər,wərd/ ▸ *n.* a concluding section in a book, typically by a person other than the author.

AG ▸ *abbr.* ■ adjutant general. ■ attorney general.

Ag[1] ▸ *symb.* the chemical element silver.

Ag[2] *Biochem.* ▸ *abbr.* antigen.

a·gain /ə'gen; ə'gān/ ▸ *adv.* another time; once more: *they were disappointed yet again.* ■ returning to a previous position or condition: *he rose, tidied the bed, and sat down again.* ■ in addition to what has already been mentioned: *the wages were low, but they made half as much again in tips.* ■ used to introduce a further point for consideration, supporting or contrasting with what has just been said: *I never saw any signs, but then again, maybe I wasn't looking.* ■ used to ask someone to repeat something: *what was your name again?* ▷Old English *ongēan, ongægn,* etc., of Germanic origin; related to German *entgegen* 'opposite.'

a·gainst /ə'genst; ə'gānst/ ▸ *prep.* **1** in opposition to: *swimming against the tide.* ■ in opposition to, with reference to legal action: *allegations against police officers.* ■ in opposition to, with reference to an athletic contest: *the championship game against Virginia.* ■ (in betting) in anticipation of the failure of: *the odds were 5–1 against Pittsburgh.* **2** in anticipation of and preparation for (a problem or difficulty): *insurance against unemployment.* ■ in resistance to; as protection from: *he turned up his collar against the wind.* ■ in relation to (an amount of money owed or due) so as to reduce or cancel it: *money was advanced against the value of the property.* **3** in conceptual contrast to: *the benefits must be weighed against the costs.* ■ in visual contrast to: *silhouetted against the light of the window.* **4** in or into physical contact with (something), typically so as to be supported by or collide with it: *his lips brushed against her hair.*
▸ □ **have something against someone** dislike or bear a grudge against someone: *I have nothing against you personally.*

a·gam·ic /ā'gamik; ə'gam-/ ▸ *adj. Biol.* asexual; reproducing asexually.

a·ga·pan·thus /,agə'panTHəs/ ▸ *n.* a South African plant (genus *Agapanthus*) of the lily family, with funnel-shaped bluish flowers that grow in rounded clusters.

a·gape[1] /ə'gāp/ ▸ *adj.* (of the mouth) wide open, esp. with surprise or wonder: *Downes stared, mouth agape with incredulity.*

a·ga·pe[2] /ä'gä,pā; 'ägə-/ ▸ *n. Christian Theol.* Christian love, as distinct from erotic or emotional affection.

a·gar /'ä,gär; 'ā,gär/ (also **a·gar-a·gar** /'ägär 'ä,gär; 'āgär 'ä,gär/) ▸ *n.* a gelatinous substance obtained from various kinds of red seaweed and used in biological culture media and as a thickener in foods.

ag·a·ric /'agərik; ə'gar-; ə'ger-/ ▸ *n.* a fungus (order Agaricales, class Basidiomycetes) with a fruiting body that resembles the ordinary mushroom, having a convex or flattened cap with gills on the underside.

ag·ate /'agit/ ▸ *n.* an ornamental stone consisting of a hard variety of chalcedony, typically banded in appearance. ■ a colored toy marble resembling a banded gemstone.

a·ga·ve /ə'gävē/ ▸ *n.* a succulent plant (genus *Agave*, family Agavaceae)

with rosettes of narrow spiny leaves and tall flower spikes, native to the southern US and tropical America.

age /āj/ ▸ *n.* **1** the length of time that a person has lived or a thing has existed: *at the age of 51 | he must be nearly 40 years of age.* ■ a particular stage in someone's life: *children of primary school age.* ■ the latter part of life or existence; old age: *with age this gland can become sluggish.* **2** a distinct period of history: *a child of the television age.* ■ *Geol.* a division of time that is a subdivision of an epoch. ■ *archaic* a lifetime taken as a measure of time; a generation: *Nestor is said to have lived three ages when he was ninety.* ■ (**ages/an age**) *inf.* a very long time: *I haven't seen her for ages | it would take an age to tell her everything.*
▸ *v.* (**ag·ing**) [*intr.*] grow old or older, esp. visibly and obviously so: *you haven't aged a lot.* ■ [*tr.*] cause to grow, feel, or appear older: *he tried aging the painting with coffee.* ■ (esp. with reference to an alcoholic drink) mature or allow to mature: [*intr.*] *the wine ages in open vats.* ■ [*tr.*] determine how old (something) is: *we didn't have a clue how to age these animals.*
▸ □ **come of age** (of a person) reach adult status. ■ (of a movement or activity) become fully established. □ **through the ages** throughout history.

aged ▸ *adj.* **1** /ājd/ having lived for a specified length of time; of a specified age: *young people aged 14 to 18 | he died aged 60.* **2** /'ājid/ having lived or existed for a long time; old: *aged men with white hair | [as pl. n.] (the aged) Methodist homes for the aged.* /ājd/ that has been subjected to aging: *stonewashed jeans have a unique aged appearance.*

age·ism /'āj,izəm/ (also **ag·ism**) ▸ *n.* prejudice or discrimination on the basis of a person's age. —**age·ist** (also **ag·ist**) *adj. & n.*

age·less /'ājlis/ ▸ *adj.* never growing or appearing to grow old: *the town retains an ageless charm.* —**age·less·ness** *n.*

a·gen·cy /'ājənsē/ ▸ *n.* **1** a business or organization established to provide a particular service, typically one that involves organizing transactions between two other parties: *an advertising agency.* ■ a department or body providing a specific service for a government or similar organization: *the Environmental Protection Agency.* **2** action or intervention, esp. such as to produce a particular effect: *a belief in supernatural agency.* ■ a thing or person that acts to produce a particular result: *the movies could be an agency molding the values of the public.*

a·gen·da /ə'jendə/ ▸ *n.* a list of items of business to be considered and discussed at a meeting: *the issue was removed from the agenda.* ■ a list or program of things to be done or problems to be addressed: *he vowed to put jobs at the top of his agenda.* ▷early 17th cent. (in the sense 'things to be done'): from Latin, neuter plural of *agendum,* gerund of *agere* 'do.'

a·gent /'ājənt/ ▸ *n.* **1** a person who acts on behalf of another, in particular: ■ a person who manages business, financial, or contractual matters for an actor, performer, or writer. ■ a person or company that provides a particular service, typically one that involves organizing transactions between two other parties: *a real-estate agent.* ■ a person who obtains information for a government or other official body, typically in secret: *an FBI agent.* **2** a person or thing that takes an active role or produces a specified effect: *bleaching agents.* ■ *Gram.* the doer of an action, typically expressed as the subject of an active verb or in a *by* phrase with a passive verb.

age-old ▸ *adj.* having existed for a very long time.

ag·glom·er·ate ▸ *v.* /ə'glämə,rāt/ collect or form into a mass or group: [*tr.*] *companies agglomerate multiple sites such as chains of stores* [*intr.*] *these small particles soon agglomerate together.*
▸ *n.* /-rit/ a mass or collection of things: *a multimedia agglomerate.* ■ *Geol.* a volcanic rock consisting of large fragments bonded together.
▸ *adj.* /-rit/ collected or formed into a mass. —**ag·glom·er·a·tion** /ə,glämə-'rāSHən/ *n.* —**ag·glom·er·a·tive** /-,rātiv; -rətiv/ *adj.*

ag·glu·ti·nate /ə'glōōtn,āt/ ▸ *v.* firmly stick or be stuck together to form a mass. ■ *Biol.* (with reference to bacteria or red blood cells) clump together: [*tr.*] *these strains agglutinate human red cells* [*intr.*] *cell fragments agglutinate and form intricate meshes.* ■ [*tr.*] *Linguistics* combine (simple words or parts of words) without change of form to express compound ideas. —**ag·glu·ti·na·tion** /ə,glōōtn'āSHən/ *n.*

ag·gran·dize /ə'gran,dīz/ ▸ *v.* [*tr.*] increase the power, status, or wealth of: *an action intended to aggrandize the Frankish dynasty.* ■ enhance the reputation of (someone) beyond what is justified by the facts. —**ag·gran·dize·ment** /-,dīzmənt; -diz-/ *n.* —**ag·gran·diz·er** *n.*

ag·gra·vate /'agrə,vāt/ ▸ *v.* [*tr.*] **1** make (a problem, injury, or offense) worse or more serious: *military action would only aggravate the situation.* **2** *inf.* annoy or exasperate (someone), esp. persistently. —**ag·gra·vat·ing·ly** *adv.* —**ag·gra·va·tion** /,agrə'vāSHən/ *n.*

ag·gre·gate ▸ *n.* /'agrigit/ **1** a whole formed by combining several (typically disparate) elements: *the council was an aggregate of three regional assemblies.* ■ the total number of points scored by a player or team in a

series of sporting contests: *the result put the sides even on aggregate.* **2 a** material or structure formed from a loosely compacted mass of fragments or particles. ■ pieces of broken or crushed stone or gravel used to make concrete, or more generally in construction work.
▶*adj.* /ˈagrigit/ formed or calculated by the combination of many separate units or items; total: *the aggregate amount of grants made.* ■ *Econ.* denoting the total supply or demand for goods and services in an economy at a particular time.
▶*v.* /-ˌgāt/ form or group into a class or cluster: [*intr.*] *the butterflies aggregate in dense groups.* —**ag·gre·ga·tion** /ˌagriˈgāSHən/ *n.* —**ag·gre·ga·tive** /-ˌgātiv/ *adj.*

ag·gre·ga·tor /ˈagriˌgātər/ ▶*n. Comput.* an Internet company that collects information about competing products and services and distributes it through a single Web site: *a travel insurance aggregator.*

ag·gres·sion /əˈgreSHən/ ▶*n.* hostile or violent behavior or attitudes toward another; readiness to attack or confront: *territorial aggression between individuals of the same species.* ■ the action of attacking without provocation, esp. in beginning a quarrel or war. ■ forceful and sometimes overly assertive pursuit of one's aims and interests.

ag·gres·sive /əˈgresiv/ ▶*adj.* ready or likely to attack or confront; characterized by or resulting from aggression: *aggressive behavior.* ■ pursuing one's aims and interests forcefully, sometimes unduly so. —**ag·gres·sive·ly** *adv.* —**ag·gres·sive·ness** *n.*

ag·gres·sor /əˈgresər/ ▶*n.* a person or country that attacks another first.

ag·grieved /əˈgrēvd/ ▶*adj.* resentful at having been unfairly treated: *she saw herself as the aggrieved party.* —**ag·griev·ed·ly** /-vidlē/ *adv.*

a·ghast /əˈgast/ ▶*adj.* filled with horror or shock: *when the news came out they were aghast.* ▷late Middle English: past participle of the obsolete verb *agast, gast* 'frighten,' from Old English *gǣsten.* The spelling with *gh* (originally Scots) became general by about 1700, probably influenced by *ghost.*

ag·ile /ˈajəl/ ▶*adj.* able to move quickly and easily: *Ruth was as agile as a monkey* | *fig. his vague manner concealed an agile mind.* —**ag·ile·ly** /ˈajə(l)lē/ *adv.* —**a·gil·i·ty** /əˈjilitē/ *n.*

ag·ing /ˈājiNG/ (also **age·ing**) ▶*n.* the process of growing old: *the external signs of aging* | [as *adj.*] *the aging process.* ■ the process of change in the properties of a material occurring over a period, either spontaneously or through deliberate action.
▶*adj.* (of a person) growing old; elderly: *looking after aging relatives.* ■ (of a thing) reaching the end of useful life; obsolescent.

ag·i·tate /ˈajiˌtāt/ ▶*v.* [*tr.*] make (someone) troubled or nervous. ■ [*intr.*] campaign to arouse public concern about an issue in the hope of prompting action: *they agitated for a reversal of the decision.* ■ stir or disturb (something, esp. a liquid) briskly. —**ag·i·tat·ed·ly** *adv.*

ag·i·ta·tion /ˌajiˈtāSHən/ ▶*n.* **1** a state of anxiety or nervous excitement. ■ the action of arousing public concern about an issue and pressing for action on it: *widespread agitation for social reform.* **2** the action of briskly stirring or disturbing something, esp. a liquid.

a·gi·ta·to /ˌajiˈtätō/ ▶*adv. & adj. Mus.* (esp. as a direction after a tempo marking) in an agitated manner: *allegro agitato.*

ag·i·ta·tor /ˈajiˌtātər/ ▶*n.* **1** a person who urges others to protest or rebel: *a communist agitator.* **2** an apparatus for stirring liquid, as in a washing machine or a photographic developing tank.

ag·it·prop /ˈajitˌpräp/ ▶*n.* political (originally communist) propaganda, esp. in art or literature: [as *adj.*] *agitprop painters.*

a·glow /əˈglō/ ▶*adj.* glowing: *his bald head aglow under the lights.*

ag·nos·tic /agˈnästik/ ▶*n.* a person who believes that nothing is known or can be known of the existence or nature of God or of anything beyond material phenomena; a person who claims neither faith nor disbelief in God.
▶*adj.* of or relating to agnostics or agnosticism. —**ag·nos·ti·cism** /-təˌsizəm/ *n.*

a·go /əˈgō/ ▶*adv.* (used after a measurement of time) before the present; earlier: *he went five minutes ago* | *as long ago as 1942* | *not long ago.*

a·gog /əˈgäg/ ▶*adj.* very eager or curious to hear or see something: *I'm all agog to see London* | *New York is agog at the gossip.*

ag·o·nist /ˈagənist/ ▶*n.* **1** *Biochem.* a substance that initiates a physiological response when combined with a receptor. Compare with **ANTAGONIST.** **2** *Anat.* a muscle whose contraction moves a part of the body directly. Often contrasted with **ANTAGONIST.** **3** another term for **PROTAGONIST.** ▷early 20th cent.: from Greek *agōnistēs* 'contestant' (a sense reflected in English in the early 17th cent.), from *agōn* 'contest.' —**ag·o·nism** /-ˌnizəm/ *n.*

ag·o·nis·tic /ˌagəˈnistik/ ▶*adj.* combative; polemical. ■ *Zool.* (of animal

behavior) associated with conflict. ■ *Biochem.* of, relating to, or acting as an agonist. —**ag·o·nis·ti·cal·ly** /-ik(ə)lē/ *adv.*

ag·o·nize /ˈagəˌnīz/ ▶*v.* [*intr.*] undergo great mental anguish through worrying about something: *I didn't agonize over the problem.* ■ [*tr.*] cause mental anguish to (someone).

ag·o·ny /ˈagənē/ ▶*n.* (*pl.* **-nies**) extreme physical or mental suffering: *he crashed to the ground in agony.* ■ the final stages of a difficult or painful death: *his last agony* | *the death agony.*

ag·o·ra·pho·bi·a /ˌagərəˈfōbēə/ ▶*n.* extreme or irrational fear of crowded spaces or enclosed public places. —**ag·o·ra·pho·bic** /-ˈfōbik/ *adj. & n.* —**ag·o·ra·phobe** /ˈagərəˌfōb/ *n.*

a·grar·i·an /əˈgre(ə)rēən/ ▶*adj.* of or relating to cultivated land or the cultivation of land. ■ relating to landed property.
▶*n.* a person who advocates a redistribution of landed property.

a·gree /əˈgrē/ ▶*v.* (**a·grees, a·greed, a·gree·ing**) [*intr.*] **1** have the same opinion about something; concur: *I completely agree with your editorial* | [*tr.*] *the authors agree that Jerusalem must remain united.* ■ (**agree with**) approve of (something) with regard to its moral correctness: *I'm not sure I agree with abortion.* **2** (**agree to** or **to do something**) consent to do something that has been suggested by another person: *she had agreed to see a movie with him.* ■ [*intr.*] reach agreement about (something), typically after a period of negotiation: *the commission agreed on a proposal.* **3** (**agree with**) be consistent with: *your body language does not agree with what you are saying.* ■ *Gram.* have the same number, gender, case, or person as: *make the verb agree with the subject.* ■ be healthy or appropriate for someone: *she's eaten something that did not agree with her.*

a·gree·a·ble /əˈgrēəbəl/ ▶*adj.* **1** enjoyable and pleasurable; pleasant: *a cheerful and agreeable companion.* **2** willing to agree to something: *they were agreeable to its publication.* ■ (of a course of action) acceptable: *a compromise that might be agreeable.* —**a·gree·a·ble·ness** *n.* —**a·gree·a·bly** /-blē/ *adv.*

a·gree·ment /əˈgrēmənt/ ▶*n.* harmony or accordance in opinion or feeling; a position or result of agreeing: *the governments failed to reach agreement* | *the two officers nodded in agreement.* ■ a negotiated and typically legally binding arrangement between parties as to a course of action: *a trade agreement.* ■ the absence of incompatibility between two things; consistency. ■ *Gram.* the condition of having the same number, gender, case, or person.

ag·ri·busi·ness /ˈagrəˌbiznis/ ▶*n.* **1** agriculture conducted on commercial principles, esp. using advanced technology. ■ an organization engaged in this. **2** the group of industries dealing with agricultural produce and services required in farming. —**ag·ri·busi·ness·man** *n.* (*pl.* **-men**).

ag·ri·cul·ture /ˈagriˌkəlCHər/ ▶*n.* the science or practice of farming, including cultivation of the soil for the growing of crops and the rearing of animals to provide food and other products. —**ag·ri·cul·tur·al** /ˌagriˈkəlCHərəl/ *adj.* —**ag·ri·cul·tur·ist** /-rist/ *n.*

ag·ro·chem·i·cal /ˌagrōˈkemikəl/ ▶*n.* a chemical used in agriculture, such as a pesticide or a fertilizer.

a·gron·o·my /əˈgränəmē/ ▶*n.* the science of soil management and crop production. —**ag·ro·nom·ic** /ˌagrəˈnämik/ *adj.* —**ag·ro·nom·i·cal** /ˌagrəˈnämikəl/ *adj.* —**ag·ro·nom·i·cal·ly** /ˌagrəˈnämik(ə)lē/ *adv.* —**a·gron·o·mist** /-mist/ *n.*

a·ground /əˈground/ ▶*adj. & adv.* (with reference to a ship) on or onto the bottom in shallow water: [as *adv.*] *the ships must slow to avoid running aground* | [as *adj.*] *a cargo ship aground in the Mediterranean.*

a·gue /ˈāˌgyo͞o/ ▶*n. archaic* malaria or some other illness involving fever and shivering. ■ a fever or shivering fit. —**a·gued** *adj.* —**a·gu·ish** *adj.*

AH ▶*abbr.* in the year of the Hegira (used in the Muslim calendar for reckoning years from Muhammad's departure from Mecca in AD 622); of the Muslim era: *a Koran dated 556 AH.*

ah /ä/ ▶*interj.* used to express a range of emotions including surprise, pleasure, sympathy, and realization: *ah, there you are!* | *ah, this is the life.*

a·ha /äˈhä/ ▶*interj.* used to express satisfaction, triumph, or surprise: *aha! So that's your secret plan!*

a·head /əˈhed/ ▶*adv.* further forward in space; in the line of one's forward motion. ■ further forward in time; in advance; in the near future: *to plan ahead.* ■ onward so as to make progress. ■ in the lead: *the Bucks were ahead by four.* ■ higher in number, amount, or value than previously: *profits were slightly ahead.*
▶ □ **ahead of one's** (or **its**) **time** innovative and radical.

a·hem /əˈhem; əˈhm/ ▶*interj.* used to represent the noise made when clearing the throat, typically to attract attention or express disapproval or embarrassment.

a·hi /ˈähē/ ▶*noun* Japanese name for YELLOWFIN.

a·him·sa /əˈhimˌsä/ ▶*n.* (in the Hindu, Buddhist, and Jain tradition) the principle of nonviolence toward all living things.

a·hoy /əˈhoi/ ▶*interj. Naut.* a call used in hailing: *ship ahoy!*

AI ▶*abbr.* ■ artificial insemination. ■ artificial intelligence.

AID ▶*abbr.* ■ Agency for International Development. ■ artificial insemination by donor.

aid /ād/ ▶*n.* help, typically of a practical nature: *he was walking with the aid of a walker.* ■ financial or material help given to a country or area in need: *700,000 tons of food aid.* ■ a person or thing that is a source of help or assistance: *exercise is an important aid to recovery after heart attacks | a teaching aid.* ■ *hist.* a grant of subsidy or tax to a king.
▶*v.* [*tr.*] help, assist, or support (someone or something) in the achievement of something: *women were aided in childbirth by midwives | [intr.] the heel was slanted to aid in climbing hilly terrain.* ■ promote or encourage (something): *diet and exercise aid healthy skin.*

aide /ād/ ▶*n.* an assistant to an important person, esp. to a political leader: *a presidential aide.* ■ short for AIDE-DE-CAMP.

aide-de-camp /ˈād də ˈkamp/ ▶*n.* (*pl.* **aides-de-camp** /ˈādz/ *pronunc.* same) a military officer acting as a confidential assistant to a senior officer.

AIDS /ādz/ ▶*n.* acquired immune deficiency syndrome, a disease in which there is a severe loss of the body's cellular immunity, greatly lowering the resistance to infection and malignancy.

ai·ki·do /ˌīkēˈdō; īˈkēdō/ ▶*n.* a Japanese form of self-defense and martial art that uses locks, holds, throws, and the opponent's own movements.

ail /āl/ ▶*v.* [*tr.*] trouble or afflict (someone) in mind or body: *exercise is good for whatever ails you.*

ai·ler·on /ˈāləˌrän/ ▶*n.* a hinged surface in the trailing edge of an airplane wing, used to control lateral balance.

ail·ing /ˈāliNG/ ▶*adj.* in poor health: *my ailing mother | fig. the ailing economy.*

ail·ment /ˈālmənt/ ▶*n.* an illness, typically a minor one.

aim /ām/ ▶*v.* **1** [*tr.*] point or direct (a weapon or camera) at a target: *aim the camcorder at some suitable object | [intr.] aim for the middle of the target.* ■ direct (an object or blow) at someone or something: *she aimed the bottle at his head.* ■ (**aim something at**) direct information or an action toward (a particular group): *the TV campaign is aimed at the 16-24 age group.* **2** [*intr.*] have the intention of achieving: *we aim to give you the best service.*
▶*n.* **1** a purpose or intention; a desired outcome: *our primary aim is to achieve financial discipline.* **2** the directing of a weapon or object at a target: *his aim was perfect.*
▶ □ **take aim** point a weapon or camera at a target.

aim·less /ˈāmlis/ ▶*adj.* without purpose or direction: *an aimless, ungratifying life.* —**aim·less·ly** *adv.* —**aim·less·ness** *n.*

ain't /ānt/ *inf.* ▶*contr. of* ■ am not; are not; is not: *if it ain't broke, don't fix it.* ■ has not; have not: *they ain't got nothing to say.*

air /e(ə)r/ ▶*n.* **1** the invisible gaseous substance surrounding the earth, a mixture mainly of oxygen and nitrogen. ■ this substance regarded as necessary for breathing: *get some fresh air.* ■ the free or unconfined space above the surface of the earth: *he tossed his hat high in the air.* ■ [as *adj.*] used to indicate that something involves the use of aircraft: *air travel.* ■ the earth's atmosphere as a medium for transmitting radio waves: *they've sold products over the air.* ■ air considered as one of the four elements in ancient philosophy and in astrology. ■ a breeze or light wind. ■ air conditioning. **2** (**air of**) an impression of a quality or manner given by someone or something: *she answered with a faint air of boredom.* ■ (**airs**) an annoyingly affected and condescending manner: *he began to put on airs and boss us around.* **3** *Mus.* a tune or short melodious composition, typically a song.
▶*v.* **1** [*tr.*] (often **be aired**) express (an opinion or grievance) publicly: *long-standing grievances were aired.* ■ broadcast (a program) on radio or television. **2** [*tr.*] expose (a room) to the open air in order to ventilate it.
▶ □ **by air** in an aircraft: *all goods must come in by air.* □ **in the air** noticeable all around; becoming prevalent: *I smell violence in the air.* □ **on** (or **off**) **the air** being (or not being) broadcast on radio or television. □ **up in the air** (of a plan or issue) still to be settled; unresolved. □ **walk on air** feel elated.

air bag ▶*n.* a safety device fitted inside a road vehicle, consisting of a cushion designed to inflate rapidly in the event of a collision and positioned so as to protect passengers from being flung forward.

air·base /ˈe(ə)rˌbās/ ▶*n.* a base for the operation of military aircraft.

air blad·der ▶*n.* an air-filled bladder or sac found in certain animals and plants. ■ another term for SWIM BLADDER.

air·borne /ˈe(ə)rˌbôrn/ ▶*adj.* transported by air: *airborne pollutants.* ■ (of an aircraft) in the air after taking off.

air brake ▶*n.* a brake worked by air pressure. ■ a movable flap or other device on an aircraft to reduce its speed.

air·brush /ˈe(ə)rˌbrəSH/ ▶*n.* an artist's device for spraying paint by means of compressed air.
▶*v.* [*tr.*] paint with an airbrush. ■ alter or conceal (a photograph or a detail in one) using an airbrush: *a picture of a man with wings airbrushed onto his shoulders.* ■ [usu. as *adj.*] (**airbrushed**) *fig.* represent or describe (someone or something) as better or more beautiful than they in fact are: *an airbrushed vision of the decade.*

airbrush

air con·di·tion·ing ▶*n.* a system for controlling the humidity, ventilation, and temperature in a building or vehicle, typically to maintain a cool atmosphere. —**air con·di·tioned** *adj.* —**air con·di·tion·er** *n.*

air·craft /ˈe(ə)rˌkraft/ ▶*n.* (*pl.* same) an airplane, helicopter, or other machine capable of flight.

air cush·ion ▶*n.* **1** an inflatable cushion. **2** the layer of air supporting a hovercraft or similar vehicle.

Aire·dale /ˈe(ə)rˌdāl/ ▶*n.* a large terrier of a rough-coated black and tan breed.

air·fare /ˈe(ə)rˌfe(ə)r/ ▶*n.* the price of a passenger ticket for travel by aircraft: *save a bundle in airfare by flying standby.*

air·field /ˈe(ə)rˌfēld/ ▶*n.* an area of land set aside for the takeoff, landing, and maintenance of aircraft.

air·flow /ˈe(ə)rˌflō/ ▶*n.* the flow of air, esp. that encountered by a moving aircraft or vehicle.

air·foil /ˈe(ə)rˌfoil/ ▶*n.* a structure with curved surfaces designed to give the most favorable ratio of lift to drag in flight, used as the basic form of the wings, fins, and horizontal stabilizers of most aircraft.

air force ▶*n.* (often **the air force** or **the Air Force**) the branch of a nation's armed services that conducts military operations in the air.

air·frame /ˈe(ə)rˌfrām/ ▶*n.* the body of an aircraft as distinct from its engine.

air·freight /ˈe(ə)rˌfrāt/ ▶*n.* the transportation of goods by aircraft. ■ goods in transit, or to be carried, by aircraft.
▶*v.* [*tr.*] carry or send (goods) by aircraft.
▶*adv.* by airfreight: *the exhibit was flown airfreight.*

air·glow /ˈe(ə)rˌglō/ ▶*n.* a glow in the night sky caused by radiation from the upper atmosphere.

air gun ▶*n.* a gun that fires pellets using compressed air.

air·head ▶*n. inf.* a silly or foolish person.

air·ing /ˈe(ə)riNG/ ▶*n.* **1** an exposure to warm or fresh air, for the purpose of ventilating or removing dampness from something: *give the place a thorough airing.* ■ a walk or outing: *taking the baby out for an airing.* **2** a public expression of an opinion or subject: *ideas that might be worth an airing.* ■ a transmission of a television or radio program.

air·less /ˈe(ə)rlis/ ▶*adj.* stuffy; not ventilated: *a dusty, airless basement.* ■ without wind or breeze; still: *a hot, airless night.* —**air·less·ness** *n.*

air·lift /ˈe(ə)rˌlift/ ▶*n.* an act of transporting supplies by aircraft, typically in a blockade or other emergency: *a massive airlift of food.*
▶*v.* [*tr.*] transport (troops or supplies) by aircraft, typically when transportation by land is difficult.

air·line /ˈe(ə)rˌlīn/ ▶*n.* an organization providing a regular public service of air transportation on one or more routes. ■ (usu. **air line**) a route that forms part of a system regularly used by aircraft.

air·lin·er /ˈe(ə)rˌlīnər/ ▶*n.* a large passenger aircraft.

air·lock /ˈe(ə)rˌläk/ (also **air lock**) ▶*n.* **1** a blockage of the flow in a pump or pipe, caused by an air bubble. **2** a compartment with controlled pressure and parallel sets of doors, to permit movement between areas at different pressures.

air·mail /ˈe(ə)rˌmāl/ ▶*n.* a system of transporting mail by aircraft, typically overseas. ■ a letter carried by aircraft.
▶*v.* [*tr.*] send (mail) by aircraft: *a recent letter that I airmailed to Miss Sifton.*

air·man /ˈe(ə)rmən/ ▶n. (pl. **-men**) a pilot or member of the crew of an aircraft, esp. in an air force. ■ a member of the U.S. Air Force of the lowest rank, below sergeant.

air mat·tress ▶n. an inflatable mattress.

air·plane /ˈe(ə)r‚plān/ ▶n. a powered flying vehicle with fixed wings and a weight greater than that of the air it displaces.

air·play /ˈe(ə)r‚plā/ ▶n. broadcasting time devoted to a particular record, performer, or musical genre.

air pock·et ▶n. a cavity containing air. ■ a region of low pressure causing an aircraft to lose height suddenly.

air·port /ˈe(ə)r‚pôrt/ ▶n. a complex of runways and buildings for the takeoff, landing, and maintenance of civil aircraft, with facilities for passengers. ■ relating to or denoting light popular fiction such as is offered for sale to travelers in airports: *another airport thriller.*

air pow·er ▶n. airborne military forces.

air raid ▶n. an attack in which bombs are dropped from aircraft onto a ground target.

air ri·fle ▶n. a rifle that fires pellets using compressed air.

air·ship /ˈe(ə)r‚SHip/ ▶n. a power-driven aircraft that is kept aloft by gas (typically helium, formerly hydrogen) that is lighter than air.

air·sick /ˈe(ə)r‚sik/ ▶adj. affected with nausea due to travel in an aircraft. **—air·sick·ness** n.

air·space /ˈe(ə)r‚spās/ ▶n. space available in the atmosphere immediately above the earth. ■ the air available to aircraft to fly in, esp. the part subject to the jurisdiction of a particular country: *the airliner was refused permission to enter Maltese airspace.* ■ *Law* the right of a private landowner to the space above his land and any structures on it, which he can use for ordinary purposes such as the erection of signposts.

air·speed /ˈe(ə)r‚spēd/ ▶n. the speed of an aircraft relative to the air through which it is moving.

air·stream /ˈe(ə)r‚strēm/ ▶n. a current of air.

air·strip /ˈe(ə)r‚strip/ ▶n. a strip of ground set aside for the takeoff and landing of aircraft.

air·tight /ˈe(ə)r‚tīt/ ▶adj. not allowing air to escape or pass through. ■ having no weaknesses; unassailable: *Scamp had an airtight alibi.*

air·time /ˈe(ə)r‚tīm/ ▶n. time during which a broadcast is being transmitted. ■ time during which a cellular phone is in use, including calls made and received.

air·waves /ˈe(ə)r‚wāvz/ ▶pl. n. the radio frequencies used for broadcasting: *football pervades the airwaves.*

air·way /ˈeər‚wā/ ▶n. **1** the passage by which air reaches a person's lungs. ■ a tube for supplying air to a person's lungs in an emergency. ■ a ventilating passage in a mine. **2** a recognized route followed by aircraft. ■ (**Airways**) in names of airlines: *British Airways.*

air·wor·thy /ˈe(ə)r‚wərTHē/ ▶adj. (of an aircraft) safe to fly. **—air·wor·thi·ness** n.

air·y /ˈe(ə)rē/ ▶adj. (**air·i·er**, **air·i·est**) **1** spacious, well lit, and well ventilated. ■ delicate, as though filled with or made of air: *airy clouds.* ■ *fig.* giving an impression of light gracefulness and elegance: *her airy presence filled the house.* **2** giving an impression of being unconcerned or not serious, typically about something taken seriously by others: *her airy unconcern.* **—air·i·ly** /-əlē/ adv. **—air·i·ness** n.

aisle /īl/ ▶n. a passage between rows of seats in a building such as a theater, an airplane, or a train. ■ a passage between shelves of goods in a supermarket or other building. ■ *Archit.* (in a church) a lower part parallel to and at the side of a nave, choir, or transept, from which it is divided by pillars. ▷late Middle English *ele, ile,* from Old French *ele,* from Latin *ala* 'wing.' The spelling change in the 17th cent. was due to confusion with *isle* and influenced by French *aile* 'wing.' **—aisled** /īld/ adj.

aitch /āCH/ ▶n. the name of the letter H.

aitch·bone /ˈāCH‚bōn/ ▶n. the buttock or rump bone of cattle. ■ a cut of beef lying over this.

a·jar /əˈjär/ ▶adv. & adj. (of a door or other opening) slightly open: [as adv.] *she had left the window ajar that morning* | [as adj.] *the door to the sitting room was ajar.*

aka ▶abbr. also known as: *John Merrick, aka the Elephant Man.*

AKC ▶abbr. American Kennel Club.

a·kim·bo /əˈkimbō/ ▶adv. with hands on the hips and elbows turned outward: *she stood with arms akimbo, frowning at the small boy.* ■ (of other limbs) flung out widely or haphazardly.

a·kin /əˈkin/ ▶adj. of similar character: *something akin to gratitude overwhelmed her* | *genius and madness are akin.* ■ related by blood.

AL ▶abbr. ■ *Baseball* American League. ■ American Legion.

Al ▶symb. the chemical element aluminum.

à la /ˈä ‚lä; ˈä lə/ ▶prep. (of a dish) cooked or prepared in a specified style or manner: *fish cooked à la meunière.* ■ *inf.* in the style or manner of: *afternoon talk shows à la Oprah.*

al·a·bas·ter /ˈalə‚bastər/ ▶n. a fine-grained, translucent form of gypsum, typically white, often carved into ornaments. ▶adj. made of alabaster. ■ *poetic/lit.* like alabaster in whiteness and smoothness.

à la carte /‚ä lä ˈkärt; lə/ ▶adj. (of a menu or restaurant) listing or serving food that can be ordered as separate items, rather than part of a set meal. ■ (of food) available on such a menu. ▶adv. as separately priced items from a menu, not as part of a set meal: *wine and good food served à la carte.*

a·lack /əˈlak/ (also **a·lack-a-day**) ▶interj. archaic an expression of regret or dismay.

a·lac·ri·ty /əˈlakritē/ ▶n. brisk and cheerful readiness: *she accepted the invitation with alacrity.*

à la mode /‚ä lä ˈmōd/ ▶adv. & adj. **1** in fashion; up to date. **2** served with ice cream. **3** (of beef) braised in wine, typically with vegetables.

A·lar /ˈā‚lär/ ▶n. trademark for **DAMINOZIDE.**

a·lar /ˈālər/ ▶adj. chiefly *Zool.* of or relating to a wing or wings. ■ *Anat.* winglike or wing-shaped.

a·larm /əˈlärm/ ▶n. an anxious awareness of danger: *the boat tilted and the boatmen cried out* **in alarm** | *he views the right-wing upsurge* **with alarm.** ■ a warning of danger: *I hammered on doors to* **raise the alarm.** ■ a warning sound or device: *a burglar alarm.* ■ an alarm clock. ▶v. **1** [tr.] cause (someone) to feel frightened, disturbed, or in danger: *the government was alarmed by an outbreak of unrest.* **2** (**be alarmed**) be fitted or protected with an alarm: *this door is locked and alarmed between 11 p.m. and 6 a.m.* ▷late Middle English (as an exclamation meaning 'to arms!'): from Old French *alarme,* from Italian *allarme,* from *all' arme!* 'to arms!' **—a·larm·ing·ly** adv.

a·larm clock ▶n. a clock with a device that can be made to sound at the time set in advance, used to wake someone up.

a·larm·ist /əˈlärmist/ ▶n. someone who is considered to be exaggerating a danger and so causing needless worry or panic. ▶adj. creating needless worry or panic. **—a·larm·ism** /-‚mizəm/ n.

a·las /əˈlas/ ▶interj. chiefly poetic/lit. or humorous an expression of grief, pity, or concern: *alas, my funds have some limitations.*

A·las·kan mal·a·mute /əˈlaskən/ (also **Alaskan mal·e·mute**) ▶n. a powerful dog of a breed with a thick, gray coat, bred by the Inuit and typically used to pull sleds.

a·late /ˈā‚lāt/ ▶adj. Bot. & Entomol. (chiefly of insects or seeds) having wings or winglike appendages.

alb /alb/ ▶n. a white vestment worn by clergy and servers in some Christian Churches.

al·ba·core /ˈalbə‚kôr/ (also **albacore tuna**) ▶n. a tuna (*Thunnus alalunga* and *Euthynus alletteratus*) that travels in large schools and is of commercial importance as a food fish.

Al·ba·ni·an /alˈbānēən; ôl-/ ▶adj. of or relating to Albania or its people or their language. ▶n. **1** a native or national of Albania, or a person of Albanian descent. **2** the language of Albania.

al·ba·tross /ˈalbə‚trôs; -‚träs/ ▶n. (pl. **albatrosses**) a large oceanic bird (genera *Diomedea* and *Phoebetria,* family Diomedeidae) whose narrow wings may span greater than 10 feet (3.3 m). ■ a source of frustration; an encumbrance (in allusion to Coleridge's *The Rime of the Ancient Mariner*).

al·be·do /alˈbēdō/ ▶n. (pl. **-dos**) chiefly Astron. the proportion of the incident light or other radiation that is reflected by a surface, typically that of a planet or moon.

al·be·it /ôlˈbē-it; al-/ ▶conj. although: *he was making progress, albeit rather slowly.*

al·bi·no /alˈbīnō/ ▶n. (pl. **-nos**) a person or animal having a congenital absence of pigment in the skin and hair (which are white) and the eyes (which are typically pink). ■ *inf.* an abnormally white animal or plant: *an albino tiger.* **—al·bi·nism** /ˈalbə‚nizəm/ n.

al·bum /ˈalbəm/ ▶n. **1** a blank book for the insertion of photographs, stamps, or pictures: *the wedding pictures had pride of place in the family album.* **2** a collection of recordings, on long-playing record, cassette, or compact disc, that are issued as a single item.

A

al·bu·men /alˈbyōōmən/ ▶ n. egg white, or the protein contained in it. —**al·bu·mi·nous** /-mənəs/ adj.

al·bu·min /alˈbyōōmən/ ▶ n. Biochem. a simple form of protein that is soluble in water and coagulable by heat, such as that found in egg white, milk, and (in particular) blood serum.

al·bu·mi·nu·ri·a /alˌbyōōməˈn(y)o͝orēə/ ▶ n. Med. the presence of albumin in the urine, typically as a symptom of kidney disease.

al·che·my /ˈalkəmē/ ▶ n. the medieval forerunner of chemistry, concerned particularly with attempts to convert base metals into gold or to find a universal elixir. ■ fig. a process by which paradoxical results are achieved or incompatible elements combined with no obvious rational explanation: his conducting managed by some alchemy to give a sense of fire and ice. —**al·chem·ic** /alˈkemik/ adj. —**al·chem·i·cal** /alˈkemikəl/ adj. —**al·che·mist** /-mist/ n. —**al·che·mize** /-ˌmīz/ v.

al·co·hol /ˈalkəˌhôl; -ˌhäl/ ▶ n. a colorless volatile flammable liquid, C₂H₅OH, that is the intoxicating constituent of wine, beer, spirits, and other drinks, and is also used as an industrial solvent and as fuel; also called ETHANOL, ETHYL ALCOHOL.. ■ drink containing this. ■ Chem. any organic compound whose molecule contains one or more hydroxyl groups attached to a carbon atom.

al·co·hol·ic /ˌalkəˈhôlik; -ˈhäl-/ ▶ adj. containing or relating to alcoholic liquor: beer is the favorite alcoholic drink. ■ caused by the excessive consumption of alcohol: alcoholic liver disease. ■ suffering from alcoholism. ▶ n. a person suffering from alcoholism.

al·co·hol·ism /ˈalkəhôˌlizəm; -hä-/ ▶ n. an addiction to the consumption of alcoholic liquor or the mental illness and compulsive behavior resulting from alcohol dependency.

al·cove /ˈalˌkōv/ ▶ n. a recess, typically in the wall of a room or of a garden.

al·de·hyde /ˈaldəˌhīd/ ▶ n. Chem. an organic compound containing the group –CHO, formed by the oxidation of alcohols. —**al·de·hy·dic** /ˌaldəˈhīdik/ adj.

al den·te /äl ˈdentā; al/ ▶ adj. & adv. (of food, typically pasta) cooked so as to be still firm when bitten.

al·der /ˈôldər/ (also **alder tree**) ▶ n. a widely distributed tree (genus Alnus) of the birch family that has toothed leaves and bears male catkins and woody female cones.

al·der·man /ˈôldərmən/ ▶ n. (pl. **-men**) an elected member of a municipal council. ■ (in England before 1974) a member of a county or borough council, next in status to the Mayor. ■ (in Anglo-Saxon England) a noble serving the king as a chief officer in a district or shire. ▷Old English aldormann (originally in the general sense 'a man of high rank'), from aldor, ealdor 'chief, patriarch,' from ald 'old' + mann 'man.' Later the sense 'warden of a guild' arose; then, as the guilds became identified with the ruling municipal body, 'local magistrate, municipal officer,' —**al·der·man·ic** /ˌôldərˈmanik/ adj. —**al·der·man·ship** /-ˌSHip/ n.

ale /āl/ ▶ n. a type of beer with a bitter flavor and higher alcoholic content: amber-colored beers, ales, and stouts.

a·le·a·tor·ic /ˌālēəˈtôrik; ˌal-/ ▶ adj. another term for ALEATORY.

a·le·a·to·ry /ˈālēəˌtôrē; ˈal-/ ▶ adj. depending on the throw of a die or on chance; random. ■ relating to or denoting music or other forms of art involving elements of random choice during their composition, production, or performance.

a·lee /əˈlē/ ▶ adv. & adj. on the side of a ship that is sheltered from the wind. ■ (of the helm) moved around to leeward in order to tack a vessel or to bring its bows up into the wind.

ale·house /ˈālˌhous/ ▶ n. dated a tavern.

a·lem·bic /əˈlembik/ ▶ n. a distilling apparatus, now obsolete, consisting of a flask and a cap with a long beak.

a·leph /ˈälif; ˈälef/ ▶ n. the first letter of the Hebrew alphabet.

a·lert /əˈlərt/ ▶ adj. quick to notice any unusual and potentially dangerous or difficult circumstances; vigilant. ■ able to think clearly; intellectually active.
▶ n. the state of being watchful for danger: forces placed **on alert**. ■ an announcement or signal warning of danger: a bomb alert. ■ a period of vigilance in response to such a warning: traffic was halted during the alert.
▶ v. [tr.] warn (someone) of a danger, threat, or problem, typically with the intention of having it avoided or dealt with: he **alerted** people **to** the dangers of smoking | police were alerted after three men drove away without paying. —**a·lert·ly** adv. —**a·lert·ness** n.
▶ □ **on the alert** vigilant and prepared.

Al·eut /əˈlōōt; ˈaləˌōōt/ ▶ n. **1** a member of a people inhabiting the Aleutian Islands, other islands in the Bering Sea, and parts of western Alaska. **2** the language of this people, related to Eskimo.
▶ adj. of or relating to this people or their language.

Al·ex·an·dri·an /ˌaligˈzandrēən/ ▶ adj. of or relating to Alexandria in Egypt. ■ belonging to or akin to the schools of literature and philosophy of ancient Alexandria. ■ (of a writer) derivative or imitative rather than creative; fond of recondite learning.

al·ex·an·drine /ˌaligˈzandrin; -ˌdrēn/ Prosody ▶ adj. (of a line of verse) having six iambic feet.
▶ n. (usu. **alexandrines**) an alexandrine line.

a·lex·i·a /əˈleksēə/ ▶ n. the inability to see words or to read, caused by a defect of the brain. Compare with DYSLEXIA.

al·fal·fa /alˈfalfə/ ▶ n. a leguminous plant (Medicago sativa) with cloverlike leaves and bluish flowers. It is widely grown for fodder.

al·fres·co /alˈfreskō; äl/ ▶ adv. & adj. in the open air: [as adj.] an alfresco luncheon.

al·ga /ˈalgə/ ▶ n. (usu. in pl. **algae** /-jē/) a simple nonflowering plant of a large assemblage that includes the seaweeds and many single-celled forms. Algae contain chlorophyll but lack true stems, roots, leaves, and vascular tissue. —**al·gal** /-gəl/ adj.

al·ge·bra /ˈaljəbrə/ ▶ n. the part of mathematics in which letters and other general symbols are used to represent numbers and quantities in formulae and equations. ■ a system of this based on given axioms. ▷late Middle English: from Italian, Spanish, and medieval Latin, from Arabic al-jabr 'the reunion of broken parts,' 'bone setting,' from jabara 'reunite, restore.' The original sense, 'the surgical treatment of fractures,' probably came via Spanish, in which it survives; the mathematical sense comes from the title of a book, 'ilm al-jabr wa'l-muḳābala 'the science of restoring what is missing and equating like with like.' —**al·ge·bra·ic** /ˌaljəˈbrāik/ adj. —**al·ge·bra·ist** /-ˌbrā-ist/ n.

al·gi·cide /ˈaljəˌsīd/ ▶ n. a substance that is poisonous to algae.

Al·gol¹ /ˈalˌgôl; -ˌgäl/ Astron. ▶ a variable star or star system in the constellation Perseus, regarded as the prototype of eclipsing binary stars.

Al·gol² ▶ n. one of the early high-level computer programming languages that was devised to carry out scientific calculations.

Al·gon·qui·an /alˈgäNGk(w)ēən/ (also **Al·gon·ki·an** /-kēən/) ▶ adj. denoting, belonging to, or relating to a family of North American Indian languages formerly spoken across a vast area from the Atlantic seaboard to the Great Lakes and the Great Plains.
▶ n. **1** this family of languages. **2** a speaker of any of these languages.

Al·gon·quin /alˈgäNGk(w)ən/ (also **Al·gon·kin**) ▶ n. **1** a member of a North American Indian people living in Canada along the Ottawa River and its tributaries and westward to the north of Lake Superior. **2** the dialect of Ojibwa spoken by this people.
▶ adj. of or relating to this people or their language.

al·go·rithm /ˈalgəˌriT͟Həm/ ▶ n. a process or set of rules to be followed in calculations or other problem-solving operations, esp. by a computer: a basic algorithm for division. —**al·go·rith·mic** /ˌalgəˈriT͟Hmik/ adj. —**al·go·rith·mi·cal·ly** /ˌalgəˈriT͟Hmik(ə)lē/ adv.

a·li·as /ˈālēəs/ ▶ adv. used to indicate that a named person is also known or more familiar under another specified name: Eric Blair, alias George Orwell. ■ inf. indicating another term or synonym: the catfish—alias bullhead—makes a mighty tasty fry-up.
▶ n. a false or assumed identity: a spy operating **under the alias** Barsad. ■ Comput. an alternative name or label that refers to a file, command, address, or other item, and can be used to locate or access it.

al·i·bi /ˈaləˌbī/ ▶ n. (pl. **-bis**) a claim or piece of evidence that one was elsewhere when an act, typically a criminal one, is alleged to have taken place: she **has an alibi** for the whole of yesterday evening | a defense of alibi. ■ inf. an excuse or pretext: a catch-all alibi for failure and inadequacy.
▶ v. (**-bis, -bied, -bi·ing**) [tr.] inf. offer an excuse or defense for (someone), esp. by providing an account of their whereabouts at the time of an alleged act. ■ [intr.] make excuses: not once do I recall him whining or alibiing.

a·li·en /ˈālyən; ˈālēən/ ▶ adj. belonging to a foreign country or nation. ■ unfamiliar and disturbing or distasteful: bossing anyone around was alien to him. ■ relating to or denoting beings supposedly from other worlds; extraterrestrial: an alien spacecraft. ■ (of a plant or animal species) introduced from another country and later naturalized.
▶ n. a foreigner, esp. one who is not a naturalized citizen of the country where they are living: an illegal alien. ■ a hypothetical or fictional being from another world. ■ a plant or animal species originally introduced from another country and later naturalized. —**al·ien·ness** n.

al·ien·a·ble /ˈālēənəbəl; ˈālyənə-/ ▶ adj. Law able to be transferred to new ownership. —**a·lien·a·bil·i·ty** /ˌālēənəˈbilitē; ˌālyən-/ n.

al·ien·ate /ˈālēəˌnāt; ˈālyə-/ ▶ v. [tr.] **1** cause (someone) to feel isolated or estranged: an urban environment that would alienate its inhabitants. ■ cause (someone) to become unsympathetic or hostile: the association does not wish to alienate its members. **2** Law transfer ownership of (property rights) to another person or group. —**al·i·en·a·tion** /ˌālēəˈnāsHən; ˈālyə-/ n.

al·i·form /ˈalə̱ˌfôrm; ˈālə-/ ▶ adj. wing-shaped.

a·light[1] /əˈlīt/ ▶ v. [intr.] (of a bird) descend from the air and settle: a lovely blue swallow alighted on a branch. ■ descend from a train, bus, or other form of transportation: the conductor alights to push the cable car around.

a·light[2] ▶ adv. & adj. on fire; burning: [as adj.] the house was alight when the firemen arrived | [as adv.] flammable liquid was set alight. ■ shining brightly: [as adj.] a lamp was alight | fig. the boy's face was **alight with** excitement.

a·lign /əˈlīn/ ▶ v. 1 [tr.] place or arrange (things) in a straight line: brush the surface to align the fibers. ■ put (things) into correct or appropriate relative positions: the fan blades are aligned | fig. aligning domestic prices with prices in world markets. ■ [intr.] lie in a straight line, or in correct relative positions: the pattern of the border at the seam should align perfectly. 2 (**align oneself with**) give support to (a person, organization, or cause): newspapers align themselves with certain political parties. ■ [intr.] come together in agreement or alliance: all of them must align against the foe. —**a·lign·ment** n.

a·like /əˈlīk/ ▶ adj. (of two or more subjects) similar to each other: the brothers were very much alike | the houses all looked alike.
▶ adv. in the same or a similar way: the girls dressed alike in black pants and jackets. ■ used to show that something applies equally to a number of specified subjects: he talked in a friendly manner to staff and patients alike.

al·i·men·ta·ry /ˌaləˈment(ə)rē/ ▶ adj. of or relating to nourishment or sustenance.

al·i·men·ta·tion /ˌaləmenˈtāsHən/ ▶ n. formal the provision of nourishment or other necessities of life.

al·i·mo·ny /ˈaləˌmōnē/ ▶ n. a husband's or wife's court-ordered provision for a spouse after separation or divorce. ▷early 17th cent. (in the sense 'nourishment, means of subsistence'): from Latin alimonia 'nutriment,' from alere 'nourish.'

A-line /ˈā ˌlīn/ ▶ adj. (of a garment) slightly flared from a narrow waist or shoulders: A-line skirts.

al·i·quot /ˈalikwət/ ▶ n. a portion of a larger whole, esp. a sample taken for chemical analysis or other treatment. ■ (also **aliquot part** or **portion**) Math. a quantity that can be divided into another an integral number of times.

A-list /ˈā ˌlist/ (or **B-list**) ▶ n. a real or imaginary list of the most (or, for B-list, second-most) celebrated or sought-after individuals, especially in show business: [as modifier] an A-list celebrity.

a·live /əˈlīv/ ▶ adj. 1 (of a person, animal, or plant) living, not dead: he was kept alive by a feeding-tube. ■ (of a feeling or quality) continuing in existence: keeping hope alive. ■ continuing to be supported or in use: militarism was kept alive by superstition. 2 (of a person or animal) alert and active; animated: Ken comes alive when he hears his music played. ■ fig. having interest and meaning: we make history come alive for the children. 3 (**alive to**) aware of and interested in; responsive to: always alive to new ideas. 4 (**alive with**) swarming or teeming with: in spring those cliffs are alive with auks and gulls. —**a·live·ness** n.
▶ □ **alive and kicking** inf. prevalent and very active: bigotry is still alive and kicking. □ **alive and well** still existing or active (often used to deny rumors or beliefs that something has disappeared or declined): Jefferson's ideas are alive and well today in Washington.

al·ka·hest /ˈalkəˌhest/ ▶ n. hist. the hypothetical universal solvent sought by alchemists.

al·ka·li /ˈalkəˌlī/ ▶ n. (pl. **-lis**) a chemical compound that neutralizes or effervesces with acids and turns litmus blue; typically, a caustic or corrosive substance of this kind such as lime or soda. Often contrasted with ACID; compare with BASE[1].

al·ka·line /ˈalkəlin; -ˌlīn/ ▶ adj. having the properties of an alkali, or containing alkali; having a pH greater than 7. —**al·ka·lin·i·ty** /ˌalkəˈlinitē/ n.

al·ka·loid /ˈalkəˌloid/ ▶ n. Chem. any of a class of nitrogenous organic compounds of plant origin that have pronounced physiological actions on humans. They include many drugs (morphine, quinine) and poisons (atropine, strychnine).

al·ka·lo·sis /ˌalkəˈlōsis/ ▶ n. Med. an excessively alkaline condition of the body fluids or tissues that may cause weakness or cramps.

al·kane /ˈalˌkān/ ▶ n. Chem. any of the series of saturated hydrocarbons having the general formula C_nH_{2n+2}, including methane, ethane, and propane.

al·kene /ˈalˌkēn/ ▶ n. Chem. any of the series of unsaturated hydrocarbons containing a double bond and having the general formula C_nH_{2n}, including ethylene and propylene. Also called OLEFIN.

al·kyd /ˈalkid/ ▶ n. Chem. any of a group of synthetic polyester resins derived from various alcohols and acids, used in paints and adhesives.

al·kyl /ˈalkəl/ ▶ n. [as adj.] Chem. of or denoting a hydrocarbon radical derived from an alkane by removal of a hydrogen atom. ▷late 19th cent.: German, from Alkohol 'alcohol' + the chemical suffix -yl.

all /ôl/ ▶ adj. & pron. used to refer to the whole quantity or extent of a particular group or thing: [as adj.] 10% of all cars sold | [as pron.] carry all of the blame | the men are all bearded. ■ [adj.] any whatever: he denied all knowledge. ■ [adj.] used to emphasize the greatest possible amount of a quality: they were **in all** probability completely unaware | **with all** due respect. ■ inf. dominated by a particular feature or characteristic: an eleven-year-old string bean, all elbows and knees. ■ [pron.] the only thing (used for emphasis): all I want is to be left alone. ■ [pron.] (used to refer to surroundings or a situation in general) everything: it was all very strange. ■ inf. used to indicate more than one person or thing: a team of specialists who all know the patient. ■ dial. consumed; finished; gone: the cake is all.
▶ adv. 1 used for emphasis; completely: she's been all around the world. ■ consisting entirely of: all leather jacket. 2 (in games) used after a number to indicate an equal score: after extra time it was still two all.
▶ n. the whole of one's possessions, energy, or interest: giving their all.
▶ □ ■ **all along** all the time; from the beginning: she'd known all along. □ **all around** (Brit. also **all round**) 1 in all respects: it was a bad day all around. 2 for or by each person: drinks all around. □ **all but** 1 very nearly: the subject was all but forgotten. 2 all except: we have support from all but one of the networks. □ **all for** inf. strongly in favor of: I was all for tolerance. □ **all in** inf. exhausted: he was all in by halftime. □ **all in all** everything considered; on the whole: all in all it's been a good year. □ **all of** as much as (typically used ironically of a quantity considered small by the speaker): the show lasted all of six weeks. □ **all out** using all one's strength or resources: going all out to win | [as adj.] an all-out effort. □ **all over** 1 completely finished: it's all over between us. 2 inf. everywhere: there were bodies all over. ■ with reference to all parts of the body: I was shaking all over. 3 inf. typical of the person mentioned: that's our management all over! 4 inf. effusively attentive to (someone): James was all over her. □ **all there** inf. in full possession of one's mental faculties: he's not quite all there. □ **all told** in total: they tried a dozen times all told. □ **all very well** inf. used to express criticism or rejection of a favorable or consoling remark: your proposal is all very well in theory. □ **at all** (used for emphasis) in any way; to any extent: I don't like him at all. □ **in all** in total number; altogether: there were about 5,000 people in all.

Al·lah /ˈälə; ˈalə/ ▶ the name of God among Muslims (and Arab Christians).

all-A·mer·i·can ▶ adj. 1 possessing qualities characteristic of American ideals, such as honesty, industriousness, and health. 2 having members or contents drawn only from America or the U.S. ■ involving or representing the whole of America or the U.S.: an all-American final. ■ (of a sports player) honored as one of the best amateur competitors in the U.S.: an all-American wrestler.
▶ n. a sports player honored as one of the best amateurs in the U.S.

all-a·round (Brit. **all-round**) ▶ adj. having many uses or abilities; versatile: an all-around artist. ■ in many or all respects: his all-around excellence. ■ comprehensive; extensive: an all-around education.

al·lay /əˈlā/ ▶ v. [tr.] diminish or put at rest (fear, suspicion, or worry): the report attempted to allay fears. ■ relieve or alleviate (pain or hunger).

all clear ▶ n. a signal that danger or difficulty is over: she was given the all-clear to travel home.

al·le·ga·tion /ˌaliˈgāsHən/ ▶ n. a claim or assertion that someone has done something illegal or wrong, typically one made without proof: he made allegations of corruption against the administration.

al·lege /əˈlej/ ▶ v. [tr.] claim or assert that someone has done something illegal or wrong, typically without proof that this is the case: he alleged that he had been assaulted. | the offenses are alleged to have been committed outside the woman's home. | (usu. **be alleged**) suppose or affirm to be the case: the first artifact ever alleged to be from Earhart's aircraft.

al·leged /əˈlejd/ ▶ adj. (of an incident or a person) said, without proof, to have taken place or to have a specified illegal or undesirable quality: the alleged conspirators. —**al·leg·ed·ly** /-ˈidlē/ adv.

al·le·giance /əˈlējəns/ ▶ n. loyalty or commitment of a subordinate to a superior or of an individual to a group or cause: those wishing to receive citizenship must swear allegiance to the republic.

al·le·gor·i·cal /ˌaliˈgôrikəl; -ˈgär-/ ▶ adj. constituting or containing allegory: an allegorical painting. —**al·le·gor·ic** adj. —**al·le·gor·i·cal·ly** adv.

al·le·go·rize /ˈaligəˌrīz/ ▶ v. [tr.] interpret or represent symbolically. —**al·le·go·ri·za·tion** /ˌaliˌgôriˈzāsHən/ n.

al·le·go·ry /ˈaləˌgôrē/ ▶ n. (pl. **-ries**) a story, poem, or picture that can be interpreted to reveal a hidden meaning, typically a moral or political one: *Pilgrim's Progress is an allegory of the spiritual journey.* ■ the genre to which such works belong. ■ a symbol. —**al·le·go·rist** /-ist/ n.

al·le·gret·to /ˌaliˈgretō/ *Mus.* ▶ adj. & adv. (esp. as a direction) at a fairly brisk tempo.

al·le·gro /əˈleɡrō/ *Mus.* ▶ adj. & adv. (esp. as a direction) at a brisk tempo.

al·lele /əˈlēl/ ▶ n. *Genetics* one of two or more alternative forms of a gene that arise by mutation and are found at the same place on a chromosome. —**al·lel·ic** /əˈlēlik; əˈlel-/ adj.

al·le·lu·ia /ˌaləˈlōōyə/ ▶ interj. variant spelling of HALLELUJAH.

Al·len wrench (also **al·len wrench**) ▶ n. an L-shaped metal bar with a hexagonal head at each end, used to turn screws.

al·ler·gen /ˈalərjən/ ▶ n. a substance that causes an allergic reaction. —**al·ler·gen·ic** /ˌalərˈjenik/ adj. —**al·ler·ge·nic·i·ty** /ˌalərjəˈnisitē/ n.

al·ler·gic /əˈlərjik/ ▶ adj. caused by or relating to an allergy: *an allergic reaction.* ■ having an allergy to (a substance): *allergic to the sting of bees.* ■ (**allergic to**) *inf.* having a strong dislike for: *I'm allergic to the hype.*

al·ler·gy /ˈalərjē/ ▶ n. (pl. **-gies**) a damaging immune response by the body to a substance, esp. pollen, fur, a particular food, or dust, to which it has become hypersensitive. ■ *inf.* an antipathy: *their allergy to free enterprise.* —**al·ler·gist** n.

al·le·vi·ate /əˈlēvēˌāt/ ▶ v. [tr.] make (suffering, deficiency, or a problem) less severe: *he couldn't prevent her pain, only alleviate it.* —**al·le·vi·a·tion** /əˌlēvēˈāSHən/ n. —**al·le·vi·a·tor** /-ˌātər/ n.

al·ley¹ /ˈalē/ ▶ n. (pl. **-leys**) a narrow passageway between or behind buildings. ■ a path lined with trees, bushes, or stones. ■ a long, narrow area in which games such as bowling are played. ■ *Tennis* either of the two areas of the court between the doubles sideline and the singles or service sideline. ■ *Baseball* the area between the outfielders in left center or right center field.

▶ □ **up one's alley** (or **right up one's alley**) *inf.* well suited to one's tastes, interests, or abilities.

al·ley² (also **al·ly**) ▶ n. (pl. **-leys**) a toy marble made of marble, alabaster, or glass.

All Fools' Day ▶ n. another term for APRIL FOOL'S DAY.

al·li·ance /əˈlīəns/ ▶ n. a union or association formed for mutual benefit, esp. between countries or organizations: *a defensive alliance between Australia and New Zealand* | *divisions within the alliance.* ■ a relationship based on an affinity in interests, nature, or qualities: *an alliance between medicine and morality.* ■ a state of being joined or associated: *his party is in alliance with the Greens.*

al·lied /əˈlīd; ˈalˌīd/ ▶ adj. joined by or relating to members of an alliance: *allied territories* | *the allied fleet.* ■ (usu. **Allied**) of or relating to the U.S. and its allies in World War I and World War II and after: *the liberation of Paris by Allied troops.* ■ (**allied to/with**) in combination or working together with: *skilled craftsmanship allied to advanced technology.* ■ connected or related: *members of the medical and allied professions.*

al·li·ga·tor /ˈaliˌgātər/ ▶ n. a large semiaquatic reptile (genus *Alligator*, family Alligatoridae, order Crocodylia) similar to a crocodile but with a broader and shorter head. ■ the skin of the alligator or material resembling it. ▷ late 16th cent.: from Spanish *el lagarto* 'the lizard,' probably based on Latin *lacerta*.

al·lit·er·ate /əˈlitəˌrāt/ ▶ v. [intr.] (of a phrase or line of verse) contain words that begin with the same sound or letter: *his first and last names alliterated.* ■ use words that begin with the same sound or letter. —**al·lit·er·a·tive** adj.

al·lit·er·a·tion /əˌlitəˈrāSHən/ ▶ n. the occurrence of the same letter or sound at the beginning of adjacent or closely connected words.

al·li·um /ˈalēəm/ ▶ n. (pl. **alliums**) a bulbous plant (genus *Allium*) of the lily family that includes the onion and its relatives (e.g., garlic and chives).

al·lo·cate /ˈaləˌkāt/ ▶ v. [tr.] distribute (resources or duties) for a particular purpose: *the authorities allocated 50,000 places to refugees.* —**al·lo·ca·ble** /-kəbəl/ adj. —**al·lo·ca·tion** /ˌaləˈkāSHən/ n. —**al·lo·ca·tor** /-ˌkātər/ n.

al·lo·cu·tion /ˌaləˈkyōōSHən/ ▶ n. a formal speech giving advice or a warning.

al·lo·morph /ˈaləˌmôrf/ ▶ n. *Linguistics* any of the versions of a morpheme, such as the plural endings /s/ (as in *bats*), /z/ (as in *bugs*), and /iz/ (as in *buses*) for the plural morpheme. —**al·lo·mor·phic** /ˌaləˈmôrfik/ adj.

al·lop·a·thy /əˈläpəTHē/ ▶ n. the treatment of disease by conventional means, i.e., with drugs having opposite effects to the symptoms. Often contrasted with HOMEOPATHY. —**al·lo·path·ic** /ˌaləˈpaTHik/ adj. —**al·lop·a·thist** /-THist/ n.

al·lo·phone /ˈaləˌfōn/ ▶ n. *Linguistics* any of the speech sounds that represent a single phoneme, such as the aspirated *k* in *kit* and the

unaspirated *k* in *skit*, which are allophones of the phoneme *k*. —**al·lo·phon·ic** /ˌaləˈfänik/ adj.

al·lot /əˈlät/ ▶ v. (**-lot·ted**, **-lot·ting**) [tr.] give or apportion (something) to someone as a share or task: *equal time was allotted to each.*

al·lot·ment /əˈlätmənt/ ▶ n. the amount of something allocated to a particular person: *the gadget shuts off the television set when a kid has used up his allotment.* ■ *chiefly hist.* a piece of land deeded by the government to an American Indian. ■ the action of allotting.

al·lo·trope /ˈaləˌtrōp/ ▶ n. *Chem.* each of two or more different physical forms in which an element can exist. Graphite, charcoal, and diamond are all allotropes of carbon. —**al·lo·trop·ic** /ˌaləˈträpik; -ˈtrōpik/ adj.

al·low /əˈlou/ ▶ v. [tr.] **1** admit (an event or activity) as legal or acceptable: *a plan to allow Sunday shopping.* ■ give (someone) permission to do something: *the dissident was allowed to leave the country.* ■ permit (someone) to have (something): *he was allowed his first sip of Scotch.* ■ permit (someone) to enter a place or go in a particular direction: *the river was patrolled and few people were allowed across.* ■ fail to prevent (something) from happening: *I could not believe that we would allow the opportunity to slip away.* **2** give the necessary time or opportunity for: *he stopped for a moment to allow his eyes to adjust.* ■ [intr.] (**allow for**) make provision or provide scope for (something): *the house was demolished to allow for road widening.* ■ [intr.] (**allow for**) take (something) into consideration when making plans or calculations: *income rose by 11 percent allowing for inflation.* ■ provide or set aside (a specified amount of something) for a specific purpose: *allow an hour or so for driving.* **3** admit the truth of; concede: *he allowed that the penalty appeared too harsh for the crime.* ■ *inf.* or *dial.* assert; be of the opinion: *Lincoln allowed that he himself could never support the man.* —**al·low·a·ble** adj. —**al·low·a·bly** /-əblē/ adv.

al·low·ance /əˈlou-əns/ ▶ n. the amount of something that is permitted, esp. within a set of regulations or for a specified purpose: *a seventy-five-pound baggage allowance.* ■ a sum of money paid regularly to a person to meet specified needs or expenses. ■ a small amount of money that a parent regularly gives a child. ■ an amount of money that can be earned or received free of tax: *a personal allowance.* ■ a reduction in price, typically for the exchange of used goods: *he made the down payment with the trade-in allowance.* ■ *archaic* tolerance.

▶ □ **make allowance(s) for 1** take into consideration when planning or making calculations: *a special circuit makes allowances for changes in the ambient temperature.* **2** regard or treat leniently on account of mitigating circumstances: *she liked them and made allowances for their faults.*

al·loy ▶ n. /ˈaˌloi/ a metal made by combining two or more metallic elements, esp. to give greater strength or resistance to corrosion: *an alloy of nickel, bronze, and zinc.* ■ an inferior metal mixed with a precious one.

▶ v. /ˈaˌloi; əˈloi/ [tr.] mix (metals) to make an alloy: *alloying tin with copper to make bronze.* ■ *fig.* debase (something) by adding something inferior.

all-pur·pose ▶ adj. having many uses, esp. all that might be expected from something of its type: *an all-purpose kitchen knife.*

all right ▶ adj. satisfactory but not especially good; acceptable: *the tea was all right.* ■ (of a person) in a satisfactory mental or physical state: *"Are you all right? You were screaming."* ■ permissible; allowable: *it's all right for you to go now.*

▶ adv. **1** in a satisfactory manner or to a satisfactory extent; fairly well: *everything will turn out all right.* **2** used to emphasize how certain one is about something: *"Are you sure it's him?" "It's him all right."*

▶ interj. expressing or asking for assent, agreement, or acceptance: *all right, I'll tell you.*

all right·y ▶ exclam. *inf.* ALL RIGHT, used especially to express agreement or acceptance.

All Souls' Day ▶ n. a festival in some Christian churches with prayers for the souls of the dead, held on November 2.

all·spice /ˈôlˌspīs/ ▶ n. **1** the dried aromatic fruit of a West Indian tree, used whole or ground as a culinary spice. **2** a tree (*Pimenta dioica*) of the myrtle family from which this spice is obtained. Also called PIMENTO. **3** an aromatic North American tree or shrub (genus *Calycanthus*, family Calycanthaceae).

all-time ▶ adj. unsurpassed: *all-time favorite.*

al·lude /əˈlōōd/ ▶ v. [intr.] (**allude to**) suggest or call attention to indirectly; hint at: *she had a way of alluding to Jean but never saying her name.* ■ mention without discussing at length: *we will allude briefly to the main points.* ■ (of an artist or a work of art) recall (an earlier work or style) in such a way as to suggest a relationship with it: *the photographs allude to Italian Baroque painting.*

al·lure /əˈlŏŏr/ ▶ n. the quality of being powerfully and mysteriously attractive or fascinating: *people for whom gold holds no allure.*

▶ v. [tr.] powerfully attract or charm; tempt: [as adj.] (**alluring**) *the town offers alluring shops and restaurants.* —**al·lure·ment** n. —**al·lur·ing·ly** adv.

al·lu·sion /ə'lōōZHən/ ▶n. an expression designed to call something to mind without mentioning it explicitly; an indirect or passing reference: *an allusion to Shakespeare | a classical allusion.* ■ the practice of making such references, esp. as an artistic device.

al·lu·sive /ə'lōōsiv/ ▶adj. (of a remark or reference) working by suggestion rather than explicit mention: *allusive references to the body.* —**al·lu·sive·ly** adv. —**al·lu·sive·ness** n.

al·lu·vi·um /ə'lōōvēəm/ ▶n. a deposit of clay, silt, sand, and gravel left by flowing streams in a river valley or delta. —**al·lu·vi·al** /-əl/ adv.

al·ly¹ ▶n. /'alī/ (pl. **-lies**) a state formally cooperating with another for a military or other purpose, typically by treaty. ■ a person or organization that cooperates with or helps another in a particular activity: *he was forced to dismiss his closest political ally.* ■ (**the Allies**) a group of nations taking military action together, in particular the countries that fought with the U.S. in World War I and World War II.
▶v. /ə'lī/ (**-lies, -lied**) [tr.] (**ally something to/with**) combine or unite a resource or commodity with (another) for mutual benefit: *he allied his racing experience with his father's business acumen.* ■ (**ally oneself with**) side with or support (someone or something): *he allied himself with the rebels.*

al·ly² ▶n. (pl. **-lies**) variant spelling of ALLEY².

al·ma·nac /'ôlmə,nak; 'al-/ (also, esp. in titles, **al·ma·nack**) ▶n. an annual calendar containing important dates and statistical information such as astronomical data and tide tables. ■ an annual handbook containing information of general interest or on a sport or pastime.

al·might·y /ôl'mītē/ ▶adj. having complete power; omnipotent: *God almighty.* ■ (**the Almighty**) a name or title for God: *I wanted to beg the Almighty for mercy.* ■ inf. very great; enormous: *an almighty roar.*

al·mond /'ä(l)mz/ /'ā(l)-/ ▶n. **1** the oval nutlike seed (kernel) of the almond tree, used as food. **2** (also **almond tree**) the widely cultivated Asian tree (*Prunus dulcis*) of the rose family that produces this nut.
▶adj. made of or flavored with almonds. ■ of an oval shape, pointed at one or both ends: *almond eyes.* ■ a pale tan color, as of an almond shell.

al·mond paste ▶n. another term for MARZIPAN.

al·most /'ôl'mōst; 'ôl,mōst/ ▶adv. not quite; very nearly: *he almost knocked Georgina over | the place was almost empty.*

alms /ä(l)mz/ ▶pl. n. (in historical contexts) money or food given to poor people. ▷Old English ælmysse, ælmesse, from Christian Latin eleemosyna, from Greek eleēmosunē 'compassion,' from eleēmōn 'compassionate,' from eleos 'mercy.'

alms·house /'ä(l)mz,hous/ ▶n. a house built originally by a charitable person or organization for poor people to live in.

al·oe /'alō/ ▶n. a succulent plant (genus *Aloe*) of the lily family, typically having a rosette of toothed fleshy leaves and bell-shaped or tubular flowers on long stems. ■ (**al·oes** or **bitter aloes**) a strong laxative obtained from the bitter juice of various kinds of aloe. ■ (also **American aloe**) another term for CENTURY PLANT.

a·loft /ə'lôft/ ▶adj. & adv. up in or into the air; overhead: *the congregation sways, hands aloft* | [as adv.] *she held her glass aloft.* ■ up the mast or into the rigging of a sailing vessel.

a·lo·ha /ə'lō,hä/ ▶interj. & n. Hawaiian word used when greeting or parting from someone.

a·lone /ə'lōn/ ▶adj. & adv. **1** having no one else present; on one's own: *she was alone that evening* | [as adv.] *he lives alone.* ■ without others' help or participation; single-handed: *team members are more effective than individuals working alone.* ■ [as adj.] isolated and lonely: *she was terribly alone and exposed.* ■ having no companions in a particular position or course of action: *they were not alone in dissenting from the advice.* **2** [as adv.] indicating that something is confined to the specified subject or recipient: *we agreed to set up such a test for him alone.* ■ used to emphasize that only one factor out of several is being considered and that the whole is greater or more extreme: *there were fifteen churches in the town center alone.* —**a·lone·ness** /ə'lōn(n)əs/ n.
▶ □ **go it alone** inf. act by oneself without assistance. □ **leave** (or **let**) **someone/something alone 1** abandon or desert someone or something. **2** stop disturbing or interfering with someone or something.

a·long /ə'lông; ə'läng/ ▶prep. **1** moving in a constant direction on (a path or any more or less horizontal surface): *soon we were driving along a narrow road* | [as adv.] *she sailed along.* ■ used metaphorically to refer to the passage of time or the making of progress: *they can be helped along the road to modernity* | [as adv.] *they asked how the construction was coming along.* **2** extending in a more or less horizontal line on: *cars were parked along the grass border.*
▶adv. in or into company with others: *he had brought along a friend of his.* ■ at hand; with one: *take along a camcorder when you visit.*

a·long·shore /ə'lông'SHôr; ə'läng-/ ▶adv. along or by the shore: *currents flowing alongshore.*

a·long·side /ə'lông'sīd; ə'läng-/ ▶prep. (also **alongside of**) close to the side of; next to: *she was sitting alongside him* | [as adv.] *the boat came alongside.* ■ together and in cooperation with: *a care assistant was working alongside him.* ■ at the same time as or in coexistence with: *alongside the development of full-time courses there had to be provision for the part-time student.*

a·loof /ə'lōōf/ ▶adj. not friendly or forthcoming; cool and distant: *courteous but aloof.* ■ conspicuously uninvolved and uninterested, typically through distaste: *he stayed aloof from the bickering.* —**a·loof·ly** adv. —**a·loof·ness** n.

a·loud /ə'loud/ ▶adv. **1** audibly; not silently or in a whisper: *he read the letter aloud.* **2** archaic loudly: *he wept aloud.*

alp /alp/ ▶n. a high mountain, esp. a snow-capped one.

al·pac·a /al'pakə/ ▶n. (pl. same or **alpacas**) a long-haired domesticated South American mammal (*Lama pacos*) of the camel family, related to the llama and valued for its wool. ■ the wool of the alpaca. ■ fabric made from this wool.

al·pen·horn /'alpən,hôrn/ ▶n. a valveless wooden horn up to 12 feet (4 m) long, used for signaling in the Alps.

al·pha /'alfə/ ▶n. **1** the first letter of the Greek alphabet (A, α), transliterated as "a." ■ [as adj.] denoting the first of a series of items or categories, e.g., forms of a chemical compound: *alpha interferon.* ■ (**Alpha**) [followed by Latin genitive] the first (typically the brightest) star in a constellation: *Alpha Centauri.* ■ [as adj.] relating to alpha decay or alpha particles: *an alpha emitter.* ■ (of animals in a group) the socially dominant individual: *he rose to be alpha male of his troop at the very early age of 16.* **2** a code word representing the letter A, used in radio communication.
▶symb. ■ (α) a plane angle.

al·pha·bet /'alfə,bet/ ▶n. a set of letters or symbols in a fixed order, used to represent the basic sounds of a language; in particular, the set of letters from A to Z. ■ the basic elements in a system which combine to form complex entities: *DNA's 4-letter alphabet.*

al·pha·bet·i·cal /,alfə'betikəl/ ▶adj. of or relating to an alphabet: *alphabetical characters.* ■ in the order of the letters of the alphabet: *an alphabetical index.* —**al·pha·bet·ic** adj. —**al·pha·bet·i·cal·ly** /-ik(ə)lē/ adv.

al·pha·bet·ize /'alfəbi,tīz/ ▶v. [tr.] arrange (words or phrases) in alphabetical order: *the listings are arranged by state and alphabetized by city.* —**al·pha·bet·i·za·tion** /,alfə,betə'zäsHən/ n.

al·pha·nu·mer·ic /,alfən(y)ōō'merik/ ▶adj. consisting of or using both letters and numerals: *alphanumeric data | an alphanumeric keyboard.*
▶n. a character that is either a letter or a number. —**al·pha·nu·mer·i·cal** adj.

al·pine /'al,pīn/ ▶adj. [usu. attrib] of or relating to high mountains: *alpine habitats.* ■ (in the names of plants and animals) growing or found on high mountains: *the alpine forget-me-not.* ■ (**Alpine**) of or relating to the Alps. ■ (also **Al·pine**) (of skiing) involving downhill racing.
▶n. a plant native to mountain districts, often suitable for growing in rock gardens.

al Qae·da /al 'kīdə; 'kādə; kä'ēdə/ (also **al-Qa'i·dah, al-Qae·da**) ▶a militant Islamic fundamentalist group. Founded in the late 1980s, its goal is to establish a pan-Islamic caliphate.

al·read·y /ôl'redē/ ▶adv. **1** before or by now or the time in question: *Anna has suffered already.* ■ as surprisingly soon or early as this: *at 31, he already suffers from arthritis.* **2** inf. used as an intensive after a word or phrase to express impatience: *enough already with these crazy kids!*

al·right /ôl'rīt/ ▶ variant spelling of ALL RIGHT.

Al·sa·tian /al'sāsHən/ ▶n. **1** chiefly Brit. another term for GERMAN SHEPHERD. **2** a native or inhabitant of Alsace.
▶adj. of or relating to Alsace or its inhabitants.

al·so /'ôlsō/ ▶adv. in addition; too: *a brilliant linguist, he was also interested in botany | also, a car is very expensive to run.*

al·so-ran ▶n. a loser in a race or contest, esp. by a large margin. ■ an undistinguished or unsuccessful person or thing.

alt. (also **alt-**) ▶combining form denoting a version of something that is intended as a challenge to the traditional version: *an alt.classical quartet.*

al·tar /'ôltər/ ▶n. the table in a Christian church at which the bread and wine are consecrated in communion services. ■ a table or flat-topped block used as the focus for a religious ritual, esp. for making sacrifices or offerings to a deity. ▷Old English altar, alter, based on late Latin altar, altarium, from Latin altus 'high.'

A

al·tar·piece /ˈôltər,pēs/ ▶n. a work of art, esp. a painting on wood, set above and behind an altar.

alt·az·i·muth /alˈtazəməTH/ ▶n. (also **altazimuth mount** or **mounting**) *Astron.* a telescope mounting that moves in azimuth (about a vertical axis) and in altitude (about a horizontal axis).

alt.coun·try /ˈôltˈkəntrē/ (also **alt-coun·try**) ▶n. a style of country music that is influenced by alternative rock.

al·ter /ˈôltər/ ▶v. [tr.] change or cause to change in character or composition, typically in a comparatively small but significant way: *Eliot was persuaded to alter the passage* | [intr.] *our outward appearance alters as we get older.* ■ make structural changes to (a building): *plans to alter the dining hall.* ■ tailor (clothing) for a better fit or to conform to fashion: *skirts with the hemlines altered a dozen different times.* ■ castrate or spay (a domestic animal). —**al·ter·a·ble** *adj.* —**al·ter·a·tion** /,ôltəˈrāSHən/ *n.*

al·ter·ca·tion /,ôltərˈkāSHən/ ▶n. a noisy argument or disagreement, esp. in public: *I had an altercation with the conductor.*

al·ter·nate ▶v. /ˈôltər,nāt/ [intr.] occur in turn repeatedly: *the governorship alternated between the Republican and Democratic parties.* ■ [tr.] do or perform in turn repeatedly: *some adults who wish to* **alternate** *work with education.*
▶adj. /ˈôltərnit/ (abbr.: **alt.**) **1** every other; every second: *she was asked to attend on alternate days.* ■ (of two things) each following and succeeded by the other in a regular pattern: *alternate bouts of intense labor and of idleness.* ■ (of a sequence) consisting of alternate items. ■ *Bot.* (of leaves or shoots) placed alternately on the two sides of the stem. **2** taking the place of; alternative: *alternate routes.*
▶n. /-nit/ (abbr.: **alt.**) a person who acts as a deputy or substitute. —**al·ter·nate·ly** /-nitlē/ *adv.* —**al·ter·na·tion** /,ôltərˈnāSHən/ *n.*

al·ter·na·tive /ôlˈtərnətiv/ ▶adj. (of one or more things) available as another possibility: *the various alternative methods for resolving disputes.* ■ (of two things) mutually exclusive: *the facts fit two alternative scenarios.* ■ of or relating to behavior that is considered unconventional and is often seen as a challenge to traditional norms: *an alternative lifestyle.*
▶n. one of two or more available possibilities: *she had no alternative but to break the law.* —**al·ter·na·tive·ly** *adv.* alternatively, you may telephone us direct.

al·ter·na·tive med·i·cine ▶n. any of a range of medical therapies that are not regarded as orthodox by the medical profession, such as herbalism, homeopathy, and acupuncture. See also COMPLEMENTARY MEDICINE.

al·ter·na·tor /ˈôltər,nātər/ ▶n. a generator that produces an alternating current.

al·though /ôlˈTHō/ ▶conj. in spite of the fact that; even though: *although the sun was shining, it wasn't that warm.* ■ however; but: *he says he has the team jersey, although I've never seen him wear it.*

al·tim·e·ter /alˈtimitər/ (abbr.: **alt.**) ▶n. an instrument for determining altitude attained, esp. a barometric or radar device used in an aircraft.

al·ti·tude /ˈalti,t(y)ōōd/ (abbr.: **alt.**) ▶n. the height of an object or point in relation to sea level or ground level: *flying at altitudes over 15,000 feet.* ■ great height: *the mechanism can freeze at altitude.* ■ *Astron.* the apparent height of a celestial object above the horizon, measured as an angle. ■ *Geom.* the length of the perpendicular line from a vertex to the opposite side of a figure. —**al·ti·tu·di·nal** /,alti't(y)ōōdn-əl/ *adj.*

al·to /ˈaltō/ ▶n. (pl. **-tos**) *Mus.* a voice, instrument, or part below the highest range and above tenor, in particular: ■ the highest adult male singing voice; countertenor. ■ the lowest female singing voice; contralto. ■ [as *adj.*] denoting the member of a family of instruments pitched second or third highest: *alto flute.*

al·to·geth·er /,ôltəˈgeTHər/ ▶adv. completely; totally: *I stopped seeing her altogether* | *I'm not altogether sure that I'd trust him.* ■ including everything or everyone; in total: *he had forty-six children altogether.* ■ taking everything into consideration; on the whole: *altogether it was a great evening.*
▶ □ **in the altogether** *inf.* without any clothes on; naked.

al·to-re·lie·vo /ˈaltō rəˈlēvō/ ▶n. (pl. **-vos**) *Sculpture* another term for HIGH RELIEF at RELIEF (sense 4). ■ a sculpture or carving in high relief.

al·tru·ism /ˈaltrōō,izəm/ ▶n. the belief in or practice of disinterested and selfless concern for the well-being of others: *some may choose to work with vulnerable elderly people out of altruism.* ■ *Zool.* behavior of an animal that benefits another at its own expense. —**al·tru·ist** *n.* —**al·tru·is·tic** /,altrōōˈistik/ *adj.* —**al·tru·is·ti·cal·ly** *adv.*

a·lum /ˈaləm/ ▶n. *Chem.* a colorless astringent compound, $AlK(SO_4)_2.12H_2O$, a hydrated double sulfate of aluminum and potassium, used in solution medicinally and in dyeing and tanning. ■ any of a number of analogous crystalline double sulfates of a monovalent metal (or group) and a trivalent metal.

a·lu·mi·na /əˈlōōmənə/ ▶n. aluminum oxide, a white solid that is a

major constituent of many rocks, esp. clays, and is found crystallized as corundum, sapphire, and other minerals.

a·lu·mi·no·sil·i·cate /ə,lōōmənəˈsilikit/ ▶n. *Chem.* a silicate in which aluminum replaces some of the silicon, esp. a rock-forming mineral such as a feldspar or a clay mineral.

a·lu·mi·num /əˈlōōmənəm/ (*Brit.* **al·u·min·i·um** /,alyəˈmineəm/) ▶n. the chemical element of atomic number 13, a light silvery-gray metal. (Symbol: **Al**)

a·lum·nus /əˈləmnəs/ ▶n. (pl. **-ni** /-nī; -nē/) a graduate or former student, esp. male, of a particular school, college, or university.

al·ve·o·lar /alˈvēələr/ ▶adj. of or relating to an alveolus, in particular: ■ *Anat.* relating to or denoting the bony ridge that contains the sockets of the upper teeth. ■ *Phonet.* (of a consonant) pronounced with the tip of the tongue on or near this ridge (e.g., *n, s, t*). ■ *Anat.* of or relating to an alveolus or the alveoli of the lung.
▶n. *Phonet.* an alveolar consonant.

al·ve·o·lus /alˈvēələs/ ▶n. (pl. **-li** /-,lī/) *chiefly Anat.* a small cavity, pit, or hollow, in particular: ■ any of the many tiny air sacs in the lungs where the exchange of oxygen and carbon dioxide takes place. ■ the bony socket for the root of a tooth. —**al·ve·o·late** /-lit; -,lāt/ *adj.*

al·ways /ˈôl,wāz; -wēz/ (*archaic* **al·way**) ▶adv. **1** at all times; on all occasions: *the sun always rises in the east.* ■ throughout a long period of the past: *she had always been an obstinate sort.* ■ for all future time; forever: *she will always be missed.* ■ repeatedly and annoyingly: *she is always making derogatory remarks.* **2** as a last resort; failing all else: *if the marriage doesn't work out, we can always get divorced.*

a·lys·sum /əˈlisəm/ ▶n. a widely cultivated plant (genera *Alyssum* and *Lobularia*) of the cabbage family that bears small flowers in a range of colors, typically white, yellow, or violet.

Alz·hei·mer's dis·ease /ˈälts,hīmərz; ˈôlts-; ˈälz-; ˈôlz-/ ▶n. progressive mental deterioration that can occur in middle or old age, due to generalized degeneration of the brain. It is the most common cause of premature senility. ▷early 20th cent.: named after Alois *Alzheimer* (1864–1915), German neurologist who first identified it.

AM ▶abbr. ■ amplitude modulation. ■ Master of Arts.

Am ▶symb. the chemical element americium.

am /am/ ▶ 1st person singular present of BE.

a.m. ▶abbr. before noon, used with times of day between midnight and noon: *we can deliver your most time-sensitive shipments by 10:30 a.m.*

AMA ▶abbr. ■ American Management Association. ■ American Medical Association. ■ American Motorcycle Association.

a·mal·gam /əˈmalgəm/ ▶n. a mixture or blend: *a curious amalgam of the traditional and the modern.* ■ *Chem.* an alloy of mercury with another metal, esp. one used for dental fillings.

a·mal·ga·mate /əˈmalgə,māt/ ▶v. combine or unite to form one organization or structure: [tr.] *he amalgamated his company with another.* | [intr.] *numerous small railroad companies amalgamated.* —**a·mal·ga·ma·tion** /ə,malgəˈmāSHən/ *n.*

a·man·u·en·sis /ə,manyōōˈensis/ ▶n. (pl. **-ses** /-,sēz/) a literary or artistic assistant, in particular one who takes dictation or copies manuscripts.

am·a·ranth /ˈamə,ranTH/ ▶n. any plant of the genus *Amaranthus* (family Amaranthaceae), typically having small green, red, or purple flowers. Certain varieties are grown as a food source.

am·a·ret·to /,aməˈretō; ,ämə-/ ▶n. a sweet, almond-flavored liqueur.

am·a·ryl·lis /,aməˈrilis/ ▶n. a bulbous plant of the lily family with showy white, pink, or red flowers and straplike leaves, in particular: ■ a South African plant (*Amaryllis belladonna*). ■ a tropical South American plant that is frequently grown as a houseplant (hybrids of the genus *Hippeastrum*, formerly *Amaryllis*).

a·mass /əˈmas/ ▶v. [tr.] gather together or accumulate (a large amount or number of valuable material or things) over a period of time: *starting from nothing he had amassed a huge fortune.* ■ [intr.] *archaic* (of people) gather together in a crowd or group. —**a·mass·er** *n.*

am·a·teur /ˈamətər; -,tər; -,CHŏŏr; -CHər/ ▶n. a person who engages in a pursuit, esp. a sport, on an unpaid basis. ■ a person considered contemptibly inept at a particular activity: *that bunch of stumbling amateurs.*
▶adj. engaging or engaged in without payment; nonprofessional: *an amateur archaeologist.* ■ inept or unskillful. —**am·a·teur·ism** /-,rizəm/ *n.*

am·a·teur·ish /,aməˈtərish; -'t(y)ŏŏr-; -'CHŏŏr-/ ▶adj. unskillful; inept: *the editing is amateurish.* —**am·a·teur·ish·ly** *adv.* —**am·a·teur·ish·ness** *n.*

am·a·to·ry /ˈamə,tôrē/ ▶adj. relating to or induced by sexual love or desire: *his amatory exploits.*

a·maze /əˈmāz/ ▶v. [tr.] (often **be amazed**) surprise (someone) greatly; fill with astonishment: *he was amazed at how modern everything was.* —**a·maze·ment** *n.*

a·maz·ing /ə'māziNG/ ▶*adj.* causing great surprise or wonder; astonishing: *an amazing number of people registered* | *it is amazing how short your memory is.* ■ *inf.* startlingly impressive: *she makes the most amazing cakes.* —**a·maz·ing·ly** *adv. an amazingly good idea.*

Am·a·zon (also **am·a·zon**) ▶*n.* a tall and strong or athletic woman. —**Am·a·zo·ni·an** *adj.*

am·bas·sa·dor /am'basədər; -,dôr/ ▶*n.* an accredited diplomat sent by a country as its official representative to a foreign country: *the French ambassador to Portugal.* ■ a person who acts as a representative or promoter of a specified activity: *he is a good ambassador for the industry.* —**am·bas·sa·do·ri·al** /am,basə'dôrēəl/ *adj.* —**am·bas·sa·dor·ship** /-,SHip/ *n.*

am·ber /'ambər/ ▶*n.* hard translucent fossilized resin produced by extinct coniferous trees of the Tertiary period, typically yellowish in color. ■ a honey-yellow color typical of this substance. ■ a yellow light used as a cautionary signal between green for "go" and red for "stop." ▶*adj.* made of amber: *amber beads.* ■ having the yellow color of amber.

am·ber·gris /'ambər,gris; -,grē(s)/ ▶*n.* a waxlike substance that originates as a secretion in the intestines of the sperm whale, found floating in tropical seas and used in perfume manufacture.

am·bi·dex·trous /,ambi'dekst(ə)rəs/ ▶*adj.* able to use the right and left hands equally well: *few of us are naturally ambidextrous.* ■ (of an implement) designed to be used by left-handed and right-handed people with equal ease. —**am·bi·dex·ter·i·ty** /-dek'steritē/ *n.* —**am·bi·dex·trous·ly** *adv.*

am·bi·ence /'ambēəns/ (also **am·bi·ance**) ▶*n.* the character and atmosphere of a place: *the relaxed ambience of the cocktail lounge is popular with guests.* ■ background noise added to a musical recording to give the impression that it was recorded live.

am·bi·ent /'ambēənt/ ▶*adj.* of or relating to the immediate surroundings of something: *the liquid is stored at below ambient temperature.* ▶*n.* (also **ambient music**) a style of instrumental music with electronic textures and no persistent beat, used to create or enhance a mood or atmosphere.

am·bi·gu·i·ty /,ambi'gyōō-itē/ ▶*n.* (*pl.* **-ties**) uncertainty or inexactness of meaning in language: *no ambiguity in this section of the Act.* ■ a lack of decisiveness or commitment resulting from a failure to make a choice between alternatives: *the film is fraught with moral ambiguity.*

am·big·u·ous /am'bigyōōəs/ ▶*adj.* (of language) open to more than one interpretation; having a double meaning: *the question is rather ambiguous.* ■ unclear or inexact because a choice between alternatives has not been made: *this whole society is morally ambiguous.* —**am·big·u·ous·ly** *adv.*

am·bit /'ambit/ ▶*n.* the scope, extent, or bounds of something: *within the ambit of federal law.*

am·bi·tion /am'bishən/ ▶*n.* a strong desire to do or to achieve something, typically requiring determination and hard work: *her ambition was to become a model.* ■ desire and determination to achieve success: *life offered few opportunities for young people with ambition.*

am·bi·tious /am'bishəs/ ▶*adj.* having or showing a strong desire and determination to succeed: *his mother was hard-working and ambitious for her four children.* ■ (of a plan or piece of work) intended to satisfy high aspirations and therefore difficult to achieve: *the scope of the book is very ambitious.* —**am·bi·tious·ly** *adv.* —**am·bi·tious·ness** *n.*

am·biv·a·lent /am'bivələnt/ ▶*adj.* having mixed feelings or contradictory ideas about something or someone: *an ambivalent attitude to terrorism.* —**am·biv·a·lence** *n.* —**am·biv·a·lent·ly** *adv.*

am·bi·vert /'ambə,vərt/ ▶*n.* *Psychol.* a person whose personality has a balance of extrovert and introvert features. —**am·bi·ver·sion** /,ambi-'vərzHən/ *n.*

am·ble /'ambəl/ ▶*v.* [*intr.*] walk or move at a slow, relaxed pace: *they ambled along the riverbank* | *he ambled into the foyer.* ▶*n.* a walk at a slow, relaxed pace, esp. for pleasure: *a peaceful riverside amble.* —**am·bler** /-blər/ *n.*

am·bro·sia /am'brōzH(ē)ə/ ▶*n.* the food of the gods. ■ something very pleasing to taste or smell: *the tea was ambrosia after the slop I'd been drinking.* ■ a dessert made with oranges and shredded coconut. ▷mid 16th cent.: via Latin from Greek, 'elixir of life,' from *ambrotos* 'immortal.' —**am·bro·sial** *adj.*

am·bu·lance /'ambyələns/ ▶*n.* a vehicle specially equipped for taking sick or injured people to and from the hospital, esp. in emergencies.

am·bu·la·to·ry /'ambyələ,tôrē/ ▶*adj.* relating to or adapted for walking. ■ *Med.* able to walk; not bedridden: *ambulatory patients.* ■ *Med.* relating to patients who are able to walk: *an ambulatory care facility.* ■ movable; mobile: *an ambulatory ophthalmic service.* ▶*n.* (*pl.* **-ries**) a place for walking, esp. an aisle around the apse or a cloister in a church or monastery.

am·bush /'am,bŏŏsH/ ▶*n.* a surprise attack by people lying in wait in a concealed position: | *terrorists waiting in ambush.* ▶*v.* [*tr.*] (often **be ambushed**) make a surprise attack on (someone) from a concealed position: *they were ambushed and taken prisoner by the enemy.*

a·me·ba /ə'mēbə/ (also **a·moe·ba**) ▶*n.* (*pl.* **amebas** or **amebae** /-bē/) a single-celled animal (phylum Rhizopoda, kingdom Protista) that catches food and moves about by extending fingerlike projections of protoplasm. —**a·me·bic** /-bik/ *adj.* —**a·me·boid** /-boid/ *adj.*

a·me·lio·rate /ə'mēlyə,rāt; ə'mēlēə-/ ▶*v.* [*tr.*] make (something bad or unsatisfactory) better: *the reform did much to ameliorate living standards.* —**a·me·lio·ra·tion** /ə,mēlyə'rāsHən/ *n.* —**a·me·lio·ra·tive** /-rətiv; -,rātiv/ *adj.* —**a·me·lio·ra·tor** /-,rātər/ *n.*

a·men /ä'men; ā'men/ ▶*interj.* uttered at the end of a prayer or hymn, meaning 'so be it.' ■ used to express agreement or assent: *amen to that!* ▶*n.* an utterance of "amen."

a·me·na·ble /ə'mēnəbəl; ə'men-/ ▶*adj.* (of a person) open and responsive to suggestion; easily persuaded or controlled: *parents who have had easy babies and amenable children.* ■ (**amenable to**) (of a thing) capable of being acted upon in a particular way; susceptible to: *the patients had cardiac failure not amenable to medical treatment.* —**a·me·na·bil·i·ty** /ə,mēnə'bilitē; ə,men-/ *n.* —**a·me·na·bly** /-blē/ *adv.*

a·mend /ə'mend/ ▶*v.* [*tr.*] make minor changes in (a text) in order to make it fairer, more accurate, or more up-to-date: *the rule was amended to apply to nonmembers.* ■ modify formally, as a legal document or legislative bill: *pressuring Panama to amend its banking laws.* ■ make better; improve: *if you can amend people's mind-set.* ■ *archaic* put right: *things had gone wrong but had been amended.* —**a·mend·a·ble** *adj.* —**a·mend·er** *n.*

a·mend·ment /ə'men(d)mənt/ ▶*n.* a minor change in a document. ■ a change or addition to a legal or statutory document: *an amendment to existing bail laws.* ■ (**Amendment**) an article added to the U.S. Constitution: *the First Amendment.* ■ something that is added to soil in order to improve its texture or fertility.

a·mends /ə'mendz/ ▶*pl. n.* [treated as *sing.*] reparation or compensation. ▶ ☐ **make amends** do something in order to make up for a wrong inflicted on someone: *try to make amends for the rude way you spoke to Lucy.*

a·men·i·ty /ə'menitē; ə'mē-/ ▶*n.* (*pl.* **-ties**) (usu. **amenities**) a desirable or useful feature or facility of a building or place: *heating is regarded as a basic amenity.* ■ the pleasantness of a place or a person: *the exertion of amenity toward the boss.*

a·men·or·rhe·a /ā,menə'rēə/ ▶*n.* an abnormal absence of menstruation.

Am·er·a·sian /,amər'āzHən/ ▶*adj.* having one American and one Asian parent. ▶*n.* a person with one American and one Asian parent.

a·merce·ment /ə'mərsmənt/ ▶*n.* *hist. English Law* a fine. —**a·merce** *v.*

A·mer·i·can /ə'merikən/ ▶*adj.* of, relating to, or characteristic of the United States or its inhabitants: *the election of a new American president.* ■ relating to or denoting the continents of America: *the American continent south of the tropic of Cancer.* ▶*n.* **1** a native or citizen of the United States. ■ a native or inhabitant of any of the countries of North, South, or Central America. **2** the English language as it is used in the United States; American English. —**A·mer·i·can·ness** *n.*

A·mer·i·ca·na /ə,meri'känə; -'kanə/ ▶*pl. n.* things associated with the culture and history of America, esp. the United States.

A·mer·i·can In·di·an ▶*n.* a member of any of the indigenous peoples of North, Central, and South America, esp. those of North America. ▶*adj.* of or relating to any of these groups. See also **NATIVE AMERICAN**.

A·mer·i·can·ism /ə'merikə,nizəm/ ▶*n.* a word or phrase peculiar to or originating from the U.S. ■ the qualities regarded as definitive of America or Americans.

A·mer·i·can·ize /ə'merikə,nīz/ ▶*v.* [*tr.*] make American in character or nationality: *trying to Americanize the immigrant children.* —**A·mer·i·can·i·za·tion** /ə,merikəni'zāsHən/ *n.*

A·mer·i·can plan ▶*n.* (in hotels) a system of paying a single daily rate that covers the room and all meals. Often contrasted with **EUROPEAN PLAN**.

a·mer·i·ci·um /amə'risHēəm/ ▶*n.* the chemical element of atomic number 95, a radioactive metal of the actinide series. (Symbol: **Am**)

Pronunciation Key ə *ago*, *up*; ər *over*, *fur*; a *hat*; ā *ate*; ä *car*; CH *chin*; e *let*; ē *see*; e(ə)r *air*; i *fit*; ī *by*; i(ə)r *ear*; NG *sing*; ō *go*; ô *law*, *for*; oi *toy*; ŏŏ *good*; ōō *goo*; ou *out*; SH *she*; TH *thin*; ŦH *then*; (h)w *why*; ZH *vision*

A

Am·er·in·di·an /ˌaməˈrindēən/ (also **Am·er·ind** /ˈamərind/) ▸*adj. & n.* another term for AMERICAN INDIAN, used chiefly in anthropological and linguistic contexts.

am·e·thyst /ˈaməθəst/ ▸*n.* a precious stone consisting of a violet or purple variety of quartz. ■ a violet or purple color. —**am·e·thys·tine** /ˌaməˈθistin; -ˌtīn/ *adj.*

a·mi·a·ble /ˈāmēəbəl/ ▸*adj.* having or displaying a friendly and pleasant manner: *an amiable, unassuming fellow.* ▷late Middle English (originally in the senses 'kind' and 'lovely, lovable'): via Old French from late Latin *amicabilis* 'amicable.' The current sense, influenced by modern French *aimable* 'trying to please,' dates from the mid 18th cent. —**a·mi·a·bil·i·ty** /ˌāmēəˈbilitē/ *n.* —**a·mi·a·bly** /-blē/ *adv.* —**a·mi·a·ble·ness** *n.*

am·i·ca·ble /ˈamikəbəl/ ▸*adj.* (of relations between people) having a spirit of friendliness; without serious disagreement or rancor: *there will be an amicable settlement of the dispute.* —**am·i·ca·bil·i·ty** /ˌamikəˈbilitē/ *n.* —**am·i·ca·bly** /-blē/ *adv.*

am·ice ▸*n.* a cap, hood, or cape worn by members of certain religious orders.

a·mid /əˈmid/ ▸*prep.* surrounded by; in the middle of: *our dream home, set amid magnificent rolling countryside.* ■ in an atmosphere or against a background of: *talks broke down amid accusations of a hostile takeover bid.*

am·ide /ˈamīd; -id/ ▸*n.* *Chem.* an organic compound containing the group —C(O)NH₂. ■ a compound containing the anion NH₂⁻.

a·mid·ships /əˈmidˌSHips/ (also **a·mid·ship**) ▸*adv. & adj.* in the middle of a ship: [as *adv.*] *the destroyer rammed her amidships* | [as *adj.*] *an amidships engine.*

a·mi·go /əˈmēgō/ ▸*n.* (*pl.* **-gos**) *inf.* used to address or refer to a friend, chiefly in Spanish-speaking areas: *I will think about it, amigo.*

a·mine /əˈmēn; ˈamēn/ ▸*n.* *Chem.* an organic compound derived from ammonia by replacement of one or more hydrogen atoms by organic radicals.

a·mi·no ac·id ▸*n.* *Biochem.* a simple organic compound containing both a carboxyl (—COOH) and an amino (—NH₂) group. They occur naturally in plant and animal tissues and form the basic constituents of proteins.

A·mish /ˈämisH/ ▸*pl. n.* the members of a strict Mennonite sect that established major settlements in Pennsylvania, Ohio, and elsewhere in North America from 1720 onward.
▸*adj.* of or relating to this sect.

a·miss /əˈmis/ ▸*adj.* not quite right; inappropriate or out of place: *there was something amiss about his calculations.*
▸*adv.* dated wrongly or inappropriately: *the danger of her loving amiss.*
▸ □ **take something amiss** be offended by something that is said, typically through misinterpreting the intentions behind it.

am·i·ty /ˈamitē/ ▸*n.* a friendly relationship: *international amity.*

am·me·ter /ˈa(m)ˌmētər/ ▸*n.* an instrument for measuring electric current in amperes.

am·mo /ˈamō/ ▸*n.* informal term for AMMUNITION.

am·mo·nia /əˈmōnyə; -nēə/ ▸*n.* a colorless gas, NH₃, with a characteristic pungent smell. It dissolves in water to give a strongly alkaline solution. ■ a solution of this gas, used as a cleaning fluid. —**am·mo·ni·at·ed** *adj.* —**am·mo·ni·a·tion** *n.*

am·mo·ni·a·cal /ˌaməˈnīəkəl/ ▸*adj.* of or containing ammonia.

am·mo·nite /ˈaməˌnīt/ ▸*n.* an ammonoid that belongs to the order *Ammonitida*, typically having elaborately frilled suture lines.

am·mo·ni·um /əˈmōnēəm/ ▸*n.* [as *adj.*] *Chem.* the cation NH₄⁺, present in solutions of ammonia and its salts derived from ammonia.

am·mo·noid /ˈaməˌnoid/ ▸*n.* *Paleontol.* an extinct mollusk with a flat-coiled spiral shell.
▸*adj.* of or relating to the ammonoids.

am·mu·ni·tion /ˌamyəˈnisHən/ ▸*n.* a supply or quantity of bullets and shells. ■ *fig.* considerations that can be used to support one's case in debate: *these figures provide ammunition to the argument for more resources.*

am·ne·sia /amˈnēZHə/ ▸*n.* a partial or total loss of memory. —**am·ne·si·ac** /amˈnēZHēˌak; -ZHə-ˌak/ *n. & adj.* —**am·ne·sic** /-zik; -sik/ *adj. & n.* —**am·nes·tic** /amˈnestik/ *adj.*

am·nes·ty /ˈamnistē/ ▸*n.* (*pl.* **-ties**) an official pardon for people who have been convicted of political offenses: *the new law granted amnesty to those who illegally left the country.* ■ an undertaking by the authorities to take no action against specified offenses or offenders during a fixed period: *a month-long weapons amnesty.*
▸*v.* (**-ties**, **-tied**) [*tr.*] grant an official pardon to.

am·ni·o·cen·te·sis /ˌamnēō-ōsenˈtēsis/ ▸*n.* (*pl.* **-ses** /-sēz/) *Med.* the sampling of amniotic fluid using a hollow needle inserted into the uterus, to screen for developmental abnormalities in a fetus.

am·ni·on /ˈamnēˌän; -ən/ ▸*n.* (*pl.* - or **-ni·a** /-nēə/) the innermost membrane that encloses the embryo of a mammal, bird, or reptile.

am·ni·ot·ic flu·id /ˌamnēˈätik/ ▸*n.* the fluid surrounding a fetus within the amnion.

a·moe·ba ▸*n.* (*pl.* **-bas** or **-bae** /-bē/) variant spelling of AMEBA. —**a·moe·bic** *adj.* —**a·moe·boid** *adj.*

a·mok /əˈmək; əˈmäk/ (also **a·muck**) ▸*adv.* (in phrase **run amok**) behave uncontrollably and disruptively: *stone-throwing anarchists running amok* | *fig.* *her feelings seemed to be running amok.* ▷mid 17th cent.: via Portuguese *amouco*, from Malay *amok* 'rushing in a frenzy.' Early use was as a noun denoting a Malay in a homicidal frenzy; the adverb use dates from the late 17th cent.

a·mong /əˈməNG/ (*chiefly Brit.* also **a·mongst** /əˈməNGst/) ▸*prep.* **1** surrounded by; in the company of: *you're among friends.* **2** being a member or members of (a larger set): *he was among the first 29 students enrolled.* **3** occurring in or practiced by (some members of a community): *a drop in tooth decay among children.* ■ involving most or all members of a group reciprocally: *members of the government bickered among themselves.* **4** indicating a division, choice, or differentiation involving three or more participants: *the king called the three princesses to divide his kingdom among them.*

a·mor·al /āˈmôrəl/ ▸*adj.* lacking a moral sense; unconcerned with the rightness or wrongness of something: *an amoral attitude to sex.* —**a·mo·ral·i·ty** /ˌāməˈralitē/ *n.* —**a·mor·al·ism** /-ˌlizəm/ *n.* —**a·mor·al·ist** /-list/ *n.*

a·mo·ro·so /ˌäməˈrōsō/ ▸*adv. & adj.* *Mus.* (esp. as a direction) in a loving or tender manner.

am·o·rous /ˈamərəs/ ▸*adj.* showing, feeling, or relating to sexual desire: *his amorous advances.* —**am·o·rous·ly** *adv.* —**am·o·rous·ness** *n.*

a·mor·phous /əˈmôrfəs/ ▸*adj.* without a clearly defined shape or form: *amorphous blue forms.* ■ vague; ill-organized; unclassifiable: *amorphous statements.* ■ (of a group of people or an organization) lacking a clear structure or focus: *an amorphous and leaderless legislature.* ■ *Mineralogy & Chem.* (of a solid) noncrystalline; having neither definite form nor apparent structure. —**a·mor·phous·ly** *adv.* —**a·mor·phous·ness** *n.*

am·or·tize /ˈamərˌtīz/ ▸*v.* [*tr.*] reduce or extinguish (a debt) by money regularly put aside: *loan fees can be amortized over the life of the mortgage.* ■ gradually write off the initial cost of (an asset): *they want to amortize the tooling costs quickly.* —**am·or·ti·za·tion** /ˌamərtiˈzāsHən; əˌmôrti-/ *n.*

a·mount /əˈmount/ ▸*n.* a quantity of something, typically the total of a thing or things in number, size, value, or extent: *the sport gives an enormous amount of pleasure to many people* | *the substance is harmless if taken in small amounts.* ■ a sum of money: *they have spent a colossal amount.*
▸*v.* [*intr.*] (**amount to**) come to be (the total) when added together: *losses amounted to over 10 million dollars.* ■ be the equivalent of: *their actions amounted to a conspiracy.* ■ develop into; become: *you'll never amount to anything.*

a·mour /əˈmo͝or; äˈmo͝or/ ▸*n.* a secret or illicit love affair or lover.

AMP ▸*Biochem. abbr.* adenosine monophosphate.

amp¹ /amp/ ▸*n.* short for AMPERE.

amp² ▸*n. inf.* short for AMPLIFIER.
▸*v.* (often **amp something up**) **1** play (music) through electric amplification: *their willingness to amp up traditional songs virtually began the folk-rock genre.* **2** [as *adj.*] (**amped** or **amped up**) *inf.* full of nervous energy.

am·per·age /ˈamp(ə)rij/ ▸*n.* the strength of an electric current in amperes.

am·pere /ˈamˌpi(ə)r/ (*abbr.:* **A**) ▸*n.* the SI base unit of electric current equal to a flow of one coulomb per second.

am·per·sand /ˈampərˌsand/ ▸*n.* the sign & (standing for *and*, as in *Smith & Co.*, or the Latin *et*, as in &c.).

am·phet·a·mine /amˈfetəˌmēn; -min/ ▸*n.* a synthetic, addictive, mood-altering drug used illegally as a stimulant and as a prescription drug to treat ADD and narcolepsy.

am·phib·i·an /amˈfibēən/ ▸*n.* *Zool.* a cold-blooded vertebrate animal of a class (Amphibia) that comprises the frogs, toads, newts, and salamanders, distinguished by having an aquatic gill-breathing larval stage followed (typically) by a terrestrial lung-breathing adult stage. ■ a seaplane, tank, or other vehicle that can operate on land and on water.
▸*adj.* *Zool.* of or relating to this class of animals.

am·phib·i·ous /amˈfibēəs/ ▸*adj.* relating to, living in, or suited for both land and water: *amphibious habitats* | *an amphibious vehicle.* ■ (of a military operation) involving forces landed from the sea: *an amphibious assault.* ■ (of forces) trained for such operations.

am·phi·bole /ˈamfəˌbōl/ ▸*n.* any of a class of rock-forming silicate or aluminosilicate minerals typically occurring as fibrous or columnar crystals.

am·phi·the·a·ter /'amfə,THēətər/ ▶n. (esp. in Greek and Roman architecture) a round building, typically unroofed, with a central space for the presentation of dramatic or sporting events. Tiers of seats surround the central space. ■ a sloping, semicircular seating gallery: *a lecture in the amphitheater of the hospital.* ■ a large circular hollow in rocks or hills.

am·pho·ra /'amfərə/ ▶n. (pl. **-rae** /-,rē/ or **-ras**) a tall ancient Greek or Roman jar with two handles and a narrow neck.

am·pi·cil·lin /,ampi'silin/ ▶n. Med. a semisynthetic form of penicillin used chiefly to treat infections of the urinary and respiratory tracts.

am·ple /'ampəl/ ▶adj. (**-pler**, **-plest**) enough or more than enough; plentiful: *ample time for discussion.* ■ large and accommodating: *his ample chair.* ■ used euphemistically to convey that someone is fat: *her ample hips.* —**am·ple·ness** n. —**am·ply** /-p(ə)lē/ adv.

am·pli·fi·er /'amplə,fīər/ ▶n. an electronic device for increasing the amplitude of electrical signals, used chiefly in sound reproduction. ■ a device of this kind combined with a loudspeaker, used to amplify electric guitars and other musical instruments.

am·pli·fy /'amplə,fī/ ▶v. (**-fies**, **-fied**) [tr.] (often **be amplified**) increase the volume of (sound), esp. using an amplifier. ■ increase the amplitude of (an electrical signal or other oscillation). ■ cause to become more marked or intense: *policy initiatives amplified social polarization.* ■ Genetics make multiple copies of (a gene or DNA sequence). ■ enlarge upon or add detail to (a story or statement). —**am·pli·fi·ca·tion** /,amplefi-'kāSHən/ n.

am·pli·tude /'ampli,t(y)ood/ ▶n. **1** Physics the maximum extent of a vibration or oscillation, measured from the position of equilibrium. ■ the maximum difference of an alternating electrical current or potential from the average value. **2** breadth, range, or magnitude: *the amplitude of the crime of manslaughter lies beneath murder.*

am·pli·tude mod·u·la·tion (abbr.: **AM**) ▶n. the modulation of a wave by varying its amplitude, used chiefly as a means of radio broadcasting, in which an audio signal is combined with a carrier wave. Often contrasted with **FREQUENCY MODULATION**. ■ the system of radio transmission using such modulation.

am·poule /'am,p(y)ool/ (also **am·pul** or **am·pule**) ▶n. a sealed glass capsule containing a liquid, esp. a measured quantity ready for injecting.

am·pu·tate /'ampyə,tāt/ ▶v. [tr.] cut off (a limb), typically by surgical operation: *surgeons had to amputate her left hand* | *the wounded had to* **have** *legs or arms* **amputated**. —**am·pu·ta·tion** /,ampyə'tāSHən/ n.

am·pu·tee /,ampyə'tē/ ▶n. a person who has had a limb amputated.

am·trac /'am,trak/ (also **am·track**, **am·trak**) ▶n. an amphibious tracked vehicle used for landing assault troops on a shore.

Am·trak /'am,trak/ ▶trademark a federal passenger railroad service in the U.S., operated by the National Railroad Passenger Corporation.

a·muck /ə'mək/ ▶adv. variant spelling of **AMOK**.

am·u·let /'amyəlit/ ▶n. an ornament or small piece of jewelry thought to give protection against evil, danger, or disease.

a·muse /ə'myooz/ ▶v. [tr.] **1** cause (someone) to find something funny; entertain: *he made faces to amuse her.* **2** provide interesting and enjoyable occupation for (someone): *the hotel has planned many activities to amuse its guests.* —**a·mus·ed·ly** /-zidlē/ adv. —**a·mus·ing** adj. —**a·mus·ing·ly** adv.

a·muse·ment /ə'myoozmənt/ ▶n. the state or experience of finding something funny: *we looked with amusement at our horoscopes.* ■ the provision or enjoyment of entertainment: *an evening's amusement.* ■ something that causes laughter or provides entertainment.

am·yl /'aməl/ ▶n. [as adj.] Chem. the straight-chain pentyl radical $-C_5H_{11}$.

am·yl·ase /'amə,lās; -,lāz/ ▶n. Biochem. an enzyme, found chiefly in saliva and pancreatic fluid, that converts starch and glycogen into simple sugars.

an /an/ ▶adj. the form of the indefinite article (see **A**) used before words beginning with a vowel sound.

An·a·bap·tism /,anə'bap,tizəm/ ▶n. the doctrine that baptism should only be administered to believing adults, held by a radical Protestant sect that emerged during the 1520s and 1530s. —**An·a·bap·tist** n. & adj.

an·a·bol·ic /,anə'bälik/ ▶adj. Biochem. relating to or promoting anabolism.

an·a·bol·ic ste·roid ▶n. a synthetic steroid hormone that resembles testosterone in promoting the growth of muscle. Such hormones are used medicinally to treat some forms of weight loss and (illegally by some athletes and others to enhance physical performance.

a·nab·o·lism /ə'nabə,lizəm/ ▶n. Biochem. the synthesis of complex molecules in living organisms from simpler ones together with the storage of energy; constructive metabolism.

a·nach·ro·nism /ə'nakrə,nizəm/ ▶n. a thing belonging or appropriate to a period other than that in which it exists, esp. a thing that is conspicuously old-fashioned: *everything was as it would have appeared in centuries past apart from one anachronism, a bright yellow construction crane.* ■ an act of attributing a custom, event, or object to a period to which it does not belong. —**a·nach·ro·nis·tic** /ə,nakrə'nistik/ adj. —**a·nach·ro·nis·ti·cal·ly** /-'nistik(ə)lē/ adv.

an·a·con·da /,anə'kändə/ ▶n. a large semiaquatic snake (genus *Eunectes*) of the boa family, native to tropical South America.

an·a·cru·sis /,anə'kroosis/ ▶n. (pl. **-ses** /-sēz/) Prosody one or more unstressed syllables at the beginning of a verse.

an·aer·obe /'anə,rōb/ ▶n. Biol. an organism that grows without air, or requires oxygen-free conditions to live. —**an·aer·o·bic** /,anə'rōbik/ adj.

an·a·glyph /'anə,glif/ ▶n. **1** Photog. a stereoscopic photograph with the two images superimposed and printed in different colors, producing a stereo effect when the photograph is viewed through correspondingly colored filters. **2** an object, such as a cameo, embossed or carved in low relief. —**an·a·glyph·ic** /,anə'glifik/ adj.

an·a·gram /'anə,gram/ ▶n. a word, phrase, or name formed by rearranging the letters of another, such as *cinema*, formed from *iceman*. —**an·a·gram·mat·ic** /,anəgrə'matik/ adj. —**an·a·gram·mat·i·cal** /,anəgrə-'matikəl/ adj.

a·nal /'ānl/ ▶adj. involving, relating to, or situated near the anus. ■ (in Freudian psychoanalysis) relating to or denoting a stage of infantile psychosexual development supposedly preoccupied with the anus and defecation. ■ inf. (of a person) excessively orderly and fussy: *he's anal about things like that.* ■ (of a person's behavior) excessively preoccupied with details: *You think that's anal?* —**a·nal·ly** adv.

an·a·lects /'anl,ek(t)s/ (also **an·a·lec·ta** /,anl'ektə/) ▶pl. n. a collection of short literary or philosophical extracts.

an·al·ge·si·a /,anl'jēzēə; -zHə/ ▶n. Med. the inability to feel pain.

an·al·ge·sic /,anl'jēzik; -sik/ Med. ▶adj. (chiefly of a drug) acting to relieve pain.
▶n. an analgesic drug.

an·a·log /'anl,ôg; -,äg/ (also **an·a·logue**) ▶n. a person or thing seen as comparable to another: *the idea that the fertilized egg contains a miniature analog of every adult structure.* ■ Chem. a compound with a molecular structure closely similar to that of another.
▶adj. relating to or using signals or information represented by a continuously variable physical quantity such as spatial position or voltage. Often contrasted with **DIGITAL** (sense 1). ■ (of a clock or watch) showing the time by means of hands rather than displayed digits.

a·nal·o·gize /ə'nalə,jīz/ ▶v. [tr.] make a comparison of (something) with something else to assist understanding.

a·nal·o·gous /ə'naləgəs/ ▶adj. (often **analogous to**) comparable in certain respects, typically in a way that makes clearer the nature of the things compared: *they saw the relationship between a ruler and his subjects as analogous to that of father and children.* ■ Biol. (of structures) performing a similar function but having a different evolutionary origin, such as the wings of insects and birds. Often contrasted with **HOMOLOGOUS**. —**a·nal·o·gous·ly** adv.

an·a·logue ▶n. & adj. variant spelling of **ANALOG**.

a·nal·o·gy /ə'naləjē/ ▶n. (pl. **-gies**) a comparison between two things, typically on the basis of their structure and for the purpose of explanation or·clarification: *an* **analogy between** *the workings of nature and those of human societies.* ■ a correspondence or partial similarity: *the syndrome is called deep dysgraphia because of its* **analogy to** *deep dyslexia.* ■ a thing that is comparable to something else in significant respects: *works of art were seen as an analogy for works of nature.* ■ Linguistics a process by which new words and inflections are created on the basis of regularities in the form of existing ones. ■ Biol. the resemblance of function between organs that have a different evolutionary origin. ▷late Middle English (in the sense 'appropriateness, correspondence'): from French *analogie*, Latin *analogia* 'proportion', from Greek, from *analogos* 'proportionate.' —**an·a·log·i·cal** /,anə'läjikəl/ adj. —**an·a·log·i·cal·ly** adv.

a·nal·y·sand /ə'nalə,sand; -,zand/ ▶n. a person undergoing psychoanalysis.

a·nal·y·sis /ə'naləsis/ ▶n. (pl. **-ses** /-,sēz/) detailed examination of the elements or structure of something, typically as a basis for discussion or

---

Pronunciation Key ə *ago*, *up*; ər *over*, *fur*; a *hat*; ā *ate*; ä *car*; CH *chin*; e *let*; ē *see*; e(ə)r *air*; i *fit*; ī *by*; i(ə)r *ear*; NG *sing*; ō *go*; ô *law*, *for*; oi *toy*; oo *good*; oo *goo*; ou *out*; SH *she*; TH *thin*; <u>TH</u> *then*; (h)w *why*; ZH *vision*

interpretation: *an analysis of popular culture.* ■ the process of separating something into its constituent elements. Often contrasted with **SYNTHESIS.** ■ the identification and measurement of the chemical constituents of a substance or specimen. ■ short for **PSYCHOANALYSIS.** ■ *Linguistics* the use of separate, short words and word order rather than inflection or agglutination to express grammatical structure. ■ *Math.* the part of mathematics concerned with the theory of functions and the use of limits, continuity, and the operations of calculus.

an·a·lyst /'anl-ist/ ▶*n.* a person who conducts analysis, in particular: ■ an investment expert, typically in a specified field: *rising consumer confidence and falling oil prices are the keys to any upturn, many analysts believe.* ■ short for **PSYCHOANALYST.** ■ a chemist who analyzes substances. ■ short for **SYSTEMS ANALYST.**

an·a·lyt·ic /,anl'itik/ ▶*adj.* another term for **ANALYTICAL.** ■ *Linguistics* (of a language) tending not to alter the form of its words and to use word order rather than inflection or agglutination to express grammatical structure.

an·a·lyt·i·cal /,anl'itikəl/ ▶*adj.* relating to or using analysis or logical reasoning: *analytical methods.* —**an·a·lyt·i·cal·ly** /-ik(ə)lē/ *adv.*

an·a·lyze /'anl,īz/ (*Brit.* **an·a·lyse**) ▶*v.* [*tr.*] examine methodically and in detail the constitution or structure of (something, esp. information), typically for purposes of explanation and interpretation: *we need to analyze our results more closely.* ■ discover or reveal (something) through such examination: *he tried to analyze exactly what was going on.* ■ psychoanalyze (someone). ■ identify and measure the chemical constituents of (a substance or specimen). ■ *Gram.* resolve (a sentence) into its grammatical elements; parse. —**an·a·lyz·a·ble** /,anə'līzəbəl/ *adj.* —**an·a·lyz·er** *n.*

an·a·pest /'anə,pest/ ▶*n.* *Prosody* a metrical foot consisting of two short or unstressed syllables followed by one long or stressed syllable. —**an·a·pes·tic** /,anə'pestik/ *adj.*

a·naph·o·ra /ə'nafərə/ ▶*n.* **1** *Gram.* the use of a word referring to or replacing a word used earlier in a sentence, to avoid repetition, such as *do* in *I like it and so do they.* **2** *Rhetoric* the repetition of a word or phrase at the beginning of successive clauses. —**an·a·phor·ic** /,anə'fôrik/ *adj.*

an·aph·ro·dis·i·ac /an,afrə'dizē,ak; -'dēzē-; -'dēzHē-/ *Med.* ▶*adj.* (chiefly of a drug) tending to reduce sexual desire.
▶*n.* an anaphrodisiac drug.

an·a·phy·lax·is /,anəfə'laksis/ ▶*n.* (also **an·a·phy·lac·tic shock** /-'laktik/) *Med.* an extreme, often life-threatening, allergic reaction to an antigen (e.g., a bee sting) to which the body has become hypersensitive following an earlier exposure. —**an·a·phy·lac·tic** /-'laktik/ *adj.*

an·ar·chism /'anər,kizəm/ ▶*n.* belief in the abolition of all government and the organization of society on a voluntary, cooperative basis without recourse to force or compulsion. ■ anarchists as a political force or movement: *socialism and anarchism emerged to offer organized protest against the injustices of Spanish society.*

an·ar·chist /'anərkist/ ▶*n.* a person who believes in or tries to bring about anarchy.
▶*adj.* relating to or supporting anarchy or anarchists: *an anarchist newspaper.* —**an·ar·chis·tic** /,anər'kistik/ *adj.*

an·ar·chy /'anərkē/ ▶*n.* a state of disorder due to absence or nonrecognition of authority. ■ absence of government and absolute freedom of the individual, regarded as a political ideal. —**an·ar·chic** /ə'närkik/ *adj.*

A·na·sa·zi /,anə'säzē/ ▶*n.* (*pl.* same or **-zis**) a member of an ancient American Indian people of the southwestern U.S., who flourished between *c.*200 BC and AD 1500.

a·nas·to·mo·sis /ə,nastə'mōsis/ ▶*n.* (*pl.* **-ses** /-sēz/) *technical* a cross-connection between adjacent channels, fibers, or other parts of a network. ■ *Med.* a connection made surgically between adjacent blood vessels, parts of the intestine, or other channels of the body, or the operation in which this is constructed. —**a·nas·to·mot·ic** /-'mätik/ *adj. & n.*

a·nas·tro·phe /ə'nastrəfē/ ▶*n.* *Rhetoric* the inversion of the usual order of words or clauses.

a·nath·e·ma /ə'naTHəmə/ ▶*n.* **1** something or someone that one vehemently dislikes: *racial hatred was anathema to her.* **2** a formal curse by a pope or a council of the Church, excommunicating a person or denouncing a doctrine. ■ *poetic/lit.* a strong curse.

a·nath·e·ma·tize /ə'naTHəmə,tīz/ ▶*v.* [*tr.*] curse; condemn: *she anathematized Tom as the despoiler of a helpless widow.*

an·a·tom·i·cal /,anə'tämikəl/ (abbr.: **anat.**) ▶*adj.* of or relating to bodily structure: *anatomical abnormalities.* ■ of or relating to anatomy: *anatomical lectures.* —**an·a·tom·i·cal·ly** /-ik(ə)lē/ *adv.*

a·nat·o·mize /ə'natə,mīz/ ▶*v.* [*tr.*] dissect (a body). ■ examine and analyze in detail: *successful comedy is notoriously difficult to anatomize.*

a·nat·o·my /ə'natəmē/ (abbr.: **anat.**) ▶*n.* (*pl.* **-mies**) the branch of science concerned with the bodily structure of humans, animals, and other living organisms, esp. as revealed by dissection and the separation of parts. ■ the bodily structure of an organism: *descriptions of the cat's anatomy and behavior.* ■ *inf., humorous* a person's body: *he left dusty handprints on his lady customers' anatomies.* ■ *fig.* a study of the structure or internal workings of something: *Machiavelli's anatomy of the art of war.*

a·nat·to /ə'nätō/ ▶*n.* (**-tos**) variant spelling of **ANNATTO.**

ANC ▶*abbr.* African National Congress.

an·ces·tor /'an,sestər/ ▶*n.* a person, typically one more remote than a grandparent, from whom one is descended. ■ an early type of animal or plant from which others have evolved. ■ an early version of a machine, artifact, system, etc., that later became more developed.

an·ces·tral /an'sestrəl/ ▶*adj.* of, belonging to, inherited from, or denoting an ancestor or ancestors: *the family's ancestral home.*

an·ces·try /'an,sestrē/ ▶*n.* (*pl.* **-tries**) one's family or ethnic descent: *his dark eyes came from his Jewish ancestry.* ■ the evolutionary or genetic line of descent of an animal or plant: *the ancestry of the rose is extremely complicated.* ■ *fig.* the origin or background of something.

an·chor /'aNGkər/ ▶*n.* **1** a heavy object attached to a rope or chain and used to moor a vessel to the sea bottom, typically one having a metal shank with a ring at one end for the rope and a pair of curved and/or barbed flukes at the other. ■ *fig.* a person or thing that provides stability or confidence in an otherwise uncertain situation: *the European Community is the economic anchor of the New Europe.* ■ (in full **anchor store**) a store, e.g., a department store, that is the principal tenant of a mall or a shopping center. **2** an anchorman or anchorwoman, esp. in broadcasting or athletics.
▶*v.* [*tr.*] **1** moor (a ship) to the sea bottom with an anchor: *the ship was anchored in the lee of the island* | [*intr.*] *we anchored in the harbor.* ■ secure firmly in position: *with cords and pitons they anchored him to the rock.* ■ provide with a firm basis or foundation: *it is important that policy be anchored to some acceptable theoretical basis.* **2** to act or serve as an anchor for (a news program or sporting event).
▶ □ **drop anchor** (of a ship) let down the anchor and moor. □ **weigh** (or **raise** or **heave**) **anchor** (of a ship) take up the anchor when ready to depart.

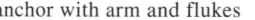

anchor with arm and flukes   mushroom anchor

anchor

an·chor·age /'aNGk(ə)rij/ ▶*n.* **1** an area that is suitable for a ship to anchor. ■ the action of securing something to a base or the state of being secured. **2** *hist.* an anchorite's dwelling place.

an·cho·rite /'aNGkə,rīt/ ▶*n.* *hist.* a religious recluse. —**an·cho·rit·ic** /,aNGkə'ritik/ *adj.*

an·chor·man /'aNGkər,man/ ▶*n.* (*pl.* **-men**) a man who presents and coordinates a live television or radio program involving other contributors. ■ a man who plays the most crucial part or is the most dependable contributor. ■ the member of a relay team who runs the last leg.

an·chor text ▶*n.* the text that appears highlighted in a hypertext link and that can be clicked to open the target Web page.

an·chor·wom·an /'aNGkər,wŏŏmən/ ▶*n.* (*pl.* **-wom·en**) a woman who presents and coordinates a live television or radio program involving other contributors.

an·cho·vy /'an,CHōvē; an'CHōvē/ ▶*n.* (*pl.* **-ies**) a small shoaling fish (genus *Engraulis*, family Engraulidae). Commercially important as a food fish, it is strongly flavored and usually preserved in salt and oil.

an·cient[1] /'änCHənt/ ▶*adj.* belonging to the very distant past and no longer in existence: *the ancient civilizations of the Mediterranean.* ■ having been in existence for a very long time: *ancient forests.* ■ *chiefly humorous* showing or feeling signs of age or wear: *an ancient pair of jeans.*

▶ *n. archaic* or *humorous* an old person: *a solitary ancient in a tweed jacket.* —**an·cient·ness** *n.*

an·cient[2] ▶ *n. archaic* a standard, flag, or ensign.

an·cil·lar·y /ˈansəˌlerē/ ▶ *adj.* providing necessary support to the primary activities or operation of an organization, institution, industry, or system: *the development of ancillary services to support its products.* ■ additional; subsidiary: *paragraph 19 was merely **ancillary** to paragraph 16.* ▶ *n.* (*pl.* **-laries**) a person whose work provides necessary support to the primary activities of an organization, institution, or industry: *specialist teachers and ancillaries.* ■ something that functions in a supplementary or supporting role: *undergraduate courses of three main subjects with related ancillaries.* ▷mid 17th cent.: from Latin *ancillaris*, from *ancilla* 'maidservant.'

and /and/ ▶ *conj.* **1** used to connect words of the same part of speech, clauses, or sentences that are to be taken jointly: *bread and butter* | *red and black tiles.* ■ used to connect two clauses when the second happens after the first: *she washed and dried her hair.* ■ used to connect two clauses, the second of which results from the first: *do that once more, and I'll skin you alive.* ■ connecting two identical comparatives, to emphasize a progressive change: *getting better and better.* ■ connecting two identical words, implying great duration or great extent: *I cried and cried.* ■ used to connect two identical words to indicate that things of the same name or class have different qualities: *all human conduct is determined or caused—but there are causes and causes.* ■ used to connect two numbers to indicate that they are being added together: *six and four make ten.* ■ *archaic* used to connect two numbers, implying succession: *a line of men marching two and two.* **2** used to introduce an additional comment or interjection: *they believe they are descended from him, and quite right, too.* ■ used to introduce a question in connection with what someone else has just said: *"I found the letter in her bag." "And did you steam it open?"* ■ (esp. in broadcasting) used to introduce a statement about a new topic: *and now to the dessert.* **3** *inf.* used after some verbs and before another verb to indicate intention, instead of "to": *I would **try and** do what he said.*
▶ *n.* (usu. **AND**) *Logic Electr.* a Boolean operator that gives the value one if and only if all the operands are one and otherwise has a value of zero. ■ (also **AND gate**) a circuit that produces an output signal only when signals are received simultaneously through all input connections.
▶ □ **and/or** either or both of two stated possibilities: *audio and/or video.*

an·dan·te /änˈdänˌtā/ *Mus.* ▶ *adj. & adv.* (esp. as a direction) in a moderately slow tempo.

an·dan·ti·no /ˌändänˈtēnō/ *Mus.* ▶ *adj. & adv.* (esp. as a direction) more lighthearted than andante, and in most cases quicker.

and·i·ron /ˈanˌdīərn/ ▶ *n.* a metal support, typically one of a pair, that holds wood burning in a fireplace.

An·drew·sar·chus /ˌandrooˈsärkəs/ ▶ *n.* a very large carnivorous mammal (*Andrewsarchus mongoliensis*, order Creodonta) of the Eocene epoch.

an·dro·gen /ˈandrəjən/ ▶ *n. Biochem.* a male sex hormone, such as testosterone. —**an·dro·gen·ic** /ˌandrəˈjenik/ *adj.*

an·drog·y·nous /anˈdräjənəs/ ▶ *adj.* partly male and partly female in appearance; of indeterminate sex. ■ having the physical characteristics of both sexes; hermaphrodite. —**an·drog·y·ny** /-nē/ *n.*

an·droid /ˈanˌdroid/ ▶ *n.* (in science fiction) a robot with a human appearance.

an·ec·dote /ˈanikˌdōt/ ▶ *n.* a short and amusing or interesting story about a real incident or person. | *he had a rich store of anecdotes.* ■ an account regarded as unreliable or hearsay: *his wife's death has long been the subject of rumor and anecdote.* ■ the depiction of a minor narrative incident in a painting.. —**an·ec·dot·al** /ˌanikˈdōtl/ *adj.*

a·ne·mi·a /əˈnēmēə/ (*Brit.* **a·nae·mi·a**) ▶ *n.* a condition marked by a deficiency of red blood cells or of hemoglobin in the blood, resulting in pallor and weariness.

a·ne·mic /əˈnēmik/ (*Brit.* **a·nae·mic**) ▶ *adj.* suffering from anemia. ■ *fig.* lacking in color, spirit, or vitality.

an·e·mom·e·ter /ˌanəˈmämitər/ ▶ *n.* an instrument for measuring the speed of the wind, or of any current of gas. —**an·e·mom·e·try** /-trē/ *n.* —**an·e·mo·met·ric** /-məˈmetrik/ *adj.*

a·nem·o·ne /əˈnemənē/ ▶ *n.* **1** a widely distributed, often cultivated plant (genus *Anemone*) of the buttercup family, typically bearing brightly colored flowers. **2** short for SEA ANEMONE. ▷mid 16th cent.: said to be from Greek *anemōnē*, literally 'daughter of the wind.'

an·er·oid /ˈanəˌroid/ ▶ *adj.* relating to or denoting a barometer that measures air pressure by the action of air in deforming the elastic lid of an evacuated box or chamber.

an·es·the·sia /ˌanəsˈthēzhə/ (*Brit.* **an·aes·the·sia**) ▶ *n.* insensitivity to pain, esp. as artificially induced by the administration of gases or the injection of drugs before surgical operations. ■ the induction of this state, or the branch of medicine concerned with it.

an·es·the·si·ol·o·gy /ˌanəsˌthēzēˈäləjē/ (also *Brit.* **an·aes·the·si·ol·o·gy**) ▶ *n.* the branch of medicine concerned with anesthesia and anesthetics. —**an·es·the·si·ol·o·gist** /-jist/ *n.*

an·es·thet·ic /ˌanəsˈthetik/ (*Brit.* **an·aes·thet·ic**) ▶ *n.* a substance that induces insensitivity to pain.
▶ *adj.* inducing or relating to insensitivity to pain.

an·es·the·tist /əˈnesthitist/ (*Brit.* **an·aes·the·tist**) ▶ *n.* a medical specialist who administers anesthetics.

an·es·the·tize /əˈnesthiˌtīz/ (*Brit.* **an·aes·the·tize**) ▶ *v.* [*tr.*] administer an anesthetic to. ■ *fig.* deprive of feeling or awareness: *tragedy of a magnitude that anesthetizes the mind.* —**an·es·the·ti·za·tion** /-THitəˈzāSHən/ *n.*

an·eu·rysm /ˈanyəˌrizəm/ (also **an·eu·rism**) ▶ *n. Med.* an excessive localized enlargement of an artery caused by a weakening of the artery wall. —**an·eu·rys·mal** /-ˌrizməl/ *adj.*

a·new /əˈn(y)oo/ ▶ *adv. chiefly poetic/lit.* in a new or different, typically more positive, way: *her career had begun anew, with a lucrative Japanese modeling contract.* ■ once more; again: *tears filled her eyes anew.*

an·gel /ˈānjəl/ ▶ *n.* **1** a spiritual being believed to act as an attendant, agent, or messenger of God, conventionally represented in human form with wings and a long robe. ■ an attendant spirit, esp. a benevolent one: *there was an angel watching over me.* ■ *inf.* a financial backer of an enterprise, typically in the theater. ■ in traditional Christian theology, a being of the lowest order of the celestial hierarchy. **2** a person of exemplary conduct or virtue: *I know I'm **no angel**.* ■ used in similes or comparisons to refer to a person's outstanding beauty, qualities, or abilities: *you sang **like an angel**.* ■ used in approval when a person has been or is expected to be kind or willing to oblige: *be an angel and let us come in.* ■ used as a term of endearment. **3** (**angels**) *inf., Aviation* an aircraft's altitude (often used with a numeral indicating thousands of feet): *we rendezvous at angels nine.*

an·gel dust ▶ *n. inf.* the hallucinogenic drug phencyclidine hydrochloride.

an·gel·fish /ˈānjəlˌfiSH/ ▶ *n.* (*pl.* same or **-fishes**) any of a number of laterally compressed deep-bodied fish with extended dorsal and anal fins, in particular: ■ the freshwater cichlid *Pterophyllum scalare*, native to the Amazon basin. ■ the **gray angelfish** (*Pomacanthus arcuatus*, family Pomacanthidae), a coastal marine fish.

an·gel·ic /anˈjelik/ ▶ *adj.* of or relating to angels: *the angelic hosts.* ■ (of a person) exceptionally beautiful, innocent, or kind: *she looks remarkably young and angelic.* —**an·gel·i·cal** *adj.* —**an·gel·i·cal·ly** /-ik(ə)lē/ *adv.*

An·ge·lus /ˈanjələs/ (also **an·ge·lus**) ▶ *n.* a Roman Catholic devotion commemorating the Incarnation of Jesus and including the Hail Mary, said at morning, noon, and sunset.

an·ger /ˈaNGgər/ ▶ *n.* a strong feeling of annoyance, displeasure, or hostility: *the colonel's anger at his daughter's disobedience.*
▶ *v.* [*tr.*] (often **be angered**) fill (someone) with such a feeling; provoke anger in: *she was angered by his terse answer.*

an·gi·na /anˈjīnə/ ▶ *n.* **1** (also **angina pec·to·ris** /ˈpektəris/) a condition marked by severe pain in the chest, caused by an inadequate blood supply to the heart. **2** any of a number of disorders in which there is an intense localized pain: *Ludwig's angina.*

an·gi·o·gram /ˈanj(ē)əˌgram/ ▶ *n.* an X-ray photograph of blood or lymph vessels, made by angiography.

an·gi·o·sperm /ˈanjēəˌspərm/ ▶ *n. Bot.* a plant that has flowers and produces seeds enclosed within a carpel. The angiosperms are a large group and include herbaceous plants, shrubs, grasses, and most trees.

An·gle /ˈaNGgəl/ ▶ *n.* a member of a Germanic people, originally inhabitants of what is now Schleswig-Holstein, who migrated to England in the 5th century AD.

an·gle[1] /ˈaNGgəl/ ▶ *n.* **1** the space (usually measured in degrees) between two intersecting lines or surfaces at or close to the point where they meet. ■ a corner, esp. an external projection or an internal recess of a part of a building or other structure: *a skylight in the angle of the roof.* ■ slope; a measure of the inclination of two lines or surfaces with respect to each other, equal to the amount that one would have to be turned in order to point in the same direction as the other: *sloping at an angle of 33° to the horizontal.* ■ a position from which something is viewed or along which it travels or acts, often as measured by its inclination from an implicit horizontal or vertical baseline: *camera angles.* **2** a particular way of approaching or considering an issue or problem:

Pronunciation Key ə *ago, up;* ər *over, fur;* a *hat;* ā *ate;* ä *car;* CH *chin;* e *let;* ē *see;* e(ə)r *air;* i *fit;* ī *by;* i(ə)r *ear;* NG *sing;* ō *go;* ô *law, for;* oi *toy;* oo *good;* ōo *goo;* ou *out;* SH *she;* TH *thin;* TH *then;* (h)w *why;* ZH *vision*

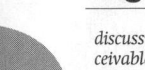

discussing the problems from every conceivable angle. ■ one part of a larger subject, event, or problem: *a black prosecutor who downplayed the racial angle.* ■ a bias or point of view: *Zimmer saw the world from an angle that few could understand.*

▶*v.* [*tr.*] direct or incline at an angle: *Anna angled her camera toward the tree.* ■ [*intr.*] move or be inclined at an angle: *the cab angled across two lanes and skidded to a stop.* ■ [*tr.*] present (information) to reflect a particular view or have a particular focus.

an·gle[2] ▶*v.* [*intr.*] fish with rod and line: *there are no big fish left to* **angle** *for.* ■ seek something desired by indirectly prompting someone to offer it: *Ralph had begun to angle for an invitation.*

an·gled /'aNGgəld/ ▶*adj.* **1** placed or inclined at an angle to something else: *a sharply angled flight of stairs.* **2** [in *comb.*] (of an object or shape) having an angle or angles of a specified type or number: *a right-angled bend.* ■ (of information) presented so as to reflect a particular view or to have a particular focus.

an·gler /'aNGglər/ ▶*n.* a person who fishes with a rod and line: *a carp angler.* ■ short for ANGLERFISH.

an·gler·fish /'aNGglər,fisH/ ▶*n.* (*pl.* same or **-fishes**) a fish (order Lophiiformes) that lures prey with a fleshy lobe attached to a filament that arises from the snout and hangs in front of the mouth.

An·gli·can /'aNGglikən/ ▶*adj.* of, relating to, or denoting the Church of England or any Church in communion with it.
▶*n.* a member of any of these Churches. —**An·gli·can·ism** /-,nizəm/ *n.*

An·gli·cism /'aNGglə,sizəm/ ▶*n.* **1** a word or phrase that is peculiar to British English. ■ the quality of being typically English or of favoring English things. **2** a word or phrase borrowed from English into a foreign language: *"purists" condemn the use of "fin de semaine" because it is an Anglicism.*

an·gli·cize /'aNGglə,sīz/ ▶*v.* [*tr.*] make English in form or character: *he anglicized his name to Goodman.* —**an·gli·ci·za·tion** /,aNGgləsə'zāsHən/ *n.*

An·glo /'aNGglō/ ▶*n.* (*pl.* **-glos**) a white, English-speaking American as distinct from a Hispanic American: [as *adj.*] *Anglo neighborhoods.*

An·glo·phile /'aNGglə,fīl/ ▶*n.* a person who is fond of or greatly admires England or Britain.
▶*adj.* fond or admiring of England or Britain. —**An·glo·phil·i·a** /,aNGglə-'filēə/ *n.*

An·glo·phobe /'aNGglə,fōb/ ▶*n.* a person who greatly hates or fears England or Britain.
▶*adj.* greatly hating or fearing England or Britain. —**An·glo·pho·bi·a** /,aNGglə'fōbēə/ *n.*

an·glo·phone /'aNGglə,fōn/ ▶*adj.* English-speaking: *anglophone students.*
▶*n.* an English-speaking person.

An·glo-Sax·on ▶*adj.* relating to or denoting the Germanic inhabitants of England from their arrival in the 5th century up to the Norman Conquest. ■ of English descent. ■ of, in, or relating to the Old English language. ■ *inf.* (of an English word or expression) plain, in particular vulgar: *using a lot of good old Anglo-Saxon expletives.*
▶*n.* **1** a Germanic inhabitant of England between the 5th century and the Norman Conquest. ■ a person of English descent. ■ any white, English-speaking person. **2** another term for OLD ENGLISH. ■ *inf.* plain English, in particular vulgar slang.

an·go·ra /aNG'gôrə/ ▶*n.* a cat, goat, or rabbit of a long-haired breed: *angora rabbits.* ■ a fabric made from the hair of the angora goat or rabbit: [as *adj.*] *an angora cardigan.*

an·gos·tu·ra /,aNGgə'st(y)ŏŏrə/ (also **angostura bark**) ▶*n.* an aromatic bitter bark from certain South American trees, used as a flavoring.

an·gry /'aNGgrē/ ▶*adj.* (**-gri·er, -gri·est**) having a strong feeling of or showing annoyance, displeasure, or hostility; full of anger: *why are you angry with me?* ■ *fig.* (of the sea or sky) stormy, turbulent, or threatening: *the wild, angry sea.* ■ (of a wound or sore) red and inflamed. —**an·gri·ly** /-grəlē/ *adv.*

angst /aNG(k)st; äNG(k)st/ ▶*n.* a feeling of deep anxiety or dread,

typically an unfocused one about the human condition or the state of the world in general: *adolescent angst.* ■ *inf.* a feeling of persistent worry about something trivial: *my hair causes me angst.*

ang·strom /'aNGstrəm/ (also **ång·ström, angstrom unit**) (abbr.: Å) ▶*n.* a unit of length equal to one hundred-millionth of a centimeter, 10^{-10} meter, used mainly to express wavelengths and interatomic distances.

an·guish /'aNGgwisH/ ▶*n.* severe mental or physical pain or suffering: *she shut her eyes in anguish* | *Philip gave a cry of anguish.*
▶*v.* suffer or cause someone to suffer anguish: *he anguished over how to reply.*

an·guished /'aNGgwisHt/ ▶*adj.* experiencing or expressing severe mental or physical pain or suffering: *he gave an anguished cry.*

an·gu·lar /'aNGgyələr/ ▶*adj.* **1** (of an object, outline, or shape) having angles or sharp corners: *angular chairs.* ■ (of a person or part of their body) lean and having a prominent bone structure: *her angular face.* ■ (of a person's way of moving) not flowing smoothly; awkward or jerky: *his movements were stiff and angular.* ■ placed or directed at an angle: *large angular writing.* **2** *chiefly Physics* denoting physical properties or quantities measured with reference to or by means of an angle, esp. those associated with rotation: *angular acceleration.* —**an·gu·lar·i·ty** /,aNGgyə'laritē/ *n.* —**an·gu·lar·ly** *adv.*

an·hy·drous /an'hīdrəs/ ▶*adj.* *Chem.* (of a substance, esp. a crystalline compound) containing no water.

an·i·line /'anl-ən/ ▶*n.* *Chem.* a colorless oily liquid, $C_6H_5NH_2$, present in coal tar. It is used in the manufacture of dyes, drugs, and plastics.
▷mid 19th cent.: from *anil* 'indigo,' ultimately from Arabic *an-nīl* (from Sanskrit *nīlī*, from *nīla* 'dark blue').

an·i·ma /'anəmə/ ▶*n.* *Psychol.* Jung's term for the feminine part of a man's personality! ■ the part of the psyche that is directed inward, and is in touch with the subconscious. Often contrasted with PERSONA.

an·i·mad·vert /,anəmad'vərt/ ▶*v.* [*intr.*] (**animadvert on/upon/against**) *formal* pass criticism or censure on; speak out against: *we shall be obliged to animadvert most severely upon you in our report.* —**an·i·mad·ver·sion** /-'vərzHən/ *n.*

an·i·mal /'anəməl/ ▶*n.* a living organism that feeds on organic matter, typically having specialized sense organs and nervous system and able to respond rapidly to stimuli: *humans are the only animals who weep.* ■ any such living organism other than a human being: *are humans superior to animals, or just different?* ■ a mammal, as opposed to a bird, reptile, fish, or insect: *the snowfall seemed to have chased all birds, animals, and men indoors.* ■ a person whose behavior is regarded as devoid of human attributes or civilizing influences, esp. someone who is very cruel, violent, or repulsive. ■ a particular type of person or thing: *a regular party animal* | *the government that followed the election was a very different animal.*
▶*adj.* of, relating to, or characteristic of animals: *the evolution of animal life* | *animal welfare.* ■ of animals as distinct from plants: *tissues of animal and vegetable protein.* ■ characteristic of the physical and instinctive needs of animals; of the flesh rather than the spirit or intellect: *a crude surrender to animal lust.*

an·i·mal·ism /'anəmə,lizəm/ ▶*n.* behavior that is characteristic of or appropriate to animals, particularly in being physical and instinctive. ■ religious worship of or concerning animals. —**an·i·mal·is·tic** /,anəmə'listik/ *adj.*

an·i·mate ▶*v.* /'anə,māt/ [*tr.*] **1** *chiefly fig.* bring to life: *the desert is like a line drawing waiting to be animated with color.* ■ give inspiration, encouragement, or renewed vigor to: *she has animated the nation with a sense of political direction.* **2** (usu. **be animated**) give (a movie or character) the appearance of movement using animation techniques.
▶*adj.* /-mit/ alive or having life (often as a contrast with INANIMATE). ■ lively and active: *party photos of animate socialites.*

an·i·mat·ed /'anə,mātid/ ▶*adj.* **1** full of life or excitement; lively: *an animated conversation.* ■ (of a movie) made using animation techniques: *an animated version of the fairy tale.* ■ moving or appearing to move as if alive: *animated life-size figures.* —**an·i·mat·ed·ly** *adv.*

an·i·ma·tion /,anə'māsHən/ ▶*n.* **1** the state of being full of life or vigor; liveliness: *they started talking with animation.* ■ *chiefly archaic* the state of being alive. **2** the technique of filming successive drawings or positions of puppets or models to create an illusion of movement when the movie is shown as a sequence. ■ (also **computer animation**) the manipulation of electronic images by means of a computer in order to create moving images. —**an·i·ma·tor** /'anə,mātər/ *n.*

an·i·mism /'anə,mizəm/ ▶*n.* **1** the attribution of a soul to plants, inanimate objects, and natural phenomena. **2** the belief in a supernatural power that organizes and animates the material universe. —**an·i·mist** *n.* —**an·i·mis·tic** /,anə'mistik/ *adj.*

[figure labels:] acute · right · obtuse · **angles**

an·i·mos·i·ty /ˌanəˈmäsitē/ ▶n. (pl. **-ties**) strong hostility: *he no longer felt any animosity toward her* | *the animosity between the King and his brother.*

an·i·mus /ˈanəməs/ ▶n. **1** hostility or ill feeling: *the author's animus toward her.* **2** motivation to do something: *the reformist animus came from within the Party.* **3** *Psychol.* Jung's term for the masculine part of a woman's personality.

an·i·on /ˈanˌīən/ ▶n. *Chem.* a negatively charged ion, i.e., one that would be attracted to the anode in electrolysis. The opposite of CATION. —**an·i·on·ic** /ˌanīˈänik/ adj.

an·ise /ˈanis/ ▶n. **1** a Mediterranean plant (*Pimpinella anisum*) of the parsley family, cultivated for its aromatic seeds, used in cooking and herbal medicine. **2** an Asian or American tree or shrub (genus *Illicium*, family Illiciaceae) that bears fruit with an aniseedlike odor, esp. **star anise** (*I. verum*), used in Chinese cooking.

an·i·seed /ˈanə(s)ˌsēd/ ▶n. the seed of the anise.

ankh /ängk/ ▶n. an object or design resembling a cross but having a loop instead of the top arm, used in ancient Egypt as a symbol of life.

an·kle /ˈaNGkəl/ ▶n. the joint connecting the foot with the leg. ■ the narrow part of the leg between the foot and the calf.
▶v. *inf.* [*tr.*] leave: *he ankled the series to do a movie.* ■ [*intr.*] walk.

an·klet /ˈaNGklit/ ▶n. **1** a sock that reaches just above the ankle. **2** an ornament worn around an ankle.

an·ky·lo·sis /ˌaNGkəˈlōsis/ ▶n. *Med.* abnormal stiffening and immobility of a joint due to fusion of the bones. —**an·ky·lot·ic** /-ˈlätik/ adj.

ankh

an·nal·ist /ˈanl-ist/ ▶n. a person who writes annals. —**an·nal·is·tic** /ˌanlˈistik/ adj.

an·nals /ˈanlz/ ▶pl. n. a record of events year by year: *eighth-century Northumberland annals.* ■ historical records: *the annals of the European discoverers.* ■ (**Annals**) used in the titles of learned journals.

an·nat·to /əˈnätō/ (also **a·nat·to**) ▶n. (pl. **-tos**) **1** an orange-red dye obtained from the pulp of a tropical fruit, used for coloring foods and fabric. **2** the tropical American tree (*Bixa orellana*, family Bixaceae) from which this fruit is obtained.

an·neal /əˈnēl/ ▶v. [*tr.*] heat (metal or glass) and allow it to cool slowly, in order to remove internal stresses and toughen it. ■ *Biochem.* recombine (DNA) in the double-stranded form following separation by heat. —**an·neal·er** n.

an·ne·lid /ˈanl-id/ ▶n. any of various segmented worms, including earthworms and leeches.
▶adj. of or relating to annelids.

an·nex ▶v. /əˈneks; ˈaneks/ [*tr.*] (often **be annexed**) append or add as an extra or subordinate part, esp. to a document: *the first ten amendments were annexed to the Constitution in 1791.* ■ add (territory) to one's own territory by appropriation: *Moldova was annexed by the Soviet Union in 1940.* ■ *inf.* take for oneself; appropriate. ■ *archaic* add or attach as a condition or consequence.
▶n. /ˈaneks; -iks/ (pl. **-nex·es**) **1** a building joined to or associated with a main building, providing additional space or accommodations. **2** an addition to a document: *an annex to the report.* —**an·nex·a·tion** /ˌanekˈsāSHən/ ; ˌanik-/ n. —**an·nex·a·tion·ist** n. & adj.

an·ni·hi·late /əˈnīəˌlāt/ ▶v. [*tr.*] destroy utterly; obliterate: *a crusade to annihilate evil.* ■ defeat utterly: *the stronger force annihilated its opponent.* —**an·ni·hi·la·tor** /-ˌlātər/ n. —**an·ni·hi·la·tion** /əˌnīəˈlāSHən/ n.

an·ni·ver·sa·ry /ˌanəˈvərsərē/ ▶n. (pl. **-ries**) the date on which an event took place in a previous year: *the 50th anniversary of the start of World War II.* ■ the date on which a country or other institution was founded in a previous year: *Canada's 125th anniversary.* ■ the date on which a couple was married in a previous year: *he forgot our tenth anniversary!* ■ *inf.* the date on which a romance began in a previous month or week.

an·no·tate /ˈanəˌtāt/ ▶v. [*tr.*] add notes to (a text or diagram) giving explanation or comment: *documentation should be annotated with explanatory notes.* —**an·no·tat·a·ble** adj. —**an·no·ta·tion** /ˌanəˈtāSHən/ n. —**an·no·ta·tor** /-ˌtātər/ n.

an·nounce /əˈnouns/ ▶v. [*tr.*] make a public and typically formal declaration about a fact, occurrence, or intention: *the president's office announced that the state of siege would be lifted* | *he announced his retirement from football.* ■ make known: *we announce our failures by warring against ourselves and others.* ■ give information about (transportation) in a station or airport via a public address system: *they were announcing her train.* ■ (of a notice, letter, sound, etc.) give information to (someone) via the senses of sight or hearing: *storms were announced by long wisps that lashed*

out from a snow cloud's body. ■ make known the arrival or imminence of (a guest or a meal) at a formal social occasion: *dinner was announced.*

an·nounce·ment /əˈnounsmənt/ ▶n. a public and typically formal statement about a fact, occurrence, or intention: *the spokesperson was about to make an announcement.* ■ the action of making such a statement: *the announcement of the decision of the president.* ■ a notice appearing in a newspaper or public place and announcing something such as a birth, death, or marriage. ■ a statement of information given over a public address system: *a loudspeaker announcement echoed across the field.*

an·nounc·er /əˈnounsər/ ▶n. a person who announces something, in particular someone who introduces or gives information about programs on radio or television.

an·noy /əˈnoi/ ▶v. [*tr.*] (often **be annoyed**) irritate (someone); make (someone) a little angry: *he was annoyed at being woken up so early* | *Kelly was annoyed with herself for feeling a pang of jealousy* | *your damned cheerfulness has always annoyed me* | [*intr.*] *rock music loud enough to annoy.* ■ *archaic* harm or attack repeatedly: *a gallant Saxon, who annoyed this Coast.* ▷Middle English (in the sense 'be hateful to'): from Old French *anoier* (verb), *anoi* (noun), based on Latin *in odio* in the phrase *mihi in odio est* 'it is hateful to me.' —**an·noy·ing** adj. —**an·noy·ing·ly** adv.

an·noy·ance /əˈnoi-əns/ ▶n. the feeling or state of being annoyed; irritation: *he turned his charm on Tara, much to Herbert's annoyance.* ■ a thing that annoys someone; a nuisance: *the Council found him an annoyance.*

an·nu·al /ˈanyo͞oəl/ ▶adj. occurring once every year: *the union's annual conference.* ■ calculated over or covering a period of a year: *annual accounts.* ■ (of a plant) living for a year or less, perpetuating itself by seed: *annual flowers.*
▶n. a book or magazine that is published once a year under the same title but with different contents. ■ an annual plant. —**an·nu·al·ly** adv.

an·nu·al·ized /ˈanyo͞oəˌlīzd/ ▶adj. (of a rate of interest, inflation, or return on an investment) recalculated as an annual rate: *an annualized yield of about 11.5%.*

an·nu·i·ty /əˈn(y)o͞oitē/ ▶n. (pl. **-ties**) a fixed sum of money paid to someone each year, typically for the rest of their life: *he left her an annuity of $1,000 in his will.* ■ a form of insurance or investment entitling the investor to a series of annual sums: [as adj.] *an annuity plan.*

an·nul /əˈnəl/ ▶v. (**-nulled, -nul·ling**) [*tr.*] (usu. **be annulled**) declare invalid (an official agreement, decision, or result): *the elections were annulled by the general amid renewed protests.* ■ declare (a marriage) to have had no legal existence. —**an·nul·ment** n.

an·nu·lar /ˈanyələr/ ▶adj. technical ring-shaped. —**an·nu·lar·ly** adv.

an·nu·lus /ˈanyələs/ ▶n. (pl. **-li** /-ˌlī/) technical a ring-shaped object, structure, or region.

an·nun·ci·ate /əˈnənsēˌāt/ ▶v. [*tr.*] archaic announce (something).

an·nun·ci·a·tion /əˌnənsēˈāSHən/ ▶n. (usu. **the Annunciation**) the announcement of the Incarnation by the angel Gabriel to Mary. ■ the church festival commemorating this, held on March 25 (Lady Day). ■ *formal* or *archaic* the announcement of something.

an·ode /ˈanōd/ ▶n. the positively charged electrode by which the electrons leave a device. The opposite of CATHODE. ■ the negatively charged electrode of a device supplying current such as a primary cell. —**an·od·al** /anˈōdl; āˈnōdl/ adj. —**an·od·ic** /anˈädik/ adj.

an·o·dize /ˈanəˌdīz/ ▶v. [*tr.*] [usu. as adj.] (**anodized**) coat (a metal, esp. aluminum) with a protective oxide layer by an electrolytic process in which the metal forms the anode. —**an·o·diz·er** n.

an·o·dyne /ˈanəˌdīn/ ▶adj. not likely to provoke dissent or offense; uncontentious or inoffensive, often deliberately so: *anodyne new age music.*
▶n. a pain-killing drug or medicine. ■ *fig.* something that alleviates a person's mental distress: *an anodyne to the misery she had put him through.*

a·noint /əˈnoint/ ▶v. [*tr.*] smear or rub with oil, typically as part of a religious ceremony: *bodies were anointed after death for burial.* ■ (**anoint something with**) smear or rub something with (any other substance): *Cuna Indians anoint the tips of their arrows with poison.* ■ ceremonially confer divine or holy office upon (a priest or monarch) by smearing or rubbing with oil. ■ *fig.* nominate or choose (someone) as successor to or leading candidate for a position: *he was anointed as the organizational candidate of the party.*

a·no·le /əˈnōlē/ ▶n. a small, mainly arboreal American lizard (genus *Anolis*) of the iguana family, with a throat fan that (in the male) is typically brightly colored. Anoles have some ability to change color. Also called CHAMELEON.

Pronunciation Key ə *ago, up*; ər *over, fur*; a *hat*; ā *ate*; ä *car*; CH *chin*; e *let*; ē *see*; e(ə)r *air*; i *fit*; ī *by*; i(ə)r *ear*; NG *sing*; ō *go*; ô *law, for*; oi *toy*; o͞o *good*; o͞o *goo*; ou *out*; SH *she*; TH *thin*; ͓TH *then*; (h)w *why*; ZH *vision*

a·nom·a·lous /ə'nämələs/ ▸ *adj.* deviating from what is standard, normal, or expected: *an anomalous situation* | *sentences that are grammatically anomalous.* —**a·nom·a·lous·ly** *adv.* —**a·nom·a·lous·ness** *n.*

a·nom·a·ly /ə'näməlē/ ▸ *n.* (*pl.* **-lies**) something that deviates from what is standard, normal, or expected: *the apparent anomaly that those who produced the wealth were the poorest.*

an·o·mie /'anə,mē/ (also **an·o·my**) ▸ *n.* lack of the usual social or ethical standards in an individual or group. —**a·nom·ic** /ə'nämik; ə'nō-/ *adj.*

a·non /ə'nän/ ▸ *adv.* archaic soon; shortly: *I'll see you anon.*

anon. ▸ *abbr.* anonymous.

a·non·y·mous /ə'nänəməs/ ▸ *adj.* (of a person) not identified by name; of unknown name: *the anonymous author of Beowulf.* ■ having no outstanding, individual, or unusual features; unremarkable or impersonal: *the anonymous black car waiting to take him to the airport.* ■ used in names of support groups for addicts of a substance or behavior to indicate the confidentiality maintained among members of the group: *Alcoholics Anonymous* | *Debtors Anonymous.* —**an·o·nym·i·ty** /,anə'nimitē/ *n.* —**a·non·y·mous·ly** *adv.*

a·noph·e·les /ə'näfəlēz/ (also **anopheles mosquito**) ▸ *n.* a mosquito (genus *Anopheles*) common in warm climates. Its many species include those that transmit the malarial parasite to humans. —**a·noph·e·line** /-,līn; -lin/ *adj. & n.*

an·o·rak /'anə,rak/ ▸ *n.* a waterproof jacket, typically with a hood, of a kind originally used in polar regions.

an·o·rex·i·a /,anə'reksēə/ ▸ *n.* a lack or loss of appetite for food (as a medical condition). ■ (also **anorexia ner·vo·sa** /nər'vōsə/) an emotional disorder characterized by an obsessive desire to lose weight by refusing to eat; compare with **BULIMIA.**

an·o·rex·ic /,anə'reksik/ (also **an·o·rec·tic** /,anə'rektik/) ▸ *adj.* relating to, characterized by, or suffering from anorexia. ■ inf. extremely thin.
▸ *n.* **1** a person suffering from anorexia. **2** (**anorectic**) a medicine that produces a loss of appetite.

an·oth·er /ə'nəTHər/ ▸ *adj. & pron.* **1** used to refer to an additional person or thing of the same type as one already mentioned or known about; one more; a further: [as *adj.*] *have another drink* | [as *pron.*] *they have two practices, one in the morning and another in the afternoon.* ■ [usu. as *adj.*] used with a proper name to indicate someone or something's similarity to the person or event specified: *this will not be another Vietnam.* **2** used to refer to a different person or thing from one already mentioned or known about: [as *adj.*] *come back another day.* | [as *pron.*] *moving from one place to another.* ■ [*adj.*] used to refer to someone sharing an attribute in common with the person already mentioned: *his kiss with another man caused a tabloid rumpus.*

an·swer /'ansər/ ▸ *n.* a thing said, written, or done to deal with or as a reaction to a question, statement, or situation. ■ a thing written or said in reaction to a question in a test or quiz: *write your answers on a postcard.* ■ the correct solution to such a question: *the answer is 280°.* ■ a solution to a problem or dilemma: *the answer to poverty and unemployment is a properly funded range of services.* ■ (**answer to**) a thing or person that imitates or fulfills the same role as something or someone else: *the press called her Britain's answer to Marilyn Monroe.* ■ Law the defendant's reply to the plaintiff's charges.
▸ *v.* **1** [*tr.*] say or write something to deal with or as a reaction to someone or something: *she answered that she would take nothing but the ring* | *she tried to answer his questions truthfully* | [*intr.*] *Steve was about to answer, but Hazel spoke first.* ■ [*tr.*] provide the required responses to (a test or quiz): *answer the questions below for a chance to win a vacation.* ■ [*intr.*] (**answer back**) respond impudently or disrespectfully to someone, esp. when being criticized or told to do something: *one couldn't argue with a parent; one couldn't answer back* | [*tr.*] *Mary resisted the temptation to answer her mother back.* ■ [*tr.*] act in reaction to (a sound such as a telephone ringing or a knock or ring on a door): *David answered the door* | [*intr.*] *she called Edward's house, hoping he would answer.* ■ [*tr.*] act in response to (a stimulus): *answering the call of nature.* ■ [*tr.*] discharge (a responsibility or claim): *they answered the call of duty in World War II.* ■ [*tr.*] defend oneself against (a charge, accusation, or criticism): *he said he would return to Spain to answer all charges.* ■ [*intr.*] (**answer for**) be responsible or to blame for: *the dust mite has a lot to answer for, especially if you are asthmatic.* ■ [*intr.*] (**answer to**) be responsible or report to (someone): *I answer to the assistant commissioner.* ■ [*intr.*] (**answer to**) be required to explain or justify oneself to (someone): *you will have the police to answer to.* **2** be suitable for fulfilling (a need); satisfy: [*tr.*] *entrepreneurship is necessary to answer the needs of national and international markets* [*intr.*] *nothing short of that would answer.* —**an·swer·er** *n.* **an·swer·less** *adj.*

an·swer·a·ble /'ansərəbəl/ ▸ *adj.* **1** (**answerable to**) required to explain or justify one's actions; responsible or having to report to: *I'm not answerable to you for my every movement.* ■ (**answerable for**) responsible for: *an employer is answerable for the negligence of his employees.* **2** (of a question) able to be answered.

ant /ant/ ▸ *n.* a small insect (family Formicidae, order Hymenoptera), often with a sting, that usually lives in a complex social colony with one or more breeding queens.

ant·ac·id /ant'asid/ ▸ *adj.* (chiefly of a medicine) preventing or correcting acidity, esp. in the stomach.
▸ *n.* an antacid medicine.

an·tag·o·nism /an'tagə,nizəm/ ▸ *n.* active hostility or opposition: *the antagonism between them.* ■ Biochem. inhibition of or interference with the action of one substance or organism by another.

an·tag·o·nist /an'tagənist/ ▸ *n.* a person who actively opposes or is hostile to someone or something; an adversary: *he turned to confront his antagonist.* ■ Biochem. a substance that interferes with or inhibits the physiological action of another. ■ Anat. a muscle whose action counteracts that of another specified muscle. —**an·tag·o·nis·tic** /an-,tagə'nistik/ *adj.*

an·tag·o·nize /an'tagə,nīz/ ▸ *v.* [*tr.*] cause (someone) to become hostile: *he antagonized many colleagues during the budget wars.*

Ant·arc·tic /ant'ärktik; -'ärtik/ ▸ *adj.* of or relating to the south polar region or Antarctica.
▸ *n.* (**the Antarctic**) the Antarctic region.

an·te /'antē/ ▸ *n.* a stake put up by a player in poker and similar games before receiving cards.
▸ *v.* (**-tes, -ted, -te·ing**) [*tr.*] (**ante something up**) put up an amount as an ante in poker and similar games. ■ inf. pay an amount of money in advance: *he anted up $925,000 of his own money.* ■ [*intr.*] (**ante up**) inf. put up one's money; pay up: *the owners have to ante up if they want to attract the best talent.*
▸ □ **up** (or **raise**) **the ante** increase what is at stake or under discussion, esp. in a conflict or dispute: *he decided to up the ante in the trade war.*

ant·eat·er /'ant,ētər/ ▸ *n.* a mammal that feeds on ants and termites, with a long snout and sticky tongue. Most anteaters are edentates of the Central and South American family Myrmecophagidae.

an·te·bel·lum /,antē'beləm/ ▸ *adj.* occurring or existing before a particular war, esp. the American Civil War.

an·te·ced·ent /,antə'sēdnt/ ▸ *n.* a thing or event that existed before or logically precedes another: *some antecedents to the African novel might exist in Africa's oral traditions.* ■ (**antecedents**) a person's ancestors or family and social background. ■ Gram. a word, phrase, clause, or sentence to which another word (esp. a following relative pronoun) refers. ■ Math. the first term in a ratio.
▸ *adj.* preceding in time or order; previous or preexisting. ■ denoting a grammatical antecedent. —**an·te·ced·ence** *n.*

an·te·cham·ber /'antē,CHāmbər/ ▸ *n.* a small room leading to a main one.

an·te·date /'antē,dāt/ ▸ *v.* [*tr.*] precede in time; come before (something) in date: *a civilization that antedated the Roman Empire.* ■ indicate that (a document or event) should be assigned to an earlier date.

an·te·di·lu·vi·an /,antēdə'loovēən/ ▸ *adj.* of or belonging to the time before the biblical Flood: *gigantic bones of antediluvian animals.* ■ chiefly humorous ridiculously old-fashioned.

an·te·lope /'antl,ōp/ ▸ *n.* (*pl.* same or **antelopes**) a swift-running deerlike ruminant of the cattle family with smooth hair and upward-pointing horns, native to Africa and Asia. ■ another term for **PRONGHORN.** ▷late Middle English (name of a mythical creature): via Old French, ultimately from late Greek *antholps.*

an·te·na·tal /,antē'nātl/ ▸ *adj.* before birth; during or relating to pregnancy; prenatal: *antenatal care.*
▸ *n.* inf. a medical examination during pregnancy. —**an·te·na·tal·ly** *adv.*

an·ten·na /an'tenə/ ▸ *n.* **1** Zool. (*pl.* **-ten·nae** /-'tenē/) either of a pair of long, thin sensory appendages on the heads of insects, crustaceans, and some other arthropods. ■ (**antennae**) fig. the faculty of instinctively detecting and interpreting subtle signs: *he has the political antennae of a party whip.* **2** (*pl.* **-ten·nas**) a rod, wire, or other device used to transmit or receive radio or television signals. —**an·ten·nal** /-'tenl/ *adj.* (in sense 1). —**an·ten·na·ry** /-'tenərē/ *adj.*

an·te·pe·nul·ti·mate /,antēpə'nəltəmit/ ▸ *adj.* last but two in a series; third last: *the antepenultimate syllable.*

an·te·ri·or /an'ti(ə)rēər/ ▸ *adj.* **1** technical, chiefly Anat. & Biol. nearer the front, esp. situated in the front of the body, or nearer to the head or forepart: *the veins anterior to the heart.* The opposite of **POSTERIOR.** **2** formal coming before in time; earlier. —**an·te·ri·or·i·ty** /an,ti(ə)rē'ôritē; -'är-/ *n.* —**an·te·ri·or·ly** *adv.*

an·te·room /'antē,rōōm; -,rŏŏm/ ▶ *n.* an antechamber, typically serving as a waiting room.

an·them /'anтнəm/ ▶ *n.* **1** a rousing or uplifting song identified with a particular group, body, or cause: *the song became the anthem for hippie activists.* ■ (also **national anthem**) a solemn patriotic song officially adopted by a country as an expression of national identity. **2** a choral composition based on a biblical passage, for singing by a choir in a church service.

an·ther /'anтнər/ ▶ *n. Bot.* the part of a stamen that contains the pollen.

ant·hill /'ant,hil/ ▶ *n.* a moundlike nest built by ants or termites.

an·thol·o·gize /an'тнälə,jīz/ ▶ *v.* [*tr.*] [usu. as *adj.*] (**anthologized**) include (an author or work) in an anthology: *the most anthologized of today's poets.*

an·thol·o·gy /an'тнäləjē/ ▶ *n.* (*pl.* **-gies**) a published collection of poems or other pieces of writing. ■ a similar collection of songs or musical compositions issued in one album. ▷mid 17th cent.: via French or medieval Latin from Greek *anthologia*, from *anthos* 'flower' + *-logia* 'collection' (from *legein* 'gather'). In Greek, the word originally denoted a collection of the "flowers" of verse, i.e., small choice poems or epigrams, by various authors. —**an·thol·o·gist** /-jist/ *n.*

an·thra·cene /'anтнrə,sēn/ ▶ *n. Chem.* a colorless crystalline aromatic hydrocarbon, $C_{14}H_{10}$, obtained by the distillation of crude oils and used in chemical manufacture.

an·thra·cite /'anтнrə,sīt/ ▶ *n.* coal of a hard variety that contains relatively pure carbon and burns with little flame and smoke. —**an·thra·cit·ic** /,anтнrə'sitik/ *adj.*

an·thrax /'an,тнraks/ ▶ *n.* a notifiable bacterial disease of sheep and cattle, typically affecting the skin and lungs. It can be transmitted to humans, causing severe skin ulceration or a form of pneumonia. ▷late Middle English: Latin, 'carbuncle' (the earliest sense in English), from Greek *anthrax, anthrak-* 'coal, carbuncle,' with reference to the skin ulceration in humans.

An·thro·po·cene /'anтнrəpə,sēn/ ▶ *n.* the current geological age, viewed as having begun about 200 years ago with the significant impact of human activity on the ecosphere.

an·thro·po·cen·tric /,anтнrəpō'sentrik/ ▶ *adj.* regarding humankind as the central or most important element of existence, esp. as opposed to God or animals. —**an·thro·po·cen·tri·cal·ly** /-trik(ə)lē/ *adv.* —**an·thro·po·cen·trism** /-,trizəm/ *n.*

an·thro·poid /'anтнrə,poid/ ▶ *adj.* resembling a human being in form. ■ *Zool.* of or relating to the group of higher primates, which includes monkeys, apes, and humans. ■ *Zool.* (of an ape) belonging to one of the families of great apes. ■ *inf., derog.* (of a person) apelike in appearance or behavior.
▶ *n. Zool.* a higher primate, esp. an ape. ■ *inf., derog.* a person that resembles an ape.

an·thro·pol·o·gy /,anтнrə'päləjē/ ▶ *n.* the study of humankind, in particular: ■ (also **cultural** or **social anthropology**) the comparative study of human societies and cultures and their development. ■ (also **physical anthropology**) the science of human zoology, evolution, and ecology. —**an·thro·po·log·i·cal** /-pə'läjikəl/ *adj.* —**an·thro·pol·o·gist** /-jist/ *n.*

an·thro·pom·e·try /,anтнrə'pämitrē/ ▶ *n.* the scientific study of the measurements and proportions of the human body. —**an·thro·po·met·ric** /-pō'metrik/ *adj.*

an·thro·po·mor·phic /,anтнrəpə'môrfik/ ▶ *adj.* relating to or characterized by anthropomorphism. ■ having human characteristics: *anthropomorphic bears and monkeys.* —**an·thro·po·mor·phi·cal·ly** /-ik(ə)lē/ *adv.*

an·thro·po·mor·phism /,anтнrəpə'môr,fizəm/ ▶ *n.* the attribution of human characteristics or behavior to a god, animal, or object. —**an·thro·po·mor·phize** /-,fīz/ *v.*

an·thro·po·mor·phous /,anтнrəpə'môrfəs/ ▶ *adj.* (of a god, animal, or object) human in form or nature.

an·thro·poph·a·gy /,anтнrə'päfəjē/ ▶ *n.* the eating of human flesh by human beings. —**an·thro·poph·a·gous** /-gəs/ *adj.*

an·ti /'an,tī; 'antē/ ▶ *prep.* opposed to; against: *I'm anti the abuse of drink.*
▶ *adj. inf.* opposed: *one big soul fight in the GOP concerns immigration—illegal and legal, anti or pro.*
▶ *n.* (*pl.* **an·tis**) *inf.* a person opposed to a particular policy, activity, or idea: *a shadow army of antis who endanger your sport.*

an·ti·a·bor·tion /,antēə'bôrsнən; ,antī-/ ▶ *adj.* opposing or legislating against medically induced abortion. —**an·ti·a·bor·tion·ist** *n.*

an·ti·air·craft /,antē'er,kraft; ,antī-/ (also **an·ti·air·craft**) (abbr.: **AA**) ▶ *adj.* (esp. of a gun or missile) used to attack enemy aircraft.

an·ti·bal·lis·tic mis·sile /,antēbə'listik; ,antī-/ (abbr.: **ABM**) ▶ *n.* a missile designed for intercepting and destroying a ballistic missile while in flight.

an·ti·bi·o·sis /,antēbī'ōsis; ,antī-/ ▶ *n. Biol.* an antagonistic association between two organisms (esp. microorganisms), in which one is adversely affected. See also SYMBIOSIS.

an·ti·bi·ot·ic /,antēbī'ätik; ,antī-/ ▶ *n.* a medicine (such as penicillin or its derivatives) that inhibits the growth of or destroys microorganisms.
▶ *adj.* relating to, involving, or denoting antibiotics.

an·ti·bod·y /'anti,bädē/ ▶ *n.* (*pl.* **-bod·ies**) a blood protein produced in response to and counteracting a specific antigen. Antibodies combine chemically with substances that the body recognizes as alien.

an·tic /'antik/ ▶ *adj. poetic/lit.* grotesque or bizarre.

An·ti·christ /'antē,krīst; 'antī-/ ▶ *n.* (**the An·ti·christ**) a great personal opponent of Christ who will spread evil throughout the world before being conquered at Christ's second coming. ■ a person or force seen as opposing Christ or the Christian Church.

an·tic·i·pate /an'tisə,pāt/ ▶ *v.* [*tr.*] **1** regard as probable; expect or predict: *she anticipated scorn on her return to the theater.* ■ guess or be aware of (what will happen) and take action in order to be prepared: *they failed to anticipate a full scale invasion.* ■ look forward to: *Stephen was eagerly anticipating the break from the routine of business.* ■ use or spend in advance. **2** act as a forerunner or precursor of: *he anticipated Bates's theories on mimicry and protective coloration.* ■ come or take place before (an event or process expected or scheduled for a later time). ■ react or respond to (someone) too quickly, without giving them a chance to do or say something. ■ pay (a debt) before it is due. —**an·tic·i·pa·tor** /-,pātər/ *n.* —**an·tic·i·pa·to·ry** /-pə,tôrē/ *adj.*

an·tic·i·pa·tion /an,tisə'pāsнən/ ▶ *n.* the action of anticipating something; expectation or prediction: *her eyes sparkled with anticipation.* ■ *Mus.* the introduction in a composition of part of a chord that is about to follow in full.

an·ti·cli·max /,antē'klī,maks; ,antī-/ ▶ *n.* a disappointing end to an exciting or impressive series of events. —**an·ti·cli·mac·tic** /-klī'maktik/ *adj.* —**an·ti·cli·mac·ti·cal·ly** /-klī'maktik(ə)lē/ *adv.*

an·ti·cline /'antī,klīn/ ▶ *n. Geol.* a ridge-shaped fold of stratified rock in which the strata slope downward from the crest. Compare with SYNCLINE. —**an·ti·cli·nal** /,antē'klīnl; ,anti-/ *adj.*

an·ti·co·ag·u·lant /,antēkō'agyələnt; ,antī-/ ▶ *adj.* having the effect of retarding or inhibiting the coagulation of the blood.
▶ *n.* an anticoagulant substance.

an·ti·con·vul·sant /,antēkən'vəlsənt; ,antī-/ ▶ *adj.* (chiefly of a drug) used to prevent or reduce the severity of epileptic fits or other convulsions.
▶ *n.* an anticonvulsant drug.

an·tics /'antiks/ ▶ *pl. n.* foolish, outrageous, or amusing behavior: *the antics of our political parties.* ▷early 16th cent.: from *antic* 'grotesque, bizarre,' from Italian *antico* 'antique.'

an·ti·cy·clone /,antē'sīklōn; ,antī-/ ▶ *n.* a weather system with high atmospheric pressure at its center, around which air slowly circulates in a clockwise (northern hemisphere) or counterclockwise (southern hemisphere) direction. —**an·ti·cy·clon·ic** /-sī'klänik/ *adj.*

an·ti·de·pres·sant /,antēdə'presnt; ,antī-/ ▶ *adj.* (chiefly of a drug) used to alleviate depression.
▶ *n.* an antidepressant drug.

an·ti·dote /'anti,dōt/ ▶ *n.* a medicine taken or given to counteract a particular poison. ■ something that counteracts or neutralizes an unpleasant feeling or situation: *laughter is an antidote to stress.*
▶ *v.* [*tr.*] (**-dotes, -dot·ed, -dot·ing**) counteract or cancel with an antidote: *What remedy will antidote Bryonia?* —**an·ti·dot·al** /,anti'dōtl/ *adj.*

an·ti·freeze /'anti,frēz/ ▶ *n.* a liquid, typically one based on ethylene glycol, which can be added to water to lower the freezing point, chiefly used in the radiator of a motor vehicle.

an·ti·gen /'antijən/ ▶ *n.* a toxin or other foreign substance that induces an immune response in the body, esp. the production of antibodies. —**an·ti·gen·ic** /,anti'jenik/ *adj.*

an·ti·glob·al·i·za·tion /,antē,glōbələ'zāsнən; ,antī-/ ▶ *n.* opposition to the agendas and actions of groups perceived to favor globalization, such as the IMF, the World Trade Organization, and the G8 countries.

an·ti·grav·i·ty /,antē'gravitē; ,antī-/ ▶ *n. Physics* a hypothetical force opposing gravity.
▶ *adj.* (chiefly of clothing for a pilot or astronaut) designed to counteract the effects of high acceleration.

an·ti·he·ro /'antē,hi(ə)rō; 'antī-/ ▶ *n.* a central character in a story, movie, or drama who lacks conventional heroic attributes.

Pronunciation Key ə *ago,* up; ər *over,* fur; a *hat;* ā *ate;* ä *car;* cн *chin;* e *let;* ē *see;* e(ə)r *air;* i *fit;* ī *by;* i(ə)r *ear;* ng *sing;* ō *go;* ô *law, for;* oi *toy;* ŏŏ *good;* ōō *goo;* ou *out;* sн *she;* тн *thin;* тн *then;* (h)w *why;* zн *vision*

an·ti·his·ta·mine /ˌantēˈhistəmin; -mēn/ ▸n. [usu. as *adj.*] a drug or other compound that inhibits the physiological effects of histamine, used esp. in the treatment of allergies: *an antihistamine injection.*

an·ti-in·flam·ma·to·ry /ˌantēinˈflaməˌtôrē; ˌantī-/ ▸adj. (chiefly of a drug) used to reduce inflammation.
▸n. (pl. **-ries**) an anti-inflammatory drug.

an·ti·knock /ˌantēˈnäk; ˌantī-/ ▸n. a substance (such as tetraethyl lead) added to gasoline to inhibit preignition.

an·ti·lock /ˌantēˈläk; ˌantī-/ (also **an·ti-lock**) ▸adj. (of brakes) designed so as to prevent the wheels from locking and the vehicle from skidding if applied suddenly.

an·ti·log·a·rithm /ˌantēˈlôgəˌriᴛHəm; -ˈläg-; ˌantī-/ ▸n. the number to which a logarithm belongs.

an·ti·ma·cas·sar /ˌantēməˈkasər/ ▸n. chiefly hist. a piece of cloth put over the back of a chair to protect it from dirt or as an ornament.

an·ti·mat·ter /ˈantēˌmatər; ˈantī-/ ▸n. Physics molecules formed by atoms consisting of antiprotons, antineutrons, and positrons. Stable antimatter does not appear to exist in our universe.

an·ti·mo·ny /ˈantəˌmōnē/ ▸n. the chemical element of atomic number 51, a brittle silvery-white metalloid. (Symbol: **Sb**) —**an·ti·mo·ni·al** /ˌantəˈmōnēəl/ —**an·ti·mo·nic** /ˌantəˈmänik/ adj. —**an·ti·mo·ni·ous** /ˌantəˈmōnēəs/ adj.

an·ti·ox·i·dant /ˌantēˈäksidənt; ˌantī-/ ▸n. a substance that inhibits oxidation, esp. one used to counteract the deterioration of stored food products. ■ a substance such as vitamin C or E that removes potentially damaging oxidizing agents in a living organism.

an·ti·par·ti·cle /ˈantēˌpärtikəl; ˈantī-/ ▸n. Physics a subatomic particle having the same mass as a given particle but opposite electric or magnetic properties. Every kind of subatomic particle has a corresponding antiparticle.

an·ti·pas·to /ˌantēˈpästō; ˌän-/ ▸n. (pl. **-pas·ti** /-ˈpästē/) (in Italian cooking) an appetizer typically consisting of olives, anchovies, cheeses, and meats.

an·tip·a·thy /anˈtipəᴛHē/ ▸n. (pl. **-thies**) a deep-seated feeling of dislike; aversion: *a thinly disguised mutual antipathy.* ▷late 16th cent. (in the sense 'opposition of feeling, nature, or disposition'): from French *antipathie* or Latin *antipathia*, from Greek *antipatheia*, from *antipathēs* 'opposed in feeling,' from *anti* 'against' + *pathos* 'feeling.'

an·ti·per·son·nel /ˌantēˌpərsəˈnel; ˌantī-/ ▸adj. (of weapons, esp. bombs) designed to kill or injure people rather than to damage buildings or equipment.

an·ti·per·spi·rant /ˌantiˈpərspərənt/ ▸n. a substance that is applied to the skin, esp. under the arms, to prevent or reduce perspiration.

an·ti·phon /ˈantəˌfän/ ▸n. (in traditional western Christian liturgy) a short sentence sung or recited before or after a psalm or canticle.

an·tiph·o·nal /anˈtifənl/ ▸adj. (in traditional western Christian liturgy) (of a short sentence or its musical setting) sung, recited, or played alternately by two groups. —**an·tiph·o·nal·ly** adv.

an·tiph·o·ny /anˈtifənē/ ▸n. antiphonal singing, playing, or chanting.

an·ti·pode /ˈantiˌpōd/ ▸n. the direct opposite of something else. —**an·tip·o·dal** /anˈtipədl/ adj.

an·tip·o·des /anˈtipədēz/ ▸pl. n. (**the An·tip·o·des**) Australia and New Zealand (used by inhabitants of the northern hemisphere). ■ the direct opposite of something. —**an·tip·o·de·an** /anˌtipəˈdēən/ adj., n.

an·ti·pro·ton /ˈantēˌprōtän; ˈantī-/ ▸n. Physics the negatively charged antiparticle of a proton.

an·ti·py·ret·ic /ˌantēpīˈretik; ˌantī-/ ▸adj. (chiefly of a drug) used to prevent or reduce fever.
▸n. an antipyretic drug.

an·ti·quar·i·an /ˌantiˈkwe(ə)rēən/ ▸adj. relating to or dealing in antiques or rare books. ■ valuable because rare or old: *antiquarian books.*
▸n. a person who studies or collects antiques or antiquities. —**an·ti·quar·i·an·ism** /-ˌnizəm/ n.

an·ti·quar·y /ˈantiˌkwerē/ ▸n. (pl. **-quar·ies**) another term for ANTIQUARIAN.

an·ti·quat·ed /ˈantiˌkwātid/ ▸adj. old-fashioned or outdated.

an·tique /anˈtēk/ ▸n. a collectible object such as a piece of furniture or work of art that has a high value because of its considerable age.
▸adj. **1** (of a collectible object) having a high value because of considerable age: *an antique clock.* ■ (of a method of finishing a wooden surface) intended to resemble the appearance of antique furniture. **2** belonging to ancient times: *antique gods.* ■ old-fashioned or outdated: *trade unions defending antique work practices.* ■ often humorous showing signs of great age or wear: *an antique divorcee in reduced circumstances.*
▸v. **1** (**-tiques**, **-tiqued**, **-ti·quing**) [tr.] [usu. as adj.] (**antiqued**) make

(something) resemble an antique by artificial means: *an antiqued door.* **2** (**go antiquing**) shop in stores where antiques are sold.

an·tiq·ui·ty /anˈtikwitē/ ▸n. (pl. **-ties**) **1** the ancient past, esp. the period before the Middle Ages: *the great civilizations of antiquity.* ■ a specified historical period during the ancient past: *cameos dating from classical antiquity.* ■ (usu. **antiquities**) an object, building, or work of art from the ancient past. **2** great age: *a church of great antiquity.*

an·ti·re·tro·vi·ral /ˌantēˌretrōˈvīrəl; ˌantī-/ ▸adj. working against or targeted against retroviruses, especially HIV: *antiretroviral therapy.*
▸n. an antiretroviral drug.

an·ti-Sem·i·tism ▸n. hostility to or prejudice against Jews. —**an·ti-Sem·ite** n. —**an·ti-Se·mit·ic** adj.

an·ti·sep·sis /ˌantiˈsepsis/ ▸n. the practice of using antiseptics to eliminate the microorganisms that cause disease. Compare with ASEPSIS.

an·ti·sep·tic /ˌantiˈseptik/ ▸adj. of, relating to, or denoting substances that prevent the growth of disease-causing microorganisms. ■ (of medical techniques) based on the use of such substances. ■ fig. scrupulously clean or pure, esp. so as to be bland or characterless.
▸n. an antiseptic compound or preparation. —**an·ti·sep·ti·cal·ly** /-ik(ə)lē/ adv.

an·ti·se·rum /ˈanti,si(ə)rəm/ ▸n. (pl. **-se·ra** /-,si(ə)rə/) a blood serum containing antibodies against specific antigens, injected to treat or protect against specific diseases.

an·ti·so·cial /ˌantēˈsōsHəl; ˌantī-/ ▸adj. **1** contrary to the laws and customs of society; devoid of or antagonistic to sociable instincts or practices. **2** not sociable; not wanting the company of others.

an·ti·ter·ror·ism /ˌantēˈterəˌrizəm; ˌantī-/ ▸n. the prevention or abatement of terrorism: *a meeting of experts on antiterrorism* | *antiterrorism measures.* —**an·ti·ter·ror·ist** n. & adj.

an·tith·e·sis /anˈtiᴛHəsis/ ▸n. (pl. **-ses** /-ˌsēz/) a person or thing that is the direct opposite of someone or something else: *love is the antithesis of selfishness.* ■ a contrast or opposition between two things. ■ a figure of speech in which an opposition or contrast of ideas is expressed by parallelism of words that are the opposites of, or strongly contrasted with, each other, such as "hatred stirs up strife, but love covers all sins."

an·ti·thet·i·cal /ˌantəˈᴛHetikəl/ ▸adj. **1** directly opposed or contrasted; mutually incompatible: *people whose religious beliefs are antithetical to mine.* **2** connected with, containing, or using the rhetorical device of antithesis. —**an·ti·thet·ic** adj. —**an·ti·thet·i·cal·ly** adv.

an·ti·tox·in /ˌantēˈtäksin/ ▸n. Physiol. an antibody that counteracts a toxin. —**an·ti·tox·ic** /-sik/ adj.

an·ti·trust /ˌantēˈtrəst; ˌantī-/ ▸adj. of or relating to legislation preventing or controlling trusts or other monopolies.

an·ti·vi·ral /ˌantēˈvīrəl; ˌantī-/ ▸adj. Med. (chiefly of a drug or treatment) effective against viruses.

ant·ler /ˈantlər/ ▸n. one of the branched horns on the head of an adult (usually male) deer, which are made of bone and are grown and cast off annually. ■ one of the branches on such a horn. —**ant·lered** adj.

ant li·on ▸n. an insect (family Myrmeleontidae) that resembles a dragonfly, with predatory larvae that construct conical pits into which insect prey, esp. ants, fall.

an·to·no·ma·sia /ˌanˌtänəˈmāᴢH(ē)ə/ ▸n. Rhetoric the substitution of an epithet or title for a proper name (e.g., *the Bard* for Shakespeare). ■ the use of a proper name to express a general idea (e.g., *a Scrooge* for a miser).

an·to·nym /ˈantəˌnim/ ▸n. Linguistics a word opposite in meaning to another (e.g., *bad* and *good*). —**an·ton·y·mous** /anˈtänəməs/ adj.

an·trum /ˈantrəm/ ▸n. (pl. **-tra** /-trə/) Anat. a natural chamber or cavity in a bone or other anatomical structure. ■ the part of the stomach just inside the pylorus. —**an·tral** /-trəl/ adj.

ant·sy /ˈantsē/ ▸adj. agitated, impatient, or restless.

a·nus /ˈānəs/ ▸n. Anat. & Zool. the opening at the end of the alimentary canal through which solid waste matter leaves the body.

an·vil /ˈanvil/ ▸n. a heavy steel or iron block with a flat top, concave sides, and typically a pointed end, on which metal can be hammered and shaped. ■ the horizontally extended upper part of a cumulonimbus cloud: [as adj.] *anvil clouds.* ■ Anat. another term for INCUS.

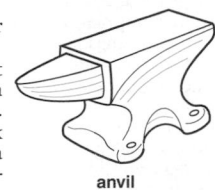

anvil

anx·i·e·ty /aNGˈzī-itē/ ▸n. (pl. **-ties**) a feeling of worry, nervousness, or unease, typically about an imminent event or something with an uncertain outcome. ■ desire to do something, typically accompanied by unease: *the housekeeper's eager anxiety to please.* ■ *Psychiatry* a nervous disorder characterized by a state of excessive uneasiness and apprehension, typically with compulsive behavior or panic attacks.

anx·ious /'aNG(k)sHəs/ ▸*adj.* **1** experiencing worry, unease, or nervousness, typically about an imminent event or something with an uncertain outcome: *she was anxious about her exams.* ■ (of a period of time or situation) causing or characterized by worry or nervousness: *some anxious moments.* **2** wanting something very much, typically with a feeling of unease: *the company was anxious to avoid any trouble.* —**anx·ious·ly** *adv.* —**anx·ious·ness** *n.*

an·y /'enē/ ▸*adj. & pron.* **1** used to refer to one or some of a thing or number of things, no matter how much or many: [as *adj.*] *I don't have any choice* | | [as *pron.*] *someone asked him for a match, but Joe didn't have any.* ■ [as *pron.*] *anyone: it ceased payments to any but the elderly.* **2** whichever of a specified class might be chosen: [as *adj.*] *visible at any hour of the night* | [as *pron.*] *the illness may be due to any of several causes.*
▸*adv.* (used for emphasis) at all; in some degree: *he wasn't any good at basketball.* ■ *inf.* used alone, not qualifying another word: *I didn't hurt you any.*
▸ □ **any time** (or **day** or **minute**, etc.) now *inf.* very soon: *we'll get them back any day now.*

an·y·bod·y /'enē,bädē; -,bədē/ ▸*pron.* **1** anyone: *there wasn't anybody around.* **2** a person of any importance: *everybody who was anybody in state government turned out to be involved.*

an·y·how /'enē,hou/ ▸*adv.* **1** another term for ANYWAY. **2** in a careless or haphazard way: *two suitcases flung anyhow.*

an·y·more /,enē·môr/ (also **any more**) ▸*adv.* [usu. with *negative* or in *questions*] to any further extent; any longer: *she refused to listen anymore* | *you don't get men like him anymore.*

an·y·one /'enē,wən/ ▸*pron.* **1** any person or people: *there wasn't anyone there* | *does anyone remember him?* ■ used for emphasis: *anyone could do it.* **2** a person of importance or authority: *they are read by anyone who's anyone.*

an·y·place /'enē,plās/ ▸*adv.* informal term for ANYWHERE.

an·y·thing /'enē,THiNG/ ▸*pron.* used to refer to a thing, no matter what: *nobody was saying anything.* ■ used for emphasis: *I was ready for anything.* ■ used to indicate a range: *he trains anything from seven to eight hours a day.*
▸ □ **anything but** not at all (used for emphasis): *he is anything but racist.* □ (**as**) — **as anything** *inf.* extremely—: *she said it out loud, clear as anything.*

an·y·way /'enē,wā/ ▸*adv.* **1** used to confirm or support a point just mentioned: *it's all right, and anyway, it was my fault.* ■ used in questions to emphasize the speaker's wish to obtain the truth: *"What are you doing here, anyway?"* **2** used in conversations: ■ to change the subject or to resume a subject: *How she lives with him is beyond me. Anyway, I really like her.* ■ to indicate that the speaker wants to end the conversation: *"Anyway, I must go."* ■ to indicate that the speaker is passing over less significant aspects in order to focus on important points: *"John always enjoyed a drink. Anyway, he died last year."* **3** used to indicate that something happened or will happen in spite of something else: *nobody invited Miss Honey to sit down so she sat down anyway.*

an·y·where /'enē,(h)we(ə)r/ ▸*adv.* in or to any place: *he couldn't be found anywhere.* ■ used for emphasis: *I could go anywhere in the world.* ■ used to indicate a range: *this iron garden seat dates anywhere from 1890 to 1920.*
▸*pron.* any place: *he doesn't have anywhere to live.*

An·zac /'an,zak/ ▸*n.* a soldier in the Australian and New Zealand Army Corps (1914–18).

A-OK (also **A-o·kay**) *inf.* ▸*adj.* in good order or condition; all right: *everything will be A-OK.*
▸*adv.* in a good manner or way; all right: *we hit it off A-OK.*

a·or·ta /ā'ôrtə/ ▸*n.* the main artery of the body, supplying oxygenated blood to the circulatory system. —**a·or·tic** /-'tik/ *adj.*

a·pace /ə'pās/ ▸*adv. poetic/lit.* swiftly; quickly: *work continues apace.*

A·pach·e ▸/ə'pasHē/ *n.* **1** (*pl.* same or **A·pach·es**) a member of a North American Indian people living chiefly in New Mexico and Arizona. **2** the Athabaskan language of this people.
▸*adj.* of or relating to the Apache or their language.

a·pache /ə'pasH; ä'päsH/ ▸*n.* (*pl.* **a·paches** pronunc. same) a violent street ruffian, originally in Paris.

a·part /ə'pärt/ ▸*adv.* **1** (of two or more people or things) separated by a distance; at a specified distance from each other in time or space: *his parents are now living apart.* **2** to or on one side; at a distance from the main body: *Isabel stepped away from Joanna and stood apart.* ■ used after a noun to indicate that someone or something has distinctive qualities that mark them out from other people or things: *wrestlers were a*

breed apart. ■ used after a noun to indicate that someone or something has been dealt with sufficiently or is being excluded from what follows: *Alaska apart, much of America's energy business concentrates on producing gas.* **3** so as to be shattered; into pieces: *he leapt out of the car just before it was blown apart.* —**a·part·ness** *n.*
▸ □ **apart from** **1** except for: *the whole world seemed to be sleeping, apart from Barbara.* **2** in addition to; as well as: *quite apart from all the work, he had such financial problems.* □ **tell apart** distinguish or separate one from another: *the twins were so identical that it was impossible to tell them apart.*

a·part·heid /ə'pärt,(h)āt; -,(h)īt/ ▸*n. hist.* (in South Africa) a policy or system of segregation or discrimination on grounds of race. ■ segregation in other contexts: *sexual apartheid.*

a·part·ment /ə'pärtmənt/ (abbr.: **apt.**) ▸*n.* a suite of rooms forming one residence, typically in a building containing a number of these. ■ a large building containing such suites; an apartment building. ■ (**apartments**) a suite of rooms in a very large or grand house set aside for the private use of a monarch or noble: *the Imperial apartments.* ▷mid 17th cent. (denoting a suite of rooms for the use of a particular person or group): from French *appartement*, from Italian *appartamento*, from *appartare* 'to separate,' from *a parte* 'apart.'

ap·a·thet·ic /,apə'THetik/ ▸*adj.* showing or feeling no interest, enthusiasm, or concern: *apathetic slackers.* —**ap·a·thet·i·cal·ly** /-ik(ə)lē/ *adv.*

ap·a·thy /'apəTHē/ ▸*n.* lack of interest, enthusiasm, or concern.

a·pa·to·saur /,apətō'sôrəs/ (also **a·pa·to·saur·us** /-'sôrəs/) ▸*n.* a huge herbivorous dinosaur (genus *Apatosaurus*, infraorder Sauropoda, order Saurischia) of the late Jurassic period, with a long neck and tail. Also called, esp. formerly, BRONTOSAUR. —**a·pa·to·sau·ri·an** *adj.*

ape /āp/ ▸*n.* a large primate (families Pongidae and Hylobatidae) that lacks a tail, including the gorilla, chimpanzees, orangutan, and gibbons. See also GIBBON. ■ used in names of macaque monkeys with short tails, e.g., **Barbary ape**. ■ (in general use) any monkey. ■ an unintelligent or clumsy person.
▸*v.* [*tr.*] imitate the behavior or manner of (someone or something), esp. in an absurd or unthinking way.
▸ □ **go ape** *inf.* express wild excitement or anger.

a·pe·ri·od·ic /,āpi(ə)rē'ädik/ ▸*adj. technical* not periodic; irregular: *aperiodic fluctuations.* —**a·pe·ri·o·dic·i·ty** /ā,pi(ə)rēə'disitē/ *n.*

a·pe·ri·tif /ä,peri'tēf; -ə,per-/ ▸*n.* an alcoholic drink taken before a meal to stimulate the appetite.

ap·er·ture /'apər,CHər/ ▸*n. chiefly technical* an opening, hole, or gap: *the bell ropes passed through apertures in the ceiling.* ■ a space through which light passes in an optical or photographic instrument, esp. the variable opening by which light enters a camera.

A·pex /'āpeks/ ▸*n.* [usu. as *adj.*] a system of reduced fares for scheduled airline flights and railroad journeys that must be booked and paid for before a certain period in advance of departure: *Apex fares.*

a·pex /'āpeks/ ▸*n.* (*pl.* **a·pex·es** or **a·pi·ces** /'āpə,sēz; 'apə-/) the top or highest part of something, esp. one forming a point: *the apex of the roof* | *fig. the apex of his career.* ■ *Geom.* the highest point in a plane or solid figure, relative to a base line or plane. ■ *Bot.* the growing point of a shoot. ■ the highest level of a hierarchy, organization, or other power structure regarded as a triangle or pyramid.
▸*v.* [*intr.*] reach a high point or climax.

a·phaer·e·sis /ə'ferəsis/ ▸*n. Linguistics* the loss of a sound or sounds at the beginning of a word, e.g., in the derivation of *adder* from *nadder*.
▸(usu. **a·pher·e·sis**) *Med.* /,afə'rēsis/ the removal of blood plasma from the body by the withdrawal of blood, its separation into plasma and cells.

a·pha·sia /ə'fāzHə/ ▸*n. Med.* loss of ability to understand or express speech, caused by brain damage. —**a·pha·sic** /-zik/ *adj. & n.*

a·phe·li·on /ə'fēlyən; ə'fēlēən/ ▸*n.* (*pl.* **a·phe·li·a** /əfēlyə; ə'fēlēə/ or **a·phe·li·ons**) *Astron.* the point in the orbit of a planet, asteroid, or comet at which it is furthest from the sun: *Mars is at aphelion.* The opposite of PERIHELION.

aph·e·sis /'afisis/ ▸*n. Linguistics* the loss of an unstressed vowel at the beginning of a word, e.g., of *a* from *around* to form *round*). —**a·phet·ic** /ə'fetik/ *adj.* —**a·phet·i·cal·ly** /ə'fetik(ə)lē/ *adv.*

a·phid /'āfid; 'af-/ ▸*n.* a minute bug (superfamily Aphidoidea) that feeds by sucking sap from plants.

a·phis /'āfis; 'af-/ ▸*n.* (*pl.* **a·phi·des** /'āfi,dēz; 'afi-/) an aphid, esp. one of the genus *Aphis*.

Pronunciation Key ə *ago, up;* ər *over, fur;* a *hat;* ā *ate;* ä *car;* CH *chin;* e *let;* ē *see;* e(ə)r *air;* i *fit;* ī *by;* i(ə)r *ear;* NG *sing;* ō *go;* ô *law, for;* oi *toy;* o͝o *good;* o͞o *goo;* ou *out;* sH *she;* TH *thin;* ∓H *then;* (h)w *why;* zH *vision*

aph·o·rism /'afə,rizəm/ ▶n. a pithy observation that contains a general truth, such as, "if it ain't broke, don't fix it." ■ a concise statement of a scientific principle, typically by an ancient classical author. —**aph·o·rist** n. —**aph·o·ris·tic** /,afə'ristik/ adj. —**aph·o·ris·ti·cal·ly** /,afə'ristik(ə)lē/ adv. —**aph·o·rize** /-,rīz/ v.

aph·ro·dis·i·ac /,afrə'dizē,ak; -'dēzē-; -'dēzнē-/ ▶n. a food, drink, or drug that stimulates sexual desire. ■ a thing that causes excitement: *for a few seconds she'd fallen for the powerful aphrodisiac of music.*

a·pi·ar·y /'āpē,erē/ ▶n. (pl. -**ar·ies**) a place where bees are kept. —**a·pi·ar·i·an** /,āpē'e(ə)rēən/ adj. —**a·pi·a·rist** /-ə,rist/ n.

a·pi·cal /'āpikəl; 'ap-/ ▶adj. technical of, relating to, or denoting an apex. ■ Phonet. (of a consonant) formed with the tip of the tongue.

a·pi·ces /'āpə,sēz; 'apə-/ ▶ plural form of APEX.

a·pi·cul·ture /'āpi'kəlснər/ ▶n. technical term for BEEKEEPING. —**a·pi·cul·tur·al** /,āpi'kəlснərəl/ adj. —**a·pi·cul·tur·ist** /,āpi'kəlснərist/ n.

a·piece /ə'pēs/ ▶adv. (used after a noun or an amount) to, for, or by each one of a group: *we sold 385 prints at $10 apiece.*

ap·ish /'āpish/ ▶adj. of or resembling an ape in appearance: *Australopithecus had an apish cranium and a humanlike jaw.* ■ resembling or likened to an ape in being foolish or silly. —**ap·ish·ly** adv. —**ap·ish·ness** n.

a·plen·ty /ə'plentē/ ▶adj. in abundance: *there are going to be disasters aplenty in the garden.*

a·plomb /ə'pläm; ə'pləm/ ▶n. self-confidence or assurance, esp. when in a demanding situation: *Diana passed the test with aplomb.*

ap·ne·a /'apnēə; ap'nēə/ (also Brit. **ap·noe·a**) ▶n. Med. temporary cessation of breathing, esp. during sleep: *thousands suffer from sleep apnea.*

APO ▶abbr. ■ (U.S.) Air Force Post Office. ■ (U.S.) Army Post Office.

a·poc·a·lypse /ə'päkə,lips/ ▶n. (often **the Apocalypse**) the complete final destruction of the world, esp. as described in the biblical book of Revelation. ■ an event involving destruction or damage on an awesome or catastrophic scale: *a stock market apocalypse.* ■ (**the Apocalypse**) (esp. in the Vulgate Bible) the book of Revelation.

a·poc·a·lyp·tic /ə,päkə'liptik/ ▶adj. describing or prophesying the complete destruction of the world. ■ resembling the end of the world; momentous or catastrophic. ■ of or resembling the biblical Apocalypse. —**a·poc·a·lyp·ti·cal·ly** /-ik(ə)lē/ adv.

A·poc·ry·pha /ə'päkrəfə/ ▶pl. n. [treated as sing. or pl.] biblical or related writings not forming part of the accepted canon of Scripture. ■ (**apocrypha**) writings or reports not considered genuine.

a·poc·ry·phal /ə'päkrəfəl/ ▶adj. (of a story or statement) of doubtful authenticity, although widely circulated as being true: *an apocryphal story about a president.* ■ (also **A·poc·ry·phal**) of or belonging to the Apocrypha.

ap·o·gee /'apəjē/ ▶n. Astron. the point in the orbit of the moon or a satellite at which it is furthest from the earth. The opposite of PERIGEE. ■ fig. the highest point in the development of something; the climax or culmination of something. ▷late 16th cent.: from French *apogée* or modern Latin *apogaeum* from Greek *apogaion (diastēma)* '(distance) away from earth,' from *apo* 'from' + *gaia, gē* 'earth.'

a·po·lit·i·cal /,āpə'litikəl/ ▶adj. not interested or involved in politics.

a·pol·o·get·ic /ə,pälə'jetik/ ▶adj. regretfully acknowledging or excusing an offense or failure: *she was very apologetic about the whole incident.* ■ of the nature of a formal defense or justification of something such as a theory or religious doctrine: *the apologetic proposition that production for profit is the same thing as production for need.*
▶n. a reasoned argument or writing in justification of something, typically a theory or religious doctrine. —**a·pol·o·get·i·cal·ly** /-ik(ə)lē/ adv.

a·po·lo·gi·a /,apə'lōj(ē)ə/ ▶n. a formal written defense of one's opinions or conduct: *an apologia for book banning.*

a·pol·o·gist /ə'päləjist/ ▶n. a person who offers an argument in defense of something controversial.

a·pol·o·gize /ə'pälə,jīz/ ▶v. [intr.] express regret for something that one has done wrong: *I must apologize for disturbing you like this.*

a·pol·o·gy /ə'päləjē/ ▶n. (pl. -**gies**) **1** a regretful acknowledgment of an offense or failure: *my apologies for the delay.* ■ a public statement of regret, such as one issued by a newspaper, government, or other organization: *the Prime Minister demanded an apology from the ambassador.* ■ (**apologies**) used to express formally one's regret at being unable to attend a meeting or social function: *apologies for absence were received from Miss Brown.* **2** (**an apology for**) a very poor or inadequate example of: *we were shown into an apology for a bedroom.* **3** a reasoned argument or writing in justification of something, typically a theory or religious doctrine.
▶ □ **with apologies to** used before the name of an author or artist to

indicate that something is a parody or adaptation of their work: *here, with apologies to Rudyard Kipling, is a more apt version of "If."*

ap·o·plec·tic /,apə'plektik/ ▶adj. inf. overcome with anger; extremely indignant: *Mark was apoplectic with rage at the decision.* —**ap·o·plec·ti·cal·ly** /-ik(ə)lē/ adv.

ap·o·plex·y /'apə,pleksē/ ▶n. (pl. -**plex·ies**) dated unconsciousness or incapacity resulting from a cerebral hemorrhage or stroke. ■ inf. incapacity or speechlessness caused by extreme anger.

a·pos·ta·sy /ə'pästəsē/ ▶n. the abandonment or renunciation of a religious or political belief.

a·pos·tate /ə'päs,tāt; -tit/ ▶n. a person who renounces a religious or political belief or principle.
▶adj. abandoning a religious or political belief or principle. —**ap·o·stat·i·cal** /,apə'statikəl/ adj.

a·pos·ta·tize /ə'pästə,tīz/ ▶v. [intr.] renounce a religious or political belief or principle.

a·pos·tle /ə'päsəl/ ▶n. (often **Apostle**) each of the twelve chief disciples of Jesus Christ. ■ any important early Christian teacher, esp. St. Paul. ■ (**Apostle of**) the first successful Christian missionary in a country or to a people: *Kiril and Metodije, the Apostles of the Slavs.* ■ a vigorous and pioneering advocate or supporter of a particular policy, idea, or cause. ■ a messenger or representative: *apostles of doom.* ■ one of the twelve administrative officers of the Mormon church. —**a·pos·tle·ship** /-,ship/ n.

ap·os·tol·ic /,apə'stälik/ ▶adj. Christian Church of or relating to the Apostles: *a simple apostolic life.* ■ of or relating to the pope, esp. when he is regarded as the successor to St. Peter: *an apostolic nuncio.*

a·pos·tro·phe¹ /ə'pästrəfē/ ▶n. a punctuation mark (') used to indicate either possession e.g., *Harry's book; boys' coats*) or the omission of letters or numbers (e.g., *can't; he's; class of '99*).

a·pos·tro·phe² ▶n. Rhetoric an exclamatory passage in a speech or poem addressed to a person (typically one who is dead or absent) or thing (typically one that is personified).

a·poth·e·car·y /ə'pätнi,kerē/ ▶n. (pl. -**car·ies**) archaic a person who prepared and sold medicines and drugs.

ap·o·thegm /'apə,тнem/ ▶n. a concise saying or maxim; an aphorism. —**ap·o·theg·mat·ic** /,apəтнeg'matik/ adj.

a·poth·e·o·sis /ə,pätнē'ōsis; ,apə'тнēəsis/ ▶n. (pl. -**ses** /-,sēz/) the highest point in the development of something; culmination or climax. ■ the elevation of someone to divine status; deification.

ap·o·tro·pa·ic /,apətrə'pā-ik/ ▶adj. supposedly having the power to avert evil influences or bad luck. —**ap·o·tro·pa·i·cal·ly** /-ik(ə)lē/ adv.

ap·pall /ə'pôl/ ▶v. (-**palled**, -**pall·ing**) [tr.] (usu. **be appalled**) greatly dismay or horrify: *bankers are appalled at the economic incompetence of some officials.* ▷Middle English: from Old French *apalir* 'grow pale,' from *a-* (from Latin *ad* 'to, at') + *palir* 'to pale.' The original sense was 'grow pale,' later 'make pale,' hence 'dismay, horrify' (late Middle English).

Ap·pa·loo·sa /,apə'lōōsə/ ▶n. a horse of a North American breed having dark spots on a light background.

ap·pa·rat·chik /,apə'räcнik/ ▶n. (pl. -**chiks** or -**chi·ki** /-снi,kē/) derog. or humorous an official in a large organization, typically a political one.

ap·pa·rat·us /,apə'ratəs; -'rātəs/ ▶n. (pl. -**us·es**) **1** the equipment needed for a particular activity or purpose: *laboratory apparatus.* ■ the organs used to perform a particular bodily function: *the specialized male and female sexual apparatus.* **2** a complex structure within an organization or system: *the apparatus of government.*

ap·par·el /ə'parəl/ ▶n. formal clothing.

ap·par·ent /ə'parənt; ə'pe(ə)r-/ ▶adj. clearly visible or understood; obvious: *for no apparent reason she laughed.* ■ seeming real or true, but not necessarily so: *his apparent lack of concern.* —**ap·par·ent·ly** adv.

ap·pa·ri·tion /,apə'risнən/ ▶n. a ghost or ghostlike image of a person. ■ the appearance of something remarkable or unexpected, typically an image of this type. —**ap·pa·ri·tion·al** /-sнənl/ adj.

ap·peal /ə'pēl/ ▶v. [intr.] **1** make a serious or urgent request, typically to the public: *she appealed to Germany for political asylum.* **2** Law apply to a higher court for a reversal of the decision of a lower court: *he said he would appeal against the conviction* | [tr.] *to appeal the decision.* ■ (**appeal to**) address oneself to (a principle or quality in someone) in anticipation of a favorable response: *I appealed to his sense of justice.* **3** be attractive or interesting: *the topics will appeal to youngsters.*
▶n. **1** a serious or urgent request, typically one made to the public. ■ an attempt to obtain financial support: *a public appeal to raise $120,000.* ■ entreaty: *a look of appeal on his face.* **2** Law an application to a higher court for a decision to be reversed: *he has 28 days in which to lodge an appeal* | *the right of appeal.* ■ an address to a principle or quality in anticipation of a favorable response: *an appeal to black pride.* **3** the quality of

being attractive or interesting: *the popular appeal of football.* —**ap·peal·er** *n.*

ap·peal·ing /ə'pēliNG/ ▶ *adj.* **1** attractive or interesting. **2** (of an expression or tone of voice) showing that one wants help or sympathy. —**ap·peal·ing·ly** *adv.*

ap·pear /ə'pi(ə)r/ ▶ *v.* [*intr.*] **1** come into sight; become visible or noticeable, typically without visible agent or apparent cause. ■ come into existence or use: *the major life forms appeared on earth.* ■ (of a book) be published: *the paperback edition didn't appear for another two years.* ■ feature or be shown: *the symbol appears in many paintings of the period.* ■ perform publicly in a movie, play, etc.: *he appeared on Broadway.* ■ (of an accused person, witness, or lawyer) make an official appearance in a court of law. ■ *inf.* arrive at a place: *by ten o'clock Bill still hadn't appeared.* **2** seem; give the impression of being: *she appeared not to know what was happening* | *it appears unlikely that interest rates will fall* | *he appeared unaware of the rebuke.*

ap·pear·ance /ə'pi(ə)rəns/ ▶ *n.* **1** the way that someone or something looks: *I like the appearance of stripped antique pine.* ■ an impression given by someone or something, although this may be misleading: *she read it with every appearance of interest.* **2** an act of performing or participating in a public event: *he is well-known for his television appearances.* **3** an act of becoming visible or noticeable; an arrival: *the sudden appearance of her daughter startled her.* ■ a process of coming into existence or use: *the appearance of the railroad.*

▶ □ **keep up appearances** maintain an impression of wealth or well-being, typically to hide the true situation. □ **make** (or **put in**) **an appearance** attend an event briefly, typically out of courtesy. □ **to** (or **by**) **all appearances** as far as can be seen.

ap·pease /ə'pēz/ ▶ *v.* [*tr.*] **1** pacify or placate (someone) by acceding to their demands. **2** relieve or satisfy (a demand or a feeling). —**ap·pease·ment** *n.* —**ap·peas·er** *n.*

ap·pel·lant /ə'pelənt/ ▶ *n.* *Law* a person who applies to a higher court for a reversal of the decision of a lower court.

ap·pel·late /ə'pelit/ ▶ *adj.* *Law* (typically of a court) concerned with or dealing with applications for decisions to be reversed.

ap·pel·la·tion /,apə'lāsHən/ ▶ *n.* *formal* a name or title. ■ the action of giving a name to a person or thing.

ap·pend /ə'pend/ ▶ *v.* [*tr.*] add (something) as an attachment or supplement: *the results of the survey are appended to this chapter.*

ap·pend·age /ə'pendij/ ▶ *n.* (often with negative connotations) a thing that is added or attached to something larger or more important: *they treat Scotland as a mere appendage of England.* ■ *Biol.* a projecting part of an invertebrate or other living organism, with a distinct appearance or function: *many species have specialized clutching appendages.*

ap·pen·dec·to·my /,apən'dektəmē/ ▶ *n.* (*pl.* **-mies**) a surgical operation to remove the appendix.

ap·pen·di·ci·tis /ə,pendə'sītis/ ▶ *n.* a serious medical condition in which the appendix becomes inflamed and painful.

ap·pen·dix /ə'pendiks/ ▶ *n.* (*pl.* **-di·ces** /-di,sēz/; **-dix·es**) **1** *Anat.* a tube-shaped sac attached to and opening into the lower end of the large intestine in humans and some other mammals. Also called **VERMIFORM APPENDIX**. **2** a section or table of additional matter at the end of a book or document.

ap·per·cep·tion /,apər'sepsHən/ ▶ *n.* *dated Psychol.* the mental process by which a person makes sense of an idea by assimilating it to the body of ideas he or she already possesses. ■ fully conscious perception. —**ap·per·cep·tive** /-tiv/ *adj.*

ap·per·tain /,apər'tān/ ▶ *v.* [*intr.*] **1** (**appertain to**) relate to; concern: *the answers appertain to improvements in standards.* **2** be appropriate or applicable: *the institutional arrangements that appertain under the system.*

ap·pe·tite /'api,tīt/ ▶ *n.* a natural desire to satisfy a bodily need, esp. for food: *he has a healthy appetite.* ■ a strong desire or liking for something: *an unquenchable appetite for life.*

ap·pe·tiz·er /'api,tīzər/ ▶ *n.* a small dish of food or a drink taken before a meal or the main course of a meal to stimulate one's appetite.

ap·pe·tiz·ing /'api,tīziNG/ (also **ap·pe·tis·ing**) ▶ *adj.* stimulating one's appetite: *the appetizing aroma of sizzling bacon.* —**ap·pe·tiz·ing·ly** *adv.*

ap·plaud /ə'plôd/ ▶ *v.* [*intr.*] show approval or praise by clapping: *the crowd whistled and applauded* | [*tr.*] *his speech was loudly applauded.* ■ [*tr.*] show strong approval of (a person or action); praise: *Jill applauded the decision.*

ap·plause /ə'plôz/ ▶ *n.* approval or praise expressed by clapping: *they gave him a round of applause.*

ap·ple /'apəl/ ▶ *n.* **1** the round fruit of a tree of the rose family, which typically has thin red or green skin and crisp flesh. ■ an unrelated fruit that resembles this in some way. **2** (also **apple tree**) the tree (genus *Malus*) bearing such fruit.

▶ □ **the apple of one's eye** a person of whom one is extremely fond and proud. □ **apples and oranges** (of two people or things) irreconcilably or fundamentally different.

ap·ple·jack /'apəl,jak/ ▶ *n.* an alcoholic drink distilled from fermented cider.

ap·pli·ance /ə'plīəns/ ▶ *n.* a device or piece of equipment designed to perform a specific task, typically a domestic one: *electrical and gas appliances.* ■ an apparatus fitted by a surgeon or a dentist for corrective or therapeutic purpose.

ap·pli·ca·ble /'aplikəbəl; ə'plik-/ ▶ *adj.* relevant or appropriate: *the same considerations are equally applicable to accident claims.* —**ap·pli·ca·bil·i·ty** /,aplikə'bilitē/ *n.* —**ap·pli·ca·bly** /-blē/ *adv.*

ap·pli·cant /'aplikənt/ ▶ *n.* a person who makes a formal application for something, typically a job.

ap·pli·ca·tion /,apli'kāsHən/ ▶ *n.* **1** a formal request to an authority for something: *an application for leave.* ■ the action or process of making such a request. **2** the action of putting something into operation: *the application of general rules to particular cases.* ■ practical use or relevance: *this principle has no application to the present case.* **3** the action of putting something on a surface: *a fresh application of makeup.* ■ a medicinal substance put on the skin. **4** sustained effort; hard work: *the job takes a great deal of patience and application.* **5** *Comput.* a program or piece of software designed and written to fulfill a particular purpose of the user: *a database application.* —**ap·pli·ca·tion·al** /-sHənl/ *adj.*

ap·pli·ca·tor /'apli,kātər/ ▶ *n.* a device used for inserting something or for applying a substance to a surface. ■ a person who applies a substance or installs something, such as house siding.

ap·plied /ə'plīd/ ▶ *adj.* (of a subject or type of study) put to practical use as opposed to being theoretical: *applied chemistry.*

ap·pli·qué /,apli'kā/ ▶ *n.* ornamental needlework in which pieces of fabric are sewn or stuck onto a large piece of fabric to form patterns.

▶ *v.* (**-qués, -quéd, -qué·ing**) [*tr.*] (usu. **be appliquéd**) decorate (a piece of fabric) in such a way: *the coat is appliquéd with exotic-looking cloth.*

ap·ply /ə'plī/ ▶ *v.* (**-plies, -plied**) **1** [*intr.*] make a formal application or request: *you need to apply to the local authorities for a grant.* ■ put oneself forward formally as a candidate for a job: *she had applied for a number of positions.* **2** [*intr.*] be applicable or relevant: *normal rules apply.* **3** [*tr.*] put or spread (something) on a surface: *the sealer can be applied to new wood.* ■ administer: *smooth over with a cloth, applying even pressure.* **4** (**apply oneself**) give one's full attention to a task; work hard. **5** [*tr.*] bring or put into operation or practical use: *the oil industry has failed to apply appropriate standards of care.*

ap·pog·gia·tu·ra /ə,päjə'tŏŏrə/ ▶ *n.* (*pl.* **-tu·ras** or **-tu·re** /-'tŏŏrā/) *Mus.* a grace note performed before a note of the melody and falling on the beat.

ap·point /ə'point/ ▶ *v.* [*tr.*] **1** assign a job or role to (someone): *she has been appointed to the board.* **2** determine or decide on (a time or a place): *they appointed a day in May for the meeting.* ■ *archaic* decree: *such laws are appointed by God.* **3** *Law* decide the disposal of (property of which one is not the owner) under powers granted by the owner. —**ap·point·ee** /ə,poin'tē/ *n.* —**ap·point·er** *n.*

ap·point·ment /ə'pointmənt/ ▶ *n.* **1** an arrangement to meet someone at a particular time and place: *she made an appointment with my receptionist.* **2** an act of appointing; assigning a job or position to someone: *his appointment as president.* ■ a job or position: *she took up an appointment as head of communications.* ■ a person appointed to a job or position. **3** (**appointments**) furniture or fittings.

ap·por·tion /ə'pôrsHən/ ▶ *v.* [*tr.*] divide and allocate: *voting power will be apportioned according to contribution.* ■ assign: *they did not apportion blame or liability to any one individual.* —**ap·por·tion·ment** *n.*

ap·po·site /'apəzit/ ▶ *adj.* apt in the circumstances or in relation to something: *an apposite quote.* —**ap·po·site·ly** *adv.* —**ap·po·site·ness** *n.*

ap·po·si·tion /,apə'zisHən/ ▶ *n.* **1** *chiefly technical* the positioning of things or the condition of being side by side or close together. **2** *Gram.* a relationship between two or more words or phrases in which the two units are grammatically parallel and have the same referent (e.g., *my friend Sue; the first U.S. President, George Washington*). —**ap·po·si·tion·al** *adj.*

ap·prais·al /ə'prāzəl/ ▶ *n.* an act of assessing something or someone: *a*

A

thorough appraisal of the patient's condition. ■ an expert estimate of the value of something.

ap·praise /əˈprāz/ ▶v. [tr.] assess the value or quality of: *she stealthily appraised him in a pocket mirror* | [intr.] *the interviewer's job is to appraise and evaluate.* ■ (of an official or expert) set a price on; value: *they appraised the painting at $200,000.* —**ap·prais·er** n. —**ap·prais·ing·ly** adv.

ap·pre·ci·a·ble /əˈprēsH(ē)əbəl/ ▶adj. large or important enough to be noticed: *tea and coffee both contain appreciable amounts of caffeine.* —**ap·pre·ci·a·bly** /-blē/ adv.

ap·pre·ci·ate /əˈprēsHē,āt/ ▶v. [tr.] **1** recognize the full worth of: *she feels that he does not appreciate her.* ■ be grateful for (something): *I'd appreciate any information you could give me.* **2** understand (a situation) fully; recognize the full implications of: *they failed to appreciate the pressure he was under.* **3** [intr.] rise in value or price: *they expected the house to appreciate in value.* —**ap·pre·cia·tive** /-sH(ə)tiv/ adj. (in sense 1). —**ap·pre·cia·tive·ly** adv. —**ap·pre·ci·a·tor** /-,ātər/ n.

ap·pre·ci·a·tion /ə,prēsHēˈāsHən/ ▶n. **1** the recognition and enjoyment of the good qualities of someone or something: *I smiled in appreciation.* ■ gratitude for something: *they would be the first to show their appreciation.* ■ a piece of writing in which the qualities of a person or the person's work are discussed and assessed. ■ sensitive understanding of the aesthetic value of something: *courses in music appreciation.* **2** a full understanding of a situation: *they have an appreciation of the needs of users.* **3** increase in monetary value: *the appreciation of the pound against the dollar.*

ap·pre·hend /,apriˈhend/ ▶v. [tr.] **1** arrest (someone) for a crime: *a warrant was issued but he has not been apprehended.* **2** understand or perceive: *great art invites us to apprehend beauty.* ■ archaic anticipate (something) with uneasiness or fear.

ap·pre·hen·sion /,apriˈhensHən/ ▶n. **1** anxiety or fear that something bad or unpleasant will happen: *he felt sick with apprehension.* **2** understanding; grasp: *the pure apprehension of the work of art.* **3** the action of arresting someone: *they acted with intent to prevent lawful apprehension.*

ap·pre·hen·sive /,apriˈhensiv/ ▶adj. **1** anxious or fearful that something bad or unpleasant will happen. **2** archaic or poetic/lit. of or relating to perception or understanding. —**ap·pre·hen·sive·ly** adv. —**ap·pre·hen·sive·ness** n.

ap·pren·tice /əˈprentis/ ▶n. a person who is learning a trade from a skilled employer, having agreed to work for a fixed period at low wages. ■ [usu. as adj.] a beginner at something: *an apprentice confidence trickster.*
▶v. [tr.] (usu. **be apprenticed**) employ (someone) as an apprentice: *Edward was apprenticed to a printer.* ■ [intr.] serve as an apprentice: *she apprenticed with midwives in San Francisco.* —**ap·pren·tice·ship** /-,sHip/ n.

ap·prise /əˈprīz/ ▶v. [tr.] inform or tell (someone): *I thought it right to apprise Chris of what had happened.*

ap·proach /əˈprōcH/ ▶v. [tr.] **1** come near or nearer to (someone or something) in distance: *the train approached the main line* | [intr.] *she hadn't heard him approach.* | ■ come near or nearer to (a future time or event): *he was approaching retirement.* ■ [intr.] (of a future time) come nearer: *the time is approaching when you will be destroyed.* ■ come close to (a number, level, or standard) in quality or quantity: *the population will approach 12 million by the end of the decade.* ■ (of an aircraft) descend toward and prepare to land on (an airfield, runway, etc.): *the single-seater plane hit a post as it was approaching the runway.* **2** speak to (someone) for the first time about something, typically with a proposal or request: *the department had been approached about funding.* **3** start to deal with (something) in a certain way: *one must approach the matter with caution.*
▶n. **1** a way of dealing with something: *we need a new approach to the job.* **2** an act of speaking to someone for the first time about something, typically a proposal or request: *the landowner made an approach to the developer.* ■ (**approaches**) dated behavior intended to propose personal or sexual relations with someone: *feminine resistance to his approaches.* **3** the action of coming near or nearer to someone or something in distance or time: *the approach of winter.* ■ (**approach to**) an approximation to something: *the past is impossible to recall with any approach to accuracy.* ■ the part of an aircraft's flight in which it descends gradually toward an airfield or runway for landing. **4** (usu. **approaches**) a road, sea passage, or other way leading to a place. ▷Middle English: from Old French *aprochier*, *aprocher*, from ecclesiastical Latin *appropiare* 'draw near,' from *ad-* 'to' + *propius* (comparative of *prope* 'near').

ap·proach·a·ble /əˈprōcHəbəl/ ▶adj. **1** friendly and easy to talk to: *managers should be approachable.* **2** (of a place) able to be reached from a particular direction or by a particular means. —**ap·proach·a·bil·i·ty** /ə,prōcHəˈbilitē/ n.

ap·pro·ba·tion /,aprəˈbāsHən/ ▶n. formal approval or praise: *the opera met with high approbation.* —**ap·pro·ba·tive** /ˈaprə,bātiv; əˈprōbətiv/ adj. —**ap·pro·ba·to·ry** /əˈprōbə,tôrē/ adj.

ap·pro·pri·ate ▶adj. /əˈprōprē-it/ suitable or proper in the circumstances: *a measure appropriate to a wartime economy.*
▶v. /-,āt/ [tr.] **1** take (something) for one's own use, typically without the owner's permission: *his images have been appropriated by advertisers.* **2** devote (money or assets) to a special purpose: *there can be problems in appropriating funds for legal expenses.* —**ap·pro·pri·ate·ly** /-itlē/ adv. —**ap·pro·pri·ate·ness** /-itnis/ n. —**ap·pro·pri·a·tor** /-,ātər/ n.

ap·pro·pri·a·tion /ə,prōprēˈāsHən/ ▶n. **1** the action of taking something for one's own use, typically without the owner's permission: *the appropriation of parish funds.* ■ often derog. the artistic practice or technique of reworking images from well-known paintings, photographs, etc., in one's own work. **2** a sum of money or total of assets devoted to a special purpose.

ap·prov·al /əˈpro͞ovəl/ ▶n. **1** the action of officially agreeing to something or accepting something as satisfactory: *the road plans have been given approval.* ■ the belief that someone or something is good or acceptable: *stepparents need to win a child's approval.* **2** (usu. **approvals**) Philately stamps sent by request to a collector or potential customer.
▶ □ **on approval** (of goods) supplied on condition that they may be returned if not satisfactory.

ap·prove /əˈpro͞ov/ ▶v. [tr.] **1** officially agree to or accept as satisfactory: *the budget was approved by Congress.* ■ [intr.] believe that someone or something is good or acceptable: *I don't approve of the way she pampers my father and brothers.* **2** archaic prove; show. —**ap·prov·ing·ly** adv.

approx. ▶abbr. approximate(ly).

ap·prox·i·mate ▶adj. /əˈpräksəmit/ close to the actual, but not completely accurate or exact: *the calculations are very approximate.*
▶v. /-,māt/ [intr.] come close or be similar to something in quality, nature, or quantity: *a leasing agreement approximating to ownership* | [tr.] *reality can be approximated by computational techniques.* ■ [tr.] estimate or calculate (a quantity) fairly accurately: *I approximated the horse's weight.* —**ap·prox·i·mate·ly** adv. —**ap·prox·i·ma·tion** /ə,präksəˈmāsHən/ n.

ap·pur·te·nance /əˈpərtn-əns/ ▶n. (usu. **appurtenances**) an accessory or other item associated with a particular activity or style of living: *all the appurtenances of luxurious travel.*

APR ▶abbr. annual or annualized percentage rate, typically of interest on loans or credit.

Apr. ▶abbr. April.

a·près-ski /,äprä ˈskē/ ▶n. the social activities and entertainment following a day's skiing: [as adj.] *the après-ski disco.* —**a·près-ski·ing** n.

ap·ri·cot /ˈapri,kät; ˈāpri-/ ▶n. **1** a juicy, soft fruit, resembling a small peach, of an orange-yellow color. ■ an orange-yellow color like the skin of a ripe apricot. **2** (also **apricot tree**) the tree (*Prunus armeniaca*) of the rose family that bears this fruit.

A·pril /ˈāprəl/ ▶n. the fourth month of the year, in the northern hemisphere usually considered the second month of spring.

A·pril Fool's Day (also **April Fools' Day**) ▶n. April 1, in many Western countries traditionally an occasion for playing tricks. Also called **ALL FOOLS' DAY**.

a pri·o·ri /,ä prē ˈôrē; prī ˈôrī; ˈä/ ▶adj. relating to or denoting reasoning or knowledge that proceeds from theoretical deduction rather than from observation or experience: *a priori assumptions about human nature.*
▶adv. in a way based on theoretical deduction rather than empirical observation: *sexuality may be a factor, but it cannot be assumed a priori.* —**a·pri·o·rism** /,äprīˈôrizəm; -prē-; ,äprē-/ n.

a·pron /ˈāprən/ ▶n. **1** a protective or decorative garment worn over the front of one's clothes and tied at the back. ■ a similar garment worn as part of official dress, as by an Anglican bishop or a Freemason. ■ a sheet of lead worn to shield the body during an X-ray examination. **2** a small area adjacent to another larger area or structure: *a tiny apron of garden.* ■ a hard-surfaced area on an airfield used for maneuvering or parking aircraft. ■ a projecting strip of stage for playing scenes in front of the curtain. ■ a broadened area of pavement at the end of a driveway. ■ the outer edge or border of a golf green. **3** an object resembling an apron, in particular: ■ a covering protecting an area or structure, for example, from water erosion. ■ an endless conveyor made of overlapping plates: [as adj.] *apron feeders bring coarse ore to a grinding mill.*
▶ □ (**tied to**) **someone's apron strings** (too much under) the influence and control of someone.

ap·ro·pos /,aprəˈpō/ ▶prep. with reference to; concerning: *she remarked apropos of the initiative, "It's not going to stop the abuse."*
▶adv. (**apropos of nothing**) used to state a speaker's belief that

someone's comments or acts are unrelated to any previous discussion or situation: *Isabel kept smiling apropos of nothing.*
▸*adj.* very appropriate to a particular situation.

apse /aps/ ▸*n.* a large semicircular or polygonal recess in a church, arched or with a domed roof, typically at the eastern end, and usually containing the altar. —**ap·si·dal** /'apsidl/ *adj.*

ap·sis /'apsis/ ▸*n.* (*pl.* **-si·des** /-si,dēz/) either of two points on the orbit of a planet or satellite that are nearest to or furthest from the body around which it moves. —**ap·si·dal** /'apsidl/ *adj.*

apt /apt/ ▸*adj.* **1** appropriate or suitable in the circumstances. **2** (**apt to do something**) having a tendency to do something: *she was apt to confuse the past with the present.* **3** quick to learn. —**apt·ly** *adv.* —**apt·ness** *n.*

ap·ti·tude /'apti,t(y)ood/ ▸ **1** *n.* (often **aptitude for**) a natural ability to do something: *he had a remarkable **aptitude for** learning words.* ■ a natural tendency: *his natural **aptitude for** failure.* **2** *archaic* suitability or fitness: *aptitude of expression.*

aq·ua /'äkwə; 'ak-/ ▸*n.* a light bluish-green color; aquamarine: *houses of yellow and aqua* | [as *adj.*] *aqua blue.*

aq·ua·cul·ture /'äkwə,kəlchər; 'ak-/ ▸*n. Bot.* the rearing of aquatic animals or the cultivation of aquatic plants for food.

aq·ua·lung /'äkwə,ləNG; 'ak-/ ▸*n.* a portable breathing apparatus for divers, consisting of cylinders of compressed air strapped on the back, feeding air automatically through a mask or mouthpiece.

aq·ua·ma·rine /,äkwəmə'rēn; ,ak-/ ▸*n.* a precious stone consisting of a light bluish-green variety of beryl. ■ a light bluish-green color: *the aquamarine of the Atlantic Ocean* | [as *adj.*] *the aquamarine water.*

aq·ua·plane /'äkwə,plān; 'ak-/ ▸*n.* a board for riding on water, pulled by a speedboat.
▸*v.* [often as *n.*] (**aquaplaning**) ride standing on an aquaplane. ■ (of a vehicle) slide uncontrollably on a wet surface.

a·quar·i·um /ə'kwe(ə)rēəm/ ▸*n.* (*pl.* **-i·ums** or **-i·a** -ēə/) a transparent tank of water in which fish and other water creatures and plants are kept. ■ a building containing such tanks, esp. one that is open to the public.

A·quar·i·us /ə'kwe(ə)rēəs/ ▸ **1** *Astron.* a large constellation, the Water-carrier or Water-bearer, said to represent a man pouring water from a jar. **2** *Astrol.* the eleventh sign of the zodiac, which the sun enters about January 21. ■ (**an Aquarius**) a person born when the sun is in this sign. —**A·quar·i·an** /-ən/ *n. & adj.*

a·quat·ic /ə'kwätik; ə'kwat-/ ▸*adj.* of or relating to water. ■ (of a plant or animal) growing or living in or near water: *the bay could support aquatic life.* ■ (of a sport) played in or on water. ■ (of a store or dealer) specializing in products for ponds or aquariums.
▸*n.* **1** an aquatic plant or animal, typically one suitable for a pond or aquarium. **2** (**aquatics**) sports played in or on water.

aq·ua·tint /'äkwə,tint; 'ak-/ ▸*n.* a print resembling a watercolor, produced from a copper plate etched with nitric acid. ■ the technique or process of making pictures in such a way.
▸*v.* [*tr.*] create (a scene or picture) in such a way.

aq·ua·vit /'äkwə,vēt; 'ak-/ (also **ak·va·vit** /'äkvä,vēt/) ▸*n.* an alcoholic spirit made from potatoes or other starchy plants.

aq·ue·duct /'äkwə,dəkt; 'ak-/ ▸*n.* an artificial channel for conveying water, typically in the form of a bridge supported by tall columns across a valley. ■ *Anat.* a small canal containing fluid. ▷mid 16th cent.: from obsolete French (now *aqueduc*), from Latin *aquae ductus* 'conduit,' from *aqua* 'water' + *ducere* 'to lead.'

a·que·ous /'äkwēəs; 'ak-/ ▸*adj.* of or containing water, typically as a solvent or medium: *an aqueous solution of potassium permanganate.* ■ *fig.* like water; watery: *a great hall of aqueous marble.*

a·que·ous hu·mor ▸*n.* the clear fluid filling the space in the front of the eyeball between the lens and the cornea. Compare with VITREOUS HUMOR.

aq·ui·fer /'äkwəfər; 'ak-/ ▸*n.* a body of permeable rock that can contain or transmit groundwater.

aq·ui·line /'akwə,līn; -lin/ ▸*adj.* like an eagle. ■ (of a person's nose) hooked or curved like an eagle's beak.

AR ▸*abbr.* ■ (also **A/R**) accounts receivable. ■ Army Regulation. ■ Autonomous Republic.

Ar ▸*symb.* the chemical element argon.

Ar·ab /'arəb/ ▸*n.* **1** a member of a Semitic people, originally from the Arabian peninsula and neighboring territories, inhabiting much of the Middle East and North Africa. **2** an Arabian horse.
▸*adj.* of or relating to Arabia and the people of Arabia: *Arab countries.*

ar·a·besque /,arə'besk/ ▸*n.* **1** an ornamental design consisting of intertwined flowing lines, originally found in Arabic or Moorish decoration. ■ *Mus.* a passage or composition with fanciful ornamentation

of the melody. **2** *Ballet* a posture in which the body is supported on one leg, with the other leg extended horizontally backward.

A·ra·bi·an /ə'rābēən/ ▸*adj. hist.* of or relating to Arabia or Arabs.
▸*n. hist.* **1** a native or inhabitant of Arabia. **2** (also **Arabian horse**) a horse of a breed originating in Arabia, with a distinctive dished face and high-set tail.

Ar·a·bic /'arəbik/ ▸*n.* the Semitic language of the Arabs, spoken by some 150 million people throughout the Middle East and North Africa.
▸*adj.* of or relating to the literature or language of Arab people.

ar·a·ble /'arəbəl/ ▸*adj.* (of land) used or suitable for growing crops. ■ (of crops) able to be grown on such land. ■ concerned with growing such crops: *arable farming.*
▸*n.* land or crops of this type.

a·rach·nid /ə'raknid/ ▸*n.* any of various arthropods having four pairs of walking legs and simple eyes, including spiders, scorpions, mites, and ticks.
▸*adj.* of or relating to arachnids.

a·rach·noid /ə'rak,noid/ ▸*adj.* like a spider or arachnid.
▸*n.* (also **arachnoid membrane** or **arachnoid mater**) *Anat.* a fine, delicate membrane, the middle one of the three membranes or meninges that surround the brain and spinal cord.

a·rach·no·pho·bi·a /ə,raknə'fōbēə/ ▸*n.* extreme or irrational fear of spiders. —**a·rach·no·phobe** /ə'raknə,fōb/ *n.* —**a·rach·no·pho·bic** /-bik/ *adj.*

Ar·a·ma·ic /,arə'māik/ ▸*n.* a Semitic language that was used as a lingua franca in the Near East from the 6th century BC. It replaced Hebrew as the language of the Jews and was itself supplanted by Arabic in the 7th century AD.
▸*adj.* of or in this language.

A·rap·a·ho /ə'rapə,hō/ ▸*n.* **1** (*pl.* same or **-hos**) a member of a North American Indian people living chiefly on the Great Plains, esp. in Wyoming. **2** the Algonquian language of this people.
▸*adj.* of or relating to this people or their language.

ar·bi·ter /'ärbitər/ ▸*n.* a person who settles a dispute or has ultimate authority in a matter: *the military acted as arbiter of conflicts between political groups.* ■ (usu. **arbiter of**) a person whose views or actions have great influence over trends in social behavior: *an arbiter of taste.*

ar·bi·trage /'ärbi,träzh/ ▸*n.* the simultaneous buying and selling of securities, currency, or commodities in different markets or in derivative forms in order to take advantage of differing prices.
▸*v.* [*intr.*] buy and sell assets in such a way.

ar·bi·tra·geur /,ärbiträ'zhər; 'ärbi,träzhər/ (also **ar·bi·tra·ger** /'ärbi,träzhər/) ▸*n.* a person who engages in arbitrage.

ar·bi·trar·y /'ärbi,trerē/ ▸*adj.* based on random choice or personal whim, rather than any reason or system: *his mealtimes were entirely arbitrary.* ■ (of power or a ruling body) unrestrained and autocratic in the use of authority. ■ *Math.* (of a constant or other quantity) of unspecified value. —**ar·bi·trar·i·ly** /,ärbi'tre(ə)rəlē/ *adv.* —**ar·bi·trar·i·ness** *n.*

ar·bi·trate /'ärbi,trāt/ ▸*v.* [*intr.*] (of an independent person or body) reach an authoritative judgment or settlement: *the board has the power to arbitrate in disputes* | [*tr.*] *it set up a commission to arbitrate border tensions.*

ar·bi·tra·tion /,ärbi'träSHən/ ▸*n.* the use of an arbitrator to settle a dispute.

ar·bi·tra·tor /'ärbi,trātər/ ▸*n.* an independent person or body officially appointed to settle a dispute.

ar·bor[1] /'ärbər/ ▸*n.* an axle or spindle on which something revolves. ■ a device holding a tool in a lathe.

ar·bor[2] (*Brit.* **ar·bour**) ▸*n.* a shady garden alcove with sides and a roof formed by trees or climbing plants trained over a wooden framework.

Ar·bor Day ▸*n.* a day dedicated annually to public tree-planting in the U.S., Australia, and other countries. It is usually observed in late April or early May.

ar·bo·re·al /är'bôrēəl/ ▸*adj.* (chiefly of animals) living in trees: *arboreal rodents.* ■ of or relating to trees. —**ar·bo·re·al·i·ty** /är,bôrē'alitē/ *n.*

ar·bo·re·tum /,ärbə'rētəm/ ▸*n.* (*pl.* **-re·tums** or **-re·ta** /-'rētə/) a botanical garden devoted to trees.

ARC /ärk/ ▸*abbr.* ■ *Med.* AIDS-related complex. ■ American Red Cross.

arc /ärk/ ▸*n.* **1** a part of the circumference of a circle or other curve. ■ a curved shape, or something shaped like a curve: *the arc of the sky.* ■ a curving trajectory: *he swung his flashlight in an arc.* ■ [as *adj.*] *Math.* indicating the inverse of a trigonometrical function. **2** (also **electric arc**) a luminous electrical discharge between two electrodes or other points.

Pronunciation Key ə *ago,* up; ər *over, fur;* a *hat;* ā *ate;* ä *car;* CH *chin;* e *let;* ē *see;* e(ə)r *air;* i *fit;* ī *by;* i(ə)r *ear;* NG *sing;* ō *go;* ô *law, for;* oi *toy;* o͝o *good;* o͞o *goo;* ou *out;* SH *she;* TH *thin;* T͟H *then;* (h)w *why;* zh *vision*

▶*v.* (**arced, arc·ing**) [*intr.*] **1** move with a curving trajectory: *the ball arced across the room.* **2** [usu. as *n.*] (**arcing**) form an electric arc: *check that switches operate properly with no sign of arcing.*

ar·cade /ärˈkād/ ▶*n.* **1** a covered passageway with arches along one or both sides. ■ a covered walk with stores along one or both sides. ■ *Archit.* a series of arches supporting a wall, or set along it. **2** short for VIDEO ARCADE. —**ar·cad·ed** *adj.* —**ar·cad·ing** *n.*

Ar·ca·di·an /ärˈkādēən/ ▶*n.* a native of Arcadia. ■ *poetic/lit.* an idealized country dweller.
▶*adj.* of or relating to Arcadia. ■ *poetic/lit.* of or relating to an ideal rustic paradise.

ar·cane /ärˈkān/ ▶*adj.* understood by few; mysterious or secret: *modern math and its arcane notation.* —**ar·cane·ly** *adv.*

arch¹ /ärCH/ ▶*n.* a curved symmetrical structure spanning an opening and typically supporting the weight of a bridge, roof, or wall above it. ■ a structure of this type forming a passageway or a ceremonial monument: *a triumphal arch.* ■ a shape resembling such a structure or a thing with such a shape: *the delicate arch of his eyebrows.* ■ the inner side of the foot.
▶*v.* **1** [*intr.*] have the curved shape of an arch: *a bridge that arched over a canal.* ■ form or cause to form the curved shape of an arch: [*intr.*] *her eyebrows arched in surprise* | [*tr.*] *she arched her back.* **2** [*tr.*] provide (a bridge, building, or part of a building) with an arch. ■ *archaic* or *poetic/lit.* span (something) by or as if by an arch.

arch² ▶*adj.* deliberately or affectedly playful and teasing: *arch observations about even the most mundane matters.* —**arch·ly** *adv.* —**arch·ness** *n.*

ar·chae·ol·o·gy /ˌärkēˈäləjē/ (also **ar·che·ol·o·gy**) ▶*n.* the study of human history and prehistory through the excavation of sites and the analysis of artifacts and other physical remains. —**ar·chae·o·log·ic** /-əˈläjik/ *adj.* —**ar·chae·o·log·i·cal** /-əˈläjikəl/ *adj.* —**ar·chae·o·log·i·cal·ly** *adv.* —**ar·chae·ol·o·gist** /-jist/ *n.*

ar·cha·ic /ärˈkāik/ ▶*adj.* very old or old-fashioned. ■ (of a word or a style of language) no longer in everyday use but sometimes used to impart an old-fashioned flavor. ■ of an early period of art or culture, esp. the 7th–6th centuries BC in Greece. —**ar·cha·i·cal·ly** *adv.*

ar·cha·ism /ˈärkē,izəm; ˈärkā-/ ▶*n.* a thing that is very old or old-fashioned. ■ an archaic word or style of language or art. ■ the use or conscious imitation of very old or old-fashioned styles or features in language or art. —**ar·cha·is·tic** /ˌärkēˈistik; ˌärkā-/ *adj.*

arch·an·gel /ˈärk,ānjəl/ ▶*n.* an angel of high rank. —**arch·an·gel·ic** /ˌärkanˈjelik/ *adj.*

arch·bish·op /ˈärCHˈbishəp/ ▶*n.* the chief bishop responsible for an archdiocese. —**arch·bish·op·ric** /-əˈprik/ *n.*

arch·dea·con /ˈärCHˈdēkən/ ▶*n.* a senior Christian cleric (in the early Church a deacon, in the modern Anglican church a priest) to whom a bishop delegates certain responsibilities. —**arch·dea·con·ry** *n.* —**ar·chi·di·ac·o·nal** *adj.* /ˌärkidīˈakənl/ —**ar·chi·di·ac·o·nate** *n.* /-nit/

arch·di·o·cese /ˈärCHˈdīəsis; -ˌsēz/ ▶*n.* the district for which an archbishop is responsible. —**arch·di·o·ce·san** /ˌärCHdīˈäsəsən/ *adj.*

arch·duke /ˈärCHˈd(y)o͞ok/ ▶*n.* *hist.* a son of the emperor of Austria. —**arch·du·cal** /ˌärCHˈd(y)o͞okəl/ *adj.*

arch·en·e·my /ˈärCHˈenəmē/ ▶*n.* a person who is extremely hostile or opposed to someone or something: *the twins were archenemies.*

ar·che·ol·o·gy ▶*n.* variant of ARCHAEOLOGY.

arch·er /ˈärCHər/ ▶*n.* a person who shoots with a bow and arrows, esp. at a target for sport. ■ (**the Archer**) the zodiacal sign or constellation Sagittarius.

ar·cher·y /ˈärCHərē/ ▶*n.* the sport or skill of shooting with a bow and arrows, esp. at a target.

ar·che·type /ˈärk(i),tīp/ ▶*n.* a very typical example of a certain person or thing: *the book is a perfect archetype of the genre.* ■ an original that has been imitated: *the archetype of faith is Abraham.* ■ a recurrent symbol or motif in literature, art, or mythology. ■ *Psychoanalysis* (in Jungian psychology) a primitive mental image inherited from the earliest human ancestors, and supposed to be present in the collective unconscious. —**ar·che·typ·al** /ˌärkiˈtipəl/ *adj.* —**ar·che·typ·i·cal** /ˌärk(i)ˈtipikəl/ *adj.*

ar·chi·e·pis·co·pal /ˌärkēəˈpiskəpəl/ ▶*adj.* of or relating to an archbishop. —**ar·chi·e·pis·co·pa·cy** /-əˈpiskəpəsē/ *n.* (*pl.* **-cies**) —**ar·chi·e·pis·co·pate** /-pit; -,pāt/ *n.*

ar·chi·pel·a·go /ˌärkəˈpelə,gō/ ▶*n.* (*pl.* **-gos** or **-goes**) a group of islands. ■ a sea or stretch of water containing many islands. ▷early 16th cent.: from Italian *arcipelago,* from Greek *arkhi-* ‘chief’ + *pelagos* ‘sea.’ The word was originally used as a proper name (*the Archipelago* ‘the Aegean Sea’): the generalization of meaning occurred because the Aegean Sea is remarkable for its large numbers of islands.

ar·chi·tect /ˈärki,tekt/ ▶*n.* a person who designs buildings and in many cases also supervises their construction. ■ a person who is responsible for inventing or realizing a particular idea or project: *a chief architect of the plan to slash income taxes.*
▶*v.* [*tr.*] (usu. **be architected**) *Comput.* design and make: *he architected applications for large pharmaceutical companies.*

ar·chi·tec·ton·ic /ˌärkitekˈtänik/ ▶*adj.* of or relating to architecture or architects. ■ (of an artistic composition or physical appearance) having a clearly defined structure, esp. one that is artistically pleasing.
▶*n.* (**architectonics**) [usu. treated as *sing.*] the scientific study of architecture. ■ musical, literary, or artistic structure: *the architectonics of Latin prose.* —**ar·chi·tec·ton·i·cal·ly** /-ik(ə)lē/ *adv.*

ar·chi·tec·ture /ˈärki,tekCHər/ ▶*n.* **1** the art or practice of designing and constructing buildings. ■ the style in which a building is designed or constructed, esp. with regard to a specific period, place, or culture: *Victorian architecture.* **2** the complex or carefully designed structure of something: *the chemical architecture of the human brain.* ■ the conceptual structure and logical organization of a computer or computer-based system: *a client-server architecture.* —**ar·chi·tec·tur·al** /ˌärkiˈtekCHərəl/ *adj.* —**ar·chi·tec·tur·al·ly** /ˌärkiˈtekCHərəlē/ *adv.*

ar·chi·trave /ˈärki,trāv/ ▶*n.* **1** (in classical architecture) a main beam resting across the tops of columns, specifically the lower third entablature. **2** the molded frame around a doorway or window. ■ a molding around the exterior of an arch.

ar·chive /ˈär,kīv/ (usu. **archives**) ▶*n.* a collection of historical documents or records providing information about a place, institution, or group of people. ■ the place where such documents or records are kept.
▶*v.* [*tr.*] place or store (something) in such a collection or place. ■ *Comput.* transfer (data) to a less frequently used storage medium such as magnetic tape. —**ar·chi·val** /ärˈkīvəl/ *adj.*

ar·chi·vist /ˈärkəvist; -,kī-/ ▶*n.* a person who maintains and is in charge of archives.

arch·lute /ˈärCH,lo͞ot/ ▶*n.* a bass lute with an extended neck and unstopped bass strings.

arch·way /ˈärCH,wā/ ▶*n.* a curved structure forming a passage or entrance.

arc light (also **arc lamp**) ▶*n.* a light source using an electric arc.

arc minute /ˈminit/ ▶*n.* see MINUTE¹ (sense 2).

Arc·tic /ˈärktik; ˈärtik/ ▶*adj.* **1** of or relating to the regions around the North Pole. ■ (of animals or plants) living or growing in such regions. ■ designed for use in such regions. **2** (**arctic**) *inf.* (of weather conditions) very cold.
▶*n.* **1** (**the Arctic**) the regions around the North Pole. **2** (**arctics**) thick waterproof overshoes. ▷late Middle English: ultimately from Greek *arktikos,* from *arktos* ‘bear, North Star.’

arc weld·ing ▶*n.* a technique in which metals are welded using heat generated by an electric arc.

ar·dent /ˈärdnt/ ▶*adj.* enthusiastic or passionate: *an ardent suitor.* ■ *archaic* or *poetic/lit.* burning; glowing: *ardent flames.* —**ar·dent·ly** *adv.*

ar·dor /ˈärdər/ (*Brit.* **ar·dour**) ▶*n.* enthusiasm or passion.

ar·du·ous /ˈärjo͞oəs/ ▶*adj.* involving or requiring strenuous effort; difficult and tiring. —**ar·du·ous·ly** *adv.* —**ar·du·ous·ness** *n.*

are¹ /är/ ▶ 2nd person singular present and 1st, 2nd, 3rd person plural present of BE.

are² /är; e(ə)r/ ▶*n.* *hist.* a metric unit of measure, equal to 100 square meters (about 119.6 square yards).

ar·e·a /ˈe(ə)rēə/ ▶*n.* **1** a region or part of a town, a country, or the world: *rural areas of New Jersey.* ■ a space allocated for a specific purpose: *the dining area.* ■ a part of an object or surface: *areas of the body.* ■ a subject or range of activity or interest: *the key areas of science.* ■ **2** the extent or measurement of a surface or piece of land: *the area of a triangle* | *the room is twelve square feet in area.* —**ar·e·al** *adj.*

a·re·ca /əˈrēkə; ˈarəkə; ˈer-/ (also **areca palm**) ▶*n.* a tropical Asian palm (genus *Areca*).

a·re·ca nut ▶*n.* the astringent seed of an areca palm (*Areca catechu*), which is often chewed with betel leaves. Also called BETEL NUT.

a·re·na /əˈrēnə/ ▶*n.* a level area surrounded by seats for spectators, in which sports, entertainments, and other public events are held. ■ a place or scene of activity, debate, or conflict: *the political arena.*

ar·e·na·ceous /ˌarəˈnāSHəs/ ▶*adj.* *Geol.* consisting of sand or sandlike particles.

aren't /är(ə)nt/ ▶*contr. of* are not: *they aren't here.* ■ am not (only used in questions): *I'm right, aren't I?* | *why aren't I being given a pay raise?*

a·re·o·la /əˈrēələ/ ▶*n.* (*pl.* **-lae** /-,lē/) *Anat.* a small circular area, in particular the ring of pigmented skin surrounding a nipple. ■ *Med.* a reddened patch around a spot or papule. —**a·re·o·lar** *adj.* —**a·re·o·late** /-lit; -,lāt/ *adj.*

a·rête /ə'rāt/ ▸*n.* a sharp mountain ridge.

ar·gent /'ärjənt/ ▸*adj.* *poetic/lit.* & *Heraldry* silvery; silvery white: *the argent moon.*

▸*n.* *Heraldry* silver as a heraldic tincture.

ar·gen·tine /'ärjən,tīn; -,tēn/ ▸*adj.* *archaic* of or resembling silver.

ar·gon /'är,gän/ ▸*n.* the chemical element of atomic number 18, an inert gaseous element of the noble gas group. (Symbol: **Ar**)

ar·go·naut /'ärgə,nôt/ ▸*n.* a small floating octopus (genus *Argonauta*), the female of which has webbed arms like sails and secretes a thin, coiled, papery shell in which the eggs are laid. Also called **PAPER NAUTILUS**.

ar·go·sy /'ärgəsē/ ▸*n.* (*pl.* **-sies**) *poetic/lit.* a large merchant ship, originally one from Ragusa (now Dubrovnik) or Venice.

ar·got /'ärgō; -gət/ ▸*n.* the jargon or slang of a particular group or class: *teenage argot.*

ar·gu·a·ble /'ärgyōōəbəl/ ▸*adj.* able to be argued or asserted: *it is arguable that egg donation raises a series of moral and practical problems.* ■ open to disagreement; not obviously correct: *a highly arguable assumption.* —**ar·gu·a·bly** *adv.*

ar·gue /'ärgyōō/ ▸*v.* (**-gues**, **-gued**, **-gu·ing**) **1** [*tr.*] give reasons or cite evidence in support of an idea, action, or theory, typically with the aim of persuading others to share one's view: *defense attorneys **argue that** the police lacked "probable cause" to arrest the driver.* ■ (**argue someone into/out of**) persuade someone to do or not to do (something) by giving reasons: *I tried to argue him out of it.* **2** [*intr.*] exchange or express diverging or opposite views, typically in a heated or angry way: *don't **argue with** me.* | [*tr.*] *she was too tired to **argue the point**.* —**ar·gu·er** *n.*

ar·gu·ment /'ärgyəmənt/ ▸*n.* **1** an exchange of diverging or opposite views, typically a heated or angry one: *I've had an **argument with** my father.* **2** a reason or set of reasons given with the aim of persuading others that an action or idea is right or wrong: *there is a strong argument for submitting a formal appeal.* **3** *Math.* an independent variable associated with a function and determining the value of the function. ■ *Comput.* a value or address passed to a procedure or function at the time of call.

ar·gu·men·ta·tion /,ärgyəmən'tāSHən/ ▸*n.* the action or process of reasoning systematically in support of an idea, action, or theory.

ar·gu·men·ta·tive /,ärgyə'mentətiv/ ▸*adj.* **1** given to expressing divergent or opposite views: *an argumentative child.* **2** using or characterized by systematic reasoning: *the highest standards of argumentative rigor.* —**ar·gu·men·ta·tive·ly** *adv.* —**ar·gu·men·ta·tive·ness** *n.*

ar·gus /'ärgəs/ ▸*n.* (**Argus**) *Greek Mythol.* a monster with a hundred eyes, used by Hera to watch over Io. ■ an alert, watchful guardian.

a·ri·a /'ärēə/ ▸*n.* *Mus.* an accompanied song for a solo voice, typically one in an opera or oratorio.

ar·id /'arid/ ▸*adj.* (of land or a climate) having little or no rain; too dry or barren to support vegetation. ■ *fig.* lacking in interest, excitement, or meaning. —**a·rid·i·ty** /ə'riditē/ *n.* —**ar·id·ly** *adv.* —**ar·id·ness** *n.*

Ar·ies /'e(ə)rēz/ ▸ **1** *Astron.* a small constellation (the Ram), said to represent the ram whose Golden Fleece was sought by Jason and the Argonauts. ■ [as *genitive*] (**A·ri·e·tis** /ə'rī-itis/) used with a preceding letter or numeral to designate stars: *the star Beta Arietis.* **2** *Astrol.* the first sign of the zodiac, which the sun enters at the vernal equinox (about March 20). ■ (**an Aries**) (*pl.* same) a person born when the sun is in this sign.

a·right /ə'rīt/ ▸*adv.* *dial.* correctly; properly: *I wondered if I'd heard aright.*

ar·il /'arəl/ ▸*n.* *Bot.* an extra seed-covering, typically hairy or fleshy, e.g., the red fleshy cup around a yew seed. —**ar·il·late** /-lit; -,lāt/ *adj.*

a·rise /ə'rīz/ ▸*v.* (*past* **a·rose** /ə'rōz/; *past part.* **a·ris·en** /ə'rizən/) [*intr.*] **1** (of a problem, opportunity, or situation) emerge; become apparent: *difficulties had arisen.* ■ come into being; originate: *the practice arose in the nineteenth century.* ■ (**arise from/out of**) occur as a result of: *most conflicts arise from ignorance or uncertainty.* **2** *formal* or *poetic/lit.* get or stand up.

ar·is·toc·ra·cy /,ari'stäkrəsē/ ▸*n.* (*pl.* **-cies**) [treated as *sing.* or *pl.*] (usu. **the aristocracy**) the highest class in certain societies, esp. those holding hereditary titles or offices. ■ a form of government in which power is held by the nobility. ■ a state governed in this way. ■ *fig.* a group regarded as privileged or superior in a particular sphere: *high-level technocrats make up a large part of this "technical aristocracy."* ▷late 15th cent.: from Old French *aristocratie*, from Greek *aristokratia*, from *aristos* 'best' + *-kratia* 'power.' The term originally denoted the government of a state by its best citizens, later by the rich and well-born, hence the sense 'nobility,' regardless of the form of government (mid 17th cent.).

a·ris·to·crat /ə'ristə,krat/ ▸*n.* a member of the aristocracy: *an aristocrat by birth.* ■ something believed to be the best of its kind: *the trout is the aristocrat of freshwater fish.*

a·ris·to·crat·ic /ə,ristə'kratik/ ▸*adj.* of or relating to the aristocracy. ■ distinguished in manners or bearing: *a stately, aristocratic manner.* ■ grand; stylish. —**a·ris·to·crat·i·cal·ly** /-ik(ə)lē/ *adv.*

Ar·is·to·te·lian /ə,ristə'tēlyən/, ˌaristə-; -lēən/ ▸*adj.* of or relating to Aristotle or his philosophy.

▸*n.* a student of Aristotle or an adherent of his philosophy.

a·rith·me·tic ▸*n.* /ə'riTHmə,tik/ the branch of mathematics dealing with the properties and manipulation of numbers: *the laws of arithmetic.* ■ the use of numbers in counting and calculation: *he could do arithmetic in his head.* ■ *fig.* those aspects of a particular situation that can be expressed in numerical terms: *some unsettling parliamentary arithmetic.*

▸*adj.* (**ar·ith·met·ic**) /,ariTH'metik/ (also **ar·ith·met·i·cal**) of or relating to arithmetic. —**ar·ith·met·i·cal·ly** *adv.*

ar·ith·met·ic pro·gres·sion /,ariTH'metik; ,er-/ (also **arithmetic series**) ▸*n.* a sequence of numbers in which each differs from the preceding by a constant quantity (e.g., 3, 6, 9, 12, etc.; 9, 7, 5, 3, etc.).

ark /ärk/ ▸*n.* **1** (**the ark**) (in the Bible) the ship built by Noah to save his family and two of every kind of animal from the Flood; Noah's ark. ■ *fig.* a vessel or sanctuary that serves as protection against extinction. ■ a large, flat-bottomed boat. **2** short for **ARK OF THE COVENANT**. ■ (also **Holy Ark**) a chest or cupboard housing the Torah scrolls in a synagogue.

Ark of the Cov·e·nant ▸the chest containing the tablets of the laws of the ancient Israelites, which was kept in the Temple at Jerusalem.

ARM ▸*abbr.* ADJUSTABLE RATE MORTGAGE.

arm[1] /ärm/ ▸*n.* **1** each of the two upper limbs of the human body from the shoulder to the hand. ■ (in technical use) each of these upper limbs from the shoulder to the elbow. ■ each of the forelimbs of an animal. ■ a flexible limb of an invertebrate animal, e.g., an octopus. ■ a sleeve of a garment. ■ an ability to throw a ball skillfully: *he has a good arm.* ■ an athlete with such an ability. ■ used to refer to the holding of a person's arm in support or companionship: *he arrived with a pretty girl on his arm.* ■ used to refer to something perceived as powerful or protective: *the comforting arms of the church.* **2** a thing resembling an arm in form or function, in particular: ■ a side part of a chair or other seat on which a sitter's arm can rest. ■ a narrow strip of water or land projecting from a larger body. ■ a large branch of a tree. ■ *fig.* a long, narrow shape or object: *a long arm of sunshine.* **3** a branch or division of a company or organization: *the political arm of the separatist group.* ■ one of the types of troops of which an army is composed, such as infantry or artillery. **4** *Math.* each of the lines enclosing an angle. —**arm·ful** /-,fŏŏl/ *n.* (*pl.* **-fuls**) —**arm·less** *adj.*

▸ □ **the long arm of the law** used to refer to the criminal justice system as far-reaching. □ **cost an arm and a leg** *inf.* be extremely expensive. □ **give one's right arm** *inf.* used to convey a strong desire to have or do something: *I'd give my right arm to go with them.* □ **keep someone/something at arm's length** avoid intimacy or close contact with someone or something. □ **with open arms** with great affection or enthusiasm.

arm[2] ▸*v.* [*tr.*] supply or provide with weapons: *both sides **armed themselves with** grenades and machine guns.* ■ supply or provide with equipment, tools, or other items in preparation or readiness for something: *she **armed** them **with** brushes and mops.* ■ activate the fuse of (a bomb or other device) so that it is ready to explode.

▸*n.* see **ARMS**.

ar·ma·da /är'mädə/ ▸*n.* a fleet of warships. ■ (**the Spanish Armada**) a Spanish naval invasion force sent against England by Philip II of Spain. It was defeated by the English and almost completely destroyed by storms.

ar·ma·dil·lo /,ärmə'dilō/ ▸*n.* (*pl.* **-os**) a nocturnal omnivorous mammal (several genera, family Dasypodidae) native to Central and South America, with large claws for digging and a body covered in bony plates.

Ar·ma·ged·don /,ärmə'gedn/ ▸*n.* (in the New Testament) the last battle between good and evil before the Day of Judgment. ■ the place where the last battle between good and evil will be fought. ■ a dramatic and catastrophic conflict, typically seen as likely to destroy the world or the human race: *nuclear Armageddon.*

ar·ma·ment /'ärməmənt/ ▸*n.* (also **armaments**) military weapons and equipment: *chemical weapons and other unconventional armaments.* ■ the

---

process of equipping military forces for war. ■ *archaic* a military force equipped for war.

ar·ma·men·tar·i·um /ˌärməmənˈte(ə)rēəm/ ▶*n.* (*pl.* **-tar·i·a** /-ˈte(ə)rēə/) the medicines, equipment, and techniques available to a medical practitioner. ■ a collection of resources available for a certain purpose.

ar·ma·ture /ˈärməCHər; -ˌCHŏŏr/ ▶*n.* **1** the rotating coil or coils of a dynamo or electric motor. ■ any moving part of an electrical machine in which a voltage is induced by a magnetic field. **2** a metal framework on which a sculpture is molded with clay or similar material. **3** *Biol.* the protective covering of an animal or plant.

arm·band /ˈärmˌband/ ▶*n.* a band worn around a person's upper arm to hold up a shirtsleeve or as a symbol.

arm·chair ▶*n.* /ˈärmˌCHe(ə)r/ a comfortable chair, typically upholstered, with side supports for a person's arms.
▶*adj.* lacking or not involving practical or direct experience of a particular subject or activity: *armchair adventurers.*

Ar·me·ni·an /ärˈmēnēən; -yən/ ▶*adj.* of or relating to Armenia, its language, or the Christian Church established there.
▶*n.* **1** a native of Armenia or a person of Armenian descent. **2** the Indo-European language of Armenia, spoken by around 4 million people.

arm·hole /ˈärmˌhōl/ ▶*n.* each of two openings in a garment through which the wearer puts their arms.

ar·mi·stice /ˈärməstis/ ▶*n.* an agreement made by opposing sides in a war to stop fighting for a certain time; a truce.

arm·let /ˈärmlit/ ▶*n.* a band or bracelet worn around the upper part of a person's arm.

arm·lock /ˈärmˌläk/ ▶*n.* a method of restraining someone by holding an arm tightly behind their back.

ar·moire /ärmˈwär; ˈärmˌwär/ ▶*n.* a wardrobe or movable cabinet, typically one that is ornate or antique.

ar·mor /ˈärmər/ (*Brit.* **ar·mour**) ▶*n.* the metal coverings formerly worn by soldiers or warriors to protect the body in battle: *knights in armor | a suit of armor.* ■ (also **armor plate**) the tough metal layer covering a military vehicle or ship to defend it from attack. ■ military vehicles collectively. ■ the protective layer or shell of some animals and plants. ■ a person's emotional, social, or other defenses: *his armor of self-confidence.*
▶*v.* [*tr.*] provide (someone) with emotional, social, or other defenses: *the knowledge armored him against her.* —**ar·mor·plat·ed** *adj.*

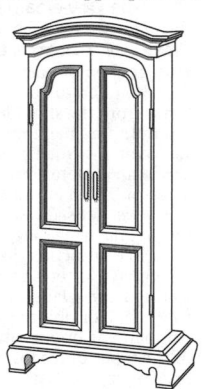
armoire

ar·mor·er /ˈärmərər/ (*Brit.* **ar·mour·er**) ▶*n.* **1** a maker, supplier, or repairer of weapons or armor. **2** an official in charge of the arms of a military unit.

ar·mo·ri·al /ärˈmôrēəl/ ▶*adj.* of or relating to heraldry or heraldic devices: *armorial shields.*

ar·mor·y[1] /ˈärmərē/ (*Brit.* **ar·mour·y**) ▶*n.* (*pl.* **-mor·ies**) **1** a place where arms are kept. ■ a supply of arms: *the most powerful weapon in our armory.* ■ a place where arms are manufactured. ■ *fig.* an array of resources available for a particular purpose: *his armory of comic routines.* **2** a place where military reservists are trained or have their headquarters.

ar·mor·y[2] ▶*n.* heraldry.

arm·pit /ˈärmˌpit/ ▶*n.* a hollow under the arm at the shoulder; also called AXILLA. ■ *inf.* a place regarded as extremely unpleasant: *they call the region the armpit of America.*

arm·rest /ˈärmˌrest/ ▶*n.* a padded or upholstered arm of a chair or other seat on which a sitter can comfortably rest.

arms /ärmz/ ▶*pl. n.* **1** weapons and ammunition; armaments: [as *adj.*] *arms exports.* **2** distinctive emblems or devices, originally borne on shields in battle and now forming the heraldic insignia of families, corporations, or countries. See also COAT OF ARMS.
▶ □ **up in arms** (**about/over**) protesting vigorously about something: *teachers are up in arms about new school tests.*

arm·twist·ing ▶*n. inf.* persuasion by the use of physical force or moral pressure: *eight years of diplomatic arm-twisting.* —**arm-twist** *v.*

ar·my /ˈärmē/ ▶*n.* (*pl.* **-mies**) an organized military force equipped for fighting on land. ■ (**the army** or **the Army**) the branch of a nation's armed services that conducts military operations on land. ■ (**an army of** or **armies of**) a large number of people or things, typically formed or organized for a particular purpose: *an army of photographers | armies of cockroaches.*

ar·ni·ca /ˈärnikə/ ▶*n.* a plant (genus *Arnica*) of the daisy family that bears yellow daisylike flowers.

a·ro·ma /əˈrōmə/ ▶*n.* a distinctive, typically pleasant smell. ■ a subtle, pervasive quality or atmosphere of a particular type: *the aroma of officialdom.*

a·ro·ma·tase /əˈrōməˌtās/ ▶*n.* an adrenal enzyme that produces estrogen. Inhibiting its action is one approach to breast cancer prevention and treatment.

a·ro·ma·ther·a·py /əˌrōməˈTHerəpē/ ▶*n.* the use of aromatic plant extracts and essential oils in massage or baths. —**a·ro·ma·ther·a·peu·tic** /-ˌTHerəˈpyŏŏtik/ *adj.* —**a·ro·ma·ther·a·pist** /-pist/ *n.*

ar·o·mat·ic /ˌarəˈmatik/ ▶*adj.* **1** having a pleasant and distinctive smell: *a massage with aromatic oils.* **2** *Chem.* (of an organic compound) containing a planar unsaturated ring of atoms that is stabilized by an interaction of the bonds forming the ring.
▶*n.* **1** a substance or plant emitting a pleasant and distinctive smell. **2** (usu. **aromatics**) *Chem.* an aromatic compound. —**ar·o·mat·i·cal·ly** *adv.* —**ar·o·ma·tic·i·ty** /-məˈtisitē/ *n.* (*Chem.*).

a·ro·ma·tize /əˈrōməˌtīz/ ▶*v.* [*tr.*] cause to have a pleasant and distinctive smell. —**a·ro·ma·ti·za·tion** /əˌrōməti'zāsHən/ *n.*

a·rose /əˈrōz/ ▶ past of ARISE.

a·round /əˈround/ ▶*adv.* **1** (*Brit.* also **round**) located or situated on every side: *the mountains towering all around.* ■ so as to surround someone or something: *everyone crowded around.* ■ *fig.* so as to give support and companionship: *if one girl is distraught, the others will rally around.* ■ with circular motion: *the boats were spun around by waterspouts.* ■ so as to cover or take in the whole area surrounding a particular center: *she paused to glance around admiringly at the décor.* ■ so as to reach everyone in a particular group or area: *he passed a newspaper clipping around.* **2** (*Brit.* also **round**) so as to rotate and face in the opposite direction: *Jack seized her by the shoulders and turned her around.* ■ so as to lead in another direction: *it was the last house before the road curved around.* ■ used in describing the position of something, typically with regard to the direction in which it is facing or its relation to other items: *the picture shows the pieces the wrong way around.* ■ used to describe a situation in terms of the relation between people, actions, or events: *it was he who was attacking her, not the other way around.* **3** (*Brit.* also **round**) so as to reach a new place or position, typically by moving from one side of something to the other: *he made his way around to the back of the building.* ■ in or to many places throughout a locality: *his only ambition is to drive around in a sports car.* ■ used to convey an ability to navigate or orient oneself: *I like pupils to find their own way around.* ■ *inf.* used to convey the idea of visiting someone else: *why don't you come around to my office?* ■ randomly or unsystematically; here and there: *one of them was glancing nervously around.* **4** (*Brit.* also **round**) in existence, in the vicinity, or in active use: *there was no one around.* ■ near at hand: *he would want to have her around as much as possible.* **5** approximately; about: *software costs would be around $1,500* | [as *prep.*] *I returned to my hotel around 3 a.m.*
▶*prep.* (*Brit.* also **round**) **1** on every side of: *the hills around the city.* ■ (of something abstract) having (the thing mentioned) as a focal point: *our entire culture is built around those loyalties.* **2** in or to many places throughout (a community or locality): *cycling around the village.* ■ on the other side of (a corner or obstacle): *Steven parked the car around the corner.* ■ so as to hit (something) in passing: *if he didn't shut up, he might get a slap around the ear.* **3** so as to encircle or embrace (someone or something): *he put his arm around her.* ■ (of a person's arm or arms) partially encircling (another person) as part of a gesture of affection: *Mike put an arm around Mary.* ■ following an approximately circular route: *he walked around the airfield.* ■ so as to cover or take in the whole area of (a place): *she went around the house and saw that all the windows were barred.*
▶ □ **have been around** *inf.* have a lot of varied experience and understanding of the world.

a·rouse /əˈrouz/ ▶*v.* [*tr.*] **1** evoke or awaken (a feeling, emotion, or response): *something about the man aroused the guard's suspicions.* ■ excite or provoke (someone) to anger or strong emotions: *an ability to influence the audience and to arouse the masses.* ■ excite (someone) sexually. **2** awaken (someone) from sleep. —**a·rous·al** /-zəl/ *n.*

ar·peg·gi·o /ärˈpejēˌō/ ▶*n.* (*pl.* **-os**) *Mus.* the notes of a chord played in succession. ▷Italian, from *arpeggiare* 'play the harp,' from *arpa* 'harp.'

ar·que·bus /ˈärk(w)əbəs/ ▶*n.* variant spelling of HARQUEBUS.

arr. ▶*abbr.* ■ (of a piece of music) arranged by: *Variations on a theme of Corelli (arr. Wild).* ■ (with reference to the arrival time of a bus, train, or airplane) arrives.

ar·rack /ˈarək; əˈrak/ (also **ar·ak**) ▶*n.* an alcoholic liquor typically distilled from the sap of the coconut palm or from rice.

ar·raign /əˈrān/ ▶*v.* (often **be arraigned**) [*tr.*] call or bring (someone) before a court to answer a criminal charge: *her sister was arraigned on attempted murder charges.* ■ find fault with (someone or something); censure. —**ar·raign·ment** *n.*

ar·range /əˈrānj/ ▶ *v.* [*tr.*] **1** put (things) in a neat, attractive, or required order: *she had just finished arranging the flowers.* **2** organize or make plans for (a future event): *they hoped to arrange a meeting.* ■ [*intr.*] reach agreement about an action or event in advance: *I arranged with my boss to have the time off.* ■ ensure that (something) is done or provided by organizing it in advance: *accommodations can be arranged if required.* **3** *Mus.* adapt (a composition) for performance with instruments or voices other than those originally specified: *songs arranged for viola and piano.* —**ar·range·a·ble** *adj.* —**ar·rang·er** *n.*

ar·range·ment /əˈrānjmənt/ ▶ *n.* **1** the action, process, or result of arranging or being arranged: *the arrangement of windows failed to take TV viewing into account.* ■ a thing that has been arranged in a neat or attractive way: *flower arrangements.* **2** (usu. **arrangements**) plans or preparations for a future event: *all the arrangements for the wedding were made.* ■ an agreement with someone: *the travel agents have an arrangement with the hotel.* **3** *Mus.* a composition adapted for performance with different instruments or voices than those originally specified: *Mozart's symphonies in arrangements for cello and piano.* **4** *archaic* a settlement of a dispute or claim.

ar·rant /ˈarənt/ ▶ *adj. dated* complete, utter: *what arrant nonsense!*

ar·ray /əˈrā/ ▶ *n.* **1** an impressive display or range of a particular type of thing: *a vast array of literature on the topic.* **2** an ordered arrangement, in particular: ■ an arrangement of troops. ■ *Math.* an arrangement of quantities or symbols in rows and columns; a matrix. ■ *Comput.* an ordered set of related elements. **3** *poetic/lit.* elaborate or beautiful clothing: *he was clothed in fine array.*

▶ *v.* **1** [*tr.*] (usu. **be arrayed**) display or arrange (things) in a particular way: *arrayed across the table was a buffet.* **2** [*tr.*] (usu. **be arrayed in**) dress someone in (the clothes specified): *they were arrayed in Hungarian national dress.*

ar·rears /əˈ ri(ə)rz/ ▶ *pl. n.* money that is owed and should have been paid earlier: *the arrears of rent.* —**ar·rear·age** /əˈri(ə)rij/ *n.*

▶ □ **in arrears** (also *chiefly Law* **in arrear**) behind in paying money that is owed: *two out of three tenants are in arrears.* ■ (of payments made or due for wages, rent, etc.) at the end of each period of work or occupancy: *you will be paid monthly in arrears.*

ar·rest /əˈrest/ ▶ *v.* [*tr.*] **1** seize (someone) by legal authority and take into custody: *the police arrested him for possession of marijuana.* **2** stop or check (progress or a process): *the spread of the disease can be arrested* | [as *adj.*] (**arrested**) *arrested development may occur.* **3** attract the attention of (someone): *his attention was arrested by a strange sound.*

▶ *n.* **1** the action of seizing someone to take into custody: *I have a warrant for your arrest* | *they placed her under arrest.* **2** a stoppage or sudden cessation of motion: *a cardiac arrest.*

ar·riv·al /əˈrīvəl/ ▶ *n.* the action or process of arriving: *he was dead on arrival at the hospital.* ■ a person who has arrived somewhere. ■ the emergence or appearance of a new development, phenomenon, or product: *the arrival of democracy.* ■ such a new development, phenomenon, or product: *sociology is a relatively new arrival on the academic scene.*

ar·rive /əˈrīv/ ▶ *v.* [*intr.*] reach a place at the end of a journey or a stage in a journey: *we arrived at his house and knocked at the door.* ■ (of a thing) be brought or delivered: *the invitation arrived a few days later.* ■ (**arrive at**) reach (a conclusion or decision): *they arrived at the same conclusion.* ■ (of an event or a particular moment) happen or come: *we will be in touch with them when the time arrives.* ■ (of a new development or product) come into existence or use: *microcomputers arrived at the start of the 1970s.* ■ (of a baby) be born. ■ *inf.* achieve success or recognition.

ar·ri·viste /ˌärēˈvēst/ ▶ *n.* an ambitious or ruthlessly self-seeking person, esp. one who has recently acquired wealth or social status.

ar·ro·gant /ˈarəgənt/ ▶ *adj.* having or revealing an exaggerated sense of one's own importance or abilities. —**ar·ro·gance** *n.* —**ar·ro·gant·ly** *adv.*

ar·ro·gate /ˈarəˌgāt/ ▶ *v.* [*tr.*] take or claim (something) for oneself without justification: *they arrogate to themselves the ability to divine the nation's true interests.* —**ar·ro·ga·tion** /ˌarəˈgāshən/ *n.*

ar·row /ˈarō/ ▶ *n.* a shaft sharpened at the front and with feathers or vanes at the back, shot from a bow as a weapon or for sport. ■ a mark or sign resembling an arrow, used to show direction or position; a pointer: *we drove in the main gate and followed a series of arrows.*

ar·row·head /ˈarōˌhed/; ˈer-/ ▶ *n.* **1** the pointed end of an arrow, typically wedge-shaped. ■ a decorative device resembling an arrowhead. **2** an aquatic or semiaquatic plant (genus *Sagittaria*, family Alismataceae) with arrow-shaped leaves and three-petaled white flowers. Several species include the common **broad-leaved arrowhead** (*S. latifolia*).

ar·row·root /ˈarōˌro͞ot; -ˌro͝ot; ˈer-/ ▶ *n.* a West Indian plant (*Maranta arundinacea*, family Marantaceae) from which a starch is prepared. ■ the fine-grained starch obtained from this plant, used in cooking and medicine. ▷late 17th cent.: alteration of Arawak *aru-aru* (literally 'meal of meals') by association with *arrow* + *root*, the tubers being used to absorb poison from arrow wounds.

ar·roy·o /əˈroi,ō/ ▶ *n.* (*pl.* **-os**) a steep-sided gully cut by running water in an arid or semiarid region.

ar·se·nal /ˈärs(ə)nl/ ▶ *n.* a collection of weapons and military equipment stored by a country, person, or group: *Britain's nuclear arsenal.* ■ a place where weapons and military equipment are stored or made. ■ *fig.* an array of resources available for a certain purpose: *an arsenal of computers at our disposal.*

ar·se·nic ▶ *n.* /ˈärs(ə)nik/ the chemical element of atomic number 33, a brittle steel-gray metalloid. (Symbol: **As**)

▶ *adj.* (**ar·sen·ic**) /ärˈsenik/ of or relating to arsenic. ■ *Chem.* of arsenic with a valence of five; of arsenic(V).

ar·sen·i·cal /ärˈsenikəl/ ▶ *adj.* of or containing arsenic.

ar·son /ˈärsən/ ▶ *n.* the criminal act of deliberately setting fire to property. —**ar·son·ist** /-nist/ *n.*

art¹ /ärt/ ▶ *n.* **1** the expression or application of human creative skill and imagination, typically in a visual form such as painting or sculpture, producing works to be appreciated primarily for their beauty or emotional power: *the art of the Renaissance.* ■ works produced by such skill and imagination: *his collection of modern art.* ■ creative activity resulting in the production of paintings, drawings, or sculpture: *she's good at art.* **2** (**the arts**) the various branches of creative activity, such as painting, music, literature, and dance: *the visual arts* | *the art of photography.* **3** (**arts**) subjects of study primarily concerned with the processes and products of human creativity and social life, such as languages, literature, and history (as contrasted with scientific or technical subjects): *the belief that the arts and sciences were incompatible.* **4** a skill at doing a specified thing, typically one acquired through practice: *the art of conversation.*

art² ▶ *archaic* or dialect 2nd person singular present of BE.

art dec·o ▶ *n.* the predominant decorative art style of the 1920s and 1930s, characterized by precise and boldly delineated geometric shapes and strong colors, and used most notably in household objects and in architecture.

ar·te·ri·al /ärˈti(ə)rēəl/ ▶ *n.* a through road: *sabotaged arterials needed for evacuation of civilians.*

▶ *adj.* of or relating to an artery or arteries. ■ denoting an important route in a system of roads, railroad lines, or rivers: *one of the main arterial routes from New York.*

ar·te·ri·ole /ärˈti(ə)rē,ōl/ ▶ *n.* *Anat.* a small branch of an artery leading into capillaries. —**ar·te·ri·o·lar** /är,ti(ə)rēˈōlər/ *adj.*

ar·te·ri·o·scle·ro·sis /är,ti(ə)rēōskləˈrōsis/ ▶ *n.* *Med.* the thickening and hardening of the walls of the arteries, occurring typically in old age. —**ar·te·ri·o·scle·rot·ic** /-ˈrätik/ *adj.*

ar·ter·y /ˈärtərē/ ▶ *n.* (*pl.* **-ter·ies**) any of the muscular-walled tubes forming part of the circulation system by which blood (mainly that which has been oxygenated) is conveyed from the heart to all parts of the body. Compare with VEIN (sense 1). ■ an important route in a system of roads, rivers, or railroad lines: *the east-west artery.*

art·ful /ˈärtfəl/ ▶ *adj.* **1** (of a person or action) clever or skillful, typically in a crafty or cunning way: *her artful wiles.* **2** showing creative skill or taste: *an artful photograph.* —**art·ful·ly** *adv.* —**art·ful·ness** *n.*

ar·thri·tis /ärˈTHrītis/ ▶ *n.* painful inflammation and stiffness of the joints. —**ar·thrit·ic** /-ˈTHritik/ *adj. & n.*

ar·thro·pod /ˈärTHrə,päd/ ▶ *n.* any of various invertebrates with a segmented body, an external skeleton, and jointed limbs, including insects, spiders, and crustaceans.

ar·thro·scope /ˈärTHrə,skōp/ ▶ *n.* *Med.* an instrument through which the interior of a joint may be inspected or operated on. —**ar·thro·scop·ic** /,ärTHrəˈskäpik/ *adj.* —**ar·thros·co·py** /ärˈTHräskəpē/ *n.*

ar·ti·choke /ˈärti,CHōk/ ▶ *n.* **1** (also **globe artichoke**) a European plant (*Cynara scolymus*) of the daisy family cultivated for its large thistlelike flowerheads. ■ the unopened flowerhead of this, of which the heart and the fleshy bases of the bracts are edible. **2** see JERUSALEM ARTICHOKE.

ar·ti·cle /ˈärtikəl/ ▶ *n.* **1** a particular item or object, typically one of a specified type: *small household articles.* **2** a piece of writing included with others in a newspaper, magazine, or other publication. **3** a separate clause or paragraph of a legal document or agreement, typically one outlining a single rule or regulation: [as *adj.*] *Article 7 of the treaty.* **4** *Gram.* see **DEFINITE ARTICLE, INDEFINITE ARTICLE.**

▶*v.* [*tr.*] (usu. **be articled**) bind by the terms of a contract, as one of apprenticeship.

▶ □ **an article of faith** a firmly held belief: *it was an article of faith that women must free themselves.* □ **the genuine article** a person or thing considered to be an authentic and excellent example of their kind.

ar·tic·u·lar /är'tikyələr/ ▶*adj.* of or relating to a joint or the joints: *articular cartilage.*

ar·tic·u·late ▶*adj.* /är'tikyəlit/ **1** (of a person or a person's words) having or showing the ability to speak fluently and coherently: *an articulate account of their experiences.* **2** having joints or jointed segments.

▶*v.* /-,lāt/ **1** [*tr.*] express (an idea or feeling) fluently and coherently: *they were unable to articulate their emotions.* ■ pronounce (something) clearly and distinctly: *he articulated each word with precision* | [*intr.*] *people who do not articulate well are more difficult to lip-read.* **2** [*intr.*] form a joint: *the mandible is a solid piece* **articulating with the head.** ■ (**be articulated**) be connected by joints: *the wing is articulated to the thorax.* —**ar·tic·u·la·ble** *adj.* —**ar·tic·u·la·cy** /-ləsē/ *n.* —**ar·tic·u·late·ly** *adv.* —**ar·tic·u·late·ness** *n.* —**ar·tic·u·la·tor** /-,lātər/ *n.* —**ar·tic·u·la·to·ry** /-lə,tôrē/ *adj.*

ar·tic·u·la·tion /är,tikyə'lāsHən/ ▶*n.* **1** the action of putting into words an idea or feeling of a specified type: *it would involve the articulation of a theory of the just war.* ■ the formation of clear and distinct sounds in speech: *the articulation of vowels.* ■ *Mus.* clarity in the production of successive notes. ■ *Phonet.* the act or manner of uttering a speech sound, esp. a consonant. **2** the state of being jointed: *the area of articulation of the lower jaw.* ■ a specified joint: *the leg articulation.*

ar·ti·fact /'ärtə,fakt/ (*Brit.* **ar·te·fact**) ▶*n.* **1** an object made by a human being, typically an item of cultural or historical interest: *gold and silver artifacts.* ■ *Archaeol.* such an object as distinguished from a similar object naturally produced. **2** something observed in a scientific investigation or experiment that is not naturally present but occurs as a result of the preparative or investigative procedure. —**ar·ti·fac·tu·al** /,ärtə'fakCHŌŌəl/ *adj.*

ar·ti·fice /'ärtəfis/ ▶*n.* clever or cunning devices or expedients, esp. as used to trick or deceive others: *artifice and outright fakery.*

ar·ti·fi·cial /,ärtə'fisHəl/ ▶*adj.* **1** made or produced by human beings rather than occurring naturally, typically as a copy of something natural: *her skin glowed in the artificial light.* ■ (of a situation or concept) not existing naturally; contrived or false: *the artificial division of people into age groups.* ■ *Bridge* (of a bid) conventional as opposed to natural. **2** (of a person or a person's behavior) insincere or affected: *an artificial smile.* —**ar·ti·fi·ci·al·i·ty** /-,fisHē'alitē/ *n.* —**ar·ti·fi·cial·ly** *adv.*

ar·til·ler·y /är'tilərē/ ▶*n.* (*pl.* **-ler·ies**) large-caliber guns used in warfare on land: *tanks and heavy artillery.* ■ a military detachment or branch of the armed forces that uses such guns. —**ar·til·ler·ist** /-rist/ *n.* —**ar·til·ler·y·man** /-mən/ *n.*

ar·ti·o·dac·tyl /,ärtē-ō'daktl/ ▶*n.* any ungulate with an even number of toes on each foot, including camels, pigs, hippopotamuses, and ruminants.

▶*adj.* of or relating to artiodactyls.

ar·ti·san /'ärtizən/ ▶*n.* a worker in a skilled trade, esp. one that involves making things by hand. —**ar·ti·san·al** /-zənl/ *adj.*

art·ist /'ärtist/ ▶*n.* a person who produces paintings or drawings as a profession or hobby. ■ a person who practices any of the creative arts, such as a sculptor, novelist, poet, or filmmaker. ■ a person skilled at a particular task or occupation: *a surgeon who is an artist with the scalpel.* ■ a performer, such as a singer, actor, or dancer. ■ *inf.* a habitual practitioner of a specified reprehensible activity: *a con artist.* —**art·ist·ry** *n.*

ar·tis·tic /är'tistik/ ▶*adj.* having or revealing natural creative skill: *my lack of artistic ability.* ■ of, relating to, or characteristic of art or artistry: *a denial of artistic freedom.* ■ aesthetically pleasing: *computer programs that produce artistic designs.* —**ar·tis·ti·cal·ly** /-ik(ə)lē/ *adv.*

art·less /'ärtlis/ ▶*adj.* without guile or deception: *an artless, naive girl* | *artless sincerity.* ■ without effort or pretentiousness; natural and simple: *an artless literary masterpiece.* ■ without skill or finesse. —**art·less·ly** *adv.*

art nou·veau /är(t) nōō'vō/ ▶*n.* a style of decorative art, architecture, and design prominent in western Europe and the U.S. from about 1890 until World War I and characterized by intricate linear designs and flowing curves based on natural forms.

arts and crafts ▶*pl. n.* decorative design and handicraft.

art·sy /'ärtsē/ (also **art·y** /'ärtē/) ▶*adj.* (**-si·er, -si·est**) *inf.* making a strong, affected, or pretentious display of being artistic or interested in the arts: *the artsy town of Taos* | *artsy French flicks.* —**art·si·ness** *n.*

art·sy-craft·sy /'kraftsē/ *inf.* ▶*adj.* interested or involved in making decorative, artistic objects, typically ones perceived as quaint or homespun: *artsy-craftsy gift shops.*

art·work /'ärt,wərk/ ▶*n.* illustrations, photographs, or other nontextual material prepared for inclusion in a publication. ■ paintings, drawings, or other artistic works: *a collection of artwork from tribal cultures* | *each artwork is reproduced in color on a full page.*

ar·um /'arəm/ ▶*n.* a North American and European plant that has arrow-shaped leaves and a broad leafy spathe enclosing a club-shaped spadix, and that bears bright red berries in late summer.The **arum family** (Araceae) includes jack-in-the-pulpit, skunk cabbage, philodendrons, and calla lilies.

Ar·y·an /'e(ə)rēən/ ▶*n.* a member of a people speaking an Indo-European language who invaded northern India in the 2nd millennium BC, displacing the Dravidian and other aboriginal peoples. ■ (in Nazi ideology) a person of Caucasian race not of Jewish descent.

▶*adj.* of or relating to this people or their language.

AS ▶*abbr.* ■ Anglo-Saxon. ■ Asperger's syndrome. ■ Associate in Science.

As ▶*symb.* the chemical element arsenic.

as[1] /az/ ▶*adv.* (usu. **as — as**) used in comparisons to refer to the extent or degree of something: *hailstones as big as tennis balls* | *go as fast as you can.* ■ used to emphasize an amount: *as many as twenty-two rare species.*

▶*conj.* **1** used to indicate that something happens during the time when something is taking place: *Frank watched him as he ambled through the crowd.* **2** used to indicate by comparison the way that something happens or is done: *dress as you would if you were having guests* | [as *adv.*] *she kissed him goodbye, as usual.* ■ used to add or interject a comment relating to the statement of a fact: *as you can see, I didn't go after all.* **3** because; since: *I must stop now as I have to go out.* **4** even though: *sweet as he is, he doesn't pay his bills.*

▶*prep.* **1** used to refer to the function or character that someone or something has: *he got a job as a cook.* **2** during the time of being (the thing specified): *he had often been sick as a child.*

▶ □ **as if!** *inf.* I very much doubt it: *You know how lottery winners always say it won't change their lives? Yeah, as if!* □ **as it were** in a way (used to be less precise): *areas that have been, as it were, pushed aside.* □ **as of** used to indicate the time or date from which something starts: *I'm on unemployment as of today.* □ **as to** with respect to; concerning: *decisions as to which patients receive treatment.* □ **as yet** until now or a particular time in the past: *the damage is as yet undetermined.*

as[2] /as/ ▶*n.* (*pl.* **as·ses**) an ancient Roman copper coin.

ASAP (also **asap**) ▶*abbr.* as soon as possible.

as·bes·tos /as'bestəs; az-/ ▶*n.* a fibrous silicate mineral that can be woven into heat-resistant fabrics, and is used in fire-resistant and insulating materials such as brake linings: [as *adj.*] *asbestos shingles.* ▷early 17th cent.: via Latin from Greek *asbestos* 'unquenchable' (applied by Dioscurides to quicklime), from *a-* 'not' + *sbestos* (from *sbennumi* 'quench').

as·bes·to·sis /,asbes'tōsis; ,az-/ ▶*n.* a lung disease resulting from the inhalation of asbestos particles, marked by severe fibrosis and a high risk of mesothelioma (cancer of the pleura).

as·cend /ə'send/ ▶*v.* **1** [*tr.*] go up or climb: *she ascended the stairs* | [*intr.*] *new magmas were created and ascended to the surface.* ■ climb to the summit of (a mountain or hill): *the first traveler to ascend the mountain.* ■ (of a fish or boat) move upstream along (a river). **2** [*intr.*] rise through the air: *we had ascended 3,000 ft.* ■ (of a road or flight of steps) slope or lead up: *the road* **ascends to** *the lake.* ■ move up the social or professional scale: *he took exams to ascend through the ranks.* ■ (**ascend to**) rise to (an important position or a higher level): *some executives ascend to top-level positions.* ■ (of a spiritual being or soul) rise into heaven: *the Prophet ascended to heaven.* ■ (of a sound) rise in pitch.

▶ □ **ascend the throne** become king or queen.

as·cend·an·cy /ə'sendənsē/ (also **as·cend·en·cy**) ▶*n.* occupation of a position of dominant power or influence: *the ascendancy of good over evil.*

as·cend·ant /ə'sendənt/ (also **as·cend·ent**) ▶*adj.* **1** rising in power or influence: *ascendant moderate factions in the party.* **2** *Astrol.* (of a planet, zodiacal degree, or sign) just above the eastern horizon.

▶*n.* *Astrol.* the point on the ecliptic at which it intersects the eastern horizon at a particular time, typically that of a person's birth.

▶ □ **in the ascendant** rising in power or influence.

as·cend·er /ə'sendər/ ▶*n.* a person or thing that ascends, in particular: ■ a part of a letter that extends above the main part (as in *b* and *h*). ■ a letter having such a part. ■ a device used in climbing that can be clipped to a rope to act as a foothold or handhold, or to keep something in position.

as·cen·sion /ə'sensHən/ ▶*n.* the act of rising to an important position or a higher level: *his **ascension** to the ranks of pop star.* ■ (**Ascension**) the ascent of Christ into heaven on the fortieth day after the Resurrection.

as·cent /ə'sent/ ▶*n.* **1** a climb or walk to the summit of a mountain or hill: *the first ascent of the Matterhorn.* ■ an upward slope or path: *the ascent grew steeper.* **2** an instance of rising through the air: *the first balloon ascent was in 1783.* ■ a rise to an important position or a higher level: *his **ascent** to power.*

as·cer·tain /ˌasər'tān/ ▶*v.* [*tr.*] find (something) out for certain; make sure of: *an attempt to ascertain the cause of the accident.* —**as·cer·tain·a·ble** *adj.* —**as·cer·tain·ment** *n.*

as·cet·ic /ə'setik/ ▶*adj.* characterized by or suggesting the practice of severe self-discipline and abstention from all forms of indulgence, typically for religious reasons.
▶*n.* a person who practices such self-discipline and abstention. —**as·cet·i·cal·ly** /-ik(ə)lē/ *adv.* —**as·cet·i·cism** /-ˌsizəm/ *n.*

ASCII /'askē/ *Comput.* ▶*abbr.* American Standard Code for Information Interchange, a set of digital codes representing letters, numerals, and other symbols, widely used as a standard format in the transfer of text between computers.

as·ci·tes /ə'sītēz/ ▶*n. Med.* the accumulation of fluid in the peritoneal cavity, causing abdominal swelling. —**as·cit·ic** /ə'sitik/ *adj.*

a·scor·bic ac·id /ə'skôrbik/ ▶*n.* a vitamin found particularly in citrus fruits and green vegetables. It is essential in maintaining healthy connective tissue, and is also thought to act as an antioxidant. Severe deficiency causes scurvy. Also called **VITAMIN C**. —**a·scor·bate** /-bāt; -bit/ *n.*

as·cot /'as,kät; -kət/ ▶*n.* (also **ascot tie**) a man's broad silk necktie.

as·cribe /ə'skrīb/ ▶*v.* [*tr.*] (**ascribe something to**) attribute something to (a cause): *he ascribed Jane's short temper to her upset stomach.* ■ (usu. **be ascribed to**) attribute (a text, quotation, or work of art) to a particular person or period: *a quotation ascribed to Thomas Cooper.* ■ (usu. **be ascribed to**) regard (a quality) as belonging to: *tough-mindedness is a quality commonly ascribed to top bosses.* —**a·scrib·a·ble** *adj.*

as·crip·tion /ə'skripSHən/ ▶*n.* the attribution of something to a cause: *an **ascription** of effect to cause.* ■ the attribution of a text, quotation, or work of art to a particular person or period: *her **ascription** of the text to Boccaccio.* ■ the action of regarding a quality as belonging to someone or something: *the author's **ascription** of human attributes to his hero.* ■ a preacher's words ascribing praise to God at the end of a sermon.

ASEAN /'äsē,än; 'as-/ ▶*abbr.* Association of Southeast Asian Nations.

a·sep·sis /ā'sepsis/ ▶*n.* the absence of bacteria, viruses, and other microorganisms. ■ the exclusion of bacteria and other microorganisms, typically during surgery. Compare with **ANTISEPSIS**.

a·sep·tic /ā'septik/ ▶*adj.* free from contamination caused by harmful bacteria, viruses, or other microorganisms. ■ (of surgical practice) aiming at the complete exclusion of harmful microorganisms. ■ (of a wound, instrument, or dressing) surgically sterile or sterilized.

a·sex·u·al /ā'seksHōōəl/ ▶*adj.* without sex or sexuality, in particular: ■ *Biol.* (of reproduction) not involving the fusion of gametes. ■ *Biol.* without sex or sexual organs: *asexual parasites.* ■ without sexual feelings or associations. —**a·sex·u·al·i·ty** /āseksHōō'alitē/ *n.* —**a·sex·u·al·ly** *adv.*

ash¹ /asH/ ▶*n.* the powdery residue left after the burning of a substance: *cigarette ash.* ■ (**ashes**) the remains of something destroyed; ruins: *democracies taking root in the ashes of the Soviet empire.* ■ (**ashes**) the remains of the human body after cremation or burning. ■ powdery material ejected by a volcano: *the plains have been showered by volcanic ash.* ■ the mineral component of an organic substance, as assessed from the residue left after burning: *coal contains higher levels of ash than premium fuels.*
▶ □ **rise** (or **emerge**) **from the ashes** be renewed after destruction: *Atlanta has risen from the ashes.*

ash² ▶*n.* **1** (also **ash tree**) a tree (genus *Fraxinus*) of the olive family, with silver-gray bark and compound leaves, widely distributed throughout north temperate regions. Its many species include the North American **white ash** (*F. americana*) and the **European ash** (*F. excelsior*). ■ the hard pale wood of this tree. **2** an Old English runic letter (so named from the word of which it was the first letter). ■ the symbol æ or Æ, used in the Roman alphabet in place of the runic letter, and as a phonetic symbol.

a·shamed /ə'sHāmd/ ▶*adj.* embarrassed or feeling guilt because of something one has done or a characteristic one has: *you should be ashamed of yourself.* ■ (**ashamed to do something**) reluctant to do something through fear of embarrassment or humiliation: *I'm ashamed to say I followed him home.* ■ embarrassed or humiliated to be associated with a person: *his clothes and manners made me ashamed of him.* —**a·sham·ed·ly** /ə'sHāmidlē/ *adv.*

ash blond (also **ash blonde**) ▶*adj.* (of a person or their hair) very pale blond.
▶*n.* a very pale blond color. ■ a person with hair of such a color.

A-shirt ▶*n.* a sleeveless undershirt, with straps over the shoulders.

Ash·ke·naz·i /ˌasHkə'nazē; ˌäsHkə'näzē/ ▶*n.* (*pl.* **-naz·im** /-'nazim; -'näzim/) a Jew of central or eastern European descent. More than 80 percent of Jews today are Ashkenazim. Compare with **SEPHARDI**. —**Ash·ke·naz·ic** /-'nazik; -'nä-/ *adj.*

ash·lar /'asHlər/ ▶*n.* masonry made of large square-cut stones, typically used as a facing on walls of brick or stone.

a·shore /ə'sHôr/ ▶*adv.* to or on the shore from the direction of the sea: *the seals come ashore to breed.* ■ on land as opposed to at sea: *we spent the day ashore.*

ash·ram /'äsHrəm/ ▶*n.* (in the Indian subcontinent) a hermitage, monastic community, or other place of religious retreat for Hindus. ■ a place of religious retreat or community life modeled on the Indian ashram.

ash·tray /'asH,trā/ ▶*n.* a receptacle for tobacco ash and cigarette butts.

ash·y /'asHē/ ▶*adj.* **1** of a pale grayish color: *the ashy shadows of the mountains.* **2** covered with, consisting of, or resembling ashes.

A·sian /'āzHən/ ▶*adj.* of or relating to Asia or its people, customs, or languages.
▶*n.* a native of Asia or a person of Asian descent.

A·si·at·ic /ˌāzHē'atik; ˌāzē-/ ▶*adj.* relating to or deriving from Asia: *Asiatic cholera* | *Asiatic coastal regions.*
▶*n. often offens.* an Asian person.

a·side /ə'sīd/ ▶*adv.* to one side; out of the way: *he pushed his plate aside* | *they stood aside to let a car pass.* ■ in reserve; for future use: *she set aside some money for rent.* ■ used to indicate that one is dismissing something from consideration, or that one is shifting from one topic or tone of discussion to another: *joking aside, I've certainly had my fill.*
▶*n.* **1** a remark or passage by a character in a play that is intended to be heard by the audience but unheard by the other characters in the play. ■ a remark not intended to be heard by everyone present: *"Does that make him a murderer?" whispered Alice in an aside to Fred.* **2** a remark that is not directly related to the main topic of discussion: *the recipe book has little asides about the importance of home and family.*
▶ □ **take** (or **draw**) **someone aside** move someone away from a group of people in order to talk privately.

as·i·nine /'asə,nīn/ ▶*adj.* extremely stupid or foolish: *Lydia ignored his asinine remark.* —**as·i·nin·i·ty** /ˌasə'ninitē/ *n.*

ask /ask/ ▶*v.* **1** [*tr.*] say something in order to obtain an answer or some information: *he asked if she wanted coffee* | *people are always asking questions* | [*intr.*] *the old man asked about her job.* ■ [*intr.*] (**ask around**) talk to various people in order to find something out: *there are fine meals to be had if you ask around.* ■ [*intr.*] (**ask after**) inquire about the health or well-being of: *Mrs. Savage asked after Iris's mother.* **2** [*tr.*] request (someone) to do or give something: *Mary asked her father for money* | [*intr.*] *don't be afraid to ask for advice.* ■ request permission to do something: *she asked if she could move in.* ■ [*intr.*] (**ask for**) request to speak to: *when I arrived, I asked for Catherine.* ■ request (a specified amount) as a price for selling something: *he was asking $250 for the guitar.* ■ expect or demand (something) of someone: *it's asking a lot, but could you look through Billy's things?* **3** [*tr.*] invite (someone) to one's home or a function: *it's about time we asked Pam to dinner.* ■ (**ask someone along**) invite someone to join one on an outing. ■ (**ask someone out**) invite someone out socially, typically on a date.
▶*n.* **1** a request, especially for a donation: *an ask for more funding.* **2** the price at which an item, esp. a financial security, is offered for sale: [as *adj.*] *ask prices for bonds.* —**ask·er** *n.*
▶ □ **be asking for it** (or **trouble**) *inf.* behave in a way that is likely to result in difficulty for oneself: *they accused me of asking for it.* □ **for the asking** used to indicate that something can be easily obtained: *the job was his for the asking.*

a·skance /ə'skans/ (also **a·skant** /ə'skant/) ▶*adv.* with an attitude or look of suspicion or disapproval: *a waiter looked askance at my jeans.*

a·skew /ə'skyōō/ ▶*adv. & adj.* not in a straight or level position: [as *adv.*] *the door was hanging askew on one twisted hinge* | [as *adj.*] *her hat was slightly askew.* ■ *fig.* wrong; awry: [as *adv.*] *the plan went sadly askew* | [as *adj.*] *outrageous humor with a decidedly askew point of view.*

a·slant /ə'slant/ ▶*adv.* at an angle or in a sloping direction: *some of the paintings hung aslant.*

Pronunciation Key ə *ago,* up; ər *over,* fur; a *hat;* ā *ate;* ä *car;* CH *chin;* e *let;* ē *see;* e(ə)r *air;* i *fit;* ī *by;* i(ə)r *ear;* NG *sing;* ō *go;* ô *law, for;* oi *toy;* ōō *good;* ōō *goo;* ou *out;* sH *she;* TH *thin;* TH *then;* (h)w *why;* zH *vision*

A

▸*prep.* across at an angle or in a sloping direction: *rays of light fell aslant a door.*

a·sleep /əˈslēp/ ▸*adj. & adv.* in or into a state of sleep: [as *adj.*] *she had been asleep for over three hours* | [as *adv.*] *Bob regularly fell asleep in his recliner.* ■ not attentive or alert; inactive: [as *adj.*] *the competition was not asleep.* ■ (of a limb) having no feeling; numb: [as *adj.*] *his legs were asleep.* ■ *poetic/lit.* used euphemistically to say that someone is dead.
▸ □ **asleep at the switch** (or **wheel**) *inf.* not attentive or alert; inactive.

a·so·cial /āˈsōsHəl/ ▸*adj.* avoiding social interaction; inconsiderate of or hostile to others.

asp /asp/ ▸*n.* (also **asp viper**) a small southern European viper (*Vipera aspis*) with an upturned snout. ■ another term for **EGYPTIAN COBRA**.

ASP ▸*abbr.* application service provider, a company providing Internet access to software applications that would otherwise have to be installed on individual computers.

as·par·a·gus /əˈsparəgəs; əˈspe(ə)r-/ ▸*n.* a tall plant (*Asparagus officinalis*) of the lily family with fine feathery foliage, cultivated for its edible shoots. ■ the tender young shoots of this plant, eaten as a vegetable.

as·par·tame /ˈaspärˌtām/ ▸*n.* a very sweet substance used as an artificial sweetener, chiefly in low-calorie products.

ASPCA ▸*abbr.* American Society for the Prevention of Cruelty to Animals.

as·pect /ˈaspekt/ ▸*n.* **1** a particular part or feature of something: *the financial aspect can be overstressed.* ■ a specific way in which something can be considered: *from every aspect, theirs was a changing world.* ■ a particular appearance or quality: *a man of decidedly foreign aspect.* **2** the positioning of a building or thing in a specified direction: *a greenhouse with a southern aspect.* ■ the side of a building facing a particular direction: *the front aspect of the hotel.* **3** *Gram.* a grammatical category or form that expresses the way in which time is denoted by the verb: *the semantics of tense and aspect.* —**as·pec·tu·al** /aˈspekCHŌŌəl/ *adj.*

as·pen /ˈaspən/ ▸*n.* a poplar tree with rounded, long-stalked, and typically coarsely-toothed leaves that tremble in even a slight breeze.

As·per·ger's syn·drome /ˈaspərgərz/ ▸*n.* a developmental disorder related to autism and characterized by higher than average intellectual ability coupled with impaired social skills and restrictive, repetitive patterns of interest and activities.

as·per·i·ty /əˈsperitē/ ▸*n.* (*pl.* **-ties**) harshness of tone or manner: *he pointed this out with some asperity.* ■ (**asperities**) harsh qualities or conditions: *the asperities of a harsh and divided society.* ■ (usu. **asperities**) a rough edge on a surface: *the asperities of the metal surfaces.*

as·per·sion /əˈspərzHən/ ▸*n.* (usu. **aspersions**) an attack on the reputation or integrity of someone or something: *I don't think anyone is casting aspersions on you.*

as·phalt /ˈasfôlt/ ▸*n.* a mixture of dark bituminous pitch with sand or gravel, used for surfacing roads, flooring, roofing, etc. ■ the pitch used in this mixture, usually made by the distillation of crude oil.
▸*v.* [*tr.*] cover with asphalt. —**as·phal·tic** /asˈfôltik/ *adj.*

as·pho·del /ˈasfəˌdel/ ▸*n.* **1** a Eurasian plant (genera *Asphodelus* and *Asphodeline*) of the lily family, typically having long slender leaves and flowers borne on a spike. **2** *poetic/lit.* an immortal flower said to grow in the Elysian fields.

as·phyx·i·a /asˈfiksēə/ ▸*n.* a condition arising when the body is deprived of oxygen, causing unconsciousness or death; suffocation. —**as·phyx·i·al** *adj.* —**as·phyx·i·ant** /-sēənt/ *adj. & n.*

as·phyx·i·ate /asˈfiksēˌāt/ ▸*v.* [*tr.*] (usu. **be asphyxiated**) kill (someone) by depriving them of air. ■ [*intr.*] die in this way: *they slowly asphyxiated.* —**as·phyx·i·a·tion** /asˌfiksēˈāsHən/ *n.*

as·pic /ˈaspik/ ▸*n.* a savory jelly, often made with meat stock, used as a garnish, or to contain pieces of food such as meat, seafood, or eggs, set in a mold. ▷late 18th cent.: from French, literally 'asp,' from the colors of the jelly as compared with those of the snake.

as·pi·dis·tra /ˌaspiˈdistrə/ ▸*n.* a bulbous plant (genus *Aspidistra*) of the lily family, with broad tapering leaves, native to eastern Asia and often grown as a houseplant.

as·pir·ant /ˈaspərənt; əˈspī-/ ▸*adj.* (of a person) having ambitions to achieve something, typically to follow a particular career.
▸*n.* a person who has ambitions to achieve something.

as·pi·rate ▸*v.* /ˈaspəˌrāt/ [*tr.*] **1** *Phonet.* pronounce (a sound) with an exhalation of breath. ■ [*intr.*] pronounce the sound *h* at the beginning of a word. **2** (usu. **be aspirated**) *Med.* draw (fluid) by suction from a vessel or cavity. ■ draw fluid in such a way from (a vessel or cavity). ■ breathe (something) in; inhale: *some drowning victims don't aspirate any water.*
▸*n.* /ˈasp(ə)rit/ *Phonet.* an aspirated consonant. ■ the sound *h* or a character used to represent this sound.

▸*adj.* /ˈasp(ə)rit/ *rare Phonet.* (of a sound) pronounced with an exhalation of breath; aspirated.

as·pi·ra·tion /ˌaspəˈrāsHən/ ▸*n.* **1** (usu. **aspirations**) a hope or ambition of achieving something: *he had nothing tangible to back up his literary aspirations.* ■ the object of such an ambition; a goal: *fabrics and oriental rugs were my aspirations.* **2** the action of pronouncing a sound with an exhalation of breath. **3** *Med.* the action of drawing fluid by suction from a vessel or cavity. —**as·pi·ra·tion·al** /-sHənl/ *adj.*

as·pi·ra·tor /ˈaspəˌrātər/ ▸*n.* *Med.* an instrument or apparatus for aspirating fluid from a vessel or cavity.

as·pire /əˈspī(ə)r/ ▸*v.* [*intr.*] direct one's hopes or ambitions toward achieving something: *we never thought that we might aspire to those heights.* ■ *poetic/lit.* rise high; tower.

as·pi·rin /ˈasp(ə)rin/ ▸*n.* a synthetic compound, $C_9H_8O_4$, used medicinally to relieve mild or chronic pain and to reduce fever and inflammation. ■ (*pl.* same or **aspirins**) a tablet containing this.

a·squint /əˈskwint/ ▸*adv. & adj.* with a glance to one side or from the corner of the eyes: [as *adv.*] *a woman looked asquint at me.*

ass¹ /as/ ▸*n.* **1** a hoofed mammal (genus *Equus*) of the horse family with a braying call, typically smaller than a horse and with longer ears. The two species are *E. africanus* of Africa, which is the ancestor of the domestic ass or donkey, and *E. hemionus* of Asia. ■ (in general use) a donkey. **2** *inf.* a foolish or stupid person.
▸*phrasal v.* □ **make an ass of oneself** *inf.* behave in a way that makes one look foolish or stupid.

ass² (*Brit.* **arse**) ▸*n.* *vulgar slang* a person's buttocks or anus. ■ a stupid, irritating, or contemptible person. ■ women regarded as a source of sexual gratification. ■ oneself (used in phrases for emphasis): *get your ass in here fast* | *the bureaucrat who wants everything in writing so as to cover his ass.* —**assed** /ast/ *adj.* [in *comb.*] *fat-assed guys.*

as·sail /əˈsāl/ ▸*v.* [*tr.*] make a concerted or violent attack on: *the Scots army assailed Edward's army from the rear.* ■ (usu. **be assailed**) (of an unpleasant feeling or physical sensation) come upon (someone) suddenly and strongly: *she was assailed by doubts and regrets.* ■ criticize (someone) strongly. —**as·sail·a·ble** *adj.*

as·sail·ant /əˈsālənt/ ▸*n.* a person who physically attacks another.

as·sas·sin /əˈsasin/ ▸*n.* a murderer of an important person in a surprise attack for political or religious reasons. ■ (**Assassin**) *hist.* a member of a sect of Muslims at the time of the Crusades.

as·sas·si·nate /əˈsasəˌnāt/ ▸*v.* (often **be assassinated**) murder (an important person) in a surprise attack for political or religious reasons. —**as·sas·si·na·tion** /əˌsasəˈnāsHən/ *n.*

as·sault /əˈsôlt/ ▸*v.* [*tr.*] make a physical attack on: *he pleaded guilty to assaulting a police officer.* ■ *fig.* attack or bombard (someone or the senses) with something undesirable or unpleasant: *her right ear was assaulted with a tide of music.* ■ carry out a military attack or raid on (an enemy position): *they left their strong position to assault the hill.* ■ rape.
▸*n.* **1** a physical attack: *his imprisonment for an assault on the film director.* ■ *Law* an act, criminal or wrongful, that threatens physical harm to a person, whether or not actual harm is done: *charged with assault.* ■ a military attack or raid on an enemy position: *troops began an assault on the city.* ■ a strong verbal attack. **2** a concerted attempt to do something demanding: *a winter assault on Mt. Everest.* —**as·sault·er** *n.*

as·sault and bat·ter·y ▸*n.* *Law* the crime of threatening a person together with the act of making physical contact with them.

as·say /ˈaˌsā; aˈsā/ ▸*n.* the testing of a metal or ore to determine its ingredients and quality: *submission of plate for assay.* ■ a procedure for measuring the biochemical or immunological activity of a sample: *each assay was performed in duplicate.*
▸*v.* [*tr.*] **1** determine the content or quality of (a metal or ore). ■ determine the biochemical or immunological activity of (a sample): *cell contents were assayed for enzyme activity.* ■ examine (something) in order to assess its nature: *stepping inside, I quickly assayed the clientele.* **2** *archaic* attempt: *I assayed a little joke of mine on him.* —**as·say·er** *n.*

as·sem·blage /əˈsemblij/ ▸*n.* a collection or gathering of things or people: *a wondrous assemblage of noble knights, cruel temptresses, and impossible loves.* ■ a machine or object made of pieces fitted together: *some vast assemblage of gears and cogs.* ■ a work of art made by grouping found or unrelated objects. ■ the action of gathering or fitting things together.

as·sem·ble /əˈsembəl/ ▸*v.* **1** [*intr.*] (of people) gather together in one place for a common purpose: *a crowd had assembled.* ■ [*tr.*] bring (people or things) together for a common purpose: *he assembled the surviving members of the group for a tour.* ■ [usu. as *n.*] (**assembling**) *Entomol.* (of male moths) gather for mating in response to a pheromone released by a female. **2** [*tr.*] fit together the separate component parts of (a machine or other object): *a factory that assembled parts for trucks.* ■ *Comput.* translate (a program) from low-level symbolic code into machine code.

as·sem·bler /əˈsemblər/ ▶ *n.* **1** a person who assembles a machine or its parts. **2** *Comput.* a program for converting instructions written in low-level symbolic code into machine code.

as·sem·bly /əˈsemblē/ ▶ *n.* (*pl.* **-blies**) **1** a group of people gathered together in one place for a common purpose: *an assembly of scholars.* ■ a group of people elected to make laws or decisions for a particular country or region, esp. the lower legislative house in some U.S. states: *the Connecticut General Assembly.* **2** the action of gathering together as a group for a common purpose: *freedom of assembly.* ■ a regular gathering of the teachers and students of a school. ■ **3** [often as *adj.*] the action of fitting together the component parts of a machine or other object: *a car assembly plant.* ■ a unit consisting of components that have been fitted together: *the tail assembly of the aircraft.* ■ [usu. as *adj.*] *Comput.* the conversion of instructions in low-level code to machine code by an assembler.

as·sent /əˈsent/ ▶ *n.* the expression of approval or agreement: *a loud murmur of assent* | *he nodded assent.* ■ official agreement or sanction: *the governor has power to withhold his assent from a bill.*
▶ *v.* [*intr.*] express approval or agreement, typically officially: *Roosevelt assented to the agreement.* **—as·sent·er** *n.*

as·sert /əˈsərt/ ▶ *v.* [*tr.*] state a fact or belief confidently and forcefully: *the company asserts that the cuts will not affect development* | *he asserted his innocence.* ■ cause others to recognize (one's authority or a right) by confident and forceful behavior: *the good librarian is able to assert authority when required.* ■ (**assert oneself**) behave or speak in a confident and forceful manner: *it was time to assert himself.* **—as·sert·er** *n.*

as·ser·tion /əˈsərSHən/ ▶ *n.* a confident and forceful statement of fact or belief: *his assertion that his father had deserted the family.* ■ the action of stating something or exercising authority confidently and forcefully: *the assertion of his legal rights.*

as·ser·tive /əˈsərtiv/ ▶ *adj.* having or showing a confident and forceful personality. **—as·ser·tive·ly** *adv.* **—as·ser·tive·ness** *n.*

as·sess /əˈses/ ▶ *v.* [*tr.*] evaluate or estimate the nature, ability, or quality of: *the committee must assess the relative importance of the issues.* ■ (usu. **be assessed**) calculate or estimate the price or value of: *the damage was assessed at $5 billion.* ■ (often **be assessed**) set the value of a tax, fine, etc., for (a person or property) at a specified level: *all empty properties will be assessed at 50 percent.* **—as·sess·a·ble** *adj.* **—as·sess·ment** *n.*

as·ses·sor /əˈsesər/ ▶ *n.* a person who assesses someone or something, in particular: ■ a person who calculates or estimates the value of something or an amount to be paid, chiefly for tax or insurance purposes. ■ a person who is knowledgeable in a particular field and is called upon for advice, typically by a judge or committee of inquiry.

as·set /ˈaset/ ▶ *n.* a useful or valuable thing, person, or quality: *the school is an asset to the community.* ■ (usu. **assets**) property owned by a person or company, regarded as having value and available to meet debts, commitments, or legacies: *growth in net assets.* ■ (**assets**) military equipment, such as planes, ships, communications and radar installations, employed or targeted in military operations.

as·sev·er·a·tion /əˌsevəˈrāSHən/ ▶ *n.* the solemn or emphatic declaration or statement of something: *I fear that you offer only unsupported asseveration.* **—as·sev·er·ate** /əˈsevəˌrāt/ *v.*

ass·hole /ˈasˌhōl/ ▶ *n. vulgar slang* the anus. ■ an irritating or contemptible person.

as·si·du·i·ty /ˌasiˈd(y)o͞oitē/ ▶ *n.* (*pl.* **-ties**) constant or close attention to what one is doing. ■ (**assiduities**) *archaic* or *poetic/lit.* constant attentions to someone.

as·sid·u·ous /əˈsijo͞oəs/ ▶ *adj.* showing great care and perseverance. **—as·sid·u·ous·ly** *adv.* **—as·sid·u·ous·ness** *n.*

as·sign /əˈsīn/ ▶ *v.* [*tr.*] **1** allocate (a job or duty): *Congress assigned the task to the agency.* ■ (often **be assigned**) appoint (someone) to a particular job, task, or organization: *she has been assigned to a new job.* **2** designate or set (something) aside for a specific purpose: *managers happily assign large sums of money to travel budgets.* ■ (**assign something to**) attribute something as belonging to: *it is difficult to decide whether to assign the victory to Goodwin.* **3** transfer (legal rights or liabilities): *they will ask you to assign your rights against the airline.*
▶ *n. Law* another term for **ASSIGNEE** (sense 1). **—as·sign·a·ble** *adj.* (in sense 3 of the *verb*). **—as·sign·er** *n.* **—as·sign·or** /əˈsīnər/ *n.*

as·sig·na·tion /ˌasigˈnāSHən/ ▶ *n.* **1** an appointment to meet someone in secret, typically one made by lovers: *his assignation with an older*

woman. **2** the allocation or attribution of someone or something as belonging to something.

as·sign·ee /əˌsīˈnē/ ▶ *n. chiefly Law* **1** a person to whom a right or liability is legally transferred. **2** a person appointed to act for another.

as·sign·ment /əˈsīnmənt/ ▶ *n.* **1** a task or piece of work assigned to someone as part of a job or course of study: *a homework assignment.* ■ the allocation of a job or task to someone. ■ the task or post to which one has been appointed. **2** the attribution of someone or something as belonging to: *the assignment of individuals to particular social positions.* **3** an act of making a legal transfer of a right, property, or liability: *an assignment of leasehold property.* ■ a document effecting such a transfer.

as·sim·i·late /əˈsiməˌlāt/ ▶ *v.* [*tr.*] **1** take in (information, ideas, or culture) and understand fully. ■ (usu. **be assimilated**) absorb and integrate (people, ideas, or culture) into a wider society or culture: *pop trends are assimilated into the mainstream with alarming speed* | [*intr.*] *the converts were assimilated into the society of their conquerors.* ■ absorb and integrate and use for one's own benefit: *the music business assimilated whatever aspects of punk it could turn into profit.* ■ (usu. **be assimilated**) (of the body or any biological system) absorb and digest (food or nutrients): *the sugars in the fruit are readily assimilated by the body.* **2** cause (something) to resemble; liken. ■ [*intr.*] come to resemble: *the churches assimilated to a certain cultural norm.* ■ *Phonet.* make (a sound) more like another in the same or next word. **—as·sim·i·la·ble** /-ləbəl/ *adj.* **—as·sim·i·la·tion** /əˌsiməˈlāSHən/ *n.* **—as·sim·i·la·tive** /-ˌlātiv; -lətiv/ *adj.* **—as·sim·i·la·tor** /-ˌlātər/ *n.* **—as·sim·i·la·to·ry** /-ləˌtôrē/ *adj.*

As·sin·i·boin /əˈsinəˌboin/ (also **As·sin·i·boine**) ▶ *n.* (*pl.* same or **-boins**) **1** a member of an American Indian people formerly living in southern Manitoba, but now living in Montana, Alberta, and Saskatchewan. **2** the Siouan language of this people.
▶ *adj.* of or relating to the Assiniboin or their language.

as·sist /əˈsist/ ▶ *v.* [*tr.*] help (someone), typically by doing a share of the work: *a senior academic would assist him in his work* | [*intr.*] *their presence would assist in keeping the peace.* ■ help by providing money or information: *they were assisting police with their inquiries* | [*intr.*] *funds to assist with capital investment.* ■ [*intr.*] be present as a helper or spectator: *two midwives who assisted at a water birth.*
▶ *n.* an act of help, typically by providing money: *the budget must have an assist from tax policies.* ■ (chiefly in ice hockey, basketball, or baseball) the act of touching the puck or ball in a play in which a teammate scores or an opposing batter is put out. ■ [in *comb.*] a mechanical device that provides help: *the implant is a ventricular-assist device.* **—as·sis·tance** *n.* **—as·sist·er** *n.*

as·sis·tant /əˈsistənt/ ▶ *n.* a person who ranks below a senior person: *the managing director and his assistant* | [as *adj.*] *an assistant manager.* ■ a person who helps in particular work: *a laboratory assistant.*

as·so·ci·ate ▶ *v.* /əˈsōsēˌāt/ [*tr.*] connect (someone or something) with something else in one's mind: *I associated wealth with freedom.* ■ (usu. **be associated**) connect (something) with something else because they occur together or one produces another: *the environmental problems associated with nuclear waste.* ■ (**associate oneself with**) allow oneself to be connected with or seen to be supportive of: *I cannot associate myself with some of the language used.* ■ (**be associated with**) be involved with: *she has been associated with the project from the first.* ■ [*intr.*] meet or have dealings with someone commonly regarded with disapproval: *she began associating with socialists.*
▶ *n.* /-it/ **1** a partner or colleague in business or at work. ■ a companion or friend. **2** a person with limited or subordinate membership in an organization. ■ a person who holds an academic degree conferred by a junior college (only in titles or set expressions): *an associate's degree in science* | *an Associate of Arts.*
▶ *adj.* /-it/ joined or connected with an organization or business: *an associate company.* ■ denoting shared function or membership but with a lesser status: *associate director.* **—as·so·ci·a·bil·i·ty** /əˌsōSH(ē)əˈbilitē; -SHē-/ *n.* **—as·so·ci·a·ble** /əˈsōSH(ē)əbəl; -SHē-/ *adj.* **—as·so·ci·ate·ship** /-ˌSHip/ *n.*

as·so·ci·a·tion /əˌsōsēˈāSHən; -SHē-/ ▶ *n.* **1** (abbr.: **assn.**) (often in names) a group of people organized for a joint purpose: *the National Association of Broadcasters.* ■ *Ecol.* a plant community defined by a characteristic group of dominant plant species. **2** a connection or cooperative link between people or organizations: *he developed a close association with the university.* ■ the action or state of becoming a member of an organization with subordinate status. ■ *Chem.* the linking of molecules through hydrogen bonding or other interaction short of full bond formation. **3** (usu. **associations**) a mental connection between ideas or things: *the word bureaucracy has unpleasant associations.* ▪ the action of making such a connection. ▪ the fact of occurring with something else; co-occurrence: *cases of cancer found in association with colitis.* —**as·so·ci·a·tion·al** /-ʃənl/ *adj.*

as·so·ci·a·tive /əˈsōsēˌātiv; -shē-; -sēətiv; -shətiv/ ▸ *adj.* **1** of or involving the action of associating ideas or things: *an associative, nonlinear mode of thought.* ▪ *Comput.* of or denoting computer storage in which items are identified by content rather than by address. **2** *Math.* involving the condition that a group of quantities connected by operators gives the same result whatever their grouping, as long as their order remains the same, e.g., $(a \times b) \times c = a \times (b \times c)$.

as·so·nance /ˈasənəns/ ▸ *n.* in poetry, the repetition of the sound of a vowel or diphthong in nonrhyming stressed syllables near enough to each other for the echo to be discernible (e.g., *penitence, reticence*). Compare with **ALLITERATION.** —**as·so·nant** *adj.* —**as·so·nate** /-ˌnāt/ *v.*

as·sort /əˈsôrt/ ▸ *v.* **1** [*intr.*] *Genetics* (of genes or characters) become distributed among cells or progeny. **2** [*tr.*] *archaic* place in a group; classify: *he would assort it with the fabulous dogs as a monstrous invention.*

as·sort·ed /əˈsôrtid/ ▸ *adj.* of various sorts put together; miscellaneous: *bowls in assorted colors.*

as·sort·ment /əˈsôrtmənt/ ▸ *n.* a miscellaneous collection of things or people: *the room was filled with an assortment of clothes.*

as·suage /əˈswāj/ ▸ *v.* [*tr.*] make (an unpleasant feeling) less intense: *the letter assuaged the fears of most members.* ▪ satisfy (an appetite or desire): *an opportunity occurred to assuage her desire for knowledge.* ▹Middle English: from Old French *assouagier, asouagier,* based on Latin *ad-* 'to' (expressing change) + *suavis* 'sweet.' —**as·suage·ment** *n.*

as·sume /əˈsōōm/ ▸ *v.* [*tr.*] **1** suppose to be the case, without proof: *you're afraid of what people are going to assume about me.* **2** take or begin to have (power or responsibility). ▪ seize (power or control): *the rebels assumed control of the capital.* **3** take on (a specified quality, appearance, or extent): *militant activity had assumed epidemic proportions.* ▪ adopt falsely: *Oliver assumed an expression of penitence* | [as *adj.*] (**assumed**) *a man living under an assumed name.* —**as·sum·ed·ly** /-midlē/ *adv.*

as·sum·ing /əˈsōōmiNG/ ▸ *conj.* used for the purpose of argument to indicate a premise on which a statement can be based: *assuming that the treaty is ratified, what is its relevance?*
▸ *adj. archaic* arrogant or presumptuous.

as·sump·tion /əˈsəm(p)sHən/ ▸ *n.* **1** a thing that is accepted as true or as certain to happen, without proof: *they made certain assumptions about the market.* **2** the action of taking or beginning to take power or responsibility: *the assumption of an active role in regional settlements.* **3** (**Assumption**) the reception of the Virgin Mary bodily into heaven. This was formally declared a doctrine of the Roman Catholic Church in 1950. ▪ the feast in honor of this, celebrated on August 15.

as·sur·ance /əˈsHŏŏrəns/ ▸ *n.* **1** a positive declaration intended to give confidence; a promise: *he gave an assurance that work would commence on Wednesday.* **2** confidence or certainty in one's own abilities. ▪ certainty about something: *assurance of faith depends on our trust in God.* **3** *chiefly Brit.* insurance, specifically life insurance.

as·sure /əˈsHŏŏr/ ▸ *v.* [*tr.*] **1** tell someone something positively or confidently to dispel any doubts they may have: *Tony assured me that there was a supermarket in the village.* | [*tr.*] *they assured him of their full confidence.* ▪ make (someone) sure of something: *you would be assured of a fine welcome.* **2** (often **be assured**) make (something) certain to happen: *victory was now assured.* —**as·sur·er** *n.*

AST ▸ *abbr.* Atlantic Standard Time (see **ATLANTIC TIME**).

as·ta·tine /ˈastəˌtēn; -tin/ ▸ *n.* the chemical element of atomic number 85, a radioactive member of the halogen group. (Symbol: **At**)

as·ter /ˈastər/ ▸ *n.* **1** a plant (genus *Aster*) of the daisy family that has bright rayed flowers, typically purple or pink. Many species, including the **New England aster** (*A. novae-angliae*), bloom in autumn. **2** *Biol.* a star-shaped structure formed during division of the nucleus of an animal cell.

as·ter·isk /ˈastəˌrisk/ ▸ *n.* a symbol (*) used to mark printed or written text, typically as a reference to an annotation or to stand for omitted matter. ▪ a thing resembling a star in shape: *soft asterisks of pollen.*
▸ *v.* [*tr.*] [usu. as *adj.*] (**asterisked**) mark (printed or written text) with an asterisk: *asterisked entries.*

a·stern /əˈstərn/ ▸ *adv.* **1** behind or toward the rear of a ship or aircraft: *the engine rooms lay astern.* **2** (of a ship) backward: *the lifeboat was carried astern by the tide.*

as·ter·oid /ˈastəˌroid/ ▸ *n.* a small rocky body orbiting the sun. Large numbers of these, ranging in size from nearly 600 miles (1,000 km)

across to dust particles, are found (as the **asteroid belt**) esp. between the orbits of Mars and Jupiter. —**as·ter·oi·dal** /ˌastəˈroidl/ *adj.*

as·the·ni·a /asˈTHēnēə/ ▸ *n. Med.* abnormal physical weakness or lack of energy.

asth·ma /ˈazmə/ ▸ *n.* a respiratory condition marked by spasms in the bronchi of the lungs, causing difficulty in breathing. It usually results from an allergic reaction or other forms of hypersensitivity.

asth·mat·ic /azˈmatik/ ▸ *adj.* relating to or suffering from asthma.
▸ *n.* a person who suffers from asthma. —**asth·mat·i·cal·ly** /-ik(ə)lē/ *adv.*

a·stig·ma·tism /əˈstigməˌtizəm/ ▸ *n.* a defect in the eye or in a lens caused by a deviation from spherical curvature, which results in distorted images, as light rays are prevented from meeting at a common focus. —**as·tig·mat·ic** /ˌastigˈmatik/ *adj.*

a·stir /əˈstər/ ▸ *adj.* in a state of excited movement: *the streets are all astir.* ▪ awake and out of bed: *he woke before anyone else was astir.*

as·ton·ish /əˈstäniSH/ ▸ *v.* [*tr.*] surprise or impress (someone) greatly: *you never fail to astonish me* | *it astonished her that he could seem so anxious.* —**as·ton·ish·ing·ly** *adv.* —**as·ton·ish·ment** *n.*

as·tound /əˈstound/ ▸ *v.* [*tr.*] shock or greatly surprise: *her bluntness astounded him.* —**as·tound·ing** *adj.*

as·tral /ˈastrəl/ ▸ *adj.* of, connected with, or resembling the stars. ▪ of or relating to a supposed nonphysical realm of existence to which various psychic and paranormal phenomena are ascribed, and in which the physical human body is said to have a counterpart.

a·stray /əˈstrā/ ▸ *adv.* **1** away from the correct path or direction: *we went astray but a man redirected us.* **2** into error or morally questionable behavior: *he was led astray by boozy colleagues.*

a·stride /əˈstrīd/ ▸ *prep.* with a leg on each side of: *he was sitting astride the bike* | *a figure astride a horse* | [as *adv.*] *he sat on the chair astride.* ▪ extending across: *the port stands astride an international route* | *why do people build their dream homes astride some seismic fault?* ▪ [as *adv.*] with legs apart: *he stood, legs astride.*

as·trin·gent /əˈstrinjənt/ ▸ *adj.* **1** causing the contraction of body tissues, typically of the skin: *an astringent skin lotion.* **2** sharp or severe in manner or style. ▪ (of taste or smell) sharp or bitter.
▸ *n.* a substance that causes the contraction of body tissues, typically used to protect the skin and to reduce bleeding from minor abrasions. —**as·trin·gen·cy** *n.* —**as·trin·gent·ly** *adv.*

as·tro·labe /ˈastrəˌlāb/ ▸ *n. chiefly hist.* an instrument formerly used to make astronomical measurements, typically of the altitudes of celestial bodies, and in navigation for calculating latitude, before the development of the sextant.

as·trol·o·gy /əˈsträləjē/ ▸ *n.* the study of the movements and relative positions of celestial bodies interpreted as having an influence on human affairs and the natural world. —**as·trol·o·ger** /-jər/ *n.* —**as·tro·log·i·cal** /ˌastrəˈläjikəl/ *adj.* —**as·trol·o·gist** /-jist/ *n.*

as·tro·naut /ˈastrəˌnôt/ ▸ *n.* a person who is trained to travel in a spacecraft. —**as·tro·nau·ti·cal** /ˌastrəˈnôtikəl/ *adj.*

as·tro·nau·tics /ˌastrəˈnôtiks/ ▸ *n.* the science and technology of human space travel and exploration.

as·tro·nom·i·cal /ˌastrəˈnämikəl/ ▸ *adj.* **1** of or relating to astronomy. **2** *inf.* (of an amount) extremely large: *he wanted an astronomical fee.* —**as·tro·nom·ic** *adj.* —**as·tro·nom·i·cal·ly** /-ik(ə)lē/ *adv.*

as·tron·o·my /əˈstränəmē/ ▸ *n.* the branch of science that deals with celestial objects, space, and the physical universe as a whole. —**as·tron·o·mer** *n.*

as·tro·phys·ics /ˌastrōˈfiziks/ ▸ *n.* the branch of astronomy concerned with the physical nature of stars and other celestial bodies, and the application of the laws and theories of physics to the interpretation of astronomical observations. —**as·tro·phys·i·cal** /-ikəl/ *adj.* —**as·tro·phys·i·cist** /-isist/ *n.*

As·tro·Turf /ˈastrōˌtərf/ ▸ *n. trademark* an artificial grass surface, used for athletic fields. —**As·tro·Turfed** *adj.*

as·tute /əˈst(y)ōōt/ ▸ *adj.* having or showing an ability to accurately assess situations or people and turn this to one's advantage: *an astute businessman.* —**as·tute·ly** *adv.* —**as·tute·ness** *n.*

a·sun·der /əˈsəndər/ ▸ *adv. archaic or poetic/lit.* apart; divided: *those whom God hath joined together let no man put asunder.* ▪ into pieces: *the desk burst asunder.*

a·sy·lum /əˈsīləm/ ▸ *n.* **1** (also **political asylum**) the protection granted by a nation to someone who has left their native country as a political refugee: *granting asylum to foreigners persecuted for political reasons.* ▪ shelter or protection from danger: *asylum for those too ill to care for themselves.* **2** *dated* an institution for the care of the mentally ill. ▹late Middle English (in the sense 'place of refuge,' esp. for criminals): via Latin from Greek *asulon* 'refuge,' from *asulos* 'inviolable,' from *a-* 'without' + *sulon* 'right of seizure.' The current senses date from the 18th cent.

a·sym·me·try /ā'simitrē/ ▶ *n.* (*pl.* **-tries**) lack of equality or equivalence between parts or aspects of something; lack of symmetry. —**a·sym·met·ric** /ˌāsi'metrik/ *adj.* —**a·sym·met·ri·cal** *adj.*

a·symp·to·mat·ic /ˌāsim(p)tə'matik/ ▶ *adj. Med.* (of a condition or a person) producing or showing no symptoms.

a·syn·chro·nous /ā'siNGkrənəs/ ▶ *adj.* **1** *Comput.* & *Telecomm.* of or requiring a form of computer control timing protocol in which a specific operation begins upon receipt of an indication (signal) that the preceding operation has been completed. **2** not going at the same rate and exactly together with something else, in particular: **3** (of two or more objects or events) not existing or happening at the same time. —**a·syn·chro·nous·ly** *adv.*

At ▶ *symb.* the chemical element astatine.

at[1] /at/ ▶ *prep.* **1** expressing location or arrival in a particular place or position: *they live at Conway House.* ■ used in speech to indicate the sign @ *the children go to bed at nine o'clock.* ■ denoting a particular period of time: *the sea is cooler at night.* ■ denoting the time spent by someone attending an educational institution, a workplace, or their home: *at work, at home, or at school.* **3** denoting a particular point or segment on a scale: *prices start at $18.* ■ referring to someone's age: *at fourteen he began to work as a mailman.* **4** expressing a particular state or condition: *placed them at a serious disadvantage.* ■ expressing a relationship between an individual and a skill: *boxing was the only sport I was any good at.* **5** expressing the object of a look, gesture, thought, action, or plan: *I looked at my watch.* ■ expressing the target of a shot from a weapon: *they tore down the main street, firing at anyone in sight.* ■ emphasizing the directing of an action toward a specified object: *she clutched at the thin gown.* **6** expressing the means by which something is done: *holding a corrections officer at knifepoint.*

▶ □ **at it** engaged in some activity, typically a reprehensible one: *the guy who faked the Hitler diaries is at it again.* □ **at that** in addition; furthermore: *it was not fog but smoke, and very thick at that.* □ **where it's at** *inf.* the fashionable place, possession, or activity: *New York is where it's at.*

at[2] /ät/ ▶ *n.* a monetary unit of Laos, equal to one hundredth of a kip.

at·a·rax·y /'atəˌraksē/ (also **at·a·rax·i·a** /ˌatə'raksēə/) ▶ *n.* a state of serene calmness. —**at·a·rac·tic** /ˌatə'raktik/ *adj.* —**at·a·rax·ic** /ˌatə'raksik/ *adj.*

at·a·vis·tic /ˌatə'vistik/ ▶ *adj.* relating to or characterized by reversion to something ancient or ancestral: *atavistic fears and instincts.* —**at·a·vism** /'atəˌvizəm/ *n.* —**at·a·vis·ti·cal·ly** /-tik(ə)lē/ *adv.*

a·tax·i·a /ə'taksēə/ (also **a·tax·y** /ə'taksē/) ▶ *n. Med.* the loss of full control of bodily movements. —**a·tax·ic** /-sik/ *adj.*

ATE ▶ *abbr.* automated test equipment.

ate /āt/ ▶ *past of* **EAT**.

at·el·ier /ˌatl'yā/ ▶ *n.* a workshop or studio, esp. one used by an artist or designer.

a tem·po /ä 'tempō/ ▶ *adv. Mus.* (esp. as a direction) in the previous or original tempo.

a·the·ism /'āthēˌizəm/ ▶ *n.* the theory or belief that God does not exist. —**a·the·ist** *n.* —**a·the·is·tic** /ˌāthē'istik/ *adj.* —**a·the·is·ti·cal** /-'istikəl/ *adj.*

a·the·mat·ic /ˌāthi'matik/ ▶ *adj.* **1** *Mus.* (of a composition) not based on the use of themes. **2** *Gram.* (of a verb form) having a suffix attached to the stem without a connecting (thematic) vowel.

ath·e·nae·um /ˌathə'nēəm/ (also **ath·e·ne·um**) ▶ *n.* used in the names of libraries or institutions for literary or scientific study: *the Boston Athenaeum.* ■ used in the titles of periodicals concerned with literature, science, and art.

ath·er·o·scle·ro·sis /ˌathərōsklə'rōsis/ ▶ *n. Med.* a disease of the arteries characterized by the deposition of plaques of fatty material on their inner walls. —**ath·er·o·scle·rot·ic** /-'rätik/ *adj.*

ath·lete /'athˌlēt/ ▶ *n.* a person who is proficient in sports and other forms of physical exercise.

ath·lete's foot ▶ *n.* a fungal infection affecting the skin between the toes. It is a form of ringworm.

ath·let·ic /ath'letik/ ▶ *adj.* **1** of or relating to athletes or athletics: *an athletic club.* **2** physically strong, fit, and active: *big, muscular, athletic boys.* —**ath·let·i·cal·ly** /-ik(ə)lē/ *adv.* —**ath·let·i·cism** /-ˌsizəm/ *n.*

ath·let·ics /ath'letiks/ ▶ *pl. n.* [usu. treated as *sing.*] physical sports and games of any kind.

a·thwart /ə'thwôrt/ ▶ *prep.* **1** from side to side of; across: *a long counter thrown athwart the entranceway.* **2** in opposition to; counter to: *these statistics run sharply athwart conventional presumptions.*

▶ *adv.* **1** across from side to side; transversely: *one table running athwart*

was all the room would hold. **2** so as to be perverse or contradictory: *our words ran athwart and we ended up at cross purposes.*

At·lan·tic time ▶ the standard time in a zone including the easternmost parts of mainland Canada, Puerto Rico, and the Virgin Islands, specifically: ■ **Atlantic Standard Time** (abbr.: **AST**) standard time based on the mean solar time at the longitude 60° W, four hours behind GMT. ■ **Atlantic Daylight Time** (abbr.: **ADT**) standard time based on the mean solar time at the longitude 60° W, four hours behind GMT.

At·las /'atləs/ *Greek Mythol.* ▶ one of the Titans, who was punished for his part in their revolt against Zeus by being made to support the heavens. —**At·lan·te·an** /ˌatlan'tēən; at'lantēən/ *adj.*

at·las /'atləs/ ▶ *n.* **1** (*pl.* **at·las·es**) a book of maps or charts: *I looked in the atlas to find a map of Italy.* ■ a book of illustrations or diagrams on any subject. **2** (*pl.* **at·las·es**) (also **atlas vertebra**) *Anat.* the topmost vertebra of the backbone, articulating with the occipital bone of the skull. **3** (*pl.* **at·lan·tes** /at'lantēz/) *Archit.* a stone carving of a male figure, used as a column to support the entablature of a Greek or Greek-style building.

ATM ▶ *abbr.* ■ automated (or automatic) teller machine.

atm *Physics* ▶ *abbr.* atmosphere(s), as a unit of pressure.

at·man /'ätmən/ (also **At·man**) ▶ *n. Hinduism* the spiritual life principle of the universe, esp. when regarded as inherent in the real self of the individual.

at·mos·phere /'atməsˌfi(ə)r/ ▶ *n.* **1** the envelope of gases surrounding the earth or another planet. ■ the air in any particular place: *the dusty atmosphere of his apartment.* ■ (abbr.: **atm**) *Physics* a unit of pressure equal to mean atmospheric pressure at sea level, 101,325 pascals. **2** the pervading tone or mood of a place, situation, or work of art: *the hotel is famous for its friendly, welcoming atmosphere.* ■ a pleasurable and interesting or exciting mood: *a superb restaurant, full of atmosphere.* ▷ mid 17th cent.: from modern Latin *atmosphaera,* from Greek *atmos* 'vapor' + *sphaira* 'ball, globe.'

at·mos·pher·ics /ˌatməs'fi(ə)riks; -'feriks/ ▶ *pl. n.* **1** electrical disturbances in the atmosphere due to lightning and other phenomena, esp. as they interfere with telecommunications. **2** effects intended to create a particular atmosphere or mood, esp. in music: *a jazz sound with spooky atmospherics.* —**at·mos·pher·ic** *adj.*

at·oll /'atˌôl; 'atˌäl; 'āˌtôl; 'āˌtäl/ ▶ *n.* a ring-shaped reef, island, or chain of islands formed of coral.

at·om /'atəm/ ▶ *n.* the basic unit of a chemical element. ■ such particles as a source of nuclear energy: *the power of the atom.* ■ an extremely small amount of a thing or quality: *I shall not have one atom of strength left.*

at·om bomb (also **a·tom·ic bomb**) ▶ *n.* a bomb that derives its destructive power from the rapid release of nuclear energy by fission of heavy atomic nuclei, causing damage through heat, blast, and radioactivity.

a·tom·ic /ə'tämik/ ▶ *adj.* of or relating to an atom or atoms: *the atomic nucleus.* ■ *Chem.* (of a substance) consisting of uncombined atoms rather than molecules: *atomic hydrogen.* ■ of or forming a single irreducible unit or component in a larger system: *a society made up of atomic individuals pursuing private interests.* ■ relating to, denoting, or using the energy released in nuclear fission or fusion: *the atomic age required a new way of political thinking | atomic weapons.* —**a·tom·i·cal·ly** /-ik(ə)lē/ *adv.*

at·om·ize /'atəˌmīz/ ▶ *v.* [*tr.*] convert (a substance) into very fine particles or droplets. ■ reduce (something) to atoms or other small distinct units: *by disrupting our ties with our neighbors, crime atomizes society.* —**at·om·i·za·tion** /ˌatəmə'zāSHən/ *n.*

at·om·iz·er /'atəˌmīzər/ (*Brit.* also **at·om·is·er**) ▶ *n.* a device for emitting water, perfume, or other liquids as a fine spray.

a·ton·al /ā'tōnl/ ▶ *adj. Mus.* not written in any key or mode.

a·tone /ə'tōn/ ▶ *v.* [*intr.*] make amends or reparation: *he was being helpful, to atone for his past mistakes.*

a·tone·ment /ə'tōnmənt/ ▶ *n.* reparation for a wrong or injury: *she wanted to make atonement for her husband's behavior.* ■ *Religion* reparation or expiation for sin: *the High Priest offered the sacrifice as atonement for all the sins of Israel.* ■ (**the Atonement**) *Christian Theol.* the reconciliation of God and humankind through Jesus Christ.

atomizer

a·ton·ic /āˈtänik/ ▸*adj. Linguistics* (of a syllable) without accent or stress. —**at·o·ny** /ˈatn-ē/ *n.*

a·top /əˈtäp/ ▸*prep.* on the top of: *the weathervane is perched atop the barn.* ▸*adv.* on the top: *the air raid siren atop of the courthouse.*

ATP ▸*abbr. Biochem.* adenosine triphosphate.

at·ra·bil·ious /ˌatrəˈbilēəs; -ˈbilyəs/ ▸*adj. poetic/lit.* melancholy or ill-tempered. —**at·ra·bil·ious·ness** *n.*

at-risk ▸*adj.* vulnerable, especially to abuse or delinquency: *a church-run school for the most at-risk children.*

a·tri·um /ˈātrēəm/ ▸*n.* (*pl.* **a·tri·a** /ˈātrēə/ or **a·tri·ums**) **1** *Archit.* an open-roofed entrance hall or central court in an ancient Roman house. ▪ a central hall or court in a modern building, with rooms or galleries opening off it, often glass-covered. **2** *Anat.* each of the two upper cavities of the heart from which blood is passed to the ventricles. The right atrium receives deoxygenated blood from the veins of the body; the left atrium receives oxygenated blood from the pulmonary vein. Also called **AURICLE**. —**a·tri·al** /ˈātrēəl/ *adj.*

a·tro·cious /əˈtrōSHəs/ ▸*adj.* horrifyingly wicked: *atrocious cruelties.* ▪ of a very poor quality; extremely bad or unpleasant: *atrocious weather.* —**a·tro·cious·ly** *adv.* —**a·tro·cious·ness** *n.*

a·troc·i·ty /əˈträsitē/ ▸*n.* (*pl.* **-ties**) an extremely wicked or cruel act, typically one involving physical violence or injury: *war atrocities* | *scenes of hardship and atrocity.* ▪ *humorous* a highly unpleasant or distasteful object: *the house was a split-level atrocity.*

at·ro·phy /ˈatrəfē/ ▸*v.* (**-phies, -phied**) [*intr.*] (of body tissue or an organ) waste away, typically due to the degeneration of cells, or become vestigial during evolution: *without exercise, the muscles will atrophy.* ▪ *fig.* gradually decline in effectiveness or vigor due to underuse or neglect: *her artistic skills atrophied from lack of use.*
▸*n.* the condition or process of atrophying: *gastric atrophy.* ▪ *fig.* the gradual decline of effectiveness or vigor due to underuse or neglect: *extensive TV viewing may lead to atrophy of children's imaginations.* —**a·troph·ic** /āˈtrōfik; āˈträfik/ *adj.*

at·ro·pine /ˈatrəˌpēn/ ▸*n. Chem.* a poisonous alkaloid compound, $C_{17}N_{23}NO_3$, found in deadly nightshade and related plants, and used in medicine.

at·tach /əˈtaCH/ ▸*v.* [*tr.*] fasten; join: *he made certain that the trailer was securely attached to the van.* ▪ fasten (a related document) to another: *I attach a copy of the memo for your information.* ▪ include (a condition) as part of an agreement: *the Commission can attach appropriate conditions to the operation of the agreement.* ▪ used to indicate that someone regards something as important or valuable: *he doesn't attach too much importance to radical ideas.* ▪ [*intr.*] (**attach to**) used to indicate someone regards something as important or valuable: *in South Korea enormous importance is attached to respect for the dead.* ▪ (**attach oneself to**) join (someone or something) without being invited: *they were all too ready to attach themselves to you for the whole day.* ▪ (usu. **be attached**) appoint (someone) for special or temporary duties: *I was attached to another department.* ▪ *Law* seize (a person's property) by legal authority: *the court attached his wages for child support.* —**at·tach·a·ble** *adj.*

at·ta·ché /ˌatəˈSHā ˌata-/ ▸*n.* a person on the staff of an ambassador, typically with a specialized area of responsibility: *military attachés.*

at·ta·ché case ▸*n.* a small, flat, rectangular case used for carrying documents.

at·tached /əˈtaCHt/ ▸*adj.* **1** joined or fastened to something: *please complete the attached form.* ▪ (of a building or room) adjacent to and typically connected with another building or room: *a ground-floor bedroom with a bathroom attached.* **2** full of affection or fondness: *during his visit, Mark became increasingly attached to Tara.* **3** (**attached to**) (of a person) appointed to an organization or group for special or temporary duties: *he was attached to military intelligence.* ▪ (of an organization or body) affiliated to another larger organization or body: *a public relations agency attached to the university.*

at·tach·ment /əˈtaCHmənt/ ▸*n.* **1** an extra part or extension that is or can be attached to something to perform a particular function: *the food processor comes with a blender attachment.* ▪ a computer file appended to an e-mail. **2** the condition of being attached to something or someone, in particular: ▪ affection, fondness, or sympathy for someone or something: *she felt a sentimental attachment to the place.* ▪ an affectionate relationship between two people: *he formed an attachment with a young widow.* **3** the action of attaching something: *the case has a loop for attachment to your belt.* ▪ legal seizure of property.

at·tack /əˈtak/ ▸*v.* [*tr.*] take aggressive action against (a place or enemy forces) with weapons or armed force, typically in a battle or war: *in December, the Japanese attacked Pearl Harbor* | [*intr.*] *the terrorists did not attack again until March.* ▪ (of a person or animal) act against (someone or

something) aggressively in an attempt to injure or kill. ▪ (of a disease, chemical substance, or insect) act harmfully on: *HIV is thought to attack certain cells in the brain.* ▪ criticize or oppose fiercely and publicly. ▪ begin to deal with (a problem or task) in a determined and vigorous way: *a plan of action to attack unemployment.* ▪ [*intr.*] make an aggressive or forceful attempt to score a goal or point, or gain or exploit an advantage in a game against an opposing team or player. ▪ *Chess* move into or be in a position to capture (an opponent's piece).
▸*n.* an aggressive and violent action against a person or place: *three classrooms were gutted in the arson attack.* ▪ destructive action by a disease, chemical, or insect: *the tissue is open to attack by fungus.* ▪ a sudden short bout of an illness or stress: *an attack of nausea.* ▪ an instance of fierce public criticism or opposition: *he launched a stinging attack on the White House.* ▪ a determined attempt to tackle a problem or task: *an attack on inflation.* ▪ *Mus.* the manner of beginning to play or sing a passage. ▪ forceful and decisive style in performing music or another art: *the sheer attack of Hendrix's playing.* ▪ an aggressive attempt to score a goal, win points, or gain or exploit an advantage in a game. —**at·tack·er** *n.*
▸ ▫ **under attack** subject to fierce public criticism or opposition: *his paintings have come under attack for their satanic content.*

at·tain /əˈtān/ ▸*v.* [*tr.*] succeed in achieving (something that one desires and has worked for): *clarify your objectives and ways of attaining them* | *he attained the rank of admiral.* ▪ reach (a specified age, size, or amount): *dolphins can attain remarkable speeds in water.* —**at·tain·a·bil·i·ty** /əˌtānə-ˈbilitē/ *n.* —**at·tain·a·ble** *adj.*

at·tain·ment /əˈtānmənt/ ▸*n.* the action or fact of achieving a goal toward which one has worked: *the attainment of a mystical state of communion with God.* ▪ (often **attainments**) a thing achieved, esp. a skill or educational achievement: *scholarly attainments.*

at·tar /ˈatər/ ▸*n.* a fragrant essential oil, typically made from rose petals.

at·tempt /əˈtem(p)t/ ▸*v.* [*tr.*] make an effort to achieve or complete (something, typically a difficult task or action): *she attempted a comeback in 1989* | *those who attempted to flee were captured at the border.* ▪ try to climb to the top of (a mountain): *the group's next plan was to attempt Everest.*
▸*n.* an act of trying to achieve something, typically one that is unsuccessful or not certain to succeed: *any attempt at talking politics ended in a fit of laughter.* ▪ an effort to surpass a record or conquer a mountain: *we made an attempt on the southwest buttress.* ▪ a bid to kill someone: *Karakozov made an attempt on the tsar's life.* ▪ a thing produced as a result of trying to make or achieve something: *her first attempt at a letter ended up in the wastebasket.*

at·tend /əˈtend/ ▸*v.* **1** [*tr.*] be present at (an event, meeting, or function): *the entire sales force attended the conference.* ▪ go regularly to (an educational, religious, social, or clinical institution): *all children are required to attend school.* **2** [*intr.*] (**attend to**) deal with: *he muttered that he had business to attend to.* ▪ give practical help and care to; look after: *the severely wounded had two medics to attend to their wounds* | [*tr.*] *each of the beds in the intensive care unit is attended by a nurse.* ▪ pay attention to: *Alice hadn't attended to a word of his sermon.* **3** [*tr.*] (usu. **be attended**) occur with or as a result of: *people feared that the switch to a peacetime economy would be attended by a severe slump.* ▪ escort or accompany (a member of royalty or other important personage) so as to assist them; wait on. —**at·tend·er** /əˈtendər/ *n.*

at·tend·ance /əˈtendəns/ ▸*n.* the action or state of going regularly to or being present at a place or event: *my attendance at church was very irregular.* ▪ the number of people present at a particular event, function, or meeting: *reports placed the attendance at 500,000.*
▸ ▫ **in attendance** present at a function or a place. ▪ accompanying a member of royalty or the aristocracy in the capacity of an assistant or servant.

at·tend·ant /əˈtendənt/ ▸*n.* **1** a person employed to provide a service to the public in a particular place: *a gas station attendant.* ▪ an assistant to an important person; a servant or courtier. **2** a person who is present at an event, meeting, or function: *a regular attendant at chapel.*
▸*adj.* occurring with or as a result of; accompanying: *the sea and its attendant attractions* | *the dangers attendant on solitary life.* ▪ (of a person or animal) accompanying another as a companion or assistant.

at·tend·ee /əˌtenˈdē; ˌaten-/ ▸*n.* a person who attends a conference or other gathering.

at·ten·tion /əˈtenSHən/ ▸*n.* **1** notice taken of someone or something; the regarding of someone or something as interesting or important: *you've never paid that much attention to her opinions.* ▪ the mental faculty of considering or taking notice of someone or something: *he turned his attention to the educational system.* **2** the action of dealing with or taking special care of someone or something: *the business needed her* *attention.* ■ (**attentions**) a person's interest in someone, esp. when unwelcome or regarded as excessive: *his aim was to avoid the attentions of the newspapers.* ■ (**attentions**) a person's actions intended to express interest of a sexual or romantic nature in someone, sometimes when unwelcome: *she felt flattered by his attentions.* **3** *Mil.* a position assumed by a soldier, standing very straight with the heels together and the arms straight down the sides of the body: *the squadron stood to attention* | *midshipmen standing at attention.* ■ [as *interj.*] an order to assume such a position. —**at·ten·tion·al** /-SHənl/ *adj.*

at·ten·tive /ə'tentiv/ ▶ *adj.* paying close attention to something: *never before had she had such an attentive audience* | *Congress should be more attentive to the interests of taxpayers.* ■ assiduously attending to the comfort or wishes of others; very polite or courteous: *the hotel has a pleasant atmosphere and attentive service.* —**at·ten·tive·ly** *adv.* —**at·ten·tive·ness** *n.*

at·ten·u·ate ▶ *v.* /ə'tenyoo,āt/ [*tr.*] (often **be attenuated**) reduce the force, effect, or value of: *her intolerance was attenuated by a rather unexpected liberalism.* ■ [usu. as *adj.*] (**attenuated**) reduce the virulence of (a pathogenic organism or vaccine): *attenuated strains of rabies virus.* ■ reduce in thickness; make thin.
▶ *adj.* /-it; -,āt/ *rare* reduced in force, effect, or physical thickness. —**at·ten·u·a·tion** /ə,tenyoo'āSHən/ *n.* —**at·ten·u·a·tor** *n.*

at·test /ə'test/ ▶ *v.* [*tr.*] provide or serve as clear evidence of: *his status is attested by his recent promotion* | [*intr.*] *his numerous drawings of ships attest to his fascination with them.* ■ [*intr.*] declare that something exists or is the case: *I can attest to his tremendous energy* | *the deceased's attorney attested that he had been about to institute divorce proceedings.* ■ be a witness to; certify formally: *the witnesses must attest and sign the will in the testator's presence.* —**at·tes·ta·tion** /,ate'stāSHən/ *n.*

At·tic /'atik/ ▶ *adj.* of or relating to Athens or Attica, or the dialect of Greek spoken there in ancient times.
▶ *n.* the dialect of Greek used by the ancient Athenians, the chief literary form of classical Greek.

at·tic /'atik/ ▶ *n.* a space or room just below the roof of a building.

at·tire /ə'tī(ə)r/ ▶ *n.* clothes, esp. fine or formal ones: *holiday attire.*
▶ *v.* (**be attired**) be dressed in clothes of a specified kind: *Donna was attired in an elaborate evening gown.*

at·ti·tude /'ati,t(y)ood/ ▶ *n.* a settled way of thinking or feeling about someone or something, typically one that is reflected in a person's behavior: *she took a tough attitude toward other people's indulgences.* ■ a position of the body proper to or implying an action or mental state: *the boy was standing in an attitude of despair, his chin sunk on his chest.* ■ *inf.* uncooperative behavior; a resentful or antagonistic manner: *I asked the waiter for a clean fork, and all I got was attitude.* ■ *inf.* individuality and self-confidence as manifested by behavior or appearance; style: *she snapped her fingers with attitude.* ■ the orientation of an aircraft or spacecraft, relative to the direction of travel. ■ *Ballet* a position in which one leg is lifted behind with the knee bent at right angles and turned out, and the corresponding arm is raised above the head, the other extended to the side. ▷late 17th cent. (denoting the placing or posture of a figure in art): from French, from Italian *attitudine* 'fitness, posture,' from late Latin *aptitudo*, from *aptus* 'fit.' —**at·ti·tu·di·nal** /,ati't(y)oodn-əl/ *adj.*

at·tor·ney /ə'tərnē/ ▶ *n.* (*pl.* **-neys**) **1** a person appointed to act for another in business or legal matters. **2** a lawyer. —**at·tor·ney·ship** /-,SHip/ *n.*

at·tor·ney gen·er·al (abbr.: **AG** or **Atty. Gen.**) ▶ *n.* (*pl.* **at·tor·neys gen·er·al**) the principal legal officer who represents a country or a state in legal proceedings and gives legal advice to the government. ■ the head of the U.S. Department of Justice.

at·tract /ə'trakt/ ▶ *v.* [*tr.*] cause to come to a place or participate in a venture by offering something of interest, favorable conditions, or opportunities: *a campaign to attract more visitors to West Virginia.* ■ evoke (a specified reaction): *I did not want to attract attention* | *his criticism of the government attracted widespread support.* ■ cause (someone) to have a liking for or interest in something: *I was attracted to the idea of working for a ballet company.* ■ cause (someone) to have a sexual or romantic interest in someone: *it was her beauty that attracted him.* ■ exert a force on (an object) that is directed toward the source of the force: *the negatively charged ions attract particles of dust.* —**at·trac·tor** /-tər/ *n.*

at·trac·tion /ə'trakSHən/ ▶ *n.* the action or power of evoking interest, pleasure, or liking for someone or something: *she has romantic ideas about sexual attraction.* ■ a quality or feature of something or someone that evokes interest, liking, or desire: *the main attraction of Peking duck is the crackling texture of its skin.* ■ a thing or place that draws visitors by providing something of interest or pleasure: *the church is the town's main tourist attraction.* ■ *Physics* a force under the influence of which objects tend to move toward each other: *gravitational attraction.* ■ *Gram.* the

influence exerted by one word on another that causes it to change to an incorrect form, e.g., *the wages of sin is* (for *are*) *death.*

at·trac·tive /ə'traktiv/ ▶ *adj.* (of a thing) pleasing or appealing to the senses: *an attractive home.* ■ (of a person) appealing to look at; sexually alluring. ■ (of a thing) having beneficial qualities or features that induce someone to accept what is being offered: *the site is close to the high-rent district, which makes it attractive to developers.* —**at·trac·tive·ly** *adv.* —**at·trac·tive·ness** *n.*

at·trib·ute ▶ *v.* /ə'tri,byoot/ [*tr.*] (**attribute something to**) regard something as being caused by (someone or something): *he attributed the firm's success to the efforts of the director.* ■ ascribe a work or remark to (a particular author, artist, or speaker): *the building was attributed to Frank Lloyd Wright.* ■ regard a quality or feature as characteristic of or possessed by (someone or something): *ancient peoples attributed magic properties to certain stones.*
▶ *n.* (**at·tri·bute**) /'atrə,byoot/ a quality or feature regarded as a characteristic or inherent part of someone or something: *flexibility and mobility are the key attributes of our army.* ■ a material object recognized as symbolic of a person, esp. a conventional object used in art to identify a saint or mythical figure. ■ *Gram.* an attributive adjective or noun. ■ *Statistics* a real property that a statistical analysis is attempting to describe. —**at·trib·ut·a·ble** /ə'tribyətəbəl/ *adj.* —**at·tri·bu·tion** /,atrə'byooSHən/ *n.*

at·trib·u·tive /ə'tribyətiv/ ▶ *adj. Gram.* (of an adjective or noun) preceding the word it qualifies or modifies and expressing an attribute, as *old* in *the old dog* (but not in *the dog is old*) and *expiration* in *expiration date* (but not in *date of expiration*). Often contrasted with PREDICATIVE. —**at·trib·u·tive·ly** *adv.*

at·tri·tion /ə'triSHən/ ▶ *n.* **1** the action or process of gradually reducing the strength or effectiveness of someone or something through sustained attack or pressure: *the council is trying to wear down the opposition by attrition.* ■ the gradual reduction of a workforce by employees' leaving and not being replaced rather than by their being laid off: *with so few retirements since March, the year's attrition was insignificant.* ■ wearing away by friction; abrasion: *the skull shows attrition of the edges of the teeth.* **2** (in scholastic theology) sorrow, but not contrition, for sin. —**at·tri·tion·al** /-SHənl/ *adj.*

at·tune /ə't(y)oon/ ▶ *v.* [*tr.*] (usu. **be attuned**) make receptive or aware: *a society more attuned to consumerism than ideology* | [as *adj.*] (**attuned**) *the department is very attuned politically.* ■ accustom or acclimatize: *students are not attuned to making decisions.* ■ [*intr.*] become receptive to or aware of: *a conscious attempt to attune to the wider audience.* ■ make harmonious: *the interests of East and West are now closely attuned.*

Atty. ▶ *abbr.* Attorney.

Atty. Gen. ▶ *abbr.* Attorney General.

ATV ▶ *abbr.* all-terrain vehicle.

a·typ·i·cal /ā'tipikəl/ ▶ *adj.* not representative of a type, group, or class: *a sample of people who are rather atypical of the target audience* | *there were somewhat atypical results in May and November.* —**a·typ·i·cal·ly** *adv.*

AU ▶ *abbr.* ■ ångström unit(s). ■ (also **a.u.**) astronomical unit(s).

Au ▶ *symb.* the chemical element gold.

au·burn /'ôbərn/ ▶ *adj.* (chiefly of a person's hair) of a reddish-brown color.
▶ *n.* a reddish-brown color.

auc·tion /'ôkSHən/ ▶ *n.* a public sale in which goods or property are sold to the highest bidder. ■ the action or process of selling something in this way: *the Ferrari sold at auction for $10 million.* ■ *Bridge* the part of the play in which players bid to decide the contract in which the hand shall be played.
▶ *v.* [*tr.*] (often **be auctioned**) sell or offer for sale at an auction: *his collection of vintage cars is to be auctioned off tomorrow.*

auc·tion·eer /,ôkSHə'ni(ə)r/ ▶ *n.* a person who conducts auctions by accepting bids and declaring goods sold. —**auc·tion·eer·ing** *n.*

au·da·cious /ô'dāSHəs/ ▶ *adj.* **1** showing a willingness to take surprisingly bold risks: *a series of audacious takeovers.* **2** showing an impudent lack of respect. —**au·da·cious·ly** *adv.* —**au·da·cious·ness** *n.* —**au·dac·i·ty** /ô'dasitē/ *n.*

au·di·ble /'ôdəbəl/ ▶ *adj.* able to be heard: *ultrasound is audible to dogs.*
▶ *n.* *Football* a change in the offensive play called by the quarterback at the line of scrimmage. —**au·di·bil·i·ty** /,ôdə'bilitē/ *n.* —**au·di·bly** /-blē/ *adv.*

au·di·ence /'ôdēəns/ ▶ *n.* **1** the assembled spectators or listeners at a

Pronunciation Key ə *ago, up;* ər *over, fur;* a *hat;* ā *ate;* ä *car;* CH *chin;* e *let;* ē *see;* e(ə)r *air;* i *fit;* ī *by;* i(ə)r *ear;* NG *sing;* ō *go;* ô *law, for;* oi *toy;* oo *good;* oo *goo;* ou *out;* SH *she;* TH *thin;* TH *then;* (h)w *why;* ZH *vision*

public event, such as a play, movie, concert, or meeting: *the orchestra was given an ovation from the audience.* ■ the people who watch or listen to a television or radio program: *the program attracted an audience of almost twenty million.* ■ the readership of a book, magazine, or newspaper: *the newspaper has a sophisticated audience.* ■ the people giving or likely to give attention to something: *there will always be an audience for romantic literature.* **2** a formal interview with a person in authority: *he demanded an audience with the pope.* **3** *archaic* formal hearing.

au·di·o /'ôdē,ō/ ▶*n.* [usu. as *adj.*] sound, esp. when recorded, transmitted, or reproduced: *audio equipment | it includes support for embedded audio.*

au·di·o·cas·sette /,ôdē-ōkə'set/ ▶*n.* a cassette of audiotape.

au·di·ol·o·gy /,ôdē'äləjē/ ▶*n.* the branch of science and medicine concerned with the sense of hearing. —**au·di·o·log·i·cal** /-ə'läjikəl/ *adj.* —**au·di·ol·o·gist** /-jist/ *n.*

au·di·om·e·try /,ôdē'ämitrē/ ▶*n.* measurement of the range and sensitivity of a person's sense of hearing. —**au·di·om·e·ter** /-itər/ *n.* —**au·di·o·met·ric** /-ə'metrik/ *adj.*

au·di·o·phile /'ôdē-ō,fīl/ ▶*n.* a hi-fi enthusiast.

au·di·o·tape /'ôdē-ō,tāp/ ▶*n.* magnetic tape on which sound can be recorded. ■ a length of this, typically in the form of a cassette.
▶*v.* [*tr.*] record (sound) on tape: *each interview was audiotaped.*

au·di·o·vis·u·al /,ôdē-ō'vizHŌŌəl/ ▶*adj.* using both sight and sound, typically in the form of slides or video and recorded speech or music.

au·dit /'ôdit/ ▶*n.* an official inspection of an individual's or organization's accounts, typically by an independent body. ■ a systematic review or assessment of something: *a complete audit of flora and fauna at the site.*
▶*v.* (**-dit·ed, -dit·ing**) [*tr.*] **1** conduct an official financial examination of (an individual's or organization's accounts): *companies must have their accounts audited.* ■ conduct a systematic review of: *auditing obstetrical care.* **2** attend (a class) informally, not for academic credit.

au·di·tion /ô'dishən/ ▶*n.* an interview for a particular role or job as a singer, actor, dancer, or musician, consisting of a practical demonstration of the candidate's suitability and skill.
▶*v.* [*intr.*] perform an audition: *he was* **auditioning for** *the lead role in the play.* ■ [*tr.*] assess the suitability of (someone) for a role by means of an audition: *she was* **auditioning** *people* **for** *her new series.*

au·di·tor /'ôditər/ ▶*n.* **1** a person who conducts an audit. **2** a listener. ■ a person who attends a class informally without working for academic credit. —**au·di·to·ri·al** /,ôdə'tôrēəl/ *adj.*

au·di·to·ri·um /,ôdi'tôrēəm/ ▶*n.* (*pl.* **-to·ri·ums** or **-to·ri·a** /-'tôrēə/) **1** the part of a theater, concert hall, or other public building in which the audience sits. **2** a large building or hall used for public gatherings, typically concerts or sports events. ■ a large room for such gatherings, esp. in a school.

au·di·to·ry /'ôdi,tôrē/ ▶*adj.* of or relating to the sense of hearing: *the auditory nerves | teaching methods use both visual and auditory stimulation.*

au fait /,ō 'fe/ ▶*adj.* (**au fait with**) having a good or detailed knowledge of something: *you should be reasonably* **au fait with** *the company.*

Aug. ▶*abbr.* August.

au·ger /'ôgər/ ▶*n.* a tool with a helical bit for boring holes in wood. ■ a similar larger tool for boring holes in the ground or in ice.

aught¹ /ôt/ (also **ought**) *archaic* ▶*pron.* anything at all: *know you aught of this fellow, young sir?*

aught² ▶*n.* the digit 0; zero.

aug·ment ▶*v.* /ôg'ment/ [*tr.*] make (something) greater by adding to it; increase: *he augmented his summer income by painting houses.*
▶*n.* /'ôg,ment; -mənt/ *Linguistics* a vowel prefixed to past tenses of verbs in Greek and other Indo-European languages.

aug·men·ta·tion /,ôgmen'tāsHən/ ▶*n.* the action or process of making or becoming greater in size or amount. ■ *Mus.* the lengthening of the time values of notes in a melodic part.

aug·ment·a·tive /ôg'mentətiv/ ▶*adj. Gram.* (of an affix or derived word) reinforcing the idea of the original word, esp. by meaning 'a large —,' as with the Italian suffix -*one* in *borrone* 'ravine,' compared with *borro* 'ditch.'

au gra·tin /,ō 'grätn; 'gratn; gra'taN/ ▶*adj.* sprinkled with breadcrumbs or grated cheese, or both, and browned: *mushrooms au gratin.*

au·gur /'ôgər/ ▶*v.* [*intr.*] (**augur well/badly/ill**) (of an event or circumstance) portend a good or bad outcome: *the end of the Cold War seemed to augur well.* ■ [*tr.*] portend or bode (a specified outcome): *they feared that these happenings augured a neo-Nazi revival.* ■ [*tr.*] (*archaic*) foresee or predict.
▶*n. hist.* (in ancient Rome) a religious official who observed natural

signs, esp. the behavior of birds, interpreting these as an indication of divine approval or disapproval of a proposed action.

au·gu·ry /'ôgyərē/ ▶*n.* (*pl.* **-ries**) a sign of what will happen in the future; an omen: *they heard the sound as an augury of death.* ■ the work of an augur; the interpretation of omens.

Au·gust /'ôgəst/ ▶*n.* the eighth month of the year, in the northern hemisphere usually considered the last month of summer.

au·gust /ô'gəst/ ▶*adj.* respected and impressive: *she was in august company.* —**au·gust·ly** *adv.*

Au·gus·tan /ô'gəstən/ ▶*adj.* connected with or occurring during the reign of the Roman emperor Augustus. ■ relating to or denoting Latin literature of the reign of Augustus, including the works of Virgil, Horace, Ovid, and Livy. ■ relating to or denoting 17th- and 18th-century English literature of a style considered refined and classical, including the works of Pope, Addison, and Swift.
▶*n.* a writer of the (Latin or English) Augustan age.

Au·gus·tin·i·an /,ôgə'stinēən/ ▶*adj.* **1** of or relating to St. Augustine of Hippo or his theological doctrines. **2** of or relating to a religious order observing a rule derived from St. Augustine's writings.
▶*n.* of St. Augustine or the Augustinians.

auk /ôk/ ▶*n.* a short-winged diving seabird found in northern oceans, typically with a black head and black and white underparts. The **auk family** (Alcidae) comprises the guillemots, puffins, and their relatives.

auld lang syne /ôld laNG 'zīn/ ▶*n.* times long past.

aunt /ant; änt/ ▶*n.* the sister of one's father or mother or the wife of one's uncle. ■ *inf.* an unrelated older woman friend, esp. of a child.

au pair /,ō 'pe(ə)r/ ▶*n.* a young foreign person, typically a woman, who helps with housework or child care in exchange for room and board.

au·ra /'ôrə/ ▶*n.* (*pl.* **au·ras**) the distinctive atmosphere or quality that seems to surround and be generated by a person, thing, or place: *the ceremony retains* **an aura** *of mystery.* ■ a supposed emanation surrounding the body of a living creature, viewed by mystics, spiritualists, and some practitioners of complementary medicine as the essence of the individual. ■ any invisible emanation, esp. a scent or odor: *a faint aura of disinfectant.* ■ *Med.* (*pl.* **au·rae** /'ôrē/) a warning sensation experienced before an attack of epilepsy or migraine. ▷late Middle English (originally denoting a gentle breeze): via Latin from Greek, 'breeze, breath.' Current senses date from the 18th cent.

au·ral /'ôrəl/ ▶*adj.* of or relating to the ear or the sense of hearing: *information held in written, aural, or database form.* —**au·ral·ly** *adv.*

au·re·ate /'ôrē-it; -,āt/ ▶*adj.* denoting, made of, or having the color of gold. ■ (of language) highly ornamented or elaborate.

au·re·ole /'ôrē,ōl/ (also **au·re·o·la** /ô'rēələ/) ▶*n.* a circle of light or brightness surrounding something, esp. as depicted in art around the head or body of a person represented as holy. ■ another term for AREOLA.

au re·voir /,ō rəv'wär/ ▶*interj.* good-bye until we meet again.

au·ri·cle /'ôrikəl/ ▶*n. Anat. & Biol.* a structure resembling an ear or earlobe. ■ another term for ATRIUM (of the heart). ■ strictly, a small muscular appendage of each atrium. ■ the external part or pinna of the ear.

au·ric·u·lar /ô'rikyələr/ ▶*adj.* **1** of or relating to the ear or hearing. **2** of, relating to, or shaped like an auricle.

au·rochs /'ourəks; 'ô,räks/ ▶*n.* (*pl.* same) a large wild Eurasian ox (*Bos taurus*) that was the ancestor of domestic cattle. It was probably exterminated in Britain in the Bronze Age.

au·ro·ra /ə'rôrə; ô'rôrə/ ▶*n.* (*pl.* **au·ro·ras** or **au·ro·rae** /ô'rôrē/) **1** a natural electrical phenomenon characterized by the appearance of streamers of reddish or greenish light in the sky, usually near the northern or southern magnetic pole (**aurora borealis** or **aurora australis**). **2** *poetic/lit.* the dawn. —**au·ro·ral** *adj.*

aus·cul·ta·tion /,ôskəl'tāsHən/ ▶*n.* the action of listening to sounds from the heart, lungs, or other organs, typically with a stethoscope, as a part of medical diagnosis. —**aus·cul·tate** /'ôskəl,tāt/ *v.* —**aus·cul·ta·to·ry** /ô'skəltə,tôrē/ *adj.*

aus·pice /'ôspis/ ▶*n. archaic* a divine or prophetic token.
▶ □ **under the auspices of** with the help, support, or protection of: *the delegation's visit was arranged under UN auspices.*

aus·pi·cious /ô'spisHəs/ ▶*adj.* conducive to success; favorable: *the most auspicious moment to hold an election.* ■ giving or being a sign of future success: *they said it was an auspicious moon—it was rising.* ■ *archaic* characterized by success. —**aus·pi·cious·ly** *adv.* —**aus·pi·cious·ness** *n.*

Aus·sie /'ôsē/ ▶*n.* (*pl.* **-sies**) & *adj.* informal term for AUSTRALIAN.

aus·tere /ô'sti(ə)r/ ▶*adj.* (**-ter·er, -ter·est**) severe or strict in manner, attitude, or appearance: *an austere man, with a rigidly puritanical outlook.* ■ (of living conditions or a way of life) having no comforts or luxuries;

harsh or ascetic: *conditions in the prison could hardly be more austere.* ■ having an extremely plain and simple style or appearance; unadorned: *the cathedral is impressive in its austere simplicity.* ■ (of an economic policy or measure) designed to reduce a budget deficit, esp. by cutting public expenditure. —**aus·tere·ly** *adv.*

aus·ter·i·ty /ô'sterĭtē/ ▶ *n.* (*pl.* **-ties**) sternness or severity of manner or attitude. ■ extreme plainness and simplicity of style or appearance: *the room was decorated with a restraint bordering on austerity.* ■ (**austeri-ties**) conditions characterized by severity, sternness, or asceticism: *his austerities had undermined his health.* ■ difficult economic conditions created by government measures to reduce a budget deficit, esp. by reducing public expenditure: *a period of austerity.*

Aus·tral·ian /ô'strālyən/ ▶ *n.* a native or national of Australia, or a person of Australian descent.
▶ *adj.* of or relating to Australia. ■ *Zool.* of, relating to, or denoting a zoogeographical region comprising Australasia together with Indonesia east of Wallace's line, in which monotremes and marsupials dominate the fauna. —**Aus·tral·ian·ism** /-,nizəm/ *n.*

au·then·tic /ô'тнentik/ (abbr.: **auth.**) ▶ *adj.* of undisputed origin; genuine: *the letter is now accepted as an authentic document.* ■ made or done in the traditional or original way, or in a way that faithfully resembles an original: *the restaurant serves authentic Italian meals* ■ based on facts; accurate or reliable: *an authentic depiction of the situation.* ■ (in existentialist philosophy) relating to or denoting an emotionally appropriate, significant, purposive, and responsible mode of human life. —**au·then·ti·cal·ly** /-ik(ə)lē/ *adv.* —**au·then·tic·i·ty** /,ôтнen'tisitē/ *n.*

au·then·ti·cate /ô'тнenti,kāt/ ▶ *v.* [*tr.*] prove or show (something, esp. a claim or an artistic work) to be true or genuine: *they were invited to authenticate artifacts from the Italian Renaissance.* ■ validate: *the nationalist statements authenticated their leadership among the local community.* ■ [*intr.*] *Comput.* (of a user or process) have one's identity verified. —**au·then·ti·ca·tion** /ô,тнenti'kāshən/ *n.* —**au·then·ti·ca·tor** /-,kātər/ *n.*

au·thor /'ôтнər/ (abbr.: **auth.**) ▶ *n.* a writer of a book, article, or report. ■ someone who writes books as a profession. ■ the writings of such a person: *I had to read authors I disliked.* ■ *fig.* an originator or creator of something, esp. a plan or idea: *the authors of the peace plan.*
▶ *v.* [*tr.*] be the author of (a book or piece of writing): *she has authored several articles on wildlife.* ■ *fig.* be the originator of; create: *the concept has been authored largely by insurance companies.* ▷Middle English (in the sense 'a person who invents or causes something'): from Old French *autor*, from Latin *auctor*, from *augere* 'increase, originate, promote.' The spelling with *th* arose in the 15th cent., and perhaps became established under the influence of *authentic.* —**au·tho·ri·al** /ô'тнôrēəl/ *adj.*

au·thor·i·tar·i·an /ə,тнôri'te(ə)rēən; ô,тнär-/ ▶ *adj.* favoring or enforcing strict obedience to authority, esp. that of the government, at the expense of personal freedom: *the transition from an authoritarian to a democratic regime.* ■ showing a lack of concern for the wishes or opinions of others; domineering; dictatorial.
▶ *n.* an authoritarian person. —**au·thor·i·tar·i·an·ism** *n.*

au·thor·i·ta·tive /ə'тнôri,tātiv; ə'тнär-/ ▶ *adj.* **1** able to be trusted as being accurate or true; reliable: *clear, authoritative information.* ■ (of a text) considered to be the best of its kind and unlikely to be improved upon: *the authoritative study of mollusks.* **2** commanding and self-confident; likely to be respected and obeyed: *she had an authoritative air.* ■ proceeding from an official source and requiring compliance or obedience: *authoritative directives.* —**au·thor·i·ta·tive·ly** *adv.* —**au·thor·i·ta·tive·ness** *n.*

au·thor·i·ty /ə'тнôritē; ô'тнär-/ (abbr.: **auth.**) ▶ *n.* (*pl.* **-ties**) **1** the power or right to give orders, make decisions, and enforce obedience: *he had absolute* **authority over** *his subordinates.* ■ the right to act in a specified way, delegated from one person or organization to another: *military forces have the legal authority to arrest drug traffickers.* ■ official permission; sanction: *the money was spent without congressional authority.* **2** (often **authorities**) a person or organization having power or control in a particular, typically political or administrative, sphere: *the health authorities* | *the Chicago Transit Authority.* **3** the power to influence others, esp. because of one's commanding manner or one's recognized knowledge about something: *he spoke* **with authority** *on the subject.* ■ the confidence resulting from personal expertise: *he hit the ball with authority.* ■ a person with extensive or specialized knowledge about a subject; an expert: *she was* **an authority on** *the stock market.* ■ a book or other source able to supply reliable information or evidence, typically to settle a dispute: *the court cited a series of authorities supporting their decision.*
▶ □ **have something on good authority** have ascertained something from a reliable source: *I have it on good authority that there is a waiting list.*

au·thor·ize /'ôтнə,rīz/ ▶ *v.* [*tr.*] give official permission for or approval to

(an undertaking or agent): *the troops were authorized to use force.* —**au·thor·i·za·tion** /,ôтнərə'zāshən/ *n.*

au·thor·ship /'ôтнər,ship/ ▶ *n.* the fact or position of someone's having written a book or other written work: *an investigation into the authorship of the Gospels.* ■ the occupation of writing: *he took to authorship.*

au·tism /'ô,tizəm/ ▶ *n. Psychiatry* a mental condition, present from early childhood, characterized by great difficulty in communicating and forming relationships with other people and in using language and abstract concepts. ■ a mental condition in which fantasy dominates over reality, as a symptom of schizophrenia and other disorders. —**au·tis·tic** /ô'tistik/ *adj. & n.*

au·to /'ôtō/ ▶ *n.* (*pl.* **-tos**) *inf.* an automobile.

au·to·bahn /'ôtə,bän/ ▶ *n.* a German, Austrian, or Swiss expressway.

au·to·bi·og·ra·phy /,ôtōbī'ägrəfē/ ▶ *n.* (*pl.* **-phies**) an account of a person's life written by that person. ■ such writing as a literary genre. —**au·to·bi·og·ra·pher** /-fər/ *n.* —**au·to·bi·o·graph·i·cal** /,ôtə,bīə'grafikəl/ *adj.*

au·toch·thon /ô'täkтнən/ ▶ *n.* (*pl.* **-thons** or **-tho·nes** /-тнə,nēz/) an original or indigenous inhabitant of a place; an aborigine. —**au·toch·thon·ous** /-тнənəs/ *adj.*

au·to·clave /'ôtə,klāv/ ▶ *n.* a strong, heated container used for chemical reactions and other processes using high pressures and temperatures, e.g., steam sterilization.
▶ *v.* [*tr.*] heat (something) in an autoclave. ▷late 19th cent.: from French, from *auto-* 'self' + Latin *clavus* 'nail' or *clavis* 'key' (so called because it is self-fastening).

au·to·com·plete /,ôtōkəm'plēt/ *Comput.* ▶ *n.* a software function that gives users the option of completing words or forms by a shorthand method on the basis of what has been typed before.
▶ *v.* [*tr.*] complete (a word or form) in this way. —**au·to·com·ple·tion** *n.* /-kəm'plēshən/

au·toc·ra·cy /ô'täkrəsē/ ▶ *n.* (*pl.* **-cies**) a system of government by one person with absolute power. ■ a regime based on such a principle of government. ■ a country, state, or society governed in such a way. ■ domineering rule or control.

au·to·crat /'ôtə,krat/ ▶ *n.* a ruler who has absolute power. ■ someone who insists on complete obedience from others. —**au·to·crat·ic** *adj.*

au·to·da·fé /,ôtō də 'fā/ ▶ *n.* (*pl.* **au·tos-da-fé**) the burning of a heretic by the Spanish Inquisition. ■ a sentence of such a kind.

au·to·dial·er /'ôtō,dī(ə)lər/ ▶ *n.* an electronic device that dials telephone numbers randomly or from a list and may also leave messages and request information.

au·to·di·dact /,ôtō'dī,dakt/ ▶ *n.* a self-taught person. —**au·to·di·dac·tic** /-,dī'daktik/ *adj.*

au·to·e·rot·ic /,ôtō-i'rätik/ ▶ *adj.* of or relating to sexual excitement generated by stimulating or fantasizing about one's own body. —**au·to·e·rot·i·cism** /-,sizəm/ *n.*

au·to·fo·cus /'ôtō,fōkəs/ ▶ *n.* a device that focuses a camera or other piece of equipment automatically. ■ automatic focusing. —**au·to·fo·cus·ing** /-sing/ *n.*

au·tog·e·nous /ô'täjənəs/ ▶ *adj.* arising from within or from a thing itself.

au·to·gi·ro /,ôtō'jīrō/ (also **au·to·gy·ro**) ▶ *n.* (*pl.* **-ros**) a form of aircraft with freely rotating horizontal vanes and a propeller. It differs from a helicopter in that the vanes are not powered but rotate in the slipstream, propulsion being by a conventional mounted engine.

au·to·graft /'ôtə,graft/ ▶ *n.* a graft of tissue from one point to another of the same individual's body.

au·to·graph /'ôtə,graf/ ▶ *n.* **1** a signature, esp. that of a celebrity written as a memento for an admirer. **2** a manuscript or musical score in the author's or musician's own handwriting. ■ a person's handwriting.
▶ *v.* [*tr.*] (of a celebrity) write one's signature on (something); sign: *the whole team autographed a shirt for him* | [as *adj.*] (**autographed**) *an autographed photo.*
▶ *adj.* written in the author's own handwriting: *an autograph manuscript.* ■ (of a painting or sculpture) done by the artist, not by a copier.

Au·to·harp /'ôtō,härp/ ▶ *n. trademark* a kind of zither with a mechanical device that allows the playing of a chord by damping all the other strings.

au·to·im·mune /,ôtōə'myōon/ ▶ *adj. Med.* of or relating to disease caused by antibodies or lymphocytes produced against substances naturally

A

present in the body: *the infection triggers an autoimmune response.* —**au·to·im·mu·ni·ty** /-nitē/ *n.*

au·to·in·tox·i·ca·tion /ˌôtō-inˌtäksiˈkāsʜən/ ▶*n.* *Med.* poisoning by a toxin formed within the body itself.

au·tol·y·sis /ôˈtäləsis/ ▶*n.* *Biol.* the destruction of cells or tissues by their own enzymes, esp. those released by lysosomes. —**au·to·lyt·ic** /ˌôtlˈitik/ *adj.*

au·to·mat /ˈôtəˌmat/ ▶*n.* *hist.* a cafeteria in which food and drink were obtained from vending machines.

au·to·mate /ˈôtəˌmāt/ ▶*v.* [*tr.*] convert (a process or facility) to largely automatic operation: *industry is investing in automating production* | [as *adj.*] (**automated**) *a fully automated process.*

au·to·mat·ic /ˌôtəˈmatik/ ▶*adj.* **1** (of a device or process) working by itself with little or no direct human control: *an automatic kettle that switches itself off when it boils.* ■ (of a firearm) self-loading and able to fire continuously until the ammunition is exhausted or the pressure on the trigger is released. ■ (of a motor vehicle or its transmission) using gears that shift by themselves according to speed and acceleration: *a four-speed automatic gearbox.* **2** done or occurring spontaneously, without conscious thought or intention: *automatic physical functions such as breathing.* ■ occurring as a matter of course and without debate: *he is the automatic choice for the senior team.* ■ (esp. of a legal sanction) given or imposed as a necessary and inevitable result of a fixed rule or particular set of circumstances: *for missing the team workout, he received an automatic one-game suspension.*
▶*n.* **1** an automatic machine or device, in particular: ■ a gun that continues firing until the ammunition is exhausted or the pressure on the trigger is released. ■ a vehicle with automatic transmission. **2** *Football* another term for AUDIBLE. —**au·to·mat·i·cal·ly** /-ik(ə)lē/ *adv.* —**au·to·ma·tic·i·ty** /-məˈtisitē/ *n.*

au·to·mat·ic pi·lot ▶*n.* a device for keeping an aircraft on a set course without the intervention of the pilot.

au·to·ma·tion /ˌôtəˈmāsʜən/ ▶*n.* the use of largely automatic equipment in a system of manufacturing or other production process: *unemployment due to the spread of automation* | *the automation of office tasks.*

au·tom·a·tism /ôˈtäməˌtizəm/ ▶*n.* the performance of actions without conscious thought or intention. ■ *Art* the avoidance of conscious intention in producing works of art, esp. by using mechanical techniques or subconscious associations. ■ an action performed unconsciously or involuntarily.

au·tom·a·tize /ôˈtäməˌtīz/ ▶*v.* [*tr.*] make automatic or habitual. —**au·tom·a·ti·za·tion** /ôˌtämətiˈzāsʜən/ *n.*

au·tom·a·ton /ôˈtämətən/ ▶*n.* (*pl.* **-ta** /-tə/ or **-tons**) a moving mechanical device made in imitation of a human being. ■ a machine that performs a function according to a predetermined set of coded instructions, esp. one capable of a range of programmed responses to different circumstances. ■ used in similes and comparisons to refer to a person who seems to act in a mechanical or unemotional way: *she went about her preparations like an automaton.*

au·to·mo·bile /ˌôtəmōˈbēl/ ▶*n.* a road vehicle, typically with four wheels, powered by an internal combustion engine or electric motor and able to carry a small number of people.

au·to·mo·tive /ˌôtəˈmōtiv/ ▶*adj.* of, relating to, or concerned with motor vehicles.

au·to·nom·ic /ˌôtəˈnämik/ ▶*adj.* *chiefly Physiol.* involuntary or unconscious; relating to the autonomic nervous system.

au·to·nom·ic nerv·ous sys·tem ▶*n.* the part of the nervous system responsible for control of the bodily functions not consciously directed, such as breathing, the heartbeat, and digestive processes.

au·ton·o·mous /ôˈtänəməs/ ▶*adj.* (of a country or region) having self-government, at least to a significant degree: *the federation included sixteen autonomous republics.* ■ acting independently or having the freedom to do so: *an autonomous committee of the school board.* —**au·ton·o·mous·ly** *adv.*

au·ton·o·my /ôˈtänəmē/ ▶*n.* (*pl.* **-mies**) (of a country or region) the right or condition of self-government, esp. in a particular sphere. ■ a self-governing country or region. ■ freedom from external control or influence; independence: *economic autonomy is still a long way off for many women.* —**au·ton·o·mist** /-mist/ *n. & adj.*

au·to·pi·lot /ˈôtōˌpīlət/ ▶*n.* short for AUTOMATIC PILOT.

au·top·sy /ˈôˌtäpsē/ ▶*n.* (*pl.* **-sies**) a postmortem examination to discover the cause of death or the extent of disease.

au·to·ra·di·o·graph /ˌôtōˈrādēōˌgraf/ ▶*n.* a photograph of an object produced by radiation from radioactive material in the object and revealing the distribution or location of labeled material in the object.

▶*v.* [*tr.*] make an autoradiograph of. —**au·to·ra·di·o·graph·ic** /-ˌrādēō-ˈgrafik/ *adj.* —**au·to·ra·di·og·ra·phy** /-ˌrādēˈägrəfē/ *n.*

au·to·sug·ges·tion /ˌôtōsə(g)ˈjescʜən/ ▶*n.* the hypnotic or subconscious adoption of an idea that one has originated oneself, e.g. through repetition of verbal statements to oneself in order to change behavior.

au·to·tox·in /ˈôtōˌtäksin/ ▶*n.* a substance produced by an organism that is toxic to the organism itself. —**au·to·tox·ic** /ˌôtōˈtäksik/ *adj.*

au·tumn /ˈôtəm/ ▶*n.* the third season of the year, when crops and fruits are gathered and leaves fall, in the northern hemisphere from September to November and in the southern hemisphere from March to May: *the countryside is ablaze with color in autumn.* | *fig. he was* **in the autumn** *of his life.* ■ *Astron.* the period from the autumnal equinox to the winter solstice.

au·tum·nal /ôˈtəmnəl/ ▶*adj.* of, characteristic of, or occurring in autumn: *chilly autumnal weather*

aux·il·ia·ry /ôgˈzilyərē, -ˈzil(ə)rē/ ▶*adj.* providing supplementary or additional help and support: *an auxiliary nurse.* ■ (of equipment) held in reserve: *an auxiliary power source.* ■ (of troops) engaged in the service of a nation at war but not part of the regular army, and often of foreign origin. ■ (of a sailing vessel) equipped with a supplementary engine.
▶*n.* (*pl.* **-ries**) a person or thing providing supplementary or additional help and support: *there are two main fuel tanks and two auxiliaries.* ■ a group of volunteers giving supplementary support to an organization or institution: *the Volunteer Fire Department's women's auxiliary.* ■ (**auxiliaries**) troops engaged in the service of a nation at war but not part of the regular army, and often of foreign origin. ■ *Gram.* an auxiliary verb. ■ a naval vessel with a supporting role, not armed for combat.

aux·in /ˈôksin/ ▶*n.* a plant hormone that causes the elongation of cells in shoots and is involved in regulating plant growth.

AV ▶*abbr.* ■ audiovisual (teaching aids). ■ Authorized Version.

Av /äv; ôv/ ▶*n.* variant spelling of AB¹.

a·vail /əˈvāl/ ▶*v.* **1** (**avail oneself of**) use or take advantage of (an opportunity or available resource): *my daughter did not avail herself of my advice.* **2** help or benefit: [*tr.*] *no amount of struggle availed Charles* | [*intr.*] *the dark and narrow hiding place did not avail to save the fugitives.*
▶ □ **of little** (or **no**) **avail** not very (or not at all) effective or successful: *Latin was of little avail in the practical affairs of life.* □ **to little** (or **no**) **avail** with little (or no) success or benefit: *he tried to get his work recognized, but to little avail.*

a·vail·a·ble /əˈvāləbəl/ ▶*adj.* able to be used or obtained; at someone's disposal: *refreshments will be available all afternoon.* ■ (of a person) not otherwise occupied; free to do something: *the nurse is only available at certain times.* ■ not currently involved in a sexual or romantic relationship: *there's a dearth of available women here.* —**a·vail·a·bil·i·ty** /əˌvāləˈbilitē/ *n.*

av·a·lanche /ˈavəˌlancʜ/ ▶*n.* a mass of snow, ice, and rocks falling rapidly down a mountainside. ■ a large mass of any material moving rapidly downhill: *an avalanche of mud.* ■ *fig.* a sudden arrival or occurrence of something in overwhelming quantities: *we have had an avalanche of applications.* ■ *Physics* a cumulative process in which a fast-moving ion or electron generates further ions and electrons by collision.
▶*v.* [*intr.*] (of a mass of snow, ice, and rocks) descend rapidly down a mountainside. ■ [*tr.*] (usu. **be avalanched**) engulf or carry off by such a mass of material: *the climbers were avalanched down the south face of the mountain.*

a·vant-garde /ˈavänt ˈgärd; ˌaväN/ ▶*n.* (usu. **the avant-garde**) new and unusual or experimental ideas, esp. in the arts, or the people introducing them: *works by artists of the Russian avant-garde.*
▶*adj.* favoring or introducing such new ideas: *a controversial avant-garde composer.* —**a·vant-gard·ism** /-ˌdizəm/ *n.* —**a·vant-gard·ist** /-dist/ *n.*

av·a·rice /ˈavəris/ ▶*n.* extreme greed for wealth or material gain. —**av·a·ri·cious** /ˌavəˈrisʜəs/ *adj.*

a·vast /əˈvast/ ▶*interj.* *archaic Naut.* stop; cease: *you, young man, avast there!*

av·a·tar /ˈavəˌtär/ ▶*n.* *chiefly Hinduism* a manifestation of a deity or released soul in bodily form on earth; an incarnate divine teacher. ■ an incarnation, embodiment, or manifestation of a person or idea: *he set himself up as a new avatar of Arab radicalism.* ■ *Comput.* a movable icon representing a person in cyberspace or virtual reality graphics.

Ave. ▶*abbr.* Avenue.

a·venge /əˈvenj/ ▶*v.* [*tr.*] inflict harm in return for (an injury or wrong done to oneself or another): *his determination to avenge the murder of his brother.* ■ inflict such harm on behalf of (oneself or someone else previously wronged or harmed): *we must avenge our dead* | *she avenged herself after he broke off their engagement* | *the warrior swore he would be avenged on their prince.* —**a·veng·er** *n.*

av·e·nue /ˈavəˌn(y)o͞o/ ▶*n.* **1** a broad road in a town or city, typically having trees at regular intervals along its sides. ■ [in *proper names*] a thoroughfare running at right angles to the streets in a city laid out on a grid pattern: *7th Avenue.* ■ a tree-lined road or path, esp. one that leads to a country house or similar building: *an avenue of limes.* **2** a way of approaching a problem or making progress toward something: *three possible avenues of research suggested themselves.*

a·ver /əˈvər/ ▸ *v.* [*tr.*] (**a·verred, a·ver·ring**) *formal* state or assert to be the case: *he averred that he was innocent of the allegations.* ■ [*tr.*] *Law* allege as a fact in support of a plea.

av·er·age /ˈav(ə)rij/ (abbr.: **avg.**) ▸ *n.* the result obtained by adding several quantities together and then dividing this total by the number of quantities; the mean: *the housing prices there are twice the national average.* ■ an amount, standard, level, or rate regarded as usual or ordinary: *the month's snowfall is below average.*
▸ *adj.* constituting the result obtained by adding together several quantities and then dividing this total by the number of quantities: *the average temperature in May was 64°F.* ■ of the usual or ordinary standard, level, or quantity: *a woman of average height.* ■ having qualities that are seen as typical of a particular person or thing: *the average teenager prefers comfort to high fashion.* ■ mediocre; not very good.
▸ *v.* [*tr.*] achieve or amount to as an average rate or amount over a period of time: *annual inflation averaged 2.4 percent.* ■ calculate or estimate the average of (figures or measurements): *their earnings, averaged out over the month, were only $62 a week.* ■ [*intr.*] (**average out**) result in an even distribution; even out: *it is reasonable to hope that the results will average out.* ■ [*intr.*] (**average out at/to**) result in an average figure of: *the cost should average out to about $6 per page.* ▷late 15th cent.: from French *avarie* 'damage to ship or cargo,' earlier 'customs duty,' from Italian *avaria,* from Arabic *'awār* 'damage to goods'; the suffix *-age* is on the pattern of *damage.* Originally denoting a charge or customs duty payable by the owner of goods to be shipped, the term later denoted the financial liability from goods lost or damaged at sea, and specifically the equitable apportionment of this between the owners of the vessel and the cargo (late 16th cent.); this gave rise to the general sense of the equalizing out of gains and losses by calculating the mean (mid 18th cent.). —**av·er·age·ly** *adv.*

a·ver·ment /əˈvərmənt/ ▸ *n. formal* an affirmation or allegation. ■ *Law* a formal statement by a party in a case of a fact or circumstance that the party offers to prove or substantiate.

a·verse /əˈvərs/ ▸ *adj.* (**averse to**) having a strong dislike of or opposition to something: *as a former CIA director, he is not averse to secrecy* | [in *comb.*] *the bank's approach has been risk-averse.*

a·ver·sion /əˈvərZHən/ ▸ *n.* a strong dislike or disinclination: *he had a deep-seated aversion to most forms of exercise.* ■ someone or something that arouses such feelings. —**a·ver·sive** /-siv; -ziv/ *adj.*

a·vert /əˈvərt/ ▸ *v.* [*tr.*] **1** turn away (one's eyes or thoughts): *she averted her eyes during the more violent scenes.* **2** prevent or ward off (an undesirable occurrence): *talks failed to avert a rail strike.*

a·vi·an /ˈāvēən/ ▸ *adj.* of or relating to birds: *avian tuberculosis.*
▸ *n.* a bird.

a·vi·an in·flu·en·za ▸ the technical name for **BIRD FLU**.

a·vi·ar·y /ˈāvēˌerē/ ▸ *n.* (*pl.* **-ar·ies**) a large cage, building, or enclosure for keeping birds in.

a·vi·a·tion /ˌāvēˈāSHən/ ▸ *n.* the flying or operating of aircraft: [as *adj.*] *the aviation industry* | *aviation engineering.*

a·vi·a·tor /ˈāvēˌātər/ ▸ *n. dated* a pilot.

av·id /ˈavid/ ▸ *adj.* having or showing a keen interest in or enthusiasm for something: *an avid reader of science fiction* | *she took an avid interest in the project.* ■ (**avid for**) having an eager desire for something: *she was avid for information about the murder inquiry.* —**a·vid·i·ty** /əˈviditē/ *n.* —**av·id·ly** *adv.*

a·vi·fau·na /ˌāvəˈfônə; ˌavə-/ ▸ *n.* the birds of a particular region, habitat, or geological period. —**a·vi·fau·nal** *adj.*

a·vi·on·ics /ˌāvēˈäniks/ ▸ *pl. n.* [usu. treated as *sing.*] electronics as applied to aviation. ■ electronic equipment fitted in an aircraft.

a·vi·ta·min·o·sis /ˌāˌvītəmiˈnōsis/ ▸ *n.* (*pl.* **-ses** /-sēz/) *Med.* a condition resulting from a deficiency of one or more particular vitamins.

av·o·ca·do /ˌavəˈkädō; ˌävə-/ ▸ *n.* (*pl.* **-os**) **1** a pear-shaped fruit with a rough leathery skin, smooth oily edible flesh, and a large stone. ■ a light green color like that of the flesh of avocados. **2** the tropical evergreen tree (*Persea americana*) of the laurel family that bears this fruit. It is native to Central America and widely cultivated elsewhere. ▷mid 17th cent.: from Spanish, alteration of *aguacate,* from Nahuatl *ahuacatl.*

av·o·ca·tion /ˌavəˈkāSHən/ ▸ *n.* a hobby or minor occupation. —**av·o·ca·tion·al** /-SHənl/ *adj.*

av·o·cet /ˈavəˌset/ ▸ *n.* a long-legged wading bird (genus *Recurvirostra,* family Recurvirostridae) with a slender upturned bill and strikingly patterned plumage.

a·void /əˈvoid/ ▸ *v.* [*tr.*] **1** keep away from or stop oneself from doing (something): *avoid excessive exposure to the sun.* ■ contrive not to meet (someone): *boys lined up to meet Gloria, but avoided her bossy sister.* ■ (of a person or a route) not go to or through (a place): *this route avoids downtown Boston.* ■ prevent from happening: *make the necessary adjustments to avoid an accident.* **2** *Law* repudiate, nullify, or render void (a decree or contract). —**a·void·a·ble** *adj.* —**a·void·a·bly** /-əblē/ *adv.* —**a·void·ance** /əˈvoidns/ *n.* —**a·void·er** *n.*

av·oir·du·pois /ˌavərdəˈpoiz/ ▸ *n.* a system of weights based on a pound of 16 ounces or 7,000 grains, widely used in English-speaking countries: [as *adj.*] *avoirdupois weights* | *a pound avoirdupois.* Compare with **TROY**. ■ *humorous* weight; heaviness.

a·vow /əˈvou/ ▸ *v.* [*tr.*] assert or confess openly: *he avowed that he had voted Republican in every election* | *he avowed his change of faith.* —**a·vow·al** /əˈvouəl/ *n.* —**a·vow·ed·ly** /əˈvou-idlē/ *adv.*

a·vun·cu·lar /əˈvəNGkyələr/ ▸ *adj.* **1** of or relating to an uncle. ■ kind and friendly toward a younger or less experienced person: *an avuncular manner.* **2** *Anthropol.* of or relating to the relationship between men and their siblings' children.

AWACS /ˈāˌwaks/ ▸ *n.* an aircraft equipped with a long-range airborne radar system for detecting enemy aircraft and missiles and directing attacks on them.

a·wait /əˈwāt/ ▸ *v.* [*tr.*] (of a person) wait for (an event): *we await the proposals with impatience* | *prisoners awaiting trial.* ■ (of an event or circumstance) be in store for (someone): *many dangers await them.*

a·wake /əˈwāk/ ▸ *v.* (*past* **a·woke** /əˈwōk/; *past part.* **a·wok·en** /əˈwōkən/) [*intr.*] stop sleeping; wake from sleep: *she awoke to find the streets covered in snow.* ■ [*tr.*] cause (someone) to wake from sleep: *my screams awoke my parents.* ■ regain consciousness: *I awoke six hours after the operation.* ■ (**awake to**) *fig.* become aware of; come to a realization of: *the authorities finally awoke to the extent of the problem.* ■ make or become active again: *there were echoes and scents that awoke some memory in me.*
▸ *adj.* not asleep: *the noise might keep you awake at night.* ■ (**awake to**) aware of: *too few are awake to the dangers.*

a·wak·en /əˈwākən/ ▸ *v.* [*tr.*] rouse from sleep; cause to stop sleeping: *Anna was awakened by the telephone.* ■ [*intr.*] stop sleeping: *he sighed but did not awaken.* ■ rouse (a feeling): *different images can awaken new emotions within us.* ■ (**awaken someone to**) make someone aware of (something) for the first time: *the movie helped to awaken the public to the horrors of apartheid.*

a·ward /əˈwôrd/ ▸ *v.* [*tr.*] give or order the giving of (something) as an official payment, compensation, or prize to (someone): *he was awarded the Purple Heart.* ■ grant or assign (a contract or commission) to (a person or organization).
▸ *n.* a prize or other mark of recognition given in honor of an achievement: *the company's annual award for high-quality service* | [as *adj.*] *an award ceremony.* ■ an amount of money paid to someone as an official payment, compensation, or grant: *a generous award given to promising young dancers.* ■ the action of giving a payment, compensation, or prize: *an award of damages.* —**a·ward·ee** /əˌwôrˈdē/ *n.* —**a·ward·er** *n.*

a·ware /əˈwe(ə)r/ ▸ *adj.* having knowledge or perception of a situation or fact: *most people are aware of the dangers of sunbathing.* ■ concerned and well-informed about a particular situation or development: *a politically aware electorate.* —**a·ware·ness** *n.*

a·wash /əˈwôSH; əˈwäSH/ ▸ *adj.* covered or flooded with water, esp. seawater or rain: *the boat rolled violently, its decks awash* | *fig. the city was awash with journalists.* ■ level with the surface of water, esp. the sea, so that it just washes over: *a rock awash outside the reef entrance.*

a·way /əˈwā/ ▸ *adv.* **1** to or at a distance from a particular place, person, or thing: *they walked away from the church in silence* | *Bernice pushed him away* | *we'll be away for four nights.* ■ at a specified distance: *when he was ten or twelve feet away, he stopped.* ■ at a specified future distance in time: *the wedding is only weeks away.* ■ toward a lower level; downward: *in front of them the land fell away to the river.* ■ conceptually to one side, so as no longer to be the focus of attention: *the museum has shifted its emphasis away from research toward exhibitions.* **2** into an appropriate place for storage or safekeeping: *he put away the lawn furniture.* ■ toward or into nonexistence: *the sound of hoofbeats died away.* **3** constantly, persistently, or continuously: *there was little Edgar crooning away.*

▸*adj.* (of a sports competition) played at the opponents' grounds: *to-morrow night's away game at Yankee Stadium.*

awe /ô/ ▸*n.* a feeling of reverential respect mixed with fear or wonder: *they gazed in awe at the small mountain of diamonds.* ■ *archaic* capacity to inspire awe: *is it any wonder that Christmas Eve has lost its awe?* ▸*v.* [*tr.*] (usu. **be awed**) inspire with awe: *they were both awed by the vastness of the forest* | [as *adj.*] (**awed**) *he spoke in a hushed, awed whisper.*

a·weigh /ə'wā/ ▸*adj. Naut.* (of an anchor) raised just clear of the sea or riverbed.

awe-in·spir·ing ▸*adj.* arousing awe through being impressive, formidable, or magnificent: *Michelangelo's awe-inspiring masterpiece.*

awe·some /'ôsəm/ ▸*adj.* extremely impressive or daunting; inspiring great admiration, apprehension, or fear: *the awesome power of the atomic bomb.* ■ *inf.* extremely good; excellent: *the band is truly awesome!* —**awe·some·ly** *adv.* —**awe·some·ness** *n.*

awe·struck /'ô,strək/ (also **awe·strick·en** /'ô,strikən/) ▸*adj.* filled with or revealing awe: *people were awestruck by the pictures sent back to earth.*

aw·ful /'ôfəl/ ▸*adj.* **1** very bad or unpleasant: *the place smelled awful* | *I look awful in a swimsuit.* ■ extremely shocking; horrific: *awful, bloody images.* ■ used to emphasize the extent of something, esp. something unpleasant or negative: *I've made an awful fool of myself.* ■ (of a person) very unwell, troubled, or unhappy: *I felt awful for being so angry with him.* **2** *archaic* inspiring reverential wonder or fear. ▸*adv. inf.* awfully; very: *we're an awful long way from the main road.* —**aw·ful·ness** *n.*

▸ □ **an awful lot** a very large amount; a great deal.

aw·ful·ly /'ôf(ə)lē/ ▸*adv.* **1** (used esp. in spoken English) very: *I'm awfully sorry to bother you so late* | *an awfully nice man.* **2** very badly or unpleasantly: *we played awfully.*

a·while /ə'(h)wīl/ ▸*adv.* for a short time: *stand here awhile.*

awk·ward /'ôkwərd/ ▸*adj.* **1** causing difficulty; hard to do or deal with: *one of the most awkward jobs is painting a ceiling.* ■ deliberately unreasonable or uncooperative: *please excuse my daughter—she's at an awkward age.* **2** causing or feeling embarrassment or inconvenience: *he had put her in a very awkward situation.* **3** not smooth or graceful; ungainly. ■ uncomfortable or abnormal: *sleeping in an awkward position.* —**awk·ward·ly** *adv.* —**awk·ward·ness** *n.*

awl /ôl/ ▸*n.* a small pointed tool used for piercing holes, esp. in leather.

awn /ôn/ ▸*n. Bot.* a stiff bristle, esp. one of those growing from the ear or flower of barley, rye, and many grasses. —**awned** *adj.*

awn·ing /'ôniNG/ ▸*n.* a sheet of canvas or other material stretched on a frame and used to keep the sun or rain off a storefront, window, doorway, or deck.

a·woke /ə'wōk/ ▸*past of* **AWAKE**.

a·wo·ken /ə'wōkən/ ▸ *past participle of* **AWAKE**.

AWOL /'ā,wôl/ ▸*adj. Mil.* absent from one's post but without intent to desert: *the men have gone AWOL* | *humorous now the parrot has gone AWOL.*

a·wry /ə'rī/ ▸*adv. & adj.* away from the appropriate, planned, or expected course; amiss: [as *adv.*] *many youthful romances go awry* | [as *adj.*] *I got the impression that something was awry.* ■ out of the normal or correct position; askew: [as *adj.*] *he was hatless, his silver hair awry.*

ax /aks/ (also **axe**) ▸*n.* **1** a tool typically used for chopping wood, usually a steel blade attached at a right angle to a wooden handle. ■ *fig.* a measure intended to reduce costs drastically, esp. one that involves elimination of staff: *thirty workers are facing the ax in the assembly department.* **2** *inf.* a musical instrument, esp. a jazz musician's saxophone or a bass guitar. ▸*v.* [*tr.*] **1** end, cancel, or dismiss suddenly and ruthlessly: *the company is axing 125 jobs.* ■ reduce (costs or services) drastically. **2** cut or strike with an ax, esp. violently or destructively: *the door had been axed by the firefighters.*

▸ □ **have an ax to grind** have a self-serving reason for doing or being involved in something: *she joined the board because she had an ax to grind.*

ax·el /'aksəl/ (also **Ax·el**) ▸*n. Figure Skating* a jump with a forward takeoff from the forward outside edge of one skate to the backward outside edge of the other, with one and a half turns in the air.

awl

ax

ax·es /'ak,sēz/ ▸ plural form of **AXIS**.

ax·i·al /'aksēəl/ ▸*adj.* of, forming, or relating to an axis: *the main axial road.* ■ around an axis: *the axial rotation rate of the earth.* —**ax·i·al·ly** *adv.*

ax·il /'aksəl/ ▸*n. Bot.* the upper angle between a leaf stalk or branch and the stem or trunk from which it is growing.

ax·il·la /ak'silə/ ▸*n.* (*pl.* **ax·il·lae** /ak'silē/) *Anat.* the space below the shoulder through which vessels and nerves enter and leave the upper arm; a person's armpit.

ax·il·lar·y /'aksə,lerē/ ▸*adj. Anat.* of or relating to the armpit: *enlargement of the axillary lymph nodes.* ■ *Bot.* in or growing from an axil: *axillary shoots.*

ax·i·om /'aksēəm/ ▸*n.* a statement or proposition that is regarded as being established, accepted, or self-evidently true: *the axiom that supply equals demand.* ■ *chiefly Math.* a statement or proposition on which an abstractly defined structure is based. ▷late 15th cent.: from French *axiome* or Latin *axioma*, from Greek *axiōma* 'what is thought fitting,' from *axios* 'worthy.'

ax·i·o·mat·ic /,aksēə'matik/ ▸*adj.* self-evident or unquestionable: *it is ax-iomatic that dividends have to be financed.* —**ax·i·o·mat·i·cal·ly** /-ik(ə)lē/ *adv.*

ax·is /'aksis/ ▸*n.* (*pl.* **ax·es** /'aksēz/) **1** an imaginary line about which a body rotates: *the earth revolves on its axis once every 24 hours.* ■ *Geom.* an imaginary straight line passing through the center of a symmetrical solid, and about which a plane figure can be conceived as rotating to generate the solid. ■ an imaginary line that divides something into equal or roughly equal halves, esp. in the direction of its greatest length. **2** *Math.* a fixed reference line for the measurement of coordinates: *the horizontal axis.* **3** a straight central part in a structure to which other parts are connected. ■ *Zool.* the skull and backbone of a vertebrate animal. **4** *Anat.* the second cervical vertebra, below the atlas at the top of the backbone. **5** an agreement or alliance between two or more countries that forms a center for an eventual larger grouping of nations: *the Anglo-American axis.* ■ (**the Axis**) the alliance of Germany and Italy formed before and during World War II, later extended to include Japan and other countries: [as *adj.*] *the Axis Powers.*

ax·le /'aksəl/ ▸*n.* a rod or spindle (either fixed or rotating) passing through the center of a wheel or group of wheels: [as *adj.*] *axle grease axle loads.*

ax·on /'ak,sän/ ▸*n.* the long threadlike part of a nerve cell along which impulses are conducted from the cell body to other cells. —**ax·on·al** /'aksənl; ak'sänl/ *adj.*

a·ya·tol·lah /,äyə'tōlə/ ▸*n.* a Shiite religious leader in Iran.

aye[1] /ī/ (also **ay**) ▸*interj. archaic* or *dial.* said to express assent; yes: *aye, you're right about that.* ■ (**aye, aye**) *Naut.* a response acknowledging an order: *aye, aye, captain.* ■ (in voting) I assent: *all in favor say, "aye."* ▸*n.* an affirmative answer or assent, esp. in voting.

▸ □ **the ayes have it** the affirmative votes are in the majority.

aye[2] /ā/ ▸*adv. archaic* or *Scot.* always or still.

▸ □ **for aye** forever: *I shall treasure the memory for aye.*

a·zal·ea /ə'zālyə/ ▸*n.* a deciduous flowering shrub (genus *Rhododendron*) of the heath family with clusters of brightly colored flowers.

az·i·muth /'azəməTH/ ▸*n.* the direction of a celestial object from the observer, expressed as the angular distance from the north or south point of the horizon to the point at which a vertical circle passing through the object intersects the horizon. ■ the horizontal angle or direction of a compass bearing. —**az·i·muth·al** /,azə'məTHəl/ *adj.*

a·zo·ic /ā'zō-ik; ə'zō-/ ▸*adj.* having no trace of life or organic remains.

AZT ▸*abbr. trademark* azidothymidine, an antiretroviral drug used to treat HIV infections.

Az·tec /'az,tek/ ▸*n.* **1** a member of the American Indian people dominant in Mexico before the Spanish conquest of the 16th century. **2** the extinct language of this people, a Uto-Aztecan language. ▸*adj.* of, relating to, or denoting this people or their language. ▷from French *Aztèque* or Spanish *Azteca*, from Nahuatl *aztecatl* 'person of Aztlan,' their legendary place of origin.

az·ure /'aZHər/ ▸*adj.* bright blue in color, like a cloudless sky. ▸*n.* **1** a bright blue color. ■ *poetic/lit.* the clear sky. **2** a small butterfly (*Celastrina* and other genera, family Lycaenidae) typically blue or purplish, with color differences between the sexes.

Bb

B[1] /bē/ (also **b**) ▶ *n.* (*pl.* **Bs** or **B's**) **1** the second letter of the alphabet. ■ the second highest class of academic mark. ■ denoting the second-highest-earning socioeconomic category for marketing purposes, including intermediate management and professional personnel. ■ (usu. **b**) the second constant to appear in an algebraic equation. ■ the human blood type (in the ABO system) containing the B antigen and lacking the A. **2** (usu. **B**) *Mus.* the seventh note of the diatonic scale of C major. ■ a key based on a scale with B as its keynote.
▶ □ **plan B** an alternative strategy: *it's time I put plan B into action.*

B[2] ▶ *abbr.* ■ black (used in describing grades of pencil lead): *2HB pencils.* ■ (in personal ads) Black. ■ bomber (in designations of U.S. aircraft types): *a B52.*
▶ *symb.* ■ the chemical element boron.

b ▶ *abbr.* ■ (**b.**) born (used to indicate a date of birth): *George Lloyd (b. 1913).* ■ billion.

BA ▶ *abbr.* ■ Bachelor of Arts: *David Brown, BA.* ■ *Baseball* batting average.

Ba ▶ *symb.* the chemical element barium.

baa /bä/ ▶ *v.* (**baas, baaed** /bäd/, **baa·ing**) [*intr.*] (of a sheep or lamb) bleat. ▶ *n.* the cry of a sheep or lamb.

ba·ba /ˈbä,bä/ (also **baba au rhum** /ō ˈrəm/) ▶ *n.* a small rich sponge cake, typically soaked in rum-flavored syrup.

bab·ble /ˈbabəl/ ▶ *v.* [*intr.*] talk rapidly and continuously in a foolish, excited, or incomprehensible way: *he would **babble on** in his gringo Spanish.* ■ [usu. as *adj.*] (**babbling**) (of a stream) make the continuous murmuring sound of water flowing over stones: *a gently babbling brook.* ▶ *n.* the sound of people talking quickly and in a way that is difficult or impossible to understand: *a babble of protest.* ■ foolish, excited, or confused talk: *her soft voice stopped his babble.* ■ [usu. in *comb.*] pretentious jargon from a specified field: *to shed light on such transatlantic psycho-babble.* ■ the continuous murmuring sound of water flowing over stones in a stream: *the babble of a brook.* —**bab·bler** *n.*

babe /bāb/ ▶ *n.* **1** *chiefly poetic/lit.* a baby: *a babe in arms, less than twelve months old.* ■ *fig.* an innocent or helpless person: *cable TV is no longer a babe in swaddling clothes.* **2** *inf.* an affectionate form of address, typically for someone with whom one has a sexual or romantic relationship: *I'm the golden boy, babe.* ■ a form of address for a young woman or girl (often considered sexist): *oh, babe, waltz with me.* ■ a sexually attractive young woman or girl: *he's been pumping up his pecs to impress the babes.*

ba·bel /ˈbabəl; ˈbā-/ ▶ *n.* a confused noise, typically that made by a number of voices: *the babel of voices on the road.*

bab·ka /ˈbäbkə/ ▶ *n.* a loaf-shaped coffee cake made with sweet yeast dough to which raisins, chocolate, or nuts may be added.

ba·boon /baˈbo͞on/ ▶ *n.* a large Old World ground-dwelling monkey (*Papio, Mandrillus,* and other genera, family Cercopithecidae) with a long doglike snout and large teeth. Species include the drill and mandrill. ■ an ugly or uncouth person. ▷Middle English: from Old French *babuin* or medieval Latin *babewynus,* perhaps from Old French *baboue* 'grimace.'

ba·bush·ka /bəˈbo͞oSHkə/ ▶ *n.* (in Poland and Russia) an old woman or grandmother. ■ a headscarf tied under the chin, typical of those worn by Polish and Russian women.

ba·by /ˈbābē/ ▶ *n.* (*pl.* **-bies**) **1** a very young child, esp. one newly or recently born. ■ a young or newly born animal. ■ the youngest member of a family or group: *Clara was the baby of the family.* ■ a timid or childish person: *"Don't be such a baby!"* ■ (**one's baby**) *fig.* one's particular responsibility, achievement, or concern: *"This is your baby, Gerry,"* she said, handing him the brief. **2** *inf.* a young woman or a person with whom one is having a romantic relationship (often as a form of address): *my baby left me for another guy* ■ a thing regarded with affection or familiarity: *this baby can reach speeds of 140 mph.*
▶ *adj.* comparatively small or immature of its kind: *a baby grand piano.* ■ (of vegetables) picked before reaching their usual size: *baby carrots.*
▶ *v.* (**-bies, -bied**) [*tr.*] treat (someone) as a baby; pamper or be overprotective toward: *her aunt babied her and fussed over her clothes.* —**ba·by·hood** /-,ho͝od/ *n.* —**ba·by·ish** *adj.*

ba·by boom ▶ *n. inf.* a temporary marked increase in the birth rate, esp. the one following World War II. —**ba·by boom·er** *n.*

ba·by car·riage ▶ *n.* a four-wheeled carriage for a baby, typically with a retractable hood, pushed by a person on foot.

ba·by grand ▶ *n.* the smallest size of grand piano, about 4.5 feet (1.5 m) long.

ba·by·sit /ˈbābē,sit/ ▶ *v.* (**-sit·ting**; *past* and *past part.* **-sat**) [*intr.*] look after a child or children while the parents are out: *I babysit for my neighbor sometimes* | [as *n.*] (**babysitting**) *part-time jobs such as babysitting.* —**ba·by·sit·ter** *n.*

ba·by talk ▶ *n.* childish talk used by or to young children.

bac·ca·lau·re·ate /,bakəˈlôrēit/ ▶ *n.* a college bachelor's degree.

bac·ca·rat /ˈbäkə,rä; ,bäkəˈrä/ ▶ *n.* a gambling card game in which players hold two- or three-card hands, the winning hand being that giving the highest remainder when its face value is divided by ten.

bac·cha·nal /,bäkəˈnäl; ,bak-; ˈbakənl/ *chiefly poetic/lit.* ▶ *n.* an occasion of wild and drunken revelry. —**bac·cha·nal·i·an** /-ēən/ *adj.*

bach·e·lor /ˈbaCH(ə)lər/ ▶ *n.* **1** a man who is not and has never been married: *Mark is a confirmed bachelor* **2** a person who holds an undergraduate degree from a university or college (only in titles or set expressions): *he graduated with a bachelor's degree in philosophy* | *a Bachelor of Arts.* —**bach·e·lor·hood** /-,ho͝od/ *n.*

ba·cil·li·form /bəˈsilə,fôrm/ ▶ *adj. chiefly Biol.* rod-shaped.

ba·cil·lus /bəˈsiləs/ ▶ *n.* (*pl.* **-cil·li** /-ˈsilī/) a disease-causing bacterium. ■ a rod-shaped bacterium. ▷late 19th cent.: from late Latin, diminutive of Latin *baculus* 'stick.' —**bac·il·lar·y** /ˈbasə,lerē/ *adj.*

back /bak/ ▶ *n.* **1** the rear surface of the human body from the shoulders to the hips: *he lay on his back.* ■ the corresponding upper surface of an animal's body. ■ the part of a chair against which the sitter's back rests. ■ the part of a garment that covers a person's back. ■ a person's torso or body regarded in terms of wearing clothes: *all he owned were the clothes on his back.* ■ a person's back regarded as carrying a load or bearing an imposition: *they wanted the government* ***off their backs.*** **2** the side or part of something that is away from the spectator or from the direction in which it moves or faces; the rear: *at the back of the hotel is a secluded garden.* ■ the position directly behind someone or something: *she unbuttoned her dress from the back.* ■ the side or part of an object opposed to the one that is normally seen or used; the less active, visible, or important part of something: *write on the back of a postcard.* **3** a player in a field game whose initial position is behind the front line: *their backs showed some impressive running and passing.*
▶ *adv.* **1** toward the rear; in the opposite direction from the one that one is facing or traveling: *she moved back a pace* | *she walked away without looking back.* ■ expressing movement of the body into a reclining position: *he leaned back in his chair* | *sit back and relax.* ■ at a distance away: *I thought you were miles back* | *the officer pushed the crowd back.* ■ (**back of**) behind: *he knew that other people were back of him.* **2** expressing a return to

an earlier or normal condition: *she put the book back on the shelf* | *drive to Montreal and back* | *I went back to sleep.* ■ fashionable again: *sideburns are back.* **3** in or into the past: *he made his fortune back in 1955.* ■ at a place previously left or mentioned: *the folks back home are counting on him.* **4** in return: *they wrote back to me.*

▶ *v.* **1** [*tr.*] give financial, material, or moral support to: *he had a newspaper empire backing him* | *go up there and tell them—I'll back you up.* ■ bet money on (a person or animal) winning a race or contest: *he backed the horse at 33–1.* ■ be in favor of: *over 97 percent backed the changes.* ■ supplement in order to reinforce or strengthen: *U.S. troops were backed up by forces from European countries.* **2** (esp. in popular music) provide musical accompaniment to (a singer or musician): *brisk guitar work backed by drums, bass, fiddle, and accordion.* **3** [*intr.*] walk or drive backward: *she tried to back away* | *backing down the stairs* | *fig. the administration backed away from the* plan | [*tr.*] *he backed the Mercedes into the yard.*

▶ *phrasal v.* □ **back down** withdraw a claim or assertion in the face of opposition: *the contenders backed down from their original pledge.* □ **back off** draw back from action or confrontation: *they backed off from fundamental reform of the system.* ■ another way of saying BACK DOWN. □ **back out** withdraw from a commitment: *if he backs out of the deal they'll sue him.* □ **back up 1** (of vehicles) form a line due to congestion: *the traffic began to back up.* **2** (of running water) accumulate behind an obstruction. □ **back something up** *Comput.* make a spare copy of data or a disk.

▶ *adj.* **1** of or at the back of something: *the back pocket of his jeans.* ■ situated in a remote or subsidiary position: *back roads.* **2** (esp. of wages or something published or released) from or relating to the past: *she was owed back pay.* **3** directed toward the rear or in a reversed course: *back currents.* **4** *Phonet.* (of a sound) articulated at the back of the mouth. —**back·er** *n.* —**back·less** *adj.*

▶ □ **back and forth** to and fro. □ **behind someone's back** without a person's knowledge and in an unfair or dishonorable way: *Carla made fun of him behind his back.* □ **get** (or **put**) **someone's back up** make someone annoyed or angry. □ **turn one's back on** ignore (someone) by turning away. ■ reject or abandon: *she turned her back on her career to devote her life to animals.* □ **with one's back to** (or **up against**) **the wall** in a desperate situation; hard-pressed.

back·ache /'bak,āk/ ▶ *n.* a prolonged pain in one's back.

back·bit·ing /'bak,bītiNG/ ▶ *n.* malicious talk about someone who is not present. —**back·bite** /-,bīt/ *v.* —**back·bit·er** /-tər/ *n.*

back·board /'bak,bôrd/ ▶ *n.* a board placed at or forming the back of something, such as a collage or piece of electronic equipment. ■ *Basketball* an upright board behind the basket, off which the ball may rebound. ■ a board used to support or straighten a person's back, esp. after an accident.

back·bone /'bak,bōn/ ▶ *n.* the series of vertebrae extending from the skull to the pelvis; the spine. ■ *fig.* the chief support of a system or organization; the mainstay: *these firms are the backbone of our industrial sector.* ■ *fig.* strength of character; firmness: *he has the backbone to see us through this difficulty.*

back·break·ing (also **back·break·ing**) ▶ *adj.* (esp. of manual labor) physically demanding: *a day's back-breaking work.*

back·coun·try /'bak,kentrē/ ▶ *n.* (**the backcountry**) sparsely inhabited rural areas; wilderness: *exploring the backcountry on horseback.*

back·date /'bak,dāt/ ▶ *v.* [*tr.*] put an earlier date to (a document or agreement) than the actual one: *they backdated the sale documents to evade a court order.*

back door ▶ *n.* the door or entrance at the back of a building.

▶ *adj.* (also **back·door**) (of an activity) clandestine; underhanded: *backdoor private deals.*

back·drop /'bak,dräp/ ▶ *n.* a painted cloth hung at the back of a theater stage as part of the scenery. ■ *fig.* the setting or background for a scene, event, or situation: *the conference took place against a backdrop of increasing diplomatic activity.*

back·field /'bak,fēld/ ▶ *n.* *Football* the area of play behind either the offensive or defensive line. ■ the players positioned in this area.

back·fill /'bak,fil/ ▶ *v.* [*tr.*] refill (an excavated hole) with the material dug out of it: *they backfill the hole to street level.*

▶ *n.* material used for backfilling.

back·fire /'bak,fi(ə)r/ ▶ *v.* [*intr.*] **1** (of an engine) undergo a mistimed explosion in the cylinder or exhaust: *a car backfired in the road.* **2** (of a plan or action) rebound adversely on the originator; have the opposite effect to what was intended: *overzealous publicity backfired on her.*

▶ *n.* **1** a mistimed explosion in the cylinder or exhaust of a vehicle or engine. **2** a fire set intentionally to arrest the progress of an approaching fire by creating a burned area in its path, thus depriving the fire of fuel.

back·gam·mon /'bak,gamən/ ▶ *n.* a board game in which two players move their pieces around twenty-four triangular points according to the throw of dice, the winner being the first to remove all their pieces from the board.

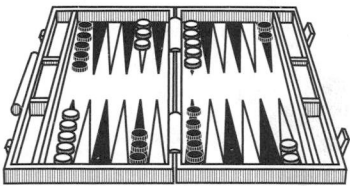

backgammon board

back·ground /'bak,ground/ ▶ *n.* **1** the area or scenery behind the main object of contemplation, esp. when perceived as a framework for it: *the house stands against a background of sheltering trees.* ■ the part of a picture or design that serves as a setting to the main figures or objects, or that appears furthest from the viewer: *the background shows a landscape of domes and minarets* | *the word is written in white on a red background.* ■ a position or function that is not prominent or conspicuous: *after that evening, Athens remained in the background.* **2** the general scene, surroundings, or circumstances: *the black cab blends beautifully into the city background.* ■ the circumstances, facts, or events that influence, cause, or explain something: *the political and economic background.* ■ a person's education, experience, and social circumstances: *she has a background in nursing* | *a mix of students from many different backgrounds.* **3** a persistent level of some phenomenon or process, against which particular events or measurements are distinguished, in particular: ■ *Physics* low-intensity radiation from radioisotopes present in the natural environment. ■ unwanted signals, such as noise in the reception or recording of sound. **4** *Comput.* used to describe tasks or processes running on a computer that do not need input from the user: *programs can be left running in the background.*

back·hand /'bak,hand/ ▶ *n.* **1** (in tennis and other racket sports) a stroke played with the back of the hand facing in the direction of the stroke, typically starting with the arm crossing the body: *he drove a backhand into the net.* **2** handwriting that slopes to the left.

▶ *v.* [*tr.*] strike with a backhanded blow or stroke: *in a flash, he backhanded Ace across the jaw.*

back·hand·ed /'bak,handid/ ▶ *adj.* made with the back of the hand facing in the direction of movement: *a backhanded pass.* ■ *fig.* indirect; ambiguous or insincere: *coming from me, teasing is a backhanded compliment.*

▶ *adv.* with the back of the hand or with the hand turned backward.

back·haul /'bak,hôl/ ▶ *n.* **1** a cargo carried on a return journey. **2** an unedited video transmission via satellite or other means to a network or station. ■ a frequency on which such transmissions occur.

▶ *v.* carry (freight) on a return journey.

back·hoe /'bak,hō/ ▶ *n.* a mechanical excavator that draws toward itself a bucket attached to a hinged boom.

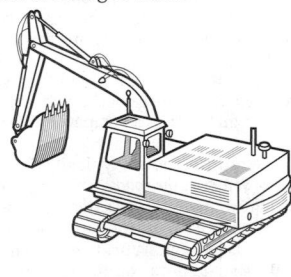

backhoe

back·ing /'bakiNG/ ▶ *n.* support or help: *he accepted the backing of the police group.* ■ a layer of material that forms, protects, or strengthens the back of something: *the fabric has a special backing for durability.* ■ (esp. in popular music) the music or singing that accompanies the main singer or soloist: *the trio provided backing to some of the most popular vocalists of the day.*

back·lash /'bak,laSH/ ▶ *n.* a strong and adverse reaction by a large number of people, esp. to a social or political development: *a public backlash against racism.*

back·list /'bak,list/ ▸n. a publisher's list of older books still in print.

back·lit /'bak,lit/ ▸adj. (esp. in photography or of a graphic display) illuminated from behind: *she was backlit by the morning sun | a backlit LCD screen.*

back·log /'bak,lôg; -,läg/ ▸n. an accumulation of something, esp. uncompleted work or matters that need to be dealt with: *the company took on extra staff to clear the backlog of work.*

back num·ber ▸n. an issue of a periodical earlier than the current one.

back·pack /'bak,pak/ ▸n. a bag, often supported by a metal frame, with shoulder straps that allow it to be carried on someone's back. ■ a knapsack used by students to carry books, or any small bag carried on the back. ■ a load or piece of equipment carried on a person's back: *a two-tank scuba backpack.*
▸v. [intr.] [usu. as n.] (**backpacking**) travel or hike carrying one's belongings in a backpack: *a week's backpacking in the Pyrenees | he has backpacked around the world.*

back·pay /'bak,pā; ,bak'pā/ ▸n. payment for work done in the past that was withheld at the time, usually because of a dispute: *Hickman should be provided backpay plus any expenses.*

back·ped·al /'bak,pedl/ ▸v. (**-ped·aled, -ped·al·ing**; Brit. **-ped·alled, -ped·al·ling**) [intr.] move the pedals of a bicycle backward in order to brake. ■ move hastily backward: *backpedaling furiously, he flipped a perfect pass.* ■ reverse one's previous action or opinion: *you've criticized him for backpedaling on budget reform.*

back·scat·ter /'bak,skatər/ ▸n. Physics deflection of radiation or particles through an angle of 180°. ■ radiation or particles that have been deflected in this way. ■ Photog. light from a flashgun or other light source that is deflected directly into a lens: *backscatter causes an underexposed picture with a blizzard effect.*
▸v. [tr.] Physics deflect (radiation or particles) through an angle of 180°: [as adj.] (**backscattered**) *backscattered sound reaches the sonar receiver.*

back·scratch·er /'bak,skraCHər/ ▸n. a rod terminating in a clawed hand for scratching one's own back.

back seat (also **back-seat**) ▸n. a seat at the back of a vehicle.
▸ □ **take a back seat** take or be given a less important position or role: *printed words will take a back seat to TV and video screens.*

back·seat driv·er /'bak'sēt/ ▸n. a passenger in a car who gives the driver unwanted advice. ■ a person who is eager to advise without taking responsibility. —**back·seat driv·ing** n.

back·side /'bak,sīd/ ▸n. inf. a person's buttocks or rump.

back·slash /'bak,slaSH/ ▸n. Comput. a backward-sloping diagonal line (\), used to separate file and folder names in a path statement.

back·slide /'bak,slīd/ ▸v. (past **-slid**; past part. **-slid** or **-slid·den** /-,slidn/) [intr.] relapse into bad ways or error: *converted vegetarians backslide to T-bones* | [as n.] (**backsliding**) *there would be no backsliding from the administration's sound policies.* —**back·slid·er** n.

back·space /'bak,spās/ ▸n. a key on a typewriter or computer keyboard that causes the carriage or cursor to move backward.
▸v. [intr.] move a typewriter carriage or computer cursor back one or more spaces.

back·spin /'bak,spin/ ▸n. a backward spin given to a moving ball, causing it to stop more quickly or rebound at a steeper angle on hitting a surface.

back·stage /'bak'stāj/ ▸n. the area in a theater out of view of the audience, esp. in the wings or dressing rooms.
▸adj. of, relating to, or situated in the area behind the stage in a theater. ■ fig. kept from public scrutiny; secret: *backstage deals.*
▸adv. in or to the backstage area in a theater. ■ fig. not known to the public; in secret: *we planned our strategies backstage.*

back·stitch /'bak,stiCH/ ▸n. sewing with overlapping stitches.
▸v. sew using backstitches.

back·stop /'bak,stäp/ ▸n. a person or thing placed at the rear of or behind something as a barrier, support, or reinforcement: *bullets volleyed into the backstop of a flood-control canal.* ■ Baseball a high fence or similar structure behind the home plate area. ■ inf. Baseball a catcher: *he tore the chest protector completely off the big Yankee backstop.* ■ fig. an emergency precaution or last resort: *the human operator has to act as the ultimate backstop when things go badly wrong.*

back·sto·ry /'bak,stôrē/ ▸n. (pl. **-ries**) a history or background created for a fictional character in a motion picture or television program. ■ similar background information about a real person or thing that promotes fuller understanding of it: *the little-known backstory about the theory of evolution.*

back·street /'bak,strēt/ ▸n. a minor street remote from a main road: *the fetid backstreets of the shanty town.*

▸adj. operating or performed secretly, and typically illegally: *a loophole that allowed backstreet chemists to make methamphetamine.*

back·stroke /'bak,strōk/ ▸n. a swimming stroke performed on the back with the arms lifted alternately out of the water in a backward circular motion and the legs extended and kicking. ■ (**the backstroke**) a race, typically of a specified length or kind, in which such a style of swimming is used: *he was fifth in the 200-meter backstroke.* —**back·strok·er** n.

back·swing /'bak,swiNG/ ▸n. a backward swing, esp. of an arm or of a golf club when about to hit a ball.

back talk ▸n. inf. rude or impertinent remarks made in reply to someone in authority: *no back talk, I'm warning you.*

back-to-back ▸adj. consecutive: *back-to-back homers in a major league baseball game.*
▸adv. (**back to back**) consecutively; in succession.

back-to-na·ture ▸adj. advocating or relating to reversion to a simpler way of life: *a back-to-nature lifestyle.*

back·track /'bak,trak/ ▸v. [intr.] retrace one's steps: *she had to bypass two closer farms and backtrack to them later | fig. to backtrack a little, the case is a complex one.* ■ fig. reverse one's previous action or opinion: *the unions have had to backtrack on their demands.*

back·up /'bak,əp/ ▸n. **1** help or support: *no police backup could be expected.* ■ a person or thing that can be called on if necessary; a reserve: *I've got a security force as backup* | [as adj.] *a backup generator.* **2** Comput. the procedure for making extra copies of data in case the original is lost or damaged: *automatic online backup* | [as adj.] *a backup system.* ■ a copy of this type: *there are long backups on all routes.* **3** an overflow caused by a stoppage, as in water or automobile traffic: *there are long backups on all routes.*

back·ward /'bakwərd/ ▸adj. **1** directed behind or to the rear: *she left the room without a backward glance.* ■ looking toward the past, rather than being progressive; retrograde: *he said the decision was a backward step.* **2** (of a person) having learning difficulties: *a lively child but a bit backward.* ■ having made less than normal progress: *economically backward countries.*
▸adv. (also **back·wards**) **1** (of a movement) away from one's front; in the direction of one's back: *he took a step backward | Harry suddenly fell backward into a somersault.* ■ in reverse of the usual direction or order: *counting backward | baseball caps turned backward.* ■ with the rear facing forward. **2** toward or into the past: *a loving look backward at his early life.* ■ toward or into a worse state: *a giant step backward for child-centered education.* —**back·ward·ly** adv. —**back·ward·ness** n.
▸ □ **bend** (or **lean**) **over backward** inf. make every effort, esp. to be fair or helpful: *Jensen bent over backward to be fair.* □ **know something backward** (**and forward**) be entirely familiar with something.

back·wash /'bak,wôSH; -,wäSH/ ▸n. the motion of receding waves. ■ a backward current of water or air created by the motion of an object through it: *the backwash of a truck on the highway.*

back·wa·ter /'bak,wôtər; -,wätər/ ▸n. a part of a river not reached by the current, where the water is stagnant. ■ an isolated or peaceful place: *a sleepy Midwest backwater.* ■ a place or condition in which no development or progress is taking place: *the country remained an economic backwater.*

back·woods /'bak'wŏŏdz/ ▸pl. n. [often as adj.] remote uncleared forest land: *backwoods homesteads.* ■ a remote or sparsely inhabited region, esp. one considered backward. —**back·woods·man** /-mən/ n.

back·yard /'bak'yärd/ ▸n. **1** a yard behind a house or other building, typically surrounded by a fence: *a tree-shaded succession of backyards* | [as adj.] *a casual backyard party.* **2** the area close to where one lives, or the territory close to a particular country, regarded with proprietorial concern: *anything was preferable to a nuclear dump in their own backyard.*

ba·con /'bākən/ ▸n. cured meat from the back or sides of a pig.
▸ □ **bring home the bacon** inf. **1** supply material provision or support; earn a living. **2** achieve success.

bac·te·ri·a /bak'ti(ə)rēə/ ▸ plural form of **BACTERIUM**.

bac·te·ri·cide /bak'ti(ə),sīd/ ▸n. a substance that kills bacteria. —**bac·te·ri·cid·al** /-,ti(ə)rə'sīdl/ adj.

bac·te·ri·ol·o·gy /bak,ti(ə)rē'äləjē/ ▸n. the study of bacteria. —**bac·te·ri·o·log·i·cal** /-,ti(ə)rēə'läjəkəl/ adj. —**bac·te·ri·ol·o·gist** /-jist/ n.

bac·te·ri·o·phage /bak'ti(ə)rēə,fāj/ ▸n. Biol. a virus that parasitizes a bacterium by infecting it and reproducing inside it.

bac·te·ri·o·stat /bak'ti(ə)rēə,stat/ ▸n. a substance that prevents the multiplying of bacteria without destroying them. **—bac·te·ri·o·sta·sis** /-,tī(ə)rēə'stāsis/ *n*. **—bac·te·ri·o·stat·ic** /-,tī(ə)rēə'statik/ *adj*. **—bac·te·ri·o·stat·i·cal·ly** *adv*.

bac·te·ri·um /bak'ti(ə)rēəm/ ▶*n*. (*pl*. **-te·ri·a** /-'ti(ə)rēə/) a member of a large group of unicellular microorganisms that have cell walls but lack organelles and an organized nucleus, including some that can cause disease. ▷mid 19th cent.: modern Latin, from Greek *baktērion*, diminutive of *baktēria* 'staff, cane' (because the first ones to be discovered were rod-shaped). **—bac·te·ri·al** /-'ti(ə)rēəl/ *adj*.

Bac·tri·an cam·el /'baktrēən/ ▶*n*. the two-humped camel (*Camelus bactrianus*).

bad /bad/ ▶*adj*. (**worse** /wərs/; **worst** /wərst/) **1** of poor quality; inferior or defective: *a bad diet*. ■ (of a person) not able to do something well; incompetent: *I'm so bad at names*. **2** unpleasant or unwelcome: *bad news*. ■ unsatisfactory or unfortunate: *bad luck* | [as *n*.] (**the bad**) *taking the good with the bad*. ■ (of an unwelcome thing) serious; severe: *bad headaches* | *a bad mistake*. ■ unfavorable; adverse: *bad reviews*. ■ harmful: *soap was bad for his face*. ■ not suitable: *morning was a bad time to ask Andy about anything*. **3** (of food) decayed; putrid: *everything in the fridge would go bad*. ■ (of the atmosphere) polluted; unhealthy: *bad air*. **4** (of parts of the body) injured, diseased, or causing pain: *a bad back*. ■ (of a person) unwell: *I feel bad*. **5** regretful, guilty, or ashamed about something: *working mothers who feel bad about leaving their children*. **6** morally depraved; wicked: *the bad guys* | *bad language* | *a bad reputation*. ■ naughty; badly behaved: *what a bad girl*. **7** worthless; not valid: *he ran up 87 bad checks*. **8** (**bad·der, bad·dest**) *inf*. good; excellent: *they want the baddest, best-looking Corvette there is*.
▶*adv*. *inf*. badly: *he beat her up real bad*. **—bad·dish** *adj*. **—bad·ness** *n*.
▶ □ **not** (or **not so**) **bad** *inf*. fairly good: *she discovered he wasn't so bad after all*. □ **too bad** *inf*. used to indicate that something is regrettable but now beyond retrieval: *too bad, but that's the way it is*.

bad blood ▶*n*. ill feeling: *there has always been bad blood between them*.

bad break ▶*n*. *inf*. a piece of bad luck: *a weird coincidence and a bad break*.

bad breath ▶*n*. unpleasant-smelling breath; halitosis.

bad debt ▶*n*. a debt that cannot be recovered.

bade /bad; bād/ ▶ past of BID².

bad faith ▶*n*. intent to deceive: *the owners have bargained in bad faith*.

badge /baj/ ▶*n*. a distinctive emblem worn as a mark of office, membership, achievement, licensed employment, etc.: *name badges* | *a Girl Scout badge*. ■ a distinguishing object or emblem: *a large gold key hung around his neck as his badge of office*. ■ a feature or sign that reveals a particular condition or quality: *my jeans had patches on the knees, like badges of courage marking encounters with barbed wire*.
▶*v*. [*tr*.] mark with a badge or other distinguishing emblem.

badg·er /'bajər/ ▶*n*. **1** a heavily built omnivorous nocturnal mammal of the weasel family, typically having a gray and black coat. Several genera and species include the North American *Taxidea taxus*, with a white stripe on the head. **2** (**Badger**) *inf*. a native of Wisconsin.
▶*v*. [*tr*.] ask (someone) repeatedly and annoyingly for something; pester: *they badgered him about the deals*.

bad·i·nage /,badn'äzH/ ▶*n*. humorous or witty conversation: *cultured badinage about art and life*. ▷mid 17th cent.: from French, from *badiner* 'to joke,' from *badin* 'fool,' based on Provençal *badar* 'gape.'

bad·lands /'bad,landz/ ▶*pl. n*. extensive tracts of deeply eroded, uncultivable land with little vegetation.

bad·ly /'badlē/ ▶*adv*. (**worse** /wərs/, **worst** /wərst/) **1** in an unsatisfactory, inadequate, or unsuccessful way: *a badly managed company* | *the war was going badly*. ■ in an unfavorable way: *try not to think badly of me*. ■ in an unacceptable or unpleasant way: *she realized she was behaving rather badly*. **2** to a great or serious degree; severely: *the building was badly damaged by fire* | *I wanted a baby so badly*.
▶*adj*. *inf*. guilty or regretful: *I felt badly about my unfriendliness of the previous evening*.

bad·min·ton /'badmintn/ ▶*n*. a game with rackets in which a shuttlecock is played back and forth across a net.

bad-mouth ▶*v*. [*tr*.] *inf*. criticize (someone or something); speak disloyally of: *no one wants to hire an individual who bad-mouths a prior employer*.

bad news ▶*n*. *inf*. an unpleasant or undesirable person or thing: *dry weather is always bad news for gardeners*.

bad-tem·pered ▶*adj*. easily annoyed or made angry: *in a heat wave, many people become increasingly bad-tempered*. ■ characterized by anger or ungraciousness: *Mary was feeling very bad-tempered* | *a bad-tempered exchange*. **—bad-tem·pered·ly** *adv*.

baf·fle /'bafəl/ ▶*v*. [*tr*.] totally bewilder or perplex: *an unexplained occurrence that baffled everyone* | [as *adj*.] (**baffling**) *the baffling murder of her sister*.
▶*n*. a device used to restrain the flow of a fluid, gas, or loose material or to prevent the spreading of sound or light in a particular direction. **—baf·fle·ment** *n*. **—baf·fling·ly** *adv*.

bag /bag/ ▶*n*. **1** a container of flexible material with an opening at the top, used for carrying things: *brown paper bags*. ■ an amount held by such a container: *a bag of apples*. ■ a thing resembling a bag in shape. ■ a woman's handbag or purse. ■ a piece of luggage: *she began to unpack her bags*. ■ *Baseball* a base. **2** the amount of game shot by a hunter. **3** (usu. **bags**) a loose fold of skin under a person's eye: *the bags under his eyes gave him a sad appearance*. **4** *inf., derog*. a woman, esp. an older one, perceived as unpleasant, bad-tempered, or unattractive: *an interfering old bag*. **5** (**one's bag**) *inf*. one's particular interest or taste: *if religion and politics are your bag, you'll find something to interest you here*.
▶*v*. (**bagged, bag·ging**) [*tr*.] **1** put (something) in a bag: *customers bagged their own groceries*. **2** (of a hunter) succeed in killing or catching an animal: *in 1979, handgun hunters bagged 677 deer*. ■ *fig*. succeed in securing (something): *we've bagged three awards for excellence*. ■ *inf*. take, occupy, or reserve (something) before someone else can do so: *get there early to bag a seat in the front row*. **3** [*intr*.] (of clothes, esp. pants) hang loosely or lose shape: *these trousers never bag at the knee*. **4** quit; give up on: *it was a drag to be in the ninth grade at 17, so he bagged it*. **—bag·ful** /-,fo͝ol/ *n*. (*pl*. **-fuls**).
▶ □ **bag and baggage** with all one's belongings: *he threw her out bag and baggage*. □ **in the bag** *inf*. **1** (of something desirable) as good as secured: *the election is in the bag*. **2** drunk: *I don't think my parents even suspected that I was half in the bag*.

bag·a·telle /,bagə'tel/ ▶*n*. **1** a thing of little importance; a very easy task: *dealing with these boats was a mere bagatelle for the world's oldest yacht club*. **2** a short, light piece of music, esp. one for the piano.

ba·gel /'bāgəl/ ▶*n*. a dense bread roll in the shape of a ring, made by boiling dough and then baking it.

bag·gage /'bagij/ ▶*n*. personal belongings packed in suitcases for traveling; luggage. ■ *fig*. past experiences or long-held ideas regarded as burdens and impediments: *the emotional baggage I'm hauling around*.

bag·gy /'bagē/ ▶*adj*. (**-gi·er, -gi·est**) (of clothing) loose and hanging in folds: *baggy pants*. ■ (of eyes) with folds of puffy skin below the eyes. **—bag·gi·ly** /'bagəlē/ *adv*. **—bag·gi·ness** *n*.

bag la·dy ▶*n*. *inf*. a homeless woman who carries her possessions in shopping bags.

bag·man /'bag,man; -mən/ ▶*n*. (*pl*. **-men**) *inf*. an agent who collects or distributes the proceeds of illicit activities: *one million dollars cash paid to the general's bagman*.

bag·pipe /'bag,pīp/ ▶*n*. (usu. **bagpipes**) a musical instrument with reed pipes that are sounded by the pressure of wind emitted from a bag squeezed by the player's arm. Bagpipes are associated esp. with Scotland, but are also used in folk music in Ireland, Northumberland, and France. **—bag·pip·er** /'bag,pīpər/ *n*.

bagpipes

ba·guette /ba'get/ ▶*n*. **1** a long, narrow loaf of French bread. **2** a gem, esp. a diamond, cut in a long rectangular shape: *a baguette diamond*.

bah /bä/ ▶*interj*. an expression of contempt or disagreement: *You think it was an accident? Bah!*

Ba·ha·'i /bə'hī/ (also **Ba·ha·i**) ▶*n*. (*pl*. **-ha·'is**) a monotheistic religion founded in the 19th century as a development of Babism, emphasizing the essential oneness of humankind and of all religions and seeking world peace. The Baha'i faith was founded by the Persian Baha'ullah (1817–92) and his son Abdul Baha (1844–1921). ■ an adherent of the Baha'i faith. **—Ba·ha·'ism** /-,izəm/ *n*.

bail¹ /bāl/ ▶*n*. the temporary release of an accused person awaiting trial, sometimes on condition that a sum of money be lodged to guarantee their appearance in court: *he has been released on bail*. ■ money paid by or for such a person as security.
▶*v*. [*tr*.] (usu. **be bailed**) release or secure the release of (a prisoner) on payment of bail: *his son called home to get bailed out of jail*. **—bail·a·ble** *adj*.
▶ □ **jump bail** *inf*. fail to appear for trial after being released on bail: *he jumped bail and was on the run until his arrest*. □ **post bail** pay a sum of money as bail: *I posted bail for him*.

bail² ▶*n*. **1** a bar that holds something in place, in particular: ■ *Fishing* a bar that guides fishing line on a reel. ■ a bar on a typewriter or computer printer that holds the paper steady. **2** an arched handle, such as on a bucket or a teapot: [as *adj.*] *drawers fitted with brass bail handles.*

bail³ ▶*v.* **1** [*tr.*] scoop water out of (a ship or boat): *the first priority is to **bail** out the boat with buckets.* ■ scoop (water) out of a ship or boat: *I started to use my hands to **bail** out the water.* **2** [*intr.*] abandon a commitment, obligation, or responsibility: *after 12 years of this, including Sunday Mass with the family, I bailed.* ■ (**bail on**) let (someone) down by failing to fulfill a commitment, obligation, or responsibility: *he looks a little like the guy who bailed on me.*
▶*phrasal v.* □ **bail out** make an emergency parachute descent from an aircraft; eject. ■ *fig.* become free of an obligation or commitment; discontinue an activity: *she felt ready to bail out of the corporate rat race.* □ **bail someone/something out** release someone or something from a difficulty; rescue: *the state will not bail out loss-making enterprises.* —**bail·er** *n.*

bai·ley /ˈbālē/ ▶*n.* (*pl.* **-leys**) the outer wall of a castle. ■ a court enclosed by this.

bail·iff /ˈbālif/ ▶*n.* a person who performs certain actions under legal authority, in particular: ■ an official in a court of law who keeps order, looks after prisoners, etc.

bail·i·wick /ˈbālə,wik/ ▶*n. inf.* one's sphere of operations or particular area of interest: *you never give the presentations—that's my bailiwick.*

bail·out /ˈbāl,out/ ▶*n. inf.* an act of giving financial assistance to a failing business or economy to save it from collapse.

bait /bāt/ ▶*n.* food used to entice fish or other animals as prey: *herrings make excellent bait for pike.* ■ *fig.* an allurement; a thing intended to tempt or entice: *many potential buyers are reluctant to take the bait.*
▶*v.* [*tr.*] **1** deliberately annoy or taunt (someone): *the other boys reveled in baiting him about his love of literature.* ■ torment (a trapped or restrained animal), esp. by allowing dogs to attack it. **2** prepare (a hook, trap, net, or fishing area) with bait to entice fish or animals as prey: *she baited a trap with carrots and corn.* ■ *fig.* lure; entice: *workers baited by your carrot powers of hiring.*
▶ □ **rise to the bait** react to a provocation or temptation exactly as intended: *Jenny was being provocatively rude, but he never rose to the bait.*

baize /bāz/ ▶*n.* a coarse, feltlike, woolen material that is typically green, used for covering billiard and card tables and for aprons.

bake /bāk/ ▶*v.* [*tr.*] **1** cook (food) by dry heat without direct exposure to a flame, typically in an oven or on a hot surface: *they bake their own bread and cakes.* ■ [*intr.*] (of food) be cooked in such a way: *the bread was baking on hot stones.* **2** (of the sun or other agency) subject (something) to dry heat, esp. so as to harden it: *the sun has baked the earth a dusty brown.* ■ [*intr.*] *inf.* (of a person or place) be or become extremely hot in prolonged sun or hot weather: *the city was baking in a heat wave*
▶*n.* a social gathering at which baked food is eaten: *lobster bakes on deserted islands.*

Ba·ke·lite /ˈbāk(ə)ˌlīt/ ▶*n. trademark* an early form of brittle plastic, typically dark brown, made from formaldehyde and phenol, used chiefly for electrical equipment.

bak·er /ˈbākər/ ▶*n.* a person who makes bread and cakes, esp. commercially. ■ an oven for a particular purpose: *a bread baker.*

bak·er's doz·en ▶*n.* a group or set of thirteen: *a baker's dozen of love songs.*

bak·er·y /ˈbāk(ə)rē/ ▶*n.* (*pl.* **-er·ies**) a place where bread and cakes are made or sold: *delicious aromas wafting from the bakery* | [as *adj.*] *an assortment of bakery goods.* ■ baked goods such as bread and cakes: *a table overflowing with homemade bakery and wine.*

bak·ing pow·der ▶*n.* a mixture of sodium bicarbonate and cream of tartar, used instead of yeast in baking.

bak·ing so·da ▶*n.* sodium bicarbonate used in cooking, for cleaning, or in toothpaste.

ba·kla·va /ˌbäkləˈvä/ ▶*n.* a dessert originating in the Middle East made of phyllo pastry filled with chopped nuts and soaked in honey.

bak·sheesh /ˈbaksHēsH; bakˈsHēsH/ ▶*n.* (in parts of Asia) a small sum of money given as alms, a tip, or a bribe.

bal·a·cla·va /ˌbaləˈklävə/ (also **balaclava helmet**) ▶*n.* a close-fitting garment covering the whole head and neck except for parts of the face, typically made of wool.

bal·a·lai·ka /ˌbaləˈlīkə/ ▶*n.* a guitarlike musical instrument with a triangular body and two, three, or four strings, popular in Russia and other Slavic countries.

bal·ance /ˈbaləns/ ▶*n.* **1** an even distribution of weight enabling someone or something to remain upright and

balalaika

steady: *slipping in the mud but keeping their balance.* ■ stability of one's mind or feelings: *the way to some kind of peace and personal balance.* **2** a condition in which different elements are equal or in the correct proportions: *overseas investments can add balance to an investment portfolio.* ■ *Art* harmony of design and proportion. ■ the relative volume of various sources of sound: *the balance of the voices is good.* **3** an apparatus for weighing, esp. one with a central pivot, beam, and a pair of scales. **4** a counteracting weight or force. ■ (also **balance wheel**) the regulating device in a mechanical clock or watch. **5** a predominating weight or amount; the majority: *the balance of opinion was that work was more important than leisure.* **6** a figure representing the difference between credits and debits in an account; the amount of money held in an account: *he accumulated a healthy balance with the savings bank.* ■ the difference between an amount due and an amount paid: *unpaid credit-card balances.* ■ an amount left over.
▶*v.* [*tr.*] **1** keep or put (something) in a steady position so that it does not fall: *a mug that she balanced on her knee.* ■ [*intr.*] remain in a steady position without falling: *Richard balanced on the ball of one foot.* **2** offset or compare the value of (one thing) with another: *the cost of obtaining such information needs to be balanced against its benefits.* ■ counteract, equal, or neutralize the weight or importance of: *he balanced his radical remarks with more familiar references.* ■ establish equal or appropriate proportions of elements in: *balancing work and family life.* **3** compare debits and credits in (an account), typically to ensure that they are equal: *the law requires the council to balance its books each year.* ■ [*intr.*] (of an account) have credits and debits equal. —**bal·anc·er** *n.*
▶ □ **balance of power 1** a situation in which nations of the world have roughly equal power. **2** the power held by a small group when larger groups are of equal strength. □ **balance of trade** the difference in value between a country's imports and exports. □ **in the balance** uncertain; at a critical stage: *his survival hung in the balance for days.* □ **on balance** with all things considered: *but on balance he was pleased.*

bal·ance beam ▶*n.* a narrow horizontal bar raised off the floor, on which a gymnast balances while performing exercises. ■ the set of exercises performed on such a piece of equipment.

bal·ance sheet ▶*n.* a statement of the assets, liabilities, and capital of a business or other organization at a particular point in time, detailing the balance of income and expenditure over the preceding period.

bal·co·ny /ˈbalkənē/ ▶*n.* (*pl.* **-nies**) **1** a platform enclosed by a wall or balustrade on the outside of a building, with access from an upper-floor window or door. **2** (**the balcony**) the upstairs seats in a theater, concert hall, or auditorium. —**bal·co·nied** *adj.*

bald /bôld/ ▶*adj.* **1** having a scalp wholly or partly lacking hair: *he had a shiny bald head* | *he was starting to go bald.* ■ (of an animal) not covered by the usual fur, hair, or feathers: *hedgehogs are born bald.* ■ (of a tire) having the tread worn away: *my car had two bald tires.* **2** without any extra detail or explanation; plain or blunt: *the bald statement in the preceding paragraph requires amplification.* —**bald·ing** *adj.* —**bald·ish** *adj.* —**bald·ly** *adv.* "I want to leave," Stephen said baldly. —**bald·ness** *n.*

bald ea·gle ▶*n.* a white-headed North American eagle (*Haliaeetus leucocephalus*) that includes fish among its prey. It is the national emblem of the U.S.

bal·der·dash /ˈbôldərˌdasH/ ▶*n.* senseless talk or writing; nonsense.

bale /bāl/ ▶*n.* a bundle of paper, hay, cotton, etc., tightly wrapped and bound with cords or hoops: *the fire destroyed 500 bales of hay.* ■ the quantity in a bale as a measure, esp. 500 pounds of cotton.
▶*v.* [*tr.*] make (something) into bales: *they baled a lot of good hay* | [as *n.*] (**baling**) *most baling and field work have been finished.*

ba·leen /bəˈlēn/ ▶*n.* whalebone.

ba·leen whale /bəˈlēn/ ▶*n.* a whale (suborder Mysticeti) that has plates of whalebone in the mouth for straining plankton from the water.

bale·ful /ˈbālfəl/ ▶*adj.* threatening harm; menacing: *Bill shot a baleful glance in her direction* | *the baleful light cast trembling shadows.* ■ having a harmful or destructive effect. —**bale·ful·ly** *adv.* —**bale·ful·ness** *n.*

Ba·li·nese /ˌbäləˈnēz; ˌbal-; -ˈnēs/ ▶*adj.* of or relating to Bali or its people or language.
▶*n.* (*pl.* same) **1** a native of Bali. **2** the Indonesian language of Bali.

balk /bôk/ (*Brit.* also **baulk**) ▶*v.* [*intr.*] **1** hesitate or be unwilling to accept an idea or undertaking: *any gardener will at first balk at enclosing the garden.* ■ (of a horse) refuse to go on. **2** *Baseball* (of a pitcher) make an illegal motion, penalized by an advance of the base runners: *the rookie balked and permitted Robinson to score.*

Pronunciation Key ə *ago*, *up*; ər *over*, *fur*; a *hat*; ā *ate*; ä *car*; CH *chin*; e *let*; ē *see*; e(ə)r *air*; i *fit*; ī *by*; i(ə)r *ear*; NG *sing*; ō *go*; ô *law*, *for*; oi *toy*; ŏŏ *good*; ōō *goo*; ou *out*; SH *she*; TH *thin*; TH *then*; (h)w *why*; ZH *vision*

▶ *n.* **1** *Baseball* an illegal motion made by a pitcher that may deceive a base runner. **2** any area on a pool or billiard table in which play is restricted in some way.

Bal·kan·ize /'bôlkə,nīz/ ▶ *v.* [*tr.*] divide (a region or body) into smaller mutually hostile states or groups. —**Bal·kan·i·za·tion** /,bôlkənə'zāsHən/ *n.*

balk·y /'bôkē/ (*Brit.* also **baulk·y**) ▶ *adj.* (**balk·i·er**, **balk·i·est**) reluctant; uncooperative: *he was trying to get his balky horse to move.*

ball¹ /bôl/ ▶ *n.* **1** a solid or hollow sphere or ovoid, esp. one that is kicked, thrown, or hit in a game: *a soccer ball.* ■ a ball-shaped object: *a ball of wool* | *he crushed the card into a ball.* ■ *hist.* a solid nonexplosive missile for a firearm. ■ a game played with a ball, esp. baseball: *young men would graduate from college and enter pro ball.* **2** *Baseball* a pitch delivered outside the strike zone that the batter does not attempt to hit: *the umpire called it a ball.* ■ *Sports* a pass of a ball from one player to another: *Whelan sent a long ball to Goddard.* **3** (in full **the ball of the foot**) the rounded protuberant part of the foot at the base of the big toe. **4** (**balls**) *vulgar slang* testicles. ■ (**ball**) an act of sexual intercourse. ■ courage or nerve. ■ nonsense; rubbish (often said to express strong disagreement).
▶ *v.* [*tr.*] **1** (usu. **ball up**) squeeze or form (something) into a rounded shape: *Robert balled up his napkin and threw it on to his plate.* ■ clench or screw up (one's fist) tightly: *she balled her fist so that the nails dug into her palms.* ■ [*intr.*] form a round shape: *the fishing nets eventually ball up and sink.* **2** *vulgar slang* have sexual intercourse with.
▶ □ **balled up 1** formed into a ball. **2** entangled; confused: *I got slightly balled up in my facts.* □ **the ball is in your court** it is up to you to make the next move. □ **a ball of fire** a person full of energy and enthusiasm. □ **on the ball** alert to new ideas, methods, and trends: *maintaining contact with customers keeps me on the ball.* □ **play ball** *inf.* work willingly with others; cooperate: *if his lawyers won't play ball, there's nothing we can do.* □ **start** (or **get** or **set**) **the ball rolling** set an activity in motion; make a start: *to start the ball rolling, the government was asked to contribute a million dollars to the fund.*

ball² ▶ *n.* a formal social gathering for dancing: *the social season was highlighted by debutante balls* | [as *adj.*] *a ball gown.*
▶ □ **have a ball** *inf.* enjoy oneself greatly; have a lot of fun: *I had a ball on my fortieth birthday.*

bal·lad /'baləd/ ▶ *n.* a poem or song narrating a story in short stanzas. Traditional ballads are typically of unknown authorship, having been passed on orally from one generation to the next as part of the folk culture. ■ a slow sentimental or romantic song. ▷late 15th cent. (denoting a light, simple song): from Old French *balade*, from Provençal *balada* 'dance, song to dance to,' from *balar* 'to dance,' from late Latin *ballare*. The sense 'narrative poem' dates from the mid 18th cent.

bal·lade /bə'läd/ ▶ *n.* **1** a poem normally composed of three stanzas and an envoi. The last line of the opening stanza is used as a refrain, and the same rhymes, strictly limited in number, recur throughout. **2** a short, lyrical piece of music, esp. one for piano.

bal·lad·eer /,balə'di(ə)r/ ▶ *n.* a singer or composer of ballads.

ball-and-sock·et joint ▶ *n.* a natural or manufactured joint or coupling, such as the hip joint, in which a partially spherical end lies in a socket, allowing multidirectional movement and rotation.

bal·last /'baləst/ ▶ *n.* **1** heavy material, such as gravel, sand, iron, or lead, placed low in a vessel to improve its stability. ■ a substance of this type carried in an airship or on a hot-air balloon to stabilize it, and jettisoned when greater altitude is required. ■ *fig.* something that gives stability or substance: *the film is an entertaining comedy with some serious ideas thrown in for ballast.* **2** gravel or coarse stone used to form the bed of a railroad track or road. ■ a mixture of coarse and fine aggregate for making concrete. **3** a passive component used in an electric circuit to moderate changes in current.
▶ *v.* [*tr.*] (usu. **be ballasted**) **1** give stability to (a ship) by putting a heavy substance in its bilge. **2** form (the bed of a railroad line or road) with gravel or coarse stone.

ball bear·ing ▶ *n.* a bearing between a wheel and a fixed axle, in which the rotating part and the stationary part are separated by a

ball-and-socket joint

ball bearing

ring of small solid metal balls that reduce friction. ■ a ball used in such a bearing.

ball boy ▶ *n.* a boy who retrieves balls that go out of play during a game such as tennis or baseball, and who supplies players or umpires with new balls.

ball cock ▶ *n.* a valve that automatically fills a tank after liquid has been drawn from it. Used, for example, in a flush toilet, a ball cock has a float on the end of a pivoting arm that opens the valve when the arm drops.

bal·le·ri·na /,balə'rēnə/ ▶ *n.* a female ballet dancer.

bal·let /ba'lā/ ▶ *n.* an artistic dance form performed to music using precise and highly formalized set steps and gestures. Classical ballet is characterized by light, graceful, fluid movements and the use of pointe shoes. ■ a creative work of this form or the music written for it. ■ a group of dancers who regularly perform such works: *the New York City Ballet.* ■ *fig.* an elaborate or complicated interaction between people: *that delicate and cautious ballet known as the planning process.*

ball game ▶ *n.* **1** a game played with a ball. ■ a baseball game. **2** *inf.* a particular situation, esp. one that is completely different from the previous situation: *making the film was a whole new ball game for her.*

bal·lis·tic /bə'listik/ ▶ *adj.* **1** of or relating to projectiles or their flight. **2** moving under the force of gravity only. —**bal·lis·ti·cal·ly** /-ik(ə)lē/ *adv.*
▶ □ **go ballistic** *inf.* fly into a rage.

bal·lis·tic mis·sile ▶ *n.* a missile with a high, arching trajectory, that is initially powered and guided but falls under gravity onto its target.

bal·lis·tics /bə'listiks/ ▶ *pl. n.* [treated as *sing.*] the science of projectiles and firearms. ■ the study of the effects of being fired on a bullet, cartridge, or gun.

bal·loon /bə'lo͞on/ ▶ *n.* **1** a brightly colored rubber sac inflated with air and then sealed at the neck, used as a children's toy or a decoration: *the room was festooned with balloons and streamers* | *fig. his derision pricked the fragile balloon of her vanity.* ■ a round or pear-shaped outline in which the words or thoughts of characters in a comic strip or cartoon are written: *a balloon reading "Ka-Pow!"* **2** a large bag filled with hot air or gas to make it rise in the air, typically carrying a basket for passengers: *a hot-air balloon.*
▶ *v.* [*intr.*] **1** swell out in a spherical shape; billow: *the trousers ballooned out below his waist.* ■ (of an amount of money) increase rapidly: *the company's debt has ballooned in the last five years* | [as *adj.*] (**ballooning**) *ballooning government spending.* ■ swell dramatically in size or number: *the public payroll ballooned from about 27,000 people to about 66,000 people.* ■ (of a person) increase rapidly and dramatically in weight: *I had ballooned on the school's starchy diet.* **2** travel by hot-air balloon: *he is famous for ballooning across oceans.*
▶ *adj.* resembling a balloon; puffed: *a flouncy balloon curtain.* ▷late 16th cent. (originally denoting a game played with a large inflated leather ball): from French *ballon* or Italian *ballone* 'large ball.'

bal·lot /'balət/ ▶ *n.* a process of voting, in writing and typically in secret: *next year's primary ballot* | *the commissioners were elected by ballot.* ■ (**the ballot**) the total number of votes cast in such a process: *he won 54 percent of the ballot.* ■ the piece of paper used to record someone's vote in such a process. ■ a list of candidates or issues to be voted on: *he agreed to have his name placed on California's primary ballot.* ■ the right to vote: *they were a contrivance to deny the ballot to Negro voters.*
▶ *v.* (**-lot·ed**, **-lot·ing**) [*tr.*] (of an organization) elicit a secret vote from (members) on a particular issue: *the union is preparing to ballot its members on the same issue.*

bal·lot box ▶ *n.* a sealed box into which voters put completed ballots. ■ (**the ballot box**) democratic principles and methods: *the proper remedy was the ballot box and not the court.*

ball·park /'bôl,pärk/ ▶ *n.* a baseball stadium or field. ■ *inf.* a particular area or range: *we can make a pretty good guess that this figure's in the ballpark.*
▶ *adj. inf.* (of prices or costs) approximate; rough: *the ballpark figure is $400–500.*

ball·point /'bôl,point/ (also **ballpoint pen**) ▶ *n.* a pen with a tiny ball as its writing point. The ball transfers ink from a cartridge to the paper.

ball·room /'bôl,ro͞om; -,ro͝om/ ▶ *n.* a large room used for dancing.

ball·room danc·ing ▶ *n.* formal social dancing in couples, popular as a recreation and also as a competitive activity. The ballroom dance repertoire includes dances such as the waltz, the tango, rumba, and cha-cha, and the foxtrot and quickstep. —**ball·room dance** *n.*

bal·ly·hoo /'balē,ho͞o/ ▶ *n.* extravagant publicity or fuss: *after all the ballyhoo, the film was a flop.*
▶ *v.* (**-hoos**, **-hooed**) [*tr.*] praise or publicize extravagantly: [as *adj.*] (**ballyhooed**) *a much-ballyhooed musical extravaganza.*

balm /bä(l)m/ ▸*n.* a fragrant ointment or preparation used to heal or soothe the skin. ■ used in names of other aromatic herbs of the mint family, e.g., **bee balm.** ■ *fig.* something that has a comforting, soothing, or restorative effect.

balm·y /'bä(l)mē/ ▸*adj.* (**balm·i·er, balm·i·est**) **1** (of the weather) pleasantly warm: *the balmy days of late summer.* **2** *inf.* extremely foolish; eccentric: *this is a balmy decision.* | *I think he's **gone balmy** again.* —**balm·i·ness** *n.*

ba·lo·ney /bə'lōnē/ ▸*n. inf.* **1** foolish or deceptive talk; nonsense: *typical salesman's baloney.* **2** variant of BOLOGNA.

bal·sa /'bôlsə/ ▸*n.* (also **balsa wood**) a very lightweight wood used in particular for making models and rafts.

bal·sam /'bôlsəm/ ▸*n.* **1** an aromatic resinous substance, such as balm, exuded by various trees and shrubs and used as a base for certain fragrances and medical preparations. ■ a tree or shrub that yields balsam. **2** a herbaceous plant (genus *Impatiens,* family Balsaminaceae) cultivated for its flowers, which are typically pink or purple and carried high on the stem. —**bal·sam·ic** /bôl'samik/ *adj.*

bal·sam fir ▸*n.* a North American fir tree (*Abies balsamea*) that yields Canada balsam.

bal·sam pop·lar ▸*n.* a North American poplar tree (*Populus balsamifera*) that yields balsam.

Bal·tic /'bôltik/ ▸*adj.* **1** of or relating to the Baltic Sea or the region surrounding it. **2** denoting, belonging to, or relating to a branch of the Indo-European family of languages consisting of Lithuanian, Latvian, and Old Prussian.
▸*n.* **1** (**the Baltic**) the Baltic Sea or the Baltic States. **2** the Baltic languages collectively.

bal·us·ter /'baləstər/ ▸*n.* a short pillar or column, typically decorative in design, in a series supporting a rail or coping. ■ [as *adj.*] (of a furniture leg or other decorative item) having the form of a baluster. ▷early 17th cent.: from French *balustre,* from Italian *balaustro,* from *balaust(r)a* 'wild pomegranate flower' (via Latin from Greek *balaustion*), so named because part of the pillar resembles the curving calyx tube of the flower.

bal·us·trade /'balə,strād/ ▸*n.* a railing supported by balusters, esp. an ornamental parapet on a balcony, bridge, or terrace. —**bal·us·trad·ed** *adj.*

bam·bi·no /bam'bēnō/ ▸*n.* (*pl.* **-ni** /-nē/) *often humorous* a baby or young child. ■ an image of the infant Jesus.

bam·boo /,bam'boo/ ▸*n.* a giant woody grass (*Bambusa* and other genera), that grows chiefly in the tropics, where it is widely cultivated. ■ the hollow jointed stem of this plant, used as a cane or to make furniture and implements.

balustrade

bam·boo shoot ▸*n.* a young shoot of bamboo, eaten as a vegetable.

bam·boo·zle /bam'boozəl/ ▸*v.* [*tr.*] *inf.* fool or cheat (someone): *Tom Sawyer bamboozled the neighborhood boys into doing it for him.* ■ (often **be bamboozled**) confound or perplex: *bamboozled by the number of savings plans being offered.*

ban /ban/ ▸*v.* (**banned, ban·ning**) [*tr.*] (often **be banned**) officially or legally prohibit: *he was **banned from** driving for a year* | *a proposal to ban all trade in ivory.* ■ officially exclude (someone) from a place: *he once was banned from a casino in Reno.*
▸*n.* **1** an official or legal prohibition: *a proposed **ban on** cigarette advertising* | *a three-year driving ban.* ■ an official exclusion of a person from an organization, country, or activity: *a **ban on** homosexuals in the armed forces.* **2** a tacit prohibition by public opinion: *Barenboim proposed to defy an unwritten ban on Wagner's works.*

ba·nal /'bānl; bə'nal; -'näl/ ▸*adj.* so lacking in originality as to be obvious and boring: *songs with banal, repeated words.* —**ba·nal·i·ty** /bə'nalitē/ *n.* (*pl.* **-ties**) —**ba·nal·ly** *adv.*

ba·nan·a /bə'nanə/ ▸*n.* **1** a long curved fruit that grows in clusters and has soft pulpy flesh and yellow skin when ripe. **2** (also **banana plant** or **banana tree**) the tropical and subtropical treelike plant (genus *Musa,* family Musaceae) that bears this fruit, with very large leaves. **3** *adj.* (**bananas**) *inf.* insane or extremely silly: *he's beginning to think I'm bananas.*
▸ □ **top banana** *inf.* the most important person in an organization or activity.

ba·nan·a re·pub·lic ▸*n. chiefly derog.* a small nation, esp. in Central America, dependent on one crop or the influx of foreign capital.

ba·nan·a split ▸*n.* a dessert made with a split banana, ice cream, sauce, whipped cream, nuts, and a cherry.

band¹ /band/ ▸*n.* **1** a flat, thin strip or loop of material put around something, typically to hold it together or to decorate it: *wads of banknotes fastened with gummed paper bands.* ■ a strip of material forming part of a garment: *hatband* | *waistband.* ■ a plain ring for the finger, esp. a gold wedding ring: *a narrow band of gold was her only jewelry.* ■ *Ornithol.* a ring of metal placed around a bird's leg to identify it. **2** a stripe or elongated area of a different color, texture, or composition than its surroundings: *a long, narrow band of cloud.* **3** a range of frequencies or wavelengths in a spectrum (esp. of radio frequencies): *channels in the UHF band.*
▸*v.* [*tr.*] (usu. **be banded**) **1** surround (an object) with something in the form of a strip or ring, typically for reinforcement or decoration: *doors are banded with iron to make them stronger.* ■ *Ornithol.* put a band on (a bird) for identification. **2** mark (something) with a stripe or stripes of a different color: *the bird's bill is banded across the middle with black* | [as *adj.*] (**banded**) *banded agate.*

band² ▸*n.* **1** a group of people who have a common interest or purpose: *guerrilla bands* | *a determined band of activists.* ■ *Anthropol.* a subgroup of a tribe. **2** a group of musicians who play together, in particular: ■ a small group of musicians and vocalists who play pop, jazz, or rock music: *the band's last two albums* | *a rock band.* ■ a group of musicians who play brass, wind, or percussion instruments: *a military band.* ■ *inf.* an orchestra. **3** a herd or flock: *moving bands of caribou.*
▸*v.* [*intr.*] (of people or organizations) form a group for a mutual purpose: *local people **banded together** to fight the company.*

band·age /'bandij/ ▸*n.* a strip of material used to bind a wound or to protect an injured part of the body: *her leg was swathed in bandages.*
▸*v.* [*tr.*] bind (a wound or a part of the body) with a protective strip of material: *bandage the foot so that the ankle is supported.*

Band-Aid /'band,ād/ ▸*n. trademark* an adhesive bandage with a gauze pad in the center, used to cover minor wounds. ■ *fig.* (also **band-aid**) a makeshift or temporary solution: [as *adj.*] *a band-aid solution to a much deeper problem.*

ban·dan·na /ban'danə/ ▸*n.* a large handkerchief or neckerchief, typically of silk or cotton, often having a colorful pattern.

b. & b. (also **B&B**) ▸*abbr.* bed and breakfast.

ban·deau /ban'dō/ ▸*n.* (*pl.* **-deaux** /-'dōz/) a narrow band worn around the head to hold the hair in position: *their dusty blonde hair smoothly combed in bandeaux.* ■ a woman's strapless top formed from a band of fabric fitting around the bust: *white two-piece bathing suit with quilted sateen bandeau top.*

ban·di·coot /'bandi,koot/ ▸*n.* a mainly insectivorous marsupial (family Peramelidae) native to Australia and New Guinea. Several genera and species, some of which are endangered or extinct, include the **short-nosed bandicoot** (*Isodon obesulus*).

ban·dit /'bandit/ ▸*n.* (*pl.* **ban·dits** or **ban·dit·ti** /ban'ditē/) a robber or outlaw belonging to a gang and typically operating in an isolated or lawless area: *the bandit produced a weapon and demanded money.* ■ *fig.* a person notably proficient at something, esp. in contrast to or at the expense of a rival or opponent: *he was no base-running bandit, but he got the job done.* ■ *military slang* an enemy aircraft. ▷late 16th cent.: from Italian *bandito,* literally 'banned,' past participle of *bandire.*
▸ □ **make out like a bandit** profit greatly from an activity.

ban·do·lier /,bandə'li(ə)r/ (also **ban·do·leer**) ▸*n.* a shoulder-belt with loops or pockets for cartridges.

band·saw /'band,sô/ (also **band saw**) ▸*n.* an endless saw, consisting of a steel band with a serrated edge running over wheels.

band·stand /'band,stand/ ▸*n.* a covered outdoor platform for a band to play on, typically in a park. ■ a raised platform for performing musicians in a restaurant or dance hall.

band·wag·on /'band,wagən/ ▸*n.* a particular activity or cause that has suddenly become fashionable or popular: *the local deejays are on the home-team bandwagon.*
▸ □ **jump** (or **climb**) **on the bandwagon** join others in doing or supporting something fashionable or likely to be successful: *scientists and doctors alike have jumped on the bandwagon.*

band·width /'band,width/ ▸*n. Electr.* a range of frequencies within a given band, in particular: ■ the range of frequencies used for transmitting a signal. ■ the transmission capacity of a computer network or other telecommunication system. ■ *fig.* the breadth of a person's interests or mental capacity.

ban·dy[1] /'bandē/ ▸*adj.* (**-di·er, -di·est**) (of a person's legs) curved so as to be wide apart at the knees. ■ (often **bandy-legged**) (of a person) having legs that are curved in such a way; bowlegged.

ban·dy[2] ▸*v.* (**-dies, -died**) [*tr.*] (usu. **be bandied about/around**) pass on or discuss an idea or rumor in a casual way: *$40,000 is the figure that has been bandied about.* ■ exchange; pass back and forth: *they bandied words and laughs from one to another.*

▸ □ **bandy words with** argue pointlessly or rudely: *don't bandy words with me, Sir!*

bane /bān/ ▸*n.* a cause of great distress or annoyance: *the bane of the decorator is the long, narrow hall.* —**bane·ful** /-fəl/ *adj. archaic.*

bang /baNG/ ▸*n.* **1** a sudden loud noise: *the door slammed with a bang.* ■ a sharp blow causing such a loud noise: *I went to answer a bang on the front door.* ■ a sudden painful blow: *a nasty bang on the head.* **2** (**bangs**) a fringe of hair cut straight across the forehead: *she brushed back her wispy bangs.* **3** *vulgar slang* an act of sexual intercourse. **4** *Comput.* the character "!"

▸*v.* [*tr.*] strike or put down (something) forcefully and noisily, typically in anger or in order to attract attention: *he began to bang the table with his fist.* ■ come into contact with (something) suddenly and sharply, typically by accident: *I banged my head on the low beams.* ■ [*intr.*] make a sudden loud noise, typically repeatedly: *the shutter was banging in the wind.* ■ (of a door) open or close violently and noisily: *he banged the kitchen door shut behind him.* ■ [*intr.*] (of a person) move around or do something noisily, esp. as an indication of anger or irritation: *she was banging around the kitchen.* ■ [*tr.*] (of a sports player) hit (a ball or a shot) forcefully and successfully: *in his second start he banged out two hits.* ■ *vulgar slang* (of a man) have sexual intercourse with (a woman).

▸*interj.* **1** used to express or imitate the sound of a sudden loud noise: *firecrackers went bang.* **2** used to convey the suddenness of an action or process: *the minute something becomes obsolete, bang, it's gone.*

▸ □ **bang for one's** (or **the**) **buck** *inf.* value for money; performance for cost: *this cross between a sports car and a family sedan gave a lot of bang for the buck.* □ **get a bang out of** *inf.* derive excitement or pleasure from: *some people get a bang out of reading that stuff.* □ **go (off) with a bang** go successfully: *the occasion went with a bang.*

ban·gle /'baNGgəl/ ▸*n.* a rigid bracelet or anklet.

bang-up ▸*adj. inf.* excellent: *for a novice, he has done a bang-up job.*

ban·ish /'baniSH/ ▸*v.* [*tr.*] (often **be banished**) send (someone) away from a country or place as an official punishment: *they were banished to Siberia for political crimes.* ■ forbid, abolish, or get rid of (something unwanted): *it's perfectly feasible to banish the smoke without banning smoking.* —**ban·ish·ment** *n.*

ban·is·ter /'banəstər/ (also **ban·nis·ter**) ▸*n.* (also **banisters**) the structure formed by uprights and a handrail at the side of a staircase. ■ a single upright at the side of the staircase: *I stuck my head between the banisters.*

ban·jo /'banjō/ ▸*n.* (*pl.* **-jos** or **-joes**) a stringed musical instrument with a long neck and a round open-backed body consisting of parchment stretched over a metal hoop like a tambourine, played by plucking or with a plectrum. It is used esp. in American folk music. ■ an object resembling this in shape: [as *adj.*] *a banjo clock.* ▷mid 18th cent.: originally a black American alteration of earlier *bandore*; probably based on Greek *pandoura* 'three-stringed lute.' —**ban·jo·ist** *n.*

bank[1] /baNGk/ ▸*n.* **1** the land alongside or sloping down to a river or lake: *willows lined the bank.* **2** a slope, mass, or mound of a particular substance: *a bank of clouds | a bank of snow.* ■ an elevation in the seabed or a riverbed; a mudbank or sandbank. ■ a transverse slope given to a road, railroad, or sports track to enable vehicles or runners to maintain speed around a curve. ■ the sideways tilt of an aircraft when turning in flight. **3** a set or series of similar things, esp. electrical or electronic devices, grouped together in rows: *the DJ had big banks of lights and speakers on either side of his console.* **4** the cushion of a pool table: [as *adj.*] *a bank shot.*

▸*v.* [*tr.*] **1** heap (a substance) into a mass or mound: *the rain banked the soil up behind the gate.* ■ [*intr.*] rise or form into a mass or mound. ■ heap a mass or mound of a substance against (something): *people were banking their houses with earth.* ■ heap (a fire) with tightly packed fuel so that it burns slowly: *she could have made a fire and banked it with dirt.* **2** (of an aircraft or vehicle) tilt or cause to tilt sideways in making a turn: [*intr.*] *the plane banked as if to return to the airport | [tr.] I banked the aircraft steeply*

banjo

and turned. ■ [*intr.*] build (a road, railroad, or sports track) higher at the outer edge of a bend to facilitate fast cornering. **3** (in pool and other games) play (a ball) so that it rebounds off a surface such as a backboard or cushion.

bank[2] ▸*n.* a financial establishment that invests money deposited by customers, pays it out when required, makes loans at interest, and exchanges currency: *I paid the money straight into my bank.* ■ a stock of something available for use when required: *a blood bank | building a bank of test items is the responsibility of teachers.* ■ a place where something may be safely kept: *the computer's memory bank.* ■ (**the bank**) the store of money or tokens held by the banker in some gambling or board games. ■ the person holding this store; the banker.

▸*v.* [*tr.*] deposit (money or valuables) in a bank: *I banked the check.* ■ [*intr.*] have an account at a particular bank: *he did not bank with the old family banks.* ■ *inf.* (esp. of a competitor in a game or race) win or earn (a sum of money): *he banked $100,000 for a hole-in-one.* ■ store (something, esp. blood, tissue, or sperm) for future use: *the sperm is banked or held in storage for the following spring.*

▸*phrasal v.* □ **bank on** base one's hopes or confidence on: *they can bank on my winning 25 games next year.*

▸ □ **break the bank** (in gambling) win more money than is held by the bank. ■ *inf.* cost more than one can afford: *Christmas need not break the bank.*

bank card ▸*n.* a card issued by a bank for the purpose of identifying a customer, as at an automated teller machine. ■ a credit card issued by a bank.

bank·er /'baNGkər/ ▸*n.* an officer or owner of a bank or group of banks. ■ the person running the table, controlling play, or acting as dealer in some gambling or board games.

bank·ing /'baNGkiNG/ ▸*n.* the business conducted or services offered by a bank: *with this account, you are entitled to free banking.* ■ the occupation of a banker: [as *adj.*] *to pursue a banking career.*

bank·note /'baNGk,nōt/ (also **bank note**) ▸*n.* a piece of paper money, constituting a central bank's promissory note to pay a stated sum to the bearer on demand: *is the $1 bill the only banknote with George Washington's picture on it?*

bank·roll /'baNGk,rōl/ ▸*n.* a roll of paper money. ■ *fig.* financial resources: *his bankroll allowed him to run campaigns all over the U.S.*

▸*v.* [*tr.*] *inf.* support (a person, organization, or project) financially.

bank·rupt /'baNGk,rəpt; -rəpt/ ▸*adj.* (of a person or organization) declared in law unable to pay outstanding debts: *the company was declared bankrupt.* ■ impoverished or depleted: *a bankrupt country with no natural resources.* ■ *fig.* completely lacking in a particular quality or value: *their cause is morally bankrupt.* —**bank·rupt·cy** *n.*

▸*n.* a person judged by a court to be insolvent, whose property is taken and disposed of for the benefit of creditors.

▸*v.* [*tr.*] reduce (a person or organization) to bankruptcy: *the strike nearly bankrupted the union.* —**bank·rupt·cy** *n.*

bank state·ment ▸*n.* a printed record of the balance in a bank account and the amounts that have been paid into and withdrawn from it, issued periodically to the holder of the account.

ban·ner /'banər/ ▸*n.* **1** a long strip of cloth bearing a slogan or design, hung in a public place or carried in a demonstration or procession: *a banner in the front window announced "Grand Reopening."* ■ a flag on a pole used as the standard of a monarch, army, or knight. ■ *fig.* an idea or principle used to rally public opinion: *the administration is flying the free trade banner.* **2** (also **banner ad**) an advertisement appearing across the top of a web page: *to get a new banner now, click Step 1.*

▸*adj.* excellent; outstanding: *I predict that 1998 will be a banner year.* —**ban·nered** *adj.*

ban·nis·ter ▸*n.* variant spelling of **BANISTER**.

banns /banz/ ▸*pl. n.* a notice read out on three successive Sundays in a parish church, announcing an intended marriage and giving the opportunity for objections.

ban·quet /'baNGkwit/ ▸*n.* an elaborate and formal evening meal for many people, often followed by speeches: *the Austrian emperor's lavish banquets* [as *adj.*] *a banquet table.* ■ an elaborate and extensive meal; a feast: *a ten-course Chinese banquet.*

▸*v.* (**-quet·ed, -quet·ing**) [*tr.*] entertain with a banquet: *there are halls for banqueting up to 3,000 people |* [as *adj.*] (**banqueting**) *a banqueting hall.* —**ban·quet·er** *n.*

ban·quette /baNG'ket/ ▸*n.* an upholstered bench along a wall, esp. in a restaurant or bar.

ban·shee /'banSHē/ ▸*n.* (in Irish legend) a female spirit whose wailing warns of an impending death in a house: *the little girl dropped her ice cream and began to howl like a banshee |* [as *adj.*] *a horrible banshee wail.*

ban·tam /'bantəm/ ▸n. a chicken of a small breed, of which the cock is noted for its aggressiveness.

ban·tam·weight /'bantəm,wāt/ ▸n. a weight in boxing and other sports intermediate between flyweight and featherweight. In boxing it ranges from 112 to 118 pounds (51 to 54 kg). ■ a boxer or other competitor of this weight.

ban·ter /'bantər/ ▸n. the playful and friendly exchange of teasing remarks: *there was much singing and good-natured banter.*
▸v. [intr.] talk or exchange remarks in a good-humored teasing way.

Ban·tu /'bantōō/ ▸n. (pl. same or **-tus**) **1** a member of an extensive group of native peoples of central and southern Africa. **2** the group of languages spoken by these peoples.
▸adj. of or relating to these peoples or their languages.

ban·yan /'banyən/ ▸n. (also **banyan tree**) an Indian fig tree (*Ficus benghalensis*) whose branches produce aerial roots that later become accessory trunks. A mature tree may cover several acres in this manner.

ban·zai /'ban'zī/ ▸interj. a Japanese battle cry.

bap·tism /'bap,tizəm/ ▸n. (in the Christian Church) the religious rite of sprinkling water onto a person's forehead or of immersion in water, symbolizing purification or regeneration and admission to the Christian Church. In many denominations, baptism is performed on young children and is accompanied by name-giving. ■ a ceremony or occasion at which this takes place. ■ a religious experience likened to this: *baptism in the Holy Spirit.* ■ fig. a person's initiation into a particular activity or role, typically one perceived as difficult: *this event constituted his baptism as a politician.* —**bap·tis·mal** /bap'tizməl/ adj.
▸ □ **baptism of fire** a difficult or painful new undertaking or experience.

bap·tist /'baptist/ ▸n. (**Baptist**) a member of a Protestant Christian denomination advocating baptism only of adult believers by total immersion.

bap·tize /'bap,tīz; bap'tīz/ ▸v. [tr.] administer baptism to (someone); christen: *he was baptized Joshua.* ■ admit (someone) into a specified church by baptism: *Mark had been baptized a Catholic.* ■ give a name or nickname to: *he baptized the science of narrative "narratology."*

bar[1] /bär/ ▸n. **1** a long rod or rigid piece of wood, metal, or similar material, typically used as an obstruction, fastening, or weapon. ■ an amount of food or another substance formed into a regular narrow block: *a bar of chocolate | gold bars.* ■ a band of color or light, esp. on a flat surface: *bars of sunlight shafting through the broken windows.* ■ see CROSSBAR. ■ a sandbank or shoal at the mouth of a harbor, bay, or estuary. **2** a counter across which alcoholic drinks or refreshments are served. ■ a room in a restaurant or hotel in which alcohol is served. ■ an establishment where alcohol and sometimes other refreshments are served. ■ a small store or booth serving refreshments or providing a service: *a dairy bar.* **3** a barrier or restriction to an action or advance: *political differences are not necessarily a bar to a good relationship.* **4** Mus. a measure of music or the time of a piece of music. **5** any kind of tribunal: *the bar of public opinion.* **6** (**the Bar**) the legal profession. ■ lawyers collectively.
▸v. (**barred, bar·ring**) [tr.] **1** fasten (something, esp. a door or window) with a bar or bars: *she bolts and bars the door.* ■ (usu. **be barred**) prevent or forbid the entrance or movement of: *boulders barred her passage | she was barred from a men-only dinner.* ■ prohibit (someone) from doing something: *journalists had been barred from covering the elections.* ■ exclude (something) from consideration: *nothing is barred in the crime novel.* **2** (usu. **be barred**) mark (something) with bars or stripes: *his face was barred with light.* —**barred** /bärd/ adj. barred windows | birds with barred breasts | [in comb.] a five-barred gate.
▸ □ **bar none** with no exceptions: *the greatest living American poet bar none.* □ **behind bars** in prison.

bar[2] ▸n. a unit of pressure equivalent to 100,000 newtons per square meter or approx. one atmosphere.

barb /bärb/ ▸n. **1** a sharp projection near the end of an arrow, fishhook, or similar item, angled away from the main point so as to make extraction difficult. ■ a cluster of spikes on barbed wire. ■ fig. a deliberately hurtful remark: *his barb hurt more than she cared to admit.* ■ a beardlike filament at the mouth of some fish, such as barbel and catfish. **2** a freshwater fish (*Barbus* and other genera) of the minnow family that typically has barbels around the mouth, popular in aquariums.

bar·bar·i·an /bär'be(ə)rēən/ ▸n. (in ancient times) a member of a community or tribe not belonging to one of the great civilizations (Greek, Roman, Christian). ■ an uncultured or brutish person.
▸adj. of or relating to ancient barbarians: *barbarian invasions | barbarian peoples.* ■ uncultured; brutish.

bar·bar·ic /bär'barik/ ▸adj. **1** savagely cruel; exceedingly brutal: *he had*

carried out barbaric acts in the name of war. **2** primitive; unsophisticated: *the barbaric splendor he found in civilizations since destroyed.* ■ uncivilized and uncultured. —**bar·bar·i·cal·ly** adv.

bar·ba·rism /'bärbə,rizəm/ ▸n. **1** absence of culture and civilization: *the collapse of civilization and the return to barbarism.* **2** extreme cruelty or brutality: *she called the execution an act of barbarism | barbarisms from the country's past.*

bar·bar·i·ty /bär'baritē/ ▸n. (pl. **-ties**) **1** extreme cruelty or brutality: *the barbarity displayed by the terrorists | the Nazi barbarities of the last war.* **2** absence of culture and civilization: *beyond the Empire lay barbarity.*

bar·ba·rous /'bärbərəs/ ▸adj. **1** savagely cruel; exceedingly brutal: *many early child-rearing practices were barbarous by modern standards.* **2** primitive; uncivilized: *a remote and barbarous country.* ■ (esp. of language) coarse and unrefined. —**bar·ba·rous·ly** adv.

Bar·ba·ry ape ▸n. a tailless macaque monkey (*Macaca sylvana*) that is native to northwestern Africa and also found on the Rock of Gibraltar.

bar·be·cue /'bärbi,kyōō/ ▸n. a meal or gathering at which meat, fish, or other food is cooked out of doors on a rack over an open fire or on a portable grill. ■ a portable grill used for the preparation of food at a barbecue, or a brick fireplace containing a grill. ■ food cooked in such a way.
▸v. (**-cued, -cu·ing**) [tr.] cook (meat, fish, or other food) on a barbecue: *fish barbecued with herbs | [as adj.] (barbecued) barbecued chicken.* ▷mid 17th cent.: from Spanish *barbacoa*, perhaps from Arawak *barbacoa* 'wooden frame on posts.' The original sense was 'wooden framework for sleeping on, or for storing meat or fish to be dried.'

bar·be·cue sauce ▸n. a highly seasoned sauce containing vinegar, spices, and usually chilies.

barbed wire ▸n. wire with clusters of short, sharp spikes set at intervals along it, used to make fences or in warfare as an obstruction.

bar·bel /'bärbəl/ ▸n. **1** a fleshy filament growing from the mouth or snout of a fish. **2** a large European freshwater fish (*Barbus barbus*) of the minnow family that has such filaments hanging from its mouth.

bar·bell /'bär,bel/ ▸n. a long metal bar to which disks of varying weights are attached at each end, used for weightlifting.

bar·be·que /'bärbi,kyōō/ ▸n. & v. a common misspelling of barbecue.

bar·ber /'bärbər/ ▸n. a person who cuts hair, esp. men's, and shaves or trims beards as an occupation.
▸v. [tr.] cut or trim (a man's hair): *his hair was neatly barbered.*

bar·ber·ry /'bär,berē/ ▸n. (pl. **-ies**) a thorny shrub (genus *Berberis*, family Berberidaceae) that bears yellow flowers and red or blue-black berries.

bar·ber·shop /'bärbər,SHäp/ ▸n. a shop where a barber works. ■ [often as adj.] a popular style of close harmony singing, typically for four male voices: *a barbershop quartet.*

bar·ber's pole (also **bar·ber pole**) ▸n. a pole painted with spiraling red and white stripes and hung outside barbershops as a business sign.

bar·bi·tal /'bärbi,tôl; -,tôl/ ▸n. a long-acting sedative and sleep-inducing drug, $C_6H_{12}O_3N_2$, of the barbiturate type.

bar·bi·tu·rate /bär'biCHərit; -ə,rāt/ ▸n. any of a class of sedative and sleep-inducing drugs derived from barbituric acid.

barb·wire /'bärb'wīr/ ▸n. barbed wire.

bar·ca·role /'bärkə,rōl/ (also **bar·ca·rolle**) ▸n. a song traditionally sung by Venetian gondoliers. ■ a musical composition in the style of such a song.

bar chart ▸n. another term for BAR GRAPH.

bar code ▸n. a machine-readable code in the form of numbers and a pattern of parallel lines of varying widths, printed on and identifying a product. Also called UNIVERSAL PRODUCT CODE.

bard /bärd/ ▸n. archaic or poetic/lit. a poet, traditionally one reciting epics and associated with a particular oral tradition. ■ (**the Bard** or the **Bard of Avon**) Shakespeare. —**bard·ic** /-dik/ adj.

bare /be(ə)r/ ▸adj. **1** (of a person or part of the body) not clothed or covered: *he was bare from the waist up | she padded in bare feet toward the door.* ■ without the appropriate, usual, or natural covering: *a clump of bare aspen trees | bare floorboards.* ■ without the appropriate or usual contents: *a bare cell with just a mattress.* ■ unconcealed; without disguise: *an ordeal that would lay bare a troubled family background.* **2** without addition; basic and simple: *he outlined the bare essentials of the story | a strange, bare production of Twelfth Night.* ■ only just sufficient: *a bare majority.* ■ surprisingly small in number or amount: *all you need to get started with this program is a bare 10K bytes of memory.*

▸ *v.* [*tr.*] uncover (a part of the body or other thing) and expose it to view: *he bared his chest to show his scar.* **—bare·ness** *n.*

▸ □ **the bare bones** the basic facts about something, without any detail: *the bare bones of the plot.* □ **bare one's soul** reveal one's innermost secrets and feelings to someone. □ **bare one's teeth** show one's teeth, typically when angry. □ **with one's bare hands** without using tools or weapons.

bare·back /'be(ə)r,bak/ ▸ *adj. & adv.* on an unsaddled horse or other animal: [as *adj.*] *a bareback circus rider* | [as *adv.*] *riding bareback.*

bare·faced /'be(ə)r,fāst/ ▸ *adj.* shameless; undisguised: *a barefaced lie.*

bare·foot /'be(ə)r,foŏt/ (also **bare·foot·ed** /-,foŏtid/) ▸ *adj. & adv.* wearing nothing on the feet: [as *adv.*] *I won't walk barefoot.*

bare·head·ed /'be(ə)r,hedid/ ▸ *adj. & adv.* without a covering for one's head: [as *adv.*] *he walked bareheaded in the teeming rain.*

bare·ly /'be(ə)rlē/ ▸ *adv.* **1** only just; almost not: *she nodded, barely able to speak* | *a barely perceptible pause.* ■ only a short time before: *they had barely sat down when forty policemen swarmed in.* **2** in a simple and sparse way: *their barely furnished house.*

barf /bärf/ *inf.* ▸ *v.* [*intr.*] vomit.
▸ *n.* vomited food.

bar·fly /'bär,flī/ ▸ *n.* (*pl.* **-flies**) *inf.* a person who spends much time drinking in bars.

bar·gain /'bärgən/ ▸ *n.* **1** an agreement between two or more parties as to what each party will do for the other: *the extraconstitutional bargain between the northern elite and the southern planters.* **2** a thing bought or offered for sale more cheaply than is usual or expected: *the secondhand table was a real bargain.*
▸ *v.* [*intr.*] negotiate the terms and conditions of a transaction: *he bargained with the city council to rent the stadium* | [as *n.*] (**bargaining**) *many statutes are passed by political bargaining.* ■ [*tr.*] (**bargain something away**) part with something after negotiation but get little or nothing in return: *his determination not to bargain away any of the province's existing economic powers.* ■ (**bargain for/on**) be prepared for; expect: *I got more information than I'd bargained for* | *he didn't bargain on this storm.* **—bar·gain·er** *n.*

▸ □ **drive a hard bargain** be uncompromising in making a deal.

bar·gain base·ment ▸ *n.* a part of a store where goods are sold cheaply, typically because they are old or imperfect: [as *adj.*] *bargain-basement prices* | *fig. a mixture of styles from pop culture's bargain basement.*

barge /bärj/ ▸ *n.* a flat-bottomed boat for carrying freight, typically on canals and rivers, either under its own power or towed by another.
▸ *v.* **1** [*intr.*] move forcefully or roughly: *we can't just barge into a private garden.* ■ (**barge in**) intrude or interrupt rudely or awkwardly: *sorry to barge in on your cozy evening.* **2** [*tr.*] convey (freight) by barge.

bar graph (also **bar chart**) ▸ *n.* a diagram in which the numerical values of variables are represented by the height or length of lines or rectangles of equal width.

bar·ite /'be(ə)rīt; 'bar-/ ▸ *n.* a mineral consisting of barium sulfate, typically occurring as colorless prismatic crystals or thin white flakes.

bar·i·tone /'bari,tōn/ ▸ *n.* **1** an adult male singing voice between tenor and bass: *he sang in a rich baritone.* ■ a singer with such a voice. ■ a part written for such a voice. **2** an instrument that is second lowest in pitch in its family. ■ a large, valved brass instrument in coiled oval form, used esp. in military or street bands.
▸ *adj.* second lowest in musical pitch.

bar·i·um /'be(ə)rēəm; 'bar-/ ▸ *n.* the chemical element of atomic number 56, a soft white reactive metal of the alkaline earth group. (Symbol: **Ba**) ■ a mixture of barium sulfate and water, opaque to X-rays, that is swallowed to permit radiological examination of the stomach or intestines: [as *adj.*] *a barium meal.*

bark¹ /bärk/ ▸ *n.* the sharp explosive cry of certain animals, esp. a dog, fox, or seal. ■ a sound resembling this cry, typically one made by someone laughing or coughing: *a short bark of laughter.*
▸ *v.* **1** [*intr.*] (of a dog or other animal) emit a bark: *a dog barked at her.* ■ (of a person) make a sound, such as a cough or a laugh, resembling a bark: *she barked with laughter.* **2** [*tr.*] utter (a command or question) abruptly or aggressively: *he began barking out his orders* | [with *direct speech*] *"Nobody is allowed up here," he barked* | [*intr.*] *he was barking at me to make myself presentable.* ■ [*intr.*] call out in order to sell or advertise something: *doormen bark at passersby, promising hot music and cold beer.*

bark² ▸ *n.* the tough, protective outer sheath of the trunk, branches, and twigs of a tree or woody shrub. ■ this material used for tanning leather, making dyestuffs, or as a mulch in gardening.
▸ *v.* [*tr.*] strip the bark from (a tree or piece of wood). ■ scrape the skin off (one's shin) by accidentally hitting it against something hard. **—barked** *adj.* [in *comb.*] *the red-barked dogwood.*

bark³ ▸ *n.* (also **barque**) a sailing ship, typically with three masts, in which the foremast and mainmast are square-rigged and the mizzenmast is rigged fore-and-aft.

bar·keep·er /'bär,kēpər/ (also **bar·keep**) ▸ *n.* a person who owns or serves drinks in a bar.

bar·ley /'bärlē/ ▸ *n.* a hardy cereal (genus *Hordeum*) that has coarse bristles extending from the ears, widely cultivated for use in brewing and stockfeed. ■ the grain of this plant. See also **PEARL BARLEY**.

bar·maid /'bär,mād/ ▸ *n.* a waitress who serves drinks in a bar.

bar mitz·vah /,bär 'mitsvə/ ▸ *n.* the religious initiation ceremony of a Jewish boy who has reached the age of 13 and is regarded as ready to observe religious precepts and eligible to take part in public worship. ■ the boy undergoing this ceremony.
▸ *v.* [*tr.*] (usu. **be bar mitzvahed**) celebrate the bar mitzvah of (a boy).

barn¹ /bärn/ ▸ *n.* a large farm building used for storing grain, hay, or straw or for housing livestock. ■ a large shed used for storing vehicles. ■ a large and unattractive building: *moved into that barn of a house.*

barn² (abbr.: **b**) ▸ *n. Physics* a unit of area, 10^{-28} square meters, used esp. in particle physics.

bar·na·cle /'bärnəkəl/ ▸ *n.* a marine crustacean (class Cirripedia) with an external shell, which attaches itself permanently to a variety of surfaces. ■ used figuratively to describe a tenacious person or thing. **—bar·na·cled** *adj.*

barn burn·er (also **barn-burn·er**) ▸ *n. inf.* an event, typically a sports contest, that is very exciting or intense.

barn dance ▸ *n.* an informal social gathering for square dancing, originally held in a barn.

barn owl ▸ *n.* an owl (genus *Tyto*, family Tytonidae) with a heart-shaped face, dark eyes, and relatively long, slender legs. It typically nests in farm buildings or in holes in trees.

barn·storm /'bärn,stôrm/ ▸ *v.* [*intr.*] tour rural districts giving theatrical performances, originally often in barns. ■ [*tr.*] make a rapid tour of (an area), typically as part of a political campaign. ■ travel around giving exhibitions of flying and performing aeronautical stunts: [as *n.*] (**barnstorming**) *barnstorming had become a popular occupation among many trained pilots.* **—barn·storm·er** *n.*

barn·yard /'bärn,yärd/ ▸ *n.* the area of open ground around a barn.
▸ *adj.* (esp. of manners or language) typical of a barnyard; earthy: *a polite way of avoiding barnyard language.*

bar·o·graph /'barə,graf/ ▸ *n.* a barometer that records its readings on a moving chart.

ba·rom·e·ter /bə'rämitər/ ▸ *n.* an instrument measuring atmospheric pressure, used esp. in forecasting the weather and determining altitude. ■ something that reflects changes in circumstances or opinions: *furniture is a barometer of changing tastes.* **—bar·o·met·ric** /,barə'metrik/ *adj.* **—bar·o·met·ri·cal** *adj.* **—ba·rom·e·try** /-'rämitrē/ *n.*

bar·on /'barən/ ▸ *n.* a member of the lowest order of the British nobility. ■ a similar member of a foreign nobility. ■ *hist.* a person who held lands or property from the sovereign or a powerful overlord. ■ an important or powerful person in a specified business or industry: *a press baron.* **—ba·ro·ni·al** /bə'rōnēəl/ *adj.* **—bar·on·y** *n.*

bar·on·age /'barənij/ ▸ *n.* [treated as *sing.* or *pl.*] barons or nobles collectively.

bar·on·ess /'barənis/ ▸ *n.* the wife or widow of a baron. ■ a woman holding the rank of baron either as a life peerage or as a hereditary rank.

bar·on·et /'barənit; ,barə'net/ ▸ *n.* a member of the lowest hereditary titled British order. **—bar·on·et·cy** *n.*

ba·roque /bə'rōk/ ▸ *adj.* relating to or denoting a style of European architecture, music, and art of the 17th and 18th centuries that followed mannerism and is characterized by ornate detail. In architecture the period is exemplified by the palace of Versailles and by the work of Bernini in Italy. Major composers include Vivaldi, Bach, and Handel; Caravaggio and Rubens are important baroque artists. ■ highly ornate and extravagant in style: *the candles were positively baroque.*
▸ *n.* the baroque style. ■ the baroque period.

barque /bärk/ ▸ *n.* variant spelling of **BARK**³.

bar·rack /'barək/ ▸ *v.* [*tr.*] (often **be barracked**) provide (soldiers) with accommodations in a building or set of buildings: *the granary in which the platoons were barracked.*

bar·ra·cu·da /,berə'koŏdə/ ▸ *n.* (*pl.* same or **barracudas**) a large, predatory tropical marine fish (genus *Sphyraena*, family Sphyraenidae) with a slender body and large jaws and teeth.

bar·rage /bə'räzн/ ▸ *n.* a concentrated artillery bombardment over a wide area. ■ *fig.* a concentrated outpouring, as of questions or blows:

she was not prepared for his **barrage** *of questions* | *a barrage of 60-second television spots.*

▶*v.* [*tr.*] (usu. **be barraged**) bombard (someone) with something: *his doctor was barraged with unsolicited advice.*

bar·ra·try /ˈbarətrē/ ▶*n. Law* vexatious litigation or incitement to it. —**bar·ra·tor** /ˈbarətər/ *n.* —**bar·ra·trous** /-trəs/ *adj.*

barre /bär/ ▶*n.* a horizontal bar at waist level on which ballet dancers rest a hand for support during exercises.

bar·ré /baˈrā/ ▶*n. Mus.* a method of playing a chord on the guitar or similar instrument with a finger laid across the strings at a particular fret, raising their pitch.

bar·rel /ˈbarəl/ ▶*n.* **1** a cylindrical container bulging out in the middle, traditionally made of wooden staves with metal hoops around them. ■ such a container together with its contents: *a barrel of beer.* ■ a measure of capacity used for oil and beer usually equal to 42 U.S. gallons (roughly 192 liters). **2** a tube forming part of an object such as a gun or a pen. **3** the belly and loins of a four-legged animal such as a horse.
▶*v.* (**-reled, -rel·ing**; *Brit.* **-relled, -rel·ling**) **1** [*intr.*] *inf.* drive or move fast, often heedless of surroundings or conditions: *we barreled across the Everglades* | *barreling along the Ventura freeway.* **2** [*tr.*] put into a barrel or barrels.
▶ □ **a barrel of laughs** *inf.* a source of fun or amusement: *life is not exactly a barrel of laughs at the moment.* □ **over a barrel** *inf.* in a helpless position; at someone's mercy. □ **with both barrels** *inf.* with unrestrained force or emotion.

bar·rel-chest·ed ▶*adj.* having a large rounded chest.

bar·rel or·gan ▶*n.* a mechanical musical instrument from which predetermined music is produced by turning a handle, played, esp. in former times; by street musicians.

bar·rel vault ▶*n. Archit.* a vault forming a half cylinder. —**bar·rel-vault·ed** *adj.*

bar·ren /ˈbarən/ ▶*adj.* **1** (of land) too poor to produce much or any vegetation. ■ (of a tree or plant) not producing fruit or seed. ■ (of a female animal) not pregnant or unable to become so. ■ showing no results or achievements; unproductive: *much of philosophy has been barren.* **2** (of a place or building) bleak and lifeless: *the sports hall turned out to be a rather barren concrete building.* ■ empty of meaning or value: *those young heads were stuffed with barren facts.* ■ (**barren of**) devoid of: *the room was barren of furniture.*
▶*n.* (usu. **barrens**) a barren tract or tracts of land: *crossing the barrens was no easy feat.* —**bar·ren·ness** *n.*

bar·rette /bəˈret/ ▶*n.* a typically bar-shaped clip or ornament for the hair.

bar·ri·cade /ˈbariˌkād/ ▶*n.* an improvised barrier erected across a street or other thoroughfare to prevent or delay the movement of opposing forces.
▶*v.* [*tr.*] block or defend with such a barrier: *he barricaded the door with a bureau* | [as *adj.*] (**barricaded**) *the heavily barricaded streets.* ■ shut (oneself or someone) into a place by blocking all the entrances: *detainees who barricaded themselves into their dormitory.*

bar·ri·er /ˈbarēər/ ▶*n.* a fence or other obstacle that prevents movement or access. ■ a circumstance or obstacle that prevents communication or that keeps people or things apart: *a language barrier.* ■ something that prevents progress or success: *the cultural barriers to economic growth.* ■ the starting gate of a racecourse. ■ (in full **barrier island**) a long narrow island lying parallel and close to the mainland, protecting the mainland from erosion and storms.
▶ □ **break the barrier** pass or exceed a significant level or amount: *the Tokyo stock exchange reopened to break the 5000-yen barrier.*

bar·ri·er reef ▶*n.* a coral reef running parallel to the shore but separated from it by a channel of deep water.

bar·ring /ˈbäriNG/ ▶*prep.* except for; if not for: *barring a miracle, he's crippled for life.*

bar·ri·o /ˈbärēˌō/ ▶*n.* (*pl.* **-os**) a district of a town in Spain and Spanish-speaking countries. ■ (in the U.S.) the Spanish-speaking quarter of a town or city. ■ a poor neighborhood populated by Spanish-speaking people.

bar·ris·ter /ˈbarəstər/ (also **bar·ris·ter-at-law**) ▶*n. chiefly Brit.* a lawyer entitled to practice as an advocate, particularly in the higher courts. Compare with **SOLICITOR**.

bar·room /ˈbärˌroŏm; -ˌroŏm/ ▶*n.* a room where alcoholic drinks are served over a counter. ■ typical of a barroom: *a barroom brawl.*

bar·row[1] /ˈbarō/ ▶*n.* a metal frame with two wheels used for transporting objects such as luggage. ■ a wheelbarrow.

bar·row[2] ▶*n. Archaeol.* an ancient burial mound.

bar·row[3] ▶*n.* a male pig castrated before maturity.

bar·tend·er /ˈbärˌtendər/ ▶*n.* a person who mixes and serves drinks at a bar.

bar·ter /ˈbärtər/ ▶*v.* [*tr.*] exchange (goods or services) for other goods or services without using money: *he often bartered a meal for drawings.*
▶*n.* the action or system of exchanging goods or services without using money: *it will be paid for by a mixture of barter and cash.* ■ the goods or services used for such an exchange: *I took a supply of coffee and cigarettes to use as barter.* —**bar·ter·er** *n.*

bar·y·on /ˈbarēˌän/ ▶*n. Physics* a subatomic particle, such as a nucleon or hyperon, that has a mass equal to or greater than that of a proton. —**bar·y·on·ic** /ˌbarēˈänik/ *adj.*

bar·y·on·ic mat·ter ▶*n.* matter composed of protons and neutrons; ordinary matter, as distinct from exotic forms.

ba·sal /ˈbāsəl; -zəl/ ▶*adj. chiefly technical* forming or belonging to a bottom layer or base.

ba·sal met·a·bol·ic rate ▶*n.* the rate at which the body uses energy while at rest to keep vital functions going, such as breathing and keeping warm. —**ba·sal me·tab·o·lism** *n.*

ba·salt /bəˈsôlt/ ▶*n.* a dark, fine-grained volcanic rock. ■ a kind of black stoneware resembling such rock. ▷early 17th cent. (in the Latin form): from Latin *basaltes* (variant of *basanites*), from Greek *basanitēs*, from *basanos* 'touchstone.' —**ba·sal·tic** /-tik/ *adj.*

base[1] /bās/ ▶*n.* **1** the lowest part or edge of something, esp. the part on which it rests or is supported: *she sat down at the base of a tree.* ■ *Archit.* the part of a column between the shaft and pedestal or pavement. ■ *Bot. & Zool.* the end at which a part or organ is attached to the trunk or main part: *a shoot is produced at the base of the stem.* ■ *Geom.* a line or surface on which a figure is regarded as standing: *the base of the triangle.* ■ *Surveying* a line of known length used in triangulation. **2** a conceptual structure or entity on which something draws or depends: *the town's economic base collapsed.* ■ something used as a foundation or starting point for further work; a basis: *uses existing data as the base for the study.* ■ a group of people regarded as supporting an organization, for example by buying its products: *a client base.* **3** the main place where a person works or stays: *he makes the studio her base.* ■ *chiefly Mil.* a place used as a center of operations by the armed forces or others; a headquarters: *he headed back to base.* ■ a place from which a particular activity can be carried out: *a base for shipping operations.* **4** a main or important element or ingredient to which other things are added: *soaps with a vegetable oil base.* **5** *Chem.* a substance capable of reacting with an acid to form a salt and water, or (more broadly) of accepting or neutralizing hydrogen ions. Compare with **ALKALI.** ■ *Biochem.* a purine or pyrimidine group in a nucleotide or nucleic acid. **6** *Electr.* the middle part of a bipolar transistor, separating the emitter from the collector. **7** *Linguistics* the root or stem of a word or a derivative. ■ the uninflected form of a verb. **8** *Math.* a number used as the basis of a numeration scale. ■ a number in terms of which other numbers are expressed as logarithms. **9** *Baseball* one of the four stations that must be reached in turn to score a run.
▶*v.* [*tr.*] **1** (often **be based**) have as the foundation for (something); use as a point from which (something) can develop: *the film is based on a novel by Pat Conroy.* **2** situate as the center of operations: *a research program based at the University of Arizona.*
▶ □ **get to first base** *inf.* achieve the first step toward one's objective. □ **first base, second base, third base** *inf.* used to refer to progressive levels of sexual intimacy. □ **off-base** *inf.* mistaken: *the boy is way off-base.* □ **touch base(s)** *inf.* briefly make or renew contact with (someone).

base[2] ▶*adj.* (of a person or a person's actions or feelings) without moral principles; ignoble: *the electorate's baser instincts of greed and selfishness.* ■ (of coins or other articles) not made of precious metal. —**base·ly** *adv.* —**base·ness** *n.*

base·ball /ˈbāsˌbôl/ ▶*n.* a ball game played between two teams of nine on a field with a diamond-shaped circuit of four bases. It is played chiefly in the U.S., Canada, Latin America, and East Asia. ■ the hard ball used in this game.

base·board /ˈbāsˌbôrd/ ▶*n.* a narrow board running along the base of an interior wall.

base hit ▶*n. Baseball* a fair ball hit such that the batter can advance safely to a base without aid of an error committed by the team in the field.

Pronunciation Key ə *ago, up;* ər *over, fur;* a *hat;* ā *ate;* ä *car;* CH *chin;* e *let;* ē *see;* e(ə)r *air;* i *fit;* ī *by;* i(ə)r *ear;* NG *sing;* ō *go;* ô *law, for;* oi *toy;* oŏ *good;* oō *goo;* ou *out;* SH *she;* TH *thin;* ṮH *then;* (h)w *why;* ZH *vision*

base·less /'bāslis/ ▸ adj. without foundation in fact: baseless allegations. —**base·less·ly** adv. —**base·less·ness** n.

base·line /'bās,līn/ ▸ n. **1** a minimum or starting point used for comparisons. **2** (in tennis, volleyball, etc.) the line marking each end of the court. ▪ Baseball the line between bases, which a runner must stay close to when running.

base·man /'bāsmən/ ▸ n. (pl. -men) Baseball a fielder designated to cover first, second, or third base.

base·ment /'bāsmənt/ ▸ n. the floor of a building partly or entirely below ground level. ▪ Geol. the oldest rocks underlying a particular area.

base on balls (abbr.: **BB**) ▸ n. Baseball another term for WALK n. 3.

ba·ses /'bāsēz/ ▸ plural form of BASIS.

base u·nit ▸ n. a fundamental unit that is defined arbitrarily and not by combinations of other units. The base units of the SI system are the meter, kilogram, second, ampere, kelvin, mole, and candela.

bash /basH/ ▸ v. [tr.] inf. strike hard and violently: bash a mosquito with a newspaper. ▪ fig. criticize severely: a remark bashing the Belgian brewing industry.
▸ n. inf. **1** a heavy blow: a bash on the head. **2** inf. a party or social event: a birthday bash.

bash·ful /'basHfəl/ ▸ adj. reluctant to draw attention to oneself; shy: don't be bashful about telling folks how you feel. —**bash·ful·ly** adv. —**bash·ful·ness** n.

BASIC /'bāsik/ ▸ n. a simple high-level computer programming language that uses familiar English words, designed for beginners and formerly widely used.

ba·sic /'bāsik/ ▸ adj. **1** forming an essential foundation or starting point; fundamental: certain basic rules must be obeyed. ▪ offering or consisting in the minimum required without elaboration or luxury; simplest or lowest in level: basic and unsophisticated resorts. ▪ common to or required by everyone; primary and ineradicable or inalienable: basic human rights. **2** Chem. having the properties of a base, or containing a base; having a pH greater than 7.
▸ n. (**basics**) the essential facts or principles of a subject or skill: learning the basics of the business. ▪ essential food and other supplies: people are facing a shortage of basics like flour. ▪ Mil. basic training.

ba·si·cal·ly /'bāsik(ə)lē/ ▸ adv. in the most essential respects; fundamentally: we started from a basically simple idea. ▪ used to indicate that a statement summarizes the most important aspects, or gives a roughly accurate account, of a more complex situation: I basically played the same tunes every night.

bas·il /'bāzəl; 'bazəl/ ▸ n. an aromatic annual herb (genus Ocimum) of the mint family, native to tropical Asia. ▪ the leaves of this plant used as a culinary herb, esp. in Mediterranean dishes.

ba·sil·i·ca /bə'silikə/ ▸ n. a large oblong hall or building with double colonnades and a semicircular apse, used in ancient Rome as a court of law or for public assemblies. ▪ a similar building used as a Christian church. ▪ the name given to certain churches granted special privileges by the pope. —**ba·sil·i·can** adj.

bas·i·lisk /'basə,lisk; 'baz-/ ▸ n. **1** a mythical reptile with a lethal gaze or breath, hatched by a serpent from a cock's egg. **2** a long, slender, and mainly bright green lizard (Basiliscus plumifrons, family Iguanidae) found in Central America, the male of which has a crest running from the head to the tail. It can swim well and is able to run on its hind legs across the surface of water.

bas·i·lo·sau·rus /,basələ'sôrəs/ ▸ n. (pl. -sau·rus·es or -sau·ri /-'sôrī/) a large marine cetacean (Basilosaurus isis) of the Eocene epoch, having a long, slender body and vestigial fore and hind limbs. Fossils were discovered in the early 1990s.

ba·sin /'bāsən/ ▸ n. **1** a bowl for washing, typically attached to a wall and having faucets connected to a water supply; a washbasin. **2** a wide, round open container, esp. one used for holding liquid. **3** a natural depression on the earth's surface, typically containing water: the Indian Ocean basin. ▪ the tract of country that is drained by a river and its tributaries or drains into a lake or sea: the Amazon basin | a drainage basin. ▪ an enclosed area of water where vessels can be moored: a yacht basin. —**ba·sin·ful** /-,fŏŏl/ n.

ba·sis /'bāsis/ ▸ n. (pl. -ses /-sēz/) the underlying support or foundation for an idea, argument, or process: trust is the only basis for a good working relationship. ▪ the system or principles according to which an activity or process is carried on: she needed coaching on a regular basis. ▪ the justification for or reasoning behind something: on the basis of these statistics, important decisions are made.

bask /bask/ ▸ v. [intr.] lie exposed to warmth and light, typically from the sun, for relaxation and pleasure: sprawled figures **basking in** the afternoon sun. ▪ (**bask in**) fig. revel in and make the most of (something pleasing): he went on **basking in** the glory of his first book.

bas·ket /'baskit/ ▸ n. **1** a container used to hold or carry things, typically made from interwoven strips of cane or wire: a laundry basket. ▪ a structure suspended from the envelope of a hot-air balloon for carrying the crew, equipment, and ballast. ▪ Finance a group or range of currencies or investments: the European currency unit is made up of **a basket of** ten currencies. **2** Basketball a net fixed on a hoop used as the goal. ▪ a goal scored.

bas·ket·ball /'baskit,bôl/ ▸ n. a game played between two teams of five players in which goals are scored by throwing a ball through a netted hoop fixed above each end of the court. ▪ the inflated ball used in this game.

bas·ket case ▸ n. inf. a person or thing regarded as useless or unable to cope.

bas·ket·ry /'baskitrē/ ▸ n. the craft of basket-making.

bas·ket weave ▸ n. a style of weave or a pattern resembling basketwork.

bas·ket·work /'baskit,wərk/ ▸ n. material woven in the style of a basket. ▪ the craft of making such material.

bas·ma·ti /bäs'mätē/ (also **basmati rice**) ▸ n. a kind of long-grain Indian rice of a high quality. ▷from Hindi bāsmatī, literally 'fragrant.'

bas mitz·vah /bäs 'mitsvə/ ▸ n. a variant of BAT MITZVAH.

Basque /bask/ ▸ n. **1** a member of a people living in the Basque Country of France and Spain. Culturally one of the most distinct groups in Europe, the Basques were largely independent until the 19th century. **2** the language of this people, which has no known relation to any other language.
▸ adj. of or relating to the Basques or their language.

bas-re·lief /,bä rə'lēf/ ▸ n. Sculpture see RELIEF (sense 4). ▪ a sculpture, carving, or molding in bas-relief.

bass[1] /bās/ ▸ n. a voice, instrument, or sound of the lowest range, in particular: ▪ the lowest adult male singing voice. ▪ [as adj.] denoting the member of a family of instruments that is the lowest in pitch: a bass clarinet | a bass drum. ▪ inf. a bass guitar or double bass. ▪ the low-frequency output of a radio or audio system, corresponding to the bass in music. —**bass·ist** n.

bass[2] /bas/ ▸ n. (pl. same or **basses**) **1** the common European freshwater perch. **2** any of a number of fish similar to or related to this, in particular: ▪ a mainly marine fish found in temperate waters (family Percichthyidae or Moronidae). ▪ an American fish (genera Ambloplites and Micropterus) of the freshwater sunfish family. ▪ a sea bass.

bass clef /bās klef/ ▸ n. a clef placing F below middle C on the second-highest line of the staff.

bas·set hound /'basit hound/ ▸ n. a sturdy hunting dog of a breed with a long body, short legs, and big ears.

bas·si·net /,basə'net/ ▸ n. a baby's wicker cradle, usually with a hood.

bas·so /'basō; bä-/ ▸ n. (pl. **bas·sos** or **bas·si** /'bäsē/) a singer with a bass voice.

bas·soon /bə'sōōn; ba-/ ▸ n. a bass instrument of the oboe family with a double reed. —**bas·soon·ist** n.

bas·so pro·fun·do /'basō prō'fəndō; 'bäsō/ ▸ n. (pl. **bas·so pro·fun·dos** or **bas·si pro·fun·di** /'bäsē prō'fəndē/) a bass singer with an exceptionally low range.

bas·so·re·lie·vo /'basō ri'lēvō/ ▸ n. (pl. -vos) Sculpture another term for BAS-RELIEF (see RELIEF sense 4).

bass·wood /'bas,wŏŏd/ ▸ n. a North American linden tree, including the large-leaved Tilia americana (also called **American linden**) of the northern U.S. and Canada.

bast /bast/ ▸ n. (also **bast fiber**) fibrous material from the phloem of a plant, used as fiber in matting, cord, etc.

bassoon

bas·tard /'bastərd/ ▸ n. **1** archaic or derog. a person born of parents not married to each other. **2** inf. an unpleasant or despicable person: he lied to me, the bastard! ▪ a person (used to suggest an emotion such as pity or envy): the poor bastard. ▪ a difficult or awkward thing, undertaking, or situation: it's been an absolute bastard of a week.
▸ adj. **1** archaic or derog. born of parents not married to each other; illegitimate: a bastard child. **2** (of a thing) no longer in its pure or original form; debased: a bastard Darwinism. ▷Middle English: via Old French from medieval Latin bastardus. —**bas·tar·dy** n.

bas·tard·ize /ˈbastərˌdīz/ ▶v. [tr.] [often as adj.] (**bastardized**) corrupt or debase (something such as a language or art form), typically by adding new elements: *a strange, bastardized form of French.* —**bas·tard·i·za·tion** /ˌbastərdiˈzāSHən/ n.

baste¹ /bāst/ ▶v. [tr.] pour juices or melted fat over (meat) during cooking in order to keep it moist.

baste² ▶v. [tr.] *Needlework* tack with long, loose stitches in preparation for sewing.

bas·ti·na·do /ˌbastəˈnādō; -ˈnädō/ *chiefly hist.* ▶n. a form of punishment or torture that involves caning the soles of someone's feet.

bas·tion /ˈbasCHən/ ▶n. a projecting part of a fortification built at an angle to the line of a wall, so as to allow defensive fire in several directions. ■ *fig.* an institution, place, or person strongly defending or upholding particular principles, attitudes, or activities: *the last bastion of male privilege.*

bat¹ /bat/ ▶n. an implement with a handle and a solid surface, usually of wood, used for hitting the ball in games such as baseball, cricket, and table tennis.
▶v. (**bat·ted**, **bat·ting**) **1** [intr.] (of a team or a player in sports such as baseball) take in turns the role of hitting rather than fielding: *Johnson will be batting in the fifth inning.* **2** [tr.] hit at (someone or something) with the palm of one's hand: *he batted the flies away.*
▶*phrasal v.* □ **bat something around** *inf.* discuss an idea or proposal casually or idly. □ **go to bat for** *inf.* defend the interests of; support: *his willingness to go to bat for his employees.*
▶ □ **right off the bat** at the very beginning.

bat² ▶n. a mainly nocturnal mammal (order Chiroptera) capable of sustained flight, with membranous wings that extend between the fingers and connecting the forelimbs to the body and the hind limbs to the tail.
▶ □ **have bats in the** (or **one's**) **belfry** *inf.* be eccentric or crazy. □ **like a bat out of hell** *inf.* very fast and wildly.

bat³ ▶v. (**bat·ted**, **bat·ting**) [tr.] flutter one's eyelashes, typically in a flirtatious manner: *she batted her long dark eyelashes at him.*
▶ □ **not bat** (or **without batting**) **an eyelid** (or **eye**) *inf.* show (or showing) no reaction: *she paid the bill without batting an eyelid.*

batch /baCH/ ▶n. a quantity or consignment of goods produced at one time: *a batch of cookies.* ■ *inf.* a number of things or people regarded as a group or set: *a batch of hostile letters came.* ■ *Comput.* a group of records processed as a single unit, usually without input from a user.
▶v. [tr.] arrange (things) in sets or groups.

ba·teau /baˈtō/ ▶n. (*pl.* **-teaux** /-ˈtōz/) a light flat-bottomed riverboat used in eastern and central North America.

bat·ed /ˈbātid/ ▶adj. (in phrase **with bated breath**) in great suspense; very anxiously or excitedly: *he waited for a reply to his offer with bated breath.*

bath /baTH/ ▶n. (*pl.* **baths** /baTHs; baTHz/) an act or process of immersing and washing one's body in a large container of water: *she took a long, hot bath.* ■ any act of washing or cleansing oneself: *sweat baths | sponge baths.* ■ (usu. **baths**) a public establishment offering bathing facilities. ■ (**baths**) a resort with a mineral spring used for medical treatment. ■ a bathroom. ■ a container holding a liquid or other substance in which something is immersed, typically when undergoing a process such as film developing.
▶v. [tr.] wash (someone) while immersing him or her in a container of water: *how to bath a baby.*
▶ □ **take a bath** *inf.* suffer a heavy financial loss.

bathe /bāTH/ ▶v. [intr.] wash by immersing one's body in water. ■ spend time in the ocean or a lake, river, or swimming pool for pleasure. ■ [tr.] soak or wipe gently with liquid to clean or soothe: *she bathed and bandaged my knee.* ■ [tr.] wash (someone) in a bath: *they bathed the baby.* ■ [tr.] (usu. **be bathed**) *fig.* suffuse or envelop in something: *the park lay bathed in sunshine | mussels bathed in garlic butter.* —**bath·er** n.

bath·house /ˈbaTHˌhous/ ▶n. **1** a building with baths for communal use. **2** a building where swimmers change clothes.

bath·ing suit ▶n. a garment worn for swimming; a swimsuit.

ba·thos /ˈbāTHäs/ ▶n. (esp. in a work of literature) an effect of anticlimax created by an unintentional lapse in mood from the sublime to the trivial or ridiculous. ▷mid 17th cent. (first recorded in the Greek sense): from Greek, literally 'depth.' The current sense was introduced by Alexander Pope in the early 18th cent. —**ba·thet·ic** /bəˈTHetik/ adj.

bath·robe /ˈbaTHˌrōb/ ▶n. a robe, typically made of terry, worn esp. before and after taking a bath.

bath·room /ˈbaTHˌro͞om; -ˌro͝om/ ▶n. a room containing a bathtub or a shower and usually also a washbasin and a toilet. ■ a set of matching units to be fitted in such a room, esp. as sold together. ■ a room containing a toilet: *I have to go to the bathroom.*

bath salts ▶*pl. n.* a crystalline substance that is dissolved in bathwater to soften or perfume the water.

bath·tub /ˈbaTHˌtəb/ ▶n. a tub, usually installed in a bathroom, in which to bathe.

ba·thym·e·ter /bəˈTHimitər/ ▶n. an instrument used to measure the depth of water in oceans, seas, or lakes.

bath·y·sphere /ˈbaTHəˌsfir/ ▶n. a manned spherical chamber for deep-sea observation, lowered by cable from a ship.

ba·tik /bəˈtēk/ ▶n. a method (originally used in Java) of producing colored designs on textiles by dyeing them, having first applied wax to the parts to be left undyed. ■ an item or piece of cloth treated in this way.

ba·tiste /bəˈtēst/ ▶n. a fine, light linen or cotton fabric resembling cambric.

bat mitz·vah /bät ˈmitsvə/ ▶n. a religious initiation ceremony for a Jewish girl aged twelve years and one day, regarded as the age of religious maturity. ■ the girl undergoing such a ceremony.

ba·ton /bəˈtän/ ▶n. a short stick or staff or something resembling one, in particular: ■ a thin stick used by a conductor to direct an orchestra or choir. ■ *Track & Field* a short stick or tube passed from runner to runner in a relay race. ■ a long stick carried and twirled by a drum major. ■ a police officer's club.
▶ □ **pass** (**on**) **the baton** hand over a particular duty or responsibility. □ **take up** (or **pick up**) **the baton** accept a duty or responsibility.

bat·tal·ion /bəˈtalyən/ ▶n. a large body of troops ready for battle, esp. an infantry unit forming part of a brigade typically commanded by a lieutenant colonel. ■ a large, organized group of people pursuing a common aim or sharing a major undertaking.

bat·ten /ˈbatn/ ▶n. a long, flat strip of squared wood or metal used to hold something in place or as a fastening against a wall. ■ a strip of wood or plastic used to stiffen and extend the leech of a sail.
▶ □ **batten down the hatches** ■ prepare for a difficulty or crisis.

bat·ter¹ /ˈbatər/ ▶v. [tr.] strike repeatedly with hard blows; pound heavily and insistently: *a prisoner was **battered to death** with a table leg | fig. their idealism has been battered.* ■ [often as n.] (**battering**) subject (one's spouse, partner, or child) to repeated violence and assault. ■ [usu. as n.] (**battering**) *fig.* censure, criticize, or defeat severely: *the movie took a battering from critics.* —**bat·ter·er** n.

bat·ter² ▶n. a semiliquid mixture of flour, egg, and milk or water used in cooking, esp. for making cakes or for coating food before frying.

bat·tered¹ /ˈbatərd/ ▶adj. injured by repeated blows or punishment: *he finished the day battered and bruised.* ■ having suffered repeated violence from a spouse, partner, or parent: *a battered wife.* ■ (of a thing) damaged by age and repeated use; shabby: *a pair of battered black boots.*

bat·tered² ▶adj. (of food) coated in batter and deep-fried until crisp.

bat·ter·ing ram ▶n. a heavy object swung or rammed against a door to break it down: *fig. a battering ram to crush opposing views.* ■ *hist.* a heavy beam, originally with an end in the form of a carved ram's head, used in breaching fortifications.

bat·ter·y /ˈbatərē/ ▶n. (*pl.* **-ter·ies**) **1** a container consisting of one or more cells, in which chemical energy is converted into electricity and used as a source of power: [as adj.] *battery power.* **2** a fortified emplacement for heavy guns. **3** a set of similar units of equipment, typically when connected together: *a battery of equipment to monitor blood pressure.* ■ an extensive series, sequence, or range of things: *children given a battery of tests.* **4** *Law* the crime or tort of unconsented physical contact with another person, even where the contact is not violent but merely menacing or offensive. See also **ASSAULT AND BATTERY**. **5** (**the battery**) *Baseball* the pitcher and the catcher in a game, considered as a unit.

bat·ting ▶n. cotton wadding prepared in sheets for use in quilts.

bat·ting or·der ▶n. *Baseball* the order in which batters take their turn at bat.

bat·tle /ˈbatl/ ▶n. a sustained fight between large, organized armed forces. ■ a lengthy and difficult conflict or struggle: *the battle over the future shape of Europe | the battle against aging.*
▶v. fight or struggle tenaciously to achieve or resist something: *he has been battling against the illness.* —**bat·tler** n.
▶ □ **battle royal** (*pl.* **battles royal**) a fiercely contested fight or dispute:

there promises to be a battle royal between the two companies. □ **half the battle** an important step toward achieving something: *he never gives in, and that's half the battle.*

bat·tle-ax (also **bat·tle-axe**) ▸*n.* **1** a large broad-bladed ax used in ancient warfare. **2** *inf.* a formidably aggressive older woman.

battle cry ▸*n.* a word or phrase shouted by soldiers going into battle to express solidarity and intimidate the enemy. ▪ a slogan expressing the ideals of people promoting a cause.

battle fa·tigue ▸*n.* another term for SHELL SHOCK.

bat·tle·field /ˈbatlˌfēld/ (also **bat·tle-ground** /-ˌground/) ▸*n.* the piece of ground on which a battle is or was fought: *death on the battlefield* | [as *adj.*] *battlefield conditions.* ▪ *fig.* a place or situation of strife or conflict: *an ideological battlefield.*

bat·tle·ment /ˈbatlmənt/ ▸*n.* (usu. **battlements**) a parapet at the top of a wall, usually of a fort or castle, that has regularly spaced, squared openings for shooting through. —**bat·tle·ment·ed** *adj.*

bat·tle·ship /ˈbatlˌSHip/ ▸*n.* a heavy warship of a type built chiefly in the late 19th and early 20th centuries, with extensive armor and large-caliber guns.

bat·ty /ˈbatē/ ▸*adj.* (**-ti·er, -ti·est**) *inf.* crazy; insane: *you'll drive me batty!* —**bat·ti·ly** /ˈbatəlē/ *adv.* —**bat·ti·ness** *n.*

bau·ble /ˈbôbəl/ ▸*n.* a small, showy trinket or decoration. ▪ *fig.* something of no importance or worth.

baud /bôd/ ▸*n.* (*pl.* same or **bauds**) *chiefly Comput.* a unit used to express the speed of transmission of electronic signals, corresponding to one information unit or event per second. ▪ a unit of data transmission speed for a modem of one bit per second (in fact there is usually more than one bit per event).

baux·ite /ˈbôksīt/ ▸*n.* an clayey rock that is the chief commercial ore of aluminum. It consists largely of hydrated alumina. —**baux·it·ic** /ˌbôkˈsitik/ *adj.*

bawd·y /ˈbôdē/ ▸*adj.* (**bawd·i·er, bawd·i·est**) dealing with sexual matters in a comical way; humorously indecent.
▸*n.* humorously indecent talk or writing. —**bawd·i·ly** /-dəlē/ *adv.* —**bawd·i·ness** *n.*

bawl /bôl/ ▸*v.* **1** shout or call out noisily and unrestrainedly: *"Move!" bawled the drill sergeant* | [*tr.*] *lustily bawling out the hymns* **2** [*intr.*] weep or cry noisily: *she began to bawl like a child* | [as *adj.*] (**bawling**) *bawling babies.*
▸*phrasal v.* □ **bawl someone out** reprimand someone angrily: *tales of how she bawled out employees.*
▸*n.* a loud, unrestrained shout.

bay[1] /bā/ ▸*n.* a broad inlet of the sea.

bay[2] ▸*n.* **1** (also **bay tree.**) an evergreen Mediterranean shrub (*Laurus nobilis*) of the laurel family, with deep green leaves and purple berries. Its aromatic leaves are used in cooking and were formerly used to make triumphal crowns for victors. **2** a similarly aromatic tree or shrub of North America, esp. the bayberry used in the preparation of bay rum.

bay[3] ▸*n.* a recessed or enclosed area, in particular: ▪ a space created by a window-line projecting outward from a wall. ▪ short for BAY WINDOW. ▪ a section of wall between two buttresses or columns, esp. in the nave of a church. ▪ a compartment with a particular function in a motor vehicle, aircraft, or ship: *an engine bay* | *a bomb bay.* ▪ an area allocated or marked off for a specified purpose: *a loading bay.* ▪ *Comput.* a cabinet, or a space in the cabinet, into which an electronic device is installed: *a drive bay.*

bay[4] ▸*n.* a brown horse with black points.

bay[5] ▸*v.* [*intr.*] (of a dog, esp. a large one) bark or howl loudly: *the dogs bayed.*
▸ □ **at bay** forced to confront one's attackers or pursuers; cornered. □ **hold** (or **keep**) **someone/something at bay** prevent someone or something from approaching or having an effect.

bay·ber·ry /ˈbāˌberē/ ▸*n.* (*pl.* **-ies**) **1** a North American shrub (genus *Myrica*, family Myricaceae) with aromatic leathery leaves and waxy berries. **2** a tropical American shrub (*Pimenta racemosa*) of the myrtle family with aromatic leaves that are used in the preparation of bay rum. Also called **bay rum tree.**

bay leaf ▸*n.* the aromatic, usually dried, leaf of the bay tree, used in cooking.

bay·o·net /ˈbāənit/ ˌbāəˈnet/ ▸*n.* **1** a swordlike stabbing blade that may be fixed to the muzzle of a rifle for use in hand-to-hand fighting.

2 [as *adj.*] denoting a fitting for a light bulb, camera lens, or other appliance that is engaged by being pushed into a socket and then twisted to lock it in place.
▸*v.* (**-net·ed, -net·ing**) [*tr.*] stab (someone) with a bayonet.

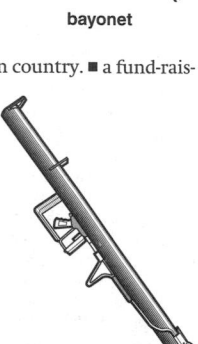

bayonet

bay·ou /ˈbīoō; ˈbīō/ ▸*n.* (*pl.* **-ous**) a slow-flowing stream in a swampy area.

bay rum ▸*n.* an aromatic liquid, used esp. for the hair or as an aftershave, typically distilled from rum and the leaves of the bayberry.

bay win·dow ▸*n.* a window built to project outward from an outside wall.

ba·zaar /bəˈzär/ ▸*n.* a market in a Middle-Eastern country. ▪ a fund-raising sale of goods, typically for charity.

ba·zoo·ka /bəˈzoōkə/ ▸*n.* **1** a short-range tubular rocket launcher used against tanks. **2** a trombonelike type of kazoo.

BB ▸*symb.* a standard size of lead pellet used in air rifles.
▸*abbr. Baseball* base on balls.

BBC ▸*abbr.* British Broadcasting Corporation.

BC ▸*abbr.* ▪ before Christ (used to indicate that a date is before the Christian Era). ▪ British Columbia (in official postal use).

bcc ▸*abbr.* blind carbon copy, a copy of an e-mail sent to someone whose name and address isn't visible to other recipients.

BCE ▸*abbr.* ▪ Bachelor of Chemical Engineering. ▪ Bachelor of Civil Engineering. ▪ before the Common Era (used of dates before the Christian era, esp. by non-Christians).

BDD ▸*abbr.* body dysmorphic disorder.

bdel·li·um /ˈdeleəm/ ▸*n.* a fragrant resin produced by a number of trees related to myrrh, used in perfumes.

BE ▸*abbr.* ▪ Bachelor of Education. ▪ Bachelor of Engineering. ▪ bill of exchange. ▪ Black English.

Be ▸*symb.* the chemical element beryllium.

be /bē/ ▸*v.* (*sing. present am* /am/; *are* /är/; *is* /iz/; *pl. present* **are**; *1st and 3rd sing. past was* /wəz; wäz/; *2nd sing. past and pl. past* **were** /wər/; *present subjunctive* **be**; *past subjunctive* **were**; *present part.* **be·ing** /ˈbēiNG/; *past part.* **been** /bin/) **1** (usu. **there is/are**) exist: *there are no easy answers.* ▪ be present: *there is a boy sitting on the step.* **2** occur; take place: *the exhibition will be in November* | *that was before the war.* ▪ occupy a position in space: *the Salvation Army store was on his left.* ▪ stay in the same place or condition: *she was here until about ten-thirty* | *he's a tough customer—let him be.* ▪ attend: *the days when she was in school.* ▪ come; go; visit: *he's from Missouri* | *I have just been to Thailand.* **3** having the state, quality, identity, nature, role, etc., specified: *Amy was 91* | *the floor was uneven* | *I want to be a teacher* | *father was not well* | *his hair's brown* | *it will be Christmas soon* | *"Be careful," Mr. Carter said.* ▪ cost: *the tickets were $25.* ▪ amount to: *one and one is two.* ▪ represent: *let A be a square matrix of order n.* ▪ signify: *we were everything to each other.* ▪ consist of; constitute: *the monastery was several three-story buildings.*
▸*phrasal v.* □ **be off** go away; leave: *he was anxious to be off.*
▸*aux. v.* **1** used with a present participle to form continuous tenses: *they are coming.* | *she will be waiting.* **2** used with a past participle to form the passive mood: *it was done.* **3** used to indicate something due to happen: *construction is to begin next summer.* ▪ used to express obligation or necessity: *you are to follow these orders.* ▪ used to express possibility: *these snakes are to be found in North America.* ▪ used to hypothesize about something that might happen: *if I were to lose.*
▸ □ **the be-all and end-all** *inf.* a feature of an activity or a way of life that is of greater importance than any other. □ **not be oneself** not feel well. □ **-to-be** [in *comb.*] of the future: *my bride-to-be.*

beach /bēCH/ ▸*n.* a pebbly or sandy shore, esp. by the ocean between high- and low-water marks.
▸*v.* [*tr.*] run or haul up (a boat or ship) onto a beach: *at the water's edge a rowboat was beached* | [*intr.*] *crews would not beach for fear of damaging craft.* ▪ [often as *adj.*] (**beached**) cause (a whale or similar animal) to become stranded out of the water. ▪ [*intr.*] (of a whale or similar animal) become stranded out of the water. ▪ (of an angler) land (a fish) on a beach. ▪ *fig.* cause (someone) to suffer a loss: *competitive procurement seems to have beached several companies.*

beach ball ▸*n.* a large inflatable ball used for playing games on the beach.

beach·comb·er /'bēcH,kōmər/ ▶n. **1** a vagrant who makes a living by searching beaches for articles of value and selling them. **2** a person who searches beaches for useful or interesting items.

beach·head /'bēcH,hed/ ▶n. a defended position on a beach taken from the enemy by landing forces, from which an attack can be launched.

bea·con /'bēkən/ ▶n. a fire or light set up in a high or prominent position as a warning, signal, or celebration: *a chain of beacons carried the news* | *fig. the prospect of a new government was a beacon of hope for millions.* ■ a light or other visible object serving as a signal, warning, or guide, esp. at sea or on an airfield. ■ a radio transmitter whose signal helps to fix the position of a ship, aircraft, or spacecraft.

bead /bēd/ ▶n. **1** a small piece of glass, stone, or similar material, typically rounded and perforated for threading with others as a necklace or rosary or for sewing onto fabric. ■ (**beads**) a necklace made of a string of beads. ■ (**beads**) a rosary. **2** something resembling a bead or a string of beads, in particular: ■ a drop of a liquid on a surface: *beads of sweat.* ■ a long, narrow strip of caulking compound, adhesive or similar material applied to a surface. ■ a small knob forming the front sight of a gun. ■ the reinforced inner edge of a pneumatic tire that grips the rim of the wheel.
▶v. [*tr.*] **1** [often as *adj.*] (**beaded**) decorate or cover with beads: *a beaded evening bag.* ■ string (beads) together. **2** (often **be beaded**) cover (a surface) with drops of moisture: *his face was beaded with perspiration.*

bead·ing /'bēdiNG/ ▶n. decoration or ornamental molding resembling a string of beads or of a semicircular cross section.

bead·y /'bēdē/ ▶adj. (of a person's eyes) small, round, and gleaming. ■ (of a look) bright and penetrating: *she fixed him with a beady stare.* —**bead·i·ly** /'bēdəlē/ adv.

bead·y-eyed ▶adj. having small, glinting eyes. ■ inf. keenly observant, typically in a sinister or hostile way.

bea·gle /'bēgəl/ ▶n. a small sturdy hound of a breed with a coat of medium length, bred esp. for hunting. —**bea·gler** /-g(ə)lər/ n.

beak /bēk/ ▶n. a bird's horny projecting jaws; a bill. ■ the similar horny projecting jaw of other animals, e.g., a turtle or squid. ■ inf. a person's nose, esp. a hooked one: *she can't wait to stick her beak in.* ▷Middle English: from Old French *bec*, from Latin *beccus*, of Celtic origin. —**beaked** adj. [in *comb.*] *a yellow-beaked alpine chough.* —**beak·y** adj.

beak·er /'bēkər/ ▶n. a lipped cylindrical glass container for laboratory use.

beam /bēm/ ▶n. **1** a long, sturdy piece of squared timber or metal spanning an opening or part of a building, usually to support the roof or floor above. ■ another term for **BALANCE BEAM**. ■ a horizontal piece of squared timber or metal supporting the deck and joining the sides of a ship. ■ *Naut.* the direction of an object visible from the port or starboard side of a ship when it is perpendicular to the center line of the vessel: *there was land in sight on the port beam.* ■ a ship's breadth at its widest point: *a cutter with a beam of 16 feet.* ■ the crossbar of a balance. ■ (esp. in a stationary steam engine) an oscillating shaft through which the vertical piston movement is transmitted to the crank or pump. **2** a ray or shaft of light: *a beam of light flashed in front of her.* ■ a directional flow of particles or radiation: *beams of electrons.* ■ a series of radio or radar signals emitted to serve as a navigational guide for ships or aircraft. **3** a radiant or good-natured look or smile: *a beam of satisfaction.*
▶v. **1** [*tr.*] transmit (a radio signal or broadcast) in a specified direction: *beaming a distress signal into space* | [*intr.*] *the TV station begins beaming into homes in the new year.* ■ [*tr.*] (**beam someone up/down**) (in science fiction) transport someone instantaneously to another place, esp. to or from a spaceship: *Scotty, beam me up!* **2** [*intr.*] (of a light or light source) shine brightly: *the sun's rays beamed down.* **3** [*intr.*] smile radiantly: *she beamed with pleasure* | [as *adj.*] (**beaming**) *a beaming smile.* ■ [*tr.*] express (an emotion) with a radiant smile: *the teacher beamed her approval.* **4** (**beamed**) construct a ceiling with exposed beams: *vaulted beamed ceilings in the family room.*
▶ □ **off** (or **way off**) **beam** inf. on the wrong track; mistaken: *you're way off beam on this one.* □ **on the beam** inf. on the right track.

bean /bēn/ ▶n. **1** an edible seed, typically kidney-shaped, growing in long pods on certain leguminous plants. ■ the hard seed of coffee, cocoa, and certain other plants. **2** a leguminous plant (*Phaseolus* and other genera) that bears such seeds in pods. **3** (**beans**) inf. a very small amount or nothing at all of something (used emphatically): *I didn't know beans about being a stepparent.* **4** inf. a person's head, typically when regarded as a source of common sense.
▶v. [*tr.*] inf. hit (someone) on the head: *Boone was nearly beaned by that wild pitch.*
▶ □ **full of beans** inf. lively; in high spirits. □ **a hill of beans** anything of any importance or value: *three little people don't amount to a hill of beans in this crazy world.*

bean·bag /'bēn,bag/ ▶n. **1** a small bag filled with dried beans and typically used in children's games. ■ *Football* a square of colored plastic with a weighted section, used as a penalty flag. **2** a large cushion, typically filled with polystyrene beads, used as a seat.

bean curd ▶n. another term for **TOFU**.

bean·ie /'bēnē/ ▶n. (pl. **-ies**) a small, close-fitting hat worn on the back of the head.

bean·pole /'bēn,pōl/ ▶n. a stick for supporting bean plants. ■ inf. a tall, thin person.

bean sprouts ▶pl. n. the sprouting seeds of certain beans, esp. mung beans, used in Asian cooking.

bear[1] /be(ə)r/ ▶v. (past **bore** /bôr/; past part. **borne** /bôrn/) [*tr.*] **1** (of a person) carry: *he was bearing a tray of brimming glasses.* ■ have or display as a visible mark or feature: *a small boat bearing a white flag.* ■ (**bear oneself**) carry or conduct oneself in a particular manner: *she bore herself with dignity.* **2** support: *walls that cannot bear a stone vault.* ■ take responsibility for: *no one likes to bear the responsibility for such decisions.* ■ be able to accept or stand up to: *it is doubtful whether either of these distinctions would bear scrutiny.* **3** endure (an ordeal or difficulty): *she bore the pain stoically.* ■ manage to tolerate (a situation or experience): *she could hardly bear his sarcasm* | *I cannot bear to see you hurt* ■ (**cannot bear someone/something**) strongly dislike: *I can't bear caviar.* **4** give birth to (a child): *she bore six daughters* | *his wife had borne him a son.* ■ (of a tree or plant) produce (fruit or flowers): *a squash that bears fruit shaped like cucumbers.* **5** [*intr.*] turn and proceed in a specified direction: *bear left and follow the old road.*
▶*phrasal v.* □ **bear down on** move quickly toward someone, in a purposeful or an intimidating manner. □ **bear on** be relevant to (something): *two kinds of theories that bear on literary studies.* ■ be a burden on (someone): *a tax that will bear heavily on poorer households.* □ **bear something out** support or confirm something: *this assumption is not borne out by any evidence.* □ **bear with** be patient or tolerant with.
▶ □ **bear arms 1** carry firearms. **2** wear or display a coat of arms. □ **bear fruit** fig. yield positive results: *plans for power-sharing may be about to bear fruit.* □ **bear witness** (or **testimony**) **to** testify: *little is left to bear witness to the past greatness of the city.* □ **bring to bear 1** muster and use to effect: *she had reservations about how much influence she could bring to bear.* **2** aim (a weapon): *bringing his rifle to bear on a distant target.*

bear[2] ▶n. **1** a large, heavy, mostly omnivorous mammal of the family Ursidae that walks on the soles of its feet, with thick fur and a very short tail. ■ a teddy bear. ■ a rough, unmannerly, or uncouth person. ■ a large, heavy, cumbersome man: *a lumbering bear of a man.* ■ (**the Bear**) the constellation Ursa Major or Ursa Minor. **2** *Stock Market* a person who forecasts that prices of stocks or commodities will fall, esp. a person who sells shares hoping to buy them back later at a lower price: [as *adj.*] *bear markets.* Often contrasted with **BULL**[1] (sense 2 of the noun).
▶ □ **loaded for bear** inf. fully prepared for any eventuality, typically a confrontation or challenge.

bear·a·ble /'be(ə)rəbəl/ ▶adj. able to be endured: *a ceiling fan made the heat bearable.* —**bear·a·bly** adv.

bear-bait·ing /'be(ə)r,bātiNG/ ▶n. hist. a form of entertainment that involved setting dogs to attack a captive bear.

beard /bi(ə)rd/ ▶n. **1** a growth of hair on the chin and lower cheeks of a man's face: *he had a black beard.* ■ a tuft of hair on the chin of certain mammals, for example a lion or goat. ■ an animal's growth or marking that is likened to a beard, e.g., the gills of an oyster, or the beak bristles of certain birds. ■ a tuft of hairs or bristles on certain plants, esp. the awn of a grass. **2** inf. a person who carries out a transaction, typically a bet, for someone else in order to conceal the other's identity. ■ a person who pretends to have a romantic or sexual relationship with someone else in order to conceal the other's true sexual orientation.
▶v. [*tr.*] boldly confront or challenge (someone formidable). —**beard·ed** adj. [in *comb.*] *a gray-bearded man.* —**beard·less** adj.
▶ □ **beard the lion in his den** (or **lair**) confront or challenge someone on their own ground.

bear·er /'be(ə)rər/ ▶n. **1** a person or thing that carries or holds something: *I'm sorry to be the bearer of bad tidings* | [in *comb.*] *a flag-bearer.* ■ a carrier of equipment on an expedition. ■ a tree or plant that bears fruit or flowers. **2** a person who presents a check or other order to pay money: *promissory notes payable to the bearer.* ■ [as *adj.*] payable to the possessor: *bearer bonds.*

bear hug ▶ *n.* a rough, tight embrace.

bear·ing /ˈbe(ə)riNG/ ▶ *n.* **1** a person's way of standing or moving: *a man of precise military bearing.* ■ the way one behaves or conducts oneself: *she has the bearing of a First Lady.* **2** relation or relevance: *the case has no direct bearing on the issues.* **3** the level to which something bad can be tolerated: *school was bad enough, but now it's past bearing.* **4** a part of a machine that bears friction, esp. between a rotating part and its housing. ■ a ball bearing. **5** *Archit.* a structural part that supports weight, such as a wall that supports a beam. **6** the direction or position of something, or the direction of movement, relative to a fixed point. It is typically measured in degrees, usually with north as zero: *the Point is on a bearing of 015°.* ■ (**one's bearings**) awareness of one's position relative to one's surroundings: *he rose unsteadily to his feet and tried to get his bearings.* **7** *Heraldry* a device or charge: *armorial bearings.* **8** the act, capability, or time of producing fruit or offspring: *I gave myself up to the bearing of children.*

bear·ish /ˈbe(ə)riSH/ ▶ *adj.* **1** resembling or likened to a bear, typically in being rough, surly, or clumsy: *a bearish figure with thick whiskers.* **2** *Stock Market* characterized by falling share prices. ■ (of a dealer) inclined to sell because of an anticipated fall in prices. —**bear·ish·ly** *adv.* —**bear·ish·ness** *n.*

bear·skin /ˈbe(ə)r.skin/ ▶ *n.* the pelt of a bear, esp. when used as a rug or wrap. ■ a tall cap of black fur worn ceremonially by certain military troops.

beast /bēst/ ▶ *n.* an animal, esp. a large or dangerous four-footed one: *a wild beast.* ■ (usu. **beasts**) a domestic animal, esp. a bovine farm animal. ■ an inhumanly cruel, violent, or depraved person: *he is a filthy drunken beast.* ■ *inf.* an objectionable or unpleasant person or thing: *a scheming, manipulative little beast.* ■ (**the beast**) a person's brutish or untamed characteristics: *the beast in you is rearing its ugly head.* ■ *inf.* a thing or concept possessing a particular quality: *that much-maligned beast, the rave record.*

beast of bur·den ▶ *n.* an animal such as a mule or donkey that is used for carrying loads.

beast of prey ▶ *n.* an animal, esp. a mammal, that kills and eats other animals.

beat /bēt/ ▶ *v.* (*past* **beat**; *past part.* **beat·en** /ˈbētn/) [*tr.*] **1** strike (a person or an animal) repeatedly and violently so as to hurt or injure them, usually with an implement such as a club or whip: *she beat me with a stick for the slightest misdemeanor.* ■ strike (an object) repeatedly so as to make a noise: *he beat the table with his hand.* ■ [*intr.*] (of an instrument) make a rhythmical sound by being struck: *drums were beating in the distance.* ■ flatten or shape (metal) by striking it repeatedly with a hammer: *pure gold can be beaten out to form very thin sheets.* ■ move across (an area of land) repeatedly striking at the ground cover in order to raise game birds for shooting. **2** defeat (someone) in a game, competition, election, or commercial venture: *she beat him easily at chess.* ■ *inf.* baffle: *it beats me how you managed to work in this heat.* ■ overcome (a problem, or disease): *they are investing their savings in hopes of beating inflation.* ■ do or be better than (a record or score): *he beat his own world record.* ■ *inf.* be better than: *you can't beat the taste of fresh raspberries.* **3** succeed in getting somewhere ahead of (someone): *I could beat him on my bicycle.* ■ take action to avoid (difficult or inconvenient effects of an event or circumstance): *they set off early to beat the traffic.* **4** [*intr.*] (of the heart) pulsate: *her heart beat faster with panic.* **5** (of a bird) move (the wings) up and down. ■ (of a bird or its wings) make rhythmic movements through (the air): *black-tipped wings beat the air.* **6** stir (cooking ingredients) vigorously with a fork, whisk, or beater to make a smooth or frothy mixture. **7** (**beat it**) *inf.* leave: [in *imper.*] *now beat it, will you!*

▶ *n.* **1** a main accent or rhythmic unit in music or poetry: *the glissando begins on the second beat.* ■ a strong rhythm in popular music: *the music changed to a funky disco beat.* ■ a regular, rhythmic sound or movement: *the beat of the windshield wipers became almost hypnotic.* ■ the sound made when something, typically a musical instrument, is struck: *he heard a regular drumbeat.* ■ a pulsation of the heart. ■ a periodic variation of sound or amplitude due to the combination of two sounds, electrical signals, or other vibrations having similar but not identical frequencies. ■ the movement of a bird's wings. **2** an area allocated to a police officer to patrol: *a patrolman who strived to make his beat a safe one* | *public clamor for more police officers on the beat.* ■ a spell of duty allocated to a police officer: *her beat ended at 6 a.m.* ■ an area regularly frequented by someone, typically a prostitute. ■ *fig.* a person's area of interest: *his*

beat is construction, property, and hotels. **3** a brief pause or moment of hesitation, typically one lasting a specified length: *she waited for a beat of three seconds.*

▶ *adj.* **1** *informal* completely exhausted: *I'm dead beat.* **2** of or relating to the beat generation or its philosophy: *beat poet Allen Ginsberg.* —**beat·a·ble** *adj.* —**beat·er** *n.* —**beat·ing** *n.*

▶ □ **beat all** be amazing or impressive: *well, that beats all.* □ **beat around the bush** discuss a matter without coming to the point. □ **beat the clock** perform a task quickly or within a fixed time limit. □ **beat a dead horse** waste energy on a lost cause or unalterable situation. □ **beat a path to someone's door** (of a large number of people) hasten to make contact with someone regarded as interesting or inspiring, or in association with whom one stands to profit. □ **beat a** (**hasty**) **retreat** withdraw, typically in order to avoid something unpleasant: *as the bombs started to go off, they beat a hasty retreat across the field.* □ **beat the system** succeed in finding a means of getting around rules, regulations, or other means of control. □ **to beat all ——s** that is infinitely better than all the things mentioned: *a PC screen saver to beat all screen savers.* □ **to beat the band** *inf.* in such a way as to surpass all competition: *they were talking to beat the band.*

beat·en /ˈbētn/ ▶ past participle of BEAT.

▶ *adj.* **1** having been defeated: *I knew when I was beaten.* ■ exhausted and dejected: *he sat feeling old and beaten.* **2** having been beaten or struck: *he trudged home like a beaten dog.* ■ (of food) whipped to a uniform consistency: *beaten eggs.* ■ (of metal) shaped by hammering, typically so as to give the surface a dimpled texture or to form thin foil for ornamental use. **3** (of a path) well trodden; much used.

▶ □ **off the beaten track** (or **path**) in or into an isolated place. ■ unusual: [as *adj.*] *off-the-beaten-track experiences.*

bea·ter bar ▶ *n.* the rotating-brush unit within the powerhead of a vacuum cleaner.

beat gen·er·a·tion ▶ a movement of young people in the 1950s who rejected conventional society and favored Zen Buddhism, modern jazz, free sexuality, and recreational drugs. Among writers associated with the movement were Jack Kerouac and Allen Ginsberg.

be·a·tif·ic /ˌbēəˈtifik/ ▶ *adj.* blissfully happy: *a beatific smile.* —**be·a·tif·i·cal·ly** /-ik(ə)lē/ *adv.*

be·at·i·fi·ca·tion /bē.atəfiˈkāSHən/ ▶ *n.* (in the Roman Catholic Church) declaration by the pope that a dead person is in a state of bliss, constituting a step toward canonization and permitting public veneration.

be·at·i·fy /bēˈatə.fī/ ▶ *v.* (**-fies, -fied**) [*tr.*] (in the Roman Catholic Church) announce the beatification of.

be·at·i·tude /bēˈati.t(y)o͞od/ ▶ *n.* supreme blessedness. ■ (**the Beatitudes**) the blessings listed by Jesus in the Sermon on the Mount.

beat·nik /ˈbētnik/ ▶ *n.* a young person in the 1950s and early 1960s belonging to a subculture associated with the beat generation.

beat-up ▶ *adj. inf.* (of a thing) worn out by overuse; in a state of disrepair.

beau /bō/ ▶ *n.* (*pl.* **beaux** /bōz/ or **beaus**) *dated* **1** a boyfriend or male admirer. **2** a rich, fashionable young man; a dandy.

Beau·fort scale /ˈbōfərt/ ▶ a scale of wind speed based on a visual estimation of the wind's effects, ranging from force 0 (less than 1 knot or 1 kph, "calm") to force 12 (64 knots or 118 kph and above, "hurricane").

beau geste /ˌbō ˈzHest/ ▶ *n.* (*pl.* **beaux gestes** *pronunc.* same) a noble and generous act.

beau i·dé·al /ˌbō ˌēdāˈal; ī'dēəl/ ▶ *n.* a person or thing representing the highest possible standard of excellence in a particular respect.

Beau·jo·lais /ˌbōzHəˈlā/ ▶ *n.* a light red or (less commonly) white burgundy wine produced in the Beaujolais district of southeastern France.

beau monde /ˌbō ˈmônd/ ▶ *n.* (**the beau monde**) fashionable society.

beaut /byo͞ot/ *inf.* ▶ *n.* a particularly fine example of something: *the idea was a beaut.* ■ a beautiful person.

beau·te·ous /ˈbyo͞otēəs/ ▶ *adj. poetic/lit.* beautiful: *his beauteous bride.*

beau·ti·cian /byo͞oˈtisHən/ ▶ *n.* a person whose job is to do hair styling, manicures, and other beauty treatments.

beau·ti·ful /ˈbyo͞otəfəl/ ▶ *adj.* pleasing the senses or mind aesthetically: *beautiful poetry* | *the mountains were calm and beautiful.* ■ of a very high standard; excellent: *the house had been left in beautiful order.* —**beau·ti·ful·ly** /-f(ə)lē/ *adv.* [as *adj.*] *the rules are beautifully simple.*

▶ □ **the beautiful people 1** fashionable, glamorous, and privileged people. **2** (in the 1960s) hippies.

beau·ti·fy /ˈbyo͞otə.fī/ ▶ *v.* (**-fies, -fied**) [*tr.*] improve the appearance of. —**beau·ti·fi·ca·tion** /ˌbyo͞otəfiˈkāsHən/ *n.* —**beau·ti·fi·er** *n.*

beau·ty /'byo͞otē/ ▶ n. (pl. **-ties**) **1** a combination of qualities, such as shape, color, or form, that pleases the aesthetic senses, esp. the sight: *I was struck by her beauty.* ■ a combination of qualities that pleases the intellect or moral sense. ■ denoting something intended to make a woman more attractive: *beauty products.* **2** a beautiful or pleasing thing or person, in particular: ■ a beautiful woman. ■ an excellent specimen or example of something: *the fish was a beauty, around 14 pounds.* ■ the best feature or advantage of something: *the beauty of keeping cats is that they don't tie you down.* ▷Middle English: from Old French *beaute*, based on Latin *bellus* 'beautiful, fine.'

beau·ty pag·eant ▶ n. see PAGEANT.

beau·ty par·lor (also **beauty salon** or **beauty shop**) ▶ n. an establishment in which hairdressing, makeup, and similar cosmetic treatments are carried out professionally.

beau·ty queen ▶ n. a woman judged most beautiful in a beauty contest.

beau·ty sleep ▶ n. *humorous* sleep considered to be sufficient to keep one looking young and beautiful.

beau·ty spot ▶ n. a small natural or artificial mark such as a mole on a woman's face, considered to enhance another feature.

beaux /bōz/ ▶ plural form of BEAU.

beaux arts /ˌbō ˈzär/ ▶ pl. n. **1** fine arts. **2** (usu. **Beaux Arts**) [as *adj.*] relating to the classical decorative style maintained by the École des Beaux-Arts in Paris, esp. in the 19th century.

bea·ver[1] /'bēvər/ ▶ n. (pl. same or **beavers**) a large semiaquatic broad-tailed rodent (genus *Castor*, family Castoridae), esp. *C. canadensis* of North America. It is noted for its habit of gnawing through tree trunks to fell the trees in order to make dams. ■ the soft light brown fur of the beaver. ■ *fig.* a very hardworking person.
▶ v. [intr.] *inf.* work hard: *Joe beavered away to keep things running.*

bea·ver[2] ▶ n. *vulgar slang* a woman's genitals or pubic area. ■ *offens.* a woman.

be·bop /'bēˌbäp/ ▶ n. a type of jazz originating in the 1940s and characterized by complex harmony and rhythms. It is associated particularly with Charlie Parker, Thelonious Monk, and Dizzy Gillespie. —**be·bop·per** n.

be·calm /bi'kä(l)m/ ▶ v. [tr.] (usu. **be becalmed**) leave (a sailing vessel) unable to move through lack of wind.

be·came /bi'kām/ ▶ past participle of BECOME.

be·cause /bi'kôz; -'kəz/ ▶ conj. for the reason that; since: *we did it because we felt it our duty.*
▶ □ **because of** on account of; by reason of: *they moved here because of the baby.*

beck ▶ n. *poetic/lit.* a gesture requesting attention, such as a nod or wave.
▶ □ **at someone's beck and call** always having to be ready to obey someone's orders immediately.

beck·on /'bekən/ ▶ v. [intr.] make a gesture with the hand, arm, or head to encourage someone to come nearer or follow: *Miranda beckoned to Adam.* ■ [tr.] attract the attention of and summon (someone) in this way: *he beckoned Christopher over.* ■ *fig.* seem to be appealing or inviting: *the going is tough, and soft options beckon.*

be·come /bi'kəm/ ▶ v. (*past* **-came**; *past part.* **-come**) **1** [intr.] begin to be: *they became angry | it is becoming clear that we are in a totally new situation.* ■ grow to be; turn into: *the child will become an adult.* ■ (of a person) qualify or be accepted as; acquire the status of: *she wanted to become a doctor.* ■ (**become of**) (in questions) happen to: *what would become of her now?* **2** [tr.] (of clothing) look good on or suit (someone): *the dress becomes her.* ■ be appropriate or suitable to (someone): *minor celebrity status did not become him.*

BEd ▶ *abbr.* Bachelor of Education.

bed /bed/ ▶ n. **1** a piece of furniture for sleep or rest, typically a framework with a mattress and coverings: *a large double bed | she was in bed by nine | getting out of bed is a real struggle.* ■ a bed and associated facilities making up a place for a patient in a hospital or for a guest at a hotel: *a round of hospital staff layoffs and bed closings.* ■ *inf.* used with reference to a bed as the typical place for sexual activity: *some men care very little about pleasing their partners in bed.* **2** an area of ground, typically in a garden, where flowers and plants are grown: *a bed of tulips.* **3** a flat base or foundation on which something rests or is supported, in particular: ■ the foundation of a road or railroad. ■ the open part of a truck, wagon, or railroad car, where goods are carried. **4** a layer or pile of something, in particular: ■ a layer of food on which other foods are served: *the salad is served on a bed of raw spinach.* ■ a layer of rock or other geological material: *a bed of clay.* ■ any mass or pile resembling a bed: *pots steaming on the fragrant bed of coals.* **5** the bottom of the sea or

a lake or river: *a riverbed.* ■ a place on the seabed where shellfish, esp. oysters or mussels, breed or are bred: *mussel beds.*
▶ v. (**bed·ded**, **bed·ding**) **1** [intr.] settle down to sleep or rest for the night, typically in an improvised place: *he usually bedded down on newspapers in the church porch.* ■ (**bed someone/something down**) settle a person or animal down to sleep or rest for the night. **2** transfer (a plant) from a pot or seed tray to a garden plot: *I bedded out these houseplants.* **3** lay or arrange (something, esp. stone) in a layer.
▶ □ **bed of roses** used in reference to a situation or activity that is comfortable or easy: *farming is no bed of roses.* □ **get up on the wrong side of the bed** start the day in a bad temper. □ **in bed with** *inf.* having sexual intercourse with: *he found his wife in bed with one of the neighbors.* ■ *fig.* in undesirably close association with: *these meetings with politicians put the gay movement in bed with the dreaded Establishment.*

bed and break·fast (also **bed-and-break·fast**; abbr.: **b. & b.**) ▶ n. sleeping accommodations for a night and a morning meal, provided in guest houses and small hotels. ■ a guest house or small hotel offering such accommodations.

be·daz·zle /bi'dazəl/ ▶ v. [tr.] (often **be bedazzled**) greatly impress (someone) with brilliance or skill: *bedazzled by him, they offered him a job in Paris.* ■ cleverly outwit. —**be·daz·zle·ment** n.

bed·bug /'bedˌbəg/ ▶ n. a bloodsucking insect (*Cimex* and other genera, family Cimicidae) that is a parasite of birds and mammals, some species of which feed mainly on humans.

bed·clothes /'bedˌklō(TH)z/ ▶ pl. n. coverings for a bed, such as sheets and blankets.

bed·ding /'bediNG/ ▶ n. **1** coverings for a bed, such as sheets and blankets. ■ straw or similar material for animals to sleep on. **2** a base or bottom layer: [as *adj.*] *a bedding course of sand.* **3** *Geol.* the stratification or layering of rocks or other geological materials: [as *adj.*] *a bedding plane.*

be·deck /bi'dek/ ▶ v. [tr.] (often **be bedecked**) decorate: *he led us into a room bedecked with tinsel.*

be·dev·il /bi'devəl/ ▶ v. (**-dev·iled**, **-dev·il·ing**; also chiefly *Brit.* **-dev·illed**, **-dev·il·ling**) [tr.] (of something bad) cause great and continual trouble to: *inconsistencies that bedevil modern English spelling.* ■ (of a person) torment or harass: *he bedeviled them with petty practical jokes.* —**be·dev·il·ment** n.

bed·fel·low /'bedˌfelō/ ▶ n. a person who shares a bed with another. ■ *fig.* a person or thing allied or closely connected with another: *the treaty will make strange bedfellows of a number of enemies.*

bed head ▶ n. *inf.* a casual hairstyle resulting from failure to comb or arrange the hair after sleep.

bed·lam /'bedləm/ ▶ n. a scene of uproar and confusion: *there was bedlam in the courtroom.* ▷late Middle English: early form of *Bethlehem*, referring to the hospital of St. Mary of Bethlehem in London, used as an asylum for the insane.

bed lin·en ▶ n. sheets, pillowcases, and duvet covers.

Bed·ou·in /'bed(ə)win/ (also **Bed·u·in**) ▶ n. (pl. same) a nomadic Arab of the desert.

bed·pan /'bedˌpan/ ▶ n. a receptacle used by a bedridden patient as a toilet.

bed·post /'bedˌpōst/ ▶ n. any of the four upright supports of a bedstead.
▶ □ **between you and me and the bedpost** *inf.* in strict confidence.

be·drag·gled /bi'dragəld/ ▶ adj. dirty and disheveled: *bedraggled refugees | we got there, tired and bedraggled.* —**be·drag·gle** v.

bed·rid·den /'bedˌridn/ ▶ adj. confined to bed by sickness or old age.

bed·rock /'bedˌräk/ ▶ n. solid rock underlying loose deposits such as soil or alluvium. ■ *fig.* the fundamental principles on which something is based: *honesty is the bedrock of a good relationship.*

bed·roll /'bedˌrōl/ ▶ n. a sleeping bag or other bedding rolled into a bundle.

bed·room /'bedˌro͞om; -ˌro͝om/ (abbr.: **bdrm.**) ▶ n. a room for sleeping in: [in *comb.*] *a three-bedroom house.* ■ [as *adj.*] relating to sexual relations: *bedroom secrets.* ■ [as *adj.*] denoting a small town or suburb whose residents travel to work in a nearby city: *a bedroom community.*

bed·side /'bedˌsīd/ ▶ n. the space beside a bed, typically that of someone who is ill: *he was summoned to the bedside of a dying man.*
▶ □ **bedside manner** a doctor's approach or attitude toward a patient.

bed·sore /'bedˌsôr/ ▶ n. a sore developed by an invalid because of pressure caused by lying in bed in one position.

B

bed·spread /'bed,spred/ ▶ n. a decorative cloth used to cover a bed.

bed·stead /'bed,sted/ ▶ n. the framework of a bed on which the bed-springs and mattress are placed.

bed·straw /'bed,strô/ ▶ n. a herbaceous plant (genus *Galium*, family Rubiaceae) with small, lightly perfumed, white or yellow flowers and whorls of slender leaves, formerly used for stuffing mattresses.

bed·time /'bed,tīm/ ▶ n. the usual time when someone goes to bed: *it was well past her bedtime.*

bed-wet·ting ▶ n. involuntary urination during sleep. **—bed-wet·ter** n.

bee /bē/ ▶ n. **1** a honeybee. **2** an insect of a large group (superfamily Apoidea) to which the honeybee belongs, including many solitary as well as social kinds. **3** a meeting for communal work or amusement: *a quilting bee.*

▶ □ **have a bee in one's bonnet** *inf.* be preoccupied or obsessed about something, esp. a scheme or plan of action:

beech /bēCH/ ▶ n. (also **beech tree**) a large tree (genera *Fagus* and *Notofagus*) with smooth gray bark, glossy leaves, and hard, pale, fine-grained timber. Its fruit, a small triangular nut (**beechnut**), is an important food for numerous wild birds and mammals. The **beech family** (Fagaceae) also includes the oaks and chestnuts.

bee-eat·er ▶ n. a brightly colored insectivorous bird (*Merops* and other genera, family Meropidae) with a large head and a long down-curved bill, and typically with long central tail feathers.

beef /bēf/ ▶ n. **1** the flesh of a cow, bull, or ox, used as food. ■ (*pl.* **beeves** /bēvz/) *Farming* a cow, bull, or ox fattened for its meat. ■ *inf.* flesh or muscle, typically when well developed: *he needs a little more beef on his bones.* ■ *inf.* strength or power: *he's been brought in to give the team more beef.* **2** (*pl.* **beefs**) *inf.* a complaint or grievance: *he has a beef with American education: it doesn't teach the basics of investing.* **3** *inf.* a criminal charge: *a drunk-driving beef.*

▶ v. [*intr.*] *inf.* complain: *he was beefing about how the recession was killing the business.*

▶ *phrasal v.* □ **beef something up** *inf.* give more substance or strength to something: *cost-cutting measures are planned to beef up performance.*

beef·cake /'bēf,kāk/ ▶ n. *inf.* an attractive man with well-developed muscles.

beef·steak /'bēf,stāk/ ▶ n. a thick slice of lean beef, typically from the rump and eaten grilled, broiled, or fried.

beef·y /'bēfē/ ▶ adj. (**beef·i·er**, **beef·i·est**) **1** *inf.* muscular or robust: *he shrugged his beefy shoulders.* ■ large and impressively powerful: *beefy skis.* **2** tasting like beef. **—beef·i·ly** /'bēfəlē/ adv. **—beef·i·ness** n.

bee·hive /'bē,hīv/ ▶ n. a structure in which bees are kept, typically in the form of a dome or box. ■ [usu. as *adj.*] something having the domed shape of a traditional wicker beehive: *beehive huts | beehive ovens.* ■ a busy, crowded place: *the church became a beehive of activity.* **2** a woman's domed and lacquered hairstyle, esp. popular in the 1960s. **—bee·hived** adj.

bee·keep·ing /'bē,kēpiNG/ ▶ n. the occupation of owning and breeding bees for their honey. **—bee·keep·er** /-,kēpər/ n.

bee·line /'bē,līn/ ▶ n. a straight line between two places.

▶ □ **make a beeline for** hurry directly to.

been /bin/ ▶ past participle of BE.

beep /bēp/ ▶ n. a short, high-pitched sound emitted by electronic equipment or a vehicle horn.

▶ v. [*intr.*] (of a horn or electronic device) produce such a sound: *radio receivers squawked and beeped.* ■ [*tr.*] summon (someone) by means of a pager: *they have themselves beeped in restaurants.*

beep·er /'bēpər/ ▶ n. another term for PAGER.

beer /bi(ə)r/ ▶ n. an alcoholic drink made from yeast-fermented malt flavored with hops: *a pint of beer | I'm dying for a beer.* ■ any of several other fermented drinks: *ginger beer.*

beer gar·den ▶ n. a garden, typically one attached to a bar or tavern, where beer is served.

bees·wax /'bēz,waks/ ▶ n. **1** the wax secreted by bees to make honeycombs and used to make wood polishes and candles: *turning pollen into beeswax.* **2** *inf.* a person's concern or business: *that's none of your beeswax.*

beet /bēt/ ▶ n. a herbaceous plant (*Beta vulgaris*) of the goosefoot family, widely cultivated as a source of food for humans and livestock, and for processing into sugar. Some varieties are grown for their leaves and some for their swollen nutritious root.

bee·tle¹ /'bētl/ ▶ n. an insect of a group distinguished by having forewings typically modified into hard wing cases (elytra) that cover and protect the hind wings and abdomen. ■ (loosely) a similar insect, esp. a black one.

▶ v. *inf.* make one's way hurriedly: *the tourist beetled off.*

bee·tle² ▶ v. [*intr.*] [usu. as *adj.*] (**beetling**) (of a person's eyebrows) project or overhang threateningly: *piercing eyes glittered beneath a great beetling brow.*

▶ *adj.* (of a person's eyebrows) shaggy and projecting. **—bee·tle-browed** *adj.*

beeves /bēvz/ ▶ plural form of BEEF (sense 1).

be·fall /bi'fôl/ ▶ v. (*past* **-fell**; *past part.* **-fall·en**) [*tr.*] *poetic/lit.* (of something bad) happen to someone: *a tragedy befell his daughter* | [*intr.*] *she was to blame for anything that befell.*

be·fit /bi'fit/ ▶ v. (**fit·ted**, **-fit·ting**) [*tr.*] be appropriate for; suit: *the ballet ends nobly, as befits a tragedy* | [as *adj.*] (**befitting**) *I answered in a befitting manner.* **—be·fit·ting·ly** adv.

be·fore /bi'fôr/ ▶ *prep., conj.,* & *adv.* **1** during the period of time preceding (a particular event, date, or time): [as *prep.*] *she had to rest before dinner* | *the day before yesterday* | [as *conj.*] *they lived rough for four days before they were arrested* **2** in front of: [as *prep.*] *Matilda stood before her, panting* | *the patterns swam before her eyes* ■ [*prep.*] in front of and required to answer to (a court of law, tribunal, or other authority): *he could be taken before a magistrate for punishment.* **3** in preference to; with a higher priority than: [as *prep.*] *a woman who placed duty before all else* | [as *conj.*] *they would die before they would cooperate with each other.*

be·fore·hand /bi'fôr,hand/ ▶ adv. before an action or event; in advance: *rooms must be booked beforehand.*

be·foul /bi'foul/ ▶ v. [*tr.*] make dirty; pollute: *they befoul our water with mining.*

be·friend /bi'frend/ ▶ v. [*tr.*] act as a friend to (someone) by offering help or support.

be·fud·dle /bi'fədl/ ▶ v. [*tr.*] [usu. as *adj.*] (**befuddled**) make (someone) unable to think clearly: *he has an air of befuddled unworldliness.* **—be·fud·dle·ment** n.

beg /beg/ ▶ v. (**begged**, **beg·ging**) **1** ask (someone) earnestly or humbly for something: [*tr.*] *a leper begged Jesus for help* | [*intr.*] *I must beg of you not to act impulsively.* ■ ask for (something) earnestly or humbly: *he begged their forgiveness* | [with *direct speech*] *"Don't leave me," she begged.* ■ ask formally for (permission to do something): *I will now beg leave to make some observations* | [*intr.*] *we beg to inform you that we are instructed to wait.* **2** [*intr.*] ask for something, typically food or money, as charity or a gift: *they had to beg for food.* ■ [*tr.*] acquire (something) from someone in this way: *a piece of bread that I begged from a farmer.* ■ live by acquiring food or money in this way. ■ (of a dog) sit up with the front paws raised expectantly in the hope of a reward.

▶ □ **beg, borrow, or steal** *fig.* do whatever may be necessary to acquire something greatly desired: *I'm gonna get the money to buy Casey's ring, even if I have to beg, borrow, or steal.* □ **beg off** request to be excused from a question or obligation: *asked to name her favorites from her films, Hepburn begs off.* □ **beg the question 1** (of a fact or action) raise a question or point that has not been dealt with; invite an obvious question. **2** avoid the question; evade the issue. **3** assume the truth of an argument or proposition to be proved, without arguing it. □ **go begging** (of an article) be available for use because unwanted by others: *half the apartments in New York go begging in the summer.* ■ (of an opportunity) not be taken: *we let so many good chances go begging.*

be·gan /bi'gan/ ▶ past of BEGIN.

be·get /bi'get/ ▶ v. (**-get·ting**; *past* **-got** /-'gat/; *past part.* **-got·ten**) [*tr.*] *poetic/lit.* **1** (typically of a man, sometimes of a man and a woman) bring (a child) into existence by the process of reproduction: *they hoped that the King might beget an heir by his new queen.* **2** give rise to; bring about: *success begets further success.* **—be·get·ter** n.

beg·gar /'begər/ ▶ n. **1** a person, typically a homeless one, who lives by asking for money or food. **2** *inf.* a person of a specified type, often one to be envied or pitied: *poor little beggars.*

▶ v. [*tr.*] reduce (someone) to poverty: *by being soft to the unfortunate, we beggared ourselves.*

beg·gar·ly /'begərlē/ ▶ adj. poverty-stricken. ■ pitifully or deplorably bad: *the beggarly physical condition to which I had been reduced.* ■ very small and mean: *the stipend was a beggarly $26.* **—beg·gar·li·ness** n.

beg·gar·y /'begərē/ ▶ n. a state of extreme poverty.

be·gin /bi'gin/ ▶ v. (**-gin·ning**; *past* **-gan** /-'gan/; *past part.* **-gun** /-'gən/) **1** [*tr.*] start; perform or undergo the first part of (an action or activity): *the Communists have just begun to fight* | (**begin to do/doing something**) *it was beginning to snow* | [*intr.*] *she began by rewriting the syllabus.* ■ [*intr.*] come into being or have its starting point at a certain time or place: *the ground campaign had begun.* ■ [*intr.*] (of a person) hold a specific position or role before holding any other: *he began as a drummer.* ■ [*intr.*] (of a thing) originate: *Watts Lake began as a marine inlet.* ■ [*intr.*] (**begin with**) have as a first element: *words beginning with a vowel.* ■ [*intr.*] (**begin**

on/upon) set to work at: *Picasso began on a great canvas.* ▪ [with *direct speech*] start speaking by saying: *"I've got to go to the hotel," she began.* ▪ [*intr.*] (**begin at**) (of an article) cost at least (a specified amount): *rooms begin at $139.* **2** [*intr.*] *inf.* not have any chance or likelihood of doing a specified thing: *circuitry that Karen could not begin to comprehend.*

be·gin·ner /bi'ginər/ ▸ *n.* a person just starting to learn a skill or take part in an activity.

▸ □ **beginner's luck** good luck supposedly experienced by a beginner at a particular activity.

be·gin·ning /bi'giniNG/ ▸ *n.* the point in time or space at which something starts: *he left at the beginning of February | they had reached the beginning of the forest.* ▪ the process of coming, or being brought into being: *the beginning of active cooperation.* ▪ the first part or earliest stage of something: *the beginning of a letter.* ▪ (usu. **beginnings**) the background or origins of anything: *the series explores the beginnings of flight.*

▸ *adj.* new or inexperienced: *a beginning gardener.* ▪ introductory or elementary: *the beginning guitar class.*

▸ □ **the beginning of the end** the event to which ending or failure can be traced.

be·go·nia /bi'gōnyə/ ▸ *n.* a herbaceous plant (genus *Begonia*, family Begoniaceae) of warm climates, the bright flowers of which have brightly colored sepals but no petals.

be·got /bi'gät/ ▸ past of BEGET.

be·got·ten /bi'gätn/ ▸ past participle of BEGET.

be·grudge /bi'grəj/ ▸ *v.* **1** envy (someone) the possession or enjoyment of (something): *she begrudged Martin his affluence.* **2** [*tr.*] give reluctantly or resentfully: *nobody begrudges a single penny spent on health.* —**be·grudg·ing·ly** *adv.*

be·guile /bi'gīl/ ▸ *v.* [*tr.*] charm or enchant (someone), sometimes in a deceptive way: *every prominent American artist has been beguiled by Maine |* [as *adj.*] (**beguiling**) *a beguiling smile.* ▪ trick (someone) into doing something: *they were beguiled into signing a peace treaty.* —**be·guile·ment** *n.* —**be·guil·er** *n.* —**be·guil·ing·ly** *adv.*

be·guine /bi'gēn/ ▸ *n.* a popular dance of West Indian origin, similar to the foxtrot.

be·gun /bi'gən/ ▸ past participle of BEGIN.

be·half /bi'haf/ ▸ *n.*

▸ □ **on** (also **in**) **behalf of** (or **on someone's behalf**) **1** in the interests of a person, group, or principle: *votes cast by labor unions on behalf of their members.* **2** as a representative of: *he had to attend the funeral on Mama's behalf.*

be·have /bi'hāv/ ▸ *v.* [*intr.*] **1** act or conduct oneself in a specified way, esp. toward others: *he always behaved like a gentleman | you should behave affectionately toward the patient.* ▪ (of a machine or natural phenomenon) work or function in a specified way: *each car behaves differently.* **2** [often in *imper.*] conduct oneself in accordance with the accepted norms of a society or group: *you can go as long as you behave |* (**behave oneself**) *they were expected to behave themselves.*

be·hav·ior /bi'hāvyər/ (*Brit.* **be·hav·iour**) ▸ *n.* the way in which one acts or conducts oneself, esp. toward others: *good behavior | his insulting behavior toward me.* ▪ the way in which an animal or person acts in response to a particular situation or stimulus: *the feeding behavior of predators.* ▪ the way in which a natural phenomenon or a machine works or functions: *the erratic behavior of the old car.*

be·hav·ior·al /bi'hāvyərəl/ ▸ *adj.* involving, relating to, or emphasizing behavior: *closely related species have similar behavioral patterns | a behavioral approach to children's language.* —**be·hav·ior·al·ly** *adv.*

be·hav·ior·ism /bi'hāvyə,rizəm/ ▸ *n.* *Psychol.* the theory that human and animal behavior can be explained in terms of conditioning, without appeal to thoughts or feelings, and that psychological disorders are best treated by altering behavior patterns. ▪ such study and treatment in practice. —**be·hav·ior·ist** *n. & adj.* —**be·hav·ior·is·tic** /bi,hāvyə'ristik/ *adj.*

be·head /bi'hed/ ▸ *v.* cut off the head of (someone), typically as a form of execution: [as *n.*] (**beheading**) *Arabs have public beheadings.*

be·held /bi'held/ ▸ past and past participle of BEHOLD.

be·he·moth /bi'hēməth; 'bēəməth/ ▸ *n.* a huge or monstrous creature. ▪ something enormous, esp. a big and powerful organization: *shoppers are now more loyal to their local stores than to faceless behemoths.*

be·hest /bi'hest/ ▸ *n.* *poetic/lit.* a person's orders or command: *they had assembled at his behest | the slaughter of the male children at the behest of Herod.*

be·hind /bi'hīnd/ ▸ *prep.* **1** at or to the far side of (something), typically so as to be hidden by it: *the recording machinery was kept behind screens.* ▪ *fig.* hidden from the observer: *the agony behind his decision to retire.* ▪ expressing movement: *Jannie instinctively hid her*

cigarette behind her back. ▪ at the back of (someone), after they have passed through a door: *she ran out of the room, slamming the door behind her.* **2** in a line or procession, following or further back than (another member of the line or procession): *stuck behind a slow-moving tractor.* **3** in support of or giving guidance to (someone else): *whatever you decide to do, I'll be behind you | the power behind the throne.* ▪ guiding, controlling, or responsible for (an event or plan): *the chances were that he was behind the death of the girl.* **4** after the departure or death of (the person referred to): *he left behind him a manuscript that was subsequently published.* **5** less advanced than (someone else) in achievement or development: *the government admitted it is ten years behind the West in PC technology.* **6** having a lower score than (another competitor): *Bergman is five baskets behind Kelley in the free-throw contest.*

▸ *adv.* **1** at or to the far side or the back side of something: *as I looked behind, my feet crashed into a basket.* **2** in a place or time already past: *the adventure lay behind them.* **3** remaining after someone or something is gone: *blocks of ice left behind by a retreating glacier | don't leave me behind.* **4** further back than other members of a group: *Bill led the way, with the others a short distance behind.* **5** (in a game or contest) having a score lower than that of the opposition: *polls showed him as much as 50 points behind.* **6** slow or late in accomplishing a task: *getting behind with my work.* ▪ in arrears: *she was behind with her rent.* **7** underlying or motivating: *behind his winning facade lurks uncertainty.*

▸ *adj.* following; lagging: *the team behind could accept a loss.*

▸ *n. inf.* the buttocks: *sitting on her behind.*

be·hold /bi'hōld/ ▸ *v.* (*past* and *past part.* **-held** /-'held/) [*tr.*] [often in *imper.*] *archaic* or *poetic/lit.* see or observe (a thing or person, esp. a remarkable or impressive one): *behold your king! | the botanical gardens were a wonder to behold.* ▷Old English *bihaldan,* from *bi-* 'thoroughly' + *haldan* 'to hold.' —**be·hold·er** *n.*

be·hold·en /bi'hōldən/ ▸ *adj.* owing thanks or having a duty to someone in return for help or a service: *I don't like to be beholden to anybody.*

be·hoove /bi'hōōv/ (*Brit.* **be·hove** /-'hōv/) ▸ *v.* [*tr.*] (**it behooves someone to do something**) *formal* it is a duty or responsibility for someone to do something; it is incumbent on: *it behooves any coach to study his predecessors.* ▪ it is appropriate or suitable; it befits: *it ill behooves the opposition constantly to decry the sale of arms to friendly countries.*

beige /bāzh/ ▸ *adj.* of a pale sandy yellowish-brown color: *the beige tiles of the kitchen floor.*

▸ *n.* a pale sandy yellowish-brown: *tones of beige, green, and orange.*

be·ing /'bēiNG/ ▸ present participle of BE.

▸ *n.* **1** existence: *the railway brought many towns into being.* ▪ living; being alive: *holism promotes a unified way of being.* **2** the nature or essence of a person: *sometimes one aspect of our being has been developed at the expense of the others.* **3** a real or imaginary living creature, esp. an intelligent one: *animals regarded as primitive beings.* ▪ a human being: *she felt anxiety about so small and vulnerable a being.* ▪ a supernatural entity: *a being who had made all things.*

be·jew·eled /bi'jōōəld/ (also **be·jew·elled**) ▸ *adj.* adorned with jewels: *a wave of his bejeweled hand.*

bel /bel/ ▸ *n.* a unit used in the comparison of power levels in electrical communication or of intensities of sound, corresponding to an intensity ratio of 10 to 1. See also DECIBEL.

be·la·bor /bi'lābər/ ▸ *v.* [*tr.*] **1** argue or elaborate (a subject) in excessive detail: *critics thought they belabored the obvious.* **2** attack or assault (someone) physically or verbally: *Tyndale seized every opportunity to belabor the Roman Church.*

be·lat·ed /bi'lātid/ ▸ *adj.* coming or happening later than should have been the case: *a belated apology.* —**be·lat·ed·ly** *adv.* —**be·lat·ed·ness** *n.*

be·lay /bi'lā/ ▸ *v.* [*tr.*] **1** fix (a running rope) around a cleat, pin, rock, or other object, to secure it. ▪ secure (a mountaineer) in this way: *he belayed his partner across the ice.* **2** [usu. in *imper.*] *Nautical slang* stop; enough!: *"Belay that, mister. Man your post."*

▸ *n.* **1** an act of belaying: *the leader may require belays to tackle more difficult sections.* **2** a spike of rock or other hard material used for belaying. —**be·lay·er** *n.*

bel can·to /bel 'käntō; 'kan-/ ▸ *n.* a lyrical style of operatic singing using a full rich broad tone and smooth phrasing: *a superb piece of bel canto |* [as *adj.*] *the bel canto arias of Bellini.*

belch /belCH/ ▸ *v.* **1** [*intr.*] emit gas noisily from the stomach through the mouth. **2** [*tr.*] (often **belch out/forth/into**) (esp. of a chimney) send (smoke or flames) out or up: *a factory chimney belches out smoke.* ▪ [*intr.*]

Pronunciation Key ə *ago, up;* ər *over, fur;* a *hat;* ā *ate;* ä *car;* CH *chin;* e *let;* ē *see;* e(ə)r *air;* i *fit;* ī *by;* i(ə)r *ear;* NG *sing;* ō *go;* ô *law, for;* oi *toy;* ŏŏ *good;* ōō *goo;* ou *out;* SH *she;* TH *thin;* ŦH *then;* (h)w *why;* ZH *vision*

(often **belch from**) (of smoke or flames) pour out from a chimney or other opening: *flames belch from the wreckage.*
▶ *n.* an act of belching: *he gave a loud belch.*

be·lea·guer /biˈlēgər/ ▶ *v.* [*tr.*] [usu. as *adj.*] (**beleaguered**) lay siege to: *he is leading a relief force to the aid of the beleaguered city.* ■ beset with difficulties: *the board is supporting the beleaguered director amid calls for his resignation.* ▷late 16th cent.: from Dutch *belegeren* 'camp around,' from *be-* '(all) around' + *leger* 'a camp.'

bel·fry /ˈbelfrē/ ▶ *n.* (*pl.* **-fries**) a bell tower or steeple housing bells, esp. one that is part of a church. ■ a space for hanging bells in a church tower.

Bel·gian /ˈbeljən/ ▶ *adj.* of or relating to Belgium.
▶ *n.* a native or national of Belgium or a person of Belgian descent.

be·lie /biˈlī/ ▶ *v.* (**-ly·ing**) [*tr.*] **1** (of an appearance) fail to give a true notion or impression of (something); disguise or contradict: *his lively alert manner belied his years.* **2** fail to fulfill or justify (a claim or expectation); betray: *the notebooks belie Darwin's later recollection.*

be·lief /biˈlēf/ ▶ *n.* **1** an acceptance that a statement is true or that something exists: *his belief in God* | *a belief that solitude nourishes creativity.* ■ something one accepts as true or real; a firmly held opinion or conviction: *we're prepared to fight for our beliefs.* ■ a religious conviction: *Christian beliefs.* **2** (**belief in**) trust, faith, or confidence in someone or something: *a belief in democratic politics.*
▶ □ **beyond belief** astonishingly good or bad; incredible: *riches beyond belief.*

be·lieve /biˈlēv/ ▶ *v.* [*tr.*] **1** accept (something) as true; feel sure of the truth of: *the superintendent believed Lancaster's story* | *Christians believe that Jesus rose from the dead.* ■ accept the statement of (someone) as true: *he didn't believe her or didn't want to know.* ■ [*intr.*] have faith, esp. religious faith: *there are those on the fringes of the Church who do not really believe.* ■ (**believe something of someone**) feel sure that (someone) is capable of a particular action: *I wouldn't have believed it of Lois—what an extraordinary woman!* **2** hold (something) as an opinion; think or suppose: *I believe we've already met* | *things were not as bad as the experts believed* | *humu-humu are, I believe, shrimp fritters* | (**believe someone/something to be**) *four men were believed to be trapped.*
▶ *phrasal v.* □ **believe in 1** have faith in the truth or existence of: *I believe in God.* **2** be of the opinion that (something) is right, proper, or desirable: *I don't believe in censorship of the arts* | *he didn't believe in sex before marriage.* **3** have confidence in (a person or a course of action): *he had finally begun to believe in her.* —**be·liev·a·ble** *adj.*

be·liev·er /biˈlēvər/ ▶ *n.* **1** a person who believes that a specified thing is effective, proper, or desirable: *a believer in ghosts.* **2** an adherent of a particular religion; someone with religious faith.

be·lit·tle /biˈlitl/ ▶ *v.* [*tr.*] make (someone or something) seem unimportant: *this is not to belittle his role* | *she felt belittled.* —**be·lit·tle·ment** *n.* —**be·lit·tler** *n.*

bell /bel/ ▶ *n.* **1** a hollow object, typically made of metal and having the shape of a deep inverted cup widening at the lip, that sounds a clear musical note when struck, typically by means of a clapper inside. ■ a device that includes or sounds like a bell, used to give a signal or warning: *a bicycle bell.* ■ the sound of a bell: *at the bell we are both giggling.* ■ (**the bell**) (in boxing and other sports) a bell rung to mark the start or end of a round: *they were dragged off each other at the final bell.* **2** a bell-shaped object or part of one, such as the end of a trumpet. ■ the corolla of a bell-shaped flower: *a flower with small, pale blue bells.* **3** (**bells**) another term for TUBULAR BELLS. **4** *Naut.* (preceded by a numeral) the time as indicated every half hour of a watch by the striking of the ship's bell one to eight times: *clean shirt for muster at five bells.*
▶ *v.* **1** [*tr.*] provide with a bell or bells; attach a bell or bells to: *the young men were belling and hobbling the horses before releasing them.* **2** [*intr.*] make a ringing sound likened to that of a bell: *the organ belling away.* **3** [*intr.*] spread or flare outward like the lip of a bell: *her shirt belled out behind.*
▶ □ **be saved by the bell** (in boxing and other sports) avoid being counted out by the ringing of the bell at the end of a round. □ **bells and whistles** *inf.* attractive additional features or trimmings: *an advocate of more bells and whistles on the income tax code.* □ (**as**) **clear as a bell** perfectly clear or sound: *Aunt Nora's words came clear as a bell.* □ **ring a bell** *inf.* revive a distant recollection; sound familiar: *the name Woodall rings a bell.* □ **with bells on** *inf.* enthusiastically: *everybody's waiting for you with bells on.*

bel·la·don·na /ˌbeləˈdänə/ ▶ *n.* deadly nightshade.

bell-bot·toms ▶ *pl. n.* trousers with a marked flare below the knee: [as *adj.*] (**bell-bottom**) *bell-bottom trousers.* —**bell-bot·tomed** *adj.*

bell-buoy /ˈbelˌbo͞oē; -ˌboi/ ▶ *n.* a buoy equipped with a bell rung by the motion of the sea, warning nearby vessels of shoal waters.

belle /bel/ ▶ *n.* a beautiful girl or woman, esp. the most beautiful at a particular event or in a particular group: *the belle of the season.*
▶ □ **belle of the ball** the most beautiful and popular girl or woman at a dance.

belle é·poque /ˌbel āˈpək/ ▶ *n.* the period of settled and comfortable life preceding World War I: [as *adj.*] *a romantic, belle-époque replica of a Paris bistro.*

belles-let·tres /ˌbel ˈletrə/ ▶ *pl. n.* [also treated as *sing.*] **1** essays, particularly of literary and artistic criticism, written and read primarily for their aesthetic effect. **2** literature considered as a fine art. —**bel·let·rism** /belˈletrizəm/ *n.* —**bel·let·rist** /belˈletrist/ *n.* —**bel·let·ris·tic** /ˌbeləˈtristik/ *adj.*

bell·flow·er /ˈbelˌflou(-ə)r/ ▶ *n.* a plant (genus *Campanula*, family Campanulaceae) with bell-shaped flowers that are usually blue, purple, pink, or white.

bell·hop /ˈbelˌhäp/ ▶ an attendant in a hotel who performs services such as carrying guests' luggage.

bel·li·cose /ˈbeliˌkōs/ ▶ *adj.* demonstrating aggression and willingness to fight: *a group of bellicose patriots.* —**bel·li·cos·i·ty** /ˌbeləˈkäsitē/ *n.*

bel·lig·er·ent /bəˈlijərənt/ ▶ *adj.* hostile and aggressive: *a bull-necked, belligerent old man.* ■ engaged in a war or conflict, as recognized by international law.
▶ *n.* a nation or person engaged in war or conflict, as recognized by international law. —**bel·lig·er·ence** *n.* —**bel·lig·er·ent·ly** *adv.*

bell jar ▶ *n.* a bell-shaped glass cover used for covering delicate objects or used in a laboratory, typically for enclosing samples.

bel·low /ˈbelō/ ▶ *v.* [*intr.*] (of a person or animal) emit a deep loud roar, typically in pain or anger: *he bellowed in agony* | [as *n.*] (**bellowing**) *the bellowing of a bull.* ■ shout something with a deep loud roar: [*tr.*] *the watchers were bellowing encouragement* | *"God send the right!" he bellowed.* ■ [*tr.*] sing (a song) loudly and tunelessly: *he got thrown out of bars for bellowing Portuguese folk songs.*
▶ *n.* a deep roaring shout or sound: *a bellow of rage.*

bel·lows /ˈbelōz/ ▶ *pl. n.* [also treated as *sing.*] **1** a device with a bag that emits a stream of air when squeezed: ■ (also **pair of bellows**) a kind with two handles used for blowing air at a fire. ■ a kind used in a harmonium or small organ. **2** an object or device with concertinaed sides to allow it to expand and contract, such as a tube joining a lens to a camera body.

bellows

bell pep·per ▶ *n.* another term for SWEET PEPPER.

bell·weth·er /ˈbelˌweᴛʜər/ ▶ *n.* the leading sheep of a flock, with a bell on its neck. ■ an indicator or predictor of something: *college campuses are often the bellwether of change.*

bel·ly /ˈbelē/ ▶ *n.* (*pl.* **-lies**) the human trunk below the ribs, containing the stomach and bowels. ■ the front of this part of the body: *he fell flat on his belly.* ■ the stomach, esp. as representing the body's need for food: *they'll fight all the better on empty bellies.* ■ the underside of a bird or other animal. ■ a cut of pork from the underside between the legs. ■ a pig's belly as food, esp. as a traded commodity. ■ the rounded underside of a ship or aircraft.
▶ *v.* (**-lies, -lied**) [*intr.*] **1** swell; bulge: *as she leaned forward her pullover bellied out.* **2** (**belly up to**) *inf.* move or sit close to (a bar or table): *regulars who first bellied up to the bar years before.* ▷Old English *belig* 'bag,' of Germanic origin, from a base meaning 'swell, be inflated.' —**bel·lied** *adj.* [usu. in *comb.*] *fat-bellied men.* —**bel·ly·ful** *n.*
▶ □ **go belly up** *inf.* go bankrupt.

bel·ly·ache /ˈbelēˌāk/ *inf.* ▶ *n.* an abdominal pain.
▶ *v.* [*intr.*] complain noisily or persistently: *heads of departments bellyaching about lack of resources* | [as *n.*] (**bellyaching**) *there was plenty of bellyaching.* —**bel·ly·ach·er** *n.*

bel·ly but·ton ▶ *n. inf.* a person's navel.

bel·ly dance ▶ *n.* a dance originating in the Middle East, typically performed by a woman and involving undulating movements of the belly and rapid gyration of the hips. —**bel·ly danc·er** *n.* —**bel·ly danc·ing** *n.*

bel·ly·flop /ˈbelēˌfläp/ *inf.* ▶ *n.* a dive into water, landing flat on one's front. ■ *fig.* a commercial failure: *the film's bellyflop at the box office is unsurprising.*
▶ *v.* (**-flopped, -flop·ping**) [*intr.*] perform such a dive.

bel·ly laugh ▶ *n.* a loud, unrestrained laugh.

be·long /bi'lông/ ▸v. [intr.] **1** (of a thing) be rightly placed in a specified position: *learning to place the blame where it belongs.* ■ be rightly classified in or assigned to a specified category: *bony fish: the vast majority of living fish belong here.* **2** (of a person) fit in a specified place or environment: *she is a stranger, and doesn't belong here* | [as n.] (**belonging**) *we feel a real sense of belonging.* ■ have the right personal or social qualities to be a member of a particular group: *young people are generally very anxious to belong.* ■ (**belong to**) be a member or part of (a particular group, organization, or class): *they belong to garden and bridge clubs.* **3** (**belong to**) be the property of: *the vehicle did not belong to him.* ■ (of a contest or period of time) be dominated by: *the race belonged completely to Ferguson.* —**be·long·ing·ness** *n.*

be·long·ings /bi'lôNGiNGz/ ▸pl. n. one's movable possessions.

Be·lo·rus·sian /ˌbelō'rəSHən/ (also **Bye·lo·rus·sian** /ˌbyelō-/) ▸adj. of or relating to Belarus, its people, or its language.
▸n. **1** a native or national of Belarus. ■ a person of Belorussian descent. **2** the East Slavic language of Belarus.

be·lov·ed /bi'ləv(i)d/ ▸adj. dearly loved. ■ (**beloved by/of**) very popular with or much used by a specified set of people: *being so close, the mountain hut is beloved of families on a day's outing.*
▸n. a much loved person: *he watched his beloved.*

be·low /bi'lō/ ▸prep. **1** extending underneath: *the tunnel below the crags* | *cables running below the floorboards* | *hanging space below a top storage shelf.* **2** at a lower level or layer than: *just below the pocket was a stain* | *blistered skin below his collar.* ■ lower in grade or rank than: *they rated its financial soundness below its competitor's.* **3** lower than (a specified amount, rate, or norm): *below average.*
▸adv. at a lower level or layer: *he jumped from the window into the moat below.* ■ under the surface of the water: *trout lying more than 20 feet below.* ■ on earth: *deflections of the stars from their proper orbits with fatal results here below.* ■ in hell: *traitors gnash their teeth below.* ■ lower than zero (esp. zero degrees Fahrenheit) in temperature: *there's a north wind blowing, and it's 30 below.* ■ (in printed text) mentioned later or further down on the same page: *our nutritionist is pictured below right* | *the most common methods are shown below.* ■ Naut. below deck: *I'll go below and fix us a drink.*

belt /belt/ ▸n. **1** a strip of leather or other material worn around the waist or across the chest, esp. in order to support clothes or carry weapons: *a sword belt* | [as adj.] *a belt buckle.* ■ short for SEAT BELT. ■ a belt worn as a sign of rank or achievement: *he was awarded the victor's belt.* ■ a belt of a specified color, marking the attainment of a particular level in judo, karate, or similar sports: [as adj.] *brown-belt level.* ■ a person who has reached such a level: *I am a karate black belt.* ■ (**the belt**) the punishment of being struck with a belt. **2** a strip of material used in various technical applications, in particular: ■ a continuous band of material used in machinery for transferring motion from one wheel to another. **3** a strip or encircling band of something having a specified nature or composition that is different from its surroundings: *the asteroid belt.* **4** a heavy blow: *she ran in to administer a good belt with her stick.* **5** *inf.* a gulp or shot of liquor: *they could probably use a few belts.*
▸v. [tr.] **1** [tr.] fasten with a belt: *she paused only to belt a robe about her waist.* ■ [intr.] be fastened with a belt: *the jacket belts at the waist.* ■ attach or secure with a belt: *he was securely belted into the passenger seat.* **2** beat or strike (someone), esp. with a belt, as a punishment. ■ hit (something) hard: *he belted the ball to the left-field fence.* **3** gulp a drink quickly: *belting down shots of gun metal drink called arrack.*
▸phrasal v. □ **belt something out** sing or play a song loudly and forcefully. —**belt·ed** *adj.* —**belt·er** *n.*
▸ □ **below the belt** unfair or unfairly; disregarding the rules: *there has been yet another below-the-belt blow to the workers of Chicago.* □ **tighten one's belt** cut one's spending; live more frugally. □ **under one's belt 1** safely or satisfactorily achieved, experienced, or acquired: *I want to get more experience under my belt.* **2** (of food or drink) consumed: *Gus already had a large brandy under his belt.*

belt·way /'belt,wā/ ▸n. a highway encircling an urban area. ■ (**Beltway**) [often as adj.] Washington, DC, esp. as representing the perceived insularity of the U.S. government: *conventional beltway wisdom.*

be·lu·ga /bə'lōōgə/ ▸n. (*pl.* same or **belugas**) **1** a small, white-toothed whale (*Delphinapterus leucas*, family Monodontidae) related to the narwhal, living in herds mainly in Arctic coastal waters. **2** a very large sturgeon (*Huso huso*) occurring in the inland seas and associated rivers of central Eurasia. ■ (also **beluga caviar**) caviar obtained from this fish.

bel·ve·dere /'belvi,di(ə)r/ ▸n. a summerhouse or open-sided gallery, usually at rooftop level, commanding a fine view.

be·ly·ing /bi'lī-iNG/ ▸ present participle of BELIE.

be·moan /bi'mōn/ ▸v. [tr.] *often humorous* express discontent or sorrow over (something): *single women bemoaning the absence of men.*

be·muse /bi'myōōz/ ▸v. [tr.] [usu. as adj.] (**bemused**) puzzle, confuse, or bewilder (someone): *her bemused expression* | *she was accepted with bemused resignation by her parents as a hippie.* —**be·mus·ed·ly** /-zidlē/ *adv.* —**be·muse·ment** *n.*

bench /benCH/ ▸n. **1** a long seat for several people, typically made of wood or stone. **2** a long, sturdy work table used by a carpenter, mechanic, scientist, or other worker. **3** (**the bench**) the office of judge or magistrate: *his appointment to the civil bench.* ■ a judge's seat in a court. ■ judges or magistrates collectively: *rulings from the bench.* **4** (**the bench**) a seat on which sports coaches and players sit during a game when they are not playing.
▸v. [tr.] withdraw (a sports player) from play; substitute: *the coach benched quarterback Randall Cunningham in favor of Jim McMahon.*
▸ □ **on the bench 1** appointed as or in the capacity of a judge or magistrate: *he retired after twenty-five years on the bench.* **2** acting as one of the possible substitutes in a sports contest.

bench·mark /'benCH,märk/ ▸n. **1** a standard or point of reference against which things may be compared or assessed: [as adj.] *a benchmark case.* ■ a problem designed to evaluate the performance of a computer system: *a graphics benchmark.* **2** a surveyor's mark cut in a wall, pillar, or building and used as a reference point in measuring elevations.
▸v. [tr.] evaluate or check (something) by comparison with a standard: *we are benchmarking our performance against external criteria.* ■ [intr.] evaluate or check something in this way: *we continue to benchmark against the competition.*

bench test *chiefly Comput.* ▸n. a test carried out on a machine, a component, or software before it is released for use, to ensure that it works properly.
▸v. (**bench-test**) [tr.] run a bench test on (something): *they are offering you the chance to bench-test their applications.* ■ [intr.] give particular results during a bench test: *it bench-tests two times faster than the previous version.*

bend /bend/ ▸v. (*past* **bent** /bent/) **1** [tr.] shape or force (something straight) into a curve or angle: *the rising wind bent the long grass.* ■ [intr.] (of something straight) be shaped or forced into a curve or angle: *the oar bent as Lance heaved angrily at it.* ■ *fig.* force or be forced to submit: [tr.] *they want to bend me to their will* | [intr.] *a refusal to bend to mob rule.* ■ [intr.] (of a road, river, or path) deviate from a straight line in a specified direction; have a sharply curved course: *the road bent left and then right.* **2** [intr.] (of a person) incline the body downward from the vertical: *he bent down and picked her up* | *I bent over my plate.* ■ [tr.] move (a jointed part of the body) to an angled position: *extend your left leg and bend your right.* **3** [tr.] interpret or modify (a rule) to suit oneself or somebody else: *we cannot bend the rules, even for Darren.* **4** [tr.] direct or devote (one's attention or energies) to a task: *Eric bent all his efforts to persuading them to donate some blankets.*
▸n. **1** a curve, esp. a sharp one, in a road, river, racecourse, or path. **2** a curved or angled part or form of something: *making a bend in the wire.* **3** a kind of knot used to join two ropes, or to tie a rope to another object, e.g. a carrick bend. **4** (**the bends**) decompression sickness, esp. in divers. —**bend·a·ble** *adj.* —**bend·y** *adj.*
▸ □ **bend someone's ear** *inf.* talk to someone, esp. with great eagerness or in order to ask a favor: *she regularly bent Michael's ear with her problems.* □ **bend one's elbow** drink alcohol. □ **bend over backward** see BACKWARD. □ **on bended knee** (or **knees**) kneeling, esp. when pleading or showing great respect. □ **around the bend** *inf.* crazy; insane: *I'd tell you if you were going around the bend.*

bend·er /'bendər/ *inf.* ▸n. [usu. in comb.] an object or person that bends something else: *a fender bender.* **2** a wild drinking spree.

be·neath /bi'nēTH/ ▸prep. **1** extending or directly underneath, typically with close contact: *in the labyrinths beneath central Moscow.* ■ underneath so as to be hidden, covered, or protected: *unaltered even after years beneath the sea.* **2** at a lower level or layer than: *beneath this floor there's a cellar.* ■ lower in grade or rank than: *relegated to the rank beneath theirs.* ■ considered of lower status or worth than: *taking jobs beneath my abilities.* ■ behind (a physical surface): *they found another layer beneath the stucco.* ■ behind or hidden behind (an appearance): *beneath the gloss of success.*
▸adv. **1** extending or directly underneath something: *a house built on stilts to allow air to circulate beneath.* **2** at a lower level or layer: *the runways had cracked open, exposing the black earth beneath.*

Ben·e·dic·tine /ˌbeni'dik,tēn; -tin/ ▸n. **1** a monk or nun of an order following the rule of St. Benedict. **2** *trademark* a liqueur based on brandy, originally made by Benedictine monks in France. ▶*adj.* of St. Benedict or the Benedictines.

ben·e·dic·tion /ˌbeniˈdikSHən/ ▶*n.* the utterance or bestowing of a blessing, esp. at the end of a religious service.

ben·e·fac·tion /ˌbenəˈfaksHən/ ▶*n.* a donation or gift.

ben·e·fac·tor /ˈbenəˌfaktər; ˌbenəˈfaktər/ ▶*n.* a person who gives money or other help to a person or cause.

ben·e·fice /ˈbenəfis/ ▶*n.* a permanent Church appointment, typically that of a rector or vicar, for which property and income are provided in respect of pastoral duties. —**ben·e·ficed** *adj.*

be·nef·i·cent /bəˈnefəsənt/ ▶*adj.* (of a person) generous or doing good. ■ resulting in good: *a beneficent democracy.* —**be·nef·i·cence** *n.* —**be·nef·i·cent·ly** *adv.*

ben·e·fi·cial /ˌbenəˈfisHəl/ ▶*adj.* favorable or advantageous; resulting in good: *the beneficial effect on the economy* | *discoveries* **beneficial to** *mankind.* ■ *Law* of or relating to rights, other than legal title: *the beneficiary will be taxed on the value of his beneficial use of the property.* —**ben·e·fi·cial·ly** *adv.*

ben·e·fi·ci·ar·y /ˌbenəˈfisHē,erē/ ▶*n.* (*pl.* **-ar·ies**) a person who derives advantage from something, esp. a trust, will, or life insurance policy.

ben·e·fit /ˈbenəfit/ ▶*n.* **1** an advantage or profit gained from something: *tenants bought their houses* **with the benefit of** *a discount* | *enjoy the benefits of being a member.* **2** a payment or gift made by an employer, the state, or an insurance company: *welfare benefits* | *wages and benefits.* **3** a public performance or other entertainment of which the proceeds go to a particular charitable cause.
▶*v.* (**-fit·ed**, **-fit·ing** or **-fit·ted**, **-fit·ting**) [*intr.*] receive an advantage; profit; gain: *areas that would* **benefit from** *regeneration.* ■ [*tr.*] bring advantage to: *the bill will benefit the nation.* ▷late Middle English (originally denoting a kind deed or something well done): from Old French *bienfet,* from Latin *benefactum* 'good deed,' from *bene facere* 'do good (to).'
▶ □ **the benefit of the doubt** a concession that a person or fact must be regarded as correct or justified, if the contrary has not been proven: *I'll* **give you the benefit of the doubt** *as to whether it was deliberate or not.*

be·nev·o·lent /bəˈnevələnt/ ▶*adj.* well meaning and kindly: *a benevolent smile.* ■ (of an organization) serving a charitable rather than a profit-making purpose: *a benevolent fund.* —**be·nev·o·lence** *n.* —**be·nev·o·lent·ly** *adv.*

be·night·ed /biˈnītid/ ▶*adj.* in a state of pitiful or contemptible intellectual or moral ignorance, typically owing to a lack of opportunity: *they saw themselves as bringers of culture to poor benighted peoples.* —**be·night·ed·ness** *n.*

be·nign /biˈnīn/ ▶*adj.* **1** gentle; kindly: *her face was calm and benign.* ■ (of a climate or environment) mild and favorable: ■ not harmful to the environment: [in comb.] *an ozone-benign refrigerant.* **2** *Med.* (of a disease) not harmful in effect: in particular, (of a tumor) not malignant. —**be·nig·ni·ty** /biˈnignitē/ *n.* —**be·nign·ly** *adv.*

bent[1] /bent/ ▶ past and past participle of **BEND**[1].
▶*adj.* **1** sharply curved or having an angle: *a piece of bent wire.* **2** (**bent on**) determined to do or have something: *a missionary bent on saving souls* | *a mob bent on violence.*
▶*n.* a natural talent or inclination: *a man of religious bent.*
▶ □ **bent out of shape** *inf.* angry or agitated: *it was just a mistake, nothing to get bent out of shape about.*

bent[2] ▶*n.* (also **bent grass**) a stiff grass (*Agrostis* and other genera) that is used for lawns and is a component of pasture and hay grasses. ■ the stiff flowering stalk of a grass.

bent·wood /ˈbent,wood/ ▶*n.* wood that is artificially shaped for use in making furniture: [as adj.] *bentwood chairs.*

ben·zene /ˈben,zēn; benˈzēn/ ▶*n.* a colorless volatile liquid hydrocarbon, C_6H_6, present in coal tar and petroleum, used in chemical synthesis.

ben·zene ring ▶*n. Chem.* the hexagonal unsaturated ring of six carbon atoms present in benzene and many other aromatic molecules.

ben·zine /ˈben,zēn; benˈzēn/ (also **ben·zin** /ˈbenzin/) ▶*n.* a mixture of liquid hydrocarbons obtained from petroleum.

ben·zo·in /ˈbenzō-in/ ▶*n.* **1** a fragrant gum resin obtained from a tropical eastern Asian tree (genus *Styrax,* family Styracaceae), used in medicines, perfumes, and incense. **2** *Chem.* a white aromatic crystalline ketone, present in this resin.

be·queath /biˈkwēTH; -ˈkwēTH/ ▶*v.* [*tr.*] leave (a personal estate or one's body) to a person or other beneficiary by a will: *he bequeathed his art collection to the town.* ■ pass (something) on or leave (something) to someone else: *he is ditching the unpopular policies bequeathed to him.* —**be·queath·er** *n.*

be·quest /biˈkwest/ ▶*n.* a legacy: *her $135,000 was the largest bequest the library ever has received.* ■ the action of bequeathing something: *a painting acquired by bequest.*

be·rate /biˈrāt/ ▶*v.* [*tr.*] scold or criticize (someone) angrily: *my son berated me for not giving him a Jewish upbringing.*

be·reave /biˈrēv/ ▶*v.* (**be bereaved**) be deprived of a loved one through a profound absence, esp. due to the loved one's death: *the year after they had been bereaved* | [as adj.] (**bereaved**) *bereaved families* | [as *pl. n.*] (**the bereaved**) *those who counsel the bereaved.* —**be·reave·ment** *n.*

be·reft /biˈreft/ ▶ archaic past participle of **BEREAVE**.
▶*adj.* deprived of or lacking something, esp. a nonmaterial asset: *her room was stark and bereft of color.* ■ (of a person) lonely and abandoned, esp. through someone's death or departure: *his death in 1990 left her bereft.*

be·ret /bəˈrā/ ▶*n.* a round flattish cap of felt or cloth.

ber·ga·mot /ˈbərgə,mät/ ▶*n.* **1** an oily substance extracted from the rind of the fruit of a dwarf variety of the Seville orange tree, used in cosmetics and as flavoring in tea. **2** (also **bergamot orange**) the tree (*Citrus aurantium bergamia*) that bears this fruit. **3** an aromatic North American herb (*Monarda didyma*) of the mint family, grown for its bright flowers and used medicinally.

ber·i·ber·i /ˈberēˌberē/ ▶*n.* a disease causing inflammation of the nerves and heart failure, caused by a deficiency of vitamin B_1.

ber·ke·li·um /bərˈkēlēəm/ ▶*n.* the chemical element of atomic number 97, an artificial radioactive metal of the actinide series. (Symbol: **Bk**)

berm /bərm/ ▶*n.* a flat strip of land, raised bank, or terrace bordering a river or canal. ■ a path or grass strip beside a road. ■ an artificial ridge or embankment, e.g., as a defense against tanks.

Ber·mu·da on·ion ▶*n.* a variety of cultivated onion with a mild flavor and a flattened shape.

Ber·mu·da shorts (also **Ber·mu·das**) ▶*pl. n.* casual knee-length shorts.

ber·ry /ˈberē/ ▶*n.* (*pl.* **-ries**) a small roundish juicy fruit without a stone: *juniper berries* | [as adj.] *berry clusters.* ■ *Bot.* any fruit that has its seeds enclosed in a fleshy pulp, for example, a banana or tomato.

ber·serk /bərˈzərk; -ˈsərk/ ▶*adj.* (of a person or animal) out of control with anger or excitement; wild or frenzied: *after she left him, he* **went berserk,** *throwing things about the apartment.* ■ (of a mechanical device or system) operating in a wild or erratic way; out of control: *the climate control went berserk and either roasted or froze us.* ■ (of a procedure, program, or activity) fluctuating wildly: *the stock market's gone berserk, with sugar at 15.27 cents a pound.* ▷early 19th cent. (originally as a noun denoting a wild Norse warrior who fought with frenzy): from Old Norse *berserkr* (noun), probably from *birn-, bjorn* 'bear' + *serkr* 'coat,' but also possibly from *berr* 'bare' (i.e., without armor).

berth /bərTH/ ▶*n.* **1** a ship's allotted place at a wharf or dock. **2** a fixed bed or bunk on a ship, train, or other means of transport. **3** *inf.* (often in a sports context) a situation or position in an organization or event: *today's victory clinched a berth for the Orioles in the playoffs.*
▶*v.* [*tr.*] moor (a ship) in its allotted place: *these modern ships can almost berth themselves.* ■ [*intr.*] (of a ship) dock: *the Dutch freighter berthed at the Brooklyn docks.*
▶ □ **give a wide berth** stay away from someone or something: *I'd sworn to give women a wide berth.*

ber·yl /ˈberəl/ ▶*n.* a transparent pale green, blue, or yellow mineral consisting of a silicate of beryllium and aluminum, sometimes used as a gemstone.

be·ryl·li·um /bəˈrilēəm/ ▶*n.* the chemical element of atomic number 4, a hard gray metal. (Symbol: **Be**)

be·seech /biˈsēCH/ ▶*v.* (*past* **-sought** /-ˈsôt/ or **-seeched**) *formal* or *literary* ask (someone) urgently and fervently to do something; implore; entreat: [*tr.*] *they beseeched him to stay* | [*tr.*] *"You have got to believe me," Gloria beseeched him* | [as adj.] (**beseeching**) *a beseeching gaze.* —**be·seech·ing·ly** *adv.*

be·set /biˈset/ ▶*v.* (**-set·ting**; *past* and *past part.* **-set**) [*tr.*] (of a problem or difficulty) trouble or threaten persistently: *the social problems that beset the inner city* | *she was beset with self-doubt.* ■ surround and harass; assail on all sides: *I was beset by clouds of flies.* ■ hem in; enclose: *the ship was beset by ice.*

be·side /biˈsīd/ ▶*prep.* **1** at the side of; next to: *he sat beside me in the front seat.* ■ compared with: *beside Beth's idealism, my priorities looked shabby.* **2** in addition to; apart from: *he commissioned work from other artists beside Rivera.*
▶ □ **beside oneself** overcome with worry or anger; distraught: *she was beside herself with anguish.* □ **beside the point** see **POINT**.

be·sides /bi'sīdz/ ▸*prep.* in addition to; apart from: *I have no other family besides my parents.*
▸*adv.* in addition; as well: *I'm capable of doing the work, and a lot more besides.* ■ moreover; anyway: *I had no time to warn you. Besides, I wasn't sure.*

be·siege /bi'sēj/ ▸*v.* [*tr.*] surround (a place) with armed forces in order to capture it or force its surrender; lay siege to: *the guerrillas continued to besiege other major cities to the north* | [as *adj.*] (**besieged**) *the besieged city.* ■ crowd around oppressively; surround and harass: *she spent the whole day besieged by newsmen.* ■ (**be besieged**) be inundated by large numbers of requests or complaints: *the television station was besieged with calls.* —**be·sieg·er** *n.*

be·smirch /bi'smərCH/ ▸*v.* [*tr.*] damage the reputation of (someone or something) in the opinion of others: *he had besmirched the good name of his family.*

be·som /'bēzəm/ ▸*n.* a broom made of twigs tied around a stick.

be·sot·ted /bi'sätid/ ▸*adj.* strongly infatuated: *he became besotted with his best friend's sister.*

be·sought /bi'sôt/ ▸ past and past participle of BESEECH.

be·speak /bi'spēk/ ▸*v.* (*past* **-spoke**; *past part.* **-spok·en**) [*tr.*] **1** (of an appearance or action) suggest; be evidence of: *the attractive tree-lined road bespoke money.* **2** order or reserve (something) in advance: *obtaining the affidavits that it has been necessary to bespeak.*

best /best/ superlative of GOOD. ▸*adj.* of the most excellent, effective, or desirable type or quality: *the best pitcher in the league.* ■ most enjoyable: *some of the best times of my life.* ■ most appropriate, advantageous, or well advised: *do whatever you think best.*
▸*adv.* superlative of WELL[1]. ■ to the highest degree; most: *the one we liked best.* ■ most excellently or effectively: *the best-dressed man in Hollywood.* ■ most suitably, appropriately, or usefully: *this is best done at home.*
▸*n.* (usu. **the best**) that which is the most excellent, outstanding, or desirable: *buy the best you can afford* | *Sarah always had to be the best at everything.* ■ the most meritorious aspect of a thing or person: *he brought out the best in people.* ■ (**one's best**) the peak of condition; the highest standard or level that a person or thing can reach: *this is jazz at its best* | *try to look your best.* ■ (**one's best**) one's finest or most formal clothes: *she dressed in her best.* ■ (in sports) a record of a specified kind, esp. a personal one: *a personal best.*
▸*v.* [*tr.*] *inf.* outwit or get the better of (someone): *she refused to allow herself to be bested.*
▸ □ **at best** taking the most optimistic or favorable view: *signs of recovery are patchy at best.* □ **be for** (or **all for**) **the best** be desirable in the end, although not at first seeming so. □ **the best part of** most of: *it took them the best part of 10 years.* □ **do** (or **try**) **one's best** do all one can: *Ruth did her best to reassure her.* □ **get the best of** overcome (someone): *his drinking got the best of him and he was fired.* □ **had best do something** find it most sensible or well advised to do the thing mentioned: *I'd best be going.* □ **make the best of** derive what limited advantage one can from (something unsatisfactory or unwelcome): *you'll just have to make the best of the situation.* ■ use (resources) as well as possible: *he tried to make the best of his talents.* □ **to the best of one's ability** (or **knowledge**) as far as one can do or know: *the text is free of factual errors, to the best of my knowledge.* □ **with the best of them** as well as or as much as anyone: *he'll be out there dancing with the best of them.*

bes·tial /'bēsCHəl; 'bes-/ ▸*adj.* of or like an animal or animals: *Darwin's revelations about our bestial beginnings.* ■ savagely cruel and depraved: *bestial and barbaric acts.* —**bes·tial·ly** *adv.*

bes·ti·al·i·ty /,bēsCHē'alitē; ,bes-/ ▸*n.* **1** savagely cruel or depraved behavior: *there seems no end to the bestiality of human beings.* **2** sexual intercourse between a person and an animal.

bes·ti·ar·y /'bēsCHē,erē; 'bes-/ ▸*n.* (*pl.* **-ar·ies**) a descriptive or anecdotal treatise on various real or mythical kinds of animals, esp. a medieval work with a moralizing tone.

be·stir /bi'stər/ ▸*v.* (**-stirred**, **-stir·ring**) (**bestir oneself**) make a physical or mental effort; exert or rouse oneself: *they rarely bestir themselves except in the most pressing of circumstances.*

best man ▸*n.* a male friend or relative chosen by a bridegroom to assist him at his wedding.

best-of /'best ,əv; əv/ ▸*n.* a list or collection comprising the best examples of something: *foodies have flocked like sheep to this critic's best-ofs.*
▸*adj.* denoting such a collection or list.

be·stow /bi'stō/ ▸*v.* [*tr.*] confer or present (an honor, right, or gift): *the office was bestowed on him by the chief of state* | *fig. she bestowed her nicest smile on Jim.* —**be·stow·al** /-əl/ *n.*

be·stride /bi'strīd/ ▸*v.* (*past* **-strode**; *past part.* **-strid·den**) [*tr.*] stand astride over; span or straddle: *fig. creatures that bestride the dividing line between*
amphibians and reptiles. ■ sit astride on: *he bestrode his horse with the easy grace of a born horseman.*

best sell·er ▸*n.* a book or other product that sells in very large numbers: *her autobiography is an international best seller.*

bet /bet/ ▸*v.* (**bet·ting**; *past* **bet** or **bet·ted**) **1** [*intr.*] risk something, usually a sum of money, against someone else's on the basis of the outcome of a future event, such as the result of a race or game: *betting on horses* | *I would be prepared to bet that what he really wanted was to settle down* | [*tr.*] *most people would bet their life savings on this prospect.* ■ [*tr.*] risk a sum of money against (someone) on the outcome or happening of a future event: *I'll bet you $15 you won't find a single scratch.* **2** *inf.* feel sure: *I bet this place is really spooky late at night* | *he'll be surprised to see me, I'll bet.*
▸*n.* an act of risking a sum of money in this way: *every Saturday she had a bet on the horses.* ■ a sum of money staked in this way: *the bookies are taking bets on his possible successor.* ■ *inf.* a candidate or course of action to choose; an option: *your best bet is to call a professional exterminator.* ■ (**one's bet**) *inf.* an opinion, typically one formed quickly or spontaneously: *my bet is that the president will veto the bill.*
▸ □ **all bets are off** *inf.* the outcome of a situation is unpredictable. □ **want to** (or **wanna**) **bet?** *inf.* used to express vigorous disagreement with a confident assertion: *"You can't be with me every moment." "Want to bet?"* □ **you bet** *inf.* you may be sure; certainly: *"Would you like this piece of pie?" "You bet!"*

be·ta /'bātə/ ▸*n.* the second letter of the Greek alphabet (Β, β), transliterated as 'b.' ■ [as *adj.*] denoting the second of a series of items, categories, forms of a chemical compound, etc.: *beta carotene* | *beta blocker.* ■ *inf.* short for BETA TEST: *their database system is currently in beta* | [as *adj.*] *a beta version.* ■ (**Beta**) [followed by Latin genitive] the second (usually second-brightest) star in a constellation: *Beta Virginis.* ■ [as *adj.*] relating to beta decay or beta particles: *beta emitters.*

be·ta block·er ▸*n.* any of a class of drugs that prevent the stimulation of the receptors responsible for increased cardiac action. Beta blockers are used to control heart rhythm, treat angina, and reduce high blood pressure.

be·ta par·ti·cle (also **beta ray**) ▸*n.* Physics a fast-moving electron emitted in radioactive decay.

be·ta test ▸*n.* a trial of machinery, software, or other products, in the final stages of its development, carried out by a party unconnected with its development.
▸*v.* (**be·ta-test**) [*tr.*] subject (a product) to such a test.

be·tel /'bētl/ ▸*n.* **1** the leaf of an Asian evergreen climbing plant, used in the East as a mild stimulant. Parings of areca nut, lime, and cinnamon are wrapped in the leaf, which is then chewed, causing the saliva to turn red and, with prolonged use, the teeth to go black. **2** the plant (*Piper betle*) of the pepper family from which these leaves are taken.

be·tel nut ▸*n.* another term for ARECA NUT.

bête noire /,bāt 'nwär; ,bet/ ▸*n.* (*pl.* **bêtes noires** *pronunc.* same or /'nwärz/) a person or thing that one particularly dislikes: *great-uncle Edward was my father's bête noire.*

be·to·ken /bi'tōkən/ ▸*v.* [*tr.*] *poetic/lit.* be a sign of; indicate: *she wondered if his cold, level gaze betokened indifference or anger.* ■ be a warning or indication of (a future event): *the falling comet betokened the true end of Merlin's powers.*

be·tray /bi'trā/ ▸*v.* [*tr.*] be disloyal to: *his friends were shocked when he betrayed them.* ■ be disloyal to (one's country, organization, or ideology) by acting in the interests of an enemy: *he could betray his country for the sake of communism.* ■ treacherously inform an enemy of the existence or location of (a person or organization): *this group was betrayed by an informer.* ■ treacherously reveal (secrets or information): *many of those employed by diplomats betrayed secrets and sold classified documents.* ■ *fig.* reveal the presence of; be evidence of: *she drew a deep breath that betrayed her indignation.* —**be·tray·al** /-əl/ *n.* —**be·tray·er** *n.*

be·troth /bə'trōTH; -'trôTH/ ▸*v.* [*tr.*] (usu. **be betrothed**) *dated* enter into a formal agreement to marry: *soon I shall be betrothed to Isabel* | [as *n.*] (**betrothed**) *how long have you known your betrothed?* —**be·troth·al** /-əl/ *n.*

bet·ter[1] /'betər/ ▸*adj.* **1** comparative of GOOD and WELL. ■ of a more excellent or effective type or quality: *hoping for better weather* | *the new facilities were far better* | *I'm better at algebra than Alice.* ■ more appropriate, advantageous, or well advised: *there couldn't be a better time to start this job.* **2** partly or fully recovered from illness or injury: *she's much better today* | *his leg was getting better.* ■ fitter and healthier; less unwell: *we'll feel a lot better after a decent night's sleep.*

▶*adv.* comparative of WELL. ■ more excellently or effectively: *Johnny could do better if he tried.* ■ to a greater degree; more: *I liked it better when we lived in the country.* ■ more suitably, appropriately, or usefully: *the money could be better spent on more urgent cases.*

▶*n.* **1** the better one; that which is better: *the Natural History Museum book is by far the better of the two | a change for the better.* **2** (one's betters) *chiefly dated* or *humorous* one's superiors in social class or ability: *amusing themselves by imitating their betters.*

▶*v.* [*tr.*] improve on or surpass (an existing or previous level or achievement): *bettering his previous time by ten minutes.* ■ make (something) better; improve: *his ideas for bettering the working conditions.* ■ (**better oneself**) achieve a better social position or status: *the residents are mostly welfare mothers who have bettered themselves.* ■ overcome or defeat (someone): *she bettered him at archery.* —**bet·ter·ment** *n.*

▶ □ **be better off** be in a better position, esp. in financial terms. □ **the —— the better** used to emphasize the importance or desirability of the quality or thing specified: *the sooner we're off, the better | the more people there the better.* □ **the better part of** almost all of; most of: *it is the better part of a mile.* □ **better than** more than: *he'd lived there for better than twenty years.* □ **the better to** —— so as to —— better: *he leaned closer the better to hear her.* □ **for better or (for) worse** whether the outcome is good or bad: *ours, for better or for worse, is the century of youth.* □ **get the better of** (often of something immaterial) win an advantage over (someone); defeat or outwit: *curiosity got the better of her.* □ **go one better** narrowly surpass a previous effort or achievement: *I want to go one better this time and score.* ■ narrowly outdo (another person): *he went one better than Jack by reaching the finals.* □ **had better do something** would find it wiser to do something; ought to do something: *you had better be careful.* □ **have the better of** be more successful in a contest: *she usually had the better of these debates.*

bet·ter² ▶*n.* variant spelling of BETTOR.

bet·ter half ▶*n. inf.* a person's wife, husband, or partner.

bet·ting /'betiNG/ ▶*n.* the act of gambling money on the outcome of a race, game, or other unpredictable event: *there was a good deal of betting on the races going on.*

bet·tor /'betər/ (also **bet·ter**) ▶*n.* a person who bets, typically regularly or habitually.

be·tween /bi'twēn/ (abbr.: **bet.**) ▶*prep.* **1** at, into, or across the space separating (two objects or regions): ■ expressing location: *traffic was at a standstill between exits 12 and 14.* ■ expressing movement to a point: *the dog crawled between us and lay down at our feet.* ■ expressing movement from one side or point to the other and back again: *traveling by train between London and Paris.* **2** in the period separating (two points in time): *they snack between meals.* **3** in the interval separating (two points on a scale): *a man aged between 18 and 30 | the difference between income and expenditure.* **4** indicating a connection or relationship involving two or more parties: *links between science and industry.* ■ with reference to a collision or conflict: *a collision in midair between two light aircraft above Geneva | the wars between Russia and Poland.* ■ with reference to a choice or differentiation involving two or more things being considered together: *if you have to choose between two or three different options.* **5** by combining the resources or actions of (two or more people or other entities): *China and India between them account for a third of the global population.* ■ shared by (two or more people or things): *they had drunk between them a bottle of Chianti.*

▶*adv.* **1** in or along the space separating two objects or regions: *layers of paper with tar in between | from Leipzig to Dresden, with the gentle Elbe flowing between.* **2** in the period separating two points in time: *sets of exercises with no rest in between.*

▶ □ **between ourselves** (or **you and me**) in confidence: *just between you and me, I don't think it is going to happen.*

be·twixt /bi'twikst/ ▶*prep.* & *adv.* archaic term for BETWEEN.

▶ □ **betwixt and between** *inf.* neither one thing nor the other.

bev·el /'bevəl/ ▶*n.* (in carpentry, metalwork and stonework) a sloping surface or edge. ■ (in full **bev·el square**) a tool for marking angles in carpentry, metalwork and stonework.

▶*v.* (**bev·eled, bev·el·ing** or **bev·elled, bev·el·ling**) [*tr.*] [often as *adj.*] (**beveled**) reduce (a square edge on an object) to a sloping edge: *a beveled mirror.* ▷late 16th cent. (as an adjective in the sense 'oblique'): from an Old French diminutive of *baif* 'open-mouthed,' from *baer* 'to gape'.

bev·el gear ▶*n.* a gear working another gear at an angle to it by means of bevel wheels.

bev·er·age /'bev(ə)rij/ ▶*n.* a drink, esp. one other than water.

bev·y /'bevē/ ▶*n.* (*pl.* **bev·ies**) a large group of people or things of a particular kind: *he was surrounded by a bevy of beautiful girls.* ■ a group of

birds, particularly when closely gathered on the ground: *a bevy of quail stayed through winter, feeding on our locust beans.*

be·wail /bi'wāl/ ▶*v.* [*tr.*] express great regret, disappointment, or bitterness over (something) by complaining about it to others: *he bewailed the fact that heart trouble had slowed him down.* ■ cry or wail loudly about (something).

be·ware /bi'we(ə)r/ ▶*v.* [*intr.*] be cautious and alert to the dangers of: *consumers were warned to beware of faulty packaging | Beware! Dangerous submerged rocks ahead | [tr.] we should beware the incompetence of legislators.*

be·wil·der /bi'wildər/ ▶*v.* [*tr.*] [often as *adj.*] (**bewildered**) cause (someone) to become perplexed and confused: *she seemed frightened and bewildered | his reaction had bewildered her | [as adj.] (bewildering) there is a bewildering array of desserts to choose from.* —**be·wil·dered·ly** *adv.* —**be·wil·der·ing·ly** *adv.* —**be·wil·der·ment** *n.*

be·witch /bi'wiCH/ ▶*v.* [*tr.*] (often **be bewitched**) cast a spell on and gain control over (someone) by magic: *his relatives were firmly convinced that he was bewitched.* ■ enchant and delight (someone): *they both were bewitched by the country and its culture | [as adj.] (bewitching) she was certainly a bewitching woman.* —**be·witch·ing·ly** *adv.* —**be·witch·ment** *n.*

be·yond /bē'änd; bi'yänd/ ▶*prep.* & *adv.* **1** at or to the further side of: [as *prep.*] *he pointed to a spot beyond the trees | passengers traveling to destinations beyond Boston | [as adv.] there was the terminal and, beyond, an endless line of warehouses.* ■ [*prep.*] outside the physical limits or range of: *the land sloped away until far beyond sight it reached the Great Plains.* ■ *fig.* more extensive or extreme than; further-reaching than: [as *prep.*] *what these children go through is far beyond what most adults endure in a lifetime. | [as adv.] pushing the laws to their limits and beyond.* **2** happening or continuing after (a specified time or event): [as *prep.*] *we can manage another two years, but beyond that the system is not viable | [as adv.] music going on into the night and beyond.* **3** having progressed or achieved more than (a specified stage or level): [as *prep.*] *we need to get beyond square one.* ■ above or greater than (a specified amount): [as *prep.*] *the absenteeism had gone beyond 15% | [as adv.] he could count up to a billion now, and beyond.* **4** [*prep.*] to a degree or condition where a specified action is impossible: *the landscape has changed beyond recognition.* ■ too much for (someone) to achieve or understand: *I did something that I thought was beyond me.* **5** [*prep.*] apart from; except: *there was little vegetation beyond scrub and brush.*

▶*n.* (**the beyond**) the unknown after death: *messages from the beyond.*

bez·el /'bezəl/ ▶*n.* a groove holding the crystal of a watch or the stone of a gem in its setting.

Bi ▶*symb.* the chemical element bismuth.

bi /bī/ ▶*abbr. inf.* bisexual.

bi·an·nu·al /bī'anyōōəl/ ▶*adj.* occurring twice a year: *the biannual meeting of the planning committee.* —**bi·an·nu·al·ly** *adv.*

bi·as /'bīəs/ ▶*n.* **1** prejudice in favor of or against one thing, person, or group compared with another, usually in a way considered to be unfair: *there was evidence of bias against foreign applicants | a systematic bias in favor of the powerful.* ■ a concentration on or interest in one particular area or subject: *a discernible bias toward philosophy.* ■ *Statistics* a systematic distortion of a statistical result due to a factor not allowed for in its derivation. **2** an edge cut obliquely across the grain of a fabric. **3** in some sports, such as lawn bowling, the irregular shape given to a ball. ■ the oblique course that such a shape causes a ball to run. **4** *Electr.* a steady voltage, magnetic field, or other factor applied to an electronic system or device to cause it to operate over a predetermined range.

▶*v.* (**bi·ased, bi·as·ing** or **bi·assed, bi·as·sing**) **1** [*tr.*] (usu. **be biased**) show prejudice for or against (someone or something) unfairly: *readers said the paper was biased toward the conservatives | [as adj.] (biased) a biased view of the world.* ■ influence unfairly to invoke favoritism: *her well-rehearsed sob story failed to bias the jury.* **2** give a bias to: *bias the ball.*

bi·ath·lon /bī'aTHlän/ ▶*n.* an athletic contest combining two events, esp. cross-country skiing and rifle shooting. —**bi·ath·lete** /-lēt/ *n.*

bib /bib/ ▶*n.* a piece of cloth or plastic fastened around a person's neck

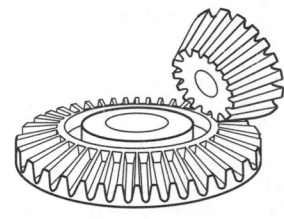

bevel gears

to keep their clothes clean while eating. ■ the part above the waist of the front of an apron or pair of overalls. ■ a loose-fitting, sleeveless garment worn for identification, esp. by competitors and officials at sporting events. ■ a patch of color on the throat of a bird or other animal: *a black bird with a white bib.*

bi·be·lot /'bib(ə),lō/ ▸ *n.* a small, decorative ornament or trinket.

Bi·ble /'bībəl/ ▸ *n.* (**the Bible**) the Christian scriptures, consisting of the 66 books of the Old and New Testaments. ■ (**the Bible**) the Jewish scriptures, consisting of the Torah or Law, the Prophets, and the Hagiographa or Writings. ■ (also **bi·ble**) a copy of the Christian or Jewish scriptures: *clutching a large black Bible under his arm.* ■ a particular edition or translation of the Bible: *the New English Bible.* ■ (**bible**) *inf.* any authoritative book: *"Larousse Gastronomique," the bible of French cooking.* ■ the scriptures of any religion. ▷Middle English: via Old French from ecclesiastical Latin *biblia,* from Greek *biblia* 'books,' from *biblion* 'book,' originally a diminutive of *biblos* 'papyrus, scroll,' of Semitic origin.

Bi·ble Belt ▸ *n.* (**the Bible Belt**) *inf.* those areas of the southern and midwestern U.S. and western Canada where Protestant fundamentalism is widely practiced.

bib·li·cal /'biblikəl/ (also **Bib·li·cal**) (abbr.: **bibl.** or **Bibl.**) ▸ *adj.* of, relating to, or contained in the Bible: *the biblical account of creation | biblical times.* ■ resembling the language or style of the Bible: *there is a biblical cadence in the last words he utters.* ■ very great; on a large scale: *they see themselves as victims of almost biblical dimensions.* —**bib·li·cal·ly** /-ik(ə)lē/ *adv.*

bib·li·og·ra·phy /,biblē'ägrəfē/ (abbr.: **bibliog.**) ▸ *n.* (*pl.* **-phies**) a list of the books referred to in a scholarly work, usually printed as an appendix. ■ a list of the books of a specific author or publisher, or on a specific subject: *a bibliography of his publications.* ■ the history or systematic description of books, their authorship, printing, publication, editions, etc.: *he regarded bibliography as a science.* ■ any book containing such information. —**bib·li·og·ra·pher** /-fər/ *n.* —**bib·li·o·graph·ic** /-lēə'grafik/ *adj.* —**bib·li·o·graph·i·cal** /-'grafikəl/ *adj.* —**bib·li·o·graph·i·cal·ly** /-ik(ə)lē/ *adv.*

bib·li·o·phile /'biblēə,fīl/ ▸ *n.* a person who collects or has a great love of books. —**bib·li·o·phil·ic** /,biblēə'filik/ *adj.* —**bib·li·oph·i·ly** /,biblē'äfəlē/ *n.*

bib·u·lous /'bibyələs/ ▸ *adj. formal* excessively fond of drinking alcohol.

bi·cam·er·al /bī'kamərəl/ ▸ *adj.* (of a legislative body) having two branches or chambers. —**bi·cam·er·al·ism** /-,lizəm/ *n.*

bi·car·bo·nate /bī'kärbə,nāt; -nit/ ▸ *n. Chem.* a salt containing the anion HCO_3^-. ■ (also **bicarbonate of soda**) sodium bicarbonate.

bi·cen·ten·ar·y /,bīsen'tenərē/ ▸ *n. & adj.* another term for **BICENTENNIAL**.

bi·cen·ten·ni·al /,bīsen'teneəl/ ▸ *n.* the two-hundredth anniversary of a significant event.
▸ *adj.* of or relating to such an anniversary: *the bicentennial celebrations.*

bi·ceps /'bī,seps/ ▸ *n.* (*pl.* same or **-ceps·es** /-sepsiz/) a muscle having two points of attachment at one end, in particular: ■ the muscle in the upper arm that turns the hand to face palm uppermost and flexes the arm and forearm: *he clenched his fist and exhibited his bulging biceps.* ■ the muscle in the back of the thigh that helps to flex the leg.

bick·er /'bikər/ ▸ *v.* [*intr.*] argue about petty and trivial matters: *whenever the phone rings, they bicker over who must answer it* | [as *n.*] (**bickering**) *the constant bickering between Edgar and his mother.*

bi·cul·tur·al /bī'kəlCHərəl/ ▸ *adj.* having or combining the cultural attitudes and customs of two nations, peoples, or ethnic groups: *there is too little recognition of the children's bilingual and bicultural status.* —**bi·cul·tur·al·ism** /-,lizəm/ *n.*

bi·cus·pid /bī'kəspid/ ▸ *adj.* having two cusps or points.
▸ *n.* a tooth with two cusps, esp. a human premolar tooth.

bi·cy·cle /'bīsikəl/ ▸ *n.* a vehicle composed of two wheels held in a frame one behind the other, propelled by pedals and steered with handlebars attached to the front wheel.
▸ *v.* [*intr.*] ride a bicycle in a particular direction: *they had spent the day bicycling around the island.* —**bi·cy·clist** /-siklist/ *n.*

bid¹ /bid/ ▸ *v.* (**bid·ding**; *past* and *past part.* **bid**) [*tr.*] offer (a certain price) for something, esp. at an auction: *a consortium of dealers bid a world record price for a snuff box* | [*intr.*] *guests will bid for pieces of fine jewelry.* ■ [*intr.*] (**bid for**) (of a contractor) offer to do (work) for a stated price; tender for: *nineteen companies have indicated their intention to bid for the contract.* ■ [*intr.*] (**bid for**) make an effort or attempt to achieve: *the two freshmen are bidding for places in the varsity swim team.* ■ *Bridge* make a bid: *North bids four hearts* | [*intr.*] *with this hand, South should not bid.*
▸ *n.* an offer of a price, esp. at an auction: *several buyers made bids for the Van Gogh sketches.* ■ an offer to buy the shares of a company in order to gain control of it: *a takeover bid.* ■ an offer to do work or supply goods at a stated price; a tender. ■ an attempt or effort to achieve something: *an investigation would be carried out in a bid to establish what had happened* | *she hesitated to help her sister with her bid for the presidency.* ■ *Bridge* an

undertaking by a player in the auction to make a stated number of tricks with a stated suit as trumps. —**bid·der** *n.*

bid² ▸ *v.* (**bid·ding**; *past* **bid** or **bade** /bad; bād/; *past part.* **bid**) [*tr.*] **1** utter (a greeting or farewell) to: *a chance to bid farewell to their president.* **2** *archaic* or *poetic/lit.* command or order (someone) to do something: *I did as he bade me.* ■ invite (someone) to do something: *he bade his companions enter.*

bid call·er ▸ *n.* one who announces the bids and recognizes bidders at an auction.

bid·ding /'bidiNG/ ▸ *n.* **1** the offering of particular prices for something, esp. at an auction: *their first sale produced a wide range of lots and some energetic bidding.* ■ the offers made in such a situation: *from a cautious opener of $30, the bidding soared to $450.* ■ (in bridge and whist) the action of stating before play how many tricks one intends to make. **2** the ordering or requesting of someone to do something: *the clandestine associations that would act at their bidding.*
▸ □ **do someone's bidding** do what someone orders or requests, typically in a way considered overly slavish.

bid·dy /'bidē/ ▸ *n.* (*pl.* **-dies**) *inf.* a woman, usually an elderly one regarded as annoying or interfering: *the old biddies were muttering in his direction.*

bide /bīd/ ▸ *v.* [*intr.*] *archaic* or *dial.* remain or stay somewhere.
▸ □ **bide one's time** wait quietly for a good opportunity to do something: *she bided her time, patiently reading a magazine and planning her escape.*

bi·det /bi'dā/ ▸ *n.* a low oval basin used for washing one's genital and anal area.

bi·en·ni·al /bī'enēəl/ ▸ *adj.* **1** taking place every other year: *summit meetings are normally biennial.* **2** (esp. of a plant) living or lasting for two years.
▸ *n.* **1** a plant that takes two years to grow from seed to fruition and die. Compare with ANNUAL, PERENNIAL. **2** an event celebrated or taking place every two years. —**bi·en·ni·al·ly** *adv.*

bi·en·ni·um /bī'enēəm/ ▸ *n.* (*pl.* **-en·ni·ums** or **-en·ni·a** /-'enēə/) (usu. **the biennium**) a specified period of two years: *the budget for the next biennium.*

bier /bi(ə)r/ ▸ *n.* a movable frame on which a coffin or a corpse is placed before burial or cremation or on which it is carried to the grave.

bi·fo·cal /'bī,fōkəl/ ▸ *adj.* (usually of a pair of eyeglasses) having lenses each with two parts with different focal lengths, one for distant vision and one for near vision.
▸ *n.* (**bifocals**) a pair of eyeglasses having two such parts.

bi·fur·cate /'bīfər,kāt/ ▸ *v.* divide into two branches or forks: *just below Cairo the river bifurcates.*

bi·fur·ca·tion /,bīfər'kāSHən/ ▸ *n.* the division of something into two branches or parts: *the bifurcation of the profession into social do-gooders and self-serving iconoclasts.* ■ a thing divided in this way or either of the branches: *the bifurcation of the aorta is a site commonly affected first.*

big /big/ ▸ *adj.* (**big·ger, big·gest**) **1** of considerable size, extent, or intensity: *big hazel eyes | big cuts in staff.* ■ of a large or the largest size: *my big toe.* ■ grown up: *I'm a big girl now.* ■ elder: *my big sister.* ■ *inf.* doing a specified action very often or on a very large scale: *a big eater.* ■ on an ambitiously large scale: *a small company with big plans.* ■ *inf.* popular or exciting interest among the public: *Latino bands that are big in Los Angeles.* ■ showing great enthusiasm: *a big tennis fan | he tells me the Inuits of the Arctic are very big on Jim Reeves.* **2** of considerable importance or seriousness: *it's a big decision | Mark's biggest problem is money | he made a big mistake.* ■ *inf.* holding an important position or playing an influential role: *as a senior in college, he was a big man on campus.* **3** *inf.* often ironic generous: *"I'm inclined to take pity on you." "That's big of you!"*
▸ *n.* (**the bigs**) *inf.* the major league in a professional sport. —**big·ness** *n.*
▸ □ **big idea** *chiefly ironic* a clever or important intention or scheme: *okay, what's the big idea?* □ **big screen** *inf.* the movies: *the play was adapted for the big screen.* □ **big shot** (also **big noise**) *inf.* an important or influential person. □ **go over big** *inf.* have a great effect; be a success: *the story went over big with the children.* □ **make it big** *inf.* become very successful or famous: *Simon had made it big in the financial world.* □ **talk big** *inf.* talk confidently or boastfully. □ **think big** *inf.* be ambitious. □ **too big for one's britches** (or **breeches**) *inf.* conceited.

big·a·my /'bigəmē/ ▸ *n.* the act of going through a marriage ceremony while already married to another person. —**big·a·mist** /-mist/ *n.* —**big·a·mous** /-məs/ *adj.*

big band ▸*n.* a large group of musicians playing jazz or dance music: [as *adj.*] *the big band sound.*

big bang (also **Big Bang**) ▸*n. Astron.* the explosion of dense matter that, according to current cosmological theories, marked the origin of the universe.

Big Broth·er ▸*n. inf.* a person or organization exercising total control over people's lives.

big busi·ness ▸*n.* large-scale or important financial or commercial activity: *the children's toy market is big business now.*

Big Dip·per ▸*n.* a prominent group of seven stars in the constellation Ursa Major (the Great Bear), containing the Pointers that indicate the direction to Polaris.

Big·foot /'big,fŏŏt/ ▸*n. (pl.* **-feet**) a large, hairy, apelike creature resembling a yeti, supposedly found in northwestern America. Also called SASQUATCH.

big game ▸*n.* large animals hunted for sport: [as *adj.*] *a big-game hunter.*

big·head /'big,hed/ ▸*n. inf.* a conceited or arrogant person. —**big·head·ed** *adj.* —**big·head·ed·ness** *n.*

big·heart·ed /'big,härtid/ ▸*adj.* (of a person or action) kind and generous.

big·horn /'big,hôrn/ ▸*n.* (in full **American bighorn sheep**) a stocky brown North American wild sheep (*Ovis canadensis*) found esp. in the Rocky Mountains.

bight /bīt/ ▸*n.* a curve or recess in a coastline, river, or other geographical feature. ■ a loop of rope, as distinct from the rope's ends.

big·mouth /'big,mouᴛʜ/ ▸*n. inf.* an indiscreet or boastful person. —**big·mouthed** *adj.*

big·ot /'bigət/ ▸*n.* a person who is bigoted: *religious bigots.* —**big·ot·ry** *n.*

big·ot·ed /'bigətid/ ▸*adj.* obstinately convinced of the superiority or correctness of one's own opinions and prejudiced against those who hold different opinions: *a bigoted group of reactionaries.* ■ expressing or characterized by prejudice and intolerance: *a thoughtless and bigoted article.*

big top ▸*n.* the main tent in a circus.

big·wig /'big,wig/ ▸*n. inf.* an important person, usually in a particular sphere. Also called **big wheel**.

bike /bīk/ *inf.* ▸*n.* a bicycle or motorcycle: *I'm going by bike* | [as *adj.*] *a bike ride.*
▸*v.* [*intr.*] ride a bicycle or motorcycle: *we hope to encourage as many people as possible to bike to work* | [as *n.*] (**biking**) *the terrain is perfect for biking.*

bik·er /'bīkər/ ▸*n. inf.* a motorcyclist: [as *adj.*] *her biker boyfriend.* ■ a member of a motorcycle gang or club. ■ a cyclist: *a mountain biker.*

bi·ki·ni /bi'kēnē/ ▸*n. (pl.* **-nis**) a very brief two-piece swimsuit for women. ■ (also **bi·ki·nis**) scanty underpants.

bi·lat·er·al /bī'latərəl/ ▸*adj.* having or relating to two sides; affecting both sides: *bilateral hearing is essential for sound location.* ■ involving two parties, usually countries: *the recently concluded bilateral agreements with Japan.* —**bi·lat·er·al·ly** *adv.*

bil·ber·ry /'bil,berē/ ▸*n. (pl.* **-ies**) a hardy dwarf shrub (genus *Vaccinium*) of the heath family, closely related to the blueberry, with red drooping flowers and dark blue edible berries. ■ the small blue edible berry of this plant.

bile /bīl/ ▸*n.* a bitter greenish-brown alkaline fluid that aids digestion and is secreted by the liver and stored in the gallbladder. ■ *fig.* anger; irritability: *that topic is sure to stir up plenty of bile.*

bile duct ▸*n.* the duct that conveys bile from the liver and the gallbladder to the duodenum.

bilge /bilj/ ▸*n.* the area on the outer surface of a ship's hull where the bottom curves to meet the vertical sides. ■ bilgewater. ■ *fig., inf.* nonsense; rubbish: *romantic bilge dreamed up by journalists.*

bi·har·zi·a /bil'härzēə/ ▸*n.* a chronic disease, endemic in parts of Africa and South America, caused by infestation with blood flukes (schistosomes).

bi·lin·gual /bī'liNGgwəl/ ▸*adj.* (of a person) speaking two languages fluently: *a bilingual secretary.* ■ (of a text or an activity) written or conducted in two languages: *bilingual dictionaries* | *bilingual education.* ■ (of a country, city, etc.) using two languages, esp. officially: *the town is virtually bilingual in Dutch and German.* —**bi·lin·gual·ism** /-,lizəm/ *n.*

bil·ious /'bilyəs/ ▸*adj.* affected by or associated with nausea or vomiting: *I had eaten something that didn't agree with me and I was a little bilious.* ■ (of a color) lurid or sickly: *a bilious olive hue.* ■ *fig.* spiteful; bad-tempered: *outbursts of bilious misogyny.* —**bil·ious·ly** *adv.* —**bil·ious·ness** *n.*

bil·i·ru·bin /'bili,rŏŏbin/ ▸*n. Biochem.* an orange-yellow pigment formed in the liver by the breakdown of hemoglobin and excreted in bile.

bilk /bilk/ *inf.* ▸*v.* [*tr.*] obtain or withhold money from (someone) by deceit or without justification; cheat or defraud: *government waste has bilked the taxpayer of billions of dollars.*

bill¹ /bil/ ▸*n.* **1** an amount of money owed for goods supplied or services rendered, set out in a printed or written statement of charges: *he was running up a bill of hundreds of dollars.* **2** a draft of a proposed law presented to parliament for discussion: *a debate over the civil rights bill.* **3** a program of entertainment, esp. at a theater: *she was top of the bill at America's leading vaudeville house.* **4** a banknote; a piece of paper money: *a ten-dollar bill.* **5** a poster or handbill: *the circus promoters were posting bills all over town.*
▸*v.* [*tr.*] **1** (usu. **be billed**) list (a person or event) in a program: *they were billed to appear but didn't show up.* ■ (**bill someone/something as**) describe someone or something in a particular, usually promotional, way, esp. as a means of advertisement: *he was billed as "the new Sean Connery."* **2** send a note of charges to (someone): *we shall be billing them for the damage caused.* ■ charge (a sum of money): *we billed her $400,000.* —**bill·a·ble** *adj.*
▸ □ **fit** (or **fill**) **the bill** be suitable for a particular purpose: *a partner is an ally or a companion, and you don't seem to fit the bill.*

bill² ▸*n.* the beak of a bird, esp. when it is slender, flattened, or weak, or belongs to a web-footed bird or a bird of the pigeon family. ■ the muzzle of a platypus. ■ *Brit.* a stiff brim at the front of a cap.
▸*v.* [*intr.*] (of birds, esp. doves) stroke bill with bill during courtship. —**billed** *adj.* [usu. in *comb.*] *the red-billed weaverbird.*
▸ □ **bill and coo** *inf.* exchange caresses or affectionate words; behave or talk in a very loving or sentimental way.

bill·board /'bil,bôrd/ ▸*n.* a large outdoor board for displaying advertisements.

bil·let¹ /'bilit/ ▸*n.* a place, usually a civilian's house or other nonmilitary facility, where soldiers are lodged temporarily.
▸*v.* (**-let·ed, -let·ing**) [*tr.*] (often **be billeted**) lodge (soldiers) in a particular place, esp. a civilian's house or other nonmilitary facility.

bil·let² ▸*n.* a thick piece of wood. ■ *Archit.* each of a series of short cylindrical pieces inserted at intervals in decorative hollow moldings.

bill·fish /'bil,fiSH/ ▸*n. (pl.* same or **-fishes**) a large, fast-swimming fish (family Istiophoridae) of open seas, with a streamlined body and a long, pointed spearlike snout. Its several species include the marlins and sailfishes.

bill·fold /'bil,fōld/ ▸*n.* a thin wallet with few compartments, typically made of leather. ■ any wallet.

bill·hook /'bil,hŏŏk/ ▸*n.* a tool with a sickle-shaped blade with a sharp inner edge, used for pruning or lopping branches or other vegetation.

bil·liard /'bilyərd/ ▸*n.* **1** (**billiards**) [usu. treated as *sing.*] a game usually for two people, played on a billiard table, in which three balls are struck into pockets around the edge of the table: *play billiards at home* | [as *adj.*] *billiard ball* | *billiard room.* ■ (**English billiards**) a game played on a billiard table with pockets, in which points are made by caroms, pocketing an object ball, or caroming the cue ball into a pocket: **2** a stroke in which the cue ball strikes two balls successively.

bil·lion /'bilyən/ ▸*cardinal number (pl.* **-lions** or (with numeral or quantifying word) same) the number equivalent to the product of a thousand and a million; 1,000,000,000 or 10⁹: *a world population of over 6 billion.* ■ (**billions**) *inf.* a very large number or amount of something: *our immune systems are killing billions of germs right now.* ■ a billion dollars (or pounds, etc.). —**bil·lionth** /-yənᴛʜ/ *ordinal number.*

bil·lion·aire /'bilyə,ne(ə)r/ ▸*n.* a person possessing assets worth at least a billion dollars (or pounds, etc.).

bill of at·tain·der ▸*n. Law* an item of legislation (prohibited by the U.S. Constitution) that inflicts attainder without judicial process: *during the Revolutionary War, bills of attainder were passed to a wide extent.*

bill of ex·change ▸*n.* a written order to a person requiring the person to make a specified payment to the signatory or to a named payee; a promissory note.

bill of fare ▸*n. dated* a menu. ■ *inf.* the selection of food available to or consumed by (a person or animal): *our bill of fare in Alaska included clams, mussels, and herring.* ■ a program for a theatrical event.

bill of goods ▸*n.* a consignment of merchandise.
▸ □ **sell someone a bill of goods** deceive someone, usually by persuading them to accept something untrue or undesirable: *she was sold a bill of goods about that dog's pedigree.*

bill of health ▸*n.* a certificate relating to the incidence of infectious disease on a ship or in the port from which it has sailed.
▸ □ **a clean bill of health** a declaration or confirmation that someone is healthy or that something is in good condition: *a survey gave the property a clean bill of health.*

bill of lad·ing ▸*n.* a detailed list of a shipment of goods in the form of a receipt given by the carrier to the person consigning the goods.

Bill of Rights ▸*n. Law* a statement of the rights of a class of people, in particular: ■ the first ten amendments to the U.S. Constitution, ratified in 1791 and guaranteeing such rights as the freedoms of speech, assembly, and worship.

bill of sale ▸ *n.* a certificate of transfer of personal property.

bil·low /ˈbilō/ ▸ *n.* a large undulating mass of something, typically cloud, smoke, or steam.

▸ *v.* [*intr.*] (of fabric) fill with air and swell outward: *her dress billowed out around her.* ■ (of smoke, cloud, etc.) move or flow outward with an undulating motion: *smoke was billowing from the chimney.* —**bil·low·y** *adj.*

bil·ly /ˈbilē/ ▸ *n.* (*pl.* **-lies**) **1** short for BILLY GOAT. **2** (also **billy club**) a truncheon; a cudgel. ▷mid 19th cent.: from *Billy*, nickname for the given name *William*.

bil·ly goat ▸ *n.* a male goat.

bim·bo /ˈbimbō/ (also **bim·bette** /bimˈbet/) ▸ *n.* (*pl.* **-bos**) *inf.* an attractive but empty-headed young woman, esp. one perceived as a willing sex object.

bi·me·tal·lic /ˌbīməˈtalik/ ▸ *adj.* made or consisting of two metals.

bi·month·ly /bīˈmən(t)Hlē/ ▸ *adj.* occurring or produced twice a month or every two months: *a bimonthly newsletter.*

▸ *adv.* twice a month or every two months: *the journal appears bimonthly.*

▸ *n.* (*pl.* **-lies**) a periodical produced twice a month or every two months.

bin /bin/ ▸ *n.* a receptacle for storing or depositing a specified substance: *a vegetable bin* | *a trash bin.* ■ *Statistics* each of a series of ranges of numerical value into which data are sorted in statistical analysis.

▸ *v.* (**binned**, **bin·ning**) [*tr.*] place (something) in a bin. ■ *Statistics* group together (data) in bins. ▷Old English *bin(n)*, *binne*, of Celtic origin; related to Welsh *ben* 'cart.' The original meaning was 'receptacle' in a general sense; also specifically 'a receptacle for provender in a stable' and 'a receptacle for storing grain, bread, or other foodstuffs.'

bi·na·ry /ˈbīˌnerē; -nərē/ ▸ *adj.* **1** relating to, using, or expressed in a system of numerical notation that has 2 rather than 10 as a base. ■ in binary format: *it is stored as a binary file.* **2** relating to, composed of, or involving two things: *testing the so-called binary, or dual-chemical, weapons.*

▸ *n.* (*pl.* **-ries**) **1** the binary system: binary notation: *the device is counting in binary.* **2** something having two parts. ■ a binary star.

bi·na·ry code ▸ *n.* *Electr.* a coding system using the binary digits 0 and 1 to represent a letter, digit, or other character in a computer or other electronic device.

bi·na·ry dig·it ▸ *n.* one of two digits (0 or 1) in a binary system of notation.

bi·na·ry star ▸ *n.* a system of two stars in which one star revolves around the other or both revolve around a common center.

bi·na·ry sys·tem ▸ *n.* **1** a system in which information can be expressed by combinations of the digits 0 and 1. **2** a system consisting of two parts: *the binary system of state and public schools.* ■ *Astron.* a star system containing two stars orbiting around each other.

bin·au·ral /bīˈnôrəl; bin-/ ▸ *adj.* of, relating to, or used with both ears: *human hearing is binaural.* ■ of or relating to sound recorded using two microphones and usually transmitted separately to the two ears of the listener.

bind /bīnd/ ▸ *v.* (*past* and *past part.* **bound**) [*tr.*] **1** tie or fasten (something) tightly. ■ restrain (someone) by the tying up of hands and feet. **2** cause (people) to feel that they belong together: *the comradeship that bound such a disparate bunch together.* ■ (**bind someone to**) cause someone to feel strongly attached to (a person or place). ■ cohere or cause to cohere in a single mass: [*tr.*] *with the protection of trees to bind soil* | [*intr.*] *clay is chiefly tiny soil particles that bind together.* ■ cause (ingredients) to cohere by adding another ingredient. ■ cause (painting pigments) to form a smooth medium by mixing them with oil. ■ hold by chemical bonding. ■ [*intr.*] (**bind to**) combine with (a substance) through chemical bonding: *these proteins bind to DNA.* **3** *formal* impose a legal or contractual obligation on. ■ (**bind oneself**) *formal* make a contractual or enforceable undertaking. ■ (**be bound by**) be hampered or constrained by. **4** fix together and enclose (the pages of a book) in a cover.

▸ *phrasal v.* □ **bind someone over** (usu. **be bound over**) (of a court of law) require someone to fulfill an obligation, typically by paying a sum of money as surety.

▸ *n.* **1** a problematical situation. **2** *formal* a statutory constraint.

bind·er /ˈbīndər/ ▸ *n.* a thing or person that binds something, in particular: ■ a cover for holding loose sheets of paper, magazines, etc., together. ■ a substance that acts cohesively. ■ a reaping machine that binds grain into sheaves. ■ a bookbinder.

bind·er·y /ˈbīndərē/ ▸ *n.* (*pl.* **-er·ies**) a workshop or factory in which books are bound.

bind·ing /ˈbīndiNG/ ▸ *n.* **1** a strong covering holding the pages of a book

together. ■ fabric such as braid used for binding the edges of a piece of material. **2** (also **ski binding**) a mechanical device fixed to a ski to grip a ski boot, esp. either of a pair used for downhill skiing that hold the toe and heel of the boot and release it automatically in a fall. **3** the action of fastening, holding together, or being linked by chemical bonds: *the binding of antibodies to cell surfaces.*

▸ *adj.* (of an agreement or promise) involving an obligation that cannot be broken: *business agreements are intended to be legally binding.*

binge /binj/ *inf.* ▸ *n.* a short period devoted to indulging in an activity, esp. drinking alcohol, to excess: *he went on a binge and was in no shape to drive* | [as *adj.*] *binge eating* | *a spending binge.*

▸ *v.* (**bing·ing** or **binge·ing**) [*intr.*] indulge in an activity, esp. eating, to excess: *some dieters say they cannot help binging on chocolate* | [as *n.*] (**binging**) *her secret binging and vomiting.* —**bing·er** *n.*

binge-purge syn·drome ▸ *n.* see BULIMIA.

bin·go /ˈbiNGgō/ ▸ *n.* a game in which players mark off numbers on cards as the numbers are drawn randomly by a caller, the winner being the first person to mark off five numbers in a row or other pattern.

▸ *interj.* used to express satisfaction or surprise at a sudden positive event or outcome: *bingo, she leapfrogged into a sales trainee position.* ■ a call by someone who wins a game of bingo.

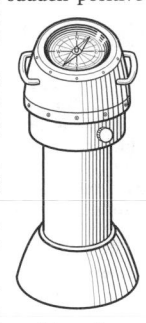

bin·na·cle /ˈbinəkəl/ ▸ *n.* a built-in housing for a ship's compass. ▷late 15th cent. (as *bittacle*): from Spanish *bitácula*, *bitácora* or Portuguese *bitacola*, from Latin *habitaculum* 'dwelling place,' from *habitare* 'inhabit.' The change to *binnacle* occurred in the mid 18th cent.

bin·oc·u·lar /biˈnäkyələr/ ▸ *adj.* adapted for or using both eyes: *a binocular microscope.*

bin·oc·u·lars /biˈnäkyələrz/ ▸ *pl. n.* an optical instrument with a lens for each eye, used for viewing distant objects.

bi·no·mi·al /bīˈnōmēəl/ ▸ *n.* **1** *Math.* an algebraic expression of the sum or the difference of two terms. **2** a two-part name, esp. the Latin name of a species of living organism.

binnacle

▸ *adj.* **1** *Math.* consisting of two terms. ■ of or relating to a binomial or to the binomial theorem. **2** having or using two names, used esp. of the Latin name of a species of living organism.

bi·o /ˈbīō/ ▸ *n.* (*pl.* **-os**) *inf.* **1** biology: *he dated a bio major in college.* **2** a biography: *the latest in a series of unauthorized bios.*

▸ *adj. inf.* **1** biological: *studying the effects of bio treatment.* **2** biographical: *it was excluded from her official bio material.*

bi·o·ac·tive /ˌbīōˈaktiv/ ▸ *adj.* (of a substance) having a biological effect. —**bi·o·ac·tiv·i·ty** /-akˈtivitē/ *n.*

bi·o·chem·is·try /ˌbīōˈkeməstrē/ ▸ *n.* the branch of science concerned with the chemical and physicochemical processes that occur within living organisms. ■ processes of this kind: *abnormal brain biochemistry.* —**bi·o·chem·i·cal** /-ˈkemikəl/ *adj.* —**bi·o·chem·i·cal·ly** *adv.* —**bi·o·chem·ist** /-ˈkemist/ *n.*

bi·o·de·grad·a·ble /ˌbīōdiˈgrādəbəl/ ▸ *adj.* (of a substance or object) capable of being decomposed by bacteria or other living organisms. —**bi·o·de·grad·a·bil·i·ty** /-ˌgrādəˈbilitē/ *n.*

bi·o·di·ver·si·ty /ˌbīōdiˈvərsitē/ ▸ *n.* the variety of life in the world or in a particular habitat or ecosystem.

bi·o·e·lec·tron·ics /ˌbīōiˈlekˈträniks; -ˌēlek-/ ▸ *pl. n.* [usu. treated as *sing.*] **1** the study and application of electronics in medicine and biological processes. **2** the integration of biological principles in electronic technology: *the impact of bioelectronics on computer hardware.* —**bi·o·e·lec·tron·ic** *adj.* —**bi·o·e·lec·tron·i·cal·ly** /-ik(ə)lē/ *adv.*

bi·o·en·gi·neer·ing /ˌbīōˌenjəˈni(ə)riNG/ ▸ *n.* **1** another term for GENETIC ENGINEERING. **2** the use of artificial tissues, organs, or organ components to replace damaged or absent parts of the body, such as artificial limbs and heart pacemakers. **3** the use in engineering or industry of biological organisms or processes. —**bi·o·en·gi·neer** *n. & v.*

bi·o·feed·back /ˌbīōˈfēd.bak/ ▸ *n.* the use of electronic monitoring of a normally automatic bodily function in order to train someone to acquire voluntary control of that function.

bi·o·gas /ˈbīōˌgas/ ▸ *n.* gaseous fuel, esp. methane, produced by the fermentation of organic matter.

bi·o·gen·e·sis /ˌbīōˈjenəsis/ ▸ *n.* the synthesis of substances by living organisms. ■ *hist.* the hypothesis that living matter arises only from other living matter. —**bi·o·ge·net·ic** /-jə'netik/ *adj.*

bi·o·gen·ic /ˌbīō'jenik/ ▶*adj.* produced or brought about by living organisms: *biogenic sediments.*

bi·og·ra·phy /bī'ägrəfē/ ▶*n.* (*pl.* **-phies**) an account of someone's life written by someone else. ■ writing of such a type as a branch of literature. ■ a human life in its course: *although their individual biographies are different, both are motivated by a similar ambition.* —**bi·og·ra·pher** /-fər/ *n.* —**bi·o·graph·ic** /ˌbīə'grafik/ *adj.* —**bi·o·graph·i·cal** /ˌbīə'grafikəl/ *adj.*

bi·o·haz·ard /'bīō,hazərd/ ▶*n.* a risk to human health or the environment arising from biological work, esp. with microorganisms.

bi·o·log·i·cal /ˌbīə'läjikəl/ (abbr.: **biol.**) ▶*adj.* of or relating to biology or living organisms. ■ genetically related; related by blood: *the alleged rights of the biological father.* ■ (of a detergent or other cleaning product) containing enzymes to assist the process of cleaning.
▶*n.* a therapeutic substance, such as a vaccine or drug, derived from biological sources: [usu. *pl.*] *an international biotechnology company with interests in biologicals, agriculture, and pharmaceutical products.* —**bi·o·log·i·cal·ly** /-ik(ə)lē/ *adv.*

bi·ol·o·gy /bī'äləjē/ (abbr.: **biol.**) ▶*n.* the study of living organisms, divided into many specialized fields that cover their morphology, physiology, anatomy, behavior, origin, and distribution. ■ the plants and animals of a particular area: *the biology of Chesapeake Bay.* ■ the physiology, behavior, and other qualities of a particular organism or class of organisms: *human biology.* —**bi·ol·o·gist** /-jist/ *n.*

bi·o·lu·mi·nes·cence /ˌbīō,lōōmə'nesəns/ ▶*n.* the biochemical emission of light by living organisms such as fireflies and deep-sea fishes. ■ the light emitted in such a way. —**bi·o·lu·mi·nes·cent** /-'nesənt/ *adj.*

bi·o·mag·ni·fi·ca·tion /ˌbīō,magnifi'kāSHən/ ▶*n.* the concentration of toxins in an organism as a result of its ingesting other plants or animals in which the toxins are more widely disbursed. —**bi·o·mag·ni·fy** *v.*

bi·o·mark·er /'bīō,märkər/ ▶*n.* a measurable substance in an organism whose presence is indicative of some phenomenon such as disease, infection, or environmental exposure: *a biomarker that may predict aggressive disease recurrence in liver transplant recipients.*

bi·o·mass /'bīō,mas/ ▶*n.* the total mass of organisms in a given area or volume. ■ organic matter used as a fuel, esp. in a power station for the generation of electricity.

bi·ome /'bī,ōm/ ▶*n. Ecol.* a large naturally occurring community of flora and fauna occupying a major habitat, e.g., forest or tundra.

bi·o·me·chan·ics /ˌbīōmə'kaniks/ ▶*pl. n.* [treated as *sing.*] the study of the mechanical laws relating to the movement or structure of living organisms.

bi·o·met·ric read·er /ˌbīō'metrik/ ▶*n.* an electronic device that determines identity by detecting and matching physical characteristics.

bi·on·ics /bī'äniks/ ▶*pl. n.* [treated as *sing.*] the study of mechanical systems that function like living organisms or parts of living organisms.

bi·o·phys·ics /ˌbīō'fiziks/ ▶*pl. n.* [treated as *sing.*] the science of the application of the laws of physics to biological phenomena. —**bi·o·phys·i·cal** /-'fizikəl/ *adj.* —**bi·o·phys·i·cist** /-'fizəsist/ *n.*

bi·op·sy /'bī,äpsē/ ▶*n.* (*pl.* **-sies**) an examination of tissue removed from a living body to discover the presence, cause, or extent of a disease.

bi·o·rhythm /'bīō,riTHəm/ ▶*n.* a recurring cycle in the physiology or functioning of an organism, such as the daily cycle of sleeping and waking. ■ a cyclic pattern of physical, emotional, or mental activity said to occur in the life of a person. —**bi·o·rhyth·mic** /ˌbīō'riTHmik/ *adj.*

bi·o·sphere /'bīə,sfi(ə)r/ ▶*n.* the regions of the surface, atmosphere, and hydrosphere of the earth (or analogous parts of other planets) occupied by living organisms. —**bi·o·spher·ic** /ˌbīə'sfi(ə)rik; -'sfer-/ *adj.*

bi·o·sur·ger·y /ˌbīō'sərjərē/ ▶*n.* the medical use of maggots to clean infected wounds, especially in cases where a patient is resistant to conventional antibiotic treatment.

bi·o·syn·the·sis /ˌbīō'sinTHəsis/ ▶*n.* the production of complex molecules within living organisms or cells. —**bi·o·syn·thet·ic** *adj.*

bi·o·ta /bī'ōtə/ ▶*n. Ecol.* the animal and plant life of a particular region, habitat, or geological period: *the biota of the river.*

bi·o·tech /ˌbīō'tek; 'bīō,tek/ ▶*n. inf.* short for BIOTECHNOLOGY.
▶*adj. inf.* genetically modified: *biotech corn.*

bi·o·tech·nol·o·gy /ˌbīōtek'näləjē/ ▶*n.* the exploitation of biological processes for industrial and other purposes, esp. the genetic manipulation of microorganisms for the production of antibiotics, hormones, etc.

bi·ot·ic /bī'ätik/ ▶*adj.* of, relating to, or resulting from living things, esp. in their ecological relations: *preserving biotic diversity.*

bi·o·tin /'bīətin/ ▶*n. Biochem.* a vitamin of the B complex, found in egg yolk, liver, and yeast. It is involved in the synthesis of fatty acids and glucose.

bi·o·weap·on /'bīō,wepən/ ▶*n.* a biological weapon.

bi·par·ti·san /bī'pärtəzən/ ▶*adj.* of or involving the agreement or cooperation of two political parties that usually oppose each other's policies: *educational reform received considerable bipartisan approval.* —**bi·par·ti·san·ship** /-,SHip/ *n.*

bi·par·tite /bī'pär,tīt/ ▶*adj.* involving or made by two separate parties: *the bipartite system of elementary and secondary schools.*

bi·ped·al /bī'pedl/ ▶*adj. Zool.* (of an animal) using only two legs for walking. —**bi·ped** /'bīped/ *n. & adj.* —**bi·ped·al·ism** /bī'pedl,izəm/ *n.* —**bi·pe·dal·i·ty** /ˌbīpi'dalitē/ *n.*

bi·plane /'bī,plān/ ▶*n.* an early type of aircraft with two pairs of wings, one above the other.

biplane

bi·po·lar /bī'pōlər/ ▶*adj.* having or relating to two poles or extremities: *a sharply bipolar division of affluent and underclasses.* ■ (of a plant or animal species) of or occurring in both polar regions. ■ (of a nerve cell) having two axons, one on either side of the cell body. —**bi·po·lar·i·ty** /ˌbīpō'laritē; -pə-/ *n.*

bi·po·lar dis·or·der ▶*n.* a mental disorder marked by alternating periods of elation and depression. Also called MANIC DEPRESSION. Compare with UNIPOLAR.

birch /bərCH/ ▶*n.* (also **birch tree**) a slender, fast-growing tree (genus *Betula*, family Betulaceae) that has thin bark (often peeling) and bears catkins. Birches grow chiefly in north temperate regions. ■ (also **birch·wood**) the hard fine-grained pale wood of any of these trees.

bird /bərd/ ▶*n.* **1** a warm-blooded egg-laying vertebrate (class Aves) distinguished by the possession of feathers, wings, and a beak and (typically) by being able to fly. ■ an animal of this type that is hunted for sport or used for food: *carve the bird at the dinner table.* ■ a clay pigeon. ■ *inf.* an aircraft, spacecraft, satellite, or guided missile: *the crews worked frantically to ready their birds for flight.* **2** *inf.* a person of a specified kind or character: *I'm a pretty tough old bird.*
▶ □ **the birds and the bees** basic facts about sex and reproduction, as told to a child. □ **flip** (or **give**) **someone the bird** stick one's middle finger up at someone as a sign of contempt or anger. □ (**strictly**) **for the birds** *inf.* not worth consideration; unimportant: *this piece of legislation is for the birds.* ■ **have a bird** *inf.* be very shocked or agitated: *the press corps would have a bird if the president-to-be appointed his wife to a real job.*

bird·brain /'bərd,brān/ ▶*n. inf.* an annoyingly stupid and shallow person. —**bird·brained** *adj.*

bird·cage /'bərd,kāj/ ▶*n.* a cage for pet birds, typically made of wire or cane.

bird call ▶*n.* a note uttered by a bird for the purpose of contact, alarm, or marking its territory. ■ an instrument imitating such a sound, used esp. by hunters.

bird flu ▶*n.* an often fatal flu virus of birds, esp. poultry, that is transmissible from them to humans, in whom it may also prove fatal.

bird·ie /'bərdē/ ▶*n.* (*pl.* **bird·ies**) **1** *inf.* a little bird. **2** *Golf* a score of one stroke under par at a hole.

bird of par·a·dise ▶*n.* **1** (*pl.* **birds of paradise**) a tropical Australasian bird (family Paradisaeidae), the male of which is noted for the beauty and brilliance of its plumage. **2** (also **bird of paradise flower**) a southern African plant (genus *Strelitzia*, family Strelitziaceae), bearing a showy irregular flower with a long projecting tongue.

bird of prey ▶*n.* a predatory bird, distinguished by a hooked bill and sharp talons and belonging to the order Falconiformes (the diurnal birds of prey) or Strigiformes (the owls), a raptor.

bird's-eye view ▶*n.* a general view from above: *we had a bird's-eye view from the attic window.* ■ a general view as if from above: *the map gives a bird's-eye view of the route.* ■ a broad, general, or superficial consideration (of something).

bird-watch·er (also **bird·watch·er**) ▶*n.* a person who observes birds in their natural surroundings as a hobby. —**bird-watch·ing** *n.*

bi·reme /ˈbīˌrēm/ ▶n. an ancient warship with two files of oarsmen on each side.

bi·ret·ta /bəˈretə/ (also **be·ret·ta**) ▶n. a square cap with three flat projections on top, worn by Roman Catholic clergymen.

Bir·ken·stock /ˈbərkənˌstäk/ ▶n. trademark a type of shoe or sandal with a contoured cork-filled sole and a thick leather upper. ■ denoting people concerned with political correctness or conservationist issues: *leave environmentalism to the Birkenstock crowd.*

birth /bərth/ ▶n. the emergence of a baby or other young from the body of its mother; the start of life as a physically separate being: *he was blind from birth | despite a difficult birth he's fit and healthy.* ■ a baby born: *the overall rate of incidence of Down syndrome is one in every 800 live births.* ■ the beginning or coming into existence of something: *the birth of democracy.* ■ origin, descent, or ancestry: *the mother is American by birth.* ■ high or noble descent: *she was proud of her beauty and her birth.*
▶v. [tr.] inf. give birth to (a baby or other young): *she had carried him and birthed him | [intr.] in spring the cows birthed.*
▶ □ **give birth** bear a child or young: *she's due to give birth in March | she gave birth to a son.*

birth cer·tif·i·cate ▶n. an official document issued to record a person's birth, including such identifying data as name, gender, date of birth, place of birth, and parentage.

birth con·trol ▶n. the practice of preventing unwanted pregnancies, typically by use of contraception.

birth con·trol pill ▶n. a contraceptive pill.

birth·date /ˈbərthˌdāt/ ▶n. **1** date of birth. **2** the anniversary of a date of birth, especially for someone dead: *the communists' symbolic vote to clear the name of Stalin came six days after Stalin's birthdate.*

birth·day /ˈbərthˌdā/ ▶n. the annual anniversary of the day on which a person was born, typically treated as an occasion for celebration and present-giving: *I'm getting a dollhouse for my birthday.* ■ the day of one's birth: *she shares a birthday with Paul McCartney.* ■ the anniversary of something starting or being founded: *the staff celebrated the twenty-fifth birthday of the paper.*
▶ □ **in one's birthday suit** humorous naked.

birth de·fect ▶n. a physical or biochemical abnormality that is present at birth and that may be inherited or the result of environmental influence.

birth·mark /ˈbərthˌmärk/ ▶n. an unusual and typically permanent brown or red mark on someone's body from birth.

birth·place /ˈbərthˌplās/ ▶n. the place where a person was born. ■ the place where something started or originated: *Florence was the birthplace of the Renaissance.*

birth rate ▶n. the number of live births per thousand of population per year.

birth·right /ˈbərthˌrīt/ ▶n. a particular right of possession or privilege one has from birth, esp. as an eldest child. ■ the possession or privilege itself: *your daddy's gold watch is your birthright.* ■ a natural or moral right, possessed by everyone: *she saw a liberal education as the birthright of every child.*

birth·stone /ˈbərthˌstōn/ ▶n. a gemstone popularly associated with the month or astrological sign of one's birth.

bis·cuit /ˈbiskit/ ▶n. **1** a small, typically round cake of bread leavened with baking powder, baking soda, or sometimes yeast. ■ Brit. a cookie or cracker. **2** another term for BISQUE³: [as adj.] biscuit ware. **3** a light brown color. **4** a small flat piece of wood used to join two mortised planks.
▶adj. light brown in color. ▷Middle English: from Old French *bescuit*, based on Latin *bis* 'twice' + *coctus*, past participle of *coquere* 'to cook' (so named because originally biscuits were cooked in a twofold process: first baked and then dried out in a slow oven so that they would keep). —**bis·cuit·y** adj.

bi·sect /bīˈsekt; ˈbīˌsekt/ ▶v. [tr.] divide into two parts: *a landscape of farmland bisected by long straight roads.* ■ Geom. divide (a line, angle, shape, etc.) into two equal parts. —**bi·sec·tion** n. —**bi·sec·tor** n.

bi·sex·u·al /bīˈsekSHōōəl/ ▶adj. sexually attracted to both men and women. ■ Biol. having characteristics of both sexes.
▶n. a person who is sexually attracted to both men and women. —**bi·sex·u·al·i·ty** /ˌbīseksHōōˈalitē/ n.

bish·op /ˈbisHəp/ ▶n. **1** a senior member of the Christian clergy, typically in charge of a diocese and empowered to confer holy orders. **2** a chess piece, typically with its top shaped like a miter, that can move in any direction along a diagonal on which it stands.

bish·op·ric /ˈbisHəprik/ ▶n. the office or rank of a bishop. ■ a district under a bishop's control; a diocese.

bis·muth /ˈbizməTH/ ▶n. the chemical element of atomic number 83, a brittle reddish-gray metal. (Symbol: **Bi**) ■ a compound of this element used medicinally.

bi·son /ˈbīsən; -zən/ ▶n. (pl. same) a humpbacked shaggy-haired wild ox (genus *Bison*) native to North America (*B. bison*) and Europe (*B. bonasus*).

bisque¹ /bisk/ ▶n. a rich, creamy soup typically made with shellfish, esp. lobster.

bisque² ▶n. an extra turn, point, or stroke allowed to a weaker player in croquet or court tennis.

bisque³ ▶n. **1** fired unglazed pottery: *using bisque for doll heads | [as adj.] bisque figurines.* **2** a light brown color: *shades of bisque and taupe.*
▶adj. light brown in color.

bis·ter /ˈbistər/ (also **bis·tre**) ▶n. a brownish-yellowish pigment made from the soot of burned wood. ■ the color of this pigment.

bis·tro /ˈbistrō; ˈbē-/ ▶n. (pl. **-tros**) a small restaurant.

bi·sul·fate /bīˈsəlˌfāt/ (chiefly Brit. also **bi·sul·phate**) ▶n. Chem. a salt of the anion HSO_4^-.

bit¹ /bit/ ▶n. **1** a small piece, part, or quantity of something: *give the duck a bit of bread.* ■ (**a bit**) a fair amount: *there's a bit to talk about there.* ■ (**a bit**) a short time or distance: *I fell asleep for a bit.* ■ inf. a set of actions or ideas associated with a specific group or activity: *she's gone off to do her theatrical bit.* **2** inf., dated a unit of 12½ cents (used in even multiples): *the sideshow admission was two bits.*
▶ □ **a bit** somewhat; to some extent: *he came back looking a bit annoyed.* □ **bit by bit** gradually: *the school was built bit by bit over the years.* □ **bits and pieces** an assortment of small items: *weird bits and pieces of paraphernalia.* □ **do one's bit** inf. make a useful contribution to an effort or cause: *she was keen to do her bit to help others.* □ **not a bit** not at all: *I'm not a bit tired.* □ **to bits** **1** into pieces: *he smashed it to bits with a hammer.* **2** inf. very much: *we've got two great kids whom I love to bits.*

bit² ▶ past of BITE.

bit³ ▶n. **1** a mouthpiece, typically made of metal, that is attached to a bridle and used to control a horse. **2** a tool or piece for boring or drilling, typically of metal: *a drill bit.* ■ the cutting or gripping part of a plane, pliers, or other tool.
▶v. [tr.] put a bit into the mouth of (a horse). ■ fig. restrain: *my own hysteria was bitted by upbringing and respect.* —**bit·ted** adj. [in comb.] *a double-bitted ax.*

drill bits

bit⁴ ▶n. Comput. a unit of information expressed as either a 0 or 1 in binary notation.

bitch /bicH/ ▶n. **1** a female dog, wolf, fox, or otter. **2** inf., derog. a woman whom one dislikes or considers to be malicious or unpleasant. ■ inf. a thing or situation that is unpleasant or difficult to deal with: *the stove is a bitch to fix.*
▶v. [intr.] inf. express displeasure; grumble: *they bitch about everything | [as n.] (bitching) we're tired of your bitching.*

bitch·y /ˈbicHē/ inf. ▶adj. (**bitchier**, **bitchiest**) (of a person's comments or behavior) malicious or unpleasant: *bitchy remarks.* —**bitch·i·ness** n.

bite /bīt/ ▶v. (past tense **bit** /bit/; past part. **bit·ten** /ˈbitn/) [intr.] **1** (of a person or animal) use the teeth to cut into something in order to eat it: *Rosa bit into a cupcake.* ■ [tr.] (of an animal or a person) use the teeth in order to inflict injury on: *she had bitten, scratched, and kicked her assailant.* ■ [tr.] (of a snake, insect, or arachnid) wound with a sting, pincers, or fangs: *getting bitten by mosquitoes.* ■ (of a fish) take the bait or lure on the end of a fishing line into the mouth. ■ fig. (of a person) be persuaded to accept a deal or offer: *a hundred or so retailers should bite.* **2** (of a tool, tire, boot, etc.) grip a surface: *once on the wet grass, my boots failed to bite.* ■ (of an object) press into a part of the body, causing pain: *the handcuffs bit into his wrists.* ■ fig. cause emotional pain: *Cheryl's betrayal had bitten deep.*
▶n. **1** an act of biting into something in order to eat it: *Stephen ate a hot dog in three big bites.* ■ a piece cut off by biting: *Robyn took a large bite out*

B

B

of her sandwich. ■ *inf.* a quick snack: *I plan to stop off in the village and have a bite to eat.* ■ a wound inflicted by an animal's or a person's teeth: *Perry's dog had given her a nasty bite.* ■ a wound inflicted by a snake, insect, or arachnid: *suspected it to be a tick bite.* ■ an act of bait being taken by a fish: *by four o'clock he still hadn't had a single bite.* ■ *Dentistry* the bringing together of the teeth in occlusion. **2** a sharp or pungent flavor: *a fresh, lemony bite.* ■ incisiveness or cogency of style: *his colorful characterizations brought added bite to the story.* ■ a feeling of cold in the air or wind: *by early October there's a bite in the air.* —**bit·er** *n.*

▸ □ **be bitten by the —— bug** develop a passionate interest in a specified activity: *Joe was bitten by the showbiz bug at the age of four.* □ **bite the bullet** decide to do something difficult or unpleasant that one has been putting off or hesitating over. □ **bite the dust** *inf.* be killed: *and the bad guys bite the dust with lead in their bellies.* ■ *fig.* fail; come to an end: *she hoped the new program would not bite the dust for lack of funding.* □ **bite one's lip** dig one's front teeth into one's lip in embarrassment, grief, or annoyance, or to prevent oneself from saying something or to control oneself when experiencing physical pain. ■ *fig.* forcing oneself to remain silent even though annoyed, provoked, or in possession of information: *he could have mocked Carol's obnoxious behavior, but he bit his lip.* □ **bite off more than one can chew** take on a commitment one cannot fulfill. □ **bite one's tongue** make a desperate effort to avoid saying something: *I had bitten my tongue and accept his explanation.* □ **put the bite on** *inf.* borrow or extort money from. □ **take a bite out of** *inf.* reduce by a significant amount: *insurance costs that can take a bite out of your retirement funds.*

bit·ing /ˈbītiNG/ ▸*adj.* (of insects and certain other animals) able to wound the skin with a sting or fangs: *ridding the premises of biting red ants.* ■ (of wind or cold) so cold as to be painful: *he leaned forward to protect himself against the biting wind.* ■ (of wit or criticism) harsh or cruel: *his biting satire on corruption and power.* —**bit·ing·ly** *adv.*

bit part ▸*n.* a small acting role in a play or a movie.

bit·ter /ˈbitər/ ▸*adj.* **1** having a sharp, pungent taste or smell; not sweet: *the raw berries have an intensely bitter flavor.* ■ (of chocolate) dark and unsweetened. **2** (of people or their feelings or behavior) angry, hurt, or resentful because of one's bad experiences or a sense of unjust treatment: *I don't feel jealous or bitter.* **3** harsh or unpleasant, in particular: ■ (often used for emphasis) painful or unpleasant to accept or contemplate: *today's decision has come as a bitter blow.* ■ (of a conflict, argument, or opponent) full of anger and acrimony: *a bitter, five-year legal battle.* ■ (of wind, cold, or weather) intensely cold: *a bitter wind blowing from the east.*
▸*n.* **1** [*mass noun*] *Brit.* beer that is strongly flavored with hops and has a bitter taste. **2** (**bitters**) [treated as *sing*] liquor that is flavored with the sharp pungent taste of plant extracts and is used in cocktails or to promote appetite or digestion. —**bit·ter·ly** *adv.* —**bit·ter·ness** *n.*
▸ □ **to the bitter end** used to say that one will continue doing something until it is finished, no matter what: *the workers would fight to the bitter end for safer conditions.*

bit·tern /ˈbitərn/ ▸*n.* a large marsh bird (genera *Botaurus* and *Ixobrychus*) of the heron family, with brown streaked plumage. The males of certain species are noted for a deep booming call during the breeding season.

bit·ter·sweet /ˈbitərˌswēt/ ▸*adj.* (of food, drink, or flavor) sweet with a bitter aftertaste. ■ arousing pleasure tinged with sadness or pain: *bittersweet memories.*
▸*n.* **1** another term for woody nightshade (see NIGHTSHADE). **2** a vinelike climbing plant (genus *Celastrus*, family Celastraceae) that bears clusters of bright orange pods.

bit·ty /ˈbitē/ *inf.* ▸*adj.* (**-tier, -tiest**) tiny: *a little bitty house.*

bi·tu·men /biˈt(y)o͞omən; bī-/ ▸*n.* a black viscous mixture of hydrocarbons obtained naturally or as a residue from petroleum distillation. It is used for road surfacing and roofing. —**bi·tu·mi·nous** *adj.*

bi·tu·mi·nous coal ▸*n.* black coal having a relatively high volatile content.

bi·valve /ˈbīˌvalv/ ▸*n.* an aquatic mollusk (class Bivalvia) that has a compressed body enclosed within two hinged shells, including oysters, clams, mussels, and scallops.

biv·ou·ac /ˈbivo͞oˌak; ˈbivwak/ ▸*n.* a temporary camp without tents or cover, used esp. by soldiers or mountaineers.
▸*v.* [*intr.*] (**-acked, -ack·ing**) stay in such a camp: *he'd bivouacked on the north side of the town* | *the battalion was now bivouacked in a field.* ▹early 18th cent. (denoting a night watch by the whole army): from French, probably from Swiss German *Biwacht* 'additional guard at night,' apparently denoting a citizens' patrol supporting the ordinary town watch.

bi·week·ly /bīˈwēklē/ ▸*adj.* & *adv.* appearing or taking place every two weeks or twice a week: [as *adj.*] *a biweekly bulletin.*
▸*n.* (*pl.* **-lies**) a periodical that appears every two weeks or twice a week.

bi·year·ly /bīˈyi(ə)rlē/ ▸*adj.* & *adv.* appearing or taking place every two years or twice a year.

biz /biz/ ▸*n.* *inf.* a business, typically one connected with entertainment: *in the music biz.*

bi·zarre /biˈzär/ ▸*adj.* very strange or unusual, esp. so as to cause interest or amusement: *her bizarre dresses and outrageous hairdos.* —**bi·zarre·ly** *adv.* —**bi·zarre·ness** *n.*

Bk ▸*symb.* the chemical element berkelium.

bk ▸*abbr.* ■ bank. ■ book. ■ brick.

blab /blab/ *inf.* ▸*v.* (**blabbed, blab·bing**) [*intr.*] reveal secrets by indiscreet talk: *she blabbed to the press.*

blab·ber /ˈblabər/ *inf.* ▸*v.* [*intr.*] talk foolishly, mindlessly, or excessively: *she blabbered on and on.*
▸*n.* a person who talks foolishly or indiscreetly. ■ foolish or mindless talk: *annoyed by their endless blabber.*

black /blak/ ▸*adj.* **1** of the very darkest color; the opposite of white; colored like coal, due to the absence of or complete absorption of light: *black smoke.* ■ (of the sky or night) completely dark due to nonvisibility of the sun, moon, or stars, normally because of dense cloud cover: *the sky was moonless and black.* ■ deeply stained with dirt: *his clothes were absolutely black.* ■ (of a plant or animal) dark in color as distinguished from a lighter variety: *Japanese black pine.* ■ (of coffee or tea) served without milk or cream. ■ or denoting the suits spades and clubs in a deck of cards. ■ (of a ski run) of the highest level of difficulty, as indicated by black markers positioned along it. **2** (also **Black**) of any human group having dark-colored skin, esp. of African or Australian Aboriginal ancestry: *black adolescents of Jamaican descent.* ■ of or relating to black people: *black culture.* **3** *fig.* (of a period of time or situation) characterized by tragic or disastrous events; causing despair or pessimism: *five thousand men were killed on the blackest day of the war.* ■ (of a person's state of mind) full of gloom or misery; very depressed: *Jean had disappeared and Mary was in a black mood.* ■ (of humor) presenting tragic or harrowing situations in comic terms: *"Good place to bury the bodies," she joked with black humor.* ■ full of anger or hatred: *Roger shot her a black look.*
▸*n.* **1** black color or pigment: *a tray decorated in black and green.* ■ black clothes or material, often worn as a sign of mourning: *dressed in widow's black.* ■ darkness, esp. of night or an overcast sky: *the only thing visible in the black was the light of the lantern.* **2** (also **Black**) a member of a dark-skinned people, esp. one of African or Australian Aboriginal ancestry: *a coalition of blacks and whites against violence.* **3** (in a game or sport) a black piece or ball, or the set of black pieces that constitute one side, in particular the black pieces in chess. ■ (often **Black**) the player of the black pieces in chess or checkers.
▸*v.* [*tr.*] make black, esp. by the application of black polish: *blacking the prize bull's hooves.*
▸*phrasal v.* □ **black out** (of a person) undergo a sudden and temporary loss of consciousness: *they knocked me around and I blacked out.* □ **black something out 1** (usu. **be blacked out**) extinguish all lights or completely cover windows, esp. for protection against an air attack or in order to provide darkness in which to show a movie: *the bombers began to come nightly and the city was blacked out.* ■ subject a place to an electricity failure: *Chicago was blacked out yesterday after a freak flood.* **2** obscure something completely so that it cannot be read or seen: *the license plate had been blacked out with masking tape.* ■ (of a television company) suppress the broadcast of a program: *they blacked out the women's finals on local television.* —**black·ish** *adj.* —**black·ly** *adv.* —**black·ness** *n.*
▸ □ **in the black** (of a person or organization) not owing any money; solvent.

black and blue ▸*adj.* discolored by bruising: *a black-and-blue mark on his arm.* ■ (of a person) covered in bruises: *they were both black and blue the day after the accident.*

black and white ▸*adj.* **1** (of a photograph, movie, television program, or illustration) in black, white, and shades of gray: *old black-and-white movies.* ■ (of a television) displaying images only in black, white, and shades of gray. **2** (of a situation or debate) involving clearly defined opposing principles or issues: *there is nothing black and white about these matters.*
▸*n.* *inf.* a police car.
▸ □ **in black and white 1** in writing or in print, and regarded as more reliable, credible, or formal than by word of mouth: *getting her contract*

down in black and white. **2** in terms of clearly defined opposing principles or issues: *children think in black and white, good and bad.*

black art ▶n. (usu. **the black art**) another term for BLACK MAGIC. ■ *often humorous* a technique or practice considered mysterious and sinister: *the black art of political news management.*

black·ball /'blak,bôl/ ▶v. [tr.] reject (someone, usually a candidate applying to become a member of a private club), typically by means of a secret ballot: *her husband was blackballed when he tried to join the country club.*

black belt ▶n. a black belt worn by an expert in judo, karate, and other martial arts. ■ a person qualified to wear this.

black·ber·ry /'blak,berē/ ▶n. (pl. **-ries**) **1** an edible soft fruit, consisting of a cluster of soft purple-black drupelets. **2** the prickly climbing shrub (*Rubus fruticosus*) of the rose family that bears this fruit and that grows extensively in the wild.

Black·Ber·ry /'blak,berē/ ▶trademark a hand-held wireless electronic device that provides Internet access along with e-mail, telephone, and text messaging services.

black·bird /'blak,bərd/ ▶n. **1** a European thrush (genus *Turdus*) with mainly black plumage. **2** an American bird (family Icteridae) with a strong pointed bill. The male has black plumage that is iridescent or has patches of red or yellow.

black·board /'blak,bôrd/ ▶n. a large board with a smooth, typically dark, surface attached to a wall or supported on an easel and used for writing on with chalk, esp. by teachers in schools.

black box ▶n. a flight recorder in an aircraft. ■ any complex piece of equipment, typically a unit in an electronic system, with contents that are mysterious to the user.

black cur·rant ▶n. **1** a small round edible black berry that grows in loose hanging clusters. **2** the shrub (genus *Ribes*) of the gooseberry family that produces this fruit.

Black Death ▶the great epidemic of bubonic plague that killed a large part of the population of Europe in the mid 14th century. It originated in central Asia and China and spread rapidly through Europe, carried by the fleas of black rats, reaching England in 1348.

black·en /'blakən/ ▶v. become or make black or dark, esp. as a result of burning, decay, or bruising: [intr.] *he set fire to the paper, watching the end blacken as it burned* | [as adj.] (**blackened**) *her smile revealed blackened teeth.* ■ [tr.] dye or color (the face or hair) black for camouflage or cosmetic effect: *in full combat gear with blackened faces.* ■ [intr.] (of the sky) become dark as night or a storm approaches. ■ [tr.] *fig.* damage or destroy (someone's good reputation); defame: *she won't thank you for blackening her husband's name.*

black Eng·lish ▶n. any of various nonstandard forms of English spoken by black people, esp. as an urban dialect in the U.S.

black eye ▶n. a bruised and discolored area around the eye resulting from a blow. ■ *fig.* a mark or source of dishonor or shame: *legislators have caused the state to suffer yet another black eye.*

black-eyed Su·san ▶n. any of a number of flowers that have yellowish petals and a dark center, in particular *Rudbeckia hirta*, a North American flower of the daisy family with bristly leaves and stems.

black fly ▶n. (pl. **-flies**) a small black, often swarming fly (*Simulium* and other genera, family Simuliidae), the female of which sucks blood and can transmit a number of serious human and animal diseases.

Black·foot /'blak,fŏŏt/ ▶n. (pl. same or **-feet**) **1** a member of a confederacy of North American Indian peoples of the northwestern plains. **2** the Algonquian language of this people.
▶adj. of or relating to the Blackfeet or their language.

black·guard /'blagərd; 'blak,gärd/ ▶n. *dated* a person, particularly a man, who behaves in a dishonorable or contemptible way.

black·head /'blak,hed/ ▶n. a plug of sebum in a hair follicle, darkened by oxidation.

black hole ▶n. *Astron.* a region of space having a gravitational field so intense that no matter or radiation can escape. ■ *inf.* a figurative place of emptiness or aloneness: *they think he's sitting in a black hole with no interaction with his people.* ■ *inf., chiefly humorous* a place where money, lost items, etc., are supposed to go, never to be seen again: *the moribund economy has been a black hole for federal funds.* ■ *inf.* (of a system, practice, or institution) a state of inadequacy or excessive bureaucracy in which hopes, progress, etc., become futile: *juveniles lost for good in the black hole of the criminal justice system.*

black ice ▶n. a transparent coating of ice, found esp. on a paved surface.

black·jack /'blak,jak/ ▶n. a gambling card game in which players try to acquire cards with a face value as close as possible to 21 without going over. Also called TWENTY-ONE.

black light ▶n. ultraviolet or infrared radiation, invisible to the eye.

black·list /'blak,list/ ▶n. a list of people or products viewed with suspicion or disapproval.
▶v. [tr.] (often **be blacklisted**) put (a person or product) on such a list: *workers were blacklisted after being quoted in the newspaper.*

black lung ▶n. pneumoconiosis caused by inhalation of coal dust.

black mag·ic ▶n. magic involving the supposed invocation of evil spirits for evil purposes.

black·mail /'blak,māl/ ▶n. the action, treated as a criminal offense, of demanding money from a person in return for not revealing compromising or injurious information about that person: *they were acquitted of charges of blackmail.* ■ money demanded in this way: *we do not pay blackmail.* ■ the use of threats or the manipulation of someone's feelings to force them to do something.
▶v. [tr.] demand money from (a person) in return for not revealing compromising or injurious information about that person: *trying to blackmail him for $400,000.* ■ force (someone) to do something by using threats or manipulating their feelings: *he had blackmailed her into sailing with him.* —**black·mail·er** n.

black mark ▶n. *inf.* used to indicate that someone is remembered and regarded with disfavor: *an arrest will be a black mark on your record.*

black mar·ket ▶n. an illegal traffic or trade in officially controlled or scarce commodities: *they planned to sell the meat on the black market.* —**black mar·ke·teer** (also **black-mar·ke·teer**) n. —**black mar·ket·er** n.

Black Mus·lim ▶n. a member of the NATION OF ISLAM.

black na·tion·al·ism ▶n. the advocacy of separate national status for black people, esp. in the U.S. —**black na·tion·al·ist** n.

black·out /'blak,out/ ▶n. **1** a period when all lights must be turned out or covered to prevent them being seen by the enemy during an air raid: *people found it difficult to travel in the blackout* | [as adj.] *she peered out through the blackout curtains.* ■ a failure of electrical power supply: *due to a power blackout, their hotel was in total darkness.* **2** a suppression of information, esp. one imposed on the media by government: *there is a total information blackout on minority interests.* ■ a period during which a particular activity is prohibited: *there are no blackout days during the travel period.* **3** a temporary loss of consciousness: *she was suffering from blackouts.*

Black Pan·ther ▶n. a member of a militant political organization set up in the U.S. in 1966 to fight for black rights.

black pan·ther ▶n. a leopard that has black fur rather than the typical spotted coat.

black pep·per ▶n. the dried black berries of the pepper (see PEPPER sense 2), which are harvested while still green and unripe. Black pepper is widely used as a spice and a condiment.

black rasp·ber·ry ▶n. **1** an edible soft fruit related to the blackberry, consisting of a cluster of black drupelets. **2** the prickly arching shrub (*Rubus occidentalis*) of the rose family that bears this fruit.

black sheep ▶n. *inf.* a member of a family or group who is regarded as a disgrace to them: *the black sheep of the family.*

black·shirt /'blak,SHərt/ ▶n. a member of a fascist organization, in particular: ■ (**Blackshirt**) (in Italy) a member of a paramilitary group founded by Mussolini. ■ (**Blackshirt**) (in Nazi Germany) a member of the SS.

black·smith /'blak,smiTH/ ▶n. a person who makes and repairs things in iron by hand. ■ a farrier.

black·thorn /'blak,THôrn/ ▶n. a thorny Eurasian shrub (*Prunus spinosa*) of the rose family that bears white flowers and astringent blue-black fruits. Also called SLOE.

black tie ▶n. a black bow tie worn with a dinner jacket. ■ formal evening dress: *the audience wears black tie.*
▶adj. (**black-tie**) (of an event) requiring formal evening dress: *evening meals were black-tie affairs.*

black·top /'blak,täp/ ▶n. asphalt used for surfacing roads. ■ a road or area surfaced with such material: *playing hopscotch on the blacktop behind the school.*
▶v. [tr.] surface (a road or area) with such material: *41 miles had been blacktopped to date.*

black wid·ow ▶n. a venomous American spider (*Latrodectus mactans*, family Theridiidae), the female of which has a black body with a red hourglass shape on its underside.

blad·der /'bladər/ ▶n. **1** a membranous sac in humans and other

---

Pronunciation Key ə *ago,* up; ər *over,* fur; a *hat;* ā *ate;* ă *car;* CH *chin;* e *let;* ē *see;* e(ə)r *air;* i *fit;* ī *by;* i(ə)r *ear;* NG *sing;* ō *go;* ô *law, for;* oi *toy;* ŏŏ *good;* ōō *goo;* ou *out;* SH *she;* TH *thin;* TH *then;* (h)w *why;* ZH *vision*

B

animals, in which urine is collected for excretion. **2** anything inflated and hollow: *an air bladder in the arch and collar of the shoe.*

blad·der·wrack /ˈbladərˌrak/ (also **bladder wrack**) ▶*n.* a common brown shoreline seaweed (*Fucus vesiculosus*, class Phaeophyceae) that has tough straplike fronds containing air bladders that give buoyancy.

blade /blād/ ▶*n.* **1** the flat cutting edge of a knife, saw, or other tool or weapon. ■ *poetic/lit.* a sword. **2** the flat, wide section of an implement or device such as an oar or a propeller. ■ a thin, flat metal runner on an ice skate. ■ a shoulder bone in a cut of meat, or the cut of meat itself. ■ the flat part of the tongue behind the tip. **3** a long, narrow leaf of grass or another similar plant: *a blade of grass.* ■ *Bot.* the broad thin part of a leaf apart from the stalk. **4** *inf., dated* a dashing or energetic young man. **—blad·ed** *adj.* [in comb.] *double-bladed paddles.*

blah /blä/ *inf.* ▶used to substitute for actual words in contexts where they are felt to be too tedious or lengthy to give in full: *the typical kid, going out every night, blah, blah, blah.*
▶*n.* **1** (also **blah-blah**) used to refer to something that is boring or without meaningful content: *talking all kinds of blah to him* | [as *adj.*] *his blah feeling.* **2** (**the blahs**) depression: *he battled a case of the blahs.*

blame /blām/ ▶*v.* [*tr.*] assign responsibility for a fault or wrong: *the inquiry blamed the engineer for the accident.*
▶*n.* responsibility for a fault or wrong: *his players had to take the blame.* **—blam·a·ble** (also **blame·a·ble**) *adj.* **—blame·ful** /-fəl/ *adj.*

blame·less /ˈblāmlis/ ▶*adj.* innocent of wrongdoing: *he led a blameless life.* **—blame·less·ly** *adv.* **—blame·less·ness** *n.*

blame·wor·thy /ˈblāmˌwərᴛᴈē/ ▶*adj.* responsible for wrongdoing and deserving of censure or blame. **—blame·wor·thi·ness** *n.*

blanch /blanᴄʜ/ ▶*v.* **1** [*tr.*] make white or pale by extracting color; bleach: *the cold light blanched her face.* ■ [*tr.*] whiten (a plant) by depriving it of light: *blanch endive by covering plants with large flowerpots.* ■ [*intr.*] *fig.* (of a person) grow pale from shock, fear, or a similar emotion: *many people blanch at the suggestion.* **2** [*tr.*] prepare (vegetables) for freezing or further cooking by immersing briefly in boiling water. [as *adj.*] (**blanched**) *blanched almonds.*

blanc·mange /bləˈmänj; -ˈmänzʜ/ ▶*n.* a sweet opaque gelatinous dessert made with cornstarch and milk.

bland /bland/ ▶*adj.* lacking strong features or characteristics and therefore uninteresting: *rebelling against the bland uniformity.* ■ (of food or drink) mild or insipid. ■ (of a person or behavior) showing no strong emotion; dull and unremarkable: *offering bland reassurance.* **—bland·ly** *adv.* **—bland·ness** *n.*

bland·ish·ment /ˈblandisʜmənt/ ▶*n.* a flattering or pleasing statement or action used to persuade someone gently to do something: *the blandishments of the travel brochure.*

blank /blaNGk/ ▶*adj.* **1** (of a surface or background) unrelieved by decorative or other features; bare, empty, or plain: *the blank skyline.* ■ not written or printed on: *a blank sheet of paper.* ■ (of a document) with spaces left for a signature or details: *blank tax-return forms.* ■ (of a recording medium) with nothing recorded on it: *blank cassettes.* **2** showing incomprehension or no reaction: *we were met by blank looks.* ■ having temporarily no knowledge or understanding: *her mind went blank.*
▶*n.* **1** a space left to be filled in a document: *this game required players to fill in the blanks in a story.* ■ a document with blank spaces to be filled. **2** (also **blank cartridge**) a cartridge containing gunpowder but no bullet, used for training or as a signal. **3** an empty space or period of time, esp. in terms of a lack of knowledge or understanding: *my mind was a total blank.* **4** an object that has no mark or design on it, in particular: ■ a roughly cut metal or wooden block intended for further shaping or finishing. ■ a plain metal disk from which a coin is made by stamping a design on it. **5** a dash written instead of a word or letter, esp. instead of an obscenity or profanity. ■ used euphemistically in place of a noun regarded as obscene, profane, or abusive.
▶*v.* [*tr.*] **1** cover up, obscure, or cause to appear blank or empty: *electronic countermeasures blanked out the radar signals.* ■ [*intr.*] become blank or empty: *the picture blanked out.* **2** *inf.* defeat (a sports opponent) without allowing the opposition to score: *Baltimore blanked Toronto in a 7–0 victory.* **—blank·ly** *adv.* **—blank·ness** *n.*
▶ □ **draw a blank** elicit no successful response; fail: *the search drew a blank.*

blank check ▶*n.* a bank check with the amount left for the payee to fill in. ■ *fig.* an unlimited freedom of action: *he effectively granted a blank check to conduct a war without congressional authorization.*

blan·ket /ˈblaNGkit/ ▶*n.* a large piece of woolen or similar material used as a bed covering or other covering for warmth. ■ *fig.* a thick mass or layer of a specified material that covers something completely: *a dense gray blanket of cloud.*
▶*adj.* covering all cases or instances; total and inclusive: *a blanket ban on tobacco advertising.*
▶*v.* (**-ket·ed**, **-ket·ing**) [*tr.*] cover completely with a thick layer of something: *the countryside was blanketed in snow.* ▷Middle English (denoting undyed woolen cloth): via Old Northern French from Old French *blanc* 'white,' ultimately of Germanic origin.

blank·e·ty /ˈblaNGkitē/ (also **blank·e·ty-blank**) ▶*adj.* & *n. inf.* used euphemistically to replace a word considered coarse or vulgar: *it's time to ditch the blankety-blank tax code.*

blank verse ▶*n.* verse without rhyme, esp. that which uses iambic pentameter.

blare /ble(ə)r/ ▶*v.* [*intr.*] sound loudly and harshly: *the ambulance arrived outside, siren blaring.*
▶*n.* a loud harsh sound: *a blare of trumpets.*

blar·ney /ˈblärnē/ ▶*n.* talk that aims to charm, pleasantly flatter, or persuade: *he had the "street charm" of an Irish politician, but this blarney concealed his inner self.* ■ amusing and harmless nonsense: *this story is perhaps just a bit of blarney.*

bla·sé /bläˈzā/ ▶*adj.* unimpressed or indifferent to something because one has experienced or seen it so often before: *she was becoming quite blasé about the dangers.*

blas·pheme /blasˈfēm; ˈblas,fēm/ ▶*v.* [*intr.*] speak irreverently about God or sacred things: *allegations that he had blasphemed against Islam.* **—blas·phem·er** /blasˈfēmər; ˈblasfəmər/ *n.* **—blas·phem·ous** /-əs/ *adj.* **—blas·phem·ous·ly** *adv.*

blas·phe·my /ˈblasfəmē/ ▶*n.* (pl. **-mies**) the act or offense of speaking sacrilegiously about God or sacred things; profane talk: *he was detained on charges of blasphemy* | *screaming incomprehensible blasphemies.*

blast /blast/ ▶*n.* **1** a destructive wave of highly compressed air spreading outward from an explosion: *they were thrown backward by the blast.* ■ an explosion or explosive firing, esp. of a bomb: *a bomb blast.* ■ *fig.* a forceful attack or assault: *he defeated his weakest opponent in such a blast that the fans left unimpressed.* **2** a strong gust of wind or air: *the icy blast hit them.* **3** a single loud note of a horn, whistle, or other noisemaking device: *a blast of the ship's siren.* **4** *inf.* a severe reprimand: *I braced myself for the inevitable blast.* **5** *inf.* an enjoyable experience or lively party: *it could turn out to be a real blast.*
▶*v.* [*tr.*] **1** blow up or break apart (something solid) with explosives: *quantities of solid rock had to be blasted away.* ■ produce (damage or a hole) by means of an explosion: *the force of the collision blasted out a tremendous crater.* ■ [*tr.*] force or throw (something) in a specified direction by impact or explosion: *the car was blasted thirty feet into the sky.* ■ *inf.* criticize fiercely: *the school was blasted by government inspectors.* **2** make or cause to make a loud continuous musical or other noise: [*intr.*] *music blasted out at full volume.* **3** kick, strike, or throw (a ball) hard: *Ripken blasted the ball into the gap in right field.* **4** *poetic/lit.* (of a wind or other natural force) wither, shrivel, or blight (a plant): *crops blasted on the eve of harvest.* ■ strike with divine anger: *damn and blast this awful place!*
▶*phrasal v.* ■ **blast off** (of a rocket or spacecraft) take off from a launching site.
▶ □ **(at) full blast** at maximum power or intensity: *the heat is on full blast.*

blast·ed /ˈblastid/ ▶*adj.* **1** *inf.* used to express annoyance: *make your own blasted coffee!* **2** *inf.* drunk: *the waiter kept bringing us free cocktails, so I got really blasted.*

blast fur·nace ▶*n.* a smelting furnace in the form of a tower into which a blast of hot compressed air can be introduced from below. Such furnaces are used chiefly to make iron from a mixture of iron ore, coke, and limestone.

blast·off /ˈblast,ôf; -,äf/ ▶*n.* the launching of a rocket or spacecraft.

blas·tu·la /ˈblasᴄʜələ/ ▶*n.* (pl. **-las** or **-lae** /-,lē/) *Embryology* an animal embryo at the early stage of development when it is a hollow ball of cells.

bla·tant /ˈblātnt/ ▶*adj.* (of bad behavior) done openly and unashamedly: *blatant lies.* ■ completely lacking in subtlety; very obvious: *forcing herself to resist his blatant charm.* ▷late 16th cent.: perhaps an alteration of Scots *blatand* 'bleating.' It was first used by Spenser as an epithet for a thousand-tongued monster, a symbol of calumny, which he called the *blatant beast.* It was subsequently used to mean 'clamorous, offensive to the ear;' the sense 'obtrusive to the eye, unashamedly conspicuous' arose in the late 19th cent. **—bla·tan·cy** /ˈblātnsē/ *n.* **—bla·tant·ly** *adv.*

blath·er /ˈblaᴛʜər/ ▶*v.* [*intr.*] talk long-windedly without making very much sense: *she began blathering on about spirituality and life after death* | [as *n.*] (**blathering**) *now stop your blathering and get back to work.*
▶*n.* long-winded talk with no real substance.

blaze[1] /blāz/ ▸*n.* **1** a very large or fiercely burning fire: *twenty fireman fought the blaze.* ■ a harsh bright light: *a lightning flash changed the gentle illumination of the office into a sudden white blaze.* ■ a very bright display of light or color: *the gardens in summer are a blaze of color.* ■ *fig.* a conspicuous display or outburst of something: *their relationship broke up in a blaze of publicity.* **2** (**blazes**) *inf.* used in various expressions of anger, bewilderment, or surprise as a euphemism for "hell": *what in blue blazes are you all talking about?*
▸*v.* [*intr.*] **1** burn fiercely or brightly: *the fire blazed merrily.* ■ shine brightly or powerfully: *the sun blazed down* | *fig. Barbara's eyes were blazing with anger.* **2** (of a gun or a person firing a gun) fire repeatedly or indiscriminately: *two terrorists burst into the house with guns blazing.* **3** *inf.* achieve something in an impressive manner: *she blazed to a gold medal in the 200-meter sprint.*
▸ □ **like (blue) blazes** *inf.* very fast or forcefully: *I ran like blazes toward home | they came at us like blue blazes.*

blaze[2] ▸*n.* **1** a white spot or stripe on the face of a mammal or bird. ■ a broad white stripe running the length of a horse's face. **2** a mark made on a tree by cutting the bark so as to mark a route.
▸*v.* (**blaze a trail**) mark out a path or route. ■ *fig.* set an example by being the first to do something; pioneer: *small firms would set the pace, blazing a trail for others to follow.*

blaze[3] ▸*v.* [*tr.*] (of a newspaper) present or proclaim (news) in a prominent, typically sensational, manner.

blaz·er /'blāzər/ ▸*n.* a lightweight jacket, typically solid-colored, often worn as part of a uniform by members of a club, sports team, or school. ■ a plain jacket, typically dark blue, not forming part of a suit but considered appropriate for formal or semiformal wear.

bla·zon /'blāzən/ ▸*v.* [*tr.*] display prominently or vividly: *they saw their company name blazoned all over the media.* ■ report (news), esp. in a sensational manner: *accounts of their ordeal blazoned to the entire nation.*

bleach /blēCH/ ▸*v.* [*tr.*] whiten by exposure to sunlight or by a chemical process: *paper products are bleached with chlorine* | [as *adj.*] (**bleached**) *permed and bleached hair.* ■ clean and sterilize: *a new formula to bleach and brighten clothing.* ■ *fig.* deprive of vitality or substance: *his contributions to the album are bleached of personality.*
▸*n.* a chemical (typically a solution of sodium hypochlorite or hydrogen peroxide) used to whiten or sterilize materials.

bleach·er /'blēCHər/ ▸*n.* (usu. **bleachers**) a cheap bench seat at a sports arena, typically in an outdoor uncovered stand.

bleak /blēk/ ▸*adj.* (of an area of land) lacking vegetation and exposed to the elements: *a bleak and barren moor.* ■ (of a building or room) charmless and inhospitable; dreary. ■ (of the weather) cold and miserable: *a bleak midwinter's day.* ■ (of a situation or future prospect) not hopeful or encouraging; unlikely to have a favorable outcome: *he paints a bleak picture of a company that has lost its way.* ■ (of a person or a person's expression) cold and forbidding: *his bleak, near vacant eyes grew remote.* —**bleak·ly** *adv.* —**bleak·ness** *n.*

blear·y /'bli(ə)rē/ ▸*adj.* (**blear·i·er**, **blear·i·est**) (of the eyes) unfocused or filmy from sleep or tiredness: *you hate to face the world with bleary, tear-soaked eyes.* —**blear·i·ly** /'bli(ə)rəlē/ *adv.* —**blear·i·ness** *n.*

blear·y-eyed (also **blear-eyed**) ▸*adj.* (of a person) having bleary eyes.

bleat /blēt/ ▸*v.* [*intr.*] (of a sheep, goat, or calf) make a characteristic wavering cry: *the lamb was bleating weakly.* | [as *n.*] (**bleating**) *the silence was broken by the plaintive bleating of sheep.* ■ speak or complain in a weak, querulous, or foolish way: *he bleated incoherently about the report.*
▸*n.* the wavering cry made by a sheep, goat, or calf: *the distant bleat of sheep in the field.* ■ a person's plaintive cry: *his despairing bleat touched her heart.* ■ *inf.* a complaint: *they're hoping that I'll bow to their idiotic arrangements without a bleat.*

bleed /blēd/ ▸*v.* (*past* and *past part.* **bled** /bled/) **1** [*intr.*] lose blood from the body as a result of injury or illness: *some casualties were left to bleed to death* | [as *n.*] (**bleeding**) *the bleeding has stopped now.* ■ (of a dye or color) seep into an adjacent color or area: *I worked loosely with the oils, allowing colors to bleed into one another.* **2** [*tr.*] draw blood from (someone), esp. as a once-common method of treatment in medicine. ■ remove blood from (an animal carcass): *the first steer rolled out on the floor to be bled, skinned, and dressed.* ■ [*tr.*] *inf.* drain (someone) of money or resources: *his policy of attempting to bleed unions of funds.* ■ [*tr.*] allow (fluid or gas) to escape from a closed system through a valve: *open the valves and bleed air from the pump chamber.*
▸*n.* an instance of bleeding: *a lot of blood was lost from the placental bleed.*
▸ □ **bleed someone dry** (or **white**) drain someone of all money or resources: *the railroads claimed that personnel costs were bleeding them dry.*

bleed·er /'blēdər/ ▸*n.* **1** *inf.* a person who bleeds easily, esp. a hemophiliac. ■ a blood vessel that bleeds freely during surgery. **2** *Baseball* a ground ball that barely passes between two infielders.

bleed·ing heart ▸*n.* **1** *inf., derog.* a person considered to be dangerously softhearted, typically someone considered too liberal in political beliefs. **2** any of a number of plants that have heart-shaped flowers, typically pink or red, in particular a popular garden plant (genus *Dicentra*, family Fumariaceae).

bleep /blēp/ ▸*n.* a short high-pitched sound made by an electronic device as a signal or to attract attention: *the autopilot sent back an acknowledgment bleep.* ■ a sound of this type used in broadcasting as a substitute for a censored word or phrase.
▸*v.* [*intr.*] (of an electronic device) make a short high-pitched sound or repeated sequence of sounds: *the screen flickered for a few moments and bleeped.* ■ [*tr.*] substitute a bleep or bleeps for (a censored word or phrase): *cable operators have bleeped out the accuser's name.* ■ used in place of an expletive: *"what the bleep are we going to do?" he asked.*

blem·ish /'blemiSH/ ▸*n.* a small mark or flaw that spoils the appearance of something: *the merest blemish on a Rolls Royce might render it unsalable.* ■ *fig.* a moral defect or fault: *local government is not without blemish.*
▸*v.* [*tr.*] [often as *adj.*] (**blemished**) spoil the appearance of (something) that is otherwise aesthetically perfect: *thousands of Web pages are blemished with embarrassing typos* | *fig. his reign as world champion has been blemished by controversy.*

blench /blenCH/ ▸*v.* [*intr.*] make a sudden flinching movement out of fear or pain: *he blenched and struggled to regain his composure.*

blend /blend/ ▸*v.* [*tr.*] mix (a substance) with another substance so that they combine together as a mass: *blend the cornstarch with a tablespoon of water.* ■ [often as *adj.*] (**blended**) mix (different types of the same substance, such as tea, coffee, liquor, etc.) together so as to make a product of the desired quality: *a blended whiskey.* ■ put or combine (abstract things) together: *blend basic information with some scientific gardening.* | [as *n.*] (**blending**) *a blending of romanticism with a more detached modernism.* ■ merge (a color) with another so that one is not clearly distinguishable from the other. ■ form a harmonious combination: *costumes, music, and lighting all blend together beautifully.* ■ (**blend in/into**) be unobtrusive or harmonious by being similar in appearance or behavior: *she would have to employ a permanent bodyguard in the house, someone who would blend in.*
▸*n.* a mixture of different things or people: *knitting yarns in mohair blends.* ■ a mixture of different types or grades of a substance, such as tea, coffee, whiskey, etc. ■ a combination of different abstract things or qualities: *a blend of Marxist and anarchist ideas.* ■ a word made up of the parts of others and combining their meanings, for example *motel* from *motor* and *hotel.*

blend·er /'blendər/ ▸*n.* a person or thing that mixes things together, in particular: ■ an electric mixing machine used in food preparation for liquefying, chopping, or puréeing.

bless /bles/ ▸*v.* [*tr.*] (of a priest) pronounce words in a religious rite, to confer or invoke divine favor upon; ask God to look favorably on: *he blessed the dying man and anointed him.* ■ consecrate (something) by a religious rite, action, or spoken formula. ■ (esp. in Christian Church services) call (God) holy; praise (God). ■ (**bless someone with**) (of God or some notional higher power) endow (someone) with a particular cherished thing or attribute: *God has blessed us with free will.* ■ express or feel gratitude to; thank: *she silently blessed the premonition which had made her pack her best dress.* ■ used in expressions of surprise, endearment, gratitude, etc.: *bless my soul, Alan, what are you doing?* ▷Old English *blēdsian, blētsian,* based on *blōd* 'blood' (i.e., originally perhaps 'mark or consecrate with blood'). The meaning was influenced by its being used to translate Latin *benedicere* 'to praise, worship,' and later by association with *bliss.*
▸ □ **bless you!** said to a person who has just sneezed.

bless·ed /blest; 'blesid/ ▸*adj.* **1** made holy; consecrated. ■ a title preceding the name of a dead person considered to have led a holy life, esp. a person formally beatified by the Roman Catholic Church: *the Convent of the Blessed Agnes.* ■ used respectfully in reference to a dead person: *a gracious lady of blessed memory.* ■ endowed with divine favor and protection: *blessed are the meek.* ■ bringing pleasure or relief as a welcome contrast to what one has previously experienced: *he half stumbled out of the room on to his bed and blessed, blessed sleep.* ■ (**blessed with**) endowed with (a particular quality or attribute): *a beautiful city, steeped in history and blessed with huge sandy beaches.* **2** *inf.* used in mild expressions of annoyance or exasperation: *there wasn't a blessed thing anybody could have done.* —**blessedly** /'blesidlē/ *adv.*

bless·ed·ness /'blesidnis/ ▸*n.* the state of being blessed with divine favor.

bless·ing /'blesiNG/ ▸*n.* God's favor and protection: *may God continue to give us his blessing.* ■ a prayer asking for such favor and protection: *a priest gave a blessing as the ship was launched.* ■ grace said before or after a meal. ■ a beneficial thing for which one is grateful; something that brings well-being: *it's a blessing we're alive.* ■ a person's sanction or support: *he gave the plan his blessing even before it was announced.*

blew /blōō/ ▸ past of BLOW¹ and BLOW³.

blight /blīt/ ▸*n.* a plant disease, esp. one caused by fungi such as mildews, rusts, and smuts: *the vines suffered blight and disease.* ■ *inf.* anything that causes a plant disease or interferes with the healthy growth of a plant. ■ a thing that spoils or damages something: *her remorse could be a blight on that happiness.* ■ an ugly, neglected, or rundown condition of an urban area: *the depressing urban blight that lies to the south of the city.*
▸*v.* [*tr.*] (usu. **be blighted**) infect (plants or a planted area) with blight: *a peach tree blighted by leaf curl.* ■ spoil, harm, or destroy: *the scandal blighted the careers of several leading politicians* | [as *adj.*] (**blighted**) *his father's blighted ambitions.* ■ [usu. as *adj.*] (**blighted**) subject (an urban area) to neglect: *plans to establish enterprise zones in blighted areas.*

blimp /blimp/ ▸*n. inf.* a small nonrigid airship. ■ an obese person: *I could work out four hours a day and still end up a blimp.* —**blimp·ish** *adj.*

blind /blīnd/ ▸*adj.* **1** unable to see; sightless: *she suffered from glaucoma, which has left her completely blind.* ■ (of an action, esp. a test or experiment) done without being able to see or without being in possession of certain information; compare with DOUBLE-BLIND: *a blind tasting of eight wines.* ■ *Aeron.* (of flying) using instruments only: *blind landings during foggy conditions.* **2** lacking perception or discernment: *he's absolutely blind where you're concerned, isn't he?* ■ (**blind to**) unwilling or unable to appreciate or notice something apparent to others: *she was blind to the realities of her position.* ■ (of an action or state of mind) not controlled by reason or judgment: *they left in blind panic.* **3** concealed or closed, in particular: ■ (of a corner or bend in a road) impossible to see around: *two trucks collided on a blind curve in the road.*
▸*v.* [*tr.*] **1** cause (someone) to be unable to see, permanently or temporarily: *the injury temporarily blinded him.* **2** (**be blinded**) deprive (someone) of understanding, judgment, or perception: *a clever tactician blinded by passion.* ■ (**blind someone with**) confuse or overawe someone with something difficult to understand: *they try to blind you with science.*
▸*n.* **1** [as *pl. n.*] (**the blind**) people who are unable to see: *guide dogs for the blind.* **2** an obstruction to sight or light, in particular: ■ a screen for a window, esp. one on a roller or made of slats: *she pulled down the blinds.* **3** something designed to conceal one's real intentions: *he phoned again from his own home: that was just a blind for his wife.* ■ a camouflaged shelter used by hunters to get close to wildlife: *a duck blind.*
▸*adv.* without being able to see clearly: *he was the first pilot in history to fly blind.* ■ without having all the relevant information; unprepared: *he was going into the interview blind.* —**blind·ly** *adv.* —**blind·ness** *n.*
▸ □ **rob** (or **steal**) **someone blind** *inf.* rob or cheat someone in a comprehensive or merciless way. □ **turn a blind eye** pretend not to notice.

blind al·ley ▸*n.* an alley or road that is closed at one end. ■ *fig.* a course of action leading nowhere: *many technologies that show early promise lead up blind alleys.*

blind date ▸*n.* a social engagement or date with a person one has not previously met: *a blind date arranged by well-meaning friends.*

blind·er /'blīndər/ ▸*n.* (**blinders**) a pair of small leather screens attached to a horse's bridle to prevent it seeing sideways and behind. Also called BLINKERS (see BLINKER). ■ *fig.* something that prevents someone from gaining a full understanding of a situation: *they will wear their cultural blinders to the grave.*

blind·fold /'blīnd,fōld/ ▸*v.* [*tr.*] (often **be blindfolded**) deprive (someone) of sight by tying a piece of cloth around the head so as to cover the eyes.
▸*n.* a piece of cloth tied around the head to cover someone's eyes.
▸*adv.* with a blindfold covering the eyes: *the reporter was driven blindfold to meet the gangster.* ■ done with great ease and confidence, as if it could have been done wearing a blindfold: *missing putts that he would normally hole blindfold.*

blind·man's bluff /'blīndmənz/ (also **blindman's buff**) ▸*n.* a children's game in which a blindfolded player tries to catch others while being pushed about by them.

blind side ▸*n.* a direction in which a person has a poor view, typically of approaching danger: *a minivan nearly clipped him on his blind side.*
▸*v.* (**blind·side**) [*tr.*] hit or attack (someone) on the blind side: *Jenkins*

blindsided Adams, knocking him to the sidewalk. ■ (often **be blindsided**) catch (someone) unprepared; attack from an unexpected position: *protection against being technologically blindsided.*

blind spot ▸*n.* **1** *Anat.* the point of entry of the optic nerve on the retina, insensitive to light. **2** an area where a person's view is obstructed: *the angle rearview mirror eliminates blind spots on both sides of the car.* ■ an area in which a person lacks understanding or impartiality: *Ed had a blind spot where these ethical issues were concerned.* **3** *Telecomm.* a point within the normal range of a transmitter where there is unusually weak reception.

blind stitch ▸*n.* a sewing stitch visible on one side only.

blink /bliNGk/ ▸*v.* [*intr.*] **1** shut and open the eyes quickly: *she blinked, momentarily blinded* | [*tr.*] *he blinked his eyes nervously.* ■ [*tr.*] clear (dust or tears) from the eyes by this action: *she blinked away her tears.* ■ [*tr.*] (**blink back**) try to control or prevent (tears) by such an action: *Elizabeth blinked back tears.* ■ (**blink at**) *fig.* react to (something) with surprise or disapproval: *he doesn't blink at the unsavory aspects of his subject.* ■ *fig.* back down from a confrontation: *it seemed that the Iraqis had blinked and that the likelihood of an immediate invasion had decreased.* **2** (of a light or light source) shine intermittently or unsteadily: *the icon for his e-mail was blinking.*
▸*n.* **1** an act of shutting and opening the eyes quickly: *he was observing her every blink.* ■ *fig.* a moment's hesitation: *Thompson would have given her all this without a blink.* **2** a momentary gleam of light.
▸ □ **not blink an eye** show no reaction. □ **in the blink of an eye** (or **in a blink**) *inf.* very quickly. □ **on the blink** *inf.* (of a machine) not working properly; out of order: *the computer's on the blink.*

blink·er /'bliNGkər/ ▸*n.* **1** a device that blinks, esp. a vehicle's turn signal. **2** (**blinkers**) another term for BLINDERS (see BLINDER).

blip /blip/ ▸*n.* **1** a short high-pitched sound made by an electronic device. **2** a flashing point of light on a radar screen representing an object, typically accompanied by a high-pitched sound. **3** an unexpected, minor, and typically temporary deviation from a general trend: *an upward blip in house prices.* **4** a brief segment, esp. of a telecast: *the media fire unrelated blips of information at us* | *the blips on the evening news.*
▸*v.* (**blipped, blip·ping**) [*intr.*] (of an electronic device) make a short high-pitched sound or succession of sounds. ▷late 19th cent. (denoting a sudden rap or tap): imitative; the noun sense 'unexpected deviation' dates from the 1970s.

bliss /blis/ ▸*n.* perfect happiness; great joy: *she gave a sigh of bliss.* ■ something providing such happiness: *the steam room was bliss.* ■ a state of spiritual blessedness, typically that reached after death. —**bliss·ful** *adj.* —**bliss·ful·ly** *adv.*

B-list /'bē ,list/ ▸*n.* see A-LIST.

blis·ter /'blistər/ ▸*n.* a small bubble on the skin filled with serum and caused by friction, burning, or other damage. ■ a similar swelling, filled with air or fluid, on the surface of a plant, heated metal, painted wood, or other object.
▸*v.* **1** [*intr.*] form swellings filled with air or fluid on the surface of something: *the surface of the door began to blister* | [as *adj.*] (**blistered**) *he had blistered feet.* ■ [*tr.*] cause blisters to form on the surface of: *a caustic liquid that blisters the skin.* **2** criticize sharply: *they came out and blistered the girls for pulling leaves off a chestnut tree.*

blis·ter pack ▸*n.* a type of packaging in which a product is sealed in plastic, often with a cardboard backing.

blithe /blīth; blīth/ ▸*adj.* showing a casual and cheerful indifference considered to be callous or improper: *a blithe disregard for the rules of the road.* ■ happy or joyous: *a blithe seaside comedy.* —**blithe·ly** *adv.* —**blithe·ness** *n.* —**blithe·some** /-səm/ *adj.* (*poetic/lit.*).

blith·er·ing /'blithəriNG/ ▸*adj. inf.* senselessly talkative; babbling: *a blithering idiot.*

blitz /blits/ ▸*n.* an intensive or sudden military attack. ■ *inf.* a sudden, energetic, and concerted effort, typically on a specific task: *a major press blitz.* ■ *Football* a charge of the passer by the defensive linebackers just after the ball is snapped. ■ (**the Blitz**) the German air raids on Britain in 1940.
▸*v.* [*tr.*] (often **be blitzed**) attack or damage (a place or building) in a blitz: *news came that Rotterdam had been blitzed* | *fig. organizations blitzed Capitol Hill with e-mails and postcards.* ■ *Football* attack (the passer) in a blitz.

blitz·krieg /'blits,krēg/ ▸*n.* an intense military campaign intended to bring about a swift victory.

bliz·zard /'blizərd/ ▸*n.* a severe snowstorm with high winds and low visibility. ■ *fig.* an overabundance; a deluge: *a blizzard of legal forms.*

bloat /blōt/ ▸*v.* [*tr.*] cause to swell with fluid or gas: *the fungus has bloated his fingers.* ■ [*intr.*] become swollen with fluid or gas: [as *n.*] (**bloating**) *she suffered from abdominal bloating.*

B

▶ *n.* a disease of livestock characterized by an accumulation of gas in the stomach.

BLOB /bläb/ ▶ *n. Comput.* binary large objects.

blob /bläb/ ▶ *n.* a drop of a thick liquid or other viscous substance: *blobs of paint.* ■ a spot of color: *a badly printed blob on shopping bags.* ■ an indeterminate mass or shape: *a leathery blob commonly known as a sea squirt.*
▶ *v.* [*tr.*] (often **be blobbed**) put small drops of thick liquid or spots of color on: *her nose was blobbed with paint.* —**blob·by** *adj.*

bloc /bläk/ ▶ *n.* a combination of countries, parties, or groups sharing a common purpose: *a center-left voting bloc.*

block /bläk/ ▶ *n.* **1** a large solid piece of hard material, esp. rock, stone, or wood, typically with flat surfaces on each side: *a block of marble.* ■ a sturdy, flat-topped block used as a work surface, typically for chopping food. ■ (usu. **blocks**) any of a set of solid cubes used as a child's toy. ■ (usu. **blocks**) a starting block: *the thrust a sprinter gets when coming out of the blocks.* ■ (also **cylinder block** or **engine block**) the main body of an internal combustion engine, containing the pistons. **2** the area bounded by four streets in a town or suburb: *she went for a run around the block.* ■ the length of one side of such an area, typically as a measure of distance: *he lives a few blocks away from the museum.* **3** a building, esp. part of a complex, used for a particular purpose: *a cell block.* ■ *chiefly Brit.* a large single building subdivided into separate rooms, apartments, or offices: *an apartment block.* **4** a large quantity or allocation of things regarded as a unit: *a block of shares* | [as *adj.*] *block grants.* ■ *Comput.* a large piece of text processed as a unit. ■ an unseparated unit of at least four postage stamps in at least two rows, generally a group of four. **5** an obstacle to the normal progress or functioning of something: *substantial demands for time off may constitute* **a block to** *career advancement.* ■ *Sports* a hindering or stopping of an opponent's movement or action. ■ *Tennis* a shot in which the racket is held stationary rather than being swung back, esp. a stop volley. **6** a flat area of something, typically a solid area of color: *cover the eyelid with a neutral block of color.* **7** a pulley or system of pulleys mounted in a case. **8** *inf.* a person's head: *"I'll knock your block off,"* he said.
▶ *v.* [*tr.*] **1** make the movement or flow in (a passage, pipe, road, etc.) difficult or impossible: *block up the holes with sticky tape.* ■ put an obstacle in the way of (something proposed or attempted): *he stood up, blocking her escape.* ■ restrict the use or conversion of (currency or any other asset). ■ *Sports* hinder or stop the movement or action of (an opponent). ■ *Sports* stop (a blow or ball) from finding its mark: *when driving for a lay-up or leaping to block a shot.* ■ *Med.* produce insensibility in (a part of the body) by injecting an anesthetic close to the nerves that supply it. ■ *Bridge* play in such a way that an opponent cannot establish (a long suit). **2** shape or reshape (a hat) using a wooden mold.
▷Middle English (denoting a log or tree stump): from Old French *bloc* (noun), *bloquer* (verb), from Middle Dutch *blok*, of unknown ultimate origin. —**block·er** *n.*
▶ □ **have been around the block (a few times)** *inf.* (of a person) have a lot of experience. □ **the new kid on the block** *inf.* a newcomer to a particular place or sphere of activity, typically someone who has yet to prove themselves. □ **on the (auction) block** for sale at auction: *the original first manuscript for Ravel's Bolero goes on the block today* | *fig. the company put its subsidiary on the block because it did not fit its core business interests.*

block·ade /blä'kād/ ▶ *n.* an act of sealing off a place to prevent goods or people from entering or leaving: *the army has imposed an economic blockade.* ■ anything that prevents access or progress: *the police pulled down blockades on the highway.*
▶ *v.* [*tr.*] seal off (a place) to prevent goods or people from entering or leaving. —**blockader** *n.*

block·age /'bläkij/ ▶ *n.* an obstruction that makes movement or flow difficult or impossible: *a blockage in the pipes.*

block and tack·le ▶ *n.* a mechanism consisting of ropes and one or more pulley-blocks, used for lifting or pulling heavy objects.

block·bust·er /'bläk,bəstər/ ▶ *n. inf.* a thing of great power or size, in particular: ■ a movie, book, or other product that is a great commercial success: [as *adj.*] *a blockbuster pay-per-view special event.* ■ a huge aerial bomb capable of destroying targets within a wide area.

block and tackle

block·head /'bläk,hed/ ▶ *n. inf.* a stupid person. —**block·head·ed** *adj.*

block·house /'bläk,hous/ ▶ *n.* a reinforced concrete shelter used as an observation point. ■ *hist.* a one-storied timber building with loopholes, used as a fort.

blog /bläg/ ▶ *n.* a Web site on which an individual or group of users produces an ongoing narrative: *Most of his work colleagues were unaware of his blog until recently.*
▶ *v.* (**blogged**, **blog·ging**) [*intr.*] add new material to or regularly update a weblog. —**blog·ger** *n.*

blog·o·sphere /'blägə,sfi(ə)r/ ▶ *n.* the community of blogs and bloggers.

blond /bländ/ ▶ *adj.* (of hair) fair or pale yellow: *short-cropped blond hair* | *her hair was dyed blond.* ■ (of a person) having hair of a fair or pale yellow color: *a slim blond woman.* ■ (of wood and other substances) light in color or tone: *a New York office full of blond wood.*
▶ *n.* a person with fair hair and skin. —**blond·ish** *adj.* —**blond·ness** *n.*

blonde /bländ/ ▶ *adj.* (of a woman or a woman's hair) blond.
▶ *n.* a blond-haired woman.

blood /bləd/ ▶ *n.* **1** the red liquid that circulates in the arteries and veins of humans and other vertebrate animals, carrying oxygen to and carbon dioxide from the tissues of the body: *drops of blood.* ■ an internal bodily fluid, not necessarily red, that performs a similar function in invertebrates. ■ *fig.* violence involving bloodshed: *a commando operation full of blood and danger.* ■ *fig.* a person's downfall or punishment, typically as retribution: *the press is baying for blood.* **2** *fig.* temperament or disposition, esp. when passionate: *a ritual that fires up his blood.* **3** family background; descent or lineage: *she must have Irish blood in her.* ■ [in *comb.*] a person of specified descent: *a mixed-blood.*
▶ □ **be like getting blood out of** (or **from**) **a stone** (or **turnip**) be extremely difficult (said in reference to obtaining something from someone): *getting a story out of her is like getting blood out of a stone!* □ **blood, sweat, and tears** extremely hard work; unstinting effort. □ **first blood 1** the first shedding of blood, esp. in a boxing match or formerly in dueling with swords. **2** the first point or advantage gained in a contest: *King drew first blood when he took the opening set.* □ **have blood on one's hands** be responsible for someone's death. □ **in one's blood** ingrained in or fundamental to one's character: *racing is in his blood.* □ **in cold blood** ruthlessly; without feeling: *proving that he can kill in cold blood.* □ **make someone's blood boil** *inf.* infuriate someone. □ **make someone's blood run cold** horrify someone. □ **taste blood** achieve an early success that stimulates further efforts: *the speculators have tasted blood and could force a devaluation of the franc.* □ **young blood** a younger member or members of a group, typically as an invigorating force.

blood bank ▶ *n.* a place where supplies of blood or plasma for transfusion are stored.

blood·bath /'bləd,baтH/ ▶ *n.* an event or situation in which many people are killed in a violent manner: *the protest sparked a bloodbath* | *fig. the bad publicity would be a media bloodbath.*

blood broth·er ▶ *n.* a brother by birth. ■ a man who has sworn to treat another man as a brother, sometimes with a ceremonial mingling of blood.

blood count ▶ *n.* a determination of the number of corpuscles in a specific volume of blood. ■ the number found in such a procedure: *a low blood count.*

blood·cur·dling /'bləd,kərd(ə)liNG/ ▶ *adj.* causing terror or horror: *the warrior's bloodcurdling cry.*

blood do·nor ▶ *n.* a person who gives blood for transfusion.

blood·ed /'blədid/ ▶ *adj.* [usu. in *comb.*] having blood or a temperament of a specified kind: *warm-blooded animals.* ■ (of horses or cattle) of good pedigree: *a blooded stallion.*

blood feud ▶ *n.* a lengthy conflict between families involving a cycle of retaliatory killings or injury.

blood group ▶ *n.* any of the various types of human blood whose antigen characteristics determine compatibility in transfusion. The best known blood groups are those of the ABO system.

blood·hound /'bləd,hound/ ▶ *n.* a large hound of a breed with a very keen sense of smell, used in tracking.

blood·less /'blədlis/ ▶ *adj.* **1** without blood: *the meat is clean and relatively bloodless.* ■ (of a revolution or conflict) without violence or killing: *a bloodless coup.* ■ (of surgery or other medical procedures) spilling little or no blood: *it is usually the drug of choice for bloodless medicine.* **2** (of the skin or a part of the body) drained of color: *his bloodless lips.* ■ (of a person) cold or unemotional. ■ lacking in vitality; feeble. —**blood·less·ly** *adv.* —**blood·less·ness** *n.*

blood·let·ting /'bləd,letiNG/ ▶ *n. chiefly hist.* the surgical removal of some of a patient's blood for therapeutic purposes. ■ the violent killing and wounding of people during a war or conflict: *gang members have halted*

Pronunciation Key ə *ago*, *up*; ər *over*, *fur*; a *hat*; ā *ate*; ä *car*; CH *chin*; e *let*; ē *see*; e(ə)r *air*; i *fit*; ī *by*; i(ə)r *ear*; NG *sing*; ō *go*; ô *law*, *for*; oi *toy*; o͞o *good*; o͞o *goo*; ou *out*; SH *she*; TH *thin*; TH *then*; (h)w *why*; ZH *vision*

their internecine bloodletting. ■ bitter division and quarreling within an organization.

blood·line /'bləd,līn/ ▶*n.* an animal's set of ancestors or pedigree, typically considered with regard to the desirable characteristics bred into it. ■ a set of ancestors or line of descent of a person.

blood·mo·bile /'blədmə,bēl/ ▶*n.* a motor vehicle equipped for collecting blood from volunteer donors.

blood mon·ey ▶*n.* money paid in compensation to the family of someone who has been killed. ■ money paid to a hired killer. ■ money paid by the police or the media for information about a killer or killing.

blood or·ange ▶*n.* an orange of a variety with red or red-streaked flesh.

blood poi·son·ing ▶*n.* the presence of microorganisms or their toxins in the blood, causing disease; septicemia.

blood pres·sure ▶*n.* the pressure of the blood in the circulatory system, often measured for diagnosis since it is closely related to the force and rate of the heartbeat and the diameter and elasticity of the arterial walls.

blood re·la·tion (also **blood rel·a·tive**) ▶*n.* a person related to another by birth rather than by marriage.

blood·shed /'bləd,sнed/ ▶*n.* the killing or wounding of people, typically on a large scale during a conflict.

blood·shot /'bləd,sнät/ ▶*adj.* (of the eyes) inflamed or tinged with blood, typically as a result of tiredness.

blood sport ▶*n.* (usu. **blood sports**) a sport involving the shedding of blood, esp. the hunting or killing of animals: *cockfighting, bullfighting, fox hunting, and other blood sports* | *fig. politics is a blood sport.*

blood·stain /'bləd,stān/ ▶*n.* a stain or a spot caused by blood. —**blood·stained** *adj.*

blood·stone /'bləd,stōn/ ▶*n.* a type of green chalcedony spotted or streaked with red, used as a gemstone.

blood·stream /'bləd,strēm/ ▶*n.* the blood circulating through the body of a person or animal.

blood·suck·er /'bləd,səkər/ ▶*n.* **1** an animal or insect that sucks blood, esp. a leech or a mosquito. **2** a person who extorts money. ■ a person who lives off others; a parasite. —**blood·suck·ing** /-,səkiNG/ *adj.*

blood sug·ar ▶*n.* the concentration of glucose in the blood.

blood·thirst·y /'bləd,тнərstē/ ▶*adj.* (-**thirst·i·er**, -**thirst·i·est**) eager to shed blood: *a bloodthirsty dictator.* —**blood·thirst·i·ly** /-stəlē/ *adv.* —**blood·thirst·i·ness** *n.*

blood type ▶*n.* another term for BLOOD GROUP.

blood ves·sel ▶*n.* a tubular structure carrying blood through the tissues and organs; a vein, artery, or capillary.

blood·y[1] /'blədē/ ▶*adj.* (**bloodier**, **bloodiest**) **1** covered, smeared, or running with blood: *a bloody body.* ■ composed of or resembling blood: *a bloody discharge.* **2** involving or characterized by bloodshed or cruelty: *the bloody tyrannies of Europe.*
▶*v.* (**blood·ies**, **blood·ied**) [*tr.*] (often **be bloodied**) cover or stain with blood: *he ended the fight with his face bloodied and battered* | *fig. she has been bloodied in her three years on the commission.* —**blood·i·ly** /'blədəlē/ *adv.* —**blood·i·ness** *n.*

blood·y[2] ▶*adj. inf., chiefly Brit.* used to express anger, annoyance, or shock, or simply for emphasis: *took your bloody time*

Blood·y Mar·y ▶*n.* a drink consisting of vodka and seasoned tomato juice.

bloom /'blōōm/ ▶*n.* **1** a flower, esp. one cultivated for its beauty: *an exotic bloom.* ■ the state or period of flowering: *the apple trees were in bloom.* ■ the state or period of greatest beauty, freshness, or vigor: *a young girl, still in the bloom of youth.* **2** a youthful or healthy glow in a person's complexion: *her face had lost its usual bloom.* **3** a delicate powdery surface deposit on certain fresh fruits, leaves, or stems. ■ a rapid growth of microscopic algae or cyanobacteria in water, often resulting in a colored scum on the surface. ■ a grayish-white appearance on chocolate caused by cocoa butter rising to the surface.
▶*v.* [*intr.*] produce flowers; be in flower: *a rose tree bloomed on a ruined wall.* ■ come into or be in full beauty or health; flourish: *she bloomed as an actress under his tutelage.*

bloom·er /'blōōmər/ ▶*n.* [usu. in comb.] a plant that produces flowers at a specified time: *fragrant night-bloomers.* ■ a person who matures or flourishes at a specified time: *he was a late bloomer.*

bloo·mers /'blōōmərz/ ▶*pl. n.* women's loose-fitting knee-length underpants, considered old-fashioned. ■ *hist.* women's and girls' loose-fitting trousers, gathered at the knee or, originally, the ankle.

bloom·ing /'blōōmiNG/ ▶*adj. & adv. Brit., inf.* used for emphasis or to express annoyance: [as *adj.*] *I didn't learn a blooming thing.*

bloop·er /'blōōpər/ ▶*n. inf.* **1** an embarrassing error: *he poked fun at his*

own tendency to utter bloopers. ■ a brief television or radio segment containing a humorous error, collected with others for broadcast as a group: *a selection of bloopers and outtakes from the evening.* **2** *Baseball* a weakly hit fly ball landing just beyond the reach of the infielders.

blos·som /'bläsəm/ ▶*n.* a flower or a mass of flowers on a tree or bush: *tiny white blossoms* | *the slopes were ablaze with almond blossom.* ■ the state or period of flowering: *fruit trees in blossom.*
▶*v.* [*intr.*] (of a tree or bush) produce flowers or masses of flowers: *the mango trees have shed their fruit and blossomed again.* ■ mature or develop in a promising or healthy way: *their friendship blossomed into romance.* ■ seem to grow or open like a flower: *the smile blossomed on his lips.* —**blos·som·y** *adj.*

blot /blät/ ▶*n.* a dark mark or stain, typically one made by ink, paint, or dirt: *an ink blot.* ■ a shameful act or quality that tarnishes an otherwise good character or reputation: *the only blot on an otherwise clean campaign.*
▶*v.* (**blot·ted**, **blot·ting**) [*tr.*] **1** dry (a wet surface or substance) using an absorbent material: *Guy blotted his face with a dust rag.* **2** mark or stain (something): [as *adj.*] (**blotted**) *the writing was messy and blotted.* ■ tarnish the good character or reputation of: *the turmoil blotted his memory of the school.* **3** (**blot something out**) cover writing or pictures with ink or paint so that they cannot be seen. ■ obscure a view: *a dust shield blotting out the sun.* ■ obliterate or disregard something painful in one's memory or existence: *the concentration necessary to her job blotted out all the feelings.*

blotch /bläcн/ ▶*n.* an irregular patch or unsightly mark on a surface, typically the skin: *red blotches on her face.*
▶*v.* (usu. **be blotched**) cover with blotches: *her face was blotched and swollen with crying.* —**blotch·y** *adj.*

blot·ter /'blätər/ ▶*n.* **1** a sheet or pad of blotting paper inserted into a frame and kept on a desk. **2** a temporary recording book, esp. a police charge sheet: *the boys ended up on police blotters for property crimes.*

blot·ting pa·per ▶*n.* absorbent paper used for soaking up excess ink when writing.

blouse /blous; blouz/ ▶*n.* a woman's loose upper garment resembling a shirt, typically with a collar, buttons, and sleeves.
▶*v.* [*tr.*] make (a garment) hang in loose folds: *I bloused my trousers over my boots* | [*intr.*] *my dress bloused out above my waist.* ▷early 19th cent. (denoting a belted loose garment worn by peasants): from French, of unknown origin.

blous·on /'blou,sän; -,zän/ ▶*n.* a top or dress, typically bloused at the waist.

blow[1] /blō/ ▶*v.* (*past* **blew** /blōō/; *past part.* **blown** /blōn/) **1** [*intr.*] (of wind) move creating an air current: *a cold wind began to blow.* ■ [*tr.*] (of wind) cause to move; propel: *a gust of wind blew a cloud of smoke into his face* | *the spire was blown down during a gale.* ■ [*intr.*] be carried, driven, or moved by the wind or an air current: *it was so windy that the tent nearly blew away.* ■ [*tr.*] *inf.* leave (a place): *I'm ready to blow town.* **2** [*intr.*] (of a person) expel air through pursed lips: *Willie took a deep breath, and blew.* ■ [*tr.*] use one's breath to propel: *he blew cigar smoke in her face.* ■ [*tr.*] cause to breathe hard; exhaust of breath. ■ [*tr.*] (of a person) force air through the mouth into (an instrument) in order to make a sound: *the umpire blew his whistle.* ■ [*tr.*] sound (the horn of a vehicle). ■ [*tr.*] force air through a tube into (molten glass) in order to create an artifact. ■ [*tr.*] remove the contents of (an egg) by forcing air through it. ■ (of flies) lay eggs in or on something: *to repel the hordes of flies that would otherwise blow on the buffalo hide.* ■ (of a whale) eject air and vapor through the blowhole. **3** [*tr.*] (of an explosion or explosive device) displace violently or send flying: *the blast had blown the windows out of the van.* ■ [*intr.*] (of a vehicle tire) burst suddenly while the vehicle is in motion. ■ burst or cause to burst due to pressure or overheating: [*intr.*] *the engines sounded as if their exhausts had blown.* ■ (of an electrical circuit) burn out or cause to burn out through overloading: [*intr.*] *the fuse in the plug had blown.* **4** [*tr.*] *inf.* spend recklessly: *they blew $100,000 in just eighteen months.* **5** *inf.* completely bungle (an opportunity): *the wider issues were to show that politicians had blown it.* ■ (usu. **be blown**) expose (a stratagem): *a man whose cover was blown.* **6** [*tr.*] *vulgar slang* perform fellatio.
▶*phrasal v.* □ **blow someone away** *inf.* **1** kill someone using a firearm. **2** (**be blown away**) be extremely impressed: *I'm blown away by his new poem.* □ **blow in** *inf.* (of a person) arrive casually and unannounced. □ **blow someone off** *inf.* fail to keep an appointment with someone. ■ end a romantic or sexual relationship with someone. □ **blow something off** *inf.* ignore or make light of something. ■ fail to attend something: *Ivy blew off class.* □ **blow out** **1** be extinguished by an air current: *the candles blew out.* **2** (of a tire) puncture while the vehicle is in motion. **3** (of an oil or gas well) emit gas suddenly and forcefully. **4** (**blow itself out**) (of a storm) finally lose its force: *fig. the recession may finally*

have *blown itself out.* □ **blow something out 1** use one's breath to extinguish a flame: *he blew out the candle.* **2** *inf.* render a part of the body useless: *he blew out his arm trying to snap a curveball.* □ **blow over** (of trouble) fade away without serious consequences. □ **blow up 1** explode. ■ (of a person) lose one's temper: *Meg blows up at Patrick for always throwing his tea bags in the sink.* **2** (of a wind or storm) begin to develop. ■ (of a scandal or dispute) emerge or become public. **3** inflate: *my stomach had started to blow up.* □ **blow something up 1** cause something to explode. **2** inflate something: *a small pump for blowing up balloons.* ■ enlarge a photograph or text.

▶ *n.* **1** a strong wind: *we're in for a blow.* **2** an act of blowing on an instrument: *a number of blows on the whistle.* ■ an act of blowing one's nose: *give your nose a good blow.* ■ *inf.* a spell of playing jazz or rock music. ■ (in steelmaking) an act of sending an air or oxygen blast through molten metal in a converter. **3** *inf.* cocaine. —**blow·y** *adj.*

▶ □ **be blown off course** *fig.* (of a project) be disrupted by some circumstance. □ **be blown out of the water** *fig.* (of a person, idea, or project) be shown to lack all credibility. □ **blow a gasket** *inf.* lose one's temper. □ **blow hot and cold** vacillate. □ **blow one's lid** (or **top** or **stack** or **cool**) *inf.* lose one's temper. □ **blow someone's mind** *inf.* affect someone very strongly. □ **blow one's nose** clear one's nose of mucus by blowing forcefully through it. □ **blow something to bits** (or **pieces** or **smithereens**) use bombs or other explosives to destroy something, typically a building, completely. □ **blow something out of proportion** exaggerate the importance of something. □ **blow up in one's face** (of an action, project, or situation) go drastically wrong with damaging effects to oneself. □ **blow with the wind** be incapable of maintaining a consistent course of action.

blow² ▶ *n.* a powerful stroke with a hand, weapon, or hard object: *he received a blow to the skull.* ■ a sudden shock or disappointment: *the news came as a crushing blow.*

▶ □ **at one blow** by a single stroke; in one operation: *the letter had destroyed his certainty at one blow.* □ **come to blows** start fighting after a disagreement. □ **strike a blow for** (or **against**) act in support of (or opposition to): *a chance to strike a blow for freedom.*

blow-by-blow ▶ *adj.* (of a description of an event) giving all the details in the order in which they occurred: *he gave them a blow-by-blow account of your rescue.*

blow-dry ▶ *v.* [*tr.*] arrange (the hair) into a particular style while drying it with a hand-held dryer.

▶ *n.* an act of arranging the hair in such a way. —**blow-dry·er** (also **blow· dri·er**) *n.*

blow·er /'blōər/ ▶ *n.* a person or thing that blows, typically a mechanical device for creating a current of air used to dry or heat something.

blow·fish /'blō,fiSH/ ▶ *n.* (*pl.* same or **-fish·es**) any of a number of fishes that are able to inflate their bodies when alarmed, such as a globefish.

blow·fly /'blō,flī/ ▶ *n.* (*pl.* **-flies**) a large and typically metallic-colored fly (family Calliphoridae) that lays its eggs on meat and carcasses.

blow·gun /'blō,gən/ ▶ *n.* a primitive weapon consisting of a long tube through which an arrow or dart is propelled by force of the breath.

blow·hard /'blō,härd/ *inf.* ▶ *n.* a person who blusters and boasts in an unpleasant way: *a bunch of pompous blowhards trying to get on the news.*

blow·hole /'blō,hōl/ ▶ *n.* a hole for blowing or breathing through, in particular: ■ the nostril of a whale on the top of its head. ■ a hole in ice to which seals, whales, and other aquatic animals come to breathe.

blown /blōn/ ▶ past participle of BLOW¹.

▶ *adj.* destroyed; spoiled: *a blown fuse | your cover is blown.*

▶ □ **blown away** extremely surprised; flabbergasted: *Sharon was blown away by the place.*

blow·out /'blō,out/ ▶ *n.* **1** a sudden rupture or malfunction of a part or apparatus due to pressure, in particular: ■ a bursting of an automobile tire. ■ *fig.* an outburst of anger; an argument: *that exchange led to a big blowout five years ago.* ■ a surge of oil or gas from a well. ■ *inf.* a melting of an electric fuse. **2** *inf.* an easy victory in a sporting contest or an election: *they had lost seven games—four by blowouts.* **3** *inf.* a large or lavish meal or social gathering. **4** a hollow eroded by the wind, esp. in a sand dune.

▶ *adj.* huge; all-consuming: *an inventory blowout sale.*

blow·pipe /'blō,pīp/ ▶ *n.* a long tube by means of which molten glass is blown into the required shape. ■ a tube used to intensify the heat of a flame by blowing air or other gas through it at high pressure.

blows·y /'blouzē/ (also **blowz·y**) ▶ *adj.* (of a woman) coarse, untidy, and red-faced: *a blowsy woman wearing Bermuda shorts.* —**blows·i·ly** /-zəlē/ *adv.* —**blows·i·ness** *n.*

blow·torch /'blō,tôrCH/ ▶ *n.* a portable device producing a hot flame that is directed onto a surface, typically to solder metal.

blow·up /'blō,əp/ (also **blow-up**) ▶ *n.* **1** an enlargement of a photograph. **2** *inf.* an outburst of anger.

▶ *adj.* inflatable: *a blowup neck pillow.*

BLT ▶ *n.* a sandwich filled with bacon, lettuce, and tomato.

blub·ber¹ /'bləbər/ ▶ *n.* the fat of sea mammals, esp. whales and seals. ■ *inf., derog.* excessive human fat. —**blub·ber·y** *adj.*

blub·ber² ▶ *v.* [*intr.*] *inf.* sob noisily and uncontrollably: *he was blubbering like a child.*

bludg·eon /'bləjən/ ▶ *n.* a thick stick with a heavy end, used as a weapon: *fig. a rhetorical bludgeon in the war against liberalism.*

▶ *v.* [*tr.*] beat (someone) repeatedly with a bludgeon or other heavy object. ■ force or bully (someone) to do something: *she was determined not to be bludgeoned into submission.*

blue /blōō/ ▶ *adj.* (**bluer, bluest**) **1** of a color intermediate between green and violet, as of the sky or sea on a sunny day. ■ (of a person's skin) having or turning such a color, esp. with cold or breathing difficulties. ■ (of a bird or other animal) having blue markings. ■ (of cats, foxes, or rabbits) having fur of a smoky gray color. ■ *Physics* denoting one of three colors of quark. **2** *inf.* (of a person or mood) melancholy, sad, or depressed. **3** *inf.* (of a movie, joke, or story) with sexual or pornographic content. ■ (of language) marked by cursing, swearing, and blasphemy. **4** *inf.* rigidly religious or moralistic; puritanical.

▶ *n.* **1** blue color or pigment. ■ blue clothes or material. ■ a blue uniform, or a person wearing a blue uniform, such as a police officer or a baseball umpire. ■ (usu. **Blue**) the Union army in the Civil War, or a member of that army. **2** a blue thing. **3** a small butterfly (family Lycaenidae), the male of which is predominantly blue while the female is typically brown.

▶ *v.* (**blues, blued, bluing** or **blueing**) **1** make or become blue: [*tr.*] *the light dims, bluing the retina* | [*intr.*] *the day would haze, the air bluing with afternoon.* ■ [*tr.*] heat (metal) so as to give it a grayish-blue finish. **2** [*tr.*] wash (white clothes) with bluing. —**blue·ness** *n.* —**blu·ish** *adj.*

▶ □ **once in a blue moon** *inf.* very rarely. □ **out of the blue** (or **out of a clear blue sky**) *inf.* without warning; unexpectedly. □ **talk a blue streak** *inf.* speak continuously and at great length.

blue ba·by ▶ *n.* a baby with a blue complexion from lack of oxygen in the blood due to a congenital defect of the heart or major blood vessels.

blue·bell /'blōō,bel/ ▶ *n.* **1** (also **English bluebell**) a widely cultivated European woodland plant (*Hyacinthoides nonscripta*) of the lily family that produces clusters of bell-shaped blue flowers in spring. **2** any of a number of other plants with blue bell-shaped flowers, in particular the bellflower and the Virginia bluebell.

blue·ber·ry /'blōō,berē/ ▶ *n.* (*pl.* **-ies**) **1** a hardy dwarf shrub (genus *Vaccinium*) of the heath family, with small, whitish drooping flowers and dark blue edible berries. **2** the small, sweet edible berry of this plant.

blue·bird /'blōō,bərd/ ▶ *n.* an American songbird (genus *Sialia*) of the thrush family, the male of which has a blue head, back, and wings.

blue blood ▶ *n.* noble birth: *blue blood is no guarantee of any particular merit, competence, or expertise.* ■ (also **blue-blood**) a person of noble birth: *a comforting figure among that crowd of blue bloods.* —**blue-blood·ed** *adj.*

blue book ▶ *n.* **1** a listing of socially prominent people. ■ (in full **Kelley Blue Book**) *trademark* a reference book listing the prices of used cars. **2** a blank book used for written examinations in high school and college.

blue·bot·tle /'blōō,bätl/ ▶ *n.* **1** a common blowfly (*Calliphora vomitoria*) with a metallic-blue body. **2** the wild cornflower.

blue cheese ▶ *n.* cheese containing veins of blue mold.

blue-chip ▶ *adj.* denoting companies or their shares considered to be a reliable investment, though less secure than gilt-edged stock. ■ of the highest quality: *blue-chip art.*

blue-col·lar ▶ *adj.* of or relating to workers who wear work clothes: *unskilled blue-collar operators.* Compare with WHITE-COLLAR.

blue crab ▶ *n.* a large edible swimming crab (*Callinectes sapidus*, family Portunidae) of the Atlantic coast of North America.

blue·fish /'blōō,fiSH/ ▶ *n.* (*pl.* same or **-fishes**) a predatory blue-colored marine fish (*Pomatomus saltatrix*, family Pomatomidae) of tropical and temperate waters, popular as a game fish.

blue·grass /'blōō,gras/ ▶ *n.* **1** (also **Kentucky bluegrass**) a bluish-green grass that was introduced into North America from northern Europe.

Pronunciation Key ə *ago,* up; ər *over,* fur; a *hat;* ā *ate;* ä *car;* CH *chin;* e *let;* ē *see;* e(ə)r *air;* i *fit;* ī *by;* i(ə)r *ear;* NG *sing;* ō *go;* ô *law, for;* oi *toy;* ŏŏ *good;* ōō *goo;* ou *out;* SH *she;* TH *thin;* TH *then;* (h)w *why;* ZH *vision*

It is widely grown for fodder, esp. in Kentucky and Virginia. **2** a kind of country music influenced by jazz and blues and characterized by virtuosic playing of banjos and guitars and high-pitched vocals.

blue-green al·gae ▶*pl. n.* another term for CYANOBACTERIA.

blue jay ▶*n.* a common North American jay (*Cyanocitta cristata*) with a blue crest, back, wings, and tail.

blue jeans ▶*n.* jeans made of blue denim.

blue mold ▶*n.* a bluish fungus (*Penicillium* and other genera, phylum Ascomycota) that grows on food. Blue molds are deliberately introduced into some cheeses, and some kinds are used to produce antibiotics such as penicillin.

blue-pen·cil ▶*v.* [*tr.*] edit or make cuts in (a manuscript, movie, or other work).

blue·print /'bloo,print/ ▶*n.* a design plan or other technical drawing. ■ *fig.* something that acts as a plan, model, or template: *a vague blueprint for fundamental land redistribution.*

blue-rib·bon ▶*adj.* of the highest quality; first-class: *blue-ribbon service.* ■ (of a jury or committee) carefully or specially selected.

blues /blooz/ ▶*pl. n.* **1** [treated as *sing.* or *pl.*] (often **the blues**) melancholic music of black American folk origin, typically in a twelve-bar sequence. **2** (**the blues**) *inf.* feelings of melancholy, sadness, or depression: *she's got the blues.* —**blues·y** *adj.*

blue·shift /'bloo,shift/ (also **blue shift**) ▶*n.* *Astron.* the displacement of the spectrum to shorter wavelengths in the light coming from distant celestial objects moving toward the observer. Compare with REDSHIFT. —**blue·shift·ed** *adj.*

blue·stock·ing /'bloo,stäkiNG/ ▶*n.* *often derog.* an intellectual or literary woman.

blue whale ▶*n.* a migratory, mottled bluish-gray rorqual (*Balaenoptera musculus*), found in all oceans of the world. It is the largest animal ever to inhabit the earth.

bluff[1] /bləf/ ▶*n.* an attempt to deceive someone into believing that one can or will do something: *the offer was denounced as a bluff.*
▶*v.* [*intr.*] try to deceive someone as to one's abilities or intentions: *he's been bluffing all along.* ■ (in a card game) bet heavily on a weak hand in order to deceive opponents. ■ (**bluff one's way**) contrive a difficult escape or other achievement by maintaining a pretense: *he bluffed his way onto an Antarctic supply vessel.* —**bluff·er** *n.*
▶ □ **call someone's bluff** challenge someone thought to be bluffing.

bluff[2] ▶*adj.* direct in speech or behavior but in a good-natured way: *a big, bluff, hearty man.* —**bluff·ly** *adv.* —**bluff·ness** *n.*

bluff[3] ▶*n.* a steep cliff, bank, or promontory.
▶*adj.* (of a cliff or a ship's bow) having a vertical or steep broad front.

blu·ing /'blooiNG/ (also **blue·ing**) ▶*n.* **1** blue powder used to preserve the whiteness of laundry. **2** a grayish-blue finish on metal produced by heating.

blun·der /'bləndər/ ▶*n.* a stupid or careless mistake.
▶*v.* [*intr.*] make such a mistake; act or speak clumsily: *the mayor and the City Council have blundered in an ill-advised campaign.* ■ move clumsily or as if unable to see: *we were blundering around in the darkness.* —**blun·der·er** *n.* —**blun·der·ing·ly** *adv.*

blun·der·buss /'bləndər,bəs/ ▶*n.* *hist.* a short-barreled large-bored gun with a flared muzzle, used at short range. ■ *fig.* an action or way of doing something regarded as lacking in subtlety and precision: *economists resort too quickly to the blunderbuss of regulation.*

blunt /blənt/ ▶*adj.* **1** (of a knife, pencil, etc.) having a worn-down edge or point; not sharp. **2** (of a person or remark) uncompromisingly forthright: *he is as blunt as a kick in the shins.*
▶*v.* make or become less sharp: [*intr.*] *the edge may blunt very rapidly.* ■ [*tr.*] *fig.* weaken or reduce (something): *their determination had been blunted.* —**blunt·ly** *adv.* —**blunt·ness** *n.*

blur /blər/ ▶*v.* (**blurred, blur·ring**) make or become unclear or less distinct: [*tr.*] *tears blurred her vision.*
▶*n.* a thing that cannot be seen or heard clearly: *the words were a blur.* ■ an indistinct memory or impression of events, typically because they happened very fast: *the day before was a blur.* —**blur·ry** *adj.*

blurb /blərb/ ▶*n.* a short description of a book, movie, or other product written for promotional purposes and appearing on the cover of a book or in an advertisement.
▶*v.* [*tr.*] *inf.* write or contribute such a passage for (a book, movie, or other product).

blurt /blərt/ ▶*v.* [*tr.*] say (something) suddenly and without careful consideration: *she wouldn't **blurt out** words she did not mean.*

blush /bləsh/ ▶*v.* [*intr.*] develop a pink tinge in the face from embarrass-

ment or shame: *she blushed at the unexpected compliment.* ■ feel embarrassed or ashamed.
▶*n.* **1** a reddening of the face as a sign of embarrassment or shame: *he had brought a faint blush to her cheeks.* ■ a pink or pale red tinge: *the roses were white with a lovely pink blush.* ■ another term for BLUSHER). **2** (also **blush wine**) a wine with a slight pink tint made in the manner of white wine but from red grape varieties.

blush·er /'bləshər/ ▶*n.* a cosmetic of a powder or cream consistency used to give a warm color to the cheeks. Also called BLUSH.

blus·ter /'bləstər/ ▶*v.* [*intr.*] talk in a loud, aggressive, or indignant way with little effect: *you threaten and bluster, but won't carry it through.* ■ (of a storm, wind, or rain) blow or beat fiercely and noisily: *a winter gale blustered against the sides of the house.*
▶*n.* loud, aggressive, or indignant talk with little effect: *their threats contained a measure of bluster.* —**blus·ter·er** *n.* —**blus·ter·y** *adj.*

blvd. ▶*abbr.* boulevard.

B-mov·ie ▶*n.* a low-budget movie, esp. one made for use as a companion to the main attraction in a double feature: [as *adj.*] *a B-movie actress.*

bo·a /'bōə/ ▶*n.* **1** a constrictor snake (family Boidae) that bears live young and may reach great size, native to America, Africa, Asia, and some Pacific islands. Its numerous species include the large **boa constrictor** (*Boa constrictor*) of tropical America. **2** a long thin stole of feathers or fur worn around a woman's neck, typically as part of evening dress.

boar /bôr/ ▶*n.* (*pl.* same or **boars**) **1** (also **wild boar**) a tusked Eurasian wild pig (*Sus scrofa*) from which domestic pigs are descended. ■ the flesh of the wild boar as food. **2** an uncastrated domestic male pig.

board /bôrd/ ▶*n.* **1** a long, thin, flat piece of wood or other hard material, used for floors or other building purposes: *loose boards creaked as I walked on them.* ■ (**the boards**) *inf.* the stage of a theater. **2** a thin, flat, rectangular piece of wood or other stiff material used for various purposes, in particular: ■ a vertical surface on which to write or pin notices. ■ a horizontal surface on which to cut things, play games, or perform other activities. ■ a flat insulating sheet used as a mounting for an electronic circuit: *a graphics board.* ■ the piece of equipment on which a person stands in surfing, skateboarding, snowboarding, and certain other sports. ■ (**boards**) the wooden structure surrounding an ice-hockey rink. ■ (usu. **boards**) *Basketball* informal term for BACKBOARD, referring specifically to rebounding: *center David Robinson dominates on the boards.* ■ (**boards**) pieces of thick stiff cardboard used for book covers. **3** [treated as *sing.* or *pl.*] a group of people constituted as the decision-making body of an organization: *he sits on the board of directors.* **4** the provision of regular meals when one stays somewhere, in return for payment or services: *your room and board will be free.*
▶*v.* **1** [*tr.*] get on or into (a ship, aircraft, or other vehicle): *we boarded the plane for Oslo* | [*intr.*] *they would not be able to board without a ticket.* ■ (**be boarding**) (of an aircraft) be ready for passengers to embark: *flight 172 to Istanbul is now boarding at gate 37.* **2** [*intr.*] live and receive regular meals in a house in return for payment or services: *the cousins boarded for a while with Ruby.* ■ (of a student) live at school during the semester in return for payment. ■ [*tr.*] (often **be boarded**) provide (a person or animal) with regular meals and somewhere to live in return for payment: *dogs may have to be boarded at kennels.* **3** [*tr.*] (**board something up**) cover or seal a window, storefront, or other structure with pieces of wood: *the shop was still boarded up.* ▷Old English *bord*, of Germanic origin; related to Dutch *boord* and German *Bort*; reinforced in Middle English by Old French *bort* 'edge, ship's side' and Old Norse *borth* 'board, table.'
▶ □ **go by the board** (of something planned or previously upheld) be abandoned, rejected, or ignored: *my education just went by the board.* □ **on board** on or in a ship, aircraft, or other vehicle. ■ *inf.* onto a team or group as a member: *the need to bring on board a young manager.*

board·er /'bôrdər/ ▶*n.* **1** a person who receives regular meals when staying somewhere, in return for payment or services. **2** a person who takes part in a sport using a board, such as surfing or snowboarding.

board·ing·house /'bôrdiNG,hous/ (also **board·ing-house** or **board·ing house**) ▶*n.* a house providing food and lodging for paying guests.

board·ing school ▶*n.* a school where students reside during the semester.

board·room /'bôrd,rōōm/ ▶*n.* a room in which the members of a board meet regularly. ■ the directors of a company or organization considered collectively.

board·walk /'bôrd,wôk/ ▶*n.* a wooden walkway across sand or marshy ground. ■ a promenade along a beach or waterfront, typically made of wood.

boast /bōst/ ▶*v.* **1** talk with excessive pride and self-satisfaction about one's achievements, possessions, or abilities: [with *direct speech*] *Ted* used to boast, "I manage ten people" **2** [tr.] (of a person, place, or thing) possess (a feature that is a source of pride): *the hotel boasts high standards of comfort.*

▶*n.* an act of talking with excessive pride and self-satisfaction: *I said I would score, and it wasn't an idle boast.* —**boast·er** *n.* —**boast·ing·ly** *adv.*

boast·ful /ˈbōstfəl/ ▶*adj.* showing excessive pride and self-satisfaction in one's achievements, possessions, or abilities. —**boast·ful·ly** *adv.* —**boast·ful·ness** *n.*

boat /bōt/ ▶*n.* **1** a small vessel propelled on water by oars, sails, or an engine: *a fishing boat.* ■ (in general use) a ship of any size. **2** a serving dish in the shape of a boat: *a gravy boat.*

▶*v.* [intr.] travel or go in a boat for pleasure: *they boated through fjords* [as *n.*] (**boating**) *she likes to go boating.* ■ [tr.] to bring a caught fish into a boat. —**boat·ful** *n.* —**boat·man** *n.*

▶ □ **be in the same boat** *inf.* be in the same unfortunate circumstances as others. □ **rock the boat** *inf.* say or do something to disturb an existing situation.

boat·house /ˈbōtˌhous/ ▶*n.* a shed at the edge of a river or lake used for housing boats.

boat·ing /ˈbōtiNG/ ▶*n.* rowing or sailing in boats as a sport or form of recreation.

boat peo·ple ▶*pl. n.* refugees who have left a country by sea, in particular the Vietnamese who fled in small boats to Hong Kong, Australia, and elsewhere after the conquest of South Vietnam by North Vietnam in 1975.

boat·swain /ˈbōsən/ (also **bo'sun** or **bo·sun**) ▶*n.* a ship's officer in charge of equipment and the crew.

bob[1] /bäb/ ▶*v.* (**bobbed**, **bob·bing**) [intr.] (of a thing) make a quick short movement up and down: *I could see his red head bobbing around | the boat bobbed up and down.* ■ [tr.] cause (something) to make such a movement: *she bobbed her head.* ■ [intr.] make a sudden move in a particular direction so as to appear or disappear: *a lady bobbed up from beneath the counter.* ■ [intr.] move up and down briefly in a curtsy.

▶*n.* a movement up and down: *she could only manage a slight bob of her head.* ■ a curtsy.

▶ □ **bob and weave** make rapid bodily movements up and down and from side to side, for example as an evasive tactic by a boxer.

bob[2] ▶*n.* **1** a style in which the hair is cut short and evenly all around so that it hangs above the shoulders. **2** a weight on a pendulum, plumb line, or kite-tail.

▶*v.* (**bobbed**, **bob·bing**) **1** [tr.] [usu. as adj.] (**bobbed**) cut (someone's hair) in a bob: *she tied a headscarf over her bobbed brown hair.* **2** [intr.] ride on a bobsled.

bob[3] *Brit., inf.* ▶*n.* (*pl.* same) a shilling. ■ used with reference to a moderately large but unspecified amount of money: *those vases are worth a few bob.*

bob·ber /ˈbäbər/ ▶*n.* a small float placed on a fishing line to hold the hook at the desired depth.

bob·bin /ˈbäbin/ ▶*n.* a cylinder or cone holding thread, yarn, or wire, used esp. in weaving, machine sewing, and lacemaking. ■ a spool or reel.

bob·ble *inf.* ▶*v.* **1** [tr.] mishandle (a ball): *Andy bobbled the ball, so his throw home was too late.* **2** [intr.] move with an irregular bouncing motion: *the glare of the snow made the landscape bobble.*

▶*n.* **1** a mishandling of a ball: *a once-a-season bobble by Jordan en route to a breakaway jam.* **2** an irregular bouncing motion.

bob·by pin ▶*n.* a kind of sprung hairpin or small clip.

▶*v.* (**bob·by-pin**) [tr.] fix (hair) in place with such a pin or clip.

bob·by socks (also **bob·by sox**) ▶*pl. n. dated* short socks reaching just above the ankle (used chiefly in the 1940s and 1950s to refer to the socks worn by teenage girls).

bob·cat /ˈbäbˌkat/ ▶*n.* a small North American cat (*Lynx rufus*) with a barred and spotted coat and a short tail.

bob·sled /ˈbäbˌsled/ ▶*n.* a mechanically steered and braked sled, typically manned by crews of two or four, used for racing down a steep ice-covered run with banked curves. —**bob·sled·ding** *n.*

bob·white /ˈbäb(h)wīt/ (also **bobwhite quail**) ▶*n.* a New World quail with mottled reddish-brown plumage, in particular the **northern** (or **common**) **bobwhite** (*Colinus virginianus*).

bock /bäk/ (also **bock beer**) ▶*n.* a strong dark beer brewed in the fall and drunk in the spring.

bo·da·cious /bōˈdāsHəs/ ▶*adj. inf.* excellent, admirable, or attractive: *the restaurant serves bodacious grilled lobster.* ■ audacious in a way considered admirable: *those bodacious dudes have an excellent time playing games with death.*

bode /bōd/ ▶*v.* [intr.] (**bode well/ill**) be an omen of a particular outcome: *their argument did not bode well for the future.*

bo·de·ga /bōˈdāgə/ ▶*n.* a grocery store in a Spanish-speaking neighborhood.

bod·ice /ˈbädis/ ▶*n.* the part of a woman's dress (excluding sleeves) that is above the waist. ■ a woman's vest, esp. a laced vest worn as an outer garment. ■ a woman's vestlike undergarment.

bod·i·ly /ˈbädl-ē/ ▶*adj.* of or concerning the body: *children learn to control their bodily functions.* ■ material or actual as opposed to spiritual or incorporeal: *God is not present in bodily form.*

▶*adv.* by taking hold of a person's body, esp. with force: *he hauled her bodily from the van.* ■ with one's whole body; with great force: *he launched himself bodily at the door.*

bod·kin /ˈbädkin/ ▶*n.* a blunt thick needle with a large eye used esp. for drawing tape or cord through a hem. ■ a small pointed instrument used to pierce cloth or leather.

bod·y /ˈbädē/ ▶*n.* (*pl.* **bod·ies**) **1** the physical structure of a person or an animal, including the bones, flesh, and organs: *it's important to keep your body in good condition.* ■ a corpse: *they found his body washed up on the beach.* ■ the physical and mortal aspect of a person as opposed to the soul or spirit: *a duality of body and soul.* ■ *inf.* a person's body regarded as an object of sexual desire: *he was just after her body.* **2** the trunk: *the blow almost severed his head from his body.* ■ (**the body of**) the main or central part of something, esp. a building or text: *information that changes regularly is kept apart from the main body of the text.* ■ the main section of a car or aircraft: *the body of the aircraft was filled with smoke.* ■ a large or substantial amount of something; a mass or collection of something: *a rich body of Canadian folklore.* ■ (in pottery) a clay used for making the main part of ceramic ware, as distinct from a glaze. **3** a group of people with a common purpose or function acting as an organized unit: *a regulatory body.* **4** *technical* a distinct material object: *the path taken by the falling body.* **5** a full or substantial quality of flavor in wine. ■ fullness or thickness of a person's hair: *designed to add body to limp and straight hair.* —**bod·ied** *adj.* [in comb.] *a wide-bodied jet.*

▶ □ **body and soul** involving every aspect of a person; completely: *the company owned them body and soul.* □ **over my dead body** *inf.* used to emphasize that one opposes something and would do anything to prevent it from happening: *she moves into our home over my dead body.*

bod·y·build·ing /ˈbädēˌbildiNG/ ▶*n.* the practice of strengthening and enlarging the muscles of the body through exercise. —**bod·y·build·er** /-ˌbildər/ *n.*

bod·y·guard /ˈbädēˌgärd/ ▶*n.* a person or group of persons hired to escort and protect another person, esp. a dignitary.

bod·y lan·guage ▶*n.* the process of communicating nonverbally through conscious or unconscious gestures and movements: *his intent was clearly expressed in his body language.*

bod·y pol·i·tic ▶*n.* (usu. **the body politic**) the people of a nation, state, or society considered collectively as an organized group of citizens.

bod·y shop ▶*n.* a garage where repairs to the bodies of vehicles are carried out.

bod·y stock·ing ▶*n.* a woman's one-piece undergarment that covers the torso and legs.

bod·y·suit /ˈbädēˌsoōt/ ▶*n.* a close-fitting one-piece stretch garment for women, typically worn for sports.

bod·y·work /ˈbädēˌwərk/ ▶*n.* **1** the metal outer shell of a vehicle. **2** therapies and techniques in complementary medicine that involve touching or manipulating the body. —**bod·y·work·er** *n.*

bod·y wrap ▶*n.* a type of beauty treatment involving the application of skin-cleansing ingredients to the body, which is then wrapped in hot towels.

Boer /bôr; boŏr/ *chiefly hist.* ▶*n.* a member of the Dutch and Huguenot population that settled in southern Africa in the late 17th century.

bog /bäg; bôg/ ▶*n.* wet muddy ground too soft to support a heavy body: *the island is a wilderness of bog | a peat bog | fig. a bog of legal complications.* ■ *Ecol.* wetland with acid, peaty soil, typically dominated by peat moss. Compare with FEN[1].

▶*v.* (**bogged**, **bog·ging**) [tr.] (usu. **be bogged down**) cause (a vehicle, person, or animal) to become stuck in mud or wet ground: *the car became bogged down on the beach road.* ■ (**be bogged down**) *fig.* (of a person or process) be unable to make progress: *you must not get bogged down in detail.* ▷Middle English: from Irish or Scottish Gaelic *bogach*, from *bog* 'soft.' —**bog·gy** *adj.* —**bog·gi·ness** *n.*

bo·gey[1] /'bōgē/ *Golf* ▶*n.* (*pl.* **-geys**) a score of one stroke over par at a hole.
▶*v.* (**-geys, -geyed**) [*tr.*] play (a hole) in one stroke over par.

bo·gey[2] /'bōōgē/ (also **bo·gy**) ▶*n.* (*pl.* **-geys**) a person or thing that causes fear or alarm: *the bogey of recession.* ■ an evil or mischievous spirit. ■ *inf.* an enemy aircraft.

bo·gey·man /'bōōgē,man; 'bō-/ (also **boo·gey·man, bo·gy·man**) ▶*n.* (*pl.* **-men**) (usu. **the bogeyman**) an imaginary evil spirit, referred to typically to frighten children: *with the blankets pulled over our heads to keep out the bogeyman.* ■ a person or thing that is widely regarded as an object of fear: *the violent criminal has replaced the communist as the bogeyman.*

bog·gle /'bägəl/ ▶*v.* [*intr.*] *inf.* (of a person or a person's mind) be astonished or overwhelmed when trying to imagine something: *the mind boggles at the spectacle.* ■ [*tr.*] cause (a person or a person's mind) to be astonished in such a way: *the inflated salary of a CEO boggles the mind*

bo·gus /'bōgəs/ ▶*adj.* not genuine or true; fake: *a bogus insurance claim.* —**bo·gus·ly** *adv.* —**bo·gus·ness** *n.*

bo·gy·man ▶*n.* variant spelling of BOGEYMAN.

Bo·he·mi·an /bō'hēmēən/ ▶*n.* **1** a native or inhabitant of Bohemia. **2** (also **bo·he·mi·an**) a person who has informal and unconventional social habits, esp. an artist or writer: *the young bohemians with their art galleries and sushi bars.*
▶*adj.* **1** of or relating to Bohemia or its people. **2** (also **bo·he·mi·an**) having informal and unconventional social habits: *the bohemian writer's drafty-garret existence.* —**Bo·he·mi·an·ism** *n.*

boil[1] /boil/ ▶*v.* **1** [*tr.*] heat (a liquid) to the temperature at which it bubbles and turns to vapor: *we tried to get people to boil their drinking water.* ■ (of a liquid) be at or reach this temperature: *he waited for the water to boil.* ■ heat (a container) until the liquid in it reaches such a temperature: [*tr.*] *she boiled the kettle and took down a couple of mugs.* ■ [*intr.*] (of a container) be heated until the liquid in it reaches such a temperature: *the kettle boiled and he filled the teapot.* **2** [*tr.*] subject (something) to the heat of boiling liquid, in particular: ■ cook (food) by immersing in boiling water: *boil the potatoes until well done* | [as *adj.*] (**boiled**) *two boiled eggs.* ■ [*intr.*] (of food) be cooked in boiling water: *make the sauce while the lobsters are boiling.* **3** [*intr.*] (of the sea or clouds) be turbulent and stormy: *a huge cliff with the black sea boiling below.* ■ (of a person or strong emotion) be stirred up or inflamed: *he was boiling with rage.*
▶*phrasal v.* ☐ **boil down to** be in essence a matter of: *everything boiled down to cash in the end.* ☐ **boil over** (of a liquid) flow over the sides of the container in boiling. ■ *fig.* (of a situation or strong emotion) become so excited or tense as to get out of control: *one woman's anger boiled over.*
▶*n.* **1** the temperature at which a liquid bubbles and turns to vapor: *stir in cream and* **bring to a boil.** ■ an act or process of heating a liquid to such a temperature. ■ *fig.* a state of vigorous activity or excitement. ■ an area of churning water. ■ *Fishing* a sudden rise of a fish at a fly. **2** an outdoor meal at which seafood is boiled: *everything for a traditional Louisiana seafood boil can be carried down to the beach.* ■ a blend of seasonings added to water to enhance the flavor of boiled seafood: *a salt-free seafood boil.*

boil[2] ▶*n.* an inflamed pus-filled swelling on the skin, typically caused by the infection of a hair follicle.

boil·er /'boilər/ ▶*n.* a fuel-burning apparatus or container for heating water, in particular: ■ a household device providing a hot-water supply or serving a central heating system. ■ a tank for generating steam under pressure in a steam engine.

boil·ing /'boiliNG/ ▶*adj.* (for fresh water at sea level) at 212°F (100°C). ■ *inf.* extremely hot: *Saturday is forecast to be boiling and sunny.* ■ (of an emotion) intensely and powerfully felt: *his boiling hatred of oppression.*
▶*n.* the action of bringing a liquid to the temperature at which it bubbles and turns to vapor. ■ the temperature at which such an event occurs: *reheat gently to just below boiling.*

boil·ing point ▶*n.* the temperature at which a liquid boils and turns to vapor. ■ *fig.* the point at which anger or excitement breaks out into violent expression: *racial tension surges to boiling point.*

bois·ter·ous /'boist(ə)rəs/ ▶*adj.* (of a person, event, or behavior) noisy, energetic, and cheerful; rowdy: *the boisterous conviviality associated with taverns of that period.* ■ (of wind, weather, or water) wild or stormy: *the boisterous wind was lulled.* —**bois·ter·ous·ly** *adv.* —**bois·ter·ous·ness** *n.*

bok choy /'bäk 'CHoi/ ▶*n.* Chinese cabbage of a variety with smooth-edged tapering leaves.

bo·la /'bōlə/ (also **bo·las**) ▶*n.* (esp. in South America) a weapon consisting of a number of balls connected by strong cord, which when thrown entangles the limbs of the quarry.

bold /bōld/ ▶*adj.* **1** (of a person, action, or idea) showing an ability to take risks; confident and courageous: *a bold attempt to solve the crisis* | *he*

was the only one bold enough to air his dislike. ■ **dated** (of a person or manner) so confident as to suggest a lack of shame or modesty: *she tossed him a bold look.* **2** (of a color or design) having a strong or vivid appearance: *a coat with bold polka dots.* ■ (of a typeface) having thick strokes. **3** (of a cliff or coastline) steep or projecting: *bold, craggy edges on the lip of the plateau.*
▶*n.* a typeface with thick strokes: *difficult words and phrases are highlighted in bold.* —**bold·ly** *adv.* —**bold·ness** *n.*

bo·le·ro /bə'le(ə)rō/ ▶*n.* (*pl.* **-ros**) **1** a Spanish dance in simple triple time. ■ a piece of music for this dance. **2** a woman's short open jacket.

bol·lard /'bälərd/ ▶*n.* a short, thick post on the deck of a ship or on a wharf, to which a ship's rope may be secured.

boll wee·vil /bōl/ ▶*n.* a small weevil (*Anthonomus grandis,* family Curculionidae) that feeds on the fibers of the rounded seed capsule (the **boll**) of a cotton plant. It is a major pest of the American cotton crop. ■ *inf.* in the U.S., a conservative Southern Democrat, esp. a member of Congress.

bo·lo·gna /bə'lōnē/ (also **bologna sausage**) ▶*n.* a large smoked, seasoned sausage made of various meats, esp. beef and pork.

bo·lo·ney ▶*n.* variant spelling of BALONEY.

Bol·she·vik /'bōlsHə,vik/ ▶*n. hist.* a member of the majority faction of the Russian Social Democratic Party, which was renamed the Communist Party after seizing power in the October Revolution of 1917. ■ *chiefly derog.* (in general use) a person with politically subversive or radical views; a revolutionary.
▶*adj.* of, relating to, or characteristic of Bolsheviks or their views or policies. —**Bol·she·vism** /-,vizəm/ *n.* —**Bol·she·vist** /-vist/ *n.*

bol·ster /'bōlstər/ ▶*n.* (also **bolster pillow**) a long, thick pillow that is placed under other pillows for support. ■ a part, as of a vehicle or tool, providing structural support.
▶*v.* [*tr.*] support or strengthen; prop up: *the fall in interest rates is starting to bolster confidence* | *he wished to bolster up his theories with hard data.* ■ provide (a seat) with padded support: [as *adj.*] (**bolstered**) *I snuggled down into the heavily bolstered seat.*

bolt[1] /bōlt/ ▶*n.* **1** a metal pin or bar, in particular: ■ a bar that slides into a socket to fasten a door or window. ■ a threaded pin that screws into a nut and is used to fasten things together. ■ the sliding piece of the breech mechanism of a rifle. ■ (in rock climbing) a long pin that is driven into a rock face so that a rope can be attached to it. **2** a short heavy arrow shot from a crossbow. **3** a flash of lightning leaving a jagged line across the sky.
▶*v.* [*tr.*] fasten (something) with a metal pin or bar, in particular: ■ fasten (a door or window) with a bar that slides into a socket: *all the doors were locked and bolted.* ■ [*tr.*] fasten (an object) to something else with a bolt: *a camera was bolted to the aircraft.*
▶ ☐ **a bolt from** (or **out of**) **the blue** a sudden and unexpected event or piece of news: *the job came like a bolt from the blue.* ☐ **bolt upright** upright, with the back rigid and straight: *she sat bolt upright in bed.*

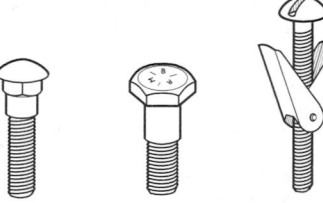

carriage bolt   hex-head bolt   toggle bolt
bolts

bolt[2] ▶*v.* **1** [*intr.*] (of a horse or other animal) run away suddenly out of control: *the horses shied and bolted.* ■ [*intr.*] (of a person) move or run away suddenly: *they bolted down the stairs.* ■ (of a plant) grow tall quickly and stop flowering as seeds develop: *the lettuce has bolted.* **2** [*tr.*] (often **bolt something down**) eat or swallow (food) quickly: *it is normal for puppies to bolt down their food.*
▶ ☐ **make a bolt for** try to escape by moving suddenly toward (something): *Ellie made a bolt for the door.*

bolt[3] ▶*n.* a roll of fabric, originally as a measure: *the room is stacked with bolts of cloth.*

bomb /bäm/ ▶*n.* **1** a container filled with explosive, incendiary material, smoke, gas, or other destructive substance, designed to explode on impact or when detonated by a time mechanism, remote-control device, or lit fuse. ■ an explosive device fitted into a specified object: *a* *package bomb.* See also **LETTER BOMB.** ■ **(the bomb)** nuclear weapons considered collectively as agents of mass destruction: *she joined the fight against the bomb.* ■ a small pressurized container that sprays liquid, foam, or gas: *an aerosol bomb.* **2** a thing resembling a bomb in impact, in particular: ■ a lump of lava thrown out by a volcano. ■ *inf.* a movie, play, or other event that fails badly: *that bomb of an old movie.* ■ a long forward pass or hit in a ball game: *a big 40-yard bomb down the middle to tight end Howard Cross.* ■ an old car. **3** *inf.* **(da** or **the) bomb)** an outstandingly good person or thing: *the site would really be da bomb if its content were updated more frequently.* **4** *inf.* a marijuana cigarette.

▶*v.* **1** [*tr.*] attack (a place or vehicle) with a bomb or bombs: *London was bombed, night after night* | [as n.] **(bombing)** *a series of bombings.* **2** [*intr.*] *inf.* (of a movie, play, or other event) fail miserably: *a big-budget movie that bombed at the box office.* ▷late 17th cent.: from French *bombe,* from Italian *bomba,* probably from Latin *bombus* 'booming, humming,' from Greek *bombos,* of imitative origin.

bom·bard /bämˈbärd/ ▶*v.* [*tr.*] attack (a place or person) continuously with bombs, shells, or other missiles: *the city was bombarded by federal forces* | *supporters* **bombarded** police **with** *bottles.* ■ assail (someone) persistently, as with questions, criticisms, or information: *they will be* **bombarded with** *complaints.* ■ *Physics* direct a high-speed stream of particles at (a substance). —**bom·bard·ment** *n.*

bom·bar·dier /ˌbämbə(r)ˈdi(ə)r/ ▶*n.* a member of a bomber crew in the U.S. Air Force responsible for sighting and releasing bombs.

bom·bast /ˈbämbast/ ▶*n.* high-sounding language with little meaning, used to impress people. —**bom·bas·tic** *adj.* —**bom·bas·ti·cal·ly** *adv.*

bombe /bäm(b)/ ▶*n.* a frozen dome-shaped dessert.

bomb·er /ˈbämər/ ▶*n.* **1** an aircraft designed to carry and drop bombs. **2** a person who plants, detonates, or throws bombs in a public place, esp. as a terrorist. **3** *inf.* a cigarette containing marijuana.

bomb·er jack·et ▶*n.* a short jacket, usually leather, gathered at the waist and cuffs by elasticized bands and typically having a zipper front.

bomb·shell /ˈbämˌSHel/ ▶*n.* **1** an overwhelming surprise or disappointment: *the news came as a bombshell.* **2** *inf.* a very attractive woman: *a twenty-year-old* **blonde bombshell.**

bo·na fide /ˈbōnə ˌfīd; ˈbänə/ ▶*adj.* genuine; real: *only bona fide members of the company are allowed to use the logo.*

bo·na fi·des /ˈbōnə ˌfīdz; ˈfīdēz; ˈbänə/ ▶*n.* a person's honesty and sincerity of intention: *he went to great lengths to establish his liberal bona fides.* ■ [treated as *pl.*] *inf.* documentary evidence showing a person's legitimacy; credentials: *are you satisfied with my bona fides?*

bo·nan·za /bəˈnanzə/ ▶*n.* a situation or event that creates a sudden increase in wealth, good fortune, or profits: *a bonanza in military sales.* ■ a large amount of something desirable: *the festive feature film bonanza.*

bon·bon /ˈbänˌbän/ ▶*n.* a piece of candy, esp. one covered with chocolate.

bond /bänd/ ▶*n.* **1** **(bonds)** physical restraints used to hold someone or something prisoner, esp. ropes or chains. ■ a thing used to tie something or to fasten things together: *she brushed back a curl that had strayed from its bonds* | *fig. chaos could result if the bonds of obedience and loyalty were broken.* ■ adhesiveness; ability of two objects to stick to each other: *a total lack of effective bond between the concrete and the steel.* ■ *fig.* a force or feeling that unites people; a common emotion or interest: *there was a bond of understanding between them.* ■ **(bonds)** *fig.* restricting forces or circumstances; obligations: *bonds of loyalty.* **2** an agreement or promise with legal force, in particular: ■ *Law* a deed by which a person is committed to make payment to another. ■ a certificate issued by a government or a public company promising to repay borrowed money at a fixed rate of interest at a specified time. ■ (of dutiable goods) storage in a bonded warehouse until the importer pays the duty owing. **3** (also **chemical bond**) a strong force of attraction holding atoms together in a molecule or crystal, resulting from the sharing or transfer of electrons. **4** short for **BOND PAPER.**

▶*v.* **1** join or be joined securely to something else, typically by means of an adhesive substance, heat, or pressure: [*tr.*] *press the material to* **bond** the layers **together** | [*intr.*] *fig.* establish a relationship with someone based on shared feelings, interests, or experiences: *the failure to properly bond with their children* | *the team has* **bonded together** *well* | [as n.] **(bonding)** *the film has some great male bonding scenes.* **2** join or be joined by a chemical bond. **3** [usu. as *n.*] **(bonding)** place (dutiable goods) in bond.

bond·age /ˈbändij/ ▶*n.* **1** the state of being a slave: *the deliverance of the Israelites from Egypt's bondage.* ■ *fig.* a state of being greatly constrained by circumstances or obligations: *young women lost to the bondage of early motherhood.* **2** sexual practice that involves the tying up or restraining of one partner.

bond·ed /ˈbändid/ ▶*adj.* **1** (of a thing) joined securely to another thing,

esp. by an adhesive, a heat process, or pressure: *bonded metal plates.* ■ *fig.* emotionally or psychologically linked: *a strongly bonded group of females.* ■ held by a chemical bond: *bonded atoms.* **2** (of a person or company) bound by a legal agreement, in particular: ■ (of a debt) secured by bonds. ■ (of a worker or workforce) obliged to work for a particular employer, often in a condition close to slavery. **3** (of dutiable goods) placed in bond.

bond pa·per ▶*n.* high-quality writing paper.

bonds·man /ˈbändzmən/ ▶*n.* (*pl.* **-men**) a person who stands surety for a bond.

bone /bōn/ ▶*n.* **1** any of the pieces of hard, whitish tissue making up the skeleton in humans and other vertebrates: *his injuries included many broken bones* | *a shoulder bone.* ■ **(bones)** a person's body: *he hauled his tired bones upright.* ■ **(bones)** a corpse or skeleton: *the diggers turned up the bones of a fifteen-year-old girl* | *bones of prehistoric mammals.* ■ **(bones)** figurative the basic or essential framework of something: *you need to put some flesh on the bones of your idea.* ■ a bone of an animal with meat on it, used as food for people or dogs: *stewed in stock made with a ham bone* | *dogs yelping over a bone.* **2** the calcified material of which bones consist: *an earring of bone.* ■ a substance similar to this such as ivory, dentin, or whalebone. ■ (often **bones**) a thing made of, or once made of, such a substance, for example a pair of dice. **3** the whitish color of bone: *the sandals she had dyed bone to match the small purse.* **4** *vulgar slang* a penis.

▶*v.* **1** [*trans.*] remove the bones from (meat or fish): *while the gumbo is simmering, bone the cooked chicken.* **2** [*intrans.*] **(bone up on)** *informal* study (a subject) intensively, often in preparation for something: *she boned up on languages she had learned long ago and went back to New Guinea.* **3** [*trans.*] *vulgar slang* (of a man) have sexual intercourse with (someone). ▷Old English *bān,* of Germanic origin; related to Dutch *been* and German *Bein.* —**bone·less** *adj.*

▶ □ **a bag of bones** see **BAG.** □ **the bare bones** see **BARE.** □ **be skin and bones** see **SKIN.** □ **a bone of contention** a subject or issue over which there is continuing disagreement: *the examination system has long been a serious bone of contention.* □ **close to** (or **near**) **the bone 1** (of a remark) penetrating and accurate to the point of causing hurt or discomfort. **2** destitute; hard up. □ **cut** (or **pare**) **something to the bone** reduce something to the bare minimum: *costs will have to be cut to the bone.* □ **(as) dry as a bone** see **DRY.** □ **have a bone to pick with someone** *informal* have reason to disagree or be annoyed with someone. □ **have not a —— bone in one's body** (of a person) have not the slightest trace of the specified quality: *there's not a conservative bone in his body.* □ **in one's bones** felt, believed, or known deeply or instinctively: *he has rhythm in his bones* | *something good was bound to happen; he could* **feel it in his bones.** □ **make no bones about something** have no hesitation in stating or dealing with something, however awkward or distasteful it is: *the film is an op-ed piece, and the director makes no bones about its biases.* □ **to the bone 1** (of a wound) so deep as to expose a person's bone: *his thigh had been axed open to the bone* | *figurative his contempt cut her to the bone.* ■ (esp. of cold) affecting a person in a penetrating way: *chilled to the bone.* **2** (or **to one's bones**) used to emphasize that a person has a specified quality in an overwhelming or fundamental way: *she's a New Englander to her bones* | *he's a cop to the bone.* □ **throw a bone to** give someone only a token concession: *was the true purpose of the minimum wage hike to throw a bone to the unions?* □ **what's bred in the bone will come out in the flesh** (or **blood**) *proverb* a person's behavior or characteristics are determined by heredity. □ **work one's fingers to the bone** work very hard: *Tracy can work her fingers to the bone, but it's Ms. Green who gets the thanks.*

bone chi·na ▶*n.* fine china made of clay mixed with bone ash.

bone-dry ▶*adj.* extremely or completely dry.

bone·head /ˈbōnˌhed/ ▶*n.* *inf.* a stupid person. —**bone·head·ed** *adj.*

bone mar·row ▶*n.* see **MARROW** (sense 1).

bone·meal /ˈbōnˌmēl/ ▶*n.* crushed or ground bones used as a fertilizer.

bon·er /ˈbōnər/ ▶*n.* **1** *inf.* a stupid mistake. **2** *vulgar slang* an erection of the penis.

bon·fire /ˈbänˌfīr/ ▶*n.* a large open-air fire used as part of a celebration, for burning trash, or as a signal.

bong[1] /bäNG/ ▶*n.* a low-pitched sound as of a bell: *the clock had struck the hour, and it was only three bongs.*

▶*v.* [*intr.*] emit such a sound.

bong[2] ▶*n.* a water pipe used for smoking marijuana or other drugs.

Pronunciation Key ə *ago, up;* ər *over, fur;* a *hat;* ā *ate;* ä *car;* CH *chin;* e *let;* ē *see;* e(ə)r *air;* i *fit;* ī *by;* i(ə)r *ear;* NG *sing;* ō *go;* ô *law, for;* oi *toy;* o͝o *good;* o͞o *goo;* ou *out;* SH *she;* TH *thin;* TH *then;* (h)w *why;* ZH *vision*

bong³ ▸*n. Mountaineering* a large piton.

bon·go¹ /'bäNGgō; 'bôNG-/ (also **bongo drum**) ▸*n.* (*pl.* **-gos** or **-goes**) either of a pair of small, long-bodied drums typically held between the knees and played with the fingers.

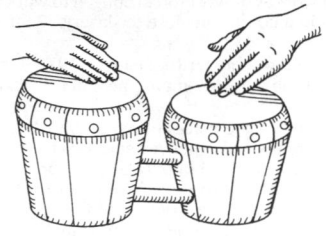

bongos

bon·go² ▸*n.* (*pl.* same or **-os**) a forest antelope (*Tragelaphus euryceros*) that has a chestnut coat with narrow white vertical stripes, native to central Africa.

bon·ho·mie /'bänə,mē; ,bänə'mē/ ▸*n.* cheerful friendliness; geniality: *he exuded good humor and bonhomie.* **—bon·hom·ous** /-məs/ *adj.*

bo·ni·to /bə'nētō/ ▸*n.* (*pl.* **-os**) a smaller relative of the tunas (*Sarda* and other genera), with dark oblique stripes on the back and important as a food and game fish.

bonk /bäNGk/ *inf.* ▸*v.* **1** [*tr.*] knock or hit (something) so as to cause a reverberating sound: *he bonked his head on the plane's low bulkhead.* **2** [*tr.*] have sexual intercourse with (someone).
▸*n.* **1** an act of knocking or hitting something that causes a reverberating sound: *give it a bonk with a hammer.* ■ a reverberating sound caused in such a way. **2** an act of sexual intercourse.

bon·kers /'bäNGkərz/ ▸*adj. inf.* mad; crazy: *and the fans go bonkers | he's driving me bonkers.*

bon mot /'bän 'mō; ,bôN 'mō/ ▸*n.* (*pl.* **bons mots** *pronunc.* same or /'mōz/) a witty remark.

bon·net /'bänit/ ▸*n.* **1** a woman's or child's hat tied under the chin, typically with a brim framing the face. ■ (also **war bonnet**) the ceremonial feathered headdress of an American Indian. **2** a protective cover or cap over a machine or object. ■ *Brit.* the hood of an automobile. **—bon·net·ed** *adj.*

bon·sai /bän'sī; 'bänsī/ ▸*n.* (*pl.* same) (also **bonsai tree**) an ornamental tree or shrub grown in a pot and artificially prevented from reaching its normal size. ■ the art of growing trees or shrubs in such a way.

bo·nus /'bōnəs/ ▸*n.* a payment or gift added to what is usual or expected, in particular: ■ an amount of money added to wages on a seasonal basis, esp. as a reward for good performance: *big Christmas bonuses.* ■ something welcome and often unexpected that accompanies and enhances something that is itself good: *good weather is an added bonus but the real appeal is the landscape.* ■ *Basketball* an extra free throw awarded to a fouled player when the opposing team has exceeded the number of team fouls allowed during a period. ▷*late 18th cent.* (probably originally London stock-exchange slang): from Latin *bonus* (masculine) 'good,' used in place of *bonum* (neuter) 'good, good thing.'

bon vi·vant /'bän vē'vänt; ,bôN vē'väN/ ▸*n.* (*pl.* **bon vi·vants** or **bons vi·vants** *pronunc.* same or /-'väNts/) a person who enjoys a sociable and luxurious lifestyle.

bon vo·yage /'bän voi'äzH; 'bôN; bôē/ ▸*interj.* used to express good wishes to someone about to go on a journey: *good luck and bon voyage!*

bon·y /'bōnē/ ▸*adj.* (**bon·i·er**, **bon·i·est**) of or like bone: *the bony plates that protect turtles and tortoises.* ■ (of a person or part of the body) so thin that the bones are prominent: *he held up his bony fingers.* ■ (of a fish eaten as food) having many bones. **—bon·i·ness** *n.*

boo /bōō/ ▸*interj.* **1** said suddenly to surprise someone: *"Boo!" she cried, jumping up to frighten him.* **2** said to show disapproval or contempt, esp. at a performance or athletic contest.
▸*n.* an utterance of "boo" to show disapproval or contempt: *the audience greeted this comment with boos and hisses.*
▸*v.* (**boos, booed**) say "boo" to show disapproval or contempt: [*intr.*] *they booed and hissed when he stepped on stage.*

boob¹ /bōōb/ *inf.* ▸*n.* a foolish or stupid person: *why was that boob given a key investigation?*

boob² ▸*n.* (usu. **boobs**) *inf.* a woman's breast.

boo-boo ▸*n. inf.* a mistake: *you could make a big boo-boo if you leap to any drastic conclusions.* ■ *inf.* a minor injury, such as a scratch.

boob tube *inf.* ▸*n.* television or a television set: *librarians are scrambling for ways to compete with the boob tube.*

boo·by¹ /'bōōbē/ ▸*n.* (*pl.* **-bies**) **1** a stupid or childish person. **2** a large tropical seabird (genus *Sula*) of the gannet family, with brown, black, or white plumage and often brightly colored feet.

boo·by² ▸*n.* (*pl.* **-bies**) (usu. **boobies**) *inf.* a woman's breast.

boo·by prize ▸*n.* a prize given as a joke to the last-place finisher in a race or competition.

boo·by trap ▸*n.* a thing designed to catch the unwary, in particular: ■ an apparently harmless object containing a concealed explosive device designed to kill or injure anyone who touches it: *miles of mines, booby traps, and underground fortifications.* ■ a trap intended as a practical joke, such as an object placed on top of a door ajar ready to fall on the next person to pass through.
▸*v.* (**boob·y-trap**) [*tr.*] place a booby trap in or on (an object or area).

boog·ey·man ▸*n.* variant spelling of **BOGEYMAN**.

boog·ie /'bōōgē/ ▸*n.* (also **boog·ie-woog·ie** /'wōōgē/) (*pl.* **boog·ies**) a style of blues played on the piano with a strong, fast beat. ■ *inf.* a dance to fast pop or rock music.
▸*v.* (**boog·ie·ing**) [*intr.*] *inf.* dance to fast pop or rock music: *ready to boogie down to the music of the house band.* ■ [*intr.*] move or leave somewhere fast: *let's boogie! | I think we'd better boogie on out of here.*

book /bŏŏk/ ▸*n.* **1** a written or printed work consisting of pages glued or sewn together along one side and bound in covers: *a book of selected poems.* ■ a literary composition that is published or intended for publication as such a work: *the book is set in the 1940s.* ■ (**the books**) used to refer to studying: *he is so deep in his books he would forget to eat.* ■ a main division of a classic literary work, an epic, or the Bible: *the Book of Genesis.* ■ (**the book**) the local telephone directory: *is your name in the book?* ■ (**the Book**) the Bible. ■ *inf.* a magazine. ■ *fig.* an imaginary record or list (often used to emphasize the thoroughness or comprehensiveness of someone's actions or experiences): *she felt every emotion in the book of love.* **2** a bound set of blank sheets for writing or keeping records in: *an accounts book.* ■ (**books**) a set of records or accounts: *he can balance the books.* ■ a bookmaker's record of bets accepted and money paid out. **3** a set of tickets, stamps, matches, checks, samples of cloth, etc., bound together: *a pattern book.* ■ (**the book**) the first six tricks taken by the declarer in a hand of bridge.
▸*v.* [*tr.*] **1** reserve (accommodations, a place, etc.); buy (a ticket) in advance: *I have booked a table at the Swan.* ■ reserve accommodations for (someone): *his secretary had booked him into the Howard Hotel.* ■ engage (a performer or guest) for an occasion or event. ■ (**be booked (up)**) have all appointments or places reserved; be full. **2** make an official record of the name and other personal details of (a criminal suspect or offender): *the cop booked me and took me down to the station.*
▶ □ **by the book** strictly according to the rules: *a cop who doesn't exactly play it by the book.* □ **close the book on** lay aside; expend no further energy on: *Congress closed the book on wool subsidies.* □ **in my book** in my opinion: *that counts as a lie in my book.* □ **one for the books** an extraordinary feat or event. □ **throw the book at** *inf.* charge or punish (someone) as severely as possible. □ **wrote the book** be the leader in the field: *John wrote the book on extreme biking.*

book·bind·er /'bŏŏk,bīndər/ ▸*n.* a person who binds books as a profession. **—book·bind·ing** /-,bīndiNG/ *n.*

book·case /'bŏŏk,kās/ ▸*n.* a set of shelves for books set in a surrounding frame or cabinet.

book·end /'bŏŏk,end/ ▸*n.* a support for the end of a row of books to keep them upright, often one of a pair.
▸*v.* [*tr.*] (usu. **be bookended**) *inf.* occur or be positioned at the end or on either side of (something): *the narrative is bookended by a pair of essays.*

book·ie /'bŏŏkē/ ▸*n.* (*pl.* **-ies**) informal term for **BOOKMAKER**.

book·ing /'bŏŏkiNG/ ▸*n.* an act of reserving accommodations, travel, etc., or of buying a ticket in advance: *the hotel does not handle group bookings.* ■ an engagement for a performance by an entertainer.

book·ish /'bŏŏkisH/ ▸*adj.* (of a person or way of life) devoted to reading and studying rather than worldly interests: *by comparison I was very bookish, intellectual, and wordy in a wrong way.* ■ (of language or writing) literary in style or allusion: *long bookish scholarship.* **—book·ish·ly** *adv.* **—book·ish·ness** *n.*

book·keep·ing /'bŏŏk,kēpiNG/ ▸*n.* the activity or occupation of keeping records of the financial affairs of a business. **—book·keep·er** *n.*

book learn·ing ▸*n.* knowledge gained from books or study; mere theory: *knowledge based on experience rather than book learning.*

book·let /'bŏŏklit/ ▸*n.* a small book consisting of a few sheets, typically with paper covers.

book·mak·er /ˈbo͝okˌmākər/ ▸n. a person who takes bets (esp. on horse races), calculates odds, and pays out winnings. —**book·mak·ing** n.

book·mark /ˈbo͝okˌmärk/ ▸n. a strip of leather, cardboard, or other material, used to mark one's place in a book. ■ Comput. a record of the address of a file, web page, or other data used to enable quick access by a user.
▸v. Comput. record the address of (a file, web page, or other data) for quick access by a user: if you think politics is the ultimate game, be sure to bookmark eVote.

book·plate /ˈbo͝okˌplāt/ ▸n. a decorative label stuck in the front of a book, bearing the name of the book's owner.

book·sell·er /ˈbo͝okˌselər/ ▸n. a person who sells books, esp. as the owner or manager of a bookstore.

book·store /ˈbo͝okˌstôr/ (also chiefly Brit. **book·shop** /-ˌSHäp/) ▸n. a store where books are sold.

book val·ue ▸n. the value of a security or asset as entered in a company's books. Often contrasted with MARKET VALUE.

book·worm /ˈbo͝okˌwərm/ ▸n. **1** inf. a person devoted to reading. **2** the larva of a wood-boring beetle that feeds on the paper and glue in books.

Bool·e·an /ˈbo͞olēən/ ▸adj. denoting a system of algebraic notation used to represent logical propositions, esp. in computing and electronics.
▸n. Comput. a binary variable, having two possible values called "true" and "false."

Bool·e·an log·ic ▸n. a system in which the logical operators 'and,' 'or,' and 'not' are used in retrieving information from a computer database.

boom¹ /bo͞om/ ▸n. a loud, deep, resonant sound: the deep boom of the bass drum. ■ the characteristic resonant call of the bittern.
▸v. [intr.] make a loud, deep, resonant sound: thunder boomed in the sky. —**boom·y** adj.

boom² ▸n. a period of great prosperity or rapid economic growth: a boom in precious metal mining | [as adj.] a boom economy.
▸v. [intr.] undergo a period of great prosperity or rapid economic growth: business is booming.

boom³ ▸n. a long pole or rod, in particular: ■ a spar to which the foot of a vessel's sail is attached. ■ [often as adj.] a movable arm over a television or movie set, carrying a microphone or camera: a boom mike. ■ a long beam extending upward at an angle from the mast of a derrick, for guiding or supporting objects being moved or suspended. ■ a floating beam used to contain oil spills or to form a barrier across the mouth of a harbor or river. ■ a retractable tube for inflight transfer of fuel from a tanker airplane to another airplane.

boom box ▸n. inf. a portable sound system, typically including radio and cassette or CD player, capable of powerful sound: teenagers dance to boom boxes on warm April nights.

boo·mer·ang /ˈbo͞oməˌraNG/ ▸n. a curved flat piece of wood that can be thrown so as to return to the thrower, traditionally used by Australian Aboriginals as a hunting weapon.
▸v. [intr.] (of a plan or action) return to the originator, often with negative consequences: misleading consumers about quality will eventually boomerang on a carmaker.

boom town (also **boom·town**) ▸n. a town undergoing rapid growth due to sudden prosperity.

boon¹ /bo͞on/ ▸n. a thing that is helpful or beneficial: the navigation system will be a boon to both civilian and military users.

boon² ▸adj. (of a companion or friend) close; intimate; favorite: he debated the question with a few boon companions in the barroom.

boomerang

boon·docks /ˈbo͞onˌdäks/ ▸pl. n. inf. rough, remote, or isolated country: we're out here in the boondocks, miles from a telephone. ▷1940s: boondock from Tagalog bundok 'mountain.'

boon·dog·gle /ˈbo͞onˌdägəl; -ˌdôgəl/ inf. ▸n. work or activity that is wasteful or pointless but gives the appearance of having value: writing off the cold fusion phenomenon as a boondoggle best buried in literature. ■ a public project of questionable merit that typically involves political patronage and graft.

boon·ies /ˈbo͞onēz/ ▸pl. n. short for BOONDOCKS.

boor /bo͝or/ ▸n. a rude, unmannerly person: at last the big obnoxious boor had been dealt a stunning blow for his uncouth and belligerent manner. ■ a clumsy person. ■ a peasant; a yokel. —**boor·ish** adj. —**boor·ish·ly** adv. —**boor·ish·ness** n.

boost /bo͞ost/ ▸v. [tr.] help or encourage (something) to increase or improve: a range of measures to boost tourism. ■ push from below; assist: people they were trying to boost over a wall. ■ amplify (an electrical signal). ■ Informal steal, esp. by shoplifting or pickpocketing.
▸n. a source of help or encouragement leading to increase or improvement: the cut in interest rates will give a further boost to the economy. ■ an increase or improvement: a boost in exports. ■ a push from below.

boost·er /ˈbo͞ostər/ ▸n. **1** a person or thing that helps increase or promote something, in particular: ■ a keen promoter of a person, organization, or cause: [as adj.] athletic booster clubs. ■ a source of help or encouragement: job fairs are a great morale booster. ■ Med. a dose of an immunizing agent increasing or renewing the effect of an earlier one. ■ the first stage of a rocket or spacecraft, used to give initial acceleration. ■ a device for increasing electrical voltage or signal strength. **2** inf. a shoplifter.

boost·er ca·ble ▸n. another term for JUMPER CABLE.

boot¹ /bo͞ot/ ▸n. **1** a sturdy item of footwear covering the foot, the ankle, and sometimes the leg below the knee: walking boots. ■ a covering or sheath to protect a mechanical connection, as on a gearshift. ■ (also **Denver boot**) a clamp placed by the police on the wheel of an illegally parked vehicle to make it immobile. **2** inf. a hard kick: I got a boot in the stomach. **3** Brit. the trunk of a car. **4** (also **boot up**) [usu. as adj.] the process of starting a computer and putting it into a state of readiness for operation: a boot disk. **5** Mil. a navy or marine recruit.
▸v. [tr.] **1** [usu. as adj.] (**booted**) place boots on (oneself, another person, or an animal): thin, booted legs. **2** [tr.] kick (something) hard in a specified direction: he ended up booting the ball into the stands. ■ (in an athletic contest) misplay (a ball); mishandle (a play). ■ (**boot someone out**) inf. force someone to leave a place, institution, or job unceremoniously: she had been booted out of school. **3** start (a computer) and put it into a state of readiness for operation: the menu will be ready as soon as you boot up your computer | [intr.] the system won't boot from the original drive.
▸ □ **get the boot** inf. be dismissed from one's job. □ **give someone the boot** inf. dismiss someone from their job.

boot² ▸n. (in phrase **to boot**) as well; in addition: images that are precise, revealing, and often beautiful to boot.

boot camp ▸n. a military training camp for new recruits, with strict discipline. ■ a prison for youthful offenders, run on military lines.

booth /bo͞oTH/ ▸n. **1** a small temporary tent or structure, used esp. for the sale or display of goods at a market or fair: there are booths offering everything from accessories to food to health care. ■ a small room where a vendor sits separated from customers by a window: a ticket booth. **2** an enclosure or compartment for various purposes, such as telephoning, broadcasting, or voting: the phone booth alongside the highway | ex-athletes in the broadcast booth. **3** a set of a table and benches in a restaurant or bar: I sat in a booth with coffee and a roll.

boot·ie /ˈbo͞otē/ (also **boot·ee**) ▸n. (pl. **-ies**) a soft shoe, typically knitted, worn by a baby. ■ any soft, socklike shoe.

boot·lace /ˈbo͞otˌlās/ ▸n. a cord or leather strip for lacing boots.

boot·leg /ˈbo͞otˌleg/ ▸adj. (esp. of liquor, computer software, or recordings) made, distributed, or sold illegally: bootleg cassettes | bootleg whiskey.
▸v. (**-legged**, **-leg·ging**) [tr.] make, distribute, or sell (illicit goods, esp. liquor, computer software, or recordings) illegally: [as n.] (**bootlegging**) domestic bootlegging was almost impossible to control.
▸n. **1** an illegal musical recording, esp. one made at a concert. **2** Football a play in which the quarterback fakes a handoff and runs with the ball hidden next to his hip. —**boot·leg·ger** n.

boot·less /ˈbo͞otlis/ ▸adj. archaic (of a task or undertaking) ineffectual; useless: words at this pass were vain and bootless.

boot·lick·er /ˈbo͞otˌlikər/ ▸n. inf. an obsequious or overly deferential person; a toady. —**boot·lick·ing** /-ˌlikiNG/ n.

boot·strap /ˈbo͞otˌstrap/ ▸n. **1** a loop at the back of a boot, used to pull it on. ■ [usu. as adj.] the technique of starting with existing resources to create something more complex and effective: her willingness to work night and day in a tiny basement office was evidence of her trademark bootstrap. **2** Comput. a technique of loading a program into a computer by means of a few initial instructions that enable the introduction of the rest of the program from an input device.
▸v. (**-strapped**, **-strap·ping**) **1** get (oneself or something) into or out of a situation using existing resources. **2** [tr.] start up (an enterprise), especially one based on the Internet, with minimal resources: they are bootstrapping their stations themselves, not with lots of dot-com venture capital.

Pronunciation Key ə ago, up; ər over, fur; a hat; ā ate; ä car; CH chin; e let; ē see; e(ə)r air; i fit; ī by; i(ə)r ear; NG sing; ō go; ô law, for; oi toy; o͝o good; o͞o goo; ou out; SH she; TH thin; TH then; (h)w why; ZH vision

▶ □ **pull oneself up by one's (own) bootstraps** improve one's position by one's own efforts.

boo·ty[1] /'bōōtē/ ▶ n. valuable stolen goods, esp. those seized in war: *the militias supply themselves with booty from the raided civilian populations.* ■ something gained or won: *now the booty: four winners will receive prizes.*

boo·ty[2] ▶ n. (pl. **-ties**) inf. a person's buttocks.

booze /bōōz/ inf. ▶ n. alcohol, esp. hard liquor: *they turn to booze to beat work pressure.*
▶ v. [intr.] drink alcohol, esp. in large quantities: *you used to booze a lot on expensive hard liquor.* —**booz·er** n. —**booz·y** adj.

bop[1] /bäp/ inf. ▶ n. short for BEBOP.
▶ v. (**bopped**, **bop·ping**) [intr.] dance to pop music: *bopping to the radio while they made breakfast.* ■ move or travel energetically: *we had been bopping around the county all morning.* —**bop·per** n.

bop[2] inf. ▶ v. (**bopped**, **bop·ping**) [tr.] hit; punch lightly: *I warned him I'd bop him on the nose if he tried it.*
▶ n. a blow or light punch.

bor·age /'bôrij; 'bär-/ ▶ n. a herbaceous plant (*Borago officinalis*, family Boraginaceae) with bright blue flowers and hairy leaves, used medicinally and as a salad green.

bo·rate /'bôrāt/ ▶ n. Chem. a salt in which the anion contains both boron and oxygen, as in borax.

bo·rax /'bôraks/ ▶ n. a white mineral, hydrated sodium borate, occurring in some alkaline salt deposits, used in making glass and ceramics, as a metallurgical flux, and as an antiseptic. —**bo·rac·ic** /bə'rasik/ adj.

bor·del·lo /bôr'delō/ ▶ n. (pl. **-los**) a brothel.

bor·der /'bôrdər/ ▶ n. 1 a line separating two political or geographical areas, esp. countries: *Iraq's northern* **border with** *Turkey.* 2 the edge or boundary of something, or the part near it: *the northern border of their distribution area.* 3 a band or strip, esp. a decorative one, around the edge of something: *put a white border around the picture.*
▶ v. [tr.] form an edge along or beside (something): *a pool bordered by palm trees.* ■ (of a country or area) be adjacent to (another country or area): *regions bordering Azerbaijan.* ■ [intr.] (**border on**) fig. be close to an extreme condition: *Sam arrived in a state of excitement bordering on hysteria.* ■ (usu. **be bordered with**) provide (something) with a decorative edge: *a curving driveway bordered with chrysanthemums.*

bor·der·land /'bôrdər,land/ ▶ n. (usu. **borderlands**) the district near a border. ■ fig. an area of overlap between two things: *the murky borderland between history and myth.*

bor·der·line /'bôrdər,līn/ ▶ n. a line marking a border. ■ fig. a division between two distinct (often extreme) conditions: *the borderline between ritual and custom.*
▶ adj. barely acceptable in quality or as belonging to a category; on the borderline: *references may be requested in borderline cases.*

bore[1] /bôr/ ▶ v. 1 [tr.] make (a hole) in something, esp. with a revolving tool: *they bored holes in the sides.* ■ [tr.] hollow out (a tube or tunnel): *try to bore the tunnel at the correct angle.* ■ [intr.] (**bore into**) fig. (of a person's eyes) stare harshly at: *your terrible blue eyes bore into me.* 2 [intr.] make one's way through (a crowd).
▶ n. the hollow part inside a gun barrel or other tube. ■ [often in comb.] the diameter of this; the caliber: *a small-bore rifle.* ■ [in comb.] a gun of a specified bore: *he shot a guard in the leg with a twelve-bore.*

bore[2] ▶ n. a person whose talk or behavior is dull and uninteresting: *a crashing bore who tells the same old jokes over and over.* ■ a tedious situation or thing: *it's such a bore cooking when one's alone.*
▶ v. [tr.] make (someone) feel weary and uninterested by tedious talk or dullness: *rather than bore you with all the details, I'll hit some of the bright spots.* —**bore·dom** n.

bore[3] ▶ n. a steep-fronted wave caused by the meeting of two tides or by the constriction of a tide rushing up a narrow estuary.

bore[4] ▶ past of BEAR[1].

bo·re·al /'bôrēəl/ ▶ adj. of the North or northern regions. ■ Ecol. relating to or characteristic of the climatic zone south of the Arctic, esp. the cold temperate region dominated by taiga and forests of birch, poplar, and conifers: *northern boreal forest.*

bore·hole /'bôr,hōl/ ▶ n. a deep, narrow hole made in the ground, esp. to locate water or oil.

bor·er /'bôrər/ ▶ n. 1 a worm, mollusk, insect, or insect larva that bores into wood, other plant material, or rock. 2 a tool for boring.

bo·ric /'bôrik/ ▶ adj. Chem. of boron: boric oxide.

bo·ric ac·id ▶ n. Chem. a weakly acid crystalline compound derived from borax and used as a mild antiseptic and in the manufacture of heat-resistant glass and enamels.

Bo·ri·cua /bô'rēkwə/ ▶ n. inf. a Puerto Rican, especially one living in the United States.

bor·ing /'bôriNG/ ▶ adj. not interesting; tedious: *I've got a boring job in an office.* —**bor·ing·ly** adv.

born /bôrn/ ▶ past participle of BEAR[1] (sense 4).
▶ adj. existing as a result of birth: *he was born in Seattle* | *she was born Margaret Roberts* | [in comb.] *a German-born philosopher.* ■ having a natural ability to do a particular job or task: *he's a born engineer.* ■ perfectly suited or trained to do a particular job or task: *they believe that they are born to rule.* ■ (of a thing) brought into existence: *her own business was born.* ■ (**born of**) existing as a result of a particular situation or feeling: *a power born of obsession.*

born-a·gain ▶ adj. converted to a personal faith in Christ: *a born-again Christian.* ■ fig. having the extreme enthusiasm of the newly converted: *born-again environmentalists.*
▶ n. a born-again Christian.

borne /bôrn/ ▶ past participle of BEAR[1].
▶ adj. [in comb.] carried or transported by: *waterborne bacteria* | *insect-borne pollen.*

bo·ron /'bôrän/ ▶ n. the chemical element of atomic number 5, a non-metallic solid. (Symbol: **B**) —**bo·ride** /-,rīd/ n.

bor·ough /'bərō/ (abbr.: **bor.**) ▶ n. a town or district that is an administrative unit. ■ an incorporated municipality in certain U.S. states.

bor·row /'bärō; 'bôrō/ ▶ v. [tr.] take and use (something that belongs to someone else) with the intention of returning it: *he had borrowed a car from one of his colleagues.* ■ take and use (money) from a person or bank under an agreement to pay it back later: *I borrowed the money for a return plane ticket* | [intr.] *lower interest rates will make it cheaper for individuals to borrow.* ■ take (a word, idea, or method) from another source and use it in one's own language or work: *the term is borrowed from Greek.* ■ take and use (a book) from a library for a fixed period of time. ■ in subtraction, take a unit from the next larger denomination. —**bor·row·er** n. —**bor·row·ing** n.
▶ □ **be (living) on borrowed time** used to say that someone has continued to survive against expectations, with the implication that this will not be for much longer.

borscht /bôrSH(t)/ (also **borsch**) ▶ n. a Russian or Polish soup made with beets and usually served with sour cream.

bor·zoi /'bôrzoi/ ▶ n. (pl. **-zois**) a large Russian wolfhound of a breed with a narrow head and silky, often white, coat.

bos·cage /'bäskij/ (also **bos·kage**) ▶ n. massed trees or shrubs: *the lush subtropical boscage.*

bo's·n ▶ n. variant spelling of BOATSWAIN.

bos·om /'bŏŏzəm/ ▶ n. a woman's chest: *the dress offered a fair display of bosom.* ■ (usu. **bosoms**) a woman's breast. ■ a part of a woman's dress covering the chest. ■ the space between a person's clothing and chest used for carrying things: *he carried a letter in his bosom.* ■ (**the bosom of**) poetic/lit. the loving care and protection of: *Bruno went home each night to the bosom of his family.* ■ used to refer to the chest as the seat of emotions: *quivering dread was settling in her bosom.*
▶ adj. (of a friend) close or intimate: *the two girls had become bosom friends.* —**bos·omed** adj. [in comb.] *her small-bosomed physique.*

boss[1] /bôs; bäs/ inf. ▶ n. a person in charge of a worker or organization: *I asked my boss for a promotion* | *union bosses.*
▶ v. [tr.] give (someone) orders in a domineering manner: *plump old battle-axes bossing everyone around.*
▶ adj. excellent; outstanding: *she's a real boss chick.* —**boss·y** adj.

boss[2] ▶ n. a round knob, stud, or other protuberance, in particular: ■ a stud on the center of a shield. ■ Archit. a piece of ornamental carving covering the point where the ribs in a vault or ceiling cross.

boss[3] (also **boss·y**) ▶ n. inf. a cow.

bos·sa no·va /'bäsə 'nōvə; ,bô-/ ▶ n. a dance like the samba, originating in Brazil. ■ a piece of music for this dance or in its rhythm.

bo·sun (also **bo'sun**) ▶ n. variant spelling of BOATSWAIN.

bot·a·ny /'bätn-ē/ ▶ n. the scientific study of plants, including their physiology, structure, genetics, ecology, distribution, classification, and economic importance. ■ the plant life of a particular region, habitat, or geological period: *the botany of North America.* —**bo·tan·ic** /bə'tanik/ adj. —**bo·tan·i·cal** adj. —**bot·a·nist** /-ist/ n.

botch /bäCH/ ▶ v. [tr.] inf. carry out (a task) badly or carelessly: *he was in a position to hire people, and he botched that up* —**botch·er** n.

bot·fly /'bät,flī/ ▶ n. (pl. **-flies**) a stout hairy-bodied fly with larvae that are internal parasites of mammals, in particular: ■ a fly (*Gasterophilus* and other genera, family Gasterophilidae) with larvae (bots) that develop within the guts of horses. ■ a fly of the warble fly family.

both /bōтн/ ▸*adj. & pron.* used to refer to two people or things, regarded and identified together: [as *adj.*] *both his parents indulged him* | [as *pron.*] *a picture of both of us together.*
▸*adv.* used before the first of two alternatives to emphasize that the statement being made applies to each (the other alternative being introduced by "and"): *they all loved to play, both the boys and the girls.*
▸ □ **have it both ways** benefit from two incompatible ways of thinking or behaving: *countries cannot have it both ways: the cost of a cleaner environment may sometimes be fewer jobs.*

both·er /'bäтнər/ ▸*v.* **1** take the trouble to do something: *nobody bothered locking the doors* | *the driver didn't bother to ask why.* **2** (of a circumstance or event) worry, disturb, or upset (someone): *secrecy is an issue that bothers journalists.* | ■ trouble or annoy (someone) by interrupting or causing inconvenience: *she didn't feel she could bother Mike with the problem.* ■ [*intr.*] feel concern about or interest in: *don't bother about me—I'll find my own way home* | [as *adj.*] (**bothered**) *I'm not particularly bothered about how I look.*
▸*n.* effort, worry, or difficulty: *he saved me the bother of having to come up with a speech.* ■ (**a bother**) a person or thing that causes worry or difficulty: *I hope she hasn't been a bother.* ■ a nuisance or inconvenience: *it's no bother, it's on my way home.* ▷late 17th cent. (as a noun in the dialect sense 'noise, chatter'): of Anglo-Irish origin; probably related to Irish *bodhaire* 'noise,' *bodhraim* 'deafen, annoy.' The verb (originally dialect) meant 'confuse with noise' in the early 18th cent.
▸ □ **hot and bothered** in a state of anxiety or physical discomfort.

both·er·some /'bäтнərsəm/ ▸*adj.* causing bother; troublesome: *most childhood stomachaches, though bothersome, aren't serious.*

bot·tle /'bätl/ ▸*n.* a container, typically made of glass or plastic and with a narrow neck, used for storing drinks or other liquids: *a bottle of soda pop.* ■ the contents of such a container: *he managed to put away a bottle of wine.* ■ (**the bottle**) *inf.* used in reference to heavy drinking: *more women are taking to the bottle.* ■ a bottle fitted with a nipple for giving milk or other drinks to babies and very young children: *a bottle of formula.* ■ (**the bottle**) the milk given to a baby from such a bottle: *the age at which parents want a baby to give up the bottle varies.* ■ a large metal cylinder holding liquefied gas.
▸*v.* [*tr.*] (usu. **be bottled**) place (drinks or other liquid) in bottles or jars: *the wine is then bottled.* ■ [usu. as *adj.*] (**bottled**) store (gas) in a container in liquefied form: *connecting the bottled gas to the stove.*
▸*phrasal v.* □ **bottle something up** repress or conceal feelings over a period of time: *learning how to express anger instead of bottling it up.* —**bot·tler** *n.*
▸ □ **hit the bottle** *inf.* drink heavily.

bot·tle-feed ▸*v.* [*tr.*] feed (a baby) with milk from a bottle instead of from the mother's breast: [as *adj.*] (**bottle-fed**) *a bottle-fed baby.*

bot·tle·neck /'bätl,nek/ ▸*n.* **1** the neck or mouth of a bottle. **2** a point of congestion or blockage, in particular: ■ a narrow section of road or a junction that impedes traffic flow: *narrow streets and a lack of parking space combine to make the town a bottleneck.* ■ a situation that causes delay in a process or system: *lack of imports is making the bottlenecks in domestic output worse than usual.* **3** a device shaped like the neck of a bottle, worn on a guitarist's finger to produce special sound effects. ■ (also **bottleneck guitar**) the style of guitar playing that uses such a device.

bot·tle-nose dol·phin /'bätl,nōz/ (also **bot·tle-nosed dolphin**) ▸*n.* a stout-bodied dolphin (*Tursiops truncatus*) with a distinct short beak, found in tropical and temperate coastal waters.

bot·tom /'bätəm/ ▸*n.* (usu. **the bottom**) **1** the lowest point or part: *the bottom of the page.* ■ the lower surface of something: *place the fruit on the bottom of the dish.* ■ the part on which a thing rests; the underside: *he sat on the bottom of an upturned bucket.* ■ the ground under a sea, river, or lake: *the liner plunged to the bottom of the sea.* ■ the seat of a chair. ■ the lowest position in a competition or ranking: *he started at the bottom and now has his own business.* ■ the basis or origin: *there's a mad scientist at the bottom of it all.* ■ (also **bot·toms**) the lower half of a two-piece garment: *pajama bottoms* | *a skimpy bikini bottom.* ■ the lowest part of the hull of a ship, esp. the relatively flat portion on either side of the keel. **2** *inf.* the buttocks: *he climbs the side of the gorge, scratching his bottom unselfconsciously.* **3** *Baseball* the second half of an inning: *the bottom of the ninth.* **4** *Physics* one of six flavors of quark.
▸*adj.* in the lowest position: *the books on the bottom shelf.* ■ in the lowest or last position in a competition or ranking: *households in the bottom income bracket.*
▸*v.* [*intr.*] (of a performance or situation) reach the lowest point before stabilizing or improving: *interest rates have bottomed out.* —**bot·tomed** *adj.* [in *comb.*] *a glass-bottomed boat.* —**bot·tom·most** /-,mōst/ *adj.*
▸ □ **bet your bottom dollar** *inf.* stake everything: *you can bet your bottom*

dollar it'll end in tears. □ **the bottom falls** (or **drops**) **out** collapse or failure occurs: *the bottom fell out of the market for classic cars.* □ **get to the bottom of** find an explanation for (a mystery): *he hopes to get to the bottom of the scam.*

bot·tom·less /'bätəmlis/ ▸*adj.* **1** without a bottom. ■ very deep: *the cold dark sea in whose bottomless depths monsters swam.* ■ *fig.* inexhaustible: *I don't have a bottomless pit of money.* **2** naked, esp. below the waist.

bot·tom line ▸*n. inf.* the final total of an account, balance sheet, or other financial document: *fig. the determination of Japanese companies to ignore the bottom line.* ■ the ultimate criterion: *the bottom line is, does it work?* ■ the underlying or ultimate outcome: *the bottom line is I'm still married to Denny.*

bot·u·lism /'bäcнə,lizəm/ ▸*n.* food poisoning caused by a bacterium (botulinum) growing on improperly sterilized canned meats and other preserved foods.

bou·clé /,boo'klā/ ▸*n.* [often as *adj.*] yarn with a looped or curled ply, or fabric woven from this yarn: *a bouclé sweater.*

bou·doir /'boo,dwär/ ▸*n.* chiefly *hist.* or *humorous* a woman's bedroom or private room.

bouf·fant /boo'fänt/ ▸*adj.* (of a person's hair) styled so as to puff out in a rounded shape: *a blonde lady with bouffant hair.*

bou·gain·vil·le·a /,boogən'vilyə; -'vēə; ,bō-/ (also **bou·gain·vil·lae·a**) ▸*n.* an ornamental climbing plant (genus *Bougainvillea*, family Nyctaginaceae) that is widely cultivated in the tropics. The insignificant flowers are surrounded by brightly colored papery bracts.

bough /bou/ ▸*n.* a main branch of a tree: *apple boughs laden with blossom.*

bought /bôt/ ▸ past and past participle of BUY.

bouil·la·baisse /,boo(l)yə'bäs; 'boo(l)yə,bäs/ ▸*n.* a rich, spicy stew or soup made with various kinds of fish, originally from Provence.

bouil·lon /'boolyən; -yän/ ▸*n.* a broth made by stewing meat, fish, or vegetables in water.

boul·der /'bōldər/ ▸*n.* a large rock, typically one that has been worn smooth by erosion. —**boul·der·y** *adj.*

boule /bool/ (also **boules** pronunc. same) ▸*n.* **1** a French lawn game, played on rough ground with metal balls. **2** a crystal, as of sapphire, synthetically manufactured by fusion and used as a gemstone. **3** a rounded loaf of bread.

boul·e·vard /'boolə,värd/ (abbr.: **blvd.**) ▸*n.* a wide street in a town or city, typically one lined with trees: [in *names*] *Sunset Boulevard.*

bounce /bouns/ ▸*v.* [*intr.*] (of an object, esp. a ball) move quickly away from a surface after hitting it; rebound: *the ball bounced off the rim* | [*tr.*] *he was bouncing the ball against the wall.* ■ rebound repeatedly: *the ball bounced away, and he chased it.* ■ (of light, sound, or an electronic signal) come into contact with an object or surface and be reflected: *short sound waves bounce off even small objects.* ■ (of a thing) move up and down while remaining essentially in the same position: *the gangplank bounced under his confident step.* ■ (of a person) jump repeatedly up and down, typically on something springy: *bouncing up and down on the mattress.* ■ [*tr.*] cause (a child) to move lightly up and down on one's knee as a game: *I remember how you used to bounce me on your knee.* ■ move in an energetic or happy manner: *Linda bounced in through the open front door.* ■ (of a vehicle) move jerkily along a bumpy surface: *the car bounced down the narrow track.* ■ (**bounce back**) *fig.* recover well after a setback: *admired for his ability to bounce back from injury.* ■ *Baseball* hit a ball that bounces before reaching a fielder: *bouncing out with the bases loaded* | [*tr.*] *bounced a grounder to third.* ■ [*tr.*] (of a check) be returned by a bank when there are insufficient funds to meet it: *my rent check bounced.* | [*tr.*] *inf.* write a (check) on insufficient funds. ■ [*tr.*] *inf.* eject (a troublemaker) forcibly from a nightclub or similar establishment.
▸*n.* a rebound of a ball or other object: *a bad bounce caused the ball to get away from the second baseman.* ■ an act of jumping or an instance of being moved up and down: *every bounce of the truck brought them into fresh contact.* ■ a sudden rise in the level of something: *economists agree that there could be a bounce in prices next year.* ■ exuberant self-confidence: *the bounce was now back in Jenny's step.* —**bounc·y** *adj.*

bounc·er /'bounsər/ ▸*n.* **1** a person employed by a nightclub or similar establishment to prevent troublemakers from entering or to eject them from the premises. **2** *Baseball* a batted ball that bounces before being fielded.

bounc·ing /'bounsɪng/ ▸*adj.* (of a ball) rebounding up and down: *an awkwardly bouncing ball.* ■ (of a baby) vigorous and healthy: *Lisa gave birth to*

Pronunciation Key ə *ago,* up; ər *over,* fur; a *hat*; ā *ate*; ä *car*; cн *chin*; e *let*; ē *see*; e(ə)r *air*; i *fit*; ī *by*; i(ə)r *ear*; ng *sing*; ō *go*; ô *law, for*; oi *toy*; oo *good*; oo *goo*; ou *out*; sh *she*; тн *thin*; тн *then*; (h)w *why*; zh *vision*

a bouncing baby boy. ■ lively and confident: *by the next day she was her usual bouncing, energetic self.*

bound¹ /bound/ ▶ *v.* [*intr.*] walk or run with leaping strides: *Louis came bounding down the stairs.*
▶ *n.* a leaping movement upward: *I went up the steps in two effortless bounds.*

bound² ▶ *n.* (often **bounds**) a territorial limit; a boundary: *the ancient bounds of the forest.* ■ a limitation or restriction on feeling or action: *it is not beyond the bounds of possibility that the issue could arise again.* ■ technical a limiting value.
▶ *v.* [*tr.*] (usu. **be bounded**) form the boundary of; enclose: *the ground was bounded by a main road on one side and a meadow on the other.* ■ place within certain limits; restrict: *freedom of action is bounded by law.*
▶ □ **out of bounds** (of a place) outside the limits of where one is permitted to be: *his kitchen was out of bounds to me at mealtimes.* ■ *Sports* outside the regular playing area. ■ *fig.* beyond what is acceptable: *Paul felt that this conversation was getting out of bounds.*

bound³ ▶ *adj.* heading toward somewhere: *trains bound for Chicago.* ■ *fig.* destined or likely to have a specified experience: *they were bound for disaster.*

bound⁴ ▶ past and past participle of **BIND**.
▶ *adj.* **1** [in *comb.*] restricted or confined to a specified place: *his job kept him city-bound.* ■ prevented from operating normally by the specified conditions: *blizzard-bound Boston.* **2** certain to do or have something: *there is bound to be a change of plan.* ■ obliged by law, circumstances, or duty to do something: *I'm bound to do what I can to help Sam.* **3** [in *comb.*] (of a book) having a specified binding: *fine leather-bound books.*

bound·a·ry /'bound(ə)rē/ ▶ *n.* (*pl.* **-ries**) a line that marks the limits of an area; a dividing line: *the eastern boundary of the wilderness.* | [as *adj.*] *a boundary wall.* ■ (often **boundaries**) *fig.* a limit of a subject or sphere of activity: *a community without class or political boundaries.*

bound·en /'boundən/ ▶ archaic past participle of **BIND**.
▶ □ **one's bounden duty** a responsibility regarded as obligatory: *the Pastor believed that it was his bounden duty to keep them on the right path.*

bound·less /'boundlis/ ▶ *adj.* unlimited; immense: *enthusiasts who devote boundless energy to their hobby.* —**bound·less·ly** *adv.* *the land was boundlessly fertile.* —**bound·less·ness** *n.*

boun·te·ous /'bountēəs/ ▶ *adj.* archaic generously given or giving; bountiful: *the earth yields a bounteous harvest.* —**boun·te·ous·ly** *adv.* —**boun·te·ous·ness** *n.*

boun·ti·ful /'bountəfəl/ ▶ *adj.* large in quantity; abundant: *the ocean provided a bountiful supply of fresh food.* ■ giving generously: *he was exceedingly bountiful to persons in distress.* —**boun·ti·ful·ly** *adv.*

boun·ty /'bountē/ ▶ *n.* (*pl.* **-ties**) **1** generosity; liberality: *fig. for millennia the people along the Nile have depended entirely on its bounty.* ■ abundance; plenty: *we ask that growers share their bounty with others.* **2** a monetary gift or reward, typically given by a government, in particular: ■ a sum paid for killing or capturing a person or animal: *there was an increased bounty on his head.* ■ a sum paid to army or navy recruits upon enlistment. ■ *poetic/lit.* something given or occurring in generous amounts: *the bounties of nature.*

boun·ty hunt·er ▶ *n.* one who pursues a criminal or seeks an achievement for the sake of the reward.

bou·quet /bō'kā; bōō-/ ▶ *n.* **1** an attractively arranged bunch of flowers, esp. one presented as a gift or carried at a ceremony. ■ *fig.* an expression of approval; a compliment: *we will happily publish the bouquets.* **2** a characteristic scent, esp. that of a wine or perfume: *the aperitif has a faint bouquet of almonds.*

bour·bon /'bərbən/ ▶ *n.* a straight whiskey distilled from a mash having at least 51 percent corn in addition to malt and rye.

bour·geois /bōōr'ZHwä/ ▶ *adj.* of or characteristic of the middle class, typically with reference to its perceived materialistic values or conventional attitudes: *a rich, bored, bourgeois family.* ■ (in Marxist contexts) upholding the interests of capitalism; not communist: *bourgeois society took for granted the sanctity of property.*
▶ *n.* (*pl.* same) a bourgeois person: *a self-confessed and proud bourgeois.* —**bour·geoi·sie** /,bōōrzHwä'zē/ *n.*

bourn (also **bourne**) ▶ *n.* *poetic/lit.* **1** a goal; a destination. **2** a limit; a boundary.

bourse /bōōrs/ ▶ *n.* a stock market in a non-English-speaking country, esp. France. ■ (**Bourse**) the Paris stock exchange. ▷mid 16th cent. (as *burse*, the usual form until the mid 19th cent.): from French, literally 'purse,' via medieval Latin from Greek *bursa* 'leather.'

bout /bout/ ▶ *n.* a short period of intense activity of a specified kind: *occasional bouts of strenuous exercise.* ■ an attack of illness or strong emotion of a specified kind: *a severe bout of flu.* ■ a wrestling or boxing match.

bou·tique /bōō'tēk/ ▶ *n.* **1** a small store selling fashionable clothes or accessories. **2** a business that serves a sophisticated or specialized clientele: *a small investment boutique.* | [as *adj.*] *a boutique film.* —**bou·tique·y** *adj.*

bou·ton·nière /,bōōtn'i(ə)r/ ▶ *n.* a spray of flowers worn in a buttonhole.

bou·zou·ki /bōō'zōōkē/ ▶ *n.* (*pl.* **-kis** or **-kia** /-kyä/) a long-necked Greek instrument similar to the mandolin.

bo·vine /'bōvīn; -vēn/ ▶ *adj.* of, relating to, or affecting cattle: *bovine tuberculosis.* ■ (of a person) slow-moving and dull-witted.
▶ *n.* an animal of the cattle group, which also includes buffaloes and bisons. —**bo·vine·ly** *adv.*

bow¹ /bō/ ▶ *n.* **1** a knot tied with two loops and two loose ends, used esp. for tying shoelaces and decorative ribbons: *a girl with long hair tied back in a bow.* ■ a decorative ribbon tied in such a knot. **2** a weapon for shooting arrows, typically made of a curved piece of wood whose ends are joined by a taut string. **3** a long, partially curved rod with horsehair stretched along its length, used for playing the violin and other stringed instruments. **4** a thing that is bent or curved in shape. ■ a side piece or lens frame of a pair of glasses.
▶ *v.* **1** [*tr.*] play (a stringed instrument or music) using a bow: *the techniques by which the pieces were bowed.* **2** bend into the shape of a bow: *the sides of the image are squeezed in or bowed out.*

bow² /bou/ ▶ *v.* [*intr.*] bend the head or upper part of the body as a sign of respect, greeting, or shame: *he turned and bowed to his father* | [*tr.*] *she knelt and bowed her head.* ■ [*tr.*] express (thanks, agreement, or other sentiments) by bending one's head respectfully: *he looked at Hector before bowing grave thanks.* ■ [*intr.*] bend the body in order to see or concentrate: [as *adj.*] *my mother sat bowed over a library book.* ■ [*tr.*] cause (something) to bend with age or under a heavy weight: *the vines were bowed down with flowers* | [*intr.*] *the grass bowed down before the wind.* ■ submit to pressure or to someone's demands: *the mayor bowed to public opinion.*
▶ *phrasal v.* □ **bow out** withdraw or retire from an activity, role, or commitment: *many artists are forced to bow out of the profession at a relatively early age.*
▶ *n.* an act of bending the head or upper body as a sign of respect or greeting: *the man gave a little bow.*
▶ □ **bow and scrape** behave in an obsequious way to someone in authority. □ **take a bow** (of an actor or entertainer) acknowledge applause after a performance by bowing: *fig. the aides do the grind work while the boss takes the bows.*

bow³ /bou/ (also **bows**) ▶ *n.* the front end of a ship: *water sprayed high over her bows.*

bowd·ler·ize /'bōdlə,rīz; 'boud-/ ▶ *v.* [*tr.*] remove material that is considered improper or offensive from (a text or account), esp. with the result that it becomes weaker or less effective: [as *adj.*] (**bowdlerized**) *a bowdlerized version of the story.* —**bowd·ler·ism** /-,rizəm/ *n.* —**bowd·ler·i·za·tion** *n.*

bow·el /'bou(ə)l/ (also **bow·els**) ▶ *n.* the part of the alimentary canal below the stomach; the intestine. ■ (**the bowels of**) the parts deep inside something large: *the train picks up speed for its final plunge into the subterranean bowels of Manhattan.*

bow·el move·ment ▶ *n.* an act of defecation. ■ the feces discharged in an act of defecation.

bow·er /'bou(-ə)r/ ▶ *n.* a pleasant shady place under trees or climbing plants in a garden or wood.

bow·er·bird /'bou(-ə)r,bərd/ ▶ *n.* a strong-billed Australasian bird (family Ptilonorhynchidae), noted for the male's habit of constructing an elaborate bower adorned with feathers, shells, and other objects to attract the female for courtship.

bow·head /'bō,hed/ (also **bowhead whale**) ▶ *n.* an Arctic right whale (*Balaena mysticetus*) with black skin, feeding by skimming the surface for plankton.

bowl¹ /bōl/ ▶ *n.* **1** a round, deep dish or basin used for food or liquid: *a mixing bowl.* ■ the contents of such a container: *huge bowls of steaming spaghetti.* ■ [usu. in *names*] a decorative round dish awarded as a prize in a competition: *the McGeorge Rose Bowl.* ■ a rounded, concave part of an object: *a toilet bowl* | *the bowl of a spoon.* ■ *Geog.* a natural basin. **2** [in *names*] a stadium for sporting or musical events: *the Hollywood Bowl.* ■ a football game played after the regular season between leading or all-star teams: [as *adj.*] *their last four bowl games.* —**bowl·ful** *n.*

bowl² ▶ *v.* **1** [*tr.*] roll (a ball or hoop) along the ground: *she snatched her hat off and bowled it ahead of her like a hoop.* **2** [*intr.*] play a game of tenpin bowling. ■ [*tr.*] achieve a score in tenpin bowling. **3** [*intr.*] move rapidly and smoothly in a specified direction: *they bowled along the country roads.*
▶ *phrasal v.* □ **bowl someone over** knock someone down: *he was almost*

bowling people over in his haste. ■ (usu. **be bowled over**) *inf.* completely overwhelm or astonish someone, for example by one's good qualities or looks: *when he met Angela, he was just bowled over by her.*

bow legs /bō/ ▸*pl. n.* legs that curve outward at the knee; bandy legs. —**bow-leg·ged** *adj.*

bowl·er[1] /ˈbōlər/ ▸*n.* **1** a player at tenpin bowling, lawn bowling, or skittles. **2** *Cricket* a member of the fielding side who bowls or is bowling.

bowl·er[2] (also **bowler hat**) ▸*n.* a man's hard felt hat with a round dome-shaped crown.

bow·line /ˈbōlin; ˈbō,līn/ ▸*n.* **1** a rope attached to the weather leech of a square sail and leading forward, thus helping the ship sail nearer the wind. **2** a nonbinding knot for forming a nonslipping nonjamming loop at the end of a rope.

bowl·ing /ˈbōliNG/ ▸*n.* the game of tenpin bowling as a sport or recreation. ■ the game of candlepin or duckpin bowling. ■ the game of lawn bowling. ■ the game of skittles.

bowl·ing ball ▸*n.* a large, heavy ball with holes for the thumb and two fingers, used in tenpin bowling.

bowl·ing green ▸*n.* an area of closely mown grass on which the game of lawn bowling is played.

bow·man[1] /ˈbōmən/ ▸*n.* (*pl.* -**men**) an archer.

bow·man[2] /ˈboumən/ ▸*n.* (*pl.* -**men**) the rower who sits nearest the bow of a boat, esp. a racing boat.

bow saw /bō/ ▸*n.* a narrow saw stretched like a bowstring on a light frame.

bow·sprit /ˈbou,sprit; ˈbō-/ ▸*n.* a spar extending forward from a ship's bow, to which the forestays are fastened.

bowsprit

bow·string /ˈbō,striNG/ ▸*n.* the string of an archer's bow, traditionally made of three strands of hemp.
▸*v.* (*past* and *past part.* -**strung**) [*trans.*] *hist.* strangle with a bowstring (a former Turkish method of execution).

bow tie /bō/ ▸*n.* a necktie in the form of a bow or a knot with two loops.

bow-wow /ˈbou ˈwou/ ▸*interj.* an imitation of a dog's bark.

box[1] /bäks/ ▸*n.* **1** a container with a flat base and sides, typically square or rectangular and having a lid: *a cereal box.* ■ the contents of such a container: *she ate a whole box of chocolates that night.* ■ *inf.* a casing containing a computer. ■ *inf.* a coffin: *I always thought I'd be in a box when I finally left here.* ■ *vulgar slang* a woman's vagina. **2** an area or space enclosed within straight lines, in particular: ■ an area on a printed page that is to be filled in or that is set off by a border: *a picture of Sandy was in the upper right-hand box.* ■ an area on a computer screen for user input or displaying information. ■ (**the box**) (also **the batter's box**) *Baseball* the rectangular area occupied by the batter. ■ *Baseball* the rectangular area behind home plate for the catcher (**catcher's box**), or those near first and third bases, in foul territory, for each base coach (**coach's box**). ■ (**the box**) *Soccer* the penalty area: *he curled in a shot from the edge of the box.* **3** a small structure or building for a specific purpose, in particular: ■ a separate section or enclosed area within a larger building, esp. one reserved for a group of people in a theater or sports ground or for witnesses or the jury in a law court: *a box at the opera* | *the jury was now in the box.* **4** a protective casing for a piece of a mechanism. **5** a mailbox at a post office, newspaper office, or other facility where a person may arrange to receive correspondence: *write to me care of PO Box 112.*
▸*v.* [*tr.*] [often as *adj.*] (**boxed**) put in or provide with a box: *the books are sold as a boxed set* | *She boxed up all of Christopher's clothes.* ■ (**box someone in**) restrict the ability of (someone) to move freely: *a van double-*

parked alongside her car and totally boxed her in. —**box·ful** *n.* —**box·like** *adj.*
▸ □ **think outside** (**of**) **the box** think in an original or creative way.

box[2] ▸*v.* [*intr.*] fight an opponent using one's fists; compete in the sport of boxing: *he boxed for England* | [*tr.*] *he had to box Bennett for the title.*
▸*n.* a slap with the hand on the side of a person's head given as a punishment or in anger: *she gave him a box on the ear.*
▸ □ **box someone's ears** slap someone on the side of the head as a punishment or in anger.

box[3] ▸*n.* **1** (also **box tree**) a slow-growing European evergreen shrub or small tree (*Buxus sempervirens*) with glossy dark green leaves, often grown as a hedge and for topiary. ■ (also **box·wood**) the hard, heavy wood of this tree, formerly widely used for engraving and for musical instruments. **2** any of a number of trees that have similar wood or foliage, including several Australian eucalyptus trees.

box·car /ˈbäks,kär/ ▸*n.* an enclosed railroad freight car, typically with sliding doors on the sides.

box el·der ▸*n.* an American maple (*Acer negundo*) of damp soils that has green or purplish twigs, and leaves similar to those of the ash.

Box·er /ˈbäksər/ ▸*n.* a member of a fiercely nationalistic Chinese secret society that flourished in the 19th century. In 1899 the society led a Chinese uprising (**the Boxer Rebellion**) against Western domination that was eventually crushed by a combined European force, aided by Japan and the U.S.

box·er /ˈbäksər/ ▸*n.* **1** a person who takes part in boxing, esp. as a sport. **2** a medium-sized dog of a breed with a smooth brown coat and puglike face.

box·er shorts (also **boxers**) ▸*pl. n.* men's loose underpants similar in shape to the shorts worn by boxers.

box·ing /ˈbäksiNG/ ▸*n.* the sport or practice of fighting with the fists, esp. with padded gloves in a roped square ring according to prescribed rules.

box·ing glove ▸*n.* a heavily padded mitten worn in boxing.

box kite ▸*n.* a tailless kite in the form of a long box open at each end.

box lunch ▸*n.* an individual lunch carried in a box rather than a bag.

box of·fice ▸*n.* a place at a theater or other arts establishment where tickets are bought or reserved. ■ used to refer to the commercial success of a movie, play, or actor in terms of the audience size or takings they command: [as *adj.*] *the movie was a huge box-office hit.*

box score ▸*n.* the tabulated results of a baseball game or other sporting event, with statistics given for each player's performance.

box seat ▸*n.* a seat in a box in a theater or sports stadium.

box spring ▸*n.* each of a set of vertical springs housed in a frame in a mattress or upholstered divan base.

box·wood /ˈbäks,wŏŏd/ ▸*n.* see BOX[3] (sense 1).

boy /boi/ ▸*n.* **1** a male child or young man: *a group of six boys.* ■ a son: *she put her little boy to bed.* ■ a male child or young man who does a specified job: *a delivery boy.* **2** used informally or lightheartedly to refer to a man: *the inspector was a local boy.* ■ *dated* used as a friendly form of address from one man to another, often from an older man to a young man: *my dear boy, don't say another word!* ■ used as a form of address to a male dog: *down boy, down!*
▸*interj. inf.* used to express strong feelings, esp. of excitement or admiration: *oh boy, that's wonderful!* —**boy·hood** *n.* —**boy·ish** *adj.*
▸ □ **the big boys** men or organizations considered to be the most powerful and successful. □ **one of the boys** an accepted member of a group, esp. a group of men: *he expected to be treated just like one of the boys.*

boy·cott /ˈboi,kät/ ▸*v.* [*tr.*] withdraw from commercial or social relations with (a country, organization, or person) as a punishment or protest. ■ refuse to buy or handle (goods) as a punishment or protest. ■ refuse to cooperate with or participate in (a policy or event).
▸*n.* a punitive ban that forbids relations with other bodies, cooperation with a policy, or the handling of goods. ▷from the name of Captain C. C. Boycott (1832–97), an English land agent in Ireland, so treated in 1880, in an attempt instigated by the Irish to get rents reduced.

boy·friend /ˈboi,frend/ ▸*n.* a regular male companion with whom one has a romantic or sexual relationship.

Boyle's law *Chem.* ▸a law stating that the pressure of a given mass of an ideal gas is inversely proportional to its volume at a constant temperature.

Boy Scout ▸*n.* A member of an organization of boys, esp. the **Boy**

Pronunciation Key ə *ago, up;* ər *over, fur;* a *hat;* ā *ate;* ä *car;* CH *chin;* e *let;* ē *see;* e(ə)r *air;* i *fit;* ī *by;* i(ə)r *ear;* NG *sing;* ō *go;* ô *law, for;* oi *toy;* ŏŏ *good;* ōō *goo;* ou *out;* SH *she;* TH *thin;* ṮH *then;* (h)w *why;* ZH *vision*

Scouts of America, that promotes character, outdoor activities, good citizenship, and service to others. ■ an honest, friendly, and typically naive man: [as adj.] his trademark Boy Scout smile.

boy·sen·ber·ry /ˈboizənˌberē/ ▸n. (pl. **-ies**) **1** a large red edible blackberrylike fruit. **2** the shrubby plant (Rubus loganobaccus) that bears this fruit, which is a hybrid of several kinds of bramble.

bo·zo /ˈbōzō/ ▸n. (pl. **-zos**) inf. a stupid, rude, or insignificant person, esp. a man.

BP ▸abbr. ■ before the present (era): 18,000 years BP. ■ blood pressure. ■ Baseball batting practice. ■ boiling point.

bp ▸abbr. ■ baptized. ■ Biochem. base pair(s), as a unit of length in nucleic acid chains. ■ Finance basis point(s). ■ (**b.p.**) boiling point.

bps Comput. ▸abbr. bits per second.

BR ▸abbr. ■ bedroom(s). ■ bills receivable.

Br ▸symb. the chemical element bromine.

bra /brä/ ▸n. an undergarment worn by women to support the breasts. ■ (also **auto bra** or **car bra**) a carbon-based cover that fits over the front bumper of a car, absorbing the microwaves used in police radar equipment to minimize the risk of detection for the speeding motorist. —**bra·less** adj.

brace /brās/ ▸n. **1** a device that clamps things tightly together or that gives support, in particular: ■ a device fitted to a weak or injured neck, leg, or other part of the body for support. ■ (**braces**) a wire device fitted in the mouth to straighten the teeth. ■ a strengthening piece of iron or timber used in building and carpentry. ■ a tool in carpentry having a crank handle and a socket to hold a bit for boring. ■ a rope leading aft from each yardarm, used for trimming the sail. ■ (**braces**) British term for SUSPENDERS. **2** either of the two marks { and }, used either to indicate that two or more items on one side have the same relationship as each other to the single item to which the other side points, or in pairs to show that words between them are connected. ■ Mus. a similar mark connecting staves to be performed at the same time.
▸v. [tr.] make (a structure) stronger or firmer with wood, iron, or other forms of support: the posts were braced by lengths of timber. ■ press (one's body or part of one's body) firmly against something in order to stay balanced: she braced her feet against a projecting shelf. ■ prepare (someone or oneself) for something difficult or unpleasant: both stations are bracing themselves for job losses. ▷Middle English (as a verb meaning 'clasp, fasten tightly'): from Old French bracier 'embrace,' from brace 'two arms,' from Latin bracchia, plural of bracchium 'arm,' from Greek brakhiōn.

brace and bit ▸n. a revolving tool with a D-shaped crank handle used for boring holes.

brace·let /ˈbrāslit/ ▸n. an ornamental band, hoop, or chain worn on the wrist or arm. ■ (**bracelets**) inf. handcuffs.

brac·er /ˈbrāsər/ ▸n. inf. an alcoholic drink intended to prepare one for something difficult or unpleasant.

bra·chi·al /ˈbrākēəl; ˈbrak-/ ▸adj. Anat. of or relating to the arm, specifically the upper arm, or an armlike structure: the brachial artery. ■ like an arm.

bra·chi·ate ▸v. /ˈbrākēˌāt; ˈbrak-/ [intr.] (of certain apes) move by using the arms to swing from branch to branch: the gibbons brachiate energetically across their enclosure. —**bra·chi·a·tion** /ˌbrākēˈāSHən/, ˌbrak-/ n. —**bra·chi·a·tor** /-ˌātər/ n.

bra·chi·o·pod /ˈbrākēəˌpäd; ˈbrak-/ ▸n. any of various marine invertebrates, esp. a fossil one, having an unhinged bivalve shell and a ciliated feeding arm.

bra·chi·o·saur /ˈbrākēəˌsôr; ˈbrak-/ (also **bra·chi·o·sau·rus** /ˌbrākēə-ˈsôrəs; ˌbrak-/) ▸n. a huge herbivorous dinosaur (genus Brachiosaurus, order Saurischia) of the late Jurassic to mid Cretaceous periods, with forelegs much longer than the hind legs. —**bra·chi·o·sau·ri·an** /-ˈsôr-ˈēən/ adj.

brack·en /ˈbrakən/ ▸n. a tall fern (Pteridium aquilinum, family Dennstaedtiaceae) with coarse lobed fronds that occurs worldwide and can cover large areas. ■ (loosely) any large coarse fern resembling this.

brack·et /ˈbrakit/ ▸n. **1** each of a pair of marks [] used to enclose words or figures so as to separate them from the context: symbols are given in brackets. **2** a category of people or things that are similar or fall between specified limits: those in a high income bracket. **3** a right-angled support attached to and projecting from a wall for holding a shelf, lamp, or other object. ■ a shelf fixed with such a support to a wall.
▸v. (**-et·ed, -et·ing**) [tr.] **1** (usu. **be bracketed**) place (one or more people

brace and bit

or things) in the same category or group: he is sometimes bracketed with the "new wave" of film directors. **2** enclose (words or figures) in brackets: [as adj.] (**bracketed**) the relevant data are included as bracketed points. ■ Math. enclose (a complex expression) in brackets to denote that the whole of the expression rather than just a part of it has a particular relation, such as multiplication or division, to another expression. **3** hold or attach (something) by means of a right-angled support: pipes should be bracketed. **4** Mil. establish the range of (a target) by firing two preliminary shots, one short of the target and the other beyond it. ■ Photog. establish (the correct exposure) by taking several pictures with slightly more or less exposure.

brack·ish /ˈbrakiSH/ ▸adj. (of water) slightly salty, as is the mixture of river water and seawater in estuaries. ■ (of fish or other organisms) living in or requiring such water. ■ unpleasant or distasteful: the lighting in the movie is brackish. —**brack·ish·ness** n.

bract /brakt/ ▸n. Bot. a modified leaf or scale, typically small, with a flower or flower cluster in its axil. Bracts are sometimes larger and more brightly colored than the true flower, as in a poinsettia. —**brac·te·ate** /-tēit; -tē,āt/ adj.

brad /brad/ ▸n. a small wire nail with a small head.

brad·y·car·di·a /ˌbradiˈkärdēə/ ▸n. Med. abnormally slow heart action.

brag /brag/ ▸v. (**bragged, brag·ging**) say in a boastful manner: [with direct speech] "I found them," she bragged. | [intr.] they were bragging about how easy it had been.
▸n. **1** a gambling card game that is a simplified form of poker. **2** a boastful statement; an act of talking boastfully.
▸adj. inf., excellent; first-rate: that was my brag heifer. —**brag·ger** n. —**brag·ging·ly** adv.
▸ □ **bragging rights** used to express pride in bettering a rival: it took the team seven games to wrest bragging rights from their interstate rivals.

brag·ga·do·ci·o /ˌbragəˈdōSHē,ō/ ▸n. boastful or arrogant behavior.

brag·gart /ˈbragərt/ ▸n. a person who boasts about achievements or possessions: [as adj.] braggart men.

Brah·ma /ˈbrämə/ ▸ **1** the creator god in later Hinduism, who forms a triad with Vishnu the preserver and Shiva the destroyer. **2** another term for BRAHMAN (sense 2).

Brah·ma bull ▸n. another term for BRAHMAN sense 3.

Brah·man /ˈbrämən/ (also **Brah·min** /-min/) ▸n. (pl. **-mans** or **-mins**) **1** a member of the highest Hindu caste, that of the priesthood. **2** (in Hinduism) the ultimate reality underlying all phenomena. **3** an ox (Bos indicus) of a humped breed originally domesticated in India that is tolerant of heat and drought. It is often included under the name B. taurus with other domestic cattle. Also called BRAHMA BULL; ZEBU. —**Brah·man·ic** /brä'manik/ adj. —**Brah·man·i·cal** /brä'manikəl/ adj.

Brah·min /ˈbrämin/ ▸n. **1** variant spelling of BRAHMAN. **2** a socially or culturally superior person, esp. a member of the upper classes from New England. —**Brah·min·i·cal** /brä'minikəl/ adj.

braid /brād/ ▸n. **1** threads of silk, cotton, or other material woven into a decorative band for edging or trimming garments: a coat trimmed with gold braid **2** a length of hair made up of three or more interlaced strands: women with long black braids. ■ a length made up of three or more interlaced strands of any flexible material: a flexible copper braid | braids of garlic.
▸v. [tr.] **1** interlace three or more strands of (hair or other flexible material) to form a length: their long hair was tightly braided. **2** [often as adj.] (**braided**) edge or trim (a garment) with braid: braided red trousers. **3** [usu. as adj.] (**braided**) (of a river or stream) flow in shallow interwoven channels divided by deposits of sediment.

Braille ▸n. a form of written language for the blind, in which characters are represented by patterns of raised dots that are felt with the fingertips.

brain /brān/ ▸n. **1** an organ of soft nervous tissue contained in the skull of vertebrates, functioning as the coordinating center of sensation and intellectual and nervous activity. ■ (**brains**) the substance of such an organ, typically that of an animal, used as food. ■ inf. an electronic device with functions comparable to those of the human brain. **2** intellectual capacity: I didn't have enough brains for the sciences. ■ (**the brains**) inf. a clever person who supplies the ideas and plans for a group of people: Tom was the brains of the outfit. ■ a person's mind: a tiny alarm bell began to ring in her brain. ■ an exceptionally intelligent person: he was known more as a snappy dresser than a brain.
▸v. [tr.] inf. hit (someone) hard on the head with an object: she brained me with a rolling pin.

brain death ▸n. irreversible brain damage causing the end of independent respiration, regarded as indicative of death.

brain drain ▸ *n. inf.* the emigration of highly trained or intelligent people from a particular country.

brain·pan /'brān,pan/ ▸ *n. inf.* a person's skull.

brain·pow·er /'brān,pouər/ ▸ *n.* mental ability; intelligence.

brain·stem /'brān,stem/ (also **brain stem**) ▸ *n. Anat.* the central trunk of the mammalian brain, consisting of the medulla oblongata, pons, and midbrain, and continuing downward to form the spinal cord, the seat of basic, reflexive bodily functions.

brain·storm /'brān,stôrm/ ▸ *n.* **1** a spontaneous group discussion to produce ideas and ways of solving problems. ▪ *inf.* a sudden clever idea. **2** *inf.* a moment in which one is suddenly unable to think clearly or act sensibly.
▸ *v.* [*intr.*] produce an idea or way of solving a problem by holding a spontaneous group discussion: [as *n.*] (**brainstorming**) *a brainstorming session.*

brain-teas·er (also **brain-twist·er**) ▸ *n. inf.* a problem or puzzle, typically one designed to be solved for amusement. —**brain-teas·ing** *adj.*

brain trust ▸ *n.* a group of experts appointed to advise a government or politician.

brain-wash /'brān,wôSH; -,wäSH/ ▸ *v.* [*tr.*] make (someone) adopt radically different beliefs by using systematic and often forcible pressure: *the organization could brainwash young people.*

brain-wave /'brān,wāv/ ▸ *n.* (usu. **brainwaves**) an electrical impulse in the brain. ▪ *inf.* a sudden clever idea.

brain·y /'brānē/ ▸ *adj.* (**brain·i·er, brain·i·est**) having or showing intelligence: *a brainy, high-powered lawyer.* —**brain·i·ly** /-nəlē/ *adv.* —**brain·i·ness** *n.*

braise /brāz/ ▸ *v.* [*tr.*] sauté (food) lightly and then stew it slowly in a closed container: [as *adj.*] (**braised**) *braised veal.*

brake[1] /brāk/ ▸ *n.* a device for slowing or stopping a moving vehicle, typically by applying pressure to the wheels: *he slammed on his brakes.* ▪ a thing that slows or hinders a process: *China's decision to* **put the brakes on** *economic reform.*
▸ *v.* [*intr.*] make a moving vehicle slow down or stop by using a brake: *drivers who brake abruptly* | [as *adj.*] (**braking**) *an anti-lock braking system.*

brake[2] (also **brake fern**) ▸ *n.* a coarse fern (genus *Pteris*, family Pteridaceae) of warm and tropical countries, frequently having the fronds divided into long linear segments. ▪ archaic term for BRACKEN.

brake[3] ▸ archaic past of BREAK.

brake drum ▸ *n.* a broad, very short cylinder attached to a wheel, against which the brake shoes press in a drum brake.

brake horse·pow·er ▸ *n.* (*pl.* same) the available power of an engine, assessed by measuring the force needed to brake it: *the net brake horsepower is only up by six.*

brake lin·ing ▸ *n.* a layer attached to a brake shoe to increase friction against the brake drum.

brake·man /'brākmən/ ▸ *n.* (*pl.* -men) **1** a railroad worker responsible for a train's brakes and other aspects of its operation. **2** a person in charge of brakes, for instance in a bobsled.

brake shoe ▸ *n.* either of the long curved blocks that press against the inside of the brake drum.

bram·ble /'brambəl/ ▸ *n.* a prickly scrambling wild shrub of the rose family, esp. a blackberry or (loosely) a dog rose. ▪ any rough, prickly vine or shrub. —**bram·bly** /-b(ə)lē/ *adj.*

bran /bran/ ▸ *n.* pieces of grain husk separated from flour after milling.

branch /branCH/ ▸ *n.* a part of a tree that grows out from the trunk or from a bough. ▪ a lateral extension or subdivision extending from the main part of something, typically one extending from a river, road, or railway: *a branch of the Susquehanna River.* ▪ a division or office of a large business or organization, operating locally or having a particular function: *he went to work at our Boston branch.* ▪ a conceptual subdivision of something, esp. a family, group of languages, or a subject: *a branch of mathematics called graph theory.* ▪ *Comput.* a control structure in which one of several alternative sets of program statements is selected for execution.
▸ *v.* [*intr.*] (of a road or path) divide. ▪ (of a tree or plant) bear or send out branches. ▪ (**branch off**) diverge from the main route or part: *the road branched off at the town.* ▪ (**branch out**) extend or expand one's activities or interests in a new direction: *the company is branching out into Europe.* —**branch·let** /-lit/ *n.* —**branch·like** *adj.* —**branch·y** *adj.*

brand /brand/ ▸ *n.* **1** a type of product manufactured by a particular company under a particular name: *a new brand of detergent.* ▪ a brand name: *the company will market computer software under its own brand.* ▪ a particular type or kind of something: *the Finnish brand of democratic socialism.* **2** an identifying mark burned on livestock or (esp. formerly) criminals or slaves with a branding iron. ▪ *fig.* a habit, trait, or quality

that causes someone public shame or disgrace: *the brand of Paula's alcoholism.* **3** a piece of burning or smoldering wood: *he took two burning brands from the fire.*
▸ *v.* [*tr.*] **1** mark (an animal, formerly a criminal or slave) with a branding iron. ▪ mark indelibly: *an ointment that branded her with unsightly violet-colored splotches.* ▪ describe (someone or something) as something bad or shameful: *the media was intent on branding us as communists* | [*tr.*] *she was branded a liar.* **2** assign a brand name to: [as *adj.*] (**branded**) *branded goods at low prices.* ▪ [as *n.*] (**branding**) the promotion of a particular product or company by means of advertising and distinctive design. —**brand·er** *n.*

bran·dish /'brandiSH/ ▸ *v.* [*tr.*] wave or flourish (something, esp. a weapon) as a threat or in anger or excitement. —**bran·dish·er** *n.*

brand name ▸ *n.* a name given by the maker to a product or range of products, esp. a trademark. ▪ a familiar or widely known name: [as *adj.*] *younger writers who clamber toward brand-name status.*

brand new ▸ *adj.* completely new.

bran·dy /'brandē/ ▸ *n.* (*pl.* -dies) a strong alcoholic spirit distilled from wine or fermented fruit juice. ▷mid 17th cent.: from earlier *brandwine, brandewine*, from Dutch *brandewijn*, from *branden* 'burn, distill' + *wijn* 'wine.'

brash[1] /braSH/ ▸ *adj.* self-assertive in a rude, noisy, or overbearing way: *he could be brash, cocky, and arrogant.* ▪ strong, energetic, or irreverent: *I like brash, vibrant flavors.* ▪ (of a place or thing) having an ostentatious or tasteless appearance: *the café was a brash new building.* —**brash·ly** *adv.* —**brash·ness** *n.*

brash[2] ▸ *n.* a mass of fragments, in particular: ▪ loose broken ice.

brass /bras/ ▸ *n.* a yellow alloy of copper and zinc: [as *adj.*] *a brass plate on the door.* ▪ a decorative object made of such an alloy: *shining brasses stood on the mantelpiece.* ▪ a memorial, typically medieval, consisting of a flat piece of inscribed brass, laid in the floor or set into the wall of a church. ▪ *Mus.* brass wind instruments (including trumpet, horn, trombone) forming a band or a section of an orchestra: *the brass and percussion were consistently too loud.* ▪ (also **top brass**) *inf.* people in authority or of high military rank. ▪ *inf.* in extended or metaphorical use referring to a person's hardness or effrontery: *he was the only one who* **had the brass to** *show his face.*
▸ □ **the brass ring** *inf.* a prize or goal that someone strives for: *Willa went for the brass ring, joining the firm at a whopping salary.*

brass band ▸ *n.* a group of musicians playing brass instruments and sometimes also percussion.

bras·se·rie /,brasə'rē/ ▸ *n.* (*pl.* -ries) an informal restaurant, esp. one in France or modeled on a French one and with a large selection of drinks.

bras·si·ca /'brasikə/ ▸ *n.* a plant of the cabbage family's genus *Brassica*, which includes cabbage, turnip, Brussels sprouts, and mustard.

bras·siere /brə'zi(ə)r/ ▸ *n.* full form of BRA.

brass knuck·les ▸ *n.* a metal guard worn over the knuckles in fighting, esp. to increase the effect of the blows.

brass·y /'brasē/ ▸ *adj.* (**brass·i·er, brass·i·est**) resembling brass, in particular: ▪ bright or harsh yellow. ▪ sounding like a brass musical instrument; harsh and loud. ▪ (of a person, typically a woman) tastelessly showy or loud in appearance or manner: *her brassy, audacious exterior.* —**brass·i·ly** /'brasəlē/ *adv.* —**brass·i·ness** *n.*

brat /brat/ ▸ *n. inf., derog.* or *humorous* a child, typically a badly behaved one. —**brat·tish** *adj.*

brat·wurst /'brät,wərst/ (also **brats**) ▸ *n.* a type of fine German pork sausage that is typically fried or grilled.

bra·va·do /brə'vädō/ ▸ *n.* a bold manner or a show of boldness intended to impress or intimidate.

brave /brāv/ ▸ *adj.* ready to face and endure danger or pain; showing courage. ▪ *poetic/lit.* fine or splendid in appearance: *his medals made a brave show.*
▸ *n.* [as *pl. n.*] (**the brave**) people who are ready to face and endure danger or pain. **2** *dated* an American Indian warrior. ▪ a young man who shows courage or a fighting spirit.
▸ *v.* [*tr.*] endure or face (unpleasant conditions or behavior) without showing fear: *we had to brave the full heat of the sun.* —**brave·ly** *adv.* —**brave·ness** *n.*

brav·er·y /'brāv(ə)rē/ ▸ *n.* courageous behavior or character.

bra·vo /'brävō/ ▸ *interj.* used to express approval when a performer or

---

Pronunciation Key ə *ago, up;* ər *over, fur;* a *hat;* ā *ate;* ä *car;* CH *chin;* e *let;* ē *see;* e(ə)r *air;* i *fit;* ī *by;* i(ə)r *ear;* NG *sing;* ō *go;* ô *law, for;* oi *toy;* o͝o *good;* o͞o *goo;* ou *out;* SH *she;* TH *thin;* T͟H *then;* (h)w *why;* ZH *vision*

other person has done something well: *people kept on clapping and shouting "bravo!"*
▸*n.* (*pl.* **-vos**) **1** a cry of bravo: *bravos rang out.* **2** a code word representing the letter B, used in radio communication.

bra·vu·ra /brəˈv(y) o͝orə/ ▸*n.* great technical skill and brilliance shown in a performance or activity: *the recital ended with a blazing display of bravura* | [as *adj.*] *a bravura performance.* ■ the display of great daring: *the show of bravura hid a guilty timidity.*

brawl /brôl/ ▸*n.* a rough or noisy fight or quarrel.
▸*v.* [*intr.*] fight or quarrel in a rough or noisy way. **—brawl·er** *n.*

brawn /brôn/ ▸*n.* physical strength in contrast to intelligence: *commando work required as much brain as brawn.* ▷Middle English: from Old French *braon* 'fleshy part of the leg,' of Germanic origin; related to German *Braten* 'roast meat.'

brawn·y /ˈbrônē/ ▸*adj.* (**brawn·i·er, brawn·i·est**) physically strong; muscular. **—brawn·i·ness** *n.*

bray /brā/ ▸*n.* the loud, harsh cry of a donkey or mule. ■ a sound, voice, or laugh resembling such a cry.
▸*v.* [*intr.*] make a loud, harsh cry or sound: *he brayed with laughter.* ■ [*tr.*] say (something) in a loud, harsh way: *vendors brayed the merits of spiced sausages* | [with *direct speech*] *"Leave," brayed a hoarse voice behind her.*

braze /brāz/ ▸*v.* [*tr.*] (often as *adj.*) (**brazed**) form, fix, or join by soldering with an alloy of copper and zinc at high temperature.
▸*n.* a brazed joint.

bra·zen /ˈbrāzən/ ▸*adj.* **1** bold and without shame: *he went about his illegal business with a brazen assurance* | *a brazen hussy!* **2** chiefly poetic/lit. made of brass. ■ harsh in sound: *the music's brazen chords.* **—bra·zen·ly** *adv.* **—bra·zen·ness** *n.*

bra·zier /ˈbrāZHər/ ▸*n.* **1** a portable heater consisting of a pan or stand for holding lighted coals. **2** a barbecue.

Bra·zil (also **bra·zil**) ▸*n.* **1** (also **Bra·zil nut**) a large three-sided nut with an edible kernel, several of which grow inside a large woody capsule, borne on a South American forest tree (*Bertholletia excelsa,* family Lecythidaceae). **2** (also **Bra·zil wood** or **bra·zil·wood**) a hard red wood obtained from a tropical tree (genus *Caesalpinia*) of the pea family, and from which dyes are obtained.

breach /brēCH/ ▸*n.* **1** an act of breaking or failing to observe a law, agreement, or code of conduct: *a breach of confidence* | *I sued for breach of contract.* ■ a break in relations: *a sudden breach between father and son.* **2** a gap in a wall, barrier, or defense, esp. one made by an attacking army.
▸*v.* [*tr.*] **1** make a gap in and break through (a wall, barrier, or defense): *the river breached its bank.* ■ break or fail to observe (a law, agreement, or code of conduct). **2** [*intr.*] (of a whale) rise and break through the surface of the water.
▸ □ **breach of promise** the action of breaking a sworn assurance to do something, formerly esp. to marry someone.

bread /bred/ ▸*n.* food made of flour, water, and yeast or another leavening agent, mixed together and baked: *a loaf of bread.* ■ the bread or wafer used in the Eucharist. ■ inf. the money or food that one needs in order to live: *I hate doing this, but I need the bread* | *his day job puts bread on the table.*
▸ □ **break bread** celebrate the Eucharist. ■ *poetic/lit.* share a meal with someone. □ **daily bread** the money or food that one needs in order to live: *she earned her daily bread by working long hours.*

bread and but·ter ▸*n.* a person's livelihood or main source of income, typically as earned by routine work: *their bread and butter is reporting local events.* ■ an everyday or ordinary person or thing: *the bread and butter of non-League soccer.*

bread·bas·ket /ˈbred,baskit/ ▸*n.* **1** a part of a region that produces cereals for the rest of it. **2** inf. a person's stomach, considered as the target for a blow.

bread·crumb /ˈbred,krəm/ ▸*n.* (usu. **breadcrumbs**) a small fragment of bread.

bread·fruit /ˈbred,fro͞ot/ ▸*n.* **1** a large, round, starchy fruit, used as a vegetable and sometimes to make a substitute for flour. **2** (also **bread·fruit tree**) the large evergreen tree (*Artocarpus altilis*) of the mulberry family that bears this fruit, widely cultivated on the islands of the Pacific and the Caribbean.

bread·line /ˈbred,līn/ ▸*n.* a line of people waiting to receive free food.

breadth /bredTH/ ▸*n.* the distance or measurement from side to side of something; width: *a black sweater outlined the breadth of his shoulders* | *the boat measured 27 feet in breadth* | *we traveled the length and breadth of India.* ■ wide range or extent: *she has the advantage of breadth of experience* | *there is a greater breadth of sound in the later recordings.* ■ the capacity to accept a wide range of ideas or beliefs: *the minister is not noted for his breadth of*

vision. ■ overall unity of artistic effect: *these masterpieces showed a new breadth of handling.*

bread·win·ner /ˈbred,winər/ ▸*n.* a person who earns money to support a family. **—bread·win·ning** /-,winiNG/ *n.*

break /brāk/ ▸*v.* (*past* **broke** /brōk/; *past part.* **brok·en** /ˈbrōkən/) **1** separate or cause to separate into pieces as a result of a blow, shock, or strain: [*intr.*] *the rope broke with a loud snap* | [*tr.*] *windows in the street were broken by the blast.* ■ [*tr.*] (of a person or animal) sustain an injury involving the fracture of a bone or bones in (a part of the body): *she had broken her leg in two places.* ■ [*tr.*] sustain such an injury to (a bone in the body). ■ [*tr.*] (of a part of the body or a bone) sustain a fracture: *what if his leg had broken?* ■ [*tr.*] cause a cut or graze in (the skin): *the bite had scarcely broken the skin.* ■ make or become inoperative: [*intr.*] *the machine has broken, and they can't fix it until next week* | [*tr.*] *he's broken the video.* ■ (of the amniotic fluid surrounding a fetus) be or cause to be discharged when the sac is ruptured in the first stages of labor: [*intr.*] *she realized her water had broken.* ■ [*tr.*] open (a safe) forcibly. ■ [*tr.*] use (a piece of paper currency) to pay for something and receive change out of the transaction: *she had to break a ten.* ■ [*tr.*] exchange (a piece of paper currency of large denomination) for the same amount in smaller denominations. ■ [*intr.*] (of two boxers or wrestlers) come out of a clinch, typically at the referee's command: *I was acting as referee and telling them to break.* ■ [*tr.*] succeed in deciphering (a code). ■ [*tr.*] open (a shotgun or rifle) at the breech. **2** [*tr.*] interrupt (a continuity, sequence, or course): *the new government broke the pattern of growth* | *his concentration was broken by a sound.* ■ put an end to (a silence) by speaking or making contact. ■ make a pause in (a journey). ■ [*intr.*] stop proceedings in order to have a pause or vacation: *at mid-morning they broke for coffee.* ■ lessen the impact of (a fall): *she put out an arm to break her fall.* ■ stop oneself from being subject to (a habit), or put an end to (a tie in a game) by making a score. ■ [*intr.*] (chiefly of an attacking player or team, or of a military force) make a rush or dash in a particular direction: *the flight broke to the right and formed a defensive circle.* ■ surpass (a record): *the movie broke box-office records.* ■ disconnect or interrupt (an electrical circuit). ■ [*intr.*] *Sports* (of a pitched or bowled ball) swerve or dip in direction. ■ [*intr.*] *Soccer* (of the ball) rebound unpredictably: *the ball broke to Craig but his shot rebounded from the post.* **3** [*tr.*] fail to observe (a law, regulation, or agreement): *the district attorney says she will prosecute retailers who break the law* | *a legally binding contract that can only be broken by mutual consent.* **4** [*tr.*] crush the emotional strength, spirit, or resistance of: *the idea was to better the prisoners, not to break them.* ■ [*intr.*] (of a person's emotional strength) give way: *her self-control finally broke.* ■ destroy the power of (a movement or organization). ■ destroy the effectiveness of (a strike), typically by bringing in other people to replace the striking workers. ■ tame or train (a horse). **5** [*intr.*] undergo a change or enter a new state, in particular: ■ (of the weather) change suddenly: *the weather broke, and thunder rumbled through a leaden sky.* ■ (of a storm) begin violently. ■ (of dawn or day) begin with the sun rising: *dawn was just breaking.* ■ (of clouds) move apart and begin to disperse. ■ (of waves) curl over and dissolve into foam: *the Caribbean sea breaking gently on the shore.* ■ (of a pitched baseball) curve or drop on its way toward the batter. ■ (of the voice) falter and change tone, due to emotion: *her voice broke as she relived the experience.* ■ (of a boy's voice) change in tone and register at puberty. ■ (of prices on the stock exchange) fall sharply. ■ (of news or a scandal) suddenly become public: *since the news broke I've received thousands of wonderful letters.* ■ [*tr.*] (**break something to someone**) make bad news known to someone. ■ make the first stroke at the beginning of a game of billiards, pool, or snooker.
▸*phrasal v.* □ **break away** (of a person) escape from someone's hold. ■ escape from the control of a person, group, or practice: *an attempt to break away from the elitism that has dominated the book trade.* ■ (of a competitor in a race) move into the lead. □ **break down 1** (of a machine or motor vehicle) suddenly cease to function: *his van broke down.* ■ (of a person) have the vehicle they are driving cease to function: *she broke down on the highway.* ■ (of a relationship, agreement, or process) cease to continue; collapse: *pay negotiations with management broke down.* ■ lose control of one's emotions when in a state of distress: *if she had tried to utter a word, she would have broken down.* ■ (of a person's health or emotional control) fail or collapse: *his health broke down under the strain of overwork.* **2** undergo chemical decomposition: *waste products that break down into low-level toxic materials.* □ **break something down 1** demolish a door or other barrier: *they had to get the police to break the door down* | *fig. race barriers can be broken down by educational reform.* **2** separate something into parts: *each tutorial is broken down into more manageable units.* ■ analyze information: *bar graphs show how the information can be broken down.* ■ convert a substance into simpler compounds by chemical action: *almost every natural substance can be broken down by*

bacteria. □ **break even** reach a point in a business venture when the profits are equal to the costs. □ **break forth** burst out suddenly; emerge. □ **break free** another way of saying BREAK AWAY. □ **break in 1** force entry to a building: *it sounded like someone trying to break in.* **2** [with *direct speech*] interject: *"I don't want to interfere," Mrs. Hendry broke in.* □ **break someone in** familiarize someone with a new job or situation: *there was no time to break in a new executive assistant.* ■ (**break a horse**) accustom a horse to a saddle and bridle, and to being ridden. □ **break something in** wear something, typically a pair of new shoes, until it becomes supple and comfortable. □ **break into 1** enter or open a (place, vehicle, or container) for the purposes of theft: *four men broke into the house.* ■ succeed in winning a share of (a market or a position in a profession): *Japanese companies failed to break into the U.S. personal-computer market.* **2** (of a person) suddenly or unexpectedly burst forth into (laughter or song). ■ (of a person's face or mouth) relax into (a smile). **3** change one's pace to (a faster one): *Greg broke into a sprint.* □ **break off** become severed: *the fuselage had broken off just behind the pilot's seat.* ■ abruptly stop talking: *she broke off, stifling a sob.* □ **break something off** remove something forcibly, typically for the purpose of or whole: *Tucker broke off a piece of bread.* ■ discontinue talks or relations: *the U.S. threatened to break off diplomatic relations.* □ **break out** (of war, fighting, or similarly undesirable things) start suddenly: *forest fires have broken out across Indonesia.* ■ (of a physical discomfort) suddenly manifest itself: *prickles of sweat had broken out along her backbone.* □ **break out in** (of a person or a part of their body) be suddenly affected by an unpleasant sensation or condition: *something had caused him to break out in a rash.* □ **break something out** *inf.* open and start using something: *it was time to break out the champagne.* □ **break through** make or force a way through (a barrier): *demonstrators attempted to break through the police lines* | *the sun might break through in a few spots.* ■ *fig.* (of a person) achieve success in a particular area: *so many talented players are struggling to break through.* □ **break up** disintegrate; disperse: *the bones had broken up into minute fragments.* ■ (of a gathering) disband; end. ■ (of a couple in a relationship) part company. ■ start laughing uncontrollably: *the whole cast broke up.* ■ become emotionally upset. □ **break something up** cause something to separate into pieces, parts, or sections: *break up the chocolate, and place it in a bowl* | *he intends to break the company up into strategic business units.* ■ bring a social event or meeting to an end by being the first person to leave: *Richard was sorry to break up the party.* ■ disperse or put an end to a gathering: *police broke up a demonstration in the capital.* □ **break with** quarrel or cease relations with (someone): *he had broken with his family long before.* ■ act in a way that is not in accordance with (a custom or tradition).

▸*n.* **1** an interruption of continuity or uniformity: *the magazine has been published without a break since 1950.* ■ an act of separating oneself from a state of affairs: *a break with the past.* ■ a change in the weather. ■ a change of line, paragraph, or page: *dotted lines on the screen show page breaks.* ■ a curve or drop in the path of a pitched baseball. ■ a change of tone in the voice due to emotion: *there was a break in her voice now.* ■ an interruption in an electrical circuit. ■ a rush or dash in a particular direction, esp. by an attacking player or team: *he made a bounce pass for a basket on the break in the second quarter.* ■ a breakout, esp. from prison. ■ a sudden decrease, typically in prices. ■ *inf.* an opportunity or chance, esp. one leading to professional success: *his big break came when a critic gave him a rave review.* ■ (also **break of serve**) *Tennis* the winning of a game against an opponent's serve. **2** a pause in work: *they take long coffee breaks.* ■ a short vacation: *the Christmas break.* **3** a gap or opening: *the spectacular vistas occasionally offered by a break in the rain forest* | *he stopped to wait for a break in the traffic.* **4** an instance of breaking; the point where something is broken: *a break in the valve was being repaired.* **5** *Billiards* a player's turn to make the opening shot of a game or a rack. ▷Old English *brecan* (verb), of Germanic origin; related to Dutch *breken* and German *brechen*, from an Indo-European root shared by Latin *frangere* 'to break.' —**break·a·ble** *adj.*

▸ □ **break of day** dawn. □ **break wind** release gas from the anus. □ **give someone a break** [usu. in *imper.*] *inf.* stop putting pressure on someone about something. ■ (**give me a break**) used to express contemptuous disagreement or disbelief about what has been said: *He's seven times as quick and he's only 20 years old. Give me a break.* □ **make a break for** make a sudden dash in the direction of, typically in a bid to escape: *he made a break for the door.* □ **make a clean break** remove oneself completely and finally from a situation or relationship.

break·age /ˈbrākij/ ▸*n.* the action of breaking something: *some breakage of bone has occurred.*

break·a·way /ˈbrākəˌwā/ ▸*n.* **1** a divergence or radical change from something established or long standing: *rock was a breakaway from pop.* ■ a secession of a number of people from an organization, typically

following conflict or disagreement and resulting in the establishment of a new organization: [as *adj.*] *the breakaway republic.* **2** *Sports* a sudden attack or forward movement, esp. in a bicycle race or in hockey or football.

break·danc·ing /ˈbrākˌdansiNG/ ▸*n.* an energetic and acrobatic style of street dancing, developed by American blacks. —**break·dance** *v. & n.* —**break·danc·er** *n.*

break·down /ˈbrākˌdoun/ ▸*n.* **1** a failure of a relationship or of communication: *the breakdown of their marriage.* ■ a collapse of a system of authority due to widespread transgression of the rules: *a breakdown in military discipline.* ■ a sudden collapse in someone's mental health. ■ a mechanical failure. ■ the chemical or physical decomposition of something: *the breakdown of ammonia to nitrites.* **2** an explanatory analysis, esp. of statistics: *a detailed cost breakdown.* **3** a lively, energetic American country dance.

break·er /ˈbrākər/ ▸*n.* **1** a heavy sea wave that breaks into white foam on the shore or a shoal. **2** a person or thing that breaks something: [in *comb.*] *a rule-breaker a code-breaker.* ■ short for CIRCUIT BREAKER.

break·fast /ˈbrekfəst/ ▸*n.* a meal eaten in the morning, the first of the day: *I often have toast for my breakfast.*

▸*v.* [*intr.*] have this meal: *she breakfasted on French toast and bacon.* —**break·fast·er** *n.* **break·fast·less** *adj.*

break-in ▸*n.* a forced or unconsented entry into a building, car, computer system, etc., typically to steal something.

break·ing point ▸*n.* the moment of greatest strain at which someone or something gives way: *the refugee crisis has **reached the breaking point**.*

break·neck /ˈbrākˌnek/ ▸*adj.* dangerously or extremely fast: *he drove at breakneck speed.*

break·out /ˈbrākˌout/ ▸*n.* **1** a forcible escape, typically from prison: *a prison breakout.* ■ (in soccer, hockey, and other sports) a sudden attack by a team that had been defending. **2** an outbreak: *a breakout of hostilities.* **3** a categorized list: *an excellent breakout of Web sites by topic.*

▸*adj. inf.* **1** suddenly and extremely popular or successful: *a breakout movie.* **2** denoting or relating to groups that break away from a conference or other larger gathering for discussion: *we divided into 15 breakout groups.*

break point ▸*n.* **1** a place or time at which an interruption or change is made. ■ (usu. **break·point**) *Comput.* a place in a computer program where the sequence of instructions is interrupted, esp. by another program or by the operator. **2** *Tennis* the state of a game when the side receiving service needs only one more point to win the game: *he hit a winner to reach break point.* **3** another term for BREAKING POINT.

break·through /ˈbrākˌTHrōō/ ▸*n.* a sudden, dramatic, and important discovery or development, esp. in science: *a major breakthrough in DNA research.* ■ a significant and dramatic overcoming of a perceived obstacle, allowing the completion of a process: *the union's agreement was the key breakthrough on pay and conditions.*

break·up /ˈbrākˌəp/ ▸*n.* an end to a relationship, typically a marriage. ■ a division of a country or organization into smaller autonomous units: *the breakup of the Soviet Union.* ■ a physical disintegration of something: *large quantities of oil are released after the breakup of a tanker* | *the spring breakup of the ice.*

break·wa·ter /ˈbrākˌwôtər; -ˌwätər/ ▸*n.* a barrier built out into a body of water to protect a coast or harbor from the force of waves.

bream /brim; brēm/ ▸*n.* (*pl.* same) a greenish-bronze deep-bodied freshwater fish (*Abramis brama*) of the minnow family, native to Europe and popular with anglers. ■ used in names of other fishes resembling or related to this, e.g., **sea bream**.

breast /brest/ ▸*n.* either of the two soft, protruding organs on the upper front of a woman's body that secrete milk after pregnancy. ■ a person's chest: *her heart was hammering in her breast.* ■ the corresponding part of a bird or mammal: [as *adj.*] *the breast feathers of the doves.* ■ a portion of poultry cut from such a part: *a grilled chicken breast.* ■ the part of a garment that covers the chest: [as *adj.*] *a breast pocket.* ■ a person's chest regarded as the seat of the emotions: *wild feelings of frustration were rising up in his breast.*

▸*v.* [*tr.*] face and move forward against or through (something): *I watched him breast the wave.* ■ reach the top of (a hill). —**breast·ed** *adj.* [in *comb.*] *a crimson-breasted bird.*

▸ □ **beat one's breast** make an exaggerated show of sorrow, despair, or regret.

breast·bone /'brest,bōn/ ▸n. a thin, flat bone running down the center of the chest and connecting the ribs. Also called STERNUM.

breast-feed ▸v. (past and past part. **-fed**) [tr.] (of a woman) feed (a baby) with milk from the breast: *she breast-fed her first child.* ■ [intr.] (of a baby) feed from the breast: *the child began to breast-feed.*

breast·plate /'brest,plāt/ ▸n. a piece of armor covering the chest.

breast·stroke /'brest,strōk/ ▸n. a style of swimming on one's front, in which the arms are pushed forward and then swept back in a circular movement, while the legs are tucked in toward the body and then kicked out in a corresponding movement. ■ (**the breaststroke**) a race, typically of a specified length or kind, in which such a style of swimming is used: *she won the 200 m breaststroke.*

breast·work /'brest,wərk/ ▸n. a low temporary defense or parapet.

breath /breTH/ ▸n. an inhalation or exhalation of air from the lungs: *she drew in a quick breath.* ■ an exhalation of air by a person or animal that can be seen, smelled, or heard: *he sighed, his breath hanging like a cloud in the icy air.* ■ the physiological process of taking air into the lungs and expelling it again, esp. the ability to breathe easily: *she paused for breath.* ■ the air taken into or expelled from the lungs: *I was gasping for breath.* ■ a brief moment; the time required for one act of respiration: *in Las Vegas, they marry you in a breath.* ■ a slight movement of air: *the weather was balmy, not a breath of wind.* ■ a sign, hint, or suggestion: *he avoided the slightest breath of scandal.*

▸ □ **a breath of fresh air** a refreshing change: *the company's no-nonsense attitude is a breath of fresh air.* □ **catch one's breath 1** cease breathing momentarily in surprise or fear. **2** rest after exercise to restore normal breathing: *she stood for a few moments, catching her breath.* □ **don't hold your breath** *inf.* used hyperbolically to indicate that something is likely to take a long time: *don't hold your breath waiting for Congress to clean up political action committees.* □ **hold one's breath** cease breathing temporarily. ■ *fig.* be in a state of suspense or anticipation: *France held its breath while the Senate chose its new president.* □ **in the same** (or **next**) **breath** at the same time: *he congratulated Simon on his victory but in the same breath dismissed it.* □ **out of breath** gasping for air, typically after exercise: *he arrived on the top floor out of breath.* □ **save one's breath** stop wasting time in futile talk: *save your breath; I know all about it.* □ **take someone's breath away** astonish or inspire someone with awed respect or delight. □ **under** (or **below**) **one's breath** in a very quiet voice; almost inaudibly: *he swore violently under his breath.* □ **waste one's breath** talk or give advice without effect: *I have better things to do than waste my breath arguing.*

breath·a·lyz·er /'breTHə,līzər/ (also *trademark* **Breath·a·lyz·er**) ▸n. a device used by police for measuring the amount of alcohol in a driver's breath.

breathe /brēTH/ ▸v. [intr.] take air into the lungs and then expel it, esp. as a regular physiological process: *she was wheezing as she breathed* | [tr.] *we are polluting the air we breathe.* ■ be or seem to be alive because of this: *at least I'm still breathing.* ■ [with *direct speech*] say something with quiet intensity: *"We're together at last," she breathed.* ■ (of an animal or plant) respire or exchange gases: *plants breathe through their roots.* ■ (of material or soil) admit or emit air or moisture: *let your lawn breathe.* ■ [tr.] allow (a horse) to rest after exertion.

▸ □ **breathe down someone's neck** follow closely behind someone. ■ constantly check up on someone.

breath·er /'brēTHər/ ▸n. **1** *inf.* a brief pause for rest: *the director is taking a breather from his furious schedule.* **2** a vent or valve to release pressure or to allow air to move freely around something. **3** a person or animal that breathes in a particular way, or breathes a particular substance: *a heavy breather* | [in *comb.*] *reptiles are lung-breathers.*

breath·ing /'brēTHiNG/ ▸n. the process of taking air into and expelling it from the lungs: *his breathing was shallow.*

breath·less /'breTHlis/ ▸adj. gasping for breath, typically due to exertion: *the climb left me breathless.* ■ short of breath or appearing this way because of excitement or other strong feelings: *a breathless story about risking death to steal the truth.* ■ (of the air or weather) unstirred by a wind or breeze; stiflingly still: *the warm, breathless air.* —**breath·less·ly** *adv.* —**breath·less·ness** *n.*

breath·tak·ing /'breTH,tākiNG/ ▸adj. astonishing or awe-inspiring in quality, so as to take one's breath away: *the scene was one of breathtaking beauty.* —**breath·tak·ing·ly** *adv.*

breath test ▸n. a test in which a driver is made to blow into a breathalyzer to check the amount of alcohol that has been drunk.

breath·y /'breTHē/ ▸adj. (**breath·i·er, breath·i·est**) producing or causing an audible sound of breathing, often related to physical exertion or strong feelings: *a breathy laugh.* —**breath·i·ly** /'breTHəlē/ *adv.* —**breath·i·ness** *n.*

brec·ci·a /'brecHēə; 'bresH-/ ▸n. *Geol.* rock consisting of angular fragments cemented together.

bred /bred/ ▸ past and participle of BREED.
▸adj. [usu. in *comb.*] (of a person or animal) reared in a specified environment or way: *a city-bred man.*

breech /brēcH/ ▸n. the part of a cannon behind the bore. ■ the back part of a rifle or gun barrel.

breech birth (also **breech delivery**) ▸n. a delivery of a baby so positioned in the uterus that the buttocks or feet are delivered first.

breech·es /'bricHiz; 'brē-/ ▸pl. n. short trousers fastened just below the knee. ■ *inf.* trousers.
▸ □ **too big for one's breeches** see BIG.

breech-load·er ▸n. a gun designed to have ammunition inserted at the breech rather than through the muzzle. —**breech-load·ing** *adj.*

breed /brēd/ ▸v. (past and past part. **bred** /bred/) [tr.] cause (an animal) to produce offspring, typically in a controlled and organized way: *bitches may not be bred from more than once a year.* ■ [intr.] (of animals) mate and then produce offspring: *toads are said to return to the pond of their birth to breed* | [as *adj.*] (**breeding**) *the breeding season.* ■ develop (a kind of animal or plant) for a particular purpose or quality: *these horses are bred for this sport.* ■ raise (livestock or animals): *they live on an island, where they breed Hanoverian horses.* ■ rear and train (someone) to behave in a particular way or have certain qualities: *Theresa had been beautifully bred.* ■ cause (something) to happen or occur, typically over a period of time: *success breeds confidence.*

▸n. a stock of animals or plants within a species having a distinctive appearance and typically having been developed by deliberate selection. ■ a sort or kind of person or thing: *a new breed of entrepreneurs.* —**breed·er** *n.*

▸ □ **a dying breed** a sort or kind of person that is slowly disappearing: *the country's dying breed of elder statesmen.*

breed·er re·ac·tor ▸n. a nuclear reactor that creates fissile material (typically plutonium-239 by irradiation of uranium-238) at a faster rate than it uses another fissile material (typically uranium-235) as fuel.

breed·ing /'brēdiNG/ ▸n. the mating and production of offspring by animals: *some worms use the moon to time their breeding.* ■ the activity of controlling the mating and production of offspring of animals: *the breeding of rats and mice for experiments.* ■ training and education, esp. in proper social behavior: *a girl of good breeding.* ■ the good manners regarded as characteristic of the aristocracy and conferred by heredity: *a lady of breeding.*

breeze /brēz/ ▸n. **1** a gentle wind. ■ a wind of force 2 to 6 on the Beaufort scale (4–27 knots or 4.5-31 mph). **2** *inf.* a thing that is easy to do or accomplish: *traveling through London was a breeze.*
▸v. [intr.] *inf.* come or go in a casual or lighthearted manner: *I breezed in as if nothing were wrong.* ■ [tr.] deal with something with apparently casual ease: *the computer has the power to breeze through huge documents.*

breez·y /'brēzē/ ▸adj. (**breez·i·er, breez·i·est**) **1** pleasantly windy: *it was a bright, breezy day.* **2** appearing relaxed, informal, and cheerily brisk: *the text is written in a breezy, matter-of-fact manner.* —**breez·i·ly** /-zəlē/ *adv.* —**breez·i·ness** *n.*

breth·ren /'breTH(ə)rin/ ▸ archaic plural form of BROTHER.
▸pl. n. fellow Christians or members of a male religious order. ■ used for humorous or rhetorical effect to refer to people belonging to a particular group: *our brethren in the popular press.*

Bret·on /'bretn/ ▸n. **1** a native of Brittany. **2** the Celtic language of Brittany, related to Cornish.
▸adj. of or relating to Brittany or its people or language.

breve /brēv; brev/ ▸n. **1** a musical note, rarely used in modern music, having the time value of two semibreves or whole notes. **2** a written or printed mark (˘) indicating a short or unstressed vowel.

bre·vet /brə'vet; 'brevit/ ▸n. [often as *adj.*] a former type of military commission conferred esp. for outstanding service by which an officer was promoted to a higher rank without the corresponding pay: *a brevet lieutenant.*

bre·vi·ar·y /'brēvē,erē; 'brev-/ ▸n. (pl. **-ar·ies**) a book containing the service for each day, to be recited by those in orders in the Roman Catholic Church.

brev·i·ty /'brevitē/ ▸n. concise and exact use of words in writing or speech. ■ shortness of time: *the brevity of human life.*

brew /broō/ ▸v. [tr.] **1** make (beer) by soaking, boiling, and fermentation. **2** make (tea or coffee) by mixing it with hot water: *I've just brewed some coffee* | [intr.] *he did a crossword while the tea brewed.* **3** [intr.] (of an unwelcome event or situation) begin to develop: *there was more trouble brewing as the airline pilots went on strike* | *a storm was brewing.*
▸n. **1** beer: *nonalcoholic brews.* ■ *inf.* a serving of beer. **2** a cup or mug of

tea or coffee. **3** a mixture of events, people, or things that interact to form a more potent whole: *a dangerous brew of political turmoil and violent conflict.* —**brew·er** *n.*

brew·er·y /'brōōərē/ ▶*n.* (*pl.* **-er·ies**) a place where beer is made commercially.

bri·ar[1] /'brī(ə)r/ ▶*n.* variant spelling of BRIER[1].

bri·ar[2] ▶*n.* variant spelling of BRIER[2].

bribe /brīb/ ▶*v.* [*tr.*] persuade (someone) to act in one's favor, typically illegally or dishonestly, by a gift of money or other inducement: [*tr.*] *you weren't willing to be good to your sister without being bribed with a lollipop.* | [*intr.*] *he has no money to bribe with.*
▶*n.* a sum of money or other inducement offered or given in this way. ▷late Middle English: from Old French *briber, brimber* 'beg,' of unknown origin. The original sense was 'rob, extort,' hence (as noun) 'theft, stolen goods,' also 'money extorted or demanded for favors,' later 'offer money as an inducement' (early 16th cent.). —**brib·a·ble** *adj.* —**brib·er** *n.* —**brib·er·y** *n.*

bric-a-brac /'brik ə ,brak/ ▶*n.* miscellaneous objects and ornaments of little value.

brick ▶*n.* a small rectangular block typically made of fired or sun-dried clay, used in building. ■ bricks collectively as a building material: *this mill was built of brick.* ■ a small, rectangular object: *a brick of ice cream.*
▶*v.* [*tr.*] (often **be bricked**) block or enclose with a wall of bricks: *the doors have been bricked up.*
▶ □ **hit** (or **run into**) **a brick wall** face an insuperable problem or obstacle while trying to do something.

brick·bat /'brik,bat/ ▶*n.* a piece of brick, typically when used as a weapon. ■ a remark or comment which is highly critical and typically insulting: *the plaudits were beginning to outnumber the brickbats.*

brick·lay·er /'brik,lāər/ ▶*n.* a person whose job is to build walls, houses, and other structures with bricks. —**brick·lay·ing** /-,lāiNG/ *n.*

bricks and mor·tar ▶*n.* used to denote a business that operates in the physical world rather than over the Internet: *the bricks-and-mortar banks.*

brick·work /'brik,wərk/ ▶*n.* the bricks in a wall, house, or other structure, typically in terms of their type or layout: *the patterned brickwork of the gables.*

brick·yard /'brik,yärd/ ▶*n.* a place where bricks are made.

brid·al /'brīdl/ ▶*adj.* of or concerning a bride or a wedding: *the bridal party came out into the church porch.*

bride /brīd/ ▶*n.* a woman on her wedding day or just before and after the event.

bride·groom /'brīd,grōōm/ ▶*n.* a man on his wedding day or just before and after the event.

brides·maid /'brīdz,mād/ ▶*n.* a girl or woman who accompanies a bride on her wedding day.

bridge[1] /brij/ ▶*n.* **1** a structure carrying a road, path, railroad, or canal across a river, ravine, road, railroad, or other obstacle: *a bridge across the river* | *a railroad bridge.* ■ something that makes a physical connection between two other things. ■ something that is intended to reconcile or form a connection between two things: *a committee that was formed to create a bridge between rival parties.* ■ a partial denture supported by natural teeth on either side. See also BRIDGEWORK. ■ the support formed by the hand for the forward part of a billiard cue. ■ a long stick with a frame at the end that is used to support a cue for a shot that is otherwise hard to reach. ■ *Mus.* an upright piece of wood on a string instrument over which the strings are stretched. ■ *Mus.* a bridge passage. **2** the elevated platform on a ship from which the captain and officers direct operations. **3** the upper bony part of a person's nose: *he pushed his spectacles further up the bridge of his nose.* ■ the central part of a pair of glasses, fitting over this: *these sunglasses have a special nose bridge for comfort.* **4** an electric circuit with two branches across which a detector or load is connected.
▶*v.* [*tr.*] be a bridge over (something): *a covered walkway that bridged the gardens.* ■ build a bridge over (something): *earlier attempts to bridge the channel had failed.* ■ make (a difference between two groups) smaller or less significant: *bridging the gap between avant garde art and popular culture.* —**bridge·a·ble** *adj.*

bridge[2] ▶*n.* a card game descended from whist, played by two partnerships of two players who at the beginning of each hand bid for the right to name the trump suit, the highest bid also representing a contract to make a specified number of tricks with a specified suit as trumps.

bridge·head /'brij,hed/ ▶*n.* a strong position secured by an army inside enemy territory from which to advance or attack: *fig. in the 1970s, academic literary theory established bridgeheads in Britain.*

bridge·work /'brij,wərk/ ▶*n.* dental bridges collectively.

bri·dle /'brīdl/ ▶*n.* the headgear used to control a horse, consisting of buckled straps to which a bit and reins are attached. ■ a line, rope, or device that is used to restrain or control the action or movement of something.
▶*v.* **1** [*tr.*] (usu. **be bridled**) put a bridle on (a horse). ■ bring (something) under control; curb: *the fact that he was their servant bridled his tongue.* **2** [*intr.*] show one's resentment or anger, esp. by throwing up the head and drawing in the chin: *ranchers have bridled at excessive federal control.*

bri·dle path ▶*n.* a path or track used for horseback riding.

Brie /brē/ ▶*n.* a kind of soft, mild, creamy cheese with a firm, white skin.

bridle

brief /brēf/ ▶*adj.* of short duration: *the president made a brief visit to Moscow.* ■ concise in expression; using few words: *introductions were brief and polite.* ■ (of a piece of clothing) not covering much of the body; scanty: *Alice sported a pair of extremely brief black shorts.*
▶*n.* a concise statement or summary: *their comments were cribbed right from industry briefs.* ■ a set of instructions given to a person about a job or task: *his brief is to turn around the country's economy.* ■ a written summary of the facts and legal points supporting one side of a case, for presentation to a court.
▶*v.* [*tr.*] instruct or inform (someone) thoroughly, esp. in preparation for a task: *she briefed him on last week's decisions.* ▷Middle English: from Old French *brief,* from Latin *brevis* 'short.' The noun is via late Latin *breve* 'note, dispatch,' hence 'an official letter.' —**brief·ing** *n.* —**brief·ly** *adv.* —**brief·ness** *n.*
▶ □ **in brief** in a few words; in short: *he is, in brief, the embodiment of evil* | *the news in brief.*

brief·case /'brēf,kās/ ▶*n.* a flat, rectangular container, typically made of leather, for carrying books and papers.

bri·er[1] /'brī(ə)r/ (also **bri·ar**) ▶*n.* any of a number of prickly scrambling shrubs, esp. the sweetbrier and other wild roses. —**bri·er·y** *adj.*

bri·er[2] (also **bri·ar**) ▶*n.* (also **brier pipe**) a tobacco pipe made from woody nodules borne at ground level by a large woody plant (*Erica arborea*) of the heath family.

brig /brig/ ▶*n.* a two-masted, square-rigged ship with an additional gaff sail on the mainmast. ■ *inf.* a prison, esp. on a warship.

Brig. ▶*abbr.* ■ brigade. ■ brigadier.

bri·gade /bri'gād/ ▶*n.* a subdivision of an army, typically consisting of a small number of infantry battalions and/or other units and often forming part of a division: *he commanded a brigade of 3,000 men.* ■ an organization with a specific purpose, typically with a military or quasi-military structure: *the local fire brigade.* ■ *inf., often derog.* a group of people with a common characteristic or dedicated to a common cause: *the anti-smoking brigade.*

brig·a·dier gen·er·al ▶*n.* (*pl.* **brigadier generals**) an officer in the U.S. Army, Air Force, or Marine Corps ranking above colonel and below major general.

brig·and /'brigənd/ ▶*n.* *poetic/lit.* a member of a gang that ambushes and robs people in forests and mountains. —**brig·and·age** /-dij/ *n.* —**brig·and·ry** /-drē/ *n.*

brig·an·tine /'brigən,tēn/ ▶*n.* a two-masted sailing ship with a square-rigged foremast and a fore-and-aft-rigged mainmast.

bright /brīt/ ▶*adj.* **1** giving out or reflecting a lot of light; shining: *I have problems seeing when the sun is bright* | *her bright, dark eyes.* ■ full of light: *the rooms are bright and spacious.* ■ (of a period of time) having sunny, cloudless weather: *the long, bright days of June.* ■ having a vivid color: *the bright flowers* | *a bright tie.* ■ (of color) vivid and bold: *the bright green leaves.* **2** (of sound) clear, vibrant, and typically high-pitched: *her voice is fresh and bright.* **3** (of a person, idea, or remark) intelligent and quick-witted: *a bright young journalist* | *a suggestion box for bright ideas.* **4** giving an appearance of cheerful liveliness: *she gave a bright smile.* ■ (of someone's future) likely to be successful and happy: *the bright prospects for her early retirement.*
▶*adv.* luminously: *a full moon shining bright.*
▶*n.* (**brights**) **1** bold and vivid colors: *gloves in neon brights.* **2** headlights

---

Pronunciation Key ə *ago, up;* ər *over, fur;* a *hat;* ā *ate;* ä *car;* CH *chin;* e *let;* ē *see;* e(ə)r *air,* i *fit;* ī *by;* i(ə)r *ear;* NG *sing;* ō *go;* ô *law, for;* oi *toy;* ōō *good;* ōō *goo;* ou *out;* SH *she;* TH *thin;* ͡TH *then;* (h)w *why;* ZH *vision*

switched to high beam: *he turned the brights on, and we drove along the dirt road.* —**bright·ly** *adv.* —**bright·ness** *n.*

▶ □ **bright and early** very early in the morning. □ **look on the bright side** be optimistic or cheerful in spite of difficulties.

bright·en /'brītn/ ▶*v.* make or become more light: [*intr.*] *the day began to brighten in the east* | [*tr.*] *the fire began to blaze fiercely, brightening the room.* ■ [*tr.*] make (something) more attractively and cheerfully colorful: *this colorful hanging ornament will brighten any room* | *daffodils* **brighten up** *many gardens and parks.* ■ make or become happier and more cheerful: [*intr.*] *Sarah* **brightened up** *considerably as she thought of Emily's words* | [*tr.*] *she seems to brighten his life.*

bright-eyed ▶*adj.* **1** having shining eyes. **2** alert and lively: *bright-eyed young lawyers* | *a bright-eyed optimism.*

▶ □ **bright-eyed and bushy-tailed** *inf.* alert and lively; eager.

Bright's dis·ease ▶*n.* a disease involving chronic inflammation of the kidneys.

brill /bril/ ▶*n.* a European flatfish (*Scophthalmus rhombus*, family Scophthalmidae) that resembles a turbot.

bril·liance /'brilyəns/ (also **bril·lian·cy** /-sē/) ▶*n.* intense brightness of light: *the nights were dark, lit only by the brilliance of Aegean stars.* ■ vividness of color. ■ exceptional talent or intelligence: *he's played the stock market with great brilliance.*

bril·liant /'brilyənt/ ▶*adj.* **1** (of light) very bright and radiant. ■ (of a color) brightly and intensely vivid. **2** exceptionally clever or talented: *a brilliant young mathematician* | *a brilliant idea.* ■ outstanding; impressive: *his brilliant career at Harvard.* ■ *Brit., inf.* very good, excellent, or marvelous: *we had a brilliant time.*

▶*n.* a diamond of brilliant cut. —**bril·liant·ly** *adv.*

brim /brim/ ▶*n.* the projecting edge around the bottom of a hat: *a soft hat with a turned-up brim.* ■ the upper edge or lip of a cup, bowl, or other container: *tankards frothing to the brim.*

▶*v.* (**brimmed, brim·ming**) [often as *adj.*] (**brimming**) fill or be full to the point of overflowing: [*intr.*] *a brimming cup* | [*tr.*] *seawater brimmed the riverbanks.* ■ fill something so completely as almost to spill out of it: *large tears brimmed in her eyes.* ■ *fig.* be possessed by or full of feelings or thoughts: *he is* **brimming with** *ideas.* —**brimmed** *adj.* [in *comb.*] : *a wide-brimmed hat.* —**brim·less** *adj.*

brim·ful /'brim,fŏŏl/ ▶*adj.* filled with something to the point of overflowing: *a jug brimful of custard.*

brim·stone /'brim,stōn/ ▶*n. archaic* sulfur.

▶ □ **fire and brimstone** see **FIRE**.

brin·dle /'brindl/ ▶*n.* a brownish or tawny color of animal fur, with streaks of other color. ■ an animal with such a coat.

▶*adj.* (also **brin·dled**) (esp. of domestic animals) brownish or tawny with streaks of other color: *a brindle pup.*

brine /brīn/ ▶*n.* water saturated or strongly impregnated with salt. ■ seawater: *dolphins and whales can't help taking in the odd gulp of brine as they swallow a fish.* ■ *technical* a strong solution of a salt or salts.

▶*v.* [*tr.*] [often as *adj.*] (**brined**) soak in or saturate with salty water: *brined anchovies.*

bring /briNG/ ▶*v.* (*past* **brought** /brôt/) [*tr.*] come to a place with (someone or something): *she brought Luke home from the hospital.* ■ cause (someone or something) to come to a place: *what brings you here?* | *a felony case brought before a jury.* ■ make (someone or something) move in a particular direction: *heavy rain* **brought down** *part of the ceiling.* ■ cause (something): *the bad weather brought famine* | *her letter* **brought forth** *a torrent of criticism.* ■ cause (someone or something) to be in or change to a particular state or condition: *I'll give you some aspirin to* **bring down** *his temperature* | *his approach* **brought** *him* **into** *conflict with government.* ■ (**bring someone in**) involve (someone) in a particular activity: *he has brought in a consultant.* ■ initiate (legal action) against someone: *riot and conspiracy charges should* **be brought against** *them.* ■ (**bring oneself to do something**) force oneself to do something unpleasant or distressing: *she could not* **bring herself to** *mention it.* ■ cause someone to receive (an amount of money) as income or profit: *two important Chippendale lots brought $10,000 each.*

▶*phrasal v.* ■ **bring something about 1** cause something to happen: *she brought about a revolution.* **2** cause a ship to head in a different direction. □ **bring something on** cause something, typically something unpleasant, to occur or develop: *ulcers are not brought on by a rich diet.* ■ (**bring something on/upon**) be responsible for something, typically something unpleasant, that happens to oneself or someone else: *the doom that he has* **brought upon** *himself.* □ **bring something out** produce and launch a new product or publication: *the band is bringing out a video.* ■ make something more evident; emphasize something: *the shawl brings out the color of your eyes* | *he* **brought out the best** *in his team.* □ **bring**

someone around 1 restore someone to consciousness. **2** persuade someone to do something, esp. to adopt one's own point of view: *my wife has brought me around to eating broiled grouper.* □ **bring someone to** restore someone to consciousness. □ **bring someone up** look after a child until it is an adult. ■ (**be brought up**) be taught as a child to adopt particular behavior or attitudes: *he had been brought up to believe that marriage was forever.* □ **bring something up** raise a matter for discussion or consideration: *she tried repeatedly to bring up the subject of marriage.* —**bring·er** *n.*

▶ □ **bring the house down** make an audience respond with great enthusiasm, typically as shown by their laughter or applause. □ **bring someone/something to mind** cause one to remember or think of someone or something: *all that marble brought to mind a mausoleum.*

brink /briNGk/ ▶*n.* an extreme edge of land before a steep or vertical slope: *the brink of the cliffs.* ■ a point at which something, typically an unwelcome or disastrous event, is about to happen: *a hapless dictator teetering on the brink.*

▶ □ **on the brink of** about to experience something, typically a disastrous or unwelcome event: *the country was on the brink of a constitutional crisis.*

brink·man·ship /'briNGkmən,SHip/ (also **brinks·man·ship** /'briNGksmən-/) ▶*n.* the art or practice of pursuing a dangerous policy to the limits of safety before stopping, typically in politics.

brin·y /'brīnē/ ▶*adj.* of salty water or the sea; salty: *the briny tang of the scallops.*

bri·o /'brēō/ ▶*n.* vigor or vivacity of style or performance: *she told her story with some brio.* See also **CON BRIO**.

bri·oche /brē'ōSH; -'ôSH/ ▶*n.* a light, sweet yeast bread typically in the form of a small, round roll.

bri·quette /bri'ket/ (also **bri·quet**) ▶*n.* a block of compressed charcoal or coal dust used as fuel.

brisk /brisk/ ▶*adj.* active, fast, and energetic: *a good brisk walk* | *business appeared to be brisk.* ■ (of the weather or wind) cold but fresh and enlivening. ■ sharp or abrupt: *the brisk, dismissive nod of her head.* —**brisk·ly** *adv.* —**brisk·ness** *n.*

bris·ket /'briskit/ ▶*n.* meat cut from the breast of an animal, typically a cow.

bris·ling /'brizliNG; 'bris-/ ▶*n.* (*pl.* same or **-lings**) a sprat, typically one seasoned and smoked in Norway and sold in a can.

bris·tle /'brisəl/ ▶*n.* (usu. **bristles**) a short stiff hair, typically one of those on an animal's skin, a man's face, or a plant. ■ a stiff animal hair, or a man-made substitute, used to make a brush: *a toothbrush with nylon bristles* | *the heads are made with natural bristle.*

▶*v.* [*intr.*] **1** (of hair or fur) stand upright away from the skin, esp. in anger or fear: *the hair on the back of his neck bristled.* ■ make one's hair or fur stand on end: *the cat bristled in annoyance.* ■ react angrily or defensively, as by drawing oneself up: *she* **bristled at** *his rudeness.* **2** (**bristle with**) be covered with or abundant in: *the roof bristled with antennas.* —**bris·tly** *adj.*

bris·tle·tail /'brisəl,tāl/ ▶*n.* a small wingless insect with bristles at the end of the abdomen, belonging to two orders: Thysanura (the three-bristled **true bristletails**, the silverfish) and Diplura (the **two-pronged bristletails**).

Brit /brit/ *inf.* ▶*n.* a British person.

Bri·tan·ni·a /bri'tanyə; -'tänēə/ ▶the personification of Britain, usually depicted as a helmeted woman with shield and trident.

Brit·i·cism /'briti,sizəm/ (also **Brit·ish·ism** /'britisH,izəm/) ▶*n.* an idiom used in Britain but not in other English-speaking countries.

Brit·ish /'britisH/ ▶*adj.* **1** of or relating to Great Britain or the United Kingdom, or to its people or language. **2** of the British Commonwealth or (formerly) the British Empire.

▶*n.* [as *pl. n.*] (**the British**) the British people. —**Brit·ish·ness** *n.*

Brit·ish Eng·lish ▶*n.* English as used in Great Britain, as distinct from that used elsewhere.

Brit·on /'britn/ ▶*n.* **1** a citizen or native of Great Britain. ■ a person of British descent. **2** one of the people of southern Britain before and during Roman times.

brit·tle /'britl/ ▶*adj.* hard but liable to break or shatter easily: *her bones became fragile and brittle.* ■ (of a sound, esp. a person's voice) unpleasantly hard and sharp and showing signs of instability or nervousness: *a brittle laugh.* ■ (of a person or behavior) appearing aggressive or hard but unstable or nervous within: *her manner was strained and brittle.*

▶*n.* a candy made from nuts and set melted sugar: *peanut brittle.* —**brit·tle·ly** (or **brit·tly**) *adv.* —**brit·tle·ness** *n.*

brit·tle·star /'britl,stär/ ▶*n.* an echinoderm (*Ophiura* and other genera, class Ophiuroidea) with long, thin, flexible arms radiating from a small central disk.

broach[1] /brōcH/ ▸v. [tr.] **1** raise (a sensitive or difficult subject) for discussion: *he broached the subject he had been avoiding all evening.* **2** pierce (a cask) to draw liquor. **3** [intr.] (of a fish or sea mammal) rise through the water and break the surface: *the salmon broach, then fall to slap the water.*

broach[2] *Naut.* ▸v. [intr.] (also **broach to**) (of a ship with the wind on the quarter) veer and pitch forward because of bad steering or a sea hitting the stern.

broad /brôd/ ▸adj. **1** having an ample distance from side to side; wide: *a broad staircase.* ▪ (after a measurement) giving the distance from side to side: *the valley is three miles long and half a mile broad.* ▪ large in area; spacious: *a broad expanse of prairie.* **2** covering a large number and wide scope of subjects or areas: *a broad range of experience.* ▪ having or incorporating a wide range of meanings, applications, or kinds of things; loosely defined: *three broad categories of mutual funds.* ▪ including or coming from many people of many kinds: *broad support for the president's foreign policy.* **3** general; without detail: *a broad outline of NATO's position.* ▪ (of a hint) clear and unambiguous; not subtle: *a broad hint.* ▪ somewhat coarse and indecent: *what we regard as broad or even bawdy is a fact of nature to him.* **4** (of a regional accent) very noticeable and strong: *his broad Bronx accent.*
▸n. *inf., chiefly derog.* a woman. —**broad·ness** n.

broad bean ▸n. **1** a large edible flat green bean that is typically eaten without the pod. **2** the plant (*Vicia faba*) that yields these beans, often cultivated in gardens.

broad·cast /'brôd,kast/ ▸v. (*past* **-cast** or **-cast·ed**; *past part.* **-cast** or **-cast·ed**) [tr.] **1** (often **be broadcast**) transmit (a program or some information) by radio or television: *the announcement was broadcast live* | [as n.] (**broadcasting**) *the 1920s saw the dawn of broadcasting.* ▪ [intr.] take part in a radio or television transmission: *the station broadcasts 24 hours a day.* ▪ tell (something) to many people; make widely known: *we don't want to broadcast our unhappiness to the world.* **2** scatter (seeds) by hand or machine rather than placing in drills or rows.
▸n. a radio or television program or transmission.
▸adj. of or relating to such programs: *a broadcast journalist.* —**broad·cast·er** n.

broad·cloth /'brôd,klôтн/ ▸n. clothing fabric of fine twilled wool or plain-woven cotton. ▷late Middle English: originally denoting cloth made 72 inches wide, as opposed to 'strait' cloth, 36 inches wide. The term now implies quality rather than width.

broad·en /'brôdn/ ▸v. [intr.] become larger in distance from side to side; widen: *her smile broadened* | *the river slowed and broadened out slightly.* ▪ expand to encompass more people, ideas, or things: *her interests broadened as she grew up.*
▸ □ **broaden one's horizons** expand one's range of interests, activities, and knowledge.

broad·loom /'brôd,lōōm/ ▸n. carpet woven in wide widths: *wall-to-wall broadloom.* —**broad·loomed** adj.

broad·ly /'brôdlē/ ▸adv. **1** in general and with the exception of minor details: *the climate is broadly similar in the two regions.* **2** widely and openly: *he was grinning broadly.*

broad-mind·ed ▸adj. tolerant or liberal in one's views and reactions; not easily offended: *a broad-minded approach to religion.* —**broad-mind·ed·ness** n. —**broad-mind·ed·ly** adv.

broad·side /'brôd,sīd/ ▸n. **1** a nearly simultaneous firing of all the guns from one side of a warship. ▪ *fig.* a strongly worded critical attack: *broadsides against the Christian faith.* **2** a sheet of paper printed on one side only, forming one large page: *a broadside of Lee's farewell address.*
▸adv. with the side turned to a particular thing: *the yacht was drifting broadside to the wind.* ▪ on the side: *her car was hit broadside by another vehicle.*
▸v. [tr.] collide with the side of (a vehicle): *I had to skid my bike sideways to avoid broadsiding her.*

broad-spec·trum ▸adj. denoting antibiotics, pesticides, etc., effective against a large variety of organisms.

broad·sword /'brôd,sôrd/ ▸n. a sword with a wide blade, used for cutting rather than thrusting.

bro·cade /brō'kād/ ▸n. a rich fabric, often silk, woven with a raised pattern, often with gold or silver thread: [as adj.] *a heavy brocade curtain.*

broc·co·li /'bräk(ə)lē/ ▸n. a cabbage of a variety similar to the cauliflower, bearing heads of green or purplish flower buds. ▪ the flower stalk and head eaten as a vegetable.

broc·co·li·ni /,bräkə'lēnē/ ▸n. a vegetable that is a hybrid of broccoli and kale, with small florets on slender stalks.

bro·chette /brō'sHet/ ▸n. a skewer or spit on which chunks of meat or fish are barbecued, grilled, or roasted: *beef and lamb en brochette.*

bro·chure /brō'sHŏŏr/ ▸n. a small book or magazine containing pictures and information about a product or service.

bro·chure·ware /brō'sHŏŏr,we(ə)r/ ▸n. Web sites or Web pages produced by converting a company's printed marketing or advertising material into an Internet format, typically providing little or no opportunity for interactive contact with prospective customers.

brogue[1] /brōg/ ▸n. a strong outdoor shoe with ornamental perforated patterns in the leather.

brogue[2] ▸n. a marked accent, esp. Irish or Scottish, when speaking English: *a fine Irish brogue.*

broil[1] /broil/ ▸v. [tr.] cook (meat or fish) by exposure to direct, intense radiant heat: *he broiled a wedge of sea bass* | [as adj.] (**broiled**) *a broiled sirloin steak.* ▪ [intr.] become very hot, esp. from the sun: *the countryside lay broiling in the sun.*

broil[2] ▸n. *archaic* a quarrel or a commotion.

broil·er /'broilər/ ▸n. **1** (also **broiler chicken**) a young chicken suitable for roasting, grilling, or barbecuing. **2** a gridiron, grill, or special part of a stove for broiling meat or fish.

broke /brōk/ ▸ past (and archaic past participle) of BREAK.
▸adj. *inf.* having completely run out of money: *many farmers went broke.*
▸ □ **go for broke** *inf.* risk everything in an all-out effort.

bro·ken /'brōkən/ ▸ past participle of BREAK. ▸adj. **1** having been fractured or damaged and no longer in one piece or in working order: *a broken arm.* ▪ rejected, defeated, or despairing: *he went to his grave a broken man* | *a broken heart.* ▪ sick or weakened: *broken health.* ▪ (of a relationship) ended, typically by betrayal or faithlessness: *a broken marriage.* ▪ disrupted or divided: *broken families.* ▪ (of an agreement or promise) not observed by one of the parties involved. **2** having gaps or intervals that break a continuity: *a broken white line across the road.* ▪ having an uneven and rough surface: *broken ground.* ▪ (of speech or a language) spoken falteringly and with many mistakes, as by a foreigner: *a young man talking in broken Italian.* ▪ spoken haltingly, as if overcome by emotion: *he whispered in a broken voice.* —**bro·ken·ly** adv. —**bro·ken·ness** n.

bro·ken-down ▸adj. worn out and dilapidated by age, use, or ill-treatment: *a broken-down car.* ▪ (of a machine or vehicle) not functioning due to a mechanical failure. ▪ (of a horse) with serious damage to the legs, in particular the tendons, caused by excessive strain.

bro·ken-heart·ed ▸adj. overwhelmed by grief or disappointment.

bro·ker /'brōkər/ ▸n. a person who buys and sells goods or assets for others.
▸v. [tr.] arrange or negotiate (a settlement, deal, or plan): *fighting continued despite attempts to broker a cease-fire.*

bro·ker·age /'brōkərij/ ▸n. the business or service of acting as a broker. ▪ a fee or commission charged by a broker: *a revenue of $1,400 less a sales brokerage of $12.50.* ▪ a company that buys or sells goods or assets for clients.

bro·me·li·ad /brō'mēlē,ad/ ▸n. a plant (*Bromelia* and other genera, family Bromeliaceae) of tropical and subtropical America, typically having short stems with rosettes of stiff, usually spiny, leaves. Some kinds are epiphytic, and many are cultivated as houseplants.

bro·mic ac·id /'brōmik/ ▸n. *Chem.* a strongly oxidizing acid, $HBrO_3$, known only in aqueous solutions. —**bro·mate** /'brō,māt/ n.

bro·mide /'brōmīd/ ▸n. **1** *Chem.* a compound of bromine with another element or group, esp. a salt containing the anion Br^- or an organic compound with bromine bonded to an alkyl radical. ▪ a reproduction or piece of typesetting on bromide paper. **2** a trite and unoriginal idea or remark, typically intended to soothe or placate: *feel-good bromides create the illusion of problem solving.* —**bro·mid·ic** /brō'midik/ adj.

bro·mine /'brōmēn/ ▸n. the chemical element of atomic number 35, a dark red fuming toxic liquid with a choking, irritating smell. It is a member of the halogen group and occurs chiefly as salts in seawater and brines. (Symbol: **Br**)

bron·chi /'bräNGkī; -kē/ ▸ plural form of BRONCHUS.

bron·chi·al /'bräNGkēəl/ ▸adj. of or relating to the bronchi or bronchioles: *bronchial pneumonia.*

bron·chi·ole /'bräNGkē,ōl/ ▸n. *Anat.* any of the minute branches into which a bronchus divides. —**bron·chi·o·lar** /,bräNGkē'ōlər/ adj.

bron·chi·tis /bräNG'kītis/ ▸n. inflammation of the mucous membrane in the bronchial tubes. It typically causes deep and severe coughing. —**bron·chit·ic** /brăNG'kitik/ *adj.* & *n.*

bron·cho·scope /'brăNGkə,skōp/ ▸*n.* a fiber-optic cable that is passed into the windpipe in order to view the bronchi. —**bron·chos·co·py** /brăNG'käskəpē/ *n.*

bron·chus /'brăNGkəs/ ▸*n.* (*pl.* **-chi** /-kī; -kē/) any of the major air passages of the lungs that diverge from the windpipe.

bron·co /'brăNGkō/ ▸*n.* (*pl.* **-cos**) a wild or half-tamed horse, esp. of the western U.S.

bron·to·saur /'brăntə,sôr/ (also **bron·to·sau·rus** /,brăntə'sôrəs/) ▸*n.* another term for APATOSAUR. —**bron·to·sau·ri·an** /-'sôrēən/ *adj.*

bron·to·there /'brăntəTHi(ə)r/ ▸*n.* a large ungulate mammal (*Embolotherium andrewsi*) of the Eocene epoch with a hornlike bony growth on the nose.

Bronx cheer ▸*n.* a sound of derision or contempt made by blowing through closed lips with the tongue between them; a raspberry.

bronze /brănz/ ▸*n.* a yellowish-brown alloy of copper with up to one-third tin. ■ a yellowish-brown color: *rich, gleaming shades of bronze.* ■ a work of sculpture or other object made of bronze.
▸*adj.* made of or colored like bronze: *a bronze statue.*
▸*v.* [tr.] (usu. **be bronzed**) make (a person or part of the body) suntanned: *Alison was bronzed by outdoor life.* ■ give a surface of bronze or something resembling bronze to: *the doors were bronzed with sculpted reliefs.* ▷mid 17th cent. (as a verb): from French *bronze* (noun), *bronzer* (verb), from Italian *bronzo*, probably from Persian *birinj* 'brass.' —**bronz·y** *adj.*

Bronze Age ▸a prehistoric period that followed the Stone Age and preceded the Iron Age, when certain weapons and tools came to be made of bronze rather than stone.

brooch /brōCH; brōōCH/ ▸*n.* an ornament fastened to clothing with a hinged pin and catch.

brood /brōōd/ ▸*n.* a family of young animals, esp. of a bird, produced at one hatching or birth: *a brood of chicks.* ■ bee or wasp larvae. ■ *inf.* all of the children in a family: *she was brought up by a loving stepfather as part of a brood of eight.* ■ a group of things or people having a similar character: *a remarkable brood of writers.*
▸*v.* **1** [intr.] think deeply about something that makes one unhappy: *he brooded over his need to find a wife.* **2** [tr.] (of a bird) sit on (eggs) to hatch them. ■ (of a fish, frog, or invertebrate) hold (developing eggs) within the body. **3** [usu. foll. by over] (of silence, a storm, etc.) hang or hover closely: *a winter storm broods over the lake.*
▸*adj.* (of an animal) kept to be used for breeding: *a brood mare.*

brood·er /'brōōdər/ ▸*n.* **1** a heated house for chicks or piglets. **2** a person who broods about something.

brook[1] /brōōk/ ▸*n.* a small stream. —**brook·let** /-lit/ *n.*

brook[2] ▸*v.* [tr.] *formal* tolerate or allow (something, typically dissent or opposition): *Jenny would brook no criticism of Matthew.*

brook trout ▸*n.* see CHAR[3].

broom /brōōm; brōōm/ ▸*n.* **1** a long-handled brush of bristles or twigs used for sweeping. **2** a shrub (genera *Cytisus* and *Genista*) of the pea family, with long, thin green stems and a profusion of flowers.

Bros ▸*pl. n.* brothers (in names of companies): *Hills Bros. coffee.*

broth /brôTH; brŏTH/ ▸*n.* **1** soup consisting of meat or vegetable chunks, and often rice, cooked in stock. ■ meat or fish stock. **2** *Microbiology* liquid medium containing proteins and other nutrients for the culture of bacteria: [as *adj.*] *broth cultures of intestinal tissue.*

broth·el /'brăTHəl; 'brŏTHəl/ ▸*n.* a house where men can visit prostitutes.

broth·er /'brəTHər/ ▸*n.* **1** a man or boy in relation to other sons and daughters of his parents. ■ a half-brother, stepbrother, or foster brother. ■ a brother-in-law. ■ a male associate or fellow member of an organization: *fraternity brothers.* ■ *inf.* a black man (chiefly used as a term of address among black people). ■ a fellow human being. ■ a thing that resembles or is connected to another thing: *the machine is almost identical to its larger brother.* **2** (*pl.* also **breth·ren** /'breTHrin/) *Christian Church* a (male) fellow Christian. ■ a member of a religious order or congregation of men: *a Benedictine brother.*
▸*interj.* used to express annoyance or surprise. ▷Old English *brōthor*, of Germanic origin; related to Dutch *broeder* and German *Bruder*, from an Indo-European root shared by Latin *frater*. —**broth·er·li·ness** *n.* —**broth·er·ly** *adj.*

broth·er·hood /'brəTHər,hŏŏd/ ▸*n.* **1** the relationship between brothers. ■ the feeling of kinship with and closeness to a group of people or all people: *a gesture of solidarity and brotherhood.* **2** an association, society, or community of people linked by a common interest, religion, or trade: *a religious brotherhood.* ■ a trade union.

broth·er-in-law ▸*n.* (*pl.* **broth·ers-in-law**) the brother of one's wife or husband. ■ the husband of one's sister or sister-in-law.

brought /brôt/ ▸ past and past participle of BRING.

brou·ha·ha /'brōōhä,hä; brōō'hähä/ ▸*n.* a noisy and overexcited critical response, display of interest, or trail of publicity: *24 members resigned over the brouhaha* | *all that election brouhaha.*

brow /brou/ ▸*n.* **1** a person's forehead: *he wiped his brow.* ■ (usu. **brows**) an eyebrow: *his brows lifted in surprise.* **2** the summit of a hill or pass: *the cottages were built on the brow of a hill.*

brow·beat /'brou,bēt/ ▸*v.* (*past* **-beat**; *past part.* **-beat·en**) [tr.] intimidate (someone), typically into doing something, with stern or abusive words: *a witness is being browbeaten under cross-examination.*

brown /broun/ ▸*adj.* of a color produced by mixing red, yellow, and black, as of dark wood or rich soil: *an old brown coat.* ■ dark-skinned or suntanned: *his face was brown from the sun.* ■ (of bread) made from a dark, unsifted, or unbleached flour.
▸*n.* brown color or pigment: *the brown of his eyes.* | *the print is rich with velvety browns.*
▸*v.* make or become brown, typically by cooking: [tr.] *a skillet in which food has been browned* | [intr.] *bake the pizza until the cheese has browned.* —**brown·ish** *adj.* —**brown·ness** *n.*

brown bag·ging ▸*n.* **1** the practice of bringing one's own packed lunch to work. **2** the practice of bringing one's own liquor to a restaurant or club that can not sell alcoholic beverages.

brown bear ▸*n.* a large bear (*Ursus arctos*) with a coat color ranging from cream to black, occurring chiefly in forests in Eurasia and North America.

Brown·i·an mo·tion /'brounēən/ ▸*n.* *Physics* the erratic random movement of microscopic particles in a fluid, as a result of continuous bombardment from molecules of the surrounding medium.

Brown·ie /'brounē/ ▸*n.* (*pl.* **-ies**) **1** a member of the junior branch of the Girl Scouts, for girls aged between about 6 and 8. **2** (**brownie**) a small square of rich cake, typically chocolate cake with nuts. **3** (**brownie**) a benevolent elf supposed to haunt houses and do housework secretly.
▸ □ **brownie point** *inf., humorous* an imaginary award given to someone who does good deeds or tries to please: *his policy will win brownie points with voters.*

brown-nose (also **brown·nose**) *inf.* ▸*n.* (also **brown-nos·er**) a person who acts in a grossly obsequious way.
▸*v.* [tr.] curry favor with (someone) by acting in such a way: *academics were brown-nosing the senior faculty.*

brown·out /'broun,out/ ▸*n.* a partial blackout.

brown rice ▸*n.* unpolished rice with only the husk of the grain removed.

Brown·shirt /'broun,SHərt/ ▸*n.* *chiefly hist.* a member of an early Nazi militia founded by Hitler in Munich in 1921, with brown uniforms resembling that of Mussolini's Blackshirts. They aided Hitler's rise to power. Also called STORM TROOPS.

brown·stone /'broun,stōn/ ▸*n.* a kind of reddish-brown sandstone used for building. ■ a building faced with such sandstone.

brown sug·ar ▸*n.* unrefined or partially refined sugar. ■ a consumer product made by adding molasses to white sugar.

browse /brouz/ ▸*v.* [intr.] **1** survey objects casually, esp. goods for sale: *he stopped to browse around a sporting goods store.* ■ scan through a book or magazine superficially to gain an impression of the contents: *she browsed through the newspaper* [tr.] *patrons can browse the shelves of the library.* ■ [tr.] *Comput.* read or survey (data files), typically via a network. **2** (of an animal) feed on leaves, twigs, or other high-growing vegetation: *they reach upward to browse on bushes.*
▸*n.* **1** an act of casual looking or reading: *the brochure is well worth a browse.* **2** vegetation, such as twigs and young shoots, eaten by animals. —**brows·a·ble** *adj.*

brows·er /'brouzər/ ▸*n.* a person who looks casually through books or magazines or at things for sale. ■ *Comput.* a program with a graphical user interface for displaying HTML files, used to navigate the World Wide Web: *a Web browser.*

bru·in /'brōōin/ ▸*n.* a bear, esp. in children's fables.

bruise /brōōz/ ▸*n.* an injury appearing as an area of discolored skin on the body, caused by a blow or impact rupturing underlying blood vessels. ■ a similar area of damage on a fruit, vegetable, or plant.
▸*v.* [tr.] [often as *adj.*] (**bruised**) inflict such an injury on (someone or something): *a bruised knee.* ■ hurt (someone's feelings): *she tried to bolster her bruised pride.* ■ [intr.] be susceptible to bruising: *potatoes bruise easily, so treat them with care.* ■ crush or pound (something): *bruise the raisins before adding to the mixture.*

bruis·er /ˈbro͞ozər/ ▶n. inf., chiefly derog. a person who is tough and aggressive and enjoys a fight or argument. ■ a professional boxer.

bruit /broōt/ ▶v. [tr.] spread (a report or rumor) widely: *I didn't want to have our relationship bruited about the office.*

brunch /brənCH/ ▶n. a late morning meal eaten instead of breakfast and lunch.

bru·nette /broō'net/ (also **bru·net**) ▶adj. having dark brown hair: *a fresh-faced brunette woman in her thirties.* ■ (of hair) dark brown: *her lustrous brunette tresses.*

▶n. a person having dark brown hair.

brunt /brənt/ ▶n. (**the brunt**) the worst part or chief impact of a specified thing: *education will bear the brunt of the cuts.*

brush¹ /brəSH/ ▶n. **1** an implement with a handle, consisting of bristles or wire set into a block, used for cleaning or scrubbing, applying a liquid or powder to a surface, arranging the hair, or other purposes: *a paint brush.* ■ an act of sweeping, applying, or arranging with such an implement or with one's hand: *he gave the seat a brush.* ■ (usu. **brushes**) a thin stick set with long wire bristles, used to make a soft hissing sound on drums or cymbals. **2** a slight and fleeting touch: *the lightest brush of his lips against her cheek.* ■ a brief and typically unpleasant or unwelcome encounter with someone or something: *a brush with death.* **3** a piece of carbon or metal serving as an electrical contact with a moving part in a motor or alternator.

▶v. **1** [tr.] remove (dust or dirt) by sweeping or scrubbing: *we'll be able to brush the mud off easily.* ■ [tr.] use a brush or one's hand to remove dust or dirt from (something): *she brushed down her best coat.* ■ [tr.] clean (one's teeth) by scrubbing with a brush. ■ [tr.] arrange (one's hair) by running a brush through it. ■ [tr.] apply a liquid to (a surface) with a brush: *brush the potatoes with oil.* ■ apply (a liquid or substance) to a surface: *brush on a floor enamel for a long-lasting base coat.* **2** [intr.] touch lightly and gently: *stems of grass brush against her legs.* ■ (**brush past**) touch fleetingly and in passing: *she brushed past him to leave the room.* ■ [tr.] push (something) away with a quick movement of the hand: *she brushed a wisp of hair away from her face.* ■ [tr.] (**brush something aside**) dismiss (something) curtly and confidently: *people brushed aside the possibility of imminent war.* ■ [tr.] (**brush someone/something off**) dismiss in an abrupt, contemptuous way: *the president brushed off a reporter's question about terrorism.*

▶phrasal v. □ **brush up on** improve one's previously good knowledge of or skill at a particular thing: *brush up on your telephone skills.*

brush² ▶n. undergrowth, small trees, and shrubs. —**brush·y** adj.

brush-off ▶n. inf. a rejection or dismissal in which someone is treated as unimportant: *he's been **giving** her the brush-off.*

brush·stroke /ˈbəSH,strōk/ ▶n. **1** the stroke of a brush, especially a hair brush or paintbrush. ■ the mark or effect created by this: *an errant brushstroke doesn't necessarily destroy a painting.* **2** an individual action that contributes to an overall effect or work: *you write in broad, inaccurate brushstrokes.*

brush·wood /ˈbrəSH,woŏd/ ▶n. undergrowth, twigs, and small branches, typically used for firewood or kindling.

brush·work /ˈbrəSH,wərk/ ▶n. the way in which painters use their brush, as evident in their paintings: *canvases characterized by lively, flowing brushwork.*

brusque /brəsk/ ▶adj. abrupt or offhand in speech or manner: *she could be brusque and impatient.* —**brusque·ly** adv. —**brusque·ness** n.

Brus·sels sprout (also **brus·sels sprout**) ▶n. a vegetable consisting of the small compact bud of a variety of cabbage. ■ the plant that yields this vegetable, bearing many such buds along a tall single stem.

brut /broōt/ ▶adj. (of sparkling wine) unsweetened; very dry.

bru·tal /ˈbroōtl/ ▶adj. savagely violent: *a brutal murder.* ■ punishingly hard or uncomfortable: *the brutal winter wind.* ■ without any attempt to disguise unpleasantness: *the brutal honesty of his observations.* —**bru·tal·i·ty** /broō'talitē/ n. —**bru·tal·ly** adv.

bru·tal·ism /ˈbroōtl,izəm/ ▶n. a style of architecture or art characterized by a deliberate plainness, crudity, or violence of imagery. The term was first applied to functionalist buildings of the 1950s and 1960s that made much use of steel and concrete in starkly massive blocks. —**bru·tal·ist** n. & adj.

bru·tal·ize /ˈbroōtl,īz/ ▶v. [tr.] attack (someone) in a savage and violent way: *they brutalize and torture persons in their custody.* ■ (often **be brutalized**) desensitize (someone) to the pain or suffering of others by exposing them to violent behavior or situations: *he had been brutalized in prison and became cynical* | [as adj.] (**brutalizing**) *the brutalizing effects of warfare.* —**bru·tal·i·za·tion** /ˌbroōtl'zāSHən/ n.

brute /broōt/ ▶n. a savagely violent person or animal: *he was a cold-blooded brute.* ■ inf. a cruel, unpleasant, or insensitive person: *what an unfeeling little brute you are.* ■ an animal as opposed to a human being. ■ something awkward, difficult, or unpleasant: *a great brute of a machine.*

▶adj. unreasoning and animal-like: *a brute struggle for social superiority.* ■ merely physical: *we achieve little by brute force.* ■ harsh, fundamental, or inescapable: *the brute necessities of basic subsistence.* —**brut·ish** adj.

brux·ism /ˈbrəksizəm/ ▶n. the involuntary or habitual grinding of the teeth, typically during sleep.

bry·o·ny /ˈbrīənē/ ▶n. (pl. **-ies**) **1** (also **white bryony**) a climbing Eurasian plant (*Bryonia dioica*) of the gourd family, with greenish-white flowers and red berries. **2** (also **black bryony**) a climbing European plant (*Tamus communis*) of the yam family, with broad glossy leaves, poisonous red berries, and black tubers.

bry·o·phyte /ˈbrīə,fīt/ ▶n. any flowerless, rootless plant of the phylum Bryophyta, including mosses and liverworts.

bry·o·zo·an /ˌbrīə'zōə/ Zool. ▶n. (pl. **-zo·a**, **-zo·ans**) a sedentary aquatic animal found chiefly in the sea, either encrusting rocks, seaweeds, or other surfaces, or forming stalked fronds.

▶adj. of or relating to bryozoa.

Bry·thon·ic /bri'THänik/ ▶adj. denoting, relating to, or belonging to the southern group of Celtic languages, consisting of Welsh, Cornish, and Breton.

▶n. these languages collectively.

BS ▶abbr. ■ Bachelor of Science. ■ balance sheet. ■ Blessed Sacrament. ■ vulgar slang used as a euphemism for "bullshit."

BSE ▶abbr. bovine spongiform encephalopathy, a usually fatal disease of cattle affecting the central nervous system, causing agitation and staggering. It is thought to be caused by an agent such as a prion or a virino, and its possible connection with Creutzfeldt–Jakob disease in humans is still much debated. Also (popularly) called **MAD COW DISEASE**.

Btu (also **BTU**) ▶abbr. British thermal unit(s).

bub /bəb/ ▶n. inf. an aggressive or rude way of addressing a boy or man: *hey, bub, I'm looking for someone.*

bub·ble /ˈbəbəl/ ▶n. **1** a thin sphere of liquid enclosing air or another gas. ■ an air- or gas-filled spherical cavity in a liquid or a solidified liquid such as glass or amber. ■ fig. a state or feeling that is unstable and unlikely to last. ■ a brief, sudden, upward change from a general trend. **2** a transparent domed cover or enclosure. ■ a place or position of isolated safety: *seeing foreign ports from a bubble.*

▶v. [intr.] (of a liquid) contain bubbles of air or gas rising to the surface. ■ [often as adj.] (**bubbling**) make a sound resembling this: *a bubbling fountain.*

▶phrasal v. □ **bubble (over) with** (of a person) be exuberantly filled with an irrepressible positive feeling.

bub·ble bath ▶n. liquid, crystals, or powder added to bathwater to make it foam and have a fragrant smell. ■ a bath of water with such a substance added.

bub·ble·gum /ˈbəbəl,gəm/ ▶n. **1** chewing gum that can be blown into bubbles. ■ (also **bubblegum pink**) the bright pink color of such gum. **2** [usu. as adj.] a thing considered to be insipid, simplistic, or adolescent in taste or style: *rockers hate bubblegum pop.*

bub·ble mem·o·ry ▶n. Comput. a type of memory in which data is stored as a pattern of magnetized regions in a thin layer of magnetic material.

bub·ble wrap (trademark **Bub·ble Wrap**) ▶n. plastic packaging material in sheets containing numerous small air cushions designed to protect fragile goods.

bub·bly /ˈbəb(ə)lē/ ▶adj. (**-bli·er**, **-bli·est**) containing bubbles: *bake until the top is crisp and bubbly.* ■ fig. (of a person) full of cheerful high spirits: *a bright and bubbly personality.*

▶n. inf. champagne.

bu·bo /ˈb(y)oōbō/ ▶n. (pl. **-boes**) a swollen, inflamed lymph node in the armpit or groin. —**bu·bon·ic** /b(y)oō'bänik/ adj.

bu·bon·ic plague ▶n. the commonest form of plague in humans, characterized by fever, delirium, and the formation of buboes.

buc·cal /ˈbəkəl/ ▶adj. technical of or relating to the mouth: *the buccal cavity.* ■ of or relating to the cheek: *the buccal side of the molars.*

buc·ca·neer /ˌbəkə'nir/ ▶n. hist. a pirate, originally off the Spanish-American coasts. ■ a daring, adventurous, and sometimes reckless person, esp. in business. ▷mid 17th cent. (originally denoting European hunters in the Caribbean): from French *boucanier*, from *boucan* 'a

---

Pronunciation Key ə *ago*, *up*; ər *over*, *fur*; a *hat*; ā *ate*; ä *car*; CH *chin*; e *let*; ē *see*; e(ə)r *air*; i *fit*; ī *by*; i(ə)r *ear*; NG *sing*; ō *go*; ô *law*, *for*; oi *toy*; oō *good*; oō *goo*; ou *out*; SH *she*; TH *thin*; TH *then*; (h)w *why*; ZH *vision*

frame on which to cook or cure meat,' from Tupi *mukem*. —**buc·ca·neer·ing** *adj.*

buck¹ /bək/ ▸*n.* **1** the male of some antlered animals, esp. the fallow deer, roe deer, reindeer, and antelopes. ▪ a male hare, rabbit, ferret, rat, or kangaroo. **2** a vertical jump performed by a horse, with the head lowered, back arched, and back legs thrown out behind. **3** a fashionable and typically hell-raising young man. **4** *inf., offens.* a black or American Indian man. **5** (**bucks**) an oxford shoe made of buckskin.
▸*v.* **1** [*intr.*] (of a horse) to perform a buck: *he's got to get his head down to buck* | [*tr.*] *she bucked them off if they tried to get on her back.* ▪ (of a vehicle) make sudden jerky movements: *the boat began to buck in the water.* **2** [*tr.*] oppose or resist (something that seems oppressive or inevitable): *the shares bucked the market trend.* **3** [*tr.*] *inf.* make (someone) more cheerful: *Bella and Jim need me to buck them up* | [*intr.*] (**buck up**) *buck up, kid, it's not the end of the world.*
▸*adj. military slang* lowest of a particular rank: *a buck private.*

buck² ▸*n. inf.* a dollar: *a run-down hotel room for five bucks a night.*
▸ □ **big bucks** a lot of money. □ **a fast** (or **quick**) **buck** easily and quickly earned money: *the pursuit of a fast buck is the cause of most losses.*

buck³ ▸*n.* an article placed as a reminder before a player whose turn it is to deal at poker.
▸ □ **pass the buck** *inf.* shift the responsibility for something to someone else.

buck·board /ˈbəkˌbôrd/ ▸*n.* an open, four-wheeled, horse-drawn carriage with seating that is attached to a plank stretching between the front and rear axles.

buck·et /ˈbəkit/ ▸*n.* a roughly cylindrical open container, typically made of metal or plastic, with a handle, used to hold and carry liquids or other material. ▪ the contents of such a container or the amount it can contain: *she emptied a **bucket** of water over them.* ▪ (**buckets**) *inf.* large quantities of liquid, typically rain or tears: *I wept buckets.* ▪ *Basketball* a basket. ▪ *Comput.* a unit of data that can be transferred from secondary storage in a single operation. ▪ a compartment on the outer edge of a waterwheel. ▪ the scoop of a dredger or grain elevator. ▪ a scoop attached to the front of a loader, digger, or tractor.
▸*v.* (**buck·et·ed**, **buck·et·ing**) [*intr.*] *inf.* rain heavily: *it was still bucketing down.* —**buck·et·ful** *n.*

buck·et·load /ˈbəkitˌlōd/ ▸*n. inf.* a large quantity: *he scoops up business donations by the bucketload.*

buck·et seat ▸*n.* a seat in a car or aircraft with a rounded back to fit one person.

buck·eye /ˈbəkˌī/ ▸*n.* **1** a North American tree or shrub (genus *Aesculus*, family Hippocastanaceae), related to the horse chestnut, with showy yellow, red, or white flowers. **2** (also **buckeye butterfly**) an orange and brown New World butterfly (*Junonia coenia*, family Nymphalidae) with conspicuous eyespots on the wings. **3** (**Buckeye**) *inf.* a native of the state of Ohio (with reference to Ohio's abundance of buckeye trees).

buck·horn /ˈbəkˌhôrn/ ▸*n.* the material of deer antlers, used typically for knife handles, small containers, or rifle sights.

buck·le /ˈbəkəl/ ▸*n.* a flat, typically rectangular frame with a hinged pin, used for joining the ends of a belt or strap. ▪ a similarly shaped ornament, esp. on a shoe.
▸*v.* **1** [*tr.*] fasten or decorate with a buckle: *he buckled his belt.* ▪ [*intr.*] (**buckle up**) fasten one's seat belt in a car or aircraft. **2** [*intr.*] bend and give way under pressure or strain: *the earth buckled under the titanic stress.* ▪ [*tr.*] bend (something) out of shape: *a giant oak buckles the sidewalk.* ▪ *fig.* (of a person) yield or collapse under pressure: *a weaker person might have buckled under the strain.*
▸*phrasal v.* □ **buckle down** tackle a task with determination: *they will buckle down to negotiations over the next few months.*

buck·ram /ˈbəkrəm/ ▸*n.* coarse linen or other cloth stiffened with gum or paste and used typically as interfacing and in bookbinding.
▸*adj.* of or like such material: *sturdy volumes in buckram bindings.*

buck·saw /ˈbəkˌsô/ ▸*n.* a type of saw typically set in an H-shaped frame and used with both hands.

buck·shot /ˈbəkˌSHät/ ▸*n.* coarse lead shot used in shotgun shells.

buck·skin /ˈbəkˌskin/ ▸*n.* **1** the skin of a male deer. ▪ grayish leather with a suede finish, traditionally made from such skin but now more commonly made from sheepskin: [as *adj.*] *a pair of buckskin moccasins.* ▪ (**buckskins**) clothes or shoes made from such leather. ▪ thick, smooth cotton or woolen fabric. **2** a horse of a grayish-yellow color. —**buck·skinned** *adj.*

buck·thorn /ˈbəkˌTHôrn/ ▸*n.* **1** a typically thorny North American shrub or small tree (genus *Rhamnus*, family Rhamnaceae). Some kinds yield dyes, and others have been used medicinally. **2** a thorny shrub or

small tree (*Bumelia lycioides*) of the sapodilla family, with clusters of small white flowers.

buck·tooth ▸*n.* an upper tooth that projects over the lower lip. —**buck·toothed** *adj.*

buck·wheat /ˈbəkˌ(h)wēt/ ▸*n.* an Asian plant (*Fagopyrum esculentum*) of the dock family. Cultivated in the U.S., it produces starchy seeds that are used for fodder and milled into flour.

bu·col·ic /byōōˈkälik/ ▸*adj.* of or relating to the pleasant aspects of the countryside and country life: *the church is lovely for its bucolic setting.*
▸*n.* (usu. **bucolics**) a pastoral poem.

bud¹ /bəd/ ▸*n.* a compact knoblike growth on a plant that develops into a leaf, flower, or shoot. ▪ *Biol.* an outgrowth from an organism that separates to form a new individual without sexual reproduction taking place. ▪ *Zool.* (of an animal) a rudimentary leg or other appendage that has not yet grown, or never will grow, to full size.
▸*v.* (**bud·ded**, **bud·ding**) [*intr.*] *Biol.* (of a plant or animal) form a bud: *new blood vessels bud out from the vascular bed.*

bud² ▸*n. inf.* a form of address, usually to a boy or man, used esp. when the name of the one being addressed is not known: *listen, bud, I saw you there with my own eyes.*

Bud·dha /ˈbōōdə; ˈbŏŏdə/ ▸a title given to the founder of Buddhism, Siddartha Gautama (*c.*563–*c.*460 BC). Born an Indian prince, he renounced wealth and family to become an ascetic, and after achieving enlightenment while meditating, taught all who came to learn from him. ▪ [as *n.*] (**a buddha**) *Buddhism* a person who has attained full enlightenment. ▪ a statue or picture of the Buddha.

Bud·dhism /ˈbōōdizəm; ˈbŏŏd-/ ▸*n.* a widespread Asian religion or philosophy, founded by Siddartha Gautama in northeastern India in the 5th century BC. —**Bud·dhist** *n. & adj.*

bud·dle·ia /ˈbədlēə; bədˈlēə/ ▸*n.* a widely cultivated shrub (genus *Buddleia*, family Loganiaceae) with fragrant lilac, white, or yellow flowers.

bud·dy /ˈbədē/ *inf.* ▸*n.* (pl. **-dies**) a close friend. ▪ a working companion with whom close cooperation is required.
▸*v.* (**-dies, -died**) [*intr.*] become friendly and spend time with: *I decided to buddy up to them.*

budge /bəj/ ▸*v.* make or cause to make the slightest movement: [*intr.*] *the line in the bank hasn't budged* | [*tr.*] *I couldn't budge the door.* ▪ change or make (someone) change an opinion: [*intr.*] *I tried to persuade him, but he wouldn't budge.*

budg·er·i·gar /ˈbəjərēˌgär/ (also **bud·gie** /ˈbəjē/) ▸*n.* a small gregarious green Australian parakeet (*Melopsittacus undulatus*) with a yellow head. Popular as a pet bird, it has been bred in a variety of colors.

budg·et /ˈbəjit/ ▸*n.* an estimate of income and expenditure for a set period of time: *keep within the household budget.* | [as *adj.*] *a budget deficit.* ▪ an annual or other regular estimate of national revenue and expenditure put forward by the government, often including details of changes in taxation. ▪ the amount of money needed or available for a purpose: *they have a limited budget.*
▸*v.* (**budg·et·ed, budg·et·ing**) [*intr.*] allow or provide for in a budget: *the university is budgeting for a deficit* | [as *adj.*] (**budgeted**) *a budgeted figure of $31,000* | [as *n.*] (**budgeting**) *corporate planning and budgeting.* ▪ [*tr.*] provide (a sum of money) for a particular purpose from a budget: *the council proposes to budget $100,000 to provide grants.*
▸*adj.* inexpensive: *a budget guitar.* ▷late Middle English: from Old French *bougette*, diminutive of *bouge* 'leather bag,' from Latin *bulga* 'leather bag, knapsack,' of Gaulish origin. The word originally meant a pouch or wallet, and later its contents. In the mid 18th cent., the Chancellor of the Exchequer in the UK, in presenting his annual statement, was said "to open the budget." In the late 19th cent. the use of the term was extended from governmental to private or commercial finances. —**budg·et·ar·y** /-ˌterē/ *adj.*
▸ □ **on a budget** with a restricted amount of money: *we're traveling on a budget.*

buff¹ /bəf/ ▸*n.* **1** a yellowish-beige color: **2** a dull yellow leather with a velvety surface.
▸*v.* [*tr.*] polish (something): *he buffed the glass until it gleamed.* ▪ give (leather) a velvety finish by removing the surface of the grain.
▸*adj.* **1** yellowish beige. **2** *Informal* being in good physical shape with fine muscle tone.
▸ □ **in the buff** *inf.* naked.

buff² ▸*n. inf.* a person who is enthusiastically interested in and very knowledgeable about a particular subject: *a computer buff.*

buf·fa·lo /ˈbəfəˌlō/ ▸*n.* (*pl.* same, **-loes** or **-los**) **1** a heavily built wild ox (genus *Bubalus*) with backswept horns, found mainly in the Old World tropics. See also WATER BUFFALO. ▪ the North American bison. **2** (also

buffalo fish) a large grayish-olive freshwater sucker (genus *Ictiobus*) with thick lips, common in North America.

▶ *v.* (**-loes, -loed**) [*tr.*] (often **be buffaloed**) *inf.* overawe or intimidate (someone): *she didn't like being buffaloed.* ▪ baffle (someone): *the problem has buffaloed the advertising staff.*

Buf·fa·lo wings (also **buf·fa·lo wings**) ▶ *pl. n.* deep-fried chicken wings coated in a spicy sauce.

buff·er /'bəfər/ ▶ *n.* **1** a person or thing that prevents incompatible or antagonistic people or things from coming into contact with or harming each other: *family and friends can provide a buffer against stress.* **2** (also **buffer solution**) *Chem.* a solution that resists changes in pH when acid or alkali is added to it. Buffers typically involve a weak acid or alkali together with one of its salts. **3** *Comput.* a temporary memory area or queue used when transferring data between devices or programs operating at different speeds.

▶ *v.* [*tr.*] **1** lessen or moderate the impact of (something): *the massage helped to buffer the strain.* **2** treat with a chemical buffer.

buff·er zone ▶ *n.* a neutral area serving to separate hostile forces or nations. ▪ an area of land designated for environmental protection: *oyster harvesters are not allowed in certain buffer zones.*

buf·fet[1] /bə'fā/ ▶ *n.* **1** a meal consisting of several dishes from which guests serve themselves: [as *adj.*] *a cold buffet lunch.* **2** a room or counter in a station, hotel, or other public building selling light meals or snacks. **3** a cabinet with shelves and drawers for keeping cutlery and table linens.

buf·fet[2] /'bəfit/ ▶ *v.* (**-fet·ed, -fet·ing**) [*tr.*] (esp. of wind or waves) strike repeatedly and violently; batter: *the rough seas buffeted the coast.* ▪ knock (someone) over or off course: *he was buffeted from side to side.* ▪ (often **be buffeted**) *fig.* (of misfortunes or difficulties) afflict or harm (someone) repeatedly or over a long period: *they were buffeted by a major recession.*

buf·fet·ing /'bəfitiNG/ ▶ *n.* the action of striking someone or something repeatedly and violently: *the roofs have survived the buffeting of worse winds than this.* ▪ *fig.* the action or result of afflicting or harming someone, typically repeatedly or over a long period: *the buffeting that people are taking in lost job status.*

buf·fo /'boōfō/ ▶ *n.* (*pl.* **-fos**) a comic actor in Italian opera or a person resembling such an actor.

▶ *adj.* of or typical of Italian comic opera: *a buffo character.*

buf·foon /bə'foōn/ ▶ *n.* a ridiculous but amusing person; a clown. —**buf·foon·er·y** *n.* —**buf·foon·ish** *adj.*

bug /bəg/ ▶ *n.* **1** a small insect. ▪ *inf.* a harmful microorganism, as a bacterium or virus. ▪ an illness caused by such a microorganism. ▪ *fig., inf.* an enthusiast, almost obsessive, interest in something: *they caught the sailing bug.* **2** (also **true bug**) *Entomol.* an insect of a large order (Hemiptera) distinguished by having mouthparts that are modified for piercing and sucking. **3** a concealed miniature microphone, used for surveillance. **4** an error in a computer program or system.

▶ *v.* (**bugged, bugging**) [*tr.*] **1** (often **be bugged**) conceal a miniature microphone in (a room, telephone, etc.) in order to monitor or record someone's conversations. ▪ record or monitor (a conversation) in this way. **2** *inf.* annoy or bother (someone).

▶ *phrasal v.* □ **bug off** *inf.* go away. □ **bug out** *inf.* **1** leave quickly. **2** *chiefly fig.* bulge outward.

bug·a·boo /'bəgə,boō/ ▶ *n.* an object of fear or alarm; a bugbear.

bug·bear /'bəg,be(ə)r/ ▶ *n.* a cause of obsessive fear, irritation, or loathing. ▪ *archaic* an imaginary being invoked to frighten children, typically a sort of hobgoblin supposed to devour them.

bug-eyed ▶ *adj. & adv.* with bulging eyes: [as *adj.*] *bug-eyed monsters* | [as *adv.*] *he stared bug-eyed at John.*

bug·ger /'bəgər; 'boōg-/ *vulgar slang chiefly Brit.* ▶ *n.* **1** a contemptible or pitied person, typically a man. ▪ a person with a particular negative quality or characteristic. ▪ used as a term of affection or respect, typically grudgingly: *all right, let the **little buggers** come in.* **2** *derog.* a person who commits buggery.

▶ *v.* [*tr.*] penetrate the anus of (someone) during sexual intercourse; sodomize.

▶ *interj.* used to express annoyance or anger.

bug·ger·y /'bəgərē; 'boōg-/ *vulgar slang chiefly Brit.* ▶ *n.* anal intercourse.

bug·gy[1] /'bəgē/ ▶ *n.* (*pl.* **-gies**) a small or light vehicle, in particular: ▪ a small motor vehicle, typically one with an open top: *a golf buggy.* ▪ *hist.* a light, horse-drawn vehicle for one or two people, with two or four wheels.

bug·gy[2] ▶ *adj.* (**-gi·er, -gi·est**) **1** infested with bugs. ▪ (of a computer program or system) faulty in operation. **2** *inf.* crazy; insane.

bu·gle[1] /'byoōgəl/ ▶ *n.* a brass instrument like a small trumpet, typically without valves or keys and used for military signals. ▪ a loud sound resembling that of a bugle, as the mating call of a bull elk.

▶ *v.* [*intr.*] sound a bugle. ▪ [*tr.*] sound (a note or call) on a bugle: *he bugled a warning.* ▪ issue a loud sound resembling that of a bugle, particularly the mating call of a bull elk. —**bu·gler** *n.*

bu·gle[2] (also **bu·gle·weed**) ▶ *n.* a creeping plant (esp. *Ajuga reptans*) of the mint family, with blue flowers held on upright stems.

bu·gle[3] ▶ *n.* (also **bugle bead**) an ornamental tube-shaped glass or plastic bead sewn on to clothing.

bu·gloss /'byoōglôs; -läs/ ▶ *n.* a bristly plant (*Anchusa, Lycopsis,* and other genera) of the borage family, with bright blue flowers.

build /bild/ ▶ *v.* (*past* and *past part.* **built** /bilt/) [*tr.*] (often **be built**) construct (something, typically something large) by putting parts or material together over a period of time: *the factory was built in 1936.* ▪ commission, finance, and oversee the building of (something): *the city council plans to build a bridge.* ▪ (**build something in/into**) incorporate (something) and make it a permanent part of a structure, system, or situation: *engineers want to build in extra traction.* ▪ *Comput.* compile (a program, database, index, etc.). ▪ [*intr.*] (of a program, database, index, etc.) be compiled. ▪ establish and develop (a business, relationship, or situation) over a period of time: *he'd built up the store from nothing.* ▪ [*intr.*] (**build on**) use as a basis for further progress or development: *the nation should build on the talents of its workforce.* ▪ increase the size, intensity, or extent of: *we built up confidence in our abilities.*

▶ *n.* **1** the dimensions or proportions of a person's or animal's body: *she was of medium height and slim build.* ▪ the style or form of construction of something, typically a vehicle. **2** *Comput.* a compiled version of a program. ▪ the process of compiling a program.

build·er /'bildər/ ▶ *n.* a person who constructs something by putting parts or material together over a period of time: *a boat builder.* ▪ a person whose job is to construct or repair houses, or to contract for their construction and repair. ▪ [usu. in *comb.*] a person or thing that creates or develops something: *breaking the record was a real confidence builder.*

build·ing /'bildiNG/ (abbr.: **bldg.**) ▶ *n.* **1** a structure with a roof and walls, such as a house, school, store, or factory. **2** the process or business of constructing something: *the building of highways* | [as *adj.*] *building materials.* ▪ the process of commissioning, financing, or overseeing the construction of something. ▪ the process of creating or developing something, typically a system or situation, over a period of time: *the building of democracy in Guatemala.* ▪ the process of increasing the intensity of a feeling: *a playwright's cunning in the building of suspense.*

build·out /'bild,out/ ▶ *n.* the growth, development, or expansion of something: *the rapid buildout of digital technology.*

build·up /'bild,əp/ ▶ *n.* **1** a gradual accumulation or increase, typically of something negative and typically leading to a problem or crisis: *the buildup of carbon dioxide in the atmosphere.* **2** a period of excitement and preparation in advance of a significant event: *the buildup to Christmas.* ▪ a favorable description in advance; publicity: *a showbiz buildup before the album release.*

built-in ▶ *adj.* forming an integral part of a structure or device: *a camera with a built-in zoom lens.* ▪ (of a characteristic) inherent; innate: *the system has a built-in resistance to change.*

built-up ▶ *adj.* **1** (of an area) densely covered by houses or other buildings. **2** increased in height by the addition of parts: *shoes with built-up heels.* ▪ (of a feeling) increasing in intensity over a period of time: *built-up frustration.*

bulb /bəlb/ ▶ *n.* **1** a rounded underground storage organ present in some plants, notably those of the lily family, consisting of a short stem surrounded by fleshy scale leaves or leaf bases and resting over winter. Compare with CORM, RHIZOME. ▪ a plant grown from an organ of this kind. ▪ a similar underground organ such as a corm or a rhizome. **2** an object with a rounded or teardrop shape like a bulb, in particular: ▪ a light bulb. ▪ an expanded part of a glass tube such as that forming the reservoir of a thermometer. ▪ a hollow flexible container with an opening through which the air can be expelled by squeezing, such as that used to fill a syringe. ▪ a spheroidal dilated part at the end of an anatomical structure.

bul·bous /'bəlbəs/ ▶ *adj.* **1** fat, round, or bulging: *a bulbous nose.* **2** (of a plant) growing from a bulb.

bul·gar /'bəlgər/ (also **bul·gur, bulgar wheat**) ▶ *n.* a cereal food made from whole wheat partially boiled then dried.

Pronunciation Key ə *ago, up;* ər *over, fur;* a *hat;* ā *ate;* ä *car;* CH *chin;* e *let;* ē *see;* e(ə)r *air;* i *fit;* ī *by;* i(ə)r *ear;* NG *sing;* ō *go;* ô *law, for;* oi *toy;* oō *good;* oō *goo;* ou *out;* SH *she;* TH *thin;* TH *then;* (h)w *why;* ZH *vision*

B

Bul·gar·i·an /ˌbəlˈge(ə)rēən; ˌbŏŏl-/ ▶ *n.* **1** a native or national of Bulgaria. **2** the South Slavic language spoken in Bulgaria.
▶ *adj.* of or relating to Bulgaria, its people, or their language.

bulge /bəlj/ ▶ *n.* a rounded swelling or protuberance that distorts a flat surface. ■ *inf.* a temporary unusual increase in number or size: *a bulge in the birth rate.*
▶ *v.* [*intr.*] swell or protrude to an unnatural or incongruous extent: *the veins in his neck bulged.* ■ be full of and distended with: *a briefcase bulging with documents.* ■ —**bulg·y** *adj.*

bul·gur /ˈbəlgər/ ▶ *n.* variant spelling of **BULGAR.**

bu·lim·i·a /bŏŏˈlimēə/ ▶ *n.* insatiable overeating as a medical condition, in particular: ■ (also **bulimia ner·vo·sa** /nərˈvōsə/) an emotional disorder involving distortion of body image and an obsessive desire to lose weight, in which bouts of extreme overeating are followed by depression and self-induced vomiting, purging, or fasting. Also called BINGE-PURGE SYNDROME. —**bu·lim·ic** /-ˈlimik; ˈlē-/ *adj. & n.*

bulk /bəlk/ ▶ *n.* the mass or magnitude of something large: *the sheer bulk of the bags.* ■ a large mass or shape, for example of a building or a heavy body: *he moved quickly in spite of his bulk.* ■ [as *adj.*] large in quantity or amount: *bulk orders of more than 100 copies.* ■ (**the bulk**) the majority or greater part of something: *the bulk of the traffic had passed.* ■ roughage in food: *bread and potatoes supply energy, essential protein, and bulk.* ■ cargo that is an unpackaged mass such as grain, oil, or milk.
▶ *v.* **1** [*intr.*] be or seem to be of great size or importance: *territorial questions bulked large in diplomatic relations.* **2** [*tr.*] treat (a product) so that its quantity appears greater than it in fact is: *traders were bulking up their flour with chalk.* ■ [*intr.*] (**bulk up**) build up body mass, typically in training for athletic events. ▷Middle English: the senses 'cargo as a whole' and 'heap, large quantity' (the earliest recorded) are probably from Old Norse *búlki* 'cargo'; the origin of other senses remains uncertain, perhaps arising by alteration of obsolete *bouk* 'belly, body.'
▶ □ **in bulk 1** (esp. of goods) in large quantities, usually at a reduced price: *buying tomatoes in bulk from a local farmer.* **2** (of a cargo or commodity) loose; not packaged: *sugar is imported in bulk and bagged on the island.*

bulk·head /ˈbəlkˌhed/ ▶ *n.* a dividing wall or barrier between compartments in a ship, aircraft, or vehicle.

bulk·y /ˈbəlkē/ ▶ *adj.* (**bulk·i·er, bulk·i·est**) taking up much space, typically inconveniently; large and unwieldy: *a bulky piece of luggage.* ■ (of a person) heavily built. ■ (of clothing) made of a thick yarn or fabric: *a bulky sweater.* —**bulk·i·ly** /-kəlē/ *adv.* —**bulk·i·ness** *n.*

bull[1] /bŏŏl/ ▶ *n.* **1** an uncastrated male bovine animal: [as *adj.*] *bull calves.* ■ a large male animal, esp. a whale or elephant. ■ (**the Bull**) the zodiacal sign or constellation Taurus. **2** *Stock Market* a person who buys shares hoping to sell them at a higher price later. Often contrasted with BEAR[2].
▶ *v.* [*tr.*] push or drive powerfully or violently: *he bulled the motorcycle clear of the tunnel.*
▶ □ **take the bull by the horns** deal bravely and decisively with a difficult, dangerous, or unpleasant situation.

bull[2] ▶ *n.* a papal edict.

bull[3] ▶ *n. inf.* stupid or untrue talk or writing; nonsense: *much of what he says is sheer bull.*

bull·dog /ˈbŏŏlˌdôg/ ▶ *n.* a dog of a sturdy smooth-haired breed with a large head and powerful protruding lower jaw, a flat wrinkled face, and a broad chest. ■ a person noted for courageous or stubborn tenacity: [as *adj.*] *the bulldog spirit.*
▶ *v.* (**-dogged, -dog·ging**) [*tr.*] wrestle (a steer) to the ground by holding its horns and twisting its neck: [as *n.*] (**bulldogging**) *cowboys compete in bulldogging and bareback riding.* —**bull·dog·ger** *n.*

bull·doze /ˈbŏŏlˌdōz/ ▶ *v.* [*tr.*] clear (ground) or destroy (buildings, trees, etc.) with a bulldozer: *developers are bulldozing the site.* ■ *fig., inf.* use insensitive force when dealing with (someone or something): *she believes that to build status you need to bulldoze everyone else.*

bull·doz·er /ˈbŏŏlˌdōzər/ ▶ *n.* a powerful tractor with a broad upright

bulldozer

blade at the front for clearing ground. ■ *fig.* a person, army, or other body exercising irresistible power, esp. in disposing of obstacles or opposition: *he was a political bulldozer.*

bul·let /ˈbŏŏlit/ ▶ *n.* **1** a projectile for firing from a rifle, revolver, or other small firearms, typically of metal, cylindrical and pointed, and sometimes containing an explosive. ■ used in similes and comparisons to refer to someone or something that moves very fast: *the ball sped across the grass like a bullet.* ■ (in a sporting context) a very fast ball. **2** *Printing* a small solid circle printed just before a line of type, such as an item in a list, to emphasize it.

bul·le·tin /ˈbŏŏlitin; -ˌtin/ ▶ *n.* a short official statement or broadcast summary of news. ■ a regular newsletter or printed report issued by an organization or society. ▷mid 17th cent. (denoting an official warrant in some European countries): from French, from Italian *bullettino,* diminutive of *bulletta* 'passport,' diminutive of *bulla* 'seal, bull.'

bul·le·tin board ▶ *n.* a board for displaying notices. ■ *Comput.* (also **bulletin board system**) an information storage system designed to permit any authorized computer user to access and add to it from a remote terminal.

bul·let·proof /ˈbŏŏlitˌprŏŏf/ ▶ *adj.* designed to resist the penetration of bullets: *a bulletproof vest.*

bull·fight /ˈbŏŏlˌfīt/ ▶ *n.* a public spectacle, particularly in Spain, Portugal, and Latin America, at which a bull is baited in a highly stylized manner and then usually killed. —**bull·fight·er** *n.* —**bull·fight·ing** *n.*

bull·finch /ˈbŏŏlˌfinCH/ ▶ *n.* a stocky Eurasian finch (genus *Pyrrhula*) with a short, thick bill, and typically with gray or pinkish plumage, dark wings, and a white rump.

bull·frog /ˈbŏŏlˌfrôg; -ˌfräg/ ▶ *n.* a very large frog (genera *Rana* and *Pyxicephalus,* family Ranidae) that has a deep booming croak and is often a predator of smaller vertebrates.

bull·head /ˈbŏŏlˌhed/ ▶ *n.* **1** (also **bullhead catfish**) an American freshwater catfish with four pairs of barbels around the mouth. **2** a small, mainly freshwater Eurasian fish (genera *Cottus* and *Taurulus*) of the sculpin family, with a broad flattened head and spiny fins. **3** (also **bullhead lily**) a North American water lily (*Nuphar variegatum*) with globular yellow flowers.

bull·head·ed /ˈbŏŏlˌhedid/ ▶ *adj.* determined in an obstinate or unthinking way: *a bullheaded belief that she is right.* —**bull·head·ed·ly** *adv.* —**bull·head·ed·ness** *n.*

bull·horn /ˈbŏŏlˌhôrn/ ▶ *n.* an electronic device for amplifying the sound of the voice so it can be heard at a distance.

bul·lion /ˈbŏŏlyən/ ▶ *n.* **1** gold or silver in bulk before coining, or valued by weight. **2** (also **bullion fringe**) ornamental braid or trimming made with twists of gold or silver thread.

bull·ish /ˈbŏŏliSH/ ▶ *adj.* **1** resembling a bull: *a sketch of his round, bullish head.* ■ stupid or oafish; bullheaded: *it's impossible to reason with such a bullish man.* ■ assertively masculine; macho: *surrounded by girls and the aura of bullish manhood.* **2** *Stock Market* characterized by rising share prices: *the market was bullish.* ■ (of a dealer) inclined to buy because of an anticipated rise in prices. **3** feeling especially hopeful; optimistic: *challenging those who are bullish on the nation's economic prospects.* —**bull·ish·ly** *adv.* —**bull·ish·ness** *n.*

bull mar·ket ▶ *n. Stock Market* a market in which share prices are rising, encouraging buying.

bul·lock ▶ *n.* another term for STEER[2].

bull·pen /ˈbŏŏlˌpen/ ▶ *n.* (also **bull pen**) an enclosure for bulls. ■ an exercise area for baseball pitchers. ■ the relief pitchers of a baseball team. ■ an open-plan office area. ■ a large cell in which prisoners are held before a court hearing.

bull·ring /ˈbŏŏlˌriNG/ ▶ *n.* an arena where bullfights are held.

bull ses·sion ▶ *n.* an informal, typically impromptu discussion, esp. among a small group.

bull's-eye ▶ *n.* (also **bulls-eye**) **1** the center of a target in sports such as archery, shooting, and darts. ■ a shot that hits such a target center. ■ *fig.* used to refer to something that achieves exactly the intended effect: *the silence told him he'd scored a bull's-eye.* **2** a large, round, hard peppermint-flavored candy.

bull·shit /ˈbŏŏlˌSHit/ *vulgar slang* ▶ *n.* stupid or untrue talk or writing; nonsense.
▶ *v.* (**-shit·ted, -shit·ting**) [*tr.*] talk nonsense to (someone), typically to be misleading or deceptive. —**bull·shit·ter** *n.*

bull ter·ri·er ▶ *n.* a short-haired dog of a breed that is a cross between a bulldog and a terrier.

bul·ly[1] /ˈbŏŏlē/ ▶ *n.* (*pl.* **-lies**) a person who uses strength or power to harm or intimidate those who are weaker.

▶ *v.* (**-lies, -lied**) [*tr.*] use superior strength or influence to intimidate (someone), typically to force him or her to do what one wants.

bul·ly² *inf.* ▶ *adj.* very good; first-rate: *the statue really looked bully.* ▶ *interj.* (**bully for**) an expression of admiration or approval: *he got away— bully for him.*

bul·ly boy ▶ *n.* a tough or aggressive man: [as *adj.*] *bully-boy tactics.*

bul·rush /ˈbo͝olˌrəSH/ (also **bull-rush**) ▶ *n.* **1** another term for CATTAIL. **2** a tall rushlike water plant (*Scirpus lacustris*) of the sedge family. Native to temperate regions of the northern hemisphere, it is used for weaving and is grown as an aid to water purification. **3** (in biblical use) a papyrus plant.

bul·wark /ˈbo͝olˌwərk/ ▶ *n.* a defensive wall. ■ *fig.* a person, institution, or principle that acts as a defense: *the security forces are a bulwark against the breakdown of society.*

bum /bəm/ *inf.* ▶ *n.* **1** a vagrant. ■ a lazy or worthless person: *you ungrateful bum.* **2** [in *comb.*] a person who devotes a great deal of time to a specified activity: *a ski bum* | *a poker bum.* ▶ *v.* (**bummed, bum·ming**) **1** [*intr.*] travel, with no particular purpose or destination: *he bummed around Florida for a few months.* ■ pass one's time idly: *we spent most of the summer just bumming around.* **2** [*tr.*] get by asking or begging: *they tried to bum money off us.* **3** [*tr.*] make (someone) feel upset or disappointed: *it really bummed me out when he forgot my birthday.* ▶ *adj.* of poor quality; bad or wrong: *not one bum note was played.* ▶ □ **give someone** (or **get**) **the bum's rush** forcibly eject someone (or be forcibly ejected) from a place or gathering. ■ abruptly dismiss someone (or be abruptly dismissed) for a poor idea or performance.

bum·ble /ˈbəmbəl/ ▶ *v.* **1** [*intr.*] move or act in an awkward or confused manner: *they bumbled around the house* | [as *adj.*] (**bumbling**) *his bumbling interventions.* **2** [*intr.*] speak in a confused or indistinct way: *the succeeding speakers bumbled.* ■ (of an insect) buzz or hum: *she watched a bee bumble among the flowers.* —**bum·bler** /-b(ə)lər/ *n.*

bum·ble·bee /ˈbəmbəlˌbē/ ▶ *n.* a large hairy bee (genus *Bombus,* family Apidae) with a loud hum, living in small colonies in holes underground.

bum·mer /ˈbəmər/ ▶ *n.* *inf.* **1** (**a bummer**) a thing that is annoying or disappointing: *the party was a real bummer.* ■ an unpleasant reaction to a hallucinogenic drug. **2** a loafer or vagrant. ▶ *interj.* *inf.* used to express frustration or disappointment, typically sympathetically: *You lost your wallet? Bummer!*

bump /bəmp/ ▶ *n.* **1** a light blow or a jolting collision: *a nasty bump on the head.* ■ the dull sound of such a blow or collision. ■ *Aeron.* a rising air current causing an irregularity in an aircraft's motion. **2** a protuberance on a level surface: *bumps in the road.* ■ a swelling on the skin, esp. one caused by illness or injury. ▶ *v.* **1** [*intr.*] knock or run into someone or something, typically with a jolt: *I almost bumped into him.* ■ (**bump into**) meet by chance: *we might just bump into each other.* ■ [*tr.*] hurt or damage (something) by striking or knocking it against something else: *she bumped her head on the sink.* ■ [*tr.*] cause to collide with something: *she went through the door, bumping the bag against it.* **2** [*intr.*] move or travel with much jolting and jarring: *the car bumped along the rutted track.* ■ [*tr.*] push (something) jerkily in a specified direction: *she had to bump the wheelchair down the steps.* **3** [*tr.*] refuse (a passenger) a reserved place on an airline flight, typically because of deliberate overbooking. ■ cause to move from a job or position, typically in favor of someone else; displace: *she was bumped for a youthful model.* ▶ *phrasal v.* □ **bump someone off** *inf.* murder someone.

bump·er /ˈbəmpər/ ▶ *n.* a horizontal bar fixed across the front or back of a motor vehicle to reduce damage in a collision or as a trim. ▶ *adj.* exceptionally large, fine, or successful: *a bumper crop.* ▶ □ **bumper-to-bumper** very close together, as cars in a traffic jam.

bump·er car ▶ *n.* a small electrically powered car with rubber bumpers all around, driven in an enclosure at an amusement park with the aim of bumping into other such cars.

bump·er stick·er ▶ *n.* a label carrying a slogan or advertisement fixed to a vehicle's bumper.

bump·kin /ˈbəmpkin/ ▶ *n.* *inf., often derog.* an unsophisticated or socially awkward person from a rural area: *a country bumpkin.*

bump·tious /ˈbəmpSHəs/ ▶ *adj.* self-assertive or proud to an irritating degree: *these bumptious young boys today.* —**bump·tious·ly** *adv.* —**bump·tious·ness** *n.*

bump·y /ˈbəmpē/ ▶ *adj.* (**bump·i·er, bump·i·est**) (of a surface) uneven, with many patches raised above the rest: *the bumpy road.* ■ (of a journey or other movement) involving sudden jolts and jerks, esp. caused by an uneven surface: *she took us all on a bumpy ride.* ■ *fig.* fluctuating and unreliable; subject to unexpected difficulties: *bumpy market conditions.* —**bump·i·ly** /-pəlē/ *adv.* —**bump·i·ness** *n.*

bum rap ▶ *n.* *inf.* a false charge, typically one leading to imprisonment: *he's been handed a bum rap for handling stolen goods.* ■ *fig.* an unfair punishment or scolding.

bum steer ▶ *n.* *inf.* a piece of false information or guidance: *apparently, those who recommended your good service gave us a bum steer.*

bun /bən/ ▶ *n.* **1** a bread roll of various shapes and flavorings, typically sweetened and often containing dried fruit. **2** a hairstyle in which the hair is drawn back into a tight coil at the back of the head. **3** (**buns**) *inf.* a person's buttocks.

bunch /bənCH/ ▶ *n.* a number of things, typically of the same kind, growing or fastened together: *a bunch of grapes.* ■ *inf.* a group of people. ■ *inf.* a large number or quantity; a lot: *I had to turn down a bunch of well-paid jobs.* ▶ *v.* [*tr.*] collect or fasten into a compact group: *she bunched the carnations together.* ■ gather (cloth) into close folds. ■ [*intr.*] form into a tight group or crowd: *he halted, forcing the rest of the field to bunch up behind him.* —**bunch·y** *adj.*

bun·co /ˈbəNGkō/ (also **bun·ko**) *inf.* ▶ *n.* (*pl.* **-cos**) [often as *adj.*] a swindle or confidence trick: *a bunco artist.*

bun·combe ▶ *n.* variant spelling of BUNKUM.

bun·dle /ˈbəndl/ ▶ *n.* a collection of things, or a quantity of material, tied or wrapped up together: *a thick bundle of envelopes.* ■ *fig.* a large quantity or collection, typically a disorganized one: *a bundle of facts.* ■ *inf.* a person displaying a specified characteristic to a very high degree: *he was an enthusiastic bundle of energy.* ■ a set of nerve, muscle, or other fibers running close together in parallel. ■ *Comput.* a set of software or hardware sold together. ■ (**a bundle**) *inf.* a large amount of money: *the new printer cost a bundle.* ▶ *v.* **1** [*tr.*] tie or roll up (a number of things) together as though into a parcel: *she quickly bundled up her clothes.* ■ [*tr.*] wrap or pack (something): *the figure was bundled in furs.* ■ (usu. **be bundled up**) dress (someone) in many clothes to keep warm: *they were bundled up in thick sweaters* | [*intr.*] *I bundled up in my parka.* ■ *Comput.* sell (items of hardware and software) as a package. **2** [*tr.*] (often **be bundled**) *inf.* push or carry forcibly: *he was bundled into a van.* ■ send (someone) away hurriedly or unceremoniously: *the old man was bundled off into exile.* ■ [*intr.*] (esp. of a group of people) move clumsily or in a disorganized way: *they bundled out into the corridor.*

Bundt cake /ˈbənt/ ▶ *n.* *trademark* a ring-shaped cake made in a fluted tube pan, called a **Bundt pan.**

bung /bəNG/ ▶ *n.* a stopper for closing a hole in a container. ▶ *v.* [*tr.*] close with a stopper: *the casks are bunged before delivery.* ■ (**bung something up**) block (something), typically by overfilling it: *you let vegetable peelings bung up the sink.* ■ ruin something.

bun·ga·low /ˈbəNGgəˌlō/ ▶ *n.* a low house having either no upper floor or upper rooms set in the roof, typically with dormer windows.

bun·gee /ˈbənjē/ ▶ *n.* (also **bungee cord**) a long nylon-cased rubber band, used typically in bungee jumping or for securing luggage. ▶ *v.* [*intr.*] (as a sport) leap from a great height, typically a bridge or crane, while secured by such a band around the ankles.

bun·gee-jump·ing ▶ *n.* the sport of leaping from a height while secured by a long nylon-cased rubber band from the ankles. —**bun·gee jump** *n.* —**bun·gee-jump·er** *n.*

bun·gle /ˈbəNGgəl/ ▶ *v.* [*tr.*] carry out (a task) clumsily or incompetently, leading to failure or an unsatisfactory outcome: *she had bungled every attempt to help* | [as *adj.*] (**bungled**) *a bungled bank raid.* ■ [*intr.*] [usu. as *adj.*] (**bungling**) make or be prone to making many mistakes: *the work of a bungling amateur.* ▶ *n.* a mistake or failure, typically one resulting from mismanagement or confusion. —**bun·gler** /-g(ə)lər/ *n.*

bun·ion /ˈbənyən/ ▶ *n.* a painful swelling on the first joint of the big toe.

bunk¹ /bəNGk/ ▶ *n.* a narrow shelflike bed, typically one of two or more arranged one on top of the other. ▶ *v.* [*intr.*] sleep in shared quarters as a temporary arrangement: *they bunk together in the dormitory.*

bunk² ▶ *n.* *inf.* nonsense: *anyone with a brain cell would never believe such bunk.*

bunk bed ▶ *n.* a piece of furniture consisting of two beds, one above the other, that form a unit.

bun·ker /ˈbəNGkər/ ▶ *n.* **1** a large container or compartment for storing

---

Pronunciation Key ə *ago,* up; ər *over,* fur; a *hat;* ā *ate;* ä *car;* CH *chin;* e *let;* ē *see;* e(ə)r *air;* i *fit;* ī *by;* i(ə)r *ear;* NG *sing;* ō *go;* ô *law, for;* oi *toy;* o͝o *good;* o͞o *goo;* ou *out;* SH *she;* TH *thin;* TH *then;* (h)w *why;* ZH *vision*

fuel: *a coal bunker.* ■ (**bunkers**) fuel for a ship. **2** a reinforced underground shelter, typically for use in wartime. **3** a hollow filled with sand, used as an obstacle on a golf course.
▶ *v.* [*tr.*] fuel (a ship).

bunk·house /'bəNGk,hous/ ▶ *n.* a building offering basic sleeping accommodations for workers, visitors, or campers.

bun·kum /'bəNGkəm/ (also **bun·combe**) ▶ *n. dated, inf.* nonsense: *they talk a lot of bunkum about their products.*

bun·ny /'bənē/ ▶ *n.* (*pl.* **-nies**) *inf.* (also **bunny rabbit**) a rabbit, esp. a young one. ■ *inf.* a person of a specified type or in a specified mood: *ski slopes crawling with snow bunnies.*

Bun·sen burn·er ▶ *n.* a small adjustable gas burner used in laboratories.

bunt[1] /bənt/ ▶ *v.* [*tr.*] *Baseball* (of a batter) gently tap (a pitched ball) without swinging in an attempt to make it more difficult to field: *the batter tried to bunt the ball down the first baseline.* ■ (of a batter) help (a base runner) to progress to a further base by tapping a ball in such a way: *he bunted Davis to third.*
▶ *n. Baseball* an act or result of tapping a pitched ball in such a way.

bunt[2] ▶ *n.* a disease of wheat caused by a smut fungus (*Tilletia caries*), the spores of which give off a smell of rotten fish.

bunt·ing[1] /'bəntiNG/ ▶ *n.* a small New World songbird (genera *Passerina* and *Cyanocompsa*, family Emberizidae) of the cardinal subfamily, the male of which is brightly colored.

bunt·ing[2] ▶ *n.* flags and other colorful festive decorations. ■ a loosely woven fabric used for such decoration.

bu·oy /'bōō-ē; boi/ ▶ *n.* an anchored float serving as a navigation mark, to show reefs or other hazards, or for mooring.
▶ *v.* [*tr.*] **1** keep (someone or something) afloat: *I let the water buoy up my weight.* ■ (often **be buoyed**) cause to become cheerful or confident: *the party was buoyed by an election victory.* ■ (often **be buoyed**) cause (a price) to rise to or remain at a high level: *the price is buoyed up by investors.* **2** mark with a buoy: [as *adj.*] (**buoyed**) *a buoyed channel.*

buoy·ant /'boi-ənt; 'bōōyənt/ ▶ *adj.* able or apt to stay afloat or rise to the top of a liquid or gas. ■ (of a liquid or gas) able to keep something afloat. ■ *fig.* (of an economy, business, or market) involving or engaged in much activity: *car sales were not buoyant.* ■ *fig.* cheerful and optimistic: *the conference ended with the party in a buoyant mood.* —**buoy·an·cy** *n.* —**buoy·ant·ly** *adv.*

bup·kis /'bŏŏpkis; 'bəp-/ ▶ *n. inf.* nothing at all: *you know bupkis about fundraising.*

bur /bər/ (also **burr**) ▶ *n.* **1** a prickly seed case or flowerhead that clings to animals and clothes. ■ [usu. as *adj.*] a plant that produces burs, e.g., *bur reed.* **2** [as *adj.*] denoting wood containing knots or other growths that show a pattern of dense swirls in the grain when sawn, used for veneers and other decorative woodwork: *bur walnut.* **3** variant spelling of **BURR** (senses 2, 3, and 5).

bur·ble /'bərbəl/ ▶ *v.* [*intr.*] make a continuous murmuring noise: *the wind burbled at his ear.* ■ speak in an unintelligible or silly way, typically at unnecessary length: *he burbled on about annuities.*
▶ *n.* continuous murmuring noise.

bur·bot /'bərbət/ ▶ *n.* an elongated bottom-dwelling fish (*Lota lota*) of Eurasia and North America. It is the only freshwater fish of the cod family.

bur·den /'bərdn/ ▶ *n.* **1** a load, esp. a heavy one. ■ *fig.* a duty or misfortune that causes hardship, anxiety, or grief: *the burden of mental illness.* ■ the main responsibility for achieving a specified aim or task: *the burden of establishing that the cost was unreasonable.* ■ a ship's carrying capacity; tonnage. **2** (**the burden**) the main theme or gist of a speech, book, or argument: *the burden of his views.*
▶ *v.* [*tr.*] (usu. **be burdened**) load heavily: *she walked forward burdened with a wooden box.* ■ *fig.* cause (someone) hardship or distress: *they were not yet burdened with adult responsibility.* —**bur·den·some** /'-səm/ *adj.*
▶ □ **burden of proof** the obligation to prove one's assertion.

bur·dock /'bərdäk/ ▶ *n.* a large herbaceous plant (genus *Arctium*) of the daisy family. The hook-bearing flowers become woody burrs after fertilization and cling to animals' coats for seed dispersal.

bu·reau /'byŏŏrō/ ▶ *n.* (*pl.* **bu·reaus** or **bu·reaux** /'byŏŏrōz/) **1** a chest of drawers. **2** (abbr.: **bur.**) an office or department for transacting particular business: *a news bureau.* ■ the office in a particular place of an organization based elsewhere: *the London bureau of the Washington*

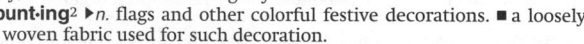

bunsen burner

Post. ■ a government department: *the intelligence bureau.* ▷late 17th cent.: from French, originally 'baize' (used to cover writing desks), from Old French *burel*, probably from *bure* 'dark brown,' based on Greek *purros* 'red.'

bu·reauc·ra·cy /byŏŏ'räkrəsē/ ▶ *n.* (*pl.* **-cies**) a system of government in which most of the important decisions are made by state officials rather than by elected representatives. ■ a state or organization governed or managed according to such a system. ■ the officials in such a system, considered as a group or hierarchy. ■ excessively complicated administrative procedure, seen as characteristic of such a system: *the unnecessary bureaucracy in local government.*

bu·reau·crat /'byŏŏrə,krat/ ▶ *n.* an official in a government department. ■ an administrator concerned with procedural correctness at the expense of people's needs. —**bu·reau·crat·ic** *adj.* —**bu·reau·crat·i·cal·ly** *adv.*

bu·rette /byŏŏ'ret/ (also **bu·ret**) ▶ *n.* a graduated glass tube with a tap at one end, for delivering known volumes of a liquid, esp. in titrations.

burg /bərg/ ▶ *n.* an ancient or medieval fortress or walled town. ■ *inf.* a town or city.

bur·geon /'bərjən/ ▶ *v.* [*intr.*] [often as *adj.*] (**burgeoning**) begin to grow or increase rapidly; flourish: *manufacturers are keen to cash in on the burgeoning demand.*

burg·er /'bərgər/ ▶ *n.* short for **HAMBURGER**. ■ a variation of a hamburger with additional or substitute ingredients: *a veggie burger.*

bur·gess /'bərjis/ ▶ *n.* a person with municipal authority or privileges, in particular: ■ a magistrate or member of the governing body of a town. ■ *hist.* a member of the assembly of colonial Maryland or Virginia.

bur·glar /'bərglər/ ▶ *n.* a person who commits burglary.

bur·glar·ize /'bərglə,rīz/ ▶ *v.* [*tr.*] (often **be burglarized**) enter (a building) illegally with intent to commit a crime, esp. theft: *our summer house has been burglarized.*

bur·gla·ry /'bərglərē/ ▶ *n.* (*pl.* **-ries**) entry into a building illegally with intent to commit a crime, esp. theft: *a two-year sentence for burglary.*

bur·gle /'bərgəl/ ▶ *v.* another term for **BURGLARIZE**.

bur·gun·dy /'bərgəndē/ (also **Bur·gun·dy**) ▶ *n.* (*pl.* **-dies**) a usually red wine from Burgundy: *a glass of Burgundy.* ■ a deep red color like that of burgundy wine: *warm shades of brown and burgundy.*

bur·i·al /'berēəl/ ▶ *n.* the action or practice of interring a dead body: *his remains were shipped home for burial.* ■ a ceremony at which someone's body is interred; a funeral: [as *adj.*] *burial rites.* ■ *Archaeol.* a grave or the remains found in it: [as *adj.*] *burial mounds.*

bu·rin /'byŏŏrin/ ▶ *n.* a steel tool used for engraving in copper or wood. ■ *Archaeol.* a flint tool with a chisel point.

Bur·kitt's lym·pho·ma /'bərkits/ ▶ *n. Med.* cancer of the lymphatic system, caused by the Epstein–Barr virus, chiefly affecting children in central Africa.

burl /bərl/ ▶ *n.* a rounded knotty growth on a tree, giving an attractive figure when polished and used esp. for handcrafted objects and veneers.

bur·lap /'bərlap/ ▶ *n.* coarse canvas woven from jute, hemp, or a similar fiber, used esp. for sacking. ■ lighter material of a similar kind used in dressmaking and upholstery.

bur·lesque /bər'lesk/ ▶ *n.* **1** a parody or comically exaggerated imitation of something, esp. in a literary or dramatic work: *the funniest burlesque of opera* | [as *adj.*] *burlesque nursery rhymes.* ■ humor that depends on comic imitation and exaggeration; absurdity: *the argument descends into burlesque.* **2** a variety show, typically including striptease: [as *adj.*] *burlesque clubs.*
▶ *v.* (**-lesques, -lesqued, -lesqu·ing**) [*tr.*] cause to appear absurd by parodying or copying in an exaggerated form: *she struck a ridiculous pose that burlesqued her own vanity.*

bur·ly /'bərlē/ ▶ *adj.* (**-li·er, -li·est**) (of a person) large and strong; heavily built. —**bur·li·ness** *n.*

Bur·mese /bər'mēz; -'mēs/ ▶ *n.* (*pl.* same) **1** a member of the largest ethnic group of Myanmar (Burma) in Southeast Asia. **2** a native or national of Myanmar. **3** the Tibeto-Burman language of the Burmese people, written in an alphabet derived from that of Pali and the official language of Myanmar. **4** (also **Burmese cat**) a cat of a short-haired breed originating in Asia.
▶ *adj.* of or relating to Myanmar, its people, or their language.

burn[1] /bərn/ ▶ *v.* (*past* and *past part.* **burned** or *chiefly Brit.* **burnt** /bərnt/) **1** [*intr.*] (of a fire) flame or glow while consuming a material such as coal or wood: *a fire burned and crackled cheerfully in the grate.* ■ (of a candle or other source of light) be alight: *a light was burning in the hall.* ■ be or cause to be destroyed by fire: *he watched his restaurant burn to the ground* ■ [*tr.*] damage or injure by heat or fire: *I burned myself on the stove.* **2** [*intr.*] (of a person, the skin, or a part of the body) become red and painful through exposure to the sun: *my skin tans easily but sometimes burns.* ■ feel or cause to feel sore, hot, or inflamed, typically as a result of illness or injury. ■ (of a person's face) feel hot and flushed from an intense emotion such as shame or indignation: *her face burned with the humiliation.* ■ (**be burning with**) be possessed by (a desire or an emotion): *Martha was burning with curiosity.* **3** [*tr.*] use (a type of fuel) as a source of heat or energy: *a diesel engine converted to burn natural gas.* ■ [*tr.*] (of a person) convert (calories) to energy: *the speed at which your body burns calories.* **4** [*tr.*] produce (a compact disc or DVD) by copying from an original or master copy. **5** [*intr.*] *inf.* drive very fast: *he burned past us like a maniac.*

▸*phrasal v.* □ **burn out** be completely consumed and thus no longer aflame: *the candle in the saucer had burned out.* ■ cease to function as a result of excessive heat or friction: *the clutch had burned out.* □ **burn (oneself) out** ruin one's health or become completely exhausted through overwork. □ **burn up** **1** (of a fire) produce brighter and stronger flames. **2** (of an object entering the earth's atmosphere) be destroyed by heat. □ **burn someone up** *inf.* make someone angry: *his thoughtless remarks really burn me up.* □ **burn something up** ■ use up the calories or energy provided by food, rather than converting these to fat: *in the typical Western diet, all the energy in protein is burned up daily.*

▸*n.* **1** an injury caused by exposure to heat or flame: *he was treated in the hospital for burns to his hands.* ■ a mark left on something as a result of being burned: *the carpet was covered with cigarette burns.* ■ a feeling of heat and discomfort on the skin caused by friction, typically by a rope or razor: *a smooth shave without razor burn.* ■ a sensation of heat experienced on swallowing spicy food, hot liquid, or strong alcoholic drink: *Kate felt the burn as the curry hit her throat.* **2** consumption of a type of fuel as an energy source: *natural gas produces the cleanest burn of the lot.* ■ a firing of a rocket engine in flight. **3** an act of clearing vegetation by burning, intentionally or by accident. ■ an area of land cleared in this way. **4** a hot, painful sensation in the muscles experienced as a result of sustained vigorous exercise: *work up a burn.*

▸ □ **burn one's bridges** do something that makes it impossible to return to an earlier state. □ **burn the candle at both ends** go to bed late and get up early, esp. to get work done. □ **burn the midnight oil** read, study, or work late into the night. □ **slow burn** *inf.* a state of slowly mounting anger or annoyance.

burn² ▸*n.* chiefly *Scot. & N. Engl.* a small stream; a brook.

burned-out (also **burnt-out**) ▸*adj.* (of a vehicle or building) destroyed or badly damaged by fire; gutted. ■ (of an electrical device or component) having failed through overheating. ■ (of a person) in a state of physical or mental collapse caused by overwork or stress: *she felt burned out, an empty shell.* ■ *inf.* (of a teenager or other person) having dropped out; drug-using.

burn·er /ˈbərnər/ ▸*n.* a thing that burns something or is burned, in particular: ■ a part of a stove, lamp, etc., that emits and shapes a flame. ■ an apparatus in which a fuel is used or an aromatic substance is heated. ■ an activity that uses something of a specified kind as energy: *uphill walking is a great calorie burner.* ■ *inf.* a handgun.

▸ □ **on the back** (or **front**) **burner** *inf.* having low (or high) priority: *he wants the matter to be put on the back burner.*

burn·ing /ˈbərniNG/ ▸*adj.* on fire: *a burning building.* ■ very hot or bright: *burning desert sands.* ■ *fig.* very keenly or deeply felt; intense: *he had a burning ambition to climb to the upper reaches of management.* ■ *fig.* of urgent interest and importance; exciting or calling for debate: *democracy remains a burning issue.* —**burn·ing·ly** *adv.*

bur·nish /ˈbərniSH/ ▸*v.* [*tr.*] [usu. as *adj.*] (**burnished**) polish (something, esp. metal) by rubbing: *highly burnished armor.* ■ *fig.* enhance or perfect (something such as a reputation or a skill).

▸*n.* the shine on a highly polished surface. —**bur·nish·er** *n.*

bur·noose /bərˈnoos/ (also **bur·nous**) ▸*n.* a long, loose hooded cloak worn by Arabs.

burn·out /ˈbərnˌout/ ▸*n.* **1** physical or mental collapse caused by overwork or stress: *high levels of professionalism that may result in burnout.* ■ *inf.* a dropout or drug abuser, esp. a teenage one. **2** failure of an electrical device or component through overheating: *an antistall mechanism prevents motor burnout.*

burn rate ▸*n.* the rate at which an enterprise spends money, especially venture capital, in excess of income.

burnt /bərnt/ ▸*adj.* chiefly British past and past participle of BURN.

burp /bərp/ *inf.* ▸*v.* [*intr.*] noisily release air from the

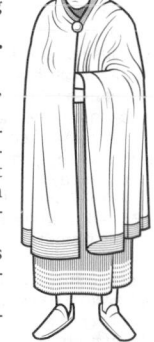

burnoose

stomach through the mouth; belch. ■ [*tr.*] make (a baby) belch after feeding, typically by patting its back.

▸*n.* a noise made by air released from the stomach through the mouth; a belch.

burr /bər/ ▸*n.* **1** a rough sounding of the sound r, esp. with a uvular trill (a "French r") as in certain Northern England accents. ■ (loosely) a regional accent characterized by such a trill: *a soft Scottish burr.* **2** (also **bur**) a rough edge or ridge left on an object (esp. of metal) by the action of a tool or machine. **3** (also **bur**) a small rotary cutting tool with a shaped end, used chiefly in woodworking, medicine, and dentistry. **4** variant spelling of BUR.

bur·ri·to /bəˈrētō/ ▸*n.* (*pl.* **-tos**) a Mexican dish consisting of a tortilla rolled around a filling, typically of beans or ground or shredded beef.

bur·ro /ˈbərō; ˈbo͝orō/ ▸*n.* (*pl.* **-ros**) a small donkey used as a pack animal.

bur·row /ˈbərō/ ▸*n.* a hole or tunnel dug by a small animal, esp. a rabbit, as a dwelling.

▸*v.* [*intr.*] (of an animal) make a hole or tunnel, esp. to use as a dwelling: *moles burrowing away underground.* ■ move underneath or press close to something in order to hide oneself or in search of comfort: *the child burrowed deeper into the bed.* ■ *fig.* make a thorough inquiry; investigate: *journalists are burrowing into the president's business affairs.* —**bur·row·er** *n.*

bur·sa /ˈbərsə/ ▸*n.* (*pl.* **-sae** /-sē/ or **-sas**) *Anat.* a fluid-filled sac or saclike cavity, esp. one countering friction at a joint. —**bur·sal** *adj.*

bur·sar /ˈbərsər/ ▸*n.* a person who manages the financial affairs of a college or university.

bur·si·tis /bərˈsītis/ ▸*n. Med.* inflammation of a bursa, typically one in the knee, elbow or shoulder.

burst /bərst/ ▸*v.* (*past* and *past part.* **burst**) [*intr.*] (of a container) break suddenly and violently apart, spilling the contents, typically as a result of an impact or internal pressure: *we inflated dozens of balloons and only one burst.* ■ [*tr.*] cause to break, esp. by puncturing: *he burst the balloon in my face.* ■ [*tr.*] (of contents) break open (a container) from the inside by growing too large to be held: *the swollen river was expected to burst its banks.* ■ [*tr.*] suffer from the sudden breaking of (a bodily organ or vessel): *he burst a blood vessel during a fit of coughing.* ■ be so full as almost to break open: *the drawers were bursting with clothes.* ■ feel a very strong or irrepressible emotion or impulse: *he was bursting with joy and excitement | she was bursting to say something.* ■ suddenly begin doing something as an expression of a strong feeling: *if anyone said anything to upset me, I'd burst out crying.* ■ issue suddenly and uncontrollably, as though from a splitting container: *an aircraft crashed and burst into flames.* ■ be opened suddenly and forcibly: *a door burst open and a girl raced out.*

▸*n.* an instance of breaking or splitting as a result of internal pressure or puncturing; an explosion. ■ a sudden issuing forth: *her breath was coming in short bursts.* ■ a sudden outbreak, typically short and often violent or noisy: *a sudden burst of activity.* ■ a short, sudden, and intense effort: *he sailed 474 miles in one 24-hour burst.*

▸ □ **burst someone's bubble** shatter someone's illusions about something or destroy someone's sense of well-being.

bur·y /ˈberē/ ▸*v.* (**bur·ies**, **bur·ied**) [*tr.*] put or hide under ground: *he buried the box in the back garden* | [as *adj.*] (**buried**) *buried treasure.* ■ (usu. **be buried**) place (a dead body) in the earth, in a tomb, or in the sea, typically with funeral rites: *he was buried in Arlington National Cemetery.* ■ *fig.* lose (someone, typically a relative) through death: *she buried her sixty-year-old husband.* ■ completely cover; cause to disappear or become inconspicuous: *the countryside has been buried under layers of concrete.* ■ move or put out of sight: *she buried her face in her hands.* ■ *fig.* deliberately forget; conceal from oneself: *they had buried their feelings of embarrassment and fear.* ■ overwhelm (an opponent) beyond hope of recovery: *he boasted that socialism would bury capitalism.* ■ (**bury oneself**) involve oneself deeply in something to the exclusion of other concerns: *he buried himself in work.*

▸ □ **bury the hatchet** end a quarrel or conflict and become friendly. □ **bury one's head in the sand** ignore unpleasant realities.

bus /bəs/ ▸*n.* (*pl.* **bus·es** or **bus·ses**) **1** a large motor vehicle carrying passengers by road, one serving the public on a fixed route and for a fare: [as *adj.*] *a bus service.* **2** *Comput.* a distinct set of conductors carrying data and control signals within a computer system, to which pieces of equipment may be connected in parallel.

▸*v.* (**bus·es**, **bused**, **bus·ing** or **bus·ses**, **bus·sed**, **bus·sing**) **1** [*tr.*] (often **be bused**) transport in a communal road vehicle: *managerial staff was bused in and out of the factory.* ■ transport (a child of one race) to a school where another race is predominant, in an attempt to promote racial integration. **2** [*tr.*] remove (dirty tableware) from a table in a restaurant or cafeteria: *I'd never bused so many dishes in one night.*

bus·boy /'bəs,boi/ ▶ *n.* a young man who clears tables in a restaurant or cafeteria.

bus·by /'bəzbē/ ▶ *n.* (*pl.* **-bies**) a tall fur hat with a colored cloth flap hanging down on the right-hand side and often a plume on the top, worn by soldiers of certain regiments of hussars and artillerymen.

bush /bŏŏsH/ ▶ *n.* a shrub or clump of shrubs with stems of moderate length: *a rose bush.* ■ a thing resembling such a shrub, esp. a clump of thick hair or fur: *a childish face with a bush of bright hair.* ■ *vulgar slang* a person's pubic hair, esp. that of a woman. ■ **(the bush)** (esp. in Australia, Africa, and Canada) wild or uncultivated country: *they have to spend a night camping in the bush.*
▶ *v.* [*intr.*] spread out into a thick clump: *her hair bushed out like a halo.*

busby

bush ba·by (also **bush-ba·by**) ▶ *n.* (*pl.* **-bies**) a small nocturnal tree-dwelling African primate (genus *Galago*) of the loris family, with very large eyes.

bushed /bŏŏsHt/ ▶ *adj. inf.* tired out: *after three days of training, the rookies were totally bushed.*

bush·el /'bŏŏsHəl/ (abbr.: **bu.**) ▶ *n.* **1** a measure of capacity equal to 64 pints (35.2 liters), used for dry goods. ■ *fig.* a large amount: *we sold it for a bushel of money.* **2** a container with the capacity of a bushel: *packing oysters into bushel baskets.* —**bush·el·ful** *n.* .

bush·ing /'bŏŏsHiNG/ ▶ *n.* a metal lining for a round hole enclosing a revolving shaft. ■ more generally, a bearing for a revolving shaft. ■ a clamp that grips and protects an electric cable where it passes through a metal panel.

Bush·man /'bŏŏsHmən/ ▶ *n.* (*pl.* **-men**) **1** a member of any of several aboriginal peoples of southern Africa, esp. of the Kalahari Desert. They are traditionally nomadic hunter-gatherers. Also called **San**. **2** the language of these peoples, now usually called **San**. **3** (**bushman**) a person who lives, works, or travels in the Australian bush.

bush·whack /'bŏŏsH,(h)wak/ ▶ *v.* **1** [*intr.*] [often as *n.*] (**bushwhacking**) live or travel in wild or uncultivated country: *I have not seen a bear yet after seven days of bushwhacking.* **2** [*tr.*] make a surprise attack on (someone) from a hidden place; ambush.

bush·whack·er /'bŏŏsH,(h)wakər/ ▶ *n.* a person who clears woods and bush country. ■ a person who lives or travels in bush country.

bush·y /'bŏŏsHē/ ▶ *adj.* (**bush·i·er, bush·i·est**) **1** growing thickly into or so as to resemble a bush: *a dense, bushy plant.* **2** covered with bush or bushes: *bushy desert areas.* —**bush·i·ly** /'bŏŏsHəlē/ *adv.* —**bush·i·ness** *n.*

busi·ness /'biznis/ (**bus.**) ▶ *n.* **1** a person's regular occupation, profession, or trade: *are you here on business?* ■ an activity that someone is engaged in: *what is your business here?* ■ a person's concern: *this is none of your business.* ■ work that has to be done or matters that have to be attended to: *government business | let's get down to business.* **2** the practice of making one's living by engaging in commerce: *the world of business.* ■ trade considered in terms of its volume or profitability: *how's business?* ■ a commercial company: *a catering business.* **3** *inf.* an affair or series of events, typically a scandalous or discreditable one: *they must be told about this blackmailing business.* ■ *inf.* a group of related or previously mentioned things: *use carrots, cauliflower, and broccoli, and serve the whole business hot.* **4** *Theater* actions other than dialogue performed by actors: *a piece of business.* **5** *inf.* a scolding; harsh verbal criticism: *the supervisor really gave him the business.* ▷Old English *bisignis*. The sense in Old English was 'anxiety'; the sense 'the state of being busy' was used from Middle English down to the 18th cent., but is now differentiated as *busyness*. The sense 'an appointed task' dates from late Middle English, and from it all the other current senses have developed.
▶ □ **business as usual** an unchanging state of affairs despite difficulties or disturbances: *apart from being under new management, it's business as usual in the department.* □ **have no business** have no right to do something or be somewhere: *he had no business tampering with social services.* □ **like nobody's business** *inf.* to an extraordinarily high degree or standard: *these weeds spread like nobody's business.* □ **mean business** be in earnest. □ **mind one's own business** refrain from meddling in other people's affairs: *he was yelling at her to get out and mind her own business.*

busi·ness card ▶ *n.* a small card printed with one's name, professional occupation, company position, business address, and other contact information.

busi·ness·like /'biznis,līk/ ▶ *adj.* (of a person) carrying out tasks

efficiently without wasting time or being distracted by personal or other concerns; systematic and practical. ■ (of clothing, furniture, etc.) designed or appearing to be practical rather than decorative. ■ excessively brisk or practical; severe or impersonal.

busi·ness·man /'biznis,man; -mən/ ▶ *n.* (*pl.* **-men**) a man who works in business or commerce, esp. at an executive level.

busi·ness mod·el ▶ *n.* a design for the successful operation of a business, identifying revenue sources, customer base, products, and details of financing: *many of the free sites have either shifted their business model or have gone out of business completely.*

busi·ness per·son (also **busi·ness-per·son**) ▶ *n.* a man or woman who works in business or commerce, esp. at an executive level.

busk /bəsk/ ▶ *v.* [*intr.*] play music or otherwise perform for voluntary donations in the street or in subways: *the group began by busking on Philadelphia sidewalks.* —**busk·er** *n.*

bus·man /'bəsmən/ ▶ *n.* (*pl.* **-men**) a driver of a bus.
▶ □ **a busman's holiday** a vacation or form of recreation that involves doing the same thing that one does at work.

bust[1] /bəst/ ▶ *n.* **1** a woman's chest as measured around her breasts: *a 36-inch bust.* ■ a woman's breasts, esp. considered in terms of their size: *selecting clothes that would minimize her large bust.* **2** a sculpture of a person's head, shoulders, and chest.

bust[2] *inf.* ▶ *v.* (*past* and *past part.* **bust·ed** or **bust**) [*tr.*] **1** break, split, or burst (something): *they bust the tunnel wide open.* ■ [*intr.*] come apart or split open. ■ cause to collapse; defeat utterly: *he promised to bust the mafia.* ■ (**bust something up**) cause (something) to break up: *men hired to bust up union rallies.* ■ strike violently: *they wanted to bust me on the mouth.* ■ (**bust out**) break out; escape: *she busted out of prison.* ■ [*intr.*] (in blackjack and similar card games) exceed the score of 21, losing one's stake. **2** raid or search (premises where illegal activity is suspected): *their house got busted.* ■ arrest: *he was busted for drugs.* ■ reduce (a soldier) to a lower rank; demote: *he was busted to private.*
▶ *n.* **1** a period of economic difficulty or depression: *the boom was followed by the present bust.* **2** a police raid: *a drug bust.* **3** a worthless thing: *as a show it was a bust.*
▶ *adj.* bankrupt: *firms will go bust.*

bus·tard /'bəstərd/ ▶ *n.* a large, heavily built Old World bird (family Otididae), in particular the **great bustard** (*Otis tarda*), which is the heaviest flying land bird.

bust·er /'bəstər/ ▶ *n. chiefly inf.* **1** a person or thing that breaks, destroys, or overpowers something: [in *comb.*] *the drug's reputation as a flu-buster.* **2** *inf.* used as a mildly disrespectful or humorous form of address, esp. to a man or boy: *your parents' decisions affect you, like it or not, buster.*

bus·tier /bŏŏs'tyā/ ▶ *n.* a close-fitting strapless top worn by women.

bus·tle[1] /'bəsəl/ ▶ *v.* [*intr.*] move in an energetic or noisy manner: *people clutching clipboards bustled about.* ■ [*tr.*] make (someone) move hurriedly in a particular direction: *she bustled us into the kitchen.* ■ [*intr.*] (of a place) be full of activity: *the small harbor bustled with boats.*
▶ *n.* excited activity and movement: *all the noise and the traffic and the bustle.*

bus·tle[2] ▶ *n. hist.* a pad or frame worn under a skirt and puffing it out behind.

bust·y /'bəstē/ ▶ *adj.* (**bust·i·er, bust·i·est**) *inf.* (of a woman) having large breasts. —**bust·i·ness** *n.*

bus·y /'bizē/ ▶ *adj.* (**bus·i·er, bus·i·est**) having a great deal to do: *he had been too busy to enjoy himself.* ■ occupied with or concentrating on a particular activity or object of attention: *the team members are busy raising money.* ■ (of a place) full of activity. ■ excessively detailed or decorated; fussy: *they papered the bedroom with a busy pattern of satyrs and dryads.* ■ (of a telephone line) in use.
▶ *v.* (**bus·ies, bus·ied**) [*tr.*] (**busy oneself**) keep occupied: *she busied herself with her new home.* —**bus·i·ly** /-lē/ *adv.* —**bus·y·ness** *n.*

bus·y·bod·y /'bizē,bädē/ ▶ *n.* (*pl.* **-bod·ies**) a meddling or prying person.

bus·y sig·nal ▶ *n.* a sound indicating that a telephone line is in use, typically a repeated single bleep.

but /bət/ ▶ *conj.* **1** used to introduce something contrasting with what has already been mentioned: *nevertheless; however: he stumbled but didn't fall.* ■ on the contrary; in contrast: *I am clean but you are dirty.* **2** used to indicate the impossibility of anything other than what is being stated: *one cannot but sympathize | there was nothing they could do but swallow their pride.* **3** used to introduce a response expressing a feeling such as surprise or anger: *but that's an incredible saving! | but why?* **4** used after an expression of apology for what one is about to say: *I'm sorry, but I can't pay you.* **5** *archaic* without its being the case that: *it never rains but it pours.*
▶ *prep.* except; apart from; other than: *I trusted no one but him.* ■ used with

repetition of certain words to give emphasis: *nobody, but nobody, was going to stop her.*

▸*adv.* no more than; only: *he is but a shadow of his former self.*

▸*n.* an argument against something; an objection: *no buts—just get out of here.*

▸ □ **but for** except for: *I walked along Broadway, deserted but for the occasional cab.* ■ if it were not for: *the game could be over but for you.* □ **but then** on the other hand; that being so: *it's a very hard exam, but then they all are.*

bu·tane /ˈbyo͞oˌtān/ ▸*n. Chem.* a flammable hydrocarbon gas, C_4H_{10}, that is a constituent of petroleum and is used in bottled form as a fuel. It is a member of the alkane series.

butch /bo͝oCH/ *inf.* ▸*adj.* manlike or masculine in appearance or behavior, typically aggressively or ostentatiously so.

▸*n.* a mannish lesbian, often contrasted with a more feminine partner.

butch·er /ˈbo͝oCHər/ ▸*n.* **1** a person whose trade is cutting up and selling meat in a shop. ■ a person who slaughters and cuts up animals for food: *a pork butcher.* ■ a person who kills or has people killed indiscriminately or brutally: *the Nazi death camp butcher.* **2** *inf.* a person selling refreshments, newspapers, and other items on a train or in a stadium or theater.

▸*v.* [*tr.*] (often **be butchered**) slaughter or cut up (an animal) for food: *the meat will be butchered for the local market.* ■ kill (someone) brutally: *they butchered 250 people.* ■ *fig.* ruin (something) deliberately or through incompetence: *the film was butchered by the studio that released it.*

butch·er·y /ˈbo͝oCHərē/ ▸*n.* (*pl.* **-er·ies**) the savage killing of large numbers of people.

but·ler /ˈbətlər/ ▸*n.* the chief manservant of a house.

butt¹ /bət/ ▸*v.* [*tr.*] (of a person or animal) hit (someone or something) with the head or horns: *she butted him in the chest with her head.* ■ strike (the head) against something: *he butts his head against a wall.*

▸*phrasal v.* □ **butt in** take part in a conversation or activity, or enter somewhere, without being invited or expected: *sorry to butt in on you.* □ **butt out** *inf.* stop interfering: *anyone who tries to cut across our policies should butt out.*

▸*n.* a push or blow, typically given with the head: *he would follow up with a butt from his head.*

▸ □ **butt heads** engage in conflict or be in strong disagreement: *the residents continue to butt heads with the mall developers.*

butt² ▸*n.* the person or thing at which criticism or humor, typically unkind, is directed: *his singing is the butt of dozens of jokes.* ■ (usu. **butts**) an archery or shooting target or range.

butt³ ▸*n.* **1** (also **butt end**) the thicker end, esp. of a tool or a weapon: *a rifle butt.* ■ the square end of a plank or plate meeting the end or side of another, as in the side of a ship. **2** (also **butt end**) the stub of a cigar or a cigarette: *the ashtray was crammed with cigarette butts.* **3** *inf.* the buttocks.

▸*v.* [*intr.*] adjoin or meet end to end: *the church **butted up against** the row of houses.* ■ [*tr.*] join (pieces of stone, lumber, and other building materials) with the ends or sides flat against each other: *the floorboards will be butted up against each other to make tight seams.*

butt⁴ ▸*n.* a cask, typically used for wine, ale, or water.

butte /byo͞ot/ ▸*n. technical* an isolated hill with steep sides and a flat top (similar to but narrower than a mesa).

but·ter /ˈbətər/ ▸*n.* a pale yellow edible fatty substance made by churning cream and used as a spread or in cooking. ■ a substance of a similar consistency: *cocoa butter.*

▸*v.* [*tr.*] spread (something) with butter: *she buttered the toast.*

▸*phrasal v.* □ **butter someone up** *inf.* flatter or otherwise ingratiate oneself with someone.

but·ter·ball /ˈbətərˌbôl/ ▸*n. inf. derog.* a fat person. ■ a plump bird, esp. a turkey.

but·ter bean ▸*n.* a lima bean, esp. one of a variety with large flat white seeds that are usually dried.

but·ter·cream /ˈbətərˌkrēm/ ▸*n.* a soft mixture of butter and powdered sugar used as a filling or topping for a cake.

but·ter·cup /ˈbətərˌkəp/ ▸*n.* a poisonous herbaceous plant (genus *Ranunculus*) with bright yellow cup-shaped flowers, common in grassland and as a garden weed. The **buttercup family** (Ranunculaceae) also includes anemones, celandines, aconites, clematises, and hellebores.

but·ter·fat /ˈbətərˌfat/ ▸*n.* the natural fat contained in milk and dairy products.

but·ter·fin·gers /ˈbətərˌfiNGgərz/ ▸*n.* (*pl.* same) *inf.* a clumsy person, esp. one who fails to hold a catch. ■ clumsiness in handling something: *fumbling for the ball with butterfingers.* —**but·ter·fin·gered** *adj.*

but·ter·fly /ˈbətərˌflī/ ▸*n.* (*pl.* **-flies**) an insect (superfamilies Papilio-

noidea and Hesperioidea, order Lepidoptera) with two pairs of large wings that are covered with tiny scales, usually brightly colored, and typically held erect when at rest. Butterflies fly by day, have clubbed or dilated antennae, and usually feed on nectar. ■ a showy or frivolous person: *a social butterfly.* ■ (**butterflies**) *inf.* a fluttering and nauseated sensation felt in the stomach when one is nervous. ■ (in full **butterfly stroke**) a stroke in swimming in which both arms are raised out of the water and lifted forward together. ■ [as *adj.*] having a two-lobed shape resembling the spread wings of a butterfly: *a butterfly clip.*

▸*v.* (**-flies, -flied**) [*tr.*] split (a piece of meat) almost in two and spread it out flat.

but·ter·fly stroke ▸*n.* another term for BUTTERFLY (in swimming).

but·ter knife ▸*n.* a blunt knife used for cutting or spreading butter or other similar spreads.

but·ter·milk /ˈbətərˌmilk/ ▸*n.* the slightly sour liquid left after butter has been churned, used in baking or consumed as a drink. ■ a pale yellow color (used esp. to describe paint or wallpaper): [as *adj.*] *buttermilk paintwork.*

but·ter·nut /ˈbətərˌnət/ ▸*n.* a soft-timbered North American walnut tree (*Juglans cinerea*) that bears oblong sticky fruits. ■ the edible oily nut of this tree.

but·ter·scotch /ˈbətərˌskäCH/ ▸*n.* a flavor created originally by combining melted butter with brown sugar: [as *adj.*] *butterscotch syrup.* ■ a candy with this flavor.

but·ter·y¹ /ˈbətərē/ ▸*adj.* containing or tasting like butter: *layers of flaky buttery pastry.* ■ covered with butter: *buttery fingers.* —**but·ter·i·ness** *n.*

but·ter·y² ▸*n.* (*pl.* **-ter·ies**) a pantry, or a room for storing wine and liquor.

but·tock /ˈbətək/ ▸*n.* either of the two round fleshy parts that form the lower rear area of a human trunk. ■ (**buttocks**) the rump of an animal.

but·ton /ˈbətn/ ▸*n.* a small disk or knob sewn on to a garment, either to fasten it by being pushed through a slit made for the purpose, or for decoration: *a blouse with five buttons in front* | [as *adj.*] *button thread.* ■ a knob on a piece of electrical or electronic equipment that is pressed to operate it. ■ a badge bearing a design or slogan and pinned to the clothing. ■ a small, round object resembling a button: *chocolate buttons.* ■ *Fencing* a knob fitted to the point of a foil to make it harmless.

▸*v.* [*tr.*] fasten (clothing) with buttons: *he **buttoned up** his jacket.* ■ [*intr.*] (of a garment) be fastened with buttons: *a dress that buttons down the front.* ■ (**button it**) [often in *imper.*] *inf.* stop talking.

▸*phrasal v.* □ **button something up 1** *inf.* complete or conclude something satisfactorily: *trying to button up a deal.* **2** [often as *adj.*] (**buttoned up**) repress or contain something: *it was repressive enough to keep public opinion buttoned up.* —**but·ton·less** *adj.* —**but·toned** *adj.* [in *comb.*] *a gold-buttoned blazer.*

▸ □ **button one's lip** *inf.* stop or refrain from talking. □ **on the button** *inf.* punctually: *it was nearly visiting hours and she would arrive on the button.* ■ exactly right: *his prediction was right on the button in terms of actual rainfall.* □ **push** (or **press**) **someone's buttons** *inf.* arouse or provoke a reaction in someone: *stay cool and don't allow them to push your buttons.*

but·ton·hole /ˈbətnˌhōl/ ▸*n.* a slit made in a garment to receive a button for fastening.

▸*v.* [*tr.*] *inf.* attract the attention of and detain (someone) in conversation, typically against his or her will.

but·tress /ˈbətris/ ▸*n.* a projecting support of stone or brick built against a wall. ■ *fig.* a source of defense or support: *there was a demand for a new stable order as a buttress against social collapse.*

▸*v.* [*tr.*] provide (a building or structure) with projecting supports built against its walls: [as *adj.*] (**buttressed**) *a buttressed wall.* ■ *fig.* increase the strength of or justification for; reinforce: *authority was buttressed by religious belief.*

bux·om /ˈbəksəm/ ▸*adj.* (of a woman) plump, esp. with large breasts. —**bux·om·ness** *n.*

buy /bī/ ▸*v.* (**buys, buy·ing**; *past* and *past part.* **bought** /bôt/) [*tr.*] **1** obtain in exchange for payment: *he had been able to **buy up** hundreds of acres* | [*intr.*] *had no interest in **buying into** an entertainment company.* ■ (**buy someone out**) pay someone to give up an ownership, interest, or share. ■ procure the loyalty and support of (someone) by bribery: *here was a man who could not be bought.* ■ be a means of obtaining (something) through exchange or payment: *money can't buy happiness.* ■ (often **be bought**) get by sacrifice or great effort: *greatness is dearly bought.* ■ [*intr.*] make a profession of purchasing goods for a store or

B

firm. **2** *inf.* accept the truth of: *I am not prepared to buy the claim that the ends justify the means* | [*intr.*] *I hate to* **buy into** *stereotypes.* **3** (**bought it**) *inf.* died: *his friends had bought it in the jungle.*

▸ *n. inf.* a purchase: *the wine is a good buy at $3.49.* ■ an act of purchasing something: *out on a produce buy for the restaurant.*

▸ □ **buy time** delay an event temporarily so as to have longer to improve one's own position.

buy·er /ˈbīər/ ▸ *n.* a person who makes a purchase. ■ a person employed to select and purchase stock or materials for a large retail or manufacturing business, etc.

▸ □ **a buyer's market** an economic situation in which goods or shares are plentiful and buyers can keep prices down.

buy·out /ˈbīˌout/ ▸ *n.* the purchase of a controlling share in a company, esp. by its own managers.

buzz /bəz/ ▸ *n.* a low, continuous humming or murmuring sound, made by or similar to that made by an insect: *the buzz of the bees.* ■ the sound of a buzzer or telephone. ■ *inf.* a telephone call: *I'll give you a buzz.* ■ *inf.* a rumor: *the buzz is that he's in big trouble.* ■ an atmosphere of excitement and activity: *there is a real buzz about the place.* ■ *inf.* a feeling of excitement or euphoria: *I got such a buzz out of seeing the kids' faces.*

▸ *v.* [*intr.*] **1** make a humming sound: *mosquitoes were buzzing all around us.* ■ (often as *n.*) (**buzzing**) (of the ears) be filled with a humming sound: *I remember a buzzing in my ears.* ■ signal with a buzzer: *the electric bell began to buzz for closing time* | [*tr.*] *he buzzed the stewardesses every five minutes.* ■ [*tr.*] *inf.* make a telephone call to (someone). **2** move quickly or busily: *she buzzed along the highway back into town.* ■ [*tr.*] *inf.* *Aeron.* fly very close to (another aircraft, the ground, etc.) at a high speed. **3** (of a place) have an air of excitement or purposeful activity: *the club is buzzing with excitement.* ■ (of a person's mind or head) be filled with excited or confused thoughts: *her mind was buzzing with ideas.*

▸ *phrasal v.* □ **buzz off** [often in *imper.*] *inf.* go away.

buz·zard /ˈbəzərd/ ▸ *n.* a large hawklike bird of prey (family Accipitridae) with broad wings and a rounded tail, typically seen soaring in wide circles, in particular the common *Buteo buteo.* ■ a North American vulture, esp. a turkey vulture. ▷late Middle English: from Old French *busard*, based on Latin *buteo* 'falcon.'

buzz·er /ˈbəzər/ ▸ *n.* an electrical device, similar to a bell, that makes a buzzing noise and is used for signaling.

buzz·word /ˈbəzˌwərd/ (also **buzz phrase**) ▸ *n. inf.* a technical word or phrase that has become fashionable, typically as a slogan.

by /bī/ ▸ *prep.* **1** identifying the agent performing an action: ■ after a passive verb: *the door was opened by my cousin Annie.* ■ after a noun denoting an action: *further attacks by the mob* | *a clear decision by the electorate.* ■ identifying the author of a text, idea, or work of art: *a book by Ernest Hemingway.* **2** indicating the means of achieving something: *malaria can be controlled by attacking the parasite.* ■ indicating a term to which an interpretation is to be assigned: *what is meant by "fair?"* ■ indicating a name according to which a person is known: *she mostly calls me by my last name.* ■ indicating the means of transport selected for a journey: *traveling by train to Boston.* ■ indicating the other parent of someone's child or children: *Richard is his son by his third wife.* ■ indicating the sire of a pedigree animal, esp. a horse: *a black filly by Goldfuerst.* ■ (followed by a noun without an adjective) in various phrases indicating how something happens: *I heard by chance that she has married again.* **3** indicating the amount or size of a margin: *the shot missed her by miles.* ■ indicating a unit of measurement: *billing is by the minute.* ■ in phrases indicating something happening repeatedly or progressively, typically with repetition of a unit of time: *colors changing minute by minute.* ■ identifying a parameter: *a breakdown of employment figures by age and occupation.* ■ expressing multiplication, often in dimensions: *a map measuring 24 by 36 inches* | *she multiplied it by 89.* **4** indicating a deadline or the end of a particular time period: *I've got to do this report by Monday.* **5** indicating location of a physical object beside a place or object: *remains were discovered by the roadside.* ■ past; beyond: *I drove by our house.* **6** indicating the period in which something happens: *this animal always hunts by night.* **7** concerning; according to: *anything you do is*

all right by me | *she had done her duty by him.* **8** used in mild oaths: *it was the least he could do, by God.*

▸ *adv.* so as to go past: *a car flashed by on the other side of the road* | *he let only a moment go by.*

▸ *n.* (*pl.* **byes**) variant spelling of BYE[1].

▸ □ **by and by** before long; eventually. □ **by the by** (or **bye**) incidentally; parenthetically: *where's Hector, by the by?* □ **by and large** on the whole; everything considered: *mammals have, by and large, bigger brains than reptiles.* □ **by oneself 1** alone: *living in that big house by himself.* **2** unaided: *the patient often learns to undress by himself.*

bye[1] /bī/ ▸ *n.* **1** the transfer of a competitor directly to the next round of a competition in the absence of an assigned opponent. **2** *Golf* one or more holes remaining unplayed after the match has been decided.

bye[2] ▸ *interj. inf.* short for GOODBYE.

bye-bye ▸ *interj.* informal way of saying GOODBYE.

Bye·lo·rus·sian ▸ *adj. & n.* variant spelling of BELORUSSIAN.

by·gone /ˈbīˌgôn/ ▸ *adj.* belonging to an earlier time: *relics of a bygone society.*

▸ *n.* (usu. **bygones**) a thing dating from an earlier time.

▸ □ **let bygones be bygones** forget past offenses or causes of conflict and be reconciled.

by·law /ˈbīˌlô/ (also **by-law**) ▸ *n.* **1** a rule made by a company or society to control the actions of its members. **2** a regulation made by a local authority; an ordinance.

by·line /ˈbīˌlīn/ ▸ *n.* a line in a newspaper naming the writer of an article.

by·name /ˈbīˌnām/ (also **by-name**) ▸ *n.* a sobriquet or nickname, esp. one given to distinguish people with the same given name.

by·pass /ˈbīˌpas/ ▸ *n.* a road passing around a town or its center to provide an alternative route for through traffic. ■ a secondary channel, pipe, or connection to allow a flow when the main one is closed or blocked. ■ an alternative passage made by surgery, typically to aid the circulation of blood. ■ a surgical operation to make such a passage: *a heart bypass.*

▸ *v.* [*tr.*] go past or around: *bypass the farm and continue to the road.* ■ provide (a town) with a route diverting traffic from its center: *the town has been bypassed.* ■ avoid or circumvent (an obstacle or problem): *a manager might bypass formal channels of communication.*

by·prod·uct ▸ *n.* (also **by-prod·uct**) an incidental or secondary product made in the manufacture or synthesis of something else: *zinc is a byproduct of the glazing process.* ■ a secondary result, unintended but inevitably produced in doing or producing something else: *he saw poverty as the byproduct of colonial prosperity.*

by·road /ˈbīˌrōd/ ▸ *n.* (also **by-road**) a minor road.

by·stand·er /ˈbīˌstandər/ ▸ *n.* a person who is present at an event or incident but does not take part.

byte /bīt/ ▸ *n. Comput.* a group of binary digits or bits (usually eight) operated on as a unit. Compare with BIT[4]. ■ such a group as a unit of memory size.

by·way /ˈbīˌwā/ ▸ *n.* a road or track not following a main route; a minor road or path. ■ a little-known area or detail: *byways of Russian music.*

by·word /ˈbīˌwərd/ ▸ *n.* a person or thing cited as a notorious and outstanding example or embodiment of something: *his name became a byword for luxury.* ■ a word or expression summarizing a thing's characteristics or a person's principles: *"Small is beautiful" may be the byword for most couturiers.*

Byz·an·tine /ˈbizənˌtēn; bəˈzan-; -ˌtīn/ ▸ *adj.* of or relating to Byzantium, the Byzantine Empire, or the Eastern Orthodox Church. ■ of an ornate artistic and architectural style that developed in the Byzantine Empire and spread esp. to Italy and Russia. The art is generally rich and stylized (as in religious icons) and the architecture typified by many-domed, highly decorated churches. ■ (of a system or situation) excessively complicated, typically involving a great deal of administrative detail: *Byzantine insurance regulations.* ■ characterized by deviousness or underhanded procedure: *Byzantine intrigues.*

▸ *n.* a citizen of Byzantium or the Byzantine Empire. —**By·zan·tin·ism** *n.*

Cc

C¹ /sē/ (also **c**) ▶*n.* (*pl.* **Cs** or **C's**) **1** the third letter of the alphabet. ■ denoting the third in a set of items, categories, sizes, etc. ■ denoting the third of three or more hypothetical people or things. ■ the third highest class of academic grades. ■ (**c**) *Chess* denoting the third file from the left of a chessboard, as viewed from White's side of the board. ■ (usu. **c**) the third fixed constant to appear in an algebraic expression, or a known constant. ■ denoting the lowest soil horizon, comprising parent materials. **2** a shape like that of a letter C: [in *comb.*] *C-springs.* **3** (usu. **C**) *Mus.* the first note of the diatonic scale of C major, the major scale having no sharps or flats. ■ a key based on a scale with C as its keynote. **4** the Roman numeral for 100. **5** (**C**) a high-level computer programming language originally developed for implementing the UNIX operating system.

C² ▶*abbr.* ■ (**C.**) Cape (chiefly on maps). ■ Celsius or centigrade. ■ (©) copyright. ■ a 1.5 volt dry cell battery size.
▶*symb.* ■ *Physics* capacitance. ■ the chemical element carbon.

c ▶*abbr.* ■ cent(s). ■ [in *comb.*] (in units of measurement) centi-: *centistokes (cS).* ■ (**c.**) century or centuries: *a watch case, 19th c.* ■ (preceding a date or amount) circa; approximately: *Isabella was born c 1759.* ■ (of water) cold: *all cabins have h & c.* ■ colt.
▶*symb. Physics* the speed of light in a vacuum: $E = mc^2$.

CA ▶*abbr.* chief accountant.

Ca ▶*symb.* the chemical element calcium.

ca (also **ca.**) ▶*abbr.* (preceding a date or amount) circa.

CAB ▶*abbr.* Civil Aeronautics Board.

cab /kab/ ▶*n.* **1** short for TAXICAB. ■ *hist.* a horse-drawn vehicle for public hire. **2** the driver's compartment in a truck, bus, or train.
▶*v.* (**cabbed**, **cab·bing**) [*intr.*] travel in a taxi: *Roger cabbed home.*

ca·bal /kə'bäl; -'bal/ ▶*n.* a secret political clique or faction. —**cab·a·lis·tic** /ˌkabə'listik/ *adj.*

ca·ban·a /kə'ban(y)ə/ ▶*n.* a cabin, hut, or shelter, esp. one at a beach or swimming pool.

cab·a·ret /ˌkabə'rā; 'kabəˌrā/ ▶*n.* entertainment held in a nightclub or restaurant while the audience eats or drinks at tables. ■ a nightclub or restaurant where such entertainment is performed. ▷mid-17th cent. (denoting a French inn): from Old French, literally 'wooden structure,' via Middle Dutch from Old Picard *camberet* 'little room.' Current senses date from the early 20th cent.

cab·bage /'kabij/ ▶*n.* a cultivated plant (*Brassica oleracea*) eaten as a vegetable, having thick green or purple leaves surrounding a spherical heart or head of young leaves. The **cabbage family** (Cruciferae, or Brassicaceae) includes the mustards and cresses together with many ornamentals. ■ the leaves of this plant, eaten as a vegetable. ■ *inf.* paper money.

cab·bage white ▶*n.* a mainly white butterfly (genus *Pieris*, family Pieridae) that has caterpillars that are pests of cabbages and related plants.

Cab·ba·la /kə'bälə; 'kabələ/ (also **Cab·a·la**) ▶*n.* variant spelling of KABBALAH.

cab·bie /'kabē/ (also **cab·by**) ▶*n.* (*pl.* **-bies**) *inf.* a taxicab driver.

cab·in /'kabən/ ▶*n.* **1** a private room or compartment on a ship. ■ the area for passengers in an aircraft. **2** a small shelter or house, made of wood and situated in a wild or remote area.

cab·i·net /'kabənit/ ▶*n.* **1** a cupboard with drawers or shelves for storing or displaying articles: *a medicine cabinet.* ■ a wooden container or piece of furniture housing a radio, television set, or speaker. **2** (in the U.S.) a body of advisers to the President, composed of the heads of the executive departments of the government: [as *adj.*] *a cabinet meeting.*

■ (also **Cabinet**) (in the UK, Canada, and other Commonwealth countries) the committee of senior ministers responsible for controlling government policy. **3** *archaic* a small private room.

cab·in fe·ver ▶*n. inf.* irritability, listlessness, and similar symptoms resulting from long confinement or isolation indoors during the winter.

ca·ble /'kābəl/ ▶*n.* **1** a thick rope of wire or nonmetallic fiber, typically used for construction, mooring ships, and towing vehicles. ■ the chain of a ship's anchor. ■ *Naut.* a length of 200 yards (182.9 m) or (in the U.S.) 240 yards (219.4 m). ■ (also **cable molding**) *Archit.* a molding resembling twisted rope. **2** an insulated wire or wires having a protective casing and used for transmitting electricity or telecommunication signals. ■ a cablegram. ■ access to television and the Internet over a system of cables: *local commissions are supposed to determine what kind of cable service best suits each community.* ■ short for CABLE TELEVISION.
▶*v.* [*tr.*] **1** contact or send a message to (someone) by cablegram. ■ transmit (a message) by cablegram. ■ [*intr.*] send a cablegram. **2** (often **be cabled**) provide (an area or community) with power lines or with the equipment necessary for cable television. ▷Middle English: from an Anglo-Norman French variant of Old French *chable*, from late Latin *capulum* 'halter.'

ca·ble car ▶*n.* **1** a transportation system, typically one traveling up and down a mountain, in which cabins are suspended on a continuous moving cable driven by a motor at one end of the route. ■ a cabin on such a system. **2** a car on a cable railroad.

ca·ble·gram /'kābəlˌgram/ ▶*n. hist.* a telegraph message sent by cable.

ca·ble mo·dem ▶*n.* a type of modem that connects a computer or local network to high-speed Internet service through the same cable that supplies cable television service. ■ the service connection made via a cable modem: *a broadband Internet connection, such as DSL or cable modem.*

ca·ble-read·y ▶*adj.* adapted for cable television.

ca·ble tel·e·vi·sion ▶*n.* a system in which television programs are transmitted to the sets of subscribers by cable rather than by a broadcast signal.

ca·ble·way /'kābəlˌwā/ ▶*n.* a transportation system in which goods are carried suspended from a continuous moving cable.

cab·man /'kabmən/ ▶*n.* (*pl.* **-men**) a taxicab driver. ■ *hist.* the driver of a horse-drawn hackney carriage.

cab·o·chon /'kabəˌSHän/ ▶*n.* a gem polished but not faceted: [as *adj.*] *a necklace of cabochon rubies.*
▶ □ **en cabochon** /äN/ (of a gem) treated in this way.

ca·boo·dle /kə'bōōdl/ (also **ka·boo·dle**) ▶*n.* (in phrase **the whole caboodle** or **the whole kit and caboodle**) *inf.* the whole number or quantity of people or things in question.

ca·boose /kə'bōōs/ ▶*n. dated* a railroad car with accommodations for the train crew, typically attached to the end of the train. ■ *inf.* (typically referring to a woman) buttocks: *she got a sexy caboose.*

cab·ri·ole /'kabrē,ōl/ ▶*n. Ballet* a jump in which one leg is extended into the air forward or backward, the other is brought up to meet it, and the dancer lands on the second foot.

cab·ri·o·let /ˌkabrēə'lā/ ▶*n.* **1** a car with a roof that folds down. **2** a light, two-wheeled carriage with a hood, drawn by one horse.

ca·ca·o /kə'kou; kə'kāō/ ▶*n.* (*pl.* **-os**) **1** (also **cacao bean**) a beanlike seed from which cocoa, cocoa butter, and chocolate are made. **2** the small tropical American evergreen tree (*Theobroma cacao*, family Sterculiaceae) that bears these seeds in large, oval pods.

cache /kaSH/ ▶*n.* a collection of items of the same type stored in a hidden or inaccessible place: *an arms cache | a cache of gold coins.* ■ a hidden or inaccessible storage place for valuables, provisions, or ammunition. ■ (also **cache memory**) *Comput.* an auxiliary memory from which high-speed retrieval is possible.

▶ *v.* [*tr.*] store away in hiding or for future use. ■ *Comput.* store (data) in a cache memory. ■ *Comput.* provide (hardware) with a cache memory.

ca·chet /ka'SHā/ ▶ *n.* **1** the state of being respected or admired; prestige: *no other shipping company had quite the cachet of Cunard.* **2** a distinguishing mark or seal. ■ *Philately* a printed design added to an envelope to commemorate a special event.

ca·cique /ka'sēk/ ▶ *n.* **1** (in Latin America or the Spanish-speaking Caribbean) a native chief. **2** (in Spain or Latin America) a local political boss.

cack·le /'kakəl/ ▶ *v.* [*intr.*] (of a bird, typically a hen or goose) give a raucous, clucking cry: *the hen was cackling as if demented.* ■ make a harsh sound resembling such a cry when laughing: *she cackled with laughter* | [*tr.*] *"Ah ha!" he cackled.*

▶ *n.* the raucous clucking cry of a bird such as a hen or a goose. ■ a harsh laugh resembling such a cry: *her delighted cackle.*

ca·cog·ra·phy /kə'kägrəfē/ ▶ *n.* archaic bad handwriting or spelling. —**ca·cog·ra·pher** /-fər/ *n.*

ca·col·o·gy /kə'käləjē/ ▶ *n.* archaic bad choice of words or poor pronunciation.

ca·coph·o·ny /kə'käfənē/ ▶ *n.* (*pl.* **-nies**) a harsh, discordant mixture of sounds: *a cacophony of alarm bells* | *fig. a cacophony of architectural styles.* —**ca·coph·o·nous** /-nəs/ *adj.*

cac·tus /'kaktəs/ ▶ *n.* (*pl.* **cacti** /'kak,tī/ *or* **cactuses**) a succulent New World plant (family Cactaceae), chiefly of arid regions, with a thick, fleshy stem that typically bears spines and has brilliantly colored flowers.

CAD /kad/ ▶ *abbr.* computer-aided design.

cad /kad/ ▶ *n.* dated *or* humorous a man who behaves dishonorably, esp. toward a woman. —**cad·dish** *adj.* —**cad·dish·ly** *adv.* —**cad·dish·ness** *n.*

ca·dav·er /kə'davər/ ▶ *n. Med.* or poetic/lit. a corpse. —**ca·dav·er·ic** /-rik/ *adj.*

ca·dav·er·ous /kə'davərəs/ ▶ *adj.* resembling a corpse in being very pale, thin, or bony: *he had a cadaverous appearance.*

cad·die /'kadē/ (also **cad·dy**) ▶ *n.* (*pl.* **-dies**) a person who carries a golfer's clubs and provides other assistance during a match.

▶ *v.* (**cad·died**, **cad·dy·ing**) [*intr.*] work as a caddie. ▷mid 17th cent. (originally Scots): from French *cadet* 'cadet.' The original term denoted a gentleman who joined the army without a commission, intending to learn the profession and follow a military career, later coming to mean 'odd-job man.' The current sense dates from the late 18th cent.

cad·dis·fly /'kadəs,flī/ (also **caddis fly**) ▶ *n.* (*pl.* **-flies** /-flīz/) a small, moth-like insect with an aquatic larva (**caddisworm**) that typically builds a protective, portable case of sticks, stones, and other particles.

cad·dis·worm /'kadis ,wərm/ (also **cad·dis worm**) ▶ *n.* the soft-bodied, aquatic larva of a caddisfly, often used as fishing bait.

Cad·do·an /'kadō-ən/ ▶ *adj.* relating to or denoting a group of American Indian peoples formerly inhabiting the Midwest, or their languages.

▶ *n.* **1** a member of any of these peoples. **2** the family of languages spoken by these peoples, which includes Pawnee and may be related to Siouan and Iroquoian. ▷from Caddo (a language of this family) *kaduhdacu*, denoting a band belonging to this group.

cad·dy[1] /'kadē/ ▶ *n.* (*pl.* **-dies**) a small storage container, typically one with divisions: *a tool caddy.* See also **TEA CADDY**.

cad·dy[2] ▶ *n.* & *v.* variant spelling of **CADDIE**.

ca·dence /'kādns/ ▶ *n.* **1** a modulation or inflection of the voice: *the measured cadences that he employed in the Senate.* ■ such a modulation in reading aloud as implied by the structure and ordering of words and phrases in written text: *the dry cadences of the essay.* ■ a fall in pitch of the voice at the end of a phrase or sentence. ■ rhythm. **2** *Mus.* a sequence of notes or chords comprising the close of a musical phrase: *the final cadence of the prelude.* —**ca·denced** *adj.*

ca·den·za /kə'denzə/ ▶ *n. Mus.* a virtuoso solo passage inserted into a movement in a concerto or other work, typically near the end.

ca·det /kə'det/ ▶ *n.* **1** a young trainee in the armed services or police force: *an air force cadet.* ■ a student in training at a military school. **2** formal *or* archaic a younger son or daughter. ■ [usu. as *adj.*] a junior branch of a family: *a cadet branch of the family.* ▷early 17th cent. (sense 2): from French, from Gascon dialect *capdet*, a diminutive based on Latin *caput* 'head.' The notion "little head" or "inferior head" gave rise to that of 'younger, junior.' —**ca·det·ship** /-,SHip/ *n.*

cadge /kaj/ ▶ *v.* [*tr.*] inf. ask for or obtain (something to which one is not

strictly entitled): *he eats whenever he can cadge a meal.* | [*intr.*] *they cadge, but timidly.* —**cadg·er** *n.*

cad·mi·um /'kadmēəm/ ▶ *n.* the chemical element of atomic number 48, a silvery-white metal. (Symbol: **Cd**)

ca·dre /'kadrē; 'kad-; -,rä/ ▶ *n.* a small group of people specially trained for a particular purpose or profession: *a small cadre of scientists.* ■ a group of activists in a communist or other revolutionary organization. ■ a member of such a group.

ca·du·ce·us /kə'd(y)ōōsēəs; -SHəs/ ▶ *n.* (*pl.* **-ce·i** /-sē,ī; -SHē,ī/) an ancient Greek or Roman herald's wand, typically one with two serpents twined around it, carried by the messenger god Hermes or Mercury. ■ a representation of this, traditionally associated with healing.

Cae·sar ▶ *n.* a title used by Roman emperors, esp. those from Augustus to Hadrian. ■ an autocrat.

cae·sar·e·an /si'ze(ə)rēən/ ▶ *adj.* & *n.* **1** (also **Cae·sar·e·an**) variant spelling of **CESAREAN**. **2** (**Caesarean**) of or connected with Julius Caesar or the Caesars.

caduceus

cae·su·ra /si'ZHŏŏrə; -'zŏŏrə/ ▶ *n.* (in Greek and Latin verse) a break between words within a metrical foot. ■ (in modern verse) a pause near the middle of a line. ■ any interruption or break. —**cae·su·ral** *adj.*

CAF ▶ *abbr.* cost and freight.

ca·fé /,ka'fā; kə-/ (also **ca·fe**) ▶ *n.* **1** a small restaurant selling light meals and drinks. **2** a bar or nightclub. **3** a serving of coffee, esp. prepared European-style; [in comb.] *an assortment of cappuccinos and café mochas.*

ca·fé au lait /,ka,fā ō 'lā/ ▶ *n.* coffee with milk. ■ the light brown color of this: [as *adj.*] *smooth café au lait skin.*

caf·e·te·ri·a /,kafi'ti(ə)rēə/ ▶ *n.* a restaurant or dining room in a school or a business in which customers serve themselves or are served from a counter and pay before eating.

caf·feine /ka'fēn; 'kaf,ēn/ ▶ *n.* an alkaloid crystalline compound found esp. in tea and coffee plants. It is a stimulant of the central nervous system.

caf·tan ▶ *n.* variant spelling of **KAFTAN**.

cage /kāj/ ▶ *n.* a structure of bars or wires in which birds or other animals are confined: *she kept a canary in a cage.* ■ a prison cell or camp. ■ an open framework forming the compartment in an elevator. ■ a structure of crossing bars or wires designed to hold or support something. ■ *Baseball* a portable backstop behind the batter during batting practice. ■ (in hockey and other games) a goal made from a network frame. ■ an indoor athletic facility with areas fenced off for security.

▶ *v.* [*tr.*] (usu. **be caged**) confine in or as in a cage: *the parrot screamed, furious at being caged* | [as *adj.*] (**caged**) *a caged bird.* ■ inf. put in prison.

cag·ey /'kājē/ (also **cag·y**) ▶ *adj.* inf. reluctant to give information owing to caution or suspicion: *manufacturers are cagey about the recipes they use.* —**cag·i·ly** /'kājilē/ *adv.* —**cag·i·ness** (also **cag·ey·ness**) *n.*

ca·hoots /kə'hōōts/ ▶ *pl. n.* (in phrase **in cahoots**) inf. colluding or conspiring together secretly: *the area is dominated by guerrillas* **in cahoots** *with drug traffickers.*

CAI ▶ *abbr.* computer-assisted (or -aided) instruction.

cai·man /'kāmən/ (also **cay·man**) ▶ *n.* a semiaquatic reptile (*Caiman* and other genera, family Alligatoridae), similar to the alligator but with a heavily armored belly, native to tropical America.

Cain /kān/ ▶ *n.* (in the Bible) the eldest son of Adam and Eve and murderer of his brother Abel.

▶ □ **raise Cain** inf. create trouble or a commotion.

cairn /ke(ə)rn/ ▶ *n.* **1** a mound of rough stones built as a memorial or landmark, typically on a hilltop or skyline. ■ a prehistoric burial mound made of stones. **2** (also **cairn terrier**) a small terrier of a breed with short legs, a longish body, and a shaggy coat.

cais·son /'kā,sän; 'kāsən/ ▶ *n.* **1** a large watertight chamber, open at the bottom from which the water is kept out by air pressure and in which construction work may be carried out under water. **2** *hist.* a chest or wagon for holding ammunition.

ca·jole /kə'jōl/ ▶ *v.* [*tr.*] (often **cajole someone into doing something**) persuade someone to do something by sustained coaxing or flattery: *he hoped to cajole her into selling the house* | [*intr.*] *she pleaded and cajoled as she tried to win his support.* —**ca·jole·ment** *n.* —**ca·jol·er·y** *n.*

cake /kāk/ ▶ *n.* an item of soft, sweet food made from a mixture of flour, shortening, eggs, sugar, and other ingredients, baked and often decorated. ■ an item of savory food formed into a flat, round shape, and typically baked or fried: *crab cakes.* ■ a flattish, compact mass of something, esp. soap: *a cake of soap.*

▶ *v.* [*tr.*] (usu. **be caked**) (of a thick or sticky substance that hardens when dry) cover and become encrusted on (the surface of an object): *a pair of boots caked with mud.* ■ [*intr.*] (of a thick or sticky substance) dry or harden into a solid mass: *the blood under his nose was beginning to cake.*

▶ □ **a piece of cake** *inf.* something easily achieved. □ **take the cake** surpass or exceed all others: *of all the hard-hearted women, she takes the cake.*

CAL ▶ *abbr.* computer-assisted (or -aided) learning.

Cal ▶ *abbr.* large calorie(s).

cal (also **cal.**) ▶ *abbr.* ■ calendar. ■ caliber. ■ calorie. ■ small calorie(s).

cal·a·bash /ˈkaləˌbaSH/ ▶ *n.* (also **calabash tree**) an evergreen tropical American tree (*Crescentia cujete*, family Bignoniaceae) that bears fruit in the form of large woody gourds. ■ a gourd from this tree. ■ a water container, tobacco pipe, or other object made from the dried shell of this or a similar gourd.

cal·a·boose /ˈkaləˌbo͞os/ ▶ *n. inf.* a prison.

ca·la·ma·ri /ˌkäləˈmärē; ˌkalə-/ ▶ *n.* squid served as food. ▷Italian, plural of *calamaro*, from medieval Latin *calamarium* 'pen case,' from Greek *kalamos* 'pen' (with reference to the squid's long tapering internal shell and its ink). The variant *calamares* is Spanish, *calamaries* being its anglicized form.

cal·a·mine /ˈkaləˌmīn/ ▶ *n.* a pink powder consisting of zinc carbonate and ferric oxide, used to make a soothing lotion or ointment.

ca·lam·i·ty /kəˈlamitē/ ▶ *n.* (*pl.* **-ties**) an event causing great and often sudden damage or distress; a disaster. ■ disaster and distress: *the journey had led to calamity.* —**ca·lam·i·tous** /-itəs/ *adj.* —**ca·lam·i·tous·ly** *adv.*

cal·ca·ne·us /kalˈkānēəs/ (also **cal·ca·ne·um** /-nēəm/) ▶ *n.* (*pl.* **-ne·i** /-nē,ī; -nē,ē/ or **-ne·a** /-nēə/) *Anat.* the large bone forming the heel.

cal·car·e·ous /kalˈke(ə)rēəs/ ▶ *adj.* containing calcium carbonate; chalky. ■ *Ecol.* (of vegetation) occurring on chalk or limestone.

cal·ce·o·lar·i·a /ˌkalsēəˈlerēə/ ▶ *n.* a South American plant (genus *Calceolaria*) of the figwort family that is cultivated for its bright slipper-shaped flowers.

cal·cif·er·ol /kalˈsifəˌrôl; -ˌrōl/ ▶ *n. Biochem.* one of the D vitamins, a sterol that is formed when its isomer ergosterol is exposed to ultraviolet light, and that is routinely added to dairy products. Also called **vi-tamin D₂** (see **vitamin D**).

cal·ci·fy /ˈkalsəˌfī/ ▶ *v.* (**-fies**, **-fied**) [*tr.*] [usu. as *adj.*] (**calcified**) harden by deposition of or conversion into calcium carbonate or some other insoluble calcium compounds: *calcified cartilage.* —**cal·cif·er·ous** /kalˈsifərəs/ *adj.* —**cal·cif·ic** /kalˈsifik/ *adj.* —**cal·ci·fi·ca·tion** /ˌkalsəfiˈkāSHən/ *n.*

cal·cine /ˈkalˌsīn/ ▶ *v.* [*tr.*] [usu. as *adj.*] (**calcined**) reduce, oxidize, or desiccate by roasting or strong heat: *calcined bone ash.* —**cal·ci·na·tion** /ˌkalsəˈnāSHən/ *n.*

cal·cite /ˈkalˌsīt/ ▶ *n.* a white or colorless mineral consisting of calcium carbonate. It is a major constituent of sedimentary rocks, can occur in crystalline form, and may be deposited in caves to form stalactites and stalagmites. —**cal·cit·ic** /kalˈsitik/ *adj.*

cal·ci·um /ˈkalsēəm/ ▶ *n.* the chemical element of atomic number 20, a soft gray metal. (Symbol: **Ca**)

cal·ci·um car·bon·ate ▶ *n.* a white, insoluble solid occurring naturally as chalk, limestone, and marble, and forming mollusk shells and stony corals.

cal·cu·late /ˈkalkyəˌlāt/ ▶ *v.* [*tr.*] **1** determine (the amount or number of something) mathematically: *Japanese land value was calculated at 2.5 times that of the U.S.* ■ determine by reasoning, experience, or common sense; reckon or judge: *I was bright enough to calculate that she had been on vacation.* ■ [*intr.*] (**calculate on**) include as an essential element in one's plans: *he may have calculated on maximizing pressure for policy revision.* **2** ■ (usu. **be calculated to do something**) intend (an action) to have a particular effect: *his last words were calculated to wound her.* ■ suppose; believe. —**cal·cu·la·tion** /ˌkalkyəˈlāSHən/ *n.* —**cal·cu·la·tive** /-ˌlātiv/ *adj.*

cal·cu·lat·ed /ˈkalkyəˌlātid/ ▶ *adj.* (of an action) done with full awareness of the likely consequences: *a calculated decision.* ■ carefully planned or intended: *vicious and calculated assaults.* ■ (of an amount or number) mathematically worked out or measured. —**cal·cu·lat·ed·ly** *adv.*

cal·cu·lat·ing /ˈkalkyəˌlātiNG/ ▶ *adj.* acting in a scheming and ruthlessly determined way. —**cal·cu·lat·ing·ly** *adv.*

cal·cu·la·tor /ˈkalkyəˌlātər/ ▶ *n.* something used for making mathematical calculations, in particular a small electronic device with a keyboard and a visual display.

cal·cu·lus /ˈkalkyələs/ ▶ *n.* **1** (*pl.* **-lus·es**) (also **infinitesimal calculus**) the branch of mathematics that deals with the finding and properties of derivatives and integrals of functions, by methods originally based on the summation of infinitesimal differences. The two main types are **differential calculus** and **integral calculus**. **2** (*pl.* **-lus·es**) *Math. & Logic* a particular method or system of calculation or reasoning. **3** (*pl.* **-li** /-ˌlī; -ˌlē/) *Med.* a concretion of minerals formed within the body, esp. in the kidney or gallbladder. ■ another term for **tartar**.

cal·de·ra /kalˈderə; kôl-; -ˈdi(ə)rə/ ▶ *n.* a large volcanic crater, typically one formed by a major eruption leading to the collapse of the mouth of the volcano.

cal·dron ▶ *n.* variant spelling of **cauldron**.

Cal·e·do·ni·an /ˌkaləˈdōnēən/ ▶ *adj.* (chiefly in names or geographical terms) of or relating to Scotland or the Scottish Highlands: *the Caledonian Railway.*

▶ *n. humorous* or *poetic/lit.* a person from Scotland.

cal·en·dar /ˈkaləndər/ (abbr.: **cal** or **cal.**) ▶ *n.* a chart or series of pages showing the days, weeks, and months of a particular year, or giving particular seasonal information. ■ a datebook. ■ a system by which the beginning, length, and subdivisions of the year are fixed. ■ a timetable of special days or events of a specified kind or involving a specified group: *the college calendar.* ■ a list of people or events connected with particular dates, esp. canonized saints and cases for trial.

▶ *v.* [*tr.*] enter (something) in a calendar or timetable. —**ca·len·dric** /kəˈlendrik/ *adj.* —**ca·len·dri·cal** /kəˈlendrikəl/ *adj.*

cal·en·dar month ▶ *n.* see **month**.

cal·en·der /ˈkaləndər/ ▶ *n.* a machine in which cloth or paper is pressed by rollers to glaze or smooth it.

▶ *v.* [*tr.*] press in such a machine.

cal·ends /ˈkalindz; ˈkā-/ (also **kal·ends**) ▶ *pl. n.* the first day of the month in the ancient Roman calendar.

ca·len·du·la /kəˈlenjələ/ ▶ *n.* a Mediterranean plant (genus *Calendula*) of the daisy family that includes the common (or pot) marigold.

calf¹ /kaf/ ▶ *n.* (*pl.* **calves** /kavz/) **1** a young bovine animal, esp. a domestic cow or bull in its first year. ■ the young of some other large mammals, such as elephants, rhinoceroses, large deer and antelopes, and whales. ■ short for **calfskin**. **2** a floating piece of ice detached from an iceberg. —**calf·like** /-ˌlīk/ *adj.*

calf² ▶ *n.* (*pl.* **calves** /kavz/) the fleshy part at the back of a person's leg below the knee.

calf·skin /ˈkafˌskin/ ▶ *n.* leather made from the hide or skin of a calf, used chiefly in bookbinding and shoemaking.

cal·i·ber /ˈkaləbər/ (*Brit.* **cal·i·bre**) (abbr.: **cal** or **cal.**) ▶ *n.* **1** the quality of someone's character or the level of someone's ability: *they could ill afford to lose a man of his caliber.* ■ the standard reached by something: *educational facilities of a high caliber.* **2** the internal diameter or bore of a gun barrel: [in *comb.*] *a .22 caliber rifle.* ■ the diameter of a bullet, shell, or rocket. ■ the diameter of a body of circular section, such as a tube, blood vessel, or fiber. —**cal·i·bered** *adj.* [also in *comb.*].

cal·i·brate /ˈkaləˌbrāt/ ▶ *v.* [*tr.*] (often **be calibrated**) mark (a gauge or instrument) with a standard scale of readings. ■ correlate the readings of (an instrument) with those of a standard in order to check the instrument's accuracy. ■ adjust (experimental results) to take external factors into account or to allow comparison with other data. —**cal·i·bra·tion** /ˌkaləˈbrāSHən/ *n.* —**cal·i·bra·tor** /-ˌbrātər/ *n.*

cal·i·co /ˈkaliˌkō/ ▶ *n.* (*pl.* **-coes** or **-cos**) printed cotton fabric: [as *adj.*] *a calico dress.*

▶ *adj.* (of an animal, typically a cat) multicolored or mottled.

cal·i·for·ni·um /ˌkaləˈfôrnēəm/ ▶ *n.* the chemical element of atomic number 98, a radioactive metal of the actinide series. (Symbol: **Cf**)

cal·i·per /ˈkaləpər/ (also **cal·li·per**) ▶ *n.* (**calipers**) an instrument for measuring external or internal dimensions resembling a pair of compasses, having two hinged legs and in-turned or out-turned points. ■ (also **caliper rule**) an instrument performing a similar function but having one linear component sliding along another, with two parallel jaws and a vernier scale. ■ (also **brake caliper**) a motor-vehicle or bicycle brake consisting of two or more hinged components.

ca·liph /ˈkālif; ˈkal-/ ▶ *n. hist.* the chief Muslim civil and religious ruler, regarded as the successor of Muhammad. —**cal·iph·ate** /ˈkāləˌfāt; ˈkal-; -fit/ *n.*

cal·is·then·ics /ˌkalisˈTHeniks/ (*Brit.* **cal·lis·then·ics**) ▶ *pl. n.* gymnastic exercises to achieve bodily fitness and grace of movement. —**cal·is·then·ic** *adj.*

Pronunciation Key ə *ago, up;* ər *over, fur;* a *hat;* ā *ate;* ä *car;* CH *chin;* e *let;* ē *see;* e(ə)r *air;* i *fit;* ī *by;* i(ə)r *ear;* NG *sing;* ō *go;* ô *law, for;* oi *toy;* o͞o *good;* o͞o *goo;* ou *out;* SH *she;* TH *thin;* TH *then;* (h)w *why;* ZH *vision*

calk ▸*n. & v.* variant spelling of **CAULK**.

call /kôl/ ▸*v.* **1** [*tr.*] cry out to (someone) in order to summon them or attract their attention: *she heard Terry calling her* | [*intr.*] *I distinctly heard you call.* ■ cry out (a word or words): *he heard an insistent voice calling his name* | *Meredith was already calling out a greeting.* ■ shout out or chant (the steps and figures) to people performing a square dance or country dance. ■ [*intr.*] (of an animal, esp. a bird) make its characteristic cry. ■ telephone (a person or telephone number): *could I call you back?* ■ summon (something, esp. an emergency service or a taxicab) by telephone: *call the police.* ■ bring (a witness) into court to give evidence. ■ [*tr.*] archaic inspire or urge (someone) to do something. ■ fix a date or time for (a meeting, strike, or election). ■ [*intr.*] guess the outcome of tossing a coin: *"You call," he said. "Heads or tails?"* ■ predict the result of (a future event, esp. an election or a vote): *in the Northeast, the race remains too close to call.* ■ *Comput.* cause the execution of (a subroutine). **2** [*intr.*] (of a person) pay a brief visit. ■ (**call for**) stop to pick up (someone) at the place where they are living or working. **3** [*tr.*] give (an infant or animal) a specified name: *they called their daughter Hannah.* ■ address or refer to (someone) by a specified name, title, endearment, or term of abuse: *please call me Lucy.* ■ refer to, consider, or describe (someone or something) as being: *he's the only person I would call a friend.* ■ (of an umpire or other official in a game) pronounce (a ball, stroke, or other action) to be the thing specified: *the linesman called the ball wide.*

▸*phrasal v.* □ **call for** make necessary: *desperate times call for desperate measures.* ■ draw attention to the need for: *the report calls for an audit of endangered species.* □ **call someone in** enlist someone's aid or services. □ **call something in** require payment of a loan or promise of money. □ **call something off** cancel an event or agreement. □ **call on 1** pay a visit to (someone): *he's planning to call on Katherine today.* **2** (also **call upon**) have recourse to: *we are able to call on academic staff with a wide variety of expertise.* ■ demand that (someone) do something: *he called on the government to hold a plebiscite.* □ **call someone up 1** inf. telephone someone. **2** summon someone to serve in the army. ■ select someone to play in a team: *he was called up from Columbus to finish the season with the Yankees.* □ **call something up** summon for use something that is stored or kept available: *icons that allow you to call up a graphic.* ■ fig. evoke something.

▸*n.* **1** a cry made as a summons or to attract someone's attention: *in response to the call, a figure appeared.* ■ the characteristic cry of a bird or other animal. ■ a series of notes sounded on a brass instrument as a signal to do something: *a bugle call to rise at 5:30.* ■ a telephone communication or conversation: *I'll give you a call at around five.* ■ (**a call for**) an appeal or demand for: *the call for action was welcomed.* ■ a summons: *his call to the throne.* ■ a vocation: *his call to be a disciple.* ■ a powerful force of attraction: *hikers can't resist the call of the Sierras.* ■ (**a call for**) a demand or need for (goods or services): *there was little call for Turkish food in Milltown.* ■ *Comput.* a command to execute a subroutine. ■ a shout by an official in a game indicating whether the ball has gone out of play, if a rule has been breached, etc.; the decision or ruling so made: *the umpire made a bad call.* ■ *Bridge* a bid, response, or double. ■ a direction in a square dance given by the caller. ■ a demand for payment of lent or unpaid capital. ■ *Stock Market* short for **CALL OPTION**. ■ a player's right or turn to make a bid in a card game. **2** a brief visit: *we paid a call on Howard.* ■ a visit or journey made in response to an emergency appeal for help: *the doctor was out on a call.*

▸ □ **call something into** (or **in**) **question** cast doubt on something: *these findings call into question the legitimacy of the proceedings.* □ **call the shots** take the initiative in deciding how something should be done. □ **call someone/something to mind** cause one to think of someone or something, esp. through similarity. ■ remember someone or something: *I cannot call to mind where I have seen you.* □ **on call 1** (of a person) able to be contacted in order to provide a professional service if necessary, but not formally on duty. **2** (of money lent) repayable on demand.

cal·la /ˈkalə/ ▸*n.* (usu. **calla lily**) a plant (genus *Zantedeschia*) of the arum family, with a large showy white spathe.

call·er /ˈkôlər/ ▸*n.* **1** a person who makes a telephone call or pays a brief visit. **2** a person who calls out numbers in a game of bingo or directions in a dance.

cal·lig·ra·phy /kəˈligrəfē/ ▸*n.* decorative handwriting or handwritten lettering. ▷early 17th cent.: from Greek *kalligraphia*, from *kalligraphos* 'person who writes beautifully,' from *kallos* 'beauty' + *graphein* 'write'. —**cal·lig·ra·pher** /-fər/ *n.* —**cal·li·graph·ic** /ˌkaləˈgrafik/ *adj.* —**cal·lig·ra·phist** /-fist/ *n.*

call·ing /ˈkôliNG/ ▸*n.* **1** the loud cries or shouts of an animal or person: *the calling of a cuckoo.* **2** a strong urge toward a particular way of life or career; a vocation: *those who have a special calling to minister to others' needs.* ■ a profession or occupation.

call·ing card ▸*n.* **1** a card bearing a person's name and address, sent or left in lieu of a formal social or business visit. ■ fig. an action or the result of an action by which someone or something can be identified: *a dog whose calling card is a savage nip at the nearest ankles.* **2** a card that allows the user to make telephone calls from any phone and charge the cost to their home telephone number. ■ a prepaid card that allows the user to make telephone calls up to a specified value.

cal·lis·then·ics /ˌkaləsˈTHeniks/ ▸*pl. n.* British spelling of **CALISTHENICS**.

call op·tion ▸*n. Stock Market* an option to buy assets at an agreed price on or before a particular date.

cal·lous /ˈkaləs/ ▸*adj.* showing or having an insensitive and cruel disregard for others: *his callous comments about the murder made me shiver.* ▸*n.* variant spelling of **CALLUS**. —**cal·lous·ly** *adv.* —**cal·lous·ness** *n.*

cal·low /ˈkalō/ ▸*adj.* (esp. of a young person) inexperienced and immature. ▷Old English *calu* 'bald '; probably from Latin *calvus* 'bald.' This was extended to mean 'unfledged,' which led to the present sense 'immature.' —**cal·low·ly** *adv.* —**cal·low·ness** *n.*

cal·lus /ˈkaləs/ (also **cal·lous**) ▸*n.* a thickened and hardened part of the skin or soft tissue, esp. in an area that has been subjected to friction. ■ *Med.* the bony healing tissue that forms around the ends of broken bone. ■ *Bot.* a hard formation of tissue, esp. new tissue formed over a wound.

calm /kä(l)m/ ▸*adj.* **1** (of a person, action, or manner) not showing or feeling nervousness, anger, or other emotions: *keep calm, she told herself* | *his voice was calm.* ■ (of a place) peaceful, esp. in contrast to recent violent activity: *the city was reported to be calm, but army patrols remained.* **2** (of the weather) pleasantly free from wind: *the night was clear and calm.* ■ (of the sea) not disturbed by large waves.

▸*n.* **1** the absence of violent or confrontational activity within a place or group: *the elections proceeded in an atmosphere of relative calm* | *an edgy calm reigned in the capital.* ■ the absence of nervousness, agitation, or excitement in a person: *his usual calm deserted him.* **2** the absence of wind: *in the center of the storm calm prevailed.* ■ still air represented by force 0 on the Beaufort scale. ■ (often **calms**) an area of the sea without wind.

▸*v.* [*tr.*] make (someone) tranquil and quiet; soothe: *I took him inside and tried to calm him down* | *he lit a cigarette to calm his nerves* | [as *adj.*] (**calming**) *a cup of tea will have a calming effect.* ■ [*intr.*] (**calm down**) (of a person) become tranquil and quiet: *gradually I calmed down and lost my anxiety.* —**calm·ly** *adv.* —**calm·ness** *n.*

ca·lor·ic /kəˈlôrik; -ˈlär-/ ▸*adj. technical* of or relating to heat; calorific: *a caloric value of 7 calories per gram.*

▸*n. hist. Physics* (in the late 18th and early 19th centuries) a hypothetical fluid substance that was thought to be responsible for the phenomena of heat. —**ca·lor·i·cal·ly** *adv.*

cal·o·rie /ˈkal(ə)rē/ (abbr.: **cal.**) ▸*n.* (pl. **-ries**) either of two units of heat energy: ■ (also **small calorie**) (abbr.: **cal**) the energy needed to raise the temperature of 1 gram of water through 1 °C (now usually defined as 4.1868 joules). ■ (also **large calorie**) (abbr.: **Cal**) the energy needed to raise the temperature of 1 kilogram of water through 1 °C, equal to one thousand small calories and often used to measure the energy value of foods.

cal·o·rif·ic /ˌkaləˈrifik/ ▸*adj. chiefly Brit.* relating to the amount of energy contained in food or fuel: *she knew the calorific contents of every morsel.* ■ (of food or drink) containing many calories and so likely to be fattening. —**cal·o·rif·i·cal·ly** /-ik(ə)lē/ *adv.*

cal·trop /ˈkaltrəp; ˈkôl-/ (also **cal·trap**) ▸*n.* a creeping plant (genus *Tribulus*, family Zygophyllaceae) with woody carpels that typically have hard spines.

cal·u·met /ˈkalyə,met; -mit; ,kalyə'met/ ▸*n.* a North American Indian peace pipe.

calumet

ca·lum·ni·ate /kəˈləmnē,āt/ ▸*v.* [*tr.*] *formal* make false and defamatory statements about. —**ca·lum·ni·a·tion** /kə,ləmnēˈāSHən/ *n.* —**ca·lum·ni·a·tor** /-,ātər/ *n.*

cal·um·ny /ˈkaləmnē/ ▶n. (pl. **-nies**) the making of false and defamatory statements in order to damage someone's reputation; slander. ■ a false and slanderous statement. —**ca·lum·ni·ous** /kəˈləmnēəs/ adj.

Cal·va·dos /ˌkalvəˈdōs/ (also **cal·va·dos**) ▶n. apple brandy, traditionally made in the Calvados region of Normandy.

calve /kav/ ▶v. **1** [intr.] (of cows and certain other large animals) give birth to a calf. **2** [intr.] (of a mass of ice) split off from an iceberg or glacier.

calves /kavz/ ▶ plural form of CALF[1], CALF[2].

Cal·vin·ism /ˈkalvəˌnizəm/ ▶n. the Protestant theological system of John Calvin and his successors, which develops Luther's doctrine of justification by faith alone and emphasizes the grace of God and the doctrine of predestination. —**Cal·vin·ist** n. —**Cal·vin·is·tic** /ˌkalvəˈnistik/ adj. —**Cal·vin·is·ti·cal** adj.

ca·lyp·so /kəˈlipsō/ ▶n. (pl. **-sos**) a kind of West Indian (originally Trinidadian) music in syncopated African rhythm, typically with words improvised on a topical theme. ■ a song in this style. —**ca·lyp·so·ni·an** /kəˌlipˈsōnēən; ˌkalip-/ adj. & n.

ca·lyx /ˈkāliks; ˈkal-/ (also **ca·lix**) ▶n. (pl. **ca·ly·ces** /ˈkāləˌsēz; ˈkal-/ or **ca·lyx·es**) **1** Bot. the sepals of a flower, typically forming a whorl that encloses the petals and forms a protective layer around a flower in bud. Compare with COROLLA. **2** Zool. a cuplike cavity or structure, in particular: ■ a portion of the pelvis of a mammalian kidney.

CAM /kam/ ▶abbr. computer-aided manufacturing.

cam /kam/ ▶n. a projection on a rotating part in machinery, designed to make sliding contact with another part while rotating and to impart reciprocal or variable motion to it. ■ short for CAMSHAFT. ■ short for CAMERA[1].

ca·ma·ra·de·rie /ˌkäm(ə)ˈrädərē; ˌkam-; -ˈrad-/ ▶n. mutual trust and friendship among people who spend a lot of time together.

cam·ber /ˈkambər/ ▶n. a slightly convex or arched shape of a road or other horizontal surface: the deck beams are curved for the camber of the deck. ■ the slight sideways inclination of the front wheels of a motor vehicle. ■ the extent of curvature of a section of an airfoil. —**cam·bered** adj.

Cam·bo·di·an /kamˈbōdēən/ ▶adj. of or relating to Cambodia, its people, or their language.
▶n. **1** a native or national of Cambodia, or a person of Cambodian descent. **2** another term for KHMER (the language).

Cam·bri·an /ˈkambrēən; ˈkäm-/ ▶adj. **1** (chiefly in names or geographical terms) Welsh. **2** Geol. of, relating to, or denoting the first period in the Paleozoic era, between the end of the Precambrian eon and the beginning of the Ordovician period. ■ [as n.] (**the Cambrian**) the Cambrian period or the system of rocks deposited during it.

cam·bric /ˈkāmbrik/ ▶n. a lightweight, closely woven white linen or cotton fabric.

cam·cord·er /ˈkamˌkôrdər/ ▶n. a portable combined video camera and video recorder.

came /kām/ ▶ past tense of COME.

cam·el /ˈkaməl/ ▶n. a large, long-necked ungulate mammal (genus Camelus) of arid country, with long slender legs, broad cushioned feet, and either one or two fat-storing humps on the back. The **camel family** (Camelidae) also includes the llama and its relatives. ■ a fabric made from camel hair. ■ a yellowish-fawn color like that of camel hair.

ca·mel·lia /kəˈmēlyə/ ▶n. an evergreen eastern Asian shrub (genus Camellia) of the tea family, grown for its showy flowers.

Cam·em·bert /ˈkaməmˌbe(ə)r/ ▶n. a kind of rich, soft, creamy cheese with a whitish rind, originally made near Camembert in Normandy.

cam·e·o /ˈkamēˌō/ ▶n. (pl. **-os**) **1** a piece of jewelry, typically oval in shape, consisting of a portrait in profile carved in relief on a background of a different color. **2** a short descriptive literary sketch that neatly encapsulates someone or something: cameos of street life. ■ a small character part in a play or movie, played by a distinguished actor or a celebrity: [as adj.] he played numerous cameo roles.

cam·er·a[1] /ˈkam(ə)rə/ ▶n. a device for recording visual images in the form of photographs, movie film, or video signals. —**cam·er·a·man** n.

cam·er·a[2] ▶n. [in names] a chamber or round building: the Radcliffe Camera.
▶ □ **in camera** chiefly Law in private, in particular taking place in the private chambers of a judge, with the press and public excluded.

cam·er·a ob·scu·ra /əbˈskyōōrə/ ▶n. a darkened box with a convex lens or aperture for projecting the image of an external object onto a screen inside. It is important historically in the development of photography. ■ a small round building with a rotating angled mirror at the apex of the roof, projecting an image of the landscape on to a horizontal surface inside.

cam·er·a-read·y ▶adj. Printing (of matter to be printed) in the right form and of good enough quality to be reproduced photographically onto a printing plate: camera-ready copy.

cam·i·sole /ˈkaməˌsōl/ ▶n. a woman's loose-fitting undergarment for the upper body, typically held up by shoulder straps and having decorative trimming.

cam·o·mile ▶n. variant spelling of CHAMOMILE.

cam·ou·flage /ˈkaməˌfläzh; -ˌfläj/ ▶n. the disguising of military personnel, equipment, and installations by painting or covering them to make them blend in with their surroundings. ■ the clothing or materials used for such a purpose: figures dressed in army camouflage. ■ an animal's natural coloring or form that enables it to blend in with its surroundings: the whiteness of polar bears provides camouflage. ■ fig. actions or devices intended to disguise or mislead: much of my apparent indifference was merely protective camouflage.
▶v. [tr.] (often **be camouflaged**) hide or disguise the presence of (a person, animal, or object) by means of camouflage: the war area had to be camouflaged with mud | fig. grievances should be discussed, not camouflaged. ▷World War I: from French, from camoufler 'to disguise,' from Italian camuffare 'disguise, deceive,' perhaps by association with French camouflet 'whiff of smoke in the face.'

camp[1] /kamp/ ▶n. **1** a place with temporary accommodations of huts, tents, or other structures, typically used by soldiers, refugees, prisoners, or travelers: the enemy camp. ■ the people lodging in such a place: the shot woke the whole camp. ■ a recreational institution providing facilities for outdoor activities, sports, crafts, and other special interests and typically featuring rustic overnight accommodations. ■ temporary overnight lodging out of doors, typically in tents: we made camp at a bend in the creek | we pitched camp at a fine spot. ■ a facility at which athletes train during the off-season. **2** the supporters of a particular party or doctrine regarded collectively: his views were rooted in the conservative camp.
▶v. [intr.] live for a time in a camp, tent, or camper, as when on vacation: parks in which you can camp or stay in a chalet | [as n.] (**camping**) camping attracts people of all ages. ■ lodge temporarily, esp. in an inappropriate or uncomfortable place: we camped out for the night in a mission schoolroom. ■ remain persistently in one place: the press will be camping on your doorstep once they get onto this story.
▶ □ **break camp** take down a tent or the tents of an encampment.

camp[2] inf. ▶adj. deliberately exaggerated and theatrical in style, typically for humorous effect. ■ (of a man or his manner) ostentatiously and extravagantly effeminate: a heavily made-up and highly camp actor. ■ innocently idealistic, conventional, or sentimental: straight camp is about the ongoing comedy of American straightness: the Mormon Tabernacle Choir, the Secret Service, the NRA.
▶n. deliberately exaggerated and theatrical behavior or style.
▶v. [intr.] (of a man) behave in an ostentatiously effeminate way: he camped it up a bit for the cameras. —**camp·i·ly** /ˈkampəlē/ adv. —**camp·i·ness** n. —**camp·y** adj.

cam·paign /kamˈpān/ ▶n. a series of military operations intended to achieve a particular objective, confined to a particular area, or involving a specified type of fighting: a desert campaign. ■ an organized course of action to achieve a particular goal: an advertising campaign | his campaign to win her heart. ■ the organized actions that a political candidate undertakes in order to win an election.
▶v. [intr.] work in an organized and active way toward a particular goal, typically a political or social one: people who campaigned against child labor. ▷early 17th cent. (denoting a tract of open country): from French campagne 'open country,' via Italian from late Latin campania, from campus 'level ground.' The change in sense arose from an army's practice of "taking the field" (i.e., moving from a fortress or town to open country) at the onset of summer. —**cam·paign·er** n.

cam·pa·ni·le /ˌkampəˈnēlē; -ˈnēl/ ▶n. an Italian bell tower, esp. a freestanding one.

cam·pa·nol·o·gy /ˌkampəˈnäləjē/ ▶n. the art or practice of bell-ringing. —**cam·pa·no·log·i·cal** /ˌkampənlˈäjikəl/ adj. —**cam·pa·nol·o·gist** /-jist/ n.

camp·er /ˈkampər/ ▶n. **1** a person who spends a vacation in a tent or camp. **2** a large motor vehicle with facilities for sleeping and cooking while camping.
▶ □ **happy camper** a comfortable, contented person.

Pronunciation Key ə ago, up; ər over, fur; a hat; ā ate; ä car; CH chin; e let; ē see; e(ə)r air; i fit; ī by; i(ə)r ear; NG sing; ō go; ô law, for; oi toy; ŏŏ good; ōō goo; ou out; SH she; TH thin; TH then; (h)w why; ZH vision

cam·phor /ˈkamfər/ ▶n. a white, volatile, crystalline substance, a terpenoid ketone with an aromatic smell and bitter taste, occurring in certain essential oils.

cam·pi·on /ˈkampēən/ ▶n. a plant (genera *Silene* and *Lychnis*) of the pink family, typically having pink or white flowers with notched petals, found in both Eurasia and North America.

camp·site /ˈkampˌsīt/ ▶n. a place used for camping.

cam·pus /ˈkampəs/ ▶n. (*pl.* **-pus·es**) the grounds and buildings of a university or college: *for the first year I had a room* **on campus**. ■ the grounds of a school, hospital, or other institution.

cam·shaft /ˈkamˌsHaft/ ▶n. a shaft with one or more cams attached to it, esp. one operating the valves in an internal combustion engine.

can[1] /kan/ ▶*modal verb* (3rd sing. present **can**; *past* **could** /kŏŏd/) **1** be able to: *they can run fast | I could hear footsteps.* ■ be able to through acquired knowledge or skill: *I can speak Italian.* ■ have the opportunity or possibility to: *there are many ways vacationers can take money abroad.* ■ used to express doubt or surprise about the possibility of something's being the case: *he can't have finished | where can she have gone?* **2** be permitted to: *you can use the phone if you want to.* ■ used to ask someone to do something: *can you open the window?* ■ used to make a suggestion or offer: *we can have another drink if you like.* **3** used to indicate that something is typically the case: *he could be very moody.*

can[2] ▶n. **1** a cylindrical metal container: *a garbage can | a can of paint.* ■ a small steel or aluminum container in which food or drink is hermetically sealed for storage over long periods: *soup cans.* ■ the quantity of food or drink held by such a container: *he drank two cans of beer.* **2** (**the can**) *inf.* prison. **3** (**the can**) *inf.* the toilet.
▶v. (**canned**, **can·ning**) [*tr.*] (often **be canned**) **1** preserve (food) in a can. **2** *inf.* dismiss (someone) from their job: *he was canned because of a fight over promotion.* ■ reject (something) as inadequate. —**can·ner** n.
▶ □ **a can of worms** a complicated matter likely to prove awkward or embarrassing: *to question the traditional model of education* **opens up a can** *of worms.*

Can·a·da goose ▶n. a common North American goose (*Branta canadensis*) with a black head and neck and a loud trumpeting call.

ca·nal /kəˈnal/ ▶n. an artificial waterway constructed to allow the passage of boats or ships inland or to convey water for irrigation. ■ a tubular duct in a plant or animal, serving to convey or contain food, liquid, or air: *the ear canal.* ■ *Astron.* any of a number of linear markings formerly reported as seen by telescope on the planet Mars.

can·a·pé /ˈkanəˌpā -ˌpē/ ▶n. a small piece of bread or pastry with a savory topping, often served with drinks at a reception or formal party.

ca·nard /kəˈnär(d)/ ▶n. **1** an unfounded rumor or story. **2** a small wing-like projection attached to an aircraft forward of the main wing to provide extra stability or control, sometimes replacing the tail.

ca·nar·y /kəˈnerē/ ▶n. (*pl.* **-ies**) **1** a mainly African finch (genus *Serinus*) with a melodious song, typically having yellowish-green plumage. ■ *inf.* an informer. **2** (also **canary yellow**) a bright yellow color resembling the plumage of a canary. **3** (also **canary wine**) *hist.* a sweet wine from the Canary Islands, similar to Madeira.

ca·nas·ta /kəˈnastə/ ▶n. a card game resembling rummy, using two packs. It is usually played by two pairs of partners, and the aim is to collect sets (or melds) of cards. ■ a meld of seven cards in this game.

can·can /ˈkanˌkan/ ▶n. a lively, high-kicking stage dance originating in 19th-century Parisian music halls.

can·cel /ˈkansəl/ ▶v. (**-celed**, **-cel·ing**; *Brit.* **-celled**, **-cel·ling**) [*tr.*] **1** decide or announce that (an arranged or planned event) will not take place: *he was forced to cancel his visit.* ■ annul or revoke (a formal arrangement which is in effect): *his visa was canceled.* ■ abolish or make void (a financial obligation): *I intend to cancel your debt to me.* ■ mark, pierce, or tear (a ticket, check, or postage stamp) to show that it has been used or invalidated: [as *adj.*] *canceled checks.* **2** (of a factor or circumstance) neutralize or negate the force or effect of (another): *the electric fields may* **cancel each other out.** ■ *Math.* delete (an equal factor) from both sides of an equation or from the numerator and denominator of a fraction. ▷late Middle English (in the sense 'obliterate or delete writing by drawing or stamping lines across it'): from Old French *canceller*, from Latin *cancellare*, from *cancelli* 'crossbars.'

can·cel·la·tion /ˌkansəˈlāSHən/ ▶n. the action of canceling something that has been arranged or planned: *train services are subject to cancellation at short notice.* ■ a crossing out of something written. ■ a visible or electronic mark placed on a postage stamp to show that it has been used.

Can·cer /ˈkansər/ ▶ **1** *Astron.* a constellation (the Crab), said to represent a crab crushed under the foot of Hercules. It is most noted for the globular star cluster of Praesepe (the Beehive cluster). **2** *Astrol.* the fourth sign of the zodiac, which the sun enters at the northern

summer solstice (about June 21). ■ (**a Cancer**) a person born when the sun is in this sign.
▶ □ **tropic of Cancer** see TROPIC[1].

can·cer /ˈkansər/ ▶n. the disease caused by an uncontrolled division of abnormal cells in a part of the body. ■ a malignant growth or tumor resulting from such a division of cells: *skin cancers.* ■ *fig.* a practice or phenomenon perceived to be evil or destructive and hard to contain or eradicate. —**can·cer·ous** /ˌkansərəs/ adj.

can·de·la·brum /ˌkandəˈläbrəm; -ˈlab-/ ▶n. (*pl.* **-la·bra** /-ˈläbrə; -ˈlabrə/) a large branched candlestick or holder for several candles or lamps.

can·did /ˈkandid/ ▶adj. **1** truthful and straightforward; frank. **2** (of a photograph of a person) taken informally, esp. without the subject's knowledge. —**can·did·ly** adv. —**can·did·ness** n.

can·di·da /ˈkandidə/ ▶n. a yeastlike, parasitic fungus (genus *Candida*, phylum Ascomycota) that can cause an infection (**candidiasis**) such as athlete's foot and vaginitis.

can·di·date /ˈkandiˌdāt; -dit/ ▶n. a person who applies for a job or is nominated for election: *the Republican candidate.* ■ a person taking an examination: *doctoral candidates in literature.* ■ a person or thing regarded as suitable for or likely to receive a particular fate, treatment, or position: *a leading* **candidate** *for the title of New York's ugliest building.* —**can·di·da·cy** /ˈkandidəsē/ n.

can·di·di·a·sis /ˌkandiˈdīəsis/ ▶n. infection with candida, esp. as causing oral or vaginal thrush.

can·dle /ˈkandl/ ▶n. a cylinder or block of wax or tallow with a central wick that is lit to produce light as it burns. ■ (also **international candle**) *Physics* a unit of luminous intensity, superseded by the candela.
▶v. [*tr.*] (often **be candled**) (of a poultry breeder) test (an egg) for freshness or fertility by holding it to the light. —**can·dler** /ˈkandlər; -dl-ər/ n.
▶ □ **be unable to hold a candle to** *inf.* be not nearly as good as: *nobody in the final could hold a candle to her.*

can·dle·pow·er /ˈkandlˌpou(ə)r/ ▶n. illuminating power expressed in candelas or candles: [as *adj.*] *a 16-candlepower lamp.*

can·dle·snuffer /ˈkandlˌsnəfər/ ▶n. see SNUFFER.

can·dle·stick /ˈkandlˌstik/ ▶n. a support or holder for one or more candles, typically one that is tall and thin.

can·dle·wick /ˈkandlˌwik/ ▶n. a thick, soft cotton fabric with a raised, tufted pattern. ■ tufted embroidery work made with heavy cotton yarn similar to that used to make wicks for candles.

can·dor /ˈkandər; -ˌdôr/ (*Brit.* **can·dour**) ▶n. the quality of being open and honest in expression; frankness: *a man of refreshing candor.*

C&W ▶abbr. country and western (music).

can·dy /ˈkandē/ ▶n. (*pl.* **-dies**) a sweet food made with sugar or syrup combined with fruit, chocolate, or nuts. ■ sugar crystallized by repeated boiling and slow evaporation.
▶v. (**-dies, -died**) [*tr.*] (often as *adj.*] (**candied**) preserve (fruit) by coating and impregnating it with a sugar syrup: *candied fruit.*

can·dy-strip·er /ˈstrīpər/ ▶n. *inf.* a teenage girl who does volunteer nursing in a hospital.

can·dy·tuft /ˈkandēˌtəft/ ▶n. a European plant (genus *Iberis*) of the cabbage family, with small heads of white, pink, or purple flowers, often cultivated as a garden plant.

cane /kān/ ▶n. **1** the hollow, jointed stem of a tall grass, esp. sugar cane, or the stem of a slender palm such as rattan. ■ any plant that produces such stems. ■ stems of bamboo, rattan, or wicker used as a material for making furniture or baskets: [as *adj.*] *a cane coffee table.* ■ short for SUGAR CANE. ■ a flexible, woody stem of the raspberry plant or any of its relatives. **2** a length of cane or a slender stick, esp. one used as a support for plants, as a walking stick, or as an instrument of punishment. ■ (**the cane**) *chiefly Brit.* a form of corporal punishment used in certain schools, involving beating with a cane.
▶v. [*tr.*] **1** (often **be caned**) beat with a cane as a punishment. **2** [usu. as *adj.*] (**caned**) make or repair (furniture) with cane: *armchairs with caned seats.* —**can·er** n.

cane sug·ar ▶n. sugar obtained from sugar cane.

can·id /ˈkanid; ˈkā-/ ▶n. *Zool.* a mammal of the dog family (Canidae).

ca·nine /ˈkāˌnīn/ ▶adj. of, relating to, or resembling a dog or dogs: *canine distemper virus.* ■ *Zool.* of or relating to animals of the dog family.
▶n. **1** a dog. ■ *Zool.* another term for CANID. **2** (also **canine tooth**) a pointed tooth between the incisors and premolars of a mammal, often greatly enlarged in carnivores.

can·is·ter /ˈkanəstər/ ▶n. a round or cylindrical container, typically one made of metal, used for storing such things as food, chemicals, or rolls of film. ■ a cylinder of pressurized gas, typically one that explodes when thrown or fired from a gun.

can·ker /ˈkaNGkər/ ▶n. **1** a necrotic, fungal disease of apple and other trees that results in damage to the bark. ■ an open lesion in plant tissue caused by infection or injury. ■ fungal rot in some fruits and vegetables, e.g., parsnips and tomatoes. **2** *Med.* an ulcerous condition or disease, in particular: ■ (also **canker sore**) a small ulcer of the mouth or lips. ■ *fig.* a malign and corrupting influence that is difficult to eradicate: *racism remains a canker.*
▶v. [tr.] [usu. as adj.] (**cankered**) infect with a pervasive and corrupting bitterness: *he hated her with a cankered, shameful abhorrence.* —**can·ker·ous** /-kərəs/ adj.

can·ker·worm /ˈkaNGkər,wərm/ ▶n. the caterpillar of a North American moth of the family Geometridae (esp. *Paleacrita vernata* and *Alsophila pometaria*) that can be a major pest of fruit and shade trees.

can·na·bis /ˈkanəbəs/ ▶n. a plant (*Cannabis sativa*, family Cannabaceae) used to produce hemp fiber and as a mildly psychotropic drug. Also called **HEMP, MARIJUANA.** ■ a dried preparation of the flowering tops or other parts of this plant, or a resinous extract of it (**cannabis resin**).

canned /kand/ ▶adj. **1** (of food or drink) preserved or supplied in a sealed can: *canned beans.* **2** *inf., often derog.* (of music, laughter, or applause) prerecorded and therefore considered to be lacking in freshness and spontaneity.

can·nel·lo·ni /ˌkanlˈōnē/ ▶n. rolls of pasta stuffed with a meat or vegetable mixture. ■ [treated as *sing.*] an Italian dish consisting of such rolls of pasta cooked in a cheese sauce.

can·ner·y /ˈkanərē/ ▶n. (*pl.* **-ner·ies**) a factory where food is canned.

can·ni·bal /ˈkanəbəl/ ▶n. a person who eats the flesh of other human beings: [as *adj.*] *cannibal tribes.* ■ an animal that feeds on flesh of its own species. —**can·ni·bal·ism** /-ˌlizəm/ n. —**can·ni·bal·is·tic** /ˌkanəbəˈlistik/ adj. —**can·ni·bal·is·ti·cal·ly** /ˌkanəbəˈlistik(ə)lē/ adv.

can·ni·bal·ize /ˈkanəbə,līz/ ▶v. [tr.] **1** use (a machine) as a source of spare parts for another, similar machine. ■ use (the creative work of others) in one's own art: *high culture should cannibalize mass culture.* ■ (of a company) reduce the sales of one of its products) by introducing a similar, competing product. **2** (of an animal) eat (an animal of its own kind). —**can·ni·bal·i·za·tion** /ˌkanəbələˈzāsHən/ n.

can·no·li /kəˈnōlē/ ▶pl. n. Italian pastries in the form of hard tubular shells filled with sweetened ricotta cheese and often containing nuts, citron, or chocolate bits.

can·non /ˈkanən/ ▶n. **1** (*pl.* usu. same) a large, heavy piece of artillery, typically mounted on wheels, formerly used in warfare. ■ an automatic heavy gun that fires shells from an aircraft or tank. **2** *Engineering* a heavy cylinder or hollow drum that is able to rotate independently on a shaft.

can·non·ade /ˌkanəˈnād/ ▶n. a period of continuous, heavy gunfire.
▶v. [intr.] discharge heavy guns continuously: [as *n.*] (**cannonading**) *the daily cannonading continued.*

can·non·ball /ˈkanən,bôl/ ▶n. a round metal or stone projectile fired from a cannon in former times. ■ (also **cannonball dive**) a jump into water performed upright with the knees clasped to the chest.

can·non fod·der ▶n. soldiers regarded merely as material to be expended in war.

can·not /kəˈnät; ˈkan,ät/ ▶contr. *of* can not.

can·nu·la /ˈkanyələ/ ▶n. (*pl.* **-lae** /-lē/ or **-las**) *Surgery* a thin tube inserted into a vein or body cavity to administer medicine, drain off fluid, or insert a surgical instrument.

can·ny /ˈkanē/ ▶adj. (**-ni·er, -ni·est**) having or showing shrewdness and good judgment, esp. in money or business matters: *canny shoppers came early for a bargain.* —**can·ni·ly** /ˈkanl-ē/ adv. —**can·ni·ness** n.

ca·noe /kəˈnōō/ ▶n. a narrow, keelless boat with pointed ends, propelled by a paddle or paddles.
▶v. (**-noes, -noed, -noe·ing**) [intr.] travel in or paddle a canoe: *he had once canoed down the Nile.* —**ca·noe·ist** /-ˈnōōist/ n.

canoe

ca·no·la /kəˈnōlə/ ▶n. oilseed rape of a variety developed in Canada and grown in North America. It yields a valuable culinary oil.

can·on¹ /ˈkanən/ ▶n. **1** a general law, rule, principle, or criterion by which something is judged: *the canons of fair play and equal opportunity.*
■ a church decree or law: *a set of ecclesiastical canons.* **2** a collection or list of sacred books accepted as genuine: *the formation of the biblical canon.* ■ the works of a particular author or artist that are recognized as genuine: *the Shakespeare canon.* ■ a list of literary or artistic works considered to be permanently established as being of the highest quality: *Hopkins was established in the canon of English poetry.* **3** (also **canon of the Mass**) (in the Roman Catholic Church) the part of the Mass containing the words of consecration. **4** *Mus.* a piece in which the same melody is begun in different parts successively, so that the imitations overlap.

can·on² ▶n. a member of the clergy who is on the staff of a cathedral, esp. one who is a member of the chapter.

ca·non·i·cal /kəˈnänikəl/ ▶adj. **1** according to or ordered by canon law. **2** included in the list of sacred books officially accepted as genuine: *the canonical Gospels of the New Testament.* ■ accepted as being accurate and authoritative. ■ (of an artist or work) belonging to the literary or artistic canon. ■ according to recognized rules or scientific laws: *canonical nucleotide sequences.* ■ *Math.* of or relating to a general rule or standard formula. **3** of or relating to a cathedral chapter or a member of it.
▶pl. n. (**canonicals**) the prescribed official dress of the clergy: *Cardinal Bea in full canonicals.* —**ca·non·i·cal·ly** /-ik(ə)lē/ adv.

can·on·ize /ˈkanə,nīz/ ▶v. [tr.] (often **be canonized**) (in the Roman Catholic Church) officially declare (a dead person) to be a saint: *he was the last English saint to be canonized prior to the Reformation.* ■ *fig.* regard as being above reproach or of great significance: *we have canonized freedom of speech.* ■ accept into the literary or artistic canon. ■ sanction by Church authority. —**can·on·i·za·tion** /ˌkanənəˈzāsHən/ n.

can·on law ▶n. ecclesiastical law, esp. (in the Roman Catholic Church) that laid down by papal pronouncements.

can·o·py /ˈkanəpē/ ▶n. (*pl.* **-pies**) an ornamental cloth covering hung or held up over something, esp. a throne or bed. ■ *fig.* something hanging or perceived as hanging over a person or scene: *the canopy of stars.* ■ *Archit.* a rooflike projection or shelter: *they mounted the steps under the concrete canopy.* ■ the transparent cover of an aircraft's cockpit. ■ the expanding, umbrellalike part of a parachute, made of silk or nylon. ■ the uppermost trees or branches of the trees in a forest, forming a more or less continuous layer of foliage.
▶v. (**-pies, -pied**) [tr.] [usu. as *adj.*] (**canopied**) cover or provide with a canopy: *a canopied bed* | *the river was canopied by overhanging trees.* ▷late Middle English: from medieval Latin *canopeum* 'ceremonial canopy,' alteration of Latin *conopeum* 'mosquito net over a bed,' from Greek *kō nōpeion* 'couch with mosquito curtains,' from *kōnōps* 'mosquito.'

canst /kanst/ ▶archaic second person singular present of CAN¹.

cant¹ /kant/ ▶n. **1** hypocritical and sanctimonious talk, typically of a moral, religious, or political nature. **2** [as *adj.*] denoting a phrase or catchword temporarily current or in fashion: *they are misrepresented as, in the cant word of our day, uncaring.* ■ language peculiar to a specified group or profession and regarded with disparagement: *thieves' cant.*
▶v. [intr.] *dated* talk hypocritically and sanctimoniously about something: *if they'd stop canting about "honest work," they might get somewhere.*

cant² ▶v. [tr.] cause (something) to be in a slanting or oblique position; tilt: *he canted his head to look at the screen.* ■ [intr.] take or have a slanting position: *mismatched slate roofs canted at all angles.*
▶n. **1** a slope or tilt: *the outward cant of the curving walls.* **2** a wedge-shaped block of wood, esp. one remaining after the better-quality pieces have been cut off.

can·ta·bi·le /känˈtäbə,lā/ *Mus.* ▶adv. & adj. in a smooth singing style.

can·ta·loupe /ˈkantl,ōp/ (also **cantaloupe melon**) ▶n. a small, round melon of a variety with orange flesh and ribbed skin.

can·tan·ker·ous /kanˈtaNGkərəs/ ▶adj. bad-tempered, argumentative, and uncooperative. —**can·tan·ker·ous·ly** adv. —**can·tan·ker·ous·ness** n.

can·ta·ta /kənˈtätə/ ▶n. a medium-length narrative or descriptive piece of music with vocal solos and usually a chorus and orchestra.

can·teen /kanˈtēn/ ▶n. **1** a restaurant provided by an organization such as a military camp, college, factory, or company for its students or staff. **2** a small water bottle, as used by soldiers or campers.

can·ter /ˈkantər/ ▶n. a three-beat gait of a horse or other quadruped between a trot and a gallop: *I rode away at a canter.* ■ a ride on a horse at such a speed.

cannon

Pronunciation Key ə *ago, up;* ər *over, fur;* a *hat;* ā *ate;* ä *car;* CH *chin;* e *let;* ē *see;* e(ə)r *air;* i *fit;* ī *by;* i(ə)r *ear;* NG *sing;* ō *go;* ô *law, for;* oi *toy;* ŏŏ *good;* ōō *goo;* ou *out;* SH *she;* TH *thin;* T͟H *then;* (h)w *why;* ZH *vision*

▶v. [intr.] (of a horse) move at a canter in a particular direction: *they cantered down into the village.* ■ [tr.] make (a horse) move at a canter.

can·thar·i·des /kanˈтнari,dēz/ ▶pl. n. see **SPANISH FLY.**

can·thus /ˈkanтнəs/ ▶n. (pl. **-thi** /-,тнī; -,тнē/) the outer or inner corner of the eye, where the upper and lower lids meet. —**can·thic** /ˈkanтнik/ adj.

can·ti·cle /ˈkantikəl/ ▶n. a hymn or chant, typically with a biblical text, forming a regular part of a church service.

can·ti·le·na /,kantlˈēnə/ ▶n. Mus. a lyrical vocal or instrumental melody in a composition.

can·ti·le·ver /ˈkantl,ēvər/ -,evər/ ▶n. a long projecting beam or girder fixed at only one end, used chiefly in bridge construction. ■ a long bracket or beam projecting from a wall to support a balcony, cornice, or similar structure.
▶v. [tr.] (usu. as adj.) (**cantilevered**) support by a cantilever or cantilevers: *a cantilevered deck.* ■ [intr.] project as or like a cantilever: *a conveyor cantilevered out over the river.*

can·ti·na /kanˈtēnə/ ▶n. (esp. in a Spanish-speaking country or the southwestern U.S.) a bar. ■ (in Italy) a wine shop.

can·to /ˈkan,tō/ ▶n. (pl. **-tos**) one of the sections into which certain long poems are divided.

can·ton /ˈkantn/ ▶n. a subdivision of a country established for political or administrative purposes. ■ a state of the Swiss Confederation. —**can·ton·al** /kanˈtänl; ˈkantnl/ adj.

Can·ton·ese /,kantnˈēz; -ˈēs/ ▶adj. of or relating to Canton (Guangzhou), its inhabitants, their dialect, or their cuisine.
▶n. (pl. same) **1** a native or inhabitant of Canton. **2** a form of Chinese spoken mainly in southeastern China (including Hong Kong).

can·ton·ment /kanˈtōnmənt; -ˈtän-/ ▶n. a military camp.

can·tor /ˈkantər/ ▶n. **1** an official who sings liturgical music and leads prayer in a synagogue. **2** (in formal Christian worship) a person who sings solo verses or passages to which the choir or congregation responds.

Ca·nuck /kəˈnək/ ▶n. inf. a Canadian, esp. a French Canadian (chiefly used by Canadians themselves and often derogatory in the U.S.).

can·vas /ˈkanvəs/ ▶n. a strong, coarse unbleached cloth made from hemp, flax, cotton, or a similar yarn, used to make items such as sails and tents and as a surface for oil painting: [as adj.] *a canvas bag.* ■ a piece of such cloth prepared for use as the surface for an oil painting. ■ an oil painting. ■ a variety of canvas with an open weave, used as a basis for tapestry and embroidery. ■ (**the canvas**) the floor of a boxing or wrestling ring, having a canvas covering.
▶v. (**-vased, -vas·ing**) [tr.] (usu. **be canvased**) cover with canvas: *the door had been canvased over.*

can·vas·back /ˈkanvəs,bak/ ▶n. a North American diving duck (*Aythya valisineria*) with a long, sloping black bill and a light gray back.

can·vass /ˈkanvəs/ ▶v. [tr.] **1** solicit votes from (electors in a constituency): *in each ward, two workers canvassed some 2,000 voters* | [intr.] *she canvassed for votes.* ■ question (someone) in order to ascertain their opinion on something. ■ ascertain (someone's opinion) through questioning: *opinions on the merger were canvassed.* ■ try to obtain; request: *they're canvassing support among shareholders.* **2** [tr.] (often **be canvassed**) discuss thoroughly: *the issues that were canvassed were still unresolved.*
▶n. an act or process of attempting to secure votes or ascertain opinions: *a house-to-house canvass.* —**can·vass·er** n.

can·yon /ˈkanyən/ ▶n. a deep gorge, typically one with a river flowing through it, as found in North America.

CAP ▶abbr. Civil Air Patrol.

cap[1] /kap/ ▶n. **1** a kind of soft, flat hat without a brim, and sometimes having a visor. ■ a kind of soft, close-fitting head covering worn for a particular purpose or as a mark of a particular profession or status: *a bathing cap.* ■ an academic mortarboard: *graduates in cap and gown.* **2** a protective lid or cover for an object such as a bottle or a camera lens. ■ *Dentistry* an artificial protective covering for a tooth. ■ the top of a bird's head when distinctively colored. ■ the broad upper part of the fruiting body of most mushrooms and toadstools, at the top of a stem. **3** an upper limit imposed on spending or other activities: *a cap on legal immigration.* **4** short for **PERCUSSION CAP.**
▶v. (**capped, cap·ping**) [tr.] **1** put a lid or cover on: *he capped his pen.* ■ (often **be capped**) form a covering layer or top part of: *several towers were capped by domes* | [as adj., in comb.] (**-capped**) *snow-capped mountains.* ■ put an artificial protective covering on (a tooth). ■ provide a fitting climax or conclusion to: *he capped a memorable season by becoming champion.* ■ follow or reply to (a story, remark, or joke) by producing a better or more apposite one: *they capped each other's stories.* **2** (often **be**

capped) place a limit or restriction on (prices, expenditure, or other activity). —**cap·ful** /-,fo͝ol/ n. (pl. **-fuls**)
▶ □ **cap** (or **hat**) **in hand** humbly asking for a favor: *we have to go cap in hand begging for funds.* □ **set one's cap for** (or **at**) *dated* (of a woman) try to attract (a particular man) as a suitor.

cap[2] /kap/ ▶n. Finance short for **CAPITALIZATION** (see **CAPITALIZE**): *mid-cap companies* | *small-cap stocks.*

ca·pa·bil·i·ty /,kāpəˈbilitē/ ▶n. (pl. **-ties**) (often **capability of doing** (or **to do**) **something**) power or ability: *the capability to increase productivity.* ■ (often **capabilities**) the extent of someone's or something's ability: *the job is beyond my capabilities.* ■ a facility on a computer for performing a specified task: *a graphics capability.* ■ forces or resources giving a country or state the ability to undertake a particular kind of military action: *nuclear capability.*

ca·pa·ble /ˈkāpəbəl/ ▶adj. (**capable of doing something**) having the ability, fitness, or quality necessary to do or achieve a specified thing: *I'm quite capable of taking care of myself.* ■ able to achieve efficiently whatever one has to do; competent. ■ open to or admitting of something: *the strange events are capable of rational explanation.* ■ ready or inclined to: *children capable of murder.* —**ca·pa·bly** /-blē/ adv.

ca·pa·cious /kəˈpāsнəs/ ▶adj. having a lot of space inside; roomy: *her capacious handbag.* —**ca·pa·cious·ly** adv. **ca·pa·cious·ness** n.

ca·pac·i·tance /kəˈpasitəns/ ▶n. Physics the ability of a system to store an electric charge. ■ the ratio of the change in an electric charge in a system to the corresponding change in its electric potential. (Symbol: **C**)

ca·pac·i·tor /kəˈpasitər/ ▶n. a device used to store an electric charge, consisting of one or more pairs of conductors separated by an insulator.

ca·pac·i·ty /kəˈpasitē/ ▶n. (pl. **-ties**) **1** the maximum amount that something can contain: *the capacity of the freezer is 1.1 cubic feet.* ■ [as adj.] fully occupying the available area or space: *they played to a capacity crowd.* ■ the amount that something can produce: *doubling its electricity-generating capacity.* ■ the total cylinder volume that is swept by the pistons in an internal combustion engine. **2** the ability or power to do, experience, or understand something: *I was impressed by her capacity for hard work.* ■ a person's legal competence: *cases where a patient's testamentary capacity is in doubt.* **3** a specified role or position: *I was engaged in a voluntary capacity.* —**ca·pac·i·tive** /-ətiv/ (also **ca·pac·i·ta·tive** /-,tātiv/) adj. (*chiefly Physics*)

ca·par·i·son /kəˈparəsən/ ▶n. an ornamental covering spread over a horse's saddle or harness.
▶v. (**be caparisoned**) (of a horse) be decked out in rich decorative coverings.

cape[1] /kāp/ ▶n. a sleeveless cloak, typically a short one. ■ a part of a longer coat or cloak that falls loosely over the shoulders from the neckband. ■ the pelt from the head and neck of an animal, for preparation as a hunting trophy.
▶v. [tr.] skin the head and neck of (an animal) to prepare a hunting trophy. —**caped** adj.

cape[2] ▶n. **1** a headland or promontory. **2** (**Cape**) (also **Cape Cod**) a type of rectangular house with a deeply gabled roof.

cap·e·lin /ˈkap(ə)lən/ ▶n. a small fish (*Mallotus villosus*) of the smelt family, found in North Atlantic coastal waters and used as food.

ca·per[1] /ˈkāpər/ ▶v. [intr.] skip or dance about in a lively or playful way: *children were capering about the room.*
▶n. **1** a playful skipping movement: *she did a little caper.* **2** inf. an activity or escapade, typically one that is illicit or ridiculous. ■ an amusing or far-fetched story, esp. one presented on film or stage: *a cop caper about intergalactic drug dealers.* —**ca·per·er** /ˈkāpərər/ n.

ca·per[2] ▶n. **1** (usu. **capers**) the cooked and pickled flower buds of a spiny southern European shrub, used to flavor food. **2** the shrub (*Capparis spinosa*, family Capparidaceae) from which these buds are taken.

cap·il·lar·y /ˈkapə,lerē/ ▶n. Anat. any of the fine branching blood vessels that form a network between the arterioles and venules. **2** (also **capillary tube**) a tube that has an internal diameter of hairlike thinness.
▶adj. of or relating to capillaries or capillarity. —**cap·il·lar·i·ty** /,kapəˈlaritē/ n.

cap·il·lar·y ac·tion ▶n. the tendency of a liquid in a capillary tube or absorbent material to rise or fall as a result of surface tension.

cap·i·tal[1] /ˈkapitl/ ▶n. **1** (also **capital city** or **town**) the most important city or town of a country or region, usually its seat of government and administrative center. ■ a place associated more than any other with a specified activity or product: *Milan is the fashion capital of the world.* **2** wealth in the form of money or other assets owned by a person or organization or available or contributed for a particular purpose such as starting a company or investing: *the senior partner would provide the initial capital.* ■ the excess of a company's assets over its liabilities. ■ people who possess wealth and use it to control a society's economic activity, considered collectively: *a conflict of interest between capital and labor.* ■ *fig.* a valuable resource of a particular kind: *investment in* **human capital. 3** (also **capital letter**) a letter of the size and form used to begin sentences and names: *he wrote the name in capitals.*

▶*adj.* **1** (of an offense or charge) liable to the death penalty: *murder was a capital crime.* **2** of or relating to wealth: *capital losses.* **3** of greatest political importance: *the capital city.* **4** (of a letter of the alphabet) large in size and of the form used to begin sentences and names. **5** *inf., dated* excellent.

▶*interj. Brit., inf., dated* used to express approval, satisfaction, or delight: *That's splendid! Capital!*

cap·i·tal[2] ▶*n. Archit.* the distinct, typically broader section at the head of a pillar or column.

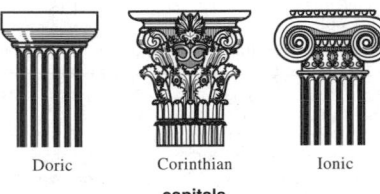

Doric   Corinthian   Ionic

capitals

cap·i·tal gain ▶*n.* (often **capital gains**) a profit from the sale of property or of an investment.

cap·i·tal·ism /ˈkapətlˌizəm/ ▶*n.* an economic and political system in which a country's trade and industry are controlled by private owners for profit, rather than by the state.

cap·i·tal·ist /ˈkapətlist/ ▶*n.* a wealthy person who uses money to invest in trade and industry for profit in accordance with the principles of capitalism.

▶*adj.* practicing, supporting, or based on the principles of capitalism: *the global economy is essentially capitalist.* —**cap·i·tal·is·tic** /ˌkapətlˈistik/ *adj.* —**cap·i·tal·is·ti·cal·ly** /ˌkapətl-əˈzāsHən/ *adv.*

cap·i·tal·ize /ˈkapətlˌīz/ ▶*v.* **1** [*intr.*] (**capitalize on**) take the chance to gain advantage from: *an attempt by the opposition to capitalize on the government's embarrassment.* **2** [*tr.*] provide (a company or industry) with capital. **3** realize (the present value of an income); convert into capital. ■ reckon (the value of an asset) by setting future benefits against the cost of maintenance: *a trader will want to capitalize repairs expenditure.* **4** [*tr.*] write or print (a word or letter) in capital letters. ■ begin (a word) with a capital letter. —**cap·i·tal·i·za·tion** /ˌkapətl-əˈzāsHən/ *n.*

Cap·i·tol /ˈkapitl/ (usu. **the Capitol**) ▶ **1** the seat of the U.S. Congress in Washington, DC. ■ (**cap·i·tol**) a building housing a legislative assembly: *50,000 people marched on New Jersey's state capitol.* **2** the temple of Jupiter on the Capitoline Hill in ancient Rome.

ca·pit·u·late /kəˈpiCHəˌlāt/ ▶*v.* [*intr.*] cease to resist an opponent or an unwelcome demand; surrender. ▷mid 16th cent. (in the sense 'parley, draw up terms'): from French *capituler,* from medieval Latin *capitulare* 'draw up under headings,' from Latin *capitulum,* diminutive of *caput* 'head.' —**ca·pit·u·la·tor** /-ˈlātər/ *n.*

ca·pit·u·la·tion /kə,piCHəˈlāsHən/ ▶*n.* the action of surrendering or ceasing to resist an opponent or demand: *a capitulation to wage demands.* ■ (**capitulations**) *hist.* an agreement or set of conditions.

cap'n /ˈkapm/ ▶*n.* informal contraction of **CAPTAIN**, used in representing speech.

ca·po[1] /ˈkāpō; ˈkäpō/ ▶*n.* (*pl.* **-pos**) a clamp fastened across all the strings of a fretted musical instrument to raise their tuning by a chosen amount.

ca·po[2] ▶*n.* (*pl.* **-pos**) the head of a crime syndicate, esp. the Mafia, or a branch of one.

ca·pon /ˈkā,pän; -pən/ ▶*n.* a castrated domestic cock fattened for eating. —**ca·pon·ize** /ˈkāpə,nīz/ *v.*

cap·puc·ci·no /ˌkapəˈCHēnō; ˌkäp-/ ▶*n.* (*pl.* **-nos**) coffee made with milk that has been frothed up with pressurized steam. ▷1940s: from Italian, literally 'Capuchin,' because its color resembles that of a Capuchin's habit.

ca·pric·ci·o /kəˈprēCHē,ō; -CHō/ ▶*n.* (*pl.* **-os**) a lively piece of music, typically one that is short and free in form. ■ a painting or other work of art representing a fantasy or a mixture of real and imaginary features.

ca·price /kəˈprēs/ ▶*n.* **1** a sudden and unaccountable change of mood or behavior. **2** *Mus.* another term for **CAPRICCIO**.

ca·pri·cious /kəˈprisHəs; -ˈprē-/ ▶*adj.* given to sudden and unaccountable changes of mood or behavior: *a capricious and often brutal administration | a capricious climate.* —**ca·pri·cious·ly** *adv.* —**ca·pri·cious·ness** *n.*

Cap·ri·corn /ˈkapri,kôrn/ *Astrol.* ▶the tenth sign of the zodiac (the Goat), which the sun enters at the northern winter solstice (about December 21). ■ (**a Capricorn**) a person born when the sun is in this sign.
▶ □ **tropic of Capricorn** see **TROPIC**[1].

cap·ri·ole /ˈkaprē,ōl/ ▶*n.* a movement performed in classical riding, in which the horse leaps from the ground and kicks out with its hind legs. ■ a leap or caper in dancing, esp. a cabriole.

ca·pri pants /kəˈprē/ (also **ca·pris**) ▶*pl. n.* close-fitting calf-length tapered trousers, usually worn by women and girls.

caps /kaps/ ▶*abbr.* capital letters.

cap·si·cum /ˈkapsikəm/ ▶*n.* (*pl.* **capsicums**) a tropical American pepper plant (genus *Capsicum*) of the nightshade family with fruits containing many seeds. Several species and varieties, in particular *C. annuum* var. *annuum,* the cultivated forms of which include sweet peppers and chili peppers.

cap·sid ▶*n. Microbiology* the protein coat or shell of a virus particle, surrounding the nucleic acid or nucleoprotein core.

cap·size /ˈkap,sīz; kapˈsīz/ ▶*v.* (of a boat) overturn in the water: [*intr.*] *the craft capsized in heavy seas* | [*tr.*] *gale-force gusts capsized the dinghies.*
▶*n.* an instance of capsizing.

cap·stan /ˈkapstən/ ▶*n.* a revolving cylinder with a vertical axis used for winding a rope or cable, powered by a motor or pushed around by levers. ■ the motor-driven spindle on a tape recorder that makes the tape travel past the head at constant speed.

cap·sule /ˈkapsəl; ˈkap,soōl/ ▶*n.* a small case or container, esp. a round or cylindrical one. ■ a small, soluble case of gelatin containing a dose of medicine, swallowed whole. ■ a top or cover for a bottle, esp. the foil or plastic covering the cork of a wine bottle. ■ short for **SPACE CAPSULE**. ■ [as *adj.*] *fig.* (of a piece of writing) shortened but retaining the essence of the original: *a capsule review of the movie.* ■ *Anat.* a tough sheath or membrane that encloses something in the body, such as a kidney, a lens, or a synovial joint. ■ *Biol.* a gelatinous layer forming the outer surface of some bacterial cells. ■ *Bot.* a dry fruit that releases its seeds by bursting open when ripe, such as a pea pod. ■ *Bot.* the spore-producing structure of mosses and liverworts, typically borne on a stalk. —**cap·su·lar** /ˈkapsələr/ *adj.* —**cap·su·late** /ˈkapsələt; -,lāt/ *adj.*

Capt. ▶*abbr.* Captain.

cap·tain /ˈkaptən/ ▶*n.* the person in command of a ship. ■ the pilot in command of a civil aircraft. ■ a naval officer of high rank, in particular (in the U.S. Navy or Coast Guard) an officer ranking above commander and below commodore. ■ an army officer of high rank, in particular (in the U.S. Army, Marine Corps, or Air Force) an officer ranking above first lieutenant and below major. ■ a police officer in charge of a precinct, ranking below a chief. ■ the head of a precinct's fire department. ■ the leader of a team, esp. in sports. ■ a powerful or influential person in a particular field: *a captain of industry.* ■ a political party leader in a local district. ■ a supervisor of waiters or bellhops.
▶*v.* [*tr.*] be the captain of (a ship, aircraft, or sports team). —**cap·tain·cy** /-tənsē/ *n.*

CAPTCHA /ˈkapsHə/ (also **captcha**) ▶*n.* a program or system intended to distinguish human from machine input, typically as a way of thwarting spam and automated extraction of data from Web sites.

cap·tion /ˈkapsHən/ ▶*n.* a title or brief explanation appended to an article, illustration, cartoon, or poster. ■ a piece of text appearing on a movie or television screen as part of a movie or broadcast.
▶*v.* [*tr.*] (usu. **be captioned**) provide (an illustration) with a title or explanation: *the drawings were captioned with humorous texts.* ▷late Middle English (in the sense 'seizing, capture'): from Latin *caption-,* from *capere* 'take, seize.' Early senses 'arrest' and 'warrant for arrest' gave rise to 'statement of where, when, and by whose authority a warrant was issued' (late 17th cent.): this was usually appended to a legal document, hence the sense 'heading or appended wording' (late 18th cent.).

cap·tious /ˈkapsHəs/ ▶*adj. formal* (of a person) tending to find fault or raise petty objections. —**cap·tious·ly** *adv.* —**cap·tious·ness** *n.*

cap·ti·vate /ˈkaptə,vāt/ ▶*v.* [*tr.*] attract and hold the interest and attention of; charm: *he was captivated by her beauty.* —**cap·ti·vat·ing·ly** /-ˌvātiNGlē/ *adv.* —**cap·ti·va·tion** /ˌkaptəˈvāSHən/ *n.*

cap·tive /ˈkaptiv/ ▶*n.* a person who has been taken prisoner or an animal that has been confined.
▶*adj.* imprisoned or confined: *a captive animal.* ■ having no freedom to choose alternatives or to avoid something: *advertisements at the movie theater reach a* **captive audience.** ■ (of a facility or service) controlled by, and typically for the sole use of, an establishment or company: *a captive power plant.*

cap·tiv·i·ty /kapˈtivitē/ ▶*n.* (*pl.* **-ties**) the condition of being imprisoned or confined: *he was released after 865 days* **in captivity** | *the third month of their captivity.*

cap·tor /ˈkaptər; -ˌtôr/ ▶*n.* a person or animal that catches or confines another.

cap·ture /ˈkapCHər/ ▶*v.* [*tr.*] take into one's possession or control by force: *the Russians captured 13,000 men* | *fig. the appeal captured the imagination of thousands.* ■ record or express accurately in words or pictures: *she did a series of sketches, trying to capture all his moods.* ■ *Physics* absorb (an atomic or subatomic particle). ■ (in chess and other board games) make a move that secures the removal of (an opposing piece) from the board. ■ *Astron.* (of a star, planet, or other celestial body) bring (a less massive body) permanently within its gravitational influence. ■ cause (data) to be stored in a computer or in a digital format.
▶*n.* the action of capturing or being captured. ■ a person or thing that has been captured. —**cap·tur·er** *n.*

Cap·u·chin /ˈkap(y)əSHən; kəˈp(y)ōō-/ ▶*n.* **1** a friar belonging to a strict branch of the Franciscan order. **2** (**capuchin** or **capuchin monkey**) a South American monkey (genus *Cebus*) with a cap of hair on the head that has the appearance of a cowl.

cap·y·ba·ra /ˈkapiˌberə; -ˌbärə/ ▶*n.* (*pl.* same or **capybaras**) a South American mammal (*Hydrochoerus hydrochaeris*, family Hydrochaeridae) that resembles a large guinea pig. It is the largest living rodent.

car /kär/ ▶*n.* a road vehicle, typically with four wheels, powered by an internal combustion engine and able to carry a small number of people. ■ a vehicle that runs on rails, esp. a railroad car. ■ a railroad car of a specified kind: *the first-class cars.* ■ the passenger compartment of an elevator, cableway, airship, or balloon. ■ *poetic/lit.* a chariot. —**car·ful** /-ˌfōōl/ *n.* (*pl.* **-fuls**).

car·a·bi·ner /ˌkarəˈbēnər/ ▶*n.* a coupling link with a safety closure, used by rock climbers.

car·a·cal /ˈkerəˌkal/ ▶*n.* a long-legged lynxlike cat (*Felis caracal*) with black tufted ears and a uniform brown coat, native to Africa and western Asia. Also called **AFRICAN LYNX** (see **LYNX**).

car·a·cole /ˈkarəˌkōl/ ▶*n.* a half turn to the right or left by a horse.
▶*v.* [*intr.*] (of a horse) perform a caracole.

car·a·cul ▶*n.* variant spelling of **KARAKUL**.

ca·rafe /kəˈraf; -ˈräf/ ▶*n.* an open-topped glass flask typically used for serving wine or water.

car·a·mel /ˈkarəməl; -ˌmel; ˈkärmel/ ▶*n.* sugar or syrup heated until it turns brown, used as a flavoring or coloring for food or drink. ■ the light brown color of this substance: *the liquid turns a pale caramel* | [as *adj.*] *a caramel sweater.* ■ a soft candy made with sugar and butter that have been melted and further heated.

car·a·mel·ize /ˈkarəməˌlīz; ˈkärmə-/ ▶*v.* [*intr.*] (of sugar or syrup) be converted into caramel. ■ [*tr.*] [usu. as *adj.*] (**caramelized**) cook (food) with sugar so that it becomes coated with caramel. —**car·a·mel·i·za·tion** /ˌkarəmələˌzāSHən/ *n.*

car·a·pace /ˈkarəˌpās/ ▶*n.* the hard upper shell of a turtle or crustacean.

car·at /ˈkarət/ ▶*n.* **1** a unit of weight for precious stones and pearls, now equivalent to 200 milligrams: *a half-carat diamond ring.* **2** chiefly British spelling of **KARAT.** ▷late Middle English (sense 2): from French, from Italian *carato*, from Arabic *ḳīrāṭ* (a unit of weight), from Greek *keration* 'fruit of the carob' (also denoting a unit of weight), diminutive of *keras* 'horn,' with reference to the elongated seedpod of the carob.

car·a·van /ˈkarəˌvan/ ▶*n.* **1** *hist.* a group of people, esp. traders or pilgrims, traveling together across a desert in Asia or North Africa. ■ any large group of people, typically with vehicles or animals traveling together, in single file: *a caravan of cars and trucks.* **2** *Brit.* a recreational vehicle; a trailer or camper. ■ a covered horse-drawn wagon: *a gypsy caravan.* ■ a covered truck; a van.

car·a·van·sa·ry /ˌkarəˈvansərē/ (*chiefly Brit.* also **car·a·van·se·rai** /-səˌrī/) ▶*n.* (*pl.* **-sa·ries** or **-se·rais** /-səˌrīz/) **1** *hist.* an inn with a central courtyard for travelers in the desert regions of Asia or North Africa. **2** a group of people traveling together; a caravan.

car·a·way /ˈkarəˌwā/ ▶*n.* (also **caraway seed**) the seeds of a

Mediterranean plant (*Carum carvi*) of the parsley family, used for flavoring and as a source of oil.

car·bide /ˈkärˌbīd/ ▶*n. Chem.* a binary compound of carbon with an element of lower or comparable electronegativity. ■ calcium carbide, used to generate acetylene by reaction with water and formerly used in portable lamps: [as *adj.*] *a carbide lamp.*

car·bine /ˈkärˌbīn; -ˌbēn/ ▶*n.* a light automatic rifle. ■ *hist.* a short rifle or musket used by cavalry.

car·bo·hy·drate /ˌkärbōˈhīˌdrāt/ ▶*n. Biochem.* any of a large group of organic compounds occurring in foods and living tissues and including sugars, starch, and cellulose. They contain hydrogen and oxygen in the same atomic ratio as water (2:1).

car·bo·load /ˈkärbō ˌlōd/ ▶*v.* [*intr.*] eat large amounts of carbohydrates, as in preparation for athletic endurance.

car·bon /ˈkärbən/ ▶*n.* the chemical element of atomic number 6, a non-metal that has two main forms (diamond and graphite) and that also occurs in impure form in charcoal, soot, and coal. (Symbol: **C**) ■ *Chem.* an atom of this element. ■ a piece of carbon paper or a carbon copy.

car·bon-14 ▶*n.* a long-lived naturally occurring radioactive carbon isotope of mass 14, used in carbon dating and as a tracer in biochemistry.

car·bo·nate ▶*n.* /ˈkärbənət; -ˌnāt/ a salt of the anion $CO_3{}^{2-}$, typically formed by reaction of carbon dioxide with bases.
▶*v.* /ˈkärbəˌnāt/ [*tr.*] [usu. as *adj.*] (**carbonated**) dissolve carbon dioxide in (a liquid): *a carbonated soft drink.* ■ *Chem.* convert into a carbonate, typically by reaction with carbon dioxide. —**car·bo·na·tion** /ˌkärbəˈnāSHən/ *n.*

car·bon cop·y ▶*n.* a copy of written or typed material made with carbon paper. ■ *fig.* a person or thing identical or very similar to another.

car·bon dat·ing ▶*n.* the determination of the age of an organic object from the relative proportions of the carbon isotopes carbon-12 and carbon-14 that it contains. The ratio between them changes as radioactive carbon-14 decays and is not replaced by exchange with the atmosphere.

car·bon di·ox·ide ▶*n.* a colorless, odorless gas, CO_2, produced by burning carbon and organic compounds and by respiration. It is naturally present in air (about 0.03 percent) and is absorbed by plants in photosynthesis.

car·bon·ic /kärˈbänik/ ▶*adj.* of or relating to carbon or its compounds, esp. carbon dioxide.

car·bon·ic ac·id ▶*n.* a very weak acid, H_2CO_3, formed in solution when carbon dioxide dissolves in water.

Car·bon·if·er·ous /ˌkärbəˈnifərəs/ ▶*adj. Geol.* of, relating to, or denoting the fifth period of the Paleozoic era, between the Devonian and Permian periods. ■ (**the Carboniferous**) [as *n.*] the Carboniferous period or the system of rocks deposited during it.

car·bon·ize /ˈkärbəˌnīz/ ▶*v.* [*tr.*] convert into carbon, typically by heating or burning, or during fossilization: *the steak was carbonized on the outside.* ■ [usu. as *adj.*] (**carbonized**) coat with carbon. —**car·bon·i·za·tion** /ˌkärbənəˈzāSHən/ *n.*

car·bon mon·ox·ide ▶*n.* a colorless, odorless, toxic flammable gas, CO, formed by incomplete combustion of carbon.

car·bon pa·per ▶*n.* thin paper coated with carbon or another pigmented substance, used for making copies of written or typed documents.

car·bon·yl /ˈkärbəˌnil/ ▶*n.* [as *adj.*] *Chem.* of or denoting the divalent radical =C=O, present in such organic compounds as aldehydes, ketones, amides, and esters, and in organic acids as part of the carboxyl group: *carbonyl compounds.*

car·bo·run·dum /ˌkärbəˈrəndəm/ ▶*n.* a very hard black solid consisting of silicon carbide, used as an abrasive.

car·box·yl /kärˈbäksəl/ ▶*n.* [as *adj.*] *Chem.* of or denoting the acid radical –COOH, present in most organic acids: *the carboxyl group.* —**car·box·yl·ic** /ˌkärbäkˈsilik/ *adj.*

car·boy /ˈkärˌboi/ ▶*n.* a large globular plastic bottle with a narrow neck, typically protected by a frame and used for holding acids or other corrosive liquids.

carbs /kärbz/ ▶*pl. n. inf.* dietary carbohydrates.

car·bun·cle /ˈkärˌbəNGkəl/ ▶*n.* **1** a severe abscess or multiple boil in the skin, typically infected with staphylococcus bacteria. **2** a bright red gem, in particular a garnet cut en cabochon. —**car·bun·cu·lar** /kärˈbəNGkyələr/ *adj.*

car·bu·re·tor /ˈkärb(y)əˌrātər/ (also **car·bu·ra·tor**, *Brit.* **car·bu·ret·tor**) ▶*n.* a device in an internal combustion engine for mixing air with a fine spray of liquid fuel.

car·bu·rize /ˈkärb(y)əˌrīz/ ▶*v.* [*trans.*] add carbon to (iron or steel), in particular by heating in the presence of carbon to harden the surface. —**car·bu·ri·za·tion** /ˌkärb(y)ərəˈzāsHən/ n.

car·ca·jou /ˈkärkəˌjōō; ˌzHōō/ ▶n. another term for the North American WOLVERINE.

car·cass /ˈkärkəs/ (Brit. also **car·case**) ▶n. the dead body of an animal. ■ the trunk of an animal such as a cow, sheep, or pig, for cutting up as meat. ■ the remains of a cooked bird after all the edible parts have been removed. ■ derog. or humorous a person's body, living or dead. ■ the structural framework of a building, ship, or piece of furniture. ■ fig. the remains of something being discarded, dismembered, or worthless: the floor is littered with the carcasses of newspapers.

car·cin·o·gen /kärˈsinəjən; ˈkärsənəˌjen/ ▶n. a substance capable of causing cancer in living tissue.

car·cin·o·gen·ic /ˌkärsənəˈjenik/ ▶adj. having the potential to cause cancer. —**car·ci·no·ge·nic·i·ty** /-ˌnōjəˈnisitē/ n.

car·ci·no·ma /ˌkärsəˈnōmə/ ▶n. (pl. **-no·mas** or **-no·ma·ta** /-ˈnōmətə/) a cancer arising in the epithelial tissue of the skin or of the lining of the internal organs. —**car·ci·no·ma·tous** /-ˈnōmətəs/ adj.

card[1] /kärd/ ▶n. **1** a piece of thick, stiff paper or thin pasteboard, in particular one used for writing or printing on: notes jotted down on a card. ■ such a piece of thick paper printed with a picture and used to send a message or greeting: a birthday card. ■ a small piece of such paper with a person's name and other details printed on it for identification, for example a business card. **2** a small rectangular piece of plastic issued by a bank, containing personal data in a machine-readable form and used chiefly to obtain cash or credit. ■ a similar piece of plastic used for other purposes such as paying for a telephone call or gaining entry to a room or building. **3** a playing card: a deck of cards. ■ (**cards**) a game played with playing cards. **4** Comput. short for EXPANSION CARD. **5** inf. a person regarded as odd or amusing. **6** a program of events at a racetrack. ■ a record of scores in a sports event; a scorecard. ■ a list of holes on a golf course, on which a player's scores are entered.
▶v. [tr.] **1** write (something) on a card, esp. for indexing. **2** check the identity card of (someone), in particular as evidence of legal drinking age. **3** inf. (in golf and other sports) score (a certain number of points on a scorecard): he carded 68 in the final round.
▶ □ **hold all the cards** be in a very strong or advantageous position. □ **in the cards** inf. very possible or likely: an overwhelming military triumph is in the cards. □ **play the —— card** exploit the specified issue or idea mentioned, esp. for political advantage: he saw an opportunity to play the peace card. □ **play one's cards right** make the best use of one's assets and opportunities. □ **put** (or **lay**) **one's cards on the table** be completely open and honest.

card[2] ▶v. [tr.] comb and clean (raw wool, hemp fibers, or similar material) with a sharp-toothed instrument in order to disentangle the fibers before spinning.
▶n. a toothed implement or machine for this purpose. —**card·er** n.

car·da·mom /ˈkärdəməm/ (also **car·da·mon** /-mən/) ▶n. **1** the aromatic seeds of a plant of the ginger family, used as a spice and also medicinally. **2** the Southeast Asian plant (Elettaria cardamomum) that bears these seeds.

card·board /ˈkärdˌbôrd/ ▶n. pasteboard or stiff paper: [as adj.] a cardboard box. ■ [as adj.] (of a character in a literary work) lacking depth and realism; artificial: its superficial, cardboard characters.

card·car·ry·ing ▶adj. registered as a member of a political party or labor union. ■ inf. humorous confirmed in or dedicated to a specified pursuit or outlook: a card-carrying pessimist.

car·di·ac /ˈkärdēˌak/ ▶adj. of or relating to the heart: a cardiac arrest.

car·di·gan /ˈkärdigən/ ▶n. a knitted sweater fastening down the front, typically with long sleeves. ▷mid 19th cent. (Crimean War): named after James Thomas Brudenel, 7th Earl of Cardigan (1797–1868), leader of the Charge of the Light Brigade, whose troops first wore such garments.

car·di·nal /ˈkärdnəl; ˈkärdn-əl/ ▶n. **1** a leading dignitary of the Roman Catholic Church, nominated by the pope and collectively forming the Sacred College. ■ (also **cardinal red**) a deep scarlet color like that of a cardinal's cassock. **2** a New World songbird of the bunting family, with a stout bill and conspicuous crest, in particular the **northern** (or **common**) **cardinal** (Cardinalis cardinalis), the male of which is scarlet with a black face.
▶adj. of the greatest importance; fundamental.

car·di·nal num·ber ▶n. a number denoting quantity (one, two, three, etc.), as opposed to an ordinal number (first, second, etc.).

car·di·nal sin ▶n. **1** another name for DEADLY SIN. **2** chiefly humorous

a serious error of judgment: the program was canceled for the biggest cardinal sin of them all—it dared to be intelligent.

car·di·o·gram /ˈkärdēəˌgram/ ▶n. a record of muscle activity within the heart made by a cardiograph.

car·di·o·graph /ˈkärdēəˌgraf/ ▶n. an instrument for recording heart muscle activity, such as an electrocardiograph. —**car·di·og·ra·pher** /ˌkärdēˈägrəfər/ n. —**car·di·og·ra·phy** /-ˈägrəfē/ n.

car·di·ol·o·gy /ˌkärdēˈäləjē/ ▶n. the branch of medicine that deals with diseases and abnormalities of the heart. —**car·di·o·log·i·cal** /ˌkärdēəˈläjikəl/ adj. —**car·di·ol·o·gist** /-jist/ n.

car·di·o·vas·cu·lar /ˌkärdēōˈvaskyələr/ ▶adj. Med. of or relating to the heart and blood vessels.

card sharp (also **card sharp·er** or **card shark**) ▶n. a person who cheats at cards in order to win money.

CARE /ke(ə)r/ ▶abbr. Cooperative for American Relief Everywhere, a large private organization that provides emergency assistance.

care /ke(ə)r/ ▶n. **1** the provision of what is necessary for the health, welfare, maintenance, and protection of someone or something: the care of the elderly. **2** serious attention or consideration applied to doing something correctly or to avoid damage or risk: he planned his departure with great care. ■ an object of concern or attention: the cares of family life. ■ a feeling of or occasion for anxiety: without a care in the world.
▶v. [intr.] **1** feel concern or interest; attach importance to something: they don't care about human life | [tr.] I don't care what she says. ■ feel affection or liking: you care very deeply for him. ■ (**care for something/care to do something**) like or be willing to do or have something: would you care for some tea? **2** (**care for**) look after and provide for the needs of: he has numerous animals to care for.
▶ □ **care of** at the address of: write to me care of Anne. □ **I** (or **he, she**, etc.) **couldn't** (or inf. also **could**) **care less** inf. used to express complete indifference: he couldn't care less about football. □ **for all you care** (or **he, she**, etc., **cares**) inf. used to indicate that someone feels no interest or concern: I could drown for all you care. □ **take care 1** [often in imper.] be cautious; keep oneself safe. ■ said to someone on leaving them: take care, see you soon. **2** make sure of doing something: he would take care to provide himself with an escape clause. □ **take care of 1** keep (someone or something) safe and provided for. **2** deal with (something).

ca·reen /kəˈrēn/ ▶v. **1** [tr.] turn (a ship) on its side for cleaning, caulking, or repair. ■ [intr.] (of a ship) tilt; lean over: a heavy flood tide caused my vessel to careen dizzily. **2** [intr.] move swiftly and in an uncontrolled way in a specified direction: an electric golf cart careened around the corner.

ca·reer /kəˈri(ə)r/ ▶n. an occupation undertaken for a significant period of a person's life and with opportunities for progress. ■ the time spent by a person in such an occupation or profession: the end of a distinguished career in the navy. ■ the progress through history of an institution or organization: the court has had a checkered career. ■ [as adj.] working permanently in or committed to a particular profession: a career diplomat. ■ [as adj.] (of a woman) interested in pursuing a profession rather than devoting all her time to child care and housekeeping.
▶v. [intr.] move swiftly and in an uncontrolled way in a specified direction: the car careered across the road and went through a hedge.

care·free /ˈke(ə)rˌfrē/ ▶adj. free from anxiety or responsibility. —**care·free·ness** n.

care·ful /ˈke(ə)rfəl/ ▶adj. **1** making sure of avoiding potential danger, mishap, or harm; cautious: I begged him to be more careful. ■ (**careful of/about**) anxious to protect (something) from harm or loss; solicitous: he was very careful of his reputation. ■ prudent in the use of something, esp. money: Ali had always been careful with money. **2** done with or showing thought and attention: a careful consideration of the facts. —**care·ful·ly** adv. —**care·ful·ness** n.

care·giv·er /ˈke(ə)rˌgivər/ ▶n. a family member or paid helper who regularly looks after a child or a sick, elderly, or disabled person. —**care·giv·ing** n. & adj.

care·less /ˈkerlis/ ▶adj. not giving sufficient attention or thought to avoiding harm or errors. ■ (of an action or its result) showing or caused by a lack of attention. ■ (**careless of/about**) not concerned or worried about: he was careless about his own safety. ■ showing no interest or effort; casual: she gave a careless shrug. —**care·less·ly** adv. —**care·less·ness** n.

ca·ress /kəˈres/ ▶v. [tr.] touch or stroke gently or lovingly: she caressed the girl's forehead | fig. [as adj.] (**caressing**) the caressing warmth of the sun.
▶n. a gentle or loving touch. —**ca·ress·ing·ly** adv.

Pronunciation Key ə ago, up; ər over, fur; ă hat; ā ate; ä car; CH chin; e let; ē see; e(ə)r air; i fit; ī by; i(ə)r ear; NG sing; ō go; ô law, for; oi toy; ŏŏ good; ōō goo; ou out; SH she; TH thin; TH then; (h)w why; ZH vision

car·et /ˈkarit/ ▸*n.* a mark (^, ⌄) placed below the line to indicate a proposed insertion in a printed or written text.

care·tak·er /ˈke(ə)rˌtākər/ ▸*n.* **1** a person employed to look after a public building or a house in the owner's absence. ■ [as *adj.*] holding power temporarily: *his was a caretaker regime.* **2** a person employed to look after people or animals. —**care·take** *v.*

care·worn /ˈke(ə)rˌwôrn/ ▸*adj.* tired and unhappy because of prolonged worry: *a careworn expression.*

car·go /ˈkärgō/ ▸*n.* (*pl.* **-goes** or **-gos**) goods carried on a ship, aircraft, or motor vehicle: *transportation of bulk cargo | a cargo of oil.*

Car·ib /ˈkarib/ ▸*n.* **1** a member of an indigenous South American people living mainly in coastal regions of French Guiana, Suriname, Guyana, and Venezuela. **2** the Cariban language of this people.
▸*adj.* of or relating to the Caribs or their language. ■ of or relating to Island Carib or Black Carib.

car·i·bou /ˈkarəˌbo͞o/ ▸*n.* (*pl.* same or **caribous**) a large North American reindeer (genus *Rangifer*), esp. the **woodland caribou** (*R. caribou*) and the **barren ground caribou** (*R. tarandus*).

car·i·ca·ture /ˈkarikəCHər/ -ˌCHŏŏr/ ▸*n.* a picture, description, or imitation of a person or thing in which certain striking characteristics are exaggerated in order to create a comic or grotesque effect. ■ the art or style of such exaggerated representation: *there are elements of caricature in the portrayal of the hero.* ■ a ludicrous or grotesque version of someone or something: *he looked like a caricature of his normal self.*
▸*v.* [*tr.*] (usu. **be caricatured**) make or give a comically or grotesquely exaggerated representation of (someone or something). —**car·i·ca·tur·al** /ˌkarikəˈCHŏŏrəl/ *adj.* —**car·i·ca·tur·ist** /-ˌCHŏŏrist/ *n.*

car·ies /ˈkerēz/ ▸*n.* decay and crumbling of a tooth or bone.

car·il·lon /ˈkarəˌlän; -lən/ ▸*n.* a set of bells in a tower, played using a keyboard or by an automatic mechanism similar to a piano roll. —**car·il·lon·neur** /ˌkarələˈnər/ *n.*

Ca·ri·na /kəˈrēnə; -ˈrī-/ *Astron.* ▸a southern constellation (the Keel) partly in the Milky Way, originally part of Argo. It contains the second brightest star in the sky, Canopus.

ca·ri·na /kəˈrēnə; -ˈrī-/ ▸*n.* (*pl.* **-nae** /-ˌnē/ or **-nas**) chiefly *Biol.* a keel-shaped structure, in particular: ■ *Zool.* the ridge of a bird's breastbone, to which the main flight muscles are attached. —**ca·ri·nal** *adj.*

car·ing /ˈke(ə)riNG/ ▸*adj.* displaying kindness and concern for others.
▸*n.* the work or practice of looking after those unable to care for themselves, esp. the sick and the elderly: [as *adj.*] *the caring professions.*

car·jack·ing /ˈkärˌjakiNG/ ▸*n.* the action of violently stealing an occupied car. —**car·jack** *v.* —**car·jack·er** /-ˌjakər/ *n.*

car·load /ˈkärˌlōd/ ▸*n.* the number of people that can travel in an automobile: *a carload of passengers.* ■ the quantity of goods that can be carried in a railroad freight car.

Car·lo·vin·gi·an /ˌkärləˈvinj(ē)ən/ ▸*adj.* & *n.* another term for CAROLIN-GIAN.

Car·mel·ite /ˈkärməˌlīt/ ▸*n.* a friar or nun of a contemplative Catholic order founded at Mount Carmel during the Crusades.
▸*adj.* of or relating to the Carmelites.

car·min·a·tive /kärˈminətiv; ˈkärməˌnātiv/ ▸*adj. Med.* (chiefly of a drug) relieving flatulence.
▸*n.* a drug of this kind.

car·mine /ˈkärmən; -ˌmīn/ ▸*n.* a vivid crimson color: [as *adj.*] *carmine roses.* ■ a vivid crimson pigment made from cochineal.

car·nage /ˈkärnij/ ▸*n.* the killing of a large number of people.

car·nal /ˈkärnl/ ▸*adj.* relating to physical, esp. sexual, needs and activities: *carnal desire.* —**car·nal·i·ty** /kärˈnalitē/ *n.* —**car·nal·ly** *adv.*

car·nal know·ledge ▸*n. dated, chiefly Law* sexual intercourse.

car·nas·si·al /kärˈnasēəl/ ▸*adj. Zool.* denoting the large upper premolar and lower molar teeth of a carnivore, adapted for shearing flesh.
▸*n.* a tooth of this type.

car·na·tion[1] /kärˈnāSHən/ ▸*n.* a double-flowered cultivated variety of clove pink (*Dianthus caryophyllus*) with gray-green leaves and showy pink, white, or red flowers.

car·na·tion[2] ▸*adj.* of a rosy pink color: *sage and carnation throw pillows.*
▸*n.* a rosy pink color.

car·nau·ba /kärˈnôbə; -ˈnoubə/ ▸*n.* a northeastern Brazilian fan palm (*Copernicia cerifera*) whose leaves exude a yellowish wax. ■ (also **car·nauba wax**) wax from this palm, formerly used as a polish and for making candles.

car·nel·ian /kärˈnēlyən/ ▸*n.* a semiprecious stone consisting of an orange or orange-red variety of chalcedony.

car·ni·val /ˈkärnəvəl/ ▸*n.* **1** a period of public revelry at a regular time each year, typically during the week before Lent in Roman Catholic countries, involving processions, music, dancing, and the use of masquerade. ■ *fig.* an exciting or riotous mixture of something: *the whole evening was a carnival of fun.* **2** a traveling amusement show or circus. —**car·ni·val·esque** /ˌkärnəvəˈlesk/ *adj.*

car·ni·vore /ˈkärnəˌvôr/ ▸*n.* an animal, esp. a mammal, that feeds on flesh.

car·niv·o·rous /kärˈnivərəs/ ▸*adj.* (of an animal) feeding on other animals. ■ (of a plant) able to trap and digest small animals, esp. insects. —**car·niv·o·rous·ly** *adv.* —**car·niv·o·rous·ness** *n.*

car·ob /ˈkarəb/ ▸*n.* **1** a powder extracted from the carob bean, used as a substitute for chocolate. **2** (also **carob tree**) a leguminous Arabian evergreen tree (*Ceratonia siliqua*) that bears long brownish-purple edible pods. Also called **locust tree**. ■ (also **carob bean**) the edible pod of this tree.

car·ol /ˈkarəl/ ▸*n.* a religious folk song or popular hymn, particularly one associated with Christmas.
▸*v.* (**car·oled, car·ol·ing; car·ol·led, car·ol·ling**) [*intr.*] sing Christmas songs or hymns, esp. in a group.

Car·o·lin·gi·an /ˌkarəˈlinj(ē)ən/ (also **Car·lo·vin·gi·an**) ▸*adj.* of or relating to the Frankish dynasty, founded by Charlemagne's father (Pepin III), that ruled in western Europe from 750 to 987. ■ denoting or relating to a style of minuscule script developed in France during the time of Charlemagne, on which modern lower-case letters are largely based.
▸*n.* a member of the Carolingian dynasty.

car·om /ˈkarəm/ ▸*n. Billiards* a stroke in which the cue ball strikes two balls successively. ■ (also **carom billiards**) any of the billiard games played on a table without pockets.
▸*v.* [*intr.*] make a carom; strike and rebound.

car·o·tene /ˈkarəˌtēn/ ▸*n. Chem.* an orange or red plant pigment found in carrots and many other plant structures. It is a terpenoid hydrocarbon with several isomers, of which one (**beta carotene**) is important in the diet as a precursor of vitamin A.

ca·rot·id /kəˈrätid/ ▸*adj.* of, relating to, or denoting the two main arteries that carry blood to the head and neck, and their two main branches.
▸*n.* each of these arteries. ▷early 17th cent.: from French *carotide* or modern Latin *carotides*, from Greek *karōtides*, plural of *karōtis* 'drowsiness,' from *karoun* 'stupefy' (because compression of these arteries was thought to cause stupor).

ca·rouse /kəˈrouz/ ▸*v.* [*intr.*] drink plentiful amounts of alcohol and enjoy oneself with others in a noisy, lively way: *they danced and caroused until the drink ran out* | [as *n.*] (**carousing**) *a night of carousing.*
▸*n.* a noisy, lively drinking party: *corporate carouses.* —**ca·rous·al** /-zəl/ *n.* —**ca·rous·er** *n.*

car·ou·sel /ˌkarəˈsel; ˈkarəˌsel/ (also **car·rou·sel**) ▸*n.* a merry-go-round. ■ a rotating machine or device, in particular a conveyor system at an airport from which arriving passengers collect their luggage.

carp[1] /kärp/ ▸*n.* (*pl.* same) a deep-bodied freshwater fish of the minnow family, typically with barbels around the mouth. Carp are farmed for food in some parts of the world.

carp[2] ▸*v.* [*intr.*] complain or find fault continually, typically about trivial matters: *I don't want to carp about the way you did it.* —**carp·er** *n.*

car·pal /ˈkärpəl/ ▸*n.* any of the eight small bones forming the wrist. See CARPUS. ■ any of the equivalent bones in an animal's forelimb.
▸*adj.* of or relating to these bones.

car·pal tun·nel syn·drome ▸*n.* a painful condition of the hand and fingers caused by compression of a major nerve where it passes over the carpal bones through a passage at the front of the wrist. It may be caused by repetitive movements over a long period, or by fluid retention.

car·pel /ˈkärpəl/ ▸*n. Bot.* the female reproductive organ of a flower, consisting of an ovary, a stigma, and usually a style. It may occur singly or as one of a group. —**car·pel·lar·y** /-ˌlerē/ *adj.*

car·pen·ter /ˈkärpəntər/ ▸*n.* a person who makes and repairs wooden objects and structures.
▸*v.* [*tr.*] (usu. **be carpentered**) make by shaping wood: *the rails were carpentered very skillfully.* ■ [*intr.*] do the work of a carpenter. ▷Middle English: from Anglo-Norman French, from Old French *carpentier, charpentier*, from late Latin *carpentarius (artifex)* 'carriage (maker),' from *carpentum* 'wagon,' of Gaulish origin; related to *car.*

car·pen·ter ant ▸*n.* a large ant (genus *Camponotus*) that burrows into wood to nest.

car·pen·try /ˈkärpəntrē/ ▸*n.* the activity or occupation of making or repairing things in wood. ■ the work made or done by a carpenter.

car·pet /ˈkärpit/ ▸*n.* a floor or stair covering made from thick woven

fabric, typically shaped to fit a particular room: *the house has fitted carpets throughout* | *the floor was covered with carpet*. ■ a large rug, typically an oriental one: *priceless Persian carpets*. ■ fig. a thick or soft expanse or layer of something: *carpets of snowdrops and crocuses*. ■ inf. a carpetlike artificial playing surface on a tennis court or an athletic field.
▶v. (-pet·ed, -pet·ing) [tr.] (usu. **be carpeted**) cover (a floor or stairs) with a carpet. ■ fig. cover with a thick or soft expanse or layer of something: *the meadows are carpeted with flowers*.

car·pet·bag /ˈkärpitˌbag/ ▶n. a traveling bag of a kind originally made of carpeting or carpetlike material.
▶v. [intr.] act as a carpetbagger: [as *adj.*] (**carpetbagging**) *rich, carpetbagging developers*.

car·pet·bag·ger /ˈkärpitˌbagər/ ▶n. derog. a political candidate who seeks election in an area where they have no local connections. ■ hist. (in the U.S.) a person from the northern states who went to the South after the Civil War to profit from Reconstruction. ■ a person perceived as an unscrupulous opportunist.

car·pool /ˈkärˌpo͞ol/ ▶n. an arrangement between people to make a regular journey in a single vehicle, typically with each person taking turns to drive the others. ■ a group of people with such an arrangement.
▶v. [intr.] form or participate in a carpool. —**car·pool·er** n.

car·port /ˈkärˌpôrt/ ▶n. a shelter for a car consisting of a roof supported on posts, built beside a house.

car·pus /ˈkärpəs/ ▶n. (*pl.* **-pi** /-ˌpī; -ˌpē/) the group of small bones between the main part of the forelimb and the metacarpus in terrestrial vertebrates. The eight bones of the human carpus form the wrist and part of the hand.

car·ra·geen /ˈkarəˌgēn/ (also **car·ra·gheen** or **carrageen moss**) ▶n. an edible red shoreline seaweed (*Chondrus crispus*) found in both Eurasia and North America and used to produce an edible thickening or emulsifying agent (**carrageenan**).

car·rel /ˈkarəl/ ▶n. a small cubicle with a desk for the use of a reader or student in a library. ■ hist. a small enclosure or study in a cloister.

car·riage /ˈkarij/ ▶n. **1** a means of conveyance, in particular: ■ a four-wheeled passenger vehicle pulled by two or more horses: *a horse-drawn carriage*. ■ a baby carriage. ■ a shopping cart. ■ a wheeled support for moving a heavy object such as a gun. ■ Brit. a passenger car of a train: *the first-class carriages*. **2** the transporting of items or merchandise from one place to another. ■ the cost of such a procedure. **3** a moving part of a machine that carries other parts into the required position: *a typewriter carriage*. **4** a person's bearing or deportment: *her carriage was graceful*.

car·riage house ▶n. a building for housing a horse-drawn carriage, typically such a building that has been converted into a dwelling.

car·ri·er /ˈkarēər/ ▶n. **1** a person or thing that carries, holds, or conveys something: *water carriers*. **2** a person or company that undertakes the professional conveyance of goods or people: *Pan Am was the third U.S. carrier to cease operations in 1991.* ■ a vessel or vehicle for transporting people or things, esp. goods in bulk: *the largest timber carrier*. ■ an aircraft carrier. ■ a company that provides facilities for conveying telecommunications messages. **3** a person or animal that transmits a disease-causing organism to others. Typically, the carrier suffers no symptoms of the disease. ■ a person or other organism that possesses a particular gene, esp. as a single copy whose effect is masked by a dominant allele, so that the associated characteristic (such as a hereditary disease) is not displayed but may be passed to offspring. **4** a substance used to support or convey another substance such as a pigment, catalyst, or radioactive material. ■ Biochem. a molecule that transfers a specified molecule or ion within the body, esp. across a cell membrane.

car·ri·er pig·eon ▶n. a homing pigeon trained to carry messages tied to its neck or leg.

car·ri·on /ˈkarēən/ ▶n. the decaying flesh of dead animals.

car·rot /ˈkarət/ ▶n. **1** a tapering orange-colored root eaten as a vegetable. **2** a cultivated plant (*Daucus carota*) of the parsley family with feathery leaves, which yields this vegetable. **3** an offer of something enticing as a means of persuasion. —**car·rot·y** adj.

car·rou·sel ▶n. variant spelling of **CAROUSEL**.

car·ry /ˈkarē/ ▶v. (-ries, -ried) [tr.] **1** support and move (someone or something) from one place to another: *medics were carrying a wounded man on a stretcher*. ■ transport: *the train service carries 20,000 passengers daily*. ■ have on one's person and take with one wherever one goes: *the money he was carrying was not enough to pay the fine* | fig. *she had carried the secret all her life*. ■ conduct; transmit: *nerves carry visual information from the eyes*. ■ be infected with (a disease) and liable to transmit it to others: *ticks can carry Lyme disease*. ■ transfer (a figure) to an adjacent

column during an arithmetical operation (esp. when a column of digits adds up to more than ten). **2** support the weight of: *the bridge is capable of carrying even the heaviest loads*. ■ be pregnant with: *she was carrying twins*. ■ (**carry oneself**) stand and move in a specified way: *she carried herself straight and tall*. ■ assume or accept (responsibility or blame). ■ be responsible for the effectiveness or success of: *they relied on dialogue to carry the plot*. **3** have as a feature or consequence: *being a combat sport, karate carries with it the risk of injury*. **4** take or develop (an idea or activity) to a specified point: *he carried the criticism much further*. ■ (of a gun or similar weapon) propel (a missile) to a specified distance. ■ (of a ball) move or be hit a specified distance: *the balls seem to carry well in that ballpark*. ■ Golf hit the ball over and beyond (a particular point). **5** (often **be carried**) approve (a proposed measure) by a majority of votes: *the resolution was carried by a two-to-one majority*. ■ persuade (colleagues or followers) to support one's policy: *he could not carry the cabinet*. ■ gain (a state or district) in an election. **6** (of a newspaper or a television or radio station) publish or broadcast: *the paper carried a detailed account of the current crisis*. ■ (of a retail outlet) keep a regular stock of (particular goods for sale). ■ have visible on the surface: *the product does not carry the "UL" symbol*. ■ be known by (a name): *some products carry the same names as overseas beers*. **7** [intr.] (of a sound or a person's voice) be audible at a distance: *his voice carried clearly across the room*.
▶phrasal v. □ **be/get carried away** lose self-control: *I got carried away when describing the final game*. □ **carry something off** succeed in doing something difficult: *he could not have carried it off without help*. □ **carry on 1** continue an activity or task: *carry on with what you were doing*. **2** inf. behave in an extreme way: *she carries on about television programming*. **3** inf. be engaged in a love affair, typically one of which the speaker disapproves: *she was carrying on with young Adam*. □ **carry something on** engage in an activity: *he could not carry on a logical conversation*. □ **carry something out** perform a task or planned operation. □ **carry over** extend beyond the normal or original area of application: *his artistic practice is clearly carrying over into his social thought*. □ **carry something over** retain something and apply or deal with it in a new context: *much of the wartime economic planning was carried over into the next decade*. ■ postpone an event: *the match had to be carried over till Sunday*. □ **carry something through** bring a project to completion. ■ bring something safely out of difficulties: *he was the only one who could carry the country through*.
▶n. (*pl.* **-ries**) **1** an act of lifting and transporting something from one place to another: *we did a carry of equipment*. ■ Football an act of running with the ball from scrimmage. ■ the action of keeping something, esp. a gun, on one's person: *this pistol is the right choice for on-duty or off-duty carry*. ■ hist. a place or route between navigable waters over which boats or supplies had to be carried. ■ the transfer of a figure into an adjacent column (or the equivalent part of a computer memory) during an arithmetical operation. ■ Finance the maintenance of an investment position in a securities market, esp. with regard to the costs or profits accruing. **2** (in golf) the distance a ball travels before reaching the ground. ■ (in golf) the distance a ball must travel to reach a certain destination. ■ the range of a gun or similar weapon.
▶ □ **carry the day** be victorious or successful. □ **carry weight** be influential or important.

car·ry·back note /ˈkarēˌbak/ ▶n. Finance a negotiable promissory note representing the value of real estate when the seller has provided the financing.

car·ry·out ▶adj. & n. another term for **TAKEOUT** (sense 1).

car·sick /ˈkärˌsik/ ▶adj. affected with nausea caused by the motion of a car or other vehicle in which one is traveling. —**car·sick·ness** n.

cart /kärt/ ▶n. a strong open vehicle with two or four wheels, typically used for carrying loads and pulled by a horse. ■ a light two-wheeled open vehicle pulled by a single horse and used as a means of transport. ■ a shallow open container on wheels that may be pulled or pushed by hand. ■ a shopping cart.
▶v. [tr.] **1** (often **be carted**) convey or put in a cart or similar vehicle: *the produce was packed in crates and carted to Kansas City*. **2** [tr.] inf. carry (a heavy or cumbersome object) with difficulty: *they carted the piano down three flights of stairs*. ■ remove or convey (someone) somewhere unceremoniously: *they carted off the refugees in the middle of the night*. —**cart·er** n.; **cart·ful** /-ˌfo͝ol/ n. (*pl.* **-fuls**).
▶ □ **put the cart before the horse** reverse the proper order or procedure of something.

cart·age /'kärtij/ ▸ n. the transporting of something in a cart or other vehicle. ■ the cost of such a procedure.

carte blanche /'kärt 'blänsh, 'blänch/ ▸ n. complete freedom to act as one wishes or thinks best: *we were given carte blanche.*

car·tel /kär'tel/ ▸ n. an association of manufacturers or suppliers with the purpose of maintaining prices at a high level and restricting competition: *the Colombian drug cartels.* ■ *chiefly hist.* a coalition or cooperative arrangement between political parties intended to promote a mutual interest.

Car·te·sian /kär'tēzhən/ ▸ adj. of or relating to Descartes and his ideas. ▸ n. a follower of Descartes. —**Car·te·sian·ism** /-,nizəm/ n.

Car·te·sian co·or·di·nates ▸ pl. n. Math. numbers that indicate the location of a point relative to a fixed reference point (the origin), being its shortest (perpendicular) distances from two fixed axes (or three planes defined by three fixed axes) that intersect at right angles at the origin.

Car·thu·sian /kär'TH(y)ōōzhən/ ▸ n. a monk or nun of an austere contemplative order founded by St. Bruno in 1084. ▸ adj. of or relating to this order.

car·ti·lage /'kärtl-ij/ ▸ n. firm, whitish, flexible connective tissue found in various forms in the larynx and respiratory tract, in structures such as the external ear, and in the articulating surfaces of joints. ■ a particular structure made of this tissue. —**car·ti·lag·i·noid** /,kärtl'ajə,noid/ adj. —**car·ti·lag·i·nous** /,kärtl'ajənəs/ adj.

car·ti·lag·i·nous fish ▸ n. a fish of a class (Chondrichthyes) distinguished by having a skeleton of cartilage rather than bone, including the sharks, rays, and chimeras.

car·tog·ra·phy /kär'tägrəfē/ ▸ n. the science or practice of drawing maps. —**car·tog·ra·pher** /-fər/ n. —**car·to·graph·ic** /,kärtə'grafik/ —**car·to·graph·i·cal** /,kärtə'grafikəl/ adj. —**car·to·graph·i·cal·ly** /,kärtə'grafik(ə)lē/ adv.

car·ton /'kärtn/ ▸ n. a light box or container, typically one made of waxed cardboard or plastic in which drinks or foodstuffs are packaged.

car·toon /kär'tōōn/ ▸ n. **1** a simple drawing showing the features of its subjects in a humorously exaggerated way, esp. a satirical one in a newspaper or magazine. ■ a comic strip. ■ *fig.* a simplified or exaggerated version or interpretation of something: *this movie is a cartoon of rural life in America.* **2** a motion picture using animation techniques to photograph a sequence of drawings rather than real people or objects. **3** a full-size drawing made by an artist as a preliminary design for a painting or other work of art. ▸ v. [tr.] (usu. **be cartooned**) make a drawing of (someone) in a simplified or exaggerated way: *she has a face with enough character to be cartooned.* —**car·toon·ish** adj. —**car·toon·ist** /-ist/ n. —**car·toon·y** adj.

car·touche /kär'tōōsh/ ▸ n. a carved tablet or drawing representing a scroll with rolled-up ends, used ornamentally or bearing an inscription. ■ *Archaeol.* an oval or oblong enclosing a group of Egyptian hieroglyphs, typically representing the name and title of a monarch.

car·tridge /'kärtrij/ ▸ n. a container holding a spool of photographic film, a quantity of ink, or other item or substance, designed for insertion into a mechanism. ■ a casing containing a charge and a bullet or shot for small arms or an explosive charge for blasting. ■ a component carrying the stylus on the pickup head of a record player.

cart·wheel /'kärt,(h)wēl/ ▸ n. **1** the wheel of a cart. **2** a circular sideways handspring with the arms and legs extended. ▸ v. [intr.] perform such a handspring or handsprings.

carve /kärv/ ▸ v. [tr.] **1** (often **be carved**) cut (a hard material) in order to produce an aesthetically pleasing object or design: *the wood was carved with runes.* ■ produce (an object) by cutting and shaping a hard material: *the altar was carved from a block of solid jade.* ■ produce (an inscription or design) by cutting into hard material: *an inscription was carved over the doorway* ‖ *fig. the river carved a series of gorges into the plain.* **2** cut (cooked meat) into slices for eating. ■ cut (a slice of meat) from a larger piece. ▸ phrasal v. □ **carve something out 1** take something from a larger whole, esp. with difficulty: *carving out a 5 percent share of the overall vote.* **2** establish or create something through painstaking effort: *he managed to carve out a successful photographic career for himself.*

carve·out /'kärv,out/ ▸ n. **1** an entity separated from a larger one and given separate treatment, in particular: ■ a small company created from a larger one. ■ a class of medical procedures treated separately with regard to insurance coverage. ■ a class of employees treated separately with regard to benefits. **2** the activity of effecting such a separation.

carv·er /'kärvər/ ▸ n. **1** a person who carves wood, stone, ivory, coral,

etc., esp. professionally. **2** a knife designed for slicing meat. **3** a person who cuts and serves the meat at a meal.

carv·ing /'kärviNG/ ▸ n. an object or design cut from a hard material as an artistic work.

car·y·at·id /,karē'atid; 'karēə,tid/ ▸ n. (pl. **car·y·at·ids** or **car·y·at·i·des** /,karē'atə,dēz/) Archit. a stone carving of a draped female figure, used as a pillar to support the entablature of a Greek or Greek-style building.

cas·bah /'kas,bä/ (also **kas·bah**) ▸ n. the citadel of a North African city. ■ (**the casbah**) the area surrounding such a citadel, typically the old part of a city.

cas·cade /kas'kād/ ▸ n. **1** a small waterfall, typically one of several that fall in stages down a steep rocky slope. ■ a mass of something that falls or hangs in copious or luxuriant quantities: *a cascade of pink bougainvillea.* ■ a large number or amount of something occurring or arriving in rapid succession: *a cascade of antiwar literature.* **2** a process whereby something, typically information or knowledge, is successively passed on: [as adj.] *the greater the number of people who are well briefed, the wider the cascade effect.* ■ a succession of devices or stages in a process, each of which triggers or initiates the next. ▸ v. [intr.] (of water) pour downward rapidly and in large quantities: *water was cascading down the stairs.* ■ fall or hang in copious or luxuriant quantities: *blonde hair cascaded down her back.*

case[1] /kās/ ▸ n. **1** an instance of a particular situation; an example of something occurring: *a case of mistaken identity.* ■ the situation affecting or relating to a particular person or thing; one's circumstances or position: *I'll make an exception in your case.* ■ an incident or set of circumstances under police investigation: *a murder case.* **2** an instance of a disease, or problem: *200,000 cases of hepatitis B.* ■ a person suffering from a disease or injury: *most breast cancer cases were older women.* ■ the circumstances or particular problem of a person who requires or receives professional attention: *the welfare office discussed his case.* ■ inf. a person whose situation is regarded as pitiable or as having no chance of improvement: *Vicky was a very sad case.* ■ inf., dated an amusing or eccentric person. **3** a legal action, esp. one to be decided in a court of law: *a former employee brought the case against the council.* ■ a set of facts or arguments supporting one side in such a legal action: *the case for the defense.* ■ a legal action that has been decided and may be cited as a precedent. ■ a set of facts or arguments supporting one side of a debate or controversy: *the case against tobacco advertising.* **4** Gram. any of the inflected forms of a noun, adjective, or pronoun that express the semantic relation of the word to other words in the sentence: *the accusative case.* ■ such a relation whether indicated by inflection or not: *English normally expresses case by the use of prepositions.* ▸ □ **as the case may be** according to the circumstances (used when referring to two or more possible alternatives): *the authorities will decide if they are satisfied or not satisfied, as the case may be.* □ **in any case** whatever happens or may have happened. ■ used to confirm or support a point or idea just mentioned: *he wasn't allowed out yet, and in any case he wasn't well enough.* □ **(just) in case 1** as a provision against something happening or being true: *we put on thick sweaters, in case it was cold.* **2** if it is true: *in case you haven't figured it out, let me explain.* □ **in case of** in the event of (a particular situation): *what to do in case of fire.* □ **in that case** if that happens or has happened; if that is the situation: *"I'm free this evening." "In that case, why not have dinner with me?"* □ **on someone's case** inf. continually criticizing or harassing someone.

case[2] ▸ n. a container designed to hold or protect something: *he placed the trumpet safely in its velvet-lined case.* ■ the outer protective covering of a natural or manufactured object: *a seed case.* ■ an item of luggage; a suitcase. ■ a box containing bottles or cans of a beverage, sold as a unit. ■ Printing a partitioned container for loose metal type. ■ each of the two forms, capital or minuscule, in which a letter of the alphabet may be written or printed. See also **UPPERCASE, LOWERCASE.** ▸ v. [tr.] (usu. **be cased**) **1** surround in a material or substance: *the towers are of steel cased in granite.* ■ enclose in a protective container. **2** inf. reconnoiter (a place) before carrying out a robbery: *I was casing the joint.*

case-hard·en ▸ v. [tr.] [often as adj.] (**case-hardened**) harden the surface of (a material). ■ give a hard surface to (iron or steel) by carburizing it: *a case-hardened steel anvil.* ■ fig. make (someone) callous or tough.

case his·to·ry ▸ n. a record of a person's background or medical history kept by a doctor or social worker.

ca·sein /kā'sēn; 'kāsēən/ ▸ n. the main protein present in milk and (in coagulated form) in cheese. It is used in processed foods and in adhesives, paints, and other industrial products.

case law ▸ *n.* (also **caselaw**) the law as established by the outcome of former cases. Compare with **COMMON LAW**.

case·load /'kās,lōd/ ▸ *n.* the amount of work (in terms of number of cases) with which a doctor, lawyer, or social worker is concerned at one time.

case·ment /'kāsmənt/ ▸ *n.* a window or part of a window set on a hinge so that it opens like a door: [as *adj.*] *casement windows.* ■ *chiefly poetic/lit.* a window. ■ the sash of a sash window.

case-sen·si·tive ▸ *adj. Comput.* (of a program or function) differentiating between capital and lowercase letters. ■ (of input) treated differently depending on whether it is in capitals or lowercase text.

case stud·y ▸ *n.* **1** a process or record of research in which detailed consideration is given to the development of a particular person, group, or situation over a period of time. **2** a particular instance of something used or analyzed in order to illustrate a thesis or principle: *deregulation provides a case study of the effects of the internal market.*

case·work[1] /'kās,wərk/ ▸ *n.* social work directly concerned with individuals, esp. that involving a study of a person's family history and personal circumstances. —**case·work·er** *n.*

case·work[2] ▸ *n.* the decorative outer case protecting the workings of a complex mechanism such as an organ or harpsichord.

cash[1] /kaSH/ ▸ *n.* money in coins or notes, as distinct from checks, money orders, or credit: *the staff were paid in cash | a discount for cash.* ■ money in any form, esp. that which is immediately available.
▸ *v.* [*tr.*] give or obtain notes or coins for (a check or money order). ■ *Bridge* lead (a high card) so as to take the opportunity to win a trick.
▸ *phrasal v.* □ **cash in** *inf.* take advantage of or exploit (a situation): *the breweries were cashing in on the rediscovered taste for real ales.* □ **cash something in** convert an insurance policy, savings account, or other investment into money. □ **cash something out** another way of saying **CASH SOMETHING IN**. —**cash·a·ble** *adj.* —**cash·less** *adj.*

cash[2] ▸ *n.* (*pl.* same) *hist.* a coin of low value from China, southern India, or Southeast Asia.

cash and car·ry ▸ *n.* a system of wholesale trading whereby goods are paid for in full at the time of purchase and taken away by the purchaser. ■ a wholesale store operating this system.

cash cow ▸ *n. inf.* a business, investment, or product that provides a steady income or profit: *traditional cash cows like cars and VCRs.* ■ a person or organization that is a source of easy profit.

cash crop ▸ *n.* a crop produced for its commercial value rather than for use by the grower. —**cash crop·ping** *n.*

cash·ew /'kaSH,ōō; kə'SHōō/ ▸ *n.* **1** (also **cashew nut**) an edible kidney-shaped nut, rich in oil and protein. **2** (also **cashew tree**) a bushy tropical American tree (*Anacardium occidentale*), bearing cashew nuts singly at the tip of each swollen fruit. The **cashew family** (Anacardiaceae) also includes the mangoes, pistachios, sumacs, and poison ivy.

cash flow ▸ *n.* the total amount of money being transferred into and out of a business, esp. as affecting liquidity.

cash·ier[1] /ka'SHi(ə)r/ ▸ *n.* a person handling payments and receipts in a store, bank, or other business.

cash·ier[2] ▸ *v.* [*tr.*] (usu. **be cashiered**) dismiss someone from the armed forces in disgrace because of a serious misdemeanor. ■ *inf.* suspend or dismiss someone from an office, position, or membership: *the team owner had been cashiered for consorting with a gambler.*

cash·mere /'kaZH,mi(ə)r; 'kaSH-/ ▸ *n.* fine soft wool, originally that from the Kashmir goat. ■ woolen material made from or resembling such wool: [as *adj.*] *a cashmere sweater.*

cash reg·is·ter ▸ *n.* a machine used in places of business for regulating money transactions with customers. It typically has a drawer for cash and totals, displays, and records the amount of each sale.

cas·ing /'kāsiNG/ ▸ *n.* **1** a cover or shell that protects or encloses something: *a waterproof casing.* **2** the frame around a door or window.

ca·si·no /kə'sēnō/ ▸ *n.* (*pl.* **-nos**) a public room or building where gambling games are played.

cask /kask/ ▸ *n.* a large barrel-like container made of wood, metal, or plastic, used for storing liquids, typically alcoholic drinks. ■ the quantity of liquid held in such a container: *a cask of cider.*

cas·ket /'kaskit/ ▸ *n.* a small ornamental box or chest for holding jewels, letters, or other valuable objects. ■ a coffin.

cas·sa·ta /kə'sätə/ ▸ *n.* a Neapolitan ice cream containing candied fruit and nuts.

cas·sa·va /kə'sävə/ ▸ *n.* **1** the starchy tuberous root of a tropical tree, used as food in tropical countries. Also called **MANIOC**. ■ a starch or flour obtained from such a root. **2** the shrubby tree (genus *Manihot*) of the spurge family from which this root is obtained, native to tropical America.

cas·se·role /'kasə,rōl/ ▸ *n.* a kind of stew that is cooked slowly in an oven: *a chicken casserole.* ■ a large covered dish, typically of earthenware or glass, used for cooking such stews.

cas·sette /kə'set/ ▸ *n.* a sealed plastic unit containing a length of audiotape wound on a pair of spools, for insertion into a recorder or playback device. ■ a similar unit containing videotape, film, or other material for insertion into a machine.

cas·sia /'kaSHə/ ▸ *n.* **1** a tree, shrub, or herbaceous plant (genus *Cassia*) of the pea family, native to warm climates and yielding a variety of products, including medicinal drugs. **2** (also **cassia bark**) the aromatic bark of an eastern Asian tree (*Cinnamomum aromaticum*) of the laurel family, yielding an inferior kind of cinnamon.

cas·sis /ka'sēs/ (also **crème de cassis** /,krem də/) ▸ *n.* a syrupy liqueur flavored with black currants and produced mainly in Burgundy.

cas·sock /'kasək/ ▸ *n.* a full-length garment of a single color worn by certain Christian clergy, members of church choirs, acolytes, and others having some particular office in a church. —**cas·socked** *adj.*

cas·sou·let /,kasə'lā/ ▸ *n.* a stew made with meat and beans.

cas·so·war·y /'kasə,werē/ ▸ *n.* (*pl.* **-ies**) a large flightless bird (genus *Casuarius*, family Casuariidae) native mainly to the forests of New Guinea.

cast[1] /kast/ ▸ *v.* [*tr.*] (*past* **cast** /kast/) **1** throw (something) forcefully in a specified direction: *lemmings cast themselves off the cliff | fig. individuals who do not accept the norms are cast out from the group.* ■ throw (something) so as to cause it to spread over an area: *the fishermen cast a large net around a school of tuna.* ■ direct (one's eyes or a look) at something: *she cast down her eyes.* ■ throw the hooked end of (a fishing line) out into the water. ■ register (a vote). ■ let down (an anchor or sounding line). ■ *Hunting* let loose (hounds) on a scent. ■ [*intr.*] *Hunting* (of a dog) search in different directions for a lost scent. **2** cause (light or shadow) to appear on a surface: *the moon cast a pale light over the cottages.* ■ cause (uncertainty or disparagement) to be associated with something: *journalists cast doubt on the government's version of events.* ■ cause (a magic spell) to take effect: *the witch cast a spell on her to turn her into a beast | fig. the city casts a spell on the visitor.* **3** discard: *the issue was cast from the list of concerns.* ■ shed (skin or horns) in the process of growth. ■ (of a horse) lose (a shoe). **4** shape (metal or other material) by pouring it into a mold while molten. ■ make (an object) in this way: *a bell was cast for the church.* ■ arrange and present in a specified form or style: *he issued statements cast in tones of reason.* ■ calculate and record details of (a horoscope). **5** [*intr.*] (in country dancing) change one's position by moving a certain number of places in a certain direction along the outside of the line in which one is dancing.
▸ *phrasal v.* □ **cast aside** discard or reject: *they cast aside the principles of their youth.* □ **cast off** (or **cast something off**) **1** *Knitting* take the stitches off the needle by looping each over the next to finish the edge. **2** set a boat or ship free from its moorings. □ **cast on** (or **cast something on**) *Knitting* make the first row of a specified number of loops on the needle.
▸ *n.* **1** an object made by shaping molten metal or similar material in a mold: *bronze casts of the sculpture.* ■ (also **plaster cast**) a mold used to make such an object. ■ (also **plaster cast**) a bandage stiffened with plaster of Paris, molded to the shape of a limb that is broken and used to support and protect it. **2** an act of throwing something forcefully. ■ *archaic* at dice, a throw or a number thrown. ■ *Fishing* a throw of a fishing line. **3** the form or appearance of something, esp. someone's features: *she had a somewhat masculine cast of countenance.* ■ the character of something: *this question is for minds of a more philosophical cast than mine.* ■ the overall appearance of someone's skin or hair as determined by a tinge of a particular color: *the olive cast of his skin.* **4** a slight squint: *he had a cast in one eye.* **5** a convoluted mass of earth or sand ejected onto the surface by a burrowing worm. ■ a pellet regurgitated by a hawk or owl. **6** a search made by a hound or pack of hounds over a wide area to find a trail.

cast[2] ▸ *n.* the actors taking part in a play, movie, or other production.
▸ *v.* (*past* and *past part.* **cast**) [*tr.*] assign a part in a play, movie, or other production to (an actor): *he was cast as the Spanish dancer | fig. a campaign for good nutrition, in which red meat is cast as the enemy.* ■ allocate parts in (a play, movie, or other production).

cas·ta·nets /,kastə'nets/ ▸ *pl. n.* small concave pieces of wood, ivory, or

---

plastic, joined in pairs by a cord and clicked together by the fingers as a rhythmic accompaniment to Spanish dancing. ▷early 17th cent.: from Spanish *castañeta*, diminutive of *castaña*, from Latin *castanea* 'chestnut.'

cast·a·way /'kastə,wā/ ▶n. a person who has been shipwrecked and stranded in an isolated place. ■ an outcast.

caste /kast/ ▶n. each of the hereditary classes of Hindu society, distinguished by relative degrees of ritual purity or pollution and of social status. ■ the system of dividing society into such classes. ■ any class or group of people who inherit privileges or are perceived as socially distinct: *those educated in private schools belong to a privileged caste.* ■ *Entomol.* (in some social insects) a physically distinct individual with a particular function in the society. ▷mid 16th cent. (in the general sense 'race, breed'): from Spanish and Portuguese *casta* 'lineage, race, breed,' feminine of *casto* 'pure, unmixed,' from Latin *castus* 'chaste.'

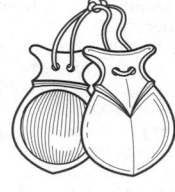

castanets

cas·tel·lat·ed /'kastə,lātid/ ▶adj. **1** having battlements: *a castellated tower.* ■ (of a nut or other mechanical part) having grooves or slots on its upper face. **2** having a castle or several castles: *the castellated hills.*

cast·er /'kastər/ ▶n. **1** a person who casts something or a machine for casting something. **2** *Fishing* a fly pupa used as bait. **3** each of a set of small wheels, free to swivel in any direction, fixed to the legs or base of a heavy piece of furniture so that it can be moved easily. **4** the angular inclination of a steering pivot or kingpin, esp. that of the front wheel of a vehicle. **5** a small container with holes in the top, esp. one used for sprinkling sugar or pepper.

cas·ti·gate /'kastə,gāt/ ▶v. [tr.] *formal* reprimand (someone) severely: *he was castigated for not setting a good example.* —**cas·ti·ga·tion** /,kastə-'gāSHən/ n. —**cas·ti·ga·tor** /-,gātər/ n. —**cas·ti·ga·to·ry** /-gə,tôrē/ adj.

cast·ing /'kasting/ ▶n. an object made by pouring molten metal or other material into a mold.

cast i·ron ▶n. a hard, relatively brittle alloy of iron and carbon that can be readily cast in a mold and contains a higher proportion of carbon than steel (typically 2.0–4.3 percent). ■ [as adj.] *fig.* firm and unchangeable: *there are no cast-iron guarantees.*

cas·tle /'kasəl/ ▶n. a large building or group of buildings fortified against attack with thick walls, battlements, towers, and in many cases a moat. ■ a magnificent and imposing mansion, esp. one that is the home or former home of a member of the nobility. [in names] *Castle Howard.* ■ *inf. Chess* old-fashioned term for **ROOK**². ▶v. [intr.] [often as n.] (**castling**) *Chess* make a special move (no more than once in a game by each player) in which the king is transferred from its original square two squares along the back rank toward the corner square of a rook, which is then transferred to the square passed over by the king. —**cas·tled** /'kasəld/ adj. (archaic).

cast·off /'kast,ôf/ ▶adj. no longer wanted; abandoned or discarded. ▶n. (usu. **castoffs**) something, esp. a garment, that is no longer wanted.

Cas·tor /'kastər/ ▶ **1** *Greek Mythol.* the twin brother of Pollux. **2** *Astron.* the second brightest star in the constellation Gemini, close to Pollux. It is a multiple star system, the three components visible in a moderate telescope being close binaries.

cas·tor oil ▶n. a pale yellow oil obtained from castor beans, used as a purgative and a lubricant and in manufacturing oil-based products.

cas·trate /'kas,trāt/ ▶v. [tr.] remove the testicles of (a male animal or man). ■ *fig.* deprive of power, vitality, or vigor: [as adj.] (**castrated**) *the nation is a castrated giant, afraid to really punish subversives.* ▶n. a man or male animal whose testicles have been removed. —**cas·tra·tion** /ka'strāSHən/ n. —**cas·tra·tor** /-,trātər/ n.

cas·tra·to /kas'trä,tō/ ▶n. (pl. **-ti** /-tē/) *hist.* a male singer castrated in boyhood so as to retain a soprano or alto voice.

ca·su·al /'kazHōōəl/ ▶adj. **1** relaxed and unconcerned: *he tried to make his voice sound casual.* ■ made or done without much thought or premeditation: *a casual remark.* ■ done or acting in a desultory way: *to the casual observer, rugby looks something like soccer.* ■ done or acting without sufficient care or thoroughness: *the casual way in which victims were treated.* **2** not regular or permanent: *the tent is ideal for casual outdoor use.* ■ (of a worker) employed on a temporary or irregular basis. ■ (of a sexual relationship or encounter) occurring between people who

are not regular or established sexual partners. **3** happening by chance; accidental: *he pretended it was a casual meeting.* **4** without formality of style, manner, or procedure, in particular: ■ (of clothes or a style of dress) suitable for everyday wear rather than formal occasions. ■ (of a social event) not characterized by particular social conventions. ■ (of a place or environment) relaxed and friendly: *the inn's casual atmosphere.* ▶n. **1** a person who does something irregularly: *a number of casuals became regular customers.* ■ a worker employed on an irregular or temporary basis. **2** (**casuals**) clothes or shoes suitable for everyday wear rather than formal occasions. —**cas·u·al·ly** adv. —**cas·u·al·ness** n.

cas·u·al·ty /'kazH(ōō)əltē/ ▶n. (pl. **-ties**) a person killed or injured in a war or accident. ■ *fig.* a person or thing badly affected by an event or situation: *the building industry has been one of the casualties of the recession.* ■ (chiefly in insurance) an accident, mishap, or disaster.

CAT /'kat/ ▶abbr. ■ clear air turbulence. ■ computer-assisted (or -aided) testing. ■ *Med.* computerized axial tomography: [as adj.] *a CAT scan.*

cat² /kat/ ▶n. **1** a small domesticated carnivorous mammal (*Felis catus*), with soft fur, a short snout, and retractile claws. The **cat family** (Felidae) also includes the ocelot, serval, margay, lynx, and the big cats. ■ a wild animal of the cat family. ■ used in names of catlike animals of other families, e.g., **ring-tailed cat.** **2** *inf.* (particularly among jazz enthusiasts) a person, esp. a man. ▶v. (**catted, catting**) [tr.] *Naut.* raise (an anchor) from the surface of the water to the cathead.

cat³ ▶n. short for **CATAMARAN.**

cat·a·chre·sis /,katə'krēsis/ ▶n. (pl. **-ses** /-sēz/) the use of a word in a way that is not correct, for example, the use of *mitigate* for *militate.* —**cat·a·chres·tic** /-'krestik/ adj.

cat·a·clysm /'katə,klizəm/ ▶n. a large-scale and violent event in the natural world. ■ a sudden violent upheaval, esp. in a political or social context: *the cataclysm of the First World War.* —**cat·a·clys·mic** /,katə-'klizmik/ adj.

cat·a·comb /'katə,kōm/ ▶n. (usu. **catacombs**) an underground cemetery consisting of a subterranean gallery with recesses for tombs, as constructed by the ancient Romans. ■ an underground construction resembling or compared to such a cemetery.

ca·tad·ro·mous /kə'tadrəməs/ ▶adj. *Zool.* (of a fish such as the eel) migrating down rivers to the sea to spawn.

cat·a·falque /'katə,fô(l)k; -,falk/ ▶n. a decorated wooden framework supporting the coffin of a distinguished person during a funeral or while lying in state.

cat·a·lep·sy /'katl,epsē/ ▶n. a medical condition characterized by a trance or seizure with a loss of sensation and consciousness accompanied by rigidity of the body. —**cat·a·lep·tic** /,katl'eptik/ adj. & n.

cat·a·log /'katl,ôg; -,äg/ (also **cat·a·logue**) ▶n. a complete list of items, typically one in alphabetical or other systematic order, in particular: ■ a list of all the books or resources in a library. ■ a publication containing details and often photographs of items for sale, esp. one produced by a mail-order company. ■ a descriptive list of works of art in an exhibition or collection giving detailed comments and explanations. ■ a list of courses offered by a university or college. ■ a series of unfortunate or bad things: *his life was a catalog of dismal failures.* ▶v. (**-logs, -loged, -log·ing**; also **-logues, -logued, -logu·ing**) [tr.] make a systematic list of (items of the same type). ■ enter (an item) in such a list. ■ list (similar situations, qualities, or events) in succession: *the report catalogs dangerous work practices.* —**cat·a·log·er** (also **cat·a·logu·er**) n.

ca·tal·pa /kə'talpə/ ▶n. a tree (genus *Catalpa*, family Bignoniaceae) with large heart-shaped leaves, clusters of trumpet-shaped flowers, and slender beanlike seedpods, native to North America and eastern Asia.

ca·tal·y·sis /kə'taləsis/ ▶n. *Chem. & Biochem.* the acceleration of a chemical reaction by a catalyst. ▷mid 19th cent.; from modern Latin, from Greek *katalusis*, from *kataluein* 'dissolve,' from *kata-* 'down' + *luein* 'loosen.'

cat·a·lyst /'katl-ist/ ▶n. a substance that increases the rate of a chemical reaction without itself undergoing any permanent chemical change. ■ *fig.* a person or thing that precipitates an event.

cat·a·lyt·ic /,katl'itik/ ▶adj. relating to or involving the action of a catalyst. —**cat·a·lyt·i·cal·ly** /-ik(ə)lē/ adv.

cat·a·lyt·ic con·vert·er ▶n. a device incorporated in the exhaust system of a motor vehicle, containing a catalyst for converting pollutant gases into less harmful ones.

cat·a·lyze /'katl,īz/ ▶v. [tr.] cause or accelerate (a reaction) by acting as a catalyst. ■ *fig.* cause (an action or process) to begin.

cat·a·ma·ran /ˌkatəməˈran; ˈkatəməˌran/ ▶n. a yacht or other boat with twin hulls in parallel.

catamaran

cat·a·mite /ˈkatəˌmīt/ ▶n. archaic a boy kept for homosexual practices.

cat·a·mount /ˈkatəˌmount/ (also **cat·a·moun·tain** /-ˌmountən/) ▶n. a medium-sized or large wild cat, esp. a cougar.

cat·a·plex·y /ˈkatəˌpleksē/ ▶n. a medical condition in which strong emotion or laughter causes a person to suffer sudden physical collapse though remaining conscious. —**cat·a·plec·tic** /ˌkatəˈplektik/ adj.

cat·a·pult /ˈkatəˌpəlt; -ˌpŏolt/ ▶n. a device in which accumulated tension is suddenly released to hurl an object some distance, in particular: ■ hist. a military machine worked by a lever and ropes for hurling large stones or other missiles. ■ a mechanical device for launching a glider or other aircraft, esp. from the deck of a ship.
▶v. [tr.] hurl or launch (something) in a specified direction with or as if with a catapult: their music catapulted them to the top of the charts. ■ [intr.] move suddenly or at great speed as though hurled by a catapult: the horse catapulted away from the fence.

cat·a·ract /ˈkatəˌrakt/ ▶n. 1 a large waterfall. ■ a sudden rush of water; a downpour: the rain enveloped us in a deafening cataract. 2 (usu. cataracts) a medical condition in which the lens of the eye becomes progressively opaque, resulting in blurred vision.

ca·tarrh /kəˈtär/ ▶n. excessive discharge or buildup of mucus in the nose or throat, associated with inflammation of the mucous membrane. —**ca·tarrh·al** /kəˈtärəl/ adj.

ca·tas·tro·phe /kəˈtastrəfē/ ▶n. an event causing great and often sudden damage or suffering; a disaster: a national economic catastrophe | leading the world to catastrophe. ■ the denouement of a classical tragedy. —**cat·as·troph·ic** /ˌkatəˈsträfik/ adj.

ca·tas·tro·phism /kəˈtastrəˌfizəm/ n. ▶Geol. the theory that changes in the earth's crust during geological history have resulted chiefly from sudden violent and unusual events. —**ca·tas·tro·phist** n. & adj.

cat·a·to·ni·a /ˌkatəˈtōnēə/ ▶n. Psychiatry abnormality of movement and behavior arising from a disturbed mental state (typically schizophrenia). It may involve repetitive or purposeless overactivity, or catalepsy, resistance to passive movement, and negativism. ■ inf. a state of immobility and stupor. —**cat·a·ton·ic** /ˌkatəˈtänik/ adj.

cat·bird /ˈkatˌbərd/ ▶n. a long-tailed North American songbird (Dumetella carolinensis) of the mockingbird family, with mainly dark gray or black plumage and catlike calls.
▶ □ **in the catbird seat** inf. in a superior or advantageous position.

cat·boat /ˈkatˌbōt/ ▶n. a sailboat with a single mast placed well forward and carrying only one sail.

cat bur·glar ▶n. a thief who enters a building by climbing to an upper story.

cat·call /ˈkatˌkôl/ ▶n. a shrill whistle or shout of disapproval, typically one made at a public meeting or performance. ■ a loud whistle or a comment of a sexual nature made by a man to a passing woman.
▶v. [intr.] make such a whistle, shout, or comment.

catch /kaCH; keCH/ ▶v. (past **caught** /kôt/) [tr.] **1** intercept and hold (something that has been thrown, propelled, or dropped). ■ intercept the fall of (someone). ■ seize or take hold of: he caught hold of her arm as she tried to push past him. ■ [intr.] (**catch at**) grasp or try to grasp: his hands caught at her arms as she tried to turn away. **2** capture (a person or animal that tries or would try to escape): we hadn't caught a single rabbit. ■ [intr.] (of an object) accidentally become entangled or trapped in something: the charm bracelet caught on her clothing. ■ [tr.] (of a person) have (a part of one's body or clothing) become entangled or trapped in something: she caught her foot in the bedspread | fig. companies face risks of being caught in a downward spiral. ■ [tr.] (usu. be caught) fix or fasten in place: her hair was caught back in a scrunchie. **3** reach in time and

board (a train, bus, or aircraft): they caught the 12:15 from Chicago. ■ reach or be in a place in time to see (a person, performance, program, etc.): hurrying downstairs to catch the news. ■ come upon (someone) unexpectedly: unexpected snow caught us by surprise. ■ (**be caught in**) (of a person) unexpectedly find oneself in (an unwelcome situation): my sister was caught in a thunderstorm. ■ (**catch it**) inf. be punished or told off. ■ (often **be caught**) surprise (someone) in an incriminating situation or in the act of doing something wrong: he was caught with bomb-making equipment. **4** engage (a person's interest or imagination). ■ perceive fleetingly: she caught a glimpse of herself in the mirror. ■ hear or understand (something said), esp. with effort: he bellowed something Jess couldn't catch. ■ succeed in evoking or representing: the program caught something of the flavor of Minoan culture. **5** [tr.] strike (someone) on a part of the body: Ben caught him on the chin. ■ accidentally strike (a part of one's body) against something: she fell and caught her head on the corner of the hearth. **6** contract (an illness) through infection or contagion. **7** [intr.] become ignited, due to contact with flame, and start burning: the rafters have caught. ■ (of an engine) fire and start running.
▶phrasal v. □ **catch on** inf. **1** (of a practice or fashion) become popular: his music never caught on in the South. **2** understand what is meant or how to do something: I caught on to what it was the guy was saying. □ **catch up** succeed in reaching a person who is ahead of one: O'Hara caught up with Stella at the bottom of the hill. ■ do work or other tasks that one should have done earlier: catch up on paperwork. □ **catch up with 1** talk to (someone) whom one has not seen for some time in order to find out what they have been doing. **2** begin to have a damaging effect on. □ **be/get caught up in** become involved in (something that one had not intended to become involved in): he had no desire to be caught up in political activities.
▶n. **1** an act of catching something, typically a ball. ■ an amount of fish caught: a record catch of 6.9 billion pounds of fish. ■ inf. a person considered attractive, successful, or prestigious and so desirable as a partner or spouse: he would be a good catch. **2** a device for securing something such as a door, window, or box. **3** a hidden problem or disadvantage in an apparently ideal situation: there's a catch in it somewhere. **4** an unevenness in a person's voice caused by emotion. **5** Mus. a round, typically one with words arranged to produce a humorous effect. ▷Middle English (also in the sense 'chase'): from Anglo-Norman French and Old Northern French cachier, variant of Old French chacier, based on Latin captare 'try to catch,' from capere 'take.' —**catch·a·ble** adj.
▶ □ **catch one's breath 1** draw one's breath in sharply as a reaction to an emotion. **2** recover one's breath after exertion. □ **catch someone's eye 1** be noticed by someone. **2** attract someone's attention by making eye contact: I caught Rhoda's eye and gave her a friendly wave. □ **catch fire** become ignited and burn. □ **catch sight of** suddenly notice; glimpse.

catch-22 ▶n. a dilemma or difficult circumstance from which there is no escape because of mutually conflicting or dependent conditions.

catch-all ▶n. [usu. as adj.] a term or category that includes a variety of different possibilities: the stigmatizing catch-all term "schizophrenia."

catch-as-catch-can ▶n. archaic wrestling in which all holds are permitted.
▶adj. using whatever methods or materials are available.

catch·er /ˈkaCHər; ˈkeCH-/ ▶n. a person or thing that catches something. ■ Baseball a fielder positioned behind home plate to catch pitches not hit by the batter and to execute other defensive plays.

catch·fly /ˈkaCHˌflī; ˈkeCH-/ ▶n. (pl. -**flies**) a campion or similar plant (Silene, Lychnis, and other genera) of the pink family, with a sticky stem.

catch·ing /ˈkaCHiNG; ˈkeCH-/ ▶adj. inf. (of a disease) infectious: Huntington's chorea isn't catching | fig. her enthusiasm is catching.

catch·line /ˈkaCHˌlīn; ˈkeCH-/ ▶n. Printing a short, eye-catching line of type, typically one at the top of a page such as a running head. ■ an advertising slogan.

catch·ment /ˈkaCHmənt; ˈkeCH-/ ▶n. the action of collecting water, esp. the collection of rainfall over a natural drainage area.

catch·pen·ny /ˈkaCHˌpenē; ˈkeCH-/ ▶adj. having a cheap superficial attractiveness designed to encourage quick sales.

catch·phrase /ˈkaCHˌfrāz; ˈkeCH-/ ▶n. a well-known sentence or phrase, typically one that is associated with a particular famous person.

catch-up (also **catch·up**) ▶n. inf. an act of catching someone up in a particular activity.
▶ □ **play catch-up 1** fall behind continually with work or financial

matters: *I'm always playing catch-up with my homework.* **2** try to equal a competitor in a sport or game.

catch·word /ˈkaCHˌwərd; ˈkeCH-/ ▶n. **1** a briefly popular or fashionable word or phrase used to encapsulate a particular concept: *"motivation" is a great catchword.* **2** a word printed or placed so as to attract attention. ■ *chiefly hist.* Printing the first word of a page given at the foot of the previous one.

catch·y /ˈkaCHē; ˈkeCHē/ ▶adj. (**catch·i·er, catch·i·est**) (of a tune or phrase) instantly appealing and memorable: *a catchy recruiting slogan.* —**catch·i·ly** /ˈkaCHəlē; ˈkeCH-/ adv. —**catch·i·ness** n.

cat·e·chism /ˈkatəˌkizəm/ ▶n. a summary of the principles of Christian religion in the form of questions and answers, used for the instruction of Christians. ■ a series of fixed questions, answers, or precepts used for instruction in other situations. —**cat·e·chis·mal** /ˌkatəˈkizəməl/ adj.

cat·e·chist /ˈkatəkist/ ▶n. a teacher of the principles of Christian religion, esp. one using a catechism.

cat·e·chize /ˈkatəˌkīz/ ▶v. [tr.] instruct (someone) in the principles of Christian religion by means of question and answer, typically by using a catechism. ■ *fig.* put questions to or interrogate (someone). —**cat·e·chiz·er** n.

cat·e·gor·i·cal /ˌkatəˈgôrikəl/ ▶adj. unambiguously explicit and direct: *a categorical assurance.* —**cat·e·gor·ic** adj. —**cat·e·gor·i·cal·ly** /-ik(ə)lē/ adv.

cat·e·go·rize /ˈkatəgəˌrīz/ ▶v. [tr.] (often **be categorized**) place in a particular class or group. —**cat·e·go·ri·za·tion** /ˌkatəgərəˈzāSHən/ n.

cat·e·go·ry /ˈkatəˌgôrē/ ▶n. (pl. **-ries**) a class or division of people or things regarded as having particular shared characteristics: *five categories of intelligence.* —**cat·e·go·ri·al** /ˌkatəˈgôrēəl/ adj.

cat·e·go·ry kill·er ▶n. a large store, typically one of a chain, that specializes in a particular type of discounted merchandise and becomes the dominant retailer in that category.

cat·e·nat·ed /ˈkatəˌnātid; ˈkatnˌātid/ ▶adj. *technical* connected in a chain or series: *catenated molecules.* —**cat·e·na·tion** /ˌkatəˈnāSHən; ˌkatnˈāSHən/ n.

ca·ter /ˈkātər/ ▶v. [tr.] provide (food and drink), typically at social events and in a professional capacity: *he catered a lunch for 20 people.* ■ (**cater to**) provide with what is needed or required: *the school caters to children with learning difficulties.* ■ (**cater to**) try to satisfy (a particular need or demand): *he catered to her every whim.* —**ca·ter·er** n.

cat·er-cor·nered /ˈkatē ˌkôrnərd; ˈkatər/ (also **cat·er-cor·ner** or **catty·cor·nered** or **kit·ty-cor·ner**) ▶adj. & adv. situated diagonally opposite someone or something: [as adj.] *a restaurant cater-cornered from the movie theater* | [as adv.] *motorcyclists cut cater-cornered across his yard.*

cat·er·pil·lar /ˈkatə(r)ˌpilər/ ▶n. **1** the larva of a butterfly or moth, having a segmented wormlike body with three pairs of true legs and several pairs of leglike appendages. ■ (in general use) any similar larva of various insects, esp. sawflies. **2** (also **caterpillar track** or **tread**) *trademark* an articulated steel band passing around the wheels of a vehicle for travel on rough ground. ■ a vehicle with such tracks. ▷late Middle English: perhaps from a variant of Old French *chatepelose*, literally 'hairy cat,' influenced by obsolete *piller* 'ravager.' The association with "cat" is found in other languages.

cat·er·waul /ˈkatərˌwôl/ ▶v. [intr.] [often as n.] (**caterwauling**) (of a cat) make a shrill howling or wailing noise: *the caterwauling of a pair of bobcats* | [as adj.] (**caterwauling**) *fig. a caterwauling guitar.*
▶n. a shrill howling or wailing noise.

cat·fish /ˈkatˌfiSH/ ▶n. (pl. same or **-fishes**) a freshwater or marine fish with whiskerlike barbels around the mouth, typically bottom-dwelling. Its many families include the Eurasian family Siluridae and the large North American family Ictaluridae.

cat·gut /ˈkatˌgət/ ▶n. a material used for the strings of musical instruments and for surgical sutures, made of the dried twisted intestines of sheep or horses, but not cats.

Cath. ▶abbr. ■ Cathedral. ■ Catholic.

ca·thar·sis /kəˈTHärsis/ ▶n. the process of releasing, and thereby providing relief from, strong or repressed emotions.

ca·thar·tic /kəˈTHärtik/ ▶adj. providing psychological relief through the open expression of strong emotions; causing catharsis: *crying is a cathartic release.*
▶n. *Med.* a purgative drug. —**ca·thar·ti·cal·ly** adv.

ca·the·dral /kəˈTHēdrəl/ ▶n. the principal church of a diocese, with which the bishop is officially associated: [in names] *St. Paul's Cathedral.*

cath·e·ter /ˈkaTHətər/ ▶n. *Med.* a flexible tube inserted through a narrow opening into a body cavity, particularly the bladder, for removing fluid.

cath·e·ter·ize /ˈkaTHitəˌrīz/ ▶v. [tr.] *Med.* insert a catheter into (a patient or body cavity). —**cath·e·ter·i·za·tion** /ˌkaTHitərəˈzāSHən/ n.

cath·ode /ˈkaTHˌōd/ ▶n. the negatively charged electrode by which electrons enter an electrical device. The opposite of ANODE. ■ the positively charged electrode of an electrical device, such as a primary cell, that supplies current. —**cath·o·dal** /ˈkaTHˌōdl/ adj. —**ca·thod·ic** /kaˈTHädik/ adj.

cath·ode ray ▶n. a beam of electrons emitted from the cathode of a high-vacuum tube.

cath·ode-ray tube (abbr.: **CRT**) (also **cath·ode ray tube**) ▶n. a high-vacuum tube in which cathode rays produce a luminous image on a fluorescent screen, used chiefly in televisions and computer terminals.

cath·o·lic /ˈkaTH(ə)lik/ ▶adj. **1** (esp. of a person's tastes) including a wide variety of things; all-embracing. **2** (**Catholic**) of the Roman Catholic faith. ■ of or including all Christians. ■ of or relating to the historic doctrine and practice of the Western Church.
▶n. (**Catholic**) a member of the Roman Catholic Church. —**Ca·thol·i·cism** /kəˈTHälˌsizəm/ n. —**cath·o·lic·i·ty** /ˌkaTH(ə)ˈlisətē/ n. —**ca·thol·ic·ly** adv.

cat·i·on /ˈkatˌīən; -ˌī,än/ ▶n. *Chem.* a positively charged ion, i.e., one that would be attracted to the cathode in electrolysis. The opposite of ANION. —**cat·i·on·ic** /ˌkatīˈänik/ adj.

cat·kin /ˈkatkin/ ▶n. a flowering spike of trees such as willow and hazel. Catkins are typically downy, pendulous, composed of flowers of a single sex, and wind-pollinated.

cat lit·ter ▶n. see LITTER (sense 3).

cat·nap /ˈkatˌnap/ ▶n. a short, light sleep; a doze.
▶v. (**-napped, -nap·ping**) [intr.] have such a sleep.

cat·nip /ˈkatˌnip/ ▶n. a plant (genus *Nepeta*) of the mint family, with downy leaves, purple-spotted white flowers, and a pungent smell attractive to cats.

cat-o'-nine-tails ▶n. *hist.* a rope whip with nine knotted cords, formerly used (esp. at sea) to flog offenders.

CAT scan ▶n. an X-ray image made using computerized axial tomography. —**CAT scan·ner** n.

cat's cra·dle ▶n. a child's game in which a loop of string is put around and between the fingers and complex patterns are formed.

cat's-eye ▶n. a semiprecious stone, esp. chalcedony or chrysoberyl.

cat's-paw ▶n. a person who is used by another, typically to carry out an unpleasant or dangerous task.

cat·sup /ˈkeCHəp; ˈkaCHəp; ˈkatsəp/ ▶n. variant spelling of KETCHUP.

cat·tail /ˈkatˌtāl/ ▶n. a tall marsh plant (genus *Typha*, family Typhaceae) with long, reedlike leaves and brown, velvety cylindrical spikes of numerous tiny flowers. Also called BULRUSH.

cat·tish /ˈkatiSH/ ▶adj. another term for CATTY. —**cat·tish·ly** adv. —**cat·tish·ness** n.

cat·tle /ˈkatl/ ▶pl. n. **1** large ruminants (*Bos taurus*) with horns and cloven hoofs, domesticated for meat or milk, or as beasts of burden; cows. **2** similar animals of a group related to domestic cattle, including yak, bison, and buffalo. The **cattle family** (Bovidae) also includes the sheep, goats, goat-antelopes, and antelopes.

cat·tle·man /ˈkatlmən; -ˌman/ ▶n. (pl. **-men**) a person who tends or rears cattle.

cat·ty /ˈkatē/ ▶adj. (**cat·ti·er, cat·ti·est**) **1** deliberately hurtful in one's remarks; spiteful. **2** of or relating to cats; catlike. —**cat·ti·ly** /ˈkatl-ē/ adv. —**cat·ti·ness** n.

CATV ▶abbr. community antenna television (i.e., cable television).

cat·walk /ˈkatˌwôk/ ▶n. a narrow walkway or platform extending into an auditorium, esp. in an industrial installation, along which models walk to display clothes in fashion shows. ■ a narrow platform or stage.

Cau·ca·sian /kôˈkāzHən/ ▶adj. **1** *often offens.* of or relating to one of the traditional divisions of humankind, covering a broad group of peoples from Europe, western Asia, and parts of India and North Africa. ■ white-skinned; of European origin. **2** of or relating to the Caucasus. **3** of or relating to a group of languages spoken in the region of the Caucasus. The most widely spoken is Georgian, of the small **South Caucasian** family, not related to the three **North Caucasian** families.
▶n. *often offens.* a Caucasian person. ■ a white person; a person of European origin.

cau·cus /ˈkôkəs/ ▶n. (pl. **-cus·es**) **1** a meeting of the members of a legislative body who are members of a particular political party, to select candidates or decide policy. ■ the members of such a body. **2** a group of people with shared concerns within a political party or larger organization. ■ a meeting of such a group.
▶v. (**-cused, -cus·ing**) [intr.] hold or form such a group or meeting. ▷mid

18th cent. (originally U.S.): perhaps from Algonquian *cau'-cau'-as'u* 'adviser.'

cau·dal /ˈkôdl/ ▸ *adj.* of or like a tail. ■ at or near the tail or the posterior part of the body. —**cau·dal·ly** *adv.*

cau·dil·lo /kôˈdēlyō; -ˈdēō; kouˈdē,(y)ō/ ▸ *n.* (*pl.* **-los**) (in Spanish-speaking regions) a military or political leader.

caught /kôt/ ▸ past and past participle of CATCH.

caul /kôl/ ▸ *n.* **1** the amniotic membrane enclosing a fetus. **2** *Anat.* the omentum.

caul·dron /ˈkôldrən/ (also **cal·dron**) ▸ *n.* a large metal pot with a lid and handle, used for cooking over an open fire. ■ *fig.* a situation characterized by instability and strong emotions: *a cauldron of repressed anger.*

cau·li·flow·er /ˈkôli,flou(-ə)r; ˈkäli-/ ▸ *n.* a cabbage of a variety that bears a large immature flowerhead of small creamy-white flower buds. ■ the flowerhead of this plant eaten as a vegetable.

cau·li·flow·er ear ▸ *n.* an ear that has become thickened or deformed as a result of repeated blows, typically in boxing.

caulk /kôk/ (also **calk**) ▸ *n.* (also **caulk·ing**) a waterproof filler and sealant, used in building work and repairs.
▸ *v.* [*tr.*] seal (a gap or seam) with such a substance. ■ stop up (the seams of a boat) with oakum and waterproofing material, or by driving plate-junctions together; make (a boat) watertight by this method. —**caulk·er** *n.*

caus·al /ˈkôzəl/ ▸ *adj.* of, relating to, or acting as a cause: *the causal factors associated with illness.* ■ *Gram. & Logic* expressing or indicating a cause: *a causal conjunction.* —**caus·al·ly** *adv.*

cau·sal·i·ty /kôˈzalətē/ ▸ *n.* **1** the relationship between cause and effect. **2** the principle that everything has a cause.

cau·sa·tion /kôˈzāSHən/ ▸ *n.* the action of causing something. ■ the relationship between cause and effect; causality.

caus·a·tive /ˈkôzətiv/ ▸ *adj.* acting as a cause: *a causative factor.* ■ *Gram.* expressing causation: *a causative verb.*
▸ *n.* a causative verb.

cause /kôz/ ▸ *n.* **1** a person or thing that gives rise to an action, phenomenon, or condition: *the cause of the accident is not clear.* ■ reasonable grounds for doing, thinking, or feeling something: *Faye's condition had given no cause for concern.* **2** a principle, aim, or movement that, because of a deep commitment, one is prepared to defend or advocate: *she devoted her life to the cause of deaf people.* ■ something deserving of one's support, typically a charity: *I'm raising money for a good cause.* **3** a matter to be resolved in a court of law. ■ an individual's case offered at law.
▸ *v.* [*tr.*] make (something) happen: *this disease can cause blindness.* —**cause·less** *adj.* —**caus·er** *n.*
▸ □ **cause and effect** the principle of causation. ■ the operation or relation of a cause and its effect. □ **make common cause** unite in order to achieve a shared aim: *nationalist movements made common cause with the reformers.*

'cause /kəz/ ▸ *conj. inf.* short for BECAUSE.

cause cé·lè·bre /ˈkôz səˈleb(rə); ˈkôz/ ▸ *n.* (*pl.* **causes cé·lè·bres** pronunc. same) a controversial issue that attracts a great deal of public attention.

cau·se·rie /ˌkôzəˈrē/ ▸ *n.* (*pl.* **-ries** pronunc. same) an informal article or talk, typically one on a literary subject.

cause·way /ˈkôz,wā/ ▸ *n.* a raised road or track across low or wet ground.

caus·tic /ˈkôstik/ ▸ *adj.* **1** able to burn or corrode organic tissue by chemical action: *a caustic cleaner.* ■ *fig.* sarcastic in a scathing and bitter way. ■ *fig.* (of an expression or sound) expressive of such sarcasm: *a caustic smile.* **2** *Physics* formed by the intersection of reflected or refracted parallel rays from a curved surface.
▸ *n.* **1** a caustic substance. **2** *Physics* a caustic surface or curve. —**caus·ti·cal·ly** /-ik(ə)lē/ *adv.* —**caus·tic·i·ty** /kôˈstisətē/ *n.*

cau·ter·ize /ˈkôtə,rīz/ ▸ *v.* [*tr.*] *Med.* burn the skin or flesh of (a wound) with a heated instrument or caustic substance, typically to stop bleeding or prevent the wound from becoming infected. —**cau·ter·i·za·tion** /ˌkôtərəˈzāSHən/ *n.*

cau·tion /ˈkôSHən/ ▸ *n.* **1** care taken to avoid danger or mistakes: *anyone receiving a suspect package should exercise caution.* ■ warning: *advisers have sounded a note of caution.* **2** *inf., dated* an amusing or surprising person.
▸ *v.* [*tr.*] say something as a warning: *the secretary cautioned that economic uncertainties remained.* ■ [*intr.*] (**caution against**) warn or advise against (doing something): *advisers have cautioned against tax increases.*

cau·tion·ar·y /ˈkôSHə,nerē/ ▸ *adj.* serving as a warning: *a cautionary tale.*

cau·tious /ˈkôSHəs/ ▸ *adj.* attentive to potential problems or dangers: *a cautious driver.* ■ (of an action) characterized by such an attitude: *the plan received a cautious welcome.* —**cau·tious·ly** *adv.* —**cau·tious·ness** *n.*

cav·al·cade /ˌkavəlˈkād/ ▸ *n.* a formal procession of people walking, on horseback, or riding in vehicles.

cav·a·lier /ˌkavəˈli(ə)r/ ▸ *n.* (**Cavalier**) *hist.* a supporter of King Charles I in the English Civil War. ■ *archaic or poetic/lit.* a courtly gentleman, esp. one acting as a lady's escort. ■ *archaic* a horseman, esp. a cavalryman.
▸ *adj.* showing a lack of proper concern; offhand: *Anne was irritated by his cavalier attitude.* —**cav·a·lier·ly** *adv.*

cav·al·ry /ˈkavəlrē/ ▸ *n.* (*pl.* **-ries**) [usu. treated as *pl.*] *hist.* soldiers who fought on horseback. ■ *hist.* a branch of an army made up of such soldiers. ■ modern soldiers who fight in armored vehicles. —**cav·al·ry·man** /-mən/ *n.* (*pl.* **-men**).

cave /kāv/ ▸ *n.* a large underground chamber, typically of natural origin, in a hillside or cliff.
▸ *v.* [*intr.*] explore caves as a sport.
▸ *phrasal v.* □ **cave in** (or **cave something in**) (with reference to a roof or similar structure) subside or collapse or cause something to do this. ■ *fig.* yield or submit under pressure: *the manager caved in to his demands.* —**cave·like** /-ˌlīk/ *adj.* —**cav·er** *n.*

ca·ve·at /ˈkavē,ät; ˈkäv-/ ▸ *n.* a warning or proviso of specific stipulations, conditions, or limitations.

ca·ve·at emp·tor /ˈemp,tôr/ ▸ *n.* the principle that the buyer alone is responsible for checking the quality and suitability of goods before a purchase is made.

cave bear ▸ *n.* a large extinct bear (*Ursus spelaeus*) of the Pleistocene epoch, whose remains have been found in caves throughout Europe.

cave dwell·er ▸ *n.* a caveman or cavewoman.

cave-in ▸ *n.* a collapse of a roof or similar structure, typically underground: *a mine cave-in.* ■ *fig.* an instance of yielding or submitting under pressure: *the government's cave-in to industry pressure.*

cave·man /ˈkāv,man/ ▸ *n.* (*pl.* **-men**) a prehistoric man who lived in caves. ■ a man whose behavior is uncivilized or violent.

cav·ern /ˈkavərn/ ▸ *n.* a cave, or a chamber in a cave, typically a large one. ■ used in similes and comparisons to refer to a vast, dark space: *rouses me from the cavern of sleep.* —**cav·ern·ous** /-ərnəs/ *adj.*

cav·i·ar /ˈkavē,är/ (also **cav·i·are**) ▸ *n.* the pickled roe of sturgeon or other large fish, eaten as a delicacy. ▷ mid 16th cent.: from Italian *caviale* (earlier *caviaro*) or French *caviar*, probably from medieval Greek *khaviari*.

cav·il /ˈkavəl/ ▸ *v.* [*intr.*] make petty or unnecessary objections: *they caviled at the cost.*
▸ *n.* an objection of this kind. —**cav·il·er** *n.*

cav·ing /ˈkāving/ ▸ *n.* another term for SPELUNKING.

cav·i·ty /ˈkavitē/ ▸ *n.* (*pl.* **-ties**) an empty space within a solid object, in particular the human body: *the abdominal cavity | a body cavity.* ■ a decayed part of a tooth. —**cav·i·tar·y** /-i,terē/ *adj.*

cav·ort /kəˈvôrt/ ▸ *v.* [*intr.*] jump or dance around excitedly: *spider monkeys leap and cavort in the branches.* ■ *inf.* apply oneself enthusiastically to sexual or disreputable pursuits: *he spent his nights cavorting with the glitterati.*

ca·vy /ˈkāvē/ ▸ *n.* (*pl.* **-ies**) a South American rodent (family Caviidae) with a sturdy body and vestigial tail. Its several species include the guinea pig.

caw /kô/ ▸ *n.* the harsh cry of a crow or similar bird.
▸ *v.* [*intr.*] utter such a cry.

cay /kē; kā/ ▸ *n.* a low bank or reef of coral, rock, or sand. Compare with KEY[2].

cay·enne /kīˈen; kā-/ (also **cayenne pepper**) ▸ *n.* a pungent hot-tasting red powder prepared from ground dried chili peppers.

cay·man ▸ *n.* variant spelling of CAIMAN.

CB ▸ *abbr.* Citizens' Band (radio frequencies).

CBC ▸ *abbr.* Canadian Broadcasting Corporation.

CBI ▸ *abbr.* computer-based instruction.

CBS ▸ *abbr.* Columbia Broadcasting System.

CC ▸ *abbr.* ■ closed-captioned. ■ Cape Cod.

cc (also **c.c.**) ▸ *abbr.* ■ carbon copy (used as an indication that a duplicate has been or should be sent to another person). ■ cubic centimeter(s).

CCTV ▸ *abbr.* closed-circuit television.

CCU ▸ *abbr.* ■ cardiac care unit. ■ coronary care unit. ■ critical care unit.

CD ▸*abbr.* ■ certificate of deposit. ■ compact disc. ■ corps diplomatique.

Cd ▸*symb.* the chemical element cadmium.

cd ▸*abbr.* ■ cord.

CD burn·er ▸*n.* a device for producing a compact disc by copying from an original or master copy.

CDC ▸*abbr.* Centers for Disease Control.

Cdr. (also **CDR**) ▸*abbr.* Commander.

Cdre. ▸*abbr.* Commodore.

CD-ROM /ˌsē ˌdē ˈräm/ ▸*n.* a compact disc used as a read-only optical memory device for a computer system.

CDT ▸*abbr.* Central Daylight Time (see **CENTRAL TIME**).

CE ▸*abbr.* ■ Chemical Engineer. ■ Church of England. ■ civil engineer. ■ Common Era. ■ Corps of Engineers.

Ce ▸*symb.* the chemical element cerium.

cease /sēs/ ▸*v.* [*intr.*] come to an end: *the hostilities had ceased and normal life was resumed.* ■ [*tr.*] bring (a specified action) to an end: *they were asked to cease all military activity.*

▸ □ **never cease to** (in hyperbolic use) do something very frequently: *her exploits never cease to amaze me.*

cease-fire ▸*n.* a temporary suspension of fighting, typically one during which peace talks take place. ■ an order or signal to stop fighting.

cease·less /ˈsēslis/ ▸*adj.* constant and unending: *the fort was subjected to ceaseless bombardment.* —**cease·less·ly** *adv.*

ce·cum /ˈsēkəm/ (*Brit.* **cae·cum**) ▸*n.* (*pl.* **-ca** /-kə/) *Anat.* a pouch connected to the junction of the small and large intestines. —**ce·cal** /-kəl/ *adj.*

ce·dar /ˈsēdər/ ▸*n.* any of a number of conifers that typically yield fragrant, durable timber, in particular: ■ a large tree (genus *Cedrus*) of the pine family, esp. the **cedar of Lebanon** (*C. libani*). ■ a tall slender North American or Asian tree (genus *Thuja*) of the cypress family, esp. the **western red cedar** (*T. plicata*) and the **northern white cedar** (*T. occidentalis*).

cede /sēd/ ▸*v.* [*tr.*] give up (power or territory).

ce·dil·la /səˈdilə/ ▸*n.* a mark (¸) written under the letter *c*, esp. in French, to show that it is pronounced like an *s* rather than a *k* (e.g., façade). ■ a similar mark under *s* in Turkish and other oriental languages.

ceil·ing /ˈsēliNG/ ▸*n.* the upper interior surface of a room or other similar compartment. ■ *fig.* an upper limit, typically one set on prices, wages, or expenditure. See also **GLASS CEILING**. ■ the maximum altitude that a particular aircraft can reach. ■ the altitude of the base of a cloud layer.

cel·an·dine /ˈselənˌdīn; -ˌdēn/ ▸*n.* a common plant (*Ranunculus ficaria*) of the buttercup family that produces yellow flowers in the early spring.

ce·leb /səˈleb/ ▸*n. inf.* a celebrity: *a TV celeb.*

cel·e·brant /ˈseləbrənt/ ▸*n.* **1** a person who performs a rite, esp. a priest at the Eucharist. **2** a person who celebrates something.

cel·e·brate /ˈseləˌbrāt/ ▸*v.* [*tr.*] **1** mark (a significant or happy day or event), typically with a social gathering. ■ [*intr.*] do something enjoyable to mark such an occasion: *she celebrated with a glass of champagne.* ■ reach (a birthday or anniversary). **2** perform (a religious ceremony) publicly and duly, in particular officiate at (the Eucharist): *he celebrated holy communion.* **3** honor or praise publicly: *a film celebrating the actor's career* | [as *adj.*] (**celebrated**) *a celebrated mathematician.* —**cel·e·bra·tion** /ˌseləˈbrāSHən/ *n.* —**cel·e·bra·tor** /-ˌbrātər/ *n.* —**cel·e·bra·to·ry** /səˈlebrəˌtôrē; ˈseləbrə-/ *adj.*

ce·leb·ri·ty /səˈlebrətē/ ▸*n.* (*pl.* **-ties**) a famous person. ■ the state of being well known: *his prestige and celebrity grew.*

ce·ler·i·ty /səˈlerətē/ ▸*n. archaic* or *poetic/lit.* swiftness of movement.

cel·er·y /ˈsel(ə)rē/ ▸*n.* a cultivated plant (*Apium graveolens* var. *dulce*) of the parsley family, with closely packed succulent stalks that are eaten raw or cooked.

ce·les·ta /səˈlestə/ ▸*n.* (also **ce·leste**) a small keyboard instrument in which felted hammers strike a row of steel plates suspended over wooden resonators, giving an ethereal bell-like sound.

ce·les·tial /səˈlesCHəl/ ▸*adj.* positioned in or relating to the sky, or outer space as observed in astronomy: *a celestial body.* ■ belonging or relating to heaven: *the celestial city.* ■ supremely good: *the celestial beauty of music.* —**ce·les·tial·ly** *adv.*

ce·les·tial e·qua·tor ▸*n.* the projection into space of the earth's equator; an imaginary circle equidistant from the celestial poles.

ce·les·tial me·rid·i·an ▸*n.* see **MERIDIAN** (sense 1).

ce·les·ti·al sphere ▸*n.* an imaginary sphere of which the observer is the center and on which all celestial objects are considered to lie.

ce·li·ac dis·ease ▸*n.* a disease in which chronic failure to digest food is triggered by hypersensitivity of the small intestine to gluten.

cel·i·bate /ˈseləbət/ ▸*adj.* abstaining from marriage and sexual relations, typically for religious reasons: *a celibate priest.* ■ having or involving no sexual relations: *I'd rather stay single and celibate.*

▸*n.* a person who abstains from marriage and sexual relations. —**cel·i·ba·cy** /-bəsē/ *n.*

cell /sel/ ▸*n.* **1** a small room in which a prisoner is locked up or in which a monk or nun sleeps. ■ a small compartment in a larger structure such as a honeycomb. **2** *Biol.* the smallest structural and functional unit of an organism, typically microscopic and consisting of cytoplasm and a nucleus enclosed in a membrane. ■ an enclosed cavity in an organism. ■ *fig.* a small group forming a nucleus of political activity, typically a secret, subversive one: *the weapons may be used to arm terrorist cells.* ■ the local area covered by one of the short-range transmitters in a cellular telephone system. **3** a device containing electrodes immersed in an electrolyte, used for current-generation or electrolysis. ■ a unit in a device for converting chemical or solar energy into electricity. —**celled** *adj.* [in *comb.*] *a single-celled organism.* —**cell-like** /-ˌlīk/ *adj.*

cel·lar /ˈselər/ ▸*n.* a room below ground level in a house, typically one used for storing wine or coal. ■ a stock of wine.

▸*v.* [*tr.*] store (wine) in a cellar.

cel·lo /ˈCHelō/ ▸*n.* (*pl.* **-los**) a bass instrument of the violin family, held upright on the floor between the legs of the seated player. —**cel·list** *n.*

cello

cel·lo·phane /ˈseləˌfān/ ▸*n.* a thin transparent wrapping material made from viscose.

cell phone ▸*n.* (also **cell·phone**) short for **CELLULAR PHONE**.

cel·lu·lar /ˈselyələr/ ▸*adj.* **1** of, relating to, or consisting of living cells: *cellular proliferation.* **2** denoting or relating to a mobile telephone system that uses a number of short-range radio stations to cover the area that it serves, the signal being automatically switched from one station to another as the user travels about. **3** consisting of small compartments or rooms: *cellular accommodations.* —**cel·lu·lar·i·ty** /ˌselyəˈlaritē/ *n.*

cel·lu·lar phone (also **cellular telephone**) ▸*n.* a telephone with access to a cellular radio system so it can be used over a wide area, without a physical connection to a network.

cel·lu·lite /ˈselyəˌlīt/ ▸*n.* persistent subcutaneous fat causing dimpling of the skin, esp. on women's hips and thighs. Not in technical use.

cel·lu·loid /ˈselyəˌloid/ ▸*n.* a transparent flammable plastic made in sheets from camphor and nitrocellulose, formerly used for cinematographic film. ■ motion pictures as a genre.

cel·lu·lose /ˈselyəˌlōs; -ˌlōz/ ▸*n.* **1** an insoluble substance that is the main constituent of plant cell walls and of vegetable fibers such as cotton. **2** paint or lacquer consisting principally of cellulose acetate or nitrate in solution. —**cel·lu·lo·sic** /ˌselyəˈlōsik; -ˈlōzik/ *adj.*

Cel·si·us (abbr.: **C**) ▸*adj.* of or denoting a scale of temperature on which water freezes at 0° and boils at 100° under standard conditions.

▸*n.* (also **Celsius scale**) this scale of temperature.

Celt /kelt; selt/ ▸*n.* a member of a group of peoples inhabiting much of Europe and Asia Minor in pre-Roman times. Their culture developed in the late Bronze Age and reached its height in the 5th to 1st centuries BC before being overrun by the Romans and various Germanic peoples. ■ a native of any of the modern nations or regions in which Celtic languages are (or were until recently) spoken; a person of Irish, Highland Scottish, Manx, Welsh, or Cornish descent.

celt /selt/ ▸*n. Archaeol.* a prehistoric stone or metal implement with a beveled cutting edge, probably used as a tool or weapon.

Celt·ic /ˈkeltik; ˈsel-/ ▸*adj.* of or relating to the Celts or their languages, which constitute a branch of the Indo-European family and include Irish, Scottish Gaelic, Welsh, Breton, Manx, Cornish, and several extinct pre-Roman languages such as Gaulish.

▸*n.* the Celtic language group. —**Celt·i·cism** /ˈkeltəˌsizəm; ˈsel-/ *n.* —**Celt·i·cist** /ˈkeltəˌsist/ *n.*

Celt·ic cross ▸*n.* a Latin cross with a circle around the center.

ce·ment /səˈment/ ▸*n.* a powdery substance made by calcining lime and clay, mixed with water to form mortar or mixed with sand, gravel, and water to make concrete. ■ a soft glue that hardens on setting: *rubber cement.* ■ *fig.* an element that unites a group of people. ■ another term for **CONCRETE**. ■ a substance for filling cavities in teeth. ■ (also **ce·men·tum** /səˈmentəm/) *Anat.* a thin layer of bony material that fixes

teeth to the jaw. ■ *Geol.* the material that binds particles together in sedimentary rock.
▶ *v.* [*tr.*] attach with cement: *wooden posts were cemented into the ground.* ■ *fig.* settle or establish firmly: *the two firms are expected to cement an agreement soon.* —**ce·ment·er** *n.*

cem·e·ter·y /ˈseməˌterē/ ▶ *n.* (*pl.* **-ter·ies**) a burial ground; a graveyard.

cen·o·taph /ˈsenəˌtaf/ ▶ *n.* a tomblike monument to someone buried elsewhere, esp. one commemorating people who died in a war.

Ce·no·zo·ic /ˌsenəˈzōik/ ▶ *adj. Geol.* relating to or denoting the most recent era, following the Mesozoic era and comprising the Tertiary and Quaternary periods. ■ [*as n.*] (**the Cenozoic**) the Cenozoic era, or the system of rocks deposited during it.

cen·ser /ˈsensər/ ▶ *n.* a container in which incense is burned, typically during a religious ceremony.

cen·sor /ˈsensər/ ▶ *n.* **1** an official who examines material that is about to be released, such as books, movies, news, and art, and suppresses any parts that are considered obscene, politically unacceptable, or a threat to security. **2** (in ancient Rome) either of two magistrates who held censuses and supervised public morals.
▶ *v.* [*tr.*] (often **be censored**) examine (a book, movie, etc.) officially and suppress unacceptable parts of it. —**cen·so·ri·al** /senˈsôrēəl/ *adj.* —**cen·sor·ship** *n.*

cen·so·ri·ous /senˈsôrēəs/ ▶ *adj.* severely critical of others. —**cen·so·ri·ous·ly** *adv.* —**cen·so·ri·ous·ness** *n.*

cen·sure /ˈsenSHər/ ▶ *v.* [*tr.*] (often **be censured**) express severe disapproval of (someone or something), typically in a formal statement: *a judge was censured in 1983 for a variety of types of injudicious conduct.*
▶ *n.* the expression of formal disapproval: *social ostracism and family censure.* —**cen·sur·a·ble** *adj.*

cen·sus /ˈsensəs/ ▶ *n.* (*pl.* **-sus·es**) an official count or survey of a population, typically recording various details of individuals: *population estimates extrapolated from the 1981 census* | [*as adj.*] *census data.* ▷ *early 17th cent.* (denoting a poll tax): from Latin, applied to the registration of citizens and property in ancient Rome, usually for taxation, from *censere* 'assess.' The current sense dates from the mid 18th cent.

cent /sent/ ▶ *n.* **1** a monetary unit of the U.S., Canada, and various other countries, equal to one hundredth of a dollar. ■ a coin of this value. ■ *inf.* a small sum of money: *she saved every cent possible.* ■ *inf.* used for emphasis to denote any money at all: *he hadn't yet earned a cent.* **2** a monetary unit of some states of the European Union, equal to one hundredth of a euro.
▶ □ **one's two cents' worth** one's opinion.

cen·taur /ˈsenˌtôr/ ▶ *n. Greek Mythol.* a creature with the head, arms, and torso of a man and the body and legs of a horse.

cen·te·nar·i·an /ˌsentnˈe(ə)rēən/ ▶ *n.* a person who is one hundred or more years old.
▶ *adj.* one hundred or more years old.

cen·ten·ar·y /senˈtenərē; ˈsentnˌerē/ *chiefly Brit.* ▶ *n.* (*pl.* **-ar·ies**) the hundredth anniversary of a significant event; a centennial. ■ a celebration of such an anniversary.
▶ *adj.* of or relating to a hundredth anniversary; centennial.

cen·ten·ni·al /senˈtenēəl/ ▶ *adj.* of or relating to a hundredth anniversary: *centennial celebrations.*
▶ *n.* a hundredth anniversary: *the museum's centennial.* ■ a celebration of such an anniversary.

cen·ter /ˈsentər/ (*Brit.* **cen·tre**) ▶ *n.* **1** the middle point of a circle or sphere, equidistant from every point on the circumference or surface. ■ a point or part that is equally distant from all sides, ends, or surfaces of something; the middle: *the center of the ceiling.* ■ a pivot or axis of rotation: *the galactic rotation of the solar system around the galactic center.* ■ a political party or group holding moderate opinions. ■ *Sports* the middle player in a line or group in many games: *Terry played center on the basketball team.* ■ *Baseball* short for **CENTER FIELD.** ■ a core, such as the filling in a piece of chocolate: *truffles with liqueur centers.* ■ a conical adjustable support for a workpiece in a lathe or similar machine. **2** a place or group of buildings where a specified activity is concentrated: *a center for medical research.* ■ a point at which an activity or quality is at its most intense and from which it spreads: *the city was a center of discontent.* ■ the point on which an activity is focused: *two issues at the center of the health-care debate.* ■ the most important place in the respect specified: *Geneva was then the center of the international world.*
▶ *v.* **1** [*intr.*] (**center around/on**) have (something) as a major concern or theme: *the case centers around the couple's children.* ■ [*tr.*] (**center**

centaur

something around/on) cause an argument or discussion to focus on (a specified issue): *he is centering his discussion on an analysis of patterns of mortality.* ■ (**be centered in**) (of an activity) occur mainly in or around (a specified place). **2** [*tr.*] place in the middle: *to center the needle, turn the knob.* ■ *Football* pass the ball back from the ground to another player to begin a down; snap. —**cen·ter·most** /-ˌmōst/ *adj.*
▶ □ **the center of attention** a person or thing that draws general attention.

cen·ter·board /ˈsentərˌbôrd/ ▶ *n.* a pivoted board that can be lowered through the keel of a sailboat to reduce sideways movement.

cen·ter field (also **cen·ter·field**) ▶ *n. Baseball* the central part of the outfield, behind second base. ■ the position of an outfielder in this area —**cen·ter field·er** *n.*

cen·ter·fold /ˈsentərˌfōld/ ▶ *n.* the two middle pages of a magazine, typically taken up by a single illustration or feature. ■ an illustration on such pages, typically a picture of a naked or scantily clad model.

cen·ter·ing /ˈsentəriNG/ ▶ *n. Archit.* framing used to support an arch or dome while it is under construction.

cen·ter of grav·i·ty ▶ *n.* a point from which the weight of a body or system may be considered to act. In uniform gravity it is the same as the center of mass.

cen·ter·piece /ˈsentərˌpēs/ ▶ *n.* a decorative piece or display placed in the middle of a dining or serving table. ■ an item or issue intended to be a focus of attention: *the tower is the centerpiece of the park.*

cen·tes·i·mal /senˈtesəməl/ ▶ *adj.* of or relating to division into hundredths. —**cen·tes·i·mal·ly** *adv.*

cen·ti·grade /ˈsentəˌgrād/ ▶ *adj.* another term for **CELSIUS**[2]. ■ having a scale of a hundred degrees.

cen·ti·gram /ˈsentəˌgram/ (abbr.: **cg**) ▶ *n.* a metric unit of mass, equal to one hundredth of a gram.

cen·ti·li·ter /ˈsentəˌlētər/ (*Brit.* **cen·ti·li·tre**) (abbr.: **cl**) ▶ *n.* a metric unit of capacity, equal to one hundredth of a liter.

cen·time /ˈsänˌtēm; ˈsent-/ ▶ *n.* a monetary unit of Switzerland and certain other countries (including France, Belgium, and Luxembourg until the introduction of the euro), equal to one hundredth of a franc or other decimal currency unit. ■ a coin of this value.

cen·ti·me·ter /ˈsentəˌmētər; ˈsän-/ (*Brit.* **cen·ti·me·tre**) (abbr.: **cm**) ▶ *n.* a metric unit of length, equal to one hundredth of a meter.

cen·ti·pede /ˈsentəˌpēd/ ▶ *n.* a predatory myriapod invertebrate (class Chilopoda, several orders) with a flattened elongated body composed of many segments. Most segments bear a single pair of legs.

cen·tral /ˈsentrəl/ ▶ *adj.* **1** of, at, or forming the center: *the station has a central courtyard.* ■ accessible from a variety of places: *coaches met at a central location.* ■ *Phonet.* (of a vowel) articulated in the center of the mouth. **2** of the greatest importance; principal or essential: *his preoccupation with history is central to his work.* ■ (of a group or organization) having controlling power over a country or another organization: *central government.* ■ (of power or authority) in the hands of such a group: *local councils subject to central control.* —**cen·tral·i·ty** /senˈtralətē/ *n.* —**cen·tral·ly** *adv.*

cen·tral·ize /ˈsentrəˌlīz/ ▶ *v.* [*tr.*] concentrate (control of an activity or organization) under a single authority. ■ bring (activities) together in one place: *the ultimate goal is to centralize boxing under one umbrella.* —**cen·tral·i·za·tion** /ˌsentrələˈzāSHən/ *n.*

cen·tral nerv·ous sys·tem ▶ *n. Anat.* the complex of nerve tissues that controls the activities of the body. In vertebrates it comprises the brain and spinal cord.

cen·tral proc·ess·ing u·nit (also **cen·tral proc·es·sor**) (abbr.: **CPU**) ▶ *n. Comput.* the part of a computer in which operations are controlled and executed.

Cen·tral time ▶ the standard time in a zone that includes the central states of the U.S. and parts of central Canada, specifically: ■ **Central Standard Time** (abbr.: **CST**) standard time based on the mean solar time at longitude 90° W., six hours behind GMT. ■ **Central Daylight Time** (abbr.: **CDT**) Central time during daylight saving, five hours behind GMT.

cen·trif·u·gal /senˈtrif(y)əgəl/ ▶ *adj. Physics* moving or tending to move away from a center. The opposite of **CENTRIPETAL.** —**cen·trif·u·gal·ly** *adv.*

cen·trif·u·gal force ▶ *n. Physics* an apparent force that acts outward on a body moving around a center, arising from the body's inertia.

Pronunciation Key ə *ago,* up; ər *over,* fur; a *hat;* ā *ate;* ä *car;* CH *chin;* e *let;* ē *see;* e(ə)r *air;* i *fit;* ī *by;* i(ə)r *ear;* NG *sing;* ō *go;* ô *law, for;* oi *toy;* oͦo *good;* oͦo *goo;* ou *out;* SH *she;* TH *thin;* TH *then;* (h)w *why;* ZH *vision*

cen·tri·fuge /ˈsentrəˌfyo͞oj/ ▶n. a machine with a rapidly rotating container that applies centrifugal force to its contents, typically to separate fluids of different densities (e.g., cream from milk) or liquids from solids.
▶v. [tr.] (usu. **be centrifuged**) subject to the action of a centrifuge. ■ separate by centrifuge: *the black liquid is centrifuged into oil and water.* —**cen·trif·u·ga·tion** /ˌsentrəˌfyo͞oˈgāSHən; senˌtrif(y)ə-/ n.

cen·trip·e·tal /senˈtripətl/ ▶adj. *Physics* moving or tending to move toward a center. The opposite of CENTRIFUGAL. —**cen·trip·e·tal·ly** adv.

cen·trip·e·tal force ▶n. *Physics* a force that acts on a body moving in a circular path and is directed toward the center around which the body is moving.

cen·trist /ˈsentrəst/ ▶adj. having moderate political views or policies.
▶n. a person with moderate political views. —**cen·trism** /-ˌtrizəm/ n.

cen·tu·ri·on /senˈt(y)o͝orēən/ ▶n. the commander of a century in the ancient Roman army.

cen·tu·ry /ˈsenCH(ə)rē/ ▶n. (pl. **-ries**) **1** a period of one hundred years: *a century ago most people walked to work.* ■ a period of one hundred years reckoned from the traditional date of the birth of Jesus Christ: *the fifteenth century* | [as adj., in *combination*] (**-century**) *a twentieth-century lifestyle.* **2** a group of one hundred things. **3** a company in the ancient Roman army, originally of one hundred men. ■ an ancient Roman political division for voting. **4** a bicycle race of one hundred miles: [as adj.] *the nation's largest single-day century ride.* ■ a score of one hundred in a sporting event. —**cen·tu·ri·al** /senˈt(y)o͝orēəl/ adj.

cen·tu·ry plant ▶n. a stemless agave (*Agave americana*) with long spiny leaves that produces a tall flowering stem after many years of growth and then dies. Also called AMERICAN ALOE (see ALOE).

CEO ▶abbr. chief executive officer.

cep /sep/ ▶n. an edible European and North American bolete mushroom (*Boletus edulis*) with a smooth brown cap, a stout white stalk, and pores rather than gills.

ce·phal·ic /səˈfalik/ ▶adj. *technical* of, in, or relating to the head.

ceph·a·lo·pod /ˈsefələˌpäd/ ▶n. any of various mollusks having a distinct tentacled head, including octopuses, squids, and cuttlefish.

ceph·a·lo·tho·rax /ˌsefəlōˈTHôraks/ ▶n. (pl. **-tho·ra·ces** /-ˈTHôrəˌsēz/ or **-tho·rax·es**) *Zool.* the fused head and thorax of arachnids, horseshoe crabs, and other related arthropods.

ce·pheid /ˈsēfēəd; ˈsef-/ (also **cepheid variable**) ▶n. *Astron.* a variable star having a regular cycle of brightness with a frequency related to its luminosity, so allowing estimation of its distance from the earth.

ce·ram·ic /səˈramik/ ▶adj. made of clay and hardened by heat: *a ceramic bowl.* ■ of or relating to the manufacture of such articles.
▶n. (**ceramics**) pots and other articles made from clay hardened by heat. ■ [usu. treated as *sing.*] the art of making such articles: *sculpting, drawing, ceramics, and fiber art.* ■ (**ceramic**) the material from which such articles are made: *tableware in ceramic.* ■ (**ceramic**) any nonmetallic solid that remains hard when heated. —**ce·ram·i·cist** /səˈraməsist/ n.

ce·re·al /ˈsi(ə)rēəl/ ▶n. a grain used for food, such as wheat, oats, or corn. ■ (usu. **cereals**) a grass producing such grain, grown as an agricultural crop: [as adj.] *cereal crops.* ■ a breakfast food made from roasted grain, typically eaten with milk: *a bowl of cereal* | [as adj.] *a cereal box.*

cer·e·bel·lum /ˌserəˈbeləm/ ▶n. (pl. **-bel·lums** or **-bel·la** /-ˈbelə/) *Anat.* the part of the brain at the back of the skull in vertebrates. Its function is to coordinate and regulate muscular activity. —**cer·e·bel·lar** adj.

ce·re·bral /səˈrēbrəl; ˈserəbrəl/ ▶adj. **1** of the cerebrum of the brain: *the cerebral cortex.* ■ intellectual rather than emotional or physical. **2** *Phonet.* another term for RETROFLEX. —**ce·re·bral·ly** adv.

ce·re·bral pal·sy ▶n. a condition marked by impaired muscle coordination (spastic paralysis) and/or other disabilities, typically caused by damage to the brain before or at birth. See also SPASTIC.

cer·e·bra·tion /ˌserəˈbrāSHən/ ▶n. *technical* or *formal* the working of the brain; thinking. —**cer·e·brate** /ˈserəˌbrāt/ v.

ce·re·bro·spi·nal /səˌrēbrōˈspīnl; ˌserəbrō-/ ▶adj. *Anat.* of or relating to the brain and spine.

ce·re·bro·vas·cu·lar /səˌrēbrōˈvaskyələr; ˌserəbrō-/ ▶adj. *Anat.* of or relating to the brain and its blood vessels.

ce·re·brum /səˈrēbrəm; ˈserə-/ ▶n. (pl. **-bra** /-brə/) *Anat.* the principal part of the brain in vertebrates, located in the front of the skull and consisting of two hemispheres, left and right.

cer·e·mo·ni·al /ˌserəˈmōnēəl/ ▶adj. **1** relating to or used for formal events of a religious or public nature: *a ceremonial Buddhist headpiece.* **2** (of a position or role) involving only nominal authority or power.
▶n. the system of rules and procedures to be observed at a formal or religious occasion: *the procedure was conducted with all due ceremonial.*

■ a rite or ceremony. —**cer·e·mo·ni·al·ism** n. —**cer·e·mo·ni·al·ist** n. —**cer·e·mo·ni·al·ly** adv.

cer·e·mo·ni·ous /ˌserəˈmōnēəs/ ▶adj. relating or appropriate to grand and formal occasions: *a Great Hall where ceremonious appearances were made.* ■ excessively polite; punctilious: *he accepted the gifts with ceremonious dignity.* —**cer·e·mo·ni·ous·ly** adv. —**cer·e·mo·ni·ous·ness** n.

cer·e·mo·ny /ˈserəˌmōnē/ ▶n. (pl. **-nies**) **1** a formal religious or public occasion, typically one celebrating a particular event or anniversary. ■ an act or series of acts performed according to a traditional or prescribed form. **2** the ritual observances and procedures performed at grand and formal occasions: *the new Queen was proclaimed with due ceremony.* ■ formal polite behavior: *Harry showed them to their table with great ceremony.* ▷late Middle English: from Old French *ceremonie* or Latin *caerimonia* 'religious worship,' (plural) 'ritual observances.'
▶ □ **stand on ceremony** insist on the observance of formalities: *we don't stand on ceremony in this house.* □ **without ceremony** without preamble or politeness: *he was pushed without ceremony into the bathroom.*

ce·ri·um /ˈsi(ə)rēəm/ ▶n. the chemical element of atomic number 58, a silvery white lanthanide metal. (Symbol: **Ce**)

ce·ro /ˈsirō/ ▶n. (pl. same or **-os**) a large fish (*Scomberomorus regalis*) of the mackerel family, valued as a food fish in the tropical western Atlantic.

cert. ▶abbr. ■ certificate. ■ certified.

cer·tain /ˈsərtn/ ▶adj. **1** known for sure; established beyond doubt: *she looks certain to win an Oscar.* ■ having complete conviction about something; confident: *are you absolutely certain about this?* **2** specific but not explicitly named or stated: *the exercise was causing him a certain amount of pain.* ■ used when mentioning the name of someone not known to the reader or hearer: *a certain General Percy captured the town.*
▶pron. (**certain of**) some but not all: *certain of his works have been edited.*
▶ □ **for certain** without any doubt: *I don't know for certain.* □ **make certain** take action to ensure that something happens or is the case: *I made certain that our paths would never cross again.* ■ establish whether something is definitely correct or true: *he probably knew her, but it didn't do any harm to make certain.*

cer·tain·ly /ˈsərtnlē/ ▶adv. undoubtedly; definitely; surely: *the prestigious address certainly adds to the firm's appeal.* ■ (in answer to a question or command) yes; by all means: *"A good idea," she agreed. "Certainly!"*

cer·tain·ty /ˈsərtntē/ ▶n. (pl. **-ties**) firm conviction that something is the case: *she knew with absolute certainty that they were dead.* ■ the quality of being reliably true: *there is a bewildering lack of certainty and clarity in the law.* ■ a fact that is definitely true or an event that is definitely going to take place: *an immediate transfer would be a certainty.* ■ a person or thing that may be relied on: *expected to be a certainty for a gold medal.*

cer·ti·fi·a·ble /ˌsərtəˈfīəbəl/ ▶adj. **1** able or needing to be certified: *little hope for certifiable progress.* **2** officially recognized as needing treatment for a mental disorder. ■ *inf.* crazy. —**cer·ti·fi·a·bly** /-blē/ adj.

cer·tif·i·cate ▶n. /sərˈtifikit/ an official document attesting a certain fact, in particular: ■ a document recording a person's birth, marriage, or death. ■ a document describing a medical condition: *certificate of immunization.* ■ a document attesting a level of achievement in a course of study or training: *graduate certificate in information technology.* ■ a document attesting ownership of a certain item: *a stock certificate.*
▶v. /-ˈtifəkāt/ [tr.] (usu. **be certificated**) provide with or attest in an official document. —**cer·ti·fi·ca·tion** /ˌsərtəfiˈkāSHən/ n.

cer·tif·i·cate of de·pos·it (abbr.: **CD**) ▶n. a certificate issued by a bank to a person depositing money for a specified length of time.

cer·ti·fied check ▶n. a check that is guaranteed by a bank.

cer·ti·fied pub·lic ac·count·ant (abbr.: **CPA**) ▶n. a member of an officially accredited professional body of accountants.

cer·ti·fy /ˈsərtəˌfī/ ▶v. (**-fies, -fied**) [tr.] (often **be certified**) attest or confirm in a formal statement: | *the medical witness certified that death was due to cerebral hemorrhage.* ■ [often as adj.] (**certified**) officially recognize (someone or something) as possessing certain qualifications or meeting certain standards: *a certified scuba instructor.* ■ officially declare insane.

cer·ti·tude /ˈsərtəˌt(y)o͞od/ ▶n. absolute certainty or conviction that something is the case: *the question may never be answered with certitude.* ■ something that someone firmly believes is true.

ce·ru·le·an /səˈro͞olēən/ *poetic/lit.* ▶adj. deep blue in color like a clear sky: *cerulean waters and golden sands.*
▶n. a deep sky-blue color.

cer·vi·cal /ˈsərvikəl/ ▶adj. *Anat.* **1** of or relating to the narrow necklike passage forming the lower end of the uterus: *cervical cancer.* **2** of or relating to the neck: *the fifth cervical vertebra.*

cer·vix /'sərviks/ ▸n. (pl. **-vices** /-və,sēz/) the narrow necklike passage forming the lower end of the uterus.

ce·sar·e·an /si'zâr(ē)ən/ (also **cae·sar·e·an, Cae·sar·e·an,** or **Cae·sar·i·an**) ▸adj. of or effected by cesarean section: *a cesarean delivery.*
▸n. a cesarean section: *two sons born by cesarean.*

ce·sar·e·an sec·tion ▸n. a surgical operation for delivering a child by cutting through the wall of the mother's abdomen.

ce·si·um /'sēzēəm/ (*Brit.* **cae·si·um**) ▸n. the chemical element of atomic number 55, a soft, silvery, extremely reactive alkali metal. (Symbol: **Cs**)

ces·sa·tion /se'sāSHən/ ▸n. a ceasing; an end: *the cessation of hostilities.* ■ a pause or interruption: *a cessation of respiration requiring resuscitation.*

ces·sion /'seSHən/ ▸n. the formal giving up of rights, property, or territory, esp. by a state: *the cession of twenty important towns.*

cess·pool /'ses,pool/ ▸n. an underground container for the temporary storage of liquid waste and sewage. ■ *fig.* a disgusting or corrupt place.

ces·tode /'ses,tōd/ ▸n. any of the group of flatworms that includes tapeworms.

ce·ta·cean /si'tāSHən/ ▸n. any of various marine mammals with a streamlined hairless body, a horizontal tail fin, and a dorsal blowhole for breathing, including whales, dolphins, and porpoises.
▸adj. of or relating to cetaceans.

ce·tane /'sētān/ ▸n. *Chem.* a colorless liquid alkane hydrocarbon used as a solvent.

ce·tane num·ber ▸n. a measure of the ignition properties of diesel fuel relative to cetane as a standard.

Cey·lon moss ▸n. a red seaweed (*Gracilaria lichenoides*) of the Indian subcontinent, the main source of agar.

CF ▸abbr. ■ carried forward. ■ cost and freight. ■ cystic fibrosis.

Cf ▸symb. the chemical element californium.

cf. ▸abbr. compare with (used to refer a reader to another written work or another part of the same written work).

CFA¹ (also **CFA franc**) ▸n. the basic monetary unit of Cameroon, Congo, Gabon, and the Central African Republic, equal to 100 centimes.

CFA² ▸abbr. chartered financial analyst.

CFC ▸abbr. *Chem.* chlorofluorocarbon.

cfm ▸abbr. cubic feet per minute.

CFS ▸abbr. chronic fatigue syndrome.

cfs ▸abbr. cubic feet per second.

CG ▸abbr. ■ Coast Guard. ■ commanding general.

cgi ▸abbr. *Comput.* common gateway interface, a script standard for writing interactive programs (such as forms and searches) generated by visitors to Web pages.

cgi-bin /'sē,jē'ī ,bin/ ▸n. *Comput.* a server directory where cgi programs are stored.

cgs ▸abbr. centimeter-gram-second.

CH ▸abbr. ■ courthouse. ■ custom house.

ch. ▸abbr. ■ chaplain. ■ chapter. ■ church.

Cha·blis /SHa'blē; SHə-; SHä-/ ▸n. a dry white burgundy wine from Chablis in eastern France.

cha-cha /'CHä ,CHä/ (also **cha-cha-cha** /-'CHä/) ▸n. a ballroom dance with small steps and swaying hip movements, performed to a Latin American rhythm. ■ music for or in the rhythm of such a dance.
▸v. (**cha-chas, cha-chaed** or **cha-cha'd, cha-cha·ing**) [intr.] dance the cha-cha.

chad·or /'CHədər; 'CHäd,ôr/ (also **chad·ar**) ▸n. a large piece of dark-colored cloth, typically worn by Muslim women, wrapped around the head and upper body to leave only the face exposed. ▷early 17th cent.: from Urdu *chādar, chaddar,* from Persian *čādar* 'sheet or veil.'

chafe /CHāf/ ▸v. **1** [tr.] (of something restrictive or too tight) make (a part of the body) sore by rubbing against it: *the collar chafed his neck.* ■ [intr.] (of a part of the body) be or become sore as a result of such rubbing. ■ [intr.] (of an object) rub abrasively against another object: *the grommet stops the cable from chafing on the metal.* **2** [tr.] rub (a part of the body) to restore warmth or sensation. ■ restore (warmth or sensation) in this way. **3** become or make annoyed or impatient because of a restriction or inconvenience: [intr.] *the bank chafed at the restrictions imposed upon it* | [tr.] *it chafed him to be confined like this.*
▸n. **1** wear or damage caused by rubbing. **2** *archaic* a state of annoyance.

chaf·er /'CHāfər/ ▸n. a flying beetle (family Scarabaeidae), the adult and larva of which can be very destructive to foliage and plant roots, respectively.

chaff¹ /CHaf/ ▸n. the husks of corn or other seed separated by winnowing or threshing. ■ chopped hay and straw used as fodder. ■ *fig.*

worthless things; trash. ■ strips of metal foil or metal filings released in the atmosphere from aircraft, or deployed as missiles, to obstruct radar detection or confuse radar-tracking missiles.
▸ □ **separate the wheat from the chaff** distinguish valuable people or things from worthless ones.

chaff² ▸n. lighthearted joking; banter.
▸v. [tr.] tease.

chaf·fer /'CHafər/ ▸v. [intr.] haggle about the terms of an agreement or price of something.
▸n. *archaic* haggling about the price of something. —**chaff·er·er** n.

chaf·ing dish /'CHāfiNG/ ▸n. a metal pan with an outer pan of hot water, used for keeping food warm. ■ a metal pan, typically one containing an alcohol lamp, used for cooking at the table.

cha·grin /SHə'grin/ ▸n. distress or embarrassment at having failed or been humiliated: *Jeff, much to his chagrin, wasn't invited.*
▸v. (**be chagrined**) feel distressed or humiliated.

chain /CHān/ ▸n. **1** a connected flexible series of metal links used for fastening or securing objects and pulling or supporting loads. ■ (**chains**) such a series of links, or a set of them, used to confine a prisoner: *kept in chains.* ■ such a series of links worn as a decoration; a necklace. ■ *chiefly Brit.* such a series of links worn as a badge of office. ■ (**chains**) *fig.* a force or factor that binds or restricts someone: *the chains of illness.* **2** a sequence of items of the same type forming a line: *he kept the chain of buckets supplied with water.* ■ a sequence or series of connected elements: *a chain of events.* ■ a group of establishments, such as hotels, stores, or restaurants, owned by the same company: *the nation's largest hotel chain.* ■ a range of mountains. ■ a part of a molecule consisting of a number of atoms (typically carbon) bonded together in a linear sequence. ■ a figure in a quadrille or similar dance, in which dancers meet and pass each other in a continuous sequence. **3** a jointed measuring line consisting of linked metal rods. ■ the length of such a measuring line (66 ft.). ■ *Football* a measuring chain of ten yards, used in the determination of first downs.
▸v. [tr.] fasten or secure with a chain: *she chained her bicycle to the railing.* ■ confine with a chain: *he had been **chained up*** | *fig. as an actuary you will not be chained to a desk.*

chain gang ▸n. a group of convicts chained together while working outside the prison.

chain let·ter ▸n. one of a sequence of letters, each recipient in the sequence being requested to send copies to a specific number of other people.

chain mail ▸n. *hist.* armor made of small metal rings linked together.

chain re·ac·tion ▸n. a chemical reaction or other process in which the products themselves promote or spread the reaction, which under certain conditions may accelerate dramatically. ■ the self-sustaining fission reaction spread by neutrons that occurs in nuclear reactors and bombs. ■ *fig.* a series of events, each caused by the previous one: *an article in one publication sets off a chain reaction in the media.*

chain·saw /'CHān,sô/ ▸n. a power-driven cutting tool with teeth set on an endless chain that moves around the edge of a blade.

chain-smoke ▸v. [intr.] smoke continually, esp. by lighting a new cigarette from the butt of the last one smoked. —**chain-smok·er** n.

chair /CHe(ə)r/ ▸n. **1** a separate seat for one person, typically with a back and four legs. ■ *hist.* a sedan chair. ■ short for **CHAIRLIFT. 2** the person in charge of a meeting or organization (used as a neutral alternative to chairman or chairwoman). ■ an official position of authority, for example on a board of directors: *the editorial chair.* ■ (also **chair umpire**) *Tennis* another term for **UMPIRE. 3** a professorship: *he held a chair in physics.* **4** a particular seat in an orchestra: [as adj., in combination] *she was fourth-chair trumpet.* **5** (**the chair**) short for **ELECTRIC CHAIR.**
▸v. [tr.] **1** act as chairperson of or preside over (an organization, meeting, or public event). **2** *Brit.* carry (someone) aloft to celebrate a victory.

chair·la·dy /'CHe(ə)r,lādē/ ▸n. (pl. **-dies**) another term for **CHAIRWOMAN.**

chair·lift /'CHe(ə)r,lift/ ▸n. **1** a series of chairs hung from a moving cable, typically used for carrying passengers up and down a mountain. **2** a device for carrying people in wheelchairs from one floor of a building to another.

chair·man /'CHe(ə)rmən/ ▸n. (pl. **-men**) **1** a person, esp. a man, designated to preside over a meeting. ■ the permanent or long-term president of a committee, company, or other organization. ■ (**Chairman**) (since 1949) the leading figure in the Chinese Communist Party. **2** a person, esp. a man, who is the administrative head of a department of instruction at a college or university. **3** *hist.* a sedan-bearer. —**chair·man·ship** /-,SHip/ *n.*

chair·per·son /'CHe(ə)r,pərsən/ ▸*n.* a chairman or chairwoman (used as a neutral alternative).

chair·wom·an /'CHe(ə)r,wŏŏmən/ ▸*n.* (*pl.* -**wom·en**) **1** a woman designated to preside over committee or board meetings. **2** a woman who is the administrative head of a department of instruction at a college or university.

chaise /SHāz/ ▸*n.* **1** *chiefly hist.* a horse-drawn carriage for one or two people, typically one with an open top and two wheels. **2** short for **CHAISE LONGUE**.

chaise longue /'SHāz 'lôNG/ ▸*n.* (*pl.* **chaises longues** /'SHāz 'lôNG(z)/) a reclining chair with a lengthened seat forming a leg-rest.

chal·ced·o·ny /kal'sedn,ē; CHal-; 'kalsə,dōnē; 'CHalsə-/ ▸*n.* (*pl.* -**nies**) a type of quartz occurring in several different forms, including onyx, agate, and jasper. —**chal·ce·don·ic** /,kalsə'dänik/ *adj.*

Chal·de·an /kal'dēən/ ▸*n.* **1** a member of an ancient people who lived in Chaldea *c.*800 BC and ruled Babylonia 625–539 BC. They were renowned as astronomers and astrologers. **2** the Semitic language of the ancient Chaldeans. ▪ a language related to Aramaic and spoken in parts of Iraq.
▸*adj.* of or relating to ancient Chaldea or its people or language.

cha·let /SHa'lā; 'SHa,lā/ ▸*n.* a wooden house or cottage with overhanging eaves, typically found in the Swiss Alps. ▪ a similar building used as a ski lodge.

chal·ice /'CHaləs/ ▸*n. hist.* a large cup or goblet, typically used for drinking wine. ▪ the wine cup used in the Christian Eucharist.

chalk /CHôk/ ▸*n.* a soft white limestone (calcium carbonate) formed from the skeletal remains of sea creatures. ▪ a similar substance (calcium sulfate), made into white or colored sticks used for drawing or writing.
▸*v.* [*tr.*] **1** draw or write with chalk. ▪ draw or write on (a surface) with chalk. **2** rub (something, esp. a pool cue) with chalk.
▸*phrasal v.* ☐ **chalk something up 1** achieve something noteworthy: *he has chalked up a box-office success.* **2** ascribe something to a particular cause: *I chalked my sleeplessness up to nerves.*

chalk·board /'CHôk,bôrd/ ▸*n.* another term for **BLACKBOARD**.

chalk-stripe ▸*adj.* (of a garment or material) having a pattern of thin white stripes on a dark background.
▸*n.* (**chalk stripe**) a pattern of this kind. —**chalk-striped** *adj.*

chalk·y /'CHôkē/ ▸*adj.* (**chalk·i·er**, **chalk·i·est**) **1** consisting of or rich in chalk: *a chalky, powdery soil.* **2** resembling chalk in texture or paleness of color: *patches of creamy or chalky white.* —**chalk·i·ness** *n.*

chal·lenge /'CHalənj/ ▸*n.* **1** a call to take part in a contest or competition, esp. a duel: *he accepted the challenge.* ▪ a task or situation that tests someone's abilities. ▪ an attempt to win a contest or championship in a sport: *a world title challenge.* **2** an objection or query as to the truth of something, often with an implicit demand for proof: *a challenge to the legality of the order.* ▪ a sentry's call for a password or other proof of identity. ▪ *Law* an objection regarding the eligibility or suitability of a jury member. **3** *Med.* exposure of the immune system to pathogenic organisms or antigens.
▸*v.* [*tr.*] **1** invite (someone) to engage in a contest: *he challenged one of my men to a duel.* ▪ enter into competition with or opposition against. ▪ make a rival claim to or threaten someone's hold on (a position): *they were challenging his leadership.* ▪ [*tr.*] invite (someone) to do something that one thinks will be difficult or impossible; dare: *I challenged them to make up their own minds.* ▪ [usu. as *adj.*] (**challenging**) test the abilities of: *challenging and rewarding employment.* **2** dispute the truth or validity of: *employees challenged the company's requirement.* ▪ *Law* object to (a jury member). ▪ (of a sentry) call on (someone) for proof of identity. **3** *Med.* expose (the immune system) to pathogenic organisms or antigens. ▷Middle English (in the senses 'accusation' and 'accuse'): from Old French *chalenge* (noun), *chalenger* (verb), from Latin *calumnia* 'calumny,' *calumniari* 'calumniate.' —**chal·lenge·a·ble** *adj.* —**chal·leng·er** *n.* —**chal·leng·ing·ly** *adv.*

chal·lis /'SHalē/ ▸*n.* a soft lightweight clothing fabric made from silk and worsted.

cham·ber /'CHāmbər/ ▸*n.* **1** a hall used by a legislative or judicial body. ▪ the body that meets in such a hall. ▪ any of the houses of a legislature: *the Senate chamber.* **2** *poetic/lit.* or *archaic* a private room, typically a bedroom. ▪ (**chambers**) *Law* a judge's room used for official proceedings not required to be held in open court. **3** an enclosed space or cavity: *an echo chamber.* ▪ a large underground cavern. ▪ the part of

a gun bore that contains the ammunition. ▪ *Biol.* a cavity in a plant, animal body, or organ: *the four chambers of the heart.* **4** [as *adj.*] *Mus.* of or for a small group of instruments: *a chamber concert.*
▸*v.* [*tr.*] place (a bullet) into the chamber of a gun. —**cham·bered** *adj.*

cham·ber·lain /'CHāmbərlən/ ▸*n. hist.* an officer who manages the household of a monarch or noble. ▪ *Brit.* the treasurer of a corporation or public body. —**cham·ber·lain·ship** /-,SHip/ *n.*

cham·ber·maid /'CHāmbər,mād/ ▸*n.* a maid who cleans bedrooms and bathrooms, esp. in a hotel.

chamber of com·merce (abbr.: **C. of C.**) ▸*n.* a local association to promote and protect the interests of the business community in a particular place.

chamber pot ▸*n.* a bowl kept in a bedroom and used as a toilet, esp. at night.

cham·bray /'SHam,brā; -brē/ ▸*n.* a linen-finished cloth with a white weft and a colored warp, producing a mottled appearance.

cha·me·le·on /kə'mēlyən; -lēən/ (*chiefly Brit.* also **cha·mae·le·on**) ▸*n.* a small Old World lizard (*Chamaeleo* and other genera, family Chamaeleonidae) with a prehensile tail, extensible tongue, and the ability to change color. Numerous species include the **common chameleon** (*C. chamaeleon*). ▪ (also **American chameleon**) an anole. ▪ *fig.* a changeable or inconstant person. —**cha·me·le·on·ic** /kə,mēlē-'änik/ *adj.*

cham·fer /'CHamfər/ ▸*v.* [*tr.*] in carpentry, cut away (a right-angled edge or corner) to make a symmetrical sloping edge.
▸*n.* a symmetrical sloping surface at an edge or corner.

cham·ois /'SHamē/ ▸*n.* **1** (*pl.* same /'SHamēz/) an agile goat-antelope (genus *Rupicapra*) with short hooked horns, found in mountainous areas of Europe from Spain to the Caucasus. **2** (*pl.* same) (also **chamois leather**) soft pliable leather made from the skin of sheep, goats, or deer. ▪ a piece of such leather, used typically for washing windows or cars.

cham·o·mile /'kamə,mēl; -,mīl/ (also **cam·o·mile**) ▸*n.* an aromatic European plant (*Anthemis* and other genera) of the daisy family, with white and yellow daisylike flowers. ▷Middle English: from Old French *camomille*, from late Latin *chamomilla*, from Greek *khamaimēlon* 'earth apple.'

champ¹ /CHamp/ ▸*v.* another term for **CHOMP**.

champ² ▸*n. inf.* a champion.

cham·pagne /SHam'pān/ ▸*n.* a white sparkling wine associated with celebration and regarded as a symbol of luxury, typically that made in the Champagne region of France. ▪ a pale cream or straw color.

cham·pi·on /'CHampēən/ ▸*n.* **1** a person who has defeated or surpassed all rivals in a competition, esp. in sports. **2** a person who fights or argues for a cause or on behalf of someone else. ▪ *hist.* a knight who fought in single combat on behalf of the monarch.
▸*v.* [*tr.*] support the cause of; defend: *priests who championed human rights.*

cham·pi·on·ship /'CHampēən,SHip/ ▸*n.* **1** a contest for the position of champion in a sport, often involving a series of games or matches. ▪ the position or title of the winner of such a contest. **2** the vigorous support or defense of someone or something: *Alan's championship of his estranged wife.*

chance /CHans/ ▸*n.* **1** a possibility of something happening: *there is little chance of his finding a job.* ▪ (**chances**) the probability of something happening: *he played down his chances of becoming chairman.* ▪ an opportunity to do or achieve something: *I gave her a chance to answer.* ▪ a ticket in a raffle or lottery. **2** the occurrence and development of events in the absence of any obvious design: *he met his brother by chance.* ▪ the unplanned and unpredictable course of events regarded as a power: *chance was offering me success.*
▸*adj.* fortuitous; accidental: *a chance meeting.*
▸*v.* **1** [*intr.*] do something by accident or without design: *if they chanced to meet.* ▪ (**chance upon/on**) find or see by accident: *he chanced upon an interesting advertisement.* **2** [*tr.*] *inf.* do (something) despite its being dangerous or of uncertain outcome: *she chanced another look.*
▸ ☐ **by any chance** possibly (used in tentative inquiries or suggestions): *were you looking for me by any chance?* ☐ **no chance** *inf.* there is no possibility of that: *I asked if we could leave early and she said, "No chance."* ☐ **on the (off) chance** just in case: *Joan phoned at noon on the off chance that he'd be home.* ☐ **stand a chance** have a prospect of success or survival: *his rivals don't stand a chance.* ☐ **take a chance** (or **chances**) behave in a way that leaves one vulnerable to danger or failure. ▪ (**take a chance on**) put one's trust in (something or someone) knowing that it may not be safe or certain. ☐ **take one's chances** do something risky with the hope of success.

chan·cel /'CHansəl/ ▸*n.* the part of a church near the altar, reserved for the clergy and choir, and typically separated from the nave by steps or a screen.

chan·cel·ler·y /ˈCHans(ə)lərē/ ▶n. (pl. **-ler·ies**) **1** the position, office, or department of a chancellor. ■ the official residence of a chancellor. **2** an office attached to an embassy or consulate.

chan·cel·lor /ˈCHans(ə)lər/ ▶n. a senior state or legal official. ■ the head of the government in some European countries, such as Germany. ■ the presiding judge of a chancery court. ■ the president or chief administrative officer of a college or university. ■ a bishop's law officer. ■ (**Chancellor**) short for CHANCELLOR OF THE EXCHEQUER. —**chan·cel·lor·ship** /-,SHip/ n.

Chan·cel·lor of the Ex·cheq·uer ▶n. the finance minister of the United Kingdom, responsible for preparing the nation's annual budgets.

chan·cer·y /ˈCHans(ə)rē/ ▶n. (pl. **-cer·ies**) **1** a court of equity. ■ equity. ■ hist. the court of a bishop's chancellor. ■ (**Chancery**) Brit. Law the Lord Chancellor's court, a division of the High Court of Justice. **2** (in the Roman Catholic Church) the office of a diocese. **3** chiefly Brit. an office attached to an embassy or consulate. **4** a public records office.

chan·cre /ˈkaNGkər; ˈSHaNG-/ ▶n. Med. a painless ulcer, particularly one developing on the genitals as a result of venereal disease.

chanc·y /ˈCHansē/ ▶adj. (**chanc·i·er**, **chanc·i·est**) inf. subject to unpredictable changes and circumstances: the screening process was likely to be chancy and unreliable. —**chanc·i·ly** /-səlē/ adv. —**chanc·i·ness** n.

chan·de·lier /,SHandəˈli(ə)r/ ▶n. a decorative hanging light with branches for several light bulbs or candles.

chan·dler /ˈCHan(d)lər/ ▶n. **1** (also **ship chandler**) a dealer in supplies and equipment for ships and boats. **2** hist. a dealer in household items such as oil, soap, paint, and groceries. ■ a person who makes and sells candles. —**chan·dler·y** n.

change /CHānj/ ▶v. **1** make or become different: [tr.] a proposal to change the law | [intr.] a Virginia creeper just beginning to **change** from green to gold. ■ make or become a different substance entirely; transform: [tr.] filters **change** the ammonia **into** nitrate [intr.] computer graphics can show cars changing into cheetahs. ■ [intr.] alter in terms of: the ferns began to **change** shape. ■ [intr.] (of traffic lights) move from one color of signal to another. ■ (of a boy's voice) become deeper with the onset of puberty. **2** [tr.] take or use another instead of: she decided to change her name. ■ move from one to another: she changed jobs. ■ exchange; trade: the sun and moon changed places. ■ [intr.] move to a different train, airplane, or subway line. ■ give up (something) in exchange for something else: we changed the shades for vertical blinds. ■ remove (something dirty or faulty) and replace it with another of the same kind: change a light bulb. ■ put a clean garment on (a baby or young child). ■ engage a different gear in a motor vehicle: [tr.] wait for a gap and then change gears. ■ exchange (a sum of money) for the same amount in smaller denominations or in coins, or for different currency. ■ [intr.] put different clothes on: he changed for dinner.
▶phrasal v. □ **change over** move from one system or situation to another: crop farmers have to **change over to** dairy farming.
▶n. **1** the act or instance of making or becoming different: environmental change. ■ the substitution of one thing for another: a change of venue. ■ an alteration or modification: a change came over Eddie's face. ■ a new or refreshingly different experience: couscous makes an interesting change from rice. ■ a clean garment or garments as a replacement for clothes one is wearing: a change of socks. ■ (**the change** or **the change of life**) inf. menopause. **2** coins as opposed to paper currency. ■ money given in exchange for the same amount in larger denominations. ■ money returned to someone as the balance of the amount paid for something. **3** (usu. **changes**) an order in which a peal of bells can be rung. ▷Middle English: from Old French change (noun), changer (verb), from late Latin cambiare, from Latin cambire 'barter,' probably of Celtic origin. —**chang·er** n.
▶ □ **change hands** (of a business or building) pass to a different owner. ■ (of money or a marketable commodity) pass to another person during a business transaction. □ **a change of heart** a move to a different opinion or plan. □ **a change of heart** a move to a different opinion or attitude. □ **change the subject** begin talking about something different, esp. to avoid embarrassment or the divulgence of confidences. □ **change one's tune 1** express a different opinion or behave in a different way. **2** change one's style of language or manner, esp. from an insolent to a respectful tone. □ **for a change** contrary to how things usually happen; for variety.

change·a·ble /ˈCHānjəbəl/ ▶adj. **1** irregular; inconstant: the weather will be changeable, with rain at times. **2** able to change or be changed. —**change·a·bil·i·ty** /,CHānjəˈbilətē/ n. —**change·a·ble·ness** n. —**change·a·bly** /-blē/ adv.

change·less /ˈCHānjlis/ ▶adj. remaining the same. —**change·less·ly** adv. —**change·less·ness** n.

change·ling /ˈCHānjliNG/ ▶n. a child believed to have been secretly substituted by fairies for the parents' real child in infancy.

change·out /ˈCHānj,out/ ▶n. the replacement of a spent, used, dysfunctional or otherwise inferior part or object with a new one.

change·o·ver /ˈCHānj,ōvər/ ▶n. a change from one system or situation to another.

chan·nel /ˈCHanl/ ▶n. **1** a length of water wider than a strait, joining two larger areas of water, esp. two seas. ■ the navigable part of a waterway. ■ a hollow bed for a natural or artificial waterway. ■ a narrow gap or passage. ■ a tubular passage or duct for liquid. ■ an electric circuit that acts as a path for a signal: an audio channel. ■ a groove or flute, esp. in a column. ■ Electr. the semiconductor region in a field-effect transistor that forms the main current path between the source and the drain. **2** a band of frequencies used in radio and television transmission, esp. as used by a particular station. ■ a service or station using such a band: a shopping channel. **3** a medium for communication or the passage of information: they didn't apply through the proper channels.
▶v. (**-neled**, **-nel·ing**; Brit. **-nelled**, **-nel·ling**) [tr.] **1** direct toward a particular end or object: advertisers channel money into radio. ■ guide along a particular route or through a specified medium. ■ (of a person) serve as a medium for (a spirit). **2** [usu. as adj.] (**channeled**) form channels or grooves in: the lower jawbone is deeply channeled.

chan·nel-surf ▶v. inf. change frequently from one television channel to another, using a remote control device. —**chan·nel-surf·er** n. —**chan·nel-surf·ing** n.

chant /CHant/ ▶n. **1** a repeated rhythmic phrase, typically one shouted or sung in unison by a crowd. ■ a monotonous or repetitive song, typically an incantation or part of a ritual. **2** Mus. a short musical passage in two or more phrases used for singing unmetrical words; a psalm or canticle sung to such music. ■ the style of music consisting of such passages: Gregorian chant.
▶v. [tr.] say or shout repeatedly in a sing-song tone: protesters were chanting slogans. ■ sing or intone (a psalm, canticle, or sacred text).

chant·er /ˈCHantər/ ▶n. **1** a person who chants. **2** Mus. the pipe of a bagpipe with finger holes, on which the melody is played.

chan·teuse /,SHänˈtōoz; ˈtœz/ ▶n. a female singer of popular songs, esp. in a nightclub.

chant·ey /ˈSHantē/ (also **chant·y**, **shant·y**, or **sea chantey**) ▶n. a song with alternating solo and chorus, of a kind originally sung by sailors while performing physical labor together.

Chan·til·ly lace ▶n. a delicate kind of bobbin lace.

chant·y ▶n. (pl. **chant·ies**) variant spelling of CHANTEY.

Cha·nu·kah ▶n. variant spelling of HANUKKAH.

cha·os /ˈkā,äs/ ▶n. complete disorder and confusion: snow caused chaos in the region. ■ Physics behavior so unpredictable as to appear random, owing to great sensitivity to small changes in conditions. ■ the formless matter supposed to have existed before the creation of the universe. ■ (**Chaos**) Greek Mythol. the first created being, from which came the primeval deities. —**cha·ot·ic** /kāˈätik/ adj.

chap[1] /CHap/ ▶v. (**chapped**, **chap·ping**) [intr.] (of the skin) become cracked, rough, or sore, typically through exposure to cold weather: ■ [tr.] [usu. as adj.] (**chapped**) (of the wind or cold) cause (skin) to crack in this way: chapped lips.
▶n. a cracked or sore patch on the skin.

chap[2] ▶n. inf., chiefly Brit. a man or a boy.

chap·ar·ral /,SHapəˈral/ ▶n. vegetation consisting chiefly of tangled shrubs and thorny bushes.

chape /CHāp/ ▶n. **1** hist. the metal point of a scabbard. **2** the metal pin of a buckle.

chap·el /ˈCHapəl/ ▶n. a small building for Christian worship, typically one attached to an institution or private house. ■ regular services held in such a building: attendance at chapel was compulsory. ■ a part of a large church or cathedral with its own altar and dedication. ■ a room or building in which funeral services are held.

chap·er·one /ˈSHapə,rōn/ (also **chap·er·on**) ▶n. a person who accompanies and looks after another person or group of people, in particular: ■ dated an older woman responsible for the decorous behavior of a young unmarried girl at social occasions. ■ a person who takes charge of a child or group of children in public.

▶ v. [tr.] accompany and look after or supervise. —**chap·er·on·age** /-ˌrōnij; ˌsHapə'rōnij/ n.

chap·lain /'cHaplən/ ▶ n. a member of the clergy attached to a private chapel, institution, ship, branch of the armed forces, etc. —**chap·lain·cy** /'cHaplənsē/ n.

chap·let /'cHaplət/ ▶ n. **1** a garland or wreath for a person's head. **2** a string of 55 beads (one third of the rosary number) for counting prayers, or as a necklace. —**chap·let·ed** adj.

chaps /cHaps; sHaps/ ▶ pl. n. leather pants without a seat, worn by a cowboy over ordinary pants to protect the legs.

chap·ter /'cHaptər/ ▶ n. **1** a main division of a book, typically with a number or title. ■ fig. a period of time or an episode in a person's life, a nation's history, etc.: a tragic chapter in history. **2** a local branch of a society. **3** the governing body of a religious community, esp. a cathedral or a knightly order. **4** a series or sequence: the latest episode in a chapter of problems.

▶ □ **chapter and verse** an exact reference or authority.

char[1] /cHär/ ▶ v. (**charred, char·ring**) [tr.] (usu. **be charred**) partially burn (an object) so as to blacken its surface: their bodies were badly charred in the fire. ■ [intr.] (of an object) become burned and discolored in such a way.

▶ n. material that has been charred.

char[2] Brit., inf. ▶ n. a charwoman.

▶ v. (**charred, char·ring**) [intr.] work as a charwoman.

char[3] (also **charr**) ▶ n. (pl. same) a freshwater or marine fish (genus Salvelinus) of the salmon family, occurring in northern countries and widely valued as a food and game fish. Its several species include the North American **brook trout** (S. fontinalis) and the red-bellied **Arctic char** (S. alpinus).

char·a·banc /'sHarəˌbang; -ˌbaNGk/ ▶ n. Brit. an early form of bus, used typically for pleasure trips.

char·ac·ter /'kariktər/ ▶ n. **1** the mental and moral qualities distinctive to an individual: running away was not in keeping with her character. ■ the distinctive nature of something: gas lamps give the area its character. ■ the quality of being individual, typically in an interesting or unusual way: the island is full of character. ■ strength and originality in a person's nature: she had character as well as beauty. ■ a person's good reputation. ■ dated a written statement of someone's good qualities; a recommendation. **2** a person in a novel, play, or movie. ■ a part played by an actor. ■ a person seen in terms of a particular aspect of character: shady characters. ■ inf. an interesting or amusing individual. **3** a printed or written letter or symbol. ■ Comput. a symbol representing a letter or number. ■ Comput. the bit pattern used to store such a symbol. **4** chiefly Biol. a characteristic, esp. one that assists in the identification of a species.

▶ v. [tr.] archaic inscribe; engrave. ■ describe; characterize. ▷Middle English: from Old French caractere, via Latin from Greek kharaktēr 'a stamping tool.' From the early sense 'distinctive mark' arose 'token, feature, or trait' (early 16th cent.), and from this 'a description, esp. of a person's qualities,' giving rise to 'distinguishing qualities.' —**char·ac·ter·ful** /-fəl/ adj. —**char·ac·ter·ful·ly** adv. —**char·ac·ter·less** adj.

▶ □ **in** (or **out of**) **character** in keeping (or not in keeping) with someone's usual pattern of behavior.

char·ac·ter·is·tic /ˌkariktə'ristik/ ▶ adj. typical of a particular person, place, or thing: large farms are characteristic of this area.

▶ n. **1** a feature or quality belonging typically to a person, place, or thing and serving to identify it: inherited characteristics such as blood groups. **2** Math. the whole number or integral part of a logarithm, which gives the order of magnitude of the original number. —**char·ac·ter·is·ti·cal·ly** adv.

char·ac·ter·ize /'kariktəˌrīz/ ▶ v. [tr.] **1** describe the distinctive nature or features of. **2** (often **be characterized**) (of a feature or quality) be typical or characteristic of: the disease is **characterized by** weakening of the immune system. —**char·ac·ter·i·za·tion** /ˌkariktərə'zāsHən/ n.

cha·rade /sHə'rād/ ▶ n. an absurd pretense intended to create a pleasant or respectable appearance: talk of unity was nothing more than a charade. ■ (**charades**) a game in which players guess a word or phrase from pantomimed clues.

char·coal /'cHärˌkōl/ ▶ n. a porous black solid, consisting of an amorphous form of carbon, obtained as a residue when wood, bone, or other organic matter is heated in the absence of air. ■ briquettes of charcoal used for barbecuing: lamb grilled on charcoal. ■ a crayon made of charcoal and used for drawing. ■ a drawing made using charcoal. ■ a dark gray color: his charcoal sweater | [as adj.] **charcoal gray**.

▶ v. [usu. as adj.] (**charcoaled**) cook over charcoal: charcoaled lobster.

chard /cHärd/ ▶ n. (also **Swiss chard**) a beet of a variety with broad white leaf stalks that may be prepared and eaten separately from the green parts of the leaf.

Char·don·nay /ˌsHärdn'ā/ ▶ n. a variety of white wine grape used for making champagne and other wines. ■ a wine made from this grape.

charge /cHärj/ ▶ v. [tr.] **1** demand (an amount) as a price from someone for a service rendered or goods supplied: the restaurant charged $15 for dinner | [intr.] museums should **charge for** admission. ■ (**charge something to**) record the cost of something as an amount payable by (someone) or on (an account): they charge the calls to their credit-card accounts. **2** accuse (someone) of something, esp. an offense under law: they were **charged with** assault. ■ make an accusation or assertion that: opponents charged that below-cost pricing would reduce safety. **3** entrust (someone) with a task as a duty or responsibility: the committee was **charged with** reshaping the educational system. **4** store electrical energy in (a battery or battery-operated device). ■ [intr.] (of a battery or battery-operated device) receive and store electrical energy. ■ technical or formal load or fill (a container, gun, etc.) to the full or proper extent. ■ (usu. **be charged with**) fig. fill or pervade (something) with a quality or emotion: the air was charged with menace. **5** [intr.] rush forward in attack. ■ move aggressively toward (someone or something) in attack. ■ move quickly and with impetus: Henry charged up the staircase.

▶ n. **1** a price asked for goods or services: an admission charge. ■ a financial liability or commitment: an asset of $550,000 should have been taken as **a charge on** earnings. **2** an accusation, typically one formally made against a prisoner brought to trial: **a charge of** attempted murder. **3** the responsibility of taking care or control of someone or something: the people **in her charge**. ■ a person or thing entrusted to the care of someone: the babysitter watched over her charges. ■ dated a responsibility or onerous duty assigned to someone. ■ an official instruction, esp. one given by a judge to a jury regarding points of law. **4** the property of matter that is responsible for electrical phenomena, existing in a positive or negative form. ■ the quantity of this carried by a body. ■ energy stored chemically for conversion into electricity. ■ the process of storing electrical energy in a battery. ■ inf. a thrill: I get a real charge out of working hard. **5** a quantity of explosive to be detonated, typically in order to fire a gun or similar weapon. **6** a headlong rush forward, typically one made by attacking soldiers in battle: a cavalry charge. ■ the signal or call for such a rush. **7** Heraldry a device or bearing placed on a shield or crest. —**charge·a·ble** adj.

▶ □ **free of charge** without any payment due. □ **in charge** in control or with overall responsibility. □ **press** (or **prefer**) **charges** accuse someone formally of a crime so that they can be brought to trial. □ **take charge** assume control or responsibility.

charge ac·count ▶ n. an account to which goods and services may be charged on credit.

charge·back /'cHärjˌbak/ ▶ n. an act or policy of allocating the cost of an organization's centrally located resources to the individuals or departments that use them.

charge card ▶ n. a credit card for use with an account that must be paid when a statement is issued.

charg·er[1] /'cHärjər/ ▶ n. **1** a horse trained for battle; a cavalry horse. **2** a device for charging a battery or battery-powered equipment. **3** a person who charges forward.

charg·er[2] (also **charger plate**) ▶ n. a large, flat dish; a platter. ■ a large plate placed under a dinner plate in some formal table settings.

char·i·ot /'cHarēət/ ▶ n. hist. a two-wheeled horse-drawn vehicle used in ancient warfare and racing. ■ hist. a four-wheeled carriage with back seats and a coachman's seat. ■ poetic/lit. a stately or triumphal carriage.

▶ v. [tr.] poetic/lit. convey in or as in a chariot.

chariot

char·i·ot·eer /ˌcHarēə'ti(ə)r/ ▶ n. a chariot driver.

cha·ris·ma /kə'rizmə/ ▶ n. **1** compelling attractiveness or charm that can inspire devotion in others. **2** (*pl.* **-ma·ta** /-ˌmətə/) (also **char·ism** /ˈkar,izəm/) a divinely conferred power or talent.

char·is·mat·ic /ˌkarizˈmatik/ ▶*adj.* **1** exercising a compelling charm that inspires devotion in others. **2** of or relating to the charismatic movement in the Christian Church. ■ (of a power or talent) divinely conferred.
▶*n.* an adherent of the charismatic movement. ■ a person who claims divine inspiration. —**char·is·mat·i·cal·ly** *adv.*

char·is·mat·ic move·ment ▶*n.* a movement within some Christian churches that emphasizes gifts believed to be conferred by the Holy Spirit, such as speaking in tongues and healing of the sick.

char·i·ta·ble /ˈCHaritəbəl/ ▶*adj.* **1** of or relating to the assistance of those in need. ■ (of an organization or activity) officially recognized as devoted to the assistance of those in need. ■ generous in giving to those in need. **2** apt to judge others leniently or favorably. —**char·i·ta·ble·ness** *n.* —**char·i·ta·bly** *adv.*

char·i·ty /ˈCHaritē/ ▶*n.* (*pl.* **-ties**) **1** the voluntary giving of help, typically in the form of money, to those in need. ■ help or money given in this way: *an unemployed teacher living on charity.* **2** an organization set up to provide help and raise money for those in need. ■ such organizations viewed collectively as the object of fund-raising or donations: *the proceeds of the sale will go to charity.* **3** kindness and tolerance in judging others. ■ *archaic* love of humankind, typically in a Christian context: *faith, hope, and charity.*

char·la·tan /ˈSHärlətən; ˈSHärlətn/ ▶*n.* a person falsely claiming to have a special knowledge or skill; a fraud. —**char·la·tan·ism** /-lətəˌnizəm; -lətn,izəm/ *n.* —**char·la·tan·ry** /ˈSHärlətənrē; -lətnrē/ *n.*

Charles·ton (also **charles·ton**) ▶*n.* a lively dance of the 1920s that involved turning the knees inward and kicking out the lower legs.
▶*v.* [*intr.*] dance the Charleston.

char·ley horse /ˈCHärlē/ ▶*n. inf.* a cramp or feeling of stiffness in an arm or leg.

charm /CHärm/ ▶*n.* **1** the power or quality of giving delight or arousing admiration: *he was captivated by her youthful charm.* ■ (usu. **charms**) an attractive or alluring characteristic: *the charms of the city.* **2** a small ornament worn on a necklace or bracelet. **3** an object, act, or saying believed to have magic power. ■ an object kept or worn to ward off evil and bring good luck. **4** *Physics* one of six flavors of quark.
▶*v.* [*tr.*] **1** delight greatly: *the books have charmed children the world over.* ■ gain or influence by charm: *he charmed her into going out.* **2** control or achieve by or as if by magic: *pretending to charm a cobra* | *she will charm your warts away.* ▷Middle English (in the senses 'incantation or magic spell' and 'to use spells'): from Old French *charme* (noun), *charmer* (verb), from Latin *carmen* 'song, verse, incantation.' —**charm·er** *n.* —**charm·less** *adj.*
▶ □ **turn on the charm** use one's ability to charm in order to influence someone. □ **work like a charm** be completely successful or effective.

charm·ing /ˈCHärmiNG/ ▶*adj.* pleasant or attractive. ■ (of a person or manner) polite, friendly, and likable. —**charm·ing·ly** *adv.*

char·nel house ▶*n. hist.* a building or vault in which corpses or bones are piled. ■ *fig.* a place associated with violent death.

chart /CHärt/ ▶*n.* **1** a sheet of information in the form of a table, graph, or diagram: *a chart showing how much do-it-yourself costs compared with retail.* ■ (usu. **the charts**) a weekly listing of the current best-selling pop records: *she topped the charts for eight weeks.* ■ a geographical map or plan, esp. one used for navigation by sea or air. ■ *Med.* a written record of information about a patient: *scribbled on a patient's chart.* ■ (also **birth chart** or **natal chart**) *Astrol.* a map, typically circular, showing the positions of the planets at the time of someone's birth, from which astrologers are said to be able to deduce character or potential.
▶*v.* **1** [*tr.*] make a map of (an area). ■ plot (a course) on a chart: *the pilot found his craft taking a route he had not charted* | *fig. the poems chart his descent into madness.* ■ (usu. **be charted**) record on a chart. **2** [*intr.*] (of a recording) enter the weekly music charts at a particular position.

chart·bust·er /ˈCHärt,bəstər/ ▶*n. inf.* a popular singer or group that makes a best-selling recording. ■ a best-selling recording.

char·ter /ˈCHärtər/ ▶*n.* **1** a written grant by a country's legislative or sovereign power, by which an institution such as a company, college, or city is created and its rights and privileges defined. ■ a written constitution or description of an organization's functions. **2** the reservation of an aircraft, boat, or bus for private use: *a plane on charter to a multinational company.* ■ an aircraft, boat, or bus reserved for private use. ■ a trip made by an aircraft, boat, or bus under charter.
▶*v.* [*tr.*] **1** grant a charter to (a city, college, or other institution). **2** reserve (an aircraft, boat, or bus) for private use.

char·ter mem·ber ▶*n.* an original or founding member of an organization.

Chart·ism /ˈCHärt,izəm/ ▶*n.* a UK parliamentary reform movement of 1837–48, the principles of which were set out in a manifesto called *The People's Charter.* —**Chart·ist** *n. & adj.*

chart·let /ˈCHärtlit/ ▶*n.* a small chart, as for navigation, highlighting a particular feature.

char·treuse /SHär'trœz; -'trōōs/ ▶*n.* a pale green or yellow liqueur made from brandy and aromatic herbs. ■ a pale yellow or green color resembling this liqueur.

char·wom·an /ˈCHär,wŏŏmən/ ▶*n.* (*pl.* **-wom·en**) *Brit., dated* a woman employed to clean houses or offices.

char·y /ˈCHe(ə)rē/ ▶*adj.* (**char·i·er, char·i·est**) cautious; wary: *most people are chary of allowing themselves to be photographed.* ■ cautious about the amount one gives or reveals. —**char·i·ly** /ˈCHe(ə)rəlē/ *adv.*

chase[1] /CHās/ ▶*v.* [*tr.*] **1** pursue in order to catch or catch up with: *police chased the stolen car* | [*intr.*] *the dog chased after the stick.* ■ seek to attain: *seventy candidates chasing a single job.* ■ seek the company of (a member of the opposite sex) in an obvious way. ■ [*tr.*] drive or cause to go in a specified direction: *she chased him out of the house.* **2** try to make contact with (someone) in order to get something owed or required: *chasing customers who had not paid their bills.* ■ make further investigation of (an unresolved matter): *investigators got a warrant to chase down the case.*
▶*n.* an act of pursuing someone or something: *they captured the youths after a brief chase.* ■ (**the chase**) hunting as a sport: *she was an ardent follower of the chase.* ■ *Brit.* an area of unenclosed land formerly reserved for hunting. ■ *archaic* a hunted animal.
▶ □ **give chase** go in pursuit.

chase[2] ▶*v.* [*tr.*] [usu. as *adj.*] (**chased**) engrave (metal, or a design on metal): *a miniature container with a delicately chased floral design.*

chase[3] ▶*n.* (in letterpress printing) a metal frame for holding the composed type and blocks being printed at one time.

chase[4] ▶*n.* **1** the part of a gun enclosing the bore. **2** a groove or furrow cut in the face of a wall or other surface to receive a pipe.

chas·er /ˈCHāsər/ ▶*n.* **1** a person or thing that chases: [in *combination*] *promotion-chasers.* **2** *inf.* a drink taken after another of a different kind, typically a weak alcoholic drink after a stronger one: *bourbon on the rocks with a beer chaser.* **3** a horse for steeplechasing.

chasm /ˈkazəm/ ▶*n.* a deep fissure in the earth, rock, or another surface. ■ *fig.* a profound difference between people, viewpoints, feelings, etc.: *the chasm between rich and poor.* —**chas·mic** /ˈkazmik/ *adj.* (*rare*).

chas·sé /SHa'sā/ ▶*n.* a gliding step in dancing in which one foot displaces the other.
▶*v.* (**chas·séd, chas·sé·ing**) [*intr.*] make such a step.

chas·sis /ˈCHasē; ˈSHasē/ ▶*n.* (*pl.* same) the base frame of a motor vehicle or other wheeled conveyance. ■ the outer structural framework of a piece of audio, radio, or computer equipment.

chaste /CHāst/ ▶*adj.* abstaining from extramarital, or from all, sexual intercourse. ■ not having any sexual nature or intention: *a chaste, consoling embrace.* ■ without unnecessary ornamentation; simple or restrained: *the dark, chaste interior.* —**chaste·ly** *adv.* —**chaste·ness** *n.*

chas·ten /ˈCHāsən/ ▶*v.* [*tr.*] (of a reproof or misfortune) have a restraining or moderating effect on: *the director was somewhat chastened by his recent flops.* —**chas·ten·er** /ˈCHās(ə)nər/ *n.*

chas·tise /CHas'tīz/ ▶*v.* [*tr.*] rebuke or reprimand severely: *he chastised his colleagues for their laziness.* ■ *dated* punish, esp. by beating. —**chas·tise·ment** /CHas'tīzmənt; ˈCHastəz-/ *n.* —**chas·tis·er** /CHas,tīzər/ *n.*

chas·ti·ty /ˈCHastətē/ ▶*n.* the state or practice of refraining from extramarital, or esp. from all, sexual intercourse: *vows of chastity.*

chas·ti·ty belt ▶*n. hist.* a garment or device designed to prevent a woman from having sexual intercourse.

chas·u·ble /ˈCHazəbəl; ˈCHazн-; ˈCHas-/ ▶*n.* a sleeveless outer vestment worn by a Catholic or High Anglican priest when celebrating Mass, typically ornate and having a simple hole for the head.

chat[1] /CHat/ ▶*v.* (**chat·ted, chat·ting**) [*intr.*] talk in a friendly and informal way: *she chatted to her mother on the phone every day.*
▶*phrasal v.* □ **chat someone up** *inf.* engage someone in flirtatious conversation. ■ talk persuasively to someone, esp. with a motive.
▶*n.* an informal conversation.

chat[2] ▶*n.* any of a number of small songbirds with harsh calls,

---

Pronunciation Key ə *ago, up*; ər *over, fur*; a *hat*; ā *ate*; ä *car*; CH *chin*; e *let*; ē *see*; e(ə)r *air*; i *fit*; ī *by*; i(ə)r *ear*; NG *sing*; ō *go*; ô *law, for*; oi *toy*; ŏŏ *good*; ōō *goo*; ou *out*; SH *she*; TH *thin*; ŦH *then*; (h)w *why*; ZH *vision*

including a New World warbler, (genera *Icteria* and *Granatellus*), that typically has a yellow or pink breast.

cha·teau /sʜaˈtō/ (also **châ·teau**) ▶ *n*. (*pl*. **-teaux** /-ˈtō(z)/) a large French country house or castle often giving its name to wine made in its neighborhood: [in *names*] *Château Margaux.*

cha·teau·bri·and /sʜaˌtōbrēˈôn/ ▶ *n*. a thick tenderloin of beef, typically served with Béarnaise sauce.

chat·e·laine /ˈsʜatlˌān/ ▶ *n*. dated a woman in charge of a large house. ■ *hist*. a set of short chains attached to a woman's belt, used for carrying keys or other items.

chat·tel /ˈsʜatl/ ▶ *n*. (in general use) a personal possession. ■ *Law* an item of property other than real estate.

chat·ter /ˈsʜatər/ ▶ *v*. [*intr*.] talk rapidly or incessantly about trivial matters. ■ (of a bird, monkey, or machine) make a series of quick high-pitched sounds. ■ (of a person's teeth) click repeatedly together, typically from cold or fear.
▶ *n*. incessant trivial talk: *a stream of idle chatter.* ■ a series of quick high-pitched sounds: *the chatter of a typewriter.* ■ undesirable vibration in a mechanism: *the windshield wipers should operate without chatter.* —**chat·ter·er** *n*. —**chat·ter·y** *adj*.

chat·ter·box /ˈsʜatərˌbäks/ ▶ *n*. inf. a person who talks at length about trivial matters.

chat·ty /ˈsʜatē/ ▶ *adj*. (**chat·ti·er**, **chat·ti·est**) (of a person) fond of talking in an easy, informal way. ■ (of a conversation, letter, etc.) informal and lively. —**chat·ti·ly** /ˈsʜatl-ē/ *adv*. —**chat·ti·ness** *n*.

chauf·feur /ˈsʜōfər, sʜōˈfər/ ▶ *n*. a person employed to drive a private or rented automobile.
▶ *v*. [*tr*.] drive (a car or a passenger in a car), typically as part of one's job.

chau·vin·ism /ˈsʜōvəˌnizəm/ ▶ *n*. exaggerated or aggressive patriotism. ■ excessive or prejudiced loyalty or support for one's own cause, group, or gender: *a bastion of male chauvinism.* ▷late 19th cent.: named after Nicolas *Chauvin*, a Napoleonic veteran noted for his extreme patriotism, popularized as a character by the Cogniard brothers in *Cocarde Tricolore* (1831).

chau·vin·ist /ˈsʜōvənist/ ▶ *n*. a person displaying aggressive or exaggerated patriotism. ■ a person displaying excessive or prejudiced loyalty or support for a particular cause, group, or gender: *what a male chauvinist that man is.*
▶ *adj*. showing or relating to such excessive or prejudiced support or loyalty: *a chauvinist slur.* —**chau·vin·is·tic** /ˌsʜōvəˈnistik/ *adj*. —**chau·vin·is·ti·cal·ly** /ˌsʜōvəˈnistik(ə)lē/ *adv*.

Ch.E ▶ *abbr*. Chemical Engineer.

cheap /cʜēp/ ▶ *adj*. (of an item for sale) low in price; worth more than its cost. ■ charging low prices: *a cheap restaurant.* ■ (of prices or other charges) low: *my rent was pretty cheap.* ■ inexpensive because of inferior or quality: *cheap, shoddy goods.* ■ inf. miserly; stingy. ■ of little worth because achieved in a discreditable way requiring little effort: *her moment of cheap triumph.* ■ deserving of contempt: *a cheap trick.*
▶ *adv*. at or for a low price: *a house that was going cheap.* —**cheap·ly** *adv*. —**cheap·ness** *n*.
▶ □ **dirt cheap** very cheap or cheaply: *the auctioneers let us have it dirt cheap.*

cheap·en /ˈcʜēpən/ ▶ *v*. [*tr*.] reduce the price of: *the depreciation of the dollar would cheapen U.S. exports.* ■ degrade: *the mass media simplify and cheapen the experience of art.*

cheap·skate /ˈcʜēpˌskāt/ ▶ *n*. inf. a stingy person. ▷late 19th cent. (originally U.S.): from *cheap* (from obsolete *good cheap* 'a good bargain,' from Old English *cēap* 'bargaining, trade,' based on Latin *caupo* 'small trader, innkeeper') + *skate* 'a worn-out horse' or 'a mean, contemptible, or dishonest person,' of unknown origin.

cheat /cʜēt/ ▶ *v*. **1** [*intr*.] act dishonestly or unfairly in order to gain an advantage, esp. in a game or examination: *she always cheats at cards.* ■ [*tr*.] deceive or trick: *he had cheated her out of everything she had.* ■ use inferior materials or methods unobtrusively in order to save time or money: *they cheat by photographing mashed potatoes instead of ice cream.* ■ inf. be sexually unfaithful: *his wife was cheating on him.* **2** [*tr*.] avoid (something undesirable) by luck or skill: *she cheated death in a spectacular crash.* ■ archaic help (time) pass.
▶ *n*. a person who behaves dishonestly in order to gain an advantage: *a liar and a cheat.* ■ an act of cheating; a fraud or deception.

cheat·er /ˈcʜētər/ ▶ *n*. **1** a person who acts dishonestly in order to gain an advantage. **2** (**cheaters**) inf. a pair of glasses or sunglasses.

check[1] /cʜek/ ▶ *v*. [*tr*.] **1** examine (something) in order to determine its accuracy, quality, or condition, or to detect the presence of something: *customs officers have the right to check all luggage* | [*intr*.] *a simple blood test to check for anemia.* ■ verify or establish to one's satisfaction: *check the expiration date on your passport.* ■ examine with a view to rectifying any

fault or problem discovered: *check the oil and fluid levels again.* ■ (**check against**) verify the accuracy of something by comparing it with (something else): *keep your receipt to check against your statement.* ■ another way of saying **CHECK SOMETHING OFF**. ■ another way of saying **CHECK SOMETHING IN**. ■ [*intr*.] agree or correspond when compared. **2** stop or slow down the progress of (something undesirable): *efforts were made to check the disease.* ■ curb or restrain (a feeling or emotion): *he learned to check his excitement.* ■ (**check oneself**) master an involuntary reaction: *Chris took one step backward then checked himself.* ■ *Hockey* hamper or neutralize (an opponent) with one's body or stick. ■ (**check against**) provide a means of preventing: *processes to check against deterioration in the quality of the data held.* **3** [*tr*.] *Chess* move a piece or pawn so that (the opposing king) is under attack. **4** [*intr*.] (in poker) choose not to make a bet when called upon, allowing the action to move to another player.
▶ *phrasal v*. □ **check in** (or **check someone in**) arrive and register at a hotel or airport. □ **check something in** have one's baggage weighed and put aside for consignment to the hold of an aircraft on which one is booked to travel. ■ register and leave baggage in a left-luggage department. □ **check into** register one's arrival at (a hotel). □ **check something off** mark an item on a list with a check mark to show that it has been dealt with. □ **check on 1** verify, ascertain, or monitor the state or condition of. **2** another way of saying **CHECK UP ON**. □ **check out** settle one's hotel bill before leaving. ■ inf. die. □ **check someone/something out 1** establish the truth or inform oneself about someone or something: *they decided to check out a local restaurant.* **2** (**check something out**) enter the price of goods in a supermarket into a cash register for addition and payment by a customer. ■ register something as having been borrowed. □ **check something over** inspect or examine something thoroughly. □ **check up on** investigate in order to establish the truth about or accuracy of.
▶ *n*. **1** an examination to test or ascertain accuracy, quality, or satisfactory condition. **2** a stopping or slowing of progress: *there was no check to the expansion of the market.* ■ a means of control or restraint: *a permanent check upon the growth of central authority.* ■ *Hockey* an act of hampering or neutralizing an opponent with one's body or stick. ■ a temporary loss of the scent in hunting. ■ a part of a piano that catches the hammer and prevents it from retouching the strings. **3** *Chess* a move by which a piece or pawn directly attacks the opponent's king. If the defending player cannot counter the attack, the king is checkmated. **4** the bill in a restaurant. ■ (also **baggage/luggage check**) a token of identification for left luggage. ■ a counter used as a stake in a gambling game. **5** short for **CHECK MARK**. **6** a crack or flaw in timber.
▶ *interj*. **1** inf. expressing assent or agreement. **2** used by a chess player to announce that the opponent's king has been placed in check. —**check·a·ble** *adj*.
▶ □ **in check 1** under control: *a way of keeping inflation in check.* **2** *Chess* (of a king) directly attacked by an opponent's piece or pawn; (of a player) having the king in this position.

check[2] (*Brit.* **cheque**) ▶ *n*. a written order to a bank to pay a stated sum from the drawer's account: *awarded a check for $1,000.* ■ the printed form on which such an order is written.

check[3] ▶ *n*. a pattern of small squares: *a fine black-and-white check.* ■ a garment or fabric with such a pattern.
▶ *adj*. having such a pattern: *a blue check T-shirt.*

check·book /ˈcʜekˌbŏŏk/ ▶ *n*. a book of blank checks with a register for recording checks written.

checked /cʜekt/ ▶ *adj*. **1** (of clothes or fabric) having a pattern of small squares: *a checked shirt.* **2** *Phonet.* (of a vowel) followed by one or more consonants in the same syllable.

check·er[1] /ˈcʜekər/ ▶ *n*. **1** a person or thing that verifies or examines something: *a spelling checker.* **2** a cashier in a supermarket.

check·er[2] (*Brit.* **chequer**) ▶ *n*. **1** (often **checkers**) a pattern of squares, typically alternately colored: [as *adj*.] *a checker design.* **2** (**checkers**) [treated as *sing*.] a game for two players, with twelve pieces each, played on a checkerboard. ■ (**checker**) a round flat piece, typically red or black, used to play checkers.

check·er·board /ˈcʜekərˌbôrd/ ▶ *n*. a board for playing checkers and certain other games, with a regular pattern of squares in alternating colors, typically black and white. ■ a pattern resembling such a board.

check·ered /ˈcʜekərd/ ▶ *adj*. having a pattern of alternating squares of different colors. ■ *fig*. marked by periods of varied fortune or discreditable incidents: *his checkered past might hurt his electability.*

check·ing ac·count (*Can.* **chequing ac·count**) ▶ *n*. an account at a bank against which checks can be drawn by the account depositor.

check·list /ˈcʜekˌlist/ ▶ *n*. a list of items required, things to be done, or points to be considered, used as a reminder.

check mark ▶*n.* a mark (✔) used to indicate that a textual item is correct or has been chosen or verified.

check·mate /'chek,māt/ ▶*n. Chess* a check from which a king cannot escape. ■ [as *interj.*] (by a player) announcing that the opponent's king is in such a position. ■ *fig.* a final defeat or deadlock.
▶*v.* [*tr.*] *Chess* put into checkmate. ■ *fig.* defeat or frustrate totally.

check·out /'chek,out/ ▶*n.* **1** a point at which goods are paid for in a supermarket or other store: [as *adj.*] *packaging that is scanned at the checkout counter.* **2** the administrative procedure followed when a guest leaves a hotel at the end of a stay: [as *adj.*] *checkout time.*

check·point /'chek,point/ ▶*n.* a barrier or manned entrance, typically at a border, where travelers are subject to security checks. ■ a place along the route of a long-distance race where the time for each competitor is recorded.

check rein ▶*n.* a bearing rein.

check·up /'chek,əp/ ▶*n.* a thorough examination, esp. a medical or dental one.

ched·dar /'chedər/ ▶*n.* a kind of firm smooth cheese, originally made in Cheddar in southern England.

cheek /chēk/ ▶*n.* **1** either side of the face below the eye: *tears rolled down her cheeks.* ■ either of the inner sides of the mouth. ■ *inf.* either of the buttocks. ■ either of two side pieces or parts of a structure. **2** impertinent talk or behavior: *he had the cheek to complain.* —**cheeked** *adj.* [in *combination*] *rosy-cheeked.*
▶ □ **cheek by jowl** close together; side by side: *the houses were packed cheek by jowl along the coast.* [from a use of *jowl* in the sense 'cheek'; the phrase was originally *cheek by cheek.*] □ **cheek to cheek** (of two people dancing) with their heads close together in an intimate way. □ **turn the other cheek** refrain from retaliating when one has been attacked or insulted. [with biblical allusion to Matt. 5:39.]

cheek·bone /'chēk,bōn/ ▶*n.* the bone below the eye.

cheek·y /'chēkē/ ▶*adj.* (**cheek·i·er**, **cheek·i·est**) impudent or irreverent, typically in an endearing or amusing way: *a cheeky grin.* —**cheek·i·ly** /-kəlē/ *adv.* —**cheek·i·ness** *n.*

cheep /chēp/ ▶*n.* a shrill squeaky cry made by a bird, typically a young one. ■ a sound resembling such a cry: *an electronic cheep from the alarm.*
▶*v.* [*intr.*] make a shrill squeaky sound.

cheer /chi(ə)r/ ▶*v.* **1** [*intr.*] shout for joy or in praise or encouragement: *she cheered from the sidelines.* ■ [*tr.*] praise or encourage with shouts: *they cheered his emotional speech* | *the cyclists were cheered on by the crowds.* **2** [*tr.*] give comfort or support to: *he seemed greatly cheered by my arrival.* ■ (**cheer someone up** or **cheer up**) make or become less miserable: [*tr.*] *I asked her out to lunch to cheer her up* | [*intr.*] *he cheered up at the sight of her.*
▶*n.* **1** a shout of encouragement, praise, or joy. ■ a brief phrase shouted in unison by a crowd, typically led by cheerleaders, in support of an athletic team. **2** (also **good cheer**) cheerfulness, optimism, or confidence: *inject a little cheer into this gloomy season.* ■ something that causes such feelings: *the sunset provided some cheer for rush-hour motorists.* ■ food and drink provided for a festive occasion: *they had partaken heartily of the Christmas cheer.* ▷Middle English: from Old French *chiere* 'face,' from late Latin *cara*, from Greek *kara* 'head.' The original sense was 'face,' hence 'expression, mood,' later specifically 'a good mood.'
▶ □ **of good cheer** *archaic* cheerful; optimistic.

cheer·ful /'chi(ə)rfəl/ ▶*adj.* noticeably happy and optimistic: *a cheerful voice.* ■ causing happiness by its nature or appearance: *a chatty, cheerful letter* | *the room was painted in cheerful colors.* —**cheer·ful·ly** *adv.* —**cheer·ful·ness** *n.*

cheer·lead·er /'chi(ə)r,lēdər/ ▶*n.* a person who leads cheers and applause, esp. at a sports event. ■ an enthusiastic and vocal supporter: *he was a cheerleader for individual initiative.* —**cheer·lead** *v.*

cheer·less /'chi(ə)rlis/ ▶*adj.* gloomy; depressing: *the corridors were ill-lit and cheerless.* —**cheer·less·ly** *adv.* —**cheer·less·ness** *n.*

cheer·y /'chi(ə)rē/ ▶*adj.* (**cheer·i·er**, **cheer·i·est**) happy and optimistic: *a cheery smile.* —**cheer·i·ly** /'chi(ə)rəlē/ *adv.* —**cheer·i·ness** *n.*

cheese¹ /chēz/ ▶*n.* **1** a food made from the pressed curds of milk. ■ a molded mass of such food with its rind, often in a round flat shape: *a 50-pound, muslin-wrapped cheese.* **2** *inf.* the quality of being too obviously sentimental: *the conversations tend too far toward cheese.*

cheese² (also **big cheese**) ▶*n. inf.* an important person.

cheese³ ▶*v. inf.* chiefly *Brit.*, exasperate, frustrate, or bore: *that really cheesed off Ricky.*
▶ □ **cheese it 1** *Brit., archaic* look out. **2** *dated* run away.

cheese·burg·er /'chēz,bərgər/ ▶*n.* a hamburger with a slice of cheese on it.

cheese·cake /'chēz,kāk/ ▶*n.* **1** a kind of rich dessert cake made with cream and soft cheese on a cookie or pastry crust. **2** *inf.* photography, a movie, or art that portrays women in a manner emphasizing stereotypical sexual attractiveness.

cheese·cloth /'chēz,klôth/ ▶*n.* thin, loosely woven cloth of cotton, used originally for making and wrapping cheese.

cheese·steak /'chēz,stāk/ ▶*n.* (also **Philadelphia cheesesteak**, **Philly cheesesteak**) a sandwich containing thin-sliced sautéed beef, melted cheese, and typically sautéed onions, served in a long roll.

chees·y /'chēzē/ ▶*adj.* (**chees·i·er**, **chees·i·est**) **1** like cheese in taste, smell, or consistency. **2** *inf.* cheap, unpleasant, or blatantly inauthentic: *a big cheesy grin.* —**chees·i·ness** *n.*

chee·tah /'chētə/ ▶*n.* a large spotted cat (*Acinonyx jubatus*) found in Africa and parts of Asia. It is the fastest animal on land.

chef /shef/ ▶*n.* a professional cook, typically the chief cook in a restaurant or hotel.
▶*v.* (**cheffed**, **chef·fing**) [*intr.*] *inf.* work as a chef.

chef-d'œu·vre /shā 'dœv(rə); 'də(r)v/ ▶*n.* (*pl.* **chefs-d'œu·vre** /shāz 'dœv(rə); 'də(r)v/) a masterpiece.

che·la¹ /'kēlə/ ▶*n.* (*pl.* **-lae** /-lē; -lī/) *Zool.* a pincerlike claw, esp. of a crab or other crustacean.

che·la² /'chālā/ ▶*n.* a follower and student of a guru.

che·late /'kē,lāt/ ▶*n. Chem.* a compound containing a ligand (typically organic) bonded to a central metal atom at two or more points.
▶*v.* [*tr.*] *Chem.* form a chelate with. —**che·la·tion** /kē'lāshən/ *n.* —**che·la·tor** /-,lātər/ *n.*

che·lo·ni·an ▶*n.* any reptile of the group including turtles and tortoises.
▶*adj.* of or relating to chelonians.

chem. ▶*abbr.* ■ chemical. ■ chemist. ■ chemistry.

chem·i·cal /'kemikəl/ (abbr.: **chem.**) ▶*adj.* of or relating to chemistry or the interactions of substances as studied in chemistry. ■ of or relating to chemicals: *chemical treatments for killing fungi.* ■ relating to, involving, or denoting the use of poison gas or other chemicals as weapons of war: *the manufacture of chemical weapons.*
▶*n.* a compound or substance that has been purified or prepared, esp. artificially: *never mix disinfectant with other chemicals* | *controversy arose over treatment of apples with this chemical.* —**chem·i·cal·ly** /-ik(ə)lē/ *adv.*

chem·i·cal el·e·ment ▶*n.* see ELEMENT (sense 2).

chem·i·cal for·mu·la ▶*n.* see FORMULA (sense 1).

chem·i·cal war·fare ▶*n.* warfare using poison gas and other chemicals.

chem·i·lum·i·nes·cence /,kemi,lōōmə'nesəns/ ▶*n.* the emission of light during a chemical reaction that does not produce significant quantities of heat. —**chem·i·lum·i·nes·cent** *adj.*

che·mise /shə'mēz; -'mēs/ ▶*n.* a dress hanging straight from the shoulders and giving the figure a uniform shape, popular in the 1920s. ■ a woman's loose-fitting undergarment or nightgown, typically of silk or satin with a lace trim. ■ a priest's alb or surplice. ■ *hist.* a smock.

chem·i·sorp·tion /,kemi'sôrpshən; -'zôrp-/ ▶*n. Chem.* adsorption in which the adsorbed substance is held by chemical bonds. —**chem·i·sorbed** /'kemi,sôrbd/ *adj.*

chem·ist /'kemist/ (abbr.: **chem.**) ▶*n.* **1** an expert in chemistry; a person engaged in chemical research or experiments. **2** *Brit.* a drugstore. ■ a pharmacist.

chem·is·try /'kemistrē/ (abbr.: **chem.**) ▶*n.* (*pl.* **-tries**) **1** the branch of science that deals with the identification of the substances of which matter is composed; the investigation of their properties and the ways in which they interact, combine, and change; and the use of these processes to form new substances. ■ the chemical composition and properties of a substance or body: *the chemistry of soil* | *the chemistries of other galaxies.* ■ *fig.* a complex entity or process: *the chemistry of politics.* **2** the emotional or psychological interaction between two people, esp. when experienced as a powerful mutual attraction: *their affair was triggered by intense sexual chemistry.*

che·mo /'kēmō/ ▶*n. inf.* chemotherapy.

che·mo·syn·the·sis /,kēmō'sinthəsəs/; ,kemō-/ ▶*n. Biol.* the synthesis of organic compounds by bacteria or other living organisms using energy derived from reactions involving inorganic chemicals, typically in the absence of sunlight. —**che·mo·syn·thet·ic** /-sin'thetik/ *adj.*

che·mo·ther·a·py /,kēmō'therəpē/; ,kemō-/ ▶*n.* the treatment of disease by the use of chemical substances, esp. the treatment of cancer by cell-killing and other drugs. —**che·mo·ther·a·pist** /-pist/ *n.*

Pronunciation Key ə *ago, up;* ər *over, fur;* a *hat;* ā *ate;* ä *car;* ch *chin;* e *let;* ē *see;* e(ə)r *air;* i *fit;* ī *by;* i(ə)r *ear;* ng *sing;* ō *go;* ô *law, for;* oi *toy;* ōō *good;* ōō *goo;* ou *out;* sh *she;* th *thin;* <u>th</u> *then;* (h)w *why;* zh *vision*

che·nille /SHə'nēl/ ▶n. a tufted velvety cord or yarn, used for trimming furniture and making carpets and clothing. ■ fabric made from such yarn.

cheong·sam /'CHŌNG,säm/ ▶n. a close-fitting dress with a high neck and a slit skirt, worn traditionally by Chinese women.

cheque ▶n. British spelling of CHECK³.

chequ·er ▶n. & v. British spelling of CHECKER².

cher·ish /'CHerisH/ ▶v. [tr.] protect and care for (someone) lovingly: *he cared for me beyond measure and cherished me in his heart.* ■ hold (something) dear: *I cherish the letters she wrote.* ■ (of a hope, idea, or memory) think of longingly or lovingly: *we will cherish your memory.*

Cher·o·kee /'CHerəkē/ ▶n. (*pl.* same or **-kees**) **1** a member of an American Indian people of the southeastern U.S., now living on reservations in Oklahoma and North Carolina. **2** the Iroquoian language of this people, which has had its own script since 1820.
▶adj. of or relating to this people or their language.

che·root /SHə'rōōt/ ▶n. a cigar with both ends open and untapered.

cher·ry /'CHerē/ ▶n. (*pl.* **-ies**) **1** a small, round stone fruit that is typically bright or dark red. **2** (also **cherry tree**) the tree (genus *Prunus*) of the rose family that bears such fruit. ■ the wood of this tree. **3** a bright or deep red color. **4** *vulgar slang* the hymen, as representing a woman's virginity.
▶ □ **a bowl of cherries** a pleasant or enjoyable situation or experience.

cher·ry pick·er ▶n. *inf.* **1** a hydraulic crane with a railed platform at the end for raising and lowering workers. **2** a person who cherry-picks.

cher·ry to·ma·to ▶n. a spherical miniature tomato (esp. *Lycopersicon lycopersicum cerasiforme*), typically eaten in salad.

cher·ub /'CHerəb/ ▶n. (*pl.* **cher·u·bim** /'CHer(y)əbim/ a winged angelic being described in biblical tradition as attending on God. ■ (*pl.* **cher·u·bim** /'CHer(y)ə,bim/ or **cher·ubs**) a representation of a cherub in art. ■ (*pl.* **cher·ubs**) a beautiful or innocent-looking child. —**che·ru·bic** /CHə'rōōbik/ adj.

cher·vil /'CHərvəl/ ▶n. a plant (*Anthriscus cerefolium*) of the parsley family, with small white flowers and delicate fernlike leaves that are used as a culinary herb.

Chesh·ire /'CHesHər/ (also **Cheshire cheese**) ▶n. a kind of firm crumbly cheese, originally made in Cheshire, England.

chess /CHes/ ▶n. a board game for two players, played on a checkered board. Each player begins with sixteen pieces that are moved according to precise rules. The object is to put the opponent's king under a direct attack from which escape is impossible.

chess·board /'CHes,bôrd/ ▶n. a square board divided into sixty-four alternating dark and light squares, used for playing chess or checkers.

chess·man /'CHes,man; -mən/ ▶n. (*pl.* **-men**) a solid figure used as a chess piece.

chest /CHest/ ▶n. **1** the front surface of a person's or animal's body between the neck and the abdomen. ■ the whole of a person's upper trunk, esp. with reference to physical size: *a 42-inch chest.* ■ *inf.* a woman's breasts. **2** a large strong box, typically made of wood and used for storage or shipping: *an oak chest.* ■ a small cabinet for medicines, toiletries, etc.: *the medicine chest.* ■ (also **chest of drawers**) a piece of furniture consisting of a set of drawers in a frame, typically used for storing clothes. —**chest·ed** adj. [in *combination*] *a bare-chested youth.*
▶ □ **get something off one's chest** *inf.* say something that one has wanted to say for a long time, resulting in a feeling of relief. □ **play** (or **keep**) **one's cards close to one's chest** *inf.* be secretive and cautious about one's intentions.

ches·ter·field /'CHestər,fēld/ ▶n. **1** a sofa with padded arms and back of the same height and curved outward at the top. ■ *chiefly Can.* any sofa or couch. **2** a man's plain straight overcoat, typically with a velvet collar.

chest·nut /'CHes(t),nət/ ▶n. **1** a glossy brown nut that may be roasted and eaten. **2** (also **chestnut tree**) the large European tree (*Castanea sativa*) of the beech family that produces the edible chestnut, which develops within a bristly case, with serrated leaves and heavy timber. ■ short for HORSE CHESTNUT. ■ used in names of trees and plants that produce similar nuts, e.g., **water chestnut**. **3** a deep reddish-brown color. ■ a horse of a reddish-brown color, with a brown mane and tail. **4** a small horny patch on the inside of each of a horse's legs. **5** *colloq.* a stale joke or anecdote.

chest·y /'CHestē/ ▶adj. *inf.* **1** (of a sound) produced deep in the chest. **2** (of a woman) having large or prominent breasts. **3** conceited and arrogant. —**chest·i·ly** /'CHestəlē/ adv. —**chest·i·ness** n.

che·val glass /SHə'val/ (also **cheval mirror**) ▶n. a tall mirror fitted at its middle to an upright frame so that it can be tilted.

chev·a·lier /,SHevə'li(ə)r/ ▶n. *hist.* a knight. ■ a chivalrous man. ■ a member of certain orders of knighthood or of modern French orders such as the Legion of Honor. ■ (**Chevalier**) *Brit., hist.* the title of James and Charles Stuart, pretenders to the British throne.

chè·vre /'SHev(rə)/ ▶n. cheese made with goat's milk.

chev·ron /'SHevrən/ ▶n. a line or stripe in the shape of a V or an inverted V, esp. one on the sleeve of a uniform indicating rank or length of service. ■ *Archit.* a molding of continuous V-shaped patterns, common in Norman architecture. ▷late Middle English (in heraldic use): from Old French, based on Latin *caper* 'goat'; compare with Latin *capreoli* (diminutive of *caper*) used to mean 'pair of rafters.'

chevron

chev·ro·tain /'SHevrə,tān/ ▶n. a small deerlike mammal (genera *Moschiola* and *Hyemoschus*, family Tragulidae) with short tusks, typically nocturnal and found in the tropical rain forests of Africa and South Asia.

chew /CHŌŌ/ ▶v. [tr.] bite and work (food) in the mouth with the teeth, esp. to make it easier to swallow: *he was chewing a mouthful of toast* | [*intr.*] *he chewed for a moment, then swallowed.* ■ gnaw at (something) persistently, typically as a result of worry or anxiety: *he chewed his lip reflectively* | [*intr.*] *she chewed at a fingernail.*
▶phrasal v. □ **chew someone out** *inf.* reprimand someone severely. □ **chew something over** discuss or consider something at length.
▶n. a repeated biting or gnawing of something. ■ something other than food that is meant for chewing: *a dog chew* | *a chew of tobacco.* —**chew·a·ble** adj. —**chew·er** n. [usu. in *combination*] *a tobacco-chewer.*
▶ □ **chew the fat** *inf.* chat in a leisurely way, esp. at length.

chew·ing gum ▶n. flavored gum for chewing, typically sold in packets of individually wrapped thin strips.

chew·y /'CHŌŌē/ ▶ **1** adj. (**chew·i·er, chew·i·est**) (of food) needing to be chewed hard or for some time. **2** suitable for chewing: *pasta should be chewy, never soft.* —**chew·i·ness** n.

Chey·enne /SHī'an/ ▶n. (*pl.* same or **-ennes**) **1** a member of an American Indian people formerly living between the Missouri and Arkansas rivers but now on reservations in Montana and Oklahoma. **2** the Algonquian language of this people.
▶adj. of or relating to the Cheyenne or their language.

chi /kī/ ▶n. the twenty-second letter of the Greek alphabet (X, χ), transliterated in the traditional Latin style as 'ch' (as in *Christ*) or in the modern style as 'kh' (as in *Khaniá*).

Chi·an·ti /kē'äntē; -'antē/ (also **chi·an·ti**) ▶n. (*pl.* **-tis**) a dry red wine, originally produced in Tuscany, Italy.

chi·a·ro·scu·ro /kē,ärə'sk(y)ŏŏrō; kē,arə-/ ▶n. the treatment of light and shade in drawing and painting. ■ an effect of contrasted light and shadow created by light falling unevenly or from a particular direction on something: *the chiaroscuro of cobbled streets.*

chic /SHēk/ ▶adj. (**chic·er, chic·est**) elegantly and stylishly fashionable.
▶n. stylishness and elegance, typically of a specified kind: *French chic* | *biker chic.* —**chic·ly** adv.

chi·cane /SHi'kān; CHi-/ ▶n. **1** an artificial narrowing or turn on a road or auto-racing course. **2** *dated* (in card games) a hand without cards of one particular suit; a void. **3** *archaic* chicanery.
▶v. *archaic* employ trickery or chicanery. ■ [*tr.*] deceive or trick (someone).

chi·can·er·y /SHi'kānərē; CHi-/ ▶n. the use of trickery to achieve a political, financial, or legal purpose.

Chi·ca·no /CHi'känō; SHi-/ (also *fem.* **Chi·ca·na**) ▶n. (*pl.* **-nos**) (in North America) a person of Mexican origin or descent.

chi·chi /'SHēSHē; 'CHēCHē/ ▶adj. attempting stylish elegance but achieving only an overelaborate affectedness: *the chichi world of Manhattan cultural privilege.*
▶n. pretentious and overelaborate refinement.

chick /CHik/ ▶n. **1** a young bird, esp. one newly hatched. ■ a newly hatched domestic fowl. **2** *inf., chiefly derog.* a young woman.

chick·a·dee /'CHikədē/ ▶n. a North American titmouse, in particular the **black-capped chickadee** (*Parus atricapillus*), with distinctive black cap and throat.

Chick·a·saw /'CHikə,sô/ ▶n. (*pl.* same or **-saws**) **1** a member of an American Indian people formerly resident in Mississippi and Alabama, and now in Oklahoma. **2** the Muskogean language of this people.
▶adj. of or relating to this people or their language.

chick·en /'CHikən/ ▸*n.* **1** a domestic fowl kept for its eggs or meat, esp. a young one. ■ meat from such a bird: *roast chicken.* **2** *inf.* a game in which the first person to lose nerve and withdraw from a dangerous situation is the loser. ■ a coward. **3** *inf.* (among homosexuals) an adolescent male.
▸*adj. inf.* cowardly: *they were too chicken to follow the murderers into the mountains.*
▸*v.* [*intr.*] (**chicken out**) *inf.* withdraw from or fail in something through lack of nerve: *the referee chickened out of giving a penalty.*
▸ □ **don't count your chickens before they're hatched** see COUNT[1].

chick·en feed ▸*n.* food for poultry. ■ *fig., inf.* an insignificant amount of money: *the pay was chicken feed for the work I put in.*

chick·en-heart·ed (also **chick·en-liv·ered**) ▸*adj.* easily frightened; cowardly.

chick·en pox (also **chick·en·pox**) ▸*n.* an infectious disease causing a mild fever and a rash of itchy inflamed blisters. It is caused by the herpes zoster virus and mainly affects children.

chick·en wire ▸*n.* light wire netting with a hexagonal mesh.

chick·pea /'CHik,pē/ ▸*n.* **1** a round yellowish seed, used widely as food. **2** the leguminous Old World plant (*Cicer arietinum*) that bears these seeds.

chic·le /'CHikəl; 'CHiklē/ ▸*n.* the milky latex of the sapodilla tree, used to make chewing gum. ■ another term for SAPODILLA.

chic·o·ry /'CHikərē/ ▸*n.* (*pl.* **-ies**) **1** a blue-flowered Mediterranean plant (*Cichorium intybus*) of the daisy family, cultivated for its edible salad leaves and carrot-shaped root. ■ the root of this plant, which is roasted and ground for use as an additive to or substitute for coffee. **2** another term for ENDIVE.

chide /CHīd/ ▸*v.* (*past* **chid·ed** or *archaic* **chid** /CHid/; *past part.* **chid·ed** or *archaic* **chid·den** /'CHidn/) [*tr.*] scold or rebuke: *she chided him for not replying to her letters.* —**chid·er** *n.* —**chid·ing·ly** *adv.*

chief /CHēf/ ▸*n.* a leader or ruler of a people or clan: *the chief of the village.* ■ the person with the highest rank in an organization: *the chief of police.* ■ an informal form of address, esp. to someone of superior rank or status: *it's quite simple, chief.*
▸*adj.* most important: *the chief reason for the spending cuts.* ■ having or denoting the highest rank or authority: *the government's chief adviser.* —**chief·dom** /-dəm/ *n.* —**chief·ship** /-,SHip/ *n.*

chief jus·tice ▸*n.* (the title of) the presiding judge in a supreme court. ■ (**Chief Justice of the United States**) (the formal title of) the chief justice of the U.S. Supreme Court.

chief·ly /'CHēflē/ ▸*adv.* above all; mainly: *remembered chiefly for his sonatas.* ■ for the most part; mostly: *consisted chiefly of communists.*

chief of staff ▸*n.* the senior staff officer of a service or command.

chief·tain /'CHēftən/ ▸*n.* the leader of a people or clan. ■ *inf.* a powerful member of an organization. —**chief·tain·cy** /-sē/ *n.* (*pl.* **-cies**) —**chief·tain·ship** /-,SHip/ *n.*

chif·fon /SHi'fän; 'SHif,än/ ▸*n.* a light, sheer fabric typically made of silk or nylon: [as *adj.*] *a chiffon blouse.* ■ [as *adj.*] (of a cake or dessert) made with beaten egg whites to give a light consistency: *chiffon cake.*

chif·fo·nier /,SHifə'ni(ə)r/ ▸*n.* a tall chest of drawers, often with a mirror on top.

chig·ger /'CHigər/ (also **jigger**) ▸*n.* a tiny mite (genus *Trombicula,* family Trombiculidae) whose parasitic larvae live on or under the skin of warm-blooded animals, where they cause irritation and dermatitis.

chi·gnon /'SHēn,yän; SHēn'yän/ ▸*n.* a knot or coil of hair arranged on the back of a woman's head.

chi·hua·hua /CHə'wäwä; SHə-; -wə/ ▸*n.* a small dog of a smooth-haired, large-eyed breed originating in Mexico.

chil·blain /'CHil,blān/ ▸*n.* a painful, itching swelling on the skin, typically on a hand or foot, caused by poor circulation in the skin when exposed to cold. —**chil·blained** *adj.*

child /CHīld/ ▸*n.* (*pl.* **chil·dren** /'CHildrən/) a young human being below the age of full physical development or below the legal age of majority. ■ a son or daughter of any age. ■ an immature or irresponsible person. ■ a person who has little or no experience in a particular area. ■ (**children**) the descendants of a family or people. ■ (**child of**) a person or thing influenced by a specified environment: *a child of the sixties.* —**child·less** *adj.* —**child·less·ness** *n.*
▸ □ **child's play** a task that is easily accomplished. □ **with child** *formal* pregnant.

child-bear·ing /'CHīld,be(ə)riNG/ ▸*n.* the process of giving birth to children: [as *adj.*] *women of childbearing age.*

child·birth /'CHīld,bərTH/ ▸*n.* the action of giving birth to a child: *she died in childbirth.*

child care ▸*n.* the action or skill of looking after children. ■ the care of children by a day-care center, babysitter, or other provider while parents are working.

child-free /'CHīld'frē/ ▸*adj.* pertaining to adults who do not have or live with children: *I'm interested in finding a childfree computer geek-girl with a worldview similar to mine.*

child·hood /'CHīld,ho͝od/ ▸*n.* the state of being a child. ■ the period during which a person is a child: [as *adj.*] *a childhood friend.*

child·ish /'CHīldiSH/ ▸*adj.* of, like, or appropriate to a child. ■ silly and immature. —**child·ish·ly** *adv.* —**child·ish·ness** *n.*

child·like /'CHīld,līk/ ▸*adj.* (of an adult) having good qualities associated with a child: *she speaks with a childlike directness.*

child·proof /'CHīld,pro͞of/ ▸*adj.* designed to prevent children from injuring themselves or doing damage.
▸*v.* [*tr.*] make inaccessible to children: *childproof those cabinets with safety latches.*

chil·dren /'CHildrən/ ▸ plural form of CHILD.

chil·i /'CHilē/ (also **chili pepper**) ▸*n.* (*pl.* **chi·lies**) a small hot-tasting pod of a variety of capsicum, used chopped (and often dried) in sauces, relishes, and spice powders. ■ short for CHILI POWDER. ■ (also **chile con car·ne** /kän 'kärnē; kən/) a spicy stew of beef and red chilies or chili powder, often with beans and tomatoes.

chil·i·ad /'kilē,ad/ ▸*n.* a thousand. ■ a group of a thousand (things). ■ a thousand years.

chil·i pow·der ▸*n.* a hot-tasting mixture of ground dried red chilies and other spices.

chill /CHil/ ▸*n.* a moderate but unpleasant coldness: *there was a chill in the air.* ■ (often **chills**) a lowered body temperature, often accompanied by shivering. ■ a feverish cold. ■ *fig.* a coldness of manner: *the sudden chill in China's relations with the West.* ■ *fig.* a depressing influence: *his statements have cast a chill over this whole country.* ■ a sudden and powerful unpleasant feeling, esp. of fear: *his words sent a chill of apprehension down my spine.*
▸*v.* [*tr.*] **1** (often **be chilled**) make (someone) cold: *I'm chilled to the bone.* ■ cool (food or drink) in a refrigerator. **2** (often **be chilled**) horrify or frighten (someone): *the city was chilled by the violence.* **3** (also **chill out**) [*intr.*] *inf.* calm down and relax. ■ pass time without a particular aim or purpose, esp. with other people: *we had a week at home and we chilled out.*
▸*adj.* chilly: *the chill gray dawn* | *fig.* the chill winds of public censure. —**chill·er** *n.* —**chill·ing·ly** *adv.* —**chill·ness** *n.*
▸ □ **take the chill off** warm slightly.

chill·y /'CHilē/ ▸*adj.* (**chill·i·er, chill·i·est**) uncomfortably cool or cold: *a chilly day.* ■ (of a person) feeling cold: *I felt a bit chilly.* ■ unfriendly: *a chilly reception.* —**chill·i·ness** *n.*

chime[1] /CHīm/ ▸*n.* (often **chimes**) a bell or a metal bar or tube, typically one of a set tuned to produce a melodious series of ringing sounds when struck. ■ a sound made by such an instrument: *I hear the chimes of the hour from the courthouse.* ■ (**chimes**) a set of tuned metal rods used as an orchestral instrument. ■ (**chimes**) a set of tuned bells used as a doorbell.
▸*v.* [*intr.*] **1** (of a bell or clock) make ringing sounds, typically to indicate the time. ■ [*tr.*] (of a clock) make such sounds in order to indicate (the time): *the clock chimed eight.* **2** be in agreement; harmonize: *his poem chimes with our modern experience of loss.*
▸*phrasal v.* □ **chime in 1** interject a remark. **2** join in harmoniously. —**chim·er** *n.*

chime[2] (also **chimb**) ▸*n.* the projecting rim at the end of a cask.

chi·me·ra /kī'mirə; kə-/ (also **chi·mae·ra**) ▸*n.* **1** (**Chimera**) (in Greek mythology) a fire-breathing female monster with a lion's head, a goat's body, and a serpent's tail. ■ any mythical animal with parts taken from various animals. **2** a thing that is hoped or wished for but in fact is illusory or impossible to achieve. **3** *Biol.* an organism containing genetically different tissues, formed by processes such as fusion of early embryos, grafting, or mutation. ■ a DNA molecule with sequences derived from two or more different organisms, formed by laboratory manipulation. **4** (usu. **chimaera**) a cartilaginous marine fish (Chimaeridae and other families) with a long tail, an erect spine before the first dorsal fin, and typically a forward projection from the snout. —**chi·mer·ic** /kī'mirik; kə-; -'merik/ *adj.* —**chi·mer·i·cal** /kī'merikəl; kə-; -'mir-/ *adj.* —**chi·mer·i·cal·ly** /kī'merik(ə)lē; kə-; -'mir-/ *adv.*

chim·ney /'CHimnē/ ▸*n.* (*pl.* **-neys**) a vertical channel or pipe that conducts smoke and combustion gases up from a fire or furnace and

---

typically through the roof of a building. ■ the part of such a structure that extends above the roof. ■ a glass tube that protects the flame of a lamp. ■ a steep narrow cleft by which a rock face may be climbed. ▷Middle English (denoting a fireplace or furnace): from Old French *cheminee* 'chimney, fireplace,' from late Latin *caminata*, perhaps from *camera caminata* 'room with a fireplace,' from Latin *caminus* 'forge, furnace,' from Greek *kaminos* 'oven.'

chim·ney sweep ▶n. a person whose job is cleaning out the soot from chimneys.

chimp /CHimp/ ▶n. informal term for CHIMPANZEE.

chim·pan·zee /ˌCHim,pan'zē; -pən'zē; -'panzē/ ▶n. a great ape (genus *Pan*) with large ears, mainly black coloration, and lighter skin on the face, native to the forests of western and central Africa.

chin /CHin/ ▶n. the protruding part of the face below the mouth, formed by the apex of the lower jaw.
▶v. [tr.] draw one's body up so as to bring one's chin level with or above (a horizontal bar) with one's feet off the ground, as an exercise. —**chinned** adj. [in *combination*] *square-chinned*.
▶ □ **keep one's chin up** inf. remain cheerful in difficult circumstances: *keep your chin up, we're not lost yet.* □ **take it on the chin** endure or accept misfortune courageously or stoically.

chi·na /'CHīnə/ ▶n. a fine white or translucent vitrified ceramic material: *a plate made of china* | [as adj.] *a china cup.* Also called PORCELAIN. ■ household tableware or other objects made from this or a similar material: *the breakfast china.*

chi·na clay ▶n. another term for KAOLIN.

Chi·na·town /'CHīnə,toun/ ▶n. a district of any non-Chinese town, esp. a city or seaport, in which the population is predominantly of Chinese origin.

chinch /CHinCH/ (also **chinch bug** /sinCH/) ▶n. a plant-eating ground bug (family Lygaeidae) that forms large swarms on grasses and rushes.

chin·chil·la /CHin'CHilə/ ▶n. a small South American rodent (genus *Chinchilla*, family Chinchillidae) with soft gray fur and a long bushy tail. ■ a cat or rabbit of a breed with silver-gray or gray fur. ■ the highly valued fur of the chinchilla, or of the chinchilla rabbit.

chine[1] /CHīn/ ▶n. a backbone, esp. that of an animal as it appears in a cut of meat. ■ a cut of meat containing all or part of this.

chine[2] ▶n. *Brit.* a deep, narrow ravine formed by running water.

Chi·nese /CHī'nēz; -'nēs/ ▶adj. of or relating to China or its language, culture, or people. ■ belonging to or relating to the people forming the dominant ethnic group of China and widely dispersed elsewhere. Also called HAN.
▶n. (pl. same) **1** the Chinese language. **2** a native or national of China, or a person of Chinese descent.

Chi·nese cab·bage ▶n. an oriental cabbage (genus *Brassica*) that does not form a firm heart. See also BOK CHOY.

Chi·nese lan·tern ▶n. **1** a collapsible paper lantern. **2** a plant (*Physalis alkekengi*) of the nightshade family with white flowers and globular orange fruits enclosed in an orange-red papery calyx.

Chink /CHiNGk/ ▶n. *inf., offens.* a Chinese person.

chink[1] /CHiNGk/ ▶n. a narrow opening or crack, typically one that admits light: *a chink in the curtains.* ■ a narrow beam or patch of light admitted by such an opening: *I noticed a chink of light under the door.*
▶ □ **a chink in someone's armor** a weak point in someone's character, arguments, or ideas, making them vulnerable to attack or criticism.

chink[2] ▶v. make or cause to make a light and high-pitched ringing sound, as of glasses or coins striking together: [intr.] *the chain joining the handcuffs chinked* | [tr.] *they chinked glasses and kissed.*
▶n. a high-pitched ringing sound: *the chink of glasses.*

chin·less /'CHinlis/ ▶adj. (of a person) lacking a well-defined chin. ■ inf. lacking strength of character; ineffectual.

chi·no /'CHēnō/ ▶n. (pl. -nos) a cotton twill fabric, typically khaki-colored. ■ (**chinos**) casual pants made from such fabric.

Chi·nook /SHə'nŏŏk; CHə-/ ▶n. (pl. same or -nooks) **1** a member of an American Indian people originally inhabiting the region around the lower Columbia River in Oregon and Washington. **2** the language of this people.
▶adj. of or relating to the Chinook or their language.

chi·nook /SHə'nŏŏk; CHə-/ ▶n. **1** (also **chinook wind**) a warm dry wind that blows down the east side of the Rocky Mountains at the end of winter. **2** (also **chinook salmon**) a large North Pacific salmon (*Oncorhynchus tshawytscha*) that is an important commercial food fish.

chintz /CHints/ ▶n. printed multicolored cotton fabric with a glazed finish, used esp. for curtains and upholstery: *a sofa upholstered in chintz* | [as adj.] *floral chintz curtains.*

chintz·y /'CHintsē/ ▶adj. (**chintz·i·er, chintz·i·est**) **1** of, like, or decorated with chintz. ■ brightly colorful but gaudy and tasteless. **2** inf. miserly. —**chintz·i·ly** adv. —**chintz·i·ness** n.

chin-up ▶n. another term for PULL-UP (sense 1).

chip /CHip/ ▶n. **1** a small piece of something removed in the course of chopping, cutting, or breaking something, esp. a hard material such as wood or stone: *mulch the shrubs with cedar chips.* ■ a hole or flaw left by the removal of such a piece: *a chip on his tooth.* **2** a thin slice of food made crisp by being fried, baked, or dried and typically eaten as a snack: *tortilla chips.* ■ a small chunk of candy added to desserts or sweet snacks, esp. of chocolate. ■ (**chips**) *chiefly Brit.* French fries: *an order of fish and chips.* **3** short for MICROCHIP. **4** a counter used in certain gambling games to represent money: *a poker chip.* **5** (in golf, soccer, and other sports) a short lofted kick or shot with the ball. ■ *Tennis* a softly sliced return intended to land between the net and the opponent's service line.
▶v. (**chipped, chip·ping**) [tr.] **1** cut or break (a small piece) from the edge or surface of a hard material: *chipping ice off the upper deck.* ■ [intr.] (of a material or object) break at the edge or on the surface: *the paint had chipped off.* ■ cut pieces off (a hard material) to alter its shape or break it up: *it required a craftsman to chip the blocks of flint to the required shape* | [intr.] *she chipped away at the ground.* **2** (in golf, soccer, and other sports) kick or strike (a ball or shot) to produce a short lobbed shot or pass: *he chipped a superb shot.*
▶phrasal v. □ **chip away** gradually and relentlessly make something smaller or weaker: *rivals may chip away at one's profits by undercutting product prices.* □ **chip in** (or **chip something in**) contribute something as one's share of a joint activity, cost, etc.
▶ □ **a chip off the old block** inf. someone who resembles his or her parent, esp. in character. □ **a chip on one's shoulder** inf. a deeply ingrained grievance, typically about a particular thing. □ **when the chips are down** inf. when a very serious and difficult situation arises.

chip·board /'CHip,bôrd/ ▶n. another term for PARTICLEBOARD.

chip·munk /'CHip,məNGk/ ▶n. a burrowing ground squirrel (genus *Tamias*) with cheek pouches and light and dark stripes running down the body. Its many species include the North American **eastern chipmunk** (*T. striatus*).

Chip·pen·dale ▶adj. (of furniture) designed, made by, or in the style of English furniture-maker Thomas Chippendale (1718–79), whose pieces were neoclassical, with elements of French rococo and Gothic revival.

chip·per[1] /'CHipər/ ▶adj. inf. cheerful and lively.

chip·per[2] ▶n. a person or thing that turns something into chips. ■ a machine for chipping the trunks and limbs of trees.

Chip·pe·wa /'CHipə,wä; -,wā; -wə/ (also **Chip·pe·way** /-,wā/) ▶n. (pl. same) another term for OJIBWA.

chip·py /'CHipē/ inf. ▶n. (also **chip·pie**) (pl. -**pies**) a promiscuous young woman, esp. a prostitute.
▶adj. touchy and irritable. ■ (of an ice-hockey game or player) rough and belligerent, with or incurring numerous penalties.

chip shot ▶n. *Golf* a stroke at which the ball is or must be chipped into the air.

chi·rog·ra·phy /kī'rägrəfē/ ▶n. handwriting, esp. as distinct from typography. —**chi·ro·graph·ic** /ˌkīrə'grafik/ adj.

chi·ro·man·cy /'kīrə,mansē/ ▶n. the prediction of a person's future from the lines on the palms of his or her hands; palmistry.

chi·rop·o·dy /kə'räpədē; SHə-/ ▶n. another term for PODIATRY. —**chi·rop·o·dist** /kə'räpədist/ n.

chi·ro·prac·tic /ˌkīrə'praktik/ ▶n. a system of complementary medicine based on the diagnosis and manipulative treatment of misalignments of the joints, esp. those of the spinal column, which are held to cause other disorders by affecting the nerves, muscles, and organs. —**chi·ro·prac·tor** /ˌprakter/ n.

chi·rop·ter·an ▶n. any mammal of the group comprising the bats.
▶adj. of or relating to chiropterans.

chirp /CHərp/ ▶v. [intr.] (typically of a small bird or an insect) utter a short, sharp, high-pitched sound. ■ (of a person) say something in a lively and cheerful way: *"Good morning!" chirped Alex.*
▶n. a short, sharp, high-pitched sound. —**chirp·er** n.

chirp·y /'CHərpē/ ▶adj. (**chirp·i·er, chirp·i·est**) inf. cheerful and lively. —**chirp·i·ly** /'CHərpəlē/ adv. —**chirp·i·ness** n.

chirr /CHər/ (also **churr**) ▶v. [intr.] (esp. of an insect) make a prolonged low trilling sound.
▶n. a low trilling sound.

chir·rup /'CHi(ə)rəp; 'CHərəp/ ▶v. (-**ruped, -ruping**) [intr.] (esp. of a small

bird) make repeated short high-pitched sounds; twitter. ■ (of a person) say something in a high-pitched voice.
▸*n.* a short, high-pitched sound. —**chir·rup·y** *adj.*

chis·el /'CHizəl/ ▸*n.* a long-bladed hand tool with a beveled cutting edge and a plain handle that is struck with a hammer or mallet, used to cut or shape wood, stone, metal, or other hard materials.
▸*v.* (**-eled, -el·ing**; *Brit.* **-elled, -el·ling**) [*tr.*] **1** cut or shape (something) with a chisel: *carefully* **chisel** *out a groove for the hinge.* **2** *inf.* cheat or swindle (someone) out of something: *he's* **chiseled** *me out of my dues.* —**chis·el·er** /'CHiz(ə)lər/ *n.*

chit[1] /CHit/ ▸*n.* a short official note, memorandum, or voucher, typically recording a sum owed.

chit[2] ▸*n.* a young woman regarded with disapproval for her immaturity or lack of respect: *a mere chit of a girl.*

chit·chat /'CHit,CHat/ *inf.* ▸*n.* inconsequential conversation.
▸*v.* [*intr.*] talk about trivial matters: *I can't stand around chitchatting.*

chi·tin /'kītn/ ▸*n. Biochem.* a fibrous substance consisting of polysaccharides and forming the major constituent in the exoskeleton of arthropods and the cell walls of fungi. —**chi·tin·ous** /'kītn-əs/ *adj.*

chi·ton /'kītn; 'kī,tän/ ▸*n.* **1** a long woolen tunic worn in ancient Greece. [from Greek *khitōn* 'tunic.'] **2** a marine mollusk (class Polyplacophora) that has an oval flattened body with a shell of overlapping plates.

chit·ter·lings /'CHitlənz/ ▸*pl. n.* the smaller intestines of a pig, cooked for food.

chiv·al·rous /'SHivəlrəs/ ▸*adj.* (of a man or his behavior) courteous and gallant, esp. toward women. ■ of or relating to the historical notion of chivalry. —**chiv·al·rous·ly** *adv.*

chiv·al·ry /'SHivəlrē/ ▸*n.* the medieval knightly system with its religious, moral, and social code. ■ *hist.* knights, noblemen, and horsemen collectively. ■ the combination of qualities expected of an ideal knight, esp. courage, honor, courtesy, justice, and a readiness to help the weak. ■ courteous behavior, esp. that of a man toward women. —**chi·val·ric** /SHə'valrik/ *adj.*

chives /CHīvz/ ▸*pl. n.* a small plant (*Allium schoenoprasum*) of the lily family, with dense tufts of long tubular leaves that taste oniony and are used as a culinary herb. ■ the leaves from this plant.

chla·myd·i·a /klə'midēə/ ▸*n.* (*pl.* same or **chlamydiae** /-'midē,ē/) a very small parasitic bacterium (genus *Chlamydia*, order Chlamydiales) that, like a virus, requires the biochemical mechanisms of another cell in order to reproduce. Bacteria of this type cause various diseases including trachoma, psittacosis, and nonspecific urethritis. —**chla·myd·i·al** *adj.*

chlo·ride /'klôr,īd/ ▸*n. Chem.* a compound of chlorine with another element or group; a salt of the anion Cl⁻ or an organic compound with chlorine bonded to an alkyl group.

chlo·ri·nate /'klôrə,nāt/ ▸*v.* [*tr.*] [usu. as *adj.*] (**chlorinated**) impregnate or treat with chlorine: *chlorinated water.* ■ *Chem.* introduce chlorine into (a compound). —**chlo·ri·na·tion** /,klôrə'nāSHən/ *n.* —**chlo·ri·na·tor** /-,nātər/ *n.*

chlo·rine /'klôr,ēn/ ▸*n.* the chemical element of atomic number 17, a toxic, irritant, pale green halogen gas. (Symbol: **Cl**)

chlo·ro·fluor·o·car·bon /,klôrō,flŏŏrō'kärbən/ (abbr.: **CFC**) ▸*n.* any of a class of compounds of carbon, hydrogen, chlorine, and fluorine, typically gases used chiefly in refrigerants and aerosol propellants. They are harmful to the ozone layer in the earth's atmosphere.

chlo·ro·form /'klôrə,fôrm/ ▸*n.* a colorless, volatile, sweet-smelling liquid, CHCl₃, used as a solvent and formerly as a general anesthetic.
▸*v.* [*tr.*] render (someone) unconscious with this substance.

chlo·ro·phyll /'klôrə,fil/ ▸*n.* a green pigment, present in all green plants and in cyanobacteria, responsible for the absorption of light to provide energy for photosynthesis. Its molecule contains a magnesium atom held in a porphyrin ring. —**chlo·ro·phyl·lous** /,klôrə'filəs/ *adj.*

chlo·ro·plast /'klôrə,plast/ ▸*n. Bot.* (in green plant cells) a plastid that contains chlorophyll and in which photosynthesis takes place.

chlo·ro·sis /klô'rōsəs/ ▸*n. Bot.* abnormal reduction or loss of the normal green coloration of leaves of plants, typically caused by iron deficiency in lime-rich soils, or by disease or lack of light. —**chlo·rot·ic** /klôr'ätik/ *adj.*

chlor·pyr·i·fos /klôr'pirə,fäs/ ▸*n.* a broad-spectrum organophosphate insecticide, widely used in food crop agriculture and to kill termites.

chock /CHäk/ ▸*n.* **1** a wedge or block placed against a wheel or rounded object, to prevent it from moving. ■ a support on which a rounded structure, such as a cask or the hull of a boat, may be placed to keep it steady. **2** a fitting with a gap at the top, through which a rope or line is run.

▸*v.* [*tr.*] (often **be chocked**) prevent the forward movement of (a wheel or vehicle) with a chock.

choc·o·late /'CHäk(ə)lit; 'CHôk-/ ▸*n.* a food preparation in the form of a paste or solid block made from roasted and ground cacao seeds, typically sweetened. ■ a candy made of or covered with this: *a box of chocolates.* ■ a drink made by mixing milk with chocolate: *sipping on hot* **chocolate.** ■ a deep brown color: [as *adj.*] *huge spiders, yellow and chocolate brown.* ▷early 17th cent. (in the sense 'a drink made with chocolate'): from French *chocolat* or Spanish *chocolate*, from Nahuatl *chocolatl* 'food made from cacao seeds,' influenced by unrelated *cacaua-atl* 'drink made from cacao.' —**choc·o·lat·y** (also **choc·o·lat·ey**) *adj.*

Choc·taw /'CHäk,tô/ ▸*n.* (*pl.* same or **-taws**) **1** a member of a native people now living mainly in Mississippi. **2** the Muskogean language of this people, closely related to Chickasaw. **3** *Figure Skating* a step from one edge of a skate to the other edge of the other skate in the opposite direction.
▸*adj.* of or relating to the Choctaw or their language.

choice /CHois/ ▸*n.* an act of selecting or making a decision when faced with two or more possibilities: *the* **choice** *between good and evil.* ■ the right or ability to make, or possibility of making, such a selection: *I had to do it, I had no choice.* ■ a range of possibilities from which one or more may be selected: *a sofa in a choice of fabrics.* ■ a course of action, thing, or person that is selected or decided upon: *this CD drive is the perfect choice.*
▸*adj.* **1** (esp. of food) of very good quality: *he picked some choice early plums.* **2** (of words, phrases, or language) rude and abusive: *he had a few choice words at his command.* —**choice·ly** *adv.* —**choice·ness** *n.*
▸ □ **by choice** of one's own volition. □ **of choice** selected as one's favorite or the best: *champagne was his drink of choice.* □ **of one's choice** that one chooses or has chosen: *the college of her choice.*

choir /'kwīər/ ▸*n.* an organized group of singers, typically one that takes part in church services or performs regularly in public: *a church choir.* ■ the part of a cathedral or large church between the altar and the nave, used by the choir and clergy.

choir·boy /'kwīr,boi/ ▸*n.* a boy who sings in a church or cathedral choir.

choke[1] /CHōk/ ▸*v.* **1** [*intr.*] (of a person or animal) have severe difficulty in breathing because of a constricted or blocked throat or a lack of air: *Willie* **choked** *on a mouthful of soda.* ■ [*tr.*] hinder or obstruct the breathing of (a person or animal) in such a way. ■ [*tr.*] retard the growth of or kill (a plant) by depriving it of light, air, or nourishment: *the bracken will* **choke** *the wild gladiolus.* ■ [*tr.*] (often **be choked with**) fill (a passage or space), esp. so as to make movement difficult or impossible: *the roads were* **choked** *with traffic.* ■ [*tr.*] prevent or suppress (the occurrence of something): *higher rates of interest* **choke off** *investment demand.* **2** [*tr.*] (often **be choked**) overwhelm and make (someone) speechless with a strong and typically negative feeling or emotion: *she was* **choked** *with angry emotion* | [*intr.*] *I just* **choked up** *reading it.* ■ [*intr.*] *inf.* (in sports) fail to perform at a crucial point of a game or contest owing to a failure of nerve. **3** [*tr.*] enrich the fuel mixture in (a gasoline engine) by reducing the intake of air.
▸*phrasal v.* □ **choke something back** suppress a strong emotion or the expression of such an emotion. □ **choke something down** swallow something with difficulty. □ **choke up** (in sports) grip (a bat, racket, etc.) further from the narrow end than is usual: *he* **choked up** *on the bat.*
▸*n.* **1** a valve in the carburetor of a gasoline engine that is used to reduce the amount of air in the fuel mixture when the engine is started. ■ a knob that controls such a valve. ■ a narrowed part of a shotgun bore, typically near the muzzle and serving to restrict the spread of the shot. **2** an action or sound of a person or animal having or seeming to have difficulty in breathing: *a little* **choke** *of laughter.*

choke[2] ▸*n.* the inedible mass of silky fibers at the center of a globe artichoke.

choke·ber·ry /'CHōk,berē/ ▸*n.* a North American shrub (genus *Aronia*) of the rose family, with white flowers and red autumn foliage, cultivated as an ornamental. ■ the bitter berrylike fruit of this shrub.

choke chain ▸*n.* a chain formed into a loop by passing one end through a ring on the other, placed around a dog's neck to exert control by causing pressure on the windpipe when the dog pulls.

chok·er /'CHōkər/ ▸*n.* **1** a close-fitting necklace or ornamental neckband. ■ a clerical or other high collar. **2** a cable looped around a log to drag it.

chol·er /'kälər/ ▸*n.* (in medieval science and medicine) one of the four bodily humors, identified with bile, believed to be associated with a peevish or irascible temperament. ■ *poetic/lit.* or *archaic* anger or irascibility.

chol·er·a /'kälərə/ ▶*n.* an infectious and often fatal bacterial disease of the small intestine, typically contracted from infected water supplies and causing severe vomiting and diarrhea.

chol·er·ic /'kälərik; kə'lerik/ ▶*adj.* bad-tempered or irritable. ■ *hist.* influenced by or predominating in the humor called choler: *a choleric disposition.* —**chol·er·i·cal·ly** *adv.*

cho·les·ter·ol /kə'lestə,rôl; -,rōl/ ▶*n.* a compound of the sterol type, C27H46O, found in most body tissues, including the blood and the nerves. High concentrations in the blood are thought to promote atherosclerosis.

cho·line /'kōlēn/ ▶*n.* *Biochem.* a strongly basic compound, HON (CH3)3CH2CH2OH, occurring widely in living tissues and important in the synthesis and transport of lipids.

chomp /CHämp; CHômp/ ▶*v.* [*intr.*] **1** munch or chew vigorously and noisily: *he chomped on his sandwich.* ■ (of a horse) make a noisy biting or chewing action. **2** fret impatiently.
▶*n.* a chewing noise or action.

choo-choo /'CHŌŌ ,CHŌŌ/ (also **choo-choo train**) ▶*n.* a child's word for a railroad train or locomotive, esp. a steam engine.

choose /CHŌŌz/ ▶*v.* (*past* **chose** /CHŌz/; *past part.* **cho·sen** /'CHŌzən/) [*tr.*] pick out or select (someone or something) as being the best or most appropriate of two or more alternatives: *he chose a seat facing the door* | [*intr.*] *now it's my turn to choose.* ■ [*intr.*] decide on a course of action, typically after rejecting alternatives: *I'll stay as long as I choose.* —**choos·er** *n.*

choos·y /'CHŌŌzē/ ▶*adj.* (**choos·i·er**, **choos·i·est**) *inf.* overly fastidious in making a choice. ■ **choos·i·ly** /-zəlē/ *adv.* —**choos·i·ness** *n.*

chop /CHäp/ ▶*v.* (**chopped**, **chop·ping**) [*tr.*] cut (something) into small pieces with repeated sharp blows using an ax or knife. ■ (**chop something off**) remove by cutting: *they chopped off all her hair.* ■ cut through the base of (something, esp. a tree) with blows from an ax or similar implement, in order to fell it: *the boy chopped down eight trees* | [*intr.*] *the men were chopping at the undergrowth with machetes.* ■ strike (a ball) with a short heavy blow, as if cutting at something. ■ (usu. **be chopped**) abolish or reduce the size or extent of (something) in a way regarded as brutally sudden: *their training courses are to be chopped.*
▶*n.* **1** a downward cutting blow or movement, typically with the hand. **2** a thick slice of meat, esp. pork or lamb, adjacent to, and typically including, a rib. **3** crushed or ground grain used as animal feed. **4** the broken motion of water, typically due to the action of the wind against the tide: *we started our run into a two-foot chop.*

chop·per /'CHäpər/ ▶*n.* **1** a person, tool, or machine that chops. ■ a butcher's cleaver. ■ (**choppers**) *inf.* teeth. **2** *inf.* a helicopter. **3** *inf.* a motorcycle, esp. one with high handlebars and the front-wheel fork extended forward. **4** *Baseball* a batted ball that makes a high bounce after hitting the ground in fair territory.

chop·py /'CHäpē/ ▶*adj.* (**chop·pi·er**, **chop·pi·est**) (of a sea or river) having many small waves. —**chop·pi·ly** /'CHäpəlē/ *adv.* —**chop·pi·ness** *n.*

chops /CHäps/ ▶*pl. n. inf.* **1** a person's or animal's mouth or jaws. ■ a person's cheeks; jowls. **2** the technical skill of a musician, esp. one who plays jazz.
▶ □ **bust one's chops** *inf.* exert oneself. □ **bust someone's chops** *inf.* nag or criticize someone.

chop shop ▶*n. inf.* a place where stolen vehicles are dismantled so that the parts can be sold or used to repair other stolen vehicles.

chop·stick /'CHäp,stik/ ▶*n.* (usu. **chopsticks**) each of a pair of small tapered sticks of wood, ivory, or plastic, held together in one hand and used as eating utensils, esp. by people in eastern Asia.

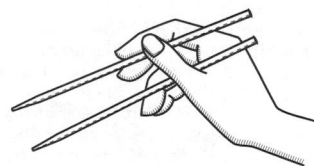

chopsticks

chop su·ey /,CHäp 'sōōē/ ▶*n.* a Chinese-style dish of meat stewed and fried with bean sprouts, bamboo shoots, and onions, and often served with rice.

cho·ral /'kôrəl/ ▶*adj.* composed for or sung by a choir or chorus. ■ engaged in or concerned with singing. —**cho·ral·ly** *adv.*

cho·rale /kə'ral; -'räl/ ▶*n.* **1** a musical composition (or part of one) consisting of or resembling a harmonized version of a simple, stately hymn tune. **2** a choir or choral society.

chord[1] /kôrd/ ▶*n.* a group of (typically three or more) notes sounded together, as a basis of harmony: *a G major chord.* —**chord·al** /'kôrdl/ *adj.*

chord[2] ▶*n.* **1** *Math.* a straight line joining the ends of an arc. **2** *Anat.* variant spelling of **CORD**. **3** *poetic/lit.* a string on a harp or other instrument.
▶ □ **strike** (or **touch**) **a chord** affect or stir someone's emotions. [with figurative reference to the emotions being the 'strings' of the mind visualized as a musical instrument.]

chor·date /'kôrdət; -,dāt/ ▶*n.* any animal of the phylum Chordata, including all vertebrates as well as the invertebrate sea squirts and lancelets, distinguished by the possession of a notochord at some stage during their development.
▶*adj.* of or related to the chordates.

chore /CHôr/ ▶*n.* a routine task, esp. a household one. ■ an unpleasant but necessary task: *he sees interviews as a chore.*

cho·re·a /kə'rēə/ ▶*n.* *Med.* a neurological disorder characterized by jerky involuntary movements affecting esp. the shoulders, hips, and face. See also **HUNTINGTON'S CHOREA**.

cho·re·o·graph /'kôrēə,graf/ ▶*v.* [*tr.*] compose the sequence of steps and moves for (a performance of dance or ice skating). ■ *fig.* plan and control (an event or operation): *the committee choreographs the movement of troops.* —**cho·re·o·graph·er** /,kôrē'ägrəfər/ *n.*

cho·re·og·ra·phy /,kôrē'ägrəfē/ ▶*n.* the sequence of steps and movements in dance or figure skating, esp. in a ballet or other staged dance. ■ the art or practice of designing such sequences. ■ the written notation for such a sequence. —**cho·re·o·graph·ic** /,kôrēə'grafik/ *adj.* —**cho·re·o·graph·i·cal·ly** /,kôrēə'grafik(ə)lē/ *adv.*

cho·re·ol·o·gy /,kôrē'äləjē/ ▶*n.* the notation of dance movement. —**cho·re·ol·o·gist** /-jist/ *n.*

chor·is·ter /'kôrəstər; 'kär-/ ▶*n.* **1** a member of a choir, esp. a child or young person singing the treble part in a church choir. **2** a person who leads the singing of a church choir or congregation. ▷late Middle English *queristre*, from an Anglo-Norman French variant of Old French *cueriste*, from *quer* 'choir,' from Latin *chorus* 'chorus,' from Greek *khoros*. The change in the first syllable in the 16th cent. was due to association with obsolete *chorist* 'member of a choir or chorus,'but the older form *quirister* long survived.

cho·roid /'kôr,oid/ (also **cho·ri·oid** /'kôrē,oid/) ▶*n.* (also **choroid coat**) the pigmented vascular layer of the eyeball between the retina and the sclera. —**cho·roi·dal** /kə'roidl/ *adj.*

chor·tle /'CHôrtl/ ▶*v.* [*intr.*] laugh in a breathy, gleeful way; chuckle.
▶*n.* a breathy, gleeful laugh: *Thomas gave a chortle.*

cho·rus /'kôrəs/ ▶*n.* (*pl.* **-rus·es**) **1** an organized group of singers, esp. one that performs together with an orchestra or opera company. ■ a piece of choral music, esp. one forming part of a larger work such as an opera or oratorio. ■ a part of a song that is repeated after each verse, typically by more than one singer. **2** (in ancient Greek tragedy) a group of performers who comment on the main action, typically speaking and moving together. ■ a simultaneous utterance of something by many people: *a growing chorus of complaint.* ■ a single character who speaks the prologue and other linking parts of the play, esp. in Elizabethan drama. ■ a section of text spoken by the chorus in drama. ■ a device used with an amplified musical instrument to give the impression that more than one instrument is being played: [as *adj.*] *a chorus pedal.*
▶*v.* (**-rused**, **-rus·ing**) [*tr.*] (of a group of people) say the same thing at the same time: *they chorused a noisy amen.*

cho·rus girl ▶*n.* a young woman who sings or dances in the chorus of a musical.

chose /CHōz/ ▶ past of **CHOOSE**.

cho·sen /'CHōzən/ ▶ past participle of **CHOOSE**.
▶*adj.* having been selected as the best or most appropriate: *music is his chosen vocation.*
▶ □ **chosen few** a group of people who are special or different, typically in a way thought to be unfair.

chow /CHou/ ▶*n.* **1** *inf.* food. **2** (also **chow chow**) a dog of a sturdy Chinese breed with a broad muzzle, a tail curled over the back, a bluish-black tongue, and typically a dense thick coat.
▶*phrasal v.* **chow down** (or **chow something down**) *inf.* eat.

chow·der /'CHoudər/ ▶*n.* a rich soup typically containing fish, clams, or corn with potatoes and onions: *clam chowder.*

chow mein /'CHou 'mān/ ▶*n.* a Chinese-style dish of shredded meat or seafood and vegetables served with fried noodles.

Chr. ▸*abbr. Bible* Chronicles.

chres·tom·a·thy /kreˈstäməTHē/ ▸*n.* (*pl.* **-thies**) *formal* a selection of passages from an author or authors, designed to help in learning a language.

chrism /ˈkrizəm/ ▸*n.* a mixture of oil and balsam, consecrated and used for anointing at baptism and in other rites of Catholic, Orthodox, and Anglican Churches.

Chris·ma·tion /krizˈmāSHən/ ▸*n.* a rite in the Orthodox and Eastern Catholic churches that is comparable and similar to confirmation in the Roman Catholic Church.

Christ /krīst/ ▸*n.* the title, also treated as a name, given to Jesus of Nazareth.
▸*interj.* an oath used to express irritation, dismay, or surprise. —**Christ·hood** /-ˌho͝od/ *n.* —**Christ·like** /-ˌlīk/ *adj.* —**Christ·ly** *adj.*
▸ □ **before Christ** full form of **BC**.

Chris·ta·del·phi·an /ˌkristəˈdelfēən/ ▸*n.* a member of a Christian sect, founded in the U.S. in 1848, that claims to return to the beliefs and practices of the earliest disciples and holds that Christ will return in power to set up a worldwide theocracy beginning at Jerusalem.
▸*adj.* of or adhering to this sect and its beliefs.

chris·ten /ˈkrisən/ ▸*v.* [*tr.*] (often **be christened**) give (a baby) a Christian name at baptism as a sign of admission to a Christian Church: *their second daughter was christened Jeanette.* ■ give to (someone or something) a name that reflects a notable quality or characteristic: *a person so creepy that his colleagues christened him "Millipede."* ■ dedicate (a vessel, building, etc.) ceremonially: *their first garbage truck was christened with a bottle of champagne.* ■ *inf.* use for the first time: *let's get steaks and christen the new grill.*

Chris·ten·dom /ˈkrisəndəm/ ▸*n.* *dated* the worldwide body or society of Christians. ■ the Christian world: *the greatest church in Christendom.*

Chris·tian ▸*adj.* of, relating to, or professing Christianity or its teachings: *the Christian Church.* ■ *inf.* having or showing qualities associated with Christians, esp. those of decency, kindness, and fairness.
▸*n.* a person who has received Christian baptism or is a believer in Jesus Christ and his teachings. —**Chris·tian·i·za·tion** /ˌkrisCHənəˈzāSHən/ *n.* —**Chris·tian·ize** /-ˌnīz/ *v.* —**Chris·tian·ly** *adv.*

Chris·tian e·ra ▸*n.* (**the Christian era**) the period of time that begins with the traditional date of Christ's birth.

Chris·ti·an·i·ty /ˌkrisCHēˈanitē/ ▸*n.* the religion based on the person and teachings of Jesus of Nazareth, or its beliefs and practices. ■ Christian quality or character: *you may know a man by his Christianity.*

Chris·tian name ▸*n.* a name given to an individual that distinguishes him or her from other members of the same family and is used as an address of familiarity; a forename, esp. one given at baptism.

Chris·tian Sci·ence ▸*n.* the beliefs and practices of the Church of Christ Scientist, a Christian sect founded by Mary Baker Eddy in 1879. Members hold that only God and the mind have ultimate reality, and that sin and illness are illusions that can be overcome by prayer and faith. —**Chris·tian Sci·en·tist** *n.*

Christ·mas /ˈkrisməs/ ▸*n.* (*pl.* **-mas·es**) the annual Christian festival celebrating Christ's birth, held on December 25. ■ the period immediately before and after December 25: *we had guests over Christmas.* —**Christ·mas·sy** /-məsē/ *adj.*

chro·ma /ˈkrōmə/ ▸*n.* purity or intensity of color.

chro·mat·ic /krōˈmatik/ ▸*adj.* **1** *Mus.* relating to or using notes not belonging to the diatonic scale of the key in which a passage is written. ■ (of a scale) ascending or descending by semitones. ■ (of an instrument) able to play all the notes of the chromatic scale. **2** of, relating to, or produced by color. —**chro·mat·i·cal·ly** /-ik(ə)lē/ *adv.* —**chro·mat·i·cism** /-əˌsizəm/ *n.*

chro·ma·tic·i·ty /ˌkrōməˈtisətē/ ▸*n.* the quality of color, independent of brightness.

chro·ma·tid /ˈkrōməˌtid/ ▸*n.* *Biol.* each of the two threadlike strands into which a chromosome divides longitudinally during cell division. Each contains a double helix of DNA.

chro·ma·tin /ˈkrōmətən/ ▸*n.* *Biol.* the material of which the chromosomes of organisms other than bacteria (i.e., eukaryotes) are composed. It consists of protein, RNA, and DNA.

chro·ma·tog·ra·phy /ˌkrōməˈtägrəfē/ ▸*n.* *Chem.* the separation of a mixture by passing it in solution or suspension or as a vapor (as in gas chromatography) through a medium in which the components move at different rates. —**chro·mat·o·graph** /krōˈmatəˌgraf/ *n.* —**chro·mat·o·graph·ic** /krō,matəˈgrafik/ *adj.*

chrome /krōm/ ▸*n.* chromium plating as a decorative or protective finish on motor-vehicle fittings and other objects: [as *adj.*] *a chrome bumper.* ■ [as *adj.*] denoting compounds or alloys of chromium: *chrome dyes.*

chro·mite /ˈkrō,mīt/ ▸*n.* a brownish-black mineral that consists of a mixed oxide of chromium and iron and is the principal ore of chromium.

chro·mi·um /ˈkrōmēəm/ ▸*n.* the chemical element of atomic number 24, a hard white metal used in stainless steel and other alloys. (Symbol: **Cr**)

chro·mo /ˈkrōmō/ ▸*n.* (*pl.* **-mos**) **1** shortened form of CHROMOLITHO-GRAPH.

chro·mo·lith·o·graph /ˌkrōmōˈliTHəˌgraf/ *hist.* ▸*n.* a colored picture printed by lithography, esp. in the late 19th and early 20th centuries. —**chro·mo·li·thog·ra·pher** /-liˈTHägrəfər/ *n.* —**chro·mo·lith·o·graph·ic** /-ˌliTHəˈgrafik/ *adj.* —**chro·mo·li·thog·ra·phy** /-liˈTHägrəfē/ *n.*

chro·mo·some /ˈkrōmə,sōm/ ▸*n.* *Biol.* a threadlike structure of nucleic acids and protein found in the nucleus of most living cells, carrying genetic information in the form of genes. —**chro·mo·so·mal** /ˌkrōmə-ˈsōməl/ *adj.*

chro·mo·sphere /ˈkrōmə,sfi(ə)r/ ▸*n.* *Astron.* a reddish gaseous layer immediately above the photosphere of the sun or another star. Together with the corona, it constitutes the star's outer atmosphere. —**chro·mo·spher·ic** /ˌkrōməˈsfi(ə)rik; -ˈsferik/ *adj.*

Chron. ▸*abbr. Bible* Chronicles.

chron·ic /ˈkränik/ ▸*adj.* (of an illness) persisting for a long time or constantly recurring: *chronic bronchitis.* Often contrasted with ACUTE. ■ (of a person) having such an illness: *a chronic asthmatic.* ■ (of a problem) long-lasting and difficult to eradicate: *the school suffers from chronic overcrowding.* ■ (of a person) having a particular bad habit: *a chronic liar.* —**chron·i·cal·ly** /-ik(ə)lē/ *adv.* —**chro·nic·i·ty** /krəˈnisətē/ *n.*

chron·i·cle /ˈkränikəl/ ▸*n.* a factual written account of important or historical events in the order of their occurrence. ■ a work of fiction or nonfiction that describes a particular series of events.
▸*v.* [*tr.*] record (a related series of events) in a factual and detailed way. —**chron·i·cler** /-iklər/ *n.*

chron·o·graph /ˈkränə,graf; ˈkrō-/ ▸*n.* an instrument for recording time with great accuracy. ■ a stopwatch. —**chron·o·graph·ic** /ˌkränəˈgrafik; ˌkrō-/ *adj.*

chron·o·log·i·cal /ˌkränlˈäjikəl/ ▸*adj.* relating to the establishment of dates and time sequences: *the diary provided a chronological framework for the events.* ■ (of a record of several events) starting with the earliest and following the order in which they occurred: *the entries are in chronological order.* ■ calculated in terms of the passage of time rather than some other criterion: *ratings are calculated by dividing a child's mental age by his or her chronological age.* —**chron·o·log·i·cal·ly** /-ik(ə)lē/ *adv.*

chro·nol·o·gy /krəˈnäləjē/ ▸*n.* (*pl.* **-gies**) the study of historical records to establish the dates of past events. ■ the arrangement of events or dates in the order of their occurrence. ■ a table or document displaying such an arrangement. —**chro·nol·o·gist** /-jist/ *n.*

chro·nom·e·ter /krəˈnämətər/ ▸*n.* an instrument for measuring time, esp. one designed to keep accurate time in spite of motion or variations in temperature, humidity, and air pressure. Chronometers were first developed for marine navigation.

chro·nom·e·try /krəˈnämətrē/ ▸*n.* the science of accurate time measurement. —**chron·o·met·ric** /ˌkränəˈmetrik; ˌkrō-/ *adj.* —**chron·o·met·ri·cal** /ˌkränəˈmetrikəl; ˌkrō-/ *adj.* —**chron·o·met·ri·cal·ly** /ˌkränə-ˈmetrik(ə)lē/ *adv.*

chrys·a·lis /ˈkrisələs/ (also **chrys·a·lid** /ˈkrisə,lid/) ▸*n.* (*pl.* **-lis·es**) a quiescent insect pupa, esp. of a butterfly or moth. ■ the hard outer case of this, esp. after being discarded. ■ *fig.* a preparatory or transitional state: *she emerged from the chrysalis of self-conscious adolescence.* ▷*early 17th cent.*: from Latin *chrysal(l)is, chrysal(l)id-*, from Greek *khrusallis*, from *khrusos* 'gold' (because of the gold color or metallic sheen of the pupae of some species).

chry·san·the·mum /kriˈsanTHəməm/ ▸*n.* (*pl.* **chrysanthemums**) a plant (genera *Chrysanthemum* and *Dendranthema*) of the daisy family, having brightly colored ornamental flowers and existing in many cultivated varieties. ■ a flower or flowering stem of this plant.

chub /CHəb/ ▸*n.* a thick-bodied European river fish (*Leuciscus cephalus*) of the minnow family, with a gray-green back and white underparts.

chub·by /ˈCHəbē/ ▸*adj.* (**-bi·er, -bi·est**) plump and rounded: *a pretty child with chubby cheeks.* —**chub·bi·ly** /ˈCHəbəlē/ *adv.* —**chub·bi·ness** *n.*

chuck¹ /CHək/ *inf.* ▸*v.* [*tr.*] throw (something) carelessly or casually:

someone chucked a brick through the window. ■ throw (something) away: *they make a living out of stuff people* **chuck out.** ■ give up (a job or activity) suddenly: *Richard chucked his cultural studies course.* ■ break off a relationship with (a partner). —**chuck·er** *n.*

▶ □ **chuck it all in** abandon a course of action or way of life, esp. for another that is radically different.

chuck² ▶*v.* [*tr.*] touch (someone) playfully or gently under the chin.
▶*n.* a playful touch under the chin.

chuck³ ▶*n.* **1** a device for holding a workpiece in a lathe or a tool in a drill, typically having three or four jaws that move radially in and out. **2** a cut of beef that extends from the neck to the ribs, typically used for stewing.

chuck⁴ ▶*n. inf.* food or provisions.

chuck·le /'CHəkəl/ ▶*v.* [*intr.*] laugh quietly or inwardly: *I chuckled at the astonishment on her face.*
▶*n.* a quiet or suppressed laugh. —**chuck·ler** /'CHəklər/ *n.*

chuck wag·on ▶*n.* a wagon with cooking facilities providing food on a ranch, workplace, or campsite.

chuff /CHəf/ ▶*v.* [*intr.*] (of a steam engine) move with a regular sharp puffing sound.

chug¹ /CHəg/ ▶*v.* (**chugged, chug·ging**) [*intr.*] emit a series of regular muffled explosive sounds, as of an engine running slowly: *he could hear the pipes chugging.* ■ [*intr.*] (of a vehicle or boat) move slowly making such sounds: *a cabin cruiser was chugging down the river.*
▶*n.* a muffled explosive sound or a series of such sounds.

chug² (also **chug·a·lug** or **chug-a-lug** /'CHəgə,ləg/) ▶*v.* (**chugged, chug·ging**) [*tr.*] *inf.* consume (a drink) in large gulps without pausing.

chuk·ker /'CHəkər/ (also **chuk·ka**) ▶*n.* each of a number of periods (typically six) into which play in a game of polo is divided.

chum¹ /CHəm/ *inf., dated* ▶*n.* a close friend. ■ a form of address expressing familiarity or friendliness: *it's your own fault, chum.*
▶*v.* (**chummed, chum·ming**) [*intr.*] be friendly to or form a friendship with someone: *they started chumming around in high school.* —**chum·mi·ly** /'CHəməlē/ *adv.* —**chum·mi·ness** *n.* —**chum·my** *adj.*

chum² ▶*n.* chopped fish, fish fluids, and other material thrown overboard as angling bait. ■ refuse from fish, esp. that remaining after expressing oil.
▶*v.* [*intr.*] use chum as bait when fishing.

chum³ (also **chum salmon**) ▶*n.* (*pl.* same or **chums**) a large North Pacific salmon (*Oncorhyncus keta*) that is commercially important as a food fish.

chump /CHəmp/ ▶*n. inf.* a foolish person: *how can this chump be a detective?* ■ an easily deceived person; a sucker.

chunk¹ /CHəNGk/ ▶*n.* a thick, solid piece of something: *huge chunks of masonry littered the street.* ■ an amount or part of something: *fuel takes a large chunk of their small income.*
▶*v.* [*tr.*] divide (something) into chunks: *chunk four pounds of pears.* ■ (in psychology or linguistic analysis) group together (connected items or words) so that they can be stored or processed as single concepts.

chunk² ▶*v.* [*intr.*] move with or make a muffled, metallic sound.

chunk·y /'CHəNGkē/ ▶*adj.* (**chunk·i·er, chunk·i·est**) **1** (of a person) short and sturdy. ■ bulky and solid: *a chunky bracelet.* ■ (of wool or a woolen garment) thick and bulky. **2** (of food) containing chunks: *fresh chunky salsa* | *a chunky soup.* —**chunk·i·ly** /-kəlē/ *adv.* —**chunk·i·ness** *n.*

chu·pa·ca·bra /,CHo͞opə'käbrə/ (also **chu·pa·ca·bras** /-brəs/) ▶*n.* a mythical beast said to kill young animals by sucking their blood.

church /CHərCH/ ▶*n.* a building used for public Christian worship: *they came to church with me.* ■ (usu. **Church**) a particular Christian organization, typically one with its own clergy, buildings, and distinctive doctrines: *the Church of England.* ■ (**the Church**) the hierarchy of clergy of such an organization, esp. the Roman Catholic Church or the Church of England. ■ institutionalized religion as a political or social force: *the separation of church and state.* ■ the body of all Christians.

church·go·er /'CHərCH,gōər/ ▶*n.* a person who goes to church, esp. one who does so regularly. —**church·go·ing** /-,gō-iNG/ *n. & adj.*

church·man /'CHərCHmən/ ▶*n.* (*pl.* -**men**) a male member of the Christian clergy or of a church.

Church of Eng·land ▶the English branch of the Western Christian Church, which combines Catholic and Protestant traditions, rejects the pope's authority, and has the monarch as its titular head.

church·y /'CHərCHē/ ▶*adj.* **1** (of a person) excessively pious and consequently narrow-minded or intolerant. **2** resembling a church: *Gothic design looks too churchy.* —**church·i·ness** *n.*

church·yard /'CHərCH,yärd/ ▶*n.* an enclosed area surrounding a church, esp. as used for burials.

churl /CHərl/ ▶*n.* an impolite and mean-spirited person. ■ *archaic* a miser. ■ *archaic* a person of low birth; a peasant.

churl·ish /'CHərlisH/ ▶*adj.* rude in a mean-spirited and surly way: *it seems churlish to complain.* —**churl·ish·ly** *adv.* —**churl·ish·ness** *n.*

churn /CHərn/ ▶*n.* a machine or container in which butter is made by agitating milk or cream.
▶*v.* **1** [*tr.*] (often **be churned**) agitate or turn (milk or cream) in a machine in order to produce butter. ■ produce (butter) in such a way. **2** [*intr.*] (of liquid) move about vigorously: *the seas churned* | *fig. her stomach was churning at the thought of the ordeal.* ■ [*tr.*] (often **be churned**) cause (liquid) to move in this way: *in high winds most of the lake is churned up.* ■ [*tr.*] break up the surface of (an area of ground): *the earth had been churned up where vehicles had passed through.* **3** [*tr.*] (of a broker) encourage frequent turnover of (investments) in order to generate commission.
▶*phrasal v.* □ **churn something out** produce something routinely or mechanically, esp. in large quantities.

churr ▶*v. & n.* variant spelling of **CHIRR**.

chur·ro /'CHo͞orō/ ▶*n.* (*pl.* **chur·ros**) a Latin American fried pastry in ridged cigar shapes.

chute¹ /SHo͞ot/ ▶*n.* a sloping channel or slide for conveying things to a lower level. ■ a water slide into a swimming pool.

chute² ▶*n. inf.* a parachute. ■ *Sailing* informal term for **SPINNAKER**. —**chut·ist** /'SHo͞otist/ *n.*

chut·ney /'CHətnē/ ▶*n.* (*pl.* -**neys**) a spicy condiment made of fruits or vegetables with vinegar, spices, and sugar, originating in India.

chutz·pah /'ho͝otspə; 'kho͝otspə; -spä/ (also **chutz·pa**) ▶*n. inf.* shameless audacity; impudence.

CI ▶*abbr.* ■ certificate of insurance. ■ Channel Islands. ■ cost and insurance.

Ci ▶*abbr.* ■ cirrus. ■ curie.

CIA ▶*abbr.* Central Intelligence Agency.

ciao /CHou/ ▶*interj. inf.* used as a greeting at meeting or parting.

ci·bo·ri·um /sə'bôrēəm/ ▶*n.* (*pl.* -**bo·ri·a** /-'bôrēə/) **1** a receptacle shaped like a shrine or a cup with an arched cover, used in the Christian Church for the reservation of the Eucharist. **2** a canopy over an altar in a church, standing on four pillars.

ci·ca·da /sə'kādə; sə'kädə/ ▶*n.* a large homopterous insect (family Cicadidae) with long transparent wings, occurring chiefly in warm countries. The male cicada makes a loud shrill droning noise after dark by vibrating two membranes on its abdomen.

ci·ca·trix /'sikə,triks/ (also **cic·a·trice** /-,tris/) ▶*n.* (*pl.* **cic·a·tri·ces** /,sikə'trīsēz; sə'kätrə,sēz/) the scar of a healed wound. ■ a scar on the bark of a tree. ■ *Bot.* a mark on a stem left after a leaf or other part has become detached. —**cic·a·tri·cial** /,sikə'trisHəl/ *adj.*

cic·e·ly /'sisilē/ (also **sweet cicely**) ▶*n.* (*pl.* -**ies**) an aromatic white-flowered plant (genera *Myrrhis* and *Osmorhiza*) of the parsley family, with fernlike leaves.

cic·e·ro·ne /,sisə'rōnē; ,CHēCHə-/ ▶*n.* (*pl.* -**ro·ni** *pronunc.* same) a guide who gives information about antiquities and places of interest to sightseers.

cich·lid /'siklid/ ▶*n.* *Zool.* a perchlike freshwater fish of a family (Cichlidae) widely distributed in tropical countries. Cichlids provide a valuable source of food in some areas, and many are popular in aquariums.

ci·der /'sīdər/ ▶*n.* (also **sweet cider**) an unfermented drink made by crushing fruit, typically apples. ■ (also **hard cider**) an alcoholic drink made from fermented crushed fruit, typically apples.

ci·de·vant /,sē də'vän/ ▶*adj.* from or in an earlier time (used to indicate that someone or something once possessed a specified characteristic but no longer does so): *her ci-devant student, now her lover.*

CIF (also **C.I.F.**) ▶*abbr.* cost, insurance, freight (as included in a price).

cig /sig/ ▶*n. inf.* a cigarette.

ci·gar /si'gär/ ▶*n.* a cylinder of tobacco rolled in tobacco leaves for smoking. ▷early 18th cent.: from French *cigare*, or from Spanish *cigarro*, probably from Mayan *sik'ar* 'smoking.'

▶ □ **close, but no cigar** *inf.* (of an attempt) almost, but not quite successful. [referring to a cigar received in congratulation.]

cig·a·rette /,sigə'ret; 'sigə,ret/ (also **cig·a·ret**) ▶*n.* a thin cylinder of

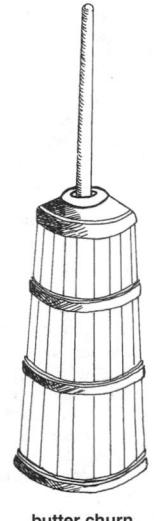

butter churn

finely cut tobacco rolled in paper for smoking. ■ a similar cylinder containing a narcotic, herbs, or a medicated substance.

cig·a·ril·lo /ˌsigəˈrilō; -ˈrē(y)ō/ ▶n. (pl. **-los**) a small cigar.

cil·i·ar·y bod·y ▶n. Anat. the part of the eye that connects the iris to the choroid.

cil·i·ate /ˈsilē‚āt; -ēət/ ▶n. Zool. a single-celled animal of the phylum Ciliophora (kingdom Protista), distinguished by the possession of cilia. The ciliates are a large and diverse group of advanced protozoans.
▶adj. Zool. (of an organism, cell, or surface) bearing cilia.

cil·i·um /ˈsilēəm/ ▶n. (usu. in pl. **cil·i·a** /ˈsilēə/ Biol. & Anat. a short hair-like vibrating structure found in large numbers on the surface of certain cells. ■ an eyelash, or a delicate hairlike structure that resembles one. —**cil·i·ar·y** /-‚erē/ adj.

CINC ▶abbr. Commander in Chief.

cinch /sinCH/ ▶n. **1** inf. an extremely easy task: the program was a cinch to use. ■ a sure thing; a certainty: he was a cinch to take a prize. **2** a girth for a Western saddle or pack.
▶v. [tr.] **1** secure (a garment) with a belt. ■ fix (a saddle) securely by means of a girth; girth up (a horse). **2** inf. make certain of: his advice cinched her decision to accept the offer.

cin·cho·na /sinˈkōnə; sinˈCHōnə/ ▶n. an evergreen South American tree or shrub (genus Cinchona) of the bedstraw family. ■ (also **cinchona bark**) the bark of this tree, a source of quinine.

cinc·ture /ˈsiNGkCHər/ ▶n. **1** poetic/lit. a girdle or belt. **2** Archit. a ring at either end of a column shaft.

cin·der /ˈsindər/ ▶n. a small piece of partly burned coal or wood that has stopped giving off flames but still has combustible matter in it. —**cin·der·y** adj.

cin·der block ▶n. a lightweight building brick made from small cinders mixed with sand and cement.

Cin·der·el·la /ˌsindəˈrelə/ ▶a fairy tale character who is exploited as a servant but enabled by a fairy godmother to attend a royal ball. She captivates Prince Charming but has to flee at midnight, leaving the prince to identify her by the glass slipper that she leaves behind. ■ [as n.] a person or thing of unrecognized or disregarded merit or beauty.

cin·e /ˈsinē/ ▶adj. chiefly Brit. cinematographic: a cine camera.

cin·e·ast /ˈsinē‚ast/ (also **cin·é·aste** or **cin·e·aste**) ▶n. a filmmaker. ■ an enthusiast for or devotee of movies or filmmaking.

cin·e·ma /ˈsinəmə/ ▶n. chiefly Brit. a movie theater. ■ the production of movies as an art or industry: the history of American cinema. —**cin·e·mat·ic** /ˌsinəˈmatik/ adj.

cin·e·ma·tog·ra·phy /ˌsinəməˈtägrəfē/ ▶n. the art of making motion pictures. —**cin·e·ma·tog·ra·pher** /-fər/ n. —**cin·e·mat·o·graph·ic** /-‚matə-ˈgrafik/ adj. —**cin·e·mat·o·graph·i·cal·ly** /-‚matəˈgrafik(ə)lē/ adv.

ci·né·ma-vé·ri·té /ˈsinəmə ‚veriˈtā/ ▶n. a style of filmmaking characterized by realistic, typically documentary motion pictures that avoid artificiality and artistic effect and are generally made with simple equipment. ■ motion pictures of this style collectively.

cin·e·plex /ˈsini‚pleks/ (also **Cin·e·plex**) ▶n. trademark a movie theater with several separate screens; a multiplex.

cin·e·rar·i·um /ˌsinəˈre(ə)rēəm/ ▶n. (pl. **-ums**) a place where the ashes of the cremated dead are kept. —**cin·e·rar·y** /ˈsinə‚rerē/ adj.

cin·na·bar /ˈsinə‚bär/ ▶n. a bright red mineral consisting of mercury sulfide. It is the only important ore of mercury and is sometimes used as a pigment.

cin·na·mon /ˈsinəmən/ ▶n. **1** an aromatic spice made from the dried bark of a Southeast Asian tree. ■ flavored with cinnamon, or having a similar flavor. ■ a reddish- or yellowish-brown color resembling that of cinnamon. **2** (also **cinnamon tree**) the tree (genus Cinnamomum) of the laurel family that yields this spice. ▷late Middle English: from Old French cinnamome (from Greek kinnamōmon), and Latin cinnamon (from Greek kinnamon), both from a Semitic language.

ci·pher /ˈsīfər/ (also **cy·pher**) ▶n. **1** a secret or disguised way of writing; a code: he was writing cryptic notes in a cipher | the information may be given in cipher. ■ a thing written in such a code. ■ a key to such a code. **2** dated a zero; a figure 0. ■ fig. a person or thing of no importance, esp. a person who does the bidding of others and seems to have no will of their own. **3** a monogram. **4** a continuous sounding of an organ pipe, caused by a mechanical defect.
▶v. **1** [tr.] put (a message) into secret writing; encode. **2** [intr.] archaic do arithmetic.

cir. (also **circ.**) ▶abbr. ■ circle. ■ circuit. ■ circular. ■ circulation. ■ circumference.

cir·ca /ˈsərkə/ ▶prep. (often preceding a date) approximately: built circa 1935.

cir·ca·di·an /sərˈkādēən/ ▶adj. Physiol. (of biological processes) recurring naturally on a twenty-four-hour cycle, even in the absence of light fluctuations: a circadian rhythm.

cir·cle /ˈsərkəl/ (abbr.: **cir.** or **circ.**) ▶n. **1** a round plane figure whose boundary (the circumference) consists of points equidistant from a fixed point (the center). ■ the line enclosing such a figure. ■ something in the shape of such a figure: the lamp spread a circle of light. ■ a group of people or things arranged to form such a figure: they all sat around in a circle. ■ a movement or series of movements that follows the approximate circumference of such a figure: the astrological houses rotate in a circle. ■ a dark circular mark below each eye, typically caused by illness or tiredness. ■ a curved upper tier of seats in a theater. See also DRESS CIRCLE. **2** a group of people with a shared profession, interests, or acquaintances: she did not normally move in such exalted circles.
▶v. [tr.] move all the way around (someone or something), esp. more than once: the two dogs circle each other with hackles raised | [intr.] we circled around the island. ■ [tr.] (from the air) move in a ring-shaped path above (someone or something), esp. more than once: they were circling the airport. ■ [intr.] (**circle back**) move in a wide loop back toward one's starting point. ■ (often **be circled**) form a ring around. ■ draw a line around: circle the correct answers.
▶ □ **come** (or **turn**) **full circle** return to a past position or situation, esp. in a way considered to be inevitable. □ **go around** (or **around and around**) **in circles** inf. do something for a long time without achieving anything but purposeless repetition. □ **run around in circles** inf. be fussily busy with little result.

cir·clet /ˈsərklət/ ▶n. a circular band, typically one made of precious metal, worn on the head as an ornament. ■ a small circular arrangement or object.

cir·cuit /ˈsərkət/ (abbr.: **cir.** or **circ.**) ▶n. **1** a roughly circular line, route, or movement that starts and finishes at the same place. ■ a complete and closed path around which a circulating electric current can flow. ■ a system of electrical conductors and components forming such a path. **2** an established itinerary of events or venues used for a particular activity, typically involving public performance: the alternative cabaret circuit. ■ a series of sporting events in which the same players regularly take part: his first season on the professional circuit. ■ a series of athletic exercises performed consecutively in one training session: [as adj.] circuit training. ■ a regular journey made by a judge around a particular district to hear cases in court: [as adj.] a circuit judge. ■ a district of this type. ■ a judicial region formerly administered by traveling judges. ■ a chain of theaters or nightclubs under a single management.
▶v. [tr.] move all the way around (a place or thing).

cir·cuit board ▶n. a thin rigid board containing an electric circuit; a printed circuit.

cir·cuit break·er ▶n. an automatic device for stopping the flow of current in an electric circuit as a safety measure.

cir·cu·i·tous /sərˈkyōōətəs/ ▶adj. (of a route or journey) longer than the most direct way: the canal followed a circuitous route | fig. a circuitous line of reasoning. —**cir·cu·i·tous·ly** adv. —**cir·cu·i·tous·ness** n.

cir·cuit·ry /ˈsərkətrē/ ▶n. (pl. **-ries**) electric circuits collectively: solid state circuitry. ■ a circuit or system of circuits performing a particular function in an electronic device: switching circuitry.

cir·cu·lar /ˈsərkyələr/ (abbr.: **cir.** or **circ.**) ▶adj. **1** having the form of a circle: the building features a circular atrium. ■ (of a movement or journey) starting and finishing at the same place and often following roughly the circumference of an imaginary circle: a circular walk. **2** Logic (of an argument) already containing an assumption of what is to be proved, and therefore fallacious.
▶n. a letter or advertisement that is distributed to a large number of people. —**cir·cu·lar·i·ty** /ˌsərkyəˈlaritē/ n. —**cir·cu·lar·ly** adv.

cir·cu·lar·ize /ˈsərkyələ‚rīz/ ▶v. [tr.] distribute a large number of letters, leaflets, or questionnaires to (a group of people) in order to advertise something or canvas opinion. —**cir·cu·lar·i·za·tion** /ˌsərkyələrə-ˈzāSHən/ n.

cir·cu·late /ˈsərkyə‚lāt/ ▶v. **1** move or cause to move continuously or freely through a closed system or area: [intr.] antibodies circulate in the bloodstream | [tr.] the fan circulates hot air around the oven. ■ [intr.] move around a social function in order to talk to many different people. **2** pass or cause to pass from place to place or person to person: [intr.] rumors of his arrest circulated | [tr.] they were circulating the list to conservation groups. —**cir·cu·la·tive** /-‚lātiv; -lətiv/ adj. —**cir·cu·la·tor** /-‚lātər/ n.

Pronunciation Key ə ago, up; ər over, fur; a hat; ā ate; ä car; CH chin; e let; ē see; e(ə)r air; i fit; ī by; i(ə)r ear; NG sing; ō go; ô law, for; oi toy; o͝o good; o͞o goo; ou out; SH she; TH thin; <u>TH</u> then; (h)w why; ZH vision

cir·cu·la·tion /ˌsərkyəˈlāSHən/ (abbr.: **cir.** or **circ.**) ▶ *n.* **1** movement to and fro or around something, esp. that of fluid in a closed system: *an extra pump for good water circulation.* ■ the continuous motion by which the blood travels through all parts of the body under the action of the heart. **2** the public availability or knowledge of something: *his music has achieved wide circulation.* ■ the movement, exchange, or availability of money in a country: *the new coins go into circulation today.* ■ the number of copies sold of a newspaper or magazine: *the magazine had a large circulation.*

▶ □ **in** (or **out of**) **circulation** available (or unavailable) to the public; in (or not in) general use: *there is a huge volume of video material in circulation.* ■ used of a person who is seen (or not seen) in public: *Anne had made a good recovery and was back in circulation.*

cir·cu·la·to·ry /ˈsərkyələˌtôrē/ ▶ *adj.* of or relating to the circulation of blood or sap.

circum. ▶ *abbr.* circumference.

cir·cum·cise /ˈsərkəmˌsīz/ ▶ *v.* [*tr.*] cut off the foreskin of (a young boy or man, esp. a baby) as a religious rite, esp. in Judaism and Islam, or as a medical treatment. ■ cut off the clitoris, and sometimes the labia, of (a girl or young woman) as a traditional practice among some peoples.

cir·cum·ci·sion /ˌsərkəmˈsizhən; ˈsərkəmˌsizhən/ ▶ *n.* the action or practice of circumcising a young boy or man.

cir·cum·fer·ence /sərˈkəmf(ə)rəns/ (abbr.: **cir.**, **circ.**, or **circum.**) ▶ *n.* the enclosing boundary of a curved geometric figure, esp. a circle. ■ the distance around something. ■ the edge or region that entirely surrounds something: *petals on the circumference are larger than those in the center.* —**cir·cum·fer·en·tial** /sərˌkəmfəˈrenCHəl/ *adj.* —**cir·cum·fer·en·tial·ly** *adv.*

cir·cum·flex /ˈsərkəmˌfleks/ ▶ *n.* (also **circumflex accent**) a mark (^) placed over a vowel in some languages to indicate contraction, length, or pitch or tone.

▶ *adj. Anat.* bending around something else; curved: *circumflex coronary arteries.*

cir·cum·lo·cu·tion /ˌsərkəmˌlōˈkyoōSHən/ ▶ *n.* the use of many words where fewer would do, esp. in a deliberate attempt to be vague or evasive: *his admission came after years of circumlocution | he used a number of poetic circumlocutions.* —**cir·cum·loc·u·to·ry** /-ˈläkyəˌtôrē/ *adj.*

cir·cum·nav·i·gate /ˌsərkəmˈnavəˌgāt/ ▶ *v.* [*tr.*] sail all the way around (something, esp. the world). ■ *humorous* go around or across (something): *he helped her to circumnavigate a frozen puddle.* —**cir·cum·nav·i·ga·tion** /-ˌnavəˈgāSHən/ *n.* —**cir·cum·nav·i·ga·tor** /-ˌgātər/ *n.*

cir·cum·scribe /ˈsərkəmˌskrīb/ ▶ *v.* [*tr.*] (often **be circumscribed**) **1** restrict (something) within limits: *their movements were strictly monitored and circumscribed.* **2** *Geom.* draw (a figure) around another, touching it at points but not cutting it. Compare with INSCRIBE. —**cir·cum·scrib·er** *n.* —**cir·cum·scrip·tion** /ˌsərkəmˈskripSHən/ *n.*

cir·cum·spect /ˈsərkəmˌspekt/ ▶ *adj.* wary and unwilling to take risks: *the officials were very circumspect in their statements.* —**cir·cum·spec·tion** /ˌsərkəmˈspekSHən/ *n.* —**cir·cum·spect·ly** *adv.*

cir·cum·stance /ˈsərkəmˌstans; -stəns/ ▶ *n.* **1** (usu. **circumstances**) a fact or condition connected with or relevant to an event or action: *we wanted to marry but circumstances didn't permit.* ■ an event or fact that causes or helps to cause something to happen, typically something undesirable: *he was found dead but there were no suspicious circumstances | they were thrown together by circumstance.* **2** one's state of financial or material welfare: *living in reduced circumstances.* —**cir·cum·stanced** *adj.*

▶ □ **under no circumstances** never, whatever the situation is or might be. □ **under** (or **in**) **the circumstances** given the difficult nature of the situation: *she had every right to be angry under the circumstances.*

cir·cum·stan·tial /ˌsərkəmˈstanSHəl/ ▶ *adj.* **1** (of evidence or a legal case) pointing indirectly toward someone's guilt but not conclusively proving it. **2** (of a description) containing full details: *the picture was circumstantial and therefore convincing.* —**cir·cum·stan·ti·al·i·ty** /-ˌstanSHēˈalətē/ *n.* —**cir·cum·stan·tial·ly** *adv.*

cir·cum·vent /ˌsərkəmˈvent/ ▶ *v.* [*tr.*] find a way around (an obstacle). ■ overcome (a problem or difficulty), typically in a clever and surreptitious way: *terrorists found the airport checks easy to circumvent.* ■ *archaic* deceive; outwit. —**cir·cum·ven·tion** /-ˈvenCHən/ *n.*

cir·cus /ˈsərkəs/ ▶ *n.* (pl. **-cus·es**) **1** a traveling company of acrobats, trained animals, and clowns that gives performances, typically in a large tent, in a series of different places. ■ (in ancient Rome) a rounded or oblong arena lined with tiers of seats, used for equestrian and other sports and games. ■ *inf.* a public scene of frenetic and noisily intrusive activity: *a media circus.* **2** [in *place names*] *Brit.* a rounded open space in a city where several streets converge: *Piccadilly Circus.*

cir·rho·sis /səˈrōsəs/ ▶ *n.* a chronic disease of the liver marked by degeneration of cells, inflammation, and fibrous thickening of tissue. It is typically a result of alcoholism or hepatitis. ▷early 19th cent.: modern Latin, from Greek *kirrhos* 'tawny' (because this is the color of the liver in many cases). —**cir·rhot·ic** /səˈrätik/ *adj.*

cir·ri·ped /ˈsirəˌped/ ▶ *n.* any crustacean of the group that includes the barnacles.

cir·rus /ˈsirəs/ ▶ *n.* (pl. **cir·ri** /ˈsirˌī; ˈsirē/) cloud forming wispy filamentous tufted streaks ("mare's tails") at high altitude, usually 16,500–45,000 feet (5–13 km).

cis·al·pine /sisˈalpīn/ ▶ *adj.* on the southern side of the Alps.

cis·at·lan·tic /ˌsisətˈlantik/ ▶ *adj.* on the same side of the Atlantic as the speaker.

cis·co /ˈsiskō/ ▶ *n.* (pl. **-oes**) a freshwater whitefish (genus *Coregonus*) of northern countries. Most species are migratory and are important food fishes.

cist /sist; kist/ ▶ *n. Archaeol.* a coffin or burial chamber made from stone or a hollowed tree.

Cis·ter·cian /sisˈtərSHən/ ▶ *n.* a monk or nun of an order founded in 1098 as a stricter branch of the Benedictines. The monks are now divided into two observances, the strict observance, whose adherents are known popularly as Trappists, and the common observance, which has certain relaxations.

▶ *adj.* of or relating to this order: *a Cistercian abbey.*

cis·tern /ˈsistərn/ ▶ *n.* a tank for storing water, esp. one supplying taps or as part of a flushing toilet. ■ an underground reservoir for rainwater.

cit. ▶ *abbr.* ■ citation. ■ cited. ■ citizen.

cit·a·del /ˈsitədl; -ˌdel/ ▶ *n.* a fortress, typically on high ground, protecting or dominating a city.

ci·ta·tion /sīˈtāSHən/ (abbr.: **cit.**) ▶ *n.* **1** a quotation from or reference to a book, paper, or author, esp. in a scholarly work. ■ a mention of a praiseworthy act or achievement in an official report, esp. that of a member of the armed forces in wartime. ■ a note accompanying an award, describing the reasons for it. ■ *Law* a reference to a former tried case, used as guidance in the trying of comparable cases or in support of an argument. **2** *Law* a summons: *a traffic citation.*

cite /sīt/ ▶ *v.* [*tr.*] (often **be cited**) **1** quote (a passage, book, or author) as evidence for or justification of an argument or statement, esp. in a scholarly work. ■ mention as an example. ■ praise (someone, typically a member of the armed forces) for a courageous act in an official dispatch. ■ *Law* adduce a former tried case as a guide to deciding a comparable case or in support of an argument. **2** *Law* summon (someone) to appear in a court of law.

▶ *n.* a citation. —**cit·a·ble** *adj.*

cit·i·fied /ˈsitiˌfīd/ (also **cit·y·fied**) ▶ *adj. often derog.* characteristic of or adjusted to an urban environment: *black-hatted, citified cowboys.* —**cit·i·fi·ca·tion** /ˌsitifiˈkāSHən/ *n.* —**cit·i·fy** /-fī/ (**-fies**, **-fied**) *v.*

cit·i·zen /ˈsitizən; -sən/ (abbr.: **cit.**) ▶ *n.* a legally recognized subject or national of a state or commonwealth, either native or naturalized: *a Polish citizen.* ■ an inhabitant of a particular town or city: *the citizens of Los Angeles.* —**cit·i·zen·ry** /-rē/ *n.* —**cit·i·zen·ship** /-ˌSHip/ *n.*

cit·i·zen's ar·rest ▶ *n.* an arrest by an ordinary person without a warrant, allowable in certain cases.

cit·ric ac·id ▶ *n. Chem.* a sharp-tasting crystalline acid, $C_6H_8O_7$, present in the juice of lemons and other sour fruits. It is made commercially by the fermentation of sugar and used as a flavoring and setting agent.

cit·ron /ˈsitrən/ ▶ *n.* a shrubby Asian citrus tree (*Citrus medica*) that bears large fruits similar to lemons, but with flesh that is less acid and peels that are thicker and more fragrant. ■ the fruit of this tree.

cit·ron·el·la /ˌsitrəˈnelə/ ▶ *n.* **1** (also **citronella oil**) a fragrant natural oil used as an insect repellent and in perfume and soap manufacture. **2** the South Asian grass (*Cymbopogon nardus*) from which this oil is obtained.

cit·rus /ˈsitrəs/ ▶ *n.* (pl. **-rus·es**) a tree of the rue family belonging to the genus *Citrus*, which includes citron, lemon, lime, orange, and grapefruit. ■ (also **citrus fruit**) a fruit from such a tree.

▶ *adj.* of or relating to these trees or their fruits. —**cit·rus·y** *adj.*

cit·y /ˈsitē/ ▶ *n.* (pl. **cit·ies**) **1** a large town: [as *adj.*] *the city center.* ■ an incorporated municipal center. **2** *inf.* a place or situation characterized by a specified attribute: *panic city.* ▷Middle English: from Old French *cite*, from Latin *civitas*, from *civis* 'citizen.' Originally denoting a town, and often used as a Latin equivalent to Old English *burh* 'borough,' the term was later applied to foreign and ancient cities and to the more important English boroughs. —**cit·y·ward** /-wərd/ *adj.* & *adv.* —**cit·y·wards** /-wərdz/ *adv.* —**cit·y·wide** /-ˌwīd/ *adj.*

cit·y·fied ▶ *adj.* variant spelling of CITIFIED.

cit·y hall (often **City Hall**) ▶*n.* the administration building of a municipal government. ■ [treated as *sing.*] municipal offices or officers collectively: *they cultivated close ties with City Hall.*

cit·y·scape /ˈsitēˌskāp/ ▶*n.* the visual appearance of a city or urban area; a city landscape. ■ a picture of a city.

cit·y slick·er /ˈslikər/ ▶*n.* chiefly derog. a person with the values generally associated with urban dwellers, typically regarded as unprincipled and untrustworthy.

cit·y-state ▶*n.* chiefly hist. a city that with its surrounding territory forms an independent state.

civ·et /ˈsivət/ ▶*n.* (also **civet cat**) a slender nocturnal carnivorous mammal (*Viverra* and other genera) with a barred and spotted coat, native to Africa and Asia. The **civet family** (Viverridae) also includes the genets, linsang, and fossa, and formerly included the mongooses. ■ a strong musky perfume obtained from the secretions of the civet's scent glands.

civ·ic /ˈsivik/ ▶*adj.* of or relating to a city or town, esp. its administration; municipal. ■ of or relating to the duties or activities of people in relation to their town, city, or local area. —**civ·i·cal·ly** /-ik(ə)lē/ *adv.*

civ·ic cen·ter ▶*n.* a municipal building or building complex, often publicly financed, with space for conventions, sports events, and theatrical entertainment.

civ·ics /ˈsiviks/ ▶*plural n.* [usu. treated as *sing.*] the study of the rights and duties of citizenship.

civ·il /ˈsivəl/ ▶*adj.* **1** of or relating to ordinary citizens and their concerns, as distinct from military or ecclesiastical matters. ■ (of disorder or conflict) occurring between citizens of the same country. ■ Law relating to private relations between members of a community; noncriminal. ■ Law of or relating to aspects of the civil (or code) law derived from European systems. **2** courteous and polite. **3** (of time measurement or a point in time) fixed by custom or law rather than being natural or astronomical: *civil twilight starts at sunset.* —**civ·il·ly** *adv.*

civ·il de·fense ▶*n.* the organization and training of civilians for the protection of lives and property during and after attacks in wartime.

civ·il dis·o·be·di·ence ▶*n.* the refusal to comply with certain laws or to pay taxes and fines, as a peaceful form of political protest.

civ·il en·gi·neer ▶*n.* an engineer who designs and maintains roads, bridges, dams, and similar structures. —**civ·il en·gi·neer·ing** *n.*

ci·vil·ian /səˈvilyən/ ▶*n.* a person not in the armed services or the police force.
▶*adj.* of, denoting, or relating to a person not belonging to the armed services or police: *military agents in civilian clothes.*

ci·vil·ian·ize /səˈvilyəˌnīz/ ▶*v.* [tr.] make (something) nonmilitary in character or function. —**ci·vil·ian·i·za·tion** /səˌvilyənəˈzāSHən/ *n.*

ci·vil·i·ty /səˈvilətē/ ▶*n.* (pl. **-ties**) formal politeness and courtesy in behavior or speech: *I hope we can treat each other with civility and respect.* ■ (**civilities**) polite remarks used in formal conversation: *she was exchanging civilities with her mother.*

civ·i·li·za·tion /ˌsivələˈzāSHən/ ▶*n.* the stage of human social development and organization that is considered most advanced. ■ the process by which a society or place reaches this stage. ■ the society, culture, and way of life of a particular area: *the great books of Western civilization.* ■ the comfort and convenience of modern life, regarded as available only in towns and cities.

civ·i·lize /ˈsivəˌlīz/ ▶*v.* [tr.] [usu. as adj.] (**civilized**) bring (a place or people) to a stage of social, cultural, and moral development considered to be more advanced: *a civilized society.* ■ [as adj.] (**civilized**) polite and well-mannered: *such an affront to civilized behavior will no longer be tolerated.* —**civ·i·liz·a·ble** *adj.* —**civ·i·liz·er** *n.*

civ·il law ▶*n.* the system of law concerned with private relations between members of a community rather than criminal, military, or religious affairs. Contrasted with CRIMINAL LAW. ■ the system of law predominant on the European continent and of which a form is in force in Louisiana, historically influenced by the codes of ancient Rome.

civ·il lib·er·ty ▶*n.* the state of being subject only to laws established for the good of the community, esp. with regard to freedom of action and speech. ■ (**civil liberties**) individual rights protected by law from unjust governmental or other interference. —**civ·il lib·er·tar·i·an** *n.*

civ·il rights ▶*plural n.* the rights of citizens to political and social freedom and equality.

civ·il serv·ant ▶*n.* a member of the civil service.

civ·il serv·ice ▶*n.* the permanent professional branches of a government's administration, excluding military and judicial branches and elected politicians.

civ·il war ▶*n.* a war between citizens of the same country.

civ·vies /ˈsivēz/ inf. ▶*plural n.* civilian clothes, as opposed to a uniform.
▶*adj.* (**civvy**) of or relating to civilians: *civvy life.*

Cl ▶*symb.* the chemical element chlorine.

cl ▶*abbr.* centiliter: *70 cl bottles.*

clack /klak/ ▶*v.* make or cause to make a sharp sound or series of such sounds as a result of a hard object striking another: [intr.] *he heard the sound of her heels clacking across flagstones* | [tr.] *he clacked the castanets in fine syncopation.* ■ [intr.] archaic chatter loudly: *he will sit clacking for hours.*
▶*n.* a sharp sound or series of sounds made in such a way: *the clack of her high heels.* ■ archaic loud chatter: *her clack would go all day.* —**clack·er** *n.*

clad[1] /klad/ ▶ past participle of CLOTHE.
▶*adj.* **1** clothed: *they were clad in T-shirts and shorts* [in comb.] *a leotard-clad instructor.* **2** provided with cladding: [in comb.] *copper-clad boards.*

clad[2] ▶*v.* (**clad·ding**; past and past part. **clad·ded** or **clad**) [tr.] provide or encase with a covering or coating.

clad·ding /ˈkladiNG/ ▶*n.* a covering or coating on a structure or material: [as adj.] *a range of roofing and cladding products.*

clade /klād/ ▶*n.* Biol. a group of organisms believed to have evolved from a common ancestor, according to the principles of cladistics.

claim /klām/ ▶*v.* [tr.] state or assert that something is the case, typically without providing evidence or proof: *he claimed that he came from a wealthy, educated family.* ■ assert that one has gained or achieved (something): *his supporters claimed victory in the presidential elections.* ■ formally request or demand; say that one owns or has earned (something): *if no one claims the items, they will become government property.* ■ make a demand for (money) under the terms of an insurance policy. ■ call for (someone's notice and thought): *a most unwelcome event claimed his attention.* ■ cause the loss of (someone's life).
▶*n.* **1** an assertion of the truth of something, typically one that is disputed or in doubt: *he was dogged by the claim that he had CIA links.* **2** a demand or request for something considered one's due: *the court had denied their claims to asylum.* ■ an application for compensation under the terms of an insurance policy. ■ a right or title to something: *they have first claim on the assets of the trust.* ■ (also **mining claim**) a piece of land allotted to or taken by someone in order to be mined. —**claim·a·ble** *adj.*
▶ □ **claim to fame** a reason for being regarded as unusual or noteworthy: *his claim to fame was bringing Garbo to Hollywood.*

claim·ant /ˈklāmənt/ ▶*n.* a person making a claim, esp. in a lawsuit or for a government-sponsored benefit.

clair·voy·ance /kle(ə)rˈvoiəns/ ▶*n.* the supposed faculty of perceiving things or events in the future or beyond normal sensory contact.

clair·voy·ant /kle(ə)rˈvoiənt/ ▶*n.* a person who claims to have a supernatural ability to perceive events in the future or beyond normal sensory contact.
▶*adj.* having or exhibiting such an ability. ▷late 17th cent. (in the sense 'clear-sighted, perceptive'): from French, from *clair* 'clear' + *voyant* 'seeing' (from *voir* 'to see'). The current sense dates from the mid 19th cent. —**clair·voy·ant·ly** *adv.*

clam /klam/ ▶*n.* **1** a marine bivalve mollusk (subclass Heterodonta) with shells of equal size. ■ inf. any of a number of edible bivalve mollusks, e.g., a scallop. **2** inf. a dollar. **3** colloq. a shy or withdrawn person.
▶*v.* (**clammed, clamming**) [intr.] **1** dig for or collect clams. **2** (**clam up**) inf. abruptly stop talking, either for fear of revealing a secret or from shyness.

clam·bake /ˈklamˌbāk/ ▶*n.* an outdoor social gathering at which clams and other seafood (and often chicken, potatoes, and sweet corn) are baked or steamed, traditionally in a pit, over heated stones and under a bed of seaweed.

clam·ber /ˈklambər; ˈklamər/ ▶*v.* [intr.] climb, move, or get in or out of something in an awkward and laborious way, typically using both hands and feet: *I clambered out of the trench.*
▶*n.* a difficult climb or movement of this sort.

clam·my /ˈklamē/ ▶*adj.* (**clam·mi·er, clam·mi·est**) unpleasantly damp and sticky or slimy to touch. ■ (of air or atmosphere) damp and unpleasant. —**clam·mi·ly** /ˈklaməlē/ *adv.* —**clam·mi·ness** *n.*

clam·or /ˈklamər/ (Brit. **clam·our**) ▶*n.* a loud and confused noise, esp. that of people shouting vehemently: *the questions rose to a clamor.* ■ a strongly expressed protest or demand, typically from a large number of people: *the growing public clamor for more policemen on the beat.*
▶*v.* [intr.] (of a group of people) shout loudly and insistently: *the surging crowds clamored for attention.* ■ make a vehement protest or demand:

---

scientists are **clamoring** *for a ban on all chlorine substances.* —**clam·or·ous** |-ərəs| *adj.* —**clam·or·ous·ly** |-ərəslē| *adv.* —**clam·or·ous·ness** |-ərəsnəs| *n.*

clamp |klamp| ▶*n.* a brace, band, or clasp used for strengthening or holding things together.
▶*v.* [*tr.*] (often **be clamped**) fasten (something) in place with a clamp. ■ fasten (two things) firmly together: *the two frames are* **clamped together.** ■ hold (something) tightly against in or another thing: *Maggie had to clamp a hand over her mouth to stop herself from laughing.*
▶*phrasal v.* □ **clamp down** suppress or prevent something, typically in an oppressive or harsh manner: *police* **clamped down on** *a pro-democracy demonstration.* —**clamp·er** *n.*

clamp·down |'klamp,doun| ▶*n. inf.* a severe or concerted attempt to suppress something: *a clampdown on crime.*

clan |klan| ▶*n.* a group of close-knit and interrelated families (esp. associated with families in the Scottish Highlands). ■ *often inf.* a family, esp. a large one: *the Kennedy clan gathered for the celebration.* ■ a group of people with a strong common interest: *New York's garrulous clan of artists.* ■ *inf.* a family or group of plants or animals.

clan·des·tine |klan'destən; -,tīn; -,tēn; 'klandes-| ▶*adj.* kept secret or done secretively, esp. because illicit. —**clan·des·tine·ly** *adv.* —**clan·des·tin·i·ty** |,klandes'tinitē| *n.*

clang |klaNG| ▶*n.* a loud, resonant metallic sound or series of sounds.
▶*v.* make or cause to make such a sound: [*intr.*] *she turned the faucet on and the plumbing clanged* | [*tr.*] *the belfry still clangs its bell at 9 p.m.*

clang·or |'klaNGər| (*Brit.* **clang·our**) ▶*n.* a continuous loud banging or ringing sound: *the clangor of the steam hammers.* —**clang·or·ous** |'klaNGərəs| *adj.* —**clang·or·ous·ly** |'klaNGərəslē| *adv.*

clank |klaNGk| ▶*n.* a loud, sharp sound or series of sounds, typically made by pieces of metal meeting or being struck together.
▶*v.* make or cause to make such a sound: [*intr.*] *I could hear the chain clanking* | [*tr.*] *Cassie bounced on the bed, clanking the springs.* —**clank·ing·ly** *adv.*

clap[1] |klap| ▶*v.* (**clapped**, **clap·ping**) [*tr.*] strike the palms of (one's hands) together repeatedly, typically in order to applaud: *Agnes clapped her hands in glee* | [*intr.*] *the crowd was clapping and cheering.* ■ show approval of (a person or action) in this way. ■ strike the palms of (one's hands) together once, esp. as a signal. ■ slap (someone) encouragingly on the back or shoulder. ■ place (a hand) briefly against or over one's mouth or forehead as a gesture of dismay or regret: *he swore and clapped a hand to his forehead.* ■ (of a bird) flap (its wings) audibly.
▶*n.* **1** an act of striking together the palms of the hands, either once or repeatedly. ■ a friendly slap or pat on the back or shoulder. **2** an explosive sound, esp. of thunder: *a clap of thunder echoed through the valley.*

clap[2] ▶*n.* (usu. **the clap**) *inf.* a venereal disease, esp. gonorrhea.

clap·per |'klapər| ▶*n.* the free-swinging metal piece inside a bell that is made to strike the bell to produce the sound.

clap·trap |'klap,trap| (also **clap-trap**) ▶*n.* absurd or nonsensical talk or ideas: *such sentiments are just pious claptrap.*

claque |klak| ▶*n.* a group of people hired to applaud (or heckle) a performer or public speaker. ■ a group of sycophantic followers.

clar·et |'klarit| ▶*n.* a red wine from Bordeaux, or wine of a similar character made elsewhere. ■ a deep purplish-red color.

clar·i·fy |'klarə,fī| ▶*v.* (**-fies**, **-fied**) [*tr.*] **1** make (a statement or situation) less confused and more clearly comprehensible. **2** [often as *adj.*] (**clarified**) melt (butter) in order to separate out the impurities. —**clar·i·fi·ca·tion** |,klarəfi'kāSHən| *n.* —**clar·i·fi·er** *n.*

clar·i·net |,klarə'net| ▶*n.* a woodwind instrument with a single-reed mouthpiece, a cylindrical tube of dark wood with a flared end, and holes stopped by keys. —**clar·i·net·ist** (*Brit.* **clar·i·net·tist**) *n.*

clar·i·on |'klarēən| ▶*n. chiefly hist.* a shrill, narrow-tubed war trumpet. ■ an organ stop with a quality resembling that of such a trumpet.
▶*adj.* loud and clear: *clarion trumpeters.*
▶ □ **clarion call** a strongly expressed demand or request for action.

clar·i·ty |'klaritē| ▶*n.* the quality of being clear, in particular:
■ the quality of coherence and intelligibility: *for the sake of clarity, each of these strategies is dealt with separately.* ■ the quality of being easy to see or hear; sharpness of image or sound: *the clarity of the picture.* ■ the

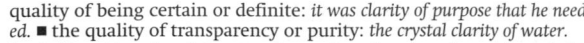

clamp

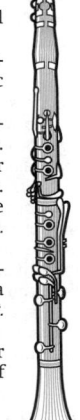

clarinet

quality of being certain or definite: *it was clarity of purpose that he needed.* ■ the quality of transparency or purity: *the crystal clarity of water.*

clash |klaSH| ▶*n.* **1** a violent confrontation: *there have been minor clashes with security forces.* ■ an incompatibility leading to disagreement: *a personality clash.* **2** a mismatch of colors. ■ an inconvenient coincidence of the timing of events or activities: *it is hoped that clashes of dates will be avoided.* **3** a loud jarring sound made by or resembling that made by metal objects being struck together: *a clash of cymbals.*
▶*v.* **1** [*intr.*] meet and come into violent conflict: *protesters demanding self-rule clashed with police.* ■ have a forceful disagreement: *Clarke has frequently clashed with his colleagues.* ■ be incompatible; be at odds: *his thriftiness clashed with Ross's largesse.* **2** [*intr.*] (of colors) appear discordant or ugly when placed close to each other. ■ inconveniently occur at the same time. **3** [*tr.*] strike (cymbals) together, producing a loud discordant sound. —**clash·er** *n.*

clasp |klasp| ▶*v.* [*tr.*] **1** grasp (something) tightly with one's hand. ■ place (one's arms) around something so as to hold it tightly: *Kate's arms were* **clasped around** *her knees.* ■ hold (someone) tightly: *he clasped Joanne in his arms.* ■ (**clasp one's hands**) press one's hands together with the fingers interlaced: *he lay on his back with his hands clasped behind his head.* **2** *archaic* fasten (something) with a small device, typically a metal one.
▶*n.* **1** a device with interlocking parts used for fastening things together: *a handbag with a golden clasp.* ■ a silver bar on a medal ribbon, inscribed with the name of the battle at which the wearer was present. **2** an embrace. ■ a grasp or handshake.

class |klas| ▶*n.* **1** a set or category of things having some property or attribute in common and differentiated from others by kind, type, or quality: *the accommodations were good for a hotel of this class.* ■ *Biol.* a principal taxonomic grouping that ranks above order and below phylum or division, such as Mammalia or Insecta. **2** the system of ordering a society in which people are divided into sets based on perceived social or economic status: *people who are socially disenfranchised by class.* ■ a set in a society ordered in such a way: *the ruling class.* ■ (**the classes**) *archaic* the rich or educated. ■ *inf.* impressive stylishness in appearance or behavior: *she's got class—she looks like a princess.* **3** a group of students who are taught together. ■ an occasion when students meet with their teacher for instruction; a lesson: *I was late for a class.* ■ a course of instruction: *I took classes in Indian music.* ■ all those graduating from a school or college in a particular year: **the class of** *1907.*
▶*v.* [*tr.*] (often **be classed as**) assign or regard as belonging to a particular category: *conduct that is classed as criminal.*
▶*adj. inf.* showing stylish excellence: *he's a class player.*
▶ □ **class act** a person or thing displaying impressive and stylish excellence. □ **in a class of** (or **on**) **its** (or **one's**) **own** unequaled, esp. in excellence or performance: *the delicacy of English roses puts them in a class of their own.*

class con·scious·ness ▶*n.* awareness of one's place in a system of social classes, esp. (in Marxist terms) as it relates to the class struggle. —**class-con·scious** *adj.*

clas·sic |'klasik| ▶*adj.* judged over a period of time to be of the highest quality and outstanding of its kind: *a classic car.* ■ (of a garment or design) of a simple elegant style not greatly subject to changes in fashion: *I had the classic symptoms.* ■ remarkably and instructively typical: *I had the classic symptoms.*
▶*n.* **1** a work of art of recognized and established value: *his books have become classics.* ■ a garment of a simple, elegant, and long-lasting style. ■ a thing that is memorable and a very good example of its kind: *he's hoping that tomorrow's game will be a classic.* **2** (usu. **Classics**) a school subject that involves the study of ancient Greek and Latin literature, philosophy, and history. ■ (usu. **the classics**) the works of ancient Greek and Latin writers and philosophers. ■ *dated* a scholar of ancient Greek and Latin. **3** a major sports tournament or competition, as in golf or tennis.

clas·si·cal |'klasikəl| ▶*adj.* **1** of or relating to ancient Greek or Latin literature, art, or culture: *classical mythology.* ■ (of art or architecture) influenced by ancient Greek or Roman forms or principles. ■ (of language) having the form used by the ancient standard authors. ■ based on the study of ancient Greek and Latin: *a classical education.* **2** (typically of a form of art) regarded as representing an exemplary standard; traditional and long-established in form or style: *a classical ballet.* **3** of or relating to the first significant period of an area of study: *classical Marxism.* ■ *Physics* relating to or based upon concepts and theories that preceded the theories of relativity and quantum mechanics; Newtonian: *classical physics.* —**clas·si·cal·ism** |-,lizəm| *n.* —**clas·si·cal·i·ty** |,klasə'kalətē| *n.* —**clas·si·cal·ly** |-ik(ə)lē| *adv.*

clas·si·cism |'klasə,sizəm| ▶*n.* the following of ancient Greek or Roman principles and style in art and literature, esp. from the Renaissance to the 18th century. Often contrasted with ROMANTICISM. ■ the following of traditional and long-established theories or styles. —**clas·si·cist** n.

clas·si·cize /ˈklasəˌsīz/ ▶v. [intr.] [usu. as adj.] (**classicizing**) imitate a classical style: *the classicizing strains in Guercino's art.*

clas·si·fied /ˈklasəˌfīd/ ▶adj. arranged in classes or categories. ■ (of newspaper or magazine advertisements or the pages on which these appear) organized in categories according to what is being advertised. ■ (of information or documents) designated as officially secret and to which only authorized people may have access.
▶n. (**classifieds**) small advertisements placed in a newspaper and organized in categories.

clas·si·fy /ˈklasəˌfī/ ▶v. (**-fies, -fied**) [tr.] (often **be classified**) arrange (a group of people or things) in classes or categories according to shared qualities or characteristics: *mountain peaks are classified according to their shape.* ■ assign (someone or something) to a particular class or category: *elements are usually classified as metals or nonmetals.* ■ designate (documents or information) as officially secret or to which only authorized people may have access. —**clas·si·fi·a·ble** /ˌklasəˈfīəbəl/ adj. —**clas·si·fi·ca·tion** /ˌklasəfiˈkāSHən/ n. —**clas·si·fi·ca·to·ry** /-fīkə,tôrē/ adj. —**class·i·fi·er** n.

class·less /ˈklasləs/ ▶adj. (of a society) not divided into social classes. ■ not showing obvious signs of belonging to a particular social class: *his voice was classless.* —**class·less·ness** n.

class·mate /ˈklasˌmāt/ ▶n. a fellow member of a class at school or college. ■ a schoolmate.

class·room /ˈklasˌro͞om; -ˌro͝om/ ▶n. a room, typically in a school, in which a class of students is taught.

class·y /ˈklasē/ ▶adj. (**class·i·er, class·i·est**) inf. stylish and sophisticated: *the hotel is classy but relaxed.* —**class·i·ly** /ˈklasəlē/ adv. —**class·i·ness** n.

clat·ter /ˈklatər/ ▶n. a continuous rattling sound as of hard objects falling or striking each other: *the horse spun around with a clatter of hooves.* ■ noisy rapid talk.
▶v. make or cause to make a continuous rattling sound: [intr.] *her coffee cup clattered in the saucer* | [tr.] *she clattered cups and saucers onto a tray.* ■ [intr.] fall or move with such a sound: *the knife clattered to the floor.*

clause /klôz/ ▶n. **1** a unit of grammatical organization next below the sentence in rank and in traditional grammar said to consist of a subject and predicate. See also MAIN CLAUSE, SUBORDINATE CLAUSE. **2** a particular and separate article, stipulation, or proviso in a treaty, bill, or contract. —**claus·al** /ˈklôzəl/ adj.

claus·tro·pho·bi·a /ˌklôstrəˈfōbēə/ ▶n. extreme or irrational fear of confined places. —**claus·tro·phobe** /ˈklôstrə,fōb/ n.

claus·tro·pho·bic /ˌklôstrəˈfōbik/ ▶adj. (of a person) suffering from claustrophobia. ■ (of a place or situation) inducing claustrophobia.
▶n. a person who suffers from claustrophobia. —**claus·tro·pho·bi·cal·ly** /-ik(ə)lē/ adv.

clave¹ /klāv/ ▶n. (usu. **claves**) Mus. one of a pair of hardwood sticks used to make a hollow sound when struck together.

clave² ▶ archaic past of CLEAVE².

clav·i·chord /ˈklavə,kôrd/ ▶n. a small, rectangular keyboard instrument, popular from the early 15th to early 19th centuries. ▷late Middle English: from medieval Latin *clavichordium*, from Latin *clavis* 'key' + *chorda* 'string.'

clav·i·cle /ˈklavikəl/ ▶n. Anat. technical term for COLLARBONE. —**cla·vic·u·lar** /kləˈvikyələr; klə-/ adj.

cla·vier /kləˈvi(ə)r; ˈklāvēər; ˈklavēər/ ▶n. **1** the keyboard of a musical instrument. **2** a keyboard instrument, esp. one with strings, such as the harpsichord.

claw /klô/ ▶n. a curved pointed horny nail on each digit of the foot in birds, lizards, and some mammals. ■ either of a pair of small hooked appendages on an insect's leg. ■ the pincer of a crab, scorpion, or other arthropod. ■ a mechanical device resembling a claw, used for gripping or lifting.
▶v. [intr.] (of an animal or person) scratch or tear something with the claws or the fingernails: *the kitten was clawing at Lowell's trouser leg* | [tr.] *her hands clawed his shoulders.* ■ clutch at something with the hands: *his fingers clawed at the air.* ■ (**claw one's way**) make one's way with difficulty by hauling oneself forward with one's hands. ■ [tr.] (**claw something away**) try desperately to move or remove something with the hands. —**clawed** adj. [often in comb.] *a short-clawed otter.* —**claw·less** adj.

claw·back /ˈklô,bak/ ▶n. the recovery of money already disbursed: *funds that are not subject to any clawback by the government.*
▶v. [tr.] retrieve or recover (funds) already allocated or dispersed.

claw ham·mer ▶n. **1** a hammer with one side of the head split and curved, used for extracting nails. **2** (**clawhammer**) a style of banjo playing in which the thumb and fingers strum or pluck the strings in a downward motion.

clay /klā/ ▶n. a stiff, sticky fine-grained earth, typically yellow, red, or bluish-gray in color and often forming an impermeable layer in the soil. It can be molded when wet, and is dried and baked to make bricks, pottery, and ceramics. ■ technical sediment with particles smaller than silt. ■ a hardened clay surface for a tennis court. ■ poetic/lit. the substance of the human body: *this lifeless clay.* —**clay·ey** /ˈklā-ē/ adj. —**clay·ish** adj. —**clay·like** /-ˌlīk/ adj.

clay pig·eon ▶n. a saucer-shaped piece of baked clay or other material thrown up in the air from a trap as a target for shooting.

-cle ▶suffix forming nouns such as *article, particle*, which were originally diminutives.

clean /klēn/ ▶adj. **1** free from dirt, marks, or stains. ■ having been washed since last worn or used: *a clean blouse.* ■ (of paper) not yet marked by writing or drawing. ■ (of a person) attentive to personal hygiene. ■ free from pollutants or unpleasant substances. ■ free from or producing relatively little radioactive contamination. **2** morally uncontaminated; pure; innocent: *clean living.* ■ not sexually offensive or obscene. ■ showing or having no record of offenses or crimes: *a clean driving license is essential for the job.* ■ played or done according to the rules: *it was a good clean fight.* ■ inf. not possessing or containing anything illegal, esp. drugs or stolen goods: *I searched his luggage, and he was clean.* ■ inf. (of a person) not taking or having taken drugs or alcohol. **3** free from irregularities; having a smooth edge or surface: *a clean fracture of the leg.* ■ having a simple, well-defined, and pleasing shape: *the clean lines of modernism.* ■ (of an action) smoothly and skillfully done: *I still hadn't made a clean takeoff.* ■ (of a taste, sound, or smell) giving a clear and distinctive impression to the senses; sharp and fresh. ■ (of timber) free from knots.
▶adv. **1** so as to be free from dirt, marks, or unwanted matter: *the room had been washed clean.* **2** inf. used to emphasize the completeness of a reported action, condition, or experience: *he was knocked clean off his feet.*
▶v. [tr.] make (something or someone) free of dirt, marks, or mess, esp. by washing, wiping, or brushing: *clean your teeth properly after meals* | [intr.] *he always expected other people to clean up after him* | [as n.] (**cleaning**) *Anne will help with the cleaning.* ■ remove the innards of (fish or poultry) prior to cooking.
▶phrasal v. □ **clean someone out** inf. use up or take all someone's money. □ **clean up** ■ make things or an area clean or neat. ■ inf. make a substantial gain or profit. ■ win all the prizes available in a sporting competition or series of events: *the Germans cleaned up at Wimbledon.* □ **clean something up** restore order or morality to: *the police chief was given the job of cleaning up a notorious district.* —**clean·ness** n.
▶ □ **a clean sweep 1** the removal of all unwanted people or things in order to start afresh: *the new leaders wanted to make a clean sweep of the old order.* **2** the winning of all of a group of similar or related competitions, events, or matches: *a clean sweep of Tuesday's primaries.* □ **clean up one's act** inf. begin to behave in a better way, esp. by giving up alcohol, drugs, or illegal activities. □ **come clean** inf. be completely honest; keep nothing hidden: *the company has refused to come clean about its pollution record.* □ **keep one's hands clean** not involve oneself in an immoral act. □ **make a clean breast of something** (or **make a clean breast of it**) confess fully one's mistakes or wrongdoings.

clean-cut ▶adj. sharply outlined: *the normally clean-cut edge between sea and land has become blurred.* ■ giving the appearance of neatness and respectability: *the ad featured two clean-cut teenagers.* ■ evoking or suggesting such respectability: *a scandal that threatens her clean-cut image.*

clean·er /ˈklēnər/ ▶n. a person or thing that cleans something, in particular: ■ a person employed to clean the interior of a building. ■ (**the cleaners**) a place of business where clothes and fabrics are dry-cleaned: *my suit's at the cleaners.* ■ a device for cleaning, such as a vacuum cleaner. ■ a chemical substance used for cleaning: *an oven cleaner.*
▶ □ **take someone to the cleaners** inf. take all someone's money or possessions in a dishonest or unfair way.

clean·ly ▶adv. /ˈklēnlē/ **1** in a way that produces no dirt, noxious gases, or other pollutants: *the engine burns cleanly.* **2** without difficulty or impediment; smoothly and efficiently.
▶adj. /ˈklenlē/ (**-li·er, -li·est**) archaic (of a person or animal) habitually clean and careful to avoid dirt. —**clean·li·ness** /ˈklenlēnis/ n.

cleanse /klenz/ ▸v. [tr.] make (something, esp. the skin) thoroughly clean: *this preparation will cleanse and tighten the skin.* ■ rid (a person, place, or thing) of something seen as unpleasant, unwanted, or defiling: *the mission to cleanse the nation of subversives.* ■ free (someone) from sin or guilt. ■ *archaic* (in biblical translations) cure (a leper).

cleans·er /'klenzər/ ▸n. a substance that cleanses, in particular: ■ a powder or liquid for scouring sinks, toilets, and bathtubs. ■ a cosmetic product for cleansing the skin.

clean slate ▸n. an absence of existing restraints or commitments: *no government starts with a clean slate.*

clean·up /'klēn,əp/ (also **clean-up**) ▸n. **1** an act of making a place clean or tidy: *an environmental cleanup.* ■ an act of removing or putting an end to disorder, immorality, or crime. **2** [usu. as *adj.*] *Baseball* the fourth position in a team's batting order, typically reserved for a power hitter likely to clear the bases by enabling any runners to score: *L.A.'s cleanup hitter* | [as *adverb*] *playing right field and batting cleanup.*

clear /'kli(ə)r/ ▸*adj.* **1** easy to perceive, understand, or interpret: *clear and precise directions.* ■ leaving no doubt; obvious or unambiguous: *a clear case of poisoning.* ■ having or feeling no doubt or confusion: *every student must be clear about what is expected.* **2** free of anything that marks or darkens something, in particular: ■ (of a substance) transparent: *a stream of clear water.* ■ free of cloud, mist, or rain: *the day was fine and clear.* ■ (of a person's skin) free from blemishes. ■ (of a person's eyes) unclouded; shining: *I looked into her clear gray eyes.* ■ (of a color) pure and intense. ■ *archaic* (of a fire) burning with little smoke. **3** free of any obstructions or unwanted objects: *I had a clear view in both directions.* ■ (of a period of time) free of any appointments or commitments: *the following Saturday Mattie had a clear day.* ■ (of a person) free of something undesirable or unpleasant: *he was clear of TB.* ■ (of a person's mind) free of something that impairs logical thought: *in the morning, with a clear head, she would tackle her problems.* ■ (of a person's conscience) free of guilt. **4** (**clear of**) not touching; away from: *the truck was wedged in the ditch, one wheel clear of the ground.* **5** (of a sum of money) net: *a clear profit of $1,100.* **6** *Phonet.* denoting a palatalized form of l (as in *salad* or *willing*) in some southern U.S. accents or as in *leaf* in Irish accents.

▸*adv.* **1** so as to be out of the way of or away from: *stand clear, I'll start the plane up.* ■ so as not to be obstructed or cluttered: *the floor had been swept clear of litter.* **2** with clarity; distinctly: *she had to toss her head to see the lake clear again.* **3** completely: *he had time to get clear away.* ■ (**clear to**) all the way to: *you could see clear to the bottom of the lagoon.*

▸*v.* **1** [*intr.*] become free of something that marks, darkens, obstructs, or covers something, in particular: ■ (of the sky or weather) become free of cloud or rain: *we'll go out if the weather clears.* ■ (of a liquid) become transparent: *a wine that refuses to clear.* ■ become free of obstructions: *the boy's lungs cleared and he began to breathe more easily.* ■ gradually go away or disappear: *the fever clears in two to four weeks.* ■ (of a person's face or expression) assume a happier aspect following previous confusion or distress: *for a moment, Sam was confused; then his expression cleared.* ■ (of a person's mind) regain the capacity for logical thought; become free of confusion: *his mind cleared and he began to reflect.* **2** [*tr.*] make (something) free of marks, obstructions, or unwanted items, in particular: ■ remove an obstruction or unwanted item or items from: *the driveway had been cleared of snow.* ■ free (land) for cultivation or building by removing vegetation or existing structures. ■ free (one's mind) of unpleasantness or confusion. ■ cause people to leave (a building or place): *the police shouted a warning and cleared the streets.* **3** [*tr.*] remove (an obstruction or unwanted item) from somewhere: *snow was cleared from the storm drains.* ■ chiefly *Soccer* send (the ball) away from the area near one's goal. ■ discharge (a debt). **4** [*tr.*] get past or over (something) safely or without touching it: *the plane rose high enough to clear the trees.* ■ jump (a specified height) in a competition: *she cleared 1.50 meters in the high jump.* **5** [*tr.*] show or declare (someone) officially to be innocent: *the commission had cleared the weightlifter of cheating.* **6** [*tr.*] give official approval or authorization to: *I cleared him to return to his squadron.* ■ get official approval for (something): *the press releases had to be cleared with the White House.* ■ (of a person or goods) satisfy the necessary requirements to pass through (customs). ■ pass (a check) through a clearinghouse so that the money goes into the payee's account. ■ [*intr.*] (of a check) pass through a clearinghouse in such a way. **7** [*tr.*] earn or gain (an amount of money) as a net profit.

▸*phrasal v.* □ **clear out** *inf.* leave quickly. □ **clear something out** remove the contents from something so as to tidy it or free it for alternative use. □ **clear up 1** (of an illness or other medical condition) become cured. **2** (of the weather) become brighter. ■ (of rain) stop. □ **clear something up 1** (also **clear up**) tidy something up by removing trash or other unwanted items. ■ remove trash or other unwanted items to

leave something tidy. **2** solve or explain something: *he wanted to clear up some misconceptions.* **3** cure an illness or other medical condition. —**clear·ly** *adv.* —**clear·ness** *n.*

▸ □ **as clear as mud** see MUD. □ **clear the air** make the air less sultry. ■ defuse or clarify an angry, tense, or confused situation by frank discussion. □ (**as**) **clear as a bell** see BELL[1]. □ (**as**) **clear as day** very easy to see or understand. □ **clear the name of** show to be innocent. □ **clear one's throat** cough slightly so as to speak more clearly, attract attention, or to express hesitancy before saying something awkward. □ **clear the way** remove an obstacle or hindrance to allow progress: *the ruling could be enough to clear the way for impeachment proceedings.* □ **in the clear** no longer in danger or suspected of something: *the latest information put her in the clear.* □ **out of a** (or **the**) **clear blue sky** as a complete surprise.

clear·ance /'kli(ə)rəns/ ▸n. **1** the action or process of removing or getting rid of something or of something's dispersing: *there will be sunny intervals after clearance of any early mist.* ■ the removal of buildings, people, or trees from land so as to free it for alternative uses: *slum clearance accelerated during the 1960s.* **2** official authorization for something to proceed or take place: *a delay in obtaining diplomatic clearance to overfly Israel.* ■ (also **security clearance**) official permission for someone to have access to classified information. ■ permission for an aircraft to take off or land at an airport. ■ the clearing of a person or ship by customs. ■ a certificate showing that such clearance has been granted. ■ the process of clearing checks through a clearinghouse. **3** clear space allowed for a thing to move past or under another: *always give cyclists plenty of clearance.*

clear·ing /'kli(ə)riNG/ ▸n. an open space in a forest, esp. one cleared for cultivation.

clear·ing·house /'kli(ə)riNG,hous/ (also **clear·ing house**) (abbr.: **c.h.** or **C.H.**) ▸n. a bankers' establishment where checks and bills from member banks are exchanged, so that only the balances need be paid in cash. ■ an agency or organization that collects and distributes something, esp. information.

clear·sto·ry ▸n. (*pl.* **-ries**) variant spelling of CLERESTORY.

cleat /klēt/ ▸n. a T-shaped piece of metal or wood, esp. on a boat or ship, to which ropes are attached. ■ one of a number of projecting pieces of metal, rubber, or other material on the sole of a shoe, designed to prevent the wearer from losing their footing. ■ (**cleats**) athletic shoes with a cleated sole, typically used when playing football. ■ a projection on a spar or other part of a ship, to prevent slipping. —**cleat·ed** *adj.*

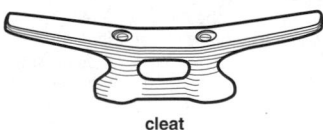

cleat

cleav·age /'klēvij/ ▸n. a sharp division; a split. ■ the hollow between a woman's breasts when supported, esp. as exposed by a low-cut garment. ■ *Biol.* cell division, esp. of a fertilized egg cell. ■ the splitting of rocks or crystals in a preferred plane or direction.

cleave[1] /klēv/ ▸v. (*past* **clove** /klōv/ or **cleft** /kleft/ or **cleaved** /klēvd/; *past part.* **clo·ven** /'klōvən/ or **cleft** or **cleaved**) [*tr.*] split or sever (something), esp. along a natural line or grain: *the large ax his father used to cleave wood for the fire.* ■ split (a molecule) by breaking a particular chemical bond. ■ make a way through (something) forcefully, as if by splitting it apart: *they watched a coot cleave the smooth water* | [*intr.*] *an unstoppable warrior clove through their ranks.* ■ [*intr.*] *Biol.* (of a cell) divide. —**cleav·a·ble** *adj.*

cleave[2] ▸v. [*intr.*] (**cleave to**) *poetic/lit.* stick fast to: *Rose's mouth was dry, her tongue cleaving to the roof of her mouth.* ■ adhere strongly to (a particular pursuit or belief): *part of why we cleave to sports is that excellence is so measurable.* ■ become very strongly involved with or emotionally attached to (someone): *it was his choice to cleave to the Brownings.*

cleav·er /'klēvər/ ▸n. a tool with a heavy broad blade, used by butchers for chopping meat.

clef /klef/ ▸n. *Mus.* any of several symbols placed at the left-hand end of a staff, indicating the pitch of the notes written on it.

cleft[1] /kleft/ ▸ past and past participle of CLEAVE[1].
▸*adj.* split, divided, or partially divided into two: *a cleft chin.*

cleft[2] ▸n. a fissure or split, esp. one in rock or the

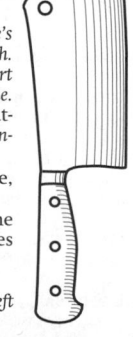

cleaver

ground. ■ a vertical indentation in the middle of a person's forehead or chin. ■ a deep division between two parts of the body.

cleft lip ▶*n.* a congenital split in the upper lip on one or both sides of the center, often associated with a cleft palate.

cleft pal·ate ▶*n.* a congenital split in the roof of the mouth.

clem·a·tis /ˈklemətəs; kləˈmatəs/ ▶*n.* a climbing plant (genus *Clematis*) of the buttercup family that bears white, pink, or purple flowers and feathery seeds.

clem·ent /ˈklemənt/ ▶*adj.* **1** (of weather) mild. **2** (of a person or a person's actions) merciful. —**clem·en·cy** /-ənsē/ *n.*

clem·en·tine /ˈklemən,tīn; -,tēn/ ▶*n.* a tangerine of a deep orange-red North African variety that is grown around the Mediterranean and in South Africa.

clench /klenCH/ ▶*v.* (with reference to the fingers or hand) close into a tight ball, esp. when feeling extreme anger: [*tr.*] *she clenched her fists, struggling for control* | [*intr.*] *John's right hand clenched into a fist.* ■ (with reference to the teeth) press or be pressed tightly together, esp. with anger or determination or so as to suppress a strong emotion: [*intr.*] *her teeth clenched in anger.* ■ [*tr.*] grasp (something) tightly, esp. with the hands or between the teeth. ■ [*intr.*] (of a muscular part of the body) tighten or contract sharply, esp. with strong emotion.
▶*n.* a contraction or tightening of part of the body: *she saw the anger rise, saw the clench of his fists.* ■ the state of being tightly closed or contracted.

clere·sto·ry /ˈklir(ə),stôrē/ (also **clear·sto·ry**) ▶*n.* (*pl.* **-ries**) the upper part of the nave, choir, and transepts of a large church, containing a series of windows.

cler·gy /ˈklərjē/ ▶*n.* (*pl.* **-gies**) [usu. treated as *pl.*] the body of all people ordained for religious duties, esp. in the Christian Church: *all marriages were to be solemnized by the clergy.*

cler·gy·man /ˈklərjēmən/ ▶*n.* (*pl.* **-men**) a male priest or minister of a Christian church.

cler·ic /ˈklerik/ ▶*n.* a priest or minister of a Christian church. ■ a priest or religious leader in any religion. ▷early 17th cent.: from ecclesiastical Latin *clericus* 'clergyman,' from Greek *klērikos* 'belonging to the Christian clergy,' from *klēros* 'lot, heritage.'

cler·i·cal /ˈklerikəl/ ▶*adj.* **1** (of a job or person) concerned with or relating to work in an office, esp. routine documentation and administrative tasks: *temps are always needed for clerical work.* **2** of or relating to the clergy: *he was still attired in his clerical outfit.* —**cler·i·cal·ly** *adv.*

clerk /klərk/ ▶*n.* **1** a person employed in an office or bank to keep records and accounts and to undertake other routine administrative duties: *a bank clerk.* ■ an official in charge of the records of a local council or court: *a clerk to the court.* ■ a person employed by a judge, or being trained by a lawyer, who does legal research, etc. ■ a lay officer of a cathedral, parish church, college chapel, etc.: *a chapter clerk.* **2** (also **desk clerk**) a receptionist in a hotel. ■ an assistant in a store; a salesclerk.
▶*v.* [*intr.*] work as a clerk: *eleven of those who left college this year are clerking in auction houses.* —**clerk·ship** *n.*

clev·er /ˈklevər/ ▶*adj.* (**clev·er·er**, **clev·er·est**) quick to understand, learn, and devise or apply ideas; intelligent. ■ skilled at doing or achieving something; talented: *she is clever with her hands.* ■ (of a thing, action, or idea) showing intelligence or skill; ingenious. ■ superficially ingenious or witty: *a story too clever to be real.* ■ *dated inf.* sensible; well-advised: *it wasn't too clever, leaving Dolly alone.* ▷Middle English (in the sense 'quick to catch hold,' only recorded in this period): perhaps from Dutch or Low German origin, and related to *cleave* 'stick fast.' In the late 16th cent. the term came to mean (probably through dialect use) 'manually skillful'; the sense 'possessing mental agility' dates from the early 18th cent. —**clev·er·ly** *adv.* —**clev·er·ness** *n.*

clev·is /ˈklevəs/ ▶*n.* a U-shaped or forked metal connector within which another part can be fastened by means of a bolt or pin passing through the ends of the connector.

clew /klōō/ ▶*n.* **1** the lower or after corner of a sail. **2** archaic variant of CLUE.

cli·ché /klēˈSHā kli-; ˈklēˌSHā/ (also **cli·che**) ▶*n.* a phrase or opinion that is overused and betrays a lack of original thought: *the old cliché "one man's meat is another man's poison."* ■ a very predictable or unoriginal thing or person: *each building is a mishmash of tired clichés.*

click /klik/ ▶*n.* **1** a short, sharp sound as of a switch being operated or of two hard objects coming quickly into contact: *she heard the click of the door.* ■ *Phonet.* an ingressive consonantal stop produced by sudden withdrawal of the tongue from the soft palate, front teeth, or back teeth and hard palate, occurring in some southern African and other languages. ■ *Comput.* an act of pressing a mouse button.

▶*v.* **1** make or cause to make a short, sharp sound: [*intr.*] *the key clicked in the lock and the door opened* | [*tr.*] *she clicked off the light.* ■ [*intr.*] move with such a sound: *Louise turned on her three-inch heels and clicked away.* ■ [*tr.*] *Comput.* press (a mouse button): *click the left mouse button twice.* ■ [*intr.*] (**click on**) *Comput.* select (an item represented on the screen or a particular function) by pressing one of the buttons on the mouse when the cursor is over the appropriate symbol. **2** [*intr.*] *inf.* become suddenly clear or understandable: *finally it clicked what all the fuss had been about.* ■ become very comfortable with someone at the first meeting: *we just clicked, and I found myself falling in love.* ■ become successful or popular: *I don't think this issue has clicked with the voters.* —**click·er** *n.*

click rate (also **click-through rate**) ▶*n. Comput.* the percentage of people visiting a Web page who access a hypertext link to a particular advertisement.

clicks and mor·tar ▶*n.* used to refer to a traditional business that has expanded its activities to operate also on the Internet: *a clicks-and-mortar strategy.*

cli·ent /ˈklīənt/ ▶*n.* **1** a person or organization using the services of a lawyer or other professional person or company. ■ a person receiving social or medical services. ■ (also **client state**) a nation that is dependent on another, more powerful nation. **2** *Comput.* (in a network) a desktop computer or workstation that is capable of obtaining information and applications from a server. ■ (also **client application** or **program**) a program that is capable of obtaining a service provided by another program. **3** (in ancient Rome) a plebeian under the protection of a patrician. ■ *archaic* a dependent; a hanger-on. —**cli·ent·ship** /-,SHip/ *n.*

cli·en·tele /,klīən'tel; ,klē-/ ▶*n.* [treated as *sing.* or *pl.*] clients collectively: *an upscale clientele.* ■ the customers of a shop, bar, or place of entertainment: *the dancers don't mix with the clientele.*

cli·ent-serv·er ▶*adj. Comput.* denoting a computer system in which a central server provides data to a number of networked workstations.

cliff /klif/ ▶*n.* a steep rock face, esp. at the edge of the sea: *a path along the top of rugged cliffs* | [as *adj.*] *the cliff face.* —**cliff·like** /-,līk/ *adj.* —**cliff·y** *adj.*

cliff·hang·er /ˈklif,haNGər/ ▶*n.* an ending to an episode of a serial drama that leaves the audience in suspense. ■ a story or event with a strong element of suspense. —**cliff·hang·ing** /-,haNGiNG/ *adj.*

cli·mac·ter·ic /klīˈmaktərik; ,klīmak'terik/ ▶*n.* a critical period or event: *the first major climacteric in twentieth-century poetry.* ■ *Med.* the period of life when fertility and sexual activity are in decline; (in women) menopause. ■ *Bot.* the ripening period of certain fruits such as apples, involving increased metabolism and only possible while on the tree.
▶*adj.* having extreme and far-reaching implications or results; critical. ■ *Med.* occurring at, characteristic of, or undergoing the climacteric; (in women) menopausal. ■ *Bot.* (of a fruit) undergoing a climacteric.

cli·mate /ˈklīmit/ ▶*n.* the weather conditions prevailing in an area in general or over a long period: *our cold, wet climate.* ■ a region with particular prevailing weather conditions: *vacationing in a warm climate.* ■ the prevailing trend of public opinion or of another aspect of public life: *the current economic climate.* ▷late Middle English: from Old French *climat* or late Latin *clima, climat-,* from Greek *klima* 'slope, zone,' from *klinein* 'to slope.' The term originally denoted a zone of the earth between two lines of latitude, then any region of the earth, and later, a region considered with reference to its atmospheric conditions. —**cli·mat·ic** /klīˈmatik/ *adj.* —**cli·mat·i·cal** /klīˈmatikəl/ *adj.* —**cli·mat·i·cal·ly** /klīˈmatikə̇lē/ *adv.*

cli·mate change ▶*n.* long-term, significant change in the climate of an area or of the earth, usually seen as resulting from human activity. Often used as a synonym for GLOBAL WARMING.

cli·ma·tol·o·gy /,klīmə'täləjē/ ▶*n.* the scientific study of climate. —**cli·ma·to·log·i·cal** /,klīmətl'läjikəl/ *adj.* —**cli·ma·tol·o·gist** /-jist/ *n.*

cli·max /ˈklī,maks/ ▶*n.* the most intense, exciting, or important point of something; a culmination or apex: *the climax of her speech.* ■ an orgasm. ■ *Ecol.* the final stage in a succession in a given environment, at which a plant community reaches a state of equilibrium: [as *adj.*] *a mixed hardwood climax forest.* ■ *Rhetoric* a sequence of propositions or ideas in order of increasing importance, force, or effectiveness of expression.
▶*v.* [*intr.*] culminate in an exciting or impressive event; reach a climax. ■ [*tr.*] bring (something) to a climax. ■ have an orgasm.

climb /klīm/ ▶*v.* **1** [*tr.*] go or come up (a slope, incline, or staircase), esp. by using the feet and sometimes the hands; ascend: *we began to climb the hill* | [*intr.*] *the air became colder as they climbed higher.* ■ [*intr.*] (of an

---

Pronunciation Key ə *ago, up;* ər *over, fur;* a *hat;* ā *ate;* ä *car;* CH *chin;* e *let;* ē *see;* e(ə)r *air;* i *fit;* ī *by;* i(ə)r *ear;* NG *sing;* ō *go;* ô *law, for;* oi *toy;* ŏŏ *good;* ōō *goo;* ou *out;* SH *she;* TH *thin;* <u>TH</u> *then;* (h)w *why;* ZH *vision*

aircraft or the sun) go upward. ■ [*intr.*] (of a road or track) slope upward or up. ■ (of a plant) grow up (a wall, tree, or trellis) by clinging with tendrils or by twining: *when ivy climbs a wall, it infiltrates any crack* | [*intr.*] *there were roses **climbing up** the walls.* ■ [*intr.*] grow in scale, value, or power: *the stock market climbed 24 points.* ■ move to a higher position in (a chart or table): *the song is climbing the Billboard charts.* **2** [*intr.*] move with effort, esp. into or out of a confined space; clamber: *I climbed down a narrow ladder.* ■ (**climb into**) put on (clothes).
▶*n.* an ascent, esp. of a mountain or hill, by climbing: *the climb up the mountain* | *fig. his climb from poverty.* ■ a mountain, hill, or slope that is climbed or is to be climbed: *the mountain is no easy climb.* ■ a recognized route up a mountain or cliff: *this may be the hardest rock climb in the world.* ■ an aircraft's flight upward: *we leveled out from the climb at 600 feet.* ■ a rise or increase in value, rank, or power. —**climb·a·ble** *adj.* —**climb·er** *n.*
▶ □ **be climbing the walls** *inf.* feel frustrated, helpless, and trapped.
climb·ing wall ▶*n.* a wall at a sports center or in a gymnasium fitted with attachments to simulate a rock face for climbing practice.
clime /klīm/ ▶*n.* (usu. **climes**) *chiefly poetic/lit.* a region considered with reference to its climate: *the Continent and its proudest climes.*
clinch /klinCH/ ▶*v.* [*tr.*] **1** confirm or settle (a contract or bargain). ■ conclusively settle (an argument or debate). ■ confirm the winning or achievement of (a game, competition, or victory): *his team clinched the title.* ■ secure (a nail or rivet) by driving the point sideways when it has penetrated. ■ fasten (a rope or fishing line) with a clinch knot. **2** [*intr.*] grapple at close quarters, esp. (of boxers) so as to be too closely engaged for full-arm blows. ■ (of two people) embrace.
▶*n.* a struggle or scuffle at close quarters, esp. (in boxing) one in which the fighters become too closely engaged for full-arm blows. ■ an embrace, esp. an amorous one.
clinch·er /klinCHər/ ▶*n.* a fact, argument, or event that settles a matter conclusively: *his two-run double was the clincher.*
cline /klīn/ ▶*n.* a continuum with an infinite number of gradations from one extreme to the other. ■ *Biol.* a gradation in one or more characteristics within a species or other taxon, esp. between different populations. —**clin·al** /'klīnl/ *adj.*
cling /kliNG/ ▶*v.* (*past* and *past part.* **clung** /kləNG/) [*intr.*] (**cling to/onto/on**) (of a person or animal) hold on tightly to: *she clung to Joe's arm* | *fig. she clung onto life.* ■ (**cling to**) adhere or stick firmly or closely to; be hard to part or remove from: *the fabric clung to her smooth skin.* ■ (**cling to**) remain very close to: *the fish cling to the line of the weed.* ■ remain persistently or stubbornly faithful to something: *she clung resolutely to her convictions.* ■ be overly dependent on someone emotionally: *you are clinging to him for security.* —**cling·er** *n.*
cling·y /'kliNGē/ ▶*adj.* (**cling·i·er**, **cling·i·est**) (of a person or garment) liable to cling; clinging. —**cling·i·ness** *n.*
clin·ic /'klinik/ ▶*n.* **1** a place or hospital department where outpatients are given medical treatment or advice, esp. of a specialist nature: *a mental health clinic.* ■ an occasion or time when such treatment or advice is given: *we're now holding regular clinics.* ■ a gathering at a hospital bedside for the teaching of medicine or surgery. **2** a conference or short course on a particular subject: *a ski clinic.* —**cli·ni·cian** /kli'niSHən/ *n.*
clin·i·cal /'klinikəl/ ▶*adj.* **1** of or relating to a clinic: *an annual clinical examination* ■ of or relating to the observation and treatment of actual patients rather than theoretical or laboratory studies: *clinical medicine.* ■ (of a disease or condition) causing observable and recognizable symptoms: *clinical depression.* **2** efficient and unemotional; coldly detached. ■ (of a room or building) bare, functional, and clean. —**clin·i·cal·ly** *adv.*
clink¹ /kliNGk/ ▶*n.* a sharp ringing sound, such as that made when metal or glass are struck: *a clink of keys* | *the clink of ice in tall glasses.*
▶*v.* [*intr.*] make such a sound: *his ring clinked against the crystal* | [as *n.*] (**clinking**) *the clinking of glasses* | [as *adj.*] (**clinking**) *clinking chains.* ■ [*tr.*] cause (something) to make such a sound: *I heard Suzie clink a piece of crockery.* ■ [*tr.*] strike (a glass or glasses) with another to express friendly feelings toward one's companions before drinking.
clink² ▶*n.* *inf.* prison: *he was put in the clink for six days.*
clink·er¹ /'kliNGkər/ ▶*n.* the stony residue from burned coal or from a furnace. ■ (also **clinker brick**) a brick with a vitrified surface.
clink·er² ▶*n.* *inf.* something that is unsatisfactory, of poor quality, or a failure. ■ a wrong musical note.
cli·nom·e·ter /klī'nämətər/ ▶*n.* *Surveying* an instrument used for measuring the angle or elevation of slopes.
clip¹ /klip/ ▶*n.* a device, typically flexible or worked by a spring, for holding an object or objects together or in place. ■ a device such as this

used to hold paper currency. ■ a piece of jewelry fastened by a clip. ■ a metal holder containing cartridges for an automatic firearm.
▶*v.* (**clipped**, **clip·ping**) fasten or be fastened with a clip or clips: [*tr.*] *she clipped on a pair of diamond earrings* | [*intr.*] *the panels simply clip on to the framework.*
clip² ▶*v.* (**clipped**, **clip·ping**) [*tr.*] **1** cut short or trim (hair, wool, nails, or vegetation) with shears or scissors. *clipping the hedge.* ■ trim or remove the hair or wool of (an animal). ■ (**clip something off**) cut off a thing or part of a thing with shears or scissors: *he clipped off a piece of wire* | *fig. she clipped nearly two seconds off the old record.* ■ cut (a section) from a newspaper or magazine. ■ pare the edge of (a coin), esp. illicitly. ■ speak (words) in a quick, precise, staccato manner. ■ *Comput.* process (an image) so as to remove the parts outside a certain area. ■ *Electr.* truncate the amplitude of (a signal) above or below predetermined levels. **2** strike briskly or with a glancing blow: *the steamroller clipped some parked cars.* ■ [*tr.*] strike or kick (something, esp. a ball) briskly in a specified direction. **3** *inf.* swindle or rob (someone). **4** [*intr.*] *inf.* move quickly in a specified direction: *we clip down the track.*
▶*n.* **1** an act of clipping or trimming something. ■ a short sequence taken from a movie or broadcast. ■ (also **wool clip**) the quantity of wool clipped from a sheep or flock. **2** *inf.* a quick or glancing blow. **3** *inf.* a specified speed or rate of movement, esp. when rapid: *we crossed the dance floor at a fast clip.*
▶ □ **at a clip** *inf.* at a time; all at once: *eight hours at a clip.* □ **clip the wings of** trim the feathers of (a bird) so as to disable it from flight. ■ prevent (someone) from acting freely; check the aspirations of.
clip·board /'klip,bôrd/ ▶*n.* a small board with a spring clip at the top, used for holding papers and providing support for writing. ■ *Comput.* a temporary storage area where text or other data cut or copied from a file is kept until it is pasted into another file.
clip·per /'klipər/ ▶*n.* **1** (usu. **clippers**) an instrument for cutting or trimming small pieces off things. **2** a person who clips or cuts: *a coupon clipper.* **3** (also **clipper chip**) a microchip that inserts an identifying code into encrypted transmissions, allowing them to be deciphered by a third party having access to a government-held key. **4** (also **clipper ship**) a fast sailing ship, esp. one of 19th-century design with concave bows and raked masts.
clip·ping /'klipiNG/ ▶*n.* (often **clippings**) a small piece trimmed from something. ■ an article cut from a newspaper or magazine.
clique /klēk; klik/ ▶*n.* a small group of people, with shared interests or other features in common, who spend time together and do not readily allow others to join them. —**cli·quey** *adj.* —**cli·quish** *adj.* —**cli·quish·ness** *n.*
clit·o·ris /'klitərəs/ ▶*n.* a small sensitive and erectile part of the female genitals at the anterior end of the vulva. —**clit·o·ral** /'klitərəl/ *adj.*
clo·a·ca /klō'ākə/ ▶*n.* (*pl.* **-cae** /-,kē; -,sē/) *Zool.* a common cavity at the end of the digestive tract for the release of both excretory and genital products in vertebrates (except most mammals) and certain invertebrates. The cloaca is present in birds, reptiles, amphibians, most fish, and monotremes. ■ *archaic* a sewer. —**clo·a·cal** *adj.*
cloak /klōk/ ▶*n.* an outdoor overgarment, typically sleeveless, that hangs loosely from the shoulders. ■ *fig.* something serving to hide or disguise something: *lifting **the cloak of secrecy** on the arms trade.*
▶*v.* [*tr.*] dress in a cloak. ■ *fig.* hide, cover, or disguise (something).
cloak-and-dag·ger ▶*adj.* involving or characteristic of mystery, intrigue, or espionage: *a cloak-and-dagger operation.*
cloak·room /'klōk,ro͞om; -,ro͝om/ ▶*n.* a room in a public building where coats and other belongings may be left temporarily.
clob·ber¹ /'kläbər/ ▶*v.* [*tr.*] *inf.* hit (someone) hard. ■ treat or deal with harshly: *the recession clobbered other parts of the business.* ■ defeat heavily.
clob·ber² ▶*v.* [*tr.*] add enameled decoration to (porcelain).
cloche /klōSH/ ▶*n.* a small translucent cover for protecting or forcing outdoor plants. ■ (also **cloche hat**) a woman's close-fitting, bell-shaped hat.
clock¹ /kläk/ ▶*n.* a mechanical or electrical device for measuring time, indicating hours, minutes, and sometimes seconds, typically by hands on a round dial or by displayed figures. ■ (**the clock**) time taken as a factor in an activity, esp. in competitive sports: *her life is ruled by the clock.* ■ *inf.* a measuring device resembling a clock for recording things other than time, such as a speedometer, taximeter, or odometer. ■ see **TIME CLOCK**.

cloche hat

▶*v.* [*tr.*] *inf.* **1** attain or register (a specified time, distance, or speed): *Thomas has clocked up forty years service* | [*intr.*] *the book clocks in at 989 pages.* ■ achieve (a victory): *he clocked up his first win of the year.* ■ record as attaining a specified time or rate: *the tower operators clocked a gust of 185 mph.* **2** *inf.* hit (someone), esp. on the head.
▶*phrasal v.* □ **clock in** (or **out**) (of an employee) punch in (or out).
▶ □ **around** (or **round**) **the clock** all day and all night. □ **run out the clock** *Sports* deliberately use as much time as possible in order to preserve one's own team's advantage. □ **stop the clock** allow extra time by temporarily ceasing to count the time left before a deadline arrives. □ **watch the clock** (of an employee) be overly strict or zealous about not working more than one's required hours.

clock² ▶*n.* *dated* an ornamental pattern woven or embroidered on the side of a stocking or sock near the ankle.

clock·wise /'kläk,wīz/ ▶*adv. & adj.* in a curve corresponding in direction to the movement of the hands of a clock: [as *adv.*] *turn the knob clockwise* | [as *adj.*] *a clockwise direction.*

clock·work /'kläk,wərk/ ▶*n.* a mechanism with a spring and toothed gearwheels, used to drive a mechanical clock, toy, or other device.
▶*adj.* driven by clockwork: *a clockwork motor.* ■ very smooth and regular: *the clockwork precision of the galaxy.* ■ repetitive and predictable.
▶ □ **like clockwork** very smoothly and easily: *the event ran like clockwork.* ■ with mechanical regularity: *these hens lay like clockwork.*

clod /kläd/ ▶*n.* **1** a lump of earth or clay. **2** *inf.* a stupid person (often used as a general term of abuse).

clod·dish /'klädiSH/ ▶*adj.* foolish, awkward, or clumsy. —**clod·dish·ly** *adv.* —**clod·dish·ness** *n.*

clod·hop·per /'kläd,häpər/ ▶*n.* **1** a large, heavy shoe. **2** *inf.* a foolish, awkward, or clumsy person.

clod·hop·ping /'kläd,häpiNG/ ▶*adj.* *inf.* foolish, awkward, or clumsy.

clog /kläg; klôg/ ▶*n.* **1** a shoe with a thick wooden sole. **2** an encumbrance or impediment: *a clog in the system.*
▶*v.* (**clogged**, **clog·ging**) [*tr.*] fill or block with an accumulation of thick, wet matter: *the gutters were clogged up with leaves.* ■ [*intr.*] become blocked in this way: *too much fatty food makes your arteries clog up.* ■ fill up or crowd (something) so as to obstruct passage: *tourists clog the roads in summer.*

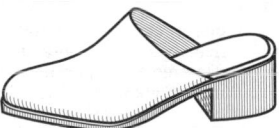

clog

cloi·son·né /,kloizə'nā; ,klwäz-/ (also **cloisonné enamel**) ▶*n.* enamel work in which the different colors are separated by strips of flattened wire placed edgeways on a metal backing.

clois·ter /'kloistər/ ▶*n.* a covered walk in a convent, monastery, college, or cathedral, typically with a wall on one side and a colonnade open to a quadrangle on the other. ■ (**the cloister**) monastic life. ■ a convent or monastery. ■ any place or position of seclusion: *college is a cloister apart from the cares of the world.*
▶*v.* [*tr.*] seclude or shut up in or as if in a convent or monastery. ▷Middle English (in the sense 'place of religious seclusion'): from Old French *cloistre*, from Latin *claustrum*, *clostrum* 'lock, enclosed place,' from *claudere* 'to close.'

cloister

clomp /klämp; klômp/ ▶*v.* [*intr.*] walk with a heavy tread: *she clomped down the steps.*

clon·al·i·ty /klō'nalitē/ ▶*n.* the fact or condition of being genetically identical, as to a parent, sibling, or other biological source.

clone /klōn/ ▶*n.* *Biol.* a group of organisms or cells produced asexually from one ancestor or stock, to which they are genetically identical. ■ an individual organism or cell so produced. ■ a person or thing regarded as identical to another: *successful women don't want to be male clones.* ■ a microcomputer designed to simulate exactly the operation of another, typically more expensive, model: *an IBM PC clone.*
▶*v.* [*tr.*] propagate (an organism or cell) as a clone. ■ make an identical copy of. ■ *Biochem.* replicate (a fragment of DNA placed in an organism) so that there is enough to analyze or use in protein production. ■ illegally copy the security codes from (a mobile phone) to one or more others as a way of obtaining free calls. —**clon·al** /'klōnl/ *adj.*

clonk /kläNGk; klôNGk/ another term for **CLUNK**. ▶*v.* **1** [*intr.*] move with or make such a sound: *the horses clonked and snorted softly.* **2** [*tr.*] *inf.* hit. —**clonk·y** *adj.*

clop /kläp/ ▶*n.* a sound or series of sounds made by a horse's hooves on a hard surface.
▶*v.* (**clopped**, **clop·ping**) [*intr.*] (of a horse) move with such a sound.

close¹ /klōs/ ▶*adj.* **1** a short distance away or apart in space or time: *the hotel is close to the sea.* ■ with very little or no space in between; dense: *cloth with a closer weave.* ■ (**close to**) very near to (being or doing something): *she was close to tears.* ■ (of a competitive situation) won or likely to be won by only a small amount or distance. ■ (of a final position in a competition) very near to the competitor immediately in front: *she finished a close second.* ■ narrowly enclosed: *animals in close confinement.* ■ (of hair or grass) very short or near the surface: *the ground will need to be level enough to allow close mowing.* ■ *Phonet.* another term for **HIGH** (sense 7). **2** denoting a family member who is part of a person's immediate family, typically a parent or sibling. ■ (of a person or relationship) on very affectionate or intimate terms. ■ (of a connection or resemblance) strong: *the college has close links with many other institutions.* **3** (of observation, examination, etc.) done in a careful and thorough way: *pay close attention to what your body is telling you about yourself.* ■ carefully guarded: *his whereabouts are a close secret.* ■ not willing to give away money or information; secretive. ■ following faithfully an original or model: *the debate about close or free translation.* **4** uncomfortably humid or airless.
▶*adv.* in a position so as to be very near to someone or something; with very little space between: *they stood close to the door* | *he was holding her close.* —**close·ly** *adv.* —**close·ness** *n.* —**clos·ish** *adj.*
▶ □ **close by** very near; nearby: *her father lives quite close by.* □ **close to** (or **close on**) (of an amount) almost; very nearly. □ **close up** very near: *close up she was no less pretty.* □ **close to the wind** *Sailing* (of a sailing vessel) pointed as near as possible to the direction from which the wind is blowing while still making headway. □ **come close** almost achieve or do: *he came close to calling the President a liar.* □ **too close for comfort** dangerously or uncomfortably near: *the friendly stranger who suddenly comes too close for comfort.*

close² /klōz/ ▶*v.* **1** move or cause to move so as to cover an opening: [*intr.*] *she jumped into the train just as the doors were closing* | [*tr.*] *they had to close the window because of the insects.* ■ [*tr.*] block up (a hole or opening): *glass doors close off the living room from the hall.* ■ [*tr.*] bring two parts of (something) together so as to block its opening or bring it into a folded state: *Ron closed the book.* ■ [*intr.*] gradually get nearer to someone or something: *a large group of aircraft about 130 miles away and closing fast.* ■ [*intr.*] (**close around/over**) come into contact with (something) so as to encircle and hold it: *my fist closed around the weapon.* ■ [*tr.*] make (an electric circuit) continuous: *this will cause a relay to operate and close the circuit.* **2** bring or come to an end: [*tr.*] *the members were thanked for attending, and the meeting was closed* | [*intr.*] *the concert closed with "Silent Night."* ■ [*intr.*] (of a business, organization, or institution) cease to be in operation or accessible to the public, either permanently or at the end of a working day or other period of time: *the factory is to close* | [*tr.*] *the country has been closed to outsiders for almost 50 years.* ■ [*intr.*] finish speaking or writing: *we close with a point about truth.* ■ [*tr.*] bring (a business transaction) to a satisfactory conclusion: *he closed a deal with a metal dealer.* ■ [*tr.*] remove all the funds from (a bank account) and cease to use it. ■ [*tr.*] *Comput.* make (a data file) inaccessible after use, so that it is securely stored until required again.
▶*phrasal v.* □ **close something down** (or **close down**) cause to cease or cease business or operation, esp. permanently. □ **close in (on)** come nearer to someone being pursued: *the police were closing in on them.* ■ gradually surround, esp. with the effect of hindering movement or

vision: *the weather has now closed in, so an attempt on the summit is unlikely.* □ **close something up** (or **close up**) **1** cause to cease or cease operation or being used: *the broker advised me to close the house up for the time being.* **2** (**close up**) (of an opening) grow smaller or become blocked by something: *she felt her throat close up.*
▸ *n.* **1** the end of an event or of a period of time or activity: *the afternoon drew to a close.* ■ (**the close**) the end of a day's trading on a stock market: *at the close the Dow Jones average was down 13.52 points.* ■ *Mus.* the conclusion of a phrase; a cadence. **2** the shutting of something, esp. a door. —**clos·a·ble** *adj.* —**clos·er** *n.*
▸ □ **close the door on** (or **to**) see DOOR. □ **close one's eyes to** see EYE. □ **close one's mind to** see MIND. □ **close ranks** see RANK[1]. □ **close up shop** see SHOP.

closed /klōzd/ ▸ *adj.* not open. ■ (of a business) having ceased trading, esp. for a short period: *he put the "Closed" sign up on the door.* ■ no longer under discussion or investigation; concluded: *closed cases of alleged contract irregularities.* ■ (of a society or system) not communicating with or influenced by others; independent. ■ limited to certain people; not open or available to all: *the UN Security Council met in closed session.* ■ unwilling to accept new ideas: *you're facing the situation with a closed mind.* ■ *Math.* (of a set) having the property that the result of a specified operation on any element of the set is itself a member of the set. ■ *Geom.* of or pertaining to a curve whose ends are joined.
▸ □ **behind closed doors** taking place secretly. □ **closed book** a subject or person about which one knows nothing.

closed cap·tion ▸ *n.* one of a series of subtitles to a television program, accessible through a decoder.
▸ *v.* (**closed-cap·tion**) [*tr.*] [usually as *noun* **closed-captioning**] provide (a program) with closed captions.

closed chain ▸ *n. Chem.* a number of atoms bonded together to form a closed loop in a molecule.

close-fist·ed /klōs/ ▸ *adj.* unwilling to spend money; stingy.

close-fit·ting /klōs/ ▸ *adj.* (of a garment) fitting tightly and showing the contours of the body.

close-knit /klōs/ ▸ *adj.* (of a group of people) united or bound together by strong relationships and common interests: *a close-knit community.*

close-mouthed /ˈklōs ˈmouᴛʜd; ˈmouᴛʜt/ ▸ *adj.* reticent; discreet.

clos·et /ˈkläzit/ ▸ *n.* **1** a small room or cupboard used for storing things. ■ *archaic* a small, private room used for prayer or study. **2** *archaic* a toilet. **3** (**the closet**) a state of secrecy or concealment, esp. about one's homosexuality: *lesbians who had come out of the closet.*
▸ *adj.* secret; covert: *a closet socialist.*
▸ *v.* (**clos·et·ed, clos·et·ing**) [*tr.*] (often **be closeted**) shut (someone) away, esp. in private conference or study. ■ in a state of concealment, esp. about one's homosexuality.

close-up /ˈklōs ˌəp/ ▸ *n.* a photograph, movie, or video taken at close range and showing the subject on a large scale: *a close-up of her face* | *they see themselves in close-up* | [as *adj.*] *a close-up view.* ■ an intimate and detailed description or study: [as *adj.*] *the book's close-up account.*

clo·sure /ˈklōzhər/ ▸ *n.* an act or process of closing something, esp. an institution, thoroughfare, or frontier, or of being closed: *road closures* | *hospitals that face closure.* ■ a thing that closes or seals something, such as a cap or zipper. ■ a resolution or conclusion to a work or process: *he brings modernist closure to his narrative.*

clot /klät/ ▸ *n.* a thick mass of coagulated liquid, esp. blood, or of material stuck together: *a flat, wet clot of dead leaves* | *fig. a clot of people.*
▸ *v.* (**clot·ted, clot·ting**) form or cause to form into clots: [*intr.*] *drugs that help blood to clot* | [*tr.*] *a blood protein known as factor VIII clots blood.* ■ [*tr.*] cover (something) with sticky matter: *its nostrils were clotted with blood.*

cloth /klôᴛʜ/ ▸ *n.* (*pl.* **cloths** /klôᴛʜz; klôᴛʜs/) **1** woven or felted fabric made from wool, cotton, or a similar fiber: ■ a piece of cloth for a particular purpose, such as a dishcloth or a tablecloth: *wipe clean with a damp cloth.* **2** (**the cloth**) the clergy; the clerical profession: *a man of the cloth.*

clothe /klōᴛʜ/ ▸ *v.* (*past* and *past part.* **clothed** or **clad** /klad/) [*tr.*] (often **be clothed in**) put clothes on (oneself or someone); dress: *she was clothed in white.* ■ provide (someone) with clothes: *they already had eight children to feed and clothe.* ■ *fig.* cover (something) as if with clothes: *luxuriant tropical forests clothed the islands.* ■ *fig.* endow (someone) with a particular quality: *he is clothed with the personality and character of Jesus.*

clothes /klōᴛʜz/ ▸ *pl. n.* **1** items worn to cover the body: *he stripped off his clothes* | *baby clothes* | [as *adj.*] *a clothes shop.* **2** bedclothes.

clothes horse ▸ *n.* a frame on which washed clothes are hung to air indoors. ■ *inf., often derog.* a determinedly fashionable person.

clothes·line /ˈklōᴛʜzˌlīn/ ▸ *n.* a rope or wire on which washed clothes are hung to dry.

clothes moth ▸ *n.* a small, drab moth (family Tineidae) whose larvae feed on a range of animal fibers and can be destructive to clothing and other domestic textiles.

clothes·pin /ˈklōᴛʜzˌpin/ (*Brit.* also **clothes peg**) ▸ *n.* a wooden or plastic clip for securing clothes to a clothes line.

cloth·ier /ˈklōᴛʜyər; -ᴛʜēər/ ▸ *n.* a person or company that makes, sells, or deals in clothes or cloth.

cloth·ing /ˈklōᴛʜiNG/ ▸ *n.* clothes collectively: *an item of clothing* | [as *adj.*] *the clothing trade.*

clo·ture /ˈklōchər/ ▸ *n.* (in a legislative assembly) a procedure for ending a debate and taking a vote: [as *adj.*] *a cloture motion.*
▸ *v.* [*tr.*] apply the cloture to (a debate or speaker) in a legislative assembly.

cloud /kloud/ ▸ *n.* **1** a visible mass of condensed water vapor floating in the atmosphere, typically high above the ground. ■ an indistinct or billowing mass, esp. of smoke or dust: *a cloud of dust.* ■ a large number of insects or birds moving together: *clouds of orange butterflies.* ■ a vague patch of color in or on a liquid or transparent surface. **2** *fig.* a state or cause of gloom, suspicion, trouble, or worry: *a black cloud hung over their lives.* ■ a frowning or depressed look.
▸ *v.* **1** [*intr.*] (of the sky) become overcast with clouds: *the blue skies clouded over abruptly.* ■ [*tr.*] (usu. **be clouded**) darken (the sky) with clouds. ■ make or become less clear or transparent: [*tr.*] *blood pumped out, clouding the water* | [*intr.*] *her eyes clouded with tears.* **2** *fig.* make or become darkened or overshadowed, in particular: ■ [*intr.*] (of someone's face or eyes) show worry, sorrow, or anger: *his expression clouded over.* ■ [*tr.*] (of such an emotion) show in (someone's face). ■ [*tr.*] make (a matter or mental process) unclear or uncertain; confuse: *don't allow your personal feelings to cloud your judgment.* ■ [*tr.*] spoil or mar (something). —**cloud·less** *adj.* —**cloud·less·ly** *adv.*
▸ □ **have one's head in the clouds** (of a person) be out of touch with reality; be daydreaming. □ **in the clouds** out of touch with reality: *this clergyman was in the clouds.* □ **on cloud nine** extremely happy. □ **under a cloud** under suspicion; discredited: *he left under something of a cloud, accused of misappropriating funds.*

cloud·burst /ˈkloudˌbərst/ ▸ *n.* a sudden, violent rainstorm.

cloud·scape /ˈkloudˌskāp/ ▸ *n.* a large cloud formation considered in terms of its visual effect.

cloud·y /ˈkloudē/ ▸ *adj.* (**cloud·i·er, cloud·i·est**) **1** (of the sky or weather) covered with or characterized by clouds; overcast. **2** (of a liquid) not transparent or clear. ■ (of a color) opaque; having white as a constituent: *cloudy reds and blues and greens.* ■ (of marble) variegated with cloudlike markings. ■ (of someone's eyes) misted with tears. ■ uncertain; unclear. —**cloud·i·ly** /ˈkloudl-ē/ *adv.* —**cloud·i·ness** *n.*

clout /klout/ ▸ *n.* **1** *inf.* a heavy blow with the hand or a hard object: *a clout on the ear.* **2** *inf.* influence or power, esp. in politics or business: *I knew he carried a lot of clout.* **3** *archaic* a piece of cloth or clothing, esp. one used as a patch. **4** *Archery* a target used in long-distance shooting, placed flat on the ground with a flag marking its center. ■ a shot that hits such a target.
▸ *v.* [*tr.*] **1** *inf.* hit hard with the hand or a hard object: *I clouted him on the head.* **2** *archaic* mend with a patch.

clove[1] /klōv/ ▸ *n.* **1** the dried flower bud of a tropical tree, used as a pungent aromatic spice. ■ (**oil of cloves**) aromatic analgesic oil extracted from these buds and used medicinally, esp. for dental pain. **2** the Indonesian tree (*Syzygium aromaticum,* or *Eugenia caryophyllus*) of the myrtle family from which these buds are obtained. **3** (also **clove pink**) a clove-scented pink (*Dianthus caryophyllus*) that is the original type from which the carnation and other double pinks have been bred.

clove[2] ▸ *n.* any of the small bulbs making up a compound bulb of garlic, shallot, etc.

clove[3] ▸ past of CLEAVE[1].

clo·ven /ˈklōvən/ ▸ past participle of CLEAVE[1].
▸ *adj.* split or divided in two.

clo·ven hoof (also **cloven foot**) ▸ *n.* the divided hoof or foot of ruminants such as cattle, sheep, goats, antelopes, and deer. —**clo·ven-hoofed** *adj.* —**clo·ven-foot·ed** *adj.*

clo·ver /ˈklōvər/ ▸ *n.* a herbaceous plant (genus *Trifolium*) of the pea family that has dense, globular flowerheads and leaves that are typically three-lobed. It is an important and widely grown fodder.
▸ □ **in clover** in ease and luxury.

clo·ver·leaf /ˈklōvərˌlēf/ ▸ *n.* a junction of roads intersecting at different levels with connecting sections forming the pattern of a four-leaf clover.
▸ *adj.* having a shape or pattern resembling a leaf of clover, esp. a four-leaf clover: *cloverleaf rolls.*

clown /kloun/ ▶*n.* **1** a comic entertainer, esp. one in a circus, wearing a traditional costume and exaggerated makeup. ■ a comical, silly, playful person: *I was always the class clown.* ■ a foolish or incompetent person. **2** *archaic* an unsophisticated country person; a rustic.
▶*v.* [*intr.*] behave in a comical way; act playfully: *Harvey clowned around pretending to be a dog.* —**clown·ish** *adj.* —**clown·ish·ly** *adv.* —**clown·ish·ness** *n.*

cloy /kloi/ ▶*v.* [*tr.*] [usu. as *adj.*] (**cloying**) disgust or sicken (someone) with an excess of sweetness, richness, or sentiment: *a romantic, rather cloying story* | *a curious bittersweetness that cloyed her senses* | [*intr.*] *the first sip gives a malty taste that never cloys.* ▷late Middle English: shortening of obsolete *accloy* 'stop up, choke,' from Old French *encloyer* 'drive a nail into,' from medieval Latin *inclavare*, from *clavus* 'a nail.' —**cloy·ing·ly** *adv.*

CLU ▶*abbr.* Civil Liberties Union.

club[1] /kləb/ ▶*n.* [treated as *sing.* or *pl.*] an association or organization dedicated to a particular interest or activity: *a photography club* | [as *adj.*] *the club secretary.* ■ the building or facilities used by such an association. ■ an organization or facility offering members social amenities, meals, and temporary residence. ■ a nightclub, esp. one playing fashionable dance music. ■ an organization constituted to play games in a particular sport: *a football club* | [as *adj.*] *the club captain.* ■ a commercial organization offering subscribers special benefits: *a shopping club.* ■ a group of people, organizations, or nations having something in common: *in cocktail lounges all over town convenes the daily meeting of the ain't-it-awful club.*
▶*v.* (**clubbed, club·bing**) [*intr.*] *inf.* go out to nightclubs: *she enjoys going clubbing in Orlando.*
▶ □ **join the club** [in *imper.*] *inf. often humorous* used as an observation that someone else is in a difficult or unwelcome situation to one's own: *if you're confused, join the club!*

club[2] ▶*n.* **1** a heavy stick with a thick end, esp. one used as a weapon. ■ short for GOLF CLUB. **2** (**clubs**) one of the four suits in a conventional pack of playing cards, denoted by a black trefoil. ■ a card of such a suit.
▶*v.* (**clubbed, club·bing**) [*tr.*] beat (a person or animal) with a club or similar implement: *the islanders clubbed whales to death.*

club·by /ˈkləbē/ ▶*adj.* (**-bi·er, -bi·est**) *inf.* friendly and sociable with fellow members of a group or organization but not with outsiders.

club foot ▶*n.* **1** a deformed foot that is twisted so that the sole cannot be placed flat on the ground. It is typically congenital or a result of polio. **2** a woodland toadstool (*Clitocybe clavipes*, family Tricholomataceae) with a grayish-brown cap, primrose-yellow gills, and a stem with a swollen woolly base, found in Eurasia and North America. —**club-foot·ed** *adj.*

club·house /ˈkləbˌhous/ ▶*n.* **1** a building or part of a building used by a sports team, esp. a baseball team, as a locker room. **2** a building or room used by a club. **3** a building in a sporting area, esp. a golf course, used for socializing and recreation.

club·man /ˈkləbmən; -ˌman/ ▶*n.* (*pl.* **-men**) a man who is a member of one or more clubs, esp. a member of a gentleman's club.

club sand·wich ▶*n.* a sandwich of meat (usually chicken and bacon), tomato, lettuce, and mayonnaise, with two layers of filling between three slices of toast or bread.

club so·da ▶*n.* trademark another term for SODA (sense 1).

cluck /klək/ ▶*n.* **1** the characteristic short, guttural sound made by a hen. ■ a similar sound made by a person to express annoyance: *Loretta gave a cluck of impatience.* **2** *inf.* a stupid or foolish person.
▶*v.* (also **cluck-cluck**) [*intr.*] (of a hen) make a short, guttural sound. ■ [*tr.*] (of a person) make such a sound with (one's tongue) to express concern or disapproval: *Michael clucked his tongue irritably.* ■ [*intr.*] (**cluck over/at/about**) express fussy concern about: *they were cluck-clucking over the dishonor he brought to the office.*

clue /kloo/ ▶*n.* **1** a piece of evidence or information used in the detection of a crime or solving of a mystery. ■ a fact or idea that serves as a guide or aid in a task or problem: *archaeological evidence can give clues about the past.* **2** a verbal formula giving an indication as to what is to be inserted in a particular space in a crossword or other puzzle.
▶*v.* (**clues, clued, clu·ing**) [*tr.*] (**clue someone in**) *inf.* inform someone about a particular matter: *Stella had clued her in about Peter.*
▶ □ **not have a clue** *inf.* know nothing about something or about how to do something.

clue·ful /ˈkloofəl/ ▶*adj. inf.* well-informed; competently intelligent.

clue·less /ˈkloolis/ ▶*adj. inf.* having no knowledge, understanding, or ability. —**clue·less·ly** *adv.* —**clue·less·ness** *n.*

clump /kləmp/ ▶*n.* **1** a compacted mass or lump of something: *clumps of earth.* ■ a small, compact group of people. ■ a small group of trees or plants growing closely together: *a clump of ferns.* ■ *Physiol.* an agglutinated mass of blood cells or bacteria, esp. as an indicator of the presence of an antibody to them. **2** a thick extra sole on a boot or shoe. **3** the sound of heavy footsteps.
▶*v.* [*intr.*] **1** form into a clump or mass: *the particles tend to clump together.* **2** (also **clomp**) walk with a heavy tread. —**clump·y** *adj.*

clum·sy /ˈkləmzē/ ▶*adj.* (**-si·er, -si·est**) awkward in movement or in handling things. ■ done awkwardly or without skill or elegance: *a clumsy attempt to park* | *a clumsy remake of an old movie.* ■ difficult to handle or use; unwieldy: *the legal procedure is far too clumsy.* ■ lacking social skills and graces. —**clum·si·ly** /-zəlē/ *adv.* —**clum·si·ness** *n.*

clung /kləNG/ ▶ past and past participle of CLING.

clunk /kləNGk/ ▶*n.* **1** a heavy, dull sound such as that made by thick pieces of metal striking together. **2** *inf.* a stupid or foolish person.
▶*v.* [*intr.*] move with or make such a sound: *the machinery clunked into life.*

clus·ter /ˈkləstər/ ▶*n.* a group of similar objects growing closely together: *clusters of creamy-white flowers.* ■ a group of people or similar objects positioned or occurring close together: *a cluster of antique shops.* ■ *Astron.* a group of stars or galaxies forming a relatively close association. ■ *Linguistics* (also **consonant cluster**) a group of consonants pronounced in immediate succession, as *str* in *strong.* ■ a natural subgroup of a population, used for statistical sampling or analysis. ■ *Chem.* a group of atoms of the same element, typically a metal, bonded closely together in a molecule.
▶*v.* [*intr.*] be or come into a cluster or close group; congregate: *the children clustered around her skirts.* ■ *Statistics* (of data points) have similar numerical values: *students tended to have scores clustering around 70 percent.*

clus·tered /ˈkləstərd/ ▶*adj.* growing or situated in a group: *the clustered roofs of the old town.* ■ *Archit.* (of pillars, columns, or shafts) positioned close together, or disposed around or half-detached from a pier.

clutch[1] /kləCH/ ▶*v.* [*tr.*] grasp or seize (something) tightly or eagerly: *he stood clutching a microphone* | [*intr.*] *fig. Mrs. Longhill clutched at the idea.*
▶*n.* **1** a tight grasp or an act of grasping something. ■ (**someone's clutches**) a person's power or control, esp. when perceived as cruel or inescapable: *he had narrowly escaped the clutches of the Nazis.* **2** a slim, flat handbag without handles or a strap. **3** (**the clutch**) an emergency or critical moment: *he came through for us in the clutch* [as *adj.*] *the best clutch hitters in baseball.* **4** a mechanism for connecting and disconnecting a vehicle engine from its transmission system. ■ the pedal operating such a mechanism. ■ an arrangement for connecting and disconnecting the working parts of any machine.

clutch[2] ▶*n.* a group of eggs fertilized at the same time, typically laid in a single session and (in birds) incubated together. ■ a brood of chicks. ■ a small group of people or things: *a clutch of young girls on roller skates.*

clut·ter /ˈklətər/ ▶*n.* a collection of things lying about in an untidy mass: *the attic is full of clutter.* ■ an untidy state: *the room was in a clutter of smelly untidiness.*
▶*v.* [*tr.*] crowd (something) untidily; fill with clutter: *his apartment was cluttered with paintings and antiques* | *luggage cluttered up the hallway.*

Cm ▶*symb.* the chemical element curium.

cm ▶*abbr.* centimeter(s).

Cmdr. ▶*abbr.* Commander.

Cmdre. ▶*abbr.* Commodore.

CMYK ▶*abbr.* cyan, magenta, yellow, and black, the colors used in most four-color printing.

cni·dar·i·an /nīˈde(ə)rēən/ ▶*n.* any aquatic invertebrate of the group including jellyfish, corals, and sea anemones, usu. having a simple body and tentacles with stinging hairs.
▶*adj.* of or relating to the cnidarians.

CNS ▶*abbr.* central nervous system.

CO ▶*abbr.* ■ Commanding Officer. ■ conscientious objector.

Co ▶*symb.* the chemical element cobalt.

Co. ▶*abbr.* ■ company: *the Consett Iron Co.* ■ county: *Hudson Co.*

coach[1] /kōCH/ ▶*n.* **1** a horse-drawn carriage, esp. a closed one. **2** a railroad car. ■ [as *adj.*] denoting economy class seating in an aircraft or train: *the cheapest coach-class fare.* **3** a bus, esp. one that is comfortably equipped and used for longer journeys. [as *adj.*]
▶*v.* [*intr.*] travel by coach: *they coached to Claude's dwelling.*
▶*adv.* in economy class accommodations in an aircraft or train: *flying coach.* —**coach·man** *n.*

coach[2] ▶*n.* an athletic instructor or trainer. ■ a tutor who gives private or specialized teaching.
  ▶*v.* [*tr.*] train or instruct (a team or player). ■ give (someone) extra or private teaching: *he was coached to speak more slowly and curb his hand gestures.* ■ teach (a subject or sport) as a coach. ■ prompt or urge (someone) with instructions: *he had improperly coached the witness to testify more credibly.*

coach house ▶*n.* an outbuilding in which a carriage is or was kept.

co·ad·ju·tor /ˌkōəˈjōōtər; kōˈajətər/ ▶*n.* a bishop appointed to assist a diocesan bishop, and often also designated as his successor.

co·ag·u·lant /kōˈagyələnt/ ▶*n.* a substance that causes blood or another liquid to coagulate.

co·ag·u·late /kōˈagyəˌlāt/ ▶*v.* [*intr.*] (of a fluid, esp. blood) change to a solid or semisolid state. ■ [*tr.*] cause (a fluid) to change to a solid or semisolid state: *epinephrine coagulates the blood.* —**co·ag·u·la·ble** /-ləbəl/ *adj.* —**co·ag·u·la·tion** /kōˌagyəˈlāSHən/ *n.* —**co·ag·u·la·tive** /-ˌlātiv/ *adj.* —**co·ag·u·la·tor** /-ˌlātər/ *n.*

coal /kōl/ ▶*n.* a combustible black or dark brown rock consisting mainly of carbonized plant matter, found mainly in underground deposits and widely used as fuel: [as *adj.*] *a coal fire.* ■ a red-hot piece of coal or other material in a fire: *the glowing coals.*
  ▶*v.* [*tr.*] provide with a supply of coal: [as *n.*] (**coaling**) *the coaling and watering of the engine.* ▷Old English *col* (in the senses 'glowing ember' and 'charred remnant'), of Germanic origin; related to Dutch *kool* and German *Kohle.* The sense 'combustible mineral used as fuel' dates from Middle English. —**coal·y** *adj.*

co·a·lesce /ˌkōəˈles/ ▶*v.* [*intr.*] come together and form one mass or whole: *the puddles had **coalesced into** shallow streams.* ■ [*tr.*] combine (elements) in a mass or whole: *to help coalesce the community, they established an office.* —**co·a·les·cence** /-ˈlesəns/ *n.* —**co·a·les·cent** /-ˈlesənt/ *adj.*

coal·field /ˈkōlˌfēld/ ▶*n.* an extensive area containing a number of underground coal deposits.

co·a·li·tion /ˌkōəˈliSHən/ ▶*n.* an alliance for combined action, especially a temporary alliance of political parties forming a government or of states: *a coalition of conservatives and disaffected Democrats.* | [as *adj.*] *a coalition government.* —**co·a·li·tion·ist** /-nist/ *n.*

coal tar ▶*n.* a thick black liquid produced by the destructive distillation of bituminous coal. It contains benzene, naphthalene, phenols, aniline, and many other organic chemicals.

coam·ing /ˈkōmiNG/ (also **coam·ings**) ▶*n.* a raised border around a ship's hatch serving to support the hatch covers and to keep out water. ■ a similar structure around the cockpit of a boat.

coarse /kôrs/ ▶*adj.* **1** rough or loose in texture or grain: *a coarse woolen cloth.* ■ made of large grains or particles: *coarse sand.* ■ (of grains or particles) large. ■ (of a person's features) not elegantly formed or proportioned. ■ (of food or drink) of inferior quality. **2** (of a person or a person's speech) rude, crude, or vulgar. —**coarse·ly** *adv.* —**coarse·ness** *n.* —**coars·ish** *adj.*

coars·en /ˈkôrsən/ ▶*v.* make or become rough: [*tr.*] *her hands were coarsened by outside work* | [*intr.*] *his facial features appeared to coarsen with age.* ■ make or become crude, vulgar, or unpleasant: [*tr.*] [as *adj.*] *people with coarsened characters* | [*intr.*] *the voice coarsened.*

coast /kōst/ ▶*n.* **1** the part of the land near the sea; the edge of the land. ■ (**the Coast**) the Pacific coast of North America. **2** a run or movement in or on a vehicle without the use of power.
  ▶*v.* **1** [*intr.*] (of a person or vehicle) move easily without using power: *the engines stopped, and the craft coasted along.* ■ act or make progress without making much effort: *he **coasted to** victory.* ■ slide down a snowy hill on a sled. **2** [*intr.*] sail along the coast, esp. in order to carry cargo. —**coast·al** *adj.*
  ▶ □ **the coast is clear** there is no danger of being observed or caught.

coast·er /ˈkōstər/ ▶*n.* **1** a ship used to carry cargo along the coast. ■ a person who inhabits a specified coast: *a West coaster.* **2** a small tray or mat placed under a bottle or glass to protect the table underneath. **3** a toboggan. ■ short for ROLLER COASTER.

coast guard /ˈkōstˌgärd/ (also **coast·guard**) ▶*n.* (**Coast Guard**) a branch of the U.S. armed forces, responsible for the enforcement of maritime law and for the protection of life and property at sea. ■ (**the coastguard**) a civilian or volunteer organization keeping watch on the sea near a coast in order to assist people or ships in danger and to prevent smuggling.

coast·line /ˈkōstˌlīn/ ▶*n.* the outline of a coast, esp. with regard to its shape and appearance: *the hotel has wonderful views of the rugged coastline.*

coast to coast ▶*adj.* & *adv.* all the way across an island or continent: [as *adv.*] *retail stores from coast to coast* | [as *adj.*] (**coast-to-coast**) *a coast-to-coast journey.*

coat /kōt/ ▶*n.* **1** an outer garment worn outdoors, having sleeves and typically extending below the hips: *a winter coat.* ■ a similar item worn indoors as a protective garment: *a laboratory coat.* ■ a man's jacket or tunic, esp. as worn when hunting or by soldiers. ■ a man's or woman's tailored jacket. **2** an animal's covering of fur or hair. **3** a structure, esp. a membrane, enclosing or lining an organ. ■ a skin, rind, or husk. ■ a layer of a plant bulb. ■ an outer layer or covering of a specified kind: *the protein coat of the virus.* **4** a covering of paint or similar material laid on a surface at one time.
  ▶*v.* [*tr.*] (often **be coated**) provide with a layer or covering of something; apply a coat to: *his boots were **coated with** mud.* ■ (of a substance) form a covering to: *a film of dust coated the floor.* —**coat·ed** *adj.* [in *comb.*] *plastic-coated wire.*

coat hang·er ▶*n.* see HANGER (sense 2).

co·a·ti /kōˈätē/ (also **co·a·ti·mun·di** /kōˌätiˈməndē/) ▶*n.* (*pl.* **coatis**, **coatimundis**) a mammal (genera *Nasua* and *Nasuella*) of the raccoon family found mainly in Central and South America, with a long, flexible snout and a ringed tail.

coat·ing /ˈkōtiNG/ ▶*n.* a thin layer or covering of something: *a coating of paint.* ■ material used for making coats.

coat of arms ▶*n.* the distinctive heraldic bearings or shield of a person, family, corporation, or country.

coat of mail ▶*n. hist.* a jacket covered with or composed of metal rings or plates, serving as armor.

coat·tail /ˈkōtˌtāl/ ▶*n.* (usu. **coattails**) each of the flaps formed by the lower back of a coat, esp. a tailcoat.
  ▶ □ **on someone's coattails** benefiting from another's success, sometimes undeservedly: *he was elected on the coattails of his predecessor.*

coax[1] /kōks/ ▶*v.* [*tr.*] persuade (someone) gradually or by flattery to do something: *the trainees were coaxed into doing hard, boring work.* ■ (**coax something from/out of**) use such persuasion to obtain something from: *we coaxed money out of my father* | *fig. coaxing more speed from the car.* ■ manipulate (something) carefully into a particular shape or position: *her lovely hair had been coaxed into ringlets.* —**coax·er** *n.* —**coax·ing·ly** *adv.*

coax[2] /ˈkō-aks; kōˈaks/ *inf.* ▶*n.* coaxial cable.
  ▶*adj.* coaxial: *coax connectors.*

co·ax·i·al /kōˈaksēəl/ ▶*adj.* having a common axis. ■ (of a cable or line) consisting of two concentric conductors separated by an insulator. —**co·ax·i·al·ly** *adv.*

COB ▶*abbr.* close of business: *you have until COB today to show us why you should not be disconnected.*

cob /käb/ ▶*n.* **1** (also **corn·cob**) the central, cylindrical, woody part of the corn ear to which the grains, or kernels, are attached. **2** (also **cob·nut**) a hazelnut or filbert, esp. one of a large variety. ■ a hazel or filbert bush. **3** a powerfully built, short-legged horse. **4** a male swan. **5** *Brit.* a roundish lump of coal.

co·balt /ˈkōˌbôlt/ ▶*n.* the chemical element of atomic number 27, a hard silvery-white magnetic metal. (Symbol: **Co**) ■ short for COBALT BLUE: [as *adj.*] *a cobalt sky.* —**co·bal·tic** /kōˈbôltik/ *adj.* —**co·bal·tous** /kōˈbôltəs/ *adj.*

co·balt blue ▶*n.* a deep blue pigment containing cobalt and aluminum oxides. ■ the deep blue color of this.

cob·ble[1] /ˈkäbəl/ ▶*n.* (usu. **cobbles**) a cobblestone.

cob·ble[2] ▶*v.* [*tr.*] **1** *dated* repair (shoes). **2** (**cobble something together**) roughly assemble or put together something from available parts or elements: *the mayor cobbled together a budget.*

cob·bler /ˈkäblər/ ▶*n.* **1** a person who mends shoes as a job. **2** an iced drink made with wine or sherry, sugar, and lemon. **3** a fruit pie with a rich crust on top.

cob·ble·stone /ˈkäbəlˌstōn/ ▶*n.* a small, round stone of a kind formerly used to cover road surfaces.

COBOL /ˈkōˌbôl/ ▶*n.* a computer programming language designed for use in commerce.

co·bra /ˈkōbrə/ ▶*n.* a highly venomous snake (*Naja* and two other genera, family Elapidae) native to Africa and Asia that spreads the skin of its neck into a hood when disturbed.

cob·web /ˈkäbˌweb/ ▶*n.* (usu. **cobwebs**) a spider's web, esp. when old and covered with dust. ■ *Zool.* a tangled three-dimensional spider's web. ■ something resembling a cobweb in delicacy or intricacy: *white cobwebs of frost.* —**cob·webbed** *adj.* —**cob·web·by** *adj.*

co·ca /ˈkōkə/ ▶*n.* a tropical American shrub (*Erythroxylum coca*, family Erythroxylaceae) that is widely grown for its leaves, which are a source of cocaine. ■ the dried leaves of this shrub, chewed as a stimulant by the native people of western South America.

co·caine /kōˈkān; ˈkōˌkān/ ▶*n.* an addictive drug derived from coca or prepared synthetically, used as an illegal stimulant and sometimes medicinally as a local anesthetic.

coc·cus /'käkəs/ ▸*n.* (*pl.* **coc·ci** /'käk,(s)ī; 'käk,(s)ē/) *Biol.* any spherical or roughly spherical bacterium. —**coc·cal** /'käkəl/ *adj.* —**coc·coid** /'käk ,oid/ *adj.*

coc·cyx /'käksiks/ ▸*n.* (*pl.* **coc·cy·ges** /'käksə,jēz/ or **coc·cyx·es** /'käksik-siz/) a small, triangular bone at the base of the spinal column in humans and some apes, formed of fused vestigial vertebrae. —**coc·cyg·e·al** /käk'sijēəl/ *adj.*

coch·i·ne·al /'käCHə,nēəl; 'kō-/ ▸*n.* a scarlet dye used chiefly for coloring food. ■ the dried bodies of a female scale insect (*Dactylopius coccus*, family Dactylopiidae), which are crushed to yield this dye.

coch·le·a /'kōklēə; 'käk-/ ▸*n.* (*pl.* **-le·ae** /-lē,ē; -lē,ī/) the spiral cavity of the inner ear containing the organ of Corti, which produces nerve impulses in response to sound vibrations. ▷mid 16th cent. (used to denote spiral objects such as a spiral staircase and an Archimedean screw): from Latin, 'snail shell or screw,' from Greek *kokhlias*. The current sense dates from the late 17th cent. —**coch·le·ar** *adj.*

cock[1] /käk/ ▸*n.* **1** a male bird, esp. a rooster. ■ [in comb.] used in names of birds, esp. game birds, e.g., **moorcock**. ■ *Brit.* a male lobster, crab, or salmon. **2** *vulgar slang* a penis. **3** a firing lever in a gun which can be raised to be released by the trigger. **4** a stopcock.
▸*v.* [*tr.*] **1** tilt (something) in a particular direction: *she cocked her head slightly to one side.* ■ bend a (limb or joint) at an angle. ■ (of a male dog) lift (a back leg) in order to urinate. **2** raise the cock of (a gun) in order to make it ready for firing.
▸ □ **at full cock** (of a gun) with the cock lifted to the position at which the trigger will act. □ **cock one's ear** (of a dog) raise its ears to an erect position. ■ (of a person) listen attentively to or for something. □ **cock of the walk** someone who dominates others within a group. □ **cock a snook** see SNOOK[2].

cock[2] ▸*n.* *dated* a cone-shaped pile of hay, straw, or other material.
▸*v.* [*tr.*] *archaic* pile (hay, straw, or other material) into such a shape.

cock·ade /kä'kād/ ▸*n.* a rosette or knot of ribbons worn in a hat as a badge of office or party, or as part of a livery. —**cock·ad·ed** *adj.*

cock and bull sto·ry ▸*n. inf.* a ridiculous and implausible story.

cock·a·poo /'käkə,poō/ ▸*n.* a dog resulting from a cross between a cocker spaniel and a miniature poodle.

cock·a·tiel /'käkə,tēl/ ▸*n.* a slender, long-crested Australian parrot (*Nymphicus hollandicus*) related to the cockatoos.

cock·a·too /'käkə,toō/ ▸*n.* a large crested parrot, with typically white plumage tinged with pink or yellow. Numerous genera and species, esp. genus *Cacatua*, are found in Australia and eastern Indonesia.

cock·a·trice /'käkətris; -,trīs/ ▸*n.* another term for BASILISK (sense 1).

cock·chaf·er /'käk,CHāfər/ ▸*n.* a large brown European beetle (*Melolontha melolontha*, family Scarabaeidae). The adults damage foliage and flowers, and the larvae are a pest of cereal and grass roots.

cock·crow /'käk,krō/ (also **cock-crow** or **cock crow**) ▸*n. poetic/lit.* dawn: *the hour of cockcrow was still far off.*

cock·er span·iel /'käkər/ (also **cock·er**) ▸*n.* a small spaniel of a breed with a silky coat.

cock·eyed /'käk'īd/ ▸*adj. inf.* crooked or askew; not level. ■ absurd; impractical: *do you expect us to believe a cockeyed story like that?* ■ drunk.

cock·fight·ing /'käk,fītiNG/ ▸*n.* the sport (illegal in certain countries) of setting two cocks to fight each other. Fighting cocks often have had their legs fitted with metal spurs. —**cock·fight** /'käk,fīt/ *n.*

cock·le[1] /'käkəl/ ▸*n.* an edible, burrowing bivalve mollusk (genus *Cardium*, family Cardiidae) with a strong ribbed shell.

cock·le[2] ▸*v.* [*intr.*] (of paper) bulge out in certain places so as to present a wrinkled or creased surface; pucker.

cock·ney /'käknē/ ▸*n.* (*pl.* **-neys**) a native of East London. ■ the dialect or accent typical of such people.
▸*adj.* of or characteristic of cockneys or their dialect or accent.

cock·pit /'käk,pit/ ▸*n.* **1** a compartment for the pilot and sometimes also the crew in an aircraft or spacecraft. ■ a similar compartment for the driver in a racing car. ■ a sunken area in the after deck of a boat providing space for members of the crew. **2** a place where a battle or other conflict takes place: *the cockpit of capitalist conflict in Europe.* ■ a place where cockfights are held.

cock·roach /'käk,rōCH/ ▸*n.* a beetlelike insect that feeds by scavenging. Among the several species that have become established worldwide as pests in homes and food service establishments is the **American cock-roach** (*Periplaneta americana*).

cocks·comb /'käk,skōm/ ▸*n.* **1** the crest or comb of a domestic cock. **2** a tropical plant (*Celosia cristata*) of the amaranth family, with a

showy crest or plume of yellow, orange, or red flowers, widely cultivated as a garden annual. **3** a colorful orchid (genus *Hexalectris*) native to southern North America.

cock·sure /'käk'SHŏŏr/ ▸*adj.* presumptuously or arrogantly confident. —**cock·sure·ly** *adv.* —**cock·sure·ness** *n.*

cock·tail /'käk,tāl/ ▸*n.* **1** an alcoholic drink consisting of a spirit or several spirits mixed with other ingredients, such as fruit juice, lemonade, or cream: [as *adj.*] *cocktail parties.* ■ a mixture of substances or factors, esp. when dangerous or unpleasant in its effects: *a cocktail of drugs that inhibits replication of HIV.* **2** a dish consisting of small pieces of seafood or fruits, typically served cold at the beginning of a meal as an hors d'oeuvre: *a shrimp cocktail.*

cock·tail lounge ▸*n.* a bar, typically in a hotel, restaurant, or airport, where alcoholic drinks are served.

cock·y /'käkē/ ▸*adj.* (**cock·i·er**, **cock·i·est**) conceited or arrogant, esp. in a bold or impudent way. —**cock·i·ly** /'käkəlē/ *adv.* —**cock·i·ness** *n.*

co·co /'kōkō/ ▸*n.* (*pl.* **-cos**) **1** [usu. as *adj.*] coconut: *coco matting* | *coco palm.* **2** *W. Indian* the root of the taro.

co·coa /'kōkō/ ▸*n.* a chocolate powder made from roasted and ground cacao seeds. ■ a hot drink made from such a powder mixed with sugar and milk or water.

co·coa but·ter ▸*n.* a fatty substance obtained from cocoa beans and used esp. in the manufacture of confectionery and cosmetics.

co·co·nut /'kōkə,nət/ ▸*n.* **1** the large, oval, brown seed of a tropical palm, consisting of a hard shell lined with edible white flesh and containing a clear liquid. ■ the flesh of a coconut, esp. when used as food. **2** (also **coconut palm** or **tree**) the tall palm tree (*Cocos nucifera*) that yields this nut.

co·coon /kə'koōn/ ▸*n.* a silky case spun by the larvae of many insects for protection as pupae. ■ a similar structure made by other animals. ■ a covering that prevents the corrosion of metal equipment. ■ something that envelops or surrounds, esp. in a protective or comforting way: *the cocoon of her kimono* | *fig. a warm cocoon of love.*
▸*v.* [*tr.*] (usu. **be cocooned**) envelop or surround in a protective or comforting way: *we were cocooned in our sleeping bags.* ■ spray with a protective coating. ■ [*intr.*] retreat from the stressful conditions of public life into the cozy private world of the family: *the movers and shakers are now cocooning.* —**co·coon·er** *n.*

co·cotte /kô'kôt; kə'kät/ ▸*n.* **1** (usu. **en cocotte**) a covered, heatproof dish or casserole in which food can be both cooked and served; a Dutch oven. **2** *dated* a fashionable prostitute.

COD ▸*abbr.* ■ cash on delivery. ■ collect on delivery.

cod /käd/ (also **codfish**) ▸*n.* (*pl.* same) a large marine fish with a small barbel on the chin. The **cod family** (Gadidae) comprises many genera and species, in particular the North Atlantic *Gadus morhua*, of great commercial importance as a food fish and as a source of cod liver oil.

co·da /'kōdə/ ▸*n. Mus.* the concluding passage of a piece or movement, typically forming an addition to the basic structure. ■ the concluding section of a dance, esp. of a pas de deux or the finale of a ballet in which the dancers parade before the audience. ■ a concluding event, remark, or section: *his new novel is a kind of **coda** to his previous books.*

cod·dle /'kädl/ ▸*v.* [*tr.*] **1** treat in an indulgent or overprotective way: *I was coddled and spoiled.* **2** cook (an egg) in water below the boiling point. —**cod·dler** /'kädlər; 'kädl-ər/ *n.*

code /kōd/ ▸*n.* **1** a system of words, letters, figures, or other symbols substituted for other words, letters, etc., esp. for the purposes of secrecy. ■ a system of signals, such as sounds, light flashes, or flags, used to send messages: *Morse code.* ■ a series of letters, numbers, or symbols assigned to something for the purposes of classification or identification: *the genetic code.* **2** *Comput.* program instructions: *hundreds of lines of code.* **3** a systematic collection of laws or regulations: *the criminal code.* ■ a set of conventions governing behavior or activity in a particular sphere *a dress code.* ■ a set of rules and standards adhered to by a society, class, or individual: *a stern code of honor.*
▸*v.* **1** [*tr.*] (usu. **be coded**) convert (the words of a message) into a particular code in order to convey a secret meaning: *only Mitch knew how to read the message—even the name was coded.* ■ express the meaning of (a statement or communication) in an indirect or euphemistic way: [as *adj.*] (**coded**) *a national campaign against "playing by ear," a coded phrase that meant jazz.* ■ assign a code to (something) for purposes of classification, analysis, or identification: *she coded the samples and sent them down for dissection.* **2** [*intr.*] (**code for**) *Biochem.* specify the genetic

sequence for (an amino acid or protein): *genes that code for human growth hormone.* ■ be the genetic determiner of (a characteristic): *one pair of homologous chromosomes that codes for eye color.* —**cod·er** *n.*

▶ □ **bring something up to code** renovate an old building or update its features in line with the latest building regulations.

co·deine /'kō,dēn/ ▶*n. Med.* a sleep-inducing and analgesic drug, $C_{18}H_{21}NO_3$, derived from morphine.

co·de·pen·den·cy /,kōdə'pendənsē/ ▶*n.* excessive emotional or psychological reliance on a partner, typically a partner who requires support due to an illness or addiction. —**co·de·pend·ence** /-dəns/ *n.* —**co·de·pend·ent** /-dənt/ *adj. & n.*

cod·er /'kōdər/ ▶*n.* a computer programmer.

code-share /'kōd,SHe(ə)r/ ▶*n.* ▶a marketing arrangement in which two airlines sell seats on a flight that one of them operates. ■ a flight or aircraft in which such an arrangement is in effect. —**code-shar·ing** *n.*

co·de·ter·mi·na·tion /,kōdi,tərmə'nāSHən/ ▶*n.* cooperation between management and workers in decision-making, esp. by the representation of workers on boards of directors.

co·dex /'kō,deks/ ▶*n.* (*pl.* **co·di·ces** /'kōdə,sēz/ 'käd-/ or **co·dex·es**) an ancient manuscript text in book form.

cod·fish /'käd,fiSH/ ▶*n.* (*pl.* same or **-fish·es**) another term for COD[1].

codg·er /'käjər/ ▶*n. often derog.* an elderly man, esp. one who is old-fashioned or eccentric: *old codgers always harp on about yesteryear.*

co·di·ces /'kōdə,sēz/ 'käd-/ ▶ plural form of CODEX.

cod·i·cil /'kädəsəl/ -,sil/ ▶*n.* an addition or supplement that explains, modifies, or revokes a will or part of one. —**cod·i·cil·la·ry** /,kädə'silərē/ *adj.*

cod·i·fy /'kädə,fī/ 'kōd-/ ▶*v.* (**-fies, -fied**) [*tr.*] arrange (laws or rules) into a systematic code. ■ arrange according to a plan or system. —**cod·i·fi·ca·tion** /,kädəfə'kāSHən/ ,kōd-/ *n.* —**cod·i·fi·er** /'kädə,fīər/ 'kōd-/ *n.*

cod·ling /'kädliNG/ ▶*n.* an immature cod.

cod liv·er oil ▶*n.* oil pressed from the fresh liver of cod, which is rich in vitamins D and A.

cod·piece /'käd,pēs/ ▶*n.* a pouch, esp. a conspicuous and decorative one, attached to a man's breeches or close-fitting hose to cover the genitals, worn in the 15th and 16th centuries.

co·ed /'kō,ed/ *inf.* ▶*n. dated* a female student at a co-educational institution.

▶*adj.* (of an institution or system) co-educational.

co·ed·u·ca·tion /,kō,ejə'kāSHən/ ▶*n.* the education of students of both sexes together. —**co·ed·u·ca·tion·al** /-SHənl/ *adj.*

co·ef·fi·cient /,kōə'fiSHənt/ ▶*n.* **1** *Math.* a numerical or constant quantity placed before and multiplying the variable in an algebraic expression (e.g., 4 in $4xy$). **2** *Physics* a multiplier or factor that measures some property: *coefficients of elasticity | the drag coefficient.*

coe·la·canth /'sēlə,kanTH/ ▶*n.* a large, bony marine fish (*Latimeria chalumnae*, family Latimeriidae), found chiefly around the Comoro Islands.

coe·len·ter·ate /si'lentə,rāt; -rət/ ▶*n. Zool.* an aquatic invertebrate animal of the phylum Cnidaria (formerly Coelenterata), which includes jellyfishes, corals, and sea anemones. They are distinguished by having a tube- or cup-shaped body. Also called CNIDARIAN.

co·en·zyme /kō'en,zīm/ ▶*n. Biochem.* a nonprotein compound that is necessary for the functioning of an enzyme.

co·e·qual /kō'ēkwəl/ ▶*adj.* equal with one another; having the same rank or importance: *coequal partners.*

▶*n.* a person or thing equal with another. —**co·e·qual·i·ty** /,kō-i'kwälitē/ *n.*

co·erce /kō'ərs/ ▶*v.* [*tr.*] persuade (an unwilling person) to do something by using force or threats: *they were coerced into silence.* ■ obtain (something) by such means: *their confessions were allegedly coerced by torture.* —**co·er·ci·ble** *adj.* —**co·er·cion** /kō'ərzHən; -SHən/ *n.* —**co·er·cive** *adj.*

co·e·val /kō'ēvəl/ ▶*adj.* having the same age or date of origin; contemporary.

▶*n.* a person of roughly the same age as oneself; a contemporary: *like so many of his coevals, he yearned for stability.* ▷early 17th cent. (as a noun): from late Latin *coaevus*, from *co-* 'jointly, in common' + Latin *aevum* 'age.' —**co·e·val·i·ty** /,kō-ē'valitē/ *n.* —**co·e·val·ly** *adv.*

co·ex·ist /,kō-ig'zist/ ▶*v.* [*intr.*] exist at the same time or in the same place: *traditional and modern values coexist in Africa.* ■ (of nations or peoples) exist in mutual tolerance despite different ideologies or interests: *the task of diplomacy was to help different states to coexist.* —**co·ex·ist·ence** /-'zistəns/ *n.* —**co·ex·ist·ent** /-'zistənt/ *adj.*

co·ex·ten·sive /,kō-ik'stensiv/ ▶*adj.* extending over the same space or time; corresponding exactly in extent: *the Caliphate, a Muslim state more*

or less **coextensive with** the Muslim world of its day. ■ (of a term) denoting the same referent as another.

cof·fee /'kôfē; 'käfē/ ▶*n.* **1** a hot drink made from the roasted and ground beanlike seeds of a tropical shrub. ■ a cup of this drink. ■ these seeds raw, roasted and ground, or processed into a powder that dissolves in hot water. ■ a pale brown color like that of coffee mixed with milk. ■ a party or reception at which coffee is served. **2** the shrub (genus *Coffea*) of the bedstraw family that yields these seeds.

cof·fee break ▶*n.* a pause from work for rest and usu. a beverage and snack.

cof·fee cake ▶*n.* a cake often cinnamon-flavored, with a drizzled white icing or crumb topping, and usually eaten with coffee.

cof·fee·house /'kôfē,hous; 'käfē-/ ▶*n.* a place where coffee is served and people gather for conversation and informal entertainment.

cof·fee ta·ble ▶*n.* a low table, typically placed in front of a sofa.

cof·fer /'kôfər; 'käfər/ ▶*n.* **1** a strongbox or small chest for holding valuables. ■ (**coffers**) the funds or financial reserves of a group or institution: *the federal government's empty coffers.* **2** a recessed panel in a ceiling. —**cof·fered** *adj.*

cof·fer·dam /'kôfər,dam; 'käfər,dam/ ▶*n.* a watertight enclosure pumped dry to permit construction work below the waterline, as when building bridges or repairing a ship.

cof·fin /'kôfən; 'käfən/ ▶*n.* a long, narrow box, typically of wood, in which a corpse is buried or cremated. ■ *inf.* an old and unsafe aircraft or vessel.

cog /käg/ ▶*n.* a wheel or bar with a series of projections on its edge that transfers motion by engaging with projections on another wheel or bar: *fig. she was only a very small cog in a big machine.* ■ each of such a series of projections. —**cogged** *adj.*

co·gent /'kōjənt/ ▶*adj.* (of an argument or case) clear, logical, and convincing. —**co·gen·cy** *n.* —**co·gent·ly** *adv.*

cog·i·tate /'käjə,tāt/ ▶*v.* [*intr.*] *formal* or *humorous* think deeply about something; meditate or reflect. —**cog·i·ta·tion** /,käjə'tāSHən/ *n.* —**cog·i·ta·tive** /-,tātiv/ *adj.* —**cog·i·ta·tor** /-,tātər/ *n.*

co·gnac /'kōn,yak; 'kän-; 'kôn-/ ▶*n.* a high-quality brandy, properly that distilled in Cognac in western France.

cog·nate /'käg,nāt/ ▶*adj.* **1** *Linguistics* (of a word) having the same linguistic derivation as another; from the same original word or root (e.g., English *is*, German *ist*, Latin *est* from Indo-European *esti*). **2** *formal* related; connected: *cognate subjects such as physics and chemistry.* ■ related to or descended from a common ancestor.

▶*n. Linguistics* a cognate word. —**cog·nate·ly** *adv.* —**cog·nate·ness** *n.*

cog·nate ob·ject ▶*n. Gram.* a direct object that has the same linguistic derivation as the verb that governs it, as in "sing a song," "live a good life." ■ a direct object that makes explicit a semantic concept that is already wholly present in the semantics of the verb which governs it, as in "ask a question," "eat some food."

cog·ni·tion /,käg'niSHən/ ▶*n.* the mental action or process of acquiring knowledge and understanding through thought, experience, and the senses. ■ a result of this; a perception, sensation, notion, or intuition. —**cog·ni·tion·al** /-SHənl/ *adj.* —**cog·ni·tive** /'kägnətiv/ *adj.*

cog·ni·za·ble /'kägnəzəbəl; käg'nīz-/ ▶*adj.* **1** *formal* perceptible; clearly identifiable. **2** *Law* within the jurisdiction of a court.

cog·ni·zance /'kägnəzəns/ (also **cog·ni·sance**) ▶*n. formal* knowledge, awareness, or notice. ■ *Law* the action of taking jurisdiction. ■ the action of taking judicial notice (of a fact beyond dispute).

▶ □ **take cognizance of** *formal* attend to; take account of.

cog·ni·zant /'kägnəzənt/ (also **cog·ni·sant**) ▶*adj. formal* having knowledge or being aware of: *statesmen must be cognizant of the political boundaries within which they work.*

cog·no·men /käg'nōmən; 'kägnəmən/ ▶*n.* an extra personal name given to an ancient Roman citizen, functioning rather like a nickname and typically passed down from father to son. ■ a name; a nickname.

cog rail·way ▶*n.* a railroad with a toothed central rail between the bearing rails that engages with a cogwheel under the locomotive, providing traction for ascending very steep slopes.

cog·wheel /'käg,(h)wēl/ ▶*n.* another term for COG.

co·hab·it /kō'habit/ ▶*v.* (**-hab·it·ed, -hab·it·ing**) [*intr.*] live together and have a sexual relationship without being married. ■ coexist. —**co·hab·it·ant** /-ənt/ *n.* —**co·hab·i·ta·tion** /kō,habə'tāSHən/ *n.* —**co·hab·it·er** *n.*

co·here /kō'hi(ə)r/ ▶*v.* [*intr.*] **1** be united; form a whole: *our mixed physical and spiritual natures cohere and mature.* **2** (of an argument or theory) be logically consistent: *this view does not cohere with their other beliefs.*

co·her·ent /kō'hi(ə)rənt/ ▶*adj.* **1** (of an argument, theory, or policy) logical and consistent. ■ (of a person) able to speak clearly and logically.

2 united as or forming a whole: *divided into a number of geographically co-herent kingdoms.* **3** *Physics* (of waves) having a constant phase relationship. —**co·her·ence** *n.* —**co·her·en·cy** *n.* (*rare*) —**co·her·ent·ly** *adv.*

co·he·sion /kōˈhēzHən/ ▶*n.* the action or fact of forming a united whole, or of sticking together: *the work at present lacks cohesion.*

co·he·sive /kōˈhēsiv; -ziv/ ▶*adj.* characterized by or causing cohesion. —**co·he·sive·ly** *adv.* —**co·he·sive·ness** *n.*

co·ho /ˈkōhō/ (also **coho salmon** or **co·hoe**) ▶*n.* (*pl.* same, **-os**, or **-oes**) a deep-bodied North Pacific salmon (*Oncorhynchus kisutch*) with small black spots.

co·hort /ˈkōˌhôrt/ ▶*n.* **1** [treated as *sing.* or *pl.*] an ancient Roman military unit, comprising six centuries, equal to one tenth of a legion. **2** [treated as *sing.* or *pl.*] a group of people banded together or treated as a group: *a cohort of civil servants.* ■ a group of people with a common statistical characteristic: *the 1940–44 birth cohort of women.* **3** a supporter or companion. ■ an accomplice or conspirator.

coif ▶*n.* /koif/ a woman's close-fitting cap, now only worn under a veil by nuns.
▶*v.* /kwäf; koif/ (**coiffed, coif·fing**; also **coifed, coif·ing**) [*tr.*] style or arrange (someone's hair), typically in an elaborate way: [as *adj.*] (**coiffed**) *elaborately coiffed hair.* ■ style or arrange the hair of (someone).

coif·feur /kwäˈfər/ ▶*n.* a hairdresser.

coif·fure /kwäˈfyŏŏr/ ▶*n.* a person's hairstyle, typically an elaborate one. —**coif·fured** *adj.*

coil¹ /koil/ ▶*n.* a length of something wound or arranged in a spiral or sequence of rings: *a coil of rope.* ■ a single ring or loop in such a sequence. ■ a roll of postage stamps, esp. one for use in a vending machine. ■ a slow-burning spiral made with the dried paste of pyrethrum powder, which produces a smoke that inhibits mosquitoes from biting. ■ (often **the coil**) an intrauterine contraceptive device in the form of a coil. ■ an electrical device consisting of a length of wire arranged in a coil for converting the level of a voltage, producing a magnetic field, or adding inductance to a circuit: *a relay coil.* ■ such a device used for transmitting high voltage to the spark plugs of an internal combustion engine. ■ a length of wire or piping wound in circles or spirals.
▶*v.* [*tr.*] arrange or wind (something long and flexible) in a joined sequence of concentric circles or rings: *he began to coil up the heavy ropes* | *he coiled a lock of her hair around his finger.* ■ [*intr.*] move or twist into such an arrangement or shape: *smoke coiled lazily toward the ceiling.*

coil² ▶*n. archaic* or *dial.* a confusion or turmoil.

coin /koin/ ▶*n.* a flat, typically round piece of metal with an official stamp, used as money. ■ money in the form of coins: *large amounts of coin and precious metal.* ■ *inf.* money. ■ (**coins**) one of the suits in some tarot packs, corresponding to pentacles in others.
▶*v.* [*tr.*] **1** make (coins) by stamping metal. ■ make (metal) into coins. **2** invent or devise (a new word or phrase). —**coin·er** *n.*
▶ □ **the other side of the coin** the opposite or contrasting aspect of a matter.

coin·age /ˈkoinij/ ▶*n.* **1** coins collectively: *the volume of coinage in circulation.* ■ the action or process of producing coins from metal. ■ a system or type of coins in use: *decimal coinage.* **2** the invention of a new word or phrase. ■ a newly invented word or phrase.

co·in·cide /ˌkōənˈsīd; ˈkōənˌsīd/ ▶*v.* [*intr.*] occur at or during the same time: *publication is timed to coincide with a major exhibition.* ■ correspond in nature; tally: *the interests of employers and employees do not always coincide.* ■ correspond in position; meet or intersect. ■ be in agreement: *the members of the College coincide in this opinion.*

co·in·ci·dence /kōˈinsədəns; -ˌdens/ ▶*n.* **1** a remarkable concurrence of events or circumstances without apparent causal connection: *they met by coincidence.* **2** correspondence in nature or in time of occurrence: *the coincidence of interest between the mining companies and certain politicians.*

co·in·ci·dent /kōˈinsədənt; -ˌdent/ ▶*adj.* occurring together in space or time: *liberty is an idea coincident with the spread of Christianity.* ■ in agreement or harmony: *the stake of defense attorneys is not always coincident with that of their clients.* —**co·in·ci·dent·ly** /kōˈinsəˈdentlē/ *adv.*

co·in·ci·den·tal /kōˌinsəˈdentl/ ▶*adj.* **1** resulting from a coincidence; done or happening by chance. **2** happening or existing at the same time: *it's convenient that his plan is coincidental with the group's closure.* —**co·in·ci·den·tal·ly** /kōˌinsəˈdentlē; -ˈdentl-ē/ *adv.*

coir /ˈkoi(ə)r/ ▶*n.* fiber from the outer husk of the coconut, used for making ropes and matting.

co·i·tus /ˈkōətəs; kōˈētəs/ ▶*n. formal* sexual intercourse. —**co·i·tal** /ˈkōətl; kōˈētl/ *adj.*

co·i·tus in·ter·rup·tus /ˌintəˈrəptəs/ ▶*n.* sexual intercourse in which the penis is withdrawn before ejaculation.

coke¹ /kōk/ ▶*n.* a solid fuel made by heating coal in the absence of air so that the volatile components are driven off. ■ carbon residue left after the incomplete combustion of gasoline or other fuels.
▶*v.* [*tr.*] [usu. as *n.*] (**coking**) convert (coal) into coke.

coke² ▶*n.* informal term for COCAINE.

coked /kōkt/ ▶*adj. inf.* having taken a large amount of cocaine.

col /käl/ ▶*n.* the lowest point of a ridge or saddle between two peaks, typically affording a pass from one side of a mountain range to another.

Col. ▶*abbr.* ■ colonel. ■ *Bible* Colossians.

col. ▶*abbr.* ■ collected. ■ college. ■ colony. ■ column.

COLA ▶*abbr.* cost-of-living adjustment, an increase made to wages or Social Security benefits to keep them in line with inflation.

co·la /ˈkōlə/ ▶*n.* **1** a brown carbonated drink that is flavored with an extract of cola nuts, or with a similar flavoring. **2** (also **kola**) a small evergreen African tree (genus *Cola*, family Sterculiaceae) that is cultivated in the tropics for its seeds (cola nuts).

col·an·der /ˈkələndər; ˈkäl-/ ▶*n.* a perforated bowl used to strain off liquid from food, esp. after cooking.

col·chi·cum /ˈkälcHikəm; ˈkälki-/ ▶*n.* (*pl.* **colchicums**) a plant of the genus *Colchicum*, which includes the autumn crocuses. ■ the dried corm or seed of meadow saffron, which has analgesic properties and is used medicinally.

cold /kōld/ ▶*adj.* **1** of or at a low or relatively low temperature, esp. when compared with the human body: *a freezing cold day.* ■ (of food or drink) served or consumed without being heated or after cooling. ■ (of an engine) not having been warmed up properly. ■ (of a person) feeling uncomfortably cold: *she was cold, and I put some more wood on the fire.* ■ feeling or characterized by fear or horror: *a cold shiver of fear.* ■ *inf.* unconscious: *she was out cold.* ■ dead. **2** lacking affection or warmth of feeling; unemotional: *cold politeness.* ■ not affected by emotion; objective: *cold statistics.* ■ sexually unresponsive; frigid. ■ depressing or dispiriting; not suggestive of warmth: *the cold, impersonal barrack-room.* ■ (of a color) containing pale blue or gray. ■ ineffective in playing a game: *Butler capitalized on Xavier's cold shooting.* **3** (of the scent or trail of a hunted person or animal) no longer fresh and easy to follow: *the trail went cold.* ■ (in children's games) far from finding or guessing what is sought, as opposed to warm or nearing success. **4** without preparation or rehearsal; unawares: *going into the test cold.*
▶*n.* **1** a low temperature, esp. in the atmosphere; cold weather; a cold environment: *my teeth chattered with the cold* | *they nearly died of cold.* **2** a common viral infection in which the mucous membrane of the nose and throat becomes inflamed, typically causing running at the nose, sneezing, a sore throat, and other similar symptoms.
▶*adv. inf.* completely; entirely: *she knew world capitals cold by age nine.* —**cold·ly** *adv.* —**cold·ness** /ˈkōl(d)nəs/ *n.*
▶ □ **catch** (or **take**) **cold** become infected with a cold. □ **cold comfort** poor or inadequate consolation. □ **cold feet** loss of nerve or confidence: *some investors got cold feet and backed out.* □ **the cold shoulder** a show of intentional unfriendliness; rejection: *why is even his own family giving him the cold shoulder?* □ **in cold blood** without feeling or mercy; ruthlessly. □ **out in the cold** ignored; neglected: *the talks left the French out in the cold.* □ **throw** (or **pour**) **cold water on** be discouraging or negative about.

cold-blood·ed ▶*adj.* **1** (of a kind of animal) having a body temperature varying with that of the environment; poikilothermic. **2** without emotion or pity; deliberately cruel or callous: *a cold-blooded murder.* —**cold-blood·ed·ly** *adv.* —**cold-blood·ed·ness** *n.*

cold cream ▶*n.* a cosmetic preparation used for cleansing and softening the skin.

cold cuts /ˈkōld ˌkəts/ ▶*pl. n.* slices of cold cooked or processed meats.

cold frame ▶*n.* a four-sided frame of boards with a removable glass or plastic top. The frame is used to house, protect, and harden off seedlings and small plants, without artificial heat.

cold front ▶*n. Meteorol.* the boundary of an advancing mass of cold air, in particular the trailing edge of the warm sector of a low-pressure system.

cold fu·sion ▶*n.* nuclear fusion occurring at or close to room temperature. Claims for its discovery in 1989 are generally held to have been mistaken.

cold-heart·ed ▶*adj.* lacking affection or warmth; unfeeling. —**cold-heart·ed·ly** *adv.* —**cold-heart·ed·ness** *n.*

---

cold sore ▸*n.* an inflamed blister in or near the mouth, caused by infection with the herpes simplex virus.

cold stor·age ▸*n.* the keeping of something in a refrigerator or other cold place for preservation. ■ *fig.* the temporary postponement of something: *the project went into cold storage.*

cold sweat ▸*n.* a state of sweating induced by fear, nervousness, or illness: *he used to break into a cold sweat when he was called on in class.*

cold tur·key *inf.* ▸*n.* the abrupt and complete cessation of taking a drug to which one is addicted.
▸*adv.* in a sudden and abrupt manner: *many banks have cut commercial builders off cold turkey.*

cold war ▸*n.* a state of political hostility existing between countries, characterized by threats, violent propaganda, subversive activities, and other measures short of open warfare, in particular: ■ (**the Cold War**) the state of political hostility that existed between the Soviet bloc countries and the U.S.-led Western powers from 1945 to 1990.

co·le·op·ter·an /ˌkōlēˈäptərən/ ▸*n.* any of various insects with front wings modified into sheaths to protect the hind wings, comprising the beetles, including weevils.
▸*adj.* of or relating to the coleopterans.

cole·slaw /ˈkōlˌslô/ ▸*n.* sliced raw cabbage mixed with mayonnaise and other vegetables, eaten as a salad.

co·le·us /ˈkōlēəs/ ▸*n.* a tropical Southeast Asian plant (genus *Solenostemon*) of the mint family that has brightly colored variegated leaves and is popular as a houseplant.

col·ic /ˈkälik/ ▸*n.* severe, often fluctuating pain in the abdomen caused by intestinal gas or obstruction in the intestines and suffered esp. by babies. —**col·ick·y** *adj.*

col·i·se·um /ˌkäləˈsēəm/ (also **col·os·se·um**) ▸*n.* [in *names*] a large theater or stadium: *the Charlotte Coliseum.*

co·li·tis /kəˈlītis; kō-/ ▸*n. Med.* inflammation of the lining of the colon.

col·lab·o·rate /kəˈlabəˌrāt/ ▸*v.* [*intr.*] work jointly on an activity, esp. to produce or create something: *he collaborated with a distinguished painter on the designs.* ■ cooperate traitorously with an enemy: *during the last war they collaborated with the Nazis.* —**col·lab·o·ra·tion** /kəˌlabəˈrāSHən/ *n.* —**col·lab·o·ra·tive** /-ˌrātiv/ *adj.* —**col·lab·o·ra·tor** /-ˌrātər/ *n.*

col·lage /kəˈläZH; kô-; kō-/ ▸*n.* a form of art in which various materials such as photographs and pieces of paper or fabric are arranged and stuck to a backing. ■ a composition made in this way. ■ a combination or collection of various things. —**col·lag·ist** /-läZHist/ *n.*

col·la·gen /ˈkäləjən/ ▸*n. Biochem.* the main structural protein found in animal connective tissue, yielding gelatin when boiled.

col·lapse /kəˈlaps/ ▸*v.* [*intr.*] **1** (of a structure) fall down or in; give way. ■ [*tr.*] cause (something) to fall in or give way: *it feels as if the slightest pressure would collapse it* | *fig. many people tend to collapse the distinction between the two concepts.* ■ (of a lung or blood vessel) fall inward and become flat and empty. ■ [*tr.*] cause (a lung or blood vessel) to do this. ■ fold or be folded to fit into a small space: [*intr.*] *some cots collapse down to fit into a bag.* **2** (of a person) fall down and become unconscious, typically through illness or injury. ■ *inf.* sit or lie down as a result of tiredness or prolonged exertion. **3** (of an institution or undertaking) fail suddenly and completely: *in the face of such resolve his opposition finally collapsed.* ■ (of a price or currency) drop suddenly in value.
▸*n.* an instance of a structure falling down or in: *the church roof is in danger of collapse.* ■ a sudden failure of an institution or undertaking: *the collapse of communism.* ■ a physical or mental breakdown: *he suffered a collapse from overwork.* ▷early 17th cent. (as *collapsed*): from medical Latin *collapsus*, past participle of *collabi*, from *col-* 'together' + *labi* 'to slip.' —**col·laps·i·ble** *adj.*

col·lar /ˈkälər/ ▸*n.* **1** a band of material around the neck of a shirt, dress, coat, or jacket, either upright or turned over and generally an integral part of the garment. ■ a band of leather or other material put around the neck of a domestic animal, esp. a dog or cat. ■ a colored marking resembling a collar around the neck of a bird or other animal. ■ a heavy rounded part of the harness worn by a draft animal, which rests at the base of its neck on the shoulders. **2** a restraining or connecting band, ring, or pipe in machinery. **3** *Bot.* the part of a plant where the stem joins the roots.
▸*v.* **1** [*tr.*] put a collar on. **2** [*tr.*] *inf.* seize, grasp, or apprehend (someone): *police collared the culprit.* ■ approach aggressively and talk to (someone who wishes to leave): *he collared a departing guest for some last words.* —**col·lared** *adj.* [in *comb.*] *a fur-collared jacket.* —**col·lar·less** *adj.*

col·lar·bone /ˈkälərˌbōn/ ▸*n.* either of the pair of bones joining the breastbone to the shoulder blades. Also called **CLAVICLE.**

col·late /kəˈlāt; ˈkōˌlāt; ˈkälˌāt/ ▸*v.* [*tr.*] collect and combine (texts, information, or sets of figures) in proper order. ■ compare and analyze

(texts or other data). ■ *Printing* verify the order of (sheets of a book) by their signatures. —**col·la·tor** *n.*

col·lat·er·al /kəˈlatərəl; kəˈlatrəl/ ▸*n.* **1** something pledged as security for repayment of a loan. **2** a person having the same descent in a family as another but by a different line.
▸*adj.* **1** descended from the same stock but by a different line: *a collateral descendant of George Washington.* **2** additional but subordinate; secondary: *the collateral meanings of a word.* ■ situated side by side; parallel: *collateral veins.* —**col·lat·er·al·i·ty** /kəˌlatəˈralitē/ *n.* —**col·lat·er·al·ly** *adv.*

col·la·tion /kəˈlāSHən; kō-; kä-/ ▸*n.* **1** the action of collating something: *data management and collation.* **2** a light, informal meal.

col·league /ˈkälˌēg/ ▸*n.* a person with whom one works, esp. in a profession or business. —**col·le·gial** /kəˈlēj(ē)əl/ *adj.*

col·lect[1] /kəˈlekt/ ▸*v.* [*tr.*] **1** bring or gather together (things, typically when scattered or widespread). ■ accumulate and store over a period of time: *collect rainwater to use on the garden.* ■ systematically seek and acquire (items of a particular kind) as a hobby: *I've started collecting stamps.* [*intr.*] *the urge to collect, to have the full set, is in us all.* ■ [*intr.*] come together and form a group or mass: *dust and dirt collect so quickly.* **2** call for and take away; fetch: *the children were collected from school.* ■ go somewhere and accept or receive (something), esp. as a right or due: *she went to Oxford to collect her honorary degree.* ■ solicit and receive (donations), esp. for charity: *collecting money for the war effort* | [*intr.*] *we collected for the United Way.* ■ receive (money that is due; be paid: [*tr.*] *they called to collect a debt* [*intr.*] *he'd come to collect.* **3** (**collect oneself**) regain control of oneself, typically after a shock. ■ bring together and concentrate (one's thoughts). **4** *archaic* conclude; infer.
▸*adv. & adj.* (with reference to a telephone call) to be paid for by the person receiving it: [as *adv.*] *I called my mother collect* | [as *adj.*] *a collect call.*

col·lect[2] /ˈkälˌekt; -likt/ ▸*n.* (in church use) a short prayer, esp. one assigned to a particular day or season.

col·lect·i·ble /kəˈlektəbəl/ (also chiefly Brit. **col·lect·a·ble**) ▸*adj.* **1** (of an item) worth collecting; of interest to a collector. **2** able to be collected: *a surplus collectible as rent by the landowner.*
▸*n.* (usu. **collectibles**) an item valued and sought by collectors. —**col·lect·i·bil·i·ty** /kəˌlektəˈbilitē/ *n.*

col·lec·tion /kəˈlekSHən/ ▸*n.* **1** the action or process of collecting someone or something. ■ a regular removal of mail for dispatch or of trash for disposal. ■ an instance of collecting money in a church service or for a charitable cause: *they took up a collection for her burial.* ■ a sum collected in this way. **2** a group of things or people: *a rambling collection of houses.* ■ an assembly of items such as works of art, pieces of writing, or natural objects, esp. one systematically ordered: *paintings from the permanent collection.* ■ (**collections**) an art museum's holdings esp. organized by medium, such as sculpture, painting, or photography. ■ a book or recording containing various texts, poems, songs, etc.: *a collection of essays.* ■ a range of new clothes produced by a fashion house: *a preview of their autumn collection.*

col·lec·tive /kəˈlektiv/ ▸*adj.* done by people acting as a group. ■ belonging or relating to all the members of a group: *ministers who share collective responsibility.* ■ (esp. of feelings or memories) common to the members of a group: *a collective sigh of relief.* ■ taken as a whole; aggregate.
▸*n.* a cooperative enterprise. ■ a collective farm. —**col·lec·tive·ly** *adv.* —**col·lec·tive·ness** *n.* —**col·lec·tiv·i·ty** /kəˌlekˈtivitē; ˌkäl,ek-/ *n.*

col·lec·tive bar·gain·ing ▸*n.* negotiation of wages and other conditions of employment by an organized body of employees.

col·lec·tive noun ▸*n. Gram.* a count noun that denotes a group of individuals (e.g., *assembly, family, crew*).

col·lec·tiv·ism /kəˈlektəˌvizəm/ ▸*n.* the practice or principle of giving a group priority over each individual in it. ■ the theory and practice of the ownership of land and the means of production by the people or the state. —**col·lec·tiv·ist** *adj. & n.* —**col·lec·tiv·is·tic** /-ˌlektəˈvistik/ *adj.*

col·lec·tor /kəˈlektər/ ▸*n.* a person or thing that collects something, in particular: ■ a person who collects things of a specified type, professionally or as a hobby: *book collectors.* ■ an official who is responsible for collecting money owed to an organization or body: *a tax collector.*

col·lec·tor's i·tem ▸*n.* an object of interest to collectors, esp. because it is rare, beautiful, or associated with someone famous.

col·lege /ˈkälij/ ▸*n.* **1** an educational institution or establishment, in particular: ■ one providing higher education or specialized professional or vocational training. ■ (within a university) a school offering a general liberal arts curriculum leading only to a bachelor's degree. ■ (in Britain) any of a number of independent institutions within certain universities, each having its own teaching staff, students, and buildings. ■ *Brit.* a private secondary school: [in *names*] *Eton College.* ■ the teaching staff and students of a college considered collectively.

■ the buildings and campus of a college. **2** an organized group of professional people with particular aims, duties, and privileges: [in names] *the electoral college.*

col·le·giate /kə'lējət/ ▶*adj.* **1** belonging or relating to a college or its students: *collegiate life.* **2** (of a university) composed of different colleges.

col·lide /kə'līd/ ▶*v.* [*intr.*] hit with force when moving: *she collided with someone | two suburban trains collided.* ■ come into conflict or opposition: *in his work, politics and metaphysics collide.*

col·lie /'kälē/ ▶*n.* (*pl.* **-lies**) a sheepdog of a breed originating in Scotland, having a long, pointed nose and thick, long hair.

col·lier·y /'kälyərē/ ▶*n.* (*pl.* **-ler·ies**) a coal mine and the buildings and equipment associated with it.

col·li·gate /'kälə,gāt/ ▶*v.* **1** *Linguistics* be or cause to be juxtaposed or grouped in a syntactic relation: [*intr.*] *the two grammatical items are said to colligate* | [*tr.*] *pronouns are regularly colligated with verbal forms.* **2** [*tr.*] connect; unite.■ *Logic* join or relate (apparently unrelated facts) into a pattern, esp. to reveal a general principle. —**col·li·ga·tion** /,kälə'gāSHən/ *n.*

col·lin·e·ar /kə'linēər; kä-/ ▶*adj. Geom.* (of points) lying in the same straight line. —**col·lin·e·ar·i·ty** /kə,linē'aritē; kä-/ *n.*

col·li·sion /kə'liZHən/ ▶*n.* **1** an instance of one moving object or person striking violently against another. ■ an instance of conflict between opposing ideas, interests, or factions: *a collision between experience and theory | cultures in collision.* **2** *Comput.* an event of two or more records being assigned the same location in memory. ■ an instance of simultaneous transmission by more than one node of a network. —**col·li·sion·al** /-ZHənl/ *adj.*

col·lo·cate /'kälə,kāt/ ▶*v.* **1** [*intr.*] *Linguistics* (of a word) be habitually juxtaposed with another with a frequency greater than chance: *"maiden" collocates with "voyage."* **2** [*tr.*] *rare* place side by side or in a particular relation.

▶*n. Linguistics* a word that is habitually juxtaposed with another with a frequency greater than chance. —**col·lo·ca·tion** /,kälə'kāSHən/ *n.*

col·loid /'käl,oid/ ▶*n.* a homogeneous, noncrystalline substance consisting of large molecules or ultramicroscopic particles of one substance dispersed through a second substance. Colloids include gels, sols, and emulsions. ■ *Anat. & Med.* a substance of gelatinous consistency.

▶*adj.* of the nature of, relating to, or characterized by a colloid or colloids. —**col·loi·dal** /kə'loidl/ *adj.*

col·lo·qui·al /kə'lōkwēəl/ ▶*adj.* (of language) used in ordinary or familiar conversation; not formal or literary. —**col·lo·qui·al·ly** *adv.*

col·lo·qui·al·ism /kə'lōkwēə,lizəm/ ▶*n.* a word or phrase that is not formal or literary, used in ordinary or familiar conversation. ■ the use of such words or phrases.

col·lo·qui·um /kə'lōkwēəm/ ▶*n.* (*pl.* **-qui·ums** or **-qui·a** /-kwēə/) an academic conference or seminar.

col·lo·quy /'käləkwē/ ▶*n.* (*pl.* **-quies**) *formal* a conversation.

col·lude /kə'lood/ ▶*v.* [*intr.*] come to a secret understanding for a harmful purpose; conspire: *university leaders colluded in price-rigging | the president accused his opponents of colluding with foreigners.* —**col·lud·er** *n.*

col·lu·sion /kə'looZHən/ ▶*n.* secret or illegal cooperation or conspiracy, esp. in order to cheat or deceive others: *collusion between media owners and political leaders.* ■ *Law* such cooperation or conspiracy, esp. between ostensible opponents in a lawsuit. —**col·lu·sive** /-siv; -ziv/ *adj.* —**col·lu·sive·ly** /-sivlē; -zivlē/ *adv.*

col·o·bus /'käləbəs/ (also **colobus monkey**) ▶*n.* (*pl.* same) a slender, leaf-eating African monkey (genera *Colobus* and *Procolobus*) with silky fur, a long tail, and very small or absent thumbs.

co·logne /kə'lōn/ ▶*n.* eau de cologne or scented toilet water.

co·lon[1] /'kōlən/ ▶*n.* a punctuation mark (:) indicating: ■ that a writer is introducing a quotation or a list of items. ■ that a writer is separating two clauses of which the second expands or illustrates the first. ■ a statement of proportion between two numbers: *a ratio of 10:1.* ■ the separation of hours from minutes (and minutes from seconds) in a statement of time given in numbers: *4:30 p.m.* ■ the number of the chapter and verse respectively in biblical references: *Exodus 3:2.*

co·lon[2] ▶*n. Anat.* the main part of the large intestine, which passes from the cecum to the rectum and absorbs water and electrolytes from food that has remained undigested. —**co·lon·ic** /kə'länik/ *adj.*

colo·nel /'kərnl/ ▶*n.* an army officer of high rank, in particular (in the U.S. Army, Air Force, and Marine Corps) an officer above a lieutenant colonel and below a brigadier general. ▷mid 16th cent.: from obsolete French *coronel* (earlier form of *colonel*), from Italian *colonnello* 'column of soldiers,' from *colonna* 'column,' from Latin *columna.* The form *coronel,* source of the modern pronunciation, was usual until the mid 17th cent. —**colo·nel·cy** /'kərnlsē/ *n.* (*pl.* **-cies**).

co·lo·ni·al /kə'lōnyəl; -nēəl/ ▶*adj.* **1** of, relating to, or characteristic of a colony or colonies. ■ relating to the period of the American colonies before independence. ■ (esp. of architecture or furniture) made during or in the style of this period. **2** (of animals or plants) living in colonies.

▶*n.* **1** a native or inhabitant of a colony. **2** a house built in colonial style. —**co·lo·ni·al·ly** *adv.*

co·lo·ni·al·ism /kə'lōnēə,lizəm; kə'lōnyə,lizəm/ ▶*n.* the policy or practice of acquiring full or partial political control over another country, occupying it with settlers, and exploiting it economically. —**co·lo·ni·al·ist** /-list/ *n. & adj.*

col·o·nist /'kälənist/ ▶*n.* a settler in or inhabitant of a colony.

col·o·nize /'kälə,nīz/ ▶*v.* [*tr.*] (of a country or its citizens) send a group of settlers to (a place) and establish political control over it: *the Greeks colonized Sicily and southern Italy.* ■ come to settle among and establish political control over (the indigenous people of an area). ■ appropriate (a place or domain) for one's own use. ■ *Ecol.* (of a plant or animal) establish itself in an area: *mussels can colonize even the most inhospitable rock surfaces* | [*intr.*] *insect borers colonize in rotted trees.* —**col·o·ni·za·tion** /,kälənə'zāSHən/ *n.* —**col·o·niz·er** *n.*

col·on·nade /,kälə'nād/ ▶*n.* a row of columns supporting a roof, an entablature, or arcade. ■ a row of trees or other tall objects. —**col·on·nad·ed** *adj.*

col·o·ny /'kälənē/ ▶*n.* (*pl.* **-nies**) **1** a country or area under the full or partial political control of another country, typically a distant one, and occupied by settlers from that country. ■ a group of people living in such a country or area, consisting of the original settlers and their descendants and successors. ■ (**the Colonies**) chiefly British term for **Thirteen Colonies.** ■ (**the colonies**) all the foreign countries or areas formerly under British political control. **2** a group of people of one nationality or ethnic group living in a foreign city or country: *the British colony in New York.* ■ a place where a group of people with similar interests live together: *an artists' colony.* **3** *Biol.* a community of animals or plants of one kind living together or forming a physically connected structure. ■ a group of fungi or bacteria grown from a single spore or cell on a culture medium. ▷late Middle English (denoting a settlement formed mainly of retired soldiers, acting as a garrison in newly conquered territory in the Roman Empire): from Latin *colonia* 'settlement, farm,' from *colonus* 'settler, farmer,' from *colere* 'cultivate.'

col·o·phon /'käləfən; -,fän/ ▶*n.* a publisher's emblem or imprint, esp. one on the title page or spine of a book. ■ *hist.* a statement at the end of a book, typically with a printer's emblem, giving information about its authorship and printing.

col·or /'kələr/ (*Brit.* **col·our**) ▶*n.* **1** the property possessed by an object of producing different sensations on the eye as a result of the way the object reflects or emits light. ■ one, or any mixture, of the constituents into which light can be separated in a spectrum or rainbow, sometimes including (loosely) black and white. ■ the use of all colors, not only black, white, and gray, in photography or television: *he has shot the whole film in color* | [as *adj.*] *color television.* ■ a substance used to give something a particular color: *lip color.* ■ *fig.* a shade of meaning: *many events in her past had taken on a different color.* ■ *fig.* character or general nature: *the hospitable color of his family.* **2** the appearance of someone's skin; in particular: ■ pigmentation of the skin, esp. as an indication of someone's race: *discrimination on the basis of color.* ■ a group of people considered as being distinguished by skin pigmentation: *all colors and nationalities.* ■ rosiness of the complexion, esp. as an indication of someone's health. ■ redness of the face as a manifestation of an emotion, esp. embarrassment or anger. **3** vividness of visual appearance resulting from the presence of brightly colored things: *for color, plant groups of winter-flowering pansies.* ■ *fig.* picturesque or exciting features that lend a particularly interesting quality to something. ■ *fig.* variety of musical tone or expression: *orchestral color.* **4** (**colors**) an item or items of a particular color or combination of colors worn to identify an individual or a member of a school, group, or organization; in particular: ■ the clothes or accoutrements worn by a jockey or racehorse to indicate the horse's owner. ■ the flag of a regiment or ship. ■ a national flag: *the armed forces of a country, as symbolized by its flag: he was called to the colors during the war.* **5** *Physics* a quantized property of quarks which can take three values (designated blue, green, and red) for each flavor.

▶*v.* **1** [*tr.*] change the color of (something) by painting or dyeing it with

---

crayons, paints, or dyes. ■ [*intr.*] take on a different color: *the foliage will not color well if the soil is too rich.* ■ use crayons to fill (a particular shape or outline) with color. ■ *fig.* make vivid or picturesque. **2** [*intr.*] (of a person or their skin) show embarrassment or shame by becoming red; blush: *everyone stared at him, and he colored slightly.* ■ [*tr.*] cause (a person or their skin) to change in color: *rage colored his pale complexion.* ■ [*tr.*] (of a particular color) imbue (a person's skin): *a pink flush colored her cheeks.* ■ [*tr.*] *fig.* (of an emotion) imbue (a person's voice) with a particular tone. **3** [*tr.*] influence, esp. in a negative way; distort: *the experiences had colored her whole existence.* ■ misrepresent by distortion or exaggeration: *witnesses might color evidence to make a story saleable.*

▶ □ **show one's true colors** reveal one's real character or intentions, esp. when these are disreputable or dishonorable.

Col·o·rad·o po·ta·to bee·tle ▶*n.* a yellow- and black-striped leaf beetle (*Leptinotarsa decemlineata*, family Chrysomelidae) native to North America. The larvae are highly destructive to potato plants.

col·o·ra·tion /ˌkələˈrāsHən/ ▶*n.* **1** a visual appearance with regard to color: *some bacterial structures take on a purple coloration.* ■ the natural color or variegated markings of animals or plants: *the red coloration of many maples.* ■ a scheme or method of applying color. **2** a specified pervading character or tone of something: *the movement has taken on a fundamentalist coloration.* ■ a variety of musical or vocal expression: *a skillful singer can do much with coloration.*

col·o·ra·tu·ra /ˌkələrəˈto͝orə/ ; ˌkäl-/ ▶*n.* elaborate ornamentation of a vocal melody, esp. in operatic singing by a soprano. ■ (also **coloratura soprano**) a soprano skilled in such singing.

col·or·blind (also **col·or·blind**) ▶*adj.* **1** unable to distinguish certain colors, or (rarely in humans) any colors at all. **2** not influenced by racial prejudice: *a color-blind society.* —**col·or·blind·ness** *n.*

col·ored /ˈkələrd/ (*Brit.* **col·oured**) ▶*adj.* **1** having or having been given a color or colors, esp. as opposed to being black, white, or neutral: *brightly colored birds* | [in *comb.*] *a peach-colored sofa.* ■ *fig.* imbued with an emotive or exaggerated quality. **2** (also **Colored**) wholly or partly of nonwhite descent (now usually offensive in the U.S.). ■ (also **Coloured**) *S. Afr.* used as an ethnic label for people of mixed ethnic origin, including African slave, Malay, Chinese, and white. ■ relating to people who are wholly or partly of nonwhite descent.

▶*n.* **1** (also **Colored**) *dated, usually offens.* a person who is wholly or partly of nonwhite descent. ■ *S. Afr.* a person of mixed ethnic origin speaking Afrikaans or English as their mother tongue. **2** (**coloreds**) clothes, sheets, etc., that are any color but white (used esp. in the context of washing and color fastness).

col·or·fast /ˈkələrˌfast/ ▶*adj.* dyed in colors that will not fade or be washed out. —**col·or·fast·ness** *n.*

col·or·ful /ˈkələrfəl/ (*Brit.* **col·our·ful**) ▶*adj.* **1** having much or varied color; bright. **2** full of interest; lively and exciting. ■ (of a person's life or background) involving various disreputable activities. ■ (of language) vulgar or rude. —**col·or·ful·ly** /-f(ə)lē/ *adv.* —**col·or·ful·ness** *n.*

col·or·ing /ˈkələriNG/ (*Brit.* **col·our·ing**) ▶*n.* **1** the process or skill of applying a substance to something so as to change its original color. ■ the process of filling in a particular shape or outline with crayons: [as *adj.*] *a coloring book.* ■ a drawing produced in this way. **2** visual appearance with regard to color, in particular: ■ the arrangement of colors and markings on an animal. ■ the natural hues of a person's skin, hair, and eyes: *her fair coloring.* ■ *fig.* the pervading character or tone of something. **3** a substance used to give a particular color to something, esp. food.

col·or·ist /ˈkələrist/ (*Brit.* **col·our·ist**) ▶*n.* an artist or designer who uses color in a special or skillful way. ■ a person who tints black-and-white prints, photographs, or movies. ■ a hairdresser who specializes in dyeing people's hair.

col·or·ize /ˈkələˌrīz/ (*Brit.* also **col·our·ize**) ▶*v.* [*tr.*] add color to (a black-and-white movie) by means of computer technology. —**col·or·i·za·tion** /ˌkələrəˈzāsHən/ *n. trademark* —**col·or·iz·er** *n. trademark*

col·or·less /ˈkələrləs/ (*Brit.* **col·our·less**) ▶*adj.* **1** (esp. of a gas or liquid) without color. ■ dull or pale in hue. **2** lacking distinctive character or interest; dull. —**col·or·less·ly** *adv.*

col·or sat·u·ra·tion ▶*n.* see SATURATION.

col·or scheme ▶*n.* an arrangement or combination of colors, esp. as used in interior decoration: *a cool, simple color scheme.*

col·or sep·a·ra·tion ▶*n. Photog. & Printing* any of three negative images of the same subject taken through green, red, and blue filters and combined to reproduce the full color of the original.

co·los·sal /kəˈläsəl/ ▶*adj.* extremely large: *a colossal mistake.* ■ *Sculpture* (of a statue) at least twice life size. —**co·los·sal·ly** *adv.*

co·los·sus /kəˈläsəs/ ▶*n.* (*pl.* **-los·si** /-ˈläs,ī/ or **-los·sus·es**) a statue that

is much bigger than life size. ■ *fig.* a person or thing of enormous size, importance, or ability. ▷late Middle English: via Latin from Greek *kolossos* (applied by Herodotus to the statues of Egyptian temples).

co·los·to·my /kəˈlästəmē/ ▶*n.* (*pl.* **-mies**) a surgical operation in which a piece of the colon is diverted to an artificial opening in the abdominal wall so as to bypass a damaged part of the colon. ■ an opening so formed: [as *adj.*] *a colostomy bag.*

co·los·trum /kəˈlästrəm/ ▶*n.* the first secretion from the mammary glands after giving birth, rich in antibodies.

col·po·scope /ˈkälpəˌskōp/ ▶*n.* a surgical instrument used to examine the vagina and the cervix. —**col·pos·co·py** /kälˈpäskəpē/ *n.*

colt /kōlt/ ▶*n.* a young, uncastrated male horse, in particular one less than four years old. —**colt·ish** *adj.*

colts·foot /ˈkōlts,fo͝ot/ ▶*n.* (*pl.* **coltsfoots**) a Eurasian medicinal plant (*Tussilago farfara*) of the daisy family, with yellow flowers followed by large, heart-shaped leaves.

co·lum·bine /ˈkäləm,bīn/ ▶*n.* a plant (genus *Aquilegia*) of the buttercup family with long-spurred flowers.

col·umn /ˈkäləm/ ▶*n.* **1** an upright pillar, typically cylindrical and made of stone or concrete, supporting an entablature, arch, or other structure or standing alone as a monument. ■ a similar vertical, roughly cylindrical thing: *a column of smoke.* ■ an upright shaft forming part of a machine and typically used for controlling it: *a Spitfire control column.* **2** a vertical division of a page or text. ■ a vertical arrangement of figures or other information. ■ a section of a newspaper or magazine regularly devoted to a particular subject or written by a particular person. **3** one or more lines of people or vehicles moving in the same direction: *we walked in a column.* ■ *Mil.* a narrow-fronted deep formation of troops in successive lines. ■ a military force deployed in such a formation. ■ a similar formation of ships in a fleet or convoy. —**col·um·nar** /kəˈləmnər/ *adj.* —**col·umned** /ˈkäləmd/ *adj.*

col·um·nist /ˈkäləmnist/ ▶*n.* a journalist contributing regularly to a newspaper or magazine.

co·ma[1] /ˈkōmə/ ▶*n.* a state of deep unconsciousness that lasts for a prolonged or indefinite period, caused esp. by severe injury or illness.

co·ma[2] ▶*n.* (*pl.* **co·mae** /ˈkōmē/) *Astron.* a diffuse cloud of gas and dust surrounding the nucleus of a comet.

Co·man·che /kəˈmanCHē/ ▶*n.* (*pl.* same or **-ches**) **1** a member of an American Indian people of the southwestern U.S. The Comanche were among the first to acquire horses (from the Spanish) and resisted white settlers fiercely. **2** the Uto-Aztecan language of this people. ▶*adj.* of or relating to this people or their language.

com·a·tose /ˈkōmə,tōs; ˈkämə-/ ▶*adj.* of or in a state of deep unconsciousness for a prolonged or indefinite period, esp. as a result of severe injury or illness. ■ *humorous* (of a person or thing) extremely exhausted, lethargic, or sleepy: *the economy remains almost comatose.*

comb /kōm/ ▶*n.* **1** a strip of plastic, metal, or wood with a row of narrow teeth, used for untangling or arranging the hair. ■ an instance of untangling or arranging the hair with such a device: *she gave her hair a comb.* ■ a short curved device of this type, worn by women to hold hair in place or as an ornament. **2** something resembling a comb in function or structure, in particular: ■ a device for removing loose hair from an animal, esp. a dog or cat. ■ a device for separating and dressing textile fibers. **3** the red fleshy crest on the head of a domestic fowl, esp. a rooster. **4** short for HONEYCOMB (sense 1). ▶*v.* [*tr.*] **1** untangle or arrange (the hair) by drawing a comb through it. ■ (**comb something out**) remove something from the hair by drawing a comb through it. ■ curry (a horse). **2** prepare (wool, flax, or cotton) for manufacture with a comb. ■ [usu. as *adj.*] (**combed**) treat (a fabric) in such a way: *soft combed cotton.* **3** search carefully and systematically: *police combed the area* | [*intr.*] *his mother combed through the boxes.* —**comb-like** /-,līk/ *adj.*

com·bat ▶*n.* /ˈkäm,bat/ fighting between armed forces: *killed in combat* | *pilots reenacted the aerial combats of yesteryear* | [as *adj.*] *a combat zone.* ■ nonviolent conflict or opposition: *intellectual combat.* ▶*v.* /kəmˈbat; ˈkäm,bat/ (**-bat·ed** or **-bat·ted**, **-bat·ing** or **-bat·ting**) [*tr.*] take action to reduce, destroy, or prevent (something undesirable): *an effort to combat drug trafficking.* ■ *archaic* engage in a fight with; oppose in battle: [*intr.*] *your men combated against the first of ours.*

com·bat·ant /kəmˈbatnt; ˈkämbətənt/ ▶*n.* a person engaged in fighting during a war. ■ a nation at war with another. ■ a person engaged in conflict or competition with another. ▶*adj.* engaged in fighting during a war.

com·bat fa·tigue ▶*n.* **1** psychological disturbance caused by prolonged exposure to active warfare, esp. being under bombardment. **2** (**combat fatigues**) a uniform of a type to be worn into combat.

com·bat·ive /kəm'bativ/ ▶ *adj.* ready or eager to fight; pugnacious. —**com·bat·ive·ly** *adv.* —**com·bat·ive·ness** *n.*

comb·er /'kōmər/ ▶ *n.* **1** a long curling sea wave. **2** a person or machine that separates and straightens the fibers of cotton or wool.

com·bi·na·tion /ˌkämbə'nāSHən/ ▶ *n.* **1** the act or an instance of combining; the process of being combined. ■ [as *adj.*] uniting different uses, functions, or ingredients: *a combination garment bag and backpack.* ■ the state of being joined or united in such a way: *these four factors work together in combination.* ■ *Chem.* the joining of substances in a compound with new properties. ■ *Chem.* the state of being in a compound. **2** a set of people or things that have been combined: *a combination of beauty and utility.* ■ an arrangement of elements: *the canvases may be arranged in any number of combinations.* ■ a sequence of numbers or letters used to open a combination lock. ■ (in various sports and games) a coordinated and effective sequence of moves. **3** *Math.* a selection of a given number of elements from a larger number without regard to their arrangement. —**com·bi·na·tion·al** /-SHənl/ *adj.* —**com·bi·na·tive** /'kämbəˌnātiv; kəm'bīnətiv/ *adj.* —**com·bi·na·to·ri·al** /ˌkämbənə'tôrēəl; kəm'bīnə-/ *adj.* (*Math.*) —**com·bi·na·to·ri·al·ly** *adv.* (*Math.*) —**com·bi·na·to·ry** /kəm'bīnəˌtôrē; 'kämbənə-/ *adj.*

com·bi·na·tion lock ▶ *n.* a lock that is opened by rotating a dial or set of dials, marked with letters or numbers, through a specific sequence.

com·bine[1] ▶ *v.* /kəm'bīn/ [*trans.*] unite; merge: *the band combines a variety of musical influences* | [*intrans.*] *high tides and winds combined to bring chaos to the East Coast.* ■ [*intrans.*] *Chem.* unite to form a compound: *oxygen and hydrogen do not combine at room temperatures.* ■ [*intrans.*] unite for a common purpose: *groups of teachers combined to tackle a variety of problems.* ■ engage in simultaneously: *combine shopping and sightseeing.*
▶ *n.* /'käm,bīn/ a group of people or companies acting together for a commercial purpose. —**com·bin·a·ble** /kəm'bīnəbəl/ *adj.*

com·bine[2] /'käm,bīn/ ▶ *n.* (in full **combine harvester**) an agricultural machine that cuts, threshes, and cleans a grain crop in one operation.
▶ *v.* [*trans.*] harvest (a crop) by means of a combine.

com·bin·er /kəm'bīnər/ ▶ *n.* any of various electronic devices that combine signals, in particular: ■ a device that couples different frequencies to a single antenna. ■ a component of a cipher that combines two data sources to encrypt text. ■ an electrical transformer comprising several smaller ones.

com·bin·ing form /kəm'bīniNG/ ▶ *n. Gram.* a linguistic element used in combination with another element to form a word (e.g., *Anglo-* 'English' in *Anglo-American*, *bio-* 'life' in *biology*).

com·bo /'kämbō/ ▶ *n.* (*pl.* **-bos**) *inf.* **1** a small jazz, rock, or pop band. **2** a combination, typically of different foods: [as *adj.*] *the combo platter.*

com·bo drive ▶ *n. Comput.* an optical disk drive that can read and record CDs and can also read DVDs.

com·bus·ti·ble /kəm'bəstəbəl/ ▶ *adj.* able to catch fire and burn easily: *highly combustible paint thinner.* ■ *fig.* excitable; easily annoyed.
▶ *n.* a combustible substance. —**com·bus·ti·bil·i·ty** /kəmˌbəstə'bilitē/ *n.*

com·bus·tion /kəm'bəsCHən/ ▶ *n.* the process of burning something: *the combustion of fossil fuels.* ■ *Chem.* rapid chemical combination of a substance with oxygen, involving the production of heat and light. —**com·bus·tive** /-'bəstiv/ *adj.*

com·bus·tion cham·ber ▶ *n.* an enclosed space in which combustion takes place, esp. in an engine or furnace.

Comdr. ▶ *abbr.* commander.

come /kəm/ ▶ *v.* (*past* **came** /kām/; *past part.* **come**) [*intrans.*] **1** move or travel toward or into a place thought of as near or familiar to the speaker: *Jessica came into the kitchen* | *they came here as immigrants* | *he came rushing out.* ■ arrive at a specified place: *we walked along till we came to a stream* | *it was very late when she came back* | *my trunk hasn't come yet.* ■ (of a thing) reach or extend to a specified point: *women in slim dresses that came all the way to their shoes* | *the path comes straight down.* ■ (**be coming**) approach: *someone was coming* | *she heard the train coming.* ■ travel in order to be with a specified person, to do a specified thing, or to be present at an event: *the police came* | *come and live with me* | *the electrician came to fix the stove* | *fig. we have certainly come a long way since Aristotle.* ■ join someone in participating in a specified activity or course of action: *do you want to come fishing tomorrow?* ■ (**come along/on**) make progress; develop: *he's coming along nicely* | *she asked them how their garden was coming on.* ■ [in *imper.*] (also **come, come!**) said to someone when correcting, reassuring, or urging them on: *"Come, come, child, no need to thank me."* **2** occur; happen; take place: *twilight had not yet come* | *waiting for a crash that never came* | *a chance like this doesn't come along every day.* ■ be heard, perceived, or experienced: *a voice came from the kitchen* | *"No," came the reply* | *it came as a great shock.* ■ (of a quality) become apparent or noticeable through actions or performance: *as an actor your style and*

personality must come through. ■ (**come across** or **off** or *Brit.* **over**) (of a person) appear or sound in a specified way; give a specified impression: *he'd always come across as a decent guy.* ■ (of a thought or memory) enter one's mind: *the basic idea came to me while reading an article* | *a passage from a novel came back to Adam.* **3** take or occupy a specified position in space, order, or priority: *prisons come far down the list of priorities* | *I make sure my kids come first.* ■ achieve a specified place in a race or contest: *she came second among sixty contestants.* **4** pass into a specified state, esp. one of separation or disunion: *his shirt had come undone.* ■ (**come to/into**) reach or be brought to a specified situation or result: *you will come to no harm* | *staff who come into contact with the public.* ■ reach eventually a certain condition or state of mind: *he had come to realize she was no puppet.* **5** be sold, available, or found in a specified form: *the cars come with a variety of extras* | *they come in three sizes.* **6** *inf.* have an orgasm.

▶ *phrasal v.* □ **come about 1** happen; take place: *the relative speed with which emancipation came about.* **2** (of a ship) change direction. □ **come across 1** meet or find by chance: *I came across these old photos recently.* **2** *inf.* hand over or provide what is wanted: *she has come across with some details.* ■ (of a woman) agree to have sexual intercourse with a man. □ **come along** [in *imper.*] said when encouraging someone or telling them to hurry up. □ **come around** (*chiefly Brit.* also **round**) **1** recover consciousness: *I'd just come around from a drunken stupor.* **2** be converted to another person's opinion: *I came around to her point of view.* **3** (of a date or regular occurrence) recur; be imminent again: *Friday had come around so quickly.* □ **come at** launch oneself at (someone); attack. □ **come away** be left with a specified feeling, impression, or result after doing something: *she came away feeling upset.* □ **come back 1** (in sports) recover from a deficit: *the Mets came back from a 3–0 deficit.* **2** reply or respond to someone, esp. vigorously: *he came back at Judy with a vengeance.* □ **come before** be dealt with by (a judge or court): *it is the most controversial issue to come before the Supreme Court.* □ **come between** interfere with or disturb the relationship of (two people): *I let my stupid pride come between us.* □ **come by 1** call casually and briefly as a visitor: *his friends came by* | *she came by the house.* **2** manage to acquire or obtain (something). □ **come down 1** (of a building or other structure) collapse or be demolished. ■ (of an aircraft) crash or crash-land. **2** be handed down by tradition or inheritance: *the name has come down from the last century.* **3** reach a decision or recommendation in favor of one side or another: *advisers and inspectors came down on our side.* **4** *inf.* experience the lessening of an excited or euphoric feeling, esp. one produced by a narcotic drug. □ **come down on** criticize or punish (someone) harshly: *she came down on me like a ton of bricks.* ■ **come down to** (of a situation or outcome) be dependent on (a specified factor): *it came down to her word against Guy's.* □ **come down with** begin to suffer from (a specified illness): *I came down with influenza.* □ **come forward** volunteer oneself for a task or post or to give evidence about a crime. □ **come from** originate in; have as its source: *the word caviar comes from the Italian caviale.* ■ be the result of: *a dignity that comes from being in control.* ■ have as one's place of birth or residence: *I come from the Bronx.* ■ be descended from: *she comes from a family of Muslim scholars.* □ **come in 1** join or become involved in an enterprise: *that's where Jack comes in* | *I agreed to come in on the project.* ■ have a useful role or function: *this is where grammar comes in.* ■ prove to have a specified good quality: *the money came in handy for treating his cronies at the tavern.* **2** finish a race in a specified position: *the favorite came in first.* **3** (of money) be earned or received regularly. **4** [in *imper.*] begin speaking or make contact, esp. in radio communication: *come in, London.* **5** (of a tide) rise; flow. □ **come into** suddenly receive (money or property), esp. by inheriting it. □ **come of** result from: *no good will come of it.* ■ be descended from: *she came of Neapolitan stock.* □ **come off 1** (of an action) succeed; be accomplished. ■ fare in a specified way in a contest: *Jeff always came off worse in an argument.* **2** become detached or be detachable from something. □ **come on 1** (of a state or condition) start to arrive or happen: *she felt a mild case of the sniffles coming on* | *it was coming on to rain.* **2** (also **come upon**) meet or find by chance. **3** [in *imper.*] said when encouraging someone to do something or to hurry up or when one feels that someone is wrong or foolish: *Come on! We must hurry!* ■ said or shouted to express support, for example for a sports team. □ **come on to** *inf.* make sexual advances toward. □ **come out 1** (of a fact) emerge; become known: *it came out that the accused had illegally registered to vote.* ■ happen as a result: *something good can come out of something that went wrong.* ■ (of a photograph) be produced satisfactorily or in a specified

---

Pronunciation Key ə *ago,* up; ər *over,* fur; a *hat;* ā *ate;* ä *car;* CH *chin;* e *let;* ē *see;* e(ə)r *air;* i *fit;* ī *by;* i(ə)r *ear;* NG *sing;* ō *go;* ô *law, for;* oi *toy;* ŏŏ *good;* ōō *goo;* ou *out;* SH *she;* TH *thin;* TH *then;* (h)w *why;* ZH *vision*

way: *I hope my photographs come out all right.* ■ (of the result of a calculation or measurement) emerge at a specified figure: *rough cider usually comes out at about eight percent alcohol.* **2** (of a book or other work) appear; be released or published. **3** declare oneself as being for or against something: *residents have come out against the proposals.* **4** achieve a specified placing in an examination or contest: *he deservedly came out the winner on points | she came out victorious.* ■ acquit oneself in a specified way: *surprisingly, it's Penn who comes out best.* **5** (of a stain) be removed or able to be removed. **6** *inf.* openly declare that one is homosexual. **7** *dated* (of a young upper-class woman) make one's debut in society. □ **come out with** say (something) in a sudden, rude, or incautious way. □ **come over 1** (of a feeling or manner) begin to affect (someone). **2** change to another side or point of view. □ **come through 1** succeed in surviving or dealing with (an illness or ordeal): *she's come through the operation very well.* **2** (of a message) be sent and received. ■ (of an official decree) be processed and notified. □ **come to 1** (also **come to oneself**) recover consciousness. **2** (of an expense) reach in total; amount to: *he hasn't the least idea of how much it will come to.* **3** (of a ship) come to a stop. □ **come under 1** be classified as or among: *they all come under the general heading of opinion polls.* **2** be subject to (an influence or authority). ■ be subjected to (pressure or aggression): *his vehicle came under mortar fire.* □ **come up** (of an issue, situation, or problem) occur or present itself, esp. unexpectedly. ■ (of a specified time or event) approach or draw near: *she's got exams coming up.* ■ (of a legal case) reach the time when it is scheduled to be dealt with. □ **come up against** be faced with or opposed by (something such as an enemy or problem). □ **come up with** produce (something), esp. when pressured or challenged. □ **come upon** attack by surprise.
▸*prep. inf.* when a specified time is reached or event happens: *I don't think that they'll be far away from honors come the new season.*
▸*n. inf.* semen ejaculated at orgasm.
▸ □ **as —— as they come** used to describe someone or something that is a supreme example of the quality specified: *Smith is as tough as they come.* □ **come again?** *inf.* used to ask someone to repeat or explain something they have said. □ **come to nothing** have no significant or successful result in the end. □ **come to pass** *chiefly poetic/lit.* happen; occur: *it came to pass that she had two sons.* □ **come to that** (or **if it comes to that**) *inf.* in fact (said to introduce an additional point): *there isn't a clock on the mantelpiece—come to that, there isn't a mantelpiece!* □ **come to think of it** on reflection (said when an idea or point occurs to one while one is speaking). □ **come what may** no matter what happens. □ **have it coming (to one)** *inf.* be due for retribution on account of something bad that one has done: *his uppity sister-in-law had it coming to her.* □ **how come?** *inf.* said when asking how or why something happened or is the case: *how come you never married, Jimmy?* □ **to come** (following a noun) in the future: *films that would inspire generations to come | in years to come.* □ **where someone is coming from** *inf.* someone's meaning, motivation, or personality.
come·back /ˈkəmˌbak/ ▸*n.* **1** a return by a well-known person, esp. an entertainer or sports player, to the activity in which they have formerly been successful. ■ a return to fashion of an item, activity, or style: *stirrup pants have **made a comeback**.* **2** *inf.* a quick reply to a critical remark. ■ the opportunity to seek redress.
co·me·di·an /kəˈmēdēən/ ▸*n.* an entertainer whose act is designed to make an audience laugh. ■ *often ironic* an amusing or entertaining person. ■ a comic actor.
co·me·di·enne /kəˌmēdēˈen/ ▸*n.* a female comedian.
come·down /ˈkəmˌdoun/ ▸*n. inf.* **1** a loss of status or importance. **2** a feeling of disappointment or depression: *it's such a comedown after Christmas is over.* ■ a lessening of the sensations generated by a narcotic drug as its effects wear off.
com·e·dy /ˈkämədē/ ▸*n.* (*pl.* **-dies**) professional entertainment consisting of jokes and satirical sketches, intended to make an audience laugh. ■ a movie, play, or broadcast program intended to make an audience laugh. ■ the style or genre of such types of entertainment. ■ the humorous or amusing aspects of something. ■ a play characterized by its humorous or satirical tone and its depiction of amusing people or incidents, in which the characters ultimately triumph over adversity. ■ the dramatic genre represented by such plays. Compare with TRAGEDY (sense 2). —**co·me·dic** /kəˈmēdik/ *adj.*
com·e·dy of man·ners ▸*n.* a comedy that satirizes behavior in a particular social group, esp. the upper classes.
come-hith·er *inf., dated* ▸*adj.* flirtatious; sexually inviting.
▸*n.* a flirtatious or enticing manner.
come·ly /ˈkəmlē/ ▸*adj.* (**-li·er, -li·est**) (typically of a woman) pleasant to look at; attractive. ■ agreeable; suitable. —**come·li·ness** *n.*

come-on ▸*n. inf.* a thing that is intended to lure or entice. ■ a gesture or remark that is intended to attract someone sexually. ■ a marketing ploy, such as a free or cheap offer.
com·er /ˈkəmər/ ▸*n.* **1** a person who arrives somewhere: *feeding every comer is still a sacred duty.* See also LATECOMER, NEWCOMER. **2** *inf.* a person or thing likely to succeed.
com·et /ˈkämit/ ▸*n.* a celestial object consisting of a nucleus of ice and dust and, when near the sun, a "tail" of gas and dust particles pointing away from the sun. —**com·et·ar·y** /ˈkämiˌterē/ *adj.*
come·up·pance /kəˈməpəns/ ▸*n. inf.* a punishment or fate that someone deserves: *he got his comeuppance.*
com·fort /ˈkəmfərt/ ▸*n.* **1** a state of physical ease and freedom from pain or constraint. ■ (**comforts**) things that contribute to physical ease and well-being. ■ prosperity and the pleasant lifestyle secured by it. **2** consolation for grief or anxiety: *a few words of comfort.* ■ reassurance: *they should **take comfort** that help is available.* ■ a person or thing that gives consolation: *his friendship was a great comfort.* ■ a person or thing that gives satisfaction: *I felt a great comfort in the relationship of the moon to my astrological sign.* **3** *dial.* a warm quilt.
▸*v.* [*tr.*] soothe in grief; console. ■ help (someone) feel at ease; reassure. —**com·fort·ing** *adj.* —**com·fort·ing·ly** *adv.* —**com·fort·less** *adj.*
com·fort·a·ble /ˈkəmfərtəbəl; ˈkəmftərbəl/ ▸*adj.* **1** (esp. of clothes or furnishings) providing physical ease and relaxation. ■ (of a person) physically relaxed and free from constraint: *they would not be comfortable in any other clothes.* ■ not in pain (used esp. of a hospital patient). ■ free from stress or fear: *they appear very comfortable in each other's company.* ■ free from financial worry; having an adequate standard of living. **2** as large as is needed or wanted: *a comfortable income.* ■ with a wide margin: *a comfortable victory.*
▸*n. dial.* a warm quilt. —**com·fort·a·ble·ness** *n.* —**com·fort·a·bly** /-blē/ *adv.*
com·fort·er /ˈkəmfərtər/ ▸*n.* **1** a warm quilt. **2** a person or thing that provides consolation. ■ (**Comforter**) the Holy Spirit. **3** *dated* a woolen scarf.
com·frey /ˈkəmfrē/ ▸*n.* (*pl.* **-eys**) a Eurasian plant (genus *Symphytum*) of the borage family, with large hairy leaves and clusters of purplish or white bell-shaped flowers. It is commonly used in herbal medicine.
com·fy /ˈkəmfē/ ▸*adj.* (**-fi·er, -fi·est**) *inf.* comfortable. —**com·fi·ly** /-fəlē/ *adv.* —**com·fi·ness** *n.*
com·ic /ˈkämik/ ▸*adj.* causing or meant to cause laughter: *comic and fantastic exaggeration.* ■ relating to or in the style of comedy: *a comic actor.*
▸*n.* **1** a comedian, esp. a professional one. **2** (**comics**) comic strips.
com·i·cal /ˈkämikəl/ ▸*adj.* amusing: *a series of comical misunderstandings.* —**com·i·cal·i·ty** /ˌkämiˈkalitē/ *n.* —**com·i·cal·ly** /-ik(ə)lē/ *adv.*
com·ic book ▸*n.* a magazine comprised of stories presented as comic strips.
com·ic op·er·a ▸*n.* an opera that portrays humorous situations and characters. ■ the genre of such opera.
com·ic strip ▸*n.* a sequence of drawings in boxes that tell an amusing story, typically printed in a newspaper or comic book.
com·ing /ˈkəmiNG/ ▸*adj.* **1** due to happen or just beginning: *work is due to start in the coming year.* **2** likely to be important or successful in the future: *he was the coming man of French racing.*
▸*n.* an arrival or an approach: *the coming of a new age.*
com·i·ty /ˈkämitē/ ▸*n.* (*pl.* **-ties**) **1** courtesy and considerate behavior toward others. **2** an association of nations for their mutual benefit. ■ (also **comity of nations**) the mutual recognition by nations of the laws and customs of others.
com·ma /ˈkämə/ ▸*n.* **1** a punctuation mark (,) indicating a pause between parts of a sentence. It is also used to separate items in a list and to mark the place of thousands in a large numeral. **2** a butterfly (genus *Polygonia*, family Nymphalidae) that has wings with irregular, ragged edges and typically a comma-shaped mark on the underside of each hind wing.
com·mand /kəˈmand/ ▸*v.* [*tr.*] **1** give an authoritative order: *a gruff voice commanded us to enter.* ■ [*intr.*] give orders: *she commands and we obey.* ■ [*intr.*] have authority: *someone born to command.* ■ *Mil.* have authority over; be in charge of (a unit). ■ dominate (a strategic position) from a superior height: *the two castles commanded the harbor.* ■ *archaic* control or restrain (oneself or one's feelings). **2** be in a strong enough position to secure: *no party commanded a majority.* ■ deserve and receive: *a moral force that commanded respect.*
▸*n.* an authoritative order. ■ *Comput.* an instruction or signal that causes a computer to perform one of its basic functions. ■ authority, esp. over armed forces: *an officer took command.* ■ the ability to use or control something: *he had a brilliant command of English.* ■ [treated as *sing.* or

pl.] *Mil.* a group of officers exercising control over a particular group or operation. ■ *Mil.* a body of troops or a district under the control of a particular officer.

▸ □ **at someone's command** at someone's disposal; available.

com·man·dant /ˈkämənˌdant; -ˌdänt/ ▸*n.* an officer in charge of a particular force or institution: *the West Point commandant of cadets.*

com·man·deer /ˌkämənˈdi(ə)r/ ▸*v.* [*tr.*] officially take possession or control of (something), esp. for military purposes. ■ take possession of (something) without authority: *he hoisted himself onto a table, commandeering it as a speaker's platform.* ■ enlist (someone) to help in a task, typically against the person's will.

com·mand·er /kəˈmandər/ (abbr.: **Comdr.**) ▸*n.* **1** a person in authority, esp. over a body of troops or a military operation. ■ a naval officer of high rank, in particular (in the U.S. Navy or Coast Guard) an officer ranking above lieutenant commander and below captain. ■ (in certain metropolitan police departments) the officer in charge of a division, district, precinct, or squad. **2** a member of a higher class in some orders of knighthood. **—com·mand·er·ship** /-ˌSHip/ *n.*

com·mand·er in chief (also **Com·mand·er in Chief**) ▸*n.* (*pl.* **com·mand·ers in chief**) a head of state or officer in supreme command of a country's armed forces. ■ an officer in charge of a major subdivision of a country's armed forces, or of its forces in a particular area.

com·mand·ing /kəˈmandiNG/ ▸*adj.* (in military contexts) having a position of authority: *a commanding officer.* ■ (of an advantage or position) controlling; superior: *a commanding 13-6 lead.* ■ indicating or expressing authority; imposing. ■ (of a place or position) dominating physically; giving a wide view: *a commanding position looking out over the sea.* **—com·mand·ing·ly** *adv.*

com·mand·ment /kəˈmandmənt/ ▸*n.* a divine rule, esp. one of the Ten Commandments. ■ a rule to be observed as strictly as one of the Ten Commandments.

com·man·do /kəˈmandō/ ▸*n.* (*pl.* **-dos**) a soldier specially trained to carry out raids. ■ a unit of such troops. ■ a group forming part of a larger organization, typically an illegal or secret one, and carrying out attacks on its behalf.

com·mand per·for·mance ▸*n.* a presentation of a play, concert, opera, or other show at the request of royalty.

com·me·dia dell'ar·te /kəˈmädēə delˈärtē/ ▸*n.* an improvised kind of popular comedy in Italian theaters in the 16th–18th centuries, based on stock characters ▷Italian, 'comedy of art.'

com·mem·o·rate /kəˈmeməˌrāt/ ▸*v.* [*tr.*] recall and show respect for (someone or something) in a ceremony: *a ceremony to commemorate the war dead.* ■ serve as a memorial to: *a stone commemorating a boy who died at sea.* ■ mark (a significant event). ■ (often **be commemorated**) celebrate (an event, a person, or a situation) by doing or building something: *it was a night commemorated in a song.* **—com·mem·o·ra·tion** /kəˌmeməˈrāSHən/ *n.* **—com·mem·o·ra·tive** /-(ə)rətiv; -ˌēˌrātiv/ *adj.* **—com·mem·o·ra·tor** /-ˌrātər/ *n.*

com·mence /kəˈmens/ ▸*v.* begin; start: [*tr.*] *his design team commenced work* | [*intr.*] *a public inquiry is due to commence on the 16th.*

com·mence·ment /kəˈmensmənt/ ▸*n.* **1** a beginning or start: *at the commencement of training.* **2** a ceremony in which degrees or diplomas are conferred on graduating students: [as *adj.*] *a commencement address.*

com·mend /kəˈmend/ ▸*v.* [*tr.*] **1** (often **be commended**) praise formally or officially: *he was commended by the judge for his courageous actions.* ■ present as suitable for approval or acceptance; recommend: *I commend her to you without reservation.* ■ cause to be acceptable or pleasing: *this recording has a lot to commend it.* **2** (**commend someone/something to**) entrust someone or something to: *I commend them to your care.*

com·mend·a·ble /kəˈmendəbəl/ ▸*adj.* deserving praise: *commendable restraint.* **—com·mend·a·bly** /-blē/ *adv.*

com·men·da·tion /ˌkämənˈdāSHən; -ˌen-/ ▸*n.* praise: *the film deserved the highest commendation* | *commendations for their kindness.* ■ an award involving special praise: *the detectives received commendations for bravery.*

com·men·sal /kəˈmensəl/ ▸*adj. Biol.* of, relating to, or exhibiting commensalism. ▸*n. Biol.* a commensal organism, such as many bacteria. **—com·men·sal·i·ty** /ˌkämənˈsalitē/ *n.*

com·men·sal·ism /kəˈmensəˌlizəm/ ▸*n. Biol.* an association between two organisms in which one benefits and the other derives neither benefit nor harm.

com·men·su·ra·ble /kəˈmensərəbəl; kəˈmensHərəbəl/ ▸*adj.* **1** measurable by the same standard: *the finite is not commensurable with the infinite.* **2** (**commensurable to**) *rare* proportionate to. **—com·men·su·ra·bil·i·ty** /kəˌmensərəˈbilitē; -ˌmensHə-/ *n.* **—com·men·su·ra·bly** /-blē/ *adv.*

com·men·su·rate /kəˈmensərət; -ˈmensHə-/ ▸*adj.* corresponding in size or degree; in proportion: *salary will be commensurate with experience.* **—com·men·su·rate·ly** *adv.*

com·ment /ˈkämˌent/ ▸*n.* a remark expressing an opinion or reaction. ■ discussion, esp. of a critical nature, of an issue or event: *the plans were sent to the council for comment.* ■ an indirect expression of the views of the creator of an artistic work: *their second single is a comment on commercialism.* ■ an explanatory note in a book or other written text. ■ *archaic* a written explanation or commentary. ■ *Comput.* a piece of specially tagged text placed within a program to help other users to understand it, which the computer ignores when running the program.

▸*v.* [*tr.*] express (an opinion or reaction): *the review commented that the book was agreeably written* | [*intr.*] *the company would not comment on the venture.* ■ *Comput.* place a piece of specially tagged explanatory text within (a program) to assist other users. ■ *Comput.* turn (part of a program) into a comment so that the computer ignores it when running the program. ▷late Middle English (in the senses 'expository treatise' and 'explanatory note'): from Latin *commentum* 'contrivance' (in late Latin also 'interpretation'), neuter past participle of *comminisci* 'devise.' **—com·ment·er** *n.*

▸ □ **no comment** used in refusing to answer a question, esp. in a sensitive situation.

com·men·tar·y /ˈkämənˌterē/ ▸*n.* (*pl.* **-tar·ies**) the expression of opinions or explanations about an event or situation: *narrative overlaid with commentary.* ■ opinion, either written or spoken. ■ a descriptive spoken account (esp. on radio or television) of an event or a performance as it happens. ■ a set of explanatory or critical notes on a text.

com·men·ta·tor /ˈkämənˌtātər/ ▸*n.* a person who comments on events, esp. on television or radio. ■ a person who writes a commentary on a text.

com·merce /ˈkämərs/ (abbr.: **comm.**) ▸*n.* **1** the activity of buying and selling, esp. on a large scale: *the possible increase of commerce by a great railroad.* **2** *dated* social dealings between people: *outside the normal commerce of civilized life.* **3** *archaic* sexual intercourse.

com·mer·cial /kəˈmərSHəl/ (abbr.: **comm.**) ▸*adj.* **1** concerned with or engaged in commerce: *a commercial agreement.* **2** making or intended to make a profit: *commercial products.* ■ having profit, rather than artistic or other value, as a primary aim. **3** (of television or radio) funded by the revenue from broadcast advertisements. **4** (of chemicals) supplied in bulk and not of the highest purity.

▸*n.* a television or radio advertisement. **—com·mer·ci·al·i·ty** /kəˌmərSHēˈalitē/ *n.* **—com·mer·cial·ly** *adv.*

com·mer·cial·ism /kəˈmərSHəˌlizəm/ ▸*n.* emphasis on the maximizing of profit. ■ *derog.* practices and attitudes that are concerned with the making of profit at the expense of quality.

com·mer·cial·ize /kəˈmərSHəˌlīz/ ▸*v.* [*tr.*] (usu. **be commercialized**) make (an organization or activity) commercial: *the museum has been commercialized.* ■ exploit or spoil for the purpose of gaining profit. **—com·mer·cial·i·za·tion** /kəˌmərSHələˈzāSHən/ *n.*

com·mer·cial space ▸*n.* see SPACE (sense 1).

com·mie /ˈkämē/ (also **Com·mie**) *inf., derog.* ▸*n.* (*pl.* **-mies**) a communist. ▸*adj.* communist.

com·mi·na·to·ry /ˈkämənəˌtôrē; kəˈminə-/ ▸*adj.* threatening, punitive, or vengeful.

com·min·gle /kəˈmiNGgəl; kä-/ ▸*v.* mix; blend: [*intr.*] *the dust had commingled with the rain* | [*tr.*] *publicly reproved for commingling funds.*

com·mi·nut·ed /ˈkäməˌn(y)ootəd/ ▸*adj. technical* reduced to minute particles or fragments. ■ *Med.* (of a fracture) producing multiple bone splinters.

com·mis·er·ate /kəˈmizəˌrāt/ ▸*v.* [*intr.*] express or feel sympathy or pity; sympathize: *she went over to commiserate with Rose on her unfortunate circumstances.* ■ [*tr.*] *archaic* feel, show, or express pity for (someone). **—com·mis·er·a·tion** /kəˌmizəˈrāSHən/ *n.* **—com·mis·er·a·tive** /-rətiv/ *adj.*

com·mis·sar·y /ˈkäməˌserē/ ▸*n.* (*pl.* **-sar·ies**) **1** a restaurant in a movie studio, military base, prison, or other institution. ■ a store that sells food and drink to members of an organization, esp. a large grocery store on a military base. **2** a deputy or delegate. **—com·mis·sar·i·al** /ˌkäməˈse(ə)rēəl/ *adj.*

com·mis·sion /kəˈmiSHən/ (abbr.: **comm.**) ▸*n.* **1** the authority to perform a task or certain duties. ■ an instruction, command, or duty given to a person or group of people: *his commission to redesign the building.* ■ an order for something, esp. a work of art, to be produced: *Mozart at last received a commission to write an opera.* ■ a work produced

---

in response to such an order. **2** a group of people officially charged with a particular function: *the United Nations High Commission for Refugees.* **3** an amount of money, typically a set percentage of the value involved, paid to an agent in a commercial transaction: *foreign banks may charge a commission.* **4** a warrant conferring the rank of officer in an army, navy, or air force: *he has resigned his commission.* **5** the action of committing a crime or offense.

▶ *v.* [*tr.*] **1** give an order for or authorize the production of (something such as a building, piece of equipment, or work of art). ■ order or authorize (a person or organization) to do or produce something: *they commissioned an architect to manage the building project.* ■ give (an artist) an order for a piece of work. **2** bring (something newly produced, such as a factory or machine) into working condition. ■ bring (a warship) into readiness for active service. **3** (usu. **be commissioned**) appoint (someone) to the rank of officer in the armed services: [as *adj.*] (**commissioned**) *a commissioned officer.* —**com·mis·sion·a·ble** *adj.*

▶ □ **in commission** (of a ship, vehicle, machine, etc.) in use or in service. □ **out of commission** not in service; not in working order. ■ (of a person) unable to work or function normally, esp. through illness or injury.

com·mis·sion·er /kəˈmiSH(ə)nər/ (abbr.: **comm.**) ▶ *n.* a person appointed by a commission to perform a specific task: *the traffic commissioner.* ■ a person appointed as a member of a government commission: *the New York State Health Commissioner.* ■ a person appointed to regulate a particular sport: *the baseball commissioner.* ■ a representative of the supreme authority in an area. —**com·mis·sion·er·ship** /-ˌSHip/ *n.*

com·mit /kəˈmit/ ▶ *v.* (**-mit·ted, -mit·ting**) [*tr.*] **1** carry out or perpetrate (a mistake, crime, or immoral act). **2** pledge or bind (a person or an organization) to a certain course or policy: *they were reluctant to commit themselves to an opinion.* ■ pledge or set aside (resources) for future use: *manufacturers will have to commit substantial funds to developing new engines.* ■ (**be committed to**) be in a long-term emotional relationship with (someone). ■ (**be committed to**) be dedicated to (something): *it is a modern Marxist party committed to democratic socialism.* **3** send, entrust, or consign, in particular: ■ consign (someone) officially to prison, esp. on remand. ■ send (a person or case) for trial. ■ send (someone) to be confined in a psychiatric hospital. ■ (**commit something to**) transfer something to (a state or place): *he composed a letter but didn't commit it to paper.* ■ refer (a legislative bill) to a committee. —**com·mit·ta·ble** *adj.* —**com·mit·ter** *n.*

com·mit·ment /kəˈmitmənt/ ▶ *n.* **1** the act of committing or the state of being committed. ■ dedication; application. ■ a pledge or undertaking: *I cannot make such a commitment at the moment.* ■ an act of pledging or setting aside something: *there must be a major commitment of money and time.* **2** (usu. **commitments**) an engagement or obligation that restricts freedom of action: *business commitments.*

com·mit·tal /kəˈmitl/ ▶ *n.* **1** the action of sending a person to an institution, esp. prison or a psychiatric hospital. **2** the burial of a corpse.

com·mit·tee /kəˈmitē/ ▶ *n.* [treated as *sing.* or *pl.*] a group of people appointed for a specific function, typically consisting of members of a larger group: *the housing committee* | [as *adj.*] *a committee meeting.* ■ such a body appointed by a legislature to consider the details of proposed legislation: *there was much scrutiny in committee.*

com·mode /kəˈmōd/ ▶ *n.* **1** a piece of furniture containing a concealed chamber pot. ■ a toilet. ■ *hist.* a movable washstand. **2** a chest of drawers or chiffonier of a decorative type popular in the 18th century.

com·mo·di·ous /kəˈmōdēəs/ ▶ *adj.* **1** *formal* (esp. of furniture or a building) roomy and comfortable. **2** *archaic* convenient. —**com·mo·di·ous·ly** *adv.* —**com·mo·di·ous·ness** *n.*

com·mod·i·ty /kəˈmäditē/ ▶ *n.* (*pl.* **-ties**) a raw material or primary agricultural product that can be bought and sold, such as copper or coffee. ■ a useful or valuable thing, such as water or time.

com·mo·dore /ˈkäməˌdôr/ ▶ *n.* a naval officer of high rank, in particular an officer in the U.S. Navy or Coast Guard ranking above captain and below rear admiral. ■ the president of a yacht club. ■ the senior captain of a shipping line.

com·mon /ˈkämən/ ▶ *adj.* (**-mon·er, -mon·est**) **1** occurring, found, or done often; prevalent. ■ (of an animal or plant) found or living in relatively large numbers; not rare. ■ ordinary; of ordinary qualities; without special rank or position: *the dwellings of common people.* ■ (of a quality) of a sort or level to be generally expected: *common decency.* ■ of the most familiar type: *the common or vernacular name.* ■ denoting the most widespread or typical species of an animal or plant: *the common blue spruce.* **2** showing a lack of taste and refinement; vulgar. **3** shared by, coming from, or done by more than one: *problems common to both communities.* ■ belonging to, open to, or affecting the whole of a community or the public: *common land.* ■ *Math.* belonging to two or more quantities. **4** *Gram.* (in Latin and certain other languages) of or

denoting a gender of nouns that are conventionally regarded as masculine or feminine, contrasting with neuter. ■ (in English) denoting a noun that refers to individuals of either sex (e.g., *teacher*). **5** *Prosody* (of a syllable) able to be either short or long.

▶ *n.* a piece of open land for public use, esp. in a village or town. —**com·mon·ly** *adv.* —**com·mon·ness** *n.*

▶ □ **the common good** the benefit or interests of all. □ **common ground** a point or argument accepted by both sides in a dispute. ■ ideas or interests shared by different people: *artists from different cultural backgrounds found common ground.* □ **common knowledge** something known by most people. □ **in common** **1** in joint use or possession; shared: *car engines have nothing in common with aircraft engines.* **2** of joint interest: *the two men had little in common.* □ **in common with** in the same way as: *in common with other officers, I had to undertake guard duties.*

com·mon·al·i·ty /ˌkämənˈalitē/ ▶ *n.* (*pl.* **-ties**) **1** the state of sharing features or attributes: *a commonality of interest.* ■ a shared feature or attribute. **2** (**the commonality**) another term for COMMONALTY.

com·mon·al·ty /ˈkämənltē/ ▶ *n.* [treated as *pl.*] (**the commonalty**) *chiefly hist.* people without special rank or position; common people: *a petition by the earls, barons, and commonalty of the realm.* ■ the general body of a group.

com·mon de·nom·i·na·tor ▶ *n. Math.* a shared multiple of the denominators of several fractions. See also LOWEST COMMON DENOMINATOR. ■ *fig.* a feature shared by all members of a group.

com·mon·er /ˈkämənər/ ▶ *n.* **1** an ordinary person, without rank or title. **2** (at some British universities) an undergraduate who does not have a scholarship.

Com·mon E·ra ▶ *n.* (**the Common Era**) another term for CHRISTIAN ERA.

com·mon law ▶ *n.* the part of English law that is derived from custom and judicial precedent rather than statutes. ■ the body of English law as adopted and modified separately by the different states of the U.S. and by the federal government. Compare with CIVIL LAW. ■ [as *adj.*] denoting a partner in a marriage by common law (which recognized unions created by mutual agreement and public behavior), not by a civil or ecclesiastical ceremony: *a common-law husband.*

com·mon mar·ket ▶ *n.* a group of countries imposing few or no duties on trade with one another and a common tariff on trade with other countries. ■ (**the Common Market**) a name for the European Economic Community or European Union, used esp. in the 1960s and 1970s.

com·mon noun ▶ *n. Gram.* a noun denoting a class of objects or a concept as opposed to a particular individual. Often contrasted with PROPER NOUN.

com·mon·place /ˈkämənˌplās/ ▶ *adj.* not unusual; ordinary: *unemployment was commonplace in his profession.* ■ not interesting or original; trite: *the usual commonplace remarks.*

▶ *n.* **1** a usual or ordinary thing. ■ a trite saying or topic; a platitude. **2** a notable quotation copied into a commonplace book. ▷mid 16th cent. (originally *common place*): translation of Latin *locus communis*, rendering Greek *koinos topos* 'general theme.' —**com·mon·place·ness** *n.*

com·mons /ˈkämənz/ ▶ *pl. n.* **1** a dining hall in a residential school or college. **2** [treated as *sing.*] land or resources belonging to or affecting the whole of a community. ■ a public park of a town or city. **3** (**the Commons**) short for HOUSE OF COMMONS. ■ *hist.* the common people regarded as a part of a political system, esp. in Britain. **4** *archaic* provisions shared in common; rations.

com·mon salt ▶ *n.* see SALT (sense 1).

com·mon sense ▶ *n.* good sense and sound judgment in practical matters: *use your common sense* | [as *adj.*] *a common-sense approach.* —**com·mon·sen·si·cal** /ˌkämənˈsensikəl/ *adj.*

com·mon stock ▶ *pl. n.* (also **com·mon stocks**) shares entitling their holder to dividends that vary in amount and may even be missed, depending on the fortunes of the company. Compare with PREFERRED STOCK.

com·mon·wealth /ˈkämənˌwelTH/ ▶ *n.* **1** an independent country or community, esp. a democratic republic. ■ an aggregate or grouping of countries or other bodies. ■ a community or organization of shared interests in a nonpolitical field: *the Christian commonwealth.* ■ a self-governing unit voluntarily grouped with the U.S., such as Puerto Rico. ■ a formal title of some of the states of the U.S., esp. Kentucky, Massachusetts, Pennsylvania, and Virginia. ■ the title of the federated Australian states. **2** (**the Commonwealth**) (in full **the Commonwealth of Nations**) an international association consisting of the UK together with states that were previously part of the British Empire, and dependencies. **3** (**the commonwealth**) *archaic* the general good.

com·mo·tion /kəˈmōSHən/ ▶ *n.* a state of confused and noisy disturbance: *she was distracted by a commotion across the street.* ■ civil insurrection.

com·mu·nal /kəˈmyōōnl/ ▶adj. **1** shared by all members of a community; for common use. ■ of, relating to, or done by a community. ■ involving the sharing of work and property: *communal living.* **2** (of conflict) between different communities, esp. those having different religions or ethnic origins. —**com·mu·nal·i·ty** /ˌkämyəˈnalitē/ n. —**com·mu·nal·ly** adv.

com·mu·nal·ism /kəˈmyōōnlˌizəm/ ▶n. **1** a principle of political organization based on federated communes. ■ the principle or practice of living together and sharing possessions and responsibilities. **2** allegiance to one's own ethnic group rather than to the wider society. —**com·mu·nal·ist** adj. & n. —**com·mu·nal·is·tic** /kəˌmyōōnlˈistik/ adj.

com·mune1 /ˈkämˌyōōn/ ▶n. **1** a group of people living together and sharing possessions and responsibilities. ■ a communal settlement in a communist country. **2** the smallest French territorial division for administrative purposes. ■ a similar division elsewhere. **3** (**the Commune**) the group that seized the municipal government of Paris in the French Revolution and played a leading part in the Reign of Terror until suppressed in 1794. ■ (also **the Paris Commune**) the municipal government organized on communalistic principles elected in Paris in 1871. It was soon brutally suppressed by government troops.

com·mune2 /kəˈmyōōn/ ▶v. [intr.] **1** (**commune with**) share one's intimate thoughts or feelings with (someone or something), esp. when the exchange is on a spiritual level: *the purpose of praying is to commune with God.* ■ feel in close spiritual contact with: *to commune with nature.* **2** *Christian Church* receive Holy Communion.

com·mu·ni·ca·ble /kəˈmyōōnikəbəl/ ▶adj. able to be communicated to others: *the value of the product must be communicable to the potential consumers.* ■ (of a disease) able to be transmitted from one sufferer to another; contagious or infectious. —**com·mu·ni·ca·bil·i·ty** /kəˌmyōōnikəˈbilitē/ n. —**com·mu·ni·ca·bly** /-blē/ adv.

com·mu·ni·cant /kəˈmyōōnikənt/ ▶n. *Christian Church* a person who receives Holy Communion.

com·mu·ni·cate /kəˈmyōōnəˌkāt/ ▶v. **1** [intr.] share or exchange information, news, or ideas. ■ [tr.] impart or pass on (information, news, or ideas): *he communicated his findings to the inspector.* ■ [tr.] convey or transmit (an emotion or feeling) in a nonverbal way. ■ succeed in conveying one's ideas or in evoking understanding in others: *the ability to communicate.* ■ (of two people) be able to share and understand each other's thoughts and feelings. ■ [tr.] (usu. **be communicated**) pass on (an infectious disease) to another person or animal. ■ [tr.] transmit (heat or motion). ■ [often as adj.] (**communicating**) (of two rooms) have a common connecting door. **2** [intr.] *Christian Church* receive Holy Communion. —**com·mu·ni·ca·tor** /-ˌkātər/ n. —**com·mu·ni·ca·to·ry** /-kəˌtôrē/ adj.

com·mu·ni·ca·tion /kəˌmyōōnəˈkāSHən/ ▶n. **1** the imparting or exchanging of information or news: *direct communication between the two countries will produce greater understanding* | *at the moment I am in communication with London.* ■ a letter or message containing such information or news. ■ the successful conveying or sharing of ideas and feelings: *there was a lack of communication between Pamela and her parents.* ■ social contact. **2** (**communications**) means of connection between people or places, in particular: ■ the means of sending or receiving information, such as telephone lines or computers: *satellite communications* | [as adj.] *a communications network.* ■ the means of traveling or of transporting goods, such as roads or railroads. ■ [treated as sing.] the field of study concerned with the transmission of information by various means. —**com·mu·ni·ca·tion·al** /-ˈkāSHənl/ adj.

com·mu·ni·ca·tive /kəˈmyōōnəˌkātiv; -nikətiv/ ▶adj. ready to talk or impart information. ■ relating to the conveyance or exchange of information: *the communicative process in literary texts.* —**com·mu·ni·ca·tive·ly** adv.

com·mun·ion /kəˈmyōōnyən/ ▶n. **1** the sharing or exchanging of intimate thoughts and feelings, esp. when the exchange is on a mental or spiritual level. ■ common participation in a mental or emotional experience: *festivals where all take part in joyous communion.* **2** (often **Communion** or **Holy Communion**) the service of Christian worship at which bread and wine are consecrated and shared. See **Eucharist.** ■ the consecrated bread and wine so administered and received: *the priests gave him Holy Communion.* ■ reception of the consecrated bread and wine at such a service. **3** a relationship of recognition and acceptance between Christian churches or denominations, or between individual Christians or Christian communities and a church (signified by a willingness to give or receive the Eucharist): *the Eastern Churches are not in communion with Rome.* ■ a group of Christian communities or churches that recognize one another's ministries or that of a central authority: *the Anglican communion.*

com·mu·ni·qué /kəˌmyōōnəˈkā; kəˈmyōōnəˌkā/ (also **com·mu·ni·que**) ▶n. an official announcement or statement, esp. one made to the media.

com·mu·nism /ˈkämyəˌnizəm/ (often **Communism**) ▶n. a political theory derived from Karl Marx, advocating class war and leading to a society in which all property is publicly owned and each person works and is paid according to their abilities and needs. See also **Marxism.** —**com·mu·nist** n. & adj. —**com·mu·nis·tic** /ˌkämyəˈnistik/ adj.

com·mu·ni·tar·i·an·ism /kəˌmyōōniˈte(ə)rēəˌnizəm/ ▶n. a theory or system of social organization based on small self-governing communities. ■ an ideology that emphasizes the responsibility of the individual to the community and the social importance of the family unit. —**com·mu·ni·tar·i·an** adj. & n.

com·mu·ni·ty /kəˈmyōōnitē/ ▶n. (pl. **-ties**) **1** a group of people living together in one place, esp. one practicing common ownership. ■ all the people living in a particular area or place: *local communities.* ■ a particular area or place considered together with its inhabitants: *a rural community.* ■ (**the community**) the people of a district or country considered collectively, esp. in the context of social values and responsibilities; society. ■ [as adj.] denoting a worker or resource designed to serve the people of a particular area: *community health services.* **2** a group of people having a religion, race, profession, or other particular characteristic in common: *the scientific community.* ■ a body of nations or states unified by common interests: [in *names*] *the European Community.* **3** a feeling of fellowship with others, as a result of sharing common attitudes, interests, and goals: *the sense of community that organized religion can provide.* ■ a similarity or identity: *writers who shared a community of interests.* ■ joint ownership or liability: *a commitment to the community of goods.* **4** *Ecol.* a group of interdependent organisms of different species growing or living together in a specified habitat: *communities of insectivorous birds.* ■ a set of species found in the same habitat or ecosystem at the same time.

com·mu·ni·ty cen·ter ▶n. a place where people from a particular community can meet for social, educational, or recreational activities.

com·mu·ni·ty col·lege ▶n. a nonresidential junior college offering courses to people living in a particular area.

com·mu·ni·ty serv·ice ▶n. voluntary work intended to help people in a particular area. ■ *Law* unpaid work, intended to be of social use, that an offender is required to do instead of going to prison.

com·mu·ni·ver·si·ty /kəˌmyōōnəˈvərsitē/ ▶n. an organization representing a liaison between a college or university and the community where it is located: *a communiversity theater.*

com·mut·a·ble /kəˈmyōōtəbəl/ ▶adj. **1** (of a place or home) sufficiently close to one's place of work that one can travel between the two on a regular basis. ■ (of a distance) sufficiently short that it can be traveled on a regular basis. **2** *rare* capable of being exchanged or converted. —**com·mut·a·bil·i·ty** /kəˌmyōōtəˈbilitē/ n.

com·mu·ta·tion /ˌkämyəˈtāSHən/ ▶n. action or the process of commuting a judicial sentence. ■ the conversion of a legal obligation or entitlement into another form, e.g., the replacement of an annuity or series of payments by a single payment.

com·mu·ta·tive /ˈkämyəˌtātiv; kəˈmyōōtətiv/ ▶adj. *Math.* involving the condition that a group of quantities connected by operators gives the same result whatever the order of the quantities involved, e.g., $a \times b = b \times a$.

com·mu·ta·tor /ˈkämyəˌtātər/ ▶n. an attachment, connected to the armature of a motor or generator, through which electrical connection is made and which ensures that the current flows as direct current.

com·mute /kəˈmyōōt/ ▶v. **1** [intr.] travel some distance between one's home and place of work on a regular basis: *she commuted from Westport in to Grand Central Station.* **2** [tr.] reduce (a judicial sentence, esp. a sentence of death) to one less severe. ■ (**commute something for/into**) change one kind of payment or obligation for (another). ■ replace (an annuity or other series of payments) with a single payment. ▶n. a regular journey of some distance to and from one's place of work. —**com·mut·er** n.

co·mor·bid·i·ty /ˌkōmôrˈbiditē/ ▶n. the simultaneous presence of two chronic diseases or conditions in a patient.

comp /kämp/ inf. ▶n. short for: ■ a composition. ■ a complimentary ticket or voucher. ■ compensation. ■ a musical accompaniment. ■ a comprehensive examination. ▶v. [tr.] **1** play (music) as an accompaniment, esp. in jazz or blues: *if someone is comping chord changes, there are more textured harmonies* | [intr.]

Pronunciation Key ə *ago*, *up*; ər *over*, *fur*; a *hat*; ā *ate*; ä *car*; CH *chin*; e *let*; ē *see*; e(ə)r *air*; i *fit*; ī *by*; i(ə)r *ear*; NG *sing*; ō *go*; ô *law*, *for*; oi *toy*; ŏŏ *good*; ōō *goo*; ou *out*; SH *she*; TH *thin*; TH *then*; (h)w *why*; ZH *vision*

he comps with an open, jangly sound. **2** give (something) away free, esp. as part of a promotion. **3** short for COMPOSITE.
▸*adj.* **1** complimentary; free. **2** compensatory: *comp time.*

com·pact[1] ▸*adj.* /kəm'pakt; käm-; 'käm,pakt/ **1** closely and neatly packed together; dense: *a compact cluster of houses.* ■ having all the necessary components or features neatly fitted into a small space: *a compact car.* ■ (of a person or animal) small, solid, and well-proportioned. ■ (of speech or writing) concise in expression. **2** (**compact of**) *archaic* composed or made up of.
▸*v.* /kəm'pakt; käm-/ [*tr.*] (often **be compacted**) exert force on (something) to make it more dense; compress: *the soil may be compacted by iron oxide.* ■ [*intr.*] (of a substance) become compressed in this way: *the snow hardened and compacted.* ■ *archaic* form (something) by pressing its component parts firmly together. ■ express in fewer words; condense: *the ideas are compacted into two sentences.*
▸*n.* /'käm,pakt/ **1** a small flat case containing face powder, a mirror, and a powder puff. **2** something that is a small and conveniently shaped example of its kind, in particular: ■ short for COMPACT CAR. —**com·pac·tion** /kəm'pakshən/ *n.* —**com·pact·ly** *adv.* —**com·pact·ness** *n.* —**com·pac·tor** /kəm'paktər; käm-; 'käm,paktər/ (also **com·pact·er**) *n.*

com·pact[2] ▸*n.* /'käm,pakt/ a formal agreement or contract between two or more parties.
▸*v.* /kəm'pakt; käm-/ [*tr.*] make or enter into (a formal agreement) with another party or parties: *the Democratic Party compacted an alliance with dissident groups.*

com·pact car ▸*n.* a medium-sized car.

com·pact disc (also **com·pact disk**) (abbr.: **CD**) ▸*n.* a small plastic disc on which music or other digital information is stored, and from which the information can be read using reflected laser light. See also **CD-ROM**.

com·pan·ion[1] /kəm'panyən/ ▸*n.* **1** a person or animal with whom one spends a lot of time or with whom one travels. ■ a person who shares the experiences of another, esp. when these are unpleasant or unwelcome: *my companions in misfortune.* ■ a person with similar tastes and interests to one's own, with whom one has a friendly relationship: *drinking companions.* ■ a person's long-term sexual partner outside marriage. ■ a person, esp. an unmarried or widowed woman, employed to live with and assist another. ■ *Astron.* a star, galaxy, or other celestial object that is close to or associated with another. **2** one of a pair of things intended to complement or match each other: [as *adj.*] *a companion volume.* ■ [usu. in *names*] a book that provides information about a particular subject: *the Oxford Companion to English Literature.* ■ *chiefly Brit., dated* a piece of equipment containing objects used in a particular activity: *a traveler's companion.* **3** (**Companion**) a member of the lowest grade of certain orders of knighthood.
▸*v.* [*tr.*] *formal* accompany: *he is companioned by a pageboy.*

com·pan·ion[2] ▸*n.* *Naut.* a covering over the hatchway leading below decks.

com·pan·ion·a·ble /kəm'panyənəbəl/ ▸*adj.* (of a person) friendly and sociable: *a companionable young man.* ■ (of a shared situation) relaxed and pleasant: *they walked in companionable silence.* —**com·pan·ion·a·ble·ness** *n.* —**com·pan·ion·a·bly** /-blē/ *adv.*

com·pan·ion·ate /kəm'panyənət/ ▸*adj.* *formal* (of a marriage or relationship) between partners or spouses as equal companions. ■ (of a person) acting as a companion.

com·pan·ion·ship /kəm'panyən,SHip/ ▸*n.* a feeling of fellowship or friendship.

com·pan·ion·way /kəm'panyən,wā/ ▸*n.* a set of steps leading from a ship's deck down to a cabin or lower deck.

com·pa·ny /'kəmpənē/ ▸*n.* (*pl.* **-nies**) **1** a commercial business. **2** the fact or condition of being with another or others, esp. in a way that provides friendship and enjoyment: *I could do with some company.* ■ a person or people seen as a source of such friendship and enjoyment: *she is excellent company.* ■ the person or group of people whose society someone is currently sharing: *he was silent among such distinguished company.* ■ a visiting person or group of people: *I'm expecting company.* **3** a number of individuals gathered together, esp. for a particular purpose. ■ a body of soldiers, esp. the smallest subdivision of an infantry battalion, typically commanded by a major or captain. ■ a group of actors, singers, or dancers who perform together.
▸*v.* (**-nies**, **-nied**) [*intr.*] (**company with**) *poetic/lit.* associate with; keep company with. ■ [*tr.*] *archaic* accompany (someone).
▸ □ **be in good company** be in the same situation as someone important or respected: *if you spot the ghost, you are in good company: King George V saw it too.* □ **in company with** together with. □ **keep someone company** accompany or spend time with someone in order to prevent

them from feeling lonely or bored. ■ engage in the same activity as someone else in order to be sociable: *I'll have a drink myself, just to keep you company.* □ **keep company with** associate with habitually. ■ have a social or romantic relationship with; date.

com·pa·ra·ble /'kämp(ə)rəbəl/ ▸*adj.* (of a person or thing) able to be likened to another; similar: *bone tools* **comparable to** *Neanderthal man's tools.* ■ of equivalent quality; worthy of comparison: *no one is comparable with this athlete.* —**com·pa·ra·bil·i·ty** /,kämp(ə)rə'bilitē/ *n.* —**com·par·a·bly** *adv.*

com·par·a·tive /kəm'parətiv/ ▸*adj.* **1** perceptible by comparison; relative: *he returned to the comparative comfort of his own home.* **2** of or involving comparison between two or more branches of science or subjects of study: *comparative religion.* **3** *Gram.* (of an adjective or adverb) expressing a higher degree of a quality, but not the highest possible (e.g., *braver; more fiercely*). Contrasted with SUPERLATIVE. ■ (of a clause) involving comparison (e.g., *their memory is not as good as it used to be*).
▸*n.* *Gram.* a comparative adjective or adverb. ■ (**the comparative**) the middle degree of comparison. —**com·par·a·tive·ly** *adv.*

com·pare /kəm'pe(ə)r/ ▸*v.* [*tr.*] **1** estimate, measure, or note the similarity or dissimilarity between: *individual schools* **compared** *their facilities* **with** *those of others in the area.* ■ (**compare something to**) point out the resemblances to; liken to: *her novel was compared to the work of Daniel Defoe.* ■ (**compare something to**) draw an analogy between one thing and (another) for the purposes of explanation or clarification: *he compared the religions to different paths toward the peak of the same mountain.* ■ [*intr.*] have a specified relationship with another thing or person in terms of nature or quality: *salaries* **compare** *favorably* **with** *those of other professions.* ■ [*intr.*] be of an equal or similar nature or quality: *sales cannot* **compare with** *the glory days of 1989.* **2** (usu. **be compared**) *Gram.* form the comparative and superlative degrees of (an adjective or an adverb): *words of one syllable are usually compared by "-er" and "-est."*
▸ □ **beyond** (or **without**) **compare** of a quality or nature surpassing all others of the same kind: *a diamond beyond compare.* □ **compare notes** (of two or more people) exchange ideas, opinions, or information about a particular subject.

com·par·i·son /kəm'parəsən/ ▸*n.* **1** the act or instance of comparing: *the two books invite comparison with one another.* ■ an analogy. ■ the quality of being similar or equivalent: *if you want a thrill, there's no comparison to climbing.* **2** *Gram.* the formation of the comparative and superlative forms of adjectives and adverbs.
▸ □ **by/in comparison** when compared: *computer-based communication is extremely fast* **in comparison** *with telephone or postal services.*

com·part·ment /kəm'pärtmənt/ ▸*n.* a separate section or part of something, in particular: ■ a division of a railroad car marked by partitions: *a first-class compartment.* ■ a section of a container in which certain items can be kept separate from others: *the freezer compartment.* ■ a watertight section of a ship: *the cargo compartment.* ■ *fig.* an area in which something can be considered in isolation from other things: *religion and politics should be kept in different compartments.*
▸*v.* [*tr.*] (usu. **be compartmented**) divide (something) into separate parts or sections. —**com·part·men·ta·tion** /kəm,pärt,men'tāshən; -mən-/ *n.*

com·part·men·tal /kəm,pärt'mentl/ ▸*adj.* characterized by division into separate sections. —**com·art·men·tal·ly** *adv.*

com·part·men·tal·ize /kəm,pärt'mentl,īz/ ▸*v.* [*tr.*] divide into sections or categories: *he had the ability to compartmentalize his life.* —**com·part·men·tal·ism** /-,izəm/ *n.* —**com·part·men·tal·i·za·tion** /kəm,pärt,mentl-ə-'zāshən/ *n.*

com·pass /'kəmpəs/ ▸*n.* **1** (also **magnetic compass**) an instrument containing a magnetized pointer that shows the direction of magnetic north and bearings from it. **2** (also **pair of compasses**) an

pair of   magnetic
compasses   compass

compasses

instrument for drawing circles and arcs and measuring distances between points, consisting of two arms linked by a movable joint, one arm ending in a point and the other usually carrying a pencil or pen. **3** the range or scope of something: *the event had repercussions that are beyond the compass of this book.* ■ the enclosing limits of an area: *this region had within its compass many types of agriculture.* ■ the range of notes that can be produced by a voice or a musical instrument.
▸*v.* [*tr.*] *archaic* **1** go around (something) in a circular course. ■ surround or enclose on all sides. **2** contrive to accomplish (something): *he compassed his end only by the exercise of violence.* ▷Middle English: from Old French *compas* (noun), *compasser* (verb), based on Latin *com-* 'together' + *passus* 'a step or pace.' Several senses ('measure,' 'artifice,' 'circumscribed area,' and 'pair of compasses') that appeared in Middle English are also found in Old French, but their development and origin are uncertain. The transference of sense to the magnetic compass is held to have occurred in the related Italian word *compasso*, from the circular shape of the compass box.
com·pass card ▸*n.* a circular rotating card showing the 32 principal bearings, forming the indicator of a magnetic compass.
com·pas·sion /kəmˈpasHən/ ▸*n.* sympathetic pity and concern for the sufferings or misfortunes of others: *victims treated with compassion.*
com·pas·sion·ate /kəmˈpasHənət/ ▸*adj.* feeling or showing sympathy and concern for others. —**com·pas·sion·ate·ly** *adv.*
com·pat·i·ble /kəmˈpatəbəl/ ▸*adj.* (of two things) able to exist or occur together without conflict: *the fruitiness of Beaujolais is compatible with a number of meat dishes.* ■ (of two people) able to have a harmonious relationship: *well-suited.* ■ (of one thing) consistent with another: *the symptoms were compatible with gastritis.* ■ (of a computer, a piece of software, or other device) able to be used with a specified piece of equipment or software without special adaptation or modification.
▸*n.* a computer that can use software designed for another make or type. —**com·pat·i·bil·i·ty** /kəmˌpatəˈbilitē/ *n.* —**com·pat·i·bly** /-blē/ *adv.*
com·pa·tri·ot /kəmˈpātrēət/ ▸*n.* a fellow citizen or national of a country.
com·pel /kəmˈpel/ ▸*v.* (**-pelled, -pel·ling**) [*tr.*] force or oblige (someone) to do something: *a sense of duty compelled Harry to answer her questions.* ■ bring about (something) by the use of force or pressure: *they may compel a witness's attendance at court.* ■ *poetic/lit.* drive forcibly.
com·pen·di·ous /kəmˈpendēəs/ ▸*adj.* *formal* containing or presenting the essential facts of something in a comprehensive but concise way. —**com·pen·di·ous·ly** *adv.* —**com·pen·di·ous·ness** *n.*
com·pen·di·um /kəmˈpendēəm/ ▸*n.* (*pl.* **-di·ums** or **-di·a** /-dēə/) a collection of concise but detailed information about a particular subject, esp. in a book or other publication. ■ a collection of things, esp. one systematically gathered: *the program is a compendium from our archives.*
com·pen·sate /ˈkämpənˌsāt/ ▸*v.* **1** [*tr.*] recompense (someone) for loss, suffering, or injury, typically by the award of a sum of money: *payments were made to farmers to compensate them for cuts in subsidies.* ■ pay (someone) for work performed: *he will be richly compensated for his efforts.* **2** [*intr.*] (**compensate for**) make up for (something unwelcome or unpleasant) by exerting an opposite force or effect: *officials have boosted levies to compensate for huge deficits.* ■ act to neutralize or correct (a deficiency or abnormality in a physical property or effect): *the output voltage rises, compensating for the original fall.* ■ *Psychol.* attempt to conceal or offset (a disability or frustration) by development in another direction: *they identified with radical movements to compensate for their inability to relate to individual human beings.* —**com·pen·sa·tive** /kəmˈpensətiv; ˈkämpənˌsātiv/ *adj.* —**com·pen·sa·tor** /-ˌsātər/ *n.*
com·pen·sa·tion /ˌkämpənˈsāsHən/ ▸*n.* something, typically money, awarded to someone as a recompense for loss, injury, or suffering: *seeking compensation for injuries suffered at work* | [as *adj.*] *a compensation claim.* ■ the action or process of making such an award: *the compensation of victims.* ■ the money received by an employee from an employer as a salary or wages. ■ something that counterbalances or makes up for an undesirable or unwelcome state of affairs: *getting older has some compensations.* ■ *Psychol.* the process of concealing or offsetting a psychological difficulty by developing in another direction. —**com·pen·sa·tion·al** /-sHənl/ *adj.*
com·pen·sa·to·ry /kəmˈpensəˌtôrē/ ▸*adj.* providing, effecting, or aiming at compensation, in particular: ■ (of a payment) intended to recompense someone who has experienced loss, suffering, or injury. ■ reducing or offsetting the unpleasant or unwelcome effects of something.
com·pete /kəmˈpēt/ ▸*v.* [*intr.*] strive to gain or win something by defeating or establishing superiority over others who are trying to do the same: *universities are competing for applicants.* ■ take part in a contest.
com·pe·tence /ˈkämpətəns/ (also **com·pe·ten·cy** /-tənsē/) ▸*n.* **1** the

ability to do something successfully or efficiently. ■ the scope of a person's or group's knowledge or ability. ■ a skill or ability. ■ the legal authority of a court or other body to deal with a particular matter. ■ the ability of a criminal defendant to stand trial, as gauged by their mental ability to understand the proceedings and to assist defense lawyers. ■ (also **linguistic** or **language competence**) *Linguistics* a speaker's subconscious, intuitive knowledge of the rules of their language. **2** *dated* an income large enough to live on, typically unearned.
com·pe·tent /ˈkämpətənt/ ▸*adj.* having the necessary ability, knowledge, or skill to do something successfully. ■ (of a person) efficient and capable: *an infinitely competent mother of three.* ■ acceptable and satisfactory, though not outstanding: *she spoke quite competent French.* ■ (chiefly of a court or other body) accepted as having legal authority to deal with a particular matter. ■ (of a criminal defendant) able to understand the charges and to aid in defending themselves. ■ *Biol. & Med.* capable of performing the normal function effectively. —**com·pe·tent·ly** *adv.*
com·pe·ti·tion /ˌkämpəˈtisHən/ ▸*n.* the activity or condition of competing: *an event or contest in which people compete: a beauty competition.* ■ the action of participating in such an event or contest: *in the heat of competition.* ■ the person or people with whom one is competing, esp. in a commercial or sporting arena; the opposition: *I walked around to check out the competition.* ■ *Ecol.* interaction between organisms, populations, or species, in which birth, growth and death depend on gaining a share of a limited environmental resource.
com·pet·i·tive /kəmˈpetətiv/ ▸*adj.* **1** of, relating to, or characterized by competition. ■ having or displaying a strong desire to be more successful than others. **2** as good as or better than others of a comparable nature: *a car industry competitive with any in the world.* ■ (of prices) low enough to compare well with those of rival merchants. —**com·pet·i·tive·ly** *adv.* —**com·pet·i·tive·ness** *n.*
com·pet·i·tor /kəmˈpetətər/ ▸*n.* an organization or country that is engaged in commercial or economic competition with others: *our main industrial competitors.* ■ a person who takes part in an athletic contest.
com·pi·la·tion /ˌkämpəˈlāsHən/ ▸*n.* **1** the action or process of producing something, esp. a list, book, or report, by assembling information collected from other sources. **2** a thing, esp. a book, record, or broadcast program, that is put together by assembling previously separate items.
com·pile /kəmˈpīl/ ▸*v.* [*tr.*] **1** produce (something, esp. a list, report, or book) by assembling information collected from other sources: *the local authority must compile a list of taxpayers.* ■ collect (information) in order to produce something. ■ accumulate (a specified score): *the 49ers have compiled a league-leading 14–2 record.* **2** *Comput.* (of a computer) convert (a program) into a machine-code or lower-level form in which the program can be executed. —**com·pil·er** *n.*
com·pla·cent /kəmˈplāsənt/ ▸*adj.* showing smug or uncritical satisfaction with oneself or one's achievements. —**com·pla·cen·cy** *n.* —**com·pla·cent·ly** *adv.*
com·plain /kəmˈplān/ ▸*v.* [*tr.*] express dissatisfaction or annoyance about a state of affairs or an event: *local authorities complained that they lacked sufficient resources* | [*intr.*] *we all complained about the food.* ■ [*intr.*] (**complain of**) state that one is suffering from (a pain or other symptom of illness): *complaining of headaches.* ■ [*intr.*] state a grievance: *they complained to the French government.* ■ [*intr.*] *poetic/lit.* make a mournful sound. ■ [*intr.*] (of a structure or mechanism) groan or creak under strain. —**com·plain·er** *n.* —**com·plain·ing·ly** *adv.*
com·plain·ant /kəmˈplānənt/ ▸*n.* *Law* a plaintiff in certain lawsuits.
com·plaint /kəmˈplānt/ ▸*n.* **1** a statement that a situation is unsatisfactory or unacceptable. ■ a reason for dissatisfaction: *I have no complaints about the hotel.* ■ the expression of dissatisfaction: *a letter of complaint.* ■ *Law* the plaintiff's reasons for proceeding in a civil action. **2** an illness or medical condition, esp. a relatively minor one: *she is receiving treatment for her skin complaint.*
com·plai·sant /kəmˈplāsənt/ ▸*adj.* willing to please others; obliging. —**com·plai·sance** *n.* —**com·plai·sant·ly** *adv.*
com·pleat /kəmˈplēt/ ▸*adj. & v.* archaic spelling of COMPLETE.
com·ple·ment ▸*n.* /ˈkämpləmənt/ **1** a thing that completes or brings to perfection: *the libretto proved a perfect complement to the music.* **2** a number or quantity of something required to make a group complete: *we have a full complement of staff.* ■ the number of people required to crew a ship: *almost half the ship's complement of 322 were wounded.* ■ *Geom.* the amount in degrees by which a given angle is less than 90°. ■ *Math.* the members of a set that are not members of a given subset. **3** *Gram.* one

or more words, phrases, or clauses governed by a verb (or by a nominalization or a predicative adjective) that complete the meaning of the predicate. ■ (in systemic grammar) an adjective or noun that has the same reference as either the subject (as *mad* in *he is mad*) or the object (as *mad* in *he drove her mad*). **4** *Physiol.* a group of proteins present in blood plasma and tissue fluid that combine with an antigen–antibody complex to bring about the lysis of foreign cells.

▶*v.* /-,ment; -mənt/ [*tr.*] add to (something) in a way that enhances or improves it; make perfect: *a classic blazer complements a look that's stylish or casual.* ■ add to or make complete. —**com·ple·men·tal** /,kämplə'mentl/ *adj.*

com·ple·men·tar·i·ty /,kämpləmen'taritē/ ▶*n.* (*pl.* **-ties**) a complementary relationship or situation: *a culture based on the complementarity of men and women.* ■ *Law* the principle that jurisdictions will not overlap in legislation, administration, or prosecution of crime.

com·ple·men·ta·ry /,kämplə'ment(ə)rē/ ▶*adj.* **1** completing; forming a complement: *backyard satellite dishes and the complementary electronic components.* ■ (of two or more different things) combining in such a way as to enhance or emphasize each other's qualities: *three guitarists playing interlocking, complementary parts.* ■ *Biochem.* (of gene sequences, nucleotides, etc.) related by the rules of base pairing. **2** of or relating to complementary medicine. —**com·ple·men·ta·ri·ly** /,kämplə'mentrəlē; -men'terəlē/ *adv.* —**com·ple·men·ta·ri·ness** *n.*

com·ple·men·ta·ry an·gle ▶*n.* either of two angles whose sum is 90°.

com·ple·men·ta·ry med·i·cine ▶*n.* any of a range of medical therapies that fall beyond the scope of scientific medicine but may be used alongside it in the treatment of disease and ill health. Examples include acupuncture and osteopathy. See also **ALTERNATIVE MEDICINE**.

com·plete /kəm'plēt/ ▶*adj.* **1** having all the necessary or appropriate parts: *a complete list of courses offered by the college.* ■ (of all the works of a particular author) collected together in one volume or edition: *the complete works of Shakespeare.* ■ entire; full: *I only managed one complete term at school.* ■ having run its full course; finished: *the restoration of the chapel is complete.* **2** (often used for emphasis) to the greatest extent or degree; total: *a complete ban on smoking | their marriage came as a complete surprise to me.* ■ (also **com·pleat**) *chiefly humorous* skilled at every aspect of a particular activity; consummate: *these articles are for the compleat mathematician.*

▶*v.* [*tr.*] **1** finish making or doing: *he completed his Ph.D. in 1983.* ■ *Football* (esp. of a quarterback) successfully throw (a forward pass) to a receiver. **2** make (something) whole or perfect: *he only needed one thing to complete his happiness.* ■ write the required information on (a form or questionnaire). —**com·plete·ly** *adv.* —**com·plete·ness** *n.* —**com·plet·er** *n.* —**com·ple·tion** /-'plēsHən/ *n.*

▶ □ **complete with** having something as an additional part or feature.

com·plex ▶*adj.* /käm'pleks; kəm'pleks; 'käm,pleks/ **1** consisting of many different and connected parts: *a complex network.* ■ not easy to analyze or understand; complicated or intricate: *a complex personality.* **2** *Math.* denoting or involving numbers or quantities containing both a real and an imaginary part.

▶*n.* /'käm,pleks/ **1** a group of similar buildings or facilities on the same site: *a new apartment complex.* ■ a group or system of different things that are linked in a close or complicated way; a network: *a complex of mountain roads.* **2** *Psychoanalysis* a related group of emotionally significant ideas that are completely or partly repressed and that cause psychic conflict leading to abnormal mental states or behavior. ■ *inf.* a disproportionate concern or anxiety about something. **3** *Chem.* an ion or molecule in which one or more groups are linked to a metal atom by coordinate bonds. ■ any loosely bonded species formed by the association of two molecules: *cross-linked protein—DNA complexes.*

▶*v.* /käm'pleks; kəm'pleks; 'käm,pleks/ [*tr.*] (usu. **be complexed**) *Chem.* make (an atom or compound) form a complex with another. —**com·plex·i·ty** /kəm'pleksitē/ *n.* —**com·plex·ly** *adv.*

com·plex·ion /kəm'pleksHən/ ▶*n.* **1** the natural color, texture, and appearance of a person's skin, esp. of the face: *an attractive girl with a pale complexion.* **2** the general aspect or character of something: *Congress's new complexion became boldly apparent last summer.* ▷Middle English: via Old French from Latin *complexio(n)-* 'combination' (in late Latin 'physical constitution'), from *complectere* 'embrace, comprise.' The term originally denoted physical constitution or temperament determined by the combination of the four bodily humors, hence sense 1 (late 16th cent.) as a visible sign of this. —**com·plex·ioned** *adj.* [often in *comb.*] *they were both fair-complexioned.*

com·plex sen·tence ▶*n.* *Gram.* a sentence containing a subordinate clause or clauses.

com·pli·ance /kəm'plīəns/ (also **com·pli·an·cy** /-'plīənsē/) ▶*n.* the action

or fact of complying with a wish or command. ■ (**compliance with**) the state or fact of according with or meeting rules or standards: *all imports of timber are in compliance with regulations.* ■ unworthy or excessive acquiescence: *the appalling compliance with government views shown by the commission.*

▶*adj.* undertaken or existing mainly in order to comply with an earlier treaty, order, or law: *WTO compliance legislation that ignores skyrocketing drug costs.*

com·pli·ant /kəm'plīənt/ ▶*adj.* inclined to agree with others or obey rules, esp. to an excessive degree; acquiescent. ■ meeting or in accordance with rules or standards: *the systems are Y2K compliant.* —**com·pli·ant·ly** *adv.*

com·pli·cate /'kämplə,kāt/ ▶*v.* [*tr.*] make (something) more difficult or confusing by causing it to be more complex. ■ *Med.* introduce complications in (an existing condition): *smoking may complicate pregnancy.*

com·pli·ca·tion /,kämplə'kāsHən/ ▶*n.* **1** a circumstance that complicates something; a difficulty. ■ an involved or confused condition or state: *to add further complication, English speakers use a different name.* **2** *Med.* a secondary disease or condition aggravating an already existing one: *she developed complications after the surgery.*

com·plic·i·ty /kəm'plisitē/ ▶*n.* the state of being involved with others in an illegal activity or wrongdoing: *accused of complicity in the attack.*

com·pli·ment ▶*n.* /'kämpləmənt/ a polite expression of praise or admiration: *she paid me an enormous compliment..* ■ an act or circumstance that implies praise or respect: *it's a compliment to the bride to dress up on her special day.* ■ (**compliments**) congratulations or praise expressed to someone: *my compliments on your cooking.* ■ (**compliments**) greetings or regards, esp. when sent as a message.

▶*v.* /'kämplə,ment/ [*tr.*] politely congratulate or praise (someone) for something. ■ praise (something) politely. ■ (**compliment someone with**) *archaic* present someone with (something) as a mark of courtesy.

▶ □ **pay one's compliments** send or express formal greetings. □ **return the compliment** give a compliment in return for another. □ **with someone's compliments** (or **the compliments of**) used to express the fact that what one is giving is free: *all drinks will be supplied with our compliments.*

com·pli·men·ta·ry /,kämplə'mentərē; -'mentrē/ ▶*adj.* **1** expressing a compliment; praising or approving. **2** given or supplied free of charge.

com·pline /'kämplin; -,plīn/ ▶*n.* a service of evening prayers forming part of the Divine Office of the Western Christian Church, traditionally said (or chanted) before retiring for the night.

com·ply /kəm'plī/ ▶*v.* (**-plies, -plied**) [*intr.*] (of a person or group) act in accordance with a wish or command: *we are unable to comply with your request.* ■ (of an article) meet specified standards: *all secondhand furniture must comply with the new standards.*

com·po·nent /kəm'pōnənt/ ▶*n.* a part or element of a larger whole, esp. a part of a machine or vehicle: *stereo components.* ■ *Physics* each of two or more forces, velocities, or other vectors acting in different directions that are together equivalent to a given vector.

▶*adj.* constituting part of a larger whole; constituent.

com·port /kəm'pôrt/ ▶*v.* **1** (**comport oneself**) *formal* conduct oneself; behave. **2** [*intr.*] (**comport with**) accord with; agree with: *the actions that comport with her own liberal views.* —**com·port·ment** *n.*

com·pose /kəm'pōz/ ▶*v.* [*tr.*] **1** write or create (a work of art, esp. music or poetry). ■ write or phrase (a letter or piece of writing) with care and thought: *the first sentence is so hard to compose.* ■ form (a whole) by ordering or arranging the parts, esp. in an artistic way: *compose and draw a still life.* ■ order or arrange (parts) to form a whole, esp. in an artistic way. **2** (usu. **be composed**) (of elements) constitute or make up (a whole): *the system is composed of a group of machines.* ■ be (a specified number or amount) of a whole: *Christians compose 40 percent of the state's population.* **3** calm or settle (oneself or one's features or thoughts): *she tried to compose herself.* **4** prepare (a text) for printing by manually, mechanically, or electronically setting up the letters and other characters in the order to be printed. ■ set up (letters and characters) in this way.

com·pos·er /kəm'pōzər/ ▶*n.* a person who writes music, esp. as a professional occupation.

com·pos·ite /kəm'päzət; käm-/ ▶*adj.* **1** made up of various parts or elements. ■ (esp. of a constructional material) made up of recognizable constituents. ■ *Math.* (of an integer) being the product of two or more factors greater than one; not prime. **2** (**Composite**) relating to or denoting a classical order of architecture consisting of elements of the Ionic and Corinthian orders. **3** *Bot.* relating to or denoting plants of the daisy family.

▶*n.* **1** a thing made up of several parts or elements. ■ a composite

photograph. ■ a composite constructional material. **2** *Bot.* a plant of the daisy family. **3** (**Composite**) the Composite order of architecture.
▶ *v.* [*tr.*] [usu. as *n.*] (**compositing**) combine (two or more images) to make a single picture, esp. electronically: *photographic compositing by computer.* ■ amalgamate (two or more similar resolutions). —**com·pos·ite·ly** *adv.* —**com·pos·ite·ness** *n.*

com·po·si·tion /ˌkämpəˈzishən/ ▶ *n.* **1** the nature of something's ingredients or constituents; the way in which a whole or mixture is made up: *the social composition of villages.* ■ the action of putting things together; formation or construction. ■ a thing composed of various elements. ■ *archaic* mental constitution; character: *persons who have a touch of madness in their composition.* ■ [often as *adj.*] a compound artificial substance, esp. one serving the purpose of a natural one: *composition flooring.* ■ *Linguistics* the formation of words into a compound word. ■ *Math.* the successive application of functions to a variable, the value of the first function being the argument of the second, and so on: *composition of functions, when defined, is associative.* **2** a work of music, literature, or art. ■ the action or art of producing such a work: *the technical aspects of composition.* ■ an essay, esp. one written by a school or college student. ■ the artistic arrangement of the parts of a picture. **3** the preparing of text for printing by setting up the characters in order. —**com·po·si·tion·al** /-SHənl/ *adj.* —**com·po·si·tion·al·ly** /-SHənl-ē/ *adv.*

com·pos·i·tor /kəmˈpäzitər/ ▶ *n. Printing* a person who arranges type for printing or keys text into a composing machine.

com·post /ˈkämˌpōst/ ▶ *n.* decayed organic material used as a plant fertilizer. ■ a mixture of this with loam and/or other ingredients, used as a growing medium.
▶ *v.* [*tr.*] make (vegetable matter or manure) into compost: *don't compost heavily infested plants.* ■ treat (soil) with compost.

com·post heap (also **compost pile**) ▶ *n.* a pile of garden and organic kitchen refuse that decomposes to produce compost.

com·po·sure /kəmˈpōzHər/ ▶ *n.* the state or feeling of being calm and in control of oneself: *she was struggling to regain her composure.*

com·pote /ˈkämˌpōt/ ▶ *n.* **1** fruit preserved or cooked in syrup. ■ a dish consisting of fruit salad or stewed fruit, often with syrup. **2** a bowl-shaped dessert dish with a stem.

com·pound[1] ▶ *n.* /ˈkämˌpound/ a thing that is composed of two or more separate elements; a mixture. ■ (also **chemical compound**) a substance formed from two or more elements chemically united in fixed proportions: *a compound of hydrogen and oxygen.* ■ a word made up of two or more existing words, such as *steamship.*
▶ *adj.* /ˈkämˌpound; kämˈpound; kəmˈpound/ made up or consisting of several parts or elements, in particular: ■ (of a word) made up of two or more existing words or elements: *a compound noun.* ■ (of interest) payable on both capital and the accumulated interest: *compound interest.* ■ *Biol.* (esp. of a leaf, flower, or eye) consisting of two or more simple parts or individuals in combination.
▶ *v.* /kəmˈpound; kämˈpound; ˈkämˌpound/ [*tr.*] **1** (often **be compounded**) make up (a composite whole); constitute: *a dialect compounded of Spanish and Dutch.* ■ mix or combine (ingredients or constituents). ■ calculate (interest) on previously accumulated interest. ■ (of a sum of money invested) increase by compound interest: *let your money compound for five years.* **2** make (something bad) worse; intensify the negative aspects of: *I compounded the problem by trying to make wrong things right.* **3** *Law* forbear from prosecuting (a felony) in exchange for money or other consideration. ■ settle (a debt or other matter) in this way. ▷late Middle English *compoune* (verb), from Old French *compoun,* present tense stem of *compondre,* from Latin *componere* 'put together.' The final -*d* was added in the 16th cent. on the pattern of *expound* and *propound.* —**com·pound·a·ble** /kəmˈpoundəbəl; käm-/ *adj.*

com·pound[2] /ˈkämˌpound/ ▶ *n.* an area enclosed by a fence, in particular: ■ an open area in which a factory or large house stands. ■ an open area in a prison, prison camp, or work camp.

com·pound eye ▶ *n.* an eye consisting of an array of numerous small visual units, as found in insects and crustaceans.

com·pound frac·ture ▶ *n.* an injury in which a broken bone pierces the skin, causing a risk of infection.

com·pound in·ter·val ▶ *n. Mus.* an interval greater than an octave.

com·pound sen·tence ▶ *n.* a sentence with more than one subject or predicate.

com·pre·hend /ˌkämpriˈhend/ ▶ *v.* [*tr.*] **1** grasp mentally; understand: *he couldn't comprehend her reasons for marrying Lovat.* **2** *formal* include, comprise, or encompass. —**com·pre·hend·er** *n.*

com·pre·hen·si·ble /ˌkämpriˈhensəbəl/ ▶ *adj.* able to be understood; intelligible: *clear and comprehensible English.* —**com·pre·hen·si·bil·i·ty** /-ˌhensəˈbilitē/ *n.* —**com·pre·hen·si·bly** /-blē/ *adv.*

com·pre·hen·sion /ˌkämpriˈhenchən/ ▶ *n.* the action or capability of understanding something.

com·pre·hen·sive /ˌkämpriˈhensiv/ ▶ *adj.* **1** complete; including all or nearly all elements or aspects of something: *a comprehensive list of sources.* ■ of large content or scope; wide-ranging: *a comprehensive collection of photographs.* ■ (of automobile insurance) providing coverage for most risks, including damage to the policyholder's own vehicle. ■ (also **comprehensive examination**) an examination testing a student's command of a special field of knowledge. **2** *archaic* of or relating to understanding. —**com·pre·hen·sive·ly** *adv.* —**com·pre·hen·sive·ness** *n.*

com·press ▶ *v.* /kəmˈpres/ [*tr.*] (often **be compressed**) flatten by pressure; squeeze; press. ■ [*intr.*] be squeezed or pressed together or into a smaller space: *the land is sinking as the soil compresses.* ■ squeeze or press (two things) together: *Violet compressed her lips together grimly.* ■ express in a shorter form; abridge. ■ *Comput.* alter the form of (data) to reduce the amount of storage necessary. ■ [as *adj.*] (**compressed**) *chiefly Biol.* having a narrow shape as if flattened, esp. sideways: *most sea snakes have a compressed tail.*
▶ *n.* /ˈkämˌpres/ a pad of absorbent material pressed onto part of the body to relieve inflammation or stop bleeding: *a cold compress.* —**com·press·i·bil·i·ty** /kəmˌpresəˈbilitē/ *n.* —**com·press·i·ble** *adj.* —**com·pres·sive** /-ˈpresiv/ *adj.*

com·pres·sion /kəmˈpreshən/ ▶ *n.* the action of compressing or being compressed. ■ the reduction in volume (causing an increase in pressure) of the fuel mixture in an internal combustion engine before ignition. —**com·pres·sion·al** /-SHənl/ *adj.*

com·pres·sor /kəmˈpresər/ ▶ *n.* an instrument or device for compressing something. ■ a machine used to supply air or other gas at increased pressure, e.g., to power a gas turbine.

com·prise /kəmˈprīz/ ▶ *v.* [*tr.*] consist of; be made up of: *the country comprises twenty states.* ■ make up; constitute: *this single breed comprises 50 percent of the Swiss cattle population* | (**be comprised of**) *documents are comprised of words.*

com·pro·mise /ˈkämprəˌmīz/ ▶ *n.* an agreement or a settlement of a dispute that is reached by each side making concessions. ■ a middle state between conflicting opinions or actions reached by mutual concession or modification: *a compromise between communism and private enterprise.* ■ the acceptance of standards that are lower than is desirable: *sexism should be tackled without compromise.*
▶ *v.* **1** [*intr.*] settle a dispute by mutual concession: *in the end we compromised and deferred the issue.* ■ [*tr.*] *archaic* settle (a dispute) by mutual concession. **2** [*tr.*] weaken (a reputation or principle) by accepting standards that are lower than is desirable: *commercial pressures could compromise safety.* ■ [*intr.*] accept standards that are lower than is desirable: *we were not prepared to compromise on safety.* ■ bring into disrepute or danger by indiscreet, foolish, or reckless behavior: *situations in which his troops could be compromised.* —**com·pro·mis·er** *n.*

comp·trol·ler /kənˈtrōlər; ˌkäm(p)ˈtrōlər; ˈkäm(p)ˌtrōlər/ ▶ *n.* a controller (used in the title of some financial officers).

com·pul·sion /kəmˈpəlshən/ ▶ *n.* **1** the action or state of forcing or being forced to do something; constraint: *the payment was made under compulsion.* **2** an irresistible urge to behave in a certain way, esp. against one's conscious wishes.

com·pul·sive /kəmˈpəlsiv/ ▶ *adj.* **1** resulting from or relating to an irresistible urge, esp. one that is against one's conscious wishes: *compulsive eating.* ■ (of a person) acting as a result of such an urge: *a compulsive liar.* **2** irresistibly interesting or exciting; compelling: *this play is compulsive viewing.* —**com·pul·sive·ly** *adv.* —**com·pul·sive·ness** *n.*

com·pul·so·ry /kəmˈpəlsərē/ ▶ *adj.* required by law or a rule; obligatory: *compulsory military service* | *it was compulsory to attend Mass.* ■ involving or exercising compulsion; coercive: *the abuse of compulsory powers.* —**com·pul·so·ri·ly** /-ˈsərəlē/ *adv.* —**com·pul·so·ri·ness** *n.*

com·punc·tion /kəmˈpəNG(k)shən/ ▶ *n.* a feeling of guilt or moral scruple that follows the doing of something bad: *spend the money without compunction.* ■ a pricking of the conscience: *he had no compunction about behaving blasphemously.* —**com·punc·tion·less** *adj.* —**com·punc·tious** /-SHəs/ *adj.* —**com·punc·tious·ly** /-SHəslē/ *adv.*

com·pu·ta·tion /ˌkämpyōōˈtāshən/ ▶ *n.* the action of mathematical calculation. ■ the use of computers, esp. as a subject of research or study. —**com·pu·ta·tion·al** *adj.*

Pronunciation Key ə *ago,* up; ər *over,* fur; a *hat;* ā *ate;* ä *car;* CH *chin;* e *let;* ē *see;* e(ə)r *air;* i *fit;* ī *by;* i(ə)r *ear;* NG *sing;* ō *go;* ô *law, for;* oi *toy;* ŏŏ *good;* ōō *goo;* ou *out;* SH *she;* TH *thin;* TH *then;* (h)w *why;* ZH *vision*

com·pute /kəmˈpyo͞ot/ ▶v. [tr.] (often **be computed**) calculate or reckon (a figure or amount): *we can compute the exact increase.* ■ [intr.] make a calculation, esp. using a computer. ■ [intr.] inf. seem reasonable; make sense: *the idea that his actions might have serious repercussions just doesn't compute.* —**com·put·a·bil·i·ty** /kəmˌpyo͞otəˈbilitē/ n. —**com·put·a·ble** adj. —**com·put·a·bly** /-blē/ adv. —**com·put·ist** /-ˈpyo͞otist/ n.

com·put·er /kəmˈpyo͞otər/ ▶n. an electronic device for storing and processing data, typically in binary form, according to instructions given to it in a variable program. ■ a person who makes calculations, esp. with a calculating machine.

com·put·er·ize /kəmˈpyo͞otəˌrīz/ ▶v. [tr.] [often as adj.] (**computerized**) convert to a system that is operated or controlled by computer. ■ convert (information) to a form that is stored or processed by computer. —**com·put·er·i·za·tion** /kəmˌpyo͞otərəˈzāSHən/ n.

com·put·er-lit·er·ate ▶adj. (of a person) having sufficient knowledge and skill to be able to use computers; familiar with the operation of computers. —**com·put·er lit·er·a·cy** n.

com·put·er vi·rus ▶n. see VIRUS.

com·rade /ˈkämˌrad; ˈkämrəd/ ▶n. a companion who shares one's activities or is a fellow member of an organization. ■ (also **com·rade-in-arms**) a fellow soldier or serviceman. ■ a fellow socialist or communist (often as a form of address): *Comrade Lenin.* —**com·rade·ly** adj. —**com·rade·ship** /-ˌSHip/ n.

con[1] /kän/ inf. ▶v. (**conned**, **con·ning**) [tr.] persuade (someone) to do or believe something, typically by use of a deception: *she was jailed for conning her aunt out of $500,000.*
▶n. an instance of deceiving or tricking someone: *when depositors, realizing that the whole thing is a con, demand repayment* | [as adj.] *a con artist.*

con[2] ▶n. a disadvantage: *weigh up the pros and cons.*

con[3] ▶n. inf. a convict.

con[4] ▶ variant spelling of CONN.

con[5] ▶v. (**conned**, **con·ning**) [tr.] archaic study attentively or learn by heart (a piece of writing).

con bri·o /kän ˈbrēō; kōn/ ▶adv. Mus. (esp. as a direction) with vigor.

con·cat·e·nate /kənˈkatnˌāt/ ▶v. [tr.] formal or technical link (things) together in a chain or series. —**con·cat·e·na·tion** /kənˌkatnˈāSHən/ n.

con·cave /känˈkāv; ˈkänˌkāv/ ▶adj. having an outline or surface that curves inward like the interior of a circle or sphere. Compare with CONVEX (sense 1). —**con·cave·ly** adv. —**con·cav·i·ty** /känˌkavitē/ n.

con·ceal /kənˈsēl/ ▶v. [tr.] keep from sight; hide: *a line of sand dunes concealed the distant sea.* ■ keep (something) secret; prevent from being known or noticed: *love that they had to conceal from others.* —**con·ceal·a·ble** adj. —**con·ceal·er** n. —**con·ceal·ment** n.

con·cede /kənˈsēd/ ▶v. [tr.] **1** admit that something is true or valid after first denying or resisting it: *that principle now seems to have been conceded.* ■ admit (defeat) in a contest: *he conceded defeat.* ■ [tr.] admit defeat in (a contest). **2** [tr.] surrender or yield (something that one possesses): *to concede all the territory he'd won.* ■ grant (a right, privilege, or demand). ■ (in sports) fail to prevent the scoring of (a goal or point) by an opponent: *the coach conceded three safeties rather than kick into the wind.* ■ allow (a lead or advantage) to slip. ■ [intr.] make a concession: *Zoe conceded with a grin and went with Jay.* —**con·ced·er** n.

con·ceit /kənˈsēt/ ▶n. **1** excessive pride in oneself. **2**. a fanciful expression in writing or speech; an elaborate metaphor: *the idea of the wind's singing is a prime romantic conceit.* ■ an artistic effect or device: *the director's brilliant conceit was to film this tale in black and white.* ■ a fanciful notion: *he is alarmed by the widespread conceit that he spent most of the 1980s drunk.*

con·ceit·ed /kənˈsētid/ ▶adj. excessively proud of oneself; vain. —**con·ceit·ed·ly** adv. —**con·ceit·ed·ness** n.

con·ceiv·a·ble /kənˈsēvəbəl/ ▶adj. capable of being imagined or grasped mentally: *photographed from every conceivable angle.* —**con·ceiv·a·bil·i·ty** /kənˌsēvəˈbilitē/ n. —**con·ceiv·a·bly** adv.

con·ceive /kənˈsēv/ ▶v. [tr.] (often **be conceived**) **1** become pregnant with (a child): *she was conceived when her father was 49.* ■ [intr.] (of a woman) become pregnant: *five months ago Wendy conceived.* **2** form or devise (a plan or idea) in the mind: *the project was originally conceived in 1977* | [as adj.] (**conceived**) *a brilliantly conceived robbery.* ■ form a mental representation of; imagine: *without society an individual cannot be conceived as having rights* | [intr.] *we could not conceive of such things happening to us.* ■ become affected by (a feeling).

con·cen·trate /ˈkänsənˌtrāt/ ▶v. **1** [intr.] focus one's attention or mental effort on a particular object or activity: *she couldn't concentrate on the movie.* ■ (**concentrate on/upon**) do or deal with (one particular thing) above all others: *Luke wants to concentrate on his film career.* **2** [tr.] (often

be concentrated) gather (people or things) together in numbers or in a mass to one point. ■ [intr.] come together in this way: *troops were concentrating at the western front.* ■ increase the strength or proportion of (a substance or solution) by removing or reducing the water or any other diluting agent or by selective accumulation of atoms or molecules.
▶n. a substance made by removing water or other diluting agent; a concentrated form of something, esp. food: *apple juice concentrate.* —**con·cen·tra·tive** /-ˌtrātiv/ adj. —**con·cen·tra·tor** /-ˌtrātər/ n.

con·cen·tra·tion /ˌkänsənˈtrāSHən/ ▶n. **1** the action or power of focusing one's attention or mental effort. ■ (**concentration on/upon**) dealing with one particular thing above all others: *concentration on the needs of the young can mean that the elderly are forgotten.* **2** a close gathering of people or things: *the largest concentration of Canada geese on earth.* ■ the action of gathering together closely: *the concentration of power.* **3** the relative amount of a given substance contained within a solution or in a particular volume of space; the amount of solute per unit volume of solution: *the gas can collect in dangerous concentrations.* ■ the action of strengthening a solution by the removal of water or other diluting agent or by the selective accumulation of atoms or molecules.

con·cen·tra·tion camp ▶n. a place where large numbers of people, esp. political prisoners or members of persecuted minorities, are deliberately imprisoned to provide forced labor or to await mass execution.

con·cen·tric /kənˈsentrik; kän-/ ▶adj. of or denoting circles, arcs, or other shapes that share the same center, the larger often completely surrounding the smaller. —**con·cen·tri·cal·ly** /-(ə)lē/ adv. —**con·cen·tric·i·ty** /ˌkänˌsenˈtrisitē/ n.

con·cept /ˈkänˌsept/ ▶n. an abstract idea; a general notion: *the concept of justice.* ■ a plan or intention; a conception: *the center has kept firmly to its original concept.* ■ an idea or invention to help sell or publicize a commodity: *a new concept in corporate hospitality.* ■ [as adj.] (of a car or other vehicle) produced as an experimental model to test the viability of new design features.

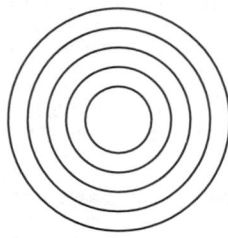

concentric circles

con·cep·tion /kənˈsepSHən/ ▶n. **1** the action of conceiving a child or of a child being conceived: *an unfertilized egg before conception.* ■ the forming or devising of a plan or idea: *the time between a product's conception and its launch.* **2** the way in which something is perceived or regarded: *our conception of how language relates to reality.* ■ a general notion; an abstract idea: *the conception of a balance of power.* ■ a plan or intention: *reconstructing Bach's original conceptions.* ■ understanding; ability to imagine: *he had no conception of politics.* —**con·cep·tion·al** /-SHənl/ adj.

con·cep·tu·al /kənˈsepCHo͞oəl/ ▶adj. of, relating to, or based on mental concepts: *philosophy deals with conceptual difficulties.* —**con·cep·tu·al·ly** adv.

con·cep·tu·al·ize /kənˈsepCHo͞oəˌlīz/ ▶v. [tr.] form a concept or idea of (something): *we can easily conceptualize speed in miles per hour.* —**con·cep·tu·al·i·za·tion** /kənˌsepCHo͞oələˈzāSHən/ n. —**con·cep·tu·al·iz·er** n.

con·cern /kənˈsərn/ ▶v. [tr.] **1** relate to; be about: *the story concerns a friend of mine* (**be concerned with**) *this fable is concerned with forgiveness and redemption.* ■ be relevant or important to; affect or involve: *they should not pry into what does not concern them.* ■ (**be concerned with**) regard it as important or interesting to do something: *I was mainly concerned with making something that children could enjoy.* ■ (**be concerned in**) formal have a specific connection with or responsibility for: *the organs concerned in digestion and in blood-making.* ■ (**concern oneself with**) interest or involve oneself in: *we need not concern ourselves with the semantics of this language.* **2** worry (someone); make anxious: *you must not concern yourself about me.*
▶n. **1** anxiety; worry. ■ a cause of anxiety or worry: *safety concerns.* **2** a matter of interest or importance to someone: *oil reserves are the concern of the Energy Department.* ■ (**concerns**) affairs; issues: *Aboriginal concerns.* **3** a business; a firm.
▶ □ **to whom it may concern** a formula placed at the beginning of a letter or document when the identity of the reader or readers is unknown.

con·cerned /kənˈsərnd/ ▶adj. worried, troubled, or anxious: *the villagers are concerned about burglaries.* —**con·cern·ed·ly** /-ˈsərnədlē/ adv.

con·cern·ing /kənˈsərniNG/ ▶prep. on the subject of or in connection with; about: *dreadful stories concerning a horrible beast.*

con·cert ▶n. /ˈkänˌsərt; ˈkänsərt/ **1** a musical performance given in public, typically by several performers or of several separate compositions: *symphony concerts* | [as adj.] *a concert pianist.* ■ [as adj.] of, relating to, or denoting the performance of music written for opera, ballet, or theater on its own without the accompanying dramatic action: *the concert version of the fourth interlude from the opera.* **2** *formal* agreement, accordance, or harmony.

▶*v.* /kənˈsərt/ [*tr.*] *formal* arrange (something) by mutual agreement or coordination. ▷late 16th cent. (in the sense 'unite, cause to agree'): from French *concerter,* from Italian *concertare* 'harmonize.' The noun use, dating from the early 17th cent. (in the sense 'a combination of voices or sounds'), is from French *concert,* from Italian *concerto,* from *concertare.*

▶ □ **in concert** acting jointly: *he made his decision* **in concert with** *his son.*

con·cert·ed /kənˈsərtəd/ ▶*adj.* **1** jointly arranged, planned, or carried out; coordinated: *determined to begin a concerted action against them.* ■ strenuously carried out; done with great effort: *it would take* **a concerted effort** *for a burglar to break into my home.* **2** (of music) arranged in several parts of equal importance: *concerted secular music for voices.*

con·cert grand ▶*n.* the largest size of grand piano, up to 12 feet (2.75 m) long.

con·cer·ti·na /ˌkänsərˈtēnə/ ▶*n.* a small musical instrument, typically polygonal in shape, played by stretching and squeezing between the hands, to work a central bellows that blows air over reeds, each note being sounded by pushing a button. ■ [as *adj.*] opening or closing in multiple folds: *concertina doors.*

concertina

con·cert·mas·ter /ˈkänsərtˌmastər/ ▶*n.* (*fem.* **con·cert·mis·tress**) the leading first-violin player in some orchestras.

con·cer·to /kənˈCHertō/ ▶*n.* (*pl.* **-tos** or **-ti** /-tē/) a musical composition for a solo instrument or instruments accompanied by an orchestra, esp. one conceived on a relatively large scale.

con·cert pitch ▶*n. Mus.* a standard for the tuning of musical instruments, internationally agreed upon in 1960, in which the note A above middle C has a frequency of 440 Hz. ■ *fig.* a state of readiness, efficiency, and keenness.

con·ces·sion /kənˈseSHən/ ▶*n.* **1** a thing that is granted, esp. in response to demands; a thing conceded. ■ the action of conceding, granting, or yielding something. ■ (**a concession to**) a gesture, esp. a token one, made in recognition of a demand or prevailing standard: *her only concession to fashion was her ornate silver ring.* **2** a preferential allowance or rate given by an organization: *tax concessions.* **3** the right to use land or other property for a specified purpose, granted by a government, company, or other controlling body: *new logging concessions.* ■ a commercial operation within the premises of a larger concern, typically selling refreshments. ■ *Can.* a piece of land into which surveyed land is divided, itself further divided into lots.

con·ces·sive /kənˈsesiv/ ▶*adj.* **1** characterized by, or tending to concession: *we must look for a more concessive approach.* **2** *Gram.* (of a preposition or conjunction) introducing a phrase or clause denoting a circumstance that might be expected to preclude the action of the main clause, but does not (e.g., *in spite of, although*). ■ (of a phrase or clause) introduced by a concessive preposition or conjunction.

conch /käNGk; känCH/ ▶*n.* (*pl.* **conchs** /käNGks/ or **conches** /ˈkänCHiz/) **1** (also **conch shell**) a tropical marine mollusk (*Strombus* and other genera, family Strombidae) with a spiral shell that may bear long projections and have a flared lip. ■ a shell of this kind blown like a trumpet to produce a musical note, often depicted as played by Tritons and other mythological figures. **2** *Archit.* the roof of a semicircular apse, shaped like half a dome.

con·cierge /kônˈsyerZH; ˌkänsēˈerZH/ ▶*n.* **1** (esp. in France) a caretaker of an apartment complex or a small hotel, typically one living on the premises. **2** a hotel employee whose job is to assist guests by arranging tours, making theater and restaurant reservations, etc.

con·cil·i·ate /kənˈsilēˌāt/ ▶*v.* [*tr.*] **1** stop (someone) from being angry or discontented; placate; pacify. ■ [*intr.*] act as a mediator. ■ *formal* reconcile; make compatible: *all complaints about charges will be conciliated if pos-*

sible. **2** *archaic* gain (esteem or goodwill). —**con·cil·i·a·tion** /kənˌsilēˈāSHən/ *n.* —**con·cil·i·a·tive** /-ˈsilēətiv; -ē.ātiv/ *adj.* —**con·cil·i·a·tor** /-ˌātər/ *n.* —**con·cil·i·a·to·ry** /kənˈsilēə.tôrē/ *adj.*

con·cise /kənˈsīs/ ▶*adj.* giving a lot of information clearly and in a few words; brief but comprehensive: *a concise account of the country's history.* —**con·cise·ly** *adv.* —**con·cise·ness** *n.* —**con·ci·sion** /-ˈsiZHən/ *n.*

con·clave /ˈkänˌklāv/ ▶*n.* a private meeting. ■ (in the Roman Catholic Church) the assembly of cardinals for the election of a pope. ■ the meeting place for such an assembly.

con·clude /kənˈklo͞od/ ▶*v.* **1** [*tr.*] bring (something) to an end: *they conclude their study with these words* | [*intr.*] *we concluded by singing carols.* ■ [*intr.*] come to an end. ■ formally and finally settle or arrange (a treaty or agreement). **2** arrive at a judgment or opinion by reasoning: *the doctors* **concluded that** *Esther had suffered a stroke.* ■ say in conclusion: *"It's a wicked old world," she concluded.* ■ with *dated* decide to do something: *I* **concluded to** *go without his knowledge.*

con·clu·sion /kənˈklo͞oZHən/ ▶*n.* **1** the end or finish of an event or process. ■ the summing-up of an argument or text. ■ the settling or arrangement of a treaty or agreement: *the conclusion of a free-trade accord.* **2** a judgment or decision reached by reasoning. ■ *Logic* a proposition that reached from given premises.

▶ □ **in conclusion** lastly; to sum up. □ **jump** (or **leap**) **to conclusions** make a hasty judgment before learning or considering all the facts.

con·clu·sive /kənˈklo͞osiv; -ziv/ ▶*adj.* (of evidence or argument) serving to prove a case; decisive or convincing. ■ (of a victory) achieved easily or by a large margin. —**con·clu·sive·ly** *adv.* —**con·clu·sive·ness** *n.*

con·coct /kənˈkäkt/ ▶*v.* [*tr.*] make (a dish or meal) by combining various ingredients. ■ create or devise (said esp. of a story or plan). —**con·coct·er** *n.* —**con·coc·tion** *n.*

con·com·i·tant /kənˈkämitənt/ *formal* ▶*adj.* naturally accompanying or associated: *she loved travel, with all its concomitant worries.*

▶*n.* a phenomenon that naturally accompanies or follows something. —**con·com·i·tance** *n.* —**con·com·i·tant·ly** *adv.*

con·cord /ˈkäNGˌkôrd; ˈkän-/ ▶*n.* **1** *formal* agreement or harmony between people or groups: *a pact of peace and concord.* ■ a treaty. **2** *Gram.* agreement between words in gender, number, case, person, or any other grammatical category that affects the forms of the words. **3** *Mus.* a chord that is pleasing or satisfactory in itself.

con·cord·ance /kənˈkôrdns/ ▶*n.* **1** an alphabetical list of the words (esp. the important ones) present in a text, usually with citations of the passages concerned: *a concordance to the Bible.* **2** *formal* agreement.

▶*v.* [*tr.*] (often as *adj.*) (**concordanced**) make a concordance of.

con·cord·ant /kənˈkôrdnt/ ▶*adj.* in agreement; consistent: *the answers were roughly concordant.* ■ *Mus.* in harmony. —**con·cord·ant·ly** *adv.*

con·course /ˈkänˌkôrs; ˈkäNG-/ ▶*n.* **1** a large open area inside or in front of a public building, as in an airport or train station. **2** *formal* a crowd or assembly of people. ■ the action of coming together or meeting.

con·crete ▶*adj.* /ˈkänˌkrēt; ˈkänˌkrēt; kənˈkrēt/ existing in a material or physical form; real or solid; not abstract: *concrete objects like stones.* ■ specific; definite: *I haven't got any concrete proof.* ■ (of a noun) denoting a material object as opposed to an abstract quality, state, or action.

▶*n.* /ˈkänˌkrēt; känˈkrēt/ a heavy, rough building material made from a mixture of broken stone or gravel, sand, cement, and water, that can be spread or poured into molds and that forms a stonelike mass on hardening: *slabs of concrete* | [as *adj.*] *the concrete sidewalk.*

▶*v.* /ˈkänˌkrēt; känˈkrēt/ [*tr.*] (often **be concreted**) **1** cover (an area) with concrete. ■ [*tr.*] fix in position with concrete. **2** *archaic* form (something) into a mass; solidify: *the juices of the plants are concreted upon the surface.* ■ make real or concrete instead of abstract. ▷late Middle English (in the sense 'formed by cohesion, solidified'): from French *concret* or Latin *concretus,* past participle of *concrescere* 'grow together.' —**con·crete·ly** *adv.* —**con·crete·ness** *n.*

▶ □ **be set in concrete** (of a policy or idea) be fixed and unalterable.

con·cre·tion /kənˈkrēSHən; kän-/ ▶*n.* a hard solid mass formed by the local accumulation of matter, esp. within the body or within a mass of sediment. ■ the formation of such a mass. —**con·cre·tion·ar·y** /-SHəˌnerē/ *adj.*

con·cu·bine /ˈkäNGkyo͝oˌbīn/ ▶*n. chiefly hist.* (in polygamous societies) a woman who lives with a man but has lower status than his wife or

Pronunciation Key ə *ago, up*; ər *over, fur*; a *hat*; ā *ate*; ä *car*; CH *chin*; e *let*; ē *see*; e(ə)r *air*; i *fit*; ī *by*; i(ə)r *ear*; NG *sing*; ō *go*; ô *law, for*; oi *toy*; o͝o *good*; o͞o *goo*; ou *out*; SH *she*; TH *thin*; <u>TH</u> *then*; (h)w *why*; ZH *vision*

wives. ■ *archaic* a mistress. —**con·cu·bi·nar·y** /kənˈkyōōbə,nerē; kän-/ *adj.*

con·cu·pis·cence /känˈkyōōpisəns; kən-/ ▶*n. formal* strong sexual desire. —**con·cu·pis·cent** *adj.*

con·cur /kənˈkər/ ▶*v.* (**-curred, -cur·ring**) [*intr.*] **1** be of the same opinion; agree: *the authors concurred with the majority.* ■ (**concur with**) agree with (a decision, opinion, or finding): *we strongly concur with this recommendation.* **2** happen or occur at the same time; coincide: *in tests, cytogenetic determination has been found to concur with enzymatic determination.* —**con·cur·rence** /-ˈkərəns/ *n.* —**con·cur·ren·cy** /-ˈkərənsē/ *n.*

con·cur·rent /kənˈkərənt/ ▶*adj.* existing, happening, or done at the same time: *there are three concurrent art fairs around the city.* ■ (of two or more prison sentences) to be served at the same time. —**con·cur·rent·ly** *adv.*

con·cus·sion /kənˈkəsHən/ ▶*n.* **1** temporary unconsciousness caused by a blow to the head. The term is also used loosely of the aftereffects such as confusion. **2** a violent shock as from a heavy blow.

con·demn /kənˈdem/ ▶*v.* [*tr.*] **1** express complete disapproval of, typically in public; censure. **2** find (someone) guilty of a criminal act or wrong. ■ sentence (someone) to a particular punishment, esp. death: *the rebels had been condemned to death.* ■ (usu. **be condemned**) officially declare (something, esp. a building) to be unfit for use. ■ prove or show the guilt of. ■ (of circumstances) force (someone) to endure something unpleasant or undesirable: *the physical ailments that condemned him to a lonely childhood.* —**con·dem·na·ble** /-ˈdem(n)əbəl/ *adj.* —**con·dem·na·tion** /,kändemˈnāsHən; -dəm-/ *n.* —**con·dem·na·to·ry** /-ˈdemnə,tôrē/ *adj.*

con·den·sa·tion /,kän,denˈsāsHən; -dən-/ ▶*n.* **1** water that collects as droplets on a cold surface when humid air is in contact with it. **2** the process of becoming more dense, in particular: ■ the conversion of a vapor or gas to a liquid. ■ (also **condensation reaction**) *Chem.* a reaction in which two molecules combine to form a larger molecule, producing a small molecule such as H_2O as a byproduct. **3** a concise version of something, esp. a text.

con·dense /kənˈdens/ ▶*v.* **1** [*tr.*] make (something) denser or more concentrated: *the limestones of the Jurassic age are condensed into a mere 11 feet.* ■ [usu. as *adj.*] (**condensed**) thicken (a liquid) by reducing the water content, typically by heating: *condensed soup.* ■ express (a piece of writing or speech) in fewer words; make concise: *he condensed the three plays into a three-hour drama.* ■ (in word processing) (of character spacing) reduced. **2** [*intr.*] be changed from a gas or vapor to a liquid: *the moisture vapor in the air condenses into droplets of water.* ■ [*tr.*] cause (a gas or vapor) to be changed to a liquid. —**con·den·sa·ble** *adj.*

con·densed milk ▶*n.* canned milk that has been thickened by evaporation and sweetened.

con·dens·er /kənˈdensər/ ▶*n.* a person or thing that condenses something, in particular: ■ an apparatus or container for condensing vapor. ■ another term for CAPACITOR.

con·de·scend /,kändəˈsend/ ▶*v.* [*intr.*] show feelings of superiority; patronize: *take care not to condescend to your reader.* ■ do something in a haughty way, as though it is below one's dignity or level of importance: *we'll be waiting for twenty minutes before she condescends to appear.* —**con·des·cend·ing** *adj.* —**con·des·cend·ing·ly** *adv.* —**con·de·scen·sion** /-ˈsenCHən/ *n.*

con·dign /kənˈdīn/ ▶*adj. formal* (of punishment or retribution) appropriate to the crime or wrongdoing; fitting and deserved. —**con·dign·ly** *adv.*

con·di·ment /ˈkändəmənt/ ▶*n.* a substance such as salt or ketchup that is used to add flavor to food.

con·di·tion /kənˈdisHən/ ▶*n.* **1** the state of something, esp. with regard to its appearance, quality, or working order: *the wiring is in good condition | the bridge is in an extremely dangerous condition.* ■ a person's or animal's state of health or physical fitness: *he is in fairly good condition | she was in a serious condition.* ■ an illness or other medical problem: *a heart condition.* ■ a particular state of existence: *a condition of misery.* ■ *archaic* social position or rank. **2** (**conditions**) the circumstances affecting the way in which people live or work, esp. with regard to their safety or well-being: *harsh living conditions.* ■ the factors or prevailing situation influencing the performance or the outcome of a process: *present market conditions.* ■ the prevailing state of the weather, ground, sea, or atmosphere at a particular time, esp. as it affects a sporting event. **3** a state of affairs that must exist or be brought about before something else is possible or permitted: *for a member to borrow money, three conditions have to be me.*

▶*v.* [*tr.*] **1** (often **be conditioned**) have a significant influence on or determine (the manner or outcome of something): *national choices are* conditioned *by the international political economy.* ■ train or accustom (someone or something) to behave in a certain way or to accept certain circumstances: *the child is conditioned to dislike food* | [as *n.*] (**conditioning**) *social conditioning.* **2** bring (something) into the desired state for use: *a product for conditioning leather.* ■ [often as *adj.*] (**conditioned**) make (a person or animal) fit and healthy: *he was six feet two of perfectly conditioned muscle and bone.* ■ apply something to (the skin or hair) to give it a healthy or attractive look or feel. ■ [*intr.*] (of a beer or stout) undergo such a process. **3** set prior requirements on (something) before it can occur or be done.

▶ □ **in** (or **out of**) **condition** in a fit (or unfit) physical state. □ **in no condition to do something** certainly not fit or well enough to do something. □ **on condition that** with the stipulation that.

con·di·tion·al /kənˈdisHənl/ ▶*adj.* **1** subject to one or more conditions or requirements being met; made or granted on certain terms: *Western aid was only granted conditional on further reform.* **2** *Gram.* (of a clause, phrase, conjunction, or verb form) expressing a condition.

▶*n.* **1** *Gram. & Philos.* a conditional clause or conjunction. ■ a statement or sentence containing a conditional clause. **2** *Gram.* the conditional mood of a verb, for example *should die* in *if I should die.* —**con·di·tion·al·i·ty** /kən,disHəˈnalitē/ *n.* —**con·di·tion·al·ly** *adv.*

con·di·tion·er /kənˈdisH(ə)nər/ ▶*n.* a substance or appliance used to improve or maintain something's condition: *add a water conditioner to neutralize chlorine.* ■ a liquid applied to the hair after shampooing to improve its condition: *conditioner will protect your hair from damage.*

con·do /ˈkändō/ ▶*n.* (*pl.* **-dos**) *inf.* short for CONDOMINIUM (sense 1).

con·dole /kənˈdōl/ ▶*v.* [*intr.*] (**condole with**) express sympathy for (someone); grieve with: *the priest came to condole with Madeleine.*

con·do·lence /kənˈdōləns/ ▶*n.* (usu. **condolences**) an expression of sympathy, esp. on the occasion of a death: *we offer our sincere condolences to his widow | letters of condolence.*

con·dom /ˈkändəm; ˈkən-/ ▶*n.* a thin rubber sheath worn on a man's penis during sexual intercourse as a contraceptive or as protection against infection. ▷early 18th cent.: of unknown origin; often said to be named after a physician who invented it, but no such person has been traced.

con·do·min·i·um /,kändəˈminēəm/ ▶*n.* (*pl.* **-ums**) **1** a building or complex of buildings containing a number of individually owned apartments or houses. ■ each of the individual apartments or houses in such a building or complex. ■ the system of ownership by which these operate, in which owners have full title to the individual apartment or house and an undivided interest in the shared parts of the property. **2** the joint control of a country's or territory's affairs by other countries. ■ a state so governed.

con·done /kənˈdōn/ ▶*v.* [*tr.*] accept and allow (behavior that is considered morally wrong or offensive) to continue: *the college cannot condone behavior that involves illicit drugs.* ■ approve or sanction (something), esp. with reluctance: *the practice is not officially condoned by any airline.* —**con·don·a·ble** *adj.* —**con·do·na·tion** /-ˈnāsHən; -dō-/ *n.* —**con·don·er** *n.*

con·dor /ˈkän,dôr; -dər/ ▶*n.* a large New World vulture with a bare head and mainly black plumage. Two species: the **Andean condor** (*Vultur gryphus*) of South America and the **California condor** (*Gymnogyps californianus*), which is close to extinction in the wild.

con·duce /kənˈd(y)ōōs/ ▶*v.* (**conduce to**) *formal* help to bring about (a particular situation or outcome): *every possible care was taken that could conduce to their health and comfort.*

con·du·cive /kənˈd(y)ōōsiv/ ▶*adj.* making a certain situation or outcome likely or possible: *the music was conducive to a relaxed atmosphere.*

con·duct ▶*n.* /ˈkän,dəkt/ **1** the manner in which a person behaves, esp. on a particular occasion or in a particular context: *the conduct of the police.* **2** the action or manner of managing an activity or organization. ■ *archaic* the action of leading; guidance.

▶*v.* /kənˈdəkt/ [*tr.*] **1** organize and carry out: *surveys conducted among students.* ■ direct the performance of (a piece of music or a musical ensemble): *my first attempt to conduct a great work* | [*intr.*] *Toscanini is coming to conduct.* ■ lead or guide (someone) to or around a particular place. ■ *Physics* transmit (a form of energy such as heat or electricity) by conduction. **2** (**conduct oneself**) behave in a specified way: *he conducted himself with the utmost propriety.* —**con·duct·i·ble** /kənˈdəktəbəl/ *adj.* —**con·duct·i·bil·i·ty** /kən,dəktəˈbilitē/ *n.*

con·duct·ance /kənˈdəktəns/ ▶*n.* the degree to which an object conducts electricity, calculated as the ratio of the current that flows to the potential difference present. This is the reciprocal of the resistance, and is measured in siemens or mhos. (Symbol: **G**)

con·duc·tion /kənˈdəksHən/ ▶*n.* the process by which heat or electricity is directly transmitted through a substance when there is a difference of temperature or of electrical potential between adjoining regions, without movement of the material. ■ the process by which sound waves travel through a medium. ■ the transmission of impulses along nerves. ■ the conveying of fluid through a pipe or other channel. —**con·duc·tive** *adj.*

con·duc·tiv·i·ty /ˌkän,dək'tivitē; kən-/ ▶*n.* (*pl.* **-ties**) (also **electrical conductivity**) the degree to which a specified material conducts electricity, calculated as the ratio of the current density in the material to the electric field that causes the flow of current. It is the reciprocal of the resistivity. ■ (also **thermal conductivity**) the rate at which heat passes through a specified material, expressed as the amount of heat that flows per unit time through a unit area with a temperature gradient of one degree per unit distance.

con·duc·tor /kən'dəktər/ ▶*n.* **1** a person who directs the performance of an orchestra or choir. **2** a person in charge of a train, streetcar, or other public conveyance, who collects fares and sells tickets. **3** *Physics* a material or device that conducts or transmits heat, electricity, or sound, esp. when regarded in terms of its capacity to do this.

con·duit /'kän,d(y) o͞oət; 'känd(w)ət/ ▶*n.* a channel for conveying water or other fluid: *fig. the office acts as a conduit for ideas to flow throughout the organization.* ■ a tube or trough for protecting electric wiring.

cone /kōn/ ▶*n.* **1** a solid or hollow object that tapers from a circular or roughly circular base to a point. ■ *Math.* a surface or solid figure generated by the straight lines that pass from a circle or other closed curve to a single point (the vertex) not in the same plane as the curve. ■ (also **traffic cone**) a plastic cone-shaped object that is used to separate off or close sections of a road. ■ an edible wafer container shaped like a cone in which ice cream is served. ■ a conical mountain or peak, esp. one of volcanic origin. ■ (also **pyrometric cone**) a ceramic pyramid that melts at a known temperature and is used to indicate the temperature of a kiln. **2** the dry fruit of a conifer, typically tapering to a rounded end and formed of a tight array of overlapping scales on a central axis that separate to release the seeds. ■ a flower resembling a pine cone, esp. that of the hop plant. **3** a light-sensitive cell of one of the two types present in the retina of the eye, responding mainly to bright light and responsible for color perception.

Con·es·to·ga wag·on /ˌkänə'stōgə/ ▶*n. hist.* a large covered wagon used for long-distance travel, typically carrying pioneers in the westward migration.

co·ney /'kōnē/ (also **co·ny**) ▶*n.* (*pl.* **-eys**) **1** a rabbit. ■ rabbit fur. **2** a small fish, esp. a grouper (*Epinephelus fulvus*), found on the coasts of the tropical western Atlantic, with variable coloration.

con·fab *inf.* ▶*n.* /'kän,fab; kən'fab/ an informal private conversation or discussion. ■ a meeting or conference of members of a particular group.
▶*v.* /kən'fab; 'kän,fab/ (**-fabbed, -fab·bing**) [*intr.*] engage in informal private conversation: *Peter was confabbing with a curly-haired guy.*

con·fab·u·late /kən'fabyə,lāt/ ▶*v.* [*intr.*] **1** *formal* engage in conversation; talk. **2** *Psychiatry* fabricate imaginary experiences as compensation for loss of memory. —**con·fab·u·la·tion** /-,fabyə'lāsHən/ *n.* —**con·fab·u·la·to·ry** /-lə,tôrē/ *adj.*

con·fec·tion /kən'feksHən/ ▶*n.* **1** a dish or delicacy made with sweet ingredients. ■ an elaborately constructed thing, esp. a frivolous one. ■ a fashionable or elaborate article of women's dress. **2** the action of mixing or compounding something. —**con·fec·tion·ar·y** /-,nerē/ *adj.*

con·fec·tion·er /kən'feksHənər/ ▶*n.* a person whose occupation is making or selling candy and other sweets.

con·fec·tion·ers' sug·ar (also **con·fec·tion·er's sug·ar**) ▶*n.* finely powdered sugar with cornstarch added, used for making icings and candy.

con·fec·tion·er·y /kən'feksHə,nerē/ ▶*n.* (*pl.* **-er·ies**) candy and other sweets considered collectively. ■ a shop that sells such items.

con·fed·er·a·cy /kən'fedərəsē/ ▶*n.* (*pl.* **-cies**) a league or alliance, esp. of confederate states. ■ (**the Confederacy**) another term for CONFEDERATE STATES OF AMERICA. ■ an alliance formed for an unlawful purpose; a conspiracy.

con·fed·er·ate ▶*adj.* /kən'fedərət/ joined by an agreement or treaty: *some local groups united to form confederate councils.* ■ (**Confederate**) of or relating to the Confederate States of America: *the Confederate flag.*
▶*n.* /kən'fedərət/ **1** a person one works with, esp. in something secret or illegal; an accomplice. **2** (**Confederate**) a supporter of the Confederate States of America.
▶*v.* /-,rāt/ [*tr.*] [usu. as *adj.*] (**confederated**) bring (states or groups of people) into an alliance: *Switzerland is a model for the new confederated Europe.*

Con·fed·er·ate States of A·mer·i·ca (also **the Con·fed·er·a·cy**) ▶the 11 Southern states (Alabama, Arkansas, Florida, Georgia, Louisiana, Mississippi, North Carolina, South Carolina, Tennessee, Texas, and

Virginia) that seceded from the U.S. in 1860–61, thus precipitating the Civil War.

con·fed·er·a·tion /kən,fedə'rāsHən/ ▶*n.* an organization that consists of a number of parties or groups united in an alliance or league. ■ a more or less permanent union of countries with some or most political power vested in a central authority: *Canada became a confederation in 1867.* ■ the action of confederating or the state of being confederated.

con·fer /kən'fər/ ▶*v.* (**-ferred, -fer·ring**) **1** [*tr.*] grant or bestow (a title, degree, benefit, or right). **2** [*intr.*] have discussions; exchange opinions: *the officials were conferring with allies.* —**con·fer·ment** *n.* (in sense 1). —**con·fer·ra·ble** *adj.* —**con·fer·ral** /-'fərəl/ *n.*

con·fer·ence /'känf(ə)rəns/ ▶*n.* **1** a formal meeting for discussion. ■ a formal meeting that typically takes place over a number of days and involves people with a shared interest, esp. one held regularly by an association or organization: *an international conference on the environment.* ■ [usu. as *adj.*] a linking of several telephones or computers, so that each user may communicate with the others simultaneously: *a conference call.* **2** an association of sports teams that play each other. **3** the governing body of some Christian churches, esp. the Methodist Church.
▶*v.* [*intr.*] [usu. as *n.*] (**conferencing**) take part in a conference or conference call: *video conferencing.*
▶ □ **in conference** in a meeting; engaged in discussions.

con·fess /kən'fes/ ▶*v.* [*tr.*] admit or state that one has committed a crime or is at fault in some way: *he confessed that he had attacked the old man* | [*intr.*] *he wants to confess to Caroline's murder.* ■ admit or acknowledge something reluctantly, typically because one feels slightly ashamed or embarrassed: *I must confess that I was slightly surprised* | [*intr.*] *he confessed to a lifelong passion for food.* ■ declare (one's religious faith): *150 people confessed faith in Christ.* ■ declare one's sins formally to a priest: *I could not confess all my sins* | [*intr.*] *he gave himself up after confessing to a priest.* ■ (of a priest) hear the confession of (someone) in such a way: *St. Ambrose would weep bitter tears when confessing a sinner.*

con·fess·ed·ly /kən'fesədlē/ ▶*adv.* by one's own admission: *many therapists have clients who, confessedly or otherwise, have fallen in love with them.*

con·fes·sion /kən'fesHən/ ▶*n.* **1** a formal statement admitting that one is guilty of a crime. ■ an admission or acknowledgment that one has done something that one is ashamed or embarrassed about: *by his own confession, he had strayed perilously close to alcoholism.* ■ a formal admission of one's sins with repentance and desire of absolution, esp. privately to a priest as a religious duty: *she still had not been to confession.* ■ (**confessions**) *often humorous* intimate revelations about a person's private life or occupation, esp. as presented in a sensationalized form in a book, newspaper, or movie. **2** (also **confession of faith**) a statement setting out essential religious doctrine. ■ (also **Confession**) the religious body or church sharing a confession of faith. ■ a statement of one's principles: *his words are a political confession of faith.* —**con·fes·sion·ar·y** /-,nerē/ *adj.*

con·fes·sion·al /kən'fesHənl/ ▶*n.* **1** an enclosed stall in a church divided by a screen or curtain in which a priest sits to hear people confess their sins. **2** an admission or acknowledgment that one has done something that one is ashamed or embarrassed about; a confession.
▶*adj.* **1** (esp. of speech or writing) in which a person reveals or admits to private thoughts or past incidents, esp. ones that cause shame or embarrassment. ■ of or relating to religious confession. **2** of or relating to confessions of faith or doctrinal systems.

con·fes·sor /kən'fesər/ ▶*n.* **1** /kən'fesər; 'kän,fesər; 'känfə,sôr/ a priest who hears confessions and gives absolution and spiritual counsel. ■ a person to whom another confides personal problems. **2** /kən'fesər; 'kän,fesər/ a person who avows religious faith in the face of opposition, but does not suffer martyrdom. **3** /kən'fesər/ a person who makes a confession.

con·fet·ti /kən'fetē/ ▶*n.* small pieces of colored paper thrown during a celebration such as a wedding.

con·fi·dant /'känfə,dant; -,dänt/ ▶*n.* (*fem.* **con·fi·dante** *pronunc.* same) a person with whom one shares a secret or private matter, trusting them not to repeat it to others.

con·fide /kən'fīd/ ▶*v.* [*tr.*] tell someone about a secret or private matter while trusting them not to repeat it to others: *he confided his fears to his mother.* ■ [*intr.*] (**confide in**) trust (someone) enough to tell them of such a secret or private matter: *he confided in friends that he and his wife planned to separate.* ■ (**confide something to**) *dated* entrust something to (some-

---

Pronunciation Key ə *ago,* up; ər *over,* fur; a *hat*; ā *ate*; ä *car*; CH *chin*; e *let*; ē *see*; e(ə)r *air*; i *fit*; ī *by*; i(ə)r *ear*; NG *sing*; ō *go*; ô *law, for*; oi *toy*; o͞o *good*; o͞o *goo*; ou *out*; SH *she*; TH *thin*; <u>TH</u> *then*; (h)w *why*; ZH *vision*

one) for safekeeping: *the property of others confided to their care was unjustifiably risked.* —**con·fid·ing·ly** *adv.*

con·fi·dence /ˈkänfədəns; -fəˌdens/ ▶ *n.* the feeling or belief that one can rely on someone or something; firm trust: *he had gained the young man's confidence.* ■ the state of feeling certain about the truth of something: *it is not possible to say with confidence how much of the increase in sea levels is due to melting glaciers.* ■ a feeling of self-assurance arising from one's appreciation of one's abilities or qualities: *she's brimming with confidence* | *he would walk up those steps with a confidence he didn't feel.* ■ the telling of private matters or secrets with mutual trust: *someone with whom you may raise your suspicions* **in confidence.** ■ (often **confidences**) a secret or private matter told to someone under such a condition of trust.

▶ □ **take someone into one's confidence** tell someone one's secrets.

con·fi·dence game (*Brit.* also **confidence trick**) ▶ *n.* a swindle in which the victim is persuaded to trust the swindler in some way.

con·fi·dence man ▶ *n.* old-fashioned term for CON MAN.

con·fi·dent /ˈkänfədənt; -fəˌdent/ ▶ *adj.* feeling or showing confidence in oneself; self-assured. ■ feeling or showing certainty about something: *this time they're* **confident of** *a happy ending* | *I am not very* **confident about** *tonight's game.*

▶ *n. archaic* a confidant. —**con·fi·dent·ly** *adv.*

con·fi·den·tial /ˌkänfəˈdenCHəl/ ▶ *adj.* intended to be kept secret: *confidential information.* ■ (of a person's tone of voice) indicating that what one says is private or secret: *a confidential whisper.* ■ entrusted with private or restricted information: *a confidential secretary.* —**con·fi·den·ti·al·i·ty** /-ˌdenCHēˈalitē/ *n.* —**con·fi·den·tial·ly** *adv.*

con·fig·u·ra·tion /kənˌfig(y)əˈrāSHən/ ▶ *n.* an arrangement of elements in a particular form, figure, or combination: *the broad configuration of the economy remains capitalist.* ■ *Chem.* the fixed three-dimensional relationship of the atoms in a molecule, defined by the bonds between them. ■ *Comput.* the arrangement in which items of computer hardware or software are interconnected. ■ *Psychol.* another term for GESTALT. —**con·fig·u·ra·tion·al** /-SHənl/ *adj.* —**con·fig·u·ra·tive** /-ˈfig(y)ərətiv/ *adj.*

con·fig·ure /kənˈfigyər/ ▶ *v.* [*tr.*] (often **be configured**) shape or put together in a particular form or configuration ■ *Comput.* arrange or order (a computer system or an element of it) so as to fit it for a designated task. —**con·fig·ur·a·ble** *adj.*

con·fine ▶ *v.* /kənˈfīn/ [*tr.*] (**confine someone/something to**) keep or restrict someone or something within certain limits of (space, scope, quantity, or time): *he does not confine his message to politics.* ■ (**confine someone to/in**) restrain or forbid someone from leaving (a place): *the troops were confined to their barracks.* ■ (**be confined to**) (of a person) be unable to leave (one's bed, home, or a wheelchair) because of illness or disability. ■ (**be confined**) *dated* (of a woman) remain in bed for a period before, during, and after the birth of a child.

▶ *n.* /ˈkänˌfīn/ (**confines**) the borders or boundaries of a place, esp. with regard to their restricting freedom of movement: *cramped within the confines of a little cabin.* ■ *fig.* the limits or restrictions of something abstract, esp. a subject or sphere of activity. —**con·fine·ment** *n.*

con·firm /kənˈfərm/ ▶ *v.* [*tr.*] **1** establish the truth or correctness of (something previously believed, suspected, or feared to be the case): *if these fears are confirmed, the outlook for the economy will be dire.* ■ state with assurance that a report or fact is true: *he confirmed that the general was in the hands of the rebels.* ■ (**confirm someone in**) reinforce someone in (an opinion, belief, or feeling): *he fueled his misogyny by cultivating women who confirmed him in this view.* ■ make (a provisional arrangement or appointment) definite. ■ make (something, esp. a person's appointment to a position or an agreement) formally valid; ratify. ■ formally declare (someone) to be appointed to a particular position: *he was confirmed as the new peace envoy.* **2** administer the religious rite of confirmation to: *he had been baptized and confirmed.* —**con·firm·a·tive** /-mətiv/ *adj.* —**con·firm·a·to·ry** /-məˌtôrē/ *adj.*

con·fir·ma·tion /ˌkänfərˈmāSHən/ ▶ *n.* **1** the action of confirming something or the state of being confirmed. **2** (in the Christian Church) the rite at which a baptized person, esp. one baptized as an infant, affirms Christian belief and is admitted as a full member of the church. ■ the Jewish ceremony of bar mitzvah or bat mitzvah.

con·firmed /kənˈfərmd/ ▶ *adj.* (of a person) firmly established in a particular habit, belief, or way of life and unlikely to change: *a confirmed bachelor* | *a confirmed teetotaler.*

con·fis·cate /ˈkänfəˌskāt/ ▶ *v.* [*tr.*] take or seize (someone's property) with authority: *the guards confiscated his camera.* ■ take (a possession, esp. land) as a penalty and give it to the public treasury: *the government confiscated his property.* —**con·fis·ca·tion** /ˌkänfəˈskāSHən/ *n.* —**con·fis·ca·tor** /-ˌskātər/ *n.* —**con·fis·ca·to·ry** /kənˈfiskəˌtôrē/ *adj.*

con·fla·gra·tion /ˌkänfləˈgrāSHən/ ▶ *n.* an extensive fire that destroys a great deal of land or property.

con·flate /kənˈflāt/ ▶ *v.* [*tr.*] combine (two or more texts, ideas, etc.) into one: *the urban crisis conflates a number of different economic and social issues.* —**con·fla·tion** /-ˈflāSHən/ *n.*

con·flict ▶ *n.* /ˈkänˌflikt/ a serious disagreement or argument, typically a protracted one. ■ a prolonged armed struggle. ■ an incompatibility between two or more opinions, principles, or interests: *there was a* **conflict between** *his business and domestic life.* ■ *Psychol.* a condition in which a person experiences a clash of opposing wishes or needs.

▶ *v.* /kənˈflikt; ˈkänˌflikt/ [*intr.*] be incompatible or at variance; clash: *parents' and children's interests sometimes conflict.* ■ [as *adj.*] (**conflicted**) having or showing confused and mutually inconsistent feelings: *my feelings are so conflicted that I hardly know how to answer.* —**con·flic·tive** /kənˈfliktiv; ˈkänˌflik-/ *adj.* —**con·flic·tu·al** /kənˈflikCHOōəl/ *adj.*

con·flu·ence /ˈkänˌflōōəns; kənˈflōōəns/ ▶ *n.* the junction of two rivers, esp. rivers of approximately equal width: *here at* **the confluence of** *the Laramie and North Platte Rivers.* ■ an act or process of merging: *a major confluence of the world's financial markets.*

con·flu·ent /ˈkänˌflōōənt; kənˈflōōənt/ ▶ *adj.* flowing together or merging.

con·flux /ˈkänˌfləks/ ▶ *n.* another term for CONFLUENCE.

con·form /kənˈfôrm/ ▶ *v.* [*intr.*] comply with rules, standards, or laws: *the kitchen does not conform to hygiene regulations.* ■ (of a person) behave according to socially acceptable conventions or standards: *the pressure to conform.* ■ be similar in form or type; agree: *the countryside should* **conform to** *a certain idea of the picturesque.* —**con·form·er** *n.*

con·form·a·ble /kənˈfôrməbəl/ ▶ *adj.* (usu. **conformable to**) (of a person) disposed or accustomed to conform to what is acceptable or expected. ■ similar in form or nature; consistent: *this proposition might be conformable to the original conjecture.* —**con·form·a·bil·i·ty** /-ˌfôrməˈbilitē/ *n.* —**con·form·a·bly** /-blē/ *adv.*

con·for·ma·tion /ˌkänfôrˈmāSHən; -fər-/ ▶ *n.* the shape or structure of something, esp. an animal. ■ *Chem.* any of the spatial arrangements that the atoms in a molecule may adopt and freely convert between, esp. by rotation about individual single bonds. —**con·for·ma·tion·al** /-SHənl/ *adj.*

con·form·ist /kənˈfôrmist/ ▶ *n.* a person who conforms to accepted behavior or established practices.

▶ *adj.* (of a person or activity) conforming to accepted behavior or established practices; conventional. —**con·form·ism** /-ˌmizəm/ *n.*

con·form·i·ty /kənˈfôrmitē/ ▶ *n.* compliance with standards, rules, or laws: *the goods were* **in conformity with** *the contract.* ■ behavior in accordance with socially accepted conventions or standards: *loyalty to one's party need not imply unquestioning conformity.* ■ similarity in form or type; agreement in character: *these changes are intended to ensure conformity between all schemes.* ■ *Geol.* (of strata in contact) a continuous sequence of deposits, typically in parallel strata.

con·found /kənˈfound/ ▶ *v.* [*tr.*] **1** cause surprise or confusion in (someone), esp. by acting against their expectations. ■ prove (a theory, expectation, or prediction) wrong. ■ defeat (a plan, aim, or hope). ■ *archaic* overthrow (an enemy). **2** (often **be confounded with**) mix up (something) with something else so that the individual elements become difficult to distinguish: *'nuke' is now a cooking technique, as microwave radiation is confounded with nuclear radiation.*

▶ *interj. dated* used to express anger or annoyance: *oh, confound it, where is the thing?*

con·found·ed /kənˈfoundəd; kän-/ ▶ *adj. inf., dated* used for emphasis, esp. to express anger or annoyance: *he was a confounded nuisance.* —**con·found·ed·ly** *adv.*

con·front /kənˈfrənt/ ▶ *v.* [*tr.*] meet (someone) face to face with hostile or argumentative intent. ■ face up to and deal with (a problem or difficult situation). ■ compel (someone) to face or consider something, esp. by way of accusation: *Tricia confronted him with her suspicions.* ■ (often **be confronted**) (of a problem, difficulty, etc.) present itself to (someone) so that dealing with it cannot be avoided: *post-czarist Russia was confronted with a Ukrainian national movement.* ■ (usu. **be confronted**) appear or be placed in front of (someone) so as to unsettle or threaten: *we were confronted with pictures of moving skeletons.* —**con·fron·ta·tion** /ˌkänfrənˈtāSHən/ *n.* —**con·fron·ta·tion·al** *adj.*

Con·fu·cian·ism /kənˈfyōōSHəˌnizəm/ ▶ *n.* a system of philosophical and ethical teachings founded by Confucious and developed by Mencius. —**Con·fu·cian** *n* & *adj.* —**Con·fu·cian·ist** *n* & *adj.*

con·fuse /kənˈfyōōz/ ▶ *v.* [*tr.*] **1** cause (someone) to become bewildered or perplexed. ■ make (something) more complex or less easy to understand. ■ identify wrongly; mistake: *purchasers might confuse the two products.* —**con·fus·a·ble** *adj.* —**con·fus·ing·ly** *adv.*

con·fu·sion /kənˈfyoōzHən/ ▸n. **1** lack of understanding; uncertainty: *there seems to be some* **confusion about** *which system does what.* ■ a situation of panic; a breakdown of order: *the shaken survivors retreated* **in confusion.** ■ a disorderly jumble: *all I can see is* **a confusion of** *brown cardboard boxes.* **2** the state of being bewildered or unclear in one's mind about something: *she looked about her* **in confusion.** ■ the mistaking of one person or thing for another: *there is some confusion between "unlawful" and "illegal."*

con·fute /kənˈfyoōt/ ▸v. [tr.] *formal* prove (a person or an assertion) to be wrong. —**con·fu·ta·tion** /ˌkänfyoōˈtāSHən/ n.

con·ga /ˈkäNGgə/ ▸n. **1** a Latin American dance of African origin, usually with several people in a single line, one behind the other. **2** (also **conga drum**) a tall, narrow, low-toned drum beaten with the hands.
▸v. (**-gas**, **-gaed** /-gəd/ or **-ga'd**, **-ga·ing** /-gə-iNG/) [intr.] dance the conga.

con·geal /kənˈjēl/ ▸v. [intr.] solidify or coagulate, esp. by cooling: *the blood had* **congealed into** *blobs* | [as adj.] (**congealed**) *congealed egg white.* ■ *fig.* take shape or coalesce, esp. to form a satisfying whole. —**con·geal·a·ble** adj. —**con·geal·ment** n. (archaic).

con·ge·la·tion /ˌkänjəˈlāSHən/ ▸n. the process of congealing or the state of being congealed: *the component of metals that causes their congelation.*

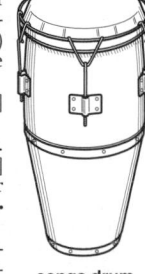

conga drum

con·gen·ial /kənˈjēnyəl/ ▸adj. (of a person) pleasant because of a personality, qualities, or interests that are similar to one's own: *his need for some congenial company.* ■ (of a thing) pleasant or agreeable because suited to one's taste or inclination: *a climate more* **congenial to** *his cold stony soul.* —**con·ge·ni·al·i·ty** /-ˌjēnēˈalitē/ n. —**con·gen·ial·ly** adv.

con·gen·i·tal /kənˈjenətl/ ▸adj. (esp. of a disease or physical abnormality) present from birth. ■ (of a person) having a particular trait from birth or by firmly established habit: *a congenital liar.* —**con·gen·i·tal·ly** adv.

con·ger /ˈkäNGgər/ (also **conger eel**) ▸n. a large edible predatory eel (*Conger* and other genera, family Congridae) of shallow coastal waters.

con·ge·ries /ˈkänjərēz/ ▸n. (pl. same) a disorderly collection; a jumble.

con·gest·ed /kənˈjestid/ ▸adj. blocked up with or too full of something, in particular: ■ (of a road or place) so crowded with traffic or people as to hinder freedom of movement. ■ (of the respiratory tract) blocked with mucus so as to hinder breathing. ■ (of a part of the body) abnormally full of blood: *congested arteries.* —**con·ges·tive** adj.

con·ges·tion /kənˈjesCHən/ ▸n. the state of being congested.

con·glom·er·ate /kənˈglämərət/ ▸n. **1** a number of different things or parts that are put or grouped together to form a whole but remain distinct entities. ■ a large corporation formed by the merging of separate and diverse firms. **2** *Geol.* a coarse-grained sedimentary rock composed of rounded fragments (> 2 mm) within a matrix of finer grained material.
▸adj. /kənˈglämərət/ of or relating to a conglomerate, esp. a large corporation: *conglomerate businesses.*
▸v. /-ˌrāt/ [intr.] gather together into a compact mass: *atoms that conglomerate at the center.* ■ form a conglomerate by merging diverse businesses. ▷late Middle English (as an adjective describing something gathered up into a rounded mass): from Latin *conglomeratus,* past participle of *conglomerare,* from *con-* 'together' + *glomus, glomer-* 'ball.' The geological sense dates from the early 19th cent.; the other noun senses are later. —**con·glom·er·a·tion** /kənˌgläməˈrāSHən/ n.

Con·go·lese /ˌkäNGgəˈlēz; -ˈlēs/ ▸adj. of or relating to the Congo or the Democratic Republic of the Congo (formerly Zaire).
▸n. (pl. same) **1** a native or inhabitant of the Congo or the Democratic Republic of the Congo. **2** any of the Bantu languages spoken in the Congo region, in particular Kikongo.

con·grat·u·late /kənˈgraCHəˌlāt; -ˈgrajə-/ ▸v. [tr.] give (someone) one's good wishes when something special or pleasant has happened to them: *I went into the living room to* **congratulate** *Bill* **on** *his marriage.* ■ praise (someone) for a particular achievement: *the operators are to be* **congratulated for** *the excellent service.* ■ (**congratulate oneself**) feel pride or satisfaction: *she* **congratulated herself on** *her powers of deduction.* —**con·grat·u·la·tor** /-ˌlātər/ n. —**con·grat·u·la·to·ry** /-lə,tôrē/ adj.

con·grat·u·la·tion /kənˌgraCHəˈlāSHən; -ˌgrajə-/ ▸n. an expression of praise for an achievement or good wishes on a special occasion; the act of congratulating: *he began pumping the hand of his son in congratulation.* ■ (**congratulations**) words expressing congratulation: *our congratulations to the winners* | [as interj.] *congratulations on a job well done!*

con·gre·gate /ˈkäNGgrəˌgāt/ ▸v. [intr.] gather into a crowd or mass: *some 4000 demonstrators had congregated at a border point.*
▸adj. /-gət; -ˌgāt/ communal: *congregate living facilities.*

con·gre·ga·tion /ˌkäNGgrəˈgāSHən/ ▸n. **1** a group of people assembled for religious worship. ■ a group of people regularly attending a particular place of worship. **2** a gathering or collection of people, animals, or things. ■ the action of gathering together in a crowd.

con·gre·ga·tion·al /ˌkäNGgrəˈgāSHənl/ ▸adj. **1** of or relating to a congregation: *congregational singing.* **2** (**Congregational**) of or adhering to Congregationalism: *the Congregational Church.*

Con·gre·ga·tion·al·ism /ˌkäNGgrəˈgāSHənl,izəm/ ▸n. a system of organization among Christian churches whereby individual local churches are largely self-governing. —**Con·gre·ga·tion·al·ist** n. & adj.

con·gress /ˈkäNGgrəs; ˈkän-/ ▸n. **1** the national legislative body of a country. ■ (**Congress**) the national legislative body of the U.S., meeting at the Capitol in Washington, DC. It is composed of the Senate and the House of Representatives. ■ a particular session of the U.S. Congress: *the 104th Congress.* **2** a formal meeting or series of meetings for discussion between delegates, esp. those from a political party or trade union or from within a particular discipline: *an international congress of mathematicians.* **3** a society or organization, esp. a political one: *the National Congress of American Indians.* **4** the action of coming together: *sexual congress.* —**con·gres·sion·al** /kənˈgreSHənl/ adj.

Con·gres·sion·al Med·al of Hon·or ▸n. see MEDAL OF HONOR.

con·gress·man /ˈkäNGgrəsmən; ˈkän-/ ▸n. (pl. **-men**) a member of the U.S. Congress (also used as a form of address), usually specifically a member of the U.S. House of Representatives.

con·gru·ent /kənˈgroōənt; ˈkäNGgroōənt/ ▸adj. **1** in agreement or harmony: *the rules are congruent with the requirements of the law.* **2** *Geom.* (of figures) identical in form; coinciding exactly when superimposed. —**con·gru·ence** n. —**con·gru·en·cy** n. —**con·gru·ent·ly** adv.

con·gru·ous /ˈkäNGgroōəs/ ▸adj. in agreement or harmony: *this explanation is* **congruous with** *earlier observations.* —**con·gru·i·ty** /kənˈgroōitē/ n. —**con·gru·ous·ly** adv.

con·ic /ˈkänik/ *chiefly Math.* ▸adj. of or like a cone.

con·i·cal /ˈkänikəl/ ▸adj. having the shape of a cone. —**con·i·cal·ly** /-ik(ə)lē/ adv.

con·ic sec·tion ▸n. a figure formed by the intersection of a plane and a circular cone whose height is perpendicular to its base. Depending on the angle of the plane with respect to the cone, a conic section may be a circle, an ellipse, a parabola, or a hyperbola.

co·ni·fer /ˈkänəfər; kō-/ ▸n. a tree that bears cones and evergreen needle-like or scalelike leaves. Its families include the pines and firs (Pinaceae) and the cypresses (Cupressaceae). —**co·nif·er·ous** /kəˈnifərəs/ adj.

con·jec·ture /kənˈjekCHər/ ▸n. an opinion or conclusion formed on the basis of incomplete information: *conjectures about the newcomer* | *the purpose of the wall is open to conjecture.* ■ an unproven mathematical or scientific theorem. ■ (in textual criticism) the suggestion or reconstruction of a reading of a text not present in the original source.
▸v. [tr.] form an opinion or supposition about (something) on the basis of incomplete information: *many conjectured that she had a second husband in mind.* ■ (in textual criticism) propose (a reading). —**con·jec·tur·a·ble** adj. —**con·jec·tur·al** adj.

con·join /kənˈjoin; kän-/ ▸v. [tr.] *formal* join; combine.

con·joined twin ▸n. either of a pair of twins who are physically joined at birth, sometimes sharing organs, and sometimes separable by surgery.

con·joint /kənˈjoint; kän-/ ▸adj. combining all or both people or things involved: *conjoint family therapy.* —**con·joint·ly** adv.

con·ju·gal /ˈkänjəgəl/ ▸adj. of or relating to marriage or the relationship between husband and wife: *conjugal loyalty.* —**con·ju·gal·i·ty** /ˌkänjəˈgalitē/ n. —**con·ju·gal·ly** adv.

con·ju·gal vis·it ▸n. *Law* a visit by the spouse of a prisoner, especially for sexual relations.

con·ju·gate ▸v. /ˈkänjəˌgāt/ **1** [tr.] *Gram.* give the different forms of (a verb in an inflected language) as they vary according to voice, mood, tense, number, and person. **2** [intr.] *Biol.* (of bacteria or unicellular organisms) become temporarily united in order to exchange genetic material: *E. coli only conjugate when one of the cells possesses fertility genes.* ■ (of gametes) become fused. **3** [tr.] *Chem.* be combined with or joined to reversibly: *bilirubin is conjugated by liver enzymes and excreted in the bile.*
▸adj. /ˈkänjigət; -jəˌgāt/ coupled, connected, or related, in particular: ■ *Chem.* (of an acid or base) related to the corresponding base or acid by loss or gain of a proton. ■ *Math.* joined in a reciprocal relation, esp.

Pronunciation Key ə *ago,* up; ər *over,* fur; a *hat;* ā *ate;* ä *car;* CH *chin;* e *let;* ē *see;* e(ə)r *air;* i *fit;* ī *by;* i(ə)r *ear;* NG *sing;* ō *go;* ô *law, for;* oi *toy;* oō *good;* oō *goo;* ou *out;* SH *she;* TH *thin;* ‖ *then;* (h)w *why;* ZH *vision*

having the same real parts and equal magnitudes but opposite signs of imaginary parts. ■ *Geom.* (of angles) adding up to 360°; (of arcs) combining to form a complete circle. ■ *Biol.* (esp. of gametes) fused.
▶*n.* /'känjigət; -jə,gāt/ a thing that is conjugate or conjugated, in particular: ■ *chiefly Biochem.* a substance formed by the reversible combination of two or more others. ■ a mathematical value or entity having a reciprocal relation with another. —**con·ju·ga·cy** /'känjəgəsē/ *n.* —**con·ju·ga·tion** *n.* —**con·ju·ga·tive** /'känjə,gātiv/ *adj.*

con·junct ▶*adj.* /kən'jəNGkt; kän-/ joined together, combined, or associated. ■ *Mus.* of or relating to the movement of a melody between adjacent notes of the scale.
▶*n.* /'känjəNGkt/ each of two or more things that are joined or associated. ■ *Gram.* an adverbial whose function is to join two sentences or other discourse units (e.g., *however, anyway, in the first place*).

con·junc·tion /kən'jəNGkSHən/ ▶*n.* **1** the act of joining or the condition of being joined: *the conjunction of floating islands.* ■ an instance of two or more events or things occurring at the same point in time or space: *a conjunction of favorable circumstances.* ■ *Astron. & Astrol.* an alignment of two planets or other celestial objects so that they appear to be in the same, or nearly the same, place in the sky. **2** *Gram.* a word used to connect clauses or sentences or to coordinate words in the same clause (e.g., *and, but, if*). —**con·junc·tion·al** /-SHənl/ *adj.*
▶ □ **in conjunction** together: *herbal medicine was used* **in conjunction with** *acupuncture and massage.*

con·junc·ti·va /,kän,jəNG(k)'tīvə; kən-/ ▶*n. Anat.* the mucous membrane that covers the front of the eye and lines the inside of the eyelids. —**con·junc·ti·val** *adj.*

con·junc·tive /kən'jəNG(k)tiv/ ▶*adj.* serving to join; connective: *the conjunctive tissue.* ■ involving the combination or co-occurrence of two or more conditions or properties: *conjunctive hypotheses are simpler to process than negative ones.* ■ *Gram.* of the nature of or relating to a conjunction.
▶*n. Gram.* a word or expression acting as a conjunction. —**con·junc·tive·ly** *adv.*

con·junc·ti·vi·tis /kən,jəNG(k)tə'vītis/ ▶*n. Med.* inflammation of the conjunctiva of the eye. Also called **PINKEYE.**

con·junc·ture /kən'jəNGKCHər/ ▶*n.* a combination of events: *the peculiar political conjunctures that led to war.* ■ a state of affairs.

con·jure /'känjər; 'kən-/ ▶*v.* [*tr.*] make (something) appear unexpectedly or seemingly from nowhere as if by magic: *Anne* **conjured up** *a most delicious homemade stew.* ■ call (an image) to mind: *conjuring up the image of her mother's face.* ■ (of a word, sound, smell, etc.) cause someone to feel or think of (something): *one scent can* **conjure up** *a childhood summer.* ■ call upon (a spirit or ghost) to appear, by means of a magic ritual. —**con·jur·or** /-jərər/ *n.*

conk[1] /käNGk; kôNGk/ ▶*v.* [*intr.*] (**conk out**) *inf.* (of a machine) break down: *my car conked out.* ■ (of a person) faint or go to sleep. ■ die.

conk[2] *inf.* ▶*v.* [*tr.*] hit (someone) on the head.
▶*n. Brit.* a person's nose.

conk[3] ▶*n.* a hairstyle in which curly or kinky hair is straightened.
▶*v.* [*tr.*] straighten curly or kinky hair.

con man ▶*n. inf.* a man who cheats or tricks someone by means of a confidence game.

con mo·to /kän 'mōtō/ ▶*adv. Mus.* (esp. as a direction) with movement: *andante con moto.*

conn /kän/ (also **con**) *Naut.* ▶*v.* [*tr.*] direct the steering of (a ship).
▶*n.* (**the conn**) the action or post of conning a ship: *I quickly took the conn and restored the channel course.*

con·nect /kə'nekt/ ▶*v.* [*tr.*] (often **be connected**) bring together or into contact so that a real or notional link is established: *the electrodes were* **connected to** *a recording device.* ■ join together so as to provide access and communication: *all the buildings are connected by underground passages* | [*intr.*] *the highway* **connects with** *major routes from all parts of the country.* ■ link to a power or water supply: *your house is* **connected to** *the main cable TV network.* ■ put (someone) into contact by telephone. ■ [*intr.*] (of a train, bus, aircraft, etc.) be timed to arrive at its destination before another train, aircraft, etc., departs so that passengers can transfer from one to the other: *the bus* **connects** *with* **trains** *from Union Station.* ■ associate or relate in some respect: *employees are rewarded with bonuses* **connected to** *their firm's performance.* ■ think of as being linked or related: *I didn't* **connect** *the two incidents at the time.* ■ (of a thing) provide or have a link or relationship with (someone or something): *there was no evidence to* **connect** *Jeff* **with** *the theft.* ■ [*intr.*] form a relationship or feel an affinity: *I* **connected with** *kids individually.* ■ [*intr.*] *inf.* (of a blow) hit the intended target. —**con·nect·a·ble** *adj.* —**con·nect·ed·ly** *adv.* —**con·nect·ed·ness** *n.* —**con·nec·tor** *n.*

con·nec·tion /kə'nekSHən/ (*Brit.* also **con·nex·ion**) ▶*n.* **1** a relationship in which a person, thing, or idea is linked or associated with something else. ■ the action of linking one thing with another: *connection to the Internet.* ■ the placing of parts of an electric circuit in contact so that a current may flow. ■ a link between pipes or electrical components: *it is important to ensure that all connections between the wires are properly made.* ■ a link between two telephones: *she replaced the receiver before the connection was made.* ■ an arrangement or opportunity for catching a connecting train, bus, aircraft, etc.: *ferry connections are sporadic.* ■ such a train, bus, etc.: *we had to wait for our connection to Frankfurt.* ■ (**connections**) people with whom one has social or professional contact or to whom one is related, esp. those with influence and able to offer one help: *he had connections with the music industry.* **2** *inf.* a supplier of narcotics. ■ a narcotics sale or purchase. —**con·nec·tion·al** /-SHənl/ *adj.*
▶ □ **in connection with** with reference to; concerning: *detectives are questioning two men in connection with alleged criminal damage.*

con·nec·tive /kə'nektiv/ ▶*adj.* connecting.
▶*n.* something that connects, in particular: ■ *Gram.* a word or phrase whose function is to link linguistic units together.

con·nec·tive tis·sue ▶*n. Anat.* tissue that connects, supports, binds, or separates other tissues or organs.

conn·ing tow·er ▶*n.* the superstructure of a submarine, from which it can be commanded when on the surface.

con·nive /kə'nīv/ ▶*v.* [*intr.*] (**connive at/in**) secretly allow (something considered immoral, illegal, wrong, or harmful) to occur: *you have it in your power to connive at my escape.* ■ conspire to do something considered immoral, illegal, or harmful: *the government had* **connived with** *security forces in permitting murder* | [as *adj.*] (**conniving**) *a heartless and conniving woman.* —**con·niv·er** *n.*

con·nois·seur /,känə'sər; -'sŏŏr/ ▶*n.* an expert judge in matters of taste: *a connoisseur of music.* —**con·nois·seur·ship** /-,SHip/ *n.*

con·note /kə'nōt/ ▶*v.* [*tr.*] (of a word) imply or suggest (an idea or feeling) in addition to the literal or primary meaning: *the term "modern science" usually connotes a complete openness to empirical testing.* ■ (of a fact) imply as a consequence or condition: *in that period a log cabin connoted hard luck.* —**con·no·ta·tion** /,känə'tāSHən/ *adj.* —**con·no·ta·tive** /'känə,tātiv/ *adj.*

con·nu·bi·al /kə'n(y)ŏŏbēəl/ ▶*adj. poetic/lit.* of or relating to marriage or the relationship of husband and wife; conjugal: *their connubial bed.* —**con·nu·bi·al·i·ty** /kə,n(y)ŏŏbē'alitē/ *n.* —**con·nu·bi·al·ly** *adv.*

con·quer /'käNGkər/ ▶*v.* [*tr.*] overcome and take control of (a place or people) by use of military force. ■ successfully overcome (a problem or weakness). ■ climb (a mountain) successfully. ■ gain the love, admiration, or respect of (a person or group of people). —**con·quer·a·ble** /-k(ə)rəbəl/ *adj.* —**con·quer·or** /-kərər/ *n.*

con·quest /'kän,kwest; 'käNG-/ ▶*n.* the subjugation and assumption of control of a place or people by use of military force. ■ a territory that has been gained in such a way: *colonial conquests.* ■ (**the Conquest**) the invasion and assumption of control of England by William of Normandy in 1066. See also **NORMAN CONQUEST.** ■ the overcoming of a problem or weakness. ■ a person whose affection or favor has been won.

con·quis·ta·dor /kôNG'kēstə,dôr; kän'k(w)istə-; kən-/ ▶*n.* (*pl.* **-quis·ta·do·res** /-,kēstə'dôrēz; -ās; -,k(w)istə-/ or **-quis·ta·dors**) a conqueror, esp. one of the Spanish conquerors of Mexico and Peru in the 16th century.

con·san·guin·e·ous /,kän,saNG'gwinēəs/ ▶*adj.* relating to or denoting people descended from the same ancestor: *consanguineous marriages.* —**con·san·guin·i·ty** /-'gwinitē/ *n.*

con·science /'känCHəns/ ▶*n.* an inner feeling or voice viewed as acting as a guide to the rightness or wrongness of one's behavior: *he had a* **guilty conscience** *about his desires.* —**con·science·less** *adj.*
▶ □ **in (good) conscience** by any reasonable standard; by all that is fair: *they have in conscience done all they could.* □ **on one's conscience** weighing heavily and guiltily on one's mind.

con·sci·en·tious /,känCHē'enCHəs/ ▶*adj.* (of a person) wishing to do what is right, esp. to do one's work or duty well and thoroughly: *a conscientious and hardworking clerk.* ■ (of work or a person's manner) showing such an attitude. ■ relating to a person's conscience. —**con·sci·en·tious·ly** *adv.* —**con·sci·en·tious·ness** *n.*

con·sci·en·tious ob·jec·tor ▶*n.* a person who for reasons of conscience objects to serving in the armed forces. —**con·sci·en·tious ob·jec·tion** *n.*

con·scious /'känCHəs/ ▶*adj.* aware of and responding to one's surroundings; awake. ■ having knowledge of something; aware: *we are* **conscious of** *the extent of the problem.* ■ (**conscious of**) painfully aware of; sensitive to: *he was very conscious of his appearance.* ■ concerned with or worried about a particular matter: *they were growing increasingly security-conscious.* ■ (of an action or feeling) deliberate and intentional. ■ (of the mind or a thought) directly perceptible to and under the control of the person concerned. —**con·scious·ly** *adv.*

con·scious·ness /ˈkänCHəsnəs/ ▸ *n.* the state of being awake and aware of one's surroundings. ■ the awareness or perception of something by a person. ■ the fact of awareness by the mind of itself and the world.

con·script ▸ *v.* /kənˈskript/ [*tr.*] (often **be conscripted**) enlist (someone) compulsorily, typically into the armed services.
▸ *n.* /ˈkänˌskript/ a person enlisted compulsorily.

con·scrip·tion /kənˈskripSHən/ ▸ *n.* compulsory enlistment for state service, typically into the armed forces. ▷ early 19th cent.: via French (conscription was introduced in France in 1798), from late Latin *conscriptio(n-)* 'levying of troops,' from Latin *conscribere* 'write down together, enroll,' from *con-* 'together' + *scribere* 'write.'

con·se·crate /ˈkänsiˌkrāt/ ▸ *v.* [*tr.*] (usu **be consecrated**) make or declare (something, typically a church) sacred; dedicate formally to a religious or divine purpose: *the present Holy Trinity church was consecrated in 1845* | [as *adj.*] (**consecrated**) *consecrated ground.* ■ (in Christian belief) make (bread or wine) into the body or blood of Christ: [as *adj.*] (**consecrated**) *the consecrated wine.* ■ ordain (someone) to a sacred office, typically that of bishop: *in 1969 he was consecrated bishop of Northern Uganda.* ■ *inf.* devote (something) exclusively to a particular purpose. —**con·se·cra·tion** /ˌkänsiˈkrāSHən/ *n.* —**con·se·cra·tor** /-ˌkrātər/ *n.* —**con·se·cra·to·ry** /-krəˌtôrē/ *adj.*

con·sec·u·tive /kənˈsekyətiv/ ▸ *adj.* following continuously: *five consecutive months of serious decline.* ■ in unbroken or logical sequence. ■ *Gram.* expressing consequence or result: *a consecutive clause.* ■ *Mus.* denoting intervals of the same kind (esp. fifths or octaves) occurring in succession between two parts or voices. —**con·sec·u·tive·ly** *adv.* —**con·sec·u·tive·ness** *n.*

con·sen·sus /kənˈsensəs/ ▸ *n.* general agreement: *a consensus of opinion among judges* | [as *adj.*] *a consensus view.*

con·sent /kənˈsent/ ▸ *n.* permission for something to happen or agreement to do something: *no change may be made without his consent.*
▸ *v.* [*intr.*] give permission for something to happen: *he consented to a search by a detective.* ■ agree to do something. —**con·sen·su·al** /-ˈsenshōōəl/ *adj.*

con·sent·ing a·dult ▸ *n.* an adult who willingly agrees to engage in an act, esp. a sexual act.

con·se·quence /ˈkänsikwəns; -ˌkwens/ ▸ *n.* **1** a result or effect of an action or condition: *many have been laid off from work as a consequence of the administration's policies.* **2** importance or relevance: *the past is of no consequence* | *he didn't say anything of great consequence.* ■ *dated* social distinction: *a woman of consequence.*
▸ □ **in consequence** as a result. □ **take the consequences** accept responsibility for the negative results of one's action.

con·se·quent /ˈkänsikwənt; -ˌkwent/ ▸ *adj.* following as a result or effect: *labor shortages would be created with a consequent increase in wages.* ■ *Geol.* (of a stream or valley) having a direction or character determined by the original slope of the land before erosion. ■ *archaic* logically consistent.
▸ *n.* a thing that follows another. ■ *Logic* the second part of a conditional proposition, whose truth is stated to be conditional upon that of the antecedent.

con·se·quen·tial /ˌkänsəˈkwenCHəl/ ▸ *adj.* **1** following as a result or effect: *a loss of confidence and a consequential withdrawal of funds.* ■ *Law* resulting from an act, but not immediately and directly: *consequential damages.* **2** important; significant. —**con·se·quen·ti·al·i·ty** /ˌkänsəˌkwenCHēˈalitē/ *n.* —**con·se·quen·tial·ly** *adv.*

con·se·quent·ly /ˈkänsikwəntlē; -ˌkwentlē/ ▸ *adv.* as a result.

con·serv·an·cy /kənˈsərvənsē/ ▸ *n.* (*pl.* **-cies**) **1** [in *names*] a body concerned with the preservation of nature, specific species, or natural resources: *the Nature Conservancy.* **2** the conservation of something, esp. wildlife and the environment.

con·ser·va·tion /ˌkänsərˈvāSHən/ ▸ *n.* the action of conserving something, in particular: ■ preservation, protection, or restoration of the natural environment, natural ecosystems, vegetation, and wildlife. ■ preservation, repair, and prevention of deterioration of archaeological, historical, and cultural sites and artifacts. ■ prevention of excessive or wasteful use of a resource. ■ *Physics* the principle by which the total value of a physical quantity (such as energy, mass, or linear or angular momentum) remains constant in a system. —**con·ser·va·tion·al** /-SHənl/ *adj.* —**con·ser·va·tion·ist** *n.*

con·ser·va·tive /kənˈsərvətiv; -vəˌtiv/ ▸ *adj.* holding to traditional attitudes and values and cautious about change or innovation, typically in relation to politics or religion. ■ (of dress or taste) sober and conventional. ■ (of an estimate) purposely low for the sake of caution. ■ (of surgery or medical treatment) intended to control rather than eliminate a condition, with existing tissue preserved as far as possible. ■ (**Conservative**) of or relating to the Conservative Party of Great Britain or a similar party in another country.
▸ *n.* a person who is averse to change and holds to traditional values and attitudes, typically in relation to politics. ■ (**Conservative**) a supporter or member of the Conservative Party of Great Britain or a similar party in another country. —**con·serv·a·tism** /kənˈsərvəˌtizəm/ *n.* —**con·serv·a·tive·ly** *adv.* —**con·serv·a·tive·ness** *n.*

con·serv·a·to·ry /kənˈsərvəˌtôrē/ ▸ *n.* (*pl.* **-ries**) **1** a college for the study of classical music or other arts. **2** a room with a glass roof and walls, attached to a house and used as a greenhouse or a sun parlor.

con·serve ▸ *v.* /kənˈsərv/ [*tr.*] protect (something, esp. an environmentally or culturally important place or thing) from harm or destruction: *the funds will help conserve endangered wetlands.* ■ prevent the wasteful or harmful overuse of (a resource): *industry should conserve water.* ■ *Physics* maintain (a quantity such as energy or mass) at a constant overall total. ■ preserve (food, typically fruit) with sugar.
▸ *n.* /ˈkänˌsərv/ a sweet food made by preserving fruit with sugar; jam.

con·sid·er /kənˈsidər/ ▸ *v.* [*tr.*] (often **be considered**) think carefully about (something), typically before making a decision: *each application is considered on its merits.* ■ think about and be drawn toward (a course of action): *he had considered giving up his job.* ■ regard (someone or something) as having a specified quality: *I consider him irresponsible.* ■ believe; think: *I don't consider that I'm to blame.* ■ take (something) into account when making an assessment or judgment: *one service area is not enough when you consider the number of cars using this highway.* ■ look attentively at.
▸ □ **all things considered** taking everything into account.

con·sid·er·a·ble /kənˈsidər(ə)bəl; -ˈsidrəbəl/ ▸ *adj.* notably large in size, amount, or extent: *a position of considerable influence.* ■ (of a person) having merit or distinction. —**con·sid·er·a·bly** /-blē/ *adv.*

con·sid·er·ate /kənˈsidərət/ ▸ *adj.* careful not to cause inconvenience or hurt to others. ■ *archaic* showing careful thought: *be considerate over your handwriting.* —**con·sid·er·ate·ly** *adv.* —**con·sid·er·ate·ness** *n.*

con·sid·er·a·tion /kənˌsidəˈrāSHən/ ▸ *n.* **1** careful thought, typically over a period of time. ■ a fact or a motive taken into account in deciding or judging something: *the idea was motivated by political considerations.* ■ thoughtfulness and sensitivity toward others: *companies should show more consideration for their employees.* **2** a payment or reward: *you can buy the books for a small consideration.* ■ *Law* (in a contractual agreement) anything given or promised or forborne by one party in exchange for the promise or undertaking of another. **3** *archaic* importance; consequence.
▸ □ **in consideration of** on account of: *a nightlight burned in consideration of Ernie's phobia.* ■ in return for: *he paid them in consideration of their services.* □ **take into consideration** take into account. □ **under consideration** being thought about.

con·sid·er·ing /kənˈsidəriNG/ ▸ *prep.* & *conj.* taking into consideration: [as *prep.*] *considering the conditions, it's very good* | [as *conj.*] *considering that he was the youngest on the field, he played well.*
▸ *adv. inf.* taking everything into account: *it's not bad, considering.*

con·sign /kənˈsīn/ ▸ *v.* [*tr.*] deliver (something) to a person's custody, typically in order for it to be sold: *he consigned three paintings to Sotheby's.* ■ send (goods) by a public carrier. ■ (**consign someone/something to**) assign; commit decisively or permanently: *she consigned the letter to the wastebasket.* ▷ late Middle English (in the sense 'mark with the sign of the cross,' esp. at baptism or confirmation, as a sign of dedication to God): from French *consigner* or Latin *consignare* 'mark with a seal.' —**con·sign·ee** /ˌkänsīˈnē; kənˌsīˈnē/ *n.* —**con·sign·ment** *n.* —**con·sign·or** /kənˈsīnər/ *n.*

con·sign·ment shop (or **consignment store**) ▸ *n.* a store that sells secondhand items on behalf of the original owner, who receives a percentage of the selling price.

con·sist ▸ *v.* /kənˈsist/ [*intr.*] **1** (**consist of**) be composed or made up of: *the exhibition consists of 180 drawings.* ■ (**consist in**) have as an essential feature: *his duties consist in taking the condition of the barometer.* **2** (**consist with**) *archaic* be consistent with: *the information consists with our account.*

con·sist·en·cy /kənˈsistənsē/ (also **con·sist·ence** /-təns/) ▸ *n.* (*pl.* **-cies**) **1** conformity in the application of something, typically that which is necessary for the sake of logic, accuracy, or fairness: *the grading system* *is to be streamlined to ensure greater consistency.* ■ the achievement of a level of performance that does not vary greatly in quality over time. **2** the way in which a substance, typically a liquid, holds together; thickness or viscosity: *the sauce has the consistency of creamed butter.*

con·sist·ent /kən'sistənt/ ▶ *adj.* (of a person, behavior, or process) unchanging in achievement or effect over a period of time: *manufacturing processes require a consistent approach.* ■ compatible or in agreement with something: *the injuries are consistent with falling from a great height.* ■ (of an argument or set of ideas) not containing any logical contradictions: *a consistent explanation.* —**con·sist·ent·ly** *adv.*

con·so·la·tion /ˌkänsə'lāsHən/ ▶ *n.* comfort received by a person after a loss or disappointment: *there was consolation in knowing that others were worse off.* ■ a person or thing providing such comfort: *the church was the main consolation in a hard life.* ■ *Sports* a round or contest for tournament entrants who have been eliminated before the finals, often to determine third and fourth place. —**con·sol·a·to·ry** /kən'sōlə,tôrē/ *adj.*

con·so·la·tion prize ▶ *n.* a prize given to a competitor who narrowly fails to win or who finishes last.

con·sole[1] /kən'sōl/ ▶ *v.* [tr.] comfort (someone) at a time of grief or disappointment. —**con·sol·a·ble** *adj.* —**con·sol·er** *n.* —**con·sol·ing·ly** *adv.*

con·sole[2] /'kän,sōl/ ▶ *n.* **1** a panel or unit accommodating a set of controls for electronic or mechanical equipment. ■ a cabinet for television or radio equipment. ■ the cabinet or enclosure containing the keyboards, stops, pedals, etc., of an organ. ■ a monitor and keyboard in a multiuser computer system. **2** an ornamented bracket with scrolls or corbel supporting a cornice, shelf, or tabletop. **3** a support between the seats of an automobile that has a compartment and indentations for holding small items.

con·sol·i·date /kən'sälə,dāt/ ▶ *v.* **1** [tr.] make (something) physically stronger or more solid: *consolidate the outside walls.* ■ reinforce or strengthen (one's position or power): *the company consolidated its position in the international market.* ■ combine (a number of things) into a single more effective or coherent whole: *all manufacturing activities have been consolidated in new premises.* ■ combine (a number of financial accounts or funds) into a single overall account or set of accounts. ■ combine (two or more legal actions involving similar questions) into one for action by a court. **2** [intr.] become stronger or more solid. —**con·sol·i·da·tion** /-,sälə'dāsHən/ *n.* —**con·sol·i·da·tor** /-,dātər/ *n.*

con·som·mé /ˌkänsə'mā/ ▶ *n.* a clear soup made with concentrated stock.

con·so·nance /'känsənəns/ ▶ *n.* agreement or compatibility between opinions or actions: *consonance between conservation measures and existing agricultural practice.* ■ the recurrence of similar sounds, esp. consonants, in close proximity (chiefly as used in prosody). ■ *Mus.* the combination of notes that are in harmony with each other due to the relationship between their frequencies.

con·so·nant /'känsənənt/ ▶ *n.* a basic speech sound in which the breath is at least partly obstructed and which can be combined with a vowel to form a syllable. Contrasted with **VOWEL**. ■ a letter representing such a sound.
▶ *adj.* **1** denoting or relating to such a sound or letter: *a consonant phoneme.* **2** (**consonant with**) in agreement or harmony with: *the findings are consonant with other research.* ■ *Mus.* making a harmonious interval or chord: *the bass is consonant with all the upper notes.* —**con·so·nan·tal** /ˌkänsə'nantl/ *adj.* —**con·so·nant·ly** *adv.*

con·sort[1] ▶ *n.* a wife, husband, or companion, in particular the spouse of a reigning monarch.
▶ *v.* /kən'sôrt; 'kän,sôrt/ [intr.] (**consort with**) habitually associate with (someone), typically with the disapproval of others: *you chose to consort with the enemy.* ■ (**consort with/to**) *archaic* agree or be in harmony with.

con·sort[2] /'kän,sôrt/ ▶ *n.* a small group of musicians performing together, typically playing instrumental music of the Renaissance period: *a consort of viols.*

con·sor·ti·um /kən'sôrsH(ē)əm; -'sôrtēəm/ ▶ *n.* (*pl.* **-ti·a** /-tēə/; **-sh**(ē)ə/ or **-ti·ums**) **1** an association, typically of several business companies. **2** *Law* the right of association and companionship with one's husband or wife.

con·spec·tus /kən'spektəs/ ▶ *n.* a summary or overview of a subject.

con·spic·u·ous /kən'spikyōōs/ ▶ *adj.* standing out so as to be clearly visible: *he was very thin, with a conspicuous Adam's apple.* ■ attracting notice or attention: *he showed conspicuous bravery.* —**con·spi·cu·i·ty** /ˌkänspi'kyōōitē/ *n.* —**con·spic·u·ous·ly** *adv.* —**con·spic·u·ous·ness** *n.*

con·spir·a·cy /kən'spirəsē/ ▶ *n.* (*pl.* **-cies**) a secret plan by a group to do something unlawful or harmful: *a conspiracy to destroy the government.* ■ the action of plotting or conspiring.

con·spir·a·tor /kən'spirətər/ ▶ *n.* a person who takes part in a conspiracy. —**con·spir·a·to·ri·al** /kən,spirə'tôrēəl/ *adj.* —**con·spir·a·to·ri·al·ly** /kən,spirə'tôrēəlē/ *adv.*

con·spire /kən'spīr/ ▶ *v.* [intr.] make secret plans jointly to commit an unlawful or harmful act: *they conspired against him.* ■ (of events or circumstances) seem to be working together to bring about a particular result, typically to someone's detriment: *everything conspires to exacerbate the situation.*

con·sta·ble /'känstəbəl/ ▶ *n.* **1** a peace officer with limited policing authority, typically in a small town. ■ *Brit.* a police officer. **2** the governor of a royal castle. ■ *hist.* the highest-ranking official in a royal household.

con·stab·u·lar·y /kən'stabyə,lerē/ ▶ *n.* (*pl.* **-lar·ies**) the constables of a district, collectively. ■ *Brit.* a police force covering a particular area or city.
▶ *adj.* of or relating to a constabulary.

con·stan·cy /'känstənsē/ ▶ *n.* the quality of being faithful and dependable. ■ the quality of being enduring and unchanging: *the trade winds are noted for constancy in speed and direction.*

con·stant /'känstənt/ ▶ *adj.* occurring continuously over a period of time: *the pain is constant.* ■ remaining the same over a period of time. ■ (of a person) unchangingly faithful and dependable.
▶ *n.* a situation or state of affairs that does not change: *the condition of struggle remained a constant.* ■ *Math.* a quantity or parameter that does not change its value whatever the value of the variables, under a given set of conditions. —**con·stant·ly** *adv.*

con·stel·la·tion /ˌkänstə'lāsHən/ ▶ *n.* a group of stars forming a recognizable pattern that is traditionally named after its apparent form or identified with a mythological figure. Modern astronomers divide the sky into eighty-eight constellations. ■ a group or cluster of related things. ▷Middle English (as an astrological term denoting the relative positions of the "stars" (planets), supposed to influence events): via Old French from late Latin *constellatio(n-)*, based on Latin *stella* 'star.'

con·ster·na·tion /ˌkänstər'nāsHən/ ▶ *n.* feelings of anxiety or dismay, typically at something unexpected: *I always welcomed clover, much to the consternation of the neighbors.*

con·sti·pat·ed /'känstə,pātid/ ▶ *adj.* (of a person or animal) affected with constipation. ■ *fig.* slow-moving; restricted or inhibited in some way. —**con·sti·pate** /-,pāt/ *v.*

con·sti·pa·tion /ˌkänstə'pāsHən/ ▶ *n.* a condition in which there is difficulty in emptying the bowels, usually associated with hardened feces. ■ *fig.* a high level of constraint or restriction; a pronounced lack of ease: *literary constipation.*

con·stit·u·en·cy /kən'stiCHōōənsē/ ▶ *n.* (*pl.* **-cies**) a body of voters in a specified area who elect a representative to a legislative body. ■ *chiefly Brit.* the area represented in this way. ■ a body of customers or supporters.

con·stit·u·ent /kən'stiCHōōənt/ ▶ *adj.* **1** being a part of a whole: *the constituent minerals of the rock.* **2** being a voting member of a community or organization and having the power to appoint or elect: *the constituent body has a right of veto.* ■ able to make or change a political constitution: *a constituent assembly.*
▶ *n.* **1** a member of a constituency. **2** a component part of something. ■ *Linguistics* the common part of two or several more complex forms, e.g., *gentle* in *gentleman, gentlemanly, ungentlemanly.* ■ *Linguistics* a word or construction that is part of a larger construction.

con·sti·tute /'känstə,t(y)ōot/ ▶ *v.* [tr.] **1** be (a part) of a whole: *single parents constitute a great proportion of the poor.* ■ (of people or things) combine to form (a whole): *there were enough members present to constitute a quorum.* ■ be or be equivalent to (something): *his failure to act constituted a breach of duty.* **2** (usu. **be constituted**) give legal or constitutional form to (an institution); establish by law.

con·sti·tu·tion /ˌkänstə't(y)ōosHən/ ▶ *n.* **1** a body of fundamental principles or established precedents according to which a state or other organization is acknowledged to be governed. ■ a written record of this: *the preamble to the constitution of UNESCO.* ■ (**the Constitution**) the basic written set of principles and precedents of federal government in the U.S., which came into operation in 1789 and has since been modified by twenty-seven amendments. **2** the composition of something: *the genetic constitution of a species.* ■ the forming or establishing of something. **3** a person's physical state with regard to vitality, health, and strength. ■ a person's mental or psychological makeup.

con·sti·tu·tion·al /ˌkänstə't(y)ōosHənl/ ▶ *adj.* **1** of or relating to an established set of principles governing a state: *a constitutional amendment.* ■ in accordance with or allowed by such principles: *a constitutional monarchy.* **2** of or relating to someone's physical or mental condition.

▶*n. dated* a walk, typically one taken regularly to maintain or restore good health. —**con·sti·tu·tion·al·i·ty** /-ˌt(y)o͞osʜə'nalitē/ *n.* —**con·sti·tu·tion·al·ly** *adv.*

con·strain /kən'strān/ ▶*v.* [*tr.*] (often **be constrained**) severely restrict the scope, extent, or activity of: *agricultural development is constrained by climate.* ■ compel or force (someone) toward a particular course of action: *children are constrained to work in the way the book dictates.* ■ [usu. as *adj.*] (**constrained**) cause to appear unnaturally forced, typically because of embarrassment: *acting in a constrained manner.* ■ *poetic/lit.* confine forcibly; imprison. ■ *archaic* bring about (something) by compulsion. —**con·strain·ed·ly** /-nədlē/ *adv.*

con·straint /kən'strānt/ ▶*n.* a limitation or restriction: *time constraints make it impossible to do everything.* ■ stiffness of manner and inhibition in relations between people: *talk without constraint.*

con·strict /kən'strikt/ ▶*v.* [*tr.*] make narrower, esp. by encircling pressure: *chemicals that constrict the blood vessels.* ■ [*intr.*] become narrower: *he felt his throat constrict.* ■ (of a snake) coil around (prey) in order to asphyxiate it. ■ *fig.* restrict: *the fear and the reality of crime constrict many people's lives.* —**con·stric·tion** /-'striksʜən/ *n.* —**con·stric·tive** /-tiv/ *adj.*

con·stric·tor /kən'striktər/ ▶*n.* **1** a snake (families Boidae and Pythonidae, and some members of other families, esp. Colubridae) that kills by coiling around its prey and asphyxiating it. **2** (also **constrictor muscle**) *Anat.* a muscle whose contraction narrows a vessel or passage. ■ each of the muscles that constrict the pharynx.

con·struct ▶*v.* /kən'strəkt/ [*tr.*] build or erect (something, typically a building, road, or machine). ■ form (an idea or theory) by bringing together various conceptual elements, typically over a period of time. ■ *Gram.* form (a sentence) according to grammatical rules. ■ *Geom.* draw or delineate (a geometric figure) accurately to given conditions. ▶*n.* /'kän,strəkt/ an idea or theory containing various conceptual elements, typically one considered to be subjective and not based on empirical evidence. ■ *Linguistics* a group of words forming a phrase. ■ a physical thing that is deliberately built or formed. —**con·struct·i·ble** *adj.* —**con·struc·tor** /-tər/ *n.*

con·struc·tion /kən'strəksʜən/ ▶*n.* the building of something, typically a large structure: *a skyscraper under construction.* ■ such activity considered as an industry. ■ the style or method used in the building of something: *the mill is of brick construction.* ■ a building or other structure. ■ the creation or formation of an abstract entity: *language plays a large part in our construction of reality.* ■ an interpretation or explanation: *you could put an honest construction upon their conduct.* ■ *Gram.* the arrangement of words according to syntactical rules: *sentence construction.* —**con·struc·tion·al** /-sʜənl/ *adj.* —**con·struc·tion·al·ly** /-sʜənl-ē/ *adv.*

con·struc·tive /kən'strəktiv/ ▶*adj.* **1** serving a useful purpose; tending to build up: *constructive criticism.* **2** *Law* derived by inference; implied by operation of law; not obvious or explicit: *constructive fraud.* **3** *Math.* relating to, based on, or denoting mathematical proofs that show how an entity may in principle be constructed or arrived at in a finite number of steps. —**con·struc·tive·ly** *adv.* —**con·struc·tive·ness** *n.*

con·strue /kən'stro͞o/ ▶*v.* (**-strues, -strued, -stru·ing**) [*tr.*] (often **be construed**) interpret (a word or action) in a particular way. ■ *dated* analyze the syntax of (a text, sentence, or word): *both verbs can be construed with either infinitive.* ■ *dated* translate (a passage or author) word for word, typically aloud. —**con·stru·a·ble** *adj.* —**con·stru·al** /-'stro͞oəl/ *n.*

con·sub·stan·tial /ˌkänsəb'stanchəl/ ▶*adj.* of the same substance or essence (used esp. of the three persons of the Trinity in Christian theology): *Christ is consubstantial with the Father.* —**con·sub·stan·ti·al·i·ty** /-ˌstanchē'alətē/ *n.*

con·sub·stan·ti·a·tion /ˌkänsəbˌstanchē'āsʜən/ ▶*n.* *Christian Theol.* the doctrine, esp. in Lutheran belief, that the substance of the bread and wine coexists with the body and blood of Christ in the Eucharist. Compare with TRANSUBSTANTIATION.

con·sul /'känsəl/ ▶*n.* **1** an official appointed by a government to live in a foreign city and protect and promote the government's citizens and interests there. **2** (in ancient Rome) one of the two annually elected chief magistrates who jointly ruled the republic. ■ any of the three chief magistrates of the first French republic (1799–1804). —**con·su·lar** /'käns(y)ələr/ *adj.* —**con·sul·ship** /-,sʜip/ *n.*

con·su·late /'känsələt/ ▶*n.* **1** the place or building in which a consul's duties are carried out. ■ the office, position, or period of office of a consul. **2** *hist.* the period of office of a Roman consul. ■ (**the consulate**) the system of government by consuls in ancient Rome. **3** (**the Consulate**) the government of the first French republic (1799–1804) by three consuls.

con·sult /kən'səlt/ ▶*v.* [*tr.*] seek information or advice from (someone with expertise in a particular area): *you should consult a financial advisor.*

■ have discussions or confer with (someone), typically before undertaking a course of action: *patients are entitled to be consulted about their treatment* | [*intr.*] *they've got to consult with their board of directors.* ■ refer for information to (a book, watch, etc.) in order to ascertain something. —**con·sul·ta·tive** /-'səltətiv/ *adj.*

con·sult·ant /kən'səltnt/ ▶*n.* a person who provides expert advice professionally.

con·sul·ta·tion /ˌkänsəl'tāsʜən/ ▶*n.* the action or process of formally consulting or discussing. ■ a meeting with an expert or professional, such as a medical doctor, in order to seek advice.

con·sult·ing /kən'səltiɴɡ/ ▶*adj.* **1** (of a senior person in a professional or technical field) engaged in the business of giving advice to others working in the same field: *a consulting engineer.* ■ (of a business or company) giving specialist advice: *an environmental consulting company.* ▶*n.* the business of giving specialist advice to other professionals, typically in financial and business matters.

con·sume /kən'so͞om/ ▶*v.* [*tr.*] eat, drink, or ingest (food or drink). ■ buy (goods or services). ■ use up (a resource). ■ (esp. of a fire) completely destroy. ■ (usu. **be consumed**) (of a feeling) absorb all of the attention and energy of (someone): *Carolyn was consumed with guilt* | [as *adj.*] (**consuming**) *a consuming passion.* —**con·sum·a·ble** *adj.* —**con·sum·ing·ly** *adv.*

con·sum·er /kən'so͞omər/ ▶*n.* a person who purchases goods and services for personal use: [as *adj.*] *consumer demand.* ■ a person or thing that eats or uses something: *Scandinavians are the largest consumers of rye.*

con·sum·er goods ▶*pl. n.* goods bought and used by consumers, rather than by manufacturers for producing other goods.

con·sum·er·ism /kən'so͞omə,rizəm/ ▶*n.* **1** the protection or promotion of the interests of consumers. **2** *often derog.* the preoccupation of society with the acquisition of consumer goods. —**con·sum·er·ist** *adj.* & *n.* —**con·sum·er·is·tic** /kən,so͞omə'ristik/ *adj.*

con·sum·mate ▶*v.* /'känsə,māt/ [*tr.*] make (a marriage or relationship) complete by having sexual intercourse. ■ complete (a transaction or attempt); make perfect. ▶*adj.* /'känsəmət; kən'səmət/ showing a high degree of skill and flair; complete or perfect: *she dressed with consummate elegance.* —**con·sum·mate·ly** /'känsəmətlē; kən'səmətlē/ *adv.* —**con·sum·ma·tor** /'känsə,mātər/ *n.*

con·sum·ma·tion /ˌkänsə'māsʜən/ ▶*n.* the point at which something is complete or finalized: *the consummation of a sale.* ■ the action of making a marriage or relationship complete by having sexual intercourse.

con·sump·tion /kən'səm(p)sʜən/ ▶*n.* **1** the using up of a resource: *we should reduce energy consumption.* ■ the eating, drinking, or ingesting of something: *liquor is sold for consumption off the premises.* ■ an amount of something that is used up or ingested: *a daily consumption of 15 cigarettes.* ■ the purchase and use of goods and services by the public: *an article for mass consumption.* ■ the reception of information or entertainment, esp. by a mass audience: *his memo was not meant for public consumption.* **2** *dated* a wasting disease, esp. pulmonary tuberculosis.

con·sump·tive /kən'səm(p)tiv/ ▶*adj.* **1** *dated* affected with a wasting disease, esp. pulmonary tuberculosis. **2** *chiefly derog.* of or relating to the using up of resources. —**con·sump·tive·ly** *adv.*

cont. ▶*abbr.* ■ contents. ■ continued.

con·tact ▶*n.* /'kän,takt/ **1** the state or condition of physical touching: *the tennis ball is in contact with the court surface for as little as 5 milliseconds.* ■ the state or condition of communicating or meeting: *he had lost contact with his friends.* ■ [as *adj.*] activated by or operating through physical touch: *contact dermatitis.* ■ a connection for the passage of an electric current from one thing to another, or a part or device by which such a connection is made. ■ (**contacts**) contact lenses. **2** a meeting, communication, or relationship with someone. ■ a person who may be communicated with for information or assistance, esp. with regard to one's job. ■ a person who has associated with a patient with a contagious disease (and so may carry the infection). ▶*v.* /'kän,takt; kən'takt/ [*tr.*] communicate with (someone), typically in order to give or receive specific information. —**con·tact·a·ble** /'kän,taktəbəl; kən'tak-/ *adj.*

con·tact lens ▶*n.* a thin plastic lens placed directly on the surface of the eye to correct visual defects.

con·tact sport ▶*n.* a sport in which the participants necessarily come into bodily contact with one another.

con·ta·gion /kən'tājən/ ▶*n.* the communication of disease from one

---

Pronunciation Key ə *ago, up;* ər *over, fur;* a *hat;* ā *ate;* ä *car;* cʜ *chin;* e *let;* ē *see;* e(ə)r *air;* i *fit;* ī *by;* i(ə)r *ear;* ɴɢ *sing;* ō *go;* ô *law, for;* oi *toy;* o͞o *good;* o͞o *goo;* ou *out;* sʜ *she;* тʜ *thin;* ᴛʜ *then;* (h)w *why;* zʜ *vision*

person to another by close contact: *the rooms held no risk of contagion.* ■ a disease spread in such a way. ■ *fig.* the spreading of a harmful idea or practice: *the contagion of disgrace.* ■ a contagium.

con·ta·gious /kən'tājəs/ ▶*adj.* (of a disease) spread from one person or organism to another by direct or indirect contact. ■ (of a person or animal) likely to transmit a disease by contact with other people or animals. ■ *fig.* (of an emotion, feeling, or attitude) likely to spread to and affect others. —**con·ta·gious·ly** *adv.* —**con·ta·gious·ness** *n.*

con·tain /kən'tān/ ▶*v.* [*tr.*] **1** have or hold (someone or something) within. ■ be made up of (a number of things); consist of: *borscht can contain mainly beets or a number of vegetables.* ■ (of a number) be divisible by (a factor) without a remainder. **2** control or restrain (oneself or a feeling). ■ prevent (a severe problem) from increasing in extent or intensity: *a new western policy to contain the conflict in Bosnia.* —**con·tain·a·ble** *adj.*

con·tain·er /kən'tānər/ ▶*n.* an object that can be used to hold or transport something: *a microwaveable glass container.* ■ a large metal box of a standard design and size used for the transportation of goods by road, rail, sea, or air: *a container ship.*

con·tain·ment /kən'tānmənt/ ▶*n.* the action of keeping something harmful under control or within limits: *the containment of the AIDS epidemic.* ■ the action or policy of preventing the expansion of a hostile country or influence: *the containment of communism.*

con·tam·i·nate /kən'tamə,nāt/ ▶*v.* [*tr.*] (often **be contaminated**) make (something) impure by exposure to or addition of a poisonous or polluting substance: *the site was found to be contaminated by radioactivity* | *fig. the entertainment industry is able to contaminate the mind of the public.* —**con·tam·i·nant** /-'tamənənt/ *n.* —**con·tam·i·na·tion** /-,tamə'nāSHən/ *n.* —**con·tam·i·na·tor** /-,nātər/ *n.*

con·tem·plate /'käntəm,plāt/ ▶*v.* [*tr.*] look thoughtfully for a long time at. ■ think about: *the results of a trade war are too horrifying to contemplate.* ■ [*intr.*] think profoundly and at length; meditate: *he sat morosely contemplating.* ■ have in mind as a probable though not certain intention: *she was contemplating a gold mining venture.* —**con·tem·pla·tion** /,käntəm'plāSHən/ *n.* —**con·tem·pla·tor** /-,plātər/ *n.*

con·tem·pla·tive /kən'templətiv/ ▶*adj.* expressing or involving prolonged thought: *she regarded me with a contemplative eye.* ■ involving or given to deep silent prayer or religious meditation.
▶*n.* a person whose life is devoted primarily to prayer, esp. in a monastery or convent. —**con·tem·pla·tive·ly** *adv.*

con·tem·po·ra·ne·ous /kən,tempə'rānēəs/ ▶*adj.* existing or occurring in the same period of time: *Pythagoras was contemporaneous with Buddha.* —**con·tem·po·ra·ne·i·ty** /-rə'nēitē; -rə'nāitē/ *n.* —**con·tem·po·ra·ne·ous·ly** *adv.* —**con·tem·po·ra·ne·ous·ness** *n.*

con·tem·po·rar·y /kən'tempə,rerē/ ▶*adj.* **1** living or occurring at the same time: *the event was recorded by a contemporary historian.* ■ dating from the same time: *this series of paintings is contemporary with other works in an early style.* **2** belonging to or occurring in the present: *the tension and complexities of our contemporary society.* ■ following modern ideas or fashion in style or design: *contemporary art.*
▶*n.* (pl. **-rar·ies**) a person or thing living or existing at the same time as another: *he was a contemporary of Darwin.* ■ a person of roughly the same age as another: *my contemporaries at school.* —**con·tem·po·rar·i·ly** /kən,tempə're(ə)rəlē/ *adv.* —**con·tem·po·rar·i·ness** *n.*

con·tempt /kən'tem(p)t/ ▶*n.* the feeling that a person or a thing is beneath consideration, worthless, or deserving scorn: *he showed his contempt for his job by doing it badly.* ■ disregard for something that should be taken into account: *an arrogant contempt for the wishes of the majority.* ■ (also **contempt of court**) the offense of being disobedient to or disrespectful of a court of law and its officers: *several unions were held to be in contempt.* ■ the offense of being similarly disobedient to or disrespectful of the lawful operation of a legislative body.
▶ □ **beneath contempt** utterly worthless or despicable. □ **hold someone/something in contempt** consider someone or something to be unworthy of respect or attention.

con·tempt·i·ble /kən'tem(p)təbəl/ ▶*adj.* deserving contempt; despicable: *a display of contemptible cowardice.* —**con·tempt·i·bly** /-blē/ *adv.*

con·temp·tu·ous /kən'tem(p)CHŌōs/ ▶*adj.* showing contempt; scornful: *she was intolerant and contemptuous of the majority of the human race.* —**con·temp·tu·ous·ly** *adv.* —**con·temp·tu·ous·ness** *n.*

con·tend /kən'tend/ ▶*v.* **1** [*intr.*] (**contend with/against**) struggle to surmount (a difficulty or danger): *she had to contend with his uncertain temper.* ■ (**contend for**) engage in a competition or campaign in order to win or achieve (something): *the local team should contend for a division championship.* **2** assert something as a position in an argument: *he contends that the judge was wrong.* —**con·tend·er** *n.*

con·tent[1] /kən'tent/ ▶*adj.* in a state of peaceful happiness: *he seemed more*

content, less bitter. ■ satisfied with a certain level of achievement, good fortune, etc., and not wishing for more: *to be content with third place.*
▶*v.* [*tr.*] satisfy (someone): *nothing would content her.* ■ (**content oneself with**) accept as adequate despite wanting more or better.
▶*n.* a state of satisfaction. —**con·tent·ment** *n.*
▶ □ **to one's heart's content** to the full extent of one's desires.

con·tent[2] /'kän,tent/ ▶*n.* **1** (usu. **contents**) the things that are held or included in something: *he picked up the correspondence and scanned the contents.* ■ the amount of a particular constituent occurring in a substance: *milk with a low-fat content.* ■ (**contents** or **table of contents**) a list of the titles of chapters or sections contained in a book or periodical. **2** the substance or material dealt with in a speech, literary work, etc., as distinct from its form or style: *the outward form and precise content of the messages.* —**con·tent·less** *adj.*

con·tent·ed /kən'tentəd/ ▶*adj.* happy and at ease. ■ expressing happiness and satisfaction. ■ willing to accept the correspondence; satisfied: *I was never contented with half measures.* —**con·tent·ed·ly** *adv.* —**con·tent·ed·ness** *n.*

con·ten·tion /kən'tenCHən/ ▶*n.* **1** heated disagreement: *the captured territory was one of the main areas of contention between the two countries.* **2** an assertion, esp. one maintained in argument: *statistics bear out his contention that many runners are not well-trained for this event.*
▶ □ **in contention** having a good chance of success in a contest.

con·ten·tious /kən'tenCHəs/ ▶*adj.* causing or likely to cause an argument; controversial. ■ involving heated argument. ■ (of a person) given to arguing or provoking argument. ■ *Law* relating to or involving differences between contending parties. —**con·ten·tious·ly** *adv.* —**con·ten·tious·ness** *n.*

con·tent pro·vid·er ▶*n.* a person or organization who supplies information for use on a Web site.

con·ter·mi·nous /kän'tərmənəs; kən-/ ▶*adj.* sharing a common boundary: *the forty-eight conterminous United States.* ■ having the same area, context, or meaning. —**con·ter·mi·nous·ly** *adv.*

con·test ▶*n.* /'kän,test/ an event in which people compete for supremacy in a sport, activity, or particular quality: *a beauty contest.* ■ a competition for a political position: *the mayoral contest.* ■ a dispute or conflict: *a contest between traditional and liberal views.*
▶*v.* /kən'test; 'kän,test/ [*tr.*] **1** engage in competition to attain (a position of power). ■ take part in (a competition or election). **2** oppose (an action, decision, or theory) as mistaken or wrong: *the former chairman contests his dismissal.* ■ engage in dispute about: *the issues have been hotly contested.* ▷late 16th cent. (as a verb in the sense 'swear to, attest'): from Latin *contestari* 'call upon to witness, initiate an action (by calling witnesses),' from *con-* 'together' + *testare* 'to witness.' The senses 'wrangle, strive, struggle for' arose in the early 17th cent., whence the current noun and verb senses. —**con·test·a·ble** /kən'testəbəl/ *adj.* —**con·test·er** /kən'testər; 'kän,tes-/ *n.*
▶ □ **no contest 1** another term for **NOLO CONTENDERE**: *he pleaded no contest to two misdemeanor counts.* **2** a competition, comparison, or choice of which the outcome is a foregone conclusion: *when the two teams faced each other it was no contest.* ■ a decision by the referee to declare a boxing match invalid on the grounds that one or both of the boxers are not making serious efforts.

con·test·ant /kən'testənt/ ▶*n.* a person who takes part in a contest or competition.

con·text /'kän,tekst/ ▶*n.* the circumstances that form the setting for an event, statement, or idea, and in terms of which it can be fully understood and assessed: *the decision was within the context of planned spending.* ■ the parts of something written or spoken that immediately precede and follow a word or passage and clarify its meaning. —**con·text·less** *adj.* —**con·tex·tu·al** /kən'teksCHŌōəl/ *adj.* —**con·tex·tu·al·ly** *adv.*
▶ □ **in context** considered together with the surrounding words or circumstances. □ **out of context** without the surrounding words or circumstances and so not fully understandable: *comments that aides have long insisted were taken out of context.*

con·tex·tu·al·ize /kən'teksCHŌōə,līz/ ▶*v.* [*tr.*] place or study in context. —**con·tex·tu·al·i·za·tion** /kən,teksCHŌōələ'zāSHən/ *n.*

con·tig·u·ous /kən'tigyōōəs/ ▶*adj.* sharing a common border; touching: *the 48 contiguous states.* ■ next or together in sequence: *five hundred contiguous dictionary entries.* —**con·ti·gu·i·ty** /,käntə'gyōoitē/ *n.* —**con·tig·u·ous·ly** *adv.*

con·ti·nent[1] /'käntn-ənt; 'käntnənt/ ▶*n.* any of the world's main continuous expanses of land (Africa, Antarctica, Asia, Australia, Europe, North America, South America). ■ a mainland contrasted with islands.

con·ti·nent[2] ▶*adj.* **1** able to control movements of the bowels and bladder. **2** exercising self-restraint, esp. sexually. —**con·ti·nence** n. —**con·ti·nent·ly** adv.

con·ti·nen·tal /ˌkäntnˈentl/ ▸adj. **1** forming or belonging to a continent: *continental Antarctica.* **2** coming from or characteristic of mainland Europe: *traditional continental cuisine.* **3** (also **Continental**) pertaining to the 13 original colonies of the U.S.
▸n. **1** an inhabitant of mainland Europe. **2** (**Continental**) a member of the colonial army in the American Revolution. **3** (also **Continental**) a piece of paper currency used at the time of the American Revolution: *the redemption of Continentals by the government.* —**con·ti·nen·tal·ly** adv.

con·ti·nen·tal break·fast ▸n. a light breakfast, typically consisting of coffee and rolls with butter and jam.

con·ti·nen·tal drift ▸n. the gradual movement of the continents across the earth's surface through geological time. See **PLATE TECTONICS**.

con·ti·nen·tal shelf ▸n. the area of seabed around a large landmass where the sea is relatively shallow.

con·tin·gen·cy /kənˈtinjənsē/ ▸n. (pl. **-cies**) a future event or circumstance that is possible but cannot be predicted with certainty. ■ a provision for such an events or circumstance: *a contingency reserve.* ■ an incidental expense. ■ the absence of certainty in events: *the island's public affairs can be invaded by contingency.*

con·tin·gent /kənˈtinjənt/ ▸adj. **1** subject to chance: *the contingent nature of the job.* ■ (of losses, liabilities, etc.) that can be anticipated to arise if a particular event occurs. ■ *Philos.* true by virtue of the way things in fact are and not by logical necessity: *that men are living creatures is a contingent fact.* **2** (**contingent on/upon**) occurring or existing only if (certain other circumstances) are the case; dependent on: *resolution of the conflict was contingent on the signing of a cease-fire agreement.*
▸n. a group of people united by some common feature, forming part of a larger group. ■ a body of troops or police sent to join a larger force in an operation. —**con·tin·gent·ly** adv.

con·tin·u·al /kənˈtinyo͞oəl/ ▸adj. frequently recurring; always happening: *his plane went down after continual attacks.* ■ having no interruptions: *some patients need continual safeguarding.* —**con·tin·u·al·ly** adv.

con·tin·u·ance /kənˈtinyo͞oəns/ ▸n. **1** *formal* the state of remaining in existence or operation. ■ the time for which a situation or action lasts: *the trademarks shall be used only during the continuance of this agreement.* ■ the state of remaining in a particular position or condition: *the king's ministers depended on his favor for their continuance in office.* **2** *Law* a postponement or adjournment.

con·tin·u·a·tion /kənˌtinyəˈwāSHən/ ▸n. the action of carrying something on over a period of time or the process of being carried on. ■ the state of remaining in a particular position or condition. ■ a part that is attached to and an extension of something else: *once a separate village, it is now a continuation of the suburbs.*

con·tin·ue /kənˈtinyo͞o/ ▸v. (**-ues, -ued, -uing**) **1** [intr.] persist in an activity or process: *prices continued to fall during April.* ■ remain in existence or operation: *discussions continued throughout the year.* ■ [tr.] carry on with (something that one has begun): *I continued my stroll.* ■ remain in a specified position or state: *they have indicated their willingness to continue in office.* ■ carry on traveling in the same direction: *he hummed to himself as they continued northward.* ■ (of a road, river, etc.) extend farther in the same direction: *the main path continued through a tunnel.* **2** recommence or resume after interruption: [tr.] *we continue the story from the point reached in Chapter 1* | [intr.] *the trial continues tomorrow.* ■ [intr.] carry on speaking after a pause or interruption. ■ [tr.] *Law* postpone or adjourn (a legal proceeding). —**con·tin·u·er** n.

con·ti·nu·i·ty /ˌkäntnˈ(y)o͞oətē/ ▸n. (pl. **-ties**) **1** the unbroken and consistent existence or operation of something over a period of time. ■ a state of stability and the absence of disruption. ■ (often **continuity between/with**) a connection or line of development with no sharp breaks: *the Church stands in direct continuity with the Old Testament people of God.* **2** the maintenance of continuous action and self-consistent detail in the various scenes of a movie or broadcast.

con·tin·u·o /kənˈtinyəˌwō/ (also **bas·so con·tin·u·o**) ▸n. (pl. **-os**) (in baroque music) an accompanying part that includes a bass line and harmonies, typically played on a keyboard instrument.

con·tin·u·ous /kənˈtinyo͞oəs/ ▸adj. **1** forming an unbroken whole; without interruption: *one continuous movement.* ■ forming a series with no exceptions or reversals: *continuous advances in design.* ■ *Math.* (of a function) of which the graph is a smooth unbroken curve, i.e., one such that as the value of *x* approaches any given value *a*, the value of *f(x)* approaches that of *f(a)* as a limit. **2** *Gram.* another term for **PROGRESSIVE** (sense 3). —**con·tin·u·ous·ly** adv. —**con·tin·u·ous·ness** n.

con·tin·u·um /kənˈtinyo͞oəm/ ▸n. (pl. **-u·a** /-yo͞oə/) a continuous sequence in which adjacent elements are not perceptibly different from each

other, although the extremes are quite distinct: *at the fast end of the fast-slow continuum.*

con·tort /kənˈtôrt/ ▸v. twist or bend out of its normal shape: [tr.] *a spasm of pain contorted his face* | [intr.] *her face contorted with anger.* —**con·tor·tion** /kənˈtôrSHən/ n.

con·tor·tion·ist /kənˈtôrSHənist/ ▸n. an entertainer who twists and bends their body into strange and unnatural positions.

con·tour /ˈkänˌto͝or/ ▸n. (usu. **contours**) an outline, esp. one representing or bounding the shape or form of something: *she traced the contours of his face with her finger.* ■ an outline of a natural feature such as a hill or valley. ■ short for **CONTOUR LINE**. ■ a line joining points on a diagram at which some property has the same value: *the map shows contours of every 10-foot difference in elevation.* ■ a way in which something varies, esp. the pitch of music or the pattern of tones in an utterance.
▸v. [tr.] **1** (usu. **be contoured**) mold into a specific shape, typically one designed to fit into something else: *the compartment has been contoured with smooth rounded corners* | [as adj.] (**contoured**) *the contoured leather seats.* **2** mark (a map or diagram) with contour lines: [as adj.] (**contoured**) *a huge contoured map.* **3** (of a road or railroad) follow the outline of (a topographical feature), esp. along a contour line: *the road contours the hillside.*

con·tour line ▸n. a line on a map joining points of equal height above or below sea level.

con·tra /ˈkäntrə/ (also **Con·tra**) ▸n. a member of a guerrilla force in Nicaragua that opposed the left-wing Sandinista government 1979–90, and was supported by the U.S. for much of that time.

con·tra·band /ˈkäntrəˌband/ ▸n. goods that have been imported or exported illegally. ■ trade in smuggled goods: *the government has declared a nationwide war on contraband.* ■ (also **contraband of war**) goods forbidden to be supplied by neutrals to those engaged in war. ■ during the U.S. Civil War, a black slave who escaped or was transported across Union lines.
▸adj. imported or exported illegally, either in defiance of a total ban or without payment of duty: *contraband drug shipments.* ■ relating to traffic in illegal goods: *the contraband market.* —**con·tra·band·ist** /-ist/ n.

con·tra·bass /ˈkäntrəˌbäs/ ▸n. another term for **DOUBLE BASS**.
▸adj. denoting a musical instrument with a range an octave lower than the normal bass range: *a contrabass clarinet.*

con·tra·cep·tion /ˌkäntrəˈsepSHən/ ▸n. the deliberate use of artificial methods or other techniques to prevent pregnancy as a consequence of sexual intercourse.

con·tra·cep·tive /ˌkäntrəˈseptiv/ ▸adj. (of a method or device) serving to prevent pregnancy. ■ of or relating to contraception.
▸n. a device or drug serving to prevent pregnancy.

con·tract ▸n. /ˈkänˌtrakt/ a written or spoken agreement, esp. one concerning employment, sales, or tenancy, that is intended to be enforceable by law. ■ the branch of law concerned with the making and observation of such agreements. ■ *inf.* an arrangement for someone to be killed by a hired assassin: *smuggling bosses routinely put out contracts on witnesses.* ■ *Bridge* the declarer's undertaking to win the number of tricks bid with a stated suit as trump. ■ *dated* a formal agreement to marry.
▸v. **1** /kənˈtrakt/ [intr.] decrease in size, number, or range. ■ (of a muscle) become shorter or tighter in order to effect movement of part of the body: *the heart is a muscle that contracts about seventy times a minute* | [tr.] *then contract your lower abdominal muscles.* ■ [tr.] shorten (a word or phrase) by combination or elision. **2** /ˈkänˌtrakt; kənˈtrakt/ [intr.] enter into a formal and legally binding agreement: *the local authority will contract with a wide range of agencies to provide services.* ■ secure specified rights or undertake specified obligations in a formal and legally binding agreement: *the paper had contracted to publish extracts from the diaries.* ■ impose an obligation on (someone) to do something by means of a formal agreement. ■ [tr.] (**contract something out**) arrange for work to be done by another organization. ■ [tr.] *dated* formally enter into (a marriage). ■ [tr.] enter into (a friendship or other relationship). **3** /kənˈtrakt/ [tr.] catch or develop (a disease or infectious agent). **4** /kənˈtrakt/ [tr.] become liable to pay (a debt). —**con·tract·ee** /ˌkänˌtrakˈtē/ n. —**con·trac·tive** /kənˈtraktiv; ˈkänˌtraktiv/ adj.

con·tract bridge /ˈkänˌtrakt/ ▸n. the standard form of the card game bridge, in which only tricks bid and won count toward the game.

con·trac·tile /kənˈtraktəl; -ˌtīl/ ▸adj. *Biol. & Physiol.* capable of or producing contraction. —**con·trac·til·i·ty** /ˌkänˌtrakˈtilitē/ n.

con·trac·tion /kən'traksHən/ ▶n. the process of becoming smaller. ■ the process in which a muscle becomes or is made shorter and tighter. ■ (usu. **contractions**) a shortening of the uterine muscles occurring at intervals before and during childbirth. ■ a word or group of words resulting from shortening an original form: *"goodbye" is a contraction of "God be with you."* ■ the process of shortening a word by combination or elision.

con·trac·tor /'kän,traktər/ ▶n. a person or company that undertakes a contract to provide materials or labor to perform a service or do a job.

con·trac·tu·al /kən'trakcHōōəl/ ▶adj. agreed in a contract: *a contractual obligation.* ■ having similar characteristics to a contract: *the contractual nature of the shareholder's rights.* —**con·trac·tu·al·ly** adv.

con·tra·dict /,käntrə'dikt/ ▶v. [tr.] deny the truth of (a statement), esp. by asserting the opposite. ■ assert the opposite of a statement made by (someone). ■ be in conflict with: *that evaporation seems to contradict one of the most fundamental principles of physics.* —**con·tra·dic·tion** /-'diksHən/ n. —**con·tra·dic·tor** /-'diktər/ n.

con·tra·dic·to·ry /,käntrə'dikt(ə)rē/ ▶adj. mutually opposed or inconsistent: *the two attitudes are contradictory.* ■ containing elements which are inconsistent or in conflict: *the committee rejected the policy as too vague and internally contradictory.* ■ Logic (of two propositions) so related that one and only one must be true.
▶n. (pl. **-ries**) Logic a contradictory proposition. —**con·tra·dic·to·ri·ly** /-'dikt(ə)rəlē/ adv. —**con·tra·dic·to·ri·ness** n.

con·tra·dis·tinc·tion /,käntrədə'stiNGksHən/ ▶n. distinction made by contrasting the different qualities of two things: *the bacterium is termed "rough" in contradistinction to its ordinary smooth form.*

con·trail /'kän,trāl/ ▶n. a trail of condensed water from an aircraft or rocket at high altitude, seen as a white streak against the sky.

con·tra·in·di·cate /,käntrə'ində,kāt/ ▶v. [tr.] (usu. **be contraindicated**) Med. (of a condition or circumstance) suggest or indicate that (a particular technique or drug) should not be used in the case in question. —**con·tra·in·di·ca·tion** /-,ində'kāsHən/ n.

con·tral·to /kən'traltō/ ▶n. (pl. **-tos**) the lowest female singing voice. ■ a singer with such a voice. ■ a part written for such a voice.

con·trap·tion /kən'trapsHən/ ▶n. a machine or device that appears strange or unnecessarily complicated, and often badly made.

con·tra·pun·tal /,käntrə'pəntl/ ▶adj. Mus. of or in counterpoint. ■ (of a piece of music) with two or more independent melodic lines.

con·trar·y ▶adj. /'kän,tre(ə)rē/ **1** opposite in nature, direction, or meaning. ■ (of two or more statements, beliefs, etc.) opposed to one another: *his mother had given him contrary messages.* ■ (of a wind) blowing in the opposite direction to one's course; unfavorable. **2** /kən'tre(ə)rē/ perversely inclined to disagree or to do the opposite of what is expected or desired.
▶n. /'kän,tre(ə)rē/ (pl. **-trar·ies**) (**the contrary**) the opposite: *the magazine has proved that the contrary is true.* —**con·trar·i·ly** /-əlē/ adv. —**con·trar·i·ness** n.
▶ □ **contrary to** conflicting with; counter to: *contrary to his expectations, he found the atmosphere exciting.* □ **on** (or **quite**) **the contrary** used to intensify a denial of what has just been implied or stated: *there was no malice in her; on the contrary, she was very kind.* □ **to the contrary** with the opposite meaning or implication: *he continued to drink despite medical advice to the contrary.*

con·trast ▶n. /'kän,trast/ the state of being strikingly different from something else, typically something in juxtaposition or close association: *a contrast between rural and urban trends.* ■ the degree of difference between tones in a television picture, photograph, or other image. ■ enhancement of the apparent brightness or clarity of a design provided by the juxtaposition of different colors or textures. ■ the action of calling attention to notable differences. ■ a thing or person having qualities noticeably different from another: *the castle is quite a contrast to other places where the singer has performed.*
▶v. /'kän,trast; kən'trast/ [intr.] differ strikingly: *his friend's success contrasted with his own failure.* ■ [tr.] compare in such a way as to emphasize differences. ▷late 17th cent. (as a term in fine art, in the sense 'juxtapose so as to bring out differences in form and color'): from French *contraste* (noun), *contraster* (verb), via Italian from medieval Latin *contrastare*, from Latin *contra-* 'against' + *stare* 'stand.' —**con·trast·ing·ly** /'kän,trastiNGlē; kən'tras-/ adv. —**con·tras·tive** /kən'trastiv; 'kän,tras-/ adj.

con·tra·vene /,käntrə'vēn/ ▶v. [tr.] violate the prohibition or order of (a law, treaty, or code of conduct): *this would contravene the rule against hearsay.* ■ conflict with (a right, principle, etc.), esp. to its detriment: *this contravened Washington's commitment to its own proposal.* —**con·tra·ven·er** n.

con·tra·ven·tion /,käntrə'vencHən/ ▶n. an action that violates a law,

treaty, or other ruling: *young persons who commit offenses bear responsibility for their contraventions.*

con·tre·coup /'käntrə,kōō/ ▶n. (pl. **-coups** /-,kōōz/) a contusion resulting from the brain contacting the skull on the side opposite from where impact occurs. Compare with **COUP**.

con·tre·temps /'käntrə,tän; ˌkôntrə'tän/ ▶n. (pl. same /-,tän(z); -'tän(z)/) an unexpected and unfortunate occurrence. ■ a minor dispute.

con·trib·ute /kən'tribyōōt; -byət/ ▶v. [tr.] give (something, esp. money) in order to help achieve or provide something: *he contributed more than $500,000 to the center* | [intr.] *she contributed to a private pension.* ■ [intr.] (**contribute to**) help to cause or bring about: *gases that contribute to global warming.* ■ supply (an article) for publication: *he contributed articles to the magazine* | [intr.] *the staff who contribute to your sports pages are doing a splendid job.* ■ [intr.] give one's views in a discussion. —**con·trib·u·tive** /-yətiv/ adj. —**con·trib·u·tor** n.

con·tri·bu·tion /,käntrə'byōōsHən/ ▶n. a gift or payment to a common fund or collection: *charitable contributions.* ■ the part played by a person or thing in bringing about a result or helping something to advance. ■ an article or other piece of writing submitted for publication in a collection.

con·trib·u·to·ry /kən'tribyə,tôrē/ ▶adj. **1** playing a part in bringing something about: *smoking may be a contributory cause of lung cancer.* **2** (of or relating to a pension or insurance plan) operated by means of a fund into which people pay: *contributory benefits.*

con·trite /kən'trīt/ ▶adj. feeling or expressing remorse or penitence; affected by guilt. —**con·trite·ly** adv. —**con·trite·ness** n. —**con·tri·tion** /-'trisHən/ n.

con·triv·ance /kən'trīvəns/ ▶n. a thing that is created skillfully and inventively to serve a particular purpose: *an assortment of electronic equipment and mechanical contrivances.* ■ the use of skill to bring something about or create something: *the requirements of the system, by happy chance and some contrivance, can be summed up in an acronym.* ■ a device, esp. in literary or artistic composition, that gives a sense of artificiality.

con·trive /kən'trīv/ ▶v. [tr.] create or bring about (an object or a situation) by deliberate use of skill and artifice: *his opponents contrived a crisis.* ■ manage to do something foolish or create an undesirable situation: *the poor guy contrived to hang himself.* —**con·triv·a·ble** adj. —**con·triv·er** n.

con·trived /kən'trīvd/ ▶adj. deliberately created rather than arising naturally or spontaneously. ■ giving a sense of artificiality.

con·trol /kən'trōl/ ▶n. **1** the power to influence or direct people's behavior or the course of events: *the whole operation is under the control of a production manager.* ■ the ability to manage a machine or other moving object: *he lost control of his car.* ■ the restriction of an activity, tendency, or phenomenon: *pest control.* ■ the power to restrain something, esp. one's own emotions or actions: *get control of your emotions.* ■ (often **controls**) a means of limiting or regulating something: *growing controls on spending.* ■ a switch or other device by which a machine is regulated: *the volume control.* ■ the place where a particular item is verified: *passport control.* ■ the base from which a system or activity is directed: *mission control.* ■ Bridge a high card that will prevent opponents from establishing a particular suit. ■ Comput. short for **CONTROL KEY**. **2** Statistics a group or individual used as a standard of comparison for checking the results of a survey or experiment. **3** a member of an intelligence organization who personally directs the activities of a spy.
▶v. (**-trolled**, **-trol·ling**) **1** [tr.] determine the behavior or supervise the running of: *he was appointed to control the company's marketing strategy.* ■ maintain influence or authority over: *you shouldn't have dogs if you can't control them.* ■ limit the level, intensity, or numbers of: *he had to control his temper.* ■ (**control oneself**) remain calm and reasonable despite provocation. ■ regulate (a mechanical or scientific process): *the airflow is controlled by a fan.* ■ [as adj.] (**controlled**) (of a drug) restricted by law with respect to use and possession. **2** Statistics [intr.] (**control for**) take into account (an extraneous factor that might affect results) when performing an experiment: *no attempt was made to control for variations.* ■ check; verify. —**con·trol·la·bil·i·ty** /kən,trōlə'bilitē/ n. —**con·trol·la·ble** adj. —**con·trol·la·bly** /-əblē/ adv.
▶ □ **in control** able to direct a situation, person, or activity. □ **out of control** no longer possible to manage. □ **under control** (of a danger or emergency) being dealt with successfully and competently: *it took two hours to bring the blaze under control.*

con·trol key ▶n. Comput. a key that alters the function of another key if both are pressed at the same time.

con·trol·ler /kən'trōlər/ ▶n. a person or thing that directs or regulates something: *the power controller on a subway train.* ■ a person in charge of an organization's finances. —**con·trol·ler·ship** /-,sHip/ n.

con·trol·ling in·ter·est ▶*n.* the holding by one person or group of a majority of the stock of a business, giving the holder a means of exercising control: *the purchase of a controlling interest in a company in California.*

con·trol tow·er ▶*n.* a tall building at an airport from which the movements of air and runway traffic are controlled.

con·tro·ver·sial /ˌkäntrəˈvərsHəl; -ˈvərsēəl/ ▶*adj.* giving rise or likely to give rise to public disagreement: *years of wrangling over a controversial bypass.* —**con·tro·ver·sial·ist** /-list/ *n.* —**con·tro·ver·sial·ly** *adv.*

con·tro·ver·sy /ˈkäntrəˌvərsē/ ▶*n.* (*pl.* -**sies**) disagreement, typically when prolonged, public, and heated.

con·tro·vert /ˈkäntrəˌvərt; ˌkäntrəˈvərt/ ▶*v.* [*tr.*] deny the truth of (something): *subsequent work from the same laboratory controverted these results.* ■ argue about (something). —**con·tro·vert·i·ble** *adj.*

con·tu·ma·cious /ˌkänt(y)əˈmāsHəs/ ▶*adj.* archaic or Law (esp. of a defendant's behavior) stubbornly or willfully disobedient to authority. —**con·tu·ma·cious·ly** *adv.* —**con·tu·ma·cy** /ˌkänt(y)əməsē/ *n.*

con·tu·me·ly /kənˈt(y)o͞oməlē; ˈkänt(y)əˌmēlē; ˈkänˌt(y)o͞omlē/ ▶*n.* (*pl.* -**lies**) insolent or insulting language or treatment. —**con·tu·me·li·ous** /ˌkänt(y)əˈmēlēəs/ *adj.*

con·tuse /kənˈto͞oz/ ▶*v.* [*tr.*] (usu. **be contused**) injure (a part of the body) without breaking the skin, forming a bruise. —**con·tu·sion** /ˈto͞ozHən/ *n.*

co·nun·drum /kəˈnəndrəm/ ▶*n.* (*pl.* -**drums**) a confusing and difficult problem or question. ■ a question asked for amusement, typically one with a pun in its answer; a riddle. ▷late 16th cent.: of unknown origin, but first recorded in a work by Thomas Nashe, as a term of abuse for a crank or pedant, later coming to denote a whim or fancy, also a pun. Current senses date from the late 17th cent.

con·ur·ba·tion /ˌkänərˈbāSHən/ ▶*n.* an extended urban area, typically consisting of several towns merging with the suburbs of one or more cities.

con·va·lesce /ˌkänvəˈles/ ▶*v.* [*intr.*] recover one's health and strength over a period of time after an illness or operation.

con·va·les·cent /ˌkänvəˈlesənt/ ▶*adj.* (of a person) recovering from an illness or operation. ■ relating to convalescence.
▶*n.* a person who is recovering after an illness or operation. —**con·va·les·cence** *n.*

con·vec·tion /kənˈveksHən/ ▶*n.* the movement caused within a fluid by the tendency of hotter and therefore less dense material to rise, and colder, denser material to sink under the influence of gravity, which consequently results in transfer of heat. —**con·vec·tion·al** /-sHənl/ *adj.* —**con·vec·tive** /-ˈvektiv/ *adj.*

con·vene /kənˈvēn/ ▶*v.* [*tr.*] call people together for (a meeting). ■ assemble or cause to assemble for a common purpose: [*tr.*] *he convened a group of well-known scientists and philosophers* | [*intr.*] *the committee had convened for its final plenary session.* —**con·ven·a·ble** *adj.* —**con·ven·er** *n.* —**con·ve·nor** /-ˈvēnər/ *n.*

con·ven·ience /kənˈvēnyəns/ ▶*n.* **1** the state of being able to proceed with something with little effort or difficulty: *the museum has a cafeteria for your convenience.* ■ the quality of contributing to such a state: *the convenience of a portable phone.* ■ a thing that contributes to an easy and effortless way of life. **2** Brit. a public toilet.
▶ □ **at one's convenience** at a time or place that suits one. □ **at one's earliest convenience** as soon as one can without difficulty.

con·ven·ience store ▶*n.* a store with extended opening hours and in a convenient location, stocking a limited range of household goods and groceries.

con·ven·ient /kənˈvēnyənt/ ▶*adj.* fitting in well with a person's needs, activities, and plans. ■ involving little trouble or effort. ■ (**convenient to**) situated so as to allow easy access to: *the 34-story building is convenient to downtown.* ■ occurring in a place or at a time that is useful. —**con·ven·ient·ly** *adv. he lived, conveniently, in Paris.*

con·vent /ˈkänˌvent/ ▶*n.* a Christian community under monastic vows, esp. one of nuns. ■ (also **convent school**) a school, esp. one for girls, attached to and run by such a community. ■ the building or buildings occupied by such a community.

con·ven·tion /kənˈvensHən/ ▶*n.* **1** a way in which something is usually done, esp. within a particular area or activity: *the woman who overturned so many conventions of children's literature.* ■ behavior that is considered acceptable or polite to most members of a society: *social conventions.* ■ Bridge an artificial bid by which a bidder tries to convey specific information about the hand to their partner. **2** an agreement between countries covering particular matters, esp. one less formal than a treaty. **3** a large meeting or conference, esp. of members of a political party or a particular profession: *a convention of retail merchants.* ■ (in the U.S.) an assembly of the delegates of a political party to select candidates for office. ■ an organized meeting of enthusiasts for a television program, movie, or literary genre: *a Star Trek convention.* ■ a body set up by agreement to deal with a particular issue.

con·ven·tion·al /kənˈvensHənl/ ▶*adj.* based on or in accordance with what is generally done or believed: *a conventional morality.* ■ (of a person) concerned with what is generally held to be acceptable at the expense of individuality and sincerity. ■ (of a work of art or literature) following traditional forms and genres: *conventional love poetry.* ■ (of weapons or power) nonnuclear. ■ Bridge (of a bid) intended to convey a particular meaning according to an agreed upon convention. —**con·ven·tion·al·ism** /-ˌizəm/ *n.* —**con·ven·tion·al·ist** /-list/ *n.* —**con·ven·tion·al·i·ty** /-ˌvenCHəˈnalitē/ *n.* —**con·ven·tion·al·ize** /-ˌīz/ *v.* —**con·ven·tion·al·ly** *adv.*

con·verge /kənˈvərj/ ▶*v.* [*intr.*] (of several people or things) come together from different directions so as eventually to meet: *fig. two separate people whose lives converge briefly from time to time.* ■ (**converge on/upon**) come from different directions and meet at (a place): *sports fans will converge on the capital.* ■ (of a number of things) gradually change so as to become similar or develop something in common: *two cultures converged as the French settled Vermont.* ■ (of lines) tend to meet at a point. ■ Math. (of a series) approximate in the sum of its terms toward a definite limit. —**con·ver·gence** *n.* —**con·ver·gent** *adj.*

con·ver·sant /kənˈvərsənt/ ▶*adj.* familiar with or knowledgeable about something: *many ladies are conversant with the merits of drill-eyed needles.* —**con·ver·sance** *n.* —**con·ver·san·cy** /-sənsē/ *n.*

con·ver·sa·tion /ˌkänvərˈsāSHən/ ▶*n.* the informal exchange of ideas by spoken words: *the two men were deep in conversation.* ■ an instance of this: *she picked up the phone and held a conversation in French.*
▶ □ **make conversation** talk for the sake of politeness without having anything to say.

con·ver·sa·tion·al /ˌkänvərˈsāSHənl/ ▶*adj.* appropriate to an informal conversation: *his tone was casual and conversational.* ■ consisting of or relating to conversation: *conversational skills.* —**con·ver·sa·tion·al·ly** *adv.*

con·ver·sa·tion·al·ist /ˌkänvərˈsāSHənl-ist/ ▶*n.* a person who is good at or fond of engaging in conversation.

con·verse[1] ▶*v.* /kənˈvərs/ [*intr.*] engage in conversation.
▶*n.* /ˈkänˌvərs/ archaic conversation. —**con·vers·er** /kənˈvərsər/ *n.*

con·verse[2] /ˈkänˌvərs/ ▶*n.* a situation, object, or statement that is the reverse of another, or that corresponds to it but with certain terms transposed: *if spirituality is properly political, the converse is also true: politics is properly spiritual.* ■ Math. a theorem whose hypothesis and conclusion are the conclusion and hypothesis of another.
▶*adj.* /ˈkänˌvərs/ having characteristics that are the reverse of something else already mentioned. —**con·verse·ly** *adv.*

con·ver·sion /kənˈvərzHən/ ▶*n.* **1** the act or an instance of converting or the process of being converted: *the conversion of food into body tissues.* ■ the fact of changing one's religion or beliefs or the action of persuading someone else to change theirs. ■ Christian Theol. repentance and change to a godly life. ■ the adaptation of a building for a new purpose. ■ Psychiatry the manifestation of a mental disturbance as a physical disorder or disease. **2** Football the act of scoring an extra point or points after having scored a touchdown. ■ the act of gaining a first down. **3** Law the action of wrongfully dealing with goods in a manner inconsistent with the owner's rights. **4** Physics the change in a quantity's numerical value as a result of using a different unit of measurement.

con·ver·sion van ▶*n.* a van in which the cargo space has been converted to a special purpose, such as a living space.

con·vert ▶*v.* /kənˈvərt/ **1** [*tr.*] cause to change in form, character, or function. ■ [*intr.*] change or be able to change from one form to another: *the seating converts to a double or two single beds.* ■ [*intr.*] change one's religious faith or other beliefs: *he converted to Catholicism.* ■ persuade (someone) to do this: *he was converted in his later years to the socialist cause.* ■ change (money, stocks, or units in which a quantity is expressed) into others of a different kind. ■ adapt (a building) to make it suitable for a new purpose. **2** [*tr.*] score from (a penalty kick, pass, or other opportunity) in a sport or game. ■ [*intr.*] Football score an extra point or points after having scored a touchdown by kicking a goal (one point) or running another play into the end zone (two points). ■ [*intr.*] Football advance the ball far enough during a down to earn a first down.

▶*n.* /'kän,vərt/ a person who has been persuaded to change their religious faith or other beliefs: *he is a recent **convert** to the church.*

con·vert·er /kən'vərtər/ (also **con·ver·tor**) ▶*n.* a person or thing that converts something. ■ a device for altering the nature of an electric current or signal, esp. from AC to DC or vice versa, or from analog to digital or vice versa. ■ *Comput.* a program that converts data from one format to another. ■ a camera lens that changes the focal length of another lens by a set amount.

con·vert·i·ble /kən'vərtəbəl/ ▶*adj.* able to be changed in form, function, or character: *a living room that is miraculously **convertible** into a bedroom.* ■ (of a car) having a folding or detachable roof. ■ (of currency) able to be converted into other forms, esp. into gold or U.S. dollars. ■ (of a bond or stock) able to be converted into ordinary or preference shares. ▶*n.* **1** a car with a folding or detachable roof. **2** (usu. **convertibles**) a convertible security. —**con·vert·i·bil·i·ty** /-,vərtə'bilitē/ *n.*

con·vex /kän'veks; 'kän,veks; kən'veks/ ▶*adj.* **1** having an outline or surface curved like the exterior of a circle or sphere. Compare with **CONCAVE**. **2** (of a polygon) having only interior angles measuring less than 180°. —**con·vex·i·ty** /kän'veksitē; kən-/ *n.* —**con·vex·ly** *adv.*

con·vey /kən'vā/ ▶*v.* [*tr.*] transport or carry to a place: *pipes were laid to **convey** water to the house.* ■ make (an idea, impression, or feeling) known or understandable to someone: *it's impossible to convey how lost I felt.* ■ communicate (a message or information). ■ *Law* transfer the title to (property). —**con·vey·a·ble** *adj.*

convex and concave

con·vey·ance /kən'vāəns/ ▶*n.* **1** the action or process of transporting someone or something from one place to another. ■ a means of transportation; a vehicle. ■ the action of making an idea, feeling, or impression known or understandable to someone: *art's conveyance of meaning is complicated.* **2** *Law* the legal process of transferring property from one owner to another. ■ a legal document effecting such a process. —**con·vey·anc·ing** *n.*

con·vey·or /kən'vāər/ (also **con·vey·er**) ▶*n.* a person or thing that transports or communicates something: *a conveyor of information.* ■ a conveyor belt.

con·vey·or belt ▶*n.* a continuous moving band of fabric, rubber, or metal used for moving objects from one place to another.

con·vict ▶*v.* /kən'vikt/ [*tr.*] (often **be convicted**) declare (someone) to be guilty of a criminal offense by the verdict of a jury or the decision of a judge in a court of law. ▶*n.* /'kän,vikt/ a person found guilty of a criminal offense and serving a sentence of imprisonment.

con·vic·tion /kən'vikSHən/ ▶*n.* **1** a formal declaration that someone is guilty of a criminal offense, made by the verdict of a jury or the decision of a judge in a court of law. **2** a firmly held belief or opinion: *his conviction that the death was no accident.* ■ the quality of showing that one is firmly convinced of what one believes or says: *his voice lacked conviction.*

con·vince /kən'vins/ ▶*v.* [*tr.*] cause (someone) to believe firmly in the truth of something: *Robert's expression had obviously **convinced** her of his innocence.* ■ persuade (someone) to do something: *she convinced my father to branch out on his own.* —**con·vinc·er** *n.* —**con·vin·ci·ble** *adj.*

con·vinc·ing /kən'vinsiNG/ ▶*adj.* capable of causing someone to believe that something is true or real: *there is no convincing evidence that advertising influences total alcohol consumption.* ■ (of a victory or a winner) leaving no margin of doubt; clear. —**con·vinc·ing·ly** *adv.*

con·viv·i·al /kən'vivēəl; kən'vivyəl/ ▶*adj.* (of an atmosphere or event) friendly, lively, and enjoyable. ■ (of a person) cheerful and friendly; jovial. —**con·viv·i·al·i·ty** /kən,vivē'alitē/ *n.* —**con·viv·i·al·ly** *adv.*

con·vo·ca·tion /,känvə'kāSHən/ ▶*n.* **1** a large formal assembly of people. ■ a formal ceremony at a college or university, as for the conferring of awards. **2** the action of calling people together for a large formal assembly. —**con·vo·ca·tion·al** /-SHənl/ *adj.*

con·voke /kən'vōk/ ▶*v.* [*tr.*] *formal* call together or summon (an assembly or meeting): *she sent messages convoking a Council of Ministers.*

con·vo·lut·ed /'känvə,lōōtid/ ▶*adj.* (esp. of an argument, story, or sentence) extremely complex and difficult to follow. ■ *chiefly technical* intricately folded, twisted, or coiled: *walnuts come in hard and convoluted shells.* —**con·vo·lut·ed·ly** *adv.*

con·vo·lu·tion /,känvə'lōōSHən/ ▶*n.* (often **convolutions**) a coil or twist, esp. one of many. ■ a thing that is complex and difficult to follow: *the convolutions of farm policy.* —**con·vo·lu·tion·al** /-SHənl/ *adj.*

con·voy /'kän,voi/ ▶*n.* a group of ships or vehicles traveling together, typically accompanied by armed troops, warships, or other vehicles for protection. ▶*v.* /'kän,voi; kən'voi/ [*tr.*] (of a warship or armed troops) accompany (a group of ships or vehicles) for protection. ▶ □ **in convoy** (of traveling vehicles) as a group; together.

con·vulse /kən'vəls/ ▶*v.* [*intr.*] (of a person) suffer violent involuntary contraction of the muscles, producing contortion of the body or limbs. ■ [*tr.*] (usu. **be convulsed**) (of an emotion, laughter, or physical stimulus) cause (someone) to make sudden, violent, uncontrollable movements: *Carlos was convulsed by a second bout of sneezing.* ■ [*tr.*] *fig.* throw (a country) into violent social or political upheaval.

con·vul·sion /kən'vəlsHən/ ▶*n.* (often **convulsions**) a sudden, violent, irregular movement of a limb or of the body, caused by involuntary contraction of muscles and associated esp. with brain disorders such as epilepsy, the presence of certain toxins or other agents in the blood, or fever in children. ■ (**convulsions**) uncontrollable laughter: *the audience collapsed in convulsions.* ■ *fig.* a violent social or political upheaval.

con·vul·sive /kən'vəlsiv/ ▶*adj.* producing or consisting of convulsions: *a convulsive disease | she gave a convulsive sob.* —**con·vul·sive·ly** *adv.*

co·ny ▶*n.* (*pl.* **-nies**) variant spelling of **CONEY**.

coo /kōō/ ▶*v.* (**coos**, **cooed**) [*intr.*] (of a pigeon or dove) make a soft murmuring sound. ■ (of a baby) make a soft murmuring sound similar to this, expressing contentment. ■ (of a person) speak in a soft gentle voice, typically to express affection: *I cruised the room, cooing at toddlers.* ▶*n.* a soft murmuring sound made by a dove or pigeon.

cook /kōōk/ ▶*v.* **1** [*tr.*] prepare (food, a dish, or a meal) by combining and heating the ingredients in various ways: *shall I cook dinner tonight? | [intr.] I told you I could cook.* ■ [*intr.*] (of food) be heated so that the condition required for eating is reached: *while the rice is cooking, add the saffron to the stock.* ■ (**cook something down**) heat food and cause it to thicken and reduce in volume. ■ [*intr.*] (**cook down**) (of food being cooked) be reduced in volume in this way. ■ (**be cooking**) *inf.* be happening or planned: *what's cooking on the alternative fuels front?* **2** [*tr.*] *inf.* alter dishonestly; falsify: *a narcotics team who cooked the evidence.* ■ (**be cooked**) be in an inescapably bad situation: *if I can't talk to him, I'm cooked.* **3** [*intr.*] *inf.* perform or proceed vigorously or well: *the band used to get up on the bandstand and really cook.* ▶*phrasal v.* □ **cook something up** concoct a story, excuse, or plan, esp. an ingenious or devious one. ▶*n.* a person who prepares and cooks food, esp. as a job or in a specified way: *I'm a good cook.* —**cook·a·ble** *adj.* ▶ □ **cook the books** *inf.* alter facts or figures dishonestly or illegally.

cook·book /'kōōk,bōōk/ ▶*n.* a book containing recipes and other information about the preparation and cooking of food.

cook·er /'kōōkər/ ▶*n. chiefly Brit.* an appliance used for cooking food.

cook·er·y /'kōōkərē/ ▶*n.* (*pl.* **-er·ies**) **1** the practice or skill of preparing and cooking food. **2** a place in which food is cooked; a kitchen.

cook·ie /'kōōkē/ ▶*n.* (*pl.* **-ies**) **1** a small sweet cake, typically round, flat, and crisp. **2** *inf.* a person of a specified kind: *a tough cookie with one eye on her bank account.* **3** *Comput.* a packet of data sent by an Internet server to a browser, which is returned by the browser each time it subsequently accesses the same server, used to identify the user or track their access to the server.

cook·ing /'kōōkiNG/ ▶*n.* the process of preparing food by heating it. ■ the practice or skill of preparing food. ■ food that has been prepared in a particular way: *authentic Italian cooking.* ■ [as *adj.*] suitable for or used in cooking: *cooking oil.*

cook·out /'kōōk,out/ ▶*n.* a party or gathering where a meal is cooked and eaten outdoors.

cook·ware /'kōōk,we(ə)r/ ▶*n.* pots, pans, or dishes for cooking food.

cool /kōōl/ ▶*adj.* **1** of or at a fairly low temperature. ■ soothing or refreshing because of its low temperature: *a cool drink | fig. the bathroom was all cool, muted blues.* ■ (esp. of clothing) keeping one from becoming too hot: *cool, comfortable shirts.* ■ showing no friendliness toward a person or enthusiasm for an idea or project: *he gave a cool reception to the suggestion.* ■ free from excitement or anxiety: *he prided himself on keeping a cool head.* ■ calmly audacious: *such an expensive strategy requires cool nerves.* ■ (of jazz, esp. modern jazz) restrained and relaxed. **2** *inf.* fashionably attractive or impressive: *I always wore sunglasses to look cool.* ■ excellent: [as *interj.*] *a computer you didn't even have to plug in. Cool!* **3** (**a cool** ——) *inf.* used to emphasize a specified quantity or amount, esp. of money: *a cool $15,000 to buy the franchise.* ▶*n.* **1** (**the cool**) a fairly low temperature: *the cool of the night air.* ■ a time or place at which the temperature is pleasantly low: *the cool of the* *evening.* ■ calmness; composure. **2** the quality of being fashionably attractive or impressive: *all the cool of high fashion.*

▶ *v.* become or cause to become less hot: [*intr.*] we dived into the river to *cool off* | *fig.* his feelings for her took a long time to *cool* | [*tr.*] *cool the pastry for five minutes.* ■ become or cause to become calm or less excited: [*intr.*] *after I'd cooled off, I realized I was being irrational* | [*tr.*] *George was trying to cool him down.* ■ [usu. in *imper.*] (**cool it**) inf. behave in a less excitable manner: *"Cool it and tell me why you're so ecstatic."* —**cooled** *adj.* —**cool·ish** *adj.* —**cool·ly** *adv.* —**cool·ness** *n.*

▶ □ **cool one's heels** be kept waiting. □ **keep** (or **lose**) **one's cool** inf. maintain (or fail to maintain) a calm and controlled attitude. □ **play it cool** see PLAY.

cool·ant /'kōōlənt/ ▶ *n.* a liquid or gas that is used to remove heat from something.

cool·er /'kōōlər/ ▶ *n.* **1** a device or container for keeping things cool, in particular: ■ an insulated container for keeping food and drink cool. ■ a refrigerated room. **2** a tall drink, esp. a mixture of wine, fruit juice, and soda water. **3** (**the cooler**) inf. prison or a prison cell.

cool·head·ed /'kōōl,hedəd/ ▶ *adj.* not easily worried or excited.

cool·ing-off pe·ri·od ▶ *n.* an interval during which two people or groups who are in disagreement can try to settle their differences before taking further action. ■ an interval after a sales contract is agreed upon during which the purchaser can decide to cancel without loss.

cool·ing tow·er ▶ *n.* a tall, open-topped, cylindrical concrete tower, used for cooling water or condensing steam from an industrial process.

coon /kōōn/ ▶ *n.* **1** short for RACCOON. **2** inf., offens. a black person.

coop /kōōp; kŏŏp/ ▶ *n.* a cage or pen for confining poultry: *a chicken coop.* ▶ *v.* [*tr.*] (usu. **be cooped up**) confine in a small space: *being cooped up indoors all day makes him fidgety.* ■ put or keep (a fowl) in a cage or pen.

co-op /'kō,äp; kō'äp/ ▶ *n.* inf. a cooperative society, business, or enterprise.

co·op·er·ate /kō'äpə,rāt/ (also **co-op·er·ate**) ▶ *v.* [*intr.*] act jointly; work toward the same end: *the leaders promised to cooperate in ending the civil war.* ■ assist someone or comply with their requests: *I was cooperating with the FBI.* —**co·op·er·ant** /-rənt/ *n.* —**co·op·er·a·tion** /kō,äpə'rāshən/ *n.* —**co·op·er·a·tor** /-,rātər/ *n.*

co·op·er·a·tive /kō'äp(ə)rətiv/ (also **co-op·er·a·tive**) ▶ *adj.* involving mutual assistance in working toward a common goal. ■ willing to be of assistance. ■ (of a farm, business, etc.) owned and run jointly by its members, with profits or benefits shared among them.

▶ *n.* a farm, business, or other organization that is owned and run jointly by its members, who share the profits or benefits. —**co·op·er·a·tive·ly** *adv.* —**co·op·er·a·tive·ness** *n.*

co·o·pe·ti·tion /kō,äpi'tishən/ ▶ *n.* collaboration between business competitors, in the hope of mutually beneficial results.

co-opt /kō'äpt; 'kō,äpt/ ▶ *v.* [*tr.*] (often **be co-opted**) appoint to membership of a committee or other body by invitation of the existing members. ■ divert to or use in a role different from the usual or original one: *social scientists were co-opted to work with the development agencies.* ■ adopt (an idea or policy) for one's own use: *the green parties have had most of their ideas co-opted by bigger parties.* —**co-op·ta·tion** /kō,äp'tāshən/ *n.* —**co-op·tion** /,kō'äpshən/ *n.* —**co-op·tive** /-'äptiv/ *adj.*

co·or·di·nate /kō-ôr·di·nate/ ▶ *v.* [*tr.*] /kō'ôrdə,nāt/ bring the different elements of (a complex activity or organization) into a relationship that will ensure efficiency or harmony. ■ [*intr.*] negotiate with others in order to work together effectively: *you will coordinate with consultants and other departments on a variety of projects.* ■ [*intr.*] match or harmonize attractively: *the stud fastenings are colored to coordinate with the shirt.*

▶ *adj.* /kō'ôrdn-ət/ **1** equal in rank or importance. ■ *Gram.* (of parts of a compound sentence) equal in rank and fulfilling identical functions. **2** *Chem.* denoting a type of covalent bond in which one atom provides both the shared electrons.

▶ *n.* /kō'ôrdənət/ **1** *Math.* each of a group of numbers used to indicate the position of a point, line, or plane. **2** (**coordinates**) matching items of clothing. —**co·or·di·na·tion** /kō,ôrdə'nāshən/ *n.* —**co·or·di·na·tive** /kō-'ôrdn-ətiv; 'ôrdn,ātiv/ *adj.* —**co·or·di·na·tor** /-'ôrdn,ātər/ *n.*

coot /kōōt/ ▶ *n.* **1** (*pl.* same) an aquatic bird (genus *Fulica*) of the rail family, with blackish plumage, lobed feet, and a bill that extends back onto the forehead as a horny shield. **2** inf. a foolish or eccentric person, typically an old man.

coot·ie /'kōōtē/ ▶ *n.* inf. a body louse. ■ a children's term for an imaginary germ or repellent quality transmitted by obnoxious or slovenly people.

cop /käp/ inf. ▶ *n.* a police officer.

▶ *v.* (**copped**, **cop·ping**) [*tr.*] **1** catch or arrest (an offender). ■ incur (something unwelcome): *the team's captain copped most of the blame.* ■

■ obtain (an illegal drug). ■ steal. ■ receive or attain (something welcome): *she copped an award for her role in the film.* **2** strike (an attitude or pose): *I copped an attitude—I acted real tough.*

▶ *phrasal v.* □ **cop out** avoid doing something that one ought to do.

▶ □ **cop a plea** engage in plea bargaining.

co·pa·cet·ic /,kōpə'setik/ (also **co·pa·set·ic**) ▶ *adj.* inf. in excellent order.

co·part·ner /'kō,pärtnər/ ▶ *n.* a partner or associate, esp. an equal partner in a business. —**co·part·ner·ship** /-,ship/ *n.*

cope[1] /kōp/ ▶ *v.* [*intr.*] (of a person) deal effectively with something difficult: *his ability to cope with stress.* ■ (of a machine or system) have the capacity to deal successfully with: *the roads are barely adequate to cope with the present traffic.* —**cop·er** *n.*

cope[2] ▶ *n.* a long, loose cloak worn by a priest or bishop on ceremonial occasions.

co·peck /'kō,pek/ ▶ *n.* chiefly British variant spelling of KOPEK.

Co·per·ni·can sys·tem /kə'pərnikən/ (also **Copernican theory**) ▶ *n.* Astron. the theory that the sun is the center of the solar system, with the planets (including the earth) orbiting around it. Compare with PTOLEMAIC SYSTEM.

cop·i·a·ble /'käpēəbəl/ ▶ *adj.* able to be copied, esp. legitimately photocopied.

cop·i·er /'käpēər/ ▶ *n.* a machine that makes exact copies of something, esp. documents, video or audio recordings, or software.

co·pi·lot /'kō,pīlət/ ▶ *n.* a second pilot in an aircraft.

▶ *v.* [*tr.*] act as the copilot of (an aircraft).

cop·ing /'kōpiNG/ ▶ *n.* the top, typically sloping, course of a brick or stone wall.

co·pi·ous /'kōpēəs/ ▶ *adj.* abundant in supply or quantity: *she took copious notes.* ■ archaic profuse in speech or ideas. —**co·pi·ous·ly** *adv.* —**co·pi·ous·ness** *n.*

co·pol·y·mer /kō'päləmər/ ▶ *n.* Chem. a polymer made by reaction of two different monomers, with units of more than one kind.

cop-out ▶ *n.* inf. an instance of avoiding a commitment or responsibility: *being 'average' is the lazy person's cop-out.*

cop·per[1] /'käpər/ ▶ *n.* **1** a red-brown metal, the chemical element of atomic number 29. A ductile metal, it is a very good conductor of heat and electricity and is used esp. for electrical wiring. (Symbol: **Cu**) **2** dated a copper coin, esp. a penny. **3** a reddish-brown color like that of copper. **4** a small, typically orange or purple butterfly (genus *Lycaena*, family Lycaenidae) of North America and Eurasia.

▶ *v.* [*tr.*] cover or coat (something) with copper.

cop·per[2] ▶ *n.* inf. a police officer.

cop·per beech ▶ *n.* a variety of European beech tree with purplish-brown leaves.

cop·per·head /'käpər,hed/ ▶ *n.* any of a number of stout-bodied venomous snakes with coppery-pink or reddish-brown coloration, in particular a North American pit viper (*Agkistrodon contortrix*).

cop·per·plate /,käpər'plāt; 'käpər,plāt/ ▶ *n.* **1** a polished copper plate with a design engraved or etched into it. ■ a print made from such a plate. **2** a style of neat, round handwriting, usually slanted and looped.

cop·per·y /'käpərē/ ▶ *adj.* like copper, esp. in color.

cop·pice /'käpəs/ chiefly Brit. ▶ *n.* an area of woodland in which the trees or shrubs are, or formerly were, periodically cut back to ground level to stimulate growth and provide firewood or timber.

▶ *v.* [*tr.*] cut back (a tree or shrub) to ground level periodically to stimulate growth: [as *adj.*] (**coppiced**) *coppiced timber.*

cop·ra /'käprə/ ▶ *n.* dried coconut kernels, from which oil is obtained.

co·pro·duce /,kōprə'd(y)ōōs/ ▶ *v.* [*tr.*] produce (a theatrical work or a radio or television program) jointly. —**co·pro·duc·er** *n.* —**co·pro·duc·tion** /-'dəkshən/ *n.*

copse /käps/ ▶ *n.* a small group of trees.

cop·ter /'käptər/ ▶ *n.* informal term for HELICOPTER.

cop·u·la /'käpyələ/ ▶ *n.* Logic & Gram. a connecting word, in particular a form of the verb *be* connecting a subject and complement. —**cop·u·lar** /'käpyələr/ *adj.*

cop·u·late /'käpyə,lāt/ ▶ *v.* [*intr.*] have sexual intercourse. —**cop·u·la·tion** /,käpyə'lāshən/ *n.* —**cop·u·la·to·ry** /-lə,tôrē/ *adj.*

cop·y /'käpē/ ▶ *n.* (*pl.* **cop·ies**) **1** a thing made to be similar or identical to another. **2** a single specimen of a particular book, record, or other publication or issue. **3** matter to be printed: *copy for the next issue must* be submitted by the beginning of the month. ■ material for a newspaper or magazine article: *bad news makes good copy.* ■ the text of an advertisement: *"No more stubble—no more trouble,"* trumpeted their ad copy.

▶*v.* (**cop·ies, cop·ied**) [*tr.*] make a similar or identical version of; reproduce. ■ *Comput.* reproduce (data stored in one location) in another location: *the command will* **copy** *a file* **from** *one disc* **to** *another.* ■ write out (information that one has read or heard): *he copied the details into his notebook.* ■ behave in a similar way to; do the same as: *she was such fun that everybody wanted to copy her.* ■ imitate or reproduce (an idea or style) rather than creating something original: *lifestyles* **copied from** *Miami and Fifth Avenue* | [*intr.*] *art students* **copied from** *approved old masters.* ■ (**copy something to**) send a copy of a letter to (a third party). ▷Middle English (denoting a transcript or copy of a document): from Old French *copie* (noun), *copier* (verb), from Latin *copia* 'abundance' (in medieval Latin 'transcript,' from such phrases as *copiam describendi facere* 'give permission to transcribe').

cop·y·book /ˈkäpēˌbook/ ▶*n.* a book containing models of handwriting for learners to imitate.
▶*adj.* exactly in accordance with established criteria; perfect. ■ tritely conventional: *out come the copybook maxims.*

cop·y·cat /ˈkäpēˌkat/ ▶*n.* *inf., derog.* (esp. in children's use) a person who copies another's behavior, dress, or ideas. ■ [as *adj.*] denoting an action, typically a crime, carried out in imitation of another.

cop·y·desk /ˈkäpēˌdesk/ ▶*n.* a desk in a newspaper office at which copy is edited for printing.

cop·y·ed·it /ˈkäpēˌedit/ (also **cop·y-ed·it**) ▶*v.* [*tr.*] edit (text to be printed) by checking its consistency and accuracy. —**cop·y·ed·i·tor** /-ˌedətər/ (also **cop·y ed·i·tor**) *n.*

cop·y·ist /ˈkäpēˌist/ ▶*n.* a person who makes copies, esp. of handwritten documents or music. ■ a person who imitates the styles of others, esp. in art.

cop·y·right /ˈkäpēˌrīt/ ▶*n.* the exclusive legal right, given to an originator or an assignee to print, publish, perform, film, or record literary, artistic, or musical material, and to authorize others to do the same.
▶*v.* [*tr.*] secure copyright for (such material).

cop·y·writ·er /ˈkäpiˌrītər/ ▶*n.* a person who writes the text of advertisements or publicity material. —**cop·y·writ·ing** /-ˌrītiNG/ *n.*

co·quette /kōˈket/ ▶*n.* a woman who flirts. —**co·quet·tish** *adj.* —**co·quet·tish·ly** *adv.* —**co·quet·tish·ness** *n.*

co·qui /ˈkōkē/ *n.* ▶a singing tree frog (*Eleutherodactylus coqui*), native to Puerto Rico, that has become an invasive pest in Hawaii.

cor·al /ˈkôrəl/ ▶*n.* **1** a hard stony substance secreted by certain marine coelenterates as an external skeleton, typically forming large reefs in warm seas. ■ precious red coral, used in jewelry. ■ the pinkish-red color of red coral. **2** a sedentary, typically colonial coelenterate of warm and tropical seas, with a calcareous, horny, or soft skeleton. **3** the unfertilized roe of a lobster or scallop. —**cor·al·loid** /-ˌloid/ *adj.* (*chiefly Biol. Zool.*).

cor·al·line /ˈkôrəˌlīn/ ▶*n.* (also **coralline alga** or **coralline seaweed**) a branching reddish seaweed (family Corallinaceae) with a calcareous stem, in particular *Corallina officinalis*, common on the coasts of the North Atlantic. ■ a sedentary colonial marine animal, esp. a bryozoan.
▶*adj.* resembling coral: *coralline sponges.* ■ of the pinkish-red color of precious red coral.

cor·al snake ▶*n.* a brightly colored venomous snake (*Micrurus* and other genera) of the cobra family, typically having conspicuous bands of red, yellow, white, and black.

cor·bel /ˈkôrbəl/ ▶*n.* a projection jutting out from a wall to support a structure above it.
▶*v.* (**-beled, -bel·ing**; *chiefly Brit.* **-belled, -bel·ling**) [*tr.*] (often **be corbeled out**) support (a structure such as an arch or balcony) on corbels.

cord /kôrd/ ▶*n.* **1** long thin flexible string or rope made from several twisted strands. ■ a length of such material, typically one used to fasten or move a specified object. ■ an anatomical structure resembling a length of cord (e.g., the spinal cord, the umbilical cord). ■ a flexible insulated cable used for carrying electric current to an appliance. **2** ribbed fabric, esp. corduroy: [as *adj.*] *cord jackets.* ■ (**cords**) *inf.* corduroy pants. ■ a cordlike rib on fabric. **3** a measure of cut wood, usually 128 cubic feet (3.62 cu m). —**cord·like** /-ˌlīk/ *adj.*

cord·age /ˈkôrdij/ ▶*n.* cords or ropes, esp. in a ship's rigging.

cor·date /ˈkôrˌdāt/ ▶*adj.* *Bot. & Zool.* heart-shaped.

cord blood ▶*n.* blood from the human umbilical cord, a source of stem cells.

cor·dial /ˈkôrjəl/ ▶*adj.* warm and friendly. ■ strongly felt.

▶*n.* **1** another term for **LIQUEUR**. **2** a comforting or pleasant-tasting medicine. —**cor·dial·i·ty** /ˌkôrjēˈalitē/ *n.* —**cor·dial·ly** *adv.*

cor·dil·le·ra /ˌkôrdlˈ(y)erə/ ▶*n.* a system or group of parallel mountain ranges together with the intervening plateaus and other features, esp. in the Andes or the Rockies.

cord·ite /ˈkôrˌdīt/ ▶*n.* a smokeless explosive made from nitrocellulose, nitroglycerine, and petroleum jelly, used in ammunition.

cord·less /ˈkôrdləs/ ▶*adj.* (of an electrical appliance or telephone) working without connection to a main supply or central unit.
▶*n.* a cordless telephone.

cor·don /ˈkôrdn/ ▶*n.* **1** a line or circle of police, soldiers, or guards preventing access to or from an area or building. **2** an ornamental cord or braid.
▶*v.* [*tr.*] (**cordon off**) prevent access to or from (an area or building) by surrounding it with police or other guards.

cor·don bleu /ˌkôrdôN ˈbloe/ ▶*adj.* *Cooking* of the highest class: *a cordon bleu chef.* ■ denoting a dish consisting of an escalope of veal or chicken rolled, filled with cheese and ham, and then fried in breadcrumbs.
▶*n.* a cook of the highest class.

cor·du·roy /ˈkôrdəˌroi/ ▶*n.* a thick cotton fabric with velvety ribs. ■ (**corduroys**) pants made of corduroy.

CORE /kôr/ ▶*abbr.* Congress of Racial Equality.

core /kôr/ ▶*n.* **1** the tough central part of various fruits, containing the seeds: *an apple core.* **2** the central or most important part of something, in particular: ■ [often as *adj.*] the part of something that is central to its existence or character: *managers can concentrate on their core activities* | *the plan has the interests of children at its core.* ■ an important or unchanging group of people forming the central part of a larger body. ■ the dense central region of a planet, esp. the nickel–iron inner part of the earth. ■ the central part of a nuclear reactor, which contains the fissile material. ■ a tiny ring of magnetic material used in a computer memory to store one bit of data, now superseded by semiconductor memories. ■ the inner strand of an electrical cable or rope. ■ a piece of soft iron forming the center of an electromagnet or an induction coil. ■ an internal mold filling a space to be left hollow in a casting. ■ a cylindrical sample of rock, ice, or other material obtained by boring with a hollow drill. ■ *Archaeol.* a piece of flint from which flakes or blades have been removed.
▶*v.* [*tr.*] remove the tough central part and seeds from (a fruit). —**cor·er** *n.*

co·re·op·sis /ˌkôrēˈäpsəs/ ▶*n.* a plant (genus *Coreopsis*) of the daisy family, cultivated for its rayed, typically yellow, flowers.

co·re·spond·ent (also **co·re·spond·ent**) ▶*n.* **1** a joint defendant in a lawsuit, esp. one on appeal. **2** a person cited in a divorce case as having committed adultery with the respondent.

cor·gi /ˈkôrgē/ ▶*n.* (*pl.* **cor·gis**) short for **WELSH CORGI**.

co·ri·an·der /ˈkôrēˌandər; ˌkôrēˈandər/ ▶*n.* an aromatic Mediterranean plant (*Coriandrum sativum*) of the parsley family, the leaves and seeds of which are used as culinary herbs.

Co·rin·thi·an /kəˈrinTHēən/ ▶*adj.* **1** belonging or relating to Corinth, esp. the ancient city. ■ relating to or denoting the lightest and most ornate of the classical orders of architecture (used esp. by the Romans), characterized by flared capitals with rows of acanthus leaves. **2** involving or displaying the highest standards of sportsmanship: *a club embodying the Corinthian spirit.*
▶*n.* **1** a native of Corinth. ■ *hist.* a wealthy amateur of sport. **2** the Corinthian order of architecture.

cork /kôrk/ ▶*n.* the buoyant, light brown substance obtained from the outer layer of the bark of the cork oak: [as *adj.*] *cork tiles.* ■ a bottle stopper, esp. one made of cork. ■ a piece of cork used as a float for a fishing line or net. ■ *Bot.* a protective layer of dead cells immediately below the bark of woody plants.
▶*v.* [*tr.*] (often **be corked**) **1** close or seal (a bottle) with a cork. ■ [as *adj.*] (**corked**) (of wine) spoiled by tannin from the cork. **2** draw with burnt cork. **3** illicitly hollow out (a baseball bat) and fill it with cork to make it lighter. —**cork·like** /-ˌlīk/ *adj.*

cork oak (also **cork tree**) ▶*n.* an evergreen Mediterranean oak (*Quercus suber*), the outer layer of the bark of which is the source of cork.

cork·screw /ˈkôrkˌskrōō/ ▶*n.* a device for pulling corks from bottles, consisting of a spiral metal rod that is inserted into the cork and a handle that extracts it. ■ [usu. as *adj.*] a thing with a spiral shape or movement: *a girl with corkscrew curls.*
▶*v.* [*intr.*] move or twist in a spiral motion.

cork·y /ˈkôrkē/ ▶*adj.* (**cork·i·er, cork·i·est**) **1** corklike. **2** (of wine) corked.

corm /kôrm/ ▶*n.* a rounded underground storage organ present in plants such as crocuses, gladioli, and cyclamens, consisting of a swollen stem base covered with scale leaves. Compare with BULB (sense 1), RHIZOME.

cor·mo·rant /'kôrmərənt/ ▶ n. a large voracious diving bird (genera *Phalacrocorax* and *Nannopterum*, family Phalacrocoracidae) with a long hooked bill, short legs, and mainly dark plumage.

corn[1] /kôrn/ ▶ n. **1** a North American cereal plant (*Zea mays*) that yields large grains, or kernels, set in rows on a cob. ■ the grains of this. ■ *Brit.* the chief cereal crop of a district, esp. (in England) wheat or (in Scotland) oats. **2** *inf.* something banal or sentimental: *the movie is pure corn.*

corn[2] ▶ n. a small, painful area of thickened skin on the foot, esp. on the toes, caused by pressure.

corn·ball /'kôrn,bôl/ *inf.* ▶ *adj.* trite and sentimental: *a cornball movie.* ▶ n. a person with trite or sentimental ideas.

corn·bread /'kôrn,bred/ (also **corn bread**) ▶ n. a type of bread made from cornmeal and typically leavened without yeast.

corn·cob /'kôrn,käb/ (also **corn cob**) ▶ n. see COB[1] (sense 1).

corn·cob pipe ▶ n. a tobacco pipe with a bowl made from a dried corncob.

cor·ne·a /'kôrnēə/ ▶ n. the transparent layer forming the front of the eye. —**cor·ne·al** *adj.*

corned beef (also **corn beef**) ▶ n. beef brisket cured in brine.

cor·ne·ous /'kôrnēəs/ ▶ *adj. formal* hornlike; horny.

cor·ner /'kôrnər/ ▶ n. **1** a place or angle where two or more sides or edges meet: *Jan sat at one corner of the table.* ■ an area inside a room, box, or square-shaped space, near the place where two or more edges or surfaces meet. ■ a place where two streets meet: *an apartment on the corner of 199th Street and Amsterdam Avenue* | [as adj.] *the corner house.* ■ *fig.* a difficult or awkward situation: *he found himself* **backed into a corner.** ■ first or third base on a baseball diamond. ■ a sharp bend in a road. **2** a part, region, or area, esp. one regarded as secluded or remote: *from all corners of the world* | *fig.* *she couldn't bear journalists prying into every corner of her life.* ■ a position in which one dominates the supply of a particular commodity. **3** *Boxing & Wrestling* each of the diagonally opposite ends of the ring, where a contestant rests between rounds. ■ a contestant's supporters or seconds. **4** *Baseball* each of the two parallel sides of home plate, which are perceived as defining the vertical edges of the strike zone.

▶ *v.* [tr.] **1** (often **be cornered**) force (a person or animal) into a place or situation from which it is hard to escape. ■ detain (someone) in conversation, typically against their will: *I managed to corner Gary for fifteen minutes.* **2** control (a market) by dominating the supply of a particular commodity: *whether they will* **corner the market** *in graphics software remains to be seen.* ■ establish a corner in (a commodity). **3** [intr.] (of a vehicle or driver) go around a bend in a road.

▶ □ **in someone's corner** on someone's side; giving someone support and encouragement. □ **on** (or **at** or **in**) **every corner** everywhere. □ **see someone or something out of** (or **from**) **the corner of one's eye** see someone or something at the edge of one's field of vision.

cor·ner·stone /'kôrnər,stōn/ ▶ n. a stone that forms the base of a corner of a building, joining two walls. ■ a stone ceremonially laid usually at the corner of a foundation to mark the occasion of a building being erected. ■ an important quality or feature on which a particular thing depends or is based.

cor·net /kôr'net/ ▶ n. **1** *Mus.* a brass instrument resembling a trumpet but shorter and wider, played chiefly in bands. ■ a compound organ stop with a powerful treble sound. **2** *Brit.* a cone-shaped wafer, esp. one filled with ice cream. —**cor·net·ist** (also **cor·net·tist**) n.

corn·flakes /'kôrn,flāks/ ▶ *pl. n.* a breakfast cereal consisting of toasted flakes made from corn.

corn·flow·er /'kôrn,flouər/ ▶ n. a slender Eurasian plant (genus *Centaurea*) of the daisy family, with flowers that are typically a deep, vivid blue. ■ (also **cornflower blue**) a deep, vivid blue color.

cor·nice /'kôrnis/ ▶ n. **1** an ornamental molding around the wall of a room just below the ceiling. ■ a horizontal molded projection crowning a building or structure, esp. the uppermost member of the entablature of an order, surmounting the frieze. **2** an overhanging mass of hardened snow at the edge of a mountain precipice. —**cor·niced** *adj.* —**cor·nic·ing** n.

Cor·nish /'kôrnisH/ ▶ *adj.* of or relating to Cornwall, or its people or language.

▶ n. **1** [as pl. n.] (**the Cornish**) the people of Cornwall collectively. **2** the extinct Brythonic language of Cornwall —**Cor·nish·man** /-mən/ n. (pl. **-men**) —**Cor·nish·wom·an** /-,wŏŏmən/ n. (pl. **-wom·en**).

corn·meal /'kôrn,mēl/ ▶ n. meal made from ground, dried corn.

corn pone ▶ n. see PONE.

▶ *adj.* (**corn-pone**) *often derog.* rustic; unsophisticated: *corn-pone humor.*

corn·rows /'kôrn,rōz/ ▶ *pl. n.* a style of braiding and plaiting the hair in narrow strips to form geometric patterns on the scalp.

corn·starch /'kôrn,stärCH/ ▶ n. finely ground corn flour, used as a thickener in cooking.

cor·nu·co·pi·a /,kôrn(y)ə'kōpēə/ ▶ n. a symbol of plenty consisting of a goat's horn overflowing with flowers, fruit, and corn. ■ an ornamental container shaped like such a horn. ■ an abundant supply of good things of a specified kind: *the festival offers* **a cornucopia** *of pleasures.* —**cor·nu·co·pi·an** *adj.*

corn·y /'kôrnē/ ▶ *adj.* (**corn·i·er**, **corn·i·est**) *inf.* trite, banal, or mawkishly sentimental. —**corn·i·ly** /'kôrnē-/ *adv.* —**corn·i·ness** n.

co·rol·la /kə'rälə; kə'rōlə/ ▶ n. *Bot.* the petals of a flower, typically forming a whorl within the sepals and enclosing the reproductive organs. Compare with CALYX.

cor·ol·lar·y /'kôrə,lerē; 'kärə-/ ▶ n. (pl. **-lar·ies**) a proposition that follows from (and is often appended to) one already proved. ■ a direct or natural consequence or result.

▶ *adj.* forming a proposition that follows from one already proved. ■ associated; supplementary. ▷late Middle English: from Latin *corollarium* 'money paid for a garland or chaplet; gratuity' (in late Latin 'deduction'), from *corolla*, diminutive of *corona* 'wreath, crown, chaplet.'

co·ro·na[1] /kə'rōnə/ ▶ n. (pl. **-nae** /-nē/; **-nī**) *Astron.* the rarefied gaseous envelope of the sun and other stars. ■ (also **corona discharge**) *Physics* the glow around a conductor at high potential. ■ a small circle of light seen around the sun or moon, due to diffraction by water droplets. —**co·ro·nal** /-'rōnl/ *adj.*

co·ro·na[2] ▶ n. a long, straight-sided cigar.

cor·o·nar·y /'kôrə,nerē; 'kär-/ ▶ *adj. Anat.* relating to or denoting the arteries that surround and supply the heart. ■ relating to or denoting a structure that encircles a part of the body.

▶ n. (pl. **-nar·ies**) short for CORONARY THROMBOSIS.

cor·o·nar·y throm·bo·sis ▶ n. a blockage of the flow of blood to the heart, caused by a blood clot in a coronary artery.

cor·o·na·tion /,kôrə'nāsHən; ,kär-/ ▶ n. the ceremony of crowning a sovereign or a sovereign's consort.

cor·o·ner /'kôrənər; 'kär-/ ▶ n. an official who investigates violent, sudden, or suspicious deaths. ■ *hist.* in England, an official responsible for safeguarding the private property of the Crown. —**cor·o·ner·ship** /-,sHip/ n.

cor·o·net /,kôrə'net; ,kär-/ ▶ n. **1** a small or relatively simple crown, esp. as worn by lesser royalty and peers or peeresses. ■ a circular decoration for the head, esp. one made of flowers. **2** the band of tissue on the lowest part of a horse's pastern, containing the horn-producing cells from which the hoof grows. —**cor·o·net·ed** *adj.*

Corp. ▶ *abbr.* ■ (**Corp**) *inf.* corporal. ■ corporation: *IBM Corp.*

cor·po·ra /'kôrpərə/ ▶ plural form of CORPUS.

cor·po·ral[1] /'kôrp(ə)rəl/ ▶ n. a low-ranking noncommissioned officer in the armed forces, in particular (in the U.S. Army) one ranking above private first class and below sergeant or (in the U.S. Marine Corps) one ranking above lance corporal and below sergeant.

cor·po·ral[2] ▶ *adj.* of or relating to the human body. —**cor·po·ral·ly** *adv.*

cor·po·ral·i·ty /,kôrpə'ralitē/ ▶ n. *rare* material or corporeal existence.

cor·po·ral pun·ish·ment ▶ n. physical punishment, such as caning or flogging. ■ punishment under law that includes imprisonment and death.

cor·po·rate /'kôrp(ə)rət/ ▶ *adj.* of or relating to a corporation, esp. a large company or group. ■ *Law* (of a company or group of people) authorized to act as a single entity and recognized as such in law. ■ of or shared by all the members of a group: *the service emphasizes the corporate responsibility of the congregation.*

▶ n. a corporate company or group. —**cor·po·rate·ly** *adv.*

cor·po·rate raid·er ▶ n. a financier who makes a practice of making hostile takeover bids for companies, either to control their policies or to resell them for a profit.

cor·po·ra·tion /,kôrpə'rāsHən/ ▶ n. a company or group of people authorized to act as a single entity (legally a person) and recognized as such in law. ■ (also **municipal corporation**) a group of people elected to govern a city, town, or borough. ■ *dated, humorous* a paunch.

cor·por·a·tive /ˈkôrp(ə)rətiv/ ▶adj. of or relating to a corporation. ■ governed by or organized in corporations.

cor·po·re·al /kôrˈpôrēəl/ ▶adj. of or relating to a person's body, esp. as opposed to their spirit. ■ having a body: *a corporeal God.* ■ *Law* consisting of material objects; tangible. —**cor·po·re·al·i·ty** /kôrˌpôrēˈalitē/ *n.* —**cor·po·re·al·ly** *adv.*

corps /kôr/ ▶*n.* (*pl.* **corps** /kôrz/) a main subdivision of an armed force in the field, consisting of two or more divisions: *the 5th Army Corps.* ■ a branch of a military organization assigned to a particular kind of work: *the U.S. Army Medical Corps.* ■ a body of people engaged in a particular activity: *the press corps.* ■ short for **CORPS DE BALLET**. —**corps·man** *n.*

corps de bal·let /ˌkôr də baˈlā/ ▶*n.* [treated as *sing.* or *pl.*] the members of a ballet company who dance together as a group.

corpse /kôrps/ ▶*n.* a dead body, esp. of a human being rather than an animal. ▷Middle English (denoting the living body of a person or animal): alteration of *corse* by association with Latin *corpus*, a change that also took place in French (Old French *cors* becoming *corps*). The *p* was originally silent, as in French; the final *e* was rare before the 19th cent., but now distinguishes *corpse* from *corps.*

cor·pu·lent /ˈkôrpyələnt/ ▶adj. (of a person) fat. —**cor·pu·lence** *n.* —**cor·pu·len·cy** *n.*

cor·pus /ˈkôrpəs/ ▶*n.* (*pl.* **-po·ra** /-pərə/ or **-pus·es**) **1** a collection of written texts, esp. the entire works of a particular author or a body of writing on a particular subject: *the Darwinian corpus.* ■ a collection of written or spoken material in machine-readable form, assembled for the purpose of studying linguistic structures, frequencies, etc. **2** *Anat.* the main body or mass of a structure.

cor·pus·cle /ˈkôrˌpəsəl/ ▶*n. Biol.* a minute body or cell in an organism, esp. a red or white cell in the blood of vertebrates. ■ *hist.* a minute particle regarded as the basic constituent of matter or light. —**cor·pus·cu·lar** /kôrˈpəskyələr/ *adj.*

cor·pus de·lic·ti /dəˈlik,tī; -ˌtē/ ▶*n. Law* the facts and circumstances constituting a breach of a law. ■ concrete evidence of a crime, such as a corpse.

cor·pus lu·te·um /ˈlootēəm/ ▶*n.* (*pl.* **cor·po·ra lu·te·a** /ˈlootēə/) *Anat.* a hormone-secreting structure that develops in an ovary after an ovum has been discharged but degenerates after a few days unless pregnancy has begun.

cor·ral /kəˈral/ ▶*n.* a pen for livestock, esp. cattle or horses, on a farm or ranch. ■ *hist.* a defensive enclosure of wagons in an encampment.
▶*v.* (**-ralled, -ral·ling**) [*tr.*] put or keep (livestock) in a corral. ■ *fig.* gather (a group of people or things) together. ■ *hist.* form (wagons) into a corral.

cor·rect /kəˈrekt/ ▶adj. free from error; in accordance with fact or truth. ■ not mistaken in one's opinion or judgment; right. ■ (of a thing or course of action) meeting the requirements of or most appropriate for a particular situation or activity. ■ (of a person or their appearance or behavior) conforming to accepted social standards; proper. ■ conforming to a particular political or ideological orthodoxy. See also **POLITICALLY CORRECT**.
▶*v.* [*tr.*] put right (an error or fault). ■ mark the errors in (a written or printed text). ■ tell (someone) that they are mistaken: *he had assumed she was married and she had not corrected him.* ■ counteract or rectify: *the problem of diminished sight can be reduced or corrected by wearing eyeglasses.* ■ adjust (an instrument) to function accurately or in accord with a standard. ■ adjust (a numerical result or reading) to allow for departure from standard conditions: *data was corrected for wind-tunnel interference.* —**cor·rect·a·ble** *adj.* —**cor·rect·ly** *adv.* —**cor·rect·ness** *n.*

cor·rec·tion /kəˈrekSHən/ ▶*n.* the action or process of correcting something: *I checked the typing for errors and sent it back for correction.* ■ a change that rectifies an error or inaccuracy. ■ used to introduce an amended version of something one has just said: *after today—correction, she thought grimly, after tonight—she'd never see him again.* ■ a quantity adjusting a numerical result to allow for a departure from standard conditions. ■ a temporary reversal in an overall trend of stock market prices, esp. a brief fall during an overall increase. ■ punishment, esp. that of criminals in prison intended to rectify their behavior. —**cor·rec·tion·al** *adj.*

cor·rec·tive /kəˈrektiv/ ▶adj. designed to correct or counteract something harmful or undesirable.
▶*n.* a thing intended to correct or counteract something else: *the move might be a corrective to some inefficient practices within hospitals.* —**cor·rec·tive·ly** *adv.*

cor·re·late ▶*v.* /ˈkôrəˌlāt; ˈkär-/ [*intr.*] have a mutual relationship or connection, in which one thing affects or depends on another: *the study found that success in the educational system correlates highly with class.* ■ [*tr.*] establish such a relationship or connection between: *we correlate general trends in public opinion with trends in the content of television news.*
▶*n.* /-lət/ each of two or more related or complementary things: *financial hardship and other correlates of poverty.*

cor·re·la·tion /ˌkôrəˈlāSHən/ ▶*n.* a mutual relationship or connection between two or more things: *research showed a clear correlation between recession and levels of property crime.* ■ *Statistics* interdependence of variable quantities. ■ *Statistics* a quantity measuring the extent of such interdependence. ■ the process of establishing a relationship or connection between two or more measures. —**cor·re·la·tion·al** /-SHənl/ *adj.*

cor·rel·a·tive /kəˈrelətiv/ ▶adj. having a mutual relationship; corresponding: *rights, whether moral or legal, can involve correlative duties.* ■ *Gram.* (of words such as *neither* and *nor*) corresponding to each other and regularly used together.
▶*n.* a word or concept that has a mutual relationship with another word or concept: *the child's right to education is a correlative of the parent's duty to send the child to school.* —**cor·rel·a·tive·ly** *adv.* —**cor·rel·a·tiv·i·ty** /kəˌrelə'tivitē/ *n.*

cor·re·spond /ˌkôrəˈspänd; ˌkär-/ ▶*v.* [*intr.*] **1** have a close similarity; match or agree almost exactly: *the carved heads described in the poem correspond to those in the drawing.* ■ be analogous or equivalent in character, form, or function: *the Inuit month corresponding to December was called Aagjulirvik.* ■ represent: *digits that correspond to certain letters of the alphabet.* **2** communicate by exchanging letters. —**cor·re·spond·ing** *adj.* —**cor·re·spond·ing·ly** *adv.*

cor·re·spond·ence /ˌkôrəˈspändəns; ˌkär-/ ▶*n.* **1** a close similarity, connection, or equivalence: *there is a simple correspondence between the distance of a focused object from the eye and the size of its image on the retina.* **2** communication by exchanging letters with someone. ■ letters sent or received: *his wife dealt with his private correspondence.* —**cor·re·spond·en·cy** /-dənsē/ *n.* (*rare*).

cor·re·spond·ence course ▶*n.* a course of study in which student and teachers communicate by mail.

cor·re·spond·ent /ˌkôrəˈspändənt; ˌkär-/ ▶*n.* a person who writes letters to a person or a newspaper, esp. on a regular basis. ■ a person employed to report for a newspaper or broadcasting organization, typically on a particular subject or from a particular country: *a White House correspondent.*
▶*adj.* corresponding.

cor·ri·da /kôˈrēdə/ ▶*n.* a bullfight.

cor·ri·dor /ˈkôrədər; ˈkär-; -ˌdôr/ ▶*n.* a long passage in a building from which doors lead into rooms. ■ a belt of land between two other areas, typically having a particular feature or giving access to a particular area: *the valley provides the principal wildlife corridor between the uplands and the central urban area.* ■ a belt of land following a road, river, or other route of passage. ▷late 16th cent. (as a military term denoting a strip of land along the outer edge of a ditch, protected by a parapet): from French, from Italian *corridore*, alteration (by association with *corridore* 'runner') of *corridoio* 'running place,' from *correre* 'to run,' from Latin *currere*. The current sense dates from the early 19th cent.

cor·ri·gen·dum /ˌkôriˈjendəm; ˌkär-/ ▶*n.* (*pl.* **-gen·da** /-ˈjendə/) a thing to be corrected, typically an error in a printed text.

cor·ri·gi·ble /ˈkôrijəbəl; ˈkär-/ ▶adj. capable of being corrected, rectified, or reformed. —**cor·ri·gi·bil·i·ty** /ˌkôrijəˈbilitē; ˌkär-/ *n.*

cor·rob·o·rate /kəˈräbəˌrāt/ ▶*v.* [*tr.*] confirm or give support to (a statement, theory, or finding): *the witness had corroborated the boy's account of the attack.* —**cor·rob·o·ra·tion** /kəˌräbəˈrāSHən/ *n.* —**cor·rob·o·ra·tive** /-ˈräb(ə)rətiv/ *adj.* —**cor·rob·o·ra·tor** /-ˌrātər/ *n.* —**cor·rob·o·ra·to·ry** /-ˈräb(ə)rə,tôrē/ *adj.*

cor·rode /kəˈrōd/ ▶*v.* [*tr.*] destroy or damage (metal, stone, or other materials) slowly by chemical action. ■ [*intr.*] (of metal or other materials) be destroyed or damaged in this way. ■ *fig.* destroy or weaken (something) gradually: *the self-centered climate corrodes ideals and concerns about social justice.* —**cor·rod·i·ble** *adj.*

cor·ro·sion /kəˈrōzhən/ ▶*n.* the process of corroding metal, stone, or other materials: *each aircraft part is sprayed with oil to prevent corrosion.* ■ damage caused by such a process.

cor·ro·sive /kəˈrōsiv; -ziv/ ▶adj. tending to cause corrosion. —**cor·ro·sive·ly** *adv.* —**cor·ro·sive·ness** *n.*

cor·ru·gate /ˈkôrəˌgāt; ˈkär-/ ▶*v.* contract or cause to contract into wrinkles or folds: [*intr.*] *Micky's brow corrugated in a simian frown.*

cor·rupt /kəˈrəpt/ ▶adj. **1** having or showing a willingness to act dishonestly in return for money or personal gain. ■ evil or morally depraved. ■ *archaic* (of organic or inorganic matter) in a state of decay; rotten or putrid. **2** (of a text or manuscript) debased or made unreliable by errors or alterations. ■ (of a computer database or program) having errors introduced.
▶*v.* [*tr.*] **1** cause to act dishonestly in return for money or personal gain. ■ cause to become morally depraved. ■ *archaic* infect; contaminate.

2 (often **be corrupted**) change or debase by making errors or unintentional alterations: *Epicurus's teachings have since been much corrupted.* ■ cause errors to appear in (a computer program or database): *a program that has somehow corrupted your system files.* —**cor·rupt·er** *n.* —**cor·rupt·i·bil·i·ty** /kə,rəptə'bilitē/ *n.* —**cor·rupt·i·ble** *adj.* —**cor·rup·tive** /-tiv/ *adj.* —**cor·rupt·ly** *adv.*

cor·rup·tion /kə'rəpsHən/ ▶*n.* **1** dishonest or fraudulent conduct by those in power, typically involving bribery. ■ the action of making someone or something morally depraved or the state of being so: *the word "addict" conjures up evil and corruption.* ■ *archaic* decay; putrefaction. **2** the process by which something, typically a word or expression, is changed from its original use or meaning to one that is regarded as erroneous or debased. ■ the process of causing errors to appear in a computer program or database.

cor·sage /kôr'säzH; -'säj/ ▶*n.* **1** a spray of flowers worn pinned to a woman's clothes. **2** the upper part of a woman's dress.

cor·sair /'kôr,se(ə)r/ ▶*n. archaic* **1** a pirate. ■ a privateer, esp. one operating along the southern coast of the Mediterranean in the 17th century. **2** a pirate ship.

cor·set /'kôrsət/ ▶*n.* a woman's tightly fitting undergarment extending from below the chest to the hips, worn to shape the figure. ■ a similar garment worn by men or women to support a weak or injured back. ■ *hist.* a tightly fitting laced or stiffened outer bodice or dress. ▷Middle English: from Old French, diminutive of *cors* 'body,' from Latin *corpus.* The sense 'close-fitting undergarment' dates from the late 18th cent., by which time the sense 'bodice' had mainly historical reference. —**cor·set·ed** *adj.* —**cor·set·ry** /-trē/ *n.*

Cor·si·can /'kôrsikən/ ▶*adj.* of or relating to Corsica, its people, or their language.
▶*n.* **1** a native of Corsica. **2** the language of Corsica, which originated as a dialect of Italian.

cor·tège /kôr'tezH; 'kôr,tezH/ ▶*n.* a solemn procession, esp. for a funeral. ■ a person's entourage or retinue.

cor·tex /'kôr,teks/ ▶*n.* (*pl.* **-ti·ces** /-tə,sēz/) *Anat.* the outer layer of the cerebrum (the **cerebral cortex**), composed of folded gray matter and playing an important role in consciousness. ■ an outer layer of another organ or body part such as a kidney (the **renal cortex**), the cerebellum, or a hair. ■ *Bot.* an outer layer of tissue immediately below the epidermis of a stem or root. —**cor·ti·cal** /'kôrtikəl/ *adj.*

cor·ti·co·ster·oid /,kôrtikō'ster,oid; -'sti(ə)r,oid/ ▶*n. Biochem.* any of a group of steroid hormones produced in the adrenal cortex or made synthetically. They have various metabolic functions and some are used to treat inflammation.

cor·ti·sone /'kôrtə,sōn/ ▶*n. Biochem.* a hormone produced by the adrenal cortex. It is also made synthetically for use as an anti-inflammatory and anti-allergy agent.

co·run·dum /kə'rəndəm/ ▶*n.* extremely hard aluminum oxide, used as an abrasive. Ruby and sapphire are varieties of corundum.

cor·us·cate /'kôrə,skāt; 'kär-/ ▶*v.* [*intr.*] *poetic/lit.* (of light) flash or sparkle. —**cor·us·ca·tion** /,kôrə'skāsHən/ *n.*

cos[1] /käs; kôs/ (also **cos le·ttuce**) ▶*n.* another term for **ROMAINE**.

cos[2] ▶*abbr.* cosine.

Co·sa Nos·tra /,kōsə 'nōstrə; ,kōzə/ ▶a U.S. criminal organization resembling and related to the Mafia.

co·se·cant /kō'sē,kant; -kənt/ ▶*n. Math.* the ratio of the hypotenuse (in a right-angled triangle) to the side opposite an acute angle; the reciprocal of sine.

co·sign /'kō,sīn/ ▶*v.* **1** sign (a document) in order to guarantee a loan or other obligation: [*tr.*] *co-sign a loan* [*intr.*] *see if your parents will co-sign for you.* **2** [*tr.*] designate with two different labels or signs.

co·sig·na·to·ry /kō'signə,tôrē/ (also **co·sig·na·to·ry**) ▶*n.* a person or state signing a treaty or other document jointly with others.

co·sine /'kō,sīn/ ▶*n. Math.* the trigonometric function that is equal to the ratio of the side adjacent to an acute angle (in a right-angled triangle) to the hypotenuse.

cos·me·ceu·ti·cal /,käzmə'sootikəl/ ▶*n.* a cosmetic that has or is claimed to have medicinal properties, esp. antiaging ones.

cos·met·ic /käz'metik/ ▶*adj.* involving or relating to treatment intended to restore or improve a person's appearance: *cosmetic surgery.* ■ designed or serving to improve the appearance of the body, esp. the face. ■ affecting only the appearance of something rather than its substance: *the reform package was merely a cosmetic exercise.*
▶*n.* (usu. **cosmetics**) a product applied to the body, esp. the face, to improve its appearance. —**cos·met·i·cal·ly** /-(ə)lē/ *adv.*

cos·me·tol·o·gy /,käzmə'täləjē/ ▶*n.* the professional skill or practice of beautifying the face, hair, and skin. —**cos·me·to·log·i·cal** /-tə'läjikəl/ *adj.* —**cos·me·tol·o·gist** /-jist/ *n.*

cos·mic /'käzmik/ ▶*adj.* of or relating to the universe or cosmos, esp. as distinct from the earth: *cosmic matter.* ■ inconceivably vast. —**cos·mi·cal** *adj.* —**cos·mi·cal·ly** /-(ə)lē/ *adv.*

cos·mic string ▶*n.* another term for **STRING** (sense 4).

cos·mog·o·ny /käz'mägənē/ ▶*n.* (*pl.* **-nies**) the branch of science that deals with the origin of the universe, esp. the solar system. ■ a theory regarding this. —**cos·mo·gon·ic** /,käzmə'gänik/ *adj.* —**cos·mo·gon·i·cal** /,käzmə'gänikəl/ *adj.* —**cos·mog·o·nist** /-nist/ *n.*

cos·mog·ra·phy /käz'mägrəfē/ ▶*n.* (*pl.* **-phies**) the science that deals with the general features of the universe, including the earth. The branches of cosmography include astronomy, geography, and geology. ■ a description or representation of the universe or the earth. —**cos·mog·ra·pher** /-fər/ *n.* —**cos·mo·graph·ic** /,käzmə'grafik/ *adj.* —**cos·mo·graph·i·cal** /,käzmə'grafikəl/ *adj.*

cos·mol·o·gy /käz'mäləjē/ ▶*n.* (*pl.* **-gies**) the science of the origin and development of the universe. ■ an account or theory of the origin of the universe. —**cos·mo·log·i·cal** /,käzmə'läjikəl/ *adj.* —**cos·mol·o·gist** /-jist/ *n.*

cos·mo·naut /'käzmə,nôt; -,nät/ ▶*n.* a Russian astronaut.

cos·mo·pol·i·tan /,käzmə'pälitn/ ▶*adj.* familiar with and at ease in many different countries and cultures. ■ including people from many different countries. ■ having an exciting and glamorous character associated with travel and a mixture of cultures: *their designs became a byword for cosmopolitan chic.* ■ (of a plant or animal) found all over the world.
▶*n.* **1** a cosmopolitan person. ■ a cosmopolitan organism or species. **2** a cocktail typically made with vodka, Cointreau, cranberry juice, and lime juice. —**cos·mo·pol·i·tan·ism** /-,izəm/ *n.* —**cos·mo·pol·i·tan·ize** /-,īz/ *v.*

cos·mos[1] /'käzməs; -,mōs; -,mäs/ ▶*n.* (**the cosmos**) the universe seen as a well-ordered whole. ■ a system of thought.

cos·mos[2] ▶*n.* an ornamental plant (genus *Cosmos*) of the daisy family with single or double dahlialike flowers.

Cos·sack /'käs,ak; -ək/ ▶*n.* a member of a people of southern Russia, Ukraine, and Siberia, noted for their horsemanship and military skill.

cost /kôst/ ▶*v.* (*past* and *past part.* **cost**) [*tr.*] **1** (of an object or an action) require the payment of (a specified sum of money) before it can be acquired or done: *the magazine costs $2.25.* ■ cause the loss of: *driving at more than double the speed limit cost the woman her driving license.* ■ involve (someone) in (an effort or unpleasant action): *the accident cost me a visit to the doctor.* ■ *inf.* be expensive for (someone): *if you want to own an island, it'll cost you.* **2** (*past* and *past part.* **cost·ed**) estimate the price of.
▶*n.* an amount that has to be paid or spent to buy or obtain something. ■ the effort, loss, or sacrifice necessary to achieve or obtain something: *she averted a train accident at the cost of her life.* ■ (**costs**) legal expenses, esp. those allowed in favor of the winning party or against the losing party in a suit.
▶ □ **at all costs** (or **at any cost**) regardless of the price to be paid or the effort needed: *he was anxious to avoid war at all costs.* □ **at cost** without profit to the seller.

co·star /'kō,stär; kō'stär/ (also **co-star**) ▶*n.* a leading actor or actress appearing in a movie, on stage, etc., with another or others of equal importance.
▶*v.* [*intr.*] appear in a production as a costar: *she costarred with Robert De Niro in the movie version.* ■ [*tr.*] (of a production) include as a costar: *his latest movie costars Meryl Streep.*

cost-ef·fec·tive ▶*adj.* effective or productive in relation to its cost. —**cost-ef·fec·tive·ly** *adv.* —**cost-ef·fec·tive·ness** *n.*

cos·tive /'kästiv; 'kôstiv/ ▶*adj.* slow or reluctant in speech or action; unforthcoming. —**cos·tive·ly** *adv.* —**cos·tive·ness** *n.*

cost·ly /'kôstlē/ ▶*adj.* (**-li·er**, **-li·est**) costing a lot; expensive. ■ causing suffering, loss, or disadvantage: *most costly mistake.* —**cost·li·ness** *n.*

cost of liv·ing ▶*n.* the level of prices relating to a range of everyday items.

cos·tume ▶*n.* /'käs,t(y)oom; -təm/ a set of clothes in a style typical of a particular country or historical period. ■ a set of clothes worn by an actor or other performer for a particular role or by someone attending a masquerade: *a nun's costume.* ■ a set of clothes, esp. a woman's ensemble, for a particular occasion or purpose; an outfit.
▶*v.* /käs't(y)oom; 'käst(y)oom; 'kästəm/ [*tr.*] dress (someone) in a particular set of clothes.

cos·tume jew·el·ry ▶*n.* jewelry made with inexpensive materials or imitation gems.

Pronunciation Key ə *ago*, *up*; ər *over*, *fur*; a *hat*; ā *ate*; ä *car*; CH *chin*; e *let*; ē *see*; e(ə)r *air*; i *fit*; ī *by*; i(ə)r *ear*; NG *sing*; ō *go*; ô *law*, *for*; oi *toy*; oͬo *good*; oo *goo*; ou *out*; sH *she*; TH *thin*; ŦH *then*; (h)w *why*; zH *vision*

cos·tum·er /ˈkäsˌt(y)o͞omər; käsˈt(y)o͞o-/ (also chiefly Brit. **cos·tu·mi·er** /käsˈt(y)o͞omēər/ ▸n. a person or company that makes or supplies theatrical or fancy-dress costumes.

cot¹ /kät/ ▸n. a type of bed, in particular: ■ a camp bed, particularly a portable, collapsible one. ■ a plain narrow bed. ■ Brit. a baby's crib.

cot² ▸n. a small shelter for livestock. ■ archaic a small, simple cottage.

cot³ Math. ▸abbr. cotangent.

co·tan·gent /kōˈtanjənt/ ▸n. Math. (in a right-angled triangle) the ratio of the side (other than the hypotenuse) adjacent to a particular acute angle to the side opposite the angle.

cote /kōt; kät/ ▸n. a shelter for mammals or birds, esp. pigeons.

co·te·rie /ˈkōtərē; ˌkōtəˈrē/ ▸n. (pl. -ries) a small group of people with shared interests or tastes, esp. one that is exclusive of other people.

co·ter·mi·nous /kōˈtərmənəs/ ▸adj. having the same boundaries or extent in space, time, or meaning. —**co·ter·mi·nous·ly** adv.

cot·tage /ˈkätij/ ▸n. a small simple house, typically one near a lake or beach. ■ a dwelling forming part of a farm establishment, used by a worker: farm cottages.

cot·tage cheese ▸n. soft, lumpy white cheese made from the curds of slightly soured milk.

cot·tage in·dus·try ▸n. a business or manufacturing activity carried on in a person's home.

cot·ter pin /ˈkätər/ (also **cot·ter**) ▸n. a metal pin used to fasten two parts of a mechanism together. ■ a split pin that is opened out after being passed through a hole.

cot·ton /ˈkätn/ ▸n. **1** a soft white fibrous substance that surrounds the seeds of a tropical and subtropical plant and is used to make textile fiber and thread for sewing. ■ cloth made from cotton fibers. **2** (also **cotton plant**) the plant (genus Gossypium) of the mallow family that is commercially grown for this product.
▸v. [intr.] inf. **1** (**cotton on**) begin to understand: he cottoned on to what I was trying to say. **2** (**cotton to**) have a liking for. —**cot·ton·y** adj.

cot·ton can·dy ▸n. a mass of fluffy spun sugar, usually pink or white, wrapped around a stick or a paper cone.

cot·ton gin ▸n. a machine for separating cotton from its seeds.

cot·ton·mouth /ˈkätnˌmou̇TH/ ▸n. a large, dangerous semiaquatic pit viper (Agkistrodon piscivorus) that inhabits lowland swamps and waterways of the southeastern U.S. When threatening, it opens its mouth wide to display the white interior. Also called **WATER MOCCASIN** (see **MOCCASIN**).

cot·ton-pick·ing (also **cot·ton-pick·in'**) ▸adj. inf. used for emphasis, esp. with disapproval or reproach: he's a cotton-pickin' liar!

cot·ton·tail /ˈkätnˌtāl/ ▸n. an American rabbit (genus Sylvilagus) that has a speckled brownish coat and a white underside to the tail.

cot·ton·wood /ˈkätnˌwo͝od/ ▸n. a North American poplar with seeds covered in white cottony hairs.

cot·y·le·don /ˌkätlˈēdn/ ▸n. Bot. an embryonic leaf in seed-bearing plants, one or more of which are the first leaves to appear from a germinating seed. —**cot·y·le·don·ar·y** /-ˈēdnˌerē/ adj.

couch /kou̇CH/ ▸n. a long upholstered piece of furniture for several people to sit on.
▸v. [tr.] **1** (usu. **be couched in**) express (something) in language of a specified style: many false claims are couched in scientific jargon. **2** [intr.] poetic/lit. lie down: two creatures, couched side by side in the deep grass. ■ [tr.] lay down; spread out: pieces of eel couched on a bed of steaming rice. **3** archaic lower (a spear) to the position for attack. **4** (in embroidery) fix (a thread) to a fabric by stitching it down flat with another thread: gold and silver threads couched by hand.

couch grass /kou̇CH; ko͞oCH/ ▸n. a coarse, often troublesome grass (genera Elymus and Agropyron) with long creeping roots.

couch po·ta·to /ˈkou̇CH/ ▸n. inf. a person who spends little or no time exercising and a great deal of time watching television.

cou·gar /ˈko͞ogər/ ▸n. a large American wild cat (Felis concolor) with a plain tawny to grayish coat, found from Canada to Patagonia. Also called **MOUNTAIN LION, PUMA, PANTHER**, and **CATAMOUNT**.

cough /kôf/ ▸v. [intr.] expel air from the lungs with a sudden sharp sound. ■ (of an engine) make a sudden harsh noise, esp. as a sign of malfunction. ■ [tr.] force (something, esp. blood) out of the lungs or throat by coughing: he coughed up bloodstained fluid. ■ [tr.] (**cough something out**) say something in a harsh, abrupt way.
▸phrasal v. □ **cough something up** (or **cough up**) give something reluctantly, esp. money or information that is due or required.
▸n. an act or sound of coughing. ■ a condition of the respiratory organs causing coughing.

cough drop ▸n. a medicated lozenge sucked to relieve a cough or sore throat.

cough syr·up ▸n. liquid medicine taken either to suppress or expectorate a cough.

could /ko͝od/ ▸modal verb past of CAN¹. ■ used to indicate possibility: they could be right. ■ used in making polite requests: could I use the phone? ■ used in making suggestions: you could always phone him. ■ used to indicate annoyance because of something that has not been done: they could have told me! ■ used to indicate a strong inclination to do something: he irritates me so much that I could scream.

could·n't /ˈko͝odnt/ ▸contr. could not.

cou·lomb /ˈko͞oˌläm; -ˌlōm/ (abbr.: C) ▸n. Physics the SI unit of electric charge, equal to the quantity of electricity conveyed in one second by a current of one ampere.

coun·cil /ˈkou̇nsəl/ ▸n. an advisory, deliberative, or legislative body of people formally constituted and meeting regularly. ■ a body of people elected to manage the affairs of a city, county, or other municipal district. ■ an ecclesiastical assembly. ■ an assembly or meeting for consultation or advice: that evening, she held a family council.

coun·cil·man /ˈkou̇nsəlmən/ ▸n. (pl. **-men**) a person, esp. a man, who is a member of a council, esp. a municipal one.

coun·ci·lor /ˈkou̇ns(ə)lər/ (also chiefly Brit. **coun·cil·lor**) ▸n. a member of a council. —**coun·ci·lor·ship** /-ˌSHip/ n.

coun·sel /ˈkou̇nsəl/ ▸n. **1** advice, esp. that given formally. ■ consultation, esp. to seek or give advice. **2** (pl. same) the lawyer or lawyers conducting a case: the counsel for the defense.
▸v. (**-seled, -sel·ing**; chiefly Brit. **-selled, -sel·ling**) [tr.] give advice to (someone). ■ give professional psychological help and advice to (someone). ■ recommend (a course of action). —**coun·sel·ing** n.
▸ □ **keep one's own counsel** say nothing about what one believes, knows, or plans ■ **take counsel** discuss a problem.

coun·se·lor /ˈkou̇ns(ə)lər/ (also chiefly Brit. **coun·sel·lor**) ▸n. **1** a person trained to give guidance on personal, social, or psychological problems: a marriage counselor. ■ a person who gives advice on a specified subject: a debt counselor. **2** a person who supervises children at a camp. **3** a trial lawyer. **4** a senior officer in the diplomatic service.

count¹ /kou̇nt/ ▸v. **1** [tr.] determine the total number of (a collection of items). ■ [intr.] recite numbers in ascending order, usually starting at the number one. ■ [intr.] (**count down**) recite or display numbers backward to zero to indicate the time remaining before the launch of a rocket or the start of an operation. **2** [tr.] take into account; include: the staff has shrunk to four, or five if you count the summer intern. ■ (**count someone in**) include someone in an activity or the plans for it. ■ consider (someone or something) to possess a specified quality or fulfill a specified role: I count myself fortunate to have known him. ■ [intr.] be regarded as possessing a specified quality or fulfilling a specified role: the rebate counts as taxable income. **3** [intr.] be significant: it did not matter what the audience thought—it was the critics that counted. ■ (of a factor) play a part in influencing opinion for or against someone or something: his sportsmanlike attitude will count in his favor. ■ (**count for**) be worth (a specified amount): his views count for little. ■ (**count toward**) be included in an assessment of (a final result or amount). ■ (**count on/upon**) rely on.
▸phrasal v. □ **count someone out 1** complete a count of ten seconds over a fallen boxer to indicate defeat. **2** inf. exclude someone from an activity or the plans for it.
▸n. **1** an act of determining the total number of something. ■ the total determined by such an action: a moderate increase in the white cell count. **2** an act of reciting numbers in ascending order, up to the specified number: hold the position for five counts. ■ Boxing an act of reciting numbers up to ten by the referee when a boxer is knocked down, the boxer being considered knocked out if still down when ten is reached. ■ Baseball the number of balls and strikes that have been charged to the batter, as recalculated with each pitch. **3** a point for discussion or consideration: the program remained vulnerable on a number of counts. ■ Law a separate charge in an indictment. **4** the measure of the fineness of a yarn expressed as the weight of a given length or the length of a given weight. ■ a measure of the fineness of a woven fabric expressed as the number of warp or weft threads in a given length.
▸ □ **count one's blessings** be grateful for what one has. □ **count the days** (or **hours**) be impatient for time to pass. □ **lose count** forget how many of something there are, esp. because the number is so high.

count² ▸n. a European nobleman whose rank corresponds to that of an English earl. —**count·ship** /-ˌSHip/ n.

count·a·ble /ˈkou̇ntəbəl/ ▸adj. able to be counted.

count·down /ˈkou̇ntˌdou̇n/ ▸n. an act of counting numerals in reverse order to zero, esp. to time the last seconds before the launching of a rocket or missile. ■ (often **countdown to**) the final moments before a significant event and the procedures carried out during this time. ■ a digital display that counts down.

coun·te·nance /'kountn-əns/ ▸ *n.* **1** a person's face or facial expression. **2** support.
▸ *v.* [*tr.*] admit as acceptable or possible: *he countenanced the use of force.*
▸ □ **keep one's countenance** maintain one's composure, esp. by refraining from laughter.

coun·ter¹ /'kountər/ ▸ *n.* **1** a long flat-topped fixture in a store or bank across which business is conducted with customers. ■ a similar structure used for serving food and drinks in a cafeteria or bar. ■ a countertop. **2** an apparatus used for counting. ■ a person who counts something, for example votes in an election. ■ *Physics* an apparatus used for counting individual ionizing particles or events. **3** a small disk used as a place marker or for keeping the score in board games. ■ a token representing a coin.
▸ □ **over the counter** by ordinary retail purchase, with no need for a prescription or license: [as *adj.*] *over-the-counter medicines.* ■ (of share transactions) taking place outside the stock exchange system. □ **under the counter** (or **table**) (with reference to goods bought or sold) surreptitiously and typically illegally: *certain labs have been peddling this drug under the counter* | [as *adj.*] *an under-the-counter deal.*

coun·ter² ▸ *v.* [*tr.*] speak or act in opposition to. ■ [*intr.*] respond to hostile speech or action: *"What would you like me to do about it?" she countered.* ■ [*intr.*] *Boxing* give a return blow while parrying: *he countered with a left hook.*
▸ *adv.* (**counter to**) in the opposite direction to or in conflict with: *some actions by the authorities* **ran counter to** *the call for leniency.*
▸ *adj.* responding to something of the same kind, esp. in opposition.
▸ *n.* a thing that opposes or prevents something else. ■ an answer to an argument or criticism. ■ *Boxing* a blow given while parrying; a counterpunch.

coun·ter³ ▸ *n.* the back part of a shoe or boot, enclosing the heel.

coun·ter·act /'kountər,akt/ ▸ *v.* [*tr.*] act against (something) in order to reduce its force or neutralize it. —**coun·ter·ac·tion** /,kountər'akshən/ *n.* —**coun·ter·ac·tive** /kountər'aktiv/ *adj.*

coun·ter·at·tack /'kountərə,tak/ ▸ *n.* an attack made in response to one by an enemy or opponent.
▸ *v.* [*intr.*] attack in response. —**coun·ter·at·tack·er** *n.*

coun·ter·bal·ance ▸ *n.* /'kountər,baləns/ a weight that balances another weight. ■ a factor having the opposite effect to that of another and so preventing it from exercising a disproportionate influence.
▸ *v.* /,kountər'baləns/ [*tr.*] (of a weight) balance (another weight). ■ neutralize or cancel by exerting an opposite influence.

coun·ter·charge /'kountər,chärj/ ▸ *n.* an accusation made in turn by someone against their accuser. ■ a charge by police or an armed force in response to one made against them.

coun·ter·claim /'kountər,klām/ ▸ *n.* a claim made to rebut a previous claim. ■ *Law* a claim made by a defendant against the plaintiff.
▸ *v.* [*intr.*] *chiefly Law* make a counterclaim for something.

coun·ter·clock·wise /,kountər'kläk,wīz/ ▸ *adv. & adj.* in the opposite direction to the way in which the hands of a clock move around.

coun·ter·cul·ture /'kountər,kəlchər/ ▸ *n.* a way of life and set of attitudes opposed to or at variance with the prevailing social norm.

coun·ter·es·pi·o·nage /,kountər'espē·ə,näzh; -,näj/ ▸ *n.* activities designed to prevent or thwart spying by an enemy.

coun·ter·feit /'kountər,fit/ ▸ *adj.* made in exact imitation of something valuable or important with the intention to deceive or defraud: *passing counterfeit $10 bills.* ■ pretended; sham.
▸ *n.* a fraudulent imitation of something else; a forgery.
▸ *v.* [*tr.*] imitate fraudulently. ■ pretend to feel or possess (an emotion or quality). ■ *poetic/lit.* resemble closely: *sleep counterfeited Death so well.* ▷Middle English (as a verb): from Anglo-Norman French *countrefeter,* from Old French *contrefet,* past participle of *contrefaire,* from Latin *contra-* 'in opposition' + *facere* 'make.' —**coun·ter·feit·er** *n.*

coun·ter·in·tel·li·gence /,kountərin'teləjəns/ ▸ *n.* activities designed to prevent or thwart spying, intelligence gathering, and sabotage by an enemy or other foreign entity.

coun·ter·mand /,kountər'mand; 'kountər,mand/ ▸ *v.* [*tr.*] revoke (an order). ■ cancel an order for (goods). ■ revoke an order issued by (another person). ■ declare (voting) invalid.

coun·ter·meas·ure /'kountər,mezhər/ ▸ *n.* an action taken to counteract a danger or threat.

coun·ter·of·fen·sive /'kountərə,fensiv/ ▸ *n.* an attack made in response

to one from an enemy, typically on a large scale or for a prolonged period.

coun·ter·pane /'kountər,pān/ ▸ *n. dated* a bedspread.

coun·ter·part /'kountər,pärt/ ▸ *n.* **1** a person or thing holding a position or performing a function that corresponds to that of another person or thing in another place: *the minister held talks with his French counterpart.* **2** *Law* one of two or more copies of a legal document.

coun·ter·point /'kountər,point/ ▸ *n.* **1** *Mus.* the art or technique of setting, writing, or playing a melody or melodies in conjunction with another, according to fixed rules. **2** an argument, idea, or theme used to create a contrast with the main element.
▸ *v.* [*tr.*] (often **be counterpointed**) emphasize by contrast: *the cream walls and maple floors are counterpointed by black accents.* ■ compensate for.

coun·ter·poise /'kountər,poiz/ ▸ *n.* a factor, force, or influence that balances or neutralizes another. ■ *archaic* a state of equilibrium. ■ a counterbalancing weight.
▸ *v.* [*tr.*] have an opposing and balancing effect on. ■ bring into contrast: *the stories counterpoise a young recruit with an old-timer.*

coun·ter·pro·duc·tive /,kountərprə'dəktiv/ ▸ *adj.* having the opposite of the desired effect: *they believe they are helping animals but their extremist behavior is actually counterproductive.*

Coun·ter-Ref·or·ma·tion ▸ the reform of the Church of Rome in the 16th and 17th centuries that was stimulated by the Protestant Reformation.

coun·ter·rev·o·lu·tion /'kountər,revə'lōōshən/ ▸ *n.* a revolution opposing a former one or reversing its results. —**coun·ter·rev·o·lu·tion·ar·y** /-,nerē/ *adj. & n.*

coun·ter·sign /'kountər,sīn/ ▸ *v.* [*tr.*] add a signature to (a document already signed by another person): *each check had to be signed and countersigned.* —**coun·ter·sig·na·ture** /,kountər'signəchər; -,choor/ *n.*

coun·ter·sink /'kountər,singk/ ▸ *v.* (*past* and *past part.* **-sunk** /-,səngk/) [*tr.*] enlarge and bevel the rim of (a drilled hole) so that a screw, nail, or bolt can be inserted flush with the surface. ■ drive (a screw, nail, or bolt) into such a hole.

coun·ter·ten·or /'kountər,tenər/ ▸ *n. Mus.* the highest male adult singing voice (sometimes distinguished from the male alto voice by its strong, pure tone). ■ a singer with such a voice.

coun·ter·ter·ror·ism /,kountər'terə,rizəm/ ▸ *n.* political or military activities designed to thwart terrorism. —**coun·ter·ter·ror·ist** /,kountər'terərist/ *n. & adj.*

coun·ter·top /'kountər,täp/ ▸ *n.* a flat surface for working on, esp. in a kitchen.

coun·ter·vail /,kountər'vāl/ ▸ *v.* [*tr.*] [usu. as *adj.*] (**countervailing**) offset the effect of (something) by countering it with something of equal force: *their dominance was mediated by a number of countervailing factors.*

coun·ter·weight /'kountər,wāt/ ▸ *n.* another term for **COUNTERBALANCE**.

count·ess /'kountəs/ ▸ *n.* the wife or widow of a count or earl. ■ a woman holding the rank of count or earl in her own right.

count·ing·house /'kounting,hous/ ▸ *n. hist.* an office or building in which the accounts and money of a person or company were kept.

count·less /'kountləs/ ▸ *adj.* too many to be counted; very many: *she'd apologized countless times before.*

coun·tri·fied /'kəntri,fīd/ (also **coun·try·fied**) ▸ *adj.* reminiscent or characteristic of the country, esp. in being unsophisticated.

coun·try /'kəntrē/ ▸ *n.* (*pl.* **-tries**) **1** a nation with its own government, occupying a particular territory. ■ (**the country**) the people of a nation. ■ the land of a person's birth or citizenship: *both my native and adopted countries are at war with yours.* **2** (often **the country**) districts and small settlements outside large towns, cities, or the capital: *the airfield is right out in the country* | [as *adj.*] *a country lane.* **3** an area or region with regard to its physical features: *a tract of wild country.* ■ a region associated with a particular person, esp. a writer, or with a particular work: *Steinbeck country includes the Monterey Peninsula.* **4** short for **COUNTRY MUSIC.**

coun·try and west·ern ▸ *n.* another term for **COUNTRY MUSIC** [as *adj.*] *country-and-western singer.*

coun·try club ▸ *n.* a club with sporting and social facilities, set in a suburban area.

coun·try·fied ▸ *adj.* variant spelling of **COUNTRIFIED**.

coun·try ham ▸ *n.* a ham that is dry-cured with salt before smoking.

coun·try·man /'kəntrēmən/ ▸ *n.* (*pl.* **-men**) **1** *Brit.* a person living or born in a rural area, esp. one engaged in a typically rural occupation. **2** a

---

Pronunciation Key ə *ago, up;* ər *over, fur;* a *hat;* ā *ate;* ä *car;* CH *chin;* e *let;* ē *see;* e(ə)r *air;* i *fit;* ī *by;* i(ə)r *ear;* NG *sing;* ō *go;* ô *law, for;* oi *toy;* ōō *good;* ōō *goo;* ou *out;* SH *she;* TH *thin;* TH *then;* (h)w *why;* ZH *vision*

person from the same country or region as someone else: *they trust a fellow countryman.*

coun·try mu·sic ▶ *n.* a form of popular music originating in the rural southern U.S. It is traditionally played characteristically on fiddle, guitar, steel guitar, drums, and keyboard. Also called COUNTRY AND WEST-ERN.

coun·try·side /'kəntrē,sīd/ ▶ *n.* the land and scenery of a rural area. ■ the inhabitants of such an area.

coun·ty /'kountē/ ▶ *n.* (*pl.* **-ties**) a political and administrative division of a state, providing certain local governmental services. ■ a territorial division of some countries, forming the chief unit of local administration. ■ [treated as *sing.* or *pl.*] the people of such a territorial division collectively. ■ —**coun·ty·wide** *adj.* & *adv.*

coun·ty seat ▶ *n.* the town that is the governmental center of a county.

coup /kōō/ ▶ *n.* (*pl.* **coups** /kōōz/) **1** (also **coup d'é·tat**) a sudden, violent, and illegal seizure of power from a government. **2** a notable or successful stroke or move. ■ an unusual or unexpected but successful tactic in card play. **3** *hist.* (among North American Indians) an act of touching an armed enemy in battle as a deed of bravery, or an act of first touching an item of the enemy's in order to claim it.

coup de grâce /,kōō də 'gräs/ ▶ *n.* (*pl.* **coups de grâce** *pronunc.* same) a final blow or shot to kill a wounded person or animal: *fig. the party won another term and delivered the coup de grâce to socialism.*

coup d'é·tat /,kōō dā'tä/ ▶ *n.* (*pl.* **coups d'é·tat** /,kōō dā 'tä(z)/) another term for **COUP** (sense 1).

coupe /kōōp/ (also **cou·pé** /kōō'pā/) ▶ *n.* a car with a fixed roof and two doors.

cou·ple /'kəpəl/ ▶ *n.* **1** two individuals of the same sort considered together: *a couple of girls.* ■ *inf.* an indefinite small number: *a couple of days* | [as *pron.*] *we got some eggs—would you like a couple?* | [as *adj.*] *just a couple more questions.* | *a couple pinches of salt.* **2** [treated as *sing.* or *pl.*] two people who are married, engaged, or otherwise closely associated romantically or sexually. ■ a pair of partners in a dance or game. ■ *Mechanics* a pair of equal and parallel forces acting in opposite directions, and tending to cause rotation about an axis perpendicular to the plane containing them.
▶ *v.* [*tr.*] (often **be coupled to/with**) combine: *a sense of hope is coupled with a palpable sense of loss.* ■ connect (a railroad vehicle or a piece of equipment) to another. ■ [*intr.*] (**couple up**) join to form a pair. ■ [*intr.*] *dated* have sexual intercourse. —**cou·ple·dom** /-dəm/ *n.*

cou·pler /'kəp(ə)lər/ ▶ *n.* something that connects two things, esp. mechanical components or systems: *a hydraulic coupler.* ■ *Mus.* a device in an organ for connecting two manuals so that they both sound when only one is played. ■ *Mus.* (also **octave coupler**) a similar device for connecting notes with their octaves above or below. ■ *Photog.* a compound in a developer or an emulsion that combines with the products of development to form an insoluble dye, part of the image.

cou·plet /'kəplət/ ▶ *n.* two lines of verse, usually in the same meter and joined by rhyme, that form a unit.

cou·pling /'kəp(ə)liNG/ ▶ *n.* **1** a device for connecting parts of machinery. ■ a fitting on the end of a railroad vehicle for connecting it to another. **2** the pairing of two items. ■ sexual intercourse. ■ an interaction between two electrical components by electromagnetic induction, electrostatic charge, or optical link.

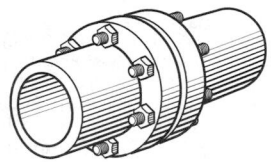

coupling

cou·pon /'k(y)ōō,pän/ ▶ *n.* **1** a voucher entitling the holder to a discount for a particular product. ■ a detachable portion of a bond that is given up in return for a payment of interest. **2** a form in a newspaper or magazine that may be filled in and sent as an application for a purchase or information.

cour·age /'kərij; 'kə-rij/ ▶ *n.* the ability to do something that frightens one: *she called on all her courage to face the ordeal.* ■ strength in the face of pain or grief. ▷*Middle English* (denoting the heart, as the seat of feelings): from Old French *corage*, from Latin *cor* 'heart.'
▶ □ **have the courage of one's convictions** act on one's beliefs despite danger or disapproval.

cou·ra·geous /kə'rājəs/ ▶ *adj.* not deterred by danger or pain; brave. —**cou·ra·geous·ly** *adv.* —**cou·ra·geous·ness** *n.*

cour·i·er /'kōōrēər; 'kərēər/ ▶ *n.* **1** a messenger who transports goods or documents, in particular: ■ a company or employee of a company that transports commercial packages and documents. ■ a messenger for an underground or espionage organization. **2** a person employed to guide and assist a group of tourists.

▶ *v.* [*tr.*] (often **be couriered**) send or transport (goods or documents) by courier.

course /kôrs/ ▶ *n.* **1** the route or direction followed by a ship, aircraft, road, or river. ■ the way in which something progresses or develops: *the course of history.* ■ a procedure adopted to deal with a situation: *the wisest course of action.* ■ the route of a race or similar sporting event. ■ an area of land set aside and prepared for racing, golf, or another sport. **2** a dish, or a set of dishes served together, forming one of the successive parts of a meal. **3** a series, in particular: ■ a series of lectures or lessons in a particular subject, typically leading to a qualification: *a business studies course.* ■ *Med.* a series of repeated treatments or doses of medication. **4** *Archit.* a continuous horizontal layer of brick, stone, or other material in a building. **5** a pursuit of game (esp. hares) with greyhounds by sight rather than scent. **6** the lowest sail on a square-rigged mast. **7** a set of adjacent strings on a guitar, lute, etc., tuned to the same note.
▶ *v.* **1** [*intr.*] (of liquid) move without obstruction; flow: *tears were coursing down her cheeks* | *fig. exultation coursed through him.* **2** [*tr.*] pursue (game, esp. hares) with greyhounds: *many of the hares coursed escaped unharmed.*
▶ □ **in the course of** — **1** undergoing the specified process: *a textbook was in the course of preparation.* **2** during the specified period: *he was a friend to many people in the course of his life.* ■ during and as a part of the specified activity: *they became friends in the course of their long walks.* □ **of course** used to introduce an idea or turn of events as being obvious or to be expected. ■ used to give or emphasize agreement or permission: *"Can I see you for a minute?" "Of course."* ■ introducing a qualification or admission: *of course we've been in touch by phone, but I wanted to see things for myself.* □ **off course** not following the intended route. □ **on course** following the intended route. □ **run** (or **take**) **its course** complete its natural development without interference: *his illness had to run its course.*

court /kôrt/ ▶ *n.* **1** (also **court of law**) a tribunal presided over by a judge, judges, or a magistrate in civil and criminal cases: *a settlement was reached during the first sitting of the court* | *she will take the matter to court* | [as *adj.*] *a court case.* ■ any of various other tribunals, such as military courts. ■ the place where such a tribunal meets. ■ (**the court**) the judge or judges presiding at such a tribunal. **2** a quadrangular area, either open or covered, marked out for ball games such as tennis or basketball: *an indoor tennis court.* ■ a quadrangular area surrounded by a building or group of buildings. ■ a subdivision of a building, usually a large hall extending to the ceiling with galleries and staircases. **3** the establishment, retinue, and courtiers of a sovereign: *the emperor is shown with his court.* ■ a sovereign and his or her councilors, constituting a ruling power: *relations between the king and the imperial court.* ■ a sovereign's residence.
▶ *v.* [*tr.*] *dated* be involved with romantically, typically with the intention of marrying: *he was courting a girl from the neighboring farm* | [*intr.*] *we went to the movies when we were courting.* ■ (of a male bird or other animal) try to attract (a mate). ■ pay special attention to (someone) in an attempt to win their support or favor: *Western politicians courted the leaders of the newly independent states.* ■ go to great lengths to win (favorable attention): *he never had to court the approval of the political elite.* ■ risk incurring (misfortune) because of the way one behaves: *he has often courted controversy.*
▶ □ **go to court** take legal action. □ **pay court to** pay flattering attention to someone in order to win favor.

cour·te·ous /'kərtēəs/ ▶ *adj.* polite, respectful, or considerate in manner. —**cour·te·ous·ly** *adv.* —**cour·te·ous·ness** *n.*

cour·te·san /'kôrtəzən; 'kər-/ ▶ *n.* a prostitute, esp. one with wealthy or upper-class clients.

cour·te·sy /'kərtəsē/ ▶ *n.* (*pl.* **-sies**) the showing of politeness in one's attitude and behavior toward others: *he had been treated with a degree of courtesy not far short of deference.* ■ (often **courtesies**) a polite speech or action, esp. one required by convention: *the superficial courtesies of diplomatic exchanges.* ■ [as *adj.*] (esp. of transport) supplied free of charge to people who are already paying for another service: *he traveled from the hotel in a courtesy car.* ■ *archaic* a curtsy.
▶ □ (**by**) **courtesy of** given or allowed by: *photograph courtesy of the Evening Star.* ■ as a result of; thanks to.

court·house /'kôrt,hous/ ▶ *n.* **1** a building in which a judicial court is held. **2** a building containing the administrative offices of a county.

cour·ti·er /'kôrtēər; 'kôrchər/ ▶ *n.* a person who attends a royal court as a companion or adviser to the king or queen. ■ a person who fawns and flatters in order to gain favor or advantage.

court·ly /'kôrtlē/ ▶ *adj.* (**-li·er, -li·est**) **1** polished or refined, as befitting a royal court: *he gave a courtly bow.* **2** given to flattery; obsequious. —**court·li·ness** *n.*

court-mar·tial ▶ *n.* (*pl.* **courts-mar·tial** or **court-mar·tials**) a judicial court for trying members of the armed services accused of offenses against military law: *they appeared before a court-martial.*
▶ *v.* (**-mar·tialed, -mar·tial·ing**; *Brit.* **-mar·tialled, -mar·tial·ling**) [*tr.*] try (someone) by such a court.

court or·der ▶ *n.* a direction issued by a court or a judge requiring a person to do or not do something.

court rec·ord ▶ *n.* see RECORD (n. sense1).

court re·port·er ▶ *n.* a stenographer who makes a verbatim record and transcription of the proceedings in a court of law.

court·room /'kôrt,rōom; -,rŏŏm/ ▶ *n.* the place or room in which a court of law meets.

court·ship /'kôrt,SHip/ ▶ *n.* a period during which a couple develop a romantic relationship, esp. with a view to marriage. ■ behavior designed to persuade someone to marry one. ■ the behavior of male birds and other animals aimed at attracting a mate. ■ the process of attempting to win a person's favor or support: *the country's courtship of foreign investors.*

court·yard /'kôrt,yärd/ ▶ *n.* an unroofed area that is completely or mostly enclosed by the walls of a building.

cous·cous /'kŏŏ,skŏŏs/ ▶ *n.* a type of North African semolina in granules made from crushed durum wheat. ■ a spicy dish made by steaming or soaking such granules and adding meat, vegetables, or fruit.

cous·in /'kəzən/ ▶ *n.* (also **first cousin**) a child of one's uncle or aunt. ■ a person belonging to the same extended family. ■ a thing related or analogous to another: *the new motorbikes are not proving as popular as their four-wheeled cousins.* ■ (usu. **cousins**) a person of a kindred culture, race, or nation. ■ *hist.* a title formerly used by a sovereign in addressing another sovereign or a noble of their own country. —**cous·in·hood** /-,hŏŏd/ *n.* —**cous·in·ly** *adj.* —**cous·in·ship** /-,SHip/ *n.*
▶ □ **first cousin once removed 1** a child of one's first cousin. **2** one's parent's first cousin. □ **first cousin twice removed 1** a grandchild of one's first cousin. **2** one's grandparent's first cousin. □ **second cousin** a child of one's parent's first cousin. □ **second cousin once removed 1** a child of one's second cousin. **2** one's parent's second cousin. □ **third cousin** a child of one's parent's second cousin.

cou·ture /kŏŏ'tŏŏr(ə)r; -'tyr/ ▶ *n.* the design and manufacture of fashionable clothes to a client's specific requirements and measurements. ■ the business of designing and making such clothes. ■ such clothes. —**cou·tu·ri·er** /-tŏŏrē,ā/ *n.*

co·va·lent /,kō'vālənt/ ▶ *adj.* *Chem.* of, relating to, or denoting chemical bonds formed by the sharing of electrons between atoms. —**co·va·lence** *n.* —**co·va·lent·ly** *adv.*

cove[1] /kōv/ ▶ *n.* **1** a small sheltered bay. **2** a sheltered recess, esp. one in a mountain. **3** *Archit.* a concave arched molding, esp. one formed at the junction of a wall with a ceiling.

cove[2] ▶ *n.* *Brit., inf., dated* a man: *he is a perfectly amiable cove.*

cov·en /'kəvən/ ▶ *n.* a group or gathering of witches who meet regularly. ■ *fig., often derog.* a secret or close-knit group of associates.

cov·e·nant /'kəvənənt/ ▶ *n.* an agreement. ■ *Law* a contract drawn up by deed. ■ *Law* a clause in a contract. ■ *Theol.* an agreement that brings about a relationship of commitment between God and his people.
▶ *v.* [*intr.*] agree, esp. by lease, deed, or other legal contract: *the landlord covenants to repair the property.* —**cov·e·nan·tal** /,kəvə'nantl/ *adj.* —**cov·e·nant·er** (also chiefly Law **cov·e·nan·tor**) *n.*

cov·er /'kəvər/ ▶ *v.* [*tr.*] **1** (often **be covered**) put something such as a cloth or lid on top of or in front of (something) in order to protect or conceal. ■ envelop in a layer of something, esp. dirt. ■ scatter a layer of loose material over (a surface, esp. a floor), leaving it completely obscured. ■ lie over or adhere to (a surface), as decoration or to conceal something. ■ protect (someone) with a garment or hat: [as *adj.*] (**covered**) *keep children covered with T-shirts.* ■ extend over (an area). ■ travel (a specified distance): *it took them four days to cover 150 miles.* **2** deal with (a subject) by describing or analyzing its most important aspects or events. ■ investigate, report on, or publish or broadcast pictures of (an event). ■ work in, have responsibility for, or provide services to (a particular area). ■ (of a rule or law) apply to (a person or situation). **3** (of a sum of money) be enough to pay (a bill or cost): *there are grants to cover the cost of materials for loft insulation.* ■ (of insurance) protect against a liability, loss, or accident involving financial consequences: *your contents are now covered against accidental loss or damage in transit.* ■ (**cover oneself**) take precautionary measures so as to protect oneself against future blame or liability. **4** disguise the sound or fact of (something) with another sound or action: *Louise laughed to cover her embarrassment.* ■ [*intr.*] (**cover for**) disguise the illicit absence or wrongdoing of (someone) in order to spare them punishment: *if the sergeant wants to know*

where you are, I'll cover for you. ■ [*intr.*] (**cover for**) temporarily take over the job of (a colleague) in their absence. **5** aim a gun at (someone) in order to prevent them from moving or escaping. ■ protect (an exposed person) by shooting at an enemy: [as *adj.*] (**covering**) *the jeeps retreated behind spurts of covering fire.* ■ (of a fortress, gun, or cannon) have (an area) within range. ■ (in team games) take up a position ready to defend against (an opposing player). ■ *Baseball* be in position at (a base) ready to catch a thrown ball. **6** *Bridge* play a higher card on (a high card) in a trick: *the ploy will fail if the ten is covered.* **7** record or perform a new version of (a song) originally performed by someone else. **8** (of a male animal, esp. a stallion) copulate with (a female animal, esp. as part of a commercial transaction between the owners of the animals).
▶ *phrasal v.* □ **cover something up** put something on, over, or around something, esp. in order to conceal or disguise it. ■ try to hide or deny the fact of an illegal or illicit action or activity.

▶ *n.* **1** a thing that lies on, over, or around something, esp. in order to protect or conceal it. ■ a thin solid object that seals a container or hole; a lid: *a manhole cover.* ■ a thick protective outer part or page of a book or magazine. ■ *Philately* a card or envelope that has traveled through the mail or that contains postal markings. ■ (**the covers**) bedclothes. **2** physical shelter or protection sought by people in danger: *the sirens wailed and people ran for cover.* ■ undergrowth, trees, or other vegetation used as a shelter by hunted animals. ■ an activity or organization used as a means of concealing an illegal or secret activity: *they use philanthropy as a cover for subsidies to terrorists.* ■ an identity or activity adopted by a person, typically a spy, to conceal their true activities. ■ military support given when someone is in danger from or being attacked by an enemy: *they provide additional naval cover.* ■ *Ecol.* the amount of ground covered by a vertical projection of the vegetation, usually expressed as a percentage. **3** short for COVER CHARGE. **4** a place setting at a table in a restaurant. **5** (also **cover version**) a recording or performance of a previously recorded song made esp. to take advantage of the original's success. —**cov·er·a·ble** *adj.*
▶ ■ **break cover** suddenly leave a place of shelter, esp. vegetation, when being hunted or pursued. □ **cover all bases** (or **cover all the bases**) include all relevant information. ■ prepare for all likely circumstances. □ **cover one's tracks** conceal evidence of what one has done. □ **take cover** protect oneself from attack by ducking down into or under a shelter. □ **under cover of** concealed by: *the yacht made landfall under cover of darkness.* □ **under separate cover** in a separate envelope.

cov·er·age /'kəv(ə)rij/ ▶ *n.* the extent to which something deals with or applies to something else: *the grammar did not offer total coverage of the language.* ■ the treatment of an issue by the media: *the program won an award for its news coverage.* ■ the amount of protection given by an insurance policy. ■ the area reached by a particular broadcasting station or advertising medium: *a network of eighty transmitters would give nationwide coverage.* ■ *Football* the manner in which a defender or a defensive team covers a player, an area, or a play.

cov·er·all /'kəvər,ôl/ ▶ *n.* (usu. **coveralls**) a full-length protective outer garment often zipped up the front. ■ [as *adj.*] inclusive: *a coverall term.*

cov·er charge ▶ *n.* a flat fee paid for admission to a restaurant, bar, club, etc.

cov·er girl ▶ *n.* a female model whose picture appears on magazine covers.

cov·er·ing /'kəv(ə)riNG/ ▶ *n.* a thing used to cover something else, typically in order to protect or conceal it. ■ a layer of something that covers something else: *a covering of cloud.*

cov·er·let /'kəvərlət/ ▶ *n.* a bedspread, typically less than floor-length.

cov·er let·ter ▶ *n.* a letter sent with, and explaining the contents of, another document or a parcel of goods.

co·vert ▶ *adj.* /'kōvərt; kō'vərt; 'kəvərt/ **1** not openly acknowledged or displayed: *covert operations against the dictatorship.* **2** *Law* (of a woman) married and under the authority and protection of her husband.
▶ *n.* /'kəv(ə)rt; 'kōvərt/ **1** a shelter or hiding place. ■ a thicket in which game can hide. **2** *Ornithol.* any of the feathers covering the bases of the main flight or tail feathers of a bird. —**co·vert·ly** /'kōvərtlē; kō'vərtlē; 'kəvərtlē/ *adv.* —**co·vert·ness** *n.*

cov·et /'kəvət/ ▶ *v.* (**cov·et·ed, cov·et·ing**) [*tr.*] yearn to possess or have (something): *the president-elect covets time for exercise and fishing* | [as *adj.*] (**coveted**) *he won the coveted Booker Prize for fiction.* —**cov·et·a·ble** *adj.*

cov·et·ous /'kəvətəs/ ▶ *adj.* having or showing a great desire to possess something, typically something belonging to someone else. —**cov·et·ous·ly** adv. —**cov·et·ous·ness** n.

cov·ey /'kəvē/ ▶ n. (pl. **-eys**) a small party or flock of birds, esp. partridge. ■ fig. a small group of people or things.

cow[1] /kou/ ▶ n. a fully grown female animal of a domesticated breed of ox, used as a source of milk or beef: *a dairy cow.* See CATTLE. ■ (loosely) a domestic bovine animal, regardless of sex or age. ■ (in farming) a female domestic bovine animal that has borne more than one calf. Compare with HEIFER. ■ the female of certain other large animals, for example elephant, rhinoceros, whale, seal, or reindeer. ■ inf., derog. a woman, esp. a fat or stupid one: *what does he see in that cow?*

▶ □ **have a cow** inf. become angry, excited, or agitated. □ **till the cows come home** inf. for an indefinitely long time.

cow[2] ▶ v. [tr.] (usu. **be cowed**) cause (someone) to submit to one's wishes by intimidation: *the intellectuals had been cowed into silence.*

cow·ard /'kou-ərd/ ▶ n. a person who lacks the courage to do or endure dangerous or unpleasant things.

▶ adj. poetic/lit. excessively afraid of danger or pain.

cow·ard·ice /'kou-ərdəs/ ▶ n. lack of bravery.

cow·ard·ly /'kou-ərdlē/ ▶ adj. lacking courage. ■ (of an action) carried out against a person who is unable to retaliate.

▶ adv. archaic in a way that shows a lack of courage. —**cow·ard·li·ness** n.

cow·bell /'kou,bel/ ▶ n. a bell hung around a cow's neck in order to help locate the animal by the noise it makes. ■ a similar bell used as a percussion instrument, typically without a clapper and struck with a stick.

cow·boy /'kou,boi/ ▶ n. **1** a man, typically one on horseback, who herds and tends cattle, esp. in the western U.S. and as represented in westerns and novels. **2** inf. a person who is reckless or careless.

▶ v. [intr.] work as a cowboy: *Sonora, Mexico, where he learned to cowboy.*

▶ □ **cowboy up** inf. mount a brave effort to overcome a formidable obstacle.

cow·catch·er /'kou,kachər; -,kechər/ ▶ n. dated a metal frame at the front of a locomotive for pushing aside cattle or other obstacles on the line.

cow·er /'kou(-ə)r/ ▶ v. [intr.] crouch down in fear.

cow·hand /'kou,hand/ ▶ n. a person employed to tend or ranch cattle; a cowboy or cowgirl.

cow·herd /'kou,hərd/ ▶ n. a person who tends grazing cattle.

cow·hide /'kou,hīd/ ▶ n. a cow's hide. ■ leather made from such a hide. ■ a whip made from such leather.

cowl /koul/ ▶ n. a large loose hood, esp. one forming part of a monk's habit. ■ a monk's hooded, sleeveless habit. ■ a cloak with wide sleeves worn by members of Benedictine orders. ■ the hood-shaped covering of a chimney or ventilation shaft. ■ the part of a motor vehicle that supports the windshield and houses the dashboard. —**cowled** adj.

cow·lick /'kou,lik/ ▶ n. a lock of hair that grows in a direction different from the rest and that resists being combed flat.

co·work·er /'kō,wərkər; kō'wərkər/ ▶ n. a fellow worker.

cow·pea /'kou,pē/ ▶ n. a plant (*Vigna unguiculata*) of the pea family, native to the Old World tropics and cultivated in the southern U.S. for animal feed and human consumption. ■ the seed of this plant as food.

cow·poke /'kou,pōk/ ▶ n. inf. a cowboy.

cow·pox /'kou,päks/ ▶ n. a viral disease of cows' udders which, when contracted by humans through contact, resembles mild smallpox, and was the basis of the first smallpox vaccines.

cow·punch·er /'kou,pənchər/ ▶ n. inf. a cowboy.

cow·rie /'kourē/ (also **cowry**) ▶ n. (pl. **-ies**) a marine mollusk (genus *Cypraea*, family Cypraeidae) that has a smooth, glossy, domed shell with a long narrow opening, typically brightly patterned. ■ the flattened yellowish shell of the **money cowrie** (*C. moneta*), formerly used as money in parts of Africa and the Indo-Pacific area.

cow·shed /'kou,shed/ ▶ n. a farm building in which cattle are kept when not in a pasture, or in which they are milked.

cow·slip /'kou,slip/ ▶ n. **1** a European primula (*Primula veris*) with clusters of drooping fragrant yellow flowers in spring. **2** any of a number of herbaceous plants, in particular the marsh marigold and the Virginia bluebell.

cox /käks/ ▶ n. a coxswain, esp. of a racing boat.

▶ v. [tr.] act as a coxswain for (a racing boat or crew): *the winning eight was coxed by a woman.*

cox·comb /'käks,kōm/ ▶ n. **1** dated a vain and conceited man; a dandy. **2** variant spelling of COCKSCOMB (sense 2). —**cox·comb·ry** n. (pl. **-ries**) —**cox·comb·er·y** /-,kōm(ə)rē/ n.

cox·swain /'käksən/ ▶ n. the steersman of a ship's boat, lifeboat, racing boat, or other boat. —**cox·swain·ship** /-,ship/ n.

coy /koi/ ▶ adj. (**coy·er**, **coy·est**) (esp. of a woman) making a pretense of shyness or modesty that is intended to be alluring but is often regarded as irritating. ■ reluctant to give details, esp. about something regarded as sensitive: *he is coy about his age.* ■ dated quiet and reserved; shy. —**coy·ly** adv. —**coy·ness** n.

coy·o·te /'kī,ōt; kī'ōtē/ ▶ n. **1** (pl. same or **coyotes**) a wolflike wild dog (*Canis latrans*) native to North America. **2** inf. a person who smuggles Latin Americans across the U.S. border, typically for a high fee.

coy·pu /'koi,pōō/ ▶ n. (pl. **-pus**) another term for NUTRIA.

co·zy /'kōzē/ (*Brit.* **co·sy**) ▶ adj. (**-zi·er**, **-zi·est**) giving a feeling of comfort, warmth, and relaxation. ■ (of a relationship or conversation) intimate and relaxed. ■ avoiding or not offering challenge or difficulty; complacent: *a rather cozy assumption among lenders that they would never go bust.* ■ (of a transaction or arrangement) working to the mutual advantage of those involved (used to convey a suspicion of corruption).

▶ n. (pl. **-zies**) a cover to keep a teapot hot.

▶ v. (**-zies**, **-zied**) [tr.] inf. impart a feeling or quality of comfort to (something). ■ [tr.] inf. give (someone) a feeling of comfort or complacency. ■ [intr.] (**cozy up to**) snuggle up to. ■ [intr.] (**cozy up to**) ingratiate oneself with. —**co·zi·ly** /-zəlē/ adv. —**co·zi·ness** n.

CP ▶ abbr. ■ cerebral palsy. ■ Command Post. ■ *Finance* commercial paper. ■ Common Pleas. ■ Communist Party. ■ (also **cp**) candlepower.

CPA ▶ abbr. certified public accountant.

cpd. ▶ abbr. compound.

CPI ▶ abbr. consumer price index.

Cpl. ▶ abbr. corporal.

CPR ▶ abbr. cardiopulmonary resuscitation, emergency medical procedures for restoring normal heartbeat and breathing to victims of heart failure, drowning, etc.

cps (also **c.p.s.**) ▶ abbr. ■ *Comput.* characters per second. ■ cycles per second.

Cpt. ▶ abbr. Captain.

CPU ▶ abbr. *Comput.* central processing unit.

Cr ▶ symb. the chemical element chromium.

cr ▶ abbr. ■ credit. ■ creditor.

crab[1] /krab/ ▶ n. **1** a crustacean with a broad carapace, stalked eyes, and five pairs of legs, the first pair of which are modified as pincers. ■ the flesh of a crab as food. ■ (**the Crab**) the zodiacal sign or constellation Cancer. **2** (also **crab louse**) a louse (*Phthirus pubis*, family Pediculidae) that infests human body hair, esp. in the genital region, causing extreme irritation. ■ (**crabs**) inf. an infestation of crab lice.

▶ v. **1** [tr.] move sideways or obliquely. **2** [intr.] fish for crabs. —**crab·ber** n. —**crab·like** /-,līk/ adj. & adv.

crab[2] ▶ n. short for CRAB APPLE.

crab[3] ▶ n. inf. an irritable person.

▶ v. (**crabbed**, **crab·bing**) inf. **1** [intr.] grumble, typically about something petty. **2** [tr.] act so as to spoil: *you're trying to crab my act.*

crab ap·ple (also **crab·ap·ple**) ▶ n. (also **crab**) **1** a small, sour apple. **2** the small tree (genus Malus) of the rose family that bears this fruit.

crab·bed /'krabəd/ ▶ adj. **1** (of handwriting) ill-formed and hard to decipher. ■ (of style) contorted and difficult to understand: *crabbed legal language.* **2** ill-humored. —**crab·bed·ly** adv. —**crab·bed·ness** n.

crab·by /'krabē/ ▶ adj. (**crab·bi·er**, **crab·bi·est**) irritable. —**crab·bi·ly** /'krabəlē/ adv. —**crab·bi·ness** n.

crab·grass /'krab,gras/ ▶ n. a creeping grass (*Digitaria* and other genera) that can become a serious weed.

crack /krak/ ▶ n. **1** a line on the surface of something along which it has split without breaking into separate parts. ■ a narrow space between two surfaces, esp. ones that have broken or been moved apart: *the door opened a tiny crack.* ■ fig. a vulnerable point; a flaw. **2** a sudden sharp or explosive noise: *a loud crack of thunder.* ■ a sharp blow, esp. one that makes a noise. ■ a sudden harshness or change in pitch in a person's voice. **3** inf. a joke, typically a critical or unkind one. **4** inf. an attempt to gain or achieve something: *I thought I had a crack at winning.* ■ a chance to attack or compete with someone: *he wanted to have a crack at the enemy.* **5** (also **crack cocaine**) a hard, crystalline form of cocaine broken into small pieces and smoked.

▶ v. **1** break or cause to break without a complete separation of the parts: [intr.] *the ice all over the lake had cracked* | [tr.] *a stone cracked the headlight glass.* ■ break or cause to break open or apart: [intr.] *the landmasses have cracked up and moved around* | fig. [intr.] *his face cracked into a smile* | [tr.] *she cracked an egg into the pan.* ■ [tr.] break (wheat or corn) into coarse pieces. ■ [tr.] open slightly: *gingerly, he cracks open his door.* ■ fig. give way

or cause to give way under torture, pressure, or strain: [*intr.*] *the witnesses cracked and the truth came out* | [*tr.*] *no one can crack them—they believe their story.* ■ [*intr.*] (**crack up**) *inf.* suffer an emotional breakdown under pressure. ■ (**crack up**) *inf.* burst or cause to burst into laughter. **2** make or cause to make a sudden sharp or explosive sound: [*intr.*] *a shot cracked across the ridge* | [*tr.*] *he cracked his whip.* ■ [*intr.*] knock against something, making a noise on impact: *she winced as her knees cracked against metal.* ■ [*tr.*] hit (someone or something) hard, making a sharp noise. ■ [*intr.*] (of a person's voice, esp. that of an adolescent boy or a person under strain) suddenly change in pitch. **3** [*tr.*] *inf.* find a solution to; decipher or interpret: *a hacker cracked the codes used in Internet software.* ■ break into (a safe). ■ succeed in achieving: *he cracked a brilliant goal.* **4** [*tr.*] tell (a joke). **5** [*tr.*] decompose (hydrocarbons) by heat and pressure with or without a catalyst to produce lighter hydrocarbons, esp. in oil refining. ▸*phrasal v.* □ **crack down on** *inf.* take severe measures against.
▸*adj.* very good, esp. at a specified activity or in a specified role: *he is a crack shot* | *crack troops.*
▸ □ **crack of dawn** a time very early in the morning; daybreak. □ **cracked up to be** *inf.* asserted to be (used to indicate that someone or something has been described too favorably): *life on tour is not as glamorous as it's cracked up to be.* □ **crack wise** *inf.* make jokes; wisecrack. □ **fall** (or **slip**) **through the cracks** escape from or be missed by something organized to catch or deal with one: *fatherless kids were not allowed to fall through the cracks.* □ **get cracking** *inf.* act quickly and energetically.
crack·down /ˈkrakˌdoun/ ▸*n.* severe measures to restrict or discourage undesirable or illegal people or behavior: *a crackdown on crime and corruption.*
cracked /krakt/ ▸*adj.* **1** damaged and showing lines on the surface from having split without coming apart. ■ (of a person's voice) having an unusual harshness or pitch, often due to distress. **2** *inf.* crazy; insane.
cracked wheat ▸*n.* grains of wheat that have been crushed into small pieces.
crack·er /ˈkrakər/ ▸*n.* **1** a thin, crisp wafer often eaten with cheese or other savory toppings. **2** a person or thing that cracks. ■ an installation for cracking hydrocarbons: *a catalytic cracker.* ■ a person who breaks into a computer system, typically for an illegal purpose. **3** *chiefly Brit.* a paper cylinder that is pulled apart at Christmas or other celebrations, making a sharp noise and releasing a small novelty. ■ a firework exploding with a sharp noise.
crack·er-bar·rel ▸*adj.* (esp. of a philosophy) simple and unsophisticated: *his cracker-barrel fascism.*
crack·er·jack /ˈkrakərˌjak/ *inf.* ▸*adj.* exceptionally good: *a crackerjack eye surgeon.*
▸*n.* an exceptionally good person or thing.
crack·ers /ˈkrakərz/ ▸*adj. inf., chiefly Brit.* insane.
crack·le /ˈkrakəl/ ▸*v.* [*intr.*] make a rapid succession of slight cracking noises: *the fire suddenly crackled and spat sparks.* ■ *fig.* give a sense of great tension or animation: *attraction and antagonism were crackling between them.*
▸*n.* **1** a sound made up of a rapid succession of slight cracking sounds. **2** a pattern of minute surface cracks on painted or varnished surfaces, glazed ceramics, or glass. —**crack·ly** /ˈkrak(ə)lē/ *adj.*
crack·ling /ˈkrakliŋ/; -liNG/ ▸*n.* the crisp, fatty skin of roast pork.
crack·pot /ˈkrakˌpät/ *inf.* ▸*n.* an eccentric or foolish person.
▸*adj.* eccentric; impractical: *his head's full of crackpot ideas.*
cra·dle /ˈkrādl/ ▸*n.* **1** an infant's bed or crib, typically one mounted on rockers. ■ *fig.* a place, process, or event in which something originates or flourishes: *he saw Greek art as the cradle of European civilization.* ■ *fig.* infancy; childhood: *a society that would secure the welfare of its citizens from cradle to grave.* **2** a framework resembling a cradle, in particular: ■ a framework on which a ship or boat rests during construction or repairs. ■ the part of a telephone on which the receiver rests when not in use.
▸*v.* [*tr.*] **1** hold gently and protectively: *she cradled his head in her arms.* ■ *fig.* be the place of origin of. **2** place (a telephone receiver) in its cradle.
cra·dle-rob·ber ▸*n. derog.* a person who marries or has a sexual relationship with a much younger person.
craft /kraft/ ▸*n.* **1** an activity involving skill in making things by hand: *the craft of bookbinding.* ■ (**crafts**) work or objects made by hand: *local crafts* | [as *adj.*] (**craft**) *a craft fair.* ■ a skilled activity or profession: *the historian's craft.* ■ skill in carrying out one's work. ■ skill used in deceiving others. ■ the members of a skilled profession. ■ (**the Craft**) the brotherhood of Freemasons. **2** (*pl.* same) a boat or ship. ■ an airplane or spaceship.
▸*v.* [*tr.*] exercise skill in making (something). ▷Old English *cræft* 'strength, skill,' of Germanic origin; related to Dutch *kracht*, German

Kraft, and Swedish *kraft* 'strength' (the change of sense to 'skill' occurring only in English). Sense 2, originally in the expression *small craft* 'small trading vessels or lighters,' may be elliptical, referring to vessels requiring a small amount of "craft" or skill to handle, as opposed to large ships. —**craft·er** *n.*
crafts·man /ˈkraf(t)smən/ ▸*n.* (*pl.* -**men**) a person who is skilled in a particular craft. ■ an artist. —**crafts·man·ship** /-,SHip/ *n.*
craft·y /ˈkraftē/ ▸*adj.* (**craft·i·er**, **craft·i·est**) **1** clever at achieving one's aims by indirect or deceitful methods: *a crafty crook.* ■ of, involving, or relating to indirect or deceitful methods: *a shameless and crafty trick.* **2** *inf.* of, involving, or relating to the making of decorative objects and other things by hand: *a market full of crafty pots.* —**craft·i·ly** /-təlē/ *adv.* —**craft·i·ness** *n.*
crag /krag/ ▸*n.* a steep or rugged cliff or rock face.
crag·gy /ˈkragē/ ▸*adj.* (-**gi·er**, -**gi·est**) (of a landscape) having many crags: *a craggy coastline.* ■ (of a cliff or rock face) rough and uneven. ■ (of a person's face, typically a man's) rugged and rough-textured in an attractive way. —**crag·gi·ly** /ˈkragəlē/ *adv.* —**crag·gi·ness** *n.*
cram /kram/ ▸*v.* (**crammed**, **cram·ming**) [*tr.*] (often **be crammed**) completely fill (a place or container) to the point that it appears to be overflowing: *the ashtray by the bed was crammed with cigarette butts.* ■ [*intr.*] (of a number of people) enter a place or space that is or seems to be too small to accommodate all of them. ■ put (something) quickly or roughly into something that is or appears to be too small to contain it: *he crammed the sandwiches into his mouth* | *fig. he had crammed so much into his short life.* ■ [*intr.*] study intensively over a short period of time just before an examination.
cramp /kramp/ ▸*n.* **1** a painful, involuntary contraction of a muscle or muscles, typically caused by fatigue or strain. ■ (**cramps**) abdominal pain caused by menstruation. **2** (also **cramp-iron**) a metal bar with bent ends for holding masonry together.
▸*v.* **1** [*tr.*] restrict or inhibit the development of: *tighter rules will cramp economic growth.* **2** [*tr.*] fasten with a cramp or cramps. **3** [*intr.*] suffer from sudden and painful contractions of a muscle or muscles.
▸ □ **cramp someone's style** *inf.* prevent a person from acting freely or naturally.
cram·pon /ˈkramˌpän/ ▸*n.* (usu. **crampons**) a metal plate with spikes fixed to a boot for walking on ice or rock climbing.
cran·ber·ry /ˈkranˌberē; -bərē/ ▸*n.* (*pl.* -**ies**) **1** a small, red, acid berry used in cooking. **2** the evergreen dwarf shrub (genus *Vaccinium*) of the heath family that yields this fruit, esp. the North American *V. macrocarpon*, which thrives in boggy places.
crane¹ /krān/ ▸*n.* a large, tall machine used for moving heavy objects, typically by suspending them from a projecting arm or beam. ■ a metal arm fastened inside a fireplace for holding cooking pots. ■ a moving platform supporting a television or movie camera.
▸*v.* **1** [*intr.*] stretch out one's neck in order to see something: *she craned forward to look more clearly.* ■ [*tr.*] stretch out (one's neck) in this way. **2** [*tr.*] move (a heavy object) with a crane.
crane² ▸*n.* a tall, long-legged, long-necked bird (*Grus* and other genera, family Gruidae), typically with white or gray plumage.

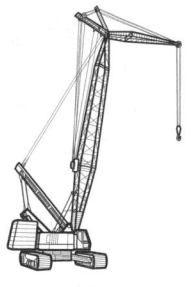
crane

crane fly ▸*n.* a slender, two-winged fly (family Tipulidae) with very long legs, in particular the large and common *Tipula maxima*.
cra·ni·al /ˈkrānēəl/ ▸*adj. Anat.* of or relating to the skull or cranium.
cra·ni·ot·o·my /ˌkrānēˈätəmē/ ▸*n.* surgical opening into the skull. ■ surgical perforation of the skull of a dead fetus to ease delivery.
cra·ni·um /ˈkrānēəm/ ▸*n.* (*pl.* -**ni·ums** or -**ni·a** /-nēə/) *Anat.* the skull, esp. the part enclosing the brain.
crank¹ /kraNGk/ ▸*v.* [*tr.*] **1** turn the crankshaft of (an internal combustion engine), typically in order to start the engine. ■ turn (a handle), typically in order to start an engine. ■ (**crank something up**) *inf.* increase the intensity of something: *he cranked up the foghorn to full volume.* ■ (**crank something out**) *inf.* produce something regularly and routinely: *an army of researchers cranked out worthy studies.* **2** [usu. as *adj.*] (**cranked**) give a bend to (a shaft, bar, etc.).
▸*n.* **1** a part of an axle or shaft bent out at right angles, for converting reciprocal to circular motion and vice versa. **2** *inf.* methamphetamine.

crank² ▸ *n.* **1** an eccentric person, esp. one who is obsessed by a particular subject or theory. ■ a bad-tempered person. **2** *poetic/lit.* a fanciful turn of speech.
▸ *adj.* originating from or denoting a malicious or mischievous person: *she was the target of a rash of crank calls.* —**crank·y** *adj.*

crank·case /'kraNGk,kās/ ▸ *n.* a case or covering enclosing a crankshaft.

crank·shaft /'kraNGk,SHaft/ ▸ *n.* a shaft driven by a crank.

cran·ny /'kranē/ ▸ *n.* (*pl.* **-nies**) a small, narrow space or opening. —**cran·nied** /'kranēd/ *adj.*

crap¹ /krap/ *vulgar slang* ▸ *n.* **1** something that is of extremely poor quality. ■ nonsense. ■ rubbish; junk. **2** excrement. ■ an act of defecation.
▸ *v.* (**crapped**, **crap·ping**) [*intr.*] defecate. —**crap·py** *adj.*

crap² ▸ *n.* a losing throw of 2, 3, or 12 in craps.
▸ *v.* [*intr.*] (**crap out**) *inf.* make a losing throw at craps. ■ withdraw from or give up on a game or activity because of fear or fatigue. ■ fail in what one is attempting to do. ■ (of a machine) break down.

crape /krāp/ ▸ *n.* archaic spelling of CREPE. —**crap·y** *adj.*

craps /kraps/ ▸ *pl. n.* [treated as *sing.*] a gambling game played with two dice. A throw of 7 or 11 is a winning throw, 2, 3, or 12 is a losing throw; any other throw must be repeated. See also CRAP².

crap·shoot /'krap,SHo͞ot/ ▸ *n.* a crap game. ■ *inf.* a risky or uncertain matter. —**crap·shoot·er** *n.*

crap·u·lent /'krapyələnt/ ▸ *adj. poetic/lit.* of or relating to the drinking of alcohol or drunkenness. —**crap·u·lence** *n.* —**crap·u·lous** /-yələs/ *adj.*

crash¹ /kraSH/ ▸ *v.* **1** [*intr.*] (of a moving object) collide violently with an obstacle or another moving object. ■ [*tr.*] cause (a moving object) to collide in this way. ■ (of an aircraft) fall from the sky and violently hit the land or sea. ■ [*tr.*] cause (an aircraft) to fall from the sky in this way. ■ *inf.* (of a business, a market, or a price) fall suddenly and disastrously in value. ■ *Comput.* [*intr.*] (of a machine, system, or software) fail suddenly. ■ *inf.* [*intr.*] go to sleep, esp. suddenly or in an improvised setting: *I'll crash in the back of the van for a couple of hours.* **2** [*intr.*] move with force, speed, and sudden loud noise: *huge waves crashed down on us.* ■ [*tr.*] move (something) in this way. ■ make a sudden loud, deep noise: *the thunder crashed.* **3** [*tr.*] *inf.* enter (a party) without an invitation or permission.
▸ *n.* **1** a violent collision, typically of one moving object with another or with an obstacle: *a car crash.* ■ an instance of an aircraft falling from the sky to hit the land or sea. ■ a sudden loud noise as of something breaking or hitting another object. **2** a sudden disastrous drop in the value or price of something, esp. shares of stock. ■ the sudden collapse of a business. ■ *Comput.* a sudden failure which puts a system out of action.
▸ *adj.* done rapidly or urgently and involving a concentrated effort: *a crash course in Italian | a crash diet.*
▸ *adv.* with a sudden loud sound: *crash went the bolt.*

crash² ▸ *n. dated* a coarse plain linen, woolen, or cotton fabric, used for curtains and towels.

crash-dive ▸ *v.* [*intr.*] (of a submarine) dive rapidly and steeply to a deeper level in an emergency.

crash hel·met ▸ *n.* a helmet worn by a motorcyclist or a race car driver to protect the head in case of a crash.

crash-land ▸ *v.* [*intr.*] (of an aircraft) land roughly in an emergency, typically without lowering the landing gear: [as *n.*] (**crash landing**) *a plane made a crash landing near the airport.*

crass /kras/ ▸ *adj.* lacking sensitivity, refinement, or intelligence. —**crass·si·tude** /'krasə,t(y)o͞od/ *n.* —**crass·ly** *adv.* —**crass·ness** *n.*

crate /krāt/ ▸ *n.* **1** a slatted wooden case used for transporting or storing goods: *a crate of bananas.* ■ a square metal or plastic container divided into small individual units, used for transporting or storing bottles: *a milk crate.* **2** *inf.* dated an old and dilapidated vehicle.
▸ *v.* [*tr.*] (often **be crated**) pack (something) in a crate for transportation. —**crate·ful** /'krāt,fo͝ol/ *n.* (*pl.* **-fuls**)

cra·ter /'krātər/ ▸ *n.* **1** a large, bowl-shaped cavity in the ground or on the surface of a planet or the moon, typically one caused by an explosion or the impact of a meteorite or other celestial body. ■ a large pit or hollow forming the mouth of a volcano. ■ a cavity or hole in any surface. **2** a large bowl used in ancient Greece for mixing wine.
▸ *v.* [*tr.*] form a crater in (the ground or a planet): *he has the offensive power to crater the enemy's runways.*

cra·vat /krə'vat/ ▸ *n.* a short, wide strip of fabric worn by men around the neck and tucked inside an open-necked shirt. ■ a necktie. ▹mid 17th cent.: from French *cravate*, from *Cravate* 'Croat' (from German *Krabat*, from Serbo-Croat *Hrvat*), because of the scarf worn by Croatian mercenaries in France. —**cra·vat·ted** *adj.*

crave /krāv/ ▸ *v.* [*tr.*] feel a powerful desire for (something): *a program to*

give the infants the human touch they crave. ■ *dated* beg for (something): *I must crave your indulgence.* —**crav·er** *n.*

cra·ven /'krāvən/ ▸ *adj.* contemptibly lacking in courage; cowardly.
▸ *n.* archaic a cowardly person. —**cra·ven·ly** *adv.* —**cra·ven·ness** *n.*

crav·ing /'krāviNG/ ▸ *n.* a powerful desire for something: *a craving for chocolate.*

craw /krô/ ▸ *n. dated* the crop of a bird or insect. ■ *chiefly humorous* the stomach of a person or animal.

crawl /krôl/ ▸ *v.* [*intr.*] **1** (of a person) move forward on the hands and knees or by dragging the body close to the ground. ■ (of an insect or small animal) move slowly along a surface. ■ (of a vehicle) move at an unusually slow pace. ■ swim using the crawl. ■ *inf.* behave obsequiously or ingratiatingly in the hope of gaining someone's favor: *don't come crawling back to me when you realize your mistake.* ■ *technical* (of paint or other liquid) move after application to form an uneven layer over the surface below: *glazes can crawl away from a crack in the piece.* **2** (**be crawling with**) be covered or crowded with insects or people, to an extent that is disgusting or objectionable: *the place was crawling with soldiers.*
▸ *n.* **1** an act of moving on one's hands and knees or dragging one's body along the ground. ■ a slow rate of movement, typically that of a vehicle: *he reduced his speed to a crawl.* **2** a swimming stroke involving alternate overarm movements and rapid kicks of the legs. —**crawl·y** *adj.*

crawl·er /'krôlər/ ▸ *n.* a thing that crawls or moves at a slow pace, esp. an insect. ■ (in full **crawler tractor**) a tractor or other vehicle moving on an endless caterpillar track. ■ *Comput.* a program that searches the World Wide Web, typically in order to create an index of data.

cray·fish /'krā,fiSH/ ▸ *n.* (*pl.* same or **-fishes**) a nocturnal freshwater crustacean (*Astacus, Cambarus,* and other genera) that resembles a small lobster and inhabits streams and rivers. ■ another term for SPINY LOBSTER.

cray·on /'krā,än; 'krāən/ ▸ *n.* a pencil or stick of colored chalk or wax, used for drawing.
▸ *v.* [*tr.*] draw with a crayon or crayons: *Jeff crayoned a picture on a legal pad* | [*intr.*] *a child crayoning in a coloring book.*

craze /krāz/ ▸ *n.* an enthusiasm for a particular activity or object that typically appears suddenly and achieves widespread but short-lived popularity: *the latest craze for bungee jumping.*
▸ *v.* [*tr.*] **1** [usu. as *adj.*] (**crazed**) wildly insane or excited: *a crazed killer* | *power-crazed tinpot dictators.* **2** (often **be crazed**) produce a network of fine cracks on (a surface): *the lake was frozen over but crazed with cracks.* ■ [*intr.*] develop such cracks.

cra·zy /'krāzē/ *inf.* ▸ *adj.* (**-zi·er, -zi·est**) **1** mentally deranged, esp. as manifested in a wild or aggressive way. ■ extremely annoyed or angry: *the noise they made was driving me crazy.* ■ foolish: *it was crazy to hope that good might come out of this mess.* **2** extremely enthusiastic: *I'm crazy about Cindy.* **3** (of an angle) appearing absurdly out of place or in an unlikely position. ■ *archaic* (of a ship or building) full of cracks or flaws; unsound or shaky.
▸ *n.* (*pl.* **-zies**) a mentally deranged person. —**cra·zi·ly** /-zilē/ *adv.* —**cra·zi·ness** *n.*
▸ □ **like crazy** to a great degree: *I was laughing like crazy.*

creak /krēk/ ▸ *v.* [*intr.*] (of an object, typically a wooden one) make a harsh, high-pitched sound when being moved or when pressure or weight is applied. ■ *fig.* show weakness or frailty under strain: *stock prices creaked to a mixed finish today.*
▸ *n.* a harsh scraping or squeaking sound: *the creak of a floorboard broke the silence.* —**creak·ing·ly** *adv.*

creak·y /'krēkē/ ▸ *adj.* (**creak·i·er, creak·i·est**) (of an object, typically a wooden one) making or liable to make a harsh, high-pitched sound when being moved or when pressure or weight is applied: *I climbed the creaky stairs.* ■ (of a voice) producing such a sound. ■ *fig.* appearing old-fashioned; decrepit: *the country's creaky legal system.* —**creak·i·ly** /-kəlē/ *adv.* —**creak·i·ness** *n.*

cream /krēm/ ▸ *n.* **1** the thick white or pale yellow fatty liquid that rises to the top when milk is left to stand and that can be eaten as an accompaniment to desserts or used as a cooking ingredient: [as *adj.*] *a cream sauce.* ■ the part of a liquid that gathers at the top. ■ *fig.* the very best of a group of people or things: *the paper's readership is the cream of American society.* ■ a sauce, soup, dessert, or similar food containing cream or milk or having the consistency of cream: *cream of mushroom soup.* ■ a candy of a specified flavor that is creamy in texture, typically covered with chocolate: *a peppermint cream.* **2** a thick liquid or semi-solid cosmetic or medical preparation applied to the skin: *shaving cream.* **3** a very pale yellow or off-white color: [as *adj.*] *a cream linen jacket.*

▶ *v.* [*tr.*] **1** work (butter, typically with sugar) to form a smooth soft paste. ■ [usu. as *adj.*] (**creamed**) mash (a cooked vegetable) and mix with milk or cream: *creamed turnips.* ■ add cream to (coffee). **2** rub a cosmetic cream into (the skin). **3** *inf.* defeat (someone) heavily, esp. in a sports contest. ■ (often **be creamed**) hit or collide heavily and violently with (someone), esp. in a car. **4** [*intr.*] *vulgar slang* (of a person) be sexually aroused, esp. to the point of producing sexual secretions. ■ [*tr.*] moisten (one's underpants) due to such arousal.

cream cheese ▶ *n.* soft, rich cheese made from unskimmed milk and cream.

cream·er /ˈkrēmər/ ▶ *n.* **1** a cream or milk substitute for adding to coffee or tea. **2** a small jug for cream. **3** a machine used for separating cream from milk.

cream·er·y /ˈkrēm(ə)rē/ ▶ *n.* (*pl.* **-er·ies**) a place where butter and cheese are produced. ■ *dated* a shop where dairy products are sold.

cream of tar·tar ▶ *n.* a white, crystalline, acidic potassium salt used chiefly in baking powder.

cream puff ▶ *n.* **1** a cake made of light pastry filled with cream. **2** *inf.* a weak or ineffectual person. ■ [as *adj.*] denoting something of little consequence or difficulty: *a cream-puff assignment.* **3** *inf.* a secondhand car or other item maintained in excellent condition.

cream·y /ˈkrēmē/ ▶ *adj.* (**cream·i·er, cream·i·est**) resembling cream in consistency or color. ■ containing a lot of cream. —**cream·i·ly** /-məlē/ *adv.* —**cream·i·ness** *n.*

crease /krēs/ ▶ *n.* **1** a line or ridge produced on paper or cloth by folding, pressing, or crushing it: *khaki trousers with knife-edge creases.* ■ a wrinkle or furrow in the skin, typically of the face, caused by age or a particular facial expression. **2** (usu. **the crease**) an area around the goal in ice hockey or lacrosse that attacking players may not normally enter unless the puck or ball has already done so. ■ *Cricket* any of a number of lines marked on the pitch at specified places.
▶ *v.* [*tr.*] **1** make a crease in (cloth or paper): *he sank into the chair, careful not to crease his dinner jacket* | [as *adj.*] (**creased**) *a creased piece of paper.* ■ cause a crease to appear temporarily in (the face or its features), typically as a result of the expression of an emotion or feeling. **2** (of a bullet) graze (someone or something), causing little damage.

cre·ate /krēˈāt/ ▶ *v.* [*tr.*] bring (something) into existence: *jobs were created.* ■ cause (something) to happen as a result of one's actions: *divorce creates problems for children.* ■ (of an actor) originate (a role) by playing a character for the first time. ■ invest (someone) with a new rank or title.

cre·a·tion /krēˈāSHən/ ▶ *n.* **1** the action or process of bringing something into existence. ■ a thing that has been made or invented, esp. something showing artistic talent: *she treats fictional creations as if they were real people.* **2** (**the Creation**) the bringing into of existence of the universe, esp. when regarded as an act of God. ■ everything so created; the universe. **3** the action or process of investing someone with a new rank or title.

cre·a·tion·ism /krēˈāSHə,nizəm/ ▶ *n.* the belief that the universe and living organisms originate from specific acts of divine creation, as in the biblical account, rather than by natural processes such as evolution. ■ another term for **CREATION SCIENCE**. —**cre·a·tion·ist** *n.* & *adj.*

cre·a·tion sci·ence ▶ *n.* the interpretation of scientific knowledge in accord with belief in the Bible, esp. the creation of matter, life, and humankind in six days.

cre·a·tive /krēˈātiv/ ▶ *adj.* relating to or involving the imagination or original ideas, esp. in the production of an artistic work: *change unleashes people's creative energy.* ■ (of a person) having good imagination or original ideas: *Homer, the creative genius of Greek epic.*
▶ *n.* a person who is creative, typically in a professional context. —**cre·a·tive·ly** *adv.* —**cre·a·tive·ness** *n.* —**cre·a·tiv·i·ty** /ˌkrēāˈtivitē/ *n.*

cre·a·tor /krēˈātər/ ▶ *n.* a person or thing that brings something into existence. ■ (**the Creator**) used as a name for God.

crea·ture /ˈkrēCHər/ ▶ *n.* an animal, as distinct from a human being. ■ an animal or person. ■ a fictional or imaginary being, typically a frightening one: *a creature from outer space.* ■ *archaic* anything living or existing: *dress, jewels, and other transitory creatures.* ■ a person of a specified kind, typically one viewed with pity, contempt, or desire: *you heartless creature!* ■ a person or organization considered to be under the complete control of another: *the village teacher was expected to be the creature of his employer.* —**crea·ture·ly** *adj.*
▶ □ **creature of habit** a person who follows an unvarying routine.

crea·ture com·forts ▶ *pl. n.* material comforts that contribute to physical ease and well-being, such as good food and accommodations.

crèche /kreSH/ ▶ *n.* **1** a model or tableau representing the scene of Jesus Christ's birth, displayed in homes or public places at Christmas.

2 *Brit.* a nursery where babies and young children are cared for during the working day.

cred·al /ˈkrēdl/ (also **creed·al**) ▶ *adj.* of or relating to a statement of Christian or other religious belief.

cre·dence /ˈkrēdns/ ▶ *n.* belief in or acceptance of something as true: *psychoanalysis finds little credence among laymen.* ■ the likelihood of something being true; plausibility: *being called upon by the media as an expert lends credence to one's opinions.*
▶ □ **give credence to** accept as true.

cre·den·tial /krəˈdenCHəl/ ▶ *n.* (usu. **credentials**) a qualification, achievement, personal quality, or aspect of a person's background, typically when used to indicate that they are suitable for something. ■ a document or certificate proving a person's identity or qualifications. ■ a letter of introduction given by a government to an ambassador before a new posting.

cre·den·tialed /krəˈdenSHəld/ ▶ *adj.* awarded or in possession of credentials: *impeccably credentialed professionals.*

cre·den·za /krəˈdenzə/ ▶ *n.* a sideboard or cupboard.

cred·i·bil·i·ty /ˌkredəˈbilitē/ ▶ *n.* the quality of being trusted and believed in: *the government's loss of credibility.* ■ the quality of being convincing or believable: *the book's anecdotes have scant regard for credibility.*

cred·i·bil·i·ty gap ▶ *n.* an apparent difference between what is said or promised and what happens or is true. ■ a lack of trust in a person's or institution's statements and motives.

cred·i·ble /ˈkredəbəl/ ▶ *adj.* able to be believed; convincing: *few people found his story credible.* ■ capable of persuading people that something will happen or be successful: *a credible threat.* —**cred·i·bly** /-blē/ *adv.*

cred·it /ˈkredit/ ▶ *n.* **1** the ability of a customer to obtain goods or services before payment, based on the trust that payment will be made in the future. ■ the money lent or made available under such an arrangement: *the bank refused to extend their credit* | [as *adj.*] *exceeding his credit limit.* **2** an entry recording a sum received, listed on the right-hand side or column of an account. The opposite of **DEBIT**. ■ a payment received. **3** public acknowledgment or praise, typically that given or received when a person's responsibility for an action or idea becomes or is made apparent: *the president claims credit for each accomplishment.* ■ a source of pride, typically someone or something that reflects well on another person or organization: *he's a credit to his mother.* ■ (usu. **credits**) an acknowledgment of a contributor's services to a movie or a television program, typically one of a list that is scrolled down the screen at the beginning or end of a movie or program. **4** the acknowledgment of a student's completion of a course that counts toward a degree or diploma as maintained in a school's records: *a student can earn one unit of academic credit.* ■ a unit of study counting toward a degree or diploma: *in his first semester he earned 17 credits.* ■ acknowledgment of merit in an examination which is reflected in the grades awarded: *students will receive credit for accuracy.* **5** *archaic* the quality of being believed or credited: *the philosophy of Cicero has lost its credit.* ■ favorable estimation; good reputation.
▶ *v.* (**cred·it·ed, cred·it·ing**) [*tr.*] (often **be credited**) **1** publicly acknowledge someone as a participant in the production of (something published or broadcast). ■ (**credit someone with**) ascribe (an achievement or good quality) to someone. **2** add (an amount of money) to an account. **3** believe (something surprising or unlikely). ▷mid 16th cent. (originally in the senses 'belief', 'credibility'): from French *crédit*, probably via Italian *credito* from Latin *creditum*, neuter past participle of *credere* 'believe, trust.'
▶ □ **do someone credit** (or **do credit to someone**) make someone worthy of praise or respect: *your concern does you credit.* □ **give someone credit for** commend someone for (a quality or achievement), esp. with reluctance or surprise: *please give me credit for some sense.* □ **have something to one's credit** have achieved something notable: *he has 65 tournament wins to his credit.* □ **on credit** with an arrangement to pay later. □ **to one's credit** used to indicate that something praiseworthy has been achieved, esp. despite difficulties: *to her credit, she had never betrayed a confidence.*

cred·it·a·ble /ˈkreditəbəl/ ▶ *adj.* (of a performance, effort, or action) deserving public acknowledgment and praise but not necessarily outstanding or successful. —**cred·it·a·bil·i·ty** /ˌkreditəˈbilitē/ *n.* —**cred·it·a·bly** /ˈkreditəblē/ *adv.*

cred·it card ▶ *n.* a small plastic card issued by a bank, business, etc., allowing the holder to purchase goods or services on credit.

---

cred·i·tor /ˈkreditər/ ▶ n. a person or company to whom money is owed.

cred·it un·ion ▶ n. a nonprofit-making money cooperative whose members can borrow from pooled deposits at low interest rates.

cre·do /ˈkrēdō; ˈkrādō/ ▶ n. (pl. **-dos**) a statement of the beliefs or aims that guide someone's actions: he announced his credo in his first editorial. ■ **(Credo)** a creed of the Christian Church in Latin.

cred·u·lous /ˈkrejələs/ ▶ adj. having or showing too great a readiness to believe things. —**cre·du·li·ty** /ˌkreˈd(y)o͞olitē/ n. —**cred·u·lous·ly** adv. —**cred·u·lous·ness** n.

Cree /krē/ ▶ n. (pl. same or **Crees**) **1** a member of a American Indian people living in a vast area of central Canada. **2** the Algonquian language of this people, closely related to Montagnais. ▶ adj. of or relating to the Cree or their language.

creed /krēd/ ▶ n. a system of Christian or other religious belief; a faith. ■ (often **the Creed**) a formal statement of Christian beliefs, esp. the Apostles' Creed or the Nicene Creed. ■ a set of beliefs or aims that guide someone's actions: liberalism was more than a political creed.

Creek /krēk/ ▶ n. (pl. same) **1** a member of a confederacy of native peoples of the southeastern U.S. in the 16th to 19th centuries whose descendants now live mainly in Oklahoma. **2** the Muskogean language of this confederacy. ▶ adj. of, relating to, or denoting this confederacy.

creek /krēk; krik/ ▶ n. a stream, brook, or minor tributary of a river. ■ an inlet in a shoreline, a channel in a marsh, or another narrow, sheltered waterway. ▶ □ **be up the creek** inf. (also **be up the creek without a paddle**) be in severe difficulty or trouble.

creel /krēl/ ▶ n. **1** a large wicker basket for carrying fish. ■ an angler's fishing basket. **2** a rack holding bobbins or spools for spinning.

creep /krēp/ ▶ v. (past and past part. **crept** /krept/) [intr.] **1** move slowly and carefully, in order to avoid being heard or noticed. ■ (of a thing) move very slowly at an inexorably steady pace: the fog was creeping up from the marsh. ■ (of a plant) grow along the ground or other surface by means of extending stems or branches. ■ (of a plastic solid) undergo gradual deformation under stress. **2** (**creep in/into**) (of an unwanted and negative characteristic or fact) occur or develop gradually and almost imperceptibly. ■ (**creep up**) increase slowly but steadily in number or amount. ▶ n. **1** inf. a detestable person. ■ a person who behaves in an obsequious way in the hope of advancement. **2** slow movement, esp. at a steady but almost imperceptible pace. ■ the tendency of a car with automatic transmission to move when in gear without the accelerator being pressed. ■ the gradual downward movement of disintegrated rock or soil due to gravitational forces. ■ the gradual deformation of a plastic solid under stress. ▶ □ **give someone the creeps** inf. induce a feeling of revulsion or fear in someone.

creep·er /ˈkrēpər/ ▶ n. **1** Bot. any plant that grows along the ground, around another plant, or up a wall by means of extending stems or branches. **2** any of a number of small birds that creep around in trees, vegetation, etc., including the North American **brown creeper** (Certhia americana, family Certhiidae). **3** a low, wheeled platform on which a mechanic lies while working on the underside of a motor vehicle.

creep·y /ˈkrēpē/ ▶ adj. (**creep·i·er, creep·i·est**) inf. causing an unpleasant feeling of fear or unease. —**creep·i·ly** /-pəlē/ adv. —**creep·i·ness** n.

creep·y-crawl·y /ˈkrôlē/ inf. ▶ n. (pl. **-crawl·ies**) a spider, worm, or other small, flightless creature, esp. when considered unpleasant or frightening. ▶ adj. causing an unpleasant feeling of fear or unease.

cre·mains /kriˈmānz/ ▶ pl. n. a person's cremated remains.

cre·mate /ˈkrēˌmāt; kriˈmāt/ ▶ v. [tr.] (usu. **be cremated**) dispose of (a dead person's body) by burning it to ashes, typically after a funeral ceremony. ■ to burn (something), typically food. —**cre·ma·tion** /kriˈmāSHən/ n. —**cre·ma·tor** /-mātər/ n.

cre·ma·to·ri·um /ˌkrēmāˈtôrēəm; ˌkrem-/ ▶ n. (pl. **-to·ri·a** /-ˈtôrēə/ or **-to·ri·ums**) another term for CREMATORY.

cre·ma·to·ry /ˈkrēmāˌtôrē; ˈkrem-/ ▶ n. (pl. **-ries**) a place where a dead person's body is cremated. ▶ adj. of or relating to cremation.

crème /krem/ (also **creme**) ▶ n. **1** cream. ■ a creamy dessert, esp. custard: crème brûlée. **2** a name for various syrupy liqueurs: crème de menthe.

crème de la crème /ˌkrem də lə ˈkrem/ ▶ n. the best person or thing of a particular kind: the crème de la crème of the dancers have left the country.

crème de menthe /ˌkrēm də ˈmenTH ˌkrēm; ˈmint/ ▶ n. a peppermint-flavored liqueur.

cren·el·late /ˈkrenlˌāt/ (also **cren·e·late**) ▶ v. [tr.] [usu. as adj.] (**crenellated**) chiefly hist. provide (a wall of a building) with battlements.

Cre·ole /ˈkrēˌōl/ (also **cre·ole**) ▶ n. **1** a person of mixed European and black descent, esp. in the Caribbean. ■ a descendant of Spanish or other European settlers in the Caribbean or Central or South America. ■ a white descendant of French settlers in Louisiana and other parts of the southern U.S. **2** a mother tongue formed from the contact of two languages through an earlier pidgin stage. ▶ adj. of or relating to a Creole or Creoles.

cre·o·sote /ˈkrēəˌsōt/ ▶ n. (also **cre·o·sote oil**) a dark brown oil distilled from coal tar and used as a wood preservative. It contains a number of phenols and other organic compounds. ▶ v. [tr.] treat (wood) with creosote.

crepe (also **crêpe**) ▶ n. **1** /krāp/ a light, thin fabric with a wrinkled surface: [as adj.] a silk crepe blouse. ■ (also **crepe rub·ber**) hard-wearing wrinkled rubber, used esp. for the soles of shoes. **2** /krāp/ black silk or imitation silk, formerly used for mourning clothes. ■ a band of such fabric formerly worn around a person's hat as a sign of mourning. **3** /krep; krāp/ a thin pancake. —**crep·ey** adj.

crepe pa·per ▶ n. thin, crinkled paper resembling crepe, used esp. for making decorations.

crêpe su·zette /ˌkrāp so͞oˈzet; ˌkrep/ ▶ n. (pl. **crêpes su·zette** pronunc. same) a thin dessert pancake with a brandy and citrus sauce, usually set aflame when served.

crept /krept/ ▶ past and past participle of CREEP.

cre·pus·cu·lar /krəˈpəskyələr/ ▶ adj. of, resembling, or relating to twilight.

cre·scen·do /krəˈSHendō/ ▶ n. (pl. **-dos** or **-di** /-dē/) Mus. a gradual increase in loudness in a piece of music. ■ the loudest point reached in a gradually increasing sound: Deborah's voice was rising to a crescendo. ■ a progressive increase in force or intensity. ■ the most intense point reached in this; a climax. ▶ v. (**-does, -doed**) [intr.] increase in loudness or intensity: the reluctant cheers began to crescendo.

cres·cent /ˈkresənt/ ▶ n. **1** the curved sickle shape of the waxing or waning moon. ■ a representation of such a shape used as an emblem of Islam or Turkey. **2** a thing that has the shape of a single curve, esp. one that is broad in the center and tapers to a point. ▶ adj. **1** in the shape of a crescent. **2** poetic/lit. growing, increasing, or developing. ▷ late Middle English cressant, from Old French creissant, from Latin crescere 'grow.' —**cres·cen·tic** /krəˈsentik/ adj.

cress /kres/ ▶ n. a plant (Barbarea and other genera) of the cabbage family, typically having small white flowers and pungent, often edible leaves.

crest /krest/ ▶ n. **1** a comb or tuft of feathers, fur, or skin on the head of a bird or other animal. ■ a thing resembling such a tuft, esp. a plume of feathers on a helmet. **2** the top of something, esp. a mountain or hill. ■ the curling foamy top of a wave. ■ the upper line of the neck of a horse or other mammal. **3** a distinctive device above the shield of a coat of arms, or separately reproduced, for example on writing paper or silverware, to represent a family or corporate body. ▶ v. [tr.] reach the top of (something such as a hill or wave). ■ [intr.] (of a river) rise to its highest level. ■ [intr.] (of a wave) form a curling foamy top. ■ (**be crested**) have attached or affixed at the top: his helmet was crested with a fan of spikes. —**crest·less** adj.

crest·fal·len /ˈkrestˌfôlən/ ▶ adj. sad and disappointed.

Cre·ta·ceous /krəˈtāSHəs/ ▶ adj. Geol. of, relating to, or denoting the last period of the Mesozoic era, between the Jurassic and Tertiary periods. ■ [as n.] (**the Cretaceous**) the Cretaceous period or the system of rocks deposited during it.

cre·tin /ˈkrētn/ ▶ n. a stupid person (used as a general term of abuse). ■ dated Med. a person who is deformed and mentally handicapped because of congenital thyroid deficiency. —**cre·tin·ism** /-ˌizəm/ n. —**cre·tin·ous** /-əs/ adj.

cre·vasse /krəˈvas/ ▶ n. a deep open crack, esp. one in a glacier.

crev·ice /ˈkrevəs/ ▶ n. a narrow opening or fissure, esp. in a rock or wall.

crew¹ /kro͞o/ ▶ n. [treated as sing. or pl.] a group of people who work on and operate a ship, boat, aircraft, spacecraft, or train. ■ such a group other than the officers. ■ the group that rows a racing shell. ■ the sport of rowing a racing shell. ■ a group of people who work closely together, in a job that is technically difficult or dangerous: an ambulance crew. ■ inf., often derog. a group of people associated in some way:

a crew of computer geeks. ■ *inf.* a group of rappers, breakdancers, or graffiti artists performing or operating together. ■ *inf.* a criminal gang.
▶ *v.* [*tr.*] (often **be crewed**) provide (a craft or vehicle) with a group of people to operate it. ■ [*intr.*] act as a member of a crew, subordinate to a captain: *I've never crewed for a world-famous yachtsman before.* —**crew·man** /ˈkrōōmən/ *n.* (*pl.* **-men**).

crew² ▶ *chiefly Brit.* past of CROW².

crew cut ▶ *n.* a very short haircut for men and boys.

crew·el /ˈkrōōəl/ ▶ *n.* a thin, loosely twisted, worsted yarn used for tapestry and embroidery.

crew neck ▶ *n.* a close-fitting, round neckline, esp. on a sweater or T-shirt: [as *adj.*] *a crew-neck sweater.* ■ a sweater with such a neckline.

crib /krib/ ▶ *n.* **1** a young child's bed with barred or latticed sides. ■ a barred container or rack for animal fodder; a manger. **2** *inf.* unfair use of notes on an examination or schoolwork. ■ *inf. Brit.* a trot: *an English crib of Caesar's Gallic Wars.* ■ a thing that has been plagiarized. **3** *inf.* an apartment or house. **4** the cards discarded by the players at cribbage, counting to the dealer. **5** (also **crib·bing**) a heavy timber framework used in foundations for a building or to line a mine shaft.
▶ *v.* (**cribbed**, **crib·bing**) [*tr.*] **1** *inf.* copy (another person's work) illicitly or without acknowledgment: *he was taking an exam and didn't want anybody to crib the answers from him* | [*intr.*] *he often cribbed from other researchers.* ■ *archaic* steal. **2** *archaic* restrain. —**crib·ber** /ˈkribər/ *n.*

crib·bage /ˈkribij/ ▶ *n.* a card game for two to four players, in which the objective is to play so that the value of one's cards played reaches exactly 15 or 31.

crib death ▶ *n.* informal term for SUDDEN INFANT DEATH SYNDROME.

crick /krik/ ▶ *n.* a painful stiff feeling in the neck or back.
▶ *v.* [*tr.*] twist or strain (one's neck or back), causing painful stiffness: [as *adj.*] (**cricked**) *he suffered a cricked neck during tackling practice.*

crick² ▶ *n.* *dial.* creek.

crick·et¹ /ˈkrikit/ ▶ *n.* an insect (family Gryllidae) related to the grasshoppers. The male produces a characteristic rhythmical chirping sound.

crick·et² ▶ *n.* an open-air game played on a large grass field with ball, bats, and two wickets, between teams of eleven players, the object of the game being to score more runs than the opposition. —**crick·et·er** *n.*
▶ □ **not cricket** *Brit., inf.* a thing contrary to traditional standards of fairness or rectitude.

crick·et³ ▶ *n.* a low stool, typically with a rectangular or oval seat and four legs splayed out.

cried /krīd/ ▶ past and past participle of CRY.

cri·er /ˈkrīər/ ▶ *n.* an officer who makes public announcements in a court of justice. ■ short for TOWN CRIER. ■ a person who shouts out announcements about their wares; a hawker.

crime /krīm/ ▶ *n.* an action or omission that constitutes an offense that may be prosecuted by the state and is punishable by law: *shoplifting was a serious crime.* ■ illegal activities: *the victims of crime.* ■ an action or activity that, although not illegal, is considered to be evil, shameful, or wrong: *they condemned apartheid as a crime against humanity.*

crime wave ▶ *n.* a sudden increase in the number of crimes committed in a country or area.

crim·i·nal /ˈkrimənl/ ▶ *n.* a person who has committed a crime.
▶ *adj.* of or relating to a crime. ■ *Law* of or relating to crime as opposed to civil matters. ■ *inf.* (of an action or situation) deplorable and shocking. —**crim·i·nal·i·ty** /ˌkriməˈnalitē/ *n.* —**crim·i·nal·ly** *adv.*

crim·i·nal law ▶ *n.* a system of law concerned with the punishment of those who commit crimes. Contrasted with CIVIL LAW. ■ a law belonging to this system.

crim·i·nal re·cord ▶ *n.* a history of being convicted for crime. ■ a list of a person's previous criminal convictions.

crim·i·nol·o·gy /ˌkriməˈnäləjē/ ▶ *n.* the scientific study of crime and criminals. —**crim·i·no·log·i·cal** /ˌkrimənlˈäjikəl/ *adj.* —**crim·i·nol·o·gist** /-jist/ *n.*

crimp /krimp/ ▶ *v.* [*tr.*] compress (something) into small folds or ridges: *she crimped the edge of the pie.* ■ squeeze (metal) so as to bend or corrugate it. ■ connect (a wire or cable) in this way. ■ make waves in (someone's hair) with a curling iron. ■ *inf.* have a limiting or adverse effect on (something): *farmers complain that the drought could crimp their income potential.*
▶ *n.* a curl, wave, or folded or compressed edge. ■ a small connecting piece for crimping wires or lines together. ■ *inf.* a restriction or limitation. —**crimp·er** *n.* —**crimp·y** *adj.*
▶ □ **put a crimp in** *inf.* have an adverse effect on.

crim·son /ˈkrimzən/ ▶ *adj.* of a rich deep red color inclining to purple.

▶ *n.* a rich deep red color inclining to purple.
▶ *v.* [*intr.*] (of a person's face) become flushed, esp. through embarrassment: *my face crimsoned and my hands began to shake.*

cringe /krinj/ ▶ *v.* (**cring·ing**) [*intr.*] bend one's head and body in fear or in a servile manner. ■ experience an inward shiver of embarrassment or disgust: *I cringed at the fellow's stupidity.*
▶ *n.* an act of cringing in fear. ■ a feeling of embarrassment or disgust. —**cring·er** *n.*

crin·kle /ˈkriNGkəl/ ▶ *v.* [*intr.*] form small creases or wrinkles in the surface of something, esp. the skin of the face as the result of a facial expression. ■ [*tr.*] cause to form such creases or wrinkles: *Burney crinkled his eyes in a smile.* ■ [*tr.*] cause (something) to make a crackling or rustling sound: *we tried hard not to crinkle the plastic as we unwrapped the pies.*
▶ *n.* a wrinkle or crease found on the surface of something. ■ the sound of crinkling. —**crin·kly** /-k(ə)lē/ *adj.*

crin·o·line /ˈkrinl-in/ ▶ *n.* **1** *hist.* a stiffened or hooped petticoat worn to make a long skirt stand out. **2** a stiff fabric made of horsehair and cotton or linen thread, typically used for stiffening petticoats or as a lining.

crip·ple /ˈkripəl/ ▶ *n.* **1** *dated, offens.* a person who is unable to walk or move properly because of disability or injury to their back or legs. **2** a person who is disabled in a specified way: *an emotional cripple.*
▶ *v.* [*tr.*] (often **be crippled**) cause (someone) to become unable to move or walk properly: *a writer who was crippled by polio at the age of eleven.* ■ cause severe and disabling damage to (a machine). ■ cause a severe and almost insuperable problem for: *developing countries are crippled by their debts.* —**crip·pler** /ˈkrip(ə)lər/ *n.*

crip·ple·ware /ˈkripəlˌwe(ə)r/ ▶ *n. inf. Comput.* software distributed with reduced functionality with a view to attracting payment for a fully functional version.

cri·sis /ˈkrīsis/ ▶ *n.* (*pl.* **-ses** /-ˌsēz/) a time of intense difficulty, trouble, or danger: *the current economic crisis.* ■ a time when a difficult or important decision must be made. ■ the turning point of a disease when an important change takes place, indicating either recovery or death. ■ the point in a play or story when a crucial conflict takes place, determining the outcome of the plot. ▷late Middle English (denoting the turning point of a disease): medical Latin, from Greek *krisis* 'decision,' from *krinein* 'decide.' The general sense 'decisive point' dates from the early 17th cent.

crisp /krisp/ ▶ *adj.* **1** (of a substance) firm, dry, and brittle, esp. in a way considered pleasing or attractive: *crisp bacon.* ■ (of a fruit or vegetable) firm, indicating freshness: *crisp lettuce.* ■ (of the weather) cool, fresh, and invigorating. ■ (of paper or cloth) smoothly and attractively stiff and uncreased. ■ (of hair) having tight curls, giving an impression of rigidity. **2** (of a way of speaking or writing) briskly decisive and matter-of-fact, without hesitation or unnecessary detail: *they were cut off with a crisp "Thank you."*
▶ *n.* a dessert of fruit baked with a crunchy topping of brown sugar, butter, and flour: *rhubarb crisp.*
▶ *v.* [*tr.*] give (something, esp. food) a crisp surface by placing it in an oven or on a grill. ■ [*intr.*] (of food) acquire a crisp surface in this way. ■ *archaic* curl into short, stiff, wavy folds or crinkles. —**crisp·ly** *adv.* —**crisp·ness** *n.*
▶ □ **burn something to a crisp** burn something completely.

crisp·er /ˈkrispər/ ▶ *n.* a compartment at the bottom of a refrigerator for storing fruit and vegetables.

crisp·y /ˈkrispē/ ▶ *adj.* (**crisp·i·er**, **crisp·i·est**) (of food, typically cooked food) having a pleasingly firm, dry, and brittle surface or texture: *crispy fried bacon.* —**crisp·i·ness** *n.*

criss·cross /ˈkris,krôs/ ▶ *n.* a pattern of intersecting straight lines or paths: *the crisscross of wrinkles on his face.*
▶ *adj.* (of a pattern) containing a number of straight lines or paths that intersect each other: *the streets ran in a regular crisscross pattern.*
▶ *adv.* in a pattern of intersecting straight lines.
▶ *v.* [*tr.*] (usu. **be crisscrossed**) form a pattern of intersecting lines or paths on (a place). ■ [*intr.*] (of straight lines or paths) intersect repeatedly. ■ move or travel around (a place) by going back and forth repeatedly: *the President crisscrossed America.*

cri·te·ri·on /krīˈti(ə)rēən/ ▶ *n.* (*pl.* **-te·ri·a** /-ˈti(ə)rēə/) a principle or standard by which something may be judged or decided: *the launch came too close to violating safety criteria.* —**cri·te·ri·al** /-ˈti(ə)rēəl/ *adj.*

crit·ic /ˈkritik/ ▶ *n.* **1** a person who expresses an unfavorable opinion of something. **2** a person who judges the merits of literary, artistic, or musical works, esp. one who does so professionally: *a film critic.*

crit·i·cal /ˈkritikəl/ ▸*adj.* **1** expressing adverse or disapproving comments or judgments. **2** expressing or involving an analysis of the merits and faults of a work of literature, music, or art: *she never won the critical acclaim she sought.* ■ (of a published literary or musical text) incorporating a literary and scholarly analysis and commentary: *a critical edition of a Bach sonata.* **3** (of a situation or problem) having the potential to become disastrous; at a point of crisis. ■ (of a person) extremely ill and at risk of death: *he had been in critical condition since undergoing surgery.* ■ having a decisive or crucial importance in the success or failure of something: *temperature is a critical factor in successful fruit storage.* . **4** *Math. & Physics* relating to or denoting a point of transition from one state to another. ■ (of a nuclear reactor or fuel) maintaining a self-sustaining chain reaction: *the reactor is due to go critical in October.* —**crit·i·cal·i·ty** /ˌkritəˈkalitē/ *n.* —**crit·i·cal·ly** /ˈkritik(ə)lē/ *adv. he's critically ill.* —**crit·i·cal·ness** *n.*

crit·i·cal mass ▸*n. Physics* the minimum amount of fissile material needed to maintain a nuclear chain reaction. ■ *fig.* the minimum size or amount of something required to start or maintain a venture: *a communication system is of no value unless there is a critical mass of users.*

crit·i·cism /ˈkritəˌsizəm/ ▸*n.* **1** the expression of disapproval of someone or something based on perceived faults or mistakes. **2** the analysis and judgment of the merits and faults of a literary or artistic work. ■ an article, book, or comment containing such analysis. ■ the scholarly investigation of literary or historical texts to determine their origin or intended form.

crit·i·cize /ˈkritəˌsīz/ ▸*v.* [*tr.*] **1** indicate the faults of (someone or something) in a disapproving way. **2** form and express a sophisticated judgment of (a literary or artistic work). —**crit·i·ciz·a·ble** *adj.* —**crit·i·ciz·er** *n.*

cri·tique /kriˈtēk/ ▸*n.* a detailed analysis and assessment of something, esp. a literary, philosophical, or political theory.
▸*v.* (**-tiques, -tiqued, -tiqu·ing**) [*tr.*] evaluate (a theory or practice) in a detailed and analytical way.

crit·ter /ˈkritər/ ▸*n. inf. or dial.* a living creature; an animal. ■ a person of a particular kind: *the old critter used to live in a shack.*

croak /krōk/ ▸*n.* a deep hoarse sound made by a frog or a crow. ■ a sound resembling this, esp. one made by a person.
▸*v.* [*intr.*] **1** (of a frog or crow) make a characteristic deep hoarse sound. ■ (of a person) make a similar sound when speaking or laughing: *"Thank you," I croaked.* ■ *archaic* prophesy evil or misfortune, esp. unjustifiably and to the irritation of others. **2** *inf.* die: *he finally croaked in 1987.* ■ [*tr.*] kill (someone).

croak·y /ˈkrōkē/ ▸*adj.* (**croak·i·er, croak·i·est**) (of a person's voice) deep and hoarse. —**croak·i·ly** /-kəlē/ *adv.*

Cro·at /ˈkrōˌat; ˈkrōˌät; krōt/ ▸*n.* **1** a native or national of Croatia, or a person of Croatian descent. **2** the South Slavic language of the Croats, almost identical to Serbian but written in the Roman alphabet. See SERBO-CROAT.
▸*adj.* of or relating to the Croats or their language.

Cro·a·tian /krōˈāSHən/ ▸*n. & adj.* another term for CROAT.

cro·chet /krōˈSHā/ ▸*n.* a handicraft in which yarn is made up into a patterned fabric by looping yarn with a hooked needle: [as *adj.*] *a crochet hook.* ■ fabric or items made in such a way: *the bikini is tiny, three triangles of cotton crochet.*
▸*v.* (**-cheted** /-ˈSHād/, **-chet·ing** /-ˈSHāiNG/) [*tr.*] make (a garment or piece of fabric) in such a way: *she had crocheted the shawl herself* | [*intr.*] *her mother had stopped crocheting.* —**cro·chet·er** /-ˈSHāər/ *n.*

crock¹ /kräk/ ▸*n.* **1** an earthenware pot or jar. ■ a broken piece of earthenware. **2** (also *vulgar slang* **crock of shit**) a thing that is considered to be complete nonsense.

crock² *inf.* ▸*n.* an old person who is feeble and useless.

crock·er·y /ˈkräkərē/ ▸*n.* plates, dishes, cups, and other similar items, esp. ones made of earthenware or china.

croc·o·dile /ˈkräkəˌdīl/ ▸*n.* a large predatory semiaquatic reptile (*Crocodylus* and two other genera) with long jaws, long tail, short legs, and a horny textured skin. ■ leather made from crocodile skin, used esp. to make bags and shoes. ▷Middle English *cocodrille, cokadrill,* from Old French *cocodrille,* via medieval Latin from Greek *krokodilos* 'worm of the stones,' from *krokē* 'pebble' + *drilos* 'worm.' —**croc·o·dil·i·an** /ˌkräkəˈdilēən/ *adj.*

croc·o·dile tears ▸*pl. n.* tears or expressions of sorrow that are insincere.

cro·cus /ˈkrōkəs/ ▸*n.* (*pl.* **crocuses** or **croci** /ˈkrōˌkī; -ˌsī/) a small, spring-flowering plant (genus *Crocus*) of the iris family that grows from a corm and bears bright yellow, purple, or white flowers.

crois·sant /k(r)wäˈsänt; -ˈsän/ ▸*n.* a French crescent-shaped roll made of flaky pastry, often eaten for breakfast.

Cro-Mag·non man /krō ˈmagnən; ˈmanyən/ ▸*n.* the earliest form of modern human in Europe. Their appearance *c.*35,000 years ago marked the beginning of the Upper Paleolithic and the apparent decline and disappearance of Neanderthal man.

crone /krōn/ ▸*n.* an old woman who is thin and ugly.

cro·ny /ˈkrōnē/ ▸*n.* (*pl.* **-nies**) *inf., often derog.* a close friend or companion: *he went gambling with his cronies.*

crook /krŏŏk/ ▸*n.* **1** the hooked staff of a shepherd. ■ a bishop's crozier. ■ a bend in something, esp. at the elbow in a person's arm: *her head was cradled in the crook of Luke's left arm.* ■ a piece of extra tubing that can be fitted to a brass instrument to lower the pitch by a set interval. ■ a metal tube on which the reed of some wind instruments (such as the bassoon) is set. **2** *inf.* a person who is dishonest or a criminal.
▸*v.* [*tr.*] bend (something, esp. a finger) as a signal.
▸*adj. inf.* (of a person or a part of the body) unwell or injured: *a crook knee.* —**crook·er·y** /ˈkrŏŏkərē/ *n.*

crook·ed /ˈkrŏŏkəd/ ▸*adj.* (**crook·ed·er, crook·ed·est**) bent or twisted out of shape or out of place: *his teeth were yellow and crooked.* ■ (of a smile or grin) with the mouth sloping down on one side; lopsided. ■ *inf.* dishonest; illegal. —**crook·ed·ly** *adv.* —**crook·ed·ness** *n.*

croon /krŏŏn/ ▸*v.* [*intr.*] hum or sing in a soft, low voice, esp. in a sentimental manner: *she was crooning to the child* | [*tr.*] *the female vocalist crooned smoky blues into the microphone.* ■ say in a soft, low voice: *"Goodbye, you lovely darling," she crooned.*
▸*n.* a soft, low voice or tone: *a gentle, highly expressive croon.* —**croon·er** *n.*

crop /kräp/ ▸*n.* **1** a cultivated plant that is grown as food, esp. a grain, fruit, or vegetable. ■ an amount of crops or their produce harvested at one time: *a heavy crop of fruit.* ■ an abundance of something, esp. a person's hair: *he had a thick crop of wiry hair.* ■ the total number of young farm animals born in a particular year on one farm. ■ a group of related people or things appearing or occurring at one time: *the current crop of politicians.* **2** a hairstyle in which the hair is cut very short. **3** short for RIDING CROP. **4** a pouch in a bird's gullet where food is stored or prepared for digestion. ■ a similar organ in an insect or earthworm.
▸*v.* (**cropped, crop·ping**) [*tr.*] **1** cut (something, esp. a person's hair) very short: [as *adj.*] (**cropped**) *cropped blond hair.* ■ (of an animal) bite off and eat the tops of (plants). ■ cut the edges of (a photograph) in order to produce a better picture or to fit a given space. **2** (often **be cropped**) harvest (plants or their produce) from a particular area. ■ sow or plant (land) with plants that will produce food or fodder, esp. on a large commercial scale.
▸*phrasal v.* ☐ **crop out** (of rock) appear or be exposed at the surface of the earth. ☐ **crop up** appear, occur, or come to one's notice unexpectedly: *some urgent business had cropped up.*

crop dust·ing ▸*n.* the spraying of powdered or liquid insecticide or fertilizer on crops, esp. from the air.

crop·per /ˈkräpər/ ▸*n.* **1** a plant that yields a crop of a specified kind or in a specified way: *the white-fleshed varieties are the heaviest croppers.* **2** a machine or person that cuts or trims something, such as wool off a sheep or the pile of a carpet during manufacture.
▸ ☐ **come a cropper** *inf.* fall heavily. ■ suffer a defeat or disaster.

crop ro·ta·tion ▸*n.* see ROTATION.

cro·quet /krōˈkā/ ▸*n.* a game played on a lawn, in which colored wooden balls are driven through a series of wickets by means of mallets: [as *adj.*] *a croquet lawn.* ■ an act of croqueting a ball.
▸*v.* (**-queted** /-ˈkād/, **-quet·ing** /-ˈkāiNG/) [*tr.*] drive away (an opponent's ball) by holding one's own ball against it and striking this with the mallet.

cro·quette /krōˈket/ ▸*n.* a small roll of chopped vegetables, meat, or fish, fried in breadcrumbs: *a potato croquette.*

cro·sier /ˈkrōZHər/ ▸*n.* variant spelling of CROZIER.

cross /krôs/ ▸*n.* **1** a mark, object, or figure formed by two short intersecting lines or pieces (+ or ×). ■ a mark of this type (×) made to represent a signature by a person who cannot write. ■ a mark of this type (×) used to show that something is incorrect or unsatisfactory. ■ an upright post with a transverse bar, as used in antiquity for crucifixion. ■ (**the Cross**) the cross on which Jesus was crucified. ■ this, or a representation of it, as an emblem of Christianity. ■ *fig.* a thing that is unavoidable and has to be endured: *she's just a cross we have to bear.* ■ short for SIGN OF THE CROSS (see SIGN). ■ a staff surmounted by a cross carried in religious processions. ■ a cross-shaped decoration awarded for

personal valor or indicating rank in some orders of knighthood: *the Military Cross.* **3** an animal or plant resulting from crossbreeding; a hybrid: *a Devon and Holstein cross.* ■ (**a cross between**) a mixture or compromise of two things: *a cross between a monorail and a conventional railroad.* **4** a sideways or transverse movement or pass, in particular: ■ *Soccer* a pass of the ball across the field toward the center close to one's opponents' goal. ■ *Boxing* a blow delivered across and over the opponent's lead.
▶*v.* [*tr.*] **1** go or extend across or to the other side of (a path, road, stretch of water, or area): *he has crossed the Atlantic twice* | *fig. a shadow of apprehension crossed her face* | [*intr.*] *we crossed over the bridge.* ■ go across or climb over (an obstacle or boundary): *he attempted to cross the border into Jordan* | [*intr.*] *we crossed over a fence.* ■ [*intr.*] (**cross over**) (esp. of an artist or an artistic style or work) begin to appeal to a different audience, esp. a wider one. **2** [*intr.*] pass in an opposite or different direction; intersect: *the two lines cross at 90°.* ■ [*tr.*] cause (two things) to intersect. ■ [*tr.*] place (something) crosswise: *Michele sat back and crossed her arms.* ■ (of a letter) be sent before receipt of another from the person being written to: *our letters crossed.* **3** draw a line or lines across; mark with a cross: *cross the t's.* ■ (**cross someone/something off**) delete a name or item on a list as being no longer required or involved. ■ (**cross something out**) delete an incorrect or inapplicable word or phrase by drawing a line through it. **4** (**cross oneself**) (of a person) make the sign of the cross in front of one's chest as a sign of Christian reverence or to invoke divine protection. **5** *Soccer* pass (the ball) across the field toward the center when attacking. **6** cause (an animal of one species, breed, or variety) to interbreed with one of another species, breed, or variety. ■ cross-fertilize (a plant): *this new rose was crossed with a hybrid tea rose.* **7** oppose or stand in the way of (someone): *no one dared cross him.*
▶*adj.* annoyed. —**cross·er** *n.* —**cross·ly** *adv.* —**cross·ness** *n.*
▶ □ **at cross purposes** misunderstanding or having different aims from one another: *we had been talking at cross purposes.* □ **cross one's fingers** (or **keep one's fingers crossed**) put one finger across another as a sign of hoping for good luck. ■ hope that someone or something will be successful. □ **cross one's mind** (of a thought) occur to one, esp. transiently: *it never crossed my mind to leave the tent and live in a house.* □ **cross someone's path** meet or encounter someone.
cross·bar /ˈkrôsˌbär/ ▶*n.* a horizontal bar fixed across another bar or between two upright bars, in particular: ■ (in sports) the bar between the two upright posts of a goal. ■ the horizontal metal bar between the handlebars and saddle on a man's or boy's bicycle.
cross·bill /ˈkrôsˌbil/ ▶*n.* a thickset finch (genus *Loxia*) with a crossed bill adapted for extracting seeds from the cones of conifers.
cross·bones /ˈkrôsˌbōnz/ ▶*n.* see SKULL AND CROSSBONES at SKULL.
cross·bow /ˈkrôsˌbō/ ▶*n.* a medieval bow of a kind that is fixed across a wooden support and has a groove for the bolt and a mechanism for drawing and releasing the string. —**cross·bow·man** /-ˌbōmən/ *n.* (*pl.* -men).
cross·breed /ˈkrôsˌbrēd/ ▶*n.* an animal or plant produced by mating or hybridizing two different species, breeds, or varieties.
▶*v.* [*tr.*] produce (an animal or plant) in this way. ■ hybridize (a breed, species, or variety) with another. ■ [*intr.*] (of an animal or plant) breed with a different breed, species, or variety.
cross·check ▶*v.* [*tr.*] **1** verify (figures or information) by using an alternative source or method: *always try to cross-check your bearings* | [as *n.*] (**cross-checking**) *no cross-checking has been done.* **2** *Ice Hockey* obstruct (an opponent) illegally with the stick held horizontally in both hands.
▶*n.* **1** an instance of verifying something by using an alternative source or method. **2** *Ice Hockey* an illegal obstruction using the stick held horizontally in both hands.
cross·claim ▶*Law* a claim brought by one defendant against another in the same proceeding.
cross·con·tam·i·na·tion ▶*n.* the process by which bacteria or other microorganisms are unintentionally transferred from one substance or object to another, with harmful effect. —**cross-con·tam·i·nate** *v.*
cross·coun·try ▶*adj.* **1** across fields or countryside, as opposed to on roads or tracks: *cross-country walking.* ■ of, relating to, or denoting the sport of running, riding, or driving along a course in the countryside, as opposed to around a track. ■ of, relating to, or denoting skiing over relatively flat or mountainous terrain, as opposed to skiing only downhill. **2** across a region or country, in particular: ■ not keeping to main or direct roads, routes, or railroad lines: *cross-country hiker* | [as *adv.*] *if you are traveling cross-country, choose where you walk with care.* ■ traveling to many different parts of a country: *a whirlwind cross-country tour.*

▶*n.* a cross-country race or competition. ■ the sport of cross-country running, riding, skiing, or driving.
cross·dress ▶*v.* [*intr.*] wear clothing typical of the opposite sex. —**cross-dress·er** *n.*
crosse /krôs/ ▶*n.* the stick used in lacrosse.
cross·ex·am·ine ▶*v.* [*tr.*] question (a witness called by the other party) in a court of law to discredit or undercut testimony already given. ■ question (someone) aggressively or in great detail. —**cross-ex·am·i·na·tion** *n.* —**cross-ex·am·in·er** *n.*
cross·eyed ▶*adj.* having one or both eyes turned inward toward the nose, either from focusing on something very close, through temporary loss of control of focus, or as a permanent condition (convergent strabismus).
cross·fer·ti·lize ▶*v.* [*tr.*] fertilize (a plant) using pollen from another plant of the same species. ■ [*intr.*] (of two plants) fertilize each other. ■ *fig.* stimulate the development of (something) with an exchange of ideas or information. —**cross-fer·ti·li·za·tion** *n.*
cross·fire /ˈkrôsˌfīr/ ▶*n.* gunfire from two or more directions passing through the same area, often killing or wounding noncombatants. ■ *fig.* used to refer to a situation in which two or more groups are attacking or arguing with each other.
cross·hairs /ˈkrôsˌhe(ə)rz/ ▶*pl. n.* a pair of fine wires or lines crossing at right angles at the focus of an optical instrument or gun sight, for use in positioning, aiming, or measuring.
cross·hatch /ˈkrôsˌhaCH/ ▶*v.* [*tr.*] [often as *n.*] (**crosshatching**) (in drawing or graphics) shade (an area) with intersecting sets of parallel lines.
cross·ing /ˈkrôsiNG/ ▶*n.* **1** a place where two roads, two railroad lines, or a road and a railroad line cross. ■ the action of moving across or over something. ■ a journey across water in a ship. ■ a place at which one may safely cross something, esp. a street. ■ a place at which one can cross a border between countries. ■ *Archit.* the intersection of a church nave and the transepts. **2** crossbreeding.
cross·leg·ged /ˈleg(ə)d/ ▶*adj.* & *adv.* (of a seated person) with the legs crossed at the ankles and the knees bent outward.
cross·match /ˈkrôsˌmaCH/ *Med.* ▶*v.* [*tr.*] [often as *n.*] (**crossmatching**) test the compatibility of (a donor's and a recipient's blood or tissue).
▶*n.* an instance of such testing.
cross·o·ver /ˈkrôsˌōvər/ ▶*n.* **1** a point or place of crossing from one side to the other. **2** the process of achieving success in a different field or style, esp. in popular music: [as *adj.*] *a jazz-classical crossover album.* **3** a person who votes for a candidate in a different political party than the one they usually support: [as *adj.*] *crossover votes.* **4** [as *adj.*] relating to or denoting trials of medical treatment in which experimental subjects and control groups are exchanged after a set period: *a crossover study.*
cross·piece /ˈkrôsˌpēs/ ▶*n.* a beam or bar fixed or placed across something else.
cross·pol·li·nate ▶*v.* [*tr.*] pollinate (a flower or plant) with pollen from another flower or plant. —**cross-pol·li·na·tion** *n.*
cross·post (also **cross·post**) *Comput.* ▶*v.* [*tr.*] post a single message to multiple Internet newsgroups or reading lists. ■ repost (a message appearing on one list or newsgroup) to another.
▶*n.* a message posted to more than one newsgroup or reading list.
cross·ques·tion ▶*v.* [*tr.*] question (someone) in great detail; cross-examine: *it seemed ungrateful to cross-question him* | [as *n.*] (**cross-questioning**) *the cross-questioning of Lopez.*
cross·rate ▶*n.* *Finance* an exchange rate between two currencies computed by reference to a third currency, usually the U.S. dollar.
cross ref·er·ence ▶*n.* a reference to another text or part of a text, typically given in order to elaborate on a point.
▶*v.* [*tr.*] (usu. **be cross-referenced**) provide with cross references to another text or part of a text: *entries are fully cross-referenced.*
cross·roads /ˈkrôsˌrōdz/ ▶*n.* an intersection of two or more roads. ■ a point at which a crucial decision must be made that will have far-reaching consequences: *we stand again at a historic crossroads.* ■ (**crossroad**) a road that crosses a main road or joins two main roads.
cross sec·tion ▶*n.* a surface or shape that is or would be exposed by making a straight cut through something, esp. at right angles to an axis. ■ a thin strip of organic tissue or other material removed by making two such cuts. ■ a diagram representing what such a cut would reveal. ■ a typical or representative sample of a larger group, esp. of

---

Pronunciation Key ə *ago, up*; ər *over, fur*; a *hat*; ā *ate*; ä *car*; CH *chin*; e *let*; ē *see*; e(ə)r *air*; i *fit*; ī *by*; i(ə)r *ear*; NG *sing*; ō *go*; ô *law, for*; oi *toy*; ŏŏ *good*; ōō *goo*; ou *out*; SH *she*; TH *thin*; ͟TH *then*; (h)w *why*; ZH *vision*

people. ■ *Physics* a quantity having the dimensions of an area which expresses the probability of a given interaction between particles.

▶ *v.* (**cross-sec·tion**) [*tr.*] make a cross section of (something): [as *n.*] (**cross-sectioning**) *complex triangular terrain models for contour cross-sectioning*. —**cross-sec·tion·al** *adj.*

cross-stitch *Needlework* ▶*n.* a stitch formed of two stitches crossing each other. ■ needlework done using such stitches.

▶ *v.* [*tr.*] sew or embroider using such stitches.

cross-walk /'krôs,wôk/ ▶*n.* a marked part of a road where pedestrians have right of way to cross.

cross-ways /'krôs,wāz/ ▶*adv.* another term for CROSSWISE.

cross-wind /'krôs,wind/ ▶*n.* a wind blowing across one's direction of travel.

cross-wise /'krôs,wīz/ ▶*adv.* in the form of a cross. ■ diagonally; transversely.

cross-word /'krôswərd/ (also **cross-word puz·zle**) ▶*n.* a puzzle consisting of a grid of squares and blanks into which words crossing vertically and horizontally are written according to clues. ▷said to have been invented by the journalist Arthur Wynne, whose puzzle (called a "word-cross") appeared in a Sunday newspaper, the *New York World*, on December 21, 1913.

crotch /krächʹ/ ▶*n.* the part of the human body between the legs where they join the torso. ■ the part of a garment that passes between the legs. ■ a fork in a tree, road, or river.

crotch·et·y /'krächətē/ ▶*adj.* irritable. —**crotch·et·i·ness** *n.*

cro·ton /'krōtn/ ▶*n.* **1** a strong-scented tree, shrub, or herbaceous plant (genus *Croton*) of the spurge family, native to tropical and warm regions. Its numerous species include *C. laccifer*, the host plant for the lac insect. **2** a small Indo-Pacific evergreen tree or shrub (genus *Codiaeum*) of the spurge family, grown for its colorful ornamental foliage.

crouch /krouCH/ ▶*v.* [*intr.*] adopt a position where the knees are bent and the upper body is brought forward and down, sometimes to avoid detection or to defend oneself.

▶*n.* a crouching stance or posture.

croup[1] /krōōp/ ▶*n.* inflammation of the larynx and trachea in children, causing breathing difficulties. —**croup·y** *adj.*

croup[2] ▶*n.* the rump or hindquarters, esp. of a horse.

croup·i·er /'krōōpē,ā; -pēər/ ▶*n.* **1** the person in charge of a gaming table, gathering in and paying out money or tokens. **2** *hist.* the assistant chairman at a public dinner, seated at the lower end of the table.

crou·ton /'krōō,tän; krōō'tän/ ▶*n.* a small piece of fried or toasted bread served with soup or used as a garnish.

Crow /krō/ ▶*n.* (*pl.* same or **Crows**) **1** a member of an American Indian people inhabiting eastern Montana. **2** the Siouan language of this people.

▶*adj.* of or relating to this people or their language.

crow[1] /krō/ ▶*n.* a large perching bird (genus *Corvus*) with mostly glossy black plumage, a heavy bill, and a raucous voice. The **crow family** (Corvidae) also includes the ravens, jays, and magpies.

▶ □ **as the crow flies** in a straight line. □ **eat crow** *inf.* be humiliated by having to admit one's defeats or mistakes.

crow[2] ▶*v.* (*past* **crowed** or *Brit.* **crew** /krōō/) [*intr.*] (of a cock) utter its characteristic loud cry. ■ (of a person) make a sound expressing a feeling of happiness or triumph. ■ say something in a tone of gloating satisfaction: *avoid crowing about your success.*

▶*n.* the cry of a cock. ■ a sound made by a person expressing triumph or happiness: *she gave a little crow of triumph.*

crow·bar /'krō,bär/ ▶*n.* an iron bar with a flattened end, used as a lever.

crowd /kroud/ ▶*n.* a large number of people gathered together, typically in a disorganized or unruly way. ■ an audience. ■ *inf., often derog.* a group of people who are linked by a common interest or activity: *I've broken away from that whole junkie crowd.* ■ (**the crowd**) the mass or multitude of people, esp. those considered to be drearily ordinary or anonymous. ■ a large number of things regarded collectively: *the crowd of tall buildings.*

▶ *v.* [*tr.*] (often **be crowded**) (of a number of people) fill (a space) almost completely, leaving little or no room for movement. ■ [*intr.*] (**crowd into**) (of a number of people) move into (a space, esp. one that seems too small). ■ [*intr.*] (**crowd around**) (of a group of people) form a tightly packed mass around (someone or something). ■ move too close to (someone), either aggressively or in a way that causes discomfort or harm. ■ (**crowd someone/something out**) exclude someone or something by taking their place: *grass invading the canyon has crowded out native plants.* ■ *Baseball* (of a batter) stand very close to (the plate) when

batting. ▷Old English *crūdan* 'press, hasten,' of Germanic origin; related to Dutch *kruien* 'push in a wheelbarrow.' In Middle English the senses 'move by pushing' and 'push one's way' arose, leading to the sense 'congregate,' and hence (mid 16th cent.) to the noun. —**crowd·ed·ness** *n.*

crowd-pleas·er ▶*n.* a person or thing with great popular appeal. —**crowd-pleas·ing** *adj.*

crow·foot /'krō,fŏŏt/ ▶*n.* a plant (genus *Ranunculus*) of the buttercup family, typically having lobed or divided leaves and white or yellow flowers. Many kinds are aquatic with flowers held above the water.

crown /kroun/ ▶*n.* **1** a circular ornamental headdress worn by a monarch as a symbol of authority, usually made of or decorated with precious metals and jewels. ■ (**the Crown**) the reigning monarch, representing a country's government. ■ (usu. **the Crown**) the power or authority residing in the monarchy. ■ an ornament, emblem, or badge shaped like a crown. ■ a wreath of leaves or flowers, esp. that worn as an emblem of victory in ancient Greece or Rome. ■ an award or distinction gained by a victory or achievement, esp. in sports: *the world heavyweight crown.* **2** the top or highest part of something: *the crown of the hill.* ■ the top part of a person's head or a hat. ■ the part of a plant just above and below the ground from which the roots and shoots branch out. ■ the upper branching or spreading part of a tree or other plant. ■ the upper part of a cut gem, above the girdle. ■ the part of a tooth projecting from the gum. ■ an artificial replacement or covering for the upper part of a tooth. ■ the point of an anchor at which the arms reach the shaft. **3** (also **crown piece**) a British coin with a face value of five shillings or 25 pence, now minted only for commemorative purposes. ■ a foreign coin with a name meaning 'crown,' esp. the krona or krone. **4** (in full **metric crown**) a paper size, now standardized at 384 × 504 mm. ■ (in full **crown octavo**) a book size, now standardized at 186 × 123 mm. ■ (in full **crown quarto**) a book size, now standardized at 246 × 189 mm.

▶*v.* [*tr.*] **1** (usu. **be crowned**) ceremonially place a crown on the head of (someone) in order to invest them as a monarch. ■ declare or acknowledge (someone) as the best, esp. at a sport: *he was crowned world champion.* ■ (in checkers) promote (a piece) to king by placing another on top of it. ■ rest on or form the top of: *the distant knoll was crowned with trees.* ■ fit a crown to (a tooth). ■ *inf.* hit on the head. **2** be the triumphant culmination of (an effort or endeavor, esp. a prolonged one): *years of struggle were crowned by a state visit to Paris.* **3** [*intr.*] (of a baby's head during labor) fully appear in the vaginal opening prior to emerging.

▶ □ **crowning glory** the best and most notable aspect of something.

crown jew·els ▶*pl. n.* the crown and other ornaments and jewelry worn or carried by the sovereign on certain state occasions. ■ (**crown jewel**) a prized asset, achievement, or person.

crown prince ▶*n.* (in some countries) a male heir to a throne.

crown prin·cess ▶*n.* the wife of a crown prince. ■ (in some countries) a female heir to a throne.

crow's-foot ▶*n.* (*pl.* **-feet**) **1** (usu. **crow's-feet**) a branching wrinkle at the outer corner of a person's eye. **2** a mark, symbol, or design formed of lines diverging from a point, resembling a bird's footprint.

crow's-nest ▶*n.* a shelter or platform fixed near the top of the mast of a vessel as a place for a lookout to stand.

cro·zier /'krōzhər/ (also **cro·sier**) ▶*n.* a hooked staff carried by a bishop as a symbol of pastoral office.

cru·ces /'krōō,sēz/ ▶ plural form of CRUX.

cru·cial /'krōōshəl/ ▶*adj.* decisive or critical, esp. in the success or failure of something: *negotiations were at a crucial stage.* ■ of great importance: *this game is crucial to our survival.* ▷early 18th cent. (in the sense 'cross-shaped'): from French, from Latin *crux, cruc-* 'cross.' The sense 'decisive' is from Francis Bacon's Latin phrase *instantia crucis* 'crucial instance,' which he explained as a metaphor from a *crux* or signpost marking a fork at a crossroad; Newton and Boyle took up the metaphor in *experimentum crucis* 'crucial experiment.' —**cru·ci·al·i·ty** /,krōōshē'alitē/ *n.* —**cru·cial·ly** *adv.*

cru·ci·ble /'krōōsəbəl/ ▶*n.* a ceramic or metal container in which metals or other substances may be melted or subjected to very high temperatures. ■ a place or occasion of severe test or trial. ■ a place or situation in which different elements interact to produce something new.

cru·cif·er·ous /krōō'sifərəs/ ▶*adj. Bot.* of, relating to, or denoting plants of the cabbage family (Brassicaceae, formerly Cruciferae).

cru·ci·fix /'krōōsə,fiks/ ▶*n.* a representation of a cross with a figure of Jesus Christ on it.

cru·ci·fix·ion /,krōōsə'fikSHən/ ▶*n. chiefly hist.* the execution of a person by nailing or binding them to a cross. ■ **(the Crucifixion)** the killing of Jesus Christ in such a way. ■ **(Crucifixion)** an artistic representation or musical composition based on this event.

cru·ci·form /'krōōsə,fôrm/ ▶adj. having the shape of a cross: *a cruciform sword.* ■ of or denoting a church having a cross-shaped plan with a nave and transepts.
▶n. a thing shaped like a cross.

cru·ci·fy /'krōōsə,fī/ ▶v. (**-fies, -fied**) [tr.] (often **be crucified**) *chiefly hist.* put (someone) to death by nailing or binding them to a cross. ■ criticize (someone) severely and unrelentingly. ■ cause anguish to (someone). —**cru·ci·fi·er** n.

crud /krəd/ ▶n. *inf.* a substance that is disgusting or unpleasant, typically because of its dirtiness. ■ nonsense. ■ a contemptible person. —**crud·dy** /'krədē/ adj.

crude /krōōd/ ▶adj. **1** in a natural or raw state; not yet processed or refined: *crude oil.* ■ *Statistics* (of figures) not adjusted or corrected: *the crude mortality rate.* ■ (of an estimate or guess) likely to be only approximately accurate. **2** constructed in a rudimentary or makeshift way. ■ (of an action) showing little finesse or subtlety and as a result unlikely to succeed. **3** (of language, behavior, or a person) offensively coarse or rude, esp. in relation to sexual matters.
▶n. natural petroleum. —**crude·ly** adv. —**crude·ness** n. —**cru·di·ty** /'krōōditē/ n.

cru·di·tés /,krōōdə'tā/ ▶pl. n. assorted raw vegetables served as an hors d'oeuvre, typically with a sauce into which they may be dipped.

cru·el /'krōōəl/ ▶adj. (**-el·er, -el·est**; *Brit.* **-el·ler, -el·lest**) causing pain or suffering: *people who are cruel to animals.* ■ having or showing a sadistic disregard for the pain or suffering of others: *a cruel face.* —**cru·el·ly** adv.

cru·el·ty /'krōōəltē/ ▶n. (pl. **-ties**) callous indifference to or pleasure in causing pain and suffering. ■ behavior that causes pain or suffering to a person or animal. ■ *Law* behavior that causes physical or mental harm to another, esp. a spouse, whether intentionally or not.

cru·el·ty-free ▶adj. (of cosmetics or other commercial products) manufactured or developed by methods that do not involve experimentation on animals.

cru·et /'krōōit/ ▶n. a small container for salt, pepper, oil, or vinegar for use at a dining table.

cruise /krōōz/ ▶v. [intr.] sail about in an area without a precise destination, esp. for pleasure: *they were cruising off the California coast* | [tr.] *she cruised the canals of France.* ■ take a vacation on a ship or boat following a predetermined course, usually calling in at several ports. ■ (of a vehicle or person) travel or move slowly around without a specific destination in mind: *a police van cruised past us* | [tr.] *aimlessly cruising the mall.* ■ (of a motor vehicle or aircraft) travel smoothly at a moderate or economical speed. ■ achieve an objective with ease, esp. in sports: *he cruised to an easy victory.* ■ [tr.] *inf.* wander or move slowly around in search of a sexual partner. ■ [tr.] *inf.* attempt to pick up (a sexual partner).
▶n. a voyage on a ship or boat taken for pleasure or as a holiday and usually calling in at several places: *a cruise down the Nile* | [as adj.] *a cruise liner.*

cruise con·trol ▶n. an electronic device in a motor vehicle that can be switched on to maintain a selected constant speed without the use of the accelerator.

cruise mis·sile ▶n. a low-flying missile that is guided to its target by an on-board computer.

cruis·er /'krōōzər/ ▶n. **1** a relatively fast warship larger than a destroyer and less heavily armed than a battleship. **2** a yacht or motorboat with passenger accommodations, designed for leisure use. ■ a person who goes on a pleasure cruise. **3** an automobile that can be driven smoothly at high speed. ■ a police patrol car.

crumb /krəm/ ▶n. **1** a small fragment of bread, cake, or cracker. ■ a very small amount of something. ■ the soft inner part of a loaf of bread. ■ a dessert topping made of brown sugar, butter, flour, and spices and crumbled over a pie or cake: [as adj.] *apple crumb pie.* ■ (usu. **crumb rub·ber**) granulated rubber, made from recycled tires. **2** *inf.* an objectionable or contemptible person.
▶v. [tr.] cover (food) with breadcrumbs.

crum·ble /'krəmbəl/ ▶v. [intr.] break or fall apart into small fragments, esp. over a period of time as part of a process of deterioration: *the plaster started to crumble.* ■ [tr.] cause (something) to break apart into small fragments. ■ (of an organization, relationship, or structure) disintegrate gradually over a period of time.
▶n. *Brit.* a mixture of flour and butter that is rubbed to the texture of breadcrumbs and cooked as a topping for fruit. ■ a dessert made with such a topping and a particular fruit: *rhubarb crumble.*

crum·bly /'krəmblē/ ▶adj. (**-bli·er, -bli·est**) consisting of or easily breaking into small fragments: *the cheese is crumbly.* —**crum·bli·ness** n.

crumb·y /'krəmē/ ▶adj. (**crumb·i·er, crumb·i·est**) **1** like or covered in crumbs. **2** variant spelling of CRUMMY.

crum·horn ▶n. variant spelling of KRUMMHORN.

crum·my /'krəmē/ (also **crumb·y**) *inf.* ▶adj. (**-mi·er, -mi·est**) dirty, unpleasant, or of poor quality: *a crummy little room.* ■ unwell; ill. —**crum·mi·ly** /'krəməlē/ adv. —**crum·mi·ness** n.

crum·pet /'krəmpət/ ▶n. *chiefly Brit.* a thick, flat, savory cake with a porous texture, made from a yeast mixture cooked on a griddle and eaten toasted.

crum·ple /'krəmpəl/ ▶v. [tr.] crush (something, typically paper or cloth) so that it becomes creased and wrinkled. ■ [intr.] become bent, crooked, or creased: *they heard the jetliner crumple moments before it crashed.* ■ [intr.] (of a person) suddenly flop down to the ground so that their body appears bent or broken. ■ [intr.] (of a person's face) suddenly sag and show an expression of desolation. ■ [intr.] suddenly lose force or effectiveness: *her composure crumpled.*
▶n. a crushed fold, crease, or wrinkle. —**crum·ply** /'krəmp(ə)lē/ adj.

crunch /krənCH/ ▶v. [tr.] **1** crush (a hard or brittle foodstuff) with the teeth, making a loud but muffled grinding sound. ■ [intr.] make such a sound, esp. when walking or driving over gravel or an icy surface. ■ strike or crush noisily: *two drivers who had just crunched fenders.* **2** process (large amounts of information) or perform (operations of great complexity), esp. by computer: *computers crunch data from real-world observations.*
▶n. **1** a loud muffled grinding sound made when crushing, moving over, or hitting something. **2** (**the crunch**) *inf.* a crucial point or situation, typically one at which a decision with important consequences must be made: *when it comes to the crunch, you chicken out.* ■ a severe shortage of money or credit: *easing America's credit crunch.* **3** a physical exercise designed to strengthen the abdominal muscles; a sit-up.

crunch·y /'krənCHē/ ▶adj. (**crunch·i·er, crunch·i·est**) **1** making a sharp noise when bitten or crushed and (of food) pleasantly crisp: *bake until the topping is crunchy.* **2** *inf.* politically and environmentally liberal. —**crunch·i·ly** /-CHəlē/ adv. —**crunch·i·ness** n.

cru·sade /krōō'sād/ ▶n. (often **Cru·sade**) a medieval military expedition, one of a series made by Europeans to recover the Holy Land from the Muslims in the 11th, 12th, and 13th centuries. ■ a war instigated by the Church for alleged religious ends. ■ an organized campaign concerning a political, social, or religious issue, typically motivated by a fervent desire for change: *a crusade against crime.*
▶v. [intr.] lead or take part in an energetic and organized campaign concerning a social, political, or religious issue. ▷late 16th cent. (originally as *croisade*): from French *croisade*, an alteration (influenced by Spanish *cruzado*) of earlier *croisée*, literally 'the state of being marked with the cross,' based on Latin *crux, cruc-* 'cross'; in the 17th cent. the form *crusado*, from Spanish *cruzado*, was introduced; the blending of these two forms led to the current spelling, first recorded in the early 18th cent. —**cru·sad·er** n.

crush /krəSH/ ▶v. [tr.] press or squeeze (someone or something) with force or violence, typically causing serious damage or injury. ■ reduce (something) to a powder or pulp by exerting strong pressure on it. ■ crease or crumple (cloth or paper). ■ (of a government or state) violently subdue (opposition or a rebellion). ■ bring about a feeling of overwhelming disappointment or embarrassment in (someone).
▶n. **1** a crowd of people pressed closely together, esp. in an enclosed space. **2** *inf.* a brief but intense infatuation for someone, esp. someone unattainable or inappropriate: *she did have a crush on Dr. Russell.* **3** a drink made from the juice of pressed fruit: *lemon crush.* —**crush·a·ble** adj. —**crush·er** n. —**crush·ing·ly** adv.

crust /krəst/ ▶n. the crisp outer part of a loaf of bread. ■ a hard, dry scrap of bread: *a kindly old woman might give her a crust.* ■ a slice of bread from the end of the loaf. ■ a layer of pastry covering a pie. ■ a hardened layer, coating, or deposit on the surface of something, esp. something soft: *a crust of snow.* ■ the outermost layer of rock of which a planet consists, esp. the part of the earth above the mantle. ■ a deposit of tartrates and other substances formed in wine aged in the bottle, esp. port.
▶v. [intr.] form into a hard outer layer: *the blisters eventually crust over.* ■ [tr.] cover with a hard outer layer. —**crus·tal** /'krəstəl/ adj.

Pronunciation Key ə *ago*, *up*; ər *over*, *fur*; a *hat*; ā *ate*; ä *car*; CH *chin*; e *let*; ē *see*; e(ə)r *air*; i *fit*; ī *by*; i(ə)r *ear*; NG *sing*; ō *go*; ô *law, for*; oi *toy*; ōō *good*; ōō *goo*; ou *out*; SH *she*; TH *thin*; TH *then*; (h)w *why*; ZH *vision*

crus·ta·cean /krəˈstāsʜən/ ▶ *n.* any arthropod of the group including crabs, lobsters, and shrimps, having a hard shell and usu. aquatic. ▶ *adj.* of or related to the crustaceans.

crust·y /ˈkrəstē/ ▶ *adj.* (**crust·i·er**, **crust·i·est**) **1** having a crisp or hard outer layer or covering: *crusty bread*. ■ (of a substance) acting as a hard outer layer or covering: *Lake Manyara was ringed by crusty salt deposits*. **2** (esp. of an old person) outspoken and irritable: *a crusty old grandfather*. —**crust·i·ly** /ˈkrəstəlē/ *adv.* —**crust·i·ness** *n.*

crutch /krəcʜ/ ▶ *n.* **1** a long stick with a crosspiece at the top, used as a support under the armpit by a lame person. ■ *fig.* a thing used for support or reassurance: *they use the Internet as a crutch for their loneliness*. **2** *archaic* another term for CROTCH (of the body or a garment). ▶ *v.* [*intr.*] move by means of or as if by means of crutches.

crux /krəks; krо̄о̄ks/ ▶ *n.* (*pl.* **crux·es** or **cru·ces** /ˈkrо̄о̄ˌsēz/) (**the crux**) the decisive or most important point at issue: *the crux of the matter is that attitudes have changed*. ■ a particular point of difficulty.

cry /krī/ ▶ *v.* (**cries**, **cried**) [*intr.*] shed tears, esp. as an expression of distress or pain: *don't cry—it'll be all right* | [*tr.*] *you'll cry tears of joy*. ■ shout or scream, esp. to express one's fear, pain, or grief: *the little girl fell down and cried for her mommy*. ■ say something in an excited or anguished tone of voice: *"Where will it end?" he cried out*. ■ (**cry out for**) *fig.* demand as a self-evident requirement or solution: *the present system cries out for reform*. ■ (of a bird or other animal) make a loud characteristic call. ■ [*tr.*] (of a hawker) proclaim (wares) for sale in the street. ▶ *n.* (*pl.* **cries**) a spell of weeping. ■ a loud inarticulate shout or scream expressing a powerful feeling or emotion: *a cry of despair*. ■ a distinctive call of a bird or other animal. ■ a loud excited utterance of a word or words: *there was a cry of "Silence!"* ■ the call of a hawker selling wares on the street. ■ an urgent appeal or entreaty. ■ a demand or opinion expressed by many people: *peace became the popular cry*.
▶ □ **cry one's eyes** (or **heart**) **out** weep bitterly and at length. □ **for crying out loud** *inf.* used to express one's irritation or impatience: *why do you have to take everything so personally, for crying out loud?*

cry·ba·by /ˈkrīˌbābē/ ▶ *n.* (*pl.* **-bies**) a person, esp. a child, who sheds tears frequently or readily.

cry·er /ˈkrīər/ ▶ *n.* archaic spelling of CRIER.

cry·ing /ˈkrī-ɪNG/ ▶ *adj.* very great: *it would be a crying shame to let some other woman have it*.

cry·o·gen·ics /ˌkrīəˈjeniks/ ▶ *pl. n.* [treated as *sing.*] the branch of physics dealing with the production and effects of very low temperatures. ■ another term for CRYONICS. —**cry·o·gen·ic** *adj.* —**cry·o·gen·i·cal·ly** /-ik(ə)lē/ *adv.*

cry·on·ics /krīˈäniks/ ▶ *pl. n.* [treated as *sing.*] the practice or technique of deep-freezing the bodies of those who have died of an incurable disease, in the hope of a future cure. —**cry·on·ic** *adj.*

crypt /kript/ ▶ *n.* an underground room or vault beneath a church, used as a chapel or burial place.

cryp·tic /ˈkriptik/ ▶ *adj.* **1** having a meaning that is mysterious or obscure. ■ (of a crossword) having difficult clues that indicate the solutions indirectly. **2** *Zool.* (of coloration or markings) serving to camouflage an animal. —**cryp·ti·cal·ly** /-(ə)lē/ *adv.*

cryp·to /ˈkriptō/ ▶ *n.* **1** short for CRYPTOGRAPHY. **2** (*pl.* **-tos**) *inf.* a person having a secret allegiance to a political creed, esp. communism.

cryp·to·gram /ˈkriptəˌgram/ ▶ *n.* **1** a text written in code. **2** a symbol or figure with secret or occult significance.

cryp·tog·ra·phy /kripˈtägrəfē/ ▶ *n.* the art of writing or solving codes. —**cryp·tog·ra·pher** /-fər/ *n.* —**cryp·to·graph·ic** /ˌkriptəˈgrafik/ *adj.* —**cryp·to·graph·i·cal·ly** /ˌkriptəˈgrafik(ə)lē/ *adv.*

crys·tal /ˈkristl/ ▶ *n.* **1** a piece of a homogeneous solid substance having a natural geometrically regular form with symmetrically arranged plane faces. ■ *Chem.* any solid consisting of a symmetrical, ordered, three-dimensional aggregation of atoms or molecules. ■ *Electr.* a crystalline piece of semiconductor used as an oscillator or transducer. ■ a clear transparent mineral, esp. quartz. ■ a piece of crystalline substance believed to have healing powers. ■ *inf.* short for CRYSTAL METH. **2** (also **crystal glass**) highly transparent glass with a high refractive index: [as *adj.*] *a crystal chandelier*. ■ articles made of such glass: *a collection of crystal*. ■ the glass over a watch face.
▶ *adj.* clear and transparent like crystal: *the clean crystal waters of the lake*.
▶ □ **crystal clear** completely transparent and unclouded. ■ unambiguous; easily understood: *the house rules are crystal clear*.

crys·tal ball ▶ *n.* a solid globe of glass or rock crystal, used by fortune-tellers and clairvoyants for crystal-gazing.

crys·tal-gaz·ing ▶ *n.* looking intently into a crystal ball with the aim of seeing images relating to future or distant events. ■ *fig.* attempting to forecast the future.

crys·tal·line /ˈkristl-in; -tl-ˌīn; -tl-ˌēn/ ▶ *adj.* having the structure and form of a crystal; composed of crystals: *a crystalline rock*. ■ *poetic/lit.* very clear: *he writes a crystalline prose*. —**crys·tal·lin·i·ty** /ˌkristlˈinitē/ *n.*

crys·tal·lize /ˈkristəˌlīz/ ▶ *v.* [*intr.*] form or cause to form crystals: *when most liquids freeze they crystallize*. ■ *fig.* make or become definite and clear: *vague feelings of unrest crystallized into something more concrete* | [*tr.*] *writing can help to crystallize your thoughts*. ■ [usu. as *adj.*] (**crystallized**) coat and impregnate (fruit or petals) with sugar as a means of preserving them: *crystallized fruits*. —**crys·tal·liz·a·ble** /ˈkristəˌlīzəbəl; ˌkristəˈlīzəbəl/ *adj.* —**crys·tal·li·za·tion** /ˌkristələˈzāsʜən/ *n.*

crys·tal·log·ra·phy /ˌkristəˈlägrəfē/ ▶ *n.* the branch of science concerned with the structure and properties of crystals. —**crys·tal·log·ra·pher** /-fər/ *n.* —**crys·tal·lo·graph·ic** /-ləˈgrafik/ *adj.* —**crys·tal·lo·graph·i·cal·ly** /-ləˈgrafik(ə)lē/ *adv.*

crys·tal meth ▶ *n.* see METH (sense 1).

Cs ▶ *symb.* the chemical element cesium.

c/s ▶ *abbr.* cycles per second.

C-sec·tion ▶ *n.* short for CESAREAN SECTION.

CST ▶ *abbr.* Central Standard Time (see CENTRAL TIME).

CT ▶ *abbr.* computerized (or computed) tomography.

C2C ▶ *abbr.* consumer-to-consumer, denoting transactions conducted via the Internet between consumers.

Cu ▶ *symb.* the chemical element copper.

cu. ▶ *abbr.* cubic (in units of measurement: for example, cu. ft. = cubic feet).

cub /kəb/ ▶ *n.* the young of a fox, bear, lion, or other carnivorous mammal. ■ *archaic* a young man, esp. one who is awkward or ill-mannered.
▶ *v.* (**cubbed**, **cub·bing**) [*intr.*] give birth to cubs.

cube /kyо̄о̄b/ ▶ *n.* a symmetrical three-dimensional shape, either solid or hollow, contained by six equal squares. ■ short for CUBICLE. ■ a block of something with six sides: *a sugar cube*. ■ *Math.* the product of a number multiplied by its square, represented by a superscript figure 3: *a body increasing in weight by the cube of its length*.
▶ *v.* [*tr.*] **1** *Math.* raise (a number or value) to its cube. **2** cut (food) into small cubes. **3** tenderize (meat) by scoring a pattern of small squares into its surface: [as *adj.*] (**cubed**) *cubed steaks*.

cube farm ▶ *n.* a large open-plan office divided into cubicles for individual workers.

cube root ▶ *n.* the number that produces a given number when cubed.

cu·bic /ˈkyо̄о̄bik/ ▶ *adj.* having the shape of a cube: *a cubic room*. ■ denoting a unit of measurement equal to the volume of a cube whose side is one of the linear unit specified: *15 billion cubic meters of water*. ■ measured or expressed in such units. ■ involving the cube (and no higher power) of a quantity or variable: *a cubic equation*. ■ of or denoting a crystal system or three-dimensional geometric arrangement having three equal axes at right angles. —**cu·bi·cal** *adj.* —**cu·bi·cal·ly** /-ik(ə)lē/ *adv.*

cu·bi·cle /ˈkyо̄о̄bikəl/ ▶ *n.* a small partitioned-off area of a room, for example one containing a bed in a dwelling or one containing a desk in an office.

cu·bi·form /ˈkyо̄о̄biˌfôrm/ ▶ *adj.* technical cube-shaped.

cub·ism /ˈkyо̄о̄ˌbizəm/ ▶ *n.* an early 20th-century style and movement in art, esp. painting, in which use was made of simple geometric shapes, interlocking planes, and, later, collage. —**cub·ist** *n. & adj.* —**cub·is·tic** /kyо̄о̄ˈbistik/ *adj.*

cuck·old /ˈkəkəld; -ōld/ ▶ *n.* archaic the husband of an adulteress, often regarded as an object of derision.
▶ *v.* [*tr.*] (of a man) make (another man) a cuckold by having a sexual relationship with his wife. ■ (of a man's wife) make (her husband) a cuckold. ▷late Old English, from Old French *cucuault*, from *cucu* 'cuckoo' (from the cuckoo's habit of laying its egg in another bird's nest). The equivalent words in French and other languages applied to both the bird and the adulterer; *cuckold* has never been applied to the bird in English. —**cuck·old·ry** /-drē/ *n.*

cuck·oo /ˈkо̄о̄kо̄о̄; ˈkо̄о̄kо̄о̄/ ▶ *n.* **1** a medium-sized long-tailed bird, typically with a gray or brown back and barred or pale underparts. The **cuckoo family** (Cuculidae) also includes roadrunners. **2** *inf.* a crazy person.
▶ *adj. inf.* crazy.

cuck·oo clock ▶ *n.* a clock that strikes the hour with a sound like a cuckoo's call and typically has a mechanical cuckoo that emerges.

cu·cum·ber /ˈkyо̄о̄ˌkəmbər/ ▶ *n.* **1** a long, green-skinned fruit with watery flesh, usually eaten raw in salads or pickled. **2** the widely cultivated climbing plant (*Cucumis sativus*) of the gourd family that yields this fruit.

▸ □ (**as**) **cool as a cucumber** untroubled by heat, stress, or exertion. ■ calm and relaxed.

cud /kəd/ ▸ *n.* partly digested food returned from the first stomach of ruminants to the mouth for further chewing.

▸ □ **chew the cud 1** (of a ruminant animal) further chew partly digested food. **2** think or talk reflectively.

cud·dle /ˈkədl/ ▸ *v.* [*tr.*] hold close in one's arms as a way of showing love or affection: *he cuddles the baby close* | [*intr.*] *the pair have been spotted kissing and cuddling.* ■ [*intr.*] lie or sit close and snug: *I love cuddling up in front of a fire.*

▸ *n.* a prolonged and affectionate hug. —**cud·dle·some** /-səm/ *adj.*

cud·dly /ˈkədlē; ˈkədl-ē/ ▸ *adj.* (**-dli·er, -dli·est**) attractive, endearing, and pleasant to cuddle, esp. as a result of being soft or plump.

cudg·el /ˈkəjəl/ ▸ *n.* a short thick stick used as a weapon.

▸ *v.* (**cudg·eled, cudg·el·ing**; *Brit.* **cudg·el·led, cudg·el·ling**) [*tr.*] beat with a cudgel.

cue[1] /kyo͞o/ ▸ *n.* a thing said or done that serves as a signal to an actor or other performer to enter or to begin their speech or performance. ■ a signal for action: *any conversational lull was my cue for asking a question.* ■ a piece of information or circumstance that aids the memory in retrieving details not recalled spontaneously. ■ *Psychol.* a feature of something perceived that is used in the brain's interpretation of the perception. ■ a hint or indication about how to behave in particular circumstances: *my teacher joked about such attitudes and I followed her cue.* ■ a facility for playing through an audio or video recording very rapidly until a desired starting point is reached.

▸ *v.* (**cues, cued, cue·ing** or **cu·ing**) [*tr.*] give a cue to or for. ■ act as a prompt or reminder. ■ set a piece of audio or video equipment in readiness to play (a particular part of the recorded material): *features make it easier to cue up a tape for editing.*

▸ □ **on cue** at the correct moment: *right on cue the door opened.* □ **take one's cue from** follow the example or advice of.

cue[2] ▸ *n.* a long, straight, tapering wooden rod for striking the ball in pool, billiards, snooker, etc.

▸ *v.* (**cues, cued, cue·ing** or **cu·ing**) [*intr.*] use such a rod to strike the ball.

cue ball ▸ *n.* the ball, usually a white one, that is to be struck with the cue in pool, billiards, snooker, etc.

cuff[1] /kəf/ ▸ *n.* **1** the end part of a sleeve, where the material of the sleeve is turned back or a separate band is sewn on. ■ the part of a glove covering the wrist. ■ the turned-up end of a trouser leg. ■ the top part of a boot, typically padded or turned down. ■ an inflatable bag wrapped around the arm when blood pressure is measured. **2** (**cuffs**) *inf.* handcuffs.

▸ *v.* [*tr.*] *inf.* secure with handcuffs. —**cuffed** *adj.* [in *comb.*] *a double-cuffed shirt.*

▸ □ **off the cuff** *inf.* without preparation: *they posed some difficult questions to answer off the cuff* | [as *adj.*] *an off-the-cuff remark.*

cuff[2] ▸ *v.* [*tr.*] strike (someone) with an open hand, esp. on the head.

▸ *n.* a blow given with an open hand.

cuff link ▸ *n.* (usu. **cuff links**) a device for fastening together the sides of a shirt cuff, often decorative.

Cu·fic /ˈk(y)o͞ofik/ ▸ *n.* & *adj.* variant spelling of **KUFIC**.

cui·rass /kwiˈras; kyo͝orˈas/ ▸ *n. hist.* a piece of armor consisting of breastplate and backplate fastened together. ■ a hard protective cover on an animal.

cui·sine /kwiˈzēn/ ▸ *n.* a style or method of cooking, esp. as characteristic of a particular country, region, or establishment: *Venetian cuisine.*

cul-de-sac /ˈkəl di ˌsak/ ▸ *n.* (*pl.* **cul-de-sacs** or **culs-de-sac** /ˈkəl(z)/) a street or passage closed at one end. ■ *fig.* a route or course leading nowhere: *the pro-democracy forces found themselves in a political cul-de-sac.*

cu·li·nar·y /ˈkələˌnerē; ˈkyo͞olə-/ ▸ *adj.* of or for cooking: *culinary skills* | *savor the culinary delights of the region.* —**cu·li·nar·i·ly** *adv.*

cull /kəl/ ▸ *v.* [*tr.*] (usu. **be culled**) select from a large quantity; obtain from a variety of sources: *anecdotes culled from Greek and Roman history.* ■ reduce the population of (a wild animal) by selective slaughter. ■ send (an inferior or surplus animal on a farm) to be slaughtered. ■ *poetic/lit.* pick (flowers or fruit): [as *adj.*] (**culled**) *fresh culled daffodils.*

▸ *n.* a selective slaughter of wild animals. ■ [usu. as *adj.*] an inferior or surplus livestock animal selected for killing: *a cull cow.* —**cull·er** *n.*

cul·mi·nate /ˈkəlməˌnāt/ ▸ *v.* [*intr.*] reach a climax or point of highest development: *the tensions and disorders which culminated in World War II.* ■ [*tr.*] be the climax or point of highest development of. —**cul·mi·na·tion** /ˌkəlməˈnāsHən/ *n.*

cu·lottes /ˈk(y)o͞oˌläts; k(y)o͞oˈläts/ ▸ *pl. n.* women's knee-length trousers, cut with very full legs to resemble a skirt.

cul·pa·ble /ˈkəlpəbəl/ ▸ *adj.* deserving blame: *sometimes you're just as culpable when you watch something as when you actually participate.* —**cul·pa·bil·i·ty** /ˌkəlpəˈbilitē/ *n.* —**cul·pa·bly** /-blē/ *adv.*

cul·prit /ˈkəlprət; ˈkəlˌprit/ ▸ *n.* a person who is responsible for a crime or other misdeed. ■ the cause of a problem or defect.

cult /kəlt/ ▸ *n.* a system of religious veneration and devotion directed toward a particular figure or object: *the cult of St. Olaf.* ■ a relatively small group of people having religious beliefs or practices regarded by others as strange or sinister: *a network of Satan-worshiping cults.* ■ a misplaced or excessive admiration for a particular person or thing: *a cult of personality surrounding the leaders.* ■ [usu. as *adj.*] a person or thing that is popular or fashionable, esp. among a particular section of society: *a cult film.* —**cul·tic** /-tik/ *adj.* —**cult·ish** *adj.* —**cult·ish·ness** *n.* —**cult·ism** /-ˌtizəm/ *n.* —**cult·ist** /-tist/ *n.*

cul·ti·var /ˈkəltəˌvär/ ▸ *n. Bot.* a plant variety that has been produced in cultivation by selective breeding. See also **VARIETY** (sense 2).

cul·ti·vate /ˈkəltəˌvāt/ ▸ *v.* [*tr.*] **1** prepare and use (land) for crops or gardening. ■ break up (soil) in preparation for sowing or planting. ■ raise or grow (plants), esp. on a large scale for commercial purposes. ■ *Biol.* grow or maintain (living cells or tissue) in culture. **2** try to acquire or develop (a quality, sentiment, or skill). ■ try to win the friendship or favor of (someone). ■ [usu. as *adj.*] (**cultivated**) apply oneself to improving or developing (one's mind or manners): *he was a remarkably cultivated and educated man.* —**cul·ti·va·ble** /-vəbəl/ *adj.* —**cul·ti·vat·a·ble** /-ˌvātəbəl/ *adj.* —**cul·ti·va·tion** /ˌkəltəˈvāsHən/ *n.*

cul·ti·va·tor /ˈkəltəˌvātər/ ▸ *n.* a person or thing that cultivates something. ■ a mechanical implement for breaking up the soil and uprooting weeds.

cul·tur·al /ˈkəlCHərəl/ ▸ *adj.* of or relating to the ideas, customs, and social behavior of a society: *cultural diversity of the world's peoples.* ■ of or relating to the arts and to intellectual achievements. —**cul·tur·al·ly** *adv.*

cul·ture /ˈkəlCHər/ ▸ *n.* **1** the arts and other manifestations of human intellectual achievement regarded collectively: *men of culture.* ■ a refined understanding or appreciation of this: *men of culture.* ■ the customs, arts, social institutions, and achievements of a particular nation, people, or other social group: *people from many different cultures.* ■ the attitudes and behavior characteristic of a particular social group: *the drug culture.* **2** *Biol.* the cultivation of bacteria, tissue cells, etc., in an artificial medium containing nutrients: *the cells proliferate readily in culture.* ■ a preparation of cells obtained in such a way: *the bacterium was isolated in two blood cultures.* ■ the cultivation of plants.

▸ *v.* [*tr.*] *Biol.* maintain (tissue cells, bacteria, etc.) in conditions suitable for growth. ▷Middle English (denoting a cultivated piece of land): the noun from French *culture* or directly from Latin *cultura* 'growing, cultivation'; the verb from obsolete French *culturer* or medieval Latin *culturare*, both based on Latin *colere* 'tend, cultivate.' In late Middle English the sense was 'cultivation of the soil' and from this (early 16th cent.) arose 'cultivation (of the mind, faculties, or manners)'; sense 1 dates from the early 19th cent.

cul·tured /ˈkəlCHərd/ ▸ *adj.* **1** characterized by refined taste and manners and good education. **2** *Biol.* (of tissue cells, bacteria, etc.) grown or propagated in an artificial medium. ■ (of a pearl) formed around a foreign body inserted into an oyster.

cul·vert /ˈkəlvərt/ ▸ *n.* a tunnel carrying a stream or open drain under a road or railroad.

cum[1] /ko͝om; kəm/ ▸ *prep.* [usu. in *comb.*] combined with; also used as (used to describe things with a dual nature or function): *a study-cum-bedroom.*

cum[2] ▸ *n. inf.* variant spelling of **COME**.

cum·ber·some /ˈkəmbərsəm/ ▸ *adj.* large or heavy and therefore difficult to carry or use; unwieldy. ■ slow or complicated and therefore inefficient: *organizations with cumbersome hierarchical structures.* —**cum·ber·some·ly** *adv.* —**cum·ber·some·ness** *n.*

cum·brous /ˈkəmbrəs/ ▸ *adj.* poetic or literary term for **CUMBERSOME**. —**cum·brous·ly** *adv.* —**cum·brous·ness** *n.*

cum·in /ˈkəmən; ˈk(y)o͞o-/ (also **cummin**) ▸ *n.* **1** the aromatic seeds of a plant of the parsley family, used as a spice, esp. ground and used in curry powder. **2** the small, slender plant (*Cuminum cyminum*) that bears this fruit and grows from the Mediterranean to central Asia.

Pronunciation Key ə *ago,* up; ər *over, fur;* a *hat;* ā *ate;* ä *car;* CH *chin;* e *let;* ē *see;* e(ə)r *air;* i *fit;* ī *by;* i(ə)r *ear;* NG *sing;* ō *go;* ô *law, for;* oi *toy;* o͝o *good;* o͞o *goo;* ou *out;* SH *she;* TH *thin;* ᴛʜ *then;* (h)w *why;* ZH *vision*

cum·mer·bund /ˈkəmərˌbənd/ ▶ n. a sash worn around the waist, esp. as part of a man's evening clothes. ▷ early 17th cent.: from Urdu and Persian *kamar-band*, from *kamar* 'waist, loins' and -*bandi* 'band.' The sash was formerly worn in the Indian subcontinent by domestic workers and low-status office workers.

cum·quat /ˈkəmˌkwät/ ▶ n. variant spelling of KUMQUAT.

cu·mu·la·tive /ˈkyoōmyələtiv; -ˌlātiv/ ▶ adj. (pl. -**nim·bi**/-ˈnimˌbī; -bē]) *Meteorol.* increasing or increased in quantity, degree, or force by successive additions: *the cumulative effect of two years of drought.* —**cu·mu·la·tive·ly** adv. —**cu·mu·la·tive·ness** n.

cu·mu·lo·nim·bus /ˌkyoōmyəlōˈnimbəs/ ▶ n. (pl. -**nim·bi** /-ˈnimˌbī; -bē]) *Meteorol.* a cloud forming a towering mass with a flat base at fairly low altitude and often a flat top, as in thunderstorms.

cu·mu·lus /ˈkyoōmyələs/ ▶ n. (pl. -**li** /-ˌlī; -lē]) *Meteorol.* a cloud forming rounded masses heaped on each other above a flat base at fairly low altitude. —**cu·mu·lous** /-ləs/ adj.

cu·ne·i·form /kyoōˈnēəˌfôrm; ˈkyoōn(ē)ə-/ ▶ adj. denoting or relating to the wedge-shaped characters used in the ancient writing systems of Mesopotamia, Persia, and Ugarit, surviving mainly impressed on clay tablets. ■ *Anat.* denoting three bones of the tarsus (ankle) between the navicular bone and the metatarsals. ■ *chiefly Biol.* wedge-shaped. ▶ n. cuneiform writing.

cun·ni·lin·gus /ˌkənlˈiNGgəs/ ▶ n. stimulation of the female genitals using the tongue or lips.

cun·ning /ˈkəniNG/ ▶ adj. **1** having or showing skill in achieving one's ends by deceit or evasion: *a cunning look came into his eyes.* ■ ingenious: *plants have evolved cunning defenses.* **2** attractive; quaint. ▶ n. skill in achieving one's ends by deceit. ■ ingenuity. —**cun·ning·ly** adv. —**cun·ning·ness** n.

cunt /kənt/ ▶ n. *vulgar slang* a woman's genitals. ■ *offens.* a woman.

cup /kəp/ ▶ n. **1** a small, bowl-shaped container for drinking from, typically having a handle and used with a matching saucer for hot drinks. ■ the contents of such a container: *a strong cup of tea.* ■ a measure of capacity used in cooking, equal to half a pint—that is, 8 ounces (0.237 l). ■ one's portion or share, as of sorrow or joy: *I submit to God's will and drink this cup for his satisfaction.* ■ an ornamental trophy in the form of a cup, usually made of gold or silver and having a stem and two handles. (**cups**) one of the suits in a tarot pack. **2** a cup-shaped thing, in particular: ■ either of the two parts of a bra shaped to contain or support one breast. ■ this as a measure of breast size: *she had grown from an A to a C cup in just six months.* ■ a jockstrap having a protective reinforcement of rigid plastic or metal. ■ *Golf* the hole on a putting green or the metal container in it. ▶ v. (**cupped**, **cup·ping**) [tr.] **1** form (one's hand or hands) into the curved shape of a cup: *"Hey!" Dad shouted, with his hands cupped around his mouth.* ■ place the curved hand or hands around: *he cupped her face in his hands.* **2** *hist. Med.* bleed (someone) by using a glass in which a partial vacuum is formed by heating. ▶ □ **in one's cups** *inf.* drunk. □ **not one's cup of tea** *inf.* not what one likes or is interested in: *cats were not her cup of tea.*

cup·board /ˈkəbərd/ ▶ n. a cabinet or closet, usually with a door and shelves, used for storage: *a kitchen cupboard.*

cup·cake /ˈkəpˌkāk/ ▶ n. **1** a small cake baked in a cup-shaped container and typically eaten cold. **2** an attractive woman (often as a term of address). ■ a weak or effeminate man.

cup·ful /ˈkəpˌfoŏl/ ▶ n. (pl. -**fuls**) the amount held by a cup: *a cupful of water.* ■ another term for CUP as a measure in cooking: *add 1 cupful of flour.*

Cu·pid /ˈkyoōpəd/ *Roman Mythol.* ▶ the god of love. He is represented as a naked, winged boy with a bow and arrows, with which he wounds his victims. ■ [as n.] (also **cupid**) a representation of a naked winged child, typically carrying a bow.

cu·pid·i·ty /kyoōˈpiditē/ ▶ n. greed for money or possessions.

cu·po·la /ˈkyoōpələ/ ▶ n. a small dome, esp. a small dome on a drum on top of a larger dome, adorning a roof or ceiling. —**cu·po·laed** adj.

cu·pric /ˈk(y)oōprik/ ▶ adj. *Chem.* of copper with a valence of two; of copper(II). Compare with CUPROUS.

cu·prous /ˈk(y)oōprəs/ ▶ adj. *Chem.* of copper with a valence of one; of copper(I). Compare with CUPRIC.

cur /kər/ ▶ n. an aggressive dog or one that is in poor condition, esp. a mongrel. ■ *inf.* a contemptible man.

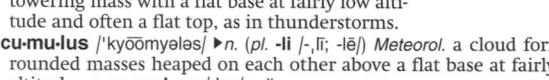

cummerbund

cur·a·ble /ˈkyoōrəbəl/ ▶ adj. able to be cured: *curable cancers.* —**cur·a·bil·i·ty** /ˌkyoōrəˈbilitē/ n.

cu·ra·re /k(y)oōˈrärē/ ▶ n. a bitter, resinous substance obtained from the bark and stems of certain South American plants. It is traditionally used by some Indian peoples to poison their arrows and darts.

cu·rate[1] /ˈkyoōrət; -ˌrāt/ ▶ n. a member of the clergy engaged as assistant to a vicar, rector, or parish priest. —**cu·ra·cy** n. /ˈkyoōrəsē/

cu·rate[2] /ˈkyoōˌrāt/ ▶ v. [tr.] select, organize, and look after the items in (a collection or exhibition). —**cu·ra·tion** /kyəˈrāsHən/ n.

cu·ra·tor /ˈkyoōr·ātər; kyoōˈrātər; ˈkyoōrətər/ ▶ n. a keeper or custodian of a museum or other collection. —**cu·ra·to·ri·al** /ˌkyoōrəˈtôrēəl/ adj. —**cu·ra·tor·ship** /-ˌsHip/ n.

curb /kərb/ ▶ n. **1** a stone or concrete edging to a street or path. **2** a check or restraint on something. **3** (also **curb bit**) a type of bit that is widely used in western riding. **4** a swelling on the back of a horse's hock, caused by spraining a ligament. ▶ v. [tr.] **1** restrain or keep in check. ■ restrain (a horse) by means of a curb. **2** lead (a dog being walked) near the curb to urinate or defecate.

curd /kərd/ ▶ n. (also **curds**) a soft, white substance formed when milk sours, used as the basis for cheese. ■ a fatty substance found between the flakes of poached salmon. —**curd·y** adj.

cur·dle /ˈkərdl/ ▶ v. separate or cause to separate into curds or lumps: [intr.] *take care not to let the soup boil or it will curdle* | [tr.] *making cheese by curdling milk.* —**cur·dler** /ˈkərdlər; ˈkərdl-ər/ n. ▶ □ **make one's blood curdle** fill one with horror.

cure /kyoōr/ ▶ v. [tr.] **1** relieve (a person or animal) of the symptoms of a disease or condition: *he was cured of the disease* | *fig. centuries of science have not cured us of our superstitions.* ■ eliminate (a disease, condition, or injury) with medical treatment: *this technology could be used to cure diabetes.* ■ solve (a problem). **2** preserve (meat, fish, tobacco, or an animal skin) by various methods such as salting, drying, or smoking: *some farmers cured their own bacon.* ■ harden (rubber, plastic, concrete, etc.) after manufacture by a chemical process such as vulcanization. ■ [intr.] undergo this process. ▶ n. **1** a substance or treatment that cures a disease or condition. ■ restoration to health: *he was beyond cure.* ■ a solution to a problem. **2** the process of curing rubber, plastic, or other material. —**cur·a·tive** /ˈkyoōrə·tiv/ adj. —**cur·er** n.

cu·ré /kyoōˈrā; ˈkyoōr·ā/ ▶ n. a parish priest in a French-speaking country or region.

cure-all ▶ n. a medicine or other remedy that will supposedly cure any ailment. ■ a solution to any problem.

cu·ret·tage /ˌkyoōrəˈtäzH/ ▶ n. *Surg.* the use of a curette, esp. on the lining of the uterus. See DILATATION AND CURETTAGE.

cu·rette /kyoōˈret/ ▶ n. a surgical instrument used to remove material by a scraping action, esp. from the uterus. ▶ v. [tr.] clean or scrape with a curette.

cur·few /ˈkərˌfyoō/ ▶ n. a regulation requiring people to remain indoors between specified hours, typically at night. ■ the hour designated as the beginning of such a restriction: *to be out after curfew without permission.* ■ the daily signal indicating this. ▷ Middle English (denoting a regulation requiring people to extinguish fires at a fixed hour in the evening, or a bell rung at that hour): from Old French *cuevrefeu*, from *cuvrir* 'to cover' + *feu* 'fire.' The current sense dates from the late 19th cent.

cu·rie /ˈkyoōrē; kyoōˈrē/ (abbr.: **Ci**) ▶ n. (pl. -**ries**) a unit of radioactivity, corresponding to 3.7×10^{10} disintegrations per second. ■ the quantity of radioactive substance that has this amount of activity.

cu·ri·o /ˈkyoōrēˌō/ ▶ n. (pl. -**os**) a rare, unusual, or intriguing object.

cu·ri·os·i·ty /ˌkyoōrēˈäsitē/ ▶ n. (pl. -**ties**) **1** a strong desire to know or learn something. **2** a strange or unusual object or fact.

cu·ri·ous /ˈkyoōrēəs/ ▶ adj. **1** eager to know or learn something. ■ expressing curiosity: *a curious stare.* **2** strange; unusual: *a curious sensation overwhelmed her.* —**cu·ri·ous·ly** adv. —**cu·ri·ous·ness** n.

cu·ri·um /ˈkyoōrēəm/ ▶ n. the chemical element of atomic number 96, an artificial radioactive metal of the actinide series. (Symbol: **Cm**)

curl /kərl/ ▶ v. **1** form or cause to form into a curved or spiral shape: [intr.] *her fingers curled around the microphone* | [tr.] *she used to curl her hair with rags.* ■ [intr.] (**curl up**) sit or lie with the knees drawn up. ■ move or cause to move in a spiral or curved course: [intr.] *a wisp of smoke curling across the sky.* ■ (with reference to one's mouth or upper lip) raise or cause to raise slightly on one side as an expression of contempt or disapproval: [intr.] *Maria saw his lip curl sardonically.* ■ (in weight training) lift (a weight) using only the hands, wrists, and forearms. **2** [intr.] play at the game of curling.

▶*n.* a lock of hair having a spiral or coiled form. ■ a thing having a spiral or inwardly curved form. ■ a curling movement. ■ (with reference to a person's hair) a state or condition of being curled. ■ a weightlifting exercise involving movement of only the hands, wrists, and forearms. —**curl·y** *adj.*

curl·er /'kərlər/ ▶*n.* **1** (usu. **curlers**) a roller or clasp around which a lock of hair is wrapped to curl it. **2** a player in the game of curling.

cur·lew /'kər,lōō; 'kərl,yōō/ ▶*n.* (*pl.* same or **curlews**) a large wading bird (genus *Numenius*) of the sandpiper family, with a long down-curved bill and brown streaked plumage.

curl·ing /'kərliNG/ ▶*n.* a game played on ice, esp. in Scotland and Canada, in which large, round, flat stones are slid toward a mark. Players use brooms to sweep the ice in the path of the stone to control it.

curl·ing stone ▶*n.* a large, polished, circular stone with an iron handle on top, used in the game of curling.

cur·mudg·eon /kər'məjən/ ▶*n.* a bad-tempered or surly person. —**cur·mudg·eon·li·ness** *n.* —**cur·mudg·eon·ly** *adj.*

cur·rant /'kərənt/ ▶*n.* **1** a small dried fruit, from a seedless variety of grape native to the eastern Mediterranean region, now widely produced in California. **2** a Eurasian shrub (genus *Ribes*) of the gooseberry family that produces small edible black, red, or white berries. ■ a berry from such a shrub.

cur·ren·cy /'kərənsē; 'kə-rənsē/ ▶*n.* (*pl.* **-cies**) **1** a system of money in general use in a particular country. **2** the fact or quality of being generally accepted or in use: *since the Gulf War, the term has gained new currency.* ■ the time during which something is in use or operation: *during the currency of the policy.*

cur·rent /'kərənt; 'kə-rənt/ ▶*adj.* belonging to the present time; happening or being used or done now: *keep abreast of current events.* ■ in common or general use: *the other meaning of the word is still current.*
▶*n.* a body of water or air moving in a definite direction, esp. through a surrounding body of water or air in which there is less movement: *ocean currents.* ■ a flow of electricity which results from the ordered directional movement of electrically charged particles. ■ a quantity representing the rate of flow of electric charge, usually measured in amperes. ■ the general tendency or course of events or opinion: *the student movement formed a distinct current of protest.*

cur·rent·ly /'kərəntlē; 'kə-rəntlē/ ▶*adv.* at the present time.

cur·ric·u·lum /kə'rikyələm/ ▶*n.* (*pl.* **-la** /-lə/ or **-lums**) the subjects comprising a course of study in a school or college. —**cur·ric·u·lar** /-lər/ *adj.*

cur·ric·u·lum vi·tae /kə'rik(y)ələm 'vē,tī; 'vītē/ (abbr.: **CV**) ▶*n.* (*pl.* **cur·ric·u·la vi·tae** /kə'rik(y)ələ/) a brief account of a person's education, qualifications, and experience, typically sent with a job application.

cur·ry[1] /'kərē; 'kə-rē/ ▶*n.* (*pl.* **-ries**) **1** a dish of meat, vegetables, etc., cooked in an Indian-style sauce of strong spices and turmeric and typically served with rice. **2** curry powder.
▶*v.* (**-ries, -ried**) [*tr.*] (usu. as *adj.*) (**curried**) prepare or flavor with a sauce of hot-tasting spices: *curried chicken.*

cur·ry[2] ▶*v.* (**-ries, -ried**) [*tr.*] **1** groom (a horse) with a rubber or plastic curry-comb. **2** *hist.* treat (tanned leather) to improve its properties.
▶ □ **curry favor** ingratiate oneself with someone through obsequious behavior.

cur·ry-comb ▶*n.* a hand-held metal device with serrated ridges, used for removing dirt out of a horse's coat or for cleaning brushes with which a horse is being groomed. ■ (also **rubber curry-comb**) a similar device of flexible rubber, used for grooming horses.

cur·ry pow·der ▶*n.* a mixture of finely ground spices, such as turmeric, ginger, and coriander, used for making curry.

curse /kərs/ ▶*n.* **1** a solemn utterance intended to invoke a supernatural power to inflict harm or punishment on someone or something: *she'd put a curse on him.* ■ a cause of harm or misery: *impatience is the curse of our day and age.* ■ (**the curse**) *inf.* menstruation. **2** an offensive word or phrase used to express anger or annoyance.
▶*v.* **1** [*tr.*] invoke or use a curse against. ■ (**be cursed with**) be afflicted with: *many owners have been cursed with a series of bankruptcies.* **2** [*intr.*] utter offensive words in anger or annoyance. ■ [*tr.*] address with such words. —**curs·er** *n.*

curs·ed /'kərsid; kərst/ ▶*adj. inf., dated* used to express annoyance or irritation: *he didn't whine about his cursed fate.* —**curs·ed·ly** /'kərsidlē/ *adv.* —**curs·ed·ness** /'kərsidnəs/ *n.*

cur·sive /'kərsiv/ ▶*adj.* written with the characters joined: *cursive script.*
▶*n.* writing with such a style. —**cur·sive·ly** *adv.*

cur·sor /'kərsər/ ▶*n.* a movable indicator on a computer screen identifying the point that will be affected by input from the user, for example showing where typed text will be inserted. ■ the transparent slide engraved with a hairline that is part of a slide rule.

cur·so·ry /'kərsərē/ ▶*adj.* hasty and therefore not thorough or detailed: *a cursory glance.* —**cur·so·ri·ly** /'kərsərəlē/ *adv.* —**cur·so·ri·ness** *n.*

curt /kərt/ ▶*adj.* rudely brief. —**curt·ly** *adv.* —**curt·ness** *n.*

cur·tail /kər'tāl/ ▶*v.* [*tr.*] (often **be curtailed**) reduce in extent or quantity; impose a restriction on. ■ (**curtail someone of**) *archaic* deprive someone of (something). —**cur·tail·ment** /kər'tālmənt/ *n.*

cur·tain /'kərtn/ ▶*n.* a piece of material suspended at the top to form a covering or screen, typically one of a pair at a window: *fig. through the curtain of falling snow, she could just make out gravestones.* ■ (**the curtain**) a screen of heavy cloth or other material that can be raised or lowered at the front of a stage. ■ a raising or lowering of such a screen at the beginning or end of an act or scene. ■ (**curtains**) *inf.* a disastrous outcome: *it looked like curtains for me.*
▶*v.* [*tr.*] provide with a curtain or curtains. ■ conceal or screen with a curtain.
▶ □ **bring down the curtain on** bring to an end.

cur·tain call ▶*n.* the appearance of one or more performers on stage after a performance to acknowledge the audience's applause.

curt·sy /'kərtsē/ (also **curt·sey**) ▶*n.* (*pl.* **-sies** or **-seys**) a woman's or girl's formal greeting made by bending the knees with one foot in front of the other: *she bobbed a curtsy to him.*
▶*v.* (**-sies, -sied** or **-seys, -seyed**) [*intr.*] perform such an action: *she curtsied onto the stage.* ▷early 16th cent.: variant of *courtesy,* from Old French *cortesie,* from *corteis* 'courtly, courteous,' based on Latin *cohors* 'yard, retinue.' Both forms were used to denote the expression of respect or courtesy by a gesture, esp. in phrases such as *do courtesy, make courtesy,* and from this arose the current use (late 16th cent.).

cur·va·ceous /kər'vāSHəs/ ▶*adj.* (esp. of a woman or a woman's figure) having an attractively curved shape. —**cur·va·ceous·ness** *n.*

cur·va·ture /'kərvəCHər; -,CHŏŏr/ ▶*n.* the fact of being curved or the degree to which something is curved: *spinal curvature.* ■ *Geom.* the degree to which a curve deviates from a straight line, or a curved surface deviates from a plane. ■ a numerical quantity expressing this.

curve /kərv/ ▶*n.* a line or outline that gradually deviates from being straight for some or all of its length. ■ a place where a road deviates from a straight path. ■ (**curves**) a curving contour of a woman's figure. ■ a line on a graph (whether straight or curved) showing how one quantity varies with respect to another: *the population curve.* ■ a system in which grades are assigned to students based on their performance relative to other students, regardless of their actual knowledge of the subject: *grades were marked on a curve.*
▶*v.* form or cause to form a curve: [*intr.*] *her mouth curved in a smile* | [*tr.*] *starting with arms outstretched, curve the body sideways.*

curve·ball /'kərv,bôl/ ▶*n. Baseball* a ball that is pitched with a snap of the wrist and a strong downward spin, which causes the ball to drop suddenly and deceptively veer away from home plate.

cur·vi·lin·e·ar /,kərvə'linēər/ ▶*adj.* contained by or consisting of a curved line or lines. —**cur·vi·lin·e·ar·ly** *adv.*

curv·y /'kərvē/ ▶*adj.* (**curv·i·er, curv·i·est**) having many curves. ■ *inf.* (esp. of a woman's figure) shapely and voluptuous. —**curv·i·ness** *n.*

cush·ion /'kŏŏSHən/ ▶*n.* a pillow or pad stuffed with a mass of soft material, used as a comfortable support for sitting or leaning on. ■ something providing support or protection against impact: *the pad forms a cushion between carpet and floor* | *fig. a poll showed the candidate with a 14-point cushion.* ■ the layer of air supporting a hovercraft or similar vehicle.
▶*v.* [*tr.*] soften the effect of an impact on: *the bag cushions equipment from inevitable knocks.* ■ *fig.* mitigate the adverse effects of: *he called for federal assistance to cushion the blow for farmers.* ▷Middle English: from Old French *cuissin,* based on a Latin word meaning 'cushion for the hip,' from *coxa* 'hip, thigh'. —**cush·ioned** *adj.* —**cush·ion·y** *adj.*

Cush·it·ic /kŏŏ'SHitik; ,kəSH-/ ▶*n.* a group of East African languages of the Afro-Asiatic family spoken mainly in Ethiopia and Somalia.
▶*adj.* of or relating to this group of languages. ▷early 20th cent.: from *Cush,* an ancient country in NE Africa..

cush·y /'kŏŏSHē/ ▶*adj.* (**cush·i·er, cush·i·est**) *inf.* **1** undemanding, easy, or secure: *cushy jobs that pay you to ski.* **2** (of furniture) comfortable. —**cush·i·ness** *n.*

cusp /kəsp/ ▶*n.* **1** a pointed end where two curves meet, in particular: ■ *Archit.* a projecting point between small arcs in Gothic tracery. ■ a cone-shaped prominence on the surface of a tooth, esp. of a molar or

Pronunciation Key ə *ago, up;* ər *over, fur;* a *hat;* ā *ate;* ä *car;* CH *chin;* e *let;* ē *see;* e(ə)r *air;* i *fit;* ī *by;* i(ə)r *ear;* NG *sing;* ō *go;* ô *law, for;* oi *toy;* ŏŏ *good;* ōō *goo;* ou *out;* SH *she;* TH *thin;* TH *then;* (h)w *why;* ZH *vision*

premolar. ■ *Anat.* a pocket or fold in the wall of the heart or a major blood vessel that fills and distends if the blood flows backward, so forming part of a valve. ■ *Math.* a point at which the direction of a curve is abruptly reversed. ■ each of the pointed ends of a crescent, esp. of the moon. **2** a point between two different situations or states, when a person or thing is poised between the two: *those on the cusp of adulthood.* —**cus·pate** /'kəspət; -,pāt/ *adj.* —**cusped** *adj.* —**cus·pi·date** /'kəspə,dāt/ *adj.*

cus·pi·dor /'kəspə,dôr/ ▶*n.* a spittoon.

cuss /kəs/ *inf.* ▶*n.* **1** an annoying or stubborn person or animal: *he was certainly an unsociable cuss.* **2** another term for CURSE (sense 2).
▶*v.* another term for CURSE (sense 2).

cuss word ▶*n. inf.* a swear word.

cus·tard /'kəstərd/ ▶*n.* a dessert or sweet sauce made with milk, eggs, and sugar.

cus·to·di·an /kəs'tōdēən/ ▶*n.* a person who has responsibility for or looks after something, such as a museum, financial assets, or a culture or tradition: *the custodians of pension and insurance funds.* ■ a person employed to clean and maintain a building. —**cus·to·di·an·ship** /-,SHip/ *n.*

cus·to·dy /'kəstədē/ ▶*n.* the protective care or guardianship of someone or something: *the property was placed in the custody of a trustee.* ■ imprisonment: *my father was being **taken into** **custody**.* ■ *Law* parental responsibility, esp. as allocated to one of two divorcing parents: *he was trying to get **custody** of their child.* —**cus·to·di·al** /kə'stōdēəl/ *adj.*

cus·tom /'kəstəm/ ▶*n.* **1** a traditional and widely accepted way of behaving or doing something that is specific to a particular society, place, or time. ■ a thing that one does habitually: *it was my custom to nap for an hour every day.* ■ *Law* established practice or usage having the force of law or right. **2** *chiefly Brit.* regular dealings with a shop or business by customers.
▶*adj.* made or done to order for a particular customer: *a custom guitar.*

cus·tom·ar·y /'kəstə,merē/ ▶*adj.* according to the customs or usual practices associated with a particular society, place, or set of circumstances. ■ according to a person's habitual practice: *I put the kettle on for our customary cup of tea.* ■ *Law* established by or based on custom rather than common law or statute. —**cus·tom·ar·i·ly** /,kəstə'me(ə)rəlē/ *adv.* —**cus·tom·ar·i·ness** *n.*

cus·tom-built ▶*adj.* another term for CUSTOM-MADE.

cus·tom·er /'kəstəmər/ ▶*n.* **1** a person or organization that buys goods or services from a store or business. **2** a person or thing of a specified kind that one has to deal with: *Jon won over Lucie's father, but her mother is a tough customer.*

cus·tom·ize /'kəstə,mīz/ ▶*v.* [*tr.*] (often **be customized**) modify (something) to suit a particular individual or task.

cus·tom-made ▶*adj.* made to a particular customer's order.

cut /kət/ ▶*v.* (**cut·ting**; *past* and *past part.* **cut**) [*tr.*] **1** make an opening, incision, or wound in (something) with a sharp-edged tool or object: *he cut his big toe on a sharp stone* | [*intr.*] *fig. his scorn cut deeper than knives.* **2** remove (something) from something larger by using a sharp implement: *I cut his photograph **out** of the paper.* ■ *inf.* castrate (an animal, esp. a horse). ■ (**cut something out**) make something by cutting: *I cut out some squares of paper.* ■ (**cut something out**) remove, exclude, or stop eating or doing something undesirable: *start today by cutting out fatty foods.* ■ (**cut something out**) separate an animal from the main herd. **3** divide into pieces with a knife or other sharp implement: *cut the beef into thin slices.* ■ make divisions in (something): *land that has been cut up by streams into forested areas.* ■ separate (something) into two; sever. ■ (**cut something down**) make something, esp. a tree, fall by cutting it through at the base. ■ (**cut someone down**) (of a weapon, bullet, or disease) kill or injure someone. **4** make or form (something) by using a sharp tool to remove material: *workmen cut a **hole in** the pipe.* ■ make or design (a garment) in a particular way: [as *adj.*] (**cut**) *an impeccably cut suit.* ■ make (a path, tunnel, or other route) by excavation, digging, or chopping: *cut a road **through** a rain forest* | [*intr.*] *investigators called for a machete to **cut through** the bush.* **5** trim or reduce the length of (something, esp. grass or a person's hair or fingernails) by using a sharp implement. **6** reduce the amount or quantity of: *buyers will bargain hard to **cut the cost** of the house they want* | [*intr.*] *the paper glut **cuts into** profits.* ■ abridge (a text, movie, or performance) by removing material. ■ *Comput.* delete (part of a text or other display) completely or so as to insert a copy of it elsewhere. See also CUT AND PASTE. ■ (in sports) remove (a player) from a team's roster. ■ end or interrupt the provision of (something, esp. power or food supplies): *we resolved to cut oil supplies to territories controlled by the rebels.* ■ (**cut something off**) block the usual means of access to a place: *the caves were **cut off** from the outside world.* ■ absent oneself deliberately from (something one should normally

attend, esp. school): *Robert was cutting class.* ■ switch off (an engine or a light). **7** (of a line) cross or intersect (another line). ■ [*intr.*] (**cut across**) pass or traverse, esp. so as to shorten one's route: *the following aircraft cut across to join him.* ■ [*intr.*] (**cut across**) have an effect regardless of (divisions or boundaries between groups): *subcultures that cut across national and political boundaries.* ■ [*intr.*] (**cut along**) *inf., dated* leave or move hurriedly. **8** *dated* ignore or refuse to recognize (someone). **9** [*intr.*, often in *imper.*] stop filming or recording. ■ move to another shot in a movie: *cut to a dentist's surgery.* ■ [*tr.*] make (a movie) into a coherent whole by removing parts or placing them in a different order. **10** make (a sound recording). **11** divide (a pack of playing cards) by lifting a portion from the top, either to reveal or draw a card at random or to place the top portion under the bottom portion. **12** *Golf* slice (the ball). **13** adulterate (a drug) or dilute (alcohol) by mixing it with another substance. **14** (**cut it**) *inf.* come up to expectations; meet requirements.

▶*phrasal v.* □ **cut in 1** interrupt someone while they are speaking: *"It's urgent," Raoul cut in.* ■ *dated* interrupt a dancing couple to take over from one partner. **2** pull in too closely in front of another vehicle after having overtaken it. **3** (of a motor or other mechanical device) begin operating, esp. when triggered automatically by an electrical signal. **4** □ **cut someone in** *inf.* include someone in a deal and give them a share of the profits. □ **cut into** interrupt the course of: *Victoria's words cut into her thoughts.* □ **cut someone off** interrupt someone while they are speaking. ■ interrupt someone during a telephone call by breaking the connection. ■ prevent someone from receiving or being provided with something, esp. power or water: *consumers cut off for nonpayment.* ■ reject someone as one's heir; disinherit someone. ■ prevent someone from having access to somewhere or someone; isolate someone from something they previously had connections with: *we were cut off from reality.* ■ *inf.* (of a driver) overtake someone and pull in too closely in front of them. □ **cut out 1** (of a motor or engine) suddenly stop operating. **2** *inf.* (of a person) leave quickly, esp. so as to avoid a boring or awkward situation. □ **cut someone out** exclude someone: *his mother cut him out of her will.* □ **cut up** *inf.* behave in a mischievous or unruly manner.

▶*n.* **1** an act of cutting, in particular: ■ a haircut. ■ a stroke or blow given by a sharp-edged implement or by a whip or cane: *he could skin an animal with a single cut of the knife.* ■ *fig.* a wounding remark or act. ■ a reduction in amount or size: *she took a 20% pay cut.* ■ (in sports) a removal of a player from a team's roster. ■ an act of removing part of a play, movie, or book, esp. to shorten the work or to delete offensive material: *the author was willing to **make cuts**.* ■ an immediate transition from one scene to another in a movie. ■ *Golf* the halfway point of a golf tournament where half of the players are eliminated. ■ *Tennis* a stroke made with a sharp horizontal or downward action of the racket, imparting spin. **2** a result of cutting something, in particular: ■ a long narrow incision in the skin made by something sharp. ■ a long narrow opening or incision made in a surface or piece of material. ■ a piece of meat cut from a carcass. ■ *inf.* a share of the profits from something: *the directors are demanding their cut.* ■ a recording of a piece of music: *a cut from his album.* ■ a version of a movie after editing: *the director's cut.* ■ a passage cut or dug out, as a railroad cutting or a new channel made for a river or other waterway. ■ a woodcut. **3** the way or style in which something, esp. a garment or someone's hair, is cut: *the elegant cut of his dinner jacket.* ▷Middle English (probably existing, although not recorded, in Old English); probably of Germanic origin and related to Norwegian *kutte* and Icelandic *kuta* 'cut with a small knife,' *kuti* 'small blunt knife.'

▶ □ **be cut out for** (or **to be**) *inf.* have exactly the right qualities for a particular role, task, or job: *I'm just not cut out to be a policeman.* □ **a cut above** *inf.* noticeably superior to. □ **cut and dried** (of a situation) completely settled or decided. □ **cut and thrust** *Fencing* the use of both the edge and the point of one's sword while fighting. ■ a spirited and rapid interchange of views: *the cut and thrust of political debate.* ■ a situation or sphere of activity regarded as carried out under adversarial conditions. □ **cut corners** undertake something in what appears to be the easiest, quickest, or cheapest way, esp. by omitting to do something important or ignoring rules. □ **cut a deal** *inf.* come to an arrangement, esp. in business; make a deal. □ **cut someone down to size** *inf.* deflate someone's exaggerated sense of self-worth. □ **cut something down to size** reduce the size or power of something, for example an organization, that is regarded as having become too large. □ **cut a —** **— figure** present oneself or appear in a particular way: *David has cut a dashing figure on the international social scene.* □ **cut from the same cloth** of the same nature; similar. □ **cut in line** push into a line of people in order to be served or dealt with before one's turn. □ **cut it fine** see

FINE[1]. □ **cut it out** [usu. in *imper.*] *inf.* used to ask someone to stop doing or saying something that is annoying or offensive: *I'm sick of that joke; cut it out, can't you?* □ **cut loose** act without restraint. □ **cut one's loss-es** abandon an enterprise or course of action that is clearly going to be unprofitable or unsuccessful before one suffers too much loss or harm. □ **cut the mustard** *inf.* come up to expectations; reach the required standard. □ **cut someone/something short** interrupt someone or something; bring an abrupt or premature end to something said or done. □ **cut a** (or **the**) **rug** *inf.* dance, typically in an energetic or accomplished way. □ **cut one's teeth** acquire initial practice or experience of a particular sphere of activity or with a particular organization. □ **cut a tooth** (usu.of a baby or child) have a tooth appear through the gum. □ **cut to the chase** *inf.* come to the point. □ **have one's work cut out** see WORK. □ **make the cut** *Golf* avoid elimination from the last two rounds of a four-round tournament.

cut and paste ▶ *n.* a process used in assembling text on a word processor or computer, in which items are removed from one part and inserted elsewhere.
▶ *v.* [tr.] move (an item of text) using this technique.

cu·ta·ne·ous /kyooˈtānēəs/ ▶ *adj.* of, relating to, or affecting the skin.

cut·a·way /ˈkətəˌwā/ ▶ *n.* [often as *adj.*] **1** a thing made or designed with a part cut out or absent, in particular: ■ a coat or jacket with the front cut away below the waist so as to curve back to the tails. ■ a diagram or drawing with some external parts left out to reveal the interior. **2** a shot in a movie that is of a different subject from those to which it is joined in editing.

cut·back /ˈkətˌbak/ ▶ *n.* an act or instance of reducing something, typically expenditures: *cutbacks in defense spending.*

cute /kyoot/ ▶ *adj.* **1** attractive in a pretty or endearing way: *a cute kitten.* ■ *inf.* sexually attractive. **2** *inf.* affectedly or superficially clever: *I don't want to be cute with you.* —**cute·ly** *adv.* —**cute·ness** *n.*

cu·ti·cle /ˈkyootikəl/ ▶ *n.* **1** the outer layer of living tissue, in particular: ■ *Bot.* & *Zool.* a protective and waxy or hard layer covering the epidermis of a plant, invertebrate, or shell. ■ the outer cellular layer of a hair. ■ *Zool.* another term for EPIDERMIS. **2** the dead skin at the base of a fingernail or toenail. —**cu·tic·u·lar** /kyooˈtikyələr/ *adj.*

cut·lass /ˈkətləs/ ▶ *n.* a short sword with a slightly curved blade, formerly used by sailors.

cutlass

cut·ler /ˈkətlər/ ▶ *n.* a person who makes or sells cutlery.

cut·ler·y /ˈkətlərē/ ▶ *n.* **1** cutting utensils, esp. knives for cutting food. **2** knives, forks, and spoons used for eating or serving food.

cut·let /ˈkətlət/ ▶ *n.* a portion of sliced meat coated in breadcrumbs and served either grilled or fried.

cut·off /ˈkətˌôf/ (also **cut-off**) ▶ *adj.* **1** of or constituting a limit: *the cutoff date to register is July 2.* **2** (of a device) producing an interruption or cessation of a power or fuel supply: *a cutoff valve.* **3** (of an item of clothing) having been cut short: *a cutoff T-shirt.*
▶ *n.* **1** a point or level that is a designated limit of something. **2** an act of stopping or interrupting the supply or provision of something. ■ a device for producing an interruption or cessation of a power or fuel supply. ■ a sudden drop in amplification or responsiveness of an electric device at a certain frequency. **3** (**cutoffs**) shorts made by cutting off the legs of a pair of jeans or other trousers above or at the knee and leaving the edges unhemmed. **4** a shortcut. **5** *Geol.* a pattern of a meandering stream in which a channel cuts a new course to bypass a meander bend.

cut·out /ˈkətˌout/ (also **cut-out**) ▶ *n.* **1** a shape of a person or thing cut out of cardboard or another material. ■ *fig.* a person perceived as characterless or as lacking in individuality: *this film's protagonists are cardboard cutouts.* **2** a hole cut in something for decoration or to allow the insertion of something else. **3** a device that automatically breaks an electric circuit for safety and either resets itself or can be reset.

cut-rate (also **cut-price**) ▶ *adj.* for sale at a reduced or unusually low price: *cut-rate tickets.* ■ offering goods at such prices.

cut·ter /ˈkətər/ ▶ *n.* **1** a person or thing that cuts something, in particular: ■ a tool for cutting something, esp. one intended for cutting a particular thing or for producing a particular shape: *a glass cutter* | (**cutters**) *a pair of bolt cutters.* ■ a person who cuts or edits movies. ■ a person in a tailoring establishment who takes measurements and cuts the cloth. ■ a person who reduces or cuts down on something, esp.

expenditures: *a determined cutter of costs.* **2** a light, fast coastal patrol boat. ■ a ship's boat used for carrying light stores or passengers. **3** *Baseball* (also **cut fastball**) a fastball that breaks somewhat on being pitched. **4** a light horse-drawn sleigh.

cut·throat /ˈkətˌThrōt/ ▶ *n.* **1** a murderer or other violent criminal. **2** (also **cutthroat trout**) a trout (*Salmo clarki*) of western North America, with red or orange markings under the jaw.
▶ *adj.* (of a competitive situation) fierce and intense; involving the use of ruthless measures. ■ (of a person) using ruthless methods in a competitive situation. ■ relating to a game or contest in which individuals score against the other players.

cut·ting /ˈkətiNG/ ▶ *n.* **1** (often **cuttings**) a piece cut off from something, esp. what remains when something is being trimmed or prepared. ■ a piece cut from a plant for propagation. ■ *Brit.* a clipping from a newspaper or periodical. **2** the action of someone or something that cuts. **3** an open passage excavated through higher ground for a railroad, road, or canal.
▶ *adj.* capable of cutting something: *the cutting blades of the hedge trimmer.* ■ *fig.* (esp. of a comment) causing emotional pain; hurtful: *a cutting remark.* ■ *fig.* (of the wind) bitterly cold. —**cut·ting·ly** *adv.*

cutting edge ▶ *n.* the edge of a tool's blade. ■ the latest or most advanced stage in the development of something: *researchers at the cutting edge of molecular biology.* ■ a person or factor that contributes a dynamic or invigorating quality to a situation and thereby puts one at an advantage: *the campaign began to lose its cutting edge.* ■ *fig.* incisiveness and directness of expression.
▶ *adj.* (**cut·ting-edge**) at the latest or most advanced stage of development; innovative or pioneering: *cutting-edge technology.*

cut·tle /ˈkətl/ ▶ *n.* a cuttlefish.

cut·tle·bone /ˈkətlˌbōn/ ▶ *n.* the internal skeleton of the cuttlefish, made of white, lightweight, chalky material. It is used as a dietary supplement for caged birds and for making casts for precious metal items.

cut·tle·fish /ˈkətlˌfiSH/ ▶ *n.* (*pl.* same or **-fishes**) a marine mollusk (*Sepia* and other genera, class Cephalopoda) with eight arms and two long tentacles that are used for grabbing prey.

cut-up (also **cut up**) ▶ *adj.* **1** divided into pieces by cutting: *cut-up vegetables.* ■ (of a soft piece of ground) having an uneven surface after the passage of heavy vehicles or animals. **2** *inf.* (of a person) very distressed.
▶ *n.* **1** a film or sound recording made by cutting and editing material from preexisting recordings. **2** (**cutup**) *inf.* a person who is fond of making jokes or playing pranks.

cut·worm /ˈkətˌwərm/ ▶ *n.* a moth caterpillar (family Noctuidae) that lives in the upper layers of the soil and eats through the stems of young plants at ground level.

CV ▶ *abbr.* ■ cardiovascular. ■ curriculum vitae.

cwt. ▶ *abbr.* hundredweight.

cy·an /ˈsīˌan; ˈsīən/ ▶ *n.* a greenish-blue color, one of the primary subtractive colors, complementary to red.

cy·a·nide /ˈsīəˌnīd/ ▶ *n.* *Chem.* a salt or ester of hydrocyanic acid, containing the anion CN^- or the group —CN. The salts are generally extremely toxic. ■ sodium or potassium cyanide used as a poison or in the extraction of gold and silver.

cy·a·no·bac·te·ri·a /ˌsīənōbakˈti(ə)rēə; sīˌanō-/ ▶ *pl. n.* *Biol.* microorganisms that are related to the bacteria but are capable of photosynthesis. They are prokaryotic and represent the earliest known form of life on the earth. Also called BLUE-GREEN ALGAE.

cy·a·no·co·bal·a·min /ˌsīənōˌkōˈbaləmin; sīˌanō-/ ▶ *n.* a vitamin found in foods of animal origin such as liver, fish, and eggs, a deficiency of which can cause pernicious anemia. Also called VITAMIN B_{12} (see VITAMIN B).

cy·a·no·sis /ˌsīəˈnōsəs/ ▶ *n.* *Med.* a bluish discoloration of the skin resulting from poor circulation or inadequate oxygenation of the blood. —**cy·a·not·ic** /ˌsīəˈnätik/ *adj.*

cy·ber·crime /ˈsībərˌkrīm/ ▶ *n.* crime conducted via the Internet or some other computer network.

cy·ber·net·ics /ˌsībərˈnetiks/ ▶ *pl. n.* [treated as *sing.*] the science of communications and automatic control systems in both machines and living things. —**cy·ber·net·ic** *adj.* —**cy·ber·ne·ti·cian** /-nəˈtiSHən/ *n.* —**cy·ber·net·i·cist** /-ˈnetəsəst/ *n.*

---

cy·ber·space /ˈsībərˌspās/ ▶n. the notional environment in which communication over computer networks occurs.

cy·ber·ter·ror·ism /ˌsībərˈterəˌrizəm/ ▶n. the politically motivated use of computers and information technology to cause severe disruption or widespread fear in society. —**cy·ber·ter·ror·ist** n.

cy·ber·war /ˈsībərˌwôr/ ▶n. acts of hostility carried out on the Internet against national interests or ethnic groups.

cy·cad /ˈsīkəd; ˈsīˌkad/ ▶n. a palmlike plant (genus *Cycas* and other genera, family Cycadaceae) of tropical and subtropical regions, bearing large male or female cones.

cy·cla·men /ˈsīkləmən; ˈsik-/ ▶n. (*pl.* same or **cyclamens**) a European plant (genus *Cyclamen*) of the primrose family, having pink, red, or white flowers with backward-curving petals.

cy·cle /ˈsīkəl/ ▶n. **1** a series of events that are regularly repeated in the same order: *the boom and slump periods of a trade cycle.* ■ the period of time taken to complete a single sequence of such events: *the cells are shed over a cycle of twenty-eight days.* ■ *technical* a recurring series of successive operations or states, as in the working of an internal combustion engine, or in the alternation of an electric current or a wave. ■ *Biol.* a recurring series of events or metabolic processes in the lifetime of a plant or animal: *the storks' breeding cycle.* ■ *Biochem.* a series of successive metabolic reactions in which one of the products is regenerated and reused. ■ *Ecol.* the movement of a simple substance through the soil, rocks, water, atmosphere, and living organisms of the earth. ■ *Comput.* a single set of hardware operations, esp. that by which memory is accessed and an item is transferred to or from it, to the point at which the memory may be accessed again. ■ *Physics* a cycle per second; one hertz. **2** a complete set or series. ■ a series of songs, stories, plays, or poems composed around a particular theme: *Wagner's Ring Cycle.* **3** a bicycle or tricycle. ■ a ride on a bicycle.
▶v. [*intr.*] **1** ride a bicycle: *she cycled to work every day.* **2** move in or follow a regularly repeated sequence of events: *economies cycle regularly between boom and slump.*

cy·clic /ˈsīklik; ˈsik-/ ▶adj. **1** occurring in cycles; regularly repeated: *the cyclic pattern of the last two decades.* ■ *Math.* (of a group) having the property that each element of the group can be expressed as a power of one particular element. ■ relating to or denoting a musical or literary composition with a recurrent theme or structural device. **2** *Math.* of or relating to a circle or other closed curve. ■ *Geom.* (of a polygon) having all its vertices lying on a circle. ■ *Chem.* (of a compound) having a molecular structure containing one or more closed rings of atoms. —**cy·cli·cal** adj. —**cy·cli·cal·ly** /-ik(ə)lē/ adv.

cy·clist /ˈsīk(ə)list/ ▶n. a person who rides a bicycle.

cy·clone /ˈsīˌklōn/ ▶n. *Meteorol.* a system of winds rotating inward to an area of low atmospheric pressure, with a counterclockwise (northern hemisphere) or clockwise (southern hemisphere) circulation; a depression. ■ another term for **TROPICAL STORM.** —**cy·clon·ic** /sīˈklänik/ adj. —**cy·clon·i·cal·ly** /sīˈklänik(ə)lē/ adv.

cy·clo·pe·di·a /ˌsīkləˈpēdēə/ (also **cy·clo·pae·di·a**) ▶n. *archaic* (except in book titles) an encyclopedia. —**cy·clo·pe·dic** /-ˈpēdik/ adj.

cy·clo·tron /ˈsīkləˌträn/ ▶n. *Physics* an apparatus in which charged atomic and subatomic particles are accelerated by an alternating electric field while following an outward spiral or circular path in a magnetic field.

cyg·net /ˈsignət/ ▶n. a young swan.

cyl·in·der /ˈsiləndər/ ▶n. a solid geometric figure with straight parallel sides and a circular or oval section. ■ a solid or hollow body, object, or part with such a shape. ■ a piston chamber in a steam or internal combustion engine. ■ a cylindrical container for liquefied gas under pressure. ■ a rotating metal roller in a printing press. ■ *Archaeol.* a cylindrical seal. —**cy·lin·dric** /səˈlindrik/ adj. —**cy·lin·dri·cal** /səˈlindrikəl/ adj. —**cy·lin·dri·cal·ly** /səˈlindrik(ə)lē/ adv.

cyl·in·der lin·er ▶n. see LINER[2].

cym·bal /ˈsimbəl/ ▶n. a musical instrument consisting of a slightly concave round brass plate that is either struck against another one or struck with a stick to make a ringing or clashing sound. —**cym·bal·ist** n.

cyn·ic /ˈsinik/ ▶n. **1** a person who believes that people are motivated purely by self-interest rather than acting for honorable or unselfish reasons. ■ a person who questions whether something will happen or whether it is worthwhile. **2** (**Cynic**) a member of a school of ancient Greek philosophers founded by Antisthenes, marked by an ostentatious contempt for ease and pleasure. —**cyn·i·cism** /ˈsinəˌsizəm/ n.

cyn·i·cal /ˈsinikəl/ ▶adj. **1** believing that people are motivated by self-interest; distrustful of human sincerity or integrity. ■ doubtful as to whether something will happen or whether it is worthwhile. ■ contemptuous; mocking. **2** concerned only with one's own interests and typically disregarding accepted or appropriate standards in order to achieve them. —**cyn·i·cal·ly** /-ik(ə)lē/ adv.

cy·no·sure /ˈsīnə,SHo͝or; ˈsin-/ ▶n. a person or thing that is the center of attention or admiration: *the Queen was the cynosure of all eyes.* ▷late 16th cent.: from French, or from Latin *cynosura*, from Greek *kunosoura* 'dog's tail' (also 'Ursa Minor'), from *kuōn, kun-* 'dog' + *oura* 'tail.' The term originally denoted the constellation Ursa Minor, or the star Polaris that it contains, long used as a guide by navigators.

cy·pher ▶n. variant spelling of CIPHER.

cy·press /ˈsīprəs/ ▶n. (also **cypress tree**) an evergreen coniferous tree (*Cupressus, Chamaecyparis*, and other genera, family Cupressaceae) with small, rounded, woody cones and flattened shoots bearing small, scalelike leaves. ■ a tree of this type, or branches from it, as a symbol of mourning. ■ used in names of similar coniferous trees of other families, e.g., **bald cypress** (*Taxodium distichum*, family Taxodiaceae).

Cyp·ri·ot /ˈsiprēət; -,ät/ ▶n. **1** a native or national of Cyprus. **2** the dialect of Greek used in Cyprus.
▶adj. of or relating to Cyprus or its people or the Greek dialect used there.

Cy·ril·lic /səˈrilik/ ▶adj. denoting the alphabet used by many Slavic peoples, chiefly those with a historical allegiance to the Orthodox Church. Ultimately derived from Greek uncials, it is used for Russian, Bulgarian, Serbian, Ukrainian, and other Slavic languages.
▶n. the Cyrillic alphabet.

cyst /sist/ ▶n. *Biol.* in an animal or plant, a thin-walled, hollow organ or cavity containing a liquid secretion; a sac, vesicle, or bladder. ■ *Med.* in the body, a membranous sac or cavity of abnormal character containing fluid. ■ a tough protective capsule enclosing the larva of a parasitic worm or the resting stage of an organism.

cys·tic /ˈsistik/ ▶adj. **1** *chiefly Med.* of, relating to, or characterized by cysts. **2** of or relating to the urinary bladder or the gallbladder.

cys·tic fi·bro·sis ▶n. a hereditary disorder affecting the exocrine glands. It causes the production of abnormally thick mucus, leading to the blockage of the pancreatic ducts, intestines, and bronchi.

cys·ti·tis /sisˈtītis/ ▶n. *Med.* inflammation of the urinary bladder. It is usually accompanied by frequent, painful urination.

cy·to·ge·net·ics /ˌsītōjəˈnetiks/ ▶pl. n. [treated as *sing.*] *Biol.* the study of inheritance in relation to the structure and function of chromosomes. —**cy·to·ge·net·ic** /-ik/ adj. —**cy·to·ge·net·i·cal** /-ikəl/ adj. —**cy·to·ge·net·i·cal·ly** /-ik(ə)lē/ adv. —**cy·to·ge·net·i·cist** /-jəˈnetəsist/ n.

cy·tol·o·gy /sīˈtäləjē/ ▶n. the branch of biology concerned with the structure and function of plant and animal cells. —**cy·to·log·i·cal** /ˌsītlˈäjikəl/ adj. —**cy·to·log·i·cal·ly** /ˌsītlˈäjik(ə)lē/ adv. —**cy·tol·o·gist** /-jist/ n.

cy·to·plasm /ˈsītəˌplazəm/ ▶n. *Biol.* the material or protoplasm within a living cell, excluding the nucleus. —**cy·to·plas·mic** /ˌsītəˈplazmik/ adj.

cy·to·sine /ˈsītəˌsēn/ ▶n. *Biochem.* a compound, $C_4H_5N_3O$, found in living tissue as a constituent base of nucleic acids.

czar /zär; (t)sär/ (also **tsar** or **tzar**) ▶n. **1** variant spelling of TSAR. **2** a person with great authority or power in a particular area: *America's new drug czar.* —**czar·dom** /-dəm/ n. —**czar·ism** /-,izəm/ n. —**czar·ist** /-ist/ n. & adj.

czar·e·vich /ˈzärə,vicH; ˈ(t)sär-/ ▶ variant spelling of TSAREVICH.

cza·ri·na /zäˈrēnə; (t)sä-/ ▶ variant spelling of TSARINA.

Czech /CHek/ ▶n. **1** a native or national of the Czech Republic or (formerly) Czechoslovakia, or a person of Czech descent. **2** the West Slavic language spoken in the Czech Republic, closely related to Slovak.
▶adj. of or relating to the Czechs or their language.

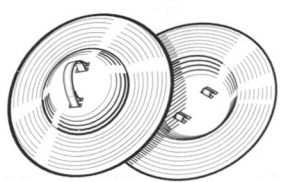

cymbals

Dd

D¹ /dē/ (also **d**) ▸ *n.* (*pl.* **Ds** or **D's**) **1** the fourth letter of the alphabet. ■ denoting the fourth in a set of items, categories, sizes, etc. ■ the fourth highest category of academic mark. **2** (**D**) a shape like that of a capital D: [in *comb.*] *the D-shaped handle.* ■ a loop or ring of this shape. **3** (usu. **D**) *Mus.* the second note of the diatonic scale of C major. ■ a key based on a scale with D as its keynote. **4** the Roman numeral for 500.

D² ▸ *abbr.* ■ Democrat or Democratic. ■ depth (in the sense of the dimension of an object from front to back). ■ (with a numeral) dimension(s) or dimensional: *a 3-D model.* ■ (in tables of sports results) drawn. ■ (on an automatic gearshift) drive. ■ (in personal ads) divorced.
▸ *symb.* ■ *Chem.* deuterium.

d ▸ *abbr.* ■ date. ■ (in genealogies) daughter. ■ day(s): *orbital period: 687.0 d.* ■ deceased. ■ deep. ■ [in *comb.*] (in units of measurement) deci-. ■ (in timetables) departs. ■ (**d.**) died (used to indicate a date of death). ■ divorced. ■ *Brit.* penny or pence (of predecimal currency): *£20 10s 6d.* ■ *Chem.* denoting electrons and orbitals possessing two units of angular momentum: *d-electrons.*
▸ *symb.* ■ *Math.* diameter. ■ *Math.* denoting a small increment in a given variable: *dy/dx.*

'd ▸ *contr. of* ■ had: *they'd already gone.* ■ would: *I'd expect that.*

DA ▸ *abbr.* ■ district attorney. ■ Doctor of Arts.

da ▸ *abbr.* [in *comb.*] (in units of measurement) deca-.

dab¹ /dab/ ▸ *v.* (**dabbed, dab·bing**) [*tr.*] **1** press against (something) lightly with absorbent material in order to clean or dry it: *he dabbed his mouth with his napkin* | [*intr.*] *she dabbed at her eyes with a handkerchief.* ■ apply (a substance) with light quick strokes. **2** aim at or strike with a light blow.
▸ *n.* a small amount of something: *she licked a dab of chocolate from her finger.* ■ a brief application of cosmetic, paint, or the like to a surface: *apply concealer with light dabs.* —**dab·ber** *n.*

dab² ▸ *n.* a small flatfish (*Limanda* and other genera, family Pleuronectidae; and genus *Citharichthys*, family Bothidae), found chiefly in the North Atlantic.

dab·ble /'dabəl/ ▸ *v.* [*tr.*] immerse (one's hands or feet) in water and move them around gently. ■ [*intr.*] (of a waterbird) move the bill around in shallow water while feeding. ■ [*intr.*] *fig.* take part in an activity in a casual or superficial way: *he dabbled in writing.* —**dab·bler** /'dab(ə)lər/ *n.*

dace /dās/ ▸ *n.* (*pl.* same) a small freshwater fish (*Leuciscus, Agosia,* and other genera) of the minnow family, typically living in running water.

da·cha /'däCHə/ ▸ *n.* a country house or cottage in Russia, typically used as a second or vacation home. ▷mid 19th cent.: Russian, originally 'grant (of land).'

dachs·hund /'däksənd; 'däks,hо̇ont/ ▸ *n.* a dog of a short-legged, long-bodied breed.

dac·tyl /'daktl/ ▸ *n. Prosody* a metrical foot consisting of one stressed syllable followed by two unstressed syllables or (in Greek and Latin) one long syllable followed by two short syllables. —**dac·tyl·ic** /dak'tilik/ *adj.*

dad /dad/ ▸ *n. inf.* one's father.

Da·da /'dädä/ ▸ *n.* an early-20th-century arts movement, repudiating and mocking conventions and emphasizing the illogical and absurd. —**Da·da·ism** /-,izəm/ *n.* —**Da·da·ist** /-ist/ *n.* & *adj.* —**Da·da·is·tic** /,dädä-'istik/ *adj.*

da·da /'dada; -də/ ▸ *n. inf.* one's father.

dad·dy /'dadē/ ▸ *n.* (*pl.* **-dies**) *inf.* one's father. ■ the oldest, best, or biggest example of something: *the daddy of all potholes.*

dad·dy long·legs ▸ *n.* any of numerous arachnids with a globular body and long thin legs. Also called **HARVESTMAN**.

da·do /'dädō/ ▸ *n.* (*pl.* **-dos**) the lower part of the wall of a room, if it has a different color or covering than the upper part. ■ a groove cut in the face of a board, into which the edge of another board is fixed. ■ *Archit.* the part of a pedestal between the base and the cornice.

dae·mon /'dēmən/ ▸ *n.* **1** (in ancient Greek belief) a divinity or supernatural being of a nature between gods and humans. ■ an inner or attendant spirit or inspiring force. **2** archaic spelling of **DEMON¹**. —**dae·mon·ic** /di'mänik/ *adj.*

daf·fo·dil /'dafə,dil/ ▸ *n.* a bulbous plant (genus *Narcissus*) of the lily family that typically bears bright yellow flowers with a long trumpet-shaped center (corona).

daf·fy /'dafē/ ▸ *adj.* (**-fi·er, -fi·est**) *inf.* silly; mildly eccentric. ■ crazy. —**daf·fi·ness** *n.*

daft /daft/ ▸ *adj. inf.,* silly; foolish. ■ crazy. ■ (**daft about**) infatuated with: *we were all daft about him.*

dag·ger /'dagər/ ▸ *n.* a short knife with a pointed and edged blade, used as a weapon. ■ *Printing* another term for **OBELUS**.
▸ □ **at daggers drawn** in bitter enmity. □ **look daggers at** glare angrily or venomously at.

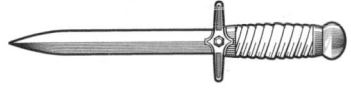

dagger

da·guerre·o·type /də'ge(ə)rə,tīp/ (also **da·guer·ro·type**) ▸ *n.* a photograph taken by an early process employing a silvered plate and mercury vapor.

dahl·ia /'dalyə; 'däl-/ ▸ *n.* a tuberous Mexican plant (genus *Dahlia*) of the daisy family, cultivated for its brightly colored flowers.

dai·ly /'dālē/ ▸ *adj.* done, produced, or occurring every day or every weekday. ■ relating to the period of a single day: *a daily rate.*
▸ *adv.* every day: *the museum is open daily.*
▸ *n.* (*pl.* **-lies**) *inf.* **1** a newspaper published every day except Sunday. **2** (**dailies**) first prints from cinematographic takes, made rapidly for movie producers or editors; rushes.

dain·ty /'dāntē/ ▸ *adj.* (**-ti·er, -ti·est**) **1** delicately small and pretty.. ■ (of a person) delicate and graceful. ■ (of food) particularly good to eat: *a dainty morsel.* **2** fastidious or difficult to please, typically concerning food..
▸ *n.* (*pl.* **-ties**) (usu. **dainties**) something good to eat; a delicacy. —**dain·ti·ly** /'dāntəlē/ *adv.* —**dain·ti·ness** *n.*

dai·qui·ri /'dakərē; 'dīkə-/ ▸ *n.* (*pl.* **-ris**) a cocktail containing rum and lime juice.

dair·y /'de(ə)rē/ ▸ *n.* (*pl.* **dair·ies**) a building, room, or establishment for the storage, processing, and distribution of milk and milk products. ■ a store where milk and milk products are sold. ■ food made from or containing milk.
▸ *adj.* containing or made from milk: *dairy products.* ■ concerned with or involved in the production of milk: *a dairy farmer.*

da·is /'dāis; 'dī-/ ▸ *n.* a low platform for a lectern, seats of honor, or a throne.

dai·sy /'dāzē/ ▸ *n.* (*pl.* **-ies**) a small grassland plant (family Compositae) that has flowers with a yellow disk and white rays. It has given rise to

D

many ornamental garden varieties. ▷Old English *dæges ēage* 'day's eye.'

▸ □ **pushing up (the) daisies** *inf.* dead and buried.

dai·sy-cut·ter ▸*n. inf.* an immensely powerful aerial bomb.

Da·ko·ta ▸*n.* (*pl.* same or **-tas**) **1** a member of a North American Indian people of the upper Mississippi valley and the surrounding plains. **2** the Siouan language of this people. Also called SIOUX.
▸*adj.* of or relating to this people or their language. ▷early 19th cent.: the name in Dakota, literally 'allies.'

Da·lai La·ma /ˈdälī ˈlämə/ ▸*n.* the spiritual head of Tibetan Buddhism and, formerly, the spiritual and temporal ruler of Tibet.

dale /dāl/ ▸*n.* a valley, esp. a broad one.

dal·li·ance /ˈdalēəns; ˈdalyəns/ ▸*n.* a casual romantic or sexual relationship. ■ brief or casual involvement with something.

dal·ly /ˈdalē/ ▸*v.* (**-lies, -lied**) [*intr.*] **1** act or move slowly. **2** have a casual romantic or sexual liaison with someone. ■ show a casual interest in something, without committing oneself seriously: *dallying with the idea of opening a new office.*

Dal·ma·tian /dalˈmāSHən/ ▸*n.* **1** a dog of a white, short-haired breed with dark spots. **2** a native or inhabitant of Dalmatia.

dam[1] ▸*abbr.* decameter(s).

dam[2] /dam/ ▸*n.* a barrier constructed to hold back water and raise its level. ■ a barrier of branches in a stream, constructed by a beaver to provide a deep pool and a lodge. ■ any barrier resembling a dam.
▸*v.* (**dammed, dam·ming**) [*tr.*] build a dam across (a river or lake). ■ hold back or obstruct (something): *the closed lock gates dammed up the canal.*

dam[3] ▸*n.* the female parent of an animal, esp. a domestic mammal.

dam·age /ˈdamij/ ▸*n.* **1** physical harm caused to something in such a way as to impair its value, usefulness, or normal function. ■ unwelcome and detrimental effects: *damage to his reputation.* **2** (**damages**) money claimed or awarded in compensation for a loss or injury.
▸*v.* [*tr.*] inflict physical harm on (something) so as to impair its value, usefulness, or normal function: *the car was badly damaged* | [as *adj.*] (**damaging**) *heat can be damaging to color film.* ■ have a detrimental effect on: *the scandal could damage his career.* —**dam·ag·ing·ly** *adv.*

▸ □ **what's the damage?** *inf., humorous* used to ask the cost of something.

dam·ask /ˈdaməsk/ ▸*n.* **1** a figured woven fabric with a pattern visible on both sides, typically used for table linen and upholstery. ■ a tablecloth made of this material. **2** short for DAMASK ROSE.
▸*adj.* made of or resembling damask. ■ *poetic/lit.* having the velvety pink or light red color of a damask rose.
▸*v.* [*tr.*] weave with figured designs. ■ *poetic/lit.* decorate with or as if with a variegated pattern.

dam·ask rose ▸*n.* a sweet-scented rose (*Rosa damascena*) that is typically pink or light red in color. The velvety petals are used to make attar.

dame /dām/ ▸*n.* **1** (**Dame**) (in the UK) the title given to a woman equivalent to the rank of knight. ■ a woman holding this title. **2** *inf.* a woman. ■ *archaic* or *humorous* an elderly or mature woman.

da·min·o·zide /dəˈminəˌzīd/ ▸*n.* a growth retardant sprayed on vegetables and fruit, esp. apples, to enhance the quality of the crop. The use of daminozide has been restricted due to potential health risks.

dam·mit /ˈdamit/ ▸*interj.* used to express anger and frustration.

damn /dam/ ▸*v.* [*tr.*] (in Christian belief) (of God) condemn (a person) to suffer eternal punishment in hell. ■ (**be damned**) be doomed to misfortune or failure: *the enterprise was damned.* ■ condemn, esp. by the public expression of disapproval. ■ curse (someone or something).
▸*interj. inf.* expressing anger, surprise, or frustration: *Damn! I forgot!*
▸*adj. inf.* used for emphasis, esp. to express anger or frustration: *turn that damn thing off!* | *don't be so damn silly!*
▸ □ **not be worth a damn** *inf.* have no value or validity at all.

dam·na·ble /ˈdamnəbəl/ ▸*adj.* **1** extremely bad or unpleasant. **2** subject to or worthy of divine condemnation. —**dam·na·bly** /-blē/ *adv.*

dam·na·tion /damˈnāSHən/ ▸*n.* (in Christian belief) condemnation to eternal punishment in hell.
▸*interj.* expressing anger or frustration.

damned /damd/ ▸*adj.* **1** (in Christian belief) condemned by God to suffer eternal punishment in hell: [as *pl. n.*] (**the damned**) *the spirits of the damned.* **2** *inf.* used for emphasis, esp. to express anger or frustration: *it's none of your damned business* | *she's too damned arrogant.* ■ (**damnedest**) used to emphasize the surprising nature of something: *the damnedest thing I ever saw.*
▸*adv.* extremely; exceedingly: *called her one damned fine pilot.*
▸ □ **do** (or **try**) **one's damnedest** do or try one's utmost.

damp /damp/ ▸*adj.* slightly wet: *hair still damp from the shower.*
▸*n.* **1** moisture diffused through the air or a solid substance or condensed on a surface, typically with detrimental or unpleasant effects. ■ foul, stifling, or poisonous gas, esp. in a mine. ■ (**damps**) *archaic* damp air or atmosphere. **2** *archaic* a check or discouragement.
▸*v.* [*tr.*] **1** make (something) slightly wet: *damp a small area with water.* **2** control or restrain (a feeling or a state of affairs): *she tried to damp down her feelings of despair.* ■ make (a fire) burn less strongly by reducing the flow of air to it. **3** restrict the amplitude of vibrations on (a piano or other musical instrument) so as to reduce sound. ■ *Physics* progressively reduce the amplitude of (an oscillation or vibration): *concrete structures damp out any vibrations.* ■ reduce the level of (a noise or sound). —**damp·ish** *adj.* —**damp·ly** *adv.* —**damp·ness** *n.*

damp·en /ˈdampən/ ▸*v.* [*tr.*] **1** make slightly wet. **2** make less strong or intense: *nothing could dampen her enthusiasm.* ■ reduce the amplitude of (a sound source). —**damp·en·er** *n.*

damp·er /ˈdampər/ ▸*n.* a person or thing that has a depressing, subduing, or inhibiting effect: *another damper on reactor development was the problem of safeguards.* ■ *Mus.* a pad that silences a piano string. ■ a device for reducing mechanical vibration, in particular a shock absorber on a motor vehicle. ■ a movable metal plate in a flue or chimney, used to regulate the draft and so control the rate of combustion.
▸ □ **put a damper on** have a depressing, subduing, or inhibiting effect on: *he put a damper on her youthful excitement.*

dam·sel /ˈdamzəl/ ▸*n. archaic* or *poetic/lit.* a young unmarried woman.

dam·sel·fly /ˈdamzəlˌflī/ ▸*n.* (*pl.* **-flies**) a slender insect related to the dragonflies, typically resting with the wings folded along the body.

dam·son /ˈdamzən; -sən/ ▸*n.* **1** a small purple-black plumlike fruit. ■ a dark purple color. **2** (also **damson tree**) the small deciduous tree of the rose family that bears this fruit.

dance /dans/ ▸*v.* [*intr.*] **1** move rhythmically to music, typically following a set sequence of steps. ■ [*tr.*] perform (a particular dance or a role in a ballet): *they danced a tango.* ■ [*tr.*] lead (someone) in a particular direction while dancing: *I danced her out of the room.* **2** (of a person) move in a quick and lively way: *Sheila danced in gaily.* ■ move up and down lightly and quickly: *midges danced over the stream.* ■ (of someone's eyes) sparkle brightly with pleasure or excitement.
▸*n.* a series of movements that match the speed and rhythm of a piece of music. ■ a particular sequence of steps and movements constituting a particular form of dancing. ■ steps and movements of this type considered as an activity or art form. ■ a social gathering at which people dance. ■ a set of lively movements resembling a dance: *he gesticulated comically and did a little dance.* ■ a piece of music for dancing to. ■ (also **dance music**) music for dancing to, esp. in a nightclub. ■ a set of stylized movements performed by certain animals. —**dance·a·bil·i·ty** *n.* —**dance·a·ble** *adj.* —**danc·er** *n.*

D and C ▸*abbr.* dilatation and curettage.

dan·de·li·on /ˈdandiˌlīən/ ▸*n.* a widely distributed plant (genus *Taraxacum*) of the daisy family, with a rosette of leaves, bright yellow flowers followed by globular heads of seeds with downy tufts, and stems containing a milky latex. ▷late Middle English: from French *dent-de-lion*, translation of medieval Latin *dens leonis* 'lion's tooth.'

dan·der[1] /ˈdandər/ ▸*n.* (in phrase **get/have one's dander up**) *inf.* lose one's temper.

dan·der[2] ▸*n.* skin flakes in an animal's fur or hair.

dan·di·fied /ˈdandiˌfīd/ ▸*adj.* (of a man) showing excessive concern about appearance. ■ self-consciously sophisticated or elaborate: *dandified prose.*

dan·dle /ˈdandl/ ▸*v.* [*tr.*] move (a baby or young child) up and down in a playful or affectionate way. ■ move (something) lightly up and down.

dan·druff /ˈdandrəf/ ▸*n.* small pieces of dead skin in a person's hair. —**dan·druff·y** *adj.*

D&X ▸*abbr.* dilation and extraction. See PARTIAL-BIRTH ABORTION.

dan·dy /ˈdandē/ ▸*n.* (*pl.* **-dies**) **1** a man unduly devoted to style, neatness, and fashion in dress and appearance. **2** *inf., dated* an excellent thing of its kind: *this umbrella is a dandy.*
▸*adj.* (**-di·er, -di·est**) **1** *inf.* excellent. **2** relating to or characteristic of a dandy. —**dan·dy·ish** *adj.* —**dan·dy·ism** /-ˌizəm/ *n.*

Dane /dān/ ▸*n.* a native or national of Denmark, or a person of Danish descent.

dan·ger /ˈdānjər/ ▸*n.* the possibility of suffering harm or injury. ■ a person or thing that is likely to cause harm or injury: *infertile soils where drought is a danger.* ■ the possibility of something unwelcome or unpleasant.
▸ □ **in danger of** likely to incur or to suffer from: *in danger of extinction.*
□ **out of danger** (of a person who has suffered a serious injury or illness) not expected to die.

dan·ger·ous /ˈdānjərəs/ ▶*adj.* able or likely to cause harm or injury. ■ likely to have adverse or unfortunate consequences; risky. ■ likely to cause problems or difficulty. ■ (of a drug) addictive or otherwise harmful. —**dan·ger·ous·ly** *adv.* —**dan·ger·ous·ness** *n.*

dan·gle /ˈdaNGgəl/ ▶*v.* [*intr.*] hang or swing loosely: *saucepans dangled from a rail* | [*tr.*] *they were dangling their legs over the water.* ■ [*tr.*] *fig.* offer (an enticing incentive) to someone. —**dan·gler** /-glər/ *n.* —**dan·gly** /-glē/ *adj.*

Dan·ish /ˈdāniSH/ ▶*adj.* of or relating to Denmark or its people or language.
▶*n.* **1** the North Germanic language of Denmark, which is also the official language of Greenland and the Faeroes. **2** [as *pl. n.*] (**the Danish**) the people of Denmark. **3** *inf.* short for DANISH PASTRY.

Dan·ish pas·try ▶*n.* a pastry made of sweetened yeast dough with toppings or fillings such as fruit, nuts, or cheese.

dank /daNGk/ ▶*adj.* disagreeably damp, musty, and typically cold. —**dank·ly** *adv.* —**dank·ness** *n.*

daph·ni·a /ˈdafnēə/ ▶*n.* (*pl.* same) a tiny and semitransparent freshwater crustacean with long antennae and prominent eyes, often used as food for aquarium fish. Also called WATER FLEA.

dap·per /ˈdapər/ ▶*adj.* (typically of a man) neat and trim in dress, appearance, or bearing. —**dap·per·ly** *adv.* —**dap·per·ness** *n.*

dap·ple /ˈdapəl/ ▶*v.* [*tr.*] (usu. **be dappled**) mark with spots or rounded patches: [as *adj.*] (**dappled**) *dappled sunlight lay upon her brown hair.*
▶*n.* a patch or spot of color or light. ■ an animal whose coat is marked with patches or spots.

dap·ple gray ▶*adj.* (of a horse) gray or white with darker ringlike markings.
▶*n.* a horse of this type.

DAR ▶*abbr.* Daughters of the American Revolution.

dare /de(ə)r/ ▶*v.* (3rd *sing. present* usu. **dare** before an expressed or implied infinitive without **to**) **1** have the courage to do something: *a story he dare not write down* | *she leaned forward as far as she dared.* **2** [*tr.*] defy or challenge (someone) to do something. **3** [*tr.*] *poetic/lit.* take the risk of; brave: *few dared his wrath.*
▶*n.* a challenge, esp. to prove courage. —**dar·er** *n.*
▶ □ **don't you dare** used to order someone not to do something. □ **how dare you** used to express indignation: *how dare you talk to me like that!* □ **I dare say** (or **daresay**) used to indicate that one believes something is probable: *I dare say you've heard about her.*

dare·dev·il /ˈde(ə)rˌdevəl/ ▶*n.* a person who enjoys doing dangerous things.
▶*adj.* reckless and daring. —**dare·dev·il·ry** /-rē/ *n.*

dar·ing /ˈde(ə)riNG/ ▶*adj.* (of a person or action) adventurous or audaciously bold: *a daring crime.* ■ boldly unconventional.
▶*n.* adventurous courage: *the zeal and daring of climbers.* —**dar·ing·ly** *adv.*

dark /därk/ ▶*adj.* with little or no light. ■ hidden from knowledge; mysterious: *a dark secret.* ■ *archaic* ignorant; unenlightened. ■ (of a theater) closed; not in use. **2** (of a color or object) not reflecting much light; approaching black in shade: *dark green.* ■ (of someone's skin, hair, or eyes) brown or black in color. ■ (of a person) having such skin, hair, or eyes: *my father and I are very dark.* ■ *fig.* (of a sound or taste) having richness or depth. ■ served or drunk with only a little or no milk or cream. **3** (of a period of time or situation) characterized by tragedy, unhappiness, or unpleasantness. ■ gloomily pessimistic. ■ (of an expression) angry; threatening: *a dark look.* ■ suggestive of or arising from evil characteristics or forces; sinister: *dark deeds.* **4** *Phonet.* denoting a velarized form of the sound of the letter *l* (as in *pull*).
▶*n.* **1** (**the dark**) the absence of light in a place: *sitting in the dark* | *scared of the dark.* ■ nightfall: *home before dark.* **2** a dark color or shade, esp. in a painting. —**dark·ish** *adj.* —**dark·ly** *adv.* —**dark·ness** *n.*
▶ □ **in the dark** in a state of ignorance about something: *we're clearly being kept in the dark.* □ **a shot** (or **stab**) **in the dark** an act whose outcome cannot be foreseen; a mere guess.

Dark Ag·es ▶the period in western Europe between the fall of the Roman Empire and the high Middle Ages, *c.*AD 500–1100, during which Germanic tribes swept through Europe and North Africa, often attacking and destroying towns and settlements. ■ a period of supposed unenlightenment. ■ (**the dark ages**) *humorous* or *derog.* an obscure or little-regarded period in the past, esp. as characterizing an outdated attitude or practice: *the judge is living in the dark ages.*

dark·en /ˈdärkən/ ▶*v.* **1** make or become dark or darker: [as *adj.*] (**darkened**) *a darkened room.* ■ [*tr.*] *fig.* cast a shadow over something; spoil: *the abuse darkened the rest of their lives.* **2** make or become gloomy, angry, or unhappy: [*intr.*] *his mood darkened.* ■ [*intr.*] (of someone's eyes or expression) show anger or another strong negative emotion: *his face*

darkened. ■ [*tr.*] (of such an emotion) show in (someone's eyes or expression): *misery darkened her gaze.* —**dark·en·er** *n.*
▶ □ **darken someone's door** visit someone's home: *never darken my door again!*

dark horse ▶*n.* **1** a person about whom little is known, esp. someone whose abilities and potential for success are concealed: [as *adj.*] *a dark-horse candidate.* **2** a competitor or candidate who has little chance of winning, or who wins against expectations.

dark·room /ˈdärkˌrōōm; -ˌrŏŏm/ ▶*n.* a room from which normal light is excluded, used for developing photographs.

dar·ling /ˈdärliNG/ ▶*n.* used as an affectionate form of address to a beloved person. ■ a lovable or endearing person. ■ a person who is particularly popular with a certain group: *the darling of the media.*
▶*adj.* beloved: *his darling wife.* ■ (esp. in affected use) pretty; charming: *a darling little pillbox hat.* —**dar·ling·ness** *n.*

darn[1] /därn/ ▶*v.* [*tr.*] mend (knitted material or a hole in this) by weaving yarn across the hole with a needle: *darn socks.*

darn[2] (also **durn**) ▶*v., adj.* & *interj. inf.* euphemism for DAMN: [as *v.*] *darn it all, Poppa* | [as *adj.*] *the darn things were expensive.*

darned /därnd/ (also **durned** /dərnd/) ▶*adj. inf.* euphemism for DAMNED: *you have to work a darned sight harder* | *they're darned good songwriters.* —**darned·est** *adj.*

dart /därt/ ▶*n.* **1** a small pointed missile that can be thrown or fired. ■ a small pointed missile with a feather or plastic tail, used in the game of darts. ■ an act of running somewhere suddenly and rapidly: *the cat made a dart for the door.* **2** a tapered tuck stitched into a garment in order to shape it.
▶*v.* [*intr.*] move or run somewhere suddenly or rapidly. ■ [*tr.*] cast (a look or one's eyes) suddenly and rapidly in a particular direction: *she darted a glance across the table.* ■ [*tr.*] *archaic* throw (a missile). ■ [*tr.*] shoot (an animal) with a dart, typically in order to administer a drug.

dart·board /ˈdärtˌbŏrd/ ▶*n.* a circular board marked with numbered segments, used as a target in the game of darts.

darts /därts/ ▶*pl. n.* [usu. treated as *sing.*] an indoor game in which small pointed missiles with feather or plastic tails are thrown at a circular target marked with numbers in order to score points.

Dar·win·i·an /därˈwinēən/ ▶*adj.* of or relating to Darwinism.
▶*n.* an adherent of Darwinism.

dash /daSH/ ▶*v.* **1** [*intr.*] run or travel somewhere in a great hurry. ■ (often **dash about/around**) move about in a great hurry, esp. in the attempt to do several things in a short period of time: *I dash about to straighten things up.* **2** [*tr.*] strike or fling (something) somewhere with great force, esp. so as to have a destructive effect; hurl: *the ship was dashed upon the rocks.* ■ [*intr.*] strike forcefully against something: *a gust of rain dashed against the bricks.* ■ [*tr.*] destroy or frustrate (a person's hopes or expectations). ■ [*tr.*] cause (someone) to lose confidence; dispirit: *I won't tell Stuart—I think he'd be dashed.*
▶*phrasal v.* □ **dash something off** write something hurriedly and without much premeditation.
▶*n.* **1** an act of running somewhere suddenly and hastily: *she made a dash for the door.* ■ a journey or period of time characterized by urgency or eager haste: *a dash to the airport.* ■ a short fast race; a sprint: *the 100-yard dash.* **2** a small quantity of a substance, esp. a liquid, added to something else: *whiskey with a dash of soda.* ■ *fig.* a small amount of a particular quality adding piquancy or distinctiveness to something else: *a dash of sophistication.* **3** a horizontal stroke in writing or printing to mark a pause or break in sense, or to represent omitted letters or words. ■ the longer signal of the two used in Morse code. Compare with DOT[1]. ■ *Mus.* a short vertical mark placed above or beneath a note to indicate that it is to be performed in a very staccato manner. **4** impetuous or flamboyant vigor and confidence; panache. **5** short for DASHBOARD.

dash·board /ˈdaSHˌbŏrd/ ▶*n.* the panel facing the driver of a vehicle, containing instruments and controls. ■ *hist.* a board of wood or leather in front of a carriage, to keep out mud.

da·shi·ki /dəˈSHēkē/ ▶*n.* (*pl.* -**kis**) a loose, brightly colored shirt or tunic, originally from West Africa.

dash·ing /ˈdaSHiNG/ ▶*adj.* attractive in a romantic, adventurous way. ■ stylish or fashionable. —**dash·ing·ly** *adv.*

das·tard·ly /ˈdastərdlē/ ▶*adj.* dated, humorous wicked and cruel: *pirates and their dastardly deeds.* —**das·tard·li·ness** *n.*

da·ta /ˈdatə; ˈdātə/ ▶*n.* [treated as *sing.* or *pl.*] facts and statistics collected

---

Pronunciation Key ə *ago*, *up*; ər *over*, *fur*; ä *hat*; ā *ate*; ä *car*; CH *chin*; e *let*; ē *see*; e(ə)r *air*; i *fit*; ī *by*; i(ə)r *ear*; NG *sing*; ō *go*; ô *law*, *for*; oi *toy*; ŏŏ *good*; ōō *goo*; ou *out*; SH *she*; TH *thin*; T͟H *then*; (h)w *why*; ZH *vision*

for reference or analysis. See also DATUM. ■ the quantities, characters, or symbols on which operations are performed by a computer, stored and transmitted in the form of electrical signals. ■ *Philos.* things known or assumed as facts, making the basis of reasoning or calculation.

da·ta·base /'datə,bās; 'dā-/ ▶*n.* a structured set of data held in a computer, esp. one that is accessible in various ways.

da·ta·link /'datə,liNGk; 'dātə-/ ▶*n.* an electronic connection for the exchange of information.

da·ta proc·ess·ing ▶*n.* a series of operations on data, esp. by a computer, to retrieve, transform, or classify information. —**da·ta proc·es·sor** *n.*

date¹ /dāt/ ▶*n.* **1** the day of the month or year as specified by a number. ■ a particular day or year when a given event occurred or will occur: *significant dates like 1776 and 1789 | they've set a date for the wedding.* ■ (**dates**) the years of a person's birth and death or of the beginning and end of a period or event. ■ the period of time to which an artifact or structure belongs. ■ a written, printed, or stamped statement on an item giving the day, month, and year of writing, publication, or manufacture. **2** *inf.* a social or romantic appointment or engagement. ■ a person with whom one has such an engagement. ■ an appointment: *a date with a specialist.* ■ a musical or theatrical engagement or performance, esp. as part of a tour: *possible live dates in the near future.*
▶*v.* [*tr.*] **1** establish or ascertain the date of (an object or event): *they* **date** *the paintings to 1460–70.* ■ mark with a date: *sign and date the document* | [as *adj.*] (**dated**) *a signed and dated painting.* ■ [*intr.*] have its origin at a particular time; have existed since: *the controversy* **dates back** *to 1986.* **2** indicate or expose as being old-fashioned: *disco—that word alone dates me.* ■ [*intr.*] seem old-fashioned: [as *adj.*] (**dated**) *his style would sound dated nowadays.* **3** *inf.* go out with (someone in whom one is romantically or sexually interested). ▷Middle English: via Old French from medieval Latin *data,* feminine past participle of *dare* 'give'; from the Latin formula used in dating letters, *data (epistola)* '(letter) given or delivered,' to record a particular time or place. —**dat·er** *n.*
▶ □ **to date** until now: *their finest work to date.*

date² ▶*n.* **1** a sweet, dark brown, oval fruit containing a hard stone. **2** (also **date palm**) the tall palm tree (*Phoenix dactylifera*) that bears clusters of this fruit, native to western Asia and North Africa.

date·book /'dāt,book/ ▶*n.* a book with spaces for each day of the year in which one notes appointments or important information for each day.

date·less /'dātlis/ ▶*adj.* **1** (of a document or stamp) having no date mark. **2** not having, or incapable of having, social or romantic appointments or engagements.

date·line /'dāt,līn/ ▶*n.* a line at the head of a dispatch or special article in a newspaper showing the date and place of writing.
▶*v.* furnish (a dispatch or article) with a dateline.

Date Line ▶ see INTERNATIONAL DATE LINE.

date rape ▶*n.* rape committed by the victim's escort.

da·tive /'dātiv/ *Gram.* ▶*adj.* (in Latin, Greek, German, and other languages) denoting a case of nouns and pronouns, and words in grammatical agreement with them, indicating an indirect object or recipient.
▶*n.* a noun or other word of this type. ■ (**the dative**) the dative case.

da·tum /'dātəm; 'datəm/ ▶*n.* (*pl.* **da·ta** /'dātə; 'datə/) See also DATA. a piece of information. ■ an assumption or premise from which inferences may be drawn.

daub /dôb/ ▶*v.* [*tr.*] coat or smear (a surface) with a substance in a carelessly rough or liberal way: *she daubed her face* **with** *cream.* ■ spread (a thick or sticky substance) on a surface in such a way: *a canvas with paint daubed on it.* ■ paint (words or drawings) on a surface in such a way.
▶*n.* **1** plaster, clay, or another substance used for coating a surface. ■ a patch or smear of a substance. **2** a painting executed without much skill.

daugh·ter /'dôtər; 'dä-/ ▶*n.* a girl or woman in relation to her parents. ■ a female offspring of an animal. ■ a female descendant: *the daughters of Adam.* ■ a woman considered as the product of a particular person, influence, or environment: *a daughter of the savannas.* ■ *archaic* used as a term of affectionate address to a woman or girl, typically by an older person. ■ *poetic/lit.* a thing personified as a daughter in relation to its origin or source: *Italian, the daughter of Latin.* ■ *Physics* a nuclide formed by the radioactive decay of another.
▶*adj.* *Biol.* originating through division or replication: *daughter cells.* ▷Old English *dohtor,* of Germanic origin; related to Dutch *dochter* and German *Tochter,* from an Indo-European root shared by Greek *thugatēr.* —**daugh·ter·hood** /-,hŏŏd/ *n.* —**daugh·ter·ly** *adj.*

daugh·ter-in-law ▶*n.* (*pl.* **daugh·ters-in-law**) the wife of one's son.

daunt /dônt; dänt/ ▶*v.* [*tr.*] make (someone) feel intimidated or apprehensive: *some people are daunted by technology.* —**daunt·ing** *adj.* —**daunt·ing·ly** *adv.*

daunt·less /'dôntlis; 'dänt-/ ▶*adj.* showing fearlessness and determination. —**daunt·less·ly** *adv.* —**daunt·less·ness** *n.*

dau·phin /'dôfin/ ▶*n.* *hist.* the eldest son of the king of France.

dav·en·port /'davən,pôrt/ ▶*n.* **1** a large upholstered sofa, typically able to be converted into a bed. **2** *Brit.* an ornamental writing desk with drawers and a sloping surface for writing.

da·vit /'davit; 'dā-/ ▶*n.* a small crane on board a ship, esp. one of a pair for suspending or lowering a lifeboat.

Da·vy Jones's lock·er /,dāvē 'jōnz(əz)/ ▶*n.* *inf.* the bottom of the sea, esp. regarded as the grave of those drowned at sea.

daw·dle /'dôdl/ ▶*v.* [*intr.*] waste time; be slow. ■ move slowly and idly. —**daw·dler** /'dôd(ə)lər/ *n.*

dawn /dôn; dän/ ▶*n.* the first appearance of light in the sky before sunrise. ■ *fig.* the beginning of a phenomenon or period of time, esp. one considered favorable: *the dawn of civilization.*
▶*v.* [*intr.*] **1** (of a day) begin: *Thursday dawned bright and sunny.* ■ *fig.* come into existence. **2** become evident to the mind; be perceived or understood: *the truth was beginning to* **dawn on** *him* | [as *adj.*] (**dawning**) *he smiled with dawning recognition.*

day /dā/ ▶*n.* **1** a period of twenty-four hours as a unit of time, reckoned from one midnight to the next, corresponding to a rotation of the earth on its axis. ■ the part of this period when it is light; the time between sunrise and sunset. ■ the time spent working during such a period: *he works an eight-hour day.* ■ *Astron.* a single rotation of a planet in relation to its primary. ■ *Astron.* the period on a planet when its primary star is above the horizon. ■ *archaic* daylight: *it was broad day.* **2** (usu. **days**) a particular period of the past; an era: *the laws were very strict in those days.* ■ (**the day**) the present time: *the issues of the day.* ■ a day associated with a particular event or purpose: *graduation day.* ■ a day's endeavor, or the period of an endeavor, esp. as bringing success: *speed and surprise would win the day.* ■ (**days**) a particular period in a person's life or career: *my student days.* ■ (**one's day**) the successful, fortunate, or influential period of a person's life or career: *a matinee idol in his day.* ■ (**one's days**) the span of someone's life: *she cared for him for the rest of his days.*
▶*adj.* carried out during the day as opposed to the evening or at night: *my day job.* ■ (of a person) working during the day as opposed to at night: *a day nurse.*
▶ □ **all in a** (or **the**) **day's work** (of something unusual or difficult) accepted as part of a normal routine or as a matter of course: *dodging sharks is all in a day's work for these scientists.* □ **any day** *inf.* at any time: *you can take me dancing* **any day** *of the week.* ■ (used to express one's strong preference for something) under any circumstances: *I'd rather live in a shack in the woods, any day.* ■ very soon: *she's expected to give birth any day.* □ **call it a day** end a period of activity, esp. resting content that enough has been done. □ **day after day** on each successive day, esp. over a long period: *the rain poured down day after day.* □ **day and night** all the time. □ **day by day** gradually and steadily. □ **day in, day out** continuously or repeatedly over a long period of time. □ **have had one's** (or **its**) **day** be no longer popular, successful, or influential. □ **in this day and age** at the present time; in the modern era. □ —— **of the day** a thing currently considered to be particularly interesting or important: *the big story of the day.* □ **one day** (or **one of these days**) at some time in the future. □ **one of those days** a day when several things go wrong. □ **that will** (or **that'll**) **be the day** *inf.* that will never happen. □ **these days** at present. □ **those were the days** used to assert that a particular past time was better than the present. □ **to the day** exactly: *four years to the day.* □ **to this day** up to the present time; still.

day·break /'dā,brāk/ ▶*n.* the time in the morning when daylight first appears; dawn: *she set off at daybreak.*

day care ▶*n.* daytime care for the needs of people who cannot be fully independent, such as children or the elderly: [as *adj.*] *a day-care center.*

day·dream /'dā,drēm/ ▶*n.* a series of pleasant thoughts that distract one's attention from the present.
▶*v.* [*intr.*] indulge in such a series of thoughts. —**day·dream·er** *n.* —**day·dream·y** *adj.*

Day-Glo /'dā ,glō/ ▶*n.* *trademark* a fluorescent paint or other coloring.
▶*adj.* (also **day-glo**) of or denoting very bright or fluorescent coloring: *wearing Day-Glo pink T-shirts.*

day·light /'dā,līt/ ▶*n.* **1** the natural light of the day: [as *adj.*] *daylight hours.* ■ the first appearance of light in the morning; dawn. ■ *fig.* distance between one person or thing and another: *the growing daylight between himself and the leading jockey.* **2** (**daylights**) used to emphasize the severity or thoroughness of an action: *he beat the living daylights out of them.*

▸ □ **see daylight** begin to understand what was previously unclear.

day·light sav·ing time (also **day·light sav·ings time**) ▸ *n.* time as adjusted to achieve longer evening daylight, esp. in summer, by setting the clocks an hour ahead of the standard time.

day·time /ˈdāˌtīm/ ▸ *n.* the time of the day between sunrise and sunset.

day-to-day ▸ *adj.* happening every day: *day-to-day management of the classroom.* ■ ordinary; everyday: *day-to-day domestic life.* ■ short-term; without consideration for the future: *the struggle for day-to-day survival.* ■ *Sports* (of a player) not playing owing to a minor injury that is being treated and evaluated on a daily basis: *their shortstop is listed as day-to-day.*
▸ *n.* an ordinary, everyday routine: *they have come to escape the day-to-day.*
▸ *adv.* on a daily basis: *the information to be traded is determined day-to-day.*

day trip ▸ *n.* a journey or excursion completed in one day. —**day-trip-per** (or **day trip-per**) *n.*

daze /dāz/ ▸ *v.* [tr.] (usu. **be dazed**) make (someone) unable to think or react properly; stupefy; bewilder.
▸ *n.* a state of stunned confusion or bewilderment: *he was walking around in a daze.* —**daz·ed·ly** /ˈdāzidlē/ *adv.*

daz·zle /ˈdazəl/ ▸ *v.* [tr.] (of a bright light) blind (a person) temporarily. ■ *fig.* amaze or overwhelm (someone) with a particular impressive quality: *dazzled by the beauty of the exhibition.*
▸ *n.* brightness that confuses someone's vision temporarily: *a dazzle of green and red spotlights.* —**daz·zle·ment** *n.* —**daz·zler** *n.* —**daz·zling** *adj.*

Db ▸ *symb.* the chemical element dubnium.

dB ▸ *abbr.* decibel(s).

DC ▸ *abbr.* ■ *Mus.* da capo. ■ direct current. ■ Doctor of Chiropractic.

DD ▸ *abbr.* ■ Department of Defense (on forms and documents): *a DD 214.* ■ *Mil.* dishonorable discharge. ■ Doctor of Divinity.

D-Day ▸ *n.* the day (June 6, 1944) in World War II on which Allied forces invaded northern France by landing in Normandy. ■ the day on which an important operation is to begin or a change to take effect.

DDT ▸ *abbr.* a synthetic chlorine-containing organic compound introduced in the 1940s as an insecticide and now widely banned.

DE ▸ *abbr.* *Football* defensive end.

dea·con /ˈdēkən/ ▸ *n.* (in Catholic, Anglican, and Orthodox churches) an ordained minister of an order ranking below that of priest. ■ (in some Protestant churches) a lay officer appointed to assist a minister, esp. in secular affairs.
▸ *v.* [tr.] appoint or ordain as a deacon. —**dea·con·ship** /-ˌSHip/ *n.*

dea·con·ess /ˈdēkənis/ ▸ *n.* (in some churches) a woman with duties similar to those of a deacon.

de·ac·ti·vate /dēˈaktəvāt/ ▸ *v.* **1** [tr.] make (something, typically technical equipment or a virus) inactive by disconnecting or destroying it. **2** [tr.] *Mil.* remove from active duty. —**de·ac·ti·va·tion** /dēˌaktəˈvāSHən/ *n.* —**de·ac·ti·va·tor** /-ˌvātər/ *n.*

dead /ded/ ▸ *adj.* **1** no longer alive. ■ (of a part of the body) having lost sensation; numb. ■ having or displaying no emotion, sympathy, or sensitivity: *a cold, dead voice.* ■ no longer current, relevant, or important: *a dead issue.* ■ devoid of living things: *a dead planet.* ■ resembling death: *a dead faint.* ■ (of a place or time) characterized by a lack of activity or excitement. ■ (of money) not financially productive. ■ (of sound) without resonance; dull. ■ (of a color) not glossy or bright. ■ (of a piece of equipment) no longer functioning: *the phone had gone dead.* ■ (of an electric circuit or conductor) carrying or transmitting no current. ■ no longer burning: *the fire had been dead for days.* ■ (of air or water) not circulating; stagnant. ■ (of the ball in a game) out of play. ■ (of a playing field, ball, or other surface) lacking springiness or bounce. **2** complete; absolute: *we sat in dead silence.*
▸ *adv.* absolutely; completely: *you're dead right.* ■ exactly: *dead on time.* ■ straight; directly: *flares were seen dead ahead.*
▸ *n.* [as *pl. n.*] (**the dead**) those who have died. —**dead·ness** *n.*
▸ □ **dead and buried** over; finished: *the incident is dead and buried.* □ **dead from the neck up** *inf.* stupid. □ **dead in the water** unable to move. ■ *fig.* unable to function effectively. □ **dead meat** *inf.* in serious trouble: *if anyone finds out, you're dead meat.* □ **the dead of night** the quietest, darkest part of the night. □ **the dead of winter** the coldest part of winter. □ **dead on** exactly right: *her judgment was dead on.* □ **dead on arrival** used to describe a person who is declared dead immediately upon arrival at a hospital. ■ *fig.* (of an idea, etc.) declared ineffective without ever having been put into effect. □ **dead on one's feet** *inf.* extremely tired. □ **dead set against** *inf.* strongly opposed to. □ **dead to rights** *inf.* in the act of doing something wrong; red-handed: *he had me dead to rights.* □ **dead to the world** *inf.* fast asleep. □ **wouldn't**

be seen (or **caught**) **dead** *inf.* used to express strong dislike for a particular thing: *wouldn't be caught dead wearing a bib.*

dead·beat /ˈdedˌbēt/ ▸ *n.* *inf.* a person who tries to evade paying debts. ■ (also **deadbeat dad**) a man who avoids paying child support. ■ an idle, feckless, or disreputable person.

dead·bolt /ˈdedˌbōlt/ ▸ *n.* a bolt engaged by turning a knob or key, rather than by spring action.

dead duck ▸ *n. inf.* **1** an unsuccessful or useless person or thing. **2** a person who is beyond help; one who is doomed.

dead·en /ˈdedn/ ▸ *v.* [tr.] make (a noise or sensation) less intense. ■ deprive of the power of sensation. ■ deprive of force or vitality; stultify: [as *adj.*] (**deadening**) *a deadening routine.* ■ make (someone) insensitive to something: *laughter might deaden us to the moral issue.* —**dead·en·er** *n.*

dead end ▸ *n.* an end of a road or passage from which no exit is possible. ■ a road or passage having such an end. ■ a situation offering no prospects of progress or development: [as *adj.*] *a dead-end job.*
▸ *v.* [intr.] (**dead-end**) (of a road or passage) come to a dead end.

dead·eye /ˈdedˌī/ ▸ *n.* **1** *Sailing* a circular wooden block with a groove around the circumference to take a lanyard, used singly or in pairs to tighten a shroud. **2** *inf.* an expert marksman.

dead·head /ˈdedˌhed/ (also **dead-head**) ▸ *n.* **1** (**Deadhead**) a fan and follower of the rock group The Grateful Dead. **2** *inf.* a commercial carrier with no paying passengers or freight on a trip. ■ a passenger or member of an audience with a free ticket. ■ *inf.* a boring or unenterprising person. **3** a sunken or partially submerged log.
▸ *v.* **1** [intr.] *inf.* (of a commercial driver, etc.) complete a trip without paying passengers or freight: *trucks deadheading into California.* ■ ride (in a plane or other vehicle) without paying for a ticket. **2** [tr.] remove dead flowerheads from (a plant) to encourage further blooming.

dead heat ▸ *n.* a situation in or result of a race in which two or more competitors are exactly even.
▸ *v.* [intr.] (**dead-heat**) run or finish a race exactly even.

dead let·ter ▸ *n.* **1** a law or treaty that has not been repealed but is ineffectual or defunct in practice. ■ *fig.* a thing that is impractical or obsolete. **2** a letter that is undeliverable and unreturnable.

dead·line /ˈdedˌlīn/ ▸ *n.* **1** the latest time or date by which something should be completed. **2** *hist.* a line drawn around a prison beyond which prisoners were liable to be shot.

dead load ▸ *n.* the intrinsic weight of a structure or vehicle, excluding the weight of passengers or goods. Often contrasted with LIVE LOAD.

dead·lock /ˈdedˌläk/ ▸ *n.* a situation, typically one involving opposing parties, in which no progress can be made.

dead·locked /ˈdedˌläkt/ ▸ *adj.* (of a situation or opposing parties) at a point where no progress can be made because of disagreement: *jurors were deadlocked.* ■ (of a contest or game) tied, esp. at a point when a winner would normally have been decided.

dead·ly /ˈdedlē/ ▸ *adj.* (**-li·er**, **-li·est**) causing or able to cause death. ■ filled with hate. ■ (typically in the context of shooting or sports) extremely accurate, effective, or skillful. ■ *inf.* extremely boring. ■ complete; total: *she was in deadly earnest.*
▸ *adv.* resembling or suggesting death: *her skin was deadly pale.* ■ extremely. —**dead·li·ness** *n.*

dead·ly night·shade ▸ *n.* a poisonous Eurasian plant (*Atropa belladonna*) of the nightshade family, with drooping purple flowers and black cherrylike fruit. Also called BELLADONNA.

dead·ly sin ▸ *n.* (in Christian tradition) a sin regarded as leading to damnation, esp. one of a traditional list of seven. See SEVEN DEADLY SINS.

dead·pan /ˈdedˌpan/ ▸ *adj.* deliberately impassive or expressionless.
▸ *adv.* in a deadpan manner.
▸ *v.* (**-panned**, **-pan·ning**) say something amusing while affecting a serious manner.

dead reck·on·ing ▸ *n.* the process of calculating one's position by estimating the direction and distance traveled rather than by using landmarks, astronomical observations, or electronic navigation methods.

dead weight (also **dead·weight**) ▸ *n.* the weight of an inert person or thing. ■ a heavy or oppressive burden: *the past was so much dead weight.* ■ the total weight of cargo, stores, etc., that a ship carries or can carry at a particular draft. ■ another term for DEAD LOAD. ■ *Farming* animals sold by the estimated weight of salable meat that they will yield.

Pronunciation Key ə *ago, up*; ər *over, fur*; a *hat*; ā *ate*; ä *car*; CH *chin*; e *let*; ē *see*; e(ə)r *air*; i *fit*; ī *by*; i(ə)r *ear*; NG *sing*; ō *go*; ô *law, for*; oi *toy*; ŏŏ *good*; ōō *goo*; ou *out*; SH *she*; TH *thin*; TH *then*; (h)w *why*; ZH *vision*

■ [usu. as *adj.*] *Econ.* losses incurred because of the inefficient allocation of resources, esp. through taxation or restriction.

dead·wood /'ded,wŏŏd/ ▶ *n.* a branch or part of a tree that is dead. ■ *fig.* people or things that are no longer useful or productive.

deaf /def/ ▶ *adj.* lacking the power of hearing or having impaired hearing: [as *pl. n.*] **(the deaf)** *subtitles for the deaf.* ■ unwilling or unable to hear or pay attention to something: *deaf to advice.* ▷Old English *dēaf*, of Germanic origin; related to Dutch *doof* and German *taub*, from an Indo-European root shared by Greek *tuphlos* 'blind.' —**deaf·ness** *n.*

▶ □ **fall on deaf ears** (of a statement or request) be ignored. □ **turn a deaf ear** refuse to listen or respond to a statement or request.

deaf·en /'defən/ ▶ *v.* [*tr.*] (usu. **be deafened**) cause (someone) to lose the power of hearing permanently or temporarily. ■ (of a loud noise) overwhelm (someone) with sound. ■ **(deafen someone to)** (of a sound) cause someone to be unaware of (other sounds).

deaf-mute *chiefly offens.* ▶ *n.* a person who is both deaf and unable to speak.

▶ *adj.* both deaf and unable to speak. ■ of or relating to such people.

deal /dēl/ ▶ *v.* (*past* and *past part.* **dealt** /delt/) **1** [*tr.*] distribute (cards) in an orderly rotation to the players for a game or round. ■ **(deal some-one in)** include a new player in a card game by giving them cards. ■ distribute or mete out (something) to a person or group. **2** [*intr.*] take part in commercial trading of a particular commodity: *directors were prohibited from dealing in the company's shares.* ■ *fig.* be concerned with: *a movie that deals in ideas and issues.* ■ *inf.* buy and sell illegal drugs. [*tr.*] *Frankie started dealing cocaine.* **3** [*intr.*] **(deal with)** take measures concerning (someone or something), esp. with the intention of putting something right: *the government had been unable to deal with the economic crisis.* ■ cope with (a difficult person or situation). ■ treat (someone) in a particular way: *life had dealt harshly with her.* ■ have relations with (a person or organization), esp. in a commercial context. ■ take or have as a subject; discuss. **4** inflict (a blow) on (someone or something): *hopes of recovery were dealt another blow.*

▶ *n.* **1** an agreement entered into by two or more parties for their mutual benefit, esp. in a business or political context. ■ an attractive price on a commodity; a bargain. ■ a particular form of treatment given or received: *working mothers get a bad deal.* **2** a significant but unspecified amount of something: *he lost a great deal of blood.* **3** the process of distributing the cards to players in a card game. ■ a player's turn to distribute cards. ■ the round of play following this. ■ the set of hands dealt to the players.

▶ □ **a big deal** *inf.* a thing considered important: *they don't make a big deal out of minor irritations.* ■ an important person; a celebrity. ■ **(big deal)** used to express one's contempt for something regarded as impressive or important by another person. □ **a raw** (or **rough**) **deal** *inf.* a situation in which someone receives unfair or harsh treatment. □ **a good** (or **great**) **deal** a large amount: *I don't know a great deal about politics.* ■ to a considerable extent.

deal·er /'dēlər/ ▶ *n.* **1** a person or business that buys and sells goods. ■ a person who buys and sells shares, securities, or other financial assets as a principal (rather than as a broker or agent). ■ *inf.* a person who buys and sells drugs. **2** the player who distributes the cards at the start of a game or hand. —**deal·er·ship** /-,SHip/ *n.*

deal·ing /'dēliNG/ ▶ *n.* **1** (usu. **dealings**) a business relation or transaction. ■ a personal connection or association with someone. ■ the activity of buying and selling a particular commodity. **2** the particular way in which someone behaves toward others.

dealt /delt/ ▶ *v.* past participle of DEAL.

dean /dēn/ ▶ *n.* **1** the head of a college or university faculty or department. ■ a college or university official, esp. one with disciplinary and advisory functions. ■ the leader or senior member of a group. **2** the head of the chapter of a cathedral or collegiate church.

dear /di(ə)r/ ▶ *adj.* **1** regarded with deep affection; cherished by someone. ■ used in speech as a way of addressing a person in a polite way. ■ used as part of the polite introduction to a letter. ■ endearing; sweet: *a dear little puppy.* **2** expensive.

▶ *n.* used as an affectionate or friendly form of address: *don't you worry, dear.* ■ a sweet or endearing person.

▶ *adv.* at a high cost: *they buy property cheaply and sell dear.*

▶ *interj.* used in expressions of surprise, dismay, or sympathy: *oh dear.* ▷Old English *dēore*, of Germanic origin; related to Dutch *dier* 'beloved,' also to Dutch *duur* and German *teuer* 'expensive.' —**dear·ly** *adv.* —**dear·ness** *n.*

dearth /dərTH/ ▶ *n.* a scarcity or lack of something: *there is a dearth of evidence.*

death /deTH/ ▶ *n.* the action or fact of dying or being killed; the end of

the life of a person or organism. ■ an instance of a person or an animal dying. ■ the state of being dead. ■ the permanent ending of vital processes in a cell or tissue. ■ **(Death)** the personification of the power that destroys life, often represented in art and literature as a skeleton or an old man holding a scythe. ■ *fig.* the destruction or permanent end of something: *the death of hopes.* ■ *fig., inf.* a damaging or destructive state of affairs: *social death.* —**death·less** *adj.* —**death·like** /-,līk/ *adj.*

▶ □ **at death's door** (esp. in hyperbolic use) so ill that one might die. □ **be the death of** (often used hyperbolically or humorously) cause someone's death: *you'll be the death of me with your questions.* □ **catch one's death** (**of cold**) *inf.* catch a severe cold or chill. □ **do something to death** perform or repeat something so frequently that it becomes tediously familiar. □ **a fate worse than death** a terrible experience. □ **like death warmed over** *inf.* extremely tired or ill.

death·bed /'deTH,bed/ ▶ *n.* the bed where someone is dying or has died. ■ used in reference to the time when someone is dying: *she visited him on his deathbed* | [as *adj.*] *a deathbed confession.*

death blow ▶ *n.* an impact or stroke that causes death. ■ *fig.* an event, circumstance, or action that ends something abruptly.

death·ly /'deTHlē/ ▶ *adj.* (**-li·er, -li·est**) resembling or suggestive of death: *a deathly hush* | *she felt deathly cold.* ■ *archaic, poetic/lit.* of, relating to, or causing death: *an eagle carrying a snake in its deathly grasp.*

death mask ▶ *n.* a plaster cast taken of a dead person's face, used to make a mask or model.

death row /'rō/ ▶ *n.* a prison section for prisoners sentenced to death.

death trap ▶ *n.* a place, structure, or vehicle that is potentially dangerous.

death wish ▶ *n.* a desire for someone's death, esp. an unconscious desire for one's own death.

deb /deb/ ▶ *n. inf.* short for DEBUTANTE.

de·ba·cle /di'bäkel; -'bäkəl/ ▶ *n.* a sudden and ignominious failure; a fiasco.

de·bar /dē'bär/ ▶ *v.* (**-barred, -bar·ring**) [*tr.*] (usu. **be debarred**) exclude or prohibit (someone) from doing something. —**de·bar·ment** *n.* /-mənt/

de·bark[1] /dē'bärk/ ▶ *v.* [*intr.*] leave a ship or aircraft. ■ [*tr.*] unload (cargo or troops) from a ship or aircraft. —**de·bar·ka·tion** /,dēbär'kāSHən/ *n.*

de·bark[2] ▶ *v.* [*tr.*] remove (the bark) from a tree.

de·base /di'bās/ ▶ *v.* [*tr.*] reduce (something) in quality or value; degrade: *the love episodes debase the drama* | [as *adj.*] **(debased)** *debased traditions of sportsmanship.* ■ lower the moral character of (someone): *war debases people.* ■ *hist.* lower the value of (coinage) by reducing the content of precious metal. —**de·base·ment** *n.* —**de·bas·er** *n.*

de·bat·a·ble /di'bātəbəl/ ▶ *adj.* open to discussion or argument. —**de·bat·a·bly** /-blē/ *adv.*

de·bate /di'bāt/ ▶ *n.* a formal discussion on a particular topic in a meeting or assembly, in which opposing arguments are put forward. ■ an argument about a particular subject, esp. one in which many people are involved: *the national debate on abortion.*

▶ *v.* [*tr.*] argue about (a subject), esp. in a formal manner. ■ consider a possible course of action before reaching a decision: *he debated whether he should leave.* —**de·bat·er** *n.*

▶ □ **be open to debate** be unproven; require further discussion. □ **under debate** being discussed or disputed.

de·bauch /di'bôCH/ ▶ *v.* [*tr.*] destroy or debase the moral purity of; corrupt. ■ *dated* seduce (a woman).

▶ *n.* a bout of excessive indulgence in sensual pleasures, esp. eating and drinking. ■ the habit or practice of such indulgence; debauchery: *his life had been spent in debauch.* —**de·bauch·er** *n.*

de·bau·chee /di,bô'CHē/ ▶ *n.* a person given to excessive indulgence in sensual pleasures.

de·bauch·er·y /di'bôCHərē/ ▶ *n.* excessive indulgence in sensual pleasures.

de·ben·ture /di'benCHər/ ▶ *n.* (also **debenture bond**) an unsecured loan certificate issued by a company, backed by general credit rather than by specified assets.

de·bil·i·tate /di'bili,tāt; dē-/ ▶ *v.* [*tr.*] [often as *adj.*] **(debilitating)** make (someone) weak and infirm: *a debilitating disease* | [as *adj.*] **(debilitated)** *chronically debilitated and unwell.* ■ hinder, delay, or weaken: *the debilitating effects of underinvestment.* —**de·bil·i·tat·ing·ly** *adv.* —**de·bil·i·ta·tion** /di,bili'tāSHən/ *n.* —**de·bil·i·ta·tive** /di'bili,tātiv/ *adj.*

de·bil·i·ty /di'bilitē/ ▶ *n.* physical weakness, esp. as a result of illness.

deb·it /'debit/ ▶ *n.* an entry recording an amount owed, listed on the left-hand side or column of an account. The opposite of CREDIT. ■ a payment made or owed.

▶ *v.* (**deb·it·ed, deb·it·ing**) [*tr.*] (usu. **be debited**) (of a bank or other financial organization) remove (an amount of money) from a customer's account, typically as payment for services or goods. ■ remove an amount of money from (a bank account).

▶ □ **on the debit side** as an unsatisfactory aspect of the situation: *on the debit side, they predict a rise in book prices.*

deb·it card ▶ *n.* a card issued by a bank allowing the holder to transfer money electronically when making a purchase.

deb·o·nair /ˌdebəˈne(ə)r/ ▶ *adj.* (esp. of a man) confident, stylish, and charming. —**deb·o·nair·ly** *adv.*

de·bouch /diˈbouCH; -ˈbōōSH/ ▶ *v.* [*intr.*] emerge from a narrow or confined space into a wide, open area: *the stream debouches into a silent pool.* —**de·bouch·ment** *n.*

de·brief /dēˈbrēf/ ▶ *v.* [*tr.*] question (someone, typically a soldier or spy) about a completed mission or undertaking: [as *n.*] (**debriefing**) *during his debriefing, he exposed two spies.* —**de·brief·er** *n.*

de·bris /dəˈbrē; ˌdā-/ ▶ *n.* scattered fragments, typically of something wrecked or destroyed. ■ loose natural material consisting esp. of broken pieces of rock: *comets and debris orbiting the sun.* ■ dirt or refuse.

debt /det/ ▶ *n.* something that is owed or due: *I paid off my debts | a way to reduce Third World debt.* ■ the state of owing money: *heavily in debt.* ■ a feeling of gratitude for a service or favor: *we owe them a debt of thanks.*

▶ □ **be in someone's debt** owe gratitude to someone for a service or favor.

debt·or /ˈdetər/ ▶ *n.* a person or institution that owes a sum of money.

de·bug /dēˈbəg/ ▶ *v.* (**-bugged, -bug·ging**) [*tr.*] **1** identify and remove errors from (computer hardware or software): [as *n.*] (**debugging**) *software debugging.* **2** detect and remove concealed microphones from (an area). **3** remove insects from (something), esp. with a pesticide.

de·bunk /diˈbəNGk/ ▶ *v.* [*tr.*] expose the falseness or hollowness of (a myth, idea, or belief). ■ reduce the inflated reputation of (someone), esp. by ridicule. —**de·bunk·er** *n.* —**de·bunk·er·y** *n.*

de·but /dāˈbyōō/ ▶ *n.* a person's first appearance or performance in a capacity or role: *his debut as a director.* ■ the first public appearance of a new product or presentation of a theatrical show. ■ [as *adj.*] denoting the first recording or publication of a group, singer, or writer: *a debut album.* ■ dated the first appearance of a debutante in society.

▶ *v.* [*intr.*] perform in public for the first time. ■ (of a new product) be launched. ■ [*tr.*] (of a company) launch (a new product).

deb·u·tante /ˈdebyōōˌtänt; ˈdebyə-/ ▶ *n.* an upper-class young woman making her first appearance in fashionable society.

Dec. ▶ *abbr.* December.

dec. ▶ *abbr.* deceased.

dec·ade /ˈdekād/ ▶ *n.* **1** a period of ten years. ■ a period of ten years beginning with a year ending in 0: *the fourth decade of the nineteenth century.* **2** a set, series, or group of ten. —**dec·a·dal** /ˈdekədl/ *adj.*

dec·a·dence /ˈdekədəns/ ▶ *n.* moral or cultural decline, esp. after a peak or culmination of achievement. ■ behavior reflecting such a decline. ■ luxurious self-indulgence.

dec·a·dent /ˈdekədənt/ ▶ *adj.* characterized by or reflecting a state of moral or cultural decline. ■ luxuriously self-indulgent.

▶ *n.* a person who is luxuriously self-indulgent. ■ (often **Decadent**) a member of a group of late 19th-cent. French and English poets associated with the Aesthetic Movement. —**dec·a·dent·ly** *adv.*

de·caf /ˈdēˌkaf/ ▶ *n.* inf. decaffeinated coffee.

de·caf·fein·ate /dēˈkafəˌnāt/ ▶ *v.* [*tr.*] [usu. as *adj.*] (**decaffeinated**) remove the caffeine from (coffee or tea). —**de·caf·fein·a·tion** /dēˌkafəˈnāSHən/ *n.*

dec·a·he·dron /ˌdekəˈhēdrən/ ▶ *n.* (*pl.* **-drons** or **-dra** /-drə/) a solid figure with ten plane faces. —**dec·a·he·dral** /-drəl/ *adj.*

de·cal /ˈdēkal/ ▶ *n.* a design prepared on special paper for transfer onto another surface such as glass, porcelain, or metal.

de·cal·co·ma·ni·a /dēˌkalkəˈmānēə/ ▶ *n.* the process of transferring designs from prepared paper on to glass or porcelain. ■ a technique used by some artists that involves pressing paint between sheets of paper.

dec·a·li·ter /ˈdekəˌlētər/ (also **dek·a·li·ter**) (abbr.: **dal** or **dkl**) ▶ *n.* a metric unit of capacity, equal to 10 liters.

Dec·a·logue /ˈdekəˌlôg; -ˌläg/ ▶ *n.* (usu. **the Decalogue**) the Ten Commandments.

dec·a·me·ter /ˈdekəˌmētər/ (also **dek·a·me·ter**) (abbr.: **dam** or **dkm**) ▶ *n.* a metric unit of length, equal to 10 meters. —**dec·a·met·ric** /ˌdekəˈmetrik/ *adj.*

de·camp /diˈkamp/ ▶ *v.* [*intr.*] depart suddenly, esp. to relocate one's business or household in another area. ■ abscond hurriedly to avoid prosecution or detection. ■ *archaic* break up or leave a military camp. —**de·camp·ment** *n.*

de·cant /diˈkant/ ▶ *v.* [*tr.*] gradually pour (liquid, typically wine or a solution) from one container into another, esp. without disturbing the sediment. ■ *fig.* empty out; move as if by pouring.

de·cant·er /diˈkantər/ ▶ *n.* a stoppered glass container into which wine is decanted.

de·cap·i·tate /diˈkapiˌtāt/ ▶ *v.* [*tr.*] cut off the head of (a person or animal): [as *adj.*] (**decapitated**) *a decapitated body.* ■ cut the end or top from (something). ■ *fig.* attempt to undermine (a group or organization) by removing its leaders. —**de·cap·i·ta·tion** /diˌkapiˈtāSHən/ *n.* —**de·cap·i·ta·tor** /-ˌtātər/ *n.*

dec·a·pod /ˈdekəˌpäd/ ▶ *n.* **1** any crustacean of the chiefly marine order Decapoda, having five pairs of walking legs, including shrimps, crabs, and lobsters. **2** any of various mollusks of the class Cephalopoda, having eight arms and two long tentacles, including squids and cuttlefish.

▶ *adj.* of or related to the decapods.

dec·a·syl·lab·ic /ˌdekəsiˈlabik/ *Prosody* ▶ *adj.* (of a metrical line) consisting of ten syllables.

▶ *n.* a metrical line of ten syllables.

de·cath·lon /diˈkaTH(ə)ˌlän/ ▶ *n.* an athletic event in which each competitor takes part in the same ten events (100-meter dash, long jump, shot put, high jump, 400-meter dash, 110-meter hurdles, discus, pole vault, javelin, and 1,500-meter run). —**de·cath·lete** /-ˈkaTH(ə)ˌlēt/ *n.*

de·cay /diˈkā/ ▶ *v.* [*intr.*] (of organic matter) rot or decompose through the action of bacteria and fungi: [as *adj.*] (**decayed**) *a decayed cabbage leaf* | [as *adj.*] (**decaying**) *the odor of decaying fish.* ■ [*tr.*] cause to rot or decompose: *the fungus will decay soft timber.* ■ (of a building or area) fall into disrepair; deteriorate. ■ decline in quality, power, or vigor: *moral authority was decaying.* ■ *Physics* (of a radioactive substance, particle, etc.) undergo change to a different form by emitting radiation. ■ *technical* (of a physical quantity) undergo a gradual decrease.

▶ *n.* the state or process of rotting or decomposition. ■ structural or physical deterioration: *the old barn fell into decay.* ■ rotten matter or tissue: *fluoride heals small spots of decay.* ■ the process of declining in quality, power, or vigor: *moral decay.* ■ *Physics* the change of a radioactive substance, particle, etc., into another by the emission of radiation. ■ *technical* gradual decrease in the magnitude of a physical quantity. ▷late Middle English: from Old French *decair*, based on Latin *decidere* 'fall down or off,' from *de-* 'from' + *cadere* 'fall.'

de·cease /diˈsēs/ ▶ *n.* formal or Law death: *his sudden decease.*

▶ *v.* [*intr.*] archaic die.

de·ceased /diˈsēst/ ▶ *n.* (**the deceased**) a person who has died.

▶ *adj.* dead; no longer living.

de·ce·dent /diˈsēdnt/ ▶ *n.* Law a person who has died: *the decedent's property.*

de·ceit /diˈsēt/ ▶ *n.* the action or practice of deceiving someone by concealing or misrepresenting the truth. ■ a dishonest act or statement. ■ deceitful disposition or character.

de·ceit·ful /diˈsētfəl/ ▶ *adj.* (of a person) deceiving or misleading others, typically on a habitual basis. ■ intended to deceive or mislead. —**de·ceit·ful·ly** *adv.* —**de·ceit·ful·ness** *n.*

de·ceive /diˈsēv/ ▶ *v.* [*tr.*] (of a person) cause (someone) to believe something that is not true, typically in order to gain some personal advantage: *I didn't intend to deceive people into thinking it was French champagne.* ■ (of a thing) give a mistaken impression: [*intr.*] *everything about him was intended to deceive.* ■ (**deceive oneself**) fail to admit to oneself that something is true. ■ be sexually unfaithful to (one's regular partner). —**de·ceiv·a·ble** *adj.* —**de·ceiv·er** *n.*

de·cel·er·ate /dēˈseləˌrāt/ ▶ *v.* [*intr.*] (of a vehicle, machine, or process) reduce speed; slow down. ■ [*tr.*] cause to move more slowly: *gravity decelerates the cosmic expansion.* —**de·cel·er·a·tion** /-ˌseləˈrāSHən/ *n.* —**de·cel·er·a·tor** /-ˌrātər/ *n.*

De·cem·ber /diˈsembər/ ▶ *n.* the twelfth month of the year, in the northern hemisphere usually considered the first month of winter.

de·cen·cy /ˈdēsənsē/ ▶ *n.* (*pl.* **-cies**) behavior that conforms to accepted standards of morality or respectability: *she had the decency to come and confess.* ■ modesty and propriety. ■ (**decencies**) the requirements of accepted or respectable behavior: *an appeal to decencies.* ■ (**decencies**) things required for a reasonable standard of life.

de·cen·ni·al /diˈsenēəl/ ▶ *adj.* recurring every ten years: *the decennial census.* ■ lasting for or relating to a period of ten years. —**de·cen·ni·al·ly** *adv.*

de·cent /ˈdēsənt/ ▶ *adj.* **1** conforming with generally accepted standards of respectable or moral behavior. ■ appropriate; fitting: *a decent waiting period.* ■ not likely to shock or embarrass others. ■ *inf.* sufficiently clothed to see visitors. **2** of an acceptable standard; satisfactory; good: *a pretty decent plot of land.* ■ kind, obliging, or generous. —**de·cent·ly** *adv.*

de·cen·tral·ize /dē'sentrə,līz/ ▸ *v.* [*tr.*] [often as *adj.*] (**decentralized**) transfer (authority) from central to local government: *decentralized governments* | [*intr.*] *countries trying to decentralize.* ■ move departments of (an organization) away from an administrative center to other locations, usually granting them some degree of autonomy. —**de·cen·tral·ist** /-list/ *n. & adj.* —**de·cen·tral·i·za·tion** /dē,sentrəli'zāsHən/ *n.*

de·cep·tion /di'sepsHən/ ▸ *n.* the action of deceiving someone. ■ a thing that deceives: *elaborate deceptions.*

de·cep·tive /di'septiv/ ▸ *adj.* giving an appearance or impression different from the true one; misleading. —**de·cep·tive·ly** *adv.* —**de·cep·tive·ness** *n.*

dec·i·bel /'desə,bel; -bəl/ (abbr.: **dB**) ▸ *n.* a unit used to measure the intensity of a sound or the power level of an electrical signal by comparing it with a given level on a logarithmic scale. ■ (in general use) a degree of loudness: *his voice went up several decibels.*

de·cide /di'sīd/ ▸ *v.* [*intr.*] come to a resolution in the mind as a result of consideration. ■ [*tr.*] cause to come to such a resolution: *this business about the letter decided me.* ■ make a choice from a number of alternatives: *she had decided on her plan of action.* ■ give a judgment concerning a matter or legal case: *the courts decided in favor of the claimants* | [*tr.*] *the judge will decide the case.* ■ [*tr.*] come to a decision about (something): *we must decide the fates of the people who headed the coup.* ■ [*tr.*] resolve or settle (a question or contest). —**de·cid·a·ble** *adj.* —**de·cid·er** *n.*

de·cid·ed /di'sīdid/ ▸ *adj.* (of a quality) definite; unquestionable: *a decided improvement.* ■ (of a person) having clear opinions; resolute. ■ (of a legal case) that has been resolved. —**de·cid·ed·ly** *adv.* —**de·cid·ed·ness** *n.*

de·cid·u·ous /di'sijŏŏəs/ ▸ *adj.* (of a tree or shrub) shedding its leaves annually. Often contrasted with **EVERGREEN**. ■ *inf.* (of a tree or shrub) broad-leaved. ■ denoting the milk teeth of a mammal, which are shed after a time. —**de·cid·u·ous·ly** *adv.* —**de·cid·u·ous·ness** *n.*

dec·i·gram /'desi,gram/ ▸ *n.* a metric unit of mass, equal to 0.1 gram.

dec·i·li·ter /'desə,lētər/ (*Brit.* **dec·i·li·tre**) (abbr.: **dl**) ▸ *n.* a metric unit of capacity, equal to one tenth of a liter.

dec·i·mal /'des(ə)məl/ ▸ *adj.* relating to or denoting a system of numbers and arithmetic based on the number ten, tenth parts, and powers of ten: *decimal arithmetic.* ■ relating to or denoting a system of currency, weights and measures, or other units in which the smaller units are related to the principal units as powers of ten: *decimal coinage.*
▸ *n.* (also **decimal fraction**) a fraction whose denominator is a power of ten and whose numerator is expressed by figures placed to the right of a decimal point. ■ the system of decimal numerical notation. —**dec·i·mal·ly** *adv.*

dec·i·mal·ize /'desəmə,līz/ ▸ *v.* [*tr.*] convert (a system of coinage or weights and measures) to a decimal system. —**dec·i·mal·i·za·tion** /,des(ə)mələ'zāsHən/ *n.*

dec·i·mal point ▸ *n.* a dot placed after the figure representing units in a decimal fraction.

dec·i·mate /'desə,māt/ ▸ *v.* [*tr.*] (often **be decimated**) **1** kill, destroy, or remove a large percentage or part of. ■ drastically reduce the strength or effectiveness of (something): *plant viruses that can decimate yields.* **2** *hist.* kill one in every ten of (a group of soldiers or others) as a punishment for the whole group. ▷late Middle English: from Latin *decimat-* 'taken as a tenth,' from the verb *decimare*, from *decimus* 'tenth.' In Middle English the term *decimation* denoted the levying of a tithe, and later the tax imposed in England by Cromwell on the Royalists (1655). The verb *decimate* originally alluded to the Roman punishment of executing one man in ten of a mutinous legion. —**dec·i·ma·tion** /,desə'māsHən/ *n.* —**dec·i·ma·tor** /-,mātər/ *n.*

dec·i·me·ter /'desə,mētər/ (*Brit.* **dec·i·me·tre**) (abbr.: **dm**) ▸ *n.* a metric unit of length, equal to one tenth of a meter. —**dec·i·met·ric** /,desə'metrik/ *adj.*

de·ci·pher /di'sīfər/ ▸ *v.* [*tr.*] convert (a text written in code, or a coded signal) into normal language. ■ succeed in understanding, interpreting, or identifying (something): *an expression she could not decipher.* —**de·ci·pher·a·ble** *adj.* —**de·ci·pher·ment** *n.*

de·ci·sion /di'sizHən/ ▸ *n.* a conclusion or resolution reached after consideration. ■ the action or process of deciding something or of resolving a question. ■ a formal judgment: *a Supreme Court decision.* ■ the ability or tendency to make decisions quickly; decisiveness: *a woman of decision.* ■ *Boxing* the awarding of a fight, in the absence of a knock-

out or technical knockout, to the boxer with the most rounds won or with the most points. ■ *Baseball* a win or a loss assigned to a pitcher.

de·ci·sive /di'sīsiv/ ▸ *adj.* settling an issue; producing a definite result: *a decisive 7–2 vote* | *decisive evidence.* ■ (of a person) having or showing the ability to make decisions quickly and effectively. —**de·ci·sive·ly** *adv.* —**de·ci·sive·ness** *n.*

deck /dek/ ▸ *n.* **1** a structure of planks or plates, approximately horizontal, extending across a ship or boat at any of various levels, esp. one of those at the highest level and open to the weather. ■ a floor or platform resembling or compared to a ship's deck, esp. the floor of a pier or a platform for sunbathing. ■ a platformlike structure, typically made of lumber and unroofed, attached to a house or other building. ■ a level of a large, open building, esp. a sports stadium. ■ (**the deck**) *inf.* the ground or floor: *there was a thud when I hit the deck.* ■ the flat part of a skateboard or snowboard. **2** a component or unit in sound-reproduction equipment that incorporates a playing or recording mechanism for discs or tapes: *a tape deck.* **3** a pack of cards. ■ *inf.* a packet of narcotics.
▸ *v.* [*tr.*] **1** (usu. **be decked**) decorate or adorn brightly or festively: *Ingrid was decked out in her Sunday best.* **2** *inf.* knock (someone) to the ground with a punch. ▷late Middle English: from Middle Dutch *dec* 'covering, roof, cloak,' *dekken* 'to cover.' Originally denoting canvas used to make a covering (esp. on a ship), the term came to mean the covering itself, later denoting a solid surface serving as roof and floor. —**decked** *adj.*
▸ □ **not playing with a full deck** *inf.* mentally deficient. □ **on deck** *fig.* ready for action or work. ■ *Baseball* next to hit in the batting order.

deck chair ▸ *n.* a folding chair of wood and canvas, typically used near the sea or on the deck of passenger ships.

deck·hand /'dek,hand/ ▸ *n.* a member of a ship's crew whose duties include maintenance of hull, decks, and superstructure, and mooring and cargo handling.

de·claim /di'klām/ ▸ *v.* utter or deliver words or a speech in a rhetorical or impassioned way, as if to an audience: [*tr.*] *she declaimed her views* | [*intr.*] *declaiming from the pulpit.* ■ [*intr.*] (**declaim against**) forcefully protest against or criticize (something). —**de·claim·er** *n.* —**de·cla·ma·tion** /,deklə'māsHən/ *n.* —**de·clam·a·to·ry** /-'klamə,tôrē/ *adj.*

dec·la·ra·tion /,deklə'rāsHən/ ▸ *n.* a formal or explicit statement or announcement. ■ the formal announcement of the beginning of a state or condition: *a declaration of independence.* ■ a listing of goods, property, income, etc., subject to duty or tax. ■ a statement asserting or protecting a legal right. ■ a written public announcement of intentions or of the terms of an agreement. ■ *Law* a plaintiff's statement of claims in proceedings. ■ *Law* an affirmation made instead of taking an oath. ■ the naming of trump in bridge, whist, or a similar card game.

de·clar·a·tive /di'kle(ə)rətiv; -'klar-/ ▸ *adj.* **1** of the nature of or making a declaration: *declarative statements.* ■ *Gram.* (of a sentence or phrase) taking the form of a simple statement. **2** *Comput.* denoting programming languages that can be used to solve problems without requiring the programmer to specify an exact procedure to be followed.
▸ *n.* a statement in the form of a declaration. ■ *Gram.* a declarative sentence or phrase. —**de·clar·a·tive·ly** *adv.*

de·clare /di'kle(ə)r/ ▸ *v.* **1** say something in a solemn and emphatic manner. ■ [*tr.*] formally announce the beginning of (a state or condition): *Spain declared war on Britain.* ■ [*tr.*] pronounce or assert (a person or thing) to be something specified: *the mansion was declared a fire hazard.* ■ [*intr.*] (**declare for/against**) openly align oneself for or against (a party or position) in a dispute. ■ [*tr.*] announce oneself as a candidate for an election: *he declared last April.* ■ (**declare oneself**) reveal one's intentions or identity. ■ (**declare oneself**) *archaic* express feelings of love to someone. **2** [*tr.*] acknowledge possession of (taxable income or dutiable goods). **3** [*tr.*] announce that one holds (certain combinations of cards) in a card game. —**de·clar·a·ble** *adj.* —**de·clar·a·to·ry** /-'kle(ə)rə,tôrē/ *adj.* —**de·clar·ed·ly** /-'kle(ə)ridlē/ *adv.* —**de·clar·er** *n.*

dé·clas·sé /,däklä'sā/ (also **dé·clas·sée**) ▸ *adj.* having fallen in social status: *his parents were poor and déclassé.*

de·clas·si·fy /dē'klasə,fī/ ▸ *v.* (**-fies**, **-fied**) [*tr.*] (often **be declassified**) officially declare (information or documents) to be no longer secret. —**de·clas·si·fi·ca·tion** /dē,klasəfi'kāsHən/ *n.*

de·clen·sion /di'klensHən/ ▸ *n.* **1** (in the grammar of Latin, Greek, and other languages) the variation of the form of a noun, pronoun, or adjective, by which its grammatical case, number, and gender are identified. ■ the class to which a noun or adjective is assigned according to this variation. **2** *poetic/lit.* a condition of decline or moral deterioration. —**de·clen·sion·al** /-sHənl/ *adj.*

dec·li·na·tion /,deklə'nāsHən/ ▸ *n.* **1** *Astron.* the angular distance of a point north or south of the celestial equator. ■ the angular deviation of a compass needle from true north (because the magnetic north pole and the geographic north pole do not coincide). **2** formal refusal. —**dec·li·na·tion·al** /-ˌSHənl/ *adj.*

de·cline /di'klīn/ ▶*v.* **1** [*intr.*] become smaller, fewer, or less; decrease. ■ diminish in strength or quality; deteriorate. [as *adj.*] (**declining**) *declining educational standards.* **2** [*tr.*] politely refuse (an invitation or offer). ■ politely refuse to do something: *the company declined to comment.* **3** [*intr.*] (esp. of the sun) move downward. ■ *archaic* bend down; droop. **4** [*tr.*] (in the grammar of Latin, Greek, and certain other languages) state the forms of (a noun, pronoun, or adjective) corresponding to cases, number, and gender.
▶*n.* a gradual and continuous loss of strength, numbers, or quality. ■ a fall in value or price. ■ *archaic* the gradual setting of the sun. ■ *archaic* any disease in which bodily strength gradually fails, esp. tuberculosis. —**de·clin·a·ble** *adj.* —**de·clin·er** *n.*

de·cliv·i·ty /di'klivitē/ ▶*n.* (pl. **-ties**) a downward slope: *a thickly wooded declivity.* —**de·cliv·i·tous** /-təs/ *adj.*

de·coc·tion /di'käkSHən/ ▶*n.* the liquor resulting from concentrating the essence of a substance by heating or boiling, esp. a medicinal preparation made from a plant: *a decoction of a root.* ■ the action or process of extracting the essence of something.

de·code /di'kōd/ ▶*v.* [*tr.*] convert (a coded message) into intelligible language. ■ analyze and interpret (a verbal or nonverbal communication or image). ■ convert (audio or video signals) into another form, e.g., to analog from digital in sound reproduction.
▶*n. inf.* a translation of a coded message. —**de·cod·a·ble** *adj.*

de·cod·er /di'kōdər/ ▶*n.* a person or thing that analyzes and interprets something, in particular: ■ an electronic device for analyzing the information components of an audio or visual signal and feeding them to separate amplifier channels. ■ an electronic device that converts a coded signal into one that can be used by other equipment.

de·col·late /'dekəˌlāt; 'dēkə-/ ▶*v.* [*intr.*] separate sheets of paper into different piles. —**de·col·la·tion** /ˌdekə'lāSHən; ˌdēkə-/ *n.* —**de·col·la·tor** /-ˌlātər/ *n.*

dé·colle·tage /dāˌkälə'täzH ˌdekələ-/ ▶*n.* a low neckline on a woman's dress or top.

dé·colle·té /dāˌkälə'tā ˌdekələ-/ ▶*adj.* (also **dé·colle·tée**) (of a woman's dress or top) having a low neckline.
▶*n.* a low neckline on a woman's dress or top.

de·col·o·nize /dē'käləˌnīz/ ▶*v.* [*tr.*] withdraw from (a colony), leaving it independent. —**de·col·o·ni·za·tion** /-ˌkälənə'zāSHən/ *n.*

de·com·mis·sion /ˌdekə'misHən/ ▶*v.* [*tr.*] withdraw (someone or something) from service, in particular: ■ make (a nuclear reactor or weapon) inoperative, and dismantle and decontaminate it to make it safe. ■ take (a ship) out of service.

de·com·pose /ˌdēkəm'pōz/ ▶*v.* [*intr.*] (of a dead body or other organic matter) decay; become rotten: [as *adj.*] (**decomposed**) *the body was decomposed.* ■ [*tr.*] cause (something) to decay or rot. ■ (of a chemical compound) break down into component elements or simpler constituents. ■ [*tr.*] break down (a chemical compound) into its component elements or simpler constituents. —**de·com·pos·a·ble** *adj.* —**de·com·po·si·tion** /dēˌkämpə'ziSHən/ *n.*

de·com·press /ˌdēkəm'pres/ ▶*v.* [*tr.*] relieve of compressing forces, in particular: ■ expand (compressed computer data) to its normal size so that it can be read and processed by a computer. ■ subject (a diver) to decompression. ■ [*intr.*] *inf.* calm down and relax.

de·com·pres·sion /ˌdēkəm'presHən/ ▶*n.* a release of compressing forces, in particular: ■ reduction in air pressure. ■ a gradual reduction of air pressure on a person who has been experiencing high pressure while diving, in order to prevent decompression sickness. ■ the process of expanding computer data to its normal size so that it can be read by a computer. ■ a surgical procedure that relieves excessive pressure on an internal part of the body such as the spinal cord.

de·com·pres·sor /ˌdēkəm'presər/ ▶*n.* an instrument or device for decompressing something. ■ a computer program that decompresses data by digitally expanding it to its original size and form.

de·con·ges·tant /ˌdēkən'jestənt/ ▶*adj.* (chiefly of a medicine) used to relieve nasal congestion.
▶*n.* a decongestant medicine.

de·con·tam·i·nate /ˌdēkən'tamə,nāt/ ▶*v.* [*tr.*] neutralize or remove dangerous substances, radioactivity, or germs from (an area, object, or person). —**de·con·tam·i·na·tion** /-ˌtamə'nāSHən/ *n.*

de·con·trol /ˌdēkən'trōl/ ▶*v.* (**-trolled, -trol·ling**) [*tr.*] release (a commodity, market, etc.) from controls or restrictions.
▶*n.* the action of decontrolling something.

de·cor /dā'kôr; di-/ ▶*n.* the furnishing and decoration of a room. ■ the decoration and scenery of a stage. —**dec·o·rous** /'dekərəs/ *adj.*

dec·o·rate /'dekə,rāt/ ▶*v.* [*tr.*] **1** make (something) look more attractive by adding ornament to it. ■ provide (a room or building) with a color scheme, paint, wallpaper, etc.. **2** confer an award or medal on (a member of the armed forces).

dec·o·ra·tion /ˌdekə'rāSHən/ ▶*n.* **1** the process or art of decorating or adorning something. ■ ornamentation. ■ a thing that serves as an ornament: *Christmas decorations.* ■ the application of paint or wallpaper in a room or building. ■ the paint or wallpaper applied. **2** a medal or award conferred as an honor.

Dec·o·ra·tion Day ▶*n.* another term for MEMORIAL DAY.

dec·o·ra·tive /'dek(ə)rətiv; 'dekəˌrātiv/ ▶*adj.* serving to make something look more attractive; ornamental. ■ relating to decoration: *a decorative artist.* —**dec·o·ra·tive·ly** *adv.* —**dec·o·ra·tive·ness** *n.*

dec·o·ra·tor /'dekəˌrātər/ ▶*n.* a person whose job is to design the interior of someone's home, by choosing colors, materials, and furnishings.

de·co·rum /di'kôrəm/ ▶*n.* behavior in keeping with good taste and propriety. ■ etiquette: *funeral decorum.* ■ (usu. **decorums**) *archaic* a particular requirement of good taste and propriety.

de·cou·page /ˌdākoo'päzH/ ▶*n.* the decoration of the surface of an object with paper cut-outs, which is then usu. varnished or lacquered.

de·cou·ple /dē'kəpəl/ ▶*v.* [*tr.*] separate, disengage, or dissociate (something) from something else: *the mountings effectively decouple the engine from the wheels.*

de·coy ▶*n.* /'dē,koi/ **1** a bird or mammal, or an imitation of one, used by hunters to attract other birds or mammals. ■ a person or thing used to lure an animal or person into a trap. ■ a fake or nonworking article, esp. a weapon, used to mislead or misdirect. **2** a pond into which wild ducks may be enticed for capture.
▶*v.* /di'koi/ [*tr.*] lure or entice (a person or animal) away from an intended course, typically into a trap. ▷mid 16th cent. (earlier as *coy*): from Dutch *de kooi* 'the decoy,' from Middle Dutch *de kouw* 'the cage,' from Latin *cavea* 'cage.' Sense 2 is from the practice of using tamed ducks to lead wild ones along channels into captivity.

de·crease ▶*v.* /di'krēs/ [*intr.*] become smaller or less in size, amount, intensity, or degree. ■ [*tr.*] make smaller or less in size, amount, intensity, or degree: *vitamin E has decreased cholesterol levels.*
▶*n.* /'dē,krēs; di'krēs/ an instance or example of becoming smaller or less. ■ the action or process of becoming smaller or fewer. —**de·creas·ing·ly** /di'krēsiNGlē/ *adv.*

de·cree /di'krē/ ▶*n.* an official order issued by a legal authority. ■ the issuing of such an order: *the king ruled by decree.* ■ a judgment or decision of certain courts of law.
▶*v.* (**-crees, -creed, -cree·ing**) [*tr.*] order (something) by decree.

dec·re·ment /'dekrəmənt/ ▶*n.* a reduction or diminution. ■ an amount by which something is reduced or diminished:.
▶*v.* [*tr.*] *chiefly Comput.* cause a discrete reduction in (a numerical quantity): *the instruction decrements the accumulator by one.*

de·crep·it /di'krepit/ ▶*adj.* (of a person) elderly and infirm. ■ worn out or ruined because of age or neglect. —**de·crep·i·tude** /-ˌt(y)ood/ *n.*

de·crim·i·nal·ize /dē'kriminl,īz/ ▶*v.* [*tr.*] cease, by legislation, to treat (something) as illegal: *a battle to decriminalize drugs.* —**de·crim·i·nal·i·za·tion** /-ˌkriminl-i'zāSHən/ *n.*

de·cry /di'krī/ ▶*v.* (**-cries, -cried**) [*tr.*] publicly denounce. —**de·cri·er** *n.*

ded·i·cate /'dedi,kāt/ ▶*v.* [*tr.*] devote (time, effort, or oneself) to a particular task or purpose. ■ devote to a particular subject or purpose. ■ (usu. **be dedicated**) cite (a book or other work) as being issued or performed in someone's honor. ■ open (a building or other facility) formally for public use. ■ (usu. **be dedicated**) ceremonially assign (a church or other building) to a deity or saint. —**ded·i·ca·tee** /ˌdedikā'tē/ *n.* —**ded·i·ca·tor** /-ˌkātər/ *n.* —**ded·i·ca·to·ry** /-kə,tôrē/ *adj.*

ded·i·ca·tion /ˌdedi'kāSHən/ ▶*n.* **1** the quality of being dedicated or committed to a task or purpose: *dedication to duties.* **2** the words with which a book or other work is dedicated. ■ the action of formally opening a building or other facility for public use: *the dedication and unveiling was attended by some 5,000 people.* ■ the action of dedicating a church or other building to a deity or saint. ■ an inscription dedicating a church or other building in this way.

de·duce /di'd(y)oos/ ▶*v.* [*tr.*] arrive at (a fact or a conclusion) by reasoning; draw as a logical conclusion: *it can be deduced from these* figures | *we deduce that the fish died because of pollution.* —**de·duc·i·ble** /-səbəl/ *adj.*

de·duct /di'dəkt/ ▶*v.* [*tr.*] subtract or take away (an amount or part) from a total: *tax has been deducted from the payments.*

de·duct·i·ble /di'dəktəbəl/ ▶*adj.* able to be deducted, esp. from taxable income or tax to be paid.
▶*n.* (in an insurance policy) a specified amount of money that the insured must pay before an insurance company will pay a claim. —**de·duct·i·bil·i·ty** /-,dəktə'bilitē/ *n.*

de·duc·tion /di'dəkSHən/ ▶*n.* **1** the action of deducting or subtracting something: *the dividend will be paid without deduction of tax.* ■ an amount that is or may be deducted from something, esp. from taxable income or tax to be paid: *tax deductions.* **2** the inference of particular instances by reference to a general law or principle: *the detective must uncover the murderer by deduction from facts.* Often contrasted with INDUCTION. ■ a conclusion that has been deduced.

de·duc·tive /di'dəktiv/ ▶*adj.* characterized by the inference of particular instances from a general law: *deductive reasoning.* ■ based on reason and logical analysis of available facts: *I used my deductive powers.* —**de·duc·tive·ly** *adv.*

deed /dēd/ ▶*n.* **1** an action that is performed intentionally or consciously. ■ a brave or noble act. ■ action or performance: *erred in both deed and manner.* **2** a legal document that is signed and delivered, esp. one regarding the ownership of property or legal rights.
▶*v.* [*tr.*] convey or transfer (property or rights) by legal deed.

dee·jay /'dē,jā/ *inf.* ▶*n.* a disc jockey.
▶*v.* (**-jays, -jayed, -jay·ing**) [*intr.*] act as, or hold a job as, a disc jockey.

deem /dēm/ ▶*v.* [*tr.*] regard or consider in a specified way: *the event was deemed a great success* | [*tr.*] *the strike was deemed to be illegal.*

de·em·pha·size /dē'emfə,sīz/ ▶*v.* [*tr.*] reduce the importance or prominence given to (something): *the reform de-emphasized central planning.* —**de·em·pha·sis** /-fə,sis/ *n.*

deep /dēp/ ▶*adj.* **1** extending far down from the top or surface: *a deep gorge* | *the lake was deep and cold.* ■ extending or situated far in or down from the outer edge or surface: *deep in the woods.* ■ (after a measurement and in questions) extending a specified distance from the top, surface, or outer edge: *the well was 200 feet deep.* ■ [in comb.] as far up or down as a specified point: *standing waist-deep in the river.* ■ in a specified number of ranks one behind another: [in comb.] *standing three-deep at the bar.* ■ taking in or giving out a lot of air: *she took a deep breath.* ■ *Baseball* far back in the outfield: *his first pitch was hit into deep left field.* **2** very intense or extreme: *a deep sleep.* ■ (of an emotion or feeling) intensely felt: *deep disappointment.* ■ profound or penetrating in awareness or understanding: *a deep analysis.* ■ difficult to understand: *this is all getting too deep for me.* ■ (**deep in**) fully absorbed or involved in (a state or activity): *they were deep in their own thoughts.* ■ (of a person) unpredictable and secretive: *that Thomas is a deep one.* **3** (of sound) low in pitch and full in tone; not shrill. **4** (of color) dark and intense.
▶*n.* (**the deep**) *poetic/lit.* the sea: *denizens of the deep.* ■ (usu. **deeps**) a deep part of the sea: *the dark and menacing deeps.* ■ (usu. **deeps**) *fig.* a remote and mysterious region: *the deeps of her imagination.*
▶*adv.* far down or in; deeply: *traveling deep into the countryside* | *fig. his passion runs deep.* ■ (in sports) distant from the start of a play or the forward line of one's team: *the defense played deep.* —**deep·ly** *adv.* —**deep·ness** *n.*
▶ □ **go off the deep end** *inf.* give way immediately to an emotional outburst, esp. of anger. ■ go mad; behave extremely strangely: *they looked at me as if I had gone off the deep end.* □ **in deep water** *inf.* in trouble or difficulty.

deep·en /'dēpən/ ▶*v.* make or become deep or deeper: [*intr.*] *the crisis deepened* ■ (of a weather system) decrease in barometric pressure. | [as *adj.*] (**deepening**) *a deepening depression.* |

deep freeze ▶*n.* (also **deep freez·er**) a refrigerated cabinet or room in which food can be quickly frozen and kept for long periods at a low temperature: *fig.* a place or situation in which progress or activity is suspended: *traditions revived after years in the deep freeze.*

deep-fry ▶*v.* [*tr.*] [as *adj.*] (**deep-fried**) fry (food) in an amount of fat or oil sufficient to cover it completely: *deep-fried onion rings.*

deep-root·ed ▶*adj.* (of a plant) deeply implanted. ■ firmly embedded in thought, behavior, or culture, and so having a persistent influence: *deep-rooted concern about declining values.* —**deep-root·ed·ness** *n.*

deep sea ▶*n.* [usu. as *adj.*] the deeper parts of the ocean, esp. those beyond the edge of the continental shelf: *deep-sea diving.*

deep-seat·ed ▶*adj.* firmly established at a deep or profound level.

deep space ▶*n.* another term for OUTER SPACE.

deer /dir/ ▶*n.* (*pl.* same) a hoofed grazing or browsing animal (family Cervidae), with branched bony antlers that are shed annually and typically borne only by the male.

deer·fly /'dir,flī/ ▶*n.* a bloodsucking horsefly (genus *Chrysops*, family Tabanidae) that can transmit various diseases, including tularemia.

deer·stalk·er /'di(ə)r,stôkər/ ▶*n.* **1** a soft cloth cap, originally worn for hunting, with bills in front and behind, and ear flaps that can be tied together over the top. **2** a person who stalks deer.

de·es·ca·late /dē'eskə,lāt/ ▶*v.* [*tr.*] reduce the intensity of (a conflict or potentially violent situation). —**de·es·ca·la·tion** /-,eskə'lāSHən/ *n.*

de·face /di'fās/ ▶*v.* [*tr.*] spoil the surface or appearance of (something), e.g., by drawing or writing on it. ■ mar; disfigure: *limestone walls defaced by the reservoir.* —**de·face·ment** *n.* —**de·fac·er** *n.*

de fac·to /di 'faktō; dā/ ▶*adv.* in fact, whether by right or not: *an island facto divided into two countries.*
▶*adj.* denoting someone or something that is such in fact.

de·fal·cate /di'falkāt; -'fôl-/ ▶*v.* [*tr.*] *formal* embezzle (funds with which one has been entrusted): *charged with defalcating government money.* —**de·fal·ca·tion** /,dēfal'kāSHən; -fôl-/ *n.* —**de·fal·ca·tor** /-kātər/ *n.*

de·fame /di'fām/ ▶*v.* [*tr.*] damage the good reputation of (someone); slander or libel: *the article defamed his family.* —**def·a·ma·tion** /,defə'māSHən/ *n.* —**de·fam·a·to·ry** /-'famə,tôrē/ *adj.* —**de·fam·er** *n.*

de·fault /di'fôlt/ ▶*n.* **1** failure to fulfill an obligation, esp. to repay a loan or appear in a court of law: *restructuring debts to avoid default.* **2** a preselected option adopted by a computer program or other mechanism when no alternative is specified by the user or programmer.
▶*v.* [*intr.*] **1** fail to fulfill an obligation, esp. to repay a loan or to appear in a court of law: *some defaulted on student loans.* ■ [*tr.*] declare (a party) in default and give judgment against that party. **2** (**default to**) (of a computer program or other mechanism) revert automatically to (a preselected option): *the system defaults to its own style.*
▶ □ **by default** because of a lack of opposition: *he won the election by default.* ■ through lack of positive action rather than conscious choice: *the proposal died by default.* □ **in default** failing to repay a loan or appear in a court of law: *a company in default on its loans.* □ **in default of** in the absence of.

de·feat /di'fēt/ ▶*v.* [*tr.*] win a victory over (someone) in a battle or other contest; overcome or beat. ■ prevent (someone) from achieving an aim: *defeated by their criticism.* ■ prevent (an aim) from being achieved: *allowing your body to droop defeats the object of the exercise.* ■ reject or block (a motion or proposal). ■ be impossible for (someone) to understand: *this line of reasoning defeats me.* ■ *Law* render null and void; annul.
▶*n.* an instance of defeating or being defeated.

de·feat·ist /di'fētist/ ▶*n.* a person who expects or is excessively ready to accept failure.
▶*adj.* demonstrating expectation or acceptance of failure: *we have a duty not to be so defeatist.* —**de·feat·ism** /-tizəm/ *n.*

def·e·cate /'defi,kāt/ ▶*v.* [*intr.*] discharge feces from the body. ▷late Middle English (in the sense 'clear of dregs, purify'): from Latin *defaecat-* 'cleared of dregs,' from the verb *defaecare*, from *de-* (expressing removal) + *faex, faec-* 'dregs.' The current sense dates from the mid 19th cent. —**def·e·ca·tion** /,defi'kāSHən/ *n.* —**def·e·ca·tor** /-,kātər/ *n.*

de·fect¹ /'dē,fekt/ ▶*n.* a shortcoming, imperfection, or lack.

de·fect² /di'fekt/ ▶*v.* [*intr.*] abandon one's country or cause in favor of an opposing one: *he defected to the Soviet Union after the war.* —**de·fec·tion** /di'fekSHən/ *n.* —**de·fec·tor** /-tər/ *n.*

de·fec·tive /di'fektiv/ ▶*adj.* imperfect or faulty. ■ lacking or deficient: *dystrophin is commonly defective in muscle tissue.* ■ *Gram.* (of a word) not having all the inflections normal for the part of speech.
▶*n. archaic* or *offens.* a mentally handicapped person. —**de·fec·tive·ly** *adv.* —**de·fec·tive·ness** *n.*

de·fend /di'fend/ ▶*v.* [*tr.*] resist an attack made on (someone or something); protect from harm or danger. ■ speak or write in favor of (an action or person); attempt to justify: *he defended his policy.* ■ conduct the case for (the party being accused or sued) in a lawsuit: *a lawyer who defends dissidents.* ■ compete to retain (a title or seat) in a contest or election: *he successfully defended his Congressional seat* | [as *adj.*] (**defending**) *the defending champion.* ■ [*intr.*] (in sports) protect one's goal rather than attempt to score against one's opponents. —**de·fend·a·ble** *adj.* —**de·fend·er** *n.*

de·fend·ant /di'fendənt/ ▶*n.* an individual, company, or institution sued or accused in a court of law. Compare with PLAINTIFF.

de·fen·es·tra·tion /dē,fenə'strāSHən/ ▶*n. formal* or *humorous* the action of throwing someone or something out of a window. —**de·fen·es·trate** /-'fenə,strāt/ *v.*

de·fense /di'fens; 'dē,fens/ (*Brit.* **de·fence**) ▶*n.* **1** the action of defending from or resisting attack. ■ attempted justification or vindication of something: *he spoke in defense of a disciplined approach.* ■ an instance of defending a title or seat in a contest or election. ■ military measures or resources for protecting a country: [as *adj.*] *defense policy.* ■ a means of protecting something from attack. ■ (**defenses**) fortifications or barriers against attack. ■ (in sports) the action or role of defending one's goal against the opposition: *we played solid defense.* ■ (**the defense**) the players in a team who perform this role. **2** the case presented by or on behalf of the party being accused or sued in a lawsuit. **3** one or more defendants in a trial. ■ (usu. **the defense**) [treated as *sing.* or *pl.*] the counsel for the defendant in a lawsuit: *the defense requested more time to prepare their case.* —**de·fense·less** *adj.*

de·fense mech·an·ism ▸ *n.* an automatic reaction of the body against disease-causing organisms. ■ a mental process (e.g., repression or projection) initiated, typically unconsciously, to avoid conscious conflict or anxiety.

de·fen·si·ble /di'fensəbəl/ ▸ *adj.* **1** justifiable by argument: *a morally defensible penal system.* **2** able to be protected: *a fort with a defensible yard at its feet.* —**de·fen·si·bil·i·ty** /di,fensə'bilitē/ *n.* —**de·fen·si·bly** /-blē/ *adv.*

de·fen·sive /di'fensiv/ ▸ *adj.* **1** used or intended to defend or protect: *troops in defensive positions.* ■ (in sports) relating to or intended as defense. **2** very anxious to challenge or avoid criticism: *he was very defensive about that side of his life.* —**de·fen·sive·ly** *adv.* —**de·fen·sive·ness** *n.*
▸ □ **on the defensive** expecting or resisting criticism or attack.

de·fer¹ /di'fər/ ▸ *v.* (**-ferred, -fer·ring**) [*tr.*] put off (an action or event) to a later time; postpone: *they deferred the decision until February.* ■ *hist.* postpone the conscription of (someone): *he was no longer deferred from the draft.* —**de·fer·ment** *n.* —**de·fer·ra·ble** *adj.* —**de·fer·ral** /-'fərəl/ *n.*

de·fer² ▸ *v.* (**-ferred, -fer·ring**) [*intr.*] (**defer to**) submit humbly to (a person or a person's wishes or qualities): *he deferred to Tim's superior knowledge.* —**de·fer·rer** *n.*

def·er·ence /'defərəns/ ▸ *n.* humble submission and respect: *he addressed her with the deference due to age.*
▸ □ **in deference to** out of respect for; in consideration of.

def·er·en·tial /,defə'renchəl/ ▸ *adj.* showing deference; respectful: *people were always deferential to him.* —**def·er·en·tial·ly** *adv.*

de·fi·ance /di'fīəns/ ▸ *n.* open resistance; bold disobedience.

de·fi·ant /di'fīənt/ ▸ *adj.* showing defiance. —**de·fi·ant·ly** *adv.*

de·fib·ril·la·tion /dē,fibrə'lāshən/ ▸ *n.* *Med.* the stopping of fibrillation of the heart by administering a controlled electric shock in order to allow restoration of the normal rhythm. —**de·fib·ril·late** /dē'fibrə,lāt/ *v.* —**de·fib·ril·la·tor** *n.*.

de·fi·cien·cy /di'fishənsē/ ▸ *n.* (*pl.* **-cies**) a lack or shortage. ■ a failing or shortcoming.

de·fi·cient /di'fishənt/ ▸ *adj.* not having enough of a specified quality or ingredient: *this diet is deficient in vitamin B.* ■ insufficient or inadequate.

def·i·cit /'defəsit/ ▸ *n.* the amount by which something, esp. a sum of money, is too small. ■ an excess of expenditure or liabilities over income or assets in a given period: *an annual operating deficit.* ■ (in sports) the amount or score by which a team or individual is losing: *came back from a 3–0 deficit.*

de·file¹ /di'fīl/ ▸ *v.* [*tr.*] sully, mar, or spoil. ■ desecrate or profane (something sacred). ■ *archaic* violate the chastity of (a woman). —**de·file·ment** *n.* —**de·fil·er** *n.*

de·file² /di'fīl; 'dē,fīl/ ▸ *n.* a steep-sided, narrow gorge or passage (originally one requiring troops to march in single file).

de·fine /di'fīn/ ▸ *v.* [*tr.*] **1** state or describe exactly the nature, scope, or meaning of. ■ give the meaning of (a word or phrase), esp. in a dictionary. ■ make up or establish the character of: *the football team defines their identity.* **2** mark out the boundary or limits of. ■ make clear the outline of; delineate. —**de·fin·a·ble** *adj.* —**de·fin·er** *n.*

def·i·nite /'defənit/ ▸ *adj.* clearly stated or decided; not vague or doubtful: *definite plans.* ■ clearly true or real; unambiguous. ■ (of a person) certain or sure about something. ■ clear or undeniable (used for emphasis): *a definite asset.* ■ having exact and discernible physical limits or form. —**def·i·nite·ness** *n.*

def·i·nite ar·ti·cle ▸ *n.* *Gram.* a determiner (*the* in English) that implies that the thing mentioned has already been mentioned, or is common knowledge, or is about to be defined (as in *the book on the table; the art of government*). Compare with **INDEFINITE ARTICLE**.

def·i·nite·ly /'defənitlē/ ▸ *adv.* without doubt (used for emphasis): *I will definitely be at the airport to meet you.* ■ in a definite manner; clearly.

def·i·ni·tion /,defə'nishən/ ▸ *n.* **1** a statement of the exact meaning of a word, esp. in a dictionary. ■ an exact statement or description of the nature, scope, or meaning of something: *our definition of poetry.* ■ the

action or process of defining something. **2** the degree of distinctness in outline of an object, image, or sound. ■ the capacity of an instrument or device for making images distinct in outline: [in *comb.*] *high-definition television.* —**def·i·ni·tion·al** /-shənl/ *adj.* —**def·i·ni·tion·al·ly** /-shənl-ē/ *adv.*
▸ □ **by definition** by its very nature; intrinsically.

de·fin·i·tive /di'finitiv/ ▸ *adj.* (of a conclusion or agreement) done or reached decisively and with authority. ■ (of a book or other text) the most authoritative of its kind: *the definitive biography of Truman.* —**de·fin·i·tive·ly** *adv.*

de·flate /di'flāt/ ▸ *v.* **1** [*tr.*] let air or gas out of (a tire, balloon, or similar object). ■ [*intr.*] be emptied of air or gas. **2** cause (someone) to suddenly lose confidence or feel less important: [as *adj.*] (**deflated**) *the news left him feeling utterly deflated.* ■ reduce the level of (an emotion or feeling): *her anger was deflated.* **3** *Econ.* bring about a general reduction of price levels in (an economy). —**de·fla·tor** /-tər/ *n.*

de·fla·tion /di'flāshən/ ▸ *n.* **1** the action or process of deflating or being deflated. **2** *Econ.* reduction of the general level of prices in an economy. —**de·fla·tion·ar·y** /-shə,nerē/ *adj.* —**de·fla·tion·ist** /-ist/ *n. & adj.*

de·flect /di'flekt/ ▸ *v.* [*tr.*] cause (something) to change direction; turn aside from a straight course: *the bullet was deflected into the ceiling* | *fig. he attempted to deflect attention away from his private life.* ■ [*intr.*] (of an object) change direction after hitting something: *the ball deflected off his body.* ■ cause (someone) to deviate from an intended purpose: *she'll not be deflected from her goals.* ■ cause (something) to change orientation. —**de·flec·tion** *n.*

de·flec·tor /di'flektər/ ▸ *n.* a device that deflects something, in particular: ■ a plate or other attachment for deflecting a flow of air, water, heat, etc. ■ an electrode in a cathode-ray tube whose magnetic field is used to deflect a beam of electrons onto a screen to form an image.

de·flow·er /dē'flou(-ə)r/ ▸ *v.* [*tr.*] **1** *dated* or *poetic/lit.* deprive (a woman) of her virginity. **2** [usu. as *adj.*] (**deflowered**) strip (a plant or garden) of flowers: *deflowered rose bushes.*

de·fo·li·ate /dē'fōlē,āt/ ▸ *v.* [*tr.*] remove leaves from (a tree, plant, or area of land). —**de·fo·li·ant** /-ənt/ *n.* —**de·fo·li·a·tion** /dē,fōlē'āshən/ *n.* —**de·fo·li·a·tor** /-,ātər/ *n.*

de·form /di'fôrm/ ▸ *v.* [*tr.*] distort the shape or form of; make misshapen: [as *adj.*] (**deformed**) *deformed hands.* ■ [*intr.*] become distorted or misshapen. —**de·form·a·ble** *adj.* —**de·for·ma·tion** /,dēfôr'māshən/ *n.*

de·form·i·ty /di'fôrmitē/ ▸ *n.* (*pl.* **-ties**) a deformed part, esp. of the body; a malformation: *children born with deformities.* ■ the state of being deformed or misshapen: *respiratory problems caused by spinal deformity.*

de·frag·ment /,dēfrag'ment/ ▸ *v.* [*tr.*] *Comput.* (of software) reduce the fragmentation of (a file) by concatenating parts stored in separate locations on a disk: *the safe way to defragment your files.* —**de·frag·men·ta·tion** /dē,fragmən'tāshən; -,men-/ *n.* —**de·frag·ment·er** *n.*

de·fraud /di'frôd/ ▸ *v.* [*tr.*] illegally obtain money from (someone) by deception: *he used a false identity to defraud the bank of thousands of dollars* | [*intr.*] *conspiracy to defraud.* —**de·fraud·er** *n.*

de·fray /di'frā/ ▸ *v.* [*tr.*] provide money to pay (a cost or expense): *the proceeds from the raffle help to defray the expenses of the evening.* ▷late Middle English (in the general sense 'spend money'): from French *défrayer,* from *dé-* (expressing removal) + obsolete *frai* 'cost, expenses' (from medieval Latin *fredum* 'a fine for breach of the peace'). —**de·fray·a·ble** *adj.* —**de·fray·al** /-'frāəl/ *n.* —**de·fray·ment** *n.*

de·frock /dē'fräk/ ▸ *v.* [*tr.*] deprive (a person in holy orders) of ecclesiastical status. ■ [usu. as *adj.*] (**defrocked**) deprive (someone) of professional status or membership in a prestigious group: *a defrocked psychiatrist.*

de·frost /di'frôst/ ▸ *v.* [*tr.*] remove frost or ice from. ■ thaw (frozen food) before cooking it. ■ [*intr.*] (of frozen food) thaw before being cooked. ■ free (the interior of a refrigerator) of accumulated ice. ■ [*intr.*] (of a refrigerator) become free of accumulated ice: *the fridge defrosts in 20 minutes.* —**de·frost·er** *n.*

deft /deft/ ▸ *adj.* neatly skillful and quick in one's movements: *a deft piece of footwork.* ■ demonstrating skill and cleverness: *the script was both deft and literate.* —**deft·ly** *adv.* —**deft·ness** *n.*

de·funct /di'fəNGkt/ ▸ *adj.* no longer existing or functioning.

de·fuse /dē'fyōoz/ ▸ *v.* [*tr.*] remove the fuse from (an explosive device) in order to prevent it from exploding. ■ *fig.* reduce the danger or tension in (a difficult situation).

de·fy /di'fī/ ▸ *v.* (**-fies, -fied**) [*tr.*] openly resist or refuse to obey. ■ (of a thing) make (an action or quality) almost impossible: *his actions defy*

D

Pronunciation Key ə *ago, up;* ər *over, fur;* a *hat;* ā *ate;* ä *car;* CH *chin;* e *let;* ē *see;* ə(ə)r *air;* i *fit;* ī *by;* i(ə)r *ear;* NG *sing;* ō *go;* ô *law, for;* oi *toy;* ōō *good;* ōō *goo;* ou *out;* SH *she;* TH *thin;* TH *then;* (h)w *why;* ZH *vision*

belief. ■ [*tr.*] appear to be challenging (someone) to do or prove something: *he glowered at her, defying her to mock him.* —**de·fi·er** *n.*

de·gen·er·ate ▸*adj.* /di'jenərit/ **1** having lost the physical, mental, or moral qualities considered normal and desirable; showing evidence of decline. **2** lacking some property, order, or distinctness of structure previously or usually present, in particular: ■ *Math.* relating to or denoting an example of a particular type of equation, curve, or other entity that is equivalent to a simpler type, often occurring when a variable or parameter is set to zero. ■ *Biol.* having reverted to a simpler form as a result of losing a complex or adaptive structure present in the ancestral form.
▸*n.* /di'jenərit/ an immoral or corrupt person.
▸*v.* /di'jenə‚rāt/ [*intr.*] decline or deteriorate physically, mentally, or morally. —**de·gen·er·a·cy** /-rəsē/ *n.* —**de·gen·er·ate·ly** /-ritlē/ *adv.* —**de·gen·er·a·tion** /di‚jenə'rāshən/ *n.*

de·gen·er·a·tive /di'jenərətiv; -ə‚rātiv/ ▸*adj.* (of a disease or symptom) characterized by progressive, often irreversible deterioration, and loss of function in the organs or tissues. ■ of or tending to decline and deterioration: *the young generation had fallen into a degenerative backslide.*

de·grade /di'grād/ ▸*v.* **1** [*tr.*] treat or regard (someone) with contempt or disrespect. ■ lower the character or quality of: *degraded radio signals.* ■ *archaic* reduce (someone) to a lower rank. **2** break down or deteriorate chemically: [*intr.*] *when exposed to light, the materials will degrade* | [*tr.*] *the bacteria will degrade hydrocarbons.* ■ [*tr.*] *Physics* reduce (energy) to a less readily convertible form. —**de·grad·a·bil·i·ty** /di‚grādə'bilitē/ *n.* —**de·grad·a·ble** *adj.* —**deg·ra·da·tion** /‚degrə'dāshən/ *n.* —**de·grad·er** *n.*

de·grad·ing /di'grādiNG/ ▸*adj.* causing a loss of self-respect; humiliating: *cruel or degrading treatment.* —**de·grad·ing·ly** *adv.*

de·gree /di'grē/ ▸*n.* **1** the amount, level, or extent to which something happens or is present: *a degree of caution.* **2** a unit of measurement of angles, one three-hundred-and-sixtieth of the circumference of a circle. (Symbol: °) **3** a stage in a scale or series, in particular: ■ a unit in any of various scales of temperature, intensity, or hardness: *water boils at 100 degrees Celsius.* (Symbol: °) ■ [in *comb.*] each of a set of grades (usually three) used to classify burns according to their severity. See FIRST-DEGREE, SECOND-DEGREE, THIRD-DEGREE. ■ [in *comb.*] a legal grade of crime or offense, esp. murder: *second-degree murder.* ■ *Mus.* a position in a musical scale, counting upward from the tonic or fundamental note: *the lowered third degree of the scale.* ■ *Math.* the class into which an equation falls according to the highest power of unknowns or variables present: *an equation of the second degree.* ■ *Gram.* any of the three steps on the scale of comparison of gradable adjectives and adverbs, namely positive, comparative, and superlative. ■ *archaic* a thing placed like a step in a series; a tier or row. **4** an academic rank conferred by a college or university after examination or after completion of a course of study, or conferred as an honor on a distinguished person. ■ *archaic* social or official rank: *persons of unequal degree.* ■ a rank in an order of Freemasonry.
▸ □ **by degrees** a little at a time; gradually. □ **to a degree** to some extent: *to a degree, it is possible to educate oneself.*

de·gree day ▸*n.* a unit used to determine the heating requirements of buildings, representing a difference of one degree below a specified average outdoor temperature (usually 18°C or 65°F) for one day.

de·hu·man·ize /dē'(h)yōōmə‚nīz/ ▸*v.* [*tr.*] deprive of positive human qualities: [as *adj.*] (**dehumanizing**) *the dehumanizing effects of war.* —**de·hu·man·i·za·tion** /dē‚(h)yōōməni'zāshən/ *n.*

de·hu·mid·i·fy /‚dē(h)yōō'midə‚fī/ ▸*v.* (**-fies, -fied**) [*tr.*] remove moisture from (the air or a gas). —**de·hu·mid·i·fi·er** *n.*

de·hy·drate /dē'hīdrāt/ ▸*v.* [*tr.*] [often as *adj.*] (**dehydrated**) cause (a person or a person's body) to lose a large amount of water. ■ [*intr.*] lose a large amount of water from the body. ■ remove water from (food) in order to preserve and store it: *dehydrated mashed potatoes.* —**de·hy·dra·tion** /‚dēhī'drāshən/ *n.* —**de·hy·dra·tor** /-tər/ *n.*

de·i·fy /'dēə‚fī/ ▸*v.* (**-fies, -fied**) [*tr.*] (usu. **be deified**) worship, regard, or treat (someone or something) as a god. —**de·i·fi·ca·tion** /‚dēəfi'kāshən/ *n.*

deign /dān/ ▸*v.* [*intr.*] do something that one considers to be beneath one's dignity: *she did not deign to answer the maid's question.*

de·ism /'dēizəm/ ▸*n.* belief in the existence of a supreme being, specifically of a creator who does not intervene in the universe. Compare with THEISM. —**de·ist** *n.* —**de·is·tic** /dē'istik/ *adj.* —**de·is·ti·cal** /dē-'istikəl/ *adj.*

de·i·ty /'dēitē/ ▸*n.* (*pl.* **-ties**) a god or goddess (in a polytheistic religion): *a deity of ancient Greece.* ■ divine status, quality, or nature: *a ruler driven by delusions of deity.* ■ (usu. **the Deity**) the creator and supreme being.

dé·jà vu /‚dāzнä 'vōō/ ▸*n.* a feeling of having already experienced the present situation. ■ tedious familiarity.

de·ject·ed /di'jektəd/ ▸*adj.* sad and depressed; dispirited. —**de·ject·ed·ly** *adv.* —**de·jec·tion** /-shən/ *n.*

de ju·re /di 'jŏōrē; dā 'jŏōrä/ ▸*adv.* according to rightful entitlement or claim; by right.
▸*adj.* denoting something or someone that is rightfully such: *the de jure king.*

Del·a·ware ▸*n.* (*pl.* same or **-wares**) **1** a member of an American Indian people formerly inhabiting the Delaware River valley of New Jersey and eastern Pennsylvania. **2** either of two Algonquian languages (Munsi and Unami) spoken by this people.
▸*adj.* of or relating to the Delaware or their languages.

de·lay /di'lā/ ▸*v.* [*tr.*] make (someone or something) late or slow: *the train was delayed.* ■ [*intr.*] be late or slow; loiter: *time being of the essence, they delayed no longer.* ■ postpone or defer (an action).
▸*n.* a period of time by which something is late or postponed. ■ the action of delaying or being delayed: *I set off without delay.* —**de·lay·er** *n.*

de·lec·ta·ble /di'lektəbəl/ ▸*adj.* (of food or drink) delicious. ■ *chiefly humorous* extremely beautiful or attractive: *the delectable Ms. Davis.* —**de·lec·ta·bil·i·ty** /-‚lektə'bilitē/ *n.* —**de·lec·ta·bly** /-blē/ *adv.*

de·lec·ta·tion /‚dēlek'tāshən/ ▸*n.* *formal, chiefly humorous* pleasure and delight: *a box of chocolates for their delectation.*

del·e·gate ▸*n.* /'deligit/ a person sent or authorized to represent others, in particular an elected representative sent to a conference. ■ a member of a committee.
▸*v.* /'delə‚gāt/ [*tr.*] entrust (a task or responsibility) to another person, typically one less senior than oneself: *the power delegated to him.* ■ [*tr.*] send or authorize (someone) to do something as a representative. —**del·e·ga·ble** /-gəbəl/ *adj.* —**del·e·ga·tor** /-‚gātər/ *n.*

del·e·ga·tion /‚deli'gāshən/ ▸*n.* [treated as *sing.* or *pl.*] a body of delegates or representatives; a deputation: *a delegation of teachers.* ■ the act or process of delegating or being delegated: *prioritizing tasks for delegation.*

de·lete /di'lēt/ ▸*v.* [*tr.*] remove or obliterate (written or printed matter), esp. by drawing a line through it or marking it with a delete sign. ■ remove (data) from a computer's memory. ■ remove (a product, esp. a recording) from the catalog of those available.
▸*n.* a command or key on a computer that erases text. —**de·le·tion** /-shən/ *n.*

del·e·te·ri·ous /‚deli'ti(ə)rēəs/ ▸*adj.* causing harm or damage: *divorce is assumed to have deleterious effects on children.* —**del·e·te·ri·ous·ly** *adv.*

delft /delft/ ▸*n.* English or Dutch tin-glazed earthenware, typically decorated by hand in blue on a white background. —**delft·ware** /-‚we(ə)r/ *n.*

del·i /'delē/ ▸*n.* (*pl.* **del·is**) *inf.* short for DELICATESSEN.

de·lib·er·ate ▸*adj.* /di'libərit/ done consciously and intentionally: *a deliberate error.* ■ fully considered; not impulsive: *a deliberate decision.* ■ done or acting in a careful and unhurried way: *a deliberate worker.*
▸*v.* /-‚rāt/ [*intr.*] engage in long and careful consideration: *she deliberated over the menu.* ■ [*tr.*] consider (a question) carefully: *jurors deliberated the fate of those charged.* —**de·lib·er·ate·ly** /-ritlē/ *adv.* —**de·lib·er·ate·ness** /-ritnis/ *n.* —**de·lib·er·a·tor** /-‚rātər/ *n.*

de·lib·er·a·tion /di‚libə'rāshən/ ▸*n.* **1** long and careful consideration or discussion. **2** slow and careful movement or thought: *he replaced the glass on the table with deliberation.*

de·lib·er·a·tive /di'libərətiv; -ə‚rātiv/ ▸*adj.* relating to or intended for consideration or discussion: *a deliberative assembly.* —**de·lib·er·a·tive·ly** *adv.*

del·i·ca·cy /'delikəsē/ ▸*n.* (*pl.* **-cies**) **1** the quality of being delicate, in particular: ■ fineness or intricacy of texture or structure. ■ susceptibility to illness or adverse conditions; fragility. ■ the quality of requiring discretion or sensitivity: *the delicacy of the situation.* ■ tact and consideration: *I have to treat this matter with delicacy.* ■ accuracy of perception; sensitiveness. **2** a choice or expensive food: *a Chinese delicacy.*

del·i·cate /'delikit/ ▸*adj.* **1** very fine in texture or structure; of intricate workmanship or quality. ■ (of a color or a scent) subtle and subdued. ■ (of food or drink) subtly and pleasantly flavored. **2** easily broken or damaged; fragile. ■ (of a person, animal, or plant) susceptible to illness or adverse conditions. ■ (of a state or condition) easily upset or damaged. **3** requiring sensitive or careful handling. ■ (of a person or an action) tactful and considerate: *delicate tact was called for.* ■ skillful and finely judged; deft. ■ (of an instrument) highly sensitive.
▸*n.* *inf.* a delicate fabric or garment made of such fabric. —**del·i·cate·ly** *adv.* —**del·i·cate·ness** *n.*

del·i·ca·tes·sen /‚delikə'tesən/ ▸*n.* a store selling cold cuts, cheeses, and a variety of salads, as well as a selection of unusual or foreign prepared foods. ■ a counter or section within a supermarket or grocery store at which a range of such foods is available. ■ foods of this type collectively.

De·li·cious /di'lishəs/ ▶n. a red or yellow variety of eating apple with a sweet flavor and a slightly elongated shape.

de·li·cious /di'lishəs/ ▶adj. highly pleasant to the taste. ■ delightful: *a delicious irony.* —**de·li·cious·ly** adv. —**de·li·cious·ness** n.

de·light /di'līt/ ▶v. [tr.] please (someone) greatly. ■ [intr.] (**delight in**) take great pleasure in: *they delight in playing tricks.*
▶n. great pleasure. ■ a cause or source of great pleasure. —**de·light·ed** adj.

de·light·ful /di'lītfəl/ ▶adj. causing delight; charming: *a delightful secluded garden.* —**de·light·ful·ly** adv. —**de·light·ful·ness** n.

de·lim·it /di'limit/ ▶v. (**-lim·it·ed, -lim·it·ing**) [tr.] determine the limits or boundaries of: *agreements delimiting fishing zones.* —**de·lim·i·ta·tion** /-,limi'tāshən/ n. —**de·lim·it·er** n.

de·lin·e·ate /di'linē,āt/ ▶v. [tr.] describe or portray (something) precisely. ■ indicate the exact position of (a border or boundary). —**de·lin·e·a·tion** /-,linē'āshən/ n. —**de·lin·e·a·tor** /-,ātər/ n.

de·link /dē'lingk/ ▶v. (**delinking**) break the connection between (something) and something else: *can we delink the past from the future?*

de·lin·quent /di'lingkwənt/ ▶adj. (typically of a young person or that person's behavior) showing or characterized by a tendency to commit crime, particularly minor crime: *delinquent children.* ■ in arrears: *delinquent accounts.* ■ formal failing in one's duty.
▶n. a delinquent person: *young delinquents.* —**de·lin·quen·cy** /-kwənsē/ n. —**de·lin·quent·ly** adv.

del·i·quesce /,deli'kwes/ ▶v. [intr.] (of organic matter) become liquid, typically during decomposition. ■ Chem. (of a solid) become liquid by absorbing moisture from the air. —**del·i·ques·cence** /-'kwesəns/ n. —**del·i·ques·cent** /-'kwesənt/ adj.

de·lir·i·ous /di'li(ə)rēəs/ ▶adj. in an acutely disturbed state of mind resulting from illness or intoxication and characterized by restlessness, illusions, and incoherence of thought and speech. ■ in a state of wild excitement or ecstasy: *a delirious crowd.* —**de·lir·i·ous·ly** adv.

de·lir·i·um /di'li(ə)rēəm/ ▶n. an acutely disturbed state of mind that occurs in fever, intoxication, and other disorders and is characterized by restlessness, illusions, and incoherence of thought and speech. ■ wild excitement or ecstasy. ▷mid 16th cent.: from Latin, from *delirare* 'deviate, be deranged' (literally 'deviate from the furrow'), from *de-* 'away' + *lira* 'ridge between furrows.'

de·lir·i·um tre·mens /di'li(ə)rēəm 'trēmənz/ (abbr.: **DTs**) ▶n. a psychotic condition typical of withdrawal in chronic alcoholics, involving tremors, hallucinations, anxiety, and disorientation.

de·liv·er /di'livər/ ▶v. [tr.] **1** bring and hand over (a letter, parcel, or ordered goods) to the proper recipient or address: *products delivered on time* | [intr.] *we deliver.* ■ formally hand over (someone). ■ obtain (a vote) in favor of a candidate or cause: *he had been able to deliver votes in huge numbers.* ■ launch or aim (a blow, a ball, or an attack). ■ provide (something promised or expected): *she's waiting for him to deliver on his promise.* ■ (**deliver someone/something from**) save, rescue, or set free from: *deliver us from misery.* **2** state in a formal manner: *the president will deliver a speech.* ■ (of a judge or court) give (a judgment or verdict). **3** assist in the birth of: *the village midwife delivered the baby.* ■ give birth to. ■ (**be delivered of**) give birth to: *she was delivered of a chestnut foal.* ■ assist (a woman) in giving birth. —**de·liv·er·a·ble** adj. —**de·liv·er·er** n.
▶ □ **deliver the goods** inf. provide what is promised or expected.

de·liv·er·ance /di'livərəns/ ▶n. **1** the act of being rescued or set free: *prayers for deliverance.* **2** a formal or authoritative utterance.

de·liv·er·y /di'livərē/ ▶n. (pl. **-er·ies**) **1** the action of delivering letters, packages, or ordered goods. ■ a regular or scheduled occasion for this. ■ an item or items delivered on a particular occasion. ■ Law the formal or symbolic handing over of property, esp. a sealed deed, to a grantee or third party. **2** the process of giving birth: *most deliveries take place in a hospital.* **3** an act of throwing or bowling a ball or striking a blow. ■ the style or manner of such an action: *hints to speed up his delivery.* **4** the manner or style of giving a speech: *her delivery was stilted.* **5** the supply or provision of something: *delivery of electricity.*

dell /del/ ▶n. poetic/lit. a small valley, usually among trees.

del·phin·i·um /del'finēəm/ ▶n. a plant (genus *Delphinium*) of the buttercup family that bears tall spikes of typically blue flowers.

del·ta¹ /'deltə/ ▶n. **1** the fourth letter of the Greek alphabet (Δ, δ), transliterated as "d." ■ [as adj.] the fourth in a series of items, categories, etc. **2** a code word representing the letter D, used in radio communication.
▶symb. ■ (δ) Math. variation of a variable or function. ■ (Δ) Math. a finite increment.

del·ta² ▶n. a triangular tract of sediment deposited at the mouth of a river, typically where it diverges into several outlets. —**del·ta·ic** /del'tāik/ adj.

del·ta wing ▶n. the single triangular swept-back wing on some aircraft, typically on military aircraft. —**del·ta-winged** adj.

del·toid /'deltoid/ ▶adj. technical triangular: *a tree with large deltoid leaves.* ■ denoting a thick triangular muscle covering the shoulder joint and used for raising the arm away from the body.

de·lude /di'lood/ ▶v. [tr.] impose a misleading belief upon (someone); deceive; fool: *too many theorists have deluded the public* | [as adj.] (**deluded**) *the poor deluded creature.* —**de·lud·ed·ly** adv. —**de·lud·er** n.

del·uge /'del(y)ooj/ ▶n. a severe flood. ■ (**the Deluge**) the biblical Flood (recorded in Genesis 6–8). ■ a heavy fall of rain. ■ fig. a great quantity of something arriving at the same time: *a deluge of complaints.*
▶v. [tr.] (usu. **be deluged**) inundate with a great quantity of something: *he has been deluged with offers of work.* ■ flood.

de·lu·sion /di'loozhən/ ▶n. an idiosyncratic belief or impression that is firmly maintained despite being contradicted by what is generally accepted as reality or rational argument, typically a symptom of mental disorder: *the delusion of being watched.* ■ the action of deluding someone or the state of being deluded. —**de·lu·sion·al** /-zhənl/ adj.
▶ □ **delusions of grandeur** a false impression of one's own importance.

de·lu·sive /di'loosiv/ ▶adj. giving a false or misleading impression: *the delusive light of Venice.* —**de·lu·sive·ly** adv. —**de·lu·sive·ness** n.

de·luxe /di'ləks/ ▶adj. luxurious or sumptuous: *a deluxe hotel.*

delve /delv/ ▶v. [intr.] reach inside a receptacle and search for something: *she delved in her pocket.* ■ research or make inquiries into something: *delving into the atom's secrets.* ■ [tr.] poetic/lit. dig; excavate. —**delv·er** n.

dem·a·gogue /'demə,gäg/ ▶n. a leader who seeks support by appealing to popular desires and prejudices rather than by using rational argument. ■ (in ancient Greece and Rome) a leader or orator who espoused the cause of the common people. ▷mid 17th cent.: from Greek *dē magōgos*, from *dēmos* 'the people' + *agōgos* 'leading' (from *agein* 'to lead'). —**dem·a·gog·ic** /,demə'gäjik; -'gägik; -'gōjik/ adj. —**dem·a·gogu·er·y** /'demə,gägərē/ n. —**dem·a·go·gy** /'demə,gäjē; -,gōjē/ n.

de·mand /di'mand/ ▶n. an insistent and peremptory request, made as if by right: *demands for reforms.* ■ (**demands**) pressing requirements: *he's got enough demands on his time already.* ■ Econ. the desire of purchasers, consumers, clients, employers, etc., for a particular commodity, service, or other item: *a slump in demand* | *a demand for specialists.*
▶v. [tr.] ask authoritatively or brusquely: *"Where is she?" he demanded* | *the police demanded that he give them the names.* ■ insist on having: *an outraged public demanded retribution* | *too much was being demanded of the top players.* ■ require; need: *activity demanding detailed knowledge.* ■ Law call into court; summon. —**de·mand·er** n.
▶ □ **in demand** sought after: *all these skills are much in demand.* □ **on demand** as soon as or whenever required: *coffee on demand.*

de·mar·ca·tion /,dēmär'kāshən/ ▶n. the action of fixing the boundary or limits of something: *the demarcation of the maritime border.* ■ a dividing line. —**de·mar·cate** /di'märkāt/ v. —**de·mar·ca·tor** /di'mär,kātər/ n.

de·mean¹ /di'mēn/ ▶v. [tr.] [often as adj.] (**demeaning**) cause a severe loss in the dignity of and respect for (someone or something): *the poster was not demeaning to women* | *I had demeaned the profession.* ■ (**demean one·self**) do something that is beneath one's dignity.

de·mean² ▶v. (**demean oneself**) archaic conduct oneself in a particular way: *no man demeaned himself so honorably.*

de·mean·or /di'mēnər/ (Brit. **de·mean·our**) ▶n. outward behavior or bearing: *a quiet, somber demeanor.*

de·ment·ed /di'mentid/ ▶adj. suffering from dementia. ■ inf. driven to behave irrationally due to anger, distress, or excitement: *a demented and sadistic Mafioso.* —**de·ment·ed·ly** adv. —**de·ment·ed·ness** n.

de·men·tia /di'menshə/ ▶n. Med. a chronic or persistent disorder of the mental processes caused by brain disease or injury and marked by memory disorders, personality changes, and impaired reasoning.

de·mer·it /di'merit/ ▶n. **1** a feature or fact deserving censure: *the merits and demerits of these proposals.* **2** a mark awarded against someone for a fault or offense. —**de·mer·i·to·ri·ous** /,meri'tôrēəs/ adj.

de·mesne /di'mān/ ▶n. hist. **1** land attached to a manor and retained for the owner's own use. ■ the lands of an estate. ■ archaic a region or domain. **2** hist. Law possession of real property in one's own right.

Pronunciation Key ə *ago, up;* ər *over, fur;* a *hat;* ā *ate;* ä *car;* CH *chin;* e *let;* ē *see;* e(ə)r *air;* i *fit;* ī *by;* i(ə)r *ear;* NG *sing;* ō *go;* ô *law, for;* oi *toy;* oo *good;* oo *goo;* ou *out;* SH *she;* TH *thin;* TH *then;* (h)w *why;* ZH *vision*

▶ □ **held in demesne** (of an estate) occupied by the owner, not by tenants.

demi- ▶*prefix* **1** half; half-size: *demisemiquaver* | *demitasse*. **2** partially; in an inferior degree: *demigod* | *demimonde*.

dem·i·god /ˈdemēˌgäd/ ▶*n.* (*fem.* **dem·i·god·dess** /ˈdemēˌgädis/) a being with partial or lesser divine status, such as a minor deity, the offspring of a god and a mortal, or a mortal raised to divine rank. ■ *fig.* a person who is greatly admired or feared.

dem·i·john /ˈdemēˌjän/ ▶*n.* a bulbous, narrow-necked bottle holding from 3 to 10 gallons of liquid, typically enclosed in a wicker cover.

de·mil·i·ta·rize /dēˈmilitəˌrīz/ ▶*v.* [*tr.*] [usu. as *adj.*] (**demilitarized**) remove all military forces from (an area): *a demilitarized zone.* —**de·mil·i·ta·ri·za·tion** /-ˌmilitərəˈzāSHən/ *n.*

dem·i·monde /ˈdemēˌmänd/ (also **dem·i-monde**) ▶*n.* (in 19th-century France) the class of women considered to be of doubtful morality and social standing. ■ a group of people considered to be on the fringes of respectable society: *the demimonde of arms deals.*

de·min·er·al·ize /dēˈminərəˌlīz/ ▶*v.* [*tr.*] [often as *adj.*] (**demineralized**) remove salts from (water). ■ deprive (teeth or bones) of minerals, causing loss of tooth enamel or softening of the skeleton. —**de·min·er·al·i·za·tion** /-ˌminərələˈzāSHən/ *n.*

de·mise /diˈmīz/ ▶*n.* **1** a person's death: *Mr. Grisenthwaite's tragic demise.* ■ the end or failure of an enterprise or institution. **2** *Law* conveyance or transfer of property or a title by demising.
▶*v.* [*tr.*] *Law* convey or grant (an estate) by will or lease. ■ transmit (a sovereign's title) by death or abdication.

dem·i·tasse /ˈdemēˌtäs; -ˌtas/ ▶*n.* a small coffee cup.

dem·o /ˈdemō/ *inf.* ▶*n.* (*pl.* **-os**) a demonstration of something, typically computer software or a musical group: [as *adj.*] *a demo tape.*

de·mo·bi·lize /dēˈmōbəˌlīz/ ▶*v.* [*tr.*] (usu. **be demobilized**) take (troops) out of active service, typically at the end of a war: *he was demobilized in 1946.* ■ [*intr.*] cease military operations: *Germany demanded that they demobilize within twelve hours.* —**de·mo·bi·li·za·tion** /-ˌmōbəliˈzāSHən/ *n.*

de·moc·ra·cy /diˈmäkrəsē/ ▶*n.* (*pl.* **-cies**) a system of government by the whole population or all eligible members of a state, typically through elected representatives. ■ a state governed in such a way. ■ control of an organization or group by the majority of its members: *industrial democracy.* ■ the practice or principles of social equality.

dem·o·crat /ˈdeməˌkrat/ ▶*n.* **1** an advocate or supporter of democracy. **2** (**Democrat**) a member of the Democratic Party.

dem·o·crat·ic /ˌdeməˈkratik/ ▶*adj.* **1** of, relating to, or supporting democracy or its principles. ■ favoring or characterized by social equality; egalitarian. **2** (**Democratic**) of or relating to the Democratic Party. —**dem·o·crat·i·cal·ly** /-ik(ə)lē/ *adv.*

Dem·o·crat·ic Par·ty ▶one of two main U.S. political parties (the other being the Republican Party), which follows a liberal program, tending to promote a strong central government and social programs.

de·moc·ra·tize /diˈmäkrəˌtīz/ ▶*v.* [*tr.*] (often **be democratized**) introduce a democratic system or democratic principles to. ■ make (something) accessible to everyone: *mass production has not democratized fashion.* —**de·moc·ra·ti·za·tion** /-ˌmäkrətəˈzāSHən/ *n.*

de·mod·u·late /dēˈmäjəˌlāt/ ▶*v.* [*tr.*] *Electr.* extract (a modulating signal) from its carrier. ■ separate a modulating signal from (its carrier). —**de·mod·u·la·tion** /-ˌmäjəˈlāSHən/ *n.* —**de·mod·u·la·tor** /-ˌlātər/ *n.*

de·mog·ra·phy /diˈmägrəfē/ ▶*n.* the study of statistics such as births, deaths, income, or the incidence of disease, which illustrate the changing structure of human populations. ■ the composition of a particular human population: *Europe's demography.* —**de·mog·ra·pher** /-fər/ *n.* —**dem·o·graph·ic** /ˌdeməˈgrafik/ *adj.*

de·mol·ish /diˈmälisH/ ▶*v.* [*tr.*] pull or knock down (a building). ■ comprehensively refute (an argument or its proponent). ■ *inf.* overwhelmingly defeat (a player or team). ■ *humorous* eat up (food) quickly: *we demolished the potato pancakes.* ▷mid 16th cent.: from French *démoliss-* lengthened stem of *démolir*, from Latin *demoliri*, from *de-* (expressing reversal) + *moliri* 'construct' (from *moles* 'mass'). —**de·mol·ish·er** *n.* —**dem·o·li·tion** /ˌdeməˈlisHən/ *n.*

de·mon¹ /ˈdēmən/ ▶*n.* **1** an evil spirit or devil, esp. one thought to possess a person or act as a tormentor in hell. ■ a cruel, evil, or destructive person or thing. ■ [often as *adj.*] a forceful, fierce, or skillful performer of a specified activity: *a demon cook* | *a demon for work.* **2** another term for DAEMON (sense 1). —**de·mon·ise** *v.*

de·mon² ▶*n.* variant spelling of DAEMON².

de·mon·e·tize /dēˈmäniˌtīz/ ▶*v.* [*tr.*] (usu. **be demonetized**) deprive (a coin or precious metal) of its status as money. —**de·mon·e·ti·za·tion** /-ˌmäniˈtäˈzāSHən/ *n.*

de·mo·ni·ac /diˈmōnēˌak/ ▶*adj.* of, like, or characteristic of a demon or demons: *a goddess with both divine and demoniac qualities* | *demoniac rage.* —**de·mo·ni·a·cal** /ˌdēməˈnīəkəl/ *adj.* —**de·mo·ni·a·cal·ly** /ˌdēməˈnīək(ə)lē/ *adv.*

de·mon·ic /diˈmänik/ ▶*adj.* of, resembling, or characteristic of demons or evil spirits: *demonic possession* | *her laughter was demonic.* ■ fiercely energetic or frenzied: *in a demonic hurry.* —**de·mon·i·cal·ly** /-ik(ə)lē/ *adv.*

de·mon·ism /ˈdēməˌnizəm/ ▶*n.* **1** belief in the power of demons. **2** action or behavior that seems too cruel or wicked to be human.

de·mon·stra·ble /diˈmänstrəbəl/ ▶*adj.* clearly apparent or capable of being logically proved. —**de·mon·stra·bil·i·ty** /-ˌmänstrəˈbilitē/ *n.* —**de·mon·stra·bly** *adv.*

dem·on·strate /ˈdemənˌstrāt/ ▶*v.* **1** [*tr.*] clearly show the existence or truth of (something) by giving proof or evidence: *their shameful silence demonstrates their ineptitude.* ■ give a practical exhibition and explanation of (how a machine, skill, or craft works or is performed). ■ show or express (a feeling or quality) by one's actions: *she began to demonstrate a new-found confidence.* **2** [*intr.*] take part in a public demonstration.

dem·on·stra·tion /ˌdemənˈstrāSHən/ ▶*n.* **1** the action or process of showing the existence or truth of something by giving proof or evidence. ■ something that proves or makes evident: *the letter was a demonstration of good faith.* ■ the outward showing of feeling: *physical demonstrations of affection.* ■ a practical exhibition and explanation of how something works or is performed. ■ a show of military force. **2** a public meeting or march protesting against something or expressing views on a political issue.

de·mon·stra·tive /diˈmänstrətiv/ ▶*adj.* **1** (of a person) tending to show feelings, esp. of affection, openly. **2** serving as conclusive evidence of something; giving proof: *demonstrative evidence.* ■ involving demonstration, esp. by scientific means. **3** *Gram.* (of a determiner or pronoun) indicating the person or thing referred to (e.g., *this, that, those*). ▶*n. Gram.* a demonstrative determiner or pronoun. —**de·mon·stra·tive·ly** *adv.* —**de·mon·stra·tive·ness** *n.*

dem·on·stra·tor /ˈdemənˌstrātər/ ▶*n.* **1** a person who takes part in a public protest meeting or march. **2** a person who shows how a particular piece of equipment works or how a skill or craft is performed. ■ a person who teaches in this way, esp. in a laboratory. ■ a piece of merchandise that can be tested by potential buyers.

de·mor·al·ize /diˈmôrəˌlīz/ ▶*v.* [*tr.*] **1** [usu. as *adj.*] (**demoralized**) cause (someone) to lose confidence or hope; dispirit: *the army was demoralized and scattered.* **2** *archaic* corrupt the morals of (someone). —**de·mor·al·i·za·tion** /-ˌmôrələˈzāSHən/ *n.* —**de·mor·al·iz·ing** *adj.* —**de·mor·al·iz·ing·ly** *adv.*

de·mote /diˈmōt/ ▶*v.* [*tr.*] give (someone) a lower rank or less senior position, usually as a punishment: *he was demoted to deputy.* —**de·mo·tion** *n.*

de·mur /diˈmər/ ▶*v.* (**-murred**, **-mur·ring**) [*intr.*] raise doubts or objections or show reluctance. ■ *dated Law* put forward a demurrer. ▶*n.* the action or process of objecting to or hesitating over something: *they accepted this ruling without demur.*

de·mure /diˈmyo͝or/ ▶*adj.* (**-mur·er**, **-mur·est**) (of a woman or her behavior) reserved, modest, and shy: *a demure little wife who sits at home minding the house.* ■ (of clothing) lending such an appearance. —**de·mure·ly** *adv.* —**de·mure·ness** *n.*

de·mur·rer /diˈmərər; -ˈmə-rər/ ▶*n.* an objection. ■ *dated Law* an objection that an opponent's point is irrelevant or invalid, while granting the factual basis of the point: *on demurrer it was held that the plaintiff's claim succeeded.*

de·mys·ti·fy /dēˈmistəˌfī/ ▶*v.* (**-fies**, **-fied**) [*tr.*] make (a difficult or esoteric subject) clearer and easier to understand. —**de·mys·ti·fi·ca·tion** /-ˌmistəfiˈkāSHən/ *n.*

den /den/ ▶*n.* a wild animal's lair or habitation. ■ *inf.* a small, comfortable room in a house where a person can pursue an activity in private. ■ a place where people meet in secret, typically to engage in some illicit activity. ■ a small subdivision of a Cub Scout pack. ▶*v.* (**denned**, **den·ning**) [*intr.*] (of a wild animal) live in or retreat to a den.

de·nar·i·us /diˈne(ə)rēəs/ ▶*n.* (*pl.* **-nar·i·i** /-ˈne(ə)rē,ī/) an ancient Roman silver coin. ■ a unit of weight equal to that of a silver denarius. ■ an ancient Roman gold coin worth 25 silver denarii.

de·na·tion·al·ize /dēˈnaSHənlˌīz/ ▶*v.* [*tr.*] **1** transfer (a nationalized industry or institution) from public to private ownership. **2** deprive (a country or person) of nationality or national characteristics. —**de·na·tion·al·i·za·tion** /-ˌnaSHənlˈzāSHən/ *n.*

de·nat·u·ral·ize /dēˈnaCHərəˌlīz/ ▶*v.* [*tr.*] **1** make (something) unnatural. **2** deprive (someone) of citizenship of a country. —**de·nat·u·ral·i·za·tion** /-ˌnaCHərələˈzāSHən/ *n.*

de·na·ture /dē'nācHər/ ▶v. [tr.] [often as adj.] (**denatured**) take away or alter the natural qualities of. ■ make (alcohol) unfit for drinking by the addition of toxic or foul-tasting substances. ■ *Biochem.* destroy the characteristic properties of (a protein or other biological macromolecule) by heat, acidity, or other effects that disrupt its molecular conformation. ■ [intr.] (of a substance) undergo this process. —**de·na·tur·a·tion** /dē,nācHə'rāsHən/ n.

den·drite /'dendrīt/ ▶n. **1** *Physiol.* a short branched extension of a nerve cell, along which impulses received from other cells at synapses are transmitted to the cell body. Compare with AXON. **2** a crystal or crystalline mass with a branching, treelike structure. ■ a natural treelike or mosslike marking on a piece of rock or mineral.

den·drit·ic /den'dritik/ ▶adj. *technical* having a branched form resembling a tree. ■ *Physiol.* of or relating to a dendrite or dendrites. —**den·drit·i·cal·ly** /-ik(ə)lē/ adv.

den·dro·chro·nol·o·gy /,dendrōkrə'näləjē/ ▶n. the science or technique of dating events, environmental change, and archaeological artifacts by using the characteristic patterns of annual growth rings in timber and tree trunks. —**den·dro·chron·o·log·i·cal** /-,kränl'äjikəl/ adj. —**den·dro·chro·nol·o·gist** /-jist/ n.

den·drol·o·gy /den'dräləjē/ ▶n. the scientific study of trees. —**den·dro·log·i·cal** /,dendrə'läjikəl/ adj. —**den·drol·o·gist** /-jist/ n.

den·gue /'deNGgē/ -gā/ (also **dengue fever**) ▶n. a debilitating viral disease of the tropics, transmitted by mosquitoes, and causing sudden fever and acute pains in the joints.

de·ni·al /di'nīəl/ ▶n. the action of declaring something to be untrue: *she shook her head in denial.* ■ the refusal of something requested or desired. ■ a statement that something is not true. ■ *Psychol.* failure to acknowledge an unacceptable truth or emotion or to admit it into consciousness, used as a defense mechanism: *you're living in denial.* ■ short for SELF-DENIAL.

de·ni·er ▶n. **1** /də'ni(ə)r; 'denyər/ a unit of weight by which the fineness of silk, rayon, or nylon yarn is measured, equal to the weight in grams of 9000 meters of the yarn and often used to describe the thickness of hosiery: *840 denier nylon.* **2** /də'ni(ə)r; dən'yā/ *hist.* a French coin, equal to one twelfth of a sou, withdrawn from use in the 19th century.

den·i·grate /'deni,grāt/ ▶v. [tr.] criticize unfairly; disparage: *there is a tendency to denigrate the poor.* —**den·i·gra·tion** /,deni'grāsHən/ n. —**den·i·gra·tor** /-,grātər/ n. —**den·i·gra·to·ry** /-grə,tôrē/ adj.

den·im /'denəm/ ▶n. a sturdy cotton twill fabric, typically blue, used for jeans, overalls, and other clothing. ■ (**denims**) clothing made of such fabric: *a pair of denims.*

den·i·zen /'denəzən/ ▶n. an inhabitant or occupant of a particular place: *denizens of field and forest.* —**den·i·zen·ship** /-,sHip/ n.

de·nom·i·nate /di'nämə,nāt/ ▶v. **1** (**be denominated**) (of sums of money) be expressed in a specified monetary unit: *the borrowings were denominated in U.S. dollars.* **2** [tr.] *formal* call; name.

de·nom·i·na·tion /di,nämə'nāsHən/ ▶n. **1** a group or branch of any religion: *clergy of all denominations.* **2** the face value of a banknote, a coin, or a postage stamp: *a hundred dollars or so, in small denominations.* ■ the rank of a playing card within a suit, or of a suit relative to others: *two cards of the same denomination.* **3** *formal* a name or designation, esp. one serving to classify a set of things. ■ the action of naming or classifying something. —**de·nom·i·na·tion·al** /-sHənl/ adj.

de·nom·i·na·tor /di'nämə,nātər/ ▶n. *Math.* the number below the line in a common fraction; a divisor. ■ a figure representing the total population in terms of which statistical values are expressed.

de·note /di'nōt/ ▶v. [tr.] be a sign of; indicate: *this mark denotes purity and quality.* ■ (often **be denoted**) stand as a name or symbol for: *the level of output per firm, denoted by X.* —**de·no·ta·tion** /,dēnō'tāsHən/ n. —**de·no·ta·tive** /'dēnō,tātiv; di'nōtətiv/ adj.

de·noue·ment /,dānoo'mäN/ ▶n. the final part of a play, movie, or narrative in which the strands of the plot are drawn together and matters are explained or resolved. ■ the climax of a chain of events, usually when something is decided or made clear.

de·nounce /di'nouns/ ▶v. [tr.] publicly declare to be wrong or evil: *the Assembly denounced the use of violence | he was widely denounced as a traitor.* ■ inform against: *some of his own priests denounced him to the King for heresy.* ▷Middle English (originally in the sense 'proclaim, announce,' also 'proclaim someone to be wicked, cursed, a rebel, etc.'): from Old French *denoncier*, from Latin *denuntiare* 'give official information,' based on *nuntius* 'messenger.' —**de·nounce·ment** n. —**de·nounc·er** n.

dense /dens/ ▶adj. closely compacted in substance: *dense volcanic rock | swirling, dense smoke.* ■ having the constituent parts crowded closely together: *an estuary dense with marine life.* ■ *fig.* (of a text) hard to understand because of complexity of ideas. ■ *inf.* (of a person) stupid. —**dense·ly** adv. —**dense·ness** n.

den·si·ty /'densitē/ ▶n. (pl. **-ties**) the degree of compactness of a substance: *a reduction in bone density.* ■ *Comput.* a measure of the amount of information on a storage medium (tape or disk). ■ *Physics* degree of consistency measured by the quantity of mass per unit volume. ■ the opacity of a photographic image. ■ the quantity of people or things in a given area or space: *a density of 10,000 per square mile.*

dent /dent/ ▶n. a slight hollow in a hard, even surface made by a blow or by the exertion of pressure. ■ a diminishing effect; a reduction: *a dent in profits.*
▶v. [tr.] mark with a dent: *the moose dented the hood of the car.* ■ have an adverse effect on; diminish: *this dented his enthusiasm.*

den·tal /'dentl/ ▶adj. **1** of or relating to the teeth: *dental health.* ■ (abbr.: **dent.**) of or relating to dentistry: *dental councils.* **2** *Phonet.* (of a consonant) pronounced with the tip of the tongue against the upper front teeth (as *th*) or the alveolar ridge (as *n, d, t*).
▶n. *Phonet.* a dental consonant. —**den·tal·ize** /'dentl,īz/ v. (*Phonet.*) —**den·tal·ly** adv.

dental floss ▶n. a soft thread of floss silk or similar material used to clean between the teeth.

dental hy·gien·ist ▶n. an ancillary dental worker specializing in scaling and polishing teeth and in giving advice on cleaning the teeth. —**dental hy·giene** n.

den·tate /'den,tāt/ ▶adj. *Bot. & Zool.* having a toothlike or serrated edge.

den·ti·frice /'dentəfris/ ▶n. a paste or powder for cleaning the teeth.

den·tin /'dentn; -tin/ (also **den·tine** /'den,tēn/) ▶n. hard, dense, bony tissue forming the bulk of a tooth beneath the enamel. —**den·tin·al** /'dentn-əl/ adj.

den·tist /'dentist/ (abbr.: **dent.**) ▶n. a doctor qualified to treat diseases and conditions that affect the teeth and gums. —**den·tist·ry** /-strē/ n.

den·ti·tion /den'tisHən/ ▶n. the arrangement or condition of the teeth in a particular species or individual.

den·ture /'dencHər/ ▶n. (usu. **dentures**) a removable plate or frame holding one or more artificial teeth.

de·nude /di'n(y)ood/ ▶v. [tr.] (often **be denuded**) strip (something) of its covering, possessions, or assets; make bare: *almost overnight the Arctic was denuded of animals.* —**de·u·da·tion** /,den(y)oo'dāsHən/ n.

de·nun·ci·a·tion /di,nənsē'āsHən/ ▶n. public condemnation of someone or something. ■ the action of informing against someone. —**de·nun·ci·a·tor** /-'nənsē,ātər/ n. —**de·nun·ci·a·to·ry** /-'nənsēə,tôrē/ adj.

de·ny /di'nī/ ▶v. (**-nies, -nied**) [tr.] refuse to admit the truth or existence of (something). ■ refuse to give (something requested or desired) to (someone): *the inquiry was denied access to intelligence sources.* ■ refuse to accept or agree to: *judges would deny the requests.* ■ refuse to acknowledge or recognize; disown: *Peter denied Jesus.* ■ (**deny oneself**) refrain from satisfying oneself.

de·o·dor·ant /dē'ōdərənt/ ▶n. a substance that removes or conceals unpleasant smells, esp. bodily odors.

de·o·dor·ize /dē'ōdə,rīz/ ▶v. [tr.] remove or conceal an unpleasant smell in: *people used dried flowers to deodorize their homes.* —**de·o·dor·i·za·tion** /-,ōdərə'zāsHən/ n. —**de·o·dor·iz·er** n.

de·ox·y·gen·ate /dē'äksijə,nāt/ ▶v. [tr.] [usu. as adj.] (**deoxygenated**) remove oxygen from. —**de·ox·y·gen·a·tion** /-,äksijə'nāsHən/ n.

de·part /di'pärt/ ▶v. [intr.] leave, typically in order to start a journey: *they departed for Germany | a contingent was departing from Cairo.* ■ (**depart from**) deviate from (an accepted, prescribed, or traditional course of action): *he departed from the precedent set by many.*

de·part·ed /di'pärtid/ ▶adj. deceased: *a dear departed relative.*
▶n. (**the departed**) a particular dead person or dead people.

de·part·ment /di'pärtmənt/ ▶n. in a large organization, a division that deals with a specific subject, commodity, or area of activity: *the English department.* ■ an administrative district in France and other countries. ■ (**one's department**) *inf.* an area of special expertise or responsibility: *that's not my department.* ■ *inf.* the specified subject under discussion: *he's average in the looks department.*

de·part·men·tal /di,pärt'mentl; ,dēpärt-/ ▶adj. concerned with or belonging to a department of an organization. —**de·part·men·tal·ize** v. —**de·part·men·tal·ly** adv.

department store ▶n. a large store stocking many varieties of goods in different departments.

de·par·ture /di'pärcHər/ ▶n. the action of leaving, typically to start a

Pronunciation Key ə *ago, up;* ər *over, fur;* a *hat;* ā *ate;* ä *car;* cH *chin;* e *let;* ē *see;* e(ə)r *air;* i *fit;* ī *by;* i(ə)r *ear;* NG *sing;* ō *go;* ô *law, for;* oi *toy;* oo *good;* oo *goo;* ou *out;* sH *she;* TH *thin;* TH *then;* (h)w *why;* zH *vision*

journey: *the day of departure* | *she made a hasty departure.* ■ a deviation from an accepted, prescribed, or traditional course of action or thought: *a departure from their usual style.*

de·pend /di'pend/ ▸ *v.* [*intr.*] **1** (**depend on/upon**) be controlled or determined by: *differences in earnings depended on a wide variety of factors.* **2** (**depend on/upon**) rely on: *the kind you could depend on.* ■ need or require for financial or other support: *a town that depended upon industry.* ■ be grammatically dependent on. **3** *archaic* or *poetic/lit.* hang down.
▸ □ **depending on** being conditioned by; contingent on: *makes 8–10 burgers (depending on size).* □ **it** (or **that**) (**all**) **depends** used to express uncertainty or qualification in answering a question: *How many people use each screen? It all depends.*

de·pend·a·ble /di'pendəbəl/ ▸ *adj.* trustworthy and reliable. —**de·pend·a·bil·i·ty** /-,pendə'bilitē/ *n.* —**de·pend·a·bly** /-blē/ *adv.*

de·pend·ence /di'pendəns/ ▸ *n.* the state of relying on or being controlled by someone or something else: *Japan's dependence on imported oil.* ■ reliance on someone or something for financial support. ■ addiction to drink or drugs: *alcohol dependence.*

de·pend·en·cy /di'pendənsē/ ▸ *n.* (*pl.* **-cies**) **1** a dependent or subordinate thing, esp. a country or province controlled by another. **2** dependence: *the country's dependency on the oil industry.*

de·pend·ent /di'pendənt/ ▸ *adj.* **1** (**dependent on/upon**) contingent on or determined by: *benefits will be dependent on length of service.* **2** requiring someone or something for financial, emotional, or other support: *households with dependent children.* ■ unable to do without: *dependent on drugs.* ■ *Gram.* (of a clause, phrase, or word) subordinate to another clause, phrase, or word.
▸ *n.* (*Brit.* also **de·pend·ant**) a person who relies on another, esp. a family member, for financial support. —**de·pend·ent·ly** *adv.*

de·pict /di'pikt/ ▸ *v.* [*tr.*] show or represent by a drawing, painting, or other art form. ■ portray in words; describe: *youth is depicted as a time of vitality and good health.* —**de·pict·er** *n.* —**de·pic·tion** /-'pikSHən/ *n.*

de·pi·late /'depə,lāt/ ▸ *v.* [*tr.*] remove the hair from. —**de·pi·la·tion** /,depə'lāSHən/ *n.*

de·pil·a·to·ry /di'pilə,tôrē/ ▸ *adj.* used to remove unwanted hair.
▸ *n.* (*pl.* **-ries**) a cream or lotion for removing unwanted hair.

de·plane /dē'plān/ ▸ *v.* [*intr.*] disembark from an aircraft.

de·plete /di'plēt/ ▸ *v.* use up the supply of; exhaust the abundance of: *fish stocks are severely depleted.* ■ [*intr.*] diminish in number or quantity: *supplies are depleting fast.* ■ exhaust. —**de·ple·tion** /-'plēSHən/ *n.*

de·plor·a·ble /di'plôrəbəl/ ▸ *adj.* deserving strong condemnation. ■ shockingly bad in quality. —**de·plor·a·bly** /-blē/ *adv.*

de·plore /di'plôr/ ▸ *v.* [*tr.*] feel or express strong disapproval of (something): *we deplore this act of violence.* —**de·plor·ing·ly** *adv.*

de·ploy /di'ploi/ ▸ *v.* [*tr.*] move (troops) into position for military action. ■ [*intr.*] (of troops) move into position for such action: *the air force began to deploy forward.* ■ bring into effective action; utilize: *they are not always able to deploy this skill.* —**de·ploy·ment** *n.*

de·po·lit·i·cize /,dēpə'liti,sīz/ ▸ *v.* [*tr.*] remove from political influence: *we have to depoliticize education.* —**de·po·lit·i·ci·za·tion** /-,litisə'zāSHən/ *n.*

de·pop·u·late /dē'päpyə,lāt/ ▸ *v.* [*tr.*] substantially reduce the population of (an area). —**de·pop·u·la·tion** /-,päpyə'lāSHən/ *n.*

de·port /di'pôrt/ ▸ *v.* **1** [*tr.*] expel (a foreigner) from a country, typically on the grounds of illegal status or for having committed a crime: *he was deported for violation of immigration laws.* ■ exile (a native) to another country. **2** (**deport oneself**) *archaic* conduct oneself in a specified manner: *he has deported himself with great dignity.* —**de·port·a·ble** *adj.* —**de·por·ta·tion** /,dēpôr'tāSHən/ *n.*

de·por·tee /,dēpôr'tē/ ▸ *n.* a person who has been or is being expelled from a country.

de·port·ment /di'pôrtmənt/ ▸ *n.* a person's behavior or manners.

de·pose /di'pōz/ ▸ *v.* [*tr.*] **1** remove from office suddenly and forcefully: *he had been deposed by a military coup.* **2** *Law* testify to or give (evidence) on oath, typically in a written statement: *every affidavit shall state the facts deposed to.* **3** *Law* to question (a witness) in deposition.

de·pos·it /di'päzit/ ▸ *n.* **1** a sum of money placed or kept in a bank account, usually to gain interest. ■ an act of placing money in a bank account: *I'd like to make a deposit.* **2** a sum payable as a first installment on the purchase of something or as a pledge for a contract, the balance being payable later: *we've saved enough for a deposit on a house.* ■ a returnable sum payable on the rental of something, to cover loss or damage. **3** a layer or body of accumulated matter: *deposits of salt on the chrome.* ■ a natural layer of sand, rock, coal, or other material.
▸ *v.* (**-it·ed, -it·ing**) **1** [*tr.*] put or set down (something or someone) in a specific place: *he deposited a pile of books on the kitchen table.* ■ (usu. **be deposited**) (of water, the wind, or other natural agency) lay down

(matter) gradually as a layer or covering: *salt is deposited by the tide.* ■ lay (an egg or group of eggs). **2** [*tr.*] store or entrust with someone for safekeeping. ■ pay (a sum of money) into a bank account. ■ pay (a sum) as a first installment or as a pledge for a contract.

dep·o·si·tion /,depə'ziSHən/ ▸ *n.* **1** the action of deposing someone, esp. a monarch. **2** *Law* the process of giving sworn evidence: *the deposition of four expert witnesses.* **3** *Law* the written record of a witness's out-of-court testimony. ■ a formal, usually written, statement to be used as evidence outside court. **4** the action of depositing something: *pebbles formed by the deposition of calcium in solution.*

de·pos·i·tor /di'päzitər/ ▸ *n.* a person who keeps money in a bank account.

de·pos·i·to·ry /di'päzi,tôrē/ ▸ *n.* (*pl.* **-ries**) a place where things are stored.

de·pot /'dēpō; 'de-/ ▸ *n.* a place for the storage of large quantities of equipment, food, or some other commodity: *an arms depot.* ■ a railroad or bus station. ■ a place where buses, trains, or other vehicles are housed and maintained.

de·prave /di'prāv/ ▸ *v.* [*tr.*] make (someone) immoral or wicked. ▷late Middle English (in the sense 'pervert the meaning of something'): from Old French *depraver* or Latin *depravare*, from *de-* 'down, thoroughly' + *pravus* 'crooked, perverse.' —**dep·ra·va·tion** /,deprə'vāSHən/ *n.* —**de·praved** *adj.*

de·prav·i·ty /di'pravitē/ ▸ *n.* (*pl.* **-ties**) moral corruption: *a tale of wickedness and depravity.* ■ a wicked or morally corrupt act.

dep·re·cate /'depri,kāt/ ▸ *v.* [*tr.*] **1** express disapproval of: [as *adj.*] (**deprecating**) *he sniffed in a deprecating way.* **2** another term for DEPRECIATE (sense 2): *he deprecates the value of children's television.* —**dep·re·cat·ing·ly** *adv.* —**dep·re·ca·tion** /,deprə'kāSHən/ *n.* —**dep·re·ca·tive** /-,kātiv/ *adj.* —**dep·re·ca·tor** /-,kātər/ *n.* —**dep·re·ca·to·ry** /-kə,tôrē/ *adj.*

de·pre·ci·ate /di'prēSHē,āt/ ▸ *v.* **1** [*intr.*] diminish in value over a period of time: *the pound is expected to depreciate against the dollar.* ■ reduce the recorded value in a company's books of (an asset) each year over a predetermined period. **2** [*tr.*] disparage or belittle (something): *she was already depreciating her own aesthetic taste.* —**de·pre·ci·a·to·ry** /-SHēə,tôrē/ *adj.*

de·pre·ci·a·tion /di,prēSHē'āSHən/ ▸ *n.* a reduction in the value of an asset with the passage of time, due in particular to wear and tear. ■ decrease in the value of a currency relative to other currencies.

dep·re·da·tion /,deprə'dāSHən/ ▸ *n.* (usu. **depredations**) an act of attacking or plundering: *protecting grain from the depredations of rats and mice.*

de·press /di'pres/ ▸ *v.* [*tr.*] **1** make (someone) feel utterly dispirited or dejected. ■ reduce the level or strength of activity in (something, esp. an economic or biological system): *fear of inflation depressed bond markets* | *alcohol depresses the nervous system.* **2** push or pull (something) down into a lower position: *depress the lever.* —**de·press·i·ble** *adj.* —**de·press·ing** *adj.* —**de·press·ing·ly** *adv.*

de·pres·sant /di'presənt/ ▸ *adj.* (chiefly of a drug) reducing functional or nervous activity.
▸ *n.* a depressant drug. ■ an influence that depresses economic or other activity: *higher taxation is a depressant.*

de·pres·sion /di'preSHən/ ▸ *n.* **1** severe despondency and dejection, typically felt over a period of time and accompanied by feelings of hopelessness and inadequacy. ■ *Med.* a condition of mental disturbance characterized by such feelings to a greater degree than seems warranted by the external circumstances, typically with lack of energy and difficulty in maintaining concentration or interest in life. ■ a long and severe recession in an economy or market. ■ (**the Depression** or **the Great Depression**) the financial and industrial slump of 1929 and subsequent years. **2** the lowering or reducing of something: *the depression of prices.* ■ the action of pressing down on something: *depression of the plunger delivers two units of insulin.* ■ a sunken place or hollow on a surface. ■ *Astron.* & *Geog.* the angular distance of an object below the horizon or a horizontal plane. ■ *Meteorol.* a region of lower atmospheric pressure, esp. a cyclonic weather system.

de·pres·sive /di'presiv/ ▸ *adj.* causing feelings of hopelessness, despondency, and dejection. ■ *Med.* relating to or tending to suffer from clinical depression. ■ causing a reduction in strength, effectiveness, or value: *steroids have a depressive effect on the immune system.*
▸ *n.* *Med.* a person suffering from or with a tendency to suffer from depression.

de·pres·sur·ize /dē'preSHə,rīz/ ▸ *v.* [*tr.*] release the pressure of the gas inside (a pressurized vehicle or container). ■ [*intr.*] (of a pressurized vehicle or container) lose pressure. —**de·pres·sur·i·za·tion** /-,preSHərə'zāSHən/ *n.*

dep·ri·va·tion /,deprə'vāSHən/ ▸ *n.* the damaging lack of material benefits considered to be basic necessities in a society. ■ the lack or denial of something considered to be a necessity: *sleep deprivation.*

de·prive /di'prīv/ ▶v. [tr.] deny (a person or place) the possession or use of something: *the city was deprived of its water supplies.* —**de·priv·al** /-vəl/ *n.*

Dept. ▶*abbr.* Department.

depth /depTH/ ▶*n.* **1** the distance from the top or surface of something to its bottom: *12 feet in depth.* ■ distance from the nearest to the farthest point of something or from the front to the back: *the depth of the wardrobe.* ■ used to specify the distance below the top or surface of something to which someone or something percolates or at which something happens: *loosen the soil to a depth of 8 inches.* ■ the apparent existence of three dimensions in a picture, photograph, or other two-dimensional representation; perspective: *texture in a picture gives it depth.* ■ lowness of pitch: *my voice had not yet acquired husky depths.* **2** complexity and profundity of thought. ■ extensive and detailed study or knowledge. ■ intensity of emotion, usually considered as a laudable quality: *a man of compassion and depth of feeling.* ■ intensity of color. **3** (**the depths**) a point far below the surface. ■ the worst or lowest part or state: *the depths to which morality has sunk.* ■ a time when one's negative feelings are at their most intense: *in the depths of despair.* ■ a place that is remote and inaccessible: *a village somewhere in the depths of Russia.* **4** *Sports* the strength of a team in its reserve of substitute players.

▶ □ **out of one's depth** *fig.* beyond one's knowledge or ability to cope.

depth charge ▶*n.* an explosive charge designed to explode under water at a preset depth, used for attacking submarines.

dep·u·ta·tion /ˌdepyə'tāshən/ ▶*n.* a group of people appointed to undertake a mission or take part in a formal process on behalf of a larger group: *he had been a member of a deputation to Napoleon III.*

de·pute /di'pyo͞ot/ ▶*v.* [tr.] appoint or instruct (someone) to perform a task for which one is responsible: *she had been deputed to look after him while Clarissa was away.* ■ delegate (authority or a task).

dep·u·tize /'depyəˌtīz/ ▶*v.* [tr.] make (someone) a deputy: *officers deputized as federal marshals.* ■ [intr.] temporarily act or speak as a deputy.

dep·u·ty /'depyətē/ ▶*n.* (*pl.* **-ties**) a person whose immediate superior is a senior figure within an organization and who is empowered to act as a substitute for this superior. ■ a parliamentary representative in certain countries. —**dep·u·ty·ship** /-ˌSHip/ *n.*

de·rail /dē'rāl/ ▶*v.* [tr.] cause (a train or trolley car) to leave its tracks. ■ [intr.] (of a train or trolley car) accidentally leave the tracks. ■ [tr.] *fig.* obstruct (a process) by diverting it from its intended course: *the plot is seen as an attempt to derail the negotiations.* —**de·rail·ment** *n.*

de·rail·leur /di'rālər/ ▶*n.* a bicycle mechanism that moves the chain out and up, allowing it to shift to different cogs.

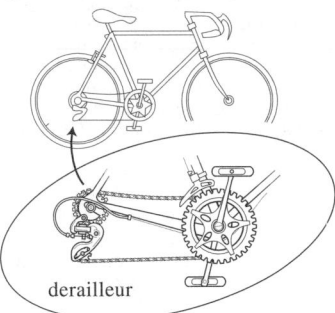

derailleur

de·range /di'rānj/ ▶*v.* [tr.] [usu. as adj.] (**deranged**) cause (someone) to become insane: *a deranged man.* ■ throw (something) into confusion; cause to act irregularly: *stress deranges the immune system.* ■ *archaic* intrude on; interrupt. —**de·range·ment** *n.*

Der·by /'derbē/ ▶*n.* (*pl.* **-bies**) **1** an annual horse race run on Epsom Downs in England in late May or early June. ■ a similar race elsewhere: *the Kentucky Derby.* ■ (**derby**) a sports contest open to the general public: *sign up for the fishing derby.* **2** (**derby**) a bowler hat.

de·reg·u·late /dē'regyəˌlāt/ ▶*v.* [tr.] remove regulations or restrictions from. —**de·reg·u·la·tion** /-ˌregyə'lāsHən/ *n.* —**de·reg·u·la·to·ry** /-lə,tôrē/ *adj.*

der·e·lict /'derəˌlikt/ ▶*adj.* in a very poor condition as a result of disuse and neglect. ■ (of a person) negligent in not having done what one should have done: *he was derelict in his duty to his country.*

▶*n.* a person without a home, job, or property: *derelicts who could fit all their possessions in a paper bag.* ■ a piece of property, esp. a ship, abandoned by the owner and in poor condition.

der·e·lic·tion /ˌderə'liksHən/ ▶*n.* the state of having been abandoned and become dilapidated. ■ (usu. **dereliction of duty**) the shameful failure to fulfill one's obligations.

de·ride /di'rīd/ ▶*v.* [tr.] express contempt for; ridicule. —**de·rid·er** *n.*

de ri·gueur /də ri'gər; rē'gœr/ ▶*adj.* required by etiquette or current fashion: *it was de rigueur for bands to grow their hair long.*

de·ri·sion /di'riZHən/ ▶*n.* contemptuous ridicule or mockery.

de·ri·sive /di'rīsiv/ ▶*adj.* expressing contempt or ridicule: *a harsh, derisive laugh.* —**de·ri·sive·ly** *adv.* —**de·ri·sive·ness** *n.*

de·ri·so·ry /di'rīsərē; -'rī-/ ▶*adj.* **1** ridiculously small or inadequate: *they were given a derisory pay rise.* **2** another term for DERISIVE.

der·i·va·tion /ˌderə'vāsHən/ ▶*n.* **1** the obtaining or developing of something from a source or origin: *the derivation of scientific laws from observation.* ■ the formation of a word from another word or from a root in the same or another language. ■ *Math.* a sequence of statements showing that a formula, theorem, etc., is a consequence of previously accepted statements. ■ *Math.* the process of deducing a new formula, theorem, etc., from previously accepted statements. **2** origin; extraction: *music of Turkish derivation.* ■ something derived; a derivative: *the derivation "sheepish" has six definitions.* —**der·i·va·tion·al** /-SHənl/ *adj.*

de·riv·a·tive /di'rivətiv/ ▶*adj.* (typically of an artist or work of art) imitative of the work of another, and usually disapproved of for that reason. ■ originating from, based on, or influenced by: *Darwin's work is derivative of the moral philosophers.* ■ (of a financial product) having a value deriving from an underlying variable asset.

▶*n.* something that is based on another source. ■ (often **derivatives**) an arrangement or instrument (such as a future, option, or warrant) whose value derives from and is dependent on the value of an underlying asset. ■ a word derived from another or from a root in the same or another language. ■ a substance that is derived chemically from a specified compound: *crack is a highly addictive cocaine derivative.* ■ *Math.* an expression representing the rate of change of a function with respect to an independent variable. —**de·riv·a·tive·ly** *adv.*

de·rive /di'rīv/ ▶*v.* [tr.] (**derive something from**) obtain something from (a specified source): *they derived great comfort from this assurance.* ■ (**derive something from**) base a concept on a logical extension or modification of (another concept): *Marx derived his philosophy of history from Hegel.* ■ [intr.] (**derive from**) (of a word) have a specified word, usually of another language) as a root or origin. ■ [intr.] (**derive from**) arise from or originate in (a specified source): *words whose spelling derives from Dr. Johnson's incorrect etymology.* ■ (**be derived from**) (of a substance) be formed or prepared by (a chemical or physical process affecting another substance): *strong acids are derived from the combustion of fossil fuels.* ■ *Math.* obtain (a function or equation) from another by a sequence of logical steps, for example by differentiation. ▷late Middle English (in the sense 'draw a fluid through or into a channel'): from Old French *deriver* or Latin *derivare*, from *de-* 'down, away' + *rivus* 'brook, stream.' —**de·riv·a·ble** *adj.*

der·ma·ti·tis /ˌdərmə'tītis/ ▶*n.* a condition of the skin in which it becomes red, swollen, and sore, resulting from direct irritation of the skin by an external agent or an allergic reaction to it.

der·ma·tol·o·gy /ˌdərmə'täləjē/ ▶*n.* the branch of medicine concerned with the diagnosis and treatment of skin disorders. —**der·ma·to·log·i·cal** /-mətl'äjikəl/ *adj.* —**der·ma·tol·o·gist** /-jist/ *n.*

der·mis /'dərmis/ ▶*n.* *technical* the skin. ■ *Anat.* the thick layer of living tissue below the epidermis that forms the true skin, containing blood capillaries, nerve endings, sweat glands, hair follicles, and other structures. —**der·mal** /-məl/ *adj.* —**der·mic** /-mik/ *adj.* (*rare*).

der·o·gate /'derə,gāt/ ▶*v.* *formal* **1** [tr.] disparage (someone or something). **2** [intr.] (**derogate from**) detract from: *this does not derogate from his duty to act honestly and faithfully.* **3** [intr.] (**derogate from**) deviate from (a set of rules or agreed form of behavior): *one country has derogated from the Rome Convention.* —**de·rog·a·tive** /di'rägətiv/ *adj.*

der·o·ga·tion /ˌderə'gāsHən/ ▶*n.* **1** an exemption from or relaxation of a rule or law: *the massive derogation of human rights.* **2** the perception or treatment of someone as being of little worth: *the derogation of women.*

de·rog·a·to·ry /di'rägə,tôrē/ ▶*adj.* showing a critical or disrespectful attitude: *his derogatory remarks are hurtful.* —**de·rog·a·to·ri·ly** /-,tôrəlē/ *adv.*

der·rick /'derik/ ▶*n.* **1** a kind of crane with a movable pivoted arm for moving or lifting heavy weights, esp. on a ship. **2** the framework over an oil well or similar boring that holds the drilling machinery.

der·ri·ère /ˌderē'e(ə)r/ ▶*n. inf.* euphemistic term for a person's buttocks.

Pronunciation Key ə *ago, up*; ər *over, fur*; a *hat*; ā *ate*; ä *car*; cH *chin*; e *let*; ē *see*; e(ə)r *air*; i *fit*; ī *by*; i(ə)r *ear*; NG *sing*; ō *go*; ô *law, for*; oi *toy*; o͞o *good*; o͞o *goo*; ou *out*; sH *she*; TH *thin*; <u>TH</u> *then*; (h)w *why*; zH *vision*

der·ring-do /ˈderiNG ˈdo͞o/ ▶n. dated, humorous action displaying heroic courage: tales of derring-do.

der·vish /ˈdərvish/ ▶n. a Muslim (specifically Sufi) religious man who has taken vows of poverty and austerity. Dervishes of the 12th century were noted for their ecstatic rituals and were known as **dancing**, **whirling**, or **howling dervishes** according to the practice of their order.

de·sal·i·nate /dēˈsaləˌnāt/ ▶v. [tr.] [usu. as adj.] (**desalinated**) remove salt from (seawater). —**de·sal·i·na·tion** /-ˌsaləˈnāSHən/ n. —**de·sal·i·na·tor** /-ˌnātər/ n.

des·cant ▶n. /ˈdesˌkant/ Mus. an independent treble melody usually sung or played above a basic melody. ■ archaic or poetic/lit. a melodious song. ■ a discourse on a theme or subject.
▶v. /desˈkant/ [intr.] talk tediously or at length: I have **descanted on** this subject before.

de·scend /diˈsend/ ▶v. [intr.] **1** move or fall downward. ■ [tr.] move down (a slope or stairs). ■ (of stairs, a road or path, or a piece of land) be on a slope or incline and extend downward: a side road descended into the forest | [tr.] stairs descended a steep slope. ■ come or go down a scale: [as adj.] (**descending**) categories listed in descending order of usefulness. ■ Mus. (of sound) become lower in pitch: [as adj.] (**descending**) descending chords. ■ (**descend to**) act in a specified way that is far below one's usual standards: she descended to self-pity. ■ (**descend into**) (of a situation or group of people) reach (a state considered undesirable or shameful). **2** (**descend on/upon**) make a sudden attack on. ■ make an unexpected and typically unwelcome visit to: treasure-seekers descended upon the site. ■ (of a feeling or atmosphere) develop suddenly and be felt throughout a place or by a person or group of people: an air of gloom descended on headquarters. ■ (of night or darkness) begin to occur: as darkness descended, the fighting ceased. **3** (**be descended from**) be a blood relative of (a specified, typically illustrious ancestor). ■ (of an asset) pass by inheritance, typically from parent to child. ▷Middle English: from Old French descendre, from Latin descendere, from de- 'down' + scandere 'to climb.' —**de·scend·ent** /-dənt/ adj.

de·scend·ant /diˈsendənt/ ▶n. a person, plant, or animal that is descended from a particular ancestor. ■ a machine, artifact, system, etc., that has developed from an earlier, more rudimentary version.

de·scend·er /diˈsendər/ ▶n. a part of a letter that extends below the level of the base of a letter such as x (as in g and p). ■ a letter having such a part.

de·scent /diˈsent/ ▶n. **1** an action of moving downward, dropping, or falling. ■ a downward slope, esp. a path or track. ■ a moral, social, or psychological decline into a specified undesirable state: the empire's descent into barbarism. **2** the origin or background of a person in terms of family or nationality: families of Hungarian descent. ■ the transmission of qualities, property, or privileges by inheritance. **3** (**descent on**) a sudden, violent attack.

de·scram·ble /dēˈskrambəl/ ▶v. [tr.] convert or restore (a signal) to intelligible form. —**de·scram·bler** /-b(ə)lər/ n.

de·scribe /diˈskrīb/ ▶v. [tr.] **1** give an account in words of (someone or something), including all the relevant characteristics, qualities, or events. ■ indicate; denote: "Jim Crow" describes a policy of segregation. **2** mark out or draw (a geometric figure). —**de·scrib·a·ble** adj. —**de·scrib·er** n.

de·scrip·tion /diˈskripSHən/ ▶n. **1** a spoken or written representation or account of a person, object, or event. ■ the action of giving such a representation or account. **2** a sort, kind, or class of people or things: ships of every description.

de·scrip·tive /diˈskriptiv/ ▶adj. **1** serving or seeking to describe. ■ Gram. (of an adjective) assigning a quality rather than restricting the application of the expression modified, e.g., blue as distinct from few. **2** describing or classifying without expressing feelings or judging. —**de·scrip·tive·ly** adv. —**de·scrip·tive·ness** n.

de·scry /diˈskrī/ ▶v. (**-scries**, **-scried**) [tr.] poetic/lit. catch sight of.

des·e·crate /ˈdesiˌkrāt/ ▶v. [tr.] (often **be desecrated**) treat (a sacred place or thing) with violent disrespect; violate: graves were desecrated. —**des·e·cra·tion** /ˌdesiˈkrāSHən/ n. —**des·e·cra·tor** /-ˌkrātər/ n.

de·seg·re·gate /dēˈsegriˌgāt/ ▶v. [tr.] end a policy of racial segregation in: actions to desegregate schools. —**de·seg·re·ga·tion** /dēˌsegriˈgāSHən/ n.

de·sen·si·tize /dēˈsensiˌtīz/ ▶v. [tr.] make less sensitive: creams to desensitize the skin. ■ make (someone) less likely to feel shock or distress at scenes of cruelty, violence, or suffering by overexposure to such images. ■ free (someone) from a phobia or neurosis by gradually exposing the person to the thing that is feared. —**de·sen·si·ti·za·tion** /dē-ˌsensitəˈzāSHən/ n. —**de·sen·si·tiz·er** n.

de·sert¹ /dəˈzərt/ ▶v. [tr.] abandon (a person, cause, or organization) in a way considered disloyal or treacherous: he deserted his wife and went back to England. ■ [usu. as adj.] (**deserted**) (of a number of people) leave (a place), causing it to appear empty: the lobby was virtually deserted. ■ (of a quality or ability) fail (someone), esp. at a crucial moment when most needed: her luck deserted her. ■ [intr.] Mil. (of a soldier) illegally run away from military service. —**de·sert·er** n. —**de·ser·tion** /-ˈzərSHən/ n.

des·ert² /ˈdezərt/ ▶n. a dry, barren area of land, esp. one covered with sand, that is characteristically desolate, waterless, and without vegetation. ■ a lifeless and unpleasant place, esp. one consisting of or covered with a specified substance: the interior of Iceland is an ice desert. ■ a situation or area considered dull and uninteresting: a cultural desert.
▶adj. like a desert. ■ uninhabited and desolate. —**de·ser·tic** adj.

de·sert³ /diˈzərt/ ▶n. (usu. **deserts**) a person's worthiness or entitlement to reward or punishment: the penal system fails to punish offenders in accordance with their deserts.
▶ □ **get** (or **receive**) **one's just deserts** receive the appropriate reward or (more usually) punishment for one's actions.

de·serve /dəˈzərv/ ▶v. [tr.] do something or have or show qualities worthy of (reward or punishment). —**de·serv·ed·ly** /-vidlē/ adv.

de·serv·ing /dəˈzərviNG/ ▶adj. worthy of being treated in a particular way, typically of being given assistance. —**de·serv·ing·ly** adv.

des·ic·cant /ˈdesikənt/ ▶n. a substance used as a drying agent.

des·ic·cate /ˈdesiˌkāt/ ▶v. [tr.] [usu. as adj.] (**desiccated**) remove the moisture from (something, esp. food), typically in order to preserve it. ■ [as adj.] (**desiccated**) fig. lacking interest, passion, or energy: desiccated ideas. —**des·ic·ca·tion** /-ˈkāSHən/ n. —**des·ic·ca·tive** /-ˌkātiv/ adj.

de·sid·er·a·tum /diˌsidəˈrätəm; -ˈrātəm; -ˌzidə-/ ▶n. (pl. **-ta** /-tə/) something that is needed or wanted: integrity was a desideratum.

de·sign /dəˈzīn/ ▶n. **1** a plan or drawing produced to show the look and function or workings of a building, garment, or other object before it is built or made: his design for the new museum. ■ the art or action of conceiving of and producing such a plan or drawing: good design can help the reader understand complicated information | the cloister is of 12-century design. ■ an arrangement of lines or shapes created to form a pattern or decoration. **2** purpose, planning, or intention that exists or is thought to exist behind an action, fact, or material object.
▶v. [tr.] decide upon the look and functioning of (a building, garment, or other object), typically by making a detailed drawing of it. ■ (often **be designed**) do or plan (something) with a specific purpose or intention in mind: [tr.] changes designed to stimulate economic growth.
▶ □ **by design** as a result of a plan; intentionally. □ **have designs on** aim to obtain (something desired), typically in a secret and dishonest way: he suspected her of having designs on the family fortune.

des·ig·nate ▶v. /ˈdezigˌnāt/ [tr.] appoint (someone) to a specified position: he was **designated as** prime minister. ■ officially assign a specified status or ascribe a specified name or quality to: [tr.] certain schools are designated "science schools." ■ signify; indicate: the term "brainstem" designates the medulla, pons, and mesencephalon.
▶adj. /-nit; -ˌnāt/ appointed to an office or position but not yet installed: the director designate. —**des·ig·na·tor** /-ˌnātər/ n.

des·ig·nat·ed driv·er ▶n. a member of a group who abstains from alcohol in order to drive the others safely.

des·ig·nat·ed hit·ter ▶n. Baseball a nonfielding player named before the start of a game to be in the batting order, typically in place of the pitcher.

des·ig·na·tion /ˌdezigˈnāSHən/ ▶n. the choosing and naming of someone to be the holder of an official position. ■ the action of choosing a place for a special purpose or giving it a special status: the designation of parts of Santa Ana as an enterprise zone. ■ a name, description, or title, typically one that is officially bestowed.

de·sign·ed·ly /dəˈzīnidlē/ ▶adv. in order to produce a specific effect.

de·sign·er /dəˈzīnər/ ▶n. a person who plans the form, look, or workings of something before its being made or built, typically by drawing it in detail. ■ [as adj.] made by or having the expensive sophistication of a famous and prestigious fashion designer: a designer label. ■ [as adj.] upscale and fashionable: designer food.

de·sign·er drug ▶n. a synthetic analog of an illegal drug, esp. one devised to circumvent drug laws. ■ a fashionable artificial drug.

de·sign·ing /dəˈzīniNG/ ▶adj. acting in a calculating, deceitful way.

de·sir·a·ble /dəˈzī(ə)rəbəl/ ▶adj. wanted or wished for as being an attractive, useful, or necessary course of action: some social control over technology is desirable. ■ (of a person) arousing sexual desire.
▶n. a desirable person, thing, or quality. —**de·sir·a·bil·i·ty** /-ˌzī(ə)rəˈbilitē/ n. —**de·sir·a·ble·ness** n. —**de·sir·a·bly** /-blē/ adv.

de·sire /də'zī(ə)r/ ▸ *n.* a strong feeling of wanting to have something or wishing for something to happen. ■ strong sexual feeling or appetite.
▸ *v.* [*tr.*] strongly wish for or want (something). ■ want (someone) sexually.

de·sir·ous /di'zīrəs/ ▸ *adj.* having or characterized by desire: *the pope was desirous of peace in Europe.*

de·sist /di'sist/ ▸ *v.* [*intr.*] cease; abstain: *a vow to **desist** from violence.*

desk /desk/ ▸ *n.* a piece of furniture with a flat or sloped surface and typically with drawers, at which one can read, write, or do other work. ■ a counter in a hotel, bank, or airport at which a customer may check in or obtain information. ■ a specified section of a news organization, esp. a newspaper: *the sports desk.*

desk·top /'desk,täp/ ▸ *n.* the working surface of a desk. ■ [as *adj.*] denoting a piece of equipment such as a microcomputer that is suitable for use at an ordinary desk. ■ a desktop computer. ■ a computer screen regarded as a representation of a notional desktop and containing icons representing items such as files and a wastebasket.

desk·top pub·lish·ing (abbr.: **DTP**) ▸ *n.* the production of printed matter by means of a printer linked to a desktop computer, with special software.

des·o·late ▸ *adj.* /'desəlit/ (of a place) deserted of people and in a state of bleak and dismal emptiness: *a desolate moor.* ■ feeling or showing misery, unhappiness, or loneliness: *I suddenly felt desolate and bereft.*
▸ *v.* /'desə,lāt/ [*tr.*] make (a place) bleakly and depressingly empty or bare. ■ (usu. **be desolated**) make (someone) feel utterly wretched and unhappy: *he was desolated by the deaths of his treasured friends.* —**des·o·late·ly** *adv.* —**des·o·late·ness** /-litnis/ *n.* —**des·o·la·tion** /,desə'lāshən/ *n.* —**des·o·la·tor** /-,lātər/ *n.*

de·spair /di'spe(ə)r/ ▸ *n.* the complete loss or absence of hope.
▸ *v.* [*intr.*] lose or be without hope. —**des·pair·ing·ly** *adv.*
▸ □ **be the despair of** be the cause of a feeling of hopelessness in (someone else): *my handwriting was the despair of my teachers.*

des·patch ▸ *v.* & *n.* variant spelling of **DISPATCH.**

des·per·a·do /,despə'rädō/ ▸ *n.* (*pl.* **-does** or **-dos**) a desperate or reckless person, esp. a criminal. —**des·per·a·do·ism** /-,izəm/ *n.*

des·per·ate /'despərit/ ▸ *adj.* feeling, showing, or involving a hopeless sense that a situation is so bad as to be impossible to deal with. ■ (of an act or attempt) tried in despair or when everything else has failed; having little hope of success: *a desperate attempt to save him.* ■ (of a situation) extremely bad, serious, or dangerous: *a desperate shortage of nurses.* ■ (of a person) having a great need or desire for something: *desperate for a cigarette.* ■ (of a person or fight) violent or dangerous. —**des·per·ate·ly** *adv.* —**des·per·ate·ness** *n.* —**des·per·a·tion** /,despə'rāshən/ *n.*

des·pi·ca·ble /di'spikəbəl/ ▸ *adj.* deserving hatred and contempt: *a despicable crime.* —**des·pi·ca·bly** /-blē/ *adv.*

de·spise /di'spīz/ ▸ *v.* [*tr.*] feel contempt or a deep repugnance for: *he despised himself for being selfish.* —**de·spis·er** *n.*

de·spite /di'spīt/ ▸ *prep.* without being affected by; in spite of: *he remains a great leader despite age and infirmity.*
▸ *n.* archaic or poetic/lit. **1** outrage; injury: *the despite done by him to the holy relics.* **2** contempt; disdain: *the theater only earns my despite.* —**de·spite·ful** /-fəl/ *adj.* (archaic or poetic/lit.).
▸ □ **despite oneself** used to indicate that one did not intend or expect to do the thing mentioned: *despite herself Fran felt a ripple of appreciation for his beauty.*

de·spoil /di'spoil/ ▸ *v.* [*tr.*] (often **be despoiled**) steal or violently remove valuable or attractive possessions from; plunder: *the church was despoiled of its marble wall covering.* —**de·spoil·er** *n.* —**de·spoil·ment** *n.* —**de·spo·li·a·tion** /-,spōlē'āshən/ *n.*

de·spond /di'spänd/ ▸ *v.* [*intr.*] archaic become dejected and lose confidence.
▸ *n.* a state of unhappiness and low spirits.

de·spond·ent /di'spändənt/ ▸ *adj.* in low spirits from loss of hope or courage. —**de·spond·en·cy** *n.* —**de·spond·ent·ly** *adv.*

des·pot /'despət/ ▸ *n.* a ruler or other person who holds absolute power, typically one who exercises it in a cruel or oppressive way. ▷mid 16th cent.: from French *despote*, via medieval Latin from Greek *despotēs* 'master, absolute ruler.' Originally (after the Turkish conquest of Constantinople) the term denoted a petty Christian ruler under the Turkish empire. The current sense dates from the late 18th cent. —**des·pot·ic** /di'spätik/ *adj.* —**des·pot·i·cal·ly** /di'spätik(ə)lē/ *adv.* —**des·pot·ism** *n.*

des·sert /di'zərt/ ▸ *n.* the sweet dish eaten at the end of a meal.

de·sta·bi·lize /dē'stābə,līz/ ▸ *v.* [*tr.*] upset the stability of; cause unrest in. —**de·sta·bi·li·za·tion** /-,stābələ'zāshən/ *n.*

des·ti·na·tion /,destə'nāshən/ ▸ *n.* the place to which someone or something is going or being sent: *a popular destination for golfers.*
▸ *adj.* being a place that people will make a special trip to visit: *a destination restaurant.*

des·tine /'destin/ ▸ *v.* [*tr.*] intend or choose (someone or something) for a particular purpose or end.

des·ti·ny /'destinē/ ▸ *n.* (*pl.* **-nies**) the events that will necessarily happen to a person or thing in the future: *unable to control her destiny.* ■ the hidden power believed to control what will happen in the future; fate.

des·ti·tute /'desti,t(y)ōōt/ ▸ *adj.* without the basic necessities of life: *the charity cares for destitute children.* ■ (**destitute of**) not having: *towns destitute of commerce.* —**des·ti·tu·tion** /,desti't(y)ōōshən/ *n.*

de·stroy /di'stroi/ ▸ *v.* [*tr.*] put an end to the existence of (something) by damaging or attacking it. ■ completely ruin or spoil (something). ■ ruin (someone) emotionally or spiritually. ■ defeat (someone) utterly. ■ (usu. **be destroyed**) kill (a sick, savage, or unwanted animal) by humane means.

de·stroy·er /di'stroiər/ ▸ *n.* a small, fast warship, esp. one equipped against submarines and aircraft. ■ someone or something that destroys.

de·struct /di'strəkt/ ▸ *v.* [*tr.*] cause deliberate, irreparable damage to (something, typically a rocket or missile).
▸ *n.* [usu. as *adj.*] the deliberate causing of terminal damage: *he had ordered him to go for the destruct button.*

de·struct·i·ble /di'strəktəbəl/ ▸ *adj.* able to be destroyed. —**de·struct·i·bil·i·ty** /-,strəktə'bilitē/ *n.*

de·struc·tion /di'strəkshən/ ▸ *n.* the action or process of causing so much damage to something that it no longer exists or cannot be repaired. ■ the action or process of killing or being killed. ■ the ruination or ending of a system or state of affairs. ■ a cause of someone's ruin: *gambling was his destruction.*

de·struc·tive /di'strəktiv/ ▸ *adj.* causing great and irreparable harm or damage. ■ tending to refute or disparage; negative and unhelpful: *destructive criticism.* —**de·struc·tive·ly** *adv.* —**de·struc·tive·ness** *n.*

des·ue·tude /'deswi,t(y)ōōd/ ▸ *n.* formal a state of disuse: *the docks fell into desuetude.*

des·ul·to·ry /'desəl,tôrē/ ▸ *adj.* lacking a plan, purpose, or enthusiasm: *dancing in a desultory fashion.* ■ (of conversation or speech) going constantly from one subject to another in a halfhearted way; unfocused: *desultory conversation.* ■ occurring randomly or occasionally: *desultory passengers.* —**des·ul·to·ri·ly** /-,tôrəlē/ *adv.* —**des·ul·to·ri·ness** *n.*

de·tach /di'tach/ ▸ *v.* [*tr.*] **1** disengage (something or part of something) and remove it. ■ [*intr.*] be easily removable: *the screen **detaches from** the keyboard.* ■ (**detach oneself from**) leave or separate oneself from (a group or place). ■ (**detach oneself from**) avoid or put an end to any connection or association with. **2** (usu. **be detached**) Mil. send (a group of soldiers or ships) on a separate mission: *our crew was detached to Puerto Rico for the exercise.* —**de·tach·a·bil·i·ty** /-,tachə'bilitē/ *n.* —**de·tach·a·ble** *adj.*

de·tach·ment /di'tachmənt/ ▸ *n.* **1** the state of being objective or aloof: *he felt a sense of detachment.* **2** Mil. a group of troops, aircraft, or ships sent away on a separate mission: *a detachment of Marines.* ■ a party of people similarly separated from a larger group. **3** the action or process of detaching; separation: *detachment of the wall.*

de·tail /di'tāl; 'dētāl/ ▸ *n.* **1** an individual feature, fact, or item: *every detail of the bill.* ■ a minor or less significant item or feature: *a detail of policy.* ■ a minor decorative feature of a building or work of art. ■ the style or treatment of such features: *the classical French detail of the facade.* ■ a small part of a picture or other work of art reproduced separately for close study. ■ (**details**) Brit. itemized information about someone; personal particulars: *they asked for my father's details.* **2** a small detachment of troops or police officers given a special duty. ■ a special duty assigned to such a detachment.
▸ *v.* [*tr.*] **1** describe item by item; give the full particulars of. **2** [*tr.*] assign (someone) to undertake a particular task: *ships were detailed to keep watch.* **3** clean (a motor vehicle) intensively.
▸ □ **go into detail** give a full account of something. □ **in detail** as regards every feature or aspect; fully: *examine the proposals in detail.*

de·tain /di'tān/ ▸ *v.* [*tr.*] keep (someone) in official custody, typically for questioning about a crime or in politically sensitive situations. ■ keep (someone) from proceeding; hold back. —**de·tain·ment** *n.*

Pronunciation Key ə *ago, up*; ər *over, fur*; a *hat*; ā *ate*; ä *car*; ch *chin*; e *let*; ē *see*; e(ə)r *air*; i *fit*; ī *by*; i(ə)r *ear*; ng *sing*; ō *go*; ô *law, for*; oi *toy*; ōō *good*; ōō *goo*; ou *out*; sh *she*; th *thin*; ᴛʜ *then*; (h)w *why*; zh *vision*

de·tain·ee /diˌtāˈnē; ˌdētāˈnē/ ▶ n. a person held in custody, esp. for political reasons.

de·tect /diˈtekt/ ▶ v. [tr.] discover or identify the presence or existence of. ■ discover or investigate (a crime or its perpetrators). ■ discern (something intangible or barely perceptible): *Paul detected a note of weariness in her voice.* —**de·tect·a·ble** *adj.* —**de·tect·a·bly** /-əblē/ *adv.* —**de·tec·tor** *n.*

de·tec·tion /diˈtekSHən/ ▶ n. the action or process of identifying the presence of something concealed. ■ the work of a detective in investigating a crime.

de·tec·tive /diˈtektiv/ ▶ n. a person, esp. a police officer, whose occupation is to investigate and solve crimes. ■ [as *adj.*] concerning crime and its investigation: *detective work.*

dé·tente /dāˈtänt/ (also **de·tente**) ▶ n. the easing of hostility or strained relations, esp. between countries.

de·ten·tion /diˈtenSHən/ ▶ n. the action of detaining someone or the state of being detained in official custody, esp. as a political prisoner. ■ the punishment of being kept in school after hours.

de·ter /diˈtər/ ▶ v. (**-terred, -ter·ring**) [tr.] discourage (someone) from doing something, typically by instilling doubt or fear of the consequences. ■ prevent the occurrence of: *strategists think about how to deter war.*

de·ter·gent /diˈtərjənt/ ▶ n. a water-soluble cleansing agent that combines with impurities and dirt to make them more soluble and differs from soap in not forming a scum with the salts in hard water. ■ any additive with a similar action, e.g., an oil-soluble substance that holds dirt in suspension in lubricating oil.
▶ *adj.* of or relating to such compounds or their action: *staining that resists detergent action.* —**de·ter·gence** *n.* —**de·ter·gen·cy** *n.*

de·te·ri·o·rate /diˈti(ə)rēəˌrāt/ ▶ v. [intr.] become progressively worse. —**de·te·ri·o·ra·tion** /-ˌti(ə)rēəˈrāSHən/ *n.* —**de·te·ri·o·ra·tive** /-ˌrātiv/ *adj.*

de·ter·mi·nant /diˈtərmənənt/ ▶ n. **1** a factor that decisively affects the nature or outcome of something: *pure force of will was the main determinant of his success.* ■ *Biol.* a gene or other factor that determines the character and development of a cell or group of cells in an organism, a set of which forms an individual's idiotype. **2** *Math.* a quantity obtained by the addition of products of the elements of a square matrix according to a given rule.
▶ *adj.* serving to determine or decide something.

de·ter·mi·nate /diˈtərmənit/ ▶ *adj.* having exact and discernible limits or form. ■ *Bot.* (of a flowering shoot) having the main axis ending in a flower bud. —**de·ter·mi·na·cy** /-minəsē/ *n.* —**de·ter·mi·nate·ly** *adv.* —**de·ter·mi·nate·ness** *n.*

de·ter·mi·na·tion /diˌtərməˈnāSHən/ ▶ n. **1** firmness of purpose; resoluteness: *unflinching determination.* **2** the process of establishing something exactly, typically by calculation or research: *determination of molecular structures.* ■ *Law* the settlement of a dispute by the decision of a judge or arbitrator. ■ *Law* a judicial decision or sentence. **3** the controlling or deciding of something's nature or outcome: *genetic sex determination.* **4** *archaic* a tendency to move in a fixed direction.

de·ter·mine /diˈtərmin/ ▶ v. [tr.] **1** cause (something) to occur in a particular way; be the decisive factor in: *your attitude may determine your future.* ■ firmly decide: *she determined to quit smoking.* **2** ascertain or establish exactly, typically as a result of research or calculation: *our aim is to determine the electric field* | *the point of our study was to **determine what** is true.* ■ *Math.* specify the value, position, or form of (a mathematical or geometric object) uniquely. —**de·ter·mi·na·ble** *adj.*

de·ter·mined /diˈtərmind/ ▶ *adj.* having made a firm decision and being resolved not to change it: *I was determined to be heard.* ■ processing or displaying resolve: *a determined child* | *a determined effort to end hunger.* —**de·ter·mined·ly** *adv.* —**de·ter·mined·ness** *n.*

de·ter·min·er /diˈtərminər/ ▶ n. **1** a person or thing that determines or decides something. **2** *Gram.* a modifying word that determines the kind of reference a noun or noun group has, for example *a, the, every*. See also **DEFINITE ARTICLE, INDEFINITE ARTICLE.**

de·ter·min·ism /diˈtərməˌnizəm/ ▶ n. *Philos.* the doctrine that all events, including human action, are ultimately determined by causes external to the will. —**de·ter·min·ist** *n. & adj.* —**de·ter·min·is·tic** /-ˌtərməˈnistik/ *adj.* —**de·ter·min·is·ti·cal·ly** /-ˌtərməˈnistik(ə)lē/ *adv.*

de·ter·rent /diˈtərənt/ ▶ n. a thing that discourages or is intended to discourage someone from doing something. ■ a nuclear weapon or weapons system regarded as deterring an enemy from attack.
▶ *adj.* able or intended to deter: *the deterrent effect of prison.* —**de·ter·rence** *n.*

de·test /diˈtest/ ▶ v. [tr.] dislike intensely. —**de·test·er** *n.*

de·test·a·ble /diˈtestəbəl/ ▶ *adj.* deserving intense dislike: *I found the film's violence detestable.* —**de·test·a·bly** /-blē/ *adv.*

de·throne /dēˈTHrōn/ ▶ v. [tr.] remove (a ruler, esp. a monarch) from power. ■ *fig.* remove from a position of authority or dominance: *he dethroned the defending title-holder.* —**de·throne·ment** *n.*

det·o·nate /ˈdetnˌāt/ ▶ v. explode or cause to explode: [intr.] *the bomb failed to detonate* | [tr.] *a trigger detonates the weapon.* ▷early 18th cent.: from Latin *detonat-* 'thundered down or forth,' from the verb *detonare*, from *de-* 'down' + *tonare* 'to thunder.' —**det·o·na·tion** /ˌdetnˈāSHən/ *n.* —**det·o·na·tive** /-ˌātiv/ *adj.* —**det·o·na·tor** /-ˌātər/ *n.*

de·tour /ˈdēˌto͝or/ ▶ n. a long or roundabout route taken to avoid something or to visit somewhere along the way. ■ an alternative route for use by traffic when the usual road is temporarily closed.
▶ v. [intr.] take a long or roundabout route: *he detoured around the walls.* ■ [tr.] avoid or bypass (something) by taking such a route.

de·tox·i·fy /dēˈtäksəˌfī/ ▶ v. (**-fies, -fied**) [tr.] remove toxic substances or qualities from: *a process to detoxify the oil.* ■ (usu. **be detoxified**) treat (an alcoholic or drug addict) to remove the effects of drink or drugs in order to help overcome addiction. ■ [intr.] abstain from drink and drugs until the bloodstream is free of toxins in order to overcome alcoholism or drug addiction. ■ [intr.] become free of poisonous substances or qualities: *the body can detoxify.* —**de·tox·i·fi·ca·tion** /dēˌtäksəfiˈkāSHən/ *n.* —**de·tox·i·fi·er** *n.*

de·tract /diˈtrakt/ ▶ v. **1** [intr.] (**detract from**) reduce or take away the worth or value of: *these quibbles in no way detract from her achievement.* ■ [tr.] deny or take away (a quality or achievement) so as to make its subject seem less impressive: *it detracts much from the credit due to them.* **2** [tr.] (**detract someone/something from**) divert or distract (someone or something) away from: *an attempt to detract attention from the issue.* —**de·trac·tion** /-ˈtrakSHən/ *n.* —**de·trac·tive** /-ˈtraktiv/ *adj.* —**de·trac·tor** /-ˈtraktər/ *n.*

det·ri·ment /ˈdetrəmənt/ ▶ n. the state of being harmed or damaged: *he is engrossed in his work **to the detriment of** his married life.* ■ a cause of harm or damage: *such tests are **a detriment to** good education.* —**det·ri·men·tal** /ˌdetrəˈmentl/ *adj.*

de·tri·tus /diˈtrītəs/ ▶ n. waste or debris of any kind. ■ gravel, sand, silt, or other material produced by erosion. ■ organic matter produced by the decomposition of organisms. —**de·tri·tal** /-tl/ *adj.*

deuce¹ /d(y)o͞os/ ▶ n. **1** a thing representing, or represented by, the number two, in particular: ■ the two on dice or playing cards. ■ a throw of two at dice. **2** *Tennis* the tie score of 40-all in a game, at which a player needs two consecutive points to win the game.

deuce² ▶ n. (**the deuce**) *inf.* used as a euphemism for "devil" in expressions of annoyance, impatience, or surprise or for emphasis: *how the deuce are we to make a profit?* | *what the deuce are you trying to do?*

deu·te·ri·um /d(y)o͞oˈti(ə)rēəm/ ▶ n. *Chem.* a stable isotope of hydrogen with a mass approximately twice that of protium, the usual isotope. (Symbol: D)

Deutsch·mark /ˈdoiCHˌmärk/ (also **Deutsch·e Mark** /ˈdoiCHə/) ▶ n. the basic monetary unit of Germany (until the introduction of the euro), equal to 100 pfennigs.

de·val·ue /dēˈvalyo͞o/ ▶ v. (**-val·ues, -val·ued, -val·u·ing**) [tr.] reduce or underestimate the worth or importance of. ■ *Econ.* reduce the official value of (a currency) in relation to other currencies: *the dinar was devalued by 20 percent.* —**de·val·u·a·tion** /dēˌvalyo͞oˈāSHən/ *n.*

De·va·na·ga·ri /ˌdāvəˈnägərē/ ▶ n. the alphabet used for Sanskrit, Hindi, and other Indian languages. ▷late 18th cent.: Sanskrit, literally 'divine town script,' from *deva* 'god' + *nāgarī* (from *nagara* 'town'), an earlier name of the script.

dev·as·tate /ˈdevəˌstāt/ ▶ v. [tr.] destroy or ruin (something). ■ cause (someone) severe and overwhelming shock or grief: *she was devastated by the loss.* —**dev·as·ta·tion** /ˌdevəˈstāSHən/ *n.* —**dev·as·ta·tor** /-ˌstātər/ *n.*

dev·as·tat·ing /ˈdevəˌstātiNG/ ▶ *adj.* highly destructive or damaging: *a devastating cyclone struck Bangladesh.* ■ causing severe shock, distress, or grief: *the news came as a devastating blow.* ■ *inf.* extremely impressive, effective, or attractive: *she had a devastating smile.* —**dev·as·tat·ing·ly** *adv.*

de·vel·op /diˈveləp/ ▶ v. (**-vel·oped, -vel·op·ing**) **1** grow or cause to grow and become more mature, advanced, or elaborate: [intr.] *motion pictures developed into mass entertainment* | [as *adj.*] (**developing**) *a rapidly developing field* | [tr.] *developing skills through trial and error.* ■ [intr.] [often as *adj.*] (**developing**) (of a poor agricultural country) become more economically and socially advanced: *the developing world.* ■ [tr.] convert (land) to a new purpose by constructing buildings or making other use of its resources. ■ construct or convert (a building). ■ [tr.] elaborate (a musical theme) by modification of the melody, harmony, or rhythm. ■ [tr.] *Chess* bring (a piece) into play from its initial position on a player's back rank. ■ *Geom.* [tr.] convert (a curved surface) conceptually into a plane figure as if by unrolling. **2** start to exist, experience, or possess: [*intr.*] *a strange closeness developed* | [*tr.*] *I developed an interest in law* | [*tr.*] *AIDS patients often develop a rare type of cancer.* **3** [*tr.*] treat (a photographic film) with chemicals to make a visible image. —**de·vel·op·a·ble** *adj.* —**de·vel·op·er** *n.*

de·vel·op·ment /dɪˈvɛləpmənt/ ▶*n.* **1** the process of developing or being developed. ■ a specified state of growth or advancement: *the wings attain full development hours after birth.* ■ a new and refined product or idea: *the latest developments in information technology.* ■ an event constituting a new stage in a changing situation: *any new developments?* ■ the process of converting land to a new purpose by constructing buildings or making use of its resources. ■ an area of land with new buildings on it: *a major housing development.* ■ *Chess* the process of bringing one's pieces into play in the opening phase of a game. **2** the process of starting to experience or suffer from an ailment or feeling. **3** the process of treating photographic film with chemicals to make a visible image.

de·vel·op·men·tal /dɪˌvɛləpˈmɛntl/ ▶*adj.* concerned with the development of someone or something. ■ concerned with the evolution of animals and plants: *developmental biology.* —**de·vel·op·men·tal·ly** *adv.*

de·vi·ant /ˈdiːvɪənt/ ▶*adj.* departing from usual or accepted standards, esp. in social or sexual behavior. ▶*n.* a deviant person or thing. —**de·vi·ance** *n.*

de·vi·ate ▶*v.* /ˈdiːvɪˌeɪt/ [*intr.*] depart from an established course: *you must not deviate from the route.* ■ depart from usual or accepted standards. ▶*n. & adj.* /ˈdiːvɪˌɪt/ old-fashioned term for DEVIANT. —**de·vi·a·tor** /-ˌeɪtər/ *n.*

de·vi·a·tion /ˌdiːvɪˈeɪʃən/ ▶*n.* **1** the action of departing from an established course or accepted standard. **2** *Statistics* the amount by which a single measurement differs from a fixed value such as the mean. **3** the deflection of a vessel's compass needle caused by iron in the vessel, which varies with the vessel's heading. —**de·vi·a·tion·ism** /-ˌɪzəm/ *n.* —**de·vi·a·tion·ist** /-ɪst/ *n.*

de·vice /dɪˈvaɪs/ ▶*n.* **1** a thing made or adapted for a particular purpose, esp. a mechanical or electronic contrivance: *a measuring device.* ■ an explosive contrivance; a bomb: *an incendiary device.* ■ *archaic* the design or look of something: *works of strange device.* **2** a plan, scheme, or trick with a particular aim: *writing a public letter is a traditional device for signaling dissent.* ■ a turn of phrase intended to produce a particular effect in speech or a literary work: *a rhetorical device.* **3** a drawing or design. ■ an emblematic or heraldic design. ▷Middle English: from Old French *devis*, based on Latin *divis-* 'divided,' from the verb *dividere.* The original sense was 'desire or intention,' found now only in *leave a person to his or her own devices* (which has become associated with sense 2).
▶ □ **leave someone to their own devices** leave someone to do as they wish without supervision.

dev·il /ˈdɛvəl/ ▶*n.* **1** (usu. **the Devil**) (in Christian and Jewish belief) the chief evil spirit; Satan. ■ an evil spirit; a demon. ■ a very wicked or cruel person. ■ a mischievously clever or self-willed person. ■ *inf.* a person with specified characteristics: *the poor devil* | *a lucky devil.* ■ (**the devil**) fighting spirit; wildness: *he was dangerous when the devil was in him.* ■ (**the devil**) a thing that is very difficult or awkward to do or deal with: *it's going to be the very devil to disentangle.* **2** (**the devil**) expressing surprise or annoyance in various questions or exclamations: *"Where the devil is he?"* **3** an instrument or machine, esp. one fitted with sharp teeth or spikes, used for tearing or other destructive work. ▶*v.* (**dev·iled, dev·il·ing**; *Brit.* **dev·illed, dev·il·ling**) [*tr.*] harass or worry (someone): *he was deviled by a new-found fear.* ▷Old English *dēofol* (related to Dutch *duivel* and German *Teufel*), via late Latin from Greek *diabolos* 'accuser, slanderer' (used in the Septuagint to translate Hebrew *śāṭān* 'Satan'), from *diaballein* 'to slander,' from *dia* 'across' + *ballein* 'to throw.'
▶ □ **devil-may-care** cheerful and reckless: *devil-may-care young pilots.* □ **like the devil** with great speed or energy: *he drove like the devil.*

dev·il·ish /ˈdɛvɪlɪʃ/ ▶*adj.* of, like, or appropriate to a devil in evil and cruelty: *devilish tortures.* ■ mischievous and rakish: *a wide, devilish grin.* ■ very difficult to deal with or use: *it turned out to be a devilish job.* ▶*adv. dated* very; extremely: *devilish clever.* —**dev·il·ish·ly** *adv.* —**dev·il·ish·ness** *n.*

dev·il·ment /ˈdɛvəlmənt/ ▶*n.* reckless mischief; wild spirits: *his eyes were blazing with devilment.*

dev·il·ry /ˈdɛvəlri/ ▶*n.* wicked activity. ■ reckless mischief: *a perverse sense of devilry urged her on.* ■ black magic; dealings with the devil.

dev·il's ad·vo·cate ▶*n.* a person who expresses a contentious opinion in order to provoke debate or test the strength of the opposing arguments.

de·vi·ous /ˈdiːvɪəs/ ▶*adj.* **1** showing a skillful use of underhanded tactics to achieve goals. **2** (of a route or journey) longer and less direct than the most straightforward way. —**de·vi·ous·ly** *adv.* —**de·vi·ous·ness** *n.*

de·vise /dɪˈvaɪz/ ▶*v.* [*tr.*] **1** plan or invent (a procedure, system, or mechanism) by careful thought: *a training program should be devised.* **2** *Law* leave (real estate) to someone by the terms of a will. ▶*n. Law* a clause in a will leaving real estate to someone. —**de·vis·a·ble** *adj.* —**de·vi·see** /dɪˌvaɪˈziː/ *n.* —**de·vis·er** *n.* —**de·vi·sor** /-ˈvaɪzər/ *n*

de·vi·tal·ize /diːˈvaɪtlˌaɪz/ ▶*v.* [*tr.*] (usu. as *adj.*) (**devitalized**) deprive of strength and vigor: *devitalized skin.* —**de·vi·tal·i·za·tion** /diːˌvaɪtlə-ˈzeɪʃən/

de·void /dɪˈvɔɪd/ ▶*adj.* (**devoid of**) entirely lacking or free from: *Lisa kept her voice devoid of emotion.*

dev·o·lu·tion /ˌdɛvəˈluːʃən/ ▶*n.* the transfer or delegation of power to a lower level, esp. by central government to local administration. ■ *formal* descent or degeneration to a lower or worse state: *the devolution of the manly ideal into a glorification of drunkenness.* ■ *Law* the legal transfer of property from one owner to another. ■ *Biol.* evolutionary degeneration. —**dev·o·lu·tion·ar·y** /-ˌnɛri/ *adj.* —**dev·o·lu·tion·ist** /-ɪst/ *n.*

de·volve /dɪˈvɑlv/ ▶*v.* [*tr.*] transfer or delegate (power) to a lower level, esp. from central government to local administration. ■ [*intr.*] (**devolve on/upon/to**) (of duties or responsibility) pass to (a body or person at a lower level): *his duties devolved on a comrade.* ■ [*intr.*] (**devolve into**) *formal* degenerate or be split into: *the Empire devolved into separate warring states.* —**de·volve·ment** *n.*

de·vote /dɪˈvoʊt/ ▶*v.* [*tr.*] (**devote something to**) give all or a large part of one's time or resources to (a person, activity, or cause): *I wanted to devote more time to my family* | *she devoted herself to fund-raising.*

de·vot·ed /dɪˈvoʊtɪd/ ▶*adj.* **1** very loving or loyal. **2** (**devoted to**) given over to the display, study, or discussion of: *a museum devoted to her work.* —**de·vot·ed·ly** *adv.* —**de·vot·ed·ness** *n.*

dev·o·tee /ˌdɛvəˈtiː; -ˈteɪ/ ▶*n.* a person who is very interested in and enthusiastic about someone or something: *a devotee of Chinese calligraphy.* ■ a strong believer in a particular religion or god: *devotees of Krishna.*

de·vo·tion /dɪˈvoʊʃən/ ▶*n.* love, loyalty, or enthusiasm for a person, activity, or cause. ■ religious worship or observance: *a life of devotion.* ■ (**devotions**) prayers or religious observances. —**de·vo·tion·al** /-ʃənl/ *adj.*

de·vour /dɪˈvaʊ(ə)r/ ▶*v.* [*tr.*] eat (food or prey) hungrily or quickly. ■ (of fire, disease, or other forces) consume (someone or something) destructively. ■ read (something) quickly and eagerly. ■ (**be devoured**) (of a person) be totally absorbed by an unpleasant feeling. —**de·vour·er** *n.* —**de·vour·ing·ly** *adv.*

de·vout /dɪˈvaʊt/ ▶*adj.* having or showing deep religious feeling or commitment. ■ totally committed to a cause or belief. —**de·vout·ly** *adv.* —**de·vout·ness** *n.*

dew /d(y)uː/ ▶*n.* tiny drops of water that form on cool surfaces at night, when atmospheric vapor condenses: *the grass was wet with dew.* ■ a beaded or glistening liquid resembling such drops: *her body had broken out in a fine dew of perspiration.* ▶*v.* [*tr.*] wet (a part of someone's body) with a beaded or glistening liquid: *sweat dewed her lashes.* —**dew·y** *adj.*

dew·ber·ry /ˈd(y)uːˌbɛri/ ▶*n.* (*pl.* **-ies**) a trailing European bramble (*Rubus caesius*) with soft prickles and edible, blackberrylike fruit, which has a dewy white bloom on the skin. ■ the fruit of this plant.

dew·claw /ˈd(y)uːˌklɔ/ ▶*n.* a rudimentary inner toe present in some dogs. ■ a false hoof on an animal such as a deer, which is formed by its rudimentary side toes.

dew·drop /ˈd(y)uːˌdrɑp/ ▶*n.* a drop of dew.

Dew·ey dec·i·mal clas·si·fi·ca·tion (also **Dewey system**) ▶*n.* an internationally applied decimal system of library classification that uses a three-figure code from 000 to 999 to represent the major branches of knowledge, and allows finer classification to be made by the addition of further figures after a decimal point.

dew·lap /ˈd(y)uːˌlap/ ▶*n.* a fold of loose skin hanging from the neck or throat of an animal or bird, esp. that present in many cattle.

dew point ▶*n.* the atmospheric temperature below which water droplets begin to condense and dew can form.

dex·ter /ˈdɛkstər/ ▶*adj. archaic* & of, on, or toward the right-hand side. The opposite of SINISTER.

Pronunciation Key ə *ago, up*; ər *over, fur*; a *hat*; ā *ate*; ä *car*; CH *chin*; e *let*; ē *see*; e(ə)r *air*; i *fit*; ī *by*; i(ə)r *ear*; NG *sing*; ō *go*; ô *law, for*; oi *toy*; ȯȯ *good*; ōō *goo*; ou *out*; SH *she*; TH *thin*; TH *then*; (h)w *why*; ZH *vision*

dex·ter·i·ty /dek'steritē/ ▶n. skill in performing tasks, esp. with the hands: *her dexterity with chopsticks | political dexterity.*

dex·ter·ous /'dekst(ə)rəs/ (also **dex·trous**) ▶adj. demonstrating neat skill, esp. with the hands. ■ mentally adroit; clever: *power users are dexterous at using software.* —**dex·ter·ous·ly** adv. —**dex·ter·ous·ness** n.

dex·trose /'dekstrōs/ ▶n. *Chem.* the predominant naturally occurring form of glucose.

DH ▶abbr. ■ Doctor of Humanities. ■ *Baseball* designated hitter.

▶v. (**DH's, DH'd, DHing**) [*intr.*] act as a designated hitter. ■ [*tr.*] use a (player) as a designated hitter.

di- ▶comb. form twice; two-; double: *dichromatic.*

▶*Chem.* containing two atoms, molecules, or groups of a specified kind: *dioxide.*

dia. ▶abbr. diameter.

di·a·be·tes /,dīə'bētēz; -tis/ ▶n. a disorder of the metabolism causing excessive thirst and the production of large amounts of urine. ▷mid 16th cent.: via Latin from Greek, literally 'siphon,' from *diabainein* 'go through.'

di·a·be·tic /,dīə'betik/ ▶adj. having diabetes. ■ relating to or designed to relieve diabetes: *a diabetic clinic | a diabetic diet.*

▶n. a person suffering from diabetes.

di·a·bol·i·cal /,dīə'bälikəl/ (also **di·a·bol·ic**) ▶adj. belonging to or so evil as to recall the Devil: *his diabolical cunning.* —**di·a·bol·i·cal·ly** /-ik(ə)lē/ adv.

di·ab·o·lism /dī'abə,lizəm/ ▶n. worship of the Devil. ■ devilish or atrociously wicked conduct. —**di·ab·o·list** n.

di·a·crit·ic /,dīə'kritik/ ▶n. a sign, such as an accent or cedilla, which when written above or below a letter indicates a difference in pronunciation from the same letter when unmarked or differently marked.

▶adj. (of a mark or sign) indicating a difference in pronunciation.

di·a·crit·i·cal /,dīə'kritikəl/ ▶adj. (of a mark or sign) serving to indicate different pronunciations of a letter above or below which it is written. —**di·a·crit·i·cal·ly** /-ik(ə)lē/ adv.

di·a·dem /'dīə,dem/ ▶n. a jeweled crown or headband worn as a symbol of sovereignty. ■ (**the diadem**) *archaic* the authority or dignity symbolized by a diadem: *the princely diadem.* —**di·a·demed** adj.

di·aer·e·sis ▶n. variant spelling of DIERESIS.

di·ag·nose /,dīəg'nōs/ ▶v. [*tr.*] identify the nature of (an illness or other problem) by examination of the symptoms. ■ (usu. **be diagnosed**) identify the nature of the medical condition of (someone). —**di·ag·nos·a·ble** adj.

di·ag·no·sis /,dīəg'nōsis/ ▶n. (pl. **-ses** /-,sēz/) **1** the identification of the nature of an illness or other problem by examination of the symptoms: *a diagnosis of Crohn's disease was made.* **2** the distinctive characterization in precise terms of a genus, species, or phenomenon.

di·ag·nos·tic /,dīəg'nästik/ ▶adj. **1** concerned with the diagnosis of illness or other problems. ■ (of a symptom) distinctive, and so indicating the nature of an illness: *fifteen infections that are diagnostic of AIDS.* **2** characteristic of a particular species, genus, or phenomenon.

▶n. **1** a distinctive symptom or characteristic. ■ *Comput.* a program or routine that helps a user to identify errors. **2** (**diagnostics**) the practice or techniques of diagnosis: *advanced medical diagnostics.* —**di·ag·nos·ti·cal·ly** /-ik(ə)lē/ adv. —**di·ag·nos·ti·cian** /-,näs'tishən/ n.

di·ag·o·nal /dī'agənl/ (abbr.: **diag.**) ▶adj. (of a straight line) joining two opposite corners of a square, rectangle, or other straight-sided shape. ■ (of a line) straight and at an angle; slanting.

▶n. a straight line joining two opposite corners of a square, rectangle, or other straight-sided shape. ■ *Math.* the set of elements of a matrix that lie on a line joining two opposite corners. ■ a slanting straight pattern or line: *bars of light made diagonals across the entrance | tiles can be laid on the diagonal.* ■ *Chess* a slanting row of squares whose color is the same. —**di·ag·o·nal·ly** adv.

di·a·gram /'dīə,gram/ (abbr.: **diag.**) a simplified drawing showing the appearance, structure, or workings of something; a schematic representation.

▶v. (**-gramed, -gram·ing**; also **-grammed, -gram·ming**) [*tr.*] represent (something) in graphic form. —**di·a·gram·mat·ic** /,dīəgrə'matik/ adj. —**di·a·gram·mat·i·cal·ly** /,dīəgrə'matik(ə)lē/ adv.

di·al /'dī(ə)l/ ▶n. a face of a clock, watch, or sundial that is marked to show units of time. ■ a similar face or flat plate with a scale and pointer for showing measurements of weight, volume, pressure, compass direction, etc. ■ a plate or disk on a radio, washing machine, or other piece of equipment that is tuned to select a wavelength or setting.

▶v. (**di·aled, di·al·ing**; *Brit.* **di·alled, di·al·ling**) [*tr.*] call (a telephone number) by turning a disk with numbered holes or pressing a set of buttons. ■ (**dial something up**) gain access to a service using a telephone line. ■ indicate or regulate by means of a dial. —**di·al·er** n.

di·a·lect /'dīə,lekt/ ▶n. a particular form of a language that is peculiar to a specific region or social group. ■ *Comput.* a particular version of a programming language. —**di·a·lec·tal** /,dīə'lektəl/ adj. —**di·a·lec·ti·cian** /,dīəlek'tishən/ n.

di·a·lec·tic /,dīə'lektik/ *Philos.* ▶n. (also **di·a·lec·tics**) [usu. treated as *sing.*] **1** the art of investigating or discussing the truth of opinions. **2** inquiry into metaphysical contradictions and their solutions. ■ the existence or action of opposing social forces, concepts, etc.

▶adj. of or relating to dialectic or dialectics; dialectical.

di·a·lec·ti·cal /,dīə'lektikəl/ ▶adj. **1** relating to the logical discussion of ideas and opinions: *dialectical ingenuity.* **2** concerned with or acting through opposing forces: *a dialectical opposition between social convention and individual libertarianism.* —**di·a·lec·ti·cal·ly** /-ik(ə)lē/ adv.

di·a·logue /'dīə,läg; -,lôg/ (also **di·a·log**) ▶n. conversation between two or more people as a feature of a book, play, or movie. ■ a discussion between two or more people or groups, esp. one directed toward exploration of a particular subject or resolution of a problem.

▶v. [*intr.*] take part in a conversation or discussion to resolve a problem. ■ [*tr.*] provide (a movie or play) with a dialogue.

di·al tone ▶n. a sound that a telephone produces indicating that a caller may start to dial.

di·al·y·sis /dī'aləsis/ ▶n. (pl. **-ses** /-sēz/) *Chem.* the separation of particles in a liquid on the basis of differences in their ability to pass through a membrane. ■ *Med.* the clinical purification of blood by this technique, as a substitute for the normal function of the kidneys. —**di·a·lyt·ic** /,dīə'litik/ adj.

di·am·e·ter /dī'amitər/ (abbr.: **diam.**) ▶n. a straight line passing from side to side through the center of a body or figure, esp. a circle or sphere. ■ the length of this line. ■ a transverse measurement of something; width or thickness. —**di·am·e·tral** /-trəl/ adj.

di·a·met·ri·cal /,dīə'metrikəl/ ▶adj. **1** used to emphasize how completely different two or more things are: *he's the diametrical opposite of Gabriel.* **2** of or along a diameter. —**di·a·met·ric** adj. —**di·a·met·ri·cal·ly** /-ik(ə)lē/ adv.

di·a·mond /'dī(ə)mənd/ ▶n. **1** a precious stone consisting of a clear and typically colorless crystalline form of pure carbon, the hardest naturally occurring substance. ■ a tool with a small stone of such a kind for cutting glass. ■ in extended and metaphorical use with reference to the brilliance, form, or hardness of diamonds: *the air glitters like diamonds.* **2** a figure with four straight sides of equal length forming two opposite acute angles and two opposite obtuse angles; a rhombus. ■ (**diamonds**) one of the four suits in a deck of playing cards, denoted by a red figure of such a shape. ■ a card of this suit. ■ the area delimited by the four bases of a baseball field, forming a square shape. ■ a baseball field. —**di·a·mond·if·er·ous** /,dī(ə)mən'difərəs/ adj.

▶ □ **diamond in the rough** a person who is generally of good character but lacks manners, education, or style.

dia·mond·back /'dī(ə)mənd,bak/ ▶n. **1** (also **diamondback rattlesnake**) a large, common North American rattlesnake (genus *Crotalus*) with diamond-shaped markings. **2** another term for TERRAPIN (sense 1).

di·an·thus /dī'anTHəs/ ▶n. (pl. **dianthuses**) a flowering plant of the pink family that belongs to the genus *Dianthus*, including the carnations.

di·a·pa·son /,dīə'pāzən; -sən/ ▶n. (also **open diapason** or **stopped diapason**) an organ stop sounding a main register of flue pipes, typically of eight-foot pitch. ■ *poetic/lit.* the entire compass, range, or scope of something.

di·a·per /'dī(ə)pər/ ▶n. **1** a piece of absorbent material wrapped around a baby's bottom and between its legs to absorb and retain urine and feces. **2** a fabric woven in a repeating pattern of small diamonds. ■ a repeating geometric or floral pattern used to decorate a surface.

▶v. [*tr.*] put a diaper on (a baby). ▷Middle English: from Old French *diapre*, from medieval Latin *diasprum*, from medieval Greek *diaspros* (adjective), from *dia* 'across' + *aspros* 'white.' The term seems originally to have denoted a costly fabric, but after the 15th cent. it was used as in noun sense 2; babies' diapers were originally made from pieces of this fabric, hence sense 1 (late 16th cent.).

di·aph·a·nous /dī'afənəs/ ▶adj. (esp. of fabric) light, delicate, and translucent: *a diaphanous dress of pale gold.*

di·a·phragm /'dīə,fram/ ▶n. **1** a muscular partition separating the thorax from the abdomen in mammals. It plays a major role in breathing. **2** a thin sheet of material forming a partition. ■ a taut, flexible membrane in mechanical or acoustic systems. ■ a thin contraceptive cap fitting over the cervix. **3** a device for varying the effective aperture of the lens in a camera or other optical system. ▷late Middle English: from late Latin *diaphragma*, from Greek, from *dia* 'through, apart' + *phragma* 'a fence.' —**di·a·phrag·mat·ic** /ˌdīəfragˈmatik/ *adj.*

di·a·rist /ˈdīərist/ ▶*n.* a person who writes a diary. —**di·a·ris·tic** /ˌdīəˈristik/ *adj.*

di·ar·rhe·a /ˌdīəˈrēə/ (*Brit.* **di·ar·rhoe·a**) ▶*n.* a condition in which liquefied feces are discharged from the bowels frequently. —**di·ar·rhe·al** *adj.* —**di·ar·rhe·ic** /-ˈrēik/ *adj.*

di·a·ry /ˈdīərē/ ▶*n.* (*pl.* **-ries**) a book in which one keeps a daily record of events and experiences. ■ a datebook.

di·as·po·ra /dīˈaspərə/ ▶*n.* (often **the Diaspora**) Jews living outside Israel. ■ the dispersion of the Jews beyond Israel. ■ the dispersion of any people from their original homeland. ■ the people so dispersed.

di·as·to·le /dīˈastl-ē/ ▶*n.* *Physiol.* the phase of the heartbeat when the heart muscle relaxes and allows the chambers to fill with blood. Often contrasted with SYSTOLE. —**di·as·tol·ic** /ˌdīəˈstälik/ *adj.*

di·a·tom /ˈdīəˌtäm/ ▶*n.* *Biol.* a single-celled alga (class Bacillariophyceae) that has a cell wall of silica. —**di·a·to·ma·ceous** /ˌdīətəˈmāsHəs/ *adj.*

di·a·tom·ic /ˌdīəˈtämik/ ▶*adj.* *Chem.* consisting of two atoms.

di·a·ton·ic /ˌdīəˈtänik/ ▶*adj.* *Mus.* (of a scale, interval, etc.) involving only notes proper to the prevailing key without chromatic alteration. ■ (of a melody or harmony) constructed from such a scale.

di·a·tribe /ˈdīəˌtrīb/ ▶*n.* a forceful and bitter verbal attack against someone or something: *a diatribe against the Roman Catholic Church.*

di·az·e·pam /dīˈazəˌpam/ ▶*n.* a tranquilizing muscle-relaxant drug, $C_{16}H_{13}N_2OCl$, used chiefly to relieve anxiety. Also called VALIUM.

dib·ble /ˈdibəl/ ▶*n.* a pointed hand tool for making holes in the ground for seeds or young plants.
▶*v.* [*tr.*] make (a hole) with a dibble. ■ sow (a seed or plant) with a dibble.

dibs /dibz/ ▶*pl. n.* *inf.* money.
▶ □ **have first dibs on** have the first right to or choice of.

dice /dīs/ ▶*pl. n.* (*sing.* **die**) small cubes with each side having a different number of spots on it, ranging from one to six, thrown and used in gambling and other games involving chance. ■ [treated as *sing.*] a game played with dice. ■ small cubes of food.
▶*v.* **1** [*intr.*] play or gamble with dice. **2** [*tr.*] cut (food or other matter) into small cubes. —**dic·er** *n.*
▶ □ **no dice** *inf.* used to refuse a request or indicate no chance of success. □ **roll** (or **throw**) **of the dice** a risky attempt to do something.

dic·ey /ˈdīsē/ ▶*adj.* (**dic·i·er**, **dic·i·est**) *inf.* unpredictable and potentially dangerous: *the lot of a wanderer is always dicey.*

di·chot·o·my /dīˈkätəmē/ ▶*n.* (*pl.* **-mies**) a division or contrast between two things that are or are represented as being opposed or entirely different: *a rigid dichotomy between science and mysticism.* —**di·chot·o·mize** /-ˌmīz/ *v.* —**di·chot·o·mous** /-məs/ *adj.*

dick¹ /dik/ ▶*n.* **1** *vulgar slang* a penis. **2** *vulgar slang* anything at all: *you don't know dick about this—you haven't a clue!*
▶*v.* [*intr.*] *vulgar slang* handle something inexpertly; meddle: *he started dicking around with the controls.*

dick² ▶*n.* *dated, inf.* a detective.

dick·ens /ˈdikinz/ ▶*n. inf., dated* used for emphasis, euphemistically invoking the Devil: *they work like the dickens.* ■ (**the dickens**) used to express annoyance or surprise: *what the dickens is going on?*

Dick·en·si·an /diˈkenzēən/ ▶*adj.* of or reminiscent of the novels of Charles Dickens, esp. in suggesting poor social conditions or comically repulsive characters: *the back streets of Dickensian London.*

dick·er /ˈdikər/ ▶*v.* [*intr.*] engage in petty argument or bargaining: *she advised him not to dicker over the extra fee.* —**dick·er·er** *n.*

dick·ey /ˈdikē/ (also **dick·y**) ▶*n.* (*pl.* **dick·eys** or **dick·ies**) *inf.* a false shirt-front.

di·cot·y·le·don /dīˌkätlˈēdn/ ▶*n.* *Bot.* a flowering plant (class Dicotyledoneae or Magnoliopsida) with an embryo that bears two cotyledons (seed leaves). Dicotyledons constitute the larger of the two divisions of flowering plants, and usu. have broad, stalked leaves with netlike veins. —**di·cot·y·le·don·ous** /-əs/ *adj.*

dic·ta /ˈdiktə/ ▶ plural form of DICTUM.

dic·tate /ˈdikˌtāt/ ▶*v.* [*tr.*] **1** lay down authoritatively; prescribe: *attempts to dictate policy* | [*intr.*] *that doesn't give you the right to dictate to me.* ■ control or decisively affect; determine: *choice is dictated by availability.* **2** say or read aloud (words to be typed, written down, or recorded on tape).
▶*n.* (usu. **dictates**) an order or principle that must be obeyed: *the dictates of fashion.*

dic·ta·tion /dikˈtāsHən/ ▶*n.* **1** (abbr.: **dict.**) the action of saying words aloud to be typed, written down, or recorded on tape. ■ the activity of taking down a passage that is read aloud by a teacher as a test of spelling, writing, or language skills: *passages for dictation.* ■ an utterance that is typed, written down, or recorded. **2** the action of giving orders authoritatively or categorically.

dic·ta·tor /ˈdikˌtātər/ ▶*n.* **1** a ruler with total power over a country, typically one who has obtained power by force. ■ a person who tells people what to do in an autocratic way or who determines behavior in a particular sphere. ■ (in ancient Rome) a chief magistrate with absolute power, appointed in an emergency. **2** a machine that records words spoken into it, used for personal or administrative purposes.

dic·ta·to·ri·al /ˌdiktəˈtôrēəl/ ▶*adj.* of or typical of a ruler with total power: *a dictatorial regime.* ■ having or showing a tendency to tell people what to do in an autocratic way: *his dictatorial manner.* —**dic·ta·to·ri·al·ly** *adv.*

dic·ta·tor·ship /dikˈtātər,sHip/ 'diktätər-/ ▶*n.* government by a dictator. ■ a country governed by a dictator. ■ absolute authority in any sphere.

dic·tion /ˈdiksHən/ ▶*n.* **1** the choice and use of words and phrases in speech or writing: *Wordsworth campaigned against exaggerated poetic diction.* **2** the style of enunciation in speaking or singing.

dic·tion·ar·y /ˈdiksHə,nerē/ (abbr.: **dict.**) ▶*n.* (*pl.* **-aries**) a book that lists the words of a language in alphabetical order and gives their meaning, or that gives the equivalent words in a different language. ■ a reference book on any subject, the items of which are arranged in alphabetical order: *a dictionary of quotations.*

dic·tum /ˈdiktəm/ ▶*n.* (*pl.* **-ta** /-tə/ or **-tums**) a formal pronouncement from an authoritative source. ■ a short statement that expresses a general truth or principle. ■ *Law* short for OBITER DICTUM.

did /did/ ▶ past of DO¹.

di·dac·tic /dīˈdaktik/ ▶*adj.* intended to teach, particularly in having moral instruction as an ulterior motive: *a didactic novel.* ■ in the manner of a teacher, particularly so as to treat someone in a patronizing way. ▷mid 17th cent.: from Greek *didaktikos*, from *didaskein* 'teach.' —**di·dac·ti·cal·ly** /-ik(ə)lē/ *adv.* —**di·dac·ti·cism** /-tə,sizəm/ *n.*

did·dle /ˈdidl/ ▶*v.* *inf.* **1** [*tr.*] cheat or swindle (someone): *he thought he'd been diddled out of his change.* ■ deliberately falsify (something). **2** [*intr.*] *inf.* pass time aimlessly or unproductively: *why diddle around?* ■ (**diddle with**) play or mess with: *he diddled with the graphics.* **3** [*tr.*] *vulgar slang* have sexual intercourse with (someone). —**did·dler** *n.*

did·dly-squat /ˈdidlē ,skwät/ (also **did·dly**, **did·dley**, or **dood·ly-squat**) ▶*pron. inf.* anything: *she didn't care diddly-squat about what Darryl thought* | *they don't know diddly about softball.*

didg·er·i·doo /ˌdijərēˈdoō/ (also **didj·er·i·doo** or **didj·er·i·du**) ▶*n.* an Australian Aboriginal wind instrument in the form of a long wooden tube, traditionally made from a hollow branch, which is blown to produce a deep, resonant sound.

did·n't /ˈdidnt/ ▶*contr. of* did not.

di·do /ˈdī,dō/ ▶*n.* (*pl.* **-does** or **-dos**) (in phrase **cut/cut up didoes**) *inf.* perform mischievous tricks or deeds.

die¹ /dī/ ▶*v.* (**dy·ing** /ˈdīiNG/) [*intr.*] **1** (of a person, animal, or plant) stop living. ■ (**die for**) be killed for (a cause). ■ have a specified status at the time of one's death: *the inventor died a pauper.* ■ (**die out**) become extinct. ■ be forgotten: *her name will never die.* ■ become less loud or strong: *the noise died down* | *the storm died away.* ■ (**die back**) (of a plant) decay from the tip toward the root. ■ (**die off**) die one after another until few or none are left. ■ be no longer under the influence of something: *we died to our former selves.* ■ (of a fire or light) stop burning or gleaming. ■ (of a machine) stop functioning. ■ *poetic/lit.* have an orgasm. **2** *inf.* used to emphasize that one wants to do or have something very much: *they must be dying for a drink* | *he's dying to meet you.* ■ *inf.* used to emphasize how keenly one feels something: *I'm dying of thirst.* **3** *inf.* used to emphasize feelings of shock, embarrassment, amusement, or misery: *I nearly died when I saw them.*
▶ □ **die hard** disappear or change very slowly: *old habits die hard.* □ **die on the vine** be unsuccessful at an early stage. □ **never say die** used to encourage someone in a difficult situation. □ **to die for** *inf.* extremely good or desirable: *the ice cream is to die for.*

die² ▶*n.* singular form of DICE

die³ ▶*n.* **1** *Archit.* the cubical part of a pedestal between the base and the cornice; a dado or plinth. **2** (*pl.* **dies**) a device for cutting or molding metal into a particular shape. ■ an engraved device for stamping a design on coins or medals.

Pronunciation Key ə *ago, up*; ər *over, fur*; a *hat*; ā *ate*; ä *car*; CH *chin*; e *let*; ē *see*; e(ə)r *air*; i *fit*; ī *by*; i(ə)r *ear*; NG *sing*; ō *go*; ô *law, for*; oi *toy*; oo͝ *good*; oo *goo*; ou *out*; sH *she*; TH *thin*; T͟H *then*; (h)w *why*; zH *vision*

D

▶ □ **the die is cast** an event has happened or a decision has been made that cannot be changed.

die-cast ▶*adj.* (of a metal object) formed by pouring molten metal into a reusable mold: *a die-cast aluminum loudspeaker chassis.*

▶*v.* [*tr.*] [usu. as *n.*] (**die-casting**) make (a metal object) in this way.

die-hard /ˈdīˌhärd/ ▶*n.* [often as *adj.*] a person who strongly opposes change or who continues to support something in spite of opposition.

die-off ▶*n.* a period in which a significant proportion of a population dies naturally, usually within a short time. ■ a process causing this. ■ the death of a significant proportion of a population in this way.

di·er·e·sis /dīˈerəsis/ (also **di·aer·e·sis**) ▶*n.* (*pl.* **-ses** /-ˌsēz/) **1** a mark (¨) placed over a vowel to indicate that it is sounded in a separate syllable, as in *naïve, Brontë.* **2** *Prosody* a natural rhythmic break in a line of verse where the end of a metrical foot coincides with the end of a word.

die·sel /ˈdēzəl; -səl/ ▶*n.* (also **diesel engine**) an internal combustion engine in which heat produced by the compression of air in the cylinder is used to ignite th ___: [as *adj.*] *a diesel locomotive.* ■ a heavy petroleum fraction used as fuel in diesel engines. —**die·sel·ize** /-ˌlīz/ *v.*

di·et¹ /ˈdī-it/ ▶*n.* the kinds of food that a person, animal, or community habitually eats: *a vegetarian diet | a specialist in diet.* ■ a special course of food to which one restricts oneself, either to lose weight or for medical reasons: *I'm going on a diet.* ■ [as *adj.*] (of food or drink) with reduced fat or sugar content: *diet soft drinks.* ■ *fig.* a regular occupation or series of activities in which one participates: *a diet of classical music.*

▶*v.* (**di·et·ed, di·et·ing**) [*intr.*] restrict oneself to small amounts or special kinds of food in order to lose weight: *it's difficult to diet.* —**di·et·er** *n.*

di·et² ▶*n.* a legislative assembly in certain countries. ■ *hist.* a regular meeting of the states of a confederation.

die·tar·y /ˈdī-iˌterē/ ▶*adj.* of or relating to diets or dieting. ■ provided by one's diet: *the average dietary calcium intake was 140 milligrams per day.*

▶*n.* (*pl.* **-tar·ies**) *dated* a regulated or restricted diet.

di·e·tet·ic /ˌdī-iˈtetik/ ▶*adj.* concerned with diet and nutrition: *experienced dietetic advice.* —**di·e·tet·i·cal·ly** /-ik(ə)lē/ *adv.*

di·e·tet·ics /ˌdī-iˈtetiks/ ▶*pl. n.* [treated as *sing.*] the branch of knowledge concerned with the diet and its effects on health, esp. with the practical application of a scientific understanding of nutrition.

di·e·ti·tian /ˌdī-iˈtishən/ (also **di·e·ti·cian**) ▶*n.* an expert on diet and nutrition.

diff /dif/ ▶*n. inf.* short for DIFFERENCE.

dif·fer /ˈdifər/ ▶*v.* [*intr.*] be unlike or dissimilar: *the second set of data differed from the first | tastes differ* | [as *adj.*] (**differing**) *widely differing circumstances.* ■ disagree: *they differed from them in ethical matters.*

▶ □ **agree to differ** cease to argue about something because neither party will be persuaded. □ **beg to differ** politely disagree.

dif·fer·ence /ˈdif(ə)rəns/ ▶*n.* a point or way in which people or things are not the same. ■ the state or condition of being dissimilar or unlike: *their difference from one another.* ■ a disagreement, quarrel, or dispute: *patching up their differences.* ■ a quantity by which amounts differ; the remainder left after subtraction of one value from another.

▶ □ **make a** (or **no**) **difference** have a significant effect (or no effect) on a person or situation: *the law will make no difference to my business.* □ **with a difference** having a new or unusual feature or treatment: *a fashion show with a difference.*

dif·fer·ent /ˈdif(ə)rənt/ ▶*adj.* **1** not the same as another or each other; unlike in nature, form, or quality: *you can play the game in different ways.* | (**different from/than**) *the car is different from anything else on the market.* ■ *inf.* novel and unusual: *something deliciously different.* **2** distinct; separate: *on different occasions.* —**dif·fer·ent·ly** *adv.* —**dif·fer·ent·ness** *n.*

dif·fer·en·tial /ˌdifəˈrenshəl/ *chiefly technical* ▶*adj.* of, showing, or depending on a difference; differing or varying according to circumstances or relevant factors: *differential achievements.* ■ constituting a specific difference; distinctive: *the differential features between tumors.* ■ *Math.* relating to infinitesimal differences or to the derivatives of functions.

▶*n.* a difference between amounts of things: **the differential between** *gasoline and diesel prices.* ■ *Math.* an infinitesimal difference between successive values of a variable. ■ (also **differential gear**) a set of gears allowing a vehicle's driven wheels to revolve at different speeds when going around corners. —**dif·fer·en·tial·ly** *adv.*

dif·fer·en·ti·ate /ˌdifəˈrenshēˌāt/ ▶*v.* [*tr.*] **1** recognize or ascertain what makes (someone or something) different: *children can differentiate the past from the present.* ■ [*intr.*] (**differentiate between**) identify differences between (two or more things or people): *unable to differentiate between fantasy and reality.* ■ make (someone or something) appear different or distinct: *Twain differentiated Huck's speech from that of other white people.* **2** *technical* make or become different in the process of growth or

development: [*tr.*] *the receptors are differentiated into sense organs* | [*intr.*] *the cells differentiate into a wide variety of cell types.* **3** *Math.* transform (a function) into its derivative. —**dif·fer·en·ti·a·tion** /-ˌrenshēˈāshən/ *n.* —**dif·fer·en·ti·a·tor** /-ˌātər/ *n.*

dif·fi·cult /ˈdifikəlt/ ▶*adj.* needing much effort or skill to accomplish, deal with, or understand: *she had a difficult decision to make* | *the questions are too difficult for the children.* ■ characterized by or causing hardships or problems: *a difficult economic climate.* ■ (of a person) not easy to please or satisfy: *Lily could be difficult.* —**dif·fi·cult·ness** *n.*

dif·fi·cul·ty /ˈdifikəltē/ ▶*n.* (*pl.* **-ties**) the state or condition of being difficult: *Guy had no difficulty in making friends | she walks with difficulty.* ■ a thing that is hard to accomplish, deal with, or understand: *there is a practical difficulty | a club with financial difficulties.* ■ a situation that is difficult or dangerous: *they went for a swim but got into difficulties.*

dif·fi·dent /ˈdifidənt/ ▶*adj.* modest or shy because of a lack of self-confidence: *a diffident youth.* —**dif·fi·dence** *n.* —**dif·fi·dent·ly** *adv.*

dif·fract /diˈfrakt/ ▶*v.* [*tr.*] *Physics* cause to undergo diffraction. —**dif·frac·tive** /-tiv/ *adj.* —**dif·frac·tive·ly** /-tivlē/ *adv.*

dif·frac·tion /diˈfrakshən/ ▶*n.* the process by which a beam of light or other system of waves is spread out as a result of passing through a narrow aperture or across an edge, typically accompanied by interference between the wave forms produced.

dif·fuse ▶*v.* /diˈfyo͞oz/ spread or cause to spread over a wide area or among a large number of people: [*intr.*] *technologies diffuse rapidly* | [*tr.*] *the problem is how to diffuse power without creating anarchy.* ■ become or cause (a fluid, gas, individual atom, etc.) to become intermingled with a substance by movement: [*intr.*] *oxygen molecules diffuse across the membrane* | [*tr.*] *gas is diffused into the bladder.* ■ [*tr.*] cause (light) to glow faintly by dispersing it in many directions.

▶*adj.* /diˈfyo͞os/ spread out over a large area; not concentrated: *the diffuse community centered on church.* ■ (of disease) not localized in the body. ■ lacking clarity or conciseness: *the second argument is more diffuse.* —**dif·fuse·ly** /-ˈfyo͞oslē/ *adv.* —**dif·fuse·ness** /-ˈfyo͞osnis/ *n.* —**dif·fus·i·ble** /-ˈfyo͞ozəbəl/ *adj.*

dif·fus·er /diˈfyo͞ozər/ (also **dif·fu·sor**) ▶*n.* a thing that diffuses something, in particular: ■ an attachment or duct for broadening an airflow and reducing its speed. ■ *Photog.* a device that spreads the light from a light source evenly and reduces harsh shadows.

dif·fu·sion /diˈfyo͞ozhən/ ▶*n.* the spreading of something more widely: *the diffusion of Marxist ideas.* ■ the action of spreading the light from a light source evenly so as to reduce glare and harsh shadows. ■ *Chem.* the intermingling of substances by the natural movement of their particles: *the rate of diffusion of a gas.* ■ *Anthropol.* the dissemination of elements of culture to another region or people. —**dif·fu·sive** /-siv/ *adj.*

dig /dig/ ▶*v.* (**dig·ging**; *past* **dug** /dəg/) **1** [*intr.*] break up and move earth with a tool or machine, or with hands, paws, snout, etc. ■ [*tr.*] make (a hole, grave, etc.) by breaking up and moving earth in such a way. ■ [*tr.*] extract from the ground by breaking up and moving earth: *they dug up fossils of.* ■ (**dig in**) (of a soldier) protect oneself by making a trench or similar ground defense. ■ [in *imper.*] (**dig in**) *inf.* used to encourage someone to start eating with gusto and have as much as they want. ■ [*tr.*] (**dig something in/into**) push or poke something in or into: *he dug his hands into his pockets.* ■ [*tr.*] excavate (an archaeological site). ■ [*tr.*] (**dig something out**) bring out something that is hidden or has been stored for a long time: *they dug out last year's notes.* ■ (**dig into**) *inf.* find money from (somewhere): *members have to dig deep into their pockets.* ■ [*intr.*] search or rummage in a specified place: *Catherine dug into her handbag and produced her card.* ■ engage in research; conduct an investigation: *digging for information.* ■ [*tr.*] (**dig something up/out**) discover information after a search or investigation: *have you dug up any information on the captain?* **2** [*tr.*] *inf., dated* like, appreciate, or understand: *I really dig heavy rock.*

▶*n.* **1** an act or spell of digging. ■ an archaeological excavation. **2** a push or poke with one's elbow, finger, etc.: *a dig in the ribs.* ■ *inf.* a remark intended to mock or criticize: *a cruel dig at Jenny.* —**dig·ger** *n.*

▶ □ **dig up dirt** *inf.* discover and reveal damaging information about someone.

di·gest ▶*v.* /diˈjest; dī-/ [*tr.*] break down (food) in the stomach and intestines into substances that can be used by the body. ■ understand or assimilate (new information or the significance of something) by a period of reflection. ■ arrange (something) in a systematic or convenient order, esp. by reduction: *the computer digested your labors into an understandable form.* ■ *Chem.* treat (a substance) with heat, enzymes, or a solvent in order to decompose it or extract essential components.

▶*n.* /ˈdīˌjest/ **1** a compilation or summary of material or information. ■ a periodical consisting of condensed versions of pieces of writing or news published elsewhere. ■ a methodical summary of a body of laws. **2** *Chem.* a substance or mixture obtained by digestion: *a digest of cloned DNA.* —**di·gest·i·ble** *adj.*

di·ges·tion /dɪ'jɛsCHən; dī-/ ▶*n.* the process of breaking down food by mechanical and enzymatic action in the stomach and intestines into substances that can be used by the body. ■ a person's capacity to break down food in such a way: *bouts of dysentery impaired his digestion.* ■ *Chem.* the process of treating a substance by means of heat, enzymes, or a solvent to promote decomposition or extract essential components.

di·ges·tive /dɪ'jɛstɪv; dī-/ ▶*adj.* of or relating to the process of digesting food: *stomach ulcers and other digestive disorders.* ■ (of food or medicine) aiding or promoting the process of digestion: *digestive mints.*
▶*n.* a food or medicine that aids or promotes the digestion of food. —**di·ges·tive·ly** *adv.*

dig·i·cam /'dijiˌkam/ ▶*n.* a digital camera.

dig·it /'dijit/ ▶*n.* **1** any of the numerals from 0 to 9, esp. when forming part of a number. **2** a finger (including the thumb) or toe. ■ *Zool.* an equivalent structure of many higher vertebrates.

dig·i·tal /'dijitl/ ▶*adj.* **1** relating to or using signals or information represented by discrete values (digits) of a physical quantity, such as voltage or magnetic polarization, to represent arithmetic numbers or approximations to numbers from a continuum or logical expressions and variables: *digital TV.* Often contrasted with **ANALOG.** ■ (of a clock or watch) showing the time by means of displayed digits rather than hands or a pointer. **2** of or relating to a finger or fingers. —**dig·it·al·ly** *adv.*

dig·i·tal au·di·o·tape (abbr.: **DAT**) ▶*n.* magnetic tape used to make digital sound recordings of very high quality.

dig·i·tal cam·er·a ▶*n.* a camera that records and stores digital images.

dig·i·tal·is /ˌdiji'talis/ ▶*n.* a drug prepared from the dried leaves of foxglove and containing substances that stimulate the heart muscle.

dig·i·tal sub·scrib·er line ▶*n. Comput.* see **DSL**

dig·i·tal tel·e·vi·sion (abbr.: **DTV**) ▶*n.* television broadcasting in which the pictures are transmitted as digital signals that are decoded by a device in or attached to the receiving television set.

dig·i·tal vid·e·o re·cord·er ▶*n.* (abbr. **DVR**) a programmable electronic device that writes audio and video input, typically from a television signal, to a rewritable hard disk.

dig·i·tize /'dijiˌtīz/ ▶*v.* [*tr.*] [usu. as *adj.*] (**digitized**) convert (pictures or sound) into a digital form that can be processed by a computer. —**dig·i·ti·za·tion** /ˌdijitə'zāsHən/ *n.* —**dig·i·tiz·er** *n.*

dig·ni·fied /'digniˌfīd/ ▶*adj.* having or showing a composed or serious manner that is worthy of respect. —**dig·ni·fied·ly** /-ˌfī(ə)dlē/ *adv.*

dig·ni·fy /'dignəˌfī/ ▶*v.* (**-fies, -fied**) [*tr.*] make (something) seem worthy and impressive. ■ (often **be dignified**) give an impressive name to (someone or something that one considers worthless): *dumps are increasingly dignified as landfills.*

dig·ni·tar·y /'digniˌterē/ ▶*n.* (*pl.* **-tar·ies**) a person considered to be important because of high rank or office.

dig·ni·ty /'dignitē/ ▶*n.* (*pl.* **-ties**) the state or quality of being worthy of honor or respect. ■ a composed or serious manner or style. ■ a sense of pride in oneself; self-respect: *it was beneath his dignity to shout.* ■ a high or honorable rank or position.

di·graph /'dīˌgraf/ ▶*n.* a combination of two letters representing one sound, as in *ph* and *ey*. ■ *Printing* a character consisting of two joined letters; a ligature. —**di·graph·ic** /dī'grafik/ *adj.*

di·gress /dī'gres/ ▶*v.* [*intr.*] leave the main subject temporarily in speech or writing. ▷early 16th cent.: from Latin *digress-* 'stepped away,' from the verb *digredi*, from *di-* 'aside' + *gradi* 'to walk.' —**di·gress·er** *n.* —**di·gres·sion** /-'gresHən/ *n.* —**di·gres·sive** /-'gresiv/ *adj.* —**di·gres·sive·ly** /-'gresivlē/ *adv.* —**di·gres·sive·ness** /-'gresivnis/ *n.*

digs ▶*pl. n. inf.* living quarters: *settled into new digs in Los Angeles.*

di·he·dral /dī'hēdrəl/ ▶*adj.* having or contained by two plane faces: *a dihedral angle.*

dike¹ /dīk/ (also **dyke**) ▶*n.* **1** a long wall or embankment built to prevent flooding from the sea. ■ a low wall or earthwork serving as a boundary or defense. ■ a causeway. ■ *Geol.* an intrusion of igneous rock cutting across existing strata. **2** a ditch or watercourse.
▶*v.* [*tr.*] provide (land) with a wall or embankment to prevent flooding.

dike² ▶*n.* variant spelling of **DYKE²**.

di·lap·i·dat·ed /dɪ'lapɪˌdātid/ ▶*adj.* (of a building or object) in a state of disrepair or ruin as a result of age or neglect.

dil·a·ta·tion /ˌdilə'tāsHən; ˌdī-/ ▶*n. chiefly Med. Physiol.* the process of becoming dilated. ■ the action of dilating a vessel or opening. ■ a dilated part of a hollow organ or vessel.

di·la·ta·tion and cu·ret·tage (also **di·la·tion and cu·ret·tage**) (abbr.: **D and C**) ▶*n. Med.* a surgical procedure involving dilatation of the cervix and curettage of the uterus, performed after a miscarriage or for the removal of cysts or tumors.

di·late /'dīˌlāt; dī'lāt/ ▶*v.* **1** make or become wider, larger, or more open: [*intr.*] *her eyes dilated with horror* | [*tr.*] *he dilated his nostrils.* **2** [*intr.*] (**dilate on**) speak or write at length on (a subject). —**di·la·tion** /dī'lāsHən/ *n.*

dil·a·to·ry /'dilə,tôrē/ ▶*adj.* slow to act: *he had been dilatory in appointing an attorney.* ■ intended to cause delay: *dilatory tactics stalled the merger.* —**dil·a·to·ri·ly** /ˌdilə'tôrəlē/ *adv.* —**dil·a·to·ri·ness** *n.*

dil·do /'dildō/ ▶*n.* (*pl.* **-dos**) an object shaped like an erect penis used for sexual stimulation. ■ *vulgar slang* a stupid or ridiculous person.

di·lem·ma /dɪ'lemə/ ▶*n.* a situation in which a difficult choice has to be made between two or more alternatives, esp. equally undesirable ones: *the people often face the dilemma of feeding themselves or their cattle.* ■ *inf.* a difficult situation or problem. ■ *Logic* an argument forcing an opponent to choose either of two unfavorable alternatives.

dil·et·tante /ˌdili'tänt/ ▶*n.* (*pl.* **-tan·ti** /-'täntē/ or **-tantes**) a person who cultivates an area of interest, such as the arts, without real commitment or knowledge. ■ *archaic* a person with an amateur interest in the arts. —**dil·et·tan·tish** *adj.* —**dil·et·tant·ism** /-ˌtizəm/ *n.*

dil·i·gence¹ /'dilejəns/ ▶*n.* careful and persistent work or effort.

dil·i·gence² ▶*n. hist.* a public stagecoach.

dil·i·gent /'dilejənt/ ▶*adj.* having or showing care and conscientiousness in one's work or duties: *a diligent search.* —**dil·i·gent·ly** *adv.*

dill /dil/ ▶*n.* an aromatic herb (*Anethum graveolens*) of the parsley family, with fine blue-green leaves and yellow flowers. The leaves and seeds are used esp. for flavoring and for medicinal purposes. ■ (also **dillweed** or **dill weed**) the fresh or dried leaves of this plant used to flavor food.

dil·ly /'dilē/ ▶*n.* (*pl.* **-lies**) *inf.* an excellent example of a particular type of person or thing: *that's a dilly of a breakfast recipe.*

dil·ly-dal·ly ▶*v.* (**-lies, -lied**) [*intr.*] *inf.* waste time through aimless wandering or indecision: *don't dilly-dally for too long.*

di·lute /dɪ'loot; dī-/ ▶*v.* [*tr.*] (often **be diluted**) make (a liquid) thinner or weaker by adding water or another solvent to it. ■ make (something) weaker in force, content, or value by modifying it or adding other elements to it. ■ reduce the value of (a shareholding) by issuing more shares in a company without increasing the values of its assets.
▶*adj.* (of a liquid) made thinner or weaker by having had water or another solvent added to it. ■ *Chem.* (of a solution) having a relatively low concentration of solute: *a dilute solution of potassium permanganate.* ■ (of color or light) weak or low in concentration. —**di·lut·er** *n.* —**di·lu·tion** *n.*

dim /dim/ ▶*adj.* (**dim·mer, dim·mest**) **1** (of a light, color, or illuminated object) not shining brightly or clearly. ■ (of an object or shape) made difficult to see by darkness, shade, or distance. ■ (of a room or space) made difficult to see in by darkness: *long dim corridors.* ■ (of the eyes) not able to see clearly. ■ (of a sound) indistinct or muffled. ■ (of prospects) not giving cause for hope or optimism. **2** not clearly recalled or formulated in the mind: *she had dim memories of that time.* ■ *inf.* stupid or slow to understand.
▶*v.* (**dimmed, dim·ming**) make or become less bright. ■ [*tr.*] lower (a vehicle's headlights) from high to low beam. ■ make or become less intense or favorable. ■ make or become less able to see clearly. ■ make or become less clear in the mind. —**dim·ly** *adv.* —**dim·mish** *adj.* —**dim·ness** *n.*
▶ □ **take a dim view of** regard with disapproval.

dime /dīm/ ▶*n.* a ten-cent coin. ■ *inf.* a small amount of money: *he didn't have a dime.* ■ *inf.* used to refer to something small in size, area, or degree: *there's not a dime's worth of difference between you and him.* ■ *inf.* short for **DIME BAG.** ▷late Middle English: from Old French *disme*, from Latin *decima pars* 'tenth part.' The word originally denoted a tithe or tenth part; the modern sense 'ten-cent coin' dates from the late 18th cent.
▶ □ **a dime a dozen** *inf.* very common and of no particular value: *experts in this field are a dime a dozen.* □ **on a dime** *inf.* used to refer to a maneuver that can be performed by a moving vehicle or person within a small area or short distance: *boats that can turn on a dime.*

dime bag ▶*n. inf.* a specified amount of an illegal drug, packaged and sold for ten dollars.

di·men·sion /dɪ'menCHən/ ▶*n.* **1** an aspect or feature of a situation, problem, or thing: *sun-dried tomatoes add a new dimension to this sauce.* **2** (usu. **dimensions**) a measurable extent of some kind, such as length,

breadth, depth, or height: *the final dimensions of the pond were 14 ft. x 8 ft.* ■ a mode of linear extension of which there are three in space and two on a flat surface, which corresponds to one of a set of coordinates specifying the position of a point. ■ *Physics* an expression for a derived physical quantity in terms of fundamental quantities such as mass, length, or time, raised to the appropriate power (acceleration, for example, having the dimension of $length \times time^{-2}$).
▶ *v.* [*tr.*] (often **be dimensioned**) cut or shape (something) to particular measurements. ■ mark (a diagram) with measurements: [as *adj.*] (**dimensioned**) *draw a dimensioned front elevation.* —**di·men·sion·al** /-CHənl/ *adj.* —**di·men·sion·al·i·ty** /di,menCHə'nalətē/ *n.* —**di·men·sion·al·ly** /-CHənl-ē/ *adj.* —**di·men·sion·less** *adj.*

di·mer /'dīmər/ ▶ *n. Chem.* a molecule or molecular complex consisting of two identical molecules linked together. —**di·mer·ic** /dī'merik/ *adj.*

di·min·ish /di'miniSH/ ▶ *v.* make or become less: [*tr.*] *a tax whose purpose is to diminish spending* | [*intr.*] *the pain will diminish.* ■ [*tr.*] make (someone or something) seem less impressive or valuable. —**di·min·ish·a·ble** *adj.*
▶ □ (**the law of**) **diminishing returns** used to refer to a point at which the level of profits or benefits gained is less than the amount of money or energy invested.

di·min·ished /di'miniSHt/ ▶ *adj.* **1** made smaller or less: *a diminished role for government.* ■ made to seem less impressive or valuable. **2** *Mus.* denoting or containing an interval that is one semitone less than the corresponding minor or perfect interval: *a diminished fifth.*

di·min·u·en·do /di,minyōō'endō/ *Mus.* ▶ *n.* (*pl.* **-dos** or **-di** /-dē/) a decrease in loudness.
▶ *adv. & adj.* (esp. as a direction) with a decrease in loudness.

dim·i·nu·tion /,dimə'n(y)ōōSHən/ ▶ *n.* a reduction in the size, extent, or importance of something: *the disease shows no signs of diminution.* ■ *Mus.* the shortening of the time values of notes in a melodic part.

di·min·u·tive /di'minyətiv/ ▶ *adj.* extremely or unusually small. ■ (of a word, name, or suffix) implying smallness, either actual or imputed in token of affection, scorn, etc., (e.g., *teeny*, *-let*, *-kins*).
▶ *n.* a smaller or shorter thing, in particular: ■ a diminutive word or suffix. ■ a shortened form of a name, typically used informally: *"Jim" is a diminutive of "James."* —**di·min·u·tive·ly** *adv.* —**di·min·u·tive·ness** *n.*

dim·mer /'dimər/ ▶ *n.* (also **dimmer switch**) a device for varying the brightness of an electric light.

dim·ple /'dimpəl/ ▶ *n.* a small depression in the flesh, either one that exists permanently or one that forms in the cheeks when one smiles. ■ a slight depression in the surface of something.
▶ *v.* [*tr.*] produce a dimple or dimples in the surface of (something): *a sucking swirl dimpled the water.* ■ [*intr.*] form or show a dimple or dimples: [as *adj.*] (**dimpled**) *a dimpled smile.* —**dim·ply** /'dimp(ə)lē/ *adj.*

dim sum /'dim 'səm/ ▶ *n.* a Chinese dish of small steamed or fried savory dumplings containing various fillings, served as a snack or main course.

dim·wit /'dim,wit/ ▶ *n. inf.* a stupid or silly person. —**dim·wit·ted** *adj.* —**dim·wit·ted·ly** *adv.* —**dim·wit·ted·ness** *n.*

din /din/ ▶ *n.* a loud, unpleasant, and prolonged noise.
▶ *v.* (**dinned**, **din·ning**) **1** [*tr.*] (**be dinned into**) (of a fact) be instilled in (someone) by constant repetition: *the doctrine that has been dinned into all our heads.* **2** [*intr.*] make a loud, unpleasant, and prolonged noise.

dine /dīn/ ▶ *v.* [*intr.*] eat dinner. ■ (**dine out**) eat dinner in a restaurant or the home of friends. ■ (**dine on**) eat (something) for dinner. ■ (**dine out on**) regularly entertain friends with (a humorous story or interesting piece of information): *a story one dines out on.*

din·er /'dīnər/ ▶ *n.* **1** a person who is eating, typically a customer in a restaurant. **2** a dining car on a train. ■ a small roadside restaurant with a long counter and booths, originally one designed to resemble a dining car on a train.

di·nette /dī'net/ ▶ *n.* a small room or part of a room used for eating meals. ■ a set of table and chairs for such an area.

ding[1] /diNG/ ▶ *v.* [*intr.*] make a ringing sound: *cash registers were dinging.*
▶ *interj.* used to imitate a metallic ringing sound resembling a bell.

ding[2] ▶ *n. inf.* a deliberate or accidental blow, esp. a mark or dent on the bodywork of a car, boat, or other vehicle.
▶ *v.* [*tr.*] *inf.* dent (something). ■ hit (someone), esp. on the head.

ding-a-ling /'diNG ə ,liNG/ ▶ *n.* **1** the ringing sound of a bell. **2** *inf.* an eccentric or stupid person.

ding·bat /'diNG,bat/ *inf.* ▶ *n.* **1** a stupid or eccentric person. **2** a typographical device other than a letter or numeral (such as an asterisk).

din·ghy /'diNGē/ ▶ *n.* (*pl.* **-ghies**) a small boat for recreation or racing, esp. an open boat with a mast and sails. ■ a small, inflatable rubber boat.

din·go /'diNGgō/ ▶ *n.* (*pl.* **-oes** or **-os**) a wild or half-domesticated dog (*Canis dingo*) with a sandy-colored coat, found in Australia.

din·gy /'dinjē/ ▶ *adj.* (**-gi·er**, **-gi·est**) gloomy and drab: *a dingy room.* —**din·gi·ly** /-əlē/ *adv.* —**din·gi·ness** *n.*

din·ing car ▶ *n.* a railroad car equipped as a restaurant.

din·ing room ▶ *n.* a room in a house or hotel in which meals are eaten.

dink·y /'diNGkē/ ▶ *adj.* (**dink·i·er**, **dink·i·est**) *inf.* small; insignificant.

din·ner /'dinər/ ▶ *n.* the main meal of the day, taken either around midday or in the evening. ■ a formal evening meal, typically one in honor of a person or event.

din·ner jack·et ▶ *n.* a man's short jacket without tails, typically a black one, worn with a bow tie for formal occasions in the evening.

di·no·saur /'dīnə,sôr/ ▶ *n.* **1** a reptile of the Mesozoic era, often reaching an enormous size. **2** a person or thing that is outdated or has become obsolete because of failure to adapt to changing circumstances. ▷mid 19th cent.: from modern Latin *dinosaurus*, from Greek *deinos* 'terrible' + *sauros* 'lizard.' —**di·no·sau·ri·an** /,dīnə'sôrēən/ *adj. & n.*

dint /dint/ ▶ *n.* **1** an impression or hollow in a surface: *the soft dints at the top of a coconut.* **2** *archaic* a blow or stroke, typically one made with a weapon in fighting. ■ force of attack; impact: *feel the dint of pity.*
▶ *v.* [*tr.*] mark (a surface) with impressions or hollows: [as *adj.*] (**dinted**) *the metal was dull and dinted.*
▶ □ **by dint of** by means of: *he got here by dint of hard work.*

di·o·cese /'dīəsis; -,sēz; -,sēs/ ▶ *n.* (*pl.* **-ces·es**) a district under the pastoral care of a bishop in the Christian Church. —**di·oc·e·san** /dī'äsisən/ *adj.*

di·ode /'dī,ōd/ ▶ *n. Electr.* a semiconductor device with two terminals, typically allowing the flow of current in one direction only. ■ a thermionic tube having two electrodes (an anode and a cathode).

di·o·ram·a /,dīə'ramə; -'rä-/ ▶ *n.* a model representing a scene with three-dimensional figures, either in miniature or as a large-scale museum exhibit. ■ *chiefly hist.* a scenic painting, viewed through a peephole, in which changes in color and direction of illumination simulate changes in the weather, time of day, etc.

di·ox·ide /dī'äk,sīd/ ▶ *n. Chem.* an oxide containing two atoms of oxygen in its molecule or empirical formula.

di·ox·in /dī'äksin/ ▶ *n.* a highly toxic and environmentally persistent compound, $C_{12}H_4O_2Cl_4$, produced as a by-product in some manufacturing processes, notably herbicide production and paper bleaching.

DIP /dip/ ▶ *abbr.* ■ *Comput.* document image processing, a system for the digital storage and retrieval of documents as scanned images. ■ *Electr.* dual in-line package, a package for an integrated circuit consisting of a rectangular sealed unit with two parallel rows of downward-pointing pins.

dip /dip/ ▶ *v.* (**dipped**, **dip·ping**) **1** [*tr.*] (**dip something in/into**) put or let something down quickly or briefly in or into (liquid): *he dipped a brush in the paint.* ■ [*intr.*] (**dip into**) put a hand or tool into (a bag or container) in order to take something out: *Ian dipped into his briefcase and pulled out a photograph.* ■ [*intr.*] (**dip into**) spend from or make use of (one's financial resources). ■ [*intr.*] (**dip into**) read only parts of (a book) in a desultory manner. ■ take (snuff). ■ immerse (sheep) in a chemical solution that kills parasites. ■ make (a candle) by immersing a wick repeatedly in hot wax: [as *adj.*] (**dipped**) *dipped candles are made using simple equipment.* **2** [*intr.*] sink or drop downward: *swallows dipped and soared.* ■ (of a level or amount) become lower or smaller, typically temporarily: *audiences dipped below 600,000 for the series.* ■ (of a road, path, or area of land) slope downward. ■ [*tr.*] lower or move (something) downward: *the plane dipped its wings.*
▶ *n.* **1** a brief swim. ■ a brief immersion in liquid. ■ a cursory read of part of a book. **2** a thick sauce in which pieces of food are dunked before eating: *garlic dip.* ■ a quantity that has been scooped up from a mass: *ice cream sold by the dip.* **3** a brief downward slope followed by an upward one: *the road's dips and turns.* ■ an act of sinking or dropping briefly before rising again: *a dip in the share price.* **4** *technical* the extent to which something is angled downward from the horizontal, in particular: ■ (also **magnetic dip**) the angle made with the horizontal at any point by the earth's magnetic field, or by a magnetic needle in response to this. ■ *Geol.* the angle a stratum makes with the horizontal: *the cliff profile tends to be dominated by the dip of the beds.* **5** *inf.* a stupid or foolish person.

diph·the·ri·a /dif'THirēə; dip-/ ▶ *n.* a highly contagious bacterial disease characterized by the formation of a breath-obstructing membrane in the throat and by a potentially fatal toxin in the blood. —**diph·the·ri·al** *adj.* —**diph·the·rit·ic** /,difTHə'ritik; ,dip-/ *adj.*

diph·thong /'dif,THäNG; 'dip-; -,THôNG/ ▶ *n.* a sound formed by the combination of two vowels in a single syllable, in which the sound begins as one vowel and moves toward another (as in *coin*, *loud*, and *side*). ■ a digraph representing the sound of a diphthong or single vowel (as in *feat*). —**diph·thon·gal** /dif'THANGgəl; dip-; -'THONG-/ *adj.*

di·plod·o·cus /di'plädəkəs/ ▶*n.* a herbivorous dinosaur (genus *Diplodocus*) of the late Jurassic period, with a long, slender neck and tail.

dip·loid /'dip,loid/ *Genetics* ▶*adj.* (of a cell or nucleus) containing two complete sets of chromosomes, one from each parent. Compare with HAPLOID. ■ (of an organism or part) composed of diploid cells. ▶*n.* a diploid cell, organism, or species. —**dip·loi·dy** /-,loidē/ *n.*

di·plo·ma /di'plōmə/ ▶*n.* a certificate awarded by an educational establishment to show that someone has successfully completed a course of study. ■ an official document or charter. ▷mid 17th cent. (in the sense 'state paper'): via Latin from Greek *diplōma* 'folded paper,' from *diploun* 'to fold,' from *diplous* 'double.'

di·plo·ma·cy /di'plōməsē/ ▶*n.* the profession, activity, or skill of managing international relations, typically by a country's representatives abroad: *an extensive round of diplomacy in the Middle East.* ■ the art of dealing with people in a sensitive and effective way.

dip·lo·mat /'diplə,mat/ ▶*n.* an official representing a country abroad. ■ a person who can deal with people in a sensitive and effective way.

dip·lo·mat·ic /,diplə'matik/ ▶*adj.* of or concerning the profession, activity, or skill of managing international relations: *diplomatic relations between the U.S. and Iran.* ■ having or showing an ability to deal with people in a sensitive and effective way. —**dip·lo·mat·i·cal·ly** /-ik(ə)lē/ *adv.*

di·pole /'dī,pōl/ ▶*n.* *Physics* a pair of equal and oppositely charged or magnetized poles separated by a distance. ■ an antenna consisting of a horizontal metal rod with a connecting wire at its center. ■ *Chem.* a molecule in which a concentration of positive electric charge is separated from a concentration of negative charge. —**di·po·lar** /dī'pōlər/ *adj.*

dip·per /'dipər/ ▶*n.* **1** a short-tailed songbird (genus *Cinclus*, family Cinclidae), frequenting fast-flowing streams and able to swim, dive, and walk under water to feed. **2** a ladle or scoop.

dip·py /'dipē/ ▶*adj.* (**dip·pi·er**, **dip·pi·est**) *inf.* stupid; foolish.

dip·so /'dipsō/ ▶*n.* (*pl.* **-sos**) *inf.* a person suffering from dipsomania.

dip·so·ma·ni·a /,dipsə'mānēə/ ▶*n.* alcoholism, specifically in a form characterized by intermittent bouts of craving for alcohol. —**dip·so·ma·ni·ac** /-nē,ak/ *n.* —**dip·so·ma·ni·a·cal** /-mə'nīəkəl/ *adj.*

dip·stick /'dip,stik/ ▶*n.* **1** a graduated rod for measuring the depth of a liquid, esp. oil in a vehicle's engine. **2** *inf.* a stupid or inept person.

dip·tych /'diptik/ ▶*n.* **1** a painting, esp. an altarpiece, on two hinged wooden panels that may be closed like a book. **2** an ancient writing tablet consisting of two hinged leaves with waxed inner sides.

dire /dīr/ ▶*adj.* (of a situation or event) extremely serious or urgent. ■ (of a warning or threat) presaging disaster. —**dire·ly** *adv.* —**dire·ness** *n.*

di·rect /di'rekt; dī-/ ▶*adj.* extending or moving from one place to another by the shortest way without changing direction or stopping. ■ without intervening factors or intermediaries. ■ (of a person or their behavior) going straight to the point; frank. ■ (of evidence or proof) bearing immediately and unambiguously upon the facts at issue. ■ (of light or heat) proceeding from a source without being reflected or blocked. ■ (of genealogy) proceeding in continuous succession from parent to child. ■ (of a quotation) taken from someone's words without being changed. ■ complete (used for emphasis): *nonviolence is the direct opposite of compulsion.* ■ perpendicular to a surface; not oblique: *a direct joint between surfaces of steel.* ■ *Astron.* & *Astrol.* (of apparent planetary motion) proceeding from west to east in accord with actual motion. ▶*adv.* with no one or nothing in between: *buy direct.* ■ by a straight route or without breaking a journey: *flying direct to Innsbruck.* ▶*v.* [*tr.*] **1** control the operations of; manage or govern. ■ supervise and control (a movie, play, or other production, or the actors in it). ■ (usu. **be directed**) train and conduct (a group of musicians). **2** [*tr.*] aim (something) in a particular direction or at a particular person: *ducts direct warm air to passengers* | *his smile was directed at Laura.* ■ tell or show (someone) how to get somewhere: *can you direct me to the station?* ■ address or give instructions for the delivery of (a letter or parcel). ■ focus or concentrate (one's attention, efforts, or feelings) on: *we direct our anger at family.* ■ (**direct something at/to**) address a comment to or aim a criticism at. ■ (**direct something at**) target a product specifically at (someone). ■ *archaic* guide or advise (someone or their judgment) in a course or decision. **3** [*tr.*] give (someone) an official order or authoritative instruction. —**di·rect·ness** *n.*

di·rect ac·cess ▶*n.* the facility of retrieving data immediately from any part of a computer file, without having to read the file from the beginning.

di·rect cur·rent (abbr.: **DC**) ▶*n.* an electric current flowing in one direction only. Compare with ALTERNATING CURRENT.

di·rec·tion /di'rekshən; dī-/ ▶*n.* **1** a course along which someone or something moves. ■ the course that must be taken in order to reach a destination: *he had a terrible sense of direction.* ■ a point to or from which a person or thing moves or faces. ■ a general way in which someone or something is developing: *new directions in architecture* | *any dialogue is a step in the right direction.* ■ general aim or purpose: *the campaign's lack of direction.* **2** the management or guidance of someone or something: *under his direction, the college has developed an international reputation.* ■ the work of supervising and controlling the actors and other staff in a movie, play, or other production. ■ (**directions**) instructions on how to reach a destination or about how to do something. ■ an authoritative order or command: *to suggest that members would* **take direction** *on how to vote is an affront.* —**di·rec·tion·less** *adj.*

di·rec·tion·al /di'rekshənl/ ▶*adj.* **1** relating to or indicating the direction in which someone or something is situated, moving, or developing. **2** having a particular direction of motion, progression, or orientation. ■ relating to, denoting, or designed for the projection, transmission, or reception of light, radio, or sound waves in or from a particular direction or directions: *a directional microphone.* —**di·rec·tion·al·i·ty** /di,rekshə'nalitē/ *n.* —**di·rec·tion·al·ly** *adv.*

di·rec·tion find·er ▶*n.* a special radio receiver with a system of antennas for locating the source of radio signals, used as an aid to navigation.

di·rec·tive /di'rektiv/ ▶*n.* an official or authoritative instruction. ▶*adj.* involving the management or guidance of operations: *he is seeking a directive role in energy policy.*

di·rect·ly /di'rektlē/ ▶*adv.* **1** without changing direction or stopping. ■ at once; immediately. ■ *dated* in a little while; soon: *I'll be back directly.* **2** with nothing or no one in between: *security forces were directly responsible for the massacre.* ■ exactly in a specified position: *the houses directly opposite.* **3** in a frank way: *she spoke simply and directly.* ▶*conj. Brit.* as soon as: *she fell asleep directly she got into bed.*

di·rect ob·ject ▶*n.* a noun or noun phrase denoting a person or thing that is the recipient of the action of a transitive verb, for example *the dog* in *Jimmy fed the dog*. Compare with INDIRECT OBJECT.

di·rec·tor /di'rektər/ (abbr.: **dir.**) ▶*n.* a person who is in charge of an activity, department, or organization. ■ a member of the board that manages or oversees the affairs of a business. ■ a person who supervises the actors, camera crew, and other staff for a movie, play, television program, or similar production. —**di·rec·to·ri·al** /di,rek'tôrēəl; ,dīrek-/ *adj.* —**di·rec·tor·ship** /-,SHip/ *n.*

di·rec·to·rate /di'rektərit/ ▶*n.* [treated as *sing.* or *pl.*] the board of directors of a company. ■ a section of a government department in charge of a particular activity.

di·rec·to·ry /di'rektərē/ ▶*n.* (*pl.* **-ries**) **1** a book listing individuals or organizations alphabetically or thematically with details such as names, addresses, and telephone numbers. ■ *Comput.* a file that consists solely of a set of other files (which may themselves be directories). **2** (**the Directory**) the French revolutionary government in France 1795–99, comprising two councils and a five-member executive.

dirge /dərj/ ▶*n.* a lament for the dead, esp. one forming part of a funeral rite. ■ a mournful song, piece of music, or poem: *singers chanted dirges* fig. *the wind howled dirges around the chimney.* —**dirge·ful** /-fəl/ *adj.*

dir·i·gi·ble /'dirijəbəl; də'rijə-/ ▶*adj.* capable of being steered, guided, or directed: *a dirigible spotlight.* ▶*n.* a dirigible airship, esp. one with a rigid structure.

dirk /dərk/ ▶*n.* a short dagger of a kind formerly carried by Scottish Highlanders.

dirn·dl /'dərndl/ ▶*n.* **1** (also **dirndl skirt**) a full, wide skirt with a tight waistband. **2** a woman's dress in the style of Alpine peasant costume, with such a skirt and a close-fitting bodice.

dirt /dərt/ ▶*n.* a substance, such as mud or dust, that soils someone or something. ■ loose soil or earth; the ground. ■ [usu. as *adj.*] earth used to make a surface for a road, floor, or other area of ground: *a dirt road.* ■ *inf.* excrement: *dog dirt.* ■ a state or quality of uncleanliness: *the sweat and dirt of industry.* ■ *inf.* gossip, esp. information about someone's activities or private life that could prove damaging if revealed: *is there any* **dirt** *on Desmond?* ■ obscene or sordid material: *we object to the dirt that television projects into homes.* ■ *inf.* a worthless or contemptible person or thing: *she treats him like dirt.* ▷Middle English: from Old Norse *drit* 'excrement,' an early sense in English. ▶ □ **do someone dirt** *inf.* harm someone's reputation maliciously.

dirt·bag /'dərt,bag/ ▶*n. inf.* a very unkempt or unpleasant person.

Pronunciation Key ə *ago*, *up*; ər *over*, *fur*; a *hat*; ā *ate*; ä *car*; CH *chin*; e *let*; ē *see*; e(ə)r *air*; i *fit*; ī *by*; i(ə)r *ear*; NG *sing*; ō *go*; ô *law*, *for*; oi *toy*; o͞o *good*; o͞o *goo*; ou *out*; SH *she*; TH *thin*; TH *then*; (h)w *why*; ZH *vision*

D

dirt bike ▶ *n.* a motorcycle designed for use on rough terrain, such as unsurfaced roads or tracks, and used esp. in scrambling.

dirt cheap ▶ *adv. & adj. inf.* extremely cheap: [as *adv.*] *the auctioneers let us have the stuff dirt cheap* | [as *adj.*] *a dirt-cheap price.*

dirt poor ▶ *adv. & adj.* extremely poor: [as *adv.*] *making people dirt poor* | [as *adj.*] *dirt-poor villages.*

dirt·y /'dərtē/ ▶ *adj.* (**dirt·i·er**, **dirt·i·est**) covered or marked with an unclean substance. ■ causing a person or environment to become unclean: *farming is a hard, dirty job.* ■ (of a nuclear weapon) producing considerable radioactive fallout. ■ (of a color) not bright, clear, or pure: *the sea was a waste of dirty gray.* ■ concerned with sex in an unpleasant or obscene way: *he told a stream of dirty jokes.* ■ *inf.* used to emphasize one's disgust for someone or something: *you dirty rat!* ■ (of an activity) dishonest; dishonorable: *he had a reputation for dirty dealing.* ■ (of weather) rough, stormy, and unpleasant. ■ (of popular music) having a distorted or rasping tone: *Nirvana's dirty guitar sound.*
▶ *v.* (**dirt·ies**, **dirt·ied**) [*tr.*] cover or mark with an unclean substance: *don't dirty another towel.* ■ cause to feel or appear morally tainted: *crime had dirtied the city.* —**dirt·i·ly** /'dərtəlē/ *adv.* —**dirt·i·ness** *n.*
▶ □ **get one's hands dirty** do manual, menial, or other hard work: *he gets his hands dirty working alongside the staff.* ■ *inf.* become involved in dishonest or dishonorable activity. □ **play dirty** *inf.* act in a dishonest or unfair way. □ **talk dirty** *inf.* speak about sex in a coarse or obscene way. □ **wash one's dirty laundry in public** see WASH.

dirt·y look ▶ *n. inf.* a facial expression of disapproval, disgust, or anger.

dirt·y trick ▶ *n.* a dishonest or unkind act. ■ (**dirty tricks**) underhanded political or commercial activity designed to discredit an opponent.

dirt·y word ▶ *n.* an offensive or indecent word. ■ *fig.* a thing regarded with dislike or disapproval: *people can talk about profit without it being a dirty word.*

dirt·y work ▶ *n.* activities or tasks that are unpleasant or dishonest and given to someone else to undertake.

dis /dis/ *inf.* ▶ *v.* (also **diss**) (**dissed**, **diss·ing**) [*tr.*] act or speak in a disrespectful way toward: *he was expelled for dissing the gym teacher.*
▶ *n.* disrespectful talk: *the airwaves bristle with the sexual dis of shock jocks.*

dis- ▶ *prefix* **1** expressing negation: *dislike* | *disquiet.* **2** denoting reversal or absence of an action or state: *dishonor* | *disintegrate.* ■ denoting separation: *discharge* | *disengage.* ■ denoting expulsion: *disbar* | *disinherit.* **3** denoting removal of the thing specified: *disbud* | *dismember.* **4** expressing completeness or intensification of an unpleasant or unattractive action: *discombobulate* | *disgruntled.*

dis·a·bil·i·ty /,disə'bilitē/ ▶ *n.* (*pl.* **-ties**) a physical or mental condition that limits a person's movements, senses, or activities. ■ a disadvantage or handicap, esp. one imposed or recognized by the law.

dis·a·ble /dis'ābəl/ ▶ *v.* [*tr.*] (of a disease, injury, or accident) limit (someone) in their movements, senses, or activities: *it's an injury that could disable somebody for life* | [*intr.*] *anxiety can disrupt and disable.* ■ put out of action: *trying to disable the alarm system.* —**dis·a·ble·ment** *n.*

dis·a·buse /,disə'byōōz/ ▶ *v.* [*tr.*] persuade (someone) that an idea or belief is mistaken: *he quickly disabused me of my fanciful notions.*

dis·ad·van·tage /,disəd'vantij/ ▶ *n.* an unfavorable circumstance or condition that reduces the chances of success or effectiveness.
▶ *v.* [*tr.*] place in an unfavorable position in relation to someone or something else: *we are disadvantaging the next generation.*

dis·ad·van·taged /,disəd'vantijd/ ▶ *adj.* (of a person or area) in unfavorable circumstances, esp. with regard to financial or social opportunities. [as *pl. n.*] (**the disadvantaged**) *we began to help the disadvantaged.*

dis·ad·van·ta·geous /,dis,advən'tājəs/ ▶ *adj.* involving or creating unfavorable circumstances that reduce the chances of success or effectiveness. —**dis·ad·van·ta·geous·ly** *adv.*

dis·af·fect·ed /,disə'fektid/ ▶ *adj.* dissatisfied with the people in authority and no longer willing to support them. —**dis·af·fect·ed·ly** *adv.* —**dis·af·fec·tion** *n.*

dis·af·fil·i·ate /,disə'filē,āt/ ▶ *v.* [*tr.*] (of a group or organization) end official connection with (a subsidiary group): *the party disaffiliated the League.* ■ [*intr.*] (of a subsidiary group) end such a connection: *a region may disaffiliate from a dominant state.* —**dis·af·fil·i·a·tion** /,disə,filē'āshən/ *n.*

dis·a·gree /,disə'grē/ ▶ *v.* (**-a·grees**, **-a·greed**, **-a·gree·ing**) [*intr.*] **1** have or express a different opinion: *who disagrees with him?* | *historians often disagree.* ■ (**disagree with**) disapprove of: *she disagreed with the system of apartheid.* **2** (of statements or accounts) be inconsistent or fail to correspond: *results that disagree with prior findings.* ■ (**disagree with**) (of food, climate, or an experience) have an adverse effect on (someone): *the North Sea crossing seemed to have disagreed with her.* —**dis·a·gree·ment** *n.*

dis·a·gree·a·ble /,disə'grēəbəl/ ▶ *adj.* unpleasant or unenjoyable. ■ unfriendly and bad-tempered. —**dis·a·gree·a·ble·ness** *n.* —**dis·a·gree·a·bly** /-blē/ *adv.*

dis·al·low /,disə'lou/ ▶ *v.* [*tr.*] (usu. **be disallowed**) refuse to declare valid: *the judge disallowed his evidence.* —**dis·al·low·ance** /,disə'louəns/ *n.*

dis·ap·pear /,disə'pi(ə)r/ ▶ *v.* [intrans.] cease to be visible: *he disappeared into the trees* | *the sun had disappeared.* ■ cease to exist or be in use: *the tension had completely disappeared.* ■ (of a thing) be lost or impossible to find. ■ (of a person) go missing or (in coded political language) be killed: *the family disappeared after being taken into custody.* —**dis·ap·pear·ance** *n.*

dis·ap·point /,disə'point/ ▶ *v.* [*tr.*] fail to fulfill the hopes or expectations of (someone). ■ prevent (hopes or expectations) from being realized: *public ownership had sadly disappointed socialist hopes.* —**dis·ap·point·ing** *adj.*

dis·ap·point·ment /,disə'pointmənt/ ▶ *n.* the feeling of sadness or displeasure caused by the nonfulfillment of one's hopes or expectations. ■ a person, event, or thing that causes such a feeling.

dis·ap·pro·ba·tion /,dis,aprə'bāshən/ ▶ *n.* strong disapproval, typically on moral grounds: *she braved her mother's disapprobation.*

dis·ap·prove /,disə'prōōv/ ▶ *v.* [*intr.*] have or express an unfavorable opinion about something: *Bob strongly disapproved of drinking and driving* | [as *adj.*] (**disapproving**) *he shot a disapproving glance at her.* ■ [*tr.*] officially refuse to agree to. —**dis·ap·prov·al** *n.* —**dis·ap·prov·ing·ly** *adv.*

dis·arm /dis'ärm/ ▶ *v.* [*tr.*] **1** take a weapon or weapons away from (a person, force, or country). ■ [*intr.*] (of a country or force) give up or reduce its armed forces or weapons. ■ remove the fuse from (a bomb), making it safe. ■ deprive (a ship, etc.) of its means of defense. **2** allay the hostility or suspicions of: *his tact will disarm critics.* ■ deprive of the power to injure or hurt: *humor acts to disarm indignation.* —**dis·arm·ing** *adj*

dis·ar·ma·ment /dis'ärməmənt/ ▶ *n.* the reduction or withdrawal of military forces and weapons.

dis·ar·range /,disə'rānj/ ▶ *v.* [*tr.*] (often **be disarranged**) make (something) untidy or disordered. —**dis·ar·range·ment** *n.*

dis·ar·ray /,disə'rā/ ▶ *n.* a state of disorganization or untidiness: *her gray hair was in disarray* | *his plans have been thrown into disarray.*
▶ *v.* [*tr.*] **1** throw (someone or something) into a state of disorganization or untidiness: *the inspection disarrayed the usual schedule.* **2** *poetic/lit.* strip (someone) of clothing: *attendant damsels to help to disarray her.*

dis·ar·tic·u·late /,disär'tikyə,lāt/ ▶ *v.* [*tr.*] separate (bones) at the joints: *the African egg-eating snake can disarticulate its lower jaw from its upper.* —**dis·ar·tic·u·la·tion** /-,tikyə'lāshən/ *n.*

dis·as·sem·ble /,disə'sembəl/ ▶ *v.* [*tr.*] take (something) to pieces: *it is disassembled for transport.* ■ *Comput.* translate (a program) from machine code into a symbolic language. —**dis·as·sem·bly** /-blē/ *n.*

dis·as·so·ci·ate /,disə'sōshē,āt; -'sōsē-/ ▶ *v.* another term for DISSOCI·ATE. —**dis·as·so·ci·a·tion** /,disə,sōshē'āshən; -,sōsē-/ *n.*

dis·as·ter /di'zastər/ ▶ *n.* a sudden event, such as an accident or a natural catastrophe, that causes great damage or loss of life. ■ an event or fact that has unfortunate consequences: *a string of personal disasters* | *financial disaster.* ■ *inf.* a person, act, or thing that is a failure.

dis·as·trous /di'zastrəs/ ▶ *adj.* causing great damage: *a disastrous fire swept through the museum.* ■ *inf.* highly unsuccessful: *the team made a disastrous start to the season.* ▷late 16th cent. (in the sense 'ill-fated'): from French *désastreux*, from Italian *disastroso*, from *disastro* 'disaster,' from *dis-* (expressing negation) + *astro* 'star' (from Latin *astrum*). —**dis·as·trous·ly** *adv.*

dis·a·vow /,disə'vou/ ▶ *v.* [*tr.*] deny any responsibility or support for: *does she disavow her communist sympathies?* —**dis·a·vow·al** /-'vouəl/ *n.*

dis·band /dis'band/ ▶ *v.* (usu. **be disbanded**) cause (an organized group) to break up. ■ [*intr.*] (of an organized group) break up and stop functioning as an organization. —**dis·band·ment** *n.*

dis·bar /dis'bär/ ▶ *v.* (**-barred**, **-bar·ring**) [*tr.*] **1** (usu. **be disbarred**) expel (a lawyer) from the Bar, so that they no longer have the right to practice law. **2** exclude (someone) from something: *competitors wearing rings will be disbarred from competition.* —**dis·bar·ment** /-mənt/ *n.*

dis·be·lief /,disbə'lēf/ ▶ *n.* inability or refusal to accept that something is true or real: *Laura shook her head in disbelief.* ■ lack of faith in something: *I'll burn in hell for disbelief.*

dis·be·lieve /,disbə'lēv/ ▶ *v.* [*tr.*] be unable to believe (someone or something). ■ [*intr.*] have no faith in God, spiritual beings, or a religious system. —**dis·be·liev·er** *n.* —**dis·be·liev·ing·ly** *adv.*

dis·burse /dis'bərs/ ▶ *v.* [*tr.*] pay out (money from a fund): *$67 million has been disbursed.* —**dis·bur·sal** /-səl/ *n.* —**dis·burse·ment** *n.* —**dis·burs·er** *n.*

disc ▶ *n.* variant spelling of DISK.

dis·card ▸*v.* /dis'kärd/ [*tr.*] get rid of (someone or something) as no longer useful or desirable: *Hilary bundled up the clothes she had discarded.* ■ (in bridge, whist, and similar card games) play (a card that is neither of the suit led nor a trump), when one is unable to follow suit.

▸*n.* /'dis,kärd/ a person or thing rejected as no longer useful or desirable. ■ (in bridge, whist, and similar card games) a card played which is neither of the suit led nor a trump, when one is unable to follow suit. —**dis·card·a·ble** /dis'kärdəbəl/ *adj.*

disc brake ▸*n.* a type of vehicle brake employing the friction of pads against a disc that is attached to the wheel.

dis·cern /di'sərn/ ▸*v.* [*tr.*] perceive or recognize (something): *I can discern no difference between the two* | *students quickly discern what is acceptable.* ■ distinguish (someone or something) with difficulty by sight or with the other senses: *she could faintly discern the shape of a skull.* —**dis·cern·er** *n.* —**dis·cern·i·ble** (also **-a·ble**) /-əblē/ *adj.* /-əblē/ *adv.*

dis·cern·ing /di'sərniNG/ ▸*adj.* having or showing good judgment: *the restaurant attracts discerning customers.* —**dis·cern·ing·ly** *adv.*

dis·cern·ment /di'sərnmənt/ ▸*n.* the ability to judge well: *an astonishing lack of discernment.*

dis·charge ▸*v.* /dis'CHärj/ [*tr.*] **1** (often **be discharged**) tell (someone) officially that they can or must leave, in particular: ■ send (a patient) out of the hospital because they are judged fit to go home. ■ dismiss or release (someone) from a job, esp. from service in the armed forces or police. ■ release (someone) from the custody or restraint of the law. ■ relieve (a juror or jury) from serving in a case. ■ *Law* relieve (a bankrupt) of liability. ■ release (a party) from a contract or obligation: *the insurer is discharged from liability.* **2** allow (a liquid, gas, or other substance) to flow out from where it has been confined: *industrial plants* **discharge** *toxic materials* **into** *rivers* | [*intr.*] *the overflow should discharge in an obvious place.* ■ (of an orifice or diseased tissue) emit (pus, mucus, or other liquid): *the swelling will eventually discharge pus* | [*intr.*] *the eyes began to discharge.* ■ (often **be discharged**) *Physics* release or neutralize the electric charge of (an electric field, battery, or other object). [*intr.*] *batteries have a tendency to discharge slowly.* ■ (of a person) fire (a gun or missile). ■ [*intr.*] (of a firearm) be fired. ■ (of a person) allow (an emotion) to be released: *he discharged his resentment in the form of memoirs.* ■ unload (cargo or passengers) from a ship. **3** do all that is required to fulfill (a responsibility) or perform (a duty). ■ pay off (a debt or other financial claim). **4** *Law* (of a judge or court) cancel (an order of a court). ■ cancel (a contract) because of completion or breach.

▸*n.* /'dis,CHärj/ **1** the action of discharging someone from a hospital or from a job. ■ *Brit.* an act of releasing someone from the custody or restraint of the law: *four days in jail and one year conditional discharge.* ■ *Law* the action of relieving a bankrupt from residual liability. **2** the action of allowing a liquid, gas, or other substance to flow out from where it is confined. ■ the quantity of material allowed to flow out in such a way. ■ the emission of pus, mucus, or other liquid from an orifice or from diseased tissue. ■ *Physics* the release of electricity from a charged object. ■ a flow of electricity through air or other gas, esp. when accompanied by emission of light. ■ the action of firing a gun or missile. ■ the action of unloading a ship of its cargo or passengers. **3** the action of doing all that is required to fulfill a responsibility or perform a duty. ■ the payment of a debt or other financial claim: *money paid* **in discharge of** *a claim.* —**dis·charge·a·ble** /dis'CHärjəbəl/ *adj.* —**dis·charg·er** /dis'CHärjər/ *n.*

dis·ci·ple /di'sīpəl/ ▸*n.* a personal follower of Jesus during his life, esp. one of the twelve Apostles. ■ a follower or student of a teacher, leader, or philosophy: *a disciple of Rousseau.* ▷Old English, from Latin *discipulus* 'learner,' from *discere* 'learn'; reinforced by Old French *deciple.* —**dis·ci·ple·ship** /-,SHip/ *n.*

dis·ci·pli·nar·i·an /,disəplə'ne(ə)rēən/ ▸*n.* a person who believes in or practices firm discipline.

dis·ci·pli·nar·y /'disəplə,nerē/ ▸*adj.* concerning or enforcing discipline.

dis·ci·pline /'disəplin/ ▸*n.* **1** the practice of training people to obey rules or a code of behavior, using punishment to correct disobedience. ■ the controlled behavior resulting from such training. ■ activity or experience that provides mental or physical training: *spiritual discipline* | *Kung fu is a discipline open to old and young.* ■ a system of rules of conduct. **2** a branch of knowledge, typically one studied in higher education.

▸*v.* [*tr.*] train (someone) to obey rules or a code of behavior, using punishment to correct disobedience. ■ punish or rebuke (someone) formally for an offense. ■ (**discipline oneself to do something**) train oneself to do something in a controlled and habitual way.

disc jock·ey (also **disk jock·ey**) ▸*n.* a person who introduces and plays recorded popular music, esp. on radio or at a disco.

dis·claim /dis'klām/ ▸*v.* [*tr.*] refuse to acknowledge; deny: *they disclaimed responsibility.* ■ *Law* renounce a legal claim to (a property or title).

dis·claim·er /dis'klāmər/ ▸*n.* a statement that denies something, esp. responsibility: *a disclaimer about the events being fictional.* ■ *Law* an act of repudiating another's claim or renouncing one's own.

dis·close /dis'klōz/ ▸*v.* [*tr.*] make (secret or new information) known. ■ allow (something) to be seen, esp. by uncovering it: *he cleared the grass and disclosed a narrow path.* —**dis·clos·er** *n.*

dis·clo·sure /dis'klōzHər/ ▸*n.* the action of making new or secret information known: *a judge ordered disclosure of the documents.* ■ a fact, esp. a secret, that is made known: *disclosures about the missiles.*

dis·co /'diskō/ *inf.* ▸*n.* (*pl.* **-cos**) **1** (also **di·sco·theque** /'diskō,tek/) a club or party at which people dance to pop music. **2** pop music intended mainly for dancing to at discos, typically soul-influenced and melodic with a regular bass beat and popular particularly in the late 1970s.

▸*v.* (**-coes, -coed**) [*intr.*] attend or dance at such a club or party.

dis·cog·ra·phy /dis'kägrəfē/ ▸*n.* (*pl.* **-phies**) a descriptive catalog of musical recordings, particularly those of a particular performer or composer.

dis·coid /'dis,koid/ ▸*adj. technical* shaped like a disc.

▸*n.* a thing that is shaped like a disc, particularly a type of ancient stone tool. —**dis·coi·dal** /dis'koidl/ *adj.*

dis·col·or /dis'kələr/ ▸*v.* [*intr.*] become a different, less attractive color: *the peeled fruit may discolor.* ■ [*tr.*] change or spoil the color of: *aluminum can discolor water* | [as *adj.*] (**discolored**) *beauty marred by discolored teeth.* —**dis·col·or·a·tion** /-,kələ'rāSHən/ *n.*

dis·com·bob·u·late /,diskəm'bäbyə,lāt/ ▸*v.* [*tr.*] *humorous* disconcert or confuse (someone): *this attitude totally discombobulated Bruce* | [as *adj.*] (**discombobulated**) *he is looking a little pained and discombobulated.*

dis·com·fit /dis'kəmfit/ ▸*v.* (**-fit·ed, -fit·ing**) [*tr.*] (usu. **be discomfited**) make (someone) feel uneasy or embarrassed: *he was not noticeably discomfited by her tone.* —**dis·com·fi·ture** /dis'kəmfi,CHŏŏr/ *n.*

dis·com·fort /dis'kəmfərt/ ▸*n.* lack of physical comfort. ■ slight pain: *the patient complained of discomfort in the left calf.* ■ a state of mental unease; worry or embarrassment: *his remarks caused her discomfort.*

▸*v.* [*tr.*] make (someone) feel anxious, anxious, or embarrassed: *she liked to discomfort my mother by her remarks.* ■ [often as *adj.*] (**discomforting**) cause (someone) slight pain: *the patient has discomforting symptoms.*

dis·com·mode /,diskə'mōd/ ▸*v.* [*tr.*] *formal* cause (someone) trouble or inconvenience: *I am sorry to have discommoded you.* —**dis·com·mo·di·ous** /-'mōdēəs/ *adj.* —**dis·com·mod·i·ty** /-'mäditē/ *n.*

dis·com·pose /,diskəm'pōz/ ▸*v.* [*tr.*] [often as *adj.*] (**discomposed**) disturb or agitate (someone): *she looked a little discomposed as she spoke.* —**dis·com·po·sure** /-'pōzHər/ *n.*

dis·con·cert /,diskən'sərt/ ▸*v.* [*tr.*] disturb the composure of; unsettle: *the abrupt change of subject disconcerted her* | [as *adj.*] (**disconcerted**) *she was amused to see a disconcerted expression on his face.* —**dis·con·cert·ed·ly** *adv.* —**dis·con·cert·ing** *adj.*

dis·con·nect /,diskə'nekt/ ▸*v.* [*tr.*] break the connection of or between: *take all violence out of television drama and you* **disconnect** *it* **from** *reality.* ■ take (an electrical device) out of action by detaching it from a power supply. ■ interrupt or terminate (a telephone conversation) by breaking the connection. ■ (usu. **be disconnected**) terminate the connection of (a household) to water, electricity, gas, or telephone, typically because of nonpayment of bills.

▸*n.* a discrepancy or lack of connection: *a disconnect between boardrooms and IT departments.* —**dis·con·nec·tion** /-'nekSHən/ *n.*

dis·con·nect·ed /,diskə'nektid/ ▸*adj.* having a connection broken: *a disconnected phone.* ■ (of a person) lacking contact with reality. ■ (of speech, writing, or thought) lacking a logical sequence; incoherent. —**dis·con·nect·ed·ly** *adv.* —**dis·con·nect·ed·ness** *n.*

dis·con·so·late /dis'känsəlit/ ▸*adj.* without consolation or comfort; unhappy. ■ (of a place or thing) causing or showing a complete lack of comfort; cheerless: *disconsolate clumps of cattails.* —**dis·con·so·late·ly** *adv.* —**dis·con·so·late·ness** *n.* —**dis·con·so·la·tion** /-,känsə'lāSHən/ *n.*

dis·con·tent /,diskən'tent/ ▸*n.* lack of contentment; dissatisfaction with one's circumstances: *popular* **discontent with** *the system.* ■ a person who is dissatisfied, typically with the prevailing social or political situation: *the cause attracted discontents and zealots.* —**dis·con·tent·ment** *n.*

dis·con·tin·ue /,diskən'tinyōō/ ▸*v.* (**-tin·ues, -tin·ued, -tin·u·ing**) [*tr.*] cease doing or providing (something), typically something provided on a

D

regular basis. ■ (usu. **be discontinued**) stop making (a particular product): *their running shoe is being discontinued* | [as *adj.*] (**discontinued**) *discontinued fabrics.* ■ cease taking (medication or a medical treatment): *many women discontinue antidepressants during pregnancy.* ■ cease taking (a newspaper or periodical) or paying (a subscription). —**dis·con·tin·u·ance** /-yōōəns/ *n.* —**dis·con·tin·u·a·tion** /-ˌtinyōō'āsHən/ *n.*

dis·con·ti·nu·i·ty /ˌdiskäntn'(y)ōōitē/ ▶*n.* (*pl.* **-ties**) a distinct break in physical continuity or sequence in time. ■ a sharp difference of characteristics between parts of something: *discontinuities in policy.* ■ *Math.* a point at which a function is discontinuous or undefined.

dis·con·tin·u·ous /ˌdiskən'tinyōōəs/ ▶*adj.* having intervals or gaps: *a person with a discontinuous employment record.* ■ *Math.* (of a function) having at least one discontinuity, and whose differential coefficient may become infinite. —**dis·con·tin·u·ous·ly** *adv.*

dis·cord /'diskôrd/ ▶*n.* **1** disagreement between people. ■ lack of agreement or harmony between things. **2** *Mus.* lack of harmony between notes sounding together: *the music faded in discord.* ■ a chord that (in conventional harmonic terms) is regarded as unpleasing or requiring resolution by another. ■ a single note dissonant with another.
▶*v.* [*intr.*] *archaic* (of people) disagree. ■ (of things) be different or in disharmony: *his views discord with ours.*

dis·cord·ant /dis'kôrdnt/ ▶*adj.* **1** disagreeing or incongruous: *the principle of meritocracy is discordant with claims of inherited worth.* ■ characterized by quarreling and conflict: *a study of children in discordant homes.* **2** (of sounds) harsh and jarring because of a lack of harmony. —**dis·cord·ance** *n.* —**dis·cor·dan·cy** /-dnsē/ *n.* —**dis·cord·ant·ly** *adv.*

dis·co·theque /'diskəˌtek/ ▶*n.* another term for DISCO (sense 1).

dis·count ▶*n.* /'diskount/ a deduction from the usual cost of something, typically given for prompt or advance payment or to a special category of buyers: *many stores will offer a discount on bulk purchases.* ■ *Finance* a percentage deducted from the face value of a bill of exchange or promissory note when it changes hands before the due date.
▶*v.* /'diskount; dis'kount/ [*tr.*] **1** deduct an amount from (the usual price of something). ■ reduce (a product or service) in price: *merchandise that was discounted up to 50 percent.* ■ buy or sell (a bill of exchange) before its due date at less than its maturity value. **2** regard (a possibility, fact, or person) as being unworthy of consideration because it lacks credibility.
▶*adj.* /'diskount/ (of a store or business) offering goods for sale at discounted prices: *a discount chain.* ■ at a price lower than the usual one: *a discount flight.* —**dis·count·a·ble** /'kountəbəl/ *adj.* —**dis·count·er** *n.*

dis·coun·te·nance /dis'kountn-əns/ ▶*v.* [*tr.*] (usu. **be discountenanced**) **1** refuse to approve of (something): *drug use is discountenanced.* **2** disturb the composure of: *Amanda was discountenanced by the accusation.*

dis·cour·age /dis'kərij; -'kə-rij/ ▶*v.* [*tr.*] **1** cause (someone) to lose confidence or enthusiasm: *I don't want to discourage you* | [as *adj.*] (**discouraging**) *the discouraging effect of poor prospects.* ■ prevent or seek to prevent (something) by showing disapproval or creating difficulties: *the plan is designed to discourage the use of private cars.* ■ persuade (someone) against an action: *we want to discourage children from smoking.* —**dis·cour·age·ment** *n.* —**dis·cour·ag·er** *n.* —**dis·cour·ag·ing·ly** *adv.*

dis·course ▶*n.* /'disˌkôrs/ written or spoken communication or debate. ■ a formal discussion of a topic in speech or writing: *a discourse on critical theory.* ■ *Linguistics* a connected series of utterances; a text or conversation.
▶*v.* /dis'kôrs/ [*intr.*] speak or write authoritatively about a topic: *she could discourse at great length on the history of Europe.* ■ engage in conversation.

dis·cour·te·ous /dis'kərtēəs/ ▶*adj.* showing rudeness and a lack of consideration for other people. —**dis·cour·te·ous·ly** *adv.* —**dis·cour·te·ous·ness** *n.*

dis·cour·te·sy /dis'kərtəsē/ ▶*n.* (*pl.* **-sies**) rude and inconsiderate behavior. ■ an impolite act or remark.

dis·cov·er /dis'kəvər/ ▶*v.* [*tr.*] **1** find (something or someone) unexpectedly or in the course of a search. ■ become aware of (a fact or situation): *it was a relief to discover that he wasn't in.* ■ be the first to find or observe (a place, substance, or scientific phenomenon): *Fleming discovered penicillin.* ■ perceive the attractions of (an activity or subject) for the first time: *a teenager who has recently discovered fashion.* ■ be the first to recognize the potential of (an actor, singer, or musician): *I discovered the band back in the 70s.* **2** *archaic* divulge (a secret): *some secrets Time will discover.* ■ disclose the identity of (someone): *she at last discovered herself to me.* ■ display (a quality or feeling): *she discovered her courage today.* —**dis·cov·er·a·ble** *adj.* —**dis·cov·er·er** *n.*

dis·cov·er·y /dis'kəvərē/ ▶*n.* (*pl.* **-ver·ies**) **1** the action or process of discovering or being discovered. ■ a person or thing discovered: *the drug*

is not a new discovery. **2** *Law* the compulsory disclosure, by a party to an action, of relevant documents referred to by the other party.

dis·cred·it /dis'kredit/ ▶*v.* (**-cred·it·ed, -cred·it·ing**) [*tr.*] harm the good reputation of (someone or something): *an effort to discredit him* | [as *adj.*] (**discredited**) *a discredited former governor.* ■ cause (an idea or piece of evidence) to seem false or unreliable: *attempts to discredit evolution.*
▶*n.* loss or lack of reputation or respect: *they committed crimes that brought discredit upon the administration.* ■ a person or thing that is a source of disgrace: *the ships were a discredit to the country.*

dis·cred·it·a·ble /dis'kreditəbəl/ ▶*adj.* tending to bring harm to a reputation: *allegations of discreditable conduct.* —**dis·cred·it·a·bly** /-blē/ *adv.*

dis·creet /dis'krēt/ ▶*adj.* (**-creet·er, -creet·est**) careful and circumspect in one's speech or actions, esp. in order to avoid causing offense or to gain an advantage: *we made some discreet inquiries.* ■ intentionally unobtrusive: *a discreet cough.* —**dis·creet·ly** *adv.* —**dis·creet·ness** *n.*

dis·crep·an·cy /dis'krepənsē/ ▶*n.* (*pl.* **-cies**) a lack of compatibility or similarity between two or more facts. —**dis·crep·ant** /-pənt/ *adj.*

dis·crete /dis'krēt/ ▶*adj.* individually separate and distinct: *speech sounds are produced as a continuous sound signal rather than discrete units.* —**dis·crete·ly** *adv.* —**dis·crete·ness** *n.*

dis·cre·tion /dis'kresHən/ ▶*n.* **1** the quality of behaving or speaking in such a way as to avoid causing offense or revealing private information: *she knew she could rely on his discretion.* **2** the freedom to decide what should be done in a particular situation: *authorities must use their discretion* | *a system used at the discretion of the department.* —**dis·cre·tion·ar·y** /-əˌnerē/ *adj.*

dis·crim·i·nate /dis'kriməˌnāt/ ▶*v.* [*intr.*] **1** recognize a distinction; differentiate: *babies can discriminate between different facial expressions of emotion.* ■ [*tr.*] perceive or constitute the difference in or between: *features that discriminate this species from other gastropods.* **2** make an unjust or prejudicial distinction in the treatment of different categories of people or things, esp. on the grounds of race, sex, or age: *existing employment policies discriminate against women.* —**dis·crim·i·nate·ly** /-nitlē/ *adv.* —**dis·crim·i·na·tive** /-ˌnātiv/ *adj.* —**dis·crim·i·na·to·ry** /-ənəˌtôrē/ *adj.*

dis·crim·i·nat·ing /dis'kriməˌnātiNG/ ▶*adj.* (of a person) having or showing refined taste or good judgment. —**dis·crim·i·nat·ing·ly** *adv.*

dis·crim·i·na·tion /disˌkrimə'nāsHən/ ▶*n.* **1** the unjust or prejudicial treatment of different categories of people or things, esp. on the grounds of race, age, or sex: *discrimination against homosexuals.* **2** recognition and understanding of the difference between one thing and another: *discrimination between right and wrong.* ■ the ability to discern what is of high quality; good judgment or taste. **3** *Electr.* the selection of a signal having a required characteristic, such as frequency or amplitude, by means of a discriminator that rejects all unwanted signals.

dis·cur·sive /dis'kərsiv/ ▶*adj.* **1** digressing from subject to subject: *dull, discursive prose.* ■ (of a style of speech or writing) fluent and expansive rather than formulaic or abbreviated: *the short story is concentrated, the novel discursive.* **2** of or relating to discourse or modes of discourse. —**dis·cur·sive·ly** *adv.* —**dis·cur·sive·ness** *n.*

dis·cus /'diskəs/ ▶*n.* (*pl.* **-cus·es**) a heavy thick-centered disk thrown by an athlete, in ancient Greek games or in modern field events. ■ the athletic event or sport of throwing the discus.

dis·cuss /dis'kəs/ ▶*v.* [*tr.*] talk about (something) with another person or group of people. ■ talk or write about (a topic) in detail, taking into account different ideas and opinions: *in Chapter Six I discuss problems that arise in applying Darwin's ideas.* ▷late Middle English (in the sense 'dispel, disperse,' also 'examine by argument'): from Latin *discuss-* 'dashed to pieces,' later 'investigated,' from the verb *discutere*, from *dis-* 'apart' + *quatere* 'shake.' —**dis·cuss·a·ble** *adj.* —**dis·cuss·er** *n.*

dis·cus·sion /dis'kəsHən/ ▶*n.* the action or process of talking about something, typically in order to reach a decision or to exchange ideas: *the proposals are just ideas for discussion* | *the content of the law is under discussion.* ■ a conversation or debate about a certain topic. ■ a detailed treatment of a particular topic in speech or writing.

dis·cus·sion board ▶*n.* *Comput.* another term for MESSAGE BOARD.

dis·dain /dis'dān/ ▶*n.* the feeling that someone or something is unworthy of one's consideration or respect; contempt.
▶*v.* [*tr.*] consider to be unworthy of one's consideration. ■ refuse or reject (something) out of feelings of pride or superiority: *she remained standing, pointedly disdaining his invitation.*

dis·dain·ful /dis'dānfəl/ ▶*adj.* showing contempt or lack of respect: *her parting, disdainful look.* —**dis·dain·ful·ly** *adv.* —**dis·dain·ful·ness** *n.*

dis·ease /di'zēz/ ▶*n.* a disorder of structure or function in a human, animal, or plant, esp. one that produces specific signs or symptoms or that affects a specific location and is not simply a direct result of physical injury. ■ *fig.* a particular quality, habit, or disposition regarded as adversely affecting a person or group of people.

dis·eased /di'zēzd/ ▶*adj.* suffering from disease: *all the diseased cattle have been removed.* ■ *fig.* abnormal and corrupt: *her diseased view of mankind.*

dis·em·bark /ˌdisem'bärk/ ▶*v.* [*intr.*] leave a ship, aircraft, or other vehicle. —**dis·em·bar·ka·tion** /ˌdisˌembär'kāSHən/ *n.*

dis·em·bar·rass /ˌdisem'barəs/ ▶*v.* (**disembarrass oneself of/from**) free oneself of (a burden or nuisance): *he would do well to disembarrass himself of his too officious advisers.* ■ [*tr.*] *rare* make (someone or something) free from embarrassment. —**dis·em·bar·rass·ment** *n.*

dis·em·bod·y /ˌdisem'bädē/ ▶*v.* (**-bod·ies**, **-bod·ied**) [*tr.*] separate or free (something) from its concrete form. —**dis·em·bod·i·ment** *n.*

dis·em·bow·el /ˌdisem'bouəl/ ▶*v.* (**-bow·eled**, **-bow·el·ing**; *Brit.* **-bow·elled**, **-bow·el·ling**) [*tr.*] cut open and remove the internal organs of. —**dis·em·bow·el·ment** *n.*

dis·en·chant /ˌdisen'CHant/ ▶*v.* [*tr.*] (usu. **be disenchanted**) free (someone) from illusion; disappoint: *he may have been disenchanted by the loss of his huge following* | [as *adj.*] (**disenchanted**) *he became disenchanted with his erstwhile ally.* —**dis·en·chant·ing·ly** *adv.* —**dis·en·chant·ment** *n.*

dis·en·cum·ber /ˌdisen'kəmbər/ ▶*v.* [*tr.*] free from or relieve of an encumbrance: *it would disencumber the world of a plague.*

dis·en·fran·chise /ˌdisen'franCHīz/ (also **dis·fran·chise** /dis'franCHīz/) ▶*v.* [*tr.*] deprive (someone) of the right to vote. ■ [as *adj.*] (**disenfranchised**) deprived of power; marginalized: *a hard core of kids who are disenfranchised and don't feel connected to the school.* ■ deprive (someone) of a right or privilege: *it would disenfranchise the disabled from using the center.* ■ *archaic* deprive (someone) of the rights and privileges of a free inhabitant of a borough, city, or country. —**dis·en·fran·chise·ment** *n.*

dis·en·gage /ˌdisen'gāj/ ▶*v.* **1** [*tr.*] detach, free, loosen, or separate (something): *I disengaged his hand from mine.* ■ detach oneself; get loose: *they clung together for a moment, then she disengaged herself.* ■ [*intr.*] become released: *the clutch will not disengage.* ■ remove (troops) from an area of conflict: *a chance to disengage their forces* | [*intr.*] *the only means by which to disengage from Korea.* **2** [*intr.*] *Fencing* pass the point of one's sword over or under the opponent's sword to change the line of attack.

dis·en·gage·ment /ˌdisen'gājmənt/ ▶*n.* **1** the action or process of withdrawing from involvement in a particular activity, situation, or group: *disengagement from politics and politicians.* ■ the withdrawal of military forces or the renunciation of military or political influence in a particular area. ■ the process of separating or releasing something or of becoming separated or released. **2** emotional detachment; objectivity.

dis·en·tan·gle /ˌdisen'taNGgəl/ ▶*v.* [*tr.*] free (something or someone) from an entanglement; extricate. ■ remove knots or tangles from (wool, rope, or hair). —**dis·en·tan·gle·ment** *n.*

dis·es·tab·lish /ˌdisi'stabliSH/ ▶*v.* [*tr.*] (usu. **be disestablished**) deprive (an organization, esp. a country's national church) of its official status. —**dis·es·tab·lish·ment** *n.*

dis·fa·vor /dis'fāvər/ (*Brit.* **dis·fa·vour**) ▶*n.* disapproval or dislike. ■ the state of being disliked: *raises could be taken away if an employee fell into disfavor.*
▶*v.* [*tr.*] regard or treat (someone or something) with disfavor.

dis·fig·ure /dis'figyər/ ▶*v.* [*tr.*] spoil the attractiveness of. —**dis·fig·u·ra·tion** /-ˌfigyə'rāSHən/ *n.* —**dis·fig·ure·ment** *n.*

dis·fran·chise /dis'franCHīz/ ▶*v.* another term for **DISENFRANCHISE**.

dis·gorge /dis'gôrj/ ▶*v.* [*tr.*] cause to pour out: *the combine disgorged a stream of grain.* ■ (of a building or vehicle) discharge (the occupants). ■ yield or give up (funds, esp. funds that have been dishonestly acquired): *they were made to disgorge the profits.* ■ eject (food) from the throat or mouth. ■ [*intr.*] (of a river) empty into a sea. —**dis·gorge·ment** *n.*

dis·grace /dis'grās/ ▶*n.* loss of reputation or respect, esp. as the result of a dishonorable action: *he left the army in disgrace* | *it brought disgrace on the family.* ■ a person or thing regarded as shameful and unacceptable: *he's a disgrace to the legal profession.*
▶*v.* [*tr.*] bring shame or discredit on (someone or something). ■ (**be disgraced**) fall from favor or lose a position of power or honor.

dis·grace·ful /dis'grāsfəl/ ▶*adj.* shockingly unacceptable: *a disgraceful waste of money.* —**dis·grace·ful·ly** *adv.*

dis·grun·tled /dis'grəntld/ ▶*adj.* angry or dissatisfied: *judges receive letters from disgruntled members of the public.* —**dis·grun·tle·ment** *n.*

dis·guise /dis'gīz/ ▶*v.* [*tr.*] give (someone or oneself) a different appearance in order to conceal one's identity: *he disguised himself as a girl* | *Brian was disguised as a priest.* ■ make (something) unrecognizable by altering its appearance, sound, taste, or smell: *does holding a handkerchief over the mouthpiece really disguise your voice?* ■ conceal the nature or existence of (a feeling or situation): *he made no effort to disguise his contempt.*
▶*n.* a means of altering one's appearance or concealing one's identity. ■ the state of having altered one's appearance in order to conceal one's identity: *I told them you were a policewoman* **in disguise.** ■ the concealing of one's true intentions or feelings: *he looked at her without disguise.*

dis·gust /dis'gəst/ ▶*n.* a feeling of revulsion or profound disapproval aroused by something unpleasant or offensive.
▶*v.* [*tr.*] (often **be disgusted**) cause (someone) to feel revulsion or profound disapproval: *I was disgusted with myself for causing so much misery* | [as *adj.*] (**disgusted**) *a disgusted look.* —**dis·gust·ed·ly** *adv.*

dis·gust·ing /dis'gəstiNG/ ▶*adj.* arousing revulsion or strong indignation. —**dis·gust·ing·ly** *adv.* —**dis·gust·ing·ness** *n.*

dish /diSH/ ▶*n.* **1** a shallow, typically flat-bottomed container for cooking or serving food. ■ the food contained or served in such a container: *a dish of oysters.* ■ a particular variety or preparation of food served as part of a meal: *pasta was served as a main dish.* ■ (**the dishes**) all the items that have been used in the preparation, serving, and eating of a meal. ■ a shallow, concave receptacle, esp. one intended to hold a particular substance: *a soap dish.* ■ (also **dish aerial**) a bowl-shaped radio antenna. See also **SATELLITE DISH**. **2** *inf.* a sexually attractive person. **3** (**the dish**) *inf.* information that is not generally known or available.
▶*v.* [*tr.*] (**dish something out/up**) put (food) onto a plate or plates before a meal. ■ (**dish something out**) dispense something in a casual or indiscriminate way: *the banks dished out loans to all and sundry.* ■ (**dish it out**) *inf.* subject others to criticism or punishment: *you can dish it out but you can't take it.* ■ [*intr.*] *inf.* gossip or share information, esp. information of an intimate or scandalous nature: *groups gather to dish about romances.* —**dish·ful** /-ˌfo͝ol/ *n.* (*pl.* **-fuls**).
▶ □ **dish the dirt** *inf.* reveal or spread scandalous information or gossip.

dis·har·mo·ny /dis'härmənē/ ▶*n.* lack of harmony or agreement. —**dis·har·mo·ni·ous** /-ˌhär'mōnēəs/ *adj.* —**dis·har·mo·ni·ous·ly** /-ˌhär'mōnēəslē/ *adv.*

dish·cloth /'diSHˌklôTH/ ▶*n.* a cloth for washing or drying dishes.

dis·heart·en /dis'härtn/ ▶*v.* [*tr.*] (often **be disheartened**) cause (someone) to lose determination or confidence: *the farmer was disheartened by the damage to his crops.* —**dis·heart·en·ing·ly** *adv.* —**dis·heart·en·ment** *n.*

di·shev·eled /di'SHevəld/ (*Brit.* **di·shev·elled**) ▶*adj.* (of a person's hair, clothes, or appearance) untidy; disordered: *a man with long, disheveled hair.* —**di·shev·el** /-'SHevəl/ *v.* —**di·shev·el·ment** *n.*

dis·hon·est /dis'änist/ ▶*adj.* behaving or prone to behave in an untrustworthy or fraudulent way. ■ intended to mislead or cheat: *a dishonest account of events.* —**dis·hon·est·ly** *adv.* —**dis·hon·es·ty** *n.*

dis·hon·or /dis'änər/ (*Brit.* **dis·hon·our**) ▶*n.* a state of shame or disgrace: *the incident brought dishonor upon the police.*
▶*v.* [*tr.*] **1** bring shame or disgrace on. ■ *archaic* violate the chastity of (a woman). **2** fail to observe or respect (an agreement or principle). ■ refuse to accept or pay (a check or a promissory note).

dis·hon·or·a·ble /dis'änərəbəl/ (*Brit.* **dis·hon·our·a·ble**) ▶*adj.* bringing shame or disgrace on someone or something: *his crimes are petty and dishonorable.* —**dis·hon·or·a·ble·ness** *n.* —**dis·hon·or·a·bly** /-blē/ *adv.*

dish·pan /'diSHˌpan/ ▶*n.* a large basin in which dishes are washed.

dish·wash·er /'diSHˌwôSHər; -ˌwäSH-/ ▶*n.* **1** a machine for washing dishes automatically. **2** a person employed to wash dishes.

dish·wa·ter /'diSHˌwôtər; -ˌwätər/ ▶*n.* dirty water in which dishes have been washed: *fig. I sipped the barely brown dishwater he passed off as coffee.*

dis·il·lu·sion /ˌdisə'lo͞oZHən/ ▶*n.* disappointment resulting from the discovery that something is not as good as one believed it to be.
▶*v.* [*tr.*] cause (someone) to realize that a belief or an ideal is false: *if they think we have a magic formula to solve the problem, don't disillusion them.* —**dis·il·lu·sion·ment** *n.*

dis·in·clined /ˌdisin'klīnd/ ▶*adj.* unwilling; reluctant. —**dis·in·cli·na·tion** /-klə'nāSHən/ *n.*

dis·in·fect /ˌdisin'fekt/ ▶*v.* [*tr.*] clean (something) with a disinfectant in order to destroy bacteria. —**dis·in·fec·tant** /-'fectənt/ *n.*

dis·in·gen·u·ous /ˌdisin'jenyo͞oəs/ ▶*adj.* not candid or sincere, typically by pretending that one knows less about something than one really does. —**dis·in·gen·u·ous·ly** *adv.* —**dis·in·gen·u·ous·ness** *n.*

dis·in·her·it /ˌdisin'herit/ ▶*v.* (**-her·it·ed**, **-her·it·ing**) [*tr.*] change one's will or take other steps to prevent (someone) from inheriting one's property. —**dis·in·her·i·tance** /-'heritəns/ *n.*

Pronunciation Key ə *ago*, *up*; ər *over*, *fur*; ä *hat*; ā *ate*; ä *car*; CH *chin*; e *let*; ē *see*; e(ə)r *air*; i *fit*; ī *by*; i(ə)r *ear*; NG *sing*; ō *go*; ô *law, for*; oi *toy*; o͝o *good*; o͞o *goo*; ou *out*; SH *she*; TH *thin*; ${\underline{TH}}$ *then*; (h)w *why*; ZH *vision*

dis·in·te·grate /dis'intə,grāt/ ▶ v. [intr.] break up into small parts, typically as the result of impact or decay: *when the missile struck, the car disintegrated.* ■ (of a society, family, or other social group) weaken or break apart. ■ *inf.* deteriorate mentally or physically: *I thought that when I finished the book I'd disintegrate.* —**dis·in·te·gra·tive** /-,grātiv/ *adj.* —**dis·in·te·gra·tor** /-,grātər/ *n.*

dis·in·te·gra·tion /dis,intə'grāshən/ ▶ n. the process of losing cohesion: *social disintegration.* ■ the process of coming to pieces: *the disintegration of cells.* ■ breakdown of the personality: *the disintegration of a proud man.* ■ *Physics* a process in which a nucleus or other subatomic particle emits a smaller particle or divides into smaller particles.

dis·in·ter /,disin'tər/ ▶ v. (-**terred**, -**ter·ring**) [tr.] dig up (something that has been buried, esp. a corpse). ■ discover (something that is well hidden). —**dis·in·ter·ment** n.

dis·in·ter·est /dis'int(ə)rist/ ▶ n. **1** the state of not being influenced by personal involvement in something; impartiality. **2** lack of interest in something: *he chided Dan for his disinterest in politics.*

dis·in·ter·est·ed /dis'intə,restid; -tristid/ ▶ adj. **1** not influenced by considerations of personal advantage. **2** having or feeling no interest in something: *her father was disinterested in her progress.* —**dis·in·ter·est·ed·ly** adv. —**dis·in·ter·est·ed·ness** n.

dis·joint /dis'joint/ ▶ v. [tr.] disturb the cohesion or organization of: *the loss of the area disjointed military plans.* ■ *dated* take apart at the joints. ▶ adj. *Math.* (of two or more sets) having no elements in common.

disk /disk/ (also **disc**) ▶ n. **1** a flat, thin, round object: *a disk of cheese.* ■ an information storage device for a computer in the shape of a round flat plate that can be rotated to give access to all parts of the surface. The data may be stored either magnetically (in a **magnetic disk**) or optically (in an **optical disk** such as a CD-ROM). ■ (**disc**) short for COMPACT DISC. ■ (**disc**) *dated* a phonograph record. ■ (**discs**) one of the suits in some tarot packs, corresponding to coins in others. **2** a shape or surface that is round and flat in appearance: *the smudged yellow disk of the moon.* **3** a roundish, flattened part in an animal or plant, in particular: ■ (**disc** or **in·ter·ver·te·bral disc**) a layer of cartilage separating adjacent vertebrae in the spine: *he suffered a prolapsed disc.* ■ *Bot.* (in a composite flowerhead of the daisy family) a close-packed cluster of disk florets in the center, forming the yellow part of the flowerhead. ▶ v. [trans.] cultivate (a field) with a disk harrow. —**disk·less** adj.

disk drive ▶ n. a device that allows a computer to read from and write to computer disks.

disk·ette /dis'ket/ ▶ n. another term for FLOPPY DISK.

disk har·row ▶ n. a harrow with cutting edges consisting of a row of concave disks set at an oblique angle.

disk jock·ey ▶ n. variant spelling of DISC JOCKEY.

dis·like /dis'līk/ ▶ v. [tr.] feel distaste for or hostility toward. ▶ n. a feeling of distaste or hostility: *her dislike of publicity | they had taken a dislike to each other.* ■ a thing to which one feels aversion: *I know all his likes and dislikes.* —**dis·lik·a·ble** (also **dis·like·a·ble**) adj.

dis·lo·cate /dis'lōkāt; 'dislō,kāt/ ▶ v. [tr.] disturb the normal arrangement or position of (something, typically a joint in the body): *he dislocated his shoulder.* ■ (often **be dislocated**) disturb the organization of; disrupt: *trade was dislocated by a famine.* ■ (often **be dislocated**) move from its proper place or position: *the symbol is dislocated from its political context.* —**dis·lo·ca·tion** n.

dis·lodge /dis'läj/ ▶ v. [tr.] remove from an established or fixed position: *the hoofs of their horses dislodged loose stones.* —**dis·lodge·a·ble** adj. —**dis·lodg·ment** (also **dis·lodge·ment**) n.

dis·loy·al /dis'loiəl/ ▶ adj. failing to be loyal to a person, country, or body to which one has obligations: *she felt that inquiring into her father's past would be disloyal to her mother.* ■ (of an action, speech, or thought) demonstrating a lack of loyalty. —**dis·loy·al·ly** adv. —**dis·loy·al·ty** /-tē/ n.

dis·mal /'dizməl/ ▶ adj. depressing; dreary: *dismal weather.* ■ (of a person or a mood) gloomy. ■ *inf.* pitifully or disgracefully bad: *he shuddered as he watched his team's dismal performance.* ▷late Middle English: from earlier *dismal* (noun), denoting the two days in each month that in medieval times were believed to be unlucky, from Anglo-Norman French *dis mal,* from medieval Latin *dies mali* 'evil days.' —**dis·mal·ly** adv. —**dis·mal·ness** n.

dis·man·tle /dis'mantl/ ▶ v. [tr.] (often **be dismantled**) take to pieces: *the engines were dismantled.* —**dis·man·tle·ment** n. —**dis·man·tler** /-t(ə)lər/ n.

dis·may /dis'mā/ ▶ v. [tr.] (usu. **be dismayed**) cause (someone) to feel consternation and distress: *they were dismayed by the U-turn in policy.* ▶ n. consternation and distress, typically that caused by something unexpected: *to his dismay, she left him.*

dis·mem·ber /dis'member/ ▶ v. [tr.] cut off the limbs of (a person or animal): [as adj.] (**dismembered**) *he buried their dismembered bodies in the back yard.* ■ partition or divide up (a territory or organization). —**dis·mem·ber·ment** n.

dis·miss /dis'mis/ ▶ v. [tr.] order or allow to leave; send away. ■ discharge from employment or office. ■ treat as unworthy of serious consideration: *it would be easy to dismiss him as all brawn and no brain.* ■ deliberately cease to think about: *he suspected a double meaning in her words, but dismissed the thought.* ■ [intr.] (of a group assembled under someone's authority) disperse. ■ *Law* refuse further hearing to (a case). ■ (in sports) defeat or end an opponent's turn. —**dis·miss·al** /-əl/ n. —**dis·miss·i·ble** adj.

dis·mis·sive /dis'misiv/ ▶ adj. feeling or showing that something is unworthy of consideration. —**dis·mis·sive·ly** adv. —**dis·mis·sive·ness** n.

dis·mount /dis'mount/ ▶ v. **1** [intr.] alight from a horse, bicycle, or other thing that one is riding. ■ [tr.] cause to fall or alight. **2** [tr.] remove (something) from its support: *we have to dismount the pump.* ■ *Comput.* make (a disk or disk drive) unavailable for use. ▶ n. *Gymnastics* a move in which a gymnast jumps off an apparatus or completes a floor exercise.

dis·o·be·di·ent /,disə'bēdēənt/ ▶ adj. refusing to obey rules or someone in authority: *disobedient employees.* —**dis·o·be·di·ence** n. —**dis·o·be·di·ent·ly** adv.

dis·o·bey /,disə'bā/ ▶ v. [tr.] fail to obey (rules, a command, or someone in authority): *1,000 soldiers had disobeyed orders.* —**dis·o·bey·er** n.

dis·o·blige /,disə'blīj/ ▶ v. [tr.] offend (someone) by not acting in accordance with their wishes: *one didn't disoblige them if one could help it.*

dis·or·der /dis'ôrdər/ ▶ n. a state of confusion. ■ the disruption of peaceful and law-abiding behavior: *periodic outbreaks of disorder.* ■ *Med.* a disruption of normal physical or mental functions; a disease or abnormal condition: *eating disorders | mental disorder.* ▶ v. [tr.] [usu. as adj.] (**disordered**) disrupt the systematic functioning or neat arrangement of: *she went to comb her disordered hair | his sleep is disordered.* ■ *Med.* disrupt the healthy or normal functioning of: *a patient who is mentally disordered.*

dis·or·der·ly /dis'ôrdərlē/ ▶ adj. lacking organization; untidy. ■ involving or contributing to a breakdown of peaceful and law-abiding behavior: *a disorderly protest.* —**dis·or·der·li·ness** n.

dis·or·gan·ize /dis'ôrgə,nīz/ ▶ v. [tr.] disrupt the systematic order or functioning of. —**dis·or·gan·i·za·tion** /-,ôrgənə'zāshən/ n.

dis·o·ri·ent /dis'ôrē,ent/ ▶ v. [tr.] [often as adj.] (**disoriented**) make (someone) lose their sense of direction. ■ make (someone) feel confused.

dis·o·ri·en·tate /dis'ôrēən,tāt/ ▶ v. another term for DISORIENT. —**dis·o·ri·en·ta·tion** /-,ôrēən'tāshən/ n.

dis·own /dis'ōn/ ▶ v. [tr.] refuse to acknowledge or maintain any connection with: *my family has disowned me.* —**dis·own·er** n. —**dis·own·ment** n.

dis·par·age /di'sparij/ ▶ v. [tr.] regard or represent as being of little worth: *he never missed an opportunity to disparage his competitors |* [as adj.] (**disparaging**) *disparaging remarks.* —**dis·par·age·ment** n. —**dis·par·ag·ing·ly** adv.

dis·pa·rate /'dispərit; di'sparit/ ▶ adj. essentially different in kind; not allowing comparison: *they inhabit disparate worlds of thought.* ■ containing elements very different from one another: *a culturally disparate country.* ▶ n. (**disparates**) *archaic* things so unlike that there is no basis for comparison. —**dis·pa·rate·ly** adv. —**dis·pa·rate·ness** n. —**dis·par·i·ty** /di'sparitē/ n.

dis·pas·sion·ate /dis'pashənit/ ▶ adj. not influenced by strong emotion, and so able to be rational and impartial. —**dis·pas·sion** /-shən/ n. —**dis·pas·sion·ate·ly** adv. —**dis·pas·sion·ate·ness** n.

dis·patch /dis'pach/ (also **des·patch**) ▶ v. [tr.] **1** send off to a destination or for a purpose: *he dispatched messages back to base | the mayor dispatched police to restore order.* **2** deal with (a task, problem, or opponent) quickly and efficiently. ■ kill: *he dispatched the snake.* ▶ n. **1** the sending of someone or something to a destination or for a purpose: *the dispatch of a peacekeeping force.* ■ speed in action: *he should proceed with dispatch.* **2** an official report on state or military affairs: *in his battle dispatch he described the gunner's bravery.* ■ a report sent in by a newspaper's correspondent from a faraway place. **3** the killing of someone or something. —**dis·patch·er** n.

dis·pel /dis'pel/ ▶ v. (-**pelled**, -**pel·ling**) [tr.] make (a feeling or belief) disappear: *the sunny day did nothing to dispel her dejection.* ■ drive (something) away; scatter: *sprinkle catnip tea to dispel beetles.*

dis·pen·sa·ble /dis'pensəbəl/ ▶ adj. able to be replaced or done without; superfluous: *tiny battlefield robots will be cheap and dispensable.* —**dis·pen·sa·bil·i·ty** /-,pensə'bilitē/ n.

dis·pen·sa·ry /dis'pensərē/ ▶ n. (pl. **-ries**) **1** a room where medicines are provided. **2** a clinic provided by public or charitable funds.

dis·pen·sa·tion /ˌdispən'sāshən; -pen-/ ▶ n. **1** exemption from a rule or requirement: *although she was too young, she was given special dispensation | they were given a dispensation to take the week off.* ▪ permission to be exempted from the laws or observances of a church. **2** a system of order, government, or organization of a nation, community, etc., esp. as existing at a particular time. **3** the action of distributing or supplying something. **—dis·pen·sa·tion·al** /-shənl/ adj.

dis·pense /dis'pens/ ▶ v. **1** [tr.] distribute or provide (a service or information) to a number of people. ▪ (of a machine) supply (a product or cash). ▪ (of a pharmacist) give out (medicine) according to a doctor's prescription. **2** [intr.] (**dispense with**) manage without; get rid of: *let's dispense with the formalities.* ▪ give special exemption from (a law or rule). ▪ [tr.] grant (someone) an exemption from a religious obligation. ▷late Middle English: via Old French from Latin *dispensare* 'continue to weigh out or disburse,' from the verb *dispendere*, based on *pendere* 'weigh.'

dis·pens·er /dis'pensər/ ▶ n. a person or thing that dispenses something. ▪ an automatic machine or container that is designed to release a specific amount of something: *a towel dispenser.*

dis·perse /dis'pərs/ ▶ v. [tr.] distribute or spread over a wide area: *storms can disperse seeds | camping sites could be **dispersed among** trees.* ▪ go or cause to go in different directions or to different destinations: [intr.] *the crowd dispersed* | [tr.] *the police used tear gas to disperse the protesters.* ▪ cause (gas, smoke, mist, or cloud) to thin out and eventually disappear: *winds dispersed the radioactive cloud high in the atmosphere.* ▪ [intr.] thin out and disappear. ▪ *Chem.* distribute (small particles) uniformly in a medium. **—dis·per·sal** /-'pərsəl/ n. **—dis·pers·er** n. **—dis·pers·i·ble** adj. **—dis·per·sion** /-'pərzhən/ n. **—dis·per·sive** /-siv/ adj.

dis·pir·it /di'spirit/ ▶ v. [tr.] (often **be dispirited**) cause (someone) to lose enthusiasm or hope: *the army was dispirited by winter conditions* | [as adj.] (**dispiriting**) *it was a dispiriting occasion.* **—dis·pir·it·ed·ly** adv. **—dis·pir·it·ed·ness** n. **—dis·pir·it·ing·ly** adv.

dis·place /dis'plās/ ▶ v. [tr.] take over the place, position, or role of (someone or something). ▪ cause (something) to move from its proper or usual place: *he seems to have displaced some vertebrae.* ▪ (usu. **be displaced**) force (someone) to leave their home, typically because of war, persecution, or natural disaster: *thousands have been displaced by the civil war.* ▪ remove (someone) from a job or position of authority against their will.

dis·placed per·son ▶ n. a person who is forced to leave their home country because of war, persecution, or natural disaster; a refugee.

dis·place·ment /dis'plāsmənt/ ▶ n. **1** the moving of something from its place or position. ▪ the removal of someone or something by someone or something else that takes their place. ▪ the enforced departure of people from their homes, typically because of war, persecution, or natural disaster. ▪ the amount by which a thing is moved from its normal position. **2** the occupation by a submerged body or part of a body of a volume that would otherwise be occupied by a fluid. ▪ the amount or weight of fluid that would fill such a volume in the case of a floating ship, used as a measure of the ship's size: *the submarine has a surface displacement of 2,185 tons.* ▪ *technical* the volume swept by a reciprocating system, as in a pump or engine. **3** *Psychoanalysis* the unconscious transfer of an intense emotion from its original object to another one: *this phobia was linked with the displacement of fear of his father.*

dis·play /dis'plā/ ▶ v. [tr.] make a prominent exhibition of (something) in a place where it can be easily seen. ▪ (of a computer or other device) show (information) on a screen. ▪ give a conspicuous demonstration of (a quality, emotion, or skill): *the aggressive kind of baseball he displayed as a player.* ▪ [intr.] (of a male bird, reptile, or fish) engage in a specialized pattern of behavior that is intended to attract a mate.
▶ n. **1** a performance, show, or event intended for public entertainment. ▪ a collection of objects arranged for public viewing: *the museum houses an informative display of rocks | work by lesser-known artists is also **on display** | [as adj.] a display case.* ▪ a notable or conspicuous demonstration of a particular type of behavior, emotion, or skill: *a display of virtuosity.* ▪ conspicuous or flashy exhibition; ostentation: *a flagrant display of wealth.* ▪ a specialized pattern of behavior by the males of some species of birds, reptiles, and fish that is intended to attract a mate: *courtship displays.* ▪ *Printing* the arrangement and choice of type in a style intended to attract attention. **2** an electronic device for the visual presentation of data: *a 17-inch color display.* ▪ the process or facility of presenting data on a computer screen or other device. ▪ the data shown on a computer screen or other device. **—dis·play·er** n.

dis·please /dis'plēz/ ▶ v. [tr.] make (someone) feel annoyed or dissatisfied: *the tone of the letter displeased him.* **—dis·pleas·ing·ly** adv.

dis·pleas·ure /dis'plezhər/ ▶ n. a feeling of annoyance or disapproval.
▶ v. [tr.] archaic annoy; displease: *not for gold would I displeasure thee.*

dis·port /dis'pôrt/ ▶ v. [intr.] archaic or humorous enjoy oneself unrestrainedly; frolic: *lords and ladies **disporting themselves** by a lake.*
▶ n. diversion from work or serious matters; recreation or amusement: *the King and all his Court were met for solace and disport.* ▪ archaic a pastime, game, or sport.

dis·pos·a·ble /dis'pōzəbəl/ ▶ adj. **1** (of an article) intended to be used and then thrown away: *disposable diapers | a disposable razor.* ▪ (of a person or idea) able to be dispensed with; easily dismissed. **2** (chiefly of financial assets) readily available for the owner's use as required.
▶ n. an article designed to be thrown away after use: *don't buy disposables, such as razors, cups, and plates.* **—dis·pos·a·bil·i·ty** /-ˌpōzə'bilitē/ n.

dis·pos·a·ble in·come ▶ n. income remaining after deduction of taxes and other mandatory charges, available to be spent or saved as one wishes.

dis·pos·al /dis'pōzəl/ ▶ n. **1** the action or process of throwing away or getting rid of something: *the disposal of radioactive waste.* ▪ (also **dis·pos·er**) *inf.* an electrically operated device fitted to the waste pipe of a kitchen sink for grinding up food waste. **2** the sale of shares, property, or other assets. **3** the arrangement or positioning of something: *she brushed her hair as if success lay in the sleek disposal of each strand.*
▶ □ **at one's disposal** available for use whenever or however one wishes.

dis·pose /dis'pōz/ ▶ v. **1** [intr.] (**dispose of**) get rid of by throwing away or giving or selling to someone else. ▪ *inf.* kill; destroy. ▪ overcome (a rival or threat): *team members were buoyant after they disposed of the champions.* ▪ *inf.* consume (food or drink) quickly or enthusiastically: *she watched him dispose of a large slice of cheese.* **2** [tr.] arrange in a particular position: *the chief disposed his attendants in a circle.* ▪ bring (someone) into a particular frame of mind: *a secondary psychological factor disposing toward happiness.* | [tr.] *fundamentalism disposes you to believe in miracles.* ▪ [intr.] *poetic/lit.* determine the course of events: *the city proposed, but the unions disposed.* **—dis·pos·er** n.

dis·po·si·tion /ˌdispə'zishən/ ▶ n. **1** a person's inherent qualities of mind and character: *a placid disposition.* ▪ an inclination or tendency: *the cattle showed a disposition to run.* **2** the way in which something is placed or arranged, esp. in relation to other things: *the plan shows the disposition of the rooms.* ▪ the action of arranging or ordering people or things in a particular way: *the disposition and control of the armed forces.* ▪ (**dispositions**) military preparations, in particular the stationing of troops ready for attack or defense. **3** the power to deal with something as one pleases: *if Napoleon had had railroads **at his disposition**, he would have been invincible.* ▪ archaic the determination of events, esp. by divine power.

dis·pos·sess /ˌdispə'zes/ ▶ v. [tr.] (often **be dispossessed**) deprive (someone) of something that they own: *they were **dispossessed of lands** and properties at the time of the Reformation* | [as pl. n.] (**the dispossessed**) *a champion of the poor and the dispossessed.* ▪ oust (a person) from a dwelling or position. **—dis·pos·ses·sion** /-'zeshən/ n.

dis·proof /dis'prŏŏf/ ▶ n. a set of facts that prove that something is untrue: *a disproof of the principle of closure.* ▪ the action of proving that something is untrue: *considerations subject to scientific verification or disproof.*

dis·pro·por·tion /ˌdisprə'pôrshən/ ▶ n. an instance of being out of proportion with something else: *a disproportion between expenditure and benefit.* **—dis·pro·por·tion·al** /-shənl/ adj. **—dis·pro·por·tion·al·i·ty** /-ˌpôrshə'nalitē/ n. **—dis·pro·por·tion·al·ly** /-shənl-ē/ adv.

dis·pro·por·tion·ate /ˌdisprə'pôrshənit/ ▶ adj. too large or too small in comparison with something else: *their sentences were disproportionate to the offenses they had committed.* **—dis·pro·por·tion·ate·ly** adv. **—dis·pro·por·tion·ate·ness** n.

dis·prove /dis'prŏŏv/ ▶ v. [tr.] prove that (something) is false: *he has given them two months to disprove the allegation.* **—dis·prov·a·ble** adj.

dis·put·a·ble /dis'pyŏŏtəbəl/ ▶ adj. not established as fact, and so open to question or debate. **—dis·put·a·bly** /-blē/ adv.

dis·pu·ta·tion /ˌdispyŏŏ'tāshən/ ▶ n. debate or argument. ▪ formal academic debate. **—dis·put·a·tive** /-'pŏŏtətiv/ adj.

dis·pu·ta·tious /ˌdispyŏŏ'tāshəs/ ▶ adj. (of a person) fond of having heated arguments: *a hangout for disputatious academics.* ▪ (of an argument or situation) motivated by or causing strong opinions: *disputatious council meetings.* —**dis·pu·ta·tious·ly** *adv.* —**dis·pu·ta·tious·ness** *n.*

dis·pute /dis'pyoot/ ▶*n.* a disagreement, argument, or debate: *a territorial dispute* | *the question* **in dispute** *is altogether insignificant.*
▶*v.* [*tr.*] argue about (something); discuss heatedly: *I disputed the charge* | [*intr.*] *he disputed with local poets.* ■ question whether (a statement or alleged fact) is true or valid. ■ compete for; strive to win: *two drivers disputing the lead.* ■ *archaic* resist (a landing or advance): *the Sudanese chose Teb as the ground upon which to dispute the advance.* —**dis·pu·tant** /-'pyoōnt/ *n.* —**dis·put·er** *n.*

dis·qual·i·fy /dis'kwälə,fī/ ▶*v.* (**-fies, -fied**) [*tr.*] (often **be disqualified**) pronounce (someone) ineligible for an office or activity because of an offense or infringement: *he was* **disqualified from** *driving for six months.* ■ eliminate (someone) from a competition because of an infringement of the rules: *he was disqualified after failing a drug test.* ■ (of a feature or characteristic) make (someone) unsuitable for an office or activity. —**dis·qual·i·fi·ca·tion** /dis,kwäləfi'kāsHən/ *n.*

dis·qui·et /dis'kwī-it/ ▶*n.* a feeling of anxiety or worry.
▶*v.* [*tr.*] [usu. as *adj.*] (**disquieted**) make (someone) worried or anxious: *she felt disquieted at the lack of interest the girl had shown.* —**dis·qui·et·ing** *adj.*

dis·qui·e·tude /dis'kwī-i,t(y)oōd/ ▶*n.* a state of uneasiness or anxiety.

dis·qui·si·tion /,diskwə'zisHən/ ▶*n.* a long or elaborate essay or discussion on a particular subject. —**dis·qui·si·tion·al** /-sHnl/ *adj.* (*archaic*).

dis·re·gard /,disri'gärd/ ▶*v.* [*tr.*] pay no attention to; ignore.
▶*n.* the action or state of disregarding or ignoring something: *blatant disregard for the law.*

dis·re·pair /,disri'pe(ə)r/ ▶*n.* poor condition of a building or structure due to neglect: *the station gradually fell into disrepair.*

dis·rep·u·ta·ble /dis'repyətəbəl/ ▶*adj.* not considered to be respectable in character or appearance: *think twice before buying cheap fireworks from disreputable sources.* —**dis·rep·u·ta·ble·ness** *n.* —**dis·rep·u·ta·bly** /-blē/ *adv.*

dis·re·pute /,disrə'pyoōt/ ▶*n.* the state of being held in low esteem by the public: *they're close to bringing the game* **into disrepute.**

dis·re·spect /,disri'spekt/ ▶*n.* lack of respect or courtesy.
▶*v.* [*tr.*] *inf.* show a lack of respect for; insult: *a young brave who disrespects his elders.* —**dis·re·spect·ful** /-fəl/ *adj.* —**dis·re·spect·ful·ly** /-fəlē/ *adv.*

dis·robe /dis'rōb/ ▶*v.* [*intr.*] take off one's clothes: *the girl disrobed and climbed into the high bed.* ■ take off the clothes worn for an official ceremony: *they walked to the vestry to disrobe.* ■ [*tr.*] undress (someone).

dis·rupt /dis'rəpt/ ▶*v.* [*tr.*] interrupt (an event, activity, or process) by causing a disturbance or problem: *a strike will disrupt service.* ■ drastically alter or destroy the structure of (something): *drugs disrupt cells.* —**dis·rupt·er** (also **dis·rup·tor** /-tər/) *n.* —**dis·rup·tion** /-'rəpsHən/ *n.* —**dis·rup·tive** *adj.* —**dis·rup·tive·ly** *adv.*

diss ▶*v.* variant spelling of DIS.

dis·sat·is·fy /dis'satis,fī/ ▶*v.* (**-fies, -fied**) [*tr.*] fail to satisfy (someone). —**dis·sat·is·fac·tion** /-,satis'faksHən/ *n.*

dis·sect /di'sekt; dī-/ ▶*v.* [*tr.*] (often **be dissected**) methodically cut up (a body, part, or plant) in order to study its internal parts. ■ analyze (something) in minute detail. —**dis·sec·tion** /-'seksHən/ *n.* —**dis·sec·tor** /-tər/ *n.*

dis·sem·ble /di'sembəl/ ▶*v.* [*intr.*] conceal one's true motives, feelings, or beliefs: *an honest, sincere person with no need to dissemble.* ■ [*tr.*] disguise or conceal (a feeling or intention): *she smiled, dissembling her true emotion.* —**dis·sem·blance** /-bləns/ *n.* —**dis·sem·bler** /-b(ə)lər/ *n.*

dis·sem·i·nate /di'semə,nāt/ ▶*v.* [*tr.*] spread or disperse (something, esp. information) widely: *officials should disseminate information.* —**dis·sem·i·na·tion** /-,semə'nāsHən/ *n.* —**dis·sem·i·na·tor** /-,nātər/ *n.*

dis·sen·sion /di'sensHən/ ▶*n.* disagreement that leads to discord.

dis·sent /di'sent/ ▶*v.* [*intr.*] hold or express opinions that are at variance with those previously, commonly, or officially expressed: *two members* **dissented from** *the majority* | [as *adj.*] (**dissenting**) *there were only a couple of dissenting voices.*
▶*n.* the expression or holding of opinions at variance with those previously, commonly, or officially held: *there was no* **dissent from** *this view.* —**dis·sent·er** *n.*

dis·ser·ta·tion /,disər'tāsHən/ ▶*n.* a long essay on a particular subject, esp. one written as a requirement for the Doctor of Philosophy degree: *Joe wrote his doctoral dissertation on Thucydides* | *fig. she went on then into a dissertation on her family's love of Ireland.* —**dis·ser·ta·tion·al** /-sHnl/ *adj.*

dis·serv·ice /dis'sərvis/ ▶*n.* a harmful action: *you have* **done a disservice** *to the African people by ignoring this fact.*

dis·si·dent /'disidənt/ ▶*n.* a person who opposes official policy, esp. that of an authoritarian state: *a dissident jailed by a military regime.*
▶*adj.* in opposition to official policy. —**dis·si·dence** *n.*

dis·sim·i·lar /dis'similər/ ▶*adj.* not alike; different: *dissimilar nations* | *the pleasures of the romance novel are* **not dissimilar from** *those of the chocolate bar.* —**dis·sim·i·lar·i·ty** /-,simə'laritē/ *n.* —**dis·sim·i·lar·ly** *adv.*

dis·sim·i·late /di'simə,lāt/ ▶*v.* [*tr.*] *Linguistics* change (a sound in a word) in order to be unlike the sounds near it: *in "pilgrim," from Latin "peregrinus," the first "r" is dissimilated to "l."* ■ [*intr.*] (of a sound) undergo such a change: *the first "r" dissimilates to "l."* —**dis·sim·i·la·tion** /-,simə'lāsHən/ *n.* —**dis·sim·i·la·to·ry** /-lə,tôrē/ *adj.*

dis·sim·u·late /di'simyə,lāt/ ▶*v.* [*tr.*] conceal or disguise (one's thoughts, feelings, or character): *a man who dissimulates his wealth beneath ragged pullovers* | [*intr.*] *now that they have power, they no longer need to dissimulate.* —**dis·sim·u·la·tion** /-,simyə'lāsHən/ *n.* —**dis·sim·u·la·tor** /-,lātər/ *n.*

dis·si·pate /'disə,pāt/ ▶*v.* **1** [*intr.*] disperse or scatter: *the cloud of smoke dissipated.* ■ (of a feeling or other intangible thing) disappear or be dispelled: *the concern she'd felt for him had wholly dissipated.* **2** [*tr.*] squander or fritter away (money, energy, or resources): *he had dissipated his entire fortune.* ■ (usu. **be dissipated**) *Physics* cause (energy) to be lost, typically by converting it to heat. —**dis·si·pa·tive** /-,pātiv/ *adj.* —**dis·si·pa·tor** /-,pātər/ (also **dis·si·pat·er**) *n.*

dis·si·pa·tion /,disə'pāsHən/ ▶*n.* **1** dissipated living: *a descent into drunkenness and sexual dissipation.* **2** squandering of money, energy, or resources: *the dissipation of the country's mineral wealth.*

dis·so·ci·ate /di'sōsHē,āt; -'sōsē-/ ▶*v.* [*tr.*] **1** disconnect or separate (used esp. in abstract contexts) : *voices should not be* **dissociated from** *their social context.* ■ (**dissociate oneself from**) declare that one is not connected with or a supporter of (someone or something): *he took pains to dissociate himself from the radicals.* ■ [*intr.*] become separated or disconnected: *the area would* **dissociate from** *the country.* **2** (usu. **be dissociated**) *Chem.* cause (a molecule) to split into separate smaller atoms, ions, or molecules, esp. reversibly: *these compounds are dissociated by solar radiation.* ■ [*intr.*] (of a molecule) undergo this process. —**dis·so·ci·a·tion** *n.* —**dis·so·ci·a·tive** /-,ātiv; -sHətiv/ *adj.*

dis·so·lute /'disə,loōt/ ▶*adj.* lax in morals; licentious. —**dis·so·lute·ly** *adv.* —**dis·so·lute·ness** *n.*

dis·so·lu·tion /,disə'loōsHən/ ▶*n.* **1** the closing down or dismissal of an assembly, partnership, or official body. ■ *technical* the action or process of dissolving or being dissolved: *minerals susceptible to dissolution.* ■ disintegration; decomposition: *the dissolution of the flesh.* ■ *formal* death. **2** debauched living; dissipation: *an advanced state of dissolution.*

dis·solve /di'zälv/ ▶*v.* **1** [*intr.*] (of a solid) become incorporated into a liquid so as to form a solution: *glucose dissolves easily.* ■ [*tr.*] cause (a solid) to become incorporated into a liquid in this way: *dissolve a bouillon cube in hot water.* ■ (of something abstract, esp. a feeling) disappear: *my courage dissolved.* ■ deteriorate or degenerate: *policy could* **dissolve into** *chaos.* ■ subside uncontrollably into (an expression of strong feelings): *she* **dissolved into** *tears.* ■ (in a movie) change gradually to (a different scene or picture): *dissolve to view down the street.* **2** [*tr.*] close down or dismiss (an assembly or official body): *the president can dissolve parliament.* ■ annul or put an end to (a partnership or marriage).
▶*n.* (in a film) an act or instance of moving gradually from one picture to another. —**dis·solv·a·ble** *adj.* —**dis·solv·er** *n.*

dis·so·nant /'disənənt/ ▶*adj.* *Mus.* lacking harmony: *irregular, dissonant chords.* ■ unsuitable or unusual in combination; clashing: *Jackson employs both harmonious and dissonant color choices..* —**dis·so·nance** *n.* —**dis·so·nant·ly** *adv.*

dis·suade /di'swād/ ▶*v.* [*tr.*] persuade (someone) not to take a particular course of action: *his friends tried to* **dissuade** *him* **from** *flying.* —**dis·suad·er** *n.* —**dis·sua·sion** /-'swāzHən/ *n.* —**dis·sua·sive** /-'swāsiv/ *adj.*

dis·taff /'distaf/ ▶*n.* a stick or spindle onto which wool or flax is wound for spinning. ■ [as *adj.*] of or concerning women.

dis·taff side ▶*n.* the female side of a family. ■ the female members of a group.

dis·tal /'distl/ ▶*adj.* *Anat.* situated away from the center of the body or from the point of attachment. The opposite of PROXIMAL. —**dis·tal·ly** *adv.*

dis·tance /'distəns/ ▶*n.* **1** an amount of space between two things or people. ■ the condition of being far off; remoteness: *distance makes things look small.* ■ a far-off point or place: *watching* **from a distance.** ■ (**the distance**) the more remote part of what is visible or discernible: *I hear sirens* **in the distance** | *they sped off* **into the distance.** ■ an interval of time: *a distance of more than twenty years.* ■ *fig.* the avoidance of familiarity; aloofness or reserve: *a mix of warmth and distance makes a good neighbor.* **2** the full length of a race: *he claimed the title in only his second race over the distance.* ■ (**the distance**) *Boxing* the scheduled length of a fight: *he has won five fights* **inside the distance.**
▶*v.* [*tr.*] make (someone or something) far off or remote in position or

nature: *her mother tried to* **distance** *her from the others.* ■ (**distance one-self from**) declare that one is not connected with or a supporter of (someone or something): *he distanced himself from the proposals.*

▶ □ **go the distance** Boxing complete a fight without being knocked out: *he went the distance after being floored in the first round.* ■ (of a boxing match) last the scheduled length. ■ last for a long time: *this amplifier should go the distance.* □ **keep one's distance** stay far away. ■ maintain one's reserve: *you had to say nothing and keep your distance.*

dis·tant /ˈdistənt/ ▶adj. **1** far away in space or time. ■ (after a measurement) at a specified distance: *the star is 30,000 light years* **distant** *from earth.* ■ (of a sound) faint or vague because far away: *the distant bark of some farm dog.* ■ fig. remote or far apart in resemblance or relationship: *a distant acquaintance.* ■ (of a person) not closely related: *a distant cousin.* **2** (of a person) not intimate; cool or reserved. ■ remote; abstracted. ▷late Middle English: from Latin *distant-* 'standing apart,' from the verb *distare*, from *dis-* 'apart' + *stare* 'stand.' —**dis·tant·ly** adv.

dis·taste /disˈtāst/ ▶n. mild dislike or aversion. —**dis·taste·ful** adj. —**dis·taste·ful·ly** adv.

dis·tem·per[1] /disˈtempər/ ▶n. **1** a viral disease of some animals, esp. dogs, causing fever, coughing, and catarrh. **2** archaic a human disease; illness. ■ fig. political disorder: *an attempt to illuminate the moral roots of the modern world's distemper.*

dis·tem·per[2] ▶n. a kind of paint using glue or size instead of an oil base, for use on walls or for scene-painting. ■ a method of mural and poster painting using this.

dis·tend /disˈtend/ ▶v. [tr.] cause (something) to swell by stretching it from inside: [as adj.] (**distended**) *a distended belly.* ■ [intr.] swell out because of pressure from inside. —**dis·ten·si·bil·i·ty** /-ˌtensəˈbilitē/ n. —**dis·ten·si·ble** /-ˈtensəbəl/ adj. —**dis·ten·sion** /-ˈtenSHən/ n.

dis·till /disˈtil/ (Brit. **distil**) ▶v. [tr.] purify (a liquid) by vaporizing it, then condensing it by cooling the vapor, and collecting the resulting liquid: [as adj.] (**distilled**) *dip the slide in distilled water.* ■ (usu. **be distilled**) make (something, esp. liquor or an essence) in this way: *whiskey is* **distilled** *from a mash of grains* | [as n.] (**distilling**) *the distilling industry.* ■ extract the essence of (something) by heating it with a solvent. ■ remove (a volatile constituent) of a mixture by using heat: *coal tar is made by* **dis-tilling out** *volatile products.* ■ (often **be distilled**) fig. extract the essential meaning or most important aspects of: *my notes were* **distilled into** *a book* | [as adj.] (**distilled**) *the report is a distilled version.* ■ [intr.] poetic/lit. emanate as a vapor or in minute drops. —**dis·til·late** /ˈdistilit/ n. —**dis·til·la·tion** /ˌdistəˈlāSHən/ n. —**dis·til·la·to·ry** /-əˌtôrē/ adj.

dis·till·er /disˈtilər/ ▶n. a person or company that manufactures liquor.

dis·till·er·y /disˈtilərē/ ▶n. (pl. **-er·ies**) a place where liquor is manufactured: *the world's oldest whiskey distillery.*

dis·tinct /disˈtiNGkt/ ▶adj. **1** recognizably different in nature from something else of a similar type: *the patterns of spoken language are* **distinct from** *those of writing.* ■ physically separate. **2** readily distinguishable by the senses: *a distinct smell of nicotine.* ■ (used for emphasis) so clearly apparent as to be unmistakable; definite: *the distinct impression that Melissa wasn't pleased.* —**dis·tinct·ly** adv. —**dis·tinct·ness** n.

dis·tinc·tion /disˈtiNGkSHən/ ▶n. **1** a difference or contrast between similar things or people: *a sharp* **distinction between** *domestic and international politics* | *unaware of class distinctions.* ■ the separation of things or people into different groups according to their attributes or characteristics: *these procedures were applied to all births, without distinction.* **2** excellence that sets someone or something apart from others: *a novelist of distinction.* ■ a decoration or honor awarded to someone in recognition of outstanding achievement. ■ recognition of outstanding achievement, such as on an examination.

dis·tinc·tive /disˈtiNGktiv/ ▶adj. characteristic of one person or thing, and so serving to distinguish it from others: *juniper berries give gin its distinctive flavor.* —**dis·tinc·tive·ly** adv. —**dis·tinc·tive·ness** n.

dis·tin·guish /disˈtiNGgwiSH/ ▶v. [tr.] recognize or treat (someone or something) as different. ■ [intr.] perceive or point out a difference: *bees are unable to* **distinguish between** *red, black, and various grays.* ■ manage to discern (something barely perceptible): *it was too dark to distinguish anything more than vague shapes.* ■ be an identifying or characteristic mark or property of: *what* **distinguishes** *sports from games?* | [as adj.] (**distinguishing**) *a yellow brick house with no distinguishing features.* ■ (**distinguish oneself**) make oneself prominent and worthy of respect through one's behavior or achievements. —**dis·tin·guish·a·ble** adj.

dis·tin·guished /disˈtiNGgwiSHt/ ▶adj. successful, authoritative, and commanding great respect: *a distinguished American educationist.* ■ showing dignity or authority in one's appearance or manner.

dis·tort /disˈtôrt/ ▶v. [tr.] pull or twist out of shape: *a grimace distorted her fine mouth* | [as adj.] (**distorted**) *his face was* **distorted with** *rage.* ■ [intr.]

become twisted out of shape: *the pipe will distort.* ■ fig. give a misleading or false account or impression of: *many factors can distort the results* | [as adj.] (**distorted**) *his report gives a distorted view of the meeting.* ■ change the form of (an electrical signal or sound wave) during transmission, amplification, or other processing. —**dis·tort·ed·ly** adv. —**dis·tort·ed·ness** n. —**dis·tor·tion** /-ˈtôrSHən/ n. —**dis·tor·tion·al** /-ˈtôrSHənl/ adj.

dis·tract /disˈtrakt/ ▶v. [tr.] prevent (someone) from giving full attention to something: *don't allow noise to* **distract** *you from your work* | [as adj.] (**distracting**) *she found his nearness distracting.* ■ divert (attention) from something. ■ (**distract oneself**) divert one's attention from something worrying or unpleasant by doing something different or more pleasurable: *I tried to distract myself by concentrating on Jane.* —**dis·tract·ing·ly** adv.

dis·trac·tion /disˈtrakSHən/ ▶n. **1** a thing that prevents someone from giving full attention to something else: *the company found passenger travel a* **distraction from** *the main business of moving freight.* ■ a diversion or recreation. **2** extreme agitation of the mind or emotions.

▶ □ **drive someone to distraction** annoy someone intensely. □ **to distraction** intensely: *she loved him to distraction.*

dis·trait /disˈtrā/ ▶adj. (fem. **dis·traite** /disˈtrāt/) distracted or absent-minded: *he seemed oddly distrait.*

dis·traught /disˈtrôt/ ▶adj. deeply upset and agitated.

dis·tress /disˈtres/ ▶n. extreme anxiety, sorrow, or pain. ■ the state of a ship or aircraft when in danger or difficulty and needing help: *vessels* **in distress.** ■ suffering caused by lack of money or the basic necessities of life. ■ Med. a state of physical strain, exhaustion, or, in particular, breathing difficulty.

▶v. [tr.] cause (someone) anxiety, sorrow, or pain: [as adj.] (**distressing**) *some very distressing news.* ■ give (furniture, leather, or clothing) simulated marks of age and wear: *leather jackets are industrially distressed.* —**dis·tress·ful** /-fəl/ adj. —**dis·tress·ing·ly** adv.

dis·tressed /disˈtrest/ ▶adj. suffering from anxiety, sorrow, or pain. ■ dated impoverished: *in distressed circumstances.* ■ (of furniture, leather, or clothing) having simulated marks of age and wear. ■ (of goods) for sale at unusually low prices or at a loss because of damage or previous use.

dis·trib·u·tar·y /disˈtribyo͞oˌterē/ ▶n. (pl. **-tar·ies**) a branch of a river that does not return to the main stream after leaving it (as in a delta).

dis·trib·ute /disˈtribyo͞ot/ ▶v. [tr.] give shares of (something); deal out. ■ supply (goods) to stores and other businesses that sell to consumers. ■ (**be distributed**) occur throughout an area: *the birds are mainly distributed in marshes and river valleys.* —**dis·trib·ut·a·ble** adj.

dis·tri·bu·tion /ˌdistrəˈbyo͞oSHən/ (abbr.: **distr.**) ▶n. the action of sharing something out among a number of recipients. ■ the way in which something is shared out among a group or spread over an area: *the distribution of wildlife.* ■ the action or process of supplying goods to stores and other businesses that sell to consumers. ■ Bridge the different number of cards of each suit in a player's hand. —**dis·tri·bu·tion·al** /-SHənl/ adj.

dis·tri·bu·tive /disˈtribyətiv/ ▶adj. **1** concerned with the supply of goods to stores and other businesses that sell to consumers. ■ concerned with the way in which things are shared between people: *distributive justice.* **2** Gram. (of a determiner or pronoun) referring to each individual of a class, not to the class collectively, e.g., *each, either.* **3** Math. (of an operation) fulfilling the condition that, when it is performed on two or more quantities already combined by another operation, the result is the same as when it is performed on each quantity individually and the products then combined.

▶n. Gram. a distributive word. —**dis·trib·u·tive·ly** adv.

dis·trib·u·tor /disˈtribyətər/ (abbr.: **distr.**) ▶n. **1** an agent who supplies goods to stores and other businesses that sell to consumers: *a wholesale liquor distributor.* **2** a device in a gasoline engine for passing electric current to each spark plug in turn.

dis·trict /ˈdistrikt/ ▶n. (abbr.: **distr.**) an area of a country or city, esp. one regarded as distinct because of a particular characteristic: *an elegant shopping district.* ■ a region defined for an administrative purpose.

▶v. [tr.] divide into districts. ▷early 17th cent. (denoting the territory under the jurisdiction of a feudal lord): from French, from medieval Latin *districtus* 'territory of) jurisdiction,' from Latin *distringere* 'draw apart.'

dis·trict at·tor·ney (abbr.: **DA**) ▶n. a public official who acts as prosecutor for the state or the federal government in a particular district.

Pronunciation Key ə *ago,* up; ər *over,* fur; a *hat;* ā *ate;* ä *car;* CH *chin;* e *let;* ē *see;* e(ə)r *air;* i *fit;* ī *by;* i(ə)r *ear;* NG *sing;* ō *go;* ô *law, for;* oi *toy;* o͝o *good;* o͞o *goo;* ou *out;* SH *she;* TH *thin;* T͟H *then;* (h)w *why;* ZH *vision*

dis·tro /'distrō/ ▸*n. Comput.* a distribution, especially of Linux software or of webzines: *I've been working on this project for a little while and decided to post this here in case anyone who runs a distro is interested.* ■ a particular distributable or distributed version of Linux software: *I was excited enough about this distro that I forked over the cash to buy it.*

dis·trust /dis'trəst/ ▸*n.* the feeling that someone or something cannot be relied on: *distrust of Soviet intentions soon followed.*
▸*v.* [*tr.*] doubt the honesty or reliability of; regard with suspicion. —**dis·trust·er** *n.* —**dis·trust·ful** /-fəl/ *adj.* —**dis·trust·ful·ly** /-fəlē/ *adv.*

dis·turb /dis'tərb/ ▸*v.* [*tr.*] interfere with the normal arrangement or functioning of: *a road disturbed by bulldozer activity.* ■ destroy the sleep or relaxation of. ■ (often **be disturbed**) cause to feel anxious: *I am disturbed by the document* | [as *adj.*] (**disturbing**) *disturbing unemployment figures.* ■ (often **be disturbed**) interrupt or intrude on (someone) when they want privacy or secrecy. —**dis·turb·er** *n.* —**dis·turb·ing·ly** *adv.*

dis·tur·bance /dis'tərbəns/ ▸*n.* the interruption of a settled and peaceful condition. ■ a breakdown of peaceful and law-abiding behavior; a riot. ■ the disruption of healthy functioning: *mental disturbance.* ■ *Law* interference with rights or property; molestation.

dis·sul·fide /dī'səl,fīd/ (*Brit.* **di·sul·phide**) ▸*n. Chem.* a sulfide containing two atoms of sulfur in its molecule or empirical formula.

dis·un·ion /dis'yōōnyən/ ▸*n.* the breaking up of something such as a federation: *his rejection of disunion was consistent with his nationalism.* —**dis·u·ni·ty** /-'yōōnitē/ *n.*

dis·use /dis'yōōs/ ▸*n.* the state of not being used.

ditch /dicH/ ▸*n.* a narrow channel dug in the ground, typically used for drainage alongside a road or the edge of a field.
▸*v.* [*tr.*] **1** provide with ditches: *he was praised for ditching the coastal areas.* ■ [*intr.*] make or repair ditches: [as *n.*] (**ditching**) *they would have to pay for hedging and ditching.* **2** *inf.* get rid of; give up: *plans for the road were ditched following a public inquiry.* ■ *inf.* end a relationship with (someone) peremptorily; abandon. ■ *inf.* be truant from (school or another obligation). **3** *inf.* bring (an aircraft) down on water in an emergency. ■ [*intr.*] (of an aircraft) make a forced landing on water: *the aircraft was obliged to ditch off the North African coast.* ■ derail (a train). —**ditch·er** *n.*

dith·er /'dithər/ ▸*v.* [*intr.*] be indecisive: *he was dithering about the election date.*
▸*n.* **1** *inf.* indecisive behavior. **2** a state of agitation: *I'm in a dither.* —**dith·er·er** *n.* —**dith·er·y** *adj.*

dit·sy ▸*adj.* variant spelling of DITZY.

dit·to /'ditō/ ▸ **1** used in accounts and lists to indicate that an item is repeated (often indicated by ditto marks under the word or figure to be repeated). ■ *inf.* used to indicate that something already said is applicable a second time: *if one folds his arms, so does the other; if one crosses his legs, ditto.* **2** a similar thing; a duplicate.

dit·to marks ▸*pl. n.* two apostrophes (") representing "ditto."

dit·ty /'ditē/ ▸*n.* (*pl.* **-ties**) a short simple song: *a lovely little music-hall ditty.*

ditz /dits/ ▸*n. inf.* a scatterbrained person.

dit·zy /'ditsē/ (also **dit·sy**) ▸*adj. inf.* silly or scatterbrained. —**dit·zi·ness** *n.*

di·u·re·sis /,dīyə'rēsis/ ▸*n. Med.* increased or excessive production of urine.

di·u·ret·ic /,dīyə'retik/ *Med.* ▸*adj.* (chiefly of drugs) causing increased urination.
▸*n.* a diuretic drug.

di·ur·nal /dī'ərnl/ ▸*adj.* **1** of or during the day. ■ *Zool.* (of animals) active in the daytime. ■ *Bot.* (of flowers) open only during the day. **2** daily; of each day: *diurnal rhythms.* —**di·ur·nal·ly** *adv.*

Div. ▸*abbr.* ■ Division. ■ divorced.

di·va /'dēvə/ ▸*n.* a famous female opera singer. ■ a female singer who has enjoyed great popular success: *a pop diva.* ■ an admired, glamorous, or distinguished woman. ■ a haughty, spoiled woman.

di·va·lent /dī'vālənt/ ▸*adj. Chem.* having a valence of two.

di·van ▸*n.* **1** /di'van; 'dī,van/ a long low sofa without a back or arms, typically placed against a wall. **2** /di'van; -'vän/ *hist.* a legislative body, council chamber, or court of justice in the Ottoman Empire or elsewhere in the Middle East.

di·var·i·cate /dī'vari,kāt; di-/ ▸*v.* [*intr.*] *technical* or *poetic/lit.* stretch or spread apart; diverge widely: *her crow's feet are divaricating like deltas.* —**di·var·i·ca·tion** /-,vari'kāsHən/ *n.*

dive /dīv/ ▸*v.* (*past* **dived** or **dove** /dōv/; *past part.* **dived**) [*intr.*] **1** plunge head first into water: *she walked to the deep end, then dived in* | *he dove off the bridge for a dare.* ■ move quickly or suddenly in a specified direction: *he dived for cover* | [as *adj.*] (**diving**) *he attempted a diving catch.* ■ (of an aircraft or bird) plunge steeply downward through the air. ■ (**dive into**) occupy oneself suddenly and enthusiastically with (a meal or an engrossing subject or activity). ■ *fig.* (of prices or profits) drop suddenly: *profits dived by 61 percent.* ■ *inf.* put one's hand quickly into something, esp. a pocket or purse, in order to find something. **2** swim under water using breathing equipment. ■ (of a fish, a submarine, or a vessel used for underwater exploration) go to a deeper level in water.
▸*n.* **1** an act of diving, in particular: ■ a plunge head first into water, esp. from a diving board in a way prescribed for competition. ■ an instance of swimming or exploring under water with breathing equipment: *divers should have a good intake of fluid before each dive.* ■ an act of going deeper under water by a fish, submarine, or diving vessel. ■ a steep descent by an aircraft or bird. See also NOSEDIVE. ■ a sudden movement in a specified direction: *she made a dive for the fridge.* ■ *fig.* a sudden and significant fall in prices or profits. **2** *inf.* a disreputable nightclub or bar.
▸ □ **dive in** help oneself to food. □ **take a dive** *Boxing* pretend to be knocked out. ■ (of prices, hopes, fortunes, etc.) fall suddenly.

dive-bomb ▸*v.* [*tr.*] bomb (a target) while diving steeply downward in an aircraft. ■ (of a bird or flying insect) attack (something) by swooping down on it: *the crow dive-bombed the vulture.* —**dive-bomb·er** *n.*

div·er /'dīvər/ ▸*n.* a person or animal that dives, in particular: ■ a person who dives as a sport. ■ a person who wears a diving suit to work under water: *a police diver.*

di·verge /di'vərj; dī-/ ▸*v.* [*intr.*] **1** (of a road, route, or line) separate from another route, esp. a main one, and go in a different direction. ■ develop in a different direction: *howler and spider monkeys diverged from a common ancestor.* ■ (of an opinion, theory, approach, etc.) differ markedly: [as *adj.*] (**diverging**) *studies from different viewpoints yield diverging conclusions.* ■ deviate from a set course or standard: *suddenly he diverged from his text.* **2** *Math.* (of a series) increase indefinitely as more terms are added. ▷mid 17th cent.: from medieval Latin *divergere*, from Latin *dis-* 'in two ways' + *vergere* 'to turn or incline.' —**di·ver·gence** *n.* —**di·ver·gent** *adj.*

di·vers /'dīvərz/ ▸*adj. archaic* or *poetic/lit.* of varying types; several: *in divers places.*

di·verse /di'vərs; dī-/ ▸*adj.* showing a great deal of variety. ■ (of two or more things) markedly different from one another: *subjects as diverse as architecture, language teaching, and the physical sciences.* —**di·verse·ly** *adv.*

di·ver·si·fy /di'vərsi,fī; dī-/ ▸*v.* (**-fies, -fied**) make or become more diverse or varied: [*intr.*] *the trilobites diversified into a great number of species* | [*tr.*] *they seek to diversify their approach to teaching* | [as *adj.*] (**diversified**) *a diversified economy.* ■ [*intr.*] (of a company) enlarge or vary its range of products or field of operation: *the company expanded rapidly and diversified into computers.* ■ [*tr.*] (often as *adj.*) (**diversified**) enlarge or vary the range of products or the field of operation of (a company): *the rise of the diversified corporation.* ■ [*tr.*] spread (investment) over several enterprises or products in order to reduce the risk of loss: *a prudent investor should diversify holdings.* —**di·ver·si·fi·ca·tion** /-,vərsifi'kāsHən/ *n.*

di·ver·sion /di'vərzHən; dī-/ ▸*n.* **1** an instance of turning aside from its course: *a diversion of resources.* ■ *Brit.* an alternative route for traffic; a detour: *the road was closed and diversions put into operation.* **2** an activity that diverts the mind from tedious or serious concerns; a recreation or pastime: *our chief diversion was reading.* ■ something intended to distract someone's attention from something more important: *a subsidiary raid was carried out on the airfield to create a diversion.* —**di·ver·sion·ar·y** /-,nerē/ *adj.*

di·ver·si·ty /di'vərsitē; dī-/ ▸*n.* (*pl.* **-ties**) the state of being diverse; variety: *there was considerable diversity in the style of the reports.* ■ a range of different things: *allow a diversity of views to be printed.*

di·vert /di'vərt; dī-/ ▸*v.* [*tr.*] **1** cause (someone or something) to change course or turn from one direction to another: *diverting water from the river to irrigate farmland.* ■ [*intr.*] (of a vehicle or person) change course: *an aircraft has diverted and will be with you shortly.* ■ reallocate (something, esp. money or resources) to a different purpose: *savings diverted into promotions.* **2** distract (someone or their attention) from something. ■ (usu. as *adj.*) (**diverting**) draw the attention of (someone) away from tedious or serious concerns; entertain or amuse: *a diverting book.* —**di·vert·er** *n.* —**di·vert·ing·ly** *adv.*

di·ver·tic·u·lum /,dīvər'tikyələm/ ▸*n.* (*pl.* **-la** /-lə/) *Anat.* & *Zool.* a blind tube leading from a cavity or passage. ■ *Med.* an abnormal sac or pouch formed at a weak point in the wall of the alimentary tract. —**di·ver·tic·u·lo·sis** /-,tikyə'lōsis/ *n.*

di·ver·ti·men·to /di,vərtə'mentō/ ▸*n.* (*pl.* **-men·ti** /-'mentē/ or **-men·tos**) *Mus.* a light and entertaining composition, typically one in the form of a suite for chamber orchestra.

di·ver·tisse·ment /di'vərtismənt/ ▸*n.* a minor entertainment or diversion. ■ *Ballet* a short dance within a ballet that displays a dancer's technical skill without advancing the plot or character development.

di·vest /di'vest; dī-/ ▶ *v.* [*tr.*] deprive (someone) of power, rights, or possessions. ■ deprive (something) of a particular quality: *he has divested the original play of its charm.* ■ [*intr.*] rid oneself of something that one no longer wants or requires, such as a business interest or investment: *it appears easier to carry on in the business than to divest* | *the government is divesting itself of state holdings.* ■ *dated* or *humorous* relieve (someone) of something being worn or carried: *she divested him of his coat.* —**di·vest·ment** *n.*

di·vide /di'vīd/ ▶ *v.* **1** separate or be separated into parts: [*tr.*] *magazines can be divided into a number of categories* | [*intr.*] *the cell clusters began to divide rapidly.* ■ [*tr.*] separate (something) into portions and distribute a share to each of a number of people: *Jack divided up the rest of the cash* | *the property was divided among his heirs.* ■ [*tr.*] allocate (different parts of one's time, attention, or efforts) to different activities or places: *the last years of her life were divided between Bermuda and Paris.* ■ [*tr.*] form a boundary between (two people or things). ■ (of a legislative assembly) separate or be separated into two groups for voting: [*intr.*] *the House divided: 287 for, 196 against.* **2** disagree or cause to disagree: [*tr.*] *the question had divided Frenchmen since the Revolution* | [as *adj.*] (**divided**) *a divided party leadership* | [*intr.*] *cities where politicians frequently divide along racial lines.* **3** [*tr.*] *Math.* find how many times (a number) contains another: *36 divided by 2 equals 18* | [*intr.*] *the program helps children to multiply and divide quickly and accurately.* ■ [*intr.*] (of a number) be susceptible to division without a remainder: *30 does not divide by 8.* ■ find how many times (a number) is contained in another: *divide 4 into 20.* ■ [*intr.*] (of a number) be contained in a number without a remainder: *3 divides into 15.*

▶ *n.* a wide divergence between two groups, typically producing tension or hostility: *there was still a profound cultural divide between the parties.* ■ a boundary between two things. ■ a ridge or line of high ground forming the division between two valleys or river systems.

▶ □ **divide and conquer** the policy of maintaining control over one's subordinates by encouraging dissent between them. □ **divided against itself** (of a group) split by factional interests.

div·i·dend /'divi,dend/ ▶ *n.* **1** a sum of money paid regularly (typically quarterly) by a company to its shareholders out of its profits (or reserves). ■ a payment divided among a number of people, e.g., members of a cooperative or creditors of an insolvent estate. ■ an individual's share of a dividend. ■ (**dividends**) a benefit from an action or policy: *persistence pays dividends.* **2** *Math.* a number to be divided by another number.

di·vid·er /di'vīdər/ ▶ *n.* **1** a person or thing that divides a whole into parts. ■ an issue on which opinions are divided: *the big divider was still nuclear weapons.* ■ (also **room divider**) a screen or piece of furniture that divides a room into two parts. **2** (**dividers**) a measuring compass, esp. one with a screw for making fine adjustments.

div·i·na·tion /,divə'nāSHən/ ▶ *n.* the practice of seeking knowledge of the future or the unknown by supernatural means. —**di·vin·a·to·ry** /di-'vinə,tôrē/ *adj.*

di·vine¹ /di'vīn/ ▶ *adj.* (**-vin·er, -vin·est**) **1** of, from, or like God or a god: *heroes with divine powers* | *paintings of shipwrecks being prevented by divine intervention.* ■ devoted to God; sacred: *divine liturgy.* **2** *inf., dated* excellent; delightful: *that plum tasted divine* | *he had the most divine smile.*

▶ *n.* (**the Divine**) providence or God. —**di·vine·ly** *adv.* —**di·vine·ness** *n.*

di·vine² ▶ *v.* [*tr.*] discover (something) by guesswork or intuition. ■ have supernatural or magical insight into (future events): *divining the future in chicken entrails.* ■ discover (water) by dowsing. —**di·vin·er** *n.*

Di·vine Of·fice ▶ *n.* see OFFICE (sense 4).

di·vin·ing rod ▶ *n.* a stick or rod used for dowsing.

di·vin·i·ty /di'vinitē/ ▶ *n.* (*pl.* **-ies**) **1** the state or quality of being divine: *Christ's divinity.* ■ the study of religion; theology: *a doctor of divinity.* ■ a divine being; a god or goddess: *Roman divinities.* ■ (**the Divinity**) God. **2** a fluffy, creamy candy made with stiffly beaten egg whites.

di·vis·i·ble /di'vizəbəl/ ▶ *adj.* capable of being divided. ■ *Math.* (of a number) capable of being divided by another number without a remainder: *24 is divisible by 4.* —**di·vis·i·bil·i·ty** /-,vizə'bilitē/ *n.*

di·vi·sion /di'viZHən/ ▶ *n.* **1** the action of separating something into parts, or the process of being separated: *the division of the land* | *cell division.* ■ the distribution of something separated into parts: *the division of his estates between the two branches of his family.* ■ an instance of members of a legislative body separating into two groups to vote for or against a bill. ■ the action of splitting the roots of a perennial plant into parts to be replanted separately, as a means of propagation. **2** disagreement between two or more groups, typically producing

tension or hostility: *ethnic and cultural divisions.* **3** the process or skill of dividing one number by another. See also LONG DIVISION. ■ *Math.* the process of dividing a matrix, vector, or other quantity by another under specific rules to obtain a quotient. **4** each of the parts into which something is divided: *the main divisions of the book.* ■ a major unit or section of an organization, typically one handling a particular kind of work: *a retail division.* ■ a group of army brigades or regiments: *an infantry division.* ■ a number of teams or competitors grouped together in a sport for competitive purposes according to such characteristics as ability, size, or geographic location. ■ a part of a county, country, or city defined for administrative or political purposes. ■ *Bot.* a principal taxonomic category that ranks above class and below kingdom, equivalent to the phylum in zoology. ■ *Zool.* any subsidiary category between major levels of classification. **5** a partition that divides two groups or things. —**di·vi·sion·al** /-zHənl/ *adj.*

▶ □ **division of labor** the assignment of different parts of a process or task to different people in order to improve efficiency.

di·vi·sive /di'vīsiv/ ▶ *adj.* tending to cause disagreement or hostility between people: *the highly divisive issue of abortion.* —**di·vi·sive·ly** *adv.* —**di·vi·sive·ness** *n.*

di·vi·sor /di'vīzər/ ▶ *n. Math.* a number by which another number is to be divided. ■ a number that divides into another without a remainder: *the greatest common divisor.*

di·vorce /di'vôrs/ ▶ *n.* the legal dissolution of a marriage by a court or other competent body: *her divorce from her first husband* | [as *adj.*] *divorce proceedings.* ■ a legal decree dissolving a marriage. ■ a separation between things that were or ought to be connected: *the bitter divorce between company and shareholders.*

▶ *v.* [*tr.*] legally dissolve one's marriage with (someone): *he divorced his first wife* | [as *adj.*] (**divorced**) *a divorced couple* | [*intr.*] *they divorced eight years later.* ■ separate or dissociate (something) from something else: *we knew how to divorce an issue from an individual.* ■ (**divorce oneself from**) distance or dissociate oneself from (something). —**di·vorce·ment** *n.*

di·vor·cée /divôr'sā -'sē/ (also **di·vor·cee**) ▶ *n.* a divorced woman.

div·ot /'divət/ ▶ *n.* a piece of turf cut out of the ground by a golf club in making a stroke.

di·vulge /di'vəlj; dī-/ ▶ *v.* [*tr.*] make known (private or sensitive information). —**div·ul·ga·tion** /,divəl'gāSHən/ *n.* —**di·vul·gence** /-jəns/ *n.*

div·vy /'divē/ *inf.* ▶ *v.* (**div·vies, div·vied**) [*tr.*] divide up and share: *they divvied up the proceeds.*

Dix·ie ▶ an informal name for the southern U.S. states.

▶ □ **whistle Dixie** engage in unrealistic fantasies; waste one's time: *until you nail down the facts, you're just whistling Dixie.*

Dix·ie·land /'diksē,land/ ▶ *n.* a kind of jazz with a strong two-beat rhythm and collective improvisation that originated in New Orleans in the early 20th century.

diz·zy /'dizē/ ▶ *adj.* (**-zi·er, -zi·est**) having or involving a sensation of spinning around and losing one's balance. ■ causing such a sensation: *dizzy flashes of light.* ■ *inf.* (of a woman) silly but attractive.

▶ *v.* (**-zies, -zied**) [*tr.*] [usu. as *adj.*] (**dizzying**) make (someone) feel unsteady, confused, or amazed: *the dizzying rate of change* | *her nearness dizzied him.* ▷Old English *dysig* 'foolish'; related to Low German *dusig, dösig* 'giddy' and Old High German *tusic* 'foolish, weak.' —**diz·zi·ly** /'dizəlē/ *adv.* —**diz·zi·ness** *n.*

DJ ▶ *n.* a disc jockey. ■ a person who uses samples of recorded music to make techno, rap, or dance music.

DL ▶ *abbr.* ■ *Football* defensive lineman. ■ disabled list.

dl ▶ *abbr.* deciliter(s).

DM (also **D-mark**) ▶ *abbr.* Deutschmark.

dm ▶ *abbr.* decimeter(s).

DMZ ▶ *abbr.* demilitarized zone, an area from which warring parties agree to remove their military forces.

DNA ▶ *n. Biochem.* deoxyribonucleic acid, a self-replicating material present in nearly all living organisms as the main constituent of chromosomes. It is the carrier of genetic information.

DNA fin·ger·print·ing (also **DNA profiling**) ▶ *n.* the analysis of DNA from samples of body tissues or fluids in order to identify individuals.

do¹ /dōō/ ▶ *v.* (**does** /dəz/; *past* **did** /did/; *past part.* **done** /dən/) **1** [*tr.*] perform (an action, the precise nature of which is often unspecified): *something must be done about traffic* | *she knew what she was doing* | *what can I do for you?* ■ perform (a particular task): *Dad always did the cooking on*

Sundays. ■ work on (something) to bring it to completion or to a required state: *she's the secretary and does the publicity.* ■ make or have available and provide: *many hotels don't do single rooms at all.* ■ solve; work out: *Joe was doing sums aloud.* ■ cook (food) to completion or to a specified degree: *the pie is done.* ■ (often in questions) work at for a living: *what does she do?* ■ produce or give a performance of (a particular play, opera, etc.): *we're doing* Macbeth *next month.* ■ perform (a particular role, song, etc.) or imitate (a particular person) in order to entertain people: *he not only does Schwarzenegger and Groucho, he becomes them.* ■ *inf.* take (a narcotic drug): *he doesn't do drugs.* ■ attend to (someone): *the barber said he'd do me next.* ■ *vulgar slang* have sexual intercourse with. ■ (**do it**) *inf.* have sexual intercourse. ■ (**do it**) *inf.* urinate; defecate. **2** [*tr.*] achieve or complete, in particular: ■ travel (a specified distance): *one car had done 112,000 miles.* ■ travel at (a specified speed): *I was speeding, doing seventy-five.* ■ make (a particular journey): *last time I did New York–Philadelphia round trip it was 80 bucks.* ■ achieve (a specified sales figure): *our CD did about a million worldwide.* ■ [*tr.*] *inf.* visit as a tourist, esp. in a superficial or hurried way: *the tourists are allotted only a day to "do"* Verona. ■ spend (a specified period of time), typically in prison or in a particular occupation: *he did five years.* ■ [*intr.*] *inf.* finish: *you must sit there and wait till I'm done* | *we're done arguing.* ■ (**be done**) be over: *when the day is done.* ■ (**be/have done with**) give up concern for: have finished with: *I'll sell the place and* **have done with it. 3** [*intr.*] act or behave in a specified way: *free to do as they please* | *you did well.* ■ make progress or perform in a specified way; get on: *the team's doing badly* | *how are you doing?* ■ [*tr.*] have a specified effect on: *the walk will do me good.* ■ [*tr.*] result in: *the years of stagnation did a lot of harm to the younger generation.* **4** [*intr.*] be suitable or acceptable: *if he's anything like you, he'll do.* **5** [*tr.*] *inf.* beat up; kill: *he's the guy who did Joey.* ■ (usu. **be done**) ruin: *once you falter, you're done.* ■ rob (a place): *we could easily do this joint.*

▶*phrasal v.* □ **do away with** *inf.* put an end to; remove. ■ kill. □ **do by** *dated* treat or deal with in a specified way: *she did well by them.* □ **do for 1** *inf.* defeat, ruin, or kill: *without that contract we're done for.* **2** suffice for: *the old version will do for now.* □ **do something** (or **nothing**) **for** *inf.* enhance (or detract from) the appearance or quality of: *that scarf does nothing for you.* □ **do someone in** *inf.* kill someone. ■ (usu. **be done in**) *inf.* tire someone out: *after hiking, I was done in.* □ **do someone out of** *inf.* deprive someone of (something) in an underhanded or unfair way. □ **do something over 1** *inf.* repeat something: *do it over until you learn it.* **2** *inf.* decorate or furnish a room or building. □ **do someone up** (usu. **be done up**) dress someone up, esp. in an elaborate or impressive way: *Agnes was all done up in a slinky black number.* □ **do something up** (usu. **be done up**) arrange one's hair in a particular way, esp. so as to be pulled back from one's face or shoulders: *her dark hair was done up in a pony tail.* ■ wrap something up: *unwieldy packages all done up with twine.* □ **do with** would find useful or would like to have or do: *I could do with a cup of coffee.* □ **do without** (usu. **can do without**) manage without: *she could do without cigarettes for a day.* ■ *inf.* would prefer not to have: *I can do without your complaints.*

▶*aux. v.* **1** used before a verb (except *be, can, may, ought, shall, will*) in questions and negative statements: *do you have any pets?* | *did he see me?* | *I don't smoke* | *it does not matter.* ■ used to make tag questions: *you write poetry, don't you?* | *I never seem to say the right thing, do I?* ■ used in negative commands: *don't be silly* | *do not forget.* **2** used to refer to a verb already mentioned: *he looks better than he did before* | *you wanted to enjoy yourself, and you did.* **3** used to give emphasis to a positive verb: *he did look tired.* ■ used in positive commands to give polite encouragement: *do tell me!* | *do sit down.* **4** used with inversion of a subject and verb when an adverbial phrase begins a clause for emphasis: *not only did the play close, the theater closed.*

▶*n.* (*pl.* **dos** or **do's**) **1** (also **'do**) *inf.* short for HAIRDO. **2** *inf.* a party or other social event: *the soccer club Christmas do.*

▶ □ **be to do with** be concerned or connected with: *the problems are usually to do with family tension.* □ **do a** —— *inf.* behave in a manner characteristic of (a specified person): *he did a Garbo after his flop in the play.* □ **do battle** enter into a conflict. □ **don't** —— **me** *inf.* do not use the word —— to me: *"Don't morning me. Where the hell've you been all night?"* □ **do or die** persist, even if death is the result. ■ used to describe a critical situation where one's actions may result in victory or defeat: *the 72nd hole was do or die.* □ **dos and don'ts** rules of behavior: *political dos and don'ts.* □ **do well for oneself** become successful or wealthy. □ **have (got)** —— **to do with** be connected with (someone or something) to the extent specified: *half the country believed rock 'n' roll had something to do with national decline.* □ **have nothing to do with** have no contact or dealings with. ■ be no business or concern of: *it's my decision—it has nothing to do with you.* ■ be unconnected with: *he says his departure has nothing to do with the calls for his resignation.* □ **it isn't done** used to

express the speaker's opinion that something contravenes custom, opinion, or propriety: *you may be rude at home, but here it isn't done.* □ **it won't do** used to express the speaker's opinion that someone's behavior is unsatisfactory and cannot be allowed to continue. □ **no you don't** *inf.* used to indicate that one intends to prevent someone from doing what they were about to do. □ **that does it!** *inf.* used to indicate that one will not tolerate something any longer.

do² /dō/ ▶*n. Mus.* (in solmization) the first and eighth note of a major scale. ■ the note C in the fixed-do system.

do. *dated* ▶*abbr.* ditto.

DOA ▶*abbr.* dead on arrival, used to describe a person who is declared dead immediately upon arrival at a hospital.

do·a·ble /'dooəbəl/ ▶*adj. inf.* within one's powers; feasible: *none of the jobs were fun, but they were doable.*

Do·ber·man /'dōbərmən/ (also **Do·ber·man pin·scher** /'pinCHər/) ▶*n.* a large dog of a German breed with powerful jaws and a smooth coat, typically black with tan markings.

doc /däk/ *inf.* ▶*abbr.* ■ doctor. ■ *Comput.* document.

do·cent /'dōsənt/ ▶*n.* **1** a person who acts as a guide, typically on a voluntary basis, in a museum, art gallery, or zoo. **2** (in certain universities and colleges) a member of the teaching staff immediately below professorial rank.

doc·ile /'däsəl/ ▶*adj.* ready to accept control or instruction; submissive. —**doc·ile·ly** *adv.* —**do·cil·i·ty** /dä'silitē/ *n.*

dock¹ /däk/ ▶*n.* a structure extending alongshore or out from the shore into a body of water, to which boats may be moored. ■ an enclosed area of water in a port for the loading, unloading, and repair of ships. ■ (**docks**) a group of such enclosed areas of water along with the wharves and buildings near them. ■ (also **loading dock**) a platform for loading or unloading trucks or freight trains.

▶*v.* [*intr.*] (of a ship) tie up at a dock, esp. in order to load or unload passengers or cargo: *the ship docked at San Francisco.* ■ [*tr.*] bring (a ship or boat) into such a place: *the riverbank where the fur traders docked their boats.* ■ (of a spacecraft) join with a space station or another spacecraft in space. ■ attach (a piece of equipment) to another.

dock² ▶*v.* [*tr.*] (usu. **be docked**) deduct (something, esp. an amount of money): *their wages are docked for public displays of affection* | *he will be docked an hour's pay.* ■ cut short (an animal's tail): *the dogs had their tails docked.* ■ cut short the tail of (an animal): *the dog had been docked.*

dock³ ▶*n.* (usu. **the dock**) the enclosure in a criminal court where a defendant is placed.

▶ □ **in the dock** (of a defendant) on trial in court.

dock⁴ ▶*n.* a coarse weed (genus *Rumex*, family Polygonaceae) of temperate regions, with inconspicuous greenish or reddish flowers.

dock·age /'däkij/ ▶*n.* accommodation or berthing of ships at docks. ■ the charge made for using docks.

dock·et /'däkit/ ▶*n.* **1** a calendar or list of cases for trial or people having cases pending. ■ an agenda or list of things to be done. **2** a document or label listing the contents of a package or delivery.

▶*v.* (**dock·et·ed, dock·et·ing**) [*tr.*] (usu. **be docketed**) **1** enter (a case or suit) onto a list of those due to be heard. **2** mark (goods or a package) with a document or label listing the contents. ■ annotate (a letter or document) with a brief summary of its contents.

dock·side /'däk,sīd/ ▶*n.* the area immediately adjacent to a dock.

dock·yard /'däk,yärd/ ▶*n.* an area or establishment with docks and equipment for repairing and maintaining ships.

doc·tor /'däktər/ ▶*n.* **1** a qualified practitioner of medicine; a physician. ■ a qualified dentist or veterinary surgeon. ■ *inf.* a person who gives advice or makes improvements: *the script doctor rewrote the original.* **2** (**Doctor**) a person who holds a doctorate: *he was made a Doctor of Divinity.* ■ *archaic* a teacher or learned person. **3** an artificial fishing fly.

▶*v.* [*tr.*] **1** change the content or appearance of (a document or picture) in order to deceive; falsify. ■ change the content of (a drink, food, or substance) by adding strong or harmful ingredients. ■ *Baseball* tamper with (a ball) so as to affect its movement when pitched. **2** [usu. as *n.*] (**doctoring**) *inf.* treat (someone) medically. —**doc·tor·ly** *adj.*

doc·tor·al /'däktərəl/ ▶*adj.* relating to or designed to achieve a doctorate: *a doctoral dissertation.*

doc·tor·ate /'däktərit/ ▶*n.* the highest degree awarded by a graduate school or other approved educational organization.

doc·tri·naire /,däktrə'ner/ ▶*adj.* seeking to impose a doctrine in all circumstances without regard to practical considerations.

▶*n.* a person who seeks to impose a theory in such a way. —**doc·tri·nair·ism** /-,izəm/ *n.*

doc·tri·nal /'däktrənl/ ▸*adj.* concerned with a doctrine or doctrines: *doctrinal disputes.* —**doc·tri·nal·ly** *adv.*

doc·trine /'däktrin/ ▸*n.* a belief or set of beliefs held and taught by a church, political party, or other group. ■ a stated principle of government policy, mainly in foreign or military affairs: *the Monroe Doctrine.* ▷late Middle English: from Old French, from Latin *doctrina* 'teaching, learning,' from *doctor* 'teacher,' from *docere* 'teach.'

doc·u·dra·ma /'däkyə,drämə/ ▸*n.* a dramatized television movie based on real events.

doc·u·ment ▸*n.* /'däkyəmənt/ a piece of written, printed, or electronic matter that provides information or evidence or that serves as an official record.
▸*v.* /'däkyə,ment/ [*tr.*] record (something) in written, photographic, or other form: *the photographer spent years documenting the lives of miners.* ■ support or accompany with documentation. —**doc·u·ment·a·ble** /,däkyə'mentəbəl/ *adj.* —**doc·u·men·tal** /,däkyə'mentl/ *adj.* —**doc·u·ment·er** /-,mentər/ *n.*

doc·u·men·ta·ry /,däkyə'mentərē/ ▸*adj.* consisting of official pieces of written, printed, or other matter: *his book is based on documentary sources.* ■ (of a movie, a television or radio program, or photography) using pictures or interviews with people involved in real events to provide a factual record or report: *documentary shorts and feature films.*
▸*n.* (*pl.* **-ries**) a movie or a television or radio program that provides a factual record or report.

doc·u·men·ta·tion /,däkyəmen'tāSHən/ ▸*n.* **1** material that provides official information or evidence or that serves as a record: *you will have to complete the relevant documentation.* ■ the written specification and instructions accompanying a computer program or hardware. **2** the process of classifying and annotating texts, photographs, etc.

dod·der¹ /'dädər/ ▸*v.* [*intr.*] tremble or totter, typically because of old age: [as *adj.*] (**doddering**) *that doddering old fool.* —**dod·der·er** *n.* —**dod·der·y** *adj.*

dod·der² ▸*n.* a widely distributed parasitic climbing plant (genus *Cuscuta*) of the morning glory family, with leafless threadlike stems that are attached to the host plant by means of suckers.

do·dec·a·he·dron /dō,deka'hēdrən/ ▸*n.* (*pl.* **-drons** or **-dra** /-drə/) a three-dimensional shape having twelve plane faces, in particular a regular solid figure with twelve equal pentagonal faces. —**do·dec·a·he·dral** /-drəl/ *adj.*

dodge /däj/ ▸*v.* [*tr.*] **1** avoid (someone or something) by a sudden quick movement: *we ducked inside to dodge shrapnel.* ■ [*intr.*] move quickly to one side or out of the way: *Adam dodged between the cars.* ■ avoid (something) in a cunning or dishonest way: *she goes after those who dodge their duties.* **2** [often as *n.*] (**dodging**) *Photog.* expose (one area of a print) less than the rest during processing or enlarging.
▸*n.* a sudden quick movement to avoid someone or something. ■ a cunning trick or dishonest act, in particular one intended to avoid something unpleasant: *bartering can be seen as a tax dodge.* —**dodg·er** *n.*

dodg·y /'däjē/ ▸*adj.* (**dodg·i·er, dodg·i·est**) *Brit., inf.* dishonest or unreliable: *a dodgy secondhand car salesman.* ■ potentially dangerous: *activities like these could be dodgy for your health.* ■ of low quality.

do·do /'dōdō/ ▸*n.* (*pl.* **-os** or **-oes**) an extinct flightless bird (*Raphus cucullatus*, family Raphidae) with a stout body, stumpy wings, a large head, and a heavy hooked bill. ■ *inf.* an old-fashioned and ineffective person or thing.

DOE ▸*abbr.* Department of Energy.

doe /dō/ ▸*n.* a female deer. ■ a female of certain other animal species, such as hare, rabbit, rat, ferret, or kangaroo.

do·er /'dooər/ ▸*n.* the person who does something: *the doer of the action.* ■ a person who acts rather than merely talking or thinking.

does /dəz/ ▸ third person singular present of DO¹.

doe·skin /'dō,skin/ ▸*n.* leather made from the skin of a female fallow deer. ■ a fine satin-weave woolen cloth resembling such leather.

does·n't /'dəzənt/ ▸*contr.* of does not.

doff /däf; dôf/ ▸*v.* [*tr.*] *dated* remove (an item of clothing): *he doffed tie and jacket.* ■ tip (one's hat) as a greeting or token of respect.

dog /dôg/ ▸*n.* **1** a domesticated carnivorous mammal (*Canis familiaris*) that typically has a long snout, an acute sense of smell, and a barking, howling, or whining voice. The **dog family** (Canidae) also includes the wolves, coyotes, jackals, and foxes. ■ a wild animal of the dog family. ■ the male of an animal of the dog family, or of some other mammals,

such as the otter. ■ (in extended and metaphorical use) referring to behavior considered to be savage, dangerous, or wildly energetic: *he bit into it like a dog.* **2** *inf.* a person regarded as unpleasant, contemptible, or wicked (used as a term of abuse). ■ used to refer to a person of a specified kind in a tone of playful reproof, commiseration, or congratulation: *you lucky dog!* ■ used in various phrases to refer to someone who is abject or miserable, esp. because they have been treated harshly: *I make him work like a dog.* ■ *inf. offens.* a woman regarded as unattractive. ■ *inf.* a thing of poor quality; a failure: *a dog of a movie.* **3** a mechanical device for gripping. **4** (**dogs**) *inf.* feet: *my tired dogs.*
▸*v.* (**dogged, dogging**) [*tr.*] **1** follow (someone or their movements) closely and persistently: *photographers dog her every step.* ■ (of a problem) cause continual trouble for: *the committee has been dogged by controversy.* **2** (**dog it**) *inf.* act lazily; fail to try one's hardest. **3** grip (something) with a mechanical device.
▸ □ **dog eat dog** used to refer to a situation of fierce competition in which people are willing to harm each other in order to succeed. □ **a dog's age** *inf.* a very long time. □ **a dog's life** an unhappy existence, full of problems or unfair treatment. □ **go to the dogs** *inf.* deteriorate shockingly: *the country is going to the dogs.* □ **put on the dog** *inf.* behave in a pretentious or ostentatious way. □ **throw someone to the dogs** discard someone as worthless.

dog days ▸*pl. n.* the hottest period of the year. ■ a period of inactivity or sluggishness.

doge /dōj/ ▸*n. hist.* the chief magistrate of Venice or Genoa.

dog-ear ▸*v.* [*tr.*] fold down the corner of (a book or magazine), typically to mark a place.
▸*adj.* (**dog-eared**) (of an object made from paper) with the corners worn or battered with use.

dog·fight /'dôg,fīt/ ▸*n.* a close combat between military aircraft. ■ a ferocious struggle for supremacy between interested parties. ■ a fight between dogs, esp. one organized illegally for public entertainment.
▸*v.* engage in a dogfight. —**dog·fight·er** *n.*

dog·fish /'dôg,fiSH/ ▸*n.* (*pl.* same or **-fishes**) **1** a small sand-colored, long-tailed bottom-dwelling shark (*Scyliorhinus canicula*, family Scyliorhinidae). **2** a small shark that resembles or is related to the dogfish.

dog·ged /'dôgid/ ▸*adj.* having or showing tenacity and grim persistence: *dogged determination.* —**dog·ged·ly** *adv.* —**dog·ged·ness** *n.*

dog·ger·el /'dôgərəl; 'däg-/ ▸*n.* comic verse composed in irregular rhythm. ■ verse or words that are badly written or expressed.

dog·gie ▸*n.* variant spelling of DOGGY.

dog·gie bag ▸*n.* a bag used by a restaurant customer or party guest to take home leftover food, supposedly for their dog.

dog·gone /'dôg,gôn/ *inf.* ▸*adj.* used to express feelings of annoyance, surprise, or pleasure: *now just a doggone minute* | *it's doggone good to be home.*
▸*v.* [*tr.*] used to express surprise, irritation, or anger: *doggone it* if *I didn't see motivation in Joey!* | *I'll be doggoned if every fourth kid is affected.*

dog·gy /'dôgē/ ▸*adj.* of or like a dog: *his doggy brown eyes.*
▸*n.* (also **dog·gie**) (*pl.* **-gies**) a child's word for a dog. —**dog·gi·ness** *n.*

dog·house /'dôg,hous/ ▸*n.* a dog's kennel.
▸ □ **(be) in the doghouse** *inf., often humorous* (be) in mild or temporary disfavor.

do·gie /'dōgē/ ▸*n.* (*pl.* **-gies**) a motherless or neglected calf.

dog in the man·ger ▸*n.* a person who has no need of, or ability to use, a possession that would be of use or value to others, but who prevents others from having it.

dog·leg /'dôg,leg/ ▸*n.* a thing that bends sharply, in particular a sharp bend in a road or route. ■ *Golf* a hole at which the player cannot aim directly at the green from the tee.
▸*adj.* (also **dog-legged**) bent like a dog's hind leg.
▸*v.* (**-legged, -leg·ging**) [*intr.*] follow a sharply bending route: *Highway 60 now doglegs northwest toward Frankfort.*

dog·ma /'dôgmə/ ▸*n.* a principle or set of principles laid down by an authority as incontrovertibly true.

dog·mat·ic /dôg'matik/ ▸*adj.* inclined to lay down principles as incontrovertibly true. —**dog·mat·i·cal·ly** /-ik(ə)lē/ *adv.*

dog·ma·tism /'dôgmə,tizəm/ ▸*n.* the tendency to lay down principles as incontrovertibly true, without consideration of evidence or the opinions of others: *a culture of dogmatism and fanaticism.* —**dog·ma·tist** *n.*

Pronunciation Key ə *ago,* up; ər *over, fur;* a *hat;* ā *ate;* ä *car;* CH *chin;* e *let;* ē *see;* e(ə)r *air;* i *fit;* ī *by;* i(ə)r *ear;* NG *sing;* ō *go;* ô *law, for;* oi *toy;* ŏŏ *good;* ōō *goo;* ou *out;* SH *she;* TH *thin;* ŦH *then;* (h)w *why;* ZH *vision*

D

do·good·er /ˈdo͞o ˌgo͝odər/ ▶n. a well-meaning but unrealistic or interfering philanthropist or reformer. —**do·good** adj. & n. —**do·good·er·y** /-ərē/ n. —**do·good·ism** /-go͝od,izəm/ n.

dog pad·dle ▶n. an elementary swimming stroke like that of a swimming dog.
▶v. (**dog-paddle**) [intr.] swim using this stroke.

dog·sled /ˈdôgˌsled/ (also **dog sled**) ▶n. a sled designed to be pulled by dogs.
▶v. [intr.] [usu. as n.] (**dogsledding**) travel by dogsled: winter activities include cross-country skiing and dogsledding.

dog tag ▶n. a metal tag attached to a dog's collar, typically giving its name and owner's address. ■ inf. a soldier's metal identity tag, worn on a chain around the neck.

dog-tired ▶adj. extremely tired; worn out: he'd gone to bed dog-tired.

dog·wood /ˈdôgˌwo͝od/ ▶n. a shrub or small tree (genus Cornus) of north temperate regions that yields hard timber and is grown for its decorative foliage and colorful berries. ■ used in names of trees that resemble the dogwood or yield similar hard timber.

doi·ly /ˈdoilē/ ▶n. (pl. **-lies**) an ornamental mat, typically made of lace and placed under decorative objects. ■ a small ornamental napkin, typically placed under a cake or other sweet foods.

do·ing /ˈdo͞oiNG/ ▶n. **1** (usu. **doings**) the activities in which a particular person engages: the latest doings of television stars. ■ deeds; accomplishments: he didn't want to trumpet his doings on an open line. ■ social events. **2** effort; activity: it would take some doing to calm him down.
▶ □ **be someone's doing** be the creation or fault of the person named: he looked at Lisa as though it was all her doing.

do-it-your·self ▶adj. (of work, esp. building, painting, or decorating) done or to be done by an amateur at home. —**do-it-your·self·er** n.

Dol·by /ˈdôlbē; ˈdôl-/ ▶n. trademark an electronic noise-reduction system used in tape recording to reduce hiss. ■ an electronic system used to provide stereophonic sound for movie theaters and television sets.

dol·ce vi·ta /ˌdôlCHä ˈvētə/ ▶n. (usu. **la dolce vita**) a life of heedless pleasure and luxury.

dol·drums /ˈdôldrəmz; ˈdäl-; ˈdōl-/ ▶pl. n. (**the doldrums**) low spirits; a feeling of boredom or depression: my February doldrums. ■ a period of inactivity or a state of stagnation: the mortgage market has been in the doldrums for three years. ■ an equatorial region of the Atlantic Ocean with calms, sudden storms, and light unpredictable winds.

dole¹ /dōl/ ▶n. **1** (usu. **the dole**) chiefly Brit., inf. benefit paid by the government to the unemployed. ■ dated a charitable gift of food, clothes, or money. **2** poetic/lit. a person's lot or destiny.
▶v. [tr.] (**dole something out**) distribute shares of something.
▶ □ **on the dole** inf. registered as unemployed and receiving benefit from the government.

dole² ▶n. archaic or poetic/lit. sorrow; mourning.

dole·ful /ˈdōlfəl/ ▶adj. expressing sorrow; mournful: a doleful look. ■ causing grief or misfortune. —**dole·ful·ly** adv. —**dole·ful·ness** n.

doll /däl/ ▶n. a small model of a human figure, used as a child's toy. ■ inf. an attractive young woman, often with connotations of unintelligence and frivolity. ■ inf. an attractive young man. ■ a generous or considerate person: would you be a doll and set the table? ■ inf. used as an affectionate, sometimes offensive, form of address: hey, doll, wanna dance?
▶v. [tr.] (**doll someone up**) inf. dress someone or oneself smartly and attractively: I got all dolled up for a party. ■ (**doll something up**) inf. decorate or dress up something. ▷mid 16th cent. (denoting a mistress): nickname for the given name Dorothy. The sense 'small model of a human figure' dates from the late 17th cent.

dol·lar /ˈdälər/ ▶n. the basic monetary unit of the U.S., Canada, Australia, and certain countries in the Pacific, Caribbean, Southeast Asia, Africa, and South America. ▷from early Flemish or Low German daler, from German T(h)aler, short for Joachimsthaler, a coin from the silver mine of Joachimsthal ('Joachim's valley'), now Jáchymov in the Czech Republic. The term was later applied to a coin used in the Spanish-American colonies, which was also widely used in the British North American colonies at the time of the American Revolution, hence adopted as the name of the U.S. monetary unit in the late 18th cent.
▶ □ **dollars to doughnuts** inf. used to emphasize one's certainty: I'd bet dollars to doughnuts he's a medical student.

dol·lar sign (also **dollar mark**) ▶n. the sign $, representing a dollar.

doll·house /ˈdäl,hous/ ▶n. a miniature toy house used for playing with dolls.

dol·lop /ˈdäləp/ ▶n. inf. a shapeless mass or blob of something, esp. soft food: great dollops of cream | fig. a dollop of romance here and there.
▶v. (**-loped, -lop·ing**) [tr.] add (a shapeless mass or blob of something) without measuring: dollop some topping on each tart.

dol·ly /ˈdälē/ ▶n. (pl. **-lies**) **1** a child's word for a doll. ■ inf., dated an attractive and stylish young woman, usually with connotations of unintelligence. **2** a small platform on wheels used for holding heavy objects, typically film or television cameras.
▶v. (**-lies, -lied**) [intr.] (of a film or television camera) be moved on a mobile platform in a specified direction: the camera dollies back to reveal hundreds of people.

dol·man sleeve ▶n. a loose sleeve cut in one piece with the body of a garment.

dol·men /ˈdōlmən; ˈdäl-/ ▶n. a megalithic tomb with a large flat stone laid on upright ones, found chiefly in Britain and France.

dol·o·mite /ˈdälə,mīt; ˈdō-/ ▶n. a translucent mineral consisting of a carbonate of calcium and magnesium. ■ a sedimentary rock formed chiefly of this mineral. —**dol·o·mit·ic** /ˌdälə'mitik/ adj.

do·lor /ˈdōlər/ (Brit. **dolour**) ▶n. poetic/lit. a state of great sorrow or distress: they squatted, hunched in their habitual dolor.

dol·or·ous /ˈdōlərəs/ ▶adj. poetic/lit. feeling or expressing great sorrow or distress. —**dol·or·ous·ly** adv.

dol·phin /ˈdälfin; ˈdôl-/ ▶n. a small gregarious and intelligent toothed whale that typically has a beaklike snout and a curved fin on the back. Dolphins inhabit seas (family Delphinidae) and rivers (family Platanistidae). ■ a dolphinlike creature depicted in heraldry or art, typically with an arched body. **2** (also **dol·phin·fish**) another term for MAHIMAHI. **3** a bollard, pile, or buoy for mooring. **4** a structure for protecting the pier of a bridge or other structure from collision with ships.

dolt /dōlt/ ▶n. a stupid person. —**dolt·ish** adj. —**dolt·ish·ly** adv. —**dolt·ish·ness** n.

do·main /dō'mān/ ▶n. an area of territory owned or controlled by a ruler or government: the French domains of the Plantagenets. ■ an estate or territory held in legal possession by a person or persons. ■ a specified sphere of activity or knowledge: the expanding domain of psychology. ■ Physics a discrete region of magnetism in ferromagnetic material. ■ Comput. a distinct subset of the Internet with addresses sharing a common suffix. ■ Math. the set of possible values of the independent variable or variables of a function. —**do·ma·ni·al** /-nēəl/ adj.

dome /dōm/ ▶n. **1** a rounded vault forming the roof of a building or structure, typically with a circular base. ■ the revolving openable hemispherical roof of an observatory. ■ [in names] a sports stadium with a domed roof. **2** a thing shaped like such a roof, in particular: ■ the rounded summit of a hill or mountain: the great dome of Mont Blanc. ■ a natural vault or canopy, such as that of the sky or trees. ■ Geol. a rounded uplifted landform or underground structure. ■ inf. the top of the head: a shaved dome. **3** poetic/lit. a stately building.
▶v. [tr.] [usu. as adj.] (**domed**) cover with or shape as a dome: a domed stadium. ■ [intr.] [often as n.] (**doming**) (of stratified rock or a surface) become rounded in formation; swell. —**dome·like** /-ˌlīk/ adj.

do·mes·tic /də'mestik/ ▶adj. **1** of or relating to the running of a home or to family relations: domestic chores | domestic violence. ■ of or for use in the home rather than in an industrial or office environment: domestic appliances. ■ (of a person) fond of family life and running a home. ■ (of an animal) tame and kept by humans. **2** existing or occurring inside a particular country; not foreign or international.
▶n. **1** (also **domestic worker** or **domestic help**) a person who is paid to help with menial tasks such as cleaning. **2** a product not made abroad. —**do·mes·ti·cal·ly** /-ik(ə)lē/ adv.

do·mes·ti·cate /də'mesti,kāt/ ▶v. [tr.] (usu. **be domesticated**) tame (an animal) and keep it as a pet or for farm produce: mammals were first domesticated for their milk. ■ cultivate (a plant) for food. ■ humorous make (someone) fond of and good at home life and the tasks that it involves: you've quite domesticated him. —**do·mes·ti·ca·ble** /-kəbəl/ adj. —**do·mes·ti·ca·tion** /-ˌmesti'kāSHən/ n.

do·mes·tic·i·ty /ˌdōme'stisitē/ ▶n. home or family life.

do·mes·tic sci·ence ▶n. dated the study of household skills such as cooking or sewing, esp. as taught at school; home economics.

dom·i·cile /ˈdämə,sīl; ˈdō-; ˈdäməsəl/ (also **dom·i·cil** /ˈdäməsəl/) ▶n. formal or Law the country that a person treats as their permanent home, or lives in and has a substantial connection with. ■ a person's residence or home: the builder I've hired to renovate my new domicile. ■ the place at which a company or other body is registered, esp. for tax purposes.
▶v. (**be domiciled**) formal or Law treat a specified country as a permanent home: the tenant is domiciled in the U.S. ■ reside; be based: he was domiciled in a frame house on the outskirts of town.

dom·i·nant /ˈdämənənt/ ▶adj. most important, powerful, or influential: they are now in an even more dominant position in the market. ■ (of a high place or object) overlooking others. ■ *Genetics* relating to or denoting heritable characteristics that are controlled by genes that are expressed in offspring even when inherited from only one parent. Often contrasted with **RECESSIVE**. ■ *Ecol.* denoting the predominant species in a plant (or animal) community.

▶ *n.* a dominant thing, in particular: ■ *Genetics* a dominant trait or gene. ■ *Ecol.* a dominant species in a plant (or animal) community. ■ *Mus.* the fifth note of the diatonic scale of any key, or the key based on this, considered in relation to the key of the tonic. —**dom·i·nance** *n.* —**dom·i·nant·ly** *adv.*

dom·i·nate /ˈdäməˌnāt/ ▶ *v.* [*tr.*] (often **be dominated**) have a commanding influence on; exercise control over. ■ be the most important or conspicuous person or thing in. ■ (of something tall or high) have a commanding position over; overlook. —**dom·i·na·tion** *n.* —**dom·i·na·tor** /-ˌnātər/ *n.*

dom·i·na·tion /ˌdäməˈnāSHən/ ▶ *n.* the exercise of control or influence over someone or something, or the state of being so controlled.

dom·i·na·trix /ˌdäməˈnātriks/ ▶ *n.* (*pl.* **-tri·ces** /-trəˌsēz/ or **-trix·es**) a dominating woman, esp. one who takes the sadistic role in sadomasochistic sexual activities.

dom·i·neer /ˌdäməˈni(ə)r/ ▶ *v.* [*intr.*] [usu. as *adj.*] (**domineering**) assert one's will over another in an arrogant way. —**dom·i·neer·ing·ly** *adv.*

Do·min·i·can[1] /dəˈminikən/ ▶ *n.* a member of the Roman Catholic order of preaching friars founded by St. Dominic, or of a religious order for women founded on similar principles.

▶ *adj.* of or relating to St. Dominic or the Dominicans.

Do·min·i·can[2] ▶ *adj.* of or relating to the Dominican Republic or its people.

▶ *n.* a native or national of the Dominican Republic.

Do·min·i·can[3] ▶ *adj.* of or relating to the island of Dominica or its people.

▶ *n.* a native or national of the island of Dominica.

do·min·ion /dəˈminyən/ ▶ *n.* **1** sovereignty; control: *man's attempt to establish dominion over nature.* **2** (usu. **dominions**) the territory of a sovereign or government. ■ (**Dominion**) *hist.* each of the self-governing territories of the British Commonwealth.

dom·i·no /ˈdäməˌnō/ ▶ *n.* (*pl.* **-noes** or **-nos**) **1** any of 28 small oblong pieces marked typically with 0–6 dots (pips) in each half. ■ (**dominoes**) [treated as *sing.*] the game played with such pieces. **2** *hist.* a loose cloak, worn with a mask for the upper part of the face at masquerades.

dom·i·no the·o·ry ▶ *n.* the theory that a political event in one country will cause similar events in neighboring countries, like a falling domino causing an entire row of upended dominoes to fall.

dominoes

don[1] /dän/ ▶ *n.* **1** (**Don**) a Spanish title prefixed to a male forename. ■ a Spanish gentleman; a Spaniard. ■ *inf.* a high-ranking member of the Mafia. **2** a university teacher, esp. a senior member of a college at Oxford or Cambridge. —**don·ship** /-ˌSHip/ *n.*

don[2] ▶ *v.* (**donned**, **don·ning**) [*tr.*] put on (an item of clothing).

do·nate /ˈdōnāt; dōˈnāt/ ▶ *v.* [*tr.*] give (money or goods) for a good cause, for example to a charity: *the proceeds will be donated to an AIDS awareness charity.* ■ allow the removal of (blood or an organ) from one's body for transplantation, transfusion, or other use. —**do·na·tor** /ˈdōnātər/ *n.*

do·na·tion /dōˈnāSHən/ ▶ *n.* something that is given to a charity, esp. a sum of money. ■ the action of donating something.

done /dən/ ▶ past participle of **DO**[1].

▶ *v. inf.* used as a nonstandard past tense of **DO**[1]: *I done a lot of rodeoin'.* ■ *inf.* used with a standard past tense verb to indicate absoluteness or completion: *I done told you to zipper your lips.*

▶ *adj.* **1** carried out, completed, or treated in a particular way: *the path needed replacing and she wanted it done in asphalt.* ■ (of food) cooked thoroughly. ■ no longer happening or existing: *her hunting days were done.* **2** *inf.* socially acceptable: *therapy was **not the done thing** then.*

▶ *interj.* used to indicate that the speaker accepts the terms of an offer: *"I'll give ten to one he misses!" called Reilly. "Done," said the conductor.*

▶ □ **a done deal** a plan or project that has been finalized. □ **done for** *inf.* in a situation so bad that it is impossible to get out: *we'll all be done for.* □ **done in** *inf.* extremely tired.

do·nee /dōˈnē/ ▶ *n.* a person who receives a gift.

don·gle /ˈdäNGgəl; ˈdôNG-/ ▶ *n. Comput.* an electronic device that must be attached to a computer in order to use protected computer software.

don·jon /ˈdänjən; ˈdən-/ ▶ *n.* the great tower or innermost keep of a castle.

don·key /ˈdôNGkē; ˈdäNG-/ ▶ *n.* (*pl.* **-eys**) **1** a domesticated hoofed mammal (*Equus asinus*) of the horse family with long ears and a braying call, used as a beast of burden; an ass. **2** *inf.* a stupid or foolish person.

▶ □ **donkey's years** *inf.* a very long time.

do·nor /ˈdōnər/ ▶ *n.* a person who donates something, esp. money to a fund or charity. ■ a person who provides blood for transfusion, semen for insemination, or an organ or tissue for transplantation. ■ *Chem.* an atom or molecule that provides electrons in forming a coordinate bond.

don't /dōnt/ ▶ *contr.* of do not. ■ *inf.* does not: *she don't drink tea.*

do·nut /ˈdōˌnət/ ▶ *n.* variant spelling of **DOUGHNUT**.

doo·dad /ˈdo͞oˌdad/ ▶ *n.* a fancy article or trivial ornament. ■ a gadget, esp. one whose name the speaker does not know or cannot recall.

doo·dle /ˈdo͞odl/ ▶ *v.* [*intr.*] scribble absentmindedly. ■ engage in idle activity; dawdle: *they could attack while we're just doodling around.*

▶ *n.* a rough drawing made absentmindedly. —**doo·dler** /-d(ə)lər/ *n.*

doo·dle·bug /ˈdo͞odlˌbəg/ ▶ *n. inf.* the larva of an ant lion.

doo·hick·ey /ˈdo͞oˌhikē/ ▶ *n.* (*pl.* **-eys**) *inf.* a small object or gadget, esp. one whose name the speaker does not know or cannot recall.

doom /do͞om/ ▶ *n.* death, destruction, or some other terrible fate.

▶ *v.* [*tr.*] (usu. **be doomed**) condemn to certain destruction or death. ■ cause to have an unfortunate and inescapable outcome: *her plan was doomed to failure* | [as *adj.*] (**doomed**) *the story of their doomed love affair.*

dooms·day /ˈdo͞omzˌdā/ (also **domes·day**) ▶ *n.* the last day of the world's existence. ■ (in Christian belief) the day of the Last Judgment. ■ *fig.* a time or event of crisis or great danger: [as *adj.*] *in all the concern over greenhouse warming, one **doomsday scenario** stands out.*

▶ □ **till doomsday** *inf.* forever.

door /dôr/ ▶ *n.* a hinged, sliding, or revolving barrier at the entrance to a building, room, or vehicle, or in the framework of a cupboard. ■ a doorway. ■ used to refer to the distance from one building in a row to another: *they lived within three doors of each other.* ■ *fig.* a means of access, admission, or exit; a means to a specified end: *that audition was the door to all my successes.* ▷Old English *duru, dor,* of Germanic origin; related to Dutch *deur* 'door' and German *Tür* 'door,' *Tor* 'gate'; from an Indo-European root shared by Latin *foris* 'gate' and Greek *thura* 'door.'

▶ □ **close** (or **shut**) **the door on** (or **to**) exclude the opportunity for. □ **lay something at someone's door** regard someone as responsible for something. □ **leave the door open** ensure that there is still an opportunity for something. □ **open the door to** create an opportunity for. □ **out of doors** in or into the open air.

door·bell /ˈdôrˌbel/ ▶ *n.* a bell in a building that can be rung by visitors outside to signal their arrival.

door·frame /ˈdôrˌfrām/ (also **door frame**) ▶ *n.* the frame in a doorway into which a door is fitted.

door·keep·er /ˈdôrˌkēpər/ ▶ *n.* a person on duty at the entrance to a building.

door·knob /ˈdôrˌnäb/ ▶ *n.* a handle on a door that is turned to release the latch.

door knock·er ▶ *n.* a metal or wooden instrument hinged to a door and rapped by visitors to attract attention and gain entry.

door·man /ˈdôrˌman; -mən/ ▶ *n.* (*pl.* **-men**) a man such as a porter, bouncer, or janitor who is on duty at the entrance to a large building.

door·mat /ˈdôrˌmat/ ▶ *n.* a mat placed in a doorway, on which people can wipe their shoes on entering a building. ■ *fig.* a submissive person who allows others to dominate them.

door·nail /ˈdôrˌnāl/ ▶ *n.* a stud set in a door for strength or as an ornament.

▶ □ (**as**) **dead as a doornail** quite dead.

door prize ▶ *n.* a prize awarded by lottery to the holder of a ticket purchased or distributed at a dance, party, or other function.

door·step /ˈdôrˌstep/ ▶ *n.* a step leading up to the outer door of a house.

▶ □ **on one's** (or **the**) **doorstep** situated very close by.

door·stop /ˈdôrˌstäp/ (also **door·stop·per**) ▶ *n.* a fixed or heavy object that keeps a door open or stops it from banging against a wall. ■ *fig.* a heavy or bulky object (used esp. in reference to a thick book).

door·way /ˈdôrˌwā/ ▶ *n.* an entrance to a room or building through a door: *Beth stood there in the doorway* | *fig. the doorway to success.*

door·yard /ˈdôrˌyärd/ ▶ *n.* a yard or garden by the door of a house.

doo·zy /ˈdo͞ozē/ (also **doo·zie**) ▶ *n.* (*pl.* **-zies**) *inf.* something outstanding or unique of its kind: *it's gonna be a doozy of a black eye.*

Pronunciation Key ə *ago,* up; ər *over, fur;* a *hat;* ā *ate;* ä *car;* CH *chin;* e *let;* ē *see;* e(ə)r *air;* i *fit;* ī *by;* i(ə)r *ear;* NG *sing;* ō *go;* ô *law, for;* oi *toy;* o͞o *good;* o͞o *goo;* ou *out;* SH *she;* TH *thin;* T͟H *then;* (h)w *why;* ZH *vision*

dope /dōp/ ▸n. **1** inf. a drug taken illegally for recreational purposes, esp. marijuana or heroin. ■ a drug given to a racehorse or greyhound to inhibit or enhance its performance. ■ a drug taken by an athlete to improve performance: [as adj.] he failed a dope test. **2** inf. a stupid person. **3** inf. information about a subject, esp. if not generally known: our reviewer will give you **the dope on** hot spots around the town.
▸v. [tr.] **1** administer drugs to (a racehorse, greyhound, or athlete) in order to inhibit or enhance sporting performance. ■ (**be doped up**) inf. be heavily under the influence of drugs, typically illegal ones. ■ treat (food or drink) with drugs. **2** smear or cover with varnish or other thick liquid: she doped the surface with photographic emulsion. **3** Electr. add an impurity to (a semiconductor) to produce a desired electrical characteristic.
▸phrasal v. □ **dope something out** inf., dated work out something: they met to dope out plans for covering the event.
▸adj. black slang very good: that suit is dope! ▷early 19th cent. (in the sense 'thick liquid'): from Dutch doop 'sauce,' from doopen 'to dip, mix.' —**dop·er** n.

dop·ey /'dōpē/ (also **dop·y**) ▸adj. (**dop·i·er**, **dop·i·est**) inf. stupefied by sleep or a drug: she was under sedation and a bit dopey. ■ idiotic: did you ever hear such dopey names? —**dop·i·ly** /'dōpəlē/ adv. —**dop·i·ness** n.

dop·pel·gäng·er /'däpəl,gaNGər/ ▸n. an apparition or double of a living person.

Dop·pler ef·fect ▸n. Physics an increase (or decrease) in the frequency of sound, light, or other waves as the source and observer move toward (or away from) each other. The effect causes the sudden change in pitch noticeable in a passing siren, as well as the redshift seen by astronomers.

dop·y /'dōpē/ ▸adj. variant spelling of DOPEY.

Dor·ic /'dôrik; 'där-/ ▸adj. **1** relating to or denoting a classical order of architecture characterized by a plain, sturdy column and a thick square abacus resting on a rounded molding. **2** relating to or denoting an ancient Greek dialect. ■ archaic (of a dialect) broad; rustic.
▸n. **1** the Doric order of architecture. **2** an ancient Greek dialect.

dork /dôrk/ ▸n. inf. a slow-witted or socially inept person. —**dork·y** adj.

dorm /dôrm/ ▸n. inf. a dormitory.

dor·mant /'dôrmənt/ ▸adj. (of an animal) having normal physical functions suspended or slowed down for a period of time; in or as if in a deep sleep: dormant butterflies | fig. memories she would rather had lain dormant. ■ (of a plant or bud) alive but not actively growing. ■ (of a volcano) temporarily inactive. ■ (of a disease) causing no symptoms but not cured and liable to recur. —**dor·man·cy** n.

dor·mer /'dôrmər/ (also **dormer window**) ▸n. a window that projects vertically from a sloping roof. ■ the projecting structure that houses such a window: the windowed dormer above the sink.

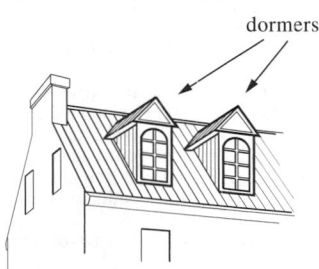

dormers

dormer

dor·mi·to·ry /'dôrmi,tôrē/ ▸n. (pl. **-ries**) a large bedroom for a number of people in a school or institution. ■ a university or college hall of residence or hostel. ■ [as adj.] chiefly Brit. denoting a small town or suburb providing a residential area for those who work in a nearby city.

dor·mouse /'dôr,mous/ ▸n. (pl. **dormice** /'dôr,mīs/) an agile mouselike rodent (family Gliridae) with a hairy or bushy tail, found in Africa and Eurasia. Some kinds are noted for spending long periods in hibernation.

dor·sal /'dôrsəl/ ▸adj. Anat., Zool., & Bot. of, on, or relating to the upper side or back of an animal, plant, or organ: a dorsal view of the body | the dorsal aorta. Compare with VENTRAL. —**dor·sal·ly** adv.

do·ry[1] /'dôrē/ ▸n. (pl. **-ies**) a narrow deep-bodied fish (families Zeidae and Oreosomatidae) with a mouth that can be opened very wide.

do·ry[2] ▸n. (pl. **-ries**) a small flat-bottomed rowboat with a high bow and stern, of a kind originally used for fishing in New England.

DOS /dôs/ Comput. ▸abbr. disk operating system, an operating system originally developed for IBM personal computers.

DoS ▸abbr. Comput. denial of service.

dos·age /'dōsij/ ▸n. the size or frequency of a dose of a medicine or drug: a dosage of 450 milligrams a day. ■ a level of exposure to or absorption of ionizing radiation.

dose /dōs/ ▸n. a quantity of a medicine or drug taken or recommended to be taken at a particular time: he took a dose of cough medicine. ■ an amount of ionizing radiation received or absorbed at one time or over a specified period. ■ inf. a venereal infection. ■ inf. a quantity of something regarded as analogous to medicine in being necessary but unpleasant: I wanted to give you a dose of the hell you put me through.
▸v. [tr.] administer a dose to (a person or animal): he dosed himself with vitamins. ■ adulterate or blend (a substance) with another substance.
▸ □ **in small doses** inf. when experienced or engaged in a little at a time: computer games are great in small doses.

do·sim·e·ter /dō'simitər/ ▸n. a device used to measure an absorbed dose of ionizing radiation. —**do·sim·et·ric** /,dōsə'metrik/ adj. —**do·sim·e·try** /-'simitrē/ n.

dos·si·er /'dôsē,ā; 'däs-/ ▸n. a collection of documents about a particular person, event, or subject: a dossier on Al | a dossier of complaints.

DOT ▸abbr. Department of Transportation.

dot[1] /dät/ ▸n. a small round mark or spot. ■ such a mark written or printed as part of an i or j, as a diacritical mark, as one of a series of marks to signify omission, or as a period. ■ Mus. such a mark used to denote the lengthening of a note or rest by half, or to indicate staccato. ■ the shorter signal of the two used in Morse code. Compare with DASH (sense 3). ■ used to refer to an object that appears tiny because it is far away. ■ used in speech to indicate the punctuation separating parts of an electronic mail or Web site address.
▸v. (**dot·ted**, **dot·ting**) [tr.] mark with a small spot or spots: wet spots of rain began to dot his shirt. ■ (of a number of items) be scattered over (an area): churches dot the countryside. ■ place a dot over (a letter): you need to dot the i. ■ Mus. mark (a note or rest) to show that the time value is increased by half: [as adj.] (**dotted**) a dotted quarter note. —**dot·ter** n.
▸ □ **dot the i's and cross the t's** inf. ensure that all details are correct. □ **on the dot** inf. exactly on time: he arrived on the dot at nine o'clock.

dot[2] ▸n. archaic a dowry, particularly one from which only the interest or annual income was available to the husband.

dot·age /'dōtij/ ▸n. the period of life in which a person is old and weak: you could live here and look after me in my dotage. ■ the state of having the intellect impaired, esp. through old age; senility.

do·tard /'dōtərd/ ▸n. an old person, esp. one who has become weak or senile.

dote /dōt/ ▸v. [intr.] **1** (**dote on/upon**) be extremely and uncritically fond of: she doted on her children | [as adj.] (**doting**) she was spoiled outrageously by her doting father. **2** archaic be silly or feebleminded, esp. as a result of old age: the parson is now old and dotes. —**dot·er** n. —**dot·ing·ly** adv.

dot ma·trix print·er ▸n. a printer that forms images of letters, numbers, etc., from a number of tiny dots.

dot·ted line ▸n. a line made up of dots or dashes (often used in reference to the space left for a signature on a contract).

dot·ty /'dätē/ ▸adj. (**dot·ti·er**, **dot·ti·est**) inf. (of a person, action, or idea) somewhat mad or eccentric. —**dot·ti·ly** /'dätəlē/ adv. —**dot·ti·ness** n.

dou·ble /'dəbəl/ ▸adj. **1** consisting of two equal, identical, or similar parts or things: the double doors. ■ having twice the usual size, quantity, or strength: she sipped a double brandy. ■ designed to be used by two people: a double bed. ■ having two different roles or interpretations, esp. in order to deceive or confuse: the furtive double life of a terrorist. **2** having some essential part or feature twice, in particular: ■ (of a flower variety) having more than one circle of petals: large double blooms. ■ (of a domino) having the same number of dots on each half. ■ used to indicate that a letter or number occurs twice in succession: "otter" is spelled with a double t. **3** Mus. lower in pitch by an octave.
▸twice as much or as many: the jail now houses almost double the number of prisoners | I'll pay double what I paid last time.
▸adv. at or to twice the amount or extent: this counts double for older people. ■ as two instead of the more usual one: she was seeing double.
▸n. **1** a thing that is twice as large as usual or is made up of two standard units or things: join the two sleeping bags together to make a double. ■ a double measure of liquor. ■ a thing designed to be used by two people, esp. a bed or a hotel room: $200 per night for a double. ■ Baseball a hit that allows the batter to reach second base safely: Sabo came home on a double. ■ a system of betting in which the winnings and stake from the first bet are transferred to a second. ■ Bridge a call that will increase the points won if the declarer is successful, or increase the

penalty points won by the defenders if the declarer fails to make the contract. **2** a person who looks exactly like another: *you could pass yourself off as his double.* ■ a person who stands in for an actor in a film. ■ an apparition of a living person: *she had seen her husband's double.* **3** (**doubles**) (esp. in tennis and badminton) a game or competition involving sides made up of two players.

▸*pron.* a number or amount that is twice as large as a contrasting or usual number or amount: *he paid double and had a room all to himself.*

▸*v.* **1** [*intr.*] become twice as much or as many: *profits doubled in one year.* ■ [*tr.*] make twice as much or as many of (something): *Clare doubled her income.* ■ [*tr.*] *archaic* amount to twice as much as: *thy fifty yet doth double five and twenty.* ■ [*intr.*] (of a member of the armed forces) move at twice the usual speed; run: *I doubled across the deck to join the others.* ■ (**double up**) share a room. ■ *Baseball* (of a batter) get a two-base hit. ■ *Bridge* make a call increasing the value of the penalty points to be scored on an opponent's bid if it wins the auction and is not fulfilled. ■ *inf.* go out on a double date: *they doubled with his sister and her boyfriend.* **2** [*tr.*] fold or bend (paper, cloth, or other material) over on itself. ■ [*intr.*] (**double up**) bend over or curl up, typically because one is overcome with pain or mirth: *we doubled up with laughter.* ■ clench (a fist): *he had one fist doubled.* ■ [*intr.*] (usu. **double back**) go back in the direction one has come. ■ *Naut.* sail around (a headland): *we struck out seaward to double the cape.* **3** [*intr.*] (of a person or thing) be used in or play another, different role: *a laser printer doubles as a photocopier.* ■ [*tr.*] (of an actor) play (two parts) in the same piece. ■ *Mus.* play two or more musical instruments. ■ [*tr.*] *Mus.* add the same note in a higher or lower octave to (a note). —**dou·bler** *n.* —**dou·bly** *adv.*

▸ □ **on the double** very fast. ■ without hesitation; immediately *he summoned his officers on the double.* □ **double or nothing** a gamble to decide whether a loss or debt should be doubled or canceled.

dou·ble a·gent ▸*n.* an agent who pretends to act as a spy for one country or organization while in fact acting on behalf of an enemy.

dou·ble-bar·reled ▸*adj.* (of a gun) having two barrels. ■ having two parts or aspects.

dou·ble bass /bās/ ▸*n.* the largest and lowest-pitched instrument of the violin family.

dou·ble-blind ▸*adj.* denoting a test or trial, esp. of a drug, in which any information that may influence the behavior of the tester or the subject is withheld until after the test.

dou·ble boil·er ▸*n.* a saucepan with a detachable upper compartment heated by boiling water in the lower one.

dou·ble-breast·ed ▸*adj.* (of a jacket or coat) having a substantial overlap of material at the front and showing two rows of buttons when fastened.

dou·ble chin ▸*n.* a roll of fatty flesh below a person's chin. —**dou·ble-chinned** *adj.*

dou·ble-cross ▸*v.* [*tr.*] deceive or betray (a person with whom one is supposedly cooperating): *he was blackmailed into double-crossing his own government.*

▸*n.* a betrayal of someone with whom one is supposedly cooperating. —**dou·ble-cross·er** *n.*

dou·ble-deal·ing ▸*n.* the practice of working for people's disadvantage behind their backs.

▸*adj.* working deceitfully to injure others. —**dou·ble-deal·er** *n.*

dou·ble-deck·er ▸*n.* something, esp. a bus, that has two floors or levels: [as *adj.*] *a double-decker bus* | *double-decker sandwiches.*

dou·ble Dutch (also **dou·ble dutch**) ▸*n.* a jump-rope game played with two long jump ropes swung in opposite directions so that they cross rhythmically: [as *adv.*] *three girls jumped double Dutch.*

dou·ble ea·gle ▸*n.* **1** a gold coin worth twenty dollars. **2** *Golf* a score of three strokes under par at a hole.

dou·ble en·ten·dre /än'tändrə/ ▸*n.* (*pl.* **dou·ble en·ten·dres** pronunc. same) a word or phrase open to two interpretations, one of which is usually risqué or indecent. ■ humor using such words or phrases.

dou·ble ex·po·sure ▸*n.* the repeated exposure of a photographic plate or film to light, often producing ghost images. ■ the photograph that results from such exposure.

dou·ble fea·ture ▸*n.* a movie program with two full-length films.

dou·ble·head·er /ˌdəbəl'hedər/ ▸*n.* (also **dou·ble-head·er**) ▸*n.* **1** a sporting event in which two games or contests are played in succession at the same venue, typically between the same teams or players. **2** a train pulled by two locomotives coupled together.

dou·ble he·lix ▸*n.* a pair of parallel helices intertwined about a common axis, esp. in that in the structure of the DNA molecule.

dou·ble in·dem·ni·ty ▸*n.* provision for payment of double the face

amount of an insurance policy under certain conditions, e.g., when death occurs as a result of an accident.

dou·ble jeop·ard·y ▸*n. Law* the prosecution of a person twice for the same offense. ■ risk or disadvantage incurred from two sources simultaneously.

dou·ble-joint·ed ▸*adj.* (of a person) having unusually flexible joints, typically those of the fingers, arms, or legs.

dou·ble-knit ▸*adj.* (of fabric) knit of two joined layers for extra thickness: *a green double-knit suit.*

dou·ble neg·a·tive ▸*n. Gram.* a negative statement containing two negative elements (for example *didn't say nothing*). ■ a positive statement in which two negative elements are used to produce the positive force, usu. for some particular rhetorical effect (for example *there is not nothing to worry about!*).

dou·ble-park ▸*v.* [*tr.*] (usu. **be double-parked**) park (a vehicle) alongside one that is already parked at the side of the road.

dou·ble play ▸*n. Baseball* a defensive play in which two players are put out.

dou·ble pneu·mo·nia ▸*n.* pneumonia affecting both lungs.

dou·ble-speak /'dəbəl,spēk/ ▸*n.* deliberately euphemistic, ambiguous, or obscure language: *the art of political doublespeak.*

dou·ble stand·ard ▸*n.* a rule or principle that is unfairly applied in different ways to different people or groups.

dou·blet /'dəblət/ ▸*n.* **1** either of a pair of similar things, in particular: ■ either of two words of the same historical source, but with two different stages of entry into the language and different resultant meanings, for example *fashion* and *faction*, *cloak* and *clock*. ■ (**doublets**) the same number on two dice thrown at once. **2** a man's short close-fitting padded jacket, commonly worn from the 14th to the 17th century.

dou·ble take ▸*n.* a delayed reaction to something unexpected, immediately after one's first reaction: *Tony glanced, then did a double take.*

dou·ble-talk ▸*n.* deliberately unintelligible speech combining nonsense syllables and actual words. ■ another term for DOUBLESPEAK.

dou·ble·think /'dəbəl,THINGk/ ▸*n.* the acceptance of two or mental capacity to accept contrary opinions or beliefs at the same time, esp. as a result of political indoctrination.

dou·bloon /də'blo͞on/ ▸*n. hist.* a Spanish gold coin.

doubt /dout/ ▸*n.* a feeling of uncertainty or lack of conviction: *some doubt has been cast upon this account* | *doubts that they would ever win.*

▸*v.* **1** [*tr.*] feel uncertain about: *I doubt my ability to do the job.* ■ question the truth or fact of (something): *who can doubt the value of these services?* | *I doubt if anyone slept that night.* ■ disbelieve (a person or their word): *I have no reason to doubt him.* ■ [*intr.*] feel uncertain, esp. about one's religious beliefs. **2** *archaic* fear; be afraid of: *I doubt not your contradictions.* —**doubt·a·ble** *adj.* —**doubt·er** *n.* —**doubt·ing·ly** *adv.*

▸ □ **beyond (a** or **a shadow of a) doubt** allowing no uncertainty. □ **in doubt** open to question: *the outcome is no longer in doubt.* ■ feeling uncertain about something: *by the age of 14 he was in no doubt about his career aims.* □ **no doubt** used to indicate the speaker's firm belief that something is true even if evidence is not given or available: *those who left were attracted, no doubt, by higher pay.* ■ used to introduce a concession that is subsequently dismissed as unimportant or irrelevant: *they no doubt did what they could to help her, but their best proved insufficient.* □ **without (a) doubt** indisputably: *he was without doubt the very worst kind of reporter.*

doubt·ful /'doutfəl/ ▸*adj.* **1** feeling uncertain about something: *he looked doubtful, but gave a nod* | *I was doubtful of my judgment.* **2** not known with certainty: *the fire was of doubtful origin.* ■ improbable: *it is doubtful whether these have any lasting effect.* ■ not established as genuine or acceptable: *of doubtful legality.* —**doubt·ful·ly** *adv.* —**doubt·ful·ness** *n.*

doubt·ing Thom·as ▸*n.* a person who is skeptical and refuses to believe something without proof.

doubt·less /'doutlis/ ▸*adv.* used to indicate the speaker's belief that a statement is certain to be true given what is known about the situation: *the company would doubtless find the reduced competition to their liking.* ■ used to refer to a desirable outcome as though it were certain: *doubtless you'll solve the problem.* —**doubt·less·ly** *adv.*

douche /do͞oSH/ ▸*n.* a shower of water: *a daily douche.* ■ a jet of liquid applied to part of the body for cleansing or medicinal purposes. ■ a device for washing out the vagina as a contraceptive measure.

Pronunciation Key ə *ago*, *up*; ər *over*, *fur*; a *hat*; ā *ate*; ä *car*; CH *chin*; e *let*; ē *see*; e(ə)r *air*; i *fit*; ī *by*; i(ə)r *ear*; NG *sing*; ō *go*; ô *law*, *for*; oi *toy*; o͝o *good*; o͞o *goo*; ou *out*; SH *she*; TH *thin*; ⊺H *then*; (h)w *why*; ZH *vision*

▸*v.* [*tr.*] spray or shower with water. ■ [*intr.*] use a douche as a method of contraception.

dough /dō/ ▸*n.* **1** a thick, malleable mixture of flour and liquid, used for baking into bread or pastry. **2** *inf.* money: *lots of dough.* ▷Old English *dāg*, of Germanic origin; related to Dutch *deeg* and German *Teig*, from an Indo-European root meaning 'smear, knead.' —**dough·i·ness** *n.* —**dough·y** *adj.* (**dough·i·er, dough·i·est**).

dough·boy /'dō,boi/ ▸*n. inf.* a U.S. infantryman, esp. one in World War I.

dough·nut /'dō,nət/ (also **do·nut**) ▸*n.* a small fried cake of sweetened dough, typically in the shape of a ball or ring.

dough·ty /'doutē/ ▸*adj.* (**-ti·er, -ti·est**) *archaic, humorous* brave and persistent. —**dough·ti·ly** /'doutl-ē/ *adv.* —**dough·ti·ness** *n.*

Doug·las fir ▸*n.* a tall, slender tree (genus *Pseudotsuga*) of the pine family, with soft foliage and, in mature trees, deeply fissured bark.

dour /dŏŏr; dou(ə)r/ ▸*adj.* relentlessly severe, stern, or gloomy in manner or appearance. —**dour·ly** *adv.* —**dour·ness** *n.*

douse /dous/ (also **dowse**) ▸*v.* [*tr.*] pour liquid over; drench. ■ extinguish (a fire or light): *fig. nothing could douse her euphoria.*

dove[1] /dəv/ ▸*n.* **1** a stocky bird of the pigeon family, with a small head, short legs, and a cooing voice. **2** a person who advocates peaceful or conciliatory policies, esp. in foreign affairs. Compare with HAWK[1] (sense 2). —**dove·like** /-,līk/ *adj.* —**dov·ish** *adj.*

dove[2] /dōv/ ▸ past of DIVE.

dove·cote /'dəv,kōt/ (also **dove·cot**) ▸*n.* a shelter with nest holes for domesticated pigeons.

dove·tail /'dəv,tāl/ ▸*n.* (also **dovetail joint**) a joint formed by one or more tapered projections (tenons) on one piece that interlock with corresponding notches or recesses (mortises) in another. ■ a tenon used in such a joint, typically wider at its extremity.

▸*v.* [*tr.*] join together by means of a dovetail. ■ fit or cause to fit together easily and conveniently: [*tr.*] *plan to enable parents to dovetail their career and family commitments* [*intr.*] *flights that dovetail with the working day.*

dow·a·ger /'douəjər/ ▸*n.* a widow with a title or property derived from her late husband. ■ *inf.* a dignified elderly woman.

dow·dy /'doudē/ ▸*adj.* (**dow·di·er, dow·di·est**) (of a person, typically a woman, or their clothes) unfashionable and without style in appearance.

▸*n.* (*pl.* **-dies**) a woman who is unfashionably and unattractively dressed. —**dow·di·ly** /'doudəlē/ *adv.* —**dow·di·ness** *n.*

dow·el /'douəl/ ▸*n.* a peg of wood, metal, or plastic without a distinct head, used for holding together components of a structure.

▸*v.* (**dow·eled, dow·el·ing**; *Brit.* **dow·elled, dow·el·ling**) [*tr.*] fasten with a dowel or dowels.

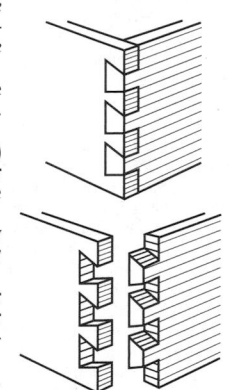

dovetail joint

dow·el·ing /'douəliNG/ (*Brit.* **dow·el·ling**) ▸*n.* cylindrical rods for cutting into dowels.

dow·er /'dou(-ə)r/ ▸*n.* a widow's share for life of her husband's estate. ■ *archaic* a dowry.

▸*v.* [*tr.*] *archaic* give a dowry to. ▷late Middle English: from Old French *douaire*, from medieval Latin *dotarium*, from Latin *dotare* 'endow,' from *dos, dot-* 'dowry'; related to *dare* 'give.'

Dow Jones In·dus·tri·al Av·er·age /'dou 'jōnz / (also **Dow Jones Average**) ▸an index of figures indicating the relative price of shares on the New York Stock Exchange, based on the average price of selected stocks.

down[1] /doun/ ▸*adv.* **1** toward or in a lower place or position, esp. to or on the ground or another surface. ■ at or to a specified distance below: *you can plainly see the bottom 35 feet down.* ■ downstairs. ■ expressing movement or position away from the north: *they're living down south.* ■ to or at a place perceived as lower (often expressing casualness or lack of hurry): *I'd rather be down at the villa | I'm going down to the arcade.* ■ (with reference to food or drink swallowed) in or into the stomach: *she couldn't keep anything down.* ■ so as to lie or be fixed flush or flat. ■ [as *interj.*] used as a command to a person or animal to sit or lie down. ■ a crossword answer that reads vertically: *how many letters in fifteen down?* **2** to or at a lower level of intensity, volume, or activity. ■ to or at a lower price, value, or rank: *output was down 20 percent.* ■ to a finer consistency, a smaller amount or size, or a simpler or more basic state: *I*

must slim down | a formal statement that can't be edited down | thin down an oil-based paint.* ■ from an earlier to a later point in time or order. **3** in or into a weaker or worse position, mood, or condition: *the scandal brought down the government | he was down with the flu.* ■ losing or at a disadvantage by a specified amount: *the Braves, down 7–6, rallied for two runs.* ■ used to express progress through a series of tasks or items: *one down and only six more to go.* ■ (of a computer system) out of action or unavailable for use (esp. temporarily): *the system went down yesterday.* ■ (**down with ——**) shouted to express strong dislike of a specified person or thing: *crowds chanted "Down with bureaucracy!"* **4** in or into writing: *I just write down whatever comes into my head | taking down notes.* ■ on or on to a list, schedule, or record: *I'll put you down for the evening shift.* **5** (with reference to partial payment of a sum of money) made initially or on the spot: *pay $500 down and the rest at the end of the month.* **6** (of sailing) with the current or the wind. ■ (of a ship's helm) moved around to leeward so that the rudder is to windward and the vessel swings toward the wind. **7** *Football* (of the ball or a player in possession) not in play, typically because forward progress has been stopped.

▸*prep.* **1** from a higher to a lower point of (something). ■ at or to a lower part of (a river or stream); nearer the sea: *a dozen miles down the Mississippi.* ■ at a point further along the course of (something): *he lived down the street.* ■ along the course or extent of: *I wandered down the road.* **2** throughout (a period of time): *down the ages.*

▸*adj.* **1** directed or moving toward a lower place or position. ■ *Physics* denoting a flavor of quark having a charge of $-\frac{1}{3}$. **2** (of a person) unhappy; depressed. ■ *inf.* (of a period of time) causing or characterized by unhappiness or depression: *up days and down days.* **3** (of a computer system) temporarily out of action or unavailable. **4** *chiefly slang* supporting or going along with someone or something: *"You going to the movies?" "Yo, I'm down."* ■ aware of and following the latest fashion: *a seriously down, hip-hop homie.*

▸*v.* [*tr.*] *inf.* **1** knock or bring to the ground. **2** consume (something, typically a drink): *he downed a six-pack.* ■ (of a golfer) sink (a putt).

▸*n.* **1** *Football* a chance for a team to advance the ball, ending when the ball carrier is tackled or the ball becomes out of play. A team must advance at least ten yards in a series of four downs in order to keep possession. **2** (**downs**) *inf.* unwelcome experiences or events. **3** *inf.* a feeling or period of unhappiness or depression: *everyone gets their downs.* ■ *inf.* short for DOWNER (sense 1).

▸ □ **be down on** *inf.* disapprove of; feel hostile or antagonistic toward. □ **be down to** to be left with only (the specified amount): *I'm down to my last few dollars.* □ **down in the mouth** *inf.* (of a person or their expression) unhappy; dejected. □ **down on one's luck** *inf.* experiencing a period of bad luck. □ **down pat** (or **cold**) memorized or mastered perfectly: *she had the routine down pat | a guy who has his art history down cold.* □ **have** (or **put**) **someone/something down as** judge someone or something to be (a particular type): *I never had Jake down as a ladies' man.* □ **down to the ground** *inf.* completely.

down[2] ▸*n.* soft fine fluffy feathers that form the first covering of a young bird or an insulating layer below the contour feathers of an adult bird. ■ such feathers taken from ducks or their nests and used for stuffing cushions, quilts, etc.; eiderdown. ■ fine soft hair on the face or body of a person. ■ short soft hairs on some leaves, fruit, or seeds.

down[3] ▸*n.* (usu. **downs**) a gently rolling hill: *the gentle green contours of the downs.*

down-and-out ▸*adj.* (of a person) without money, a job, or a place to live; destitute: *a down-and-out homeless vagrant.*

▸*n.* (also **down-and-out·er**) a person without money, a job, or a place to live.

down-at-the-heels (also **down-at-the-heel** or **down-at-heel**) ▸*adj.* (of a person, thing, or place) showing signs of neglect and deterioration; shabby: *a down-at-the-heels house.*

down·beat /'doun,bēt/ ▸*adj.* pessimistic; gloomy.

▸*n. Mus.* an accented beat, usually the first of the bar.

down·cast /'doun,kast/ ▸*adj.* **1** (of a person's eyes) looking downward: *her modestly downcast eyes.* **2** (of a person) feeling despondent.

down·code /'doun,kōd/ ▸*v.* [*tr./syntax*>.] **1** designate (a medical procedure or insurance claim) with a lower value. **2** *Comput.* rewrite or convert (programs or software) into a lower level language. —**down·cod·ing** *n.*

down·draft /'doun,draft/ ▸*n.* a downward current or draft of air, esp. one down a chimney into a room.

down·er /'dounər/ ▸*n. inf.* **1** (usu. **downers**) a depressant or tranquilizing drug, esp. a barbiturate. **2** a dispiriting or depressing experience or factor. ■ a period of consistent failure: *the Red Sox enter the season on* *a downer.* **3** a cow or other animal that is sick or injured and cannot get to its feet unaided.

down·fall /ˈdounˌfôl/ ▶*n.* a loss of power, prosperity, or status. ■ the cause of such a loss: *his intractability will prove to be his downfall.*

down·grade /ˈdounˌgrād/ ▶*v.* [*tr.*] (usu. **be downgraded**) reduce to a lower grade, rank, or level of importance.
▶*n.* **1** an instance of reducing someone or something's rank, status, or level of importance. **2** a downward gradient, typically on a railroad track or road.

down·heart·ed /ˈdounˈhärtid/ ▶*adj.* discouraged; in low spirits. —**down·heart·ed·ly** *adv.* —**down·heart·ed·ness** *n.*

down·hill /ˈdounˈhil/ ▶*adv.* toward the bottom of a slope: *follow the road downhill.* ■ *fig.* into a steadily worsening situation: *his marriage continued to slide downhill.* ■ *fig.* used to describe easy or quick progress toward an objective after initial difficulties have been overcome: *up by six runs in the eighth inning—it should have been **downhill all the way**.*
▶*adj.* leading down toward the bottom of a slope: *the route is downhill for part of the way.* ■ *fig.* leading to a steadily worsening situation: *the downhill road to delinquency.* ■ *fig.* without difficulty or challenge: *we'll not take the easy road, the downhill road.* ■ of or relating to the sport of skiing or cycling downhill.
▶*n.* **1** a downward slope. **2** *Skiing* a downhill race. ■ the activity of downhill skiing.
▶ □ **go downhill** become worse; deteriorate.

down·lev·el /ˈdounˌlevəl/ ▶*adj.* using an earlier version of software, hardware, or an operating system.

down·load /ˈdounˌlōd/ *Comput.* ▶*v.* [*tr.*] copy (data) from one computer system to another or to a disk. Compare with UPLOAD.
▶*n.* the act or process of copying data in such a way. ■ a computer file transferred in such a way. —**down·load·a·ble** *adj.*

down·mar·ket /ˈdounˌmärkit/ (also **down-mar·ket**) ▶*adj. & adv.* toward or relating to the cheaper or less prestigious sector of the market.

down pay·ment ▶*n.* an initial payment made when something is bought on credit.

down·play /ˈdounˌplā/ ▶*v.* [*tr.*] make (something) appear less important than it really is: *this report downplays the seriousness of global warming.*

down·pour /ˈdounˌpôr/ ▶*n.* a heavy rainfall.

down·right /ˈdounˌrīt/ ▶*adj.* **1** (of something bad or unpleasant) utter; complete (used for emphasis): *it's a downright disgrace.* **2** (of a person's manner or behavior) straightforward; so direct as to be blunt: *her common sense and downright attitude to life surprised him.*
▶*adv.* to an extreme degree; thoroughly. —**down·right·ness** *n.*

down·scale /ˈdounˌskāl/ ▶*v.* [*tr.*] reduce in size, scale, or extent.
▶*adj.* at the lower end of a scale, esp. a social scale; downmarket: *these brands appeal to downscale shoppers who are looking for a low price.*

down·shift /ˈdounˌSHift/ ▶*v.* [*intr.*] change to a lower gear in a motor vehicle or bicycle. ■ slow down; slacken off. ■ change a financially rewarding but stressful career or lifestyle for a less pressured and less highly paid but more fulfilling one: *they want to downshift from full-time work.*

down·side /ˈdounˌsīd/ ▶*n.* **1** the negative aspect of something, esp. something regarded as in general good or desirable: *a magazine feature on the downside of fashion modeling.* **2** [often as *adj.*] a downward movement of share prices: *each fund aims to reduce the downside risk.*

down·size /ˈdounˌsīz/ ▶*v.* [*tr.*] make (something) smaller: *downsize the wheel to 26 inches.* ■ make (a company or organization) smaller by eliminating staff positions. ■ [*intr.*] (of a company) eliminate staff positions.

down·stage /ˈdounˈstāj/ ▶*adj. & adv.* at or toward the front of a stage.

down·stairs /ˈdounˈste(ə)rz/ ▶*adv.* down a flight of stairs: *I tripped over the cat and fell downstairs.* ■ on or to a lower floor.
▶*adj.* situated downstairs: *the downstairs bathroom.*
▶*n.* the ground floor or lower floors of a building.

down·state /ˈdounˈstāt/ ▶*adj. & adv.* of, in, or to the southern part of a state. —**down·stat·er** *n.*

down·stream /ˈdounˈstrēm/ ▶*adv. & adj.* situated or moving in the direction in which a stream or river flows. ■ *Biol.* situated in or toward the part of a sequence of genetic material where transcription takes place later than at a given point: *a termination signal was found downstream from the coding region.* ■ at a stage in the process of gas or oil extraction and production after the raw material is ready for refining.

Down syn·drome /ˈdoun ˈsindrōm/ (also **Down's syn·drome**) ▶*n. Med.* a congenital disorder arising from a chromosome defect, causing intellectual impairment and physical abnormalities including short stature and a broad face.

down·time /ˈdounˌtīm/ (also **down time**) ▶*n.* time during which a machine, esp. a computer, is out of action or unavailable for use. ■ *fig.* a time of reduced activity or inactivity.

down-to-earth ▶*adj.* with no illusions or pretensions; practical and realistic: *a down-to-earth view of marriage.* —**down-to-earth·ness** *n.*

down·town /ˈdounˈtoun/ ▶*adj.* of, in, or characteristic of the central area or main business and commercial area of a town or city.
▶*adv.* in or into such an area: *I drove downtown.*
▶*n.* such an area of a town or city. —**down·town·er** *n.*

down·trod·den /ˈdounˌträdn/ ▶*adj.* oppressed or treated badly by people in power: *a downtrodden proletarian struggling for social justice.*

down·turn /ˈdounˌtərn/ ▶*n.* a decline in economic, business, or other activity: *a downturn in the housing market.*
▶*v.* [*tr.*] [usu. as *adj.*] (**downturned**) turn (something) downward.

Down Un·der (also **down un·der**) *inf.* ▶*adv.* in or to Australia or New Zealand: *talking as they do Down Under.*
▶*n.* Australia and New Zealand: *thousands of men from Down Under.*

down·ward /ˈdounwərd/ ▶*adv.* (also **down·wards**) toward a lower place, point, or level. ■ used to indicate that something applies to everyone in a certain hierarchy or set: *it affects us all, from managers downward.*
▶*adj.* moving or leading toward a lower place or level: *the downward curve of the stairs | a downward trend in inflation.* —**down·ward·ly** *adv.*

down·wind /ˈdounˈwind/ ▶*adv. & adj.* in the direction in which the wind is blowing: [as *adv.*] *I'm downwind of the fire* | [as *adj.*] *downwind landings.*

down·y /ˈdounē/ ▶*adj.* (**down·i·er**, **down·i·est**) covered with fine soft hair or feathers: *her downy cheek.* ■ filled with soft feathers: *a downy pillow.* ■ soft and fluffy: *downy hair.* —**down·i·ly** /-nəlē/ *adv.* —**down·i·ness** *n.*

dow·ry /ˈdou(ə)rē/ ▶*n.* (*pl.* **-ries**) property or money brought by a bride to her husband on their marriage.

dowse[1] /douz/ ▶*v.* [*intr.*] perform dowsing. ■ [*tr.*] search for or discover by dowsing: *he dowsed a spiral of energy on the stone.* —**dows·er** *n.*

dowse[2] ▶*v.* variant spelling of DOUSE.

dows·ing /ˈdouziNG/ ▶*n.* a technique for searching for underground water, minerals, or anything invisible, by observing the motion of a pointer (traditionally a forked stick, now often paired bent wires) or the changes in direction of a pendulum, supposedly in response to unseen influences: [as *adj.*] *a dowsing rod.*

dox·ol·o·gy /däkˈsäləjē/ ▶*n.* (*pl.* **-gies**) a liturgical formula of praise to God. —**dox·o·log·i·cal** /ˌdäksəˈläjikəl/ *adj.*

doy·en /ˈdoi·en; ˈdoi-en/ ▶*n.* the most respected or prominent person in a particular field: *the doyen of Canadian poetry.*

doz. ▶*abbr.* dozen.

doze /dōz/ ▶*v.* [*intr.*] sleep lightly. ■ (**doze off**) fall lightly asleep.
▶*n.* a short light sleep. ▷mid 17th cent. (in the sense 'stupefy, bewilder, or make drowsy'): perhaps related to Danish *døse* 'make drowsy.'

doz·en /ˈdəzən/ (*abbr.*: **dz.**) ▶*n.* **1** (*pl.* same) a group or set of twelve: *a dozen bottles of sherry.* ■ (**dozens**) *inf.* a lot: *she has dozens of admirers.* **2** (**the dozens**) an exchange of insults engaged in as a game or ritual among black Americans.
▶ □ **by the dozen** in large quantities.

do·zy /ˈdōzē/ ▶*adj.* (**do·zi·er**, **do·zi·est**) drowsy and lazy: *he grew dozy at the end of a long day.* —**do·zi·ly** /-zəlē/ *adv.* —**do·zi·ness** *n.*

DPT (also **DTP**) ▶*abbr.* diphtheria, pertussis (whooping cough), and tetanus, a combined vaccine given to small children.

Dr. ▶*abbr.* ■ (as a title) Doctor: *Dr. Russell.* ■ (in street names) Drive.

dr. ▶*abbr.* ■ debit. ■ drachma(s). ■ dram(s).

drab[1] /drab/ ▶*adj.* (**drab·ber**, **drab·best**) **1** lacking brightness or interest; drearily dull. **2** of a dull light brown color.
▶*n.* fabric of a dull brownish color. —**drab·ly** *adv.* —**drab·ness** *n.*

drab[2] ▶*n. archaic* **1** a slovenly woman. **2** a prostitute.

drach·ma /ˈdräkmə/ ▶*n.* (*pl.* **-mas** or **-mae** /-mē/) the basic monetary unit of Greece (until the introduction of the euro), notionally equal to 100 lepta. ■ a silver coin of ancient Greece.

dra·co·ni·an /drəˈkōnēən; drā-/ ▶*adj.* (of laws or their application) excessively harsh and severe. —**dra·con·ic** /-ˈkänik/ *adj.*

draft /draft/ ▶*n.* **1** a preliminary version of a piece of writing. ■ a plan, sketch, or rough drawing. ■ (in full **draft mode**) *Comput.* a mode of operation of a printer in which text is produced rapidly but with relatively low definition. **2** (**the draft**) compulsory recruitment for military service. ■ a procedure whereby new or existing sports players are made available for selection or reselection by the teams in a league, usually with the earlier choices being given to the weaker

teams. ■ *rare* a group or individual selected from a larger group for a special duty, e.g., for military service. **3** (*Brit.* **draught**) a current of cool air in a room or other confined space. **4** (*Brit.* **draught**) the action or act of pulling something along, esp. a vehicle or farm implement. **5** a written order to pay a specified sum; a check. **6** (*Brit.* **draught**) a single act of drinking or inhaling. ■ the amount swallowed or inhaled in one such act. **7** (*Brit.* **draught**) the depth of water needed to float a ship: *the shallow draft enabled her to get close to shore.* **8** (*Brit.* **draught**) the drawing in of a fishing net. ■ the fish taken at one drawing; a catch.
▶*v.* (*Brit.* **draught**) [*tr.*] **1** prepare a preliminary version of (a text). **2** select (a person or group of people) for a certain purpose. ■ conscript (someone) for military service. ■ select (a player) for a sports team through the draft. **3** pull or draw. **4** [*intr.*] *Auto Racing* benefit from reduced wind resistance by driving very closely behind another vehicle.
▶*adj.* (*Brit.* **draught**) **1** denoting beer or other drink that is kept in and served from a barrel or tank rather than from a bottle or can. **2** denoting an animal used for pulling heavy loads. —**draft·ee** /draf'tē/ *n.* —**draft·er** *n.* —**draft·y** *adj.*
▶ □ **on draft** (of beer or other drink) on tap; ready to be drawn from a barrel or tank; not bottled or canned.

drag /drag/ ▶*v.* (**dragged, drag·ging**) **1** [*tr.*] pull (someone or something) along forcefully, roughly, or with difficulty. ■ take (someone) to or from a place or event, despite their reluctance. ■ (**drag oneself**) go somewhere wearily, reluctantly, or with difficulty: *I have to drag myself out of bed each day.* ■ move (an icon or other image) across a computer screen using a tool such as a mouse. ■ [*intr.*] (of a person's clothes or an animal's tail) trail along the ground. ■ [*intr.*] (**drag at**) catch hold of and pull (something). ■ [*intr.*] engage in a drag race: *they were caught dragging on Francis Lewis Blvd.* ■ [*tr.*] (of a ship) trail (an anchor) along the seabed, causing the ship to drift. ■ [*tr.*] search the bottom of (a river, lake, or the sea) with grapnels or nets. **2** [*tr.*] (**drag something up**) *inf.* deliberately mention an unwelcome or unpleasant fact. ■ (**drag someone/something into**) involve someone or something in (a situation or matter), typically when such involvement is inappropriate or unnecessary. ■ (**drag something in/into**) introduce an irrelevant or inappropriate subject. ■ (**drag someone/something down**) bring someone or something to a lower level or standard. **3** [*intr.*] (of time, events, or activities) pass slowly and tediously. ■ (of a process or situation) continue at tedious and unnecessary length: *the dispute dragged on for years.* ■ [*tr.*] (**drag something out**) protract something unnecessarily. **4** [*intr.*] (**drag on**) *inf.* (of a person) inhale the smoke from (a cigarette).
▶*phrasal v.* □ **drag something out** extract information from someone against their will: *the truth was being dragged out of us.*
▶*n.* **1** the action of pulling something forcefully or with difficulty: *the drag of the current.* ■ the longitudinal retarding force exerted by air or other fluid surrounding a moving object. ■ a person or thing that impedes progress or development: *Larry was turning out to be **a drag on** her career.* ■ *Fishing* unnatural motion of a fishing fly caused by the pull of the line. ■ *archaic* an iron shoe that can be applied as a brake to the wheel of a cart or wagon. **2** *inf.* a boring or tiresome person or thing. **3** *inf.* an act of inhaling smoke from a cigarette. **4** clothing more conventionally worn by the opposite sex, esp. women's clothes worn by a man: *men in drag* | [as *adj.*] *a live drag show.* **5** short for DRAG RACE. ■ *inf.* a street or road: *the main drag.* ■ *hist.* a private vehicle like a stagecoach, drawn by four horses. **6** a thing that is pulled along the ground or through water, in particular: ■ *hist.* a harrow used for breaking up the surface of land. ■ an apparatus for dredging a river or for recovering the bodies of drowned people from a river, a lake, or the sea. **7** *inf.* influence over other people: *they had the education but they didn't have the drag.* **8** a strong-smelling lure drawn before hounds as a substitute for a fox or other hunted animal. ■ a hunt using such a lure. **9** *Mus.* one of the basic patterns (rudiments) of drumming, consisting of a stroke preceded by two grace notes, which are usually played with the other stick. See also RUFF².
▶ □ **drag one's feet** walk slowly and wearily or with difficulty. ■ (also **drag one's heels**) *fig.* (of a person or organization) be deliberately slow or reluctant to act. □ **drag someone/something through the mud** make damaging allegations about someone or something.

drag·net /'drag,net/ ▶*n.* a net drawn through a river or across ground to trap fish or game. ■ *fig.* a systematic search for someone or something, esp. criminals or criminal activity.

drag·on /'dragən/ ▶*n.* **1** a mythical monster like a giant reptile. ■ *derog.* a fierce and intimidating person, esp. a woman. **2** *hist.* a short musket carried on the belt of a soldier, a mounted infantryman. ■ a soldier armed with such a musket.

drag·on·fly /'dragən,flī/ ▶*n.* (*pl.* **-flies**) a fast-flying long-bodied predatory insect with two pairs of large transparent wings that are spread out sideways at rest.

dra·goon /drə'gōōn/ ▶*n.* a member of any of several cavalry regiments in the household troops of the British army. ■ *hist.* a mounted infantryman armed with a short rifle or musket.
▶*v.* [*tr.*] coerce (someone) into doing something: *dragooned into helping with the housework.* ▷early 17th cent. (denoting a kind of carbine or musket, thought of as breathing fire): from French *dragon* 'dragon.'

drag queen ▶*n.* a man who dresses up in women's clothes, typically for the purposes of entertainment. ■ a male homosexual transvestite.

drag race ▶*n.* a race between two or more cars over a short distance, usually a quarter of a mile, as a test of acceleration. —**drag rac·er** *n.* —**drag rac·ing** *n.*

drag·ster /'dragstər/ ▶*n.* a car built or modified to take part in drag races.

drain /drān/ ▶*v.* [*tr.*] **1** cause the water or other liquid in (something) to run out, leaving it empty, dry, or drier. ■ cause or allow (liquid) to run off or out of something: *fry the pork and **drain off** any excess fat.* ■ make (land) drier by providing channels for water to flow away in. ■ (of a river) carry off the superfluous water from (a district). ■ [*intr.*] (of water or another liquid) flow away from, out of, or into something. ■ [*intr.*] become dry or drier as liquid runs off or away. ■ (of a person) drink the entire contents of (a glass or other container). ■ [*intr.*] *fig.* (of a feeling or emotion) become progressively less strongly felt: *gradually the tension drained away.* **2** deprive of strength or vitality: *his limbs were drained of energy* | *Ruth slumped in her seat, drained by all that had happened.* ■ cause (money, energy, or another valuable resource) to be lost, wasted, or used up: *hospital bills are draining my income.* ■ [*intr.*] (of such a resource) be lost, wasted, or used up. **3** *inf. Golf* (of a player) hole (a putt).
▶*n.* **1** a channel or pipe carrying off surplus liquid, esp. rainwater or liquid waste. ■ a tube for drawing off accumulating fluid from a body cavity or an abscess. **2** a thing that uses up a particular resource: *a **drain on** the public purse.* ■ the continuous loss or expenditure of a particular resource.
▶ □ **go down the drain** *inf.* be totally wasted.

drain·age /'drānij/ ▶*n.* the action or process of draining something: *the pot must have holes in the base for good drainage.* ■ the means of removing surplus water or liquid waste; a system of drains.

drain·board /'drān,bôrd/ ▶*n.* a sloping grooved board or surface, on which washed dishes are left to drain, typically into a sink.

drain·er /'drānər/ ▶*n.* a device used to drain things, in particular a rack placed on a drainboard to hold washed dishes while they drain. ■ a drainboard. ■ a person or device that drains a flooded area.

drain·pipe /'drān,pīp/ ▶*n.* a pipe for carrying off rainwater or liquid refuse from a building.

drake /drāk/ ▶*n.* a male duck: *ducks and drakes* | [as *adj.*] *a drake mallard.*

DRAM /'dē,ram/ ▶*n. Electr.* a memory chip that depends upon an applied voltage to keep the stored data.

dram¹ /dram/ ▶*n.* a small drink of whiskey or other spirits.

dram² ▶*n.* the basic monetary unit of Armenia, equal to 100 luma.

dra·ma /'drämə/ ▶*n.* **1** a play for theater, radio, or television. ■ such works as a genre or style of literature. **2** an exciting, emotional, or unexpected series of events or set of circumstances.

dra·mat·ic /drə'matik/ ▶*adj.* **1** of or relating to drama or the performance or study of drama. **2** (of an event or circumstance) sudden and striking: *a dramatic increase in crime.* ■ exciting or impressive. ■ (of a person or their behavior) intending or intended to create an effect; theatrical. —**dra·mat·i·cal·ly** /-ik(ə)lē/ *adv.*

dra·mat·ic i·ro·ny ▶*n.* see IRONY¹.

dra·mat·ics /drə'matiks/ ▶*pl. n.* **1** [often treated as *sing.*] the study or practice of acting in and producing plays: *amateur dramatics.* **2** theatrically exaggerated or overemotional behavior: *cut out the dramatics.*

dram·a·tis per·so·nae /'drämətis pər'sōnē/ ▶*pl. n.* the characters of a play, novel, or narrative. ■ the participants in a series of events.

dram·a·tist /'drämə,tist/ ▶*n.* a person who writes plays.

dram·a·tize /'drämə,tīz/ ▶*v.* [*tr.*] adapt (a novel) or present (a particular incident) as a play or movie. ■ present in a vivid or striking way: *he used scare tactics to dramatize the deficit.* ■ exaggerate the seriousness or importance of (an incident or situation): *they have a tendency to dramatize things.* —**dram·a·ti·za·tion** /,dräməti'zāSHən/ *n.*

dra·me·dy /'drämədē/ ▶*n.* (*pl.* **-dies**) a movie, play, or broadcast program that combines elements of drama and comedy: *it's a dramedy about a working-class dance prodigy.* ■ the style or genre of such types of entertainment: *the slapstick of his early career rarely shows up in the comedy he delivers today.*

drank /draNGk/ ▶ past of DRINK.

drape /drāp/ ▶ v. [tr.] arrange (cloth or clothing) loosely or casually on or around something. ■ (usu. **be draped**) adorn, cover, or wrap (someone or something) loosely with folds of cloth: *the body was draped in a blanket.* ■ let (oneself or a part of one's body) rest somewhere in a casual or relaxed way: *he draped an arm around her.* ■ [intr.] (of fabric) hang or be able to hang in loose, graceful folds: *velvet drapes beautifully.*
▶n. **1** (**drapes**) long curtains: *Katherine pulled back the heavy velvet drapes.* ■ *inf.* a man's suit consisting of a long jacket and narrow trousers: *dressed in Edwardian-style drapes and suede shoes.* **2** the way in which a garment or fabric hangs: *by fixing the band you obtain a fuller drape in the fabric.*

dra·per·y /'drāpərē/ ▶n. (*pl.* **-per·ies**) cloth coverings hanging in loose folds. ■ (**draperies**) long curtains of heavy fabric. ■ the artistic arrangement of clothing in sculpture or painting.

dras·tic /'drastik/ ▶ adj. likely to have a strong or far-reaching effect; radical and extreme. —**dras·ti·cal·ly** /-ik(ə)lē/ adv.

drat /drat/ ▶ interj. (often **drat someone/something**) a mild expression of anger or annoyance: *"Drat!" said Mitch, kicking the fence.* —**drat·ted** adj.

Dra·vid·i·an /drə'vidēən/ ▶ adj. of, relating to, or denoting a family of languages spoken in southern India and Sri Lanka, or the peoples who speak them.
▶n. **1** this family of languages. **2** a member of any of the peoples speaking a Dravidian language. ▷from Sanskrit *drāviḍa* 'relating to the Tamils' (from *Dravida* 'Tamil').

draw /drô/ ▶ v. (*past* **drew** /drōō/; *past part.* **drawn** /drôn/) [tr.] **1** produce (a picture or diagram) by making lines and marks, esp. with a pen or pencil, on paper. ■ produce an image of (someone or something) in such a way: *I asked her to draw me.* ■ trace or produce (a line or mark) on a surface. **2** pull or drag (something such as a vehicle) so as to make it follow behind: *a cart drawn by two horses.* ■ pull or move (something) in a specified direction: *I drew back the blanket.* ■ [tr.] gently pull or guide (someone) in a specified direction: *"David," she whispered, drawing him aside.* ■ [intr.] move in a slow steady way: *the train drew into the station.* ■ [intr.] come to or arrive at a point in time or a specified point in a process: *the campaign drew to a close.* ■ pull (curtains, blinds, or other such coverings) shut or open. ■ make (wire) by pulling a piece of metal through successively smaller holes. **3** extract (an object or liquid) from a container or receptacle: *he drew his gun | the children went down to the pond to draw water | the syringe drew off most of the fluid | [as adj.] (**drawn**) he met them with a drawn sword.* ■ run (a bath). ■ (**draw something from**) obtain something from (a particular source): *an independent panel drawn from members of the public | he draws inspiration from ordinary scenes.* ■ (**draw on**) use (one's experience, talents, or skills) as a resource. ■ obtain or withdraw (money) from a bank or other source. ■ *Bridge* (of player) force the opponents to play (cards in a particular suit) by leading cards in that suit: *before establishing his diamonds, declarer must draw trumps.* ■ [intr.] suck smoke from (a cigarette or pipe). ■ [intr.] (of a chimney, flue, or fire) allow air to flow in and upward freely, so that a fire can burn. ■ take in (a breath). ■ disembowel: *he was hanged, drawn, and quartered.* **4** be the cause of (a specified response): *he drew criticism for lavish spending.* ■ attract (someone) to come to a place or an event: *you really drew the crowds with your playing.* ■ (usu. **be drawn**) induce (someone) to reveal or do something: *I would rather not be drawn into your argument.* ■ direct or attract (someone's attention) to something. ■ reach (a conclusion) by deduction or inference from a set of circumstances: *the moral to be drawn is that spending wins votes.* ■ formulate or perceive (a comparison or distinction): *the law drew a clear distinction between innocent and fraudulent misrepresentation.* **5** *Golf* hit (the ball) so that it travels slightly to the left (for a left-handed player, the right), usually as a result of spin given to the ball: *he had to learn to draw the ball.* ■ *Billiards* impart backspin to (the cue ball), making it move backwards after hitting an object ball. **6** (of a ship) require (a specified depth of water) to float in; have (a certain draft): *boats that draw only a few inches of water.* **7** [intr.] (of a sail) be filled with wind.
▶ *phrasal v.* □ **draw back** choose not to do something that one was expected to do. □ **draw on** (of a period of time) pass by and approach its end: *evening drew on.* □ **draw someone out** gently or subtly persuade someone to talk or become more expansive. □ **draw something out** make something last longer. □ **draw something up** prepare a plan, proposal, agreement, or other document in detail: *they instructed an attorney to draw up a sales agreement.*
▶n. **1** an act of selecting names randomly, typically by extracting them from a bag or other container, to match competitors in a game or

tournament: *the draw for this year's tournament.* **2** a game that ends with the score even; a tie. **3** a person or thing that is very attractive or interesting: *the big city was a powerful draw.* **4** an act of inhaling smoke from a cigar or cigarette. **5** an act of removing a gun from its holster in order to shoot. **6** *Golf* a shot causing the ball to deviate to the left (or, for a left-handed golfer, the right). ■ *Billiards* backspin imparted to a cue ball, causing it to move backwards after hitting an object ball.
▶ □ **draw blood** cause someone to bleed, esp. in the course of a fight. □ **draw fire** attract hostile criticism, usually away from a more important target. □ **draw the line at** set a limit of what one is willing to do or accept, beyond which one will not go. □ **quick on the draw** very fast in taking one's gun from its holster. ■ *fig.* very fast in acting or reacting.

draw·back /'drô,bak/ ▶n. **1** a feature that renders something less acceptable; a disadvantage or problem: *the main drawback is the cost.* **2** an amount of excise or import duty remitted on imported goods that the importer reexports rather than sells domestically.

draw·bridge /'drô,brij/ ▶n. *hist.* a bridge, esp. one over a castle's moat, that is hinged at one end so that it may be raised to prevent people's crossing or to allow vessels to pass under it.

draw·er /'drô(ə)r/ ▶n. **1** a boxlike storage compartment without a lid, made to slide horizontally in and out of a desk, chest, or other piece of furniture. **2** (**drawers**) *dated* or *humorous* underpants. **3** a person who draws something, in particular: ■ a person who writes a check. ■ a person who produces a drawing or design.

draw·ing /'drô-iNG/ ▶n. **1** a picture or diagram made with a pencil, pen, or crayon rather than paint, esp. one drawn in monochrome. ■ the art or skill of making such pictures or diagrams. **2** the selection of a winner or winners in a lottery or raffle.

draw·ing board ▶n. a large flat board on which paper may be spread for artists or designers to work on.
▶ □ **back to the drawing board** used to indicate that an idea, scheme, or proposal has been unsuccessful and that a new one must be devised.

draw·ing room ▶n. a room in a large private house in which guests can be received and entertained. ■ a private compartment in a train, typically one that accommodates two or three people.
▶ adj. consciously refined, lighthearted, and elegant: *drawing-room small talk.* ■ (of a song or play) characterized by a polite observance of social proprieties: *a stock figure of Thirties drawing-room comedy.*

drawl /drôl/ ▶ v. [intr.] speak in a slow, lazy way with prolonged vowel sounds: [with *direct speech*] *"Suits me fine,"* he drawled.
▶n. a slow, lazy way of speaking or an accent with unusually prolonged vowel sounds: *a Texas drawl.* —**drawl·er** n. —**drawl·y** adj.

drawn /drôn/ ▶ past participle of DRAW.
▶ adj. (of a person or a person's face) looking strained from illness, exhaustion, anxiety, or pain: *Cathy was pale and drawn.*

draw·string /'drô,striNG/ ▶n. a string in the seam of the material of a garment or a bag, which can be pulled to tighten or close it.

dray /drā/ ▶n. a truck or cart for delivering beer barrels or other heavy loads, esp. a low one without sides.

dray horse ▶n. a large, powerful horse used to pull heavy loads.

dread /dred/ ▶ v. [tr.] anticipate with great apprehension or fear: *I was dreading the party.* ■ *archaic* regard with great awe or reverence.
▶n. **1** great fear or apprehension. **2** *inf.* a person with dreadlocks. ■ (**dreads**) dreadlocks.
▶ adj. greatly feared; dreadful: *AIDS and other dread diseases.* ■ *archaic* regarded with awe; greatly revered: *the great and dread creature.*

dread·ful /'dredfəl/ ▶ adj. causing or involving great suffering, fear, or unhappiness; extremely bad or serious. ■ extremely disagreeable. ■ used to emphasize the degree to which something is the case, esp. something regarded with sadness or disapproval: *you're a dreadful flirt.* ■ (of a person or their feelings) troubled. ■ (of a person or their appearance) feeling or looking ill. —**dread·ful·ly** adv. —**dread·ful·ness** n.

dread·locks /'dred,läks/ ▶ pl. n. a hairstyle in which the hair is washed but not combed and twisted while wet into tight braids or ringlets hanging down on all sides. —**dread·locked** adj.

dread·nought /'dred,nôt/ (also **dread·naught**) ▶n. *hist.* a type of battleship introduced in the early 20th century, larger and faster than its predecessors and equipped entirely with large-caliber guns.

dream /drēm/ ▶n. a series of thoughts, images, and sensations occurring in a person's mind during sleep. ■ a state of mind in which someone is or seems to be unaware of their immediate surroundings: *he had* *been walking around* **in a dream** all day. ■ a cherished aspiration, ambition, or ideal. ■ an unrealistic or self-deluding fantasy. ■ a person or thing perceived as wonderful or perfect.

▶*v.* (*past* and *past part.* **dreamed** or **dreamt** /dremt/) [*intr.*] **1** experience dreams during sleep. ■ [*tr.*] see, hear, or feel (something) in a dream: *maybe you dreamed it.* ■ indulge in daydreams or fantasies, typically about something greatly desired. ■ [*tr.*] (**dream time away**) waste one's time in a lazy, unproductive way. **2** contemplate the possibility of doing something or that something might be the case: *I wouldn't dream of imposing.*

▶*phrasal v.* □ **dream on** [in *imper.*] *inf.* used, esp. in spoken English, as an ironic comment on the unlikely or impractical nature of a plan or aspiration: *Dean thinks he's going to get the job. Dream on, babe.* □ **dream something up** imagine or invent something. ▷Middle English: of Germanic origin, related to Dutch *droom* and German *Traum*, and probably also to Old English *drēam* 'joy, music.' —**dream·ful** /-fəl/ *adj.* (*poetic/lit.*) —**dream·less** *adj.* —**dream·like** /-ˌlīk/ *adj.*

▶ □ **in your dreams** used in spoken English to assert that something much desired is not likely ever to happen. □ **like a dream** *inf.* very well or successfully.

dream·boat /'drēmˌbōt/ ▶*n. inf.* a very attractive person, esp. a man.

dream·er /'drēmər/ ▶*n.* a person who dreams or is dreaming. ■ a person who is unpractical or idealistic: *a rebellious young dreamer.*

dream·land /'drēmˌland/ ▶*n.* sleep regarded as a world of dreams. ■ an imagined and unrealistically ideal world.

dream·y /'drēmē/ ▶*adj.* (**dream·i·er**, **dream·i·est**) reflecting a preoccupation with pleasant thoughts that distract one from one's present surroundings: *a dreamy smile.* ■ (of a person) not practical; given to daydreaming: *a dreamy boy who grew up absorbed in poetry.* ■ having a magical or dreamlike quality; peacefully gentle and relaxing. ■ *inf.* delightful; gorgeous. —**dream·i·ly** /-məlē/ *adv.* —**dream·i·ness** *n.*

drear /dri(ə)r/ ▶*adj.* poetic/literary term for **DREARY**.

drear·y /'dri(ə)rē/ ▶*adj.* (**drear·i·er**, **drear·i·est**) dull, bleak, and lifeless; depressing. —**drear·i·ly** /'dri(ə)rəlē/ *adv.* —**drear·i·ness** *n.*

dredge[1] /drej/ ▶*v.* [*tr.*] clean out the bed of (a harbor, river, or other area of water) by scooping out mud, weeds, and rubbish with a dredge. ■ bring up or clear (something) from a river, harbor, or other area of water with a dredge. ■ (**dredge something up**) *fig.* bring to people's attention an unpleasant or embarrassing fact or incident that had been forgotten: *I don't understand why you had to dredge up this story.*

▶*n.* an apparatus for bringing up objects or mud from a river or seabed by scooping or dragging. ■ a dredger.

dredge[2] ▶*v.* [*tr.*] sprinkle (food) with a powdered substance, typically flour or sugar: *dredge the bananas with sugar and cinnamon.*

dredg·er /'drejər/ ▶*n.* a barge or other vessel designed for dredging harbors or other bodies of water.

dregs /dregz/ ▶*n.* the remnants of a liquid left in a container, together with any sediment or grounds: *coffee dregs.* ■ *fig.* the most worthless part or parts of something: *the dregs of society.* —**dreg·gy** /'dregē/ *adj.*

drench /drenCH/ ▶*v.* [*tr.*] **1** (usu. **be drenched**) wet thoroughly; soak: *I fell in the stream and got drenched* | [as *n.*] (**drenching**) *another drenching would kill the wheat.* ■ *fig.* cover (something) liberally or thoroughly: *drenched in flowers* | [as *adj.*, in *comb.*] (**-drenched**) *a sun-drenched clearing.* **2** forcibly administer a drug in liquid form orally to (an animal).

dress /dres/ ▶*v.* **1** [*intr.*] put on one's clothes: *I'll go and* **get dressed**. ■ wear clothes in a particular way or of a particular type: *she's nice-looking and dresses well* | (**be dressed**) *he was dressed in jeans and a thick sweater.* ■ [*tr.*] put clothes on (someone). ■ put on clothes appropriate for a formal occasion. ■ [*tr.*] design or supply clothes for (a celebrity): *for over four decades he dressed the royal family.* ■ [*tr.*] decorate (something) in an artistic or attractive way. **2** [*tr.*] treat or prepare (something) in a certain way, in particular: ■ clean, treat, or apply a dressing to (a wound). ■ clean and prepare (food, esp. poultry or shellfish) for cooking or eating: [as *adj.*] (**dressed**) *dressed crab.* ■ add a dressing to (a salad). ■ apply a fertilizing substance to (a field, garden, or plant). ■ complete the preparation or manufacture of (leather or fabric) by treating its surface in some way. ■ smooth the surface of (stone): [as *adj.*] (**dressed**) *a tower of dressed stone.* ■ arrange or style (one's own or someone else's hair), esp. in an elaborate way. **3** [*tr.*] *Mil.* draw up (troops) in the proper alignment. ■ [*intr.*] (of troops) come into such an alignment. **4** [*tr.*] prepare (an artificial fly) for use in fishing: [as *adj.*] (**dressed**) *a dressed wet fly.*

▶*phrasal v.* □ **dress down** dress informally. □ **dress someone down** *inf.* reprimand someone. □ **dress up** dress in smart or formal clothes. ■ dress in a special costume for fun or as part of an entertainment: *he*

dressed up as a gorilla. □ **dress something up** present something in such a way that it appears better than it really is.

▶*n.* **1** a one-piece garment for a woman or girl that covers the body and extends down over the legs. **2** clothing of a specified kind for men or women: *traditional African dress.* ■ [as *adj.*] denoting military uniform or other clothing used on formal or ceremonial occasions: *a dress suit.*

▶ □ **dressed to kill** wearing glamorous clothes intended to create a striking impression. □ **dressed to the nines** dressed very elaborately.

dres·sage /drə'säzH/ ▶*n.* the art of riding and training a horse in a manner that develops obedience, flexibility, and balance.

dress cir·cle ▶*n.* the first level of seats above the ground floor in a theater.

dress code ▶*n.* a set of rules, usually written and posted, specifying the required manner of dress at a school, office, club, restaurant, etc. ■ the customary style of dress of a specified group.

dres·ser[1] /'dresər/ ▶*n.* a chest of drawers. ■ a sideboard with shelves above for storing and displaying plates and kitchen utensils.

dres·ser[2] ▶*n.* **1** a person who dresses in a specified way: *a snappy dresser.* ■ a person who habitually dresses in a smart or elegant way: *she's gorgeous—and she's a dresser.* **2** a person whose job is to look after theatrical costumes and help actors to dress. **3** a person who prepares, treats, or finishes a material or piece of equipment.

dress·ing /'dresiNG/ ▶*n.* **1** (also **sal·ad dress·ing**) a sauce for salads, typically one consisting of oil and vinegar mixed together with herbs or other flavorings. ■ stuffing: *turkey with apple dressing.* **2** a piece of material placed on a wound to protect it: *an antiseptic dressing.* **3** a fertilizing substance such as compost or manure spread over or plowed into land.

dress·ing-down ▶*n. inf.* a severe reprimand.

dress·ing gown ▶*n.* a long loose robe, typically worn after getting out of bed or bathing.

dress·ing room ▶*n.* a room in which actors change clothes before and after their performance. ■ a small room or cubicle in a clothing store, used by customers to try on clothes.

dress·ing ta·ble ▶*n.* a table with a mirror and drawers for cosmetics, etc., used while dressing or applying makeup.

dress·mak·er /'dresˌmākər/ ▶*n.* a person whose job is making women's clothes. —**dress·mak·ing** /-kiNG/ *n.*

dress·y /'dresē/ ▶*adj.* (**dress·i·er**, **dress·i·est**) (of clothes) suitable for a festive or formal occasion. ■ requiring or given to wearing such clothes. —**dress·i·ly** /'dresəlē/ *adv.* —**dress·i·ness** *n.*

drew /drŌŌ/ ▶ past of **DRAW**.

drib·ble /'dribəl/ ▶*v.* **1** [*intr.*] (of a liquid) fall slowly in drops or a thin stream. ■ [*tr.*] pour (a liquid) in such a way: *he dribbled cream into his coffee.* ■ [*intr.*] allow saliva to run from the mouth: *his mouth was open and he was dribbling.* **2** [*tr.*] (chiefly in soccer, field hockey, and basketball) take (the ball) forward past opponents with slight touches of the feet or the stick, or (in basketball) by continuous bouncing: *dribble the ball from the goal area* | [*intr.*] *he dribbled past Amos.*

▶*n.* **1** a thin stream of liquid; a trickle: *a dribble of blood.* ■ saliva running from the mouth. **2** *fig.* foolish talk or ideas; nonsense. **3** (in soccer, hockey, and basketball) an act or instance of taking the ball forward with repeated slight touches or bounces. —**drib·bler** /-b(ə)lər/ *n.*

dribs and drabs /'dribz ən 'drabz/ ▶*pl. n.* (**in dribs and drabs**) *inf.* in small scattered or sporadic amounts: *doing the work in dribs and drabs.*

dried /drīd/ ▶ past and past participle of **DRY**.

dri·er[1] /'drīər/ ▶*adj.* comparative of **DRY**.

dri·er[2] ▶*n.* variant spelling of **DRYER**.

dri·est /'drīəst/ ▶*adj.* superlative of **DRY**.

drift /drift/ ▶*v.* [*intr.*] **1** be carried slowly by a current of air or water. ■ (of a person) walk slowly, aimlessly, or casually: *people began to drift away.* ■ move passively, aimlessly, or involuntarily into a certain situation or condition: *I was drifting off to sleep* | *Lewis and his father drifted apart.* ■ (of a person or their attention) digress or stray to another subject: *I noticed my audience's attention drifting.* **2** (esp. of snow or leaves) be blown into heaps by the wind.

▶*n.* **1** a continuous slow movement from one place to another: *there was a drift to the towns.* ■ the deviation of a vessel, aircraft, or projectile from its intended or expected course as the result of currents or winds. ■ a steady movement or development from one thing toward another, esp. one that is perceived as unwelcome: *the drift toward a more repressive style of policing.* ■ a state of inaction or indecision. **2** the general intention or meaning of an argument or someone's remarks: *he didn't understand much Greek, but he* **got her drift**. **3** a large mass of snow, leaves, or other material piled up or carried along by the wind.

■ *Geol.* glacial deposits left by retreating ice sheets. **4** *Mining* a horizontal or inclined passage following a mineral vein or coal seam. —**drift·y** *adj.*

drift·er /'driftər/ ▶ *n.* a person who is continually moving from place to place, without any fixed home or job.

drift net (also **drift·net**) ▶ *n.* a large net for herring and similar fish, kept upright by weights at the bottom and floats at the top and allowed to drift with the tide. —**drift net·ter** *n.* —**drift net·ting** *n.*

drift·wood /'drift,wŏŏd/ ▶ *n.* pieces of wood that are floating on the sea or have been washed ashore.

drill¹ /dril/ ▶ *n.* **1** a hand tool, power tool, or machine with a rotating cutting tip or reciprocating hammer or chisel, used for making holes. ■ such a tool used by a dentist for cutting away part of a tooth before filling it. **2** instruction or training in military exercises. ■ intensive instruction or training in something, typically by means of repeated exercises. ■ a rehearsal of the procedure to be followed in an emergency. ■ (**the drill**) *inf.* the correct or recognized procedure or way of doing something: *he didn't know the drill.* **3** a predatory mollusk (family Muricidae) that bores into the shells of other mollusks in order to feed on the soft tissue.
▶ *v.* [*tr.*] **1** produce (a hole) in something by or as if by boring with a drill. ■ make a hole in (something) by boring

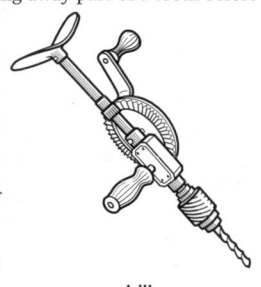

drill

with a drill. ■ [*intr.*] make a hole in or through something by using a drill. ■ [*intr.*] sink a borehole in order to obtain a certain substance, typically oil or water. ■ (of a dentist) cut away part of (a tooth) before filling it. ■ [*tr.*] *inf.* (of a sports player) hit, throw, or kick (a ball or puck) hard and in a straight line. **2** subject (someone) to military training exercises. ■ [*intr.*] (of a person) take part in such exercises. ■ instruct (someone) in something by the means of repeated exercises or practice. ■ (**drill something into**) cause (someone) to learn something by repeating it regularly. —**drill·er** *n.*

drill² ▶ *n.* a machine that makes small furrows, sows seed in them, and then covers the sown seed. ■ a small furrow, esp. one made by such a machine. ■ a ridge with such a furrow on top. ■ a row of plants sown in such a furrow: *drills of lettuce.*
▶ *v.* [*tr.*] (of a person or machine) sow (seed) with a drill: *crops drilled in autumn.* ■ plant (the ground) in furrows: *we drill next week.*

drill³ ▶ *n.* a dark brown baboon (*Mandrillus leucophaeus*) with a short tail, found in the rain forests of West Africa.

drill⁴ ▶ *n.* a coarse twilled cotton or linen fabric.

drill·ing rig ▶ *n.* a large structure with equipment for drilling an oil well.

drill·mas·ter /'dril,mastər/ ▶ *n.* one who instructs or leads others, esp. recruits, in military drills and marching. ■ a rigorous, exacting, or severe instructor; a martinet.

drill press ▶ *n.* a machine tool for drilling holes, set on a fixed stand.

drill ser·geant ▶ *n.* a noncommissioned officer who trains soldiers in basic military skills.

drink /driNGk/ ▶ *v.* (*past* **drank** /draNGk/; *past part.* **drunk** /drəNGk/) [*tr.*] take (a liquid) into the mouth and swallow. ■ [*intr.*] consume or be in the habit of consuming alcohol, esp. to excess: *she doesn't drink or smoke.* ■ [*intr.*] (**drink up**) consume the rest of a drink, esp. in a rapid manner. ■ (**drink something in**) *fig.* watch or listen to something with eager pleasure or interest: *she strolled to the window to drink in the view.* ■ *inf.* (of a plant or a porous substance) absorb (moisture).
▶ *n.* a liquid that can be swallowed as refreshment or nourishment. ■ a quantity of liquid swallowed: *a drink of water.* ■ alcohol, or the habitual or excessive consumption of alcohol: *the effects of too much drink.* ■ a glass of liquid, esp. when alcoholic: *we went for a drink.* ■ (**the drink**) *inf.* the sea or another large area of water. —**drink·a·ble** *adj.* —**drink·er** *n.*
▶ □ **drink deep** take a large draft or drafts of something: *fig. he learned to drink deep of the Catholic tradition.* □ **drink someone under the table** *inf.* consume as much alcohol as one's drinking companion without becoming as drunk. □ **I'll drink to that** uttered to express one's agreement with or approval of a statement.

drink·ing foun·tain ▶ *n.* a device producing a small jet of water for drinking.

drip /drip/ ▶ *v.* (**dripped, drip·ping**) [*intr.*] let fall or be so wet as to shed small drops of liquid. ■ (of liquid) fall in small drops: *water dripped from her clothing.* ■ [*tr.*] cause or allow (a liquid) to fall in such a way: *the candle*

was dripping wax down one side. ■ *fig.* display a copious amount or degree of a particular quality or thing: *the women were dripping with gold and diamonds* | [*tr.*] *her voice dripped sarcasm.*
▶ *n.* **1** a small drop of a liquid. ■ the action or sound of liquid falling steadily in small drops. **2** *inf.* a weak and ineffectual person. **3** *Archit.* a projection or groove on the underside of a cornice, windowsill, or molding that prevents rain from running down the wall below.

drip-dry ▶ *adj.* (of a fabric or garment) capable of drying without creasing when hung up after washing: *drip-dry shirts.*
▶ *v.* [*intr.*] (of fabric or a garment) become dry without forming creases when hung up after washing. ■ [*tr.*] dry (fabric or a garment) by hanging it up in this way: *it's easy to wash and simple to drip-dry.*

drip·ping /'dripiNG/ ▶ *n.* (**drippings**) fat and juices that have dripped from roasting meat, used in cooking. ■ wax, fat, or other liquid produced from something by the effect of heat.
▶ *adj.* extremely wet: *dripping wet hair.*

drip·py /'dripē/ ▶ *adj.* (**drip·pi·er, drip·pi·est**) **1** *inf.* weak, ineffectual, or sloppily sentimental: *a drippy love song.* **2** tending to drip: *drippy food.* —**drip·pi·ly** /'dripilē/ *adv.* —**drip·pi·ness** *n.*

drive /drīv/ ▶ *v.* (*past* **drove** /drōv/; *past part.* **driv·en** /'drivən/) **1** [*intr.*] operate and control the direction and speed of a motor vehicle: *he got into his car and drove off* | [*tr.*] *he drove the van onto the sidewalk.* ■ [*tr.*] own or use (a specified type of motor vehicle): *Sue drives an old Chevy.* ■ [*intr.*] be licensed or competent to drive a motor vehicle: *can you drive?* ■ [*tr.*] convey (someone) in a vehicle, esp. a private car: *Shelley drove him to the store.* **2** [*tr.*] propel or carry along by force in a specified direction: *the wind will drive you onshore.* ■ [*intr.*] (of wind, water, or snow) move or fall with great force. ■ [*tr.*] (of a source of power) provide the energy to set and keep (an engine or piece of machinery) in motion: *turbines driven by steam.* ■ *Electr.* (of a device) power or operate (another device): *the interface can be used to drive a printer.* ■ [*tr.*] force (a stake or nail) into place by hitting or pushing it: *nails are driven through the boards.* ■ [*tr.*] bore (a tunnel). ■ (in ball games) hit or kick (the ball) hard with a free swing of the bat, racket, or foot. ■ [*tr.*] *Golf* strike (a ball) from the tee, typically with a driver. **3** [*tr.*] urge or force (animals or people) to move in a specified direction. ■ [*tr.*] urge forward and direct the course of (an animal drawing a vehicle or plow). ■ [*tr.*] chase or frighten (wild animals) into nets, traps, or into a small area where they can be killed or captured. ■ compel to leave. **4** [*tr.*] (usu. **be driven**) (of a fact or feeling) compel (someone) to act in a particular way, esp. one that is considered undesirable or inappropriate: *he was driven by ambition* | [as *adj.*] (**driven**) *my husband is a driven man.* ■ [*tr.*] bring (someone) forcibly into a specified negative state: *the thought drove him to despair.* ■ [*tr.*] force (someone) to work to an excessive extent.
▶ *n.* **1** a trip or journey in a car. ■ [in *names*] a street or road: *Hammond Drive.* ■ short for DRIVEWAY. **2** *Psychol.* an innate, biologically determined urge to attain a goal or satisfy a need: *sexual drives.* ■ the determination and ambition of a person to achieve something: *drive sustained her through some shattering experiences.* **3** an organized effort by a number of people to achieve a particular purpose, often to raise money. ■ *Football* a series of offensive plays that advance the ball for the purpose of a score: *an 80-yard scoring drive.* **4** the transmission of power to machinery or to the wheels of a motor vehicle. ■ (in a car with automatic transmission) the position of the gear selector in which the car will move forward, shifting gears automatically as required. ■ *Comput.* short for DISK DRIVE. **5** (in ball games) a forceful stroke made with a free swing of the bat, racket, or foot against the ball. ■ *Golf* a shot from the tee. **6** an act of driving a group of animals to a particular destination. —**driv·a·bil·i·ty** /,drīvə'bilitē/ (also **drive·a·bil·i·ty**) *n.* —**driv·a·ble** (also **drive·a·ble**) *adj.*
▶ □ **drive something home** see HOME. □ **what someone is driving at** the point that someone is attempting to make.

drive-by ▶ *adj.* (of a shooting or other act) carried out from a passing vehicle. ■ *inf.* superficial or casual: *drive-by journalism.* ■ *inf.* (of a medical procedure in a hospital or clinic) involving a brief duration of on-site care for the patient. ■ *inf.* denoting a facility that performs such procedures as a customary practice.
▶ *n.* a shooting carried out from a passing vehicle.

drive-in ▶ *adj.* denoting a facility such as a restaurant that one can visit without leaving one's car.
▶ *n.* a facility of this type.

driv·el /'drivəl/ ▶ *n.* silly nonsense.

D

▸ v. (**driv·eled**, **driv·el·ing**; *Brit.* **driv·elled**, **driv·el·ling**) [*intr.*] **1** talk nonsense. **2** *archaic* let saliva or mucus flow from the mouth or nose; dribble. —**driv·el·er** (*Brit.* **driv·el·ler**) *n.*

driv·en /'drivən/ ▸ past participle of DRIVE.
▸ *adj.* **1** [in *comb.*] moved or controlled by a specified person or source of power: *a chauffeur-driven limousine* | *wind-driven sand.* ■ motivated or determined by a specified factor or feeling: *a market-driven response.* **2** (of snow) piled into drifts or made smooth by the wind.

driv·er /'drīvər/ ▸ *n.* **1** a person who drives a vehicle. ■ a person who drives a specified kind of animal: *mule drivers.* **2** a wheel or other part in a mechanism that receives power directly and transmits motion to other parts. ■ *Electr.* a device or part of a circuit that provides power for output. ■ *Comput.* a program that controls the operation of a device such as a printer or scanner. **3** a golf club with a flat face and wooden head, used for driving from the tee. —**driv·er·less** *adj.*
▸ □ **in the driver's seat** in control of or dominating a situation.

drive·shaft /'drīv‚SHaft/ ▸ *n.* a rotating shaft that transmits torque in an engine.

drive·train /'drīv‚trān/ ▸ *n.* the system in a motor vehicle that connects the transmission to the drive axles.

drive·way /'drīv‚wā/ ▸ *n.* a short road leading from a public road to a house or garage.

driv·ing /'drīvɪNG/ ▸ *adj.* (of rain or snow) falling and being blown by the wind with great force: *driving rain.* ■ having a strong and controlling influence: *Macmillan was the driving force behind the plan* | *a driving ambition.* ■ energetic; dynamic: *driving dance rhythms.*
▸ *n.* the control and operation of a motor vehicle.

driv·ing range ▸ *n.* an area where golfers can practice drives.

driz·zle /'drizəl/ ▸ *n.* light rain falling in very fine drops. ■ *Cooking* a thin stream of a liquid ingredient trickled over something.
▸ *v.* [*intr.*] (**it drizzles**, **it is drizzling**, etc.) rain lightly: [as *adj.*] (**drizzling**) *the drizzling rain.* ■ [*tr.*] *Cooking* cause a thin stream of (a liquid ingredient) to trickle over food: *drizzle the clarified butter over the top.* ■ [*tr.*] cause a liquid ingredient to trickle over (food) in this way. —**driz·zly** /-z(ə)lē/ *adj.*

droll /drōl/ ▸ *adj.* curious or unusual in a way that provokes dry amusement.
▸ *n. archaic* a jester or entertainer; a buffoon. —**droll·er·y** /'drōlərē/ *n.* —**droll·ness** *n.* —**drol·ly** *adv.*

drom·e·dar·y /'drämə‚derē/ ▸ *n.* (*pl.* **-dar·ies**) an Arabian camel, esp. one of a light and swift breed trained for riding or racing. ▷Middle English: from Old French *dromedaire* or late Latin *dromedarius (camelus)* 'swift camel,' based on Greek *dromas, dromad-* 'runner.'

drone /drōn/ ▸ *v.* [*intr.*] make a continuous low humming sound: *a machine droned.* ■ speak tediously in a dull monotonous tone. ■ move with a continuous humming sound: *traffic droned up and down the street.*
▸ *n.* **1** a low continuous humming sound. ■ *inf.* a monotonous speech. ■ a continuous musical note, typically of low pitch. ■ a musical instrument, or part of one, sounding such a continuous note, in particular (also **drone pipe**) a pipe in a bagpipe or (also **drone string**) a string in an instrument such as a hurdy-gurdy or a sitar. **2** a male bee in a colony of social bees, which does no work but can fertilize a queen. ■ *fig.* a person who does no useful work and lives off others. **3** a remote-controlled pilotless aircraft or missile.

drool /drool/ ▸ *v.* [*intr.*] drop saliva uncontrollably from the mouth: *the baby begins to drool, then to cough.* ■ *inf.* make an excessive and obvious show of pleasure or desire: *I could imagine his being drooled over.*
▸ *n.* saliva falling from the mouth.

droop /droop/ ▸ *v.* [*intr.*] bend or hang downward limply. ■ sag down from or as if from weariness or dejection. ■ [*tr.*] cause to bend or hang downward: *James drooped his head.*
▸ *n.* an act or instance of drooping; a limp or weary attitude: *the exhausted droop of her shoulders.*

droop·y /'droopē/ ▸ *adj.* (**droop·i·er**, **droop·i·est**) hanging down limply; drooping: *a droopy mustache.* ■ lacking strength or spirit. —**droop·i·ly** /-pəlē/ *adv.* —**droop·i·ness** *n.*

drop /dräp/ ▸ *v.* (**dropped**, **drop·ping**) [*tr.*] **1** let or make (something) fall vertically. ■ deliver (supplies or troops) by parachute: *the airlift dropped food into the camp.* ■ *Rugby* score (a goal) by a drop kick. ■ (of an animal, esp. a mare, cow, or ewe) give birth to (young). ■ *inf.* take (a drug, esp. LSD) orally. **2** [*intr.*] fall vertically: *the spoon dropped clatter from her hand.* ■ (of a person) allow oneself to fall; let oneself down without jumping: *they escaped by dropping to the ground.* ■ (of a person or animal) sink to or toward the ground: *he dropped to his knees in the mud.* ■ *inf.* collapse or die from exhaustion: *he looked ready to drop.* ■ (of ground) slope steeply down: *the cliff drops to the valley below.* **3** become or make lower,

weaker, or less: [*tr.*] *he dropped his voice as she came into the room* | [*intr.*] *profits dropped by 37 percent* | *tourism has dropped off in the last few years.* **4** abandon or discontinue (a course of action or study): *the charges against him were dropped last year* | *drop everything and get over here!* ■ discard or exclude (someone or something): *they were dropped from the team.* ■ *inf.* stop associating with: *I was under pressure from friends to drop Barbara.* ■ omit (a letter or syllable) in speech: *our au pair drops her h's.* **5** set down or unload (a passenger or goods), esp. on the way to somewhere else. ■ [*tr.*] put or leave in a particular place without ceremony or formality: *just drop it in the mail when you've got time.* ■ mention in passing, typically in order to impress: *she dropped a remark about having been included in the selection.* **6** (in sports) fail to win (a point, game, or match). ■ *inf.* lose (money), esp. through gambling.
▸ *phrasal v.* □ **drop back/behind** fall back or get left behind: *the colt was struggling and started to drop back.* □ **drop by/in** call informally and briefly as a visitor: *they would unexpectedly drop in on us.* □ **drop into 1** call casually and informally at (a place). **2** pass quickly and easily into (a habitual state or manner): *she couldn't help dropping into a Brooklyn accent.* □ **drop off** fall asleep easily, esp. without intending to. □ **drop out 1** cease to participate in a race or competition. **2** abandon a course of study: *kids who had dropped out of college.* **3** reject conventional society to pursue an alternative lifestyle.
▸ *n.* **1** a small round or pear-shaped portion of liquid that hangs or falls or adheres to a surface: *drops of rain splashed on the ground.* ■ a very small amount of liquid: *there was not a drop of water in sight.* ■ a drink of alcoholic liquor: *he doesn't touch a drop during the week.* ■ (**drops**) liquid medicine to be measured or applied in very small amounts. **2** an instance of falling or dropping: *the drop of the curtain.* ■ an act of dropping supplies or troops by parachute: *the planes finally managed to make the drop.* ■ a fall in amount, quality, or rate: *a drop in consumer spending.* ■ an abrupt fall or slope: *standing on the lip of a sixty-foot drop.* **3** something that drops or is dropped, in particular: ■ a section of theatrical scenery lowered from the flies; a drop cloth or drop curtain. ■ a trapdoor on a gallows, the opening of which causes the prisoner to fall and thus be hanged. ■ (**the drop**) execution by hanging. **4** something resembling a drop of liquid in shape, in particular: ■ a piece of candy or a lozenge. ■ a pendant earring. **5** *inf.* a delivery: *I got to the depot and made the drop.* ■ a mailbox. ■ a hiding place for stolen, illicit, or secret things. —**drop·pa·ble** *adj.* —**drop·let** /-lit/ *n.*
▸ □ **at the drop of a hat** *inf.* without delay or good reason. □ **drop the ball** *inf.* make a mistake; mishandle things. □ **drop dead** die suddenly and unexpectedly. ■ [in *imper.*] *inf.* used as an expression of intense scorn or dislike. □ **drop a** (or **the**) **dime on** *inf.* inform on (someone) to the police. □ **drop like flies** see FLY². □ **drop one's guard** abandon one's habitual defensive or protective stance. □ **drop a hint** (or **drop hints**) let fall a hint or hints, as if casually or unconsciously. □ **a drop in the bucket** (or *Brit.* **ocean**) a very small amount compared with what is needed or expected. □ **drop someone a line** send someone a note or letter in a casual manner: *drop me a line at the usual address.* □ **drop names** see NAME-DROPPING. □ **drop a stitch** let a stitch fall off the end of a knitting needle. □ **drop one's trousers** deliberately let one's trousers fall down, esp. in a public place. □ **have the drop on** *inf.* have the advantage over.

drop cur·tain ▸ *n.* a curtain or painted cloth lowered vertically on to a theater stage.

drop kick ▸ *n.* (formerly, in football) a kick for a goal made by dropping the ball and kicking after it touches the ground. ■ (chiefly in martial arts) a flying kick made against an opponent while dropping to the ground.
▸ *v.* (**drop-kick**) [*tr.*] kick using a drop kick.

drop leaf ▸ *n.* a hinged table leaf.

drop·out /'dräp‚out/ ▸ *n.* a person who has abandoned a course of study or who has rejected conventional society to pursue an alternative lifestyle: *a college dropout.*

drop·per /'dräpər/ ▸ *n.* a short glass tube with a rubber bulb at one end and a tiny hole at the other, for measuring out drops of medicine or other liquids.

drop·pings /'dräpɪNGz/ ▸ *pl. n.* the excrement of certain animals, such as rodents, sheep, birds, and insects.

drop shot ▸ *n.* (chiefly in tennis or squash) a softly hit shot, usually with backspin, which drops abruptly to the ground.

drop·sy /'dräpsē/ ▸ *n.* (*pl.* **-sies**) old-fashioned or less technical term for EDEMA. —**drop·si·cal** /-sikəl/ *adj.*

dro·soph·i·la /drə'säfələ/ ▸ *n.* a small fruit fly (genus *Drosophila*, family Drosophilidae), used extensively in genetic research because of its large chromosomes, numerous varieties, and rapid rate of reproduction.

dross /drôs; dräs/ ▶n. something regarded as worthless; rubbish. ■ foreign matter, dregs, or mineral waste, in particular scum formed on the surface of molten metal. —**dross·y** *adj.*

drought /drout/ ▶n. a prolonged period of abnormally low rainfall; a shortage of water resulting from this. ■ *fig.* a prolonged absence of something specified: *he ended a five-game hitting drought.* ■ *archaic* thirst. —**drought·i·ness** *n.* —**drought·y** *adj.*

drove[1] /drōv/ ▶ past of DRIVE.

drove[2] ▶n. a herd or flock of animals being driven in a body: *a drove of cattle.* ■ a large number of people or things doing or undergoing the same thing: *tourists have stayed away* **in droves** *this summer.* —**dro·ver** *n.*

drown /droun/ ▶v. [intr.] die through submersion in and inhalation of water. ■ [tr.] deliberately kill (a person or animal) in this way. ■ [tr.] submerge or flood (an area). ■ [tr.] (of a sound) make (another sound) inaudible by being much louder: *his voice was* **drowned out** *by engine noise.*
▶*phrasal v.* □ **drowned in** be overwhelmed or enveloped by: *drowned in his work.* ■ (of food) immersed in or covered by: *ham drowned in syrup.*
▶ □ **drown one's sorrows** forget one's problems by getting drunk. □ **like a drowned rat** extremely wet and bedraggled.

drowse /drouz/ ▶v. [intr.] be half asleep; doze intermittently. ■ *archaic* be sluggish or inactive: *let not your prudence drowse.*
▶*n.* a light sleep; a condition of being half asleep.

drow·sy /ˈdrouzē/ ▶*adj.* (-**si·er**, -**si·est**) sleepy and lethargic; half asleep. ■ causing sleepiness: *the drowsy heat.* ■ (esp. of a place) very peaceful and quiet. —**drow·si·ly** /-zəlē/ *adv.* —**drow·si·ness** *n.*

drub /drəb/ ▶v. (**drubbed**, **drub·bing**) [tr.] hit or beat (someone) repeatedly. ■ *inf.* defeat thoroughly in a match or contest. —**drub·bing** *n.*

drudge /drəj/ ▶n. a person made to do hard, menial, or dull work.
▶*v.* [intr.] *archaic* do such work. —**drudg·er·y** *n.*

drug /drəg/ ▶n. a substance that has a physiological effect when ingested or otherwise introduced into the body, in particular: ■ a medicine, esp. a pharmaceutical preparation. ■ a substance taken for its narcotic or stimulant effects, often illegally.
▶*v.* (**drugged**, **drug·ging**) [tr.] administer a drug to (someone) in order to induce stupor or insensibility: *they were drugged to keep them quiet.* ■ add a drug to (food or drink): [as *adj.*] (**drugged**) *he offered them drugged wine.* ■ [intr.] [usu. as *n.*] (**drugging**) *inf.* take illegally obtained drugs: *fifteen years of drinking and drugging.* ▷Middle English: from Old French *drogue*, possibly from Middle Dutch *droge vate*, literally 'dry vats,' referring to the contents (i.e., dry goods).
▶ □ **do drugs** *inf.* take illegal drugs. □ **on drugs** under the influence of or habitually taking illegal drugs.

drug ad·dict ▶n. a person who is addicted to one or more narcotic drugs.

drug·gie /ˈdrəgē/ (also **drug·gy**) ▶n. *inf.* a drug addict.

drug·gist /ˈdrəgist/ ▶n. a pharmacist or retailer of medicinal drugs.

drug·store /ˈdrəgˌstôr/ ▶n. a pharmacy that also sells toiletries and other articles.

Dru·id /ˈdrōoid/ ▶n. a priest, magician, or soothsayer in the ancient Celtic religion. ■ a member of a present-day group claiming to represent or be derived from this religion. —**Dru·id·ic** /drōoˈidik/ *adj.* —**Dru·id·i·cal** /drōoˈidikəl/ *adj.* —**Dru·id·ism** /-ˌizəm/ *n.*

drum[1] /drəm/ ▶n. **1** a percussion instrument sounded by being struck with sticks or the hands, typically cylindrical, barrel-shaped, or bowl-shaped with a taut membrane over one or both ends. ■ (**drums**) a set of drums. ■ (**drums**) the percussion section of a band or orchestra. ■ a sound made by or resembling that of a drum: *the drum of their feet.* **2** something resembling or likened to a drum in shape, in particular: ■ a cylindrical container or receptacle. ■ a rotating cylindrical part in a washing machine, in which the laundry is placed. ■ a similar cylindrical part in certain other appliances. ■ *Archit.* the circular vertical wall supporting a dome. ■ *Archit.* a stone block forming part of a column.
▶*v.* (**drummed**, **drum·ming**) [intr.] play on a drum. ■ make a continuous rhythmic noise: [as *n.*] (**drumming**) *the drumming of hooves.* ■ [tr.] beat (the fingers, feet, etc.) repeatedly on a surface, esp. as a sign of impatience or annoyance. ■ (of a woodpecker) strike the bill rapidly on a dead trunk or branch. ■ (of a snipe) vibrate the outer tail feathers in a diving display flight, making a throbbing sound.
▶*phrasal v.* □ **drum something into** drive a lesson into (someone) by constant repetition: *it had been drummed into them to dress correctly.* □ **drum someone out** expel or dismiss someone with ignominy from a place or institution: *he was drummed out of the air force.* □ **drum something**

up attempt to obtain something by canvassing or soliciting: *hoping to drum up support.*
▶ □ **beat** (or **bang**) **the drum for** (or **against**) be ostentatiously in support of (or in opposition to): *beating the drum against PACs.*

drum[2] (also **drumfish**) ▶n. (*pl.* same or **drums**) a fish (family Sciaenidae) that makes a drumming sound by vibrating its swim bladder, found mainly in estuarine and shallow coastal waters.

drum·beat /ˈdrəmˌbēt/ ▶n. a stroke or pattern of strokes on a drum.

drum brake ▶n. a type of vehicle brake in which brake shoes press against the inside of a drum on the wheel.

drum·head /ˈdrəmˌhed/ ▶n. the membrane or skin of a drum.
▶*adj.* carried out by or as if by an army in the field; improvised or summary: *a drumhead court-martial.*

drum·lin /ˈdrəmlin/ ▶n. *Geol.* a low oval mound or small hill, typically one of a group, consisting of compacted boulder clay molded by past glacial action.

drum ma·jor ▶n. **1** a noncommissioned officer commanding the drummers of a regimental band. **2** the male leader of a marching band, who often twirls a baton. ■ a male member of a baton-twirling parading group.

drum ma·jor·ette ▶n. the female leader of a marching band. ■ a girl or woman who twirls a baton, typically with a marching band or drum corps.

drum·mer /ˈdrəmər/ ▶n. **1** a person who plays a drum or drums. **2** *inf.* a traveling sales representative.

drum·stick /ˈdrəmˌstik/ ▶n. a stick, typically with a shaped or padded head, used for beating a drum. ■ the lower joint of the leg of a cooked chicken, turkey, or other fowl.

drunk /drəNGk/ ▶ past participle of DRINK.
▶*adj.* affected by alcohol to the extent of losing control of one's faculties or behavior. ■ (**drunk with**) *fig.* overcome with (a strong emotion): *the crowd was high on euphoria and drunk with patriotism.*
▶*n.* a person who is drunk or who habitually drinks to excess. ■ *inf.* a drinking bout; a period of drunkenness: *he used to go on drunks.*

drunk·ard /ˈdrəNGkərd/ ▶n. a person who is habitually drunk.

drunk·en /ˈdrəNGkən/ ▶*adj.* drunk or intoxicated. ■ habitually or frequently drunk: *his violent, drunken father.* ■ caused by or showing the effects of drink: *the man's drunken, slurred speech.* —**drunk·en·ly** *adv.* —**drunk·en·ness** *n.*

drupe /drōop/ ▶n. *Bot.* a fleshy fruit with thin skin and a central stone containing the seed, e.g., a plum, cherry, almond, or olive. ▷mid 18th cent.: from Latin *drupa* 'overripe olive,' from Greek *druppa* 'olive.' —**dru·pa·ceous** /drōoˈpāSHəs/ *adj.*

drupe·let /ˈdrōoplit/ ▶n. *Bot.* any of the small individual drupes forming a fleshy aggregate fruit such as a blackberry or raspberry.

druse /drōoz/ ▶n. *Geol.* a rock cavity lined with a crust of projecting crystals. ■ the crust of crystals lining such a cavity. —**drus·y** *adj.*

druth·er /ˈdrəTHər/ *inf.* ▶n. (usu. **one's druthers**) a person's preference in a matter: *if I had my druthers, I would prefer to be a writer.*

dry /drī/ ▶*adj.* (**dri·er**, **dri·est**) **1** free from moisture or liquid; not wet or moist. ■ having lost all wetness or moisture over a period of time: *dry paint.* ■ for use without liquid: *dry latrines.* ■ with little or no rainfall or humidity: *two dry winters in a row.* ■ (of a river, lake, or stream) empty of water as a result of evaporation and lack of rainfall. ■ (of a source) not yielding a supply of water or oil: *a dry well.* ■ thirsty or thirst-making: *working in the hot sun is making me dry | dry work.* ■ (of a cow or other domestic animal) having stopped producing milk. ■ without grease or other moisturizer or lubricator: *dry hair.* ■ (of bread or toast) without butter or other spreads: *only dry bread and water.* **2** *fig.* bare or lacking adornment: *the dry facts.* ■ unexciting; dull. ■ unemotional, undemonstrative, or impassive. ■ (of a joke or sense of humor) subtle, expressed in a matter-of-fact way, and having the appearance of being unconscious or unintentional. **3** prohibiting the sale or consumption of alcoholic drink: *the country is dry, in accordance with Islamic law.* ■ (of a person) no longer addicted to or drinking alcohol. **4** (of an alcoholic drink) not sweet: *a dry red wine.*
▶*v.* (**dries**, **dried**) [intr.] **1** become dry: *waiting for the socks to dry.* ■ [tr.] cause to become dry: *dry your hair.* ■ [tr.] wipe tears from (the eyes): *she dried her eyes and blew her nose.* ■ wipe dishes dry with a cloth after they have been washed. ■ [tr.] [usu. as *adj.*] (**dried**) preserve by allowing or encouraging evaporation of moisture from: *dried flowers.* **2** *theatrical slang* forget one's lines: *he dried in the middle of a scene.*

▶**phrasal v.** □ **dry out** *inf.* (of an alcoholic) abstain from alcoholic drink, esp. as part of a detoxification program. □ **dry up** (of something perceived as a continuous flow or source) decrease and stop: *his commissions began to dry up.*

▶**n.** (*pl.* **dries** or **drys**) a person in favor of the prohibition of alcohol. —**dry·ly** *adv.* —**dry·ness** *n.*

▶ □ **come up dry** be unsuccessful. □ (**as**) **dry as a bone** extremely dry. □ (**as**) **dry as dust** extremely dry. ■ extremely dull; lacking emotion, expression, or interest.

dry·ad /'drī,ad; -əd/ ▶*n.* (in folklore and Greek mythology) a nymph inhabiting a forest or a tree, esp. an oak tree.

dry cell ▶*n.* an electric cell in which the electrolyte is absorbed in a solid to form a paste, preventing spillage. Compare with WET CELL.

dry-clean ▶*v.* [*tr.*] (usu. **be dry-cleaned**) clean (a garment) with an organic solvent, without using water. [as *n.*] (**dry cleaning**) *premises that offered dry cleaning.* —**dry clean·er** *n.*

dry dock ▶*n.* a dock that can be drained of water to allow the inspection and repair of a ship's hull.

▶*v.* (**dry-dock**) [*tr.*] place (a ship) in a dry dock.

dry·er /'drīər/ (also **dri·er**) ▶*n.* **1** a machine or device for drying something, esp. the hair or laundry. **2** a substance mixed with oil paint or ink to promote drying.

dry fly ▶*n.* an artificial fishing fly that is made to float lightly on the water.

▶*v.* (**dry-fly**) fish using a dry fly.

dry goods ▶*pl. n.* fabric, thread, clothing, and related merchandise, esp. as distinct from hardware and groceries.

dry ice ▶*n.* solid carbon dioxide, used as a refrigerant. ■ the cold dense white mist produced by this in air, used for theatrical effects.

dry meas·ure ▶*n.* a measure of volume for loose dry commodities such as grain, tea, and sugar.

dry rot ▶*n.* **1** fungal timber decay occurring in poorly ventilated conditions in buildings, resulting in cracking and powdering of the wood. **2** (also **dry rot fungus**) the fungus (*Serpula lacrymans*, family Corticiaceae) that causes this.

dry run ▶*n. inf.* a rehearsal of a performance or procedure before the real one: *the president went through a dry run of his speech.*

dry·wall /'drī,wôl/ ▶*n.* a type of board made from plaster, wood pulp, or other material, used esp. to form the interior walls of houses.

DSL ▶*abbr.* ■ digital subscriber line. See also ADSL.

DST ▶*abbr.* daylight saving time.

DTD ▶*abbr. Comput.* document type definition; a template that sets out the format and tag structure of an XML- or SGML-compliant document.

DTP ▶*abbr.* desktop publishing.

DTs ▶*pl. n.* (usu. **the DTs**) *inf.* delirium tremens.

DTV ▶*abbr.* digital television.

du·al /'d(y)ōōəl/ ▶*adj.* consisting of two parts, elements, or aspects: *their dual role at work and home.* ■ *Gram.* (in some languages) denoting an inflection that refers to exactly two people or things (as distinct from singular and plural).

▶*n.* **1** *Gram.* a dual form of a word. ■ the dual number. **2** *Math.* a theorem, expression, etc., that is dual to another. —**du·al·i·ty** /d(y)ōō'alitē/ *n.* —**du·al·ize** /-,līz/ *v.* —**du·al·ly** *adv.*

du·al·ism /'d(y)ōōə,lizəm/ ▶*n.* **1** the division of something conceptually into two opposed or contrasted aspects, or the state of being so divided: *a dualism between man and nature.* **2** the quality or condition of being dual; duality. —**du·al·ist** *n. & adj.* —**du·al·is·tic** /,d(y)ōōə'listik/ *adj.* —**du·al·is·ti·cal·ly** /,d(y)ōōə'listik(ə)lē/ *adv.*

dub[1] /dəb/ ▶*v.* (**dubbed, dub·bing**) [*tr.*] give an unofficial name or nickname to (someone or something): *the media dubbed anorexia "the slimming disease."* ■ make (someone) a knight by the ritual touching of the shoulder with a sword: *he should be dubbed Sir Hubert.*

dub[2] ▶*v.* (**dubbed, dub·bing**) [*tr.*] **1** provide (a film) with a soundtrack in a different language from the original: *a film dubbed into French.* ■ add (sound effects or music) to a film or a recording: *background sound can be dubbed in at the editing stage.* **2** make a copy of (a sound or video recording). ■ transfer (a recording) from one medium to another. ■ combine (two or more sound recordings) into one composite soundtrack.

▶*n.* **1** an instance of dubbing sound effects or music. **2** a style of popular music originating from the remixing of recorded music (esp. reggae), typically with the removal of some vocals and instruments and the exaggeration of bass guitar.

dub[3] *inf.* ▶*n.* an inexperienced or unskillful person.

▶*v.* (**dubbed, dub·bing**) [*tr.*] *Golf* misplay (a shot).

du·bi·ous /'d(y)ōōbēəs/ ▶*adj.* **1** hesitating or doubting: *Alex looked dubious.* **2** not to be relied upon; suspect: *dubious assumptions.* ■ morally suspect: *dubious sales methods.* ■ of questionable value: *the dubious distinction of being the lowest-paid teacher.* —**du·bi·ous·ly** *adv.* —**du·bi·ous·ness** *n.*

du·cal /'d(y)ōōkəl/ ▶*adj.* of, like, or relating to a duke or dukedom: *the ducal palace in Rouen.*

duc·at /'dəkət/ ▶*n.* **1** a gold coin formerly current in most European countries. ■ (**ducats**) *inf.* money: *their production of* Hamlet *has kept the ducats pouring in.* **2** *inf.* a ticket, esp. an admission ticket.

duch·ess /'dəCHis/ ▶*n.* the wife or widow of a duke. ■ a woman holding a rank equivalent to duke in her own right.

duch·y /'dəCHē/ ▶*n.* (*pl.* **duch·ies**) the territory of a duke or duchess; a dukedom.

duck[1] /dək/ ▶*n.* (*pl.* same or **ducks**) a waterbird with a broad blunt bill, short legs, webbed feet, and a waddling gait. The **duck family** (Anatidae) also includes geese and swans, from which ducks are distinguished by their generally smaller size and shorter necks. ■ the female of such a bird. Contrasted with DRAKE[1]. ■ such a bird as food.

▶ □ **get** (or **have**) **one's ducks in a row** get (or have) one's facts straight; get (or have) everything organized. □ **take to something like a duck to water** take to something very readily. □ **water off a duck's back** a potentially hurtful or harmful remark or incident that has no apparent effect on the person mentioned.

duck[2] ▶*v.* **1** [*intr.*] lower the head or the body quickly to avoid a blow or so as not to be seen: *spectators ducked for cover* | *she* **ducked into** *the doorway* | [*tr.*] *he ducked his head and entered.* ■ (**duck out**) depart quickly: *I thought I saw you duck out.* ■ [*tr.*] avoid (a blow) by moving down quickly: *he ducked a punch from an angry first baseman.* ■ [*tr.*] *inf.* evade or avoid (an unwelcome duty or undertaking): *a less courageous man might have ducked* | [*intr.*] *I was engaged twice and* **ducked out** *both times.* **2** [*intr.*] plunge one's head or body under water briefly.

▶*n.* a quick lowering of the head. —**duck·er** *n.*

duck[3] (also **ducks**) ▶*n. Brit.* dear; darling (used as an informal or affectionate form of address, esp. among cockneys).

duck[4] ▶*n.* a strong untwilled linen or cotton fabric, used chiefly for casual or work clothes and sails. ■ (**ducks**) pants made of such a fabric.

duck·bill /'dək,bil/ ▶*n.* an animal with jaws resembling a duck's bill, e.g., a platypus or a duck-billed dinosaur.

▶*adj.* shaped like a duck's bill: *duckbill pliers.*

duck·ling /'dəkliNG/ ▶*n.* a young duck. ■ the flesh of a young duck as food.

duck soup ▶*n. inf.* an easy task, or someone easy to overcome.

duck·weed /'dək,wēd/ ▶*n.* a tiny aquatic flowering plant (family Lemnaceae, esp. the genus *Lemna*) that floats in large quantities on still water.

duck·y /'dəkē/ *inf.* ▶*n.* (*pl.* **duck·ies**) *Brit.* darling; dear (used as a form of address): *come and sit down, ducky.*

▶*adj.* charming; delightful: *everything here is just ducky.*

duct /dəkt/ ▶*n.* a channel or tube for conveying something, in particular: ■ (in a building or a machine) a tube or passageway for air, liquid, cables, etc. ■ (in the body) a vessel for conveying lymph or glandular secretions such as tears or bile. ■ (in a plant) a vessel for conveying water, sap, or air.

▶*v.* [*tr.*] (usu. **be ducted**) convey through a duct: *a ventilation system that must be ducted through the wall* | [as *adj.*] (**ducted**) *a ducted air system.* —**duct·less** *adj.*

duc·tile /'dəktl; -,tīl/ ▶*adj.* (of a metal) able to be drawn out into a thin wire. ■ able to be deformed without losing toughness; pliable, not brittle. ■ *fig.* (of a person) docile or gullible. —**duc·til·i·ty** /dək'tilitē/ *n.*

duct·ing /'dəktiNG/ ▶*n.* a system of ducts. ■ tubing or piping forming such a system.

duct·work /'dəkt,wərk/ ▶*n.* a system or network of ducts.

dud /dəd/ *inf.* ▶*n.* **1** a thing that fails to work properly or is otherwise unsatisfactory or worthless: *all three bombs were duds.* ■ an ineffectual person. **2** (**duds**) clothes: *buy yourself some new duds.*

▶*adj.* not working or meeting standards; faulty: *a dud ignition switch.* ■ counterfeit: *charged with issuing dud checks.*

dude /dōōd/ *inf.* ▶*n.* a man; a guy: *if some dude smacked me, I'd smack him back.* ■ a stylish, fastidious man: *cool dudes.* ■ a city-dweller, esp. one vacationing on a ranch in the western U.S.

▶*v.* [*intr.*] (**dude up**) dress up elaborately. —**dud·ish** *adj.*

dude ranch ▶*n.* (in the western U.S.) a cattle ranch converted to a vacation resort for tourists.

dudg·eon /'dəjən/ ▸ *n.* a feeling of offense or deep resentment: *the manager walked out in high dudgeon.*

due /d(y)oō/ ▸ *adj.* **1** expected at or planned for at a certain time: *the baby's due in August | he is due back soon | talks are due to adjourn tomorrow.* ■ (of a payment) required at a certain time. ■ (of a person) having reached a point where the thing mentioned is required or owed: *she was due for a raise.* ■ (of a thing) required or owed as a legal or moral obligation: *he was only taking back what was due to him | you must pay any income tax due.* **2** of the proper quality or extent; adequate: *driving without due care and attention.*
▸ *n.* **1** (**one's due**) a person's right; what is owed to someone: *he attracts more criticism than is his due.* **2** (**dues**) an obligatory payment; a fee.
▸ *adv.* (with reference to a point of the compass) exactly; directly: *we'll head due south again on the same road.* ▷Middle English (in the sense 'payable'): from Old French *deu* 'owed,' based on Latin *debitus* 'owed,' from *debere* 'owe.'
▸ □ **due to 1** caused by or ascribable to: *unemployment due to automation.* **2** because of; owing to: *he had to withdraw due to a knee injury.* □ **give someone their due** be fair to someone: *to give him his due, he was a generous employer.* □ **in due course** at the appropriate time: *Reynolds will respond in due course.* □ **pay one's dues** fulfill one's obligations. ■ experience difficulties before achieving success: *this drummer has paid his dues with the best.*

du·el /'d(y)oōəl/ ▸ *n.* chiefly *hist.* a contest with deadly weapons arranged between two people in order to settle a point of honor. ■ (in modern use) a contest or race between two parties: *two eminent critics engaged in a verbal duel.*
▸ *v.* (**du·eled, du·el·ing**; *Brit.* **du·elled, du·el·ling**) [*intr.*] fight a duel or duels. ▷late 15th cent.: from Latin *duellum*, archaic form of *bellum* 'war,' used in medieval Latin with the meaning 'combat between two persons,' partly influenced by *dualis* 'of two.' The original sense was 'single combat used to decide a judicial dispute'; the sense 'contest to decide a point of honor' dates from the early 17th cent. —**du·el·er** (*Brit.* **du·el·ler**) *n.* —**du·el·ist** /-ist/ (*Brit.* **du·el·list**) *n.*

duen·de /doō'endā/ ▸ *n.* a quality of passion and inspiration. ■ a spirit.

du·en·na /d(y)oō'enə/ ▸ *n.* an older woman acting as a governess and companion in charge of girls, esp. in a Spanish family; a chaperone.

due proc·ess (also **due process of law**) ▸ *n.* fair treatment through the normal judicial system, esp. as a citizen's entitlement.

du·et /d(y)oō'et/ ▸ *n.* a performance by two people, esp. singers, instrumentalists, or dancers. ■ a musical composition for two performers.

duff[1] ▸ *n.* decaying vegetable matter covering the ground under trees.

duff[2] ▸ *n. inf.* a person's buttocks: *I didn't get where I am by sitting on my duff.*

duf·fel /'dəfəl/ (also **duf·fle**) ▸ *n.* **1** a coarse woolen cloth with a thick nap. **2** sporting or camping equipment. ■ short for DUFFEL BAG.

duf·fel bag ▸ *n.* a cylindrical canvas bag closed by a drawstring and carried over the shoulder.

duf·fer /'dəfər/ ▸ *n. inf.* an incompetent or stupid person, esp. an elderly one. ■ a person inexperienced at something, esp. at playing golf.

dug[1] /dəg/ ▸ past and past participle of DIG.

dug[2] ▸ *n.* (usu. **dugs**) the udder, teat, or nipple of a female animal. ■ *archaic* a woman's breast.

du·gong /'doōgäNG; -gôNG/ ▸ *n.* (*pl.* same or **dugongs**) an aquatic mammal (*Dugong dugon*, family Dugongidae) with a forked tail, found on the coasts of the Indian Ocean from eastern Africa to northern Australia.

dug·out /'dəg,out/ ▸ *n.* **1** a shelter that is dug in the ground and roofed over, esp. one used by troops in warfare. ■ a low shelter at the side of a baseball field, with seating from which a team's coaches and players not taking part can watch the game. **2** (also **dugout canoe**) a canoe made from a hollowed tree trunk.

duke /d(y)oōk/ ▸ *n.* **1** a male holding the highest hereditary title in the British and certain other peerages. ■ *chiefly hist.* (in some parts of Europe) a male ruler of a small independent state. **2** (**dukes**) *inf.* the fists, esp. when raised in a fighting attitude.
▸ □ **duke it out** *inf.* fight it out.

duke·dom /'d(y)oōkdəm/ ▸ *n.* a territory ruled by a duke. ■ the rank of duke.

dul·cet /'dəlsit/ ▸ *adj.* (esp. of sound) sweet and soothing (often used ironically): *record the dulcet tones of your family and friends.*

dul·ci·fy /'dəlsə,fī/ ▸ *v.* (**-fies, -fied**) [*tr.*] *poetic/lit.* sweeten. ■ calm or soothe: *his voice dulcified the panic.* —**dul·ci·fi·ca·tion** /,dəlsəfi'kāSHən/ *n.*

dul·ci·mer /'dəlsəmər/ ▸ *n.* (also **hammered dulcimer**) a musical instrument with a sounding board or box, typically trapezoidal in shape, over which strings of graduated length are stretched, played by being struck with hand-held hammers. ■ (**Appalachian dulcimer**) a musical instrument with a long rounded body and a fretted fingerboard, played by bowing, plucking, and strumming.

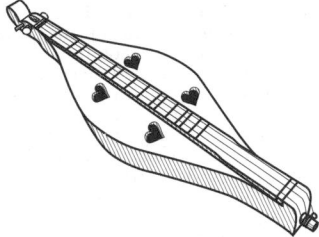

Appalachian dulcimer

dull /dəl/ ▸ *adj.* **1** lacking interest or excitement. ■ *archaic* (of a person) feeling bored and dispirited: *she said she wouldn't be dull and lonely.* **2** lacking brightness, vividness, or sheen. ■ (of the weather) overcast; gloomy. ■ (of sound) not clear; muffled: *a dull thud.* ■ (of pain) indistinctly felt; not acute. ■ (of an edge or blade) blunt. **3** (of a person) slow to understand; stupid. ■ *archaic* (of a person's senses) not perceiving things distinctly; insensitive. ■ (of activity) sluggish, slow-moving.
▸ *v.* make or become dull or less intense: [*tr.*] *time dulls the memory* | [*intr.*] *Albert's eyes dulled a little.* —**dull·ness** (also **dul·ness**) *n.* —**dul·ly** *adv.*
▸ □ (**as**) **dull as dishwater** extremely dull. □ **dull the edge of** cause to be less keenly felt; reduce the intensity or effectiveness of.

dull·ard /'dələrd/ ▸ *n.* a slow or stupid person.

du·ly /'d(y)oōlē/ ▸ *adv.* in accordance with what is required or appropriate; following proper procedure or arrangement: *a document duly signed and authorized by the inspector | the ceremony duly began at midnight.* ■ as might be expected or predicted: *I used the tent and was duly impressed.*

dumb /dəm/ ▸ *adj.* **1** *chiefly offens.* (of a person) unable to speak, most typically because of congenital deafness: *he was born deaf, dumb, and blind.* ■ (of animals) unable to speak as a natural state and thus regarded as helpless or deserving pity. ■ temporarily unable or unwilling to speak: *she stood dumb while he poured out a stream of abuse.* ■ resulting in or expressed by speechlessness: *they stared in dumb amazement.* **2** *inf.* stupid. ■ (of a computer terminal) able only to transmit data to or receive data from a computer; having no independent processing capability.
▸ *v.* [*tr.*] **1** (**dumb something down**) *inf.* simplify or reduce the intellectual content of something so as to make it accessible to a larger number of people: *critics have accused publishers of dumbing down books.* ■ [*intr.*] (**dumb down**) become less intellectually challenging: *the need to dumb down for mass audiences.* **2** *poetic/lit.* make dumb or unheard; silence: *a splendor that dumbed the tongue.* —**dumb·ly** *adv.* —**dumb·ness** *n.*

dumb·bell /'dəm,bel/ ▸ *n.* **1** a short bar with a weight at each end, used typically in pairs for exercise or muscle-building. ■ [as *adj.*] shaped like a dumbbell: *a dumbbell molecule.* **2** *inf.* a stupid person.

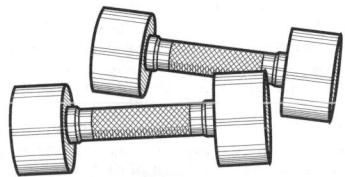

dumbbells

dumb·found /'dəm,found/ (also **dum·found**) ▸ *v.* [*tr.*] (usu. **be dumbfounded**) greatly astonish or amaze.

dum·bo /'dəmbō/ ▸ *n.* (*pl.* **-bos**) *inf.* a stupid person.

dumb·struck /'dəm,strək/ ▸ *adj.* so shocked or surprised as to be unable to speak: *he was dumbstruck with terror.*

dumb·wait·er ▸ *n.* **1** a small elevator for carrying things, esp. food and dishes, between the floors of a building. **2** *Brit.* a movable table, typically with revolving shelves, used in a dining room.

D

dum·dum /'dəm,dəm/ (also **dumdum bullet**) ▶ *n.* a kind of soft-nosed bullet that expands on impact and inflicts laceration.

dum·my /'dəmē/ ▶ *n.* (*pl.* **-mies**) **1** a model or replica of a human being. ■ a figure used for displaying or fitting clothes: *a tailor's dummy.* ■ a ventriloquist's doll. ■ a person taking no real part or present only for appearances; a figurehead. ■ *Bridge* the declarer's partner, whose cards are exposed on the table after the opening lead and played by the declarer. ■ *Bridge* the exposed hand of the declarer's partner. ■ an imaginary fourth player in whist: [as *adj.*] *dummy whist.* **2** an object designed to resemble and serve as a substitute for the real or usual one. ■ an enterprise existing mainly on paper, set up to facilitate fraud: [mainly as *adj.*] *a dummy corporation.* ■ a prototype or mock-up, esp. of a book or the layout of a page. ■ a blank round of ammunition. ■ [as *adj.*] *Gram.* denoting a word that has no semantic content but is used to maintain grammatical structure: *a dummy subject, as in "it is" or "there are."* **3** *inf.* a stupid person.
▶ *v.* (**-mies**, **-mied**) [*tr.*] create a prototype or mock-up of a book or page: *officials dummied up a set of photos.*
▶ *phrasal v.* □ **dummy up** *inf.* keep quiet; give no information.

dump /dəmp/ ▶ *n.* **1** a site for depositing garbage. ■ a place where a particular kind of waste, esp. dangerous waste, is left: *a nuclear waste dump.* ■ a heap of garbage left at a dump. ■ *inf.* an unpleasant or dreary place: *the town has become a dump.* ■ *inf.* an act of defecation. **2** *Comput.* a copying of stored data to a different location, performed typically as a protection against loss. ■ a printout or list of the contents of a computer's memory, occurring typically after a system failure.
▶ *v.* [*tr.*] **1** deposit or dispose of (garbage, waste, or unwanted material), typically in a careless or hurried way: *trucks dumped 1,900 tons of refuse here* | [*intr.*] *an attempt to prevent people from dumping on vacant lots.* ■ put down or abandon (something) hurriedly in order to make an escape. ■ put (something) down firmly or heavily and carelessly. ■ *inf.* abandon or desert (someone). ■ send (goods unsalable in the home market) to a foreign market for sale at a low price. ■ *inf.* sell off (assets) rapidly. **2** *Comput.* copy (stored data) to a different location, esp. so as to protect against loss. ■ print out or list the contents of (a store), esp. after a system failure. **3** *Football* tackle (a quarterback) before he can throw a pass.
▶ *phrasal v.* □ **dump on** *inf.* criticize or abuse (someone); treat badly.

dump·ling /'dəmplɪNG/ ▶ *n.* a small savory ball of dough that may be boiled, fried, or baked in a casserole. ■ a pastry consisting of apples or other fruit enclosed in a sweet dough and baked. ■ *humorous* a small, fat person: *he was a 250-pound dumpling.*

dumps /dəmps/ ▶ *pl. n.* (in phrase (**down**) **in the dumps**) *inf.* (of a person) depressed or unhappy.

dump·ster /'dəmpstər/ (also **Dump·ster** *trademark*) ▶ *n.* a large trash receptacle designed to be hoisted and emptied into a truck.

dump truck ▶ *n.* a truck with a body that tilts or opens at the back for unloading.

dump·y /'dəmpē/ ▶ *adj.* (**dump·i·er**, **dump·i·est**) **1** (of a person) short and stout. **2** (of a room or building) ugly, dirty, and run-down: *a dumpy little diner.* —**dump·i·ly** /-pəlē/ *adv.* —**dump·i·ness** *n.*

dun[1] /dən/ ▶ *adj.* of a dull grayish-brown color: *a dun cow.* ■ *poetic/lit.* dark; dusky: *when the dun evening comes.*
▶ *n.* **1** a dull grayish-brown color. **2** a thing that is dun in color, in particular: ■ a horse with a sandy or sandy-gray coat, black mane, tail, and lower legs, and a dark dorsal stripe.

dun[2] ▶ *v.* (**dunned**, **dun·ning**) [*tr.*] make persistent demands on (someone), esp. for payment of a debt: *they would very likely start dunning you for payment of your taxes* | [as *adj.*] (**dunning**) *dunning letters.*
▶ *n. archaic* a debt collector or an insistent creditor. ■ a demand for payment.

dunce /dəns/ ▶ *n.* a person who is slow at learning; a stupid person.

dunce cap (*Brit.* also **dunce's cap**) ▶ *n.* a paper cone formerly put on the head of a dunce at school as a mark of disgrace.

dun·der·head /'dəndər,hed/ ▶ *n. inf.* a stupid person. —**dun·der·head·ed** *adj.*

dune /d(y)oon/ ▶ *n.* a mound or ridge of sand or other loose sediment formed by the wind, esp. on the sea coast or in a desert: *a sand dune.*

dung /dəNG/ ▶ *n.* the excrement of animals; manure.
▶ *v.* [*tr.*] drop or spread dung on (a piece of ground).

dun·ga·rees /,dəNGgə'rēz/ ▶ *pl. n.* **1** blue jeans or overalls. **2** (**dungaree**) blue denim.

dung bee·tle ▶ *n.* a beetle (esp. families Scarabaeidae and Geotrupidae) whose larvae feed on dung.

dun·geon /'dənjən/ ▶ *n.* a strong underground prison cell, esp. in a castle. ■ *archaic* term for DONJON.

dung·hill /'dəNG,hil/ (also **dung·heap**) ▶ *n.* a heap of dung or refuse, esp. in a farmyard.

dunk /dəNGk/ ▶ *v.* **1** [*tr.*] dip (bread or other food) into a drink or soup before eating it. ■ immerse or dip in water. **2** [*intr.*] *Basketball* score by shooting the ball down through the basket with the hands above the rim.
▶ *n. Basketball* a shot downward into the basket with the hands above the rim. ▷ early 20th cent.: from Pennsylvania Dutch *dunke* 'dip,' from German *tunken* 'dip or plunge.' —**dunk·er** *n.*

dun·lin /'dənlin/ ▶ *n.* (*pl.* same or **dunlins**) a migratory sandpiper (*Calidris alpina*) with a down-curved bill and (in the breeding season) a reddish-brown back and black belly.

dun·nage /'dənij/ ▶ *n.* pieces of wood, matting, or similar material used to keep a cargo in position in a ship's hold.

dun·no /də'nō/ ▶ *contr. of* (I) do not know.

du·o /'d(y)oo-ō/ ▶ *n.* (*pl.* **du·os**) **1** a pair of people or things, esp. in music or entertainment. **2** *Mus.* a duet: *a duo for violin and viola.*

du·o·dec·i·mal /,d(y)ooə'desəməl; ,d(y)oo-ō-/ ▶ *adj.* relating to or denoting a system of counting or numerical notation that has twelve as a base. —**du·o·dec·i·mal·ly** *adv.*

du·o·de·num /,d(y)ooə'dēnəm; d(y)oo'ädn-əm/ ▶ *n.* (*pl.* **-nums** or **-na** /-nə/) *Anat.* the first part of the small intestine immediately beyond the stomach, leading to the jejunum. —**du·o·de·nal** /-'dēnl; -'ädnəl/ *adj.*

dupe[1] /d(y)oop/ ▶ *v.* [*tr.*] deceive; trick: *the newspaper was duped into publishing an untrue story.*
▶ *n.* a victim of deception. —**dup·a·ble** *adj.* —**dup·er** *n.* —**dup·er·y** /-pərē/ *n.*

dupe[2] ▶ *v. & n.* short for DUPLICATE, esp. in photography.

du·ple /'d(y)oopəl/ ▶ *adj. Mus.* (of rhythm) based on two main beats to the measure: *duple time.*

du·plex /'d(y)oopleks/ ▶ *n.* something having two parts, in particular: ■ a house divided into two apartments, with a separate entrance for each. ■ an apartment on two floors.
▶ *adj.* **1** having two parts, in particular: ■ (of a house) having two apartments. ■ (of an apartment) on two floors. ■ (of paper or board) having two differently colored layers or sides. ■ *Biochem.* consisting of two polynucleotide strands linked side by side. ■ (of a printer or its software) capable of printing on both sides of the paper. **2** (of a communications system, computer circuit, etc.) allowing the transmission of two signals simultaneously in opposite directions. Compare with MULTIPLEX, SIMPLEX.

du·pli·cate ▶ *adj.* /'d(y)ooplikit/ **1** exactly like something else, esp. through having been copied. **2** having two corresponding or identical parts: *a duplicate form.* ■ twice as large or many; doubled.
▶ *n.* /'d(y)ooplikit/ one of two or more identical things: *books may be disposed of if they are duplicates.* ■ a copy of an original.
▶ *v.* /'d(y)oopl ,kāt/ [*tr.*] make or be an exact copy of: *fig. they can't duplicate his successes.* ■ (often **be duplicated**) make or supply copies of (a document): *information sheets had to be typed and duplicated* | [as *adj.*] (**duplicating**) *a duplicating machine.* ■ multiply by two; double. ■ do (something) again unnecessarily: *most of these proposals duplicated work already done.* —**du·pli·ca·ble** /-plikəbəl/ *adj.* —**du·pli·ca·tion** /,d(y)ooplə'kāSHən/ *n.* —**du·pli·ca·tive** /-,kātiv/ *adj.*
▶ □ **in duplicate** consisting of two exact copies: *forms in duplicate.*

du·pli·ca·tor /'d(y)ooplə,kātər/ ▶ *n.* a machine or device for making copies of something, in particular a machine that makes copies of documents by means of fluid ink and a stencil.

du·plic·i·ty /d(y)oo'plisitē/ ▶ *n.* **1** deceitfulness; double-dealing. **2** *archaic* doubleness. —**du·plic·i·tous** /-itəs/ *adj.*

du·ra /'d(y)oorə/ (in full **dura mater**) ▶ *n. Anat.* the tough outermost membrane enveloping the brain and spinal cord. —**du·ral** *adj.*

du·ra·ble /'d(y)oorəbəl/ ▶ *adj.* able to withstand wear, pressure, or damage; hard-wearing. ■ (of a person) having endurance.
▶ *n.* (**durables**) short for DURABLE GOODS. —**du·ra·bil·i·ty** /,d(y)oorə'bilitē/ *n.* —**du·ra·ble·ness** *n.* —**du·ra·bly** *adv.*

du·ra·ble goods ▶ *plural n.* goods not for immediate consumption and able to be kept for a period of time.

du·ra ma·ter /'d(y)oorə'mätər; 'mä-/ ▶ *n.* see DURA.

du·ra·tion /d(y)oo'rāSHən/ ▶ *n.* the time during which something continues: *the duration of the convention.* —**du·ra·tion·al** *adj.*
▶ □ **for the duration** until the end of something, esp. a war: *he was in the navy for the duration plus six.* ■ *inf.* for a very long time: *some stains may be there for the duration.*

du·ress /d(y)oo'res/ ▶ *n.* threats, violence, constraints, or other action brought to bear on someone to do something against their will or better judgment. ■ *Law* constraint illegally exercised to force someone to perform an act. ■ *archaic* forcible restraint or imprisonment.

dur·ing /ˈd(y)ŏŏriNG/ ▸*prep.* throughout the course or duration of (a period of time). ▪ used to indicate constant development throughout a period: *the period during which he grew to adulthood.* ▪ at a particular point in the course of: *the stabbing took place during an argument.*

du·rum /ˈd(y)ŏŏrəm/ (also **durum wheat**) ▸*n.* a kind of hard wheat (*Triticum durum*) yielding flour that is used to make pasta.

dusk /dəsk/ ▸*n.* the darker stage of twilight: *working the land from dawn to dusk.* ▪ semidarkness: *in the dusk of an Istanbul nightclub.*
▸*v.* [*intr.*] *poetic/lit.* grow dark: [as *adj.*] (**dusking**) *the dusking sky.*
▸*adj. poetic/lit.* shadowy, dim, or dark.

dusk·y /ˈdəskē/ ▸*adj.* (**dusk·i·er, dusk·i·est**) darkish in color: *dusky red* | *a dusky complexion.* ▪ *dated* used in euphemistic or poetic reference to black or other dark-skinned people: *a dusky maiden.* ▪ *poetic/lit.* dim. ▪ used in names of animals with dark coloration, e.g., **dusky dolphin, dusky warbler.** /-kələ/ *adv.* —**dusk·i·ness** *n.*

dust /dəst/ ▸*n.* **1** fine, dry powder consisting of tiny particles of earth or waste matter lying on the ground or on surfaces or carried in the air. ▪ any material in the form of tiny particles: *coal dust.* ▪ a fine powder: *ground into a fine dust.* ▪ a cloud of dust. ▪ *poetic/lit.* a dead person's remains: *scatter my dust and ashes.* ▪ *poetic/lit.* the mortal human body: *the soul that dwells within your dust.* **2** an act of dusting: *a quick dust, to get rid of the cobwebs.*
▸*v.* [*tr.*] **1** remove the dust from the surface of (something) by wiping or brushing it. ▪ (**dust something off**) bring something out for use again after a long period of neglect. ▪ *Baseball* (**dust someone off**) deliver a pitch very near a batter so they must fall to the dirt to avoid being hit by it. **2** (usu. **be dusted**) cover lightly with a powdered substance. ▪ sprinkle (a powdered substance) onto something. **3** *inf.* beat up or kill someone: *they dusted him up a bit.* —**dust·less** *adj.*
▸ □ **the dust settles** things quiet down: *she hoped that the dust would settle quickly and the episode be forgotten.* □ **eat someone's dust** *inf.* fall far behind someone in a competitive situation. □ **gather** (or **collect**) **dust** remain unused. □ **leave someone/something in the dust** surpass someone or something easily.

dust bowl ▸*n.* an area of land where vegetation has been lost and soil reduced to dust and eroded, esp. as a consequence of drought or unsuitable farming practice.

dust cov·er ▸*n.* **1** a dust jacket. **2** a drop cloth.

dust dev·il ▸*n.* a small whirlwind or air vortex over land, visible as a column of dust and debris.

dust·er /ˈdəstər/ ▸*n.* **1** a cloth or brush for dusting furniture. **2** (also **duster coat**) a woman's loose, lightweight, full-length coat without buttons, of a style originally worn in the 1920s when traveling in an open car. ▪ a short, light housecoat. **3** *inf.* a dust storm.

dust jack·et ▸*n.* a removable paper cover, generally with a decorative design, used to protect a book from dirt or damage.

dust·pan /ˈdəst,pan/ ▸*n.* a flat hand-held receptacle into which dust and waste can be swept from the floor.

dust storm ▸*n.* a strong, turbulent wind that carries clouds of fine dust, soil, and sand over a large area.

dust·y /ˈdəstē/ ▸*adj.* (**dust·i·er, dust·i·est**) covered with, full of, or resembling dust: *dusty old records* | *a hot, dusty road.* ▪ (of a color) dull or muted: *patches of dusty pink.* —**dust·i·ly** /ˈdəstəlē/ *adv.* —**dust·i·ness** *n.*

Dutch /dəCH/ ▸*adj.* of or relating to the Netherlands or its people or their language.
▸*n.* **1** the West Germanic language of the Netherlands. **2** [as *pl. n.*] (**the Dutch**) the people of the Netherlands collectively. ▷from Middle Dutch *dutsch* 'Dutch, Netherlandish, German': the English word originally denoted speakers of both High and Low German, but became more specific after the United Provinces adopted the Low German of Holland as the national language on independence in 1579.
▸ □ **go dutch** share the cost of something, esp. a meal, equally. □ **in dutch** *inf., dated* in trouble: *he's been getting in dutch at school.*

Dutch door ▸*n.* a door divided into two parts horizontally, allowing one half to be shut and the other left open.

Dutch elm dis·ease ▸*n.* a disease of elm trees caused by the fungus *Ceratocystis ulmi* (phylum Ascomycota) and spread by bark beetles.

Dutch·man /ˈdəCHmən/ ▸*n.* (*pl.* **-men**) a native or national of the Netherlands,

Dutch door

or a person of Dutch descent. ▪ a Dutch ship. ▪ a wedge or piece used to conceal a flaw in construction. ▪ *archaic* a German.

Dutch ov·en ▸*n.* a large, heavy cooking pot with a lid. ▪ *chiefly hist.* a large metal box serving as a simple oven, heated by being placed under or next to hot coals.

Dutch treat ▸*n.* an outing, meal, or other special occasion at which each participant pays for their share of the expenses.

Dutch un·cle ▸*n. inf.* a person giving firm but benevolent advice.

du·ti·a·ble /ˈd(y)ŏŏtēəbəl/ ▸*adj.* liable to customs or other duties.

dut·i·ful /ˈd(y)ŏŏtəfəl/ ▸*adj.* conscientiously or obediently fulfilling one's duty: *a dutiful daughter.* ▪ motivated by duty rather than desire or enthusiasm: *dutiful applause.* —**du·ti·ful·ly** *adv.* —**du·ti·ful·ness** *n.*

du·ty /ˈd(y)ŏŏtē/ ▸*n.* (*pl.* **-ties**) **1** a moral or legal obligation; a responsibility: *a strong sense of duty.* ▪ [as *adj.*] (of a visit or other undertaking) done from a sense of moral obligation rather than for pleasure: *a fifteen-minute duty visit.* **2** (often **duties**) a task or action that someone is required to perform. ▪ military service: *combat duty.* ▪ [as *adj.*] (of a person) engaged in their regular work: *a duty nurse.* **3** a payment due and enforced by law or custom, in particular: ▪ a payment levied on the import, export, manufacture, or sale of goods: *a 6 percent duty on imports* | *goods subject to excise duty.* **4** *technical* the measure of an engine's effectiveness in units of work done per unit of fuel.
▸ □ **on** (or **off**) **duty** engaged (or not engaged) in one's regular work.

du·ty-bound ▸*adj.* morally or legally obliged to do something: *legitimate news stories that the press is duty-bound to report.*

du·ty-free ▸*adj. & adv.* exempt from payment of duty: [as *adj.*] *duty-free goods* | [as *adv.*] *some goods enter duty-free.* ▪ [as *adj.*] (of a shop or area) trading in goods that are exempt from payment of duty.

du·vet /ˌd(y)ŏŏˈvā/ ▸*n.* a soft quilt filled with down, feathers, or a synthetic fiber, used instead of an upper sheet and blankets.

DVD ▸*n.* a high-density videodisc that stores large amounts of data, esp. high-resolution audio-visual material. ▷abbreviation of *digital videodisc* or *digital versatile disc.*

DVD-R ▸*n.* a blank DVD on which data, including music and movies, can be permanently recorded and read using the DVD-R format. ▪ a format for recordable DVDs used by some companies.

DVD+R ▸*n.* a blank DVD on which data, including music and movies, can be permanently recorded and read using the DVD+R format. ▪ a format for recordable DVDs used by some companies.

DVD-RAM ▸*n.* a blank DVD on which data, including music and movies, can be permanently recorded and read using the DVD-RAM format. A DVD-RAM discs can be recorded over many times, but will only play back in a DVD-RAM drive. ▪ a format for recordable DVDs used by some companies.

DVD-ROM ▸*n.* a DVD used as a read-only optical memory device for a computer system.

DVD-RW ▸*n.* a blank DVD that can be recorded, erased, and rerecorded with data many times and read by systems using the DVD-RW format. ▪ a format for rewritable DVDs used by some companies. ▪ a disc drive that can read and record DVDs.

DVD+RW ▸*n.* a blank DVD that can be recorded, erased, and rerecorded with data many times and read by systems using the DVD+RW format. ▪ a format for rewritable DVDs used by some companies. ▪ a disc drive that can read and record DVDs.

DVM ▸*abbr.* ▪ Doctor of Veterinary Medicine.

DVR ▸*abbr.* digital video recorder.

dwarf /dwôrf/ ▸*n.* (*pl.* **dwarfs** or **dwarves** /dwôrvz/) **1** (in folklore or fantasy literature) a member of a mythical race of short, stocky human-like creatures. ▪ *often offens.* an abnormally small person. ▪ [as *adj.*] denoting something, esp. an animal or plant, that is much smaller than the usual size for its type or species: *a dwarf conifer.* **2** (also **dwarf star**) *Astron.* a star of relatively small size and low luminosity, including the majority of main sequence stars.
▸*v.* [*tr.*] cause to seem small or insignificant in comparison: *the trees dwarf our cabin.* ▪ stunt the growth or development of. —**dwarf·ish** *adj.*

dweeb /dwēb/ ▸*n. inf.* a boring, studious, or socially inept person. —**dweeb·ish** *adj.* —**dweeb·y** *adj.*

dwell /dwel/ ▸*v.* (*past* and *past part.* **dwelled** or **dwelt** /dwelt/) [*intr.*] **1** *formal* live in or at a specified place: *groups of gypsies still dwell in these caves.* **2** (**dwell on/upon**) think, speak, or write at length about (a particular subject, esp. one that is a source of unhappiness, anxiety, or

dissatisfaction): *dwell on the past.* ■ **(dwell on/upon)** (of one's eyes or attention) linger on (a particular object or place).
▶ *n. technical* a slight regular pause in the motion of a machine. —**dwell·er** *n.* [in *comb.*] *city-dwellers.*

dwell·ing /ˈdweliNG/ (also **dwelling place**) ▶ *n. formal* a house, apartment, or other place of residence.

dwin·dle /ˈdwindl/ ▶ *v.* [*intr.*] diminish gradually in size, amount, or strength. ▷late 16th cent.: frequentative of Scots and dialect *dwine* 'fade away,' from Old English *dwīnan*, of Germanic origin; related to Middle Dutch *dwīnen* and Old Norse *dvína.*

Dy ▶ *symb.* the chemical element dysprosium.

dye /dī/ ▶ *n.* a natural or synthetic substance used to add a color to or change the color of something.
▶ *v.* (**dyed, dye·ing**) [*tr.*] add a color to or change the color of (something) by soaking it in a solution impregnated with a dye: *I dyed my hair red* ■ [*intr.*] take color well or badly during such a process: *material that dyes well.* —**dye·a·ble** *adj.* —**dy·er** *n.*
▶ □ **dyed in the wool** unchanging in a particular belief or opinion; inveterate: *she's a dyed-in-the-wool conservative.*

dye·stuff /ˈdī,stəf/ ▶ *n.* a substance that yields a dye or that can be used as a dye, esp. when in solution.

dy·ing /ˈdī-iNG/ ▶ *adj.* on the point of death. ■ occurring at or connected with the time that someone dies: *dying words.* ■ gradually ceasing to exist or function; in decline and about to disappear.
▶ □ **to one's dying day** for the rest of one's life.

dyke¹ ▶ *n.* variant spelling of DIKE¹.

dyke² /dīk/ ▶ *n. offens.* a lesbian. —**dyke·y** *adj.*

dyn ▶ *abbr.* dyne.

dy·nam·ic /dīˈnamik/ ▶ *adj.* **1** (of a process or system) characterized by constant change, activity, or progress: *a dynamic economy.* ■ (of a person) positive in attitude and full of energy and new ideas. ■ (of a thing) stimulating development or progress: *the dynamic forces of nature.* ■ *Physics* of or relating to forces producing motion. ■ *Linguistics* (of a verb) expressing an action, activity, event, or process. ■ *Electr.* (of a memory device) needing to be refreshed by the periodic application of a voltage. ■ *Electr.* of or relating to the volume of sound produced by a voice, instrument, or sound recording equipment. **2** *Mus.* relating to the volume of sound produced by an instrument, voice, or recording.
▶ *n.* **1** a force that stimulates change or progress within a system or process: *the basic dynamic of the project.* **2** *Mus.* another term for DYNAMICS (sense 3). —**dy·nam·i·cal** *adj.* —**dy·nam·i·cal·ly** /-ik(ə)lē/ *adv.*

dy·nam·ics /dīˈnamiks/ ▶ *pl. n.* **1** [treated as *sing.*] the branch of mechanics concerned with the motion of bodies under the action of forces. ■ the branch of any science in which forces or changes are considered: *chemical dynamics.* **2** the forces or properties that stimulate growth, development, or change within a system or process: *the dynamics of changing social relations.* **3** *Mus.* the varying levels of volume of

sound in different parts of a musical performance. —**dy·nam·i·cist** /-ˈnaməsist/ *n.*

dy·na·mism /ˈdīnə,mizəm/ ▶ *n.* the quality of being characterized by vigorous activity and progress: *the dynamism and strength of the economy.* ■ the quality of being dynamic and positive in attitude. —**dy·na·mist** *n.*

dy·na·mite /ˈdīnə,mīt/ ▶ *n.* a high explosive consisting of nitroglycerine mixed with an absorbent material and typically molded into sticks. ■ *fig.* something that has the potential to generate extreme reactions or to have devastating repercussions: *that policy is political dynamite.* ■ *inf.* an extremely impressive or exciting person or thing: *both her albums are dynamite* | [as *adj.*] *a chick with a dynamite figure.*
▶ *v.* [*tr.*] blow up (something) with dynamite. —**dy·na·mit·er** *n.*

dy·na·mo /ˈdīnə,mō/ ▶ *n.* (*pl.* **-mos**) a machine for converting mechanical energy into electrical energy; a generator. ■ *inf.* an extremely energetic person: *she was a dynamo in London politics.*

dy·nas·ty /ˈdīnəstē/ ▶ *n.* (*pl.* **-ties**) a line of hereditary rulers of a country: *the Tang dynasty.* ■ a succession of people from the same family who play a prominent role in business, politics, or another field: *the Ford dynasty.* —**dy·nas·tic** /dīˈnastik/ *adj.* —**dy·nas·ti·cal·ly** /dīˈnastik(ə)lē/ *adv.*

dyne /dīn/ ▶ *n. Physics* a unit of force that, acting on a mass of one gram, increases its velocity by one centimeter per second every second along the direction that it acts.

dys·en·ter·y /ˈdisən,terē/ ▶ *n.* infection of the intestines resulting in severe diarrhea with the presence of blood and mucus in the feces. —**dys·en·ter·ic** /,disənˈterik/ *adj.*

dys·func·tion /disˈfəNGkSHən/ ▶ *n.* abnormality or impairment in the function of a specified bodily organ or system: *bowel dysfunction.* ■ deviation from the norms of social behavior in a way regarded as bad. —**dys·func·tion·al** /-SHənl/ *adj.*

dys·lex·i·a /disˈleksēə/ ▶ *n.* a general term for disorders that involve difficulty in learning to read or interpret words, letters, and other symbols, but that do not affect general intelligence. —**dys·lec·tic** /-ˈlektik/ *adj. & n.* —**dys·lex·ic** /-ˈleksik/ *adj. & n.*

dys·men·or·rhe·a /,dismenəˈrēə/ (*Brit.* **dys·men·or·rhoe·a**) ▶ *n. Med.* painful menstruation, typically involving abdominal cramps.

dys·pep·sia /disˈpepsēə; -ˈpepSHə/ ▶ *n.* indigestion.

dys·pha·sia /disˈfāZHə/ ▶ *n. Med.* language disorder marked by deficiency in the generation of speech, and sometimes also in its comprehension, due to brain disease or damage. —**dys·pha·sic** /-ˈfāzik/ *adj.*

dys·pla·sia /disˈplāZHə/ ▶ *n. Med.* the enlargement of an organ or tissue by the proliferation of cells of an abnormal type, as a developmental disorder or an early stage in the development of cancer. —**dys·plas·tic** /disˈplastik/ *adj.*

dys·pro·si·um /disˈprōzēəm/ ▶ *n.* the chemical element of atomic number 66, a soft, silvery-white metal of the lanthanide series. (Symbol: **Dy**)

Ee

E¹ /ē/ (also **e**) ▶*n.* (*pl.* **Es** or **E's**) **1** the fifth letter of the alphabet. ■ denoting the fifth in a set of items, categories, sizes, etc. ■ (**e**) *Chess* denoting the fifth file from the left, as viewed from White's side of the board. ■ denoting the lowest-earning socioeconomic category for marketing purposes. **2** (**E**) a shape like that of a capital E: [in *comb.*] *an E-shaped stately home.* **3** (usu. **E**) *Mus.* the third note of the diatonic scale of C major. ■ a key based on a scale with E as its keynote.

E² ▶*abbr.* ■ Earth. ■ East or Eastern: *139° E.* ■ Easter. ■ *inf.* the drug Ecstasy or a tablet of Ecstasy. ■ engineer or engineering. ■ English. ■ [in *comb.*] (also **e**) electronic: *E-commerce.*
▶*symb.* *Physics* ■ electromotive force. ■ energy: $E = mc^2$.

E³ ▶*symb.* (**€**) euro(s).

e ▶*symb.* ■ (also **e**−) *Chem.* an electron. ■ (**e**) *Math.* the transcendental number that is the base of Napierian or natural logarithms, approximately equal to 2.71828.

e³ /ē/ ▶*n.* (*pl.* **e's**) an e-mail system, message, or messages.
▶*v.* (**e'd, e'ing**) [*tr.*] **1** send an e-mail to (someone): *e me to make an offer.* **2** send (a message) by e-mail.

ea. ▶*abbr.* each (used esp. when giving retail prices): *T-shirts for $9.95 ea.*

each /ēCH/ ▶*adj. & pron.* used to refer to every one of two or more people or things, regarded and identified separately: [as *adj.*] *each battery is in a separate compartment* | [as *pron.*] *Doug had money from each of his five uncles.*
▶*adv.* to, for, or by every one of a group (used after a noun or an amount): *they cost $35 each.*

ea·ger /ˈēgər/ ▶*adj.* (of a person) wanting to do or have something very much: *the man was eager to please.* ■ (of a person's expression or tone of voice) characterized by keen expectancy or interest: *small eager faces looked up and listened.* ▷Middle English (also in the sense 'sharp to the senses, pungent, sour'): from Old French *aigre* 'keen,' from Latin *acer, acr-* 'sharp, pungent.' —**ea·ger·ly** *adv.* —**ea·ger·ness** *n.*

ea·gle /ˈēgəl/ ▶*n.* **1** a large bird of prey (family Accipitridae, esp. the genus *Aquila*) with a massive hooked bill and long broad wings, renowned for its keen sight and powerful soaring flight. ■ one of a pair of officer's insignia in the shape of an eagle. **2** *Golf* a score of two strokes under par at a hole.
▶*v.* [*tr.*] *Golf* play (a hole) in two strokes under par.

ea·gle eye ▶*n.* a keen or close watch: *she was keeping an eagle eye on Laura.* —**ea·gle-eyed** /ˈˌēgəl ˈīd/ *adj.*

ea·glet /ˈēglit/ ▶*n.* a young eagle.

ear¹ /i(ə)r/ ▶*n.* the organ of hearing and balance in humans and other vertebrates, esp. the external part of this. ■ an organ sensitive to sound in other animals. ■ an ability to recognize, appreciate, and reproduce sounds, esp. music or language: *an ear for melody.* ■ used to refer to a person's willingness to listen and pay attention to something: *she offers a sympathetic ear to worried pet owners.* ■ an ear-shaped thing, esp. the handle of a jug. —**eared** *adj.* [in *comb.*] *long-eared.* —**ear·less** *adj.*
▶ □ **be all ears** *inf.* be listening eagerly and attentively. □ **one's ears are burning** one is subconsciously aware of being talked about or criticized. □ **have something coming out of one's ears** *inf.* have a substantial or excessive amount of something: *that man's got money coming out of his ears.* □ **have someone's ear** have access to and influence with someone: *he claimed to have the prime minister's ear.* □ **have** (or **keep**) **an ear to the ground** be well informed about events and trends. □ **in one ear and out the other** heard but disregarded or quickly forgotten: *whatever he tells me seems to go in one ear and out the other.* □ **up to one's**

ears in *inf.* very busy with or deeply involved in: *I'm up to my ears in work here.*

ear² ▶*n.* the seed-bearing head or spike of a cereal plant. ■ a head of corn.

ear·ache /ˈi(ə)r,āk/ ▶*n.* pain inside the ear.

ear·drum /ˈi(ə)r,drəm/ ▶*n.* a membrane between the outer and middle ear that vibrates in response to sound waves; the tympanic membrane.

earl /ərl/ ▶*n.* a British nobleman ranking above a viscount and below a marquess. —**earl·dom** *n.*

ear·lobe /ˈi(ə)r,lōb/ ▶*n.* the soft, fleshy lower part of the external ear.

ear·ly /ˈərlē/ ▶*adj.* (**ear·li·er, ear·li·est**) **1** happening or done before the usual or expected time: *we ate an early lunch.* ■ (of a plant or crop) flowering or ripening before other varieties: *early potatoes.* **2** happening, belonging to, or done near the beginning of a particular time or period: *an early goal secured victory.*
▶*adv.* **1** before the usual or expected time: *I was planning to finish work early today.* **2** near the beginning of a particular time or period: *we lost a couple of games early in the season.* ■ (**earlier**) before the present time or before the time one is referring to: *you met my husband earlier.*
▶ □ **at the earliest** not before the time or date specified: *the table won't be delivered until next week at the earliest.* □ **early bird** *humorous* a person who rises, arrives, or acts before the usual or expected time. □ **an early grave** a premature or untimely death: *he worked himself into an early grave.* □ **early** (or **earlier**) **on** at an early (or earlier) stage in a particular time or period: *they discovered early on that the published data were wrong.*

ear·mark /ˈi(ə)r,märk/ ▶*n.* a mark on the ear of a domesticated animal indicating ownership or identity. ■ a characteristic or identifying feature: *this car has all the earmarks of a classic.*
▶*v.* [*tr.*] (usu. **be earmarked**) designate (something, typically funds or resources) for a particular purpose: *the new money will be earmarked for cancer research.*

ear·muffs /ˈi(ə)r,məfs/ ▶*pl. n.* a pair of soft fabric coverings, connected by a band across the top of the head, that are worn over the ears to protect them from cold or noise.

earn /ərn/ ▶*v.* [*tr.*] (of a person) obtain (money) in return for labor or services: *they earn $35 per hour* ■ (of an activity or action) cause (someone) to obtain (money): *this latest win earned them $50,000 in prize money.* ■ (of capital invested) gain (money) as interest or profit. ■ gain or incur deservedly in return for one's behavior or achievements: *through the years she has earned affection and esteem.*

ear·nest¹ /ˈərnist/ ▶*adj.* resulting from or showing sincere and intense conviction: *an earnest student.* —**ear·nest·ly** *adv.* —**ear·nest·ness** *n.*
▶ □ **in earnest** occurring to a greater extent or more intensely than before: *after Labor Day the campaign begins in earnest.* ■ (of a person) sincere and serious in behavior or convictions.

ear·nest² ▶*n.* a thing intended or regarded as a sign or promise of what is to come: *the presence of the troops is an earnest of the world's desire not to see the conflict repeated elsewhere.*

earn·ings /ˈərniNGz/ ▶*pl. n.* money obtained in return for labor or services. ■ income derived from an investment or product: *savers who are attracted by the tax-free earnings.*

ear·phone /ˈi(ə)r,fōn/ ▶*n.* (usu. **earphones**) an electrical device worn on the ear to receive radio or telephone communications or to listen to a radio or tape recorder without other people hearing.

ear·piece /ˈi(ə)r,pēs/ ▶*n.* **1** the part of a telephone, radio receiver, or other aural device that is applied to the ear during use. **2** the part of a pair of glasses that fits around the ear.

ear·plug /'i(ə)r,pləg/ ▶n. (usu. **earplugs**) a piece of wax, rubber, or cotton placed in the ear as protection against noise or water.

ear·ring /'i(ə)r,(r)iNG/ ▶n. a piece of jewelry worn on the lobe or edge of the ear.

ear·shot /'i(ə)r,SHät/ ▶n. the range or distance over which one can hear or be heard: *she waited until he was* ***out of earshot*** *before continuing.*

earth /ərTH/ ▶n. **1** (also **Earth**) the planet on which we live, the third from the sun; the world: *the diversity of life* ***on earth***. ■ the surface of the world as distinct from the sky or water: *it plummeted back to earth at 60 mph*. ■ the present abode of humankind, as distinct from heaven or hell: *God's will be done on earth as it is in heaven*. **2** the substance of the land surface; soil: *a layer of earth*. ■ one of the four elements in ancient and medieval philosophy and in astrology. ■ a stable, dense, non-volatile inorganic substance found in the ground. **3** the underground lair or habitation of a badger or fox.

▶ ■ **come** (or **bring**) **back to earth** return or cause to return to reality after a period of daydreaming or excitement. □ **on earth** used for emphasis: *who on earth would venture out in weather like this?*

earth·en /'ərTHən/ ▶adj. (of a floor or structure) made of compressed earth: *the hillside adjacent to the earthen dam.* ■ (of a pot) made of baked or fired clay.

earth·en·ware /'ərTHən,wer/ ▶n. [often as adj.] pottery made of clay fired to a porous state that can be made impervious to liquids by the use of a glaze: *an earthenware jug.*

earth·ling /'ərTHliNG/ ▶n. an inhabitant of the earth (used esp. in science fiction by members of alien species).

earth·ly /'ərTHlē/ ▶adj. **1** of or relating to the earth or human life on the earth: *water is liquid at normal earthly temperatures.* ■ of or relating to humankind's material existence as distinct from a spiritual or heavenly one: *all earthly happiness is but vanity.* **2** *inf.* used for emphasis: *there was no earthly reason why she should not come too.*

earth·quake /'ərTH,kwāk/ ▶n. a sudden and violent shaking of the ground, sometimes causing great destruction, as a result of movements within the earth's crust or volcanic action. ■ *fig.* a great convulsion or upheaval: *a political earthquake.*

earth sci·ence ▶n. the branch of science dealing with the physical constitution of the earth and its atmosphere. ■ (**earth sciences**) the various branches of this subject, e.g., geology, oceanography, and meteorology.

earth-shat·ter·ing ▶adj. (in hyperbolic use) very important, momentous, or traumatic: *tell me this earth-shattering news of yours.* —**earth-shat·ter·ing·ly** *adv.*

earth·work /'ərTH,wərk/ ▶n. **1** a large artificial bank of soil, esp. one made as a defense. **2** the process of excavating soil in civil engineering work. **3** a work of art consisting of modification of a large piece of land.

earth·worm /'ərTH,wərm/ ▶n. a burrowing annelid (*Lumbricus, Allolobophora*, and other genera, family Lumbricidae) that lives in the soil.

earth·y /'ərTHē/ ▶adj. (**earth·i·er, earth·i·est**) resembling or suggestive of earth or soil: *an earthy smell.* ■ (of a person) direct and uninhibited; hearty: *the storefront is given over to a young, earthy crowd.* ■ (of humor) somewhat coarse or crude: *their good-natured vulgarity and earthy humor.* —**earth·i·ly** *adv.* —**earth·i·ness** *n.*

ear·wax /'i(ə)r,waks/ ▶n. the protective yellow waxy substance secreted in the passage of the outer ear.

ear·wig /'ir,wig/ ▶n. a small elongated insect with a pair of terminal appendages that resemble pincers.

ease /ēz/ ▶n. absence of difficulty or effort: *he gave up tobacco and alcohol with ease.* ■ absence of rigidity or discomfort; poise: *I was always vexed by her self-contained ease.* ■ freedom from worries or problems, esp. about one's material situation: *a life of wealth and ease.*

▶*v.* **1** [*tr.*] make (something unpleasant, painful, or intense) less serious or severe: *a huge road-building program to ease congestion.* ■ [*intr.*] become less serious or severe: *the pain doesn't usually ease off for several hours.* ■ [*intr.*] (**ease up**) relax one's efforts; do something with more moderation: *I'd ease up on the hard stuff if I were you.* ■ make (something) happen more easily; facilitate. ■ [*intr.*] *Finance* (of share prices, interest rates, etc.) decrease in value or amount: *these shares should be bought and tucked away for when interest rates ease* | [as *n.*] (**easing**) *a slight easing of inflation.* **2** [*intr.*] move carefully, gradually, or gently: *I eased down the slope with care* | [*tr.*] *the pilot eased the throttle back.* ■ [*tr.*] (**ease someone out**) gradually exclude someone from a post or place, esp. by devious or subtle maneuvers: *after the scandal he was eased out of his job.*

▶ □ **at** (**one's**) **ease** free from worry, awkwardness, or problems; relaxed: *she was never quite at ease with Phil.* ■ (**at ease**) *Mil.* in a relaxed attitude with the feet apart and the hands behind the back (often as a command). □ **ease someone's mind** alleviate someone's anxiety.

ea·sel /'ēzəl/ ▶n. a self-supporting wooden frame for holding an artist's work while it is being painted or drawn. ■ a similar frame for displaying charts, promotional materials, announcements, etc. ▷late 16th cent.: from Dutch *ezel* 'ass.' The word "horse" is used in English in a similar way to denote a supporting frame.

easel

ease·ment /'ēzmənt/ ▶n. *Law* a right to cross or otherwise use someone else's land for a specified purpose.

eas·i·ly /'ēz(ə)lē/ ▶adv. **1** without difficulty or effort: *he climbed the mountain easily.* ■ in a relaxed manner: *he shrugged easily.* ■ more quickly or frequently than is usual: *they get bored easily.* **2** without doubt; by far: *English is easily the reigning language in the financial world.* ■ very probably: *events that could easily become stodgy and predictable.*

east /ēst/ ▶n. (usu. **the east**) **1** the direction toward the point of the horizon where the sun rises at the equinoxes, on the right-hand side of a person facing north, or the point on the horizon itself: *a gale was blowing from the east.* ■ the compass point corresponding to this. **2** the eastern part of the world or of a specified country, region, or town: *a factory in the east of the city.* ■ (usu. **the East**) the regions or countries lying to the east of Europe, esp. China, Japan, and India. **3** (**East**) *Bridge* the player sitting to the left of North and partnering West.

▶*adj.* **1** lying toward, near, or facing the east: *the hospital's east wing.* ■ (of a wind) blowing from the east. **2** (often **East**) of or denoting the eastern part of a specified area, city, or country or its inhabitants: *East Texas* | *East African.*

▶*adv.* to or toward the east: *traveling east, he met two men.*

east·bound /'ēs(t),bound/ ▶adj. leading or traveling toward the east: *the eastbound lane.*

Eas·ter /'ēstər/ ▶n. the most important and oldest festival of the Christian Church, celebrating the resurrection of Jesus Christ and held (in the Western Church) between March 21 and April 25, on the first Sunday after the first full moon following the northern spring equinox. ■ the period in which this occurs, esp. the weekend from Good Friday to Easter Monday.

east·er·ly /'ēstərlē/ ▶adj. & adv. in an eastward position or direction: [as *adj.*] *the captain ordered an easterly course.* ■ (of a wind) blowing from the east: [as *adj.*] *the light easterly breeze.*

east·ern /'ēstərn/ ▶adj. **1** situated in the east, or directed toward or facing the east: *the eastern slopes of the mountain.* **2** (usu. **Eastern**) living in or originating from the east, in particular the regions or countries lying to the east of Europe: *an Eastern mystic.* —**east·ern·most** /'ēstərn,mōst/ *adj.*

East·ern·er /'ēstərnər/ (also **east·ern·er**) ▶n. a native or inhabitant of the east, esp. of the eastern U.S.

East·ern time ▶the standard time in a zone including the eastern states of the U.S. and parts of Canada, specifically: ■ (**Eastern Standard Time**, abbrev.: **EST**), standard time based on the mean solar time at the meridian 75° W, five hours behind GMT. ■ (**Eastern Daylight Time**, abbrev.: **EDT**) Eastern time during daylight saving time, four hours behind GMT.

east-north-east ▶n. the direction or compass point midway between east and northeast.

east-south-east ▶n. the direction or compass point midway between east and southeast.

east·ward /'ēs(t)wərd/ ▶adj. in an easterly direction: *they followed an eastward course.*

▶*adv.* (also **eastwards**) toward the east: *the bus rattled its way eastward.* —**east·ward·ly** *adv.*

eas·y /'ēzē/ ▶adj. (**eas·i·er, eas·i·est**) **1** achieved without great effort; presenting few difficulties: *an easy way of retrieving information.* ■ (of an object of attack or criticism) having no defense; vulnerable: *he was vulnerable and an easy target.* ■ *inf., derog.* (of a woman) open to sexual advances; sexually available: *her reputation at school for being easy.* **2** (of a period of time or way of life) free from worries or problems: *promises of an easy life in the New World.* ■ (of a person) lacking anxiety or awkwardness; relaxed: *his easy and agreeable manner.*

▶*interj.* be careful: *easy, girl—you'll knock me over!* —**eas·i·ness** *n.*

▶ □ **be easier said than done** be more easily talked about than put into practice. □ **easy come, easy go** used to indicate that a relationship or possession acquired without effort may be abandoned or lost casually and without regret. □ **easy does it** used esp. in spoken English to advise someone to approach a task carefully and slowly. □ **easy on the eye** (or **ear**) *inf.* pleasant to look at (or listen to). □ **go** (or **be**) **easy on someone** *inf.* refrain from being harsh with or critical of someone. □ **go easy on something** *inf.* be sparing or cautious in one's use or consumption of something: *go easy on fatty foods.* □ **have it easy** *inf.* be free from difficulties; be fortunate. □ **rest** (or **sleep**) **easy** be untroubled by (or go to sleep without) worries: *this insurance policy will let you rest easy.* □ **take it easy** proceed calmly and in a relaxed manner. ■ make little effort; rest.

eas·y chair ▶ *n.* a large, comfortable chair, typically an armchair.

eas·y·go·ing /ˈēzēˌgōiNG/ (also **easy-go·ing**) ▶ *adj.* relaxed and tolerant in approach or manner: *an outwardly easygoing but fiercely competitive youngster.*

eat /ēt/ ▶ *v.* (*past* **ate** /āt/; *past part.* **eat·en** /ˈētn/) [*tr.*] put (food) into the mouth and chew and swallow it: *he was eating a hot dog* | [*intr.*] *she watched her son as he ate.* ■ have (a meal): *we ate dinner in a noisy café.* ■ [*intr.*] (**eat out**) have a meal in a restaurant. ■ [*intr.*] (**eat in**) have a meal at home rather than in a restaurant. ■ [*intr.*] follow a diet of a specified kind or quality: *she was very thin, although she was eating properly now.* ■ *inf.* bother; annoy: *she knew what was eating him.* ■ *inf.* absorb (financial loss or cost)

▶ *phrasal v.* □ **eat away at something** (or **eat something away**) erode or destroy something gradually: *the sun and wind eat away at the ice.* ■ use up (profits, resources, or time), esp. when they are intended for other purposes: *inflation can eat away at the annuity's value over the years.* □ **eat someone up** [usu. as *adj.*] (**eaten up**) dominate the thoughts of someone completely: *I'm eaten up with guilt.* □ **eat something up** use resources or time in very large quantities: *an operating system that eats up 200Mb of disk space.*

▶ *n.* (**eats**) *inf.* food or snacks: *people would stop for soft drinks or eats.* —**eat·er** *n.*

▶ □ **eat someone alive** *inf.* (of insects) bite someone many times: *we were eaten alive by mosquitoes.* ■ exploit someone's weakness and completely dominate them: *he expects manufacturers to be eaten alive by lawyers in liability suits.* □ **eat one's heart out** suffer from excessive longing, esp. for someone or something unattainable. ■ [in *imper.*] *inf.* used to encourage feelings of jealousy or regret: *eat your heart out, I'm having a ball!* □ **eat like a bird** (or **a horse**) *inf.* eat very little (or a lot). □ **eat someone out of house and home** *inf.* eat a lot of someone else's food. □ **eat one's words** retract what one has said, esp. in a humiliated way: *they will eat their words when I win.* □ **have someone eating out of one's hand** have someone completely under one's control.

eat·er·y /ˈētərē/ ▶ *n.* (*pl.* **-er·ies**) *inf.* a restaurant or other place where people can be served food.

eau de co·logne /ˌō də kəˈlōn/ ▶ *n.* a toilet water with a strong, characteristic scent, originally made in Cologne, Germany.

eau de toi·lette /ˌō də twäˈlet/ ▶ *n.* a dilute form of perfume; toilet water.

eaves /ēvz/ ▶ *pl. n.* the part of a roof that meets or overhangs the walls of a building.

eaves·drop /ˈēvzˌdräp/ ▶ *v.* (**-dropped, -drop·ping**) [*intr.*] secretly listen to a conversation: *she opened the window just enough to eavesdrop on the conversation outside.* ▷ early 17th cent.: back-formation from *eavesdropper* (late Middle English) 'a person who listens from under the eaves,' from the obsolete noun *eavesdrop* 'the ground on to which water drips from the eaves,' probably from Old Norse *upsardropi*, from *ups* 'eaves' + *dropi* 'a drop.' —**eaves·drop·per** *n.*

ebb /eb/ ▶ *n.* (usu. **the ebb**) the movement of the tide out to sea: *I knew the tide would be on the ebb* | [as *adj.*] *the ebb tide.*

▶ *v.* [*intr.*] (of tidewater) move away from the land; recede: *the tide began to ebb.* Compare with **FLOW**. ■ *fig.* (of an emotion or quality) gradually lessen or reduce: *my enthusiasm was ebbing away.*

▶ □ **ebb and flow** a recurrent or rhythmical pattern of coming and going or decline and regrowth.

E·bon·ics /ēˈbäniks/ ▶ *pl. n.* [treated as *sing.*] American black English regarded as a language in its own right rather than as a dialect of standard English.

eb·on·y /ˈebənē/ ▶ *n.* heavy blackish or very dark brown timber from a mainly tropical tree (genera *Diospyros* and *Euclea*). ■ a very dark brown or black color. ▷ late Middle English: from earlier *ebon* (via Old French and Latin from Greek *ebenos* 'ebony tree'.

e·bul·lient /iˈbo͝olyənt; iˈbəlyənt/ ▶ *adj.* cheerful and full of energy: *she sounded ebullient and happy.* —**e·bul·lience** *n.* —**e·bul·lient·ly** *adv.*

e-busi·ness ▶ another term for **E-COMMERCE**.

EC ▶ *abbr.* ■ European Commission. ■ European Community. ■ executive committee.

ec·cen·tric /ikˈsentrik/ ▶ *adj.* **1** (of a person or behavior) unconventional and slightly strange: *my favorite aunt is very eccentric.* **2** *technical* (of a thing) not placed centrally or not having its axis or other part placed centrally. ■ (of a circle) not centered on the same point as another. ■ (of an orbit) not circular.

▶ *n.* **1** a person of unconventional and slightly strange views or behavior: *he enjoys a colorful reputation as an engaging eccentric.* **2** a disc or wheel mounted eccentrically on a revolving shaft in order to transform rotation into backward-and-forward motion, e.g., a cam in an internal combustion engine. —**ec·cen·tri·cal·ly** *adv.* —**ec·cen·tric·i·ty** /ˌeksənˈtrisitē/ *n.*

ec·cle·si·as·tic /iˌklēzēˈastik/ *formal* ▶ *n.* a priest or clergyman.

▶ *adj.* another term for **ECCLESIASTICAL**.

ec·cle·si·as·ti·cal /iˌklēzēˈastikəl/ ▶ *adj.* of or relating to the Christian Church or its clergy: *the ecclesiastical hierarchy.* —**ec·cle·si·as·ti·cal·ly** *adv.*

ECG ▶ *abbr.* ■ electrocardiogram. ■ electrocardiograph.

ech·e·lon /ˈeSHəˌlän/ ▶ *n.* **1** a level or rank in an organization, a profession, or society: *the upper echelons of the business world.* ■ a part of a military force differentiated by position in battle or by function: *the rear echelon.* **2** *Mil.* a formation of troops, ships, aircraft, or vehicles in parallel rows with the end of each row projecting further than the one in front.

e·chid·na /əˈkidnə/ ▶ *n.* a spiny insectivorous egg-laying mammal (family Tachyglossidae) with a long snout and claws, native to Australia and New Guinea.

e·chi·no·derm /iˈkīnəˌdərm; ˈekənəˌdərm/ ▶ *n.* any marine invertebrate of the phylum Echinodermata, usu. having a spiny skin, including starfish and sea urchins.

e·chi·noid /iˈkīˌnoid; ˈekəˌnoid/ ▶ *n.* any echinoderm of the class Echinoidea, comprising the sea urchins.

▶ *adj.* of or related to the echinoids.

ech·o /ˈekō/ ▶ *n.* (*pl.* **ech·oes**) **1** a sound or series of sounds caused by the reflection of sound waves from a surface back to the listener: *the walls threw back the echoes of his footsteps.* ■ a reflected radio or radar beam. ■ the deliberate introduction of reverberation into a sound recording. ■ *Linguistics* the repetition in structure and content of one speaker's utterance by another. ■ a close parallel or repetition of an idea, feeling, style, or event: *his love for her found an echo in her own feelings.* ■ (often **echoes**) a detail or characteristic that is suggestive of something else: *the cheese has a sharp rich aftertaste with echoes of salty, earthy pastures.* **2** *Bridge* a play by a defender of a higher card in a suit followed by a lower one in a subsequent trick, used as a signal to request a further lead of that suit by their partner. **3** a code word representing the letter E, used in radio communication.

▶ *v.* (**ech·oes, ech·oed**) [*intr.*] **1** (of a sound) be repeated or reverberate after the original sound has stopped: *their footsteps echoed on the metal catwalks.* ■ (of a place) resound with or reflect back a sound or sounds: *the house echoed with shouts and thundering feet.* ■ *fig.* have a continued significance or influence: *illiteracy echoed through the whole fabric of society.* ■ [*tr.*] (often **be echoed**) repeat (someone's words or opinions), typically to express agreement: *these criticisms are echoed in a number of other studies* ■ [*tr.*] *Comput.* send a copy of (an input signal or character) back to its source or to a screen for display: *for security reasons, the password will not be echoed to the screen.* **2** *Bridge* (of a defender) play a higher card followed by a lower one in the same suit, as a signal to request one's partner to lead that suit. —**ech·o·er** *n.* —**ech·o·ey** /ˈekō-ē/ *adj.*

ech·o·car·di·o·gram /ˌekōˈkärdēəˌgram/ ▶ *n.* *Med.* a test of the action of the heart using ultrasound waves to produce a visual display, used for the diagnosis or monitoring of heart disease.

ech·o·ic /eˈkō-ik/ ▶ *adj.* of or like an echo. —**ech·o·i·cal·ly** *adv.*

ech·o·lo·ca·tion /ˌekōlōˈkāSHən/ ▶ *n.* the location of objects by reflected sound, in particular that used by animals such as dolphins and bats.

ech·o sound·er ▶ *n.* a device for determining the depth of the seabed or detecting objects in water by measuring the time taken for sound echoes to return to the listener. —**ech·o sound·ing** (also **ech·o-sound·ing**) *n.*

ech·o·vi·rus /ˈekōˌvīrəs/ (also **ECHO vi·rus**) ▶ *n.* *Med.* any of a group of enteroviruses that can cause a range of diseases, including respiratory infections and a mild form of meningitis.

Pronunciation Key ə *ago*, *up*; ər *over*, *fur*; a *hat*; ā *ate*; ä *car*; CH *chin*; e *let*; ē *see*; e(ə)r *air*; i *fit*; ī *by*; i(ə)r *ear*; NG *sing*; ō *go*; ô *law*, *for*; oi *toy*; o͞o *good*; o͞o *goo*; ou *out*; SH *she*; TH *thin*; T͟H *then*; (h)w *why*; ZH *vision*

é·clair /ā'kler; ĭ'kler/ (also **e-clair**) ▶ *n.* a small, soft, log-shaped pastry filled with cream and typically topped with chocolate icing.

é·clat /ā'klä/ ▶ *n.* brilliant display or effect: *she came into prominence briefly but with éclat.* ■ social distinction or conspicuous success: *such action bestows more éclat upon a warrior than success by other means.*

ec·lec·tic /ĭ'klektĭk/ ▶ *adj.* **1** deriving ideas, style, or taste from a broad and diverse range of sources: *her musical tastes are eclectic.* **2** (**Eclectic**) *Philos.* of, denoting, or belonging to a class of ancient philosophers who did not belong to or found any recognized school of thought but selected such doctrines as they wished from various schools. —**ec·lec·ti·cal·ly** *adv.* —**ec·lec·ti·cism** /-tĭ,sizəm/ *n.*

e·clipse /ĭ'klips/ ▶ *n.* an obscuring of the light from one celestial body by the passage of another between it and the observer or between it and its source of illumination: *an eclipse of the sun.* ■ *fig.* a loss of significance, power, or prominence in relation to another person or thing: *the election result marked the eclipse of the traditional right and center.*
▶ *v.* [*tr.*] (often **be eclipsed**) (of a celestial body) obscure the light from or to (another celestial body): *as the last piece of the sun was eclipsed by the moon.* ■ deprive (someone or something) of significance, power, or prominence: *the state of the economy has eclipsed the environment as the main issue.*
▶ □ **in eclipse** losing or having lost significance, power, or prominence: *his political power was in eclipse.*

e·clip·tic /ĭ'kliptĭk/ ▶ *n. Astron.* a great circle on the celestial sphere representing the sun's apparent path during the year, so called because lunar and solar eclipses can occur only when the moon crosses it.
▶ *adj.* of an eclipse or the ecliptic.

ec·o·cen·trism /,ekō'sen,trizəm; ,ēkō-/ ▶ *n.* a point of view that recognizes the ecosphere, rather than the biosphere, as central in importance, and attempts to redress the imbalance created by anthropocentrism. —**ec·o·cen·tric** /-'sentrĭk/ *adj.*

ec·o·con·sum·er /'ekōkən,sōōmər; 'ēkō-/ ▶ *n.* a consumer who makes purchasing decisions partly or largely on the basis of ecological issues: *sophisticated ecoconsumers are descending upon some unusual destinations.*

ecol. ▶ *abbr.* ■ ecological. ■ ecology.

E. co·li /ē 'kōlĭ/ ▶ *n.* a bacterium (*Escherichia coli*) commonly found in the intestines of humans and other animals, where it usually causes no harm. Some strains can cause severe food poisoning.

ec·o·lodge /'ekō,läj; 'ēkō-/ ▶ *n.* a type of tourist accommodation designed to have the least possible impact on the natural environment in which it is situated.

e·col·o·gy /ĭ'käləjē/ ▶ *n.* **1** the branch of biology that deals with the relations of organisms to one another and to their physical surroundings. ■ (also **human ecology**) the study of the interaction of people with their environment. **2** (also **E·col·o·gy**) the political movement that seeks to protect the environment, esp. from pollution. —**ec·o·log·i·cal** /,ekə'läjikəl; ,ēkə-/ *adj.* —**ec·o·log·i·cal·ly** *adv.* —**e·col·o·gist** /-jist/ *n.*

e·com·merce ▶ *n.* commercial transactions conducted electronically on the Internet.

econ. ▶ *abbr.* ■ economics. ■ economy.

ec·o·nom·ic /,ekə'nämĭk; ,ēkə-/ ▶ *adj.* of or relating to economics or the economy: *the government's economic policy.* ■ justified in terms of profitability: *many organizations must become larger if they are to remain economic.* ■ requiring fewer resources or costing less money: *solar power may provide a more economic solution.* ■ (of a subject) considered in relation to trade, industry, and the creation of wealth: *economic history.*

ec·o·nom·i·cal /,ekə'nämĭkəl; ,ēkə-/ ▶ *adj.* giving good value or service in relation to the amount of money, time, or effort spent: *a small, economical car.* ■ (of a person or lifestyle) careful not to waste money or resources. ■ using no more of something than is necessary: *this chassis is economical in metal and therefore light in weight.* —**ec·o·nom·i·cal·ly** *adv.*

ec·o·nom·ics /,ekə'nämĭks; ,ēkə-/ ▶ *pl. n.* [often treated as *sing.*] the branch of knowledge concerned with the production, consumption, and transfer of wealth. ■ the condition of a region or group as regards material prosperity: *he is responsible for the island's modest economics.*

e·con·o·mist /ĭ'känəmist/ ▶ *n.* an expert in economics.

e·con·o·mize /ĭ'känə,mīz/ ▶ *v.* [*intr.*] spend less; reduce one's expenses: *I have to economize where I can.* —**e·con·o·mi·za·tion** /ĭ,känəmə'zāsHən/ *n.* —**e·con·o·miz·er** *n.*

e·con·o·my /ĭ'känəmē/ ▶ *n.* (*pl.* **-mies**) **1** the wealth and resources of a country or region, esp. in terms of the production and consumption of goods and services. ■ a particular system or stage of an economy: *a free-market economy.* **2** careful management of available resources: *even heat distribution and fuel economy.* ■ sparing or careful use of something:

economy of words. ■ (usu. **economies**) a financial saving: *there were many economies to be made by giving up our offices in Manhattan.* ■ (also **economy class**) the cheapest class of air or rail travel: *we flew economy.*
▶ *adj.* (of a product) offering the best value for the money: [in *comb.*] *an economy pack.* ■ designed to be economical to use: *an economy car.* ▷late 15th cent. (in the sense 'management of material resources'): from French *économie*, or via Latin from Greek *oikonomia* 'household management,' based on *oíkos* 'house' + *nemein* 'manage.' Current senses date from the 17th cent.

ec·o·re·gion /'ekō,rējən; 'ēkō-/ ▶ *n.* a major ecosystem defined by distinctive geography and receiving uniform solar radiation and moisture: *the Columbia Basin ecoregion.*

ec·o·sphere /'ekō,sfi(ə)r; 'ēkō/ ▶ *n.* the biosphere of the earth or another planet, esp. when the interaction between the living and nonliving components is emphasized.

ec·o·sys·tem /'ekō,sistəm; 'ēkō-/ ▶ *n. Ecol.* a biological community of interacting organisms and their physical environment.

ec·ru /'ekrōō/ ▶ *n.* the light beige color of unbleached linen.

ec·sta·sy /'ekstəsē/ ▶ *n.* (*pl.* **-sies**) **1** an overwhelming feeling of great happiness or joyful excitement: *there was a look of ecstasy on his face.* **2** (**Ecstasy**) an illegal amphetamine-based synthetic drug with euphoric and hallucinatory effects, originally promoted as an adjunct to psychotherapy. (abbr.: **MDMA**).

ec·stat·ic /ek'statik/ ▶ *adj.* **1** feeling or expressing overwhelming happiness or joyful excitement: *ecstatic fans filled the stadium.* **2** involving an experience of mystic self-transcendence: *an ecstatic vision of God.*
▶ *n.* a person subject to mystical experiences. —**ec·stat·i·cal·ly** *adv.*

ECT ▶ *abbr.* electroconvulsive therapy.

ec·to·derm /'ektə,dərm/ ▶ *n. Zool. & Embryology* the outermost layer of cells or tissue of an embryo in early development, or the parts derived from this, which include the epidermis, nerve tissue, and nephridia. Compare with **ENDODERM** and **MESODERM**. —**ec·to·der·mal** /,ektō'dərməl/ *adj.*

ec·to·morph /'ektə,môrf/ ▶ *n. Physiol.* a person with a lean and delicate body build. Compare with **ENDOMORPH** and **MESOMORPH**. —**ec·to·mor·phic** /,ektə'môrfik/ *adj.* —**ec·to·morph·y** *n.*

ec·top·ic preg·nan·cy ▶ *n.* a pregnancy in which the fetus develops outside the uterus, typically in a Fallopian tube.

ec·to·plasm /'ektə,plazəm/ ▶ *n.* **1** *Biol.* the more viscous, clear outer layer of the cytoplasm in ameboid cells. Compare with **ENDOPLASM**. **2** a supernatural viscous substance that is supposed to exude from the body of a medium during a spiritualistic trance and form the material for the manifestation of spirits. —**ec·to·plas·mic** /,ektə'plazmik/ *adj.*

ec·u·men·i·cal /,ekyə'menikəl/ ▶ *adj.* representing a number of different Christian churches: ■ promoting or relating to unity among the world's Christian churches: *ecumenical dialogue.* —**ec·u·men·i·cal·ly** *adv.*

ec·ze·ma /'egzəmə; 'eksə-; ig'zēmə/ ▶ *n.* a medical condition in which patches of skin become rough and inflamed, with blisters that cause itching and bleeding, sometimes resulting from a reaction to irritation but more typically having no obvious external cause. —**ec·zem·a·tous** /ig'zemətəs; ik'sem-; ig'zē-/ *adj.*

ed. ▶ *abbr.* ■ edited by. ■ edition. ■ editor. ■ education.

E·dam /'ēdəm/ ▶ *n.* a round Dutch cheese, typically pale yellow with a red wax coating.

ed·a·ma·me /,edə'mämā/ ▶ *n.* a dish of green soybeans boiled or steamed in their pods.

ed·dy /'edē/ ▶ *n.* (*pl.* **-dies**) a circular movement of water, counter to a main current, causing a small whirlpool. ■ a movement of wind, fog, or smoke resembling this.
▶ *v.* (**-dies, -died**) [*intr.*] (of water, air, or smoke) move in a circular way: *the mists from the river eddied around the banks.*

e·del·weiss /'ādl,wīs; -,vīs/ ▶ *n.* a European mountain plant (*Leontopodium alpinum*) of the daisy family that has woolly white bracts.

e·de·ma /ĭ'dēmə/ ▶ *n.* a condition characterized by an excess of watery fluid collecting in the cavities or tissues of the body. Also called **DROPSY**. —**e·dem·a·tous** /ĭ'dēmətəs/ *adj.*

E·den (also **Garden of Eden**) ▶ the place where Adam and Eve lived in the biblical account of the Creation, from which they were expelled for disobediently eating the fruit of the tree of the knowledge of good and evil. ■ [as *n.*] (**an Eden**) a place or state of great happiness; an unspoiled paradise: *the lost Eden of his childhood.*

e·den·tate /ē'den,tāt/ ▶ *n. Zool.* a mammal of an order (Xenarthra, or Edentata) distinguished by the lack of incisor and canine teeth. All edentates, including anteaters, sloths, and armadillos, are native to Central and South America.

edge /ej/ ▶ *n.* **1** the outside limit of an object, area, or surface; a place or part farthest away from the center of something: *a willow tree at the water's edge.* ■ an area next to a steep drop: *the cliff edge.* ■ the point or state immediately before something unpleasant or momentous occurs: *the economy was teetering on **the edge of** recession.* **2** the sharpened side of the blade of a cutting implement or weapon: *a knife with a razor-sharp edge.* ■ the line along which two surfaces of a solid meet. ■ a sharp, threatening, or bitter tone of voice, usually indicating the speaker's annoyance or tension: *she was still smiling, but there was **an edge** to her voice.* ■ an intense, sharp, or striking quality: *a flamenco singer brings a primitive edge to the music.* ■ a quality or factor that gives superiority over close rivals or competitors: *the veal had the edge on flavor.*
▶ *v.* [*tr.*] **1** (often **be edged**) provide with a border or edge: *the pool is edged with paving.* **2** [*intr.*] move gradually, carefully, or furtively in a particular direction: *she tried to edge away from him.* ■ [*tr.*] *inf.* defeat by a small margin: *Connecticut avoided an upset and edged Yale 49–48.* ▷Old English *ecg* 'sharpened side of a blade,' of Germanic origin; related to Dutch *egge* and German *Ecke*, also to Old Norse *eggja*, from an Indo-European root shared by Latin *acies* 'edge' and Greek *akis* 'point.' —**edged** *adj.* [in *comb.*] *a black-edged handkerchief.*
▶ □ **on edge** tense, nervous, or irritable: *never had she felt so on edge before an interview.* □ **set someone's teeth on edge** (esp. of an unpleasantly harsh sound) cause someone to feel intense discomfort or irritation. □ **take the edge off** reduce the intensity or effect of (something unpleasant or severe): *the tablets will take the edge off the pain.*
edge·wise /ej,wīz/ (also **edge·ways** /-,wāz/) ▶ *adv.* & *adj.* with the edge uppermost or toward the viewer.
▶ □ **get a word in edgewise** contribute to a conversation with difficulty because the other speaker talks almost without pause.
edg·ing /ejiNG/ ▶ *n.* a thing forming an edge or border: *the crocheted edging of the cloth.* ■ the process of providing something with an edge or border.
edg·y /ejē/ ▶ *adj.* (**edg·i·er, edg·i·est**) tense, nervous, or irritable: *he became edgy and defensive.* ■ having an intense or sharp quality. —**edg·i·ly** /ejəlē/ *adv.* —**edg·i·ness** *n.*
ed·i·ble /edəbəl/ ▶ *adj.* fit to be eaten (often used to contrast with unpalatable or poisonous examples): *nasturtium seeds are edible.*
▶ *n.* (**edibles**) items of food. —**ed·i·bil·i·ty** /,edə'bilitē/ *n.*
e·dict /ēdikt/ ▶ *n.* an official order or proclamation issued by a person in authority. —**e·dic·tal** /i'diktl/ *adj.*
ed·i·fice /edəfis/ ▶ *n. formal* a building, esp. a large, imposing one. ■ *fig.* a complex system of beliefs: *the edifice of capitalism.*
ed·i·fy /edə,fī/ ▶ *v.* (**-fies, -fied**) [*tr.*] *formal* instruct or improve (someone) morally or intellectually. ▷Middle English: from Old French *edifier*, from Latin *aedificare* 'build,' from *aedis* 'dwelling' + *facere* 'make'. The word originally meant 'construct a building,' also 'strengthen,' hence to "build up" morally or spiritually. —**ed·i·fi·ca·tion** /-fi'kāshən/ *n.* —**ed·i·fy·ing** *adj.*
ed·it /edit/ ▶ *v.* (**ed·it·ed, ed·it·ing**) [*tr.*] (often **be edited**) prepare (written material) for publication by correcting, condensing, or otherwise modifying it: *Volume I was edited by J. Johnson.* ■ choose material for (a movie or a radio or television program) and arrange it to form a coherent whole: *the footage wasn't good enough to be edited into broadcast form.* ■ be editor of (a newspaper or magazine). ■ (**edit something out**) remove unnecessary or inappropriate words, sounds, or scenes from a text, movie, or radio or television program.
▶ *n.* a change or correction made as a result of editing.
e·di·tion /i'dishən/ ▶ *n.* a particular form or version of a published text: *a paperback edition.* ■ a particular version of a text that has been revised or created from a substantially new setting of type: *a first edition.* ■ the total number of copies of a book, newspaper, or other published material issued at one time. ■ a particular version or instance of a regular program or broadcast: *the Monday edition will be repeated on Wednesdays.* ■ *fig.* a person or thing that is compared to another as a copy to an original: *the building was a simpler edition of its namesake.*
ed·i·tor /editər/ ▶ *n.* a person who is in charge of and determines the final content of a text, particularly a newspaper or magazine: *a sports editor.* ■ a person who works for a publishing company, commissioning or preparing material for publication. ■ a computer program enabling the user to alter or rearrange text. —**ed·i·tor·ship** *n.*
ed·i·to·ri·al /,edi'tôrēəl/ ▶ *adj.* **1** of or relating to the commissioning or preparing of material for publication: *a pillar of editorial excellence.* ■ of or relating to the part of a newspaper or magazine that contains news, information, or comment as opposed to advertising. **2** of or relating to a section in a newspaper, often written by the editor, that expresses an opinion: *buoyed by yesterday's editorial endorsement.*
▶ *n.* a newspaper article written by or on behalf of an editor that gives an opinion on a topical issue. ■ the parts of a newspaper or magazine that are not advertising. —**ed·i·to·ri·al·ist** *n.* —**ed·i·to·ri·al·ize** *v.* —**ed·i·to·ri·al·ly** *adv.*
EDP ▶ *abbr.* electronic data processing.
EDT ▶ *abbr.* Eastern Daylight Time (see **EASTERN TIME**).
ed·u·cate /'ejə,kāt/ ▶ *v.* [*tr.*] (often **be educated**) give intellectual, moral, and social instruction to (someone, esp. a child), typically at a school or university. ■ provide or pay for instruction for (one's child), esp. at a school. ■ give (someone) training in or information on a particular field: [*tr.*] *the need to educate people to conserve water.* —**ed·u·ca·bil·i·ty** /,ejəkə'bilitē/ *n.* —**ed·u·ca·ble** /-kəbəl/ *adj.* —**ed·u·ca·tive** /-,kātiv/ *adj.* —**ed·u·ca·tor** *n.*
ed·u·cat·ed /'ejə,kātid/ ▶ *adj.* having been educated: [in *comb.*] *a Harvard-educated lawyer.* ■ resulting from or having had a good education: *educated tastes.*
ed·u·ca·tion /,ejə'kāshən/ ▶ *n.* the process of receiving or giving systematic instruction, esp. at a school or university: *a new system of public education.* ■ the theory and practice of teaching: *colleges of education.* ■ a body of knowledge acquired while being educated: *his education is encyclopedic and eclectic.* ■ information about or training in a particular field or subject: *health education.* ■ a particular stage in the process of being educated: *a high-school education.* ■ (**an education**) *fig.* an enlightening experience: *the wares in the shops are an education in quality.* —**ed·u·ca·tion·al** /-shənl/ *adj.*
e·duce /i'd(y)ōōs/ ▶ *v.* [*tr.*] *formal* bring out or develop (something latent or potential): *out of love obedience is to be educed.* ■ infer (something) from data: *more information can be educed from these statistics.* —**e·duc·i·ble** /ē'd(y)ōōsəbəl; i'd(y)ōōs-/ *adj.* —**e·duc·tion** /i'dəkshən/ *n.*
Ed·ward·i·an /ed'wôrdēən; -'wär-/ ▶ *adj.* of, relating to, or characteristic of the reign of King Edward VII: *the Edwardian era | a fine Edwardian house.*
EE ▶ *abbr.* ■ electrical engineer. ■ electrical engineering.
EEG ▶ *abbr.* ■ electroencephalogram. ■ electroencephalograph. ■ electroencephalography.
eel /ēl/ ▶ *n.* a snakelike fish (order Anguilliformes, esp. the family Anguillidae) with a slender elongated body and poorly developed fins. ■ used in names of unrelated fishes that resemble the true eels, e.g., **electric eel, moray eel.** —**eel·like** /-,līk/ *adj.*
EEOC ▶ *abbr.* Equal Employment Opportunity Commission.
ee·rie /'i(ə)rē/ ▶ *adj.* (**ee·ri·er, ee·ri·est**) strange and frightening: *an eerie green glow in the sky.* —**ee·ri·ly** *adv.* *it was eerily quiet.* —**ee·ri·ness** *n.*
ef·face /i'fās/ ▶ *v.* [*tr.*] erase (a mark) from a surface: *with time, the words are effaced by the frost and the rain.* ■ (**efface oneself**) *fig.* make oneself appear insignificant or inconspicuous. —**ef·face·ment** *n.*
ef·fect /i'fekt/ ▶ *n.* **1** a change that is a result or consequence of an action or other cause: *the lethal effects of hard drugs.* ■ used to refer to the state of being or becoming operative: *they succeeded in **putting** their strategies **into effect**.* ■ the extent to which something succeeds or is operative: *wind power can be used to great effect.* ■ *Physics* a physical phenomenon, typically named after its discoverer: *the Doppler effect.* ■ an impression produced in the mind of a person: *gentle music can have a soothing effect.* **2** (**effects**) the lighting, sound, or scenery used in a play, movie, or broadcast: *the production relied too much on spectacular effects.* **3** (**effects**) personal belongings: *the insurance covers personal effects.*
▶ *v.* [*tr.*] (often **be effected**) cause (something) to happen; bring about: *budget cuts that were quietly effected over four years.*
▶ □ **for effect** in order to impress people: *I suspect he's controversial for effect.* □ **in effect** in operation; in force: *a moratorium in effect since 1985 has been lifted.* ■ used to convey that something is the case in practice even if it is not formally acknowledged to be so: *additional payments which are in effect an entrance tax.* □ **to that effect** having that result, purpose, or meaning: *she thought it a foolish rule and put a notice to that effect in a newspaper.*
ef·fec·tive /i'fektiv/ ▶ *adj.* **1** successful in producing a desired or intended result: *effective solutions to environmental problems.* ■ (esp. of a law or policy) operative: *the agreements will be effective from November.* **2** fulfilling a specified function in fact, though not formally acknowledged as such: *the companies were under effective Soviet control.* ■ assessed according to actual rather than face value: *an effective price of $176 million.* ■ impressive; striking: *an effective finale.* —**ef·fec·tive·ly** *adv.* —**ef·fec·tive·ness** *n.* —**ef·fec·tiv·i·ty** /,efek'tivitē; ,ēfek-/ *n.*
ef·fec·tu·al /i'fekchōōəl/ ▶ *adj.* (typically of something inanimate or

abstract) successful in producing a desired or intended result; effective: *tobacco smoke is the most effectual protection against the mosquito.* **—ef·fec·tu·al·i·ty** /i,fekCHŌō'alitē/ *n.* **—ef·fec·tu·al·ly** *adv.* **—ef·fec·tu·al·ness** *n.*

ef·fem·i·nate /i'femənət/ ▶*adj.* (of a man) having or showing characteristics regarded as typical of a woman; unmanly. **—ef·fem·i·na·cy** /i-'femənəsē/ *n.* **—ef·fem·i·nate·ly** *adv.*

ef·fer·vesce /,efər'ves/ ▶*v.* [*intr.*] (of a liquid) give off bubbles. ▪ *fig.* (of a person) be vivacious and enthusiastic. **—ef·fer·ves·cence** *n.* **—ef·fer·ves·cent** *adj.*

ef·fete /i'fēt/ ▶*adj.* (of a person) affected, overrefined, and ineffectual: *effete trendies from art college.* **—ef·fete·ness** *n.*

ef·fi·ca·cious /,efi'kāSHəs/ ▶*adj. formal* (typically of something inanimate or abstract) successful in producing a desired or intended result; effective: *the vaccine has proved both efficacious and safe.* **—ef·fi·ca·cious·ly** *adv.* **—ef·fi·ca·cious·ness** *n.* **—ef·fi·ca·cy** /'efikəsē/ *n.*

ef·fi·cien·cy /i'fisHənsē/ ▶*n.* (*pl.* **-cies**) the state or quality of being efficient: *greater energy efficiency.* ▪ an action designed to achieve this: *to increase efficiencies and improve earnings.* ▪ *technical* the ratio of the useful work performed by a machine or in a process to the total energy expended or heat taken in. ▪ short for EFFICIENCY APARTMENT.

ef·fi·cien·cy a·part·ment (also **efficiency**) ▶*n.* an apartment in which one room typically contains the kitchen, living, and sleeping quarters, with a separate bathroom.

ef·fi·cient /i'fisHənt/ ▶*adj.* (esp. of a system or machine) achieving maximum productivity with minimum wasted effort or expense: *fluorescent lamps are efficient at converting electricity into light.* ▪ (of a person) working in a well-organized and competent way: *an efficient administrator.* ▪ [in comb.] preventing the wasteful use of a particular resource: *an energy-efficient heating system.* **—ef·fi·cient·ly** *adv.*

ef·fi·gy /'efijē/ ▶*n.* (*pl.* **-gies**) a sculpture or model of a person: *coins bearing the effigy of Maria Theresa of Austria.* ▪ a roughly made model of a particular person, made in order to be damaged or destroyed as a protest or expression of anger: *the senator was* **burned in effigy.** ▷mid 16th cent.: from Latin *effigies,* from *effingere* 'to fashion (artistically),' from *ex-* 'out' + *fingere* 'to shape.'

ef·flo·resce /,eflə'res/ ▶*v.* **1** [*intr.*] (of a substance) lose moisture and turn to a fine powder upon exposure to air. ▪ (of salts) come to the surface of brickwork, rock, or other material and crystallize there. ▪ (of a surface) become covered with salt particles. **2** reach an optimum stage of development; blossom: *simple concepts that effloresce into testable conclusions.* **—ef·flo·res·cence** /-'resəns/ *n.* **—ef·flo·res·cent** *adj.*

ef·flu·ent /'eflōōənt/ ▶*n.* liquid waste or sewage discharged into a river or the sea: *the bay was contaminated with the effluent from an industrial plant.* **—ef·flu·ence** *n.*

ef·flu·vi·um /i'flōōvēəm/ ▶*n.* (*pl.* **-vi·a** /-vēə/) an unpleasant or harmful odor, secretion, or discharge: *the unwholesome effluvia of decaying vegetable matter.*

ef·fort /'efərt/ ▶*n.* a vigorous or determined attempt: *millions more birds have been culled* **in an effort** *to stem the spread of the virus.* ▪ the result of an attempt: *thanks to Vicki's efforts, Edmeston has a Haunted House.* ▪ strenuous physical or mental exertion: *the doctor spared no effort in helping my father.* ▪ *technical* a force exerted by a machine or in a process. ▪ the activities of a group of people with a common purpose: *the war effort.* **—ef·fort·ful** *adj.* **—ef·fort·ful·ly** *adv.* **—ef·fort·less** *adj.* **—ef·fort·less·ly** *adv.*

ef·fron·ter·y /i'frəntərē/ ▶*n.* insolent or impertinent behavior: *one juror had the effrontery to challenge the coroner's decision.*

ef·ful·gent /i'fŏŏljənt; i'fəl-/ ▶*adj. poetic/lit.* shining brightly; radiant. ▪ (of a person or their expression) emanating joy or goodness. **—ef·ful·gence** *n.* **—ef·ful·gent·ly** *adv.*

ef·fu·sion /i'fyŏŏzHən/ ▶*n.* an instance of giving off something such as a liquid, light, or smell: *a massive effusion of poisonous gas.* ▪ *Med.* an escape of fluid into a body cavity. ▪ an act of talking or writing in an unrestrained or heartfelt way: *literary effusions.* **—ef·fuse** *v.*

ef·fu·sive /i'fyŏŏsiv/ ▶*adj.* expressing feelings of gratitude, pleasure, or approval in an unrestrained or heartfelt manner: *an effusive welcome.* **—ef·fu·sive·ly** *adv.* **—ef·fu·sive·ness** *n.*

E-fit /'ē ,fit/ ▶*n.* an electronic picture of a person's face made from composite photographs of facial features, created by a computer program.

e.g. ▶*abbr.* for example.

e·gal·i·tar·i·an /i,galə'terēən/ ▶*adj.* of, relating to, or believing in the principle that all people are equal and deserve equal rights and opportunities: *a fairer, more egalitarian society.*

▶*n.* a person who advocates or supports such a principle. **—e·gal·i·tar·i·an·ism** *n.*

egg¹ /eg/ ▶*n.* **1** an oval or round object laid by a female bird, reptile, fish, or invertebrate, usually containing a developing embryo. The eggs of birds are enclosed in a chalky shell, while those of reptiles are in a leathery membrane. ▪ an infertile egg, typically of the domestic hen, used for food. ▪ *Biol.* the female reproductive cell in animals and plants; an ovum. ▪ a thing resembling a bird's egg in shape: *chocolate eggs.* ▪ *Archit.* a decorative oval molding, used alternately with triangular figures. **2** *inf., dated* a person possessing a specified quality: *she was a good egg.* **—egg·y** *adj.*

▶ □ **lay an egg** *inf.* be completely unsuccessful; fail badly. □ **with egg on one's face** *inf.* appearing foolish or ridiculous.

egg² ▶*v.* [*tr.*] (**egg someone on**) urge or encourage someone to do something, esp. something foolish or risky.

egg·beat·er /'eg,bētər/ ▶*n.* a kitchen utensil used for beating ingredients such as eggs or cream. ▪ *informal* a helicopter.

egg·head /'eg,hed/ ▶*n. inf., often derog.* a person who is highly academic or studious; an intellectual. **—egg·head·ed** *adj.*

egg·nog /'eg,näg; -,nôg/ ▶*n.* a drink made from a mixture of eggs, cream, and flavorings, often with alcohol.

egg·plant /'eg,plant/ ▶*n.* **1** the large egg-shaped fruit of a tropical Old World plant, eaten as a vegetable. ▪ a dark purple color like the typical skin of this fruit. **2** the large plant (*Solanum melongena*) of the nightshade family that bears this fruit.

egg·shell /'eg,sHel/ ▶*n.* the thin, hard outer layer of an egg, esp. a hen's egg. ▪ used in similes and metaphors to refer to the fragile nature of something: *the truck would crush his car like an eggshell.* ▪ (also **eggshell paint**) an oil-based paint that dries with a slight sheen: *the woodwork was painted in eggshell.* ▪ a pale yellowish-white color.

e·go /'ēgō/ ▶*n.* (*pl.* **e·gos**) a person's sense of self-esteem or self-importance: *a boost to my ego.* ▪ *Psychoanalysis* the part of the mind that mediates between the conscious and the unconscious and is responsible for reality testing and a sense of personal identity. Compare with ID and SUPEREGO. ▪ an overly high opinion of oneself: *some major players with really big egos.* ▪ *Philos.* (in metaphysics) a conscious thinking subject. **—e·go·less** *adj.*

e·go·cen·tric /,ēgō'sentrik/ ▶*adj.* thinking only of oneself, without regard for the feelings or desires of others; self-centered. ▪ centered in or arising from a person's own existence or perspective: *egocentric spatial perception.*

▶*n.* an egocentric person. **—e·go·cen·tric·al·ly** *adv.* **—e·go·cen·tric·i·ty** /,ēgōsen'trisitē/ *n.* **—e·go·cen·trism** /,ēgō'sentrizəm/ *n.*

e·go·ism /'ēgō,izəm/ ▶*n. Ethics* an ethical theory that treats self-interest as the foundation of morality. ▪ another term for EGOTISM. **—e·go·ist** *n.* **—e·go·is·tic** *adj.* **—e·go·is·ti·cal** *adj.* **—e·go·is·ti·cal·ly** *adv.*

e·go·ma·ni·a /,ēgō'mānēə/ ▶*n.* obsessive egotism or self-centeredness. **—e·go·ma·ni·ac** /-nē,ak/ *n.* **—e·go·ma·ni·a·cal** /-mə'nīəkəl/ *adj.*

e·go·surf /'ēgō,sərf/ ▶*v.* [*intr.*] *inf.* search the Internet for instances of one's own name or links to one's own Web site. **—e·go·surf·ing** *n.*

e·go·tism /'ēgə,tizəm/ ▶*n.* the practice of talking and thinking about oneself excessively because of an undue sense of self-importance. **—e·go·tist** *n.* **—e·go·tis·tic** *adj.* **—e·go·tis·ti·cal** *adj.* **—e·go·tis·ti·cal·ly** *adv.* **—e·go·tize** /-,tīz/ *v.*

e·go trip ▶*n. inf.* an activity done in order to increase one's sense of self-importance: *driving that car was the biggest ego trip I'd ever had.*

e·gre·gious /i'grējəs/ ▶*adj.* outstandingly bad; shocking: *egregious abuses of copyright.* **—e·gre·gious·ly** *adv.* **—e·gre·gious·ness** *n.*

e·gress /'ē,gres/ ▶*n.* the action of going out of or leaving a place: *direct means of access and egress for passengers.* ▪ a way out: *a narrow egress.* ▪ *Law* the right or freedom to come out or go out.

e·gret /'ēgrit; 'ē,gret; 'egrit/ ▶*n.* a heron (genera *Egretta* and *Bubulcus*) with mainly white plumage, having long plumes in the breeding season.

E·gyp·tian /i'jipsHən/ ▶*adj.* of or relating to Egypt or its people. ▪ of or relating to Egyptian antiquities: *a large Egyptian collection was sold at Sotheby's.* ▪ of or relating to the language of ancient Egypt.

▶*n.* **1** a native of ancient or modern Egypt, or a person of Egyptian descent. **2** the Afro-Asiatic language used in ancient Egypt, attested from *c.*3000 BC. It is represented in its oldest stages by hieroglyphic inscriptions and in its latest form by Coptic; it has been replaced in modern use by Arabic. **—E·gyp·tian·i·za·tion** /i,jipsHəni'zāsHən/ *n.* **—E·gyp·tian·ize** /-,nīz/ *v.*

E·gyp·tian co·bra ▶*n.* a large nocturnal African cobra (*Naja haje*) with a thick body and large head. Also called ASP.

EIDE ▶*n. Comput.* enhanced integrated drive electronics. See IDE.

ei·der /'īdər/ ▶*n.* (also **eider duck**) (*pl.* same or **eiders** /'īdərz/) a northern sea duck (genera *Somateria* and *Polysticta*), of which the male has mainly black and white plumage with a colored head, and the brown female has soft down feathers that are used to line the nest, in particular the **common eider** (*S. mollissima*). ■ another term for **EIDERDOWN**.

ei·der·down /ˈīdərˌdoun/ ▶ *n.* small, soft feathers from the breast of the female eider duck. ■ *chiefly Brit.* a quilt filled with down (originally from the eider) or some other soft material.

eight /āt/ ▶ *cardinal number* equivalent to the product of two and four; one more than seven, or two less than ten; 8. (Roman numeral: **viii** or **VIII**.) ■ a group or unit of eight people or things: *the win placed Canada closer to the final eight.* ■ eight years old: *children as young as eight.* ■ eight o'clock: *in time for dinner at eight.* ■ a size of garment or other merchandise denoted by eight. ■ an eight-cylinder engine or a motor vehicle with such an engine. ■ a playing card with eight pips. ■ an eight-oared rowing shell or its crew. ▷Old English *ehta, eahta*, of Germanic origin; related to Dutch and German *acht*, from an Indo-European root shared by Latin *octo* and Greek *oktō*.

eigh·teen /āˈtēn; ˈāˌtēn/ ▶ *cardinal number* equivalent to the product of two and nine; one more than seventeen, or eight more than ten; 18. (Roman numeral: **xviii** or **XVIII**.) ■ a set or team of eighteen individuals. ■ eighteen years old: *he was barely eighteen.* —**eight·eenth** /āˈtēnтʜ; ˈāˌtēnтʜ / *ordinal number.*

eigh·teen-wheel·er ▶ *n.* a large tractor-trailer with eighteen wheels.

eight·fold /ˈātˌfōld/ ▶ *adj.* eight times as great or as numerous: *an eightfold increase in costs.* ■ having eight parts or elements: *an eightfold shape.* ▶ *adv.* by eight times; to eight times the number or amount: *claims have grown eightfold in ten years.*

eighth /ˈā(t)тʜ/ ▶ *ordinal number* constituting number eight in a sequence; 8th. ■ (**an eighth/one eighth**) each of eight equal parts into which something is or may be divided: *an eighth of an inch.* ■ the eighth finisher or position in a race or competition: *she finished eighth of the eleven runners.* ■ the eighth grade of a school. —**eighth·ly** *adv.*

eighth note ▶ *n. Mus.* a note having the time value of an eighth of a whole note or half a quarter note, represented by a large dot with a hooked stem.

eight·y /ˈātē/ ▶ *cardinal number* (*pl.* **eight·ies**) equivalent to the product of eight and ten; ten less than ninety; 80. (Roman numeral: **lxxx** or **LXXX**.) ■ (**eighties**) the numbers from 80 to 89, esp. the years of a century or of a person's life: *his grandmother was in her eighties.* ■ eighty years old: *he was over eighty at the time.* ■ eighty miles an hour: *roaring down the highway doing eighty.* —**eight·i·eth** /ˈātēiтʜ/ *ordinal number*

eigh·ty-six /ˌātēˈsiks/ (also **86**) ▶ *n. inf.* someone regarded as undesirable as a restaurant or bar patron. ▶ *v.* [*trans.*] **1** refuse to serve someone: *He got 86ed from a reservation casino.* **2** reject, discard, or cancel: *the passwords will be 86ed by next October.*

ein·stein·i·um /īnˈstīnēəm/ ▶ *n.* the chemical element of atomic number 99, a radioactive metal of the actinide series. Einsteinium does not occur naturally and was discovered in 1953 in debris from the first hydrogen bomb explosion. (Symbol: **Es**) ▷1950s: from the name of Albert *Einstein* + *-ium* (suffix forming names of metallic elements).

ei·ther /ˈēтʜər; ˈīтʜər/ ▶ *conj. & adv.* **1** used before the first of two (or occasionally more) alternatives that are being specified (the other being introduced by "or"): *either I accompany you to your room, or I wait here.* **2** [*adv.*] used to indicate a similarity or link with a statement just made: *it won't do any harm, but won't really help, either.* ■ for that matter; moreover (used to add information): *I was too tired to go. And I couldn't have paid my way, either.*

▶ *adj. & pron.* one or the other of two people or things: [as *adj.*] there were no children of either marriage | [as *pron.*] they have a mortgage that will be repaid if *either* of them dies. ■ [*adj.*] each of two: *the road was straight with fields of grass on either side.*

▶ □ **either way** whichever of two given alternatives is the case: *I'm not sure whether he is trying to be clever or controversial, but either way, such writing smacks of racism.*

e·jac·u·late ▶ *v.* /iˈjakyəˌlāt/ **1** [*intr.*] (of a man or male animal) eject semen from the body at the moment of sexual climax. **2** *dated* utter suddenly (a short prayer). ■ [with *direct speech*] say something quickly and suddenly: *"Indeed?" ejaculated the stranger.*

▶ *n.* /-lit/ semen that has been ejected from the body. —**e·jac·u·la·tion** /iˌjakyəˈlāsʜən/ *n.* —**e·jac·u·la·tor** /-ˌlātər/ *n.* —**e·jac·u·la·to·ry** /-lə,tôrē/ *adj.*

e·ject /iˈjekt/ ▶ *v.* [*tr.*] (often **be ejected**) force or throw (something) out, typically in a violent or sudden way: *many types of rock are ejected from volcanoes as solid, fragmentary material.* ■ cause (something) to drop out or be removed, usually mechanically: *he ejected the spent cartridge.* ■ [*intr.*] (of a pilot) escape from an aircraft by being explosively propelled out of it: *he flew on open sea, put the plane in a nosedive, and ejected.* ■ compel (someone) to leave a place: *angry supporters were forcibly*

ejected from the court. ■ dismiss (someone), esp. from political office. ■ emit; give off: *plants utilize carbon dioxide in the atmosphere that animals eject.* ■ dispossess (a tenant) by legal process. —**e·jec·tion** /iˈjeksʜən/ *n.*

e·jec·tor /iˈjektər/ ▶ *n.* a device that causes something to be removed or to drop out: *a built-in drill ejector.*

eke /ēk/ ▶ *v.* [*tr.*] (**eke something out**) manage to support oneself or make a living with difficulty: *they eked out their livelihoods from the soil.* ■ make an amount or supply of something last longer by using or consuming it frugally: *the remains of yesterday's stew could be eked out to make another meal.* ■ obtain or create, but just barely: *Tennessee eked out a 74–73 overtime victory.*

EKG ▶ *abbr.* ■ electrocardiogram. ■ electrocardiograph. ■ electrocardiography.

e·lab·o·rate ▶ *adj.* /iˈlab(ə)rit/ involving many carefully arranged parts or details; detailed and complicated in design and planning: *elaborate security precautions.* ■ (of an action) lengthy and exaggerated: *he made an elaborate pretense of yawning.*

▶ *v.* /iˈlabəˌrāt/ **1** [*tr.*] develop or present (a theory, policy, or system) in detail: *the key idea of the book is expressed in the title and elaborated in the text.* ■ [*intr.*] add more detail concerning what has already been said: *he would not elaborate on his news.* **2** [*tr.*] *Biol.* (of a natural agency) produce (a substance) from its elements or simpler constituents. —**e·lab·o·rate·ly** *adv.* —**e·lab·o·rate·ness** *n.* —**e·lab·o·ra·tion** /iˌlabəˈrāsʜən/ *n.* —**e·lab·o·ra·tive** /-ˌrātiv/ *adj.* —**e·lab·o·ra·tor** /-tər/ *n.*

é·lan /āˈlän; āˈlan/ ▶ *n.* energy, style, and enthusiasm: *a rousing march, played with great élan.*

e·land /ˈēlənd/ ▶ *n.* a spiral-horned African antelope (genus *Taurotragus*) that lives in open woodland and grassland. It is the largest of the antelopes.

e·lapse /iˈlaps/ ▶ *v.* [*intr.*] (of time) pass or go by: *weeks elapsed before anyone was charged with the attack.*

e·las·tic /iˈlastik/ ▶ *adj.* (of an object or material) able to resume its normal shape spontaneously after contraction, dilatation, or distortion. ■ able to encompass variety and change; flexible and adaptable: *the definition of nationality is elastic in this cosmopolitan country.* ■ springy and buoyant: *Annie returned with beaming eyes and elastic step.* ■ *Econ.* (of demand or supply) sensitive to changes in price or income: *the labor supply is very elastic.* ■ *Physics* (of a collision) involving no decrease of kinetic energy.

▶ *n.* cord, tape, or fabric, typically woven with strips of rubber, that returns to its original length or shape after being stretched. —**e·las·ti·cal·ly** *adv.* —**e·las·tic·i·ty** /iˌlaˈstisitē; ēˌla-/ *n.* —**e·las·ti·cize** /iˈlastəˌsīz/ *v.*

e·late /iˈlāt/ ▶ *v.* [*tr.*] [usu. as *adj.*] (**elated**) make (someone) ecstatically happy: *I felt elated at beating Dennis.* —**e·lat·ed·ly** *adv.* —**e·lat·ed·ness** *n.* —**e·la·tion** *n.*

el·bow /ˈel,bō/ ▶ *n.* the joint between the forearm and the upper arm. ■ the part of the sleeve of a garment covering the elbow. ■ a thing resembling an elbow, in particular a piece of piping bent through an angle.

▶ *v.* [*tr.*] strike (someone) with one's elbow: *one player had elbowed another in the face.* ■ [*intr.*] move by pushing past people with one's elbows: *people elbowed past each other to the door.* ■ *fig.* get rid of or disregard (a person or idea) in a cursory and dismissive way: *his new TV talk show was elbowed aside in the ratings war.*

el·bow grease ▶ *n. inf.* hard physical work, esp. vigorous polishing or cleaning: *you can get the rust off with a wire brush and elbow grease.*

el·bow room ▶ *n. inf.* adequate space to move or work in: *the car has elbow room for four adults* | *fig. Quebec wants more elbow room within the federation.*

eld·er¹ /ˈeldər/ ▶ *adj.* (of one or more out of a group of related or otherwise associated people) of a greater age: *the elder of the two sons.* ■ (**the Elder**) used to distinguish between related famous people with the same name: *Pliny the Elder.*

▶ *n.* (usu. **elders**) a person of greater age than someone specified: *schoolchildren were no less fascinated than their elders.* ■ a person of advanced age. ■ (often **elders**) a leader or senior figure in a tribe or other group: *a council of village elders.* ■ an official in the early Christian Church, or of various Protestant Churches and sects. —**eld·er·ship** *n.*

eld·er² ▶ *n.* (also **elderberry**) a small tree or shrub (genus *Sambucus*) of the honeysuckle family, with pithy stems, typically having white flowers and bluish-black or red berries.

eld·er·ber·ry /ˈeldərˌberē/ ▶ *n.* the bluish-black or red berry of the elder, used esp. for making jelly or wine. ■ an elder tree or shrub.

Pronunciation Key ə *ago, up*; ər *over, fur*; a *hat*; ā *ate*; ä *car*; cʜ *chin*; e *let*; ē *see*; e(ə)r *air*; i *fit*; ī *by*; i(ə)r *ear*; nɢ *sing*; ō *go*; ô *law, for*; oi *toy*; ōō *good*; ōō *goo*; ou *out*; sʜ *she*; тʜ *thin*; т̱ʜ *then*; (h)w *why*; zʜ *vision*

eld·er·ly /'eldərlē/ ▸adj. (of a person) old or aging: *she was elderly and silver-haired* [as *pl. n.*] (**the elderly**) *teams of volunteers to carry out home repairs for the elderly.* ■ (of a machine or similar object) showing signs of age: *a couple of elderly cars.* —**eld·er·li·ness** *n.*

eld·est /'eldəst/ ▸adj. (of one out of a group of related or otherwise associated people) of the greatest age; oldest: *Swift left the company to his eldest son, Charles.*

elec. ▸abbr. ■ electric, electrical. ■ electrician. ■ electricity.

e·lect /i'lekt/ ▸v. [*tr.*] (often **be elected**) choose (someone) to hold public office or some other position by voting: *the members who were elected to the committee* | [*tr.*] *they elected him leader.* ■ opt for or choose to do (something): *freshman year you could elect Industrial Arts.*
▸adj. [usu. as *pl. n.*] (**the elect**) (of a person) chosen or singled out: *one of the century's elect.* ■ elected to or chosen for a position but not yet in office: *the president-elect.* —**e·lect·a·ble** *adj.* —**e·lect·a·bil·i·ty** *n.*

e·lec·tion /i'leksʜən/ ▸n. **1** a formal and organized process of electing or being elected, esp. of members of a political body: *the 1860 presidential election* | *the first of his family to* **run for election.** ■ the act or an instance of electing: *his election to the House of Representatives.* **2** (in Calvinist theology) predestined salvation.

e·lec·tive /i'lektiv/ ▸adj. **1** related to or working by means of election: *an elective democracy.* ■ (of a person or office) appointed or filled by election: *he had never held elective office.* ■ (of a body or position) possessing or giving the power to elect. **2** (of a course of study) chosen by the student rather than compulsory. ■ (of surgical or medical treatment) chosen by the patient rather than urgently necessary.
▸n. an optional course of study: *up to half the credits in many public high schools are electives.* —**e·lec·tive·ly** *adv.*

e·lec·tor /i'lektər; -,tôr/ ▸n. a person who has the right to vote in an election. ■ a member of the electoral college. —**e·lec·tor·ship** *n.*

e·lec·tor·al /i'lektərəl/ ▸adj. of or relating to elections or electors: *electoral reform.* —**e·lec·tor·al·ly** *adv.*

e·lec·tor·al col·lege ▸n. (also **E·lec·tor·al Col·lege**) a body of people representing the states of the U.S., who formally cast votes for the election of the president and vice president. ■ a body of electors chosen or appointed by a larger group.

e·lec·tor·ate /i'lektərət/ ▸n. [treated as *sing.* or *pl.*] all the people in a country or area who are entitled to vote in an election.

E·lec·tra com·plex ▸n. *Psychoanalysis* old-fashioned term for the Oedipus complex as manifested in young girls.

e·lec·tric /i'lektrik/ ▸adj. of, worked by, charged with, or producing electricity: *an electric current.* ■ *fig.* having or producing a sudden sense of thrilling excitement: *the atmosphere was electric.* ■ (of a musical instrument) amplified through a loudspeaker: *electric bass guitar.* ■ (of a color) brilliant and vivid: *images shot through with jagged streaks of electric blue.* ▷mid 17th cent.: from modern Latin *electricus*, from Latin *electrum* 'amber,' from Greek *ēlektron* (because rubbing amber causes electrostatic phenomena).

e·lec·tri·cal /i'lektrikəl/ ▸adj. operating by or producing electricity: *an electrical appliance.* ■ concerned with electricity: *an electrical engineer.* —**e·lec·tri·cal·ly** *adv.*

e·lec·tric chair ▸n. a chair in which criminals sentenced to death are executed by electrocution.

e·lec·tric eel ▸n. an eellike freshwater fish (*Electrophorus electricus*) of South America, using pulses of electricity to kill prey, to assist in navigation, and for defense.

e·lec·tri·cian /ilek'trisʜən; ,ēlek-/ ▸n. a person who installs and maintains electrical equipment.

e·lec·tric·i·ty /ilek'trisitē; ,ēlek-/ ▸n. a form of energy resulting from the existence of charged particles (such as electrons or protons), either statically as an accumulation of charge or dynamically as a current. ■ the supply of electric current to a house or other building for heating, lighting, or powering appliances: *the electricity was back on.* ■ *fig.* a state or feeling of thrilling excitement: *the atmosphere was charged with a dangerous sexual electricity.*

e·lec·tric shock ▸n. a sudden discharge of electricity through a part of the body.

e·lec·tri·fy /i'lektrə,fī/ ▸v. (**-fies, -fied**) [*tr.*] charge with electricity; pass an electric current through: [as *adj.*] (**electrified**) *an electrified fence.* ■ (often **be electrified**) convert (a machine or system, esp. a railroad line) to the use of electrical power. ■ *fig.* impress greatly; thrill: *he electrified the most sophisticated of audiences.* —**e·lec·tri·fi·ca·tion** /i,lektrəfi'kāsʜən/ *n.* —**e·lec·tri·fi·er** /-,fī(ə)r/ *n.*

e·lec·tro /i'lektrō/ ▸n. (*pl.* **-tros**) a style of dance music with a fast beat and synthesized backing track.

e·lec·tro·car·di·o·gram /i,lektrō'kärdēə,gram/ (abbr.: **ECG** or **EKG**) ▸n. *Med.* a record or display of a person's heartbeat produced by electrocardiography.

e·lec·tro·car·di·o·graph /i,lektrō'kärdiə,graf/ (abbr.: **ECG** or **EKG**) ▸n. a machine used for electrocardiography.

e·lec·tro·car·di·og·ra·phy /i,lektrō,kärdē'ägrəfē/ (abbr.: **ECG** or **EKG**) ▸n. the measurement of electrical activity in the heart and the recording of such activity as a visual trace (on paper or on an oscilloscope screen), using electrodes placed on the skin of the limbs and chest. —**e·lec·tro·car·di·o·graph·ic** /-,kärdiə'grafik/ *adj.*

e·lec·tro·con·vul·sive /i,lektrōkən'vəlsiv/ ▸adj. of or relating to the treatment of mental illness by the application of electric shocks to the brain.

e·lec·tro·cute /i'lektrə,kyōōt/ ▸v. [*tr.*] (often **be electrocuted**) injure or kill someone by electric shock: *a man was electrocuted when he switched on the Christmas tree lights.* ■ execute (a convicted criminal) by means of the electric chair. —**e·lec·tro·cu·tion** /i,lektrə'kyōōsʜən/ *n.*

e·lec·trode /i'lektrōd/ ▸n. a conductor through which electricity enters or leaves an object, substance, or region.

e·lec·tro·dy·nam·ics /i,lektrōdī'namiks/ ▸pl. n. [usu. treated as *sing.*] the branch of mechanics concerned with the interaction of electric currents with magnetic fields or with other electric currents. —**e·lec·tro·dy·nam·ic** *adj.*

e·lec·tro·en·ceph·a·lo·gram /i,lektrōən'sefələ,gram/ (abbr.: **EEG**) ▸n. a test or record of brain activity produced by electroencephalography.

e·lec·tro·en·ceph·a·lo·graph /i,lektrōən'sefələ,graf/ (abbr.: **EEG**) ▸n. a machine used for electroencephalography.

e·lec·tro·en·ceph·a·log·ra·phy /i,lektrōən,sefə'lägrəfē/ (abbr.: **EEG**) ▸n. the measurement of electrical activity in different parts of the brain and the recording of such activity as a visual trace (on paper or on an oscilloscope screen).

e·lec·tro·fu·sion /i,lektrō'fyōōzʜən/ ▸n. fusion (in cells or other materials) that is induced by the application of electric current.

e·lec·trol·y·sis /ilek'träləsis; ,ēlek-/ ▸n. **1** *Chem.* chemical decomposition produced by passing an electric current through a liquid or solution containing ions. **2** the removal of hair roots or small blemishes on the skin by the application of heat using an electric current. —**e·lec·tro·lyt·ic** /i,lektrə'litik/ *adj.* —**e·lec·tro·lyt·i·cal** /i,lektrə'litikəl/ *adj.* —**e·lec·tro·lyt·i·cal·ly** /i,lektrə'litik(ə)lē/ *adv.*

e·lec·tro·lyte /i'lektrə,līt/ ▸n. a liquid or gel that contains ions and can be decomposed by electrolysis, e.g., that present in a battery. ■ (usu. **electrolytes**) *Physiol.* the ionized or ionizable constituents of a living cell, blood, or other organic matter.

e·lec·tro·mag·net /i,lektrō'magnit/ ▸n. *Physics* a soft metal core made into a magnet by the passage of electric current through a coil surrounding it.

e·lec·tro·mag·net·ic /i,lektrōmag'netik/ ▸adj. of or relating to the interrelation of electric currents or fields and magnetic fields. —**e·lec·tro·mag·net·i·cal·ly** /-(ə)lē/ *adv.*

e·lec·tro·mag·net·ism /i,lektrō'magnə,tizəm/ ▸n. the interaction of electric currents or fields and magnetic fields. ■ the branch of physics concerned with this.

e·lec·tro·me·chan·i·cal /i,lektrōmə'kanikəl/ ▸adj. of, relating to, or denoting a mechanical device that is electrically operated.

e·lec·tro·mo·tive /i,lektrə'mōtiv/ ▸adj. *Physics* producing or tending to produce an electric current.

e·lec·tron /i'lek,trän/ ▸n. *Physics* a stable subatomic particle with a charge of negative electricity, found in all atoms and acting as the primary carrier of electricity in solids.

e·lec·tron-dense ▸adj. (of biological specimens) allowing the passage of few electrons, and so appearing dark in electron micrographs.

e·lec·tron·ic /ilek'tränik; ,ēlek-/ ▸adj. **1** (of a device) having or operating with the aid of many small components, esp. microchips and transistors, that control and direct an electric current: *an electronic calculator.* ■ (of music) produced by electronic instruments. ■ of or relating to electronics: *a degree in electronic engineering.* **2** of or relating to electrons. **3** relating to or carried out using a computer or other electronic device, esp. over a network: *electronic banking.* —**e·lec·tron·i·cal·ly** /-(ə)lē/ *adv.*

e·lec·tron·ic mail ▸n. another term for E-MAIL.

e·lec·tron·ics /ilek'träniks; ,ēlek-/ ▸pl. n. [usu. treated as *sing.*] the branch of physics and technology concerned with the design of circuits using transistors and microchips, and with the behavior and movement of electrons in a semiconductor, conductor, vacuum, or gas: *electronics is* seen as a growth industry | [as adj.] electronics engineers. ■ [treated as pl.] circuits or devices using transistors, microchips, and other components.

e·lec·tron mi·cro·scope ▶ n. Physics a microscope with high magnification and resolution, employing electron beams in place of light and using electron lenses.

e·lec·tron volt (abbr.: eV) ▶ n. Physics a unit of energy equal to the work done on an electron in accelerating it through a potential difference of one volt.

e·lec·tro·pho·re·sis /i,lektrəfə'rēsis/ ▶ n. Physics & Chemistry the movement of charged particles in a fluid or gel under the influence of an electric field. ▷early 20th cent.: from electro- 'of, relating to, or caused by electricity' + Greek phorēsis 'being carried.' —e·lec·tro·pho·rese /-'rēs/ v. —e·lec·tro·pho·ret·ic /-'retik/ adj. —e·lec·tro·pho·ret·i·cal·ly /-'retik(ə)lē/ adv.

e·lec·tro·plate /i'lektrə,plāt/ ▶ v. [tr.] [usu. as n.] (**electroplating**) coat (a metal object) by electrolytic deposition with chromium, silver, or another metal. —e·lec·tro·plat·er n.

e·lec·tro·shock /i'lektrə,SHäk/ ▶ adj. of or relating to medical treatment by means of electric shocks: electroshock therapy.

e·lec·tro·stat·ic /i,lektrə'statik/ ▶ adj. Physics of or relating to stationary electric charges or fields as opposed to electric currents.

e·lec·tro·ther·a·py /i,lektrō'THerəpē/ ▶ n. the use of electric currents passed through the body to stimulate nerves and muscles, chiefly in the treatment of various forms of paralysis. —e·lec·tro·ther·a·peu·tic /-,THerə'pyOōtik/ adj. —e·lec·tro·ther·a·pist /-pist/ n.

e·lec·tro·type /i'lektrə,tīp/ ▶ n. a copy made by the electrolytic deposition of copper on a mold. —e·lec·tro·typ·er n.

el·e·gant /'eləgənt/ ▶ adj. pleasingly graceful and stylish in appearance or manner: she will look elegant in black. ■ (of a scientific theory or solution to a problem) pleasingly ingenious and simple: the grand unified theory is compact and elegant in mathematical terms. —el·e·gance n. —el·e·gant·ly adv.

el·e·gi·ac /,elə'jīək; e'lējē,ak/ ▶ adj. (esp. of a work of art) having a mournful quality: the movie score is a somber effort, elegiac in its approach. ■ (of a poetic meter) used for elegies. —el·e·gi·a·cal·ly /,elə'jīək(ə)lē/ adv.

el·e·gy /'eləjē/ ▶ n. (pl. -gies) a poem of serious reflection, typically a lament for the dead. ■ a piece of music in a mournful style. ▷early 16th cent.: from French élégie, or via Latin, from Greek elegeia, from elegos 'mournful poem.'

el·e·ment /'eləmənt/ ▶ n. **1** a part or aspect of something abstract, esp. one that is essential or characteristic: the death had **all the elements** of a great tabloid story. ■ a small but significant presence of a feeling or abstract quality: it was **the element** of danger he loved in flying. ■ (**elements**) the rudiments of a branch of knowledge: legal training may include the elements of economics and political science. ■ (often **elements**) a group of people of a particular kind within a larger group or organization: extreme right-wing elements in the army. ■ Math. & Logic an entity that is a single member of a set. **2** (also **chemical element**) each of more than one hundred substances that cannot be chemically interconverted or broken down into simpler substances and are primary constituents of matter. Each element is distinguished by its atomic number, i.e., the number of protons in the nuclei of its atoms. ■ any of the four substances (earth, water, air, and fire) regarded as the fundamental constituents of the world in ancient and medieval philosophy. ■ one of these substances considered as a person's or animal's natural environment: for the islanders, the sea is their kingdom, water their element | fig. she was **in her element** with doctors and hospitals. ■ (**the elements**) the weather, esp. strong winds, heavy rain, and other kinds of bad weather: there was no barrier against the elements. **3** a part in an electric teapot, heater, or stove that contains a wire through which an electric current is passed to provide heat.

el·e·men·tal /,elə'mentl/ ▶ adj. **1** primary or basic: elemental features from which all other structures are compounded. ■ concerned with chemical elements or other basic components: elemental analysis. ■ consisting of a single chemical element. **2** related to or embodying the powers of nature: a thunderstorm is the inevitable outcome of battling elemental forces. ■ fig. (of a human emotion or action) having the primitive and inescapable character of a force of nature: the urge for revenge was too elemental to be ignored.

el·e·men·ta·ry /,elə'ment(ə)rē/ ▶ adj. of or relating to the most rudimentary aspects of a subject: the six stages take students from elementary to advanced level. ■ easily dealt with; straightforward and uncomplicated: it's interesting, nevertheless, although a lot of it is elementary. ■ not decomposable into elements or other primary constituents. —el·e·men·tar·i·ly /-rəlē/ adv. —el·e·men·ta·ri·ness n.

el·e·men·ta·ry par·ti·cle ▶ n. any of various fundamental subatomic particles, including those that are the smallest and most basic constituents of matter (leptons and quarks) or are combinations of these (hadrons, which consist of quarks), and those that transmit one of the four fundamental interactions in nature (gravitational, electromagnetic, strong, and weak). Compare with SUBATOMIC PARTICLE.

el·e·men·ta·ry school ▶ n. a school for the first four to six grades, and usually including kindergarten.

el·e·phant /'eləfənt/ ▶ n. (pl. same or **elephants**) a heavy plant-eating mammal (family Elephantidae) with a prehensile trunk, long curved ivory tusks, and large ears, native to Africa and southern Asia. It is the largest living land animal.

el·e·phan·ti·a·sis /,eləfən'tīəsis/ ▶ n. Med. a condition in which a limb or other part of the body becomes grossly enlarged due to obstruction of the lymphatic vessels, typically by nematode parasites.

el·e·phan·tine /,elə'fantēn; -,tīn; 'eləfən,tēn; -,tīn/ ▶ adj. of, resembling, or characteristic of an elephant or elephants, esp. in being large, clumsy, or awkward: there was an elephantine thud from the bathroom.

el·e·vate /'elə,vāt/ ▶ v. [tr.] raise or lift (something) up to a higher position. ■ raise to a more important or impressive level: in the 1920s he was **elevated to** secretary of state. ■ increase the level or amount of (something).: high amounts of the drug can elevate blood pressure. —el·e·va·to·ry /-və,tôrē/ adj.

el·e·va·tion /,elə'vāSHən/ ▶ n. **1** the action or fact of elevating or being elevated: her sudden elevation to the cabinet. ■ augmentation of or increase in the amount or level of something: ■ (in a Christian Mass) the raising of the consecrated elements for adoration. **2** height above a given level, esp. sea level: a network of microclimates created by sharp differences in elevation | a total elevation gain of 3,995 feet. ■ a high place or position: most early plantation development was at the higher elevations. ■ the angle of something with the horizontal, esp. of a gun or of the direction of a celestial object. ■ Ballet the ability of a dancer to attain height in jumps. **3** a particular side of a building: a burglar alarm was prominently displayed on the front elevation. ■ a drawing of the front, side, or back of a house or other building: a set of plans and elevations. —el·e·va·tion·al adj.

el·e·va·tor /'elə,vātər/ ▶ n. **1** a platform or compartment housed in a shaft for raising and lowering people or things to different floors or levels. ■ a machine consisting of an endless belt with scoops attached, used typically for raising grain to be stored in bins: a grain elevator. ■ a tall building used for storing large quantities of grain. **2** a hinged flap on the horizontal stabilizer of an aircraft, typically one of a pair, used to control the motion of the aircraft about its lateral axis. **3** a muscle whose contraction raises a part of the body. **4** (also **elevator shoe**) a shoe with a raised insole designed to make the wearer appear taller.

e·lev·en /i'levən/ ▶ cardinal number equivalent to the sum of six and five; one more than ten; 11. (Roman numeral: xi or XI.) ■ eleven years old: the eldest is only eleven. ■ eleven o'clock: she often worked until eleven at night. ■ a size of garment or other merchandise denoted by eleven. ■ a group or unit of eleven people or things. ■ a sports team of eleven players. —e·lev·en·fold /-,fōld/ adj. & adv.

e·lev·enth /i'levənTH/ ▶ ordinal number constituting number eleven in a sequence; 11th: the eleventh century. ■ (**an eleventh/one eleventh**) each of eleven equal parts into which something is or may be divided. ■ the eleventh grade of a school. ■ Mus. an interval or chord spanning an octave plus a fourth in the diatonic scale, or a note separated from another by this interval.

▶ □ **the eleventh hour** the latest possible moment: he refused to take a public stand until the eleventh hour of the campaign.

ELF ▶ abbr. extremely low frequency.

elf /elf/ ▶ n. (pl. **elves** /elvz/) a supernatural creature of folk tales, typically represented as a small, elusive figure in human form with pointed ears, magical powers, and a capricious nature. —elf·ish adj. —elv·en /'elvən/ adj. (poetic/lit.). —elv·ish /'elviSH/ adj.

elf·in /'elfən/ ▶ adj. small and delicate, typically with an attractively mischievous or strange charm.

e·lic·it /i'lisit/ ▶ v. (-it·ed, -it·ing) [tr.] evoke or draw out (a response, answer, or fact) from someone in reaction to one's own actions or questions: they invariably elicit exclamations of approval from guests. —e·lic·i·ta·tion /i,lisi'tāSHən/ n. —e·lic·i·tor /-tər/ n.

e·lide /i'līd/ ▶ v. [tr.] omit (a sound or syllable) when speaking. ■ join together; merge: whole periods of time are elided into a few seconds of screen time.

---

el·i·gi·ble /'eləjəbəl/ ▶*adj.* having the right to do or obtain something; satisfying the appropriate conditions: *customers who are* **eligible** *for discounts.* ■ (of a person) desirable or suitable as a partner in marriage: *the world's most eligible bachelor.* —**el·i·gi·bil·i·ty** /ˌeləjə'bilitē/ *n.* —**el·i·gi·bly** /-blē/ *adv.*

e·lim·i·nate /i'limə,nāt/ ▶*v.* [*tr.*] completely remove or get rid of (something): *a policy that would eliminate inflation.* ■ exclude (someone or something) from consideration: *the police have eliminated Larry from their inquiries.* ■ murder (a rival or political opponent). ■ *Math.* remove (a variable) from an equation, typically by substituting another that is shown by another equation to be equivalent. ■ *Physiol.* expel (waste matter) from the body. —**e·lim·i·na·tion** /i,limə'nāsнən/ *n.* —**e·lim·i·na·tor** /-,nātər/ *n.*

e·li·sion /i'lizнən/ ▶*n.* the omission of a sound or syllable when speaking (as in *I'm, let's, e'en*). ■ an omission of a passage in a book, speech, or film: *the movie's elisions and distortions have been carefully thought out.* ■ the process of joining together or merging things, esp. abstract ideas: *unease at the elision of so many vital questions.*

e·lite /ə'lēt; ā'lēt/ ▶*n.* **1** a group of people considered to be the best in a particular society or category, esp. because of their power, talent, or wealth: *China's educated elite* | [as *adj.*] *an elite combat force.* **2** a size of letter in typewriting, with 12 characters to the inch.

e·lit·ism /ə'lē,tizəm; ā'lē-/ ▶*n.* the advocacy or existence of an elite as a dominating element in a system or society. ■ the attitude or behavior of a person or group who regard themselves as belonging to an elite: *he accused her of racism and white elitism.* —**e·lit·ist** *n.*

e·lix·ir /i'liksər/ ▶*n.* a magical or medicinal potion: *an elixir guaranteed to induce love.* ■ a preparation that was supposedly able to change metals into gold, sought by alchemists. ■ (also **elixir of life**) a preparation supposedly able to prolong life indefinitely. ■ a medicinal solution of a specified type: *a natural herbal cough elixir.*

E·liz·a·be·than /i,lizə'bēтнən/ ▶*adj.* of, relating to, or characteristic of the reign of Queen Elizabeth I: *a lady in Elizabethan dress.*
▶*n.* a person, esp. a writer, of the time of Queen Elizabeth I.

elk /elk/ ▶*n.* **1** (*pl.* same or **elks**) a red deer (*Cervus canadensis*) of a large race native to North America. Also called **WAPITI.** ■ British term for **MOOSE.** **2** (**Elk**) (*pl.* **Elks**) a member of a fraternal organization, the Benevolent and Protective Order of Elks.

el·lipse /i'lips/ ▶*n.* a regular oval shape, traced by a point moving in a plane so that the sum of its distances from two other points (the foci) is constant, or resulting when a cone is cut by an oblique plane that does not intersect the base.

el·lip·sis /i'lipsis/ ▶*n.* (*pl.* **-ses** /-sēz/) the omission from speech or writing of a word or words that are superfluous or able to be understood from contextual clues. ■ a set of dots indicating such an omission.

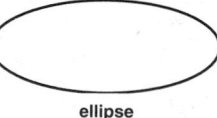
ellipse

el·lip·tic /i'liptik/ ▶*adj.* **1** of, relating to, or having the form of an ellipse. **2** (of speech or writing) lacking a word or words, esp. when the sense can be understood from contextual clues. —**el·lip·ti·cal** *adj.* —**el·lip·ti·cal·ly** /-(ə)lē/ *adv.*

elm /elm/ (also **elm tree**) ▶*n.* a tall deciduous tree (genus *Ulmus*) that typically has rough serrated leaves and propagates from root suckers. ■ (also **elm·wood**) the wood of this tree.

El Ni·ño /el 'nēnyō/ ▶*n.* (*pl.* **-ños**) an irregularly occurring and complex series of climatic changes affecting the equatorial Pacific region and beyond every few years, characterized by the appearance of unusually warm, nutrient-poor water off northern Peru and Ecuador, typically in late December. ▷late 19th cent.: Spanish, literally 'the (Christ) child,' because of the occurrence near Christmas.

el·o·cu·tion /ˌelə'kyōōsнən/ ▶*n.* the skill of clear and expressive speech, esp. of distinct pronunciation and articulation. ■ a particular style of speaking. —**el·o·cu·tion·ar·y** /-,nerē/ *adj.* —**el·o·cu·tion·ist** /-ist/ *n.*

e·lon·gate /i'lôɴɡāt; i'läɴɡ-/ ▶*v.* [*tr.*] make (something) longer, esp. unusually so in relation to its width. ■ [*intr.*] chiefly *Biol.* grow longer.
▶*adj.* chiefly *Biol.* long in relation to width; elongated: *elongate, fishlike creatures.* —**e·lon·ga·tion** *n.*

e·lon·gat·ed /i'lôɴɡātid; i'läɴɡ-/ ▶*adj.* unusually long in relation to its width: *the creature had two sets of arms and an elongated face.* ■ having grown or been made longer.

e·lope /i'lōp/ ▶*v.* [*intr.*] run away secretly in order to get married, esp. without parental consent: *later he eloped with one of the maids.* ■ run away with a lover. —**e·lope·ment** *n.* —**e·lop·er** *n.*

el·o·quence /'eləkwəns/ ▶*n.* fluent or persuasive speaking or writing: *a preacher of great power and eloquence.* ■ the art or manner of such speech or writing.

el·o·quent /'eləkwənt/ ▶*adj.* fluent or persuasive in speaking or writing: *an eloquent speech.* ■ clearly expressing or indicating something: *the touches of fatherliness are* **eloquent** *of the real man.* —**el·o·quent·ly** *adv.*

else /els/ ▶*adv.* **1** in addition; besides: *anything else you need to know?* **2** different; instead: *isn't there anyone else you could ask?*
▶ □ **or else** used to introduce the second of two alternatives: *she felt tempted either to shout at him or else to let his tantrums slide by.* ■ in circumstances different from those mentioned; if it were not the case: *they can't want it, or else they'd request it.* ■ used to warn what will happen if something is not carried out: *you go along with this or else you're going to jail.* ■ used after a demand as a threat: *she'd better shape up, or else.*

else·where /'els,(h)wer/ ▶*adv.* in, at, or to some other place or other places: *he is seeking employment elsewhere.*
▶*pron.* some other place: *all Hawaiian plants originally came from elsewhere.*

e·lu·ci·date /i'lōōsi,dāt/ ▶*v.* [*tr.*] make (something) clear; explain: *work such as theirs will help to elucidate this matter* | [*intr.*] *they would not elucidate further.* —**e·lu·ci·da·tion** /i,lōōsi'dāsнən/ *n.* —**e·lu·ci·da·tor** *n.* —**e·lu·ci·da·tor·y** /-,dātiv/ *adj.*

e·lude /i'lōōd/ ▶*v.* [*tr.*] evade or escape from (a danger, enemy, or pursuer), typically in a skillful or cunning way: *he managed to elude his pursuers by escaping into an alley.* ■ (of an idea or fact) fail to be grasped or remembered by (someone): *the logic of this eluded most people.* ■ (of an achievement, or something desired or pursued) fail to be attained by (someone): *sleep still eluded her.* ▷mid 16th cent. (in the sense 'delude, baffle'): from Latin *eludere,* from *e-* (variant of *ex-*) 'out, away from' + *ludere* 'to play.' —**e·lu·sion** /i'lōōzнən/ *n.*

e·lu·sive /i'lōōsiv/ (also rare **e·lu·so·ry** /-sərē; -zə-/) ▶*adj.* difficult to find, catch, or achieve. ■ difficult to remember or recall. —**e·lu·sive·ly** *adv.* —**e·lu·sive·ness** *n.*

E·ly·si·um /i'lizнēəm; i'lizēəm; i'lē-/ *Greek Mythol.* ▶the place at the ends of the earth to which certain favored heroes were conveyed by the gods after death. ■ [as *n.*] a place or state of perfect happiness. —**E·ly·si·an** /-ən/ *adj.*

el·y·tron /'elə,trän/ ▶*n.* (*pl.* **-tra** /-trə/) *Entomol.* each of the two wing cases of a beetle. —**el·y·trous** /-trəs/ *adj.*

EM ▶*abbr.* ■ electromagnetic. ■ enlisted man (men).

em /em/ ▶*n. Printing* a unit for measuring the width of printed matter, equal to the height of the type size being used. ■ a unit of measurement equal to twelve points.

e·ma·ci·ate /i'māsнē,āt/ ▶*v.* [*tr.*] [usu. as *adj.*] (**emaciated**) make abnormally thin or weak, esp. because of illness or a lack of food: *she was so emaciated she could hardly stand.* —**e·ma·ci·a·tion** /i,māsнē'āsнən/ *n.*

e-mail /'ē ,māl/ (also **e·mail, E·mail**) ▶*n.* messages distributed by electronic means from one computer user to one or more recipients via a network: [as *adj.*] *e-mail messages.* ■ the system of sending messages by such electronic means: *a contract communicated by e-mail.*
▶*v.* [*tr.*] send an e-mail to (someone): *you can e-mail me at my normal address.* ■ send (a message) by e-mail: *employees can e-mail the results.* —**e-mail·er** *n.*

em·a·nate /'emə,nāt/ ▶*v.* [*intr.*] (**emanate from**) (of something abstract but perceptible) issue or spread out from (a source): *warmth emanated from the fireplace.* ■ originate from; be produced by: *the proposals emanated from a committee.* ■ [*tr.*] give out or emit (something abstract but perceptible): *he emanated a powerful brooding air.* ▷mid 18th cent.: from Latin *emanat-* 'flowed out,' from the verb *emanare,* from *e-* (variant of *ex-*) 'out' + *manare* 'to flow.' —**em·a·na·tion** *n.* —**em·a·na·tive** /-,nātiv/ *adj.* —**em·a·na·tor** *n.*

e·man·ci·pate /i'mansə,pāt/ ▶*v.* [*tr.*] set free, esp. from legal, social, or political restrictions: *the citizen must be* **emancipated** *from the obsessive secrecy of government.* ■ *Law* set (a child) free from the authority of its father or parents. ■ free from slavery: *it is estimated that he emancipated 8,000 slaves.* —**e·man·ci·pa·tion** /i,mansə'pāsнən/ *n.* —**e·man·ci·pa·tor** *n.* —**e·man·ci·pa·to·ry** /-pə,tôrē/ *adj.*

e·mas·cu·late /i'maskyə,lāt/ ▶*v.* [*tr.*] make (a person, idea, or piece of legislation) weaker or less effective: *our winner-take-all elections emasculate fringe parties like neo-Nazis.* ■ [usu. as *adj.*] (**emasculated**) deprive (a man) of his male role or identity: *he feels emasculated because he cannot control his sons' behavior.* ■ *archaic* castrate (a man or male animal). —**e·mas·cu·la·tion** /i,maskyə'lāsнən/ *n.* —**e·mas·cu·la·tor** /-,lātər/ *n.* —**e·mas·cu·la·to·ry** /-lə,tôrē/ *adj.*

em·balm /em'bä(l)m/ ▶*v.* [*tr.*] [often as *n.*] (**embalming**) preserve (a corpse) from decay, originally with spices and now usually by arterial injection of a preservative: *the Egyptian method of embalming.* ■ *fig.*

preserve (someone or something) in an unaltered state: *the band was all about revitalizing pop greats and embalming their legacy.* —**em·balm·er** n.

em·bank /em'baNGk/ ▶ v. [tr.] construct a wall or bank of earth or stone in order to confine (a river) within certain limits. ■ construct a bank of earth or stone to carry (a road or railroad) over an area of low ground.

em·bank·ment /em'baNGkmənt/ ▶ n. a wall or bank of earth or stone built to prevent a river flooding an area. ■ a bank of earth or stone built to carry a road or railroad over an area of low ground.

em·bar·go /em'bärgō/ ▶ n. (pl. -**goes**) an official ban on trade or other commercial activity with a particular country: *an embargo on grain sales.* ■ an official prohibition on any activity. ■ hist. an order of a state forbidding foreign ships to enter, or any ships to leave, its ports.

▶ v. (-**goes**, -**goed**) [tr.] (usu. **be embargoed**) impose an official ban on (trade or a country or commodity): *the country has been virtually embargoed by most of the noncommunist world.* ■ officially ban the publication of: *documents of national security importance are routinely embargoed.*

em·bark /em'bärk/ ▶ v. [intr.] go on board a ship, aircraft, or other vehicle: *he embarked for India in 1817.* ■ [tr.] put or take on board a ship or aircraft: *its passengers were ready to be embarked.* ■ (**embark on/upon**) begin (a course of action, esp. one that is important or demanding): *he embarked on a new career.* —**em·bar·ka·tion** /ˌembär'kāSHən/ n. —**em·bark·ment** n.

em·bar·rass /em'barəs/ ▶ v. [tr.] cause (someone) to feel awkward, self-conscious, or ashamed: *she wouldn't embarrass either of them by making a scene.* ■ (**be embarrassed**) be caused financial difficulties: *he would be embarrassed by an inheritance tax.* —**em·bar·rass·ing** adj. —**em·bar·rass·ment** n.

em·bas·sy /'embəsē/ ▶ n. (pl. -**sies**) **1** the official residence or offices of an ambassador: *the Chilean embassy in Moscow.* ■ the staff working in such a building. ■ the position or function of an ambassador. **2** chiefly hist. a deputation or mission sent by one ruler or state to another.

em·bat·tled /em'batld/ ▶ adj. (of a place or people) involved in or prepared for war, esp. because surrounded by enemy forces: *the embattled Yugoslavian republics.* ■ (of a person) beset by problems or difficulties: *the worst may not be over for the embattled senator.*

em·bed /em'bed/ ▶ v. (-**bed·ded**, -**bed·ding**) [tr.] (often **be embedded**) fix (an object) firmly and deeply in a surrounding mass: *he had an operation to remove a nail embedded in his chest.* ■ fig. implant (an idea or feeling) within something else so it becomes an ingrained or essential characteristic of it: *the Victorian values embedded in Tennyson's poetry.* ■ Linguistics place (a phrase or clause) within another clause or sentence. ■ Comput. incorporate (a text or code) within the body of a file or document. ■ design and build (a microprocessor) as an integral part of a system or device. ■ permit a journalist to travel with a military unit: *embedded with the 24th Marine Expeditionary Unit.*

▶ n. /'em,bed/ an embedded journalist: *most of the embeds found themselves covering construction and civil works projects.* —**em·bed·ment** n.

em·bel·lish /em'beliSH/ ▶ v. [tr.] make (something) more attractive by the addition of decorative details or features: *blue silk embellished with golden embroidery.* ■ make (a statement or story) more interesting or entertaining by adding extra details, esp. ones that are not true: *she had difficulty telling the truth because she liked to embellish things.* —**em·bel·lish·er** n. —**em·bel·lish·ment** n.

em·ber /'embər/ ▶ n. (usu. **embers**) a small piece of burning or glowing coal or wood in a dying fire: *the dying embers in the fireplace* | fig. *the flickering embers of nationalism.*

em·bez·zle /em'bezəl/ ▶ v. [tr.] steal or misappropriate (money placed in one's trust or belonging to the organization for which one works): *she had embezzled $5,600,000 in company funds.* —**em·bez·zle·ment** n. —**em·bez·zler** n.

em·bit·ter /em'bitər/ ▶ v. [tr.] [usu. as adj.] (**embittered**) cause (someone) to feel bitter or resentful: *he died an embittered man.* —**em·bit·ter·ment** n.

em·bla·zon /em'blāzn/ ▶ v. [tr.] (often **be emblazoned**) conspicuously inscribe or display (a design) on something: *T-shirts emblazoned with the names of baseball teams.* ■ depict (a heraldic device): *the Cardinal's coat of arms is emblazoned on the door panel.* —**em·bla·zon·ment** n.

em·blem /'embləm/ ▶ n. a heraldic device or symbolic object as a distinctive badge of a nation, organization, or family: *America's national emblem, the bald eagle.* ■ a thing serving as a symbolic representation of a particular quality or concept: *our child would be a dazzling emblem of our love.* —**em·blem·at·ic** /,emblə'matik/ adj. —**em·blem·at·i·cal** adj.

em·bod·y /em'bädē/ ▶ v. (-**bod·ies**, -**bod·ied**) [tr.] **1** be an expression of or give a tangible or visible form to (an idea, quality, or feeling): *a team that embodies competitive spirit and skill.* ■ provide (a spirit) with a physical form. **2** include or contain (something) as a constituent part: *the*

changes in law *embodied in* the Freedom of Information Act. —**em·bod·i·ment** n.

em·bold·en /em'bōldən/ ▶ v. [tr.] **1** (often **be emboldened**) give (someone) the courage or confidence to do something or to behave in a certain way: *emboldened by robust passenger traffic, the airlines put through major fare increases.* **2** cause (a piece of text) to appear in a bold typeface: *center, embolden, and underline the heading.*

em·bo·lism /'embə,lizəm/ ▶ n. **1** Med. obstruction of an artery, typically by a clot of blood or an air bubble. **2** the periodic insertion of days or a month to correct the accumulating discrepancy between the calendar year and the solar year, as in a leap year.

em·bo·lus /'embələs/ ▶ n. (pl. -**li** /-,lī; -,lē/) a blood clot, air bubble, piece of fatty deposit, or other object that has been carried in the bloodstream to lodge in a vessel and cause an embolism.

em·boss /em'bôs; -'bäs/ ▶ v. [tr.] [usu. as adj.] (**embossed**) carve or mold a design on (a surface) so that it stands out in relief: *an embossed brass dish.* ■ decorate (a surface) with a raised design. —**em·boss·er** n. —**em·boss·ment** n.

em·brace /em'brās/ ▶ v. [tr.] hold (someone) closely in one's arms, esp. as a sign of affection: *Aunt Sophie embraced her warmly* | [intr.] *the two embraced, holding each other tightly.* ■ accept or support (a belief, theory, or change) willingly and enthusiastically: *much of the population quickly embraced the new laws.* ■ include or contain (something) as a constituent part: *his career embraces a number of activities—composing, playing, and acting.*

▶ n. an act of holding someone closely in one's arms: *they were locked in an embrace.* ■ fig. used to refer to something that is regarded as surrounding or holding someone securely, esp. in a restrictive or comforting way: *the first of the former Soviet republics to free itself from the embrace of Moscow.* —**em·brace·a·ble** adj. —**em·brace·ment** n. —**em·brac·er** n.

em·broi·der /em'broidər/ ▶ v. [tr.] decorate (cloth) by sewing patterns on it with thread: [as adj.] (**embroidered**) *an embroidered handkerchief* | [intr.] *she was teaching one of the girls how to embroider.* ■ produce (a design) on cloth in this way. ■ fig. add fictitious or exaggerated details to (an account) to make it more interesting: *she embroidered her stories with colorful detail.* —**em·broi·der·er** n.

em·broi·der·y /em'broid(ə)rē/ ▶ n. (pl. -**der·ies**) the art or process of embroidering cloth. ■ cloth decorated in this way. ■ fig. embellishment or exaggeration in the description or reporting of an event: *fanciful embroidery of the facts.*

em·broil /em'broil/ ▶ v. [tr.] [often as adj.] (**embroiled**) involve (someone) deeply in an argument, conflict, or difficult situation: *she became embroiled in a dispute between two women she hardly knew.* ■ bring into a state of confusion or disorder. —**em·broil·ment** n.

em·bry·o /'embrē,ō/ ▶ n. (pl. -**os**) an unborn or unhatched offspring in the process of development. ■ an unborn human baby, esp. in the first eight weeks from conception, after implantation but before all the organs are developed. Compare with FETUS. ■ Bot. the part of a seed that develops into a plant, consisting (in the mature embryo of a higher plant) of a plumule, a radicle, and one or two cotyledons. ■ fig. a thing at a rudimentary stage that shows potential for development: *a simple commodity economy is merely the embryo of a capitalist economy.* —**em·bry·on·ic** /,embrē'änik/ adj.

em·bry·o·gen·e·sis /,embrē-ō'jenəsis/ ▶ n. Biol. the formation and development of an embryo. —**em·bry·o·ge·net·ic** /-jə'netik/ adj. —**em·bry·o·gen·ic** /-'jenik/ adj. —**em·bry·o·ge·ny** /,embrē'äjənē/ n..

em·bry·ol·o·gy /,embrē'äləjē/ ▶ n. the branch of biology and medicine concerned with the study of embryos and their development. —**em·bry·o·log·ic** /,embrēə'läjik/ adj. —**em·bry·o·log·i·cal** adj. —**em·bry·ol·o·gist** /-jist/ n.

em·cee /,em'sē/ inf. ▶ n. a master of ceremonies.

▶ v. (**em·cees**, **em·ceed**, **em·cee·ing**) [tr.] perform the role of a master of ceremonies at (a public entertainment or a large social occasion).

e·mend /i'mend/ ▶ v. [tr.] make corrections and improvements to (a text). ■ alter (something) in such a way as to correct it: *the year of his death might need to be emended to 652.* —**e·mend·a·ble** adj. —**e·men·da·tion** /,ēmen'dāSHən/ ;,emən-/ n. —**e·mend·er** n.

em·er·ald /'em(ə)rəld/ ▶ n. **1** a bright green precious stone consisting of a chromium-rich variety of beryl. **2** a bright green color like that of an emerald.

▶ adj. bright green in color.

e·merge /i'mərj/ ▶ v. [intr.] move out of or away from something and

---

Pronunciation Key ə *ago, up*; ər *over, fur*; a *hat*; ā *ate*; ä *car*; CH *chin*; e *let*; ē *see*; e(ə)r *air*; i *fit*; ī *by*; i(ə)r *ear*; NG *sing*; ō *go*; ô *law, for*; oi *toy*; ōō *good*; o͞o *goo*; ou *out*; SH *she*; TH *thin*; TH *then*; (h)w *why*; ZH *vision*

come into view: *black ravens emerged from the fog.* ■ become apparent, important, or prominent: *Philadelphia has emerged as the clear favorite.* ■ (of facts or circumstances) become known: *reports of a deadlock emerged during preliminary discussions.* ■ recover from or survive a difficult or demanding situation: *the economy has started to emerge from recession.* ■ (of an insect or other invertebrate) break out from an egg, cocoon, or pupal case. —**e·mer·gence** *n.*

e·mer·gen·cy /i'mərjənsē/ ▶*n.* (*pl.* -**cies**) a serious, unexpected, and often dangerous situation requiring immediate action: *your quick response in an emergency could be a lifesaver.* ■ [as *adj.*] arising from or needed or used in an emergency: *an emergency exit.* ■ a person with a medical condition requiring immediate treatment. ■ short for EMERGENCY ROOM: *he was rushed into emergency.*

e·mer·gen·cy med·i·cal tech·ni·cian (abbr.: **EMT**) ▶*n.* a person who is specially trained and certified to administer basic emergency services to victims of trauma or acute illness before and during transportation to a hospital or other healthcare facility.

e·mer·gen·cy room ▶*n.* the department of a hospital that provides immediate treatment for acute illnesses and trauma.

e·mer·gent /i'mərjənt/ ▶*adj.* **1** in the process of coming into being or becoming prominent: *the emergent democracies of eastern Europe.* ■ *Bot.* of or denoting a plant that is taller than the surrounding vegetation, esp. a tall tree in a forest. **2** arising and existing only as a phenomenon of independent parts working together, and not predictable on the basis of their properties: *one such emergent property is the ability, already described, of an established ecosystem to repel an invading species.*

e·mer·i·tus /i'merətəs/ ▶*adj.* (of the former holder of an office, esp. a college professor) having retired but allowed to retain their title as an honor: *emeritus professor of microbiology | the gallery's director emeritus.*

em·er·y /'em(ə)rē/ ▶*n.* a grayish-black mixture of corundum and magnetite, used in powdered form as an abrasive. ■ [as *adj.*] denoting materials coated with emery for polishing, smoothing, or grinding: *emery paper.* ▷late 15th cent.: from French *émeri,* from Old French *esmeri,* from Italian *smeriglio,* based on Greek *smuris, smiris* 'polishing powder.'

em·er·y board ▶*n.* a strip of thin wood or card coated with emery or another abrasive and used as a nail file.

e·met·ic /i'metik/ ▶*adj.* (of a substance) causing vomiting. ■ *inf.* nauseating or revolting: *that emetic music in department stores.*
▶*n.* a medicine or other substance that causes vomiting.

em·i·grant /'emigrənt/ ▶*n.* a person who leaves their own country in order to settle permanently in another: *the first emigrants to America* | [as *adj.*] *emigrant workers.*
▶*adj.* used by emigrants: *an emigrant ship.*

em·i·grate /'emi,grāt/ ▶*v.* [*intr.*] leave one's own country in order to settle permanently in another: *Rosa's parents emigrated from Argentina.* —**em·i·gra·tion** /,emi'grāSHən/ *n.*

é·mi·gré /'emə,grā/ (also **e·mi·gre**) ▶*n.* a person who has left their own country in order to settle in another, usually for political reasons.

em·i·nence /'emənəns/ ▶*n.* **1** fame or recognized superiority, esp. within in a particular sphere or profession: *her eminence in cinematography.* ■ [*count noun*] an important, influential, or distinguished person: *the Lord Chancellor canvassed the views of various legal eminences.* ■ (**His/Your Eminence**) a title given to a Roman Catholic cardinal, or used in addressing him: *His Eminence, Cardinal Thomas Wolsey.* **2** *formal* or *poetic/lit.* a piece of rising ground: *an eminence commanding the River Emme.*

em·i·nent /'emənənt/ ▶*adj.* (of a person) famous and respected within a particular sphere or profession: *one of the world's most eminent statisticians.* ■ used to emphasize the presence of a positive quality: *the guitar's eminent suitability for recording studio work.* —**em·i·nent·ly** *adv. an eminently readable textbook.*

em·i·nent do·main ▶*n. Law* the right of a government or its agent to expropriate private property for public use, with payment of compensation.

e·mir /ə'mi(ə)r/ ▶*n.* a title of various Muslim (mainly Arab) rulers: *the emir of Kuwait.* ■ *hist.* a Muslim (usually Arab) military commander or local chief.

e·mir·ate /ə'mi(ə)r,āt; ə'mi(ə)rit; 'emərit/ ▶*n.* the rank, lands, or reign of an emir.

em·is·sar·y /'emə,serē/ ▶*n.* (*pl.* -**sar·ies**) a person sent on a special mission, usually as a diplomatic representative.

e·mis·sion /i'misHən/ ▶*n.* the production and discharge of something, esp. gas or radiation: *cuts in carbon dioxide emissions.* ■ a thing emitted: *choking on the noxious emission.* ■ an ejaculation of semen. ■ the action of giving off radiation or particles; a flow of electrons from a cathode-ray tube or other source.

e·mit /i'mit/ ▶*v.* (**e·mit·ted, e·mit·ting**) [*tr.*] produce and discharge (something, esp. gas or radiation): *coal-fired power stations continue to emit large quantities of sulfur dioxide.* ■ make (a sound): *she emitted a sound like laughter.* ■ issue formally and with authority; put into circulation, esp. currency. —**e·mit·ter** *n.*

e·mol·lient /i'mälyənt/ ▶*adj.* having the quality of softening or soothing the skin: *an emollient cream.* ■ attempting to avoid confrontation or anger; soothing or calming: *the president's emollient approach to differences.*
▶*n.* a preparation that softens the skin: *formulated with rich emollients.* —**e·mol·lience** *n.*

e·mol·u·ment /i'mälyəmənt/ ▶*n.* (usu. **emoluments**) *formal* a salary, fee, or profit from employment or office: *the directors' emoluments.*

e·mote /i'mōt/ ▶*v.* [*intr.*] (esp. of an actor) portray emotion in a theatrical manner. —**e·mot·er** *n.*

e·mo·tion /i'mōsHən/ ▶*n.* a natural instinctive state of mind deriving from one's circumstances, mood, or relationships with others: *she was attempting to control her emotions.* ■ any of the particular feelings that characterize such a state of mind, such as joy, anger, love, hate, horror, etc.: *fear had become his dominant emotion.* ■ instinctive or intuitive feeling as distinguished from reasoning or knowledge: *responses have to be based on historical insight, not simply on emotion.* —**e·mo·tion·less** *adj.*

e·mo·tion·al /i'mōsHənəl/ ▶*adj.* of or relating to a person's emotions: *children with emotional difficulties.* ■ arousing or characterized by intense feeling: *an emotional speech.* ■ (of a person) having feelings that are easily excited and openly displayed: *he was a strongly emotional young man.* —**e·mo·tion·al·ism** /-,izəm/ *n.* —**e·mo·tion·al·ize** /-,līz/ *v.* —**e·mo·tion·al·ly** *adv.*

e·mo·tive /i'mōtiv/ ▶*adj.* arousing or able to arouse intense feeling: *animal experimentation is an emotive subject | the issue has proved highly emotive.* ■ expressing a person's feelings rather than being neutrally or objectively descriptive: *the comparisons are emotive rather than analytic.* —**e·mo·tive·ly** *adv.* —**e·mo·tive·ness** *n.* —**e·mo·tiv·i·ty** /,ēmō'tivitē/ *n.*

em·pan·el /em'panl/ ▶*v.* variant spelling of IMPANEL. —**em·pan·el·ment** *n.*

em·pa·thize /'empə,THīz/ ▶*v.* [*intr.*] understand and share the feelings of another: *counselors need to be able to empathize with people.*

em·pa·thy /'empəTHē/ ▶*n.* the ability to understand and share the feelings of another. —**em·pa·thet·ic** /,empə'THetik/ *adj.* —**em·pa·thet·i·cal·ly** /,empə'THetik(ə)lē/ *adv.* —**em·path·ic** /em'paTHik/ *adj.* —**em·path·i·cal·ly** /em'paTHik(ə)lē/ *adv.*

em·per·or /'emp(ə)rər/ ▶*n.* **1** a sovereign ruler of great power and rank, esp. one ruling an empire. **2** (also **emperor butterfly**) an orange and brown North American butterfly (genus *Asterocampa,* family Nymphalidae) with a swift dodging flight.

em·pha·sis /'emfəsis/ ▶*n.* (*pl.* -**ses** /-,sēz/) special importance, value, or prominence given to something: *they placed great emphasis on the individual's freedom.* ■ stress laid on a word or words to indicate special meaning or particular importance. ■ vigor or intensity of expression: *he spoke with emphasis and complete conviction.*

em·pha·size /'emfə,sīz/ ▶*v.* [*tr.*] give special importance or prominence to (something) in speaking or writing: *he jabbed a finger into the tabletop to emphasize his point.* ■ lay stress on (a word or phrase) when speaking. ■ make (something) more clearly defined: *a one-piece bathing suit that emphasized her build.*

em·phat·ic /em'fatik/ ▶*adj.* showing or giving emphasis; expressing something forcibly and clearly: *the children were emphatic that they would like to repeat the experience.* ■ (of an action or event or its result) definite and clear: *he walked stiffly, with an emphatic limp.* ■ (of word or syllable) bearing the stress. —**em·phat·i·cal·ly** *adv.*

em·phy·se·ma /,emfə'sēmə; -'zēmə/ ▶*n. Med.* **1** (also **pulmonary emphysema**) a condition in which the air sacs of the lungs are damaged and enlarged, causing breathlessness. **2** a condition in which air is abnormally present within the body tissues. —**em·phy·sem·a·tous** /,emfə'semətəs/ *adj.* —**em·phy·se·mic** *adj.*

em·pire /'em,pī(ə)r/ ▶*n.* **1** an extensive group of states or countries under a single supreme authority, formerly esp. an emperor or empress: *the Roman Empire.* ■ a government in which the head of state is an emperor or empress. ■ a large commercial organization owned or controlled by one person or group: *her business empire grew.* ■ an extensive operation or sphere of activity controlled by one person or group: *the kitchen had once been the ladies' empire.* ■ supreme political power over several countries when exercised by a single authority: *he encouraged the Greeks in their dream of empire in Asia Minor.* **2** a variety of apple.
▶*adj.* also /ăm'pi(ə)r/ (usu. **Empire**) denoting a style of furniture, decoration, or dress fashionable during the First or (less commonly) the Second Empire in France. The decorative style was neoclassical but

marked by an interest in Egyptian and other ancient motifs probably inspired by Napoleon's Egyptian campaigns. ■ (of a dress) having a high waist.

em·pir·i·cal /em'pirikəl/ (also **em·pir·ic**) ▶*adj.* based on, concerned with, or verifiable by observation or experience rather than theory or pure logic: *they provided considerable empirical evidence to support their argument.* —**em·pir·i·cal·ly** *adv.* —**em·pir·i·cism** /-,sizəm/ *n.*

em·place·ment /em'plāsmənt/ ▶*n.* a structure on or in which something is firmly placed. ■ a platform or defended position where a gun is placed for firing.

em·ploy /em'ploi/ ▶*v.* [*tr.*] **1** give work to (someone) and pay them for it: *the firm employs 150 people.* ■ keep occupied: *most of the newcomers are employed in developing the technology into a product.* **2** make use of: *the methods they have employed to collect the data.*
▶*n.* the state or fact of being employed for wages or a salary: *I started work in the employ of a grocer and wine merchant.* —**em·ploy·a·bil·i·ty** *n.* —**em·ploy·a·ble** *adj.* —**em·ploy·er** *n.*

em·ploy·ee /em'ploi-ē; ,emploi'ē/ ▶*n.* a person employed for wages or salary, esp. at nonexecutive level.

em·ploy·ment /em'ploimənt/ ▶*n.* the condition of having paid work: *a fall in the numbers in full-time employment.* ■ a person's trade or profession. ■ the action of giving work to someone: *the employment of a full-time tutor.*

em·po·ri·um /em'pôrēəm/ ▶*n.* (*pl.* **-po·ri·ums** or **-po·ri·a** /-'pôrēə/) a large retail store selling a wide variety of goods. ■ a business establishment that specializes in products or services on a large scale (often used for humorously formal effect): *a Chinese food emporium.* ▷late 16th cent.: from Latin, from Greek *emporion*, from *emporos* 'merchant,' based on a stem meaning 'to journey.'

em·pow·er /em'pou(-ə)r/ ▶*v.* [*tr.*] give (someone) the authority or power to do something: *nobody was empowered to sign checks on her behalf.* ■ enable (someone) to do (something): *cryptography will empower individuals to control their information.* ■ [*tr.*] make (someone) stronger and more confident, esp. in controlling their life and claiming their rights: *movements to empower the poor.* —**em·pow·er·ment** *n.*

em·press /'empris/ ▶*n.* a female emperor. ■ the wife or widow of an emperor.

emp·ty /'em(p)tē/ ▶*adj.* (**-ti·er**, **-ti·est**) containing nothing; not filled or occupied: *the room was empty of furniture.* ■ *fig.* (of words or a gesture) having no meaning or likelihood of fulfillment; insincere: *empty threats.* ■ *fig.* having no value or purpose: *her life felt empty and meaningless.* ■ *inf.* hungry. ■ *Math.* (of a set) containing no members or elements. ■ emotionally exhausted: *at the funeral he stood feeling drained and empty.*
▶*v.* (**-ties**, **-tied**) [*tr.*] remove all the contents of (a container): *we empty the cash register each night at closing time.* ■ remove (the contents) from a container: *he emptied out the contents of his briefcase.* ■ [*intr.*] (of a place) be vacated by people in it: *the bar suddenly seemed to empty.* ■ [*intr.*] (**empty into**) (of a river) discharge itself into (the sea or a lake).
▶*n.* (*pl.* **-ties**) (usu. **empties**) *inf.* a container (esp. a bottle or glass) left empty of its contents. —**emp·ti·ly** /-təlē/ *adv.* —**emp·ti·ness** *n.*
▶ □ **running on empty** exhausted of all one's resources or sustenance.

emp·ty-hand·ed ▶*adj.* having failed to obtain or achieve what one wanted: *the burglars fled empty-handed.*

EMT ▶*abbr.* emergency medical technician.

EMU ▶*abbr.* European Monetary Union.

e·mu /'ēm(y)o͞o/ ▶*n.* a large flightless fast-running Australian bird (*Dromaius novaehollandiae*, family Dromaiidae) resembling the ostrich, with shaggy gray or brown plumage, bare blue skin on the head and neck, and three-toed feet.

em·u·late /'emyə,lāt/ ▶*v.* [*tr.*] match or surpass (a person or achievement), typically by imitation: *lesser men trying to emulate his greatness.* ■ imitate: *hers is not a hairstyle I wish to emulate.* ■ *Comput.* reproduce the function or action of (a different computer or software system). —**em·u·la·tion** *n.* —**em·u·la·tive** /-,lātiv/ *adj.* —**em·u·la·tor** *n.*

e·mul·si·fi·er /i'məlsə,fi(ə)r/ ▶*n.* a substance that stabilizes an emulsion, in particular a food additive used to stabilize processed foods.

e·mul·si·fy /i'məlsə,fī/ ▶*v.* (**-fies**, **-fied**) make into or become an emulsion: [*tr.*] *mustard helps to emulsify a vinaigrette.* —**e·mul·si·fi·ca·tion** *n.*

e·mul·sion /i'məlsHən/ ▶*n.* a fine dispersion of minute droplets of one liquid in another in which it is not soluble or miscible.

en /en/ ▶*n. Printing* a unit of measurement equal to half an em and approximately the average width of typeset characters, used esp. for estimating the total amount of space a text will require.

en·a·ble /en'ābəl/ ▶*v.* [*tr.*] give (someone or something) the authority or means to do something: *the evidence would enable us to arrive at firm*

conclusions. ■ [*tr.*] make possible: *a number of courses are available to enable an understanding of a broad range of issues.* ■ [*tr.*] chiefly *Comput.* make (a device or system) operational; activate. —**en·a·ble·ment** *n.* —**en·a·bler** *n.*

en·act /en'akt/ ▶*v.* [*tr.*] **1** (often **be enacted**) make (a bill or other proposal) law. ■ put into practice (a belief, idea, or suggestion). **2** act out (a role or play) on stage. —**en·act·a·ble** *adj.* —**en·ac·tion** /en'aksHən/ *n.* —**en·ac·tor** /-tər/ *n.*

en·act·ment /en'aktmənt/ ▶*n.* **1** the process of passing legislation. ■ a law that is passed. **2** a process of acting something out: *the story becomes an enactment of his fantasies.* —**en·ac·tive** /-tiv/ *adj.*

e·nam·el /i'naməl/ ▶*n.* an opaque or semitransparent glossy substance applied to metallic or other hard surfaces for ornament or as a protective coating. ■ a work of art executed in such a substance. ■ the hard glossy substance that covers the crown of a tooth. ■ (also **enamel paint**) a paint that dries to give a smooth, hard coat.
▶*v.* (**-eled**, **-el·ing**; *Brit.* **-elled**, **-el·ling**) [*tr.*] [often as *adj.*] (**enameled**) coat or decorate (a metallic or hard object) with enamel: *an enameled roasting pan.* —**e·nam·el·er** *n.* —**e·nam·el·ist** /-ist/ *n.* —**e·nam·el·work** *n.*

e·nam·el·ware /i'naməl,wer/ ▶*n.* enameled kitchenware.

en·am·or /i'namər/ (*chiefly Brit.* **en·am·our**) ▶*v.* (**be enamored of/with/by**) be filled with a feeling of love for: *it is not difficult to see why Edward is enamored of her.* ■ have a liking or admiration for: *she was truly enamored of New York.*

en·camp /en'kamp/ ▶*v.* [*intr.*] settle in or establish a camp, esp. a military one: *we encamped for the night by the side of a river.*

en·camp·ment /en'kampmənt/ ▶*n.* a place with temporary accommodations consisting of huts or tents, typically for troops or nomads. ■ the process of setting up a camp.

en·cap·su·late /en'kaps(y)ə,lāt/ ▶*v.* [*tr.*] enclose (something) in or as if in a capsule. ■ express the essential features of (someone or something) succinctly: *the conclusion is encapsulated in one sentence.* ■ *Comput.* enclose (a message or signal) in a set of codes that allow use by or transfer through different computer systems or networks. ■ *Comput.* provide an interface for (a piece of software or hardware) to allow or simplify access for the user. —**en·cap·su·la·tion** *n.*

en·case /en'kās/ ▶*v.* [*tr.*] (often **be encased**) enclose or cover in a case or close-fitting surround. —**en·case·ment** *n.*

en·ceph·a·li·tis /en,sefə'lītis/ ▶*n.* inflammation of the brain, caused by infection or an allergic reaction. —**en·ceph·a·lit·ic** /-'litik/ *adj.*

en·ceph·a·lo·gram /en'sefələ,gram/ ▶*n. Med.* an image, trace, or other record of the structure or electrical activity of the brain.

en·ceph·a·lop·a·thy /en,sefə'läpəTHē/ ▶*n.* (*pl.* **-thies**) *Med.* a disease in which the functioning of the brain is affected by some agent or condition (such as viral infection or toxins in the blood).

en·chant /en'cHant/ ▶*v.* [*tr.*] (often **be enchanted**) fill (someone) with great delight; charm: *Isabel was enchanted with the idea.* ■ put (someone or something) under a spell. —**en·chant·ed·ly** *adv.* —**en·chant·er** *n.* —**en·chant·ing** *adj.* —**en·chant·ment** *n.*

en·chi·la·da /,encHə'lädə/ ▶*n.* a rolled tortilla with a filling typically of meat and served with a chili sauce.
▶ □ **the whole enchilada** *inf.* the whole situation; everything.

en·ci·pher /en'sīfər/ ▶*v.* [*tr.*] convert (a message or piece of text) into a coded form; encrypt. —**en·ci·pher·ment** *n.*

en·cir·cle /en'sərkəl/ ▶*v.* [*tr.*] form a circle around; surround: *the town is encircled by fortified walls.* —**en·cir·cle·ment** *n.*

encl. (also **enc.**) ▶*abbr.* ■ enclosure.

en·clave /'en,klāv; 'äNG-/ ▶*n.* a portion of territory within or surrounded by a larger territory whose inhabitants are culturally or ethnically distinct. ■ a secured area within another secured area. ■ *fig.* a place or group that is different in character from those surrounding it: *the engineering department is traditionally a male enclave.* ▷mid 19th cent.: from French, from Old French *enclaver* 'enclose, dovetail,' based on Latin *clavis* 'key.'

en·close /en'klōz/ ▶*v.* [*tr.*] **1** (often **be enclosed**) surround or close off on all sides: *the entire estate was enclosed with walls.* ■ [usu. as *adj.*] (**enclosed**) seclude (a religious order or other community) from the outside world. ■ *chiefly Math.* bound on all sides; contain. **2** place (something) in an envelope together with a letter: *I enclose a copy of the job description.*

en·clo·sure /en'klōzHər/ ▶*n.* **1** an area that is sealed off with an artificial or natural barrier. ■ an artificial or natural barrier that seals off an area. **2** the state of being enclosed, esp. in a religious community:

Pronunciation Key ə *ago, up;* ər *over, fur;* a *hat;* ā *ate;* ä *car;* cH *chin;* e *let;* ē *see;* e(ə)r *air;* i *fit;* ī *by;* i(ə)r *ear;* NG *sing;* ō *go;* ô *law, for;* oi *toy;* o͞o *good;* o͞o *goo;* ou *out;* sH *she;* TH *thin;* TH *then;* (h)w *why;* zH *vision*

the nuns kept strict enclosure. ■ *hist.* the process or policy of fencing in waste or common land so as to make it private property, as pursued in much of Britain in the 18th and early 19th centuries: *one of the chief effects of enclosure was to increase the number of landless workers.* **3** a document or object placed in an envelope together with a letter.

en·code /enˈkōd/ ▶ *v.* [*tr.*] convert into a coded form. ■ *Comput.* convert (information or an instruction) into a digital form. ■ *Biochem.* (of a gene) be responsible for producing (a substance or behavior). **—en·cod·a·ble** *adj.* **—en·cod·er** *n.* **—en·code·ment** *n.*

en·co·mi·um /enˈkōmēəm/ ▶ *n.* (*pl.* **-mi·ums** or **-mi·a** /-mēə/) *formal* a speech or piece of writing that praises someone or something highly.

en·com·pass /enˈkəmpəs/ ▶ *v.* [*tr.*] surround and have or hold within: *a vast halo encompassing the Milky Way galaxy.* ■ include comprehensively: *no studies encompass all aspects of medical care.* **—en·com·pass·ment** *n.*

en·core /ˈänˌkôr/ ▶ *n.* a repeated or additional performance of an item at the end of a concert, as called for by an audience.
▶ *interj.* called out by an audience at the end of a concert to request such a performance.
▶ *v.* [*tr.*] (often **be encored**) give or call for a repeated or additional performance of (an item) at the end of a concert.

en·coun·ter /enˈkoun(t)ər/ ▶ *v.* [*tr.*] unexpectedly experience or be faced with (something difficult or hostile): *we have encountered one small problem.* ■ meet unexpectedly and confront (an adversary): *the soldiers encountered a crowd of demonstrators.* ■ meet (someone) unexpectedly.
▶ *n.* an unexpected or casual meeting with someone or something. ■ a confrontation or unpleasant struggle: *his close encounter with death.*

en·cour·age /enˈkərij, -ˈkə-rij/ ▶ *v.* [*tr.*] give support, confidence, or hope to (someone): *we were encouraged by the success of this venture* | [as *adj.*] (**encouraging**) *the results are very encouraging* | [as *adj.*] (**encouraged**) *I feel much encouraged.* ■ give support and advice to (someone) so that they will do or continue to do something: [*tr.*] *pupils are encouraged to be creative.* ■ help or stimulate (an activity, state, or view) to develop: *the intention is to encourage new writing talent.* **—en·cour·age·ment** *n.* **—en·cour·ag·er** *n.* **—en·cour·ag·ing·ly** *adv.*

en·croach /enˈkrōch/ ▶ *v.* [*intr.*] (**encroach on/upon**) intrude on (a person's territory or a thing considered to be a right): *rather than encroach on his privacy, she might have kept to her room.* ■ advance gradually and in a way that causes damage: *the sea has encroached all around the coast.* **—en·croach·er** *n.* **—en·croach·ment** *n.*

en·crust /enˈkrəst/ ▶ *v.* [*tr.*] cover (something) with a hard surface layer: *the mussels encrust navigation buoys.* ■ overlay (something) with an ornamental crust of gems or other precious material: *a crown encrusted with rubies.* ■ [*intr.*] form a crust.

en·crus·ta·tion /ˌenkrəsˈtāSHən/ (also **in·crus·ta·tion**) ▶ *n.* the action of encrusting or state of being encrusted. ■ a crust or hard coating on the surface of something: *the sides are white with encrustations of salt.* ■ an outer layer or crust of ornamentation.

en·crypt /enˈkript/ ▶ *v.* [*tr.*] convert (information or data) into a cipher or code, esp. to prevent unauthorized access. ■ (**encrypt something in**) conceal information or data in something by this means. **—en·cryp·tion** /-ˈkripSHən/ *n.* **—en·cryp·tor** /-ˈkriptər/ *n.*

en·cum·ber /enˈkəmbər/ ▶ *v.* [*tr.*] (often **be encumbered**) restrict or burden (someone or something) in such a way that free action or movement is difficult: *she was encumbered by her heavy skirts.*

en·cum·brance /enˈkəmbrəns/ ▶ *n.* a burden or impediment. ■ *Law* a mortgage or other charge on property or assets.

en·cyc·li·cal /enˈsiklikəl/ ▶ *n.* a papal letter sent to all bishops of the Roman Catholic Church.

en·cy·clo·pe·di·a /enˌsīkləˈpēdēə/ (also *chiefly Brit.* **en·cy·clo·pae·di·a**) ▶ *n.* a book or set of books giving information on many subjects or on many aspects of one subject and typically arranged alphabetically.

en·cy·clo·pe·dic /enˌsīkləˈpēdik/ (also *chiefly Brit.* **en·cy·clo·pae·dic**) ▶ *adj.* comprehensive in terms of information: *he has an almost encyclopedic knowledge of food.* ■ relating to or containing names of famous people and places and information about words that is not simply linguistic: *a dictionary with encyclopedic material.* **—en·cy·clo·pe·di·cal·ly** /-(ə)lē/ *adv.*

en·cyst /enˈsist/ ▶ *v. Zool.* enclose or become enclosed in a cyst. **—en·cys·ta·tion** /ˌensiˈstāSHən/ *n.* **—en·cyst·ment** *n.*

end /end/ ▶ *n.* **1** a final part of something, esp. a period of time, an activity, or a story: *the end of the year.* ■ a termination of a state or situation: *the party called for an end to violence.* ■ used to emphasize that something, typically a subject of discussion, is considered finished: *you will go to church and that's the end of it.* ■ death or ruin: *if she's caught stealing again, it will be the end of her career.* ■ *archaic* (in biblical use) an ultimate state or condition: *the end of that man is peace.* **2** the furthest or most extreme part or point of something: *a length of wire with a hook*

at the end | [as *adj.*] *the end house.* ■ a specified extreme point on a scale: *buyers at the lower end of the market.* ■ the part or share of an activity with which someone is concerned: *you're going to honor your end of the deal.* **3** a goal or result that one seeks to achieve: *each would use the other to further his own ends.* **4** *Football* an offensive or defensive lineman positioned nearest to the sideline.
▶ *v.* come or bring to a final point; finish: [*intr.*] *when the war ended, policy changed* | [*tr.*] *she wanted to end the relationship.* ■ [*intr.*] perform a final act: *the man ended by attacking a police officer.* ■ [*intr.*] (**end in**) have as its final part, point, or result: *one in three marriages is now likely to end in divorce.* ■ [*intr.*] (**end up**) eventually reach or come to a specified place, state, or course of action: *I ended up in Connecticut.*
▶ □ **at the end of the day** *inf.* when everything is taken into consideration: *at the end of the day, I'm responsible for what happens in the school.* □ **end it all** commit suicide. □ **the end of the road** (or **line**) the point beyond which progress or survival cannot continue: *if the lawsuit is not dropped it could be the end of the road for the publisher.* □ **the end of one's rope** (or **tether**) having no patience or energy left to cope with something: *after enduring four years of mice in the house, we were at the end of our rope.* □ **the end of the world** ■ *inf.* a complete disaster: *it's not the end of the world if you're not great at sports.* □ **in the end** eventually or on reflection: *in the end, I saw that she was right.* □ **keep** (or **hold**) **one's end up** *inf.* perform well in a difficult or competitive situation. □ **make** (**both**) **ends meet** earn enough money to live without getting into debt. □ **never** (or **not**) **hear the end of** be continually reminded of (an unpleasant topic or cause of annoyance). □ **no end** *inf.* to a great extent; very much: *this cheered me up no end.* □ **no end of** *inf.* a vast number or amount of (something): *we shared no end of good times.* □ **on end** **1** continuing without stopping for a specified period of time: *sometimes they'll be gone for days on end.* **2** in an upright position: *he brushed his hair, leaving a tuft standing on end.*

en·dan·ger /enˈdānjər/ ▶ *v.* [*tr.*] put (someone or something) at risk or in danger: *his driving was likely to endanger life.* **—en·dan·ger·ment** *n.*

en·dear /enˈdi(ə)r/ ▶ *v.* [*tr.*] cause to be loved or liked: *Flora's spirit and character endeared her to everyone who met her.*

en·dear·ing /enˈdi(ə)riNG/ ▶ *adj.* inspiring love or affection: *an endearing little grin.* **—en·dear·ing·ly** *adv.*

en·dear·ment /enˈdi(ə)rmənt/ ▶ *n.* a word or phrase expressing love or affection: *love or affection: a term of endearment.*

en·deav·or /enˈdevər/ (*Brit.* **en·deav·our**) ▶ *v.* [*intr.*] try hard to do or achieve something: *he is endeavoring to help the Third World.*
▶ *n.* an attempt to achieve a goal: *an endeavor to reduce serious injury.* ■ earnest and industrious effort, esp. when sustained over a period of time: *enthusiasm is a vital ingredient in all human endeavor.* ■ an enterprise or undertaking: *a political endeavor.*

en·dem·ic /enˈdemik/ ▶ *adj.* **1** (of a disease or condition) regularly found among particular people or in a certain area: *areas where malaria is endemic.* ■ denoting an area in which a particular disease is regularly found. **2** (of a plant or animal) native or restricted to a certain country or area: *a marsupial endemic to northeastern Australia.*
▶ *n.* an endemic plant or animal. **—en·dem·i·cal·ly** /-(ə)lē/ *adv.*

end·game /ˈen(d)ˌgām/ (also **end game**) ▶ *n.* the final stage of a game such as chess or bridge, when few pieces or cards remain: *the knight was trapped in the endgame* | *fig. the retaliatory endgame of nuclear warfare.*

end·ing /ˈendiNG/ ▶ *n.* an end or final part of something, esp. a period of time, an activity, or a book or movie: *the ending of the Cold War.* ■ the furthest part or point of something: *a nerve ending.* ■ the final part of a word, constituting a grammatical inflection or formative element.

en·dive /ˈenˌdīv; ˈänˌdēv/ ▶ *n.* **1** an edible Mediterranean plant (*Cichorium endivia*) of the daisy family whose bitter leaves may be blanched and used in salads. **2** (also **Belgian endive**) a young, typically blanched chicory plant, eaten as a cooked vegetable or in salads.

end·less /ˈen(d)ləs/ ▶ *adj.* having or seeming to have no end or limit: *endless ocean wastes.* ■ countless; innumerable: *we smoked endless cigarettes.* ■ (of a belt, chain, or tape) having the ends joined to form a loop allowing continuous action. **—end·less·ly** *adv.* **—end·less·ness** *n.*

end·most /ˈen(d)ˌmōst/ ▶ *adj.* nearest to the end.

en·do·car·di·tis /ˌendōˌkärˈdītis/ ▶ *n. Med.* inflammation of the endocardium. **—en·do·car·dit·ic** /-ˈditik/ *adj.*

en·do·car·di·um /ˌendōˈkärdēəm/ ▶ *n.* the thin, smooth membrane that lines the inside of the chambers of the heart and forms the surface of the valves.

en·do·crine /ˈendəkrin/ ▶ *adj. Physiol.* of, relating to, or denoting glands that secrete hormones or other products directly into the blood.

en·do·cri·nol·o·gy /ˌendəkrəˈnäləjē/ ▶ *n.* the branch of physiology and medicine concerned with endocrine glands and hormones. —**en·do·crin·o·log·i·cal** /-ˌkrinəˈläjikəl/ adj. —**en·do·cri·nol·o·gist** /-jist/ n.

en·do·derm /ˈendəˌdərm/ ▶ n. Zoology & Embryology the innermost layer of cells or tissue of an embryo in early development, or the parts derived from this, which include the lining of the gut and associated structures. Compare with ECTODERM and MESODERM. —**en·do·der·mal** adj. —**en·do·der·mic** adj.

en·dog·a·my /enˈdägəmē/ ▶ n. Anthropol. the custom of marrying only within the limits of a local community, clan, or tribe. Compare with EXOGAMY. ■ Biol. the fusion of reproductive cells from related individuals; inbreeding; self-pollination. —**en·do·gam·ic** /ˌendōˈgamik/ adj. —**en·dog·a·mous** /-gəməs/ adj.

en·dog·e·nous /enˈdäjənəs/ ▶ adj. having an internal cause or origin: the expected rate of infection is endogenous to the system. Often contrasted with EXOGENOUS. ■ Biol. growing or originating from within an organism: endogenous gene sequences. ■ chiefly Psychiatry (of a disease or symptom) not attributable to any external or environmental factor: endogenous depression. ■ confined within a group or society.

en·do·me·tri·um /ˌendōˈmētrēəm/ ▶ n. Anat. the mucous membrane lining the uterus. —**en·do·me·tri·al** /-trēəl/ adj.

en·do·morph /ˈendəˌmôrf/ ▶ n. Physiol. a person with a soft round body build and a high proportion of fat tissue. Compare with ECTOMORPH and MESOMORPH. —**en·do·mor·phic** /ˌendəˈmôrfik/ adj. —**en·do·mor·phy** /-ˌmôrfē/ n.

en·do·plasm /ˈendōˌplazəm/ ▶ n. dated Biol. the more fluid, granular inner layer of the cytoplasm in ameboid cells. Compare with ECTOPLASM.

en·dor·phin /enˈdôrfin/ ▶ n. Biochem. any of a group of hormones secreted within the brain and nervous system that activate the body's opiate receptors, causing an analgesic effect.

en·dorse /enˈdôrs/ ▶ v. [tr.] **1** declare one's public approval or support of: the report was endorsed by the college. ■ recommend (a product) in an advertisement. **2** sign (a check or bill of exchange) on the back as payee or to make it payable to someone other than the stated payee. ■ (usu. **be endorsed on**) write (a comment) on the front or back of a document. —**en·dors·a·ble** adj. —**en·dor·see** /ˌendôrˈsē/ n. —**en·dors·er** n.

en·dorse·ment /enˈdôrsmənt/ ▶ n. **1** an act of giving one's public approval or support to someone or something. ■ a recommendation of a product in an advertisement. **2** a clause in an insurance policy detailing an exemption from or change in coverage. **3** the action of endorsing a check or bill of exchange.

en·do·scope /ˈendəˌskōp/ ▶ n. Med. an instrument that can be introduced into the body to give a view of its internal parts. —**en·do·scop·ic** /ˌendəˈskäpik/ adj. —**en·do·scop·i·cal·ly** adv. —**en·dos·co·py** /enˈdäskəpē/ n.

en·do·skel·e·ton /ˌendōˈskelitn/ ▶ n. Zool. an internal skeleton, such as the bony or cartilaginous skeleton of vertebrates. Compare with EXOSKELETON. —**en·do·skel·e·tal** /-ˈskelitl/ adj.

en·do·sperm /ˈendəˌspərm/ ▶ n. Bot. the part of a seed that acts as a food store for the developing plant embryo, usually containing starch with protein and other nutrients.

en·do·the·li·um /ˌendəˈтНēlēəm/ (pl. **-li·a** /-lēə/) ▶ n. the tissue that forms a single layer of cells lining various organs and cavities of the body, esp. the blood vessels, heart, and lymphatic vessels. It is formed from the embryonic mesoderm. Compare with EPITHELIUM. ▷late 19th cent.: modern Latin, from ENDO- 'within' (from Greek endon) + Greek thēlē 'nipple.' —**en·do·the·li·al** /-lēəl/ adj.

en·dow /enˈdou/ ▶ v. [tr.] give or bequeath an income or property to (a person or institution): he endowed the church with lands. ■ establish (a college post, annual prize, or project) by donating the funds needed to maintain it. ■ (usu. **be endowed with**) provide with a quality, ability, or asset: he was endowed with tremendous physical strength. —**en·dow·er** n.

en·dow·ment /enˈdoumənt/ ▶ n. the action of endowing something or someone: he tried to promote the endowment of a Chair of Psychiatry. ■ an income or form of property given or bequeathed to someone. ■ (usu. **endowments**) a quality or ability possessed or inherited by someone. ■ [usu. as adj.] a form of life insurance involving payment of a fixed sum to the insured person on a specified date, or to their estate should they die before this date: an endowment policy.

end·pa·per /ˈen(d)ˌpāpər/ (also **end pa·per**) ▶ n. a blank or decorated leaf of paper at the beginning or end of a book, esp. one fixed to the inside of the cover.

en·dur·ance /enˈd(y)o͝orəns/ ▶ n. the fact or power of enduring an unpleasant or difficult process or situation without giving way: she was close to the limit of her endurance. ■ the capacity of something to last or to withstand wear and tear.

en·dure /enˈd(y)o͝or/ ▶ v. **1** [tr.] suffer (something painful or difficult) patiently: it seemed impossible that anyone could endure such pain. ■ tolerate (someone or something): I was a fool to endure him for so long. **2** [intr.] remain in existence; last: these cities have endured through time. —**en·dur·a·ble** adj. —**en·dur·er** n.

end·ways /ˈen(d)ˌwāz/ (also **end·wise** /-ˌwīz/) ▶ adv. with its end facing upward, forward, or toward the viewer. ■ in a row with the end of one object touching that of another: strips of rubber cemented endways.

ENE ▶ abbr. east-northeast.

en·e·ma /ˈenəmə/ ▶ n. (pl. **-mas**) a procedure in which liquid or gas is injected into the rectum, typically to expel its contents, but also to introduce drugs or permit X-ray imaging. ■ a quantity of fluid or a syringe used in such a procedure.

en·e·my /ˈenəmē/ ▶ n. (pl. **-mies**) a person who is actively opposed or hostile to someone or something. ■ (**the enemy**) [treated as sing. or pl.] a hostile nation or its armed forces or citizens, esp. in time of war: the enemy shot down four helicopters | [as adj.] enemy aircraft. ■ a thing that harms or weakens something else: routine is the enemy of art. ▷Middle English: from Old French enemi, from Latin inimicus, from in- 'not' + amicus 'friend.'

en·er·get·ic /ˌenərˈjetik/ ▶ adj. showing or involving great activity or vitality: energetic exercise. ■ powerfully operative; forceful. ■ Physics characterized by a high level of energy (in the technical sense): energetic X-rays. —**en·er·get·i·cal·ly** /-(ə)lē/ adv.

en·er·gize /ˈenərˌjīz/ ▶ v. [tr.] give vitality and enthusiasm to: people were energized by his ideas. ■ supply energy, typically kinetic or electrical energy, to (something). —**en·er·giz·er** n.

en·er·gy /ˈenərjē/ ▶ n. (pl. **-gies**) **1** the strength and vitality required for sustained physical or mental activity: changes in the levels of vitamins can affect energy and well-being. ■ a feeling of possessing such strength and vitality. ■ force or vigor of expression. ■ (**energies**) a person's physical and mental powers, typically as applied to a particular task or activity. **2** power derived from the utilization of physical or chemical resources, esp. to provide light and heat or to work machines. **3** Physics the property of matter and radiation that is manifest as a capacity to perform work (such as causing motion or the interaction of molecules): a collision in which no energy is transferred. ■ a degree or level of this capacity possessed by something or required by a process.

en·er·vate /ˈenərˌvāt/ ▶ v. [tr.] cause (someone) to feel drained of energy or vitality; weaken. —**en·er·va·tion** /ˌenərˈvāSHən/ n. —**en·er·va·tor** /-ˌvātər/ n.

en·fant ter·ri·ble /änˌfän teˈrēbl(ə)/ ▶ n. (pl. **en·fants ter·ri·bles** pronunc. same) a person whose unconventional or controversial behavior or ideas shock, embarrass, or annoy others.

en·fee·ble /enˈfēbəl/ ▶ v. [tr.] make weak or feeble: [as adj.] (**enfeebled**) trade unions are in an enfeebled state. —**en·fee·ble·ment** n.

en·fi·lade /ˈenfəˌlād; -ˌläd/ ▶ n. a volley of gunfire directed along a line from end to end.

en·fold /enˈfōld/ ▶ v. [tr.] **1** surround; envelop: he shut off the engine and silence enfolded them. ■ hold or clasp (someone) lovingly in one's arms. **2** fold or shape into folds. —**en·fold·ment** n.

en·force /enˈfôrs/ ▶ v. [tr.] compel observance of or compliance with (a law, rule, or obligation). ■ cause (something) to happen by necessity or force: there is no outside agency to enforce cooperation between the players. —**en·force·a·ble** /-əbəl/ adj. —**en·force·ment** n. —**en·forc·er** n.

en·fran·chise /enˈfranˌCHīz/ ▶ v. [tr.] give the right to vote to: a proposal that foreigners should be enfranchised for local elections. ■ hist. free (a slave). —**en·fran·chise·ment** n.

en·gage /enˈgāj/ ▶ v. **1** [tr.] occupy, attract, or involve (someone's interest or attention): he tried to engage Sutton's attention. ■ (**engage someone in**) cause someone to become involved in (a conversation or discussion). ■ arrange to employ or hire (someone): he was engaged as a trainee copywriter. ■ pledge or enter into a contract to do something: he engaged to pay them $10,000 against a bond. ■ dated reserve (accommodations, a place, etc.) in advance: he had engaged a small sailboat. **2** [intr.] (**engage in**) participate or become involved in: organizations engage in a variety of activities | (**be engaged in**) some are actively engaged in crime. ■ (**engage with**) establish a meaningful contact or connection with: the teams needed to engage with local communities. ■ (of a part of a machine or engine) move into position so as to come into operation: the clutch will not engage. ■ [tr.] cause (a part of a machine or engine) to do this. ■ [tr.] enter into conflict or combat with (an adversary).

Pronunciation Key ə ago, up; ər over, fur; a hat; ā ate; ä car; CH chin; e let; ē see; e(ə)r air; i fit; ī by; i(ə)r ear; NG sing; ō go; ô law, for; oi toy; o͝o good; o͞o goo; ou out; SH she; TH thin; TH then; (h)w why; ZH vision

en·gaged /enˈgājd/ ▶adj. **1** busy; occupied: *I told him I was otherwise engaged.* ■ Brit. (of a telephone line) unavailable because already in use. **2** having formally agreed to marry. **3** Archit. (of a column) attached to or partly let into a wall.

en·gage·ment /enˈgājmənt/ ▶n. **1** a formal agreement to get married. ■ the duration of such an agreement: *a good long engagement to give you time to be sure.* **2** an arrangement to do something or go somewhere at a fixed time: *a dinner engagement.* ■ a period of paid employment. **3** the action of engaging or being engaged: *Britain's continued engagement in open trading.* **4** a fight or battle between armed forces.

en·gag·ing /enˈgājiNG/ ▶adj. charming and attractive: *Sophie had a sunny, engaging personality.* —**en·gag·ing·ly** adv. —**en·gag·ing·ness** n.

en·gen·der /enˈjendər/ ▶v. [tr.] cause or give rise to (a feeling, situation, or condition): *the issue engendered continuing controversy.* ■ [intr.] come into being; arise.

en·gine /ˈenjən/ ▶n. **1** a machine with moving parts that converts power into motion. ■ a thing that is the agent or instrument of a particular process: *exports used to be the engine of growth.* **2** a railroad locomotive. ■ hist. a mechanical device or instrument, esp. one used in warfare: *a siege engine.* —**en·gined** adj. [in comb.] *a twin-engined helicopter.*

en·gi·neer /ˌenjəˈni(ə)r/ ▶n. a person who designs, builds, or maintains engines, machines, or public works. ■ a person qualified in a branch of engineering, esp. as a professional: *aeronautical engineer.* ■ the operator or supervisor of an engine, esp. a railroad locomotive or the engine on an aircraft or ship. ■ a skillful contriver or originator of something: *the prime engineer of the approach.*
▶v. [tr.] design and build (a machine or structure): *the men who engineered the tunnel.* ■ skillfully or artfully arrange for (an event or situation) to occur: *she engineered another meeting with him.* ■ modify (an organism) by manipulating its genetic material: *genetically engineered plants.*

en·gi·neer·ing /ˌenjəˈni(ə)riNG/ ▶n. the branch of science and technology concerned with the design, building, and use of engines, machines, and structures. ■ the work done by, or the occupation of, an engineer. ■ the action of working artfully to bring something about: *if not for Keegan's shrewd engineering, the election would have been lost.*

Eng·lish /ˈiNG(g)lish/ ▶adj. of or relating to England or its people or language.
▶n. **1** the West Germanic language of England, now widely used in many varieties throughout the world. **2** [as pl. n.] (**the English**) the people of England. **3** spin given to a ball, esp. in pool or billiards. —**Eng·lish·man** n. —**Eng·lish·ness** n. —**Eng·lish·wom·an** n.

Eng·lish horn ▶n. Mus. an alto woodwind instrument of the oboe family, having a bulbous bell and sounding a fifth lower than the oboe.

Eng·lish muf·fin ▶n. a flat circular spongy bread roll made from yeast dough and eaten split, toasted, and buttered.

en·gorge /enˈgôrj/ ▶v. [tr.] cause to swell with blood, water, or another fluid: *the river was engorged by a day-long deluge.* ■ [intr.] become swollen in this way. —**en·gorge·ment** n.

en·grave /enˈgrāv/ ▶v. [tr.] (usu. **be engraved**) cut or carve (a text or design) on the surface of a hard object: *my name was engraved on the ring.* ■ cut or carve a text or design on (such an object). ■ cut (a design) as lines on a metal plate for printing. ■ (**be engraved on** or **in**) be permanently fixed in (one's memory or mind): *the image would be forever engraved in his memory.* —**en·grav·er** n.

en·grav·ing /enˈgrāviNG/ ▶n. a print made from an engraved plate, block, or other surface. ■ the process or art of cutting or carving a design on a hard surface, esp. so as to make a print.

en·gross /enˈgrōs/ ▶v. [tr.] **1** absorb all the attention or interest of: *the notes totally engrossed him.* **2** Law produce (a legal document) in its final or definitive form.

en·gross·ing /enˈgrōsiNG/ ▶adj. absorbing all one's attention or interest: *the most engrossing parts of the book.* —**en·gross·ing·ly** adv.

en·gulf /enˈgəlf/ ▶v. [tr.] (often **be engulfed**) (of a natural force) sweep over (something) so as to surround or cover it completely: *the café was engulfed in flames* | fig. *Europe might be engulfed by war.* ■ eat or swallow (something) whole. —**en·gulf·ment** n.

en·hance /enˈhans/ ▶v. [tr.] intensify, increase, or further improve the quality, value, or extent of: *his refusal does nothing to enhance his reputation.* ▷Middle English (formerly also as *inhance*): from Anglo-Norman French *enhauncer*, based on Latin *in-* (expressing intensive force) + *altus* 'high.' The word originally meant 'elevate' (literally and figuratively),

English horn

later 'exaggerate, make appear greater,' also 'raise the value or price of something.' Current senses date from the early 16th cent. —**en·hance·ment** n. —**en·hanc·er** n.

e·nig·ma /iˈnigmə/ ▶n. (pl. **-mas** or **-ma·ta** /-mətə/) a person or thing that is mysterious, puzzling, or difficult to understand. ■ a riddle or paradox. —**en·ig·mat·ic** /ˌenigˈmatik/ adj.

en·join /enˈjoin/ ▶v. [tr.] instruct or urge (someone) to do something: *the code enjoined members to trade fairly.* ■ [tr.] prescribe (an action or attitude) to be performed or adopted: *the charitable deeds enjoined on him by religion.* ■ [tr.] (**enjoin someone from**) Law prohibit someone from performing (a particular action) by issuing an injunction. —**en·join·er** n. —**en·join·ment** n.

en·joy /enˈjoi/ ▶v. [tr.] **1** take delight or pleasure in (an activity or occasion): *Joe enjoys reading Icelandic family sagas.* ■ (**enjoy oneself**) have a pleasant time: *I could never enjoy myself, knowing you were in your room alone.* ■ [intr.] inf. used to urge someone to take pleasure in what is about happen or be done: *your love life and love for life get stronger after the 28th—enjoy!* **2** possess and benefit from: *the security forces enjoy legal immunity from prosecution.* —**en·joy·er** n. —**en·joy·ment** n.

en·joy·a·ble /enˈjoi-əbəl/ ▶adj. (of an activity or occasion) giving delight or pleasure: *the decision is aimed at making shopping more enjoyable.* —**en·joy·a·bil·i·ty** /en,joi-ə-ˈbilitē/ n. —**en·joy·a·ble·ness** n. —**en·joy·a·bly** /-əblē/ adv.

en·kin·dle /enˈkindl/ ▶v. [tr.] set on fire. ■ arouse or inspire (an emotion): *fresh remembrance of vexation must still enkindle rage.* ■ inflame with passion: *he confidently believed it would enkindle Clara's cold temperament.*

en·large /enˈlärj/ ▶v. make or become bigger or more extensive: [tr.] *recently my son enlarged our garden pond* | [as adj.] (**enlarged**) *an enlarged spleen.* ■ [tr.] (often **be enlarged**) develop a bigger print of (a photograph).

en·large·ment /enˈlärjmənt/ ▶n. the action or state of enlarging or being enlarged. ■ a photograph that is larger than the negative from which it is produced or than a print that has already been made from it.

en·light·en /enˈlītn/ ▶v. [tr.] give (someone) greater knowledge and understanding about a subject or situation: *Christopher had not enlightened Frances as to their relationship.* ■ give (someone) spiritual knowledge or insight. ■ fig. illuminate or make clearer (a problem or area of study): *this will enlighten the studies of origins of myths.* —**en·light·en·er** n.

en·light·en·ment /enˈlītnmənt/ ▶n. **1** the action of enlightening or the state of being enlightened: *Robbie looked to me for enlightenment.* ■ the action or state of attaining or having attained spiritual knowledge or insight. **2** (**the Enlightenment**) a European intellectual movement of the late 17th and 18th centuries emphasizing reason and individualism rather than tradition.

en·list /enˈlist/ ▶v. enroll or be enrolled in the armed services: [intr.] *he enlisted in the army* | [tr.] *hundreds of thousands of recruits had been enlisted.* ■ [tr.] engage (a person or their help or support): *the company enlisted the help of independent consultants.* —**en·list·er** n. —**en·list·ment** n.

en·liv·en /enˈlīvən/ ▶v. [tr.] make (something) more entertaining, interesting, or appealing: *the wartime routine was enlivened by a series of concerts.* ■ make (someone) more cheerful or animated: *the visit had clearly enlivened my mother.* —**en·liv·en·er** n. —**en·liv·en·ment** n.

en masse /än ˈmas/ ▶adv. in a group; all together: *the board of directors resigned en masse.*

en·mesh /enˈmesh/ ▶v. [tr.] (usu. **be enmeshed in**) cause to become entangled in something: *whales enmeshed in drift nets* | fig. *she is enmeshed in an adulterous affair.* —**en·mesh·ment** n.

en·mi·ty /ˈenmitē/ ▶n. (pl. **-ties**) the state or feeling of being actively opposed or hostile to someone or something: *enmity between Protestants and Catholics.*

en·no·ble /enˈnōbəl/ ▶v. [tr.] give (someone) a noble rank or title. ■ lend greater dignity or nobility of character to: *the theater is a moral instrument to ennoble the mind.* —**en·no·ble·ment** n.

en·nui /änˈwē/ ▶n. a feeling of listlessness and dissatisfaction arising from a lack of occupation or excitement.

e·nol·o·gy /ēˈnälējē/ ▶n. the study of wines. —**e·no·log·i·cal** /ˌēnəˈläjikəl/ adj. —**e·nol·o·gist** /-jist/ n.

e·nor·mi·ty /iˈnôrmitē/ ▶n. (pl. **-ties**) **1** (**the enormity of**) the great or extreme scale, seriousness, or extent of something perceived as bad or morally wrong: *the full enormity of the crime.* ■ (in neutral use) the large size or scale of something: *the enormity of his intellect.* **2** a grave crime or sin: *the enormities of the Hitler regime.* ▷late Middle English: via Old French from Latin *enormitas*, from *enormis*, from *e-* (variant of *ex-*) 'out of' + *norma* 'pattern, standard.' The word originally meant 'deviation from legal or moral rectitude' and 'transgression.'.

e·nor·mous /i'nôrməs/ ▶*adj.* very large in size, quantity, or extent: *her enormous blue eyes.* —**e·nor·mous·ly** *adv.* —**e·nor·mous·ness** *n.*

e·nough /i'nəf/ ▶*adj. & pron.* as much or as many as required: [as *adj.*] *too much work and not enough people to do it* | [as *pron.*] *they ordered more than enough for five people* ■ used to indicate that one is unwilling to tolerate any more of something undesirable: [as *adj.*] *we've got enough problems without that* | [as *pron.*] *I've had enough of this arguing.*
▶*adv.* **1** to the required degree or extent (used after an adjective, adverb, or verb); adequately: *before he was old enough to shave.* **2** to a moderate degree; fairly: *he can get there easily enough.* **3** used for emphasis: *curiously enough, there is no mention of him.*
▶*interj.* used to express an impatient desire for the cessation of undesirable behavior or speech: *Enough! After all of your arguing, I've had it!*
▶ □ **enough is enough** no more will be tolerated. □ **enough said** there is no need to say more; all is understood.

en·rage /en'rāj/ ▶*v.* [tr.] (usu. **be enraged**) make very angry: *the students were enraged at these new rules.*

en·rap·ture /en'rapCHər/ ▶*v.* [tr.] (usu. **be enraptured**) give intense pleasure or joy to: *Ruth was enraptured by the child who was sleeping in her arms so peacefully.*

en·rich / en'riCH/ ▶*v.* [tr.] **1** improve or enhance the quality or value of: *her exposure to museums enriched her life in France.* ■ (often **be enriched**) add to the nutritive value of (food) by adding vitamins or nutrients: *cereal enriched with extra oat bran.* ■ add to the cultural, intellectual, or spiritual wealth of: *the collection was enriched by a bequest of graphic works.* ■ [usu. as *adj.*] (**enriched**) increase the proportion of a particular isotope in (an element), esp. that of the fissile isotope U-235 in uranium so as to make it more powerful or explosive. ■ *Archit.* embellish a molding by carving or otherwise forming a sculpted, ornamental pattern, such as egg and dart. **2** make (someone) wealthy or wealthier: *top party members had enriched themselves.* —**en·rich·ment** *n.*

en·roll /en'rōl/ (*Brit.* **en·rol**) ▶*v.* (**-rolled, -rol·ling**) [intr.] officially register as a member of an institution or a student on a course: *he enrolled in drama school.* ■ [tr.] register (someone) as a member or student: *the school enrolls approximately 1,000 students.* ■ [tr.] recruit (someone) to perform a service: *a campaign to enroll more foster carers.*

en·roll·ment /en'rōlmənt/ (*Brit.* **en·rol·ment**) ▶*n.* the action of enrolling or being enrolled: *the amount due must be paid on enrollment in October.* ■ the number of people enrolled, typically at a school or college.

en route /än 'rōōt; en; äN/ ▶*adv.* during the course of a journey; on the way: *he stopped in Turkey en route to Geneva.*

en·sconce /en'skäns/ ▶*v.* [tr.] establish or settle (someone) in a comfortable, safe, or secret place: *Agnes ensconced herself in their bedroom.*

en·sem·ble /än'sämbəl/ ▶*n.* **1** a group of musicians, actors, or dancers who perform together. ■ a scene or passage written for performance by a whole cast, choir, or group of instruments. ■ the coordination between performers executing such a passage: *a high level of tuning and ensemble is guaranteed.* **2** a group of items viewed as a whole rather than individually: *the buildings in the square present a charming provincial ensemble.* ■ a set of clothes chosen to harmonize when worn together.

en·shrine /en'SHrīn/ ▶*v.* [tr.] (usu. **be enshrined**) place (a revered or precious object) in an appropriate receptacle: *relics are enshrined under altars.* ■ preserve (a right, tradition, or idea) in a form that ensures it will be protected and respected: *the right of all workers to strike was enshrined in the new constitution.* —**en·shrine·ment** *n.*

en·shroud /en'SHroud/ ▶*v.* [tr.] *poetic/lit.* envelop completely and hide from view: *heavy gray clouds enshrouded the city.*

en·sign ▶*n.* **1** /'ensən; 'en,sīn/ a flag or standard, esp. a military or naval one indicating nationality. **2** /'ensən/ a commissioned officer of the lowest rank in the U.S. Navy and Coast Guard, ranking above chief warrant officer and below lieutenant. ■ *hist.* a standard-bearer.

en·slave /en'slāv/ ▶*v.* [tr.] make (someone) a slave. ■ cause (someone) to lose their freedom of choice or action: *they were enslaved by their need to take drugs.* —**en·slave·ment** *n.* —**en·slav·er** *n.*

en·snare /en'sner/ ▶*v.* [tr.] catch in or as in a trap: *they were ensnared in downtown traffic.* —**en·snare·ment** *n.*

en·sue /en'sōō/ ▶*v.* (**en·sues, en·sued, en·su·ing**) [intr.] happen or occur afterward or as a result: *the difficulties that ensued from their commitment to Cuba.*

en·sure /en'SHŏŏr/ ▶*v.* [tr.] make certain that (something) shall occur or be the case. ■ make certain of obtaining or providing (something): *she would ensure him a place in society.* ■ [intr.] (**ensure against**) make sure that (a problem) shall not occur.

ENT ▶*abbr.* ear, nose, and throat (as a department in a hospital).

en·tab·la·ture /en'tabləCHər; -,CHŏŏr/ ▶*n. Archit.* a horizontal,

continuous lintel on a classical building supported by columns or a wall, comprising the architrave, frieze, and cornice.

en·tail ▶*v.* /en'tāl/ [tr.] **1** involve (something) as a necessary or inevitable part or consequence: *a situation that entails considerable risks.* **2** *Law* settle the inheritance of (property) over a number of generations so that ownership remains within a particular group, usually one family: *her father's estate was entailed on a cousin.*
▶*n.* /'en,tāl/ *Law* a settlement of the inheritance of property over a number of generations so that it remains within a family or other group. ■ property that is bequeathed under such conditions. —**en·tail·ment** *n.*

en·tan·gle /en'taNGgəl/ ▶*v.* [tr.] (usu. **be entangled**) cause to become twisted together with or caught in. ■ involve (someone) in difficulties or complicated circumstances from which it is difficult to escape.

en·tan·gle·ment /en'taNGgəlmənt/ ▶*n.* the action or fact of entangling or being entangled: *many dolphins die from entanglement in fishing nets.* ■ a complicated or compromising relationship or situation: *romantic entanglements.* ■ an extensive barrier, typically made of interlaced barbed wire and stakes, erected to impede enemy soldiers or vehicles: *the attackers were caught up on wire entanglements.*

en·tente /än'tänt/ ▶*n.* (also **entente cor·diale** /kôr'dyäl/) a friendly understanding or informal alliance between states or factions: *the growing entente between former opponents.* ■ a group of states in such an alliance. ■ (**the Entente Cordiale**) the understanding between Britain and France reached in 1904, forming the basis of Anglo-French cooperation in World War I.

en·ter /'entər/ ▶*v.* **1** come or go into (a place): [tr.] *she entered the kitchen* | [intr.] *the door opened and Karl entered* | *fig. reading the Bible, we enter into an amazing new world of thoughts.* ■ [intr.] used as a stage direction to indicate when a character comes on stage: *enter Hamlet.* ■ [tr.] (of a man) insert the penis into the vagina of (a woman). **2** [tr.] begin to be involved in: *in 1941 America entered the war.* ■ become a member of or start working in (an institution or profession): *that autumn, he entered college.* ■ register as a competitor or participant in (a tournament, race, or examination). ■ register (a person, animal, or thing) to compete or participate in a tournament, race, or examination. ■ [intr.] (of a particular performer in an ensemble) start or resume playing or singing. **3** write or key (information) in a book, computer, etc., so as to record it: *children can enter the data into the computer.* ■ *Law* submit (a statement) in an official capacity, usually in a court of law: *an attorney entered a plea of guilty on her behalf.*
▶*phrasal v.* □ **enter into** become involved in (an activity, situation, or matter): *they have entered into a relationship.* ■ undertake to bind oneself by (an agreement or other commitment): *the council entered into an agreement with a private firm.* ■ form part of or be a factor in: *medical ethics also enter into the question.* □ **enter on/upon 1** *formal* begin (an activity or job); start to pursue (a particular course in life): *he entered upon a turbulent political career.* **2** *Law* (as a legal entitlement) go freely into property as or as if the owner.
▶*n.* (also **enter key**) a key on a computer keyboard that is used to perform various functions, such as executing a command or selecting options on a menu.

en·ter·ic /en'terik/ ▶*adj.* of, relating to, or occurring in the intestines. —**en·te·ri·tis** /,entə'rītis/ *n.*

en·ter·o·vi·rus /,entərō'vīrəs/ ▶*n. Med.* any of a group of RNA viruses (including those causing polio and hepatitis A) that typically occur in the gastrointestinal tract, sometimes spreading to the central nervous system or other parts of the body.

en·ter·prise /'entər,prīz/ ▶*n.* **1** a project or undertaking, typically one that is difficult or requires effort. ■ initiative and resourcefulness: *success came quickly, thanks to a mixture of talent, enterprise, and luck.* **2** a business or company: *a state-owned enterprise.* ■ entrepreneurial economic activity. —**en·ter·pris·er** *n.*

en·ter·pris·ing /'entər,prīziNG/ ▶*adj.* having or showing initiative and resourcefulness: *some enterprising teachers have started their own recycling programs.* —**en·ter·pris·ing·ly** *adv.*

en·ter·tain /,entər'tān/ ▶*v.* [tr.] **1** provide (someone) with amusement or enjoyment: *a tremendous game that thoroughly entertained the crowd.* ■ receive (someone) as a guest and provide them with food and drink: *a private dining room where members could entertain groups of friends.* **2** give attention or consideration to (an idea, suggestion, or feeling): *Washington entertained little hope of an early improvement in relations.*

Pronunciation Key ə *ago,* up; ər *over,* fur; a *hat;* ā *ate;* ä *car;* CH *chin;* e *let;* ē *see;* e(ə)r *air;* i *fit;* ī *by;* i(ə)r *ear;* NG *sing;* ō *go;* ô *law, for;* oi *toy;* ŏŏ *good;* ōō *goo;* ou *out;* SH *she;* TH *thin;* <u>TH</u> *then;* (h)w *why;* ZH *vision*

en·ter·tain·er /ˌentərˈtānər/ ▶n. a person, such as a singer, dancer, or comedian, whose job is to entertain others.

en·ter·tain·ing /ˌentərˈtāniNG/ ▶adj. providing amusement or enjoyment: *the magazine is both entertaining and informative.*

en·ter·tain·ment /ˌentərˈtānmənt/ ▶n. the action of providing or being provided with amusement or enjoyment: *everyone just sits in front of the TV for entertainment.* ■ an event, performance, or activity designed to entertain others: *a theatrical entertainment.* ■ the action of receiving a guest or guests and providing them with food and drink.

en·thal·py /ˈenˌTHalpē; enˈTHalpē/ ▶n. *Physics* a thermodynamic quantity equivalent to the total heat content of a system. It is equal to the internal energy of the system plus the product of pressure and volume. (Symbol: **H**) ■ the change in this quantity associated with a particular chemical process. ▷1920s: from Greek *enthalpein* 'warm in,' from *en-* 'within' + *thalpein* 'to heat.'

en·thrall /enˈTHrôl/ (*Brit.* also **en·thral**) ▶v. (**-thralled, -thrall·ing**) [*tr.*] (often **be enthralled**) capture the fascinated attention of: *she had been so enthralled by the adventure that she had hardly noticed the cold.* —**en·thrall·ment** (*Brit* also **en·thral·ment**) *n.*

en·throne /enˈTHrōn/ ▶v. [*tr.*] (usu. **be enthroned**) install (a monarch) on a throne, esp. during a ceremony to mark the beginning of their rule. ■ *fig.* give or ascribe a position of authority to: *he was enthroned as the guru of the avant-garde.* —**en·throne·ment** *n.*

en·thuse /enˈTHo͞oz/ ▶v. say something that expresses one's eager enjoyment, interest, or approval: [*intr.*] *they both enthused over my new look* | [with *direct speech*] *"This place is superb!" she enthused.* ■ [*tr.*] make (someone) interested and eagerly appreciative: *public art is a tonic that can enthuse alienated youth.*

en·thu·si·asm /enˈTHo͞ozēˌazəm/ ▶n. intense and eager enjoyment, interest, or approval. ■ a thing that arouses such feelings: *the three enthusiasms of his life were politics, religion, and books.*

en·thu·si·ast /enˈTHo͞ozēˌast/ ▶n. a person who is highly interested in a particular activity or subject: *a sports car enthusiast.*

en·thu·si·as·tic /enˌTHo͞ozēˈastik/ ▶adj. having or showing intense and eager enjoyment, interest, or approval: *the promoter was enthusiastic about the concert venue.* —**en·thu·si·as·ti·cal·ly** *adv.*

en·tice /enˈtīs/ ▶v. [*tr.*] attract or tempt by offering pleasure or advantage: *a show that should entice a new audience into the theater* | [*tr.*] *the whole purpose of bribes is to entice governments to act against the public interest.* —**en·tice·ment** *n.* —**en·tic·er** *n.* —**en·tic·ing·ly** *adv.*

en·tire /enˈtīr/ ▶adj. with no part left out; whole: *my plans are to travel the entire world.* ■ not broken or decayed. ■ without qualification or reservations; absolute: *an ideological system with which he is in entire agreement.* ■ *Bot.* (of a leaf) without indentations or division into leaflets. ▷late Middle English (formerly also as *intire*): from Old French *entier*, based on Latin *integer* 'untouched, whole,' from *in-* 'not' + *tangere* 'to touch.'

en·tire·ly /enˈtīrlē/ ▶adv. completely (often used for emphasis): *the juries were made up entirely of men* | *we have an entirely different outlook.* ■ solely: *eight coaches entirely for passenger transport.*

en·tire·ty /enˈtī(ə)rtē; -ˈtīritē/ ▶n. the whole of something: *she would have to stay in her room over the entirety of the weekend.*

en·ti·tle /enˈtītl/ ▶v. [*tr.*] (usu. **be entitled**) give (someone) a legal right or a just claim to receive or do something: *employees are normally entitled to severance pay.* —**en·ti·tle·ment** *n.*

en·ti·ty /ˈentitē/ ▶n. (*pl.* **-ties**) a thing with distinct and independent existence: *church and empire were fused in a single entity.* ■ existence; being: *entity and nonentity.* —**en·ti·ta·tive** /-ˌtātiv/ *adj.* (*chiefly Philos.*)

en·tomb /enˈto͞om/ ▶v. [*tr.*] (usu. **be entombed**) place (a dead body) in a tomb. ■ bury or trap in or under something: *many people died, most entombed in collapsed buildings.* —**en·tomb·ment** *n.*

en·to·mol·o·gy /ˌentəˈmäləjē/ ▶n. the branch of zoology concerned with the study of insects. —**en·to·mo·log·i·cal** /-məˈläjikəl/ *adj.* —**en·to·mol·o·gist** /-jist/ *n.*

en·tou·rage /ˌänto͞oˈräzH/ ▶n. a group of people attending or surrounding an important person: *an entourage of bodyguards.*

en·tr'acte /ˈänˌtrakt; änˈtrakt/ ▶n. an interval between two acts of a play or opera. ■ a piece of music or a dance performed during such an interval.

en·trails /ˈentrālz; ˈentrəlz/ ▶pl. n. a person or animal's intestines or internal organs, esp. when removed or exposed. ■ *fig.* the innermost parts of something: *digging copper out of the entrails of the earth.* ▷Middle English: from Old French *entrailles*, from medieval Latin *intralia*, alteration of Latin *interanea* 'internal things,' based on *inter* 'among.'

en·trance¹ /ˈentrəns/ ▶n. an opening, such as a door, passage, or gate, that allows access to a place. ■ an act or instance of going or coming in. ■ the coming of an actor or performer onto a stage: *her final entrance is as a triumphant princess.* ■ an act of becoming involved in something: *their entrance into the political arena.* ■ the right, means, or opportunity to enter somewhere or be a member of an institution, society, or other body: *about fifty people attempted to gain entrance* | [as *adj.*] *an entrance examination.*

▶ □ **make an** (or **one's**) **entrance** (of an actor or performer) come on stage. ■ enter somewhere in a conspicuous or impressive way: *she slowly counted to ten before making her entrance.*

en·trance² /enˈtrans/ ▶v. [*tr.*] (often **be entranced**) fill (someone) with wonder and delight, holding their entire attention: *I was entranced by a cluster of trees that were lit up by fireflies.* ■ cast a spell on: *Orpheus entranced the wild beasts.* —**en·trance·ment** *n.* —**en·tranc·ing·ly** *adv.*

en·trant /ˈentrənt/ ▶n. a person or group that enters, joins, or takes part in something.

en·trap /enˈtrap/ ▶v. (**-trapped, -trap·ping**) [*tr.*] catch (someone or something) in or as in a trap: *she was entrapped by family expectations.* ■ trick or deceive (someone), esp. by inducing them to commit a crime in order to secure their prosecution. —**en·trap·ment** *n.* —**en·trap·per** *n.*

en·treat /enˈtrēt/ ▶v. ask someone earnestly or anxiously to do something: [*tr.*] *his friends entreated him not to go.* ■ [*tr.*] ask earnestly or anxiously for (something): *a message had been sent, entreating aid for the Navajos.* —**en·treat·ing·ly** *adv.* —**en·treat·ment** *n.*

en·treat·y /enˈtrētē/ ▶n. (*pl.* **-treat·ies**) an earnest or humble request: *the king turned a deaf ear to his entreaties.*

en·trée /ˈänˌtrā; ˌänˈtrā/ (also **en·tree**) ▶n. the main course of a meal.

en·trench /enˈtrenCH/ ▶v. [*tr.*] (often **be entrenched**) establish (an attitude, habit, or belief) so firmly that change is very difficult or unlikely: *ageism is entrenched in our society.* ■ establish (a person or their authority) in a position of great strength or security. ■ establish (a military force, camp, etc.) in trenches or other fortified positions. —**en·trench·ment** *n.*

en·tre·pre·neur /ˌäntrəprəˈno͝or; -ˈnər/ ▶n. a person who organizes and operates a business or businesses, taking on greater than normal financial risks in order to do so. ■ a promoter in the entertainment industry. —**en·tre·pre·neur·i·al** *adj.* —**en·tre·pre·neur·i·al·ism** *n.*

en·tro·py /ˈentrəpē/ ▶n. *Physics* a thermodynamic quantity representing the unavailability of a system's thermal energy for conversion into mechanical work, often interpreted as the degree of disorder or randomness in the system. (Symbol: **S**) ■ lack of order or predictability; gradual decline into disorder: *a marketplace where entropy reigns supreme.* ■ (in information theory) a logarithmic measure of the rate of transfer of information in a particular message or language. —**en·tro·pic** /enˈträpik/ *adj.* —**en·tro·pi·cal·ly** *adv.*

en·trust /enˈtrəst/ ▶v. [*tr.*] assign the responsibility for doing something to (someone): *I've been entrusted with the task of getting him safely back.* ■ put (something) into someone's care or protection: *you persuade people to entrust their savings to us.* —**en·trust·ment** *n.*

en·try /ˈentrē/ ▶n. (*pl.* **-tries**) **1** an act of going or coming in: *the door was locked, but he forced an entry.* ■ a place of entrance, such as a door or lobby. ■ the right, means, or opportunity to enter a place or be a member of something: *the flood of refugees seeking entry to western Europe.* ■ *Mus.* the point in a piece of music at which a particular performer in an ensemble starts or resumes playing or singing. **2** an item written or printed in a diary, list, ledger, or reference book. ■ the action of recording such an item: *sophisticated features to help ensure accurate data entry.* **3** a person or thing competing in a race or competition: *from the hundreds of entries we received, twelve winners were finally chosen.* ■ the number of competitors in a particular race or competition. ■ the action of participating in a race or competition.

en·try in·hib·i·tor ▶n. a class of anti-HIV drugs that work by blocking the entry of the virus into a host cell.

en·twine /enˈtwīn/ ▶v. [*tr.*] (often **be entwined**) wind or twist together; interweave: *they lay entwined in each other's arms.* —**en·twine·ment** *n.*

e·nu·mer·ate /iˈn(y)o͞oməˌrāt/ ▶v. [*tr.*] mention (a number of things) one by one: *there is not space to enumerate all his works.* ■ *formal* establish the number of: *the 2000 census enumerated 10,493 households living in the county.* —**e·nu·mer·a·tion** *n.* —**e·nu·mer·a·tive** /-rətiv; -ˌrātiv/ *adj.*

e·nu·mer·a·tor /iˈn(y)o͞oməˌrātər/ ▶n. a person employed in taking a census of the population.

e·nun·ci·ate /iˈnənsēˌāt/ ▶v. [*tr.*] say or pronounce clearly: *she enunciated each word slowly.* ■ express (a proposition or theory) in clear or definite terms: *a written document enunciating this policy.* ■ proclaim: *a prophet enunciating the Lord's wisdom.* —**e·nun·ci·a·tion** /iˌnənsēˈāSHən/ *n.* —**e·nun·ci·a·tive** /iˈnənsēˌātiv; -ˌātiv/ *adj.* —**e·nun·ci·a·tor** /-ˌātər/ *n.*

en·u·re·sis /ˌenyəˈrēsis/ ▸ *n. Med.* involuntary urination, esp. by children at night. —**en·u·ret·ic** /-ˈretik/ *adj. & n.*

en·vel·op /enˈveləp/ ▸ *v.* (**-vel·oped, -vel·op·ing**) [*tr.*] wrap up, cover, or surround completely: *a figure enveloped in a black cloak.* ■ make obscure; conceal. ■ (of troops) surround (an enemy force). —**en·vel·op·ment** *n.*

en·ve·lope /ˈenvəˌlōp; ˈänvə-/ ▸ *n.* **1** a flat paper container with a sealable flap, used to enclose a letter or document. **2** a covering or containing structure or layer: *the external envelope of the swimming pool.* ■ *Math.* a curve or surface tangent to each of a family of curves or surfaces.

▸ □ **push the envelope** *inf.* approach or extend the limits of what is possible: *these are extremely witty and clever stories that consistently push the envelope of TV comedy.*

en·vi·a·ble /ˈenvēəbəl/ ▸ *adj.* arousing or likely to arouse envy: *an enviable reputation for academic achievement.* —**en·vi·a·bly** /-əblē/ *adv.*

en·vi·ous /ˈenvēəs/ ▸ *adj.* feeling or showing envy: *I'm envious of their happiness.* —**en·vi·ous·ly** *adv.*

en·vi·ron·ment /enˈvīrənmənt; -ˈvī(ə)rn-/ ▸ *n.* **1** the surroundings or conditions in which a person, animal, or plant lives or operates. ■ the setting or conditions in which a particular activity is carried on: *a good learning environment.* ■ *Comput.* the overall structure within which a user, computer, or program operates: *a desktop development environment.* **2** (**the environment**) the natural world, as a whole or in a particular geographical area, esp. as affected by human activity.

en·vi·ron·men·tal·ist /enˌvīrənˈmen(t)l-ist; -ˌvī(ə)rn-/ ▸ *n.* **1** a person who is concerned with or advocates the protection of the environment. **2** a person who considers that environment, as opposed to heredity, has the primary influence on the development of a person or group. —**en·vi·ron·men·tal** *adj.* —**en·vi·ron·men·tal·ism** *n.* —**en·vi·ron·men·tal·ly** *adv.*

en·vi·rons /enˈvīrənz; -ˈvī(ə)rnz/ ▸ *pl. n.* the surrounding area or district: *the picturesque environs of the lake.*

en·vis·age /enˈvizij/ ▸ *v.* [*tr.*] contemplate or conceive of as a possibility or a desirable future event: *the Rome Treaty envisaged free movement across frontiers.* ■ form a mental picture of (something not yet existing or known): *he knew what he liked but had difficulty envisaging it.*

en·vi·sion /enˈvizhən/ ▸ *v.* [*tr.*] imagine as a future possibility; visualize: *she envisioned the admiring glances of guests seeing her home.*

en·voi /ˈen,voi; ˈän,voi/ (also **en·voy**) ▸ *n.* **1** a short stanza concluding a ballade. **2** *archaic* an author's concluding words.

en·voy /ˈen,voi; ˈän,voi/ ▸ *n.* a messenger or representative, esp. one on a diplomatic mission.

en·vy /ˈenvē/ ▸ *n.* (*pl.* **-vies**) a feeling of discontented or resentful longing aroused by someone else's possessions, qualities, or luck: *she felt a twinge of envy for the people on board.* ■ (**the envy of**) a person or thing that inspires such a feeling: *their national health service is the envy of many in Europe.*

▸ *v.* (**-vies, -vied**) [*tr.*] desire to have a quality, possession, or other desirable attribute belonging to (someone else): *he envied people who did not have to work on weekends.* ■ desire for oneself (something possessed or enjoyed by another): *a lifestyle that most of us would envy.* —**en·vi·er** /ˈenvēər/ *n.*

en·zyme /ˈenzīm/ ▸ *n. Biochem.* a substance produced by a living organism that acts as a catalyst to bring about a specific biochemical reaction. —**en·zy·mat·ic** /ˌenzəˈmatik/ *adj.* —**en·zy·mic** /enˈzīmik; -ˈzimik/ *adj.*

E·o·cene /ˈēə,sēn/ ▸ *adj. Geol.* of, relating to, or denoting the second epoch of the Tertiary period, between the Paleocene and Oligocene epochs. ■ [as *n.*] (**the Eocene**) the Eocene epoch or the system of rocks deposited during it.

E·o·lith·ic /ˌēəˈliTHik/ ▸ *adj. dated Archaeol.* of, relating to, or denoting a period at the beginning of the Stone Age, preceding the Paleolithic and characterized by the earliest crude stone tools. ■ [as *n.*] (**the Eolithic**) the Eolithic period.

e·on /ˈēən; ˈē,än/ (*chiefly Brit.* also **ae·on**) ▸ *n.* (often **eons**) an indefinite and very long period of time, often a period exaggerated for humorous or rhetorical effect: *he reached the crag eons before I arrived.* ■ *Astron. & Geol.* a unit of time equal to a billion years. ■ *Geol.* a major division of geological time, subdivided into eras: *the Precambrian eon.*

EPA ▸ *abbr.* Environmental Protection Agency.

ep·au·let /ˈepə,let; ,epəˈlet/ (also **ep·au·lette**) ▸ *n.* an ornamental shoulder piece on an item of clothing, typically on the coat or jacket of a military uniform. ▷late 18th cent.: from

epaulet

French *épaulette*, diminutive of *épaule* 'shoulder,' from Latin *spatula* in the late Latin sense 'shoulder blade.'

é·pée /ˌeˈpā/ ▸ *n.* a sharp-pointed dueling sword, designed for thrusting and used, with the end blunted, in fencing. ■ the sport of fencing with an épée. —**é·pée·ist** /-ist/ *n.*

e·phed·rine /əˈfedrin; ˈefəˌdrēn/ ▸ *n. Med.* a crystalline alkaloid drug, $C_{10}H_{15}NO$, obtained from certain Asiatic shrubs of the genus *Ephedra.* It causes constriction of the blood vessels and widening of the bronchial passages and is used to relieve asthma and hay fever.

e·phem·er·a /əˈfem(ə)rə/ ▸ *pl. n.* things that exist or are used or enjoyed for only a short time. ■ items of collectible memorabilia, typically written or printed ones, that were originally expected to have only short-term usefulness or popularity: *Mickey Mouse ephemera.*

e·phem·er·al /əˈfem(ə)rəl/ ▸ *adj.* lasting for a very short time: *fashions are ephemeral.* ■ (chiefly of plants) having a very short life cycle. —**e·phem·er·al·ly** *adv.* —**e·phem·er·al·ness** *n.*

ep·ic /ˈepik/ ▸ *n.* a long poem, typically one derived from ancient oral tradition, narrating the deeds and adventures of heroic or legendary figures or the history of a nation. ■ the genre of such poems: *the romances display gentler emotions not found in Greek epic.* ■ a long film, book, or other work portraying heroic deeds and adventures or covering an extended period of time: *a Hollywood biblical epic.*

▸ *adj.* of, relating to, or characteristic of an epic or epics: *England's national epic poem Beowulf.* ■ heroic or grand in scale or character: *his epic journey around the world.* —**ep·i·cal** *adj.* —**ep·i·cal·ly** *adv.*

ep·i·cen·ter /ˈepi,sentər/ (*Brit.* **ep·i·cen·tre**) ▸ *n.* the point on the earth's surface vertically above the focus of an earthquake. ■ *fig.* the central point of something, typically a difficult or unpleasant situation: *the patient was at the epicenter of concern.* —**ep·i·cen·tral** /ˌepiˈsentrəl/ *adj.*

ep·i·cure /ˈepi,kyŏŏr/ ▸ *n.* a person who takes particular pleasure in fine food and drink. —**ep·i·cur·ism** /-,rizəm; ˌepiˈkyŏŏ-/ *n.*

Ep·i·cu·re·an /ˌepikyəˈrēən; ˌepiˈkyŏŏrēən/ ▸ *n.* a disciple or student of the Greek philosopher Epicurus. ■ (**epicurean**) a person devoted to sensual enjoyment, esp. that derived from fine food and drink.

▸ *adj.* of or concerning Epicurus or his ideas: *Epicurean philosophers.* ■ (**epicurean**) relating to or suitable for an epicure: *epicurean feasts.*

ep·i·cy·cle /ˈepi,sīkəl/ ▸ *n. Geom.* a small circle whose center moves around the circumference of a larger one. ■ *hist.* a circle of this type used to describe planetary orbits in the Ptolemaic system. —**ep·i·cy·clic** /ˌepiˈsīklik; ˈepi-/ *adj.*

ep·i·dem·ic /ˌepiˈdemik/ ▸ *n.* a widespread occurrence of an infectious disease in a community at a particular time: *a flu epidemic.* ■ a disease occurring in such a way. ■ a sudden, widespread occurrence of a particular undesirable phenomenon: *an epidemic of violent crime.*

▸ *adj.* of, relating to, or of the nature of an epidemic: *shoplifting has reached epidemic proportions.*

ep·i·de·mi·ol·o·gy /ˌepi,dēmēˈäləjē/ ▸ *n.* the branch of medicine that deals with the incidence, distribution, and possible control of diseases and other factors relating to health. —**ep·i·de·mi·o·log·i·cal** /-əˈläjikəl/ *adj.* —**ep·i·de·mi·ol·o·gist** /-jist/ *n.*

ep·i·der·mis /ˌepiˈdərmis/ ▸ *n. Biol.* the outer layer of cells covering an organism, in particular: ■ *Zool. & Anat.* the surface epithelium of the skin of an animal, overlying the dermis. ■ *Bot.* the outer layer of tissue in a plant, except where it is replaced by periderm. —**ep·i·der·mal** /-ˈdərməl/ *adj.* —**ep·i·der·mic** *adj.* —**ep·i·der·moid** *adj.*

ep·i·did·y·mis /ˌepiˈdidəməs/ ▸ *n.* (*pl.* **-did·y·mi·des** /-ˈdidəmi,dēz; -di'dimi-,dēz/) *Anat.* a highly convoluted duct behind the testis, along which sperm passes to the vas deferens. —**ep·i·did·y·mal** /-məl/ *adj.*

ep·i·du·ral /ˌepiˈd(y)ŏŏrəl/ ▸ *adj. Anat. & Med.* on or around the dura mater, in particular, (of an anesthetic) introduced into the space around the dura mater of the spinal cord.

▸ *n.* an epidural anesthetic, used esp. in childbirth to produce loss of sensation below the waist.

ep·i·glot·tis /ˌepiˈglätəs/ ▸ *n.* a flap of cartilage at the root of the tongue, which is depressed during swallowing to cover the opening of the windpipe. —**ep·i·glot·tal** /-ˈglätl/ *adj.* —**ep·i·glot·tic** /-ˈglätik/ *adj.*

ep·i·gram /ˈepi,gram/ ▸ *n.* a pithy saying or remark expressing an idea in a clever and amusing way. ■ a short poem, esp. a satirical one, having a witty or ingenious ending. —**ep·i·gram·mat·ic** /ˌepigrəˈmatik/ *adj.* —**ep·i·gram·ma·tist** /ˌepiˈgramətist/ *n.* —**ep·i·gram·ma·tize** /ˌepiˈgramə,tīz/ *v.*

ep·i·graph /ˈepi,graf/ ▸ *n.* an inscription on a building, statue, or coin.

■ a short quotation or saying at the beginning of a book or chapter, intended to suggest its theme.

ep·i·la·tion /,epə'lāsHən/ ▶ *n.* the removal of hair by the roots. —**ep·i·late** /'epə,lāt/ *v.* —**ep·i·la·tor** /'epə,lātər/ *n.*

ep·i·lep·sy /'epə,lepsē/ ▶ *n.* a neurological disorder marked by sudden recurrent episodes of sensory disturbance, loss of consciousness, or convulsions, associated with abnormal electrical activity in the brain. —**ep·i·lep·tic** /,epə'leptik/ *adj.*

ep·i·logue /'epə,lôg; -,läg/ (also **ep·i·log**) ▶ *n.* a section or speech at the end of a book or play that serves as a comment on or a conclusion to what has happened.

ep·i·neph·rine /,epi'nefrin/ ▶ *n. Biochem.* a hormone secreted by the adrenal glands, esp. in conditions of stress, increasing rates of blood circulation, breathing, and carbohydrate metabolism and preparing muscles for action. Also called ADRENALINE.

e·piph·a·ny /i'pifənē/ ▶ *n.* (*pl.* **-nies**) (also **E·piph·a·ny**) the manifestation of Christ to the Gentiles as represented by the Magi. ■ the festival commemorating this on January 6. ■ a manifestation of a divine or supernatural being. ■ a moment of sudden revelation or insight. —**ep·i·phan·ic** /,epə'fanik/ *adj.*

ep·i·phyte /'epə,fīt/ ▶ *n. Bot.* a plant that grows on another plant but is not parasitic, such as the numerous ferns, bromeliads, air plants, and orchids growing on tree trunks in tropical rain forests. —**ep·i·phyt·al** /,epə'fītl/ *adj.* —**ep·i·phyt·ic** /,epə'fitik/ *adj.*

e·pis·co·pa·cy /i'piskəpəsē/ ▶ *n.* (*pl.* **-cies**) government of a church by bishops. ■ (**the episcopacy**) the bishops of a region or church collectively. ■ another term for EPISCOPATE.

e·pis·co·pal /i'piskəpəl/ ▶ *adj.* of a bishop or bishops: *episcopal power.* ■ (of a church) governed by or having bishops. —**e·pis·co·pal·ism** /-,lizəm/ *n.* —**e·pis·co·pal·ly** *adv.*

E·pis·co·pal Church ▶ the Anglican Church in the U.S. and Scotland.

e·pis·co·pa·lian /i,piskə'pālēən/ ▶ *adj.* of or advocating government of a church by bishops. ■ of or belonging to an episcopal church. ■ (**Episcopalian**) of or belonging to the Episcopal Church.
▶ *n.* an adherent of episcopacy. ■ (**Episcopalian**) a member of the Episcopal Church. —**e·pis·co·pa·lian·ism** /-,nizəm/ *n.*

e·pis·co·pate /i'piskəpət; -,pāt/ ▶ *n.* the office or term of office of a bishop. ■ (**the episcopate**) the bishops of a church or region collectively.

e·pi·si·ot·o·my /i,pēzē'ätəmē/ ▶ *n.* (*pl.* **-mies**) a surgical cut made at the opening of the vagina during childbirth, to prevent rupture of tissues.

ep·i·sode /'epi,sōd/ ▶ *n.* an event or a group of events occurring as part of a larger sequence: *the latest episode in the feud.* ■ each of the separate installments into which a serialized story or radio or television program is divided. ■ a finite period in which someone is affected by a specified illness: *acute psychotic episodes.* —**ep·i·sod·ic** /,epi'sädik/ *adj.*

ep·i·some /'epi,sōm/ ▶ *n. Microbiol.* a genetic element inside some bacterial cells, esp. the DNA of some bacteriophages, that can replicate independently of the host and also in association with a chromosome with which it becomes integrated.

e·pis·tle /i'pisəl/ ▶ *n. formal* a letter. ■ a poem or other literary work in the form of a letter or series of letters. ■ (also **E·pis·tle**) a book of the New Testament in the form of a letter from an Apostle: *St. Paul's epistle to the Romans.* ■ an extract from an Epistle (or another New Testament book not a Gospel) that is read in a church service. ▷Old English, via Latin from Greek *epistolē*, from *epistellein* 'send news,' from *epi* 'upon, in addition' + *stellein* 'send.' The word was reintroduced in Middle English from Old French.

e·pis·to·lar·y /i'pistə,lerē/ ▶ *adj.* relating to or denoting the writing of letters or literary works in the form of letters: *an epistolary novel.*

ep·i·taph /'epi,taf/ ▶ *n.* a phrase or statement written in memory of a person who has died, esp. as an inscription on a tombstone.

ep·i·the·li·um /,epə'THēlēəm/ ▶ *n.* (*pl.* **-li·a** /-lēə/) *Anat.* the thin tissue forming the outer layer of a body's surface and lining the alimentary canal and other hollow structures. ■ more specifically, the part of this derived from embryonic ectoderm and endoderm, as distinct from endothelium and mesothelium. —**ep·i·the·li·al** /-lēəl/ *adj.*

ep·i·thet /'epə,THet/ ▶ *n.* an adjective or descriptive phrase expressing a quality characteristic of the person or thing mentioned: *old men are often unfairly awarded the epithet "dirty."* ■ such a word or phrase as a term of abuse: *he felt an urge to hurl epithets in his face.* ■ a descriptive title: *the epithet "Father of Waters," poetically used for the Mississippi River.* —**ep·i·thet·ic** /,epə'THetik/ *adj.*

e·pit·o·me /i'pitəmē/ ▶ *n.* **1** a person or thing that is a perfect example of a particular quality or type: *she looked the **epitome of** elegance and good taste.* **2** a summary of a written work; an abstract.

e·pit·o·mize /i'pitə,mīz/ ▶ *v.* [*tr.*] be a perfect example of: *Hearst's newspapers epitomized bare-knuckle yellow journalism.* —**e·pit·o·mi·za·tion** /i-,pitəmi'zāsHən/ *n.*

ep·och /'epək/ ▶ *n.* a period of time in history or a person's life, typically one marked by notable events or particular characteristics: *the Victorian epoch.* ■ the beginning of a distinctive period in the history of someone or something: *Jewish reimmigration to Palestine marked an epoch in the history of Jewry.* ■ *Geol.* a division of time that is a subdivision of a period and is itself subdivided into ages: *the Pliocene epoch.* —**ep·o·chal** /-əkəl/ *adj.*

ep·o·nym /'epə,nim/ ▶ *n.* a person after whom a discovery, invention, place, etc., is named or thought to be named. ■ a name or noun formed in such a way. —**e·pon·y·mous** /ə'pänəməs/ *adj.* —**e·pon·y·my** /-mē/ *n.*

ep·ox·ide /e'päk,sīd/ ▶ *n. Chem.* an organic compound whose molecule contains a three-membered ring involving an oxygen atom and two carbon atoms.

ep·ox·y /i'päksē/ ▶ *n.* (*pl.* **-ox·ies**) (also **epoxy resin**) an adhesive, plastic, paint, or other material made from a class of synthetic thermosetting polymers containing epoxide groups.
▶ *adj.* consisting of or denoting such a material: *epoxy cement.*
▶ *v.* (**-ox·ies, -ox·ied**) [*tr.*] glue (something) using epoxy resin.

ep·si·lon /'epsi,län/ ▶ *n.* the fifth letter of the Greek alphabet (Ε, ε), transliterated as 'e.' ■ [as *adj.*] denoting the fifth in a series of items, categories, etc.

Ep·som salts ▶ *pl. n.* crystals of hydrated magnesium sulfate used as a purgative or for other medicinal use.

EQ ▶ *abbr.* ■ educational quotient ■ emotional quotient. ■ equalizer, specifically a graphic equalizer.

equ·a·ble /'ekwəbəl/ ▶ *adj.* (of a person) not easily disturbed or angered; calm and even-tempered. ■ not varying or fluctuating greatly: *an equable climate.* —**equ·a·bil·i·ty** /,ekwə'bilitē/ *n.* —**equ·a·bly** /-blē/ *adv.*

e·qual /'ēkwəl/ ▶ *adj.* **1** being the same in quantity, size, degree, or value: *add equal amounts of water and flour.* ■ (of people) having the same status, rights, or opportunities. ■ uniform in application or effect; without discrimination on any grounds: *a dedicated campaigner for equal rights.* ■ evenly or fairly balanced: *it was hardly an equal contest.* **2** (**equal to**) having the ability or resources to meet (a challenge): *the players proved equal to the task.*
▶ *n.* a person or thing considered to be the same as another in status or quality: *we all treat each other as equals.*
▶ *v.* (**e·qualed, e·qual·ing**; also *chiefly Brit.* **e·qualled, e·qual·ling**) [*tr.*] be the same as in number or amount: *the total debits should equal the total credits.* ■ match or rival in performance or extent: *he equaled the world record of 9.93 seconds.* ■ be equivalent to: *his work is concerned with why private property equals exploitation.*

e·qual·i·ty /i'kwälitē/ ▶ *n.* the state of being equal, esp. in status, rights, and opportunities: *an organization aiming to promote racial equality.* ■ *Math.* the condition of being equal in number or amount. ■ *Math.* a symbolic expression of the fact that two quantities are equal; an equation. ▷late Middle English: via Old French from Latin *aequalitas*, from *aequalis*, from *aequus* 'even, level, equal.'

e·qual·ize /'ēkwə,līz/ ▶ *v.* [*tr.*] make the same in quantity, size, or degree throughout a place or group: *incentives to equalize funding for school districts.* ■ [*intr.*] become equal to a specified or standard level: *equal volumes tend to equalize in temperature.* ■ [*tr.*] make uniform in application or effect: *the act was structured to equalize the status of a defendant.* ■ [*tr.*] *Electr.* correct or modify (a signal, etc.) with an equalizer ■ [*tr.*] *Electr.* compensate for by means of an equalizer. —**e·qual·i·za·tion** /-,lī‐/ *n.*

e·qual·iz·er /'ēkwə,līzər/ ▶ *n.* a thing that has an equalizing effect: *education is the **great equalizer**.* ■ *inf.* a weapon, esp. a gun. ■ *Electr.* a passive network designed to modify a frequency response, esp. to compensate for distortion.

e·qual·ly /'ēkwəlē/ ▶ *adv.* **1** in the same manner: *all children should be treated equally.* ■ in amounts or parts that are the same in size: *the money can be divided equally between you.* **2** to the same extent or degree: *follow-up discussion is equally important.* ■ in addition and having the same importance (used to introduce a further comment on a topic): *not all who live in inner cities are poor; equally, many poor people live outside inner cities.*

e·qual op·por·tu·ni·ty ▶ *n.* the policy of treating employees and others without discrimination, esp. on the basis of their sex, race, or age: [as *adj.*] *an equal opportunity employer.*

e·quals sign (also **e·qual sign**) ▶ *n.* the symbol =.

e·qua·nim·i·ty /,ēkwə'nimitē; ,ekwə-/ ▶ *n.* mental calmness, composure, and evenness of temper, esp. in a difficult situation: *she accepted both the good and the bad **with equanimity**.* —**e·quan·i·mous** /i'kwänəməs/ *adj.*

e·quate /i'kwāt/ ▶ *v.* [*tr.*] consider (one thing) to be the same as or

equation 303 **ergot**

equivalent to another: *customers* **equate** *their name* **with** *quality.* ■ [*intr.*] (**equate to/with**) (of one thing) be the same as or equivalent to (another): *that sum equates to half a million pounds today.* ■ [*tr.*] cause (two or more things) to be the same in quantity or value: *the level of prices will move to equate supply and demand.* —**e·quat·a·ble** /-təbəl/ *adj.*

e·qua·tion /i'kwāzʜən/ ▶*n.* **1** *Math.* a statement that the values of two mathematical expressions are equal (indicated by the sign =). **2** the process of equating one thing with another: *the equation of science with objectivity.* ■ (**the equation**) a situation or problem in which several factors must be taken into account: *money also came into the equation.* **3** *Chem.* a symbolic representation of the changes that occur in a chemical reaction, expressed in terms of the relative quantities and formulae of the molecules or other species involved.

e·qua·tor /i'kwātər/ ▶*n.* an imaginary line drawn around the earth equally distant from both poles, dividing the earth into northern and southern hemispheres and constituting the parallel of latitude 0°. ■ a corresponding line on a planet or other body. —**e·qua·to·ri·al** /ˌekwə'tôrēəl/ *adj.*

e·ques·tri·an /i'kwestrēən/ ▶*adj.* of or relating to horse riding: *his amazing equestrian skills.* ■ depicting or representing a person on horseback: *an equestrian statue.*
▶*n.* (*fem.* **e·ques·tri·enne** /iˌkwestrē'en/) a rider or performer on horseback.

e·qui·dis·tant /ˌēkwi'distənt; ˌekwi-/ ▶*adj.* at equal distances: *equidistant from both political parties.* —**e·qui·dis·tance** *n.* —**e·qui·dis·tant·ly** *adv.*

e·qui·lat·er·al /ˌēkwə'latərəl; ˌekwə-/ ▶*adj.* having all its sides of the same length: *an equilateral triangle.*

e·qui·lib·ri·um /ˌēkwə'librēəm; ˌekwə-/ ▶*n.* (*pl.* **-lib·ri·a** /-'librēə/) a state in which opposing forces or influences are balanced: *the maintenance of social equilibrium.* ■ a state of physical balance: *I stumbled over a rock and recovered my equilibrium.* ■ a calm state of mind: *his intensity could unsettle his equilibrium.* ■ *Chem.* a state in which a process and its reverse are occurring at equal rates so that no overall change is taking place: *ice is in equilibrium with water.* ■ *Econ.* a situation in which supply and demand are matched and prices stable. —**e·qui·lib·ri·al** /-'librēəl/ *adj.*

e·quine /'ekwīn; 'ē,kwīn/ ▶*adj.* of, relating to, or affecting horses or other members of the horse family: *equine infectious anemia.* ■ resembling a horse: *her somewhat equine features.*
▶*n.* a horse or other member of the horse family.

e·qui·nox /'ekwə,näks; 'ēkwə-/ ▶*n.* the time or date (twice each year) at which the sun crosses the celestial equator, when day and night are of equal length (about September 22 and March 20).

e·quip /i'kwip/ ▶*v.* (**e·quipped**, **e·quip·ping**) [*tr.*] supply with the necessary items for a particular purpose: *all bedrooms are* **equipped with** *a color TV.* ■ prepare (someone) mentally for a particular situation or task: *I don't think he's equipped for the modern age.* ▷early 16th cent.: from French *équiper*, probably from Old Norse *skipa* 'to man (a ship),' from *skip* 'ship.'

eq·ui·page /'ekwəpij/ ▶*n.* **1** *archaic* the equipment for a particular purpose. **2** *hist.* a carriage and horses with attendants.

e·quip·ment /i'kwipmənt/ ▶*n.* the necessary items for a particular purpose: *office equipment.* ■ the process of supplying someone or something with such necessary items: *the construction and equipment of new harbor facilities.* ■ mental resources: *they lacked the intellectual equipment to recognize the jokes.*

e·qui·poise /'ekwə,poiz/ ▶*n.* balance of forces or interests: *this temporary equipoise of power.* ■ a counterbalance or balancing force: *capital flows act as an* **equipoise to** *international imbalances in savings.*
▶*v.* [*tr.*] balance or counterbalance (something).

eq·ui·ta·ble /'ekwitəbəl/ ▶*adj.* **1** fair and impartial: *an equitable balance of power.* **2** *Law* valid in equity as distinct from law: *the beneficiaries have an equitable interest in the property.* —**eq·ui·ta·bil·i·ty** /ˌekwitə'bilitē/ *n.* —**eq·ui·ta·ble·ness** *n.* —**eq·ui·ta·bly** /-blē/ *adv.*

eq·ui·ty /'ekwitē/ ▶*n.* (*pl.* **-ties**) **1** the quality of being fair and impartial: *equity of treatment.* ■ *Law* a branch of law that developed alongside common law in order to remedy some of its defects in fairness and justice, formerly administered in special courts. **2** the value of the shares issued by a company: *he owns 62% of the group's equity.* ■ (**equities**) stocks and shares that carry no fixed interest. **3** the value of a mortgaged property after deduction of charges against it.

e·quiv·a·lent /i'kwivələnt/ ▶*adj.* equal in value, amount, function, meaning, etc.: *one unit is* **equivalent to** *one glass of wine.* ■ (**equivalent to**) having the same or a similar effect as: *some regulations are equivalent to censorship.*
▶*n.* a person or thing that is equal to or corresponds with another in value, amount, function, meaning, etc.: *the French equivalent of the FBI.* ■ (also **equivalent weight**) *Chem.* the mass of a particular substance that can combine with or displace one gram of hydrogen or eight

grams of oxygen, used in expressing combining powers, esp. of elements. —**e·quiv·a·lence** *n.* —**e·quiv·a·len·cy** *n.* —**e·quiv·a·lent·ly** *adv.*

e·quiv·o·cal /i'kwivəkəl/ ▶*adj.* open to more than one interpretation; ambiguous: *the equivocal nature of her remarks.* ■ uncertain or questionable in nature: *the results of the investigation were equivocal.* —**e·quiv·o·cal·i·ty** /iˌkwivə'kalitē/ *n.* —**e·quiv·o·cal·ly** *adv.* —**e·quiv·o·cal·ness** *n.*

e·quiv·o·cate /i'kwivə,kāt/ ▶*v.* [*intr.*] use ambiguous language so as to conceal the truth or avoid committing oneself: [with *direct speech*] "*Not that we are aware of,*" *she equivocated.* —**e·quiv·o·ca·tion** /iˌkwivə'kāsʜən/ *n.* —**e·quiv·o·ca·tor** /-,kātər/ *n.* —**e·quiv·o·ca·to·ry** /-kə,tôrē/ *adj.*

ER ▶*abbr.* ■ emergency room. ■ Queen Elizabeth.

Er ▶*symb.* the chemical element erbium.

er /ə; ər/ ▶*interj.* expressing hesitation: "*Are you OK?*" "*Er . . . yes.*"

ERA ▶*abbr.* ■ *Baseball* earned run average. ■ Equal Rights Amendment.

e·ra /'i(ə)rə; 'erə/ ▶*n.* a long and distinct period of history with a particular feature or characteristic: *the era of glasnost.* ■ a system of chronology dating from a particular noteworthy event: *the dawn of the Christian era.* ■ *Geol.* a major division of time that is a subdivision of an eon and is itself subdivided into periods: *the Mesozoic era.*

e·rad·i·cate /i'radi,kāt/ ▶*v.* [*tr.*] destroy completely; put an end to: *this disease has been eradicated from the world.* —**e·rad·i·ca·ble** /-kəbəl/ *adj.* —**e·rad·i·cant** /-kənt/ *n.* —**e·rad·i·ca·tion** *n.* —**e·rad·i·ca·tor** /-,kātər/ *n.*

e·rase /i'rās/ ▶*v.* [*tr.*] rub out or remove (writing or marks): *graffiti had been erased from the wall.* ■ destroy or obliterate (someone or something) so as to leave no trace: *over twenty years, the last vestiges of a rural economy were erased.* ■ remove recorded material from (a magnetic tape or medium); delete (data) from a computer's memory. —**e·ras·a·ble** /-əbəl/ *adj.* —**e·ra·sure** /i'rāsʜər/ *n.*

e·ras·er /i'rāsər/ ▶*n.* an object, typically a piece of soft rubber or plastic, used to rub out something written.

er·bi·um /'ərbēəm/ ▶*n.* the chemical element of atomic number 68, a soft, silvery-white metal of the lanthanide series. (Symbol: **Er**)

ere /e(ə)r/ ▶*prep.* & *conj. poetic/lit.* or *archaic* before (in time): [as *prep.*] *we hope you will return ere long* | [as *conj.*] *I was driven for some half mile ere we stopped.*

e·rect /i'rekt/ ▶*adj.* rigidly upright or straight: *she stood erect with her arms by her sides.* ■ (of the penis, clitoris, or nipples) enlarged and rigid, esp. in sexual excitement. ■ (of hair) standing up from the skin; bristling.
▶*v.* [*tr.*] construct (a building, wall, or other upright structure): *the guest house was erected in the eighteenth century.* ■ put into position and set upright (a barrier, statue, or other object): *the police had erected roadblocks.* ■ create or establish (a theory or system): *the party that erected the welfare state.* —**e·rect·a·ble** *adj.* —**e·rect·ly** *adv.* —**e·rect·ness** *n.*

e·rec·tile /i'rektl; -,tīl/ ▶*adj.* able to become erect: *erectile spines.* ■ denoting tissues that are capable of becoming temporarily engorged with blood, particularly those of the penis or other sexual organs. ■ relating to this process: *men with erectile dysfunction.*

e·rec·tile dys·func·tion ▶*n.* inability of a man to maintain an erection sufficient for satisfying sexual activity.

e·rec·tion /i'reksʜən/ ▶*n.* **1** the action of erecting a structure or object: *fees will be levied for the erection of monuments.* ■ a building or other upright structure. **2** an enlarged and rigid state of the penis, typically in sexual excitement.

erg /ərg/ ▶*n.* *Physics* a unit of work or energy, equal to the work done by a force of one dyne when its point of application moves one centimeter in the direction of action of the force.

er·go /'ərgō; 'ergō/ ▶*adv.* therefore: *she was the sole beneficiary of the will, ergo the prime suspect.*

er·go·nom·ics /ˌergə'nämiks/ ▶*pl. n.* [treated as *sing.*] the study of people's efficiency in their working environment. —**er·go·nom·ic** *adj.* —**er·gon·o·mist** /ər'gänəmist/ *n.*

er·gos·ter·ol /ər'gästə,rôl; -,räl/ ▶*n. Biochem.* a compound present in ergot and many other fungi. A steroid alcohol, it is converted to vitamin D_2 when irradiated with ultraviolet light. ▷early 20th cent.: from *ergot*, on the pattern of *cholesterol.*

er·got /'ərgət; -,gät/ ▶*n.* a fungal disease of rye and other cereals in which black, elongated, fruiting bodies grow in the ears of the cereal. Eating contaminated food can result in headache, vomiting, diarrhea, and gangrene of the fingers and toes. ■ a fruiting body of this fungus. ■ these fruiting bodies used as a source of certain medicinal alkaloids, esp. for inducing uterine contractions or controlling post-partum

---

Pronunciation Key ə *ago,* up; ər *over,* fur; ə *hat;* ā *ate;* ä *car;* ᴄʜ *chin;* e *let;* ē *see;* ə(ə)r *air;* i *fit;* ī *by;* i(ə)r *ear;* ɴɢ *sing;* ō *go;* ô *law, for;* oi *toy;* o͝o *good;* o͞o *goo;* ou *out;* sʜ *she;* тʜ *thin;* ᴛ͟ʜ *then;* (h)w *why;* zʜ *vision*

bleeding. ▷late 17th cent.: from French, from Old French *argot* 'cock's spur' (because of the appearance produced by the disease).

er·mine /'ərmən/ ▶*n.* (*pl.* same or **ermines**) a stoat, esp. when in its white winter coat. ■ the white fur of the stoat, used for trimming garments, esp. ceremonial robes. ▷Middle English: from Old French *hermine*, probably from medieval Latin *(mus) Armenius* 'Armenian (mouse).'

erne /ərn/ ▶*n. poetic/lit.* the sea eagle.

e·rode /i'rōd/ ▶*v.* [*tr.*] (often **be eroded**) (of wind, water, or other natural agents) gradually wear away (soil, rock, or land): *the cliffs have been eroded by the sea.* ■ [*intr.*] (of soil, rock, or land) be gradually worn away by such natural agents. ■ *fig.* gradually destroy or be gradually destroyed: [*tr.*] *this humiliation has eroded what confidence Jean has* | [*intr.*] *profit margins are eroding.* ■ *Med.* (of a disease) gradually destroy (bodily tissue). —**e·rod·i·ble** *adj.* —**e·ro·sion** /i'rōzʜən/ *n.*

e·rog·e·nous /i'räjənəs/ ▶*adj.* (of a part of the body) sensitive to sexual stimulation: *erogenous zones.*

e·rot·ic /i'rätik/ ▶*adj.* of, relating to, or tending to arouse sexual desire or excitement. —**e·rot·i·cal·ly** /-ik(ə)lē/ *adv.*

e·rot·i·ca /i'rätikə/ ▶*n.* literature or art intended to arouse sexual desire.

e·rot·i·cism /i'räti,sizəm/ (also **er·o·tism** /'erə,tizəm/) ▶*n.* the quality or character of being erotic. ■ sexual desire or excitement.

e·ro·to·gen·ic /i,rätə'jenik; -rōtə-/ (also **e·ro·tog·e·nous** /erə'täjənəs/) ▶*adj.* another term for EROGENOUS.

e·ro·to·ma·ni·a /i,rätə'mānēə; -,rōtə-/ ▶*n. Psychiatry* a delusion in which a person (typically a woman) believes that another person (typically of higher social status) is in love with them. ■ excessive sexual desire. —**e·ro·to·ma·ni·ac** /-'mānē,ak/ *n.*

err /ər; er/ ▶*v.* [*intr.*] *formal* be mistaken or incorrect; make a mistake: *the judge had erred in ruling that the evidence was inadmissible.* ■ [often as *adj.*] (**erring**) sin; do wrong: *the erring brother who had wrecked his life.*

▶ □ **err on the side of** display more rather than less of (a specified quality) in one's actions: *it is better to err on the side of caution.*

er·rand /'erənd/ ▶*n.* a short journey undertaken in order to deliver or collect something, often on someone else's behalf: *she asked Tim to run an errand for her.* ■ *archaic* the purpose or object of such a journey: *she knew that if she stated her errand, she would not be able to see him.*

er·rant /'erənt/ ▶*adj.* **1** erring or straying from the proper course or standards: *he could never forgive his daughter's errant ways.* **2** *archaic* or *poetic/lit.* traveling in search of adventure: *that same lady errant.*

er·rat·ic /i'ratik/ ▶*adj.* not even or regular in pattern or movement; unpredictable: *her breathing was erratic.* ■ deviating from the normal or conventional in behavior or opinions: *neighbors were alarmed by increasingly erratic behavior.*

▶*n.* (also **erratic block** or **boulder**) *Geol.* a rock or boulder that differs from the surrounding rock and is believed to have been brought from a distance by glacial action. —**er·rat·i·cal·ly** /-(ə)lē/ *adv.*

er·ra·tum /i'rätəm; -'rä-/ ▶*n.* (*pl.* -**ta** /-tə/) an error in printing or writing. ■ (**errata**) a list of corrected errors appended to a book or published in a subsequent issue of a journal.

er·ro·ne·ous /i'rōnēəs/ ▶*adj.* wrong; incorrect: *employers sometimes make erroneous assumptions.* —**er·ro·ne·ous·ly** *adv.* —**er·ro·ne·ous·ness** *n.*

er·ror /'erər/ ▶*n.* a mistake: *spelling errors.* ■ the state or condition of being wrong in conduct or judgment: *the crash was caused by human error.* ■ *Baseball* a misplay by a fielder that allows a batter to reach base or a runner to advance. ■ *technical* a measure of the estimated difference between the observed or calculated value of a quantity and its true value. ■ *Law* a mistake of fact or of law in a court's opinion, judgment or order. ■ *Philately* a postage stamp or item of postal stationery showing a major printing or perforation mistake.

▶ □ **see the error of one's ways** realize or acknowledge one's wrongdoing.

er·satz /'er,säts; -,zäts/ ▶*adj.* (of a product) made or used as a substitute, typically an inferior one, for something else: *ersatz coffee.* ■ not real or genuine: *ersatz emotion.*

Erse /ərs/ ▶*n.* the Scottish or Irish Gaelic language.

erst·while /'ərst,(h)wīl/ ▶*adj.* former: *his erstwhile rivals.*
▶*adv. archaic* formerly: *Mary Anderson, erstwhile the queen of America's stage.*

er·u·dite /'er(y)ə,dīt/ ▶*adj.* having or showing great knowledge or learning. —**er·u·dite·ly** *adv.* —**er·u·di·tion** /'er(y)o͞o,disʜən/ *n.*

e·rupt /i'rəpt/ ▶*v.* [*intr.*] (of a volcano) become active and eject lava, ash, and gases. ■ be ejected from an active volcano: *hot lava erupted from the crust.* ■ (of an object) explode with fire and noise resembling an active volcano: *smoke bombs erupted everywhere.* ■ break out or burst forth suddenly and dramatically: *fierce fighting erupted between the army and guerrillas.* ■ give vent to anger, enthusiasm, amusement, or other feelings in a sudden and noisy way: *the soldiers erupted in fits of laughter.* ■ (of a pimple, rash, or other prominent mark) suddenly appear on the skin. ■ (of the skin) suddenly develop such a pimple, rash, or mark. ■ (of a tooth) break through the gums during normal development. —**e·rup·tion** *n.* —**e·rup·tive** *adj.*

er·y·the·ma /,erə'ʜēmə/ ▶*n. Med.* superficial reddening of the skin, usually in patches, as a result of injury or irritation causing dilatation of the blood capillaries. —**er·y·the·mal** /-məl/ *adj.* —**er·y·them·a·tous** /-'ʜemətəs; -'ʜēmətəs/ *adj.*

e·ryth·ro·cyte /i'riʜrə,sīt/ ▶*n.* a red blood cell that (in humans) that contains hemoglobin and and transports oxygen and carbon dioxide to and from the tissues. —**e·ryth·ro·cyt·ic** /i,riʜrə'sitik/ *adj.*

Es ▶*symb.* the chemical element einsteinium.

es·ca·late /'eskə,lāt/ ▶*v.* [*intr.*] increase rapidly: *the price of tickets escalated.* ■ become or cause to become more intense or serious: [*intr.*] *the disturbance escalated into a full-scale riot* | [*tr.*] *we do not want to escalate the war.* —**es·ca·la·tion** *n.*

es·ca·la·tor /'eskə,lātər/ ▶*n.* a moving staircase consisting of an endlessly circulating belt of steps driven by a motor, conveying people between the floors of a public building.

es·ca·pade /'eskə,pād/ ▶*n.* an act or incident involving excitement, daring, or adventure.

es·cape /i'skāp/ ▶*v.* [*intr.*] break free from confinement or control: *two burglars have just escaped from prison.* ■ [*tr.*] elude or get free from (someone): *he drove along I-84 to escape the police.* ■ succeed in avoiding or eluding something dangerous, unpleasant, or undesirable: *the driver escaped with a broken knee* | [*tr.*] *a baby boy narrowly escaped death.* ■ [*tr.*] fail to be noticed or remembered by (someone): *the name escaped him.* ■ (of a gas, liquid, or heat) leak from a container. ■ [*tr.*] (of words or sounds) issue involuntarily or inadvertently from (someone or their lips): *a sob escaped her lips.*

▶*n.* an act of breaking free from confinement or control: *the story of his escape from a POW camp.* ■ an act of successfully avoiding something dangerous, unpleasant, or unwelcome: *the couple had a **narrow escape** from serious injury.* ■ a form of temporary distraction from reality or routine: *romantic novels should present an escape from the dreary realities of life.* ■ a leakage of gas, liquid, or heat from a container. ■ (also **escape key**) *Comput.* a key on a computer keyboard that either interrupts the current operation or converts subsequent characters to a control sequence. ■ a garden plant or pet animal that has gone wild and (esp. in plants) become naturalized.

es·cap·ee /i,skā'pē; ,eskā'pē/ ▶*n.* a person who has escaped from somewhere, esp. prison.

es·cape·ment /i'skāpmənt/ ▶*n.* a mechanism in a clock or watch that alternately checks and releases the train by a fixed amount and transmits a periodic impulse from the spring or weight to the balance wheel or pendulum. ■ the part of the mechanism in a piano that enables the hammer to fall back as soon as it has struck the string.

es·cape ve·loc·i·ty ▶*n.* the lowest velocity that a body must have in order to escape the gravitational attraction of a particular planet or other object.

es·cap·ism /i'skāp,izəm/ ▶*n.* the tendency to seek distraction and relief from unpleasant realities, esp. by seeking entertainment or engaging in fantasy. —**es·cap·ist** *n.* & *adj.*

es·car·got /,eskär'gō/ ▶*n.* a snail, esp. as an item on a menu.

es·carp·ment /i'skärpmənt/ ▶*n.* a long, steep slope, esp. one at the edge of a plateau or separating areas of land at different heights.

es·cha·tol·o·gy /,eskə'täləjē/ ▶*n.* the part of theology concerned with death, judgment, and the final destiny of the soul and of humankind. —**es·cha·to·log·i·cal** /e,skatl'äjikəl; ,eskətl-/ *adj.* —**es·cha·tol·o·gist** *n.*

es·chew /es'cʜo͞o/ ▶*v.* [*tr.*] deliberately avoid using; abstain from: *he appealed to the crowd to eschew violence.* —**es·chew·al** *n.*

es·cort ▶*n.* /'es,kôrt/ a person, vehicle, ship, or aircraft, or a group of these, accompanying another for protection, security, or as a mark of rank: *a police escort.* ■ a man who accompanies a woman to a particular social event. ■ a person, typically a woman, who may be hired to accompany someone socially: [as *adj.*] *an escort agency.*
▶*v.* /i'skôrt/ [*tr.*] accompany (someone or something) somewhere, esp. for protection or security, or as a mark of rank: *Shiona escorted Janice to the door.*

es·cri·toire /,eskri'twär/ ▶*n.* a small writing desk with drawers and compartments.

es·crow /'eskrō/ *Law* ▶*n.* a bond, deed, or other document kept in the custody of a third party, taking effect only when a specified condition has been fulfilled. ■ [usu. as *adj.*] a deposit or fund held in trust or as a security: *an escrow account.* ■ the state of being kept in custody or trust in this way: *the board holds funds in escrow.*

es·cutch·eon /i'skəCHən/ ▶*n.* **1** a shield or emblem bearing a coat of arms. **2** (also **escutcheon plate**) a flat piece of metal for protection and often ornamentation, around a keyhole, door handle, or light switch. —**es·cutch·eoned** *adj.*

ESE ▶*abbr.* east-southeast.

es·ker /'eskər/ ▶*n.* Geol. a long ridge of gravel and other sediment, typically having a winding course, deposited by meltwater from a retreating glacier or ice sheet.

Es·ki·mo /'eskə,mō/ ▶*n.* (*pl.* same or **-mos**) **1** *often offens.* a member of an indigenous people inhabiting northern Canada, Alaska, Greenland, and eastern Siberia, traditionally living by hunting and fishing. **2** either of the two main languages of this people (Inuit and Yupik), forming a major division of the Eskimo-Aleut family.
▶*adj.* of or relating to the Eskimos or their languages. ▷via French *Esquimaux,* possibly from Spanish *esquimao, esquimal,* from Montagnais *ayaškimew* 'netter of snowshoes,' probably applied first to the Micmac and later to the Eskimo.

ESL ▶*abbr.* English as a second language.

e·soph·a·gus /i'säfəgəs/ ▶*n.* (*pl.* **-gi** /-,gī/ or **-gus·es**) the part of the alimentary canal that connects the throat to the stomach; the gullet. In vertebrates it is a muscular tube lined with mucous membrane. —**e·soph·a·ge·al** /i,säfə'jēəl/ *adj.*

es·o·ter·ic /,esə'terik/ ▶*adj.* intended for or likely to be understood by only a small number of people with a specialized knowledge or interest: *esoteric philosophical debates.* —**es·o·ter·i·cal·ly** *adv.* —**es·o·ter·i·cism** /-'terə,sizəm/ *n.*

ESP ▶*abbr.* ■ electrostatic precipitator. ■ extrasensory perception.

es·pa·drille /'espə,dril/ ▶*n.* a light canvas shoe with a plaited fiber sole.

es·pal·ier /i'spalyər/ ▶*n.* a fruit tree or ornamental shrub whose branches are trained to grow flat against a wall, supported on a framework.

espadrille

es·pe·cial /i'speSHəl/ ▶*adj.* better or greater than usual; special: *these traditions are of especial interest to feminists.* ■ for or belonging chiefly to one person or thing: *her outburst was for my especial benefit.*

es·pe·cial·ly /i'speSHəlē/ ▶*adv.* **1** used to single out one person, thing, or situation over all others: *a new song, written especially for Jonathan.* **2** to a great extent; very much: *he didn't especially like dancing.*

Es·pe·ran·to /,espə'räntō/ ▶*n.* an artificial language devised in 1887 as an international medium of communication, based on roots from the chief European languages. —**Es·pe·ran·tist** /-'tist/ *n.*

es·pi·o·nage /'espēə,näZH; -,näj/ ▶*n.* the practice of spying or of using spies, typically by governments to obtain political and military information.

es·pla·nade /'esplə,näd; -,nād/ ▶*n.* a long, open, level area, typically beside the sea, along which people may walk for pleasure.

es·pous·al /i'spouzəl; -səl/ ▶*n.* **1** an act of adopting or supporting a cause, belief, or way of life: *his espousal of the leftist cause.* **2** *archaic* a marriage or engagement.

es·pouse /i'spouz/ ▶*v.* [*tr.*] **1** adopt or support (a cause, belief, or way of life): *she espoused communism.* **2** *archaic* marry: *Edward had espoused the Lady Grey.* —**es·pous·er** *n.*

es·pres·so /e'spresō/ ▶*n.* (*pl.* **-sos**) strong black coffee made by forcing steam through ground coffee beans.

es·prit de corps /e,sprē də 'kôr/ ▶*n.* a feeling of pride, fellowship, and common loyalty shared by the members of a particular group.

es·py /i'spī/ ▶*v.* (**-pies**, **-pied**) [*tr.*] *poetic/lit.* catch sight of: *she espied her daughter rounding the corner.*

Esq. ▶*abbr.* Esquire.

es·quire /'eskwīr; i'skwī(ə)r/ ▶*n.* **1** (**Esquire**) a title appended to a lawyer's surname (abbr.: **Esq.**) ■ *Brit.* a polite title appended to a man's name when no other title is used, typically in the address of a letter or other documents: *Robert A. Pearson Esquire.* **2** *hist.* a young nobleman who, in training for knighthood, acted as an attendant to a knight. ■ a landed proprietor or country squire.

ess /es/ ▶*n.* a thing shaped like the letter S.

es·say ▶*n.* /'esā/ **1** a short piece of writing on a particular subject.

2 *formal* an attempt or effort: *a misjudged essay.* ■ a trial design of a postage stamp yet to be accepted.
▶*v.* /e'sā/ [*tr.*] *formal* attempt or try: *essay a smile.* —**es·say·ist** *n.*

es·sence /'esəns/ ▶*n.* the intrinsic nature or indispensable quality of something, esp. something abstract, that determines its character: *conflict is the essence of drama.* ■ *Philos.* a property or group of properties of something without which it would not exist or be what it is. ■ something that exists; in particular, a spiritual entity: *the position that names express essences.* ■ an extract or concentrate obtained from a particular plant or other matter and used for flavoring or scent.

es·sen·tial /i'senSHəl/ ▶*adj.* **1** absolutely necessary; extremely important: *it is essential to keep up-to-date records.* ■ fundamental or central to the nature of something or someone: *the essential weakness of the plaintiff's case.* ■ *Biochem.* (of an amino acid or fatty acid) required for normal growth but not synthesized in the body and therefore necessary in the diet. **2** *Med.* (of a disease) with no known external stimulus or cause; idiopathic: *essential hypertension.*
▶*n.* (usu. **essentials**) a thing that is absolutely necessary: *we had only the bare essentials in the way of gear.* ■ (**essentials**) the fundamental elements or characteristics of something: *he was quick to grasp the essentials of an opponent's argument.* —**es·sen·ti·al·i·ty** /i,senSHē'alitē/ *n.* —**es·sen·tial·ly** *adv.* —**es·sen·tial·ness** *n.*

essential oil ▶*n.* a natural oil typically obtained by distillation and having the characteristic fragrance of the plant or other source from which it is extracted.

EST ▶*abbr.* Eastern Standard Time (see **EASTERN TIME**).

est /est/ ▶*n.* a system for self-improvement aimed at developing a person's potential through intensive group awareness and training.

es·tab·lish /i'stabliSH/ ▶*v.* [*tr.*] **1** set up (an organization, system, or set of rules) on a firm or permanent basis: *the British established a rich trade with Portugal.* ■ initiate or bring about (contact or communication): *the two countries established diplomatic relations.* **2** achieve permanent acceptance for (a custom, belief, practice, or institution). ■ achieve recognition or acceptance for (someone) in a particular capacity: *he had established himself as a film star.* ■ [*intr.*] (of a plant) take root and grow. ■ introduce (a character, set, or location) into a film or play and allow its identification: *establish the location with a wide shot.* **3** show (something) to be true or certain by determining the facts: *the police established that the two passports were forgeries.* **4** *Bridge* ensure that one's remaining cards in (a suit) will be winners (if not trumped) by playing off the high cards in that suit. —**es·tab·lish·er** *n.*

es·tab·lish·ment /i'stabliSHmənt/ ▶*n.* **1** the action of establishing something or being established: *the establishment of a Palestinian state.* ■ the recognition by the state of a national church or religion: *Congress shall make no law respecting an establishment of religion.* **2** a business organization, public institution, or household: *hotels or catering establishments.* ■ the premises or staff of such an organization: *she entered this establishment as our housemaid.* **3** (usu. **the Establishment**) a group in a society exercising power and influence over matters of policy or taste, and seen as resisting change. ■ an influential group within a specified profession or area of activity: *rumblings of discontent among the medical establishment.*

es·tate /i'stāt/ ▶*n.* **1** an area or amount of land or property, in particular: ■ an extensive area of land in the country, usually with a large house, owned by one person or organization. ■ all the money and property owned by a particular person, esp. at death: *in his will, he divided his estate between his wife and daughter.* ■ *Brit.* a housing or commercial development. **2** *archaic* or *poetic/lit.* a particular state, period, or condition in life: *programs for the improvement of man's estate.* ■ grandeur, pomp, or state.

es·teem /i'stēm/ ▶*n.* respect and admiration, typically for a person: *he was held in high esteem by colleagues.*
▶*v.* [*tr.*] (usu. **be esteemed**) respect and admire: *many of these qualities are esteemed by managers* ■ *formal* consider; deem: *I should esteem it a favor if you could speak to them.*

es·ter /'estər/ ▶*n.* Chem. an organic compound made by replacing the hydrogen of an acid by an alkyl or other organic group. Many naturally occurring fats and essential oils are esters of fatty acids.

es·thet·ic, etc. ▶*adj.* **AESTHETIC**, etc.

es·ti·ma·ble /'estəməbəl/ ▶*adj.* worthy of great respect. —**es·ti·ma·bly** /-blē/ *adv.*

es·ti·mate ▶*v.* /'estə,māt/ [*tr.*] roughly calculate or judge the value,

number, quantity, or extent of: *the aim is to estimate the effects of macroeconomic policy on the economy.*
▸*n.* /ˈestəmit/ an approximate calculation or judgment of the value, number, quantity, or extent of something: *at a rough estimate, our staff is recycling a quarter of the paper used.* ■ a written statement indicating the likely price that will be charged for specified work or repairs: *compare costs by getting estimates from at least two firms.* ■ a judgment of the worth or character of someone or something: *his high estimate of the poem.* —**es·ti·ma·tive** /ˈestəˌmātiv/ *adj.*

es·ti·ma·tion /ˌestəˈmāSHən/ ▸*n.* a rough calculation of the value, number, quantity, or extent of something: *estimations of protein concentrations.* ■ a judgment of the worth or character of someone or something: *the pop star rose in my estimation.*

es·ti·val /ˈestəvəl; eˈstī-/ ▸*adj.* technical belonging to or appearing in summer.

es·ti·vate /ˈestəˌvāt/ ▸*v.* [*intr.*] *Zool.* (of an animal, particularly an insect, fish, or amphibian) spend a hot or dry period in a prolonged state of torpor or dormancy. ▷early 17th cent. (in the sense 'pass the summer'): from Latin *aestivat-*, from *aestivare* 'spend the summer,' from *aestus* 'heat.'

Es·to·ni·an /eˈstōnēən/ ▸*adj.* of or relating to Estonia or its people or their language.
▸*n.* **1** a native or national of Estonia, or a person of Estonian descent. **2** the Finno-Ugric language of Estonia, closely related to Finnish.

es·tra·di·ol /ˌestrəˈdīˌol; -ˌäl/ ▸*n.* *Biochem.* a major estrogen produced in the ovaries.

es·trange /iˈstrānj/ ▸*v.* [*tr.*] cause (someone) to be no longer close or affectionate to someone; alienate: *are you deliberately seeking to estrange your readers?* —**es·trange·ment** *n.*

es·tro·gen /ˈestrəjən/ ▸*n.* any of a group of steroid hormones that promote the development and maintenance of female characteristics of the body. Such hormones are also produced artificially for use in oral contraceptives or to treat menopausal and menstrual disorders. —**es·tro·gen·ic** /ˌestrəˈjenik/ *adj.*

es·trone /ˈestrōn/ ▸*n.* *Biochem.* an estrogen similar to but less potent than estradiol.

es·trus /ˈestrəs/ ▸*n.* a recurring period of sexual receptivity and fertility in many female mammals; heat: *a mare in estrus.* —**es·trous** *adj.*

es·tu·ar·y /ˈesCHo͞oˌerē/ ▸*n.* (*pl.* **-ar·ies**) the tidal lower reaches of a large river, where the tide meets the stream. —**es·tu·ar·i·al** /ˌesCHo͞oˈe(ə)rēəl/ *adj.* —**es·tu·a·rine** /ˈesCHo͞oəˌrīn; -əˌrēn/ *adj.*

ET ▸*abbr.* ■ Eastern time. ■ extraterrestrial.

ETA ▸*abbr.* estimated time of arrival, in particular the time at which an aircraft or ship is expected to arrive at its destination.

e·ta /ˈātə; ˈētə/ ▸*n.* the seventh letter of the Greek alphabet (**H**, η), transliterated as 'e' or 'ē.'

et al. /ˌet ˈal; ˌet ˈäl/ ▸*abbr.* and others (used esp. in referring to academic books or articles that have more than one author): *the conclusions of Gardner et al.* ▷from Latin *et alii.*

etc. ▸*abbr.* et cetera.

et cet·er·a /et ˈsetərə; ˈsetrə/ (also **et·cet·er·a**) ▸*adv.* used at the end of a list to indicate that further, similar items are included: *we're trying to resolve problems of obtaining equipment, drugs, et cetera.* ■ indicating that a list is too tedious or clichéd to give in full: *we've all got to do our duty, pull our weight, et cetera, et cetera.* ▷Latin, from *et* 'and' and *cetera* 'the rest' (neuter plural of *ceterus* 'left over').

etch /eCH/ ▸*v.* [*tr.*] **1** engrave (metal, glass, or stone) by coating it with a protective layer, drawing on it with a needle, and then covering it with acid to attack the parts the needle has exposed, esp. in order to produce prints from it. ■ use such a process to produce (a print or design). ■ (of an acid or other solvent) corrode or eat away the surface of (something). ■ selectively dissolve the surface of (a semiconductor or printed circuit) with a solvent, laser, or stream of electrons. **2** (usu. **be etched**) cut or carve (a text or design) on a surface: *her initials were etched on the table* | *fig. his name is etched in baseball history.* ■ cause to stand out or be clearly defined or visible: *Jo watched the outline of the town etched against the sky* | *fig. the incident was etched indelibly in her mind.* —**etch·er** *n.*

etch·ing /ˈeCHiNG/ ▸*n.* a print produced by the process of etching: *etchings of animals and wildflowers.* ■ the art or process of producing etched plates or objects.

ETD ▸*abbr.* estimated time of departure.

e·ter·nal /iˈtərnl/ ▸*adj.* lasting or existing forever; without end or beginning: *the secret of eternal youth.* ■ (of truths, values, or questions) valid for all time; essentially unchanging: *eternal truths of art and life.*

■ *inf.* seeming to last or persist forever, esp. on account of being tedious or annoying: *eternal nagging demands.* ■ used to emphasize expressions of admiration, gratitude, or other feelings: *to his eternal credit, he maintained his dignity throughout.* ■ (**the Eternal**) used to refer to an everlasting or universal spirit, as represented by God. ▷late Middle English: via Old French from late Latin *aeternalis*, from Latin *aeternus*, from *aevum* 'age.' —**e·ter·nal·ize** /iˈtərnlˌīz/ *v.* —**e·ter·nal·ly** *adv.* —**e·ter·nal·ness** *n.*

e·ter·ni·ty /iˈtərnitē/ ▸*n.* (*pl.* **-ties**) infinite or unending time: *lasted for all eternity.* ■ a state to which time has no application; timelessness. ■ *Theol.* endless life after death: *immortal souls destined for eternity.* ■ used euphemistically to refer to death: *he could have crashed the car and taken them both to eternity.* ■ (**an eternity**) *inf.* a period of time that seems very long, esp. on account of being tedious or annoying: *a silence that lasted an eternity.*

eth /eTH/ (also **edh**) ▸*n.* an Old English letter, ð or Ð, representing the dental fricatives /TH/ and /ᵺ/. Compare with **THORN** (sense 3).

eth·ane /ˈeTHˌān/ ▸*n.* *Chem.* a colorless, odorless, flammable gas, C_2H_6, of the alkane series, that is a constituent of petroleum and natural gas.

eth·a·nol /ˈeTHəˌnôl; -ˌnäl/ ▸*n.* systematic chemical name for **ETHYL ALCOHOL**.

e·ther /ˈēTHər/ ▸*n.* **1** *Chem.* a pleasant-smelling, highly flammable, colorless, volatile liquid, $C_2H_5OC_2H_5$, used as an anesthetic and as a solvent or intermediate in industrial processes. ■ any organic compound with a similar structure to this, having an oxygen atom linking two alkyl or other organic groups. **2** *chiefly poetic/lit.* the clear sky; the upper regions of air beyond the clouds. **3** *Physics, archaic* a very rarefied and highly elastic substance formerly believed to permeate all space and to be the medium whose vibrations constituted light and other electromagnetic radiation. —**e·ther·ic** /iˈTHerik; iˈTH(ē)rik/ *adj.*

e·the·re·al /iˈTHi(ə)rēəl/ ▸*adj.* **1** extremely delicate and light in a way that seems too perfect for this world: *her ethereal beauty.* ■ heavenly or spiritual: *ethereal, otherworldly visions.* **2** *Chem.* (of a solution) having ether as a solvent. —**e·the·re·al·ize** /-ˌlīz/ *v.* —**e·the·re·al·ly** *adv.*

eth·ic /ˈeTHik/ ▸*n.* a set of moral principles, esp. ones relating to or affirming a specified group, field, or form of conduct: *the puritan ethic was being replaced by the hedonist ethic.*

eth·i·cal /ˈeTHikəl/ ▸*adj.* of or relating to moral principles or the branch of knowledge dealing with these: *ethical issues in nursing.* ■ morally correct: *can a profitable business be ethical?* ■ (of a medicine) legally available only on a doctor's prescription and usually not advertised to the general public. —**eth·i·cal·i·ty** /ˌeTHəˈkalitē/ *n.* —**eth·i·cal·ly** /-ik(ə)lē/ *adv.*

eth·ics /ˈeTHiks/ ▸*pl. n.* **1** [usu. treated as *pl.*] moral principles that govern a person's or group's behavior: *Judeo-Christian ethics.* ■ the moral correctness of specified conduct: *the ethics of euthanasia.* **2** [usu. treated as *sing.*] the branch of knowledge that deals with moral principles. —**eth·i·cist** /ˈeTHisist/ *n.*

E·thi·o·pi·an /ˌēTHēˈōpēən/ ▸*n.* a native or national of Ethiopia, or a person of Ethiopian descent.
▸*adj.* **1** of or relating to Ethiopia or its people. **2** *Zool.* of, relating to, or denoting a zoogeographical region comprising Africa south of the Sahara, together with the tropical part of the Arabian peninsula and (usually) Madagascar. Distinctive animals include the giraffes, hippopotamuses, aardvark, elephant shrews, and lemurs.

eth·nic /ˈeTHnik/ ▸*adj.* of or relating to a population subgroup (within a larger or dominant national or cultural group) with a common national or cultural tradition: *leaders of ethnic communities.* ■ of or relating to national and cultural origins: *we recruit our employees regardless of ethnic origin.* ■ denoting origin by birth or descent rather than by present nationality: *ethnic Albanians in Kosovo.* ■ characteristic of or belonging to a non-Western cultural tradition: *folk and ethnic music.*
▸*n.* a member of an ethnic minority. —**eth·ni·cal·ly** /-(ə)lē/ *adv.* —**eth·nic·i·ty** /eTHˈnisitē/ *n.*

eth·nic cleans·ing ▸*n.* the mass expulsion or killing of members of an unwanted ethnic or religious group in a society.

eth·no·cen·tric /ˌeTHnōˈsentrik/ ▸*adj.* evaluating other peoples and cultures according to the standards of one's own culture. —**eth·no·cen·tri·cal·ly** *adv.* —**eth·no·cen·tric·i·ty** /-ˌsenˈtrisitē/ *n.* —**eth·no·cen·trism** /-ˌtrizəm/ *n.*

eth·nog·ra·phy /eTHˈnägrəfē/ ▸*n.* the scientific description of the customs of individual peoples and cultures. —**eth·nog·ra·pher** /-fər/ *n.* —**eth·no·graph·ic** /ˌeTHnəˈgrafik/ *adj.* —**eth·no·graph·i·cal** *adj.* —**eth·no·graph·i·cal·ly** *adv.*

eth·nol·o·gy /eTHˈnäləjē/ ▸*n.* the study of the characteristics of various peoples and the differences and relationships between them.

—**eth·no·log·ic** /ˌeᴛʜnəˈläjik/ *adj.* —**eth·no·log·i·cal** /ˌeᴛʜnəˈläjikəl/ *adj.* —**eth·no·log·i·cal·ly** /ˌeᴛʜnəˈläjik(ə)lē/ *adv.* —**eth·nol·o·gist** /-jist/ *n.*

e·thol·o·gy /ēˈᴛʜäləjē/ ▸ *n.* the science of animal behavior. ▪ the study of human behavior and social organization from a biological perspective. —**e·tho·log·i·cal** /ēᴛʜəˈläjikəl/ *adj.* —**e·thol·o·gist** /-jist/ *n.*

e·thos /ˈēᴛʜäs/ ▸ *n.* the characteristic spirit of a culture, era, or community as manifested in its beliefs and aspirations: *a challenge to the ethos of the 1960s.*

eth·yl /ˈeᴛʜəl/ ▸ *n.* [usu. as *adj.*] *Chem.* of or denoting the hydrocarbon radical $-C_2H_5$, derived from ethane and present in many organic compounds: *ethyl acetate | an ethyl group.*

eth·yl al·co·hol ▸ *n.* see ALCOHOL.

eth·yl·ene /ˈeᴛʜəˌlēn/ ▸ *n.* *Chem.* a flammable hydrocarbon gas, C_2H_4, of the alkene series, occurring in natural gas, coal gas, and crude oil and given off by ripening fruit. It is used in chemical synthesis, esp. in the manufacture of polyethylene.

eth·yl·ene gly·col ▸ *n.* *Chem.* a colorless viscous hygroscopic liquid alcohol used as an antifreeze, in the manufacture of polyesters, and in the preservation of ancient waterlogged timbers.

e·ti·o·lat·ed /ˈētēəˌlātid/ ▸ *adj.* (of a plant) pale and drawn out due to a lack of light. ▪ having lost vigor or substance; feeble: *a tone of etiolated nostalgia.* —**e·ti·o·la·tion** *n.*

e·ti·ol·o·gy /ˌētēˈäləjē/ ▸ *n.* (pl. **-gies**) **1** *Med.* the cause, set of causes, or manner of causation of a disease or condition: *a disease of unknown etiology | a group of distinct diseases with different etiologies.* ▪ the causation of diseases and disorders as a subject of investigation. **2** the investigation or attribution of the cause or reason for something, often expressed in terms of historical or mythical explanation. —**e·ti·o·log·ic** /ˌētēəˈläjik/ *adj.* —**e·ti·o·log·i·cal** *adj.* —**e·ti·o·log·i·cal·ly** *adv.*

et·i·quette /ˈetikit; -ˌket/ ▸ *n.* the customary code of polite behavior in society or among members of a particular profession or group.

E·trus·can /iˈtrəskən/ ▸ *adj.* of or relating to ancient Etruria, its people, or their language. The Etruscan civilization was at its height *c.*500 BC and was an important influence on the Romans, who subdued the Etruscans by the end of the 3rd century BC.
▸ *n.* **1** a native of ancient Etruria. **2** the language of ancient Etruria, of unknown affinity, written in an alphabet derived from Greek.

et seq. (also **et seqq.**) ▸ *adv.* and what follows (used in page references): *see volume 35, p. 329 et seq.*

é·tude /āˈt(y)ōōd/ ▸ *n.* a short musical composition, typically for one instrument, designed as an exercise to improve the technique or demonstrate the skill of the player.

et·y·mol·o·gy /ˌetəˈmäləjē/ ▸ *n.* (pl. **-gies**) the study of the origin of words and the way in which their meanings have changed throughout history. ▪ the origin of a word and the historical development of its meaning. —**et·y·mo·log·i·cal** /-məˈläjikəl/ *adj.* —**et·y·mo·log·i·cal·ly** *adv.* —**et·y·mol·o·gist** /-jist/ *n.*

EU ▸ *abbr.* European Union.

Eu ▸ *symb.* the chemical element europium.

eu·ca·lyp·tus /ˌyōōkəˈliptəs/ (also **eu·ca·lypt** /-ˈlipt/) ▸ *n.* (pl. **-tus·es** or **-ti** /-tī/) a fast-growing evergreen Australasian tree (genus *Eucalyptus*) of the myrtle family that has been widely introduced elsewhere. It is valued for its timber, oil, gum, and resin, and as an ornamental tree. Also called GUM TREE. ▪ (also **eucalyptus oil**) the oil from eucalyptus leaves, chiefly used for its medicinal properties.

Eu·cha·rist /ˈyōōkərist/ ▸ *n.* the Christian ceremony commemorating the Last Supper, in which bread and wine are consecrated and consumed. ▪ the consecrated elements, esp. the bread. —**Eu·cha·ris·tic** /ˌyōōkəˈristik/ *adj.*

Eu·clid·e·an /yōōˈklidēən/ ▸ *adj.* of or relating to Euclid, in particular: ▪ of or denoting the system of geometry based on the work of Euclid and corresponding approximately to the geometry of ordinary experience. ▪ of such a nature that the postulates of this system of geometry are valid.

eu·gen·ics /yōōˈjeniks/ ▸ *pl. n.* [treated as *sing.*] the science of improving a human population by controlled breeding to increase the occurrence of desirable heritable characteristics. Developed largely by Francis Galton as a method of improving the human race, it fell into disfavor only after the perversion of its doctrines by the Nazis. —**eu·gen·ic** *adj.* —**eu·gen·i·cal·ly** /-ik(ə)lē/ *adv.* —**eu·gen·i·cist** /-ˈjenisist/ *n.* & *adj.* —**eu·gen·ist** /-ˈjenist/ *n.* & *adj.*

eu·kar·y·ote /yōōˈkarēˌōt; -ēət/ (also **eu·car·y·ote**) ▸ *n.* *Biol.* an organism consisting of a cell or cells in which the genetic material is DNA in the form of chromosomes contained within a distinct nucleus. Compare with PROKARYOTE. —**eu·kar·y·ot·ic** /-ˌkarēˈätik/ *adj.*

eu·lo·gize /ˈyōōləˌjīz/ ▸ *v.* [*tr.*] praise highly in speech or writing: *Cotton Mather eulogized him as the embodiment of Christian altruism.* —**eu·lo·gist** /-jist/ *n.* —**eu·lo·gis·tic** /ˌyōōləˈjistik/ *adj.* —**eu·lo·gis·ti·cal·ly** *adv.*

eu·lo·gy /ˈyōōləjē/ ▸ *n.* (pl. **-gies**) a speech or piece of writing that praises someone or something highly, typically someone who has just died: *his good friend delivered a brief eulogy.* ▷late Middle English (in the sense 'high praise'): from medieval Latin *eulogium*, *eulogia* (from Greek *eulogia* 'praise'), apparently influenced by Latin *elogium* 'inscription on a tomb' (from Greek *elegia* 'elegy'). The current sense dates from the late 16th cent.

eu·nuch /ˈyōōnək/ ▸ *n.* a man who has been castrated, esp. (in the past) one employed to guard the women's living areas at an oriental court. ▪ an ineffectual person: *a nation of political eunuchs.* ▷Old English, via Latin from Greek *eunoukhos*, literally 'bedroom guard,' from *eunē* 'bed' + a second element related to *ekhein* 'to hold.'

eu·phe·mism /ˈyōōfəˌmizəm/ ▸ *n.* a mild or indirect word or expression substituted for one considered to be too harsh or blunt when referring to something unpleasant or embarrassing: *"downsizing" as a euphemism for cuts.*

eu·phe·mis·tic /ˌyōōfəˈmistik/ ▸ *adj.* using or of the nature of a euphemism: *the euphemistic terms she uses to describe her relationships.* —**eu·phe·mis·ti·cal·ly** /-(ə)lē/ *adv.*

eu·pho·ni·ous /yōōˈfōnēəs/ ▸ *adj.* (of sound, esp. speech) pleasing to the ear: *this successful candidate delivers a stream of fine, euphonious phrases.* —**eu·pho·ni·ous·ly** *adv.*

eu·pho·ni·um /yōōˈfōnēəm/ ▸ *n.* a valved brass musical instrument resembling a small tuba, played mainly in military and brass bands.

eu·pho·ny /ˈyōōfənē/ ▸ *n.* (pl. **-nies**) the quality of being pleasing to the ear, esp. through a harmonious combination of words. ▪ the tendency to make phonetic change for ease of pronunciation. —**eu·phon·ic** /yōōˈfänik/ *adj.* —**eu·pho·nize** /-ˌnīz/ *v.*

eu·pho·ri·a /yōōˈfôrēə/ ▸ *n.* a feeling or state of intense excitement and happiness: *the euphoria of success will fuel your desire to continue training.* —**eu·phor·ic** *adj.*

Eur·a·sian /yōōrˈāzʜən/ ▸ *adj.* **1** of mixed European (or European-American) and Asian parentage. **2** of or relating to Eurasia.
▸ *n.* a person of mixed European (or European-American) and Asian parentage.

eu·re·ka /yōōˈrēkə; yə-/ ▸ *interj.* a cry of joy or satisfaction when one finds or discovers something.

eu·ro /ˈyərō; ˈyōōrō/ ▸ *n.* (pl. **-ros** or **-ro**) (also **Eu·ro**) the single European currency adopted in 1999 by eleven countries in the European Union (Belgium, Austria, Finland, Spain, Ireland, Portugal, Germany, France, Netherlands, Italy, Luxembourg) as an alternative currency in noncash transactions. In 2002 it replaced the national currencies of twelve member countries (the original eleven, plus Greece). (Symbol: €)

Eu·ro·pe·an /ˌyərəˈpēən; ˌyōōrə-/ ▸ *adj.* of, relating to, or characteristic of Europe or its inhabitants. ▪ of or relating to the European Union: *a single European currency.*
▸ *n.* a native or inhabitant of Europe. ▪ a national of a state belonging to the European Union. ▪ a person who is committed to the European Union: *they claimed to be the party of good Europeans.* ▪ a person who is white or of European parentage, esp. in a country with a large non-white population. —**Eu·ro·pe·an·ism** /-ˌnizəm/ *n.*

Eu·ro·pe·an Com·mu·ni·ty (abbr.: **EC**) ▸ an economic and political association of certain European countries, incorporated since 1993 in the European Union.

Eu·ro·pe·an plan ▸ *n.* a system of charging for a hotel room only, without meals. Often contrasted with AMERICAN PLAN.

eu·ro·pi·um /yəˈrōpēəm/ ▸ *n.* the chemical element of atomic number 63, a soft silvery-white metal of the lanthanide series. Europium oxide is used with yttrium oxide as a red phosphor in color television screens. (Symbol: **Eu**)

Eu·sta·chian tube /yōōˈstāsʜ(ē)ən; -kēən/ ▸ *n.* *Anat.* a narrow passage leading from the pharynx to the cavity of the middle ear, permitting the equalization of pressure on each side of the eardrum.

eu·tha·na·sia /ˌyōōᴛʜəˈnāzʜə/ ▸ *n.* the painless killing of a patient suffering from an incurable and painful disease or in an irreversible coma. The practice is illegal in most countries. ▷early 17th cent. (in the sense 'easy death'): from Greek, from *eu* 'well' + *thanatos* 'death.'

eu·troph·ic /yōōˈtrafik; -trō-/ ▸ *adj.* *Ecol.* (of a lake or other body of water)

Pronunciation Key ə *ago, up*; ər *over, fur*; ă *hat*; ā *ate*; ä *car*; cʜ *chin*; e *let*; ē *see*; e(ə)r *air*; i *fit*; ī *by*; i(ə)r *ear*; ɴɢ *sing*; ō *go*; ô *law, for*; oi *toy*; ŏŏ *good*; ōō *goo*; ou *out*; sʜ *she*; ᴛʜ *thin*; ᴛʜ *then*; (h)w *why*; zʜ *vision*

rich in nutrients and so supporting a dense plant population, the decomposition of which kills animal life by depriving it of oxygen.

EVA ▸ *abbr.* ▪ ethyl vinyl acetate, a material used as cushioning in running shoes, consisting of a rubbery copolymer of ethylene and vinyl acetate. ▪ (in space) extravehicular activity.

e·vac·u·ate /i'vakyŏŏ,āt/ ▸ *v.* [*tr.*] **1** remove (someone) from a place of danger to a safe place: *several families were evacuated from their homes.* ▪ leave or cause the occupants to leave (a place of danger): *fire alarms forced staff to evacuate the building.* **2** *technical* remove air, water, or other contents from (a container): *when it springs a leak, evacuate the pond.* ▪ empty (the bowels or another bodily organ). ▪ discharge (feces or other matter) from the body. —**e·vac·u·a·tion** /i,vakyŏŏ'āsHən/ *n.*

e·vac·u·ee /i,vakyŏŏ'ē/ ▸ *n.* a person evacuated from a place of danger to somewhere safe.

e·vade /i'vād/ ▸ *v.* escape or avoid, esp. by cleverness or trickery: *friends helped him to evade capture for a time.* ▪ (of an abstract thing) elude (someone): *sleep still evaded her.* ▪ avoid giving a direct answer to (a question): *he denied evading the question.* ▪ avoid dealing with or accepting; contrive not to do (something morally or legally required): *difficulties to be faced and not evaded.* ▪ escape paying (tax or duty), esp. by illegitimate presentation of one's finances. —**e·vad·a·ble** *adj.* —**e·vad·er** *n.*

e·val·u·ate /i'valyŏŏ,āt/ ▸ *v.* [*tr.*] form an idea of the amount, number, or value of; assess: *when you evaluate any hammer, look for precision machining.* ▪ *Math.* find a numerical expression or equivalent for (an equation, formula, or function). —**e·val·u·a·tion** *n.* —**e·val·u·a·tive** /-yŏŏ,ātiv; -ətiv/ *adj.* —**e·val·u·a·tor** /-yŏŏ,ātər/ *n.*

ev·a·nes·cent /,evə'nesənt/ ▸ *adj.* *chiefly poetic/lit.* soon passing out of sight, memory, or existence; quickly fading or disappearing: *a shimmering evanescent bubble.* —**ev·a·nes·cence** *n.* —**ev·a·nes·cent·ly** *adv.*

e·van·gel·i·cal /,ivan'jelikəl/ ▸ *adj.* of or according to the teaching of the gospel or the Christian religion. ▪ of or denoting a tradition within Protestant Christianity emphasizing the authority of the Bible, personal conversion, and the doctrine of salvation by faith in the Atonement. ▪ zealous in advocating something.
▸ *n.* a member of the evangelical tradition in the Christian Church. —**e·van·gel·ic** *adj.* —**e·van·gel·i·cal·ism** *n.* —**e·van·gel·i·cal·ly** *adv.*

e·van·ge·lism /i'vanjə,lizəm/ ▸ *n.* the spreading of the Christian gospel by public preaching or personal witness. ▪ zealous advocacy of a cause.

e·van·ge·list /i'vanjəlist/ ▸ *n.* **1** a person who seeks to convert others to the Christian faith, esp. by public preaching. ▪ a layperson engaged in Christian missionary work. ▪ a zealous advocate of something: *he is an evangelist of junk bonds.* **2** the writer of one of the four Gospels (Matthew, Mark, Luke, or John): *St. John the Evangelist.* —**e·van·ge·lis·tic** /i,vanjə'listik/ *adj.*

e·van·ge·lize /i'vanjə,līz/ ▸ *v.* [*tr.*] convert or seek to convert (someone) to Christianity. ▪ [*intr.*] preach the Christian gospel: *the Church's mission to evangelize and declare the faith.* —**e·van·ge·li·za·tion** *n.* —**e·van·ge·liz·er** *n.*

e·vap·o·rate /i'vapə,rāt/ ▸ *v.* turn from liquid into vapor: [*intr.*] *cook until most of the liquid has evaporated* | [*tr.*] *this gets the oil hot enough to evaporate any moisture.* ▪ lose or cause to lose moisture or solvent as vapor: [*tr.*] *the solution was evaporated to dryness.* ▪ [*intr.*] (of something abstract) cease to exist: *the militancy of earlier years had evaporated in the wake of defeat.* —**e·vap·o·ra·ble** /-rəbəl/ *adj.* —**e·vap·o·ra·tion** /i,vapə'rāsHən/ *n.* —**e·vap·o·ra·tor** /-,rātər/ *n.*

e·va·sion /i'vāzHən/ ▸ *n.* the action of evading something: *their adroit evasion of almost all questions.* ▪ an indirect answer; a prevaricating excuse: *the protestations and evasions of a witness.*

e·va·sive /i'vāsiv/ ▸ *adj.* tending to avoid commitment or self-revelation, esp. by responding only indirectly: *she was evasive about her phone number.* ▪ directed toward avoidance or escape: *they decided to take evasive action.* —**e·va·sive·ly** *adv.* —**e·va·sive·ness** *n.*

Eve /ēv/ ▸ (in the Bible) the first woman, wife of Adam and mother of Cain and Abel.

eve /ēv/ ▸ *n.* the day or period of time immediately before an event or occasion: *on the eve of her departure he gave her a little parcel.* ▪ the evening or day before a religious festival: *the service for Passover eve.* ▪ *chiefly poetic/lit.* evening: *a bitter winter's eve.*

e·ven /'ēvən/ ▸ *adj.* (**e·ven·er**, **e·ven·est**) **1** flat and smooth: *prepare the site, then lay an even bed of mortar.* ▪ in the same plane or line; level: *run a file along the saw to make all of the teeth **even with** each other.* ▪ having little variation in quality; regular: *they traveled at an even and leisurely pace.* ▪ equal in number, amount, or value: *an even gender balance among staff and students.* ▪ equally balanced: *it's not an even fight.* ▪ exactly equal to a round number; not having any fractions: *the Dow Jones ended at an even 10,000.* ▪ (of a person's temper or disposition) equable; calm: *a man of*

good humor and even temper. **2** (of a number, such as 2, 6, or 108) divisible by two without a remainder. ▪ bearing such a number: *headers can be placed on odd or even pages or both.*
▸ *v.* make or become even: [*tr.*] *she cut the hair again to even up the ends.*
▸ *adv.* used to emphasize something surprising or extreme: *they have never even heard of the U.S.* ▪ used in comparisons for emphasis: *he knows even less about it than I do.* —**e·ven·ly** *adv.* —**e·ven·ness** *n.*
▸ □ **even as** at the very same time as: *even as he spoke, their baggage was being unloaded.* □ **even if** despite the possibility that; no matter whether: *always try everything even if it turns out to be a dud.* ▪ despite the fact that: *he is a great President, even if he has many enemies.* □ **even now** (or **then**) **1** now (or then) as well as before: *even now, after all these years, it upsets me.* **2** in spite of what has (or had) happened: *even then he never raised his voice to me.* **3** at this (or that) very moment: *very likely you are even now picking up the telephone to call.* □ **even so** in spite of that; nevertheless: *not the most exciting of places, but even so I was having a good time.* □ **even though** despite the fact that: *even though he was bigger, he never looked down on me.* □ **get** (or **be**) **even** *inf.* inflict trouble or harm on someone similar to that which they have inflicted on oneself: *I'll get even with you for this.*

e·ven·hand·ed /'ēvən'handid/ ▸ *adj.* fair and impartial in treatment or judgment: *an even-handed approach.* —**e·ven·hand·ed·ly** *adv.* —**e·ven-hand·ed·ness** *n.*

eve·ning /'ēvniNG/ ▸ *n.* the period of time at the end of the day, usually from about 6 p.m. to bedtime: *it was seven o'clock **in the evening*** | [as *adj.*] *the evening meal.* ▪ this time characterized by a specified type of activity or particular weather conditions: *they could have a relaxing evening.* ▪ [as *adj.*] prescribed by fashion as suitable for relatively formal social events held in the evening: *a couple in evening dress.*
▸ *adv.* (**evenings**) *inf.* in the evening; every evening: *Saturday evenings he invariably fell asleep.*

eve·ning star ▸ *n.* (**the evening star**) the planet Venus, seen shining in the western sky after sunset.

e·ven·song /'ēvən,sôNG; -,säNG/ (also **E·ven·song**) ▸ *n.* (in the Christian Church) a service of evening prayers, psalms, and canticles, conducted according to a set form, esp. that of the Anglican Church: *choral evensong.*

e·vent /i'vent/ ▸ *n.* a thing that happens, esp. one of importance. ▪ a planned public or social occasion: *events to raise money for charity.* ▪ each of several particular contests making up a sports competition: *a star sprinter in the 100- and 200-meter events.* ▷from Latin *eventus,* from *evinire* 'result, happen,' from *e-* 'out of (from *ex-*) + *venire* 'come.'
▸ □ **in any event** (or **at all events**) whatever happens or may have happened: *in any event, there was one promise the trickster did keep.*

e·vent cre·a·tion ▸ *n.* **1** the activity of planning, organizing, and staging public events. **2** (in computer programming) the activity of or facility for creating an event that will unfold in real time when conditions for it have been met.

e·vent·ful /i'ventfəl/ ▸ *adj.* marked by interesting or exciting events: *his long and eventful life.* —**e·vent·ful·ly** *adv.* —**e·vent·ful·ness** *n.*

e·vent ho·ri·zon ▸ *n.* *Astron.* a theoretical boundary around a black hole beyond which no light or other radiation can escape. ▪ *fig.* any point of no return: *we're nearing the event horizon of the presidential election.*

e·ven·tide /'ēvən,tīd/ ▸ *n.* *archaic* or *poetic/lit.* the end of the day; evening: *the moon flower opens its white, trumpetlike flowers at eventide.*

e·vent·ing /i'ventiNG/ ▸ *n.* an equestrian sport in which competitors must take part in each of several contests, usually cross-country, dressage, and show jumping. ▷1960s: from *event,* in *three-day event,* horse trials held on three consecutive days.

e·ven·tu·al /i'venCHŏŏəl/ ▸ *adj.* occurring at the end of or as a result of a series of events; final; ultimate: *it's impossible to predict the eventual outcome of the competition.* —**e·ven·tu·al·ly** *adv.*

e·ven·tu·al·i·ty /i,venCHŏŏ'alitē/ ▸ *n.* (*pl.* **-ties**) a possible event or outcome: *you must be prepared for all eventualities.*

ev·er /'evər/ ▸ *adv.* **1** at any time: *nothing ever seemed to ruffle her.* ▪ used in comparisons for emphasis: *they felt better than ever before.* **2** at all times; always: *it remains as popular as ever* | [in *comb.*] *he toyed with his ever-present cigar.* **3** increasingly; constantly: *having to borrow ever larger sums.* **4** used for emphasis in questions expressing astonishment or outrage: *who ever heard of a grown man being frightened of the dark?*
▸ □ **ever since** throughout the period since: *she had lived alone ever since her husband died.*

ev·er·green /'evər,grēn/ ▸ *adj.* of or denoting a plant that retains green leaves throughout the year: *the glossy laurel is hardy and evergreen* | *evergreen shrubs.* Often contrasted with **DECIDUOUS**.
▸ *n.* a plant that retains green leaves throughout the year: *evergreens planted to cut off the east wind.*

ev·er·last·ing /ˌevərˈlastiNG/ ▶*adj.* lasting forever or for a very long time: *the damned would suffer everlasting torment.* —**ev·er·last·ing·ly** *adv.* —**ev·er·last·ing·ness** *n.*

ev·er·more /ˌevərˈmôr/ ▶*adv.* (chiefly used for rhetorical effect or in ecclesiastical contexts) always: *we pray that we may evermore dwell in him and he in us.*

eve·ry /ˈevrē/ ▶*adj.* (preceding a singular noun) used to refer to all the individual members of a set without exception: *the hotel assures every guest of personal attention.* ■ used before an amount to indicate something happening at specified intervals: *tours are every thirty minutes.* ■ (used for emphasis) all possible; the utmost: *you have every reason to be disappointed.*
▶ □ **every other** each second in a series; each alternate: *I train with weights every other day.* □ **every so often** from time to time; occasionally: *every so often I need a laugh to stay sane.* □ **every which way** *inf.* in all directions: *you can see cracks moving every which way.*

eve·ry·bod·y /ˈevrēˌbädē; -ˌbədē/ ▶*pron.* every person: *everybody agrees with his views.*

eve·ry·day /ˈevrēˌdā/ ▶*adj.* happening or used every day; daily: *everyday chores like shopping and housework.* ■ commonplace: *everyday drugs like aspirin.*

Eve·ry·man /ˈevrēˌman/ ▶*n.* an ordinary or typical human being: *it is Everyman's dream car.*

eve·ry·one /ˈevrēˌwən/ ▶*pron.* every person: *he knew everyone in the business.*

eve·ry·thing /ˈevrēˌTHiNG/ ▶*pron.* **1** all things; all the things of a group or class: *he taught me everything I know.* ■ the most important thing or aspect: *money isn't everything.* **2** the current situation; life in general: *everything is going okay.*
▶ □ **and everything** *inf.* used to refer vaguely to other things associated with what has been mentioned: *you'll still get paid and everything.*

eve·ry·where /ˈevrēˌ(h)wer/ ▶*adv.* in or to all places: *I've looked everywhere.* ■ in many places; common or widely distributed: *sandwich bars are everywhere.*
▶*n.* all places or directions: *everywhere was in darkness.*

e·vict /iˈvikt/ ▶*v.* [*tr.*] expel (someone) from a property, esp. with the support of the law: *he had court orders to evict the trespassers from three camps.* —**e·vic·tion** /iˈvikSHən/ *n.* —**e·vic·tor** /-tər/ *n.*

ev·i·dence /ˈevədəns/ ▶*n.* the available body of facts or information indicating whether a belief or proposition is true or valid: *the study finds little evidence of overt discrimination.* ■ *Law* information given personally, drawn from a document, or in the form of material objects, tending or used to establish facts in a legal investigation or admissible as testimony in court: *without evidence, they can't bring a charge.* ■ signs; indications: *there was no obvious evidence of a break-in.*
▶*v.* [*tr.*] (usu. **be evidenced**) be or show evidence of: *that it has been populated from prehistoric times is evidenced by the remains of Neolithic buildings.*
▶ □ **in evidence** noticeable; conspicuous: *his dramatic flair is still very much in evidence.*

ev·i·dent /ˈevədənt/ ▶*adj.* plain or obvious; clearly seen or understood: *she ate the cookies with evident enjoyment.* ▷late Middle English: from Old French, or from Latin *evidens, evident-* 'obvious to the eye or mind,' from *e-* (variant of *ex-*) 'out' + *videre* 'to see.'

ev·i·den·tial /ˌeviˈdenCHəl/ ▶*adj.* *formal* of or providing evidence: *the evidential value of the record.* —**ev·i·den·ti·al·i·ty** /ˌeviˌdenCHēˈalitē/ *n.* —**ev·i·den·tial·ly** *adv.*

ev·i·dent·ly /ˈevidəntlē; ˈeviˌdentlē; ˌevəˈdentlē/ ▶*adv.* **1** plainly or obviously; in a way that is clearly seen or understood: *a work so evidently laden with significance.* **2** it is plain that; it would seem that: *evidently Mrs. Smith thought differently.* ■ used as an affirmative response or reply: *"Were they old pals or something?" "Evidently."*

e·vil /ˈēvəl/ ▶*adj.* profoundly immoral and malevolent: *his evil deeds.* ■ (of something seen or smelled) extremely unpleasant: *a bathroom with an evil smell.*
▶*n.* profound immorality, wickedness, and depravity, esp. when regarded as a supernatural force: *good and evil in eternal opposition.* —**e·vil·ly** /ˈēvəl(l)ē/ *adv.* —**e·vil·ness** *n.*
▶ □ **the evil eye** a gaze or stare superstitiously believed to cause material harm: *he gave me the evil eye as I walked down the corridor.* □ **the Evil One** *archaic* the Devil. □ **speak evil of** slander: *it is a sin to speak evil of the king.*

e·vince /iˈvins/ ▶*v.* [*tr.*] *formal* reveal the presence of (a quality or feeling): *his letters evince the excitement he felt at undertaking this journey.* ■ be evidence of; indicate: *man's inhumanity to man as evinced in the use of torture.*

e·vis·cer·ate /iˈvisəˌrāt/ ▶*v.* [*tr.*] *formal* disembowel (a person or animal): *the goat had been skinned and eviscerated.* ■ *fig.* deprive (something) of its

essential content: *myriad little concessions that would eviscerate the project.* —**e·vis·cer·a·tion** *n.*

e·voc·a·tive /iˈväkətiv/ ▶*adj.* bringing strong images, memories, or feelings to mind: *powerfully evocative lyrics.* —**e·voc·a·tive·ly** *adv.* —**e·voc·a·tive·ness** *n.*

e·voke /iˈvōk/ ▶*v.* [*tr.*] bring or recall to the conscious mind: *the sight of American asters evokes pleasant memories of childhood.* ■ elicit (a response): *the awkward kid who evoked giggles from his sisters.* —**ev·o·ca·tion** /ˌēvōˈkāSHən; ˌevə-/ *n.* —**e·vok·er** *n.*

ev·o·lu·tion /ˌevəˈlōōSHən/ ▶*n.* **1** the process by which different kinds of living organisms are thought to have developed and diversified from earlier forms during the history of the earth. **2** the gradual development of something, esp. from a simple to a more complex form: *the forms of written languages undergo constant evolution.* **3** *Chem.* the giving off of a gaseous product, or of heat. —**ev·o·lu·tion·al** /-SHənl/ *adj.* —**ev·o·lu·tion·al·ly** *adv.* —**ev·o·lu·tion·ar·i·ly** /ˌevəˌlōōSHəˈne(ə)rəlē/ *adv.* —**ev·o·lu·tion·ar·y** /-ˌnerē/ *adj.* —**ev·o·lu·tive** /-ˈlōōtiv/ *adj.*

ev·o·lu·tion·ist /ˌevəˈlōōSHənist/ ▶*n.* a person who believes in the theories of evolution and natural selection.
▶*adj.* of or relating to the theories of evolution and natural selection: *an evolutionist model.* —**ev·o·lu·tion·ism** /-ˌnizəm/ *n.*

e·volve /iˈvälv/ ▶*v.* **1** develop gradually, esp. from a simple to a more complex form: [*intr.*] *the company has evolved into a major chemical manufacturer.* ■ (with reference to an organism or biological feature) develop over successive generations, esp. as a result of natural selection. **2** [*tr.*] *Chem.* give off (gas or heat). —**e·volve·ment** *n.*

ewe /yōō/ ▶*n.* a female sheep.

ew·er /ˈyōōər/ ▶*n.* a large jug with a wide mouth, formerly used for carrying water for someone to wash in.

ex¹ /eks/ ▶*prep.* **1** (of goods) sold direct from: *carpet tiles offered at a special price, ex stock.* **2** without; excluding: *the discount and market price are ex dividend.*

ex² ▶*n.* *inf.* a former husband, wife, or partner in a relationship: *I don't want my ex to spoil what I have now.*

ex·ac·er·bate /igˈzasərˌbāt/ ▶*v.* [*tr.*] make (a problem, bad situation, or negative feeling) worse: *the forest fire was exacerbated by the lack of rain.* —**ex·ac·er·ba·tion** /igˌzasərˈbāSHən/ *n.*

ex·act /igˈzakt/ ▶*adj.* not approximated in any way; precise: *the exact details were still being worked out.* ■ accurate or correct in all details: *an exact replica was constructed.* ■ (of a person) tending to be accurate and careful about minor details: *she was an exact, clever manager.* ■ (of a subject of study) permitting precise or absolute measurements as a basis for rigorously testable theories: *psychomedicine isn't an exact science yet.*
▶*v.* [*tr.*] demand and obtain (something, esp. a payment) from someone: *tributes exacted from the Slavic peoples.* ■ inflict (revenge) on someone: *a frustrated woman bent on exacting a cruel revenge for his rejection.* —**ex·act·a·ble** *adj.* —**ex·ac·ti·tude** /-tə,t(y)ōōd/ *n.* —**ex·act·ness** *n.* —**ex·ac·tor** /-tər/ *n.*

ex·act·ing /igˈzaktiNG/ ▶*adj.* making great demands on one's skill, attention, or other resources: *living up to such exacting standards.*

ex·ac·tion /igˈzakSHən/ ▶*n.* *formal* the action of demanding and obtaining something from someone, esp. a payment or service: *he supervised the exaction of tolls at various ports.* ■ a sum of money demanded in such a way. ■ an act of demanding unfair and exorbitant payment; an act of extortion.

ex·act·ly /igˈzak(t)lē/ ▶*adv.* **1** without discrepancy (used to emphasize the accuracy of a figure or description): *fold the second strip of paper in exactly the same way.* **2** in exact terms; without vagueness: *what exactly are you looking for?* **3** used as a reply to confirm or agree with what has just been said: *"You mean that you're going to tell me the truth?" "Exactly."*
▶ □ **not exactly** *inf.* **1** not at all: *that was not exactly convincing.* **2** not quite but close to being: *he was not exactly agitated, but disturbed.*

ex·ag·ger·ate /igˈzajəˌrāt/ ▶*v.* [*tr.*] represent (something) as being larger, greater, better, or worse than it really is: *they were apt to exaggerate any aches and pains.* ▷mid 16th cent.: from Latin *exaggerat-* 'heaped up,' from the verb *exaggerare,* from *ex-* 'thoroughly' + *aggerare* 'heap up' (from *agger* 'heap'). The word originally meant 'pile up, accumulate,' later 'intensify praise or blame,' 'dwell on a virtue or fault,' giving rise to current senses. —**ex·ag·ger·at·ed·ly** *adv.* —**ex·ag·ger·a·tion** *n.* —**ex·ag·ger·a·tive** /-ˌrātiv/ *adj.* —**ex·ag·ger·a·tor** /-ˌrātər/ *n.*

ex·alt /igˈzôlt/ ▶*v.* [*tr.*] hold (someone or something) in very high regard; think or speak very highly of: *to exalt their hero.* ■ raise to a higher rank or a position of greater power: *this naturally exalts the peasant above his brethren in the same rank of society.* ■ make noble in character; dignify: *romanticism liberated the imagination and exalted the emotions.*

ex·al·ta·tion /ˌegzôlˈtāsHən/ ˌeksôl-/ ▶*n.* **1** a feeling or state of extreme happiness: *she beams with exaltation.* **2** the action of elevating someone in rank, power, or character. ■ the action of praising someone or something highly: *the exaltation of the army as a place for brotherhood.*

ex·am /igˈzam/ ▶*n.* **1** short for EXAMINATION (sense 2): *he was likely to fail his exams again* | [as *adj.*] *exam results.* **2** a medical test of a specified kind: *routine eye exams.*

ex·am·i·na·tion /igˌzaməˈnāsHən/ ▶*n.* **1** a detailed inspection or investigation: *an examination of marketing behavior.* ■ the action or process of conducting such an inspection or investigation: *the treaty is under examination by the Senate Foreign Relations Committee.* **2** a formal test of a person's knowledge or proficiency in a particular subject or skill: *he scraped through the examinations at the end of his first year.* **3** *Law* the formal questioning of a defendant or witness in court.

ex·am·ine /igˈzamən/ ▶*v.* [*tr.*] **1** inspect (someone or something) in detail to determine their nature or condition; investigate thoroughly: *this forced us to examine every facet of our business.* **2** test the knowledge or proficiency of (someone) by requiring them to answer questions or perform tasks: *the colleges set standards by examining candidates.* ■ *Law* formally question (a defendant or witness) in court. Compare with CROSS-EXAMINE. —**ex·am·in·a·ble** *adj.* —**ex·am·i·nee** /igˌzaməˈnē/ *n.* —**ex·am·in·er** *n.*

ex·am·ple /igˈzampəl/ ▶*n.* **1** a thing characteristic of its kind or illustrating a general rule: *it's a good example of how European action can produce results.* ■ a printed or written problem or exercise designed to illustrate a rule. **2** a person or thing regarded in terms of their fitness to be imitated or the likelihood of their being imitated: *it is vitally important that parents should set an example.*
▶ □ **for example** used to introduce something chosen as a typical case: *many, like Helen, for example, come from very poor backgrounds.* □ **make an example of** punish as a warning to others.

ex·as·per·ate /igˈzaspəˌrāt/ ▶*v.* [*tr.*] irritate intensely; infuriate: *this futile process exasperates prison officials.* —**ex·as·per·at·ed·ly** *adv.* —**ex·as·per·at·ing·ly** *adv.* —**ex·as·per·a·tion** *n.*

ex ca·the·dra /ˌeks kəˈTHēdrə/ ▶*adv. & adj.* with the full authority of office (esp. of the pope's infallibility as defined in Roman Catholic doctrine): [as *adv.*] *the pope spoke ex cathedra.*

ex·ca·vate /ˈekskəˌvāt/ ▶*v.* [*tr.*] make (a hole or channel) by digging: *the cheapest way of doing this was to excavate a long trench.* ■ dig out material from (the ground): *the ground was largely excavated by hand.* ■ extract (material) from the ground by digging: *a very large amount of gravel would be excavated to form the channel.* —**ex·ca·va·tion** /ˌekskəˈvāsHən/ *n.* —**ex·ca·va·tor** /-ˌvātər/n.

ex·ceed /ikˈsēd/ ▶*v.* [*tr.*] be greater in number or size than (a quantity, number, or other measurable thing): *production costs have exceeded $60,000.* ■ go beyond what is allowed or stipulated by (a set limit, esp. of one's authority): *the Tribunal's decision clearly exceeds its powers under the statute.* ■ be better than; surpass: *catalog sales have exceeded expectations.*

ex·ceed·ing /ikˈsēdiNG/ *archaic or poetic/lit.* ▶*adj.* very great: *she spoke warmly of his exceeding kindness.*
▶*adv.* extremely; exceedingly: *an ale of exceeding poor quality.*

ex·ceed·ing·ly /ikˈsēdiNGlē/ ▶*adv.* **1** extremely: *the team played exceedingly well.* **2** *archaic* to a great extent: *the supply multiplied exceedingly.*

ex·cel /ikˈsel/ ▶*v.* (**ex·celled**, **ex·cel·ling**) [*intr.*] be exceptionally good at or proficient in an activity or subject: *a sturdy youth who excelled at football.*

ex·cel·lence /ˈeksələns/ ▶*n.* the quality of being outstanding or extremely good: *the award for excellence in engineering.* ■ *archaic* an outstanding feature or quality.

ex·cel·len·cy /ˈeksələnsē/ ▶*n.* (*pl.* **-cies**) (**His**, **Your**, etc., **Excellency**) a title given to certain high officials of state, esp. ambassadors, or of the Roman Catholic Church, or used in addressing them: *His Excellency the Indian Consul General.*

ex·cel·lent /ˈeksələnt/ ▶*adj.* extremely good; outstanding: *a 3-bedroom house in excellent condition.*
▶*interj.* used to indicate approval or pleasure: *"What a lovely idea! Excellent!"* —**ex·cel·lent·ly** *adv.*

ex·cept /ikˈsept/ ▶*prep.* not including; other than: *they work every day except Sunday.*
▶*conj.* used before a statement that forms an exception to one just made: *I didn't tell him anything, except that I needed the money.*
▶*v.* [*tr.*] *formal* specify as not included in a category or group; exclude: *he excepted from his criticism a handful of distinguished writers.*

ex·cept·ing /ikˈseptiNG/ ▶*prep. formal* except for; apart from: *excepting some of the dialogue, the book is in every way superior to the movie.*

ex·cep·tion /ikˈsepsHən/ ▶*n.* a person or thing that is excluded from a general statement or does not follow a rule: *the drives between towns are a delight, and the journey to Graz is no exception.*
▶ □ **take exception to** object strongly to; be offended by: *they took exception to his bohemian demeanor.* □ **with the exception of** except; not including. □ **without exception** with no one or nothing excluded.

ex·cep·tion·a·ble /ikˈsepsHənəbəl/ ▶*adj. formal* open to objection; causing disapproval or offense: *his drawings are almost the only exceptionable part of his work.*

ex·cep·tion·al /ikˈsepsHənəl/ ▶*adj.* unusual; not typical: *crimes of exceptional callousness and cruelty.* ■ unusually good; outstanding: *a pepper offering exceptional flavor.* ■ (of a child) mentally or physically disabled so as to require special schooling: *helping parents of exceptional children.* —**ex·cep·tion·al·i·ty** /ikˌsepsHəˈnalitē/ *n.* —**ex·cep·tion·al·ly** *adv.*

ex·cerpt ▶*n.* /ˈek.sərpt/ a short extract from a film, broadcast, or piece of music or writing.
▶*v.* /ikˈsərpt/ [*tr.*] take (a short extract) from a text: *the notes are excerpted from his forthcoming biography.* ■ take an excerpt or excerpts from (a text). —**ex·cerpt·i·ble** *adj.* —**ex·cerp·tion** *n.*

ex·cess /ikˈses; ˈekses/ ▶*n.* **1** an amount of something that is more than necessary, permitted, or desirable: *are you suffering from an excess of stress in your life?* ■ the amount by which one quantity or number exceeds another: *the excess of imports over exports rose $1.4 billion.* **2** lack of moderation in an activity, esp. eating or drinking: *bouts of alcoholic excess.* ■ (**excesses**) outrageous or immoderate behavior: *the worst excesses of the French Revolution.* **3** the action of exceeding a permitted limit: *there is no issue as to excess of jurisdiction.*
▶*adj.* exceeding a prescribed or desirable amount: *trim any excess fat off the meat.*
▶ □ **in** (or **to**) **excess** exceeding the proper amount or degree: *she insisted that he did not drink to excess.* □ **in excess of** more than; exceeding: *a top speed in excess of 20 knots.*

ex·ces·sive /ikˈsesiv/ ▶*adj.* more than is necessary, normal, or desirable; immoderate: *he was drinking excessive amounts of brandy.* —**ex·ces·sive·ly** *adv.* *excessively high taxes.* —**ex·ces·sive·ness** *n.*

ex·change /iksˈCHānj/ ▶*n.* an act of giving one thing and receiving another (esp. of the same type or value) in return: *negotiations should eventually lead to an exchange of land for peace.* ■ a visit or visits in which two people or groups from different countries stay with each other or do each other's jobs: [as *adj.*] *an exchange visit to Germany.* ■ a short conversation; an argument: *there was a heated exchange.* ■ the giving of money for its equivalent in the money of another country. ■ the fee or percentage charged for converting the currency of one country into that of another. ■ a system or market in which commercial transactions involving currency, shares, commodities, etc., can be carried out within or between countries. See also FOREIGN EXCHANGE. ■ a central office or station of operations providing telephone service: *private branch exchanges to automate internal telephone networks.* ■ *Chess* a move or short sequence of moves in which both players capture material of comparable value, or particularly (**the exchange**) in which one captures a rook in return for a knight or bishop (and is said to *win the exchange*). ■ a building or institution used for the trading of a particular commodity or commodities: *the New York Stock Exchange.*
▶*v.* [*tr.*] give something and receive something of the same kind in return: *we exchanged addresses.* ■ give or receive one thing in place of another: *we regret that tickets cannot be exchanged.* —**ex·change·a·bil·i·ty** /iksˌCHānjəˈbilitē/ *n.* —**ex·change·a·ble** *adj.* —**ex·chang·er** *n.*

ex·change rate ▶*n.* (also **rate of exchange**) the value of one currency for the purpose of conversion to another.

ex·cheq·uer /eksˈCHekər; iks-/ ▶*n.* a royal or national treasury.

ex·cise¹ ▶*n.* /ˈek.sīz/ [usu. as *adj.*] a tax levied on certain goods and commodities produced or sold within a country and on licenses granted for certain activities: *excise taxes on cigarettes.*
▶*v.* /ikˈsīz; ek-/ [*tr.*] [usu. as *adj.*] (**excised**) charge excise on (goods): *excised goods.*

ex·cise² /ikˈsīz/ ▶*v.* [*tr.*] cut out surgically: *the precision with which surgeons can excise brain tumors.* ■ remove (a section) from a text or piece of music: *the clauses were excised from the treaty.* —**ex·ci·sion** /-ˈsizHən/ *n.*

ex·cit·a·ble /ikˈsītəbəl/ ▶*adj.* responding rather too readily to something new or stimulating; too easily excited: *Chip could be a bit wayward and excitable.* ■ (of tissue or a cell) responsive to stimulation. —**ex·cit·a·bil·i·ty** /ikˌsītəˈbilitē/ *n.* —**ex·cit·a·bly** /-əblē/ *adv.*

ex·cite /ikˈsīt/ ▶*v.* [*tr.*] **1** cause strong feelings of enthusiasm and eagerness in (someone): *flying still excites me.* ■ arouse (someone) sexually: *his* *kiss thrilled and excited her.* **2** bring out or give rise to (a feeling or reaction): *the ability to excite interest in others.* **3** produce a state of increased energy or activity in (a physical or biological system): *the energy of an electron is sufficient to excite the atom.* —**ex·cit·ed·ly** /ik'sītidlē/ *adv.* —**ex·cite·ment** *n.* —**ex·cit·er** *n.*

ex·cit·ing /ik'sītiNG/ ▶ *adj.* causing great enthusiasm and eagerness: *an exciting breakthrough.* ■ sexually arousing. —**ex·cit·ing·ly** *adv.*

ex·claim /ik'sklām/ ▶ *v.* [*intr.*] often with *direct speech*] cry out suddenly, esp. in surprise, anger, or pain: *"Well, I never," she exclaimed | she looked in the mirror, exclaiming in dismay at her appearance.*

ex·cla·ma·tion /,eksklə'māSHən/ ▶ *n.* a sudden cry or remark, esp. expressing surprise, anger, or pain: *an exclamation of amazement.*

ex·cla·ma·tion point (also **exclamation mark**) ▶ *n.* a punctuation mark (!) indicating an exclamation.

ex·clam·a·to·ry /ik'sklamə,tôrē/ ▶ *adj.* of or relating to a sudden cry or remark, esp. one expressing surprise, anger, or pain.

ex·clude /ik'sklood/ ▶ *v.* [*tr.*] deny (someone) access to or bar (someone) from a place, group, or privilege: *women had been **excluded from** many scientific societies.* ■ keep (something) out of a place: *apply flux to exclude oxygen.* ■ (often **be excluded**) remove from consideration; rule out: *please note software is excluded from this warranty.* ■ prevent the occurrence of; preclude: *clauses seeking to exclude liability for loss or damage.* —**ex·clud·a·ble** *adj.* —**ex·clud·er** *n.*

ex·clu·sion /ik'sklooZHən/ ▶ *n.* the process or state of excluding or being excluded: *drug users are subject to exclusion from the military.* —**ex·clu·sion·ar·y** /-,nerē/ *adj.*

▶ □ **to the exclusion of** so as to exclude something specified: *don't revise a few topics to the exclusion of all others.*

ex·clu·sive /ik'skloosiv/ ▶ *adj.* **1** excluding or not admitting other things: *my exclusive focus is on San Antonio issues.* ■ unable to exist or be true if something else exists or is true: *these approaches are not exclusive; many students will combine them.* ■ (of terms) excluding all but what is specified. **2** restricted or limited to the person, group, or area concerned: *the couple had exclusive possession of the condo.* ■ (of an item or story) not published or broadcast elsewhere: *an exclusive interview.* ■ (of a commodity) not obtainable elsewhere: *exclusive designer jewelry.* **3** catering or available to only a few, select persons; high class and expensive: *an exclusive Georgetown neighborhood.* **4** (**exclusive of**) not including; excepting: *prices are exclusive of tax and delivery.*

▶ *n.* an item or story published or broadcast by only one source. —**ex·clu·sive·ly** *adv.* —**ex·clu·sive·ness** *n.* —**ex·clu·siv·i·ty** /,ekskloo'sivitē/ *n.*

ex·com·mu·ni·cate ▶ *v.* /,ekskə'myooni,kāt/ [*tr.*] officially exclude (someone) from participation in the sacraments and services of the Christian Church.

▶ *n.* /,ekskə'myooni,kit/ an excommunicated person. —**ex·com·mu·ni·ca·tion** /,ekskə,myooni'kāSHən/ *n.* —**ex·com·mu·ni·ca·tive** /-,kātiv/ *adj.* —**ex·com·mu·ni·ca·tor** /-,kātər/ *n.* —**ex·com·mu·ni·ca·to·ry** /-kə,tôrē/ *adj.*

ex·con ▶ *n. inf.* an ex-convict; a former inmate of a prison.

ex·co·ri·ate /ik'skôrē,āt/ ▶ *v.* [*tr.*] **1** *formal* censure or criticize severely: *the papers that had been excoriating him were now lauding him.* **2** *chiefly Med.* damage or remove part of the surface of (the skin). ▷late Middle English: from Latin *excoriat-* 'skinned,' from the verb *excoriare*, from *ex-* 'out, from' + *corium* 'skin, hide.' —**ex·co·ri·a·tion** /ik,skôrē'āSHən/ *n.*

ex·cre·ment /'ekskrəmənt/ ▶ *n.* waste matter discharged from the bowels; feces. —**ex·cre·men·tal** /,ekskrə'men(t)l/ *adj.*

ex·cres·cence /ik'skresəns/ ▶ *n.* a distinct outgrowth on a human or animal body or on a plant, esp. one that is the result of disease or abnormality. ■ an unattractive or superfluous addition or feature: *removing the excrescences of later interpretation.* —**ex·cres·cent** *adj.*

ex·cre·ta /ik'skrētə/ ▶ *n.* [treated as *sing.* or *pl.*] waste matter discharged from the body, esp. feces and urine.

ex·crete /ik'skrēt/ ▶ *v.* [*tr.*] (of a living organism or cell) separate and expel as waste (a substance, esp. a product of metabolism): *excess bicarbonate is excreted by the kidney.* —**ex·cret·er** *n.* —**ex·cre·tion** /-'krēSHən/ *n.* —**ex·cre·tive** /'ekskritiv; ik'skrētiv/ *adj.* —**ex·cre·to·ry** /'ekskri,tôrē/ *adj.*

ex·cru·ci·at·ing /ik'skrooSHē,ātiNG/ ▶ *adj.* intensely painful: *excruciating back pain.* ■ mentally agonizing; very embarrassing, awkward, or tedious: *excruciating boredom.* —**ex·cru·ci·at·ing·ly** *adv. the sting can prove excruciatingly painful.*

ex·cul·pate /'ekskəl,pāt/ ▶ *v.* [*tr.*] *formal* show or declare that (someone) is not guilty of wrongdoing: *the article exculpated the mayor.* —**ex·cul·pa·tion** /,ekskəl'pāSHən/ *n.* —**ex·cul·pa·to·ry** /eks'kəlpə,tôrē/ *adj.*

ex·cur·sion /ik'skərZHən/ ▶ *n.* a short journey or trip, esp. one engaged in as a leisure activity: *an excursion to Mount Etna | fig. an excursion into theology.* ■ [usu. as *adj.*] a trip at reduced rates: *a popular excursion fare for*

travel during the next two weeks. **2** *technical* an instance of the movement of something along a path or through an angle. ■ a deviation from a regular pattern, path, or level of operation. **3** *archaic* a digression. **4** *archaic* a military sortie (see ALARUM). —**ex·cur·sion·ist** /-ist/ *n.*

ex·cuse ▶ *v.* /ik'skyooz/ [*tr.*] **1** attempt to lessen the blame attaching to (a fault or offense); seek to defend or justify: *he did nothing to hide or excuse Jacob's cruelty.* ■ forgive (someone) for a fault or offense: *you must excuse my sister.* ■ overlook or forgive (a fault or offense): *sit down—excuse the mess.* ■ (of a fact or circumstance) serve in mitigation of (a person or act): *his ability excuses most of his faults.* **2** release (someone) from a duty or requirement: *it will not be possible to excuse you from jury duty.* ■ (used in polite formulas) allow (someone) to leave a room or gathering: *now, if you'll excuse us, we have to be getting along.* ■ (**excuse oneself**) say politely that one is leaving. ■ (**be excused**) (used esp. by school pupils) be allowed to leave the room, esp. to go to the bathroom: *please, can I be excused?*

▶ *n.* /ik'skyoos/ **1** a reason or explanation put forward to defend or justify a fault or offense: *there can be no possible **excuse for** any further delay.* ■ a reason put forward to conceal the real reason for an action; a pretext: *they use their hunting as an excuse to get away from their wives.* **2** (**an excuse for**) *inf.* a poor or inadequate example of: *that pathetic excuse for a man!* —**ex·cus·a·ble** /-zəbəl/ *adj.* —**ex·cus·a·bly** /-zəblē/ *adv.* —**ex·cus·a·to·ry** /-zə,tôrē/ *adj.*

▶ □ **excuse me** said politely in various contexts, for example when attempting to get someone's attention, asking someone to move, or interrupting or disagreeing with a speaker. ■ said when asking someone to repeat what they have just said. □ **make one's excuses** say politely that one is leaving or cannot be present.

ex·ec /eg'zek/ ▶ *n. inf.* an executive: *top execs.*

ex·e·cra·ble /'eksikrəbəl/ ▶ *adj.* extremely bad or unpleasant: *execrable cheap wine.* —**ex·e·cra·bly** /-blē/ *adv.*

ex·e·crate /'eksi,krāt/ ▶ *v.* [*tr.*] feel or express great loathing for: *they were execrated as dangerous and corrupt.* —**ex·e·cra·tion** /,eksi'krāSHən/ *n.* —**ex·e·cra·tive** /-,krātiv/ *adj.* —**ex·e·cra·to·ry** /-krə,tôrē/ *adj.*

ex·e·cute /'eksi,kyoot/ ▶ *v.* [*tr.*] **1** carry out or put into effect (a plan, order, or course of action): *the corporation executed a series of financial deals.* ■ perform (an activity or maneuver requiring care or skill): *they had to execute their dance steps with the greatest precision.* ■ *Law* make (a legal instrument) valid by signing or sealing it. ■ *Law* carry out (a judicial sentence, the terms of a will, or other order): *police executed a search warrant.* ■ *Comput.* carry out an instruction or a program. **2** (often **be executed**) carry out a sentence of death on (a legally condemned person): *he was convicted of treason and executed.* ■ kill (someone) as a political act. —**ex·e·cut·a·ble** *adj.*

ex·e·cu·tion /,eksi'kyooSHən/ ▶ *n.* **1** the carrying out or putting into effect of a plan, order, or course of action: *he was fascinated by the entire operation and its execution.* ■ the technique or style with which an artistic work is produced or carried out: *the opera's creative execution.* ■ *Law* the putting into effect of a legal instrument or order. ■ *Comput.* the performance of an instruction or a program. **2** the carrying out of a sentence of death on a condemned person: *the place of execution.* ■ the killing of someone as a political act.

ex·e·cu·tion·er /,eksi'kyooSH(ə)nər/ ▶ *n.* an official who carries out a sentence of death on a legally condemned person.

ex·ec·u·tive /ig'zekyətiv; eg-/ ▶ *adj.* having the power to put plans, actions, or laws into effect: *an executive chairman.* ■ relating to managing an organization or political administration and putting into effect plans, policies, or laws: *the executive branch of government.* Often contrasted with LEGISLATIVE.

▶ *n.* **1** a person with senior managerial responsibility in a business organization. ■ [as *adj.*] suitable or appropriate for a senior business executive: *an executive jet.* ■ an executive committee or other body within an organization: *the union executive.* **2** (**the executive**) the person or branch of a government responsible for putting policies or laws into effect. —**ex·ec·u·tive·ly** *adv.*

ex·ec·u·tor ▶ *n.* **1** /ig'zekyətər/ *Law* a person or institution appointed by a testator to carry out the terms of their will. **2** /'eksə,kyootər/ a person who produces something or puts something into effect: *the makers and executors of policy.* —**ex·ec·u·to·ry** /-,tôrē/ *adj.*

ex·e·ge·sis /,eksi'jēsis/ ▶ *n.* (*pl.* **-ses** /-sēz/) critical explanation or interpretation of a text, esp. of scripture: *the task of biblical exegesis.* —**ex·e·get·ic** /-'jetik/ *adj.* —**ex·e·get·i·cal** /-'jetikəl/ *adj.*

Pronunciation Key ə *ago, up*; ər *over, fur*; a *hat*; ā *ate*; ä *car*; CH *chin*; e *let*; ē *see*; e(ə)r *air*; i *fit*; ī *by*; i(ə)r *ear*; NG *sing*; ō *go*; ô *law, for*; oi *toy*; ŏŏ *good*; ōō *goo*; ou *out*; SH *she*; TH *thin*; ṮH *then*; (h)w *why*; ZH *vision*

ex·em·plar /ig'zemplər; -,plär/ ▶ n. a person or thing serving as a typical example or excellent model: *he became the leading exemplar of conservative philosophy.*

ex·em·pla·ry /ig'zemplərē/ ▶ adj. **1** serving as a desirable model; representing the best of its kind: *an award for exemplary community service.* ▪ characteristic of its kind or illustrating a general rule: *her works are exemplary of certain feminist arguments.* **2** (of a punishment) serving as a warning or deterrent: *exemplary sentencing may discourage the ultraviolent minority.* ▪ *Law* (of damages) exceeding the amount needed for simple compensation. —**ex·em·pla·ri·ly** /-əlē/ *adv.* —**ex·em·pla·ri·ness** *n.* —**ex·em·plar·i·ty** /,egzəm'plaritē/ *n.*

ex·em·pli·fy /ig'zemplə,fī/ ▶ v. (**-fies**, **-fied**) [tr.] be or give an example of: *rock bands that best exemplify the spirit of the age.* ▪ *Law* make an attested copy of (a document) under an official seal. —**ex·em·pli·fi·ca·tion** /ig-,zempləfi'kāSHən/ *n.*

ex·empt /ig'zem(p)t/ ▶ adj. free from an obligation or liability imposed on others: *these patients are exempt from all charges.*
▶ v. [tr.] free (a person or organization) from an obligation or liability imposed on others: *they were exempted from paying the tax.*
▶ n. a person who is exempt from something, esp. the payment of tax. —**ex·emp·tion** *n.*

ex·er·cise /'eksər,sīz/ ▶ n. **1** activity requiring physical effort, carried out esp. to sustain or improve health and fitness: *exercise improves your heart and lung power.* ▪ a task or activity done to practice or test a skill: *there are exercises at the end of each chapter to check comprehension.* ▪ a process or activity carried out for a specific purpose, esp. one concerned with a specified area or skill: *an exercise in public relations.* ▪ (**exercises**) ceremonies: *graduation exercises.* **2** the use or application of a faculty, right, or process: *the free exercise of religion.*
▶ v. [tr.] **1** use or apply (a faculty, right, or process): *anyone receiving a suspect package should exercise extreme caution.* **2** [intr.] engage in physical activity to sustain or improve health and fitness; take exercise: *she still exercised every day.* ▪ exert (part of the body) to promote or improve muscular strength: *raise your knee to exercise the upper leg and hip muscles.* ▪ cause (an animal) to engage in exercise: *she exercised her dogs before breakfast.* **3** occupy the thoughts of; worry or perplex: *the knowledge that a larger margin was possible still exercised him.* —**ex·er·cis·a·ble** /-əbəl/ *adj.*

ex·er·cise ball ▶ n. a lightweight, inflated plastic ball with a diameter of 18–36 inches (45–91 cm), used in various fitness and physiotherapeutic exercises. Also called STABILITY BALL.

ex·ert /ig'zərt/ ▶ v. [tr.] **1** apply or bring to bear (a force, influence, or quality): *the moon exerts a force on the Earth.* **2** (**exert oneself**) make a physical or mental effort: *he needs to exert himself to try to find an answer.* —**ex·er·tion** *n.*

ex·e·unt /'eksēənt; 'eksē,ȯ͝ont/ ▶ v. used as a stage direction in a printed play to indicate that a group of characters leave the stage: *exeunt Hamlet and Polonius.*

ex·fo·li·ate /eks'fōlē,āt/ ▶ v. [intr.] (of a material) come apart or be shed from a surface in scales or layers: *the bark exfoliates in papery flakes.* ▪ [tr.] cause to do this: *salt solutions exfoliate rocks on evaporating.* ▪ [tr.] wash or rub (a part of the body) with a granular substance to remove dead cells from the surface of the skin: *exfoliate your legs to get rid of dead skin.* ▪ [tr.] (often **be exfoliated**) shed (material) in scales or layers. —**ex·fo·li·a·tion** *n.* —**ex·fo·li·a·tive** /-,ātiv/ *adj.* —**ex·fo·li·a·tor** *n.*

ex·ha·la·tion /,eks(h)ə'lāSHən/ ▶ n. the process or action of exhaling. ▪ an expiration of air from the lungs: *he let his breath out in a long exhalation of relief.* ▪ an amount of vapor or fumes given off.

ex·hale /eks'hāl; 'eks,hāl/ ▶ v. breathe out in a deliberate manner: [intr.] *she sat back and exhaled deeply* | [tr.] *he exhaled the smoke toward the ceiling.* ▪ [tr.] give off (vapor or fumes): *the jungle exhaled mists of early morning.* —**ex·hal·a·ble** *adj.*

ex·haust /ig'zôst/ ▶ v. [tr.] **1** drain (someone) of their physical or mental resources; tire out: *her day trip had exhausted her.* **2** use up (resources or reserves) completely: *the country has exhausted its treasury reserves.* ▪ expound on, write about, or explore (a subject or options) so fully that there is nothing further to be said or discovered: *she seemed to have exhausted all permissible topics of conversation.*
▶ n. waste gases or air expelled from an engine, turbine, or other machine in the course of its operation: *buses spewing out black clouds of exhaust* | [as adj.] *exhaust fumes.* ▪ the system through which such gases are expelled: [as adj.] *an exhaust pipe.* —**ex·haust·er** *n.* —**ex·haust·i·bil·i·ty** /ig,zôstə'bilitē/ *n.* —**ex·haust·i·ble** *adj.* —**ex·haust·ing·ly** *adv.*

ex·haus·tion /ig'zôsCHən/ ▶ n. **1** a state of extreme physical or mental fatigue: *he was pale with exhaustion.* **2** the action or state of using something up or of being used up completely: *the rapid exhaustion of fossil fuel*

reserves. ▪ the action of exploring a subject or options so fully that there is nothing further to be said or discovered: *the total exhaustion of viable systematic alternatives.*

ex·haus·tive /ig'zôstiv/ ▶ adj. examining, including, or considering all elements or aspects; fully comprehensive: *she has undergone exhaustive tests since becoming ill.* —**ex·haus·tive·ly** *adv.* —**ex·haus·tive·ness** *n.*

ex·hib·it /ig'zibit/ ▶ v. [tr.] **1** publicly display (a work of art or item of interest) in an art gallery or museum or at a trade fair: *only one sculpture was exhibited in the artist's lifetime.* ▪ [intr.] (of an artist) display one's work to the public in an art gallery or museum: *she was invited to exhibit at several French museums.* ▪ (usu. **be exhibited**) publicly display the work of (an artist) in an art gallery or museum: *no foreign painters were exhibited.* **2** manifest or deliberately display (a quality or a type of behavior): *he could exhibit a saintlike submissiveness.* ▪ show as a sign or symptom: *patients with alcoholic liver disease exhibit many biochemical abnormalities.*
▶ n. an object or collection of objects on public display in an art gallery or museum or at a trade fair: *the museum is rich in exhibits.* ▪ an exhibition: *people flocked to the exhibit in record-breaking numbers.* ▪ *Law* a document or other object produced in a court as evidence.

ex·hi·bi·tion /,eksə'biSHən/ ▶ n. **1** a public display of works of art or other items of interest, held in an art gallery or museum or at a trade fair: *an exhibition of French sculpture.* **2** a display or demonstration of a particular skill: *a supreme exhibition of the farm worker's skills* | [as adj.] *exhibition games.* ▪ an ostentatious or insincere display of a particular quality or emotion: *a false but convincing exhibition of concern for smaller nations.*

ex·hi·bi·tion·ism /,eksə'biSHə,nizəm/ ▶ n. extravagant behavior that is intended to attract attention to oneself. ▪ *Psychiatry* a mental condition characterized by the compulsion to display one's genitals in public. —**ex·hi·bi·tion·ist** *n.* —**ex·hi·bi·tion·is·tic** /-,biSHə'nistik/ *adj.*

ex·hib·i·tor /ig'zibitər/ ▶ n. a person who displays works of art or other items of interest at an exhibition.

ex·hil·a·rate /ig'zilə,rāt/ ▶ v. (usu. **be exhilarated**) make (someone) feel very happy, animated, or elated: *the children were exhilarated by a sense of purpose.* —**ex·hil·a·rat·ing·ly** *adv.* —**ex·hil·a·ra·tion** *n.*

ex·hort /ig'zôrt/ ▶ v. [tr.] strongly encourage or urge (someone) to do something: *the media have been exhorting people to turn out for the demonstration.* ▷late Middle English: from Old French *exhorter* or Latin *exhortari*, from *ex-* 'thoroughly' + *hortari* 'encourage.' —**ex·hor·ta·tion** /,eksər'tāSHən; ,egzər-/ *n.* —**ex·hor·ta·tive** /-tətiv/ *adj.* —**ex·hor·ta·to·ry** /-tə,tôrē/ *adj.* —**ex·hort·er** *n.*

ex·hume /ig'z(y)o͞om; ek's(y)o͞om/ ▶ v. [tr.] dig out (something buried, esp. a corpse) from the ground. —**ex·hu·ma·tion** /,egz(y)o͞o'māSHən; ,eks(h)yo͞o-/ *n.*

ex·i·gen·cy /'eksijənsē; ig'zijənsē/ ▶ n. (pl. **-cies**) an urgent need or demand: *he put financial exigency before personal sentiment.* —**ex·i·gent** /-jənt/ *adj.*

ex·ig·u·ous /ig'zigyo͞oəs; ik'sig-/ ▶ adj. formal very small in size or amount: *my exiguous musical resources.* —**ex·i·gu·i·ty** /,eksi'gyo͝oitē/ *n.* —**ex·ig·u·ous·ly** *adv.* —**ex·ig·u·ous·ness** *n.*

ex·ile /'eg,zīl; 'ek,sīl/ ▶ n. the state of being barred from one's native country, typically for political or punitive reasons: *he knew now that he would die in exile.* ▪ a person who lives away from their native country, either from choice or compulsion: *the return of political exiles.*
▶ v. [tr.] (usu. **be exiled**) expel and bar (someone) from their native country, typically for political or punitive reasons: *he was exiled to Tasmania in 1849.*

ex·ist /ig'zist/ ▶ v. [intr.] **1** have objective reality or being: *there existed no organization to cope with espionage.* ▪ be found, esp. in a particular place or situation: *two conflicting stereotypes of housework exist in popular thinking today.* **2** live, esp. under adverse conditions: *how am I going to exist without you?*

ex·ist·ence /ig'zistəns/ ▶ n. the fact or state of living or having objective reality: *the need to acknowledge the existence of a problem.* ▪ continued survival: *she helped to keep the company alive when its very existence was threatened.* ▪ a way of living: *living in a city was more expensive than a rural existence.* ▪ any of a person's supposed current, future, or past lives on this earth: *reaping the consequences of evil deeds sown in previous existences.*

ex·ist·ent /ig'zistənt/ ▶ adj. formal having reality or existence: *the technique has been existent for some years.*

ex·is·ten·tial /,egzi'stenCHəl/ ▶ adj. of or relating to existence. ▪ *Philos.* concerned with existence, esp. human existence as viewed in the theories of existentialism. —**ex·is·ten·tial·ly** *adv.*

ex·is·ten·tial·ism /,egzi'stenCHə,lizəm/ ▶ n. a philosophical theory or approach that emphasizes the existence of the individual person as a free and responsible agent determining their own development through acts of the will. —**ex·is·ten·tial·ist** *n. & adj.*

ex·it /ˈegzit; ˈeksit/ ▸*n.* **1** a way out, esp. of a public building, room, or passenger vehicle: *a fire exit.* ■ a ramp where traffic can leave a highway, major road, or traffic circle: *he pulled off at an exit.* **2** an act of going out of or leaving a place: *he made a hasty exit from the room.*

▸*v.* (**ex·it·ed, ex·it·ing**) [*intr.*] go out of or leave a place or situation: *they exited from the aircraft* | [*tr.*] *elephants enter and exit the forest on narrow paths.* ■ (of an actor) leave the stage. ■ (**exit**) used as a stage direction in a printed play to indicate that a character leaves the stage: *exit Pamela.* ■ *Comput.* terminate a process or program, usually returning to an earlier or more general level of interaction: *while in multiplayer, pressing ESC will exit the player from the game.* ■ *Bridge* relinquish the lead.

ex·it poll ▸*n.* a poll of people leaving a polling place, asking how they voted.

ex·it vi·sa (also **exit permit**) ▸*n.* a document giving authorization to leave a particular country.

ex·o·crine /ˈeksəˌkrin; ˈeksəˌkrēn/ ▸*adj. Physiol.* relating to or denoting glands that secrete their products through ducts opening onto an epithelium rather than directly into the bloodstream. Often contrasted with ENDOCRINE.

Ex·o·dus /ˈeksədəs/ ▸the second book of the Bible, which recounts the departure of the Israelites from slavery in Egypt, their journey across the Red Sea and through the wilderness led by Moses, and the giving of the Ten Commandments. The events have been variously dated by scholars between about 1580 and 1200 BC.

ex·o·dus /ˈeksədəs/ ▸*n.* a mass departure of people, esp. emigrants. ■ (**the Exodus**) the departure of the Israelites from Egypt.

ex of·fi·ci·o /ˈeks əˈfisHēō/ ▸*adv. & adj.* by virtue of one's position or status: [as *adj.*] *an ex officio member of the committee.*

ex·og·a·my /ekˈsägəmē/ ▸*n. Anthropol.* the custom of marrying outside a community, clan, or tribe. Compare with ENDOGAMY. ■ *Biol.* the fusion of reproductive cells from distantly related or unrelated individuals; outbreeding; cross-pollination. —**ex·og·a·mous** /-məs/ *adj.*

ex·og·e·nous /ekˈsäjənəs/ ▸*adj.* of, relating to, or developing from external factors. Often contrasted with ENDOGENOUS. ■ *Biol.* growing or originating from outside an organism: *an exogenous hormone.* ■ chiefly *Psychiatry* (of a disease, symptom, etc.) caused by an agent or organism outside the body: *exogenous depression.* ■ relating to an external group or society: *exogenous marriage.*

ex·on·er·ate /igˈzänəˌrāt/ ▸*v.* [*tr.*] **1** (esp. of an official body) absolve (someone) from blame for a fault or wrongdoing, esp. after due consideration of the case: *the court-martial exonerated me.* **2** (**exonerate someone from**) release someone from (a duty or obligation). —**ex·on·er·a·tion** *n.* —**ex·on·er·a·tive** /-ˌrātiv/ *adj.*

ex·or·bi·tant /igˈzôrbitənt/ ▸*adj.* (of a price or amount charged) unreasonably high: *the exorbitant price of tickets.* —**ex·or·bi·tance** *n.* —**ex·or·bi·tant·ly** *adv.*

ex·or·cise /ˈeksôrˌsīz; ˈeksər-/ (also **ex·or·cize**) ▸*v.* [*tr.*] drive out or attempt to drive out (an evil spirit) from a person or place: *an attempt to exorcise an unquiet spirit.* ■ (often **be exorcised**) rid (a person or place) of an evil spirit: *infants were exorcised prior to baptism.* ▷late Middle English: from French *exorciser* or ecclesiastical Latin *exorcizare*, from Greek *exorkizein*, from *ex-* 'out' + *horkos* 'oath.' The word originally meant 'conjure up or command (an evil spirit)'; the specific sense of driving out an evil spirit dates from the mid 16th cent. —**ex·or·cism** *n.*

ex·o·skel·e·ton /ˌeksōˈskelitn/ ▸*n. Zool.* a rigid external covering for the body in some invertebrate animals, esp. arthropods, providing both support and protection. Compare with ENDOSKELETON. —**ex·o·skel·e·tal** /ˌeksōˈskelətl/ *adj.*

ex·ot·ic /igˈzätik/ ▸*adj.* originating in or characteristic of a distant foreign country: *exotic birds.* ■ attractive or striking because colorful or out of the ordinary: *an exotic outfit* | [as *n.*] (**the exotic**) *there was a touch of the exotic in her appearance.* ■ of a kind not used for ordinary purposes or not ordinarily encountered: *exotic elementary particles as yet unknown to science.*

▸*n.* an exotic plant or animal: *he planted exotics in the sheltered garden.* ■ a thing that is imported or unusual: *the market in exotics has gone crazy with speculators.* —**ex·ot·i·cal·ly** /-(ə)lē/ *adv.* —**ex·ot·i·cism** /igˈzätəˌsizəm/ *n.*

ex·ot·ic danc·er ▸*n.* a striptease dancer.

ex·pand /ikˈspand/ ▸*v.* become or make larger or more extensive: [*intr.*] *their business expanded into other hotels and properties* | [*tr.*] *baby birds cannot expand and contract their lungs.* ■ [*intr.*] *Physics* (of the universe) undergo a continuous change whereby, according to theory based on observed redshifts, all the galaxies recede from one another. ■ [*intr.*] (**expand on**) give a fuller version or account of: *Anne expanded on the theory.*

—ex·pand·a·ble *adj.* **—ex·pand·er** *n.* **—ex·pan·si·bil·i·ty** /ikˌspansə-ˈbilitē/ *n.* **—ex·pan·si·ble** /-ˈspansəbəl/ *adj.*

ex·panse /ikˈspans/ ▸*n.* an area of something, typically land or sea, presenting a wide continuous surface: *the green expanse of the forest.* ■ the distance to which something expands or can be expanded: *the moth has a wing expanse of 20 to 24 mm.*

ex·pan·sion /ikˈspansHən/ ▸*n.* the action of becoming larger or more extensive: *the rapid expansion of suburban Washington.* ■ extension of a state's territory by encroaching on that of other nations, pursued as a political strategy: *German expansion in the 1930s.* ■ a thing formed by the enlargement, broadening, or development of something: *the book is an expansion of a lecture given last year.* ■ the increase in the volume caused by combustion in the cylinder of an engine, or the piston stroke in which this occurs. —**ex·pan·sion·ar·y** /-SHəˌnerē/ *adj.* —**ex·pan·sion·ism** *n.*

ex·pan·sion card (also **expansion board**) ▸*n. Comput.* a circuit board that can be inserted in a computer to give extra facilities or memory.

ex·pan·sive /ikˈspansiv/ ▸*adj.* **1** covering a wide area in terms of space or scope; extensive or wide-ranging: *deep, expansive canyons.* **2** (of a person or their manner) open, demonstrative, and communicative: *she felt expansive and inclined to talk.* **3** tending toward economic or political expansion: *expansive domestic economic policies.* —**ex·pan·sive·ly** *adv.* —**ex·pan·sive·ness** *n.* —**ex·pan·siv·i·ty** /ˌekspanˈsivitē/ *n.*

ex·pa·ti·ate /ikˈspāsHēˌāt/ ▸*v.* [*intr.*] speak or write at length or in detail: *she expatiated on working-class novelists.* —**ex·pa·ti·a·tion** *n.*

ex·pa·tri·ate ▸*n.* /ˌeksˈpātrēit/ a person who lives outside their native country: *American expatriates in London.*

▸*adj.* /ˌeksˈpātrēit/ (of a person) living outside their native country: *expatriate writers and artists.*

▸*v.* /ˌeksˈpātrēˌāt/ [*intr.*] settle oneself abroad: *candidates should be willing to expatriate.* —**ex·pa·tri·a·tion** /eksˌpātrēˈāSHən/ *n.*

ex·pect /ikˈspekt/ ▸*v.* [*tr.*] regard (something) as likely to happen: *we expect the best.* ■ require (someone) to fulfill an obligation: [*tr.*] *we expect employers to pay a reasonable salary.* ■ (**I expect**) *inf.* used to indicate that one supposes something to be so, but has no firm evidence or knowledge: *they're just friends of his, I expect.* —**ex·pect·a·ble** *adj.*

▸ □ **be expecting (a baby)** *inf.* be pregnant. □ **to be expected** completely normal: *wild swings in the weather are to be expected.*

ex·pect·an·cy /ikˈspektənsē/ ▸*n.* (*pl.* **-cies**) the state of thinking or hoping that something, esp. something pleasant, will happen or be the case: *they waited with an air of expectancy.*

ex·pect·ant /ikˈspektənt/ ▸*adj.* having or showing an excited feeling that something is about to happen, esp. something pleasant and interesting: *an expectant conference crowd.* ■ (of a woman) pregnant: *an expectant mother.* —**ex·pect·ant·ly** *adv.*

ex·pec·ta·tion /ˌekspekˈtāSHən/ ▸*n.* a strong belief that something will happen or be the case in the future: *reality had not lived up to expectations.* ■ a belief that someone will or should achieve something: *students had high expectations for their future.* ■ (**expectations**) *archaic* one's prospects of inheritance.

ex·pec·to·rant /ikˈspektərənt/ ▸*n.* a medicine that promotes the secretion of sputum by the air passages, used esp. to treat coughs.

ex·pec·to·rate /ikˈspektəˌrāt/ ▸*v.* [*intr.*] cough or spit out phlegm from the throat or lungs. ■ [*tr.*] spit out (phlegm) in this way. —**ex·pec·to·ra·tion** /ikˌspektəˈrāSHən/ *n.*

ex·pe·di·ent /ikˈspēdēənt/ ▸*adj.* (of an action) convenient and practical, although possibly improper or immoral: *either side could break the agreement if it were expedient to do so.* ■ (of an action) suitable or appropriate: *holding a public inquiry into the scheme was not expedient.*

▸*n.* a means of attaining an end, esp. one that is convenient but considered improper or immoral: *the current policy is a political expedient.* —**ex·pe·di·ence** *n.* —**ex·pe·di·en·cy** *n.* —**ex·pe·di·ent·ly** *adv.*

ex·pe·dite /ˈekspiˌdīt/ ▸*v.* [*tr.*] make (an action or process) happen sooner or be accomplished more quickly: *he promised to expedite economic reforms.* —**ex·pe·dit·er** (also **ex·pe·di·tor** /-ˌdītər/) *n.*

ex·pe·di·tion /ˌekspəˈdisHən/ ▸*n.* **1** a journey or voyage undertaken by a group of people with a particular purpose, esp. that of exploration, scientific research, or war: *an expedition to the jungles of the Orinoco* | *inf. a shopping expedition.* ■ the people involved in such a journey or voyage: *many of the expedition have passed rigorous courses.* **2** *formal* promptness or speed in doing something: *the landlord shall remedy the defects with all possible expedition.* —**ex·pe·di·tion·ar·y** /-ˈdisHəˌnerē/ *adj.*

Pronunciation Key ə *ago, up*; ər *over, fur*; a *hat*; ā *ate*; ä *car*; CH *chin*; e *let*; ē *see*; e(ə)r *air*; i *fit*; ī *by*; i(ə)r *ear*; NG *sing*; ō *go*; ô *law, for*; oi *toy*; o͞o *good*; o͞o *goo*; ou *out*; SH *she*; TH *thin*; ṯH *then*; (h)w *why*; ZH *vision*

ex·pe·di·tious /ˌekspə'dishəs/ ▸*adj.* done with speed and efficiency: *an expeditious investigation.* —**ex·pe·di·tious·ly** *adv.* —**ex·pe·di·tious·ness** *n.*

ex·pel /ik'spel/ ▸*v.* (**ex·pelled, ex·pel·ling**) [*tr.*] (often **be expelled**) deprive (someone) of membership of or involvement in a school or other organization: *she was expelled from school.* ■ force (someone) to leave a place, esp. a country. ■ force out or eject (something), esp. from the body: *she expelled a shuddering breath.* —**ex·pel·la·ble** *adj.* —**ex·pel·lee** /ˌekspel'lē/ *n.* —**ex·pel·ler** *n.*

ex·pend /ik'spend/ ▸*v.* [*tr.*] spend or use up (a resource such as money, time, or energy): *we do not need to expend energy working on our marriage.*

ex·pend·a·ble /ik'spendəbəl/ ▸*adj.* (of an object) designed to be used only once and then abandoned or destroyed: *the need for unmanned and expendable launch vehicles.* ■ of little significance when compared to an overall purpose, and therefore able to be abandoned: *the region is expendable in the wider context of national politics.* —**ex·pend·a·bil·i·ty** /ik-ˌspendə'bilitē/ *n.* —**ex·pend·a·bly** /-əblē/ *adv.*

ex·pend·i·ture /ik'spendiCHər/ ▸*n.* the action of spending funds: *the expenditure of taxpayers' money.* ■ an amount of money spent: *cuts in public expenditure.*

ex·pense /ik'spens/ ▸*n.* the cost required for something; the money spent on something: *we had ordered suits at great expense.* ■ (**expenses**) the costs incurred in the performance of one's job or a specific task, esp. one undertaken for another person: *his hotel and travel expenses.* ■ a thing on which one is required to spend money: *tolls are a daily expense.*
▸*v.* [*tr.*] (usu. **be expensed**) offset (an item of expenditure) as an expense against taxable income.
▸ □ **at someone's expense** paid for by someone: *the document was printed at the taxpayer's expense.* ■ with someone as the victim, esp. of a joke: *my friends all had a good laugh at my expense.* □ **at the expense of** so as to cause harm to or neglect of: *the pursuit of profit at the expense of the environment.*

ex·pense ac·count ▸*n.* an arrangement under which sums of money spent in the course of business by an employee are later reimbursed by their employer.

ex·pen·sive /ik'spensiv/ ▸*adj.* costing a lot of money: *keeping a horse is expensive.* —**ex·pen·sive·ly** *adv.* —**ex·pen·sive·ness** *n.*

ex·pe·ri·ence /ik'spi(ə)rēəns/ ▸*n.* practical contact with and observation of facts or events: *he had already learned his lesson by painful experience.* ■ the knowledge or skill acquired by such means over a period of time, esp. that gained in a particular profession by someone at work: *candidates with the necessary experience.* ■ an event or occurrence that leaves an impression on someone: *for the younger players it has been a learning experience.*
▸*v.* [*tr.*] encounter or undergo (an event or occurrence): *the company is experiencing difficulties.* ■ feel (an emotion): *an opportunity to experience the excitement of New York.* —**ex·pe·ri·ence·a·ble** *adj.* —**ex·pe·ri·enc·er** *n.*

ex·pe·ri·enced /ik'spi(ə)rēənst/ ▸*adj.* having knowledge or skill in a particular field, esp. a profession or job, gained over a period of time: *an experienced social worker.*

ex·pe·ri·en·tial /ek,spi(ə)rē'enCHəl/ ▸*adj.* involving or based on experience and observation: *the experiential learning associated with employment.* —**ex·pe·ri·en·tial·ly** *adv.*

ex·per·i·ment ▸*n.* /ik'sperəmənt/ a scientific procedure undertaken to make a discovery, test a hypothesis, or demonstrate a known fact: *laboratory experiments on guinea pigs.* ■ a course of action tentatively adopted without being sure of the eventual outcome: *the previous experiment in liberal democracy had ended in disaster.*
▸*v.* /ik'sperə,ment/ [*intr.*] perform a scientific procedure, esp. in a laboratory, to determine something: *she experimented on chickens as well as mice.* ■ try out new concepts or ways of doing things: *the designers experimented with new ideas in lighting.* —**ex·per·i·men·ta·tion** /ik-ˌsperəmən'tāSHən/ *n.* —**ex·per·i·ment·er** *n.*

ex·per·i·men·tal /ik,sperə'men(t)l/ ▸*adj.* (of a new invention or product) based on untested ideas or techniques and not yet established or finalized: *an experimental drug.* ■ (of a work of art or an artistic technique) involving a radically new and innovative style: *experimental music.* ■ of or relating to scientific experiments: *experimental results.* —**ex·per·i·men·tal·ly** *adv.*

ex·pert /'ek,spərt/ ▸*n.* a person who has a comprehensive and authoritative knowledge of or skill in a particular area: *a financial expert.*
▸*adj.* having or involving such knowledge or skill: *an expert witness.* —**ex·pert·ly** *adv.* —**ex·pert·ness** *n.*

ex·per·tise /ˌekspər'tēz; -'tēs/ ▸*n.* expert skill or knowledge in a particular field: *technical expertise.*

ex·pi·ate /'ekspē,āt/ ▸*v.* [*tr.*] atone for (guilt or sin): *their sins must be*

expiated by sacrifice. —**ex·pi·a·ble** /'ekspēəbəl/ *adj.* —**ex·pi·a·tion** /ˌekspē-'āSHən/ *n.* —**ex·pi·a·tor** /-,ātər/ *n.* —**ex·pi·a·to·ry** /'ekspēə,tôrē/ *adj.*

ex·pi·ra·tion /ˌekspə'rāSHən/ ▸*n.* **1** the ending of the fixed period for which a contract is valid: *the expiration of the lease.* ■ the end of a period of time: *the expiration of three years.* **2** *technical* exhalation of breath.

ex·pire /ik'spīr/ ▸*v.* **1** [*intr.*] (of a document, authorization, or agreement) cease to be valid, typically after a fixed period of time: *the old contract had expired.* ■ (of a period of time) come to an end: *the three-year period has expired.* ■ (of a person) die. **2** [*tr.*] exhale (air) from the lung.

ex·plain /ik'splān/ ▸*v.* make (an idea, situation, or problem) clear to someone by describing it in more detail or revealing relevant facts or ideas: *they explained that their lives centered on the religious rituals.* ■ [*tr.*] account for (an action or event) by giving a reason as excuse or justification: *Callie found it necessary to explain her blackened eye* —**ex·plain·a·ble** *adj.*
▸ □ **explain oneself** expand on what one has said in order to make one's meaning clear. ■ give an account of one's motives or conduct in order to excuse or justify oneself: *he was too panicked to stay and explain himself to the policeman.*

ex·pla·na·tion /ˌeksplə'nāSHən/ ▸*n.* a statement or account that makes something clear: *the birth rate is central to any explanation of population trends.* ■ a reason or justification given for an action or belief: *my application was rejected without explanation.*

ex·plan·a·to·ry /ik'splanə,tôrē/ ▸*adj.* serving to explain something: *explanatory notes.* —**ex·plan·a·to·ri·ly** /ik,splanə'tôrəlē/ *adv.*

ex·ple·tive /'eksplitiv/ ▸*n.* an oath or swear word. ■ *Gram.* a word or phrase used to fill out a sentence or a line of verse without adding to the sense.
▸*adj. Gram.* (of a word or phrase) serving to fill out a sentence or line of verse. ▷late Middle English (as an adjective): from late Latin *expletivus*, from *explere* 'fill out,' from *ex-* 'out' + *plere* 'fill.' The general noun sense 'word used merely to fill out a sentence' (early 17th cent.) was applied specifically to an oath or swear word in the early 19th cent.

ex·pli·ca·ble /ek'splikəbəl; 'eksplik-/ ▸*adj.* able to be accounted for or understood: *the English class system is not entirely explicable in terms of money.*

ex·pli·cate /'ekspli,kāt/ ▸*v.* [*tr.*] analyze and develop (an idea or principle) in detail: *attempting to explicate the relationship between crime and economic forces.* ■ analyze (a literary work) in order to reveal its meaning. —**ex·pli·ca·tion** /ˌekspli'kāSHən/ *n.* —**ex·pli·ca·tive** /-,kātiv/ *adj.* —**ex·pli·ca·tor** /-,kātər/ *n.*

ex·plic·it /ik'splisit/ ▸*adj.* stated clearly and in detail, leaving no room for confusion or doubt: *the speaker's intentions were not made explicit.* ■ (of a person) stating something in such a way: *let me be explicit.* ■ describing or representing sexual activity in a graphic fashion: *explicit photos showing poses and acts.* —**ex·plic·it·ly** *adv.* —**ex·plic·it·ness** *n.*

ex·plode /ik'splōd/ ▸*v.* [*intr.*] **1** burst or shatter violently and noisily as a result of rapid combustion, decomposition, excessive internal pressure, or other process, typically scattering fragments widely: *a large bomb exploded in a park.* ■ [*tr.*] cause (a bomb) to do this: *the USSR had not yet exploded its first nuclear weapon.* ■ (of a person) suddenly give expression to violent and uncontainable emotion, esp. anger: *he can explode with anger.* ■ (of a violent emotion or a situation) arise or develop suddenly: *tension that could explode into violence at any time.* ■ increase suddenly or rapidly in size, number, or extent: *the car population of Warsaw has exploded.* ■ [as *adj.*] (**exploded**) (of a diagram or drawing) showing the components of a mechanism as if separated by an explosion but in the normal relative positions: *an exploded diagram of the rifle's parts.* **2** [*tr.*] (often **be exploded**) show (a belief or theory) to be false or unfounded: *the myths that link smoking with glamour need to be exploded.*

ex·ploit ▸*v.* /ik'sploit/ [*tr.*] make full use of and derive benefit from (a resource): *500 companies sprang up to exploit this new technology.* ■ use (a situation or person) in an unfair or selfish way: *the company was exploiting a legal loophole.* ■ benefit unfairly from the work of (someone), typically by overworking or underpaying them: *making money does not always mean exploiting others.*
▸*n.* /'ek,sploit/ a bold or daring feat: *the most heroic and secretive exploits of the war.* —**ex·ploit·a·ble** *adj.* —**ex·ploi·ta·tion** /ˌeksploi'tāSHən/ *n.* —**ex·ploit·a·tive** /ik'sploitətiv/ *adj.* —**ex·ploit·er** /ik'sploitər/ *n.* —**ex·ploit·ive** *adj.*

ex·plo·ra·tion /ˌeksplə'rāSHən/ ▸*n.* the action of traveling in or through an unfamiliar area in order to learn about it: *voyages of exploration.* ■ thorough analysis of a subject or theme: *an exploration of the religious dimensions of our lives.* —**ex·plo·ra·tion·al** /-'rāSHənl/ *adj.*

ex·plor·a·to·ry /ik'splôrə,tôrē/ ▸*adj.* relating to or involving exploration or investigation: *exploratory talks.*

ex·plore /ik'splôr/ ▸*v.* [*tr.*] travel in or through (an unfamiliar country or area) in order to learn about or familiarize oneself with it: *the best way to explore Iceland's northwest.* ■ [*intr.*] (**explore for**) search for resources such as mineral deposits: *the company explored for oil.* ■ inquire into or discuss (a subject or issue) in detail: *he sets out to explore fundamental questions.* ■ examine by touch: *her fingers explored his hair.* ■ *Med.* surgically examine (a wound or body cavity). ▷mid 16th cent. (in the sense 'investigate (why)'): from French *explorer*, from Latin *explorare* 'search out,' from *ex-* 'out' + *plorare* 'utter a cry.' —**ex·plor·a·tive** /-rətiv/ *adj.* —**ex·plor·er** *n.*

ex·plo·sion /ikˈsplōzhən/ ▶*n.* a violent and destructive shattering or blowing apart of something, as is caused by a bomb. ■ a sudden outburst of something such as noise, light, or violent emotion, esp. anger: *an explosion of anger.* ■ a sudden political or social upheaval. ■ a rapid or sudden increase in amount or extent: *an explosion in the adder population.*

ex·plo·sive /ikˈsplōsiv/ ▶*adj.* able or likely to shatter violently or burst apart, as when a bomb explodes: *an explosive device.* ■ likely to cause an eruption of anger or controversy: *the idea was politically explosive.* ■ of or relating to a sudden and dramatic increase in amount or extent: *the explosive growth of personal computers in the 1980s.* ■ (of a vocal sound) produced with a sharp release of air.
▶*n.* (often **explosives**) a substance that can be made to explode, esp. any of those used in bombs or shells. —**ex·plo·sive·ly** *adv.* —**ex·plo·sive·ness** *n.*

ex·po /ˈekspō/ ▶*n.* (*pl.* -**pos**) a large exhibition.

ex·po·nent /ikˈspōnənt; ˈekspōnənt/ ▶*n.* **1** a person who believes in and promotes the truth or benefits of an idea or theory: *an early exponent of the teachings of Thomas Aquinas.* ■ a person who has and demonstrates a particular skill, esp. to a high standard: *he's the world's leading exponent of country rock guitar.* **2** *Math.* a quantity representing the power to which a given number or expression is to be raised, usually expressed as a raised symbol beside the number or expression (e.g., 3 in $2^3 = 2 \times 2 \times 2$).

ex·po·nen·tial /ˌekspəˈnenCHəl/ ▶*adj. Math.* of or expressed by a mathematical exponent: *an exponential curve.* ■ (of an increase) becoming more and more rapid: *the budget was rising at an exponential rate.* —**ex·po·nen·tial·ly** *adv.*

ex·port ▶*v.* /ikˈspôrt; ˈekspôrt/ [*tr.*] send (goods or services) to another country for sale: *we exported $16 million worth of mussels to Japan.* ■ spread or introduce (ideas and beliefs) to another country: *the Greeks exported Hellenic culture around the Mediterranean basin.* ■ *Comput.* transfer (data) in a format that can be used by other programs.
▶*n.* /ˈekˌspôrt/ (usu. **exports**) a commodity, article, or service sold abroad: *wool and mohair were the principal exports.* ■ the selling and sending out of goods or services to other countries: *the export of Western technology.* ■ [as *adj.*] of a high standard suitable for export: *high-grade export coal.* —**ex·port·a·bil·i·ty** /ikˌspôrtəˈbilitē/ *n.* —**ex·port·a·ble** /ikˈspôrtəbəl/ *adj.* —**ex·por·ta·tion** /ˌekspôrˈtāshən/ *n.* —**ex·port·er** *n.*

ex·pose /ikˈspōz/ ▶*v.* [*tr.*] (often **be exposed**) make (something) visible, typically by uncovering it: *at low tide the sands are exposed.* ■ subject (photographic film) to light, esp. when operating a camera. ■ (**expose oneself**) publicly and indecently display one's genitals. ■ leave or put (someone) in an unprotected and vulnerable state: *Miranda felt exposed and lonely.* ■ (**expose someone to**) cause someone to experience or be at risk of: *he exposed himself unnecessarily to gunfire in the war.* ■ make (something embarrassing or damaging) public: *investigations exposed a vast network of illegalities.* ■ (**expose someone to**) introduce (someone) to (a subject or area of knowledge): *students were exposed to probability and statistics in high school.* ■ leave (a child) in the open to die.

ex·po·sé /ˌekspōˈzā/ ▶*n.* a report of the facts about something, esp. a journalistic report that reveals something scandalous: *a shocking exposé of a medical cover-up.*

ex·po·si·tion /ˌekspəˈziSHən/ ▶*n.* **1** a comprehensive description and explanation of an idea or theory: *an exposition and defense of Marx's writings.* ■ *Mus.* the part of a movement, esp. in sonata form, in which the principal themes are first presented. ■ the part of a play or work of fiction in which the background to the main conflict is introduced. **2** a large public exhibition of art or trade goods. ■ *archaic* the action of making public; exposure: *the country squires dreaded the exposition of their rustic conversation.* —**ex·po·si·tion·al** /-zishənl/ *adj.*

ex·pos·i·to·ry /ikˈspäziˌtôrē/ ▶*adj.* intended to explain or describe something: *formal expository prose.*

ex·pos·tu·late /ikˈspäsCHəˌlāt/ ▶*v.* [*intr.*] express strong disapproval or disagreement: *I expostulated with him in vain.* —**ex·pos·tu·la·tion** /ikˌspäsCHəˈlāSHən/ *n.* —**ex·pos·tu·la·tor** /-lātər/ *n.* —**ex·pos·tu·la·to·ry** /ikˌspäsCHələˌtôrē/ *adj.*

ex·po·sure /ikˈspōzhər/ ▶*n.* **1** the state of being exposed to contact with something: *the dangers posed by exposure to asbestos.* ■ an act or instance of being uncovered or unprotected: *thick exposures of ice in the western Arctic islands.* ■ a physical condition resulting from being outside in severe weather conditions without adequate protection: *he died of exposure at 8,000 feet.* ■ experience of something: *his exposure to the banking system.* ■ the action of exposing a photographic film to light or other radiation: *a camera which would give a picture immediately after exposure.* ■ the quantity of light or other radiation reaching a photographic film, as determined by shutter speed and lens aperture. ■ the action of placing oneself at risk of financial losses, e.g., through making loans, granting credit, or underwriting insurance. **2** the publicizing of information or an event: *scientific findings receive regular exposure in the media.* **3** the direction in which a building faces; an outlook: *the exposure is perfect—a gentle slope to the southwest.*

ex·pound /ikˈspound/ ▶*v.* [*tr.*] present and explain (a theory or idea) systematically and in detail: *he was expounding a powerful argument* | [*intr.*] *he declined to expound on his decision.* —**ex·pound·er** *n.*

ex·press[1] /ikˈspres/ ▶*v.* [*tr.*] **1** convey (a thought or feeling) in words or by gestures and conduct: *he expressed complete satisfaction.* ■ (**express oneself**) say what one thinks or means: *with a diplomatic smile, she expressed herself more subtly.* ■ *chiefly Math.* represent (a number, relation, or property) by a figure, symbol, or formula: *constants can be expressed in terms of the Fourier transform.* ■ (usu. **be expressed**) *Genetics* cause (an inherited characteristic or gene) to appear in a phenotype. **2** squeeze out (liquid or air). —**ex·press·er** *n.* —**ex·press·i·ble** *adj.*

ex·press[2] ▶*adj.* operating at high speed: *an express airmail service.* ■ (of a train or other vehicle of public transportation) making few intermediate stops and so reaching its destination quickly: *an express train.* | *an express elevator.* Compare with LOCAL. ■ denoting a company undertaking the transportation of letters and packages, esp. one promising overnight or other rapid delivery: *the nation's biggest express package shipper.* ■ *chiefly Brit.* denoting a service in which messages or goods are delivered by a special messenger to ensure speed or security: *an express letter.*
▶*adv.* by express train or delivery service: *I got my wife to send my gloves express to the hotel.*
▶*n.* **1** an express train or other vehicle of public transportation: *we embarked for the south of France on an overnight express.* **2** an overnight or rapid delivery service: *the books arrived by express.*
▶*v.* [*tr.*] send by express delivery or messenger: *I expressed my clothes to my destination.*

ex·press[3] ▶*adj.* definitely stated, not merely implied: *it was his express wish that the celebration continue.* ■ precisely and specifically identified to the exclusion of anything else: *the schools were founded for the express purpose of teaching deaf children.* —**ex·press·ly** *adv.*

ex·pres·sion /ikˈspreSHən/ ▶*n.* **1** the process of making known one's thoughts or feelings: *she accepted his expressions of sympathy.* ■ the conveying of opinions publicly without interference by the government: *the right to freedom of expression.* ■ the ability to put an emotion into words: *envious beyond expression.* ■ a word or phrase, esp. an idiomatic one, used to convey an idea: *nowhere is the expression "garbage in, garbage out" any truer.* ■ the conveying of feeling in the face or voice, in a work of art, or in the performance of a piece of music: *eyes empty of expression.* ■ *Math.* a collection of symbols that jointly express a quantity: *the expression for the circumference of a circle is $2\pi r$.* ■ *Genetics* the appearance in a phenotype of a characteristic or effect attributed to a particular gene. **2** the production of something, esp. by pressing or squeezing it out: *essential oils obtained by distillation or expression.* —**ex·pres·sion·al** /ekˈspreSHnəl/ *adj.* —**ex·pres·sion·less** *adj.* —**ex·pres·sion·less·ly** *adv.* —**ex·pres·sion·less·ness** *n.*

ex·pres·sion·ism /ikˈspreSHəˌnizəm/ ▶*n.* a style of painting, music, or drama in which the artist or writer seeks to express emotional experience rather than impressions of the external world. —**ex·pres·sion·ist** *n.* & *adj.* —**ex·pres·sion·is·tic** /ikˌspreSHəˈnistik/ *adj.* —**ex·pres·sion·is·ti·cal·ly** /ikˌspreSHəˈnistik(ə)lē/ *adv.*

ex·pres·sive /ikˈspresiv/ ▶*adj.* effectively conveying thought or feeling. ■ (**expressive of**) conveying (the specified quality or idea): *the spires are expressive of religious aspiration.* —**ex·pres·sive·ly** *adv.* —**ex·pres·sive·ness** *n.* —**ex·pres·siv·i·ty** /ˌekspreˈsivitē/ *n.*

ex·press·way /ikˈspresˌwā/ ▶*n.* a highway designed for fast traffic, with controlled entrance and exit, a dividing strip between the traffic in opposite directions, and typically two or more lanes in each direction.

ex·pro·pri·ate /ˌeks'prōprē,āt/ ▶v. [tr.] (esp. of the state) take away (property) from its owner: *government plans to expropriate farmland.* ■ dispossess (someone) of property: *the land reform expropriated the Irish landlords.* —**ex·pro·pri·a·tion** /ˌeks,prōprē'āSHən/ n. —**ex·pro·pri·a·tor** /-,ātər/ n.

ex·pul·sion /ik'spəlSHən/ ▶n. the action of depriving someone of membership in an organization: *expulsion from school.* ■ the process of forcing someone to leave a place, esp. a country: *mass expulsions of Croats during the savage fighting.* ■ the process of forcing something out of the body. —**ex·pul·sive** /ik'spəlsiv/ adj.

ex·punge /ik'spənj/ ▶v. [tr.] erase or remove completely (something unwanted or unpleasant): *the communists had expunged references to the Hitler-Stalin pact.* —**ex·punc·tion** /ik'spəNG(k)SHən/ n. —**ex·punge·ment** n. —**ex·pung·er** n.

ex·pur·gate /'ekspər,gāt/ ▶v. [tr.] remove matter thought to be objectionable or unsuitable from (a book or account): *the expurgated* Arabian Nights. —**ex·pur·ga·tion** /ˌekspər'gāSHən/ n. —**ex·pur·ga·tor** n. —**ex·pur·ga·to·ry** /ik'spərgə,tôrē/ adj.

ex·quis·ite /ek'skwizit; 'ekskwizit/ ▶adj. extremely beautiful and, typically, delicate: *exquisite portraits.* ■ intensely felt: *the most exquisite kind of agony.* ■ highly sensitive or discriminating: *her exquisite taste in painting.* ▷late Middle English (in the sense 'carefully ascertained, precise'): from Latin *exquisit-* 'sought out,' from the verb *exquirere*, from *ex-* 'out' + *quaerere* 'seek.' —**ex·quis·ite·ly** adv. —**ex·quis·ite·ness** n.

ex·tant /'ekstənt; ek'stant/ ▶adj. (esp. of a document) still in existence; surviving: *the original manuscript is no longer extant.*

ex·tem·po·ra·ne·ous /ik,stempə'rānēəs/ ▶adj. spoken or done without preparation: *an extemporaneous speech.* —**ex·tem·po·ra·ne·ous·ly** adv. —**ex·tem·po·ra·ne·ous·ness** n.

ex·tem·po·rar·y /ik'stempə,rerē/ ▶adj. another term for EXTEMPORANEOUS. —**ex·tem·po·rar·i·ly** /ik,stempə'rerəlē/ adv. —**ex·tem·po·rar·i·ness** n.

ex·tem·po·re /ik'stempərē/ ▶adj. & adv. spoken or done without preparation: [as adj.] *extempore public speaking* | [as adv.] *he recited the poem extempore.*

ex·tem·po·rize /ik'stempə,rīz/ ▶v. [intr.] compose, perform, or produce something such as music or a speech without preparation; improvise: *he extemporized at the piano.* —**ex·tem·po·ri·za·tion** /ik,stempəri'zāSHən/ n.

ex·tend /ik'stend/ ▶v. [tr.] **1** cause to cover a larger area; make longer or wider: *the Forest Service plans to extend a gravel road nearly a mile.* ■ expand in scope, effect, or meaning: *we have continued to extend our range of specialist services.* ■ cause to last longer: *high schools may consider extending the class day to seven periods.* ■ postpone (a starting or ending time) beyond the original limit: *he extended the deadline to 4 p.m. today.* ■ straighten or spread out (the body or a limb) at full length: *she is unable to extend her thumb.* ■ [intr.] occupy a specified area or stretch to a specified point: *the mountains extend over the western end of the island* | *a fault that may extend to a depth of 12 miles.* ■ [intr.] (**extend to**) include within one's scope; be applicable to: *her generosity did not extend to all adults.* ■ (**extend oneself**) exert or exercise oneself to the utmost: *you have to extend yourself to change rather than keep on doing the same thing.* **2** hold (something) out toward someone: *I nod and extend my hand.* ■ offer: *she extended an invitation to her to stay.* ■ make (a resource) available to someone: *I can't extend credit indefinitely.* —**ex·tend·a·bil·i·ty** /ik,stendə'bilitē/ n. —**ex·tend·a·ble** adj. —**ex·tend·i·bil·i·ty** /ik,stendə'bilitē/ n. —**ex·tend·i·ble** /-əbəl/ adj. —**ex·ten·si·bil·i·ty** /ik,stensə'bilitē/ n. —**ex·ten·si·ble** /-'stensəbəl/ adj.

ex·tend·ed fam·i·ly ▶n. a family that extends beyond the nuclear family, including grandparents, aunts, uncles, and other relatives, who all live nearby or in one household.

ex·tend·er /ik'stendər/ ▶n. a person or thing that extends something. ■ a substance added to a product such as paint, ink, or glue, to dilute its color or increase its bulk.

ex·ten·sion /ik'stenSHən/ ▶n. **1** a part that is added to something to enlarge or prolong it; a continuation: *the railroad's southern extension.* ■ a room or set of rooms added to an existing building. ■ the action or process of becoming or making something larger: *the extension of the president's powers.* ■ an increase in the length of time given to someone to hold office, complete a project, or fulfill an obligation. ■ Comput. an optional suffix to a file name, typically consisting of a period followed by several characters, indicating the file's content or function. **2** (also **extension cord**) a length of electric cord that permits the use of an appliance at some distance from a fixed socket. ■ an extra telephone on the same line as the main one. **3** [usu. as adj.] instruction by a university or college for students who do not attend full time: *extension courses.* **4** (**extensions**) lengths of real or artificial hair woven into a person's own hair. **5** the action of moving a limb from a bent to a straight position: *seizures with sudden rigid extension of the limbs.* ■ the muscle action controlling this: *triceps extension.* ■ Ballet the ability of a dancer to raise one leg above the waist, or an instance of this. ■ Med. the application of traction to a fractured or dislocated limb or to an injured or diseased spinal column to restore it to its normal position. ■ the lengthening of a horse's stride within a particular gait. —**ex·ten·sion·al** /-SHənl/ adj.

▶ □ **by extension** taking the same line of argument further: *the disclosures raised serious questions about his credibility and, by extension, the credibility of the company.*

ex·ten·sive /ik'stensiv/ ▶adj. **1** covering or affecting a large area: *an extensive garden.* ■ large in amount or scale: *an extensive collection of silver.* **2** (of agriculture) obtaining a relatively small crop from a large area with a minimum of attention and expense: *extensive farming techniques.* —**ex·ten·sive·ly** adv. —**ex·ten·sive·ness** n.

ex·ten·sor /ik'stensər; -sôr/ (also **extensor muscle**) ▶n. Anat. a muscle whose contraction extends or straightens a limb or other part of the body. ■ any of a number of specific muscles in the arm, hand, leg, and foot.

ex·tent /ik'stent/ ▶n. the area covered by something: *an enclosure ten acres in extent.* ■ the degree to which something has spread; the size or scale of something: *the extent of AIDS infection.* ■ the amount to which something is or is believed to be the case: *everyone will have to compromise to some extent.*

ex·ten·u·ate /ik'stenyōō,āt/ ▶v. [tr.] **1** [usu. as adj.] (**extenuating**) make (guilt or an offense) seem less serious or more forgivable: *there were extenuating circumstances that caused me to say the things I did.* **2** [usu. as adj.] (**extenuated**) poetic/lit. make (someone) thin: *drawings of extenuated figures.* —**ex·ten·u·a·tion** /ik,stenyōō'āSHən/ n. —**ex·ten·u·a·to·ry** /-ə,tôrē/ adj.

ex·te·ri·or /ik'sti(ə)rēər/ ▶adj. forming, situated on, or relating to the outside of something: *exterior and interior walls.* ■ coming from outside: *exterior noise.*

▶n. the outer surface or structure of something: *a jar with floral designs on the exterior.* ■ a person's behavior and appearance, often contrasted with their true character: *beneath that assured exterior, she's vulnerable.* ■ (in filming) an outdoor scene.

ex·ter·mi·nate /ik'stərmə,nāt/ ▶v. [tr.] (often **be exterminated**) destroy completely: *leftist ideals had not been totally exterminated.* ■ kill (a pest): *they use poison to exterminate moles.* —**ex·ter·mi·na·tion** /ik,stərmə'nāSHən/ n. —**ex·ter·mi·na·tor** /-,nātər/ n.

ex·ter·nal /ik'stərnl/ ▶adj. **1** belonging to or forming the outer surface or structure of something: *the external walls.* ■ relating to or denoting a medicine or similar substance for use on the outside of the body: *for external application only.* **2** coming or derived from a source outside the subject affected: *for many people the church was a symbol of external authority.* ■ coming from or relating to a foreign country or an outside institution: *responsibility for defense and external affairs.* ■ existing outside the mind: *the child learns to form conceptions of the external world.* ■ Comput. (of hardware) not contained in the main computer; peripheral. ■ Comput. (of storage) using a disk or tape drive rather than the main memory.

▶n. (**externals**) the outward features of something. ■ features which are only superficial; inessentials. —**ex·ter·nal·ly** adv.

ex·ter·nal·ize /ik'stərnə,līz/ ▶v. [tr.] (usu. **be externalized**) give external existence or form to: *elements of the internal construction were externalized onto the facade.* ■ express (a thought or feeling) in words or actions: *an urgent need to externalize the experience.* ■ Psychol. project (a mental image or process) onto a figure outside oneself: *such neuroses are externalized as interpersonal conflicts.* —**ex·ter·nal·i·za·tion** /ik,stərnəli'zāSHən/ n.

ex·tinct /ik'stiNG(k)t/ ▶adj. no longer in existence: *trilobites and dinosaurs are extinct.* ■ (of a volcano) not having erupted in recorded history.

ex·tinc·tion /ik'stiNG(k)SHən/ ▶n. the state or process of being or becoming extinct: *the extinction of the great auk.* ■ the state or process of ceasing or causing something to cease to exist: *the extinction of liberalism.* ■ the wiping out of a debt.

ex·tin·guish /ik'stiNGgwiSH/ ▶v. [tr.] cause (a fire or light) to cease to burn or shine: *firemen were soaking everything to extinguish the blaze.* ■ (often **be extinguished**) put an end to; annihilate: *hope is extinguished little by little.* ■ (often **be extinguished**) cancel (a debt) by full payment: *the debt was absolutely extinguished.* —**ex·tin·guish·a·ble** adj. —**ex·tin·guish·ment** n. (Law).

ex·tir·pate /'ekstər,pāt/ ▸v. [tr.] root out and destroy completely. —**ex·tir·pa·tion** /,ekstər'pāsʜən/ n. —**ex·tir·pa·tor** /-,pātər/ n.

ex·tol /ik'stōl/ ▸v. (**ex·tolled, ex·tol·ling**) [tr.] praise enthusiastically: *he extolled the virtues of the Russian peoples.* —**ex·tol·ler** n. —**ex·tol·ment** n.

ex·tort /ik'stôrt/ ▸v. obtain (something) by force, threats, or other unfair means: *he was convicted of trying to extort $1 million from a developer.* —**ex·tort·er** n. —**ex·tor·tive** /-tiv/ adj.

ex·tor·tion /ik'stôrsʜən/ ▸n. the practice of obtaining something, esp. money, through force or threats. —**ex·tor·tion·er** n. —**ex·tor·tion·ist** /-ist/ n.

ex·tor·tion·ate /ik'stôrsʜənit/ ▸adj. **1** (of a price) much too high; exorbitant: *extortionate ticket prices.* **2** using or given to extortion: *the extortionate power of the unions.* —**ex·tor·tion·ate·ly** adv. *lobster is extortionately expensive here.*

ex·tra /'ekstrə/ ▸adj. added to an existing or usual amount or number: *they offered him an extra thirty-five cents an hour.*
▸adv. **1** to a greater extent than usual; especially: *he is trying to be extra good.* **2** in addition: *installation will cost about $60 extra.*
▸n. an item in addition to what is usual or strictly necessary: *I had an education with all the extras.* ■ an item for which an additional charge is made: *the price you pay includes all major charges—there are no hidden extras.* ■ a person engaged temporarily to fill out a scene in a movie or play, esp. as one of a crowd. ■ *dated* a special issue of a newspaper.

extra- ▸prefix outside; beyond: *extracellular* | *extraterritorial.* ■ beyond the scope of: *extracurricular.*

ex·tract ▸v. /ik'strakt/ [trans.] (often **be extracted**) remove or take out, esp. by effort or force: *the decayed tooth will have to be extracted.* ■ obtain (something such as money or an admission) from someone in the face of initial unwillingness: *I won't let you go without trying to extract a promise from you.* ■ obtain (a substance or resource) from something by a special method: *lead was extracted from the copper.* ■ derive (an idea or the evidence for it) from a body of information: *the desire to extract meaningful lessons from a few experiments.* ■ *Math.* calculate (a root of a number).
▸n. /'ek,strakt/ **1** a short passage taken from a piece of writing, music, or film: *an extract from a historical film.* **2** a preparation containing the active ingredient of a substance in concentrated form: *vanilla extract.* —**ex·tract·a·bil·i·ty** /ik,straktə'bilitē/ n. —**ex·tract·a·ble** adj. —**ex·trac·tor** /ik'straktər/ n.

ex·trac·tion /ik'straksʜən/ ▸n. **1** the action of taking out something, esp. using effort or force: *mineral extraction.* **2** the ethnic origin of someone's family: *a worker of Polish extraction.*

ex·trac·tive /ik'straktiv/ ▸adj. of or involving extraction, esp. the extensive extraction of natural resources without provision for their renewal: *extractive industry.*

ex·tra·cur·ric·u·lar /,ekstrəkə'rikyələr/ ▸adj. (of an activity at a school or college) pursued in addition to the normal course of study: *extracurricular activities include sports, drama, music, chess.* ■ *often humorous* outside the normal routine, esp. that provided by a job or marriage: *Harriet's extracurricular sweetheart.* —**ex·tra·cur·ric·u·lar·ly** adv.

ex·tra·dite /'ekstrə,dīt/ ▸v. [tr.] hand over (a person accused or convicted of a crime) to the jurisdiction of the foreign state in which the crime was committed: *Greece refused to extradite him to Italy.* —**ex·tra·dit·a·ble** adj. —**ex·tra·di·tion** /,ekstrə'disʜən/ n.

ex·tra·mar·i·tal /,ekstrə'maritl/ ▸adj. (esp. of sexual relations) occurring outside marriage: *an extramarital affair.* —**ex·tra·mar·i·tal·ly** adv.

ex·tra·ne·ous /ik'strānēəs/ ▸adj. irrelevant or unrelated to the subject being dealt with. ■ of external origin: *when the transmitter pack is turned off, no extraneous noise is heard.* ■ separate from the object to which it is attached: *other insects attach extraneous objects or material to themselves.* —**ex·tra·ne·ous·ly** adv. —**ex·tra·ne·ous·ness** n.

ex·traor·di·nar·y /ik'strôrdn,erē ; ,ekstrə'ôrdn-/ ▸adj. very unusual or remarkable: *the extraordinary plumage of the male.* ■ unusually great: *young children need extraordinary amounts of attention.* ■ (of a meeting) specially convened: *an extraordinary session of the Congress.* ■ (of an official) additional; specially employed: *his appointment as Ambassador Extraordinary in London.*
▸n. (usu. **extraordinaries**) an item in a company's accounts not arising from its normal activities. —**ex·traor·di·nar·i·ly** /-,erəlē/ adv. —**ex·traor·di·nar·i·ness** n.

ex·trap·o·late /ik'strapə,lāt/ ▸v. [tr.] extend the application of (a method or conclusion, esp. one based on statistics) to an unknown situation by assuming that existing trends will continue or similar methods will be applicable: *the results cannot be extrapolated to other patient groups.* | [intr.] *it is always dangerous to extrapolate from a sample.* ■ estimate or conclude (something) in this way: *attempts to extrapolate likely human cancers from laboratory studies.* ■ *Math.* extend (a graph, curve, or range of values) by inferring unknown values from trends in the known data: [as adj.] (**extrapolated**) *a set of extrapolated values.* —**ex·trap·o·la·tion** n. —**ex·trap·o·la·tive** /-,lātiv/ adj. —**ex·trap·o·la·tor** /-,lātər/ n.

ex·tra·sen·so·ry per·cep·tion /,ekstrə'sensərē/ (abbr.: **ESP**) ▸n. the faculty of perceiving things by means other than the known senses, e.g., by telepathy or clairvoyance.

ex·tra·ter·res·tri·al /,ekstrətə'restrēəl/ ▸adj. of or from outside the earth or its atmosphere: *searches for extraterrestrial intelligence.*
▸n. a hypothetical or fictional being from outer space, esp. an intelligent one.

ex·trav·a·gant /ik'stravəgənt/ ▸adj. lacking restraint in spending money or using resources: *it was rather extravagant to buy both.* ■ costing too much money: *extravagant gifts like computer games.* ■ exceeding what is reasonable or appropriate; absurd: *extravagant claims for its effectiveness.* ▷late Middle English (in the sense 'unusual, abnormal, unsuitable'): from medieval Latin *extravagant-* 'diverging greatly,' from the verb *extravagari,* from Latin *extra-* 'outside' + *vagari* 'wander.' —**ex·trav·a·gance** n. —**ex·trav·a·gant·ly** adv.

ex·trav·a·gan·za /ik,stravə'ganzə/ ▸n. an elaborate and spectacular entertainment or production: *an extravaganza of dance in many forms.*

ex·tra·ve·hic·u·lar /,ekstrəvē'hikyələr/ ▸adj. of or relating to an activity performed in space outside a spacecraft.

ex·treme /ik'strēm/ ▸adj. **1** reaching a high or the highest degree; very great: *extreme cold.* ■ not usual; exceptional: *in extreme cases the soldier may be discharged.* ■ very severe or serious: *expulsion is an extreme sanction.* ■ (of a person or their opinions) advocating severe or drastic measures; far from moderate, esp. politically: *their more extreme socialist supporters.* ■ denoting or relating to a sport performed in a hazardous environment and involving great physical risk, such as parachuting or white-water rafting. **2** furthest from the center or a given point; outermost: *the extreme northwest of Scotland.*
▸n. either of two abstract things that are as different from each other as possible. ■ the highest degree of something: *extremes of temperature.* ■ a very severe or serious act: *he was unwilling to go to the extreme of civil war.* —**ex·treme·ly** adv. —**ex·treme·ness** n.

ex·treme unc·tion ▸n. (in the Roman Catholic Church) a former name for the sacrament of anointing of the sick, esp. when administered to the dying.

ex·trem·ist /ik'strēmist/ ▸n. a person who holds extreme or fanatical political or religious views, esp. one who resorts to or advocates extreme action: *political extremists* | [as adj.] *an extremist conspiracy.* —**ex·trem·ism** /-,mizəm/ n.

ex·trem·i·ty /ik'stremitē/ ▸n. (pl. **-ties**) **1** the furthest point or limit of something: *the peninsula's western extremity.* ■ (**extremities**) the hands and feet: *tingling and numbness in the extremities.* **2** the extreme degree or nature of something: *the extremity of the violence concerns us.* ■ a condition of extreme adversity or difficulty: *the terror of an animal in extremity.*

ex·tri·cate /'ekstri,kāt/ ▸v. [tr.] free (someone or something) from a constraint or difficulty: *he was trying to extricate himself from official duties.* —**ex·tri·ca·ble** /'ekstrikəbəl; ik'strik-/ adj. —**ex·tri·ca·tion** n.

ex·trin·sic /ik'strinzik; -sik/ ▸adj. not part of the essential nature of someone or something; coming or operating from outside: *extrinsic factors that might affect time budgets.* ■ (of a muscle, such as any of the eye muscles) having its origin some distance from the part that it moves. —**ex·trin·si·cal·ly** /-(ə)lē/ adv.

ex·tro·vert /'ekstrə,vərt/ (also **ex·tra·vert**) ▸n. an outgoing, overtly expressive person. ■ *Psychol.* a person predominantly concerned with external things or objective considerations. Compare with **INTROVERT**. —**ex·tro·ver·sion** /,ekstrə'vərzʜən/ n. —**ex·tro·vert·ed** adj.

ex·trude /ik'strōōd/ ▸v. [tr.] (usu. **be extruded**) thrust or force out: *lava was being extruded from the volcano.* ■ shape (a material such as metal or plastic) by forcing it through a die. —**ex·trud·a·ble** adj. —**ex·tru·sile** /ik-'strōōsəl; -,sīl/ adj. —**ex·tru·sion** /ik'strōōzʜən/ n. —**ex·tru·sive** /ik-'strōōsiv/ adj.

ex·u·ber·ant /ig'zōōbərənt/ ▸adj. filled with or characterized by a lively energy and excitement: *giddily exuberant crowds.* ■ growing luxuriantly or profusely: *exuberant foliage.* —**ex·u·ber·ance** n. —**ex·u·ber·ant·ly** adv.

ex·ude /ig'zōōd/ ▸v. [tr.] discharge (moisture or a smell) slowly and steadily: *the beetle exudes a caustic liquid.* ■ [intr.] (of moisture or a smell) be discharged by something in such a way: *slime exudes from the fungus.*

■ *fig.* (of a person) display (an emotion or quality) strongly and openly: *Mr. Thomas exuded friendship and goodwill.* —**ex·u·date** /'eks(y)ə,dāte/ *n.* —**ex·u·da·tion** /,eksyōō'dāsHən; ,eksə-/ *n.* —**ex·u·da·tive** /ig'zōōdətiv; 'eks(y)ə,dātiv/ *adj.*

ex·ult /ig'zəlt/ ▶*v.* [*intr.*] show or feel elation or jubilation, esp. as the result of a success: *exulting in her escape, Annie closed the door behind her.* —**ex·ul·tant** /-'zəltənt/ *adj.* —**ex·ul·ta·tion** /,eksəl'tāsHən; ,egzəl-/ *n.* —**ex·ult·ing·ly** *adv.*

eye /ī/ ▶*n.* **1** each of a pair of globular organs in the head through which people and vertebrate animals see. ■ the corresponding visual or light-detecting organ of many invertebrate animals. ■ used to refer to someone's power of vision and in descriptions of the manner or direction of someone's gaze: *his sharp eyes had missed nothing.* ■ used to refer to someone's opinion or attitude toward something: *in the eyes of his younger colleagues, Mr. Arnett was an eccentric.* **2** a thing resembling an eye in appearance, shape, or relative position, in particular: ■ the small hole in a needle through which the thread is passed. ■ *Naut.* a loop at the end of a rope, esp. one at the top end of a shroud or stay. ■ a rounded eyelike marking on an animal, such as those on the tail of a peacock; an eyespot. ■ a round, dark spot on a potato from which a new shoot can grow. ■ a center cut of meat: *eye of round.* ■ the center of a flower, esp. when distinctively colored. ■ the calm region at the center of a storm or hurricane.

▶*v.* (**eye·ing** or **ey·ing**) [*tr.*] look at or watch closely or with interest: *Rose eyed him warily.* —**eyed** /īd/ *adj.* [in *comb.*] *a brown-eyed girl.* —**eye·less** *adj.*

▶ □ **all eyes** used to convey that a particular person or thing is currently the focus of public interest or attention: *all eyes are on the hot spots of eastern Europe.* □ **close** (or **shut**) **one's eyes to** refuse to notice or acknowledge something unwelcome or unpleasant: *he couldn't close his eyes to the truth—he had cancer.* □ **give someone the eye** *inf.* look at someone in a way that clearly indicates one's sexual interest in them: *this blonde was giving me the eye.* □ **have** (or **keep**) **one's eye on** keep under careful observation. ■ hope or plan to acquire: *the county sheriff has his eye on retirement.* □ **have** (or **with**) **an eye to** have (or having) as one's objective: *with an eye to transatlantic business, he made a deal in New York.* ■ consider (or be considering) prudently; look (or be looking) ahead to: *the charity must have an eye to the future.* □ (**only**) **have eyes for** be (exclusively) interested in or attracted to: *he has eyes for no one but you.* □ **keep an eye** (or **a sharp eye**) **on** keep under careful observation: *dealers are keeping an eye on the currency markets.* □ **keep one's eyes open** be on the alert; watch carefully or vigilantly for something: *visitors should keep their eyes peeled for lions.* □ **lay** (or **set** or **clap**) **eyes on** *inf.* see: *Harry has not laid eyes on Alice for twenty years.* □ **make eyes at someone** look at someone in a way that indicates one's sexual interest. □ **open someone's eyes** enlighten someone about certain realities; cause someone to realize or discover something: *the letter finally opened my eyes to the truth.* □ **see eye to eye** have similar views or attitudes to something; be in full agreement: *Mr. Trumble and I do not always see eye to eye.* □ **with one eye on** giving some but not all one's attention to: *I sat with one eye on the clock, waiting for my turn.*

eye·ball /'ī,bôl/ ▶*n.* the round part of the eye of a vertebrate, within the eyelids and socket.

▶*v.* [*tr.*] *inf.* look or stare at closely: *we eyeballed one another.*

▶ □ **up to the** (or **one's**) **eyeballs** *inf.* used to emphasize the extreme degree of an undesirable situation or condition: *he's up to his eyeballs in debt.*

eye·brow /'ī,brou/ ▶*n.* the strip of hair growing on the ridge above a person's eye socket.

eye con·tact ▶*n.* the act of looking directly into one another's eyes: *make eye contact with your interviewers.*

eye·ful /'ī,fŏŏl/ ▶*n.* *inf.* a long, steady look at something: *they wanted to get an eyeful of Lily.* ■ a visually striking person or thing: *she was quite an eyeful.* ■ a quantity or piece of something thrown or blown into the eye: *an eyeful of fluid.*

eye·glass /'ī,glas/ ▶*n.* a single lens for correcting or assisting defective eyesight, esp. a monocle. ■ (**eyeglasses**) another term for GLASSES.

eye·hole /'ī,hōl/ ▶*n.* a hole to look through, esp. in a curtain or mask. ■ the eye socket. ■ an eyelet.

eye·lash /'ī,lasH/ ▶*n.* each of the short curved hairs growing on the edges of the eyelids, serving to protect the eyes from dust particles.

eye·let /'īlit/ ▶*n.* a small round hole in leather or cloth for threading a lace, string, or rope through. ■ a metal ring used to reinforce such a hole. ■ a fabric pierced with holes in an ornamental pattern.

eye lev·el ▶*n.* the level of the eyes looking straight ahead: *pictures hung at eye level.*

eye·lid /'ī,lid/ ▶*n.* each of the upper and lower folds of skin that cover the eye when closed.

eye·lin·er /'ī,līnər/ ▶*n.* a cosmetic applied to the edges of the eyelids to make the eyes appear larger or more noticeable.

eye·piece /'ī,pēs/ ▶*n.* the lens or group of lenses that is closest to the eye in a microscope, telescope, or other optical instrument.

eye·shade /'ī,sHād/ ▶*n.* a translucent visor used to protect the eyes from strong light.

eye·shad·ow /'ī,sHadō/ ▶*n.* a colored cosmetic, typically in powder form, applied to the eyelids or to the skin around the eyes to accentuate them.

eye·shot /'ī,sHät/ ▶*n.* the distance for which one can see: *he is within eye-shot.*

eye·sight /'ī,sīt/ ▶*n.* a person's ability to see: *poor eyesight ended his plans for a naval career.*

eye·sore /'ī,sôr/ ▶*n.* a thing that is very ugly, esp. a building that disfigures a landscape.

eye·spot /'ī,spät/ ▶*n.* **1** *Zool.* a light-sensitive pigmented spot on the bodies of invertebrate animals such as flatworms, starfishes, and microscopic crustaceans, and also in some unicellular organisms. **2** a rounded eyelike marking on an animal, esp. on the wing of a butterfly or moth.

eye strain ▶*n.* fatigue of the eyes, such as that caused by reading or looking at a computer screen for too long.

eye·stripe /'ī,strīp/ ▶*n.* a stripe on a bird's head that encloses or appears to run through the eye.

eye·tooth /'ī,tŏŏTH/ ▶*n.* (*pl.* **-teeth**) a canine tooth, esp. one in the upper jaw.

eye track·ing (also **eye-track·ing**) ▶*n.* a technology that monitors eye movements as a means of detecting abnormalities or of studying how people interact with text or online documents: *a company that uses eye tracking to evaluate visual products.*

eye·wear /'ī,wer/ ▶*n.* things worn on the eyes, such as spectacles and contact lenses.

eye·wit·ness /'ī'witnəs/ ▶*n.* [often as *adj.*] a person who has personally seen something happen and so can give a first-hand description of it: *eyewitness accounts of the London blitz.*

ey·rie /'e(ə)rē; 'i(ə)rē/ ▶*n.* variant spelling of AERIE.

Ff

F¹ /ef/ (also **f**) ▶ *n.* (*pl.* **Fs** or **F's**) **1** the sixth letter of the alphabet. ■ denoting the next after E in a set of items, categories, etc. ■ the sixth highest or lowest class of academic marks (also used to represent "Fail"). **2** (usu. **F**) *Mus.* the fourth note of the diatonic scale of C major. ■ a key based on a scale with F as its keynote.

F² ▶ *abbr.* ■ Fahrenheit: 60°F. ■ failure. ■ false. ■ farad(s). ■ *Chem.* faraday(s). ■ February. ■ Fellow. ■ female. ■ fighter (in designations of U.S. aircraft types): *the F117 Stealth fighter.* ■ forint. ■ Franc(s). ■ France. ■ French.
▶ *symb.* ■ the chemical element fluorine. ■ *Physics* force: *F = ma.*

f ▶ *abbr.* ■ farad. ■ farthing. ■ father. ■ fathom. ■ feet. ■ *Gram.* feminine. ■ female. ■ [in comb.] (in units of measurement) femto- (10⁻¹⁵). ■ filly. ■ fine. ■ (in textual references) folio. ■ following. ■ foot. ■ form. ■ *Mus.* forte. ■ (in racing results) furlong(s). ■ franc. ■ from. ■ *Chem.* denoting electrons and orbitals possessing three units of angular momentum: *f-orbitals.*
▶ *symb.* ■ focal length: *apertures of f/5.6 to f/11.* See also **F-NUMBER.** ■ *Math.* a function of a specified variable: *the value of f(x).* ■ *Electr.* frequency.

f/ ▶ *abbr. Symbol* f-number.

fa /fä/ ▶ *n. Mus.* (in solmization) the fourth note of a major scale. ■ the note F in the fixed-do system.

FAA ▶ *abbr.* Federal Aviation Administration.

fab /fab/ ▶ *adj. inf.* fabulous; wonderful.

fa·ble /ˈfābəl/ ▶ *n.* a short story, typically with animals as characters, conveying a moral. ■ a story, typically a supernatural one incorporating elements of myth and legend. ■ myth and legend: *monsters of fable.* ■ a false statement or belief.
▶ *v.* [intr.] *archaic* tell fictitious tales. ■ [*tr.*] fabricate or invent (an incident, person, or story). ▷Middle English: from Old French *fable* (noun), from Latin *fabula* 'story,' from *fari* 'speak.' —**fa·bler** /ˈfāb(ə)lər/ *n.*

fab·ric /ˈfabrik/ ▶ *n.* **1** cloth, typically produced by weaving or knitting textile fibers. **2** the walls, floor, and roof of a building. ■ *fig.* the essential structure of anything: *the fabric of society.*

fab·ri·cate /ˈfabrəˌkāt/ ▶ *v.* [*tr.*] invent or concoct (something), typically with deceitful intent: *officers fabricated evidence.* ■ construct or manufacture (something, esp. an industrial product), esp. from prepared components. —**fab·ri·ca·tion** /ˌfabrəˈkāSHən/ *n.* —**fab·ri·ca·tor** *n.*

fab·u·list /ˈfabyəlist/ ▶ *n.* a person who composes or relates fables. ■ a liar, esp. a person who invents elaborate, dishonest stories.

fab·u·lous /ˈfabyələs/ ▶ *adj.* extraordinary, esp. extraordinarily large. ■ *inf.* amazingly good; wonderful: *a fabulous two-week vacation.* ■ having no basis in reality; mythical: *fabulous creatures.* —**fab·u·los·i·ty** *n.* —**fab·u·lous·ly** *adv.* —**fab·u·lous·ness** *n.*

fa·cade /fəˈsäd/ (also **fa·çade**) ▶ *n.* the face of a building, esp. the principal front that looks onto a street or open space. ■ *fig.* an outward appearance maintained to conceal a less pleasant or creditable reality.

face /fās/ ▶ *n.* **1** the front part of a person's head from the forehead to the chin, or the corresponding part in an animal. ■ the face as expressing emotion; an expression shown on the face: *the happy faces of children.* ■ a manifestation or outward aspect of something. ■ a person conveying a particular quality or association: *this season's squad has a lot of old faces.* **2** the surface of a thing, esp. one that is presented to the view or has a particular function, in particular: ■ *Geom.* each of the surfaces of a solid: *the faces of a cube.* ■ a vertical or sloping side of a mountain or cliff. ■ the side of a planet or moon facing the observer. ■ the front of a building. ■ the plate of a clock or watch bearing the digits or hands. ■ the distinctive side of a playing card. ■ the side of a coin showing the head or principal design.
▶ *v.* [*tr.*] **1** be positioned with the face or front toward (someone or something): *he turned to face her.* ■ [*intr.*] have the face or front pointing in a specified direction. ■ [*intr.*] (of a soldier) turn in a particular direction. **2** confront and deal with or accept: *honesty forced her to face facts.* ■ (**face someone/something down**) overcome someone or something by a show of determination: *he faced down hecklers at the rally.* ■ have (a difficult event or situation) in prospect: *each defendant faced a 10-year sentence.* ■ (of a problem or difficult situation) present itself to and require action from (someone): *suddenly faced with an emergency.* **3** (usu. **be faced with**) cover the surface of (a thing) with a layer of a different material: *basement walls faced with granite slabs.*
▶ *phrasal v.* □ **face off** take up an attitude of confrontation, esp. at the start of a fight or game. —**faced** /fāst/ *adj.* [in comb.] red-faced.
▶ □ **face down** with the face or surface turned toward the ground: *he lay face down on his bed.* □ **face the music** be confronted with the unpleasant consequences of one's actions. □ **face up** with the face or surface turned upward to view: *place the panel face up before cutting.* □ **get out of someone's face** [usu. as *imper.*] *inf.* stop harassing or annoying someone: *shut up and get out of my face.* □ **in one's face** directly at or against one; as one approaches: *she slammed the door in my face.* □ **in the face of** when confronted with: *resolution in the face of the enemy.* ■ in spite of: *reform introduced in the face of considerable opposition.* □ **lose face** suffer a loss of respect; be humiliated: *the code of conduct required that he strike back or lose face.* □ **make a face** (or **faces**) produce an expression on one's face that shows dislike, disgust, or some other negative emotion, or that is intended to be amusing. □ **put a good** (or **brave** or **bold**) **face on** something act as if something unpleasant or upsetting is not as bad as it really is: *he tried to put a good face on the financial picture.* □ **save face** retain respect; avoid humiliation: *an outcome that allows them all to save face.* □ **throw something back in someone's face** reject something in a brusque or ungracious manner. □ **to one's face** openly in one's presence: *you're telling me to my face I'm a liar.*

face card ▶ *n.* a playing card that is a king, queen, or jack of a suit.

face·less /ˈfāsləs/ ▶ *adj.* remote and impersonal; anonymous: *the faceless bureaucrats who made the rules.* —**face·less·ness** *n.*

face-lift (also **face·lift**) ▶ *n.* a surgical operation to remove unwanted wrinkles by tightening the skin of the face. ■ *fig.* a procedure carried out to improve the appearance of something.

face-off ▶ *n.* a direct confrontation between two people or groups: *a face-off for the championship title.* ■ *Ice Hockey* the start or a restart of play, in which the referee drops the puck between two opposing players.

face pow·der ▶ *n.* flesh-tinted cosmetic powder used to improve the appearance of the face by reducing shine and concealing blemishes.

face-sav·ing ▶ *adj.* preserving one's reputation, credibility, or dignity: *a face-saving solution for both sides.* —**face-sav·er** *n.*

fac·et /ˈfasət/ ▶ *n.* one side of something many-sided, esp. of a cut gem. ■ a particular aspect or feature of something: *participation by the laity in all facets of church life.* ■ *Zool.* any of the individual units that make up the compound eye of an insect or crustacean. —**fac·et·ed** /ˈfasətid/ *adj.* [in comb.] multifaceted.

fa·ce·tious /fəˈsēSHəs/ ▶ *adj.* treating serious issues with deliberately inappropriate humor. —**fa·ce·tious·ly** *adv.* —**fa·ce·tious·ness** *n.*

face val·ue ▶ *n.* the value printed or depicted on a coin, banknote, postage stamp, ticket, etc. ■ *fig.* the superficial appearance or implication of something: *she felt the lie was unconvincing, but he seemed to take it at face value.*

fa·cial /ˈfāSHəl/ ▶adj. of or affecting the face: *facial expressions.*
▶n. a beauty treatment for the face. —**fa·cial·ly** adv.

fa·ci·es /ˈfā,SHēz; ˈfāSHē,ēz/ ▶n. (pl. same) **1** *Med.* the appearance or facial expression of an individual that is typical of a particular disease or condition. **2** *Geol.* the character of a rock expressed by its formation, composition, and fossil content.

fac·ile /ˈfasəl/ ▶adj. **1** (esp. of a theory or argument) appearing neat and comprehensive only by ignoring complexities; superficial. ■ having a superficial or simplistic knowledge or approach: *a facile and shallow intellect.* **2** easily achieved; effortless: *a facile victory.* ■ acting or done in a quick, fluent, and easy manner: *a facile liar.* ▷late 15th cent. (in the sense 'easily accomplished': from French, or from Latin *facilis* 'easy,' from *facere* 'do, make.' —**fac·ile·ly** adv. —**fac·ile·ness** n.

fa·cil·i·tate /fəˈsili,tāt/ ▶v. [tr.] make (an action or process) easy or easier. —**fa·cil·i·ta·tion** /fə,sili'tāSHən/ n —**fa·cil·i·ta·tive** /-,tātiv/ adj. —**fa·cil·i·ta·tor** /-,tātər/ n.

fa·cil·i·ty /fəˈsilətē/ ▶n. (pl. **-ties**) **1** space or equipment necessary for doing something: *cooking facilities.* ■ an amenity or resource, esp. one connected with leisure or hygiene. ■ (**the facilities**) a public toilet. ■ an establishment set up to fulfill a particular function or provide a particular service, typically an industrial or medical one: *a manufacturing facility.* ■ an option or service that gives the opportunity to do or benefit from something: *the program includes a help facility.* **2** an ability to do or learn something well and easily; a natural aptitude: *a facility for languages.* ■ absence of difficulty or effort: *the pianist played with great facility.*

fac·ing /ˈfāSiNG/ ▶n. **1** a layer of material covering part of a garment and providing contrast, decoration, or strength. **2** an outer layer covering the surface of a wall.
▶adj. positioned with the front toward a certain direction; opposite: *printed on facing pages* | [in comb.] *a south-facing garden.*

fac·sim·i·le /fakˈsiməlē/ ▶n. an exact copy, esp. of written or printed material. ■ another term for **FAX**.
▶v. (**-led, -le·ing**) [tr.] make a copy of: *the ride was facsimiled for Disney World.*

fact /fakt/ ▶n. a thing that is indisputably the case. ■ a piece of information used as evidence or as part of a report or news article. ■ *chiefly Law* the truth about events as opposed to interpretation: *a question of fact as to whether they had received the letter.*
▶ □ **before** (or **after**) **the fact** before (or after) the committing of a crime: *an accessory before the fact.* □ **a fact of life** something that must be accepted as true and unchanging, even if it is unpleasant. □ **facts and figures** precise details. □ **the facts of life** information about sexual functions and practices, esp. as given to children. □ **the fact of the matter** the truth. □ **in** (**point of**) **fact** used to emphasize the truth of an assertion: *Aunt Madeline isn't in fact my aunt but a family friend.*

fac·tion /ˈfakSHən/ ▶n. a small, organized, dissenting group within a larger one, esp. in politics: *the left-wing faction of the party.* ■ conflict within an organization; dissension. —**fac·tion·al** /-SHənl/ adj. —**fac·tion·al·ize** v.

fac·tious /ˈfakSHəs/ ▶adj. relating or inclined to a state of faction: *a factious country.* —**fac·tious·ly** adv. —**fac·tious·ness** n.

fac·ti·tious /fakˈtiSHəs/ ▶adj. artificially created or developed: *a largely factitious national identity.* —**fac·ti·tious·ly** adv. —**fac·ti·tious·ness** n.

fac·toid /ˈfak,toid/ ▶n. a brief or trivial item of news or information. ■ an assumption or speculation that is reported and repeated so often that it becomes accepted as fact.

fac·tor /ˈfaktər/ ▶n. **1** a circumstance, fact, or influence that contributes to a result or outcome: *his legal problems were not a **factor in** his decision* | *she worked fast, conscious of the time factor.* ■ *Biol.* a gene that determines a hereditary characteristic: *the Rhesus factor.* **2** a number or quantity that when multiplied with another produces a given number or expression. ■ *Math.* a number or algebraic expression by which another is exactly divisible. **3** *Physiol.* any of a number of substances in the blood, mostly identified by numerals, which are involved in coagulation. **4** a business agent; a merchant buying and selling on commission. ■ a company that buys a manufacturer's invoices at a discount and takes responsibility for collecting the payments due on them. ■ *archaic* an agent, deputy, or representative. —**fac·tor·ize** v.
▶v. [tr.] *Math.* express (a number or expression) as a product of factors.
▶phrasal v. □ **factor something in** (or **out**) include (or exclude) something as a relevant element when making a calculation or decision: *when the psychological costs are factored in, a different picture will emerge.* —**fac·tor·a·ble** adj.

fac·to·ri·al /fakˈtôrēəl/ ▶n. *Math.* the product of an integer and all the integers below it; e.g., factorial four (4!) is equal to 24. (Symbol: !) ■ the product of a series of factors in an arithmetic progression.

▶adj. chiefly *Math.* relating to a factor or such a product: *a factorial design.* —**fac·to·ri·al·ly** adv.

fac·to·ry /ˈfakt(ə)rē/ ▶n. (pl. **-ries**) **1** a building or group of buildings where goods are manufactured or assembled chiefly by machine. ■ *fig.* a person, group, or institution that produces a great quantity of something on a regular basis or in a short space of time: *a huge factory of lying, slander, and bad English.* **2** *hist.* an establishment for traders carrying on business in a foreign country.

fac·to·tum /fakˈtōtəm/ ▶n. an employee who does all kinds of work: *he was employed as the general factotum.*

fac·tu·al /ˈfakCHōōəl/ ▶adj. concerned with what is actually the case rather than interpretations of or reactions to it: *a mixture of comment and factual information.* ■ actually occurring: *cases mentioned are factual.* —**fac·tu·al·i·ty** /,fakCHōō'alitē/ n. —**fac·tu·al·ly** adv. —**fac·tu·al·ness** n.

fac·ul·ty /ˈfakəltē/ ▶n. (pl. **-ties**) **1** an inherent mental or physical power: *critical faculties.* ■ an aptitude or talent for doing something: *the author's faculty for philosophical analysis.* **2** the teaching staff of a university or college, or of one of its departments or divisions, viewed as a body. ■ a group of university departments concerned with a major division of knowledge: *the Faculty of Arts and Sciences.*

fad /fad/ ▶n. an intense and widely shared enthusiasm for something, esp. one that is short-lived and without basis in the object's qualities; a craze: *the latest gardening fad.* —**fad·dish** adj. —**fad·dish·ly** adv. —**fad·dish·ness** n. —**fad·dism** /-,izəm/ n. —**fad·dist** /-ist/ n.

fade /fād/ ▶v. [intr.] **1** gradually grow faint and disappear: *the noise faded away.* ■ lose or cause to lose color or brightness: [intr.] | [tr.] [usu. as adj.] (**faded**) *faded jeans.* ■ (of a flower) lose freshness and wither. ■ gradually become thin and weak, esp. to the point of death. ■ (of a racehorse, runner, etc.) lose strength or drop back, esp. after a promising start: *she faded near the finish.* ■ (of a radio signal) gradually lose intensity: *the signal faded away.* **2** (with reference to film and television images) come or cause to come gradually into or out of view, or to merge into another shot. ■ (with reference to recorded sound) increase or decrease in volume or merge into another recording. **3** *Golf* (of the ball) deviate to the right (or, for a left-handed golfer, the left), typically as a result of spin given to the ball. ■ [tr.] cause (the ball) to move in such a way.
▶phrasal v. □ **fade back** *Football* move back from the scrimmage line.
▶n. **1** the process of becoming less bright: *the sun can cause color-fade.* ■ an act of causing a film or television picture to darken and disappear gradually: *a fade to black.* **2** *Golf* a shot causing the ball to deviate to the right (or, for a left-handed golfer, the left), usually purposely.

fade-in ▶n. a filmmaking and broadcasting technique whereby an image is made to appear gradually or the volume of sound is gradually increased from zero.

fade-out ▶n. a filmmaking and broadcasting technique whereby an image is made to disappear gradually or the sound volume is gradually decreased to zero. ■ a gradual and temporary loss of a broadcast signal: *radio fade-outs.*

fa·e·rie /ˈferē/ (also **fa·e·ry**) ▶n. *archaic* or *poetic/lit.* fairyland: *the world of faerie.* ■ a fairy. ■ [as adj.] imaginary; mythical: *faerie dragons.*

fag[1] /fag/ ▶n. *inf. chiefly Brit.* a tiring or unwelcome task. ■ *Brit.* a junior pupil at a private school who works and runs errands for a senior pupil.

fag[2] ▶n. *inf., chiefly offens.* a male homosexual. —**fag·gy** adj.

fag[3] ▶n. *Brit., inf.* a cigarette.

fag·got /ˈfagət/ ▶n. **1** *inf., chiefly offens.* a male homosexual. **2** British spelling of **FAGOT**. —**fag·got·y** adj.

fag·ot /ˈfagət/ (*Brit.* **fag·got**) ▶a bundle of sticks or twigs bound together as fuel. ■ a bundle of iron rods bound together for reheating, welding, and hammering into bars.

fag·ot·ing /ˈfagətiNG/ (*Brit.* **fag·got·ing**) ▶n. embroidery in which threads are fastened together in bundles.

Fahr·en·heit /ˈfarən,hīt/ (abbr.: **F**) ▶adj. of or denoting a scale of temperature on which water freezes at 32° and boils at 212° under standard conditions.
▶n. (also **Fahrenheit scale**) this scale of temperature. ▷mid 18th cent.: named after Gabriel Daniel *Fahrenheit* (1686–1736), German physicist.

fa·ience /fīˈäns; fā-/ ▶n. glazed ceramic ware, in particular decorated tin-glazed earthenware.

fail /fāl/ ▶v. [intr.] **1** be unsuccessful in achieving one's goal: *they failed to be ranked in the top ten.* ■ [tr.] be unsuccessful in (an examination, test, or interview): *she failed her finals.* ■ [tr.] (of a person or a commodity) be unable to meet the standards set by (a test of quality or eligibility): *the player has failed a drug test.* ■ [tr.] judge (someone, esp. in an examination

not to have passed. **2** neglect to do something: *failed to give adequate warnings.* ■ behave in a way contrary to hopes or expectations by not doing something: *commuter chaos has again failed to materialize.* ■ (**cannot fail to be/do something**) used to express a strong belief that something must be the case: *you cannot fail to be deeply impressed.* ■ (**never fail to do something**) used to indicate that something invariably happens: *such comments never failed to annoy him.* ■ [*tr.*] desert or let down (someone): *at the last moment her nerve failed her.* **3** break down; cease to work well: *a truck whose brakes had failed.* ■ become weaker or of poorer quality; die away: *the light began to fail.* ■ (esp. of a rain or a crop or supply) be lacking or insufficient when needed or expected. ■ (of a business or a person) become bankrupt.
▶*n.* a grade that is not high enough to pass an examination or test.
▷Middle English: from Old French *faillir* (verb), *faille* (noun), based on Latin *fallere* 'deceive.' An earlier sense of the noun was 'failure to do or perform a duty,' surviving in the phrase *without fail.*
▶ □ **without fail** absolutely predictably; with no exception: *he writes every week without fail.*
failed /fāld/ ▶*adj.* **1** (of an undertaking or a relationship) not achieving its end or not lasting; unsuccessful: *a failed coup attempt.* ■ (of a person) unsuccessful in a particular activity, esp. not good enough to make a living by it: *a failed writer.* **2** (of a mechanism) not functioning properly; broken-down: *an aircraft with a failed engine.*
fail·ing /'fāliNG/ ▶*n.* a weakness, esp. in character; a shortcoming.
▶*prep.* in default of; in the absence of: *she longed to be with him and, failing that, to be on her own.*
fail-safe ▶*adj.* causing a piece of machinery or other mechanism to revert to a safe condition in the event of a breakdown or malfunction. ■ unlikely or unable to fail: *that computer is supposed to be fail-safe.*
▶*n.* a system or plan that comes into operation when something goes wrong or prevents such an occurrence.
fail·ure /'fālyər/ ▶*n.* **1** lack of success: *an economic policy that is doomed to failure.* ■ an unsuccessful person, enterprise, or thing: *crop failures.* ■ lack of success in passing an examination or test. **2** the omission of expected or required action: *their failure to comply with the basic rules.* ■ a lack or deficiency of a desirable quality: *a failure of imagination.* **3** the action or state of not functioning: *symptoms of heart failure.* ■ the collapse of a business.
fain /fān/ *archaic* ▶*adj.* pleased or willing under the circumstances: *the traveler was fain to proceed.* ■ compelled by the circumstances; obliged.
▶*adv.* with pleasure; gladly: *I am weary and would fain get a little rest.*
faint /fānt/ ▶*adj.* **1** (of a sight, smell, or sound) barely perceptible: *the faint murmur of voices.* ■ (of a hope, chance, or possibility) slight; remote: *there is a faint chance that the enemy may flee.* **2** weak and dizzy; close to losing consciousness: *the heat made him feel faint.* ■ appearing feeble or lacking in strength: *the faint beat of a butterfly's wing.*
▶*v.* [*intr.*] lose consciousness for a short time because of a temporarily insufficient supply of oxygen to the brain.
▶*n.* a sudden loss of consciousness: *she hit the floor in a dead faint.* —**faint·ly** *adv.* —**faint·ness** *n.*
▶ □ **not have the faintest** *inf.* have no idea: *I haven't the faintest what it means.*
faint-heart·ed ▶*adj.* lacking courage; timid: *they were feeling faint-hearted at the prospect of war.* —**faint-heart·ed·ly** *adv.* —**faint-heart·ed·ness** *n.*
fair[1] /fe(ə)r/ ▶*adj.* **1** in accordance with the rules or standards; legitimate: *fair and equal representation.* ■ just or appropriate in the circumstances: *to be fair, this subject poses special problems.* ■ *Baseball* (of a batted ball) within the field of play marked by the first and third baselines. **2** (of hair or complexion) light; blond. ■ (of a person) having such a complexion or hair. **3** considerable though not outstanding in size or amount. ■ moderately good though not outstandingly so: *he believes he has a fair chance of success.* **4** (of weather) fine and dry. **5** *archaic* beautiful; attractive: *the fairest of her daughters.*
▶*adv.* **1** without cheating or trying to achieve unjust advantage: *no one could say he played fair.* **2** *dial.* to a high degree: *she'll be fair delighted to see you.* —**fair·ish** *adj.* —**fair·ness** *n.*
▶ □ **fair and square** honestly and straightforwardly: *we won the match fair and square.* □ **a fair deal** equitable treatment. □ **fair enough** *inf.* used to admit that something is reasonable or acceptable: *"I can't come because I'm working late." "Fair enough."* □ **fair-to-middling** slightly above average: *she manages to capitalize on some fair-to-middling material.* □ **the fair sex** *dated* or *humorous* women. □ **in a fair way to do something** *dated* having nearly done something, and likely to achieve it: *he is in a fair way to get well.* □ **no fair** *inf.* unfair (often used in or as a petulant protestation): *no fair—we're the only kids in the whole school who don't get to watch TV on school nights.*

fair[2] ▶*n.* a gathering of stalls and amusements for public entertainment. ■ a competitive exhibition of livestock, agricultural products, and household skills held annually by a town, county, or state and also featuring entertainment and educational displays. ■ an exhibition to promote particular products: *the Contemporary Art Fair.*
fair game ▶*n.* a person or thing that is considered a reasonable target for criticism, exploitation, or attack.
fair·ground /'fer,ground/ (often **fair·grounds**) ▶*n.* an outdoor area where a fair is held.
fair·ly /'ferlē/ ▶*adv.* **1** with justice: *he could not fairly be accused of wasting police time.* **2** to quite a high degree: *I was fairly certain she had nothing to do with the affair.* ■ to an acceptable extent: *I get along fairly well with everybody.*
fair-mind·ed ▶*adj.* impartial in judgment; just: *a fair-minded employer.* —**fair-mind·ed·ly** *adv.* —**fair-mind·ed·ness** *n.*
fair play ▶*n.* respect for the rules or equal treatment of all concerned.
fair·way /'fer,wā/ ▶*n.* **1** the part of a golf course between a tee and the corresponding green, where the grass is kept short. **2** a navigable channel in a river or harbor.
fair-weath·er friend ▶*n.* a person who stops being a friend in times of difficulty.
fair·y /'fe(ə)rē/ ▶*n.* (*pl.* **fair·ies**) **1** a small imaginary being of human form that has magical powers, esp. a female one. **2** *inf.*, *offens.* a male homosexual.
▶*adj.* belonging to, resembling, or associated with fairies: *fairy gold.*
fair·y·land /'ferē,land/ ▶*n.* the imaginary home of fairies. ■ a beautiful or seemingly enchanted place. ■ an imagined ideal place; a utopia.
fair·y tale (also **fairy story**) ▶*n.* a children's story about magical and imaginary beings and lands. ■ [as *adj.*] denoting something regarded as resembling a fairy story in being magical, idealized, or extremely happy: *a fairy-tale romance.*
fait ac·com·pli /'fet əkäm'plē; 'fāt/ ▶*n.* a thing that has already happened or been decided before those affected hear about it, leaving them with no option but to accept.
faith /fāTH/ ▶*n.* **1** complete trust or confidence in someone or something: *this restores one's faith in politicians.* **2** strong belief in God or in the doctrines of a religion. ■ a system of religious belief: *the Christian faith.* ■ a strongly held belief or theory: *the faith that life will expand until it fills the universe.*
faith·ful /'fāTHfəl/ ▶*adj.* **1** loyal, constant, and steadfast: [as *pl. n.*] (**the faithful**) *the struggle to please the party faithful.* ■ (of a spouse or partner) never having a sexual relationship with anyone else:. ■ (of an object) reliable: *my faithful compass.* **2** [usu. as *pl. n.*] (**the faithful**) having a strong belief in a particular religion. **3** true to the facts or the original: *the rugs they make today remain faithful to their ancestors' methods.* —**faith·ful·ness** *n.*
faith·ful·ly /'fāTHfəlē/ ▶*adv.* **1** in a loyal manner. **2** in a manner that is true to the facts or the original: *she translated the novel faithfully.*
faith heal·ing ▶*n.* healing achieved by religious belief and prayer, rather than by medical treatment. —**faith heal·er** *n.*
faith·less /'fāTHlis/ ▶*adj.* **1** disloyal, esp. to a spouse or partner; untrustworthy: *her faithless lover.* **2** without religious faith. —**faith·less·ly** *adv.* —**faith·less·ness** *n.*
fa·ji·ta /fə'hētə/ ▶*n.* a dish of Mexican origin consisting of strips of spiced beef or chicken, chopped vegetables, and grated cheese, wrapped in a soft tortilla and often served with sour cream.
fake /fāk/ ▶*n.* a thing that is not genuine; a forgery or sham. ■ a person who appears or claims to be something that they are not. ■ a pretense or trick: *his excuse for coming was a fake.*
▶*adj.* not genuine; counterfeit: *expressing fake emotions.* ■ (of a person) claiming to be something that one is not: *a fake doctor.*
▶*v.* [*tr.*] forge or counterfeit (something). ■ pretend to feel or suffer from (an emotion or illness): *to fake a stomach ache.* ■ make (an event) appear to happen: *he faked his own death.* ■ accomplish (a task) by improvising: *all the experts agree that you can't fake it* ■ *Mus.* improvise. —**fak·er** *n.* —**fak·er·y** /'fākərē/ *n.*
fa·kir /fə'ki(ə)r; 'fākər/ (also **fa·keer**, **fa·quir**) ▶*n.* a Muslim (or, loosely, a Hindu) religious ascetic who lives solely on alms.
fa·la·fel /fə'läfəl/ (also **fe·la·fel**) ▶*n.* a Middle Eastern dish of spiced mashed chickpeas formed into balls or fritters and deep-fried, usually eaten with or in pita bread.

fal·con /ˈfalkən; ˈfôl-/ ▶n. a diurnal bird of prey (family Falconidae, esp. the genus *Falco*) with long pointed wings and a notched beak, typically catching prey by diving on it from above. Compare with HAWK¹ (sense 1). ■ one of these birds kept and trained to hunt small game for sport. ■ *Falconry* the female of such a bird, esp. a peregrine.

fal·con·er /ˈfalkənər; ˈfôl-/ ▶n. a person who keeps, trains, or hunts with falcons, hawks, or other birds of prey.

fal·con·ry /ˈfalkənrē; ˈfôl-/ ▶n. the sport of hunting with falcons or other birds of prey; the keeping and training of such birds.

fall /fôl/ ▶v. (past **fell** /fel/; past part. **fall·en** /ˈfôlən/) [intr.] **1** move downward, typically rapidly and freely without control, from a higher to a lower level. ■ (**fall off**) become detached accidentally and drop to the ground: *my sunglasses fell off and broke on the pavement.* ■ hang down: *hair that was allowed to fall to the shoulders.* ■ (of land) slope downward; drop away: *the land fell away in a steep bank.* ■ (**fall into**) (of a river) flow or discharge itself into. ■ [intr.] (of someone's face) show dismay or disappointment by appearing to sag or droop: *her face fell as she thought about her life with George.* ■ *fig.* occur, arrive, or become apparent as if by dropping suddenly: *when night fell we managed to crawl back to our lines | the information might fall into the wrong hands.* **2** (of a person) lose one's balance and collapse: *she fell down at school today.* ■ throw oneself down, typically in order to worship or implore someone: *they fell on their knees.* ■ (of a tree, building, or other structure) collapse to the ground: *the house looked as if it were going to fall down at any moment.* ■ die in battle: *an English leader who had fallen at the hands of the Danes.* **3** decrease in number, amount, intensity, or quality: *we're worried that standards are falling.* ■ find a lower level; subside or abate: *the water table in the Rift Valley fell.* ■ (of a measuring instrument) show a lower reading: *the barometer had fallen ten points.* **4** pass into a specified state: *many of the buildings fell into disrepair.* ■ be drawn accidentally into: *you must not fall into this common error.* ■ occur at a specified time: *Mother's birthday fell on Flag Day.* ■ be classified or ordered in the way specified: *canals fall within the Minister's brief.*
▶*phrasal v.* □ **fall apart** (or **to pieces**) break up, come apart, or disintegrate: *their marriage is likely to fall apart.* ■ (of a person) lose one's capacity to cope: *Angie fell to pieces because she had lost everything.* □ **fall back** move or turn back; retreat. □ **fall back on** have recourse to when in difficulty: *they normally fell back on one of three arguments.* □ **fall behind** fail to keep up with one's competitors. ■ fail to meet a commitment to make a regular payment: *borrowers falling behind with their mortgage payments.* □ **fall down** be shown to be inadequate or false; fail: *the deal fell down partly because there were a lot of unanswered questions.* □ **fall for** inf. **1** be captivated by; fall in love with. **2** be deceived by (something): *he should have known better than to expect Duncan to fall for a cheap trick like that.* □ **fall in with 1** meet by chance and become involved with: *he fell in with thieves.* **2** act in accordance with (someone's ideas or suggestions); agree to: *falling in with other people's views.* □ **fall on** (or **upon**) **1** attack fiercely or unexpectedly: *the army fell on the besiegers.* ■ seize enthusiastically: *she fell on the sandwiches as though she had not eaten in weeks.* **2** (of someone's eyes or gaze) be directed toward: *her gaze fell on the mud-stained coverlet.* **3** (of a burden or duty) be borne or incurred by: *the cost of tuition should not fall on the student.* □ **fall out 1** (of the hair, teeth, etc.) become detached and drop out. **2** have an argument: *he had fallen out with his family.* **3** happen; turn out: *matters fell out as Stephen arranged.* □ **fall through** come to nothing; fail: *the project fell through due to lack of money.* □ **fall to** (of a task) become the duty or responsibility of: *it fell to me to write to Shephard.* ■ (of property) revert to the ownership of.
▶n. **1** an act of falling or collapsing; a sudden uncontrollable descent: *his mother had a fall.* ■ a state of hanging or drooping downward: *the fall of her hair.* ■ a downward difference in height between parts of a surface. ■ a sudden onset or arrival as if by dropping: *the fall of darkness.* **2** a thing that falls or has fallen: *in October came the first thin fall of snow | a rock fall.* ■ (usu. **falls**) a waterfall or cascade. **3** a decrease in size, number, rate, or level; a decline: *a big fall in unemployment.* **4** a loss of office: *the fall of the government.* ■ the loss of a city or fortified place during battle: *the fall of Jerusalem.* ■ a person's moral descent, typically through succumbing to temptation. **5** (also **Fall**) autumn.
▶ □ **fall in** (or **into**) **line** conform with others or with accepted behavior. □ **fall into place** (of a series of events or facts) begin to make sense or cohere: *once he knew what to look for, the theory fell quickly into place.* □ **fall short** (**of**) (of a missile) fail to reach its target. ■ *fig.* be deficient or inadequate; fail to reach a required goal: *the total vote fell short of the required two-thirds majority.*

fal·la·cy /ˈfaləsē/ ▶n. (pl. **-cies**) a mistaken belief, esp. one based on unsound argument. ■ *Logic* a failure in reasoning that renders an

argument invalid. ■ faulty reasoning; misleading or unsound argument: *the potential for fallacy which lies behind the notion of self-esteem.* —**fal·la·cious** /fəˈlāsHəs/ adj. —**fal·la·cious·ness** /fəˈlāsHəsnəs/ n.

fall·back /ˈfôlˌbak/ ▶n. **1** an alternative plan that may be used in an emergency: *teaching was a last resort, a fallback.* **2** a reduction or retreat.

fall·en /ˈfôlən/ ▶ past participle of FALL.
▶adj. **1** *Theol.* subject to sin or depravity: *fallen human nature.* ■ *dated* (of a woman) regarded as having lost her honor through engaging in a sexual relationship outside marriage: *a fallen woman with a checkered past.* **2** (of a soldier) killed in battle: *fallen heroes.*

fall guy ▶n. inf. a scapegoat: *he contends that he was set up as a fall guy.*

fal·li·ble /ˈfaləbəl/ ▶adj. capable of making mistakes or being erroneous: *experts say the fallible.* —**fal·li·bil·i·ty** /ˌfaləˈbilətē/ n. —**fal·li·bly** /-blē/ adv.

falling star ▶n. a meteor or shooting star.

fal·lo·pi·an tube /fəˈlōpēən/ (also **Fal·lo·pi·an**) ▶n. *Anat.* (in a female mammal) either of a pair of tubes along which eggs travel from the ovaries to the uterus.

fall·out /ˈfôlˌout/ ▶n. radioactive particles that are carried into the atmosphere after a nuclear explosion or accident and gradually fall back as dust or in precipitation. ■ *fig.* the adverse side effects or results of a situation: *the growing political fallout.*

fal·low¹ /ˈfalō/ ▶adj. (of farmland) plowed and harrowed but left unsown for a period in order to restore its fertility as part of a crop rotation or to avoid surplus production: *incentives for farmers to let the land lie fallow in order to reduce grain surpluses.* ■ *fig.* inactive: *long fallow periods.* ■ (of a sow) not pregnant.
▶v. [tr.] leave (land) fallow. —**fal·low·ness** n.

fal·low² ▶n. a pale brown or reddish yellow color.

false /fôls/ ▶adj. **1** not according to truth or fact; incorrect: *false results | the allegations were false.* ■ not according to rules or law: *false imprisonment.* **2** deliberately made or meant to deceive: *the trunk has a false bottom | a false passport.* ■ artificial: *false eyelashes.* ■ feigned: *a horribly false smile.* **3** illusory; not actually so: *sunscreens give users a false sense of security.* **4** treacherous; unfaithful: *a false lover.* —**false·ly** adv. —**false·ness** n. —**fal·si·ty** /ˈfôlsətē/ n.

false·hood /ˈfôlsˌho͝od/ ▶n. the state of being untrue: *the truth or falsehood of the many legends that surround her.* ■ a lie.

fal·set·to /fôlˈsetō/ ▶n. (pl. **-tos**) *Mus.* a method of voice production used by male singers, esp. tenors, to sing notes higher than their normal range: *he sang in a piercing falsetto.* ■ a voice or sound that is unusually or unnaturally high.

fals·ies /ˈfôlsēz/ ▶pl. n. inf. pads of material in women's clothing used to increase the apparent size of the breasts.

fal·si·fy /ˈfôlsəˌfī/ ▶v. (**-fies, -fied**) [tr.] **1** alter (information or evidence) so as to mislead. ■ forge or alter (a document) fraudulently. **2** prove (a statement or theory) to be false: *the hypothesis is falsified by the evidence.* ■ fail to fulfill (a hope, fear, or expectation): *changes falsify individual expectations.* —**fal·si·fi·a·bil·i·ty** /ˌfôlsəˌfīəˈbilətē/ n. —**fal·si·fi·a·ble** /ˌfôlsəˈfīəbəl/ adj. —**fal·si·fi·ca·tion** /ˌfôlsəfəˈkāsHən/ n.

fal·ter /ˈfôltər/ ▶v. [intr.] start to lose strength or momentum: [as adj.] (**faltering**) *his faltering career.* ■ speak in a hesitant or unsteady voice. ■ move unsteadily or in a way that shows lack of confidence: *he faltered and finally stopped.* —**fal·ter·ing·ly** adv.

fame /fām/ ▶n. **1** the condition of being known or talked about by many people, esp. on account of notable achievements: *the Olympic title brought her fame and fortune.* **2** archaic reputation. **3** archaic public report; rumor. ▷Middle English (also in the sense 'reputation,' which survives in the phrase *house of ill fame*): via Old French from Latin *fama.*

famed /fāmd/ ▶adj. known about by many people; renowned: *he is famed for his eccentricities.* ■ archaic widely reported or rumored.

fa·mil·ial /fəˈmilēəl; -ˈmilyəl/ ▶adj. of, relating to, or occurring in a family or its members: *the familial Christmas dinner.*

fa·mil·iar /fəˈmilyər/ ▶adj. **1** well known from long or close association: *a familiar voice.* ■ often encountered or experienced; common: *the situation was all too familiar.* ■ (**familiar with**) having a good knowledge of: *be sure that you are familiar with the controls.* **2** in close friendship; intimate: *she hadn't realized they were on such familiar terms.* ■ informal to an inappropriate degree.
▶n. **1** (also **familiar spirit**) a demon supposedly attending and obeying a witch, often said to assume the form of an animal. **2** a close friend or associate. —**fa·mil·iar·ly** adv.

fa·mil·iar·i·ty /fəˌmilēˈaritē; -milˈyar-/ ▶n. (pl. **-ties**) close acquaintance with or knowledge of something. ■ the quality of being well known; recognizability based on long or close association: *the reassuring familiarity of his parents' home.* ■ relaxed friendliness or intimacy between people. ■ inappropriate and often offensive informality of behavior or language: *the unnecessary familiarity made me dislike him at once.*

fa·mil·iar·ize /fə'milyə,rīz/ ▶*v.* [*tr.*] give (someone) knowledge or understanding of something: *to familiarize students with the microscope and its uses.* ■ make (something) better known or more easily grasped: *exercises which will help to familiarize the terms used.* —**fa·mil·iar·i·za·tion** *n.*

fam·i·ly /'fam(ə)lē/ ▶*n.* (*pl.* **-lies**) **1** [treated as *sing.* or *pl.*] a group consisting of parents and children living together in a household. ■ a group of people related to one another by blood or marriage: *friends and family can provide support.* ■ the children of a person or couple: *she has the sole responsibility for a large family.* ■ a group of people united by an activity or affiliation. ■ *Biol.* a principal taxonomic category that ranks above genus and below order, usually ending in *-idae* (in zoology) or *-aceae* (in botany). ■ a group of objects united by a significant shared characteristic. **2** all the descendants of a common ancestor. ■ a race or group of peoples from a common stock. ■ all the languages ultimately derived from a particular early language, regarded as a group: *the Austronesian language family.*
▶*adj.* designed to be suitable for children as well as adults: *a family newspaper.*
▶ □ **in the family way** *inf.* pregnant.

fam·i·ly plan·ning ▶*n.* [often as *adj.*] the practice of controlling the number of children in a family and the intervals between their births, particularly by means of artificial contraception or voluntary sterilization: *family-planning clinics.* ■ artificial contraception.

fam·i·ly tree ▶*n.* a diagram showing the relationships between people in several generations of a family; a genealogical tree. ■ all of the descendants and ancestors in a family.

fam·ine /'famən/ ▶*n.* extreme scarcity of food. *the famine of 1921–22.* ■ a shortage: *the cotton famine of the 1860s.* ■ *archaic* hunger.

fam·ished /'famiSHt/ ▶*adj.* *inf.* extremely hungry.

fa·mous /'fāməs/ ▶*adj.* known about by many people: *the country is famous for its natural beauty | a famous star.*

fa·mous·ly /'fāməslē/ ▶*adv.* **1** *inf.* excellently: *he wasn't difficult at all—we got on famously.* **2** indicating that the fact asserted is widely known: *they have famously reclusive lifestyles.*

Fan /fan/ /fän/ ▶*n.* & *adj.* variant spelling of **FANG**.

fan[1] /fan/ ▶*n.* **1** an apparatus with rotating blades that creates a current of air for cooling or ventilation. **2** a device, typically folding and shaped like a segment of a circle when spread out, that is held in the hand and waved so as to cool the person holding it by causing the air to move. ■ a thing or shape resembling such a device when open. **3** a device for winnowing grain.
▶*v.* (**fanned**, **fan·ning**) **1** [*tr.*] cool (esp. a person or a part of the body) by waving something to create a current of air: *he fanned himself with his hat.* ■ (of breath or a breeze) blow gently on. ■ [*tr.*] brush or drive away with a waving movement: *a veil of smoke which she fanned away with a jeweled hand.* ■ [*intr.*] *Baseball & Ice Hockey* swing at and miss the ball or puck. ■ [*intr.*] *Baseball* (of a batter) strike out. ■ *Baseball* (of a pitcher) strike out (a batter). **2** [*tr.*] increase the strength of (a fire) by blowing on it or stirring up the air near it: *gusty wind fanned fires in Yellowstone Park.* ■ cause (a belief or emotion) to become stronger or more widespread: *long-range weather forecasts fanned fears of drought damage.* **3** [*intr.*] disperse or radiate from a central point to cover a wide area: *the arriving passengers began to fan out through the town in search of lodgings.* ■ spread out or cause to spread out into a semicircular shape.

fan[2] ▶*n.* a person who has a strong interest in or admiration for a particular sport, art form, or famous person: *football fans.* —**fan·dom** *n.*

fa·nat·ic /fə'natik/ ▶*n.* a person filled with excessive and single-minded zeal, esp. for an extreme cause. ■ *inf.* a person with an obsessive interest in and enthusiasm for something, esp. an activity: *a fitness fanatic.*
▶*adj.* filled with or expressing excessive zeal: *his fanatic energy.* —**fa·nat·i·cal** *adj.* —**fa·nat·i·cism** /fə'natə,sizəm/ *n.*

fan belt ▶*n.* (in a motor-vehicle engine) a belt that transmits motion from the driveshaft to the radiator fan and the generator or alternator.

fan·ci·er /'fansēər/ ▶*n.* a connoisseur or enthusiast of something, esp. someone who has a special interest in or breeds a particular animal: *a pigeon fancier.*

fan·ci·ful /'fansəfəl/ ▶*adj.* (of a person or their thoughts and ideas) overimaginative and unrealistic: *a fanciful story about a pot of gold.* ■ existing only in the imagination or fancy: *designed to be exotically ornamental rather than practical: fanciful bonnets.* —**fan·ci·ful·ly** /-f(ə)lē/ *adv.* —**fan·ci·ful·ness** *n.*

fan·cy /'fansē/ ▶*adj.* (**-ci·er**, **-ci·est**) elaborate in structure or decoration: *a fancy computerized system.* ■ designed to impress: *converted fishing boats*

with fancy new names. ■ (esp. of foodstuffs) of high quality: *fancy molasses.* ■ (of flowers) of two or more colors. ■ (of an animal) bred to develop particular points of appearance: *fancy goldfish.*
▶*v.* (**-cies**, **-cied**) [*tr.*] **1** feel a desire or liking for: *do you fancy a drink?* ■ (**fancy oneself**) *inf.* have an unduly high opinion of oneself, or of one's ability in a particular area: *he fancied himself an amateur psychologist.* **2** imagine; think: *he fancied he could smell the perfume of roses.*
▶*n.* (*pl.* **-cies**) **1** a feeling of liking or attraction, typically one that is superficial or transient: *this does not mean that the law should change with every passing fancy.* **2** the faculty of imagination: *my research assistant is prone to flights of fancy.* ■ a thing that one supposes or imagines, typically an unfounded or tentative belief or idea; notion or whim: *scientific fads and fancies.* —**fan·ci·ly** /'fansəlē/ *adv.* —**fan·ci·ness** *n.*
▶ □ **take** (or **catch**) **someone's fancy** appeal to someone: *she'll grab any toy that takes her fancy.*

fan·cy-free ▶*adj.* free from emotional involvement or commitment to anyone: *her recent divorce meant that she was footloose and fancy-free.*

fan·dan·go /fan'danggō/ ▶*n.* (*pl.* **-goes** or **-gos**) **1** a lively Spanish dance for two people, typically accompanied by castanets or tambourine. **2** a foolish or useless act or thing: *the Washington inaugural fandango.*

fan·fare /'fan,fer/ ▶*n.* a short ceremonial tune or flourish played on brass instruments, typically to introduce something or someone important. ■ *fig.* an ostentatious or noisy display: *he turned 25 on Saturday with little fanfare.*

Fang /faNG/ /fäNG/ (also **Fan** /fan/ /fän/) ▶*n.* (*pl.* same or **Fangs**) **1** a member of a people inhabiting parts of Cameroon, Equatorial Guinea, and Gabon. **2** the Bantu language of this people.
▶*adj.* of or relating to this people or their language.

fang /faNG/ ▶*n.* a large, sharp tooth, esp. a canine tooth of a dog or wolf. ■ the tooth of a venomous snake, by which poison is injected. ■ the biting mouthpart of a spider. —**fanged** *adj.* [also in *comb.*]

fan·light /'fan,līt/ ▶*n.* a small semicircular or rectangular window over a door or another window.

fan·ny /'fanē/ ▶*n.* (*pl.* **-nies**) *inf.* a person's buttocks.

fan·ny pack ▶*n.* a small pouch on a belt, for money and small articles, worn around the waist or hips.

fan·ta·sia /fan'tāzHə; fantə'zēə/ ▶*n.* a musical composition with a free form and often an improvisatory style. ■ a musical composition that is based on several familiar tunes. ■ a thing that is composed of a mixture of different forms or styles: *that theater is a Moorish fantasia.*

fan·ta·size /'fantə,sīz/ ▶*v.* [*intr.*] indulge in daydreaming about something desired: *he fantasized about leaving.* ■ [*tr.*] imagine (something that one wants to happen): *fantasize destruction.* —**fan·ta·sist** /-sist/ *n.*

fan·tas·tic /fan'tastik/ ▶*adj.* **1** imaginative or fanciful; remote from reality: *novels capable of mixing fantastic and realistic elements.* ■ of extraordinary size or degree: *fantastic reductions.* ■ (of a shape or design) bizarre or exotic: *visions of a fantastic, mazelike building.* **2** *inf.* extraordinarily good or attractive: *your support has been fantastic.* —**fan·tas·ti·cal** *adj.* —**fan·tas·ti·cal·ly** /-(ə)lē/ *adv.*

fan·ta·sy /'fantəsē/ ▶*n.* (*pl.* **-sies**) **1** the faculty or activity of imagining things, esp. things that are impossible or improbable: *his research had moved into the realm of fantasy.* ■ the product of this faculty or activity: *the scene is clearly fantasy.* ■ a fanciful mental image, typically one on which a person dwells at length or repeatedly and which reflects their conscious or unconscious wishes. ■ an idea with no basis in reality: *it is a misleading fantasy to suggest that the bill can be implemented.* ■ a genre of imaginative fiction involving magic and adventure, esp. in a setting other than the real world. **2** a musical composition, free in form, typically involving variation on an existing work or the imaginative representation of a situation or story; a fantasia.

fan·zine /'fan,zēn; fan'zēn/ ▶*n.* a magazine, usually produced by amateurs, for fans of a particular performer, group, or form of entertainment.

fa·quir ▶*n.* variant spelling of **FAKIR**.

far /fär/ ▶*adv.* (**far·ther** /'färTHər/, **far·thest** /'färTHəst/ or **fur·ther** /'fərTHər/, **fur·thest** /'fərTHəst/) **1** at, to, or by a great distance (used to indicate the extent to which one thing is distant from another): *it was not too far away.* **2** over a large expanse of space or time: *he had not traveled far.* **3** by a great deal: *the reality has fallen far short of expectations.*
▶*adj.* situated at a great distance in space or time: *the far reaches of the universe.* ■ more distant than another object of the same kind: *he was standing in the far corner.* ■ distant from a point seen as central;

extreme: *the far north of Scotland* | *electoral success for the far right.* ▷Old English *feorr*; from an Indo-European root shared by Sanskrit *para* and Greek *pera* 'further.'

▶ □ **as far as** for as great a distance as: *the river stretched away as far as he could see.* ■ for a great enough distance to reach: *I decided to walk as far as the village.* ■ to the extent that: *as far as I am concerned, it is no big deal.* □ **be a far cry from** be very different from: *the hotel's royal suite is a far cry from the poverty of his home country.* □ **by far** by a great amount: *this was by far the largest city in the area.* □ **far and away** by a great amount: *he is far and away the most accomplished player.* □ **far and near** (also **near and far**) everywhere: *they came from far and near.* □ **far and wide** over a large area: *the plains where bison roamed far and wide.* □ **far be it from me** to used to express reluctance, esp. to do something that one thinks may be resented: *far be it from me to speculate on his reasons.* □ **far from** very different from being; tending to the opposite of: *conditions were far from satisfactory.* □ **far gone** in a bad or worsening state, esp. so as to be beyond recovery. ■ advanced in time: *the legislative session is too far gone for lengthy hearings.* □ **go far** **1** achieve a great deal: *he was the bright one, and everyone was sure he would go far.* **2** contribute greatly: *a book that goes far toward bridging the gap.* **3** be worth or amount to much: *the money would not go far at this year's prices.* □ **go too far** exceed the limits of what is reasonable or acceptable. □ **how far** **1** used to ask how great a distance is: *they wanted to know how far he could travel.* **2** to what extent: *he was not sure how far she was committed.* □ **so far** **1** to a certain limited extent: *the commitment to free trade goes only so far.* **2** (of a trend that seems likely to continue) up to this time: *we've only had one honest man so far.*

far·ad /ˈfarəd; -ˌad/ (abbr.: **F**) ▶n. the SI unit of electrical capacitance, equal to the capacitance of a capacitor in which one coulomb of charge causes a potential difference of one volt.

far·a·day /ˈfarəˌdā/ (abbr.: **F**) ▶n. *Chem.* a unit of electric charge.

far·a·way /ˈfärəˌwā/ ▶adj. distant in space or time: *exotic and faraway locations.* ■ seeming remote from the immediate surroundings; dreamy: *she had a strange faraway look in her eyes.*

farce /färs/ ▶n. a comic dramatic work using buffoonery and horseplay and typically including crude characterization and ludicrously improbable situations. ■ the genre of such works. ■ an absurd event: *the debate turned into a drunken farce.* —**far·ci·cal** *adj.* *a farcical tangle of events.*

fare /fer/ ▶n. **1** the money a passenger on public transportation has to pay. ■ a passenger paying to travel in a vehicle, esp. a taxicab. **2** a range of food, esp. of a particular type: *delicious Provençal fare.* ■ *fig.* performance or entertainment of a particular style: *Hollywood fare.*
▶v. [intr.] **1** perform in a specified way in a particular situation or over a particular period of time: *the party fared badly in the spring elections.* **2** *archaic* travel: *a young knight fares forth.*

fare·well /ferˈwel/ ▶interj. used to express good wishes on parting: *farewell, Albert!*
▶n. an act of parting or of marking someone's departure: *the dinner had been arranged as a farewell.* ■ parting good wishes: *he had come on the pretext of bidding her farewell* | *I bade him a fond farewell.*

far-fetched ▶adj. (of an explanation or theory) contrived and unconvincing; unlikely. ■ (of a story or idea) implausible or exaggerated.

far-flung ▶adj. distant or remote. ■ widely distributed: *newsletters provided an important link to a far-flung membership.*

fa·ri·na /fəˈrēnə/ ▶n. flour or meal made of cereal grains, nuts, or starchy roots. ■ *archaic* starch. —**far·i·na·ceous** /ˌfarəˈnāSHəs/ *adj.*

farm /färm/ ▶n. an area of land and its buildings used for growing crops and rearing animals, typically under the control of one owner or manager. ■ a place for breeding a particular type of animal or producing a specified crop: *a fish farm.* ■ an establishment at which something is produced or processed: *an energy farm.*
▶v. **1** [intr.] make one's living by growing crops or keeping livestock: *he has farmed organically for five years.* ■ [tr.] use (land) for growing crops and rearing animals, esp. commercially. ■ [tr.] breed or grow commercially (a type of livestock or crop, esp. one not normally domesticated or cultivated). **2** [tr.] (**farm someone/something out**) send out or subcontract work to others: *it saves time and money to farm out some writing work to specialized companies.* ■ arrange for a child or other dependent person to be looked after by someone, usually for payment. **3** [tr.] *hist.* allow someone to collect and keep the revenues from (a tax) on payment of a fee: *the customs had been farmed to the collector for a fixed sum.* —**farm·a·ble** /ˈfärməbəl/ *adj.* —**farm·ing** *n.*

farm·er /ˈfärmər/ ▶n. **1** a person who owns or manages a farm. **2** *hist.* a person to whom the collection of taxes was contracted for a fee.

farm·hand /ˈfärmˌhand/ ▶n. a worker on a farm.

farm·house /ˈfärmˌhous/ ▶n. a house attached to a farm, esp. the main house in which the farmer lives.

farm·land /ˈfärmˌland/ ▶n. (also **farmlands**) land used for farming.

farm·stead /ˈfärmˌsted/ ▶n. a farm and its buildings.

farm·yard /ˈfärmˌyärd/ ▶n. a yard or enclosure attached to a farmhouse.

far·o /ˈferō/ ▶n. a gambling card game in which players bet on the order in which the cards will appear.

far-off ▶adj. remote in time or space: *a far-off country.*

far-out ▶adj. unconventional or avant-garde: *far-out politics.* ■ [often as interj.] *inf.* excellent: *it's really far-out!*

far-reach·ing ▶adj. having important and widely applicable effects or implications: *a series of far-reaching political reforms.*

far·ri·er /ˈfarēər/ ▶n. a craftsman who trims and shoes horses' hooves.

far·row /ˈfarō/ ▶n. a litter of pigs.
▶v. [tr.] (of a sow) give birth to (piglets): *a litter of nine farrowed in July.*

far-see·ing ▶adj. having or showing shrewd judgment and an ability to predict and plan for future eventualities.

Far·si /ˈfärsē/ ▶n. the modern Persian language that is the official language of Iran.

far-sight·ed /ˈfärˌsītid; -ˈsītid/ ▶adj. unable to see things clearly, esp. if they are relatively close to the eyes. ■ seeing or able to see for a great distance. ■ *fig.* having imagination or foresight: *a farsighted businessman.* —**far·sight·ed·ly** *adv.* —**far·sight·ed·ness** *n.*

fart /färt/ *inf.* ▶v. [intr.] emit gas from the anus. ■ (**fart about/around**) waste time on silly or trivial things.
▶n. an emission of gas from the anus. ■ a boring or contemptible person: *he was such an old fart.*

far·ther /ˈfärT͟Hər/ (also **fur·ther**) ▶ used as comparative of FAR.
▶adv. **1** at, to, or by a greater distance (used to indicate the extent to which one thing or person is or becomes distant from another): *fig. his action pushes Haiti even farther away from democratic rule.* **2** over a greater expanse of space or time; for a longer way: *the stream fills the passage, and only a cave diver can explore farther* | *fig. people were trying to get their food dollars to go farther.*
▶adj. more distant in space than another item of the same kind: *the farther side of the mountain.* ■ more remote from a central point: *the farther stretches of the diocese.* —**far·ther·most** *adj.*

far·thest /ˈfärT͟Hist/ (also **fur·thest**) ▶ used as superlative of FAR.
▶adj. situated at the greatest distance from a specified or understood point: *fig. it was the farthest thing from my mind.* ■ covering the greatest area or distance: *his record for the farthest flight.* ■ extremely remote: *the farthest ends of the earth.*
▶adv. **1** at or by the greatest distance (used to indicate how far one thing or person is or becomes distant from another): *the bed farthest from the window.* **2** over the greatest distance or area: *his group probably had farthest to ride* | *fig. the areas where prices have fallen the farthest.* ■ used to indicate the most distant point reached in a specified direction: *the farthest north.* ■ to the most extreme or advanced point: *the farthest he'll go is to admit a sort of resentment.*
▶ □ **at the farthest** at the greatest distance; at most.

far·thing /ˈfärT͟HiNG/ ▶n. a former monetary unit and coin of the UK, withdrawn in 1961, equal to a quarter of an old penny. ■ the least possible amount: *she didn't care a farthing for the woman.*

Far West ▶the region of North America west of the Great Plains.

fas·ces /ˈfasˌēz/ ▶pl. n. (in ancient Rome) a bundle of rods with a projecting ax blade, as a symbol of a magistrate's power. ■ (in Fascist Italy) such items used as emblems of authority.

fas·ci·a /ˈfaSH(ē)ə; ˈfā-/ ▶n. **1** a wooden board or other flat piece of material such as that covering the ends of rafters. ■ a covering, typically a detachable one, for the front part of a cellular phone. ■ (in classical architecture) a long flat surface between moldings on an architrave. **2** (pl. **fas·ci·ae** /-SHē,ē/) *Anat.* a thin sheath of fibrous tissue enclosing a muscle or other organ.

fas·ci·cle /ˈfasikəl/ ▶n. **1** a separately published installment of a book or other printed work. **2** *Anat. & Biol.* a bundle of structures, such as nerve or muscle fibers or conducting vessels in plants. —**fas·ci·cled** *adj.* —**fas·cic·u·lar** /fəˈsikyələr/ *adj.* —**fas·cic·u·late** /fəˈsikyə,lāt; -yəlit/ *adj.*

fas·ci·nate /ˈfasə,nāt/ ▶v. [tr.] (usu. **be fascinated**) draw irresistibly the attention and interest of (someone): *I've always been fascinated by other cultures.* ■ *archaic* (esp. of a snake) deprive (a person or animal) of the ability to resist or escape by the power of a look or gaze. —**fas·ci·nat·ing** *adj.* —**fas·ci·na·tion** /ˌfasəˈnāSHən/ *n.* —**fas·ci·na·tor** /-ˌnātər/ *n.*

fas·cism /ˈfaSHˌizəm/ (also **Fas·cism**) ▶n. an authoritarian and nationalistic right-wing system of government and social organization. ■ (in general use) extreme right-wing, authoritarian, or intolerant views or practice. —**fas·cist** *n. & adj.* —**fa·scis·tic** /faˈSHistik/ *adj.*

fash·ion /ˈfasHən/ ▸*n.* **1** a popular trend, esp. in styles of dress or manners of behavior: *his hair is cut in the latest fashion.* ■ the production and marketing of new styles of goods, esp. clothing and cosmetics: [as *adj.*] *a fashion magazine.* **2** a manner of doing something: *the work is done in a rather casual fashion.*

▸*v.* [*tr.*] make into a particular or the required form: *the bottles were fashioned from green glass.* ■ (**fashion something into**) use materials to make into: *the skins were fashioned into boots and shoes.* ▷Middle English (in the sense 'make, shape, appearance,' also 'a particular make or style'): from Old French *façon,* from Latin *factio(n-),* from *facere* 'do, make.'

▸ □ **after a fashion** to a certain extent but imperfectly or unsatisfactorily: *he could read after a fashion.* □ **in** (or **out of**) **fashion** popular (or unpopular) and considered (or not considered) to be attractive at the time in question.

fash·ion·a·ble /ˈfasH(ə)nəbəl/ ▸*adj.* characteristic of, influenced by, or representing a current popular trend or style: *fashionable clothes.* ■ (of a person) dressing or behaving according to the current trend. —**fash·ion·a·bly** /-əblē/ *adv.*

fast[1] /fast/ ▸*adj.* **1** moving or capable of moving at high speed. ■ performed or taking place at high speed; taking only a short time: *the journey was fast and enjoyable.* ■ allowing people or things to move at high speed: *a wide, fast road.* ■ performing or able to perform a particular type of action quickly: *a fast reader.* ■ *Sports* (of a playing field) likely to make the ball bounce or run quickly or to allow competitors to reach a high speed. ■ (of a person or lifestyle) engaging in or involving exciting or shocking activities: *the fast life she led in London.* **2** (of a clock or watch) showing a time ahead of the correct time: *I keep my watch fifteen minutes fast.* **3** firmly fixed or attached: *he made a rope fast to each corner.* ■ (of friends) close and loyal. ■ (of a dye) not fading in light or when washed. **4** *Photog.* (of a film) needing only a short exposure.

▸*adv.* **1** at high speed: *he was driving too fast.* ■ within a short time: *they think they're going to get rich fast.* **2** so as to be hard to move; firmly or securely: *the ship was held fast by the anchor chain.* ■ (of someone or something sleeping) so as to be hard to wake: *they were too fast asleep to reply.*

▸ □ **pull a fast one** *inf.* try to gain an unfair advantage: *Joey **pulled a fast one** on us.*

fast[2] ▸*v.* [*intr.*] abstain from all or some kinds of food or drink, esp. as a religious observance.

▸*n.* an act or period of fasting: *a five-day fast.*

fast·back /ˈfas(t)ˌbak/ ▸*n.* a car with a roofline that slopes continuously down at the back.

fast·ball /ˈfas(t)ˌbôl/ ▸*n.* a baseball pitch thrown at or near a pitcher's maximum speed.

fas·ten /ˈfasən/ ▸*v.* [*tr.*] close or join securely: *fasten your seat belts.* ■ [*intr.*] be closed or done up in a particular place or part or in a particular way: *a blouse that fastens down the back.* ■ [*tr.*] fix or hold in place: *she fastened her locket around her neck.* ■ (**fasten something on/upon**) direct one's eyes, thoughts, feelings, etc., intently at: *Maggie fastened her eyes on him.* ■ (**fasten something on/upon**) ascribe responsibility to: *blame hadn't been fastened on anyone.* —**fas·ten·er** *n.*

fast·en·ing /ˈfasəniNG/ ▸*n.* a device that closes or secures something.

fast food ▸*n.* food that can be prepared quickly and easily and is sold in restaurants and snack bars as a quick meal or to be taken out: [as *adj.*] *a fast-food restaurant.*

fas·tid·i·ous /fasˈtidēəs/ ▸*adj.* very attentive to and concerned about accuracy and detail: *he chooses his words with fastidious care.* ■ very concerned about cleanliness: *the child seemed fastidious about getting her fingers sticky or dirty.* —**fas·tid·i·ous·ly** *adv.* —**fas·tid·i·ous·ness** *n.*

fast·ness /ˈfas(t)nəs/ ▸*n.* **1** a secure refuge, esp. a place well protected by natural features: *a remote Himalayan fastness.* **2** the ability of a material or dye to maintain its color without fading or washing away.

fast-talk ▸*v.* [*tr.*] *inf.* pressure (someone) into doing something using rapid or misleading speech: [as *adj.*] (**fast-talking**) *a fast-talking confidence trickster.*

fast track ▸*n.* a route, course, or method that provides for more rapid results than usual: *a career in the fast track of the civil service.*

▸*v.* (**fast-track**) [*tr.*] accelerate the development or progress of (a person or project): *fast-tracked to the top of the corporate ladder.*

fat /fat/ ▸*n.* a natural oily or greasy substance occurring in animal bodies, esp. when deposited as a layer under the skin or around certain organs. ■ a substance of this type, or a similar one made from plant products, used in cooking. ■ the presence of an excessive amount of such a substance in a person or animal, causing them to become corpulent. ■ *Chem.* any of a group of natural esters of glycerol and various fatty acids, which are solid at room temperature and are the main

constituents of animal and vegetable fat. ■ something excessive or unnecessary: *fat in the state budget.*

▸*adj.* (**fat·ter, fat·test**) (of a person or animal) having a large amount of excess flesh: *the driver was a fat, wheezing man.* ■ (of an animal bred for food) made plump for slaughter. ■ containing much fat: *fat bacon.* ■ large in bulk or circumference: *a fat cigarette.* ■ *inf.* (of an asset or opportunity) financially substantial or desirable: *a fat profit.* ■ *inf.* used ironically to express the belief that there is none or very little of something: *fat chance she had of influencing him | a **fat lot** of good that'll do him.* ■ (of wood) containing a lot of pitch: *fat pine.*

▸*v.* (**fat·ted, fat·ting**) *archaic* make or become fat: [as *adj.*] (**fatted**) *a fatted duck.* —**fat·ness** *n.* —**fat·tish** *adj.*

▸ □ **live off** (or **on**) **the fat of the land** have the best of everything.

fa·tal /ˈfātl/ ▸*adj.* causing death: *a fatal accident.* ■ leading to failure or disaster: *there were three fatal flaws in the strategy.* —**fa·tal·ly** *adv.*

fa·tal·ism /ˈfātlˌizəm/ ▸*n.* the belief that all events are predetermined and therefore inevitable. ■ a submissive attitude to events, resulting from such a belief. —**fa·tal·ist** *n.* —**fa·tal·is·tic** /ˌfātlˈistik/ *adj.* —**fa·tal·is·ti·cal·ly** *adv.*

fa·tal·i·ty /fāˈtalətē; fə-/ ▸*n.* (*pl.* **-ties**) **1** an occurrence of death by accident, in war, or from disease. ■ a person killed in this way. **2** helplessness in the face of fate: *the plot needs a darker sense of fatality to cover its absurdities.*

fat cat ▸*n. derog.* a wealthy and powerful person, esp. a businessman or politician: [as *adj.*] *a fat-cat developer.*

fate /fāt/ ▸*n.* **1** the development of events beyond a person's control, regarded as determined by a supernatural power: *his injury is a cruel twist of fate.* ■ the course of someone's life, or the outcome of a particular situation for someone or something, seen as beyond their control: *he suffered the same fate as his companion.* ■ the inescapable death of a person: *the guards led her to her fate.* **2** (**the Fates**) *Greek & Roman Mythol.* the three goddesses who preside over the birth and life of humans.

▸*v.* (**be fated**) be destined to happen, turn out, or act in a particular way. ▷late Middle English: from Italian *fato* or Old French *fator* (later) from their source, Latin *fatum* 'that which has been spoken,' from *fari* 'speak.'

▸ □ **seal someone's fate** make it inevitable that something unpleasant will happen to someone.

fate·ful /ˈfātfəl/ ▸*adj.* having far-reaching and typically disastrous consequences or implications: *a fateful oversight.* —**fate·ful·ly** *adv.* —**fate·ful·ness** *n.*

fat·head /ˈfatˌhed/ ▸*n. inf.* a stupid person. —**fat·head·ed** *adj.* —**fat·head·ed·ness** *n.*

fa·ther /ˈfäTHər/ ▸*n.* **1** a man in relation to his natural child or children. ■ a man who has continuous care of a child, esp. by adoption; an adoptive father, stepfather, or foster father. ■ a father-in-law. ■ a male animal in relation to its offspring. ■ (usu. **fathers**) *poetic/lit.* an ancestor. ■ (also **founding father**) an important figure in the origin and early history of something. ■ a man who gives care and protection to someone or something: *the prince is widely regarded as **the father of** the nation.* ■ the oldest or most respected member of a society or other body. ■ (**the Father**) (in Christian belief) the first person of the Trinity; God. ■ (**Father**) *poetic/lit.* used in proper names, esp. when personifying time or a river, to suggest an old and venerable character: *Father Thames.* **2** (also **Fa·ther**) (often as a title or form of address) a priest: *pray for me, Father.*

▸*v.* [*tr.*] be the father of: *he fathered three children.* ■ treat with the protective care usually associated with a father. ■ be the source or originator of: *a culture which has fathered half the popular music in the world.* ■ (**father someone on**) make (a woman) pregnant: *he fathered a child on a one-night stand.* ▷Old English *fæder;* from an Indo-European root shared by Latin *pater* and Greek *patēr.* —**fa·ther·hood** /-ˌho͝od/ *n.* —**fa·ther·less** *adj.* —**fa·ther·li·ness** *n.*

fa·ther-in-law ▸*n.* (*pl.* **fa·thers-in-law**) the father of one's spouse.

fa·ther·land /ˈfäTHərˌland/ ▸*n.* (often **the Fatherland**) a person's native country, esp. when referred to in patriotic terms.

fa·ther·ly /ˈfäTHərlē/ ▸*adj.* of, resembling, or characteristic of a father, esp. in being protective and affectionate: *he gave me such a kind and fatherly look.* —**fath·er·li·ness** *n.*

Fa·ther Time ▸*n.* see TIME (sense 1).

fath·om /ˈfaTHəm/ ▸ n. a unit of length equal to six feet (approx. 1.8 m), chiefly used in reference to the depth of water and to the length of rope, cable or chain: *sonar says that we're in eighteen fathoms.*
▸ v. [tr.] **1** understand (a difficult problem or an enigmatic person) after much thought: *he couldn't fathom why she was being so anxious.* **2** measure the depth of (water). —**fath·om·a·ble** adj. —**fath·om·less** adj.

fa·tigue /fəˈtēg/ ▸ n. **1** extreme tiredness, typically resulting from mental or physical exertion or illness: *he was nearly dead with fatigue.* ■ a reduction in the efficiency of a muscle or organ after prolonged activity. ■ weakness in materials, esp. metal, caused by repeated variations of stress: *metal fatigue.* ■ a lessening in one's response to or enthusiasm for something, typically as a result of overexposure to it: *museum fatigue.* **2** (also **fatigue detail**) a group of soldiers ordered to perform menial, nonmilitary tasks, sometimes as a punishment. ■ (**fatigues**) loose-fitting clothing, typically khaki, olive drab, or camouflaged, of a sort worn by soldiers: *battle fatigues.*
▸ v. (**-tigues, -tigued, -ti·guing**) [tr.] (often **be fatigued**) cause (someone) to feel tired or exhausted: *they were fatigued by their journey.* ■ reduce the efficiency of (a muscle or organ) by prolonged activity. ■ weaken (a material, esp. metal) by repeated variations of stress.

fat·so /ˈfatsō/ ▸ n. (pl. **-sos**) inf., derog. a fat person.

fat·ten /ˈfatn/ ▸ v. [tr.] make (a person or animal) fat or fatter: *he could do with some good food to fatten him up.* ■ [intr.] become fat or fatter.

fat·ty /ˈfatē/ ▸ adj. (**-ti·er, -ti·est**) containing a large amount of fat: *go easy on fatty foods* | *fatty tissue.* ■ Med. (of a disease or lesion) marked by abnormal deposition of fat in cells: *fatty degeneration of the liver.*
▸ n. (pl. **-ties**) inf. a fat person (esp. as a nickname). —**fat·ti·ness** n.

fat·ty ac·id ▸ n. Chem. a carboxylic acid consisting of a hydrocarbon chain with a terminal carboxyl group, esp. any of those occurring as esters in fats and oils.

fat·u·ous /ˈfaCHo͞oəs/ ▸ adj. silly and pointless: *a fatuous comment.* —**fa·tu·i·ty** /fəˈt(y)o͞oitē/ n. (pl. **-ties**) —**fat·u·ous·ly** adv. —**fat·u·ous·ness** n.

fat·wa /ˈfätwä/ ▸ n. a ruling on a point of Islamic law given by a recognized authority.

fau·cet /ˈfôsit; ˈfäs-/ ▸ n. a device by which a flow of liquid or gas from a pipe or container can be controlled; a tap.

fault /fôlt/ ▸ n. **1** an unattractive or unsatisfactory feature, esp. in a piece of work or in a person's character: *my worst fault is impatience.* ■ a break or other defect in an electrical circuit or piece of machinery: *a fire caused by an electrical fault.* ■ a misguided or dangerous action or habit. ■ (in tennis and similar games) a service of the ball not in accordance with the rules. **2** responsibility for an accident or misfortune: *an ordinary man thrust into peril through no fault of his own.* **3** Geol. an extended break in a body of rock, marked by relative displacement and discontinuity of strata on either side of a particular surface.
▸ v. [tr.] criticize for inadequacy or mistakes: *you cannot fault him for the professionalism of his approach.*
▸ □ **at fault 1** responsible for an undesirable situation or event; in the wrong: *we recover compensation from the person at fault.* **2** mistaken or defective: *he suspected that his calculator was at fault.* □ **find fault** make an adverse criticism or objection, sometimes unfairly or destructively: *he finds fault with everything I do.* □ **— to a fault** (of someone who displays a particular commendable quality) to an extent verging on excess: *you're kind, caring and generous to a fault.*

fault-find·ing ▸ n. **1** continual criticism, typically concerning trivial things. **2** the investigation of the cause of malfunction in machinery, esp. electronic equipment. —**fault-find·er** n.

fault·less /ˈfôltləs/ ▸ adj. free from defect or error: *your logic is faultless.* —**fault·less·ly** adv. —**fault·less·ness** n.

fault·y /ˈfôltē/ ▸ adj. (**fault·i·er, fault·i·est**) working badly or unreliably because of imperfections: *a car with faulty brakes.* ■ (of reasoning and other mental processes) mistaken or misleading because of flaws: *faulty logic.* ■ having or displaying weaknesses. —**fault·i·ly** /ˈfôltəlē/ adv. —**fault·i·ness** n.

faun /fôn/ ▸ n. Roman Mythol. one of a class of lustful rural gods, represented as a man with a goat's horns, ears, legs, and tail.

fau·na /ˈfônə; ˈfänə/ ▸ n. (pl. **-nas** /-nəz/ or **-nae** /-nē/) the animals of a particular region, habitat, or geological period: *the flora and fauna of Siberia* | *islands that support one of the richest of all marine faunas.* Compare with FLORA. ■ a book or other work describing or listing the animal life of a region. —**fau·nal** /ˈfônl; ˈfänl/ adj. —**fau·nis·tic** /fôˈnistik; fä-/ adj.

Fauv·ism /ˈfō,vizəm/ (also **fauv·ism**) ▸ n. a style of painting with vivid expressionistic use of color that flourished in Paris from 1905 and, although short-lived, had an important influence on subsequent artists. Matisse was regarded as the movement's leading figure. —**fauv·ist** n. & adj.

faux /fō/ ▸ adj. artificial or imitation; false: *a string of faux pearls.*

faux pas /fō ˈpä; fō ˌpä/ ▸ n. (pl. same) an embarrassing or tactless act or remark in a social situation.

fave /fāv/ ▸ n. & adj. inf. short for FAVORITE.

fa·vi·con /ˈfāvəˌkän/ ▸ n. an icon associated with a URL that is variously displayed, as in a browser's address bar or next to the site name in a bookmark list.

fa·vor /ˈfāvər/ (Brit. **fa·vour**) ▸ n. **1** an attitude of approval or liking: *the legislation is viewed with favor.* ■ support or advancement given as a sign of approval: *a struggle for presidential favor.* ■ overgenerous preferential treatment: *showing favor to one of the players.* ■ a small gift or souvenir: *party favors.* **2** an act of kindness beyond what is due or usual: *I've come to ask you a favor.* ■ (**one's favors**) dated used with reference to a woman allowing a man to have sexual intercourse with her: *she had granted her favors to him.*
▸ v. [tr.] **1** feel or show approval or preference for. ■ give unfairly preferential treatment to: *critics argued that the policy favored the private sector.* ■ work to the advantage of: *natural selection has favored bats.* **2** inf. resemble (a parent or relative) in facial features: *she's pretty, and she favors you.* **3** treat (an injured limb) gently, not putting one's full weight on it: *he favors his sore leg.*
▸ □ **do someone a favor** do something for someone as an act of kindness. □ **in favor 1** meeting with approval: *they were not in favor with the party.* **2** having or showing approval: *the appeals court ruled 2-1 in favor of his extradition.* □ **in one's favor** to one's advantage: *events were moving in his favor.* □ **in favor of 1** to be replaced by: *he stepped down as leader in favor of his rival.* **2** to the advantage of: *the final score was 25-16 in favor of Washington.*

fa·vor·a·ble /ˈfāv(ə)rəbəl/ (Brit. **fa·vour·a·ble**) ▸ adj. **1** expressing approval: *favorable reviews.* ■ giving consent: *their demands rarely received a favorable response.* **2** to the advantage of someone or something: *they made a settlement favorable to the unions.* ■ (of weather, or a period of time judged in terms of its weather) fine. ■ suggesting a good outcome: *a favorable prognosis.* —**fa·vor·a·ble·ness** n. —**fa·vor·a·bly** /-r(ə)blē/ adv.

fa·vor·ite /ˈfāv(ə)rət/ (Brit. **fa·vour·ite**) ▸ adj. preferred before all others of the same kind: *their favorite Italian restaurant.*
▸ n. a person or thing that is especially popular or particularly well liked by someone: *the song is still a favorite after 20 years.* ■ the competitor thought most likely to win a game or contest, esp. by people betting on the outcome: *he was the early favorite to win the Ohio caucuses.*

fa·vor·it·ism /ˈfāv(ə)rəˌtizəm/ ▸ n. the practice of giving unfair preferential treatment to one person or group at the expense of another.

fawn[1] /fôn; fän/ ▸ n. **1** a young deer in its first year. **2** a light yellowish-brown color.
▸ v. [intr.] (of a deer) produce young.

fawn[2] ▸ v. [intr.] give a servile display of exaggerated flattery or affection, typically in order to gain favor or advantage: *congressmen fawn over the President.* —**fawn·ing·ly** adv.

fax /faks/ ▸ n. an image of a document made by electronic scanning and transmitted as data by telecommunication links. ■ the production or transmission of documents in this way: *he received the report by fax.* ■ (also **fax machine**) a machine for transmitting and receiving such documents.
▸ v. [tr.] send (a document) by such means. ■ contact (someone) by such means: *to obtain a brochure, fax the agent.*

fay /fā/ ▸ n. poetic/lit. a fairy.

faze /fāz/ ▸ v. [tr.] (often **be fazed**) inf. disturb or disconcert (someone): *she was not fazed by his show of anger.*

FBI ▸ abbr. Federal Bureau of Investigation.

FCC ▸ abbr. Federal Communications Commission.

F clef ▸ n. another term for bass clef.

FDA ▸ abbr. Food and Drug Administration.

FDIC ▸ abbr. Federal Deposit Insurance Corporation, a body that underwrites most private bank deposits.

Fe ▸ symb. the chemical element iron.

fe·al·ty /ˈfēltē/ ▸ n. hist. a feudal tenant's or vassal's sworn loyalty to a lord: *they owed fealty to the Earl rather than the King.* ■ formal acknowledgment of this: *a property for which she did fealty.*

fear /fi(ə)r/ ▸ n. an unpleasant emotion caused by the belief that someone or something is dangerous, likely to cause pain, or a threat: *fear of increasing unemployment* | *he is prey to irrational fears.* ■ archaic a mixed feeling of dread and reverence: *the love and fear of God.* ■ (**fear for**) a feeling of anxiety concerning the outcome of something or the safety and well-being of someone: *police launched a search for the family amid fears for*

their safety. ■ the likelihood of something unwelcome happening: *she could observe the other guests without fear of attracting attention.*
▶ *v.* [*tr.*] be afraid of (someone or something) as likely to be dangerous, painful, or threatening: *farmers fear that they will lose business.* ■ [*intr.*] (**fear for**) feel anxiety or apprehension on behalf of: *I fear for the city with this madman let loose in it.* ■ avoid or put off doing something because one is afraid: *they aim to make war so horrific that potential aggressors will fear to resort to it.* ■ used to express regret or apology: *I'll buy her book, though not, I fear, the hardback version.*
▶ □ **for fear of** (or **that**) to avoid the risk of (or that): *no one dared refuse the order for fear of losing their job.*
fear·ful /ˈfi(ə)rfəl/ ▶ *adj.* **1** feeling afraid; showing fear or anxiety. ■ causing or likely to cause people to be afraid; horrifying: *a fearful accident.* **2** *inf.* very great: *he could cause a fearful commotion.* —**fear·ful·ly** *adv.* —**fear·ful·ness** *n.*
fear·less /ˈfi(ə)rlis/ ▶ *adj.* lacking fear: *a fearless defender of freedom.* —**fear·less·ly** *adv.* —**fear·less·ness** *n.*
fear·some /ˈfi(ə)rsəm/ ▶ *adj.* frightening, esp. in appearance: *the cat growled, displaying a fearsome set of teeth.* —**fear·some·ly** *adv.* —**fear·some·ness** *n.*
fea·si·ble /ˈfēzəbəl/ ▶ *adj.* possible to do easily or conveniently: *it is not feasible to put most finds from excavations on public display.* ■ *inf.* likely; probable: *the most feasible explanation.* —**fea·si·bil·i·ty** *n.* —**fea·si·bly** /-zəblē/ *adv.*
feast /fēst/ ▶ *n.* a large meal, typically one in celebration of something. ■ a plentiful supply of something enjoyable, esp. for the mind or senses: *the concert season offers a feast of classical music.* ■ an annual religious celebration: *the feast of St. Joseph.*
▶ *v.* [*intr.*] eat and drink sumptuously. ■ (**feast on**) eat large quantities of: *feasting on barbecued chicken.*
▶ □ **feast one's eyes on** gaze at with pleasure. □ **feast or famine** either too much of something or too little.
feat /fēt/ ▶ *n.* an achievement that requires great courage, skill, or strength: *the new printing presses were considerable feats of engineering.*
feath·er /ˈfeT͟Hər/ ▶ *n.* any of the flat appendages growing from a bird's skin and forming its plumage, consisting of a partly hollow horny shaft fringed with vanes of barbs. ■ (often **feathers**) one of these appendages as decoration. ■ one of the feathers or featherlike vanes fastened to the shaft of an arrow or a dart. ■ (**feathers**) a fringe of long hair on the legs of a dog, horse, or other animal.
▶ *v.* **1** [*tr.*] rotate the blades of (a propeller) about their own axes in such a way as to lessen the air or water resistance. ■ vary the angle of attack of (rotor blades). ■ *Rowing* turn (an oar) so that it passes through the air edgewise: *he turned, feathering one oar slowly.* **2** [*intr.*] float, move, or wave like a feather: *the green fronds feathered against a blue sky.* **3** [*tr.*] shorten or taper the hair by cutting or trimming: *my sister had her hair feathered.* ▷Old English *fether*, from an Indo-European root shared by Latin *penna* 'feather' and Greek *pteron* 'wing.' —**feath·ered** *adj.* —**feath·er·i·ness** *n.*
▶ □ **a feather in one's cap** an achievement to be proud of. □ **feather one's** (**own**) **nest** make money illicitly and at someone else's expense.
feath·er·bed /ˈfeT͟Hərˌbed/ ▶ *n.* (also **feath·er bed**) a bed that has a mattress stuffed with feathers.
▶ *v.* (also **feath·er-bed**) [*tr.*] provide (someone) with advantageous economic or working conditions. ■ [usu. as *n.*] (**featherbedding**) deliberately limit production or retain excess staff in (a business) in order to create jobs or prevent unemployment, typically as a result of a union contract.
feath·er·brain /ˈfeT͟Hərˌbrān/ (also **feath·er·head**) ▶ *n.* a silly or absent-minded person. —**feath·er·brained** *adj.*
feath·er edge ▶ *n.* a fine edge produced by tapering a board or other object.
feath·er·ing /ˈfeT͟HəriNG/ ▶ *n.* the plumage of a bird or part of a bird. ■ featherlike markings or structure: *traditional finishes such as marbling and feathering.* ■ the feathers of an arrow. ■ fringes of hairs on the appendages or body of a dog.
feath·er·stitch /ˈfeT͟HərˌstiCH/ ▶ *n.* ornamental zigzag sewing.
feath·er·weight /ˈfeT͟Hərˌwāt/ ▶ *n.* a weight in boxing and other sports intermediate between bantamweight and lightweight. It ranges from 118 to 126 pounds (54 to 57 kg). ■ a boxer or other competitor of this weight. ■ a very light person or thing. ■ a person or thing not worth serious consideration: *he is an intellectual featherweight.*
fea·ture /ˈfēCHər/ ▶ *n.* **1** a distinctive attribute of something: *safety features like dual air bags.* ■ (usu. **features**) a part of the face, such as the mouth or eyes, making a significant contribution to its overall appearance. **2** a newspaper or magazine article or a broadcast program devoted to the treatment of a particular topic: *a feature on*

Detroit's downtown fishery. ■ (also **feature film**) a full-length film intended as the main item in a movie program.
▶ *v.* [*tr.*] have as a prominent attribute or aspect: *the hotel features a large lounge.* ■ have as an important actor or participant: *the film featured Glenn Miller and his Orchestra.* ■ [*intr.*] (often **be featured**) be a significant characteristic of or take an important part in: *this famous photograph is prominently featured in art collections.* —**fea·ture·less** *adj.*
Feb. ▶ *abbr.* February.
fe·brile /ˈfeb.rīl; ˈfē.brīl/ ▶ *adj.* having or showing the symptoms of a fever: *a febrile illness.* ■ having or showing a great deal of nervous excitement or energy: *a febrile imagination.* —**fe·bril·i·ty** /fēˈbrilətē/ *n.*
Feb·ru·ar·y /ˈfebrооˌerē; ˈfebyоō-/ ▶ *n.* (*pl.* **-ar·ies**) the second month of the year, in the northern hemisphere usually considered the last month of winter.
fe·ces /ˈfēsēz/ ▶ *pl. n.* waste matter discharged from the bowels after food has been digested; excrement. —**fe·cal** /ˈfēkəl/ *adj.*
feck·less /ˈfekləs/ ▶ *adj.* (of a person) lacking in efficiency or vitality: *a feckless mama's boy.* ■ unthinking and irresponsible: *feckless exploitation of the world's natural resources.* —**feck·less·ly** *adv.* —**feck·less·ness** *n.*
fec·u·lent /ˈfekyələnt/ ▶ *adj.* of or containing dirt, sediment, or waste matter: *their feet were slipping on the feculent bog.* —**fec·u·lence** *n.*
fe·cund /ˈfekənd; ˈfē-/ ▶ *adj.* producing or capable of producing an abundance of offspring or new growth; fertile: *a lush and fecund garden* | *fig. her fecund imagination.* ■ (of a woman) capable of becoming pregnant and giving birth. —**fe·cun·di·ty** /fiˈkəndətē/ *n.*
Fed /fed/ ▶ *n. inf.* **1** a federal agent or official, esp. a member of the FBI: *I don't think he has any friends since he ratted to the Feds.* **2** (usu. **the Fed**) short for FEDERAL RESERVE.
fed /fed/ ▶ past and past participle of FEED.
fed·er·al /ˈfed(ə)rəl/ ▶ *adj.* having or relating to a system of government in which several states form a unity but remain independent in internal affairs: *Russia's federal and local governments.* ■ of, relating to, or denoting the central government as distinguished from the separate units constituting a federation: *the federal agency that provides legal services to the poor.* ■ of, relating to, or denoting the central government of the U.S. ■ (**Federal**) *hist.* of the Northern States in the Civil War. —**fed·er·al·ism** *n.* —**fed·er·al·ist** *n. & adj.* —**fed·er·al·i·za·tion** *n.* —**fed·er·al·ize** *v.* —**fed·er·al·ly** *adv.*
Fed·er·al Re·serve ▶ the federal banking authority in the U.S. that performs the functions of a central bank and is used to implement the country's monetary policy, providing a national system of reserve cash available to banks.
Fed·er·al Un·ion ▶ see UNION (sense 3).
fed·er·ate ▶ *v.* /ˈfedəˌrāt/ [*intr.*] (of a number of states or organizations) form a single centralized unit, within which each keeps some internal autonomy. ■ [*tr.*] [usu. as *adj.*] (**federated**) form (states or organizations) into a centralized unit: *the 20 federated states in Mindanao.*
▶ *adj.* /ˈfedərit/ of or relating to such an arrangement: *federate armies.* —**fed·er·a·tive** /-ˌrātiv; -rətiv/ *adj.*
fed·er·a·tion /ˌfedəˈrāSHən/ ▶ *n.* a group of states with a central government but independence in internal affairs. ■ an organization or group within which smaller divisions have some degree of internal autonomy: [in *names*] *the best tag team in the World Wrestling Federation.* ■ the action of forming states or organizations into a single group with centralized control: *a first step in the federation of Europe.*
fe·do·ra /fəˈdôrə/ ▶ *n.* a low, soft felt hat with a curled brim and the crown creased lengthwise. ▷late 19th cent. (originally U.S.): from *Fédora*, the title of a drama (1882) written by the French dramatist Victorien Sardou (1831–1908).
fed up ▶ *adj.* annoyed or upset at a situation or treatment: *he was fed up with doing all the work.*
fee /fē/ ▶ *n.* **1** a payment made to a professional person or to a professional or public body in exchange for advice or services. ■ money paid as part of a special transaction, e.g., for a privilege or for admission to something: *an admission fee.* ■ (usu. **fees**) money regularly paid (esp. to a school or similar institution) for continuing services: *high tuition fees.*

fedora

Pronunciation Key ə *ago*, *up*; ər *over*, *fur*; a *hat*; ā *ate*; ä *car*; CH *chin*; e *let*; ē *see*; e(ə)r *air*; i *fit*; ī *by*; i(ə)r *ear*; NG *sing*; ō *go*; ô *law*, *for*; oi *toy*; o͝o *good*; o͞o *goo*; ou *out*; SH *she*; TH *thin*; T͟H *then*; (h)w *why*; ZH *vision*

2 *hist. Law* an estate of land, esp. one held on condition of feudal service.

fee·ble /ˈfēbəl/ ▶ *adj.* (**-bler, -blest**) lacking physical strength, esp. as a result of age or illness: *my legs are very feeble after the flu.* ■ (of a sound) faint: *his voice sounded feeble and far away.* ■ lacking strength of character: *she overreacted in such a feeble, juvenile way.* ■ failing to convince or impress: *a feeble excuse.* ▷Middle English: from Old French *fieble*, earlier *fleible*, from Latin *flebilis* 'lamentable,' from *flere* 'weep.' —**fee·ble·ness** *n.* —**fee·bly** /ˈfēb(ə)lē/ *adv.*

fee·ble-mind·ed /ˈfēbəlˌmīndəd/ ▶ *adj.* (of a person) unable to make intelligent decisions or judgments. ■ (of an idea or proposal) lacking in sense or clear direction: *a feebleminded policy.* ■ *dated* (of a person) having less than average intelligence. —**fee·ble-mind·ed·ly** *adv.* —**fee·ble-mind·ed·ness** *n.*

feed /fēd/ ▶ *v.* (*past* **fed** /fed/) [*tr.*] **1** give food to: *the raiders fed the guard dog to keep it quiet.* ■ [*intr.*] (esp. of an animal or baby) take food; eat something: *morays emerge at night to feed.* ■ provide an adequate supply of food for: *the island's simple agriculture could hardly feed its inhabitants.* ■ [*intr.*] (**feed on/off**) derive regular nourishment from (a particular substance): *fig. his powerful mind fed off political discussion.* ■ encourage the growth of: *I could feed my melancholy by reading Romantic poetry.* ■ give fertilizer to (a plant). ■ put fuel on (a fire). **2** supply (a machine) with material, power, or other things necessary for its operation: *the programs are fed into the computer.* ■ supply (someone) with (information, ideas, etc.): *I think he is feeding his old employer commercial secrets.* ■ supply water to (a body of water): *the pond is fed by a small stream* | [*intr.*] *water feeds into the lower pool.* ■ distribute (a broadcast) to local television or radio stations via satellite or network: *programs that the national networks feed to local stations.*
▶ *n.* **1** an act of giving food, esp. to animals or a baby, or of having food given to one. ■ *inf.* a meal: *a nice hot feed.* ■ food for domestic animals: *cow feed.* **2** a device or conduit for supplying material to a machine: *the plotter has a continuous paper feed.* ■ the supply of raw material to a machine or device: [as *adj.*] *a feed pipe.* ■ a broadcast distributed by satellite or network from a central source to a large number of radio or television stations: *a satellite feed from Washington.*

feed·back /ˈfēdˌbak/ ▶ *n.* **1** information about reactions to a product, a person's performance of a task, etc., used as a basis for improvement. **2** the modification or control of a process or system by its results or effects, e.g., in a biochemical pathway or behavioral response. ■ the return of a fraction of the output signal from an amplifier, microphone, or other device to the input of the same device; sound distortion produced by this.

feed·er /ˈfēdər/ ▶ *n.* **1** a person or animal that eats a particular food or in a particular manner: *a plankton feeder.* **2** a container filled with food for birds or mammals. **3** a person or thing that supplies something, in particular: ■ a device supplying material to a machine: *the automatic sheet feeder holds 10 sheets of paper.* ■ a tributary stream. ■ [usu. as *adj.*] a branch road or railroad line linking outlying districts with a main communication system. ■ a transmission line carrying electricity to a distribution point. ■ [usu. as *adj.*] a school, sports team, etc., from which members move on to one more advanced: *a feeder school for Florida State University.*

feel /fēl/ ▶ *v.* (*past* **felt** /felt/) [*tr.*] **1** be aware of (a person or object) through touching or being touched: *she felt someone touch her shoulder.* ■ be aware of (something happening) through physical sensation: *she felt the ground give way beneath her.* ■ examine or search by touch: *he felt her hair* | [*intr.*] *he felt around for the matches.* ■ [*intr.*] be capable of sensation. ■ [*intr.*] give a sensation of a particular physical quality when touched: *the wool feels soft.* ■ (**feel one's way**) find one's way by touch rather than sight: *she plunged into the dark tunnel, feeling her way along the walls.* ■ (**feel one's way**) *fig.* act cautiously, esp. in an area with which one is unfamiliar: *she was new in the job, still feeling her way.* ■ (**feel something out**) *inf.* investigate something cautiously: *they want to feel out the situation.* **2** experience (an emotion or sensation): *I felt a sense of excitement* | [*intr.*] *I felt angry and humiliated.* ■ [*intr.*] consider oneself to be in a particular state or exhibiting particular qualities: *he doesn't feel obliged to visit every weekend.* ■ (**feel up to**) have the strength and energy to do or deal with: *she didn't feel up to driving.* ■ (**feel oneself**) be healthy and well: *Ruth was not quite feeling herself.* ■ be emotionally affected by: *he didn't feel the loss of his mother so keenly.* ■ [*intr.*] have a specified reaction or attitude, esp. an emotional one, toward something: *we feel very strongly about freedom of expression.* ■ (**feel for**) have compassion for: *poor woman—I feel for her.* **3** have a belief or impression, esp. without an identifiable reason: *she felt that the woman positively disliked her.* ■ hold an opinion: *I felt I could make a useful contribution.*

▶ *n.* **1** an act of touching something to examine it. ■ the sense of touch: *he worked by feel rather than using his eyes.* **2** a sensation given by an object or material when touched: *nylon cloth with a cotton feel.* ■ the impression given by something: *the restaurant has a modern bistro feel.*
▶ □ **feel free** (**to do something**) have no hesitation or shyness (often used as an invitation or for reassurance): *feel free to say what you like.* □ **feel like** (**doing**) **something** be inclined to have or do: *I feel like celebrating.* □ **get a** (or **the**) **feel for** (or **of**) familiarize oneself with: *you can explore to get a feel of the place.* □ **have a feel for** have a sensitive appreciation or an intuitive understanding of: *you have to have a feel for animals.* □ **make oneself** (or **one's presence**) **felt** make people keenly aware of one; have a noticeable effect: *the economic crisis began to make itself felt.*

feel·er /ˈfēlər/ ▶ *n.* an animal organ such as an antenna that is used for testing things by touch or for searching for food. ■ *fig.* a tentative proposal intended to ascertain someone's attitude or opinion: *he put out feelers about seeking the party nomination.*

feel·ing /ˈfēliNG/ ▶ *n.* **1** an emotional state or reaction: *a feeling of joy.* ■ (**feelings**) the emotional side of someone's character; emotional responses or tendencies to respond: *I don't want to hurt her feelings.* ■ strong emotion: *"God bless you!" she said with feeling.* **2** a belief, esp. a vague or irrational one: *he had the feeling that he was being watched.* ■ an opinion, typically one shared by several people: *a feeling that justice had not been done.* **3** the capacity to experience the sense of touch: *a loss of feeling in the hands.* ■ the sensation of touching or being touched by a particular thing: *the feeling of water against your skin.* **4** (**feeling for**) a sensitivity to or intuitive understanding of: *he seems to have little feeling for art.*
▶ *adj.* showing emotion or sensitivity: *he had a warm and feeling heart.* —**feel·ing·ly** *adv.*

feet /fēt/ ▶ plural form of **FOOT**.

feign /fān/ ▶ *v.* [*tr.*] pretend to be affected by (a feeling, state, or injury): *she feigned nervousness.* ■ *archaic* invent (a story or excuse). ■ [*intr.*] *archaic* indulge in pretense.

feint /fānt/ ▶ *n.* a deceptive or pretended blow, thrust, or other movement, esp. in boxing or fencing: *a feint at the base.* ■ a mock attack or movement in warfare, made to distract or deceive an enemy.
▶ *v.* [*intr.*] make a deceptive or distracting movement, typically during a fight. ■ [*tr.*] pretend to throw a (punch or blow) in order to deceive or distract an opponent: *feinting a left, I bobbed to the right.*

feist·y /ˈfīstē/ ▶ *adj.* (**feist·i·er, feist·i·est**) *inf.* having or showing exuberance and strong determination: *a feisty, outspoken, streetwise teenager.* ■ touchy and aggressive: *he got a bit feisty and tried to hit me.* —**feist·i·ly** /ˈfīstəlē/ *adv.* —**feist·i·ness** *n.*

fe·la·fel ▶ *n.* variant spelling of **FALAFEL**.

feld·spar /ˈfel(d)ˌspär/ ▶ *n.* an abundant rock-forming mineral typically occurring as colorless or pale-colored crystals and consisting of aluminosilicates of potassium, sodium, and calcium. —**feld·spath·ic** /fel(d)ˈspaTHik/ *adj.*

fe·lic·i·tate /fəˈlisəˌtāt/ ▶ *v.* [*tr.*] congratulate: *the award winner was felicitated by the cultural association.* —**fe·lic·i·ta·tion** /fəˌlisiˈtāSHən/ *n.*

fe·lic·i·tous /fəˈlisətəs/ ▶ *adj.* well chosen or suited to the circumstances: *a felicitous phrase.* ■ pleasing and fortunate: *the view was the room's only felicitous feature.* —**fe·lic·i·tous·ly** *adv.* —**fe·lic·i·tous·ness** *n.*

fe·lic·i·ty /fəˈlisətē/ ▶ *n.* (*pl.* **-ties**) **1** intense happiness: *domestic felicity.* **2** the ability to find appropriate expression for one's thoughts: *speech that pleased by its felicity and fluency.* ■ a particularly effective feature of a work of literature or art: *felicities of language.*

fe·line /ˈfēˌlīn/ ▶ *adj.* of, relating to, or affecting cats or other members of the cat family: *feline leukemia.* ■ catlike: *her face was feline in shape.*
▶ *n.* a cat or other member of the cat family. —**fe·lin·i·ty** /fēˈlinətē/ *n.*

fell[1] /fel/ ▶ past of **FALL**.

fell[2] ▶ *v.* [*tr.*] (usu. **be felled**) cut down (a tree). ■ knock down: *strong winds felled power lines* | *fig. corruption that felled the financial system in Thailand.*
▶ *n.* an amount of timber cut.

fell[3] ▶ *n.* a hill or stretch of high moorland, esp. in northern England. *an area of fell and moor.*

fell[4] ▶ *adj.* *poetic/lit.* of terrible evil or ferocity; deadly: *sorcerers use spells to achieve their fell ends.*
▶ □ **in one fell swoop** all at one time: *nothing can topple the government in one fell swoop.*

fell[5] ▶ *n.* *archaic* an animal's hide or skin with its hair.

fel·la·ti·o /fəˈlāSH(ē)ˌō/ ▶ *n.* oral stimulation of a man's penis. —**fel·late** /ˈfelāt/ *v.* —**fel·la·tor** /ˈfelˌātər/ *n.*

fell·er[1] /ˈfelər/ ▶ *n.* nonstandard spelling of **FELLOW**, used in representing speech in various dialects.

fell·er² ▶ *n.* a person who cuts down trees.

fel·low /ˈfelō/ ▶ *n.* **1** *inf.* a man or boy: *he was an extremely obliging fellow.* **2** (usu. **fellows**) a person in the same position, involved in the same activity, or otherwise associated with another: *he was learning with a rapidity unique among his fellows.* ■ a thing of the same kind as or otherwise associated with another: *the page has been torn away from its fellows.* **3** a member of a learned society: *he was elected a fellow of the Geological Society.* ■ (also **research fellow**) a student or graduate receiving a fellowship for a period of research. ■ a member of the governing body in some universities.
▶ *adj.* sharing a particular activity, quality, or condition with someone or something: *fellow citizens.*

fel·low feel·ing ▶ *n.* sympathy and fellowship existing between people based on shared experiences or feelings.

fel·low·ship /ˈfelōˌSHip/ ▶ *n.* **1** friendly association, esp. with people who share one's interests: *they valued fun and good fellowship as the cement of the community.* ■ a group of people meeting to pursue a shared interest or aim. **2** an endowment established or a sum of money awarded to support a scholar or student engaged in advanced research in a particular field: *a four-year postdoctoral fellowship.* ■ the status of a fellow of a college or society: *she held the Faulkner fellowship.*

fel·low trav·el·er ▶ *n.* a person who travels with another. ■ a person who is not a member of a particular group or political party (esp. the Communist Party), but who sympathizes with the group's aims and policies.

fel·on /ˈfelən/ ▶ *n.* a person who has been convicted of a felony.
▶ *adj. archaic* cruel; wicked: *the felon hand of dark corruption.*

fe·lo·ni·ous /fəˈlōnēəs/ ▶ *adj.* of, relating to, or involved in crime: *they turned their felonious talents to the smuggling trade.* ■ *Law* relating to or of the nature of felony: *his conduct was felonious.* —**fe·lo·ni·ous·ly** *adv.*

fel·o·ny /ˈfelənē/ ▶ *n.* (*pl.* **-nies**) a crime, typically one involving violence, regarded as more serious than a misdemeanor: *he pleaded guilty to six felonies* | *an accusation of felony.*

felt¹ /felt/ ▶ *n.* a kind of cloth made by rolling and pressing wool or another textile accompanied by the application of moisture or heat, which causes the fibers to mat together to create a smooth surface.
▶ *v.* [*tr.*] make into felt; mat together: *the wood fibers are shredded and felted together.* ■ [*intr.*] become matted: *care must be taken in washing, or the wool will shrink and felt.*

felt² ▶ past and past participle of FEEL.

fe·male /ˈfēˌmāl/ ▶ *adj.* of or denoting the sex that can bear offspring or produce eggs. ■ relating to or characteristic of women or female animals: *a female audience.* ■ (of a plant or flower) having a pistil but no stamens. ■ (of parts of machinery, fittings, etc.) manufactured hollow so that a corresponding male part can be inserted.
▶ *n.* a female person, animal, or plant. —**fe·male·ness** *n.*

fem·i·nine /ˈfemənin/ ▶ *adj.* **1** having qualities or appearance traditionally associated with women, esp. delicacy and prettiness: *a feminine frilled blouse.* ■ of or relating to women; female: *he enjoys feminine company.* **2** *Gram.* of or denoting a gender of nouns and adjectives, conventionally regarded as female. **3** *Mus.* (of a cadence) occurring on a metrically weak beat. —**fem·i·nine·ly** *adv.* —**fem·i·nin·i·ty** /ˌfemə-ˈninətē/ *n.*

fem·i·nism /ˈfeməˌnizəm/ ▶ *n.* the advocacy of women's rights on the grounds of political, social, and economic equality to men. —**fem·i·nist** *n. & adj.*

fem·i·nize /ˈfeməˌnīz/ ▶ *v.* [*tr.*] make (something) more characteristic of or associated with women: *as office roles changed, clerical work was increasingly feminized.* ■ induce female sexual characteristics in (a male). —**fem·i·ni·za·tion** /ˌfemənəˈzāSHən/ *n.*

femme fa·tale /ˌfem fəˈtal; fəˈtäl/ ▶ *n.* (*pl.* **femmes fa·tales** *pronunc.* same) an attractive and seductive woman, esp. one who will ultimately bring disaster to a man who becomes involved with her.

fe·mur /ˈfēmər/ ▶ *n.* (*pl.* **fe·murs** or **fem·o·ra** /ˈfemərə/) *Anat.* the bone of the thigh or upper hind limb, articulating at the hip and the knee. —**fem·o·ral** /ˈfemərəl/ *adj.*

fen¹ /fen/ ▶ *n.* a low and marshy or frequently flooded area of land. ■ *Ecol.* wetland with alkaline, neutral, or only slightly acid peaty soil. Compare with BOG.

fen² ▶ *n.* (*pl.* same) a monetary unit of China, equal to one hundredth of a yuan.

fence /fens/ ▶ *n.* **1** a barrier, railing, or other upright structure, typically of wood or wire, enclosing an area of ground to mark a boundary, control access, or prevent escape. ■ a large upright obstacle used in equestrian jumping events. **2** *inf.* a person who deals in stolen goods.
▶ *v.* **1** [*tr.*] surround or protect with a fence: *our garden was not fully fenced.* ■ (**fence something in/off**) enclose or separate with a fence for protection or to prevent escape: *everything is fenced in to keep out the wolves.* ■ (**fence someone/something out**) use a barrier to exclude someone or something: *Idaho law requires people to fence out cows.* **2** [*tr.*] *inf.* deal in (stolen goods): *after stealing the ring, he didn't even know how to fence it.* **3** [*intr.*] fight with swords, esp. as a sport. ■ *fig.* conduct a discussion or argument in such a way as to avoid the direct mention of something: *we were fencing instead of not talking about the subject we had come to talk about.* —**fenc·er** *n.*
▶ □ **side of the fence** either of the opposing positions involved in a conflict: *whatever side of the fence you are on, the issue is here to stay.* □ **sit on the fence** avoid making a decision or choice.

fenc·ing /ˈfensiNG/ ▶ *n.* **1** the sport of fighting with swords, esp. foils, épées, or sabers, according to a set of rules, in order to score points against an opponent: [as *adj.*] *a fencing foil.* ■ *fig.* the action of conducting a discussion or argument so as to avoid the direct mention of something. **2** a series of fences: *security fencing.* ■ material used for the construction of fences. ■ the erection of fences.

fend /fend/ ▶ *v.* **1** [*intr.*] (**fend for oneself**) look after and provide for oneself, without any help from others: *you're old enough to fend for yourself.* **2** [*tr.*] (**fend someone/something off**) defend oneself from a blow, attack, or attacker. ■ evade someone or something: *he fended off the awkward questions.*

fend·er /ˈfendər/ ▶ *n.* **1** a thing used to keep something off or prevent a collision, in particular: ■ the mudguard or area around the wheel well of a vehicle. ■ a plastic cylinder, tire, etc., hung over a ship's side to protect it against impact. ■ a metal frame at the front of a locomotive or streetcar for pushing aside obstacles on the tracks; a cowcatcher. **2** a low frame bordering a fireplace to contain burning materials.

fen·nel /ˈfenl/ ▶ *n.* an aromatic yellow-flowered European plant (*Foeniculum vulgare*) of the parsley family, with feathery leaves. The seeds and leaves of the perennial fennel are used as culinary herbs. The swollen leaf bases of **sweet fennel**, an annual, are eaten as a vegetable. ▷Old English *finule, fenol,* from Latin *faeniculum,* diminutive of *faenum* 'hay.'

fe·ral /ˈfi(ə)rəl; ˈferəl/ ▶ *adj.* (esp. of an animal) in a wild state, esp. after escape from captivity or domestication: *a feral cat.* ■ resembling or characteristic of a wild animal: *a feral snarl.*

fer de lance /ˌferdlˈäns; -ˈäns/ ▶ *n.* (*pl.* **fers de lance** /ˌfer(z)-/ or **fer de lances**) a large and dangerous pit viper (genus *Bothrops*) native to Central and South America.

fer·ma·ta /fərˈmätə; fer-/ ▶ *n. Music* a pause of unspecified length on a note or rest. ■ a mark (𝄐) designating such a pause.

fer·ment ▶ *v.* /fərˈment/ **1** [*intr.*] (of a substance) undergo fermentation. ■ [*tr.*] cause the fermentation of (a substance). **2** [*tr.*] incite or stir up (trouble or disorder): *the politicians and warlords who are fermenting this chaos.* ■ [*intr.*] (of a negative feeling or memory) fester and develop into something worse: *it had been fermenting in my subconscious for a while.*
▶ *n.* /ˈfərˌment/ **1** agitation and excitement among a group of people, typically concerning major change and leading to trouble or violence: *Germany at this time was in a state of religious ferment.* **2** *archaic* a fermenting agent or enzyme. —**fer·ment·a·ble** *adj.* —**fer·ment·er** *n.*

fer·men·ta·tion /ˌfərmənˈtāSHən/ ▶ *n.* the chemical breakdown of a substance by bacteria, yeasts, or other microorganisms, typically involving effervescence and the giving off of heat. ■ the process of this kind involved in the making of beer, wine, and liquor, in which sugars are converted to ethyl alcohol. —**fer·men·ta·tive** /fərˈmentətiv/ *adj.*

fer·mi·um /ˈfermēəm; ˈfər-/ ▶ *n.* the chemical element of atomic number 100, an artificial radioactive metal of the actinide series. (Symbol: **Fm**)

fern /fərn/ ▶ *n.* (*pl.* same or **ferns**) a flowerless plant (class Filicopsida, division Pteridophyta) that has feathery or leafy fronds and reproduces by spores released from the undersides of the fronds. —**fern·y** *adj.*

fe·ro·cious /fəˈrōSHəs/ ▶ *adj.* savagely fierce, cruel, or violent: *the wolverine is nature's most ferocious animal.* ■ (of a conflict) characterized by or involving aggression, bitterness, and determination: *a ferocious argument.* ■ extreme and unpleasant: *a ferocious headache.* —**fe·ro·cious·ly** *adv.* —**fe·ro·cious·ness** *n.*

fe·roc·i·ty /fəˈräsətē/ ▶ *n.* (*pl.* **-ties**) the state or quality of being ferocious: *the ferocity of the storm caught them by surprise.*

Pronunciation Key ə *ago,* up; ər *over, fur;* a *hat;* ā *ate;* ä *car;* CH *chin;* e *let;* ē *see;* e(ə)r *air;* i *fit;* ī *by;* i(ə)r *ear;* NG *sing;* ō *go;* ô *law, for;* oi *toy;* o͝o *good;* o͞o *goo;* ou *out;* SH *she;* TH *thin;* <u>TH</u> *then;* (h)w *why;* ZH *vision*

fer·rate /ˈferˌāt/ ▶n. Chem. a salt in which the anion contains both iron (typically ferric iron) and oxygen.

fer·ret /ˈferət/ ▶n. a domesticated polecat (*Mustela putorius furo*), typically albino or brown.
▶v. (**-ret·ed**, **-ret·ing**) [*intr.*] (of a person) hunt with ferrets, typically for rabbits. ■ look around in a place or container in search of something: *he went to the desk and ferreted around.* ■ [*tr.*] (**ferret something out**) search tenaciously for and find something: *ferret out the facts.* —**fer·ret·er** *n.*

fer·ric /ˈferik/ ▶adj. of or relating to iron. ■ Chem. of iron with a valence of three; of iron(III).

Fer·ris wheel /ˈferis/ ▶n. an amusement-park or fairground ride consisting of a giant vertical revolving wheel with passenger cars suspended on its outer edge.

fer·ro·mag·net·ic /ˌferōˌmagˈnetik/ ▶adj. Physics (of a body or substance) having a high susceptibility to magnetization, the strength of which depends on that of the applied magnetizing field, and that may persist after removal of the applied field. This is the kind of magnetism displayed by iron and is associated with parallel magnetic alignment of neighboring atoms. —**fer·ro·mag·ne·tism** /ˌferōˈmagnəˌtizəm/ *n.*

Ferris wheel

fer·rous /ˈferəs/ ▶adj. (chiefly of metals) containing or consisting of iron. ■ Chem. of iron with a valence of two; of iron(II).

fer·rule /ˈferəl/ ▶n. a ring or cap, typically a metal one, that strengthens the end of a handle, stick, or tube and prevents it from splitting or wearing. ■ a metal band strengthening or forming a joint.

fer·ry /ˈferē/ ▶n. (*pl.* **-ries**) (also **fer·ry·boat**) a boat or ship for conveying passengers and goods, esp. over a relatively short distance and as a regular service. ■ a service for conveying passengers or goods in this way. ■ a similar service using another mode of transportation, esp. aircraft.
▶v. (**-ries**, **-ried**) [*tr.*] convey in a boat, esp. across a short stretch of water: *riverboats ferried weekend picnickers to the park.* ■ transport (someone or something) from one place to another: *helicopters ferried 4,000 men into the desert.*

fer·tile /ˈfərtl/ ▶adj. (of soil or land) producing or capable of producing abundant vegetation or crops: *fields along the fertile flood plains of the river.* ■ (of a seed or egg) capable of becoming a new individual. ■ (of a person, animal, or plant) able to conceive young or produce seed. ■ (of a person's mind or imagination) producing many new and inventive ideas with ease. ■ (of a situation or subject) fruitful and productive in generating new ideas: *a series of fertile debates within the social sciences.* —**fer·til·i·ty** /fərˈtilitē/ *n.*

fer·til·i·za·tion /ˌfərtl-iˈzāSHən/ ▶n. Biol. the action or process of fertilizing an egg, female animal, or plant, involving the fusion of male and female gametes to form a zygote. ■ the action or process of applying a fertilizer to soil or land.

fer·ti·lize /ˈfərtlˌīz/ ▶v. [*tr.*] cause (an egg, female animal, or plant) to develop a new individual by introducing male reproductive material. ■ make (soil or land) more fertile or productive by adding suitable substances to it. —**fer·ti·liz·a·ble** *adj.*

fer·ti·liz·er /ˈfərtlˌīzər/ ▶n. a chemical or natural substance added to soil or land to increase its fertility: *a nitrogenous fertilizer.*

fer·vent /ˈfərvənt/ ▶adj. having or displaying a passionate intensity: *a fervent disciple of tax reform.* ■ archaic hot, burning, or glowing. ▷Middle English: via Old French from Latin *fervent-* 'boiling,' from the verb *fervere.* —**fer·ven·cy** /-vənsē/ *n.* —**fer·vent·ly** *adv.*

fer·vid /ˈfərvid/ ▶adj. intensely enthusiastic or passionate, esp. to an excessive degree: *a letter of fervid thanks.* ■ poetic/lit. burning, hot, or glowing. —**fer·vid·ly** *adv.*

fer·vor /ˈfərvər/ (Brit. **fer·vour**) ▶n. intense and passionate feeling: *he talked with all the fervor of a new convert.* ■ archaic intense heat.

fes·cue /ˈfeskyo͞o/ ▶n. any of a number of narrow-leaved grasses, esp. a perennial grass (genus *Festuca*) used for lawns, pasture, and fodder, and an annual grass (genus *Vulpia*) of drier soils.

fes·tal /ˈfestəl/ ▶adj. of, like, or relating to a celebration or festival: *he appeared in festal array.* —**fes·tal·ly** *adv.*

fes·ter /ˈfestər/ ▶v. [*intr.*] (of a wound or sore) become septic; suppurate: [as *adj.*] (**festering**) *a festering abscess.* ■ (of food or garbage) become rotten and offensive to the senses: *a gully full of garbage that festered in the sun.* ■ (of a negative feeling or a problem) become worse or more intense, esp. through neglect or indifference: *anger which festers and grows*

in his heart. ■ (of a person) undergo physical and mental deterioration in isolated inactivity: *I might be festering in jail now.*

fes·ti·val /ˈfestəvəl/ ▶n. a day or period of celebration, typically a religious commemoration. ■ an annual celebration or anniversary: *highlights of this year's pumpkin festival.* ■ an organized series of concerts, plays, or movies, typically one held annually: *traditional jazz festivals.*

fes·tive /ˈfestiv/ ▶adj. of or relating to a festival: *parties are held and festive food is served.* ■ cheerful and jovially celebratory: *the somber atmosphere has given way to a festive mood.* —**fes·tive·ly** *adv.* —**fes·tive·ness** *n.*

fes·tiv·i·ty /feˈstivitē/ ▶n. (*pl.* **-ties**) the celebration of something in a joyful and exuberant way: *the season of festivity and goodwill.* ■ (**festivities**) activities or events celebrating a special occasion: *the Chinese New Year is celebrated with a multitude of festivities.*

fes·toon /fesˈto͞on/ ▶n. a chain or garland of flowers, leaves, or ribbons, hung in a curve as a decoration. ■ a carved or molded ornament representing such a garland.
▶v. [*tr.*] adorn (a place) with chains, garlands, or other decorations: *the room was festooned with balloons and streamers.*

fet·a /ˈfetə/ (also **feta cheese**) ▶n. a white salty Greek cheese made from the milk of ewes or goats.

fetch[1] /feCH/ ▶v. [*tr.*] **1** go for and then bring back (someone or something): *he ran to fetch help.* **2** achieve (a particular price) when sold: *handwoven blankets and rugs that can fetch as much as $45,000.* **3** inf. inflict (a blow or slap) on (someone).
▶n. **1** an act of going for something and then bringing it back: *he thought the best part of the fetch was wrestling over the stick.* **2** the distance traveled by wind or waves across open water. **3** archaic a contrivance, dodge, or trick.

fetch[2] ▶n. chiefly archaic the apparition or double of a living person, formerly believed to be a warning of that person's impending death.

fetch·ing /ˈfeCHiNG/ ▶adj. attractive: *a fetching little dress of pink satin.* —**fetch·ing·ly** *adv.*

fête /fāt; fet/ (also **fete**) ▶n. a celebration or festival.
▶v. [*tr.*] (usu. **be fêted**) honor or entertain (someone) lavishly: *she was an instant celebrity, fêted by the media.*

fet·id /ˈfetid/ (Brit. also **foet·id**) ▶adj. smelling extremely unpleasant: *the fetid water of the marsh.* —**fet·id·ly** *adv.* —**fet·id·ness** *n.*

fet·ish /ˈfetiSH/ ▶n. an inanimate object worshiped for its supposed magical powers or because it is considered to be inhabited by a spirit. ■ a course of action to which one has an excessive and irrational commitment: *he had a fetish for writing more opinions each year than any other justice.* ■ a form of sexual desire in which gratification is linked to a particular object, item of clothing, part of the body, etc. ▷early 17th cent. (originally denoting an object used by the peoples of West Africa as an amulet or charm): from French *fétiche*, from Portuguese *feitiço* 'charm, sorcery' (originally an adjective meaning 'made by art'), from Latin *facticius*, from *facere* 'do, make.' —**fet·ish·ism** *n.* —**fet·ish·ist** *n.* —**fet·ish·is·tic** *adj.*

fet·lock /ˈfetˌläk/ (also **fetlock joint**) ▶n. the joint of a horse's or other quadruped's leg between the cannon bone and the pastern. ■ the tuft of hair that grows at this joint.

fet·ter /ˈfetər/ ▶n. (usu. **fetters**) a chain or manacle used to restrain a prisoner, typically placed around the ankles. ■ a restraint or check on someone's freedom to do something, typically one considered unfair or overly restrictive: *the fetters of discipline and caution.*
▶v. [*tr.*] restrain with chains or manacles, typically around the ankles: [as *adj.*] (**fettered**) *a ragged and fettered prisoner.* ■ restrict or restrain (someone) in an unfair or undesirable fashion: *he was not fettered by tradition.*

fet·tle /ˈfetl/ ▶n. condition: *although old, the aircraft remains in fine fettle.* —**fet·tler** /ˈfetl-ər/ *n.*

fet·tuc·ci·ne /ˌfetəˈCHēnē/ (also **fet·tu·ci·ni**) ▶n. pasta made in ribbons.

fe·tus /ˈfētəs/ ▶n. (*pl.* **-tus·es**) an unborn offspring of a mammal, in particular an unborn human baby more than eight weeks after conception. —**fe·tal** /ˈfētl/ *adj.*

feud /fyo͞od/ ▶n. a state of prolonged mutual hostility, typically between two families or communities, characterized by violent assaults in revenge for previous injuries. ■ a prolonged and bitter quarrel or dispute: *one of the most volatile feuds that currently rock the scientific community.*
▶v. [*intr.*] take part in such a quarrel or violent conflict: *Hoover feuded with the CIA for decades.*

feu·dal /ˈfyo͞odl/ ▶adj. according to, resembling, or denoting the system of feudalism: *feudal barons.* —**feu·dal·i·za·tion** /ˌfyo͞odl-iˈzāSHən/ *n.*

feu·dal·ism /ˈfyo͞odlˌizəm/ ▶n. historical the dominant social system in medieval Europe, in which the nobility held lands from the Crown in exchange for military service, and vassals were in turn tenants of the nobles, while the peasants (villeins or serfs) were obliged to live on their lord's land and give him homage, labor, and a share of the produce, notionally in exchange for military protection. **—feu·dal·ist** *n.* **—feu·dal·is·tic** *adj.*

fe·ver /ˈfēvər/ ▸*n.* an abnormally high body temperature, usually accompanied by shivering, headache, and in severe instances, delirium. ■ a state of nervous excitement or agitation: *I was mystified, and in a fever of expectation.* ■ the excitement felt by a group of people about a particular public event: *election fever reaches its climax tomorrow.*

fe·ver·few /ˈfēvərˌfyo͞o/ ▸*n.* a bushy aromatic plant (*Tanacetum parthenium*) of the daisy family, with feathery leaves and daisylike flowers. It is used in herbal medicine to treat headaches.

fe·ver·ish /ˈfēv(ə)riSH/ ▸*adj.* having or showing the symptoms of a fever. ■ displaying frenetic excitement or energy: *the month was spent in a whirl of feverish activity.* **—fe·ver·ish·ly** *adv.* **—fe·ver·ish·ness** *n.*

few /fyo͞o/ ▸*adj. & pron.* **1** (**a few**) a small number of: [as *adj.*] *may I ask a few questions?* | [as *pron.*] *I will recount a few of the stories told me.* **2** used to emphasize how small a number of people or things is: [as *adj.*] *he had few friends* | [as *pron.*] *few thought to challenge these assumptions* | *one of the few who survived* | [*comparative*] *a population of fewer than two million.*
▸*n.* [as *pl. n.*] (**the few**) the minority of people; the elect: *a world that increasingly belongs to the few.* ▷Old English *fēawe, fēawa*; from an Indo-European root shared by Latin *paucus* and Greek *pauros* 'small.'
▸ □ **every few** once in every small group of (typically units of time): *she visits every few weeks.* □ **few and far between** scarce; infrequent: *my inspired moments are few and far between.* □ **no fewer than** used to emphasize a surprisingly large number: *there are no fewer than seventy different brand names.* □ **not a few** a considerable number: *his fiction has caused not a few readers to see red.* □ **quite a few** a fairly large number: *quite a few people can do it.*

fey /fā/ ▸*adj.* giving an impression of vague unworldliness: *his mother was a strange, fey woman.* ■ having supernatural powers of clairvoyance.

fez /fez/ ▸*n.* (*pl.* **fez·zes**) a flat-topped conical red hat with a black tassel on top, worn by men in some Muslim countries (formerly the Turkish national headdress). **—fezzed** *adj.*

ff *Mus.* ▸*abbr.* fortissimo.

ff. ▸*abbr.* ■ folios. ■ following pages.

FHA ▸*abbr.* Federal Housing Administration.

fi·an·cé /ˌfēänˈsā; fēˈänsā/ ▸*n.* a man who is engaged to be married.

fi·an·cée /ˌfēänˈsā; fēˈänsā/ ▸*n.* a woman who is engaged to be married.

fi·as·co /fēˈaskō/ ▸*n.* (*pl.* **-cos**) a thing that is a complete failure, esp. in a ludicrous or humiliating way: *his plans turned into a fiasco.*

fi·at /ˈfēət; ˈfēˌät/ ▸*n.* a formal authorization or proposition; a decree: *trying to regulate by fiat.* ■ an arbitrary order: *worthless by bureaucratic fiat.*

fib /fib/ ▸*n.* a lie, typically an unimportant one.
▸*v.* (**fibbed, fib·bing**) [*intr.*] tell such a lie. **—fib·ber** *n.*

fi·ber /ˈfībər/ (*Brit.* **fi·bre**) ▸*n.* **1** a thread or filament from which a vegetable tissue, mineral substance, or textile is formed. ■ a substance formed of such threads or filaments: *ordinary synthetics don't breathe as well as natural fibers* | *high strength carbon fiber.* ■ a threadlike structure forming part of the muscular, nervous, connective, or other tissue in the human or animal body: *muscle fibers* | *fig.* *she wanted him with every fiber of her being.* | *fig.* strength of character: *a weak person with no moral fiber.* **2** dietary material containing substances such as cellulose, lignin, and pectin, which are resistant to the action of digestive enzymes: *cereals high in fiber.*

fi·ber·board /ˈfībərˌbôrd/ (*Brit.* **fi·bre·board**) ▸*n.* a building material made of wood or other plant fibers compressed into boards.

fi·ber·glass /ˈfībərˌglas/ (*Brit.* **fi·bre·glass**) (also *trademark* **Fi·ber·glas**) ▸*n.* **1** a reinforced plastic material composed of glass fibers embedded in a resin matrix. **2** a woollike mass of glass filaments, used in insulation. **3** a textile fabric made from woven glass filaments.

fi·ber op·tics ▸*pl. n.* [treated as *sing.*] the use of thin flexible fibers of glass or other transparent solids to transmit light signals, chiefly for telecommunications or for internal examination of the body. ■ [treated as *pl.*] the fibers and associated devices so used. **—fi·ber-op·tic** *adj.*

Fi·bo·nac·ci se·ries (also **Fibonacci sequence**) ▸*n. Math.* a series of numbers in which each number (**Fibonacci number**) is the sum of the two preceding numbers. The simplest is the series 1, 1, 2, 3, 5, 8, etc.

fez

fi·bril /ˈfībrəl; ˈfib-/ ▸*n. technical* a small or slender fiber: *each fiber is subdivided into smaller fibrils.* **—fi·bril·lar** /-lər/ *adj.* **—fi·bril·lar·y** /-ˌlerē/ *adj.*

fi·bril·late /ˈfībrəˌlāt/ ▸*v.* [*intr.*] **1** (of a muscle, esp. in the heart) make a quivering movement due to uncoordinated contraction of the individual fibrils. **2** (of a fiber) split up into fibrils. ■ [*tr.*] break (a fiber) into fibrils. **—fi·bril·la·tion** /ˌfībrəˈlāSHən/ *n.*

fi·broid /ˈfīˌbroid/ ▸*adj.* of or characterized by fibers or fibrous tissue.
▸*n. Med.* a benign tumor of muscular and fibrous tissues, typically developing in the wall of the uterus.

fi·bro·my·al·gia /ˌfībrōmīˈalj(ē)ə/ ▸*n.* a chronic disorder characterized by musculoskeletal pain, fatigue, and tenderness in localized areas.

fi·bro·sis /fīˈbrōsəs/ ▸*n. Med.* the thickening and scarring of connective tissue, usually as a result of injury. **—fi·brot·ic** /fīˈbrätik/ *adj.*

fi·brous /ˈfībrəs/ ▸*adj.* consisting of or characterized by fibers: *lignin is the fibrous material that gives wood its strength.*

fib·u·la /ˈfibyələ/ ▸*n.* (*pl.* **-lae** /-ˌlē; -ˌlī/ or **-las**) *Anat.* the outer and usually smaller of the two bones between the knee and the ankle in humans (or equivalent joints in other terrestrial vertebrates), parallel with the tibia. **—fib·u·lar** /ˈfibyələr/ *adj.*

FICA ▸*abbr.* Federal Insurance Contributions Act.

fiche /fēSH/ ▸*n.* short for MICROFICHE.

fick·le /ˈfikəl/ ▸*adj.* changing frequently, esp. as regards one's loyalties, interests, or affection: *the weather is forever fickle.* **—fick·le·ness** *n.*

fic·tile /ˈfiktl; -ˌtīl/ ▸*adj.* made of earth or clay by a potter. ■ of or relating to pottery or its manufacture. ■ capable of being molded; plastic.

fic·tion /ˈfikSHən/ ▸*n.* literature in the form of prose, esp. short stories and novels, that describes imaginary events and people. ■ invention or fabrication as opposed to fact: *he dismissed the allegation as absolute fiction.* ■ a belief or statement that is false, but that is often held to be true because it is expedient to do so: *the notion of that country being a democracy is a polite fiction.* **—fic·tion·al** /-SHənl/ *adj.* **—fic·tion·al·ly** *adv.* **—fic·tion·ist** *n.*

fic·ti·tious /fikˈtiSHəs/ ▸*adj.* not real or true, being imaginary or having been fabricated: *she pleaded guilty to having a fictitious employee on her payroll.* ■ of, relating to, or denoting the imaginary characters and events found in fiction: *the people in this novel are fictitious; the background of public events is not.* **—fic·ti·tious·ly** *adv.* **—fic·ti·tious·ness** *n.*

fic·tive /ˈfiktiv/ ▸*adj.* creating or created by imagination: *the novel's fictive universe.* **—fic·tive·ness** *n.*

fid·dle /ˈfidl/ ▸*n.* **1** *inf.* a violin, esp. when used to play folk music. **2** *inf.*, chiefly *Brit.* an act of defrauding, cheating, or falsifying: *a major mortgage fiddle.*
▸*v. inf.* **1** [*intr.*] play the fiddle: (**fiddling**) *country music with lots of fiddling and banjo playing.* ■ [*tr.*] play (a tune) on the fiddle. **2** [*intr.*] touch or fidget with something in a restless or nervous way: *Laura fiddled with her cup.* ■ tinker with something in an attempt to make minor adjustments or improvements: *never fiddle with an electric machine that's plugged in.* ■ (**fiddle around**) pass time aimlessly, without doing or achieving anything of substance. **3** [*tr.*] falsify (figures, data, or records), typically in order to gain money: *everyone is fiddling their expenses.* **—fid·dler** *n.*
▸ □ (**as**) **fit as a fiddle** in good health. □ **play second fiddle to** take a subordinate role to someone or something in a way often considered demeaning: *she had to play second fiddle to the interests of her husband.*

fid·dle-de-dee /ˌfidl dē ˈdē/ ▸*n.* [often as *interj.*] *dated* nonsense.

fid·dle-fad·dle /ˈfidl ˌfadl/ ▸*n.* trivial matters: nonsense.
▸*v.* [*intr.*] bother with trifles; fuss: *you haven't time to fiddle-faddle about like that.*

fid·dle·head /ˈfidlˌhed/ ▸*n.* (also **fiddlehead fern**) the young, curled, edible frond of certain ferns.

fid·dle·stick /ˈfidlˌstik/ ▸*interj.* (**fiddlesticks**) nonsense.
▸*n. inf.* a violin bow.

fi·del·i·ty /fəˈdelətē/ ▸*n.* faithfulness to a person, cause, or belief, demonstrated by continuing loyalty and support. ■ sexual faithfulness to a spouse or partner. ■ the degree of exactness with which something is copied or reproduced: *the 1949 recording provides reasonable fidelity.*

fidg·et /ˈfijit/ ▸*v.* (**fidg·et·ed, fidg·et·ing**) [*intr.*] make small movements, esp. of the hands and feet, through nervousness or impatience: *the audience had begun to fidget on their chairs.*
▸*n.* a quick, small movement, typically a repeated one, caused by

nervousness or impatience: *he disturbed other people with convulsive fidgets.* ■ a person given to such movements, esp. one whom other people find irritating. ■ (usu. **fidgets**) a state of mental or physical restlessness or uneasiness: *a marketing person full of nervous energy and fidgets.* —**fidg·et·er** n. —**fidg·et·y** adj.

fi·du·ci·ar·y /fəˈdo͞oSHē,erē; -SHərē/ ▶ adj. Law involving trust, esp. with regard to the relationship between a trustee and a beneficiary: *the company has a fiduciary duty to shareholders.* ■ archaic held or given in trust: *fiduciary estates.* ■ Finance (of a paper currency) depending for its value on securities (as opposed to gold) or the reputation of the issuer. ▶ n. (pl. -**ar·ies**) a trustee.

fie /fī/ ▶ interj. archaic or humorous used to express disgust or outrage: *if people don't answer your first letter, fie on them!*

fief /fēf/ ▶ n. **1** hist. an estate of land, esp. one held on condition of feudal service. **2** a person's sphere of operation or control.

fief·dom /ˈfēfdəm/ ▶ n. a fief.

field /fēld/ ▶ n. **1** an area of open land, esp. one planted with crops or pasture, typically bounded by hedges or fences: *a wheat field | a field of corn.* ■ a piece of land used for a particular purpose, esp. an area marked out for a game or sport: *a football field.* ■ Baseball defensive play or the defensive positions collectively: *he is fast in the field and on the bases.* ■ a large area of land or water completely covered in a particular substance, esp. snow or ice. ■ an area rich in a natural product, typically oil or gas: *an oil field.* ■ an area on which a battle is fought: *a field of battle.* ■ an area on a flag with a single background color: *fifty white stars on a blue field.* ■ a place where a subject of scientific study or artistic representation can be observed in its natural location or context. **2** a particular branch of study or sphere of activity or interest: *we talked to professionals in various fields.* ■ Comput. a part of a record, representing an item of data. **3** (usu. **the field**) all the participants in a contest or sport: *he destroyed the rest of the field with a devastating injection of speed.* **4** Physics the region in which a particular condition prevails, esp. one in which a force or influence is effective regardless of the presence or absence of a material medium. ■ the force exerted or potentially exerted in such an area: *the variation in the strength of the field.*
▶ v. **1** [intr.] Baseball play as a fielder. ■ [tr.] catch or stop (the ball): *he fielded the ball cleanly, but threw it down the right-field line.* **2** [tr.] send out (a team or individual) to play in a game: *a high school that traditionally fielded mediocre teams.* ■ (of a political party) nominate (a candidate) to run in an election: *a radical political party that is beginning to field candidates in local elections.* ■ deploy (an army): *the small gulf sheikhdoms fielded 11,500 troops with the Saudis.* **3** [tr.] deal with (a difficult question, telephone call, etc.): *she has fielded five calls from salespeople.*
▶ adj. carried out or working in the natural environment, rather than in a laboratory or office: *field observations.* ■ (of an employee or work) away from the home office; remote: *a field representative.* ■ (of military equipment) light and mobile for use on campaign: *field artillery.* ■ denoting a game played outdoors on a marked field. —**field·er** n.
▶ ▫ **play the field** inf. indulge in a series of sexual relationships without committing oneself to anyone.

field day ▶ n. **1** Mil. a review or an exercise, esp. in maneuvering. **2** a day devoted to athletic contests or other sporting events, typically at a school. **3** an opportunity for action, success, or excitement, esp. at the expense of others: *shoplifters are **having a field day** in the store.*

field glass·es ▶ pl. n. binoculars for outdoor use.

field goal ▶ n. **1** Football a goal scored by a placekick, scoring three points. **2** Basketball a basket scored while the clock is running and the ball is in play.

field hock·ey ▶ n. a game played between two teams of eleven players who use hooked sticks to drive a hard ball toward the goals.

field hos·pi·tal ▶ n. a temporary hospital set up near a combat zone to provide emergency care for the wounded.

field mar·shal ▶ n. an officer of the highest rank in the British and other armies.

field mouse ▶ n. a dark brown mouse (genus *Apodemus*) with a long tail and large eyes.

field of vi·sion ▶ n. the entire area that a person or animal is able to see when their eyes are fixed in one position.

field·work /ˈfēldˌwərk/ ▶ n. practical work conducted by a researcher in the natural environment. —**field·work·er** n.

fiend /fēnd/ ▶ n. an evil spirit or demon. ■ a wicked or cruel person: *a fiend thirsty for blood and revenge.* ■ a person causing mischief or annoyance: *you little fiend!* ■ inf. a person who is excessively fond of or addicted to something: *a wine fiend.* ▷Old English *fēond* 'an enemy, the devil, a demon,' of Germanic origin; related to Dutch *vijand* and German *Feind* 'enemy.' —**fiend·ish** adj.

fierce /fi(ə)rs/ ▶ adj. (**fierc·er, fierc·est**) having or displaying an intense or ferocious aggressiveness: *the fierce air battles that ensued over the Pacific.* ■ (of a feeling, emotion, or action) showing a heartfelt and powerful intensity: *a fierce, demanding passion.* ■ (of the weather or temperature) powerful and destructive in extent or intensity: *fierce storms lashed the country.* —**fierce·ly** adv. —**fierce·ness** n.

fier·y /ˈfī(ə)rē/ ▶ adj. (**fier·i·er, fier·i·est**) consisting of fire or burning strongly and brightly: *the sun was a fiery ball low on the hills | fig. a fiery hot chili sauce.* ■ having the bright color of fire: *the car was painted a fiery red.* ■ (of a person) having a passionate, quick-tempered nature: *a fiery, imaginative Aries.* ■ (of behavior or words) passionately angry and deeply felt: *a fiery speech.* —**fier·i·ly** adv. —**fier·i·ness** n.

fi·es·ta /fēˈestə/ ▶ n. (in Spanish-speaking regions) a religious festival. ■ an event marked by festivities or celebration: *a balloon fiesta.*

fife /fīf/ ▶ n. a kind of small shrill flute used esp. in military bands.

fife

fif·teen /fifˈtēn; ˈfifˌtēn/ ▶ cardinal number equivalent to the product of three and five; one more than fourteen, or five more than ten; 15. (Roman numeral: **xv** or **XV**.) ■ fifteen years old: *she must be fifteen by now.* —**fif·teenth** adj.

fifth /fifTH/ ▶ ordinal number constituting number five in a sequence; 5th: *the fifth century* BC. ■ (**a fifth/one fifth**) each of five equal parts into which something is or may be divided. ■ the fifth finisher or position in a race or competition: *he finished fifth.* ■ (in some vehicles) the fifth (and typically highest) in a sequence of gears. ■ fifthly (used to introduce a fifth point or reason). ■ Mus. an interval spanning five consecutive notes in a diatonic scale, in particular (also **perfect fifth**) an interval of three whole steps and a half step (e.g., C to G). ■ Mus. the note that is higher by such an interval than the root of a diatonic scale. ■ a fifth of a gallon, as a measure of liquor, or a bottle of this capacity: *a fifth of whiskey.* ■ the fifth grade of a school. —**fifth·ly** adv.

fifth col·umn ▶ n. a group within a country at war who are sympathetic to or working for its enemies. —**fifth col·umn·ist** n.

fifth wheel ▶ n. **1** an extra wheel for a four-wheeled vehicle. ■ inf. a superfluous person or thing. **2** a coupling between a trailer and a vehicle used for towing.

fif·ty /ˈfiftē/ ▶ cardinal number (pl. **-ties**) the number equivalent to the product of five and ten; half of one hundred; 50. (Roman numeral: **l** or **L**.) ■ (**fifties**) the numbers from 50 to 59, esp. the years of a century or of a person's life: *Elvis is the icon of the Fifties.* ■ fifty years old: *she looked about fifty.* ■ fifty miles an hour: *doing about fifty.* ■ a fifty-dollar bill. —**fif·ti·eth** /ˈfiftē-iTH/ ordinal number

fif·ty-fif·ty ▶ adj. the same in share or proportion; equal: *fifty-fifty partners.* ■ used to refer to one of two possibilities that are equally likely to happen: *he has a fifty-fifty chance of surviving the operation.*
▶ adv. equally; half and half: *they divided the spoils fifty-fifty.*

fig¹ /fig/ ▶ n. **1** a soft pear-shaped fruit with sweet dark flesh and many small seeds, eaten fresh or dried. **2** (also **fig tree**) the deciduous Old World tree or shrub (*Ficus carica*) of the mulberry family that bears this fruit.

fig² inf. ▶ n. (in phrase **full fig**) smart clothes, esp. those appropriate to a particular occasion or profession: *a soldier walking up the street in full fig.*
▶ v. (**figged, fig·ging**) [tr.] archaic dress up (someone) to look smart: *he was figged out in the latest modes.*

fig. ▶ abbr. figure: see *fig.* 34.

fight /fīt/ ▶ v. (past and past part. **fought** /fôt/) [intr.] take part in a violent struggle involving the exchange of physical blows or the use of weapons: *the men were fighting.* ■ [tr.] engage in (a war or battle): ■ [intr.] *we fought and died for this country.* ■ quarrel or argue: *they were fighting over who pays the bill.* ■ [tr.] struggle to put out (a fire, esp. a large one): *two fire trucks raced to the scene to fight the blaze.* ■ [tr.] endeavor vigorously to win (an election or other contest). ■ campaign determinedly for or against something, esp. to put right what one considers unfair or unjust: *I will fight for more equitable laws.* ■ [tr.] struggle or campaign against (something): *the best way to fight fascism abroad and racism at home.* ■ [tr.] attempt to repress (a feeling or an expression of a feeling): *she had to fight back tears of frustration.* ■ [intr.] take part in a boxing match against (an opponent). ■ (**fight one's way**) move forward with difficulty, esp. by pushing through a crowd or overcoming physical obstacles: *she watched him fight his way across the room.*
▶ phrasal v. □ **fight back** counterattack or retaliate in a fight, struggle, or contest. □ **fight it out** settle a dispute by fighting or competing aggressively: *they fought it out with a tug-of-war.* □ **fight someone/some-**

thing off defend oneself against an attack by someone or something: *well-fed people are better able to fight off infectious disease.*

▶ *n.* a violent confrontation or struggle. ■ a boxing match. ■ a battle or war: *the country was not eager for a fight with the U.S.* ■ a vigorous struggle or campaign for or against something: *a long fight against cancer.* ■ an argument or quarrel: *she had a fight with her husband.* ■ the inclination or ability to fight or struggle: *Ginny felt the fight trickle out of her.*

▶ □ **fight fire with fire** use the weapons or tactics of one's enemy or opponent, even if one finds them distasteful. □ **fight a losing battle** be fated to fail in one's efforts: *he was fighting a losing battle to stem the tears.* □ **fight or flight** the instinctive physiological response to a threatening situation, which readies one either to resist forcibly or to run away.

fight·er /ˈfītər/ ▶ *n.* **1** a person or animal that fights, esp. as a soldier or a boxer. ■ a person who does not easily admit defeat in spite of difficulties or opposition. **2** a fast military aircraft designed for attacking other aircraft: *designers employ stealth to render a fighter invisible to radar.*

fight·ing chance ▶ *n.* a possibility of success if great effort is made: *they still have a fighting chance of clinching the title.*

fig·ment /ˈfigmənt/ ▶ *n.* a thing that someone believes to be real but that exists only in their imagination: *it really was Ross and not a figment of her overheated **imagination**.*

fig·u·ra·tion /ˌfigyəˈrāSHən/ ▶ *n.* **1** ornamentation by means of figures or designs. ■ *Mus.* use of florid counterpoint: *the figuration of the accompaniment comes out too strongly.* **2** allegorical representation: *the opening parable may be read as a figuration of the main idea behind the novel.*

fig·ur·a·tive /ˈfigyərətiv/ ▶ *adj.* **1** departing from a literal use of words; metaphorical: *gold, in figurative language, was "the tears wept by the sun."* **2** (of an artist or work of art) representing forms that are recognizably derived from life. —**fig·ur·a·tive·ly** *adv.* —**fig·ur·a·tive·ness** *n.*

fig·ure /ˈfigyər/ ▶ *n.* **1** a number, esp. one that forms part of official statistics or relates to the financial performance of a company: *official census figures.* ■ a numerical symbol, esp. any of the ten in Arabic notation: *the figure 7.* ■ one of a specified number of digits making up a larger number, used to give a rough idea of the order of magnitude: *their market price runs into five figures* | [in comb.] *a six-figure salary.* ■ an amount of money: *a figure of two thousand dollars.* ■ (**figures**) arithmetical calculations: *she has no **head for figures**.* **2** a person's bodily shape, esp. that of a woman: *she had always been so proud of her figure.* ■ a person of a particular kind, esp. one who is important or distinctive in some way: *Williams became something of a cult figure.* ■ a representation of a human or animal form in drawing or sculpture: *starkly painted figures.* **3** a shape defined by one or more lines in two dimensions (such as a circle or a triangle), or one or more surfaces in three dimensions (such as a sphere): *a red ground with white and blue geometric figures.* ■ a diagram or illustrative drawing, esp. in a book or magazine. ■ *Figure Skating* a movement or series of movements following a prescribed pattern and often beginning and ending at the same point. ■ a pattern formed by the movements of a group of people, for example in square dancing or synchronized swimming, as part of a longer dance or display. ■ *archaic* the external form or shape of a thing. **4** *Mus.* a short succession of notes producing a single impression.

▶ *v.* [*intr.*] **1** be a significant and noticeable part of something: *the issue of nuclear policy figured prominently in the talks.* ■ (of a person) play a significant role in a situation or event: *he figured largely in opposition to the bill.* **2** [*tr.*] calculate or work out (an amount or value) arithmetically. **3** *inf.* think, consider, or expect to be the case: [*tr.*] *for years, teachers had figured him for a dullard.* ■ (of a recent event or newly discovered fact) be logical and unsurprising: *well, she supposed **that figured**.*

▶ *phrasal v.* □ **figure on** *inf.* count or rely on something happening or being the case in the future: *anyone thinking of salmon fishing should figure on paying $200 a day.* □ **figure something out** *inf.* solve or discover the cause of a problem: *he was trying to figure out why the camera wasn't working.* □ **figure someone out** reach an understanding of a person's actions, motives, or personality. ▷Middle English (in the senses 'distinctive shape of a person or thing,' 'representation of something material or immaterial,' and 'numerical symbol,' among others): from Old French *figure* (noun), *figurer* (verb), from Latin *figura* 'shape, figure, form'; related to *fingere* 'form, contrive.'

▶ □ **figure of speech** a word or phrase used in a nonliteral sense to add rhetorical force to a spoken or written passage: *calling her a crab is just a figure of speech.*

fig·ure eight ▶ *n.* an object or movement having the shape of the number eight.

fig·ure·head /ˈfigyərˌhed/ ▶ *n.* **1** a nominal leader or head without real power. **2** *hist.* a carving, typically a bust or a full-length figure, set at the prow of a sailing ship.

fig·ure skat·ing ▶ *n.* the competitive sport of ice skating in prescribed patterns (*figures*) and choreographed free skating. —**fig·ure skat·er** *n.*

fig·ur·ine /ˌfigyəˈrēn/ ▶ *n.* a statuette, esp. one of a human form.

fig·wort /ˈfigˌwərt; -ˌwôrt/ ▶ *n.* a widely distributed herbaceous plant (genus *Scrophularia*) with purplish-brown two-lobed flowers. The **figwort family** (Scrophulariaceae) includes the snapdragons, toadflaxes, foxgloves, and mulleins.

fil·a·ment /ˈfiləmənt/ ▶ *n.* a slender threadlike object or fiber, esp. one found in animal or plant structures: *a filament of cellulose.* ■ a conducting wire or thread with a high melting point, forming part of an electric bulb or vacuum tube and heated or made incandescent by an electric current. —**fil·a·men·ta·ry** /ˌfiləˈmentərē/ *adj.* —**fil·a·men·tous** /-ˌmentəs/ *adj.*

fil·a·ri·a·sis /ˌfiləˈrīəsəs/ ▶ *n. Med.* a tropical disease caused by the presence of threadlike parasitic nematodes, esp. in the lymph vessels, where heavy infestation can result in elephantiasis. The worms are transmitted by biting flies and mosquitoes.

fil·bert /ˈfilbərt/ ▶ *n.* a cultivated hazel tree (genus *Corylus*) that bears edible oval nuts. ■ the nut of this tree.

filch /filCH/ ▶ *v.* [*tr.*] *inf.* pilfer or steal (something, esp. a thing of small value) in a casual way. —**filch·er** *n.*

file[1] /fīl/ ▶ *n.* a folder or box for holding loose papers that are typically arranged in a particular order for easy reference: *a file of correspondence.* ■ the contents of such a folder or box. ■ *Comput.* a collection of data, programs, etc., stored in a computer's memory or on a storage device under a single identifying name: *do you want to save this file?*

▶ *v.* [*tr.*] place (a document) in a cabinet, box, or folder in a particular order for preservation and easy reference: *fig. he still had the moment filed away in his memory.* ■ submit (a legal document, application, or charge) to be placed on record by the appropriate authority: *criminal charges were filed against the firm* | [*intr.*] *the company had filed for bankruptcy.* ■ (of a reporter) send (a story) to a newspaper or news organization.

▶ □ **on file** in a file or filing system.

file[2] ▶ *n.* a line of people or things one behind another: *Plains Cree warriors riding in file down the slopes.* ■ *Mil.* a small detachment of men: *a file of English soldiers had ridden out from Perth.*

▶ *v.* [*intr.*] (of a group of people) walk one behind the other, typically in an orderly and solemn manner: *the mourners filed into the church.*

file[3] ▶ *n.* a tool with a roughened surface used for smoothing or shaping a hard material: *it is possible to make the necessary notch with a file.*

▶ *v.* [*tr.*] smooth or shape (something) with such a tool: *when I have nothing else to do, I file my nails.* ■ (**file something away/off**) remove something by grinding it off with a file: *the engine numbers were filed away.*

fi·lé /fiˈlā; ˈfēlā/ ▶ *n.* pounded or powdered sassafras leaves used to flavor and thicken soup, esp. gumbo. ▷mid 19th cent.: from French, past participle of *filer* 'to twist.'

file-shar·ing ▶ *n.* the practice of or ability to transmit files from one computer to another over a network or the Internet: *file-sharing software.*

fi·let /fiˈlā; ˈfilā/ ▶ *n.* **1** French spelling of FILLET, used esp. in the names of French or French-sounding dishes: *filet de boeuf.* **2** a kind of net or lace with a square mesh.

figurehead

fi·let mi·gnon /fi,lā mēn'yōN/ ▸ *n.* a small tender piece of beef from the end of the tenderloin.

fil·i·al /'filēəl; 'filyəl/ ▸ *adj.* of or due from a son or daughter: *a display of filial affection.* ■ *Biol.* denoting the generation or generations after the parental generation. —**fil·i·al·ly** *adv.*

fil·i·bus·ter /'filə,bəstər/ ▸ *n.* **1** an action such as a prolonged speech that obstructs progress in a legislative assembly while not technically contravening the required procedures: *it was defeated by a Senate filibuster in June.* **2** *hist.* a person engaging in unauthorized warfare against a foreign country.
▸ *v.* [intr.] [often as *n.*] (**filibustering**) act in an obstructive manner in a legislature, esp. by speaking at inordinate length: *several measures were killed by Republican filibustering.* ■ [tr.] obstruct (a measure) in such a way.

fil·i·gree /'filə,grē/ (also **fil·a·gree**) ▸ *n.* ornamental work of fine (typically gold or silver) wire formed into delicate tracery: [as *adj.*] *delicate silver filigree earrings.* ■ a thing resembling such fine ornamental work. —**fil·i·greed** *adj.*

fil·ing /'fīliNG/ ▸ *n.* (usu. **filings**) a small particle rubbed off by a file when smoothing or shaping something: *iron filings.*

Fil·i·pi·no /,filə'pēnō/ (also **Pil·i·pi·no**) ▸ *adj.* of or relating to the Philippines, the Filipinos, or their language.
▸ *n.* (pl. **-nos**) **1** (fem. **Fil·i·pi·na** /,filə'pēnə/) a native or national of the Philippines, or a person of Filipino descent. **2** the national language of the Philippines, a standardized form of Tagalog.

fill /fil/ ▸ *v.* [tr.] put someone or something into (a space or container) so that it is completely or almost completely full: *I filled up the bottle with water.* ■ [intr.] (**fill with**) become full of. ■ become an overwhelming presence in: *the smell of garlic filled the air.* ■ cause (someone) to have an intense experience of an emotion or feeling: *his presence filled us with foreboding.* ■ appoint a person to hold (a vacant position). ■ hold and perform the expected duties of (a position or role). ■ occupy or take up (a period of time): *the next few days were filled with meetings.* ■ be supplied with the items described in (a prescription or order): *she needed to fill a prescription.* ■ [intr.] (of a sail) curve out tautly as the wind blows into it.
▸ *phrasal v.* □ **fill in** act as a substitute for someone when they are unable to do their job. □ **fill someone in** inform someone more fully of a matter, giving all the details: *the cab driver filled me in on the latest gossip.* □ **fill something in** put material into a hole, trench, or space so that it is completely full: *the canal is now abandoned and partly filled in.* ■ complete a drawing by adding color or shade to the spaces within an outline. □ **fill something out** add information to complete an official form or document: *he filled out the requisite forms.* ■ give more details to add to someone's understanding of something: *he filled out the background by going into historical questions.* □ **fill up** become completely full: *the dining car filled up.* ■ fill the fuel tank of a car.
▸ *n.* (**one's fill**) an amount of something that is as much as one wants or can bear: *I've had my fill of surprises for one day.* ■ an amount of something that will occupy all the space in a container. ■ material, loose or compacted, that fills a space, esp. in building or engineering work: *loose polystyrene fill.* ■ the action of filling something, esp. of shading or color in a region of a computer graphics display.
▸ □ **fill someone's shoes** *inf.* take over someone's function or duties and fulfill them satisfactorily.

fill·er[1] /'filər/ ▸ *n.* **1** a thing put in a space or container to fill it. ■ a substance used for filling cracks or holes in a surface, esp. before painting it: *quick-hardening wood filler.* ■ material used to fill a cavity or increase bulk. ■ an item serving only to fill space or time, esp. in a newspaper, broadcast, or recording. **2** [in *comb.*] a person or thing that fills a space or container: *supermarket shelf-fillers.*

fill·er[2] ▸ *n.* (pl. same) a monetary unit of Hungary, equal to one hundredth of a forint.

fil·let ▸ *n.* **1** /'filā; 'filā/ (also **fi·let**) a fleshy boneless piece of meat from near the loins or the ribs of an animal: *a chicken breast fillet.* ■ (also **fillet steak**) a beef steak cut from the lower part of a sirloin. ■ a boned side of a fish. **2** /'filit/ a band or ribbon worn around the head, esp. for binding the hair. ■ *Archit.* a narrow flat band separating two moldings. ■ *Archit.* a small band between the flutes of a column. **3** /'filit/ a concave strip of material roughly triangular in cross section that rounds off an interior angle between two surfaces: *a splayed mortar fillet at the junction of the roof with the chimney stack.*
▸ *v.* /fi'lā; 'filā/ (**-leted** /-'lād/, **-let·ing** /-'lāiNG/) [tr.] remove the bones from (a fish). ■ cut (fish or meat) into boneless strips.

fill·ing /'filiNG/ ▸ *n.* a quantity of material that fills or is used to fill something: *a cushion with polyester filling.* ■ a piece of material used to fill a cavity in a tooth: *a gold filling.* ■ an edible substance placed between the layers of a sandwich, cake, or other foodstuff: *a Swiss roll with a chocolate filling.* ■ another term for **WEFT**.
▸ *adj.* (of food) leaving one with a pleasantly satiated feeling: *a filling spicy bean soup.*

fil·lip /'filəp/ ▸ *n.* **1** something that acts as a stimulus or boost to an activity: *the halving of the automobile tax would provide a fillip to sales.* **2** *archaic* a movement made by bending the last joint of a finger against the thumb and suddenly releasing it; a flick of the finger.
▸ *v.* (**-liped, -lip·ing**) [tr.] *archaic* propel (a small object) with a flick of the finger. ■ strike (someone or something) slightly and smartly: *he filliped him on the nose.*

fil·ly /'filē/ ▸ *n.* (pl. **-lies**) a young female horse, esp. one less than four years old. ■ *dated* a lively girl or young woman.

film /film/ ▸ *n.* **1** a thin flexible strip of plastic or other material coated with light-sensitive emulsion for exposure in a camera, used to produce photographs or motion pictures. *a new range of films and cameras.* ■ material in the form of a thin flexible sheet: *clear plastic film between the layers.* ■ a thin layer covering a surface: *she quickly wiped away the light film of sweat.* **2** a motion picture; a movie: *a horror film* | [as *adj.*] *a film director.* ■ movies considered as an art or industry: *a critical overview of feminist writing on film.*
▸ *v.* **1** [tr.] capture on film as part of a series of moving images; make a movie of (a story or event): *she glowered at the television crew who were filming them.* **2** [intr.] become or appear to become covered with a thin layer of something: *his eyes had filmed over.*

film·mak·er /'film,mākər/ ▸ *n.* a person who directs or produces movies for the theater or television. —**film·mak·ing** *n.*

film·og·ra·phy /fil'mägrəfē/ ▸ *n.* (pl. **-phies**) a list of films by one director or actor, or on one subject.

film stock ▸ *n.* see **STOCK** (sense 1).

film·strip /'film,strip/ ▸ *n.* a series of transparencies in a strip for projection, used esp. as a teaching aid.

film·y /'filmē/ ▸ *adj.* (**film·i·er, film·i·est**) thin and translucent: *filmy white voile.* ■ covered with or forming a thin layer of something. —**film·i·ness** *n.*

fil·ter /'filtər/ ▸ *n.* a porous device for removing impurities or solid particles from a liquid or gas passed through it: *an oil filter.* ■ a screen, plate, or layer of a substance that absorbs light or other radiation or selectively absorbs some of its components: *filters used in photography to reduce haze.* ■ a device for suppressing electrical or sound waves of frequencies not required. ■ *Comput.* a piece of software that processes text, for example to remove unwanted spaces or to format it for use in another application.
▸ *v.* **1** [tr.] pass (a liquid, gas, light, or sound) through a device to remove unwanted material: *fig. a secretary whose job it is to filter calls.* ■ [intr.] move slowly or in small quantities or numbers through something or in a specified direction: *people filtered out of the concert during the last set.* ■ [intr.] (of information) gradually become known: *the news began to filter in from the hospital.* **2** *Comput.* [tr.] process or treat with a filter.

fil·ter·a·ble /'filtərəbəl/ (also **fil·tra·ble** /-trəbəl/) ▸ *adj.* **1** capable of passing through a filter. **2** capable of being separated out by a filter: *filterable solids.* —**fil·ter·a·bil·i·ty** *n.*

fil·ter feed·ing ▸ *n.* *Zool.* (of an aquatic animal) feeding by filtering out plankton or nutrients suspended in the water. —**fil·ter feed·er** *n.*

fil·ter tip ▸ *n.* a filter attached to a cigarette for removing some components from the smoke. ■ a cigarette with such a filter. —**fil·ter-tipped** *adj.*

filth /filTH/ ▸ *n.* disgusting dirt: *stagnant pools of filth.* ■ obscene and offensive language or printed material. ■ corrupt behavior; decadence.

filth·y /'filTHē/ ▸ *adj.* (**filth·i·er, filth·i·est**) disgustingly dirty: *a filthy floor.* ■ obscene and offensive: *filthy language.* ■ *inf.* used to express one's anger and disgust: *you filthy beast.*
▸ *adv. inf.* to an extreme and often disgusting extent: *he has become filthy rich.* —**filth·i·ness** *n.*

fil·trate /'fil,trāt/ ▸ *n.* a liquid that has passed through a filter. —**fil·tra·tion** /fil'trāSHən/ *n.*

fin /fin/ ▸ *n.* a flattened appendage on various parts of the body of many aquatic vertebrates and some invertebrates, including fish and cetaceans, used for propelling, steering, and balancing. ■ a flipper for underwater swimming. ■ a small flattened projecting surface or attachment on an aircraft, rocket, or automobile, providing aerodynamic stability or serving as a design element. ■ a flattened projection on a device, such as a radiator, used for increasing heat transfer. ▷Old English *finn, fin,* of Germanic origin; related to Dutch *vin* and probably ultimately to Latin *pinna* 'feather, wing.' —**finned** *adj.* [in *comb.*] *primitive ray-finned fishes.*

fin. ▸ *abbr.* ■ finance. ■ financial. ■ finish.

fi·na·gle /fəˈnāgəl/ ▸v. [tr.] inf. obtain (something) by devious or dishonest means: *Ted attended all the football games he could finagle tickets for.* ■ [intr.] act in a devious or dishonest manner: *they wrangled and finagled over the fine points.* —**fi·na·gler** n.

fi·nal /ˈfīnl/ ▸adj. coming at the end of a series: *the final version of the report.* ■ reached or designed to be reached as the outcome of a process or a series of events: *the final cost will run into six figures.* ■ allowing no further doubt or dispute: *the decision of the panel is final.*
▸n. **1** the last game in a sports tournament or other competition, which decides the winner. ■ (**finals**) a series of games constituting the final stage of a competition. **2** an examination at the end of a term, academic year, or particular class. **3** *Mus.* the principal note in a mode.

fi·na·le /fəˈnalē; -ˈnälē/ ▸n. the last part of a piece of music, a performance, or a public event, esp. when particularly dramatic or exciting: *the festival ends with a grand finale.*

fi·nal·ist /ˈfīnl-ist/ ▸n. a competitor or team in the final or finals of a competition.

fi·nal·i·ty /fīˈnalətē; fi-/ ▸n. (pl. **-ties**) the fact or impression of being an irreversible ending: *the abrupt finality of death.* ■ a tone or manner that indicates that no further comment or argument is possible: *"No," she said with finality.* ■ the quality of being complete or conclusive. ■ an action or event that ends something irreversibly.

fi·nal·ize /ˈfīnlˌīz/ ▸v. [tr.] complete (a transaction, esp. in commerce or diplomacy) after discussion of the terms: *the two countries had yet to finalize a peace treaty.* ■ produce or agree on a finished and definitive version of: *efforts intensified to finalize plans for postwar reconstruction.* —**fi·nal·i·za·tion** n.

fi·nal·ly /ˈfin(ə)lē/ ▸adv. after a long time, typically involving difficulty or delay: *he finally arrived to join us.* ■ as the last in a series of related events or objects: *a referendum followed by local, legislative, and, finally, presidential elections.* ■ used to introduce a final point or reason: *finally, it is common knowledge that travel broadens the horizons.* ■ in such a way as to put an end to doubt and dispute: *to dispel finally the belief that auditors were clients of the company.*

fi·nance /ˈfīnans; fəˈnans/ ▸n. the management of large amounts of money, esp. by governments or large companies. ■ monetary support for an enterprise: *housing finance.* ■ (**finances**) the monetary resources and affairs of a country, organization, or person.
▸v. [tr.] provide funding for (a person or enterprise): *the city originally financed the project.*

fi·nan·cial /fəˈnanCHəl; fī-/ ▸adj. of or relating to finance: *an independent financial adviser.* —**fi·nan·cial·ly** adv.

fin·an·cier /ˌfinənˈsi(ə)r; fəˈnanˌsi(ə)r/ ▸n. a person concerned with the management of large amounts of money.

fin·back /ˈfinbak/ (also **finback whale**) ▸n. a large baleen whale (*Balaenoptera physalus*) with a small dorsal fin, a dark gray back, and white underparts.

finch /finCH/ ▸n. a seed-eating songbird that typically has a stout bill and colorful plumage. The true finches belong to the family Fringillidae (the **finch family**), which includes canaries and crossbills. Other finches belong to the bunting or sparrow families.

find /fīnd/ ▸v. (past **found**) [tr.] **1** discover or perceive by chance or unexpectedly: *Lindsey looked up to find Neil watching her.* ■ discover (someone or something) after a deliberate search: *in this climate it could be hard to find a buyer.* ■ (**find oneself**) discover oneself to be in a surprising or unexpected situation: *phobia sufferers often find themselves virtual prisoners in their own home.* ■ succeed in obtaining (something): *she also found the time to raise five children.* ■ summon up (a quality, esp. courage) with an effort: *I found the courage to speak.* **2** (often **be found**) recognize or discover (something) to be present: *vitamin B12 is found in dairy products.* ■ become aware of; discover to be the case: [tr.] *the majority of staff find the magazine to be informative and useful.* ■ ascertain (something) by study, calculation, or inquiry: *attempts to find solutions.* ■ (**find oneself**) discover the fundamental truths about one's own character and identity: *I did psychotherapy for years—I wanted to find myself.* ■ *Law* (of a court) officially declare to be the case: [tr.] *he was found guilty of speeding | the court found that a police lab expert had fabricated evidence.* **3** (of a thing) reach or arrive at, either of its own accord or without the human agent being known: *water finds its own level.* ■ (**find one's way**) reach one's destination by one's own efforts, without knowing in advance how to get there: *he found his way to the front door.* ■ (**find one's way**) come to be in a certain situation: *each and every boy found his way into a suitable occupation.*
▸phrasal v. □ **find against** *Law* (of a court) make a decision against or judge to be guilty. □ **find for** (or **find in favor of**) *Law* (of a court) make

a decision in favor of or judge to be innocent: *a jury found for the plaintiff.* □ **find something out** (or **find out about something**) discover a fact: *he hadn't time to find out what was bothering her.*
▸n. a discovery of something valuable, typically something of archaeological interest: *he made his most spectacular finds in the Valley of the Kings | this resort is **a real find**.* ■ a person who is discovered to be useful or interesting in some way: *Paul had been a real find—he could design the whole hotel complex.* —**find·er** n.
▸ □ **find favor** be liked or prove acceptable: *the ballets did not **find favor** with the public.* □ **find God** experience a religious conversion or awakening.

find·ing /ˈfīndiNG/ ▸n. the action of finding someone or something. ■ (often **findings**) a conclusion reached as a result of an inquiry, investigation, or trial: *experimental findings.*

fine¹ /fīn/ ▸adj. **1** of high quality: *fine wines.* ■ worthy of or eliciting admiration: *what a fine human being he is.* ■ good; satisfactory: *relations in the group were fine.* ■ used to express one's agreement with or acquiescence to something: *he said such a solution would be fine.* ■ in good health and feeling well: *"I'm fine, just fine. And you?"* ■ (of the weather) bright and clear: *it was another fine winter day.* ■ (of speech or writing) sounding impressive and grand but ultimately insincere: *fine words seemed to produce few practical benefits.* ■ denoting or displaying a state of good, though not excellent, preservation in stamps, books, coins, etc. ■ (of gold or silver) containing a specified high proportion of pure metal: *the coin is struck in .986 fine gold.* **2** (of a thread, filament, or person's hair) thin: *I have always had fine and dry hair.* ■ (of a point) sharp: *I sharpened the leads to a fine point.* ■ consisting of small particles: *the soils were all fine silt.* ■ having or requiring an intricate delicacy of touch: *exquisitely fine work.* ■ (of something abstract) subtle and therefore perceived only with difficulty and care: *the fine distinctions between the new and old definitions of refugee.* ■ (of feelings) refined; elevated: *you might appeal to their finer feelings.*
▸adv. inf. in a satisfactory or pleasing manner; very well: *"And how's the job-hunting going?" "Oh, fine."*
▸v. make or become thinner. —**fine·ly** adv. —**fine·ness** n.
▸ □ **do fine** be entirely satisfactory: *an omelet will do fine.* ■ be healthy or well: *the baby's doing fine.* ■ do something in a satisfactory manner: *he was doing fine acquiring all the necessary disciplines in finance.* □ **the finer points** of the more complex or detailed aspects of: *he went on to discuss the finer points of his work.* □ **——'s finest** inf. the police of a particular city: *Moscow's finest.* □ **one's finest hour** the time of one's greatest success. □ **one fine day** at some unspecified or unknown time: *you want to be the Chancellor one fine day.*

fine² /fīn/ ▸n. a sum of money exacted as a penalty by a court of law or other authority: *a parking fine.*
▸v. [tr.] (often **be fined**) punish (someone) by making them pay a sum of money, typically as a penalty for breaking the law. —**fine·a·ble** /ˈfīnəbəl/ adj.

fi·ne³ /ˈfēnā/ ▸n. (in musical directions) the place where a piece of music finishes (when this is not at the end of the score but at the end of an earlier section that is repeated at the end of the piece).

fine art ▸n. (also **fine arts**) creative art, esp. visual art, whose products are to be appreciated primarily or solely for their imaginative, aesthetic, or intellectual content. **2** an activity requiring great skill or accomplishment: *he'll have to learn **the fine art of** persuasion.*

fine print ▸n. printed matter in small type. ■ inconspicuous details or conditions printed in an agreement or contract, esp. ones that may prove unfavorable: *the fine print of the loan document.*

fin·er·y /ˈfīnərē/ ▸n. expensive or ostentatious clothes or decoration.

fines herbes /ˌfēn ˈ(z)erb/ ▸pl. n. mixed herbs used in cooking.

fi·nesse /fəˈnes/ ▸n. intricate and refined delicacy: *orchestral playing of great finesse.* ■ artful subtlety, typically that needed for tactful handling of a difficulty: *clients want advice and action that calls for considerable finesse.* ■ subtle or delicate manipulation.
▸v. [tr.] **1** do (something) in a subtle and delicate manner. ■ slyly attempt to avoid blame or censure when dealing with (a situation or action): *the administration's attempts to finesse its mishaps.* **2** (in bridge and whist) play (a card that is not a certain winner) in the hope of winning a trick with it.

fine-tooth comb (also **fine-toothed comb**) ▸n. a comb with narrow teeth that are close together. ■ used with reference to a very thorough search or analysis of something: *you should check the small print with a fine-tooth comb.*

fine-tune ▸ *v.* [*tr.*] make small adjustments to (something) in order to achieve the best or a desired performance.

fin·ger /ˈfiNGɡər/ ▸ *n.* each of the four slender jointed parts attached to either hand (or five, if the thumb is included). ■ a part of a glove intended to cover a finger. ■ a measure of liquor in a glass, based on the breadth of a finger: *he poured three fingers of vodka into a juice glass.* ■ an object that has roughly the long, narrow shape of a finger: *a shortbread finger.*
▸ *v.* [*tr.*] **1** touch or feel (something) with the fingers: *the thin man fingered his mustache.* ■ play (a musical instrument) with the fingers, esp. in a tentative or casual manner: *the woman fingered her lute.* **2** *inf.* inform on (someone) to the police: *you fingered me for those burglaries.* —**fin·gered** *adj.* [in *comb.*] *a two-fingered whistle*
▸ □ **have a finger in every pie** be involved in a large and varied number of activities or enterprises. □ **have** (or **keep**) **one's finger on the pulse** be aware of all the latest news or developments: *he keeps his finger on the pulse of world music.* □ **lay a finger on someone** touch someone, esp. with the intention of harming them. □ **put one's finger on something** identify something exactly: *he cannot put his finger on what has gone wrong.*

fin·ger·board /ˈfiNGɡərˌbôrd/ ▸ *n.* a flat or roughly flat strip on the neck of a stringed instrument, against which the strings are pressed.

fin·ger bowl ▸ *n.* a small bowl holding water for rinsing the fingers during or after a meal.

fin·ger·ing /ˈfiNGɡəriNG/ ▸ *n.* a manner or technique of using the fingers, esp. to play a musical instrument: *keyboard fingering.*

fin·ger·nail /ˈfiNGɡərˌnāl/ ▸ *n.* the flattish horny part on the upper surface of the tip of each finger.

fin·ger paint ▸ *n.* thick paint designed to be applied with the fingers, used esp. by young children.
▸ *v.* (**fin·ger-paint**) [*intr.*] (esp. of children) apply paint with the fingers. —**fin·ger paint·ing** *n.*

fin·ger·print /ˈfiNGɡərˌprint/ ▸ *n.* an impression or mark made on a surface by a person's fingertip, esp. as used for identifying individuals from the unique pattern of whorls and lines: *the police had his fingerprints on file.* ■ *fig.* a distinctive identifying characteristic: *the faint chemical fingerprint of plastic explosives.*
▸ *v.* [*tr.*] record the fingerprints of (someone).

fin·ger·spell·ing /ˈfiNGɡərˌspeliNG/ ▸ *n.* a form of sign language in which individual letters are formed by the fingers to spell out words.

fin·ger·tip /ˈfiNGɡərˌtip/ ▸ *n.* the tip of a finger.
▸ *adj.* using or operated by the fingers: *fingertip electronic controls.* ■ reaching to the fingertips: *fingertip length.*
▸ □ **at one's fingertips** (esp. of information) readily available; accessible: *until we have more facts at our fingertips, there is no use in speculating.*

fin·i·al /ˈfinēəl/ ▸ *n.* a distinctive ornament at the apex of a roof, pinnacle, canopy, or similar structure in a building. ■ an ornament at the top, end, or corner of an object: *ornate curtain poles with decorative finials.*

fin·ick·y /ˈfinikē/ ▸ *adj.* (of a person) fussy about one's needs or requirements: *a finicky eater.* ■ showing or requiring great attention to detail: *a finicky, almost fetishistic collector.* —**fin·ick·i·ness** *n.*

fin·is /ˈfinis; fiˈnē/ ▸ *n.* the end (printed at the end of a book or shown at the end of a film).

fin·ish /ˈfiniSH/ ▸ *v.* [*tr.*] **1** bring (a task or activity) to an end; complete: *finished the job* | [*intr.*] *the musician finished to thunderous applause.* ■ consume or get through the final amount or portion of (something, esp. food or drink): *Jerry finished off a margarita.* ■ [*intr.*] (of an activity) come to an end: *the war has finished but nothing has changed.* ■ [*intr.*] (**finish with**) have no more need for or nothing more to do with: *"I've finished with Tom," Gloria said.* ■ reach the end of a race or other sporting competition, typically in a particular position: *she finished third in the 3-meter springboard diving.* **2** (usu. **be finished**) complete the manufacture or decoration of (a material, object, or place) by giving it an attractive or protective surface: *the interior was finished with V-jointed American oak.*
▸ *phrasal v.* □ **finish someone off** kill, destroy, or comprehensively defeat someone. □ **finish up** complete an action or process: *he hadn't finished up the paperwork.* ■ end a period of time or course of action by doing something or being in a particular position: *we finished up with a plate of sweets.*

finial

▸ *n.* **1** an end or final part or stage of something: *I really enjoyed the film from start to finish.* ■ a point or place at which a race or competition ends: *he surged into a winning lead 200 meters from the finish.* **2** the manner in which the manufacture of an article is completed in detail: *wide variation in specification and finish.* ■ the surface appearance of a manufactured material or object, or the material used to produce this: *lightweight nylon with a shiny finish.* —**fin·ish·er** *n.*

fin·ish·ing school ▸ *n.* a private school where girls are prepared for entry into fashionable society.

fi·nite /ˈfīnīt/ ▸ *adj.* **1** having limits or bounds: *every computer has a finite amount of memory.* **2** *Gram.* (of a verb form) having a specific tense, number, and person. —**fi·nite·ly** *adv.* —**fi·nite·ness** *n.* —**fin·i·tude** /ˈfiniˌt(y)o͞od/ *n.*

fink /fiNGk/ *inf.* ▸ *n.* an unpleasant or contemptible person, in particular: ■ a person who informs on people to the authorities: *he was assumed by some to be the management's fink.* ■ *dated* a strikebreaker.
▸ *v.* [*intr.*] **1** (**fink on**) inform on to the authorities: *people willing to fink on their neighbors.* **2** (**fink out**) fail to do something promised or expected because of a lack of courage or commitment.

Finn /fin/ ▸ *n.* a native or national of Finland or a person of Finnish descent.

fin·nan had·die /ˈfinən ˈhadē/ (also **finnan haddock**) ▸ *n.* haddock cured with the smoke of green wood, turf, or peat.

Finn·ish /ˈfiniSH/ ▸ *adj.* of or relating to the Finns or their language.
▸ *n.* the Finno-Ugric language of the Finns, spoken in Finland and in parts of Russia and Sweden.

Fin·no-U·gric /ˈfinō ˈ(y)o͞oɡrik/ (also **Fin·no-U·gri·an** /ˈ(y)o͞oɡrēən/) ▸ *adj.* of or relating to the major group of Uralic languages, whose main branches are Finnic and Ugric.
▸ *n.* this group of languages.

fiord ▸ *n.* variant spelling of FJORD.

fir /fər/ ▸ *n.* (also **fir tree**) an evergreen coniferous tree (genus *Abies*) of the pine family, with upright cones and flat needle-shaped leaves, an important source of timber and resins. —**fir·ry** *adj.*

fire /fīr/ ▸ *n.* **1** combustion or burning, in which substances combine chemically with oxygen from the air and typically give out bright light, heat, and smoke. ■ one of the four elements in ancient and medieval philosophy and in astrology. ■ a destructive burning of something: *a fire at a hotel.* ■ a collection of fuel, esp. wood or coal, burned in a controlled way to provide heat or a means for cooking: *our kettle was kept constantly on the fire.* ■ a burning sensation in the body: *the whiskey lit a fire in the back of his throat.* ■ fervent or passionate emotion or enthusiasm: *the fire of their religious conviction.* **2** the shooting of projectiles from weapons, esp. bullets from guns: *a burst of machine-gun fire.* ■ strong criticism or antagonism: *he directed his fire against policies promoting capital flight.*
▸ *v.* [*tr.*] **1** discharge a gun or other weapon in order to explosively propel (a bullet or projectile). ■ discharge (a gun or other weapon). [*intr.*] *troops fired on crowds.* ■ [*intr.*] (of a gun) be discharged. ■ direct (questions or statements, esp. unwelcome ones) toward someone in rapid succession: *they fired questions at me for what seemed like ages.* ■ (**fire something off**) send a message aggressively: *he fired off a series of letters.* **2** *inf.* dismiss (an employee) from a job: *having to fire men who've been with me for years | you're fired!* **3** supply (a furnace, engine, boiler, or power station) with fuel. ■ [*intr.*] (of an internal combustion engine, or a cylinder in one) undergo ignition of its fuel when started. **4** stimulate or excite (the imagination or an emotion): *India fired my imagination.* ■ fill (someone) with enthusiasm: *in the locker room they were really fired up.* **5** bake or dry (pottery, bricks, etc.) in a kiln. **6** start (an engine or other device): *with a flick of his wrist he fired up the chainsaw.*
▸ □ **catch fire** begin to burn. ■ *fig.* become interesting or exciting: *the show never caught fire.* □ **fire and brimstone** the torments of hell: *his father was preaching fire and brimstone sermons.* □ **fire away** *inf.* used to give someone permission to begin speaking, typically to ask questions. □ **go through fire (and water)** face any peril. □ **light a fire under someone** stimulate someone to work or act more quickly or enthusiastically. □ **on fire** in flames; burning. ■ in a state of excitement. □ **set fire to** (or **set something on fire**) cause to burn; ignite. □ **set the world on fire** do something remarkable or sensational: *the film hasn't exactly set the world on fire.* □ **under fire** being shot at: *observers sent to look for the men came under heavy fire.* ■ being rigorously criticized: *the president was under fire from all sides.*

fire·arm /ˈfī(ə)r,ärm/ ▸ *n.* a rifle, pistol, or other portable gun.

fire·ball /ˈfīr,bôl/ ▸ *n.* a ball of flame or fire. ■ an extremely hot, luminous ball of gas generated by a nuclear explosion. ■ a large bright meteor. ■ *fig.* a person with a fiery temper or a great deal of energy.

fire·bomb /'fir,bäm/ ▶n. a bomb designed to cause a fire.
▶v. [tr.] attack or destroy (something) with such a bomb.

fire·brand /'fir,brand/ ▶n. **1** a person who is passionate about a particular cause, typically inciting change and taking radical action: *a political firebrand.* **2** a piece of burning wood.

fire·break /'fir,brāk/ ▶n. an obstacle to the spread of fire, esp. an open strip in a forest or other area of dense vegetation: *fig. a firebreak against the spread of revolution.*

fire·bug /'fir,bəg/ ▶n. inf. an arsonist.

fire·crack·er /'fir,krakər/ ▶n. a loud, explosive firework, typically wrapped in paper and lit with a fuse.

fire·damp /'fir,damp/ ▶n. methane, esp. as forming an explosive mixture with air in coal mines.

fire de·part·ment ▶n. the department of a local or municipal authority in charge of preventing and fighting fires.

fire drill ▶n. a practice of the emergency procedures to be used in case of fire.

fire en·gine ▶n. a vehicle carrying firefighters and equipment for fighting large fires.

fire es·cape ▶n. a staircase or other apparatus used for escaping from a building on fire.

fire ex·tin·guish·er ▶n. a portable device that discharges a jet of water, foam, powder, or other material to extinguish a fire.

fire·fight·er /'fir,fitər/ ▶n. a person whose job is to extinguish fires. —**fire·fight·ing** n.

fire·fly /'fir,flī/ ▶n. (pl. **-flies**) a soft-bodied beetle (family Lampyridae) related to the glowworm, the winged male and flightless female of which both have luminescent organs. The light is chiefly produced as a signal between the sexes, esp. in flashes.

fire·light /'fir,līt/ ▶n. light from a fire in a fireplace.

fire·man /'firmən/ ▶n. (pl. **-men** /-mən/) **1** a firefighter. **2** a person who tends a furnace or the fire of a steam engine or steamship; a stoker.

fire·place /'fir,plās/ ▶n. a place for a domestic fire, esp. a grate or hearth at the base of a chimney. ■ a structure surrounding such a place.

fire·plug /'fir,pləg/ ▶n. a hydrant for a fire hose.

fire·pow·er /'fir,pou(-ə)r/ ▶n. the destructive capacity of guns, missiles, or a military force: *fig. the well-funded firepower of the tobacco companies.*

fire·proof /'fir,pro͞of/ ▶adj. able to withstand fire or great heat.
▶v. [tr.] make (something) fireproof: *the new museum building was fireproofed.*

fire·side /'fir,sid/ ▶n. the area around a fireplace (used esp. with reference to a person's home or family life): *the warmth of his own fireside.*

fire·stone /'fir,stōn/ ▶n. stone that can withstand fire and great heat, used esp. for lining furnaces and ovens.

fire·storm /'fir,stôrm/ ▶n. an intense and destructive fire in which strong currents of air are drawn into the blaze, making it burn more fiercely: *fig. the incident ignited a firestorm of controversy.*

fire·wall /'fir,wôl/ ▶n. a wall or partition designed to inhibit or prevent the spread of fire. ■ any barrier that is intended to thwart the spread of a destructive agent. ■ Comput. a part of a computer system or network that is designed to block unauthorized access while permitting outward communication.

fire·wa·ter /'fir,wôtər; -,wätər/ ▶n. inf. strong liquor.

FireWire /'fi(ə)r,wi(ə)r/ ▶n. trademark Comput. a technology that allows high-speed communication and data exchange between a computer and a peripheral or between two computers.

fire·wood /'fir,wo͝od/ ▶n. wood burned as fuel.

fire·work /'fir,wərk/ ▶n. a device containing gunpowder and other combustible chemicals that causes a spectacular explosion when ignited, used typically for display or in celebrations. ■ (**fireworks**) a display of fireworks: *watching the fireworks.* ■ (**fireworks**) fig. an outburst of anger or other emotion, or a display of brilliance or energy.

fir·ing /'firiNG/ ▶n. the action of setting fire to something. ■ the discharging of a gun or other weapon: *no missile firings were planned.* ■ the dismissal of an employee from a job. ■ the baking or drying of pottery or bricks in a kiln.

fir·ing line ▶n. the line of positions from which gunfire is directed at targets. ■ a situation where one is subject to criticism because of one's responsibilities or position.

fir·ing squad ▶n. a group of soldiers detailed to shoot a condemned person. ■ a group of soldiers that fire the salute at a military funeral.

fir·kin /'fərkən/ ▶n. chiefly hist. a small cask used chiefly for liquids, butter, or fish.

firm¹ /fərm/ ▶adj. **1** having a solid, almost unyielding surface or structure: *the bed should be reasonably firm, but not too hard.* ■ solidly in place and stable: *firm foundations* | *fig. a firm financial footing.* ■ having steady but not excessive power or strength. ■ (of a person, action, or attitude) showing resolute determination and strength of character. **2** strongly felt and unlikely to change: *a firm belief in the efficacy of prayer.* ■ (of a person) steadfast and constant: *firm friends.* ■ decided upon and fixed or definite: *firm plans.* ■ (of a currency, a commodity, or shares) having a steady value or price that is more likely to rise than fall: *the dollar was firm against the yen.*
▶v. [tr.] make (something) physically solid or resilient: *an exercise program designed to firm up muscle tone.* ■ fix (a plant) securely in the soil. ■ [intr.] (of a price) reach a level considered secure. ■ make (an agreement or plan) explicit and definite.
▶adv. in a resolute and determined manner: *she will stand firm.* —**firm·ly** adv. —**firm·ness** n.
▶ □ **be on firm ground** be sure of one's facts or secure in one's position, esp. in a discussion. □ **a firm hand** strict discipline or control.

firm² ▶n. a business concern, esp. one involving a partnership of two or more people: *a law firm.*

fir·ma·ment /'fərməmənt/ ▶n. poetic/lit. the heavens or the sky, esp. when regarded as a tangible thing. ■ fig. a sphere or world viewed as a collection of people: *the American golfing firmament.* —**fir·ma·men·tal** adj.

firm·ware /'fərm,wer/ ▶n. Comput. permanent software programmed into a read-only memory.

first /fərst/ ▶ordinal number **1** coming before all others in time or order; earliest; 1st. ■ never previously done or occurring: *her first day at school.* ■ coming next after a specified or implied time or occurrence: *I didn't take the first bus.* ■ met with or encountered before any others: *the first house I came to.* ■ originally. ■ before doing something else specified or implied: *do you mind if I take a shower first?* ■ for the first time. ■ firstly; in the first place (used to introduce a first point or reason). ■ with a specified part or person in a leading position: *it plunged nose first into the river.* ■ inf. the first occurrence of something notable: *a first for both of us.* ■ the first in a sequence of a vehicle's gears. ■ Baseball first base. ■ the first grade of a school. ■ a first edition of a book. **2** foremost in position, rank, or importance. ■ the most likely, pressing, or suitable: *his first problem is where to live.* ■ the first finisher or position in a race or competition. ■ Mus. performing the highest or chief of two or more parts for the same instrument or voice: *the first violins.* ■ (**firsts**) goods of the best quality: *factory firsts.* ■ Brit. a place in the top grade in an examination, esp. that for a degree: *he took a first in Classics.* ■ Brit. a person having achieved such a place. ▷Old English *fyr(e)st*; of Germanic origin, related to Old Norse *fyrstr* and German *Fürst* 'prince,' from an Indo-European root shared by Sanskrit *prathama*, Latin *primus*, and Greek *prōtos*.
▶ □ **at first** at the beginning; in the initial stage or stages. □ **first and foremost** most importantly; more than anything else: *I'm first and foremost a writer.* □ **first of all** before doing anything else; at the beginning: *first of all, let me ask you something.* ■ most importantly: *German unity depends first of all on the German people.* □ **first thing** early in the morning; before anything else: *I have to meet Josh first thing tomorrow.* □ **first things first** used to assert that important matters should be dealt with before other things. □ **from the (very) first** from the beginning or the early stages: *he should have realized it from the first.* □ **in the first place** as the first consideration or point: *political reality was not quite that simple—in the first place, divisions existed within the parties.* ■ at the beginning; to begin with (esp. in reference to the time when an action was being planned or discussed): *I should have told you in the first place.* □ **of the first order** (or **magnitude**) used to denote something that is excellent or considerable of its kind: *it is a media event of the first order.*

first aid ▶n. help given to a sick or injured person until full medical treatment is available: [as adj.] *a first-aid kit.*

first-born /'fərst,bôrn/ ▶adj. (of a person's child) the first to be born; the eldest: *his new album and his firstborn child are due in the same week.*
▶n. a person's first child: *their firstborn arrived.*

first class ▶n. a set of people or things grouped together as the best. ■ the best accommodations in a plane, train, or ship. ■ Brit. the highest division in the results of the examinations for a university degree. ■ the highest division in an examination.
▶adj. & adv. of the best quality: [as adj.] *a full-scale grand opera needs a first-class orchestra.* ■ of or relating to the best accommodations in a train, ship, or plane: [as adj.] *first-class air transportation* | [as adv.] *you can travel*

Pronunciation Key ə *ago, up*; ər *over, fur*; a *hat*; ā *ate*; ä *car*; CH *chin*; e *let*; ē *see*; e(ə)r *air*; i *fit*; ī *by*; i(ə)r *ear*; NG *sing*; ō *go*; ô *law, for*; oi *toy*; o͝o *good*; o͞o *goo*; ou *out*; SH *she*; TH *thin*; <u>TH</u> *then*; (h)w *why*; ZH *vision*

first class on any train. ■ of or relating to a class of mail given priority: [as *adj.*] *first-class mail* | [as *adv.*] *send it first class.*

first cous·in ▶*n.* see COUSIN.

first-de·gree ▶*adj.* **1** *Med.* denoting burns that affect only the surface of the skin and cause reddening. **2** *Law* denoting the most serious category of a crime, esp. murder.

first·hand /'fərst'hand/ ▶*adj. & adv.* (of information or experience) from the original source or personal experience; direct: [as *adj.*] *firsthand knowledge* | [as *adv.*] *this is something you have to hear firsthand.*

first la·dy ▶*n.* (**First La·dy**) the wife of the president of the U.S. or other head of state. ■ the leading woman in a particular activity or profession: *the first lady of rock.*

first·ly /'fərstlē/ ▶*adv.* used to introduce a first point or reason.

first mate ▶*n.* the officer second in command to the master of a merchant ship.

first name ▶*n.* a personal name given to someone at birth or baptism and used before a family name.
▶ □ **on a first-name basis** having a friendly and informal relationship.

first per·son ▶*n.* see PERSON (sense 2).

first-rate ▶*adj.* of the best class or quality; excellent: *first-rate musicians.* ■ in good health or condition; very well: *I think you look first-rate.*

firth /fərTH/ ▶*n.* a narrow inlet of the sea; an estuary.

fis·cal /'fiskəl/ ▶*adj.* of or relating to government revenue, esp. taxes: *monetary and fiscal policy.* ■ of or relating to financial matters. ■ used to denote a fiscal year: *the budget for fiscal 1996.* —**fis·cal·ly** *adv.*

fis·cal year ▶*n.* a year as reckoned for taxing or accounting purposes.

fish 1 /fiSH/ ▶*n.* (*pl.* same or **fish·es**) a limbless cold-blooded vertebrate animal with gills and fins and living wholly in water. ■ the flesh of such animals as food. ■ (**the Fish** or **Fishes**) the zodiacal sign or constellation Pisces. ■ used in names of invertebrate animals living wholly in water, e.g., **cuttlefish**, **shellfish**, **jellyfish**. ■ *inf.* a person who is strange in a specified way: *he is generally thought to be a bit of a cold fish.* ■ *inf.* a torpedo.
▶*v.* [*intr.*] catch or try to catch fish, typically by using a net or hook and line. ■ [*tr.*] catch or try to catch fish in (a particular body of water): *they fished the mountain streams when game grew scarce.* ■ search, typically by groping or feeling for something concealed. ■ try subtly or deviously to elicit a response or some information from someone: *I was not fishing for compliments.* ■ [*tr.*] (**fish something out**) pull or take something out of water or a container: *the body of a woman had been fished out of the river.*
▶ □ **a big fish** an important or influential person: *a big fish in the world of politics.* □ **drink like a fish** drink excessive amounts of alcohol. □ **a fish out of water** a person in a completely unsuitable environment or situation. □ **fished out** depleted of fish: *the grayling here have hardly been fished out.* □ **have other** (or **bigger**) **fish to fry** have other (or more important) matters to attend to. □ **neither fish nor fowl** of indefinite character and difficult to identify or classify.

fish2 /fiSH/ ▶*n.* a flat plate of metal, wood, or another material that is fixed on a beam or across a joint in order to give additional strength, esp. on a ship's damaged mast or spar as a temporary repair.
▶*v.* [*tr.*] mend or strengthen (a beam, joint, mast, etc.) with a fish. ■ join (rails in a railroad track) with a fishplate.

fish and chips ▶*n.* a dish of fried fish fillets served with French fries.

fish·er /'fiSHər/ ▶*n.* **1** a fisherman. **2** a large brown marten (*Martes pennanti*) valued for its fur, found in North American woodland.

fish·er·man /'fiSHərmən/ ▶*n.* (*pl.* **-men**) a person who catches fish for a living or for sport. ■ a fishing boat.

fish·er·y /'fiSHərē/ ▶*n.* (*pl.* **-er·ies**) a place where fish are reared for commercial purposes. ■ a fishing ground or area where fish are caught. ■ the occupation or industry of catching or rearing fish.

fish·eye /'fiSH,ī/ ▶*n.* **1** (also **fisheye lens**) a wide-angle lens with a field of vision covering up to 180°, the scale being reduced toward the edges. **2** *inf.* a suspicious or unfriendly look: *Wally gave him the fisheye.*

fish hawk ▶*n.* another term for OSPREY.

fish·hook /'fiSH,ho͝ok/ ▶*n.* see HOOK (sense 1).

fish·ing /'fiSHiNG/ ▶*n.* the activity of catching fish, either for food or as a sport.
▶ □ **fishing expedition** a search or investigation undertaken with the hope, though not the stated purpose, of discovering information.

fish·ing rod ▶*n.* a long, tapering rod to which a fishing line is attached, typically on a reel.

fish meal (also **fish·meal**) ▶*n.* ground dried fish used as fertilizer or animal feed.

fish·net /'fiSH,net/ ▶*n.* a fabric with an open mesh resembling a fishing net: [as *adj.*] *black fishnet stockings.*

fish·plate /'fiSH,plāt/ ▶*n.* a flat piece of metal used to connect adjacent rails in a railroad track. ■ a flat piece of metal with ends like a fish's tail, used to position masonry.

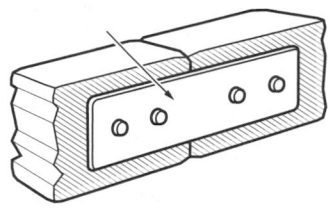

fishplate

fish sauce ▶*n.* a Thai and Vietnamese sauce used as a flavoring or condiment, prepared from fermented anchovies and salt.

fish stick ▶*n.* a small, oblong piece of fish fillet, usually coated in breadcrumbs and fried.

fish sto·ry ▶*n.* an incredible or far-fetched story.

fish·tail /'fiSH,tāl/ ▶*n.* [usu. as *adj.*] an object that is forked like a fish's tail. ■ an uncontrolled sideways movement of the back of a motor vehicle: *he hit the brakes, sending the car into a fishtail.*
▶*v.* [*intr.*] (of a vehicle) make such a movement: *the vehicle fishtailed from one side of the road to the other.* ■ [*tr.*] cause (a vehicle) to make such a movement.

fish·wife /'fiSH,wīf/ ▶*n.* (*pl.* **-wives** /-,wīvz/) **1** a coarse-mannered woman who is prone to shouting. **2** *archaic* a woman who sells fish.

fish·y /'fiSHē/ ▶*adj.* (**fish·i·er**, **fish·i·est**) **1** of, relating to, or resembling fish or a fish: *a fishy smell.* **2** *inf.* arousing feelings of doubt or suspicion: *I'm convinced there is something fishy going on.* —**fish·i·ness** *n.*

fis·sile /'fisəl; 'fis,īl/ ▶*adj.* (of an atom or element) able to undergo nuclear fission. ■ (chiefly of rock) easily split. —**fis·sil·i·ty** /fi'silətē/ *n.*

fis·sion /'fiSHən; 'fiZHən/ ▶*n.* the action of dividing or splitting something into two or more parts. ■ short for NUCLEAR FISSION. ■ *Biol.* reproduction by means of a cell or organism dividing into two or more new cells or organisms: *bacteria divide by transverse binary fission.* —**fis·sion·a·ble** *adj.*

fis·sure /'fiSHər/ ▶*n.* a long, narrow opening or line of breakage made by cracking or splitting, esp. in rock or earth. ■ *chiefly Anat.* a long narrow opening in the form of a crack or groove, e.g., any of the spaces separating convolutions of the brain. ■ a state of incompatibility or disagreement.
▶*v.* [*tr.*] [usu. as *adj.*] (**fissured**) split or crack (something) to form a long narrow opening: *the skin becomes dry, fissured, and cracked.* ▶late Middle English: from Old French, or from Latin *fissura*, from *findere* 'to split.'

fist /fist/ ▶*n.* a person's hand when the fingers are bent in toward the palm and held there tightly, typically in order to strike a blow.
▶*v.* [*tr.*] hit with or as with the fists or a fist. —**fist·ed** *adj.* [in *comb.*] *bare-fisted.* —**fist·ful** /-,fo͝ol/ *n.*

fist·fight /'fist,fīt/ ▶*n.* a fight with bare fists.

fist·i·cuffs /'fisti,kəfs/ ▶*pl. n.* fighting with the fists.

fis·tu·la /'fisCHələ/ ▶*n.* (*pl.* **-las** or **-lae** /-lē/) *Med.* an abnormal or surgically made passage between a hollow or tubular organ and the body surface, or between two hollow or tubular organs. —**fis·tu·lar** /-lər/ *adj.* —**fis·tu·lous** /-ləs/ *adj.*

fit1 /fit/ ▶*adj.* (**fit·ter**, **fit·test**) **1** (of a thing) of a suitable quality, standard, or type to meet the required purpose: *the meat is fit for human consumption* | *is the water clean and fit to drink?* ■ (of a person) having the requisite qualities or skills to undertake something competently: *he felt himself quite fit for battle.* ■ *Biol.* possessing or conferring the ability to survive and reproduce in a particular environment: *survival of the fittest.* ■ suitable and correct according to accepted social standards: *a fit subject on which to correspond.* ■ *inf.* (of a person or thing) having reached such an extreme condition as to be on the point of doing the thing specified: *he baited even his close companions until they were fit to kill him.* **2** in good health, esp. because of regular physical exercise: *I swim regularly to keep fit.*
▶*v.* (**fit·ted** or **fit** /fit/, **fit·ting**) [*tr.*] **1** be of the right shape and size for: *those jeans still fit me.* ■ (usu. **be fitted for**) try clothing on (someone) in order to make or alter it to the correct size: *she was fitted for her costume.* ■ [*intr.*] be of the right size, shape, or number to occupy a particular position or place: *we can all fit in her car.* **2** fix or put (something) into place. ■ (often **be fitted with**) provide (something) with a particular

component or article: *fitted with a new handle.* ■ join or cause to join together to form a whole: [*tr.*] *many physicists tried to* **fit together** *the various pieces of the puzzle.* **3** be in agreement or harmony with; match: *the punishment should fit the crime.* ■ (of an attribute, qualification, or skill) make (someone) suitable to fulfill a particular role or undertake a particular task.

▶ *phrasal v.* □ **fit in** (of a person) be socially compatible with other members of a group: *he feels he should become tough to* **fit in with** *his friends.* ■ (of a thing) be in harmony with other things within a larger structure: *produce ideas that* **fit in with** *an established approach.* ■ (also **fit into**) (of a person or thing) constitute part of a particular situation or larger structure: *where do your sisters fit in?* □ **fit someone/something in** (or **into**) find room or have sufficient space for someone or something: *can you fit any more books into the box?* ■ succeed in finding time in a busy schedule to see someone or do something: *you're never too busy to fit exercise into your life.* □ **fit someone/something out** (or **up**) provide with the necessary equipment, supplies, clothes, or other items for a particular situation: *the cabin had been fitted out to a high standard.*

▶ *n.* the particular way in which something, esp. a garment or component, fits around or into something: *the dress was a perfect fit.* ■ the particular way in which a thing matches something else: *a close fit between teachers' qualifications and their teaching responsibilities.* —**fit·ly** /ˈfitlē/ *adv.* —**fit·ness** *n.*

▶ □ **fit to be tied** *inf.* very angry: *Daddy was fit to be tied when I separated from Hugh.* □ **see** (or **think**) **fit** consider it correct or acceptable to do something: *why did the company see fit to give you the job?*

fit² ▶ *n.* a sudden uncontrollable outbreak of intense emotion, laughter, coughing, or other action or activity: *in a fit of temper.* ■ a sudden attack of convulsions and/or loss of consciousness, typical of epilepsy and some other medical conditions.

▶ □ **have** (or **throw**) **a fit** *inf.* be very surprised or angry: *my mother would have a fit if she heard that.* □ **in fits** (**of laughter**) *inf.* highly amused: *he had us all in fits.* □ **in** (or **by**) **fits and starts** with irregular bursts of activity: *the machine tends to go forward in fits and starts.*

fit·ful /ˈfitfəl/ ▶ *adj.* active or occurring spasmodically or intermittently; not regular or steady: *a few hours' fitful sleep.* —**fit·ful·ly** *adv.* —**fit·ful·ness** *n.*

fit·ted /ˈfitid/ ▶ *adj.* **1** made or shaped to fill a space or to cover something closely or exactly: *the blouse has a fitted bodice | navy blue fitted sheets.* **2** attached to or provided with a particular component or article: *a pistol fitted with a match-grade barrel.* **3** having the appropriate qualities or skills to do something: *physicists may not be fitted for involvement in industrial processes.*

fit·ter /ˈfitər/ ▶ *n.* **1** a person who puts together or installs machinery, engine parts, or other equipment: *a pipe fitter.* **2** a person who supervises the cutting, fitting, or alteration of garments or shoes.

fit·ting /ˈfitiNG/ ▶ *n.* **1** (often **fittings**) a small part on or attached to a piece of furniture or equipment: *wooden fittings made of walnut.* **2** the action of fitting something, in particular: ■ the installing, assembling, and adjusting of machine parts. ■ an occasion when one tries on a garment that is being made or altered: *she's coming tomorrow for a fitting.*

▶ *adj.* **1** suitable or appropriate under the circumstances; right or proper: *a fitting reward | it was fitting that he should reply.* **2** [in *comb.*] fitted around or to something or someone in a specified way: *loose-fitting trousers.* —**fit·ting·ly** *adv.* —**fit·ting·ness** *n.*

five /fīv/ ▶ *cardinal number* equivalent to the sum of two and three; one more than four, or half of ten; 5. (Roman numeral: **v** or **V**.) ■ a group or unit of five people or things: *the bulbs are planted in threes or fives.* ■ five years old. ■ five o'clock. ■ a size of garment or other merchandise denoted by five. ■ a playing card or domino with five spots or pips. ■ a five-dollar bill. ▷Old English *fīf,* of Germanic origin; related to Dutch *vijf* and German *fünf,* from an Indo-European root shared by Latin *quinque* and Greek *pente.*

five·fold /ˈfīvˌfōld/ ▶ *adj.* five times as great or as numerous: *a fivefold increase in funding.* ■ having five parts or elements.

▶ *adv.* by five times; to five times the number or amount: *the unemployment rate rose almost fivefold.*

Five Na·tions ▶ *pl. n. hist.* the original Iroquois confederacy, comprising the Mohawk, Oneida, Onondaga, Cayuga and Seneca peoples. Compare with **Six Nations**.

five o'clock shad·ow ▶ *n.* a dark appearance on a man's face caused by the slight growth of beard that has occurred since he last shaved.

fiv·er /ˈfīvər/ ▶ *n. inf.* a five-dollar bill. ■ *Brit.* a five-pound note.

five-star ▶ *adj.* (esp. of a hotel or restaurant) given five stars in a grading system, typically one in which this denotes the highest class or quality: *a luxury five-star hotel.* ■ (in the U.S. armed forces) having or

denoting the highest military rank (awarded only in wartime), distinguished by five stars on the uniform: *a five-star general.*

fix /fiks/ ▶ *v.* [*tr.*] **1** [*tr.*] fasten (something) securely in a particular place or position: *fix the clamp on a rail.* ■ *fig.* lodge or implant (an idea, image, or memory) firmly in a person's mind: *he turned back to fix the scene in his mind.* **2** (**fix something on/upon**) direct one's eyes, attention, or mind steadily or unwaveringly toward: *I fixed my attention on the tower.* ■ [*intr.*] (**fix on/upon**) (of a person's eyes, attention, or mind) be directed steadily or unwaveringly toward: *her gaze fixed on Jess.* ■ attract and hold (a person's attention or gaze): *their tense relationship fixes your attention.* ■ (**fix someone with**) look at someone unwaveringly: *she fixed her nephew with an unwavering stare.* **3** mend; repair. ■ (**fix something up**) do the necessary work to improve or adapt something: *we want to fix up the house before we sell it.* ■ make arrangements for (something); organize: *he's sent her on ahead to fix things up.* ■ *inf.* restore order or tidiness to (something, esp. one's hair, clothes, or makeup): *Laura was fixing her hair.* ■ *inf.* prepare or arrange for the provision of (food or drink): *they were fixing him breakfast.* ■ (**fix someone up**) *inf.* arrange for someone to have something; provide someone with something: *I'll fix you up with a room.* ■ (**fix someone up**) *inf.* arrange for someone to meet or go out with someone. ■ (**be fixing to do something**) *inf.* be intending or planning to do something: *you're fixing to get into trouble.* **4** decide or settle on (a specific price, date, course of action, etc.): *no date has yet been fixed for a hearing.* ■ discover the exact location of (something) by using radar or visual bearings or astronomical observation: *he fixed his position.* **5** make (something) permanent or static in nature: *the rate of interest is fixed for the life of the loan.* ■ make (a dye, photographic image, or drawing) permanent. ■ *Biol.* preserve or stabilize (a specimen) with a chemical substance prior to microscopy or other examination: *specimens were fixed in buffered formalin.* **6** *inf.* influence the outcome of (something, esp. a race, contest, or election) by illegal or underhanded means: *the foundation denies fixing races.* ■ put (an enemy or rival) out of action, esp. by killing them: *don't you tell, or I'll fix you good!* **7** *inf.* [*intr.*] take an injection of a narcotic drug. **8** castrate or spay (an animal); neuter.

▶ *n.* **1** *inf.* a difficult or awkward situation from which it is hard to extricate oneself; a predicament: *how on earth did you get into such a fix?* **2** *inf.* a dose of a narcotic drug to which one is addicted: *he hadn't had his fix.* **3** *inf.* a solution to a problem, esp. one that is hastily devised or makeshift: *representatives trying to find cheap fixes to meet their obligations.* —**fix·a·ble** /ˈfiksəbəl/ *adj.* —**fixed** /fikst/ *adj.* —**fix·ed·ly** /ˈfiksidlē/ *adv.*

▶ □ **get a fix on** determine the position of (something) by visual or radio bearings or astronomical observation. ■ *inf.* assess or determine the nature or facts of; obtain a clear understanding of: *it is hard to get a fix on their ages.*

fix·ate /ˈfikˌsāt/ ▶ *v.* [*tr.*] **1** (usu. **be fixated on/upon**) cause (someone) to acquire an obsessive attachment to someone or something. ■ [*intr.*] (**fixate on/upon**) acquire such an obsessive attachment to: *it is important not to fixate on animosity.* ■ (in Freudian theory) arrest (a person or their libidinal energy) at an immature stage, causing an obsessive attachment. **2** *technical* direct one's eyes toward.

fix·a·tion /fik'sāSHən/ ▶ *n.* **1** an obsessive interest in or feeling about someone or something. ■ *Psychoanalysis* the arresting of part of the libido at an immature stage, causing an obsessive attachment. ■ the action of making something firm or stable. ■ *Biochem.* the process by which some plants and microorganisms incorporate gaseous nitrogen or carbon dioxide to form nongaseous compounds: *his work on nitrogen fixation in plants.* ■ *Biol.* the process of preserving or stabilizing (a specimen) with a chemical substance prior to microscopy or other examination. **3** *technical* the action of concentrating the eyes directly on something.

fix·a·tive /ˈfiksətiv/ ▶ *n.* **1** a chemical substance used to preserve or stabilize biological material prior to microscopy or other examination. ■ a substance used to stabilize the volatile components of perfume. ■ a liquid sprayed on to a pastel or charcoal drawing to fix colors or prevent smudging. **2** a substance used to keep things in position or stick them together.

▶ *adj.* (of a substance) used to fix or stabilize something.

fix·er /ˈfiksər/ ▶ *n.* **1** a person who makes arrangements for other people, esp. of an illicit or devious kind. **2** a substance used for fixing a photographic image.

fix·i·ty /ˈfiksitē/ ▶ *n.* the state of being unchanging or permanent.

F

Pronunciation Key ə *ago,* up; ər *over,* fur; a *hat;* ā *ate;* ä *car;* CH *chin;* e *let;* ē *see;* e(ə)r *air;* i *fit;* ī *by;* i(ə)r *ear;* NG *sing;* ō *go;* ô *law, for;* oi *toy;* o͝o *good;* o͞o *goo;* ou *out;* SH *she;* TH *thin;* <u>TH</u> *then;* (h)w *why;* ZH *vision*

fix·ture /ˈfiksCHər/ ▶ n. a piece of equipment or furniture that is fixed in position in a building or vehicle: *a light fixture.* ■ (**fixtures**) articles attached to a house or land and considered legally part of it so that they normally remain in place when an owner moves. ■ *inf.* a person or thing that is established in a particular place or situation: *palm readers were a fixture in most '40s nightclubs.*

fizz /fiz/ ▶ v. [intr.] (of a liquid) produce bubbles of gas and make a hissing sound. ■ make a buzzing or crackling sound. ■ *fig.* move with or display excitement, exuberance, or liveliness: *anticipation began to fizz through his veins.*
▶ n. effervescence: *the champagne had lost its fizz.* ■ *inf.* an effervescent drink, esp. sparkling wine. ■ *fig.* exuberance; liveliness. ■ a buzzing or crackling sound: *the fizz of 300 sparklers.*

fiz·zle /ˈfizəl/ ▶ v. [intr.] end or fail in a weak or disappointing way: *the revolt fizzled out at yesterday's meeting.* ■ make a feeble hissing or spluttering sound: *the lights fizzled and flickered.*
▶ n. a failure: *in the end the fireworks were a fizzle.* ■ a feeble hissing or spluttering sound.

fizz·y /ˈfizē/ ▶ adj. (**fizz·i·er, fizz·i·est**) (of a beverage) containing bubbles of gas; effervescent. —**fizz·i·ly** /ˈfizəlē/ adv. —**fizz·i·ness** n.

fjord /fēˈôrd; fyôrd/ (also **fiord**) ▶ n. a long, narrow, deep inlet of the sea between high cliffs, as in Norway and Iceland, typically formed by submergence of a glaciated valley.

flab /flab/ ▶ n. *inf.* soft loose flesh on a person's body.

flab·ber·gast /ˈflabərˌgast/ ▶ v. [tr.] [usu. as adj.] (**flabbergasted**) *inf.* surprise (someone) greatly; astonish: *the news left me totally flabbergasted.*

flab·by /ˈflabē/ ▶ adj. (**-bi·er, -bi·est**) (of a part of a person's body) soft, loose, and fleshy. ■ (of a person) having soft loose flesh. ■ *fig.* not tightly controlled, powerful, or effective: *the play was uncommitted and flabby.* —**flab·bi·ly** /ˈflabəlē/ adv. —**flab·bi·ness** n.

flac·cid /ˈfla(k)səd/ ▶ adj. (of part of the body) soft and hanging loosely or limply, esp. so as to look or feel unpleasant. ■ (of plant tissue) drooping or inelastic through lack of water. ■ *fig.* lacking force or effectiveness: *the flaccid leadership campaign was causing concern.* —**flac·cid·i·ty** /fla(k)ˈsidətē/ n. —**flac·cid·ly** adv.

flack¹ /flak/ *inf.* ▶ n. a publicity agent: *a public relations flack.*
▶ v. [tr.] publicize or promote (something or someone). —**flack·er·y** /-ərē/ n.

flack² ▶ n. variant spelling of FLAK.

flag¹ /flag/ ▶ n. **1** a piece of cloth or similar material, typically oblong or square, attachable by one edge to a pole or rope and used as the symbol or emblem of a country or institution. ■ used in reference to the country to which a person has allegiance: *every soldier under the flag.* ■ a small piece of cloth, typically attached at one edge to a pole, used as a marker or signal in various sports. ■ the ensign carried by a flagship as an emblem of an admiral's rank. **2** a device, symbol, or drawing typically resembling a flag, used as a marker. ■ *Comput.* a variable used to indicate a particular property of the data in a record. **3** a hook attached to the stem of a musical note, determining the rhythmic value of the note.
▶ v. (**flagged, flag·ging**) [tr.] **1** (often **be flagged**) mark (an item) for attention or treatment in a specified way. ■ *fig.* draw attention to. **2** direct (someone) to go in the specified direction by waving a flag or using hand signals: *have him flagged off the course.* ■ (**flag someone/something down**) signal to a vehicle or driver to stop, esp. by waving one's arm. ■ [intr.] (of an official in football, soccer, and other sports) raise or throw a flag to indicate a breach of the rules. **3** register (a vessel) in a specific country, under whose flag it then sails: *the flagging out of the fleet.* —**flag·ger** n.
▶ □ **wrap oneself in the flag** make an excessive show of one's patriotism, esp. for political ends.

flag² ▶ n. a flat stone slab, typically rectangular or square, used for paving. —**flagged** adj. [often in comb.] *stone-flagged steps.*

flag³ ▶ n. a plant with sword-shaped leaves that grow from a rhizome, in particular: ■ a plant of the iris family, esp. blue flag or yellow flag. ■ sweet flag.

flag⁴ ▶ v. (**flagged, flag·ging**) [intr.] (of a person) become tired, weaker, or less enthusiastic. ■ [often as adj.] (**flagging**) (esp. of an activity or quality) become weaker or less dynamic: *her flagging career.*

Flag Day ▶ n. June 14, the anniversary of the adoption of the Stars and Stripes as the official U.S. flag in 1777.

flag·el·lant /ˈflajələnt; fləˈjelənt/ ▶ n. a person who subjects themselves or others to flogging, either as a religious discipline or for sexual gratification.

flag·el·late¹ /ˈflajəˌlāt/ ▶ v. [tr.] flog (someone), either as a religious discipline or for sexual gratification. —**flag·el·la·tion** /ˌflajəˈlāSHən/ n. —**flag·el·la·tor** /-ˌlātər/ n. —**flag·el·la·to·ry** /fləˈjeləˌtôrē/ adj.

flag·el·late² /ˈflajəlit; -ˌlāt/ *Zool.* ▶ n. a protozoan that has one or more flagella used for swimming.
▶ adj. (of a cell or single-celled organism) bearing one or more flagella.

fla·gel·lum /fləˈjeləm/ ▶ n. (pl. **-gel·la** /-ˈjelə/) *Biol.* a slender threadlike structure, esp. a microscopic whiplike appendage that enables many protozoa, bacteria, etc., to swim. —**fla·gel·lar** /fləˈjelər/ adj.

flag·on /ˈflagən/ ▶ n. a large container in which drink is served, typically with a handle and spout. ■ the amount of liquid held in such a container.

flag·pole /ˈflagˌpōl/ ▶ n. a pole used for flying a flag.
▶ □ **run something up the flagpole** test the popularity of a new idea or proposal.

fla·grant /ˈflāgrənt/ ▶ adj. (of something considered wrong or immoral) conspicuously or obviously offensive: *his flagrant bad taste | a flagrant violation of the law.* ▷ late 15th cent. (in the sense 'blazing, resplendent'): from French, or from Latin *flagrant-* 'blazing,' from the verb *flagrare.* —**fla·gran·cy** /-grənsē/ n. —**fla·grant·ly** adv.

flag·ship /ˈflagˌSHip/ ▶ n. the ship in a fleet that carries the commanding admiral. ■ the best or most important thing owned or produced by a particular organization: [as adj.] *their flagship product.*

flag·staff /ˈflagˌstaf/ ▶ n. another term for FLAGPOLE.

flag·stone /ˈflagˌstōn/ ▶ n. a flat stone slab, typically rectangular or square, used for paving. —**flag·stoned** adj.

flag-wav·ing ▶ n. the expression of patriotism in a populist and emotional way. —**flag-wav·er** n.

flail /flāl/ ▶ n. a threshing tool consisting of a wooden staff with a short heavy stick swinging from it. ■ a similar device used as a weapon or for flogging. ■ a machine for threshing or slashing.
▶ v. **1** wave or swing or cause to wave or swing wildly: [intr.] *his arms were flailing helplessly* | [tr.] *he flailed his arms and drove her away.* ■ [intr.] flounder; struggle uselessly: *flailing about in the water.* **2** [tr.] beat; flog.

flair /fler/ ▶ n. **1** a special or instinctive aptitude or ability for doing something well: *a flair for languages | artistic flair.* **2** stylishness and originality: *she dressed with flair.*

flak /flak/ (also **flack**) ▶ n. antiaircraft fire. ■ strong criticism.

flake¹ /flāk/ ▶ n. **1** a small, flat, thin piece of something, typically one that has broken away or been peeled off from a larger piece. ■ a snowflake. ■ *Archaeol.* a piece of hard stone chipped off for use as a tool by prehistoric humans. ■ thin pieces of crushed dried food or bait for fish. **2** *inf.* a crazy or eccentric person.
▶ v. **1** [intr.] come or fall away from a surface in thin pieces: *the paint was flaking off.* ■ lose small fragments from the surface: *my nails have started to flake.* **2** [tr.] break or divide (food) into thin pieces. ■ [intr.] (of food, esp. when well cooked) come apart in thin pieces.

flake² ▶ v. [intr.] (**flake out**) *inf.* fall asleep; drop from exhaustion.

flak jack·et (also **flak vest**) ▶ n. a sleeveless jacket made of heavy reinforced fabric, worn as protection against bullets and shrapnel.

flak·y /ˈflākē/ (also **flak·ey**) ▶ adj. (**flak·i·er, flakiest**) **1** breaking or separating easily into small thin pieces. ■ (esp. of skin or paint) tending to crack and come away from a surface in small pieces. **2** *inf.* crazy or eccentric: *flaky ideas about taxes.* ■ *inf.* (of a device or software) prone to break down; unreliable. —**flak·i·ness** n. —**flak·i·ly** /-kəlē/ adv.

flam·bé /flämˈbā/ ▶ adj. (of food) covered with liquor and set alight briefly: *crêpes flambé.*
▶ v. (**-bés, -béed** /-ˈbād/, **-bé·ing**) [tr.] cover (food) with liquor and set it alight briefly.

flam·boy·ant /flamˈboiənt/ ▶ adj. **1** (of a person or their behavior) tending to attract attention because of their exuberance, confidence, and stylishness. ■ (esp. of clothing) noticeable because brightly colored, highly patterned, or unusual in style. **2** *Archit.* of or denoting a style of French Gothic architecture marked by wavy flamelike tracery and ornate decoration. —**flam·boy·ance** n. —**flam·boy·an·cy** n. —**flam·boy·ant·ly** adv.

flame /flām/ ▶ n. **1** a hot glowing body of ignited gas that is generated by something on fire. **2** *figurative* used in similes and metaphors to refer to something resembling a flame in various respects, in particular: ■ a thing resembling a flame in heat, shape, or brilliance. ■ a brilliant orange-red color: [in *combination*] *a flame-red trench coat.* ■ a thing compared to a flame's ability to burn fiercely or be extinguished: *the flame of hope.* ■ a very intense emotion. ■ a cause that generates passionate feelings. ■ *Comput.* a vitriolic or abusive message sent via electronic mail.

▶ *v.* [*intr.*] burn and give off flames. ■ [*trans.*] set (something) alight. ■ *figurative* shine or glow like a flame: *her hair flamed against the light.* ■ *figurative* (of an intense emotion) appear suddenly and fiercely. ■ (of a person's face) suddenly become red with intense emotion, esp. anger or embarrassment. ■ [*trans.*] *Comput.* send (someone) abusive or vitriolic electronic mail messages.
▶ *phrasal v.* □ **flame out** (of a jet engine) lose power through the extinction of the flame in the combustion chamber. ■ *inf.* fail, esp. conspicuously. —**flame·less** *adj.* —**flame·like** /-‚līk/ *adj.*
▶ □ **in flames** on fire; burning fiercely: *the plane plunged to the ground in flames.* □ **old flame** *inf.* a former lover.

fla·men·co /fləˈmeNGkō/ ▶ *n.* a style of Spanish music, played esp. on the guitar and accompanied by singing and dancing. ■ a style of spirited, rhythmical dance performed to such music, often with castanets.

flame·proof /ˈflām‚prōōf/ ▶ *adj.* (esp. of a fabric) treated so as to be nonflammable.
▶ *v.* [*tr.*] make (something) flameproof.

flame·throw·er /ˈflām‚THrōər/ ▶ *n.* a weapon that sprays out burning fuel.

flam·ing /ˈflāmiNG/ ▶ *adj.* **1** burning fiercely and emitting flames. ■ very hot. ■ glowing with a bright orange or red color: *flaming autumn maples.* ■ (of red or orange) brilliant or intense: *flaming red hair.* ■ (esp. of an argument) passionate: *flaming jealousy.* **2** *inf.* used for emphasis to express annoyance: *a flaming nuisance.* —**flam·ing·ly** *adv.*

fla·min·go /fləˈmiNGgō/ ▶ *n.* (pl. **-gos** or **-goes**) a tall wading bird (family Phoenicopteridae) with mainly pink or scarlet plumage. It has a heavy bent bill used to filter-feed on small organisms.

flam·ma·ble /ˈflaməbəl/ ▶ *adj.* easily set on fire: *the use of highly flammable materials.* —**flam·ma·bil·i·ty** /‚flaməˈbilətē/ *n.*

flan /flan/ ▶ *n.* **1** a baked dish consisting of an open-topped pastry case with a savory or sweet filling. ■ a custard with a caramel topping. **2** a disk of metal such as one from which a coin is made.

flange /flanj/ ▶ *n.* a projecting flat rim, collar, or rib on an object, serving to strengthen or attach or (on a wheel) to maintain position on a rail. —**flanged** *adj.*

flank /flaNGk/ ▶ *n.* **1** the side of a person's or animal's body between the ribs and the hip. ■ a cut of meat from such a part of an animal. ■ the side of something large, such as a mountain, building, or ship: *the northern flank of the volcano.* **2** the right or left side of a body of people such as an army, a naval force, or a soccer team.
▶ *v.* [*tr.*] (often **be flanked**) be situated on each side of or on one side of (someone or something): *the fireplace is flanked by long shelves.* ■ [usu. as *adj.*] (**flanking**) guard or strengthen (a military force or position) from the side: *walls defended by flanking towers.* ■ [usu. as *adj.*] attack down or from the sides, or rake with gunfire from the sides: *a flanking attack.*

flank·er /ˈflaNGkər/ ▶ *n.* a person or thing situated on the flank of something, in particular: ■ *Football* an offensive back who lines up to the outside of an end.

flan·nel /ˈflanl/ ▶ *n.* **1** a kind of soft-woven fabric, typically made of wool or cotton and slightly milled and raised: [as *adj.*] *a flannel nightgown.* ■ (**flannels**) men's trousers made of such material. **2** *Brit.* a washcloth.

flap /flap/ ▶ *v.* (**flapped, flapping**) [*tr.*] (of a bird) move (its wings) up and down when flying or preparing to fly. ■ [*intr.*] (of something attached at one point or loosely fastened) flutter or wave around: *the corners flapped furiously.* ■ move (one's arms or hands) up and down or back and forth. ■ [*trans.*] strike or attempt to strike (something) loosely with one's hand, a cloth, or a broad implement, esp. to drive it away. ■ wave (something, esp. a cloth) around or at someone or something.
▶ *n.* **1** a piece of something thin, such as cloth, paper, or metal, hinged or attached only on one side, that covers an opening or hangs down from something. ■ a hinged or sliding section of an aircraft wing used to control lift. ■ the part of a dust jacket that folds inside a book's cover. **2** a movement of a wing or an arm from side to side or up and down. ■ the sound of something making such a movement. **3** *informal* a state of agitation; a panic: *they're in a flap over who's going to take Henry's lectures.* —**flap·py** *adj.*

flap·doo·dle /ˈflap‚dōōdl/ ▶ *n.* *inf.* nonsense. ■ a fool.

flap·jack /ˈflap‚jak/ ▶ *n.* a pancake.

flap·per /ˈflapər/ ▶ *n.* **1** *inf.* (in the 1920s) a fashionable young woman intent on enjoying herself and flouting conventional standards of behavior. **2** a thing that flaps, esp. a movable seal inside a toilet tank.

flare /fler/ ▶ *n.* **1** a sudden brief burst of bright flame or light. ■ a device producing a bright flame, used esp. as a signal or marker: [as *adj.*] *a flare gun.* ■ a sudden burst of intense emotion: *a flare of anger.* ■ a sudden explosion in the chromosphere and corona of the sun or another star, resulting in an intense burst of radiation. ■ *Photog.*

extraneous illumination on film caused by internal reflection in the camera. **2** a gradual widening, esp. of a skirt or pants.
▶ *v.* [*intr.*] **1** burn with a sudden intensity. ■ (of a light or a person's eyes) glow with a sudden intensity. ■ (of an emotion) suddenly become manifest in a person or their expression: *tempers flared.* ■ (**flare up**) (of an illness or chronic medical complaint) recur unexpectedly and cause further discomfort. ■ (esp. of an argument, conflict, or trouble) suddenly become more violent or intense: *the crisis flared up again.* ■ (**flare up**) (of a person) suddenly become angry. **2** [often as *adj.*] (**flared**) gradually become wider at one end: *a flared skirt.* ■ (of a person's nostrils) dilate. ■ [*tr.*] (of a person) cause (the nostrils) to dilate.

flare-up ▶ *n.* a sudden outburst of something, esp. violence or a medical condition: *a flare-up between the two countries.*

flash /flaSH/ ▶ *v.* **1** [*intr.*] (of a light or something that reflects light) shine in a bright but brief, sudden, or intermittent way. ■ [*tr.*] cause to shine briefly or suddenly: *the oncoming car flashed its lights.* ■ [*tr.*] shine or show a light to send (a signal): *to flash a warning.* ■ [*tr.*] give (a swift or sudden look): *Carrie flashed him a withering look.* ■ express a sudden burst of emotion, esp. anger, with such a look. **2** [*tr.*] display (an image, words, or information) suddenly on a television or computer screen or electronic sign, typically briefly or repeatedly. ■ [*intr.*] (of an image or message) be displayed in such a way: *results flashed on the screen.* ■ *inf.* hold up or show (something, often proof of one's identity) quickly before replacing it: *she flashed her ID.* ■ make a conspicuous display of (something) so as to impress or attract attention: *they all flash their money around.* ■ [*intr.*] [often as *n.*] (**flashing**) *inf.* (esp. of a man) show one's genitals briefly in public. **3** [*intr.*] move or pass very quickly. ■ (of a thought or memory) suddenly come into or pass through the mind. ■ [*tr.*] send (news or information) swiftly by means of telegraphy or telecommunications: *the story was flashed around the world.*
▶ *phrasal v.* □ **flash back** (of a person's thoughts or mind) briefly and suddenly recall a previous time or incident.
▶ *n.* **1** a sudden brief burst of bright light or a sudden glint from a reflective surface. **2** a thing that occurs suddenly and within a brief period of time, in particular: ■ a sudden instance or manifestation of a quality, understanding, or humor: *a flash of inspiration.* ■ a fleeting glimpse of something, esp. something eye-catching: *the blue flash of a kingfisher.* ■ a news flash. **3** a camera attachment that produces a brief very bright light, used for taking photographs in poor light.
▶ *adj.* *inf., chiefly Brit.* (of a thing) ostentatiously expensive, elaborate, or up to date. ■ (of a person) superficially attractive because stylish and full of brash charm: *carrying money around and trying to be flash.*
▶ □ **flash in the pan** a thing or person whose sudden but brief success is not repeated or repeatable. □ **in** (or **like**) **a flash** very quickly; immediately.

flash·back /ˈflaSH‚bak/ ▶ *n.* a scene in a movie, novel, etc., set in a time earlier than the main story. ■ a sudden and disturbing vivid memory of an event in the past, typically as the result of psychological trauma or taking LSD.

flash·bulb /ˈflaSH‚bəlb/ ▶ *n.* a light bulb that flashes in order to illuminate a photographic subject, of a type that is used only once.

flash card ▶ *n.* a card containing a small amount of information, held up for students to see, as an aid to learning.

flash drive ▶ *n.* *Comput.* a data storage device containing flash memory that has no moving parts and does not need batteries or a power supply. See also **USB FLASH DRIVE**.

flash·er /ˈflaSHər/ ▶ *n.* **1** an automatic device causing a light to flash on and off rapidly. ■ a signal using such a device, for example a car's turn signal. **2** *inf.* a person, esp. a man, who exposes his genitals in public.

flash flood ▶ *n.* a sudden local flood, typically due to heavy rain.

flash·gun /ˈflaSH‚gən/ ▶ *n.* a device that gives a brief flash of intense light, used for taking photographs indoors or in poor light.

flash·ing /ˈflaSHiNG/ ▶ *n.* a strip of metal used to stop water from penetrating the junction of a roof with another surface.

flash·light /ˈflaSH‚līt/ ▶ *n.* **1** a battery-operated portable light. **2** a flashing light used for signals and in lighthouses. **3** a light giving an intense flash, used for photographing at night or indoors.

flash point (also **flash·point**) ▶ *n.* **1** a place, event, or time at which trouble, such as violence or anger, flares up. **2** *Chem.* the minimum temperature at which a particular organic compound gives off sufficient vapor to ignite in air.

Pronunciation Key ə *ago*, *up*; ər *over*, *fur*; a *hat*; ā *ate*; ä *car*; CH *chin*; e *let*; ē *see*; e(ə)r *air*; i *fit*; ī *by*; i(ə)r *ear*; NG *sing*; ō *go*; ô *law*, *for*; oi *toy*; ōō *good*; ōō *goo*; ou *out*; SH *she*; TH *thin*; TH *then*; (h)w *why*; zH *vision*

flash·y /ˈflashē/ ▶adj. (**flash·i·er, flash·i·est**) ostentatiously attractive or impressive: *a flashy car.* —**flash·i·ly** /ˈflashəlē/ adv. —**flash·i·ness** n.

flask /flask/ ▶n. a container or bottle, in particular: ■ a narrow-necked glass container, typically conical or spherical, used in a laboratory to hold reagents or samples. ■ a metal container for storing a small amount of liquor, typically to be carried in one's pocket. ■ a narrow-necked bulbous glass container, typically with a covering of wicker-work, for storing wine or oil. ■ a small glass bottle for perfume. ■ a vacuum flask. ▷Middle English (in the sense 'cask'): from medieval Latin *flasca*. From the mid 16th cent. the word denoted a case of horn, leather, or metal for carrying gunpowder. The sense 'glass container' (late 17th cent.) was influenced by Italian *fiasco*, from medieval Latin *flasco*.

flat[1] /flat/ ▶adj. (**flat·ter, flat·test**) **1** smooth and even; without marked lumps or indentations. ■ (of land) without hills. ■ (of an expanse of water) calm and without waves. ■ not sloping: *the flat roof of a garage.* ■ having a broad level surface but little height or depth; shallow: *a flat rectangular box.* ■ (of the foot) having an arch that is lower than usual. ■ (of shoes) without heels or with very low heels. **2** lacking interest or emotion; dull and lifeless: *her drawings were flat and unimaginative.* ■ (of a person) without energy; dispirited. ■ (of a market, prices, etc.) showing little activity; sluggish. ■ (of a sparkling drink) having lost its effervescence: *flat champagne.* ■ (of something kept inflated, esp. a tire) having lost some or all of its air, typically because of a puncture. ■ (of a color) uniform: *a deadly, flat shade of gray.* ■ (of paint) without gloss; matte. ■ (of a photographic print or negative) lacking contrast. **3** (of a fee, wage, or price) the same in all cases, not varying with changed conditions or in particular cases: *a $30 flat fare.* ■ (of a denial, contradiction, or refusal) completely definite and firm; absolute: *a flat denial that he had misbehaved.* **4** (of musical sound) below true or normal pitch. ■ [in comb.] (of a note) a semitone lower than a specified note: *a low E-flat.* ■ (of a key) having a flat or flats in the signature.
▶adv. **1** in or to a horizontal position: *lying flat on his back | knocked flat by the blast.* ■ lying in close juxtaposition, esp. against another surface. ■ so as to become smooth and even: *I hammered the metal flat.* **2** inf. completely; absolutely: *I'm turning you down flat | flat broke.* ■ after a phrase expressing a period of time to emphasize how quickly something can be done or has been done: *you can prepare a healthy meal* **in ten minutes flat.** **3** below the true or normal pitch of musical sound: *singing flat.*
▶n. **1** the flat part of something: *the flat of her hand.* **2** a flat object, in particular: ■ (often **flats**) an upright section of painted stage scenery mounted on a frame. ■ inf. a flat tire. ■ a shallow container in which seedlings are grown and sold. ■ (often **flats**) a shoe with a very low heel or no heel. **3** (usu. **flats**) an area of low level ground, esp. near water: *the Utah salt flats.* **4** a musical note lowered a half step below natural pitch. ■ the sign ( ) indicating this.
▶v. (**flat·ted, flat·ting**) [tr.] **1** [usu. as adj.] (**flatted**) *Mus.* lower (a note) by a semitone. **2** archaic make flat; flatten. —**flat·ly** adv. —**flat·ness** n. —**flat·tish** /ˈflatish/ adj.
▶ □ **fall flat** fail completely to produce the intended or expected effect: *his jokes fell flat.* □ **flat out 1** as fast or as hard as possible: *working flat out to satisfy demand |* [as adj.] (**flat-out**) *the album lacks the flat-out urgency of its predecessor.* **2** inf. without hesitation or reservation; unequivocally: [as adj.] (**flat-out**) *flat-out perjury.* **3** lying completely stretched out, esp. asleep or exhausted.

flat[2] ▶n. British term for **APARTMENT**. —**flat·let** /-lət/ n.

flat·car /ˈflatˌkär/ ▶n. a railroad freight car without a roof or sides.

flat·fish /ˈflatˌfish/ ▶n. (pl. same or **-fishes**) a flattened marine fish (order Pleuronectiformes) that swims on its side with both eyes on the upper side.

flat·foot /ˈflatˌfoot/ ▶n. (also **flat foot**) a condition in which the foot has an arch that is lower than usual. ■ (pl. **-foots** or **-feet** /-ˌfēt/) inf., dated a police officer.

flat·foot·ed ▶adj. **1** having flat feet. **2** having one's feet flat on the ground: *he landed with a flat-footed thud.* ■ inf. unable to move quickly and smoothly; clumsy. ■ inf. not clever or imaginative; uninspired. —**flat·foot·ed·ly** adv. —**flat·foot·ed·ness** n.
▶ □ **catch someone flat-footed** inf. take someone by surprise.

flat·i·ron /ˈflatˌīərn/ ▶n. hist. an iron that was heated externally and used for pressing clothes.

flat·ten /ˈflatn/ ▶v. **1** make or become flat or flatter: [tr.] *flatten into cakes, and fry until brown |* [intr.] *the ground flattened out and became marshy.* ■ [tr.] press (oneself or one's body) against a surface, typically to get away from something or to let someone pass: *they flattened themselves on the pavement as a bomb came whistling down.* ■ [tr.] Mus. lower (a note) in pitch

by a half step. **2** [tr.] raze (a building or settlement) to the ground. ■ inf. knock someone down with power and vigor. ■ inf. defeat (someone) completely, esp. in a sports contest.
▶phrasal v. □ **flatten out 1** (of an increasing quantity or rate) show a less marked rise; slow down. **2** make an aircraft fly horizontally after a dive or climb. —**flat·ten·er** n.

flat·ter /ˈflatər/ ▶v. [tr.] lavish insincere praise and compliments upon (someone), esp. to further one's own interests. ■ give an unrealistically favorable impression of. ■ (usu. **be flattered**) make (someone) feel honored and pleased: [tr.] *I was very flattered to be given the commission.* ■ (**flatter oneself**) make oneself feel pleased by believing something favorable about oneself, typically something that is unfounded: *I flatter myself I'm the best dressed man here.* ■ (of a color or a style of clothing) make (someone) appear more attractive or to the best advantage. ■ archaic please (the ear or eye). —**flat·ter·er** n. —**flat·ter·ing** adj.

flat·ter·y /ˈflatərē/ ▶n. (pl. **-ter·ies**) excessive and insincere praise, esp. that given to further one's own interests.

flat·top /ˈflatˌtäp/ ▶n. **1** inf. an aircraft carrier. **2** a man's hairstyle in which the hair is cropped short so that it bristles up into a flat surface.

flat·u·lent /ˈflachələnt/ ▶adj. suffering from or marked by an accumulation of gas in the alimentary canal. ■ fig. inflated or pretentious in speech or writing. —**flat·u·lence** n. —**flat·u·len·cy** n. —**flat·u·lent·ly** adv.

fla·tus /ˈflātəs/ ▶n. formal gas in or from the stomach or intestines, produced by swallowing air or by bacterial fermentation.

flat·ware /ˈflatˌwer/ ▶n. eating utensils such as knives, forks, and spoons. ■ relatively flat dishes such as plates and saucers.

flat·worm /ˈflatˌwərm/ ▶n. a worm of a phylum (Platyhelminthes) that includes the planarians together with the parasitic flukes and tapeworms. They are distinguished by having a simple flattened body.

flaunt /flônt; flänt/ ▶v. [tr.] display (something) ostentatiously, esp. in order to provoke envy or admiration or to show defiance. ■ (**flaunt oneself**) dress or behave in a sexually provocative way. —**flaunt·er** n. —**flaunt·y** adj.

flau·tist /ˈflôtist; ˈflou-/ ▶n. a flutist.

fla·vi·vi·rus /ˈflāvəˌvīrəs/ ▶n. a virus whose genome consists of positive RNA, that is capable of reproducing in its arthropod vector, and that causes a number of serious human diseases including yellow fever, dengue, Japanese encephalitis, and West Nile virus.

fla·vone /ˈflāˌvōn/ ▶n. Chem. a colorless crystalline compound, $C_{15}H_{10}O_2$, that is the basis of a number of white or yellow plant pigments. ■ any of these pigments.

fla·vor /ˈflāvər/ (Brit. **fla·vour**) ▶n. **1** the distinctive quality of a particular food or drink as perceived by the taste buds and the sense of smell. ■ the general quality of taste in a food. ■ a substance used to alter or enhance the taste of food or drink; a flavoring. ■ fig. an indefinable distinctive quality of something: *this year's seminars have a European flavor.* ■ fig. an indication of the essential character of something: *the extracts give a flavor of the conversation.* **2** Physics a quantized property of quarks that differentiates them into at least six varieties (up, down, charmed, strange, top, bottom). Compare with **COLOR**.
▶v. [tr.] alter or enhance the taste of (food or drink) by adding a particular ingredient. ■ fig. give a distinctive quality to. —**fla·vor·ful** /-fəl/ adj. —**fla·vor·less** adj. —**fla·vor·some** /-səm/ adj.
▶ □ **flavor of the month** a person or thing that enjoys a short period of great popularity.

fla·vor·ing /ˈflāvəriNG/ (Brit. **flavouring**) ▶n. a substance used to give a different, stronger, or more agreeable taste to food or drink.

flaw[1] /flô/ ▶n. a mark, fault, or other imperfection that mars a substance or object. ■ a fault or weakness in a person's character. ■ a mistake or shortcoming in a plan, theory, or legal document that causes it to fail or reduces its effectiveness: *there were fundamental flaws in the case for reforming local government.*
▶v. [tr.] (usu. **be flawed**) (of an imperfection) mar, weaken, or invalidate (something): *the computer game was flawed by poor programming.* —**flaw·less** adj.

flaw[2] ▶n. poetic/lit. a squall of wind; a short storm.

flax /flaks/ ▶n. a blue-flowered herbaceous plant (Linum usitatissimum, family Linaceae) cultivated for its seed and for textile fiber made from its stalks. ■ textile fiber obtained from this plant. ■ used in names of other plants of the flax family or plants that yield similar fiber. ▷Old English *flæx*, related to German *Flachs*, from an Indo-European root shared by Latin *plectere* and Greek *plekein* 'to plait, twist.'

flax·en /ˈflaksən/ ▶adj. of flax. ■ (esp. of hair) of a pale yellow color.

flax·seed /ˈflak(s)ˌsēd/ ▶n. another term for **LINSEED**.

flay /flā/ ▸v. [tr.] peel the skin off (a corpse or carcass). ▪ peel (the skin) off a corpse or carcass. ▪ whip or beat (someone) harshly. ▪ fig. criticize severely and brutally. —**flay·er** n.

F lay·er ▸n. the highest and most strongly ionized region of the ionosphere.

flea /flē/ ▸n. a small wingless jumping insect (order Siphonaptera) that feeds on the blood of mammals and birds, including the **human flea** (*Pulex irritans*) and the **cat flea** (*Ctenocephalides felis*). ▪ a water flea (see **DAPHNIA**).

flea·bag /'flē,bag/ ▸n. inf. a seedy, run-down hotel or lodging house. ▪ a shabby and unpleasant person or thing.

flea-bit·ten ▸adj. bitten by or infested with fleas. ▪ sordid or shabby.

flea col·lar ▸n. a collar for a cat or dog that is impregnated with insecticide in order to keep the pet free of fleas.

flea mar·ket ▸n. a usu. outdoor market selling secondhand goods.

fleck /flek/ ▸n. a very small patch of color or light *his blue eyes had gray flecks in them.* ▪ a small particle or speck of something: *flecks of dandruff.* ▸v. [tr.] (often **be flecked**) mark or dot with small patches of color or particles of something: *the minarets are flecked with gold leaf.*

fled /fled/ ▸ past and past participle of **FLEE**.

fledge /flej/ ▸v. [intr.] **1** (of a young bird) develop wing feathers that are large enough for flight. ▪ [tr.] bring up (a young bird) until its wing feathers are developed enough for flight. **2** [tr.] provide (an arrow) with feathers.

fledg·ling /'flejliNG/ (also **fledge·ling**) ▸n. a young bird that has just fledged. ▪ [usu. as adj.] a person or organization that is immature, inexperienced, or underdeveloped.

flee /flē/ ▸v. (**flees, flee·ing**; past and past part. **fled** /fled/) [intr.] run away from a place or situation of danger. ▪ [tr.] run away from (someone or something).

fleece /flēs/ ▸n. **1** the woolly covering of a sheep or goat. ▪ the amount of wool shorn from a sheep in a single piece at one time. **2** a thing resembling a sheep's woolly covering, in particular: ▪ a soft warm fabric with a texture similar to sheep's wool, often used as a lining material. ▪ a jacket or other garment made from such a fabric.
▸v. [tr.] **1** inf. obtain a great deal of money from (someone), typically by overcharging or swindling them. **2** fig. cover as if with a fleece: *the sky was half fleeced with white clouds.* —**fleeced** adj.

fleec·y /'flēsē/ ▸adj. (**fleec·i·er, fleec·i·est**) **1** (esp. of a towel or garment) made of or lined with a soft, warm fabric: *a fleecy sweatshirt.* **2** (esp. of a cloud) white and fluffy. —**fleec·i·ly** /-səlē/ adv. —**fleec·i·ness** n.

fleet¹ /flēt/ ▸n. the largest group of naval vessels under one commander, organized for specific tactical or other purposes. ▪ (**the fleet**) a country's navy. ▪ a group of ships sailing together, engaged in the same activity, or under the same ownership: *a fishing fleet.* ▪ a number of ships, vehicles, or aircraft operating together or under the same ownership: *a fleet of ambulances.*

fleet² ▸adj. fast and nimble in movement: *fleet of foot.* —**fleet·ly** adv. —**fleet·ness** n.

fleet³ ▸v. [intr.] poetic/lit. move or pass quickly: *a variety of expressions fleeted across his face | time may fleet and youth may fade.* ▪ [tr.] pass (time) rapidly. ▪ fade away; be transitory: *the cares of boyhood fleet away.*

Fleet Ad·mi·ral ▸n. an admiral of the highest rank in the U.S. Navy.

fleet·ing /'flētiNG/ ▸adj. lasting for a very short time: *hoping to get a fleeting glimpse of a whale.* —**fleet·ing·ly** adv.

Flem·ing ▸n. **1** a native of Flanders. **2** a member of the Flemish-speaking people inhabiting northern and western Belgium. Compare with **WALLOON**.

Flem·ish /'flemish/ ▸adj. of or relating to Flanders, its people, or their language.
▸n. **1** the Dutch language as spoken in Flanders, one of the two official languages of Belgium. **2** (**the Flemish**) [as pl. n.] the people of Flanders.

flesh /flesh/ ▸n. the soft substance consisting of muscle and fat that is found between the skin and bones of an animal or a human. ▪ this substance in an animal or fish, regarded as food: [in comb.] *a flesh-eater.* ▪ the pulpy substance of a fruit or vegetable, esp. the part that is eaten. ▪ fat. ▪ the skin or surface of the human body with reference to its color, appearance, or sensual properties: *she gasped as the cold water hit her flesh.* ▪ (**the flesh**) the human body and its physical needs and desires, esp. as contrasted with the mind or the soul: *the pleasures of the flesh.* ▪ flesh color.
▸v. **1** [intr.] (**flesh out**) put weight on. ▪ [tr.] (**flesh something out**) add more details to something that exists only in a draft or outline form: *fleshed out a variety of scenarios.* **2** [tr.] [often as n.] (**fleshing**) remove the

flesh adhering to (a skin or hide). —**fleshed** /flesht/ adj. [usu. in comb.] *a white-fleshed fish.*
▸ □ **in the flesh** in person rather than via a telephone, a movie, the written word, or other means: *they decided that they should meet Alexander in the flesh.* □ **sins of the flesh** archaic or humorous sins related to physical indulgence, esp. sexual gratification.

flesh and blood ▸n. used to emphasize that a person is a physical, living being with human emotions or frailties, often in contrast to something abstract, spiritual, or mechanical: [as adj.] *he seemed more like a creature from a dream than a flesh-and-blood father.*
▸ □ **one's (own) flesh and blood** a near relative or one's close family: *he felt as much for that girl as if she had been his own flesh and blood.*

flesh·ly /'fleshlē/ ▸adj. (**-li·er, -li·est**) **1** of or relating to human desire or bodily appetites; sensual: *fleshly pleasures.* **2** having an actual physical presence.

flesh·pots /'flesh,päts/ ▸pl. n. places providing luxurious or hedonistic living: *he had lived the life of a roué in the fleshpots of London and Paris.*

flesh·y /'fleshē/ ▸adj. (**flesh·i·er, flesh·i·est**) **1** (of a person or part of the body) having a substantial amount of flesh; plump. ▪ (of plant or fruit tissue) soft and thick: *fleshy, green-gray leaves.* ▪ (of a wine) full-bodied. **2** resembling flesh in appearance or texture. —**flesh·i·ness** n.

fleur-de-lis /ˌflər dlˈē; ˌflōr-/ (also **fleur-de-lys** /ˌflər dlˈē(z); ˌflōr-/) ▸n. (pl. **fleurs-de-lis** /ˌflər dlˈē(z); ˌflōr-/) **1** Art a stylized lily composed of three petals bound together near their bases. **2** a European iris.

flew /floo/ ▸ past of **FLY¹**.

flex /fleks/ ▸v. [tr.] bend (a limb or joint). ▪ [intr.] (of a limb or joint) become bent *prevent the damaged wrist from flexing.* ▪ cause (a muscle) to stand out by contracting or tensing it: *bodybuilders flexing their muscles.* ▪ [intr.] (of a muscle) contract or be tensed. ▪ [intr.] (of a material) be capable of warping or bending and then reverting to shape.
▸n. the action or state of flexing: *add rigidity and eliminate brake flex.*

flex-fu·el ▸adj. denoting a motor vehicle that will run on gasoline, ethanol, or these two in any combination: *flex-fuel subcompacts have captured 20% of Brazil's new car market.*

fleur-de-lis

flex·i·ble /'fleksəbəl/ ▸adj. capable of bending easily without breaking. ▪ able to be easily modified to respond to altered circumstances or conditions. ▪ (of a person) ready and able to change so as to adapt to different circumstances. —**flex·i·bil·i·ty** /ˌfleksəˈbilətē/ n. —**flex·i·bly** /-blē/ adv.

flex·ile /'fleksəl; -ˌsīl/ ▸adj. archaic pliant and flexible: *the serpent's flexile body.* —**flex·il·i·ty** /flekˈsilətē/ n.

flex·or /'flek,sər; -sôr/ (also **flexor muscle**) ▸n. Anat. a muscle whose contraction bends a limb or other part of the body. ▪ any of a number of specific muscles in the arm, hand, leg, or foot.

flex·time /'fleks,tīm/ (Brit. **flex·i·time** /'fleksi-/) ▸n. a system of working a set number of hours with the starting and finishing times chosen within agreed limits by the employee.

flick /flik/ ▸n. **1** a sudden sharp movement. ▪ the sudden release of a bent finger or thumb. ▪ esp. to propel a small object: *he sent his cigarette spinning away with a flick of his fingers.* ▪ a light, sharp, quickly retracted blow, esp. with a whip. **2** inf. a motion picture. ▪ (**the flicks**) chiefly Brit. the movies.
▸v. [tr.] propel (something) with a sudden sharp movement, esp. of the fingers: *Emily flicked some ash off her sleeve.* ▪ (**flick something on/off**) turn something electrical on or off by means of a switch. ▪ [intr.] make a sudden sharp movement. ▪ [tr.] move (a whip) so as to strike.

flick·er¹ /'flikər/ ▸v. [intr.] (of light or a source of light) shine unsteadily; vary rapidly in brightness. ▪ (of a flame) burn fitfully, alternately flaring up and dying down: [as adj.] (**flickering**) *the flickering flames of the fire.* ▪ fig. (of a feeling or emotion) be experienced or show itself briefly and faintly, in someone's eyes. **2** make small, quick movements; flutter rapidly: *her eyelids flickered.* ▪ (of someone's eyes) move quickly in a particular direction in order to look at something. ▪ (of a facial expression) appear briefly: *a look of horror flickered across his face.*
▸phrasal v. **flicker out** (of a flame or light) die away and go out after a series of flickers. ▪ fig. (of a feeling) die away and finally disappear.
▸n. **1** an unsteady movement of a flame or light that causes rapid

variations in brightness. ▪ fluctuations in the brightness of a movie or cathode ray tube image. **2** a tiny movement: *a flicker of movement caught his eye.* ▪ a faint indication of a facial expression: *a flicker of a smile.* ▪ *fig.* a very brief and faint experience of an emotion or feeling: *she felt a small flicker of alarm.*

flick·er² ▸*n.* an American woodpecker (genus *Colaptes*) that often feeds on ants on the ground, esp. the **common flicker** (*C. auratus*).

fli·er /'flīər/ (also **fly·er**) ▸*n.* **1** a person or thing that flies, esp. in a particular way: *a nervous flier.* ▪ a person who flies something, esp. an aircraft. **2** a small handbill advertising an event or product. **3** a speculative investment.

flight /flīt/ ▸*n.* **1** the action or process of flying through the air. ▪ an act of flying; a journey made through the air or in space, esp. a scheduled journey made by an airline. ▪ the movement or trajectory of a projectile or ball through the air. ▪ *poetic/lit.* swift passage of time. **2** a group of creatures or objects flying together, in particular: ▪ a flock or large body of birds or insects in the air, esp. when migrating: *flights of Canada geese.* ▪ a group of aircraft operating together, esp. an air force unit of about six aircraft. **3** the action of fleeing or attempting to escape. **4** a series of steps between floors or levels: *four flights of stairs.* **5** an extravagant or far-fetched idea or account: *ridiculous flights of fancy.*
▸ □ **in full flight** escaping as fast as possible. ▪ having gained momentum in a run or activity: *when this jazz pianist is in full flight he can be mesmerizing.* □ **take flight** **1** (of a bird) take off and fly.| *fig. my celebrityhood took flight.* **2** flee.

flight at·tend·ant ▸*n.* a steward or stewardess on an aircraft.

flight deck ▸*n.* **1** the cockpit of a large aircraft. **2** the deck of an aircraft carrier, used for takeoff and landing.

flight·less /'flītlis/ ▸*adj.* (of a bird or an insect) naturally unable to fly. —**flight·less·ness** *n.*

flight·y /'flītē/ ▸*adj.* (**flight·i·er**, **flight·i·est**) fickle and irresponsible. —**flight·i·ly** /'flītl-ē/ *adv.* —**flight·i·ness** *n.*

flim·flam /'flim,flam/ *inf.* ▸*n.* nonsensical or insincere talk. ▪ a confidence game.
▸*v.* (**-flammed**, **-flam·ming**) [*tr.*] swindle (someone) with a confidence game. —**flim·flam·mer** *n.* —**flim·flam·mer·y** /-,flamərē/ *n.*

flim·sy /'flimzē/ ▸*adj.* (**-si·er**, **-si·est**) comparatively light and insubstantial; easily damaged: *flimsy boats.* ▪ (of clothing) light and thin. ▪ (of a pretext or account) weak and unconvincing: *a pretty flimsy excuse.*
▸*n.* (*pl.* **-sies**) *Brit.* a document, esp. a copy, made on very thin paper. ▪ very thin paper: *sheets of yellow flimsy.* —**flim·si·ly** /'flimzəlē/ *adv.* —**flim·si·ness** *n.*

flinch /flinCH/ ▸*v.* [*intr.*] make a quick, nervous movement of the face or body as an instinctive reaction to surprise, fear, or pain. ▪ (**flinch from**) *fig.* avoid doing or becoming involved in (something) through fear or anxiety.
▸*n.* an act of flinching. —**flinch·er** *n.* —**flinch·ing·ly** *adv.*

fling /fliNG/ ▸*v.* (*past* **flung** /fləNG/) [*tr.*] throw or hurl forcefully: *fig. I was flung into jail.* ▪ move or push (something) suddenly or violently. ▪ (**fling oneself**) throw oneself headlong: *he flung himself down at her feet.* ▪ (**fling oneself into**) wholeheartedly engage in or begin on (an enterprise). ▪ (**fling something on/off**) put on or take off clothes carelessly or rapidly. ▪ utter (words) forcefully.
▸*n.* **1** a short period of enjoyment or wild behavior. ▪ a short, spontaneous sexual relationship. **2** short for **HIGHLAND FLING.** —**fling·er** *n.*

flint /flint/ ▸*n.* a hard gray rock occurring chiefly as nodules in chalk. ▪ a piece of this stone, esp. as flaked or ground in ancient times to form a tool or weapon. ▪ a piece of flint used with steel to produce an igniting spark or (in modern use) a piece of an alloy used similarly, esp. in a cigarette lighter. ▪ used to express how hard and unyielding something or someone is: *mean faces with eyes like flints.* —**flint·y** *adj.*

flint·lock /'flint,läk/ ▸*n.* **1** an old-fashioned type of gun fired by a spark from a flint. **2** [usu. as *adj.*] the lock on such a gun.

flip¹ /flip/ ▸*v.* (**flipped**, **flip·ping**) **1** turn over or cause to turn over with a sudden sharp movement. **2** [*tr.*] move, push, or throw (something) with a sudden sharp movement: *she flipped a few coins on the bar.* ▪ [*tr.*] turn (an electrical appliance or switch) on or off. ▪ [*tr.*] toss (a coin) to decide an issue: [*intr.*] *do you want to flip for it?* **3** [*tr.*] buy and sell (a property) quickly and profitably using a fraudulent evaluation of its worth. **4** [*intr.*] *inf.* suddenly become deranged or very angry: *he had clearly flipped under the pressure.* ▪ suddenly become very enthusiastic: *I saw it and just flipped.*
▸*phrasal v.* □ **flip through** look or search quickly through (a volume or a collection of papers): *just flip through the phone book and pick a lawyer.*
▸*n.* a sudden sharp movement.
▸*adj.* glib; flippant.

▸ □ **flip one's lid** (or **one's wig**) *inf.* suddenly become deranged or lose one's self-control.

flip² ▸*n.* another term for **EGGNOG.**

flip chart ▸*n.* a large pad of paper bound so that each page can be turned over at the top to reveal the next, used at presentations.

flip-flop ▸*n.* **1** a light sandal, typically of plastic or rubber, with a thong between the big and second toes. **2** a backward somersault or handspring. **3** *inf.* an abrupt reversal of policy. **4** *Electr.* a switching circuit that works by changing from one stable state to another, or through an unstable state back to its stable state, in response to a triggering pulse.
▸*v.* [*intr.*] **1** perform a backward somersault or handspring: *fig. Julie's stomach flip-flopped.* **2** *inf.* make an abrupt reversal of policy.

flip-flop

flip·pant /'flipənt/ ▸*adj.* not showing a serious or respectful attitude: *a flippant remark.* —**flip·pan·cy** /'flipənsē/ *n.* —**flip·pant·ly** *adv.*

flip·per /'flipər/ ▸*n.* a broad flat limb without fingers, used for swimming by various sea animals such as seals, whales, and turtles. ▪ a flat rubber attachment worn on the foot for underwater swimming. ▪ a pivoted arm in a pinball machine, controlled by the player and used for sending the ball back up the table. ▪ *inf.* a hand.

flip side ▸*n. inf.* the less important side of a pop single record. ▪ another aspect or version of something, esp. its reverse or its unwanted concomitant: *virtues are the flip side of vices.*

flirt /flərt/ ▸*v.* [*intr.*] behave as though attracted to or trying to attract someone, but without serious intentions: *it amused him to flirt with her.* ▪ (**flirt with**) experiment with or show a superficial interest in (an idea, activity, or movement) without committing oneself to it seriously: *a painter who had flirted briefly with Cubism.* ▪ (**flirt with**) deliberately expose oneself to (danger or difficulty): *to flirt with death.*
▸*n.* a person who habitually flirts. —**flir·ta·tion** /-'tāSHən/ *n.* —**flir·ta·tious** *adj.* —**flir·ta·tious·ly** *adv.* —**flir·ta·tious·ness** *n.* —**flirt·y.**

flit /flit/ ▸*v.* (**flit·ted**, **flit·ting**) [*intr.*] move swiftly and lightly.

flit·ter /'flitər/ ▸*v.* [*intr.*] move quickly in an apparently random or purposeless manner.
▸*n.* a fluttering movement.

float /flōt/ ▸*v.* [*intr.*] **1** rest or move on or near the surface of a liquid without sinking. ▪ [*tr.*] cause (a buoyant object) to rest or move in such a way: *trees were felled and floated downstream.* ▪ be suspended freely in a liquid or gas. **2** move or hover slowly and lightly in a liquid or the air; drift. ▪ (**float about/around**) (of a rumor, idea, or substance) circulate. ▪ (of a sight or idea) come before the eyes or mind. ▪ [*tr.*] (in sports) make (the ball) travel lightly and effortlessly through the air: *he floated the kick into the net.* **3** [*tr.*] put forward (an idea) as a suggestion or test of reactions. ▪ [*tr.*] offer the shares of (a company) for sale on the stock market for the first time. **4** (of a currency) fluctuate freely in value in accordance with supply and demand in the financial markets: *a policy of letting the pound float.* ▪ [*tr.*] allow (a currency) to fluctuate in such a way.
▸*n.* **1** a thing that is buoyant in water, in particular: ▪ a small object attached to a fishing line to indicate when a fish bites. ▪ a cork or buoy supporting the edge of a fishing net. ▪ a hollow or inflated organ enabling an organism (such as the Portuguese man-of-war) to float in the water. ▪ a hollow structure fixed underneath an aircraft enabling it to take off and land on water. ▪ a device floating on the surface of a liquid that forms part of a valve apparatus controlling flow in and out of the enclosing container, e.g., in a toilet tank or a carburetor. **2** a platform mounted on a truck and carrying a display in a parade. **3** a hand tool with a rectangular blade used for smoothing plaster or concrete. **4** a soft drink with a scoop of ice cream floating in it: *root-beer floats.* —**float·a·ble** *adj.* —**float·er** *n.*

float·a·tion /flō'tāSHən/ ▸*n.* variant spelling of **FLOTATION.**

float·ing /'flōtiNG/ ▸*adj.* **1** buoyant or suspended in water or air. **2** not settled in a definite place; fluctuating or variable.

float·ing rib ▸*n.* any of the lower ribs that are not attached directly to the breastbone.

floc·cule /'fläk,yo͞ol/ ▸*n.* a small clump of material that resembles a tuft of wool.

floc·cu·lent /ˈfläkyələnt/ ▸adj. having or resembling tufts of wool. ■ having a loosely clumped texture. —**floc·cu·lence** n.

flock[1] /fläk/ ▸n. a number of birds of one kind feeding, resting, or traveling together. ■ a number of domestic animals, esp. sheep, goats, or geese, that are kept together. ■ (**flocks**) large crowds of people: *flocks of young people hung around at twilight.* ■ a Christian congregation, esp. one under the charge of a particular minister: *Thomas addressed his flock.*
▸v. [*intr.*] congregate or mass in a large group: *students flocked to spring break sites.*

flock[2] (also **flock·ing**) ▸n. [often as *adj.*] a soft material for stuffing cushions, quilts, and other soft furnishings, made of wool refuse or torn-up cloth. ■ powdered wool or cloth, sprinkled on wallpaper, cloth, or metal to make a raised pattern.

floe /flō/ (also **ice floe**) ▸n. a sheet of floating ice.

flog /fläg/ ▸v. (**flogged**, **flog·ging**) [*tr.*] beat (someone) with a whip or stick as punishment or torture. | [as n.] (**flogging**) *public floggings.* ■ *inf.* promote or talk about (something) repetitively or at excessive length.

flood /fləd/ ▸n. **1** an overflowing of a large amount of water beyond its normal confines, esp. over what is normally dry land: [as *adj.*] *a flood barrier.* ■ (**the Flood**) the biblical flood brought by God upon the earth because of the wickedness of the human race. ■ *poetic/lit.* a river, stream, or sea. **2** an outpouring of tears or emotion. ■ a very large quantity of people or things that appear or need to be dealt with: *a constant flood of callers.* **3** short for FLOODLIGHT.
▸v. **1** [*tr.*] cover or submerge (a place or area) with water. ■ [*intr.*] become covered or submerged in this way. ■ (usu. **be flooded out**) drive someone out of their home or business with a flood: *most of the families who have been flooded out will receive compensation.* ■ (of a river or sea) become swollen and overflow (its banks). ■ overfill the carburetor of (an engine) with fuel, causing the engine to fail to start. **2** [*intr.*] arrive in overwhelming amounts or quantities: *messages flooded in | his old fears came flooding back.* ■ [*tr.*] overwhelm or swamp with large amounts or quantities: *our switchboard was flooded with calls.* ■ [*tr.*] fill or suffuse completely: *flooded with light.*
▸ □ **be in full flood** (of a river) be swollen and overflowing its banks. ■ *fig.* (of a person or action) have gained momentum; be at the height of activity.

flood·gate /ˈflədˌgāt/ ▸n. a gate that can be opened or closed to admit or exclude water, esp. the lower gate of a lock. ■ (usu. **the floodgates**) *fig.* a last restraint holding back an outpouring of something powerful or substantial: *his lawsuit could open the floodgates for similar claims.*

flood·light /ˈflədˌlīt/ ▸n. a large, powerful light, typically one of several used to illuminate a sports field, a stage, or the exterior of a building. ■ the illumination provided by such a light.
▸v. (*past* and *past part.* **-lit**) [*tr.*] [usu. as *adj.*] (**floodlit**) illuminate (a building or outdoor area) with such lights: *floodlit football fields.*

flood·plain /ˈflədˌplān/ ▸n. an area of low-lying ground adjacent to a river, formed mainly of river sediments and subject to flooding.

flood tide ▸n. a rising tide. ■ a powerful surge or flow of something: *the trickle of tourists has become a flood tide.*

flood·wa·ter /ˈflədˌwôtər; -ˌwätər/ (also **flood·wa·ters**) ▸n. water overflowing as the result of a flood.

floor /flôr/ ▸n. **1** the lower surface of a room, on which one may walk: *the kitchen floor.* ■ all the rooms or areas on the same level of a building; a story: [as *adj.*, in *comb.*] *a third-floor apartment.* ■ a level area or space used or designed for a particular activity. ■ *fig.* the minimum level of prices or wages. ■ the bottom of the sea, a cave, or an area of land: *the ocean floor.* **2** (**the floor**) (in a legislative assembly) the part of the house in which members sit and from which they speak. ■ the right or opportunity to speak next in debate: *other speakers have the floor.* ■ (of the stock exchange) the large central hall where trading takes place.
▸v. [*tr.*] **1** (often **be floored**) provide (a room or area) with a floor: [as *adj.*, in *comb.*] (**-floored**) *a stone-floored building.* **2** *inf.* knock (someone) to the ground, esp. with a punch. ■ baffle or confound (someone) completely: *that question floored him.*
▸ □ **from the floor** (of a speech or question) delivered by an individual member at a meeting, not by a representative on the platform: *questions from the floor will be invited.* □ **take the floor 1** begin to dance. **2** speak in a debate or assembly.

floor·board /ˈflôrˌbôrd/ ▸n. a long plank making up part of a wooden floor in a building. ■ the floor of a motor vehicle.

floor ex·er·cise ▸n. a routine of gymnastic exercises performed without the use any of apparatus.

floor·ing /ˈflôriNG/ ▸n. the boards or other material of which a floor is made.

floor lamp ▸n. a tall lamp designed to stand on the floor.

floor plan ▸n. a scale diagram of the arrangement of rooms in one story of a building.

floor show ▸n. an entertainment, such as singing or comedy, presented at a nightclub, restaurant, or similar venue.

floor-walk·er /ˈflôrˌwôkər/ ▸n. a senior employee of a large store who assists customers and supervises salespeople.

floo·zy /ˈflo͞ozē/ (also **floo·zie**) ▸n. (*pl.* **-zies**) *inf.* a girl or a woman who has a reputation for promiscuity.

flop /fläp/ ▸v. (**flopped**, **flop·ping**) **1** [*intr.*] fall, move, or hang in a heavy, loose, and ungainly way. ■ sit or lie down heavily or suddenly in a specified place, esp. when very tired: *Liz flopped down into the armchair.* ■ *inf.* rest or sleep in a specified place. **2** [*intr.*] *inf.* (of a performer or show) be completely unsuccessful; fail totally. **3** [*tr.*] *Photog.* invert (a negative) so that the right and left sides of a photograph are reversed.
▸n. **1** a heavy, loose, and ungainly movement, or a sound made by it. ■ *inf.* a cheap place to sleep. **2** *inf.* a total failure: *the play was a flop.*

flop·house /ˈfläpˌhous/ ▸n. *inf.* a cheap hotel or rooming house.

flop·py /ˈfläpē/ ▸adj. (**-pi·er**, **-pi·est**) tending to hang or move in a limp, loose, or ungainly way: *the dog had floppy ears | floppy hats.*
▸n. (*pl.* **-pies**) *Comput.* short for FLOPPY DISK. —**flop·pi·ly** /ˈfläpəlē/ *adv.* —**flop·pi·ness** n.

flop·py disk ▸n. *Comput.* a flexible removable magnetic disk, typically encased in hard plastic, used for storing data. Also called DISKETTE. Compare with HARD DISK.

flo·ra /ˈflôrə/ ▸n. (*pl.* **flo·ras** or **flo·rae** /ˈflôrē; ˈflôrī/) the plants of a particular region, habitat, or geological period: *desert flora | the river's flora and fauna.* Compare with FAUNA. ■ a treatise on or list of such plant life.

flo·ral /ˈflôrəl/ ▸adj. of flowers. ■ decorated with or depicting flowers: *a floral pattern.* ■ *Bot.* of flora or floras: *faunal and floral evolution.*
▸n. a fabric with a floral design. —**flo·ral·ly** *adv.*

Flor·en·tine /ˈflôrənˌtēn; -tīn/ ▸adj. **1** of or relating to Florence, Italy. **2** (**florentine**) (of food) served or prepared on a bed of spinach.

flo·res·cence /flôˈresəns; fləˈres-/ ▸n. the process of flowering: *fig. a spectacular cultural florescence.*

flo·ret /ˈflôrət/ ▸n. *Bot.* one of the small flowers making up a composite flowerhead. ■ one of the flowering stems making up a head of cauliflower or broccoli.

flo·ri·at·ed /ˈflôrēˌātid/ ▸adj. decorated with floral designs.

flo·ri·bun·da /ˌflôrəˈbəndə/ ▸n. a plant, esp. a rose, that bears dense clusters of flowers.

flor·id /ˈflôrid; ˈflär-/ ▸adj. **1** having a red or flushed complexion. **2** elaborately or excessively intricate or complicated: *florid operatic-style music.* ■ (of language) using unusual words or complicated rhetorical constructions: *the florid prose of the nineteenth century.* **3** *Med.* (of a disease or its manifestations) occurring in a fully developed form. —**flo·rid·i·ty** /fləˈriditē/ n. —**flor·id·ly** *adv.* —**flor·id·ness** n.

flo·rist /ˈflôrist/ ▸n. a person who sells and arranges plants and cut flowers. —**flo·rist·ry** /-trē/ n.

flo·ru·it /ˈflôr(y)o͞oit/ (abbr. **fl.** or **flor.**) ▸v. used in conjunction with a specified period or set of dates to indicate when a particular historical figure lived, worked, or was most active.

floss /flôs; fläs/ ▸n. the rough silk enveloping a silkworm's cocoon. ■ untwisted silk fibers used in embroidery. ■ the silky down in corn and other plants: *milkweed floss.* ■ short for DENTAL FLOSS.
▸v. [*tr.*] clean between (one's) teeth with dental floss: *I flossed my teeth.* ▷mid 18th cent.: from French (*soie*) *floche* 'floss (silk),' from Old French *flosche* 'down, nap of velvet,' of unknown origin.

floss·y /ˈflôsē; ˈfläsē/ ▸adj. (**floss·i·er**, **floss·i·est**) **1** of or like floss. **2** *inf.* excessively showy: *flossy friends.*

flo·ta·tion /flōˈtāSHən/ (also **float·a·tion**) ▸n. the action of floating in a liquid or gas: *modified to assist in flotation.* ■ the process of offering a company's shares for sale on the stock market for the first time. ■ the process of separating small particles of various materials by treatment with chemicals in water in order to make some particles adhere to air bubbles and rise to the surface for removal while others remain in the water. ■ the capacity to float; buoyancy.

flo·til·la /flōˈtilə/ ▸n. a fleet of ships or boats: *a flotilla of cargo boats.*

flot·sam /ˈflätsəm/ ▸ *n.* the wreckage of a ship or its cargo found floating on or washed up by the sea. Compare with JETSAM. ■ *fig.* people or things that have been rejected and are regarded as worthless.
▸ □ **flotsam and jetsam** useless or discarded objects.

flounce[1] /flouns/ ▸ *v.* [*intr.*] go or move in an exaggeratedly impatient or angry manner: *he stood up in a fury and flounced out.* ■ move with exaggerated motions: *she flounced around, flirting.*
▸ *n.* an exaggerated action, typically intended to express one's annoyance or impatience: *she left the room with a flounce.*

flounce[2] ▸ *n.* a wide ornamental strip of material gathered and sewn to a piece of fabric, typically on a skirt or dress; a frill.
▸ *v.* [as *adj.*] (**flounced**) trimmed with a flounce or flounces: *a flounced skirt.* —**flounc·y** /ˈflounsē/ *adj.*

floun·der[1] /ˈfloundər/ ▸ *v.* [*intr.*] struggle or stagger helplessly or clumsily in water or mud. ■ struggle mentally; show or feel great confusion. ■ *fig.* be in serious difficulty: *many firms are floundering.* —**floun·der·er** *n.*

floun·der[2] ▸ *n.* a small flatfish (families Pleuronectidae and Bothidae) that typically occurs in shallow coastal water. See FLATFISH.

flour /ˈflou(ə)r/ ▸ *n.* a powder obtained by grinding grain, typically wheat, and used to make bread, cakes, and pastry. ■ fine soft powder obtained by grinding the seeds or roots of starchy vegetables: *corn flour.* ■ any fine powder: *wood flour.* —**flour·y** *adj.*
▸ *v.* [*tr.*] sprinkle (something, esp. a work surface or cooking utensil) with a thin layer of flour: *grease and flour two round cake pans.*

flour·ish /ˈflərisH/ ▸ *v.* **1** [*intr.*] (of a person, animal, or other living organism) grow or develop in a healthy or vigorous way, esp. as the result of a particularly favorable environment: *wild plants flourish on the banks of the lake.* ■ develop rapidly and successfully: *the organization has continued to flourish.* ■ (of a person) be working or at the height of one's career during a specified period: *the caricaturist who flourished in the early years of this century.* **2** [*tr.*] (of a person) wave (something) around to attract the attention of others: *flourishing a bottle of whiskey.*
▸ *n.* **1** a bold or extravagant gesture or action, made esp. to attract the attention of others: *with a flourish, she ushered them inside.* ■ an instance of suddenly performing or developing in an impressively successful way. ■ an elaborate rhetorical or literary expression. ■ an ornamental flowing curve in handwriting or scrollwork. **2** *Mus.* a fanfare played by brass instruments: *a flourish of trumpets.* ■ an ornate musical passage. ■ an improvised addition played esp. at the beginning or end of a composition. ▷Middle English: from Old French *floriss-*, lengthened stem of *florir*, based on Latin *florere*, from *flos, flor-* 'a flower.' The noun senses 'ornamental curve' and 'florid expression' come from an obsolete sense of the verb, 'adorn' (originally with flowers). —**flour·ish·er** *n.*

flout /flout/ ▸ *v.* [*tr.*] openly disregard (a rule, law or convention): *these same companies still flout basic ethical practices.* ■ [*intr.*] *archaic* mock; scoff.

flow /flō/ ▸ *v.* [*intr.*] (esp. of a fluid) move along or out steadily and continuously in a current or stream. ■ (of the sea or a tidal river) move toward the land; rise. Compare with EBB. ■ (of clothing or hair) hang loosely in an easy and graceful manner: *her red hair flowed over her shoulders.* ■ circulate continuously within a particular system: *an electric current flows through it.* ■ (of people or things) go from one place to another in a steady stream, typically in large numbers: *orders keep flowing in.* ■ proceed or be produced smoothly, continuously, and effortlessly. ■ (**flow from**) result from; be caused by: *certain advantages may flow from that decision.* ■ be available in copious quantities. ■ (of a solid) undergo a permanent change of shape under stress, without melting.
▸ *n.* the action or fact of moving along in a steady, continuous stream. ■ the rate or speed at which such a stream moves. ■ the rise of a tide or a river. Compare with EBB. ■ a steady, continuous stream of something: *the flow of traffic.* ■ menstrual discharge. ■ the gradual permanent deformation of a solid under stress, without melting.
▸ □ **go with the flow** *inf.* be relaxed and accept a situation, rather than trying to alter or control it. □ **in full flow** talking fluently and easily and showing no sign of stopping. ■ performing vigorously and enthusiastically.

flow chart (also **flow·chart** or **flow diagram**) ▸ *n.* a diagram of the sequence of movements or actions of people or things involved in a complex system or activity. ■ a graphic representation of a computer program in relation to its sequence of functions.

flow·er /ˈflou(-ə)r/ ▸ *n.* *Bot.* the seed-bearing part of a plant, consisting of reproductive organs (stamens and carpels) that are typically surrounded by a brightly colored corolla (petals) and a green calyx (sepals). ■ a brightly colored and conspicuous example of such a part of a plant together with its stalk, typically used with others as a decoration or gift. ■ the state or period in which a plant's flowers have developed and opened: *the roses were just coming into flower.*

▸ *v.* [*intr.*] (of a plant) produce flowers; bloom. ■ *fig.* be in or reach an optimum stage of development; develop fully and richly: | [as *n.*] (**flowering**) *the flowering of Viennese intellectual life.* —**flow·ered** *adj.*
▸ □ **the flower of 1** the finest individuals out of a number of people or things: *the flower of college swimmers.* **2** the period of optimum development: *in the flower of his life.*

flow·er·et /ˈflou(-ə)rət/ ▸ *n.* a floret, esp. of cauliflower or broccoli.

flow·er girl ▸ *n.* **1** a young girl attending the bride at a wedding. **2** *Brit., dated* a woman or girl who sells flowers, esp. in the street.

flow·er·head /ˈflou(ə)r,hed/ (also **flow·er head**) ▸ *n.* a compact mass of flowers at the top of a stem.

flow·er·pot /ˈflou(-ə)r,pät/ ▸ *n.* a usu. ceramic container, used for growing a plant in.

flow·er·y /ˈflou(-ə)rē/ ▸ *adj.* full of, resembling, or smelling of flowers. ■ (of a style of speech or writing) full of elaborate or literary words and phrases: *flowery language.* —**flow·er·i·ness** *n.*

flow·ing /ˈflōiNG/ ▸ *adj.* (esp. of long hair or clothing) hanging or draping loosely and gracefully. ■ (of a line or contour) smoothly continuous: *the flowing curves of the lawn.* ■ (of language, movement, or style) graceful and fluent. —**flow·ing·ly** *adv.*

flown /flōn/ ▸ past participle of FLY[1].

fl. oz. ▸ *abbr.* fluid ounce.

flu /flo͞o/ ▸ *n.* short for INFLUENZA: *I had a bad case of the flu.* —**flu·like** *adj.*

flub /fləb/ *inf.* ▸ *v.* (**flubbed**, **flub·bing**) [*tr.*] botch or bungle (something): *she flubbed her lines.*
▸ *n.* a thing badly or clumsily done; a blunder.

fluc·tu·ate /ˈfləkCHo͞o,āt/ ▸ *v.* [*intr.*] rise and fall irregularly in number or amount: [as *adj.*] (**fluctuating**) *a fluctuating level of demand.* —**fluc·tu·a·tion** *n.*

flue /flo͞o/ ▸ *n.* a duct for smoke and waste gases produced by a fire, a gas heater, a power station, or other fuel-burning installation: [as *adj.*] *flue gases.* ■ a channel for conveying heat.

flu·ent /ˈflo͞oənt/ ▸ *adj.* (of a person) able to express oneself easily and articulately: *a fluent speaker.* ■ (of a person) able to speak or write a particular foreign language easily and accurately: *fluent in French and German.* ■ (of a foreign language) spoken accurately and with facility: *he spoke fluent Spanish.* ■ (of speech, language, movement, or style) smoothly graceful and easy. ■ able to flow freely; fluid. —**flu·en·cy** *n.* —**flu·ent·ly** *adv.*

fluff /fləf/ ▸ *n.* **1** soft fibers from fabrics such as wool or cotton that accumulate in small light clumps. ■ any soft downy substance, esp. the fur or feathers of a young mammal or bird. ■ *fig.* entertainment or writing perceived as trivial or superficial: *typical Hollywood fluff.* **2** *inf.* a mistake made in speaking or playing music, or by an actor in delivering lines.
▸ *v.* [*tr.*] **1** make (something) appear fuller and softer, typically by shaking or brushing it: *I fluffed up the pillows.* **2** *inf.* fail to perform or accomplish (something) successfully or well: *the extra fluffed his only line.*

fluff·y /ˈfləfē/ ▸ *adj.* (**fluff·i·er**, **fluff·i·est**) **1** of, like, or covered with fluff. ■ (of food) light in texture and containing air. **2** *inf.* lacking substance, depth, or seriousness. ■ (of a person, esp. a woman) frivolous, silly, or vague. —**fluff·i·ly** /ˈfləfəlē/ *adv.* —**fluff·i·ness** *n.*

flu·gel·horn /ˈflo͞ogəl,hôrn/ (also **flü·gel·horn**) ▸ *n.* a valved brass musical instrument like a cornet but with a mellower tone.

flu·id /ˈflo͞oid/ ▸ *n.* a substance that has no fixed shape and yields easily to external pressure; a gas or (esp.) a liquid: *a cleaning fluid.*
▸ *adj.* (of a substance) able to flow easily: *a fluid medium.* ■ not settled or stable; likely or able to change: *our plans are still fluid.* ■ smoothly elegant or graceful: *her movements were fluid and beautiful to watch.* ■ (of a clutch or coupling) using a liquid to transmit power. —**flu·id·ic** /ˈflo͞o-'idik/ *adj.* —**flu·id·i·ty** /flo͞o'idətē/ *n.* —**flu·id·ly** *adv.*

flu·id·ize /ˈflo͞oə,dīz/ ▸ *v.* [*tr.*] *technical* cause (a finely divided solid) to acquire the characteristics of a fluid by passing a gas upward through it. —**flu·id·i·za·tion** /,flo͞oədiˈzāsHən/ *n.*

flu·id ounce (abbr.: **fl. oz.**) ▸ *n.* a unit of capacity equal to one sixteenth of a pint (approx. 0.03 liter).

fluke[1] /flo͞ok/ ▸ *n.* unlikely chance occurrence, esp. a surprising piece of luck: *their triumph was no fluke.* —**fluk·y** *adj.*

fluke[2] ▸ *n.* **1** a parasitic flatworm (classes Trematoda and Monogenea, phylum Platyhelminthes) that typically has suckers and hooks for attachment to the host. **2** a flatfish, esp. a flounder.

fluke[3] ▸ *n.* a broad triangular plate on the arm of an anchor. ■ either of the lobes of a whale's tail.

flum·mox /ˈfləməks/ ▸ *v.* [*tr.*] (usu. **be flummoxed**) *inf.* perplex (someone) greatly; bewilder: *he was completely flummoxed by the question.*

flung /fləNG/ ▶ past and past participle of FLING.

flunk /fləNGk/ *inf.* ▶ *v.* [*tr.*] fail to reach the required standard in (an examination, test, or course of study): *I flunked biology* | [*intr.*] *I didn't flunk but I didn't do well.* ■ judge (a student or examination candidate) to have failed to reach the required standard. ■ [*intr.*] (**flunk out**) (of a student) leave or be dismissed from school or college as a result of failing to reach the required standard: *he had flunked out of college.*

flun·ky /'fləNGkē/ (also **flun·key**) ▶ *n.* (*pl.* **-kies** or **-keys**) *chiefly derog.* a liveried manservant or footman. ■ a person who performs relatively menial tasks for someone else, esp. obsequiously. —**flun·ky·ism** *n.*

fluo·resce /flŏŏ(ə)'res, flôr'es/ ▶ *v.* [*intr.*] shine or glow brightly due to fluorescence: *the molecules fluoresce when excited by ultraviolet radiation.*

fluo·res·cence /flŏŏ(ə)'resəns; flôr'esəns/ ▶ *n.* the visible or invisible radiation emitted by certain substances as a result of incident radiation of a shorter wavelength such as X-rays or ultraviolet light. ■ the property of absorbing light of short wavelength and emitting light of longer wavelength. —**fluo·res·cent** *adj.*

fluo·res·cent tube (also **fluorescent bulb** or **fluorescent lamp**) ▶ *n.* a glass tube that radiates light when phosphor on its inside surface is made to fluoresce by ultraviolet radiation from mercury vapor.

fluor·i·date /'flŏŏrə,dāt, 'flôr-/ ▶ *v.* [*tr.*] add traces of fluorides to (something, esp. a water supply): [as *adj.*] (**fluoridated**) *fluoridated toothpaste.* —**fluor·i·da·tion** /,flŏŏrə'dāsHən; ,flôr-/ *n.*

fluor·ide /'flŏŏr,īd; 'flôr-/ ▶ *n. Chem.* a compound of fluorine with another element or group. ■ sodium fluoride or another fluorine-containing salt added to water supplies or toothpaste in order to reduce tooth decay.

fluor·i·nate /'flŏŏrə,nāt; 'flôr-/ ▶ *v.* [*tr.*] *Chem.* introduce fluorine into (a compound). ■ another term for FLUORIDATE. —**fluor·i·na·tion** /,flŏŏrə'nāsHən; ,flôr-/ *n.*

fluor·ine /'flŏŏr,ēn; flôr-/ ▶ *n.* the chemical element of atomic number 9, a poisonous, highly reactive, pale yellow gas of the halogen series. (Symbol: **F**)

fluo·rite /'flŏŏr,īt; flôr-/ ▶ *n.* a mineral consisting of calcium fluoride that typically occurs as cubic crystals often colored by impurities.

fluor·o·car·bon /,flŏŏrō'kärbən; ,flôrō-/ ▶ *n. Chem.* a compound formed by replacing one or more of the hydrogen atoms in a hydrocarbon with fluorine atoms.

fluor·o·quin·o·lone /,flŏŏrō'kwinl,ōn; ,flôrō-/ ▶ *n.* any of a class of therapeutic antibiotics that are active against a range of bacteria associated with human and animal diseases. Their use in livestock has sparked concerns about the spread of bacteria resistant to them in humans.

fluor·o·scope /'flŏŏrə,skōp; 'flôr-/ ▶ *n.* an instrument with a fluorescent screen used for viewing X-ray images without taking and developing X-ray photographs. —**fluor·o·scop·ic** /,flŏŏrə'skäpik; ,flôr-/ *adj.* —**fluor·o·scop·i·cal·ly** *adv.* —**fluo·ros·co·py** /flŏŏr'äskəpē; flôr-/ *n.*

flur·ry /'flərē; 'flə-rē/ ▶ *n.* (*pl.* **-ries**) a small swirling mass of something, esp. snow or leaves, moved by sudden gusts of wind. ■ a sudden short period of commotion or excitement: *flurry of activity.* ■ a number of things arriving or happening during the same period: *a flurry of editorials.*
▶ *v.* (**-ries**, **-ried**) [*intr.*] (esp. of snow or leaves) be moved in small swirling masses by sudden gusts of wind. ■ (of a person) move quickly in a busy or agitated way.

flush¹ /fləsH/ ▶ *v.* **1** [*intr.*] (of a person's skin or face) become red and hot, typically as the result of illness or strong emotion. ■ [*tr.*] cause (a person's skin or face) to become red and hot. ■ glow or cause to glow with warm color or light: *the sky was flushed with the gold of dawn.* ■ (**be flushed with**) *fig.* be excited or elated by: *flushed with success.* **2** [*tr.*] cleanse (something, esp. a toilet) by causing large quantities of water to pass through it. ■ [*intr.*] (of a toilet) be cleansed in such a way. ■ [*tr.*] remove or dispose of (an object or substance) in such a way: *the kidneys require more water to flush out waste products.* ■ [*tr.*] cause (a liquid) to flow through something. **3** [*tr.*] drive (a bird, esp. a game bird, or an animal) from its cover. ■ *fig.* cause to be revealed; force into the open: *they're trying to flush Tilton out of hiding.*
▶ *n.* **1** a reddening of the face or skin that is typically caused by illness or strong emotion. ■ an area of warm color or light. **2** a sudden rush of intense emotion: *a flush of enthusiasm.* ■ a sudden abundance or spate of something. ■ *fig.* a period when something is new or particularly fresh and vigorous: *he is no longer in the first flush of youth.* ■ a fresh growth of leaves, flowers, or fruit. **3** an act of cleansing something, esp. a toilet, with a sudden flow of water. ■ [as *adj.*] denoting a type of toilet that has such a device: *a flush toilet.* ■ a sudden flow. —**flush·er** *n.*

flush² ▶ *adj.* **1** completely level or even with another surface: *the gates are flush with the adjoining fencing.* ■ (of printed text) not indented or

protruding: *each line is flush with the margin.* ■ (of a door) having a smooth surface, without indented or protruding panels or moldings. **2** *inf.* having plenty of something, esp. money: *the banks are flush with funds.* ■ (of money) plentiful: *the years when cash was flush.*
▶ *adv.* so as to be level or even: *the screw must fit flush with the surface.* ■ so as to be directly centered; squarely: *hit Bruno flush on the jaw.* —**flush·ness** *n.*

flush³ ▶ *n.* (in poker) a hand of cards all of the same suit.

flust·er /'fləstər/ ▶ *v.* [*tr.*] [often as *adj.*] (**flustered**) make (someone) agitated or confused: *can you work under pressure and not get flustered?*
▶ *n.* an agitated or confused state: *all in a fluster.*

flute /flŏŏt/ ▶ *n.* **1** a wind instrument made from a tube with holes along it that are stopped by the fingers or keys, held vertically or horizontally so that the player's breath strikes a narrow edge. ■ a modern orchestral instrument of this type, typically of metal, held horizontally, with the mouthpiece near one end, which is closed. ■ an organ stop with wooden or metal flue pipes producing a similar tone. **2** *Archit.* an ornamental vertical groove in a column. ■ a trumpet-shaped frill on a dress or other garment. ■ any similar cylindrical groove, as on pastry. **3** a tall, narrow wine glass: *a flute of champagne.*
▶ *v.* **1** [with *direct speech*] speak in a melodious way reminiscent of the sound of a flute. ■ [*intr.*] *poetic/lit.* play a flute or pipe. **2** [*tr.*] [often as *adj.*] (**fluted**) make flutes or grooves in: *fluted columns.* —**flut·ing** *n.* —**flut·ist** *n.* —**flut·y** *adj.*

flute

flut·ter /'flətər/ ▶ *v.* [*intr.*] (of a bird or other winged creature) fly unsteadily or hover by flapping the wings quickly and lightly: *butterflies fluttered around the garden.* ■ (with reference to a bird's wings) flap in such a way. ■ move or fall with a light irregular or trembling motion: *the remaining petals fluttered to the ground.* ■ (of a person) move restlessly or uncertainly. ■ (of a pulse or heartbeat) beat feebly or irregularly.
▶ *n.* an act of fluttering: *a flutter of wings at the window.* ■ a state or sensation of tremulous excitement. ■ *Med.* disturbance of the rhythm of the heart that is less severe than fibrillation: *atrial flutter.* ■ *Electr.* rapid variation in the pitch or amplitude of a signal, esp. of recorded sound. Compare with WOW². —**flut·ter·er** *n.* —**flut·ter·ing·ly** *adv.* —**flut·ter·y** *adj.*

flu·vi·al /'flŏŏvēəl/ ▶ *adj. chiefly Geol.* of or found in a river.

flux /fləks/ ▶ *n.* **1** the action or process of flowing or flowing out. ■ *Med.* an abnormal discharge of blood or other matter from or within the body. ■ (usu. **the flux**) *archaic* diarrhea or dysentery. **2** continuous change: *the whole political system is in a state of flux.* **3** *Physics* the rate of flow of a fluid, radiant energy, or particles across a given area. ■ the amount of radiation or number of particles incident on an area in a given time. ■ the total electric or magnetic field passing through a surface. **4** a substance mixed with a solid to lower its melting point, used esp. in soldering. ■ a substance added to a furnace during metal smelting or glassmaking that combines with impurities to form slag.

fly¹ /flī/ ▶ *v.* (**flies** /flīz/; *past* **flew**; *past part.* **flown**) [*intr.*] **1** (of a bird or other winged creature) move through the air under control: *the bird can fly enormous distances.* ■ (of an aircraft or its occupants) travel through the air: *I fly back to New York this evening.* ■ [*tr.*] control the flight of (an aircraft); pilot. ■ [*tr.*] transport in an aircraft: *helicopters flew the injured to a hospital.* **2** move or be hurled quickly through the air: *balls kept flying over her hedge.* ■ (*past* **flied**) *Baseball* hit a ball high into the air. ■ go or move quickly: *she flew along the path.* ■ *inf.* depart hastily: *I must fly!* ■ (of time) pass swiftly. ■ (of a report) be circulated among many people: *rumors were flying around Chicago.* ■ (of accusations or insults) be exchanged swiftly and heatedly: *the accusations flew thick and fast.* **3** (esp. of hair) wave or flutter in the wind: *hair flying everywhere.* ■ (of a flag) be displayed, esp. on a flagpole. ■ [*tr.*] display (a flag). **4** *archaic* flee; run away. ■ [*tr.*] flee from; escape from in haste.
▶ *phrasal v.* □ **fly at** attack (someone) verbally or physically.
▶ *n.* (*pl.* **flies**) **1** an opening at the crotch of a pair of pants, closed with a zipper or buttons and typically covered with a flap. ■ a flap of material covering the opening or fastening of a garment or of a tent. ■ (**the flies**) the space over the stage in a theater. **3** *Baseball* short for FLY BALL. **4** (*pl.* usu. **flys**) *Brit. & hist.* a one-horse hackney carriage. —**fly·a·ble** *adj.*

F

▶ □ **fly the coop** *inf.* make one's escape. □ **fly high** be very successful; prosper. □ **fly in the face of** be openly at variance with (what is usual or expected): *to fly in the face of convention.* □ **fly into a rage** (or **temper**) become suddenly or violently angry. □ **fly off the handle** *inf.* lose one's temper suddenly and unexpectedly. □ **on the fly** while in motion or progress: *his deep shot was caught on the fly.* ■ *Comput.* during the running of a computer program without interrupting the run.

fly² ▶ *n.* (*pl.* **flies** /flīz/) a flying insect of a large group characterized by a single pair of transparent wings and sucking mouthparts. ■ [usu. in comb.] used in names of flying insects of other orders, e.g., **butterfly, dragonfly, firefly.** ■ a natural or artificial flying insect used as bait in fishing.

▶ □ **drop like flies** die or collapse in large numbers. □ **a fly in the ointment** a minor irritation that spoils the success or enjoyment of something. □ **fly on the wall** an unnoticed observer of a particular situation.

fly³ ▶ *adj.* (**fly·er, fly·est**) *inf.* **1** stylish and fashionable: *fly clothes.* **2** *Brit.* knowing and clever. —**fly·ness** *n.*

fly·a·way /'flīə,wā/ ▶ *adj.* (of a person's hair) fine and difficult to control.

fly ball ▶ *n. Baseball* a ball batted high into the air.

fly-by-night ▶ *adj.* unreliable or untrustworthy, esp. in business or financial matters: *fly-by-night operators.*

▶ *n.* (also **fly-by-nighter**) an unreliable or untrustworthy person.

fly·catch·er /'flī,kaCHər; -,keCHər/ ▶ *n.* a bird that catches flying insects, esp. in short flights from a perch. Old World flycatchers belong to the families Muscicapidae and Monarchidae. Most New World species belong to the family Tyrannidae (the **tyrant flycatchers**).

fly·er /'flīər/ ▶ *n.* variant spelling of **FLIER.**

fly·fish·ing ▶ *n.* the sport of fishing using a rod and an artificial fly as bait. —**fly-fish** *v.*

fly·ing /'flī-iNG/ ▶ *adj.* moving or able to move through the air with wings: *a flying ant.* ■ relating to airplanes or aviators. ■ done while hurling oneself through the air: *a flying kick.* ■ moving rapidly, esp. through the air: *cut by flying glass.* ■ hasty; brief: *a flying visit.* ■ used in names of animals that can glide by using winglike membranes or other structures, e.g., **flying squirrel.**

▶ *n.* flight, esp. in an aircraft: *she hates flying.*

▶ □ **with flying colors** with distinction: *passed with flying colors.*

fly·ing but·tress ▶ *n. Archit.* a buttress slanting from a separate pier, typically forming an arch with the wall it supports.

fly·ing fish ▶ *n.* a fish (family Exocoetidae, in particular *Exocoetus volitans*) of warm seas that leaps out of the water and uses its winglike pectoral fins to glide over the surface for some distance.

fly·ing sau·cer ▶ *n.* a disk-shaped flying craft supposedly piloted by aliens; a UFO.

fly·ing squir·rel ▶ *n.* a small squirrel that has skin joining the fore and hind limbs for gliding from tree to tree. The two species of the genus *Glaucomys* are native to North America.

fly·leaf /'flī,lēf/ ▶ *n.* (*pl.* **-leaves** /-,lēvz/) a blank page at the beginning or end of a book.

fly·pa·per /'flī,pāpər/ ▶ *n.* sticky, poison-treated strips of paper that are hung indoors to catch and kill flies.

fly·sheet /'flī,SHēt/ ▶ *n.* **1** a tract or circular of two or four pages. **2** a fabric cover pitched outside and over a tent to give extra protection against bad weather.

fly swat·ter (also **fly-swat·ter**) ▶ *n.* an implement used for swatting insects, typically a square of plastic mesh attached to a wire handle.

fly·trap /'flī,trap/ ▶ *n.* see **VENUS FLYTRAP.**

fly·weight /'flī,wāt/ ▶ *n.* a weight in boxing and other sports intermediate between light flyweight and bantamweight. In boxing it ranges from 108 to 112 pounds (48 to 51 kg). ■ a boxer or other competitor of this weight.

fly·wheel /'flī,(h)wēl/ ▶ *n.* a heavy revolving wheel in a machine that is used to increase the machine's momentum and thereby provide greater stability or a reserve of available power during interruptions in the delivery of power to the machine.

FM ▶ *abbr.* frequency modulation: *an FM radio station.*

Fm ▶ *symb.* the chemical element fermium.

f-num·ber ▶ *n. Photog.* the ratio of the focal length of a camera lens to the diameter of the aperture being used for a particular shot (e.g., *f8*, indicating that the focal length is eight times the diameter).

foal /fōl/ ▶ *n.* a young horse or related animal.

▶ *v.* [*intr.*] (of a mare) give birth to a foal. ■ (**be foaled**) (of a foal) be born.

foam /fōm/ ▶ *n.* a mass of small bubbles formed on or in liquid, typically by agitation or fermentation. ■ a thick preparation containing many small bubbles. ■ a lightweight form of rubber or plastic made by solidifying such a liquid. ■ (**the foam**) *poetic/lit.* the sea.

▶ *v.* [*intr.*] form or produce a mass of small bubbles; froth. ■ *fig., inf.* be very angry: *foaming at the mouth, venting outrage.* —**foam·y** *adj.*

foam rub·ber ▶ *n.* a spongy material made of rubber or plastic in the form of foam, used for cushioning and in upholstery.

fob¹ /fäb/ ▶ *n.* (also **fob chain**) a chain attached to a pocket watch. ■ a small ornament attached to a watch chain. ■ (also **fob pocket**) a small pocket for carrying a watch.

fob² ▶ *v.* (**fobbed, fob·bing**) [*tr.*] (**fob someone off**) deceitfully attempt to satisfy someone by making excuses or giving them something inferior: *fob off callers by saying the boss is in a meeting.* ■ (**fob something off on**) give (someone) something inferior to or different from what they want.

fo·cal /'fōkəl/ ▶ *adj.* of or relating to the center or main point of interest. ■ *Optics* of or relating to the focus of a lens. ■ (of a disease or medical condition) occurring in one particular site in the body. —**fo·cal·ly** *adv.*

fo·cal length ▶ *n.* the distance between the center of a lens or curved mirror and its focus.

fo·cal point ▶ *n.* the point at which rays or waves meet after reflection or refraction, or the point from which diverging rays or waves appear to proceed. ■ the center of interest or activity.

fo'c'sle /'fōksəl/ ▶ *n.* variant spelling of **FORECASTLE.**

fo·cus /'fōkəs/ ▶ *n.* (*pl.* **fo·cus·es** or **fo·ci** /'fō,sī; -,kī/) **1** the center of interest or activity. ■ an act of concentrating interest or activity on something: *our focus on the customer.* ■ *Geol.* the point of origin of an earthquake. Compare with **EPICENTER.** ■ *Med.* the principal site of an infection or other disease. **2** the state or quality of having or producing clear visual definition: *his face is out of focus.* ■ the point at which an object must be situated with respect to a lens or mirror for an image of it to be well defined. ■ a device on a lens that can be adjusted to produce a clear image. **3** *Geom.* one of the fixed points from which the distances to any point of a given curve, such as an ellipse or parabola, are connected by a linear relation.

▶ *v.* (**fo·cused, fo·cus·ing** or **fo·cussed, fo·cus·sing**) [*intr.*] **1** (of a person or their eyes) adapt to the prevailing level of light and become able to see clearly. ■ [*tr.*] bring (one's eyes) into such a state. ■ [*tr.*] adjust the focus of (a telescope, camera, or other instrument): *focusing a telescope on a star.* ■ (of rays or waves) meet at a single point. ■ [*tr.*] (of a lens) make (rays or waves) meet at a single point. ■ [*intr.*] (of light, radio waves, or other energy) become concentrated into a sharp beam of light or energy. ■ [*tr.*] (of a lens) concentrate (light, radio waves, or energy) into a sharp beam. **2** (**focus on**) pay particular attention to: *the study will focus on areas in Wales.* ■ [*tr.*] concentrate: *the course helps to focus your thoughts.* —**fo·cus·er** *n.*

fo·cus group ▶ *n.* a diverse group of people assembled to participate in a guided discussion about a product before it is launched, or to provide ongoing feedback on a political campaign, television series, etc.

fod·der /'fädər/ ▶ *n.* food, esp. dried hay or feed, for cattle and other livestock. ■ a person or thing regarded only as material for a specific use: *factory fodder.* See also **CANNON FODDER.**

▶ *v.* [*tr.*] give fodder to (cattle or other livestock).

foe /fō/ ▶ *n.* an enemy or opponent: *join forces against the common foe.*

foet·id ▶ *adj.* variant spelling of **FETID.**

fog /fôg; fäg/ ▶ *n.* a thick cloud of tiny water droplets suspended in the atmosphere at or near the earth's surface that obscures or restricts visibility: *the collision occurred in thick fog.* ■ an opaque mass of something in the atmosphere: *a whirling fog of dust.* ■ *fig.* something that obscures and confuses a situation or someone's thought processes: *lost in a fog of detail.* ■ *Photog.* cloudiness that obscures the image on a developed negative or print.

▶ *v.* (**fogged, fog·ging**) [*tr.*] **1** cause (a glass surface) to become covered with steam. ■ [*intr.*] (of a glass surface) become covered with steam: *the windshield was starting to fog up.* ■ *fig.* bewilder or puzzle (someone): *she stared at him, confusion fogging her brain.* ■ *fig.* make (an idea or situation) difficult to understand: *fogging the issue.* ■ *Photog.* make (a film, negative, or print) obscure or cloudy. **2** treat with something, esp. an insecticide, in the form of a spray: *fogging for mosquitoes.*

▶ □ **in a fog** in a state of perplexity; unable to think clearly or understand something.

fog bank ▶ *n.* a dense mass of fog, esp. at sea.

fo·gey /'fōgē/ (also **fo·gy**) ▶ *n.* (*pl.* **-geys** or **-gies**) a person, typically an old one, who is considered to be old-fashioned or conservative in attitude or tastes. —**fo·gey·dom** /-dəm/ *n.* —**fo·gey·ish** *adj.* —**fo·gey·ism** /-,izəm/ *n.*

fog·gy /'fôgē; 'fägē/ ▶ *adj.* (**fog·gi·er, fog·gi·est**) full of or accompanied by fog. ■ unable to think clearly; confused: *foggy with sleep.* ■ indistinctly expressed or perceived; obscure: *exactly what the company hopes to achieve is still foggy.* —**fog·gi·ness** *n.*

fog·horn /'fôg,hôrn; 'fäg-/ ▶ *n.* a device making a loud, deep sound as a warning to ships in fog. ■ *inf.* a loud penetrating voice.

fo·gy /'fōgē/ ▶ *n.* variant spelling of FOGEY.

foi·ble /'foibəl/ ▶ *n.* **1** a minor weakness or eccentricity in someone's character: *they have to tolerate each other's little foibles.* **2** *Fencing* the weaker part of a sword blade, from the middle to the point.

foie gras /fwä 'grä/ ▶ *n.* short for PÂTÉ DE FOIE GRAS.

foil[1] /foil/ ▶ *v.* [tr.] prevent (something considered wrong or undesirable) from succeeding. ■ frustrate the efforts or plans of.
▶ *n. archaic* a setback in an enterprise; a defeat.

foil[2] ▶ *n.* **1** metal hammered or rolled into a thin flexible sheet, used chiefly for covering or wrapping food: *aluminum foil.* **2** a person or thing that contrasts with and so emphasizes and enhances the qualities of another. ■ a thin leaf of metal placed under a precious stone to increase its brilliance. **3** *Archit.* a leaf-shaped curve formed by the cusping of an arch or circle, typically occurring in groups of three or more in Gothic tracery.

foil[3] ▶ *n.* a light fencing sword without cutting edges but with a button on its point. ■ the sport of fencing with a foil.

foil[4] ▶ *n.* each of the winglike structures fitted to a hydrofoil's hull to lift it clear of the water at speed.

foist /foist/ ▶ *v.* [tr.] (**foist someone/something on**) impose an unwelcome or unnecessary person or thing on. ■ (**foist someone/something into**) introduce someone or something surreptitiously or unwarrantably into: *he attempted to foist a new delegate into the conference.*

fold[1] /fōld/ ▶ *v.* [tr.] **1** bend (something flexible and relatively flat) over on itself so that one part of it covers another: *she folded her clothes and packed her bags.* ■ (**fold something in/into**) mix an ingredient gently with (another ingredient), esp. by lifting a mixture with a spoon so as to enclose it without stirring or beating. ■ [intr.] (of a piece of furniture or equipment) be able to be bent or rearranged into a flatter or more compact shape, typically in order to make it easier to store or carry: *the deck chair folds flat* | [as *adj.*] (**folding**) *a folding chair.* ■ bend or rearrange (a piece of furniture or equipment) in such a way: *he folded up his tripod.* ■ [intr.] (**fold out**) be able to be opened out; unfold: *the sofa folds out.* ■ (of a bird) collapse (its wings) and lay them flat against its body. ■ (often **be folded**) *Geol.* cause (rock strata) to undergo bending or curvature: [as *n.*] (**folding**) *igneous activity caused intense folding.* **2** cover or wrap something in (a soft or flexible material): *plastic was folded around the book.* ■ hold or clasp (someone) closely in one's arms. **3** [intr.] *inf.* (of an enterprise or organization) cease operating as a result of financial problems or a lack of support. ■ (esp. of a sports player or team) suddenly stop performing well or effectively: *he folded in the second round.* ■ (of a poker player) drop out of a hand: *knowing when to fold and when to stay in.*
▶ *n.* **1** (usu. **folds**) a form or shape produced by the gentle draping of a loose, full garment or piece of cloth: *the fabric fell in soft folds.* ■ an area of skin that sags or hangs loosely. ■ *chiefly Brit.* an undulation or gentle curve of the ground; a slight hill or hollow: *a fold of the hills.* ■ *Geol.* a bend or curvature of strata. **2** a line or crease produced in paper or cloth as the result of folding it. ■ a piece of paper or cloth that has been folded. —**fold·a·ble** *adj.*
▶ □ **fold one's arms** bring one's arms together and cross them over one's chest. □ **fold one's hands** bring or hold one's hands together.

fold[2] ▶ *n.* a pen or enclosure in a field where livestock, esp. sheep, can be kept. ■ (**the fold**) a group or community, esp. when perceived as the locus of a particular set of aims and values: *accepted into the fold.*
▶ *v.* [tr.] shut (livestock) in a fold.

fold·a·way /'fōldə,wā/ ▶ *adj.* adapted or designed to be folded up for ease of storage or transport: *a foldaway table.*

fold·er /'fōldər/ ▶ *n.* a folding cover or holder, usu. of stiff paper or cardboard, for storing loose papers. ■ an icon on a computer screen that can be used to access a directory containing related files or documents. ■ a folded leaflet or a booklet made of folded sheets of paper.

fold·ing mon·ey ▶ *n. inf.* paper money; banknotes.

fo·li·a·ceous /,fōlē'āsHəs/ ▶ *adj.* of or resembling a leaf or leaves.

fo·li·age /'fōl(ē)ij/ ▶ *n.* plant leaves, collectively: *healthy green foliage.* ▷late Middle English *foilage* (in the sense 'design resembling leaves'): from Old French *feuillage,* from *feuille* 'leaf,' from Latin *folium.*

fo·li·ar /'fōlēər/ ▶ *adj. technical* of or relating to leaves.

fo·li·ate ▶ *adj.* /'fōlēət; -,āt/ decorated with leaves or leaflike motifs.
▶ *v.* /'fōlē,āt/ [tr.] **1** decorate with leaves or leaflike motifs: *the dome is to*

be foliated. **2** number the leaves of (a book) rather than the pages. —**fo·li·a·tion** /,fōlē'āSHən/ *n.*

fo·lic ac·id /'fōlik; 'fä-/ ▶ *n. Biochem.* a vitamin of the B complex, found esp. in leafy green vegetables, liver, and kidney. A deficiency of folic acid causes megaloblastic anemia. —**fo·late** /'fō,lāt/ *n.*

fo·li·o /'fōlē'ō/ ▶ *n.* (pl. **-os**) an individual leaf of paper or parchment, numbered on the recto or front side only, occurring either loose as one of a series or forming part of a bound volume. ■ *Printing* the leaf number in a printed book. ■ a sheet of paper folded once to form two leaves (four pages) of a book. ■ a size of book made up of such sheets: *copies in folio.* ■ a book or manuscript made up of sheets of paper folded in such a way; a volume of the largest standard size.

folk /fōk/ ▶ *pl. n.* **1** (also **folks**) *inf.* people in general. ■ a specified group of people: *city folk.* ■ (**folks**) used as a friendly form of address to a group of people: *meanwhile, folks, why not relax and enjoy the show?* ■ (**one's folks**) the members of one's family, esp. one's parents. **2** folk music: *a mixture of folk and reggae.*
▶ **1** *adj.* of or relating to the traditional art or culture of a community or nation: *folk customs* | *a folk museum.* ■ relating to or originating from the beliefs and opinions of ordinary people: *a folk hero* | *folk wisdom.* **2** of or relating to folk music.
▶ □ **just (plain) folks** ordinary, down-to-earth, unpretentious people.

folk dance ▶ *n.* a popular dance, considered as part of the tradition or custom of a particular people. —**folk danc·er** *n.* —**folk danc·ing** *n.*

folk·lore /'fōk,lôr/ ▶ *n.* the traditional beliefs, customs, and stories of a community, passed through the generations by word of mouth. ■ a body of popular myth and beliefs relating to a particular place, activity, or group of people: *Hollywood folklore.* —**folk·lor·ic** /-,lôrik/ *adj.* —**folk·lor·ist** /-ist/ *n.* —**folk·lor·is·tic** /,fōklə'ristik/ *adj.*

folk mu·sic ▶ *n.* music that originates in traditional popular culture or that is written in such a style.

folk rock ▶ *n.* popular music resembling or derived from folk music but incorporating the stronger beat of rock music and using electric instruments.

folk sing·er (also **folk·sing·er**) ▶ *n.* a person who sings folk songs.

folk song ▶ *n.* a song that originates in traditional popular culture or that is written in such a style.

folk·son·o·my /,fōk'sänəmē/ ▶ *n.* (pl. **-mies**) the activity of sorting information into categories derived from the consensus of the information users. ■ a taxonomy so derived.

folk·sy /'fōksē/ ▶ *adj.* (**-si·er, -si·est**) having the characteristics of traditional culture and customs, esp. in a contrived or artificial way: *folksy, small-town image.* ■ (of a person) informal and unpretentious: *folksy oratory.* —**folk·si·ness** *n.*

folk tale ▶ *n.* a story originating in popular culture, typically passed on by word of mouth.

fol·li·cle /'fälikəl/ ▶ *n. Anat.* a small secretory cavity, sac, or gland, in particular: ■ (also **hair follicle**) the sheath of cells and connective tissue that surrounds the root of a hair. ▷late Middle English: from Latin *folliculus* 'little bag,' diminutive of *follis* 'bellows.' —**fol·lic·u·lar** /fə'likyələr/ *adj.* —**fol·lic·u·late** /fə'likyələt; -,lāt/ *adj.*

fol·low /'fälō/ ▶ *v.* [tr.] **1** go or come after (a person or thing proceeding ahead); move or travel behind. ■ go after (someone) in order to observe or monitor. ■ *archaic* strive after; aim at: *I follow fame.* ■ go along (a route or path). ■ (of a route or path) go in the same direction as or parallel to (another): *the road follows a brook.* **2** come after in time or order. ■ happen after (something else) as a consequence: *laughter followed the remark* | [intr.] *retribution soon followed.* ■ [intr.] be a logical consequence: *it follows from this equation that the value must be negative.* ■ [tr.] (of a person) do something after (something else). **3** act according to (an instruction or precept): *difficulty in following written instructions.* ■ conform to: *the film faithfully follows Shakespeare's plot.* ■ act according to the lead or example of (someone): *he follows Aristotle in believing this.* ■ treat as a teacher or guide: *follow Jesus Christ.* **4** pay close attention to (something): *following this discussion.* ■ keep track of; trace the movement or direction of: *she followed his gaze.* ■ maintain awareness of the current state or progress of (events in a particular sphere or account): *follow football.* ■ (of a person or account) be concerned with the development of (something). ■ understand the meaning or tendency of (a speaker or argument): *I still don't follow you.* **5** practice (a trade or profession). ■ undertake or carry out (a course of action or study): *she followed a strict diet.*

▶*phrasal v.* □ **follow through** (in golf, baseball, and other sports) continue one's movement after the ball has been struck or thrown. □ **follow something through** continue an action or task to its conclusion. □ **follow something up** pursue or investigate something further.

▶ □ **follow in someone's footsteps** (or **steps**) do as another person did before, esp. in following a particular career. □ **follow one's nose 1** trust to one's instincts. **2** move along guided by one's sense of smell. □ **follow suit** conform to another's actions.

fol·low·er /ˈfälō-ər/ ▶*n.* an adherent or devotee of a particular person, cause, or activity: *a freethinker and follower of Voltaire.* ■ a person who moves or travels behind someone or something.

fol·low·ing /ˈfälō-iNG/ ▶*prep.* coming after or as a result of: *police are hunting for two men following a spate of robberies in the area.*

▶*n.* **1** a body of supporters or admirers: *he attracted a worldwide following.* **2** (**the following**) [treated as *sing.* or *pl.*] what follows or comes next.

▶*adj.* **1** next in time: *the following day.* ■ about to be mentioned: *required to provide the following information.* **2** (of a wind or sea) blowing or moving in the same direction as the course of a vehicle or vessel.

fol·low-through ▶*n.* the continuing of an action or task to its conclusion. ■ a continuation of the movement of an arm, bat, racket, or club after a ball has been thrown or struck: *he has a characteristic swing and follow-through.*

fol·low-up ▶*n.* a continuation or repetition of something that has already been started or done, in particular: ■ an activity carried out in order to monitor or further develop earlier work: [as *adj.*] *follow-up interviews.* ■ further observation or treatment of a patient, esp. to monitor earlier treatment. ■ a piece of work that builds on or exploits the success of earlier work.

fol·ly /ˈfälē/ ▶*n.* (*pl.* **-lies**) **1** lack of good sense; foolishness: *an act of sheer folly.* ■ a foolish act, idea, or practice. **2** a costly building or undertaking with no practical purpose. **3** (**Follies**) a theatrical revue, typically with glamorous female performers: [in *names*] *the Ziegfeld Follies.*

fo·ment /ˈfō,ment; fōˈment/ ▶*v.* [*tr.*] instigate or stir up (an undesirable or violent sentiment or course of action): *fomenting political unrest.* —**fo·ment·er** *n.*

fo·men·ta·tion /ˌfōmenˈtāSHən; -mən-/ ▶*n.* **1** the action of instigating or stirring up undesirable sentiment or actions. **2** an herbal preparation for external use.

fond /fänd/ ▶*adj.* (**fond of**) having an affection or liking for: *I'm very fond of Mike.* ■ affectionate; loving: *waving a fond farewell | fond memories of our childhood.* ■ (of a hope or belief) foolishly optimistic; naive. —**fond·ly** *adv.* —**fond·ness** *n.*

fon·dant /ˈfändənt/ ▶*n.* a thick paste made of sugar and water and often flavored or colored, used in the making of candy and the icing and decoration of cakes. ■ a candy made of such a paste.

fon·dle /ˈfändl/ ▶*v.* [*tr.*] stroke or caress lovingly or erotically: *charges that he fondled a patient during an examination.*

▶*n.* an act of fondling. —**fon·dler** *n.*

fon·due /fänˈd(y)o͞o/ ▶*n.* a dish in which small pieces of food are dipped into a hot sauce or a hot cooking medium such as oil or broth: *a Swiss cheese fondue.*

font[1] /fänt/ ▶*n.* **1** a receptacle in a church for the water used in baptism, typically a freestanding stone structure. **2** a fount: *the font of wisdom.* —**font·al** /ˈfäntl/ *adj.*

font[2] (*Brit.* also **fount**) ▶*n.* Printing a set of type of one particular face and size for printing or for display on a computer screen.

fon·ta·nel /ˌfäntnˈel/ (also **fon·ta·nelle**) ▶*n.* a space between the bones of the skull in an infant or fetus, where ossification is not complete.

food /fo͞od/ ▶*n.* any nutritious substance that people or animals eat or drink, or that plants absorb, in order to maintain life and growth: *baby foods.*

▶ □ **food for thought** something that warrants serious consideration.

food bank ▶*n.* a place supplying food to poor or displaced people.

food chain ▶*n.* a hierarchical series of organisms each dependent on the next as a source of food.

food·ie /ˈfo͞odē/ ▶*n. inf.* a person with a particular interest in food; a gourmet.

food proc·es·sor ▶*n.* an electric kitchen appliance used for chopping, mixing, or puréeing foods.

food·stuff /ˈfo͞od,stəf/ ▶*n.* a substance suitable for consumption as food.

food sup·ple·ment ▶*n.* see SUPPLEMENT.

foo fight·er /fo͞o/ ▶*n.* an unidentified flying object of a kind reported by

U.S. pilots during World War II, usually described as a bright light or ball of fire.

fool[1] /fo͞ol/ ▶*n.* a person who acts unwisely or imprudently; a silly person. ■ *hist.* a jester or clown, esp. one retained in a noble household. ■ *inf.* a person devoted to a particular activity: *he is a running fool.* ■ *archaic* a person who is duped.

▶*v.* [*tr.*] trick or deceive (someone); dupe. ■ [*intr.*] act in a joking, frivolous, or teasing way: *to stop fooling around.* ■ [*intr.*] (**fool around**) engage in casual or extramarital sexual activity.

▶*phrasal v.* □ **fool with** toy with; play idly with. ■ tease (a person).

▶*adj. inf.* foolish or silly: *that damn fool waiter.*

▶ □ **be no** (or **nobody's**) **fool** be a shrewd or prudent person. □ **make a fool of** trick or deceive (someone) so that they look foolish. ■ (**make a fool of oneself**) behave in an incompetent or inappropriate way that makes one appear foolish. □ **play** (or **act**) **the fool** behave in a playful or silly way.

fool[2] ▶*n. chiefly Brit.* a cold dessert made of puréed fruit mixed or served with cream or custard: *raspberry fool with cream.*

fool·har·dy /ˈfo͞ol,härdē/ ▶*adj.* (**-di·er, -di·est**) recklessly bold or rash: *it would be foolhardy to go into the scheme without support.* —**fool·har·di·ly** /-,härdl-ē/ *adv.* —**fool·har·di·ness** *n.*

fool·ish /ˈfo͞oliSH/ ▶*adj.* (of a person or action) lacking good sense or judgment; unwise: *it was foolish of you to enter into correspondence.* ■ silly; ridiculous: *he'd been made to look foolish.* —**fool·ish·ly** *adv.* —**fool·ish·ness** *n.*

fool·proof /ˈfo͞ol,pro͞of/ ▶*adj.* incapable of going wrong or being misused.

fool's gold ▶*n.* a brassy yellow mineral, esp. pyrite, that can be mistaken for gold.

foot /fo͝ot/ ▶*n.* (*pl.* **feet** /fēt/) **1** the lower extremity of the leg below the ankle, on which a person stands or walks. ■ a corresponding part of the leg in vertebrate animals. ■ *Zool.* a locomotory or adhesive organ of an invertebrate. ■ the part of a sock or stocking that covers the foot. ■ *poetic/lit.* a person's manner or speed of walking or running: *fleet of foot.* **2** the lower or lowest part of something standing or perceived as standing vertically; the base or bottom: *the foot of the stairs.* ■ the end of a table that is farthest from where the host sits. ■ the end of a bed, couch, or grave where the occupant's feet normally rest. ■ a device on a sewing machine for holding the material steady as it is sewn. ■ the lower edge of a sail. **3** a unit of linear measure equal to 12 inches (30.48 cm). (Symbol: ′) **4** *Prosody* a group of syllables constituting a metrical unit.

▶*v.* [*tr.*] **1** *inf.* pay (the bill) for something, esp. when the bill is considered large or unreasonable. **2** (**foot it**) cover a distance, esp. a long one, on foot: *left to foot it ten miles back to camp.* ▷Old English *fōt*, of Germanic origin; related to Dutch *voet* and German *Fuss*, from an Indo-European root shared by Sanskrit *pad, pāda,* Greek *pous, pod-,* and Latin *pes, ped-* 'foot.' —**foot·ed** /ˈfo͝otəd/ *adj.* [in *comb.*] *the black-footed ferret.*

▶ □ **get one's feet wet** begin to participate in an activity. □ **get** (or **start**) **off on the right** (or **wrong**) **foot** make a good (or bad) start at something, esp. a task or relationship. □ **have something at one's feet** have something in one's power or command: *the world at their feet.* □ **have** (or **keep**) **one's** (or **both**) **feet on the ground** be (or remain) practical and sensible. □ **have** (or **get**) **a foot in the door** gain or have a first introduction to a profession or organization. □ **on** (or **by**) **foot** walking rather than traveling by car or using other transport. □ **put one's best foot forward** embark on an undertaking with as much effort and determination as possible. □ **put one's foot down** *inf.* adopt a firm policy when faced with opposition or disobedience. □ **put one's foot in it** (or **put one's foot in one's mouth**) *inf.* say or do something tactless or embarrassing; commit a blunder or indiscretion. □ **set foot on** (or **in**) enter; go into. □ **sweep someone off their feet** charm someone quickly and overpoweringly. □ **think on one's feet** react to events decisively, effectively, and without prior thought or planning.

foot·age /ˈfo͝otij/ ▶*n.* **1** a length of film made for movies or television: *film footage.* **2** size or length measured in feet: *square footage.*

foot-and-mouth dis·ease ▶*n.* a contagious viral disease of cattle and sheep, causing ulceration of the hoofs and around the mouth.

foot·ball /ˈfo͝ot,bôl/ ▶*n.* **1** a form of team game played in North America with an oval ball on a field marked out as a gridiron. ■ British term for SOCCER. **2** an oval ball used in such a game, made of leather and filled with compressed air. ■ *fig.* a topical issue or problem that is the subject of continued argument or controversy: *political football.* ■ *Brit.* a soccer ball. —**foot·ball·er** *n.*

foot·board /'foŏt,bôrd/ ▸n. an upright panel forming the foot of a bed.

foot·bridge /'foŏt,brij/ ▸n. a bridge designed to be used by pedestrians.

foot·er /'foŏtər/ ▸n. **1** [in *comb.*] a person or thing of a specified number of feet in length or height: *a tall, sturdy six-footer.* **2** a line or block of text appearing at the foot of each page of a book or document. Compare with HEADER.

foot·fall /'foŏt,fôl/ ▸n. the sound of a footstep or footsteps.

foot·hill /'foŏt,hil/ ▸n. (usu. **foothills**) a low hill at the base of a mountain or mountain range: *the camp lies in the foothills of the Andes.*

foot·hold /'foŏt,hōld/ ▸n. a place where a person's foot can be lodged to support them securely, esp. while climbing. ■ *fig.* a secure position from which further progress may be made: *the company is attempting to gain **a foothold** in the Russian market.*

foot·ing /'foŏtiNG/ ▸n. **1** (**one's footing**) a secure grip with one's feet. ■ the condition of a piece of ground for walking or running: *uneven footing.* **2** the basis on which something is established or operates: *a firm financial footing.* ■ the position or status of a person in relation to others: *the suppliers are on an equal footing with the buyers.* **3** (usu. **footings**) the bottommost part of a foundation wall, with a course of concrete wider than the base of the wall.

foot·lights /'foŏt,līts/ ▸pl. n. (usu. **the footlights**) a row of spotlights along the front of a stage at the level of the actors' feet.

foot·lock·er /'foŏt,läkər/ ▸n. a small trunk or storage chest.

foot·loose /'foŏt,loŏs/ ▸adj. able to travel freely and do as one pleases due to a lack of responsibilities or commitments: *I am **footloose and fancy-free**—I can follow my job wherever it takes me.*

foot·man /'foŏtmən/ ▸n. (pl. **-men**) **1** a liveried servant whose duties include admitting visitors and waiting at table. **2** *hist.* a soldier in the infantry.

foot·note /'foŏt,nōt/ ▸n. an ancillary piece of information printed at the bottom of a page. ■ *fig.* a thing that is additional or less important: *this incident seemed destined to become a mere footnote in history.* ▸v. [intr.] add a footnote or footnotes to (a piece of writing). ■ [tr.] make note of something in that way.

foot·path /'foŏt,paTH/ ▸n. a path for people to walk along.

foot·print /'foŏt,print/ ▸n. **1** the impression left by a foot or shoe on the ground or a surface. **2** the area covered by something, in particular: ■ the area in which a broadcast signal from a particular source can be received. ■ the space taken up on a surface by a piece of computer hardware. ■ the area of ground taken up by a building.

foot·rest /'foŏt,rest/ ▸n. a support for the feet or a foot, used when sitting.

foot sol·dier ▸n. a soldier who fights on foot; an infantryman. ■ a person who carries out important work but does not have a role of authority in an organization or field.

foot·step /'foŏt,step/ ▸n. a step taken by a person in walking, esp. as heard by another person.

foot·stool /'foŏt,stoŏl/ ▸n. a low stool for resting the feet on when sitting.

foot·wear /'foŏt,wer/ ▸n. outer coverings for the feet, such as shoes, boots, and sandals.

foot·work /'foŏt,wərk/ ▸n. the manner in which one moves one's feet in various activities such as sports and dancing. ■ adroit response to sudden danger or new opportunities: *the company had to do a lot of nimble footwork to stay alive.*

fop /fäp/ ▸n. a man who is concerned with his clothes and appearance in an affected and excessive way; a dandy. —**fop·per·y** /'fäpərē/ *n.* —**fop·pish** *adj.* —**fop·pish·ly** *adv.* —**fop·pish·ness** *n.*

for /fôr; fər/ ▸prep. **1** in support of or in favor of (a person or policy). **2** affecting, with regard to, or in respect of (someone or something): *the demand for money.* **3** on behalf of or to the benefit of (someone or something). ■ employed by: *a good firm to work for.* **4** having (the thing mentioned) as a purpose or function: *searching for enlightenment.* **5** having (the thing mentioned) as a reason or cause: *I could dance for joy.* **6** having (the place mentioned) as a destination: *leaving for Maine.* **7** representing (the thing mentioned): *the "F" is for Fascinating.* **8** in place of or in exchange for (something): *swap these two bottles for that one.* ■ charged as (a price): *copies are available for only a buck.* **9** in relation to the expected norm of (something): *tall for her age.* **10** indicating the length of (a period of time): *in prison for 12 years.* **11** indicating the extent of (a distance): *he crawled for 300 yards.* **12** indicating an occasion in a series: *failed for the third time.* ▸conj. *poetic/lit.* because; since: *he felt guilty, for he knew that he was responsible.*

▸ □ **oh for** —— I long for ——: *oh for a cup of coffee!* □ **there's** (or **that's**)

—— **for you** used ironically to indicate a particularly poor example of (a quality mentioned): *there's gratitude for you.*

for·age /'fôrij; 'fär-/ ▸v. [intr.] (of a person or animal) search widely for food or provisions. ■ [tr.] obtain (food or provisions): *foraging grass for oxen.* ■ [tr.] obtain food or provisions from (a place): *foraging a dumpster.* ■ [tr.] *archaic* supply (an animal or person) with food. ▸n. **1** bulky food such as grass or hay for horses and cattle; fodder. **2** a wide search over an area in order to obtain something, esp. food or provisions. —**for·ag·er** *n.*

for·ay /'fôr,ā; 'fär,ā/ ▸n. a sudden attack or incursion into enemy territory, esp. to obtain something; a raid: *fig. he made another foray to the bar.* ■ an attempt to become involved in a new activity or sphere: *my first foray into journalism.* ▸v. [intr.] make or go on a foray. —**for·ay·er** *n.*

for·bade /fər'bad; fôr-; -'bād/ (also **for·bad** /-'bad/) ▸ past of FORBID.

for·bear[1] /fər'ber; fôr-/ ▸v. (*past* **-bore**; *past part.* **-borne**) [intr.] *poetic/lit.* or *formal* politely or patiently restrain an impulse to do something; refrain: *forbore from touching anything.* ■ [tr.] refrain from doing or using (something): *Rebecca could not forbear a smile.*

for·bear[2] ▸n. variant spelling of FOREBEAR.

for·bear·ance /fôr'berəns; fər-/ ▸n. *formal* patient self-control; restraint and tolerance: *forbearance from taking action.* ■ *Law* the action of refraining from exercising a legal right, esp. enforcing the payment of a debt.

for·bid /fər'bid; fôr-/ ▸v. (**-bid·ding**; *past* **-bade** or **forbad**; *past part.* **-bid·den**) [tr.] refuse to allow (something). ■ order (someone) not to do something: [tr.] *my doctor has forbidden me to eat sugar.* ■ refuse (someone or something) entry to a place or area. ■ (of a circumstance or quality) make (something) impossible; prevent: *the cliffs forbid any turning movement.*

▸ □ **God** (or **Heaven**) **forbid** used to express a fervent wish that something does not happen: *God forbid that this should happen again.*

for·bid·den /fər'bidn; fôr-/ ▸adj. not allowed; banned: *a list of forbidden books.*

▸ □ **forbidden fruit** a thing that is desired all the more because it is not allowed.

for·bid·ding /fər'bidiNG; fôr-/ ▸adj. unfriendly or threatening in appearance: *a grim and forbidding building.* —**for·bid·ding·ly** *adv.*

for·bore /fər'bôr; fôr-/ ▸ past of FORBEAR[1].

for·borne /fər'bôrn; fôr-/ ▸ past participle of FORBEAR[1].

force /fôrs/ ▸n. **1** strength or energy as an attribute of physical action or movement: *the force of the explosion.* ■ *Physics* an influence tending to change the motion of a body or produce motion or stress in a stationary body. ■ a person or thing regarded as exerting power or influence: *a force for peace and unity.* ■ [in *comb.*] used with a number as a measure of wind strength on the Beaufort scale: *a force-nine gale.* **2** coercion or compulsion, esp. with the use or threat of violence: *they ruled by force.* **3** mental or moral strength or power: *the force of popular opinion.* ■ the state of being in effect or valid: *the law came into force in January.* ■ the powerful effect of something: *the force of her writing is undiminished.* **4** an organized body of military personnel or police: *peacekeeping force.* ■ (**forces**) troops and weaponry: *enemy forces* | *fig. the forces of good and evil.* ■ a group of people brought together and organized for a particular activity: *a sales force.* ■ (**the force**) *inf.* a police department.

▸v. [tr.] **1** make a way through or into by physical strength; break open by force. ■ [tr.] drive or push into a specified position or state using physical strength or against resistance: *Sabine forced a smile.* ■ achieve or bring about (something) by coercion or effort. ■ push or strain (something) to the utmost: *she knew if she forced it she would rip it.* ■ artificially hasten the development or maturity of (a plant). **2** (often **be forced**) make (someone) do something against their will: *forced into early retirement.* ■ *Baseball* put out (a runner), or cause (a runner) to be put out, at the base to which they are advancing when they are forced to run on a batted ball: *I was forced at second.* ■ (in cards) make a play or bid that compels another player to make (a particular response).

▸phrasal v. □ **force something down 1** manage to swallow food or drink when one does not want to: *I forced down a slice of toast.* **2** compel an aircraft to land. □ **force oneself on/upon** rape (a woman). □ **force something on/upon** impose or press something on (a person or organization): *economic cutbacks were forced on the government.* ▷Middle

English: from Old French *force* (noun), *forcer* (verb), based on Latin *fortis* 'strong.' —**force·a·ble** *adj.*

▶ □ **by force of** by means of: *exercising authority by force of arms.* □ **force someone's hand** make someone do something. □ **force the issue** compel the making of an immediate decision. □ **in force 1** in great strength or numbers: *birdwatchers were out in force.* **2** in effect; valid.

force-feed ▶*v.* [*tr.*] force (a person or animal) to eat. ▪ *fig.* impose or force (information or ideology) upon (someone).

force field ▶*n.* (chiefly in science fiction) an invisible barrier of exerted strength or impetus: *an electromagnetic force field.*

force·ful /'fôrsfəl/ ▶*adj.* (esp. of a person or argument) strong and assertive; vigorous and powerful: *forceful, imaginative marketing.* —**force·ful·ly** *adv.* —**force·ful·ness** *n.*

force-meat /'fôrs,mēt/ ▶*n.* a mixture of meat or vegetables chopped and seasoned for use as a stuffing or garnish.

for·ceps /'fôrsəps; -,seps/ ▶*pl. n.* a pair of pincers or tweezers used in surgery or in a laboratory. ▪ a large instrument of such a type with broad blades, used to encircle a baby's head and assist in birth: [as *adj.*] *a forceps delivery.*

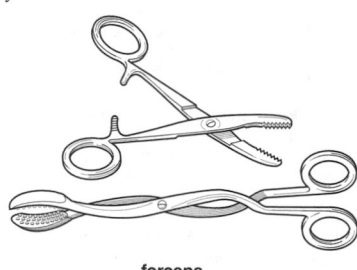

forceps

for·ci·ble /'fôrsəbəl/ ▶*adj.* done by force: *forcible entry.* ▪ vigorous and strong; forceful: *forcible appeals.* —**for·ci·bly** /-blē/ *adv.*

ford /fôrd/ ▶*n.* a shallow place in a river or stream allowing one to walk or drive across.
▶*v.* [*tr.*] (of a person or vehicle) cross (a river or stream) at a shallow place. —**ford·a·ble** *adj.* —**ford·less** *adj.*

fore /fôr/ ▶*adj.* situated or placed in front: *the fore and hind wings.*
▶*interj.* called out as a warning to people in the path of a golf ball.
▶*prep.* (also **'fore**) nonstandard form of BEFORE.
▶ □ **to the fore** in or to a conspicuous or leading position.

fore and aft ▶*adv.* at the front and rear (often used with reference to a ship or plane): *we're moored fore and aft.* ▪ backward and forward.
▶*adj.* backward and forward: *the fore-and-aft motion of the handles.* ▪ (of a sail or rigging) set lengthwise, not on transverse yards: *a fore-and-aft-rigged yacht.*

fore·arm¹ /'fôr,ärm/ ▶*n.* the part of a person's arm extending from the elbow to the wrist or the fingertips.

fore·arm² /fôr'ärm/ ▶*v.* [*tr.*] (usu. **be forearmed**) prepare (someone) in advance for danger, attack, or another undesirable future event.

fore·bear /'fôr,ber/ (also **for·bear**) ▶*n.* (usu. **one's forebears**) an ancestor.

fore·bode /fôr'bōd/ ▶*v.* [*tr.*] *archaic* or *poetic/lit.* (of a situation or occurrence) act as a warning of (something bad). ▪ have a presentiment of (something bad): *I foreboded mischief.*

fore·bod·ing /fôr'bōdiNG/ ▶*n.* fearful apprehension; a feeling that something bad will happen: *a sense of foreboding.*
▶*adj.* implying or seeming to imply that something bad is going to happen: *his voice was dark and foreboding.* —**fore·bod·ing·ly** *adv.*

fore·brain /'fôr,brān/ ▶*n. Anat.* the anterior part of the brain, including the cerebral hemispheres, the thalamus, and the hypothalamus.

fore·cast /'fôr,kast/ ▶*v.* (past **-cast** or **-cast·ed**) [*tr.*] predict or estimate (a future event or trend): [*tr.*] *coal consumption is forecast to increase.*
▶*n.* a prediction or estimate of future events, esp. coming weather or a financial trend. —**fore·cast·er** *n.*

fore·cas·tle /'fōksəl; 'fôr,kasəl/ (also **fo'c'sle**) ▶*n.* the forward part of a ship below the deck, traditionally used as the crew's living quarters. ▪ a raised deck at the bow of a ship.

fore·close /fôr'klōz/ ▶*v.* **1** [*intr.*] take possession of a mortgaged property as a result of the mortgagor's failure to keep up their mortgage payments: *the bank was threatening to foreclose on his mortgage.* ▪ [*tr.*] take away someone's power of redeeming (a mortgage) and take possession of the mortgaged property. **2** [*tr.*] rule out or prevent (a course of

action): *the decision effectively foreclosed any possibility of his early rehabilitation.* —**fore·clo·sure** /-'klōZHər/ *n.*

fore·court /'fôr,kôrt/ ▶*n.* **1** an open area in front of a large building. **2** *Tennis* the part of the court between the service line and the net.

fore·doom /fôr'dōōm/ ▶*v.* [*tr.*] (usu. **be foredoomed**) condemn beforehand to certain failure or destruction: *the policy is foredoomed to failure.*

fore·fa·ther /'fôr,fäTHər/ ▶*n.* (usu. **one's forefathers**) a member of the past generations of one's family or people; an ancestor. ▪ a precursor of a particular movement: *the forefathers of rock 'n' roll.*

fore·fin·ger /'fôr,fiNGgər/ ▶*n.* the finger next to the thumb; the first or index finger.

fore·foot /'fôr,fŏŏt/ ▶*n.* (*pl.* **-feet**) each of the front feet of a four-footed animal.

fore·front /'fôr,frənt/ ▶*n.* (**the forefront**) the leading or most important position or place: *we are at the forefront of developments.*

fore·gath·er ▶*v.* variant spelling of FORGATHER.

fore·go¹ ▶*v.* variant spelling of FORGO.

fore·go² /fôr'gō/ ▶*v.* (**fore·goes**; past **fore·went**; past part. **fore·gone**) [*tr.*] *archaic* precede in place or time. —**fore·go·er** /fôr'gōər/ *n.*

fore·go·ing /fôr'gōiNG/ *formal* ▶*adj.* just mentioned or stated; preceding: *the foregoing discussion.*
▶*n.* (**the foregoing**) [treated as *sing.* or *pl.*] the things just mentioned.

fore·gone /'fôr,gôn/ ▶ past participle of FOREGO².
▶*adj. archaic* past: *poets dream of lives foregone.*
▶ □ **foregone conclusion** a result that can be predicted with certainty.

fore·ground /'fôr,ground/ ▶*n.* (**the foreground**) the part of a view that is nearest to the observer, esp. in a picture or photograph. ▪ the most prominent or important position or situation.
▶*v.* [*tr.*] make (something) the most prominent or important feature.

fore·hand /'fôr,hand/ ▶*n.* **1** (in tennis and other racket sports) a stroke played with the palm of the hand facing in the direction of the stroke. Compare with BACKHAND **2** the part of a horse in front of the saddle.

fore·head /'fôrəd; 'fôr,hed/ ▶*n.* the part of the face above the eyebrows.

for·eign /'fôrən; 'fär-/ ▶*adj.* **1** of, from, in, or characteristic of a country or language other than one's own. ▪ dealing with or relating to other countries: *foreign policy.* ▪ of or belonging to another district or area. ▪ coming or introduced from outside: *a foreign element imported into the work.* ▪ (of a law or restriction) outside the local jurisdiction. **2** strange and unfamiliar: *feels pretty foreign.* ▪ (**foreign to**) not belonging to or characteristic of: *crime and brutality are foreign to our nature.* —**for·eign·ness** *n.*

for·eign·er /'fôrənər; 'fär-/ ▶*n.* a person born in or coming from a country other than one's own. ▪ *inf.* a person not belonging to a particular place or group; a stranger or outsider.

foreign ex·change ▶*n.* the currency of other countries. ▪ an institution or system for dealing in such currency.

foreign min·is·ter ▶*n.* (in many countries) a government minister in charge of relations with other countries.

fore·knowl·edge /fôr'näləj/ ▶*n.* awareness of something before it happens or exists.

fore·leg /'fôr,leg/ ▶*n.* either of the front legs of a four-footed animal.

fore·limb /'fôr,lim/ ▶*n.* either of the front limbs of an animal.

fore·lock /'fôr,läk/ ▶*n.* a lock of hair growing just above the forehead. ▪ the part of the mane (of a horse or similar animal) that grows above or on the forehead.

fore·man /'fôrmən/ ▶*n.* (*pl.* **-men**) a worker, esp. a man, who supervises and directs other workers. ▪ (in a court of law) a person, esp. a man, who presides over a jury and speaks on its behalf.

fore·mast /'fôr,mast; -məst/ ▶*n.* the mast of a ship nearest the bow.

fore·most /'fôr,mōst/ ▶*adj.* the most prominent in rank, importance, or position: *one of the foremost art collectors of his day.*
▶*adv.* before anything else in rank, importance, or position; in the first place: *O'Keeffe's work was, foremost, an expression of feelings.*

fore·name /'fôr,nām/ ▶*n.* another term for FIRST NAME.

fo·ren·sic /fə'renzik; -sik/ ▶*adj.* of, relating to, or denoting the application of scientific methods and techniques to the investigation of crime: *forensic evidence.* ▪ of or relating to courts of law.
▶*n.* (**forensics**) scientific tests or techniques used in connection with the detection of crime. ▪ [treated as *sing.* or *pl.*] *inf.* a laboratory or department responsible for such tests. —**fo·ren·si·cal·ly** /-(ə)lē/ *adv.*

fore·or·dain /,fôrôr'dān/ ▶*v.* [*tr.*] (of God or fate) appoint or decree (something) beforehand: *progress is not foreordained.* —**fore·or·di·na·tion** /fôr-,ôrdn'āSHən/ *n.*

fore·paw /'fôr,pô/ ▶*n.* either of the front paws of a quadruped.

F

fore·play /'fôr,plā/ ▶n. sexual activity that precedes intercourse.

fore·run·ner /'fôr,rənər/ ▶n. a person or thing that precedes the coming or development of someone or something else. ■ a sign or warning of something to come.

fore·sail /'fôr,sāl; -səl/ ▶n. the principal sail on a foremast.

fore·see /fôr'sē/ ▶v. (**-sees, -see·ing**; past **-saw**; past part. **-seen**) [tr.] be aware of beforehand; predict: *we did not foresee any difficulties.* —**fore·see·a·ble** *adj.*

fore·shad·ow /fôr'SHadō/ ▶v. [tr.] be a warning or indication of (a future event): *it foreshadowed my preoccupation with jazz.*

fore·short·en /fôr'SHôrtn/ ▶v. [tr.] portray or show (an object or view) as closer than it is or as having less depth or distance, as an effect of perspective or the angle of vision: *seen from the road, the mountain is greatly foreshortened.* ■ prematurely or dramatically shorten or reduce (something) in time or scale: [as *adj.*] (**foreshortened**) *foreshortened reports.*

fore·sight /'fôr,sīt/ ▶n. the ability to predict or the action of predicting what will happen or be needed in the future. —**fore·sight·ed** *adj.*

fore·skin /'fôr,skin/ ▶n. the retractable roll of skin covering the end of the uncircumcised penis. Also called PREPUCE.

for·est /'fôrəst; 'fär-/ ▶n. a large area covered chiefly with trees and undergrowth. ■ a large number or dense mass of vertical or tangled objects: *a forest of connecting wires.* ■ hist. (in England) an area, typically owned by the sovereign and partly wooded, kept for hunting.
▶v. [tr.] [usu. as *adj.*] (**forested**) cover (land) with forest; plant with trees: *a forested area.* ▷Middle English (in the sense 'wooded area kept for hunting,' also denoting any uncultivated land): via Old French from late Latin *forestis (silva)*, literally '(wood) outside,' from Latin *foris* 'outside'. —**for·est·a·tion** /,fôrə'stāSHən/, ,fär-/ *n.*

fore·stall /fôr'stôl/ ▶v. [tr.] prevent or obstruct (an anticipated event or action) by taking action ahead of time. ■ act in advance of (someone) in order to prevent them from doing something. ■ hist. buy up (goods) in order to profit by an enhanced price. —**fore·stall·er** *n.* —**fore·stall·ment** *n.*

fore·stay /'fôr,stā/ ▶n. a stay leading forward and down to support a ship's foremast.

for·est·er /'fôrəstər; 'fär-/ ▶n. **1** a person in charge of a forest or skilled in planting, managing, or caring for trees. **2** *chiefly archaic* a person or animal living in a forest. **3** a small, black, day-flying moth (family Agaristidae) with two white or yellow spots on each wing.

for·est·ry /'fôrəstrē; 'fär-/ ▶n. the science or practice of planting, managing, and caring for forests.

fore·taste /'fôr,tāst/ ▶n. a sample or suggestion of something that lies ahead: *the freezing rain was a foretaste of winter.*

fore·tell /fôr'tel/ ▶v. (past and past part. **-told**) [tr.] predict (the future or a future event). *a seer had foretold that she would assume the throne.* —**fore·tell·er** *n.*

fore·thought /'fôr,THôt/ ▶n. careful consideration of what will be necessary or may happen in the future: *Jim had the forethought to book in advance.*

fore·to·ken ▶v. /'fôr,tōkən/ [tr.] *poetic/lit.* be a sign of (something to come): *a shiver in the night air foretokening December.*
▶n. /'fôr,tōkən/ a sign or warning of something to come.

fore·told /fôr'tōld/ ▶ past and past participle of FORETELL.

for·ev·er /fə'revər; fô-/ ▶adv. **1** for all future time; for always. ■ a very long time (used hyperbolically): *it took forever to get a passport.* **2** continually: *forever pushing her hair out of her eyes.*

fore·warn /fôr'wôrn/ ▶v. [tr.] inform (someone) of a danger or possible problem: *he had been forewarned of a coup plot.* —**fore·warn·ing** *n.*

fore·went /fôr'went/ ▶ past of FOREGO¹, FOREGO².

fore·wing /'fôr,wiNG/ ▶n. either of the two front wings of a four-winged insect.

fore·wom·an /'fôr,wŏŏmən/ ▶n. (pl. **-wom·en**) a female worker who supervises and directs other workers. ■ (in a court of law) a woman who presides over a jury and speaks on its behalf.

fore·word /'fôr,wərd/ ▶n. a short introduction to a book, typically by a person other than the author.

for·feit /'fôrfit/ ▶v. (**-feit·ed, -feit·ing**) [tr.] lose or be deprived of (property or a right or privilege) as a penalty for wrongdoing. ■ lose or give up (something) as a necessary consequence of something else: *she didn't mind forfeiting an extra hour in bed to get up and feed the horses.*
▶n. a fine or penalty for wrongdoing or for a breach of the rules in a club or game. ■ *Law* an item of property or a right or privilege lost as a legal penalty. ■ (**forfeits**) a game in which trivial penalties are exacted. ■ the action of forfeiting something.

▶adj. lost or surrendered as a penalty for wrongdoing or neglect: *the lands which he had acquired were automatically forfeit.* —**for·feit·a·ble** *adj.* —**for·feit·er** /'fôrfitər/ *n.* —**for·fei·ture** /'fôrfəCHər/ *n.*

for·fend /fôr'fend/ ▶v. [tr.] **1** *archaic* avert, keep away, or prevent (something evil or unpleasant). **2** (also **fore·fend**) protect (something) by precautionary measures.

for·gath·er /fôr'gaTHər/ (also **fore·gath·er**) ▶v. [intr.] *formal* assemble or gather together.

for·gave /fər'gāv/ ▶ past of FORGIVE.

forge¹ /fôrj/ ▶v. [tr.] **1** make or shape (a metal object) by heating it in a fire or furnace and beating or hammering it. ■ *fig.* create (a relationship or new conditions): *the two women forged a close bond.* **2** produce a copy or imitation of (a document, signature, banknote, or work or art) for the purpose of deception.
▶n. a blacksmith's workshop; a smithy. ■ a furnace or hearth for melting or refining metal. ■ a workshop or factory containing such a furnace. —**forge·a·ble** *adj.* —**forg·er** *n.*

forge² ▶v. [intr.] move forward gradually or steadily: *he forged through the crowded streets.*
▶phrasal v. □ **forge ahead** move forward or take the lead in a race. ■ continue or make progress with a course or undertaking: *the government is forging ahead with reforms.*

for·ger·y /'fôrjərē/ ▶n. (pl. **-ger·ies**) the action of forging or producing a copy of a document, signature, banknote, or work of art. ■ a forged or copied document, signature, banknote, or work of art.

for·get /fər'get/ ▶v. (**-get·ting**; past **-got**; past part. **-got·ten** or **-got**) [tr.] fail to remember. ■ inadvertently neglect to attend to, do, or mention something: *she forgot to lock her door.* ■ inadvertently omit to bring or retrieve: *I forgot my raincoat.* ■ put out of one's mind; cease to think of or consider: [intr.] *she had struggled to forget about him.* ■ (**forget oneself**) act improperly or unbecomingly. —**for·get·ta·ble** *adj.*

for·get·ful /fər'getfəl/ ▶adj. apt or likely not to remember: *forgetful of the time.* —**for·get·ful·ly** *adv.* —**for·get·ful·ness** *n.*

for·get-me-not ▶n. a low-growing plant (*Myosotis* and other genera) of the borage family that typically has blue flowers.

for·give /fər'giv/ ▶v. (past **-gave**; past part. **-giv·en**) [tr.] stop feeling angry or resentful toward (someone) for an offense, flaw, or mistake. ■ (usu. **be forgiven**) stop feeling angry or resentful toward someone for (an offense, flaw, or mistake): *all is forgiven* | [intr.] *not easy to forgive and forget.* ■ used in polite expressions as a request to excuse or regard indulgently one's foibles, ignorance, or impoliteness: *you will have to forgive my suspicious mind.* ■ cancel (a debt). —**for·giv·a·ble** *adj.* —**for·giv·a·bly** /-əblē/ *adv.*

for·give·ness /fər'givnəs/ ▶n. the action or process of forgiving or being forgiven: *she is quick to ask forgiveness when she has overstepped the line.*

for·giv·ing /fər'giviNG/ ▶adj. ready and willing to forgive: *Taylor was in a forgiving mood.* ■ tolerant: *these flooring planks are more durable and forgiving of heavy traffic than real wood.* —**for·giv·ing·ly** *adv.*

for·go /fôr'gō/ (also **fore·go**) ▶v. (**-goes**; past **-went**; past part. **-gone**) [tr.] omit or decline to take (something pleasant or valuable); go without: *forgo the dessert.* ■ refrain from: *forgo comparison.*

for·got /fər'gät/ ▶ past of FORGET.

for·got·ten /fər'gätn/ ▶ past participle of FORGET.

fork /fôrk/ ▶n. **1** an implement with two or more prongs used for lifting food to the mouth or holding it when cutting. ■ a tool of larger but similar form used for digging or lifting in a garden or farm. **2** a device, component, or part with two or more prongs, in particular: ■ a unit consisting of a pair of supports in which a bicycle or motorcycle wheel revolves. ■ a flash of forked lightning. **3** the point where something, esp. a road or river, divides into two parts.
▶v. **1** [intr.] (esp. of a road or other route) divide into two parts. ■ [intr.] take or constitute one part or the other at the point where a road or other route divides: *a minor road forked left.* **2** [tr.] dig, lift, or manipulate (something) with a fork: *fork in some compost.* **3** [tr.] *Chess* attack (two pieces) simultaneously with one piece.
▶phrasal v. □ **fork something over/out/up** (or **fork over/out/up**) *inf.* pay money for something, esp. reluctantly. —**fork·ful** /-,fŏŏl/ *n.* (pl. **-fuls**).

forked /fôrkt/ ▶adj. having a divided or pronged end or branches: *a deeply forked tail.*

---

fork·lift /'fôrk,lift/ ▸*n.* (also **forklift truck**) a vehicle with a pronged device in front for lifting and carrying heavy loads.
▸*v.* [*tr.*] lift and carry (a heavy load) with such a vehicle.

forklift

for·lorn /fər'lôrn; fôr-/ ▸*adj.* **1** pitifully sad and abandoned or lonely. **2** (of an aim or endeavor) unlikely to succeed or be fulfilled; hopeless: *a forlorn attempt to escape.* —**for·lorn·ly** *adv.* —**for·lorn·ness** *n.*
▸ □ **forlorn hope** a persistent or desperate hope that is unlikely to be fulfilled.

form /fôrm/ ▸*n.* **1** the visible shape or configuration of something. ■ arrangement of parts; shape. ■ the body or shape of a person or thing: *his eyes scanned her slender form.* ■ arrangement and style in literary or musical composition: *a triumph of form over content.* **2** a mold, frame, or block in or on which something is shaped. ■ a temporary structure for holding fresh concrete in shape while it sets. **3** a particular way in which a thing exists or appears; a manifestation: *her obsession has taken the form of compulsive exercise.* ■ any of the ways in which a word may be spelled, pronounced, or inflected: *an adjectival form.* ■ the structure of a word, phrase, sentence, or discourse: *a distinction in form.* **4** a type or variety of something: *sponsorship is a form of advertising.* ■ an artistic or literary genre. ■ *Bot.* a taxonomic category that ranks below variety, which contains organisms differing from the typical kind in some trivial, frequently impermanent, character, e.g., a color variant. Compare with SUBSPECIES and VARIETY. **5** the customary or correct method or procedure; what is usually done: *legal form and precedent.* ■ a set order of words; a formula. ■ a formality or item of mere ceremony: *the outward forms of religion.* **6** a printed document with blank spaces for information to be inserted: *an application form.* **7** *chiefly Brit.* a class or year in a school, usually given a specifying number: *the fifth form.* **8** the state of an athlete or sports team with regard to their current standard of performance: *illness has affected his form* | *they've been in good form this season.* ■ details of previous performances by a racehorse or greyhound: *studying the form.*
▸*v.* [*tr.*] **1** bring together parts or combine to create (something): *the company was formed in 1982.* ■ (**form people/things into**) organize people or things into (a group or body). ■ go to make up or constitute: *the precepts that form the basis of the book.* ■ [*intr.*] gradually appear or develop: *a thick mist was forming all around.* ■ conceive (an idea or plan) in one's mind. ■ enter into or contract (a relationship): *the women would form supportive friendships.* ■ articulate (a word, speech sound, or other linguistic unit). ■ construct (a new word) by derivation or inflection. **2** make or fashion into a certain shape or form: *form the dough into balls.* ■ shape or develop by training or discipline. ■ influence or shape (something abstract): *the role of the news media in forming public opinion.*

for·mal /'fôrməl/ ▸*adj.* **1** done in accordance with rules of convention or etiquette; suitable for or constituting an official or important situation or occasion. ■ (of a person or their manner) prim or stiff. ■ of or denoting a style of writing or public speaking characterized by more elaborate grammatical structures and more conservative and technical vocabulary. ■ (esp. of a house or garden) arranged in a regular, classical, and symmetrical manner. **2** officially sanctioned or recognized: *a formal complaint.* ■ having a conventionally recognized form, structure, or set of rules: *he had little formal education.* **3** of or concerned with outward form or appearance, esp. as distinct from content or matter. ■ of or relating to linguistic or logical form as opposed to function or meaning.
▸*n.* an evening gown. ■ an occasion on which evening dress is worn. —**for·mal·ly** *adv.*

form·al·de·hyde /fôr'maldə,hīd; fər-/ ▸*n. Chem.* a colorless pungent gas, CH_2O, in solution.

for·ma·lin /'fôrməlin/ ▸*n.* a colorless solution of formaldehyde in water, used chiefly as a preservative for biological specimens.

for·mal·ism /'fôrmə,lizəm/ ▸*n.* excessive adherence to prescribed forms: *academic formalism.* ■ concern or excessive concern with form and

technique rather than content in artistic creation. —**for·mal·ist** *n.* —**for·mal·is·tic** /,fôrmə'listik/ *adj.*

for·mal·i·ty /fôr'malətē/ ▸*n.* (*pl.* **-ties**) the rigid observance of rules of convention or etiquette. ■ stiffness of behavior or style: *disconcerting formality.* ■ (usu. **formalities**) a thing that is done simply to comply with requirements of etiquette, regulations, or custom: *legal formalities.* ■ (**a formality**) something that is done as a matter of course and without question; an inevitability: *her saying no was just a formality.*

for·mal·ize /'fôrmə,līz/ ▸*v.* [*tr.*] give (something) legal or formal status. ■ give (something) a definite structure or shape: *we became able to formalize our thoughts.* —**for·mal·i·za·tion** /,fôrməli'zāsнən/ *n.*

for·mat /'fôr,mat/ ▸*n.* the way in which something is arranged or set out: *the format of the funeral service.* ■ the shape, size, and presentation of a book or periodical. ■ the medium in which a sound recording is made available: *the album is available as a CD as well as on LP and cassette formats.* ■ *Comput.* a defined structure for the processing, storage, or display of data: *a data file in binary format.*
▸*v.* (**-mat·ted, -mat·ting**) [*tr.*] (esp. in computing) arrange or put into a format. ■ prepare (a storage medium) to receive data.

for·ma·tion /fôr'māsнən/ ▸*n.* **1** the action of forming or process of being formed. **2** a structure or arrangement of something: *a cloud formation.* ■ a formal arrangement of aircraft in flight or troops. ■ *Geol.* an assemblage of rocks or series of strata having some common characteristic. —**for·ma·tion·al** /-sнənl/ *adj.*

for·ma·tive /'fôrmətiv/ ▸*adj.* serving to form something, esp. having a profound and lasting influence on a person's development: *his formative years.* ■ of or relating to a person's development: *a formative assessment.* ■ *Linguistics* denoting or relating to any of the smallest meaningful units that are used to form words in a language, typically combining forms and inflections. —**for·ma·tive·ly** *adv.*

form·er[1] /'fôrmər/ ▸*adj.* **1** having previously filled a particular role or been a particular thing: *her former boyfriend.* ■ of or occurring in the past or an earlier period: *in former times.* **2** (**the former**) denoting the first or first mentioned of two people or things.

for·mer·ly /'fôrmərlē/ ▸*adv.* in the past; in earlier times: *Bangladesh, formerly East Pakistan* | *the building formerly housed their offices.*

for·mic ac·id /'fôrmik/ ▸*n. Chem.* a colorless irritant volatile acid, HCOOH, made catalytically from carbon monoxide and steam.

for·mi·da·ble /'fôrmədəbəl; fər'midə-/ ▸*adj.* inspiring fear or respect through being impressively large, powerful, intense, or capable: *a formidable opponent.* —**for·mi·da·ble·ness** *n.* —**for·mi·da·bly** /-əblē/ *adv.*

form·less /'fôrmləs/ ▸*adj.* without a clear or definite shape or structure: *a dark and formless idea.* —**form·less·ly** *adv.* —**form·less·ness** *n.*

form let·ter ▸*n.* a standardized letter to deal with frequently occurring matters.

for·mu·la /'fôrmyələ/ ▸*n.* (*pl.* **-las** or **-lae** /-,lē; -,lī/) **1** a mathematical relationship or rule expressed in symbols. ■ (also **chemical formula**) a set of chemical symbols showing the elements present in a compound and their relative proportions, and in some cases the structure of the compound. **2** (*pl.* **-las**) a fixed form of words, esp. one used in particular contexts or as a conventional usage: *a legal formula.* ■ a method, statement, or procedure for achieving something, esp. reconciling different aims or positions: *a peace formula.* ■ a rule or style unintelligently or slavishly followed. ■ a stock epithet, phrase, or line repeated for various effects in literary composition, esp. epic poetry. **3** (*pl.* **-las**) a list of ingredients for or constituents of something: *secret formula.* ■ a formulation: *a coal tar formula that helps prevent dandruff.* ■ an infant's liquid food preparation based on cow's milk or soy protein, given as a substitute for breast milk. —**for·mu·la·ic** /,fôrmyə'lāik/ *adj.*

for·mu·lar·y /'fôrmyə,lerē/ ▸*n.* (*pl.* **-lar·ies**) **1** a collection of formulas or set forms, esp. for use in religious ceremonies. **2** an official list giving details of prescribable medicines.
▸*adj.* relating to or using officially prescribed formulas. —**for·mu·la·rize** /-lə,rīz/ *v.*

for·mu·late /'fôrmyə,lāt/ ▸*v.* [*tr.*] create or devise methodically (a strategy or a proposal). ■ express (an idea) in a concise or systematic way: *it can be formulated mathematically.* —**for·mu·la·tion** /,fôrmyə'lāsнən/ *n.*

for·ni·cate /'fôrni,kāt/ ▸*v.* [*intr.*] *formal* or *humorous* (of two people not married to each other) have sexual intercourse. ▷Middle English (as *fornication*): from ecclesiastical Latin *fornicat-* 'arched,' from *fornicari*, from Latin *fornix*, *fornic-* 'vaulted chamber,' later 'brothel.' —**for·ni·ca·tion** /,fôrni'kāsнən/ *n.* —**for·ni·ca·tor** /-,kātər/ *n.*

for·sake /fər'sāk; fôr-/ ▸*v.* (*past* **-sook** /-'soŏk/; *past part.* **-sak·en** /-'sākən/) [*tr.*] *chiefly poetic/lit.* abandon (someone or something). ■ renounce or give up (something valued or pleasant): *I won't forsake my vegetarian principles.* —**for·sak·en·ness** *n.* —**for·sak·er** *n.*

for·sooth /fər'sŏŏTH/ ▶adv. archaic or humorous indeed (often used ironically or to express surprise or indignation). ■ used to give an ironic politeness to questions: *what, forsooth, induced this transformation?*

for·swear /fôr'swe(ə)r/ ▶v. (past **-swore**; past part. **-sworn**) [tr.] formal agree to give up or do without (something). ■ (**forswear oneself/be forsworn**) swear falsely; commit perjury: *I do not mean to be forsworn.*

for·syth·i·a /fər'sĭTHēə/ ▶n. a widely cultivated ornamental Eurasian shrub (genus *Forsythia*) of the olive family, whose bright yellow flowers appear in early spring before the leaves.

fort /fôrt/ ▶n. a fortified building or strategic position. ■ a permanent army post. ■ hist. a trading post.

for·te[1] /'fôr,tā; fôrt/ ▶n. **1** a thing at which someone excels: *small talk was not his forte.* **2** *Fencing* the stronger part of a sword blade, from the hilt to the middle.

for·te[2] /'fôr,tā/ Mus. ▶adv. & adj. (esp. as a direction) loud or loudly.

for·te·pi·an·o /,fôrtāpē'anō; -pē'änō/ ▶n. (pl. **-an·os**) Mus. a piano, esp. of the kind made in the 18th and early 19th centuries.

forth /fôrTH/ ▶adv. chiefly archaic out from a starting point and forward or into view: *the plants will bush forth.* ■ onward in time: *from that day forth.*
▶ □ **and so forth** and so on: *services like education, housing, and so forth.*

forth·com·ing /fôrTH'kəmiNG; 'fôrTH,kəmiNG/ ▶adj. **1** planned for or about to happen in the near future. **2** (of something required) ready or made available when wanted or needed: *financial support was not forthcoming.* ■ (of a person) willing to divulge information. —**forth·com·ing·ness** n.

forth·right /'fôrTH,rīt/ ▶adj. **1** (of a person or their manner or speech) direct and outspoken; straightforward and honest: *his most forthright attack yet on the reforms.* **2** archaic proceeding directly forward.
▶adv. archaic directly forward. ■ immediately. —**forth·right·ly** adv. —**forth·right·ness** n.

forth·with /fôrTH'wiTH/ ▶adv. (esp. in official use) immediately; without delay: *we undertake to pay forthwith the money required.*

for·ti·fi·ca·tion /,fôrtə,fə'kāSHən/ ▶n. (often **fortifications**) a defensive wall or other reinforcement built to strengthen a place against attack. ■ the action of fortifying or process of being fortified.

for·ti·fy /'fôrtə,fī/ ▶v. (**-fies**, **-fied**) [tr.] strengthen (a place) with defensive works so as to protect it against attack. ■ strengthen or invigorate (someone) mentally or physically: *I was fortified by the knowledge that I was in a sympathetic house.* ■ [often as adj.] (**fortified**) strengthen (a drink) with alcohol: *fortified wine.* ■ increase the nutritive value of (food), esp. with vitamins. —**for·ti·fi·a·ble** adj. —**for·ti·fi·er** n.

for·tis·si·mo /fôr'tisə,mō/ Mus. ▶adv. & adj. very loud or loudly.

for·ti·tude /'fôrtə,tŏŏd/ ▶n. courage in pain or adversity.

fort·night /'fôrt,nīt/ ▶n. chiefly Brit. a period of two weeks. ■ inf. used after the name of a day to indicate that something will take place two weeks after that day.

For·tran /'fôr,tran/ (also **FORTRAN**) ▶n. a high-level computer programming language used esp. for scientific computation.

for·tress /'fôrtrəs/ ▶n. a military stronghold, esp. a strongly fortified town fit for a large garrison. ■ a heavily protected and impenetrable building. ■ fig. a person or thing not susceptible to outside influence or disturbance: *he had proved himself to be a fortress of moral rectitude.*

for·tu·i·tous /fôr'tŏŏətəs/ ▶adj. happening by accident or chance rather than design. ■ inf. happening by a lucky chance; fortunate: *from a cash standpoint, the timing is fortuitous.* —**for·tu·i·tous·ly** adv. —**for·tu·i·tous·ness** n.

for·tu·nate /'fôrCHənət/ ▶adj. favored by or involving good luck or fortune; lucky: *she'd been fortunate to escape more serious injury.* ■ auspicious or favorable. ■ materially well off; prosperous.

for·tu·nate·ly /'fôrCHənətlē/ ▶adv. it is fortunate that: *fortunately, no shots were fired and no one was hurt.*

for·tune /'fôrCHən/ ▶n. **1** chance or luck as an external, arbitrary force affecting human affairs. ■ luck, esp. good luck: *this piece of good fortune.* ■ (**fortunes**) the success or failure of a person or enterprise over a period of time or in the course of a particular activity. **2** a large amount of money or assets: *he inherited a substantial fortune.* ■ (**a fortune**) inf. a surprisingly high price or amount of money: *I spent a fortune on food.*
▶ □ **a small fortune** inf. a large amount of money.

for·tune hunt·er ▶n. a person who seeks to become rich through marrying someone wealthy.

for·tune-tell·er ▶n. a person who makes predictions about a person's future by palmistry, using a crystal ball, reading tarot cards, or similar divining methods. —**for·tune-tell·ing** n.

for·ty /'fôrtē/ ▶cardinal number (pl. **-ties**) the number equivalent to the product of four and ten; ten less than fifty; 40. (Roman numeral: **xl** or **XL**.) ■ (**forties**) the numbers from forty to forty-nine, esp. the years of a century or of a person's life. ■ forty years old. ■ forty miles an hour: *they were doing about forty.* —**for·ti·eth** /-tēəTH/ ordinal number —**for·ty·fold** /-,fōld/ adj. & adv.
▶ □ **forty winks** inf. a short sleep or nap, esp. during the day.

for·ty-nin·er /,fôrtē 'nīnər/ ▶n. a prospector in the California gold rush of 1849.

fo·rum /'fôrəm/ ▶n. (pl. **fo·rums**) **1** a place, meeting, or medium where ideas and views on a particular issue can be exchanged. **2** a court or tribunal. **3** (pl. **fo·ra** /'fôrə/) (in an ancient Roman city) a public square or marketplace used for judicial and other business.

for·ward /'fôrwərd/ ▶adv. (also **for·wards**) **1** toward the front; in the direction that one is facing or traveling. ■ in, near, or toward the bow or nose of a ship or aircraft. ■ in the normal order or sequence. **2** onward so as to make progress; toward a successful conclusion: *there's no way forward for the relationship.* ■ into a position of prominence or notice. **3** toward the future; ahead in time: *from that day forward.* ■ to an earlier time: *the special issue has been moved forward to winter.*
▶adj. **1** directed or facing toward the front or the direction that one is facing or traveling. ■ positioned near the enemy lines. ■ (in sports) moving toward the opponents' goal. ■ in, near, or toward the bow or nose of a ship or aircraft. ■ fig. moving or tending onwards to a successful conclusion: *the decision is a forward step.* **2** relating to or concerned with the future: *forward planning.* **3** (of a person) bold or familiar in manner, esp. in a presumptuous way. **4** developing or acting earlier than expected or required; advanced or precocious: *an alarmingly forward child.* ■ (of a plant or crop) well advanced or early. ■ progressing toward or approaching maturity or completion.
▶n. an attacking player in basketball, hockey, or other sports.
▶v. [tr.] **1** send (a letter) on to a further destination: [as adj.] (**forwarding**) *a forwarding address.* ■ hand over or send (an official document). ■ dispatch (goods): [as adj.] (**forwarding**) *a freight forwarding company.* **2** help to advance (something); promote: *forwarding the development of biotechnology.* —**for·ward·er** n. —**for·ward·ly** adv. —**for·ward·ness** n.

for·ward-look·ing ▶adj. favoring innovation and development; progressive.

for·wards /'fôrwərdz/ ▶adv. variant spelling of FORWARD.

for·went /fôr'went/ ▶ past of FORGO.

fos·sa ▶n. a large nocturnal reddish-brown catlike mammal of the civet family, found in the rain forests of Madagascar.

fos·sil /'fäsəl/ ▶n. the remains or impression of a prehistoric organism preserved in petrified form or as a mold or cast in rock. ■ derog. or humorous an antiquated or stubbornly unchanging person or thing: *a cantankerous old fossil.* ■ a word or phrase that has become obsolete except in set phrases or forms, e.g., *hue* in *hue and cry.* ▷mid 16th cent. (denoting a fossilized fish found, and believed to have lived, underground): from French *fossile*, from Latin *fossilis* 'dug up,' from *fodere* 'dig.' —**fos·sil·i·za·tion** /,fäsələ'zāSHən/ n. —**fos·sil·ize** v.

fos·sil fu·el ▶n. a natural fuel such as coal or gas, formed in the geological past from the remains of living organisms.

fos·ter /'fôstər; 'fäs-/ ▶v. [tr.] **1** encourage or promote the development of (something, typically something regarded as good): *to foster learning.* ■ develop (a feeling or idea) in oneself: *appropriate praise helps a child foster a sense of self-worth.* **2** bring up (a child that is not one's own by birth).
▶adj. denoting someone that has a specified family connection through fostering rather than birth. ■ involving or concerned with fostering a child: *foster care.* —**fos·ter·age** /-rij/ n. —**fos·ter·er** n.

fought /fôt/ ▶ past and past participle of FIGHT.

foul /foul/ ▶adj. **1** offensive to the senses, esp. through having a disgusting smell or taste or being unpleasantly soiled. ■ inf. very disagreeable or unpleasant: *a foul mood.* ■ (of the weather) wet and stormy. **2** wicked or immoral: *murder most foul.* ■ (of language) obscene or profane. ■ done contrary to the rules of a sport. **3** containing or charged with noxious matter; polluted: *foul, swampy water.* ■ (**foul with**) clogged or choked with: *a garden foul with weeds.* ■ Naut. (of a rope or anchor) entangled. ■ (of a ship's bottom) encrusted with algae, barnacles, or other marine growth. ■ Printing (of a first copy or proof) defaced by corrections.
▶n. (in sports) an unfair or invalid stroke or piece of play, esp. one

---

involving interference with an opponent. ■ a collision or entanglement in riding, rowing, or running.
▸ *adv.* unfairly; contrary to the rules. ■ (in sports) in foul territory.
▸ *v.* [*tr.*] **1** make foul or dirty; pollute. ■ disgrace or dishonor. ■ (of an animal) make (something) dirty with excrement. ■ (**foul oneself**) (of a
person) defecate involuntarily. **2** (in sports) commit a foul against (an
opponent). ■ *Baseball* hit a foul ball. **3** (of a ship) collide with or interfere with the passage of (another). ■ cause (a cable, anchor, or other
object) to become entangled or jammed. ■ [*intr.*] become entangled in
this way.
▸ *phrasal v.* □ **foul out** *Basketball* be put out of the game for exceeding the
permitted number of fouls. ■ *Baseball* (of a batter) be made out by hitting a foul ball that is caught by an opposing player. □ **foul something
up** (or **foul up**) make a mistake with or spoil something. ▷Old English
fūl, of Germanic origin; related to Old Norse *fúll* 'foul,' Dutch *vuil*
'dirty,' and German *faul* 'rotten, lazy,' from an Indo-European root
shared by Latin *pus*, Greek *puos* 'pus,' and Latin *putere* 'to stink.' —**foul·
ly** /'fou(l)lē/ *adv.* —**foul·ness** *n.*

fou·lard /foō'lärd/ ▸ *n.* a thin, soft material of usu. of silk, typically having a printed pattern. ■ a tie or handkerchief made of such material.

foul ball ▸ *n. Baseball* a ball struck so that it falls or will fall outside the
lines extending from home plate past first and third bases.

foul play ▸ *n.* **1** unfair play in a game or sport. **2** unlawful or dishonest behavior, in particular violent crime resulting in another's death.

foul shot ▸ *n. Basketball* another term for FREE THROW.

foul-up ▸ *n.* a mistake resulting in confusion.

found[1] /found/ ▸ past and past participle of FIND.
▸ *adj.* having been discovered by chance or unexpectedly, in particular:
■ (of an object or sound) collected in its natural state and presented in
a new context as part of a work of art or piece of music. ■ (of art) comprising or making use of such objects. ■ (of poetry) formed by reinter-
preting metrically the structure of a nonpoetic text.

found[2] ▸ *v.* [*tr.*] **1** establish or originate (an institution or organization).
[as *adj.*] (**founding**) *the three founding partners.* ■ plan and begin the
building of (a town or colony). **2** (usu. **be founded on/upon**) construct
or base (a principle or other abstract thing) according to a particular
principle or grounds: *founded on the highest principles.* ■ (of a thing) serve
as a basis for: *the company's fortunes are founded on its minerals business.*

foun·da·tion /foun'dāsHən/ ▸ *n.* **1** (often **foundations**) the lowest load-
bearing part of a building, typically below ground level. ■ *fig.* a body
or ground on which other parts rest or are overlaid. ■ (also **foundation
garment**) a woman's supporting undergarment, such as a girdle. ■ a
cream or powder used as a base to even out facial skin tone before applying other cosmetics. **2** an underlying basis or principle for something. ■ justification or reason: *accusations with no foundation.* **3** the action of establishing an institution or organization on a permanent
basis. ■ an institution established with an endowment, for example a
college or a body devoted to financing research or charity. —**foun·da·
tion·al** /-sHənl/ *adj.*

found·er[1] ▸ *n.* a person who manufactures articles of cast metal; the
owner or operator of a foundry: *an iron founder.*

found·er[2] ▸ *v.* [*intr.*] (of a ship) fill with water and sink. ■ *fig.* (of a plan or
undertaking) fail or break down, typically as a result of a particular
problem or setback: *the talks foundered on the issue of reform.* ■ (of a
hoofed animal, esp. a horse or pony) succumb to laminitis.
▸ *n.* laminitis in horses, ponies, or other hoofed animals.

found·ing fa·ther ▸ *n.* a person who starts or helps to start a movement
or institution. ■ (**Founding Father**) a member of the convention that
drew up the U.S. Constitution in 1787.

found·ling /'foundliNG/ ▸ *n.* an infant that has been abandoned by its
parents and is discovered and cared for by others.

found·ry /'foundrē/ ▸ *n.* (*pl.* **-ries**) a workshop or factory for casting
metal.

fount[1] /fänt; fount/ ▸ *n.* a source of a desirable quality or commodity: *our
courier was a fount of knowledge.* ■ *poetic/lit.* a spring or fountain.

fount[2] ▸ *n. Brit.* variant spelling of FONT[2].

foun·tain /'fountn/ ▸ *n.* **1** an ornamental structure in a pool or lake from
which one or more jets of water are pumped into the air. ■ short for
DRINKING FOUNTAIN. ■ *fig.* a thing that spurts or cascades into the air.
2 *chiefly poetic/lit.* a natural spring of water. ■ a source of a desirable
quality: *the government always quotes this report as the fountain of truth.*
▸ *v.* [*intr.*] spurt or cascade like a fountain.

foun·tain·head /'fountn,hed/ ▸ *n.* the headwaters or source of a stream.
■ an original source of something: *he was the fountainhead of patronage.*

foun·tain pen ▸ *n.* a pen with a reservoir or cartridge from which ink
flows continuously to the nib.

fountain pen

four /fôr/ ▸ *cardinal number* equivalent to the product of two and two; one
more than three, or six less than ten; 4. (Roman numeral: **iv**, **IV**, archaic **iiii** or **IIII**.) ■ a group or unit of four people or things. ■ four years
old. ■ four o'clock. ■ a playing card or domino with four spots or pips.

four-by-four (also **4X4**) ▸ *n. inf.* a vehicle with four-wheel drive.

four-eyes ▸ *n. derog.* a person who wears glasses.

four flush ▸ *n.* a poker hand of little value, having four cards of the
same suit and one of another.
▸ *v.* (**four-flush**) [*intr.*] *inf.* (in poker) bluff when holding a weak hand, particularly a four flush. ■ keep up a pretense; bluff. —**four-flush·er** *n.*

four·fold /'fôr,fōld/ ▸ *adj.* four times as great or as numerous: *a fourfold increase in break-ins.* ■ having four parts or elements: *fourfold symmetry.*
▸ *adv.* by four times; to four times the number or amount.

four-leaf clo·ver (also **four-leafed clover**) ▸ *n.* a clover leaf with four
leaflets, rather than the typical three, thought to bring good luck.

four-let·ter word ▸ *n.* any of several short words referring to sexual or
excretory functions, regarded as coarse or offensive.

four-post·er (also **four-poster bed**) ▸ *n.* a bed with a post at each corner,
sometimes supporting a canopy.

four·score /'fôr'skôr/ ▸ *cardinal number archaic* eighty.

four·some /'fôrsəm/ ▸ *n.* a group of four people. ■ a golf match between
two pairs of players, with partners playing the same ball.

four-square ▸ *adj.* (of a building or structure) having a square shape
and solid appearance. ■ (of a person or quality) firm and resolute.
▸ *adv.* squarely and solidly: *standing four-square on a peninsula.* ■ firmly or
resolutely, esp. in support of someone or something.

four-stroke ▸ *adj.* denoting an internal combustion engine having a
cycle of four strokes (intake, compression, combustion, and exhaust).
■ denoting a vehicle having such an engine.
▸ *n.* an engine or vehicle of this type.

four·teen /,fôr'tēn; 'fôr,tēn/ ▸ *cardinal number* equivalent to the product
of seven and two; one more than thirteen, or six less than twenty; 14.
(Roman numeral: **xiv** or **XIV**.) ■ a size of garment or other merchandise denoted by fourteen. ■ fourteen years old. —**four·teenth** /,fôr-
'tēnTH; 'fôr,tēnTH/ *ordinal number.*

fourth /fôrTH/ ▸ *ordinal number* constituting number four in a sequence;
4th. ■ (**a fourth/one fourth**) a quarter: *nearly three fourths of that money is
now gone.* ■ the fourth finisher or position in a race or competition.
■ the fourth (and often highest) in a sequence of a vehicle's gears.
■ the fourth grade of a school. ■ fourthly (used to introduce a fourth
point or reason): *third, visit popular attractions during lunch; fourth, stay
late.* ■ *Mus.* an interval spanning four consecutive notes in a diatonic
scale, in particular (also **perfect fourth**) an interval of two tones and a
semitone (e.g., C to F). ■ *Mus.* the note that is higher by this interval
than the tonic of a diatonic scale or root of a chord. —**fourth·ly** *adv.*

fourth es·tate ▸ *n.* the press; the profession of journalism.

Fourth of Ju·ly ▸ *n.* another term for INDEPENDENCE DAY.

four-wheel drive ▸ *n.* a transmission system that provides power directly to all four wheels of a vehicle. ■ a vehicle with such a system,
typically designed for off-road driving.

fowl /foul/ ▸ *n.* (*pl.* same or **fowls**) (also **domestic fowl**) a gallinaceous bird
kept chiefly for its eggs and flesh; a domestic cock or hen. ■ any other
domesticated bird kept for its eggs or flesh, e.g., the turkey, duck,
goose, and guinea fowl. ■ the flesh of birds, esp. of the domestic cock
or hen, as food; poultry. ■ birds collectively, esp. as the quarry of
hunters. ■ *archaic* a bird.

Fox ▸ *n.* (*pl.* same) **1** a member of an American Indian people formerly
living in southern Wisconsin, and now mainly in Iowa, Nebraska, and
Kansas. **2** the Algonquian language of this people.
▸ *adj.* of or relating to this people or their language.

fox /fäks/ ▸ *n.* **1** a carnivorous mammal (*Vulpes* and other genera) of the
dog family with a pointed muzzle and bushy tail, proverbial for its
cunning. ■ the fur of a fox. **2** *inf.* a cunning or sly person. ■ a sexually
attractive woman.
▸ *v.* **1** [*tr.*] *inf.* baffle or deceive (someone). **2** [*tr.*] repair (a boot or shoe)

by renewing the upper leather. ■ ornament (the upper of a boot or shoe) with a strip of leather.

fox·glove /ˈfäks,gləv/ ▸ n. a tall Eurasian plant (genus *Digitalis*) of the figwort family, with erect spikes of flowers, typically pinkish-purple or white, shaped like fingers. It is a source of the drug digitalis.

fox·hole /ˈfäks,hōl/ ▸ n. a hole in the ground used by troops as a shelter against enemy fire or as a firing point. ■ a place of refuge or concealment.

fox·hound /ˈfäks,hound/ ▸ n. a dog of a smooth-haired breed with drooping ears, often trained to hunt foxes in packs over long distances.

fox hunt·ing ▸ n. the sport of hunting a fox across country with a pack of hounds by people on foot and horseback. —**fox hunt·er** n.

fox·tail /ˈfäks,tāl/ ▸ n. a common meadow grass (genus *Alopecurus*) that has soft brushlike flowering spikes.

fox ter·ri·er ▸ n. a terrier of a short-haired or wire-haired breed originally used for unearthing foxes.

fox·trot /ˈfäks,trät/ ▸ n. 1 a ballroom dance in 4/4 time, with alternation of two slow and two quick steps. ■ a piece of music written for such a dance. ■ a gait in which a horse walks with its front legs and trots with its hind legs. 2 a code word representing the letter F, used in radio communication.

▸ v. (**-trot·ted, -trot·ting**) [*intr.*] perform such a ballroom dance.

fox·y /ˈfäksē/ ▸ adj. (**fox·i·er, fox·i·est**) resembling or likened to a fox: *a foxy expression.* ■ *inf.* cunning or sly in character. ■ *inf.* (chiefly of a woman) sexually attractive. ■ reddish brown in color. ■ (of paper or other material) marked with spots. —**fox·i·ly** adv. —**fox·i·ness** n.

foy·er /ˈfoiər; ˈfoi,ā/ ▸ n. an entrance hall or other open area in a building used by the public, esp. a hotel or theater. ■ an entrance hall in a house or apartment. ▷late 18th cent. (denoting the center of attention or activity): from French, 'hearth, home,' based on Latin *focarius* 'kitchen servant,' from *focus* 'domestic hearth.'

Fr. ▸ abbr. ■ Father (as a courtesy title of priests): *Fr. Buckley.* ■ France. ■ French. ■ Friday.

▸ symb. the chemical element francium.

fr. ▸ abbr. franc(s).

fra·cas /ˈfrākəs; ˈfrak-/ ▸ n. (pl. **-cas·es**) a noisy disturbance or quarrel.

frac·tion /ˈfraksʜən/ ▸ n. a numerical quantity that is not a whole number (e.g., $\frac{1}{2}$, 0.5). ■ a small or tiny part, amount, or proportion of something: *he hesitated for **a fraction** of a second.* ■ a dissenting group within a larger one. ■ each of the portions into which a mixture may be separated by a process in which the individual components behave differently according to their physical properties.

frac·tion·al /ˈfraksʜənl/ ▸ adj. of, relating to, or expressed as a numerical value that is not a whole number, esp. a fraction less than one. ■ small or tiny in amount. ■ *Chem.* relating to or denoting the separation of components of a mixture by making use of their differing physical properties: *fractional crystallization.* —**frac·tion·al·ize** v. —**frac·tion·al·ly** adv.

frac·tious /ˈfraksʜəs/ ▸ adj. easily irritated; bad-tempered. ■ (of an organization) difficult to control; unruly. —**frac·tious·ly** adv. —**frac·tious·ness** n.

frac·ture /ˈfrakCHər/ ▸ n. the cracking or breaking of a hard object or material. ■ a crack or break in a hard object or material, typically a bone or a body of rock. ■ the physical appearance of a freshly broken rock or mineral, esp. as regards the shape of the surface formed.

▸ v. break or cause to break: [*intr.*] *the stone has fractured* ■ [*tr.*] sustain a fracture of (a bone): [as adj.] (**fractured**) *a fractured skull.* ■ *fig.* (with reference to an organization or other abstract thing) split or fragment so as to no longer function or exist. ■ [as adj.] (**fractured**) (of speech or a language) broken.

frag·ile /ˈfrajəl; -,jīl/ ▸ adj. (of an object) easily broken or damaged. ■ flimsy or insubstantial; easily destroyed: *you have a fragile grip on reality.* ■ (of a person) not strong or sturdy; delicate and vulnerable. —**frag·ile·ly** adv. —**fra·gil·i·ty** /frəˈjilitē/ n.

frag·ment ▸ n. /ˈfragmənt/ a small part broken or separated off something. ■ an isolated or incomplete part of something.

▸ v. /ˈfrag,ment/ break or cause to break into fragments: [*intr.*] *his followers fragmented into sects.* —**frag·men·tal** /fragˈmentl/ adj.

frag·men·tar·y /ˈfragmən,terē/ ▸ adj. consisting of small parts that are disconnected or incomplete. —**frag·men·tar·i·ly** /,fragmənˈterəlē/ adv.

frag·men·ta·tion /,fragmənˈtāsʜən/ ▸ n. the process or state of breaking or being broken into small or separate parts. ■ *Comput.* the storing of a file in separate areas of memory scattered throughout a hard disk.

fra·grance /ˈfrāgrəns/ ▸ n. a pleasant, sweet smell: *the bushes fill the air with fragrance.* ■ a perfume or aftershave.

fra·grant /ˈfrāgrənt/ ▸ adj. having a pleasant or sweet smell. —**fra·grant·ly** adv.

frail /frāl/ ▸ adj. (of a person) weak and delicate. ■ easily damaged or broken; fragile or insubstantial: *the frail Russian economy.* ■ weak in character or morals. —**frail·ly** adv. —**frail·ness** n.

frail·ty /ˈfrāltē/ ▸ n. (pl. **-ties**) the condition of being weak and delicate: *the increasing frailty of old age.* ■ weakness in character or morals: *human frailty.*

frame /frām/ ▸ n. 1 a rigid structure that surrounds or encloses something such as a door or window. ■ (**frames**) a metal or plastic structure holding the lenses of a pair of glasses. ■ a case or border enclosing a mirror or picture. ■ the rigid supporting structure of an object such as a vehicle, building, or piece of furniture. ■ a person's body with reference to its size or build: *a shiver shook her slim frame.* ■ a boxlike structure of glass or plastic in which seeds or young plants are grown. ■ *archaic* or *poetic/lit.* the universe, or part of it, regarded as an embracing structure. ■ *archaic* or *poetic/lit.* the structure, constitution, or nature of someone or something: *we have in our inward frame various affections.* 2 a basic structure that underlies or supports a system, concept, or text: *a frame for interpretation.* ■ the genre or form of a literary text determining its expected style and content: *poems with a classical frame.* 3 a single complete picture in a series forming a movie, television, or video film. ■ a single picture in a comic strip. ■ *Comput.* a graphic panel in a display window, especially in an Internet browser, that encloses a self-contained section of data and permits multiple independent document viewing. 4 a round of play in bowling. ■ *inf.* an inning in a baseball game: *he closed out the game by pitching two hitless frames.*

▸ v. [*tr.*] 1 place (a picture or photograph) in a frame. ■ surround so as to create a sharp or attractive image: *a short style cut to frame the face.* 2 erect the framework of a building. 3 create or formulate (a concept, plan, or system): *framing the proposals.* ■ form or articulate (words): *frame a reply.* ■ *archaic* make or construct (something) by fitting parts together or in accordance with a plan: *what immortal hand or eye could frame thy fearful symmetry?* 4 *inf.* produce false evidence against (an innocent person) so that they appear guilty: *he claims he was framed.*

▸ □ **frame of mind** a particular mood that influences one's attitude or behavior.

frame of ref·er·ence ▸ n. a set of criteria or stated values in relation to which measurements or judgments can be made. ■ (also **reference frame**) a system of geometric axes in relation to which measurements of size, position, or motion can be made.

frame-up ▸ n. *inf.* a conspiracy to falsely incriminate someone.

frame·work /ˈfrām,wərk/ ▸ n. an essential supporting structure of a building, vehicle, or object. ■ a basic structure underlying a system, concept, or text: *the theoretical framework of political sociology.*

franc /franGk/ ▸ n. the basic monetary unit of Switzerland and several other countries (including France, Belgium, and Luxembourg until the introduction of the euro), equal to 100 centimes.

fran·chise /ˈfran,CHīz/ ▸ n. 1 an authorization granted by a government or company to an individual or group enabling them to carry out specified commercial activities. ■ a business or service given such authorization to operate. ■ an authorization given by a league to own a sports team. ■ *inf.* a professional sports team. 2 (usu. **the franchise**) the right to vote. ■ the rights of citizenship.

▸ v. [*tr.*] grant a franchise to (an individual or group). ■ grant a franchise for the sale of (goods) or the operation of (a service): *all the catering was franchised out.* —**fran·chi·see** /,fran,CHīˈzē/ n. —**fran·chis·er** (also **fran·chi·sor**) n.

Fran·cis·can /franˈsiskən/ ▸ n. a friar, sister, or lay member of a Christian religious order founded in 1209 by St. Francis of Assisi.

▸ adj. of, relating to, or denoting St. Francis or the Franciscans.

fran·ci·um /ˈtransēəm/ ▸ n. the chemical element of atomic number 87, a radioactive member of the alkali metal group. Francium occurs naturally as a decay product in uranium and thorium ores. (Symbol: **Fr**)

Fran·co·phile /ˈfranGkə,fīl/ ▸ n. a person who is fond of or greatly admires France or the French.

fran·co·phone /ˈfranGkə,fōn/ (also **Fran·co·phone**) ▸ adj. French-speaking: *a summit of francophone countries.*

▸ n. a person who speaks French.

fran·gi·ble /ˈfranjəbəl/ ▸ adj. *formal* fragile; brittle.

Frank ▸ n. a member of a Germanic people that conquered Gaul in the 6th century and controlled much of western Europe for several

---

centuries afterward. ■ (in the eastern Mediterranean region) a person of western European nationality or descent.

frank[1] /fraNGk/ ▸adj. open, honest, and direct in speech or writing, esp. when dealing with unpalatable matters: *a long and frank discussion.* ■ open, sincere, or undisguised in manner or appearance: *frank admiration.* ■ *Med.* unmistakable; obvious. —**frank·ness** *n.*

frank[2] ▸v. [tr.] (often **be franked**) stamp an official mark on (a letter or parcel), esp. to indicate that postage has been paid or does not need to be paid. ■ *hist.* sign (a letter or parcel) to ensure delivery free of charge. ■ *archaic* facilitate or pay the passage of (someone).
▸n. an official mark or signature on a letter or parcel, esp. to indicate that postage has been paid or does not need to be paid. —**frank·er** *n.*

frank[3] ▸n. short for FRANKFURTER.

Frank·en·stein /'fraNGkən,stīn/ ▸a character in the novel *Frankenstein, or the Modern Prometheus* (1818) by Mary Shelley. Baron Frankenstein is a scientist who creates and brings to life a manlike monster that eventually turns on him and destroys him. ■ (also **Frankenstein's monster**) [as n.] a thing that becomes terrifying or destructive to its maker.

frank·furt·er /'fraNGkfərtər; -,fərtər/ ▸n. a seasoned smoked sausage typically made of beef and pork.

frank·in·cense /'fraNGkən,sens/ ▸n. an aromatic gum resin obtained from an African tree (*Boswellia sacra*, family Burseraceae) and burned as incense.

Frank·lin stove ▸n. a cast-iron stove for heating a room, resembling an open fireplace in shape.

Franklin stove

frank·ly /'fraNGklē/ ▸adv. in an open, honest, and direct manner: *she talks frankly about herself.* ■ used to emphasize the truth of a statement, however unpalatable or shocking this may be: *frankly, I was pleased to leave.*

fran·tic /'frantik/ ▸adj. wild or distraught with fear, anxiety, or other emotion: *she was frantic with worry.* ■ conducted in a hurried, excited, and chaotic way, typically because of the need to act quickly: *frantic attempts to resuscitate the girl.* —**fran·ti·cal·ly** /-(ə)lē/ adv. —**fran·tic·ness** n.

frap·pé /fra'pā/ ▸adj. (of a drink) iced or chilled: *a crème de menthe frappé.*
▸n. a drink served with ice or frozen to a slushy consistency. ■ (usu. **frappe** /frap/) a milk shake, esp. one made with ice cream.

frat /frat/ ▸n. [usu. as adj.] *inf.* a students' fraternity: *a frat party.*

fra·ter·nal /frə'tərnl/ ▸adj. **1** of or like a brother or brothers: *fraternal feeling.* ■ of or denoting an organization or order for people, esp. men, that have common interests or beliefs. **2** (of twins) developed from separate ova and therefore genetically distinct and not necessarily of the same sex or more similar than other siblings. Compare with IDENTICAL (sense 1). —**fra·ter·nal·ism** n. —**fra·ter·nal·ly** adv.

fra·ter·ni·ty /frə'tərnətē/ ▸n. (pl. **-ties**) **1** a group of people sharing a common profession or interests: *members of the hunting fraternity.* ■ a male students' society in a university or college. ■ a religious or masonic society or guild. **2** the state or feeling of friendship and mutual support within a group.

frat·er·nize /'fratər,nīz/ ▸v. [intr.] associate or form a friendship with someone, esp. when one is not supposed to: *fraternizing with the enemy.* —**frat·er·ni·za·tion** /,fratərni'zāSHən/ n.

frat·ri·cide /'fratrə,sīd/ ▸n. the killing of one's brother or sister. ■ a person who kills their brother or sister. —**frat·ri·cid·al** /,fratrə'sīdl/ adj.

fraud /frôd/ ▸n. wrongful or criminal deception intended to result in financial or personal gain. ■ a person or thing intended to deceive others, typically by unjustifiably claiming or being credited with accomplishments or qualities. ▷Middle English: from Old French *fraude*, from Latin *fraus, fraud-* 'deceit, injury.'

fraud·u·lent /'frôjələnt/ ▸adj. obtained, done by, or involving deception,

esp. criminal deception: *the fraudulent copying of American software.* ■ unjustifiably claiming or being credited with particular accomplishments or qualities. —**fraud·u·lence** n. —**fraud·u·lent·ly** adv.

fraught /frôt/ ▸adj. **1** (**fraught with**) (of a situation or course of action) filled with or destined to result in (something undesirable): *fraught with danger.* **2** causing or affected by great anxiety or stress: *there was a fraught silence.*

fray[1] /frā/ ▸v. [intr.] (of a fabric, rope, or cord) unravel or become worn at the edge, typically through constant rubbing. ■ *fig.* (of a person's nerves or temper) show the effects of strain.

fray[2] ▸n. (**the fray**) a situation of intense activity, typically one incorporating an element of aggression or competition: *nineteen companies bid for the contract, with more expected to enter the fray.* ■ a battle or fight.

fraz·zle /'frazəl/ *inf.* ▸v. [tr.] [usu. as adj.] (**frazzled**) cause to feel completely exhausted; wear out. ■ fray: *fig. it's enough to frazzle the nerves.*
▸n. the state of being completely exhausted or worn out: *I'm tired, worn to a frazzle.*

freak /frēk/ ▸n. **1** a very unusual and unexpected event or situation: [as adj.] *a freak storm.* ■ (also **freak of nature**) a person, animal, or plant with an unusual physical abnormality. ■ *inf.* a person regarded as strange because of unusual appearance or behavior. ■ *inf.* a person who is obsessed with or unusually enthusiastic about a specified interest: *a fitness freak.* ■ *inf.* a person addicted to a drug of a particular kind: *cocaine freaks.* **2** *archaic* a sudden arbitrary change of mind; a whim.
▸v. **1** [intr.] *inf.* react or behave in a wild and irrational way, typically because of the effects of extreme emotion, mental illness, or drugs: *I freaked out and started smashing the place up.* ■ [tr.] cause to act in such a way. **2** [tr.] *archaic* fleck or streak randomly: *the pansy freaked with jet.*

freak·ish /'frēkiSH/ ▸adj. bizarre or grotesque; abnormal: *freakish and mischievous elves.* ■ capricious or whimsical; unpredictable: *freakish weather.* —**freak·ish·ly** adv. —**freak·ish·ness** n.

freak·y /'frēkē/ ▸adj. (**freak·i·er, freak·i·est**) *inf.* very odd, strange, or eccentric. —**freak·i·ly** /-kəlē/ adv. —**freak·i·ness** n.

freck·le /'frekəl/ ▸n. a small patch of light brown color on the skin, often becoming more pronounced through exposure to the sun.
▸v. cover or become covered with freckles. —**freck·ly** adj.

free /frē/ ▸adj. (**fre·er** /'frēər/, **fre·est** /'frēəst/) **1** not under the control or in the power of another; able to act or be done as one wishes. ■ (of a state or its citizens or institutions) subject neither to foreign domination nor to despotic government: *a free press.* ■ not or no longer confined or imprisoned. ■ *hist.* not a slave. ■ able or permitted to take a specified action: *you are free to leave.* **2** not physically restrained, obstructed, or fixed; unimpeded: *she lifted the cat free.* ■ *Physics & Chem.* not bound in an atom, a molecule, or a compound: *the atmosphere contained virtually no free oxygen.* See also FREE RADICAL. **3** not subject to or constrained by engagements or obligations: *free time.* ■ (of a facility or piece of equipment) not occupied or in use: *the bathroom was free.* **4** (**free of/from**) not subject to or affected by (a specified thing, typically an undesirable one): *membership is free of charge.* **5** given or available without charge: *free health care.* **6** using or expending something without restraint; lavish: *she was free with her money.* ■ frank or unrestrained in speech, expression, or action. ■ *archaic* overfamiliar or forward in manner. **7** (of a literary style) not observing the strict laws of form. ■ (of a translation) conveying only the broad sense; not literal. **8** *Sailing* (of the wind) blowing from a favorable direction to the side or stern of a vessel.
▸adv. **1** without cost or payment: *ladies were admitted free | giving their time for free.* **2** *Sailing* with the sheets eased.
▸v. (**frees, freed, free·ing**) [tr.] make free, in particular: ■ from captivity, confinement, or slavery. ■ from physical obstruction, restraint, or entanglement. ■ from restriction or excessive regulation. ■ from something undesirable: *free your body of excess tension.* ■ so as to become available for a particular purpose: *free up funds for development.* ▷Old English *frēo* (adjective), *frēon* (verb), of Germanic origin; related to Dutch *vrij* and German *frei*, from an Indo-European root meaning 'to love.' —**free·ly** adj. —**free·ness** n.
▸ □ **free and easy** informal and relaxed. □ **a free hand** freedom to act at one's own discretion. □ **free on board** (abbr.: **f.o.b.**) including or assuming delivery without charge to the buyer's named destination. □ **a free ride** a situation in which someone benefits without having to make a fair contribution. □ **the free world** the noncommunist countries of the world, as formerly opposed to the Soviet bloc. □ **make free with** treat without ceremony or proper respect.

free·base /'frē,bās/ (also **freebase cocaine**) ▸n. cocaine that has been converted to its base form by heating with ether or boiling with sodium bicarbonate, taken by inhaling the fumes or smoking the residue. ▸ *v.* [*tr.*] prepare or take (cocaine) in such a way.

free·bie /'frēbē/ (also **free-bee**) ▸ *n. inf.* a thing given free of charge.

free·boot·er /'frē,bōōtər/ ▸ *n.* a pirate or lawless adventurer. —**free·boot** *v.*

free-born /'frē,bôrn/ ▸ *adj.* not born in slavery. ■ of or befitting a free-born person.

freed·man /'frēdmən/ -,man/ ▸ *n.* (*pl.* -**men**) *hist.* an emancipated slave.

free·dom /'frēdəm/ ▸ *n.* the power or right to act, speak, or think as one wants without hindrance or restraint: *freedom of choice.* ■ absence of subjection to foreign domination or despotic government: *a champion of Irish freedom.* ■ the state of not being imprisoned or enslaved. ■ the state of being physically unrestricted and able to move easily: *freedom of movement.* ■ (**freedom from**) the state of not being subject to or affected by (a particular undesirable thing): *freedom from want.* ■ the power of self-determination attributed to the will; the quality of being independent of fate or necessity. ■ unrestricted use of something: *the dog has the freedom of the house.* ■ *archaic* familiarity or openness in speech or behavior.

free·dom fight·er ▸ *n.* a person who takes part in a violent struggle to achieve a political goal, esp. in order to overthrow their government.

free en·ter·prise ▸ *n.* an economic system in which private business operates in competition and largely free of state control.

free fall ▸ *n.* downward movement under the force of gravity only. ■ the part of a parachute-descent before the parachute opens. ■ the movement of a spacecraft in space without thrust from the engines. ▸ *v.* (**free-fall**) [*intr.*] move under the force of gravity only; fall rapidly.

free-for-all ▸ *n.* a disorganized or unrestricted situation or event in which everyone may take part, esp. a fight or discussion.

free-form ▸ *adj.* not conforming to a regular or formal structure or shape: *a free-form jazz improvisation.*

free·hand /'frē,hand/ ▸ *adj. & adv.* (esp. with reference to drawing) done manually without the aid of instruments such as rulers.

free-hand·ed ▸ *adj.* generous, esp. with money. —**free-hand·ed·ly** *adv.* —**free-hand·ed·ness** *n.*

free·hold /'frē,hōld/ ▸ *n.* permanent and absolute tenure of land or property with freedom to dispose of it at will. ■ (**the freehold**) the ownership of a piece of land or property by such tenure. ■ a piece of land or property held by such tenure. ▸ *adj.* held by or having the status of freehold. —**free·hold·er** *n.*

free·lance /'frē,lans/ (also **free-lance**) ▸ *adj.* working for different companies at different times rather than being permanently employed by one company: *a freelance journalist.* ■ independent or uncommitted in politics or personal life. ▸ *adv.* earning one's living in such a way: *I work freelance from home.* ▸ *n.* **1** a person who earns a living in such a way. **2** *hist.* (often **free lance**) a medieval mercenary. ▸ *v.* [*intr.*] earn one's living as a freelance. —**free·lanc·er** *n.*

free·load·er /'frē,lōdər/ ▸ *n. inf.* a person who takes advantage of others' generosity without giving anything in return. —**free·load** /'frē,lōd/ *v.*

free love ▸ *n.* the idea or practice of having sexual relations according to choice, without being restricted by marriage or other long-term relationships.

free·man /'frēmən/ -,man/ ▸ *n.* (*pl.* -**men**) **1** a person who is entitled to full political and civil rights. **2** *hist.* a person who is not a slave or serf.

free mar·ket ▸ *n.* an economic system in which prices are determined by unrestricted competition between privately owned businesses. —**free mar·ket·eer** (also **free-mar·ket·eer**) *n.*

Free·ma·son /'frē,māsən/ ▸ *n.* a member of an international order established for mutual help and fellowship, which holds elaborate secret ceremonies. —**free·ma·son·ry** /-rē/ *n.*

fre·er /'frēər/ ▸ *adj.* comparative of FREE.

free rad·i·cal ▸ *n. Chem.* an uncharged molecule (typically highly reactive and short-lived) having an unpaired valence electron.

free-range ▸ *adj.* (of livestock, esp. poultry) kept in natural conditions, with freedom of movement. ■ (of eggs) produced by birds reared under such conditions.

free·sia /'frēzhə/ ▸ *n.* a small southern African plant (genus *Freesia*) of the iris family, with fragrant, colorful, tubular flowers, many varieties of which are cultivated for use by florists.

free speech ▸ *n.* the right to express any opinions without censorship or restraint.

free-spo·ken ▸ *adj.* speaking candidly and openly.

fre·est /'frēəst/ ▸ *adj.* superlative of FREE.

free·stand·ing /'frē'standiNG/ (also **free-stand·ing**) ▸ *adj.* not supported by another structure. ■ not relying on or linked to anything else; independent: *if extracts are used, they should be freestanding and coherent.*

free·style /'frē,stīl/ ▸ *adj.* denoting a contest or version of a sport in which there are few restrictions on the moves or techniques that competitors employ: *freestyle wrestling.* ▸ *n.* a contest of such a kind, in particular a swimming race in which competitors may use any stroke. —**free·styl·er** *n.*

free·think·er /'frē'THiNGkər/ ▸ *n.* a person who rejects accepted opinions, esp. those concerning religious belief. —**free·think·ing** *n. & adj.*

free throw ▸ *n. Basketball* an unimpeded attempt at a basket (worth one point) awarded to a player following a foul or other infringement.

free verse ▸ *n.* poetry that does not rhyme or have a regular meter. Also called VERS LIBRE.

free·ware /'frē,weər/ ▸ *n.* software that is available free of charge.

free·way /'frē,wā/ ▸ *n.* an express highway, esp. one with controlled access. ■ a toll-free highway.

free·wheel /'frē,(h)wēl/ ▸ *n.* a device in a motor vehicle transmission allowing the drive shaft to spin faster than the engine. ■ a device that allows a bicycle wheel to revolve forward while the crank is stationary. ▸ *v.* [*intr.*] ride a bicycle with the pedals at rest, esp. downhill. ■ [usu. as *adj.*] (**freewheeling**) act without concern for rules, conventions, or the consequences of one's actions: *the freewheeling drug scene of the sixties.*

free will ▸ *n.* the power of acting without the constraint of necessity or fate; the ability to act at one's own discretion. ▸ *adj.* (esp. of a donation) given readily; voluntary: *free-will offerings.*

freeze /frēz/ ▸ *v.* (*past* **froze** /frōz/; *past part.* **fro·zen** /'frōzən/) **1** [*intr.*] (of a liquid) be turned into ice or another solid as a result of extreme cold. ■ [*tr.*] turn (a liquid) into ice or another solid in such a way. ■ (of something wet or containing liquid) become blocked, covered, or rigid with ice: *the pipes had frozen.* ■ [*tr.*] cause (something wet or containing liquid) to become blocked, covered, or rigid with ice: *the ground was frozen hard.* ■ [*tr.*] (of the weather) cause (someone) to feel so cold that they are near death. ■ (of the weather) be at or below freezing. ■ [*tr.*] deprive (a part of the body) of feeling, esp. by the application of a chilled anesthetic substance. ■ [*tr.*] treat (someone) with a cold manner; stare coldly at (someone): *freeze him with a look.* **2** [*tr.*] store (something) at a very low temperature in order to preserve it: *the cake can be frozen.* ■ [*intr.*] (of food) be able to be preserved in such a way: *this soup freezes well.* **3** [*intr.*] become suddenly motionless or paralyzed with fear or shock. ■ stop moving when ordered or directed. **4** [*tr.*] hold (something) at a fixed level or in a fixed state for a period of time. ■ prevent (assets) from being used for a period of time. ■ stop (a moving image) at a particular frame when filming or viewing: *freeze the action.* ■ [*intr.*] (of a computer screen) become temporarily locked because of system problems. ▸ *phrasal v.* □ **freeze someone out** *inf.* behave in a hostile or obstructive way so as to exclude someone from something. ▸ *n.* **1** an act of holding or being held at a fixed level or in a fixed state: *workers faced a pay freeze.* **2** *inf.* a period of very cold weather. ▷ Old English *frēosan* (in the phrase *hit frēoseth* 'it is freezing, it is so cold that water turns to ice'), of Germanic origin; related to Dutch *vriezen* and German *frieren*, from an Indo-European root shared by Latin *pruina* 'hoarfrost' and frost. —**freez·a·ble** /-zəbəl/ *adj.* —**fro·zen·ly** *adv.* ▸ □ **freeze one's blood** (or **one's blood freezes**) fill (or be filled) with a sudden feeling of great fear or horror.

freeze-dry ▸ *v.* [*tr.*] [usu. as *adj.*] (**freeze-dried**) preserve (something) by rapidly freezing it and then subjecting it to a high vacuum that removes ice by sublimation: *freeze-dried beef stew.*

freeze-frame ▸ *n.* the facility of stopping a film or videotape in order to view a motionless image. ■ a motionless image obtained with such a facility. ▸ *v.* [*tr.*] use such a facility on (an image or a recording).

freez·er /'frēzər/ ▸ *n.* a refrigerated compartment, cabinet, or room for preserving food at very low temperatures. ■ a device for making frozen desserts such as ice cream or sherbet.

freeze-up ▸ *n.* a period of extreme cold. ■ the freezing over of a body of water such as a lake or river: *until freeze-up, the caribou stay near the lake.*

freez·ing point ▸ *n.* the temperature at which a liquid turns into a solid when cooled.

freight /frāt/ ▸ *n.* **1** goods transported by truck, train, ship, or aircraft.

■ the transport of goods by truck, train, ship, or aircraft. ■ a charge for such transport. **2** (in full **freight train**) a train of freight cars. **3** a load or burden.

▶*v.* [*tr.*] transport (goods) in bulk by truck, train, ship, or aircraft. ■ (**be freighted with**) *fig.* be laden or burdened with: *each word was freighted with anger.*

freight car ▶*n.* a railroad car for carrying freight.

freight·er /'frātər/ ▶*n.* a ship or aircraft designed to carry goods in bulk. ■ a person who loads, receives, or forwards goods for transport.

French /frenCH/ ▶*adj.* of or relating to France or its people or language.
▶*n.* **1** the Romance language of France, also used in parts of Belgium, Switzerland, and Canada, in several countries of northern and western Africa and the Caribbean, and elsewhere. **2** [as *pl. n.*] (**the French**) the people of France collectively. —**French·i·fy** /-ə,fī/ *v.* —**French·ness** *n.*

French bread ▶*n.* white bread in a long, crisp loaf.

French Ca·na·di·an ▶*n.* **1** a Canadian whose principal language is French. **2** the form of French spoken in Canada.
▶*adj.* of or relating to French-speaking Canadians or their language.

French cuff ▶*n.* a shirt cuff that is folded back before fastening, creating a double-layered cuff.

French curve ▶*n.* a template used for drawing curved lines.

French curve

French door ▶*n.* a door with glass panes throughout its length. ■ a French window.

French dress·ing ▶*n.* a salad dressing of vinegar, oil, and seasonings. ■ a sweet, creamy salad dressing commercially prepared from oil, tomato purée, and spices.

French fries (also **French fried potatoes**) ▶*pl. n.* potatoes cut into strips and deep-fried.

French horn ▶*n.* a brass instrument with a coiled tube, valves, and a wide bell, played with the right hand in the bell.

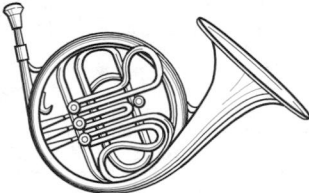

French horn

French kiss ▶*n.* a kiss with contact between tongues. —**French kiss·ing** *n.*

French leave ▶*n. inf., dated* an unauthorized or unannounced departure; absence without permission: *he seems to have taken French leave.*

French·man /'frenCHmən/ ▶*n.* (*pl.* **-men**) a person, esp. a man, who is French by birth or descent.

French toast ▶*n.* bread coated in egg and milk and fried.

French·wom·an /'frenCH,wŏŏmən/ ▶*n.* (*pl.* **-wom·en**) a female who is French by birth or descent.

fre·net·ic /frə'netik/ ▶*adj.* fast and energetic in a rather wild and uncontrolled way: *a frenetic pace of activity.* —**fre·net·i·cal·ly** /-ik(ə)lē/ *adv.*

fren·zy /'frenzē/ ▶*n.* (*pl.* **-zies**) a state or period of uncontrolled excitement or wild behavior: *a frenzy of rage.* —**fren·zied** *adj.*

Fre·on /'frē,än/ (also **fre·on**) ▶*n. trademark* an aerosol propellant, refrigerant, or organic solvent consisting of one or more of a group of chlorofluorocarbons and related compounds.

fre·quen·cy /'frēkwənsē/ ▶*n.* (*pl.* **-cies**) **1** the rate at which something occurs or is repeated over a particular period of time or in a given sample: *increasing frequency.* ■ the fact of being frequent or happening often. ■ *Statistics* the ratio of the number of actual to possible occurrences of an event. ■ *Statistics* the (relative) number of times something occurs in a given sample. **2** the rate at which a vibration occurs that constitutes a wave, either in a material (as in sound waves),

or in an electromagnetic field (as in radio waves and light), usually measured per second. (Symbol: **f** or *ν*) ■ the particular waveband at which a radio station or other system broadcasts or transmits signals.

fre·quen·cy mod·u·la·tion (abbr.: **FM**) ▶*n.* the modulation of a radio or other wave by variation of its frequency, esp. to carry an audio signal. Often contrasted with **AMPLITUDE MODULATION.** ■ the system of radio transmission using such modulation.

fre·quent ▶*adj.* /'frēkwənt/ occurring or done on many occasions, in many cases, or in quick succession. ■ (of a person) doing something often; habitual: *a frequent visitor.* ■ found at short distances apart: *frequent roadblocks.*
▶*v.* /frē'kwent/ [*tr.*] visit (a place) often or habitually: *bars frequented by soldier.* —**fre·quen·ta·tion** /,frēkwən'tāsHən/ *n.* —**fre·quent·ly** *adv.*

fre·quen·ta·tive /frē'kwentətiv/ *Gram.* ▶*adj.* (of a verb or verbal form) expressing frequent repetition or intensity of action.
▶*n.* a verb or verbal form of this type, e.g., *chatter* in English.

fres·co /'freskō/ ▶*n.* (*pl.* **-coes** or **-cos**) a painting done rapidly in watercolor on wet plaster on a wall or ceiling. ■ this method of painting, used in Roman times and by the great masters of the Italian Renaissance including Giotto, Masaccio, and Michelangelo.
▶*v.* [*tr.*] paint in fresco: [as *adj.*] *frescoed ceilings.*

fresh /fresH/ ▶*adj.* **1** not previously known or used; new or different: *fresh evidence.* **2** recently created or experienced and not faded or impaired: *the memory was still fresh.* ■ (of food) recently made or obtained; not canned, frozen, or otherwise preserved. ■ (of a person) full of energy and vigor. ■ (of a color or a person's complexion) bright or healthy in appearance. ■ (of a person) attractively youthful and inexperienced. ■ (**fresh from/out of**) (of a person) having just had (a particular experience) or come from (a particular place): *fresh out of art school.* **3** (of water) not salty. ■ pleasantly clean, pure, and cool: *fresh air.* **4** (of the wind) cool and fairly strong. **5** *inf.* presumptuous or impudent toward someone, esp. in a sexual way: *some of the men tried to get fresh with the girls.*
▶*adv.* [usu. in *comb.*] newly; recently: *fresh-cut grass.* ▷Old English *fersc* 'not salt, fit for drinking,' superseded in Middle English by forms from Old French *freis, fresche;* both ultimately of Germanic origin and related to Dutch *vers* and German *frisch.* —**fresh·ly** *adv.* —**fresh·ness** *n.*
▶ □ **be fresh out of** *inf.* have just sold or run out of (something).

fresh·en /'fresHən/ ▶*v.* **1** [*tr.*] make (something) newer, cleaner, or more attractive: *it didn't take long to freshen her makeup.* ■ add more liquid to (a drink); top off. **2** [*intr.*] (of wind) become stronger and colder.
▶*phrasal v.* □ **freshen up** revive oneself by washing or changing into clean clothes.

fresh·et /'fresHət/ ▶*n.* the flood of a river from heavy rain or melted snow. ■ a rush of fresh water flowing into the sea.

fresh·man /'fresHmən/ ▶*n.* (*pl.* **-men**) a first-year student at a university, college, or high school. ■ a newcomer or novice.

fresh·wa·ter /'fresH'wôtər; -'wätər/ ▶*adj.* **1** of or found in fresh water; not of the sea: *freshwater and marine fish.* **2** *inf.* (esp. of a school or college) situated in a remote or obscure area; provincial.

fret[1] /fret/ ▶*v.* (**fret·ted, fret·ting**) **1** [*intr.*] be constantly or visibly worried or anxious. ■ [*tr.*] cause (someone) worry or distress. **2** [*tr.*] gradually wear away (something) by rubbing or gnawing: *black waves fret the seawall.* ■ form (a channel or passage) by rubbing or wearing away. ■ [*intr.*] flow or move in small waves: *soft clay fretted between his toes.*

fret[2] ▶*n. Art & Archit.* a repeating ornamental design of interlaced vertical and horizontal lines, such as the Greek key pattern.
▶*v.* (**fret·ted, fret·ting**) [*tr.*] [usu. as *adj.*] (**fretted**) decorate with fretwork.

fret[3] ▶*n.* each of a sequence of bars or ridges on the fingerboard of some stringed musical instruments (such as the guitar), used for fixing the positions of the fingers to produce the desired notes.
▶*v.* (**fret·ted, fret·ting**) [*tr.*] [often as *adj.*] (**fretted**) **1** provide (a stringed instrument) with frets. **2** play (a note) while pressing the string down against a fret: *fretted notes.* —**fret·less** *adj.*

frets

fret·ful /ˈfretfəl/ ▶*adj.* feeling or expressing distress or irritation: *the baby was crying with a fretful whimper.* —**fret·ful·ly** *adv.* —**fret·ful·ness** *n.*

fret·saw /ˈfretˌsô/ ▶*n.* a saw with a narrow blade stretched vertically on a frame, for cutting thin wood in patterns.

fret·work /ˈfretˌwərk/ ▶*n.* ornamental design in wood, typically openwork, done with a fretsaw.

Freud·i·an /ˈfroidēən/ *Psychol.* ▶*adj.* relating to or influenced by Sigmund Freud and his methods of psychoanalysis, esp. with reference to the importance of sexuality in human behavior. ■ susceptible to analysis in terms of unconscious desires: *deep Freudian significance.* ▶*n.* a follower of Freud or his methods. —**Freud·i·an·ism** *n.*

Freud·i·an slip ▶*n.* an unintentional error regarded as revealing subconscious feelings.

Fri. ▶*abbr.* Friday.

fri·a·ble /ˈfrīəbəl/ ▶*adj.* easily crumbled: *the soil was friable between her fingers.* —**fri·a·bil·i·ty** /ˌfrīəˈbilətē/ *n.* —**fri·a·ble·ness** *n.*

fri·ar /ˈfrīər/ ▶*n.* a member of any of certain religious orders of men, esp. the four mendicant orders (Augustinians, Carmelites, Dominicans, and Franciscans).

fric·as·see /ˌfrikəˈsē/ ▶*n.* a dish of stewed or fried pieces of meat served in a thick white sauce.

fric·a·tive /ˈfrikətiv/ *Phonet.* ▶*adj.* denoting a consonant made by the friction of breath in a narrow opening, producing a turbulent air flow. ▶*n.* a consonant made in this way, e.g., *f* and *th.*

fric·tion /ˈfrikSHən/ ▶*n.* the resistance that one surface or object encounters when moving over another. ■ the action of one surface or object rubbing against another. ■ conflict or animosity caused by a clash of wills, temperaments, or opinions: *friction between father and son.* —**fric·tion·al** /-SHənl/ *adj.*

Fri·day /ˈfrīdā; -dē/ ▶*n.* the day of the week before Saturday and following Thursday. ▶*adv.* on Friday. ■ (**Fridays**) on Fridays; each Friday: *he goes there Fridays.*

fridge /frij/ ▶*n. inf.* a refrigerator.

friend /frend/ ▶*n.* a person whom one knows and with whom one has a bond of mutual affection, typically exclusive of sexual or family relations. ■ a person who acts as a supporter of a cause, organization, or country by giving financial or other help. ■ a person who is not an enemy or who is on the same side: *unsure whether he was friend or foe.* ■ a familiar or helpful thing. ■ (often as a polite form of address or in ironic reference) an acquaintance or a stranger one comes across: *my friends, let me introduce myself.* ■ (**Friend**) a member of the Religious Society of Friends; a Quaker. ▷Old English *frēond*, of Germanic origin; related to Dutch *vriend* and German *Freund*, from an Indo-European root meaning 'to love.' —**friend·less** *adj.* ▶ □ **be** (or **make**) **friends with** be (or become) on good or affectionate terms with (someone).

friend·ly /ˈfrendlē/ ▶*adj.* (**-li·er, -li·est**) kind and pleasant. ■ (of a person) on good or affectionate terms: *I was friendly with one of the local farmers.* ■ (of a contest) not seriously or unpleasantly competitive or divisive. ■ [in *comb.*] denoting something that is adapted for or is not harmful to a specified thing: *environment-friendly.* ■ favorable or serviceable. ■ *Mil.* (of troops or equipment) of, belonging to, or in alliance with one's own forces. ▶*adv.* (also **friend·li·ly** /-əlē/) in a friendly manner. —**friend·li·ness** *n.*

friend·ly fire ▶*n. Mil.* weapon fire coming from one's own side, esp. fire that causes accidental injury or death to one's own forces.

friend·ship /ˈfrendˌSHip/ ▶*n.* the emotions or conduct of friends; the state of being friends. ■ a relationship between friends. ■ a state of mutual trust and support between allied nations.

fri·er ▶*n.* variant spelling of FRYER.

frieze[1] /frēz/ ▶*n.* a broad horizontal band of sculpted or painted decoration, esp. on a wall near the ceiling. ■ a horizontal paper strip mounted on a wall to give a similar effect. ■ *Archit.* the part of an entablature between the architrave and the cornice.

frieze[2] ▶*n.* heavy, coarse woolen cloth with a nap, usu. on one side.

frig /frig/ *vulgar slang* ▶*v.* (**frigged, frig·ging**) [*tr.*] used as a euphemism for 'fuck.' ■ masturbate. ▶*interj.* expressing extreme anger, annoyance, or contempt.

frig·ate /ˈfrigit/ ▶*n.* a warship with a mixed armament, generally heavier than a destroyer. ■ *hist.* a sailing warship.

frig·ate bird ▶*n.* a predatory tropical seabird (genus *Fregata*, family Fregatidae) with dark plumage, long narrow wings, a deeply forked tail, and a long hooked bill.

fright /frīt/ ▶*n.* **1** a sudden intense feeling of fear. ■ an experience that causes one to feel sudden intense fear. **2** a person or thing looking grotesque or ridiculous. ▶*v.* [*tr.*] *archaic* frighten: *come, be comforted, he shan't fright you.* ▶ □ **take fright** suddenly become frightened or panicked.

fright·en /ˈfrītn/ ▶*v.* [*tr.*] make (someone) afraid or anxious. ■ (**frighten someone/something off**) deter someone or something from involvement or action by making them afraid. ■ [*intr.*] (of a person) become afraid or anxious: *at his age, he doesn't frighten any more.* —**fright·en·ing·ly** *adv.*

fright·ful /ˈfrītfəl/ ▶*adj.* very unpleasant, serious, or shocking: *a frightful accident.* ■ *inf.* used for emphasis, esp. of something bad: *a frightful mess.* —**fright·ful·ly** *adv.* —**fright·ful·ness** *n.*

frig·id /ˈfrijid/ ▶*adj.* very cold in temperature: *frigid water.* ■ (esp. of a woman) unable or unwilling to be sexually aroused and responsive. ■ showing no friendliness or enthusiasm; stiff or formal in behavior or style: *a frigid calm.* —**fri·gid·i·ty** /frəˈjidətē/ *n.* —**frig·id·ly** *adv.* —**frig·id·ness** *n.*

fri·jo·les /frēˈhōlēz/ ▶*pl. n.* (in Mexican cooking) beans.

frill /fril/ ▶*n.* a strip of gathered or pleated material sewn by one side onto a garment or larger piece of material as a decorative edging or ornament. ■ a thing resembling such a strip in appearance or function. ■ a natural fringe of feathers or hair on a bird or other animal. ■ (usu. **frills**) *fig.* an unnecessary extra feature or embellishment: *a comfortable apartment with no frills.* —**frilled** *adj.* —**frill·er·y** /ˈfrilərē/ *n.* —**frill·y** *adj.*

frilled liz·ard (also **frill-necked lizard**) ▶*n.* a large Australian lizard (*Chlamydosaurus kingii*, family Agamidae) with a neck membrane that forms an erect ruff for defensive display.

fringe /frinj/ ▶*n.* **1** an ornamental border or edge of threads left loose or formed into tassels or twists. **2** chiefly British term for BANGS (see BANG sense 2). ■ a natural border of hair or fibers in an animal or plant. **3** (often **the fringes**) the outer, marginal, or extreme part of an area, group, or sphere of activity: *on the fringes of crooked activity.* ■ (**the fringe**) the unconventional, extreme, or marginal wing of a group or sphere of activity: *rap music is no longer on the fringe.* **4** short for FRINGE BENEFIT. ▶*adj.* not part of the mainstream; unconventional, peripheral, or extreme: *fringe theater.* ▶*v.* [*tr.*] decorate (clothing or material) with a fringe. ■ (often **be fringed**) form a border around (something): *the sea is fringed by palm trees.* ■ [as *adj.*] (**fringed**) (of a plant or animal) having a natural border of hair or fiber. —**fring·y** /ˈfrinjē/ *adj.*

fringe ben·e·fit ▶*n.* an extra benefit supplementing an employee's salary, for example, a company car, health insurance, etc.

frip·per·y /ˈfripərē/ ▶*n.* (*pl.* **-per·ies**) showy or unnecessary ornament in architecture, dress, or language. ■ a tawdry or frivolous thing.

Fris·bee /ˈfrizbē/ (also **fris·bee**) ▶*n. trademark* a concave plastic disk designed for skimming through the air as an outdoor game or amusement. ■ the game or amusement of skimming such a disk.

frisk /frisk/ ▶*v.* **1** [*tr.*] (of a police officer or other official) pass the hands over (someone) in a search for hidden weapons, drugs, or other items. **2** [*intr.*] (of an animal or person) skip or leap playfully; frolic. ■ [*tr.*] (of an animal) move or wave (its tail or legs) playfully: *frisking his back legs like a colt.* ▶*n.* **1** an act of frisking someone. **2** a playful skip or leap.

frisk·y /ˈfriskē/ ▶*adj.* (**frisk·i·er, frisk·i·est**) playful and full of energy: *he bounds about like a frisky pup.* —**frisk·i·ly** /ˈfriskəlē/ *adv.* —**frisk·i·ness** *n.*

frit·il·lar·y /ˈfritlˌerē/ ▶*n.* **1** a Eurasian plant (genus *Fritillaria*) of the lily family, with hanging bell-like flowers. **2** a butterfly (*Argynnis, Speyeria,* and other genera, family Nymphalidae) with orange-brown wings that are checkered with black.

frit·ter[1] /ˈfritər/ ▶*v.* [*tr.*] **1** (**fritter something away**) waste time, money, or energy on trifling matters. ■ [*intr.*] dwindle; diminish. **2** *archaic* divide (something) into small pieces. —**frit·ter·er** *n.*

frit·ter[2] ▶*n.* a piece of fruit, vegetable, or meat that is coated in batter and deep-fried.

fritz /frits/ ▶*n.* (in phrase **go** or **be on the fritz**) *inf.* (of a machine) stop working properly.

friv·o·lous /ˈfrivələs/ ▶*adj.* not having any serious purpose or value: *rules to stop frivolous lawsuits.* ■ (of a person) carefree and not serious. —**fri·vol·i·ty** /friˈvälətē/ *n.* —**friv·o·lous·ly** *adv.* —**friv·o·lous·ness** *n.*

frizz /friz/ ▶*v.* [*tr.*] form (hair) into a mass of small, tight curls or tufts.

Pronunciation Key ə *ago,* u*p;* ər *over, fur;* a *hat;* ā *ate;* ä *car;* CH *chin;* e *let;* ē *see;* e(ə)r *air;* i *fit;* ī *by;* i(ə)r *ear;* NG *sing;* ō *go;* ô *law, for;* oi *toy;* ŏŏ *good;* ōō *goo;* ou *out;* SH *she;* TH *thin;* T͟H *then;* (h)w *why;* ZH *vision*

F

■ [*intr.*] (of hair) form itself into such a mass.
▶*n.* the state of being formed into such a mass of curls or tufts: *a perm designed to add curl without frizz.* —**frizz·y** *adj.*

friz·zle¹ /ˈfrizəl/ ▶*v.* [*intr.*] fry or grill with a sizzling noise. ■ [*tr.*] fry until crisp, shriveled, or burned: [as *adj.*] (**frizzled**) *add diced frizzled salt pork.*
▶*n.* the sound or act of frying: *the frizzle of the pan.*

friz·zle² ▶*v.* [*tr.*] form (hair) into tight curls.
▶*n.* a tight curl in hair. —**friz·zly** /ˈfriz(ə)lē/ *adj.*

fro /frō/ ▶*adv.* see TO AND FRO.

frock /fräk/ ▶*n.* **1** a woman's or girl's dress. **2** a loose outer garment, in particular: ■ a long gown with flowing sleeves worn by monks, priests, or clergy. ■ *hist.* a field laborer's smock.
▶*v.* [*tr.*] provide with or dress in a frock: [as *adj.*, in *comb.*] *a black-frocked Englishman.*

frog¹ /frôg; fräg/ ▶*n.* **1** a tailless amphibian with a short squat body, moist smooth skin, and very long hind legs for leaping. Frogs are found in most families of the order Anura, but the 'true frogs' are confined to the large family Ranidae. **2** (**Frog**) *derog.* a French person.
▶*v.* [*intr.*] hunt for or catch frogs.
▶ □ **have a frog in one's throat** *inf.* lose one's voice or find it hard to speak because of hoarseness.

frog² ▶*n.* a thing used to hold or fasten something, in particular: ■ an ornamental coat fastener or braid consisting of a spindle-shaped button and a loop through which it passes. ■ an attachment to a belt for holding a sword, bayonet, or similar weapon. ■ a perforated or spiked device for holding the stems of flowers in an arrangement. ■ the piece into which the hair is fitted at the lower end of the bow of a stringed instrument.

frog³ ▶*n.* an elastic horny pad growing in the sole of a horse's hoof, helping to absorb the shock when the hoof hits the ground. ■ a raised or swollen area on a surface.

frog·man /ˈfrôgˌman; ˈfräg-; -mən/ ▶*n.* (*pl.* **-men**) a person who swims underwater wearing a rubber suit, flippers, and an oxygen supply.

frog·march /ˈfrôgˌmärch; ˈfräg-/ ▶*v.* [*tr.*] force (someone) to walk forward while holding and pinning their arms from behind.

frol·ic /ˈfrälik/ ▶*v.* (**frol·icked, frol·ick·ing**) [*intr.*] (of an animal or person) play and move about cheerfully, excitedly, or energetically.
▶*n.* (often **frolics**) a playful action or movement: *his injuries were inflicted by the frolics of a young filly | the days of fun and frolic were gone for good.*
▶*adj.* *archaic* cheerful, merry, or playful. ▷early 16th cent. (as an adjective): from Dutch *vrolijk* 'merry, cheerful.' —**frol·ick·er** *n.*

frol·ic·some /ˈfräliksəm/ ▶*adj.* lively and playful. —**frol·ic·some·ly** *adv.* —**frol·ic·some·ness** *n.*

from /frəm/ ▶*prep.* **1** indicating the point in space at which a journey, motion, or action starts: *she walked away from him.* ■ indicating the distance between a particular place and another place used as a point of reference: ■ *the ambush occurred 50 yards from a checkpoint.* **2** indicating the point in time at which a particular process, event, or activity starts: *the show will run from 10 to 2.* **3** indicating the source or provenance of someone or something: *I'm from Hartford.* ■ indicating the date at which something was created: *dating from the thirteenth century.* **4** indicating the starting point of a specified range on a scale: *ranged in age from seventeen to eighty-four.* ■ indicating one extreme in a range of conceptual variations: *anything from geography to literature.* **5** indicating the point at which an observer is placed: *fig. the ability to see things from another's point of view.* **6** indicating the raw material out of which something is manufactured: *a dye made from coal tar.* **7** indicating separation or removal: *the party was ousted from power.* **8** indicating prevention: *saved from death.* **9** indicating a cause: *suffering from asthma.* **10** indicating a source of knowledge or the basis for one's judgment: *information obtained from papers, books, and presentations.* **11** indicating a distinction: *viewed in a different light from that of a manual worker.*
▶ □ **from now on** now and in the future: *they were friends from that day on.* □ **from time to time** occasionally.

frond /fränd/ ▶*n.* the leaf or leaflike part of a palm, fern, or similar plant: *fronds of bracken.* —**frond·ed** *adj.*

front /frənt/ ▶*n.* **1** the side or part of an object that presents itself to view or that is normally seen or used first; the most forward part of something. ■ the position directly ahead of someone or something; the most forward position or place: *turned to face the front.* ■ the forward-facing part of a person's body, on the opposite side to their back. ■ the part of a garment covering this: *his shirt front.* ■ any face of a building, esp. that of the main entrance: *the west front of the cathedral.* **2** the foremost line or part of an armed force; the furthest position that an army has reached and where the enemy is or may be engaged. ■ the direction toward which a line of troops faces when formed. ■ a

particular formation of troops for battle. ■ a particular situation or sphere of operation: *good news on the job front.* ■ *Meteorol.* the forward edge of an advancing mass of air. See COLD FRONT. **3** an appearance or form of behavior assumed by a person to conceal genuine feelings: *she put on a brave front.* ■ a person or organization serving as a cover for subversive or illegal activities: *a front for a terrorist group.* ■ a well-known or prestigious person who acts as a representative, rather than an active member, of an organization. See also FRONTMAN. **4** *archaic* a person's face or forehead.
▶*adj.* **1** of or at the front: *the front yard.* **2** *Phonet.* (of a vowel sound) formed by raising the body of the tongue, excluding the blade and tip, toward the hard palate.
▶*v.* [*tr.*] **1** (of a building or piece of land) have the front facing or directed toward: *the houses that front Beacon Street | [intr.] we sold the land that fronted on the road.* ■ be or stand in front of: *the hedge fronting the garden.* **2** (usu. **be fronted**) provide (something) with a front or facing of a particular type or material: [as *adj.*, in *comb.*] (**-fronted**) *a glass-fronted bookcase.* **3** lead or be the most prominent member in (an organization, activity, or group of musicians). ■ present or host (a television or radio program). ■ [*intr.*] act as a front or cover for someone or something acting illegally or wishing to conceal something: *he fronted for them in illegal property deals.* —**fron·ting** *n.* —**front·ward** /-wərd/ *adj.* & *adv.* —**front·wards** *adv.*
▶ □ **in front 1** in a position just ahead of or further forward than someone or something else: *the car in front stopped suddenly.* ■ in the lead in a game or contest. **2** on the part or side that normally first presents itself to view: *a house with a wide porch in front.* ■ **in front of 1** in a position just ahead or at the front part of someone or something else. ■ in a position facing someone or something: *she sat in front of the mirror.* **2** in the presence of: *in front of the class.* □ **out front** at or to the front; in front: *two cars stopped out front.* □ **up front 1** at or near the front: *an open living area up front.* **2** in advance: *every fee must be paid up front.* **3** open and direct; frank: *I vowed to be up front with her.*

front·age /ˈfrəntij/ ▶*n.* the facade of a building. ■ the direction this faces: *beautiful homes with river frontage.* ■ a strip or extent of land abutting on a street or water: *our lot has a frontage of 153 feet.*

front·age road ▶*n.* a subsidiary road running parallel to a main road or highway and giving access to houses and businesses. Also called SERVICE ROAD.

fron·tal /ˈfrəntl/ ▶*adj.* of or at the front. ■ (of an attack) delivered directly on the front, not the side or back. ■ of or relating to the forehead or front part of the skull: *the frontal sinuses.* —**fron·tal·ly** *adv.*

front and center ▶*adv.* prominently; at the forefront: *standing front and center here today are our bravest heroes.*
▶*adj.* prominent; of the greatest importance: *why is this matter suddenly front and center? | my front-and-center concerns.*

front court ▶*n.* the part of a basketball court where each team tries to score against its opponent. ■ the players on a team who usually play closest to the other team's basket when trying to score.

fron·tier /ˌfrənˈti(ə)r/ ▶*n.* a line or border separating two countries. ■ the district near such a line. ■ the extreme limit of settled land beyond which lies wilderness, esp. referring to the western U.S. before Pacific settlement. ■ the extreme limit of understanding or achievement in a particular area: *extending the frontiers of knowledge.* —**fron·tier·less** *adj.*

fron·tiers·man /ˌfrənˈti(ə)rzmən/ ▶*n.* (*pl.* **-men**) a person, esp. a man, living in the region of a frontier, esp. that between settled and unsettled country.

fron·tis·piece /ˈfrəntisˌpēs/ ▶*n.* **1** an illustration facing the title page of a book. **2** *Archit.* the principal face of a building. ■ a decorated entrance. ■ a pediment over a door or window.

front line (also **front·line**) ▶*n.* (usu. **the front line**) the military line or part of an army that is closest to the enemy. ■ the most important or influential position in a debate or movement.

front·man /ˈfrəntˌman; -mən/ ▶*n.* (*pl.* **-men**) a person who leads or represents a group or organization, in particular: ■ the leader of a group of musicians, esp. the lead singer of a pop group. ■ (also **front**) a person who represents an illegal or disreputable organization to give it an air of legitimacy.

front of·fice ▶*n.* the management or administrative officers of a business or other organization.

fron·ton /ˈfränˌtän/ ▶*n.* a building where pelota or jai alai is played.

front run·ner ▶*n.* the contestant that is leading in a race or other competition. ■ an athlete or horse that runs best when in the front of the field.

front-wheel drive ▶*n.* a transmission system that provides power to the front wheels of a motor vehicle.

frost /frôst/ ▶ n. a deposit of small white ice crystals formed on the ground or other surfaces when the temperature falls below freezing. ■ a period of cold weather when such deposits form. ■ fig. a chilling or dispiriting quality, esp. one conveyed by a cold manner: *a frost of anger in Jack's tone.* ■ inf., chiefly Brit. a failure.
▶ v. [tr.] cover (something) with or as if with small ice crystals; freeze: *each windowpane was frosted along its edges.* ■ [intr.] become covered with small ice crystals. ■ decorate (a cake, cupcake, or other baked item) with icing. ■ tint hair strands to change the color of isolated strands. ■ injure (a plant) by freezing weather. ■ inf. anger or annoy.

frost·bite /'frôs(t),bīt/ ▶ n. injury to body tissues caused by exposure to extreme cold, typically affecting the nose, fingers, or toes and sometimes resulting in gangrene.

frost heave ▶ n. the uplift of water-saturated soil or other surface deposits due to expansion on freezing. ■ a mound formed in this way, esp. when broken through the pavement of a road. —**frost heav·ing** n.

frost·ing /'frôstiNG/ ▶ n. icing.

frost·y /'frôstē/ ▶ adj. (**frost·i·er, frost·i·est**) **1** (of the weather) very cold with frost forming on surfaces: *a cold and frosty morning.* ■ covered with or as if with frost. **2** cold and unfriendly in manner: *a frosty look.* —**frost·i·ly** /'frôstəlē/ adv. —**frost·i·ness** n.

froth /frôTH/ ▶ n. a mass of small bubbles in liquid caused by agitation, fermentation, etc.; foam. ■ impure matter that rises to the surface of liquid. ■ fig. a thing that rises or overflows in a soft, light mass: *a froth of black lace.* ■ worthless or insubstantial talk, ideas, or activities: *the froth of party politics.*
▶ v. [intr.] form or contain a rising or overflowing mass of small bubbles: *beer frothed out of the can.* ■ fig. rise or overflow in a soft, light mass. ■ [tr.] agitate (a liquid) so as to produce a mass of small bubbles. —**froth·i·ly** /-THəlē; THəlē/ adv. —**froth·i·ness** /-THənis; THēnis/ n. —**froth·y** adj.
▶ □ **froth at the mouth** emit a large amount of saliva from the mouth in a bodily seizure. ■ fig. display intense anger.

frou·frou /'froō,froō/ (also **frou-frou**) ▶ n. a rustling noise made by someone walking in a dress. ■ frills or other ornamentation, particularly of women's clothes: [as adj.] *a little froufrou skirt.*

fro·ward /'frō(w)ərd/ ▶ adj. (of a person) difficult to deal with; contrary. —**fro·ward·ly** adv. —**fro·ward·ness** n.

frown /froun/ ▶ v. [intr.] furrow one's brow in an expression of disapproval, displeasure, or concentration. ■ (**frown on/upon**) disapprove of: *frowned on private enterprise.*
▶ n. a facial expression or look characterized by such a furrowing of one's brows: *a frown of disapproval.* ▷late Middle English: from Old French *froignier*, from *froigne* 'surly look,' of Celtic origin.

frowz·y /'frouzē/ (also **frows·y**) ▶ adj. (**frowz·i·er, frowz·i·est**) scruffy and neglected in appearance. ■ dingy and stuffy. —**frowz·i·ness** n.

froze /frōz/ ▶ past of FREEZE.

fro·zen /'frōzən/ ▶ past participle of FREEZE.
▶ adj. Billiards (of a ball) resting against another ball or a cushion.

fruc·tose /'frək,tōs; 'frŏŏk-; -,tōz/ ▶ n. Chem. a simple sugar found esp. in honey and fruit.

fru·gal /'frŏŏgəl/ ▶ adj. sparing or economical with regard to money or food: *a frugal existence.* ■ simple and plain and costing little: *a frugal meal.* —**fru·gal·i·ty** /frŏŏ'galətē/ n. —**fru·gal·ly** adv. —**fru·gal·ness** n.

fruit /froōt/ ▶ n. **1** the sweet and fleshy product of a tree or other plant that contains seed and can be eaten as food. ■ Bot. the seed-bearing structure of a plant, e.g., an acorn. ■ the result or reward of work or activity: *the fruits of their labors.* ■ archaic or poetic/lit. natural produce that can be used for food: *the fruits of the earth.* ■ archaic offspring: *the fruit of her womb.* **2** inf., offens. a male homosexual.
▶ v. [intr.] (of a tree or other plant) produce fruit, typically at a specified time. —**fruit·ed** adj.
▶ □ **bear fruit** have good results. □ **in fruit** (of a tree or plant) at the stage of producing fruit.

fruit bat ▶ n. a bat (family Pteropodidae) with a long snout and large eyes, feeding chiefly on fruit or nectar and found mainly in the Old World tropics.

fruit·cake /'froōt,kāk/ ▶ n. a cake containing dried fruit and nuts. ■ inf. an eccentric or insane person.

fruit fly ▶ n. a small fly (families Drosophilidae and Tephritidae) that feeds on fruit in both its adult and larval stages.

fruit·ful /'froōtfəl/ ▶ adj. (of a tree, a plant, or land) producing much fruit; fertile. ■ producing good or helpful results; productive. ■ (of a person) producing many offspring. —**fruit·ful·ly** adv. —**fruit·ful·ness** n.

fru·i·tion /froō'ishən/ ▶ n. the point at which a plan or project is realized: *the plans have come to fruition.* ■ the realization of a plan or project.

fruit·less /'froōtləs/ ▶ adj. **1** failing to achieve the desired results; unproductive or useless: *his fruitless attempts to publish poetry.* **2** (of a tree or plant) not producing fruit. —**fruit·less·ly** adv. —**fruit·less·ness** n.

fruit·y /'froōtē/ ▶ adj. (**fruit·i·er, fruit·i·est**) **1** (esp. of food or drink) of, resembling, or containing fruit. **2** (of a voice or sound) mellow, deep, and rich. **3** inf., offens. relating to or associated with homosexuals. **4** inf. eccentric or crazy. —**fruit·i·ly** /'froōtl-ē/ adv. —**fruit·i·ness** n.

frump /frəmp/ ▶ n. an unattractive woman who wears dowdy old-fashioned clothes. —**frump·i·ly** /'frəmpəlē/ adv. —**frump·i·ness** n. —**frump·ish** adj. —**frump·ish·ly** adv. —**frump·y** adj.

frus·trate /'frəs,trāt/ ▶ v. [tr.] prevent (a plan or attempted action) from progressing, succeeding, or being fulfilled. ■ prevent (someone) from doing or achieving something: *an increasingly popular way to frustrate car thieves.* ■ cause (someone) to feel upset or annoyed, typically as a result of being unable to change or achieve something: [as adj.] (**frustrating**) *it can be very frustrating to find that the size you want isn't there.* —**frus·trat·ing·ly** adv. —**frus·tra·tion** /frəs'trāshən/ n.

fry¹ /frī/ ▶ v. (**fries, fried**) [tr.] cook (food) in hot fat or oil, typically in a shallow pan. ■ [intr.] (of food) be cooked in such a way. ■ [intr.] inf. (of a person) burn or overheat. ■ inf. execute or be executed by electrocution.
▶ n. (pl. **fries**) a meal of meat or other food cooked in such a way. ■ a social gathering where fried food is served: *we'll explore islands and stop for a fish fry.* ■ (**fries**) another term for FRENCH FRIES.

fry² ▶ pl. n. young fish, esp. when newly hatched. ■ the young of other animals produced in large numbers, such as frogs.

fry·er /'frīər/ (also **fri·er**) ▶ n. **1** a large, deep container for frying food. **2** a small young chicken suitable for frying.

fry·ing pan (also **fry·pan**) ▶ n. a shallow pan with a long handle, used for cooking food in hot fat or oil.

FSH ▶ abbr. follicle-stimulating hormone.

FSLIC ▶ Federal Savings and Loan Insurance Corporation.

f-stop ▶ n. Photog. a camera setting corresponding to a particular f-number.

FT ▶ abbr. ■ Basketball free throw. ■ full-time.

Ft. ▶ abbr. Fort: *Ft. Lauderdale.*

ft. ▶ abbr. foot; feet.

FTC ▶ abbr. Federal Trade Commission.

FTP Comput. ▶ abbr. file transfer protocol, a standard for the exchange of program and data files across a network.
▶ v. (**FTP'd** or **FTPed, FTPing**) [trans.] informal transfer (a file) from one computer or system to another, esp. over the Internet.

fu·bar /'foō,bär/ ▶ adj. out of working order; seriously, perhaps irreparably, damaged: *the clock in the hall is fubar.*

fuch·sia /'fyoōshə/ ▶ n. **1** a shrub (genus *Fuchsia*, family Onagraceae) with pendulous tubular flowers that are typically of two contrasting colors. **2** a vivid purplish-red color.
▶ adj. purplish red.

fuck /fək/ vulgar slang ▶ v. [tr.] **1** have sexual intercourse with (someone). ■ [intr.] (of two people) have sexual intercourse. **2** ruin or damage (something).
▶ phrasal v. **fuck around** spend time doing unimportant or trivial things. ■ have sexual intercourse with a variety of partners. ■ (**fuck around with**) meddle with. □ **fuck someone over** treat someone in an unfair or humiliating way. □ **fuck someone up** damage or confuse someone emotionally. □ **fuck something up** (or **fuck up**) do something badly or ineptly.
▶ n. an act of sexual intercourse. ■ a sexual partner.

fuck-up ▶ n. vulgar slang a mess or muddle. ■ a person who has a tendency to make a mess of things.

fud·dle /'fədl/ ▶ v. [tr.] (usu. as adj.) (**fuddled**) confuse or stupefy (someone), esp. with alcohol. ■ [intr.] archaic go on a drinking bout.
▶ n. a state of confusion or intoxication.

fud·dy-dud·dy /'fədē ,dədē/ ▶ n. (pl. **-dies**) inf. a person who is old-fashioned and fussy: *he probably thinks I'm an old fuddy-duddy.*

fudge /fəj/ ▶ n. **1** a soft candy made from sugar, butter, and milk or cream. ■ rich chocolate, used esp. as a filling for cakes or a sauce on ice cream: [as adj.] *a fudge cake.* **2** an instance of faking or ambiguity. ■ archaic nonsense.

Pronunciation Key ə *ago, up;* ər *over, fur;* a *hat;* ā *ate;* ä *car;* CH *chin;* e *let;* ē *see;* e(ə)r *air;* i *fit;* ī *by;* i(ə)r *ear;* NG *sing;* ō *go;* ô *law, for;* oi *toy;* ŏŏ *good;* ōŏ *goo;* ou *out;* SH *she;* TH *thin;* TH *then;* (h)w *why;* ZH *vision*

▶ *v.* [*tr.*] present or deal with (something) in a vague, noncommittal, or inadequate way, esp. so as to conceal the truth or mislead: *a temptation to fudge the issue.* ■ adjust or manipulate (facts or figures) so as to present a desired picture.
▶ *interj. dated* nonsense (expressing disbelief or annoyance).

fueh·rer /ˈfyoŏrər/ ▶ *n.* variant spelling of FÜHRER.

fu·el /ˈfyoŏəl/ ▶ *n.* material such as coal, gas, oil or nuclear material that is used to produce heat or power. ■ food, drink, or drugs as a source of energy. ■ a thing that sustains or inflames passion, argument, or other emotion or activity: *add fuel to the debate.*
▶ *v.* (**fu·eled, fu·el·ing**; *Brit.* **fu·elled, fu·el·ling**) [*tr.*] **1** supply or power (an industrial plant, vehicle, or machine) with fuel: *fig. a big novel that is fueled by anger and revenge.* ■ fill up (a vehicle, aircraft, or ship) with oil or gasoline. ■ [*intr.*] (**fuel up**) (of a person) eat a meal. **2** cause (a fire) to burn more intensely. ■ sustain or inflame (a feeling or activity): *private pain fueled his passion as an actor.* ▷ Middle English: from Old French *fouaille*, based on Latin *focus* 'hearth' (in late Latin 'fire').

fu·el cell ▶ *n.* a cell producing an electric current directly from a chemical reaction.

fu·el in·jec·tion ▶ *n.* the direct introduction of fuel under pressure into the combustion units of an internal combustion engine. —**fu·el-in·ject·ed** *adj.*

fu·gi·tive /ˈfyoŏjətiv/ ▶ *n.* a person who has escaped from a place or is in hiding, esp. to avoid arrest or persecution: *fugitives from justice.* ■ [as *adj.*] *fig.* quick to disappear; fleeting.

fugue /fyoŏg/ ▶ *n.* **1** *Mus.* a contrapuntal composition in which a short melody or phrase is introduced by one part and successively taken up by others and developed by interweaving the parts. **2** *Psychiatry* a state or period of loss of awareness of one's identity, often coupled with flight from one's usual environment, associated with certain forms of hysteria and epilepsy. —**fugu·ist** /ˈfyoŏgist/ *n.*

füh·rer /ˈfyoŏrər/ (also **feuh·rer**) ▶ *n.* a ruthless, tyrannical leader.

ful·crum /ˈfoŏlkrəm; ˈfəl-/ ▶ *n.* (*pl.* **-cra** /-krə/ or **-crums**) the point on which a lever is supported and on which it pivots. ■ a thing that plays a central or essential role in an activity, event, or situation: *research is the fulcrum of the academic community.*

ful·fill /foŏlˈfil/ (*Brit.* **ful·fil**) ▶ *v.* **1** bring to completion or reality; achieve or realize (something desired, promised, or predicted). ■ (**fulfill oneself**) gain happiness or satisfaction by fully developing one's abilities or character. ■ *archaic* complete (a period of time or piece of work). **2** carry out (a task, duty, or role) as required, pledged, or expected: *they could not fulfill their duties.* ■ satisfy or meet (a requirement or condition). —**ful·fill·ment** *n.*

full¹ /foŏl/ ▶ *adj.* **1** containing or holding as much or as many as possible; having no empty space. ■ having eaten or drunk to one's limits or satisfaction. ■ (**full of**) containing or holding much or many; having a large number of: *his diary is full of entries about her.* ■ (**full of**) having a lot of (a particular quality): *she was full of confidence.* ■ (**full of**) completely engrossed with; unable to stop talking or thinking about: *full of her day.* ■ filled with intense emotion. ■ involving a lot of activities: *he lived a full life.* **2** not lacking or omitting anything; complete: *full details on request.* ■ (often used for emphasis) reaching the utmost limit; maximum: *turned it up to full power | John made full use of all the tuition provided.* ■ having all the privileges and status attached to a particular position: *applied for full membership in the European Community.* ■ (of a report or account) containing as much detail or information as possible. ■ used to emphasize an amount or quantity: *he kept his fast pace going for the full 14-mile distance.* **3** (of a person or part of their body) plump or rounded: *she had full lips | the fuller figure.* ■ (of the hair) having body. ■ (of a garment) made using much material arranged in folds or gathers: *a full skirt.* ■ (of a sound) strong and resonant. ■ (of a flavor or color) rich or intense.
▶ *adv.* **1** straight; directly: *looked full into his face.* **2** very: *he knew full well she was too polite to barge in.*
▶ □ **full of oneself** very self-satisfied and with an exaggerated sense of self-worth. □ **full out** as much or as far as possible; with maximum effort or power: *the car raced full out.* □ **full steam** (or **speed**) **ahead** used to indicate that one should proceed with as much speed or energy as possible. □ **full up** filled to capacity. ■ having eaten or drunk so much that one is replete. □ **in full** with nothing omitted. ■ to the full amount due: *paid in full.* ■ to the utmost; completely.

full² ▶ *v.* [*tr.*] (often as *n.*] (**fulling**) clean, shrink, and felt (cloth) by heat, pressure, and moisture. —**full·er** *n.*

full·back /ˈfoŏlˌbak/ ▶ *n.* **1** *Football* an offensive player in the backfield. ■ an offensive position in the backfield: *he played fullback against us last*

year. **2** (in a game such as soccer or field hockey) a player in a defensive position near the goal. ■ a defensive position near the goal.

full-blood·ed ▶ *adj.* **1** of unmixed race: *a full-blooded Cherokee.* ■ *fig.* genuine; pure: *his belief in full-blooded socialism.* **2** vigorous, enthusiastic, and without compromise: *a full-blooded argument.* —**full-blood·ed·ly** *adv.* —**full-blood·ed·ness** *n.*

full-blown ▶ *adj.* fully developed: *the onset of full-blown AIDS in persons infected with HIV.* ■ (of a flower) in full bloom.

full-bod·ied ▶ *adj.* rich and satisfying in flavor or sound.

full-court press ▶ *n. Basketball* a defensive tactic in which members of a team cover their opponents throughout the court and not just near their own basket. ■ *fig.* an instance of aggressive pressure.

full·er's earth ▶ *n.* a type of clay used in fulling cloth and as an adsorbent.

full-fledged ▶ *adj.* completely developed or established; of full status.

full-grown ▶ *adj.* having reached maturity.

full house ▶ *n.* **1** an audience, or a group of people attending a meeting, that fills the venue for the event to capacity. **2** a poker hand with three of a kind and a pair, beating a flush and losing to four of a kind.

full-length ▶ *adj.* of the standard length: *a full-length Disney cartoon.* ■ (of a garment or curtain) extending to, or almost to, the ground. ■ (of a mirror or portrait) showing the whole human figure.
▶ *adv.* (usu. **full length**) (of a person) with the body lying stretched out and flat: *Lucy flung herself full length on the floor.*

full moon ▶ *n.* the phase of the moon in which its whole disk is illuminated. ■ the time when this occurs: *it was several days after full moon.*

full·ness /ˈfoŏlnəs/ (also **ful·ness**) ▶ *n.* **1** the state of being filled to capacity. ■ the state of having eaten enough or more than enough and feeling full. ■ the state of being complete or whole: *the honesty and fullness of the information they provide.* **2** (of a person's body or part of it) the state of being filled out so as to produce a rounded shape. ■ richness or intensity of flavor, sound, or color: *the coffee is of a luxurious fullness.*

full-scale ▶ *adj.* of the same size as the thing represented. ■ unrestricted in size, extent, or intensity; complete and thorough: *a full-scale invasion.*

full-time ▶ *adj.* occupying or using the whole of someone's available working time, typically 40 hours in a week: *a full-time job.*
▶ *adv.* on a full-time basis: *both parents were employed full-time.*

ful·ly /ˈfoŏlē/ ▶ *adv.* **1** completely or entirely; to the furthest extent: *I fully understand the fears of the workers.* ■ without lacking or omitting anything: *this issue is discussed more fully in chapter seven | a fully equipped gymnasium.* **2** no less or fewer than (used to emphasize an amount): *fully 65 percent of all funerals are by cremation.*

ful·mi·nate /ˈfoŏlməˌnāt; ˈfəl-/ ▶ *v.* [*intr.*] express vehement protest: *all fulminated against the new curriculum.* ■ *poetic/lit.* explode violently or flash like lightning. —**ful·mi·na·tion** *n.*

ful·some /ˈfoŏlsəm/ ▶ *adj.* **1** complimentary or flattering to an excessive degree: *they are almost embarrassingly fulsome in their appreciation.* **2** of large size or quantity; generous or abundant: *a fulsome harvest.* —**ful·some·ly** *adv.* —**ful·some·ness** *n.*

fum·ble /ˈfəmbəl/ ▶ *v.* [*intr.*] use the hands clumsily while doing or handling something: *she fumbled with the lock.* ■ (of the hands) do or handle something clumsily. ■ (**fumble around/about**) move clumsily in various directions using the hands to find one's way: *Greg fumbled around in the closet and found his black jacket.* ■ [*tr.*] use the hands clumsily to move (something) as specified. ■ [*tr.*] *Football* drop or lose control of (the ball), sometimes causing a turnover: *he seldom fumbled a ball.* ■ [*tr.*] (in other ball games) fail to catch or field (the ball, a pass, a shot, etc.) cleanly. ■ express oneself or deal with something clumsily or nervously: *asked for explanations, Michael had fumbled for words.*
▶ *n.* an act of using the hands clumsily while doing or handling something. ■ *Football* an act of dropping or losing control of the ball, sometimes causing a turnover. ■ (in other ball games) an act of failing to catch or field the ball cleanly. ■ an act of managing or dealing with something clumsily: *we are not talking about subtle errors of judgment, but major fumbles.* —**fum·bler** *n.* —**fum·bling·ly** *adv.*

fume /fyoŏm/ ▶ *n.* (usu. **fumes**) gas, smoke, or vapor that smells strongly or is dangerous to inhale: *clouds of exhaust fumes spewed by cars.* ■ a pungent odor of a particular thing or substance: *he breathed fumes of wine.* ■ *poetic/lit.* a watery vapor, steam, or mist rising from the earth or sea.
▶ *v.* [*intr.*] **1** emit gas, smoke, or vapor: *fragments of lava hit the ground, fuming and sizzling.* ■ [*tr.*] [usu. as *adj.*] (**fumed**) expose (esp. wood) to ammonia fumes in order to produce dark tints: *fumed oak.* **2** feel, show, or

express great anger: *he is fuming over the interference in his work.* —**fum·ing·ly** *adv.* —**fum·y** *adj.*

fu·mi·gate /ˈfyo͞oməˌgāt/ ▸ *v.* [*tr.*] apply the fumes of certain chemicals to (an area) to disinfect it or to rid it of vermin. —**fu·mi·gant** /-gənt/ *n.* —**fu·mi·ga·tion** /ˌfyo͞oməˈgāsʜən/ *n.* —**fu·mi·ga·tor** /-ˌgātər/ *n.*

fun /fən/ ▸ *n.* enjoyment, amusement, or lighthearted pleasure. ■ a source of this: *people-watching is great fun.* ■ playful behavior or good humor: *she's full of fun.* ■ behavior or an activity that is intended purely for amusement: *harmless fun.* ■ (of a place or event) providing entertainment or leisure activities for children: *a movie-themed fun park.*
▸ *adj.* (**fun·ner fun·nest**) *inf.* amusing, entertaining, or enjoyable: *it was a fun evening.* ▷late 17th cent. (denoting a trick or hoax): from obsolete *fun* 'to cheat or hoax,' dialect variant of late Middle English *fon* 'make a fool of, be a fool,' related to *fon* 'a fool,' of unknown origin.
▸ □ **fun and games** amusing and enjoyable activities: *teaching isn't all fun and games.* □ **in fun** not intended seriously; as a joke: *his speech was all in fun.* □ **make fun of** (or **poke fun at**) tease, laugh at, or joke about (someone) in a mocking or unkind way.

func·tion /ˈfəNGKsʜən/ ▸ *n.* **1** an activity or purpose natural to or intended for a person or thing. ■ practical use or purpose in design: *building designs that prioritize style over function.* ■ a basic task of a computer, esp. one that corresponds to a single instruction from the user. **2** *Math.* a relationship or expression involving one or more variables: *the function (bx + c).* ■ a variable quantity regarded in relation to one or more other variables in terms of which it may be expressed or on which its value depends. **3** a thing dependent on another factor or factors: *class shame is a function of social power.* **4** a large or formal social event or ceremony: *he was obliged to attend party functions.*
▸ *v.* [*intr.*] work or operate in a proper or particular way: *functioning normally.* ■ (**function as**) fulfill the purpose or task of (a specified thing): *the museum intends to function as an educational and study center.*

func·tion·al /ˈfəNGKsʜənl/ ▸ *adj.* **1** of or having a special activity, purpose, or task; relating to the way in which something works or operates: *important functional differences between left and right brain.* ■ designed to be practical and useful, rather than attractive. ■ working or operating: *the museum will be fully functional from the opening of the festival.* ■ (of a disease) affecting the operation, rather than the structure, of an organ. ■ (of a mental illness) having no discernible organic cause: *functional psychosis.* **2** *Math.* of or relating to a variable quantity whose value depends on one or more other variables. —**func·tion·al·i·ty** /ˌfəNGKsʜəˈnalitē/ *n.* —**func·tion·al·ly** *adv.*

func·tion·al·ism /ˈfəNGKsʜənlˌizəm/ ▸ *n.* belief in or stress on the practical application of a thing, in particular: ■ (in the arts) the doctrine that the design of an object should be determined solely by its function, rather than by aesthetic considerations, and that anything practically designed will be inherently beautiful. ■ (in the social sciences) the theory that all aspects of a society serve a function and are necessary for the survival of that society. —**func·tion·al·ist** *n.* & *adj.*

func·tion·ar·y /ˈfəNGKsʜəˌnerē/ ▸ *n.* (*pl.* **-ar·ies**) a person who has to perform official functions or duties; an official.

fund /fənd/ ▸ *n.* a sum of money saved or made available for a particular purpose. ■ (**funds**) financial resources: *the misuse of public funds.* ■ a large stock or supply of something: *a vast fund of information.* ■ (**the funds**) *Brit.* the stock of the national debt (as a mode of investment). ■ an organization set up for the administration and management of a monetary fund.
▸ *v.* [*tr.*] provide with money for a particular purpose. [in *comb.*] *government-funded research.*

fun·da·men·tal /ˌfəndəˈmentl/ ▸ *adj.* forming a necessary base or core; of central importance: *fundamental human rights.* ■ affecting or relating to the essential nature of something or the crucial point about an issue: *the fundamental problem remains that of the housing shortage.* ■ so basic as to be hard to alter, resolve, or overcome: *a fundamental error.*
▸ *n.* (usu. **fundamentals**) a central or primary rule or principle on which something is based: *the fundamentals of microbiology.* —**fun·da·men·tal·ly** *adv.*

fun·da·men·tal·ism /ˌfəndəˈmentlˌizəm/ ▸ *n.* a form of Protestant Christianity that upholds belief in the strict and literal interpretation of the Bible, including its narratives, doctrines, prophecies, and moral laws. ■ strict maintenance of ancient or fundamental doctrines of any religion or ideology, notably Islam. —**fun·da·men·tal·ist** *n.* & *adj.*

fund-rais·er ▸ *n.* a person whose job or task is to seek financial support for a charity, institution, or other enterprise. ■ an event held to generate financial support for such an enterprise. —**fund-rais·ing** *n.*

fu·ner·al /ˈfyo͞on(ə)rəl/ ▸ *n.* the ceremonies honoring a dead person, typically involving burial or cremation.

fu·ner·al home (also **funeral parlor**) ▸ *n.* an establishment where the dead are prepared for burial or cremation.

fu·ner·ar·y /ˈfyo͞onəˌrerē/ ▸ *adj.* relating to a funeral or the commemoration of the dead: *funerary ceremonies.*

fu·ne·re·al /fyəˈni(ə)rēəl; fyo͞o-/ ▸ *adj.* having the mournful, somber character appropriate to a funeral: *funereal gloominess.* —**fu·ne·re·al·ly** *adv.*

fun·gi /ˈfən, jī; -, gī/ ▸ plural form of FUNGUS.

fun·gi·cide /ˈfənjəˌsīd; ˈfəNGGə-/ ▸ *n.* a chemical that destroys fungus. —**fun·gi·cid·al** /ˌfənjəˈsīdl; ˌfəNGGə-/ *adj.*

fun·goid /ˈfəNG, goid/ ▸ *adj.* of or caused by a fungus or fungi: *a fungoid disease.* ■ resembling a fungus in shape, texture, or speed of growth.

fun·gous /ˈfəNGGəs/ ▸ *adj.* resembling, caused by, or having the nature of a fungus.

fun·gus /ˈfəNGGəs/ ▸ *n.* (*pl.* **-gi** /-jī; -gī/ or **-gus·es**) any of a group of unicellular, multicellular, or syncytial spore-producing organisms feeding on organic matter, including molds, yeast, mushrooms, and toadstools. ■ fungal infection. ■ used to describe something that has appeared or grown rapidly and is considered unpleasant or unattractive. —**fun·gal** /ˈfəNGGəl/ *adj.* —**fun·gi·form** /ˈfənjəˌfôrm/ *adj.*

fu·nic·u·lar /fyo͞oˈnikyələr/ ▸ *adj.* (of a railroad, esp. one on a mountainside) operating by cable with ascending and descending cars counterbalanced.

funk[1] /fəNGk/ *inf.* ▸ *n.* (also **blue funk**) a state of depression: *I sat absorbed in my own blue funk.* ■ *chiefly Brit.* a state of fear or panic.

funk[2] ▸ *n.* **1** a style of popular dance music of U.S. black origin, based on elements of blues and soul and having a strong rhythm that typically accentuates the first beat in the bar. **2** *inf., dated* a strong musty smell of sweat or tobacco.
▸ *phrasal v.* □ **funk something up** give music elements of such a style.

funk·y[1] /ˈfəNGkē/ ▸ *adj.* (**funk·i·er, funk·i·est**) *inf.* **1** (of music) having or using a strong dance rhythm. ■ modern and stylish in an unconventional or striking way: *funky clothes.* **2** strongly musty. —**funk·i·ly** /ˈfəNGkəlē/ *adv.* —**funk·i·ness** *n.*

funk·y[2] ▸ *adj.* (**funk·i·er, funk·i·est**) *Brit., archaic* or *inf.* frightened, panicky, or cowardly.

fun·nel /ˈfənl/ ▸ *n.* a tube or pipe that is wide at the top and narrow at the bottom, used for guiding liquid or powder into a small opening. ■ a thing resembling such a tube or pipe in shape or function: *a funnel of light.* ■ a metal chimney on a ship or steam engine.
▸ *v.* (**-neled, -nel·ing**; *Brit.* **-nelled, -nel·ling**) guide or channel (something) through or as if through a funnel: *some $12.8 billion was funneled through the Marshall Plan.* ■ [*intr.*] move or be guided through or as if through a funnel: *the wind funneled down through the valley.* [*intr.*] assume the shape of a funnel by widening or narrowing at the end.

fun·ny /ˈfənē/ ▸ *adj.* (**-ni·er, -ni·est**) **1** causing laughter or amusement; humorous. ■ *inf.* used to emphasize that something is unpleasant or wrong and should be regarded seriously or avoided: *stealing other people's work isn't funny.* **2** difficult to explain or understand; strange: *I had a funny feeling you'd be around.* ■ unusual or odd; curious: *a funny little stammer.* ■ unusual in such a way as to arouse suspicion: *there was something funny going on.* ■ used to draw attention to or express surprise at a curious or interesting fact or occurrence: *that's funny!—that vase of flowers has been moved.* ■ *inf.* (of a person or part of the body) not in wholly good health or order; slightly ill: *my stomach felt funny.*
▸ *n.* (*pl.* **-nies**) (**funnies**) *inf.* ■ the comic strips in newspapers. —**fun·ni·ly** /ˈfənl-ē/ *adv.* —**fun·ni·ness** /ˈfənēnis/ *n.*

fun·ny bone ▸ *n. inf.* the part of the elbow over which the ulnar nerve passes. A knock on the funny bone may cause a tingle, numbness, and pain along the forearm and hand. ■ a person's sense of humor, as located in an imaginary physical organ.

fun·ny busi·ness ▸ *n.* deceptive, disobedient, or lecherous behavior.

fun·ny farm ▸ *n. inf., offens.* a psychiatric hospital.

fun·ny mon·ey ▸ *n. inf.* currency that is forged or otherwise worthless.

fur /fər/ ▸ *n.* **1** the short, fine, soft hair of certain animals. ■ the skin of an animal with such hair on it. ■ skins of this type, or fabrics resembling these, used as material for making, trimming, or lining clothes: [as *adj.*] *a fur coat.* ■ a garment made of, trimmed, or lined with fur. **2** *Brit.* a coating formed by hard water on the inside surface of a pipe, kettle, or other container. ■ a coating formed on the tongue as a symptom of sickness.
▸ *v.* (**furred, fur·ring**) [*tr.*] **1** [as *adj.*, often in *comb.*] (**furred**) covered with

---

Pronunciation Key ə *ago,* up; ər *over,* fur; a *hat;* ā *ate;* ä *car;* cʜ *chin;* e *let;* ē *see;* e(ə)r *air;* i *fit;* ī *by;* i(ə)r *ear;* NG *sing;* ō *go;* ô *law, for;* oi *toy;* o͝o *good;* o͞o *goo;* ou *out;* sʜ *she;* ᴛʜ *thin;* <u>ᴛʜ</u> *then;* (h)w *why;* zʜ *vision*

or made from a particular type of fur: *silky-furred lemurs.* **2** fix strips of wood to (floor joists, wall studs, etc.) in order to level them or increase their depth.

▶ □ **make the fur fly** *inf.* cause serious, perhaps violent, trouble.

fur·be·low /ˈfərbəˌlō/ ▶ *n.* a gathered strip or pleated border of a skirt or petticoat. ■ (**furbelows**) showy ornaments or trimmings: *frills and furbelows.*

▶ *v.* [*tr.*] [usu. as *adj.*] (**furbelowed**) *poetic/lit.* adorn with trimmings.

fur·bish /ˈfərbiSH/ ▶ *v.* [*tr.*] [usu. as *adj.*] (**furbished**) give a fresh look to (something old or shabby); renovate: *the newly furbished church.* ■ *archaic* brighten up (esp. a weapon) by polishing it. **—fur·bish·er** *n.*

fur·cate *technical* ▶ *v.* /ˈfərˌkāt; fərˈkāt/ [*intr.*] divide into two or more branches; fork: *lines of descent furcating from a common source.*

▶ *adj.* /ˈfər,kāt; -kit/ divided into two or more branches; forked. **—fur·ca·tion** /fərˈkāSHən/ *n.*

fu·ri·ous /ˈfyoŏrēəs/ ▶ *adj.* extremely angry: *she was furious at this attempt to manipulate her.* ■ full of anger or energy; violent or intense: *he drove at a furious speed.* **—fu·ri·ous·ly** *adv.* **—fu·ri·ous·ness** *n.*

furl /fərl/ ▶ *v.* [*tr.*] roll or fold up and secure neatly (a flag, sail, umbrella, or other piece of fabric): [as *adj.*] (**furled**) *a tightly furled umbrella.* ■ [*intr.*] *poetic/lit.* become rolled up; curl: [as *adj.*] (**furled**) *furled leaves.* **—furl·a·ble** *adj.*

fur·long /ˈfər,lôNG; -,läNG/ ▶ *n.* an eighth of a mile, 220 yards.

fur·lough /ˈfərlō/ ▶ *n.* leave of absence, esp. that granted to a member of the armed services. ■ a temporary release of a convict from prison: *weekend furloughs.* ■ a layoff, esp. a temporary one, from a place of employment.

▶ *v.* [*tr.*] grant such leave of absence to. ■ lay off (workers), esp. temporarily.

fur·nace /ˈfərnəs/ ▶ *n.* an enclosed structure in which material can be heated to very high temperatures, e.g., for smelting metals. ■ an appliance fired by gas, oil, or wood in which air or water is heated to be circulated throughout a building in a heating system. ■ used to describe a very hot place: *her car was a furnace.*

fur·nish /ˈfərniSH/ ▶ *v.* [*tr.*] provide (a house or room) with furniture and fittings. ■ (**furnish someone with**) supply someone with (something); give (something) to someone: *she was able to furnish me with details.* ■ be a source of; provide: *fish furnish protein.*

fur·nished /ˈfərniSHt/ ▶ *adj.* (of accommodations) available to be rented with furniture.

fur·nish·ing /ˈfərniSHiNG/ ▶ *n.* **1** (usu. **furnishings**) furniture, fittings, and other decorative accessories, such as curtains and carpets, for a house or room. **2** the action of decorating a house or room and providing it with furniture and fittings.

fur·ni·ture /ˈfərniCHər/ ▶ *n.* **1** large movable equipment, such as tables and chairs, used to make a house, office, or other space suitable for living or working. ■ *fig.* a person's habitual attitude, outlook, and way of thinking: *the mental furniture of the European.* **2** small accessories or fittings for a particular use or piece of equipment.

▶ □ **part of the furniture** *inf.* a person or thing that has been somewhere so long as to seem a permanent, unquestioned, or invisible feature.

fu·ror /ˈfyoŏr,ôr; -ər/ ▶ *n.* an outbreak of public anger or excitement: *the article raised a furor among mathematicians.* ■ *archaic* a wave of enthusiastic admiration; a craze.

fur·ri·er /ˈfərēər/ ▶ *n.* a person who prepares or deals in furs.

fur·row /ˈfərō; ˈfə-rō/ ▶ *n.* a long narrow trench made in the ground by a plow, esp. for planting seeds or for irrigation. ■ a rut, groove, or trail in the ground or another surface. ■ a line or wrinkle on a person's face.

▶ *v.* [*tr.*] make a rut, groove, or trail in (the ground or the surface of something): *gorges furrowing the deep-sea floor.* ■ (with reference to the forehead or face) mark or be marked with lines or wrinkles caused by frowning, anxiety, or concentration. ■ (with reference to the eyebrows) tighten or be tightened and lowered in anxiety, concentration, or disapproval, so wrinkling the forehead: [*tr.*] *she furrowed her brows, thinking hard.* ■ [usu. as *adj.*] (**furrowed**) use a plow to make a long narrow trench in (land or earth): *acres of furrowed fields.* ▷Old English *furh,* of Germanic origin; related to Dutch *voor* and German *Furche,* from an Indo-European root shared by Latin *porca* 'ridge between furrows.' **—fur·row·y** *adj.*

fur·ry /ˈfərē/ ▶ *adj.* (**-ri·er, -ri·est**) covered with fur. ■ having a soft surface like fur: *furry apple-green leaves.* **—fur·ri·ness** *n.*

fur·ther /ˈfərTHər/ ▶ used as comparative of FAR.

▶ *adv.* **1** (also **far·ther**) at, to, or by a greater distance (used to indicate the extent to which one thing or person is or becomes distant from another): *fig. moved further away from its original aims.* ■ used to emphasize the difference between a supposed or suggested fact or state of mind and the truth: *nothing could be further from the truth.* **2** (also **far·ther**) over a greater expanse of space or time; for a longer way: *fig. wages have been driven down even further.* ■ beyond the point already reached or the distance already covered: *before going any further we need to define our terms.* **3** beyond or in addition to what has already been done: *ways to further increase customer satisfaction | I shall not trouble you any further.* ■ used to introduce a new point relating to or reinforcing a previous statement: *Ethnic minorities are more prone to unemployment. Further, this disadvantage extends to other areas of life.* ■ at or to a more advanced, successful, or desirable stage: *at the end of three years they were no further on.*

▶ *adj.* **1** (also **far·ther**) more distant in space than something else of the same kind. ■ more remote from a central point: *the further reaches of the town.* **2** additional to what already exists or has already taken place, been done, or been accounted for: *cook for a further ten minutes.*

▶ *v.* [*tr.*] help the progress or development of (something); promote: *using them to further his own career.* **—fur·ther·er** *n.* **—fur·ther·most** *adj.*

▶ □ **not go any further** (of a secret) not be told to anyone else. □ **until further notice** used to indicate that a situation will not change until another announcement is made: *closed to the public until further notice.*

fur·ther·ance /ˈfərTHərəns/ ▶ *n.* the advancement of a scheme or interest: *acts in furtherance of an industrial dispute.*

fur·ther·more /ˈfərTHər,môr/ ▶ *adv.* in addition; besides (used to introduce a fresh consideration in an argument): *this species has a quiet charm and, furthermore, is an easy garden plant.*

fur·thest /ˈfərTHist/ ▶ *adj. & adv.* variant form of FARTHEST.

fur·tive /ˈfərtiv/ ▶ *adj.* attempting to avoid notice or attention, typically because of guilt or a belief that discovery would lead to trouble; secretive: *they spent a furtive day together | a furtive glance.* ■ suggestive of guilty nervousness: *the look in his eyes became furtive.* **—fur·tive·ly** *adv.* **—fur·tive·ness** *n.*

fu·ry /ˈfyoŏrē/ ▶ *n.* (*pl.* **-ries**) **1** wild or violent anger: *tears of fury.* ■ (**a fury**) a surge of violent anger or other feeling: *in a fury, he lashed the horse on.* ■ violence or energy displayed in natural phenomena or someone's actions: *the fury of a gathering storm.* **2** (**Fury**) *Greek Mythol.* a spirit of punishment, often represented as one of three goddesses who executed the curses pronounced upon criminals, tortured the guilty with stings of conscience, and inflicted famines and pestilences.

▶ □ **like fury** *inf.* with great energy or effort: *she fought like fury in his arms.*

fuse¹ /fyoōz/ ▶ *n.* a safety device consisting of a strip of wire that melts and breaks an electric circuit if the current exceeds a safe level.

▶ *v.* [*tr.*] join or blend to form a single entity: *intermarriage had fused the families.* ■ [*intr.*] (of groups of atoms or cellular structures) join or coalesce: *the two nuclei move together and fuse into one nucleus.* ■ melt (a material or object) with intense heat, esp. so as to join it with something else: *powdered glass was fused to a metal base.*

▶ □ **blow a fuse** use too much power in an electrical circuit, causing a fuse to melt. ■ *inf.* lose one's temper.

fuse² (also **fuze**) ▶ *n.* a length of material along which a small flame moves to explode a bomb or firework. ■ a device in a bomb, shell, or mine that makes it explode on impact, after an interval, at set distance from the target, or when subjected to magnetic or vibratory stimulation.

▶ *v.* [*tr.*] fit a fuse to (a bomb, shell, or mine). **—fuse·less** *adj.*

▶ □ **light the** (or **a**) **fuse** set something tense or exciting in motion: *the event lit the fuse for the revolution.* □ **a short fuse** a tendency to lose one's temper quickly.

fuse box ▶ *n.* a box housing the fuses for circuits in a building.

fu·se·lage /ˈfyoōsə,läzH; -zə-/ ▶ *n.* the main body of an aircraft.

fu·si·ble /ˈfyoōzəbəl/ ▶ *adj.* able to be fused or melted easily. **—fu·si·bil·i·ty** /ˌfyoōzəˈbilətē/ *n.*

fu·sil·lade /ˈfyoōsə,läd; -,lād/ ▶ *n.* a series of shots fired or missiles thrown all at the same time or in quick succession: *fig. a fusillade of accusations.*

fu·sion /ˈfyoōzHən/ ▶ *n.* the process or result of joining two or more things together to form a single entity. ■ *Physics* short for NUCLEAR FUSION. ■ the process of causing a material or object to melt with intense heat, esp. so as to join with another: *the fusion of resin and glass fiber in the molding process.* ■ music that is a mixture of different styles, esp. jazz and rock.

▶ *adj.* referring to food or cooking that incorporates elements of diverse cuisines. **—fu·sion·al** /-zHənl/ *adj.*

fuss /fəs/ ▶ *n.* a display of unnecessary or excessive excitement, activity, or interest. ■ a protest or dispute of a specified degree or kind: *he didn't put up too much of a fuss.* ■ elaborate or complex procedures; trouble or difficulty: *they settled in with very little fuss.*

▶*v.* [*intr.*] show unnecessary or excessive concern about something: *she's always fussing about her food.* ■ move around or busy oneself restlessly.
▶ □ **make a fuss** become angry and complain. □ **make a fuss over** treat (a person or animal) with excessive attention or affection.

fuss·budg·et /ˈfəsˌbəjit/ ▶*n.* a person who habitually frets over minor matters.

fuss·pot /ˈfəsˌpät/ ▶*n. inf.* a fussy person.

fuss·y /ˈfəsē/ ▶*adj.* (**fuss·i·er, fuss·i·est**) (of a person) fastidious about one's needs or requirements; hard to please. ■ showing excessive or anxious concern about detail. ■ full of unnecessary detail or decoration: *fussy clothes.* —**fuss·i·ly** /ˈfəsəlē/ *adv.* —**fuss·i·ness** *n.*

fus·tian /ˈfəsCHən/ ▶*n.* **1** thick, durable twilled cloth with a short nap, usually dyed in dark colors. **2** pompous or pretentious speech or writing: *a smoke screen of fustian and fantasy.*

fus·ty /ˈfəstē/ ▶*adj.* (**fus·ti·er, fus·ti·est**) smelling stale, damp, or stuffy. ■ old-fashioned in attitude or style: *a fusty notion.* —**fus·ti·ly** /ˈfəstəlē/ *adv.* —**fus·ti·ness** *n.*

fu·tile /ˈfyoōtl; -ˌtil/ ▶*adj.* incapable of producing any useful result; pointless: *a futile attempt to keep fans from mounting the stage.* —**fu·tile·ly** *adv.* —**fu·til·i·ty** /fyoōˈtilətē/ *n.*

fu·ton /ˈfoōˌtän/ ▶*n.* a cotton-filled mattress rolled out on the floor for use as a bed. ■ a type of low wooden sofa bed having such a mattress.

fu·ture /ˈfyoōCHər/ ▶*n.* **1** (usu. **the future**) the time or a period of time following the moment of speaking or writing; time regarded as still to come. ■ events that will or are likely to happen in the time to come: *nobody can predict the future.* ■ used to refer to what will happen to someone or something in the time to come: *the future of American fast food.* ■ a prospect of success or happiness: *a future as an artist.* ■ *Gram.* a tense of verbs expressing events that have not yet happened. **2** (**futures**) *Finance* short for **FUTURES CONTRACT**.
▶*adj.* at a later time; going or likely to happen or exist: *future generations.* ■ (of a person) planned or destined to hold a specified position: *his future wife.* ■ existing after death: *expectation of a future life.* ■ *Gram.* (of a tense) expressing an event yet to happen. ▷late Middle English: via Old French from Latin *futurus,* future participle of *esse* 'be' (from the stem *fu-,* ultimately from a base meaning 'grow, become').

fu·ture per·fect ▶*n. Gram.* a tense of verbs expressing expected completion in the future, in English exemplified by *will have done.*

fu·tures con·tract ▶*n. Finance* an agreement traded on an organized exchange to buy or sell assets, esp. commodities or shares, at a fixed price but to be delivered and paid for later.

fu·ture shock ▶*n.* a state of distress or disorientation due to rapid social or technological change.

fu·tur·ism /ˈfyoōCHəˌrizəm/ ▶*n.* concern with events and trends of the future or which anticipate the future. ■ (**Futurism**) an artistic movement begun in Italy in 1909 that violently rejected traditional forms so as to celebrate and incorporate into art the energy and dynamism of modern technology.

fu·tur·ist /ˈfyoōCHərist/ ▶*n.* **1** (**Futurist**) an adherent of futurism. **2** a person who studies the future and makes predictions about it based on current trends.
▶*adj.* **1** (often **Futurist**) of or relating to futurism or the Futurists. **2** relating to a vision of the future, esp. one involving the development of technology.

fu·tur·is·tic /ˌfyoōCHəˈristik/ ▶*adj.* having or involving modern technology or design: *a swimming pool and futuristic dome.* ■ (of a film or book) set in the future, typically in a world of advanced or menacing technology. ■ *dated* of or characteristic of Futurism. —**fu·tur·is·ti·cal·ly** *adv.*

fu·tu·ri·ty /fyoōˈtoŏrətē; -ˈCHoŏrətē/ ▶*n.* (*pl.* **-ties**) the future time. ■ a future event. ■ renewed or continuing existence: *the snowdrops were a promise of futurity.*

fuze /fyoōz/ ▶*n.* variant spelling of FUSE[2].

fuzz[1] /fəz/ ▶*n.* a fluffy or frizzy mass of hair or fiber. ■ a blurred image or area. ■ a buzzing or distorted sound, esp. one deliberately produced as an effect on an electric guitar.
▶*v.* **1** make or become blurred or indistinct. **2** [*intr.*] (of hair) become fluffy or frizzy: *her hair fuzzed out in the heat.*

fuzz[2] ▶*n.* (**the fuzz**) *inf.* the police.

fuzz·y /ˈfəzē/ ▶*adj.* (**fuzz·i·er, fuzz·i·est**) **1** having a frizzy, fluffy, or frayed texture or appearance. **2** difficult to perceive clearly or understand and explain precisely; indistinct or vague: *that fuzzy line between right and wrong.* ■ (of a person or the mind) unable to think clearly; confused: *my mind felt fuzzy.* **3** *Comput. & Logic* of or relating to a form of set theory and logic in which predicates may have degrees of applicability, rather than simply being true or false. It has important uses in artificial intelligence and the design of control systems. —**fuzz·i·ly** /ˈfəzəlē/ *adv.* —**fuzz·i·ness** *n.*

F

Gg

G[1] /jē/ (also **g**) ▶ *n.* (*pl.* **Gs** or **G's**) **1** the seventh letter of the alphabet. **2** *Mus.* the fifth note in the diatonic scale of C major.

G[2] ▶ *abbr.* ■ *Physics* gauss. ■ German. ■ [in *comb.*] (in units of measurement) giga- (10[9]). ■ *inf.* grand (a thousand dollars). ■ a unit of gravitational force equal to that exerted by the earth's gravitational field.
▶ *symb.* ■ *Chem.* Gibbs free energy. ■ general audiences, a rating in the Voluntary Movie Rating System that all ages may be admitted. ■ *Physics* the gravitational constant, equal to $6.67 \times 10^{-11} \text{N m}^2 \text{ kg}^{-2}$.

g ▶ *abbr.* ■ *Chem.* gas. ■ gelding. ■ gram(s).
▶ *symb. Physics* the acceleration due to gravity, equal to 9.81 m s^{-2}.

G8 ▶ *abbr.* Group of Eight.

GA ▶ *abbr.* ■ Gamblers Anonymous. ■ General Assembly. ■ general aviation. ■ General of the Army.

Ga[1] /gǎ/ ▶ *symb.* the chemical element gallium.

Ga[2] ▶ *abbr. Bible* Galatians.

gab /gab/ *inf.* ▶ *v.* (**gabbed, gab·bing**) [*intr.*] talk, typically at length, about trivial matters: *Franny walked right past a woman gabbing on the phone.*
▶ *n.* talk; chatter.

gab·ar·dine /ˈgabərˌdēn/ ▶ *n.* a smooth, durable twill-woven cloth, typically of worsted or cotton.

gab·ble /ˈgabəl/ ▶ *v.* [*intr.*] talk rapidly and unintelligibly; utter meaningless sounds.
▶ *n.* rapid, unintelligible talk. —**gab·bler** /ˈgablər/ *n.*

gab·by /ˈgabē/ ▶ *adj.* (**gab·bi·er, gab·bi·est**) *inf.* excessively or annoyingly talkative.

ga·bi·on /ˈgābēən/ ▶ *n.* a wirework container filled with rock, broken concrete, or other material, used in the construction of dams, retaining walls, etc. —**ga·bi·on·age** /ˈgābēəˌnäZH/ *n.*

ga·ble /ˈgābəl/ ▶ *n.* the part of a wall that encloses the end of a pitched roof. ■ (also **gable end**) a wall topped with a gable. ■ a gable-shaped canopy over a window or door. —**ga·bled** *adj.*

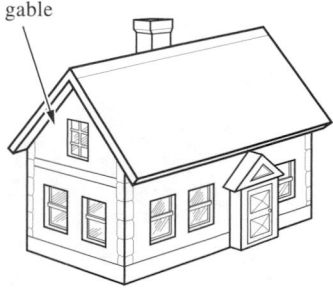

gable

gable

Gad /gad/ ▶ (in the Bible) a Hebrew patriarch, son of Jacob and Zilpah. ■ the tribe of Israel traditionally descended from him.

gad /gad/ ▶ *v.* (**gad·ded, gad·ding**) [*intr.*] *inf.* go around in the pursuit of pleasure or entertainment: *gadding about the countryside.*

gad·a·bout /ˈgadəˌbout/ ▶ *n.* a habitual pleasure-seeker.

gad·fly /ˈgadˌflī/ ▶ *n.* (*pl.* **-flies**) a fly that bites livestock, esp. a horsefly, warble fly, or botfly. ■ *fig.* an annoying person, esp. one who provokes others into action by criticism.

gadg·et /ˈgajit/ ▶ *n.* a small mechanical device or tool, esp. an ingenious or novel one: *a state-of-the-art kitchen with every conceivable gadget.* ▷late 19th cent. (originally in nautical use): probably from French *gâchette* 'lock mechanism' or from the French dialect word *gagée* 'tool.' —**gadg·e·teer** /ˌgaji'ti(ə)r/ *n.* —**gadg·et·ry** /-trē/ *n.* —**gadg·et·y** *adj.*

gad·o·lin·i·um /ˌgadl'inēəm/ ▶ *n.* the chemical element of atomic number 64, a soft silvery-white metal of the lanthanide series. (Symbol: **Gd**)

gad·wall /ˈgadˌwôl/ ▶ *n.* (*pl.* same or **gad·walls**) a brownish-gray freshwater duck (*Anas strepera*) found across Eurasia and North America.

Gad·zooks /ˌgad'zo͞oks/ (also **gad·zooks**) ▶ *interj. dated* or *humorous* an exclamation of surprise or annoyance.

Gael /gāl/ ▶ *n.* a Gaelic-speaking person. ■ a person whose ancestors spoke Gaelic. —**Gael·dom** /-dəm/ *n.*

Gael·ic /ˈgālik/ ▶ *adj.* of or relating to the Goidelic languages, particularly the Celtic language of Scotland, and the culture associated with speakers of these languages and their descendants.
▶ *n.* (also **Scottish Gaelic**) a Goidelic language brought from Ireland in the 5th and 6th centuries AD and spoken in the highlands and islands of western Scotland. ■ (also **Irish Gaelic**) another term for IRISH (the language).

gaff[1] /gaf/ ▶ *n.* **1** a stick with a hook, or a barbed spear, for landing large fish. **2** *Sailing* a spar to which the head of a fore-and-aft sail is bent.
▶ *v.* [*tr.*] seize or impale with a gaff.

gaff[2] ▶ *n.* rough treatment; criticism: *if wages increase, perhaps we can stand the gaff.*

gaffe /gaf/ ▶ *n.* an unintentional act or remark causing embarrassment to its originator; a blunder: *an unforgivable social gaffe.*

gaf·fer /ˈgafər/ ▶ *n.* **1** the chief electrician in a motion-picture or television production unit. **2** *inf.* an old man.

gag[1] /gag/ ▶ *n.* a thing, typically a piece of cloth, put in or over a person's mouth to prevent speaking or crying out. ■ *fig.* a restriction on freedom of speech or dissemination of information. ■ a device for keeping the patient's mouth open during a dental or surgical operation.
▶ *v.* (**gagged, gag·ging**) **1** [*tr.*] (often **be gagged**) put a gag on (someone). ■ *fig.* (of a person or body with authority) prevent (someone) from speaking freely or disseminating information: *the administration is trying to gag its critics.* **2** [*intr.*] choke or retch.

gag[2] ▶ *n.* a joke or an amusing story or scene, esp. one forming part of a comedian's act or in a film or play.
▶ *v.* [*intr.*] tell jokes.

ga·ga /ˈgäˌgä/ ▶ *adj. inf.* overexcited or irrational, typically as a result of infatuation or excessive enthusiasm; mentally confused; senile.

gage[1] /gāj/ *archaic* ▶ *n.* a valued object deposited as a guarantee of good faith.
▶ *v.* [*tr.*] offer (a thing or one's life) as a guarantee of good faith.

gage[2] ▶ *n.* & *v.* variant spelling of GAUGE.

gag·gle /ˈgagəl/ ▶ *n.* a flock of geese. ■ *inf.* a disorderly or noisy group of people: *the gaggle of reporters and photographers that dogged his every step.*

gag rule ▶ *n.* a regulation or directive that prohibits public discussion of a particular matter.

gai·e·ty /ˈgāitē/ (also **gay·e·ty**) ▶ *n.* (*pl.* **-ties**) the state or quality of being lighthearted or cheerful: *the sudden gaiety of children's laughter.* ■ merrymaking or festivity.

gai·ly /ˈgālē/ ▶ *adv.* in a cheerful or lighthearted way: *he waved gaily to the crowd.* ■ without thinking of the consequences. ■ with a bright or cheerful appearance: *gaily colored sailboats dot the lake.*

gain /gān/ ▶ v. [tr.] **1** obtain or secure (something desired, favorable, or profitable). ■ reach or arrive at (a desired destination): *we gained the ridge.* ■ [intr.] (**gain on**) come closer to (a person or thing pursued): *a huge bear gaining on him with every stride.* **2** increase the amount or rate of (something, typically weight or speed). ■ [intr.] increase in value. ■ [intr.] (**gain in**) improve or advance in some respect.
▶ n. an increase in wealth or resources: *the mayor was accused of using municipal funds for personal gain.* ■ a thing that is achieved or acquired: *a balance between water loss and water gain.* ■ the factor by which power or voltage is increased in an amplifier or other electronic device, usually expressed as a logarithm. —**gain·a·ble** *adj.* —**gain·er** *n.*

gain·ful /'gānfəl/ ▶ *adj.* serving to increase wealth or resources: *he soon found gainful employment.* —**gain·ful·ly** *adv.* —**gain·ful·ness** *n.*

gain·say /ˌgānˈsā; ˌgānˌsā/ ▶ v. (*past* and *past part.* **-said**) [tr.] *formal* deny or contradict (a fact or statement). ■ speak against or oppose (someone). —**gain·say·er** *n.*

gain·shar·ing /'gānˌSHe(ə)riNG/ ▶ *n.* an incentive plan in which employees or customers receive benefits directly as a result of cost-saving measures that they initiate or participate in.

'gainst /genst/ ▶ *prep. poetic/lit.* short for AGAINST.

gait /gāt/ ▶ *n.* a person's manner of walking: *the easy gait of an athlete.* ■ the paces of an animal, esp. a horse or dog.
▶ v. [intr.] (of a dog or horse) walk in a trained gait, as at a show: *the dogs are gaiting in a circle.*

gait·er /'gātər/ ▶ *n.* (usu. **gaiters**) a garment similar to leggings, worn to cover or protect the ankle and lower leg. —**gait·ered** *adj.*

gal /gal/ ▶ *n. inf.* a girl or young woman.

Gal. ▶ *abbr. Bible* Galatians.

gal. ▶ *abbr.* gallon(s).

ga·la /'gālə; 'galə/ ▶ *n.* a social occasion with special entertainments or performances: [as *adj.*] *a black-tie gala that begins with a cocktail reception.*

ga·lac·tic /gəˈlaktik/ ▶ *adj.* of or relating to a galaxy or galaxies, esp. the Milky Way galaxy.

gal·ax·y /'galəksē/ ▶ *n.* (*pl.* **-ax·ies**) a system of millions or billions of stars, together with gas and dust, held together by gravitational attraction. ■ (**the Galaxy**) the galaxy of which the solar system is a part; the Milky Way. ■ *fig.* a large or impressive group of people or things: *a galaxy of boundless young talent.* ▷late Middle English (originally referring to the Milky Way): via Old French from medieval Latin *galaxia,* from Greek *galaxias (kuklos)* 'milky (vault),' from *gala, galakt-* 'milk.'

gale /gāl/ ▶ *n.* a very strong wind: *it was almost blowing a gale* | [as *adj.*] *gale-force winds.* ■ *Meteorol.* a wind of force 7 to 10 on the Beaufort scale (28-55 knots or 32-63 mph). ■ a storm at sea. ■ (**a gale of/gales of**) *fig.* a burst of sound, esp. of laughter: *she collapsed into gales of laughter.*

ga·lette /gəˈlet/ ▶ *n.* a flat round cake. ■ a pancake made from potatoes or buckwheat.

Gal·i·le·an /ˌgaləˈlēən/ ▶ *adj.* of or relating to Galileo or his methods.

Gal·i·le·an sat·el·lites *Astron.* ▶ the four largest moons of Jupiter.

gall[1] /gôl/ ▶ *n.* **1** bold, impudent behavior: *the bank had the gall to demand a fee.* **2** the contents of the gallbladder; bile (proverbial for its bitterness). ■ an animal's gallbladder. ■ used to refer to something bitter or cruel: *accept life's gall without blaming others.*

gall[2] ▶ *n.* **1** annoyance; irritation. **2** (esp. of a horse) a sore on the skin made by chafing.
▶ v. [tr.] **1** make (someone) feel annoyed: *he knew he was losing, and it galled him.* **2** make sore by rubbing: *the straps galled their shoulders.*

gall[3] ▶ *n.* an abnormal growth formed on plants and trees, esp. oaks, in response to the presence of insect larvae, mites, or fungi.

gal·lant ▶ *adj.* **1** /'galənt/ (of a person or their behavior) brave; heroic: *she had made gallant efforts to pull herself together.* ■ *archaic* grand; fine. **2** /'galənt/ (of a man or his behavior) giving special attention and respect to women; chivalrous. —**gal·lant·ly** /'galəntlē/ *adv.*

gal·lant·ry /'galəntrē/ ▶ *n.* (*pl.* **-ries**) **1** courageous behavior, esp. in battle. **2** polite attention or respect given by men to women. ■ (**gallantries**) actions or words used when paying such attention.

gall·blad·der /'gôl,bladər/ (also **gall blad·der**) ▶ *n.* the small sac-shaped organ beneath the liver, in which bile is stored after secretion by the liver and before release into the intestine.

gal·le·on /'galēən/ ▶ *n.* a sailing ship in use (esp. by Spain) from the 15th through 17th centuries.

gal·le·ri·a /ˌgaləˈrēə/ ▶ *n.* a covered or enclosed area, esp. one with commercial establishments for shopping, dining, etc.

gal·ler·y /'galərē/ ▶ *n.* (*pl.* **-ler·ies**) **1** a room or building for the display or sale of works of art. **2** a balcony, esp. a platform or upper floor, projecting from the back or sidewall inside a church or hall, providing space for an audience or musicians. ■ (**the gallery**) the highest of such balconies in a theater, containing the cheapest seats. **3** a long room or passage, typically one that is partly open at the side to form a portico or colonnade. —**gal·ler·ied** *adj.*

gal·ley /'galē/ ▶ *n.* (*pl.* **-leys**) **1** *hist.* a low, flat ship with sails and oars, chiefly used for warfare, trade, and piracy. **2** the kitchen in a ship or aircraft. **3** (also **galley proof**) a printer's proof usually in the form of long single-column strips, not in sheets or pages.

gal·liard /'galyərd/ ▶ *n. hist.* a lively dance in triple time for two people, including complicated turns and steps.

Gal·lic /'galik/ ▶ *adj.* **1** French or typically French. **2** of or relating to the Gauls. —**Gal·li·cize** /'galə,sīz/ *v.*

gal·lic ac·id /'galik; 'gôlik/ ▶ *n. Chem.* an acid, $C_6H_2(OH)_3COOH$, formerly used in making ink.

gal·li·na·ceous /ˌgaləˈnāSHəs/ ▶ *adj. dated* of or relating to birds of an order (Galliformes) which includes domestic poultry and game birds.

gal·li·um /'galēəm/ ▶ *n.* the chemical element of atomic number 31, a soft, silvery-white metal. (Symbol: **Ga**)

gal·li·vant /'galə,vant/ ▶ *v.* [intr.] *inf.* go around from one place to another in the pursuit of pleasure or entertainment.

gal·lon /'galən/ ▶ *n.* **1** a unit of volume for liquid measure equal to four quarts, in particular: ■ equivalent to 3.79 liters. **2** (**gallons of**) *inf.* a large volume. —**gal·lon·age** /-nij/ *n.*

gal·lop /'galəp/ ▶ *n.* the fastest pace of a horse or other quadruped, with all the feet off the ground together in each stride: *riding at full gallop.* ■ a ride on a horse at this pace: *Will went for a gallop on the beach.* ■ a very fast pace of running or moving.
▶ v. (**gal·loped, gal·lop·ing**) [intr.] (of a horse) go at the pace of a gallop. ■ [tr.] make (a horse) gallop. ■ (of a person) run fast and rather boisterously. ■ *fig.* (of a process or time) progress rapidly in a seemingly uncontrollable manner: [as *adj.*] (**galloping**) *galloping inflation.* —**gal·lop·er** *n.*

Gal·lo·way /'galə,wā/ ▶ *n.* an animal of a breed of cattle that originated in Galloway, Scotland.

gal·lows /'galōz/ ▶ *pl. n.* [usu. treated as *sing.*] a structure, typically of two uprights and a crosspiece, for the hanging of criminals. ■ (**the gallows**) execution by hanging. ▷Old English *galga, gealga,* of Germanic origin; related to Dutch *galg* and German *Galgen;* reinforced in Middle English by Old Norse *gálgi.*

gall·stone /'gôl,stōn/ ▶ *n.* a small, hard crystalline mass formed abnormally in the gallbladder or bile ducts from bile pigments, cholesterol, and calcium salts.

Gal·lup poll /'galəp/ ▶ *n. trademark* an assessment of public opinion by the questioning of a statistically representative sample.

gall wasp ▶ *n.* a small winged insect (superfamily Cynipoidea) of antlike appearance. The female lays its egg in plant tissue, which swells to form a gall when the larva hatches.

ga·loot /gəˈlōōt/ ▶ *n. inf.* a clumsy or oafish person.

gal·op /'galəp/ ▶ *n.* a lively ballroom dance in duple time, popular in the late 18th century.

ga·lore /gəˈlôr/ ▶ *adj.* in abundance: *there were prizes galore.*

ga·losh /gəˈläSH/ ▶ *n.* (usu. **galoshes**) a waterproof overshoe, typically made of rubber.

ga·lumph /gəˈləmf/ ▶ *v.* [intr.] *inf.* move in a clumsy, ponderous, or noisy manner: [as *adj.*] (**galumphing**) *a galumphing tortoise.*

gal·van·ic /galˈvanik/ ▶ *adj.* **1** relating to or involving electric currents produced by chemical action. **2** sudden and dramatic: *hurry with awkward galvanic strides.* —**gal·van·i·cal·ly** /-ik(ə)lē/ *adv.*

gal·va·nize /'galvə,nīz/ ▶ *v.* [tr.] **1** shock or excite (someone), typically into taking action: *the urgency of his voice galvanized them into action.* **2** [often as *adj.*] (**galvanized**) coat (iron or steel) with a protective layer of zinc. —**gal·va·nism** /'galvə,nizəm/ *n.* —**gal·va·ni·za·tion** /ˌgalvəni-ˈzāSHən/ *n.* —**gal·va·niz·er** *n.*

gal·va·nom·e·ter /ˌgalvəˈnämitər/ ▶ *n.* an instrument for detecting and measuring small electric currents.

gam·bit /'gambit/ ▶ *n.* (in chess) an opening in which a player makes a sacrifice, typically of a pawn, for the sake of some compensating advantage. ■ a device, action, or opening remark, typically one entailing a degree of risk, that is calculated to gain an advantage.

gam·ble /'gambəl/ ▶ *v.* [intr.] play games of chance for money; bet: *she was fond of gambling on cards and horses.* ■ [tr.] bet (a sum of money) in such

---

a way. ■ *fig.* take risky action in the hope of a desired result: *the British could only gamble that something would turn up.*

▸ *n.* an act of gambling; an enterprise attempted with a risk of loss and a chance of profit or success. —**gam·bler** /-blər/ *n.*

gam·bol /'gambəl/ ▸ *v.* (**-boled, -bol·ing**) [*intr.*] run or jump about playfully.

▸ *n.* an act of running or jumping about playfully.

gam·brel /'gambrəl/ (also **gambrel roof**) ▸ *n.* a roof with two sides, each of which has a shallower slope above a steeper one.

game /gām/ ▸ *n.* **1** a form of play or sport, esp. a competitive one played according to rules and decided by skill, strength, or luck. ■ a complete episode or period of play, typically ending in a definite result: *a baseball game.* ■ a single portion of play forming a scoring unit in a match, esp. in tennis. ■ *Bridge* a score of 100 points for tricks bid and made. ■ a person's performance in a game; a person's standard or method of play: *he will attempt to raise his game to another level.* ■ (**games**) a meeting for sporting contests, esp. track and field: *the Olympic Games.* ■ the equipment for a game, esp. a board game or a computer game. **2** a type of activity or business, esp. when regarded as a game. ■ a secret and clever plan or trick. ■ a thing that is frivolous or amusing: *a Tarot reading is not a game or a stunt.* **3** wild mammals or birds hunted for sport or food. ■ the flesh of these mammals or birds, used as food.

▸ *adj.* eager and willing to do something new or challenging: *they were game for anything after the traumas of Monday.*

▸ *v.* [*intr.*] [often as *adj.*] (**gaming**) play games of chance for money: *the gaming tables of Monte Carlo.* ■ play video or computer games. —**game·ly** *adv.* —**game·ness** *n.* —**game·ster** /-stər/ *n.*

▸ □ **ahead of the game** ahead of one's competitors or peers in the same sphere of activity. □ **game over** *inf.* said when a situation is regarded as hopeless or irreversible. □ **the only game in town** *inf.* the best, the most important, or the only thing worth considering. □ **play games** deal with someone or something in a way that lacks due seriousness or respect: *Don't play games with me!*

game·cock /'gām,käk/ ▸ *n.* a rooster bred and trained for cockfighting.

game·keep·er /'gām,kēpər/ ▸ *n.* a person employed to breed and protect game, typically for a large estate. —**game·keep·ing** /-,kēpiNG/ *n.*

game plan ▸ *n.* a strategy worked out in advance, esp. in sports, politics, or business.

game point ▸ *n.* (in tennis and other sports) a point that, if won by one contestant, will also win the game.

games·man·ship /'gāmzmən,SHip/ ▸ *n.* the art of winning games by using various ploys and tactics to gain a psychological advantage. —**games·man** *n.* (*pl.* **-men**).

game·some /'gāmsəm/ ▸ *adj.* playful and merry. —**game·some·ly** *adv.* —**game·some·ness** *n.*

gam·ete /'gamēt; gə'mēt/ ▸ *n. Biol.* a mature haploid male or female germ cell that is able to unite with another of the opposite sex in sexual reproduction to form a zygote. —**ga·met·ic** /gə'metik/ *adj.*

game the·o·ry ▸ *n.* the analysis of strategies for dealing with competitive situations where the outcome of a participant's choice of action depends critically on the actions of other participants.

ga·me·to·cyte /gə'mētə,sīt/ ▸ *n. Biol.* a cell that divides (by meiosis) to form gametes.

gam·e·to·gen·e·sis /gə,mētə'jenəsis/ ▸ *n. Biol.* the process in which cells undergo meiosis to form gametes. —**ga·me·to·gen·ic** /-'jenik/ *adj.* —**gam·e·tog·e·ny** /,gamə'täjənē/ *n.*

ga·me·to·phyte /gə'mētə,fīt/ ▸ *n. Bot.* the gamete-producing and usually haploid phase, producing the zygote from which the sporophyte arises. —**ga·me·to·phyt·ic** /gə,mētə'fitik/ *adj.*

game war·den ▸ *n.* a person who is employed to supervise game and hunting in a particular area.

gam·ma /'gamə/ ▸ *n.* the third letter of the Greek alphabet (Γ, γ), transliterated as 'g.' ■ [as *adj.*] denoting the third in a series of items, categories, etc. ■ [as *adj.*] relating to gamma rays: *gamma detector.*

gam·ma rays ▸ *pl. n.* penetrating electromagnetic radiation of shorter wavelength than X-rays.

gam·mon[1] /'gamən/ ▸ *n. Brit.* ham that has been cured or smoked like bacon.

gam·mon[2] ▸ *n.* a victory in backgammon (carrying a double score) in which the winner removes all his pieces before the loser has removed any.

▸ *v.* [*tr.*] defeat (a backgammon opponent) in such a way.

gam·ut /'gamət/ ▸ *n.* (**the gamut**) **1** the complete range or scope of something: *the whole gamut of human emotion.* **2** *Mus.* a complete scale of musical notes; the compass or range of a voice or instrument.

▸ □ **run the gamut** experience, display, or perform the complete range of something: *wines that run the gamut from dry to sweet.*

gam·y /'gāmē/ (also **gam·ey**) ▸ *adj.* (**gam·i·er, gam·i·est**) (of meat) having the strong flavor or smell of game, esp. when it is slightly tainted. —**gam·i·ly** /'gāməlē/ *adv.* —**gam·i·ness** *n.*

gan·der /'gandər/ ▸ *n.* **1** a male goose. **2** *inf.* a look or glance: *take a gander at that luggage.*

gang /gaNG/ ▸ *n.* **1** an organized group of criminals. ■ a group of young people involved in petty crime or violence. ■ *inf.* a group of people, esp. young people, who regularly associate together. ■ an organized group of people doing manual work: *ninety days of hard labor on the road gang.* **2** a set of electrical or mechanical devices grouped together.

▸ *v.* **1** [*intr.*] (**gang together**) (of a number of people) form a group or gang: *the smaller supermarket chains are ganging together to beat the big boys.* ■ (**gang up**) (of a number of people) join together, typically in order to intimidate someone: *he is being unfairly ganged up on.* **2** [*tr.*] (often be **ganged**) arrange together to work in coordination.

gang·bust·er /'gaNG,bəstər/ ▸ *n. inf.* a police officer or other person who takes part in breaking up criminal gangs. ■ [as *adj.*] very successful, esp. commercially: *the restaurant did a gangbuster business.*

▸ □ **go** (or **like**) **gangbusters** used to refer to great vigor, speed, or success: *it's growing like gangbusters.*

gan·gling /'gaNGliNG/ ▸ *adj.* (of a person) tall, thin, and awkward in movements or bearing.

gan·gli·on /'gaNGlēən/ ▸ *n.* (*pl.* **-gli·a** /-glēə/ or **-gli·ons**) **1** *Anat.* a structure containing a number of nerve cell bodies, typically linked by synapses, and often forming a swelling on a nerve fiber. ■ a network of cells forming a nerve center in the nervous system of an invertebrate. **2** *Med.* an abnormal benign swelling on a tendon sheath. ▷late 17th cent.: from Greek *ganglion* 'tumor on or near sinews or tendons,' used by the Greek physician Galen to denote the complex nerve centers. —**gan·gli·on·ic** /,gaNGglē'änik/ *adj.*

gan·gly /'gaNGglē/ ▸ *adj.* (**gan·gli·er, gan·gli·est**) another term for GAN-GLING.

gang·plank /'gaNG,plaNGk/ ▸ *n.* a movable plank used as a ramp to board or disembark from a ship or boat.

gan·grene /'gaNGgrēn; gaNG'grēn/ ▸ *n. Med.* localized death and decomposition of body tissue, resulting from either obstructed circulation or bacterial infection.

▸ *v.* [*intr.*] become affected with gangrene. —**gan·gre·nous** /'gaNGgrənəs/ *adj.*

gang·ster /'gaNGstər/ ▸ *n.* a member of a gang of violent criminals. —**gang·ster·ism** /-,rizəm/ *n.*

gang·way ▸ *n.* /'gaNG,wā/ a raised platform or walkway providing a passage. ■ a movable bridge linking a ship to the shore.

▸ *interj.* /'gaNG'wā/ make way!; get out of the way!

gan·ja /'gänjə/ ▸ *n.* marijuana.

gan·net /'ganit/ ▸ *n.* a large seabird (genus *Morus*, family Sulidae) with mainly white plumage, known for catching fish by diving.

gan·try /'gantrē/ ▸ *n.* (*pl.* **-tries**) a bridgelike overhead structure with a platform supporting equipment such as a crane, railroad signals, lights, or cameras. ■ a movable framework for supporting and servicing a rocket prior to launching.

gaol /jāl/ ▸ *n. Brit.* variant spelling of JAIL. —**gaol·er** *n.*

gap /gap/ ▸ *n.* **1** a break or hole in an object or between two objects. **2** an unfilled space or interval; a break in continuity: *there are many gaps in our understanding of what happened.* ■ a difference, esp. an undesirable one, between two views or situations. —**gapped** *adj.* —**gap·py** *adj.*

gape /gāp/ ▸ *v.* [*intr.*] stare with one's mouth open wide, typically in amazement or wonder: *they gaped at her as if she were an alien.* ■ be or become wide open: *a large duffel bag gaped open by her feet* | [as *adj.*] (**gaping**) *there was a gaping hole in the wall.*

▸ *n.* a wide opening or breach: *a gape of the jaws.* ■ an open-mouthed stare. —**gap·ing·ly** *adv.*

ga·rage /gə'räzH; -'räj/ ▸ *n.* **1** a building or shed for housing a motor vehicle or vehicles. ■ an establishment that provides services and repairs for motor vehicles. **2** (also **garage rock**) a style of unpolished energetic rock music associated with suburban amateur bands. [as *adj.*] *garage band.*

▸ *v.* [*tr.*] put or keep (a motor vehicle) in a garage.

ga·ram ma·sa·la /,gärəm mə'sälə/ ▸ *n.* a spice mixture used in Indian cooking.

garb /gärb/ ▸ *n.* clothing or dress, esp. of a distinctive or special kind: *the black and brown garb of a Franciscan friar.*

▶ *v.* [*tr.*] (usu. **be garbed**) dress in distinctive clothes: *she was garbed in Indian shawls.*

gar·bage /'gärbij/ ▶ *n.* wasted or spoiled food and other refuse, as from a kitchen or household. ■ a thing that is considered worthless or meaningless: *a store full of overpriced garbage.*

▶ □ **garbage in, garbage out** (abbr.: **GIGO**) used to express the idea that in computing and other spheres, incorrect or poor quality input will always produce faulty output.

gar·ble /'gärbəl/ ▶ *v.* [*tr.*] reproduce (a message, sound, or transmission) in a confused and distorted way: *the connection was awful and kept garbling his voice* | [as *adj.*] (**garbled**) *I got a garbled set of directions.*

▶ *n.* a garbled account or transmission. —**gar·bler** /-b(ə)lər/ *n.*

gar·den /'gärdn/ ▶ *n.* **1** a piece of ground, often near a house, used for growing flowers, fruit, or vegetables. ■ (**gardens**) ornamental grounds laid out for public enjoyment and recreation: *botanical gardens.* **2** [in *names*] a large public hall: *Madison Square Garden.*

▶ *v.* [*intr.*] cultivate or work in a garden.

gar·den·er /'gärdnər/ ▶ *n.* a person who tends and cultivates a garden as a pastime or for a living: *cultivars grown by amateur gardeners* | *a topiary gardener.* —**gar·den·ing** /'gärdniNG; -dn-iNG/ *n.*

gar·de·nia /gär'dēnyə/ ▶ *n.* a widely cultivated tree or shrub (genus *Gardenia*) of the bedstraw family, with large fragrant white or yellow flowers.

Gar·den of E·den ▶ *n.* see EDEN.

gar·fish /'gärˌfiSH/ ▶ *n.* (*pl.* same or **-fishes**) any of a number of long, slender fish with elongated beaklike jaws containing sharply pointed teeth, esp. a North American freshwater fish (genus *Lepisosteus*, Lepisosteidae)

gar·gan·tu·an /gär'ganCHŌŌən/ ▶ *adj.* enormous: *a gargantuan appetite.*

gar·gle /'gärgəl/ ▶ *v.* [*intr.*] wash one's mouth and throat with a liquid kept in motion by exhaling through it: *instruct patients to gargle with warm water.*

▶ *n.* an act or instance or the sound of gargling: *a swig and gargle of mouthwash.* ■ a liquid used for gargling.

gar·goyle /'gärˌgoil/ ▶ *n.* a grotesque carved human or animal face or figure projecting from the gutter of a building, typically acting as a spout to carry water clear of a wall. —**gar·goyled** *adj.*

gar·ish /'gariSH/ ▶ *adj.* obtrusively bright and showy; lurid: *garish shirts in all sorts of colors.* —**gar·ish·ly** *adv.* —**gar·ish·ness** *n.*

gar·land /'gärlənd/ ▶ *n.* a wreath of flowers and leaves, worn on the head or hung as a decoration.

▶ *v.* [*tr.*] adorn or crown with a garland: *they were garlanded with flowers.*

gargoyle

gar·lic /'gärlik/ ▶ *n.* **1** a strong-smelling pungent-tasting bulb, used as a flavoring in cooking and in herbal medicine. **2** the plant (*Allium sativum*) of the lily family that produces this bulb. ▷Old English *gārlēac*, from *gār* 'spear' + *lēac* 'leek.' —**gar·lick·y** *adj.*

gar·ment /'gärmənt/ ▶ *n.* an item of clothing.

gar·ner /'gärnər/ ▶ *v.* [*tr.*] gather or collect (something, esp. information or approval): *the police struggled to garner sufficient evidence.*

▶ *n. archaic* a storehouse; a granary.

gar·net /'gärnit/ ▶ *n.* a precious stone consisting of a deep red vitreous silicate mineral. ■ *Mineralogy* any of a class of silicate minerals including this, which belong to the cubic system.

gar·nish /'gärniSH/ ▶ *v.* [*tr.*] **1** decorate or embellish (something, esp. food): *salad garnished with an orange slice.* **2** *Law* serve with a garnishment. ■ seize (money, esp. part of a person's salary) to settle a debt or claim: *the IRS garnished his earnings.*

▶ *n.* a decoration or embellishment for something, esp. food.

gar·nish·ee /ˌgärni'SHē/ *Law* ▶ *n.* a third party who is served notice by a court to surrender money in settlement of a debt or claim: [as *adj.*] a *garnishee order.*

▶ *v.* (**-ees, -eed**) another term for GARNISH (sense 2).

gar·nish·ment /'gärniSHmənt/ ▶ *n.* **1** a decoration or embellishment. **2** *Law* a court order directing that money or property of a third party (usually wages paid by an employer), be seized to satisfy a debt owed.

ga·rotte *v.* & *n.* variant spelling of GARROTE.

gar·ret /'garit/ ▶ *n.* a top-floor or attic room, esp. a small dismal one.

gar·ri·son /'garəsən/ ▶ *n.* the troops stationed in a fortress or town to defend it. ■ the building occupied by such troops.

▶ *v.* [*tr.*] provide (a place) with a body of troops: *troops are garrisoned in the various territories.* ■ [*tr.*] station (troops) in a particular place.

gar·rote /gə'rät/; -'rōt/ (also **gar·rotte** or **ga·rotte**) ▶ *v.* [*tr.*] kill (someone) by strangulation, typically with an iron collar or a length of wire or cord.

▶ *n.* a wire, cord, or apparatus used for such a killing.

gar·ru·lous /'gar(y)ələs/ ▶ *adj.* excessively talkative, esp. on trivial matters. —**gar·ru·li·ty** /gə'rōōlitē/ *n.* —**gar·ru·lous·ly** *adv.* —**gar·ru·lous·ness** *n.*

gar·ter /'gärtər/ ▶ *n.* a band worn around the leg to keep up a stocking or sock. —**gar·tered** *adj.*

gar·ter belt ▶ *n.* a belt with attached garters or fasteners, worn as an undergarment to hold up stockings.

gar·ter snake ▶ *n.* a harmless North American snake (genus *Thamnophis*) that typically has well-defined longitudinal stripes.

gas /gas/ ▶ *n.* (*pl.* **gas·es** or **gas·ses**) **1** an airlike fluid substance which expands freely to fill any space available, irrespective of its quantity: *hot balls of gas that become stars.* ■ *Physics* a substance of this type that cannot be liquefied by the application of pressure alone. Compare with VAPOR. ■ a flammable substance of this type used as a fuel. ■ a gaseous anesthetic such as nitrous oxide, used in dentistry. ■ gas or vapor used as a poisonous agent to kill or disable an enemy in warfare. ■ gas generated in the alimentary canal; flatulence. **2** *inf.* short for GASOLINE. **3** (**a gas**) *inf.* a person or thing that is entertaining or amusing: *the party would be a gas.*

▶ *v.* (**gas·es, gassed, gas·sing**) [*tr.*] **1** attack with or expose to poisonous gas. ■ kill by exposure to poisonous gas. **2** fill the tank of (an engine or motor vehicle) with gasoline. **3** [*intr.*] *inf.* talk, esp. excessively, idly, or boastfully: *I thought you'd never stop gassing.* ▷mid 17th cent.: invented by J. B. van Helmont (1577–1644), Belgian chemist, to denote an occult principle that he believed to exist in all matter; suggested by Greek *khaos* 'chaos,' with Dutch *g* representing Greek *kh.*

gas·bag /'gasˌbag/ ▶ *n.* **1** *inf.* a person who talks too much, typically about unimportant things. **2** the container holding the gas in a balloon or airship.

gas cham·ber ▶ *n.* an airtight room that can be filled with poisonous gas as a means of execution.

gas·e·ous /'gasēəs; 'gaSHəs/ ▶ *adj.* of, relating to, or having the characteristics of a gas: *gaseous emissions from motor vehicles* | *gaseous oxygen.* —**gas·e·ous·ness** *n.*

gas guz·zler /'gəzˌ(ə)lər/ ▶ *n. inf.* an automobile with high fuel consumption.

gash /gaSH/ ▶ *n.* a long deep slash, cut, or wound: *a bad gash in one leg became infected.* ■ a cleft made as if by a slashing cut: *the blast ripped a 25-foot gash in the hull.*

▶ *v.* [*tr.*] make a gash in; cut deeply: *the jagged edges gashed their fingers.*

gas·ket /'gaskit/ ▶ *n.* a shaped piece or ring of rubber or other material sealing the junction between two surfaces in an engine or other device.

▶ □ **blow a gasket** *inf.* lose one's temper.

gas·light /'gasˌlīt/ ▶ *n.* a type of lamp in which an incandescent mantle is heated by a jet of burning gas. —**gas·lit** /-ˌlit/ *adj.*

gas mask ▶ *n.* a protective mask used to cover a person's face as a defense against poisonous gas.

gasket

gas·o·line /ˌgasə'lēn; 'gasəlēn/ ▶ *n.* refined petroleum used as fuel for internal combustion engines.

gasp /gasp/ ▶ *v.* [*intr.*] inhale suddenly with the mouth open, out of pain or astonishment: *a woman gasped in horror at the sight of him.* ■ [*tr.*] say (something) while catching one's breath, esp. as a result of strong emotion: *Jeremy gasped out an apology* | [with *direct speech*] "*It's beautiful!," she gasped, much impressed.* ■ strain to take a deep breath: *she surfaced and gasped for air.*

▶ *n.* a convulsive catching of breath: *his breath was coming in gasps.*

gas·ser /'gasər/ ▶ *n. inf.* **1** an idle talker; a chatterer. **2** a very attractive or impressive person or thing: *that story you wrote for me is a gasser!*

gas sta·tion ▶ *n.* a service station.

gas·sy /'gasē/ ▶ *adj.* (**-si·er, -si·est**) **1** of, like, or full of gas: *the carbonated water has a gassy, soda-pop character* | *gassy planets like Jupiter.* **2** *inf.* (of people or language) inclined to be verbose: *a long and gassy book.* **3** (of people) flatulent. —**gas·si·ness** *n.*

gas·trec·to·my /ga'strektəmē/ ▶ *n.* (*pl.* **-mies**) surgical removal of a part or the whole of the stomach.

---

gas·tric /ˈgastrik/ ▸*adj.* of the stomach.

gastric juice ▸*n.* a thin, clear, virtually colorless acidic fluid secreted by the stomach glands and active in promoting digestion.

gas·tri·tis /gaˈstrītis/ ▸*n. Med.* inflammation of the lining of the stomach.

gas·tro·en·ter·i·tis /ˌgastrō͞enˈtrītis/ ▸*n.* inflammation of the stomach and intestines.

gas·tro·en·ter·ol·o·gy /ˌgastrō͞enˈtäləjē/ ▸*n.* the branch of medicine that deals with disorders of the stomach and intestines. **—gas·tro·en·ter·o·log·i·cal** /-terˈläjikəl/ *adj.* **—gas·tro·en·te·rol·o·gist** /-jist/ *n.*

gas·tro·nome /ˈgastrəˌnōm/ (also **gas·tron·o·mer** /gaˈstränəˌmər/ or **gas·tron·o·mist** /gaˈstränəˌmist/) ▸*n.* a gourmet.

gas·tron·o·my /gaˈstränəmē/ ▸*n.* the practice or art of choosing, cooking, and eating good food. ■ the cooking of a particular area. **—gas·tro·nom·ic** /ˌgastrəˈnämik/ *adj.* **—gas·tro·nom·i·cal** /ˌgastrəˈnämikəl/ *adj.* **—gas·tro·nom·i·cal·ly** /ˌgastrəˈnämik(ə)lē/ *adv.*

gas·tro·pod /ˈgastrəˌpäd/ ▸*n.* any mollusk of the group including snails, slugs, and whelks, often with a spiral shell, and that moves by means of a large muscular foot.

gas·works /ˈgasˌwərks/ ▸*pl. n.* [treated as *sing.*] a place where gas is manufactured and processed.

gat /gat/ ▸*n. inf.* a revolver or pistol.

gate /gāt/ ▸*n.* **1** a hinged barrier used to close an opening in a wall, fence, or hedge. ■ a gateway: *she went out through the gate.* ■ *fig.* a means of entrance or exit: *they were opening the gates of their country wide to the enemy.* ■ an exit from an airport building to an aircraft. **2** the number of people who pay to enter a sports facility, exhibition hall, etc., for any one event: [as *adj.*] *gate receipts.* ■ the money taken for admission. **3** a device resembling a gate in structure or function, in particular: ■ a hinged or sliding barrier for controlling the flow of water: *a sluice gate.* ■ *Skiing* an opening through which a skier must pass in a slalom course, typically marked by upright poles. **4** an electric circuit with an output that depends on the combination of several inputs: *a logic gate.*

ga·teau /gäˈtō; ga-/ ▸*n.* (*pl.* **-teaux** *pronunc.* same or /-ˈtōz/) a rich cake, typically one containing layers of cream or fruit.

gate·crash·er ▸*n.* a person who attends a party or other gathering without an invitation or ticket. **—gate-crash** *v.*

gate·fold /ˈgātˌfōld/ ▸*n.* an oversized page in a book or magazine folded to the same size as the other pages but intended to be opened out.

gate·house /ˈgātˌhous/ ▸*n.* a house or enclosure near a gateway.

gate·keep·er /ˈgātˌkēpər/ ▸*n.* an attendant at a gate who is employed to control who goes through it. ■ *fig.* a person or thing that controls access to something.

gate·keep·ing /ˈgātˌkēpiNG/ ▸*n.* **1** the activity of controlling, and usually limiting, general access to something: *Wal-Mart's cultural gatekeeping has served to narrow the mainstream for entertainment offerings.* **2** *Comput.* a function or system that controls access or operations to files, computers, networks, or the like: *a gatekeeping mechanism that allows reads under some circumstances and blocks them under others.*

gate·leg ta·ble /ˈgātˌleg/ ▸*n.* a table with hinged legs that swing out from the frame to support drop leaves that make the surface of the table larger. **—gate·legged** /ˈgātˌlegəd/ *adj.*

gate·way /ˈgātˌwā/ ▸*n.* an opening that can be closed by a gate. ■ a frame or arch built around or over a gate. ■ a means of access or entry to a place: *Mombasa, the gateway to East Africa.* ■ a means of achieving a state or condition: *death as the gateway to life.* ■ *Comput.* a device used to connect two different networks, esp. a connection to the Internet.

gath·er /ˈgaTHər/ ▸*v.* **1** [*intr.*] come together; assemble or accumulate: *a crowd gathered in the square.* **2** [*tr.*] bring together and take in from scattered places or sources. ■ pick up from the ground or a surface: *they gathered up the dirty plates and cups.* ■ collect (grain or other crops) as a harvest. ■ collect (plants, fruits, etc.) for food. ■ draw together or toward oneself. ■ draw and hold together (fabric or a part of a garment) by running thread through it: *the front is gathered at the waist.* **3** [*tr.*] infer; understand: *her clients were, I gathered, a prosperous group.* **4** [*tr.*] develop a higher degree of: *the green movement is gathering pace.* **5** [*tr.*] summon up (a mental or physical attribute such as one's thoughts or strength) for a purpose: *he gathered himself for a tremendous leap.* **—gath·er·er** *n.*

gath·er·ing /ˈgaTHəriNG/ ▸*n.* **1** an assembly or meeting, esp. a social or festive one or one held for a specific purpose: *a family gathering.* **2** a set of printed signatures of a book, gathered for binding.

Gat·ling gun /ˈgatliNG/ (also **Gat·ling**) ▸*n.* a rapid-fire, crank-driven machine gun with a cylindrical cluster of several barrels.

ga·tor /ˈgātər/ ▸*n. inf.* an alligator.

gauche /gōsH/ ▸*adj.* lacking ease or grace; unsophisticated and socially awkward. **—gauche·ly** *adv.* **—gauche·ness** *n.*

gau·che·rie /ˌgōsHəˈrē/ ▸*n.* awkward, embarrassing, or unsophisticated ways: *she had long since gotten over gaucheries such as blushing.*

gau·cho /ˈgouCHō/ ▸*n.* (*pl.* **-chos**) a South American cowboy.

gaud·y /ˈgôdē/ ▸*adj.* (**gaud·i·er**, **gaud·i·est**) extravagantly bright or showy, typically so as to be tasteless: *silver bows and gaudy ribbons.* **—gaud·i·ly** /-dəlē/ *adv.* **—gaud·i·ness** *n.*

gauge /gāj/ (*chiefly technical* also **gage**) ▸*n.* **1** an instrument or device for measuring the magnitude, amount, or contents of something, typically with a visual display of such information. ■ *fig.* a means of estimating something; a criterion or test: *emigration is perhaps the best gauge of public unease.* **2** the thickness, size, or capacity of something, esp. as a standard measure, in particular: ■ the diameter of a string, fiber, tube, etc.: [as *adj.*] *a fine 0.018-inch gauge wire.* ■ [in comb.] a measure of the diameter of a gun barrel, or of its ammunition, expressed as the number of spherical pieces of shot of the same diameter as the barrel that can be made from 1 pound (454 g) of lead: [as *adj.*] *a 12-gauge shotgun.* ■ [in comb.] the thickness of sheet metal or plastic: [as *adj.*] *500-gauge polyethylene.* ■ the distance between the rails of a line of railroad track: *the line was laid to a gauge of 2 ft. 9 in.*

▸*v.* [*tr.*] **1** estimate or determine the magnitude, amount, or volume of: *astronomers can gauge the star's intrinsic brightness.* ■ form a judgment or estimate of (a situation, mood, etc.) **2** measure the dimensions of (an object) with a gauge. ■ [as *adj.*] (**gauged**) made in standard dimensions: *gauged sets of strings.* **—gauge·a·ble** *adj.* **—gaug·er** *n.*

Gaul ▸*n.* a native or inhabitant of ancient Gaul.

gaunt /gônt/ ▸*adj.* (of a person) lean and haggard, esp. because of suffering, hunger, or age. ■ (of a building or place) grim or desolate in appearance. **—gaunt·ly** *adv.* **—gaunt·ness** *n.*

gaunt·let[1] /ˈgôntlit; ˈgänt-/ ▸*n.* a stout glove with a long loose wrist. ■ the part of a glove covering the wrist.

▸ □ **take up** (or **throw down**) **the gauntlet** accept (or issue) a challenge.

gaunt·let[2] ▸*n.* (in phrase **run the gauntlet**) go through an intimidating or dangerous crowd, place, or experience in order to reach a goal: *they had to run the gauntlet of television cameras.*

gauss /gous/ (abbr.: **G**) ▸*n.* (*pl.* same or **gauss·es**) a unit of magnetic induction, equal to one ten-thousandth of a tesla.

Gauss·i·an dis·tri·bu·tion /ˈgou̇sēən/ ▸*n. Statistics* another term for NORMAL DISTRIBUTION.

gauze /gôz/ ▸*n.* a thin translucent fabric of silk, linen, or cotton. ■ (also **wire gauze**) a very fine wire mesh. ■ *Med.* thin, loosely woven cloth used for dressing and swabs. ■ *fig.* a transparent haze or film. **—gauz·i·ly** /-zəlē/ *adv.* **—gauz·i·ness** *n.* **—gauz·y** *adj.*

gave /gāv/ ▸ past of GIVE.

gav·el /ˈgavəl/ ▸*n.* a small mallet with which an auctioneer, a judge, or the chair of a meeting hits a surface to call for attention or order.

▸*v.* (**gav·eled**, **gav·el·ing**) bring (a hearing or person) to order by use of such a mallet: *he gaveled the convention to order.*

ga·votte /gəˈvät/ ▸*n.* a medium-paced French dance, popular in the 18th century. ■ a piece of music accompanying or in the rhythm of such a dance, composed in common time beginning on the third beat of the bar.

gawk /gôk/ ▸*v.* [*intr.*] stare openly and stupidly: *they were gawking at some pinup.*

▸*n.* an awkward or shy person. **—gawk·er** *n.* **—gawk·ish** *adj.*

gawk·y /ˈgôkē/ ▸*adj.* (**gawk·i·er**, **gawk·i·est**) nervously awkward and ungainly: *a gawky teenager.* **—gawk·i·ly** /-kəlē/ *adv.* **—gawk·i·ness** *n.*

gay /gā/ ▸*adj.* (**gay·er**, **gay·est**) **1** (of a person, esp. a man) homosexual: *that friend of yours, is he gay?* ■ relating to or used by homosexuals: *feminist, black, and gay perspectives.* **2** lighthearted and carefree: *Nan had a gay disposition and a very pretty face.* ■ characterized by cheerfulness or pleasure: *we had a gay old time.* ■ brightly colored; showy; brilliant.

▸*n.* a homosexual, esp. a man. **—gay·ness** *n.*

ga·za·ni·a /gəˈzānēə/ ▸*n.* a tropical herbaceous plant (genus *Gazania*) of the daisy family, with flowers that are typically orange or yellow.

gaze /gāz/ ▸*v.* [*intr.*] look steadily and intently, esp. in admiration, surprise, or thought: *he could only gaze at her in astonishment.*

▸*n.* a steady intent look: *he turned, following her gaze* | *offices screened from the public gaze.* ■ (in literary theory) a particular perspective taken to embody certain aspects of the relationship between observer and observed, esp. as reflected in the way in which an author or film director (unconsciously or otherwise) directs attention. **—gaz·er** *n.*

ga·ze·bo /gə'zēbō/ ▸ n. (pl. **-bos** or **-boes**) a roofed structure that offers an open view of the surrounding area, typically used for relaxation or entertainment.

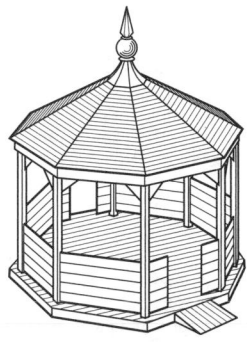

gazebo

ga·zelle /gə'zel/ ▸ n. (pl. same or **gazelles**) a small slender antelope (*Gazella* and other genera) that typically has curved horns and a fawn-colored coat, found in open country in Africa and Asia. ▷early 17th cent.: from French, probably via Spanish from Arabic *ghazāl*.

ga·zette /gə'zet/ ▸ n. (used in the names of periodicals) a journal or newspaper.

gaz·et·teer /,gazi'ti(ə)r/ ▸ n. a geographical index or dictionary.

gaz·pa·cho /gä'späCHō/ ▸ n. (pl. **-chos**) a Spanish-style soup made from tomatoes and other vegetables and spices, served cold.

GB ▸ abbr. ■ *Comput.* (also **Gb**) gigabyte(s). ■ Great Britain.

G clef ▸ n. another term for treble clef.

GDP ▸ abbr. gross domestic product.

gear /gi(ə)r/ ▸ n. **1** (often **gears**) one of a set of toothed wheels that work together to alter the relation between the speed of a driving mechanism (such as the engine of a vehicle or the crank of a bicycle) and the speed of the driven parts (the wheels). ■ a particular function or state of adjustment of engaged gears: *he was tooling along in fifth gear.* **2** *inf.* equipment that is used for a particular purpose.
▸ v. [tr.] design or adjust the gears in (a machine) to give a specified speed or power output: *it's geared too high for serious off-road use.* ■ (**gear something to**) adjust or adapt something to suit a special purpose or need.
▸ phrasal v. ▢ **gear up** equip or prepare oneself: *the region started to gear up for the tourist season.*
▸ ▢ **in gear** with a gear engaged: *the captain revved the engines and put them in gear.* ■ *fig.* done with more energy or effort: *I've got to get my act in gear.*

gear·box /'gi(ə)r,bäks/ ▸ n. a set of gears with its casing, esp. in a motor vehicle; the transmission.

gear·ing /'gi(ə)riNG/ ▸ n. the set or arrangement of gears in a machine: *the mill's internal waterwheel and gearing survive.*

gear·shift /'gi(ə)r,SHift/ ▸ n. a device used to engage or disengage gears in a transmission or similar mechanism.

gear·wheel /'gi(ə)r,(h)wēl/ ▸ n. a toothed wheel in a set of gears. ■ (on a bicycle) a cogwheel driven directly by the chain.

geck·o /'gekō/ ▸ n. (pl. **-os** or **-oes**) a nocturnal and often highly vocal lizard (Gekkonidae and related families) that has adhesive pads on the feet to assist in climbing on smooth surfaces.

gee[1] /jē/ (also **gee-whiz** /'(h)wiz/) ▸ interj. *inf.* a mild expression, typically of surprise, enthusiasm, or sympathy: *Gee, Linda looks great!*

gee[2] ▸ interj. (**gee up**) a command to a horse to go faster.
▸ v. (**gees, geed, gee·ing**) [tr.] command (a horse) to go faster. ■ encourage (someone) to work more quickly: *I was geeing people up.*

gee[3] ▸ n. *inf.* a thousand dollars: *we paid five gees.*

geek /gēk/ ▸ n. *inf.* **1** an unfashionable or socially inept person. ■ a person with an eccentric devotion to a particular interest: *a computer geek.* **2** a carnival performer who does wild or disgusting acts. —**geek·y** adj.

geese /gēs/ ▸ plural form of GOOSE.

geez /jēz/ ▸ interj. variant spelling of JEEZ.

gee·zer /'gēzər/ ▸ n. *inf.* an old man (used as a disparaging term).

Gei·ger count·er (also **Gei·ger-Mül·ler counter** /'mələr; 'myōōlər/) ▸ n. a device for measuring radioactivity by detecting and counting ionizing particles.

gei·sha /'gāSHə; 'gē-/ ▸ n. (pl. same or **-shas**) a Japanese hostess trained to entertain men with conversation, dance, and song.

gel /jel/ ▸ n. a jellylike substance containing a cosmetic, medicinal, or other preparation: *try rubbing some teething gel onto sore gums.* ■ a substance of this consistency used for setting the hair. ■ *Chem.* a semisolid colloidal suspension of a solid dispersed in a liquid.
▸ v. (**gelled, gel·ling**) [intr.] *Chem.* form into a gel: *the mixture gelled at 7 degrees Celsius.* ■ [tr.] treat (the hair) with gel.

gel·a·tin /'jelətn/ ▸ n. a virtually colorless and tasteless water-soluble protein used in food preparation as the basis of jellies, in photographic processes, and in glue. ■ (usu. **blasting gelatin**) a high explosive consisting chiefly of a gel of nitroglycerine with added cellulose nitrate.

ge·lat·i·nous /jə'latn-əs/ ▸ adj. having a jellylike consistency: *a sweet, gelatinous drink.* ■ of or like the protein gelatin: *tooth enamel is coated with a gelatinous layer of protein.* —**ge·lat·i·nous·ly** adv.

ge·la·to /jə'lätō/ ▸ n. (pl. **-ti** /-tē/) an Italian-style ice cream.

geld /geld/ ▸ v. [tr.] castrate (a male animal).

geld·ing /'geldiNG/ ▸ n. a castrated animal, esp. a male horse.

gem /jem/ ▸ n. a precious or semiprecious stone, esp. when cut and polished or engraved. ■ a person or thing considered to be outstandingly good or special in some respect: *this architectural gem of a palace.*
▸ v. (**gemmed, gem·ming**) [tr.] [usu. as adj.] (**gemmed**) *rare* decorate with or as with gems. —**gem·like** /-,līk/ adj.

Ge·ma·ra /gə'märə/ ▸ n. (**the Gemara**) a rabbinical commentary on the Mishnah, forming the second part of the Talmud.

gem·i·nate *Phonet.* ▸ adj. /'jemənit/ consisting of identical adjacent speech sounds, esp. consonants; doubled.
▸ v. /'jemə,nāt/ [tr.] double or repeat (a speech sound). —**gem·i·na·tion** /,jemə'nāSHən/ n.

Gem·i·ni /'jemə,nī; -,nē/ ▸ **1** *Astron.* a northern constellation (the Twins), said to represent the mythological twins Castor and Pollux, whose names are given to its two brightest stars. **2** *Astrol.* the third sign of the zodiac, which the sun enters about May 21. ■ (**a Gemini**) (pl. **-nis**) a person born when the sun is in this sign. **3** a series of twelve manned orbiting space missions, launched by the U.S. in the 1960s in preparation for the Apollo program.

gem·ol·o·gy /je'mäləjē/ ▸ n. the study of precious stones. —**gem·o·log·i·cal** /,jemə'läjikəl/ adj. —**gem·ol·o·gist** /-jist/ n.

gem·stone /'jem,stōn/ ▸ n. a precious or semiprecious stone, esp. one cut, polished, and used in a piece of jewelry.

Gen. ▸ abbr. ■ General: *Gen. Eisenhower.* ■ *Bible* Genesis.

gen·darme /'zHändärm/ ▸ n. an armed police officer in France and other French-speaking countries.

gen·der /'jendər/ ▸ n. **1** *Gram.* (in languages such as Latin, Greek, Russian, and German) each of the classes (typically masculine, feminine, common, neuter) of nouns and pronouns distinguished by the different inflections that they have and require in words syntactically associated with them. ■ the property (in nouns and related words) of belonging to such a class: *adjectives usually agree with the noun in gender and number.* **2** the state of being male or female (typically used with reference to social and cultural differences rather than biological ones): *traditional concepts of gender* | [as adj.] *gender roles.* ■ the members of one or other sex. ▷late Middle English: from Old French *gendre* (modern *genre*), based on Latin *genus* 'birth, family, nation.' The earliest meanings were 'kind, sort, genus' and 'type or class of noun, etc.' (which was also a sense of Latin *genus*).

gen·der bend·er ▸ n. *inf.* a person who dresses and behaves in a way characteristic of the opposite sex.

gene /jēn/ ▸ n. *Biol.* (in informal use) a unit of heredity that consists of a distinct sequence of nucleotides forming part of a chromosome and is transferred from a parent to offspring. It determines some characteristic of the offspring: *proteins coded directly by genes.*

ge·ne·a·log·i·cal /,jēnēə'läjikəl/ ▸ adj. of or relating to the study or tracing of lines of family descent: *genealogical research.* —**ge·ne·a·log·i·cal·ly** /-ik(ə)lē/ adv.

ge·ne·al·o·gy /,jēnē'äləjē; -'al-/ ▸ n. (pl. **-gies**) a line of descent traced continuously from an ancestor: *combing through the birth records and genealogies.* ■ the study and tracing of lines of descent or development. —**ge·ne·al·o·gist** /-jist/ n. —**ge·ne·al·o·gize** /-,jīz/ v.

gene doping ▸ n. the nontherapeutic use of gene therapy to enhance athletic performance, such as the supplementation of muscle-building genes.

Pronunciation Key ə *ago,* up; ər *over,* fur; a *hat;* ā *ate;* ä *car;* CH *chin;* e *let;* ē *see;* e(ə)r *air;* i *fit;* ī *by;* i(ə)r *ear;* NG *sing;* ō *go;* ô *law, for;* oi *toy;* ŏŏ *good;* ōō *goo;* ou *out;* SH *she;* TH *thin;* TH *then;* (h)w *why;* zH *vision*

gen·er·a /ˈjenərə/ ▸ plural form of GENUS.

gen·er·al /ˈjenərəl/ ▸adj. **1** affecting or concerning all or most people, places, or things; widespread: *books of general interest.* ■ not specialized or limited in range of subject, application, activity, etc.: *brush up on your general knowledge.* ■ (of a rule, principle, etc.) true for all or most cases. ■ normal or usual: *it is not general practice to confirm or deny such reports.* **2** considering or including the main features or elements of something, and disregarding exceptions; overall: *they fired in the general direction of the enemy | a general introduction to the subject.* **3** chief or principal: *a general manager.*

▸n. a commander of an army, or an army officer of very high rank. ■ an officer in the U.S. Army, Air Force, or Marine Corps ranking above lieutenant general.

▸ □ **in general 1** usually; mainly: *in general, Alexander was a peaceful, loving man.* **2** as a whole: *our understanding of culture in general and of literature in particular.*

gen·er·al an·es·the·sia ▸n. anesthesia that affects the whole body and usually induces a loss of consciousness. Compare with LOCAL ANESTHESIA.

gen·er·al e·lec·tion ▸n. a regular election of candidates for office, as opposed to a primary election. ■ a regular election for state or national offices.

gen·er·al·is·si·mo /ˌjenərəˈlisəˌmō/ ▸n. (*pl.* **-mos**) the commander of a combined military force consisting of army, navy, and air force units.

gen·er·al·ist /ˈjenərəlist/ ▸n. a person competent in several different fields or activities: *with a generalist's education and some specific skills.*

▸adj. able to carry out a range of activities, or adapt to different situations: *a generalist doctor.*

gen·er·al·i·ty /ˌjenəˈralitē/ ▸n. (*pl.* **-ties**) **1** a statement or principle having general rather than specific validity or force: *he confined his remarks to generalities.* **2** (**the generality**) the majority: *appropriate to the generality of laymen.*

gen·er·al·i·za·tion /ˌjenərəliˈzāSHən/ ▸n. a general statement or concept obtained by inference from specific cases: *he was making sweeping generalizations.* ■ the action of generalizing.

gen·er·al·ize /ˈjenərəˌlīz/ ▸v. **1** [*intr.*] infer general principles from specific cases: *it is tempting to generalize from these conclusions.* ■ make general or broad statements: *it is not easy to generalize about the poor.* ■ make or become more widely or generally applicable: [*tr.*] *what we have observed in this field can be generalized to other fields* | [*intr.*] *many of the results generalize to more complex structures.* **2** [*tr.*] make (something) more widespread or common: *attempts to generalize an elite education.* ■ [as adj.] (**generalized**) *Med.* (of a disease) affecting much or all of the body; not localized: *a generalized rash and fever.* —**gen·er·al·i·za·bil·i·ty** /ˌjenərəˌlīzəˈbilitē/ n. —**gen·er·al·iz·a·ble** adj. —**gen·er·al·iz·er** n.

gen·er·al·ly /ˈjenərəlē/ ▸adv. **1** in most cases; usually: *the term of a lease is generally 99 years.* **2** in general terms; without regard to particulars or exceptions: *a decade when France was moving generally to the left.* **3** widely: *the best scheme is generally reckoned to be the Canadian one.*

gen·er·al prac·ti·tion·er (abbr.: **GP**) ▸n. a medical doctor who is trained to provide primary health care to patients of either sex and any age.

gen·er·al·ship /ˈjenərəlˌSHip/ ▸n. the skill or practice of exercising military command.

gen·er·al store ▸n. a store, usu. located in a rural area, that carries a wide variety of merchandise, such as food, household items, hardware, and dry goods, without being divided into departments.

gen·er·ate /ˈjenəˌrāt/ ▸v. [*tr.*] cause (something, esp. an emotion or situation) to arise or come about: *changes that are likely to generate controversy.* ■ produce (energy, esp. electricity). ■ produce (a set or sequence of items) by performing specified mathematical or logical operations on an initial set. ▹early 16th cent. (in the sense 'beget, procreate'): from Latin *generat-* 'created,' from the verb *generare*, from *genus, gener-* 'stock, race.' —**gen·er·a·ble** /ˈjenərəbəl/ adj.

gen·er·a·tion /ˌjenəˈrāSHən/ ▸n. **1** all of the people born and living at about the same time, regarded collectively: *one of his generation's finest songwriters.* ■ the average period, generally considered to be about thirty years, during which children are born and grow up, become adults, and begin to have children of their own: [as adj., in comb.] *a third-generation Canadian.* ■ a single stage in the development of a type of product: *a new generation of rear-engined sports cars.* **2** the production of something: *methods of electricity generation | the generation of wealth.* ■ the propagation of living organisms; procreation. —**gen·er·a·tion·al** /-SHənl/ adj. —**gen·er·a·tion·al·ly** /-SHənl-ē/ adv.

gen·er·a·tion gap ▸n. (usu. **the generation gap**) differences of outlook or opinion between people of different generations.

Gen·er·a·tion X ▸n. the generation born after that of the baby boomers (roughly from the early 1960s to mid 1970s), often perceived to be disaffected and directionless. —**Gen·er·a·tion X-er** /ˈeksər/ n.

gen·er·a·tive /ˈjenərətiv; -ˌrātiv;/ ▸adj. of or relating to reproduction. ■ able to produce: *the generative power of the life force.*

gen·er·a·tor /ˈjenəˌrātər/ ▸n. a thing that generates something, in particular: ■ a dynamo or similar machine for converting mechanical energy into electricity. ■ an apparatus for producing gas, steam, or another product. ■ a facility that generates electrical power. ■ *Comput.* a routine that constructs other routines or subroutines using given parameters, for specific applications: *a report generator.*

ge·ner·ic /jəˈnerik/ ▸adj. **1** characteristic of or relating to a class or group of things; not specific: *chèvre is a generic term for all goat's milk cheese.* ■ (of goods, esp. medicinal drugs) having no brand name; not protected by a registered trademark: *generic aspirin.* **2** *Biol.* of or relating to a genus.

▸n. a consumer product having no brand name or registered trademark. —**ge·ner·i·cal·ly** /-ik(ə)lē/ adv.

gen·er·ous /ˈjenərəs/ ▸adj. (of a person) showing a readiness to give more of something, as money or time, than is strictly necessary or expected: *she was generous with her money.* ■ showing kindness toward others. ■ (of a thing) larger or more plentiful than is usual or necessary: *a generous sprinkle of pepper.* —**gen·er·os·i·ty** /ˌjenəˈräsitē/ n. —**gen·er·ous·ly** adv. —**gen·er·ous·ness** n.

Gen·e·sis /ˈjenəsis/ ▸the first book of the Bible, which includes the stories of the creation of the world, Noah's Ark, the Tower of Babel, and the patriarchs Abraham, Isaac, Jacob, and Joseph.

gen·e·sis /ˈjenəsis/ ▸n. the origin or mode of formation of something: *this tale had its genesis in fireside stories.*

gen·et /ˈjenit/ ▸n. a nocturnal, catlike mammal of the civet family with short legs, spotted fur, and a long bushy ringed tail, found in Africa, southwestern Europe, and Arabia. ■ the fur of the genet. ▹Middle English (used in the plural meaning 'genet skins'): from Old French *genete*, probably via Catalan, Portuguese, or Spanish from Arabic *jarnaiṭ.*

gene ther·a·py ▸n. the transplantation of normal genes into cells in place of missing or defective ones in order to correct genetic disorders.

ge·net·ic /jəˈnetik/ ▸adj. **1** of or relating to genes or heredity: *all the cells in the body contain the same genetic information.* ■ of or relating to genetics: *an attempt to control mosquitoes by genetic techniques.* **2** of or relating to origin; arising from a common origin: *the genetic relations between languages.* —**ge·net·i·cal** adj. —**ge·net·i·cal·ly** /-ik(ə)lē/ adv.

ge·net·ic blue·print ▸n. a gene map, or a genome map.

ge·net·ic code ▸n. the nucleotide triplets of DNA and RNA molecules that carry genetic information in living cells. See TRIPLET CODE.

ge·net·ic en·gi·neer·ing ▸n. the deliberate modification of the characteristics of an organism by manipulating its genetic material.

ge·net·ic fin·ger·print·ing (also **genetic profiling**) ▸n. another term for DNA FINGERPRINTING.

ge·net·ics /jəˈnetiks/ ▸pl. n. [treated as *sing.*] the study of heredity and the variation of inherited characteristics. ■ [treated as *sing.* or *pl.*] the genetic properties or features of an organism, characteristic, etc.: *the effects of family genetics on the choice of career.* —**ge·net·i·cist** /-ˈnetəsist/ n.

ge·net·ic test·ing ▸n. the sequencing of human DNA in order to discover genetic differences, anomalies, or mutations that may prove pathological.

ge·ni·al /ˈjēnyəl; -nēəl/ ▸adj. friendly and cheerful: *waved to them in genial greeting.* ■ (esp. of air or climate) pleasantly mild and warm. —**ge·ni·al·i·ty** /ˌjēnēˈalitē/ n. —**gen·ial·ly** adv.

gen·ic /ˈjenik/ ▸adj. *Biol.* of or relating to genes: *a genic mutation.*

ge·nie /ˈjēnē/ ▸n. (*pl.* **-nies** or **-ni·i** /-nē,ī/) a spirit of Arabian folklore, as traditionally depicted imprisoned within a bottle or oil lamp, and capable of granting wishes when summoned.

ge·ni·i /ˈjēnē,ī/ ▸ plural form of GENIE, GENIUS.

gen·i·tal /ˈjenitl/ ▸adj. of or relating to the human or animal reproductive organs: *conditions of the lower genital tract.*

▸n. (**genitals**) a person or animal's external organs of reproduction.

gen·i·ta·li·a /ˌjeniˈtālēə; -ˈtālyə/ ▸pl. n. formal or technical the genitals.

gen·i·tive /ˈjenitiv/ *Gram.* ▸adj. relating to or denoting a case of nouns and pronouns indicating possession or close association.

▸n. a word in the genitive case. ■ (**the genitive**) the genitive case. —**gen·i·ti·val** /ˌjeniˈtīvəl/ adj. —**gen·i·ti·val·ly** /ˌjeniˈtīvəlē/ adv.

gen·ius /ˈjēnyəs/ ▸n. (*pl.* **gen·ius·es**) **1** exceptional intellectual or creative power or other natural ability: *Gardner had a real genius for tapping* *wealth.* **2** a person who is exceptionally intelligent or creative, either generally or in some particular respect: *musical genius.* **3** (*pl.* **gen·i·i** /'jēnē͵ī/) (in some mythologies) a guardian spirit associated with a person, place, or institution. ■ a person regarded as exerting a powerful influence over another for good or evil. **4** (*pl.* **gen·i·i**) the prevalent character or spirit of something such as a nation or age: *Boucher's paintings did not suit the austere genius of neoclassicism.*

gen·o·cide /'jenə͵sīd/ ▶*n.* the deliberate killing of a large group of people, esp. those of a particular ethnic group or nation. —**gen·o·cid·al** /͵jenə'sīdl/ *adj.*

ge·nome /'jē͵nōm/ ▶*n. Biol.* the complete set of genes or genetic material present in a cell or organism. —**ge·no·mic** /jē'nämik; -'nō-; ji-/ *adj.*

gen·o·type /'jenə͵tīp; 'jē-/ ▶*n. Biol.* the genetic constitution of an individual organism. —**gen·o·typ·ic** /͵jenə'tipik; ͵jē-/ *adj.*

gen·re /'zнänrə/ ▶*n.* a category of artistic composition characterized by similarities in form, style, or subject matter.

gens /jenz/ ▶*n.* (*pl.* **gen·tes** /'jentēz/) **1** a group of families in ancient Rome who shared a name and claimed a common origin. **2** *Anthropol.* a group of people who are related through their male ancestors.

gent /jent/ ▶*n. inf.* a gentleman.

gen·teel /jen'tēl/ ▶*adj.* polite, refined, or respectable, often in an affected or ostentatious way. ▷late 16th cent. (in the sense 'fashionable, stylish'): from French *gentil* 'well-born.' From the 17th cent. to the 19th cent. the word was used in such senses as 'of good social position,' 'having the manners of a well-born person,' 'well-bred.' The ironic or derogatory implication dates from the 19th cent. —**gen·teel·ly** *adv.* —**gen·teel·ness** *n.*

gen·tes /'jentēz/ ▶ plural form of **GENS**.

gen·tian /'jenchən/ ▶*n.* a plant (genera *Gentiana* and *Gentianella*, family Gentianaceae) of temperate and mountainous regions, typically with violet or vivid blue trumpet-shaped flowers.

gen·tile /'jen͵tīl/ ▶*adj.* (**Gentile**) not Jewish. ■ (of a person) not belonging to one's own religious community.
▶*n.* (**Gentile**) a person who is not Jewish.

gen·til·i·ty /jen'tilitē/ ▶*n.* social superiority as demonstrated by genteel manners, behavior, or appearances: *her grandmother's pretensions to gentility.* ■ genteel manners, behavior, or appearances.

gen·tle /'jentl/ ▶*adj.* (**gen·tler, gen·tlest**) **1** (of a person) mild in temperament or behavior; kind or tender: *he was a gentle, sensitive man.* **2** moderate in action, effect, or degree; not harsh or severe: *a little gentle persuasion* | *a gentle breeze.*
▶*v.* make or become gentle; calm or pacify: [*intr.*] *Cobb's tone gentled a little.* ■ [*tr.*] touch gently: *her lips were gentling his cheek.* ■ [*tr.*] make (an animal) docile by gentle handling: *a bird that has been gentled enough to sit on the hand.* —**gen·tle·ness** *n.* —**gen·tly** /-tlē/ *adv.*

gent·le·man /'jentlmən/ ▶*n.* (*pl.* **-men**) **1** a chivalrous, courteous, or honorable man: *he behaved like a perfect gentleman.* ■ a man of good social position, esp. one of wealth and leisure. **2** a polite or formal way of referring to a man.

gen·tle·man·ly /'jentlmənlē/ ▶*adj.* (of a man) befitting a gentleman; chivalrous, courteous, or honorable: *a paragon of gentlemanly conduct.* —**gen·tle·man·li·ness** *n.*

gen·too /'jentOO/ (also **gentoo penguin**) ▶*n.* a tall penguin (*Pygoscelis papua*) breeding on subantarctic islands.

gen·tri·fy /'jentrə͵fī/ ▶*v.* (**-fies, -fied**) [*tr.*] renovate and improve (esp. a house or district) so that it conforms to middle-class taste. ■ [usu. as *adj.*] (**gentrified**) make (someone or their way of life) more refined or dignified. —**gen·tri·fi·ca·tion** /͵jentrəfi'kāSHən/ *n.* —**gen·tri·fi·er** *n.*

gen·try /'jentrē/ ▶*n.* (often **the gentry**) people of good social position: *the landed gentry.* ■ people of a specified class or group: *a New Orleans family of Creole gentry.* —**gen·tri·fy** /-trə͵fī/ *v.*

gen·u·flect /'jenyə͵flekt/ ▶*v.* [*intr.*] lower one's body briefly by bending one knee to the ground, typically in worship or as a sign of respect: *she genuflected and crossed herself.* —**gen·u·flec·tion** /͵jenyə'flekSHən/ *n.* —**gen·u·flec·tor** /-tər/ *n.*

gen·u·ine /'jenyOOin/ ▶*adj.* truly what something is said to be; authentic. ■ (of a person, emotion, or action) sincere: *she had no doubts as to whether Tom was genuine.* —**gen·u·ine·ly** *adv.* —**gen·u·ine·ness** *n.*

ge·nus /'jēnəs/ ▶*n.* (*pl.* **gen·er·a** /'jenərə/ or **ge·nus·es**) *Biol.* a grouping of organisms having common characteristics distinct from those of other such groupings. The genus is a principal taxonomic category that ranks above species and below family, and is denoted by a capitalized Latin name, e.g., *Leo.* ■ (in philosophical and general use) a class of things that have common characteristics and that can be divided into subordinate kinds.

Gen-X·er /'jen 'eksər/ ▶*n.* a member of Generation X (born in the 1960s and 1970s). Also called **XER**.

Geo. *dated* ▶ *abbr.* George.

ge·o·cen·tric /͵jēō'sentrik/ ▶*adj.* having or representing the earth as the center, as in former astronomical systems. Compare with **HELIOCENTRIC.** ■ *Astron.* measured from or considered in relation to the center of the earth. —**ge·o·cen·tri·cal·ly** /-trik(ə)lē/ *adv.* —**ge·o·cen·trism** /-͵trizəm/ *n.*

ge·o·chem·is·try /͵jēō'keməstrē/ ▶*n.* the study of the chemical composition of the earth and its constituent materials. —**ge·o·chem·i·cal** /-'kemikəl/ *adj.* —**ge·o·chem·ist** /-'kemist/ *n.*

ge·ode /'jēōd/ ▶*n.* a cavity in rock lined with crystals or other mineral matter. —**ge·od·ic** /jē'ädik/ *adj.*

ge·o·des·ic /͵jēō'desik; -'dē-/ ▶*adj.* of, relating to, or denoting the shortest possible line between two points on a sphere or other curved surface.

ge·o·des·ic dome ▶*n.* a dome constructed of short struts following geodesic lines and forming an open framework of triangles or polygons.

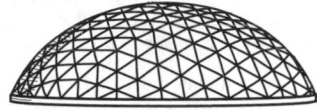

geodesic dome

ge·od·e·sy /jē'ädəsē/ ▶*n.* the branch of mathematics dealing with the shape and area of the earth. —**ge·od·e·sist** /-sist/ *n.*

ge·o·det·ic /͵jēō'detik/ ▶*adj.* of or relating to geodesy, esp. as applied to land surveying.

ge·o·graph·i·cal /͵jēə'grafikəl/ ▶*adj.* of or relating to geography. —**ge·o·graph·ic** *adj.* —**ge·o·graph·i·cal·ly** /-ik(ə)lē/ *adv.*

ge·og·ra·phy /jē'ägrəfē/ ▶*n.* the study of the physical features of the earth and its atmosphere, and of human activity as it affects and is affected by these, including the distribution of populations and resources, land use, and industries. ■ the nature and relative arrangement of places and physical features: *knowing the geography and topology of the battlefield.* —**ge·og·ra·pher** /-fər/ *n.*

geol. ▶*abbr.* ■ geologic. ■ geological. ■ geologist. ■ geology.

ge·ol·o·gy /jē'äləjē/ ▶*n.* the science that deals with the earth's physical structure and substance, its history, and the processes that act on it. ■ the geological features of an area: *the geology of the Outer Hebrides.* ■ the geological features of a planetary body. —**ge·o·log·ic** /͵jēə'läjik/ *adj.* —**ge·o·log·i·cal** /͵jēə'läjikəl/ *adj.* —**ge·o·log·i·cal·ly** /͵jēə'läjik(ə)lē/ *adv.* —**ge·ol·o·gist** /-jist/ *n.* —**ge·ol·o·gize** /-͵jīz/ *v.*

geom. ▶*abbr.* ■ geometric. ■ geometrical. ■ geometry.

ge·o·mag·net·ism /͵jēō'magni͵tizəm/ ▶*n.* the branch of geology concerned with the magnetic properties of the earth. —**ge·o·mag·net·ic** /-͵mag'netik/ *adj.* —**ge·o·mag·net·i·cal·ly** /-͵mag'netik(ə)lē/ *adv.*

ge·o·met·ric /͵jēə'metrik/ ▶*adj.* **1** of or relating to geometry, or according to its methods. **2** (of a design) characterized by or decorated with regular lines and shapes: *traditional Hopi geometric forms.* —**ge·o·met·ri·cal** *adj.* —**ge·o·met·ri·cal·ly** /-ik(ə)lē/ *adv.*

ge·o·met·ric pro·gres·sion ▶*n.* a progression of numbers with a constant ratio between each number and the one before.

ge·om·e·try /jē'ämətrē/ ▶*n.* the branch of mathematics concerned with the properties and relations of points, lines, surfaces, solids, and higher dimensional analogs. ■ the shape and relative arrangement of the parts of something: *the geometry of spiders' webs.*

ge·o·mor·phol·o·gy /͵jēō͵môr'fäləjē/ ▶*n.* the study of the physical features of the surface of the earth and their relation to its geological structures. —**ge·o·mor·pho·log·i·cal** /-͵môrfə'läjikəl/ *adj.* —**ge·o·mor·phol·o·gist** /-jist/ *n.*

ge·oph·a·gy /jē'äfəjē/ ▶*n.* the practice of eating earth, esp. chalk or clay in famine-stricken regions.

ge·o·phys·ics /͵jēō'fiziks/ ▶*pl. n.* [treated as *sing.*] the physics of the earth. —**ge·o·phys·i·cal** /-'fizikəl/ *adj.* —**ge·o·phys·i·cist** /-'fizisist/ *n.*

ge·o·pol·i·tics /͵jēō'päli͵tiks/ ▶*pl. n.* [treated as *sing.* or *pl.*] politics, esp. international relations, as influenced by geographical factors. ■ [treated as *sing.*] the study of politics of this type. —**ge·o·po·lit·i·cal**

/-pə'litikəl/ *adj.* —**ge·o·po·lit·i·cal·ly** /-pə'litik(ə)lē/ *adv.* —**ge·o·pol·i·ti·cian** /-,pälə'tiSHən/ *n.*

Geor·gian[1] /'jôrjən/ ▶*adj.* **1** of or characteristic of the reigns of the British kings George I–IV (1714–1830). ■ of or relating to British architecture of this period that was characterized esp. by restrained elegance and the use of neoclassical styles. **2** of or characteristic of the reigns of the British kings George V and VI (1910–52).

Geor·gian[2] ▶*adj.* of or relating to the country of Georgia, its people, or their language.
▶*n.* **1** a native or national of Georgia, or a person of Georgian descent. **2** the South Caucasian (or Kartvelian) language, having its own alphabet, that is the official language of Georgia.

Geor·gian[3] ▶*adj.* of or relating to the state of Georgia in the U.S.
▶*n.* a native of Georgia.

ge·o·sphere /'jēō,sfir/ ▶*n.* any of the almost spherical concentric regions of matter that make up the earth and its atmosphere, as the lithosphere and hydrosphere.

ge·o·sta·tion·ar·y /,jēō'stāSHə,nerē/ ▶*adj.* (of an artificial satellite of the earth) moving in a geosynchronous orbit in the plane of the equator, so that it remains stationary in relation to a fixed point on the surface.

ge·o·stroph·ic /,jēə'strȧfik/ ▶*adj. Meteorol. & Oceanography* relating to or denoting the component of a wind or current that arises from a balance between pressure gradients and Coriolis forces.

ge·o·syn·chro·nous /,jēō'siNGkrənəs/ ▶*adj.* (of an earth satellite or its orbit) having a period of rotation synchronous with that of the earth's rotation.

ge·o·ther·mal /,jēō'THərməl/ (also **ge·o·ther·mic** /-mik/) ▶*adj.* of, relating to, or produced by the internal heat of the earth: *some 70% of Iceland's energy needs are met from geothermal sources.*

ge·ot·ro·pism /jē'ätrə,pizəm/ ▶*n. Bot.* the growth of the parts of plants with respect to the force of gravity. The upward growth of plant shoots is an instance of **negative geotropism**; the downward growth of roots is **positive geotropism**. —**ge·o·trop·ic** /,jēə'träpik; -'trō-/ *adj.*

ge·ra·ni·um /jə'rānēəm/ ▶*n.* a herbaceous plant or small shrub of the genus *Geranium* (family Geraniaceae), which comprises the cranesbills and their relatives. ■ (in general use) a cultivated pelargonium. ■ the scarlet color of many cultivated pelargoniums.

ger·bil /'jərbəl/ ▶*n.* a burrowing mouselike rodent (subfamily Gerbillinae) that is specially adapted to living in arid conditions, found in Africa and Asia.

ger·i·at·ric /,jerē'atrik/ ▶*adj.* of or relating to old people, esp. with regard to their health care: *a geriatric hospital.*

ger·i·at·rics /,jerē'atriks/ ▶*pl. n.* [treated as *sing.* or *pl.*] the branch of medicine or social science dealing with the health and care of old people. —**ger·i·a·tri·cian** /,jerēə'triSHən/ *n.*

germ /jərm/ ▶*n.* **1** a microorganism, esp. one that causes disease. **2** a portion of an organism capable of developing into a new one or part of one. ■ the embryo in a cereal grain or other plant seed. ■ an initial stage from which something may develop: *the germ of a brilliant idea.* —**germ·y** *adj.*

Ger·man /'jərmən/ ▶*n.* **1** a native or national of Germany. ■ a person of German descent: *Sudeten Germans.* **2** a West Germanic language used in Germany, Austria, and parts of Switzerland, and by communities in the U.S. and elsewhere.
▶*adj.* of or relating to Germany, its people, or their language. ▷from Latin *Germanus*, used to designate related peoples of central and northern Europe, a name perhaps given by Celts to their neighbors; compare with Old Irish *gair* 'neighbor.'

ger·mane /jər'mān/ ▶*adj.* relevant to a subject under consideration: *that is not germane to our theme.* —**ger·mane·ly** *adv.* —**ger·mane·ness** *n.*

Ger·man·ic /jər'manik/ ▶*adj.* **1** of, relating to, or denoting the branch of the Indo-European language family that includes English, German, Dutch, Frisian, the Scandinavian languages, and Gothic. ■ of, relating to, or denoting the peoples of ancient northern and western Europe speaking such languages. **2** having characteristics of or attributed to Germans or Germany: *she had an almost Germanic regard for order.*
▶*n.* the Germanic languages collectively.

ger·ma·ni·um /jər'mānēəm/ ▶*n.* the chemical element of atomic number 32, a shiny gray semimetal. (Symbol: **Ge**)

Ger·man·ize /'jərmə,nīz/ ▶*v.* [*tr.*] make German; cause to adopt German language and customs: *the Poles had Germanized their family names.* —**Ger·man·i·za·tion** /,jərməni'zāSHən/ *n.*

Ger·man mea·sles ▶*pl. n.* [usu. treated as *sing.*] another term for RUBELLA.

Ger·man shep·herd (also **German shepherd dog**) ▶*n.* a large dog of a breed often used as guard dogs or guide dogs or for police work.

ger·mi·cide /'jərmə,sīd/ ▶*n.* an agent that destroys harmful microorganisms; an antiseptic. —**ger·mi·cid·al** /,jərmə'sīdl/ *adj.*

ger·mi·nal /'jərmənl/ ▶*adj.* relating to or of the nature of a germ cell or embryo. ■ in the earliest stage of development. ■ providing material for future development. —**ger·mi·nal·ly** *adv.*

ger·mi·nate /'jərmə,nāt/ ▶*v.* [*intr.*] (of a seed or spore) begin to grow and put out shoots after a period of dormancy. ■ [*tr.*] cause (a seed or spore) to sprout in such a way. ■ *fig.* come into existence and develop: *the idea germinated and slowly grew into an obsession.* —**ger·mi·na·ble** /-nəbəl/ *adj.* —**ger·mi·na·tion** /,jərmə'nāSHən/ *n.* —**ger·mi·na·tive** /-,nātiv/ *adj.* —**ger·mi·na·tor** /-,nātər/ *n.*

ger·on·tol·o·gy /,jerən'täləjē/ ▶*n.* the scientific study of old age, the process of aging, and the particular problems of old people. —**ge·ron·to·log·i·cal** /jə,räntl'äjikəl/ *adj.* —**ger·on·tol·o·gist** /-jist/ *n.*

ger·ry·man·der /'jerē,mandər/ ▶*v.* [*tr.*] (often as *n.*] (**gerrymandering**) manipulate the boundaries of (an electoral constituency) so as to favor one party or class. ■ achieve (a result) by such manipulation. ▷early 19th cent.: from the name of Governor Elbridge *Gerry* of Massachusetts + *salamander*, from the supposed similarity between a salamander and the shape of a new voting district on a map drawn when he was in office (1812), the creation of which was felt to favor his party: the map (with claws, wings, and fangs added), was published in the Boston *Weekly Messenger*, with the title *The Gerry-Mander*. —**ger·ry·man·der·er** *n.*

ger·und /'jerənd/ ▶*n. Gram.* a form that is derived from a verb but that functions as a noun, in English ending in -*ing*, e.g., *asking* in *do you mind my asking you?*.

ger·un·dive /jə'rəndiv/ ▶*n. Gram.* (in Latin) a form that is derived from a verb but that functions as an adjective, denoting something "that should or must be done."

ge·stalt /gə'SHtält; -'SHtôlt/ (also **Ge·stalt**) ▶*n.* (*pl.* **-stalt·en** /-'SHtältn; -'SHtôltn/ or **-stalts**) *Psychol.* an organized whole that is perceived as more than the sum of its parts. —**ge·stalt·ism** *n.* —**ge·stalt·ist** *n.*

Ge·sta·po /gə'stäpō/ ▶*the* German secret police under Nazi rule. It ruthlessly suppressed opposition to the Nazis in Germany and occupied Europe and sent Jews and others to concentration camps.

ges·tate /'je,stāt/ ▶*v.* [*tr.*] carry (a fetus) in the womb from conception to birth. [*intr.*] *rabbits gestate for approximately twenty-eight days.* ■ [*intr.*] (of a fetus) undergo gestation. ■ *fig.* develop (something) in the mind over a long period. —**ges·ta·tive** /je'stātiv; 'jestətiv/ *adj.*

ges·ta·tion /je'stāSHən/ ▶*n.* the process of carrying or being carried in the womb between conception and birth. ■ the duration of such a process. ■ *fig.* the development of something over a period of time: *various ideas are in the process of gestation.* —**ges·ta·tion·al** /-SHənl/ *adj.*

ges·tic·u·late /je'stikyə,lāt/ ▶*v.* [*intr.*] use gestures, esp. dramatic ones, instead of speaking or to emphasize one's words. —**ges·tic·u·la·tion** /je-,stikyə'lāSHən/ *n.* —**ges·tic·u·la·tive** /-,lātiv/ *adj.* —**ges·tic·u·la·tor** /-,lātər/ *n.* —**ges·tic·u·la·to·ry** /-lə,tôrē/ *adj.*

ges·ture /'jesCHər/ ▶*n.* a movement of part of the body, esp. a hand or the head, to express an idea or meaning: *Alex made a gesture of apology | so much is conveyed by gesture.* ■ an action performed to convey one's feelings or intentions: *Maggie was touched by the kind gesture.* ■ an action performed for show in the knowledge that it will have no effect.
▶*v.* [*intr.*] make a gesture: *she gestured meaningfully with the pistol.* ■ [*tr.*] express (something) with a gesture or gestures: *he gestured his dissent at this.* ■ [*tr.*] direct or invite (someone) to move somewhere specified: *he gestured her to a chair.* —**ges·tur·al** *adj.*

ge·sund·heit /gə'zŏŏntīt/ ▶*interj.* used to wish good health to a person who has just sneezed.

get /get/ ▶*v.* (**get·ting**; *past* **got** /gät/; *past part.* **got** or **got·ten** /'gätn/) **1** [*tr.*] come to have or hold (something); receive: *I got the impression that she wasn't happy.* ■ experience, suffer, or be afflicted with (something bad): *I got a sudden pain in my left eye.* ■ receive as a punishment or penalty: *I'll get the sack if things go wrong.* ■ contract (a disease or ailment): *I might be getting the flu.* ■ receive (a communication): *I got a letter from my fiancé.* **2** [*tr.*] succeed in attaining, achieving, or experiencing; obtain: *I need all the sleep I can get.* ■ move in order to pick up or bring (something); fetch: *get another chair | I'll get you a drink.* ■ [*tr.*] tend to meet with or find in a specified place or situation: *it was nothing like the winters we get in Florida.* ■ travel by or catch (a bus, train, or other form of transport): *I'll get a taxi and be home in an hour.* ■ obtain (a figure or answer) as a result of calculation. ■ respond to a ring of (a telephone or doorbell) or the knock on (a door): *I'll get it!* ■ [in *imper.*] *inf.* said as an invitation to notice or look at someone, esp. to criticize or ridicule them: *get her!*

3 [*intr.*] enter or reach a specified state or condition; become: *he got very worried* | *it's getting late* ■ [as *auxiliary v.*] used with a past participle to form the passive mood: *the cat got groomed.* ■ [*tr.*] cause to be treated in a specified way: *get the form signed by a doctor.* ■ [*tr.*] induce or prevail upon (someone) to do something: *Sophie got Beth to make a fire.* ■ [*intr.*] have the opportunity to do: *he got to try out a few of these new cars.* ■ [*intr.*] begin to be or do something, esp. gradually or by chance: *we got talking one evening.* **4** [*intr.*] come, go, or make progress eventually or with some difficulty: *I got to the airport* | *they weren't going to get anywhere.* ■ [*intr.*] move or come into a specified position, situation, or state: *she got into the car.* ■ [*tr.*] succeed in making (someone or something) come, go, or make progress: *my honesty often gets me into trouble.* ■ [*intr.*] *inf.* reach a specified point or stage: *it's getting so I can't even think.* ■ [usu. in *imper.*] *inf.* go away. **5** (**have got**) see HAVE. **6** [*tr.*] catch or apprehend (someone): *the police have got him.* ■ strike or wound (someone) with a blow or missile: *you got me in the eye!* ■ *inf.* punish, injure, or kill (someone), esp. as retribution: *I'll get you for this!* ■ (**get it**) *inf.* be punished, injured, or killed: *wait until Dad comes home, then you'll get it!* ■ (**get mine, his,** etc.) *inf.* be killed or appropriately punished or rewarded: *I'll get mine, you get yours, we'll all get wealthy.* ■ *inf.* annoy or amuse (someone) greatly: *cleaning the same things all the time, that's what gets me.* ■ *inf.* baffle (someone): *"What's a 'flowery boundary tree'?" "You got me."* **7** [*tr.*] *inf.* understand (an argument or the person making it): *What do you mean? I don't get it.*

▶*phrasal v.* □ **get something across** manage to communicate an idea clearly. □ **get ahead** become successful in one's life or career: *how to get ahead in advertising.* □ **get along 1** have a harmonious or friendly relationship: *they seem to get along pretty well.* **2** manage to live or survive: *don't worry, we'll get along without you.* □ **get around 1** coax or persuade (someone) to do or allow something that they initially do not want to. **2** deal successfully with (a problem). ■ evade (a regulation or restriction) without contravening it: *the company changed its name to get around the law.* □ **get around to** deal with (a task) in due course: *I didn't get around to putting all the photos in frames.* □ **get at 1** reach or gain access to (something): *it's difficult to get at the screws.* ■ bribe or unfairly influence (someone): *he had been got at by government officials.* **2** *inf.* imply (something): *I can see what you're getting at.* □ **get away** escape: *Stevie was caught, but the rest of us got away* | *he was very lucky to get away with his life.* ■ leave one's home or work for a time of rest or recreation; go on a vacation: *it will be nice to get away.* □ **get away with** escape blame, punishment, or undesirable consequences for (an act that is wrong or mistaken): *you'll never get away with this.* □ **get back at** take revenge on (someone): *I wanted to get back at them for what they did.* □ **get back to** contact (someone) later to give a reply or return a message: *I'll find out and get back to you.* □ **get by** manage with difficulty to live or accomplish something: *he had just enough money to get by.* □ **get down** *inf.* enjoy oneself by being uninhibited, esp. with friends in a social setting: *get down and party!* □ **get someone down** depress or demoralize someone. □ **get something down 1** write something down. **2** swallow food or drink, esp. with difficulty. □ **get down to** begin to do or give serious attention to: *let's get down to business.* □ **get in 1** (of a train, aircraft, or other transport) arrive at its destination: *the train got in late.* ■ (of a person) arrive at one's destination: *what time did you get in?* **2** (of a political party or candidate) be elected. □ **get in on** become involved in (a profitable or exciting activity). □ **get into** (of a feeling) affect, influence, or take control of (someone): *I don't know what's got into him.* □ **get in with** become friendly with (someone), esp. in order to gain an advantage: *I hope he doesn't get in with the wrong crowd.* □ **get off 1** *inf.* escape a punishment; be acquitted: *she got off lightly* | *you'll get off with a warning.* **2** *vulgar slang* have an orgasm. □ **get off on** *inf.* be excited or aroused by (something): *he was obviously getting off on the adrenaline of performing before the crowd.* □ **get on 1** perform or make progress in a specified way: *how are you getting on?* ■ continue doing something, esp. after an interruption: *I've got to get on with this job.* **2** (**be getting on**) *inf.* be old or comparatively old: *we are both getting on a bit.* □ **get out 1** (of something previously secret) become known: *news got out that we were coming.* **2** (also **get out of here**) *inf.* [in *imper.*] used to express disbelief: *get out, you're a liar.* ■ [usu. in *imper.*] *inf.* go away; leave. □ **get something out** succeed in uttering, publishing, or releasing something: *we need to get this report out by Friday.* □ **get out of** contrive to avoid or escape (a duty or responsibility): *they wanted to get out of paying.* □ **get something out of** achieve benefit from (an undertaking or exercise): *we never got any money out of it.* □ **get over 1** recover from (an ailment or an upsetting or startling experience): *the trip will help him get over Sal's death.* **2** overcome (a difficulty). □ **get something over 1** manage to communicate an idea or theory: *the company is keen to get the idea over.* **2** complete an unpleasant or tedious but necessary task promptly:

Come on, let's get it over with. □ **get through 1** (also **get someone through**) pass or assist (someone) in passing (a difficult or testing experience or period): *I need these lessons to get me through my exam.* ■ (also **get something through**) (with reference to a piece of legislation) become or cause to become law. **2** make contact by telephone: *after an hour of busy signals, I finally got through.* ■ succeed in communicating with someone in a meaningful way: *I just don't think anyone can get through to these kids.* □ **get to 1** *inf.* annoy or upset (someone) by persistent action: *he started crying—we were getting to him.* **2** another way of saying GET AROUND TO above. □ **get up 1** (also **get someone up**) rise or cause to rise from bed after sleeping. **2** (of wind or the sea) become strong or agitated. □ **get something up 1** prepare or organize a project or piece of work: *we used to get up little plays.* **2** enhance or refine one's knowledge of a subject. —**get·ta·ble** *adj.*

▶ □ — **as all get out** *inf.* to a great or extreme extent: *he was stubborn as all get out.* ■ **be out to get someone** be determined to punish or harm someone, esp. in retaliation: *he thinks the media are out to get him.* □ **get in there** *inf.* take positive action to achieve one's aim (often said as an exhortation): *you get in there, son, and you work.* □ **get it on** *inf.* have sexual intercourse. □ **get-rich-quick** *derog.* designed or concerned to make a lot of money fast: *another one of your get-rich-quick schemes.* □ **get-up-and-go** *inf.* energy, enthusiasm, and initiative.

get·a·way /ˈgetəˌwā/ ▶*n.* **1** an escape or quick departure, esp. after committing a crime: *the thugs made their getaway* | [as *adj.*] *a getaway car.* ■ a fast start by a racing car. **2** *inf.* a vacation: *a perfect family getaway.* ■ the destination or accommodations for a vacation: *a popular island getaway.*

get-to-geth-er ▶*n.* an informal gathering.

get-up /ˈgetəp/ (also **get-up**) ▶*n. inf.* a style or arrangement of dress, esp. an elaborate or unusual one: *she looks ridiculous in that getup.*

gew-gaw /ˈg(y)ōōˌgô/ ▶*n.* (usu. **gewgaws**) a showy thing, esp. one that is useless or worthless.

gey·ser /ˈgīzər/ ▶*n.* a hot spring in which water intermittently boils, sending a tall column of water and steam into the air. ■ a jet or stream of liquid: *the pipe sent up a geyser of sewer water into the street.*
▶*v.* [*intr.*] (esp. of water or steam) gush or burst out with great force.

ghast·ly /ˈgastlē/ ▶*adj.* (**-li·er, -li·est**) **1** causing great horror or fear; frightful or macabre: *she was overcome with horror at the ghastly spectacle.* ■ *inf.* objectionable; unpleasant: *we had to wear ghastly old-fashioned dresses.* **2** extremely unwell. ■ deathly white or pallid: *he turned ghastly pale and rushed to the bathroom.* —**ghast·li·ness** *n.*

gha·zi /ˈgäzē/ (also **Gha·zi**) ▶*n.* (*pl.* **gha·zis**) a Muslim fighter against non-Muslims.

ghee /gē/ ▶*n.* clarified butter made from the milk of a buffalo or cow, used in Indian cooking.

gher·kin /ˈgərkin/ ▶*n.* a small variety of cucumber, or a young green cucumber used for pickling. ■ a pickle made from such a cucumber. ▷early 17th cent.: from Dutch *augurkie, gurkje,* diminutive of *augurk, gurk,* from Slavic, based on medieval Greek *angourion* 'cucumber.'

ghet·to /ˈgetō/ ▶*n.* (*pl.* **-tos** or **-toes**) a part of a city, esp. a slum area, occupied by a minority group or groups. ■ *hist.* the Jewish quarter in a city: *the Warsaw Ghetto.* ■ an isolated or segregated group or area: *the relative security of the gay ghetto.*

ghost /gōst/ ▶*n.* an apparition of a dead person that is believed to appear or become manifest to the living, typically as a nebulous image: *the building is haunted by the ghost of a monk* | *fig.* the ghosts of communism returned to haunt the living.* ■ [as *adj.*] appearing or manifesting but not actually existing: *the Flying Dutchman is the most famous ghost ship.* ■ a faint trace of something: *she gave the ghost of a smile.* ■ *archaic* a spirit or soul. ■ a faint secondary image produced by a fault in an optical system or on a cathode-ray screen, e.g., by faulty television reception or internal reflection in a mirror or camera.
▶*v.* **1** [*tr.*] act as ghostwriter of (a work). **2** [*intr.*] glide smoothly and effortlessly: *they ghosted up the river.* —**ghost·like** /-ˌlīk/ *adj.*
▶ □ **give up the ghost** die. ■ (of a machine) stop working.

ghost·ly /ˈgōstlē/ ▶*adj.* (**-li·er, -li·est**) of or like a ghost in appearance or sound; eerie and unnatural: *a ghostly figure.* —**ghost·li·ness** *n.*

ghost town ▶*n.* a deserted town with few or no remaining inhabitants.

ghost·writ·er /ˈgōstˌrītər/ ▶*n.* a person whose job it is to write material for someone else who is the named author. —**ghost·write** *v.*

ghoul /gōōl/ ▶*n.* an evil spirit or phantom, esp. one supposed to rob graves and feed on dead bodies. ■ a person morbidly interested in

---

death or disaster. —**ghoul·ish** *adj.* —**ghoul·ish·ly** *adv.* —**ghoul·ish·ness** *n.*

GHQ ▸*abbr.* general headquarters.

ghrel·in /ˈgrelin/ ▸*n.* an enzyme produced by stomach lining cells that stimulates appetite.

GI ▸*n.* (*pl.* **GIs**) a private soldier in the U.S. Army.

gi /gē/ ▸*n.* (*pl.* **gis**) a lightweight two-piece white garment worn in judo and other martial arts.

gi·ant /ˈjīənt/ ▸*n.* **1** an imaginary or mythical being of human form but superhuman size. ■ an abnormally tall or large person, animal, or plant. ■ a very large company or organization. ■ a person of exceptional talent or qualities: *a giant among sportsmen.* **2** *Astron.* a star of relatively great size and luminosity compared to ordinary stars of the main sequence, and 10–100 times the diameter of the sun.
▸*adj.* of very great size or force; gigantic: *giant multinational corporations | a giant meteorite.* ■ used in names of very large animals and plants, e.g., **giant tortoise.** —**gi·ant·ism** *n.* —**gi·ant·like** /-ˌlīk/ *adj.*

gib·ber /ˈjibər/ ▸*v.* [*intr.*] speak rapidly and unintelligibly, typically through fear or shock: *they shrieked and gibbered as flames surrounded them* | [as *adj.*] (**gibbering**) *a gibbering idiot.*

gib·ber·el·lin /ˌjibəˈrelin/ ▸*n.* any of a group of plant hormones that stimulate stem elongation, germination, and flowering.

gib·ber·ish /ˈjibərisH/ ▸*n.* unintelligible or meaningless speech or writing; nonsense: *he talks gibberish.*

gib·bet /ˈjibit/ *hist.* ▸*n.* a gallows. ■ an upright post with an arm on which the bodies of executed criminals were left hanging as a warning or deterrent to others. ■ (**the gibbet**) execution by hanging.
▸*v.* (**-bet·ed, -bet·ing**) [*tr.*] execute (someone) by hanging.

gib·bon /ˈgibən/ ▸*n.* a small, slender tree-dwelling ape (genus *Hylobates,* family Hylobatidae) with long powerful arms and loud hooting calls, native to the forests of Southeast Asia.

gib·bous /ˈgibəs/ ▸*adj.* (of the moon) having the observable illuminated part greater than a semicircle and less than a circle. ■ convex or protuberant: *gibbous eyes.*

gibe /jīb/ (also **jibe**) ▸*n.* an insulting or mocking remark; a taunt.
▸*v.* [*intr.*] make insulting or mocking remarks; jeer: *some cynics in the media might gibe.*

gib·lets /ˈjiblits/ ▸*pl. n.* the liver, heart, gizzard, and neck of a chicken or other fowl, often used to make gravy, stuffing, or soup.

gid·dy /ˈgidē/ ▸*adj.* (**-di·er, -di·est**) having a sensation of whirling and a tendency to fall or stagger; dizzy: *I felt giddy and had to steady myself | Luke felt almost giddy with relief.* ■ disorienting and alarming, but exciting. ■ excitable and frivolous: *her giddy young sister-in-law.*
▸*v.* (**-dies, -died**) [*tr.*] make (someone) feel excited to the point of disorientation: [as *adj.*] *the giddying speed of the revolving doors.* ▹Old English *gidig* 'insane,' literally 'possessed by a god,' related to Old English *god* 'God.' Current senses date from late Middle English. —**gid·di·ly** /ˈgidəlē/ *adv.* —**gid·di·ness** *n.*

gift /gift/ ▸*n.* **1** a thing given willingly to someone without payment; a present: *a Christmas gift* | [as *adj.*] *a gift shop.* ■ an act of giving something as a present: *his mother's gift of a pen.* ■ *inf.* a very easy task or unmissable opportunity: *that touchdown was an absolute gift.* **2** a natural ability or talent: *he has a gift for comedy.*
▸*v.* [*tr.*] give (something) as a gift, esp. formally or as a donation or bequest: *the company gifted 2,999 shares to a charity.* ■ present (someone) with a gift or gifts: *the director gifted her with a heart-shaped brooch.* ■ (**gift someone with**) endow someone with (something): *she was gifted with a powerful clairvoyance.*
▸ □ **look a gift horse in the mouth** find fault with something that has been received as a gift or favor.

gift cer·tif·i·cate ▸*n.* a voucher given as a present that is exchangeable for a specified cash value of goods or services from a particular place of business.

gift·ed /ˈgiftid/ ▸*adj.* having exceptional talent or natural ability: *a gifted amateur musician.* ■ having exceptional intelligence: *scholarships for gifted students.* —**gift·ed·ness** *n.*

gift wrap ▸*n.* decorative paper for wrapping presents. Also called **gift-wrapping.**
▸*v.* (**gift-wrap**) [*tr.*] [usu. as *adj.*] (**gift-wrapped**) wrap (a present) in decorative paper. ■ *fig.* hand over (something) as if a gift: *his first on-screen role came gift-wrapped.*

gig¹ /gig/ ▸*n.* **1** *chiefly hist.* a light two-wheeled carriage pulled by one horse. **2** a light, fast, narrow boat adapted for rowing or sailing.

gig² *inf.* ▸*n.* a live performance by or engagement for a musician or group playing popular or jazz music. ■ a job, esp. one that is temporary or that has an uncertain future: *his first gig as an NFL coach.*
▸*v.* (**gigged, gig·ging**) [*intr.*] perform a gig or gigs. ■ [*tr.*] use (a piece of musical equipment) at a gig.

gig³ ▸*n.* a harpoonlike device used for catching fish or frogs.
▸*v.* (**gigged, gig·ging**) [*intr.*] catch fish or frogs using such a device.

gig⁴ ▸*n. inf. Comput.* short for **GIGABYTE.**

gig·a·bit /ˈgigəˌbit; ˈjig-/ ▸*n. Comput.* a unit of information equal to one billion (10^9) or, strictly, 2^{30} bits.

gig·a·byte /ˈgigəˌbīt; ˈjig-/ (abbr.: **GB**) ▸*n. Comput.* a unit of information equal to one billion (10^9) or, strictly, 2^{30} bytes.

gi·gan·tic /jīˈgantik/ ▸*adj.* of very great size or extent; huge or enormous: *a gigantic concrete tower.* —**gi·gan·ti·cal·ly** /-ik(ə)lē/ *adv.*

gi·gan·tism /jīˈgantizəm/ ▸*n. chiefly Biol.* unusual or abnormal largeness. ■ *Med.* excessive growth due to hormonal imbalance.

gig·gle /ˈgigəl/ ▸*v.* [*intr.*] laugh lightly in a nervous, affected, or silly manner: *they giggled at some private joke.*
▸*n.* a laugh of such a kind. ■ (**the giggles**) continuous uncontrollable giggling: *I got a fit of the giggles.* —**gig·gler** *n.* —**gig·gly** *adj.* (**-gli·er, -gli·est**)

GIGO /ˈgiˌgō/ *chiefly Comput.* ▸*abbr.* garbage in, garbage out. See **GARBAGE.**

gig·o·lo /ˈjigəˌlō/ ▸*n.* (*pl.* **-los**) *chiefly derog.* a young man paid or financially supported by an older woman to be her escort or lover. ■ a professional male dancing partner or escort. ▹1920s (in the sense 'dancing partner'): from French, formed as the masculine of *gigole* 'dance hall woman,' from colloquial *gigue* 'leg.'

gigue /zHēg/ ▸*n. Music* a lively piece of music in the style of a dance, typically of the Renaissance or baroque period.

Gi·la mon·ster /ˈhēlə/ ▸*n.* a venomous lizard (*Heloderma suspectum*) native to the southwestern U.S. and Mexico.

gild /gild/ ▸*v.* [*tr.*] cover thinly with gold. ■ give a specious or false brilliance to: *the martyrs' deaths of the pilots gilded the operation.* —**gild·er** *n.*
▸ □ **gild the lily** try to improve what is already beautiful or excellent.

gild·ing /ˈgildiNG/ ▸*n.* the process of applying gold leaf or gold paint. ■ the material used in, or the surface produced by, this process.

gill¹ /gil/ ▸*n.* (often **gills**) **1** the paired respiratory organ of fishes and some amphibians, by which oxygen is extracted from water flowing over surfaces within or attached to the walls of the pharynx. **2** the vertical plates arranged radially on the underside of mushrooms and many toadstools. **3** the wattles or dewlap of a fowl. ■ (**gills**) the flesh below a person's jaws and ears: *we stuffed ourselves to the gills.* —**gilled** *adj.* [in *comb.*] *a six-gilled shark.*
▸ □ **green around** (or **at**) **the gills** (of a person) sickly-looking.

gill² /jil/ ▸*n.* a unit of liquid measure, equal to a quarter of a pint.

gilt¹ /gilt/ ▸*adj.* covered thinly with gold leaf or gold paint. ■ gold-colored.
▸*n.* gold leaf or gold paint applied in a thin layer to a surface.

gilt² ▸*n.* a young sow.

gim·bal /ˈgimbəl; ˈjim-/ ▸*n.* (often **gimbals**) a mechanism for keeping an instrument such as a compass horizontal in a moving vessel or aircraft. —**gim·baled** (or **gim·balled**) *adj.*

gim·crack /ˈjimˌkrak/ ▸*adj.* flimsy or poorly made but deceptively attractive: *plastic gimcrack cookware.* —**gim·crack·er·y** /-ˌkrakərē/ *n.*

gim·let /ˈgimlit/ ▸*n.* **1** a small tool with a T-shaped handle and a screw-tip for boring holes. **2** a cocktail of gin (or vodka) and lime juice.

gim·mick /ˈgimik/ ▸*n.* a trick or device intended to attract attention, publicity, or business. —**gim·mick·ry** /-rē/ *n.* —**gim·mick·y** *adj.*

gimp¹ /gimp/ ▸*n.* twisted silk, worsted, or cotton with cord or wire running through it, used chiefly as upholstery trimming.

gimp² *inf., often offens.* ▸*n.* a physically handicapped or lame person. ■ a limp. ■ a feeble or contemptible person. —**gimp·y** *adj.*

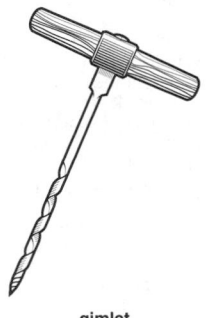

gimlet

gin¹ /jin/ ▸*n.* **1** a clear alcoholic spirit distilled from grain or malt and flavored with juniper berries. **2** (also **gin rummy**) a two-handed form of the card game rummy in which players are dealt ten cards each and attempt to produce a hand in which the point value of unmatched cards adds up to ten or less.

gin² ▸*n.* **1** a machine for separating cotton from its seeds. **2** a machine for raising and moving heavy weights. **3** (also **gin trap**) a snare for catching game.

▸ *v.* (**ginned, gin·ning**) [*tr.*] **1** treat (cotton) in a gin. **2** trap (a person or animal) in a gin. —**gin·ner** *n.*

gin·ger /ˈjinjər/ ▸ *n.* **1** a hot fragrant spice made from the rhizome of a plant. ▪ spirit; mettle. **2** the Southeast Asian plant (*Zingiber officinale*, family Zingiberaceae) from which this rhizome is taken.

▸ *adj.* (chiefly of hair or fur) of a light reddish-yellow color.

▸ *v.* [*tr.*] **1** flavor with ginger. **2** stimulate; enliven: *she slapped his hand lightly to* **ginger him up**. —**gin·ger·y** *adj.*

gin·ger ale ▸ *n.* a clear, effervescent nonalcoholic drink flavored with ginger extract.

gin·ger·bread /ˈjinjərˌbred/ ▸ *n.* cake made with molasses and flavored with ginger. ▪ fancy decoration, esp. on a building: [as *adj.*] *a high-gabled gingerbread house.*

gin·ger·ly /ˈjinjərlē/ ▸ *adv.* in a careful or cautious manner.

▸ *adj.* showing great care or caution: *with strangers the preliminaries are taken at a gingerly pace.* —**gin·ger·li·ness** *n.*

gin·ger snap ▸ *n.* a thin brittle cookie flavored with ginger.

ging·ham /ˈgiNGəm/ ▸ *n.* lightweight plain-woven cotton cloth, typically checked in a white and a bold color: [as *adj.*] *gingham curtains.*

gin·gi·va /jinˈjīvə; ˈjinjəvə/ ▸ *n.* (*pl.* **gin·gi·vae** /jinˈjīvē; ˈjinjəˌvē/) *Med.* the gum. —**gin·gi·val** *adj.*

gin·gi·vi·tis /ˌjinjəˈvītis/ ▸ *n.* *Med.* inflammation of the gums.

gink·go /ˈgiNGkō/ (also **ging·ko**) ▸ *n.* (*pl.* **-oes** or **-os**) a deciduous Chinese tree (*Ginkgo biloba*, family Ginkgoaceae) related to the conifers, with fan-shaped leaves and yellow flowers.

gi·nor·mous /jiˈnôrməs; jī-/ ▸ *adj. inf., humorous* extremely large; enormous: *a ginormous five-volume treatment of Greek and Arabic medicine.*

gin rum·my ▸ *n.* see GIN[1].

gin·seng /ˈjinseNG/ ▸ *n.* **1** a plant tuber credited with various tonic and medicinal properties. **2** the plant (genus *Panax*, family Araliaceae) from which this tuber is obtained, native to eastern Asia and North America.

gip·sy ▸ *n.* variant spelling of GYPSY.

gi·raffe /jəˈraf/ ▸ *n.* (*pl.* same or **giraffes**) a large African mammal (*Giraffa camelopardalis*, family Giraffidae) with a very long neck and forelegs, having a coat patterned with brown patches separated by lighter lines.

gir·an·dole /ˈjirənˌdōl/ ▸ *n.* **1** a branched support for candles or other lights. **2** an earring or pendant with a large central stone surrounded by small ones.

gird /gərd/ ▸ *v.* (*past* and *past part.* **gird·ed** or **girt** /gərt/) [*tr.*] *poetic/lit.* encircle (a person or part of the body) with a belt or band: *a young man was to be girded with the belt of knighthood.* ▪ secure (a garment or sword) on the body with a belt or band: *a white robe girded with a magenta sash.* ▪ surround; encircle: *the mountains girding Kabul.*

▸ □ **gird (up) one's loins** prepare and strengthen oneself for what is to come.

gird·er /ˈgərdər/ ▸ *n.* a large iron or steel beam or compound structure used for building bridges and the framework of large buildings.

gir·dle /ˈgərdl/ ▸ *n.* a belt or cord worn around the waist. ▪ a woman's elasticized corset extending from waist to thigh. ▪ a thing that surrounds something like a belt or girdle: *a communications girdle around the world.*

▸ *v.* [*tr.*] **1** encircle (the body) with or as a girdle or belt: *the Friar loosened the rope that girdled his waist.* ▪ surround; encircle: *the chain of volcanoes that girdles the Pacific.* **2** cut through the bark all the way around (a tree or branch).

girl /gərl/ ▸ *n.* **1** a female child. ▪ a person's daughter, esp. a young one: *he was devoted to his little girl.* **2** a young or relatively young woman. ▪ a young woman of a specified kind or having a specified job: *a chorus girl.* ▪ (**girls**) *inf.* women who mix socially or belong to a particular group, team, or profession: *I look forward to having lunch with the girls.* ▪ a person's girlfriend: *his girl eloped with an accountant.* —**girl·hood** *n.*

girl·friend /ˈgərlˌfrend/ ▸ *n.* a regular female companion with whom a person has a romantic or sexual relationship: *his girlfriend is Australian.* ▪ a woman's female friend.

girl·ish /ˈgərlisH/ ▸ *adj.* of, like, or characteristic of a girl: *girlish giggles.* —**girl·ish·ly** *adv.* —**girl·ish·ness** *n.*

Girl Scout ▸ *n.* a member of an organization of girls, esp. the **Girl Scouts of America**, that promotes character, outdoor activities, good citizenship, and service to others.

girt /gərt/ ▸ past participle of GIRD[1].

girth /gərTH/ ▸ *n.* **1** the measurement around the middle of something,

esp. a person's waist. **2** a band attached to a saddle, used to secure it on a horse by being fastened around its belly.

GIS ▸ *abbr.* geographic information system, a system for storing and manipulating geographical information on computer.

gist /jist/ ▸ *n.* **1** the substance or essence of a speech or text: *she noted the gist of each message.* **2** *Law* the real point of an action: *damage is the gist of the action and without it the plaintiff must fail.*

give /giv/ ▸ *v.* (*past* **gave** /gāv/; *past part.* **giv·en** /ˈgivən/) **1** freely transfer the possession of (something) to (someone); hand over to: *they gave her water to drink* | *the check given to the jeweler proved worthless* | [*tr.*] *he gave the papers back.* ▪ bestow (love, affection, or other emotional support): *his parents gave him the encouragement he needed to succeed* | [as *adj.*] (**giving**) *he was very giving and supportive.* ▪ administer (medicine): *she was given antibiotics.* ▪ hand over (an amount) in exchange or payment; pay: *how much did you give for that?* ▪ (**give something for**) place a specified value on (something): *he never gave anything for French painting.* ▪ [*tr.*] used hyperbolically to express how greatly one wants to have or do something: *I'd give my right arm to be in Othello.* ▪ communicate or impart (a message) to (someone): *give my love to all the girls.* ▪ [*tr.*] commit, consign, or entrust: *a baby given into their care.* ▪ freely devote, set aside, or sacrifice for a purpose: *all who have given thought to the matter agree* | [*intr.*] *committee members who give so generously of their time.* ▪ [*tr.*] (of a man) sanction the marriage of (his daughter) to someone: *he gave her in marriage to an English noble.* ▪ pass on (an illness or infection) to (someone): *I hope I don't give you my cold.* ▪ [*usu. in imper.*] make a connection to allow (someone) to speak to (someone else) on the telephone: *give me the police.* ▪ cite or present when making a toast or introducing a speaker or entertainer: *for your entertainment this evening I give you … Mister Albert DeNiro!* **2** cause or allow (someone or something) to have (something, esp. something abstract); provide or supply with: *you gave me such a fright* | [*tr.*] *this leaflet gives our opening times.* ▪ allot or assign (a score) to: *I gave it five out of ten.* ▪ sentence (someone) to (a specified penalty): *for the first offense I was given a fine.* ▪ concede or yield (something) as valid or deserved in respect of (someone): *give him his due.* ▪ allow (someone) to have (a specified amount of time) for an activity or undertaking: *give me a second to bring the car around* | [*tr.*] *I'll give you until tomorrow morning.* ▪ *inf.* predict that (an activity, undertaking, or relationship) will last no longer than (a specified time): *this will not improve with time—I give it three weeks.* ▪ [*tr.*] yield as a product or result: *milk is sometimes added to give a richer cheese.* ▪ [*tr.*] (**give something off/out/forth**) emit odor, vapor, or similar substances: *it can be burned without giving off toxic fumes.* **3** [*tr.*] carry out or perform (a specified action): *I gave a bow.* ▪ utter or produce (a sound): *he gave a gasp.* ▪ provide (a party or social meal) as host or hostess: *a dinner given in honor of a Canadian diplomat* | *Korda gave him a going-away party.* **4** [*tr.*] state or put forward (information or argument): *he did not give his name.* ▪ pledge or assign as a guarantee: *I give you my word.* ▪ say to (someone) as an excuse or inappropriate answer: *don't give me any of your back talk.* ▪ deliver (a judgment) authoritatively: *I gave my verdict.* ▪ present (an appearance or impression): *he gave no sign of life.* ▪ [*intr.*] *inf.* tell what one knows: *okay, give—what's that all about?* **5** [*intr.*] alter in shape under pressure rather than resist or break: *that cushion doesn't give.* ▪ yield or give way to pressure: *the heavy door didn't give until the fifth push* | *fig. when two people who don't get on are thrust together, something's got to give.* ▪ [*intr.*] *inf.* concede defeat; surrender: *I give!*

▸ *phrasal v.* □ **give someone away 1** reveal the true identity of someone: *his strangely shaped feet gave him away.* ▪ reveal information that incriminates someone. **2** hand over a bride ceremonially to her bridegroom as part of a wedding ceremony. □ **give something away** reveal something secret or concealed. □ **give in** cease fighting or arguing; yield; surrender: *he reluctantly gave in to the pressure.* □ **give out** be completely used up: *her energy was on the verge of giving out.* ▪ stop functioning; break down: *he curses and swears till his voice gives out.* □ **give something out** distribute or broadcast something: *I've been giving out leaflets.* □ **give up** cease making an effort; resign oneself to failure. □ **give it up** [usu. in *imper.*] *inf.* applaud a performer or entertainer. □ **give oneself up to** surrender oneself to law-enforcement agents. □ **give someone up** deliver a wanted person to authority: *a voice told him to come out and give himself up.* □ **give something up** part with something that one would prefer to keep: *she would have given up everything for love.* ▪ stop the habitual doing or consuming of something: *I've decided to give up drinking.*

Pronunciation Key ə *ago,* up; ər *over,* fur; a *hat;* ā *ate;* ä *car;* CH *chin;* e *let;* ē *see;* e(ə)r *air;* i *fit;* ī *by;* i(ə)r *ear;* NG *sing;* ō *go;* ô *law, for;* oi *toy;* o͝o *good;* o͞o *goo;* ou *out;* SH *she;* TH *thin;* TH *then;* (h)w *why;* ZH *vision*

☐ **give up on** stop having faith or belief in: *they weren't about to give up on their heroes so easily.*

▶ *n.* capacity to bend or alter in shape under pressure; elasticity: *plastic pots that have enough give to accommodate the vigorous roots.* ■ *fig.* ability to adapt or comply; flexibility: *there is no give in the British position.* —**giv·er** *n.*

▶ ☐ **give and take** mutual concessions and compromises. ■ [as *v.*] make concessions and compromises. ☐ **give as good as one gets** respond with equal force or vehemence when attacked. ☐ **give it to someone** *inf.* scold or punish someone. ☐ **give me** —— I prefer or admire ——: *give me the mainland any day!* ☐ **give me a break** *inf.* used to express exasperation, protest, or disbelief. ☐ **give or take** —— *inf.* to within —— (used to express the degree or accuracy of a figure): *three hundred and fifty years ago, give or take a few.* ■ apart from: *give or take a handful of machine tools, there are few new products.* ☐ **not give a damn** (or **hoot**, etc.) *inf.* not care at all: *people who don't give a damn about the environment.* ☐ **what gives?** *inf.* what's the news?; what's happening?.

give·a·way /'givˌwā/ *inf.* ▶ *n.* **1** a thing that is given free, esp. for promotional purposes: *a preelection tax giveaway.* **2** a thing that makes an inadvertent revelation: *the shape of the parcel was a dead giveaway.*
▶ *adj.* **1** free of charge: *giveaway goodies.* ■ (of prices) very low. **2** revealing: *small giveaway mannerisms.*

giv·en /'givən/ ▶ past participle of GIVE.
▶ *adj.* **1** specified or stated: *our level of knowledge on any given subject.* **2** (**given to**) inclined or disposed to: *she was not often given to anger.* **3** conferred or bestowed as a gift: *she squandered what was a given opportunity.*
▶ *prep.* taking into account: *given the task, they were able to do a good job.*
▶ *n.* a known or established fact or situation: *attentive service is a given.*

giz·mo /'gizmō/ (also **gis·mo**) ▶ *n.* (*pl.* **-mos**) *inf.* a gadget, esp. one whose name the speaker does not know or cannot recall.

giz·zard /'gizərd/ ▶ *n.* a muscular, thick-walled part of a bird's stomach for grinding food, typically with grit. ■ a muscular stomach of some fish, insects, mollusks, and other invertebrates. ▷late Middle English *giser*: from Old French, based on Latin *gigeria* 'cooked entrails of fowl.' The final *-d* was added in the 16th cent.

gla·cé /gla'sā/ ▶ *adj.* **1** (of fruit) having a glossy surface due to preservation in sugar: *a glacé cherry.* **2** (of cloth or leather) smooth and highly polished.
▶ *v.* (**-cés, -céed** /-'sād/ or **-céd, -cé·ing**) [*tr.*] glaze with a thin sugar-based coating: [as *adj.*] *glacéed cape gooseberries.*

gla·cial /'glāSHəl/ ▶ *adj.* **1** relating to, resulting from, or denoting the presence or agency of ice, esp. in the form of glaciers: *thick glacial deposits* | *a glacial lake.* **2** of ice; icy: *the glacial mountains of New Zealand* | *fig. glacial blue eyes.* ■ extremely cold: *glacial temperatures.* ■ extremely slow: *an official described progress in the talks as glacial.*
▶ *n. Geol.* a glacial period. —**gla·cial·ly** *adv.*

gla·cial pe·ri·od ▶ *n.* a period in the earth's history when polar and mountain ice sheets were unusually extensive across the earth's surface.

gla·ci·at·ed /'glāSHēˌātid/ ▶ *adj.* covered or having been covered by glaciers or ice sheets: *a glaciated valley.* ▷mid 19th cent.: past participle of obsolete *glaciate*, from Latin *glaciare* 'freeze,' from *glacies* 'ice.'

gla·cier /'glāSHər/ ▶ *n.* a slowly moving mass of ice formed by the accumulation and compaction of snow on mountains or near the poles.

gla·ci·ol·o·gy /ˌglāSHē'äləjē/ ▶ *n.* the study of the internal dynamics and effects of glaciers. —**gla·ci·o·log·i·cal** /-SHēə'läjikəl/ *adj.* —**gla·ci·ol·o·gist** /-jist/ *n.*

glad¹ /glad/ ▶ *adj.* (**glad·der, glad·dest**) pleased; delighted: *I'm really glad to hear that.* ■ happy for someone's good fortune: *I'm so glad for you.* ■ causing happiness: *glad tidings.* ■ grateful: *he was glad for the excuse to put it off.* ■ willing and eager (to do something): *he will be glad to carry your bags.* —**glad·ly** *adv.* —**glad·ness** *n.* —**glad·some** *adj.*

glad² ▶ *n. inf.* a gladiolus.

glade /glād/ ▶ *n.* an open space in a forest.

glad·i·a·tor /'gladēˌātər/ ▶ *n.* **1** (in ancient Rome) a man trained to fight with weapons against other men or wild animals in an arena. **2** a person defending or opposing a cause; a controversialist: *he chose not to be a gladiator in the presidential arena.* —**glad·i·a·to·ri·al** /ˌgladēə'tôrēəl/ *adj.*

glad·i·o·lus /ˌgladē'ōləs/ ▶ *n.* (*pl.* **gladioli** /-lī/ or **gladioluses**) a widely cultivated plant (genus *Gladiolus*) of the iris family, with sword-shaped leaves and spikes of brightly colored flowers.

glad rags ▶ *pl. n. inf.* clothes for a special occasion; one's best clothes.

Glad·stone bag ▶ *n.* a bag like a briefcase having two equal compartments joined by a hinge.

glair /gle(ə)r/ ▶ *n.* a preparation made from egg white, used esp. as an adhesive for bookbinding and gilding. —**glair·y** *adj.*

glam·or·ize /'glaməˌrīz/ (also **glam·our·ize**) ▶ *v.* [*tr.*] make (something) seem glamorous or desirable, esp. spuriously so: *the lyrics glamorize drugs.* —**glam·or·i·za·tion** /ˌglaməri'zāSHən/ *n.*

glam·our /'glamər/ (also **glam·or**) ▶ *n.* the attractive or exciting quality that makes certain people or things seem appealing or special: *the glamour of Monte Carlo* | [as *adj.*] *the glamour days of Old Hollywood.* ■ beauty or charm that is sexually attractive. —**glam·o·rous** *adj.*

glance /glans/ ▶ *v.* [*intr.*] **1** take a brief or hurried look: *Ginny glanced at her watch.* ■ (**glance at/through**) read quickly or cursorily: *I glanced through your personnel file last night.* **2** hit something at an angle and bounce off obliquely: *he saw a stone glance off a crag and hit Tom on the head.* ■ (esp. of light) reflect off something with a brief flash: *sunlight glanced off the curved body of a dolphin.*
▶ *n.* a brief or hurried look: *Sean and Michael exchanged glances.* **2** *poetic/lit.* a flash or gleam of light. —**glanc·ing** *adj.* —**glanc·ing·ly** *adv.*

▶ ☐ **at a glance** immediately upon looking: *she saw at a glance what had happened.* ☐ **at first glance** when seen or considered for the first time, esp. briefly: *good news, at first glance, for frequent travelers.*

gland¹ /gland/ ▶ *n.* an organ in the human or animal body that secretes particular chemical substances for use in the body or for discharge into the surroundings. ■ a structure resembling this, esp. a lymph node.

gland² ▶ *n.* a sleeve used to produce a seal around a piston rod or other shaft.

glan·du·lar /'glanjələr/ ▶ *adj.* of, relating to, or affecting a gland or glands.

glan·du·lar fe·ver ▶ another term for INFECTIOUS MONONUCLEOSIS.

glans /glanz/ ▶ *n.* (*pl.* **glan·des** /'glandēz/) *Anat.* the rounded part forming the end of the penis (**glans penis**) or clitoris (**glans clitoridis**).

glare /gle(ə)r/ ▶ *v.* [*intr.*] **1** stare in an angry or fierce way: *she glared at him, her cheeks flushing.* ■ [*tr.*] express (a feeling, esp. defiance) by staring in such a way: *he glared defiance at the pistols pointing down at him.* **2** (of the sun or an electric light) shine with a strong or dazzling light: *the sun glared out of a clear blue sky.*
▶ *n.* **1** a fierce or angry stare. **2** strong and dazzling light: *Murray narrowed his eyes against the glare of the sun.* ■ *fig.* oppressive public attention or scrutiny: *he carried on his life in the full glare of publicity.* —**glar·y** *adj.*

glare ice ▶ *n.* smooth, glassy ice.

glar·ing /'gle(ə)riNG/ ▶ *adj.* **1** giving out or reflecting a strong or dazzling light: *the glaring sun.* ■ staring fiercely or fixedly. **2** highly obvious or conspicuous: *a glaring omission.* —**glar·ing·ly** *adv.*

glas·nost /'glazˌnôst; 'glas-; 'gläz-; 'gläs-/ ▶ *n.* (in the former Soviet Union) the policy or practice of more open consultative government and wider dissemination of information.

glass /glas/ ▶ *n.* **1** a hard, brittle substance, typically transparent or translucent, made by fusing sand with soda, lime, and sometimes other ingredients and cooling rapidly: *a piece of glass* | *a glass door.* ■ any similar substance that has solidified from a molten state without crystallizing. **2** a thing made from, or partly from, glass, in particular: ■ a container to drink from: *a beer glass.* ■ glassware. **3** a lens, or an optical instrument containing a lens or lenses, in particular a monocle or a magnifying lens. **4** the liquid or amount of liquid contained in a glass; a glassful: *a glass of lemonade.*
▶ *v.* [*tr.*] **1** cover or enclose with glass: *the inn has a long balcony, now glassed in.* **2** (esp. in hunting) scan (one's surroundings) with binoculars: *the first day was spent glassing the rolling hills.* —**glass·ful** /-ˌfo͝ol/ *n.* (*pl.* **-fuls**.) —**glass·less** *adj.* —**glass·like** /-ˌlīk/ *adj.*

glass ceil·ing ▶ *n.* an unofficially acknowledged barrier to advancement in a profession, esp. affecting women and members of minorities.

glass·es /'glasiz/ ▶ *pl. n.* a pair of lenses set in a frame resting on the nose and ears, used to correct or assist defective eyesight or protect the eyes. ■ a pair of binoculars.

glass·ine /gla'sēn/ ▶ *n.* [usu. as *adj.*] a glossy transparent paper: *glassine envelopes.*

glass·ware /'glasˌwe(ə)r/ ▶ *n.* ornaments and articles made from glass.

glass·wort /'glasˌwərt; -ˌwôrt/ ▶ *n.* a widely distributed salt-marsh plant (genus *Salicornia*) of the goosefoot family, with fleshy scalelike leaves.

glass·y /'glasē/ ▶ *adj.* (**glass·i·er, glass·i·est**) **1** of or resembling glass in some way, in particular: ■ having the physical properties of glass; vitreous: *glassy lavas.* ■ (of water) having a smooth surface. ■ (of sound) resembling the sharp or ringing noise made when glass is struck: *a glassy clink.* ■ (of a building) having glass walls. **2** (of a person's eyes or expression) showing no interest or animation; dull and glazed. —**glass·i·ly** /ˈglasəlē/ adv. —**glass·i·ness** n.

Glau·ber's salt /ˈgloubərz/ ▶n. (also **Glauber's salts**) a crystalline hydrated form of sodium sulfate, used chiefly as a laxative.

glau·co·ma /glôˈkōmə/ ▶n. Med. a condition of increased pressure within the eyeball, causing gradual loss of sight. ▷mid 17th cent.: via Latin from Greek glaukōma, based on glaukos 'bluish-green, bluish-gray' (because of the gray-green haze in the pupil). —**glau·co·ma·tous** /-mətəs/ adj.

glau·cous /ˈglôkəs/ ▶adj. technical or poetic/lit. **1** of a dull grayish-green or blue color. **2** covered with a powdery bloom.

glaze /glāz/ ▶v. [tr.] **1** fit panes of glass into (a window or doorframe or similar structure): windows can be glazed using laminated glass. ■ enclose or cover with glass: the verandas were glazed in. **2** (often **be glazed**) cover with a glaze or similar finish. **3** [intr.] lose brightness and animation: the prospect makes my eyes glaze over with boredom | [as adj.] (**glazed**) she had that glazed look in her eyes again.
▶n. **1** a substance used to give a smooth, shiny surface to something, in particular: ■ a vitreous substance fused on to the surface of pottery. ■ a liquid such as milk or beaten egg, used to form a smooth shiny coating on food. ■ chiefly Art a thin topcoat of transparent paint used to modify the tone of an underlying color. **2** a smooth, shiny surface formed esp. by glazing: the glaze of the white cups. ■ a thin, glassy coating of ice. —**glaz·er** n.

gla·zier /ˈglāzhər/ ▶n. a person whose profession is fitting glass into windows and doors.

glaz·ing /ˈglāziNG/ ▶n. the action of installing windows. ■ glass windows: sealed protective glazing. ■ a material used to produce a glaze.

GLBT ▶abbr. gay, lesbian, bisexual, and transgendered: a planned GLBT cable channel.

gleam /glēm/ ▶v. [intr.] shine brightly, esp. with reflected light: light gleamed on the china cats. ■ (of a smooth surface or object) reflect light because well polished. | [as adj.] (**gleaming**) sleek and gleaming black limousines. ■ (of an emotion or quality) appear or be expressed through the brightness of someone's eyes or expression: a hint of mischief gleaming in her eyes.
▶n. a faint or brief light, esp. one reflected from something. ■ a brief or faint instance of a quality or emotion, esp. a desirable one: the gleam of hope vanished. ■ a brightness in a person's eyes taken as a sign of a particular emotion. —**gleam·ing·ly** adv. —**gleam·y** adj. (archaic).

glean /glēn/ ▶v. [tr.] extract (information) from various sources: the information is gleaned from press clippings. ■ collect gradually and bit by bit: objects gleaned from local markets. —**glean·er** n. —**glean·ing** n.

glee /glē/ ▶n. **1** great delight: his face lit up with impish glee. **2** a song for men's voices in three or more parts.

glee club ▶n. a group organized to sing short choral works, esp. part-songs.

glee·ful /ˈglēfəl/ ▶adj. exuberantly or triumphantly joyful: she gave a gleeful chuckle. —**glee·ful·ly** adv. —**glee·ful·ness** n.

glen /glen/ ▶n. a narrow valley.

glen·gar·ry /glenˈgarē/ ▶n. (pl. **-ries**) a brimless boat-shaped hat with a cleft down the center worn as part of Scottish Highland dress.

glib /glib/ ▶adj. (**glib·ber**, **glib·best**) (of words or the person speaking them) fluent and voluble but insincere and shallow: she was careful not to sound too glib. —**glib·ly** adv. —**glib·ness** n.

glide /glīd/ ▶v. **1** [intr.] move with a smooth continuous motion, typically with little noise: a few gondolas glided past. ■ [tr.] cause to move with a smooth continuous motion. **2** [intr.] make an unpowered flight, either in a glider or in an aircraft with engine failure. ■ (of a bird) fly through the air with very little movement of the wings.

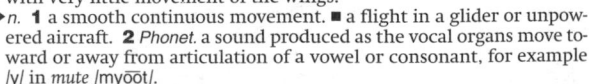

glengarry

▶n. **1** a smooth continuous movement. ■ a flight in a glider or unpowered aircraft. **2** Phonet. a sound produced as the vocal organs move toward or away from articulation of a vowel or consonant, for example /y/ in mute /myoōt/.

glid·er /ˈglīdər/ ▶n. **1** a light aircraft that is designed to fly for long periods without using an engine. **2** a person or thing that glides. **3** a long swinging seat suspended from a frame in a porch.

glim·mer /ˈglimər/ ▶v. [intr.] shine faintly with a wavering light: the moonlight glimmered on the lawn | [as adj.] (**glimmering**) pools of glimmering light.

▶n. a faint or wavering light. ■ a faint sign of a feeling or quality, esp. a desirable one: there is one glimmer of hope for Becky. —**glim·mer·ing·ly** adv.

glim·mer·ing /ˈgliməriNG/ ▶n. a glimmer: the glimmering of an idea.

glimpse /glimps/ ▶n. a momentary or partial view: she caught a glimpse of the ocean | a glimpse into the world of the wealthy.
▶v. [tr.] see or perceive briefly or partially: he glimpsed a figure standing in the shade.

glint /glint/ ▶v. [intr.] give out or reflect small flashes of light: her glasses were glinting in the firelight. ■ (of a person's eyes) shine with a particular emotion: his eyes glinted angrily.
▶n. a small flash of light, esp. as reflected from a shiny surface. ■ a brightness in someone's eyes seen as a sign of enthusiasm or a particular emotion: she saw the glint of excitement in his eyes.

glis·san·do /gliˈsändō/ ▶n. (pl. **-di** /-dē/ or **-dos**) Mus. a continuous slide upward or downward between two notes.

glis·ten /ˈglisən/ ▶v. [intr.] (of something wet or greasy) shine; glitter: his cheeks glistened with tears | [as adj.] (**glistening**) the glistening pool.
▶n. a sparkling light reflected from something wet: there was a glisten of perspiration across her top lip. —**glis·ten·ing·ly** adv.

glis·ter /ˈglistər/ poetic/lit. ▶v. [intr.] sparkle; glitter.
▶n. a sparkle.

glitch /gliCH/ inf. ▶n. a sudden, usually temporary malfunction or irregularity of equipment: a draft version was lost in a computer glitch. ■ an unexpected setback in a plan.
▶v. [intr.] suffer a sudden malfunction or irregularity: her job involves troubleshooting when systems glitch. —**glitch·y** adj.

glit·ter /ˈglitər/ ▶v. [intr.] shine with a bright, shimmering, reflected light: trees and grass glittered with dew. ■ shine as a result of strong feeling: her eyes were glittering with excitement.
▶n. bright, shimmering, reflected light. ■ tiny pieces of sparkling material used for decoration: sneakers trimmed with sequins and glitter. ■ fig. an attractive, exciting, often superficial, quality: he avoids the glitter of show business. ■ a glint in a person's eye indicating a particular emotion: the scathing glitter in his eyes. —**glit·ter·ing·ly** adv. —**glit·ter·y** adj.

glit·te·ra·ti /ˌglitəˈrätē/ ▶pl. n. inf. the fashionable set of people engaged in show business or some other glamorous activity. ▷1950s (originally U.S.): blend of glitter + literati (from Latin literatus 'acquainted with letters,' from littera 'letter').

glitz /glits/ inf. ▶n. extravagant but superficial display: the glitz and sophisticated night life of Ibiza.
▶v. [tr.] make (something) glamorous or showy: glitz up the program.

glitz·y /ˈglitsē/ ▶adj. (**glitz·i·er**, **glitz·i·est**) inf. ostentatiously attractive (often used to suggest superficial glamour): I wanted something glitzy to wear to the launch party. —**glitz·i·ly** /-səlē/ adv. —**glitz·i·ness** n.

gloam·ing /ˈglōmiNG/ ▶n. (**the gloaming**) poetic/lit. twilight; dusk.

gloat /glōt/ ▶v. [intr.] contemplate or dwell on one's own success or another's misfortune with smugness or malignant pleasure: his enemies gloated over his death.
▶n. inf. an act of gloating. ▷late 16th cent.: of unknown origin; perhaps related to Old Norse glotta 'to grin' and Middle High German glotzen 'to stare.' The original sense was 'give a sideways or furtive look,' hence 'cast amorous or admiring glances'; the current sense dates from the mid 18th cent. —**gloat·er** n. —**gloat·ing·ly** adv.

glob /gläb/ ▶n. inf. a lump of a semiliquid substance: thick globs of melted mozzarella cheese.

glob·al /ˈglōbəl/ ▶adj. of or relating to the whole world; worldwide: the downturn in the global economy. ■ of or relating to the entire earth as a planet: global environmental change. ■ relating to or embracing the whole of something, or of a group of things: a global picture of what is involved in the task. ■ Comput. operating or applying through the whole of a file, program, etc.: global searches. —**glob·al·ly** adv.

glo·bal com·mon ▶n. any of the earth's ubiquitous and unowned natural resources, such as the oceans, the atmosphere, and space: [usually pl.] financial speculators and other abusers of our global commons.

glob·al·ize /ˈglōbəˌlīz/ ▶v. develop or be developed so as to make possible international influence or operation: [trans.] communication globalizes capital markets [intrans.] building facilities overseas is part of the strategy of every company that aims to globalize. —**glob·al·i·za·tion** /ˌglōbəliˈzāSHən/ n.

glob·al warm·ing ▶n. the gradual increase in the overall temperature of the earth's atmosphere due to the greenhouse effect caused by

---

Pronunciation Key ə ago, up; ər over, fur; a hat; ā ate; ä car; CH chin; e let; ē see; e(ə)r air; i fit; ī by; i(ə)r ear; NG sing; ō go; ô law, for; oi toy; oō good; oō goo; ou out; SH she; TH thin; TH then; (h)w why; ZH vision

increased levels of carbon dioxide, methane, and other gases. See CLI-MATE CHANGE.

globe /glōb/ ▶n. **1** (**the globe**) the earth: *collecting goodies from all over the globe.* ■ a spherical representation of the earth or of the constellations with a map on the surface. **2** a spherical or rounded object: *orange trees clipped into giant globes.* ■ a glass sphere protecting a light. ■ a drinking glass shaped approximately like a sphere: *a brandy globe.*
▶v. [tr.] *poetic/lit.* form (something) into a globe. —**globe·like** /-ˌlīk/ *adj.* —**glo·boid** /'glōboid/ *adj. & n.* —**glo·bose** /'glōbōs/ *adj.*

globe·fish /'glōbˌfisH/ (*pl.* same or **-fish·es**) ▶n. **1** a pufferfish or a porcupine fish. **2** an ocean sunfish. See SUNFISH (sense 1).

glob·u·lar /'gläbyələr/ ▶*adj.* **1** globe-shaped; spherical. **2** composed of globules.

glob·ule /'gläbyōōl/ ▶n. a small round particle of a substance; a drop: *globules of fat.* —**glob·u·lous** /-yələs/ *adj.*

glock·en·spiel /'gläkən,spēl/ ; -,sHpēl/ ▶n. a musical percussion instrument having a set of tuned metal pieces mounted in a frame and struck with small hammers.

glom /gläm/ ▶v. (**glommed, glom·ming**) *inf.* [tr.] steal: *I thought he was about to glom my wallet.* ■ [intr.] (**glom onto**) become stuck or attached to.

glo·mer·u·lus /glō'meryələs/ ▶n. (*pl.* **-li** /-ˌlī/) *Anat. & Biol.* a cluster of nerve endings, spores, or small blood vessels, in particular: ■ a cluster of capillaries around the end of a kidney tubule, where waste products are filtered from the blood. —**glo·mer·u·lar** /-lər/ *adj.*

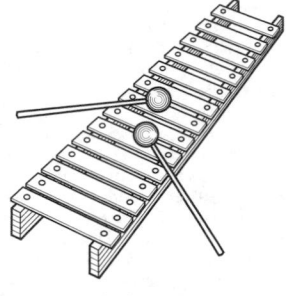
glockenspiel

gloom /glōōm/ ▶n. **1** partial or total darkness: *he strained his eyes peering into the gloom.* ■ *poetic/lit.* a dark or shady place. **2** a state of depression or despondency: *a year of economic gloom for the car industry.*
▶v. [intr.] **1** *poetic/lit.* have a dark or somber appearance: *the black gibbet glooms beside the way.* ■ [tr.] cover with gloom; make dark or dismal: *a black yew gloom'd the stagnant air.* **2** be or look depressed or despondent: *Charles was always glooming about money.*

gloom·y /'glōōmē/ ▶*adj.* (**gloom·i·er, gloom·i·est**) dark or poorly lit, esp. so as to appear depressing or frightening: *a gloomy corridor.* ■ feeling distressed or pessimistic. ■ causing distress or depression: *a gloomy atmosphere.* —**gloom·i·ly** /-məlē/ *adv.* —**gloom·i·ness** *n.*

glop /gläp/ ▶n. *inf.* a sticky and amorphous substance, typically something unpleasant. ■ a soft, shapeless lump of something: *a glop of creamy dressing.* ■ *fig.* worthless or overly sentimental writing, music, or other material: *commercialized glop, not worth thinking about.* —**glop·py** *adj.* (**-pi·er, -pi·est**).

Glo·ri·a /'glôrēə/ ▶n. a Christian liturgical hymn or formula beginning (in the Latin text) with *Gloria,* in particular: ■ the hymn beginning *Gloria in excelsis Deo.* ■ a musical setting of this: *Vivaldi's Gloria.*

glo·ri·fy /'glôrəˌfī/ ▶v. (**-fies, -fied**) [tr.] **1** reveal or make clearer the glory of (God) by one's actions: *God can be glorified through a life of scholarship.* ■ give praise to (God). **2** describe or represent as admirable, esp. unjustifiably or undeservedly: *a football video glorifying violence.* —**glo·ri·fi·ca·tion** /ˌglôrəfi'kāsHən/ *n.* —**glo·ri·fi·er** *n.*

glo·ri·ous /'glôrēəs/ ▶*adj.* **1** having, worthy of, or bringing fame or admiration. **2** having a striking beauty or splendor: *a glorious autumn day.* —**glo·ri·ous·ly** *adv.* —**glo·ri·ous·ness** *n.*

glo·ry /'glôrē/ ▶n. (*pl.* **-ries**) **1** high renown or honor won by notable achievements: *to fight and die for the glory of one's nation.* ■ praise, worship, and thanksgiving offered to God. **2** magnificence; great beauty: *the train has been restored to all its former glory.* ■ (often **glories**) a thing that is beautiful or distinctive; a special cause for pride, respect, or delight: *the glories of Paris.* ■ the splendor and bliss of heaven: *with the saints in glory.*
▶v. [intr.] (**glory in**) take great pride or pleasure in: *they were individuals who gloried in their independence.* ■ exult in unpleasantly or boastfully.
▶ □ **in one's glory** in a state of extreme joy or exaltation.

gloss¹ /gläs; glôs/ ▶n. shine or luster on a smooth surface. ■ a type of paint that dries to a bright shiny surface. ■ a superficially attractive appearance or impression: *beneath the gloss of success was a tragic private life.*
▶v. [tr.] apply a cosmetic gloss to. ■ apply gloss paint to. ■ (**gloss over**) try to conceal or disguise by treating briefly or representing as misleading: *the social costs of this growth are glossed over.* —**gloss·er** *n.*

gloss² ▶n. a translation or explanation of a word or phrase.
▶v. [tr.] (usu. **be glossed**) provide an explanation, interpretation, or paraphrase for (a text, word, etc.).

glos·sa·ry /'gläsərē; 'glô-/ ▶n. (*pl.* **-ries**) an alphabetical list of terms or words found in or relating to a specific subject, text, or dialect, with explanations. —**glos·sar·i·al** /glä'se(ə)rēəl; glô-/ *adj.* —**glos·sa·rist** /-rist/ *n.*

gloss·y /'gläsē; 'glô-/ ▶*adj.* (**gloss·i·er, gloss·i·est**) shiny and smooth: *thick, glossy, manageable hair.* ■ (of paint) drying to a bright shiny surface. ■ (of a magazine or photograph) printed on high-quality smooth shiny paper. ■ superficially attractive and stylish, and suggesting wealth or expense: *glossy TV miniseries and soaps.*
▶n. (*pl.* **gloss·ies**) *inf.* a magazine printed on glossy paper, expensively produced with many color photographs. ■ a photograph printed on glossy paper. —**gloss·i·ly** /-səlē/ *adv.* —**gloss·i·ness** *n.*

glot·tal /'glätl/ ▶*adj.* of or produced by the glottis.

glot·tis /'glätis/ ▶n. the part of the larynx consisting of the vocal cords and the slitlike opening between them. —**glot·tic** /'glätik/ *adj.*

glove /gləv/ ▶n. a covering for the hand worn for protection against cold or dirt and typically having separate parts for each finger and the thumb. ■ a padded protective covering for the hand used in boxing, baseball, and other sports. —**gloved** *adj.* —**glove·less** *adj.*
▶ □ **fit like a glove** (of clothes) fit exactly. □ **the gloves are off** (or **with the gloves off** or **take the gloves off**) used to express the notion that something will be done in an uncompromising or brutal way: *for the banks chasing this growing business, the gloves are now definitely off.*

glove box (also **glove-box**) ▶n. **1** another term for GLOVE COMPARTMENT. **2** a closed chamber into which a pair of gloves projects from openings in the side, used esp. in laboratories and incubators in hospitals to prevent contamination.

glove com·part·ment ▶n. a recess with a hinged door in the dashboard of a motor vehicle, used for storing small items.

glow /glō/ ▶v. [intr.] give out steady light without flame: *the tips of their cigarettes glowed in the dark.* ■ have an intense color and a slight shine: *faces that glowed red with the cold.* ■ have a heightened color or a bloom on the skin as a result of warmth or health. ■ feel deep pleasure or satisfaction and convey it through one's expression and bearing: *Katy always glowed when he praised her.*
▶n. a steady radiance of light or heat. ■ a feeling of warmth in the face or body; the visible effects of this as a redness of the cheeks: *he could feel the brandy filling him with a warm glow.* ■ a strong feeling of pleasure or well-being: *with a glow of pride, Mildred walked away.*

glow·er /'glouər/ ▶v. [intr.] have an angry or sullen look on one's face; scowl: *she glowered at him suspiciously.*
▶n. an angry or sullen look. —**glow·er·ing** *adj.* —**glow·er·ing·ly** *adv.*

glow·worm /'glō,wərm/ ▶n. a soft-bodied beetle (families Lampyridae and Phengodidae) with luminescent organs in the abdomen.

glox·in·i·a /gläk'sinēə/ ▶n. a tropical American plant (genera *Gloxinia* and *Sinningia,* family Gesneriaceae) with large, velvety, bell-shaped flowers.

glu·ca·gon /'glōōkə,gän/ ▶n. *Biochem.* a hormone formed in the pancreas that promotes the breakdown of glycogen to glucose in the liver.

glu·cose /'glōōkōs/ ▶n. *Biochem.* a hexose sugar, $C_6H_{12}O_6$, that is an important energy source in living organisms and is a component of many carbohydrates. ■ a syrup containing glucose and other sugars, used in the food industry.

glu·co·side /'glōōkə,sīd/ ▶n. *Biochem.* a glycoside derived from glucose. —**glu·co·sid·ic** /ˌglōōkə'sidik/ *adj.*

glue /glōō/ ▶n. an adhesive substance used for sticking objects or materials together.
▶v. (**glues, glued, glu·ing** or **glue·ing**) [tr.] fasten or join with or as if with glue. ■ (**be glued to**) *inf.* be paying very close attention to (something, esp. a television or computer screen): *I was glued to the television when the Olympics were on.* —**glue·like** /-ˌlīk/ *adj.* —**glue·y** *adj.*

glug /gləg/ *inf.* ▶v. (**glugged, glug·ging**) [tr.] drink or pour (liquid) with a hollow gurgling sound: *he glugs down half his beer.*
▶n. a hollow gurgling sound or series of sounds as of liquid being poured from a bottle. ■ an amount of liquid poured from a bottle.

glum /gləm/ ▶*adj.* (**glum·mer, glum·mest**) looking or feeling dejected; morose. —**glum·ly** *adv.* —**glum·ness** *n.*

glut /glət/ ▶n. an excessively abundant supply of something: *there is a glut of cars on the market.*
▶v. (**glut·ted, glut·ting**) [tr.] (usu. **be glutted**) supply or fill to excess.

glu·ten /'glōōtn/ ▶n. a substance present in cereal grains, esp. wheat, that is responsible for the elastic texture of dough. Gluten causes illness in people with celiac disease.

glu·te·us /ˈglo͞otēəs/ (also **gluteus muscle**) ▶n. (pl. **-te·i** /-tē,ī/) any of three muscles in each buttock that move the thigh, the largest of which is the **gluteus maximus.** —**glu·te·al** /-tēəl/ adj.

glu·ti·nous /ˈglo͞otn-əs/ ▶adj. like glue in texture; sticky: glutinous mud. —**glu·ti·nous·ly** adv. —**glu·ti·nous·ness** n.

glut·ton /ˈglətn/ ▶n. **1** an excessively greedy eater. ■ a person who is excessively fond of or always eager for something: a glutton for adventure. **2** another term for WOLVERINE, esp. the European species. ▷Middle English: from Old French gluton, from Latin glutton-, related to gluttire 'to swallow,' gluttus 'greedy,' and gula 'throat.' —**glut·ton·ize** /-,īz/ v. —**glut·ton·ous** /-əs/ adj. —**glut·ton·ous·ly** /-əslē/ adv.

▶ □ **a glutton for punishment** a person who is always eager to undertake hard or unpleasant tasks.

glut·ton·y /ˈglətn-ē/ ▶n. habitual greed or excess in eating.

gly·ce·mic in·dex /glīˈsēmik/ ▶n. a scale that ranks foods from 1 to 100 based on their effect on blood-sugar levels.

glyc·er·ide /ˈglisə,rīd/ ▶n. a fatty acid ester of glycerol.

glyc·er·in /ˈglisərin/ (also **glyc·er·ine** /-rin/ -,rēn; ,glisə'rēn/) ▶n. another term for GLYCEROL.

glyc·er·ol /ˈglisə,rôl; -,räl/ ▶n. a colorless, sweet, viscous liquid alcohol used for making explosives and antifreeze.

gly·cine /ˈglīsēn/ ▶n. Biochem. the simplest naturally occurring amino acid, H_2NCH_2COOH. It is a constituent of most proteins.

gly·co·bi·ol·o·gy /ˌglīkōbī'äləjē/ ▶n. the scientific study of carbohydrates and their role in biology. ■ this field limited to the study of sugars.

gly·co·gen /ˈglīkəjən/ ▶n. Biochem. a substance deposited in bodily tissues as a store of carbohydrates. —**gly·co·gen·ic** /ˌglīkə'jenik/ adj.

gly·co·gen·e·sis /ˌglīkə'jenəsis/ ▶n. Biochem. the formation of glycogen from sugar.

gly·col /ˈglīkôl; -kōl/ ▶n. short for ETHYLENE GLYCOL.

gly·col·y·sis /glī'käləsis/ ▶n. Biochem. the breakdown of glucose by enzymes, releasing energy and pyruvic acid. —**gly·co·lyt·ic** /ˌglīkə'litik/ adj.

gly·co·pro·tein /ˌglīkō'prōtēn/ ▶n. Biochem. any of a class of proteins that have carbohydrate groups attached to the polypeptide chain. Also called **gly·co·pep·tide.**

gly·co·side /ˈglīkə,sīd/ ▶n. Biochem. a compound formed from a simple sugar and another compound by replacement of a hydroxyl group in the sugar molecule. —**gly·co·sid·ic** /ˌglīkə'sidik/ adj.

gly·cos·u·ri·a /ˌglīkōsyo͝o'rēə/ ▶n. Med. a condition characterized by an excess of sugar in the urine, typically associated with diabetes or kidney disease. —**gly·cos·u·ric** /-'syo͝orik/ adj.

glyp·tic /ˈgliptik/ ▶adj. of or concerning carving or engraving. ▶n. (usu. **glyptics**) the art of carving or engraving, esp. on precious stones.

GM ▶abbr. ■ general manager. ■ Chess grand master. ■ genetically modified. ■ General Motors.

gm ▶abbr. gram(s).

G-man ▶n. (pl. **G-men**) inf. an FBI agent.

GMT ▶abbr. Greenwich Mean Time.

gnarled /närld/ ▶adj. knobbly, rough, and twisted, esp. with age.

gnash /nasH/ ▶v. [tr.] grind (one's teeth) together, typically as a sign of anger: no doubt he is gnashing his teeth in rage. ■ [intr.] (of teeth) strike together; grind: the dog's jaws were primed to gnash.

gnat /nat/ ▶n. a small two-winged fly (Simuliidae, Ceratopogonidae, and other families). Gnats include both biting and nonbiting forms, and they typically form large swarms.

gnaw /nô/ ▶v. [intr.] bite at or nibble something persistently: picking up the pig's foot, he gnawed at it. ■ fig. (of something painful to the mind or body) cause persistent and wearing distress or anxiety: the doubts continued to gnaw at me | [as adj.] (**gnawing**) that gnawing pain in her stomach. —**gnaw·ing·ly** adv.

gneiss /nīs/ ▶n. a metamorphic rock with a banded or foliated structure, typically coarse-grained and consisting mainly of feldspar, quartz, and mica. —**gneiss·ic** /-sik/ adj. —**gneiss·oid** /-soid/ adj.

gnoc·chi /ˈnäkē/ ▶pl. n. (in Italian cooking) small dumplings made from potato, semolina, or flour, usually served with a sauce.

gnome[1] /nōm/ ▶n. a legendary dwarfish creature supposed to guard the earth's treasures underground. ■ inf. a small ugly person. ■ (also **garden gnome**) a small garden ornament in the form of a bearded man with a pointed hat. —**gnom·ish** adj.

gnome[2] ▶n. a short statement encapsulating a general truth; a maxim.

gno·mic /ˈnōmik/ ▶adj. expressed in or of the nature of short, pithy maxims or aphorisms: that most gnomic form, the aphorism. ■ enigmatic; ambiguous. —**gno·mi·cal·ly** /-ik(ə)lē/ adv.

gnos·tic /ˈnästik/ ▶adj. of or relating to knowledge, esp. esoteric mystical knowledge. ■ (**Gnostic**) of or relating to Gnosticism.
▶n. (**Gnostic**) an adherent of Gnosticism.

Gnos·ti·cism /ˈnästə,sizəm/ ▶n. a prominent heretical movement of the 2nd-century Christian Church, partly of pre-Christian origin. Gnostic doctrine taught that the world was created and ruled by a lesser divinity, and that Christ was an emissary of the remote supreme divine being, esoteric knowledge of whom enabled the redemption of the human spirit.

GNP ▶abbr. gross national product.

gnu /n(y)o͞o/ ▶n. a large dark antelope (genus Connochaetes) with a long head, a beard and mane, and a sloping back. Also called WILDEBEEST.

go[1] /gō/ ▶v. (**goes, go·ing**; past **went** /went/; past part. **gone** /gôn; gän/) **1** [intr.] move from one place or point to another; travel: he went out to the store | she longs to go back home | we've got a long way to go. ■ travel a specified distance: you just have to go a few miles to get to the road. ■ travel or move in order to engage in a specified activity or course of action: let's go and have a beer | we went to see her. ■ (**go to**) attend or visit for a particular purpose: we went to the movies | he went to Brown University. ■ (**go to**) provide access to: that door goes to the garage. ■ [in imper.] begin motion (used in a starter's order to begin a race): ready, set, go! ■ (**go to**) (of a rank or honor) be allotted or awarded: the top prize went to a twenty-four-year-old sculptor. ■ (**go into/to/toward**) (of a thing) contribute to or be put into (a whole); be used for or devoted to: considerable effort went into making the operation successful. ■ pass a specified amount of time in a particular way or under particular circumstances: sometimes they went for two months without talking. ■ used to indicate how many people a supply of food, money, or another resource is sufficient for or how much can be achieved using it: the sale will go a long way toward easing the huge debt burden | a little luck can go a long way. ■ (of a thing) lie or extend in a certain direction: the scar started just above her ankle and went all the way up inside her leg. ■ change in level, amount, or rank in a specified direction: prices went up by 15 percent. ■ inf. used to emphasize the speaker's annoyance at a specified action or event: then he goes and spoils it all. ■ inf. said in various expressions when angrily or contemptuously dismissing someone: go and get stuffed. **2** [intr.] leave; depart: I really must go. ■ (of time) pass or elapse: the hours went by | three years went past. ■ come to an end; cease to exist: a golden age that has now gone for good | 11,500 jobs are due to go by next year. ■ leave or resign from a post: I tried to persuade the Chancellor not to go. ■ be lost or stolen: when he returned minutes later, all his equipment was gone. ■ die (used euphemistically): I'd like to see my grandchildren before I go. ■ (of a thing) be sold: all the produce went to the farmers' market in Germantown. ■ (of money) be spent, esp. in a specified way: the rest of his money went into medical expenses. **3** (**be going to be/do something**) intend or be likely or intended to be or do something; be about to (used to express a future tense): I'm going to be late for work | she's going to have a baby. **4** [intr.] pass into a specified state, esp. an undesirable one: the food is going bad | her mind immediately went blank | he's gone crazy. ■ (**go to/into**) enter into a specified state, institution, or course of action: she turned over and went back to sleep | the car went into a spin. ■ happen, proceed, or be for a time in a specified condition: no one went hungry in our house. ■ make a sound of a specified kind: the engine went bang. ■ (of a bell or similar device) make a sound in functioning: I heard the buzzer go four times. ■ [with direct speech] inf. say: the kids go, "Yeah, sure." ■ (**go by/under**) be known or called by (a specified name): he now goes under the name Charles Perez. **5** [intr.] proceed in a specified way or have a specified outcome; turn out: how did the weekend go? | it all went off smoothly. ■ be successful, esp. in being enjoyable or exciting: the hosts had to struggle to make things go. ■ be acceptable or permitted: underground events where anything goes. ■ (of a song, account, verse, etc.) have a specified content or wording: if you haven't heard it, the story goes like this. **6** [intr.] be harmonious, complementary, or matching: rosemary goes with roast lamb | the earrings and the scarf don't really go. ■ be found in the same place or situation; be associated: cooking and eating go together. **7** [intr.] (of a machine or device) function: my car won't go. ■ continue in operation or existence: the committee was kept going even when its existence could no longer be justified. **8** [intr.] (of an article) be regularly kept or put in a particular place: remember which card goes in which slot. ■ fit or be able to be accommodated in a particular place or space: you're trying to fit a round peg into a

---

Pronunciation Key ə ago, up; ər over, fur; a hat; ā ate; ä car; CH chin; e let; ē see; e(ə)r air; i fit; ī by; i(ə)r ear; NG sing; ō go; ô law, for; oi toy; o͞o good; o͞o goo; ou out; SH she; TH thin; TH then; (h)w why; ZH vision

square hole, and it just won't go. **9** [*intr.*] *inf.* use a toilet; urinate or defecate. **10** [*tr.*] bid, bet, or pay.

▸*phrasal v.* □ **go about 1** begin or carry on work at (an activity); busy oneself with: *you are going about this in the wrong way.* **2** *Sailing* change to the opposite tack. □ **go against** oppose or resist: *he refused to go against the unions.* ■ be contrary to (a feeling or principle): *these tactics go against many of our instincts.* ■ (of a judgment, decision, or result) be unfavorable for: *the tribunal's decision went against them.* □ **go ahead** proceed or be carried out without hesitation: *the project will go ahead.* □ **go along with** give one's consent or agreement to (a person or their views): *the group has decided to go along with the committee's proposal.* □ **go around 1** spin: revolve: *the wheels were going around.* **2** (esp. of food) be sufficient to supply everybody present: *there was barely enough food to go around.* **3** (of an aircraft) abort an approach to landing and prepare to make a fresh approach. □ **go around with** be regularly in the company of: *he goes around with some of the neighborhood kids.* □ **go at** energetically attack or tackle: *he went at things with a daunting eagerness.* □ **go back** (of two people) have known each other for a specified, typically long, period of time: *Victor and I go back longer than I care to admit.* □ **go back on** fail to keep (a promise): *he wouldn't go back on his word.* □ **go down 1** (of a ship or aircraft) sink or crash: *he saw eleven B-17s go down.* ■ be defeated in a contest: *they went down 2–1.* **2** (of a person, period, or event) be recorded or remembered in a particular way: *his name will now go down in history.* **3** be swallowed: *solids can sometimes go down much easier than liquids.* **4** (of a person, action, or work) elicit a specified reaction: *my slide shows went down reasonably well.* **5** *inf.* happen: *you really don't know what's going down?* □ **go down on** *vulgar slang* perform oral sex on. □ **go for 1** decide on; choose: *I wished that we had gone for plan B.* ■ tend to find (a particular type of person) attractive: *Dionne went for the outlaw type.* **2** attempt to gain or attain: *he went for a job as a delivery driver.* ■ (**go for it**) strive to the utmost to gain or achieve something (frequently said as an exhortation): *sounds like a good idea—go for it!* **3** launch oneself at (someone); attack: *she went for him with clawed hands.* **4** end up having a specified value or effect: *my good intentions went for nothing.* **5** apply to; have relevance for: *the same goes for money-grubbing lawyers.* □ **go in for** like or habitually take part in (something, esp. an activity): *I don't go in for partying as much as Jesse and Rachel do.* □ **go into 1** take up in study or as an occupation: *he went into bankruptcy law.* **2** investigate or inquire into (something): *there's no need to go into it now.* **3** (of a whole number) be capable of dividing another, typically without a remainder: *six will go into eighteen, but not into five.* □ **go off 1** (of a gun, bomb, or similar device) explode or fire. ■ (of an alarm) begin to sound. ■ *inf.* become suddenly angry; lose one's temper: *if you got in an argument with him, he'd just go off.* **2** go to sleep: *I went off as soon as my head hit the pillow.* □ **go on 1** continue or persevere: *I can't go on protecting you.* ■ talk at great length, esp. tediously or angrily: *she went on about how lovely it would be to escape from the city.* ■ continue speaking or doing something after a short pause: [with *direct speech*] *"I don't understand," she went on.* ■ *inf.* said when encouraging someone or expressing disbelief: *go on, tell him!* **2** happen; take place: *God knows what went on there.* **3** proceed to do: *she went on to do postgraduate work.* □ **go out 1** (of a fire or light) be extinguished. ■ cease operating or functioning: *the power went out on our block last night.* **2** (of the tide) ebb; recede to low tide. **3** leave one's home to go to an entertainment or social event, typically in the evening: *I'm going out for dinner.* ■ carry on a regular romantic, and sometimes sexual, relationship: *he was going out with her best friend.* **4** used to convey someone's deep sympathy or similar feeling: *the boy's heart went out to the pitiful figure.* □ **go over 1** examine, consider, or check the details of (something): *I want to go over these plans with you again.* **2** change one's allegiance or religion: *he went over to the Democratic Party.* **3** (esp. of an action or performance) be received in a specified way: *his earnestness would go over well in a courtroom.* □ **go through 1** undergo (a difficult or painful period or experience): *the country is going through a period of economic instability.* **2** search through or examine carefully or in sequence: *she started to go through the bundle of letters.* **3** (of a proposal or contract) be officially approved or completed: *the sale of the building is set to go through.* **4** *inf.* use up or spend (available money or other resources): *within two years it went through thirty-one editions.* □ **go through with** perform (an action or process) to completion despite difficulty or unwillingness: *he bravely went through with the ceremony.* □ **go under** (of a business) become bankrupt. ■ (of a person) die or suffer an emotional collapse. □ **go up 1** (of a building or other structure) be built: *housing developments went up.* **2** explode or suddenly burst into flames: *last night two factories went up in flames.* □ **go with 1** give one's consent or agreement to (a person or their views). **2** have a romantic or sexual relationship with (someone).

□ **go without** suffer lack or deprivation: *I like to give my children what they want, even if I have to go without.*

▸*n.* (*pl.* **goes**) *inf.* an attempt or trial at something: *I thought I'd give it a go.* ■ a project or undertaking that has been approved: *tell them the project is a go.*

▸*adj. inf.* functioning properly: *all systems go.*

▸ □ **as** (or **so**) **far as it goes** bearing in mind its limitations (said when qualifying praise of something): *the book is a useful catalog as far as it goes.* □ **as —— go** compared to the average or typical one of the specified kind: *as castles go, it is small and old.* □ **from the word go** *inf.* from the very beginning. □ **go halves** share something equally. □ **going!, (going!,) gone!** an auctioneer's announcement that bidding is closing or closed. □ **going on ——** approaching a specified time, age, or amount: *I was going on fourteen when I went to my first gig.* □ **go to show** (or **prove**) (of an occurrence) serve as evidence or proof of something specified. □ **have a go at** make an attempt at; try: *let me have a go at straightening the rim.* □ **have —— going for one** *inf.* used to indicate how much someone has in their favor or to their advantage: *Why did she do it? She had so much going for her.* □ **make a go of** *inf.* be successful in (something): *he's determined to make a go of his marriage.* □ **on the go** *inf.* very active or busy: *he's been on the go all evening.* □ **to go** (of food or drink from a restaurant or cafe) to be eaten or drunk off the premises: *order one large cheese-and-peppers pizza, to go.* □ **who goes there?** said by a sentry as a challenge.

go² ▸*n.* a Japanese board game of territorial possession and capture.

goad /gōd/ ▸*n.* a spiked stick used for driving cattle. ■ a thing that stimulates someone into action: *for him the visit was a goad to renewed effort.*
▸*v.* [*tr.*] provoke or annoy (someone) so as to stimulate some action or reaction: *he goaded her on to more daring revelations.* ■ [*tr.*] drive or urge (an animal) on with a goad.

goal /gōl/ ▸*n.* **1** (in football, soccer, rugby, hockey, and some other games) a pair of posts linked by a crossbar and often with a net attached behind it, forming a space into or over which the ball has to be sent in order to score. ■ an instance of sending the ball into or over this space, esp. as a unit of scoring in a game: *the decisive opening goal.* ■ a cage or basket used similarly in other sports. **2** the object of a person's ambition or effort; an aim or desired result. ■ the destination of a journey. —**goal·less** *adj.*

goal·ie /ˈgōlē/ ▸*n.* informal term for GOALTENDER or GOALKEEPER.

goal·keep·er /ˈgōlˌkēpər/ ▸*n.* another term for GOALTENDER. —**goal·keep·ing** /-ˌkēpiNG/ *n.*

goal line ▸*n. Sports* a line between each pair of goals or goalposts, extended across the playing field to form the end boundary of the field of play. ■ *Football* either of two lines, one at each end of the football field, across which the ball must be carried or caught for a touchdown.

goal·post /ˈgōlˌpōst/ ▸*n.* either of the two upright posts of a goal.
▸ □ **move the goalposts** unfairly alter the conditions or rules of a procedure during its course.

goal·tend·er /ˈgōlˌtendər/ ▸*n.* a player in soccer or hockey whose special role is to stop the ball or puck from entering the goal.

goat /gōt/ ▸*n.* **1** a hardy domesticated ruminant (*Capra hircus*) of the cattle family that has backward curving horns and (in the male) a beard. ■ (**the Goat**) the zodiacal sign Capricorn or the constellation Capricornus. **2** a person likened to a goat, in particular: ■ a lecherous man. ■ a scapegoat. ▷Old English *gāt* 'nanny goat,' of Germanic origin; related to Dutch *geit.* —**goat·ish** *adj.* —**goat·y** *adj.*
▸ □ **get someone's goat** *inf.* irritate someone: *I've tried to get along with her, but sometimes she really gets my goat.*

goat·an·te·lope ▸*n.* a ruminant of the cattle family that belongs to a group that combines the characteristics of both goats and antelopes.

goat·ee /gōˈtē/ ▸*n.* a small pointed beard. —**goat·eed** *adj.*

goat·herd /ˈgōtˌhərd/ ▸*n.* a person who tends goats.

goat's-beard (also **goats·beard**) ▸*n.* a plant (*Tragopogon pratensis*) of the daisy family, with slender grasslike leaves, yellow flowers, and downy fruits that resemble those of a dandelion.

goat·skin /ˈgōtˌskin/ ▸*n.* the skin of a goat. ■ such a skin, or leather made from it, as a material. ■ a garment or object made out of goatskin.

gob /gäb/ *inf.* ▸*n.* **1** a lump or clot of a slimy or viscous substance: *a gob of phlegm.* ■ a small lump. **2** (**gobs of**) a lot of: *he wants to make gobs of money selling cassettes.*

gob·ble¹ /ˈgäbəl/ ▸*v.* [*tr.*] eat (something) hurriedly and noisily: *one man gobbled up a burger.* | [*intr.*] *they don't eat, they gobble.* ■ use a large amount of (something) very quickly. ■ (of a large organization or other body) incorporate or take over (a smaller one).

gob·ble² ▶*v.* [*intr.*] (of a male turkey) make a characteristic swallowing sound in the throat. ■ (of a person) make such a sound when speaking, esp. when excited or angry: *she was gobbling to herself in distress.* ▶*n.* the gurgling sound made in the throat by a male turkey.

gob·ble·dy·gook /ˈgäbəldēˌgo͝ok; -ˌgo͞ok/ (also **gob·ble·de·gook**) ▶*n. inf.* language that is meaningless or is made unintelligible by excessive use of abstruse technical terms; nonsense.

gob·bler¹ /ˈgäblər/ ▶*n.* a person who eats greedily and noisily.

gob·bler² ▶*n. inf.* a turkey cock.

gob·let /ˈgäblit/ ▶*n.* a drinking glass with a foot and a stem.

gob·lin /ˈgäblin/ ▶*n.* a mischievous, ugly, dwarflike creature of folklore.

go·by /ˈgōbē/ ▶*n.* (*pl.* **-ies**) a small, usually marine fish (family Gobiidae) that typically has a suction disk on the underside.

go-cart ▶*n.* variant spelling of GO-KART.

God /gäd/ ▶*n.* **1** [without *article*] (in Christianity and other monotheistic religions) the creator and ruler of the universe and source of all moral authority; the supreme being. **2** (**god**) (in certain other religions) a superhuman being or spirit worshiped as having power over nature or human fortunes; a deity: *a moon god* | *an incarnation of the god Vishnu.* ■ an image, idol, animal, or other object worshiped as divine or symbolizing a god. ■ used as a conventional personification of fate: *he dialed the number and, the gods relenting, got through at once.* **3** (**god**) an adored, admired, or influential person: *he has little time for the fashion victims for whom he is a god.* ■ a thing accorded the supreme importance appropriate to a god: *don't make money your god.* ▶*interj.* used to express a range of emotions such as surprise, anger, and distress: *God, what did I do to deserve this?* | *my God! Why didn't you tell us sooner?* ■ to give emphasis to a statement or declaration: *God, how I hate that woman!*

god·child /ˈgädˌCHīld/ ▶*n.* (*pl.* **-chil·dren** /-ˌCHildrən/) a person in relation to a godparent.

god·damn /ˈgädˌdam/ (also **god·dam** or **god·damned**) ▶*adj., adv.,* & *n. inf.* used for emphasis, esp. to express anger or frustration: [as *adj.*] *we're sick of this goddamn weather* | [as *n.*] *I don't give a goddamn what you do!*

god·daugh·ter /ˈgädˌdôtər/ ▶*n.* a female godchild.

god·dess /ˈgädis/ ▶*n.* a female deity: *a temple to Athena Nike, goddess of victory.* ■ a woman who is adored, esp. for her beauty: *he had an affair with a screen goddess.*

god·fa·ther /ˈgädˌfäT͟Hər/ ▶*n.* **1** a male godparent. **2** a man who is influential in a movement or organization, through providing support for it or through playing a leading or innovatory part in it: *the godfather of alternative comedy.* ■ a person directing an illegal organization, esp. a leader of a Mafia family.

god·for·sak·en /ˈgädfərˌsākən/ ▶*adj.* lacking any merit or attraction; dismal: *what are you doing in this godforsaken place?*

god·head /ˈgädˌhed/ ▶*n.* (usu. **the Godhead**) God. ■ divine nature. ■ *inf.* an adored, admired, or influential person; an idol.

god·less /ˈgädlis/ ▶*adj.* not recognizing or obeying God: *the godless forces of communism.* ■ without a god: *humanity coming to terms with a godless world.* ■ profane; wicked. —**god·less·ness** *n.*

god·like /ˈgädˌlīk/ ▶*adj.* resembling God or a god in qualities such as power, beauty, or benevolence: *our parents are godlike figures to our childish eyes.* ■ befitting or appropriate to a god: *we act as though we have godlike powers to decide our own destiny.*

god·ly /ˈgädlē/ ▶*adj.* (**-li·er**, **-li·est**) devoutly religious; pious: *how to live the godly life.* —**god·li·ness** *n.*

god·moth·er /ˈgädˌməT͟Hər/ ▶*n.* a female godparent. ■ a woman who is influential in a movement or organization, through providing support for it or through playing a leading or innovatory part in it.

god·par·ent /ˈgädˌpe(ə)rənt; -ˌpar-/ ▶*n.* a person who presents a child at baptism and responds on the child's behalf, promising to take responsibility for the child's religious education.

god·send /ˈgädˌsend/ ▶*n.* a very helpful or valuable event, person, or thing: *this highway is a godsend to the local community.*

god·son /ˈgädˌsən/ ▶*n.* a male godchild.

god·wit /ˈgädwit/ ▶*n.* a large, long-legged wader (genus *Limosa*) of the sandpiper family, with a long, slightly upturned or straight bill, and typically a reddish-brown head and breast in the breeding male.

go·er /ˈgōər/ ▶*n.* **1** a person or thing that goes: *the natives are friendly to tourists, whom they call "comers and goers."* **2** [in *comb.*] a person who attends a specified place or event, esp. regularly: *a churchgoer* | *conferencegoers.* ■ a person or thing that goes in a specified way: *horse no. 7 is a fast goer.* ■ a project likely to be accepted or to succeed: *if the business is a goer, the entrepreneur moves on.*

goes /gōz/ ▶ third person singular present of GO¹.

go·fer /ˈgōfər/ (also **go·pher**) ▶*n. inf.* a person who runs errands, esp. on a movie set or in an office.

go-get·ter ▶*n. inf.* an aggressively enterprising person. —**go-get·ting** *adj.*

gog·gle /ˈgägəl/ ▶*v.* [*intr.*] look with wide open eyes, typically in amazement or wonder. ■ (of the eyes) protrude or open wide. ▶*adj.* (of the eyes) protuberant or rolling. ▶*n.* **1** (**goggles**) close-fitting eyeglasses with side shields, for protecting the eyes from glare, dust, water, etc. ■ *inf.* eyeglasses. **2** a stare with protruding eyes. —**gog·gled** *adj.*

go-go ▶*adj.* **1** relating to or denoting an unrestrained and erotic style of dancing to popular music: *a go-go bar* | *go-go dancers.* **2** assertively dynamic: *the go-go bravado of the 1980s.*

Goi·del·ic /ɡoiˈdelik/ ▶*adj.* of, relating to, or denoting the northern group of Celtic languages, including Irish, Scottish Gaelic, and Manx.

go·ing /ˈgōiNG/ ▶*n.* **1** an act or instance of leaving a place; a departure: *his going left an enormous gap in each of their lives.* **2** the condition of the ground viewed in terms of suitability for walking, riding, or other travel (used esp. in the context of horse racing): *the going was ideal here, with short turf and a level surface.* ■ progress affected by such a condition. ■ conditions for, or progress in, an endeavor: *when the going gets tough, the tough get going.* ▶*adj.* (esp. of a price) generally accepted as fair or correct; current: *people willing to work for the going rate.*

go·ing-o·ver ▶*n. inf.* a thorough treatment, esp. in cleaning or inspection: *give the place a going-over with the vacuum cleaner.* ■ a beating.

goi·ter /ˈgoitər/ ▶*n.* a swelling of the neck resulting from enlargement of the thyroid gland: *a woman with a goiter.* —**goi·tered** *adj.* —**goi·trous** /ˈgoitrəs/ *adj.*

go-kart (also **go-cart**) ▶*n.* a small racing car with a lightweight or skeleton body. —**go-kart·ing** *n.*

gold /gōld/ ▶*n.* **1** a yellow precious metal, the chemical element of atomic number 79, valued esp. for use in jewelry and decoration, and to guarantee the value of currencies. (Symbol: **Au**) ■ an alloy of this: *9-carat gold.* **2** a deep lustrous yellow or yellow-brown color: *her eyes were light green and flecked with gold.* **3** coins or articles made of gold. ■ money in large sums; wealth: *he proved to be a rabid seeker for gold and power.* ■ a thing that is precious, beautiful, or brilliant: *they scout continents in search of the new green gold.* ■ short for GOLD MEDAL. ▷Old English, of Germanic origin; related to Dutch *goud* and German *Gold*, from an Indo-European root shared by *yellow.*
▶ □ **pot of gold** a large but distant or imaginary reward.

gold brick *inf.* ▶*n.* a thing that looks valuable, but is in fact worthless. ■ (also **gold-brick** or **gold-brick·er**) a con man. ■ a lazy person: [as *adj.*] *hardworking Amos and goldbrick Andy.* ▶*v.* (usu. **goldbrick**) [*intr.*] invent excuses to avoid a task; shirk: *he wasn't goldbricking; he was really sick.*

gold dig·ger ▶*n. inf.* a person who dates others purely to extract money from them, esp. a woman who strives to marry a wealthy man.

gold dust ▶*n.* fine particles of gold.

gold·en /ˈgōldən/ ▶*adj.* **1** colored or shining like gold: *curls of glossy golden hair* | *bake until golden.* **2** made or consisting of gold: *a golden crown.* **3** rare and precious, in particular: ■ (of a period) very happy and prosperous: *those golden days before World War I.* ■ (of an opportunity) very favorable: *a golden opportunity to boost foreign trade.* ■ (of a person) popular, talented, and successful: *Einstein was the golden boy of the "Second Scientific Revolution."* **4** (of a voice) rich and smooth: *a choir of young golden voices.* **5** denoting the fiftieth year of something: *the American Ballet Theater's golden anniversary extravaganza.* —**gold·en·ly** *adv.*

gold·en age ▶*n.* an idyllic, often imaginary past time of peace, prosperity, and happiness. ■ the period when a specified art, skill, or activity is at its peak: *the golden age of cinema.*

gold·en calf ▶*n.* a false god, esp. wealth as an object of worship.

gold·en ea·gle ▶*n.* a large Eurasian and North American eagle (*Aquila chrysaetos*) with yellow-tipped head feathers in the mature adult.

Gold·en Fleece *Greek Mythol.* ▶the fleece of a golden ram, guarded by an unsleeping dragon. ■ a goal that is highly desirable but difficult to achieve.

gold·en goose ▶*n.* a continuing source of wealth or profit that may be exhausted if it is misused: *they were killing the golden goose of tourism.*

Pronunciation Key ə *ago*, *up*; ər *over*, *fur*; a *hat*; ā *ate*; ä *car*; CH *chin*; e *let*; ē *see*; e(ə)r *air*; i *fit*; ī *by*; i(ə)r *ear*; NG *sing*; ō *go*; ô *law*, *for*; oi *toy*; o͝o *good*; o͞o *goo*; ou *out*; SH *she*; TH *thin*; T͟H *then*; (h)w *why*; ZH *vision*

gold·en old·ie ▸*n. inf.* an old song or movie that is still well known and popular.

gold·en rai·sin ▸*n.* a raisin made from a white grape.

gold·en re·triev·er ▸*n.* a retriever of a breed with a thick golden-colored coat.

gold·en·rod /ˈgōldən‚räd/ ▸*n.* a plant (genus *Solidago*) of the daisy family that bears tall spikes of small bright yellow flowers.

gold·en rule ▸*n.* a basic principle that should be followed to ensure success in general or in a particular activity: *one of the golden rules in this class is punctuality.* ■ (often **Golden Rule**) the biblical rule of "do unto others as you would have them do unto you."

gold·field /ˈgōld‚fēld/ ▸*n.* a district in which gold is found as a mineral.

gold·finch /ˈgōld‚finCH/ ▸*n.* a brightly colored finch (genus *Carduelis*) with yellow feathers in the plumage.

gold·fish /ˈgōld‚fiSH/ ▸*n.* (*pl.* same or **-fishes**) a small reddish-golden Eurasian carp (*Carassius auratus*), popular in ponds and aquariums.

gold·fish bowl ▸*n.* a spherical glass container for goldfish. ■ *fig.* a place or situation lacking privacy: *a goldfish bowl of publicity.*

gold leaf ▸*n.* gold that has been beaten into a very thin sheet.

gold med·al ▸*n.* a medal made of or colored gold, customarily awarded for first place in a race or competition. —**gold med·al·ist** *n.*

gold mine ▸*n.* a place where gold is mined. ■ *fig.* a source of wealth, valuable information, or resources: *this book is a gold mine of information.* —**gold min·er** *n.*

gold plate ▸*n.* a thin layer of gold, electroplated or otherwise applied as a coating to another metal. ■ objects coated with gold.

▸*v.* (**gold-plate**) [*tr.*] cover (something) with a thin layer of gold.

gold rush ▸*n.* a rapid movement of people to a newly discovered goldfield. The first major gold rush, to California in 1848–49, was followed by others in the U.S., Australia (1851–53), South Africa (1884), and Canada (Klondike, 1897–98).

gold·smith /ˈgōld‚smiTH/ ▸*n.* a person who makes gold articles.

gold stand·ard ▸*n. hist.* the system by which the value of a currency was defined in terms of gold, for which the currency could be exchanged. ■ *fig.* the best, most reliable, or most prestigious thing of its type: *you can't rely on lab tests as being the gold standard.*

golf /gälf; gôlf/ ▸*n.* **1** a game played on a large open-air course, in which a small hard ball is struck with a club into a series of small holes in the ground, the object being to use the fewest possible strokes to complete the course. **2** a code word representing the letter G, used in radio communication.

▸*v.* [*intr.*] play golf: [as *n.*] (**golfing**) *a week's golfing.* —**golf·er** *n.*

golf ball ▸*n.* a small hard ball used in the game of golf.

golf cart ▸*n.* a small motorized vehicle for golfers and their equipment.

golf club ▸*n.* **1** a club used to hit the ball in golf, with a heavy wooden or metal head on a slender shaft. **2** an organization of members for playing golf. ■ the premises used by such an organization.

golf course ▸*n.* a course on which golf is played.

Gol·gi ap·pa·rat·us (also **Golgi body**) ▸*n. Biol.* a complex of vesicles and folded membranes within the cytoplasm of most eukaryotic cells, involved in secretion and intracellular transport.

gol·ly /ˈgälē/ (also **by golly**) ▸*interj. inf., dated* used to express surprise or delight: *"Golly! Is that the time?"*

go·nad /ˈgōnad/ ▸*n. Physiol. & Zool.* an organ that produces gametes; a testis or ovary. —**go·nad·al** /gōˈnadl/ *adj.*

go·nad·o·trop·ic hor·mone /gō‚nadəˈträpik; -ˈtrōpik/ ▸*n.* another term for GONADOTROPIN.

go·nad·o·tro·pin /gō‚nadəˈtrōpin/ ▸*n. Biochem.* any of a group of hormones secreted by the pituitary that stimulate the activity of the gonads.

gon·do·la /ˈgändələ; gänˈdōlə/ ▸*n.* a light flat-bottomed boat used on Venetian canals, high at each end and worked by one oar at the stern. ■ a cabin on a suspended ski lift. ■ (also **gondola car**) an open, flat-bottomed railroad freight car. ■ an enclosed compartment suspended from an airship or balloon.

gondola

gon·do·lier /‚gändlˈi(ə)r/ ▸*n.* a person who propels and steers a gondola.

gone /gôn/ ▸ past participle of GO[1].

▸*adj.* no longer present; departed: *while you were gone* | *the bad old days are gone.* ■ no longer in existence; dead or extinct: *an aunt of mine, long since gone.* ■ no longer available: *all 35,000 tickets will be gone by next weekend.* ■ *inf.* in a trance or stupor, esp. through exhaustion, drink, or drugs: *she sat, half-gone, on a folding chair.* ■ lost; hopeless: *spending time and effort on a gone sucker like Galindez.*

gon·er /ˈgônər/ ▸*n. inf.* a person or thing that is doomed or cannot be saved.

gong /gäNG; gôNG/ ▸*n.* a metal disk with a turned rim, giving a resonant note when struck: *a dinner gong.*

▸*v.* [*intr.*] sound a gong or make a sound like that of a gong being struck.

go·ni·om·e·ter /‚gōnēˈämitər/ ▸*n.* an instrument for the precise measurement of angles, esp. one used to measure the angles between the faces of crystals. —**go·ni·o·met·ric** /-nēəˈmetrik/ *adj.* —**go·ni·o·met·ri·cal** /-nēəˈmetrikəl/ *adj.* —**go·ni·om·e·try** /-trē/ *n.*

gon·na /ˈgônə; ˈgənə/ *inf.* ▸*contr. of* going to: *we're gonna win this game.*

gon·o·coc·cus /‚gänəˈkäkəs/ ▸*n.* (*pl.* **gon·o·coc·ci** /-ˈkäk‚sī/) a bacterium (*Neisseria gonorrhoeae*) that causes gonorrhea. —**gon·o·coc·cal** /-ˈkäkəl/ *adj.*

gon·or·rhe·a /‚gänəˈrēə/ ▸*n.* a venereal disease involving inflammatory discharge from the urethra or vagina. —**gon·or·rhe·al** *adj.*

goo /gōō/ ▸*n. inf.* **1** a sticky or slimy substance. **2** sickly sentiment.

good /gōōd/ ▸*adj.* (**bet·ter** /ˈbetər/, **best** /best/) **1** to be desired or approved of: *a good quality of life.* ■ pleasing and welcome: *she was pleased to hear good news about him.* ■ expressing approval: *the play had good reviews.* **2** having the qualities required for a particular role: *the schools here are good.* ■ functioning or performed well: *good health.* ■ appropriate to a particular purpose: *this is a good month for planting seeds.* ■ (of language) with correct grammar and pronunciation: *she speaks good English.* ■ strictly adhering to or fulfilling all the principles of a particular cause, religion, or party: *a good Catholic girl.* ■ (of a ticket) valid: *the ticket is good for travel from May to September.* **3** possessing or displaying moral virtue: *I've met many good people who made me feel ashamed of my own shortcomings* | [as *pl. n.*] (**the good**) *the rich and the good shared the same fate as the poor and the bad.* ■ showing kindness: *you are good—thank you.* ■ obedient to rules or conventions: *accustom the child to being rewarded for good behavior.* ■ used to address or refer to people, esp. in a patronizing or humorous way: *the good people of the city were disconcerted.* ■ commanding respect. ■ belonging or relating to a high social class: *he comes from a good family.* **4** giving pleasure; enjoyable or satisfying: *the streets fill up with people looking for a good time.* ■ pleasant to look at; attractive: *you're looking pretty good.* ■ (of food and drink) having a pleasant taste: *the scampi was very good.* ■ (of clothes) smart and suitable for formal wear. **5** thorough: *the attic needed a good cleaning* | *have a good look around.* ■ used to emphasize that a number is at least as great as one claims: *they're a good twenty years younger.* ■ used to emphasize a following adjective: *we had a good long hug.* ■ fairly large: *a good crowd* | *fig. there's a good chance that we may be able to help you.* **6** used in conjunction with the name of God or a related expression as an exclamation of extreme surprise or anger: *good heavens!*

▸*n.* **1** that which is morally right; righteousness: *a mysterious balance of good and evil.* **2** benefit or advantage to someone or something: *he is too clever for his own good.* **3** (**goods**) merchandise or possessions: *imports of luxury goods.* ■ (**the goods**) *inf.* the genuine article.

▸*adv. inf.* well: *my mother could never cook this good.* —**good·ish** *adj.*

▸ □ **all to the good** to be welcomed without qualification: □ **as good as —** very nearly —: *she's as good as here.* ■ used of a result which will inevitably follow: *if we pass on the information, he's as good as dead.* □ **be any** (or **no**) **good** have some (or none or much) merit: *tell me whether that picture is any good.* ■ be of some (or none or much) help in dealing with a situation: *it was no good trying to ward things off.* □ **be so good as** (or **be good enough**) **to do something** used to make a polite request: *would you be so good as to answer.* □ **come up with** (or **deliver**) **the goods** *inf.* do what is expected or required of one. □ **do good** **1** act virtuously, esp. by helping others. **2** make a helpful contribution to a situation: *could the discussion do any good?* □ **do someone good** be beneficial to someone, esp. to their health: *the walk will do you good.* □ **for good** (**and all**) forever; definitively: *the experience almost frightened me away for good.* □ **get** (or **have**) **the goods on** *inf.* obtain (or possess) information about (someone) that may be used to their detriment. □ **good and —** *inf.* used as an intensifier before an adjective or adverb: *it'll be good and dark by then.* □ (**as**) **good as gold** (esp. of a child) extremely well behaved. □ (**as**) **good as new** in a very good condition or state, close to the original state again after damage, injury, or illness: *the skirt looked as good as new.* □ **the Good Book** the Bible. □ **good for 1** having a beneficial effect on: *smoking is not good for the lungs.* **2** reliably providing: *they found him good for a laugh.* ■ sufficient to pay for: *his money was good for a bottle of whiskey.* □ **good for** (or **him**, **her**, etc.) ! used as an exclamation of approval toward a person, esp. for something that they have achieved: *"I'm taking my driving test next month." "Good for you!"* □ **the Good Shepherd** a name for Jesus. □ a **good word** words in recommendation or defense of a person: *I hoped you might put in a good word for me with your friends.* □ **in good time 1** with no risk of being late: *I arrived in good time.* **2** (also **all in good time**) in due course but without haste: *you shall have a puppy all in good time.* □ **make good** be successful: *a college friend who made good in Hollywood.* □ **make something good 1** compensate for loss, damage, or expense: *if I scratched the table, I'd make good the damage.* ■ repair or restore after damage: *make good the wall where you have buried the cable.* **2** fulfill a promise or claim: *I challenged him to make good his boast.* □ **up to no good** doing something wrong.

good·bye /ˌgo͝odˈbī/ (also **good-bye** or **good·by** or **good-by**) ▶ *interj.* used to express good wishes when parting or at the end of a conversation.
▶ *n.* (*pl.* **-byes** or **-bys**) an instance of saying "goodbye"; a parting.

Good Fri·day ▶ *n.* the Friday before Easter Sunday, on which the Crucifixion of Jesus Christ is commemorated in the Christian Church.

good-heart·ed ▶ *adj.* kind and well meaning. —**good-heart·ed·ly** *adv.* —**good-heart·ed·ness** *n.*

good-hu·mored ▶ *adj.* genial; cheerful. —**good-hu·mored·ly** *adv.*

good-look·ing ▶ *adj.* (chiefly of a person) attractive. —**good-look·er** *n.*

good·ly /ˈgo͝odlē/ ▶ *adj.* (**-li·er**, **-li·est**) considerable in size or quantity: *we ran up a goodly bar bill.* —**good·li·ness** *n.*

good na·ture ▶ *n.* a kind and unselfish disposition: *your boy has a good nature.* —**good-na·tured** *adj.* —**good-na·tured·ly** *adv.*

good·ness /ˈgo͝odnis/ ▶ *n.* the quality of being good, in particular: ■ virtue; moral excellence: *a belief in the basic goodness of mankind.* ■ kindness; generosity: *he did it out of the goodness of his heart.* ■ the beneficial or nourishing element of food.
▶ *interj.* (as a substitution for "God") expressing surprise, anger, etc.: *goodness knows what her rent will be.*

good night (also **good·night** or **good-night**) ▶ *exclam.* expressing good wishes on parting at night or before going to bed.

good·will /ˌgo͝odˈwil/ (also **good will**) ▶ *n.* **1** friendly, helpful, or cooperative feelings or attitude: *the plan is dependent on goodwill between the two sides* | [as *adj.*] *a goodwill gesture.* **2** the established reputation of a business regarded as a quantifiable asset, e.g., as represented by the excess of the price paid at a takeover for a company over its fair market value.

good·y /ˈgo͝odē/ ▶ *n.* (also **good·ie**) (*pl.* **good·ies**) *inf.* (usu. **goodies**) something attractive or desirable, esp. something tasty or pleasant to eat.
▶ *interj.* expressing childish delight: *goody, we can have a party.*

good·y-good·y *inf.* ▶ *n.* a smug or obtrusively virtuous person.
▶ *adj.* smug or obtrusively virtuous.

goo·ey /ˈgo͝oē/ ▶ *adj.* (**goo·i·er**, **goo·i·est**) *inf.* soft and sticky. ■ mawkishly sentimental. —**goo·ey·ness** *n.*

goof /go͝of/ *inf.* ▶ *n.* **1** a mistake: *he made one of the most embarrassing goofs of his tenure.* **2** a foolish or stupid person.
▶ *v.* [*intr.*] **1** spend time idly or foolishly; fool around: *I was goofing around and broke my arm.* ■ (**goof off**) evade a duty; idle or shirk: *he was goofing off from his math homework.* ■ (**goof on**) make fun of; ridicule: *Lew and I started goofing on Alison's friend.* **2** make a mistake; blunder: *you're scared to say yes in case you goof up.*

goof·ball /ˈgo͝ofˌbôl/ ▶ *n. inf.* **1** a naive, silly, or stupid person. **2** a narcotic drug in pill form, esp. a barbiturate.
▶ *adj. inf.* foolish; silly: *Yvonne and her goofball antics.*

goof·y /ˈgo͝ofē/ ▶ *adj.* (**goof·i·er**, **goof·i·est**) *inf.* **1** foolish; harmlessly eccentric. **2** (in surfing and other board sports) with the right leg in front of the left on the board. —**goof·i·ly** /-fəlē/ *adv.* —**goof·i·ness** *n.*

goo·gle /ˈgo͝ogəl/ (also **Goo·gle**) ▶ *v. inf.* [*intr.*] use an Internet search engine, particularly Google.com: *she spent the afternoon googling aimlessly.* ■ [*tr.*] search for the name of (someone) on the Internet to find out information about them.

goo·gol /ˈgo͝oˌgôl/ ▶ *cardinal number* equivalent to ten raised to the power of a hundred (10^{100}).

gook¹ /go͝ok; go͞ok/ ▶ *n. inf., offens.* a foreigner, esp. a person of Philippine, Korean, or Vietnamese descent.

gook² ▶ *n. inf.* a sloppy wet or viscous substance: *all that gook she kept putting on her face.*

goon /go͞on/ ▶ *n. inf.* **1** a silly, foolish, or eccentric person. **2** a bully or thug, esp. one hired to terrorize or do away with opposition.

goose /go͞os/ ▶ *n.* (*pl.* **geese** /gēs/) **1** a large waterbird (esp. the genera *Anser* and *Branta*), with a long neck, short legs, webbed feet, and a short broad bill. ■ the female of such a bird. ■ the flesh of a goose as food. **2** *inf.* a foolish person.
▶ *v.* [*tr.*] *inf.* **1** poke (someone) between the buttocks. **2** give (something) a boost; invigorate; increase: *goosing up ticket sales.* ▷Old English *gōs*, of Germanic origin.

goose·ber·ry /ˈgo͞osˌberē/ ▶ *n.* (*pl.* **-ies**) **1** a round edible yellowish-green or reddish berry with a thin translucent hairy skin. **2** the thorny shrub (*Ribes grossularia*, family Grossulariaceae) that bears this fruit.

goose·bumps /ˈgo͞osˌbəmps/ ▶ *pl. n.* another term for GOOSE PIMPLES.

goose egg *inf.* ▶ *n.* **1** zero, esp. a zero score in a game: *once again, our team goes home with a big goose egg.* **2** a lump, typically on the head, from a blow.

goose·flesh /ˈgo͞osˌfleSH/ ▶ *n.* a pimply state of the skin with the hairs erect, produced by cold or fright.

goose·foot /ˈgo͞osˌfo͝ot/ ▶ *n.* (*pl.* **goosefoots**) a plant (genus *Chenopodium*, family Chenopodiaceae) of temperate regions, with divided leaves that are said to resemble the foot of a goose.

goose pim·ples ▶ *pl. n.* the pimples that form gooseflesh.

goose step ▶ *n.* a military marching step in which the legs are not bent at the knee.
▶ *v.* (**goose-step**) [*intr.*] march with such a step.

GOP ▶ *abbr.* Grand Old Party (Republican Party).

go·pher¹ /ˈgōfər/ ▶ *n.* **1** (also **pocket gopher**) a burrowing rodent (family Geomyidae) with fur-lined pouches on the outside of the cheeks, found in North and Central America. ■ *inf.* another term for GROUND SQUIRREL. **2** (also **gopher tortoise**) a tortoise (*Gopherus polyphemus*, family Testudinidae) of dry sandy regions that excavates tunnels, native to the southern U.S.

go·pher² ▶ *n.* variant spelling of GOFER.

go·ral /ˈgôrəl/ ▶ *n.* a long-haired goat-antelope (genus *Nemorhaedus*) with backward curving horns, found in mountainous regions of eastern Asia.

Gor·di·an knot /ˈgôrdēən/ ▶ *n.* a difficult or involved problem.

gore¹ /gôr/ ▶ *n.* blood that has been shed, esp. as a result of violence: *the film omitted the blood and gore in order to avoid controversy.*

gore² ▶ *v.* [*tr.*] (of an animal such as a bull) pierce or stab with a horn or tusk.

gore³ ▶ *n.* a triangular or tapering piece of material used in making a garment, sail, or umbrella. ■ a small, triangular piece of land, esp. one lying in the fork of a road.
▶ *v.* [*tr.*] make with a gore-shaped piece of material: [as *adj.*] (**gored**) *a gored skirt.*

gorge /gôrj/ ▶ *n.* **1** a narrow valley between hills or mountains, typically with steep rocky walls and a stream running through it. **2** a mass of ice obstructing a narrow passage, esp. a river.
▶ *v.* [*intr.*] eat a large amount greedily; fill oneself with food: *we used to go to all the little restaurants there and gorge ourselves.* —**gorg·er** *n.*

gor·geous /ˈgôrjəs/ ▶ *adj.* beautiful; very attractive: *gorgeous colors and exquisite decoration.* ■ *inf.* very pleasant: *a short but gorgeous hot summer.* —**gor·geous·ly** *adv.* —**gor·geous·ness** *n.*

gor·get /ˈgôrjit/ ▶ *n. hist.* an article of clothing or armor that covered the throat. ■ a patch of color on the throat of a bird or other animal, esp. a hummingbird.

Gor·gon /ˈgôrgən/ (also **gor·gon**) ▶ *n.* Greek Mythol. each of three sisters with snakes for hair, who had the power to turn anyone who looked at them to stone.

Gor·gon·zo·la /ˌgôrgənˈzōlə/ ▶ *n.* a type of rich, strong-flavored Italian cheese with bluish-green veins.

go·ril·la /gəˈrilə/ ▶ *n.* a powerfully built great ape (*Gorilla gorilla*) with a large head and short neck, found in the forests of central Africa. It is the largest living primate. ■ *inf.* a heavily built, aggressive-looking man.

gor·mand·ize ▶ *v.* variant spelling of GOURMANDIZE. —**gor·mand·iz·er** *n.*

gorse /gôrs/ ▶ *n.* a yellow-flowered shrub (genus *Ulex*) of the pea family, the leaves of which are modified to form spines, native to western Europe and North Africa. —**gors·y** adj.

gor·y /'gôrē/ ▶adj. (**gor·i·er, gor·i·est**) involving or showing violence and bloodshed: *a gory horror film.* ■ covered in blood. —**gor·i·ly** /-rəlē/ adv. —**gor·i·ness** n.

▶ □ **the gory details** *humorous* the explicit details of something.

gosh /gäsH/ ▶interj. *inf.* used to express surprise or give emphasis: *gosh, we envy you.* ■ used as a euphemism for "God": *a gosh-awful team.*

gos·ling /'gäzliNG/ ▶n. a young goose.

gos·pel /'gäspəl/ ▶n. **1** the teaching or revelation of Christ: *it is the Church's mission to preach the gospel.* ■ (also **gospel truth**) a thing that is absolutely true: *they say it's sold out, but don't take that as gospel.* ■ a set of principles or beliefs: *the new economics unit has produced what it reckons to be the approved gospel.* **2** (**Gospel**) the record of Jesus' life and teaching in the first four books of the New Testament. ■ each of these books. ■ a portion from one of these read at a church service. **3** (also **gospel music**) a fervent style of black American evangelical religious singing, developed from spirituals sung in Southern Baptist and Pentecostal churches: *gospel singers.*

gos·sa·mer /'gäsəmər/ ▶n. a fine, filmy substance consisting of cobwebs spun by small spiders. ■ used to refer to something very light, thin, and insubstantial or delicate: *his hair was blond gossamer.* ▶adj. made of or resembling gossamer. —**gos·sa·mer·y** adj.

gos·sip /'gäsəp/ ▶n. casual or unconstrained conversation or reports about other people, typically involving details that are not confirmed as being true: *he became the subject of much local gossip.* ■ *chiefly derog.* a person who likes talking about other people's private lives.

▶v. (**-siped, -sip·ing**) [*intr.*] engage in gossip: *they would start gossiping about her as soon as she left.* —**gos·sip·er** n. —**gos·sip·y** adj.

gos·sip col·umn ▶n. a section of a newspaper devoted to gossip about well-known people. —**gos·sip col·um·nist** n.

gos·sip·mon·ger /'gäsəp,məNGgər; -,mäNG-/ ▶n. *derog.* a person who habitually passes on confidential information or spreads rumors.

got /gät/ ▶ past and past participle of **GET**.

Goth /gäTH/ ▶n. **1** a member of a Germanic people that invaded the Roman Empire from the east between the 3rd and 5th centuries. **2** (**goth**) a style of rock music derived from punk. ■ a member of a subculture favoring black clothing, white and black makeup, and goth music.

Goth·ic /'gäTHik/ ▶adj. **1** of or relating to the Goths or their extinct East Germanic language, which provides the earliest manuscript evidence of any Germanic language (4th–6th centuries AD). **2** of or in the style of architecture prevalent in western Europe in the 12th–16th centuries, characterized by pointed arches, rib vaults, and flying buttresses, together with large windows and elaborate tracery. **3** belonging to or redolent of the Dark Ages; portentously gloomy or horrifying: *19th-century Gothic horror.* **4** (of lettering) of or derived from the angular style of handwriting with broad vertical downstrokes used in western Europe from the 13th century. **5** (**gothic**) of or relating to goths or their rock music.

▶n. **1** the language of the Goths. **2** the Gothic style of architecture. —**Goth·i·cal·ly** /-ik(ə)lē/ adv. —**Goth·i·cism** /'gäTHə,sizəm/ n.

got·ta /'gätə/ ▶contr. of *have got to* (not acceptable in standard use): *you gotta be careful.*

got·ten /'gätn/ ▶ past participle of **GET**.

gouache /gwäsH; gōō'äsH/ ▶n. a method of painting using opaque pigments ground in water and thickened with a gluelike substance. ■ paint of this kind; opaque watercolor. ■ a picture painted in this way.

Gou·da /'gōōdə/ ▶n. a flat round cheese with a yellow rind, originally made in the town of Gouda in the Netherlands.

gouge /gouj/ ▶n. **1** a chisel with a concave blade, used in carpentry, sculpture, and surgery. **2** an indentation or groove made by gouging.

▶v. [*tr.*] **1** make (a groove, hole, or indentation) with or as if with a gouge. ■ make a rough hole or

gouge

indentation in (a surface), esp. so as to mar or disfigure it. ■ (**gouge something out**) cut or force something out roughly or brutally: *one of his eyes had been gouged out.* **2** *inf.* overcharge; swindle. —**goug·er** n.

gou·lash /'gōō,läsH/ ▶n. a highly seasoned Hungarian soup or stew of meat and vegetables, flavored with paprika.

gourd /gôrd/ ▶n. **1** a fleshy, typically large fruit with a hard skin, some varieties of which are edible. ■ a container or ornament made from the hollowed and dried skin of this fruit. **2** a climbing or trailing plant that bears this fruit. The **gourd family** (Cucurbitaceae) also includes the squashes, pumpkins, melons, and cucumbers. —**gourd·ful** /-,fōōl/ n. (pl. **-fuls**).

▶ □ **out of one's gourd** *inf.* out of one's mind; crazy.

gour·mand /gōōr'mänd/ ▶n. a person who enjoys eating and often eats too much. ■ a connoisseur of good food.

gour·man·dize /'gōōrmən,dīz/ ▶v. [*intr.*] indulge in good eating; eat greedily. —**gour·man·dism** /'gōōrmən,dizəm/ n.

gour·met /gôr'mā; ,gōōr-/ ▶n. a connoisseur of good food; a person with a discerning palate. ■ [as adj.] of a kind or standard suitable for a gourmet: *a gourmet meal.*

gout /gout/ ▶n. a disease in which defective metabolism of uric acid causes arthritis, esp. in the smaller bones of the feet, and episodes of acute pain. —**gout·i·ness** /-tēnis/ n. —**gout·y** adj.

gov. ▶abbr. ■ government. ■ governor.

gov·ern /'gəvərn/ ▶v. [*tr.*] **1** conduct the policy, actions, and affairs of (a state, organization, or people): *he was incapable of governing the country* | [as adj.] (**governing**) *the governing coalition.* ■ control, influence, or regulate (a person, action, or course of events): *the future of Jamaica will be governed by geography, not history.* ■ (**govern oneself**) conduct oneself, esp. with regard to controlling one's emotions. ■ regulate the speed of (a motor or engine) by a governor. **2** constitute a law, rule, standard, or principle for: *constant principles govern the poetic experience.* ■ serve to decide (a legal case). **3** *Gram.* (of a word) require that (another word or group of words) be in a particular case: *the Latin preposition "cum" governs nouns in the ablative.* **4** regulate the speed of (a motor or machine) with a governor. ▷Middle English: from Old French *governer,* from Latin *gubernare* 'to steer, rule,' from Greek *kubernan* 'to steer.' —**gov·ern·a·bil·i·ty** /,gəvərnə'bilitē/ n. —**gov·ern·a·ble** adj.

gov·ern·ance /'gəvərnəns/ ▶n. the action or manner of governing: *a more responsive system of governance will be required.*

gov·ern·ess /'gəvərnis/ ▶n. a woman employed to teach children in a private household.

gov·ern·ment /'gəvər(n)mənt/ ▶n. **1** [treated as *sing.* or *pl.*] the governing body of a nation, state, or community: *an agency of the federal government* | [as adj.] *government controls.* ■ the system by which a nation, state, or community is governed: *a secular, pluralistic, democratic government.* ■ the group of persons in office at a particular time; administration: *the election of the new government.* ■ another term for **POLITICAL SCIENCE.** ■ (**governments**) all bonds issued by the U.S. Treasury or other federal agencies. **2** *Gram.* the relation between a governed and a governing word. —**gov·ern·men·tal** /,gəvər(n)'mentl/ adj. —**gov·ern·men·tal·ly** /,gəvər(n)'mentl-ē/ adv.

gov·er·nor /'gəvə(r)nər/ ▶n. **1** the elected executive head of a state of the U.S. ■ an official appointed to govern a town or region. **2** a device automatically regulating the supply of fuel, steam, or water to a machine, ensuring uniform motion or limiting speed. —**gov·er·nor·ship** /-,sHip/ n.

govt. ▶abbr. government: *local govt.*

gown /goun/ ▶n. a long dress, typically having a close-fitting bodice and a flared or flowing skirt, worn on formal occasions: *a silk ball gown.* ■ a nightgown. ■ a dressing gown. ■ a protective garment worn in a hospital, either by a staff member during surgery or by a patient. ■ a loose cloak indicating one's profession or status, worn by a lawyer, teacher, academic, or college student. ■ the members of a college as distinct from the permanent residents of the college town: *efforts are underway to improve town-gown relations.*

▶v. (**be gowned**) be dressed in a gown: *she was gowned in luminous silk.*

goy /goi/ ▶n. (pl. **goy·im** /'goi-im/ or **goys**) *inf., often offens.* a Jewish name for a non-Jew. —**goy·ish** adj.

GPA ▶abbr. grade point average.

GPO ▶abbr. ■ general post office. ■ Government Printing Office.

gr (also **gr.**) ▶abbr. ■ grain(s). ■ gram(s). ■ gray. ■ gross.

grab /grab/ ▶v. (**grabbed, grab·bing**) [*tr.*] **1** grasp or seize suddenly and roughly: *she grabbed him by the shirt collar.* ■ [*intr.*] (**grab at/for**) make a sudden snatch at: *he grabbed at the handle, missed, and nearly fell.* ■ *inf.* obtain or get (something) quickly or opportunistically, sometimes unscrupulously: *I'll grab another drink while there's still time.* ■ [*intr.*] (of a brake on a vehicle) grip the wheel harshly or jerkily. **2** *inf.* attract the attention of; make an impression on: *how does that grab you?*

▶n. **1** a quick, sudden clutch or attempt to seize: *he made a grab at the pistol.* ■ an act of obtaining something opportunistically or unscrupulously: *they used the law to effect a land grab.* **2** a mechanical device for clutching, lifting, and moving things, esp. materials in bulk. ■ [as *adj.*] denoting a bar or strap for people to hold on to for support or in a moving vehicle: *for elderly people, grab rails are likely to prevent accidents.* **3** *Comput.* a frame of video or television footage, digitized and stored as a still image in a computer memory for subsequent display, printing, or editing: *a screen grab.* —**grab·ber** *n.*

▸ □ **up for grabs** *inf.* available; obtainable: *great prizes up for grabs.*

grab bag ▸ *n.* a container from which a person chooses a wrapped item at random, without knowing the contents. ■ an assortment of miscellaneous items.

grab·by /ˈgrabē/ ▸ *adj.* (**-bi·er, -bi·est**) *inf.* having or showing a selfish desire for something; greedy. ■ attracting attention; arousing people's interest: *a grabby angle on a news story.*

grace /grās/ ▸ *n.* **1** simple elegance or refinement of movement: *she moved through the water with effortless grace.* ■ courteous goodwill. ■ (**graces**) an attractively polite manner of behaving: *the social graces.* **2** (in Christian belief) the free and unmerited favor of God, as manifested in the salvation of sinners and the bestowal of blessings. ■ a divinely given talent or blessing. ■ the condition or fact of being favored by someone: *he fell from grace because of drug use.* **3** (also **grace period**) a period officially allowed for payment of a sum due or for compliance with a law or condition, esp. an extended period: *another three days' grace.* **4** a short prayer of thanks said before or after a meal. **5** (**His, Her,** or **Your Grace**) used as forms of description or address for a duke, duchess, or archbishop: *His Grace, the Duke of Atholl.*

▸ *v.* [*tr.*] do honor or credit to (someone or something) by one's presence: *the sport she has graced for two decades.* ■ [*tr.*] (of a person or thing) be an attractive presence in or on; adorn: *Ms. Pasco has graced the front pages of magazines like Elle and Vogue.*

▸ □ **be in someone's good** (or **bad**) **graces** be regarded by someone with favor (or disfavor). □ **the** (**Three**) **Graces** *Greek Mythol.* three beautiful goddesses, daughters of Zeus. They were believed to personify and bestow charm, grace, and beauty. □ **with good** (or **bad**) **grace** in a willing and happy (or reluctant and resentful) manner.

grace·ful /ˈgrāsfəl/ ▸ *adj.* having or showing grace or elegance: *she was a tall girl, slender and graceful.* —**grace·ful·ly** *adv.* —**grace·ful·ness** *n.*

grace·less /ˈgrāslis/ ▸ *adj.* lacking grace, elegance, or charm. —**grace·less·ly** *adv.* —**grace·less·ness** *n.*

gra·cious /ˈgrāSHəs/ ▸ *adj.* **1** courteous, kind, and pleasant: *gracious in defeat.* ■ pleasantly indulgent, esp. toward an inferior. ■ elegant and tasteful, esp. as exhibiting wealth and high social status: *gracious Victorian interiors | gracious living.* **2** (in Christian belief) showing divine grace: *God's gracious intervention on my behalf.*

▸ *interj.* dated expressing polite surprise. —**gra·cious·ly** *adv.* —**gra·cious·ness** *n.*

grack·le /ˈgrakəl/ ▸ *n.* **1** a songbird (esp. *Quiscalus quiscula*) of the American blackbird family, the male of which has shiny black plumage with a blue-green sheen. **2** another term for an Asian mynah or starling (*Gracula* and other genera), with mainly black plumage.

grad /grad/ ▸ *n.* informal term for GRADUATE.

gra·date /ˈgrādāt/ ▸ *v.* pass or cause to pass by gradations from one shade of color to another: [*intr.*] *the black background gradated toward a dark purple.* ■ [*tr.*] arrange in steps or grades of size, amount, or quality.

gra·da·tion /grāˈdāSHən/ ▸ *n.* a scale or a series of successive changes, stages, or degrees: *within the woodpecker family, there is a gradation of drilling ability.* ■ a stage or change in a such a scale or series: *minute gradations of distance.* ■ a minute change from one shade, tone, or color to another: *subtle gradations of green and blue.* —**gra·da·tion·al** /-SHənl/ *adj.* —**gra·da·tion·al·ly** /-SHənl-ē/ *adv.*

grade /grād/ ▸ *n.* **1** a particular level of rank, quality, proficiency, intensity, or value: *sea salt is usually available in coarse or fine grades.* ■ a level in a salary or employment structure. ■ a mark indicating the quality of a student's work: *I got good grades last semester.* ■ (with specifying ordinal number) those students in a school or school system who are grouped by age or ability for teaching at a particular level for a year: *she teaches first grade.* ■ a level of quality or size for food or other products: *grade AA butter.* **2** a gradient or slope: *a long seven percent grade.* **3** [usu. as *adj.*] a variety of cattle produced by crossing with a superior breed: *grade stock.*

▸ *v.* [*tr.*] (usu. **be graded**) **1** arrange in or allocate to grades; class or sort: *they are graded according to thickness* | [as *adj.*] (**graded**) *carefully graded exercises.* ■ give a mark to (a student or a piece of work). **2** [*intr.*] pass gradually from one level, esp. a shade of color, into another: *the sky graded from blue to white on the horizon.* **3** reduce (a road) to an easy gradient. **4** cross (livestock) with a superior breed. —**grad·a·ble** *adj.*

▸ □ **make the grade** *inf.* succeed; reach the desired standard.

grade cross·ing ▸ *n.* a place where a railroad and a road, or two railroad lines, cross at the same level.

grade point ▸ *n.* a numerical value assigned to a letter grade received in a course at a college or university, multiplied by the number of credits awarded for the course.

grade point av·er·age (abbr.: **GPA**) ▸ *n.* an indication of a student's academic achievement at a college or university, calculated as the total number of grade points received over a given period divided by the total number of credits awarded.

grad·er /ˈgrādər/ ▸ *n.* **1** a person or thing that grades. ■ a wheeled machine for leveling the ground, esp. in making roads. **2** [in *comb.*] a student of a specified grade in a school: *first-grader.*

grade school ▸ *n.* an elementary school. —**grade school·er** *n.*.

gra·di·ent /ˈgrādēənt/ ▸ *n.* **1** an inclined part of a road or railway; a slope: *fail-safe brakes for use on steep gradients.* ■ the degree of such a slope: *the path becomes very rough as the gradient increases.* ■ *Math.* the degree of steepness of a graph at any point. **2** *Physics* an increase or decrease in the magnitude of a property (e.g., temperature, pressure, or concentration) observed in passing from one point or moment to another. ■ the rate of such a change.

grad·u·al /ˈgrajōōəl/ ▸ *adj.* taking place or progressing slowly or by degrees. ■ (of a slope) not steep or abrupt.

▸ *n.* (in the Western Christian Church) a response sung or recited between the Epistle and Gospel in the Mass. ■ a book of plainsong for the Mass. —**grad·u·al·ly** *adv.* —**grad·u·al·ness** *n.*

grad·u·al·ism /ˈgrajōōə,lizəm/ ▸ *n.* a policy of gradual reform rather than sudden change or revolution. ■ *Biol.* the hypothesis that evolution proceeds chiefly by the accumulation of gradual changes. —**grad·u·al·ist** *n.* —**grad·u·al·is·tic** /,grajəwə'listik/ *adj.*

grad·u·ate ▸ *n.* /ˈgrajōōit/ **1** a person who has successfully completed a course of study or training, esp. a person who has been awarded an undergraduate academic degree. ■ a person who has received a high school diploma: *she is 19, a graduate of Lincoln High.* **2** a graduated cup, tube, flask, or measuring glass.

▸ *v.* /ˈgrajōō,āt/ **1** [*intr.*] successfully complete an academic degree, course of training, or high school: *I graduated from West Point in 1965.* ■ [*tr.*] *inf.* receive an academic degree from. ■ [*tr.*] confer a degree or other academic qualification on: *the school graduated more than one hundred arts majors in its first year.* ■ (**graduate to**) move up to (a more advanced level or position): *he started with motorbikes but now he's graduated to his first car.* **2** [*tr.*] arrange in a series or according to a scale: [as *adj.*] (**graduated**) *a graduated tax.* ■ mark out (an instrument or container) in degrees or other proportionate divisions: *the stem was graduated with marks for each hour* | [as *adj.*] *graduated cylinders.* **3** [*tr.*] change (something, typically color or shade) gradually or step by step.

▸ *adj.* /ˈgrajōōit/ relating to graduate school education: *the graduate faculty.* ■ having graduated from a school or academic program. ▷late Middle English: from medieval Latin *graduat-* 'graduated,' from *graduare* 'take a degree,' from Latin *gradus* 'degree, step.'

grad·u·ate school ▸ *n.* a division of a university offering advanced programs beyond the bachelor's degree.

grad·u·a·tion /,grajōō'āSHən/ ▸ *n.* **1** the receiving or conferring of an academic degree or diploma. ■ the ceremony at which degrees are conferred. **2** the action of dividing into degrees or other proportionate divisions on a graduated scale. ■ a mark on a container or instrument indicating a degree of quantity.

graf·fi·ti /grəˈfētē/ ▸ *pl. n.* (*sing.* **-to** /-tō/) [treated as *sing.* or *pl.*] writing or drawings scribbled, scratched, or sprayed illicitly on a wall or other surface in a public place: *the walls were covered with graffiti | a graffiti artist.*

▸ *v.* [*tr.*] write or draw graffiti on (something): *he graffitied an entire train.* ■ write (words or drawings) as graffiti. —**graf·fi·tist** /-tist/ *n.*

graft[1] /graft/ ▸ *n.* **1** *Hort.* a shoot or scion inserted into a slit of stock, from which it receives sap. ■ an instance of inserting a shoot or scion in this way. **2** *Med.* a piece of living tissue that is transplanted surgically. ■ a surgical operation in which tissue is transplanted.

▸ *v.* [*tr.*] **1** *Hort.* insert (a scion) as a graft: *graft different varieties onto a single tree trunk.* ■ insert a graft on (a stock). **2** *Med.* transplant (living tissue) as a graft: *they can graft a new hand onto the arm.* ■ *fig.* insert or fix (something) permanently to something else: *western-style government could not easily be grafted onto a profoundly different country.*

graft[2] ▶*n.* practices, esp. bribery, used to secure illicit gains in politics or business; corruption: *sweeping measures to curb official graft.* ■ such gains: *government officials grow fat off bribes and graft.*
▶*v.* [*intr.*] make money by shady or dishonest means. —**graft·er** *n.*

Grail /grāl/ (also **Holy Grail**) ▶*n.* (in medieval legend) the cup or platter used by Jesus at the Last Supper, and in which Joseph of Arimathea received Christ's blood at the Cross. ■ *fig.* (also **grail**) a thing that is being earnestly pursued or sought after: *profit has become the holy grail.*

grain /grān/ ▶*n.* **1** wheat or any other cultivated cereal crop used as food. ■ the seeds of such cereals: [as *adj.*] *grain exports.* **2** a single fruit or seed of a cereal: *a few grains of corn.* ■ a small hard particle of a substance such as salt or sand: *a grain of salt.* ■ the smallest possible quantity or amount of a quality: *there wasn't a grain of truth in what he said.* ■ a discrete particle or crystal in a metal, rock, etc. **3** (abbr.: **gr.**) the smallest unit of weight in the troy and avoirdupois systems, equal to 1/5760 of a pound troy and 1/7000 of a pound avoirdupois (approx. 0.0648 grams). **4** the arrangement or pattern of fibers in wood, paper, etc.: *he scored along the grain of the table with the knife.* ■ roughness in texture of wood, stone, etc.; the arrangement and size of constituent particles: *the lighter, finer grain of the wood is attractive.* ■ the rough or textured outer surface of leather, or of a similar artificial material.
▶*v.* [*tr.*] **1** (usu. **be grained**) give a rough surface or texture to: *her fingers were grained with chalk dust.* ■ [*intr.*] form into grains. **2** [usu. as *n.*] (**graining**) paint (esp. furniture or interior surfaces) in imitation of the grain of wood or marble: *the art of graining and marbling.* **3** remove hair from (a hide): [as *adj.*] (**grained**) *the boots were of best grained leather.* **4** feed (a horse) on grain. —**grained** *adj.* [usu. in comb.] *coarse-grained sandstone.* —**grain·er** *n.* —**grain·less** *adj.*
▶ □ **against the grain** contrary to the natural inclination or feeling of someone or something: *it goes against the grain to tell outright lies.*

grain·y /grānē/ ▶*adj.* (**grain·i·er, grain·i·est**) **1** granular: *a grainy texture.* ■ *Photog.* showing visible grains of emulsion, as characteristic of old photographs or modern high-speed film. ■ (of sound, esp. recorded music or a voice) having a rough or gravelly quality: *the grainy sound of bootleg cassettes.* ■ (of food) containing whole grains. **2** (of wood) having prominent grain. —**grain·i·ness** *n.*

gram[1] /gram/ (abbr.: **g**) ▶*n.* a metric unit of mass equal to one thousandth of a kilogram.

gram[2] ▶*n.* short for **GRANDMA**.

gram·i·na·ceous /ˌgraməˈnāshəs/ ▶*adj. Bot.* of, relating to, or denoting plants of the grass family (Gramineae).

gram·ma·logue /ˈgramə,läg/ ▶*n.* (in shorthand) a word represented by a single sign or symbol.

gram·mar /ˈgramər/ ▶*n.* the whole system and structure of a language or of languages in general, usually taken as consisting of syntax and morphology (including inflections) and sometimes also phonology and semantics. ■ a particular analysis of the system and structure of language or of a specific language. ■ a book on grammar: *my old Latin grammar.* ■ a set of actual or presumed prescriptive notions about correct use of a language: *it was not bad grammar, just dialect.* ■ the basic elements of an area of knowledge or skill: *the grammar of wine.* ■ *Comput.* a set of rules governing what strings are valid or allowable in a language or text.

gram·mar·i·an /grəˈme(ə)rēən/ ▶*n.* a person who studies and writes about grammar.

grammar school ▶*n.* another term for **ELEMENTARY SCHOOL**.

gram·mat·i·cal /grəˈmatikəl/ ▶*adj.* of or relating to grammar: *grammatical analysis | the grammatical function of a verb.* ■ well formed; in accordance with the productive rules of the grammar of a language: *a grammatical sentence.* —**gram·mat·i·cal·i·ty** /-ˌmati'kalitē/ *n.* —**gram·mat·i·cal·ly** /-ik(ə)lē/ *adv.* —**gram·mat·i·cal·ness** *n.*

gram·o·phone /ˈgramə,fōn/ ▶*n.* old-fashioned term for **RECORD PLAYER**.

gram·pus /ˈgrampəs/ ▶*n.* (*pl.* **-pus·es**) a cetacean of the dolphin family. ■ another term for **RISSO'S DOLPHIN**.

gra·na·ry /ˈgrānərē; ˈgran-/ ▶*n.* (*pl.* **-ries**) a storehouse for threshed grain. ■ a region producing large quantities of corn.

grand /grand/ ▶*adj.* **1** magnificent and imposing in appearance, size, or style: *a grand country house | the dinner party was very grand.* ■ designed to impress through scale or splendor: *a grand gesture.* ■ (of a person) of high rank and with an appearance and manner appropriate to it: *she was such a grand lady.* ■ large or ambitious in scope or scale: *his grand design for the future of Europe | collecting on a grand scale.* ■ used in names of places or buildings to suggest size or splendor: *the Grand Canyon | the Grand Hotel.* **2** denoting the largest or most important item of its kind: *the grand entrance.* ■ of the highest rank (used esp. in official titles): *the grand duke.* ■ *Law* (of a crime) serious: *grand theft.* Compare with **PETTY**

(sense 2). **3** *inf.* very good or enjoyable; excellent: *we had a grand day.* **4** [in comb.] (in names of family relationships) denoting one generation removed in ascent or descent: *a grand-niece.*
▶*n.* **1** (*pl.* same) *inf.* a thousand dollars or pounds: *he gets thirty-five grand a year.* **2** a grand piano. —**grand·ly** *adv.* —**grand·ness** *n.*

gran·dad /ˈgran,dad/ ▶*n.* variant spelling of **GRANDDAD**.

gran·dam /ˈgran,dam; -dəm/ (also **grand-dam, gran·dame**) ▶*n.* archaic term for **GRANDMOTHER**. ■ an old woman. ■ a female ancestor.

grand·child /ˈgran(d)CHīld/ ▶*n.* (*pl.* **-child·ren** /-,CHildrən/) a child of one's son or daughter.

grand·dad /ˈgran,dad/ (also **gran·dad**) ▶*n. inf.* one's grandfather.

grand·dad·dy /ˈgran,dadē/ (also **gran·dad·dy**) ▶*n.* (*pl.* **-dies**) another term for **GRANDDAD**. ■ (**the granddaddy of**) used to denote a person or thing that is considered to be the best, largest, or most notable of a particular kind: *that young fellow is going to have the granddaddy of all headaches.*

grand·daugh·ter /ˈgran,dôtər/ ▶*n.* a daughter of one's son or daughter.

grande dame /ˈgran ˈdam; ˈgrän ˈdäm/ ▶*n.* a woman of influential position within a particular sphere: *the grande dame of British sculpture.*

gran·dee /granˈdē/ ▶*n.* a Spanish or Portuguese nobleman of the highest rank. ■ a person of high rank or eminence.

gran·deur /ˈgranjər; ˈgran,dyŏŏr/ ▶*n.* splendor and impressiveness, esp. of appearance or style: *the austere grandeur of mountain scenery.* ■ high rank or social importance.

grand·fa·ther /ˈgran(d),fäTHər/ ▶*n.* the father of one's father or mother. ■ the person who founded or originated something.
▶*v.* [*tr.*] *inf.* exempt (someone or something) from a new law or regulation: *smokers who worked here before the ban have been grandfathered.* —**grand·fa·ther·ly** *adj.*

grand·fa·ther clock ▶*n.* a clock in a tall freestanding wooden case, driven by weights.

gran·di·flo·ra /ˌgrandəˈflôrə/ ▶*adj.* (of a cultivated plant) bearing large flowers.
▶*n.* a grandiflora plant.

gran·dil·o·quent /granˈdiləkwənt/ ▶*adj.* pompous or extravagant in language, style, or manner, esp. in a way that is intended to impress: *a grandiloquent celebration of Spanish glory.* —**gran·dil·o·quence** *n.* —**gran·dil·o·quent·ly** *adv.*

gran·di·ose /ˈgrandē,ōs; ˌgrandē'ōs/ ▶*adj.* impressive or magnificent in appearance or style, esp. pretentiously so. ■ excessively grand or ambitious. —**gran·di·ose·ly** *adv.* —**gran·di·os·i·ty** /ˌgrandē'äsitē/ *n.*

grand ju·ry ▶*n. Law* a jury, normally of twenty-three jurors, selected to examine the validity of an accusation before trial.

grand lar·ce·ny ▶*n. Law* theft of personal property having a value above a legally specified amount.

grand·ma /ˈgran(d),mä; ˈgram-/ ▶*n. inf.* one's grandmother.

grand mal /ˌgran(d) ˈmäl; ˈmal/ ▶*n.* a serious form of epilepsy with muscle spasms and prolonged loss of consciousness. Compare with **PETIT MAL**. ■ an epileptic fit of this kind.

grand·moth·er /ˈgran(d),məTHər/ ▶*n.* the mother of one's father or mother. —**grand·moth·er·ly** *adj.*

grand·moth·er clock ▶*n.* a clock similar to a grandfather clock but about two-thirds the size.

grand·pa /ˈgran(d),pä; ˈgram-/ ▶*n. inf.* one's grandfather.

grand·par·ent /ˈgran(d),pe(ə)rənt; -,par-/ ▶*n.* a parent of one's father or mother; a grandmother or grandfather. —**grand·pa·ren·tal** /ˌgran(d)pə'rentl/ *adj.* —**grand·par·ent·hood** /-,hŏŏd/ *n.*

grand pi·an·o ▶*n.* a large, full-toned piano that has the body, strings, and soundboard arranged horizontally and in line with the keys and is supported by three legs.

Grand Prix /ˌgrän ˈprē; ˌgran/ ▶*n.* (*pl.* **Grands Prix** *pronunc.* same) an important sporting event in which participants compete for a major prize.

grand slam ▶*n.* the winning of each of a group of major championships or matches in a particular sport in the same year, in particular in tennis or golf. ■ *Bridge* the bidding and winning of all thirteen tricks. ■ *Baseball* a home run hit when each of the three bases is occupied by a runner, thus scoring four runs.

grand·son /ˈgran(d),sən/ ▶*n.* the son of one's son or daughter.

grand·stand /ˈgran(d),stand/ ▶*n.* the main seating area, usually roofed, commanding the best view for spectators at racetracks stadiums.
▶*v.* [*intr.*] [usu. as *n.*] (**grandstanding**) *derog.* seek to attract applause or favorable attention from spectators or the media.

grand to·tal ▶*n.* the final amount after everything is added up; the sum of other totals.

grange /grānj/ ▸ n. (**the Grange**) (in the U.S.) a farmers' association organized in 1867. ■ a local lodge of this association.

gran·ite /'granit/ ▸ n. a very hard, granular, crystalline, igneous rock consisting mainly of quartz, mica, and feldspar and often used as a building stone. ■ used in similes and metaphors to refer to something very hard and impenetrable: [as adj.] a man with granite determination. ▷ mid 17th cent.: from Italian granito, literally 'grained,' from grano 'grain,' from Latin granum. —**gra·nit·ic** /grə'nitik/ adj. —**gran·it·oid** /'grani,toid/ adj. & n.

gran·ny /'granē/ (also **gran·nie**) ▸ n. (pl. **-nies**) inf. one's grandmother.

Gran·ny Smith ▸ n. a dessert apple of a bright green variety with crisp, sharp-flavored flesh, originating in Australia.

gra·no·la /grə'nōlə/ ▸ n. a kind of breakfast cereal consisting typically of rolled oats, brown sugar or honey, dried fruit, and nuts. ■ [as adj.] chiefly derog. denoting those with liberal or environmentalist political views, typified as eating health foods.

grant /grant/ ▸ v. **1** agree to give or allow (something requested) to. ■ give (a right, power, property, etc.) formally or legally to. **2** agree or admit to (someone) that (something) is true: he hasn't made much progress, I'll grant you that.
▸ n. a sum of money given by an organization, esp. a government, for a particular purpose. ■ formal the action of granting something. ■ Law a legal conveyance or formal conferment: a grant of land | a grant of probate. —**grant·a·ble** adj. —**gran·tee** /gran'tē/ n. —**grant·er** or **grant·or** n.
▸ □ **take someone/something for granted** fail to appreciate someone or something that is very familiar or obvious: the comforts that people take for granted. **take something for granted** assume that something is true without questioning it: people no longer took for granted everything about Christianity.

gran·u·lar /'granyələr/ ▸ adj. resembling or consisting of small grains or particles. ■ having a roughened surface or structure. —**gran·u·lar·i·ty** /,granyə'laritē/ n.

gran·u·late /'granyə,lāt/ ▸ v. **1** [tr.] [usu. as adj.] (**granulated**) form (something) into grains or particles: granulated sugar. ■ [intr.] (of a substance) take the form of grains or particles. **2** [intr.] [often as adj.] (**granulating**) Med. (of a wound or lesion) form a grainy surface as part of the healing process. —**gran·u·la·tion** /,granyə'lāsнən/ n. —**gran·u·la·tor** /-,lātər/ n.

gran·ule /'granyōōl/ ▸ n. a small compact particle of a substance: coffee granules.

grape /grāp/ ▸ n. a berry, typically green (classified as white), purple, red, or black, eaten as fruit and used in making wine. ■ (**the grape**) inf. wine. —**grap·ey** (also **grap·y**) adj. (**grap·i·er**, **grap·i·est**)

grape·fruit /'grāp,frōōt/ ▸ n. (pl. same) **1** a large, round, yellow citrus fruit with an acid, juicy pulp. **2** the tree (Citrus paradisi) bearing this fruit.

grape·shot /'grāp,sнät/ ▸ n. hist. ammunition consisting of a number of small iron balls fired together from a cannon.

grape·vine /'grāp,vīn/ ▸ n. **1** a vine (genus Vitis, family Vitaceae) native to both Eurasia and North America, esp. one bearing fruit (grapes) used for eating or winemaking. **2** inf. used to refer to the circulation of rumors and unofficial information: I heard it **through the grapevine**.

graph[1] /graf/ ▸ n. a diagram showing the relation between variable quantities, typically of two variables, each measured along one of a pair of axes at right angles. ■ Math. a collection of points whose coordinates satisfy a given relation.
▸ v. [tr.] plot or trace on a graph.

graph[2] ▸ n. Linguistics a visual symbol, esp. a letter of the alphabet, representing a unit of sound or other feature of speech.

graph·eme /'grafēm/ ▸ n. Linguistics the smallest meaningful contrastive unit in a writing system. —**gra·phe·mic** /grə'fēmik/ adj. —**gra·phe·mi·cal·ly** /grə'fēmik(ə)lē/ adv. —**gra·phe·mics** /grə'fēmiks/ n.

graph·ic /'grafik/ ▸ adj. **1** of or relating to visual art, esp. involving drawing, engraving, or lettering: his mature graphic work. ■ giving a vivid picture with explicit detail: he gave a graphic description of the torture. ■ Comput. of, relating to, or denoting a visual image: graphic information such as charts and diagrams. **2** of or in the form of a graph.
▸ n. Comput. a graphical item displayed on a screen or stored as data. —**graph·i·cal·ly** /-ik(ə)lē/ adv.

graph·i·cal /'grafikəl/ ▸ adj. **1** of, relating to, or in the form of a graph: flow charts are graphical presentations. **2** of or relating to visual art or computer graphics. —**graph·i·cal·ly** /-ik(ə)lē/ adv.

graph·ic arts ▸ pl. n. the visual arts based on the use of line and tone rather than three-dimensional work or the use of color. ■ (**graphic art**) the activity of practicing these arts, esp. as a subject of study. —**graph·ic art·ist** n.

graph·ics /'grafiks/ ▸ pl. n. [usu. treated as sing.] **1** the products of the graphic arts, esp. commercial design or illustration. **2** the use of diagrams in calculation and design. **3** (also **computer graphics**) [treated as pl.] visual images produced by computer processing. ■ [treated as sing.] the use of computers linked to display screens to generate and manipulate visual images.

graph·ite /'gra,fīt/ ▸ n. a gray, crystalline, allotropic form of carbon that occurs as a mineral in some rocks and can be made from coke. It is used as a solid lubricant, in pencils, and as a moderator in nuclear reactors. ▷ late 18th cent.: coined in German (Graphit), from Greek graphein 'write' (because of its use as pencil "lead"). —**gra·phit·ic** /grə'fitik/ adj.

graph·ol·o·gy /gra'fäləjē/ ▸ n. the study of handwriting, for example, as used to infer a person's character. —**graph·o·log·i·cal** /,grafə'läjikəl/ adj. —**graph·ol·o·gist** /-jist/ n.

grap·nel /'grapnəl/ ▸ n. a small anchor with several flukes.

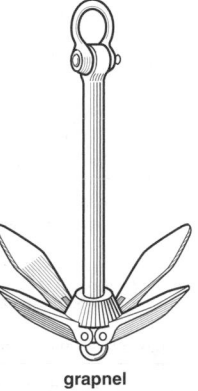
grapnel

grap·ple /'grapəl/ ▸ v. [intr.] engage in a close fight or struggle without weapons; wrestle: passersby **grappled with** the man after the knife attack. ■ [tr.] seize hold of (someone). ■ (**grapple with**) struggle with or work hard to deal with or overcome (a difficulty or challenge): other towns are still grappling with the problem.
▸ n. an act of grappling. ■ an instrument for catching hold of or seizing something. —**grap·pler** /'graplər/ n.

grasp /grasp/ ▸ v. [tr.] seize and hold firmly: she grasped the bottle. ■ [intr.] (**grasp at**) try to seize hold of: they had grasped at any means to overthrow him. ■ get mental hold of; comprehend fully: children grasp complex ideas. ■ act decisively to the advantage of (something).
▸ n. a firm hold or grip. ■ a person's power or capacity to attain something: he knew success was within his grasp. ■ a person's understanding: his grasp of detail. —**grasp·a·ble** adj. —**grasp·er** n.

grasp·ing /'graspiNG/ ▸ adj. greedy; avaricious: grasping, power-hungry individuals. —**grasp·ing·ly** adv. —**grasp·ing·ness** n.

grass /gras/ ▸ n. **1** vegetation consisting of typically short plants with long narrow leaves, growing wild or cultivated on lawns and pasture, and as a fodder crop. ■ ground covered with grass: he sat down on the grass. **2** the mainly herbaceous plant that constitutes such vegetation. The **grass family** (Gramineae) forms the dominant vegetation of many areas of the world. **3** inf. marijuana. —**grass·less** adj. —**grass·like** /-,līk/ adj.

grass·hop·per /'gras,häpər/ ▸ n. a plant-eating insect (family Acrididae) with long hind legs that are used for jumping and for producing a chirping sound.

grass·land /'gras,land/ ▸ n. (also **grass·lands**) a large open area of country covered with grass, esp. one used for grazing: rough grassland.

grass roots (also **grass·roots** /'gras,rōōts/) ▸ pl. n. the most basic level of an activity or organization: the whole campaign would be conducted **at the grass roots**. | [as adj.] improve the sport's image **at the grass-roots level**. ■ ordinary people regarded as the main body of an organization's membership: you have lost touch with the grass roots of the party.

grass·y /'grasē/ ▸ adj. (**grass·i·er**, **grass·i·est**) of or covered with grass: grassy slopes. ■ characteristic of grass: an intense grassy green. ■ tasting or smelling like grass: try the pleasant, grassy Chablis. —**grass·i·ness** n.

grate[1] /grāt/ ▸ v. **1** [tr.] reduce (something, esp. food) to small shreds by rubbing it on a grater. [as adj.] (**grated**) grated cheese. **2** [intr.] make an unpleasant rasping sound. ■ (**grate against**) rub against something with such a sound: his helmet grated against the top of the door. ■ have an irritating effect: he had a juvenile streak that **grated on** her nerves.

grate[2] ▸ n. **1** the recess of a fireplace or furnace. ■ a metal frame confining fuel in a fireplace or furnace. **2** a grating.

grate·ful /'grātfəl/ ▸ adj. feeling or showing an appreciation of kindness; thankful. —**grate·ful·ly** adv. —**grate·ful·ness** n.

grat·er /'grātər/ ▸ n. a device having a surface covered with holes edged by slightly raised cutting edges, used for grating cheese and other foods.

grat·i·fy /ˈgratəˌfī/ ▶v. (-fies, -fied) [tr.] (often be gratified) give (someone) pleasure or satisfaction: *I was gratified to see the coverage in May's issue* | [as adj.] (**gratifying**) *the results were gratifying.* ■ indulge or satisfy (a desire): *not all the sexual impulses can be gratified.* —**grat·i·fi·ca·tion** /ˌgratəfiˈkāSHən/ n. —**grat·i·fi·er** n. —**gra·ti·fy·ing·ly** adv.

grat·ing¹ /ˈgrātiNG/ ▶adj. sounding harsh and unpleasant: *her high, grating voice.* ■ irritating. —**grat·ing·ly** adv.

grat·ing² ▶n. a framework of parallel or crossed bars, typically preventing access through an opening while permitting communication or ventilation. ■ (also **diffraction grating**) *Optics* a set of equally spaced parallel wires, or a surface ruled with equally spaced parallel lines, used to produce spectra by diffraction.

grat·is /ˈgratis/ ▶adv. without charge; free: *a program was issued gratis.* ▶adj. given or done for nothing; free: *gratis copies.*

grat·i·tude /ˈgratəˌt(y)ōōd/ ▶n. the quality of being thankful; readiness to show appreciation for and to return kindness: *she expressed her gratitude to the committee for their support.*

gra·tu·i·tous /grəˈt(y)ōōitəs/ ▶adj. **1** uncalled for; lacking good reason; unwarranted: *gratuitous violence.* **2** given or done free of charge: *solicitors provide a form of gratuitous legal advice.* —**gra·tu·i·tous·ly** adv. —**gra·tu·i·tous·ness** n.

gra·tu·i·ty /grəˈt(y)ōōitē/ ▶n. (pl. **-ties**) money given in return for some service or favor, in particular: ■ *formal* a tip given to a waiter, taxicab driver, etc.

grave¹ /grāv/ ▶n. a place of burial for a dead body, typically a hole dug in the ground and marked by a stone or mound: *the coffin was lowered into the grave.* ■ (**the grave**) used as an allusive term for death: *life beyond the grave.*
▶ □ **dig one's own grave** do something foolish that causes one to fail or be ruined. □ **turn** (also **turn over**) **in one's grave** used to express the opinion that something would have caused anger or distress to someone who is now dead.

grave² ▶adj. giving cause for alarm; serious: *a matter of grave concern.* ■ serious or solemn in manner or appearance; somber: *his face was grave.*
▶n. /gräv/ another term for **GRAVE ACCENT.** —**grave·ly** adv. —**grave·ness** n.

grave³ ▶v. (past part. **grav·en** /ˈgrāvən/ or **graved**) [tr.] *archaic* engrave (an inscription or image) on a surface. ■ *poetic/lit.* fix (something) indelibly in the mind: *the times are graven on my memory.*

gra·ve⁴ /ˈgräˌvā/ ▶adj. *Mus.* slowly; with solemnity.

grave ac·cent /grāv; gräv/ ▶n. a mark (`) placed over certain letters in some languages to indicate an alteration of a sound, as of quality, quantity, or pitch.

grave-dig·ger /ˈgrāvˌdigər/ ▶n. a person who digs graves.

grav·el /ˈgravəl/ ▶n. a loose aggregation of small, rounded stones. ■ a mixture of such stones with coarse sand, used for paths and roads and as an aggregate.
▶v. (**grav·eled, grav·el·ing**) [tr.] **1** cover (an area of ground) with gravel. **2** *inf.* make (someone) angry or annoyed: *this was a bad strike, and it graveled him to involve himself in it.*

grav·el·ly /ˈgravəlē/ ▶adj. resembling, containing, or consisting of gravel: *a dry gravelly soil.* ■ (of a voice) deep and rough-sounding.

grav·en /ˈgrāvən/ ▶ past participle of **GRAVE**³.

grav·en im·age ▶n. a carved idol or representation of a god used as an object of worship.

grav·er /ˈgrāvər/ ▶n. a burin or other engraving tool.

Graves' dis·ease ▶n. a swelling of the neck and protrusion of the eyes resulting from an overactive thyroid gland.

grave·stone /ˈgrāvˌstōn/ ▶n. an inscribed headstone marking a grave.

grave·yard /ˈgrāvˌyärd/ ▶n. a burial ground, esp. one beside a church.

grave·yard shift ▶n. a work shift that runs through the early morning hours, typically covering the period between midnight and 8 a.m.

gra·vim·e·ter /grəˈvimitər/ ▶n. an instrument for measuring the difference in the force of gravity from one place to another.

grav·i·met·ric /ˌgraviˈmetrik/ ▶adj. of or relating to the measurement of weight.

grav·i·tate /ˈgraviˌtāt/ ▶v. [intr.] move toward or be attracted to a place, person, or thing: *they gravitated to the Catholic faith in their hour of need.* ■ *Physics* move, or tend to move, toward a center of gravity or other attractive force.

grav·i·ta·tion /ˌgraviˈtāSHən/ ▶n. movement, or a tendency to move, toward a center of attractive force, as in the falling of bodies to the earth. ■ *Physics* a force of attraction exerted by each particle of matter in the universe on every other particle: *the law of universal gravitation.*

■ *fig.* movement toward or attraction to something: *a tentative gravitation toward higher prices.* —**grav·i·ta·tion·al** /-SHənl/ adj. —**grav·i·ta·tion·al·ly** /-SHənl-ē/ adv.

grav·i·ty /ˈgravitē/ ▶n. **1** *Physics* the force that attracts a body toward the center of the earth, or toward any other physical body having mass. ■ the degree of intensity of this, measured by acceleration. **2** extreme or alarming importance; seriousness: *crimes of the utmost gravity.*

gra·vure /grəˈvyōōr/ ▶n. an image produced from etching a plate through an intaglio process and producing a print from it.

gra·vy /ˈgrāvē/ ▶n. (pl. **-vies**) **1** the fat and juices exuding from meat during cooking. ■ a sauce made from these juices together with stock and other ingredients. **2** *inf.* unearned or unexpected money.

gra·vy train ▶n. *inf.* used to refer to a situation in which someone can make a lot of money for very little effort: *come to Hollywood and get on the gravy train.*

gray /grā/ (*Brit.* **grey**) ▶adj. **1** of a color intermediate between black and white, as of ashes or an overcast sky: *gray flannel trousers.* ■ (of hair) turning gray or white with age: *a gray beard.* ■ (of a person) having gray hair: *a gray, fatherly gentleman.* ■ *inf.* relating to old people, esp. when seen as an oppressed group: *gray power.* ■ (of the weather) cloudy and dull; without sun: *a cold, gray November day.* ■ (of a person's face) pale, as through tiredness, age, or illness: *a few people, their faces gray and bitter.* **2** dull and nondescript; without interest or character: *gray, faceless men* | *the gray daily routine.* **3** (of financial or trading activity) not accounted for in official statistics: *the gray economy.*
▶n. **1** gray color or pigment: *dirty intermediate tones of gray.* ■ gray clothes or material: *the gentleman in gray.* ■ gray hair: *he sighed at the amount of gray at his temple.* ■ (usu. **Gray**) the Confederate army in the Civil War, or a member of that army. **2** a gray thing or animal, in particular a gray or white horse.
▶v. [intr.] (esp. of hair) become gray with age: *he had put on weight and grayed somewhat* | [as adj.] (**graying**) *a man of about fifty with graying hair.* ■ (of a person or group) become older; age: [as adj.] (**graying**) *a graying workforce.* —**gray·ish** adj. —**gray·ly** adv. —**gray·ness** n.

gray ar·e·a ▶n. an ill-defined situation or field not readily conforming to a category or to an existing set of rules: *gray areas in the legislation have still to be clarified.*

gray·ling /ˈgrāliNG/ ▶n. an edible freshwater fish (genus *Thymallus*) of the salmon family that is silvery-gray with horizontal violet stripes and has a long, high dorsal fin.

gray mat·ter ▶n. the darker tissue of the brain and spinal cord, consisting mainly of nerve cell bodies and branching dendrites. ■ *inf.* intelligence: *I wish I had a little of her gray matter.*

graze¹ /grāz/ ▶v. [intr.] (of cattle, sheep, etc.) eat grass in a field: *cattle graze on the open meadows.* ■ [tr.] (of an animal) feed on (grass or land covered by grass): *llamas graze the tufts of grass.* ■ [tr.] put (cattle, sheep, etc.) to feed on land covered by grass: *shepherds who grazed animals on common land.* ■ *inf.* (of a person) eat small quantities of food at frequent but irregular intervals: *graze on snacks or sweets.* ■ *inf.* casually sample something: *we grazed up and down the channels.* —**graz·er** n.

graze² ▶v. [tr.] scrape the skin of (a part of the body) so as to break the surface but cause little or no bleeding: *she fell down and grazed her knees.* ■ touch or scrape lightly in passing: *his hands just grazed hers.*
▶n. a slight injury where the skin is scraped: *it'll be fine, it's only a graze.*

graz·ing /ˈgrāziNG/ ▶n. grassland suitable for pasturage.

grease ▶n. /grēs/ oily or fatty matter, in particular: ■ a thick oily substance used as a lubricant: *axle grease.* ■ oil or fat used or produced in cooking. ■ oily matter in the hair, esp. when used for styling. ■ the oily matter in unprocessed wool; lanolin.
▶v. /grēs; grēz/ [tr.] smear or lubricate with grease: [as adj.] (**greased**) *place on a greased baking sheet.* ▷Middle English: from Old French *graisse*, based on Latin *crassus* 'thick, fat.' —**grease·less** adj.
▶ □ **grease the wheels** help something go smoothly: *it is inadequate to grease the wheels of recovery.* □ **like greased lightning** *inf.* extremely fast.

grease gun ▶n. a device for pumping grease under pressure to a particular point.

grease mon·key ▶n. *inf.*, *derog.* a mechanic.

grease·paint /ˈgrēsˌpānt/ ▶n. a waxy substance used as makeup by actors.

greas·er /ˈgrēsər; -zər/ ▶n. a mechanic. ■ *inf.* a rough young man, esp. one who greases his hair back and is a member of a motorcycle gang.

greas·y /ˈgrēsē; -zē/ ▶adj. (**greas·i·er, greas·i·est**) covered with an oily substance: *he wiped his greasy fingers.* ■ producing more body oils than average: *greasy skin.* ■ containing or cooked with too much oil or fat: *greasy food.* ■ of or like grease: *their moisturizers don't feel greasy.*

slippery: *the floor was greasy.* ■ *fig.* (of a person or their manner) effusively polite in a way that is felt to be insincere and repulsive: *the greasy little man from the newspaper.* —**greas·i·ly** /-səlē; -zəlē/ *adv.* —**greas·i·ness** *n.*

greas·y spoon ▶ *n. inf.* a cheap, run-down café or restaurant serving fried foods.

great /grāt/ ▶ *adj.* **1** of an extent, amount, or intensity considerably above the normal or average: *the article was of great interest* | *she showed great potential as an actor.* ■ very large and imposing: *a great ocean between them.* ■ used to reinforce another adjective of size or extent: *a great big grin.* ■ used to express surprise, admiration, or contempt, esp. in exclamations: *you great oaf!* ■ (also **greater**) used in names of animals or plants that are larger than similar kinds, e.g., **greater flamingo.** ■ (**Greater**) (of a city) including adjacent urban areas: *Greater Cleveland.* **2** of ability, quality, or eminence considerably above the normal or average: *the great Italian conductor* | *we obeyed our great men and leaders* | *great art has the power to change lives.* ■ (**the Great**) a title denoting the most important person of the name: *Alexander the Great.* ■ *inf.* very good or satisfactory; excellent: *this has been another great year* | *what a great guy* | *wouldn't it be great to have him back?* | [as *interj.*] *"Great!" said Tom.* ■ *inf.* (of a person) very skilled or capable in a particular area: *a brilliant man, great at mathematics.* **3** denoting the element of something that is the most important or the most worthy of consideration: *the great thing is the challenge.* ■ used to indicate that someone or something particularly deserves a specified description: *I was a great fan of Hank's.* **4** [in *comb.*] (in names of family relationships) denoting one degree further removed upward or downward: *great-aunt* | *great-granddaughter* | *great-great-grandfather.*
▶ *n.* a great or distinguished person: *the Beatles, Bob Dylan, all the greats.* ■ [as *pl. n.*] (**the great**) great people collectively: *the lives of the great, including Churchill and Newton.*
▶ *adv. inf.* excellently; very well: *we played awful, they played great.* —**great·ness** *n.*

great di·vide ▶ *n.* a distinction regarded as significant and very difficult to ignore or overcome: *the great divide between workers and management.* ■ an event, date, or place seen as the point at which significant and irrevocable change occurs: *to our parents, the war was the great divide.* ■ the boundary between life and death: *she is still on the human side of the great divide.*

great-heart·ed ▶ *adj. dated* having a noble, generous, and courageous spirit. —**great-heart·ed·ness** *n.*

great horned owl ▶ *n.* a large owl (*Bubo virginianus*, family Strigidae) found throughout North and South America, with hornlike ear tufts.

great·ly /'grātlē/ ▶ *adv.* by a considerable amount; very much: *I admire him greatly* | *they now have greatly increased powers.*

Great War ▶ another name for WORLD WAR I.

grebe /grēb/ ▶ *n.* a diving waterbird (family Podicipedidae) with a long neck, lobed toes, and almost no tail, typically having bright breeding plumage used in display.

Gre·cian /'grēSHən/ ▶ *adj.* of or relating to ancient Greece, esp. its architecture.

Gre·cism /'grēsizəm/ ▶ *n.* a Greek idiom or grammatical feature, esp. as imitated in another language. ■ the Greek spirit, style, or mode of expression, esp. as imitated in a work of art.

Gre·co-Ro·man /'grekō/ ▶ *adj.* of or relating to the ancient Greeks and Romans. ■ denoting a style of wrestling in which holds below the waist are prohibited.

greed /grēd/ ▶ *n.* intense and selfish desire for something, esp. wealth, power, or food.

greed·y /'grēdē/ ▶ *adj.* (**greed·i·er, greed·i·est**) having or showing an intense and selfish desire for something, esp. wealth or power: *greedy thieves who plundered a defense contractor.* ■ having an excessive desire or appetite for food. —**greed·i·ly** /-dəlē/ *adv.* —**greed·i·ness** *n.*

Greek /grēk/ ▶ *adj.* of or relating to Greece, its people, or their language.
▶ *n.* **1** a native or national of modern Greece, or a person of Greek descent. ■ a Greek-speaking person in the ancient world, typically a native of one of the city-states of Greece and the eastern Mediterranean. **2** the ancient or modern language of Greece, the only representative of the Hellenic branch of the Indo-European family. **3** a member of a fraternity or sorority having a Greek-letter name. —**Greek·ness** *n.*
▶ □ **it's (all) Greek to me** *inf.* I can't understand it at all.

green /grēn/ ▶ *adj.* **1** of the color between blue and yellow in the spectrum; colored like grass or emeralds: *the leaves are bright green.* ■ consisting of fresh vegetables of this color: *a green salad.* ■ denoting a light or flag of this color used as a signal to proceed. ■ (of a ski run) of the lowest level of difficulty, as indicated by colored markers on the run.

2 covered with grass, trees, or other plants: *proposals that would smother green fields with development.* ■ (usu. **Green**) concerned with or supporting protection of the environment as a political principle: *a Green candidate for the European parliament.* ■ (of a product) not harmful to the environment. **3** (of a plant or fruit) young or unripe: *green shoots.* ■ (of wood) unseasoned. ■ (of food or leather) not dried, smoked, or tanned. ■ (of a person) inexperienced, naive, or gullible: *a green recruit fresh from college.* ■ (of a memory) not fading. ■ still strong or vigorous: *first there was green old age, hardly different from middle age.* **4** (of the complexion or a person) pale and sickly-looking. ■ as a sign of jealousy or envy.
▶ *n.* **1** green color or pigment: *major roads are marked in green.* ■ green clothes or material: *two girls in red and green.* ■ green foliage or growing plants. ■ *inf., dated* money: *you'll save yourself some green.* **2** a green thing, in particular: ■ a green light. **3** a piece of public or common grassy land, esp. in the center of a town: *a house overlooking the green.* ■ an area of smooth, very short grass immediately surrounding a hole on a golf course. **4** (**greens**) green leafy vegetables: *salad greens* | *beet greens.* **5** (usu. **Green**) a member or supporter of an environmentalist group or party.
▶ *v.* make or become green, in particular: ■ [*tr.*] make (an urban or desert area) more verdant by planting or encouraging trees or other greenery: *greening the desert.* ■ [*tr.*] make less harmful or more sensitive to the environment: *the importance of greening this industry.* ■ [*intr.*] become green in color, through age or by becoming covered with plants: *the roof was greening with lichen.* ▷Old English *grēne* (adjective), *grēnian* (verb), of Germanic origin; related to Dutch *groen,* German *grün,* also to *grass* and *grow.* —**green·ish** *adj.* —**green·ly** *adv.* —**green·ness** *n.*

green·back /'grēn,bak/ ▶ *n. inf.* a dollar bill; a dollar: *the pot she purchased with our last greenback.*

green bean ▶ *n.* the immature pod of any of various bean plants, eaten as a vegetable. See also STRING BEAN.

Green Be·ret ▶ *n. inf.* a member of the U.S. Army Special Forces.

green·bot·tle /'grēn,bätl/ ▶ *n.* a metallic green fly (genus *Lucilia,* family Calliphoridae) that sometimes lays eggs in the wounds of animals.

green card ▶ *n.* a permit allowing a foreign national to live and work permanently in the U.S.

green·er·y /'grēnərē/ ▶ *n.* green foliage, growing plants, or vegetation.

green-eyed mon·ster ▶ *n.* (**the green-eyed monster**) *inf., humorous* jealousy personified.

green·fly /'grēn,flī/ ▶ *n.* (*pl.* same or **-flies**) a green aphid that is a common pest of crops and garden plants.

green·gage /'grēn,gāj/ ▶ *n.* **1** (also **greengage plum**) a sweet, greenish fruit resembling a small plum. **2** the tree (*Prunus domestica italica*) of the rose family bearing this fruit.

green·horn /'grēn,hôrn/ ▶ *n. inf.* a person who is new to or inexperienced at a particular activity.

green·house /'grēn,hous/ ▶ *n.* a glass building in which plants are grown that need protection from cold weather.

green·house ef·fect ▶ *n.* the trapping of the sun's warmth in a planet's lower atmosphere due to the greater transparency of the atmosphere to visible radiation from the sun than to infrared radiation emitted from the planet's surface.

green·house gas ▶ *n.* a gas that contributes to the greenhouse effect by absorbing infrared radiation, e.g., carbon dioxide and methane.

Green·ing /'grēniNG/ ▶ *n.* an apple of a variety that is green when ripe.

green·keep·er /'grēn,kēpər/ ▶ *n.* another term for GREENSKEEPER.

green light ▶ *n.* a green traffic light giving permission to proceed. ■ *fig.* permission to go ahead with a project: *the commission has given the green light for the new development.*
▶ *v.* (**green-light**) [*tr.*] give permission to go ahead with (a project, esp. a movie).

green room ▶ *n.* a room in a theater or studio in which performers can relax when they are not performing.

greens·keep·er /'grēnz,kēpər/ (also **green·keep·er**) ▶ *n.* a person employed to look after a golf course.

green·stone /'grēn,stōn/ ▶ *n. Geol.* a greenish igneous rock containing feldspar and hornblende.

green tea ▶ *n.* tea that is made from unfermented leaves and is pale in color and slightly bitter in flavor, produced mainly in China and Japan.

G

Pronunciation Key ə *ago,* up; ər *over,* fur; a *hat;* ā *ate;* ä *car;* CH *chin;* e *let;* ē *see;* e(ə)r *air;* i *fit;* ī *by;* i(ə)r *ear;* NG *sing;* ō *go;* ô *law, for;* oi *toy;* oͧo *good;* oōo *goo;* ou *out;* SH *she;* TH *thin;* <u>TH</u> *then;* (h)w *why;* ZH *vision*

green thumb ▶*n. inf.* natural talent for growing plants: *you don't need a green thumb to grow them.*

Green·wich Mean Time (abbr.: **GMT**) (also **Green·wich time**) ▶the mean solar time at the Greenwich meridian, adopted as the standard time in a zone that includes the British Isles, now replaced by **universal time** in technical and scientific use.

green·y /ˈgrēnē/ ▶*adj.* [often in *comb.*] slightly green: *the greeny-brown surface of the stone.*

greet¹ /grēt/ ▶*v.* [*tr.*] give a polite word or sign of welcome or recognition to (someone) on meeting. ■ [*tr.*] receive or acknowledge (something) in a specified way: *everyone present greeted this idea warmly.* ■ (of a sight or sound) become apparent to or be noticed by (someone) on arrival somewhere: *flowers and cheers greeted the shipyard workers.* —**greet·er** *n.*

greet² ▶*v.* [*intr.*] *Scot.* weep; cry: *he sat down on the armchair and started to greet.*

greet·ing /ˈgrētiNG/ ▶*n.* a polite word or sign of welcome or recognition: *Mandy shouted a greeting.* ■ the action of giving such a sign: *she raised her hand in greeting.* ■ (usu. **greetings**) a formal expression of goodwill, said on meeting or in a written message: *warm greetings to you all.*

greet·ing card ▶*n.* a decorative card sent to convey good wishes on some occasion.

gre·gar·i·ous /griˈge(ə)rēəs/ ▶*adj.* (of a person) fond of company; sociable: *he was a popular and gregarious man.* ■ (of animals) living in flocks or loosely organized communities: *gregarious species forage in flocks from colonies or roosts.* ■ (of plants) growing in open clusters or in pure associations. —**gre·gar·i·ous·ly** *adv.* —**gre·gar·i·ous·ness** *n.*

Gre·go·ri·an cal·en·dar /grəˈgôrēən/ ▶*n.* the calendar introduced in 1582 by Pope Gregory XIII, as a modification of the Julian calendar.

Gre·go·ri·an chant ▶*n.* church music sung as a single vocal line in free rhythm and a restricted scale (plainsong), in a style developed for the medieval Latin liturgy.

grem·lin /ˈgremlin/ ▶*n. inf.* an imaginary mischievous sprite regarded as responsible for an unexplained problem or fault, esp. a mechanical or electronic one. ■ such a problem or fault.

gre·nade /grəˈnād/ ▶*n.* a small bomb thrown by hand or launched mechanically.

gren·a·dier /ˌgrenəˈdi(ə)r/ ▶*n.* **1** a soldier armed with grenades or a grenade launcher. **2** a common bottom-dwelling fish (family Macrouridae) with a large head, a long tapering tail, and typically a luminous gland on the belly.

gren·a·dine¹ /ˈgrenəˌdēn; ˌgrenəˈdēn/ ▶*n.* a sweet syrup made from pomegranates.

gren·a·dine² ▶*n.* dress fabric of loosely woven silk or silk and wool.

grew /grōō/ ▶ past of **GROW**.

grey ▶*adj.* British spelling of **GRAY**¹.

grey·hound /ˈgrāˌhound/ ▶*n.* a dog of a tall, slender breed having keen sight and capable of high speed, used since ancient times for hunting small game and now chiefly in racing and coursing. ▷Old English *grīghund*; the first element, related to Old Norse *grey* 'bitch,' is of unknown origin.

grid /grid/ ▶*n.* **1** a framework of spaced bars that are parallel to or cross each other; a grating: *the metal grids had been pulled across the foyer.* **2** a network of lines that cross each other to form a series of squares or rectangles: *a grid of tree-lined streets.* ■ a football field. ■ a network of cables or pipes for distributing power, esp. high-voltage transmission lines for electricity. ■ a network of regularly spaced lines on a map that cross one another at right angles and are numbered to enable the precise location of a place. ■ a pattern of lines marking the starting places on a auto-racing track: *first away from the grid.* **3** a number of computers linked together via the Internet so that their combined power may be harnessed to work on processing-intensive problems. ▶*v.* [*tr.*] [usu. as *adj.*] (**gridded**) put into or set out as a grid: *a well-planned core of gridded streets.*

grid·dle /ˈgridl/ ▶*n.* a heavy, flat iron plate that is heated and used for cooking food.

grid·i·ron /ˈgridˌī(ə)rn/ ▶*n.* **1** a frame of parallel bars or beams, typically in two sets arranged at right angles, in particular: **2** a field for football, marked with regularly spaced parallel lines. **3** another term for **GRID** (sense 2).

grid·lock /ˈgridˌläk/ ▶*n.* **1** a traffic jam affecting a whole network of intersecting streets. **2** another term for **DEADLOCK** (sense 1). —**grid·locked** *adj.*

grief /grēf/ ▶*n.* deep sorrow, esp. that caused by someone's death: *she was overcome with grief.* ■ *inf.* trouble or annoyance: *they won't give you any grief in the next few days.*

▶ □ **come to grief** have an accident; meet with disaster: *many a ship has come to grief along this shore.* □ **good grief!** an exclamation of irritation, frustration, or surprise.

griev·ance /ˈgrēvəns/ ▶*n.* a real or imagined wrong or other cause for complaint or protest, esp. unfair treatment: *failure to redress genuine grievances.* ■ an official statement of a complaint over something believed to be wrong or unfair: *three pilots have filed grievances against the company.*

grieve /grēv/ ▶*v.* [*intr.*] suffer grief: *she grieved for her father.* ■ [*tr.*] feel grief for or because of: *she did not have the opportunity to grieve her mother's death.* ■ [*tr.*] cause great distress to (someone): *what grieves you, my son?* —**griev·er** *n.*

griev·ous /ˈgrēvəs/ ▶*adj. formal* (of something bad) very severe or serious: *his death was a grievous blow* | *the American fleet suffered grievous losses.* —**griev·ous·ly** *adv.* —**griev·ous·ness** *n.*

grif·fin /ˈgrifin/ (also **gryph·on, grif·fon** /ˈgrifən/) ▶*n.* a mythical creature with the head and wings of an eagle and the body of a lion.

griffin

grif·fon /ˈgrifən/ ▶*n.* **1** a dog of any of several terrierlike breeds originating in northwestern Europe. ■ (also **Brussels griffon**) a dog of a toy breed with a flat face and upturned chin. **2** variant spelling of **GRIFFIN**.

grill¹ /gril/ ▶*n.* a metal framework used for cooking food over an open fire; a gridiron. ■ a portable device for cooking outdoors, consisting of such a framework placed over charcoal or gas fuel. ■ a large griddle. ■ a dish of food, esp. meat, cooked using a grill. ■ (also **grill room**) a restaurant serving grilled food. ▶*v.* **1** [*tr.*] cook (something) using a grill: *grill the trout for about five minutes.* **2** [*tr.*] *inf.* subject (someone) to intense questioning or interrogation: *my father grilled us about what we had been doing* | [as *n.*] (**grilling**) *they faced a grilling over the latest results.* —**grill·er** *n.*

grill² ▶*n.* variant spelling of **GRILLE**.

grille /gril/ (also **grill**) ▶*n.* a grating or screen of metal bars or wires, placed in front of something as protection or to allow ventilation or discreet observation. ■ a grating at the front of a motor vehicle allowing air to circulate to the radiator to cool it.

grill·work /ˈgrilˌwərk/ ▶*n.* metal bars or wires arranged to form a grille.

grim /grim/ ▶*adj.* (**grim·mer, grim·mest**) forbidding or uninviting: *his grim expression.* ■ (of humor) lacking genuine levity; mirthless; black: *some moments of grim humor.* ■ allowing no compromise; stern; relentless: *grim determination to succeed.* —**grim·ly** *adv.* —**grim·ness** *n.*

grim·ace /ˈgriməs; griˈmās/ ▶*n.* an ugly, twisted expression on a person's face, typically expressing disgust, pain, or wry amusement. ▶*v.* [*intr.*] make a grimace: *I sipped the coffee and grimaced.* ▷mid 17th cent.: from French, from Spanish *grimazo* 'caricature,' from *grima* 'fright.'

grime /grīm/ ▶*n.* dirt ingrained on the surface of something.

grim·y /ˈgrīmē/ ▶*adj.* (**grim·i·er, grim·i·est**) covered with or characterized by grime: *a grimy industrial city.* —**grim·i·ly** /-məlē/ *adv.* —**grim·i·ness** *n.*

grin /grin/ ▶*v.* (**grinned, grin·ning**) [*intr.*] smile broadly, esp. in an unrestrained manner and with the mouth open: *Dennis appeared, grinning cheerfully.* ■ [*tr.*] express with a broad smile. ■ grimace or appear to grimace grotesquely in a way that reveals the teeth: [as *adj.*] (**grinning**) *a grinning skull.* ▶*n.* a broad smile. —**grin·ner** *n.* —**grin·ning·ly** *adv.*

grind /grīnd/ ▶*v.* (past **ground** /ground/) **1** [*tr.*] reduce (something) to small particles or powder by crushing it: *grind some black pepper over the salad* | *they grind up fish for fertilizer.* ■ [*intr.*] (of a mill or machine) work with a crushing action: *the old mill was grinding again.* ■ sharpen, smooth, or produce (something) by crushing or by friction: *power from a waterwheel was used to grind cutlery.* ■ operate (a mill or machine) by turning the handle: *she was grinding a coffee mill.* **2** rub or cause to rub together gratingly: [*intr.*] *tectonic plates that inexorably grind against each other.* ■ [*intr.*] move noisily and laboriously, esp. against a countering

force: *the truck was grinding slowly up the hill.* **3** [*intr.*] *inf.* (of a dancer) rotate the hips: *go-go girls grinding to blaring disco.*
▸*n.* **1** a crushing or grating sound or motion: *the crunch and grind of bulldozers.* ■ hard dull work: *relief from the daily grind.* ■ *inf.* an excessively hard-working student. ■ the size of ground particles: *only the right grind gives you all the fine flavor.* **2** *inf.* a dancer's rotary movement of the hips: *a bump and grind.*
grind·er /ˈgrīndər/ ▸*n.* **1** a machine used for grinding something: *a coffee grinder.* ■ a person employed to grind cutlery, tools, or cereals. **2** a molar tooth. ■ (**grinders**) *inf.* the teeth. **3** *inf.* another term for SUBMARINE SANDWICH.
grind·stone /ˈgrīndˌstōn/ ▸*n.* a thick disk of stone or other abrasive material mounted so as to revolve, used for grinding, sharpening, or polishing metal objects. ■ *rare* another term for MILLSTONE.
grin·go /ˈgriNGgō/ ▸*n.* (*pl.* **-gos**) *inf., often offens.* a white person from an English-speaking country (used in Spanish-speaking regions, chiefly Latin America). ▷mid 19th cent.: Spanish, literally 'foreign, foreigner, or gibberish,' perhaps an alteration of *griego* 'Greek.'
grip /grip/ ▸*v.* (**gripped, grip·ping**) [*tr.*] **1** take and keep a firm hold of; grasp tightly: *his knuckles were white as he gripped the steering wheel.* ■ [*intr.*] maintain a firm contact, esp. by friction: *a sole that really grips well on wet rock.* **2** (of a feeling or emotion) deeply affect (someone): *she was gripped by a feeling of excitement.* ■ (of an illness or unwelcome situation) afflict strongly: *the country was gripped by recession.* ■ compel the attention or interest of: [as adj.] (**gripping**) *a gripping TV thriller.*
▸*n.* **1** a firm hold; a tight grasp or clasp: *his arm was held in a vicelike grip* | *fig. the icy grip of winter.* ■ a manner of grasping or holding something: *I've changed my grip and my backswing.* ■ the ability of something, esp. a wheel or shoe, to maintain a firm contact with a surface: *these shoes have got no grip.* ■ an effective form of control over something: *our firm grip on inflation.* ■ an intellectual understanding of something: *you've got a pretty good* **grip on** *what's going on.* **2** a part or attachment by which something is held in the hand: *handlebar grips.* **3** a traveling bag: *a grip crammed with new clothes.* **4** an assistant in a theater; a stagehand. ■ a member of a camera crew responsible for moving and setting up equipment. —**grip·per** *n.* —**grip·ping·ly** *adv.*
▸ □ **come to grips with** engage in combat with: *they never came to grips with the enemy.* ■ begin to deal with or understand: *a real tough problem to come to grips with.* □ **get a grip** [usu. in *imper.*] *inf.* keep or recover one's self-control: *get a grip, guys!* □ **get a grip on** take control of: *the Fed will have to act to get a grip on inflation.* □ **in the grip of** dominated or affected by something undesirable or adverse: *people caught in the grip of a drug problem.*
gripe /grīp/ ▸*v.* **1** *inf.* express a complaint or grumble about something, esp. something trivial: [*intr.*] *they gripe about the paperwork* | [with *direct speech*] *"Holidays make no difference to Simon,"* Pat griped. **2** [*tr.*] affect with gastric or intestinal pain: *it gripes my belly like a green apple.* **3** [*intr.*] *Sailing* (of a ship) turn to face the wind in spite of the helm.
▸*n.* **1** *inf.* a complaint, esp. a trivial one: *his biggest gripe is that he has lost his sense of privacy.* **2** (usu. **gripes**) gastric or intestinal pain; colic. —**grip·er** *n.*
gris·ly /ˈgrizlē/ ▸*adj.* (**-li·er, -li·est**) causing horror or disgust: *the town was shaken by a series of grisly crimes.* —**gris·li·ness** *n.*
grist /grist/ ▸*n.* grain that is ground to make flour. ■ malt crushed to make mash for brewing. ■ *fig.* useful material, esp. to back up an argument.
▸ □ **grist for the mill** useful experience, material, or knowledge.
gris·tle /ˈgrisəl/ ▸*n.* cartilage, esp. when found as tough, inedible tissue in meat. —**gris·tly** /ˈgris(ə)lē/ *adj.*
grit /grit/ ▸*n.* **1** small, loose particles of stone or sand: *she had a bit of grit in her eye.* ■ [as *adj.*] (with numeral) indicating the grade of fineness of an abrasive: *220-grit paper.* **2** courage and resolve; strength of character.
▸*v.* (**grit·ted, grit·ting**) [*tr.*] clench (the teeth), esp. in order to keep one's resolve when faced with an unpleasant or painful duty: *fig. Congress must grit its teeth and take action* | [as *adj.*] (**gritted**) *"Not here," he said through gritted teeth.* —**grit·ty** *adj.*
grits /grits/ ▸*pl. n.* [also treated as *sing.*] a dish of coarsely ground corn kernels boiled with water or milk.
griz·zled /ˈgrizəld/ ▸*adj.* having or streaked with gray hair: *grizzled hair.*
griz·zly /ˈgrizlē/ ▸*n.* (*pl.* **-ies**) (also **grizzly bear**) a bear (*Ursus arctos horribilis*) of a large race of the North American brown bear.
groan /grōn/ ▸*v.* [*intr.*] make a deep inarticulate sound in response to pain or despair: *Marty groaned and pulled the blanket over his head.* ■ [with *direct speech*] say something in a despairing or miserable tone: *"Oh God!" I groaned.* ■ complain; grumble: *they were moaning and groaning*

about management. ■ (of a thing) make a low creaking or moaning sound when pressure or weight is applied: *James slumped back into his chair, making it groan and bulge.* ■ (**groan under/beneath**) *fig.* be oppressed by: *families groaning under mortgage increases.*
▸*n.* a deep, inarticulate sound made in pain or despair. ■ a complaint: *to listen with sincerity to everyone's moans and groans.* ■ a low creaking or moaning sound made by an object or device under pressure: *the protesting groan of timbers.* —**groan·er** *n.* —**groan·ing·ly** *adv.*
gro·cer /ˈgrōsər/ ▸*n.* a person who sells food and small household goods.
gro·cer·y /ˈgrōs(ə)rē/ ▸*n.* (*pl.* **-cer·ies**) (also **grocery store**) a grocer's store or business. ■ (**groceries**) items of food sold in such a store.
grog /gräg/ ▸*n.* spirits (originally rum) mixed with water. ■ *inf.*, alcoholic drink, esp. beer. ■ crushed unglazed pottery or brick used as an additive in plaster or clay.
grog·gy /ˈgrägē/ ▸*adj.* (**-gi·er, -gi·est**) dazed, weak, or unsteady, esp. from illness, intoxication, sleep, or a blow: *the sleeping pills had left her feeling groggy.* —**grog·gi·ly** /ˈgrägəlē/ *adv.* —**grog·gi·ness** *n.*
grog·ram /ˈgrägrəm/ ▸*n.* a coarse fabric made of silk, often combined with mohair or wool and stiffened with gum.
groin[1] /groin/ ▸*n.* **1** the area between the abdomen and the thigh on either side of the body. ■ *inf.* the region of the genitals. **2** *Archit.* a curved edge formed by two intersecting vaults.
groin[2] (also **groyne**) ▸*n.* a low barrier built out into the sea from a beach to check erosion and drifting.
grom·met /ˈgrämit/ ▸*n.* an eyelet placed in a hole in a sheet or panel to protect or insulate a rope or cable passed through it or to prevent the sheet or panel from being torn.
groom /grōōm; grŏŏm/ ▸*v.* [*tr.*] **1** look after the coat of (a horse, dog, or other animal) by brushing and cleaning it: *you must be prepared to spend time grooming your dog.* ■ (of an animal) clean the fur or skin of. ■ give a neat and tidy appearance to (someone): [as *n.*] (**grooming**) *she pays great attention to makeup, grooming, and clothes.* **2** prepare or train (someone) for a particular purpose or activity: *star pupils who are* **groomed for** *higher things.*
▸*n.* **1** a person employed to take care of horses. **2** a bridegroom.
groove /grōōv/ ▸*n.* **1** a long, narrow cut or depression, esp. one made to guide motion or receive a corresponding ridge. **2** an established routine or habit: *his thoughts were slipping* **into a** *familiar* **groove.** **3** *inf.* a rhythmic pattern in popular or jazz music.
▸*v.* **1** [*tr.*] make a groove or grooves in: *deep lines grooved her face.* **2** [*intr.*] *inf.* dance or listen to popular or jazz music, esp. that with an insistent rhythm: *they were* **grooving to** *Motown.* ■ enjoy oneself: *Harley relaxed and began to groove.*
▸ □ **in** (or **into**) **the groove** *inf.* performing consistently well or confidently: *it might take me a couple of races to get back into the groove.* ■ indulging in relaxed and spontaneous enjoyment, esp. dancing: *get into the groove!*
groov·y /ˈgrōōvē/ ▸*adj.* (**groov·i·er, groov·i·est**) *inf., dated* or *humorous* fashionable and exciting: *sporting a groovy new haircut.* ■ enjoyable and excellent. —**groov·i·ly** /-vəlē/ *adv.* —**groov·i·ness** *n.*
grope /grōp/ ▸*v.* **1** [*intr.*] feel about or search blindly or uncertainly with the hands: *she got up and groped for her spectacles.* ■ (**grope for**) search mentally with hesitation or uncertainty for (a word or answer): *she was groping for the words which would express what she thought* | [as *adj.*] (**groping**) *their groping attempts to create a more meaningful existence.* ■ move along with difficulty by feeling objects as one goes: *she blew out the candle and groped her way to the door.* **2** [*tr.*] *inf.* feel or fondle (someone) for sexual pleasure, esp. against their will.
▸*n.* an act of fondling someone for sexual pleasure: *she and Steve sneaked off for a quick grope.* —**grop·ing·ly** *adv.*
gros·grain /ˈgrōˌgrān/ ▸*n.* a heavy, ribbed fabric, typically of silk or rayon.
gros point /grō/ ▸*n.* a type of needlepoint embroidery consisting of stitches crossing two or more threads of the canvas in each direction.
gross /grōs/ ▸*adj.* **1** unattractively large or bloated: *I feel fat, gross—even my legs feel flabby.* ■ large-scale; not fine or detailed: *at the gross anatomical level.* ■ complete; blatant: *a gross exaggeration.* ■ vulgar; unrefined: *the duties we felt called upon to perform toward our inferiors were only gross, material ones.* ■ *inf.* very unpleasant; repulsive. **2** (of income, profit, or interest) without deduction of tax or other contributions; total: *the*

gross amount of the gift was $1,000 | the current rate of interest is about 6.1 percent gross. Often contrasted with NET[2] (sense 1).
▶ *adv.* without tax or other contributions having been deducted.
▶ *v.* [*tr.*] produce or earn (an amount of money) as gross profit or income.
▶ *phrasal v.* □ **gross someone out** *inf.* disgust someone, typically with repulsive or obscene behavior or appearance.
▶ *n.* **1** (*pl.* same) an amount equal to twelve dozen; 144: *fifty-five gross of tins of processed milk.* **2** (*pl.* **gross·es**) a gross profit or income: *the box-office grosses mounted.* ▷Middle English (in the sense 'thick, massive, bulky'): from Old French *gros, grosse* 'large,' from late Latin *grossus*. —**gross·ly** *adv. Freda was grossly overweight.* —**gross·ness** *n.*

gross do·mes·tic prod·uct (abbr.: **GDP**) ▶ *n.* the total value of goods produced and services provided in a country during one year.

gross na·tion·al prod·uct (abbr.: **GNP**) ▶ *n.* the total value of goods produced and services provided by a country during one year, equal to the gross domestic product plus the net income from foreign investments.

gro·tesque /grōˈtesk/ ▶ *adj.* comically or repulsively ugly or distorted: *grotesque facial distortions.* ■ incongruous or inappropriate to a shocking degree: *a lifestyle of grotesque luxury.*
▶ *n.* a very ugly or comically distorted figure, creature, or image: *the rods are carved in the form of a series of gargoyle faces and grotesques.* ■ (**the grotesque**) that which is grotesque: *images of the macabre and the grotesque.* ■ a style of decorative painting or sculpture consisting of the interweaving of human and animal forms with flowers and foliage. —**gro·tesque·ly** *adv.* —**gro·tesque·ness** *n.*

grot·to /ˈgrätō/ ▶ *n.* (*pl.* **-toes** or **-tos**) a small picturesque cave, esp. an artificial one in a park or garden. —**grot·toed** *adj.*

grouch /grouCH/ ▶ *n.* a habitually grumpy person: *rock's foremost poet and ill-mannered grouch.* ■ a complaint or grumble: *my only real grouch was that the children's chorus was far less easy on the ear.* ■ a fit of grumbling or sulking: *he's in a thundering grouch.*
▶ *v.* [*intr.*] voice one's discontent in an ill-tempered manner; grumble.

grouch·y /ˈgrouCHē/ ▶ *adj.* (**grouch·i·er, grouch·i·est**) irritable and bad-tempered; grumpy; complaining: *the old man grew sulky and grouchy.* —**grouch·i·ly** /-CHəlē/ *adv.* —**grouch·i·ness** *n.*

ground[1] /ground/ ▶ *n.* **1** the solid surface of the earth: *he lay on the ground.* ■ a limited or defined extent of the earth's surface; land: *an adjoining area of ground had been purchased.* ■ land of a specified kind: *my feet squelched over marshy ground.* ■ an area of land or sea used for a specified purpose: *shore dumping can pollute fishing grounds and beaches.* ■ (**grounds**) an area of enclosed land surrounding a large house or other building: *the house stands in seven acres of grounds.* ■ [as *adj.*] (in aviation) of or relating to the ground rather than the air (with particular reference to the maintenance and servicing of an aircraft on the ground): *ground staff | ground crew.* ■ [as *adj.*] (of an animal) living on or in the ground. ■ [as *adj.*] (of a fish) bottom-dwelling. ■ [as *adj.*] (of a plant) low-growing, esp. in relation to similar plants. **2** an area of knowledge or subject of discussion or thought: *third-year courses typically* **cover** *less* **ground** *and go into more depth | he shifted the argument onto theoretical grounds of his own choosing.* **3** (**grounds**) factors forming a basis for action or the justification for a belief: *there are some* **grounds** *for optimism | they called for a retrial* **on the grounds of** *the new evidence.* **4** *chiefly Art* a prepared surface to which paint or decoration is applied. **5** (**grounds**) solid particles, esp. of ground coffee, that form a residue; sediment. **6** electrical connection of a circuit or conductor to the earth or other body, such as the frame of a vehicle, whose potential is taken as zero.
▶ *v.* [*tr.*] **1** (often **be grounded**) prohibit or prevent (a pilot or an aircraft) from flying: *a bitter wind blew from the northeast, and the bombers were grounded.* ■ *inf.* (of a parent) refuse to allow (a child) to go out socially as a punishment: *he was grounded for hitting her on the head.* **2** run (a ship) aground. **3** (usu. **be grounded in**) give (something abstract) a firm theoretical or practical basis: *the study of history must be grounded in a thorough knowledge of the past.* ■ instruct (someone) thoroughly in a subject. **4** place or lay (something) on the ground or hit the ground with it:. **5** connect (an electrical device) with the ground. **6** [*intr.*] *Baseball* (of a batter) hit a pitched ball so that it bounces on the ground: *he grounded to second.* ■ (**ground out**) (of a batter) be put out by hitting a ball on the ground to a fielder who throws it to or touches first base before the batter touches that base: *he grounded out to shortstop.*
▶ □ **break new** (or **fresh**) **ground** do something innovative that is considered an advance or positive benefit. □ **from the ground up** *inf.* completely or complete: *they needed to learn the business from the ground up.* □ **gain ground** become more popular or accepted: *new moral attitudes are gaining ground.* □ **get off the ground** (or **get something off the**

ground) start or cause to start happening or functioning successfully: *he doesn't appreciate the steps he must take to get the negotiations off the ground.* □ **give** (or **lose**) **ground** retreat or lose one's advantage during a conflict or competition: *he refused to give ground on this issue.* □ **hold** (or **stand**) **one's ground** not retreat or lose one's advantage during a conflict or competition: *you will be able to hold your ground and resist the enemy's attack.* □ **work oneself into the ground** exhaust oneself by working very hard.

ground[2] ▶ past and past participle of GRIND.
▶ *adj.* reduced to fine particles by crushing or mincing: *ground cumin.* ■ shaped, roughened, or polished by grinding: *the thick opaque ground perimeter of the lenses.*

ground ball ▶ *n. Baseball* a ball hit along the ground. Also called **grounder**.

ground·break·ing /ˈground,brākiNG/ ▶ *adj.* breaking new ground; innovative; pioneering. —**ground·break·er** /-,brākər/ *n.*

ground con·trol ▶ *n.* [treated as *sing.* or *pl.*] the ground-based personnel and equipment that monitor and direct the flight and landing of aircraft or spacecraft. —**ground con·trol·ler** *n.*

ground cov·er ▶ *n.* low-growing, spreading plants that help to stop weeds from growing.

ground glass ▶ *n.* **1** glass with a smooth ground surface that renders it nontransparent while retaining its translucency. **2** glass ground into an abrasive powder.

ground·hog /ˈground,häg; -,hôg/ ▶ *n.* another term for WOODCHUCK.

ground·ing /ˈgroundiNG/ ▶ *n.* basic training or instruction in a subject: *every child needs a good* **grounding in** *science and technology.*

ground·less /ˈground-lis/ ▶ *adj.* not based on any good reason: *your fears are quite groundless.* —**ground·less·ly** *adv.* —**ground·less·ness** *n.*

ground·mass /ˈground,mas/ ▶ *n.* [in *sing.*] *Geol.* the compact, finer-grained material in which the crystals are embedded in a porphyritic rock.

grounds·keep·er /ˈgroun(d)z,kēpər/ ▶ *n.* a person who maintains an athletic field, a park, or the grounds of a school or other institution.

ground·speed /ˈground,spēd/ ▶ *n.* an aircraft's speed relative to the ground.

ground squir·rel ▶ *n.* a burrowing squirrel (*Spermophilus* and other genera) that is typically highly social, found chiefly in North America and northern Eurasia, where it usually hibernates in winter.

ground·swell /ˈgroun(d),swel/ ▶ *n.* a buildup of opinion or feeling in a large section of the population: *an unexpected groundswell of opposition developed.*

ground·wa·ter /ˈground,wôtər; -,wätər/ ▶ *n.* water held underground in the soil or in pores and crevices in rock.

ground·work /ˈground,wərk/ ▶ *n.* preliminary or basic work.

ground ze·ro ▶ *n.* the point on the earth's surface directly above or below an exploding nuclear bomb. ■ the site of the former World Trade Center in New York City in the wake of the terrorist attacks of September 11, 2001. ■ *fig.* a starting point or base for some activity: *if you're starting at ground zero in terms of knowledge, go to the library.*

group /grōōp/ ▶ *n.* [treated as *sing.* or *pl.*] a number of people or things that are located close together or are considered or classed together: *these bodies fall into four distinct groups.* ■ a number of people who work together or share certain beliefs: *I now belong to my local drama group.* ■ a commercial organization consisting of several companies under common ownership. ■ a number of musicians who play popular music together. ■ *Chem.* a combination of atoms having a recognizable identity in a number of compounds. ■ *Math.* a set of elements, together with an associative binary operation, that contains an inverse for each element and an identity element.
▶ *v.* [*tr.*] (often **be grouped**) put together or place in a group or groups: *three wooden chairs were grouped around a dining table.* ■ put into categories; classify. ■ [*intr.*] form a group or groups.

group dy·nam·ics ▶ *pl. n.* [also treated as *sing.*] *Psychol.* the processes involved when people in a group interact with each other, or the study of these.

group·er /ˈgrōōpər/ ▶ *n.* a large heavy-bodied fish (*Epinephelus, Mycteroperca,* and other genera) of the sea bass family, with a big head and wide mouth, found in warm seas.

group·ie /ˈgrōōpē/ ▶ *n. inf.* a person, esp. a young woman, who regularly follows a pop music group or other celebrity in the hope of meeting or getting to know them. ■ *often derog.* an enthusiastic or uncritical follower: *the contemporary art groupie.*

group·ing /ˈgrōōpiNG/ ▶ *n.* a set of people acting together with a common interest or purpose, esp. within a larger organization: *a grouping* *of Protestant churches.* ■ the arrangement or formation of people or things in a group or groups: *an alternative form of ability grouping.*

group ther·a·py ▶ *n.* a form of psychotherapy in which a group of patients meet to describe and discuss their problems together under the supervision of a therapist.

grouse[1] /grous/ ▶ *n.* (*pl.* same) a game bird (*Lagopus, Tetrao,* and other genera) with a plump body and feathered legs, the male being larger and more conspicuously colored than the female. The **grouse family** (Tetraonidae, or Phasianidae) also includes ptarmigans.

grouse[2] ▶ *v.* [*intr.*] complain pettily; grumble.
▶ *n.* a grumble or complaint. —**grous·er** *n.*

grout /grout/ ▶ *n.* a mortar or paste for filling crevices, esp. the gaps between wall or floor tiles.
▶ *v.* [*tr.*] fill in with grout: *the gaps are grouted afterward.*

grove /grōv/ ▶ *n.* a small wood, orchard, or group of trees: *an olive grove.*

grov·el /'grävəl; 'grə-/ ▶ *v.* (**grov·eled, grov·el·ing**) [*intr.*] lie or move abjectly on the ground with one's face downward: *she was groveling on the floor in fear.* ■ act in an obsequious manner in order to obtain someone's forgiveness or favor: *everyone expected me to grovel with gratitude.* —**grov·el·er** *n.* —**grov·el·ing·ly** *adv.*

grow /grō/ ▶ *v.* (*past* **grew** /grōō/; *past part.* **grown** /grōn/) [*intr.*] **1** (of a living thing) undergo natural development by increasing in size and changing physically; progress to maturity: *he would watch Nick grow to manhood* | [as *adj.*] (**growing**) *the linguistic skills acquired by the growing child* | [as *adj.*] (**grown**) *the stupidity of grown men hitting a ball with a stick.* ■ (of a plant) germinate and develop: *seaweed grows in the ocean.* ■ [*tr.*] produce by cultivation: *more and more land was needed to grow crops for export.* ■ [*tr.*] allow or cause (a part of the body) to grow or develop: [*tr.*] *she grew her hair long.* ■ (of something abstract) come into existence and develop: *the Vietnamese diaspora grew out of their national tragedy.* **2** become larger or greater over a period of time; increase: *turnover grew to more than $100,000 within three years* | [as *adj.*] (**growing**) *a growing number of people are coming to realize this.* ■ [*tr.*] cause (something, esp. a business) to expand or increase. **3** become gradually or increasingly: *sharing our experiences, we grew braver.* ■ (of a person) come to feel or know something over time: *she grew to like the friendly, quiet people at the farm.* ■ (**grow apart**) (of two or more people) become gradually estranged.
▶ *phrasal v.* □ **grow on** become gradually more appealing to (someone): *a house has to grow on you.* □ **grow out of** become too large to wear (a garment): *blazers that they grew out of.* ■ become too mature to retain (a childish habit): *most children grow out of tantrums by the time they're three.* □ **grow up** advance to maturity; spend one's childhood and adolescence: *a young Muslim woman who grew up in Philadelphia.* ■ [often in *imper.*] begin to behave or think sensibly and realistically: *grow up, sister, and come into the real world.* —**grow·a·ble** *adj.*
▶ □ **grow on trees** *inf.* be plentiful or easily obtained: *money doesn't grow on trees.*

grow·er /'grōər/ ▶ *n.* **1** a person who grows a particular type of crop: *a fruit grower.* **2** a plant that grows in a specified way.

grow·ing pains ▶ *pl. n.* neuralgic pains that occur in the limbs of some young children. ■ *fig.* the difficulties experienced in the early stages of an enterprise: *the growing pains of a young republic.*

growl /groul/ ▶ *v.* [*intr.*] (of an animal, esp. a dog) make a low guttural sound of hostility in the throat: *the dogs yapped and growled about his heels.* ■ [with *direct speech*] (of a person) say something in a low grating voice, typically in a threatening manner: *"Keep out of this," he growled.* ■ (of a thing) make a low or harsh rumbling sound, typically one that is felt to be threatening.
▶ *n.* a low guttural sound made in the throat, esp. by a dog. ■ a low throaty sound made by a machine or engine: *the growl of diesel engines.* —**growl·ing·ly** *adv.*

growl·er /'groulər/ ▶ *n.* **1** a person or thing that growls. **2** a small iceberg that rises little above the water. **3** *inf.* a pail or other container used for carrying drink, esp. draft beer.

grown /grōn/ ▶ past participle of **GROW**.

grown-up ▶ *adj.* adult: *Joe is married with two grown-up daughters.* ■ suitable for or characteristic of an adult: *it seems a grown-up thing to do.*
▶ *n.* an adult (esp. a child's word).

growth /grōtH/ ▶ *n.* **1** the process of increasing in physical size: *the upward growth of plants* | *the growth of the city affects the local climate.* ■ the process of developing or maturing physically, mentally, or spiritually: *keeping a journal can be a vital step in our personal growth.* ■ the increase in number and spread of small or microscopic organisms: *some additives slow down the growth of microorganisms.* ■ the process of increasing in amount, value, or importance: *the rates of population growth are lowest in the north.* ■ increase in economic value or activity: *the government aims*

to get growth back into the economy. **2** something that has grown or is growing: *a day's growth of unshaven stubble on his chin.* ■ *Med. & Biol.* a tumor or other abnormal formation. **3** a vineyard or crop of grapes of a specified classification of quality, or a wine from it.

grub /grəb/ ▶ *n.* **1** the larva of an insect, esp. a beetle. ■ a maggot or small caterpillar. **2** *inf.* food: *a popular bar serving excellent grub.*
▶ *v.* (**grubbed, grub·bing**) [*intr.*] **1** dig or poke superficially at the earth; dig shallowly in soil. ■ [*tr.*] remove (something) from the earth by digging it up. ■ [*tr.*] clear (the ground) of roots and stumps: [as *n.*] (**grub·bing**) *construction operations including clearing and grubbing.* **2** search for something in a clumsy and unmethodical manner; rummage. ■ do demeaning or humiliating work in order to achieve something. ■ [*tr.*] achieve or acquire (something) in such a way. —**grub·ber** *n.*

grub·by /'grəbē/ ▶ *adj.* (**-bi·er, -bi·est**) dirty; grimy: *the grubby face of a young boy.* ■ *fig.* disreputable; sordid: *grubby little moneylenders.* —**grub·bi·ly** /-bəlē/ *adv.* —**grub·bi·ness** *n.*

grub·stake /'grəb,stāk/ *inf.* ▶ *n.* an amount of material, provisions, or money supplied to an enterprise (originally a prospector for ore) in return for a share in the resulting profits.
▶ *v.* [*tr.*] provide with a grubstake.

grudge /grəj/ ▶ *n.* a persistent feeling of ill will or resentment resulting from a past insult or injury: *she held a grudge against her former boss.*
▶ *v.* [*tr.*] be resentfully unwilling to give, grant, or allow (something): *he grudged the work and time that the meeting involved.* ■ feel resentful that (someone) has achieved (something): *I don't grudge him his moment of triumph.* —**grudg·er** *n.* —**grudg·ing** *adj.* —**grudg·ing·ly** *adv.*

gruel /'grōōəl/ ▶ *n.* a thin liquid food of oatmeal or other meal boiled in milk or water.

gruel·ing /'grōōəliNG/ (*Brit.* **gruel·ling**) ▶ *adj.* extremely tiring and demanding: *a grueling schedule.* —**gruel·ing·ly** *adv.*

grue·some /'grōōsəm/ ▶ *adj.* causing repulsion or horror; grisly: *a most gruesome murder.* ■ *inf.* extremely unpleasant: *gruesome working hours.* —**grue·some·ly** *adv.* —**grue·some·ness** *n.*

gruff /grəf/ ▶ *adj.* abrupt or taciturn in manner: *penetrate a gruff exterior and you will find him affable.* ■ (of a voice) rough and low in pitch. —**gruff·ly** *adv.* —**gruff·ness** *n.*

grum·ble /'grəmbəl/ ▶ *v.* complain or protest about something in a bad-tempered but typically muted way: *his father was grumbling that he hadn't heard a word from him* | [*tr.*] *he grumbled something about the decision being unnecessary.* ■ [*intr.*] make a low rumbling sound: *thunder was grumbling somewhere in the distance.* ■ [*intr.*] (of an internal organ) give intermittent discomfort.
▶ *n.* a complaint: *the main grumble is that he spends too much time away.* ■ a low rumbling sound. —**grum·bler** /-blər/ *n.* —**grum·bling·ly** /-bliNGlē/ *adv.* —**grum·bly** /-blē/ *adj.*

grump /grəmp/ *inf.* ▶ *n.* a grumpy person. ■ a fit of sulking.
▶ *v.* [*intr.*] act in a sulky, grumbling manner: *he grumped at me when I moved the papers.* —**grump·ish** *adj.* —**grump·ish·ly** *adv.*

grump·y /'grəmpē/ ▶ *adj.* (**grump·i·er, grump·i·est**) bad-tempered and sulky. —**grump·i·ly** /-pəlē/ *adv.* —**grump·i·ness** *n.*

grunge /grənj/ ▶ *n.* **1** grime; dirt. **2** (also **grunge rock**) a style of rock music characterized by a raucous guitar sound and lazy vocal delivery. ■ the fashion associated with this music, including loose, layered clothing and ripped jeans. —**grun·gi·ness** *n.* —**grun·gy** *adj.*

grun·ion /'grənyən/ ▶ *n.* a small, slender Californian fish (*Leuresthes tenuis,* family Atherinidae) that swarms onto beaches at night to spawn.

grunt /grənt/ ▶ *v.* [*intr.*] (of an animal, esp. a pig) make a low, short guttural sound. ■ (of a person) make a low inarticulate sound resembling this, typically to express effort or indicate assent.
▶ *n.* **1** a low, short guttural sound made by an animal or a person. **2** *inf.* a low-ranking or unskilled soldier or other worker. **3** an edible shoaling fish (family Pomadasyidae) of tropical inshore waters and coral reefs, able to make a loud noise by grinding its teeth. ▷Old English *grunnettan,* of Germanic origin and related to German *grunzen;* probably originally imitative.

grunt·er /'grəntər/ ▶ *n.* a fish that makes a grunting noise, esp. when caught, in particular: ■ a mainly marine fish (family Theraponidae) of warm waters. ■ another term for **GRUNT** (sense 3).

gryph·on ▶ *n.* variant spelling of **GRIFFIN**.

GSA ▶ *abbr.* ■ General Services Administration. ■ Girl Scouts of America.

Pronunciation Key ə *ago,* up; ər *over,* fur; a *hat;* ā *ate;* ä *car;* CH *chin;* e *let;* ē *see;* e(ə)r *air;* i *fit;* ī *by;* i(ə)r *ear;* NG *sing;* ō *go;* ô *law, for;* oi *toy;* ŏŏ *good;* ōō *goo;* ou *out;* SH *she;* TH *thin;* TH *then;* (h)w *why;* ZH *vision*

G-string (also **gee-string**) ▶*n.* a garment consisting of a narrow strip of cloth that covers the genitals and is attached to a waistband, worn as underwear or by striptease performers.

G-suit ▶*n.* a garment with pressurized pouches that are inflatable with air or fluid, worn by fighter pilots and astronauts to enable them to withstand high forces of acceleration.

GT ▶*adj.* denoting a high-performance car: *GT cars.*
▶*n.* a high-performance car.

gua·ca·mo·le /ˌgwäkəˈmōlē/ ▶*n.* a dish of mashed avocado mixed with chopped onion, tomatoes, chili peppers, and seasoning.

guai·ac /ˈgwīak/ ▶*n.* brown resin obtained from guaiacum trees, used as a flavoring and in varnishes.

guai·a·cum /ˈgwīəkəm/ ▶*n.* an evergreen tree (*Guaiacum officinale* and *G. sanctum*) of the Caribbean and tropical America, known for its hard, heavy, oily timber.

gua·nine /ˈgwänēn/ ▶*n. Biochem.* a purine derivative, one of the four constituent bases of nucleic acids.

gua·no /ˈgwänō/ ▶*n.* (*pl.* **-nos**) the excrement of seabirds, occurring in thick deposits notably on the islands off Peru and Chile, and used as fertilizer.

Gua·ra·ni /ˌgwärəˈnē/ ▶*n.* (*pl.* same) **1** a member of an American Indian people of Paraguay and adjacent regions. **2** the language of this people. **3** (**guarani**) the basic monetary unit of Paraguay, equal to 100 centimos.

guar·an·tee /ˌgarənˈtē/ ▶*n.* a formal promise or assurance (typically in writing) that certain conditions will be fulfilled, esp. that a product will be repaired or replaced if not of a specified quality and durability: *we offer a 10-year* **guarantee against** *rusting.* ■ something that gives a certainty of outcome: *past performance is no* **guarantee** *of future results.* ■ variant spelling of GUARANTY. ■ less common term for GUARANTOR.
▶*v.* (**-tees, -teed, -tee·ing**) [*intr.*] provide a formal assurance or promise, esp. that certain conditions shall be fulfilled relating to a product, service, or transaction: *the con artist guarantees that the dirt pile will yield at least 20 ounces of gold.* ■ [*tr.*] provide such an assurance regarding (something, esp. a product): *the repairs will be guaranteed for three years* | [as *adj.*] (**guaranteed**) *the guaranteed bonus is not very high.* ■ [*tr.*] provide financial security for; underwrite: *a demand that $100,000 be deposited to guarantee their costs.* ■ [*tr.*] promise with certainty.

guar·an·tor /ˌgarənˈtôr; ˈgarəntər/ ▶*n.* a person, organization, or thing that guarantees something: *the role of the police as guarantors of public order.* ■ *Law* a person or organization who provides a guaranty.

guar·an·ty /ˈgarənˌtē/ (also **guar·an·tee**) ▶*n.* (*pl.* **-ties**) a formal pledge to pay another person's debt or to perform another person's obligation in the case of default. ■ a thing serving as security for a such a pledge.

guard /gärd/ ▶*v.* [*tr.*] watch over to keep safe. ■ watch over in order to control entry and exit: *the gates were guarded by uniformed soldiers.* ■ watch over (someone) to prevent them from escaping. ■ [*intr.*] (**guard against**) take precautions against. ■ protect against damage or harm: *the company fiercely guarded its independence.* ■ *Basketball* stay close to (an opponent) in order to prevent a good shot, pass, or drive. ■ cover or equip (a part of a machine) with a device to protect the operator.
▶*n.* **1** a person who keeps watch, esp. a soldier or other person formally assigned to protect a person or to control access to a place: *a security guard* | [as *adj.*] *he distracted the soldier on guard duty.* ■ [treated as *sing.* or *pl.*] a body of soldiers serving to protect a place or person. ■ *Football* each of two offensive players positioned either side of the center. ■ *Basketball* each of two players chiefly responsible for running the team's offense. **2** a device worn or fitted to prevent injury or damage: *a retractable blade guard.* **3** a defensive posture adopted in a boxing, fencing, or martial arts contest or in a fight. ■ a state of caution, vigilance, or preparedness against adverse circumstances.
▶ □ **lower** (or **let down**) **one's guard** relax one's defensive posture, leaving oneself vulnerable to attack. ■ reduce one's level of vigilance or caution: *she was not ready to let down her guard and confide in him.* □ **off guard** unprepared for some surprise or difficulty: *the government was caught off guard by the announcement.* □ **on guard** on duty to protect or defend something. ■ (also **on one's guard**) prepared for any contingency; vigilant: *we must be* **on guard against** *such temptation.* □ **under guard** being guarded.

guard·ed /ˈgärdid/ ▶*adj.* cautious and having possible reservations: *he has given a guarded welcome to the idea.* ■ (of a person's medical condition) serious and of uncertain outcome: *the surviving crewman was in stable but guarded condition.* —**guard·ed·ly** *adv.* —**guard·ed·ness** *n.*

guard·house /ˈgärdˌhous/ ▶*n.* a building used to accommodate a military guard or to detain military prisoners. ■ a building accommodating a guard who controls entrance to the grounds of a house, housing development, school, or other facility.

guard·i·an /ˈgärdēən/ ▶*n.* a defender, protector, or keeper: *self-appointed guardians of public morality.* ■ a person who looks after and is legally responsible for someone who is unable to manage their own affairs, esp. an incompetent or disabled person or a child whose parents have died. —**guard·i·an·ship** /-ˌSHip/ *n.*

guard·i·an an·gel ▶*n.* a spirit that is believed to watch over and protect a person or place.

guard·rail /ˈgärdˌrāl/ ▶*n.* a rail that prevents people from falling off or being hit by something. ■ a strong fence at the side of a road or in the middle of an expressway, intended to reduce the risk of serious accidents.

guard·room /ˈgärdˌro͞om; -ˌro͝om/ ▶*n.* a room in a military base used to accommodate a guard or detain prisoners.

guards·man /ˈgärdzmən/ ▶*n.* (*pl.* **-men**) a member of the National Guard.

gua·va /ˈgwävə/ ▶*n.* **1** an edible pale orange tropical fruit with pink, juicy flesh and a strong, sweet aroma. **2** the small tropical American tree (genus *Psidium*) of the myrtle family that bears this fruit.

gu·ber·na·to·ri·al /ˌgo͞obərnəˈtôrēəl/ ▶*adj.* of or relating to a state governor or the office of state governor: *a gubernatorial election.*

gudg·eon ▶*n.* a pivot or spindle on which a rudder, a bell or other object swings or rotates.

guel·der rose /ˈgeldər/ ▶*n.* a deciduous Eurasian shrub (*Viburnum opulus*) of the honeysuckle family with flattened heads of fragrant, creamy-white flowers, followed by clusters of bitter translucent red berries.

guer·ril·la /gəˈrilə/ (also **gue·ril·la**) ▶*n.* a member of a small independent group taking part in irregular fighting, typically against larger regular forces: *this small town fell to the guerrillas.*

guess /ges/ ▶*v.* [*tr.*] estimate or suppose (something) without sufficient information to be sure of being correct: *she guessed the child's age to be 14 or 15* | *he took her aside, and I guessed that he was offering her a job.* ■ (**guess at**) make a conjecture about: *their motives he could only guess at.* ■ correctly conjecture or perceive: *she's guessed where we're going.* ■ [in *imper.*] used to introduce something considered surprising or exciting: *guess what I've just seen!* ■ (**I guess**) *inf.* used to indicate that although one thinks or supposes something, it is without any great conviction or strength of feeling: *I guess I'd better tell you everything.*
▶*n.* an estimate or conjecture. —**guess·a·ble** *adj.* —**guess·er** *n.*

guess·ti·mate (also **gues·ti·mate**) *inf.* ▶*n.* /ˈgestəmit/ an estimate based on a mixture of guesswork and calculation.
▶*v.* /ˈgestəˌmāt/ [*tr.*] form such an estimate of.

guess·work /ˈgesˌwərk/ ▶*n.* the process or results of guessing.

guest /gest/ ▶*n.* a person who is invited to visit the home of or take part in a function organized by another: *I have two guests coming to dinner tonight* | [as *adj.*] *a guest bedroom.* ■ a person invited to participate in an official event: *the bishop went to Cuba as a guest of the Catholic Church* | [as *adj.*] *a guest speaker.* ■ a person invited to take part in a radio or television program, sports event, or other entertainment: *a regular guest on the morning show* | [as *adj.*] *a guest appearance.* ■ a person lodging at a hotel or boardinghouse: *a reduction for guests staying seven nights or more.*
▶*v.* [*intr.*] *inf.* appear as a guest: *he* **guested on** *one of her early albums.* ▷Middle English: from Old Norse *gestr*, of Germanic origin; related to Dutch *gast* and German *Gast*, from an Indo-European root shared by Latin *hostis* 'enemy' (originally 'stranger').
▶ □ **be my guest** *inf.* please do: *May I choose the restaurant? Be my guest!* □ **guest of honor** the most important guest at an occasion.

guest book (also **guest·book**) ▶*n.* a book in which visitors to a public building or to a private home write their names and addresses, and sometimes remarks. ■ a Web page where visitors to a site may leave their names and comments.

guest house (also **guest·house**) ▶*n.* a private house offering accommodations to paying guests. ■ a small, separate house on the grounds of a larger house or establishment, used for accommodating guests.

guff /gəf/ ▶*n. inf.* trivial, worthless, or insolent talk or ideas.

guf·faw /gəˈfô/ ▶*n.* a loud and boisterous laugh.
▶*v.* [*intr.*] laugh in such a way: *both men guffawed at the remark.*

gug·gul /ˈgo͞ogəl/ ▶*n.* an herbal preparation made from the sticky gum of various myrrh trees that has been alleged to aid in lowering serum cholesterol.

guid·ance /ˈgīdəns/ ▶*n.* **1** advice or information aimed at resolving a problem or difficulty, esp. as given by someone in authority: *he looked to his father for inspiration and guidance.* **2** the directing of the motion or position of something, esp. a missile: *a surface-to-air missile guidance system.*

guide /gīd/ ▶*n.* **1** a person who advises or shows the way to others: *this lady is going to act as our guide for the rest of the tour.* ■ a professional mountain climber in charge of a group. **2** a thing that helps someone to form an opinion or make a decision or calculation: *here is a **guide to** the number of curtain hooks you will need.* **3** a structure or marking that directs the motion or positioning of something: *the guides for the bolt needed straightening.* **4** a soldier, vehicle, or ship whose position determines the movements of others.
▶*v.* **1** [*tr.*] show or indicate the way to (someone): *he guided her to the front row and sat beside her.* **2** [*tr.*] direct or have an influence on the course of action of (someone or something): *he guided the team to a second successive win in the tournament.* —**guid·a·ble** *adj.* —**guid·er** *n.*

guide·book /'gīd,bŏŏk/ ▶*n.* a book of information about a place, designed for the use of visitors or tourists.

guide dog ▶*n.* a dog trained to lead a blind person.

guide·line /'gīd,līn/ ▶*n.* a general rule, principle, or piece of advice.

guild /gild/ (also **gild**) ▶*n.* a medieval association of craftsmen or merchants, often having considerable power. ■ an association of people for mutual aid or the pursuit of a common goal.

guild·er /'gildər/ ▶*n.* (*pl.* same or **-ers**) the basic monetary unit of the Netherlands (until the introduction of the euro), equal to 100 cents.

guild·hall /'gild,hôl/ ▶*n.* a building used as the meeting place of a guild or corporation.

guile /gīl/ ▶*n.* sly or cunning intelligence: *he used all his guile and guts to free himself.* —**guile·ful** /-fəl/ *adj.* —**guile·ful·ly** /-fəlē/ *adv.* —**guile·less** *adj.*

guil·le·mot /'gilə,mät/ ▶*n.* a black-breasted auk (genus *Cepphus*) with a narrow pointed bill, typically nesting on cliff ledges.

guil·lo·tine /'gilə,tēn; 'gēə-/ ▶*n.* a machine with a heavy blade sliding vertically in grooves, used for beheading people. ■ a device for cutting that incorporates a descending or sliding blade, used typically for cutting paper, card, or sheet metal.
▶*v.* [*tr.*] execute (someone) by guillotine. ▷late 18th cent.: from French, named after Joseph-Ignace *Guillotin* (1738–1814), the French physician who recommended its use for executions in 1789.

guilt /gilt/ ▶*n.* the fact of having committed a specified or implied offense or crime: *it is the duty of the prosecution to prove the prisoner's guilt.* ■ a feeling of having done wrong or failed in an obligation.
▶*v.* [*tr.*] *inf.* make (someone) feel guilty, especially in order to induce them to do something: *Celeste had been **guilted into** going by her parents.*

guilt·less /'giltlis/ ▶*adj.* having no guilt; innocent: *you don't need a pardon if you're guiltless.* —**guilt·less·ly** *adv.* —**guilt·less·ness** *n.*

guilt·y /'giltē/ ▶*adj.* (**guilt·i·er**, **guilt·i·est**) culpable of or responsible for a specified wrongdoing: *the police will soon discover who the guilty party is* | *he was found **guilty of** manslaughter* | *he found them **guilty on** a lesser charge.* ■ justly chargeable with a particular fault or error. ■ conscious of or affected by a feeling of guilt. ■ involving a feeling or a judgment of guilt. —**guilt·i·ly** /-təlē/ *adv.* —**guilt·i·ness** *n.*
▶ □ **not guilty** innocent, esp. of a formal charge: *he pled not guilty to murder.*

guin·ea /'ginē/ (abbr.: **gn.**) ▶*n. Brit.* the sum of £1.05 (21 shillings in pre-decimal currency), now used mainly for determining professional fees and auction prices.

guin·ea fowl ▶*n.* (*pl.* same) a large African game bird (family Numididae, or Phasianidae) with slate-colored, white-spotted plumage and a loud call. It is sometimes domesticated.

guin·ea pig ▶*n.* a tailless South American cavy (*Cavia porcellus*) typically kept as a pet or for laboratory research. ■ a person or thing used as a subject for experiment.

guise /gīz/ ▶*n.* an external form, appearance, or manner of presentation, typically concealing the true nature of something: *he visited **in the guise of** an inspector* | *telemarketing **under the guise of** market research.*

gui·tar /gi'tär/ ▶*n.* a stringed musical instrument with a fretted fingerboard, typically incurved sides, and six or twelve strings, played by plucking or strumming with the fingers or a plectrum. —**gui·tar·ist** *n.*

gulch /gəlCH/ ▶*n.* a narrow and steep-sided ravine marking the course of a fast stream.

gulf /gəlf/ ▶*n.* **1** a deep inlet of the sea almost surrounded by land, with a narrow mouth. **2** a deep ravine, chasm, or abyss. ■ *fig.* a large difference or division between two people or groups, or between viewpoints, concepts, or situations: *a **wide gulf** between theory and practice.*

gull¹ /gəl/ ▶*n.* a long-winged, web-footed seabird (*Larus* and other genera, family Laridae) with a raucous call, typically having white plumage with a gray or black mantle.

gull² ▶*v.* [*tr.*] fool or deceive (someone).
▶*n.* a person who is fooled or deceived.

Gul·lah /'gələ/ ▶*n.* **1** a member of a black people living on the coast of South Carolina and nearby islands. **2** the Creole language of this people, having an English base with elements from various West African languages.

gul·let /'gəlit/ ▶*n.* the passage by which food passes from the mouth to the stomach; the esophagus.

gul·li·ble /'gələbəl/ ▶*adj.* easily persuaded to believe something; credulous. —**gul·li·bil·i·ty** /,gələ'bilitē/ *n.* —**gul·li·bly** /-blē/ *adv.*

gul·ly /'gəlē/ (also **gul·ley**) ▶*n.* (*pl.* **-lies**) a water-worn ravine. ■ a deep artificial channel serving as a gutter or drain.
▶*v.* [*tr.*] [usu. as *adj.*] (**gullied**) erode gullies into (land) by water action: *he began to pick his way over the gullied landscape.*

gulp /gəlp/ ▶*v.* [*tr.*] swallow (drink or food) quickly or in large mouthfuls, often audibly: *he smiled and gulped his milk.* ■ breathe (air) deeply and quickly: *we emerged to gulp great lungfuls of cold night air.* ■ [*intr.*] make effortful breathing or swallowing movements, typically in response to strong emotion: *she **gulped back** the tears.*
▶*n.* an act of gulping food or drink: *she swallowed the rest of the coffee with a gulp.* ■ a large mouthful of liquid hastily drunk: *Titch took a gulp of beer and wiped his mouth on his sleeve.* ■ a large quantity of air breathed in. ■ a swallowing movement of the throat. —**gulp·y** *adj.*

gum¹ /gəm/ ▶*n.* **1** a viscous secretion of some trees and shrubs that hardens on drying but is soluble in water, and from which adhesives and other products are made. ■ a resinous secretion. Compare with **RESIN.** ■ glue that is used for sticking paper or other light materials together. ■ short for **CHEWING GUM** or **BUBBLEGUM.** **2** *dated* a long rubber boot.
▶*v.* (**gummed**, **gum·ming**) [*tr.*] cover with gum or glue: [as *adj.*] (**gummed**) *gummed paper.* ■ [*tr.*] fasten with gum or glue: *I was gumming small green leaves to a paper tree.* ■ (**gum something up**) clog up a mechanism and prevent it from working properly: *fig. there was no winner and they debated the factors that could have **gummed up** the works.*

gum² ▶*n.* the firm area of flesh around the roots of the teeth in the upper or lower jaw: *gum disease.*
▶*v.* (**gummed**, **gum·ming**) [*tr.*] chew with toothless gums.

gum³ ▶*n.* (in phrase **by gum!**) an exclamation used for emphasis.

gum ar·a·bic ▶*n.* a gum exuded by some kinds of acacia and used as an emulsifier, in glue, as the binder for watercolor paints, and in incense.

gum·bo /'gəmbō/ ▶*n.* (*pl.* **-bos**) **1** (in Cajun cooking) a spicy chicken or seafood soup thickened typically with okra or rice. **2** (**Gumbo**) a French-based patois spoken by some blacks and Creoles in Louisiana. **3** a fine, clayey soil that becomes sticky and impervious when wet. **4** a type of Cajun music consisting of a lively blend of styles and sounds.

electric guitar   acoustic guitar

guitars

Pronunciation Key ə *ago, up*; ər *over, fur*; a *hat*; ā *ate*; ä *car*; CH *chin*; e *let*; ē *see*; e(ə)r *air*; i *fit*; ī *by*; i(ə)r *ear*; NG *sing*; ō *go*; ô *law, for*; oi *toy*; ŏŏ *good*; ōō *goo*; ou *out*; SH *she*; TH *thin*; TH *then*; (h)w *why*; ZH *vision*

gum·drop /'gəm,dräp/ ▸n. a firm, jellylike, translucent candy made with gelatin or gum arabic.

gum·ma /'gəmə/ ▸n. (pl. **gum·mas** or **gum·ma·ta** /'gəmətə/) Med. a small, soft swelling that is characteristic of the late stages of syphilis and occurs in the connective tissue of the liver, brain, testes, and heart. —**gum·ma·tous** /'gəmətəs/ adj.

gum·my[1] /'gəmē/ ▸adj. (**-mi·er**, **-mi·est**) viscous; sticky. ■ covered with or exuding a viscous substance: *his eyes are all gummy.* —**gum·mi·ness** n.

gum·my[2] ▸adj. (**-mi·er**, **-mi·est**) toothless: *a gummy grin.* —**gum·mi·ly** /'gəməlē/ adv.

gump·tion /'gəmpsHən/ ▸n. inf. shrewd or spirited initiative and resourcefulness.

gum·shoe /'gəm,sHoō/ ▸n. inf. a detective.

gum tree ▸n. a tree that exudes gum, esp. a eucalyptus.

gun /gən/ ▸n. a weapon incorporating a metal tube from which bullets, shells, or other missiles are propelled by explosive force, typically making a characteristic loud, sharp noise. ■ a device for discharging something (e.g., insecticide, grease, or electrons) in a required direction. ■ a gunman: *a hired gun.* ■ a starting pistol used in track and field events. ■ the firing of a piece of artillery as a salute or signal.
▸v. (**gunned**, **gun·ning**) [tr.] **1** (**gun someone down**) shoot someone with a gun: *they were gunned down by masked snipers.* **2** inf. cause (an engine) to race. ■ [tr.] accelerate (a vehicle).
▸phrasal v. □ **gun for** pursue or act against (someone) with hostility: *the Republican candidate was gunning for his rival over campaign finances.* —**gun·less** adj. —**gunned** adj. [in comb.] *a heavy-gunned ship.*
▸ □ **big gun** inf. an important or powerful person. □ **jump the gun** inf. act before the proper time. □ **stick to one's guns** inf. refuse to compromise or change, despite criticism: *we have stuck to our guns on that issue.* □ **top gun** a (or the) most important person: *the top guns in contention for the coveted post of chairman.* □ **under the gun** inf. under great pressure: *manufacturers are under the gun to offer alternatives.*

gun·boat /'gən,bōt/ ▸n. a small, fast ship mounting guns, for use in shallow coastal waters and rivers.

gun·boat di·plo·ma·cy ▸n. foreign policy that is supported by the use or threat of military force.

gun dog ▸n. a dog trained to retrieve game for a hunter.

gun·fight /'gən,fīt/ ▸n. a fight involving an exchange of fire with guns. —**gun·fight·er** n.

gun·fire /'gən,fī(ə)r/ ▸n. the repeated firing of a gun or guns.

gung-ho /'gəNG 'hō/ ▸adj. unthinkingly enthusiastic and eager, esp. about taking part in fighting or warfare.

gunk /gəNGk/ ▸n. inf. unpleasantly sticky or messy substance.

gun·lock /'gən,läk/ ▸n. a mechanism by which the charge of a gun is exploded.

gun·man /'gənmən/ ▸n. (pl. **-men**) a man who uses a gun to commit a crime or terrorist act: *a gang of masked gunmen.*

gun·met·al /'gən,metl/ ▸n. a gray, corrosion-resistant form of bronze containing zinc, formerly used for making cannon. ■ (also **gunmetal gray**) a dark blue-brown gray color.

gun moll ▸n. inf. another term for MOLL (sense 1).

gun·nel ▸n. variant spelling of GUNWALE.

gun·ner /'gənər/ ▸n. a serviceman who operates or specializes in guns, in particular: ■ a member of an aircraft crew who operates a gun, esp. (formerly) in a gun turret on a bomber.

gun·ner·y /'gənərē/ ▸n. the design, manufacture, or firing of heavy guns: *a pioneer of naval gunnery.*

gun·ny /'gənē/ ▸n. coarse fabric, typically made of jute fiber and used esp. for sacks.

gun·point /'gən,point/ ▸n. (in phrase **at gunpoint**) while threatening someone or being threatened with a gun.

gun·pow·der /'gən,poudər/ ▸n. an explosive consisting of a powdered mixture of saltpeter, sulfur, and charcoal.

gun·run·ner /'gən,rənər/ ▸n. a person engaged in the illegal sale or importing of firearms. —**gun·run·ning** /-,rəniNG/ n.

gun·ship /'gən,sHip/ ▸n. an airplane or a helicopter heavily armed with machine guns or cannon, providing air support for ground troops in combat.

gun·shot /'gən,sHät/ ▸n. a shot fired from a gun.

gun·sling·er /'gən,sliNGər/ ▸n. inf. a man who carries a gun and shoots well. ■ fig. a forceful and adventurous participant in a particular sphere. —**gun·sling·ing** /-,sliNGiNG/ n.

gun·smith /'gən,smiTH/ ▸n. a person who makes, sells, and repairs small firearms.

gun·stock /'gən,stäk/ ▸n. the stock or support to which the barrel of a gun is attached.

gun·wale /'gənl/ (also **gun·nel**) ▸n. (often **gunwales**) the upper edge of the side of a boat or ship.
▸ □ **to the gunwales** inf. so as to be almost overflowing.

gup·py /'gəpē/ ▸n. (pl. **-ies**) a small, livebearing freshwater fish (*Poecilia reticulata*, family Poeciliidae) native to tropical America and widely kept in aquariums.

gur·gle /'gərgəl/ ▸v. [intr.] make a hollow bubbling sound like that made by water running out of a bottle: *my stomach gurgled* | [as adj.] (**gurgling**) *a faint gurgling noise.* ■ (of a liquid) run or flow with such a sound: *chemicals gurgle down a drain straight into the sewers.*
▸n. a gurgling sound: *Catherine gave a gurgle of laughter.*

Gur·kha /'goŏrkə/ ▸n. a member of any of several peoples of Nepal noted for their military prowess. ■ a member of units of the British army established specifically for Nepalese recruits in the mid 19th century.

gur·ney /'gərnē/ ▸n. (pl. **-neys**) a wheeled stretcher used for transporting hospital patients. ▷late 19th cent.: apparently named after J. T. *Gurney* of Boston, Massachusetts, patentee of a new cab design in 1883.

gu·ru /'goŏroō; goō'roō/ ▸n. (pl. **-rus**) (in Hinduism and Buddhism) a spiritual teacher, esp. one who imparts initiation. ■ each of the ten first leaders of the Sikh religion. ■ an influential teacher or popular expert.

gush /gəsH/ ▸v. [intr.] **1** (of a liquid) flow out in a rapid and plentiful stream, often suddenly: *fig. millions of dollars gushed out of that office.* ■ [tr.] send out in a rapid and plentiful stream. **2** speak or write with effusiveness or exaggerated enthusiasm.
▸n. **1** a rapid and plentiful stream or burst. **2** exaggerated effusiveness or enthusiasm. —**gush·ing·ly** adv.

gush·er /'gəsHər/ ▸n. **1** an oil well from which oil flows profusely without being pumped. ■ a thing from which a liquid flows profusely. **2** an effusive person.

gush·y /'gəsHē/ ▸adj. (**gush·i·er**, **gush·i·est**) excessively effusive: *her gushy manner.* —**gush·i·ly** /-sHəlē/ adv. —**gush·i·ness** n.

gus·set /'gəsit/ ▸n. a piece of material sewn into a garment to strengthen or enlarge a part of it. ■ a bracket strengthening an angle of a structure. —**gus·set·ed** adj.

gust /gəst/ ▸n. a brief, strong rush of wind. ■ a burst of something such as rain, sound, or emotion: *gusts of rain lashed down the narrow alleys.*

gust·na·do /gəst'nädō/ ▸n. (pl. **-does** or **-dos**) a strong whirlwind at the leading edge of a storm front or squall line.

gus·to /'gəstō/ ▸n. (pl. **-tos** or **-toes**) enjoyment or vigor in doing something; zest: *she sang it with gusto.*

gust·y /'gəstē/ ▸adj. (**gust·i·er**, **gust·i·est**) **1** characterized by or blowing in gusts: *a gusty morning.* **2** having or showing gusto: *gusty female vocals.* —**gust·i·ly** /'gəstəlē/ adv. —**gust·i·ness** n.

gut /gət/ ▸n. **1** (also **guts**) the stomach or belly: *a painful stabbing feeling in his gut.* ■ Med. & Biol. the lower alimentary canal or a part of this; the intestine. ■ (**guts**) entrails that have been removed or exposed in violence or by a butcher. ■ (**guts**) the internal parts or essence of something: *the guts of a modern computer.* **2** (**guts**) inf. personal courage and determination; toughness of character: *she had both more brains and more guts than her husband.* ■ [as adj.] inf. (of a feeling or reaction) based on a deep-seated emotional response rather than considered thought; instinctive: *a gut feeling.* **3** fiber made from the intestines of animals, used esp. for violin or racket strings or for surgical use: [as adj.] *gut strings.* **4** a narrow passage or strait.
▸v. (**gut·ted**, **gut·ting**) [tr.] take out the intestines and other internal organs of (a fish or other animal) before cooking it. ■ remove or destroy completely the internal parts of (a building or other structure): *the fire gutted most of the factory.* ■ remove or extract the most important parts of (something) in a damaging or destructive manner.
▸ □ **bust a gut** inf. make a strenuous effort: *a problem which nobody is going to bust a gut trying to solve.*

gut·less /'gətləs/ ▸adj. inf. lacking courage or determination. —**gut·less·ly** adv. —**gut·less·ness** n.

guts·y /'gətsē/ ▸adj. (**guts·i·er**, **guts·i·est**) inf. showing courage, determination, and spirit. ■ (of food or drink) strongly flavorsome. —**guts·i·ly** /-səlē/ adv. —**guts·i·ness** n.

gut·ter /'gətər/ ▸n. a shallow trough fixed beneath the edge of a roof for carrying off rainwater. ■ a channel at the side of a street for carrying off rainwater. ■ (**the gutter**) used to refer to a poor or squalid background or environment: *only moneyed privilege had kept him out of the gutter.* ■ the blank space between facing pages of a book or between

adjacent columns of type or stamps in a sheet. ■ a channel on either side of a lane in a bowling alley.
▶ *v.* [*intr.*] (of a candle or flame) flicker and burn unsteadily: *the candles had almost guttered out.*

gut·ter·snipe /ˈgətərˌsnīp/ ▶ *n. derog.* a street urchin.

gut·tur·al /ˈgətərəl/ ▶ *adj.* (of a speech sound) produced in the throat; harsh-sounding. ■ (of a manner of speech) characterized by the use of such sounds: *his parents' guttural central European accent.*
▶ *n.* a guttural consonant (e.g., k, g) or other speech sound. —**gut·tur·al·ly** *adv.*

gut-wrench·ing ▶ *adj. inf.* extremely unpleasant or upsetting.

guy[1] /gī/ ▶ *n. inf.* a man: *he's a nice guy.* ■ (**guys**) people of either sex: *you guys want some coffee?*
▶ *v.* [*tr.*] make fun of; ridicule: *he didn't realize I was guying the whole idea.*

guy[2] ▶ *n.* a rope or line fixed to the ground to secure a tent or other structure.
▶ *v.* [*tr.*] secure with a line or lines.

guz·zle /ˈgəzəl/ ▶ *v.* [*tr.*] eat or drink (something) greedily: *we guzzle our beer and devour our pizza* | *fig. this car guzzles gas.* —**guz·zler** /-z(ə)lər/ *n.*

gybe ▶ *v. & n.* variant spelling of JIBE[2].

gym /jim/ ▶ *n. inf.* **1** a gymnasium. **2** a membership organization that provides a range of facilities designed to improve and maintain physical fitness and health. **3** physical education.

gym·na·si·um /jimˈnāzēəm/ ▶ *n.* (*pl.* **-si·ums** or **-si·a** /-zēə/) a room or building equipped for gymnastics, games, and other physical exercise. ▷ late 16th cent.: via Latin from Greek *gumnasion*, from *gumnazein* 'exercise naked,' from *gumnos* 'naked.'

gym·nast /ˈjimnist/ ▶ *n.* a person trained in or skilled in gymnastics.

gym·nas·tic /jimˈnastik/ ▶ *adj.* of or relating to gymnastics: *a gymnastic display.* —**gym·nas·ti·cal·ly** /-ik(ə)lē/ *adv.*

gym·nas·tics /jimˈnastiks/ ▶ *pl. n.* [also treated as *sing.*] exercises developing or displaying physical agility and coordination. The modern sport of gymnastics typically involves exercises on uneven bars, balance beam, floor, and vaulting horse (for women), and horizontal and parallel bars, rings, floor, and pommel horse (for men). ■ other physical or mental agility of a specified kind.

gym·no·sperm /ˈjimnəˌspərm/ ▶ *n. Bot.* a plant that has seeds unprotected by an ovary or fruit. Gymnosperms include the conifers, cycads, and ginkgo.

gy·ne·col·o·gy /ˌgīnəˈkäləjē; ˌjinə-/ ▶ *n.* the branch of physiology and medicine that deals with the functions and diseases specific to women and girls, esp. those affecting the reproductive system. —**gyn·e·co·log·ic** /-kəˈläjik/ *adj.* —**gyn·e·co·log·i·cal** /-kəˈläjikəl/ *adj.* —**gyn·e·co·log·i·cal·ly** /-kəˈläjik(ə)lē/ *adv.* —**gy·ne·col·o·gist** /-jist/ *n.*

gyn·e·co·mas·ti·a /ˌgīnəkōˈmastēə/ ▶ *n. Med.* enlargement of a man's breasts, usually due to hormone imbalance or hormone therapy.

gy·noe·ci·um /jiˈnēshēəm; gī-; -sēəm/ ▶ *n.* (*pl.* **-ci·a** /-shēə; -sēə/) *Bot.* the female part of a flower, consisting of one or more carpels.

gyp /jip/ *inf.* ▶ *v.* (**gypped, gyp·ping**) [*tr.*] cheat or swindle (someone).
▶ *n.* (also **gip**) an act of cheating; a swindle.

gyp·sum /ˈjipsəm/ ▶ *n.* a soft white or gray mineral consisting of hydrated calcium sulfate. —**gyp·sif·er·ous** /jipˈsifərəs/ *adj.*

gyp·sy /ˈjipsē/ (also **gip·sy**) ▶ *n.* (*pl.* **-sies**) a member of a traveling people with dark skin and hair who speak Romany and traditionally live by seasonal work, itinerant trade, and fortune-telling. ■ the language of the gypsies; Romany. ■ a person who leads an unconventional life. ■ a person who moves from place to place as required by employment.
▶ *adj.* (of a business or business person) nonunion or unlicensed: *gypsy trucking firms.* —**gyp·sy·ish** *adj.*

gyp·sy moth ▶ *n.* a tussock moth (*Lymantria dispar*) having a brown male and larger white female.

gy·rate /ˈjīrāt/ ▶ *v.* move or cause to move in a circle or spiral, esp. quickly. ■ [*intr.*] dance in a wild or suggestive manner. —**gy·ra·tion** /jīˈrāshən/ *n.* —**gy·ra·tor** /-ˌrātər/ *n.*

gyre /jīr/ ▶ *n.* a spiral; a vortex. ■ *Geog.* a circular pattern of currents in an ocean basin.

gy·ro[1] /ˈjīrō/ ▶ *n.* (*pl.* **-ros**) short for GYROSCOPE or GYROCOMPASS.

gy·ro[2] /ˈyērō; ˈzhirō/ ▶ *n.* (*pl.* **-ros**) a sandwich made with slices of spiced meat cooked on a spit, served with salad in pita bread.

gy·ro·com·pass /ˈjīrōˌkəmpəs/ ▶ *n.* a nonmagnetic compass in which the direction of true north is maintained by a continuously driven gyroscope whose axis is parallel to the earth's axis of rotation.

gy·ro·mag·net·ic /ˌjīrōmagˈnetik/ ▶ *adj.* (of a compass) combining a gyroscope and a magnetic compass.

gy·ro·scope /ˈjīrəˌskōp/ ▶ *n.* a device consisting of a wheel or disk mounted so that it can spin rapidly about an axis that is itself free to change direction. The orientation of the axis is not affected by tilting of the mounting, so gyroscopes can be used to provide stability or maintain a reference direction in navigation systems, automatic pilots, and stabilizers. —**gy·ro·scop·ic** /ˌjīrəˈskäpik/ *adj.* —**gy·ro·scop·i·cal·ly** /ˌjīrəˈskäpik(ə)lē/ *adv.*

G

Hh

H[1] /āCH/ (also **h**) ▶*n.* (*pl.* **Hs** or **H's** /'āCHiz/) **1** the eighth letter of the alphabet. **2** (**H**) a shape like that of a capital H.

H[2] ▶*abbr.* ■ hard (used in describing grades of pencil lead): *a 2H pencil.* ■ height (in giving the dimensions of an object). ■ *Physics* henry(s). ■ *inf.* heroin.
▶*symb.* ■ *Chem.* enthalpy. ■ the chemical element hydrogen.

h /āCH/ ▶*abbr.* ■ (in measuring the height of horses) hand(s). ■ [in *comb.*] (in units of measurement) hecto-: *wine production reached 624,000 hl last year.* ■ horse. ■ hour(s): *breakfast at 0700 h.*

ha[1] /hä/ (also **hah**) ▶*interj.* used to express surprise, suspicion, triumph, or some other emotion.

ha[2] ▶*abbr.* hectare(s).

ha·be·as cor·pus /'hābēəs 'kôrpəs/ ▶*n. Law* a writ requiring a person under arrest to be brought before a judge or into court, esp. to secure the person's release unless lawful grounds are shown for their detention. ■ the legal right to apply for such a writ.

hab·er·dash·er /'habər,dashər/ ▶*n.* **1** a dealer in men's clothing. **2** *Brit.* a dealer in goods for dressmaking and sewing. **—hab·er·dash·er·y** /-ərē/ *n.*

ha·bil·i·ment /hə'biləmənt/ ▶*n.* (usu. **habiliments**) *archaic* clothing.

hab·it /'habit/ ▶*n.* **1** a settled or regular tendency or practice, esp. one that is hard to give up. ■ *inf.* an addictive practice, esp. one of taking drugs: *a cocaine habit.* ■ *Psychol.* an automatic reaction to a specific situation. ■ general shape or mode of growth, esp. of a plant or a mineral: *a shrub of spreading habit.* **2** a long, loose garment worn by a member of a religious order or congregation. ■ *archaic* dress; attire. ▷Middle English: from Old French *abit*, *habit*, from Latin *habitus* 'condition, appearance,' from *habere* 'have, consist of.' The term originally meant 'dress, attire,' later coming to denote physical or mental constitution.
▶ □ **break** (or *inf.* **kick**) **the habit** stop engaging in a habitual practice.

hab·it·a·ble /'habitəbəl/ ▶*adj.* suitable or good enough to live in. **—hab·it·a·bil·i·ty** /,habətə'bilətē/ *n.*

hab·i·tant /'habitənt; 'habətnt/ ▶*n.* **1** [often as *adj.*] an early French settler in Canada (esp. Quebec) or Louisiana: *habitant farmhouses.* **2** *archaic* an inhabitant.

hab·i·tat /'habi,tat/ ▶*n.* the natural home or environment of an animal, plant, or other organism. ■ a particular type of environment regarded as a home for organisms. ■ *inf.* a person's usual or preferred surroundings.

hab·i·ta·tion /,habi'tāSHən/ ▶*n.* the state or process of living in a particular place. ■ *formal* a place in which to live; a house or home. **—hab·i·ta·tive** /'habitə,tiv/ *adj.*

hab·it-form·ing ▶*adj.* (of a drug or activity) addictive.

ha·bit·u·al /hə'biCHOOəl/ ▶*adj.* done or doing constantly or as a habit. ■ regular; usual: *his habitual dress.* **—ha·bit·u·al·ly** *adv.*

ha·bit·u·ate /hə'biCHOO,āt/ ▶*v.* make or become accustomed or used to something. **—ha·bit·u·a·tion** /hə,biCHOO'āSHən/ *n.*

ha·bit·u·é /hə'biCHOO,ā/ ▶*n.* a resident of or frequent visitor to a particular place: *his uncle was a habitué of the French theater.*

ha·ček /'ha,CHek/ (also **há·ček**) ▶*n.* a diacritic mark (˘) placed over a letter to indicate modification of the sound in Slavic and other languages.

ha·ci·en·da /,häsē'endə/ ▶*n.* (in Spanish-speaking regions) a large estate or plantation with a dwelling house. ■ the main house on such an estate.

hack[1] /hak/ ▶*v.* **1** [*tr.*] cut with rough or heavy blows. **2** [*intr.*] use a computer to gain unauthorized access to data in a system: *they **hacked** into a bank's computer.* ■ [*tr.*] gain unauthorized access to (data in a computer). **3** (**hack it**) *inf.* manage; cope: *people leave because they **can't** hack it.*
▶*n.* **1** a rough cut, blow, or stroke. ■ (in sports) a kick or hit inflicted on another player. ■ a cut or gash. ■ a tool for rough striking or cutting, e.g., a miner's pick. **2** *inf.* an act of computer hacking. ■ a piece of computer code that performs some function, esp. an unofficial alternative or addition to a commercial program.
▶ □ **hacking cough** a short, dry, frequent cough.

hack[2] ▶*n.* **1** a writer or journalist producing dull, unoriginal work. ■ a person who does dull routine work. **2** a horse for ordinary riding. ■ an inferior or worn-out horse. ■ a horse rented out for riding. **3** a taxicab.
▶*v.* [*intr.*] [usu. as *n.*] (**hacking**) ride a horse for pleasure or exercise. **—hack·er·y** /'hakərē/ *n.*

hack·er /'hakər/ ▶*n.* **1** *inf.* an enthusiastic and skillful computer programmer or user. ■ a person who uses computers to gain unauthorized access to data. **2** a person or thing that hacks or cuts roughly. **3** a person who plays amateur sports without talent or skill.

hack·le /'hakəl/ ▶*n.* **1** (**hackles**) erectile hairs along the back of a dog or other animal that rise when it is angry or alarmed. ■ the hairs on the back of a person's neck, thought of as being raised when the person is angry or hostile. **2** (often **hackles**) a long, narrow feather on the neck or saddle of a domestic rooster or other bird. ■ *Fishing* a feather wound around a fishing fly so that its filaments are splayed out. ■ such feathers collectively. ■ a steel comb for separating flax fibers.
▶*v.* [*tr.*] dress or comb with a hackle.

hack·ney /'haknē/ ▶*n.* (*pl.* **-neys**) *hist.* a horse or pony of a light breed with a high-stepping trot, used in harness. ■ [usu. as *adj.*] a horse-drawn vehicle kept for hire: *a hackney coach.*

hack·neyed /'haknēd/ ▶*adj.* (of a phrase or idea) lacking significance through having been overused; trite: *hackneyed sayings.*

hack·saw /'hak,sô/ ▶*n.* a saw with a narrow fine-toothed blade set in a frame, used esp. for cutting metal.
▶*v.* (*past part.* **-sawn** or **-sawed**) [*tr.*] cut (something) using a hacksaw.

had /had/ ▶ past and past participle of **HAVE**.

had·dock /'hadək/ ▶*n.* (*pl.* same) a silvery-gray bottom-dwelling food fish (*Melanogrammus aeglefinus*) of the cod family, inhabiting North Atlantic coastal waters.

Ha·des /'hādēz/ *Greek Mythol.* ▶the underworld; the abode of the spirits of the dead. ■ the god of the underworld. **—Ha·de·an** /'hādēən/ *adj.*

Ha·dith /hə'dēTH/ ▶*n.* (*pl.* same or **-diths**) a collection of traditions containing sayings of the prophet Muhammad that constitute a major source of guidance for Muslims apart from the Koran. ■ one of these sayings. ▷from Arabic ḥadīṯ 'tradition.'

had·n't /'hadnt/ ▶*contr. of* had not.

had·ron /'had,rän/ ▶*n. Physics* a subatomic particle of a type including the baryons and mesons that can take part in the strong interaction. **—ha·dron·ic** /had'ränik/ *adj.*

haf·ni·um /'hafnēəm/ ▶*n.* the chemical element of atomic number 72, a hard silver-gray metal of the transition series, resembling and often occurring with zirconium. (Symbol: **Hf**)

haft /haft/ ▶*n.* the handle of a knife, ax, or spear.
▶*v.* [*tr.*] [often as *adj.*] (**hafted**) provide (a blade, ax head, or spearhead) with a haft.

hag /hag/ ▶*n.* a witch, esp. one in the form of an ugly old woman (often used as a term of disparagement for a woman). **—hag·gish** *adj.*

hag·fish /'hag,fiSH/ ▶n. (*pl.* same or **-fishes**) a primitive jawless marine vertebrate (*Myxine* and other genera, family Myxinidae) distantly related to the lampreys, with a slimy eellike body, a slitlike mouth surrounded by barbels, and a rasping tongue used for feeding on dead or dying fish.

hag·gard /'hagərd/ ▶adj. **1** looking exhausted and unwell, esp. from fatigue, worry, or suffering. **2** (of a hawk) caught for training as a wild adult of more than twelve months.
▶n. a haggard hawk. —**hag·gard·ly** adv. —**hag·gard·ness** n.

hag·gle /'hagəl/ ▶v. [*intr.*] dispute or bargain persistently, esp. over the cost of something.
▶n. a period of such bargaining. —**hag·gler** /'haglər/ n.

Hag·i·og·ra·pha /,hagē'ägrəfə; ,hāgē-/ ▶pl. n. the books of the Bible comprising the last of the three major divisions of the Hebrew scriptures, other than the Law and the Prophets. The books of the Hagiographa are: Ruth, Psalms, Job, Proverbs, Ecclesiastes, Song of Solomon, Lamentations, Daniel, Esther, Ezra, Nehemiah, and Chronicles.

hag·i·og·ra·pher /,hagē'ägrəfər; ,hāgē-/ ▶n. **1** a writer of the lives of the saints. ■ *derog.* a person who writes in an adulatory way, esp. in a biography. **2** *Theol.* a writer of any of the Hagiographa.

hag·i·og·ra·phy /,hagē'ägrəfē; ,hāgē-/ ▶n. the writing of the lives of saints. ■ *derog.* adulatory writing about another person. ■ a biography idealizing its subject. —**hag·i·o·graph·ic** /,hagēə'grafik; ,hāgēə-/ adj. —**hag·i·o·graph·i·cal** /,hagēə'grafəkəl; ,hāgēə-/ adj.

hag·i·ol·a·try /,hagē'älətrē; ,hāgē-/ ▶n. the worship of saints. ■ *derog.* undue veneration of a famous person.

hag·i·ol·o·gy /,hagē'äləjē; ,hāgē-/ ▶n. literature dealing with the lives and legends of saints. —**hag·i·o·log·i·cal** /,hagēə'läjəkəl; ,hāgēə-/ adj. —**hag·i·ol·o·gist** /-jist/ n.

hah ▶*interj.* variant spelling of HA¹.

ha-ha /'hä ,hä; ,hä 'hä/ ▶n. a ditch with a wall on its inner side below ground level, forming a boundary to a park or garden without interrupting the view.

hahn·i·um /'hänēəm/ ▶n. the name formerly proposed by the American Chemical Society for the chemical element of atomic number 105 (**dubnium**), and by IUPAC for element 108 (**hassium**).

hai·ku /'hī,kōō; 'hī'kōō/ ▶n. (*pl.* same or **-kus**) a Japanese poem of seventeen syllables, in three lines of five, seven, and five, traditionally evoking images of the natural world. ■ an English imitation of this.

hail¹ /hāl/ ▶n. pellets of frozen precipitation that fall in showers. ■ a large number of things hurled forcefully through the air, esp. with intent to harm: *a hail of bullets.*
▶v. [*intr.*] (**it hails, it is hailing,** etc.) hail falls: *it hailed so hard we had to stop.*

hail² ▶v. **1** [*tr.*] call out to (someone) to attract attention. ■ signal (an approaching taxicab) to stop. **2** [*tr.*] (often **be hailed**) acclaim enthusiastically as being a specified thing. **3** [*intr.*] (**hail from**) have one's home or origins in (a place).
▶*interj.* archaic expressing greeting or acclaim: *hail, Caesar!*
▶n. a shout or call used to attract attention. —**hail·er** n.
▶ □ **within hail** (or **within hailing distance**) at a distance within which someone may be called to; within earshot.

Hail Mar·y ▶n. (*pl.* **Hail Ma·rys**) **1** a prayer to the Virgin Mary used chiefly by Roman Catholics. ■ a recitation of such a devotional phrase or prayer. **2** [usu. as *adj.*] *Football* a desperation long pass to try to score late in the game. ■ any attempt with a small chance of success: *a Hail Mary plan.*

hail·stone /'hāl,stōn/ ▶n. a pellet of hail.

hail·storm /'hāl,stôrm/ ▶n. a storm of heavy hail.

hair /he(ə)r/ ▶n. **1** any of the fine threadlike strands growing from the skin of humans, mammals, and some other animals. ■ a similar strand growing from the epidermis of a plant, or forming part of a living cell. ■ (**a hair**) a very small quantity or extent. **2** such strands collectively, esp. those growing on a person's head. ■ the styling or dressing of a person's hair: *hair and makeup by Terry.* —**haired** adj. —**hair·less** adj. —**hair·like** adj.
▶ □ **hair of the dog** *inf.* an alcoholic drink taken to cure a hangover. □ **a hair's breadth** a very small amount or margin. ■ **in** (or **out of**) **some·one's hair** *inf.* annoying (or ceasing to annoy) someone. □ **let one's hair down** *inf.* behave in an uninhibited or relaxed manner. □ **make someone's hair stand on end** alarm or horrify someone. □ **put hair on one's chest** *inf.* (of an alcoholic drink) be very strong. □ **split hairs** make small and overfine distinctions.

hair·ball /'he(ə)r,bôl/ ▶n. (also **hair ball**) ▶n. a compact ball of hair that

accumulates in the stomach of a cat or other animal that grooms itself by licking its fur.

hair·breadth /'he(ə)r,bre(d)TH/ ▶n. see A HAIR'S BREADTH at HAIR.

hair·brush /'he(ə)r,brəsH/ ▶n. a brush for arranging or smoothing a person's hair.

hair·cloth /'he(ə)r,klôTH/ ▶n. stiff cloth woven with a cotton or linen warp and horsehair weft.

hair·cut /'heər,kət/ ▶n. the style in which a person's hair is cut. ■ an act of cutting a person's hair.

hair·do /'he(ə)r,dōō/ ▶n. (*pl.* **-dos**) *inf.* the style of a person's hair. ■ an act of styling a person's hair (used esp. of a woman's hair).

hair·dress·er /'he(ə)r,dresər/ ▶n. a person who cuts and styles hair as an occupation. —**hair·dress·ing** /-,dresiNG/ n.

hair dry·er (also **hair dri·er**) ▶n. an electrical device for drying a person's hair by blowing warm air over it.

hair·line /'he(ə)r,līn/ ▶n. **1** the edge of a person's hair, esp. on the forehead. **2** a very thin or fine line: *a hairline fracture.*

hair·net /'he(ə)r,net/ ▶n. a piece of fine mesh fabric for confining the hair.

hair·piece /'he(ə)r,pēs/ ▶n. a quantity or switch of detached hair used to augment a person's natural hair.

hair·pin /'he(ə)r,pin/ ▶n. a U-shaped pin for fastening the hair. ■ a sharp U-shaped curve in a road.
▶adj. shaped like a hairpin; forming a U: *along a slippery hairpin path.*

hair-rais·ing ▶adj. extremely alarming, astonishing, or frightening: *hair-raising adventures.* —**hair-rais·er** n.

hair·split·ting /'he(ə)r,splitiNG/ ▶adj. characterized by or fond of small and overfine distinctions.
▶n. the action of making small and overfine distinctions; quibbling. —**hair·split·ter** /-,splitər/ n.

hair spray (also **hair·spray**) /'he(ə)r,sprā/ ▶n. a solution sprayed onto a person's hair to keep it in place.

hair·spring /'he(ə)r,spriNG/ ▶n. a slender flat coiled spring regulating the movement of the balance wheel in a watch.

hair·style /'he(ə)r,stīl/ ▶n. a particular way in which a person's hair is cut or arranged.

hair trig·ger ▶n. a trigger of a firearm set for release at the slightest pressure. ■ [as *adj.*] (**hair-trigger**) *fig.* liable to change suddenly and violently: *a hair-trigger temper.*

hair·y /'he(ə)rē/ ▶adj. (**hair·i·er, hair·i·est**) **1** covered with hair, esp. thick or long hair. ■ having a rough feel or appearance suggestive of coarse hair. **2** *inf.* alarming and difficult: *we drove up a hairy mountain road.* —**hair·i·ly** /'he(ə)rəlē/ adv. —**hair·i·ness** n.

haj·i /'hajē/ (also **haj·ji** or **had·ji**) ▶n. (*pl.* **haj·is**) a Muslim who has been to Mecca as a pilgrim: [as *title*] *Haji Hadi.*

hajj /haj/ (also **haj** or **hadj**) ▶n. the Muslim pilgrimage to Mecca that takes place in the last month of the year, and that all Muslims are expected to make at least once during their lifetime.

hake /hāk/ (*pl.* same or **hakes**) ▶n. **1** a large-headed elongated food fish (genus *Merluccius*, family Merlucciidae) with long jaws and strong teeth. **2** any of a number of similar related fishes, esp. those of the northwestern Atlantic genus *Urophycis*, family Phycidae.

ha·lal /hə'läl; hə'lal/ ▶adj. denoting or relating to meat prepared as prescribed by Muslim law. ■ religiously acceptable according to Muslim law.
▶n. halal meat.

hal·berd /'halbərd; 'hôl-/ (also **hal·bert** /-bərt/) ▶n. *hist.* a combined spear and battle-ax.

hal·cy·on /'halsēən/ ▶adj. denoting a period of time in the past that was idyllically happy and peaceful.
▶n. **1** a tropical Asian and African kingfisher (genus *Halcyon*) with brightly colored plumage. **2** a mythical bird said by ancient writers to breed in a nest floating at sea at the winter solstice, charming the wind and waves into calm. ▶late Middle English: via Latin from Greek *alkuōn* 'kingfisher.'

halberd

hale[1] /hāl/ ▶*adj.* (of a person, esp. an elderly one) strong and healthy: *very hale and hearty.*

hale[2] ▶*v.* [tr.] *archaic* drag or draw forcibly.

half /haf/ ▶*n.* (*pl.* **halves** /havz/) either of two equal or corresponding parts into which something is or can be divided. ■ either of two equal periods of time into which a sports game or a performance is divided. ■ *Baseball* either of the two parts of one inning: *the top half of the third.* ▶*pron.* & *adj.* an amount equal to a half: [as *pron.*] *half of the lectures are delivered by him* | [as *adj.*] *the last half century.* ■ amounting to a part thought of as roughly a half: [as *pron.*] *half of them are gate-crashers.* ▶*adv.* to the extent of half: *the glass was half full.* ■ [often in *comb.*] to a certain extent; partly: *the chicken is half-cooked.* ▶ □ **go halves** share something equally. □ **the half of it** *inf.* the most important part or aspect of something: *you don't know the half of it.* □ **half past one** (**two**, etc.) thirty minutes after one (two, etc.) o'clock. □ **not half 1** not nearly: *not half such a fool as they thought.* **2** *inf.* not at all: *the players are not half bad.*

half-and-half ▶*adv.* & *adj.* in equal parts. | [as *adj.*] *a half-and-half mixture.* ▶*n.* a mixture of milk and cream. ■ a mixture of equal parts of beer and stout or of ale and porter.

half·back /'haf,bak/ ▶*n.* *Football* an offensive back usually positioned behind the quarterback and to the side of the fullback. ■ a usually defensive player in a ball game such as soccer or field hockey whose position is between the line or the forward.

half-baked ▶*adj.* (of an idea or philosophy) not fully thought through; lacking a sound basis.

half blood ▶*n.* **1** *dated* the relationship between people having one parent in common. ■ a person related to another in this way. **2** (**half-blood**) *offens.* another term for **HALF-BREED.** —**half-blood·ed** *adj.*

half-breed ▶*n.* *offens.* a person whose parents are of different races, esp. the offspring of an American Indian and a person of white European ancestry. ▶*adj.* denoting a person of such ancestry.

half-broth·er (also **half brother**) ▶*n.* a brother with whom one has only one parent in common.

half-doz·en (also **half a dozen**) ▶*n.* a set or group of six.

half-heart·ed /'haf'härtid/ ▶*adj.* without enthusiasm or energy. —**half·heart·ed·ly** *adv.* —**half·heart·ed·ness** *n.*

half hitch ▶*n.* a knot formed by passing the end of a rope around its standing part and then through the loop, often used in pairs.

half hour ▶*n.* (also **half an hour**) a period of thirty minutes. ■ a point in time thirty minutes after any half hour of the clock: *the clock struck the half hour.* —**half-hour·ly** *adj.* & *adv.*

half-life ▶*n.* the time taken for the radioactivity of a specified isotope to fall to half its original value. ■ the time required for any specified property (e.g., the concentration of a substance in the body) to decrease by half.

half-mast ▶*n.* the position of a flag that is being flown some way below the top of its staff as a mark of respect for a person who has died.

half-moon ▶*n.* the moon when only half of its illuminated surface is visible from the earth; the first or last quarter. ■ the time when this occurs. ■ a semicircular or crescent-shaped object.

half note (*Brit.* **min·im**) ▶*n.* *Mus.* a note having the time value of two quarter notes or half of a whole note, represented by a ring with a stem.

half-sis·ter (also **half sister**) ▶*n.* a sister with whom one has only one parent in common.

half step ▶*n.* *Mus.* a semitone.

half·time /'haf,tīm/ ▶*n.* the time at which half of a game or contest is completed, esp. when marked by an intermission.

half·tone /'haf,tōn/ ▶*n.* [usu. as *adj.*] a reproduction of a photograph or other image in which the various tones of gray or color are produced by variously sized dots of ink: *halftone illustrations.*

half-truth ▶*n.* a statement that conveys only part of the truth, esp. one used deliberately in order to deceive someone.

half·way /'haf'wā/ ▶*adv.* & *adj.* at or to a point equidistant between two others. ■ in the middle of a period of time: [as *adv.*] *halfway through the night.* ■ [as *adv.*] to some extent: *halfway decent.* ▶ □ **meet someone halfway** compromise; concede some points in order to gain others.

half·way house ▶*n.* a center for helping former drug addicts, prisoners, psychiatric patients, or others to adjust to life in general society. ■ the halfway point in a progression. ■ *hist.* an inn midway between two towns.

half·wit /'haf,wit/ ▶*n.* *inf.* a foolish or stupid person. —**half-wit·ted** *adj.* —**half-wit·ted·ly** *adv.* —**half-wit·ted·ness** *n.*

hal·i·but /'haləbət/ ▶*n.* (*pl.* same) a northern marine food fish (genus *Hippoglossus*, family Pleuronectidae) that is the largest of the flatfishes.

hal·ide /'ha,līd; 'hā-/ ▶*n.* *Chem.* a binary compound of a halogen with another element or group.

hal·ite /'ha,līt; 'hā,līt/ ▶*n.* sodium chloride as a mineral, typically occurring as colorless cubic crystals; rock salt.

hal·i·to·sis /,hali'tōsəs/ ▶*n.* technical term for **BAD BREATH.**

hall /hôl/ ▶*n.* **1** an area in a building onto which rooms open; a corridor. ■ the room or space just inside the front entrance of a house or apartment. **2** a large room for meetings, concerts, or other events. ■ a large public room in a mansion or palace used for receptions and banquets. ■ *Brit.* the room used for meals in a college, university, or school: *he dined in hall.* ■ a college or university building containing classrooms, residences, or rooms for other purposes. ■ the principal living room of a medieval house. **3** [usu. in *names*] *Brit.* a large country house, esp. one with a landed estate: *Darlington Hall.*

hal·le·lu·jah /,halə'lōōyə/ (also **al·le·lu·ia**) ▶*interj.* God be praised (uttered in worship or as an expression of rejoicing). ▶*n.* an utterance of the word "hallelujah" as an expression of worship or rejoicing. ■ (usu. **alleluia**) a piece of music or church liturgy containing this.

hall·mark /'hôl,märk/ ▶*n.* a mark stamped on articles of gold, silver, or platinum in Britain, certifying their standard of purity. ■ a distinctive feature, esp. one of excellence. ▶*v.* [tr.] stamp with a hallmark. ■ designate as distinctive, esp. for excellence.

hal·lo /hə'lō/ ▶*exclam.*, *n.*, & *v.* variant spelling of **HELLO.**

Hall of Fame ▶*a* national memorial in New York City containing busts and memorials honoring famous Americans. ■ [as *n.*] a similar establishment commemorating the achievements of a particular group of people, esp. athletes: *the Hockey Hall of Fame.* —**Hall of Fam·er** *n.*

hal·loo /hə'lōō/ ▶*interj.* used to attract someone's attention. ■ used to incite dogs to the chase during a hunt. ▶*n.* a cry of "halloo." ▶*v.* (**-loos**, **-looed**) [intr.] cry or shout "halloo" to attract attention or to give encouragement to dogs in hunting. ■ [tr.] shout to (someone) to attract their attention.

hal·low /'halō/ ▶*v.* [tr.] honor as holy. ■ *formal* make holy; consecrate. ■ [as *adj.*] (**hallowed**) greatly revered or respected: *a hallowed tradition.*

Hal·low·een /,halə'wēn; ,hälə-; -ō'ēn/ (also **Hal·low·e'en**) ▶*n.* the night of October 31, the eve of All Saints' Day, commonly celebrated by children who dress in costume and solicit treats door-to-door.

hal·lu·ces /'hal(y)ə,sēz/ ▶ plural form of **HALLUX.**

hal·lu·ci·nate /hə'lōōsən,āt/ ▶*v.* [intr.] experience a seemingly real perception of something not actually present, typically as a result of a mental disorder or of taking drugs. ■ [tr.] experience a hallucination of (something). —**hal·lu·ci·nant** /-sənənt/ *adj.* & *n.* —**hal·lu·ci·na·tor** /-,ātər/ *n.* —**hal·lu·ci·na·to·ry** /-sənə,tôrē/ *adj.*

hal·lu·ci·na·tion /hə,lōōsən'āshən/ ▶*n.* an experience involving the apparent perception of something not present.

hal·lu·ci·no·gen /hə'lōōsənə,jən/ ▶*n.* a drug that causes hallucinations, such as LSD. —**hal·lu·ci·no·gen·ic** /hə,lōōsənə'jenik/ *adj.*

hal·lux /'haləks/ ▶*n.* (*pl.* **hal·lu·ces** /'hal(y)ə,sēz/) *Anat.* a person's big toe. ■ *Zool.* the innermost digit of the hind foot of vertebrates.

hall·way /'hôl,wā/ ▶*n.* another term for **HALL** (sense 1).

ha·lo /'hālō/ ▶*n.* (*pl.* **-loes** or **-los**) a disk or circle of light shown surrounding or above the head of a saint or holy person to represent their holiness. ■ *fig.* the glory associated with an idealized person or thing. ■ a circle or ring of something resembling a halo. ■ a circle of white or colored light around the sun, moon, or other luminous body caused by refraction through ice crystals in the atmosphere. ■ *Astron.* a tenuous sphere of hot gas and old stars surrounding a spiral galaxy. ▶*v.* (**-loes**, **-loed**) [tr.] (usu. **be haloed**) surround with or as if with a halo. ▷mid 16th cent. (denoting a circle of light around the sun, etc.): from medieval Latin, from Latin *halos*, from Greek *halōs* 'disk of the sun or moon.'

hal·o·gen /'haləjən/ ▶*n.* *Chem.* any of the elements fluorine, chlorine, bromine, iodine, and astatine, occupying group VIIA (17) of the periodic table. ■ [as *adj.*] denoting lamps and radiant heat sources using a filament surrounded by the vapor of iodine or another halogen: *halogen headlights.* —**hal·o·gen·ic** /,halə'jenik/ *adj.*

hal·o·gen·ate /'haləjə,nāt; hə'läjə-/ ▶*v.* [tr.] [usu. as *adj.*] (**halogenated**) *Chem.* introduce one or more halogen atoms into (a compound or molecule), usually in place of hydrogen. —**hal·o·gen·a·tion** /ˌhaləjə-ˈnāSHən; həˌlājə-/ n.

hal·on /ˈhāˌlän/ ▶ n. any of a number of unreactive gaseous compounds of carbon with bromine and other halogens, used in fire extinguishers, but now known to damage the ozone layer.

hal·o·phyte /ˈhaləˌfīt/ ▶ n. Bot. a plant adapted to growing in saline conditions, as in a salt marsh.

halt[1] /hôlt/ ▶ v. bring or come to an abrupt stop. ■ [in imper.] used as a military command to bring marching soldiers to a stop.
▶ n. a suspension of movement or activity, typically a temporary one.

halt[2] archaic ▶ adj. lame.
▶ v. [intr.] walk with a limp. ■ hesitate; waver.

halt·er /ˈhôltər/ ▶ n. 1 a rope or strap with a noose or headstall placed around the head of a horse or other animal, used for leading or tethering it. ■ archaic a rope with a noose for hanging a person. 2 [usu. as adj.] a strap by which the bodice of a sleeveless dress or top is fastened or held behind at the neck, leaving the shoulders and back bare. ■ a top with such a neck.

halt·ing /ˈhôltiNG/ ▶ adj. slow and hesitant, esp. through lack of confidence; faltering. —**halt·ing·ly** adv.

hal·vah /ˈhälvä/ (also **hal·va**) ▶ n. a Middle Eastern confection made of sesame flour and honey.

halve /hav; häv/ ▶ v. [tr.] divide into two parts of equal or roughly equal size. ■ reduce or be reduced by half. ■ share (something) equally with another person: halving the bill. ■ Golf use the same number of strokes as one's opponent and thus tie (a hole or match).

halves /havz; hävz/ ▶ plural form of HALF.

hal·yard /ˈhalyərd/ ▶ n. a rope used for raising and lowering a sail, spar, flag, or yard on a sailing ship.

Ham /ham/ ▶ (in the Bible) a son of Noah, traditional ancestor of the Hamites.

ham /ham/ ▶ n. 1 meat from the upper part of a pig's leg salted and dried or smoked. 2 (**hams**) the backs of the thighs or the thighs and buttocks.

ham[2] ▶ n. 1 an excessively theatrical actor. 2 inf. an amateur radio operator.
▶ v. (**hammed**, **ham·ming**) [intr.] inf. overact.

ham·a·dry·ad /ˌhaməˈdrīəd/ ▶ n. (also **Ham·a·dry·ad**) Greek & Roman Mythol. a nymph who lives in a tree and dies when the tree dies.

ham·burg·er /ˈhamˌbərgər/ ▶ n. a round patty of ground beef, fried or grilled and typically served on a bun or roll. ■ ground beef.

ham-fist·ed /ˈhamˌfistid/ ▶ adj. another term for HAM-HANDED. —**ham-fist·ed·ly** adv. —**ham-fist·ed·ness** n.

ham-hand·ed ▶ adj. inf. clumsy; bungling: a ham-handed attempt. —**ham-hand·ed·ly** adv. —**ham-hand·ed·ness** n.

Ham·it·ic /həˈmitik/ ▶ adj. hist. of or denoting a hypothetical language family formerly proposed to comprise Berber, ancient Egyptian, the Cushitic languages, and the Chadic languages. These are now recognized as independent branches of the Afro-Asiatic family.

Ham·let /ˈhamlit/ ▶ a legendary prince of Denmark, hero of a tragedy by Shakespeare.

ham·let /ˈhamlit/ ▶ n. a small settlement, generally one smaller than a village.

ham·mer /ˈhamər/ ▶ n. 1 a tool with a heavy metal head mounted at right angles at the end of a handle, used for jobs such as breaking things and driving in nails. ■ a machine with a metal block for giving a heavy blow to something. ■ an auctioneer's mallet for indicating by a sharp tap that an article is sold. ■ a part of a mechanism that hits another part to make it work, such as one exploding the charge in a gun or one striking the strings of a piano. 2 a metal ball, typically weighing 16 pounds (7.3 kg), attached to a wire for throwing in an athletic contest. ■ (**the hammer**) the sport of throwing such a ball. 3 another term for MALLEUS.
▶ v. [tr.] 1 hit or beat (something) with a hammer or similar object. ■ [intr.] strike or knock at or on something violently: she hammered on his door. ■ [intr.] (**hammer away**) work hard and persistently: I have been hammering away at a plot. ■ [tr.] drive or secure (something) by striking with or as if with a hammer. ■ (**hammer something in/into**) instill (an attitude, idea, or habit) forcefully or repeatedly. 2 inf. attack or criticize forcefully and relentlessly: he got hammered for an honest mistake. ■ utterly defeat in a game or contest.
▶ phrasal v. □ **hammer something out** laboriously work out the details of a plan or agreement. ▷Old English hamor, hamer, of Germanic origin: related to Dutch hamer, German Hammer, and Old Norse hamarr 'rock.'

The original sense was probably 'stone tool.' —**ham·mer·er** n. —**ham·mer·less** adj.

▶ □ **come** (or **go**) **under the hammer** be sold at an auction. □ **hammer and tongs** inf. energetically, enthusiastically, or with great vehemence.

ham·mer and sick·le ▶ n. the symbols of the industrial worker and the peasant used as the emblem of the former Soviet Union and of international communism.

ham·mer·head /ˈhamərˌhed/ ▶ n. 1 (also **hammerhead shark**) a shark (genus Sphyrna, family Sphyrnidae) of tropical and temperate oceans that has flattened bladelike extensions on either side of the head, with the eyes and nostrils placed at or near the ends. 2 the striking head of a hammer.

ham·mer·lock /ˈhamərˌläk/ ▶ n. an armlock in which a person's arm is bent up behind the back.

ham·mer·toe /ˈhamərˌtō/ ▶ n. a toe that is bent permanently downward, typically as a result of pressure from footwear.

ham·mock /ˈhamək/ ▶ n. a bed made of canvas or of rope mesh and suspended by cords at the ends.

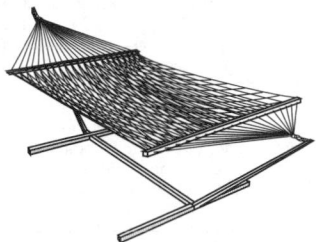

hammock

ham·per[1] /ˈhampər/ ▶ n. a large basket with a lid used for laundry: a laundry hamper. ■ a basket with a carrying handle and a hinged lid, used for food, cutlery, and plates on a picnic: a picnic hamper.

ham·per[2] ▶ v. [tr.] (often **be hampered**) hinder or impede the movement or progress of: their work is hampered by lack of funds.

ham·ster /ˈhamstər/ ▶ n. a solitary burrowing rodent (family Muridae) with a short tail and large cheek pouches for carrying food, native to Europe and northern Asia. Its several species include the **golden hamster** (Mesocricetus auratus), often kept as a pet or laboratory animal.

ham·string /ˈhamˌstriNG/ ▶ n. any of five tendons at the back of a person's knee. ■ the large tendon at the back of a quadruped's hock. ■ (also **hamstring muscle**) any of three long muscles at the back of a person's thigh.

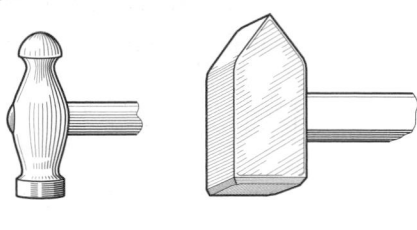

ball-peen hammer   sledge hammer

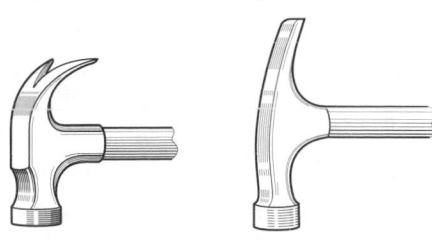

claw hammer   tack hammer

hammers

▸ *v.* (*past* and *past part.* **-strung**) [*tr.*] cripple (a person or animal) by cutting their hamstrings. ■ severely restrict the efficiency or effectiveness of: *we were hamstrung by a total lack of knowledge.*

Han /han/ ▸ **1** the Chinese dynasty that ruled from 206 BC until AD 220 with only a brief interruption. During this period Chinese rule was extended over Mongolia, Confucianism was recognized as the state philosophy, and detailed historical records were kept. **2** the dominant ethnic group in China.

hand /hand/ ▸ *n.* **1** the end part of a person's arm beyond the wrist, including the palm, fingers, and thumb: *he was leading her by the hand.* ■ a similar prehensile organ forming the end part of a limb of various mammals, such as that on all four limbs of a monkey. ■ [as *adj.*] operated by or held in the hand. ■ [as *adj.* or in *comb.*] done or made manually rather than by machine. ■ *inf.* a round of applause: *fans gave him a big hand.* ■ *dated* a pledge of marriage by a woman: *he wrote to request the hand of her daughter.* **2** something resembling a hand in form or position, in particular: ■ a pointer on a clock or watch indicating the passing of units of time. **3** (**hands**) used in reference to the power to direct something: *taking the law into their own hands.* ■ (**usu. a hand**) an active role in influencing something: *he had a hand in organizing the event.* ■ help in doing something: *do you need a hand?* ■ (usu. **hands**) (in sports) skill and dexterity: *a receiver with very good hands.* ■ a person's workmanship, esp. in artistic work: *attributing other work to his hand.* ■ a person's handwriting. ■ a person who does something to a specified standard: *I'm a great hand at inventing.* **4** a person who engages in manual labor, esp. in a factory, on a farm, or on board a ship. **5** the set of cards dealt to a player in a card game. ■ a round or short spell of play in a card game. ■ *Bridge* the cards held by declarer as opposed to those in the dummy. **6** a unit of measurement of a horse's height, equal to 4 inches (10.16 cm). **7** the feel of goods, esp. textiles, when handled: *fabrics with a softer hand.*
▸ *v.* **1** pick (something) up and give to (someone): *he handed each man a glass.* ■ *inf.* make (abusive, untrue, or otherwise objectionable) remarks to (someone): *all the yarns she'd been handing me.* ■ *inf.* make (something) easily obtainable for (someone): *a win handed to him on a plate.* **2** [*tr.*] hold the hand of (someone) in order to help them move in the specified direction: *he handed him into a carriage.*
▸ *phrasal v.* □ **hand something down 1** pass something on to a younger person or a successor. **2** announce something, esp. a judgment or sentence, formally or publicly. □ **hand something in** give something to a person in authority for their attention. □ **hand something on** pass something to the next person in a series or succession. ■ pass responsibility for something to someone else; delegate. □ **hand something out 1** give a share of something or one of a set of things to each of a number of people; distribute. **2** impose or inflict a penalty or misfortune on someone. □ **hand someone/something over** give someone or something, or the responsibility for someone or something, to someone else. □ **hand something around** offer something to each of a number of people in turn. —**hand·less** *adj.*
▸ □ **at hand** nearby. ■ readily accessible when needed. ■ close in time; about to happen: *a breakthrough in combating the disease may be at hand.* □ **at** (or **by**) **the hands** (or **hand**) **of** through the agency of. □ **bind** (or **tie**) **someone hand and foot** tie someone's hands and feet together. □ **by hand** by a person and not a machine. □ **give** (or **lend**) **a hand** assist in an action or enterprise. □ **hand in glove** in close collusion or association. □ **hand in hand** (of two people) with hands joined, esp. as a mark of affection. ■ *fig.* closely associated: *she had the confidence that usually goes hand in hand with experience.* □ (**from**) **hand to mouth** satisfying only one's immediate needs because of lack of money for future plans and investments. □ **hands down** easily and decisively; without question. □ **hands off** used as a warning not to touch or interfere with something. ■ [as *adj.*] (**hands-off**) not involving or requiring direct control or intervention. □ **hands-on** involving or offering active participation rather than theory. □ **hands up!** used as an instruction to raise one's hands in surrender or to signify assent or participation. □ **have one's hands full** have as much work as one can do. □ **have one's hands tied** *inf.* be unable to act freely. □ **have to hand it to someone** *inf.* used to acknowledge the merit or achievement of someone: *I've got to hand it to you—you've got the magic touch.* □ **in hand 1** receiving or requiring immediate attention: *the work in hand.* ■ in progress. **2** ready for use if required; in reserve. **3** under one's control: *the police had the situation in hand.* □ **in safe hands** protected by someone trustworthy from harm or damage. □ **keep one's hand in** become (or remain) practiced in something. □ **make** (or **lose** or **spend**) **money hand over fist** *inf.* make (or lose or spend) money very rapidly. □ **off someone's hands** not having to be dealt with or looked after by the person specified. □ **on every hand** all around. □ **on hand** present, esp. for a

specified purpose. ■ readily available. ■ needing to be dealt with. □ **on someone's hands** used to indicate that someone is responsible for dealing with someone or something: *he has a difficult job on his hands.* ■ used to indicate that someone is to blame for something: *he has blood on his hands.* ■ at someone's disposal: *I've had more time on my hands.* □ **on the one** (or **the other**) **hand** used to present factors that are opposed or that support opposing opinions. □ **out of hand 1** not under control. **2** without taking time to think: *they rejected negotiations out of hand.* □ **set** (or **put**) **one's hand to** start work on. □ **stay someone's hand** restrain someone from acting. □ **take a hand** become influential in determining something; intervene: *take a hand in the outcome.* □ **to hand** within easy reach. □ **turn one's hand to** undertake (an activity different from one's usual occupation: *a music teacher who turned his hand to writing books.* □ **wait on someone hand and foot** attend to all someone's needs or requests, esp. when this is regarded as unreasonable. □ **with one hand** (**tied**) **behind one's back** with serious limitations or restrictions. ■ used to indicate that one could do something without any difficulty: *I could do her job with one hand tied behind my back.*

hand·bag /'han(d),bag/ ▸ *n.* a woman's purse.

hand·ball /'han(d),bôl/ ▸ *n.* **1** a game similar to squash in which a ball is hit with the hand in a walled court. ■ (also **team handball**) a team game similar to soccer in which the ball is thrown or hit with the hands rather than kicked. ■ the ball used in these games. **2** (as **hand-ball**) *Soccer* a touching of the ball with the hand or arm, constituting a foul.

hand·bell /'han(d),bel/ ▸ *n.* a small bell with a handle or strap, esp. one of a set tuned to a range of notes and played by a group of people.

hand·bill /'han(d),bil/ ▸ *n.* a small printed advertisement or other notice distributed by hand.

hand·book /'han(d),bŏŏk/ ▸ *n.* a book giving information such as facts on a particular subject or instructions for operating a machine.

hand·brake /'han(d),brāk/ ▸ *n.* the emergency or parking brake on a motor vehicle. ■ a brake operated by hand, as on a bicycle.

hand·cart /'han(d),kärt/ ▸ *n.* a small cart pushed or drawn by hand.

hand·clap /'han(d),klap/ ▸ *n.* a clap of the hands.

hand·craft /'han(d),kraft/ ▸ *v.* [*tr.*] [usu. as *adj.*] (**handcrafted**) make skillfully by hand.
▸ *n.* another term for HANDICRAFT.

hand·cuff /'han(d),kəf/ ▸ *n.* (**handcuffs**) a pair of lockable linked metal rings for securing a prisoner's wrists.
▸ *v.* [*tr.*] put handcuffs on (someone). ■ *fig.* restrain; hamper.

hand·ful /'han(d),fŏŏl/ ▸ *n.* (*pl.* **-fuls**) **1** a quantity that fills the hand. ■ a small number or amount. **2** *inf.* a person who is very difficult to deal with or control.

hand gre·nade ▸ *n.* a hand-thrown grenade.

hand·grip /'han(d),grip/ ▸ *n.* **1** a handle for holding onto something. **2** a grasp with the hand, esp. considered in terms of its strength, as in a handshake.

hand·gun /'han(d),gən/ ▸ *n.* a gun designed for use by one hand, chiefly either a pistol or a revolver.

hand-held (also **hand·held**) ▸ *adj.* designed to be held in the hand: *a hand-held computer.*

hand·hold /'hand,hōld/ ▸ *n.* something for a hand to grip. ■ a secure grip with a hand or the hands.

hand·i·cap /'handē,kap/ ▸ *n.* a condition that markedly restricts a person's ability to function physically, mentally, or socially. ■ a circumstance that makes progress or success difficult. ■ a disadvantage imposed on a superior competitor in sports such as golf, horse racing, and competitive sailing in order to make the chances more equal. ■ a race or contest in which such a disadvantage is imposed. ■ the extra weight to be carried in a race by a racehorse on the basis of its previous performance to make its chances of winning the same as those of the other horses. ■ the number of strokes by which a golfer normally exceeds par for a course (used as a method of enabling players of unequal ability to compete with each other). —**han·di·cap·per** *n.*
▸ *v.* (**-capped**, **-cap·ping**) [*tr.*] act as an impediment to. ■ place (someone) at a disadvantage.

hand·i·capped /'handē,kapt/ ▸ *adj.* having a condition that markedly restricts one's ability to function physically, mentally, or socially.

hand·i·craft /'handē,kraft/ ▸ *n.* a particular skill of making decorative objects by hand: *teachers of drawing, design, and handicraft* | [as *adj.*] *handicraft workshops.* ■ an object made using a skill of this kind: *handicrafts decorate the hallways.*

hand·i·work /'handē,wərk/ ▸ *n.* **1** (**one's handiwork**) something that one has made or done. **2** making things by hand, considered as a subject of instruction.

hand·ker·chief /'haNGkərCHif; -CHēf/ ▶ *n.* a square of cotton or other finely woven material, typically carried one's pocket and intended for blowing or wiping one's nose.

han·dle /'handl/ ▶ *v.* [*tr.*] **1** feel or manipulate with the hands. ■ drive or control (a vehicle). ■ [*intr.*] (of a vehicle) respond in a specified manner when being driven or controlled. **2** manage (a situation or problem). ■ *inf.* deal with (someone or something). ■ have the resources to cope with: *more than I can handle.* ■ control or manage commercially. ■ (**handle oneself**) conduct oneself in a specified manner: *he handled himself with aplomb.* ■ (**handle oneself**) *inf.* defend oneself physically or verbally: *I can handle myself in a fight.* **3** process: *the airport expects to handle almost 250,000 passengers.*
▶ *n.* **1** the part by which a thing is held, carried, or controlled. ■ (**a handle on**) *fig.* a means of understanding, controlling, or approaching a person or situation: *it'll give people some kind of handle on these issues.* **2** *inf.* the name of a person or place: *that's some handle for a baby.* **3** *inf.* the total amount of money bet over a particular time (typically at a casino) or at a particular sporting event. —**han·dle·a·bil·i·ty** /,handl-ə'bilitē/ *n.* —**han·dle·a·ble** *adj.* —**han·dled** *adj.* —**han·dle·less** *adj.*

han·dle·bar /'handl,bär/ ▶ *n.* (usu. **handlebars**) the steering bar of a bicycle, motorcycle, scooter, or other vehicle, with a handgrip at each end.

han·dle·bar mus·tache ▶ *n.* a wide, thick mustache with the ends curving slightly upward.

han·dler /'handlər/ ▶ *n.* **1** a person who handles or deals with certain articles or commodities. ■ a device that handles certain articles or substances. **2** a person who trains or has charge of an animal. **3** a person who trains or manages another person, in particular: ■ a person who trains and acts as second to a boxer. ■ a publicity agent. ■ a person who advises on and directs the activities of a politician or other public figure.

hand·made /'han(d)'mād/ ▶ *adj.* made by hand, not by machine, and typically therefore of superior quality.

hand·maid·en /'han(d),mādn/ (also **hand·maid**) ▶ *n.* a female servant. ■ a subservient partner or element.

hand-me-down ▶ *n.* (often **hand-me-downs**) a garment or other item that has been passed on from another person.
▶ *adj.* passed on from another person.

hand·off /'hand,ôf; -,äf/ ▶ *n. Football* an exchange made by handing the ball to a teammate.

hand·out /'hand,out/ ▶ *n.* **1** something given free to a needy person or organization. **2** printed information provided free of charge, esp. to accompany a lecture or advertise something.

hand·pick /'hand'pik/ (also **hand-pick**) ▶ *v.* [*tr.*] select carefully with a particular purpose in mind. | [as *adj.*] (**handpicked**) *a handpicked team.*

hand·print /'hand,print/ ▶ *n.* the mark left by the impression of a hand.

hand·rail /'han(d),rāl/ ▶ *n.* a rail fixed to posts or a wall for people to hold onto for support.

hand·saw /'han(d),sô/ ▶ *n.* a wood saw worked by one hand.

hand·set /'han(d),set/ ▶ *n.* the part of a telephone that is held up to speak into and listen to. ■ a hand-held controller for a piece of electronic equipment, such as a television or video recorder.

hand·shake /'han(d),SHāk/ ▶ *n.* an act of shaking a person's hand with one's own, used as a greeting or to finalize an agreement. ■ a person's particular way of doing this. ■ *Comput.* an exchange of standardized signals between devices in a computer network regulating the transfer of data. —**hand·shak·ing** /-,SHākiNG/ *n.*

hand·some /'hansəm/ ▶ *adj.* (**-som·er**, **-som·est**) **1** (of a man) good-looking. ■ (of a woman) striking and imposing in good looks rather than conventionally pretty. ■ (of a thing) well made, imposing, and of obvious quality. **2** (of a number, sum of money, or margin) substantial: *elected by a handsome majority.* ■ generous; liberal. —**hand·some·ly** *adv.* —**hand·some·ness** *n.*

hand·spring /'hand,spriNG/ ▶ *n.* an acrobatic jump through the air onto one's hands followed by springing onto one's feet.

hand·stand /'hand,stand/ ▶ *n.* an act of balancing on one's hands with one's feet in the air or against a wall.

hand-to-hand ▶ *adj.* (of fighting) at close quarters.

hand·work /'hand,wərk/ ▶ *n.* work done with the hands: *the transition from handwork to machine production.* —**hand·worked** *adj.*

hand·wo·ven /'han(d)'wōvən/ ▶ *adj.* made on a hand-operated loom: *handwoven linens.* ■ woven by hand.

hand·writ·ing /'han(d),rītiNG/ ▶ *n.* writing with a pen or pencil. ■ a person's particular style of writing.

▶ □ **the handwriting** (or **writing**) **is on the wall** there are clear signs that something unpleasant or unwelcome is going to happen: *the handwriting was on the wall for the old system.*

hand·writ·ten /'han(d),ritn/ ▶ *adj.* written with a pen, pencil, or other hand-held implement.

hand·y /'handē/ ▶ *adj.* (**hand·i·er**, **hand·i·est**) **1** convenient to handle or use; useful. **2** close at hand: *keep credit cards handy.* ■ placed or occurring conveniently. **3** skillful: *he's handy with a needle.* —**hand·i·ly** /'handl-ē; 'handələ/ *adv.* —**hand·i·ness** *n.*

▶ □ **come in handy** *inf.* turn out to be useful: *the sort of junk that might come in handy one day.*

hand·y·man /'handē,man/ ▶ *n.* (*pl.* **-men**) a person able or employed to do occasional domestic repairs and minor renovations.

hang /haNG/ ▶ *v.* (*past* **hung** /həNG/ except in sense 2) **1** suspend or be suspended from above with the lower part dangling free. ■ attach or be attached to a wall. ■ (**be hung with**) be adorned with pictures or other decorations. ■ exhibit or be exhibited, as in a museum. ■ attach or be attached so as to allow free movement about the point of attachment: [*tr.*] *a long time was spent hanging a couple of doors.* ■ [*intr.*] droop: *she just sat with her mouth hanging open.* ■ [*intr.*] (of fabric or a garment) be arranged in folds so as to droop in a specified way: *this blend of silk and wool hangs well.* ■ [*tr.*] paste (wallpaper) to a wall. ■ informal way of saying HANG AROUND (sense 2) or HANG OUT (sense 3). **2** (*past* **hanged**) [*tr.*] kill (someone) by tying a rope attached from above around the neck and removing the support from beneath (used as a form of capital punishment). ■ [*intr.*] be killed in such a way: *both men were sentenced to hang.* ■ *dated* used in expressions as a mild oath: [*intr.*] *they could all go hang* | *I'm hanged if I know.* **3** [*intr.*] remain static in the air: *a haze of smoke hung below the ceiling.* ■ be present or imminent, esp. oppressively or threateningly: *a sense of dread hung over him for days.* ■ [*tr.*] *Baseball* deliver (a breaking pitch) that does not change direction as intended. **4** [*tr.*] (of a juror) prevent (a jury) from reaching a verdict by a dissenting vote. **5** *Comput.* come or cause to come unexpectedly to a state in which no further operations can be carried out.

▶ *phrasal v.* □ **hang around 1** loiter; wait around. **2** (**hang around with**) associate (with someone). □ **hang back** remain behind. ■ show reluctance to act or move. □ **hang in** *inf.* remain persistent and determined in difficult circumstances: *we just had to hang in there.* □ **hang on 1** hold tightly. ■ *inf.* remain firm or persevere, esp. in difficult circumstances. ■ (**hang on to**) keep; retain. **2** *inf.* wait for a short time: *hang on a minute.* **3** be contingent or dependent on: *the future of Europe should not hang on a referendum.* **4** listen closely to: *she hung on his every word.* □ **hang something on** *inf.* attach the blame for something to (someone). □ **hang out 1** (of laundry) hang from a clothesline to dry. **2** (of a shirttail or other piece of clothing) protrude and hang loosely downward. **3** *inf.* spend time relaxing or enjoying oneself. □ **hang together 1** make sense; be consistent. **2** (of people) remain associated; help or support each other. ■ **hang up 1** hang from a hook, hanger, etc. **2** end a telephone conversation by cutting the connection. ■ (**hang up on**) end a telephone conversation with (someone) by abruptly cutting the connection. □ **hang up something** hang something on a hook. ■ *inf.* cease or retire from the activity associated with the garment or object specified: *he will soon have to hang up his referee's whistle.*

▶ *n.* a downward droop or bend: *the hang of his head.* ■ the way in which something hangs: *the hang of one's clothes.* ■ the way in which pictures are displayed in an exhibition.

▶ □ **get the hang of** *inf.* learn how to operate or do (something). □ **hang by a thread** see THREAD. □ **hang fire** delay or be delayed in taking action or progressing. □ **hang one's hat** *inf.* be resident. □ **hang heavily** (or **heavy**) (of time) pass slowly. □ **hang a left** (or **right**) *inf.* make a left (or right) turn. □ **hang loose** see LOOSE. □ **hang someone out to dry** *inf.* leave someone in a difficult or vulnerable situation. □ **hang tough** be or remain inflexible or firmly resolved. □ **let it all hang out** *inf.* be very relaxed or uninhibited.

hang·ar /'haNGər/ ▶ *n.* a large building with extensive floor area, typically for housing aircraft. ▷*late 17th cent.* (in the sense 'shelter'): from French; probably from Germanic bases meaning 'hamlet' and 'enclosure.' —**hang·ar·age** /-rij/ *n.*

hang·dog /'haNG,dôg; -,däg/ ▶ *adj.* having a dejected or guilty appearance; shamefaced.

hang·er /'haNGər/ ▶ *n.* **1** [*in comb.*] a person who hangs something: *a wallpaper hanger.* **2** (also **coat hanger**) a shaped piece of wood, plastic, or metal with a hook at the top, from which clothes may be hung in order to keep them in shape and free of creases. **3** something from which another thing hangs, such as a hook.

hang·er-on ▶ *n.* (*pl.* **hang·ers-on**) a person who associates with another person or a group in a sycophantic manner or for the purpose of gaining some personal advantage.

hang glid·er ▶ *n.* an unpowered flying apparatus for a single person, consisting of a frame with a fabric airfoil stretched over it. The operator is suspended from a harness below and controls flight by body movement. ■ a person flying such an apparatus. —**hang-glide** *v.* —**hang glid·ing** *n.*

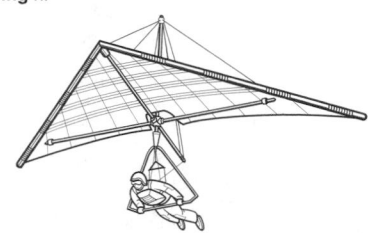

hang glider

hang·ing /'haNGiNG/ ▶ *n.* **1** the practice of hanging condemned people as a form of capital punishment. **2** a decorative piece of fabric or curtain hung on the wall of a room or around a bed.
▶ *adj.* suspended in the air: *hanging palls of smoke.* ■ situated or designed so as to appear to hang down: *hanging gardens.*

hang·man /'haNGmən; -,man/ ▶ *n.* (*pl.* **-men**) an executioner who hangs condemned people. ■ a game for two in which one player tries to guess the letters of a word, and failed attempts are recorded by drawing a gallows and someone hanging on it, line by line.

hang·nail /'haNG,nāl/ ▶ *n.* a piece of torn skin at the root of a fingernail.

hang·out /'haNG,out/ ▶ *n.* *inf.* a place one frequently visits.

hang·o·ver /'haNG,ōvər/ ▶ *n.* a severe headache or other after effects caused by drinking an excess of alcohol. ■ a thing that has survived from the past.

hang-up ▶ *n.* *inf.* an emotional problem or inhibition.

hank /haNGk/ ▶ *n.* a coil or skein of yarn, hair, rope, or other material.

hank·er /'haNGkər/ ▶ *v.* [*intr.*] (**hanker after/for/to do something**) feel a strong desire for or to do something. —**hank·er·er** *n.*

han·ky /'haNGkē/ (also **han·kie**) ▶ *n.* (*pl.* **-kies**) *inf.* a handkerchief.

han·ky-pan·ky /'paNGkē/ ▶ *n.* *inf., humorous* behavior, in particular sexual or legally dubious behavior, considered improper but not seriously so.

han·som /'hansəm/ (also **han·som cab**) ▶ *n.* *hist.* a two-wheeled horse-drawn carriage accommodating two inside, with the driver seated behind.

Ha·nuk·kah /'KHänəkə; 'hänəkə/ (also **Cha·nu·kah**) ▶ *n.* a lesser Jewish festival, lasting eight days from the 25th day of Kislev (in December) and commemorating the rededication of the Temple in 165 BC by the Maccabees after its desecration by the Syrians. It is marked by the successive kindling of eight lights.

hap·haz·ard /,hap'hazərd/ ▶ *adj.* lacking any obvious principle of organization. —**hap·haz·ard·ly** *adv.* —**hap·haz·ard·ness** *n.*

hap·less /'haplis/ ▶ *adj.* (esp. of a person) unfortunate. —**hap·less·ly** *adv.* —**hap·less·ness** *n.*

hap·loid /'hap,loid/ *Genetics* ▶ *adj.* (of a cell or nucleus) having a single set of unpaired chromosomes. Compare with DIPLOID. ■ (of an organism or part) composed of haploid cells.
▶ *n.* a haploid organism or cell. —**hap·loi·dy** *n.*

hap·pen /'hapən/ ▶ *v.* [*intr.*] **1** take place; occur. ■ ensue as an effect or result of an action or event. ■ chance to do something or come about: *we just happened to meet Paul.* ■ come about by chance. ■ (**happen on**) find or come across by chance. ■ used as a polite formula in questions: *do you happen to know?* **2** (**happen to**) be experienced by (someone); befall: *the same thing happened to me.* ■ become of: *I don't care what happens to the money.*
▶ □ **as it happens** actually; as a matter of fact.

hap·pen·ing /'hap(ə)niNG/ ▶ *n.* **1** an event or occurrence. ■ a noteworthy or exciting event. **2** a partly improvised or spontaneous piece of theatrical or other artistic performance, typically involving audience participation: *a multimedia happening.*
▶ *adj.* *inf.* fashionable; trendy: *nightclubs for the young are the happening thing.*

hap·pen·stance /'hapən,stans/ ▶ *n.* coincidence.

hap·py /'hapē/ ▶ *adj.* (**-pi·er, -pi·est**) **1** feeling or showing pleasure or contentment. ■ (**happy about**) having a sense of confidence in or satisfaction with (a person, arrangement, or situation). ■ (**happy with**) satisfied with the quality or standard of. ■ willing to do something. ■ (of an event or situation) characterized by happiness. ■ used in greetings: *happy birthday.* ■ fortunate and convenient: *the happy knack of making people like him.* **2** [in *comb.*] *inf.* inclined to use a specified thing excessively or at random: *litigation-happy.* —**hap·pi·ly** *adv.* —**hap·pi·ness** *n.*

hap·py-go-luck·y ▶ *adj.* cheerfully unconcerned about the future.

hap·py hour ▶ *n.* a period of the day when drinks are sold at reduced prices in a bar or restaurant.

hap·py me·di·um ▶ *n.* a satisfactory compromise: *you have to strike a happy medium.*

ha·ra-ki·ri /,härə 'ki(ə)rē; ,harə-; ,harē 'karē/ ▶ *n.* ritual suicide by disembowelment with a sword, formerly practiced in Japan by samurai as an honorable alternative to disgrace or execution. ■ *fig.* ostentatious or ritualized self-destruction.

ha·rangue /hə'raNG/ ▶ *n.* a lengthy and aggressive speech.
▶ *v.* [*tr.*] lecture (someone) at length in an aggressive and critical manner. —**ha·rangu·er** *n.*

ha·rass /hə'ras; 'harəs/ ▶ *v.* [*tr.*] subject to aggressive pressure or intimidation. ■ make repeated small-scale attacks on (an enemy). ■ [as *adj.*] (**harassed**) feeling or looking strained by having too many demands made on one. ▷early 17th cent.: from French *harasser*, from *harer* 'set a dog on,' from Germanic *hare*, a cry urging a dog to attack. —**ha·rass·er** *n.* —**ha·rass·ing·ly** *adv.* —**ha·rass·ment** *n.*

har·bin·ger /'härbənjər/ ▶ *n.* a person or thing that announces or signals the approach of another. ■ a forerunner of something: *these works were the most important harbinger of opera.*

har·bor /'härbər/ (*Brit.* **har·bour**) ▶ *n.* a place on the coast where vessels may find shelter, esp. one protected from rough water by piers, jetties, and other artificial structures. ■ *fig.* a place of refuge.
▶ *v.* [*tr.*] **1** keep (a thought or feeling, typically a negative one) in one's mind, esp. secretly: *to harbor doubts.* **2** give a home or shelter to. ■ shelter or hide (a criminal or wanted person): *harboring an escaped prisoner.* ■ carry the germs of (a disease). —**har·bor·er** *n.* —**har·bor·less** *adj.*

hard /härd/ ▶ *adj.* **1** solid, firm, and resistant to pressure; not easily broken, bent, or pierced. ■ (of a person) not showing any signs of weakness; tough. ■ (of information) reliable, esp. because based on something true or substantiated: *hard facts.* ■ (of a subject of study) dealing with precise and verifiable facts: *hard science.* ■ (of water) containing mineral salts that make lathering difficult. ■ (of prices of stock, commodities, etc.) stable or firm in value. ■ (of a consonant) pronounced as *c* in *cat* or *g* in *go.* **2** requiring a great deal of endurance or physical or mental effort: *hard work.* ■ putting a lot of energy into an activity: *a hard worker.* ■ difficult to bear; causing suffering: *times were hard.* ■ not showing sympathy or affection; strict. ■ (of a season or the weather) severe: *a long, hard winter.* ■ harsh or unpleasant to the senses: *the hard light of morning.* **3** done with a great deal of force or strength: *a hard blow to the head.* **4** potent, powerful, or intense, in particular: ■ (of liquor) strongly alcoholic; denoting distilled spirits rather than beer or wine. ■ (of apple cider) having alcoholic content from fermentation. ■ (of a drug) potent and addictive. ■ denoting an extreme or dogmatic faction within a political party: *the hard left.* ■ (of radiation) highly penetrating. ■ (of pornography) highly obscene and explicit.
▶ *adv.* **1** with a great deal of effort. ■ with a great deal of force; violently: *it was raining hard.* **2** so as to be solid or firm. **3** to the fullest extent possible: *put the wheel **hard** over to starboard.* —**hard·ness** *n.*
▶ □ **be hard on 1** treat or criticize (someone) severely. **2** be difficult for or unfair to. **3** be likely to hurt or damage: *hard on the eyes.* ■ **be hard put** find it very difficult: *you'll be hard put to find a better compromise.* □ **give someone a hard time** *inf.* deliberately make a situation difficult for someone. □ **go hard with** *dated* turn out to (someone's) disadvantage. □ **hard and fast** (of a rule or a distinction made) fixed and definitive. □ **hard at it** *inf.* busily working or occupied. □ **hard going** difficult to understand or enjoy. □ **hard hit** badly affected. □ **hard of hearing** not able to hear well. □ **hard on** (or **upon**) close to; following soon after: *we followed hard on their tracks.* □ **hard up** *inf.* short of money. □ **the hard way** through suffering or learning from the unpleasant consequences of mistakes: *his reputation was earned the hard way.* □ **play hard to get** deliberately adopt an aloof or uninterested attitude, typically in order to make oneself more attractive or interesting.

hard·back /'härd,bak/ ▶ *adj. & n.* another term for HARDCOVER.

hard·ball /'härd,bôl/ ▸ n. baseball, esp. as contrasted with softball. ■ inf. uncompromising and ruthless methods or dealings, esp. in politics: *the leadership played hardball to win the vote.*

hard·bit·ten (also **hard·bit·ten**) ▸ adj. tough and cynical.

hard·board /'härd,bôrd/ ▸ n. stiff board made of compressed and treated wood pulp.

hard·boiled ▸ adj. **1** (of an egg) boiled until the white and the yolk are solid. **2** (of a person) tough and cynical. ■ denoting a tough, realistic style of detective fiction set in a world permeated by corruption and deceit: *a hard-boiled thriller.* —**hard·boil** v.

hard cash ▸ n. negotiable coins and paper money as opposed to other forms of payment.

hard cop·y ▸ n. a printed version on paper of data held in a computer.

hard core ▸ n. the most active, committed, or doctrinaire members of a group or movement. | [as adj.] *a hard core following.* ■ popular music that is experimental in nature and typically characterized by high volume and aggressive presentation. ■ pornography of an explicit kind.

hard·cov·er /'härd,kəvər/ ▸ adj. (of a book) bound between rigid boards covered in cloth, paper, leather, or film.

hard disk ▸ n. Comput. a rigid nonremovable magnetic disk with a large data storage capacity, as distinct from the smaller capacity floppy disk.

hard drive ▸ n. Comput. a high-capacity, self-contained storage device containing a read-write mechanism plus one or more hard disks, inside a sealed unit. Also called **hard disk drive**.

hard·en /'härdn/ ▸ v. make or become hard or harder. ■ make or become more severe and less sympathetic. ■ make or become tougher and more clearly defined. ■ [intr.] (of prices of stocks, commodities, etc.) rise and remain steady at a higher level.
▸ phrasal v. □ **harden something off** inure a plant to cold by gradually increasing its exposure to it. —**hard·en·er** n.

hard hat ▸ n. a rigid protective helmet, as worn by factory and building workers. ■ inf. a worker who wears a hard hat. ■ inf. a person with reactionary or conservative views.

hard·head·ed /'härd,hedid/ ▸ adj. practical and realistic; not sentimental. —**hard·head·ed·ly** adv. —**hard·head·ed·ness** n.

hard·heart·ed ▸ adj. incapable of being moved to pity or tenderness; unfeeling. —**hard·heart·ed·ly** adv. —**hard·heart·ed·ness** n.

hard·hit·ting ▸ adj. **1** uncompromisingly direct and honest, esp. in revealing unpalatable facts. **2** (of an athlete or athletes) aggressive and physical.

har·di·hood /'härdē,hŏŏd/ ▸ n. dated boldness; daring.

hard line ▸ n. an uncompromising adherence to a firm policy: *to take a hard line on sentencing policy.* —**hard-lin·er** n.
▸ adj. uncompromising; strict: *a hard-line party activist.*

hard·ly /'härdlē/ ▸ adv. scarcely (used to qualify a statement by saying that it is true to an insignificant degree): *it is hardly bigger than a credit card.* ■ only a very short time before: *the party had hardly started.* ■ only with great difficulty: *she could hardly sit up straight.* ■ no or not (suggesting surprise at or disagreement with a statement): *I hardly think so.*
▸ □ **hardly any** almost no: *they sold hardly any books.* ■ almost none. □ **hardly ever** very rarely: *we hardly ever see them.*

hard-nosed ▸ adj. inf. realistic and determined; tough-minded.

hard-pressed ▸ adj. **1** closely pursued. **2** burdened with urgent business: *training centers are hard-pressed.* ■ (also **hard pressed**) in difficulties: *the hard-pressed construction industry.*

hard·scrab·ble /'härd,skrabəl/ ▸ adj. **1** returning little in exchange for great effort: *her uncle's hardscrabble peanut farm.* **2** characterized by chronic poverty and hardship: *the hardscrabble coal town of Grundy.*

hard sell ▸ n. a policy or technique of aggressive salesmanship or advertising.

hard·ship /'härd, SHip/ ▸ n. severe suffering or privation.

hard·tack /'härd,tak/ ▸ n. hard dry bread or biscuit, esp. as rations for sailors.

hard·ware /'härd,we(ə)r/ ▸ n. tools, machinery, and other durable equipment. ■ the machines, wiring, and other physical components of a computer or other electronic system. Compare with SOFTWARE. ■ tools, implements, and other items used in home life and activities such as gardening.

hard-wired ▸ adj. Electr. involving or achieved by permanently connected circuits. ■ inf. genetically determined or compelled. —**hard-wire** v. & adj.

hard·wood /'härd,wŏŏd/ ▸ n. the wood from a broad-leaved tree (such as oak, ash, or beech) as distinguished from that of conifers. ■ a tree producing such wood.

har·dy /'härdē/ ▸ adj. (**-di·er**, **-di·est**) robust; capable of enduring difficult conditions. ■ (of a plant) able to survive outside during winter. —**har·di·ly** /-dəlē/ adv. —**har·di·ness** /-dēnis/ n.

hare /he(ə)r/ ▸ n. a fast-running, long-eared mammal (*Lepus* and other genera, family Leporidae) that resembles a large rabbit, having long hind legs and occurring typically in grassland or open woodland.

hare·bell /'her,bel/ ▸ n. a widely distributed bellflower (*Campanula rotundifolia*) with slender stems and pale blue flowers. Also called BLUEBELL.

hare·brained /'he(ə)r,brānd/ ▸ adj. rash; ill-judged: *a harebrained scheme.*

hare·lip /'he(ə)r,lip/ ▸ n. offens. another term for CLEFT LIP. —**hare-lipped** adj.

har·em /'he(ə)rəm; 'har-/ ▸ n. **1** the separate part of a Muslim household reserved for wives, concubines, and female servants. **2** the wives (or concubines) of a polygamous man. ■ a group of female animals sharing a single mate.

har·i·cot /'hari,kō/ (also **haricot bean**) ▸ n. **1** a bean of a variety with small white seeds, esp. the kidney bean. **2** the dried seed of this bean used as a vegetable.

hark /härk/ ▸ v. [intr.] poetic/lit. listen: *Hark! He knocks.*
▸ phrasal v. □ **hark back** mention or remember something from the past. □ **hark back to** (evoke an older style or genre).

hark·en ▸ v. variant spelling of HEARKEN.

har·le·quin /'härlək(w)ən/ ▸ n. **1** (**Harlequin**) a mute character in traditional pantomime, typically masked and dressed in a diamond-patterned costume. ■ hist. a stock comic character in Italian *commedia dell'arte.* **2** (also **harlequin duck**) a small duck (*Histrionicus histrionicus*) of fast-flowing streams around the Arctic and North Pacific, the male having mainly gray-blue plumage with bold white markings.
▸ adj. in varied colors; variegated.

har·lot /'härlət/ ▸ n. archaic a prostitute or promiscuous woman. —**har·lot·ry** /-trē/ n.

harm /härm/ ▸ n. physical injury, esp. that which is deliberately inflicted. ■ material damage. ■ actual or potential ill effect or danger: *I can't see any harm in it.*
▸ v. [tr.] physically injure:. ■ damage the health of. ■ have an adverse effect on.
▸ □ **no harm done** used to reassure someone that what they have done has caused no real damage. □ **out of harm's way** in a safe place.

harm·ful /'härmfəl/ ▸ adj. causing or likely to cause harm. —**harm·ful·ly** adv. —**harm·ful·ness** n.

harm·less /'härmlis/ ▸ adj. not able or likely to cause harm. ■ inoffensive: *he's pretty harmless.* —**harm·less·ly** adv. —**harm·less·ness** n.

har·mon·ic /här'mänik/ ▸ adj. **1** of, relating to, or characterized by musical harmony. ■ Mus. relating to or denoting a harmonic or harmonics. **2** Math. of or relating to a harmonic progression.
▸ n. Mus. an overtone accompanying a fundamental tone at a fixed interval, produced by vibration of a string, column of air, etc., in an exact fraction of its length. ■ a note produced on a musical instrument as an overtone, e.g., by lightly touching a string while sounding it. —**har·mon·i·cal·ly** /-ik(ə)lē/ adv.

har·mon·i·ca /här'mänikə/ ▸ n. a small rectangular wind instrument with a row of metal reeds along its length, held against the lips and moved from side to side to produce different notes by blowing or sucking. Also called MOUTH ORGAN.

har·mon·ic pro·gres·sion ▸ n. **1** Music a series of chord changes forming the underlying harmony of music. **2** Mathematics a sequence of quantities whose reciprocals are in arithmetic progression (e.g., 1, $\frac{1}{3}$, $\frac{1}{5}$, $\frac{1}{7}$, etc.).

har·mo·ni·ous /här'mōnēəs/ ▸ adj. tuneful; not discordant. ■ forming a pleasing or consistent whole: *a harmonious blend of traditional and modern.* ■ free from disagreement or dissent: *harmonious relationships.* —**har·mo·ni·ous·ly** adv. —**har·mo·ni·ous·ness** n.

har·mo·ni·um /här'mōnēəm/ ▸ n. a keyboard instrument in which the notes are produced by air driven through metal reeds by foot-operated bellows.

har·mo·nize /'härmə,nīz/ ▸ v. [tr.] add notes to (a melody) to produce harmony. ■ [intr.] sing in harmony. ■ [intr.] produce a pleasing visual combination. ■ make consistent: *the group founded to harmonize development plans.* —**har·mo·ni·za·tion** /,härmənə'zāSHən/ n.

har·mo·ny /'härmənē/ ▸ n. (pl. **-nies**) **1** the combination of simultaneously sounded musical notes to produce chords and chord progressions having a pleasing effect. ▪ the study or composition of musical harmony. ▪ the quality of forming a pleasing and consistent whole: *cities where old and new blend in harmony.* **2** agreement or concord: *man and machine in perfect harmony.*

har·ness /'härnis/ ▶*n.* a set of straps and fittings by which a horse or other draft animal is fastened to a cart, plow, etc., and is controlled by its driver. ▪ an arrangement of straps for fastening something to a person's body, such as a parachute, or for restraining a young child. ▶*v.* [*tr.*] **1** put a harness on (a horse or other draft animal). ▪ (**harness something to**) attach a draft animal to (something) by a harness. **2** control and make use of (natural resources), esp. to produce energy: *attempts to harness solar energy.* —**har·ness·er** *n.*

harp /härp/ ▶*n.* **1** a musical instrument, roughly triangular in shape, consisting of a frame supporting a graduated series of parallel strings, played by plucking with the fingers. **2** *inf.* short for HARMONICA. —**harp·ist** *n.*
▶*v.* [*intr.*] **1** talk or write persistently and tediously on a particular topic. **2** *archaic* play on a harp.

har·poon /,här'po͞on/ ▶*n.* a barbed spearlike missile attached to a long rope and thrown by hand or fired from a gun, used for catching whales and other large sea creatures.
▶*v.* [*tr.*] spear (something) with a harpoon. ▷early 17th cent. (denoting a barbed dart or spear): from French *harpon*, from *harpe* 'dog's claw, clamp,' via Latin from Greek *harpē* 'sickle.' —**har·poon·er** *n.*

harp [caption]

har·poon gun ▶*n.* a type of gun used for firing harpoons.
harp seal ▶*n.* a slender North Atlantic true seal (*Phoca groenlandica*) that typically has a dark harp-shaped mark on its gray back.
harp·si·chord /'härpsi,kôrd/ ▶*n.* a keyboard instrument with horizontal strings that run perpendicular to the keyboard in a long tapering case and are plucked by points of quill, leather, or plastic operated by depressing the keys. —**harp·si·chord·ist** *n.*
har·py /'härpē/ ▶*n.* (*pl.* **-pies**) *Greek and Roman Mythol.* a rapacious monster described as having a woman's head and body and a bird's wings and claws or depicted as a bird of prey with a woman's face. ▪ a grasping, unscrupulous woman.
har·que·bus /'(h)ärk(w)əbəs/ (also **ar·que·bus**) ▶*n.* *hist.* an early type of portable gun supported on a tripod or a forked rest.
har·ri·dan /'haridn/ ▶*n.* a strict, bossy, or belligerent old woman.
har·ri·er[1] /'harēər/ ▶*n.* a person who engages in persistent attacks on others or incursions into their land.
har·ri·er[2] ▶*n.* a hound of a breed used for hunting hares. ▪ a cross-country runner.
har·ri·er[3] ▶*n.* a long-winged, slender-bodied bird of prey (genus *Circus*, family Accipitridae) with low circling flight.
har·row /'harō/ ▶*n.* an implement consisting of a heavy frame set with teeth or tines that is dragged over plowed land to break up clods, remove weeds, and cover seed.
▶*v.* [*tr.*] **1** draw a harrow over (land). **2** cause distress to: [as *adj.*] (**harrowing**) *a harrowing film about racism and violence.* —**har·row·er** *n.* —**har·row·ing·ly** *adv.*
har·ry /'harē/ ▶*v.* (**-ries, -ried**) [*tr.*] persistently carry out attacks on (an enemy or an enemy's territory). ▪ persistently harass.
harsh /härsh/ ▶*adj.* **1** unpleasantly rough or jarring to the senses: *drenched in a harsh white neon light* | *harsh guttural shouts.* **2** cruel or severe: *harsh military discipline.* ▪ (of a climate or conditions) difficult to survive in; hostile. ▪ (of reality or a fact) grim and unpalatable. ▪ having an undesirably strong effect. —**harsh·en** /-SHən/ *v.* —**harsh·ly** *adv.* —**harsh·ness** *n.*
hart /härt/ ▶*n.* an adult male deer, esp. a red deer over five years old.
har·te·beest /'härtə,bēst; 'härt-/ ▶*n.* a large African antelope (genera *Alcelaphus, Damaliscus,* and *Sigmoceros*) with a long head and sloping back, related to the gnus.
har·um-scar·um /'he(ə)rəm 'ske(ə)rəm/ ▶*adj.* reckless; impetuous.
har·vest /'härvist/ ▶*n.* the process or period of gathering in crops. ▪ the season's yield or crop. ▪ a quantity of animals caught or killed for human use. ▪ *fig.* the product or result of an action.
▶*v.* [*tr.*] gather (a crop) as a harvest. ▪ catch or kill (animals) for human consumption or use. ▪ remove (cells, tissue, or an organ) from a person or animal for transplantation or experimental purposes.

▪ *fig.* gain (something) as the result of an action. —**har·vest·a·ble** *adj.* —**har·vest·er** *n.*
har·vest·man /'härvəstmən/ ▶*n.* (*pl.* **-men**) another term for DADDY LONGLEGS (sense 1).
has /haz/ ▶ third person singular present of HAVE.
has-been ▶*n. inf., derog.* a person or thing considered to be outmoded or no longer of any significance.
hash[1] /hash/ ▶*n.* a dish of cooked meat cut into small pieces and re-cooked, usually with potatoes. ▪ a finely chopped mixture. ▪ a mixture of jumbled incongruous things; a mess.
▶*v.* [*tr.*] **1** make (meat or other food) into a hash. **2** (**hash something out**) come to agreement on something after lengthy and vigorous discussion.
▶ □ **make a hash of** *inf.* make a mess of; bungle. □ **settle someone's hash** *inf.* deal with and subdue someone in no uncertain manner.
hash[2] ▶*n. inf.* short for HASHISH.
hash[3] (also **hash mark, hash sign**) ▶*n.* the sign #.
hash·ish /'ha,shēsh/ ▶*n.* an extract of the cannabis plant, containing concentrations of the psychoactive resins.
Ha·sid /KHä'sēd; 'KHäsid; 'häsid/ (also **Has·sid**) ▶*n.* (*pl.* **Ha·si·dim** /KHäsē'dēm; hä'sēdim/) a member of a strictly orthodox Jewish sect. —**Ha·sid·ic** /KHä'sedik; häsēdik/ *adj.*
has·n't /'haznt/ ▶*contr.* of has not.
hasp /hasp/ ▶*n.* a slotted hinged metal plate that forms part of a fastening for a door or lid and is fitted over a metal loop and secured by a pin or padlock. ▪ a similar metal plate on a trunk or suitcase with a projecting piece that is secured by the lock.
▶*v.* [*tr.*] *archaic* lock (a door, window, or lid) by securing the hasp over the loop of the fastening.

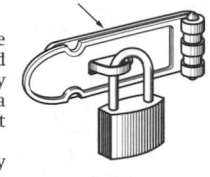

hasp [caption]

has·sle /'hasəl/ *inf.* ▶*n.* irritating inconvenience. ▪ deliberate harassment. ▪ a disagreement; a quarrel.
▶*v.* [*tr.*] harass; pester.
has·sock /'hasək/ ▶*n.* **1** a thick, firmly padded cushion, in particular: ▪ a footstool. **2** a firm clump of grass or matted vegetation in marshy or boggy ground.
haste /hāst/ ▶*n.* excessive speed or urgency of movement or action; hurry.
has·ten /'hāsən/ ▶*v.* [*intr.*] be quick to do something: *he hastened to refute the assertion.* ▪ move or travel hurriedly: *we hastened back to Paris.* ▪ [*tr.*] cause (something) to happen sooner than it otherwise would: *a move that could hasten peace talks.*
hast·y /'hāstē/ ▶*adj.* (**hast·i·er, hast·i·est**) done or acting with excessive speed or urgency; hurried: *a hasty attempt to defuse the situation.* ▪ *archaic* quick-tempered. —**hast·i·ly** /'hāstəlē/ *adv.* —**hast·i·ness** *n.*
hat /hat/ ▶*n.* a shaped covering for the head worn for warmth, as a fashion item, or as part of a uniform. ▪ used to refer to a particular role or occupation of someone who has more than one: *wearing her scientific hat.* —**hat·ful** /-,fo͝ol/ *n.* (*pl.* **-fuls.**) —**hat·less** *adj.* —**hat·ted** *adj.*
▶ □ **hat in hand** used to indicate an attitude of humility. □ **keep something under one's hat** keep something a secret. □ **pass the hat** collect contributions of money for a specific purpose. □ **pick something out of a hat** select something at random. □ **take one's hat off to** (or **hats off to**) used to state one's admiration for (someone who has done something praiseworthy): *hats off to emergency services for prompt work in the storms.* □ **throw one's hat in** (or **into**) **the ring** express willingness to take up a challenge, esp. to enter a political race.
hat·band /'hat,band/ ▶*n.* a decorative ribbon encircling a hat, held in position above the brim.
hat·box /'hat,bäks/ ▶*n.* a large cylindrical box used to protect a hat when being transported or stored.
hatch[1] /hach/ ▶*n.* an opening of restricted size allowing for passage from one area to another, in particular: ▪ a door in an aircraft, spacecraft, or submarine. ▪ an opening in the deck of a boat or ship: *a cargo hatch.* ▪ an opening in a ceiling leading to a loft or attic. ▪ an opening in a kitchen wall for serving or selling food through. ▪ the rear door of a hatchback car.
▶ □ **down the hatch** *inf.* used in a toast; drink up.
hatch[2] ▶*v.* **1** [*intr.*] (of a young bird, fish, or reptile) emerge from its egg. ▪ (of an egg) open and produce a young animal. ▪ [*tr.*] incubate (an egg). ▪ [*tr.*] cause (a young animal) to emerge from its egg. **2** [*tr.*] conspire to devise (a plot or plan): *the little plot that you and Sylvia hatched up last night.*
▶*n.* a newly hatched brood.

hatch³ ▶*v.* [*tr.*] (in fine art and technical drawing) shade (an area) with closely drawn parallel lines.

hatch·back /'hacн,bak/ ▶*n.* a car with a door across the full width at the back end that opens upward to provide easy access for loading.

hatch·er·y /'hacнərē/ ▶*n.* (*pl.* **-er·ies**) a place where the hatching of fish or poultry eggs is artificially controlled for commercial purposes.

hatch·et /'hacнit/ ▶*n.* a small ax with a short handle for use in one hand. ▷Middle English: from Old French *hachette*, diminutive of *hache* 'ax,' from medieval Latin *hapia*, of Germanic origin.

hatch·et job ▶*n. inf.* a fierce attack on someone or their work, esp. in print.

hatch·et man ▶*n. inf.* a person employed to carry out controversial or disagreeable tasks, such as the dismissal of people from employment. ■ a person who writes fierce attacks on others or their work.

hatch·way /'hacн,wā/ ▶*n.* an opening or hatch, esp. in a ship's deck.

hate /hāt/ ▶*v.* [*tr.*] feel intense or passionate dislike for (someone). ■ have a strong aversion to (something): *he hates flying.* ■ used politely to express one's regret or embarrassment at doing something: *I hate to bother you.*
▶*n.* intense or passionate dislike. ■ [as *adj.*] denoting hostile actions motivated by intense dislike or prejudice: *a hate campaign.* —**hat·a·ble** /'hātəbəl/ (also **hate·a·ble**) —**hat·er** *n.*

hate·ful /'hātfəl/ ▶*adj.* arousing, deserving of, or filled with hatred. ■ *inf.* very unpleasant: *I don't have to stay in this hateful place.* —**hate·ful·ly** *adv.* —**hate·ful·ness** *n.*

hat·pin /'hat,pin/ ▶*n.* a long pin, typically with an ornamental head, that holds a woman's hat in position by securing it to her hair.

ha·tred /'hātrid/ ▶*n.* intense dislike or ill will.

hat·ter /'hatər/ ▶*n.* a person who makes and sells hats.

hat trick ▶*n.* three successes of the same kind, esp. consecutive ones within a limited period. ■ (chiefly in ice hockey or soccer) the scoring of three goals in a game by one player. ■ (in cricket) the taking of three wickets by the same bowler with successive balls.

haugh·ty /'hôtē/ ▶*adj.* (**haugh·ti·er, haugh·ti·est**) arrogantly superior and disdainful. —**haugh·ti·ly** -*təlē/ adv.* —**haugh·ti·ness** *n.*

haul /hôl/ ▶*v.* **1** [*tr.*] (of a person) pull or drag with effort or force. ■ *Naut.* pull on (a rope). ■ (**haul oneself**) propel or pull oneself with difficulty. ■ *inf.* force (someone) to appear for reprimand or trial. ■ [*intr.*] (of a person) pull hard. **2** [*tr.*] (of a vehicle) pull (an attached trailer or load) behind it: *the train was hauling a cargo of liquid chemicals.* ■ transport in a truck or cart: *Bennie hauls trash in North Philadelphia.*
▶*n.* **1** an amount of something gained or acquired. ■ a quantity of something that was stolen or is possessed illegally. ■ the number of points, medals, or titles won by a person or team in a sporting event or over a period. ■ a number of fish caught. **2** a distance to be traversed. See also **LONG HAUL, SHORT HAUL.** —**haul·er**
▶ □ **haul off** *inf.* withdraw a little in preparation for some action: *he hauled off and smacked the kid.*

haul·age /'hôlij/ ▶*n.* the action or process of hauling. ■ the commercial transport of goods: *road haulage.* ■ a charge for such transport.

haunch /hôncн; häncн/ ▶*n.* **1** a buttock and thigh considered together, in a human or animal. **2** *Archit.* the side of an arch, between the crown and the pier.
▶ □ **sit on one's haunches** squat with the haunches resting on the backs of the heels.

haunt /hônt; hänt/ ▶*v.* [*tr.*] (of a ghost) manifest itself at (a place) regularly. ■ (of a person) frequent (a place). ■ be persistently and disturbingly present in (something): *cities haunted by the shadow of cholera.* ■ be persistently in the mind of (someone).
▶*n.* a place frequented by a specified person or group of people: *I revisited my old haunts.* —**haunt·er** *n.*

haunt·ing /'hôntiнg; 'hän-/ ▶*adj.* poignant and evocative; difficult to ignore or forget. —**haunt·ing·ly** *adv.*

Hau·sa /'housə; 'houzə/ ▶*n.* (*pl.* same or **-sas**) **1** a member of a people of northern Nigeria and adjacent regions. **2** the Chadic language of this people, spoken mainly in Nigeria and Niger, and widely used as a lingua franca in parts of West Africa.
▶*adj.* of or relating to this people or their language.

haute cou·ture /,ōt ,kōō'tōōr/ ▶*n.* the designing and making of high-quality fashionable clothes by leading fashion houses, esp. to order. ■ fashion houses that engage in such work. ■ clothes of this kind.

haute cui·sine /,ōt ,kwə'zēn/ ▶*n.* the preparation and cooking of high-quality food following the style of traditional French cuisine. ■ food produced in such a way.

hau·teur /hō'tər/ ▶*n.* haughtiness of manner; disdainful pride.

have /hav/ ▶*v.* (**has** /haz/; (h)əz/; *past* **had** /had/; (h)əd/) [*tr.*] **1** (also **have got**) possess, own, or hold. ■ possess or be provided with (a quality, characteristic, or feature). ■ (**have oneself**) *inf.* provide or indulge oneself with (something): *he had himself two highballs.* ■ be made up of; comprise: *the party had 10,000 members.* ■ used to indicate a particular relationship: *do you have a client named Pedersen?* ■ be able to make use of (something available) or at one's disposal): *how much time have I got?* ■ have gained (a qualification). ■ possess as an intellectual attainment; know (a language or subject): *I had only a little French.* **2** experience; undergo: *I had a good time | I was having difficulty staying awake.* ■ (also **have got**) suffer from (an illness, ailment, or disability). ■ (also **have got**) let (a feeling or thought) come into one's mind; hold in the mind: *he had the strong impression that someone was watching him.* ■ experience or suffer the specified action happening or being done to (something): *she had her bag stolen.* ■ cause (someone or something) to be in a particular state or condition: *I want to have everything ready in good time | I had the TV on.* ■ (also **have got**) *inf.* have put (someone) at a disadvantage in an argument (said either to acknowledge that one has no answer to a point or to show that one knows one's opponent has no answer). ■ cause (something) to be done for one by someone else: *have your carpet laid by a professional.* ■ tell or arrange for something to be done: *she had her long hair cut.* ■ (usu. **be had**) *inf.* cheat or deceive (someone): *I realized I'd been had.* ■ *vulgar slang* engage in sexual intercourse with (someone). **3** (**have to do something** or **have got to do something**) be obliged or find it necessary to do the specified thing. ■ need or be obliged to do (something). ■ be strongly recommended to do something. ■ be certain or inevitable to happen or be the case: *there has to be a catch.* **4** perform the action indicated by the noun specified (used esp. in spoken English as an alternative to a more specific verb): *the color green has a restful effect.* ■ organize and bring about: *are you going to have a party?* ■ eat or drink. ■ give birth to or be due to give birth to: *she's going to have a baby.* **5** (also **have got**) show (a personal attribute or quality) by one's actions or attitude: *he had little patience with technological gadgetry.* ■ [often in *imper.*] exercise or show (mercy, pity, etc.) toward another person: *God have mercy on me!* ■ not accept; refuse to tolerate: *I can't have you insulting Tom like that.* **6** (also **have got**) place or keep (something) in a particular position: *Mary had her back to me | I soon had the trout in a net.* ■ hold or grasp (someone or something) in a particular way: *he had me by the throat.* **7** be the recipient of (something sent, given, or done): *she had a letter from Mark.*
▶*phrasal v.* □ **have at** attempt or attack forcefully or aggressively.
▶*aux. v.* used with a past participle to form the perfect, pluperfect, and future perfect tenses, and the conditional mood: *I have finished | he had asked her | she will have left by now | I could have helped, had I known | "Have you seen him?" "Yes, I have."*
▶*n.* (**the haves**) *inf.* people with plenty of money and possessions: *an increasing gap between the haves and have-nots.*
▶ □ **have had it** *inf.* **1** be in a very poor condition; be beyond repair or past its best. ■ be extremely tired. ■ have lost all chance of survival. **2** be unable to tolerate someone or something any longer: *I've had it with him!* □ **have it 1** express the view that (used to indicate that the speaker is reporting something that they do not necessarily believe to be fact): *rumor had it that he was really very wealthy.* **2** win a decision, esp. after a vote: *the ayes have it.* **3** have found the answer to something: *"I have it!" Rosa exclaimed.* □ **have it coming** deserve punishment or downfall. □ **have (got) it in for** *inf.* feel a particular dislike of (someone) and behave in a hostile manner toward them. □ **have it out** *inf.* attempt to resolve a contentious matter by confronting someone and engaging in a frank discussion or argument. □ **have (got) nothing on** *inf.* **1** be not nearly as good as (someone or something), esp. in a particular respect: *bright though his three sons were, they had nothing on Sally.* **2** have nothing (or **something**) **on someone** know nothing (or something) discreditable or incriminating about someone.

ha·ven /'hāvən/ ▶*n.* a place of safety or refuge: *a haven for wildlife.* ■ an inlet providing shelter for ships or boats; a harbor or small port.

have-nots ▶*pl. n.* (usu. **the have-nots**) *inf.* economically disadvantaged people.

have·n't /'havənt/ ▶*contr. of* have not.

hav·er·sack /'havər,sak/ ▶*n.* a small, sturdy bag carried on the back or over the shoulder, esp. by soldiers and hikers.

hav·oc /'havək/ ▶*n.* widespread destruction. ■ great confusion or disorder: *schoolchildren wreaking havoc in the classroom.*

Pronunciation Key ə *ago,* up; ər *over,* fur; a *hat;* ā *ate;* ä *car;* cн *chin;* e *let;* ē *see;* ə(ə)r *air;* i *fit;* ī *by;* i(ə)r *ear;* ng *sing;* ō *go;* ô *law, for;* oi *toy;* ōō *good;* ōō *goo;* ou *out;* sн *she;* тн *thin;* тн *then;* (h)w *why;* zн *vision*

▶*v.* (**hav·ocked, hav·ocking**) [*tr.*] *archaic* lay waste to; devastate.
▶ □ **play havoc with** completely disrupt; cause serious damage to.

haw¹ /hô/ ▶*n.* the red fruit of the hawthorn. ▷Old English *haga,* of Germanic origin; probably related to *hedge* (compare with Dutch *haag* 'hedge').

haw² ▶*v.* see HEM AND HAW at HEM².

Ha·wai·ian /həˈwīən; -ˈwoi-ən/ ▶*n.* **1** a native or inhabitant of Hawaii. **2** the Austronesian language of Hawaii.
▶*adj.* of or relating to Hawaii, its people, or their language. ■ *Geol.* relating to or denoting a type of volcanic eruption in which fluid basaltic lava is produced, as is typical of volcanoes in Hawaii.

ha·wa·la /həˈwälə; -ˈvälə/ ▶*n.* a system or agency for transferring money traditionally used in the Muslim world, whereby the money is paid to an agent who then instructs a remote associate to pay the final recipient.

hawk¹ /hôk/ ▶*n.* **1** a diurnal bird of prey (*Accipiter* and other genera) with broad rounded wings and a long tail. Compare with FALCON. ■ a bird of prey related to the buteos. ■ *Falconry* any diurnal bird of prey used in falconry. **2** a person who advocates an aggressive or warlike policy, esp. in foreign affairs. Compare with DOVE¹ (sense 2).
▶*v.* [*intr.*] (of a person) hunt game with a trained hawk. —**hawk·ish** *adj.* —**hawk·ish·ly** *adv.* —**hawk·ish·ness** *n.*
▶ □ **have eyes like a hawk** miss nothing of what is going on around one. □ **watch someone like a hawk** keep a vigilant eye on someone.

hawk² ▶*v.* [*tr.*] carry around and offer (goods) for sale, typically advertising them by shouting.

hawk³ ▶*v.* [*intr.*] clear the throat noisily: *he hawked and spat into the flames.* ■ [*tr.*] (**hawk something up**) bring phlegm up from the throat.

hawk·er /ˈhôkər/ ▶*n.* a person who travels around selling goods, typically advertising them by shouting.

hawk-eyed ▶*adj.* having very good eyesight. ■ watching carefully; vigilant.

hawk moth (also **hawk·moth**) ▶*n.* a large swift-flying moth (family Sphingidae) with a stout body and narrow forewings, typically feeding on nectar while hovering. Also called SPHINX.

hawks·bill /ˈhôksˌbil/ (also **hawksbill turtle**) ▶*n.* a small tropical sea turtle (*Eretmochelys imbricata*) with hooked jaws and overlapping horny plates on the shell, extensively hunted as the traditional source of tortoiseshell.

hawk·weed /ˈhôkˌwēd/ ▶*n.* a widely distributed plant (genus *Hieracium*) of the daisy family, typically having small dandelionlike flowerheads.

haw·ser /ˈhôzər/ ▶*n.* a thick rope or cable for mooring or towing a ship.

haw·thorn /ˈhôˌTHôrn/ ▶*n.* a thorny shrub or tree (genus *Crataegus*) of the rose family, with white, pink, or red blossoms and small dark red fruits (haws). Native to north temperate regions, it is commonly used for hedges.

hay /hā/ ▶*n.* grass that has been mown and dried for use as fodder.
▶ □ **hit the hay** *inf.* go to bed.

hay fe·ver ▶*n.* an allergy caused by pollen or dust in which the mucous membranes of the eyes and nose are itchy and inflamed, causing a runny nose and watery eyes.

hay·mak·er /ˈhāˌmākər/ ▶*n.* *inf.* a forceful blow: *he caught him on the side of the head with a stinging haymaker.*

hay·rick /ˈhāˌrik/ ▶*n.* another term for HAYSTACK.

hay·seed /ˈhāˌsēd/ ▶*n.* **1** grass seed obtained from hay. **2** *inf.* a person from the country, esp. a simple, unsophisticated one.

hay·stack /ˈhāˌstak/ ▶*n.* a packed pile of hay, typically with a pointed or ridged top.

hay·wire /ˈhāˌwīr/ ▶*adj.* *inf.* erratic; out of control.

haz·ard /ˈhazərd/ ▶*n.* **1** a danger or risk: *the hazards of smoking.* ■ a potential source of danger: *a health hazard.* ■ a permanent feature of a golf course that presents an obstruction to playing a shot, such as a bunker or stream. **2** *poetic/lit.* chance; probability. **3** a gambling game using two dice, in which the chances are complicated by arbitrary rules.
▶*v.* [*tr.*] **1** venture to say (something): *he hazarded a guess.* **2** put (something) at risk of being lost: *business too risky to hazard money on.*

haz·ard·ous /ˈhazərdəs/ ▶*adj.* risky; dangerous. —**haz·ard·ous·ly** *adv.* —**haz·ard·ous·ness** *n.*

haze¹ /hāz/ ▶*n.* a slight obscuration of the lower atmosphere, typically caused by fine suspended particles. ■ a tenuous cloud of something such as vapor or smoke in the air. ■ *fig.* a state of mental obscurity or confusion: *an alcoholic haze.*

haze² ▶*v.* [*tr.*] force (a new or potential recruit to the military, a college

fraternity, etc.) to perform strenuous, humiliating, or dangerous tasks.

ha·zel /ˈhāzəl/ ▶*n.* **1** a temperate shrub or small tree (genus *Corylus*) of the birch family, bearing round hard-shelled edible nuts in autumn. **2** a reddish-brown or greenish-brown color, esp. of someone's eyes. ▷Old English *hæsel,* related to German *Hasel,* Latin *corylus.*

ha·zel·nut /ˈhāzəlˌnət/ ▶*n.* a round brown hard-shelled nut that is the edible fruit of the hazel.

ha·zy /ˈhāzē/ ▶*adj.* (**ha·zi·er, ha·zi·est**) covered by a haze. ■ vague, indistinct, or ill-defined. —**ha·zi·ly** /-zilē/ *adv.* —**ha·zi·ness** *n.*

Hb ▶*symb.* hemoglobin.

H-bomb ▶*n.* another term for HYDROGEN BOMB.

HDTV ▶*abbr.* high-definition television, using more lines per frame to give a sharper image than a conventional television.

He ▶*symb.* the chemical element helium.

he /hē/ ▶*pron.* [*third person sing.*] used to refer to a man, boy, or male animal previously mentioned or easily identified: *he was the perfect gentleman.* ■ used to refer to a person or animal of unspecified sex (in modern use, now chiefly replaced by "he or she" or "they": *every child needs to know that he is loved.* ■ any person (in modern use, now chiefly replaced by "anyone" or "the person"): *he who is silent consents.*
▶*n.* a male; a man: *is that a he or a she?* ■ [in *comb.*] male: *a he-goat.*

head /hed/ ▶*n.* **1** the upper part of the human body, or the front or upper part of the body of an animal, typically separated from the rest of the body by a neck, and containing the brain, mouth, and sense organs. ■ the head regarded as the location of intellect, imagination, and memory. ■ (**head for**) an aptitude for or tolerance of: *she had a good head for business.* ■ the height or length of a head as a measure: *half a head taller than he was.* ■ [usu. in *comb.*] a habitual user of an illicit drug. ■ [usu. in *comb.*] a fan or enthusiast: *Deadheads.* ■ (**heads**) the obverse side of a coin (used when tossing a coin): *heads or tails?* **2** a thing having the appearance of a head either in form or in relation to a whole, in particular: ■ the cutting, striking, or operational end of a tool, weapon, or mechanism. ■ the flattened or knobbed end of a nail, pin, screw, or match. ■ the ornamented top of a pillar or column. ■ a compact mass of leaves or flowers at the top of a stem. ■ the edible leafy part at the top of the stem of such green vegetables as cabbage and lettuce. ■ one saleable unit of certain vegetables, such as cabbage or cauliflower. **3** the front, forward, or upper part or end of something, in particular: ■ the upper end of a table or bed. ■ the flat end of a cask or drum. ■ the front of a line or procession. ■ the top of a page. ■ short for HEADLINE. ■ the top of a flight of stairs or steps. ■ the source of a river or stream. ■ the end of a lake or inlet at which a river enters. ■ the top of a ship's mast. ■ the top of a sail. ■ the bows of a ship. ■ the fully developed top of a pimple, boil, or abscess. ■ the foam on top of a glass of beer, or the cream on the top of milk. **4** a person in charge of something; a director or leader. **5** *Gram.* the word that governs all the other words in a phrase in which it is used, having the same grammatical function as the whole phrase. **6** a person considered as a numerical unit: *they paid fifty dollars a head.* ■ [treated as *pl.*] a number of cattle or game as specified. **7** a component in an audio, video, or information system by which information is transferred from an electrical signal to the recording medium, or vice versa. **8** a body of water kept at a particular height in order to provide a supply at sufficient pressure: *an 8 m head of water in the shafts.* ■ the pressure exerted by such water or by a confined body of steam. **9** *Naut., slang* a toilet, esp. on a boat or ship.
▶*adj.* chief; principal.
▶*v.* [*tr.*] **1** be in the leading position on: *the procession was headed by the two servants.* ■ be in charge of: *an organizational unit headed by a line manager.* **2** (usu. **be headed**) give a title or caption to: *an article headed "The Protection of Human Life."* **3** [*intr.*] (also **be headed**) move in a specified direction. ■ (**head for**) appear to be moving inevitably toward (something, esp. something undesirable): *the company seems to be heading for disaster.* ■ [*tr.*] direct or steer in a specified direction. **4** *Soccer* shoot or pass (the ball) with the head: *a corner kick that he headed into the net.* **5** lop off the upper part or branches of (a plant or tree). **6** [*intr.*] (of a lettuce or cabbage) form a head.
▶*phrasal v.* □ **head someone/something off** intercept and turn aside. ■ forestall: *they headed off a fight.* □ **head up** *Sailing* steer toward the wind. —**head·ed** *adj.* —**head·less** *adj.*
▶ □ **be hanging over someone's head** (of something unpleasant) threaten to affect someone at any moment. □ **be on someone's (own) head** be someone's sole responsibility. □ **come to a head** reach a crisis: *the violence came to a head with the deaths of six youths.* ■ suppurate; fester. □ **from head to toe** (or **foot**) all over one's body. □ **go to someone's head** make someone dizzy or slightly drunk. ■ (of success) make

someone conceited. □ **get something into one's** (or **someone's**) **head** come or cause (someone) to realize or understand. □ —— **one's head off** talk, laugh, etc., unrestrainedly: *singing his head off.* □ **head over heels 1** turning over completely in forward motion, as in a somersault. **2** (also **head over heels in love**) madly in love. □ **a head start** an advantage granted or gained at the beginning of something: *our fine traditions give us a head start on the competition.* □ **head to head** in open, direct conflict or competition. □ **in one's head** by mental process without use of physical aids: *the piece he'd already written in his head.* □ **keep one's head** remain calm. □ **keep one's head above water** avoid succumbing to difficulties, typically debt. □ **lose one's head** lose self-control. □ **make head or tail of** (or **heads or tails**) understand at all: *we couldn't make head or tail of his answer.* □ **off** (or **out of**) **one's head** *inf.* crazy. ■ extremely drunk or severely under the influence of drugs. □ **off the top of one's head** without careful thought or investigation. □ **over someone's head 1** (also **above someone's head**) beyond someone's ability to understand. **2** without someone's knowledge or involvement, esp. when they have a right to it. ■ with disregard for someone else's (stronger) claim: *his promotion over the heads of more senior colleagues.* □ **put their** (or **our** or **your**) **heads together** consult and work together. □ **turn someone's head** make someone conceited. □ **turn heads** attract a great deal of attention or interest.

head·ache /'hed,āk/ ▶*n.* a continuous pain in the head. ■ *inf.* a thing or person that causes worry or trouble; a problem. —**head·ach·y** /-,āke/ *adj.*

head·band /'hed,band/ ▶*n.* a band of fabric worn around the head as a decoration or to keep the hair or perspiration off the face.

head·board /'hed,bôrd/ ▶*n.* an upright panel forming or placed behind the head of a bed.

head count ▶*n.* an instance of counting the number of people present. ■ a total number of people, esp. the number of people employed in a particular organization.

head·dress /'hed,dres/ ▶*n.* an ornamental covering or band for the head, esp. one worn on ceremonial occasions.

head·er /'hedər/ ▶*n.* **1** *Soccer* a shot or pass made with the head. **2** *inf.* a headlong fall or dive. **3** a brick or stone laid at right angles to the face of a wall. **4** a line or block of text appearing at the top of each page of a book or document. Compare with FOOTER (sense 2). **5** a beam crossing and supporting the ends of joists, studs, or rafters. **6** (also **header tank**) a raised tank of water maintaining pressure in a plumbing system.

head·gear /'hed,gi(ə)r/ ▶*n.* hats, helmets, and other items worn on the head. ■ orthodontic equipment worn on the head and attached to braces on the teeth. ■ the parts of a harness around a horse's head.

head·hunt·er /'hed,həntər/ ▶*n.* **1** a person who identifies and approaches suitable candidates employed elsewhere to fill business positions. ■ a member of a society that collects the heads of dead enemies or animals as trophies. —**head·hunt** *v.* —**head·hunt·ing** /-,həntiNG/ *n.*

head·ing /'hediNG/ ▶*n.* **1** a title at the head of a page or section of a book. ■ a division or section of a subject; a class or category. **2** a direction or bearing: *he crawled on a heading of 90 degrees.* ■ a horizontal passage made in preparation for building a tunnel. ■ *Mining* a horizontal or inclined passage following a mineral vein or coal seam.

head·land /'hedlənd; 'hed,land/ ▶*n.* **1** a narrow piece of land that projects from a coastline into the sea. **2** a strip of land left unplowed at the end of a field.

head·light /'hed,līt/ (also **head·lamp**) ▶*n.* a powerful light at the front of a motor vehicle or railroad engine.

head·line /'hed,līn/ ▶*n.* a heading at the top of an article or page in a newspaper or magazine. ■ **(the headlines)** the most important items of news in a newspaper or in a broadcast news bulletin. ▶*v.* **1** [*tr.*] provide with a headline. **2** [*tr.*] appear as the star performer at (a concert).

head·lin·er /'hed,līnər/ ▶*n.* a performer or act that is promoted as the star attraction on a program or advertisement.

head·lock /'hed,läk/ ▶*n.* a method of restraining someone by holding an arm firmly around their head, esp. as a hold in wrestling.

head·long /'hed,lôNG; -,läNG/ ▶*adv. & adj.* **1** [as *adv.*] with the head foremost. **2** in a rush; with reckless haste: *a headlong dash through the house.*

head·mas·ter /'hed,mastər/ ▶*n.* (esp. in private schools) the man in charge of a school; the principal. —**head·mas·ter·ly** *adj.*

head·mis·tress /'hed,mistris/ ▶*n.* (esp. in private schools) the woman in charge of a school; the principal.

head-on ▶*adj. & adv.* **1** with or involving the front of a vehicle: *a head-*

on collision | [as *adv.*] *they hit a bus head-on.* **2** with or involving direct confrontation: *trying to avoid a head-on clash.*

head·phones /'hed,fōnz/ ▶*pl. n.* a pair of earphones typically joined by a band placed over the head, for listening to audio signals such as music or speech.

head·piece /'hed,pēs/ ▶*n.* **1** a device worn on the head as an ornament or to serve a function: *her headpiece was a wreath of silk flowers* | *headpieces for carrying water.* **2** an illustration or ornamental motif printed at the head of a chapter in a book. **3** the part of a halter or bridle that fits over the top of a horse's head behind the ears.

headphones

head·quar·ters /'hed,kwôrtərz/ ▶*n.* [treated as *sing.* or *pl.*] the premises occupied by a military commander and the commander's staff. ■ the place or building serving as the managerial and administrative center of an organization.

head·rest /'hed,rest/ ▶*n.* a padded part extending from or fixed to the back of a seat or chair, designed to support the head.

head·room /'hed,rōōm; -,rŏŏm/ ▶*n.* the space above a driver's or passenger's head in a vehicle. ■ the space or clearance between the top of a vehicle and the underside of a bridge or other structure above it.

head·sail /'hed,sāl/ ▶*n.* a sail on a ship's foremast or bowsprit.

head·set /'hed,set/ ▶*n.* a set of headphones, typically with a microphone attached, used esp. in telephone and radio communication.

head·shrink·er /'hed,sHriNGkər/ ▶*n.* *hist. inf.* a clinical psychiatrist, psychologist, or psychotherapist.

head·stall /'hed,stôl/ ▶*n.* the part of a bridle or halter that fits around a horse's head.

head·stone /'hed,stōn/ ▶*n.* a slab of stone set up at the head of a grave, typically inscribed with the name of the dead person.

head·strong /'hed,strôNG/ ▶*adj.* self-willed and obstinate.

head·wa·ter /'hed,wôtər; -,wätər/ ▶*n.* (usu. **headwaters**) a tributary stream of a river close to or forming part of its source.

head·way /'hed,wā/ ▶*n.* **1** forward movement or progress: *they appear to be making headway.* **2** the average interval of time between vehicles moving in the same direction on the same route.

head·wind /'hed,wind/ ▶*n.* a wind blowing from directly in front, opposing forward motion.

head·word /'hed,wərd/ ▶*n.* a word that begins a separate entry in a reference work such as a dictionary.

head·y /'hedē/ ▶*adj.* (**head·i·er, head·i·est**) (of liquor) potent; intoxicating. ■ having a strong or exhilarating effect: *the heady days of the birth of the women's movement.* —**head·i·ly** /'hedl-ē/ *adv.* —**head·i·ness** *n.*

heal /hēl/ ▶*v.* [*tr.*] (of a person or treatment) cause (a wound, injury, or person) to become sound or healthy again. ■ [*intr.*] become sound or healthy again. ■ alleviate (a person's distress or anguish): *time can heal the pain of grief.* ■ correct or put right (an undesirable situation): *the rift between them was never really healed.* —**heal·a·ble** *adj.* —**heal·er** *n.*

health /helTH/ ▶*n.* the state of being free from illness or injury. ■ a person's mental or physical condition: *bad health forced him to retire.* ■ *fig.* soundness, esp. financial or moral. ■ used to express friendly feelings toward one's companions before drinking.

health·care /'helTH,ke(ə)r/ (also **health care**) ▶*n.* the maintenance and improvement of physical and mental health, esp. through the provision of medical services.

health food ▶*n.* natural food that is thought to have health-giving qualities.

health·ful /'helTHfəl/ ▶*adj.* having or conducive to good health. —**health·ful·ly** *adv.* —**health·ful·ness** *n.*

health main·te·nance or·ga·ni·za·tion (abbr.: **HMO**) ▶*n.* a health insurance organization to which subscribers pay a predetermined fee in return for a range of medical services from physicians and healthcare workers registered with the organization.

health sav·ings ac·count ▶*n.* a savings account used in conjunction with a high-deductible health insurance policy that allows users to save money tax-free against medical expenses. (abbr. **HSA**)

health·y /'helTHē/ ▶*adj.* (**health·i·er, health·i·est**) in good health. ■ (of a part of the body) not diseased. ■ indicative of, conducive to, or promoting good health. ■ (of a person's attitude) sensible and well balanced. ■ *fig.* in a good condition. ■ desirable; beneficial. ■ of a satisfactory size or amount. —**health·i·ly** /ˈhelтнəlē/ *adv.* —**health·i·ness** *n.*

heap /hēp/ ▶ *n.* an untidy collection of things piled up haphazardly. ■ a mound or pile of a particular substance. ■ *inf.* an untidy or dilapidated place or vehicle. ■ (**a heap of/heaps of**) *inf.* a large amount or number of something: *we have heaps of room.*
▶ *v.* [*tr.*] put in a pile or mound. ■ (**heap something with**) load something copiously with: *he heaped his plate with rice.* ■ (**heap something on/upon**) bestow praise, abuse, or criticism liberally on. ■ [*intr.*] form a heap: *clouds heaped higher in the west.*
▶ □ **at the top** (or **bottom**) **of the heap** (of a person) at the highest (or lowest) point of a society or organization. □ **in a heap** (of a person) with the body completely limp: *he landed in a heap at the bottom of the stairs.*

hear /hi(ə)r/ ▶ *v.* (*past* **heard** /hərd/) [*tr.*] perceive with the ear the sound made by (someone or something). [*intr.*] *he did not hear very well.* ■ be told or informed of: *have you heard the news?* | [*intr.*] *I was shocked to hear of her death.* ■ [*intr.*] (**have heard of**) be aware of; know of the existence of. ■ [*intr.*] (**hear from**) be contacted by (someone), esp. by letter or telephone. ■ listen or pay attention to: *she just doesn't hear what I'm telling her.* ■ (**hear someone out**) listen to all that someone has to say. ■ [*intr.*] (**will/would not hear of**) will or would not allow or agree to. ■ *Law* listen to and judge (a case or plaintiff): *an all-woman jury heard the case.* ■ listen to and grant (a prayer). —**hear·a·ble** *adj.* —**hear·er** *n.*
▶ □ **hear! hear!** used to express one's wholehearted agreement, esp. with something said in a speech.

hear·ing /ˈhi(ə)riNG/ ▶ *n.* **1** the faculty of perceiving sounds. ■ the range within which sounds may be heard; earshot: *she had moved out of hearing.* **2** an opportunity to state one's case: *I think I had a fair hearing.* ■ *Law* an act of listening to evidence in a court of law or before an official, esp. a trial before a judge without a jury.

hear·ing aid ▶ *n.* a small device that fits in or on the ear, worn by a partially deaf person to amplify sound.

hark·en /ˈhärkən/ (also **hark·en**) ▶ *v.* [*intr.*] *archaic* listen: *hearken to Thomas's words of wisdom.*
▶ *phrasal v.* □ **hearken back** another way of saying HARK BACK (see HARK).

hear·say /ˈhi(ə)rˌsā/ ▶ *n.* information received from other people that one cannot adequately substantiate; rumor. ■ *Law* the report of another person's words by a witness, usually disallowed as evidence in a court of law: *hearsay evidence.*

hearse /hərs/ ▶ *n.* a vehicle for conveying the coffin at a funeral.

heart /härt/ ▶ *n.* **1** a hollow muscular organ that pumps the blood through the circulatory system by rhythmic contraction and dilation. The human heart has two atria and two ventricles. ■ the region of the chest above the heart: *hand on heart for the Pledge of Allegiance.* ■ the heart regarded as the center of a person's thoughts and emotions, esp. love or compassion: *he poured out his heart* | *he has no heart.* ■ one's mood or feeling: *a change of heart.* ■ courage or enthusiasm: *they may lose heart as the work mounts up* | *Mary took heart from the encouragement.* **2** the central or innermost part of something: *right in the heart of the city.* ■ the vital part or essence: *the heart of the matter.* ■ the close compact head of a cabbage or lettuce. **3** a conventional representation of a heart with two equal curves meeting at a point at the bottom and a cusp at the top. ■ (**hearts**) one of the four suits in a conventional pack of playing cards, denoted by a red figure of such a shape. ■ a card of this suit. ■ (**hearts**) a card game similar to whist, in which players attempt to avoid taking tricks containing a card of this suit. ▷Old English *heorte,* of Germanic origin; related to Dutch *hart* and German *Herz,* from an Indo-European root shared by Latin *cor, cord-* and Greek *kēr, kardia.* —**heart·ed** *adj.* [in *comb.*] *a generous-hearted woman.*
▶ □ **after one's own heart** of the type that one likes or understands best; sharing one's tastes. □ **at heart** in one's real nature, in contrast to how one may appear: *he's a good guy at heart.* □ **break someone's heart** overwhelm someone with sadness. □ **by heart** from memory. □ **from the** (**bottom of one's**) **heart** with sincere feeling: *their warmth and hospitality is right from the heart.* □ **have a heart** [often in *imper.*] be merciful; show pity. □ **have a heart of gold** have a generous nature. □ **have the heart to do something** be insensitive or hard-hearted enough to do something: *I don't have the heart to tell her.* □ **have one's heart in the right place** be sincere or well intentioned. □ **one's heart's desire** a person or thing that one greatly wishes for. □ **take something to heart** take criticism seriously and be affected or upset by it. □ **wear one's heart on one's sleeve** make one's feelings apparent. □ **with all one's heart** (or **one's whole heart**) sincerely; completely.

heart·ache /ˈhärtˌāk/ ▶ *n.* emotional anguish or grief, typically caused by the loss or absence of someone loved.

heart at·tack ▶ *n.* a sudden and sometimes fatal occurrence of coronary thrombosis, typically resulting in the death of part of a heart muscle.

heart·beat /ˈhärtˌbēt/ ▶ *n.* the pulsation of the heart. ■ (usu. **heartbeats**) a single pulsation of the heart. ■ *fig.* a person or thing providing or representing an animating or vital unifying force: *conflict is the heartbeat of fiction.*
▶ □ **a heartbeat away from** very close to; on the verge of.

heart·break /ˈhärtˌbrāk/ ▶ *n.* overwhelming distress.

heart·break·er /ˈhärtˌbrākər/ ▶ *n.* **1** a person who is very attractive but who is irresponsible in emotional relationships. **2** a story or event that causes overwhelming distress. —**heart·break·ing** *adj.*

heart·burn /ˈhärtˌbərn/ ▶ *n.* a form of indigestion felt as a burning sensation in the chest, caused by acid regurgitation into the esophagus.

heart·en /ˈhärtn/ ▶ *v.* [*tr.*] (usu. **be heartened**) make more cheerful or confident. —**heart·en·ing·ly** *adv.*

heart·felt /ˈhärtˌfelt/ ▶ *adj.* (of a feeling or its expression) sincere; deeply and strongly felt.

hearth /härтн/ ▶ *n.* the floor of a fireplace. ■ the area in front of a fireplace. ■ used as a symbol of one's home: *he left hearth and home.* ■ the base or lower part of a furnace, where molten metal collects.

hearth·rug /ˈhärтнˌrəg/ ▶ *n.* a rug laid in front of a fireplace to protect the carpet or floor.

heart·i·ly /ˈhärtl-ē/ ▶ *adv.* **1** in a hearty manner. **2** very; to a great degree (esp. with reference to personal feelings): *they were heartily sick of the whole subject.*

heart·land /ˈhärtˌland/ ▶ *n.* the central or most important part of a country, area, or field of activity. ■ the center of support for a belief or movement: *the heartland of the rebel cause.* ■ (**the heartland**) the central part of the U.S.; the Midwest.

heart·less /ˈhärtlis/ ▶ *adj.* displaying a complete lack of feeling or consideration. —**heart·less·ly** *adv.* —**heart·less·ness** *n.*

heart-rend·ing ▶ *adj.* (of a story or event) causing great sadness or distress. —**heart-rend·ing·ly** *adv.*

heart·sick /ˈhärtˌsik/ ▶ *adj.* despondent, typically from grief or loss of love. —**heart·sick·ness** *n.*

heart·throb /ˈhärtˌтнräb/ ▶ *n.* *inf.* a man, typically a celebrity, whose good looks excite immature romantic feelings in women.

heart-to-heart ▶ *adj.* (of a conversation) candid and intimate.
▶ *n.* such a conversation: *engrossed in a heart-to-heart.*

heart·warm·ing /ˈhärtˌwôrmiNG/ ▶ *adj.* emotionally rewarding or uplifting.

heart·wood /ˈhärtˌwo͝od/ ▶ *n.* the dense inner part of a tree trunk, yielding the hardest timber.

heart·y /ˈhärtē/ ▶ *adj.* (**heart·i·er, heart·i·est**) **1** (of a person or their behavior) loudly vigorous and cheerful. ■ (of a feeling or an opinion) heartfelt: *hearty congratulations.* ■ (of a person) strong and healthy. **2** (of food) wholesome and substantial. ■ (of a person's appetite) robust and healthy.
▶ *n. Brit., inf.* **1** a vigorously cheerful and sporty person. **2** (usu. **hearties**) a form of address ascribed to sailors. —**heart·i·ness** *n.*

heat /hēt/ ▶ *n.* **1** the quality of being hot; high temperature. ■ hot weather conditions. ■ a source or level of heat for cooking: *remove from the heat and beat in the butter.* ■ a spicy quality in food that produces a burning sensation in the mouth: *chili peppers add taste and heat to food.* ■ *Physics* heat seen as a form of energy arising from the random motion of the molecules of bodies, which may be transferred by conduction, convection, or radiation. ■ *technical* the amount of heat that is needed to cause a specific process or is evolved in such a process: *the heat of formation.* **2** intensity of feeling, esp. of anger or excitement: *words few men would dare use to another, even in the heat of anger.* ■ (**the heat**) *inf.* intensive and unwelcome pressure or criticism, esp. from the authorities. **3** a preliminary round in a race or contest.
▶ *v.* make or become hot or warm. ■ [*intr.*] (**heat up**) (of a person) become excited or impassioned. ■ [*intr.*] (**heat up**) become more intense and exciting: *the action really begins to heat up.* ■ [*tr.*] *archaic* inflame; excite.
▶ □ **in the heat of the moment** while temporarily angry, excited, or engrossed, and without stopping for thought. □ **in heat** (of a female mammal) in the receptive period of the sexual cycle; in estrus.

heat·ed /ˈhētid/ ▶ *adj.* **1** made warm or hot. **2** inflamed with passion or conviction: *she had a heated argument with an official.* —**heat·ed·ly** *adv.*

heat·er /ˈhētər/ ▶ *n.* **1** a person or thing that heats, in particular a device for warming the air or water. **2** *Baseball* a fastball. **3** *inf., dated* a gun.

heat ex·haus·tion ▶ *n.* a condition caused by prolonged exposure to heat during activity and characterized by weakness, profuse sweating, dizziness, and nausea. Also called HEAT PROSTRATION.

heath /hēтн/ ▶n. **1** an area of open uncultivated land, esp. in Britain, with characteristic vegetation of heather, gorse, and coarse grasses. ■ *Ecol.* vegetation dominated by dwarf shrubs of the heath family. **2** a dwarf shrub (*Erica* and related genera) with small leathery leaves and small pink or purple bell-shaped flowers, characteristic of heathland and moorland. The **heath family** (Ericaceae) also includes azalea, blueberry, and cranberry. —**heath·y** adj.

heath·en /'hēтнən/ ▶n. chiefly derog. a person who does not belong to a widely held religion (esp. one who is not a Christian, Jew, or Muslim) as regarded by those who do. ■ a follower of a polytheistic religion; a pagan. ■ **(the heathen)** heathen people collectively, esp. (in biblical use) those who did not worship the God of Israel. ■ *inf.* an unenlightened person; a person regarded as lacking culture or moral principles. ▶adj. of or relating to heathens.

heath·er /'heтнər/ ▶n. a purple-flowered Eurasian heath (*Calluna vulgaris*) that grows abundantly on moorland and heathland. ■ *inf.* any similar plant of this family; a heath.

heath·land /'hēтн,land/ ▶n. (also **heath·lands**) an extensive area of heath: *1,000 acres of heathland.*

heat·ing /'hētiNG/ ▶n. the imparting or generation of heat. ■ equipment or devices used to provide heat, esp. to a building: *baseboard heating.*

heat light·ning ▶n. a flash or flashes of light seen near the horizon, esp. on warm evenings, believed to be the reflection of distant lightning on high clouds.

heat·proof /'hēt,proōf/ ▶adj. able to resist great heat.

heat pros·tra·tion ▶n. another term for HEAT EXHAUSTION.

heat-seek·ing /'hēt,sēkiNG/ ▶adj. (of a missile) able to detect and home in on infrared radiation emitted by a target, such as the exhaust vent of a jet aircraft.

heat·stroke /'hēt,strōk/ ▶n. a condition marked by fever and often by unconsciousness, caused by failure of the body's temperature-regulating mechanism when exposed to excessively high temperatures.

heat wave ▶n. a prolonged period of abnormally hot weather.

heave /hēv/ ▶v. (past **heaved** or chiefly Naut. **hove** /hōv/) **1** [tr.] lift or haul (a heavy thing) with great effort. ■ *Naut.* pull, raise, or move (a boat or ship) by hauling on a rope or ropes. ■ *inf.* throw (something heavy). **2** [tr.] produce (a sigh). **3** [intr.] rise and fall rhythmically or spasmodically: *his shoulders heaved as he panted.* ■ make an effort to vomit; retch. ▶phrasal v. □ **heave to** Naut. (of a boat or ship) come to a stop, esp. by turning across the wind leaving the headsail backed: *he hove to and dropped anchor.* ▶n. **1** an act of heaving, esp. a strong pull. **2** (**the heaves**) inf. a case of retching or vomiting. **3** (**heaves**) a disease of horses, with labored breathing. —**heav·er** n.

heave-ho ▶interj. a cry emitted when doing in unison actions that take physical effort. ▶n. such an exclamation. ■ **(the heave-ho)** expulsion or elimination from an institution, association, or contest: *who'll get the heave-ho?*

heav·en /'hevən/ ▶n. **1** a place regarded in various religions as the abode of God (or the gods) and the angels, and of the good after death, often traditionally depicted as being above the sky. ■ God (or the gods). ■ *Theol.* a state of being eternally in the presence of God after death. ■ *inf.* a place, state, or experience of supreme bliss. ■ used in various exclamations as a substitute for "God": *Heaven knows!* **2** (often **heavens**) poetic/lit. the sky, esp. perceived as a vault in which the sun, moon, stars, and planets are situated: *Galileo used a telescope to observe the heavens.* —**heav·en·ward** /-wərd/ adj. & adv. —**heav·en·wards** /-wərdz/ adv. ▶ □ **in seventh heaven** in a state of ecstasy. □ **move heaven and earth to do something** make extraordinary efforts to do a specified thing. □ **stink** (or **smell**) **to high heaven** have a very strong and unpleasant odor.

heav·en·ly /'hevnlē/ ▶adj. **1** of heaven; divine. **2** of the heavens or sky. **3** inf. very pleasing; wonderful. —**heav·en·li·ness** n.

heav·en·ly bod·y ▶n. a planet, star, or other celestial body.

heav·en-sent ▶adj. (of an event or opportunity) occurring at a favorable time; opportune.

heav·y /'hevē/ ▶adj. (**heav·i·er**, **heav·i·est**) **1** of great weight; difficult to lift or move. ■ used in questions about weight: *how heavy is it?* ■ (of a class of thing) above the average weight; large of its kind. ■ weighed down; full of something: *branches heavy with blossoms.* ■ (of a person's head or eyes) feeling weighed down by weariness. ■ *Physics* of or containing atoms of an isotope of greater than the usual mass. See also HEAVY WATER. **2** of great density; thick or substantial: *heavy gray cloud.* ■ (of food or a meal) hard to digest; too filling. ■ (of ground or soil) hard to travel over or work with because muddy or full of clay. ■ not

delicate or graceful; coarse: *he had a big mustache and heavy features.* ■ moving slowly or with difficulty. ■ (of a smell) overpowering. ■ (of the sky) full of dark clouds; oppressive. **3** of more than the usual size, amount, or force: *traffic was heavy.* ■ doing something to excess: *a heavy smoker.* ■ (**heavy on**) using a lot of: *stories heavy on melodrama.* **4** striking or falling with force: *a heavy blow to the head.* ■ causing a strong impact: *a heavy fall.* ■ (of music, esp. rock) having a strong bass component and a forceful rhythm. **5** needing much physical effort: *heavy work.* ■ mentally oppressive; hard to endure. ■ important or serious: *a heavy discussion.* ■ (of a literary work) hard to read or understand because overly serious or difficult. ■ feeling or expressing grief: *a heavy heart.* ■ *inf.* (of a situation) serious and hard to deal with: *things were getting pretty heavy.* ■ *inf.* (of a person) strict or harsh: *the police were really getting heavy.* ▶n. (pl. **heav·ies**) **1** a large, strong man, esp. one hired for protection: *an important person: music business heavies.* **2** a villainous role or actor in a book, movie, etc.: *we've got to have this guy play the heavy.* ▶adv. heavily: *his words hung heavy in the air* —**heav·i·ly** /'hevəlē/ adv. —**heav·i·ness** n. —**heav·y·ish** adj.

heav·y-du·ty ▶adj. (of material or an article) designed to withstand the stresses of demanding use. ■ *inf.* intense, important, or abundant.

heav·y-foot·ed ▶adj. slow and laborious in movement.

heav·y go·ing ▶n. a person or situation that is difficult or boring.

heav·y-hand·ed ▶adj. clumsy or insensitive. ■ overly forceful or oppressive: *the government's most heavy-handed efforts to muzzle social protest.* —**heav·y-hand·ed·ly** adv. —**heav·y-hand·ed·ness** n.

heav·y-heart·ed ▶adj. feeling depressed or melancholy.

heav·y in·dus·try ▶n. the manufacture of large, heavy articles and materials in bulk.

heav·y met·al ▶n. **1** a type of highly amplified harsh-sounding rock music with a strong beat, characteristically using violent or fantastic imagery. **2** a metal of relatively high density, or of high atomic weight.

heav·y wa·ter ▶n. water in which the hydrogen in the molecules is partly or wholly replaced by the isotope deuterium, used esp. as a moderator in nuclear reactors.

heav·y·weight /'hevē,wāt/ ▶n. **1** a weight in boxing and other sports, typically the heaviest category. In the amateur boxing scale it ranges from 178 to 200 pounds (81 to 91 kg). ■ a boxer or other competitor of this weight. **2** a person or thing of above-average weight. ■ a person of influence or importance, esp. in a particular sphere: *a political heavyweight.* ▶adj. of above-average weight. ■ serious, important, or influential.

He·brew /'hēbrōō/ ▶n. **1** a member of an ancient people living in what is now Israel and Palestine and, according to biblical tradition, descended from the patriarch Jacob, grandson of Abraham. After the Exodus (c.1300 BC) they established the kingdoms of Israel and Judah, and their scriptures and traditions form the basis of the Jewish religion. ■ old-fashioned and sometimes offensive term for JEW. **2** the Semitic language of this people, in its ancient or modern form. ▶adj. **1** of the Hebrews or the Jews. **2** of or in Hebrew.

heck /hek/ ▶interj. A euphemism for HELL used to express surprise, frustration, or dismay: *oh heck, I can't for the life of me remember.* ■ **(the heck)** used for emphasis in questions and exclamations: *what the heck's the matter?* ▶ □ **a heck of a** —— used for emphasis in various statements or exclamations: *it was a heck of a lot of money.*

heck·le /'hekəl/ ▶v. [tr.] (often **be heckled**) interrupt (a public speaker) with derisive or aggressive comments or abuse. —**heck·ler** /'hek(ə)lər/ n.

hec·tare /'hek,te(ə)r/ (abbr.: **ha**) ▶n. a metric unit of square measure, equal to 100 ares (2.471 acres or 10,000 square meters). —**hec·tar·age** /'hektərij/ n.

hec·tic /'hektik/ ▶adj. full of incessant or frantic activity. ▷late Middle English *etik*, via Old French from late Latin *hecticus*, from Greek *hektikos* 'habitual,' from *hexis* 'habit, state of mind or body.' The original specific association with the symptoms of tuberculosis (*hectic fever*) gave rise to the early 20th-cent. sense 'characterized by feverish activity.' —**hec·ti·cal·ly** /-tik(ə)lē/ adv.

hec·to·gram /'hektə,gram/ (Brit. also **hec·to·gramme**) (abbr.: **hg**) ▶n. a metric unit of mass equal to one hundred grams.

hec·to·li·ter /'hektə,lētər/ (Brit. **hec·to·li·tre**) (abbr.: **hl**) ▶n. a metric unit of capacity equal to one hundred liters, used esp. for wine, beer, grain, and other agricultural produce.

hec·to·me·ter /ˈhektəˌmētər/ (Brit. **hec·to·me·tre**) (abbr.: **hm**) ▸*n.* a metric unit of length equal to one hundred meters.

hec·tor /ˈhektər/ ▸*v.* [tr.] talk to (someone) in a bullying way: [as *adj.*] (**hectoring**) *a brusque, hectoring manner.* —**hec·tor·ing·ly** /ˈhekt(ə)riNGlē/ *adv.*

he'd /hēd/ ▸*contr. of* ■ he had. ■ he would.

hedge /hej/ ▸*n.* a fence or boundary formed by closely growing bushes or shrubs. ■ a contract entered into or asset held as a protection against possible financial loss. ■ a word or phrase used to allow for additional possibilities or to avoid overprecise commitment, for example, *etc.*, *often, usually,* or *sometimes.*
▸*v.* [tr.] **1** surround or bound with a hedge. ■ (**hedge something in**) enclose. **2** limit or qualify (something) by conditions or exceptions: *experts usually hedge their predictions.* ■ [intr.] avoid making a definite decision, statement, or commitment. **3** protect (one's investment or an investor) against loss by making balancing or compensating contracts or transactions. —**hedg·er** *n.*
▸ □ **hedge one's bets** avoid committing oneself when faced with a difficult choice.

hedge·hog /ˈhej.hôg; ˈhej.häg/ ▸*n.* a nocturnal insectivorous Old World mammal (family Erinaceidae) with a spiny coat and short legs, able to roll itself into a ball for defense. ■ any other animal covered with spines, esp. a porcupine.

hedge·row /ˈhej.rō/ ▸*n.* a hedge of wild shrubs and trees, typically bordering a road or field.

he·don·ism /ˈhēdnˌizəm/ ▸*n.* the pursuit of pleasure; sensual self-indulgence. ■ the ethical theory that pleasure (in the sense of the satisfaction of desires) is the highest good and proper aim of human life. —**he·don·ist** *n.* —**he·don·is·tic** /ˌhēdnˈistik/ *adj.* —**he·don·is·ti·cal·ly** /ˌhēdnˈistik(ə)lē/ *adv.*

hee·bie-jee·bies /ˈhēbē ˈjēbēz/ ▸*pl. n.* (**the heebie-jeebies**) *inf.* a state of nervous fear or anxiety.

heed /hēd/ ▸*v.* [tr.] pay attention to; take notice of: *he should have heeded the warnings.* —**heed·ful** *adj.* —**heed·less** *adj.*
▸*n.* careful attention: *he paid no heed* | *take heed of the suggestions.*

hee-haw /ˈhē ˌhô/ ▸*n.* the loud, harsh cry of a donkey or mule. ■ [as *adj.*] *inf.* relating to or denoting unsophisticated rural humor and attitudes.
▸*v.* [intr.] make the loud, harsh cry of a donkey or mule.

heel[1] /hēl/ ▸*n.* **1** the back part of the foot below the ankle. ■ a corresponding part of the foot in vertebrate animals. ■ the part of the palm of the hand next to the wrist. ■ the part of a shoe or boot supporting the heel. ■ the part of a sock covering the heel. ■ (**heels**) high-heeled shoes. **2** a thing resembling a heel in form or position, in particular: ■ the end of a violin bow at which it is held. ■ the part of the head of a golf club nearest the shaft. ■ a crusty end of a loaf of bread, or the rind of a cheese. ■ a piece of the main stem of a plant left attached to the base of a cutting. **3** *inf.* an inconsiderate or untrustworthy person. **4** [as *interj.*] a command to a dog to walk close behind its owner.
▸*v.* [tr.] **1** fit or renew a heel on (a shoe or boot). **2** (of a dog) follow closely behind its owner. **3** [intr.] touch the ground with the heel when dancing. —**heeled** /hēld/ *adj.* —**heel·less** *adj.*
▸ □ **at the heels of** (or **at someone's heels**) following closely behind: *he headed off with Sammy at his heels.* □ **bring someone to heel** bring someone under control. □ **down at heel** (of a shoe) with the heel worn down. ■ having a poor, shabby appearance. □ **kick up one's heels** have a lively, enjoyable time. □ **on the heels of** following closely after. □ **set someone back on their heels** astonish or discomfit someone. □ **under the heel of** dominated or controlled by.

heel[2] ▸*v.* [intr.] (of a boat or ship) be tilted temporarily by the pressure of wind or by an uneven distribution of weight on board. ■ [tr.] cause (a boat or ship) to lean over in such a way.
▸*n.* the degree of incline of a ship's leaning measured from the vertical.

heel·tap /ˈhēlˌtap/ ▸*n.* one of the layers of leather or other material of which a shoe heel is made.

heft /heft/ ▸*v.* [tr.] lift or carry (something heavy). ■ lift or hold (something) in order to test its weight.
▸*n.* the weight of someone or something. ■ *fig.* ability or influence: *his colleagues wonder if he has the intellectual heft for his new job.*

heft·y /ˈheftē/ ▸*adj.* (**heft·i·er**, **heft·i·est**) large, heavy, and powerful. ■ (of a number or amount) impressively large. —**heft·i·ly** /-təlē/ *adv.* —**heft·i·ness** *n.*

he·gem·o·ny /həˈjemənē; ˈhejəˌmōnē/ ▸*n.* leadership or dominance, esp. by one country or social group over others.

He·gi·ra /hiˈjīrə; ˈhejərə/ (also **He·ji·ra** or **Hij·ra** /ˈhijrə/) ▸*n.* Muhammad's departure from Mecca to Medina in AD 622 marking the consolidation of the first Muslim community. ■ the Muslim era reckoned from this date: *the second century of the Hegira.* See also **AH.** ■ (**hegira**) an exodus or migration.

heif·er /ˈhefər/ ▸*n.* a young female cow that has not borne a calf.

height /hīt/ ▸*n.* **1** the measurement from base to top or (of a standing person) from head to foot. ■ elevation above ground or a recognized level (typically sea level). ■ the quality of being tall or high: *his height seems to work to his advantage.* **2** a high place or area: *he's terrified of heights.* **3** the most intense part or period of something: *the height of the tourist season.* ■ an extreme instance or example of something: *the height of bad manners.*

height·en /ˈhītn/ ▸*v.* [tr.] make (something) higher. ■ make or become more intense: [as *adj.*] (**heightened**) *the heightened color of her face.*

Heim·lich ma·neu·ver /ˈhīmlik; ˈhīmlikH/ ▸*n.* a first-aid procedure for dislodging an obstruction from a person's windpipe in which a sudden strong pressure is applied on the abdomen, between the navel and the rib cage.

hei·nous /ˈhānəs/ ▸*adj.* (of a person or wrongful act, esp. a crime) utterly odious or wicked. —**hei·nous·ly** *adv.* —**hei·nous·ness** *n.*

heir /e(ə)r/ ▸*n.* a person legally entitled to the property or rank of another on that person's death. ■ *fig.* a person inheriting and continuing the legacy of a predecessor. —**heir·dom** /-dəm/ *n.* —**heir·less** *adj.* —**heir·ship** /-ˌSHip/ *n.*

heir ap·par·ent ▸*n.* (*pl.* **heirs ap·par·ent**) an heir whose claim cannot be set aside by the birth of another heir. ■ *fig.* a person who is most likely to succeed to the place of another.

heir·ess /ˈe(ə)ris/ ▸*n.* a female heir, esp. to vast wealth: *an oil heiress.*

heir·loom /ˈe(ə)rˌlo͞om/ ▸*n.* a valuable object that has belonged to a family for several generations.

heist /hīst/ *inf.* ▸*n.* a robbery.
▸*v.* [tr.] steal: *he heisted a Pontiac.*

He·ji·ra ▸*n.* variant spelling of **HEGIRA**.

held /held/ ▸ past and past participle of **HOLD**[1].

he·li·an·thus /ˌhēlēˈanTHəs/ ▸*n.* a plant of the genus *Helianthus* in the daisy family, esp. (in gardening) a sunflower.

hel·i·cal /ˈhelikəl; ˈhē-/ ▸*adj.* having the shape or form of a helix; spiral: *helical molecules.* —**hel·i·cal·ly** /-ik(ə)lē/ *adv.*

hel·i·ces /ˈhēləˌsēz/ ▸ plural form of **HELIX**.

hel·i·cop·ter /ˈheliˌkäptər/ ▸*n.* a type of aircraft that derives both lift and propulsion from one or two sets of horizontally revolving overhead rotors. It is capable of moving vertically and horizontally, the direction of motion being controlled by the pitch of the rotor blades.
▸*v.* [tr.] transport by helicopter. ■ [intr.] fly somewhere in a helicopter.
▷late 19th cent.: from French *hélicoptère*, from Greek *helix* 'spiral' + *pteron* 'wing.'

helicopter

he·li·o·cen·tric /ˌhēlēōˈsentrik/ ▸*adj.* having or representing the sun as the center, as in the accepted astronomical model of the solar system. Compare with **GEOCENTRIC.** ■ *Astron.* measured from or considered in relation to the center of the sun. —**he·li·o·cen·tri·cal·ly** /-trik(ə)lē/ *adv.*

he·li·o·graph /ˈhēlēəˌgraf/ ▸*n.* a signaling device by which sunlight is reflected in flashes from a movable mirror. —**he·li·o·graph·ic** /ˌhēlēə-ˈgrafik/ *adj.* —**he·li·og·ra·phy** /ˌhēlēˈägrəfē/ *n.*

he·li·o·trope /ˈhēlēəˌtrōp/ ▸*n.* a plant (genus *Heliotropium*) of the borage family, cultivated for its fragrant purple or blue flowers, which are used in perfume. ■ a light purple color, similar to that typical of heliotrope flowers.

hel·i·port /ˈheləˌpôrt/ ▸*n.* an airport or landing place for helicopters.

he·li·um /ˈhēlēəm/ ▸*n.* the chemical element of atomic number 2, an inert gas that is the lightest member of the noble gas series. (Symbol: **He**)

he·lix /ˈhēliks/ ▸*n.* (*pl.* **-li·ces** /-ləˌsēz/) an object having a three-dimensional shape like that of a wire wound uniformly in a single layer around a cylinder or cone, as in a corkscrew or spiral staircase. ■ *Geom.*

a curve on a conical or cylindrical surface that would become a straight line if the surface were unrolled into a plane. ■ *Biochem.* an extended spiral chain of atoms in a protein, nucleic acid, or other polymeric molecule. ■ *Archit.* a spiral ornament. —**hel·i·coid** /ˈhēliˌkoid/ *n. & adj.*

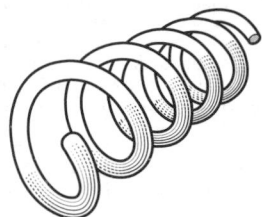

helix

hell /hel/ ▶*n.* a place regarded in various religions as a spiritual realm of evil and suffering, often traditionally depicted as a place of perpetual fire beneath the earth where the wicked are punished after death. ■ a state or place of great suffering; an unbearable experience.
▶*interj.* used to express annoyance or surprise or for emphasis: *hell, no, we were all married.* ■ (**the hell**) *inf.* expressing anger, contempt, or disbelief: *the hell you are!* ▷Old English *hel, hell,* of Germanic origin; related to Dutch *hel* and German *Hölle,* from an Indo-European root meaning 'to cover or hide.' —**hell·ward** /-wərd/ *adv. & adj.*
▶ □ **catch** (or **get**) **hell** *inf.* be severely reprimanded: *Paul kept his mouth shut and looked apologetic—we got hell.* □ **come hell or high water** whatever difficulties may occur. □ **for the hell of it** *inf.* just for fun: *she walked on window ledges for the hell of it.* □ ——— **from hell** *inf.* an extremely unpleasant or troublesome instance or example of something: *I've got a hangover from hell.* □ **give someone hell** *inf.* severely reprimand or make things very unpleasant for someone.

he'll /hēl/ ▶*contr. of* he shall; he will.

hell-bent ▶*adj.* determined to achieve something at all costs: *why are you hell-bent on leaving?*

hel·le·bore /ˈheləˌbôr/ ▶*n.* a poisonous winter-flowering Eurasian plant (genus *Helleborus*) of the buttercup family, typically having coarse divided leaves and large white, green, or purplish flowers.

Hel·lene /ˈhelēn/ ▶*n.* an ancient Greek. ■ a native of modern Greece. —**Hel·len·ic** /heˈlenik/ *adj.*

Hel·len·ism /ˈheləˌnizəm/ ▶*n.* the national character or culture of Greece, esp. ancient Greece. ■ the study or imitation of ancient Greek culture. —**Hel·len·ist** *n.* —**Hel·len·i·za·tion** /ˌhelənəˈzāSHən/ *n.* —**Hel·len·ize** /-ˌnīz/ *v.* —**Hel·len·iz·er** /-ˌnīzər/ *n.*

Hel·len·is·tic /ˌheləˈnistik/ ▶*adj.* of or relating to Greek history, language, and culture from the death of Alexander the Great to the defeat of Cleopatra and Mark Antony by Octavian in 31 BC. During this period Greek culture flourished, spreading through the Mediterranean and into the Near East and Asia and centering on Alexandria in Egypt and Pergamum in Turkey.

hell·fire /ˈhelˌfīr/ ▶*n.* the fire or fires regarded as existing in hell.

hell·hole /ˈhelˌhōl/ ▶*n.* an oppressive or unbearable place.

hell·hound /ˈhelˌhound/ ▶*n.* a demon in the form of a dog.

hell·ish /ˈheliSH/ ▶*adj.* of or like hell. ■ *inf.* extremely difficult or unpleasant: *it had been a hellish week.* —**hell·ish·ly** *adv.* —**hell·ish·ness** *n.*

hel·lo /heˈlō; həˈlō; ˈheˌlō/ (also **hal·lo** or *chiefly Brit.* **hul·lo**) ▶*interj.* used as a greeting. ■ *Brit.* used to express surprise: *hello, what's all this then?* ■ used as a cry to attract someone's attention: *"Hello below!"* ■ /həˈlō; heˈlō/ [often pronounced with a rising–falling intonation pattern and a prolonged final vowel] expressing sarcasm or anger: *hello! did you even get what the play was about?*
▶*n.* (*pl.* **-los**) an utterance of "hello"; a greeting: *polite nods and hellos.*
▶*v.* (**-loes, -loed**) [*intr.*] say or shout "hello"; greet someone.

hell-rais·er ▶*n.* a person who causes trouble by drinking, being violent, or otherwise behaving outrageously. —**hell-rais·ing** *adj. & n.*

helm[1] /helm/ ▶*n.* (**the helm**) a tiller or wheel and any associated equipment for steering a ship or boat: *she stayed at the helm.* ■ *fig.* a position of leadership: *they remain at the helm.* ■ *Naut.* a helmsman.
▶*v.* [*tr.*] steer (a boat or ship).

helm[2] ▶*n. archaic* a helmet. —**helmed** *adj.*

hel·met /ˈhelmit/ ▶*n.* a hard or padded protective hat, various types of which are worn by soldiers, police officers, motorcyclists, athletes, and others. —**hel·met·ed** *adj.*

helms·man /ˈhelmzmən/ ▶*n.* (*pl.* **-men**) a person who steers a ship or boat.

help /help/ ▶*v.* [*tr.*] **1** make it easier for (someone) to do something by offering one's services or financial or material aid. ■ improve (a situation or problem); be of benefit to: *upbeat comments helped confidence* | [*intr.*] *legislation will help.* ■ [*tr.*] assist (someone) to move in a specified direction: *I helped her up.* ■ (**help someone on/off with**) assist someone to put on or take off (a garment). ■ relieve the symptoms of (an ailment): *sore throats can be helped by gargling.* **2** (**help someone to**) serve someone with (food or drink): *she helped herself to a cookie.* ■ (**help oneself**) take something without permission. **3** (**can/could not help**) cannot or could not avoid.
▶*n.* assistance. ■ a person or thing that helps: *he was a great help.* ■ a domestic servant or employee. ■ [as *pl. n.*] (**the help**) a group of such employees working for one employer. ■ [as *adj.*] giving assistance to a computer user in the form of displayed instructions: *a help menu.*
▶*interj.* used as an appeal for urgent assistance: *Help! I'm drowning!* —**help·er** *n.*

help·ful /ˈhelpfəl/ ▶*adj.* giving or ready to give help: *people are friendly and helpful* | *helpful staff.* ■ useful: *we find it very helpful to receive comments.* —**help·ful·ly** *adv.* —**help·ful·ness** *n.*

help·ing /ˈhelpiNG/ ▶*n.* a portion of food served to one person.

help·less /ˈhelplis/ ▶*adj.* unable to defend oneself or to act without help. ■ uncontrollable: *they burst into helpless laughter.* —**help·less·ly** *adv.* —**help·less·ness** *n.*

help·mate /ˈhelpˌmāt/ (also **help·meet** /-ˌmēt/) ▶*n.* a helpful companion or partner, esp. one's husband or wife.

hel·ter-skel·ter /ˈheltər ˈskeltər/ ▶*adj. & adv.* in disorderly haste or confusion.
▶*n.* disorder; confusion.

hem[1] /hem/ ▶*n.* the edge of a piece of cloth or clothing that has been turned under and sewn.
▶*v.* (**hemmed, hem·ming**) [*tr.*] **1** turn under and sew the edge of (a piece of cloth or clothing). **2** (**hem someone/something in**) (usu. **be hemmed in**) surround and restrict the space or movement of.

hem[2] ▶*interj.* used in writing to indicate a sound made when coughing or clearing the throat to attract someone's attention or express hesitation.
▶*n.* an utterance of such a sound.
▶*v.* (**hemmed, hem·ming**) [*intr.*] *archaic* make such a sound when hesitating or as a signal.
▶ □ **hem and haw** hesitate; be indecisive.

he-man ▶*n. inf.* a well-built, muscular man, esp. one who is ostentatiously so.

he·ma·tite /ˈhēməˌtīt/ (*Brit.* **hae·ma·tite**) ▶*n.* a reddish-black mineral consisting of ferric oxide. It is an important ore of iron.

he·mat·o·cele /hiˈmatəˌsēl/ (*Brit.* **hae·mat·o·cele**) ▶*n. Med.* a swelling caused by blood collecting in a body cavity.

he·ma·tol·o·gy /ˌhēməˈtäləjē/ (*Brit.* **hae·ma·tol·o·gy**) ▶*n.* the study of the physiology of the blood. —**he·ma·to·log·ic** /-təˈläjik/ *adj.* —**he·ma·to·log·i·cal** /-təˈläjikəl/ *adj.* —**he·ma·tol·o·gist** /-jist/ *n.*

hem·i·ple·gi·a /ˌhemiˈplēj(ē)ə/ ▶*n. Med.* paralysis of one side of the body. —**hem·i·ple·gic** /-ˈplējik/ *n. & adj.*

hem·i·sphere /ˈheməˌsfi(ə)r/ ▶*n.* a half of a sphere. ■ a half of the earth or other celestial body, usually as divided into northern and southern halves by the equator, or into western and eastern halves by an imaginary line passing through the poles. ■ a half of the celestial sphere. ■ (also **cerebral hemisphere**) each of the two parts of the cerebrum (left and right) in the brain of a vertebrate. —**hem·i·spher·ic** /ˌheməˈsfi(ə)rik, -ˈsferik/ *adj.* —**hem·i·spher·i·cal** *adj.* —**hem·i·spher·i·cal·ly** *adv.*

hem·line /ˈhemˌlīn/ ▶*n.* the level of the lower edge of a garment such as a skirt, dress, or coat.

hem·lock /ˈhemˌläk/ ▶*n.* **1** a highly poisonous European plant (*Conium maculatum*) of the parsley family, with spotted stems, fernlike leaves, small white flowers, and a foul smell. ■ a sedative or poisonous potion obtained from this plant. **2** a coniferous North American tree (genus *Tsuga*) of the pine family, with dark green foliage that is said to smell like the hemlock plant when crushed.

he·mo·glo·bin /ˈhēməˌglōbin/ (*Brit.* **hae·mo·glo·bin**) ▶*n. Biochem.* a red protein responsible for transporting oxygen in the blood of vertebrates.

he·mo·lyt·ic /ˌhēməˈlitik/ (*Brit.* **hae·mo·lyt·ic**) ▶*adj. Med.* relating to or involving the rupture or destruction of red blood cells: *a case of hemolytic anemia.*

he·mo·phil·i·a /ˌhēməˈfilēə/ (*Brit.* **hae·mo·phil·i·a**) ▶*n.* a medical condition, usually hereditary, in which the ability of the blood to clot is severely reduced, causing the sufferer to bleed severely from even a slight injury. —**he·mo·phil·i·ac** /-ˈfilē‚ak/ *n.* —**he·mo·phil·ic** /-ˈfilik/ *adj.*

hem·or·rhage /ˈhem(ə)rij/ (*Brit.* **haem·or·rhage**) ▶*n.* an escape of blood from a ruptured blood vessel, esp. when profuse. ■ a damaging loss of valuable people or resources.

▶*v.* [*intr.*] (of a person) suffer a hemorrhage: *he had begun hemorrhaging in the night.* ■ [*tr.*] expend (money) in large amounts in a seemingly uncontrollable manner: *the business was hemorrhaging cash.*

hem·or·rhoid /ˈhem(ə)‚roid/ (*Brit.* **haem·or·rhoid**) ▶*n.* (usu. **hemorrhoids**) a swollen vein or group of veins in the region of the anus. Also (collectively) called **PILES.** —**hem·or·rhoi·dal** /ˌhem(ə)ˈroidl/ *adj.*

he·mo·sta·sis /ˌhēməˈstāsəs; hemeˈ/ (*Brit.* **hae·mo·sta·sis**) ▶*n. Med.* the stopping of a flow of blood. —**he·mo·stat·ic** /-ˈstatik/ *adj.*

hemp /hemp/ ▶*n.* the cannabis plant, esp. when grown for fiber. ■ the fiber of this plant, extracted from the stem and used to make rope, stout fabrics, fiberboard, and paper. ■ used in names of other plants that yield fiber, e.g., **Manila hemp.** ■ marijuana. ▷Old English *henep, hænep,* of Germanic origin; related to Dutch *hennep* and German *Hanf,* also to Greek *kannabis.*

hemp·en /ˈhempən/ ▶*adj.* made from hemp fiber.

hem·stitch /ˈhem‚stiCH/ ▶*n.* a decoration used on woven fabric, esp. alongside a hem, in which several adjacent threads are pulled out and the crossing threads are tied into bunches, making a row of small openings.

▶*v.* [*tr.*] incorporate such a decoration in the hem of (a piece of cloth or clothing).

hen /hen/ ▶*n.* a female bird, esp. of a domestic fowl. ■ (**hens**) domestic fowls of either sex. ■ used in names of birds, esp. waterbirds of the rail family, e.g., **moorhen.** ■ a female lobster, crab, or salmon.

▶ □ **as rare** (or **scarce**) **as hen's teeth** extremely rare.

hence /hens/ ▶*adv.* **1** as a consequence; for this reason. **2** in the future (used after a period of time).

hence·forth /ˈhens‚fôrTH/ (also **hence·for·ward** /hensˈfôrwərd/) ▶*adv.* from this time on or from that time on.

hench·man /ˈhenCHmən/ ▶*n.* (*pl.* **-men**) *chiefly derog.* a faithful follower or political supporter, esp. one prepared to engage in crime or dishonest practices by way of service. ■ *hist.* a squire or page of honor to a person of rank.

hen·na /ˈhenə/ ▶*n.* **1** the powdered leaves of a tropical shrub, used as a dye to color the hair and decorate the body. **2** the Old World shrub (*Lawsonia inermis,* family Lythraceae) that produces these leaves, with small pink, red, or white flowers.

▶*v.* (**hennas, hennaed** /ˈhenəd/, **hennaing**) [*tr.*] dye (hair) with henna.

▶*adj.* reddish-brown.

hen·peck /ˈhen‚pek/ ▶*v.* [*tr.*] [usu. as *adj.*] (**henpecked**) (of a woman) continually criticize and give orders to (her husband or other male partner).

hen·ry /ˈhenrē/ (abbr.: **H**) ▶*n.* (*pl.* **hen·ries** or **hen·rys**) *Physics* the SI unit of inductance, equal to an electromotive force of one volt in a closed circuit with a uniform rate of change of current of one ampere per second.

hep /hep/ ▶*adj.* old-fashioned term for **HIP**³.

hep·a·rin /ˈhepərin/ ▶*n. Biochem.* a compound occurring in the liver and other tissues that inhibits blood coagulation. A sulfur-containing polysaccharide, it is used as an anticoagulant in the treatment of thrombosis.

he·pat·ic /həˈpatik/ ▶*adj.* of or relating to the liver.

▶*n. Bot.* less common term for **LIVERWORT.**

he·pat·i·ca /həˈpatikə/ ▶*n.* a plant (genus *Hepatica*) of the buttercup family, with anemonelike flowers, native to north temperate regions.

hep·a·ti·tis /ˌhepəˈtītis/ ▶*n.* a disease characterized by inflammation of the liver.

hep·ta·gon /ˈheptə‚gän/ ▶*n.* a plane figure with seven straight sides and angles. —**hep·tag·o·nal** /hepˈtagənl/ *adj.*

hep·tath·lon /hepˈtaTH‚län/ ▶*n.* a track and field event, in particular one for women, in which each competitor takes part in the same prescribed seven events (100-meter hurdles, high jump, shot put, 200-meter dash, long jump, javelin, and 800-meter run). —**hep·tath·lete** /-ˈtaTHlēt/ *n.*

her /hər/ ▶*pron.* [*third person sing.*] used as the object of a verb or preposition to refer to a female person or animal previously mentioned or easily identified: *she knew I hated her* | *I told Hannah I would wait for her.* Compare with **SHE.** ■ referring to a ship, country, or other inanimate thing regarded as female. ■ often used in place of "she" after the verb "to be" and after "than" or "as" to refer to a female person or animal: *it must be her* | *he was younger than her.*

▶*possessive adj.* **1** belonging to or associated with a female person or animal previously mentioned or easily identified: *Patricia loved her job* | *how the mother crane treats her babies.* ■ belonging to or associated with a ship, country, or other inanimate thing regarded as female. **2** (**Her**) used in titles: *Her Royal Highness.*

her·ald /ˈherəld/ ▶*n.* **1** an official messenger bringing news. **2** a person or thing viewed as a sign that something is about to happen: *primroses as the herald of spring.* **3** *hist.* an official employed to oversee state ceremony, precedence, and the use of armorial bearings, and to make proclamations, carry ceremonial messages, and oversee tournaments.

▶*v.* [*tr.*] be a sign that (something) is about to happen: *the speech heralded a change in policy.* ■ (usu. **be heralded**) acclaim.

he·ral·dic /heˈraldik/ ▶*adj.* of or relating to heraldry. —**he·ral·di·cal·ly** /-ik(ə)lē/ *adv.*

her·ald·ry /ˈherəldrē/ ▶*n.* the system by which coats of arms and other armorial bearings are devised, described, and regulated. ■ armorial bearings or other heraldic symbols. ■ colorful ceremony: *all the pomp and heraldry provided a splendid pageant.* —**her·ald·ist** /ˈherəldist/ *n.*

herb /(h)ərb/ ▶*n.* **1** any plant with leaves, seeds, or flowers used for flavoring, food, medicine, or perfume. ■ a part of such a plant as used in cooking: *a potato base topped with tomatoes, cheese, and herbs.* **2** *Bot.* any seed-bearing plant that does not have a woody stem and dies down to the ground after flowering. ▷Middle English: via Old French from Latin *herba* 'grass, green crops, herb.' Although *herb* has always been spelled with an *h,* pronunciation without it was usual in British English until the 19th cent. and is still standard in the U.S.

her·ba·ceous /(h)ərˈbāSHəs/ ▶*adj.* of, denoting, or relating to herbs (in the botanical sense).

herb·al /ˈ(h)ərbəl/ ▶*adj.* relating to or made from herbs, esp. those used in cooking and medicine: *herbal remedies.*

▶*n.* a book that describes herbs and their properties.

herb·al·ism /ˈ(h)ərbə‚lizəm/ ▶*n.* the study or practice of the medicinal and therapeutic use of plants, now esp. as a form of alternative medicine.

herb·al·ist /ˈ(h)ərbəlist/ ▶*n.* a practitioner of herbalism. ■ a dealer in medicinal herbs. ■ an early botanical writer.

her·bar·i·um /(h)ərˈbe(ə)rēəm/ ▶*n.* (*pl.* **-bar·i·ums** or **-bar·i·a** /-ˈbe(ə)rēə/) a systematically arranged collection of dried plants. ■ a room or building housing such a collection.

herb·i·cide /ˈ(h)ərbə‚sīd/ ▶*n.* a substance that is toxic to plants and is used to destroy unwanted vegetation.

her·bi·vore /ˈ(h)ərbə‚vôr/ ▶*n.* an animal that feeds on plants. —**her·biv·o·rous** /(h)ərˈbiv(ə)rəs/ *adj.*

Her·cu·le·an /ˌhərkyəˈlēən; hərˈkyōōlēən/ ▶*adj.* requiring great strength or effort: *a Herculean task.* ■ (of a person) muscular and strong.

herd /hərd/ ▶*n.* a large group of animals, esp. hoofed mammals, that live, feed, or migrate together or are kept together as livestock: *a herd of elephants* | *large farms with big dairy herds.* ■ *derog.* a large group of people, typically with a shared characteristic: *I dodged herds of joggers.*

▶*v.* move in a particular direction: [*tr.*] *Nick herded me through the baggage claim and into his Jaguar* | [*intr.*] *we all herded into a storage room.* ■ [*tr.*] keep or look after (livestock): *Hunter and Tripp herded sheep.* —**herd·er** *n.*

herds·man /ˈhərdzmən/ ▶*n.* (*pl.* **-men**) the owner or keeper of a herd of domesticated animals.

here /hi(ə)r/ ▶*adv.* **1** in, at, or to this place or position: *they have lived here most of their lives* | *come here and let me look at them* | [after *prep.*] *I'm getting out of here* | *it's too hot in here.* ■ used when pointing or gesturing to indicate the place in mind: *sign here* | *I have here a letter from the chief of police.* ■ used to draw attention to someone or something that has just arrived: *here's my brother.* ■ used to indicate one's role in a particular situation: *I'm here to help you.* ■ used to refer to existence in the world in general: *what are we all doing here?* **2** (usu. **here is/are**) used when introducing something or someone: *here's a dish that is simple and quick to make* | *here's what you have to do.* ■ used when giving something to someone: *here is my address.* **3** used when indicating a time or situation that has arrived or is happening: *here is your opportunity* | *here comes summer.* ■ used to refer to a particular point or aspect reached in an argument, situation, or activity: *here we encounter the main problem.*

▶*interj.* **1** used to attract someone's attention: *here, let me hold it.* **2** indicating one's presence in a roll call.

▸ □ **here and now** at this very moment; at the present time: *we're going to settle this here and now* | [as *n.*] *our obsession with* **the here and now.** □ **here and there** in various places. □ **here's to someone/something** used to wish health or success before drinking: *here's to us!* | *here's to your safe arrival.* □ **neither here nor there** irrelevant.

here·a·bouts /ˈhirəˌbouts/ (also **here·a·bout**) ▸*adv.* near this place: *there is little natural water hereabouts.*

here·af·ter /hi(ə)rˈaftər/ ▸*adv. formal* from now on. ■ at some time in the future: *this court is in no way prejudging any such defense which may hereafter be raised.* ■ after death: *a sermon about hope of life hereafter.*
▸*n.* (**the hereafter**) life after death: *suffering is part of our preparation for the hereafter.*

here·by /ˌhi(ə)rˈbī; ˈhi(ə)rˌbī/ ▸*adv. formal* as a result of this document or utterance: *the Port Authority hereby solicits proposals from developers.*

he·red·i·tar·y /həˈrediˌterē/ ▸*adj.* (of a title, office, or right) conferred by or based on inheritance. ■ (of a person) holding a position by inheritance: *I am the hereditary chief of the Piscataway people.* ■ (of a characteristic or disease) determined by genetic factors and therefore able to be passed on from parents to their offspring or descendants: *cystic fibrosis is our most common fatal hereditary disease.* ■ of or relating to inheritance. ■ *Math.* (of a set) defined such that every element that has a given relation to a member of the set is also a member of the set. —**he·red·i·tar·i·ly** /həˌrediˈte(ə)rəlē/ *adv.* —**he·red·i·tar·i·ness** /həˌrediˈte(ə)rēnis/ *n.*

he·red·i·ty /həˈreditē/ ▸*n.* **1** the passing on of physical or mental characteristics genetically from one generation to another: *few scientists dispute that heredity can create a susceptibility to alcoholism.* ■ a person's ancestry. **2** inheritance of title, office, or right: *membership is largely based on heredity.*

Her·e·ford /ˈhərfərd; ˈherə-/ ▸*n.* an animal of a breed of red and white beef cattle.

here·in /ˌhi(ə)rˈin/ ▸*adv. formal* in this document or book: *the author herein recounts his travel adventures.* ■ in this matter; arising from this: *the statues are sensual to the point of erotic and herein lies their interest.*

here·in·af·ter /ˌhi(ə)rinˈaftər/ ▸*adv. formal* further on in this document.

her·e·sy /ˈherəsē/ ▸*n.* (*pl.* **-sies**) belief or opinion contrary to orthodox religious (esp. Christian) doctrine: *Huss was burned for heresy* | *the doctrine was denounced as a heresy by the pope.* ■ opinion profoundly at odds with what is generally accepted: *the politician's heresies became the conventional wisdom of the day.* ▷Middle English: from Old French *heresie*, based on Latin *haeresis*, from Greek *hairesis* 'choice' (in ecclesiastical Greek 'heretical sect'), from *haireisthai* 'choose.'

her·e·tic /ˈheretik/ ▸*n.* a person believing in or practicing religious heresy. ■ a person holding an opinion at odds with what is generally accepted. —**he·ret·i·cal** /həˈretikəl/ *adj.* —**he·ret·i·cal·ly** *adv.*

here·to /ˌhi(ə)rˈtōō/ ▸*adv. formal* to this matter or document: *the written consent of each of the parties hereto* | *hereto is appended an estimate of the cost.*

here·to·fore /ˈhi(ə)rtəˌfôr/ ▸*adv. formal* before now.

here·up·on /ˌhi(ə)rəˈpän/ ▸*adv.* after or as a result of this.

here·with /ˌhirˈwiTH; -ˈwiTH/ ▸*adv. formal* with this letter: *I send you herewith fifteen dollars.*

her·it·a·ble /ˈheritəbəl/ ▸*adj.* able to be inherited, in particular: ■ *Biol.* (of a characteristic) transmissible from parent to offspring. ■ *Law* (of property) capable of being inherited by heirs. —**her·it·a·bil·i·ty** /ˌheritəˈbilitē/ *n.* —**her·it·a·bly** /-blē/ *adv.*

her·it·age /ˈheritij/ ▸*n.* property that is or may be inherited; an inheritance. ■ valued objects and qualities such as cultural traditions, unspoiled countryside, and historic buildings that have been passed down from previous generations. ■ [as *adj.*] (of a plant variety) not hybridized with another; old-fashioned: *heritage roses.*

her·maph·ro·dite /hərˈmafrədīt/ ▸*n.* a person or animal having both male and female sex organs or other sexual characteristics, either abnormally or (in the case of some organisms) as the normal condition. ■ *Bot.* a plant having stamens and pistils in the same flower. ■ *archaic* a person or thing combining opposite qualities or characteristics.
▸*adj.* of or denoting a person, animal, or plant of this kind: *hermaphrodite creatures in classical sculpture.* —**her·maph·ro·dit·ic** /-ˌmafrəˈditik/ *adj.* —**her·maph·ro·dit·i·cal** /-ˌmafrəˈditikəl/ *adj.* —**her·maph·ro·dit·ism** /hərˈmafrədiˌtizəm/ (or **her·maph·ro·dism** /-ˌdizəm/) *n.*

her·me·neu·tics /ˌhərməˈn(y)ōōtiks/ ▸*pl. n.* [usu. treated as *sing.*] the branch of knowledge that deals with interpretation, esp. of the Bible or literary texts. —**her·me·neu·tic** *adj.*

her·met·ic /hərˈmetik/ ▸*adj.* (of a seal or closure) complete and airtight. ■ insulated or protected from outside influences: *a hermetic society.* —**her·met·i·cal·ly** /hərˈmetiklē; -ik(ə)lē/ *adv.* —**her·met·i·cism** /hərˈmetiˌsizəm/ *n.*

her·mit /ˈhərmit/ ▸*n.* a person living in solitude as a religious discipline. ■ any person living in solitude or seeking to do so. —**her·mit·ic** /hərˈmitik/ *adj.*

her·mit·age /ˈhərmitij/ ▸*n.* the dwelling of a hermit, esp. when small and remote.

her·mit crab ▸*n.* a crab with a soft asymmetrical abdomen that lives in a castoff mollusk shell for protection.

her·ni·a /ˈhərnēə/ ▸*n.* (*pl.* **-ni·as** or **-ni·ae** /-nē,ē/) a condition in which part of an organ is displaced and protrudes through the wall of the cavity containing it (often involving the intestine at a weak point in the abdominal wall). —**her·ni·al** *adj.*

he·ro /ˈhi(ə)rō/ ▸*n.* (*pl.* **-roes**) a person, typically a man, who is admired or idealized for courage, outstanding achievements, or noble qualities: *a war hero.* ■ the chief male character in a book, play, or movie, who is typically identified with good qualities, and with whom the reader is expected to sympathize. ■ (in mythology and folklore) a person of superhuman qualities and often semidivine origin, in particular one of those whose exploits and dealings with the gods were the subject of ancient Greek myths and legends. ■ (also **hero sandwich**) another term for SUBMARINE SANDWICH.

he·ro·ic /həˈrōik/ ▸*adj.* having the characteristics of a hero or heroine; very brave: *heroic deeds* | *a few heroic individuals.* ■ of or representing heroes or heroines: *early medieval heroic poetry.* ■ (of language or a work of art) grand or grandiose in scale or intention: *one passes under pyramids and obelisks, all on a heroic scale.* ■ *Sculpture* (of a statue) larger than life-size but less than colossal.
▸*n.* (**heroics**) behavior or talk that is bold or dramatic, esp. excessively or unexpectedly so: *the makeshift team performed heroics.* —**he·ro·i·cal·ly** /-ik(ə)lē/ *adv.*

her·o·in /ˈherəwin/ ▸*n.* a highly addictive analgesic drug derived from morphine, often used illicitly as a narcotic producing euphoria.

her·o·ine /ˈherō-in/ ▸*n.* a woman admired or idealized for her courage, outstanding achievements, or noble qualities. ■ the chief female character in a book, play, or movie, who is typically identified with good qualities, and with whom the reader is expected to sympathize. ■ (in mythology and folklore) a woman of superhuman qualities and often semidivine origin, in particular one whose dealings with the gods were the subject of ancient Greek myths and legends.

her·o·ism /ˈherō,izəm/ ▸*n.* great bravery.

her·on /ˈherən/ ▸*n.* a large fish-eating wading bird (family Ardeidae) with long legs, a long S-shaped neck, and a long pointed bill. Its numerous species include the **great blue heron** (*Ardea herodias*).

her·on·ry /ˈherənrē/ ▸*n.* (*pl.* **-ries**) a breeding colony of herons, typically in a group of trees.

he·ro·wor·ship ▸*n.* excessive admiration for someone. ■ (in ancient Greece) the worship of superhuman heroes.
▸*v.* [*tr.*] admire (someone) excessively. —**he·ro·wor·ship·er** *n.*

her·pes /ˈhərpēz/ ▸*n.* any of a group of viral diseases caused by herpes viruses, affecting the skin (often with blisters) or the nervous system. —**her·pet·ic** /hərˈpetik/ *adj.*

her·pes sim·plex ▸*n.* a viral infection, caused by a group of herpes viruses, that may produce cold sores, genital inflammation, or conjunctivitis.

her·pes zos·ter /ˈzästər/ ▸*n.* medical name for SHINGLES. ■ a herpes virus that causes shingles and chicken pox.

her·pe·tol·o·gy /ˌhərpəˈtäləjē/ ▸*n.* the branch of zoology concerned with reptiles and amphibians. —**her·pe·to·log·i·cal** /-təˈläjəkəl/ *adj.* —**her·pe·tol·o·gist** /-jist/ *n.*

her·ring /ˈheriNG/ ▸*n.* a silvery fish (*Clupea* and other genera) that is most abundant in coastal waters and is of great commercial importance as a food fish in many parts of the world. The **herring family** (Clupeidae) also includes the sprats, shads, and pilchards.

her·ring·bone /ˈheriNG,bōn/ ▸*n.* [usu. as *adj.*] **1** an arrangement or design consisting of columns of short parallel lines, with all the lines in one column sloping one way and all the lines in the next column sloping the other way so as to resemble the bones in a fish, used esp. in the weave of cloth or the placing of bricks: *a brown wool herringbone jacket.* **2** *Skiing* a method of

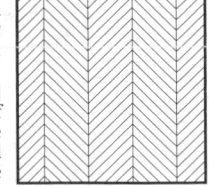
herringbone

Pronunciation Key ə *ago, up;* ər *over, fur;* a *hat;* ā *ate;* ä *car;* CH *chin;* e *let;* ē *see;* e(ə)r *air;* i *fit;* ī *by;* i(ə)r *ear;* NG *sing;* ō *go;* ô *law, for;* oi *toy;* ōō *good;* ōō *goo;* ou *out;* SH *she;* TH *thin;* TH *then;* (h)w *why;* ZH *vision*

ascending a slope by walking forward in alternate steps with each ski angled outward.

▶ *v.* [*intr.*] *Skiing* ascend a slope using the herringbone technique.

hers /hərz/ ▶ *possessive pron.* used to refer to a thing or things belonging to or associated with a female person or animal previously mentioned: *his eyes met hers | the choice was hers | friends of hers warned her.*

her·self /hər'self/ ▶ *pron.* [third person sing.] **1** [*reflexive*] used as the object of a verb or preposition to refer to a female person or animal previously mentioned as the subject of the clause: *Jo made herself a cup of tea.* **2** she or her personally (used to emphasize a particular female person or animal mentioned): *she told me herself.*

hertz /hərts/ (abbr.: **Hz**) ▶ *n.* (*pl.* same) the SI unit of frequency, equal to one cycle per second.

he's /hēz/ ▶ *contr. of* ■ he is: *he's going to speak.* ■ he has: *he's given up his job.*

hes·i·tant /'hezitənt/ ▶ *adj.* tentative, unsure, or slow in acting or speaking. —**hes·i·tance** *n.* —**hes·i·tan·cy** /-tənsē/ *n.* —**hes·i·tant·ly** *adv.*

hes·i·tate /'hezi,tāt/ ▶ *v.* [*intr.*] pause before saying or doing something, esp. through uncertainty: *she hesitated, unsure of what to say.* ■ be reluctant to do something: *he hesitated to spoil the mood by being inquisitive.* —**hes·i·tat·er** /-,tātər/ *n.* —**hes·i·tat·ing·ly** /-,tātiNGlē/ *adv.* —**hes·i·ta·tion** /,hesi'tāSHən/ *n.*

het·er·o /'hetərō/ ▶ *adj. & n. inf.* short for **HETEROSEXUAL**.

het·er·o·cy·clic /,hetərō'sīklik; -'siklik/ ▶ *adj. Chem.* denoting a compound whose molecule contains a ring of atoms of at least two elements (one of which is generally carbon).

het·er·o·dox /'hetərə,däks/ ▶ *adj.* not conforming with accepted or orthodox standards or beliefs. ▷ *early 17th cent. (originally as a noun denoting an unorthodox opinion): via late Latin from Greek heterodoxos, from heteros 'other' + doxa 'opinion.'* —**het·er·o·dox·y** *n.*

het·er·o·dyne /'hetərə,dīn/ ▶ *adj. Electr.* of or relating to the production of a lower frequency from the combination of two almost equal high frequencies, as used in radio transmission.

het·er·o·ge·ne·ous /,hetərə'jēnēəs/ ▶ *adj.* diverse in character or content: *a large and heterogeneous collection.* ■ *Chem.* of or denoting a process involving substances in different phases (solid, liquid, or gaseous). —**het·er·o·ge·ne·i·ty** /-jə'nēətē/ *n.* —**het·er·o·ge·ne·ous·ly** *adv.* —**het·er·o·ge·ne·ous·ness** *n.*

het·er·ol·o·gous /,hetə'räləgəs/ ▶ *adj. chiefly Med. Biol.* not homologous. —**het·er·ol·o·gy** /-'räləjē/ *n.*

het·er·o·mor·phic /,hetərə'môrfik/ ▶ *adj. Biol.* occurring in two or more different forms, esp. at different stages in the life cycle. —**het·er·o·morph** /'hetərə,môrf/ *n.* —/'hetərə,môrfik/ **het·er·o·mor·phy** *n.*

het·er·o·sex·u·al /,hetərō'sekSHOŌəl/ ▶ *adj.* (of a person) sexually attracted to people of the opposite sex. ■ involving or characterized by sexual attraction between people of the opposite sex.

▶ *n.* a heterosexual person. —**het·er·o·sex·u·al·i·ty** /-,sekSHOŌ'alitē/ *n.* —**het·er·o·sex·u·al·ly** *adv.*

heu·ris·tic /hyoō'ristik/ ▶ *adj.* enabling a person to discover or learn something for themselves. ■ *Comput.* proceeding to a solution by trial and error or by rules that are only loosely defined.

▶ *n.* a heuristic process or method. ■ (**heuristics**) [usu. treated as *sing.*] the study and use of heuristic techniques. —**heu·ris·ti·cal·ly** *adv.*

HEW ▶ *abbr.* (Department of) Health, Education, and Welfare.

hew /hyoō/ ▶ *v.* (past part. **hewn** /hyoōn/ or **hewed**) **1** [*tr.*] chop or cut (something, esp. wood) with an ax, pick, or other tool: *we have finished hauling and hewing timber.* ■ (usu. **be hewn**) make or shape (something) by cutting or chopping a material such as wood or stone: *a seat hewn out of a fallen tree trunk.* **2** [*intr.*] (**hew to**) conform or adhere to.

hex[1] /heks/ ▶ *v.* [*tr.*] cast a spell on; bewitch: *he hexed her with his fingers.* ▶ *n.* a magic spell; a curse: *a death hex.* ■ a witch.

hex[2] ▶ *adj. & n.* **1** short for **HEXADECIMAL**. **2** short for **HEXAGONAL** (see **HEXAGON**).

hex·ad /'hek,sad/ ▶ *n. technical* a group or set of six.

hex·a·dec·i·mal /,heksə'des(ə)məl/ ▶ *adj. Comput.* relating to or using a system of numerical notation that has 16 rather than 10 as its base. —**hex·a·dec·i·mal·ly** *adv.*

hex·a·gon /'heksə,gän/ ▶ *n.* a plane figure with six straight sides and angles. —**hex·ag·on·al** /hek'sagənl/ *adj.*

hex·a·gram /'heksə,gram/ ▶ *n.* a figure formed of six straight lines, in particular: ■ a star-shaped figure formed by two intersecting equilateral triangles. ■ any of a set of sixty-four figures made up of six parallel whole or broken lines, occurring in the ancient Chinese *I Ching.*

hex·a·he·dron /,heksə'hēdrən/ ▶ *n.* (*pl.* -**drons** or -**dra** /-drə/) a solid figure with six plane faces. —**hex·a·he·dral** /-drəl/ *adj.*

hex·am·e·ter /hek'samitər/ ▶ *n. Prosody* a line of verse consisting of six metrical feet, esp. of six dactyls. —**hex·a·met·ric** /,heksə'metrik/ *adj.*

hex·ane /'hek,sān/ ▶ *n. Chem.* a colorless liquid hydrocarbon, C_6H_{14}, of the alkane series.

hex·a·va·lent /,heksə'vālənt/ ▶ *adj. Chem.* having a valence of six.

hex·ose /'hek,sōs/ ▶ *n. Chem.* any of the class of simple sugars whose molecules contain six carbon atoms, such as glucose and fructose. They generally have the chemical formula $C_6H_{12}O_6$.

hey /hā/ ▶ *interj. inf.* used to attract attention, to express surprise, interest, or annoyance, or to elicit agreement.

▶ □ **what the hey** *inf.* used as a euphemism for "what the hell."

hey·day /'hā,dā/ ▶ *n.* (usu. **one's heyday**) the period of a person's or thing's greatest success, popularity, or vigor.

HF *Physics* ▶ *abbr.* high frequency.

Hf ▶ *symb.* the chemical element hafnium.

Hg ▶ *symb.* the chemical element mercury.

hg ▶ *abbr.* hectogram(s).

hgt. ▶ *abbr.* height.

H-hour ▶ *n.* the time of day at which an attack, landing, or other military operation is scheduled to begin.

HHS ▶ *abbr.* Department of Health and Human Services.

hi /hī/ ▶ *interj. inf.* used as a friendly greeting or to attract attention.

hi·a·tus /hī'ātəs/ ▶ *n.* (*pl.* -**tus·es**) a pause or gap in a sequence, series, or process: *there was a brief hiatus in the war with France.* ■ *Prosody & Gram.* a break between two vowels coming together but not in the same syllable, as in *the ear* and *cooperate.* —**hi·a·tal** /-'ātəl/ *adj.*

hi·ba·chi /hə'bächē/ ▶ *n.* (*pl.* -**chis**) a portable cooking apparatus consisting of a small grill over a brazier.

hi·ber·nate /'hībər,nāt/ ▶ *v.* [*intr.*] (of an animal or plant) spend the winter in a dormant state. ■ *fig.* (of a person) remain inactive or indoors for an extended period. —**hi·ber·na·tion** /,hībər'nāSHən/ *n.* —**hi·ber·na·tor** /-,nātər/ *n.*

Hi·ber·ni·an /hī'bərnēən/ ▶ *adj.* of or concerning Ireland (now chiefly used in names): *the Royal Hibernian Academy.*

▶ *n.* a native of Ireland (now chiefly used in names): *the Ancient Order of Hibernians.*

hi·bis·cus /hī'biskəs/ ▶ *n.* a plant (genus *Hibiscus*) of the mallow family, grown in warm climates esp. for its large brightly colored flowers.

hic·cup /'hikəp/ (also **hic·cough**) ▶ *n.* an involuntary spasm of the diaphragm and respiratory organs, with a sudden closure of the glottis and a characteristic sound like that of a cough. ■ (**hiccups**) an attack of such spasms occurring repeatedly for some time: *he got the hiccups.* ■ a temporary or minor difficulty or setback.

▶ *v.* (-**cuped**, -**cup·ing**) [*intr.*] suffer from or make the sound of a hiccup or series of hiccups. —**hic·cup·y** *adj.*

hick /hik/ ▶ *n. inf., chiefly derog.* a person who lives in the country, regarded as being unintelligent or provincial: *wondering what a hick from the sticks was doing there* | [as *adj.*] *a hick town.*

hick·ey /'hikē/ ▶ *n.* (*pl.* -**eys**) *inf.* a skin blemish, esp. a mark caused by a lover biting or sucking the skin.

hick·o·ry /'hik(ə)rē/ ▶ *n.* a chiefly North American tree (genus *Carya*) of the walnut family that yields useful timber and typically bears edible nuts. ■ a stick made of hickory wood.

hid /hid/ ▶ past of **HIDE**[1].

hi·dal·go /hi'dälgō/ ▶ *n.* (*pl.* -**gos**) (in Spanish-speaking regions) a gentleman.

hid·den /'hidn/ ▶ past participle of **HIDE**[1].

▶ *adj.* kept out of sight; concealed. —**hid·den·ness** *n.*

hide[1] /hīd/ ▶ *v.* (past **hid** /hid/; past part. **hid·den** /'hidn/) [*tr.*] put or keep out of sight; conceal from the view or notice of others: *he hid the money in the house* | *the sacred relic had been hidden away in a sealed cavern.* ■ (of a thing) prevent (someone or something) from being seen: *clouds hid the moon.* ■ keep secret or unknown: *Hal could hardly hide his dislike.* ■ [*intr.*] conceal oneself. ■ [*intr.*] (**hide behind**) use (someone or something) to protect oneself from criticism or punishment, esp. in a way considered cowardly or unethical.

▶ *n. Brit.* a camouflaged shelter used to get a close view of wildlife. —**hid·er** *n.*

hide[2] ▶ *n.* the skin of an animal, esp. when tanned or dressed. ■ used to refer to a person's ability to withstand criticisms or insults: *"I'm sorry I called you a pig." "My hide's thick enough; it didn't bother me."* —**hid·ed** *adj.*

▶ □ **hide or hair of someone** the slightest sight or trace of someone: *I could find neither hide nor hair of him.*

hide[3] ▶ *n.* a former measure of land used in England, typically equal to between 60 and 120 acres, being the amount that would support a family and its dependents.

hide-and-seek ▸ *n.* a children's game in which one player tries to find other players who have hidden themselves.

hide·a·way /'hīdə,wā/ ▸ *n.* a place used as a retreat or a hiding place. ▸ *adj.* designed to be concealed when not in use: *a hideaway bed.*

hide·bound /'hīd,bound/ ▸ *adj.* unwilling or unable to change because of tradition or convention. ■ (of cattle) with their skin clinging close to their back and ribs as a result of bad feeding. ▷mid 16th cent. (as a noun denoting a condition of cattle): from *hide* 'animal skin' + *bound* 'restricted or confined.' The earliest sense of the adjective (of cattle) was extended to emaciated human beings, and then applied figuratively in the sense 'narrow, cramped, or bigoted in outlook.'

hide·ous /'hīdēəs/ ▸ *adj.* ugly or disgusting to look at. ■ extremely unpleasant: *the whole hideous story.* —**hide·ous·ly** *adv. a hideously expensive camera.* —**hide·ous·ness** *n.*

hide·out /'hīd,out/ ▸ *n.* a hiding place, esp. one used by someone who has broken the law.

hid·ey-hole /'hīdē ,hōl/ ▸ *n. inf.* a place for hiding something or oneself in, esp. as a retreat from other people.

hid·ing[1] /'hīdiNG/ ▸ *n. inf.* a physical beating: *they took off after him, caught him, and gave him a hiding.* ■ *fig.* a severe defeat.

hid·ing[2] ▸ *n.* the action of concealing someone or something. ■ the state of being hidden: *the shipowner had gone into hiding.*

hie /hī/ ▸ *v.* (**hies, hied, hie·ing** or **hy·ing**) [*intr.*] go quickly: *I hied down to New Orleans* | *I hied myself to a screenwriters' conference.*

hi·er·ar·chy /'hī(ə),rärkē/ ▸ *n.* (*pl.* **-chies**) a system or organization in which people or groups are ranked one above the other according to status or authority. ■ (**the hierarchy**) the upper echelons of a hierarchical system; those in authority. ■ an arrangement or classification of things according to relative importance or inclusiveness: *a taxonomic hierarchy of phyla, classes, orders, families, genera, and species.* ■ (**the hierarchy**) the clergy of the Catholic or Episcopal Church; the religious authorities. ■ *Theol.* the traditional system of orders of angels and other heavenly beings. —**hi·er·ar·chic** /,hī(ə)'rärkik/ —**hi·er·ar·chi·cal** *adj.* —**hi·er·ar·chi·za·tion** /,hī(ə),rärkə'zāsHən/ *n.* —**hi·er·ar·chize** /-,kīz/ *v.*

hi·er·at·ic /,hī(ə)'ratik/ ▸ *adj.* of or concerning priests. —**hi·er·at·i·cal·ly** /-ik(ə)lē/ *adv.*

hi·er·o·glyph /'hī(ə)rə,glif/ ▸ *n.* a stylized picture of an object representing a word, syllable, or sound, as found in ancient Egyptian and other writing systems.

hi·er·o·glyph·ic /,hī(ə)rə'glifik/ ▸ *n.* (**hieroglyphics**) writing consisting of hieroglyphs. ■ enigmatic or incomprehensible symbols or writing. ▸ *adj.* of or written in hieroglyphs. ■ (esp. in art) stylized, symbolic, or enigmatic in effect. —**hi·er·o·glyph·i·cal** *adj.* —**hi·er·o·glyph·i·cal·ly** *adv.*

hi-fi /'hī 'fī/ *inf.* ▸ *adj.* of, used for, or relating to the reproduction of music or other sound with high fidelity. ▸ *n.* (*pl.* **-fis**) a set of equipment for high-fidelity sound reproduction, esp. a radio or phonograph.

hig·gle·dy-pig·gle·dy /'higəldē 'pigəldē/ ▸ *adv.* & *adj.* in confusion or disorder.

high /hī/ ▸ *adj.* **1** of great vertical extent: *the top of a high mountain* | *the mast was higher than the tallest building in the city.* ■ (after a measurement and in questions) measuring a specified distance from top to bottom: *a tree forty feet high* | *how high is the fence?* ■ far above ground, sea level, or another point of reference: ■ extending above the normal or average level: *a round face with a high forehead.* ■ (of territory or landscape) inland and well above sea level. ■ near to the top of a real or notional list in order of rank or importance. ■ performed at, to, or from a considerable height: *high diving.* ■ *Baseball* (of a pitched ball) above a certain level, such as the batter's armpits, as it crosses home plate, and thus outside the strike zone. **2** great or greater than normal, in quantity, size, or intensity: *a high temperature* | *fudge is high in calories.* ■ of large numerical or monetary value: *playing for high stakes.* ■ very favorable: *an admirably high opinion of himself.* ■ (of a period or movement) at its peak: *high summer.* ■ (of latitude) close to 90°; near the North or South Pole: *high southern latitudes.* **3** great in rank or status: *he held high office.* ■ ranking above others of the same kind. ■ morally or culturally superior: *they believed that nature was driven by something higher than mere selfishness.* **4** (of a sound or note) having a frequency at the upper end of the auditory range: *a high, squeaky voice.* ■ (of a singer or instrument) producing notes of relatively high pitch: *a high soprano voice.* **5** *inf.* excited; euphoric: *he was high on an idea.* ■ intoxicated with drugs: *some of them were already* **high** *on alcohol and Ecstasy.* **6** unpleasantly strong-

smelling, in particular (of food) beginning to go bad. ■ (of game) slightly decomposed and so ready to cook. **7** *Phonet.* (of a vowel) produced with the tongue relatively near the palate. ▸ *n.* **1** a high point, level, or figure: *commodity prices were at a rare high.* ■ a notably happy or successful moment: *the highs and lows of life.* ■ a high-frequency sound or musical note. ■ an area of high atmospheric pressure; an anticyclone. **2** *inf.* a state of high spirits or euphoria: *the highs I got from cocaine always ended in despair* | *the team is still* **on a high** *from Saturday's victory.* **3** a high power setting: *the vent blower was* **on high.** ■ top gear in a motor vehicle. ▸ *adv.* **1** at or to a considerable or specified height: *the sculpture stood about five feet high.* **2** highly: *he ranked high among the pioneers.* ■ at a high price: *buying shares low and selling them high.* **3** (of a sound) at or to a high pitch. ▸ □ **from on high** from a very high place. ■ from remote high authority or heaven. □ **high and dry** out of the water, esp. the sea as it retreats: *when the tide goes out, a lot of boats are* **left high and dry.** ■ in a difficult position, esp. without resources. □ **high and low** in many different places: *we* **searched high and low** *for a new teacher.* □ **high and mighty** *chiefly derog.* important and influential: *the accursed high and mighty elite.* ■ *inf.* thinking or acting as though one is more important than others. □ **it is high time that** —— it is past the time when something should have happened or been done: *it was high time that she faced the facts.* □ **on high** in or to heaven or a high place: *a spotter plane circling on high.* □ **run high** (of a river) be full and close to overflowing, with a strong current. ■ (of feelings) be intense: *passions run high when marriages break up.*

high·ball /'hī,bôl/ ▸ *n.* **1** a drink consisting of whiskey and a mixer such as soda or ginger ale, served with ice in a tall glass. **2** *inf.* a railroad signal to proceed. ▸ *v.* [*intr.*] *inf.* travel fast: *they highballed north.*

high beam ▸ *n.* the brightest setting of a vehicle's headlights. ■ (**high beams**) the headlights of a vehicle when set on high beam.

high·born /'hī,bôrn/ ▸ *adj.* having noble parents.

high·boy /'hī,boi/ ▸ *n.* a tall chest of drawers on legs.

high·brow /'hī,brou/ ▸ *adj. often derog.* scholarly or rarefied in taste. ▸ *n.* a person of this type.

high chair ▸ *n.* a small chair with long legs for a baby or small child, fitted with a tray that is used as a table at mealtimes.

high-class ▸ *adj.* of a high standard, quality, or social class.

high court ▸ *n.* a supreme court of justice. ■ the U.S. Supreme Court. ■ (in the U.S.) the supreme court in a state.

high·er-up ▸ *n. inf.* a senior person in an organization: *he was looking for a way to impress the higher-ups.*

high·fa·lu·tin /,hīfə'lootn/ (also **high·fa·lu·ting** /-'lootiNG/) ▸ *adj. inf.* (esp. of speech, writing, or ideas) pompous or pretentious.

high fi·del·i·ty ▸ *n.* the reproduction of sound with little distortion, giving a result very similar to the original.

high five ▸ *n. inf.* a gesture of celebration or greeting in which two people slap each other's palms with their arms raised: *they gave each other an exuberant high five.* ▸ *v.* (**high-five**) [*tr.*] greet with such a gesture.

high-fli·er /'hīflīər/ (also **high-fli·er, high-fly·er, high-fly·er**) ▸ *n.* a person who is or has the potential to be very successful, esp. academically or in business: *the company cannot expect to recruit many highfliers.* —**high·fly·ing** /-'flī-iNG/ *adj.*

high-flown ▸ *adj.* (esp. of language or ideas) extravagant and lofty.

high fre·quen·cy ▸ *n.* (in radio) a frequency of 3–30 megahertz.

high-grade ▸ *adj.* of very good quality: *high-grade printing papers.* ■ (of ore) rich in metal value and commercially profitable.

high-hand·ed ▸ *adj.* using power or authority without considering the feelings of others. —**high-hand·ed·ly** *adv.* —**high-hand·ed·ness** *n.*

high hat ▸ *n.* **1** a tall hat, esp. a top hat. ■ *inf.* a snobbish or supercilious person. **2** (**high-hat**) variant spelling of HI-HAT. ▸ *adj.* (**high-hat**) *inf.* snobbish. ▸ *v.* (**high-hat**) (**-hat·ted, -hat·ting**) [*tr.*] *inf.* act in a snobbish or supercilious manner toward (someone).

high jinks /jiNGks/ ▸ *pl. n.* boisterous fun.

high jump ▸ *n.* (**the high jump**) an athletic event in which competitors jump over a bar that is raised until only one competitor can jump over it without dislodging it. —**high jump·er** *n.*

high·land /'hīlənd/ ▸ n. (also **high·lands**) an area of high or mountainous land: *the highlands of Scotland* | [as adj.] *a highland region of Vietnam.* —**high·land·er** n. —**high·land·man** n. (pl. **-men**)

High·land fling ▸ n. a vigorous Scottish dance consisting of a series of complex steps performed solo, originally to celebrate victory.

high-lev·el ▸ adj. at or of a level above that which is normal or average: *high-level crop production.* ■ relating to or involving people of high administrative rank or great authority: *high-level negotiations.* ■ Comput. denoting a programming language (e.g., BASIC or Pascal) that is relatively accessible to the user, having instructions that resemble an existing language such as English.

high life ▸ n. **1** (also **high living**) an extravagant social life as enjoyed by the wealthy. **2** (usu. **high·life**) a style of dance music of West African origin, influenced by rock and jazz.

high·light /'hī,līt/ ▸ n. **1** an outstanding part of an event or period of time: *the highlight of his career.* ■ (**highlights**) the best parts of a sporting or other event edited for broadcasting or recording: *he never watches TV highlights of games he has umpired.* **2** a bright or reflective area in a painting, picture, or design. ■ (usu. **highlights**) a bright tint in the hair, esp. one produced by bleaching or dyeing.
▸ v. [tr.] **1** (often **be highlighted**) pick out and emphasize: *speakers highlighted additional problems faced by women with AIDS.* ■ make visually prominent: *a vast backdrop with the colorful logo highlighted with lasers.* ■ mark with a highlighter. **2** create highlights in (hair).

high·light·er /'hī,līter/ ▸ n. **1** a broad felt-tipped pen used to overlay transparent fluorescent color on text or a part of an illustration, leaving it legible and emphasized. **2** a cosmetic that is lighter than the wearer's foundation or skin, used to emphasize features such as the eyes or cheekbones.

high·ly /'hīlē/ ▸ adv. to a high degree: *a highly dangerous substance* | *highly paid people.* ■ high in a hierarchy: *a highly placed official.* ■ favorably: *he was highly regarded by his colleagues.*

high-main·te·nance ▸ adj. needing a lot of work to keep in good condition. ■ inf. (of a person or relationship) demanding a lot of attention.

high-mind·ed ▸ adj. having strong moral principles. —**high-mind·ed·ly** adv. —**high-mind·ed·ness** n.

high·ness /'hīnis/ ▸ n. **1** the state of being high: *the highness of her cheekbones.* **2** (**His/Your**, etc., **Highness**) a title given to a person of royal rank, or used in addressing them: *I am most grateful, Your Highness.*

high-oc·cu·pan·cy ve·hi·cle (abbr.: **HOV**) ▸ n. a car, van, or bus that is carrying passengers.

high-oc·tane ▸ adj. denoting gasoline having a high octane number and thus good anti-knock properties. ■ fig. powerful or dynamic.

high-pitched ▸ adj. **1** (of a sound) high in pitch. **2** (of a roof) steep. **3** (of a battle or dispute) intense.

high-pow·ered (also **high-pow·er**) ▸ adj. (of a machine or device) having greater than normal strength or capabilities: *a high-powered rifle.* ■ dynamic and capable: *a high-powered delegation.*

high-pres·sure ▸ adj. **1** involving a high degree of activity and exertion; stressful: *he worked in a high-pressure advertising job.* ■ (of a salesperson or sales pitch) employing a high degree of coercion; insistent: *high-pressure marketing tactics.* **2** involving or using much physical force: *high-pressure jets of freezing water.* **3** denoting a condition of the atmosphere with the pressure above average (e.g., in an anticyclone).

high priest ▸ n. a chief priest of a non-Christian religion, in particular: ■ the chief priest of the historic Jewish religion. ■ fig. a chief advocate of a belief or practice: *the high priest of the drug culture.*

high pro·file ▸ n. a position of attracting much attention or publicity: *people who have a high profile in the community.*
▸ adj. attracting much attention or publicity: *a high-profile presence.*

high-rise ▸ adj. (of a building) having many stories: *office towers and high-rise apartments.* ■ taller or set higher than normal: *high-rise handlebars.*
▸ n. a building with many stories.

high roll·er ▸ n. inf. a person who gambles or spends large amounts of money. —**high-roll·ing** adj.

high school ▸ n. a school that typically comprises grades 9 through 12, attended after primary school or middle school. —**high school·er** n.

high seas ▸ pl. n. (**the high seas**) the open ocean, esp. that not within any country's jurisdiction.

high sign ▸ n. inf. a surreptitious gesture, often prearranged, giving warning or indicating that all is well: *I'm getting the high sign—gotta go.*

high so·ci·e·ty ▸ n. see SOCIETY (sense 1).

high-speed ▸ adj. moving, operating, or happening very quickly: *high-speed travel.* ■ (of photographic film) needing little light or only short exposure.

high spir·its ▸ pl. n. lively and cheerful behavior or mood: *the team returned in high spirits.* —**high-spir·it·ed** adj. —**high-spir·it·ed·ness** n.

high-strung ▸ adj. nervous and easily upset.

high·tail /'hī,tāl/ ▸ v. [intr.] inf. move or travel fast: *I hightailed it home.*

high tea ▸ n. Brit. a meal eaten in the late afternoon or early evening, typically consisting of a cooked dish, bread and butter, and tea.

high-tech (also **hi-tech**) ▸ adj. employing, requiring, or involved in high technology: *a high-tech security system.* ■ (chiefly in architecture and interior design) using styles and materials, such as steel, glass, and plastic, that are more usual in industry.
▸ n. (**high tech**) short for HIGH TECHNOLOGY.

high tech·nol·o·gy ▸ n. advanced technological development, esp. in electronics: [as adj.] *high-technology weapons.*

high tide ▸ n. the state and time of the tide when at its highest level. ■ the highest point of something: *the high tide of nationalism.*

high-top (also **high-top**) ▸ adj. denoting a sneaker with a laced upper that extends some distance above the wearer's ankle.
▸ n. (**high-tops**) a pair of such sneakers.

high trea·son ▸ n. see TREASON.

high·way /'hī,wā/ ▸ n. a main road, esp. one connecting major towns or cities. ■ another term for EXPRESSWAY. ■ (chiefly in official use) a public road. ■ Comput. a pathway connecting parts of one computer system or between different systems.

high·way·man /'hī,wāmən/ ▸ n. (pl. **-men**) hist. a man, typically on horseback, who held up travelers at gunpoint in order to rob them.

high wire ▸ n. a high tightrope. ■ [as adj.] fig. requiring great skill or judgment: *it will take a high-wire balancing act to fund the requirements.*

hi-hat (also **high-hat**) ▸ n. a pair of foot-operated cymbals forming part of a drum kit.

hi·jack /'hī,jak/ (also **high·jack**) ▸ v. [tr.] illegally seize (an aircraft, ship, or vehicle) in transit and force it to go to a different destination or use it for one's own purposes: *three armed men hijacked a white van* | [as n.] (**hijacking**) *an eight-hour hijacking.* ■ steal (goods) by seizing them in transit. ■ take over (something) and use it for a different purpose: *the organization had been hijacked by extremists.*
▸ n. an incident or act of hijacking. —**hi·jack·er** n.

hike /hīk/ ▸ n. **1** a long walk, esp. in the country or wilderness. ■ inf. a long distance. **2** a sharp increase; rise in price. **3** Football a snap: *he takes the hike, drops back, and fakes to his right.*
▸ v. **1** [intr.] walk for a long distance, esp. across country or in the woods: *we planned to hike another mile up a steep trail.* | [as n.] (**hiking**) *she enjoys hiking and climbing in her spare time.* **2** [tr.] pull or lift up (something, esp. clothing): *he hiked up his sweatpants and marched to the door.* ■ increase (something, esp. a price) sharply: *some of the local merchants hiked the price of goods.* **3** Football snap (a football). —**hik·er** n.

hi·lar·i·ous /hə'le(ə)rēəs/ ▸ adj. extremely amusing. ■ boisterously merry: *hilarious conversation.* —**hi·lar·i·ous·ly** adv. —**hi·lar·i·ty** -'le(ə)rit/ n.

hill /hil/ ▸ n. a naturally raised area of land, not as high or craggy as a mountain. ■ a sloping piece of road or trail: *they were climbing a steep hill in low gear.* ■ a heap or mound of something: *a hill of sliding shingle.*
▸ v. [tr.] form (something) into a heap. ■ bank up (a plant) with soil: *if frost threatens our new plants, we hill them up.*
▸ □ **over the hill** inf. old and past one's prime.

hill·bil·ly /'hil,bilē/ ▸ n. (pl. **-lies**) **1** inf., chiefly derog. an unsophisticated country person, associated originally with the remote regions of the Appalachians. **2** old-fashioned term for COUNTRY MUSIC.

hill·ock /'hilək/ ▸ n. a small hill or mound. —**hill·ock·y** adj.

hill·side /'hil,sīd/ ▸ n. the sloping side of a hill.

hill·top /'hil,täp/ ▸ n. the summit of a hill.

hill·y /'hilē/ ▸ adj. (**hill·i·er**, **hill·i·est**) having many hills. —**hill·i·ness** n.

hilt /hilt/ ▸ n. the handle of a weapon or tool, esp. a sword, dagger, or knife. —**hilt·ed** adj.
▸ □ (**up**) **to the hilt** completely: *we're mortgaged to the hilt.*

HIM Brit. ▸ abbr. Her or His Imperial Majesty.

him /him/ ▸ pron. [third person sing.] **1** used as the object of a verb or preposition to refer to a male person or animal previously mentioned or easily identified: *his wife survived him* | *he took the children with him.* Compare with HE. ■ referring to a person or animal of unspecified sex (in modern use chiefly replaced by "him or her" or "them"). ■ often used in place of "he" after the verb "to be" and after "than" or "as" to refer to a male person or animal: *that's him all right* | *I could never be as good as him.* **2** archaic or dial. himself: *in the depths of him, he too didn't want to go.*

him·self /him'self/ ▸ pron. [third person sing.] **1** [reflexive] used as the object of a verb or preposition to refer to a male person or animal previously mentioned as the subject of the clause: *the steward introduced himself as Pete | he ought to be ashamed of himself.* **2** he or him personally (used to emphasize a particular male person or animal mentioned): *Thomas himself laid down what we should do | he said so himself.*

hind[1] /hīnd/ ▸ *adj.* (esp. of a bodily part) situated at the back; posterior: *he snagged a calf by the hind leg.*

hind[2] ▸ *n.* **1** a female deer, esp. a red deer or sika in and after its third year. **2** any of several large edible groupers with spotted markings.

hind·er[1] /'hindər/ ▸ *v.* [tr.] create difficulties for (someone or something), resulting in delay or obstruction.

hind·er[2] /'hindər/ ▸ *adj.* (esp. of a bodily part) rear; hind: *the hinder end of its body.*

Hin·di /'hindē/ ▸ *n.* a form of Hindustani written in Devanagari and with many loanwords from Sanskrit, an official language of India, and the most widely spoken language of northern India.
▸ *adj.* of or relating to Hindi.

hind·most /'hīn(d),mōst/ ▸ *adj.* farthest back.

hind·quar·ters /'hīn(d),kwôrtərz/ ▸ *pl. n.* the hind legs and adjoining parts of a quadruped.

hin·drance /'hindrəns/ ▸ *n.* a thing that provides resistance, delay, or obstruction to something or someone: *a hindrance to the process.*

hind·sight /'hīn(d),sīt/ ▸ *n.* understanding of a situation or event only after it has happened or developed: *with hindsight, I should have gone.*

Hin·du /'hindōō/ ▸ *n.* (*pl.* **-dus**) a follower of Hinduism.
▸ *adj.* of or relating to Hindus or Hinduism.

Hin·du·ism /'hindōō,izəm/ ▸ *n.* a major religious and cultural tradition of the Indian subcontinent, developed from Vedic religion. —**Hin·du·ize** /-,īz/ *v.*

Hin·du·sta·ni /,hindōō'stänē/ ▸ *n.* a group of Indic dialects spoken in northwestern India, principally Hindi and Urdu. ■ the Delhi dialect of Hindi, widely used throughout India as a lingua franca.
▸ *adj.* of or relating to the culture of northwestern India.

hinge /hinj/ ▸ *n.* a movable joint or mechanism on which a door, gate, or lid swings as it opens and closes, or that connects linked objects. ■ *Biol.* a natural joint that performs a similar function, for example that of a bivalve shell. ■ a central point or principle on which everything depends. ■ a small piece of gummed transparent paper used to affix a stamp to a page in an album.
▸ *v.* (**hing·ing**) [tr.] (usu. **be hinged**) attach or join with or as if with a hinge: *the ironing board was hinged at the bottom | [as adj.] (**hinged**) a pocket watch with a hinged lid.* ■ [intr.] (of a door or part of a structure) hang and turn on a hinge: *the jaw hinged down.* ■ [intr.] (**hinge on**) depend entirely on: *the future of the industry could hinge on next month's election.* —**hinge·less** *adj.*

hin·ny /'hinē/ ▸ *n.* (*pl.* **-nies**) the offspring of a female donkey and a male horse.

hinge

hint /hint/ ▸ *n.* a slight or indirect indication or suggestion: *he has given no hint of his views.* ■ a small piece of practical information or advice. ■ a very small trace of something: *Randy smiled with a hint of mockery.*
▸ *v.* [intr.] suggest or indicate something indirectly or covertly: *Edwards has hinted that he will retire next year.* ■ (**hint at**) (of a thing) be a slight or possible indication of: *the restrained fronts of the terraced houses only hinted at the wealth within.*
▸ □ **take a** (or **the**) **hint** understand and act on a hint: *she tried to put him off but he didn't take the hint.*

hin·ter·land /'hintər,land/ (also **hin·ter·lands**) ▸ *n.* the often uncharted areas beyond a coastal district or a river's banks. ■ an area surrounding a town or port and served by it. ■ the remote areas of a region: *the mountain hinterland.* ■ *fig.* an area lying beyond what is visible or known: *in the hinterland of his mind these things rose, dark and ominous.*

hip[1] /hip/ ▸ *n.* **1** a projection of the pelvis and upper thigh bone on each side of the body in human beings and quadrupeds. ■ (**hips**) the circumference of the body at the buttocks: *a sweater tied around the hips.* ■ a person's hip joint: *she ran into a fence and dislocated her hip.* **2** the sharp edge of a roof from the ridge to the eaves where two sides meet.

hip[2] (also **rose hip**) ▸ *n.* the fruit of a rose, esp. a wild kind.

hip[3] ▸ *adj.* (**hip·per**, **hip·pest**) *inf.* following the latest fashion, esp. in popular music and clothes: *it's becoming hip to be environmentally conscious.* ■ understanding; aware. —**hip·ly** *adv.* —**hip·ness** *n.*

hip[4] ▸ *interj.* introducing a communal cheer: *hip, hip, hooray!*

hip·bone /'hip,bōn/ ▸ *n.* a large bone forming the main part of the pelvis on each side of the body and consisting of the fused ilium, ischium, and pubis.

hip-hop ▸ *n.* a style of popular music of U.S. black and Hispanic origin, featuring rap with an electronic backing.

hip-hug·gers (also **hip·hug·gers**) ▸ *pl. n.* pants hanging from the hips rather than from the waist.

hip joint ▸ *n.* the ball-and-socket joint connecting a leg to the trunk of the body, in which the head of the thigh bone fits into the socket of the ilium.

hip·pie /'hipē/ (also **hip·py**) ▸ *n.* (esp. in the 1960s) a person of unconventional appearance, typically having long hair and wearing beads, associated with a subculture involving a rejection of conventional values and the taking of hallucinogenic drugs.
▸ *adj.* of or relating to hippies or the subculture associated with them. —**hip·pie·dom** /-dəm/ *n.* —**hip·pi·ness** *n.* —**hip·py·ish** /'hipē-ish/ *adj.*

hip·po /'hipō/ ▸ *n.* (*pl.* same or **-pos**) informal term for HIPPOPOTAMUS.

Hip·po·crat·ic oath /'hipə'kratik/ ▸ *n.* an oath stating the obligations and proper conduct of doctors, formerly taken by those beginning medical practice. Parts of the oath are still used in most medical schools.

hip·po·drome /'hipə,drōm/ ▸ *n.* **1** an arena used for equestrian or other sporting events. **2** (in ancient Greece or Rome) a course for chariot or horse races.

hip·po·pot·a·mus /,hipə'pätəməs/ ▸ *n.* (*pl.* **hippopotamuses** or **hippopotami** /-mī; -mē/) a large thick-skinned semiaquatic African mammal (family Hippopotamidae) with massive jaws and large tusks.

hip·py[1] ▸ *n.* & *adj.* variant spelling of HIPPIE.

hip·py[2] ▸ *adj.* having large hips.

hip·ster /'hipstər/ ▸ *n.* *inf.* a person who follows the latest trends and fashions. —**hip·ster·ism** /-,rizəm/ *n.*

hire /hīr/ ▸ *v.* [tr.] **1** employ (someone) for wages. ■ employ for a short time to do a particular job: *don't hire a babysitter who's under 16 | [as adj.] (**hired**) a hired assassin.* ■ (**hire oneself out**) make oneself available for temporary employment: *he hired himself out as a laborer.* **2** *chiefly Brit.* obtain the temporary use of (something) for an agreed payment; rent: *she had to hire a dress for the wedding.* ■ (**hire something out**) grant the temporary use of something for an agreed payment.
▸ *n.* **1** the action of hiring someone or something. **2** a recently recruited employee: *new hires go through six months of training.* —**hire·a·ble** (also **hir·a·ble**) *adj.* —**hir·er** *n.*
▸ □ **for** (or **on**) **hire** available to be hired.

hire·ling /'hīrliNG/ ▸ *n.* *chiefly derog.* a person employed to undertake menial work, esp. on a casual basis.

hir·sute /'hər,sōōt; hər'sōōt; 'hi(ə)r,sōōt/ ▸ *adj.* hairy. —**hir·sute·ness** *n.*

his /hiz/ ▸ *possessive adj.* **1** belonging to or associated with a male person or animal previously mentioned or easily identified: *James sold his business.* ■ belonging to or associated with a person or animal of unspecified sex (in modern use chiefly replaced by "his or her" or "their"): *any child with delayed speech should have his hearing checked.* **2** (**His**) used in titles: *His Honor | His Lordship.*
▸ *possessive pron.* used to refer to a thing or things belonging to or associated with a male person or animal previously mentioned: *he took my hand in his | some friends of his.*

His·pan·ic /hi'spanik/ ▸ *adj.* of or relating to Spain or to Spanish-speaking countries, esp. those of Latin America. ■ of or relating to Spanish-speaking people or their culture, esp. in the U.S.
▸ *n.* a Spanish-speaking person living in the U.S., esp. one of Latin American descent. —**His·pan·i·cize** /hi'spani,sīz/ *v.*

hiss /his/ ▸ *v.* [intr.] make a sharp sibilant sound as of the letter *s*. ■ (of a person) make such a sound as a sign of disapproval or derision: *the audience hissed at the mention of his name.* ■ [tr.] express disapproval of (someone) by making such a sound: *he was hissed off the stage.* ■ whisper something in an urgent or angry way: *"Get back!" he hissed.*
▸ *n.* a sharp sibilant sound. ■ a sound such as this used as an expression of disapproval or derision: *a hiss of annoyance.* ■ electrical interference at audio frequencies: *tape hiss.*

his·ta·mine /'histə,mēn; -,min/ ▸ *n.* *Biochem.* a heterocyclic amine, $C_5H_9N_3$, that is released by cells in response to injury and in allergic and inflammatory reactions, causing contraction of smooth muscle and dilation of capillaries. —**his·ta·min·ic** /,histə'minik/ *adj.*

his·to·gram /ˈhistəˌgram/ ▸*n. Statistics* a diagram consisting of rectangles whose area is proportional to the frequency of a variable.

his·tol·o·gy /hiˈstäləjē/ ▸*n. Biol.* the study of the microscopic structure of tissues. —**his·to·log·ic** /ˌhistəˈläjik/ *adj.* —**his·to·log·i·cal** /ˌhistəˈläjikəl/ *adj.* —**his·tol·o·gist** /-jist/ *n.*

his·tol·y·sis /hiˈstäləsis/ ▸*n. Biol.* the breaking down of tissues (e.g., during animal metamorphosis). —**his·to·lyt·ic** /ˌhistəˈlitik/ *adj.*

his·to·ri·an /hiˈstôrēən/ ▸*n.* an expert in or student of history, esp. that of a particular period, geographical region, or social phenomenon.

his·tor·ic /hiˈstôrik; -ˈstär-/ ▸*adj.* famous or important in history, or potentially so: *we are standing on a historic site | a time of historic change.* ■ *archaic* of or concerning history; of the past: *eruptions in historic times.*

his·tor·i·cal /hiˈstôrikəl; -ˈstär-/ ▸*adj.* of or concerning history; concerning past events: *the historical background to such studies.* ■ belonging to the past, not the present: *famous historical figures.* ■ (esp. of a novel or movie) set in the past. ■ (of the study of a subject) based on an analysis of its development over a period. —**his·tor·i·cal·ly** *adv.*

his·tor·i·cism /hiˈstôrəˌsizəm; -ˈstär-/ ▸*n.* the theory that social and cultural phenomena are determined by history. ■ the belief that historical events are governed by laws. —**his·tor·i·cist** *n.*

his·to·ric·i·ty /ˌhistəˈrisitē/ ▸*n.* historical authenticity.

his·to·ri·og·ra·phy /hiˌstôrēˈägrəfē/ ▸*n.* the study of historical writing. ■ the writing of history. —**his·to·ri·og·ra·pher** /-ˈägrəfər/ *n.* —**his·to·ri·o·graph·ic** /-ēˈgrafik/ *adj.* —**his·to·ri·o·graph·i·cal** /-əˈgrafikəl/ *adj.*

his·to·ry /ˈhist(ə)rē/ ▸*n. (pl.* **-ries)** **1** the study of past events, particularly in human affairs: *medieval European history.* ■ the past considered as a whole: *letters that have changed the course of history.* **2** the whole series of past events connected with someone or something: *the history of Aegean painting.* ■ an eventful past: *the group has quite a history.* ■ a past characterized by a particular thing: *his family had a history of insanity.* **3** a continuous, typically chronological, record of important or public events or of a particular trend or institution: *a history of the labor movement.* ■ a historical play: *Shakespeare's comedies, histories, and tragedies.* ▷late Middle English (also as a verb): via Latin from Greek *historia* 'finding out, narrative, history,' from *histōr* 'learned, wise man,' from an Indo-European root shared by *wit* 'have knowledge.'
▸ ☐ **be history** be perceived as no longer relevant to the present: *the mainframe will soon be history.* ■ *inf.* used to indicate imminent departure, dismissal, or death: *an inch either way and you'd be history.*

his·tri·on·ic /ˌhistrēˈänik/ ▸*adj.* overly theatrical or melodramatic in character or style: *a histrionic outburst.*
▸*n.* (**histrionics**) exaggerated dramatic behavior designed to attract attention. ■ dramatic performance; theater. —**his·tri·on·i·cal·ly** /-ik(ə)lē/ *adv.*

hit /hit/ ▸*v.* (**hit·ting;** *past* **hit)** [*tr.*] **1** bring one's hand or a tool or weapon into contact with (someone or something) quickly and forcefully: *the woman hit the mugger with her umbrella | the police hit out with billy clubs.* ■ accidentally strike (part of one's body) against something, often causing injury: *she hit her head on the metal bedstead.* ■ (of a moving object or body) come into contact with (someone or something stationary) quickly and forcefully: *a car hit the barrier.* ■ *inf.* touch or press (part of a machine or other device) in order to work it: *he picked up the phone and hit several buttons.* **2** cause harm or distress to. ■ [*intr.*] (**hit out**) make a strongly worded criticism or attack: *she hit out at suppliers for hyping their products.* ■ (of a disaster) occur in and cause damage to (an area) suddenly: *the country was hit by a major earthquake.* ■ *inf.* attack and rob or kill. ■ *inf.* be affected by (an unfortunate and unexpected circumstance or event): *the opening of the town center hit a snag.* **3** (of a missile or a person aiming one) strike (a target). ■ *inf.* reach (a particular level, point, or figure): *his career hit rock bottom.* ■ arrive at (a place): *it was still night when we hit the outskirts of Chicago.* ■ *inf.* go to (a place): *we hit a diner for coffee and doughnuts.* ■ be suddenly and vividly realized by: [*tr.*] *it hit her that I wanted to settle down here.* ■ [*intr.*] *inf.* (of a piece of music, film, or play) be successful: *actors are promised a pay increase if a show hits.* ■ [*intr.*] take effect: *we sat waiting for the caffeine to hit.* ■ *inf.* give (someone) a dose of a drug or an alcoholic drink. ■ *inf.* (of a product) become available and make an impact on: *the latest board game to hit the market.* ■ (**hit someone for/up for**) *inf.* ask someone for: *she was waiting for the right moment to hit her mother for some cash.* **4** propel (a ball) with a bat, racket, stick, etc., to score or attempt to score runs or points in a game. ■ score (runs or points) in this way: *he had hit 25 home runs.* ■ *Baseball* [*intr.*] (of a batter) make a base hit.
▸*phrasal v.* ☐ **hit on** (or **upon) 1** discover or think of, esp. by chance: *she hit on a novel idea for fund-raising.* **2** *inf.* make sexual advances toward.

☐ **hit up** attempt to get something, typically money, from (someone): *he hit up some family members.*
▸*n.* **1** an instance of striking or being struck: *few structures can withstand a hit from a speeding car.* ■ *inf.* a murder, typically one planned and carried out by a criminal organization. ■ *Baseball* short for **BASE HIT.** **2** an instance of striking the target aimed at: *one of the bombers had scored a direct hit.* ■ a successful venture, esp. in entertainment: *he was the director of many big hits | [as adj.] a hit comedy.* ■ a successful pop record or song. ■ *inf.* a successful and popular person or thing: *handsome, smiling, and smart, he was an immediate hit.* ■ *Comput.* an instance of identifying an item of data that matches the requirements of a search. ■ an instance of a particular Web site being accessed by a user: *the site gets 350,000 hits per day.* **3** *inf.* a dose of a psychoactive drug. —**hit·ter** *n.*
▸ ☐ **hit-and-miss** done or occurring at random: *picking a remedy can be a bit hit-and-miss.* ☐ **hit someone below the belt** *Boxing* give one's opponent an illegal low blow. ■ behave unfairly, esp. so as to gain an unfair advantage. ☐ **hit the hay** ☐ see HAY[1]. ☐ **hit home** see HOME. ☐ **hit it off** *inf.* be naturally friendly or well suited. ☐ **hit the jackpot** see JACKPOT. ☐ **hit the nail on the head** find exactly the right answer. ☐ **hit-or-miss** /ˌhid ôr ˈmis/ *as* likely to be unsuccessful as successful: *her work can be hit-or-miss.* ☐ **hit the road** (or **trail)** *inf.* set out on a journey. ☐ **make a hit** be successful or popular: *you made a big hit with her.*

hitch /hiCH/ ▸*v.* **1** [*tr.*] move (something) into a different position with a jerk: *she hitched the blanket around him | he hitched his pants up.* **2** [*intr.*] *inf.* travel by hitchhiking. ■ [*tr.*] obtain (a ride) by hitchhiking. **3** [*tr.*] fasten or tether with a rope: *he returned to where he had hitched his horse.* ■ harness (a draft animal or team): *Thomas hitched the pony to his cart.*
▸*n.* **1** a temporary interruption or problem: *everything went without a hitch.* **2** a knot used for fastening a rope to another rope or something else. ■ a device for attaching one thing to another, esp. the tow bar of a motor vehicle: *a trailer hitch.* **3** *inf.* an act of hitchhiking. **4** *inf.* a period of service: *his 12-year hitch in the navy.*
▸ ☐ **get hitched** *inf.* marry.

hitch·hike /ˈhiCHˌhīk/ ▸*v.* [*intr.*] travel by getting free rides in passing vehicles: *he dropped out in 1976 and hitchhiked west.*
▸*n.* a journey made by hitchhiking. —**hitch·hik·er** *n.*

hi-tech /ˈhī ˈtek/ ▸*adj.* variant spelling of HIGH-TECH.

hith·er /ˈhiT͟Hər/ ▸*adv. archaic* or *poetic/lit.* to or toward this place.

hith·er·to /ˈhiT͟Hərˌtoō; ˌhiT͟Hərˈtoō/ ▸*adv.* until now or until the point in time under discussion.

hit list ▸*n.* a list of people to be killed for criminal or political reasons: *a terrorist hit list.* ■ a list of things to be attacked or opposed.

hit man ▸*n. inf.* a person who is paid to kill someone, esp. for a criminal or political organization.

hit pa·rade ▸*n. dated* a weekly listing of the current best-selling pop records. ■ any list of popular things.

Hit·tite /ˈhitīt/ ▸*n.* **1** a member of an ancient people who established an empire in Asia Minor and Syria that flourished from *c.*1700 to *c.*1200 BC. **2** the Anatolian language of the Hittites, the earliest attested Indo-European language. Written in both hieroglyphic and cuneiform scripts, it was deciphered in the early 20th century.

HIV ▸*abbr.* human immunodeficiency virus, a retrovirus that causes AIDS.

hive /hīv/ ▸*n.* a beehive. ■ the bees in a hive. ■ a thing that has the domed shape of a beehive. ■ *fig.* a place in which people are busily occupied: *the kitchen became a hive of activity.*
▸*v.* [*tr.*] place (bees) in a hive. ■ [*intr.*] (of bees) enter a hive.

hives /hīvz/ ▸*pl. n.* [treated as *sing.* or *pl.*] another term for URTICARIA.

HL ▸*abbr.* (in the UK) House of Lords.

hl ▸*abbr.* hectoliter(s).

HM ▸*abbr.* headmaster or headmistress. ■ (in the UK) Her (or His) Majesty('s): *HM Forces.*

hm ▸*abbr.* hectometer(s).

HMO ▸*abbr.* health maintenance organization.

Ho ▸*symb.* the chemical element holmium.

ho[1] /hō/ (also **hoe**) ▸*n.* (*pl.* **hos** or **hoes**) *inf.* a prostitute. ■ *derog.* a woman.

ho[2] /hō/ ▸*interj.* **1** an expression of surprise, admiration, triumph, or derision: *Ho! I'll show you.* ■ [in *comb.*] used as the second element of various exclamations: *what ho! | heave ho.* **2** used to call for attention: *ho there!* ■ [in *comb.*] *dated, chiefly Naut.* used to draw attention to something seen: *land ho!*

hoa·gie /ˈhōgē/ ▸*n.* (also **hoa·gy**) (*pl.* **-gies**) another term for SUBMARINE SANDWICH.

hoard /hôrd/ ▸*n.* a stock or store of money or valued objects, typically

one that is secret or carefully guarded: *he came back to rescue his little hoard of gold.* ■ an ancient store of coins or other valuable artifacts: *a hoard of Romano-British bronzes.* ■ an amassed store of useful information or facts, retained for future use: *a hoard of secret information about his work.*
▶*v.* [*tr.*] amass (money or valued objects) and hide or store away. ■ accumulate a supply of (something) in a time of scarcity. ■ reserve in the mind for future use: *a year's worth of hoarded resentments and grudges.* —**hoard·er** *n.*

hoar·frost /ˈhôrˌfrôst; -ˌfräst/ ▶*n.* a grayish-white crystalline deposit of frozen water vapor formed in clear still weather on vegetation, fences, etc.

hoarse /hôrs/ ▶*adj.* (of a person's voice) sounding rough and harsh, typically as the result of a sore throat or of shouting: *a hoarse whisper | he shouted himself hoarse.* —**hoarse·ly** *adv.* —**hoars·en** /ˈhôrsən/ *v.* —**hoarse·ness** *n.*

hoar·y /ˈhôrē/ ▶*adj.* (**hoar·i·er, hoar·i·est**) **1** grayish-white: *hoary cobwebs.* **2** old and trite: *that hoary American notion that bigger is better.* —**hoar·i·ly** /ˈhôrəlē/ *adv.* —**hoar·i·ness** *n.*

hoax /hōks/ ▶*n.* a humorous or malicious deception: *they recognized the plan as a hoax | [as adj.] he was accused of making hoax calls.*
▶*v.* [*tr.*] deceive with a hoax. —**hoax·er** *n.*

hob·bit /ˈhäbit/ ▶*n.* a member of an imaginary race similar to humans, of small size and with hairy feet, in stories by J. R. R. Tolkien.

hob·ble /ˈhäbəl/ ▶*v.* **1** [*intr.*] walk in an awkward way, typically because of pain from an injury: *he was hobbling around on crutches.* ■ *fig.* proceed haltingly in action or speech: *inertia will keep it hobbling along.* **2** [*tr.*] (often **be hobbled**) tie or strap together (the legs of a horse or other animal) to prevent it from straying. ■ cause (a person or animal) to limp: *Johnson was still hobbled slightly by an ankle injury.* ■ *fig.* be or cause a problem for.
▶*n.* **1** an awkward way of walking, typically due to pain from an injury. **2** a rope or strap used for hobbling a horse or other animal. —**hob·bler** /ˈhäb(ə)lər/ *n.*

hob·by /ˈhäbē/ ▶*n.* (*pl.* **-bies**) **1** an activity done regularly in one's leisure time for pleasure: *her hobbies are reading and gardening.* **2** *archaic* a small horse or pony. ■ *hist.* an early type of velocipede. —**hob·by·ist** *n.*

hob·by·horse /ˈhäbēˌhôrs/ ▶*n.* **1** a child's toy consisting of a stick with a model of a horse's head at one end. ■ a rocking horse. **2** a preoccupation; a favorite topic.

hob·gob·lin /ˈhäbˌgäblən/ ▶*n.* (in mythology and fairy tales) a mischievous imp or sprite. ■ a fearsome mythical creature.

hob·nail /ˈhäbˌnāl/ ▶*n.* a short heavy-headed nail used to reinforce the soles of boots. ■ a blunt projection, esp. in cut or molded glassware. —**hob·nailed** *adj.*

hob·nob /ˈhäbˌnäb/ ▶*v.* (**-nobbed, -nob·bing**) [*intr.*] *inf.* mix socially, esp. with those of higher social status.

ho·bo /ˈhōˌbō/ ▶*n.* (*pl.* **-boes** or **-bos**) a homeless person; a tramp. ■ a migrant worker.

Hob·son's choice /ˈhäbsənz/ ▶*n.* a choice of taking what is available or nothing at all.

hock[1] /häk/ ▶*n.* **1** the joint in a quadruped's hind leg between the knee and the fetlock, the angle of which points backward. **2** a knuckle of meat, esp. of pork or ham.

hock[2] ▶*v.* [*tr.*] informal term for PAWN[2].
▶ □ **in hock** having been pawned. ■ in debt.

hock[3] ▶*n. Brit.* a dry white wine from the German Rhineland.

hock·ey /ˈhäkē/ ▶*n.* **1** short for ICE HOCKEY. **2** short for FIELD HOCKEY.

ho·cus-po·cus /ˈpōkəs/ ▶*n.* meaningless talk or activity, often designed to draw attention away from and disguise what is actually happening: *some people still view psychology as a lot of hocus-pocus.* ■ a form of words often used by a person performing magic tricks. ■ deception; trickery.
▶*v.* (**-po·cused, -po·cus·ing** or *Brit.* **-po·cussed, -po·cus·sing**) [*intr.*] play tricks. ■ [*tr.*] play tricks on; deceive. ▷*early 17th cent.*: from *hax pax max Deus adimax,* a pseudo-Latin phrase used as a magic formula by conjurors.

hod /häd/ ▶*n. dated* a builder's V-shaped open trough on a pole, used for carrying bricks, mortar and other building materials. ■ a coal scuttle.

hodge·podge /ˈhäjˌpäj/ (*Brit.* **hotch·potch**) ▶*n.* a confused mixture: *Rob's living room was a hodgepodge of modern furniture and antiques.*

hoe /hō/ ▶*n.* a long-handled gardening tool with a thin metal blade, used mainly for weeding and breaking up soil.
▶*v.* (**hoes, hoed, hoe·ing**) [*tr.*] use a hoe to dig (earth) or thin out or dig up (plants). ■ [*intr.*] use a hoe. —**ho·er** *n.*

hoe·cake /ˈhōˌkāk/ ▶*n.* a coarse cake made of cornmeal.

hoe·down /ˈhōˌdoun/ ▶*n.* a social gathering at which lively folk dancing takes place. ■ a lively folk dance.

hog /hôg; häg/ ▶*n.* **1** a domesticated pig, esp. one over 120 pounds (54 kg) and reared for slaughter. ■ a feral pig. ■ a wild animal of the pig family, for example, a warthog. ■ *inf.* a greedy person. **2** *inf.* a large, heavy motorcycle.
▶*v.* (**hogged, hog·ging**) [*tr.*] *inf.* keep or use all of (something) for oneself in an unfair or selfish way: *he never hogged the limelight.* —**hog·ger** *n.* —**hog·ger·y** /ˈhôgərē; ˈhäg-/ *n.* —**hog·gish** *adj.* —**hog·gish·ly** *adv.* —**hog·like** /-ˌlīk/ *adj.*
▶ □ **go (the) whole hog** *inf.* do something completely or thoroughly. □ **live high on (or off) the hog** *inf.* have a luxurious lifestyle.

ho·gan /ˈhōˌgän; -gən/ ▶*n.* a traditional Navajo hut of logs and earth.

hogan

hog·back /ˈhôgˌbak; ˈhäg-/ ▶*n.* a long hill or mountain ridge with steep sides.

hogs·head /ˈhôgzˌhed; ˈhägz-/ (*abbr.*: **hhd**) ▶*n.* a large cask. ■ a measure of capacity, equal to 63 gallons (238.7 liters) for wine and 64 gallons (245.5 liters) for beer.

hog-tie (also **hog·tie**) ▶*v.* [*tr.*] secure by fastening together the hands and feet (of a person) or all four feet (of an animal): *they gagged him and hog-tied him to the front pew.* ■ *fig.* impede or hinder greatly: *an economy hog-tied by entrenched Stalinism.*

hog·wash /ˈhôgˌwôsh; ˈhäg-ˌwäsh/ ▶*n. inf.* nonsense.

ho-hum /ˈhō ˈhəm/ ▶*interj.* used to express boredom or resignation.
▶*adj.* boring: *a ho-hum script.*

hoi pol·loi /ˈhoi pəˌloi/ ▶*pl. n.* (usu. **the hoi polloi**) *derog.* the masses; the common people: *avoid mixing with the hoi polloi.*

hoist /hoist/ ▶*v.* [*tr.*] raise (something) by means of ropes and pulleys: *high overhead great cranes hoisted girders.* ■ [*tr.*] raise or haul up.
▶*n.* an act of raising or lifting something. ■ an apparatus for lifting or raising something. ▷*late 15th cent.*: alteration of dialect *hoise,* probably from Dutch *hijsen* or Low German *hiesen,* but recorded earlier. —**hoist·er** *n.*

hoi·ty-toi·ty /ˈhoitē ˈtoitē/ ▶*adj.* **1** haughty; snobbish: *the moneyed, hoity-toity inhabitants of the island.* **2** *archaic* frolicsome.

hok·ey /ˈhōkē/ ▶*adj.* (**hok·i·er, hok·i·est**) *inf.* mawkishly sentimental: *a good-hearted, slightly hokey song.* ■ noticeably contrived: *a hokey southern accent.* —**hok·ey·ness** (also **hok·i·ness**) *n.*

ho·key-po·key ▶*n.* **1** (**the hokey-pokey**) a circle dance with a synchronized shaking of the limbs in turn, accompanied by a simple song. **2** hocus-pocus; trickery.

ho·kum /ˈhōkəm/ ▶*n. inf.* nonsense: *they dismissed such corporate homilies as boardroom hokum.* ■ trite, sentimental, or unrealistic situations and dialogue in a movie, play, or piece of writing: *classic B-movie hokum.*

hold[1] /hōld/ ▶*v.* (*past* **held** /held/) **1** [*tr.*] grasp, carry, or support with one's arms or hands: *she was holding a brown leather suitcase | [intr.] he held onto the back of a chair.* ■ [*tr.*] keep or sustain in a specified position: *I held the door open for him fig. the people are held down by a repressive military regime.* ■ embrace (someone): *Mark pulled her into his arms and held her close.* ■ (**hold something up**) support and prevent from falling: *concrete pillars hold up the elevated section of the railroad.* ■ be able to bear (the weight of a person or thing): *I reached up to the nearest branch that seemed likely to hold my weight.* ■ (of a vehicle) maintain close contact with (the road), esp. when driven at speed: *the car holds the corners very well.* ■ (of a ship or an aircraft) continue to follow (a particular course): *the ship is holding a southeasterly course.* ■ [*intr.*] *archaic* keep going in a particular direction. **2** [*tr.*] keep or detain (someone): *the police were holding him on a murder charge.* ■ keep possession of (something), typically in the face of a challenge or attack. | [*intr.*] *White managed to hold onto his lead.* ■ keep (someone's interest or attention). ■ (of a singer or musician) sustain (a note). ■ stay or cause to stay at a certain value or level: [*intr.*] *the savings rate held at 5%* | [*tr.*] *he is determined to hold down inflation.* **3** [*intr.*] remain secure, intact, or in position without breaking or giving way: *the boat's anchor would not hold.* ■ (of a favorable condition or situation) continue without changing: *let's hope her luck holds.* ■ be or remain valid or available: *I'll have that coffee now, if the offer still holds.* ■ (of an argument or theory) be logical, consistent, or convincing: *their views still seem to hold up extremely well.* ■ (**hold to**) refuse to abandon or change (a principle or opinion). ■ [*tr.*] (**hold someone to**) cause someone to adhere to (a commitment). **4** [*tr.*] contain or be capable of containing (a specified amount): *the tank held twenty-four gallons.* ■ have or be characterized by: *I don't know what the future holds.* **5** [*tr.*] have in one's possession: *the managing director still holds fifty shares in the company.* ■ [*intr.*] *inf.* be in possession of illegal drugs: *he was holding, and the police hauled him off to jail.* ■ have or occupy (a job or position). ■ have or adhere to (a belief or opinion). | *they hold that all literature is empty of meaning.* ■ [*tr.*] consider (someone) to be responsible or liable for a particular situation: *you can't hold yourself responsible for what happened.* ■ (**hold someone/something in**) regard someone or something with (a specified feeling): *the speed limit is held in contempt by many drivers.* ■ (of a judge or court) rule; decide. **6** [*tr.*] keep or reserve for someone: *a reservation can be held for twenty-four hours.* ■ prevent from going ahead or occurring: *hold your fire!* ■ maintain (a telephone connection) until the person one has telephoned is free to speak: *please hold, and I'll see if he's available.* ■ *inf.* refrain from adding or using (something, typically an item of food or drink): *a strawberry margarita, but hold the tequila.* ■ (**hold it**) *inf.* used as a way of exhorting someone to wait or to stop doing something: *hold it right there, pal!* **7** [*tr.*] arrange and take part in (a meeting or conversation): *a meeting was held at the church.*

▸*phrasal v.* □ **hold something against** allow past actions or circumstances to have a negative influence on one's present attitude toward (someone): *he knew that if he failed her, she would hold it against him forever.* □ **hold someone/something back** prevent or restrict the advance, progress, or development of someone or something: *Jane struggled to hold back her laughter.* ■ (**hold something back**) refuse or be unwilling to make something known: *you're not holding anything back from me, are you?* □ **hold forth** talk lengthily, assertively, or tediously about a subject: *he was holding forth on the merits of the band's debut album.* □ **hold off** (of bad weather) fail to occur. ■ delay or postpone an action or decision. □ **hold on 1** [often in *imper.*] wait; stop; *hold on a minute, I'll be right back!* **2** endure or keep going in difficult circumstances: *if only they could hold on a little longer.* □ **hold out** resist or survive in dangerous or difficult circumstances: *Russian troops held out against constant attacks.* ■ continue to be sufficient: *we can stay here for as long as our supplies hold out.* □ **hold out for** continue to demand (a particular thing), refusing to accept what has been offered: *he is holding out for a guaranteed 7 percent raise.* □ **hold something out** offer a chance or hope: *a new drug may hold out hope for patients with lung cancer.* □ **hold together** (or **hold something together**) remain or cause to remain united: *if your party holds together, you will probably win.* □ **hold up** remain strong or vigorous: *the dollar held up well against the yen.* □ **hold someone/something up 1** delay or block the movement or progress of someone or something: *our return flight was held up for seven hours.* **2** rob someone or something using the threat of force or violence: *a masked gunman held up the post office.* **3** present or expose someone or something as an example or for particular treatment: *they were held up to public ridicule.* □ **hold with** *inf.* approve of: *I don't hold with fighting or violence.*

▸*n.* an act or manner of grasping something; a grip. ■ a place where one can grip with one's hands and feet while climbing: *he felt carefully with his feet for a hold.* ■ a way of influencing someone: *Tom had some kind of **hold over** his father.* ■ a degree of power or control: *military forces tightened their **hold on** the capital.* —**hold·a·ble** *adj.*

▸ □ **be left holding the bag** (or **baby**) *inf.* be left with an unwelcome responsibility, typically without warning. □ **get hold of** grasp (someone or something) physically. ■ grasp (something) intellectually; understand. ■ *inf.* obtain: *if you can't get hold of ripe tomatoes, add some tomato purée.* ■ *inf.* find or manage to contact (someone): *I'll try and get hold of Mark.* □ **hold court** be the center of attention amid a crowd of one's admirers. □ **hold the fort** take responsibility for a situation while another person is temporarily absent. □ **hold hands** (of two or more people) clasp each other by the hand, typically as a sign of affection. □ **hold someone/something harmless** *Law* indemnify someone or something. □ **hold one's horses** [usu. as *imper.*] *inf.* wait a moment. □ **hold the line** not yield to the pressure of a difficult situation: *France's central bank would hold the line.* □ **hold one's tongue** [often in *imper.*] *inf.* remain silent. □ **hold true** (or **good**) remain true or valid: *his views still hold true today.* □ **hold water** (of a statement, theory, or line of

reasoning) appear to be valid, sound, or reasonable: *this argument just does not hold water.* □ **no holds barred** (in wrestling) with no restrictions on the kinds of holds that are used. ■ *fig.* used to convey that no rules or restrictions apply in a conflict or dispute: *no-holds-barred military action.* □ **on hold** waiting to be connected while making a telephone call. ■ temporarily not being dealt with or pursued: *he put his career on hold.* □ **take hold** start to have an effect: *the reforms of the late nineteenth century had taken hold.*

hold² ▸*n.* a compartment in the lower part of a ship or aircraft in which cargo is stowed.

hold·er /'hōldər/ ▸*n.* **1** a device or implement for holding something: *a cigarette holder.* **2** a person who holds something: *U.S. passport holders* | *holders of two American hostages.* ■ the possessor of a trophy, championship, or record: *the record holder in the 100-meter dash.*

hold·ing /'hōldiNG/ ▸*n.* **1** an area of land held by lease. ■ the tenure of such land. **2** (**holdings**) stocks, property, and other financial assets in someone's possession. ■ books, periodicals, magazines, and other material in a library. **3** (in certain team sports such as football, basketball, and ice hockey) an illegal move that prevents an opponent from moving freely. **4** a court's ruling on a matter of law essential to a judicial decision. ■ the legal principle drawn from such a ruling.

hold·ing com·pa·ny ▸*n.* a company created to buy and possess the shares of other companies, which it then controls.

hold·up /'hōld,əp/ ▸*n.* **1** a situation that causes delay, esp. to a journey. **2** a robbery conducted with the use of threats or violence.

hole /hōl/ ▸*n.* **1** a hollow place in a solid body or surface. ■ an animal's burrow. ■ an aperture passing through something: *he had a hole in his sock.* ■ a cavity or receptacle on a golf course, typically one of eighteen or nine, into which the ball must be hit. ■ a cavity of this type as representing a division of a golf course or of play in golf: *Stephen lost the first three holes to Eric.* ■ *Physics* a position from which an electron is absent, esp. one regarded as a mobile carrier of positive charge in a semiconductor. ■ [in *place names*] a valley: *Jackson Hole.* **2** *inf.* a small or unpleasant place: *she had wasted a whole lifetime in this hole of a town.* ■ *inf.* an awkward situation: *get yourself out of a hole.*

▸*v.* [*tr.*] **1** make a hole or holes in: *a fuel tank was holed by the attack.* **2** *Golf* hit (the ball) so that it falls into a hole: [*intr.*] *he holed in one at the third.*

▸*phrasal v.* □ **hole out** *Golf* send the ball into a hole. □ **hole up** *inf.* hide oneself: *I holed up for two days in a tiny cottage in Pennsylvania.* —**hol·ey** /'hōlē/ *adj.*

▸ □ **in the hole** *inf.* in debt: *we're still three thousand dollars in the hole.*

hole in one ▸*n.* (*pl.* **holes in one**) *Golf* a shot that enters the hole from the tee with no intervening shots.

hole in the wall ▸*n.* *inf.* a small dingy place, esp. a bar or restaurant.

hol·i·day /'häli,dā/ ▸*n.* a day of festivity or recreation when no work is done: *December 25 is an official public holiday.* ■ [as *adj.*] characteristic of a holiday; festive: *a holiday atmosphere.* ■ *chiefly Brit.* (often **holidays**) a vacation: *I spent my summer holidays on a farm* | *Fred was on holiday in Spain.*

▸*v.* [*intr.*] *chiefly Brit.* spend a holiday in a specified place: *he is holidaying in Italy.*

ho·li·er-than-thou ▸*adj.* characterized by an attitude of moral superiority: *they had quite a critical, holier-than-thou approach.*

ho·li·ness /'hōlēnis/ ▸*n.* the state of being holy. ■ (**His/Your Holiness**) a title given to the pope, Orthodox patriarchs, and the Dalai Lama, or used in addressing them.

ho·lism /'hōl,izəm/ ▸*n.* *chiefly Philos.* the theory that parts of a whole are in intimate interconnection, such that they cannot exist independently of the whole, or cannot be understood without reference to the whole, which is thus regarded as greater than the sum of its parts. Holism is often applied to mental states, language, and ecology. ■ *Med.* the treating of the whole person, taking into account mental and social factors, rather than just the physical symptoms of a disease. —**ho·list** *adj. & n.* —**ho·lis·tic** /hō'listik/ *adj.*

hol·land /'hälənd/ ▸*n.* a kind of smooth, durable linen fabric, used chiefly for window shades and furniture covering.

hol·lan·daise sauce /'hälən,dāz/ ▸*n.* a creamy sauce of melted butter, egg yolks, and lemon juice or vinegar.

hol·ler /'hälər/ *inf.* ▸*v.* [*intr.*] (of a person) give a loud shout or cry: *he hollers when he wants feeding* | [with *direct speech*] *"I can't get down," she hollered.*
▸*n.* a loud cry or shout.

hol·low /'hälō/ ▸*adj.* **1** having a hole or empty space inside. ■ (of a thing) having a depression in its surface; concave: *hollow cheeks.* ■ (of a sound) echoing, as though made in or on an empty container. **2** without significance: *the result was a hollow victory.* ■ insincere: *a hollow promise.*

▶ *n.* a hole or depression in something: *a hollow at the base of a large tree.* ■ a small valley: *the house fell behind as they climbed out of the hollow.*
▶ *v.* [*tr.*] form by making a hole: *a tunnel was hollowed out in a mountain range.* ■ make a depression in. —**hol·low·ly** *adv.* —**hol·low·ness** *n.*
▶ □ **beat someone hollow** defeat or surpass someone completely or thoroughly.

hol·low·ware /ˈhälōˌwe(ə)r/ ▶ *n.* serving dishes and accessories, esp. of silver, that are hollow or concave. Contrast with **FLATWARE**.

hol·ly /ˈhälē/ ▶ *n.* a widely distributed shrub (genus *Ilex,* family Aquifoliaceae), typically evergreen and having prickly dark green leaves, small white flowers, and red berries. ■ the branches, foliage, and berries of this plant used as Christmas decorations.

hol·ly·hock /ˈhälēˌhäk/ ▶ *n.* a tall Eurasian plant (*Alcea rosea*) of the mallow family, widely cultivated for its large showy flowers.

hol·mi·um /ˈhōlmēəm/ ▶ *n.* the chemical element of atomic number 67, a soft silvery-white metal of the lanthanide series. (Symbol: **Ho**)

hol·o·caust /ˈhäləˌkôst; ˈhōlə-/ ▶ *n.* **1** destruction or slaughter on a mass scale, esp. caused by fire or nuclear war. ■ (**the Holocaust**) the mass murder of Jews by the German Nazi regime during the period 1941–45. **2** *hist.* a Jewish sacrificial offering that is burned completely on an altar. ▷Middle English: from Old French *holocauste,* via late Latin from Greek *holokauston,* from *holos* 'whole' + *kaustos* 'burned' (from *kaiein* 'burn').

Hol·o·cene /ˈhäləˌsēn; ˈhōlə-/ ▶ *adj.* *Geol.* of, relating to, or denoting the present epoch, which is the second epoch in the Quaternary period and followed the Pleistocene. Also called **RECENT**. ■ [as *n.*] (**the Holocene**) the Holocene epoch or the system of deposits laid down during this time.

hol·o·gram /ˈhäləˌgram; ˈhōlə-/ ▶ *n.* a three-dimensional image formed by the interference of light beams from a laser or other coherent light source. ■ a photograph of an interference pattern that, when suitably illuminated, produces a three-dimensional image.

hol·o·graph /ˈhäləˌgraf; ˈhōlə-/ ▶ *n.* a manuscript handwritten by the person named as its author: [as *adj.*] *a holograph letter by Abraham Lincoln.*

hol·og·ra·phy /həˈlägrəfē/ ▶ *n.* the study or production of holograms. —**hol·o·graph·ic** /ˌhäləˈgrafik; ˌhōlə-/ *adj.*

hol·ster /ˈhōlstər/ ▶ *n.* a holder for carrying a handgun or other firearm, typically made of leather and worn on a belt or under the arm.
▶ *v.* [*tr.*] put (a gun) into its holster.

holster

ho·ly /ˈhōlē/ ▶ *adj.* (**ho·li·er, ho·li·est**) **1** dedicated or consecrated to God or a religious purpose; sacred: *the Holy Bible* | *the holy month of Ramadan.* ■ (of a person) devoted to the service of God: *saints and holy men.* ■ morally and spiritually excellent. **2** *inf.* used as an intensifier: *having a holy good time.* **3** *dated* or *humorous* used in exclamations of surprise or dismay: *holy smoke!* —**ho·li·ly** /ˈhōləlē/ *adv.*

Ho·ly Ghost ▶ *n.* another term for **HOLY SPIRIT**.

Ho·ly Ro·man Em·pire ▶ the empire set up in western Europe following the coronation of Charlemagne as emperor in the year 800.

Ho·ly Spir·it ▶ *n.* (in Christianity) the third person of the Trinity; God as spiritually active in the world.

Ho·ly Trin·i·ty ▶ *n.* see **TRINITY**.

ho·ly war ▶ *n.* a war declared or waged in support of a religious cause.

ho·ly wa·ter ▶ *n.* water blessed by a priest and used in religious ceremonies.

Ho·ly Week ▶ *n.* the week before Easter, starting on Palm Sunday.

hom·age /ˈ(h)ämij/ ▶ *n.* special honor or respect shown publicly: *they paid homage to the local boy who became president* | *a masterly work written in homage to Beethoven.* ■ *hist.* formal public acknowledgment of feudal allegiance: *a man doing homage to his personal lord.*

hom·bre /ˈämbrā; -brē/ ▶ *n.* *inf.* a man, esp. one of a particular type: *the Raiders quarterback is one tough hombre.*

hom·burg /ˈhämbərg/ ▶ *n.* a man's felt hat having a narrow curled brim and a tapered crown with a lengthwise indentation.

home /hōm/ ▶ *n.* **1** the place where one lives permanently, esp. as a member of a family or household. ■ the family or social unit occupying such a place: *he came from a good home.* ■ a house or an apartment considered as a commercial property: *low-cost homes for first-time buyers.* ■ a place where something flourishes, is most typically found, or from which it originates: *Piedmont is the home of Italy's finest red wines.* ■ *inf.* a place where an object is kept. **2** an institution for people needing professional care or supervision: *an old people's home.* **3** *Sports* the goal or end point. ■ the place where a player is free from attack. ■ *Baseball* short for **HOME PLATE**.
▶ *adj.* **1** of or relating to the place where one lives: *I don't have your home address.* ■ relating to one's own country and its domestic affairs: *Japanese competitors are selling cars for lower prices in the U.S. than in their home market.* **2** (of a sports team or player) belonging to the country or locality in which a sporting event takes place: *the home team.* ■ played on or connected with a team's own ground: *their first home game.* **3** denoting the administrative center of an organization: *the home office.*
▶ *adv.* to the place where one lives: *what time did he get home last night?* ■ in or at the place where one lives: *I stayed home with the kids.* ■ to the end or conclusion of a race or something difficult: *the favorite romped home six lengths clear.* ■ *Baseball* to or toward home plate. ■ to the intended or correct position: *he drove the bolt home noisily.*
▶ *v.* [*intr.*] **1** (of an animal) return by instinct to its territory after leaving it: *geese homing to their nesting grounds.* ■ (of a pigeon bred for long-distance racing) fly back to or arrive at its loft after being released at a distant point. **2** (**home in on**) move or be aimed toward (a target or destination) with great accuracy. ■ focus attention on: *a teaching style that homes in on what is of central importance for each student.* —**home·like** /ˈhōmˌlīk/ *adj.*
▶ □ **at home** in one's own house. ■ in one's own neighborhood, town, or country: *he has been successful at home and abroad.* ■ comfortable and at ease in a place or situation: *make yourself at home.* ■ confident or relaxed about doing or using something. ■ ready to receive and welcome visitors. ■ (with reference to sports) at a team's own ground: *Houston lost at home to Phoenix.* □ **bring something home to someone** make someone realize the full significance of something. □ **close** (or **near**) **to home** (of a remark or topic of discussion) relevant or accurate to the point that one feels uncomfortable or embarrassed. □ **drive** (or **hammer** or **press** or **ram**) **something home** make something clearly and fully understood by the use of repeated or forcefully direct arguments. □ **hit** (or **strike**) **home** (of a blow or a missile) reach an intended target. ■ (of words) have the intended, esp. unsettling or painful, effect on their audience: *she could see that her remark had hit home.* ■ (of the significance or true nature of a situation) become fully realized by someone: *the full impact of life as a celebrity began to hit home.* □ **home free** having successfully achieved or being within sight of achieving one's objective: *at 7–0 they should have been home free.*

home·bod·y /ˈhōmˌbädē/ ▶ *n.* (*pl.* **-bod·ies**) *inf.* a person who likes to stay at home, esp. one who is perceived as unadventurous.

home·boy /ˈhōmˌboi/ ▶ *n.* *inf.* a young acquaintance from one's own town or neighborhood, or from the same social background. ■ (esp. among urban black people) a member of a peer group or gang.

home·com·ing /ˈhōmˌkəmiNG/ ▶ *n.* an instance of returning home. ■ a high school, college, or university game, dance, or other event to which alumni are invited.

home ec·o·nom·ics ▶ *pl. n.* [often treated as *sing.*] cooking and other aspects of household management, esp. as taught at school.

home·grown /ˈhōmˈgrōn/ ▶ *adj.* grown or produced in one's own garden or country. ■ belonging to one's own particular locality or country.

home·land /ˈhōmˌland/ ▶ *n.* a person's or a people's native land. ■ an autonomous or semiautonomous state occupied by a particular people: *their political aim is a separate Tamil homeland.*

home·less /ˈhōmlis/ ▶ *adj.* (of a person) without a home, and therefore typically living on the streets: *the plight of young homeless people* | [as *n.*] (**the homeless**) *charities for the homeless.* —**home·less·ness** *n.*

home·ly /ˈhōmlē/ ▶ *adj.* (**home·li·er, home·li·est**) **1** (of a person) unattractive in appearance. **2** *Brit.* (of a place or surroundings) simple but cozy and comfortable, as in one's own home. ■ unsophisticated and unpretentious: *homely pleasures.* —**home·li·ness** *n.*

home·made /ˈhō(m)ˈmād/ ▶ *adj.* made at home, rather than in a store or factory: *homemade apple pies* | *it sounds like the homemade album that it is.*

home·mak·er /ˈhōmˌmākər/ ▶ *n.* a person, esp. a housewife, who manages a home.

home mov·ie ▶ *n.* a film made at home or without professional equipment or expertise, esp. a movie featuring one's own activities.

ho·me·o·path /ˈhōmēəˌpath/ (also **ho·me·op·a·thist** /ˌhōmēˈäpəthist/, *Brit.* **ho·moe·o·path**) ▶ *n.* a person who practices homeopathy.

ho·me·op·a·thy /ˌhōmēˈäpəthē/ (*Brit.* **ho·moe·op·a·thy**) ▶ *n.* the treatment of disease by minute doses of natural substances that in a healthy person would produce symptoms of disease. Often contrasted with **ALLOPATHY**. —**ho·me·o·path·ic** /ˌhōmēəˈpaᴛʜɪk/ adj. —**ho·me·o·path·i·cal·ly** /ˌhōmēəˈpaᴛʜɪk(ə)lē/ adv.

ho·me·o·therm /ˈhōmēə,ᴛʜərm/ ▶n. Zool. an organism that maintains its body temperature at a constant level, usually above that of the environment, by its metabolic activity. —**ho·me·o·ther·mal** /ˌhōmēəˈᴛʜərməl/ adj. —**ho·me·o·ther·mic** /ˌhōmēəˈᴛʜərmik/ adj. —**ho·me·o·ther·my** n.

home·own·er /ˈhōm,ōnər/ ▶n. a person who owns their own home. —**home·own·er·ship** /-SHip/ n.

home page (also **home-page**) ▶n. Comput. the introductory document of an individual's or organization's Web site. It typically serves as a table of contents to the site's other pages or provides links to other sites.

home plate ▶n. Baseball the five-sided flat white rubber base next to which the batter stands and over which the pitcher must throw the ball for a strike. A runner must touch home plate after having reached all the other bases to score a run.

ho·mer /ˈhōmər/ ▶n. **1** Baseball a home run. **2** a homing pigeon. **3** inf. a referee or official who is thought to favor the team playing at home. ▶v. [intr.] Baseball hit a home run.

home rule ▶n. the government of a colony, dependent country, or region by its own citizens.

home run ▶n. Baseball a hit that allows the batter to make a complete circuit of the bases without stopping and score a run.

home·sick /ˈhōm,sik/ ▶adj. experiencing a longing for one's home during a period of absence from it. —**home·sick·ness** n.

home·spun /ˈhōm,spən/ ▶adj. **1** simple and unsophisticated: homespun philosophy. **2** (of cloth or yarn) made or spun at home. ■ denoting a coarse handwoven fabric similar to tweed. ▶n. cloth of this type: clad in homespun.

home·stead /ˈhōm,sted/ ▶n. **1** a house, esp. a farmhouse, and outbuildings. **2** Law a person's or family's residence, which comprises the land, house, and outbuildings, and in most states is exempt from forced sale for collection of debt. **3** hist. (as provided by the federal Homestead Act of 1862) an area of public land in the West (usually 160 acres) granted to any U.S. citizen willing to settle on and farm the land for at least five years. —**home·stead·er** n.

home·stretch /ˈhōm'streᴄʜ/ (also **home stretch**) ▶n. the concluding straight part of a racecourse: he drifted in back of the pack halfway down the homestretch. ■ fig. the last part of an activity or campaign: this was his last term, the home stretch.

home·town /ˈhōm'toun/ ▶n. the town where one was born or grew up, or the town of one's present fixed residence.

home·ward /ˈhōmwərd/ ▶adv. (also **home·wards** /-wərdz/) toward home: setting off homeward. ▶adj. going or leading toward home: their homeward journey.

home·work /ˈhōm,wərk/ ▶n. schoolwork that a student is required to do at home. ■ work or study done in preparation for a certain event or situation: he had done his homework and read his predecessor's reports. ■ paid work carried out in one's own home, esp. low-paid piecework.

home·wreck·er /ˈhōm,rekər/ ▶n. inf. one who is blamed for the breakup of a marriage or family, such as an adulterous partner.

hom·ey /ˈhōmē/ (also **hom·y**) ▶adj. (**hom·i·er**, **hom·i·est**) (of a place or surroundings) pleasantly comfortable and cozy. ■ unsophisticated; unpretentious. —**hom·ey·ness** (also **hom·i·ness**) n.

hom·i·cide /ˈhämə,sīd; ˈhōmə-/ ▶n. the deliberate and unlawful killing of one person by another; murder: he was charged with homicide | two thirds of homicides in the county were drug-related. ■ (**Homicide**) the police department that deals with such crimes: a detective from Homicide. ■ dated a murderer. —**hom·i·cid·al** /-ˌsīdl/ adj.

hom·ie /ˈhōmē/ (also **hom·ey**) ▶n. (pl. **hom·ies**) inf. a homeboy or homegirl.

hom·i·let·ic /ˌhäməˈletik/ ▶adj. of the nature of or characteristic of a homily: homiletic literature. ▶n. (**homiletics**) the art of preaching or writing sermons.

hom·i·ly /ˈhäməlē/ ▶n. (pl. **-lies**) a religious discourse that is intended primarily for spiritual edification rather than doctrinal instruction; a sermon. ▷late Middle English: via Old French from ecclesiastical Latin homilia, from Greek, 'discourse, conversation' (in ecclesiastical use, 'sermon'), from homilos 'crowd.' —**hom·i·list** /-list/ n.

hom·ing /ˈhōmɪNG/ ▶adj. relating to an animal's ability to return to a place or territory after traveling a distance away from it: a strong homing instinct. ■ (of a pigeon) trained to fly home from a great distance and bred for long-distance racing. ■ (of a weapon or piece of

equipment) fitted with an electronic device that enables it to find and hit a target.

hom·i·nid /ˈhämə,nid/ ▶n. Zool. a primate of the family (Hominidae) that includes humans and their fossil ancestors.

hom·i·noid /ˈhämə,noid/ Zool. ▶n. a primate of a group that includes humans, their fossil ancestors, and the great apes. ▶adj. of or relating to primates of this group; hominid or pongid.

hom·i·ny /ˈhämənē/ ▶n. coarsely ground corn used to make grits: [as adj.] hominy grits.

Ho·mo /ˈhōmō/ ▶the genus of primates of which modern humans (Homo sapiens) are the present-day representatives. ■ denoting kinds of modern human, often humorously: a textbook example of Homo neuroticus.

ho·mo /ˈhō,mō/ offens. ▶n. (pl. **-mos**) a homosexual man. ▶adj. homosexual.

ho·mo·ge·ne·ous /ˌhōmə'jēnēəs/ ▶adj. of the same kind; alike. ■ consisting of parts all of the same kind: the farmers constitute an extremely homogeneous group. ■ Math. containing terms all of the same degree. —**ho·mo·ge·ne·i·ty** /ˌhōmōjə'nēitē; ˌhämə-/ n. —**ho·mo·ge·ne·ous·ly** adv. —**ho·mo·ge·ne·ous·ness** n.

ho·mog·e·nize /hə'mäjə,nīz/ ▶v. [tr.] **1** subject (milk) to a process in which the fat droplets are emulsified and the cream does not separate: [as adj.] (**homogenized**) homogenized milk. ■ Biol. prepare a suspension of cell constituents from (tissue) by physical treatment in a liquid. **2** make uniform or similar. —**ho·mog·e·ni·za·tion** /hə,mäjəni'zāSHən/ n. —**ho·mog·e·niz·er** n.

ho·mo·graft /ˈhōmə,graft; ˈhämə-/ ▶n. a tissue graft from a donor of the same species as the recipient.

hom·o·graph /ˈhämə,graf; ˈhōmə-/ ▶n. each of two or more words spelled the same but not necessarily pronounced the same and having different meanings and origins (e.g., BOW[1] and BOW[2]). —**hom·o·graph·ic** /ˌhämə'grafik; ˌhōmə-/ adj.

ho·mol·o·gous /hə'mäləgəs; hə-/ ▶adj. having the same relation, relative position, or structure, in particular: ■ Biol. (of organs) similar in position, structure, and evolutionary origin but not necessarily in function: a seal's flipper is **homologous** with the human arm. ■ Biol. (of chromosomes) pairing at meiosis and having the same structural features and pattern of genes. ■ Chem. (of a series of chemical compounds) having the same functional group but differing in composition by a fixed group of atoms.

ho·mo·logue /ˈhōmə,lôg; -,läg/ (also **ho·mo·log**) ▶n. technical a homologous thing.

ho·mol·o·gy /hō'mäləjē; hə-/ ▶n. the quality or condition of being homologous. ■ Biol. similarity in sequence of a protein or nucleic acid between organisms of the same or different species.

hom·o·nym /ˈhämə,nim; ˈhōmə-/ ▶n. each of two words having the same pronunciation but different meanings, origins, or spelling (e.g., TO, TOO, and TWO); a homophone. ■ each of two or more words having the same spelling but different meanings and origins (e.g., POLE[1] and POLE[2]); a homograph. ■ Biol. a Latin name that is identical to that of a different organism, the newer of the two names being invalid. —**hom·o·nym·ic** /ˌhämə'nimik; ˌhōmə-/ adj. —**ho·mon·y·mous** /hō'mänəməs; hə-/ adj. —**ho·mon·y·my** /hō'mänəmē/ n.

ho·mo·pho·bi·a /ˌhōmə'fōbēə/ ▶n. an extreme and irrational aversion to homosexuality and homosexual people. —**ho·mo·phobe** /ˈhōmə,fōb/ n. —**ho·mo·pho·bic** /-'fōbik/ adj.

ho·mo·phone /ˈhämə,fōn; ˈhōmə-/ ▶n. each of two or more words having the same pronunciation but different meanings, origins, or spelling, e.g., NEW and KNEW. ■ each of a set of symbols denoting the same sound or group of sounds.

ho·mo·phon·ic /ˌhämə'fänik; ˌhōmə-/ ▶adj. **1** Mus. characterized by the movement of accompanying parts in the same rhythm as the melody. Often contrasted with POLYPHONIC. **2** another term for HOMOPHONOUS. —**ho·mo·phon·i·cal·ly** /-ik(ə)lē/ adv.

ho·moph·o·nous /hō'mäfənəs; hə-/ ▶adj. (of a word or words) having the same pronunciation as another or others but different meaning, origin, or spelling. —**ho·moph·o·ny** /-'mäfənē/ n.

ho·mop·ter·an /hō'mäptərən/ ▶n. any insect of the group including aphids and cicadas, having wings of uniform texture. ▶adj. of or related to the homopterans. —**ho·mop·ter·ous** /-tərəs/ adj.

Ho·mo sa·pi·ens /ˈhōmō 'sāpēenz/ ▶the primate species to which modern humans belong; humans regarded as a species. See also HOMO. ■ a member of this species.

ho·mo·sex·u·al /ˌhōmə'seksʜOOəl/ ▶adj. (of a person) sexually attracted to people of one's own sex. ■ involving or characterized by sexual attraction between people of the same sex: homosexual desire.

▶ *n.* a person who is sexually attracted to people of their own sex. —**ho·mo·sex·u·al·i·ty** /-,sekSHŌŌ'alitē/ *n.* —**ho·mo·sex·u·al·ly** *adv.*

hom·y ▶ *adj.* variant spelling of **HOMEY**¹.

hon /hən/ ▶ *n. inf.* short for **HONEY** (as a form of address).

Hon. ▶ *abbr.* ■ (in official job titles) Honorary: *the Hon. Secretary.* ■ (in titles of some government officials and judges) Honorable: *the Hon. Charles Rothschild.*

hon·cho /'hänCHŌ/ *inf.* ▶ *n.* (*pl.* **-chos**) a leader or manager; the person in charge: *the company's* **head honcho** *in the U.S.* ▷1940s: from Japanese *hanchō* 'group leader,' a term brought back to the U.S. by servicemen stationed in Japan during the occupation following World War II.

hone /hōn/ ▶ *v.* [*tr.*] sharpen with a whetstone. ■ (usu. **be honed**) make sharper or more focused or efficient: *appetites honed by fresh air.*
▶ *n.* a whetstone, esp. one used to sharpen razors. ■ the stone of which whetstones are made.

hon·est /'änist/ ▶ *adj.* free of deceit and untruthfulness; sincere. ■ morally correct or virtuous: *the only right and honest thing.* ■ fairly earned, esp. through hard work: *an honest living.* ■ (of an action) blameless or well intentioned even if unsuccessful or misguided: *an honest mistake.* ■ simple, unpretentious, and unsophisticated.
▶ *adv. inf.* used to persuade someone of the truth of something: *you'll like it when you get there, honest.*

hon·est·ly /'änistlē/ ▶ *adv.* **1** in a truthful, fair, or honorable way. **2** used to emphasize the sincerity of an opinion, belief, or feeling: *she honestly believed that she was making life easier for Jack.* ■ used to emphasize the sincerity or truthfulness of a statement: *honestly, I'm not upset.* ■ used to indicate the speaker's disapproval, annoyance, or impatience: *honestly, that man is the absolute limit!*

hon·es·ty /'änistē/ ▶ *n.* **1** the quality of being honest. **2** a European plant (genus *Lunaria*) of the cabbage family, with purple or white flowers and round, flat, translucent seedpods that are used for indoor flower arrangements.

hon·ey /'hənē/ ▶ *n.* (*pl.* **-eys**) **1** a sweet, sticky, yellowish-brown fluid made by bees and other insects from nectar collected from flowers. ■ this substance used as food, typically as a sweetener. ■ a yellowish-brown or golden color: [as *adj.*] *her honey skin.* ■ any sweet substance similar to bees' honey. **2** *inf.* an excellent example of something: *it's one* **honey** *of an adaptation.* ■ darling; sweetheart.

hon·ey·bee /'hənē,bē/ ▶ *n.* a stinging winged insect (genus *Apis*, family Apidae), esp. the widespread *A. mellifera*. It collects nectar and pollen, produces wax and honey, and lives in large communities.

hon·ey·comb /'hənē,kōm/ ▶ *n.* **1** a structure of hexagonal cells of wax, made by bees to store honey and eggs. **2** a structure of adjoining cavities or cells: *a honeycomb of caves.* ■ a mass of cavities produced by corrosion or dissolution: [as *adj.*] *honeycomb weathering.*
▶ *v.* [*tr.*] fill with cavities or tunnels: *whole hillsides were honeycombed with mines.* ■ corrode (something) internally, forming small cavities in it.

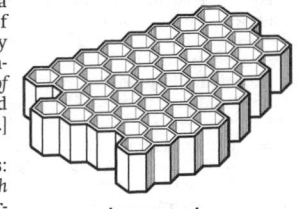
honeycomb

hon·ey·dew /'hənē,d(y)ōō/ ▶ *n.* **1** a sweet, sticky substance excreted by aphids and often deposited on leaves and stems. ■ *poetic/lit.* an ideally sweet substance. **2** (also **honeydew melon**) a melon of a variety with smooth pale skin and sweet green flesh.

hon·eyed /'hənēd/ (also **hon·ied**) ▶ *adj.* (of food) containing or coated with honey. ■ having a rich sweetness of taste or smell. ■ having a golden or warm yellow color. ■ *fig.* (of a person's words or tone of voice) soothing, soft, and intended to please or flatter.

hon·ey·moon /'hənē,mōōn/ ▶ *n.* a vacation spent together by a newly married couple. ■ [often as *adj.*] *fig.* an initial period of enthusiasm or goodwill, typically at the start of a new job.
▶ *v.* [*intr.*] spend a honeymoon: *they are honeymooning in the south of France.* —**hon·ey·moon·er** *n.*

hon·ey·suck·le /'hənē,səkəl/ ▶ *n.* a widely distributed climbing shrub (genera *Lonicera* and *Diervilla*) with tubular fragrant flowers. The **honeysuckle faimly** (Caprifoliaceae) also includes such berry-bearing shrubs as elder and snowberry.

honk /hāNGk; hôNGk/ ▶ *n.* the cry of a wild goose. ■ the harsh sound of a car horn. ■ any similar sound.
▶ *v.* [*intr.*] emit such a cry or sound. ■ [*tr.*] cause (a car horn) to make such a sound. ■ [*tr.*] express by sounding a car horn: *taxi drivers honking their support.*

hon·ky /'hāNGkē; 'hôNG-/ ▶ *n.* (*pl.* **-kies**) *inf.*, often *offens.* a contemptuous term used by black people for a white person or for white people collectively.

hon·ky-tonk /'hāNGkē ,tāNGk; 'hôNGkē ,tôNGk/ ▶ *n. inf.* **1** a cheap or disreputable bar, club, or dance hall, typically where country music is played. ■ [as *adj.*] squalid and disreputable: *a honky-tonk beach resort.* **2** country music. **3** [often as *adj.*] ragtime piano music.

hon·or /'änər/ (*Brit.* **hon·our**) ▶ *n.* **1** high respect; esteem: *his portrait hangs in the place of honor.* ■ a person or thing that brings credit: *you are an honor to our profession.* ■ adherence to what is right or to a conventional standard of conduct: *I must as a matter of honor avoid any taint of dishonesty.* **2** a privilege: *the great poet of whom it is my honor to speak tonight.* ■ an exalted position: *the honor of being horse of the year.* ■ a thing conferred as a distinction, esp. an official award for bravery or achievement: *the highest military honors.* ■ (**honors**) a special distinction for proficiency in an examination: *she passed with honors.* ■ (**honors**) a class or course of degree studies more specialized than that of the ordinary level. ■ (**His**, **Your**, etc., **Honor**) a title of respect given to or used in addressing a judge or a mayor. ■ *Golf* the right of teeing off first, having won the previous hole. **3** *dated* a woman's chastity or her reputation for this: *she died defending her honor.* **4** *Bridge* an ace, king, queen, or jack. ■ (**honors**) possession in one's hand of at least four of the ace, king, queen, and jack of trumps, or of all four aces in no trumps, for which a bonus is scored. —**hon·o·ree** /'änə'rē/ *n.*
▶ *v.* [*tr.*] **1** regard with great respect: *Joyce has now learned to honor her father's memory* | [as *adj.*] (**honored**) *an honored guest.* ■ (often **be honored**) pay public respect to: *talented writers were honored at a special ceremony.* ■ grace; privilege: *the Princess honored the ball with her presence* | [as *adj.*] (**honored**) *I felt honored to be invited.* ■ (in square dancing) salute (another dancer) with a bow. **2** fulfill (an obligation) or keep (an agreement). ■ accept (a bill) or pay (a check) when due: *the bank informed him that the check would not be honored.*
▶ □ **do the honors** *inf.* perform a social duty or small ceremony for others (often used to describe the serving of food or drink to a guest). □ **in honor of** as a celebration of or expression of respect for. □ **on one's honor** under a moral obligation: *they are on their honor as gentlemen not to cheat.*

hon·or·a·ble /'änərəbəl/ (*Brit.* **hon·our·a·ble**) ▶ *adj.* **1** bringing or worthy of honor: *this is the only honorable course* | *a decent and honorable man.* ■ *formal* or *humorous* (of the intentions of a man courting a woman) directed toward marriage: *the young man's intentions had been honorable.* **2** (**Honorable**) used as a title indicating eminence or distinction, given esp. to judges and certain high officials. —**hon·or·a·ble·ness** *n.* —**hon·or·a·bly** *adv.*

hon·or·a·ble men·tion ▶ *n.* a commendation given to a candidate in an examination or competition who is not awarded a prize.

hon·o·rar·i·um /,änə're(ə)rēəm/ ▶ *n.* (*pl.* **-rar·i·ums** or **-rar·i·a** /-'re(ə)rēə/) a payment given for professional services that are rendered nominally without charge.

hon·or·ar·y /'änə,rerē/ ▶ *adj.* conferred as an honor, without the usual requirements or functions: *an honorary doctorate.* ■ (of a person) holding such a title or position: *an honorary member of the club.*

hon·or·if·ic /,änə'rifik/ ▶ *adj.* given as a mark of respect. ■ (of an office or position) given as a mark of respect, but having few or no duties. ■ denoting a form of address showing politeness or respect: *an honorific title.*
▶ *n.* a title or word implying or expressing high status, politeness, or respect: *he will be able to put the honorific after his name.* —**hon·or·if·i·cal·ly** /ik(ə)lē/ *adv.*

hon·or roll ▶ *n.* a list of people who have attained an honor, esp. a list of students who have earned excellent grades.

hon·or sys·tem ▶ *n.* a system of payment or examination that relies solely on the honesty of those concerned.

hooch¹ /hōōCH/ (also **hootch**) ▶ *n. inf.* alcoholic liquor, esp. inferior or illicit whiskey.

hooch² /hōōCH/ ▶ *n. inf.* a shelter or improvised dwelling.

hood¹ /hŏŏd/ ▶ *n.* **1** a covering for the head and neck with an opening for the face, typically forming part of a coat or sweatshirt. ■ a separate garment similar to this worn over a college gown or a surplice to indicate the wearer's degree. **2** a thing resembling a hood in shape or use, in particular: ■ a metal part covering the engine of an automobile. ■ a canopy to protect users of machinery or to remove fumes from it. ■ a hoodlike structure or marking on the head or neck of an animal. ■ a tubular attachment to keep stray light out of a camera lens: *a lens hood.*

▸ *v.* [*tr.*] put a hood on or over. —**hood·ed** *adj.* —**hood·less** *adj.* —**hood·like** /-,līk/ *adj.*

hood² ▸ *n. inf.* a gangster or similar violent criminal.

hood³ (also **'hood**) ▸ *n. inf.* a neighborhood, esp. one's own neighborhood: *I've lived in the hood for 15 years.*

hood·lum /'hŏŏdləm; 'hŏŏd-/ ▸ *n.* a person who engages in crime and violence; a hooligan or gangster.

hoo·doo /'hŏŏ,dŏŏ/ ▸ *n.* **1** voodoo; witchcraft. ■ a run of bad luck associated with a person or activity: *when is this hoodoo going to end?* ■ a person or thing that brings or causes bad luck. **2** a column or pinnacle of weathered rock: *a towering sandstone hoodoo.*

▸ *v.* (**-doos, -dooed**) [*tr.*] bewitch. ■ bring bad luck to.

hood·wink /'hŏŏd,wiNGk/ ▸ *v.* [*tr.*] deceive or trick (someone).

hoo·ey /'hŏŏē/ ▸ *n. inf.* nonsense: *your interest is just a lot of hooey.*

hoof /hŏŏf; hŏŏf/ ▸ *n.* (*pl.* **hoofs** or **hooves** /hŏŏvz; hŏŏvz/) the horny part of the foot of an ungulate animal, esp. a horse.

▸ *v.* [*tr.*] *inf.* (**hoof it**) *inf.* dance: *we hoof it fancily.* —**hoofed** *adj.*
▸ □ **on the hoof** (of livestock) not yet slaughtered.

hook /hŏŏk/ ▸ *n.* **1** a piece of metal or other material, curved or bent back at an angle, for catching hold of or hanging things on: *a picture hook.* ■ (also **fish·hook**) a bent piece of metal, typically barbed and baited, for catching fish. ■ a cradle on which a telephone receiver rests. ■ *fig.* a thing designed to catch people's attention: *a sales hook.* ■ a chorus or repeated instrumental passage in a piece of music, esp. a pop or rock song, that gives it immediate appeal and makes it easy to remember. **2** a curved cutting instrument, esp. as used for reaping or shearing. **3** a short swinging punch made with the elbow bent, esp. in boxing. ■ *Golf* a stroke that makes the ball deviate in flight in the direction of the follow-through (from right to left for a right-handed player), typically inadvertently. Compare with SLICE. **4** *Mus.* an added stroke transverse to the stem in the symbol for an eighth note or other note. **5** [usu. in *place names*] a curved promontory or sand spit.

▸ *v.* **1** [*tr.*] attach or fasten with a hook or hooks. ■ [*intr.*] be or become attached with a hook: *a ladder that hooks over the roof ridge.* ■ bend or be bent into the shape of a hook so as to fasten around or to an object. **2** [*tr.*] catch with a hook: *he hooked a 24-lb pike.* ■ (usu. **be hooked**) *inf.* captivate: *I was hooked by John's radical zeal.* ■ *archaic, inf.* steal. **3** [*tr.*] *Golf* strike (the ball) or play (a stroke) so that the ball deviates in the direction of the follow-through, typically inadvertently. ■ [*intr.*] *Boxing* punch one's opponent with the elbow bent. —**hook·less** *adj.* —**hook·like** /-,līk/ *adj.*

▸ □ **by hook or by crook** by any possible means. □ **hook, line, and sinker** used to emphasize that someone has been completely deceived or tricked: *he fell hook, line, and sinker for this year's April Fool joke.* □ **off the hook 1** *inf.* no longer in difficulty or trouble: *I lied to get him off the hook.* **2** (of a telephone receiver) not on its rest, and so preventing incoming calls. □ **on the hook for** *inf.* (in a financial context) responsible for: *he's on the hook for about $9.5 million.* □ **on one's own hook** *inf., dated* on one's own account; by oneself.

hook·ah /'hŏŏkə; 'hŏŏkä/ ▸ *n.* an oriental tobacco pipe with a long, flexible tube that draws the smoke through water contained in a bowl.

hooked /hŏŏkt/ ▸ *adj.* **1** having a hook or hooks: *a hooked gold earring.* ■ curved like a hook: *a golden eagle with hooked beak.* **2** *inf.* captivated; absorbed: *he was hooked on a video game.* ■ addicted. **3** (of a rug or mat) made by pulling yarn through canvas with a hook.

hook·er /'hŏŏkər/ ▸ *n. inf.* a prostitute.

hook·up /'hŏŏk,əp/ ▸ *n.* a connection to a public electric, water, or sewer line, or to a similar service. ■ an interconnection of broadcasting equipment for special transmissions: *a satellite hookup.*

hook·worm /'hŏŏk,wərm/ ▸ *n.* a parasitic nematode that inhabits the intestines of humans and other animals. It has hooklike mouthparts with which it attaches itself to the wall of the gut. ■ a disease caused by an infestation of hookworms, often resulting in severe anemia.

hook·y /'hŏŏkē/ (also **hook·ey**) ▸ *n.* (in phrase **play hooky**) *inf.* stay away from school or work without permission or explanation.

hoo·li·gan /'hŏŏləgən/ ▸ *n.* a violent young troublemaker, typically one of a gang.: *late 19th cent.*: perhaps from *Hooligan*, the surname of a fictional rowdy Irish family in a music-hall song of the 1890s, also of a character in a cartoon. —**hoo·li·gan·ism** /-,nizəm/ *n.*

hoop /hŏŏp/ ▸ *n.* a circular band of metal, wood, or similar material, esp. one used for binding the staves of barrels or forming part of a framework. ■ the round metal rim from which a basketball net is suspended. ■ (**hoops**) *inf.* the game of basketball. ■ a large ring used as a toy by being bowled along. ■ a large ring, typically with paper stretched over

it, for circus performers to jump through. ■ one of a pair of rings that hold fabric taut while it is being embroidered. ■ *hist.* a circle of flexible material used for expanding a woman's petticoat or skirt.

▸ *v.* [*tr.*] bind or encircle with or as with hoops. —**hooped** *adj.*

▸ □ **jump through hoops** perform a difficult and grueling series of tests at someone else's request or command: *we had to jump through all sorts of hoops to win accreditation.* □ **shoot hoops** play basketball.

hoop·la /'hŏŏ,plä; 'hŏŏp,lä/ ▸ *n. inf.* excitement surrounding an event or situation, esp. when considered to be unnecessary fuss.

hoo·ray /hə'rā; hŏŏ-/ ▸ *interj.* another term for HURRAH.

hoose·gow /'hŏŏs,gou/ ▸ *n. inf.* a prison.

hoot /hŏŏt/ ▸ *n.* a deep or medium-pitched musical sound, often wavering or interrupted, that is the typical call of many kinds of owl. ■ a similar but typically more raucous sound made by a horn, siren, or steam whistle. ■ a shout expressing scorn or disapproval: *there were hoots of derision.* ■ a short outburst of laughter. ■ (**a hoot**) *inf.* an amusing situation or person: *your mom's a real hoot.*

▸ *v.* [*intr.*] (of an owl) utter a hoot. ■ (of a person) make loud sounds of scorn, disapproval, or merriment. ■ [*tr.*] (**hoot something down**) express loud scornful disapproval of something: *his questions were hooted down.* ■ (of a horn, siren, etc.) make a hoot. ■ [*tr.*] (of the driver of a vehicle) sound (the horn).

hoot·en·an·ny /'hŏŏtn,anē/ ▸ *n.* (*pl.* **-nies**) *inf.* an informal gathering with folk music and sometimes dancing.

hoot·er /'hŏŏtər/ ▸ *n.* **1** *inf.* a person's nose. **2** (**hooters**) *vulgar slang* a woman's breasts.

hooves /hŏŏvz; hŏŏvz/ ▸ plural form of HOOF.

hop¹ /häp/ ▸ *v.* (**hopped, hop·ping**) [*intr.*] (of a person) move by jumping on one foot. ■ (of a bird or other animal) move by jumping with two or all feet at once. ■ spring or leap a short distance with one jump: *he hopped down from the rock.* ■ [*tr.*] jump over (something): *the cow hopped the fence.* ■ *inf.* make a quick trip: *let's hop over to the bar.* ■ make a quick change of position, location, or activity: *he hopped from one department to another.* ■ [in *comb.*] visit a succession of things or places: *regulars liked to table-hop.* ■ [*tr.*] *inf.* board (a bus, airplane, or other mode of transportation). ■ [*tr.*] *inf.* jump onto (a moving vehicle). ■ [usu. as *n.* in *comb.*] (**-hopping**) (of an aircraft or ferry) pass quickly from one place to another: *island-hopping packages.*

▸ *phrasal v.* □ **hop in** (or **out**) *inf.* get into (or out of) a car.

▸ *n.* **1** a hopping movement. ■ a short journey or distance: *a short hop by cab from Soho.* **2** an informal dance.

hop² ▸ *n.* a twining climbing plant (*Humulus lupulus,* family Cannabaceae) native to north temperate regions. ■ (**hops**) the dried conelike flowers of this plant, used in beer-brewing to give a bitter flavor and as a mild disinfectant.

▸ *v.* (**hopped, hopping**) **1** [*tr.*] flavor with hops. **2** (**be hopped up**) *inf.* be stimulated or intoxicated by or as if by a psychoactive drug. —**hop·py** *adj.*

hope /hōp/ ▸ *n.* a feeling of expectation and desire for a certain thing to happen: *he looked in the hope of coming across some information | I had hopes of making the Olympic team.* ■ a person or thing that may help or save someone: *their only hope is surgery.* ■ grounds for believing that something good may happen: *he does see some hope for the future.*

▸ *v.* [*intr.*] want something to happen or be the case: *he's hoping for an offer of compensation | I hope that the kids are OK.* ■ intend if possible to do something: *we're hoping to address all these issues.* —**hop·er** *n.*

▸ □ **hope against hope** cling to a mere possibility. □ **in hopes of** with the aim of: *I lay on a towel in the park in hopes of getting a tan.* □ **in hopes that** hoping that: *they are screaming in hopes that a police launch will pick us up.* □ **not a hope** *inf.* no chance at all.

hope chest ▸ *n.* a chest containing household linen and clothing stored by a woman in preparation for her marriage.

hope·ful /'hōpfəl/ ▸ *adj.* feeling or inspiring optimism about a future event.

▸ *n.* a person likely or hoping to succeed: *a leading gubernatorial hopeful.* —**hope·ful·ness** *n.*

hope·ful·ly /'hōpfəlē/ ▸ *adv.* **1** in a hopeful manner. **2** it is to be hoped that: *hopefully, it should be finished by next year.*

hope·less /'hōplis/ ▸ *adj.* **1** feeling or causing despair about something. **2** inadequate; incompetent: *I'm hopeless at names.* —**hope·less·ly** *adv.* —**hope·less·ness** *n.*

Ho·pi /'hōpē/ ▸ *n.* (*pl.* same or **Ho·pis**) **1** a member of a Pueblo Indian people living chiefly in northeastern Arizona. **2** the Uto-Aztecan language of this people.

hop·per /'häpər/ ▸ *n.* **1** a container for a bulk material such as grain, rock, or trash, typically one that tapers downward and is able to discharge its contents at the bottom. ■ (in full **hopper car**) a railroad car able to discharge coal or other bulk material through its floor. ■ a box in which bills are put for consideration by a legislature. **2** a person or thing that hops. ■ *inf.* a person who makes a series of short trips: *an island hopper.* ■ a hopping insect, esp. a grasshopper.

hop·scotch /'häp,skäcH/ ▸ *n.* a children's game in which each child by turn hops into and over squares marked on the ground to retrieve a marker thrown into one of these squares.
▸ *v.* [*intr.*] skip from place to place; move erratically.

horde /hôrd/ ▸ *n.* **1** *chiefly derog.* a large group of people: *he was surrounded by a horde of tormenting relatives.* ■ an army or tribe of nomadic warriors: *Tartar hordes.* **2** *Anthropol.* a loosely knit small social group typically consisting of about five families. ▷mid 16th cent. (originally denoting a tribe or troop of Tartar or other nomads): from Polish *horda,* from Turkish *ordu* '(royal) camp.'

hore·hound /'hôr,hound/ ▸ *n.* either of two strong-smelling hairy plants of the mint family: **white horehound** (*Marrubium vulgare*) and **black horehound** (*Ballota nigra*). ■ the bitter aromatic juice of white horehound, used esp. in the treatment of coughs and colds.

ho·ri·zon /hə'rīzən/ ▸ *n.* **1** the line at which the earth's surface and the sky appear to meet. ■ (also **apparent** or **visible horizon**) the circular boundary of the part of the earth's surface visible from a particular point, ignoring irregularities and obstructions. ■ (also **celestial horizon**) *Astron.* a great circle of the celestial sphere, the plane of which passes through the center of the earth and is parallel to that of the apparent horizon of a place. **2** (often **horizons**) the limit of a person's mental perception, experience, or interest: *she wanted to broaden her horizons.* **3** *Geol.* a layer of soil or rock, or a set of strata, with particular characteristics. ■ *Archaeol.* a level of an excavated site representing a particular period.
▸ □ **on the horizon** imminent or becoming apparent.

hor·i·zon·tal /,hôrə'zän(t)l/ ▸ *adj.* **1** parallel to the plane of the horizon; at right angles to the vertical. ■ (of machinery) having its parts working in a horizontal direction: *a horizontal steam engine.* **2** combining companies engaged in the same stage or type of production: *a horizontal merger.* ■ involving social groups of equal status.
▸ *n.* a horizontal line, plane, etc. —**hor·i·zon·tal·i·ty** /-,zän'talitē/ *n.* —**hor·i·zon·tal·ly** *adv.*

hor·mone /'hôr,mōn/ ▸ *n. Physiol.* a regulatory substance produced in an organism and transported in tissue fluids such as blood or sap to stimulate specific cells or tissues into action. ■ a synthetic substance with a similar effect. ■ (**hormones**) a person's sex hormones as held to influence behavior or mood. —**hor·mo·nal** /hôr'mōnl/ *adj.*

horn /hôrn/ ▸ *n.* **1** a hard permanent outgrowth, often curved and pointed, found in pairs on the heads of cattle, sheep, goats, giraffes, etc., and consisting of a core of bone encased in keratinized skin. Compare with ANTLER. ■ a woolly keratinized outgrowth, occurring singly or one behind another, on the snout of a rhinoceros. ■ a deer's antler. ■ a hornlike projection on the head of another animal, e.g., a snail's tentacle or the tuft of a horned owl. ■ (**horns**) *archaic* a pair of horns as an emblem of a cuckold. **2** the substance of which horns are composed: *powdered rhino horn.* ■ a receptacle or instrument made of horn, such as a drinking container or powder flask. **3** a thing resembling or compared to a horn in shape. ■ a horn-shaped projection. ■ a sharp promontory or mountain peak. ■ a raised projection on the pommel of a Western saddle: *slung from the horn of his saddle was a leather bag.* ■ an arm or branch of a river or bay. ■ the extremity of the moon or other crescent. **4** a wind instrument, conical in shape or wound into a spiral, originally made from an animal horn (now typically brass) and played by lip vibration. ■ short for FRENCH HORN. **5** an instrument sounding a warning or other signal: *a car horn.*
▸ *v.* [*tr.*] (of an animal) butt or gore with the horns.
▸ *phrasal v.* □ **horn in** *inf.* intrude; interfere. —**horn·ist** *n.* —**horn·less** *adj.* —**horn·like** /-,līk/ *adj.*
▸ □ **on the horns of a dilemma** faced with a decision involving equally unfavorable alternatives.

horn·beam /'hôrn,bēm/ ▸ *n.* a deciduous tree (genera *Carpinus* and *Ostrya*) of the birch family, of north temperate regions, with oval serrated leaves, inconspicuous drooping flowers, and tough winged nuts. It yields hard pale timber. Also called IRONWOOD.

horn·bill /'hôrn,bil/ ▸ *n.* a medium to large tropical Old World bird (*Buceros* and other genera, family Bucerotidae), having a very large curved bill that typically has a large horny or bony casque.

horn·blende /'hôrn,blend/ ▸ *n.* a dark brown, black, or green mineral of the amphibole group containing calcium, sodium, magnesium, and iron, occurring in many igneous and metamorphic rocks.

horned /hôrnd/ ▸ *adj.* **1** having a horn or horns: *horned cattle* | [in *comb.*] *a long-horned bison.* **2** *poetic/lit.* crescent-shaped: *the horned moon.*

horned toad ▸ *n.* an American lizard (*Phrynosoma*) that somewhat resembles a toad, with spiny skin and large spines on the head, typically occurring in dry open country.

hor·net /'hôrnit/ ▸ *n.* a large stinging wasp (*Vespa* and other genera) that typically nests in hollow trees.
▸ □ **a hornets' nest** a situation fraught with difficulties or complications.

horn of plen·ty ▸ *n.* a cornucopia.

horn·pipe /'hôrn,pīp/ ▸ *n.* a lively dance associated with sailors, typically performed by one person.

horn-rimmed ▸ *adj.* (of glasses) having rims made of horn or a similar substance.

horn·swog·gle /'hôrn,swägəl/ ▸ *v.* [*tr.*] (usu. **be hornswoggled**) *inf.* get the better of (someone) by cheating or deception.

horn·y /'hôrnē/ ▸ *adj.* (**horn·i·er**, **horn·i·est**) **1** of or resembling horn: *a horny beak* | *horny nails.* ■ hard and rough: *horny, dry skin.* **2** *inf.* feeling or arousing sexual excitement. —**horn·i·ness** *n.*

hor·o·scope /'hôrə,skōp/ 'härə-/ ▸ *n. Astrol.* a forecast of a person's future, typically including a delineation of character and circumstances, based on the relative positions of the stars and planets at the time of that person's birth. ■ a short forecast for people born under a particular sign, esp. as published in a newspaper or magazine. ■ a birth chart. See CHART. —**hor·o·scop·ic** /,hôrə'skäpik/ ,härə-/ *adj.* —**ho·ros·co·py** /hə'räskəpē/ *n.*

hor·ren·dous /hə'rendəs/ hô-/ ▸ *adj.* extremely unpleasant, horrifying, or terrible: *she suffered horrendous injuries.* —**hor·ren·dous·ly** *adv.*

hor·ri·ble /'hôrəbəl/ 'här-/ ▸ *adj.* causing or likely to cause horror; shocking: *a horrible massacre.* ■ *inf.* very unpleasant: *the tea tasted horrible.* —**hor·ri·ble·ness** *n.* —**hor·ri·bly** /-blē/ *adv.*

hor·rid /'hôrid/ 'här-/ ▸ *adj.* causing horror: *a horrid nightmare.* ■ *inf.* very unpleasant or disagreeable. —**hor·rid·ly** *adv.* —**hor·rid·ness** *n.*

hor·ri·fic /hô'rifik/ hə-/ ▸ *adj.* causing horror: *horrific injuries.* —**hor·rif·i·cal·ly** /ik(ə)lē/ *adv.*

hor·ri·fy /'hôrə,fī/ 'här-/ ▸ *v.* (**-fies, -fied**) [*tr.*] (usu. **be horrified**) fill with horror; shock greatly: *they were horrified by the very idea* | [as *adj.*] (**horrified**) *the horrified spectators* | [as *adj.*] (**horrifying**) *a horrifying incident.* —**hor·ri·fi·ca·tion** /hô,rifi'kāsHən/ hə-/ *n.* —**hor·ri·fied·ly** /-,fī(ə)dlē/ *adv.* —**hor·ri·fy·ing·ly** *adv.*

hor·ror /'hôrər/ 'här-/ ▸ *n.* **1** an intense feeling of fear, shock, or disgust: *children screamed in horror.* ■ a thing causing such a feeling: *the horrors of civil war.* ■ a literary or film genre concerned with arousing such feelings: [as *adj.*] *a horror movie.* ■ intense dismay: *to her horror she found that a thief had stolen the machine.* ■ [as *interj.*] (**horrors**) *chiefly humorous* used to express dismay: *horrors, two buttons were missing!* ■ intense dislike: *many have a horror of consulting a dictionary.* ■ (**the horrors**) an attack of extreme nervousness or anxiety. **2** *inf.* a bad or mischievous person, esp. a child.

hors d'oeuvre /ôr 'dərv/ 'dœvrə/ ▸ *n.* (*pl.* same or **hors d'oeuvres** *pronunc.* same or /'dərvz/) a small savory dish, typically one served as an appetizer at the beginning of a meal.

horse /hôrs/ ▸ *n.* **1** a solid-hoofed plant-eating domesticated mammal (*Equus caballus*) with a flowing mane and tail, used for riding, racing, and to carry and pull loads. The **horse family** (Equidae) also includes the asses and zebras. ■ an adult male horse; a stallion or gelding. ■ a wild mammal of the horse family. ■ *hist.* [treated as *sing.* or *pl.*] cavalry: *forty horse and sixty foot.* **2** a frame or structure on which something is mounted or supported, esp. a sawhorse. ■ short for POMMEL HORSE or VAULTING HORSE. **3** *inf.* heroin. **4** *inf.* a unit of horsepower: *the huge 63-horse 701-cc engine.* —**horse·less** *adj.* —**horse·like** /-līk/ *adj.*
▸ *phrasal v.* □ **horse around** *inf.* fool around.
▸ □ **from the horse's mouth** (of information) from the person directly concerned or another authoritative source.

horse-and-bug·gy ▸ *adj.* old-fashioned: *horse-and-buggy technology.* ■ of a time when horses and buggies were a common mode of transportation: *he had lived in the horse-and-buggy era.*

horse·back /'hôrs,bak/ ▸ *adj. & adv.* mounted on a horse: [as *adj.*] *a horseback rider* | [as *adv.*] *they rode horseback along the trail.*
▸ □ **on** (or **by**) **horseback** mounted on a horse.

horse chest·nut ▸ *n.* a deciduous tree (genus *Aesculus,* family

Hippocastanaceae) with large leaves of five leaflets, upright conical clusters of white, pink, or red flowers, and seeds enclosed in fleshy, thorny husks. ■ the unpalatable chestnutlike seed of this tree.

horse·flesh /'hôrs,fleSH/ ▶n. horses considered collectively. ■ the flesh of a horse, esp. when used as food.

horse·fly /'hôrs,flī/ ▶n. (pl. **-flies**) a stoutly built fly (genus *Tabanus*, family Tabanidae), the female of which is a bloodsucker and inflicts painful bites on horses and other mammals.

horse·hair /'hôrs,he(ə)r/ ▶n. hair from the mane or tail of a horse, typically used in furniture for padding.

horse·man /'hôrsmən/ ▶n. (pl. **-men**) a rider on horseback, esp. a skilled one.

horse·man·ship /'hôrsmən,SHip/ ▶n. the art or practice of riding on horseback.

horse·play /'hôrs,plā/ ▶n. rough, boisterous play.

horse·pow·er /'hôrs,pou(-ə)r/ (abbr.: **hp**) ▶n. (pl. same) a unit of power equal to 550 foot-pounds per second (745.7 watts). ■ the power of an engine measured in terms of this: *a strong 140-horsepower engine.* ■ power; ability to perform strenuous tasks.

horse race ▶n. **1** a race between two or more horses ridden by jockeys. **2** a very close contest: *the election was still a horse race.* —**horse rac·ing** n.

horse·rad·ish /'hôrs,radiSH/ ▶n. a European plant (*Armoracia rusticana*) of the cabbage family, grown for its pungent root. ■ this root, which is scraped or grated as a condiment and often made into a sauce.

horse sense ▶n. *inf.* common sense.

horse·shoe /'hôr(s),SHŏŏ/ ▶n. a shoe for a horse formed of a narrow band of iron in the form of an extended circular arc and secured to the hoof with nails. ■ a shoe of this kind or a representation of one, regarded as bringing good luck. ■ something resembling this in shape: [as adj.] *a horseshoe bend.* ■ (**horseshoes**) [treated as *sing.*] a game in which horseshoes are thrown at a stake in the ground.

horse·shoe crab ▶n. a large marine arthropod (class Merostomata) with a domed horseshoe-shaped shell, a long tail-spine, and ten legs, little changed since the Devonian period.

horse·tail /'hôrs,tāl/ ▶n. a nonflowering plant (genus *Equisetum*, family Equisetaceae) with a hollow jointed stem that bears whorls of narrow leaves, producing spores in cones at the tips of the shoots.

horse-trad·ing (also **horse trad·ing**) ▶n. the buying and selling of horses. ■ hard and shrewd bargaining, typically in politics. —**horse-trade** v. —**horse-trad·er** n.

horse·whip /'hôrs,(h)wip/ ▶n. a long whip used for driving and controlling horses.
▶v. (**-whipped, -whip·ping**) [tr.] beat with such a whip.

horse·wom·an /'hôrs,wŏŏmən/ ▶n. (pl. **-wom·en**) a woman who rides on horseback, esp. a skilled one.

hors·ey /'hôrsē/ (also **hors·y**) ▶adj. (**hors·i·er, hors·i·est**) **1** of or resembling a horse: *wide eyes and big, horsey teeth.* **2** concerned with or devoted to horses or horse racing: *the horsey fraternity.* —**hors·i·ly** /'hôrsəlē/ adv. —**hors·i·ness** n.

hor·ta·to·ry /'hôrtə,tôrē/ ▶adj. tending or aiming to exhort: *the central bank relied on hortatory messages and voluntary compliance.* —**hor·ta·tion** /,hôr'tāSHən/ n. —**hor·ta·tive** /'hôrtətiv/ adj.

hor·ti·cul·ture /'hôrti,kəlCHər/ ▶n. the art or practice of garden cultivation and management. —**hor·ti·cul·tur·al** /,hôrti'kəlCHərəl/ adj. —**hor·ti·cul·tur·al·ist** /,hôrti',kəlCHərəlist/ n. —**hor·ti·cul·tur·ist** /,hôrtə-,kəlCHərist/ n.

ho·san·na /hō'zanə; -'zä-/ (also **ho·san·nah**) ▶interj. (esp. in biblical, Judaic, and Christian use) used to express adoration, praise, or joy.
▶n. an expression of adoration, praise, or joy.

hose /hōz/ ▶n. **1** a flexible tube conveying water, used esp. for watering plants and in firefighting. **2** [treated as *pl.*] stockings, socks, and tights (esp. in commercial use): *a chorus girl's fishnet hose.* ■ *hist.* breeches: *Elizabethan doublet and hose.*
▶v. [tr.] water, spray, or drench with a hose: *he was **hosing down** the driveway.* ▷Old English *hosa*, of Germanic origin; related to Dutch *hoos* 'stocking' and German *Hosen* 'trousers.' Originally singular, the term denoted a covering for the leg, sometimes including the foot but sometimes reaching only as far as the ankle.

ho·sier /'hōzHər/ ▶n. a manufacturer or seller of hosiery.

ho·sier·y /'hōzHərē/ ▶n. stockings, socks, and tights collectively.

hos·pice /'häspis/ ▶n. a home providing care for the sick, esp. the terminally ill. ■ *archaic* a lodging for travelers, esp. one run by a religious order.

hos·pi·ta·ble /hä'spitəbəl; 'häspitəbəl/ ▶adj. friendly and welcoming to

strangers or guests. ■ (of an environment) pleasant and favorable for living in: *the Sonoran desert is one of the least hospitable places on earth.* —**hos·pi·ta·bly** /-blē/ adv.

hos·pi·tal /'hä,spitl/ ▶n. an institution providing medical and surgical treatment and nursing care for sick or injured people.

hos·pi·tal·i·ty /,häspi'talitē/ ▶n. the friendly and generous reception and entertainment of guests, visitors, or strangers.
▶adj. denoting a suite or room in a hotel where visitors are entertained, typically at a convention. ■ relating to or denoting the business of housing or entertaining visitors: *the hospitality industry.*

hos·pi·tal·ize /'häspitl,īz/ ▶v. [tr.] (usu. **be hospitalized**) admit or cause (someone) to be admitted to a hospital for treatment: *Casey was hospitalized for chest pains.* —**hos·pi·tal·i·za·tion** /,häspitl-li'zāSHən/ n.

host¹ /hōst/ ▶n. **1** a person who receives or entertains other people as guests. ■ a person, place, or organization that holds and organizes an event to which others are invited: *Innsbruck once **played host** to the Winter Olympics.* ■ an area in which particular living things are found: *Australia is host to some of the world's most dangerous animals.* ■ *often humorous* the landlord or landlady of a pub: *mine host raised his glass of whiskey.* ■ the moderator or emcee of a television or radio program. **2** *Biol.* an animal or plant on or in which a parasite or commensal organism lives. ■ (also **host cell**) a living cell in which a virus multiplies. ■ a person whose immune system has been invaded by a pathogenic organism. ■ a person or animal that has received transplanted tissue or a transplanted organ. **3** (also **host computer**) a computer that mediates multiple access to databases mounted on it or provides other services to a computer network.
▶v. [tr.] act as host at (an event) or for (a television or radio program). ■ [intr.] act as host.

host² ▶n. (**a host of** or **hosts of**) a large number of people or things: *a host of memories rushed into her mind.* ■ *archaic* an army. ■ *poetic/lit.* (in biblical use) the sun, moon, and stars: *the starry host of heaven.*

host³ ▶n. (usu. **the Host**) the bread consecrated in the Eucharist.

hos·ta /'hōstə; 'hästə/ ▶n. an eastern Asian plant (genus *Hosta*) of the lily family, widely cultivated for its shade-tolerant foliage.

hos·tage /'hästij/ ▶n. a person seized or held as security for the fulfillment of a condition.
▶ □ **hold** (or **take**) **someone hostage** seize and keep someone as a hostage: *they were held hostage by armed rebels* | *taken hostage at gunpoint.*

hos·tel /'hästl/ ▶n. an establishment that provides cheap food and lodging for a specific group of people, such as students, workers, or travelers. ■ short for YOUTH HOSTEL. ■ *archaic* an inn providing accommodations.

host·ess /'hōstis/ ▶n. a woman who receives or entertains guests. ■ a woman employed at a restaurant to welcome and seat customers. ■ a woman employed to entertain customers at a nightclub, bar, or dance hall. ■ a stewardess on an aircraft, train, etc. ■ a woman who introduces a television or radio program: *a game-show hostess.*
▶v. [tr.] act as a hostess at (an event). ■ [intr.] act as a hostess.

hos·tile /'hästl; 'hä,stīl/ ▶adj. unfriendly; antagonistic. ■ of or belonging to a military enemy: *hostile aircraft.* ■ opposed: *people are very hostile to the idea.* ■ (of a takeover bid) opposed by the company to be bought. —**hos·tile·ly** adv.

hos·til·i·ty /hä'stilitē/ ▶n. (pl. **-ties**) hostile behavior; unfriendliness or opposition: *their hostility to all outsiders.* ■ (**hostilities**) acts of warfare: *he called for an immediate cessation of hostilities.*

hos·tler /'(h)äslər/ (also **os·tler**) ▶n. *hist.* a man employed to look after the horses of people staying at an inn.

hot /hät/ ▶adj. (**hot·ter, hot·test**) **1** having a high degree of heat or a high temperature. ■ feeling or producing an uncomfortable sensation of heat. ■ (of food or drink) prepared by heating and served without cooling. ■ *inf.* (of an electric circuit) at a high voltage; live. ■ *inf.* radioactive. **2** (of food) containing or consisting of pungent spices or peppers that produce a burning sensation when tasted: *a very hot dish cooked with green chili.* **3** passionately enthusiastic, eager, or excited: *the idea had been nurtured in his hot imagination.* ■ lustful, amorous, or erotic. ■ angry, indignant, or upset: *hot with rage.* ■ (of music, esp. jazz) strongly rhythmical and excitingly played: *hot salsa and lambada dancing.* **4** involving much activity, debate, or intense feeling: *a very hot issue.* ■ (esp. of news) fresh or recent and therefore of great interest: *have I got some hot gossip for you!* ■ currently popular, fashionable, or in demand: *they know the hottest dance moves.* ■ difficult to deal with; awkward or dangerous: *he found my story too hot to handle.* ■ (of a hit or return in ball games) difficult for an opponent to deal with: *fielding a hot grounder at third.* ■ *Hunting* (of the scent) fresh and strong, indicating that the quarry has passed recently. ■ *inf.* (of goods) stolen and difficult to dispose of because easily identifiable. ■ *inf.* (of a person) wanted by the police. ■ (in children's games) very close to finding or guessing something. **5** *inf.* knowledgeable or skillful: *Tony is very hot on local history.* ■ good; promising: *this is not so hot for business.* ■ (**hot on**) *inf.* considering as very important; strict about: *local customs officers are hot on confiscations.* —**hot·ly** *adv.* —**hot·ness** *n.* —**hot·tish** *adj.*

▶ □ **have the hots for** *inf.* be sexually attracted to. □ **hot and heavy** *inf.* intense; with intensity: *the competition became very hot and heavy.* □ **hot on the heels of** following closely. □ **hot under the collar** *inf.* angry, resentful, or embarrassed. □ **in hot pursuit** following closely and eagerly. □ **in hot water** *inf.* in a situation of difficulty, trouble, or disgrace. □ **make it** (or **things**) **hot for someone** *inf.* make things unpleasant for someone; persecute.

hot air ▶ *n. inf.* empty talk that is intended to impress: *they dismissed the theory as a load of hot air.*

hot·bed /ˈhätˌbed/ ▶ *n.* a bed of earth heated by fermenting manure, for raising or forcing plants. ■ an environment promoting the growth of something, esp. something unwelcome: *the country was a hotbed of revolt and dissension.*

hot-blood·ed ▶ *adj.* lustful; passionate.

hot·cake /ˈhätˌkāk/ ▶ *n.* a pancake.

▶ *phrasal v.* □ **like hotcakes** quickly and in great quantity, esp. because of popularity: *his latest CD is selling like hotcakes.*

hot dog ▶ *n.* **1** a hot sausage served in a long, soft roll and typically topped with various condiments. **2** *inf.* a person who shows off, esp. a skier or surfer who performs stunts or tricks.

▶ *interj. inf.* used to express delight or enthusiastic approval: *hot dog! I've finally found something I can do that you can't.*

▶ *v.* (**hot-dog**) (**-dogged, -dog·ging**) [*intr.*] *inf.* perform stunts or tricks; show off. —**hot·dog·ger** *n.*

ho·tel /hōˈtel/ ▶ *n.* an establishment providing accommodations, meals, and other services for travelers and tourists.

ho·te·lier /ˌōtelˈyā; hōtlˈi(ə)r/ ▶ *n.* a person who owns or manages a hotel.

hot flash ▶ *n.* a sudden feeling of feverish heat, typically as a symptom of menopause.

hot·foot /ˈhätˌfŏŏt/ ▶ *n.* a practical joke in which a match is inserted into the victim's shoe and then lit.

▶ *v.* [*tr.*] (**hotfoot it**) walk or run quickly and eagerly: *we hotfooted it after him.*

▶ *adv.* in eager haste: *he rushed hotfoot to the planning office to object.*

hot·head /ˈhätˌhed/ (also **hot-head**) ▶ *n.* a person who is impetuous or who easily becomes angry and violent. —**hot·head·ed** *adj.* —**hot·head·ed·ly** *adv.* —**hot·head·ed·ness** *n.*

hot·house /ˈhätˌhous/ ▶ *n.* a heated building, typically made largely of glass, for rearing plants out of season or in a climate colder than is natural for them. ■ *fig.* an environment that encourages the rapid growth or development of someone or something, esp. in a stifling or intense way: [as *adj.*] *the hothouse atmosphere of the college.*

▶ *v.* [*tr.*] educate (a child) to a high level at an earlier age than is usual.

hot·line /ˈhätˌlīn/ (also **hot line**) ▶ *n.* a direct telephone line set up for a specific purpose, esp. for use in emergencies or for communication between heads of government. ■ a telephone line to a source of information or emergency help.

hot plate ▶ *n.* a flat heated surface (or a set of these), typically portable, used for cooking food or keeping it hot.

hot po·ta·to ▶ *n. inf.* a controversial issue or situation that is awkward or unpleasant to deal with.

hot rod ▶ *n.* a motor vehicle that has been specially modified to give it extra power and speed.

▶ *v.* (**hot-rod**) (**-rod·ded, -rod·ding**) **1** [*intr.*] drive a hot rod. **2** [*tr.*] modify (a vehicle or other device) to make it faster or more powerful. —**hot rod·der** (also **hot-rod·der**) *n.*

hot seat ▶ *n.* (**the hot seat**) *inf.* **1** the position of a person who carries full responsibility for something, including facing criticism or being answerable for decisions or actions. **2** the electric chair.

hot·shot /ˈhätˌSHät/ ▶ *n. inf.* an important or exceptionally able person: *these three hotshots decide what's what at the firm.* ■ a show-off; an exhibitionist: *the hotshots whizz by on their snowboards.*

▶ *adj.* aggressive and skillful: *a hotshot broker angling for a partnership.*

hot spot ▶ *n.* a small area or region with a relatively hot temperature in comparison to its surroundings. ■ *Geol.* an area of volcanic activity, esp. where this is isolated. ■ *fig.* a place of significant activity or danger: *the hotel was the hot spot in town, with its all-night coffee shop.* ■ *Computing* an area where a usable Wi-Fi signal is available for personal computer use.

hot spring ▶ *n.* a spring of naturally hot water, typically heated by subterranean volcanic activity.

hot stuff ▶ *n. inf.* used to refer to a person or thing of outstanding quality, interest, or talent: *he's hot stuff at arithmetic.* ■ used to refer to a sexually exciting person, movie, book, etc.: *Jill was reputed to be hot stuff.*

hot-tem·pered ▶ *adj.* easily angered; quick-tempered.

Hot·ten·tot /ˈhätnˌtät/ ▶ *n. & adj.* used to refer to Khoikhoi peoples.

hot tub ▶ *n.* a large tub filled with hot aerated water used for recreation or physical therapy.

hot-wa·ter bot·tle (also **hot-water bag**) ▶ *n.* a flat, oblong container, typically made of rubber, that is filled with hot water and used for warmth.

hot-wire ▶ *v.* [*tr.*] *inf.* start the engine of (a vehicle) by bypassing the ignition system, typically in order to steal it.

hound /hound/ ▶ *n.* a dog of a breed used for hunting, esp. one able to track by scent. ■ any dog. ■ a person who avidly pursues something: *a publicity hound.* ■ *inf., dated* a despicable or contemptible man.

▶ *v.* [*tr.*] harass or persecute (someone) relentlessly. ■ pursue relentlessly: *he led the race from start to finish but was hounded all the way by Phillips.* ▷Old English *hund* (in the general sense 'dog'), of Germanic origin; related to Dutch *hond* and German *Hund*, from an Indo-European root shared by Greek *kuōn, kun-* 'dog.'

hounds·tooth /ˈhoun(d)zˌtōōth/ ▶ *n.* a large checked pattern with notched corners suggestive of a canine tooth, typically used in cloth for jackets and suits.

houndstooth

hour /ou(ə)r/ ▶ *n.* **1** a period of time equal to a twenty-fourth part of a day and night and divided into 60 minutes. ■ a less definite period of time: *during the early hours of the morning.* ■ the distance traveled in one hour: *Ocean City is less than an hour away.* **2** a point in time: *I wondered if my last hour had come.* ■ a time of day or night: *you can't turn him away at this hour.* ■ a time of day specified as an exact number of hours from midnight or midday. ■ (**hours**) a time so specified on the 24-hour clock: *the first bomb fell at 0051 hours.* ■ the time as formerly reckoned from sunrise: *it was about the ninth hour.* ■ the appropriate time for some specific action: *now that the hour had come, David decided he could not face it.* **3** a period set aside for some purpose or marked by some activity: *leisure hours.* ■ (**hours**) a fixed period of time for an activity, such as work, use of a building, etc.: *shortened working hours.* **4** (usu. **hours**) (in the Western Church) a short service of psalms and prayers to be said at a particular time of day, esp. in religious communities. **5** *Astron.* 15° of longitude or right ascension (one twenty-fourth part of a circle).

▶ □ **all hours** any time, esp. outside the time considered usual for something: *intruders had access at all hours.* □ **keep late hours** get up and go to bed late. □ **keep regular hours** do the same thing at the same time every day. □ **on the hour** at an exact hour, or on each hour, of the day or night. □ **within the hour** after less than an hour.

hour·glass /ˈou(ə)rˌglas/ ▶ *n.* an invertible device with two connected glass bulbs containing sand that takes an hour to pass from the upper to the lower bulb. ■ [as *adj.*] shaped like such a device: *her hourglass figure.*

hour·ly /ˈou(ə)rlē/ ▶ *adj.* **1** done or occurring every hour: *there is an hourly bus service.* ■ (with numeral or fraction) occurring at intervals measured in hours: *trains run at half-hourly intervals.* **2** reckoned hour by hour: *to introduce standard fees instead of hourly rates.*

▶ *adv.* **1** every hour. ■ (with numeral or fraction) at intervals measured in hours: *temperature should be recorded four-hourly.* **2** by the hour: *hourly paid workers.* **3** frequently; continually: *her curiosity was mounting hourly.*

house ▶ *n.* /hous/ (*pl.* **hous·es** /ˈhouziz/) **1** a building for human habitation, esp. one that is lived in by a family or small group of people. ■ the people living in such a building; a household: *do you want the whole house woken up?* ■ (often **House**) a family or family lineage, esp. a noble or royal one; a dynasty: *the house of Stewart.* ■ a building in which animals live or in which things are kept: *a reptile house.* **2** a building in which people meet for a particular activity: *a house of prayer.* ■ a business or institution: *a publishing house.* ■ a restaurant or inn: [as *adj.*] *I ordered a bottle of their house wine.* ■ a residential hall at a

school or college, or its residents. ■ a gambling establishment or its management. ■ a host or proprietor: *help yourself to a drink, compliments of the house!* ■ a theater: *a hundred musicians performed in front of a full house.* ■ an audience in a theater or concert venue: *the house burst into applause.* ■ *dated* a brothel. **3** a legislative or deliberative assembly. ■ **(the House)** the House of Representatives or (in the UK or Canada) the House of Commons or Lords. **4** (also **house music**) a style of popular dance music typically using synthesized drum and bass lines, sparse repetitive vocals, and a fast beat. **5** *Astrol.* any of the twelve divisions of the celestial sphere.
▸*adj.* /hous/ **1** (of an animal or plant) kept in, frequenting, or infesting buildings. **2** of or relating to resident medical staff at a hospital. **3** of or relating to a business, institution, or society: *a house journal.* ■ (of a band or group) resident or regularly performing in a club or other venue.
▸*v.* /houz/ [*tr.*] **1** provide (a person or animal) with shelter or living quarters. **2** provide space for; accommodate. ■ enclose or encase (something): *housed in a pod beneath the engine.* ■ insert or fix (something) in a socket or mortise. **—house·ful** /-ˌfool/ *n.* (*pl.* **-fuls**)
▸ □ **house of cards** a structure built out of playing cards precariously balanced together. ■ an insubstantial or insecure situation or scheme: *his case was a house of cards until Attorney Jabowski stepped in.* □ **on the house** (of a drink or meal in a bar or restaurant) at the management's expense; free. □ **put** (or **set** or **get**) **one's house in order** make necessary reforms: *to get their own economic house in order.*
house ar·rest ▸*n.* the state of being kept as a prisoner in one's own house, rather than in a prison: *she was placed under house arrest.*
house·boat /ˈhousˌbōt/ ▸*n.* a boat that is or can be moored for use as a dwelling.
house·bound /ˈhousˌbound/ ▸*adj.* unable to leave one's house, typically due to illness or old age.
house·boy /ˈhousˌboi/ ▸*n.* a boy or man employed to undertake domestic duties.
house·break /ˈhousˌbrāk/ (*past.* **-broke**; *past part.* **-bro·ken**) ▸*v.* [*tr.*] train (a pet) to urinate and defecate outside the house or only in a special place. ■ *inf.* or *humorous* teach (someone) good manners or neatness.
house·break·ing /ˈhousˌbrākiNG/ ▸*n.* the action of breaking into a building to commit a crime. **—house·break·er** /-ˌbrākər/ *n.*
house·coat /ˈhousˌkōt/ ▸*n.* a woman's long, loose, lightweight robe for informal wear around the house.
house·dress /ˈhousˌdres/ ▸*n.* a simple, usually washable, dress suitable for wearing while doing housework.
house·fa·ther /ˈhousˌfäTHər/ ▸*n.* a man in charge of and living in a boarding school dormitory or other group residence.
house·fly /ˈhousˌflī/ (also **house fly**) ▸*n.* (*pl.* **-flies**) a common small fly (*Musca domestica*, family Muscidae) occurring worldwide in and around human habitation.
house guest (also **house·guest**) ▸*n.* a guest staying for some days in a private house.
house·hold /ˈhousˌ(h)ōld/ ▸*n.* a house and its occupants regarded as a unit. ■ the affairs related to keeping a house: *it is mostly women who are responsible for running households* | [as *adj.*] *household appliances.*
house·hold·er /ˈhousˌ(h)ōldər/ ▸*n.* a person who owns or rents a house; the head of a household.
house·hold name (also **household word**) ▸*n.* a person or thing that is well known by the public.
house·hus·band /ˈhousˌhəzbənd/ ▸*n.* a man who lives with a partner and carries out household duties traditionally done by a housewife rather than working outside the home.
house·keep·er /ˈhousˌkēpər/ ▸*n.* a person, typically a woman, employed to manage a household. **—house·keep** *v.* (*dated*).
house·keep·ing /ˈhousˌkēpiNG/ ▸*n.* **1** the management of household affairs. ■ money set aside or given for such a purpose: *writing barely pays my part of the housekeeping.* ■ a department within a hotel or other residential facility that oversees the cleaning of rooms and the provision of necessities such as towels and glassware: *you'll never have to nag housekeeping for a set of dry towels.* **2** operations such as record-keeping or maintenance in an organization or a computer that make work possible but do not directly constitute its performance. ■ *Biol.* the regulation of metabolic functions that are common to all cells.
▸*adj.* (of cabins, cottages, or other rental properties) having basic facilities such as a stove and refrigerator.
house lights (also **house·lights**) ▸*pl. n.* the lights in the area of a theater where the audience sits: *the show ended and the house lights came up.*

house·maid /ˈhousˌmād/ ▸*n.* a female domestic employee, esp. one who cleans reception rooms and bedrooms.
house·moth·er /ˈhousˌməTHər/ ▸*n.* a woman in charge of and living in a boarding school dormitory or children's home.
house mu·sic ▸*n.* see HOUSE (sense 4).
House of Com·mons ▸(in the UK and Canada) the elected chamber of Parliament.
House of Rep·re·sent·a·tives ▸the lower house of the U.S. Congress and other legislatures, including most U.S. state governments.
house·par·ent /ˈhousˌpe(ə)rənt; -ˌparənt/ ▸*n.* a housemother or housefather.
house·plant /ˈhousˌplant/ (also **house plant**) ▸*n.* a plant grown indoors.
house·wares /ˈhousˌwe(ə)rz/ ▸*pl. n.* small articles for furnishing a home, such as dishes, kitchen utensils, and small appliances.
house·warm·ing /ˈhousˌwôrmiNG/ ▸*n.* [usu. as *adj.*] a party celebrating a move to a new home: *a housewarming gift.*
house·wife /ˈhousˌwīf/ ▸*n.* (*pl.* **-wives**) **1** a married woman whose main occupation is caring for her family, managing household affairs, and doing housework. **2** /ˈhəzif/ a small case for needles, thread, and other small sewing items. **—house·wife·ly** *adj.* **—house·wif·er·y** /-ˌwīfərē/ *n.*
house·work /ˈhousˌwərk/ ▸*n.* regular work done in housekeeping, such as cleaning, shopping, and cooking.
hous·ing /ˈhouziNG/ ▸*n.* **1** houses and apartments considered collectively. ■ the provision of accommodations: *the sector that offers housing to the poorest.* **2** a rigid casing that encloses and protects a piece of moving or delicate equipment. ■ a structure that supports and encloses the bearings at the end of an axle or shaft. **3** a recess or groove cut in one piece of wood to allow another piece to be attached to it.
HOV ▸*abbr.* high-occupancy vehicle.
hove /hōv/ *chiefly Naut.* ▸ past of HEAVE.
hov·el /ˈhəvəl; ˈhävəl/ ▸*n.* a small, squalid, unpleasant, or simply constructed dwelling.
hov·er /ˈhəvər/ ▸*v.* [*intr.*] remain in one place in the air. ■ remain poised in one place, typically with slight but undirected movement: *her hand hovered over the console.* ■ (of a person) wait or linger close at hand in a tentative or uncertain manner: *she hovered anxiously in the background.* ■ remain at or near a particular level: *inflation will hover around the 4 percent mark.* ■ remain in a state that is between two specified states or kinds of things: *his expression hovered between cynicism and puzzlement.*
▸*n.* an act of remaining in the air in one place. **—hov·er·er** *n.*
hov·er·craft /ˈhəvərˌkraft/ ▸*n.* (*pl.* same) a vehicle or craft that travels over land or water on a cushion of air provided by a downward blast.
how¹ /hou/ ▸*adv.* [usu. *interrog. adv.*] **1** in what way or manner; by what means. **2** used to ask about the condition or quality of something: *how was your vacation?* | *how did they play?* ■ used to ask about someone's physical or mental state: *how are the children?* | *I asked how he was doing.* **3** used to ask about the extent or degree of something: *how old are you?* | *how long will it take?* | *I wasn't sure how fast to go.* ■ used to express a strong feeling such as surprise about the extent of something: *how kind it was of him* | *how I wish I had been there!* **4** the way in which; that: *she told us how she had lived out of a suitcase for a week.* ■ in any way in which; however: *I'll be dubious however I like.*
▸ □ **and how!** *inf.* very much so (used to express strong agreement): *"Did you miss me?" "And how!"* □ **how about 1** used to make a suggestion or offer: *how about a drink?* **2** used when asking for information or an opinion on something: *how about your company?* □ **how do you do?** a formal greeting. □ **how's that for ——?** isn't that a remarkable instance of ——?: *how's that for stereotypical thinking?*
how² ▸*interj.* a greeting attributed to North American Indians (used in humorous imitation).
how·dah /ˈhoudə/ ▸*n.* (in the Indian subcontinent) a seat for riding on the back of an elephant or camel, typically with a canopy.
how·dy /ˈhoudē/ ▸*interj.* an informal friendly greeting, particularly associated with the western states: *howdy, stranger.*
how·ev·er /houˈevər/ ▸*adv.* **1** used to introduce a statement that contrasts with or seems to contradict something that has been said previously: *People tend to put on weight in middle age. However, gaining weight is not inevitable.* **2** in whatever way; regardless of how: *however you look at it, you can't criticize that.* ■ to whatever extent: *he was hesitant to take the risk, however small.*
how·itz·er /ˈhouətsər/ ▸*n.* a short gun for firing artillery shells on high

trajectories at low velocities. ▷late 17th cent.: from Dutch *houwitser*, from German *Haubitze*, from Czech *houfnice* 'catapult.'

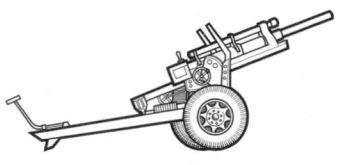
howitzer

howl /houl/ ▶*n.* a long, loud, doleful cry uttered by an animal such as a dog or wolf. ■ a loud cry of pain, fear, anger, amusement, or derision: *he let out a **howl** of anguish | fig. I got **howls** of protest from readers.* ■ a prolonged wailing noise such as that made by a strong wind: *they listened to the **howl** of the gale.*
▶*v.* [*intr.*] make a howling sound. ■ weep and cry out loudly: *a baby started to howl.* ■ [*tr.*] (**howl someone down**) shout in disapproval in order to prevent a speaker from being heard.

howl·er /'houlər/ ▶*n.* **1** *inf.* a stupid or glaring mistake, esp. an amusing one. **2** a person or animal that howls. **3** (also **howler monkey**) a fruit-eating monkey (genus *Alouatta*) with a prehensile tail and a loud howling call, native to the forests of tropical America.

howl·ing /'houliNG/ ▶*adj.* **1** producing a long, loud, doleful cry or wailing sound. ■ *archaic* filled with or characterized by such sounds: *the howling wilderness.* **2** *inf.* extreme; great: *the meal was a howling success.*

h.p. (also **HP**) ▶*abbr.* ■ high pressure. ■ horsepower.

HQ ▶*abbr.* headquarters.

HR ▶*abbr.* ■ House of Representatives. ■ human resources.

hr ▶*abbr.* hour.

HTML ▶*n. Comput.* Hypertext Markup Language, a standardized system for tagging text files to achieve font, color, graphic, and hyperlink effects on World Wide Web pages.

hub /həb/ ▶*n.* the central part of a wheel, rotating on or with the axle, and from which the spokes radiate. ■ a place or thing that forms the effective center of an activity, region, or network: *the kitchen was the **hub** of family life.*
▶ □ **hub-and-spoke** denoting a system of air transportation in which local airports offer flights to a central airport where international or long-distance flights are available.

Hub·ble Space Tel·e·scope /'həbəl/ ▶an orbiting astronomical observatory launched in 1990. The telescope's high-resolution images are far better than can be obtained from the earth's surface.

hub·bub /'həbəb/ ▶*n.* a chaotic din caused by a crowd of people. ■ a busy, noisy situation: *she fought through the hubbub.*

hub·by /'həbē/ ▶*n.* (pl. -**bies**) *inf.* a husband.

hub·cap /'həb,kap/ ▶*n.* a metal or plastic cover for the hub of a motor vehicle's wheel.

hu·bris /'(h)yōōbris/ ▶*n.* excessive pride or self-confidence. ■ (in Greek tragedy) excessive pride toward or defiance of the gods, leading to nemesis. —**hu·bris·tic** /(h)yōō'bristik/ *adj.*

huck·a·back /'həkə,bak/ ▶*n.* a strong linen or cotton fabric with a rough surface, used for toweling.

huck·le·ber·ry /'həkəl,berē/ ▶*n.* **1** a small, round, edible blue-black berry related to the blueberry. **2** the low-growing North American shrub (genus *Gaylussacia*) of the heath family that bears this fruit.

huck·ster /'həkstər/ ▶*n.* a person who sells small items, either door-to-door or from a stall or small store. ■ a mercenary person eager to make a profit out of anything. ■ a publicity agent or advertising copywriter, esp. for radio or television.
▶*v.* [*tr.*] promote or sell (something, typically a product of questionable value). ■ [*intr.*] bargain; haggle. —**huck·ster·ism** /-izəm/ *n.*

HUD /həd/ ▶*abbr.* ■ (Department of) Housing and Urban Development.

hud·dle /'hədl/ ▶*v.* [*intr.*] crowd together; nestle closely: *they **huddled** together for warmth.* ■ curl one's body into a small space: *the watchman remained, huddled under his canvas shelter.* ■ draw together for an informal, private conversation: *selection committee members huddled with attorneys.*
▶*n.* a crowded or confused mass of people or things. ■ a brief gathering of players during a game to receive instructions, esp. in football. ■ a small group of people holding an informal, private conversation.

hue /(h)yōō/ ▶*n.* a color or shade: *her face lost its golden hue | verdigris is greenish-yellow in hue.* ■ the attribute of a color by virtue of which it is discernible as red, green, etc., and which is dependent on its dominant wavelength, and independent of intensity or lightness. ■ *fig.* character; aspect: *men of all political hues submerged their feuds.* ▷Old

English *hīw*, *hēow* (also 'form, appearance,' obsolete except in Scots), of Germanic origin; related to Swedish *hy* 'skin, complexion.' The sense 'color, shade' dates from the mid 19th cent. —**hued** *adj.* [in *comb.*] *rainbow-hued.* —**hue·less** *adj.*

hue and cry ▶*n.* a loud clamor or public outcry. ■ *hist.* a loud cry calling for the pursuit and capture of a criminal.

huff /həf/ ▶*v.* [*intr.*] **1** breathe out loudly; puff. ■ [*tr.*] express (one's annoyance or offense): *he huffed out his sudden irritation.* **2** [*tr.*] sniff fumes from (gasoline or solvents) for a euphoric effect.
▶*n.* a fit of petty annoyance: *she walked off **in a huff**.* —**huff·ish** *adj.*
▶ □ **huff and puff** breathe heavily with exhaustion. ■ express one's annoyance in an obvious or threatening way.

huff·y /'həfē/ ▶*adj.* (**huff·i·er, huff·i·est**) annoyed or irritated and quick to take offense at petty things: *ask writers for more than a second draft and they get huffy.* —**huff·i·ly** *adv.* —**huff·i·ness** *n.*

hug /həg/ ▶*v.* (**hugged, hug·ging**) [*tr.*] squeeze (someone) tightly in one's arms, typically to express affection. ■ hold (something) closely or tightly around or against part of one's body: *he hugged his knees to his chest.* ■ fit tightly around: *jeans that hugged the contours of his body.* ■ keep close to: *I headed north, hugging the coastline all the way.* ■ (**hug oneself**) congratulate or be pleased with oneself: *she hugged herself with secret joy.* ■ cherish or cling to (something such as a belief): *a boy hugging a secret.*
▶*n.* an act of holding someone tightly in one's arms, typically to express affection: *there were hugs and tears as they were reunited.* —**hug·ga·ble** *adj.*

huge /(h)yōōj/ ▶*adj.* (**hug·er, hug·est**) extremely large; enormous: *a huge area | he made a huge difference to the team.* —**huge·ness** *n.*

huge·ly /'(h)yōōjlē/ ▶*adv.* very much; to a great extent: *a hugely expensive house.*

Hu·gue·not /'hyōōgə,nät/ ▶*n.* a French Protestant of the 16th–17th centuries. Largely Calvinist, the Huguenots suffered severe persecution at the hands of the Catholic majority, and many thousands emigrated.

huh /hə/ ▶*interj.* used to express scorn, anger, disbelief, surprise, or amusement: *"Huh," she snorted, "Over my dead body!"* ■ used in questions to invite agreement or further comment or to express a lack of understanding: *pretty devastating, huh?*

hu·la /'hōōlə/ (also **hu·la-hu·la**) ▶*n.* a dance performed by Hawaiian women, characterized by undulating hips and gestures symbolizing natural phenomena or historical or mythological subjects.

hu·la hoop (also *trademark* **Hu·la-Hoop**) ▶*n.* a large hoop spun around the body by gyrating the hips, for play or exercise.

hulk /həlk/ ▶*n.* **1** an old ship stripped of fittings and permanently moored, esp. for use as storage or (formerly) as a prison. ■ any large structure no longer in use: *hulks of abandoned machinery.* **2** a large or unwieldy boat or other object. ■ a large, clumsy-looking person: *a six-foot hulk of a man.*
▶*v.* [*intr.*] appear large or threatening: *mile-high cliffs, hulking above wild-rushing glacial streams.* ■ move heavily or clumsily.

hulk·ing /'həlkiNG/ ▶*adj. inf.* (of a person or object) large, heavy, or clumsy: *a hulking young man.*

hull[1] /həl/ ▶*n.* the main body of a ship or other vessel, including the bottom, sides, and deck but not the masts, superstructure, rigging, engines, and other fittings.
▶*v.* [*tr.*] (usu. **be hulled**) hit and pierce the hull of (a ship) with a shell or other missile. —**hulled** *adj.*

hull[2] ▶*n.* the outer covering of a fruit or seed, esp. the pod of peas and beans, or the husk of grain. ■ the green calyx of a strawberry or raspberry.
▶*v.* [*tr.*] (usu. as *adj.*) (**hulled**) remove the hulls from (fruit, seeds, or grain).

hul·la·ba·loo /'hələbə,lōō; ,hələbə'lōō/ ▶*n. inf.* a commotion; a fuss: *remember all the hullabaloo over the golf ball?*

hul·lo /hə'lō/ ▶*exclam.* variant spelling of **HELLO.**

hum[1] /həm/ ▶*v.* (**hummed, hum·ming**) [*intr.*] make a low, steady continuous sound like that of a bee: *the computers hummed.* ■ sing with closed lips: *she was humming a cheerful tune.* ■ (of a place) be filled with a low, steady continuous sound: *the room **hummed with** an expectant murmur.* ■ *inf.* be in a state of great activity: *the repair shops are humming.*
▶*n.* a low, steady, continuous sound. ■ an unwanted low-frequency noise in an amplifier caused by variation of electric current. —**hum·ma·ble** *adj.* —**hum·mer** *n.*

hum[2] ▶*interj.* used to express hesitation or dissent: *"Ah, hum, I think it's Elaine, isn't it?"*

---

hu·man /'(h)yōōmən/ ▶*adj.* of, relating to, or characteristic of people or human beings. ■ of or characteristic of people as opposed to God or animals or machines: *they are only human, and therefore mistakes do occur | the risk of human error.* ■ of or characteristic of people's better qualities, such as kindness or sensitivity: *the human side of politics is getting stronger.* ■ *Zool.* of or belonging to the genus *Homo.*
▶*n.* a human being, esp. a person as distinguished from an animal or (in science fiction) an alien. —**hu·man·ness** *n.*

hu·man be·ing ▶*n.* a man, woman, or child of the species *Homo sapiens,* distinguished from other animals by superior mental development, power of articulate speech, and upright stance.

hu·mane /(h)yōō'mān/ ▶*adj.* **1** having or showing compassion or benevolence: *regulations ensuring the humane treatment of animals.* ■ inflicting the minimum of pain: *humane methods of killing.* **2** *formal* (of a branch of learning) intended to have a civilizing or refining effect on people: *economics as a humane discipline.* —**hu·mane·ly** *adv.* —**hu·mane·ness** *n.*

hu·man in·ter·est ▶*n.* the aspect of a story in the media that interests people because it describes the experiences or emotions of individuals: [as *adj.*] *dry and distant matters are often treated from a human-interest angle.*

hu·man·ism /'(h)yōōmə,nizəm/ ▶*n.* an outlook or system of thought attaching prime importance to human rather than divine or supernatural matters. Humanist beliefs stress the potential value and goodness of human beings, emphasize common human needs, and seek solely rational ways of solving human problems. ■ (often **Humanism**) a Renaissance cultural movement that turned away from medieval scholasticism and revived interest in ancient Greek and Roman thought. ■ (among some contemporary writers) a system of thought criticized as being centered on the notion of the rational, autonomous self and ignoring the unintegrated and conditioned nature of the individual. —**hu·man·ist** *n. & adj.* —**hu·man·is·tic** /,(h)yōōmə'nistik/ *adj.* —**hu·man·is·ti·cal·ly** /,(h)yōōmə'nistik(ə)lē/ *adv.*

hu·man·i·tar·i·an /(h)yōō,mani'te(ə)rēən/ ▶*adj.* concerned with or seeking to promote human welfare.
▶*n.* a person who seeks to promote human welfare; a philanthropist. —**hu·man·i·tar·i·an·ism** /-,nizəm/ *n.*

hu·man·i·ty /(h)yōō'manitē/ ▶*n.* (*pl.* **-ties**) **1** the human race; human beings collectively: *appalling crimes against humanity.* ■ the fact or condition of being human; human nature. **2** humaneness; benevolence: *he praised them for their standards of humanity, care, and dignity.* **3** (**humanities**) learning or literature concerned with human culture, esp. literature, history, art, music, and philosophy.

hu·man·ize /'(h)yōōmə,nīz/ ▶*v.* [*tr.*] **1** make (something) more humane or civilized: *his purpose was to humanize prison conditions.* **2** give (something) a human character. —**hu·man·i·za·tion** /,hyōōməni'zāsHən/ *n.*

hu·man·kind /'(h)yōōmən,kīnd/ ▶*n.* human beings considered collectively (used as a neutral alternative to "mankind").

hu·man·ly /'(h)yōōmənlē/ ▶*adv.* **1** from a human point of view; in a human manner: *they can grow both humanly and spiritually.* ■ by human means; within human ability: *we did all that was humanly possible.* **2** *chiefly archaic* with human feeling or kindness.

hu·man na·ture ▶*n.* the general psychological characteristics, feelings, and behavioral traits of humankind: *he had a poor opinion of human nature.*

hu·man re·sourc·es ▶*pl. n.* the personnel of a business or organization, esp. when regarded as a significant asset. ■ the department of a business or organization that deals with the administration, management, and training of personnel.

hu·man right ▶*n.* (usu. **human rights**) a right that is believed to belong justifiably to every person: *a flagrant disregard for basic human rights | communication is a fundamental human right.*

hum·ble /'həmbəl/ ▶*adj.* (**hum·bler, hum·blest**) **1** having or showing a modest or low estimate of one's own importance. ■ (of an action or thought) offered with or affected by such an estimate of one's own importance: *my humble apologies.* **2** of low social, administrative, or political rank: *she came from a humble background.* ■ (of a thing) of modest pretensions or dimensions: *he built the business empire from humble beginnings.*
▶*v.* [*tr.*] lower (someone) in dignity or importance: *I knew he had **humbled** himself to ask for my help.* ■ (usu. **be humbled**) decisively defeat (another team or competitor, typically one that was previously thought to be superior): *humbled by his political opponents.* ▷Middle English: from Old French, from Latin *humilis* 'low, lowly,' from *humus* 'ground.' —**hum·ble·ness** *n.* —**hum·bly** /-blē/ *adv.*

hum·bug /'həm,bəg/ ▶*n.* deceptive or false talk or behavior: *his comments are sheer humbug.* ■ a hypocrite: *you see what a humbug I am.*

▶*v.* (**-bugged, -bug·ging**) [*tr.*] deceive; trick. ■ [*intr.*] *dated* act like a fraud or sham. —**hum·bug·ger·y** /-,bəg(ə)rē/ *n.*

hum·ding·er /'həm'diNGər/ ▶*n. inf.* a remarkable or outstanding person or thing of its kind: *a humdinger of a funny story.*

hum·drum /'həm,drəm/ ▶*adj.* lacking excitement or variety; dull; monotonous: *humdrum routine work.*
▶*n.* dullness; monotony: *an escape from the humdrum of his life.*

hu·mec·tant /(h)yōō'mektənt/ ▶*adj.* retaining or preserving moisture.
▶*n.* a substance, esp. a skin lotion or a food additive, used to reduce the loss of moisture.

hu·mer·us /'(h)yōōmərəs/ ▶*n.* (*pl.* **-mer·i** /-mə,rī/) *Anat.* the bone of the upper arm or forelimb, forming joints at the shoulder and the elbow. —**hu·mer·al** /-mərəl/ *adj.*

hu·mid /'(h)yōōmid/ ▶*adj.* marked by a relatively high level of water vapor in the atmosphere: *a hot and humid day.* —**hu·mid·ly** *adv.*

hu·mid·i·fi·er /(h)yōō'midə,fī(ə)r/ ▶*n.* a device for keeping the atmosphere moist in a room.

hu·mid·i·fy /(h)yōō'midə,fī/ ▶*v.* (**-fies, -fied**) [*tr.*] [often as *adj.*] (**humidified**) increase the level of moisture in (air): *a regulated flow of humidified air.* —**hu·mid·i·fi·ca·tion** /-,midəfi'kāsHən/ *n.*

hu·mid·i·ty /(h)yōō'miditē/ ▶*n.* (*pl.* **-ties**) the state or quality of being humid. ■ a quantity representing the amount of water vapor in the atmosphere or a gas: *the temperature is seventy-seven, the humidity in the low thirties.* ■ atmospheric moisture.

hu·mi·dor /'(h)yōōmi,dôr/ ▶*n.* an airtight container for keeping cigars or tobacco moist.

hu·mil·i·ate /(h)yōō'milē,āt/ ▶*v.* [*tr.*] make (someone) feel ashamed and foolish by injuring their dignity and self-respect, esp. publicly. —**hu·mil·i·at·ing·ly** /-,ātiNGlē/ *adv.* —**hu·mil·i·a·tion** /-,milē'āsHən/ *n.* —**hu·mil·i·a·tor** /-,ātər/ *n.*

hu·mil·i·ty /(h)yōō'militē/ ▶*n.* a modest or low view of one's own importance; humbleness.

hum·mer /'həmər/ ▶*n. inf.* a **Humvee**.

hum·ming·bird /'həmiNG,bərd/ ▶*n.* a small nectar-feeding, mainly tropical American bird (family Trochilidae) that is able to hover and fly backward, typically having colorful iridescent plumage.

hum·mock /'həmək/ ▶*n.* a hillock, knoll, or mound. ■ a hump or ridge in an ice field. ■ a piece of forested ground rising above a marsh. —**hum·mock·y** *adj.*

hum·mus /'hŏŏməs; 'həm-/ ▶*n.* a thick paste or spread made from ground chickpeas and sesame seeds, olive oil, lemon, and garlic, made originally in the Middle East.

hu·mon·gous /(h)yōō'mäNGgəs; -'məNG-/ (also **hu·mun·gous**) ▶*adj. inf.* huge; enormous: *a humongous steak.*

hu·mor /'(h)yōōmər/ (*Brit.* **hu·mour**) ▶*n.* **1** the quality of being amusing or comic, esp. as expressed in literature or speech. ■ the ability to perceive or express humor or to appreciate a joke: *she has a great **sense of humor.*** **2** a mood or state of mind: *her good **humor** vanished | the clash hadn't improved his humor.* **3** (also **cardinal humor**) *hist.* each of the four chief fluids of the body (blood, phlegm, yellow bile [choler], and black bile [melancholy]) that were thought to determine a person's physical and mental qualities by the relative proportions in which they were present.
▶*v.* [*tr.*] comply with the wishes of (someone) in order to keep them content, however unreasonable such wishes might be: *she was always humoring him to prevent trouble.* ■ *archaic* adapt or accommodate oneself to (something). ▷Middle English (as *humour*): via Old French from Latin *humor* 'moisture,' from *humere* 'be moist.' The original sense was 'bodily fluid' (surviving in *aqueous humor* and *vitreous humor,* fluids in the eyeball); it was used specifically for any of the cardinal humors (sense 3), whence 'mental disposition' (thought to be caused by the relative proportions of the humors). This led, in the 16th cent., to the senses 'state of mind, mood' (sense 2) and 'whim, fancy,' hence *to humor someone* 'to indulge a person's whim.' Sense 1 dates from the late 16th cent. —**hu·mor·ist** *n.* —**hu·mor·less** *adj.* —**hu·mor·less·ly** *adv.* —**hu·mor·less·ness** *n.*

hu·mor·ous /'(h)yōōmərəs/ ▶*adj.* causing lighthearted laughter and amusement; comic. ■ having or showing a sense of humor: *his humorous gray eyes.* —**hu·mor·ous·ly** *adv.* —**hu·mor·ous·ness** *n.*

hump /həmp/ ▶*n.* a rounded protuberance found on the back of a camel or other animal or as an abnormality on a person's back. ■ a rounded raised mass of earth or land.
▶*v.* **1** [*tr.*] *inf.* lift or carry (a heavy object) with difficulty: *he continued to hump cases up and down the hotel corridor.* ■ [*intr.*] move heavily and awkwardly. **2** [*tr.*] make hump-shaped: *the cat humped himself into a different*

shape and purred. **3** [*intr.*] *vulgar slang* have sexual intercourse. ■ [*tr.*] have sexual intercourse with (someone). —**humped** *adj.* —**hump·less** *adj.* —**hump·y** *adj.* (**hump·i·er, hump·i·est**).
▶ □ **over the hump** over the worst or most difficult part of something.

hump·back /ˈhəmpˌbak/ ▶*n.* **1** (also **humpback whale**) a baleen whale (*Megaptera novaeangliae*) that has a hump and long white flippers and is noted for its lengthy vocalizations or "songs." **2** another term for HUNCHBACK. —**hump·backed** *adj.*

hu·mus /ˈ(h)yōōməs/ ▶*n.* the organic component of soil, formed by the decomposition of leaves and other plant material by soil microorganisms.

Hum·vee /ˈhəmˈvē/ ▶*n.* *trademark* a modern military vehicle. ▷late 20th cent.: alteration, from the initials of *high-mobility multipurpose vehicle.*

Hun /hən/ ▶*n.* **1** a member of a warlike Asiatic nomadic people who ravaged Europe in the 4th–5th centuries. ■ a reckless or uncivilized destroyer of something. **2** *inf., derog.* a German (esp. in military contexts during World War I and World War II). —**Hun·nish** *adj.*

hunch /hənCH/ ▶*v.* [*tr.*] raise (one's shoulders) and bend the top of one's body forward. ■ [*intr.*] bend one's body into a huddled position: *I hunched up as small as I could.*
▶*n.* **1** a feeling or guess based on intuition rather than known facts: *she was acting on a hunch.* **2** a humped position or thing: *the hunch of his back.* **3** *chiefly dial.* a thick piece; a hunk: *a hunch of bread.*

hunch·back /ˈhənCHˌbak/ ▶*n.* a back deformed by a sharp forward angle, forming a hump, typically caused by collapse of a vertebra. ■ *often offens.* a person with such a deformity. —**hunch·backed** *adj.*

hun·dred /ˈhəndrid/ ▶*n.* (*pl.* **-dreds** or (with numeral or quantifying word) **-dred**) (**a/one hundred**) the number equivalent to the product of ten and ten; ten more than ninety; 100. (Roman numeral: **c** or **C.**) ■ (**hundreds**) the numbers from 100 to 999: *an unknown number, probably in the hundreds, had already been lost.* ■ (**hundreds**) several hundred things or people: *it cost hundreds of dollars.* ■ (usu. **hundreds**) *inf.* an unspecified large number: *hundreds of letters poured in.* ■ (**the —— hundreds**) the years of a specified century: *the early nineteen hundreds.* ■ one hundred years old: *you must be over a hundred!* ■ one hundred miles per hour. ■ a hundred-dollar bill. ■ (chiefly in spoken English) used to express whole hours in the twenty-four-hour system: *thirteen hundred hours.* ▷late Old English, from noun 'hundred' (from an Indo-European root shared with Latin *centum* and Greek *hekaton*) + a second element meaning 'number'; of Germanic origin and related to Dutch *honderd* and German *hundert*. —**hun·dred·fold** /-ˌfōld/ *adj. & adv.* —**hun·dredth** /ˈhəndridTH; ˈhəndritTH/ *ordinal number.*

hun·dred·weight /ˈhəndridˌwāt/ (abbr.: **cwt**) ▶*n.* (*pl.* same or **-weights**) a unit of weight equal to one twentieth of a ton.

hung /həNG/ ▶ past and past participle of HANG.
▶*adj.* **1** (of a jury) unable to agree on a verdict. **2** (**hung up**) *inf.* emotionally confused or disturbed: *people are hung up in all sorts of ways.* ■ (**hung up about/on**) have a psychological or emotional obsession or problem about: *guys are so hung up about the way they look.* ■ delayed or detained. **3** *vulgar slang* used esp. in similes to refer to the size of a man's penis: *he's hung like a horse.*

Hun·gar·i·an /həNGˈge(ə)rēən/ ▶*adj.* of or relating to Hungary, its people, or their language.
▶*n.* **1** a native or national of Hungary. ■ a person of Hungarian descent. **2** an Ugric language, the official language of Hungary. Also called MAGYAR.

hun·ger /ˈhəNGgər/ ▶*n.* a feeling of discomfort or weakness caused by lack of food, coupled with the desire to eat: *she was faint with hunger.* ■ a severe lack of food: *they died from cold and hunger.* ■ a strong desire or craving: *her hunger for knowledge.*
▶*v.* [*intr.*] **1** (**hunger after/for**) have a strong desire or craving for: *all actors hunger for such a role.* **2** *archaic* feel or suffer hunger through lack of food.

hun·ger strike ▶*n.* a prolonged refusal to eat, carried out as a protest, typically by a prisoner. —**hun·ger strik·er** *n.*

hung·o·ver /ˈhəNGˈgōvər/ (also **hung over**) ▶*adj.* suffering from a hangover after drinking alcohol.

hun·gry /ˈhəNGgrē/ ▶*adj.* (**-gri·er, -gri·est**) feeling or displaying the need for food. ■ having a strong desire or craving: *he was hungry for any kind of excitement* | [in comb.] grasping, *power-hungry individuals.* —**hun·gri·ly** /-grəlē/ *adv.* —**hun·gri·ness** *n.*

hunk /həNGk/ ▶*n.* **1** a large piece of something, esp. one of food cut or broken off a larger piece: *a hunk of bread.* **2** *inf.* a sexually attractive man, esp. a large, strong one. —**hunk·y** *adj.* (**hunk·i·er, hunk·i·est**).

hunk·y-do·ry /ˈhəNGkē ˈdôrē/ ▶*adj.* *inf.* fine; going well: *everything is hunky-dory.*

hunt /hənt/ ▶*v.* [*tr.*] pursue and kill (a wild animal) for sport or food: [*intr.*] *they hunted and fished.* ■ (of an animal) chase and kill (its prey): *mice are hunted by weasels and foxes* | [*intr.*] *lionesses hunt in groups.* ■ [*intr.*] try to find someone or something by searching carefully. ■ (**hunt something out/up**) search for something until it is found. ■ [*tr.*] (of the police) search for (a criminal): [*intr.*] *police are hunting for her attacker.* ■ (**hunt someone down**) pursue and capture someone.
▶*n.* an act of hunting wild animals or game. ■ an association of people who meet regularly to hunt, esp. with hounds. ■ an area where hunting takes place. ■ a search.

hunt·er /ˈhən(t)ər/ ▶*n.* a person or animal that hunts: *a deer hunter.* ■ a person searching for something: *a bargain hunter.* ■ a horse of a breed developed for stamina in fox hunting and ability to jump obstacles. ■ (**the Hunter**) the constellation Orion.

hunt·ing /ˈhəntiNG/ ▶*n.* the activity of hunting wild animals or game, esp. for food or sport.

Hun·ting·ton's cho·re·a /ˈhəntiNGtənz kəˈrēə/ ▶*n.* a hereditary disease marked by degeneration of the brain cells and causing chorea and progressive dementia.

hunts·man /ˈhəntsmən/ ▶*n.* (*pl.* **-men**) a person who hunts. ■ a hunt official in charge of hounds.

hur·dle /ˈhərdl/ ▶*n.* **1** an upright frame, typically one of a series, that athletes in a race must jump over. ■ (**hurdles**) a hurdle race: *the women's 100-meter hurdles.* **2** an obstacle or difficulty: *there are many hurdles to overcome.* **3** *chiefly Brit.* a portable rectangular frame strengthened with willow branches or wooden bars, used as a temporary fence. ■ a horse race over a series of such frames: *a handicap hurdle.* ■ *hist.* a frame on which traitors were dragged to execution.
▶*v.* **1** [*intr.*] [often as *n.*] (**hurdling**) take part in a race that involves jumping hurdles. ■ [*tr.*] jump over (a hurdle or other obstacle) while running. **2** [*tr.*] enclose or fence off with hurdles. —**hur·dler** *n.*

hur·dy-gur·dy /ˈhərdē ˌgərdē/ ▶*n.* (*pl.* **-dies**) a musical instrument with a droning sound played by turning a handle, which is typically attached to a rosined wheel sounding a series of drone strings, with keys worked by the left hand. ■ *inf.* a barrel organ.

hurl /hərl/ ▶*v.* [*tr.*] throw (an object) with great force: *rioters hurled a brick through the windshield of a car.* ■ push or impel (someone) violently. ■ utter (abuse) vehemently: *they were hurling insults over a back fence.* ■ [*intr.*] *inf.* vomit: *it made me want to hurl.*

hurl·y-burl·y /ˈhərlē ˈbərlē/ ▶*n.* busy, boisterous activity: *the hurly-burly of school life.*

Hu·ron /ˈhyŏŏˌrän/ ▶*n.* (*pl.* same or **-rons**) **1** a member of a confederation of native North American peoples formerly living in the region east of Lake Huron and now settled mainly in Oklahoma and Quebec. **2** the extinct Iroquoian language of any of these peoples.
▶*adj.* of or relating to these peoples or their language.

hur·rah /hŏŏˈrä; hə-/ (also **hoo·ray, hur·ray** /-ˈrä/) ▶*interj.* used to express joy or approval: *Hurrah! She's here at last!*
▶*n.* an utterance of the word "hurrah."
▶*v.* [*intr.*] shout "hurrah."

hur·ri·cane /ˈhəriˌkān; ˈhə-ri-/ ▶*n.* a storm with a violent wind, in particular a tropical cyclone in the Caribbean. ■ a wind of force 12 on the Beaufort scale (equal to or exceeding 64 knots or 74 mph). ■ *fig.* a violent uproar or outburst.

hur·ri·cane lamp ▶*n.* an oil lamp with a glass chimney, designed to protect the flame even in high winds.

hur·ry /ˈhərē; ˈhə-rē/ ▶*v.* (**-ries, -ried**) [*intr.*] move or act with haste; rush. ■ [often in *imper.*] (**hurry up**) do something more quickly: *hurry up and finish your meal.* ■ [*tr.*] cause to move or proceed with haste: *she hurried him across the landing.* ■ [*tr.*] (often **be hurried**) do or finish (something) quickly, typically too quickly: [as *adj.*] (**hurried**) *I ate a hurried breakfast.*
▶*n.* great haste: *in my hurry to leave, I knocked over a pile of books.* ■ a need for haste; urgency: *there's no hurry to get back* | *relax, what's the hurry?* —**hur·ried·ly** *adv.* —**hur·ried·ness** *n.*
▶ □ **in a hurry** rushed; in a rushed manner. ■ eager to get a thing done quickly. ■ *inf.* easily; readily: *an experience you won't forget in a hurry.*

hurt /hərt/ ▶*v.* (past and past part. **hurt**) [*tr.*] cause physical pain or injury to: *Ow! You're hurting me!* | [*intr.*] *does acupuncture hurt?* ■ [*intr.*] (of a part of the body) suffer pain: *my back hurts.* ■ cause mental pain or distress to (a person or their feelings): *she didn't want to hurt his feelings.* ■ [*intr.*]

Pronunciation Key ə *ago, up;* ər *over, fur;* a *hat;* ā *ate;* ä *car;* CH *chin;* e *let;* ē *see;* e(ə)r *air;* i *fit;* ī *by;* i(ə)r *ear;* NG *sing;* ō *go;* ô *law, for;* oi *toy;* ŏŏ *good;* ōō *goo;* ou *out;* SH *she;* TH *thin;* <u>TH</u> *then;* (h)w *why;* ZH *vision*

(of a person) feel mental pain or distress. ■ be detrimental to: *high interest rates are hurting the local economy.* ■ [intr.] (**hurt for**) *inf.* have a pressing need for: *Frank wasn't hurting for money.*
▶*n.* physical injury; harm. ■ mental pain or distress.

hurt·ful /ˈhərtfəl/ ▶*adj.* causing distress to someone's feelings: *his hurtful remarks.* —**hurt·ful·ly** *adv.* —**hurt·ful·ness** *n.*

hur·tle /ˈhərtl/ ▶*v.* [intr.] move at a great speed, typically in a wildly uncontrolled manner. ■ [tr.] cause to move in such a way.

hus·band /ˈhəzbənd/ ▶*n.* a married man considered in relation to his wife: *she and her husband are both retired.*
▶*v.* [tr.] use (resources) economically; conserve: *to husband his remaining strength.* ▷late Old English (in the senses 'male head of a household' and 'manager, steward'), from Old Norse *húsbóndi* 'master of a house,' from *hús* 'house' + *bóndi* 'occupier and tiller of the soil.' The original sense of the verb was 'till, cultivate.' —**hus·band·er** *n.* (*rare*). —**hus·band·hood** /-ˌho͝od/ *n.* —**hus·band·less** *adj.* —**hus·band·ly** *adj.*

hus·band·ry /ˈhəzbəndrē/ ▶*n.* **1** the care, cultivation, and breeding of crops and animals: *crop husbandry.* **2** management and conservation of resources.

hush /həSH/ ▶*v.* [tr.] make (someone) be quiet or stop talking: *he placed a finger before pursed lips to hush her.* ■ [intr.] be quiet: *Hush! Someone will hear you.* ■ (**hush something up**) suppress public mention of something.
▶*n.* a silence: *a hush descended over the crowd.*

hush-hush ▶*adj. inf.* (esp. of an official plan or project) highly secret or confidential: *a hush-hush research unit.*

hush mon·ey ▶*n. inf.* money paid to someone to prevent them from disclosing embarrassing or discreditable information.

hush pup·py ▶*n.* cornmeal dough that has been quickly deep-fried.

husk /həsk/ ▶*n.* the dry outer covering of some fruits or seeds. ■ a dry or rough outer layer or coating, esp. when empty of its contents.
▶*v.* [tr.] remove the husk or husks from.

husk·y¹ /ˈhəskē/ ▶*adj.* (**husk·i·er, husk·i·est**) **1** (of a voice or utterance) sounding low-pitched and slightly hoarse. **2** strong; hefty: *Patrick looked a husky, strong guy.* **3** like or consisting of a husk or husks. —**husk·i·ly** /ˈhəskəlē/ *adv.* —**husk·i·ness** *n.*

husk·y² (also **hus·kie**) ▶*n.* (*pl.* **husk·ies**) a powerful dog of a breed with a thick double coat that is typically gray, used in the Arctic for pulling sleds.

hus·sar /həˈzär/ ▶*n. hist.* (in the 15th century) a Hungarian light horseman. ■ a soldier in a light cavalry regiment that had adopted a dress uniform modeled on that of the Hungarian hussars.

hus·sy /ˈhəsē; ˈhəzē/ ▶*n.* (*pl.* **-sies**) an impudent or immoral girl or woman: *that brazen little hussy!*

hust·ings /ˈhəstiNGz/ ▶*n.* (*pl.* same) a meeting at which candidates in an election address potential voters. ■ the campaigning associated with an election: *a formidable political operator at his best* **on the hustings.**

hus·tle /ˈhəsəl/ ▶*v.* **1** [tr.] force (someone) to move hurriedly or unceremoniously in a specified direction: *they hustled him into the back of a horse-drawn wagon.* ■ [tr.] push roughly; jostle. ■ [intr.] hurry; bustle: *he had to hustle back to first.* **2** [tr.] *inf.* obtain by forceful action or persuasion. ■ (**hustle someone into**) coerce or pressure someone into doing or choosing something: *don't be hustled into anything.* ■ sell aggressively: *he hustled his company's oil around the country.* ■ obtain by illicit action; swindle; cheat: *Linda hustled money from men she met.* **3** [intr.] *inf.* engage in prostitution.
▶*n.* **1** busy movement and activity: *the* **hustle and bustle** *of the big cities.* ■ energetic effort. **2** *inf.* a fraud or swindle.

hus·tler /ˈhəslər/ ▶*n. inf.* an aggressively enterprising person; a go-getter. ■ an enterprising and often dishonest person, esp. one trying to sell something. ■ an expert player, esp. at pool or billiards, who pretends to be less skillful than they are and lures or challenges less skilled, esp. amateur, players into games in order to win money from them. ■ a female prostitute. ■ a male prostitute, esp. for homosexual clients.

hut /hət/ ▶*n.* a small single-story building of simple or crude construction, serving as a poor, rough, or temporary house or shelter. ▷mid 16th cent. (in the sense 'temporary wooden shelter for troops'): from French *hutte*, from Middle High German *hütte*. —**hut·like** /-ˌlīk/ *adj.*

hutch /həCH/ ▶*n.* **1** a box or cage, typically with a wire mesh front, for keeping rabbits, ferrets, or other small domesticated animals: *a rabbit hutch.* **2** a storage chest. ■ a cupboard or dresser typically with open shelves above.

hwy ▶*abbr.* highway.

hy·a·cinth /ˈhīə,sinTH/ ▶*n.* **1** a bulbous plant (genus *Hyacinthus*) of the lily family, with straplike leaves and a compact spike of bell-shaped fragrant flowers. ■ a light purplish-blue color typical of some hyacinth

flowers. **2** a reddish-orange gem variety of zircon. —**hy·a·cin·thine** /ˌhīəˈsinTHin; -ˌTHīn/ *adj.*

hy·a·lin /ˈhīəlin/ ▶*n. Physiol.* a clear substance produced esp. by the degeneration of epithelial or connective tissues.

hy·a·line /ˈhīəlin; -ˌlīn/ ▶*adj. Anat. & Zool.* having a glassy, translucent appearance. ■ relating to, consisting of, or characterized by hyaline material.

hy·brid /ˈhī,brid/ ▶*n.* a thing made by combining two different elements; a mixture. ■ *Biol.* the offspring of two plants or animals of different species or varieties, such as a mule (a hybrid of a donkey and a horse): *a hybrid of wheat and rye.* ■ *offens.* a person of mixed racial or cultural origin. ■ a word formed from elements taken from different languages, for example *television* (*tele-* from Greek, *vision* from Latin). ■ a hybrid car.
▶*adj.* of mixed character; composed of mixed parts. ■ bred as a hybrid from different species or varieties. —**hy·brid·ism** /ˈhībrə,dizəm/ *n.* —**hy·brid·i·ty** /hīˈbriditē/ *n.*

hy·brid car ▶*n.* a car with a gasoline engine and an electric motor, each of which can propel it.

hy·brid·ize /ˈhībri,dīz/ ▶*v.* **1** [tr.] crossbreed (individuals of two different species or varieties). ■ [intr.] (of an animal or plant) breed with an individual of another species or variety. **2** [intr.] *Biochem.* form a double-stranded nucleic acid structure from a single-stranded mixture by complementary base pairing. —**hy·brid·iz·a·ble** *adj.* —**hy·brid·i·za·tion** /ˌhībrədiˈzāSHən/ *n.*

Hy·dra /ˈhīdrə/ ▶*Greek Mythol.* a many-headed snake whose heads grew again as they were cut off. ■ [as *n.*] (**hydra**) a thing that is hard to overcome or resist because of its pervasive or enduring quality or its many aspects.

hy·dra /ˈhīdrə/ ▶*n.* a minute freshwater coelenterate (genus *Hydra*) with a stalklike tubular body and a ring of tentacles around the mouth.

hy·dran·gea /hīˈdrānjə/ ▶*n.* a shrub or climbing plant (genus *Hydrangea*, family Hydrangeaceae) with rounded or flattened flowering heads of small florets, the outer ones of which are typically infertile.

hy·drant /ˈhīdrənt/ ▶*n.* an upright water pipe, esp. one in a street, with a nozzle to which a fire hose can be attached.

hy·drate /ˈhī,drāt/ ▶*n. Chem.* a compound, typically a crystalline one, in which water molecules are chemically bound to another compound or an element.
▶*v.* [tr.] cause to absorb water. ■ *Chem.* combine chemically with water molecules: [as *adj.*] (**hydrated**) *hydrated silicate crystals.* —**hy·drat·a·ble** *adj.* —**hy·dra·tion** /hīˈdrāSHən/ *n.* —**hy·dra·tor** /-tər/ *n.*

hy·drau·lic /hīˈdrôlik/ ▶*adj.* **1** denoting, relating to, or operated by a liquid moving in a confined space under pressure: *hydraulic fluid | hydraulic lifting gear.* **2** of or relating to the science of hydraulics. **3** (of cement) hardening under water. —**hy·drau·li·cal·ly** /-(ə)lē/ *adv.*

hy·drau·lics /hīˈdrôliks/ ▶*pl. n.* **1** [usu. treated as *sing.*] the branch of science and technology concerned with the conveyance of liquids through pipes and channels, esp. as a source of mechanical force or control. **2** hydraulic systems, mechanisms, or forces.

hy·dra·zine /ˈhīdrə,zēn/ ▶*n. Chem.* a colorless volatile alkaline liquid, N_2H_4, with powerful reducing properties, used in chemical synthesis and rocket fuels.

hy·dride /ˈhī,drīd/ ▶*n. Chem.* a binary compound of hydrogen with a metal.

hy·dro /ˈhīdrō/ ▶*n.* (*pl.* **-dros**) a hydroelectric power plant. ■ hydroelectricity. ■ *Can.* electricity.

hy·dro·car·bon /ˈhīdrə,kärbən/ ▶*n. Chem.* a compound of hydrogen and carbon, such as those that are the chief components of petroleum and natural gas.

hy·dro·ceph·a·lus /ˌhīdrōˈsefələs/ ▶*n. Med.* a condition in which fluid accumulates in the brain, typically in young children, enlarging the head and sometimes causing brain damage. —**hy·dro·ce·phal·ic** /ˌhīdrōsəˈfalik/ *adj.* —**hy·dro·ceph·a·ly** /-ˈsefəlē/ *n.*

hy·dro·chlo·ric ac·id /ˌhīdrəˈklôrik/ ▶*n. Chem.* a strongly acidic solution of the gas hydrogen chloride, HCl, in water.

hy·dro·chlo·ride /ˌhīdrəˈklô,rīd/ ▶*n.* a compound of a particular organic base with hydrochloric acid: *cocaine hydrochloride.*

hy·dro·cor·ti·sone /ˌhīdrəˈkôrti,zōn/ ▶*n. Biochem.* a steroid hormone produced by the adrenal cortex and used medicinally to treat inflammation resulting from eczema and rheumatism.

hy·dro·cy·an·ic ac·id /ˌhīdrōsīˈanik/ ▶*n. Chem.* a highly poisonous acidic solution of hydrogen cyanide in water.

hy·dro·dy·nam·ics /ˌhīdrōdīˈnamiks/ ▶*pl. n.* [treated as *sing.*] the branch of science concerned with forces acting on or exerted by fluids (esp.

liquids). **—hy·dro·dy·nam·ic** *adj.* **—hy·dro·dy·nam·i·cal·ly** /-'namik(ə)lē/ *adj.* **—hy·dro·dy·nam·i·cist** /-'namisist/ *n.*

hy·dro·e·lec·tric /ˌhīdrōə'lektrik/ ▶*adj.* relating to or denoting the generation of electricity using flowing water (typically from a reservoir held behind a dam or other barrier) to drive a turbine that powers a generator. **—hy·dro·e·lec·tric·i·ty** /-ələk'trisitē/ *n.*

hy·dro·foil /'hīdrəˌfoil/ ▶*n.* a boat whose hull is fitted underneath with shaped vanes (foils) that lift the hull clear of the water to increase the boat's speed. ■ another term for FOIL⁴.

hy·dro·gen /'hīdrəjən/ ▶*n.* a colorless, odorless, highly flammable gas, the chemical element of atomic number 1. (Symbol: **H**) **—hy·drog·e·nous** /hī'dräjənəs/ *adj.*

hy·dro·gen·ate /'hīdrəjəˌnāt; hī'dräjənāt/ ▶*v.* [*tr.*] [often as *adj.*] (**hydrogenated**) charge with or cause to combine with hydrogen. **—hy·dro·gen·a·tion** /ˌhīdrəjə'nāsHən; hīˌdräjə-/ *n.*

hy·dro·gen bomb ▶*n.* an immensely powerful bomb whose destructive power comes from the rapid release of energy during the nuclear fusion of isotopes of hydrogen (deuterium and tritium), using an atomic bomb as a trigger.

hy·dro·gen per·ox·ide ▶*n.* *Chem.* a colorless unstable liquid, H_2O_2, with strong oxidizing properties, commonly used in diluted form in disinfectants and bleaches.

hy·drog·ra·phy /hī'drägrəfē/ ▶*n.* the science of surveying and charting bodies of water, such as seas, lakes, and rivers. **—hy·drog·ra·pher** /-fər/ *n.* **—hy·dro·graph·ic** /ˌhīdrə'grafik/ *adj.* **—hy·dro·graph·i·cal** /ˌhīdrə-'grafikəl/ *adj.* **—hy·dro·graph·i·cal·ly** /ˌhīdrə'grafik(ə)lē/ *adv.*

hy·droid /'hīˌdroid/ *Zool.* ▶*n.* a coelenterate of an order that includes the hydras.

hy·drol·o·gy /hī'drälǝjē/ ▶*n.* the branch of science concerned with the properties of the earth's water, esp. its movement in relation to land. **—hy·dro·log·ic** /ˌhīdrə'läjik/ *adj.* **—hy·dro·log·i·cal** /ˌhīdrə'läjikəl/ *adj.* **—hy·dro·log·i·cal·ly** /ˌhīdrə'läjik(ə)lē/ *adv.* **—hy·drol·o·gist** /-jist/ *n.*

hy·drol·y·sis /hī'dräləsis/ ▶*n.* *Chem.* the chemical breakdown of a compound due to reaction with water. **—hy·dro·lyt·ic** /ˌhīdrə'litik/ *adj.*

hy·dro·lyze /'hīdrəˌlīz/ (*Brit.* **hy·dro·lyse**) ▶*v.* [*tr.*] *Chem.* break down (a compound) by chemical reaction with water. ■ [*intr.*] undergo this process.

hy·drom·e·ter /hī'drämitər/ ▶*n.* an instrument for measuring the density of liquids. **—hy·dro·met·ric** /ˌhīdrə'metrik/ *adj.* **—hy·drom·e·try** /-itrē/ *n.*

hy·drop·a·thy /hī'dräpəTHē/ ▶*n.* the treatment of illness through the use of water, either internally or through external means such as steam baths (not now a part of orthodox medicine). Also called HYDROTHERAPY. **—hy·dro·path·ic** /ˌhīdrə'paTHik/ *adj.* **—hy·drop·a·thist** /-THist/ *n.*

hy·dro·phil·ic /ˌhīdrə'filik/ ▶*adj.* having a tendency to mix with, dissolve in, or be wetted by water. The opposite of HYDROPHOBIC. **—hy·dro·phi·lic·i·ty** /-fə'lisitē/ *n.*

hy·dro·pho·bi·a /ˌhīdrə'fōbēə/ ▶*n.* extreme or irrational fear of water, esp. as a symptom of rabies in humans. ■ rabies, esp. in humans.

hy·dro·pho·bic /ˌhīdrə'fōbik/ ▶*adj.* **1** tending to repel or fail to mix with water. The opposite of HYDROPHILIC. **2** of or suffering from hydrophobia. **—hy·dro·pho·bic·i·ty** /-fō'bisitē/ *n.*

hy·dro·plane /'hīdrəˌplān/ ▶*n.* **1** a light fast motorboat designed to skim over the surface of water. **2** a finlike attachment that enables a moving submarine to rise or fall in the water.
▶*v.* [*intr.*] **1** (of a vehicle) slide uncontrollably on the wet surface of a road: *a motorist whose car hydroplaned and crashed into a tree.* **2** (of a boat) skim over the surface of water with its hull lifted.

hy·dro·pon·ics /ˌhīdrə'päniks/ ▶*pl. n.* [treated as *sing.*] the process of growing plants in sand, gravel, or liquid, with added nutrients but without soil. **—hy·dro·pon·ic** *adj.* **—hy·dro·pon·i·cal·ly** /-'pänik(ə)lē/ *adv.*

hy·dro·sphere /'hīdrəˌsfir/ ▶*n.* (usu. **the hydrosphere**) all the waters on the earth's surface, such as lakes and seas, and sometimes including water over the earth's surface, such as clouds.

hy·dro·stat·ic /ˌhīdrə'statik/ ▶*adj.* relating to or denoting the equilibrium of liquids and the pressure exerted by liquid at rest. **—hy·dro·stat·i·cal** *adj.* **—hy·dro·stat·i·cal·ly** /ik(ə)lē/ *adv.*

hy·dro·stat·ics /ˌhīdrə'statiks/ ▶*n.* [treated as *sing.*] the branch of mechanics concerned with the hydrostatic properties of liquids.

hy·dro·ther·a·py /ˌhīdrə'THerəpē/ ▶*n.* another term for HYDROPATHY. ■ the use of exercises in a pool as part of treatment for conditions such as arthritis or partial paralysis. **—hy·dro·ther·a·pist** /-pist/ *n.*

hy·dro·ther·mal /ˌhīdrə'THərməl/ ▶*adj.* of, relating to, or denoting the action of heated water in the earth's crust. **—hy·dro·ther·mal·ly** *adv.*

hy·drous /'hīdrəs/ ▶*adj.* chiefly *Chem. Geol.* containing water as a constituent: *a hydrous lava flow.*

hy·drox·ide /hī'dräkˌsīd/ ▶*n.* *Chem.* a compound of a metal with the hydroxide ion OH⁻ (as in many alkalis) or the group −OH.

hy·drox·yl /hī'dräksəl/ ▶*n.* [as *adj.*] *Chem.* of or denoting the radical −OH, present in alcohols and many other organic compounds: *a hydroxyl group.*

hy·dro·zo·an /ˌhīdrə'zōən/ ▶*n.* (*pl.* **-zo·a**, **-zo·ans**) any cnidarian of the class Hydrozoa, including hydras and Portuguese men-of-war.
▶*adj.* of or relating to the hydrozoa.

hy·e·na /hī'ēnə/ (*Brit.* **hyaena**) ▶*n.* a doglike African mammal (genera *Hyaena* and *Crocuta*, family Hyaenidae) with an erect mane and forelimbs that are longer than the hind limbs. Hyenas are noted as scavengers but most are also effective hunters.

hy·giene /'hīˌjēn/ ▶*n.* conditions or practices conducive to maintaining health and preventing disease, esp. through cleanliness: *poor standards of food hygiene* | *personal hygiene.*

hy·gi·en·ic /hī'jenik; -'jē-/ ▶*adj.* conducive to maintaining health and preventing disease, esp. by being clean; sanitary: *hygienic conditions.* **—hy·gi·en·i·cal·ly** /-(ə)lē/ *adv.*

hy·gien·ist /hī'jenəst; -jē-/ ▶*n.* **1** a specialist in the promotion of clean conditions for the preservation of health: *an industrial hygienist.* **2** short for DENTAL HYGIENIST.

hy·grom·e·ter /hī'grämitər/ ▶*n.* an instrument for measuring the humidity of the air or other gas. **—hy·gro·met·ric** /ˌhīgrə'metrik/ *adj.* **—hy·grom·e·try** /-trē/ *n.*

hy·gro·scope /'hīgrəˌskōp/ ▶*n.* an instrument that gives an indication of the humidity of the air. **—hy·gro·scop·ic** /ˌhīgrə'skopik/ *adj.*

hy·ing /'hī-iNG/ ▶ present participle of HIE.

hy·men /'hīmən/ ▶*n.* a membrane that partially closes the opening of the vagina and whose presence is traditionally taken to be a mark of virginity. **—hy·men·al** /'hīmənl/ *adj.*

hy·me·nop·ter·an /ˌhīmə'näptərən/ ▶*n.* (*pl.* **-ter·a**, **-ter·ans**) any insect of the order Hymenoptera, having four transparent wings and often having a sting, including bees, wasps, and ants.
▶*adj.* of or relating to the hymenoptera.

hymn /him/ ▶*n.* a religious song or poem, typically of praise to God or a god: *a Hellenistic hymn to Apollo.* ■ a formal song sung during Christian worship, typically by the whole congregation. ■ a song, text, or other composition praising or celebrating someone or something.
▶*v.* [*tr.*] praise or celebrate (something): *Johnson's reply hymns education.* **—hym·nic** /'himnik/ *adj.*

hym·nal /'himnəl/ ▶*n.* a book of hymns.
▶*adj.* of hymns: *hymnal music.*

hym·no·dy /'himnədē/ ▶*n.* the singing or composition of hymns. **—hym·no·dist** /-dist/ *n.*

hype¹ /hīp/ *inf.* ▶*n.* extravagant or intensive publicity or promotion. ■ a deception carried out for the sake of publicity.
▶*v.* [*tr.*] promote or publicize (a product or idea) intensively, often exaggerating its importance or benefits: *an industry quick to hype its products.*

hype² *inf.* ▶*n.* a hypodermic needle or injection. ■ a drug addict.
▶*v.* [*tr.*] (usu. **be hyped up**) stimulate or excite (someone).

hy·per /'hīpər/ ▶*adj. inf.* hyperactive or unusually energetic.

hyper- ▶*prefix* over; beyond; above. ■ exceeding: *hypersonic.* ■ excessively; above normal: *hyperthyroidism.*

hy·per·ac·tive /ˌhīpər'aktiv/ ▶*adj.* abnormally or extremely active: *a hyperactive pituitary gland.* ■ (of a child) showing constantly active and sometimes disruptive behavior. **—hy·per·ac·tiv·i·ty** /-ˌak'tivitē/ *n.*

hy·per·bo·la /hī'pərbələ/ ▶*n.* (*pl.* **-bo·las** or **-bo·lae** /-bəˌlē/) a symmetrical open curve formed by the intersection of a cone with a plane at a smaller angle with its axis than the side of the cone. ■ *Math.* the pair

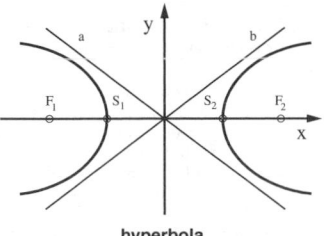

hyperbola

of such curves formed by the intersection of a plane with two equal cones on opposites of the same vertex.

hy·per·bo·le /hī'pərbəlē/ ▶ *n.* exaggerated statements or claims not meant to be taken literally. —**hy·per·bol·ic** /ˌhīpər'bälik/ *adj.* —**hy·per·bol·i·cal·ly** /ˌhīpər'bälik(ə)lē/ *adv.* —**hy·per·bo·lism** /-ˌlizəm/ *n.*

hy·per·crit·i·cal /ˌhīpər'kritikəl/ ▶ *adj.* excessively and unreasonably critical, esp. of small faults. —**hy·per·crit·i·cal·ly** /-ik(ə)lē/ *adv.*

hy·per·e·mi·a /ˌhīpə'rēmēə/ (*Brit.* **hy·per·ae·mi·a**) ▶ *n. Med.* an excess of blood in the vessels supplying an organ or other part of the body. —**hy·per·e·mic** /-'rēmik/ *adj.*

hy·per·es·the·sia /ˌhīpərəs'тнēzнə/ (*Brit.* **hy·per·aes·the·si·a**) ▶ *n. Med.* excessive physical sensitivity, esp. of the skin. —**hy·per·es·thet·ic** /-'тнetik/ *adj.*

hy·per·gly·ce·mi·a /ˌhīpərglī'sēmēə/ (*Brit.* **hy·per·gly·cae·mi·a**) ▶ *n. Med.* an excess of glucose in the bloodstream, often associated with diabetes. —**hy·per·gly·ce·mic** /-'sēmik/ *adj.*

hy·per·gol·ic /ˌhīpər'gälik/ ▶ *adj.* (of a rocket propellant) igniting spontaneously on mixing with another substance.

hy·per·ki·ne·sis /ˌhīpərki'nēsis/ (also **hy·per·ki·ne·sia** /-'nēzнə/) ▶ *n.* **1** *Med.* muscle spasm. **2** *Psychiatry* a disorder of children marked by hyperactivity and inability to concentrate.

hy·per·ki·net·ic /ˌhīpərkə'netik/ ▶ *adj.* frenetic; hyperactive. ■ of or affected with hyperkinesis.

hy·per·link /'hīpər,liNGk/ *Comput.* ▶ *n.* a link from a hypertext file or document to another location or file, typically activated by clicking on a highlighted word or image on the screen.
▶ *v.* [*tr.*] link (a file) in this way: *thumbnail images that are hyperlinked to a larger image.*

hy·per·on /'hīpə,rän/ ▶ *n. Physics* an unstable subatomic particle classified as a baryon, heavier than the neutron and proton.

hy·per·sen·si·tive /ˌhīpər'sensitiv/ ▶ *adj.* abnormally or excessively sensitive, either psychologically or in physical response. —**hy·per·sen·si·tive·ness** *n.* —**hy·per·sen·si·tiv·i·ty** /-ˌsensi'tivitē/ *n.*

hy·per·son·ic /ˌhīpər'sänik/ ▶ *adj.* relating to speeds of more than five times the speed of sound (Mach 5). —**hy·per·son·i·cal·ly** /-ik(ə)lē/ *adv.*

hy·per·ten·sion /ˌhīpər'tensнən/ ▶ *n. Med.* abnormally high blood pressure. ■ a state of great psychological stress. —**hy·per·ten·sive** *adj.*

hy·per·text /'hīpər,tekst/ ▶ *n. Comput.* a software system that links topics on the screen to related information and graphics, which are typically accessed by a point-and-click method. ■ a document presented on a computer in this way.

hy·per·ther·mi·a /ˌhīpər'тнərmēə/ ▶ *n. Med.* the condition of having a body temperature greatly above normal. —**hy·per·ther·mic** /-'тнərmik/ *adj.*

hy·per·thy·roid·ism /ˌhīpər'тнīroi,dizəm/ ▶ *n. Med.* overactivity of the thyroid gland, resulting in a rapid heartbeat and an increased rate of metabolism. —**hy·per·thy·roid** *adj.* —**hy·per·thy·roid·ic** /-тнī'roidik/ *adj.*

hy·per·ton·ic /ˌhīpər'tänik/ ▶ *adj.* having increased pressure or tone, in particular: ■ *Biol.* having a higher osmotic pressure than a particular fluid, typically a body fluid or intracellular fluid. ■ *Physiol.* of or in a state of abnormally high muscle tone. —**hy·per·to·ni·a** /-'tōnēə/ *n.* —**hy·per·to·nic·i·ty** /ˌhīpərtə'nisitē/ *n.*

hy·per·tro·phy /hī'pərtrəfē/ ▶ *n. Physiol.* the enlargement of an organ or tissue from the increase in size of its cells. ■ excessive growth.
▶ *v.* (**-phies**, **-phied**) [*intr.*] (of a body or an organ) become enlarged due to an increase in cell size. —**hy·per·troph·ic** /ˌhīpər'träfik; -'trō-/ *adj.* —**hy·per·troph·ied** /-trəfēd/ *adj.*

hy·per·ven·ti·late /ˌhīpər'ventl,āt/ ▶ *v.* [*intr.*] breathe at an abnormally rapid rate, so increasing the rate of loss of carbon dioxide. ■ [*tr.*] (usu. **be hyperventilated**) cause to breathe in such a way: *the patients were hyperventilated for two minutes.* ■ [as *adj.*] (**hyperventilated**) *fig.* inflated or pretentious in style; overblown: *hyperventilated prose.* —**hy·per·ven·ti·la·tion** /-ˌventl'āsнən/ *n.*

hy·pha /'hīfə/ ▶ *n.* (*pl.* **-phae** /-fē/) *Bot.* each of the branching filaments that make up the mycelium of a fungus. —**hy·phal** *adj.*

hy·phen /'hīfən/ ▶ *n.* the sign (-) used to join words to indicate that they have a combined meaning or that they are linked in the grammar of a sentence (as in *pick-me-up*, *rock-forming*), to indicate the division of a word at the end of a line, or to indicate a missing or implied element (as in *short- and long-term*).
▶ *v.* another term for **HYPHENATE**. ▷early 17th cent.: via late Latin from Greek *huphen* 'together,' from *hupo* 'under' + *hen* 'one.'

hy·phen·ate ▶ *v.* /'hīfə,nāt/ [*tr.*] write with a hyphen: [as *adj.*] (**hyphenated**) *a hyphenated surname.*
▶ *n.* /'hīfənit/ a person who is active in more than one occupation or

sphere: *as a supreme hyphenate, she was prepared to carry a heavy load as the director-producer-star of her new film.* —**hy·phen·a·tion** /ˌhīfə'nāsнən/ *n.*

hyp·na·gog·ic /ˌhipnə'gäjik; -'gō-/ (also **hyp·no·gog·ic**) ▶ *adj. Psychol.* of or relating to the state immediately before falling asleep. —**hyp·na·gog·i·a** *n.*

hyp·no·gog·ic ▶ a variant spelling of **HYPNAGOGIC**. —**hyp·no·gog·i·a** *n.*

hyp·no·sis /hip'nōsis/ ▶ *n.* the induction of a state of consciousness in which a person apparently loses the power of voluntary action and is highly responsive to suggestion or direction. ■ this state of consciousness.

hyp·no·ther·a·py /ˌhipnō'тнerəpē/ ▶ *n.* the use of hypnosis as a therapeutic technique. —**hyp·no·ther·a·pist** /-pist/ *n.*

hyp·not·ic /hip'nätik/ ▶ *adj.* **1** of, producing, or relating to hypnosis: *a hypnotic state.* ■ exerting a compelling, fascinating, or soporific effect: *her voice had a hypnotic quality.* **2** *Med.* (of a drug) sleep-inducing.
▶ *n.* **1** *Med.* a sleep-inducing drug. **2** a person under or open to the influence of hypnotism. —**hyp·not·i·cal·ly** /-(ə)lē/ *adv.*

hyp·no·tism /'hipnə,tizəm/ ▶ *n.* the study or practice of hypnosis. —**hyp·no·tist** *n.*

hyp·no·tize /'hipnə,tīz/ ▶ *v.* (often **be hypnotized**) [*tr.*] produce a state of hypnosis in (someone). ■ capture the whole attention of (someone); fascinate: *hypnotized by the rain, Eric stared across the street.* —**hyp·no·tiz·a·ble** /-,tīzəbəl/ ; ˌhipnə'tīzəbəl/ *adj.*

hy·po[1] /'hīpō/ ▶ *n. Photog.* the chemical sodium thiosulphate (formerly called hyposulphite) used as a photographic fixer.

hy·po[2] ▶ *n.* (*pl.* **-pos**) informal term for **HYPODERMIC**.

hy·po·al·ler·gen·ic /ˌhīpō-alər'jenik/ ▶ *adj.* (esp. of cosmetics and textiles) relatively unlikely to cause an allergic reaction.

hy·po·chlo·rous ac·id /ˌhīpə'klôrəs/ ▶ *n. Chemistry* a weak acid with oxidizing properties formed when chlorine dissolves in cold water, used in bleaching and water treatment. —**hy·po·chlo·rite** /-,rīt/ *n.*

hy·po·chon·dri·a /ˌhīpə'kändrēə/ ▶ *n.* abnormal anxiety about one's health, esp. with an unwarranted fear that one has a serious disease.

hy·po·chon·dri·ac /ˌhīpə'kändrē,ak/ ▶ *n.* a person who is abnormally anxious about their health.

hy·poc·ri·sy /hi'päkrisē/ ▶ *n.* (*pl.* **-sies**) the practice of claiming to have moral standards or beliefs to which one's own behavior does not conform; pretense.

hyp·o·crite /'hipə,krit/ ▶ *n.* a person who indulges in hypocrisy. —**hyp·o·crit·i·cal** /ˌhipə'kritikəl/ *adj.* —**hyp·o·crit·i·cal·ly** /ˌhipə'kritik(ə)lē/ *adv.*

hy·po·der·mic /ˌhīpə'dərmik/ ▶ *adj.* of or relating to the region immediately beneath the skin. ■ (of a needle or syringe) used to inject a drug or other substance beneath the skin. ■ (of a drug or other substance or its application) injected beneath the skin.
▶ *n.* a hypodermic syringe or injection. —**hy·po·der·mi·cal·ly** /-(ə)lē/ *adv.*

hy·po·ge·um /ˌhīpə'jēəm/ ▶ *n.* (*pl.* **-ge·a** /-'jēə/) an underground chamber.

hy·po·gly·ce·mi·a /ˌhīpōglī'sēmēə/ (*Brit.* **hy·po·gly·cae·mi·a**) ▶ *n. Med.* deficiency of glucose in the bloodstream. —**hy·po·gly·ce·mic** /-'sēmik/ *adj.*

hy·po·ma·ni·a /ˌhīpə'mānēə/ ▶ *n. Psychiatry* a mild form of mania, marked by elation and hyperactivity. —**hy·po·man·ic** /-'manik/ *adj.*

hy·pos·ta·sis /hī'pästəsis/ ▶ *n.* (*pl.* **-ses** /-,sēz/) *Med.* the accumulation of fluid or blood in the lower parts of the body or organs under the influence of gravity, as occurs in cases of poor circulation or after death.

hy·po·style /'hīpə,stīl/ ▶ *adj. Archit.* (of a building) having a roof supported by pillars, typically in several rows.
▶ *n.* a building having such a roof.

hy·po·tax·is /ˌhīpə'taksis/ ▶ *n. Gram.* the subordination of one clause to another. —**hy·po·tac·tic** /ˌhīpə'taktik/ *adj.*

hy·po·ten·sion /ˌhīpə'tensнən/ ▶ *n.* abnormally low blood pressure. —**hy·po·ten·sive** *adj.*

hy·pot·e·nuse /hī'pätn,(y)ōōs/ ▶ *n.* the longest side of a right triangle, opposite the right angle.

hy·po·thal·a·mus /ˌhīpə'тнaləməs/ ▶ *n.* (*pl.* **-mi** /-,mī/) *Anat.* a region of the forebrain below the thalamus that coordinates both the autonomic nervous system and the activity of the pituitary. —**hy·po·tha·lam·ic** /ˌhīpō,тнə'lamik/ *adj.*

hy·po·ther·mi·a /ˌhīpə'тнərmēə/ ▶ *n.* the condition of having an abnormally low body temperature, typically one that is dangerously low.

hy·poth·e·sis /hī'päтнəsis/ ▶ *n.* (*pl.* **-ses** /-,sēz/) a supposition or proposed explanation made on the basis of limited evidence as a starting point for further investigation. ■ *Philos.* a proposition made as a basis for reasoning, without any assumption of its truth. ▷late 16th cent.:

via late Latin from Greek *hupothesis* 'foundation,' from *hupo* 'under' + *thesis* 'placing.'

hy·poth·e·size /hīˈpäTHəˌsīz/ ▸*v.* [*tr.*] put (something) forward as a hypothesis. —**hy·poth·e·siz·er** *n.*

hy·po·thet·i·cal /ˌhīpəˈTHetikəl/ ▸*adj.* of, based on, or serving as a hypothesis: *that option is merely hypothetical at this juncture.* ▪ supposed but not necessarily real or true: *the hypothetical tenth planet.*
▸*n.* (usu. **hypotheticals**) a hypothetical proposition or statement. —**hy·po·thet·i·cal·ly** /-ik(ə)lē/ *adv.*

hy·po·thy·roid·ism /ˌhīpōˈTHīroiˌdizəm/ ▸*n. Med.* abnormally low activity of the thyroid gland, resulting in retardation of growth and mental development in children and adults. —**hy·po·thy·roid** *n. & adj.*

hy·pox·i·a /hīˈpäksēə/ ▸*n. Med.* deficiency in the amount of oxygen reaching the tissues. ▪ oxygen deficiency in a biotic environment leading to this: *aquatic hypoxia.* —**hy·pox·ic** /-sik/ *adj.*

hy·rax /ˈhīˌraks/ ▸*n.* a small herbivorous mammal (family Procaviidae) with a compact body and a very short tail, found in arid country in Africa and Arabia.

hys·sop /ˈhisəp/ ▸*n.* a small bushy aromatic plant (*Hyssopus officinalis*) of the mint family, the bitter minty leaves of which are used in cooking and herbal medicine.

hys·ter·ec·to·my /ˌhistəˈrektəmē/ ▸*n.* (*pl.* **-mies**) a surgical operation to remove all or part of the uterus.

hys·te·ri·a /hiˈsterēə; -ˈsti(ə)rēə/ ▸*n.* exaggerated or uncontrollable emotion or excitement, esp. among a group of people: *mass hysteria characterizes the week before Christmas.* ▪ *Psychiatry* a psychological disorder (not now regarded as a single definite condition) whose symptoms include conversion of psychological stress into physical symptoms (somatization), selective amnesia, shallow volatile emotions, and overdramatic or attention-seeking behavior.

hys·ter·ic /hiˈsterik/ ▸*n.* **1** (**hysterics**) *inf.* a wildly emotional and exaggerated reaction. ▪ uncontrollable laughter: *this started them both giggling and they fled upstairs in hysterics.* **2** a person suffering from hysteria.
▸*adj.* another term for **HYSTERICAL** (sense 2). ▷mid 17th cent. (as an adjective): via Latin from Greek *husterikos* 'of the womb,' from *hustera* 'womb' (hysteria being thought to be specific to women and associated with the womb), related to *uterus*.

hys·ter·i·cal /hiˈsterikəl/ ▸*adj.* **1** deriving from or affected by uncontrolled extreme emotion. ▪ *inf.* extremely funny: *her attempts to teach them to dance were hysterical.* **2** *Psychiatry* relating to, associated with, or suffering from hysteria. —**hys·ter·i·cal·ly** *adv.*

Hz ▸*abbr.* hertz.

Ii

I[1] /ī/ (also **i**) ▸*n.* (*pl.* **Is** or **I's**) **1** the ninth letter of the alphabet. ■ denoting the next after H in a set of items, categories, etc. **2** the Roman numeral for one.

I[2] ▸*pron.* [*first person sing.*] used by a speaker to refer to himself or herself: *accept me for what I am.*

I[3] ▸*abbr.* ■ (preceding a highway number) Interstate. ■ (**I.**) Island(s) or Isle(s) (chiefly on maps).
▸*symb.* ■ electric current: $V = I/R.$ ■ the chemical element iodine.

i ▸*symb.* (*i*) *Math.* the imaginary quantity equal to the square root of minus one.

i·amb /ˈī,am(b)/ ▸*n. Prosody* a metrical foot consisting of one short (or unstressed) syllable followed by one long (or stressed) syllable.

i·am·bic /ˈīˈambik/ ▸*adj. Prosody* of or using iambs: *iambic pentameters.*
▸*n.* a verse using iambs. ■ (**iambics**) verse of this kind.

ib. ▸*adv.* short for IBID.

I-beam ▸*n.* a girder that has the shape of an I when viewed in section.

I·be·ri·an /ˈīˈbi(ə)rēən/ ▸*adj.* relating to or denoting Iberia, or the countries of Spain and Portugal.
▸*n.* **1** a native of Iberia, esp. in ancient times. **2** the extinct Romance language spoken in the Iberian peninsula in late classical times. **3** the extinct Celtic language spoken in the Iberian peninsula in ancient times.

i·bex /ˈī,beks/ ▸*n.* (*pl.* **ibexes**) a wild goat (genus *Capra*, esp. *C. ibex*) with long, thick ridged horns that curve back, found in the mountains of the Alps, Pyrenees, central Asia, and Ethiopia.

ibid. /ˈibid/ (also **ib.**) ▸*adv.* in the same source (used to save space in textual references to a quoted work that has been mentioned in a previous reference).

i·bis /ˈībis/ ▸*n.* (*pl.* **ibises**) a large wading bird (family Threskiornithidae) with a long down-curved bill, long neck, and long legs.

i·bu·pro·fen /,ībyōōˈprōfən/ ▸*n.* a synthetic compound ($C_{13}H_{18}O_2$) used widely as an analgesic and anti-inflammatory drug.

ICBM ▸*abbr.* intercontinental ballistic missile.

ICC ▸*abbr.* ■ Interstate Commerce Commission. ■ International Criminal Court.

ICE /īs/ ▸*n.* an entry stored in one's cellular phone that provides emergency contact information: *paramedics failed to check his phone for ICE* | [as *adj.*] *a newer phone may have an ICE key.*
▸*v.* [*tr.*] program (a cellular phone) with such information: *frequent flyers are among those who routinely ICE their cell phones.* ▷2000s: acronym from *in case of emergency.*

ice /īs/ ▸*n.* frozen water, a brittle, transparent crystalline solid: *the pipes were blocked with ice.* ■ a frozen mixture of fruit juice or flavored water and sugar. ■ *inf.* diamonds. ■ *inf.* methamphetamine.
▸*v.* [*tr.*] **1** decorate (a cake) with icing. **2** *inf.* clinch (something such as a victory or deal). **3** *Ice Hockey* shoot (the puck) so as to commit icing.
▸ □ **break the ice** do or say something to relieve tension or get conversation going at the start of a party or when people meet for the first time. ■ *fig.* (esp. of a plan or proposal) held in reserve for future consideration: *the recommendation was put on ice.* □ **on thin ice** in a precarious or risky situation: *you're skating on thin ice.*

ice age ▸*n.* a glacial episode during a past geological period. See GLACIAL PERIOD. ■ (**the Ice Age**) the series of glacial episodes during the Pleistocene period.

ice·berg /ˈīs,bərg/ ▸*n.* a large floating mass of ice detached from a glacier or ice sheet and carried out to sea. ▷late 18th cent.: from Dutch *ijsberg,* from *ijs* 'ice' + *berg* 'hill.'
▸ □ **the tip of the iceberg** the small, perceptible part of a much larger situation or problem that remains hidden: *the statistics represent just the tip of the iceberg.*

ice·berg let·tuce ▸*n.* a lettuce of a variety having a dense, round head of crisp, pale leaves.

ice·bound /ˈīs,bound/ ▸*adj.* completely surrounded or covered by ice: *the lake was icebound.*

ice·break·er /ˈīs,brākər/ ▸*n.* a ship designed for breaking a channel through ice. ■ a thing that serves to relieve inhibitions or tension between people, or start a conversation. ■ a thing that breaks up moving ice so as to lessen its impact, esp. a structure protecting the upstream end of a bridge pier.

ice cap (also **ice-cap**) ▸*n.* a covering of ice over a large area, esp. on the polar region of a planet.

ice cream ▸*n.* a soft frozen food made with sweetened and flavored milk fat. ■ a serving of this, typically in a bowl or a wafer cone or on a stick.

ice cube ▸*n.* a small block of ice made in a freezer, esp. for adding to drinks.

iced tea (also **ice tea**) ▸*n.* a chilled drink of sweetened tea, typically flavored with lemon.

ice-fish ▸*v.* [*intr.*] fish through holes in the ice on a lake or river.
▸*n.* (**ice-fish**) (*pl.* same or **-fish·es**) **1** another term for CAPELIN. **2** a scaleless Antarctic fish (*Chaenocephalus aceratus,* family Chaenichthyidae) of pallid appearance with spiny gill covers and a snout shaped like a duck's bill. —**ice fish·ing** *n.*

ice floe ▸*n.* see FLOE.

ice hock·ey ▸*n.* a fast contact sport played on an ice rink between two teams of six skaters, who attempt to drive a small rubber disk (the puck) into the opposing goal with hooked or angled sticks.

Ice·land·er /ˈīsləndər/ ▸*n.* a native or national of Iceland. ■ a person of Icelandic descent.

Ice·lan·dic /īsˈlandik/ ▸*adj.* of or relating to Iceland or its language.
▸*n.* the North Germanic language of Iceland.

ice pick ▸*n.* a sharp, straight, pointed implement with a handle.

ice rink ▸*n.* see RINK.

ice skate ▸*n.* a boot with a blade attached to the bottom, used for skating on ice.
▸*v.* [*intr.*] skate on ice as a sport or pastime.
—**ice skat·er** *n.* —**ice skat·ing** *n.*

I Ching /ˈē ˈCHiNG; ˈjiNG/ ▸*n.* an ancient Chinese manual of divination based on eight symbolic trigrams and sixty-four hexagrams, interpreted in terms of the principles of yin and yang.

ich·thy·ol·o·gy /,iKTHēˈäləjē/ ▸*n.* the branch of zoology that deals with fishes. —**ich·thy·o·log·i·cal** /-əˈläjikəl/ *adj.* —**ich·thy·o·lo·gist** /-jist/ *n.*

ich·thy·o·saur /ˈiKTHēə,sôr/ (also **ich·thy·o·sau·rus** /,iKTHēəˈsôrəs/) ▸*n.* an extinct marine reptile (order Ichthyosauria) of the Mesozoic era resembling a dolphin, with a long pointed head, four flippers, and a vertical tail. —**ich·thy·o·sau·ri·an** /,iKTHēə-ˈsôrēən/ *adj.*

figure skate

hockey skate

ice skates

i·ci·cle /ˈīsikəl/ ▸*n.* a hanging, tapering piece of ice formed by the freezing of dripping water.

ic·ing /ˈīsiNG/ ▸*n.* **1** a mixture of sugar with liquid or butter, typically flavored and colored, and used as a coating for cakes or cookies. **2** the formation of ice on an aircraft, ship, or other vehicle, or in an engine. **3** *Ice Hockey* the action of shooting the puck from one's own end of the rink to the other but not into the goal, for which the referee calls a face-off in one's own end.

▶ □ **the icing** (or **frosting**) **on the cake** an attractive but inessential addition or enhancement: *being a scientist is enjoyable, and winning a Nobel is icing on the cake.*

ick·y /ˈikē/ ▶*adj.* (**ick·i·er, ick·i·est**) *inf.* sticky, esp. unpleasantly so. ▪ distastefully sentimental: *a romantic subplot that is just plain icky.* ▪ nasty or repulsive (used as a general term of disapproval): *icky boys with all their macho strutting.* —**ick·i·ness** *n.*

i·con /ˈīˌkän/ ▶*n.* a painting of Jesus Christ or another holy figure, typically in a traditional style on wood, venerated and used as an aid to devotion in the Byzantine and other Eastern Churches. ▪ a person or thing regarded as a representative symbol of something: *this iron-jawed icon of American manhood.* ▪ *Comput.* a symbol or graphic representation on a video display terminal of a program, option, or window, esp. one of several for selection.

i·con·ic /īˈkänik/ ▶*adj.* of, relating to, or of the nature of an icon. ▪ (of a classical Greek statue) depicting a victorious athlete in a conventional style. —**i·con·i·cal·ly** /-ik(ə)lē/ *adv.* —**i·con·ic·i·ty** /ˌīkəˈnisitē/ *n.* (esp. in linguistics).

i·con·o·clasm /īˈkänəˌklazəm/ ▶*n.* **1** the action of attacking or assertively rejecting cherished beliefs and institutions or established values and practices. **2** the rejection or destruction of religious images as heretical: the doctrine of iconoclasts.

i·con·o·clast /īˈkänəˌklast/ ▶*n.* **1** a person who attacks cherished beliefs or institutions. **2** a destroyer of images used in religious worship. —**i·con·o·clas·tic** /īˌkänəˈklastik/ *adj.* —**i·con·o·clas·ti·cal·ly** /īˌkänəˈklastik(ə)lē/ *adv.*

i·co·nog·ra·phy /ˌīkəˈnägrəfē/ ▶*n.* (*pl.* **-phies**) the use or study of images or symbols in visual arts. ▪ the visual images, symbols, or modes of representation collectively associated with a person, cult, or movement: *the iconography of pop culture.* **2** the illustration of a subject by drawings or figures. —**i·co·nog·ra·pher** /-fər/ *n.* —**i·con·o·graph·ic** /īˌkänəˈgrafik/ *adj.* —**i·con·o·graph·i·cal** /īˌkänəˈgrafikəl/ *adj.* —**i·con·o·graph·i·cal·ly** /īˌkänəˈgrafik(ə)lē/ *adv.*

i·co·nol·o·gy /ˌīkəˈnäləjē/ ▶*n.* the study of visual imagery and its symbolism and interpretation, esp. in social or political terms. ▪ symbolism: *the iconology of a work of art.* —**i·con·o·log·i·cal** /īˌkänəˈläjikəl/ *adj.*

i·co·sa·he·dron /īˌkōsəˈhēdrən; īˌkäsə-/ ▶*n.* (*pl.* **-drons** or **-dra** /-drə/) a solid figure with twenty plane faces, esp. equilateral triangular ones. —**i·co·sa·he·dral** /-drəl/ *adj.*

ic·ter·us /ˈiktərəs/ ▶*n.* *Med.* technical term for **JAUNDICE**. —**ic·ter·ic** /ikˈterik/ *adj.*

ic·tus /ˈiktəs/ ▶*n.* (*pl.* same or **ic·tus·es**) **1** *Prosody* a rhythmical or metrical stress. **2** *Med.* a stroke or seizure; a fit.

ICU ▶*abbr.* intensive care unit.

i·cy /ˈīsē/ ▶*adj.* (**i·ci·er, i·ci·est**) covered with or consisting of ice: *icy patches on the roads.* ▪ very cold: *an icy wind.* ▪ *fig.* (of a person's tone or manner) very unfriendly; hostile. —**i·ci·ly** /ˈīsilē/ *adv.* —**i·ci·ness** *n.*

ID ▶*abbr.* identification or identity: *they weren't carrying any ID* | [as *adj.*] *an ID card.*

I'd /īd/ ▶*contr. of* I would or I should: *I'd like a bath.* ▪ I had: *I'd already agreed to go.*

id /id/ ▶*n.* *Psychoanalysis* the part of the mind in which innate instinctive impulses and primary processes are manifest. Compare with **EGO** and **SUPEREGO**.

IDE *Comput.* ▶*abbr.* Integrated Drive Electronics, a standard for interfacing computers and their peripherals.

i·de·a /īˈdēə/ ▶*n.* **1** a thought or suggestion as to a possible course of action: *they don't think it's a very good idea.* ▪ a concept or mental impression: *our menu list will give you some idea of how interesting a low-fat diet can be.* ▪ an opinion or belief: *nineteenth-century ideas about drinking.* ▪ a feeling that something is probable or possible: *he had an idea that she must feel the same.* **2** (**the idea**) the aim or purpose: *I took a job with the idea of getting some money together.*

▶ □ **have** (**got**) **no idea** *inf.* not know at all: *she had no idea where she was going.* □ **that's an idea** *inf.* that suggestion or proposal is worth considering. □ **that's the idea** *inf.* used to confirm to someone that they have understood something correctly or they are doing something correctly.

i·de·al /īˈdē(ə)l/ ▶*adj.* **1** satisfying one's conception of what is perfect; most suitable: *the swimming pool is ideal for a quick dip* | *this is an ideal opportunity to save money.* **2** existing only in the imagination; desirable or

perfect but not likely to become a reality: *in an ideal world, we might have made a different decision.*

▶*n.* a person or thing regarded as perfect: *you're my ideal of how a man should be.* ▪ a standard of perfection; a principle to be aimed at: *tolerance and freedom, the liberal ideals.* —**i·de·al·ly** *adv.*

i·de·al gas ▶*n.* *Chem.* a hypothetical gas that, by definition, obeys the gas laws exactly.

i·de·al·ism /īˈdē(ə)ˌlizəm/ ▶*n.* **1** the practice of forming or pursuing ideals, esp. unrealistically: *the idealism of youth.* Compare with **REALISM**. ▪ (in art or literature) the representation of things in ideal or idealized form. Often contrasted with **REALISM** (sense 2). **2** *Philos.* any of various systems of thought in which the objects of knowledge are held to be in some way dependent on the activity of mind. —**i·de·al·ist** *n.* —**i·de·al·is·tic** /īˌdē(ə)ˈlistik/ *adj.* —**i·de·al·is·ti·cal·ly** /īˌdē(ə)ˈlistik(ə)lē/ *adv.*

i·de·al·ize /īˈdē(ə)ˌlīz/ ▶*v.* [*tr.*] [often as *adj.*] (**idealized**) regard or represent as perfect or better than in reality: *Helen's idealized accounts of their life together.* —**i·de·al·i·za·tion** /īˌdē(ə)liˈzāsHən/ *n.* —**i·de·al·iz·er** *n.*

i·de·ate /ˈīdēˌāt/ ▶*v.* [*tr.*] [often as *adj.*] (**ideated**) form an idea of; imagine or conceive. ▪ [*intr.*] form ideas; think. —**i·de·a·tion** /ˌīdēˈāsHən/ *n.*

i·dée fixe /ēdā ˈfēks/ ▶*n.* (*pl.* **i·dées fixes** *pronunc.* same) an idea or desire that dominates the mind; an obsession.

i·den·ti·cal /īˈdentikəl/ ▶*adj.* **1** similar in every detail; exactly alike: *four girls in identical green outfits* | *the passage on the second floor was **identical to** the one below.* ▪ (of twins) developed from a single fertilized ovum, and therefore of the same sex and usually very similar in appearance. Compare with **FRATERNAL** (sense 2). ▪ (of something encountered on separate occasions) the same: *the identical excuse that he gave last time.* **2** *Logic & Math.* expressing an identity: *an identical proposition.* —**i·den·ti·cal·ly** /-ik(ə)lē/ *adv.*

i·den·ti·fi·ca·tion /īˌdentəfiˈkāsHən/ ▶*n.* the action or process of identifying someone or something or the fact of being identified: *it may be impossible for relatives to make positive identifications.* ▪ a means of proving a person's identity, esp. in the form of official papers: *I asked to see his identification.* ▪ a person's sense of identity with someone or something: *children's **identification with** storybook characters.* ▪ the association or linking of one thing with another: *the identification of democracy with anarchy.*

i·den·ti·fi·er /īˈdentəˌfīər/ ▶*n.* a person or thing that identifies something. ▪ *Comput.* a sequence of characters used to identify or refer to a program or an element, such as a variable or a set of data, within it.

i·den·ti·fy /īˈdentəˌfī/ ▶*v.* (**-fies, -fied**) [*tr.*] **1** (often **be identified**) establish or indicate who or what (someone or something) is: *the judge ordered that the girl not be identified.* ▪ recognize or distinguish (esp. something considered worthy of attention): *the student's real needs are identified.* **2** (**identify someone/something with**) associate (someone) closely with; regard (someone) as having strong links with: *he was too closely identified with the peace movement.* ▪ equate (someone or something) with: *because of my upstate accent, people identified me with a farmer's wife.* ▪ [*intr.*] (**identify with**) regard oneself as sharing the same characteristics or thinking as someone else: *I liked Fromm and identified with him.* —**i·den·ti·fi·a·ble** /-ˌfīəbəl/ *adj.* —**i·den·ti·fi·a·bly** /-ˌfīəblē/ *adv.*

i·den·ti·ty /īˈdentitē/ ▶*n.* (*pl.* **-ties**) **1** the fact of being who or what a person or thing is: *he knows the identity of the bombers* | *a victim of mistaken identity.* ▪ the characteristics determining this: *attempts to define a distinct Canadian identity.* **2** a close similarity or affinity: *an identity of goals.* **3** *Math.* (also **identity operation**) a transformation that leaves an object unchanged. ▪ (also **identity element**) an element of a set that, if combined with another element by a specified binary operation, leaves that element unchanged. **4** *Math.* the equality of two expressions for all values of the quantities expressed by letters, or an equation expressing this, e.g., $(x + 1)^2 = x^2 + 2x + 1$. ▷late 16th cent. (in the sense 'quality of being identical'): from late Latin *identitas,* from Latin *idem* 'same.'

i·den·ti·ty cri·sis ▶*n.* *Psychiatry* a period of uncertainty and confusion in which a person's sense of identity becomes insecure, typically due to a change in their expected aims or role in society.

i·den·ti·ty theft ▶*n.* the fraudulent acquisition and use of a person's private identifying information, usually for financial gain.

id·e·o·gram /ˈidēəˌgram; ˈīdēə-/ ▶*n.* a written character symbolizing the idea of a thing without indicating the sounds used to say it, e.g., numerals and Chinese characters.

Pronunciation Key ə *ago,* up; ər *over, fur;* a *hat;* ā *ate;* ä *car;* CH *chin;* e *let;* ē *see;* e(ə)r *air;* i *fit;* ī *by;* i(ə)r *ear;* NG *sing;* ō *go;* ô *law, for;* oi *toy;* o͝o *good;* o͞o *goo;* ou *out;* SH *she;* TH *thin;* <u>TH</u> *then;* (h)w *why;* ZH *vision*

id·e·o·graph /ˈidēəˌgraf; ˈīdēə-/ ▶ *n.* another term for IDEOGRAM. —**id·e·o·graph·ic** /ˌidēəˈgrafik; ˌīdēə-/ *adj.* —**id·e·og·ra·phy** /ˌidēˈägrəfē; ˌīdē-/ *n.*

i·de·o·logue /ˈidēəˌlôg; -ˌläg; ˈīdēə-/ ▶ *n.* an adherent of an ideology, esp. one who is uncompromising and dogmatic: *a Nazi ideologue.*

i·de·ol·o·gy /ˌīdēˈäləjē; ˌidē-/ ▶ *n.* (*pl.* **-gies**) a system of ideas and ideals, esp. one that forms the basis of economic or political theory and policy. ▪ the ideas and manner of thinking characteristic of a group, social class, or individual. —**i·de·o·log·i·cal** /-əˈläjikəl/ *adj.* —**i·de·o·log·i·cal·ly** /-əˈläjik(ə)lē/ *adv.* —**i·de·ol·o·gist** /-jist/ *n.*

ides /īdz/ ▶ *pl. n.* (in the ancient Roman calendar) a day falling roughly in the middle of each month (the 15th day of March, May, July, and October, and the 13th of other months), from which other dates were calculated.

id·i·o·cy /ˈidēəsē/ ▶ *n.* (*pl.* **-cies**) extremely stupid behavior: *the idiocy of decimating rain forests.*

id·i·om /ˈidēəm/ ▶ *n.* **1** a group of words established by usage as having a meaning not deducible from those of the individual words (e.g., *rain cats and dogs, see the light*). ▪ a form of expression natural to a language, person, or group of people. ▪ the dialect of a people or part of a country. **2** a characteristic mode of expression in music or art.

id·i·o·mat·ic /ˌidēəˈmatik/ ▶ *adj.* **1** using, containing, or denoting expressions that are natural to a native speaker: *idiomatic dialogue.* **2** appropriate to the style of art or music associated with a particular period, individual, or group. —**id·i·o·mat·i·cal·ly** /-ik(ə)lē/ *adv.*

id·i·o·path·ic /ˌidēəˈpaTHik/ ▶ *adj. Med.* relating to or denoting any disease or condition that arises spontaneously or for which the cause is unknown.

id·i·o·syn·cra·sy /ˌidēəˈsiNGkrəsē/ ▶ *n.* (*pl.* **-sies**) (usu. **idiosyncrasies**) a mode of behavior or way of thought peculiar to an individual. ▪ a distinctive or peculiar feature or characteristic of a place or thing: *the idiosyncrasies of the prison system.* ▪ *Med.* an abnormal physical reaction by an individual to a food or drug. —**id·i·o·syn·crat·ic** /ˌidēəsiNGˈkratik/ *adj.*

id·i·ot /ˈidēət/ ▶ *n. inf.* a stupid person. —**id·i·ot·ic** /ˌidēˈätik/ *adj.* —**id·i·ot·i·cal·ly** /ˌidēˈätik(ə)lē/ *adv.*

id·i·ot sa·vant ▶ *n.* (*pl.* **id·i·ot sa·vants** or **id·i·ots sa·vants**) a person who is considered to be mentally handicapped but displays brilliance in a specific area, esp. one involving memory. ▷late 20th cent.: French, literally 'learned idiot.'

id·i·o·type /ˈidēəˌtīp/ ▶ *n. Biol.* the set of genetic determinants of an individual. ▪ *Immunol.* a set of antigen-binding sites that characterizes the antibodies produced by a particular clone of antibody-producing cells.

i·dle /ˈīdl/ ▶ *adj.* (**i·dler, i·dlest**) **1** (esp. of a machine or factory) not active or in use: *assembly lines standing idle for lack of spare parts.* ▪ (of a person) not working; unemployed. ▪ (of a person) avoiding work; lazy. ▪ (of time) characterized by inaction or absence of significant activity: *an idle moment.* ▪ (of money) held in cash or in accounts paying no interest. **2** without purpose or effect; pointless: *idle chatter.* ▪ (esp. of a threat or boast) without foundation: *idle threats.*
▶ *v.* [*intr.*] be idle. ▪ (of an engine) run slowly while disconnected from a load or out of gear: *the car is noisily idling in the street.* ▪ [*tr.*] cause (an engine) to idle. —**i·dle·ness** *n.* —**i·dler** *n.* —**i·dly** *adv.*

i·dol /ˈīdl/ ▶ *n.* an image or representation of a god used as an object of worship. ▪ a person or thing that is greatly admired, loved, or revered: *movie idol Robert Redford.*

i·dol·a·ter /īˈdälətər/ ▶ *n.* a person who worships an idol or idols.

i·dol·a·try /īˈdälətrē/ ▶ *n.* worship of idols. ▪ extreme admiration, love, or reverence for something or someone. —**i·dol·a·trous** /-trəs/ *adj.*

i·dol·ize /ˈīdlˌīz/ ▶ *v.* [*tr.*] admire, revere, or love greatly or excessively: *he idolized his mother.* —**i·dol·i·za·tion** /ˌīdlɪˈzāSHən/ *n.* —**i·dol·iz·er** *n.*

i·dyll /ˈīdl/ (also **i·dyl**) ▶ *n.* an extremely happy, peaceful, or picturesque episode or scene, typically an idealized or unsustainable one. ▪ a short description in verse or prose of a picturesque scene or incident, esp. in rustic life.

i·dyl·lic /īˈdilik/ ▶ *adj.* (esp. of a time or place) like an idyll; extremely happy, peaceful, or picturesque: *an attractive hotel in an idyllic setting.* —**i·dyl·li·cal·ly** /-ik(ə)lē/ *adv.*

IE ▶ *abbr.* Indo-European.

if /if/ ▶ *conj.* **1** introducing a conditional clause: ▪ on the condition or supposition that; in the event that: *if you have a complaint, write to the director* | *if you like, I'll put in a word for you.* ▪ (with past tense) introducing a hypothetical situation: *if you had stayed, this would never have happened.* ▪ whenever; every time: *if I go out, she gets nasty.* **2** despite the possibility that; no matter whether: *if it takes me seven years, I will do it.* **3** (often used in indirect questions) whether: *he asked if we would like*

some coffee | see if you can track it down. **4** expressing a polite request: *if you wouldn't mind giving him a message?* **5** expressing an opinion: *if you ask me, he's in love.* **6** expressing surprise or regret: *well, if it isn't Frank!* | *if I could just be left alone.* **7** with implied reservation: ▪ and perhaps not: *the teachers have little if any control.* ▪ used to admit something as being possible but regarded as relatively insignificant: *if I hurt you, I didn't mean to* | *so what if he did?* ▪ despite being (used before an adjective or adverb to introduce a contrast): *she was honest, if a little brutal.*
▶ *n.* a condition or supposition: *there are so many ifs and buts in the policy.*
▶ □ **if and only if** used to introduce a condition that is necessary as well as sufficient: *witches are real if and only if there are criteria for identifying witches.* □ **if and when** at a future time (should it arise): *if and when the film gets the green light, be sure you've read the book first.* □ **if anything** used to suggest tentatively that something may be the case (often the opposite of something previously implied): *I haven't made much of this—if anything, I've played it down.* □ **if I were you** used to accompany a piece of advice: *I would go to see him if I were you.* □ **if not** perhaps even (used to introduce a more extreme term than one first mentioned): *hundreds if not thousands of germs.* □ **if only 1** even if for no other reason than: *Willy would have to tell George more, if only to keep him from pestering.* **2** used to express a wish, esp. regretfully: *if only I had listened to you.* □ **if so** if that is the case.

if·fy /ˈifē/ ▶ *adj.* (**if·fi·er, if·fi·est**) *inf.* full of uncertainty; doubtful: *the prospects for recovery are iffy.* ▪ of doubtful quality or legality.

ig·loo /ˈiglōō/ ▶ *n.* a dome-shaped Eskimo house, typically built from blocks of solid snow.

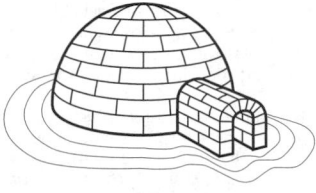

igloo

ig·ne·ous /ˈignēəs/ ▶ *adj. Geol.* (of rock) having solidified from a molten state.

ig·nite /igˈnīt/ ▶ *v.* catch fire or cause to catch fire: [*intr.*] *the fabric gives off lethal fumes when it ignites* | [*tr.*] *sparks flew out and ignited the dry scrub.* ▪ [*tr.*] *fig.* arouse (an emotion): *the words ignited fury.* ▪ [*tr.*] *fig.* inflame or instigate (a situation): *they were about to ignite a socialist revolution.* —**ig·nit·a·ble** *adj.*

ig·ni·ter /igˈnītər/ ▶ *n.* a device for igniting a fuel mixture in an engine.

ig·ni·tion /igˈnisHən/ ▶ *n.* the action of setting something on fire or starting to burn. ▪ the process of starting the combustion of fuel in the cylinders of an internal combustion engine. ▪ (usu. **the ignition**) the mechanism for bringing this about, typically activated by a key or switch.

ig·no·ble /igˈnōbəl/ ▶ *adj.* (**-no·bler, -no·blest**) **1** not honorable in character or purpose: *ignoble feelings of intense jealousy.* **2** of humble origin or social status. —**ig·no·bil·i·ty** /ˌignōˈbilitē/ *n.* —**ig·no·bly** /-blē/ *adv.*

ig·no·min·i·ous /ˌignəˈminēəs/ ▶ *adj.* deserving or causing public disgrace or shame. —**ig·no·min·i·ous·ly** *adv.* —**ig·no·min·i·ous·ness** *n.*

ig·no·min·y /ˈignəˌminē; igˈnäminē/ ▶ *n.* public shame or disgrace.

ig·no·ra·mus /ˌignəˈrāməs; -ˈraməs/ ▶ *n.* (*pl.* **-mus·es**) an ignorant or stupid person. ▷late 16th cent.: Latin, literally 'we do not know' (in legal use 'we take no notice of it'), from *ignorare* 'not know, ignore.'

ig·no·rance /ˈignərəns/ ▶ *n.* lack of knowledge or information: *he acted in ignorance of basic procedures.*

ig·no·rant /ˈignərənt/ ▶ *adj.* lacking knowledge or awareness in general; uneducated or unsophisticated: *he's ignorant but not stupid.* ▪ lacking knowledge, information, or awareness about something in particular: *they were ignorant of astronomy.* ▪ *inf.* easily angered. —**ig·no·rant·ly** *adv.*

ig·nore /igˈnôr/ ▶ *v.* [*tr.*] refuse to take notice of or acknowledge; disregard intentionally: *he ignored her question.* ▪ fail to consider (something significant): *satellite broadcasting ignores national boundaries.* ▪ *Law* (of a grand jury) reject (an indictment) as groundless. ▷late 15th cent. (in the sense 'be ignorant of'): from French *ignorer* or Latin *ignorare* 'not know, ignore,' from *in-* 'not' + *gno-*, a base meaning 'know.' Current senses date from the early 19th cent. —**ig·nor·a·ble** *adj.* —**ig·nor·er** *n.*

i·gua·na /iˈgwänə/ ▶ *n.* a large, arboreal, tropical American lizard (genus *Iguana*, family Iguanidae), esp. the **green iguana** (*I. iguana*) with a spiny crest along the back and greenish coloration. ▪ any iguanid lizard.

i·gua·nid /i'gwänid/ ▶*n. Zool.* a lizard of the iguana family (Iguanidae). Iguanids are found mainly in the New World but also occur in Madagascar and on some Pacific islands.

i·guan·o·don /i'gwänə,dän/ ▶*n.* a large, partly bipedal, herbivorous dinosaur (genus *Iguanodon*) of the early to mid Cretaceous period, with a broad, stiff tail and the thumb developed into a spike.

il·e·um /'ilēəm/ ▶*n.* (*pl.* **il·e·a** /'ilēə/) *Anat.* the third portion of the small intestine, between the jejunum and the cecum. —**il·e·ac** /-,ak/ *adj.* —**il·e·al** /-əl/ *adj.*

il·i·ac /'ilē,ak/ ▶*adj.* of or relating to the ilium or the nearby regions of the lower body: *the iliac artery.*

il·i·um /'ilēəm/ ▶*n.* (*pl.* **il·i·a** /'ilēə/) the large broad bone forming the upper part of each half of the pelvis.

ilk /ilk/ ▶*n.* a type of people or things similar to those already referred to: *bosses of his ilk | fascists, racists, and others of that ilk.*

I'll /il/ ▶*contr.* of I shall; I will: *I'll arrange it.*

ill /il/ ▶*adj.* **1** not in full health; sick: *a terminally ill patient.* **2** poor in quality: *ill judgment dogs the unsuccessful.* ■ harmful: *she suffered no ill effects.* ■ hostile: *I bear you no ill will.* ■ (esp. of fortune) not favorable.
▶*adv.* **1** [usu. in comb.] badly, wrongly, or imperfectly: *ill-chosen words | it ill becomes one so beautiful to be gloomy.* ■ unfavorably or unpropitiously. **2** only with difficulty; hardly: *she could ill afford the cost of new curtains.*
▶*n.* **1** [as pl. n.] (**the ill**) people who are ill: *the mentally ill.* **2** (usu. **ills**) a problem or misfortune: *the ills of society.* ■ evil; harm: *how could I wish him ill?*
▶ □ **ill at ease** uncomfortable or embarrassed. □ **speak** (or **think**) **ill of** say (or think) something critical about.

ill-ad·vised ▶*adj.* (of a person) unwise or imprudent: *you would be ill-advised to go on your own.* ■ badly thought out: *ill-advised financial ventures.* —**ill-ad·vis·ed·ly** *adv.*

ill-bred ▶*adj.* badly brought up or rude. —**ill breed·ing** *n.*

il·le·gal /i(l)'lēgəl/ ▶*adj.* contrary to or forbidden by law, esp. criminal law: *illegal drugs.*
▶*n.* an illegal immigrant. —**il·le·gal·i·ty** /,i(l)li'galitē/ *n.* (*pl.* **-ties**) —**il·le·gal·ly** *adv.*

il·leg·i·ble /i(l)'lejəbəl/ ▶*adj.* not clear enough to be read: *his handwriting is totally illegible.* —**il·leg·i·bil·i·ty** /i(l),lejə'bilitē/ *n.* —**il·leg·i·bly** /-blē/ *adv.*

il·le·git·i·mate /,i(l)lə'jitəmit/ ▶*adj.* not authorized by the law; not in accordance with accepted standards or rules: *an illegitimate exercise of power by the military.* ■ (of a child) born of parents not lawfully married to each other.
▶*n.* a person who is illegitimate by birth. —**il·le·git·i·ma·cy** /-məsē/ *n.* —**il·le·git·i·mate·ly** *adv.*

ill-fat·ed ▶*adj.* destined to fail or have bad luck: *an ill-fated expedition.*

ill-found·ed ▶*adj.* (esp. of an idea or belief) not based on fact or reliable evidence: *ill-founded criticism | her fear may be ill-founded.*

ill-got·ten ▶*adj.* acquired by illegal or unfair means.

ill hu·mor ▶*n.* irritability or bad temper. —**ill-hu·mored** *adj.*

il·lib·er·al /i(l)'lib(ə)rəl/ ▶*adj.* opposed to liberal principles; restricting freedom of thought or behavior: *illiberal and anti-democratic policies.* —**il·lib·er·al·i·ty** /-,libə'ralitē/ *n.* —**il·lib·er·al·ly** *adv.*

il·lic·it /i(l)'lisit/ ▶*adj.* forbidden by law, rules, or custom: *illicit drugs | illicit sex.* —**il·lic·it·ly** *adv.* —**il·lic·it·ness** *n.*

il·lit·er·ate /i(l)'litərit/ ▶*adj.* unable to read or write: *his parents were illiterate.* ■ ignorant in a particular subject or activity: *the voters are politically illiterate.* ■ uncultured or poorly educated: *the ignorant, illiterate town council.* ■ (esp. of a piece of writing) showing a lack of education, esp. an inability to read or write well.
▶*n.* a person who is unable to read or write. —**il·lit·er·a·cy** /-əsē/ *n.* —**il·lit·er·ate·ly** *adv.* —**il·lit·er·ate·ness** *n.*
▶ □ **functionally illiterate** lacking the literacy necessary for coping with most jobs and many everyday situations.

ill-man·nered ▶*adj.* having bad manners; rude.

ill-na·tured ▶*adj.* (of a person) mean and irritable.

ill·ness /'ilnis/ ▶*n.* a disease or period of sickness affecting the body or mind: *a long illness | I've never missed a day's work through illness.*

il·log·i·cal /i(l)'läjikəl/ ▶*adj.* lacking sense or clear, sound reasoning. —**il·log·i·cal·i·ty** /i(l),läji'kalitē/ *n.* (*pl.* **-ties**) —**il·log·i·cal·ly** /-ik(ə)lē/ *adv.*

ill-starred ▶*adj.* destined to fail or have many difficulties; unlucky: *an ill-starred expedition.*

ill-treat ▶*v.* [*tr.*] act cruelly toward (a person or animal). —**ill-treat·ment** *n.*

il·lu·mi·nance /i'lōōmənəns/ ▶*n. Physics* the amount of luminous flux per unit area.

il·lu·mi·nate /i'lōōmə,nāt/ ▶*v.* [*tr.*] light up: *a flash of lightning illuminated the house | fig. his face was illuminated by a smile.* ■ decorate (a building or structure) with lights for a special occasion. ■ [often as *adj.*] (**illuminated**) decorate (a page or initial letter in a manuscript) with gold, silver, or colored designs. ■ [usu. as *adj.*] (**illuminating**) *fig.* help to clarify or explain (a subject or matter): *a most illuminating discussion.* —**il·lu·mi·nat·ing·ly** *adv.* —**il·lu·mi·na·tion** /i,lōōmə'nāSHən/ *n.* —**il·lu·mi·na·tive** /-,nātiv; -nətiv/ *adj.* —**il·lu·mi·na·tor** /-,nātər/ *n.*

il·lu·sion /i'lōōZHən/ ▶*n.* a false idea or belief: *he had no illusions about his chances.* ■ a deceptive appearance or impression: *the illusion of family togetherness | tension between illusion and reality.* ■ a thing that is or is likely to be wrongly perceived or interpreted by the senses: *an optical illusion.* —**il·lu·sion·al** /-ZHənl/ *adj.*
▶ □ **be under the illusion that** believe mistakenly that: *the world is under the illusion that the painting still hangs in the Winter Palace.* □ **be under no illusion** (or **illusions**) be fully aware of the true state of affairs.

il·lu·sion·ist /i'lōōZHənist/ ▶*n.* a person who performs tricks that deceive the eye; a magician. —**il·lu·sion·ism** *n.*

il·lu·so·ry /i'lōōsərē; -zərē/ ▶*adj.* based on illusion; not real: *she knew the safety of her room was illusory.* —**il·lu·so·ri·ness** *n.*

il·lus·trate /'ilə,strāt/ ▶*v.* [*tr.*] provide (a book, newspaper, etc.) with pictures: *the guide is illustrated with full-color photographs.* ■ explain or make (something) clear by using examples, charts, pictures, etc.: *the results are illustrated in Figure 7.* ■ serve as an example of: *a collection of pieces that illustrate Bach's techniques.* ▷early 16th cent. (in the sense 'illuminate, shed light on'): from Latin *illustrat-* 'lit up,' from the verb *illustrare*, from *in-* 'upon' + *lustrare* 'illuminate.'

il·lus·tra·tion /,ilə'strāSHən/ ▶*n.* a picture illustrating a book, newspaper, etc.: *an illustration of a yacht.* ■ an example serving to clarify or prove something: *this accident is a graphic illustration of the disaster that's waiting to happen.* ■ the action or fact of illustrating something, either pictorially or by exemplification. —**il·lus·tra·tion·al** /-SHənl/ *adj.*

il·lus·tra·tive /i'ləstrətiv; 'ilə,strātiv/ ▶*adj.* serving as an example or explanation: *timetable for illustrative purposes only.* —**il·lus·tra·tive·ly** *adv.*

il·lus·tra·tor /'ilə,strātər/ ▶*n.* a person who draws or creates pictures for magazines, books, advertising, etc.

il·lus·tri·ous /i'ləstrēəs/ ▶*adj.* well known, respected, and admired for past achievements: *his illustrious predecessor | an illustrious career.* —**il·lus·tri·ous·ly** *adv.* —**il·lus·tri·ous·ness** *n.*

ill will ▶*n.* animosity or bitterness: *he didn't bear his ex-wife any ill will.*

IM ▶*v.* (**IM's, IM'd, IM'ing**) [*tr.*] send a message to (someone) by using an instant messaging system:.

I'm /īm/ ▶*contr.* of I am: *I'm a busy woman.*

im·age /'imij/ ▶*n.* a representation of the external form of a person or thing in sculpture, painting, etc. ■ a visible impression obtained by a camera, telescope, microscope, or other device, or displayed on a video screen. ■ an optical appearance or counterpart produced by light or other radiation from an object reflected in a mirror or refracted through a lens. ■ *Math.* a point or set formed by mapping from another point or set. ■ a mental representation or idea: *the public's image of actors' lives.* ■ a simile or metaphor: *he uses the image of a hole to describe emotional emptiness.* ■ the general impression that a person, organization, or product presents to the public: *she strives to project an image of youth.* ■ a person or thing that closely resembles another: *he's the image of his father.*
▶*v.* [*tr.*] (usu. **be imaged**) make a visual representation of (something) by scanning it with a detector or electromagnetic beam: *every point on the Earth's surface was imaged by the satellite | [as n.]* (**imaging**) *medical imaging.* —**im·age·less** *adj.*

im·age·ry /'imij(ə)rē/ ▶*n.* visually descriptive or figurative language, esp. in a literary work. ■ visual images collectively: *computer-generated imagery.* ■ visual symbolism: *the film's religious imagery.*

im·ag·in·a·ble /i'maj(ə)nəbəl/ ▶*adj.* possible to be thought of or believed: *the most spectacular views imaginable.* —**i·mag·i·na·bly** /-blē/ *adv.*

im·ag·i·nar·y /i'majə,nerē/ ▶*adj.* **1** existing only in the imagination: *Chris had imaginary conversations with her.* **2** *Math.* (of a number or quantity) expressed in terms of the square root of a negative number (usually the square root of −1, represented by *i* or *j*). See also **COMPLEX**. —**im·ag·i·nar·i·ly** /i,majə'ne(ə)rəlē/ *adv.*

im·ag·i·na·tion /i,majə'nāSHən/ ▶*n.* the faculty or action of forming new

---

ideas, or images or concepts of external objects not present to the senses: *a vivid imagination.* ■ the ability of the mind to be creative or resourceful: *the chance to use your imagination.* ■ the part of the mind that imagines things: *a girl who existed only in my imagination.*

im·ag·i·na·tive /i'maj(ə)nətiv/ ▶*adj.* having or showing creativity or inventiveness: *making imaginative use of computer software | an imaginative architect.* —**i·mag·i·na·tive·ly** *adv.* —**i·mag·i·na·tive·ness** *n.*

im·ag·ine /i'majən/ ▶*v.* [*tr.*] **1** form a mental image or concept of: *imagine a road trip from Philadelphia to Chicago | I couldn't imagine what she expected to tell them.* ■ [often as *adj.*] (**imagined**) believe (something unreal or untrue) to exist or be so: *they suffered from ill health, real or imagined, throughout their lives.* **2** suppose or assume: *after Ned died, everyone imagined that Mabel would move away.* ■ [as *interj.*] just suppose: *imagine! to win the championship!* —**i·mag·in·er** *n.*

im·ag·in·ings /i'majəninGZ/ ▶*pl. n.* thoughts or fantasies: *this was quite beyond his worst imaginings.*

i·ma·go /i'māgō; i'mä-/ ▶*n.* (*pl.* **i·ma·gos**, **i·ma·goes** or **i·ma·gi·nes** /i'māgə,nēz/) **1** *Entomol.* the final and fully developed adult stage of an insect, typically winged. **2** *Psychoanalysis* an unconscious, idealized mental image of someone, esp. a parent, that influences a person's behavior.

i·mam /i'mäm/ ▶*n.* the person who leads prayers in a mosque. ■ (**Imam**) a title of various Muslim leaders, esp. of one succeeding Muhammad as leader of Shiite Islam: *Imam Khomeini.* —**i·mam·ate** /-,māt/ *n.*

im·bal·ance /im'baləns/ ▶*n.* lack of proportion or relation between corresponding things: *the condition is caused by a hormonal imbalance.*

im·be·cile /'imbəsəl; -,sil/ ▶*n. inf.* a stupid person.
▶*adj.* stupid; idiotic: *imbecilic remarks.* —**im·be·cil·ic** /,imbə'silik/ *adj.* —**im·be·cil·i·ty** /,imbə'silitē/ *n.* (*pl.* **-ties**).

im·bibe /im'bīb/ ▶*v.* [*tr.*] *formal, often humorous* drink (alcohol): *they were imbibing far too many pitchers of beer | [intr.] having imbibed too freely, he fell over.* —**im·bib·er** *n.*

im·bro·glio /im'brōlyō/ ▶*n.* (*pl.* **-glios**) an extremely confused, complicated, or embarrassing situation.

im·bue /im'byōō/ ▶*v.* (**-bues**, **-bued**, **-bu·ing**) [*tr.*] inspire or permeate with a feeling or quality.

IMF ▶*abbr.* International Monetary Fund.

im·i·tate /'imi,tāt/ ▶*v.* (often **be imitated**) take or follow as a model: *his style was imitated by many other writers.* ■ copy (a person's speech or mannerisms), esp. for comic effect: *she imitated my laugh.* ■ copy or simulate: *synthetic fabrics can now imitate everything from silk to rubber.* —**im·i·ta·ble** /'imitəbəl/ *adj.* —**im·i·ta·tor** /-,tātər/ *n.*

im·i·ta·tion /,imi'tāSHən/ ▶*n.* a thing intended to simulate or copy something else: [as *adj.*] *an imitation diamond.* ■ the action of using someone or something as a model: *a child learns to speak by imitation.* ■ an act of imitating a person's speech or mannerisms, esp. for comic effect: *an atrocious imitation of an English accent.* ■ *Mus.* the repetition of a phrase or melody in another part or voice, usually at a different pitch.

im·i·ta·tive /'imi,tātiv/ ▶*adj.* **1** copying or following a model or example. ■ following a model or example without any attempt at originality. **2** (of a word) reproducing a natural sound (e.g., *fizz*) or pronounced in a way that is thought to correspond to the appearance or character of the object or action described (e.g., *blob*). —**im·i·ta·tive·ly** *adv.* —**im·i·ta·tive·ness** *n.*

im·mac·u·late /i'makyəlit/ ▶*adj.* (esp. of a person or their clothes) perfectly clean, neat, or tidy: *an immaculate white suit.* ■ free from flaws or mistakes; perfect: *an immaculate safety record.* ■ *Theol.* (in the Roman Catholic Church) free from sin. —**im·mac·u·la·cy** /-ləsē/ *n.* —**im·mac·u·late·ly** *adv.* —**im·mac·u·late·ness** *n.*

Im·mac·u·late Con·cep·tion ▶*n.* the doctrine that God preserved the Virgin Mary from the taint of original sin from the moment she was conceived. ■ the feast commemorating the Immaculate Conception on December 8.

im·ma·nent /'imənənt/ ▶*adj.* existing or operating within; inherent. ■ (of God) permanently pervading and sustaining the universe. Often contrasted with TRANSCENDENT. —**im·ma·nence** *n.* —**im·ma·nen·cy** *n.* —**im·ma·nent·ism** /-,tizəm/ *n.* —**im·ma·nent·ist** /-tist/ *n.*

im·ma·te·ri·al /,imə'ti(ə)rēəl/ ▶*adj.* **1** unimportant under the circumstances; irrelevant. **2** *Philos.* spiritual, rather than physical. —**im·ma·te·ri·al·i·ty** /-,ti(ə)rē'alitē/ *n.* —**im·ma·te·ri·al·ly** *adv.*

im·ma·ture /,imə'CHoŏr; -'t(y)oŏr/ ▶*adj.* not fully developed: *many of the fish caught are immature | immature fruit.* ■ (of a person or their behavior) having or showing emotional or intellectual development appropriate to someone younger: *his immature sense of humor.* —**im·ma·ture·ly** *adv.* —**im·ma·tu·ri·ty** /-itē/ *n.*

im·meas·ur·a·ble /i'mezHərəbəl/ ▶*adj.* too large, extensive, or extreme to measure: *immeasurable suffering.* —**im·meas·ur·a·bil·i·ty** /-,mezHərə'bilitē/ *n.* —**im·meas·ur·a·bly** *adv.*

im·me·di·ate /i'mēdē-it/ ▶*adj.* **1** occurring or done at once; instant: *the authorities took no immediate action | the book's success was immediate.* ■ relating to or existing at the present time: *an immediate concern.* **2** nearest in time, relationship, or rank: *her immediate family.* ■ nearest or next to in space: *roads in the immediate vicinity of the port.* ■ (of a relation or action) without an intervening medium or agency; direct: *the immediate cause of death.* —**im·me·di·a·cy** /-dēəsē/ *n.* —**im·me·di·ate·ness** *n.*

im·me·di·ate·ly /i'mēdē-itlē/ ▶*adv.* **1** at once; instantly: *I called immediately for an ambulance.* **2** without any intervening time or space: *she was sitting immediately behind me.* ■ in direct or very close relation: *they would be the states most immediately affected by any such action.*

im·me·mo·ri·al /,i(m)mə'môrēəl/ ▶*adj.* originating in the distant past; very old: *an immemorial custom.* —**im·me·mo·ri·al·ly** *adv.*

im·mense /i'mens/ ▶*adj.* extremely large or great, esp. in scale or degree: *the cost has been immense | an immense building.* —**im·mense·ly** *adv.* —**im·men·si·ty** /-sitē/ *n.*

im·merse /i'mərs/ ▶*v.* **1** dip or submerge in a liquid. ■ baptize (someone) by immersion in water. **2** (**immerse oneself** or **be immersed**) *fig.* involve oneself deeply in a particular activity or interest: *she immersed herself in her work.* ▷early 17th cent.: from Latin *immers-* 'dipped into,' from the verb *immergere*, from *in-* 'in' + *mergere* 'to dip.'

im·mer·sion /i'mərzHən; -sHən/ ▶*n.* the action of immersing someone or something in a liquid. ■ deep mental involvement: *his total immersion in Marxism.* ■ a method of teaching a foreign language by the exclusive use of that language, usually at a special school. ■ baptism by immersing a person bodily (but not necessarily completely) in water.

im·mi·grant /'imigrənt/ ▶*n.* a person who comes to live permanently in a foreign country. ■ *Biol.* an animal or plant living or growing in a region to which it has migrated.

im·mi·grate /'imi,grāt/ ▶*v.* [*intr.*] come to live permanently in a foreign country: *the Mennonites immigrated to western Canada in the 1870s.* —**im·mi·gra·tion** /,imi'grāSHən/ *n.*

im·mi·nent /'imənənt/ ▶*adj.* **1** about to happen: *imminent danger.* **2** *archaic* overhanging. —**im·mi·nence** *n.* —**im·mi·nent·ly** *adv.*

im·mis·ci·ble /i(m)'misəbəl/ ▶*adj.* (of liquids) not forming a homogeneous liquid when mixed together: *water is immiscible with suntan oil.* —**im·mis·ci·bil·i·ty** /-,misə'bilitē/ *n.* —**im·mis·ci·bly** /-blē/ *adv.*

im·mo·bile /i(m)'mōbəl; -bēl; -bīl/ ▶*adj.* not moving; motionless: *she sat immobile for a long time.* ■ incapable of moving or being moved: *an immobile work force.* —**im·mo·bil·i·ty** /,i(m)mō'bilitē/ *n.*

im·mo·bi·lize /i(m)'mōbə,līz/ ▶*v.* [*tr.*] prevent (something or someone) from moving or operating as normal: *I want you to immobilize their vehicle | fear had immobilized her.* ■ restrict the movements of (a limb or patient) to allow healing. —**im·mo·bi·li·za·tion** /-,mōbəli'zāSHən/ *n.*

im·mod·er·ate /i(m)'mädərit/ ▶*adj.* not sensible or restrained; excessive. —**im·mod·er·ate·ly** *adv.* —**im·mod·er·a·tion** /-,mädə'rāSHən/ *n.*

im·mod·est /i(m)'mädist/ ▶*adj.* lacking humility or decency. —**im·mod·est·ly** *adv.* —**im·mod·es·ty** *n.*

im·mo·late /'imə,lāt/ ▶*v.* [*tr.*] kill or offer as a sacrifice, esp. by burning. —**im·mo·la·tion** /,imə'lāSHən/ *n.* —**im·mo·la·tor** /-,lātər/ *n.*

im·mor·al /i(m)'môrəl; -'märəl/ ▶*adj.* not conforming to accepted standards of morality: *an immoral and unwinnable war.* —**im·mo·ral·i·ty** /,imə'ralitē; ,imô-/ *n.* (*pl.* **-ties**) —**im·mor·al·ly** *adv.*

im·mor·tal /i(m)'môrtl/ ▶*adj.* living forever; never dying or decaying. ■ deserving to be remembered forever.
▶*n.* an immortal being, esp. a god of ancient Greece or Rome. ■ a person of enduring fame. —**im·mor·tal·i·ty** /,i(m),môr'talitē/ *n.* —**im·mor·tal·ly** *adv.* —**im·mor·tal·ize** *v.*

im·mov·a·ble /i(m)'mōōvəbəl/ ▶*adj.* not able to be moved. ■ (of a person) not yielding to argument or pressure. ■ *Law* (of property) consisting of land, buildings, or other permanent items.
▶*n.* (**immovables**) *Law* immovable property. —**im·mov·a·bil·i·ty** /-,mōōvə'bilitē/ *n.* —**im·mov·a·bly** /-blē/ *adv.*

im·mune /i'myōōn/ ▶*adj.* resistant to a particular infection or toxin owing to the presence of specific antibodies or sensitized white blood cells: *they were naturally immune to hepatitis B.* ■ protected or exempt, esp. from an obligation or the effects of something: *they are immune from legal action.* ■ not affected or influenced by something. ■ *Biol.* of or relating to immunity: *the body's immune system.*

im·mune re·sponse ▶*n.* the reaction of the cells and fluids of the body to the presence of a substance that is not recognized as a constituent of the body itself.

im·mu·ni·ty /i'myōōnitē/ ▶n. (pl. **-ties**) the ability of an organism to resist a particular infection or toxin by the action of specific antibodies or sensitized white blood cells. ■ protection or exemption from something, esp. an obligation or penalty: *immunity from prosecution.* ■ *Law* officially granted exemption from legal proceedings. ■ (**immunity to**) lack of susceptibility, esp. to something unwelcome or harmful: *exercises designed to build an immunity to fatigue.*

im·mu·nize /'imyə,nīz/ ▶v. [tr.] make (a person or animal) immune to infection, typically by inoculation: *the vaccine immunizes children against measles.* —**im·mu·ni·za·tion** /,imyəni'zāSHən/ n. —**im·mu·niz·er** n.

im·mu·no·de·fi·cien·cy /,imyənōdə'fiSHənsē; i,myōō-/ ▶n. failure of the immune system to protect the body adequately from infection, due to the absence or insufficiency of some component process or substance.

im·mu·no·glob·u·lin /,imyənō'gläbyələn; i,myōō-/ ▶n. *Biochem.* any of a class of proteins present in the serum and cells of the immune system, that function as antibodies.

im·mu·nol·o·gy /,imyə'näləjē/ ▶n. the branch of medicine and biology concerned with immunity. —**im·mu·no·log·ic** /,imyənə'läjik; i,myōō-/ adj. —**im·mu·no·log·i·cal** /,imyənōdə'fiSHənsē; i,myōō-/ adj. —**im·mu·no·log·i·cal·ly** /,imyənə'läjik(ə)lē; i,myōō-/ adv. —**im·mu·nol·o·gist** /-jist/ n.

im·mu·no·sup·pres·sion /,imyənōsə'preSHən; i,myōō-/ ▶n. *Med.* the partial or complete suppression of the immune response of an individual. It is induced to help the survival of an organ after a transplant operation. —**im·mu·no·sup·pres·sant** /-sə'presənt/ n. —**im·mu·no·sup·pressed** /-sə'prest/ adj.

im·mu·no·ther·a·py /,imyənō'THerəpē/ i,myōō-/ ▶n. *Med.* the prevention or treatment of disease with substances that stimulate the immune response.

im·mu·ta·ble /i'myōōtəbəl/ ▶adj. unchanging over time or unable to be changed: *an immutable fact.* —**im·mu·ta·bil·i·ty** /i,myōōtə'bilitē/ n. —**im·mu·ta·bly** /-blē/ adv.

imp /imp/ ▶n. a mischievous child. ■ a small, mischievous devil or sprite.

im·pact ▶n. /'im,pakt/ the action of one object coming forcibly into contact with another: *there was the sound of a third impact | bullets that expand on impact.* ■ the effect or influence of one person, thing, or action, on another: *measures that have had a significant impact on unemployment.*
▶v. /im'pakt/ [intr.] come into forcible contact with another object: *the shell impacted twenty yards away.* ■ [tr.] come into forcible contact with: *an asteroid impacted the earth some 60 million years ago.* ■ have a strong effect: *the move is not expected to impact the company's employees.*

im·pair /im'pe(ə)r/ ▶v. [tr.] weaken or damage (esp. a human faculty or function): *drug use that impairs job performance.* —**im·pair·ment** n.

im·pa·la /im'palə; -'pälə/ ▶n. (pl. same) an antelope (*Aepyceros melampus*) often seen in large herds in open woodland in southern and East Africa.

im·pale /im'pāl/ ▶v. [tr.] pierce or transfix with a sharp instrument: *a head impaled on a pike.* —**im·pale·ment** n. —**im·pal·er** n.

im·pal·pa·ble /im'palpəbəl/ ▶adj. unable to be felt by touch. ■ not easily comprehended. —**im·pal·pa·bil·i·ty** /-,palpə'bilitē/ n. —**im·pal·pa·bly** /-blē/ adv.

im·pan·el /im'panl/ ▶v. (-pan·eled, -pan·el·ing; *Brit.* -pan·elled, -pan·el·ling) [tr.] enlist or enroll (a jury). ■ enroll (someone) on to a jury. —**im·pan·el·ment** n.

im·part /im'pärt/ ▶v. [tr.] make (information) known; communicate: *they try to impart strong morals to their students.* ■ bestow (a quality): *it imparts a high gloss to wood.* —**im·par·ta·tion** /,impär'tāSHən/ n.

im·par·tial /im'pärSHəl/ ▶adj. treating all rivals or disputants equally; fair and just: *independent and impartial advice.* —**im·par·ti·al·i·ty** /-,pärSHē'alitē/ n. —**im·par·tial·ly** adv.

im·pass·a·ble /im'pasəbəl/ ▶adj. impossible to travel along or over: *the narrow channels are impassable to cruise ships.* —**im·pass·a·bil·i·ty** /-,pasə'bilitē/ n. —**im·pass·a·ble·ness** n. —**im·pass·a·bly** /-blē/ adv.

im·passe /'im,pas; im'pas/ ▶n. a situation in which no progress is possible, esp. because of disagreement; a deadlock.

im·pas·sioned /im'paSHənd/ ▶adj. filled with or showing great emotion: *she made an impassioned plea for help.*

im·pas·sive /im'pasiv/ ▶adj. not feeling or showing emotion. —**im·pas·sive·ly** adv. —**im·pas·sive·ness** n. —**im·pas·siv·i·ty** /,impə'sivitē/ n.

im·pas·to /im'pastō; -'pästō/ ▶n. *Art* the process or technique of laying on paint or pigment thickly so that it stands out from a surface. ■ paint applied thickly.

im·pa·tiens /im'pāSHənz/ ▶n. an East African plant (genus *Impatiens*) of the balsam family, with abundant red, pink, or white flowers, often grown as a houseplant or bedding plant.

im·pa·tient /im'pāSHənt/ ▶adj. **1** having or showing a tendency to be quickly irritated or provoked: *an impatient driver | she was impatient with her children.* ■ (**impatient of**) intolerant of: *a man impatient of bureaucracy.* **2** restlessly eager: *they are impatient for change | he was impatient to be on his way.* —**im·pa·tience** n. —**im·pa·tient·ly** adv.

im·peach /im'pēCH/ ▶v. [tr.] call into question the integrity or validity of (a practice): *there is no basis to his motion to impeach the verdict.* ■ charge (the holder of a public office) with misconduct: *the governor served only one year before being impeached and convicted for fiscal fraud.* —**im·peach·a·ble** adj. —**im·peach·ment** n.

im·pec·ca·ble /im'pekəbəl/ ▶adj. (of behavior, performance, or appearance) in accordance with the highest standards of propriety; faultless: *a man of impeccable character.* —**im·pec·ca·bil·i·ty** /-,pekə'bilitē/ n. —**im·pec·ca·bly** /-blē/ adv.

im·pe·cu·ni·ous /,impə'kyōōnēəs/ ▶adj. having little or no money. —**im·pe·cu·ni·os·i·ty** /-,kyōōnē'äsitē/ n. —**im·pe·cu·ni·ous·ness** n.

im·ped·ance /im'pēdns/ ▶n. the effective resistance of an electric circuit or component to alternating current, arising from the combined effects of ohmic resistance and reactance.

im·pede /im'pēd/ ▶v. [tr.] delay or prevent (someone or something) by obstructing them; hinder: *swelling that can impede breathing.*

im·ped·i·ment /im'pedəmənt/ ▶n. a hindrance or obstruction in doing something: *a serious impediment to scientific progress.* ■ (also **speech impediment**) a defect in a person's speech, such as a lisp or stammer. —**im·ped·i·men·tal** /-,pedə'mentl/ adj.

im·pel /im'pel/ ▶v. (-pelled, -pel·ling) [tr.] drive, force, or urge (someone) to do something: *financial difficulties impelled him to desperate measures.* ■ drive forward; propel. ▷late Middle English (in the sense 'propel'): from Latin *impellere*, from in- 'toward' + *pellere* 'to drive.' —**im·pel·ler** n.

im·pend /im'pend/ ▶v. [intr.] (usu. as adj.) (**impending**) be about to happen: *my impending departure.* ■ (of something bad) loom.

im·pen·e·tra·ble /im'penətrəbəl/ ▶adj. **1** impossible to pass through or enter: *a dark, impenetrable forest.* ■ (of a club or group) secretive and exclusive: *an impenetrable clique.* **2** impossible to understand: *impenetrable interviews with French intellectuals.* —**im·pen·e·tra·bil·i·ty** /-,penətrə'bilitē/ n. —**im·pen·e·tra·bly** /-blē/ adv.

im·pen·i·tent /im'penitnt/ ▶adj. not feeling shame or regret about one's actions or attitudes. —**im·pen·i·tence** n. —**im·pen·i·tent·ly** adv.

im·per·a·tive /im'perətiv/ ▶adj. **1** of vital importance; crucial: *immediate action was imperative | it is imperative that standards be maintained.* **2** giving an authoritative command; peremptory. ■ *Gram.* denoting the mood of a verb that expresses a command or exhortation, as in *come here!*
▶n. **1** an essential or urgent thing: *an economic imperative.* ■ a factor or influence making something necessary. ■ a thing felt as an obligation: *moral imperative.* **2** *Gram.* a verb or phrase in the imperative mood. ■ (**the imperative**) the imperative mood. —**im·per·a·ti·val** /-,perə'tīvəl/ adj. —**im·per·a·tive·ly** adv. —**im·per·a·tive·ness** n.

im·per·cep·ti·ble /,impər'septəbəl/ ▶adj. impossible to perceive. —**im·per·cep·ti·bil·i·ty** /-,septə'bilitē/ n. —**im·per·cep·ti·bly** /-blē/ adv.

im·per·fect /im'pərfikt/ ▶adj. **1** not perfect; faulty: *an imperfect grasp of English.* ■ not fully formed or done; incomplete: *imperfect census records.* **2** *Gram.* (of a tense) denoting a past action in progress but not completed at the time in question. **3** *Mus.* (of a cadence) ending on the dominant chord. **4** *Law* (of a gift, title, etc.) transferred without all the necessary conditions or requirements being met.
▶n. (**the imperfect**) *Gram.* the imperfect tense. —**im·per·fect·ly** adv.

im·per·fec·tion /,impər'fekSHən/ ▶n. a fault, blemish, or undesirable feature: *the imperfections in our political system.* ■ the state of being faulty or incomplete: *he accepted me in all my imperfection.*

im·pe·ri·al /im'pi(ə)rēəl/ ▶adj. **1** of or relating to an empire: *Britain's imperial era.* ■ of or relating to an emperor: *the imperial family.* ■ majestic; magnificent. ■ imperious or domineering. **2** of, relating to, or denoting the system of nonmetric weights and measures (the ounce, pound, stone, inch, foot, yard, mile, acre, pint, gallon, etc.) formerly used for all measures in the UK, and still used for some.
▶n. a small pointed beard growing below the lower lip (associated with Napoleon III of France). —**im·pe·ri·al·ly** adv.

im·pe·ri·al·ism /im'pi(ə)rēə,lizəm/ ▶n. a policy of extending a country's power and influence through diplomacy or military force. ■ *chiefly hist.* rule by an emperor. —**im·pe·ri·al·is·tic** /-,pi(ə)rēə'listik/ adj. —**im·pe·ri·al·is·ti·cal·ly** adv.

---

im·pe·ri·al·ist /im'pi(ə)rēəlist/ ▶adj. of, relating to, supporting, or practicing imperialism: an imperialist regime.
▶n. chiefly derog. a person who supports or practices imperialism.

im·per·il /im'perəl/ ▶v. (-per·iled, -per·il·ing) [tr.] put at risk of being harmed, injured, or destroyed. —**im·per·il·ment** n.

im·pe·ri·ous /im'pi(ə)rēəs/ ▶adj. assuming power or authority without justification; arrogant and domineering: his imperious demands. —**im·pe·ri·ous·ly** adv. —**im·pe·ri·ous·ness** n.

im·per·ish·a·ble /im'perishəbəl/ ▶adj. enduring forever. —**im·per·ish·a·bil·i·ty** /-,perishə'bilitē/ n. —**im·per·ish·a·ble·ness** n. —**im·per·ish·a·bly** adv.

im·per·ma·nent /im'pərmənənt/ ▶adj. not permanent. —**im·per·ma·nence** n. —**im·per·ma·nen·cy** n. —**im·per·ma·nent·ly** adv.

im·per·me·a·ble /im'pərmēəbəl/ ▶adj. not allowing fluid to pass through: an impermeable membrane. ▪ not liable to be affected by pain or distress; insusceptible or imperturbable. —**im·per·me·a·bil·i·ty** /-,pərmēə'bilitē/ n.

im·per·mis·si·ble /,impər'misəbəl/ ▶adj. too bad to be allowed: impermissible behavior. —**im·per·mis·si·bil·i·ty** /-,misə'bilitē/ n.

im·per·son·al /im'pərsənl/ ▶adj. **1** not influenced by, showing, or involving personal feelings: the law is impersonal. ▪ (of a place or organization) large, featureless, and anonymous: impersonal institutions. ▪ not betraying any personal information about the user or subject: the room was bare, cramped, and impersonal. **2** not existing as a person; having no personality: an impersonal God. **3** Gram. (of a verb) used only with a formal subject (in English usually it) and expressing an action not attributable to a definite subject (as in it is snowing). —**im·per·son·al·i·ty** /-,pərsə'nalitē/ n. —**im·per·son·al·ly** adv.

im·per·son·ate /im'pərsə,nāt/ ▶v. [tr.] pretend to be (another person) as entertainment or in order to deceive someone. —**im·per·son·a·tion** /-,pərsə'nāshən/ n. —**im·per·son·a·tor** /-,nātər/ n.

im·per·ti·nent /im'pərtn-ənt/ ▶adj. not showing proper respect; rude: an impertinent question. —**im·per·ti·nence** n. —**im·per·ti·nent·ly** adv.

im·per·turb·a·ble /,impər'tərbəbəl/ ▶adj. unable to be upset or excited; calm. —**im·per·turb·a·bil·i·ty** /-tərbə'bilitē/ n. —**im·per·turb·a·bly** adv.

im·per·vi·ous /im'pərvēəs/ ▶adj. not allowing fluid to pass through: an impervious layer of clay. ▪ (**impervious to**) unable to be affected by: he seemed impervious to the heat. —**im·per·vi·ous·ly** adv. —**im·per·vi·ous·ness** n.

im·pet·u·ous /im'pechōōəs/ ▶adj. acting or done quickly and without thought or care. —**im·pet·u·os·i·ty** /-,pechōō'äsitē/ n. —**im·pet·u·ous·ly** adv. —**im·pet·u·ous·ness** n.

im·pe·tus /'impitəs/ ▶n. the force or energy with which a body moves. ▪ the force that makes something happen or happen more quickly: an impetus for change.

im·pi·e·ty /im'pī-itē/ ▶n. (pl. -ties) lack of piety or reverence, esp. for a god.

im·pinge /im'pinj/ ▶v. (-ping·ing) [intr.] have an effect or impact, esp. a negative one: she hoped that the tragedy would **impinge** as little as possible on Constance's life. ▪ advance over an area belonging to someone or something else; encroach. —**im·pinge·ment** n. —**im·ping·er** n.

im·pi·ous /'impēəs; im'pī-/ ▶adj. not showing respect or reverence, esp. for a god. —**im·pi·ous·ly** adv. —**im·pi·ous·ness** n.

imp·ish /'impish/ ▶adj. inclined to do slightly naughty things for fun; mischievous. —**imp·ish·ly** adv. —**imp·ish·ness** n.

im·plac·a·ble /im'plakəbəl/ ▶adj. unable to be placated: an implacable enemy. ▪ relentless; unstoppable. —**im·plac·a·bil·i·ty** /-,plakə'bilitē/ n. —**im·plac·a·bly** /-blē/ adv.

im·plant ▶v. /im'plant/ [tr.] insert or fix (tissue or an artificial object) in a person's body, esp. by surgery: electrodes had been **implanted** in his brain. ▪ [intr.] (of a fertilized egg) become attached to the wall of the uterus. ▪ fig. establish or fix (an idea) in a person's mind. —**im·plan·ta·tion** /,implan'tāshən/ n.
▶n. /'im,plant/ a thing implanted in something else, esp. a piece of tissue, prosthetic device, or other object implanted in the body.

im·plant·a·ble /im'plantəbəl/ ▶adj. capable of or designed for being implanted in living tissue.

im·plau·si·ble /im'plôzəbəl/ ▶adj. (of an argument or statement) not seeming reasonable or probable; failing to convince. —**im·plau·si·bil·i·ty** /-,plôzə'bilitē/ n. —**im·plau·si·bly** /-blē/ adv.

im·ple·ment ▶n. /'impləmənt/ a tool, utensil, or other piece of equipment, esp. as used for a particular purpose: agricultural implements.
▶v. /-,ment/ [tr.] put (a decision, plan, agreement, etc.) into effect: the regulations implement a 1954 treaty. —**im·ple·men·ta·tion** /,impləmən-'tāshən/ n. —**im·ple·ment·er** (also **im·ple·men·tor** /-,mentər/) n.

im·pli·cate /'impli,kāt/ ▶v. [tr.] show (someone) to be involved in a crime: police claims implicated him in many more killings. ▪ (**be implicated in**) bear some of the responsibility for (an action or process, esp. a criminal or harmful one): he is heavily implicated in the bombing | a chemical implicated in ozone depletion. —**im·pli·ca·tive** /'impli,kātiv; im'plikətiv/ adj. —**im·pli·ca·tive·ly** adv.

im·pli·ca·tion /,impli'kāshən/ ▶n. **1** the conclusion that can be drawn from something, although it is not explicitly stated: the implication is that he's guilty. ▪ a likely consequence of something: a victory that had important political implications. **2** the action or state of being involved in something: our implication in the problems. —**im·pli·ca·tion·al** /-shənl/ adj.
▶ □ **by implication** by what is implied or suggested rather than by formal expression: he criticized her and, by implication, her country.

im·pli·ca·ture /'implikəchər/ ▶n. the action of implying a meaning beyond the literal sense of what is explicitly stated, e.g., saying the frame is nice and implying I don't like the picture in it. ▪ a meaning so implied.

im·plic·it /im'plisit/ ▶adj. **1** implied though not plainly expressed: implicit criticism. ▪ (**implicit in**) essentially or very closely connected with; always to be found in: the values implicit in democracy. **2** with no qualification or question; absolute: an implicit faith in God. **3** Math. (of a function) not expressed directly in terms of independent variables. —**im·plic·it·ly** adv. —**im·plic·it·ness** n.

im·plode /im'plōd/ ▶v. collapse or cause to collapse violently inward: [intr.] the windows on both sides of the room had imploded. ▪ [intr.] fig. suffer sudden economic or political collapse. ▪ Phonet. [tr.] utter or pronounce (a consonant) with a sharp intake of air. —**im·plo·sion** /-zhən/ n. —**im·plo·sive** /-'plōsiv/ adj.

im·plore /im'plôr/ ▶v. beg someone earnestly or desperately to do something: [tr.] he implored her to change her mind | [with direct speech] "Please don't talk that way," Ellen implored. ▪ [tr.] archaic beg earnestly for: I implore mercy. —**im·plor·ing·ly** adv.

im·ply /im'plī/ ▶v. (-plies, -plied) [tr.] strongly suggest the truth or existence of (something not expressly stated): the report implies that two million jobs might be lost. ▪ (of a fact or occurrence) suggest (something) as a logical consequence: the forecasted traffic increase implied more roads and more air pollution. ▷late Middle English: from Old French emplier, from Latin implicare, from in- 'in' + plicare 'to fold.' The original sense was 'entwine, entangle'; in the 16th and 17th centuries the word also meant 'employ.' —**im·plied·ly** /-'plī-idlē/ adv.

im·po·lite /,impə'līt/ ▶adj. not having or showing good manners; rude: it would have been impolite to refuse. —**im·po·lite·ly** adv. —**im·po·lite·ness** n.

im·pol·i·tic /im'päli,tik/ ▶adj. failing to possess or display prudence; unwise. —**im·pol·i·tic·ly** adv.

im·pon·der·a·ble /im'pändərəbəl/ ▶n. a factor that is difficult or impossible to estimate or assess.
▶adj. difficult or impossible to estimate, assess, or answer: an imponderable problem of metaphysics. —**im·pon·der·a·bil·i·ty** /-,pändərə'bilitē/ n. —**im·pon·der·a·bly** /-blē/ adv.

im·port ▶v. /im'pôrt/ [tr.] bring (goods or services) into a country from abroad for sale: Japan's reluctance to import more cars. ▪ introduce (an idea) from a different place or context: new beliefs were often imported by sailors. ▪ Comput. transfer (data) into a file or document.
▶n. /'im,pôrt/ **1** (usu. **imports**) a commodity, article, or service brought in from abroad for sale. ▪ (**imports**) sales of goods or services brought in from abroad, or the revenue from such sales: an overall rise in imports. ▪ the action or process of importing goods or services: the import of live cattle from Canada. **2** the meaning or significance of something, esp. when not directly stated: the import of her message is clear. ▪ great significance; importance: pronouncements of great import. —**im·port·a·ble** adj. —**im·port·er** n.

im·por·tant /im'pôrtnt/ ▶adj. of great significance or value; likely to have a profound effect on success, survival, or well-being: important habitats for wildlife | it is important to avoid debt | the speech had passion and, more important, compassion. ▪ (of a person) having high rank or status. ▪ (of an artist or artistic work) significantly original and influential. —**im·por·tance** n. —**im·por·tant·ly** adv.

im·por·tu·nate /im'pôrchənit/ ▶adj. persistent, esp. to the point of annoyance or intrusion: importunate creditors. —**im·por·tu·nate·ly** adv. —**im·por·tu·ni·ty** /,impôr't(y)ōōnitē/ n. (pl. -ties).

im·por·tune /,impôr't(y)ōōn; im'pôrchən/ ▶v. [tr.] ask (someone) pressingly and persistently to do or to do something.

im·pose /im'pōz/ ▶v. **1** [tr.] force (something unwelcome or unfamiliar) to be accepted or put in place: the decision was theirs and was not imposed on them by others. ▪ forcibly put (a restriction) in place: sanctions *imposed on South Africa.* ■ require (a duty, charge, or penalty) to be undertaken or paid. **2** take advantage of someone by demanding their attention or commitment: *I don't mean to impose on you.* ■ (**impose oneself**) exert control over something in a domineering way: *the director was unable to impose himself on the production.* **3** [*tr.*] *Printing* arrange (pages of type) so that they will be in the correct order after printing and folding. ▷late 15th cent. (in the sense 'impute'): from French *imposer*, from Latin *imponere* 'inflict, deceive' (from *in-* 'in, upon' + *ponere* 'put'), but influenced by *impositus* 'inflicted' and Old French *poser* 'to place.'

im·pos·ing /imˈpōziNG/ ▶*adj.* grand and impressive in appearance: *the Johnsons have built an imposing house up on Bert White Road.* —**im·pos·ing·ly** *adv.*

im·po·si·tion /ˌimpəˈziSHən/ ▶*n.* **1** the action or process of imposing something or of being imposed: *the imposition of martial law.* **2** a thing that is imposed, in particular: ■ an unfair or resented demand or burden. ■ a tax or duty. ■ an inappropriate addition to an artistic or other work. **3** *Printing* the imposing of pages of type. ■ a particular arrangement of imposed pages: *some samples of 16-page impositions.*

im·pos·si·ble /imˈpäsəbəl/ ▶*adj.* not able to occur, exist, or be done: *a seemingly impossible task* | *it was almost impossible to keep up with him.* ■ very difficult to deal with: *she was in an impossible situation.* ■ *inf.* (of a person) very unreasonable. —**im·pos·si·bil·i·ty** /im,päsəˈbilitē/ *n.* —**im·pos·si·bly** *adv.*

im·pos·tor /imˈpästər/ (also **im·post·er**) ▶*n.* a person who pretends to be someone else in order to deceive others, esp. for fraudulent gain.

im·po·tent /ˈimpətnt/ ▶*adj.* **1** unable to take effective action; helpless or powerless. **2** (of a man) abnormally unable to achieve a sexual erection. ■ (of a male animal) unable to copulate. —**im·po·tence** *n.* —**im·po·ten·cy** *n.* —**im·po·tent·ly** *adv.*

im·pound /imˈpound/ ▶*v.* [*tr.*] **1** seize and take legal custody of (something, esp. a vehicle, goods, or documents) because of an infringement of a law or regulation. **2** shut up (domestic animals) in a pound or enclosure. ■ (of a dam) hold back or confine (water). —**im·pound·a·ble** *adj.* —**im·pound·er** *n.* —**im·pound·ment** *n.*

im·pov·er·ish /imˈpäv(ə)riSH/ ▶*v.* [*tr.*] make (a person or area) poor: *they discourage investment and impoverish their people* | | [as *adj.*] (**impoverished**) *impoverished farmers.* ■ exhaust the strength, vitality, or natural fertility of: *the soil was impoverished by annual burning.* —**im·pov·er·ish·ment** *n.*

im·prac·ti·ca·ble /imˈpraktikəbəl/ ▶*adj.* (of a course of action) impossible in practice to do or carry out: *it was impracticable to widen the road here.* —**im·prac·ti·ca·bil·i·ty** /-,praktikəˈbilitē/ *n.* —**im·prac·ti·ca·bly** /-blē/ *adv.*

im·prac·ti·cal /imˈpraktikəl/ ▶*adj.* **1** (of an object or course of action) not adapted for use or action; not sensible or realistic: *impractical high heels* | *his impractical romanticism.* ■ (of a person) not skilled or interested in practical matters: *Paul was impractical and dreamy.* **2** impossible to do; impracticable. —**im·prac·ti·cal·i·ty** /-,prakti'kalitē/ *n.* —**im·prac·ti·cal·ly** /-ik(ə)lē/ *adv.*

im·pre·ca·tion /ˌimpriˈkāSHən/ ▶*n.* *formal* a spoken curse. —**im·pre·ca·to·ry** /ˈimprikəˌtôrē/ *adj.*

im·pre·cise /ˌimpriˈsīs/ ▶*adj.* lacking exactness and accuracy of expression or detail. —**im·pre·cise·ly** *adv.* —**im·pre·cise·ness** *n.* —**im·pre·ci·sion** /-ˈsiZHən/ *n.*

im·preg·na·ble /imˈpregnəbəl/ ▶*adj.* (of a fortified position) unable to be captured or broken into. —**im·preg·na·bil·i·ty** /-,pregnəˈbilitē/ *n.* —**im·preg·na·bly** /-blē/ *adv.*

im·preg·nate /imˈpregˌnāt/ ▶*v.* [*tr.*] **1** make (a woman or female animal) pregnant. ■ *Biol.* fertilize (a female reproductive cell or ovum). **2** (usu. **be impregnated with**) soak or saturate (something) with a substance: *wood that had been impregnated with preservative.* —**im·preg·na·tion** /ˌimpregˈnāSHən/ *n.*

im·pre·sa·ri·o /ˌimprəˈsärēˌō; -ˈse(ə)r-/ ▶*n.* (*pl.* **-ri·os**) a person who organizes and often finances concerts, plays, or operas. ■ *chiefly hist.* the manager of a musical, theatrical, or operatic company.

im·press¹ /imˈpres/ ▶*v.* [*tr.*] **1** make (someone) feel admiration and respect: *they immediately impressed the judges* | | [*intr.*] *he has to put on an act to impress.* **2** make a mark or design on (an object) using a stamp or seal; imprint. ■ apply (a mark) to something with pressure. ■ (**impress something on**) *fig.* fix an idea in (someone's mind): *nobody impressed on me the need to save.*
▶*n.* /ˈim,pres/ a mark made by a seal or stamp. —**im·press·i·ble** *adj.*

im·press² /imˈpres/ ▶*v.* [*tr.*] *hist.* force (someone) to serve in an army or navy. ■ commandeer (goods or equipment) for public service.

im·pres·sion /imˈpreSHən/ ▶*n.* **1** an idea, feeling, or opinion about something or someone, esp. one formed without conscious thought or on the basis of little evidence: *his first impressions of the college were very*

positive | *they give the impression that everything is fine.* ■ an effect produced on someone: *her courtesy and quick wit had made a good impression.* ■ a difference made by the action or presence of someone or something: *the floor was too dirty for the mop to make much impression.* **2** an imitation of a person or thing, esp. one done to entertain: *he did an impression of Frank Sinatra.* ■ a graphic or pictorial representation of someone or something: *the police have issued an artist's impression of the attacker.* **3** a mark impressed on a surface by something. ■ *Dentistry* a negative copy of the teeth or mouth made by pressing them into a soft substance. **4** the printing of a number of copies of a book, periodical, or picture for issue at one time. ■ a particular printed version of a book or other publication, esp. one reprinted from existing type, plates, or film with no or only minor alteration. Compare with EDITION. ■ a print taken from an engraving. **5** an instance of a pop-up or other Web advertisement being seen on computer users' monitors. —**im·pres·sion·al** /-SHənl/ *adj.*
▶ □ **under the impression that** believing, mistakenly or on the basis of little evidence, that something is the case: *he was under the impression that they had become friends.*

im·pres·sion·a·ble /imˈpreSH(ə)nəbəl/ ▶*adj.* easily influenced because of a lack of critical ability: *a girl of eighteen is highly impressionable.* —**im·pres·sion·a·bil·i·ty** /-,preSH(ə)nəˈbilitē/ *n.* —**im·pres·sion·a·bly** /-blē/ *adv.*

Im·pres·sion·ism /imˈpreSHəˌnizəm/ ▶*n.* a style or movement in painting originating in France in the 1860s, characterized by a concern with depicting the visual impression of the moment, esp. in terms of the shifting effect of light and color. ■ a literary or artistic style that seeks to capture a feeling or experience rather than to achieve accurate depiction. ■ *Mus.* a style of composition (associated esp. with Debussy) in which clarity of structure and theme is subordinate to harmonic effects, characteristically using the whole-tone scale. —**im·pres·sion·ist** *n. & adj.* —**im·pres·sion·is·tic** /im,preSHəˈnistik/ *adj.*

im·pres·sive /imˈpresiv/ ▶*adj.* evoking admiration through size, quality, or skill: grand, imposing, or awesome: *an impressive view of the mountains* | *impressive achievements.* —**im·pres·sive·ly** *adv.* —**im·pres·sive·ness** *n.*

im·pri·ma·tur /ˌimprəˈmätər; -ˈmātər/ ▶*n.* an official license by the Roman Catholic Church to print an ecclesiastical or religious book. ■ a person's acceptance or guarantee that something is of a good standard.

im·print ▶*v.* /imˈprint/ **1** [*tr.*] impress or stamp (a mark or outline) on a surface or body. ■ make an impression or mark on (something). ■ *fig.* fix (an idea) firmly in someone's mind. **2** [*intr.*] (**imprint on**) *Zool.* (of a young animal) come to recognize (another animal, person, or thing) as a parent or other object of habitual trust.
▶*n.* /ˈim,print/ **1** a mark made by pressing something on to a softer substance so that its outline is reproduced. ■ *fig.* a lasting impression or effect: *years in jail had left their imprint.* **2** a printer's or publisher's name, address, and other details in a book or other printed item. ■ a brand name under which books are published, typically the name of a former publishing house that is now part of a larger group.

im·pris·on /imˈprizən/ ▶*v.* [*tr.*] (usu. **be imprisoned**) put or keep in prison or a place like a prison. —**im·pris·on·ment** *n.*

im·prob·a·ble /imˈpräbəbəl/ ▶*adj.* not likely to be true or to happen: *a highly improbable story.* —**im·prob·a·bil·i·ty** /-,präbəˈbilitē/ *n.* (*pl.* **-ties**) —**im·prob·a·bly** /-blē/ *adv.*

im·promp·tu /imˈpräm(p)ˌt(y)o͞o/ ▶*adj. & adv.* done without being planned, organized, or rehearsed: [as *adj.*] *an impromptu press conference* | [as *adv.*] *he spoke impromptu.*
▶*n.* (*pl.* **-tus**) a short piece of instrumental music, esp. a solo, that is reminiscent of an improvisation.

im·prop·er /imˈpräpər/ ▶*adj.* not in accordance with accepted rules or standards, esp. of morality or honesty: *improper behavior in his business dealings.* ■ lacking in modesty or decency. —**im·prop·er·ly** *adv.*

im·prop·er frac·tion ▶*n.* a fraction in which the numerator is greater than the denominator, such as $^5/_4$.

im·pro·pri·e·ty /ˌimprəˈprī-itē/ ▶*n.* (*pl.* **-ties**) a failure to observe standards or show due honesty or modesty; improper language, behavior, or character.

im·prove /imˈpro͞ov/ ▶*v.* make or become better: [*tr.*] *efforts to improve relations between the two countries* | [as *adj.*] (**improved**) *improved road and rail links* | [*intr.*] *his condition improved.* ■ [*intr.*] (**improve on/upon**) achieve or produce something better than: *they are trying to improve on the tired old style.* ■ increase the value of (real property) by renovation, construction, landscaping, etc. ▷early 16th cent. (as *emprowe* or *improwe*): from Anglo-Norman French *emprower* (based on Old French *prou* 'profit,' ultimately from Latin *prodest* 'is of advantage'); *-owe* was changed to *-ove* under the influence of *prove*. The original sense was 'make a profit, increase the value of'; subsequently 'make greater in amount or degree.' —**im·prov·a·bil·i·ty** /-ˌprōōvəˈbilitē/ *n.* —**im·prov·a·ble** *adj.* —**im·prov·er** *n.*

im·prove·ment /imˈprōōvmənt/ ▶ *n.* an example or instance of improving or being improved: *an improvement in East–West relations.* ■ the action of improving or being improved: *there's still room for improvement.* ■ a thing that makes something better or is better than something else: *home improvements | it's an improvement on the last cake I made.*

im·prov·i·dent /imˈprävidənt/ ▶ *adj.* not having or showing foresight; spendthrift or thoughtless: *improvident behavior.* —**im·prov·i·dence** *n.* —**im·prov·i·dent·ly** *adv.*

im·pro·vise /ˈimprəˌvīz/ ▶ *v.* [*tr.*] create and perform (music, drama, or verse) spontaneously or without preparation. ■ produce or make (something) from whatever is available. [as *adj.*] (**improvised**) *T.J. slept on the floor, using a can of Chinese noodles as an improvised pillow.* —**im·prov·i·sa·tion** /imˌprävi'zāSHən/ *n.* —**im·prov·i·sa·tion·al** /imˌprävi'zāSHənl/ *adj.* —**im·pro·vi·sa·to·ry** /imˈprävizəˌtôrē/ *adj.* —**im·pro·vis·er** *n.*

im·pru·dent /imˈprōōdnt/ ▶ *adj.* not showing care for the consequences of an action; rash. —**im·pru·dence** *n.* —**im·pru·dent·ly** *adv.*

im·pu·dent /ˈimpyəd(ə)nt/ ▶ *adj.* not showing due respect for another person; impertinent. —**im·pu·dence** *n.* —**im·pu·dent·ly** *adv.*

im·pugn /imˈpyōōn/ ▶ *v.* [*tr.*] dispute the truth, validity, or honesty of (a statement or motive); call into question. —**im·pugn·a·ble** *adj.*

im·pulse /ˈimˌpəls/ ▶ *n.* **1** a sudden strong and unreflective urge or desire to act: *I had an almost irresistible impulse to giggle* | [as *adj.*] *impulse buying.* ■ the tendency to act in this way: *a man of impulse.* **2** a driving or motivating force; an impetus: *an added impulse to this process of renewal.* **3** a pulse of electrical energy; a brief current: *nerve impulses.* **4** *Physics* a force acting briefly on a body and producing a finite change of momentum.
▶ □ **on impulse** (or **on an impulse**) suddenly and without forethought; impulsively.

im·pul·sive /imˈpəlsiv/ ▶ *adj.* acting or done without forethought: *they had married as young impulsive teenagers | perhaps he's regretting his impulsive offer.* —**im·pul·sive·ly** *adv.* —**im·pul·sive·ness** *n.* —**im·pul·siv·i·ty** /ˌimˌpəlˈsivitē/ *n.*

im·pu·ni·ty /imˈpyōōnitē/ ▶ *n.* exemption from punishment or freedom from the injurious consequences of an action: *protesters burned flags on the streets with impunity.*

im·pure /imˈpyŏŏr/ ▶ *adj.* **1** mixed with foreign matter; adulterated: *bullets cast from an impure lead.* ■ dirty: *a parasite that thrives in impure water.* ■ (of a color) mixed with another color. **2** morally wrong, esp. in sexual matters: *impure thoughts.* ■ defiled or contaminated according to ritual prescriptions. —**im·pure·ly** *adv.* —**im·pure·ness** *n.*

im·pu·ri·ty /imˈpyŏŏritē/ ▶ *n.* (pl. **-ties**) the quality or condition of being impure. ■ a thing or constituent that impairs the purity of something: *aluminum and lead are impurities frequently found in tap water.* ■ *Electr.* a trace element deliberately added to a semiconductor.

im·pute /imˈpyŏŏt/ ▶ *v.* [*tr.*] represent (something, esp. something unde-

sirable) as being done, caused, or possessed by someone; attribute: *the crimes imputed to Richard.* ■ *Finance* assign (a value) to something by inference from the value of the products or processes to which it contributes: [as *adj.*] (**imputed**) *recovering the initial outlay plus imputed interest.* —**im·put·a·ble** *adj.* —**im·pu·ta·tion** /ˌimpyə'tāSHən/ *n.*

In ▶ *symb.* the chemical element indium.

in /in/ ▶ *prep.* **1** expressing the situation of something that is or appears to be enclosed or surrounded by something else: *living in Alabama | dressed in a red shirt | soak it in warm soapy water | she saw it in the rearview mirror.* ■ expressing motion with the result that something ends up within or surrounded by something else: *don't put dye in the bathtub | he got in his car and drove off.* **2** expressing a period of time during which an event takes place or a situation remains the case: *they met in 1885 | at one o'clock in the morning | I hadn't seen him in years.* **3** expressing the length of time before a future event is expected to take place: *I'll see you in fifteen minutes.* **4** expressing a state or condition: *to be in love | I've got to put my affairs in order | a woman in her thirties | laid out in a straight line.* ■ indicating the quality or aspect with respect to which a judgment is made: *a difference in quality.* **5** expressing inclusion or involvement: *I read it in a book | acting in a film.* **6** indicating someone's occupation or profession: *she works in publishing.* **7** indicating the language or medium used: *say it in Polish | put it in writing.* ■ indicating the key in which a piece of music is written: *Mozart's Piano Concerto in E flat.* **8** as an integral part of (an activity): *in planning public expenditure it is better to be prudent.*
▶ *adv.* **1** expressing movement with the result that someone or something becomes enclosed or surrounded by something else: *come in | bring it in | presently the admiral breezed in.* **2** expressing the situation of being enclosed or surrounded by something: *we were locked in.* **3** expressing arrival at a destination: *the train got in very late.* **4** (of the tide) rising or at its highest level. **5** *Baseball* (of an infielder or outfielder) playing closer to home plate than usual: *they brought the infield in.* ■ (of a pitch) very close to the batter: *he threw a fastball in and up a little.*
▶ *adj.* **1** (of a person) present at one's home or office: *we knocked at the door but there was no one in.* **2** *inf.* fashionable: *pastels are in this year | the in thing to do.* **3** (of the ball in tennis and similar games) landing within the designated playing area.
▶ *n.* a position of influence: *he would ensure an in with the nominee.*
▶ □ **be in for** have good reason to expect (typically something unpleasant): *it looks as if we're in for a storm.* ■ (**be in for it**) have good reason to expect trouble or retribution. □ **in and out of** being a frequent visitor to (a house) or frequent inmate of (an institution): *he was in and out of jail for most of his twenties.* □ **in on** privy to (a secret): *they were in on the conspiracy.* □ **in that** for the reason that (used to specify the respect in which a statement is true): *I was fortunate in that I had friends.* □ **in with** *inf.* enjoying friendly relations with. □ **the ins and outs** *inf.* all the details (of something).

in. ▶ *abbr.* inch(es).

in- ▶ *prefix* **1** (added to adjectives) not: *inanimate | intolerant.* **2** (added to nouns) without; lacking: *inadvertence | inappreciation.*

---

in·a·bil·i·ty *n.*
in·ac·ces·si·bil·i·ty *n.*
in·ac·ces·si·ble *adj.*
in·ac·cu·ra·cy *n.*
in·ac·cu·rate *adj.*
in·ac·cu·rate·ly *adv.*
in·ac·tive *adj.*
in·ac·tiv·i·ty *n.*
in·ad·e·qua·cy *n.*
in·ad·e·quate *adj.*
in·ad·e·quate·ly *adv.*
in·ad·mis·si·ble *adj.*
in·ad·vis·a·ble *adj.*
in·ap·pre·ci·a·ble *adj.*
in·ap·pre·ci·a·tive *adj.*
in·ap·pro·pri·ate *adj.*
in·ap·pro·pri·ate·ly *adv.*
in·apt *adj.*
in·apt·ly *adv.*
in·ar·gu·a·ble *adj.*
in·ar·gu·a·bly *adv.*
in·ar·tis·tic *adj.*
in·at·ten·tion *n.*
in·at·ten·tive *adj.*

in·at·ten·tive·ly *adv.*
in·at·ten·tive·ness *n.*
in·au·di·ble *adj.*
in·au·di·bly *adv.*
in·aus·pi·cious *adj.*
in·aus·pi·cious·ly *adv.*
in·au·then·tic *adj.*
in·ca·pa·ble *adj.*
in·cau·tious *adj.*
in·cau·tious·ly *adv.*
in·ci·vil·i·ty *n.*
in·cog·ni·zance *n.*
in·cog·ni·zant *adj.*
in·com·mu·ni·ca·ble *adj.*
in·com·mu·ni·ca·tive *adj.*
in·com·plet·a·ble *adj.*
in·com·pre·hen·si·ble *adj.*
in·com·pre·hen·si·bly *adv.*
in·con·sec·u·tive *adj.*
in·cor·rect *adj.*
in·cor·rect·ly *adv.*
in·cor·rect·ness *n.*
in·cur·a·ble *adj.*
in·dec·o·rous *adj.*

in·dec·o·rous·ly *adv.*
in·de·fin·a·ble *adj.*
in·de·fin·a·bly *adv.*
in·dis·cern·i·ble *adj.*
in·dis·put·a·ble *adj.*
in·dis·put·a·bly *adv.*
in·dis·tinct *adj.*
in·dis·tinc·tive *adj.*
in·dis·tinc·tive·ly *adv.*
in·dis·tinct·ly *adv.*
in·dis·tinct·ness *n.*
in·dis·tin·guish·a·ble *adj.*
in·di·vis·i·ble *adj.*
in·ed·i·ble *adj.*
in·ed·u·ca·ble *adj.*
in·ef·fec·tive *adj.*
in·ef·fec·tive·ly *adv.*
in·ef·fec·tive·ness *n.*
in·ef·fi·ca·cious *adj.*
in·ef·fi·ca·cy *n.*
in·e·las·tic *adj.*
in·el·i·gi·ble *adj.*
in·e·rad·i·ca·ble *adj.*
in·ex·act *adj.*

in·ex·act·ness *n.*
in·ex·pe·di·ence *n.*
in·ex·pe·di·en·cy *n.*
in·ex·pe·di·ent *adj.*
in·ex·pen·sive *adj.*
in·ex·plic·it *adj.*
in·ex·plic·it·ly *adv.*
in·ex·ten·si·ble *adj.*
in·fea·si·ble *adj.*
in·fer·tile *adj.*
in·fu·si·ble *adj.*
in·hu·mane *adj.*
in·ju·di·cious *adj.*
in·op·por·tune *adj.*
in·op·por·tune·ly *adv.*
in·so·bri·e·ty *n.*
in·suf·fi·cien·cy *n.*
in·suf·fi·cient *adj.*
in·suf·fi·cient·ly *adv.*
in·sus·cep·ti·ble *adj.*
in·tan·gi·ble *adj.*
in·vi·a·bil·i·ty *n.*
in·vi·a·ble *adj.*
in·vol·a·tile *adj.*

in·a·bil·i·ty /ˌinəˈbilitē/ ▶*n.* the state of being unable to do something: *his inability to accept new ideas.*

in ab·sen·tia /ˌin əbˈsensH(ē)ə/ ▶*adv.* while not present at the event being referred to: *two foreign suspects will be tried in absentia.*

in·ac·tion /inˈaksHən/ ▶*n.* lack of action where some is expected or appropriate: *future generations will condemn us for inaction.*

in·ac·ti·vate /inˈaktəˌvāt/ ▶*v.* [*tr.*] make inactive or inoperative: *household bleach does not inactivate the virus* | [as *adj.*] (**inactivated**) *an inactivated polio vaccine.* —**in·ac·ti·va·tion** /-ˌaktəˈvāsHən/ *n.* —**in·ac·ti·va·tor** /-ˌvātər/ *n.*

in·ad·vert·ent /ˌinədˈvərtnt/ ▶*adj.* not resulting from or achieved through deliberate planning. ■ (of a mistake) made through lack of care. —**in·ad·vert·ence** *n.* —**in·ad·vert·en·cy** *n.* —**in·ad·vert·ent·ly** *adv.*

in·al·ien·a·ble /inˈālēənəbəl/ ▶*adj.* unable to be taken away from or given away by the possessor: *freedom of religion, the most inalienable of all human rights.* —**in·al·ien·a·bil·i·ty** /-ˌālēənəˈbilitē/ *n.* —**in·al·ien·a·bly** /-blē/ *adv.*

in·ane /iˈnān/ ▶*adj.* silly; stupid. —**in·ane·ly** *adv.* —**in·ane·ness** *n.* —**in·an·i·ty** /iˈnanitē/ *n.* (*pl.* **-ties**).

in·an·i·mate /inˈanəmit/ ▶*adj.* not alive, esp. not in the manner of animals and humans: *inanimate objects like stones.* ■ showing no sign of life; lifeless. —**in·an·i·mate·ly** *adv.*

in·ap·pli·ca·ble /inˈaplikəbəl; ˌinəˈplik-/ ▶*adj.* not relevant or appropriate: *the details are likely to be inapplicable to other designs.* —**in·ap·pli·ca·bil·i·ty** /-ˌaplikəˈbilitē/ *n.* —**in·ap·pli·ca·bly** /-blē/ *adv.*

in·ar·tic·u·late /ˌinärˈtikyəlit/ ▶*adj.* unable to speak distinctly or express oneself clearly. ■ not clearly expressed or pronounced: *inarticulate complaints.* ■ having no distinct meaning; unintelligible: *inarticulate cries.* —**in·ar·tic·u·la·cy** /-ləsē/ *n.* —**in·ar·tic·u·late·ly** *adv.* —**in·ar·tic·u·late·ness** *n.*

in·as·much /ˌinəzˈməCH/ ▶*adv.* (**inasmuch as**) to the extent that; insofar as: *these provisions apply only inasmuch as interstate trade is affected.* ■ considering that; since (used to specify the respect in which a statement is true): *a most unusual composer inasmuch as he was deaf.*

in·au·gu·ral /inˈôg(y)ərəl/ ▶*adj.* marking the beginning of an institution, activity, or period of office: *the inaugural ball.*
▶*n.* an inaugural speech, esp. one made by an incoming U.S. president. ■ an inaugural ceremony: *preparations for the inaugural.*

in·au·gu·rate /inˈôg(y)əˌrāt/ ▶*v.* [*tr.*] begin or introduce (a system, policy, or period). ■ admit (someone) formally to public office: *the new president will be inaugurated on January 20.* ■ mark the beginning or first public use of (an organization or project): *the museum was inaugurated on September 12.* —**in·au·gu·ra·tion** /-ˌôg(y)əˈrāsHən/ *n.* —**in·au·gu·ra·tor** *n.* —**in·au·gu·ra·to·ry** /-əˌtôrē/ *adj.*

in-be·tween *inf.* ▶*adj.* situated somewhere between two extremes or recognized categories; intermediate.
▶*n.* an intermediate thing: *successes, failures and in-betweens.*

in·board /ˈinˌbôrd/ ▶*adv. & adj.* within a ship, aircraft, or vehicle: [as *adv.*] *the spray was coming inboard now* | [as *adj.*] *the uncovered inboard engine.* ■ toward the center of a ship, aircraft, or vehicle: [as *adv.*] *move the clew inboard along the boom* | [as *adj.*] *the inboard ailerons on the wings were dead.*
▶*n.* a boat's engine housed inside its hull. ■ a boat with such an engine.

in·born /ˈinˈbôrn/ ▶*adj.* existing from birth: *an inborn defect.* ■ natural to a person or animal: *inborn instincts.*

in-box ▶*n.* a box on someone's desk for letters addressed to them and other documents that they have to deal with. ■ *Comput.* the window in which an individual user's incoming e-mail messages and similar communications are displayed.

in·bred /ˈinˌbred/ ▶*adj.* **1** produced by inbreeding: *a classic inbred Englishman.* **2** existing in a person, animal, or plant from birth; congenital: *inbred disease resistance in crops.*

in·breed /ˈinˌbrēd/ ▶*v.* (*past* and *past part.* **-bred**) [*intr.*] [often as *n.*] (**inbreeding**) breed from closely related people or animals, esp. over many generations: *persistent inbreeding has produced an unusually high frequency of sufferers from this disease.*

Inc. /iNGk/ ▶*abbr.* ■ incorporated: *Northeast Airlines Inc.* ■ (also **inc.**) incomplete.

In·ca /ˈiNGkə/ ▶*n.* **1** a member of a South American Indian people living in the central Andes before the Spanish conquest. **2** the supreme ruler of this people. —**In·ca·ic** /inˈkāik; iNG-/ *adj.* —**In·can** *adj.*

in·cal·cu·la·ble /inˈkalkyələbəl; iNG-/ ▶*adj.* **1** too great to be calculated or estimated: *an archive of incalculable value.* **2** not able to be calculated or estimated: *the cost is incalculable but colossal.* —**in·cal·cu·la·bil·i·ty** /-ˌkalkyələˈbilitē/ *n.* —**in·cal·cu·la·bly** /-blē/ *adv.*

in·can·des·cent /ˌinkənˈdesənt/ ▶*adj.* emitting light as a result of being heated: *plumes of incandescent liquid rock.* ■ (of an electric light) containing a filament that glows white-hot when heated by a current passed through it. ■ extremely angry: *she was incandescent at the way the IRS acted.* ■ of outstanding and exciting quality; brilliant: *an incandescent performance.* —**in·can·des·cence** *n.* —**in·can·des·cent·ly** *adv.*

in·can·ta·tion /ˌinkanˈtāsHən/ ▶*n.* a series of words said as a magic spell or charm. ■ the use of such words. —**in·can·ta·to·ry** /-ˈkantəˌtôrē/ *adj.*

in·ca·pac·i·tate /ˌinkəˈpasiˌtāt/ ▶*v.* [*tr.*] prevent from functioning in a normal way: *he was incapacitated by a heart attack.* ■ *Law* deprive (someone) of their legal capacity. —**in·ca·pac·i·tant** /-ˈpasətnt/ *n.* —**in·ca·pac·i·ta·tion** /-ˌpasiˈtāsHən/ *n.*

in·ca·pac·i·ty /ˌinkəˈpasitē/ ▶*n.* (*pl.* **-ties**) physical or mental inability to do something or to manage one's affairs. ■ legal disqualification: *they are not subject to any legal incapacity.*

in·car·cer·ate /inˈkärsəˌrāt/ ▶*v.* [*tr.*] (usu. **be incarcerated**) imprison: *many are incarcerated for property offenses.* ■ [*tr.*] confine (someone) in a particular place. —**in·car·cer·a·tion** /-ˌkärsəˈrāsHən/ *n.* —**in·car·cer·a·tor** /-ˌrātər/ *n.*

in·car·nate ▶*adj.* /inˈkärnit; -ˌnāt/ embodied in flesh; in human form: *God incarnate* | *he chose to be incarnate as a man.* ■ represented in the ultimate or most extreme form: *capitalism incarnate.*
▶*v.* /-ˌnāt/ [*tr.*] embody or represent (a deity or spirit) in human form: *the idea that God incarnates himself in man.* ■ put (an idea or other abstract concept) into concrete form. ■ (of a person) be the living embodiment of (a quality): *the man who incarnates the suffering which has affected every Mozambican.* ▷late Middle English: from ecclesiastical Latin *incarnat-* 'made flesh,' from the verb *incarnare*, from *in-* 'into' + *caro, carn-* 'flesh.'

in·car·na·tion /ˌinkärˈnāsHən/ ▶*n.* **1** a person who embodies in the flesh a deity, spirit, or abstract quality: *Rama was Vishnu's incarnation on earth.* ■ (**the Incarnation**) (in Christian theology) the embodiment of God the Son in human flesh as Jesus Christ. **2** (with reference to reincarnation) one of a series of lifetimes that a person spends on earth. ■ the form in which a person spends such a lifetime.

in·cen·di·ar·y /inˈsendēˌerē/ ▶*adj.* (of a device or attack) designed to cause fires. ■ tending to stir up conflict. ■ very exciting.
▶*n.* (*pl.* **-ar·ies**) an incendiary bomb or device. ■ a person who starts fires, esp. in a military context. ■ a person who stirs up conflict. —**in·cen·di·a·rism** /-dēəˌrizəm/ *n.*

in·cense[1] ▶*n.* /ˈinˌsens/ a gum, spice, or other substance that is burned for the sweet smell it produces. ■ the smoke or perfume of such a substance.
▶*v.* /inˈsens/ [*tr.*] perfume with incense or a similar fragrance. ▷Middle English (originally as *encense*): from Old French *encens* (noun), *encenser* (verb), from ecclesiastical Latin *incensum* 'something burned, incense,' neuter past participle of *incendere* 'set fire to,' from *in-* 'in' + the base of *candere* 'to glow.' —**in·cen·sa·tion** /ˌinsenˈsāsHən/ *n.*

in·cense[2] /inˈsens/ ▶*v.* [*tr.*] make very angry.

in·cen·tive /inˈsentiv/ ▶*n.* a thing that motivates or encourages one to do something: *there is no incentive for customers to conserve water.* ■ a payment or concession to stimulate greater output or investment: *tax incentives for investing in depressed areas* | [as *adj.*] *incentive payments.*

in·cep·tion /inˈsepsHən/ ▶*n.* the establishment or starting point of an institution or activity: *she has been on the board since its inception.*

in·ces·sant /inˈsesənt/ ▶*adj.* (of something regarded as unpleasant) continuing without pause or interruption: *the incessant beat of the music.* —**in·ces·san·cy** *n.* —**in·ces·sant·ly** *adv.* —**in·ces·sant·ness** *n.*

in·cest /ˈinˌsest/ ▶*n.* sexual relations between people classed as being too closely related to marry each other. ■ the crime of having sexual intercourse with a parent, child, sibling, or grandchild.

in·ces·tu·ous /inˈsescHōōəs/ ▶*adj.* **1** involving or guilty of incest: *the child of an incestuous relationship.* **2** (of human relations generally) excessively close and resistant to outside influence: *the incestuous nature of literary journalism.* —**in·ces·tu·ous·ly** *adv.* —**in·ces·tu·ous·ness** *n.*

inch /inCH/ ▶*n.* **1** a unit of linear measure equal to one twelfth of a foot (2.54 cm). (Symbol: ″) ■ a very small amount or distance: *I had no intention of budging an inch.* **2** a unit used to express other quantities, in particular: ■ (as a unit of rainfall) a quantity that would cover a horizontal surface to a depth of one inch. ■ (also **inch of mercury**) (as a unit of atmospheric pressure) an amount that would support a column of mercury one-inch high in a barometer (equal to 33.86 millibars, 29.5 inches being equal to one bar).
▶*v.* [*intr.*] move slowly and carefully in a specified direction: *the mourners*

Pronunciation Key ə *ago, up;* ər *over, fur;* a *hat;* ā *ate;* ä *car;* CH *chin;* e *let;* ē *see;* e(ə)r *air;* i *fit;* ī *by;* i(ə)r *ear;* NG *sing;* ō *go;* ô *law, for;* oi *toy;* ŏŏ *good;* ōō *goo;* ou *out;* SH *she;* TH *thin;* TH *then;* (h)w *why;* ZH *vision*

inched along narrow country lanes | *the stock market inched ahead today.* ■ [*tr.*] cause (something) to move in this manner: *he inched the car forward.*

▸ □ **by inches 1** only just: *the shot missed her by inches.* **2** very slowly and gradually; bit by bit. □ **every inch 1** the whole surface, distance, or area: *they know every inch of the country.* **2** entirely; very much so: *he's every inch the gentleman.* □ **inch by inch** gradually; bit by bit: *inch by inch he crept along the wall.* □ **within an inch of** very close to.

in·cho·ate /in'kō-it; -āt/ ▸ *adj.* just begun and so not fully formed or developed; rudimentary: *inchoate democracy.* —**in·cho·ate·ly** *adv.* —**in·cho·ate·ness** *n.*

in·ci·dence /'insidəns/ ▸ *n.* the occurrence, rate, or frequency of a disease or something else undesirable: *an increased incidence of cancer.* ■ the way in which the burden of a tax falls upon the population.

in·ci·dent /'insidənt/ ▸ *n.* an event or occurrence: *several amusing incidents.* ■ a violent event, such as a fracas or assault: *one person was stabbed in the incident.* ■ a hostile clash between forces of rival countries. ■ (**incident of**) a case or instance of something happening. ■ the occurrence of dangerous or exciting things: *the winter passed without incident.* ■ a distinct piece of action in a play or a poem.

▸ *adj.* **1** (**incident to**) likely to happen because of; resulting from: *the changes incident to economic development.* ■ *Law* attaching to: *the costs properly incident to a suit for foreclosure.* **2** (esp. of light or other radiation) falling on or striking something.

in·ci·den·tal /ˌinsi'dentl/ ▸ *adj.* **1** accompanying but not a major part of something: *incidental expenses.* ■ occurring by chance in connection with something else: *the incidental catch of dolphins in the pursuit of tuna.* **2** (**incidental to**) liable to happen as a consequence of (an activity): *the ordinary risks incidental to a fireman's job.*

▸ *n.* (usu. **incidentals**) an incidental detail, expense, event, etc.: *an allowance to cover meals, taxis, and other incidentals.*

in·ci·den·tal·ly /ˌinsi'dent(ə)lē/ ▸ *adv.* **1** used when a person has something more to say, or is about to add a remark unconnected to the current subject; by the way: *incidentally, it was many months before the truth was discovered.* **2** in an incidental manner; as chance occurrence: *the infection was discovered incidentally at a postmortem examination.*

in·ci·den·tal mu·sic ▸ *n.* music used in a film or play as a background to create or enhance a particular atmosphere.

in·cin·er·ate /in'sinə,rāt/ ▸ *v.* [*tr.*] destroy (something, esp. waste material) by burning. —**in·cin·er·a·tion** /-ˌsinə'rāSHən/ *n.*

in·cin·er·a·tor /in'sinə,rātər/ ▸ *n.* an apparatus for burning waste material, esp. industrial waste, at high temperatures until it is reduced to ash.

in·cip·i·ent /in'sipēənt/ ▸ *adj.* in an initial stage; beginning to happen or develop: *he could feel incipient anger building up.* ■ (of a person) developing into a specified type or role: *we seemed more like friends than incipient lovers.* —**in·cip·i·ence** *n.* —**in·cip·i·en·cy** *n.* —**in·cip·i·ent·ly** *adv.*

in·cise /in'sīz/ ▸ *v.* [*tr.*] mark or decorate (an object or surface) with a cut or a series of cuts: *a button incised with a skull.* ■ cut (a mark or decoration) into a surface. ■ cut (skin or flesh) with a surgical instrument.

in·ci·sion /in'siZHən/ ▸ *n.* a surgical cut made in skin or flesh. ■ a mark or decoration cut into a surface. ■ the action or process of cutting into something. —**in·ci·sion·al** /-ZHənl/ *adj.*

in·ci·sive /in'sīsiv/ ▸ *adj.* (of a person or mental process) intelligently analytical and clear-thinking: *she was an incisive critic.* ■ (of an account) accurate and sharply focused: *the songs offer incisive pictures of American ways.* —**in·ci·sive·ly** *adv.* —**in·ci·sive·ness** *n.*

in·ci·sor /in'sīzər/ ▸ *n.* (also **incisor tooth**) a narrow-edged tooth at the front of the mouth, adapted for cutting.

in·cite /in'sīt/ ▸ *v.* [*tr.*] encourage or stir up (violent or unlawful behavior): *the offense of inciting racial hatred.* ■ urge or persuade (someone) to act in a violent or unlawful way: *he incited loyal subjects to rebellion.* —**in·ci·ta·tion** /ˌinsī'tāSHən/ *n.* —**in·cite·ment** *n.* —**in·cit·er** *n.*

in·clem·ent /in'klemənt/ ▸ *adj.* (of the weather) unpleasantly cold or wet. —**in·clem·en·cy** *n.* (*pl.* -**cies**).

in·cli·na·tion /ˌinklə'nāSHən; ˌiNGklə-/ ▸ *n.* **1** a person's natural tendency or urge to act or feel in a particular way; a disposition or propensity: *John was a scientist by training and inclination.* ■ an interest in or liking for (something): *Burger King and Wendy's didn't show any inclination to jump into a price war with McDonald's.* **2** a slope or slant. ■ a bending of the body or head in a bow. **3** the angle at which a straight line or plane is inclined to another. ■ *Astron.* the angle between the orbital plane of a planet, comet, etc., and the ecliptic, or between the orbital plane of a satellite and the equatorial plane of its primary. ■ *Astron.* the angle between the axis of an astronomical object and a fixed reference angle.

in·cline ▸ *v.* /in'klīn/ **1** (**be inclined to/toward/to do something**) feel willing or favorably disposed to (an action, belief, or attitude): *he was inclined to accept the offer* | *Lucy was inclined to a belief in original sin.* ■ (esp. as a polite formula) tend toward holding a specified opinion: *I'm inclined to agree with you.* ■ [*tr.*] make (someone) willing or disposed to do something: *his prejudice inclines him to overlook obvious facts.* ■ [*intr.*] feel favorably disposed to someone or something: *I incline to the view that this conclusion is untenable.* **2** (**be inclined to/to do something**) have a tendency to do something: *she's inclined to gossip with complete strangers.* ■ have a specified disposition or talent: *some people are very mathematically inclined.* **3** [*intr.*] lean or turn away from a given plane or direction, esp. the vertical or horizontal: *the bunker doors incline outward* | [as *adj.*] (**inclined**) *an inclined ramp.* ■ [*tr.*] bend (one's head) forward and downward.

▸ *n.* /'in,klīn/ an inclined surface or slope, esp. on a road, path, or railway. ■ an inclined plane. —**in·clin·a·ble** *adj.* —**in·clin·er** *n.*

in·clude /in'klood/ ▸ *v.* [*tr.*] **1** comprise or contain as part of a whole: *the price includes dinner, bed, and breakfast.* **2** make part of a whole or set: *we have included some hints for beginners in this section.* ■ allow (someone) to share in an activity or privilege. —**in·clu·sion** /-'kloozHən/ *n.*

in·clu·sion·a·ry /in'kloozHə,nerē/ ▸ *adj.* designed or intended to accommodate diversity in age, income, race, or some other category: *several clubs prefer not to adhere to the new, inclusionary policies.*

in·clu·sive /in'kloosiv/ ▸ *adj.* including or covering all the services, facilities, or items normally expected or required: *the price is inclusive.* ■ (**inclusive of**) containing (a specified element) as part of a whole: *all prices are inclusive of taxes.* ■ with the inclusion of the extreme limits stated: *between the ages of 55 and 59 inclusive.* ■ not excluding any section of society or any party involved in something. ■ (of language) deliberately nonsexist, esp. avoiding the use of masculine pronouns to refer to both men and women. —**in·clu·sive·ly** *adv.* —**in·clu·sive·ness** *n.* —**in·clu·siv·ist** *n.*

in·clu·siv·i·ty /ˌinkloo'sivitē/ ▸ *n.* an intention or policy of including people who might otherwise be excluded or marginalized, such as the handicapped, learning-disabled, or racial and sexual minorities.

in·cog·ni·to /ˌinkäg'nētō; in'kägni,tō/ ▸ *adj. & adv.* (of a person) having one's true identity concealed: [as *adj.*] *in order to observe you have to be incognito* | [as *adv.*] *he is now operating incognito.*

▸ *n.* (*pl.* -**tos**) an assumed or false identity.

in·co·her·ent /ˌinkō'hi(ə)rənt; ˌiNG-; -'her-/ ▸ *adj.* **1** (of spoken or written language) expressed in an incomprehensible or confusing way; unclear. ■ (of a person) unable to speak intelligibly. ■ (of an ideology, policy, or system) internally inconsistent; illogical. **2** *Physics* (of waves) having no definite or stable phase relationship. —**in·co·her·ence** *n.* —**in·co·her·en·cy** *n.* (*pl.* -**cies**) —**in·co·her·ent·ly** *adv.*

in·come /'in,kəm; 'iNG-/ ▸ *n.* money received, esp. on a regular basis, for work or through investments: *he has a nice home and an adequate income.*

in·come tax ▸ *n.* tax levied by a government directly on income, esp. an annual tax on personal income.

in·com·ing /'in,kəmiNG/ ▸ *adj.* in the process of coming in: *incoming passengers.* ■ (of a message or communication) being received rather than sent: *an incoming call.* ■ (of an official or administration) having just been elected or appointed to succeed another: *the incoming president.* ■ approaching with hostile intent; attacking: *incoming jets.*

▸ *n.* (**incomings**) revenue; income.

in·com·men·su·rate /ˌinkə'mensərit; -sHə-/ ▸ *adj.* (**incommensurate with**) out of keeping or proportion with: *man's influence on the earth's surface seems incommensurate with his scale.* —**in·com·men·su·rate·ly** *adv.* —**in·com·men·su·rate·ness** *n.*

in·com·mode /ˌinkə'mōd/ ▸ *v.* [*tr.*] *formal* inconvenience (someone).

in·com·mu·ni·ca·do /ˌinkə,myooni'kädō/ ▸ *adj.* not able, wanting, or allowed to communicate with other people: *they were separated and detained incommunicado.*

in·com·mut·a·ble /ˌinkə'myootəbəl/ ▸ *adj.* not capable of being changed or exchanged. —**in·com·mut·a·bly** /-blē/ *adv.*

in·com·pa·ra·ble /in'kämp(ə)rəbəl/ ▸ *adj.* **1** without an equal in quality or extent; matchless: *the incomparable beauty of Venice.* **2** unable to be compared; totally different in nature or extent: *censorship still exists, but now it's absolutely incomparable with what it was.* —**in·com·pa·ra·bil·i·ty** /-ˌkämp(ə)rə'bilitē/ *n.* —**in·com·pa·ra·bly** /-blē/ *adv.*

in·com·pat·i·ble /ˌinkəm'patəbəl; ˌiNG-/ ▸ *adj.* (of two things) so opposed in character as to be incapable of existing together: *cleverness and femininity were seen as incompatible.* ■ (of two people) unable to live together harmoniously. ■ (**incompatible with**) (of one thing or person) not consistent or able to coexist with (another): *long hours are simply incompatible with family life.* ■ (of equipment, machinery, computer programs, etc.) not capable of being used in combination. —**in·com·pat·i·bil·i·ty** /-ˌpatə'bilitē/ *n.* —**in·com·pat·i·bly** /-blē/ *adv.*

in·com·pe·tent /in'kämpətənt; ɪNG-/ ▶*adj.* not having or showing the necessary skills to do something successfully. ■ *Law* not qualified to act in a particular capacity: *the patient is deemed legally incompetent.* ■ *Med.* (esp. of a valve or sphincter) not able to perform its function.
▶*n.* an incompetent person. —**in·com·pe·tence** *n.* —**in·com·pe·ten·cy** *n.* —**in·com·pe·tent·ly** *adv.*

in·com·plete /,inkəm'plēt; ,ɪNG-/ ▶*adj.* not having all the necessary or appropriate parts. ■ not full or finished: *the analysis remains incomplete.* —**in·com·plete·ly** *adv.* —**in·com·plete·ness** *n.*

in·com·pre·hen·sion /,inkämprə'henʃən; in,käm-/ ▶*n.* failure to understand something: *they gave him a look of complete incomprehension.*

in·con·ceiv·a·ble /,inkən'sēvəbəl/ ▶*adj.* not capable of being imagined or grasped mentally; unbelievable: *it seemed inconceivable that the president had been unaware of what was going on.* —**in·con·ceiv·a·bil·i·ty** /-,sēvə'bilitē/ *n.* —**in·con·ceiv·a·ble·ness** *n.* —**in·con·ceiv·a·bly** /-blē/ *adv.*

in·con·clu·sive /,inkən'klōōsiv; ,ɪNG-/ ▶*adj.* not leading to a firm conclusion; not ending doubt or dispute: *the medical evidence is inconclusive.* —**in·con·clu·sive·ly** *adv.* —**in·con·clu·sive·ness** *n.*

in·con·gru·ous /in'käNGgrōōəs/ ▶*adj.* not in harmony or keeping with the surroundings or other aspects of something. —**in·con·gru·i·ty** /,inkən'grōō-itē; ,ɪNG-; -käNG-/ *n.* (*pl.* **-ties**) —**in·con·gru·ous·ly** *adv.*

in·con·se·quen·tial /,inkänsə'kwenCHəl/ ▶*adj.* not important or significant. —**in·con·se·quen·ti·al·i·ty** /-,kwenCHē'alitē/ *n.* (*pl.* **-ties**) —**in·con·se·quen·tial·ly** *adv.* —**in·con·se·quen·tial·ness** *n.*

in·con·sid·er·a·ble /,inkən'sidərəbəl/ ▶*adj.* of small size, amount, or extent: *a not inconsiderable amount of money.* ■ unimportant or insignificant: *a not inconsiderable artist.*

in·con·sid·er·ate /,inkən'sidərit/ ▶*adj.* thoughtlessly causing hurt or inconvenience to others: *it's inconsiderate of her to go away without telling us.* —**in·con·sid·er·ate·ly** *adv.* —**in·con·sid·er·ate·ness** *n.* —**in·con·sid·er·a·tion** /-,sidə'rāsHən/ *n.*

in·con·sist·ent /,inkən'sistənt/ ▶*adj.* not staying the same throughout; having self-contradictory elements: *police interpretation of the law was often inconsistent.* ■ acting at variance with one's own principles or former conduct. ■ (**inconsistent with**) not compatible or in keeping with: *he had done nothing inconsistent with his morality.* ■ erratic in behavior or action. —**in·con·sis·ten·cy** *n.* —**in·con·sist·ent·ly** *adv.*

in·con·sol·a·ble /,inkən'sōləbəl/ ▶*adj.* (of a person or their grief) not able to be comforted or alleviated: *his widow, Jane, was inconsolable.* —**in·con·sol·a·bil·i·ty** /-,sōlə'bilitē/ *n.* —**in·con·sol·a·bly** /-blē/ *adv.*

in·con·spic·u·ous /,inkən'spikyōōəs/ ▶*adj.* not clearly visible or attracting attention; not conspicuous: *an inconspicuous red-brick building.* —**in·con·spic·u·ous·ly** *adv.* —**in·con·spic·u·ous·ness** *n.*

in·con·stant /in'känstənt/ ▶*adj.* frequently changing; variable or irregular. ■ (of a person or their behavior) not faithful and dependable. —**in·con·stan·cy** *n.* (*pl.* **-cies**) —**in·con·stant·ly** *adv.*

in·con·test·a·ble /,inkən'testəbəl/ ▶*adj.* not able to be disputed. —**in·con·test·a·bil·i·ty** /-,testə'bilitē/ *n.* —**in·con·test·a·bly** /-blē/ *adv.*

in·con·ti·nent /in'käntənənt; -'käntn-ənt/ ▶*adj.* **1** having no or insufficient voluntary control over urination or defecation. **2** lacking self-restraint; uncontrolled. —**in·con·ti·nence** *n.* —**in·con·ti·nent·ly** *adv.*

in·con·tro·vert·i·ble /,in,käntrə'vərtəbəl/ ▶*adj.* not able to be denied or disputed: *incontrovertible proof.* —**in·con·tro·vert·i·bil·i·ty** /-,vərtə'bilitē/ *n.* —**in·con·tro·vert·i·bly** /-blē/ *adv.*

in·con·ven·ience /,inkən'vēn-yəns/ ▶*n.* trouble or difficulty caused to one's personal requirements or comfort: *the inconvenience of having to change trains.* ■ a cause or instance of such trouble: *the inconveniences of life in a remote city.*
▶*v.* [*tr.*] cause such trouble or difficulty to.

in·con·ven·ient /,inkən'vēn-yənt/ ▶*adj.* causing trouble, difficulties, or discomfort. —**in·con·ven·ient·ly** *adv.*

in·cor·po·rate ▶*v.* /in'kôrpə,rāt/ [*tr.*] **1** put or take in (something) as part of a whole; include: *he has incorporated in his proposals a large number of measures.* ■ contain or include (something) as part of a whole: *the guide incorporates all the recent changes in legislation.* ■ combine (ingredients) into one substance. **2** (often **be incorporated**) constitute (a company, city, or other organization) as a legal corporation. ▷late Middle English: from late Latin *incorporat-* 'embodied,' from the verb *incorporare*, from *in-* 'into' + Latin *corporare* 'form into a body' (from *corpus, corpor-* 'body'). —**in·cor·po·ra·tion** /-,kôrpə'rāsHən/ *n.* —**in·cor·po·ra·tor** /-,rātər/ *n.*

in·cor·po·re·al /,inkôr'pôrēəl/ ▶*adj.* not composed of matter; having no material existence: *millions believe in a supreme but incorporeal being they call God.* ■ *Law* having no physical existence. —**in·cor·po·re·al·i·ty** /-,pôrē'alitē/ *n.* —**in·cor·po·re·al·ly** *adv.* —**in·cor·po·re·i·ty** /-pə'rēitē/ *n.*

in·cor·ri·gi·ble /in'kôrijəbəl; -'kär-/ ▶*adj.* (of a person or their tendencies) not able to be corrected, improved, or reformed: *she's an incorrigible flirt.*
▶*n.* a person of this type. —**in·cor·ri·gi·bil·i·ty** /-,kôrijə'bilitē; -,kär-/ *n.* —**in·cor·ri·gi·ble·ness** *n.* —**in·cor·ri·gi·bly** /-blē/ *adv.*

in·cor·rupt·i·ble /,inkə'rəptəbəl/ ▶*adj.* **1** not susceptible to corruption, esp. by bribery. **2** not subject to death or decay; everlasting. —**in·cor·rupt·i·bil·i·ty** /-,rəptə'bilitē/ *n.* —**in·cor·rupt·i·bly** /-blē/ *adv.*

in·crease ▶*v.* /in'krēs/ become or make greater in size, amount, intensity, or degree: [*intr.*] *an alarming rate* | [*tr.*] *increase awareness of social issues* | [as *adj.*] (**increasing**) *the increasing numbers of students.*
▶*n.* /'in,krēs/ an instance of growing or making greater. —**in·creas·a·ble** *adj.* —**in·creas·ing·ly** *adv.*
▶ □ **on the increase** becoming greater, more common, or more frequent.

in·cred·i·ble /in'kredəbəl/ ▶*adj.* **1** impossible to believe: *an almost incredible tale of triumph and tragedy.* **2** difficult to believe; extraordinary: *the noise from the crowd was incredible.* ■ *inf.* amazingly good or beautiful: *I was mesmerized: she looked so incredible.* —**in·cred·i·bil·i·ty** /-,kredə'bilitē/ *n.* —**in·cred·i·bly** *adv.*

in·cred·u·lous /in'krejələs/ ▶*adj.* (of a person or their manner) unwilling or unable to believe something: *an incredulous gasp.* —**in·cre·du·li·ty** /,inkre'd(y)ōōlitē/ *n.* —**in·cred·u·lous·ly** *adv.* —**in·cred·u·lous·ness** *n.*

in·cre·ment /'iNGkrəmənt; 'in-/ ▶*n.* an increase or addition, esp. one of a series on a fixed scale: *the inmates' pay can escalate in five-cent increments to a maximum of 90 cents an hour.* ■ a regular increase in salary on such a scale: *he had waived his right to the second increment of $18 million so that it could be distributed among 40 employees.* ■ *Math.* a small positive or negative change in a variable quantity or function. —**in·cre·men·tal** /,iNGkrə'mentl; ,in-/ *adj.* —**in·cre·men·tal·ly** /,iNGkrə'mentl-ē; ,in-/ *adv.*

in·crim·i·nate /in'krimə,nāt/ ▶*v.* [*tr.*] make (someone) appear guilty of a crime or wrongdoing; strongly imply the guilt of (someone): *he refused to answer questions in order not to incriminate himself* | [as *adj.*] (**incriminating**) *incriminating evidence.* —**in·crim·i·na·tion** /-,krimə'nāsHən/ *n.* —**in·crim·i·na·to·ry** /-nə,tôrē/ *adj.*

in·crus·ta·tion ▶*n.* variant spelling of ENCRUSTATION.

in·cu·bate /'inkyə,bāt; 'iNG-/ ▶*v.* [*tr.*] (of a bird) sit on (eggs) in order to keep them warm and bring them to hatching. ■ (esp. in a laboratory) keep (eggs, cells, bacteria, embryos, etc.) at a suitable temperature so that they develop: *the samples were incubated at 80°C for three minutes.* ■ (**be incubating something**) have an infectious disease developing inside one before symptoms appear: *the possibility that she was incubating early syphilis.* ■ [*intr.*] develop slowly without outward or perceptible signs: *unfortunately the BSE bug incubates for around three years.*

in·cu·ba·tion /,inkyə'bāsHən; ,iNG-/ ▶*n.* the process of incubating eggs, cells, bacteria, a disease, etc. —**in·cu·ba·tive** /'inkyə,bātiv; 'iNG-/ *adj.* —**in·cu·ba·to·ry** /in'kyōōbə,tôrē; iNG-/ *adj.*

in·cu·ba·tor /'inkyə,bātər; 'iNG-/ ▶*n.* an enclosed apparatus providing a controlled environment for the care and protection of premature or unusually small babies. ■ an apparatus used to hatch eggs or grow microorganisms under controlled conditions. ■ a place, esp. with support staff and equipment, made available at low rent to new small businesses.

in·cu·bus /'iNGkyəbəs; 'in-/ ▶*n.* (*pl.* **-bi** /-,bī/) a male demon believed to have sexual intercourse with sleeping women. ■ *fig.* a cause of distress or anxiety. ■ *archaic* a nightmare.

in·cul·cate /in'kəl,kāt; 'inkəl-/ ▶*v.* [*tr.*] instill (an attitude, idea, or habit) by persistent instruction: *inculcate a sense of moral responsibility.* ■ teach (someone) an attitude, idea, or habit by such instruction. —**in·cul·ca·tion** /,inkəl'kāsHən/ *n.* —**in·cul·ca·tor** /-,kātər/ *n.*

in·cum·ben·cy /in'kəmbənsē/ ▶*n.* (*pl.* **-cies**) the holding of an office or the period during which one is held.

in·cum·bent /in'kəmbənt/ ▶*adj.* **1** (**incumbent on/upon**) necessary for (someone) as a duty or responsibility: *it is incumbent on all decent people to concentrate on destroying this evil.* **2** (of an official or regime) currently holding office: *the incumbent president had been defeated.*
▶*n.* the holder of an office or post.

in·cu·nab·u·la /,inkə'nab-yələ; ,iNG-/ ▶*pl. n.* (*sing.* **in·cu·nab·u·lum** /,inkə'nabyələm; ,iNG-/ or **in·cu·na·ble** /in'kyōōnəbəl/) early printed books, esp. those printed before 1501. ■ *archaic* the early stages of the development of something. —**in·cu·nab·u·list** /-list/ *n.*

in·cur /in'kər; iNG-/ ▶*v.* (**-curred**, **-cur·ring**) [*tr.*] become subject to (something unwelcome or unpleasant) as a result of one's own behavior or actions: *I will pay any expenses incurred.* —**in·cur·rence** /-əns/ *n.*

in·cur·sion /in'kərzHən/ ▶*n.* an invasion or attack, esp. a sudden or brief one: *incursions into enemy territory.* —**in·cur·sive** /-siv/ *adj.*

in·cus /'iNGkəs/ ▶*n.* (*pl.* **in·cu·des** /in'kyōō,dēz/) *Anat.* a small anvil-shaped bone in the middle ear, transmitting vibrations between the malleus and stapes.

Ind. ▶*abbr.* ■ Independent. ■ Indian.

in·debt·ed /in'detid/ ▶*adj.* owing money: *heavily indebted countries.* ■ owing gratitude for a service or favor: *I am **indebted** to her for her help in indexing my book.* ▷Middle English *endetted*, from Old French *endette* 'involved in debt,' past participle of *endetter*. The spelling change in the 16th cent. was due to association with medieval Latin *indebitare* (based on Latin *debitum* 'debt'). —**in·debt·ed·ness** *n.*

in·de·cent /in'dēsənt/ ▶*adj.* not conforming with generally accepted standards of behavior or propriety; obscene. ■ not appropriate or fitting: *they leaped on the suggestion with indecent haste.* —**in·de·cen·cy** /-sənsē/ *n.* —**in·de·cent·ly** *adv.*

in·de·cent ex·po·sure ▶*n.* the crime of intentionally showing one's sexual organs in public. ■ the act of outraging public decency by being naked in a public place.

in·de·ci·pher·a·ble /,indi'sīfərəbəl/ ▶*adj.* not able to be read or understood: *indecipherable scrawls.*

in·de·ci·sion /,indi'sizHən/ ▶*n.* the inability to make a decision quickly.

in·de·ci·sive /,indi'sīsiv/ ▶*adj.* **1** not settling an issue. **2** (of a person) not having or showing the ability to make decisions quickly and effectively. —**in·de·ci·sive·ly** *adv.* —**in·de·ci·sive·ness** *n.*

in·deed /in'dēd/ ▶*adv.* **1** used to emphasize a statement or response confirming something already suggested: *it was not expected to last long, and indeed it took less than three weeks.* ■ used to emphasize a description, typically of a quality or condition: *it was a very good buy indeed | thank you very much indeed.* **2** used to introduce a further and stronger or more surprising point: *the idea is attractive to many men and indeed to many women.* **3** used in a response to express interest, incredulity, or contempt: *"His neck was broken." "Indeed?"* ■ expressing interest of an ironical kind with repetition of a question just asked: *"Who'd believe it?" "Who indeed?"*

in·de·fat·i·ga·ble /,ində'fatigəbəl/ ▶*adj.* (of a person or their efforts) persisting tirelessly: *an indefatigable defender of human rights.* —**in·de·fat·i·ga·bil·i·ty** /-,fatigə'bilitē/ *n.* —**in·de·fat·i·ga·bly** /-blē/ *adv.*

in·de·fen·si·ble /,ində'fensəbəl/ ▶*adj.* **1** not justifiable by argument: *the policy was morally indefensible.* **2** not able to be protected against attack. —**in·de·fen·si·bil·i·ty** /-,fensə'bilitē/ *n.* —**in·de·fen·si·bly** /-blē/ *adv.*

in·def·i·nite /in'defənit/ ▶*adj.* lasting for an unknown or unstated length of time. ■ not clearly expressed or defined; vague: *their status remains indefinite.* ■ *Gram.* (of a word, inflection, or phrase) not determining the person, thing, time, etc., referred to. —**in·def·i·nite·ness** *n.*

in·def·i·nite ar·ti·cle ▶*n. Gram.* a determiner (*a* and *an* in English) that introduces a noun phrase and implies that the thing referred to is nonspecific (as in *she bought me a book; government is an art; he went to a public school*). Typically, the indefinite article is used to introduce new concepts into a discourse. Compare with **DEFINITE ARTICLE**.

in·def·i·nite·ly /in'defənitlē/ ▶*adv.* for an unlimited or unspecified period of time: *talks cannot go on indefinitely.* ■ to an unlimited or unspecified degree or extent: *an indefinitely large number of channels.*

in·del·i·ble /in'deləbəl/ ▶*adj.* (of ink or a pen) making marks that cannot be removed. ■ not able to be forgotten or removed: *his story made an indelible impression on me.* —**in·del·i·bil·i·ty** /-,delə'bilitē/ *n.* —**in·del·i·bly** /-blē/ *adv.*

in·del·i·cate /in'delikit/ ▶*adj.* having or showing a lack of sensitive understanding or tact. ■ slightly indecent: *an earthy, often indelicate sense of humor.* —**in·del·i·ca·cy** /-kəsē/ *n.* (*pl.* **-cies**) —**in·del·i·cate·ly** *adv.*

in·dem·ni·fy /in'demnə,fī/ ▶*v.* (**-fies, -fied**) [*tr.*] compensate (someone) for harm or loss: *insurance may be carried to indemnify the owner in the event of a loss.* ■ secure (someone) against legal responsibility for their actions. —**in·dem·ni·fi·ca·tion** /-,demnəfi'kāsHən/ *n.* —**in·dem·ni·fi·er** *n.*

in·dem·ni·ty /in'demnitē/ ▶*n.* (*pl.* **-ties**) security or protection against a loss or other financial burden: *no indemnity will be given for loss of cash.* ■ security against or exemption from legal responsibility for one's actions. ■ a sum of money paid as compensation, esp. a sum exacted by a victor in war as one condition of peace.

in·dent¹ ▶*v.* /in'dent/ [*tr.*] **1** start (a line of text) or position (a block of text, table, etc.) further from the margin than the main part of the text. **2** form deep recesses in (a line or surface): *a coastline indented by many fjords.* ■ make toothlike notches in. **3** *hist.* divide (a document

drawn up in duplicate) into its two copies with a zigzag line, thus ensuring identification.

▶*n.* /in'dent; 'in,dent/ **1** a space left by indenting a line or block of text. **2** an indentation: *every indent in the coastline.* **3** an indenture. —**in·den·tor** /-tər/ *n.*

in·dent² ▶*v.* [*tr.*] make a dent or depression in (something): *his chin was firm and slightly indented.* ■ impress (a mark) on something.

in·den·ta·tion /,inden'tāsHən/ ▶*n.* **1** the action of indenting or the state of being indented: *paragraphs are marked off by indentation.* **2** a deep recess in a surface or coastline. ■ a toothlike notch: *the leaves are covered in indentations.*

in·den·ture /in'denCHər/ ▶*n.* a formal legal agreement, contract, or document, in particular: ■ *hist.* a deed of contract of which copies were made for the contracting parties with the edges indented for identification. ■ a formal list, certificate, or inventory. ■ an agreement binding an apprentice to a master. ■ *hist.* a contract by which a person agreed to work for a set period for a landowner in a British colony in exchange for passage to the colony.

▶*v.* [*tr.*] (usu. **be indentured to**) *chiefly hist.* bind (someone) by an indenture as an apprentice or laborer. —**in·den·ture·ship** /-,SHip/ *n.*

in·de·pend·ence /,ində'pendəns/ ▶*n.* the fact or state of being independent: *Argentina gained independence from Spain in 1816.*

In·de·pend·ence Day ▶*n.* a national holiday observed on July 4, celebrating the anniversary of the adoption of the Declaration of Independence in 1776. Also called **FOURTH OF JULY**.

in·de·pend·ent /,ində'pendənt/ ▶*adj.* **1** free from outside control; not depending on another's authority: *the study is totally **independent** of central government.* ■ (of a country) self-governing: *India became independent in 1947.* ■ not belonging to or supported by a political party: *the independent candidate.* ■ (of broadcasting, a school, etc.) not supported by public funds. ■ not influenced or affected by others; impartial: *a thorough and independent investigation of the case.* **2** not depending on another for livelihood or subsistence. ■ capable of thinking or acting for oneself. ■ (of income or resources) making it unnecessary to earn one's living: *a woman of independent means.* **3** not connected with another or with each other; separate: *we need two independent witnesses to testify.* ■ not depending on something else for strength or effectiveness; freestanding: *an independent electric shower.* ■ *Math.* (of one of a set of axioms, equations, or quantities) incapable of being expressed in terms of, or derived or deduced from, the others.

▶*n.* an independent person or body. ■ an independent political candidate, voter, etc. —**in·de·pend·ent·ly** *adv.*

in-depth ▶*adj.* comprehensive and thorough: *in-depth interviews.*

in·de·scrib·a·ble /,indi'skrībəbəl/ ▶*adj.* too unusual, extreme, or indefinite to be adequately described: *indescribable hardship.* —**in·de·scrib·a·bil·i·ty** /-,skrībə'bilitē/ *n.* —**in·de·scrib·a·bly** /-blē/ *adv.*

in·de·struct·i·ble /,indi'strəktəbəl/ ▶*adj.* not able to be destroyed. —**in·de·struct·i·bil·i·ty** /-,strəktə'bilitē/ *n.* —**in·de·struct·i·bly** /-blē/ *adv.*

in·de·ter·mi·na·ble /,indi'tərmənəbəl/ ▶*adj.* not able to be definitely ascertained, calculated, or identified: *a woman of indeterminable age.* ■ (of a dispute or difficulty) not able to be resolved. —**in·de·ter·mi·na·bly** /-blē/ *adv.*

in·de·ter·mi·nate /,indi'tərmənit/ ▶*adj.* not certain, known, or established: *the date of manufacture is indeterminate.* ■ left doubtful; vague. ■ *Math.* (of a quantity) having no definite or definable value. ■ *Med.* (of a condition) from which a diagnosis of the underlying cause cannot be made: *indeterminate colitis.* ■ *Bot.* (of a plant shoot) not having all the axes terminating in a flower bud and so producing a shoot of indefinite length. —**in·de·ter·mi·na·cy** /-nəsē/ *n.* —**in·de·ter·mi·nate·ly** *adv.* —**in·de·ter·mi·nate·ness** *n.*

in·dex /'in,deks/ ▶*n.* (*pl.* **-dex·es** or esp. in technical use **-di·ces** /-də,sēz/) **1** an alphabetical list of names, subjects, etc., with references to the places where they occur, typically found at the end of a book. ■ an alphabetical list by title, subject, author, or other category of a collection of books or documents, e.g., in a library. ■ *Comput.* a set of items each of which specifies one of the records of a file and contains information about its address. **2** an indicator, sign, or measure of something: *exam results may serve as an **index** of the teacher's effectiveness.* ■ a figure in a system or scale representing the average value of specified prices, shares, or other items as compared with some reference figure: *the hundred-shares index closed down 9.3.* ■ a pointer on an instrument, showing a quantity, a position on a scale, etc. ■ a number giving the magnitude of a physical property or another measured phenomenon in terms of a standard: *the oral hygiene index was calculated as the sum of the debris and calculus indices.* **3** *Math.* an exponent or other superscript or subscript number appended to a quantity. **4** *Printing* a symbol

shaped like a pointing hand, typically used to draw attention to a note.
▶*v.* [*tr.*] **1** record (names, subjects, etc.) in an index: *the list indexes theses under regional headings.* ■ provide an index to. **2** link the value of (prices, wages, or other payments) automatically to the value of a price index: *the Supreme Soviet passed legislation indexing wages to prices.* **3** [*intr.*] [often as *n.*] (**indexing**) (of a machine or part of one) rotate or otherwise move from one predetermined position to another in order to carry out a sequence of operations. —**in·dex·a·ble** *adj.* —**in·dex·a·tion** /ˌindekˈsāSHən/ *n.* —**in·dex·er** *n.* —**in·dex·i·ble** *adj.*

in·dex fin·ger ▶*n.* the finger next to the thumb; the forefinger.

In·di·a ink ▶*n.* deep black ink containing dispersed carbon particles, used esp. in drawing and technical graphics.

In·di·an /ˈindēən/ ▶*adj.* **1** of or relating to the indigenous peoples of America. **2** of or relating to India or to the subcontinent comprising India, Pakistan, and Bangladesh.
▶*n.* **1** an American Indian. **2** a native or national of India, or a person of Indian descent. —**In·di·an·i·za·tion** /ˌindēəniˈzāSHən/ *n.* —**In·di·an·ize** /-ˌnīz/ *v.* —**In·di·an·ness** *n.*

In·di·an el·e·phant ▶*n.* the elephant of southern Asia (*Elephas maximus*), smaller than the African elephant, with smaller ears and only one lip to the trunk.

In·di·an sum·mer ▶*n.* a period of unusually dry, warm weather occurring in late autumn. ■ a period of happiness or success occurring late in life.

In·dic /ˈindik/ ▶*adj.* relating to or denoting the group of Indo-European languages comprising Sanskrit and the modern Indian languages that are its descendants.
▶*n.* this language group. ▷via Latin from Greek *Indikos*, from *India*.

in·di·cate /ˈindiˌkāt/ [*tr.*] ▶*v.* **1** point out; show: *dotted lines indicate the text's margins.* ■ be a sign or symptom of; strongly imply: *sales indicate a growing market for such art.* ■ admit to or state briefly: *the president indicated his willingness to use force against the rebels.* ■ (of a person) direct attention to (someone or something) by means of a gesture: *he indicated Cindy with a brief nod of the head.* ■ (of a gauge or meter) register a reading of (a quantity, dimension, etc.). **2** suggest as a desirable or necessary course of action: *the treatment is likely to be indicated in severely depressed patients.* ▷early 17th cent.: from Latin *indicat-* 'pointed out,' from the verb *indicare*, from *in-* 'toward' + *dicare* 'make known.'

in·di·ca·tion /ˌindiˈkāSHən/ ▶*n.* a sign or piece of information that indicates something. ■ a reading given by a gauge or meter. ■ a symptom that suggests certain medical treatment is necessary: *heavy bleeding is a common indication for hysterectomy.*

in·dic·a·tive /inˈdikətiv/ ▶*adj.* **1** serving as a sign or indication of something: *having recurrent dreams is not necessarily indicative of any psychological problem.* **2** *Gram.* denoting a mood of verbs expressing simple statement of a fact. Compare with SUBJUNCTIVE.
▶*n. Gram.* a verb in the indicative mood. ■ (**the indicative**) the indicative mood. —**in·dic·a·tive·ly** *adv.*

in·di·ca·tor /ˈindiˌkātər/ ▶*n.* **1** a thing, esp. a trend or fact, that indicates the state or level of something. **2** a device providing specific information on the state or condition of something, in particular: ■ a gauge or meter of a specified kind: *a speed indicator.* **3** *Chem.* a compound that changes color at a specific pH value or in the presence of a particular substance and can be used to monitor acidity, alkalinity, or the progress of a reaction. **4** (also **indicator species**) an animal or plant species that can be used to infer conditions in a particular habitat.

in·di·ces /ˈindiˌsēz/ ▶ plural form of INDEX.

in·dict /inˈdīt/ ▶*v.* [*tr.*] formally accuse or charge (someone) with a serious crime: *his former manager was indicted for fraud.* ▷Middle English *endite, indite,* from Anglo-Norman French *enditer,* based on Latin *indicere* 'proclaim, appoint,' from *in-* 'toward' + *dicere* 'pronounce, utter.' —**in·dict·ee** /ˌindīˈtē/ *n.* —**in·dict·er** *n.*

in·dict·a·ble /inˈdītəbəl/ ▶*adj.* (of an offense) rendering the person who commits it liable to be charged with a serious crime that warrants a trial by jury. ■ (of a person) liable to be charged with a crime.

in·dict·ment /inˈdītmənt/ ▶*n.* **1** *Law* a formal charge or accusation of a serious crime: *an indictment for conspiracy.* ■ the action of indicting or being indicted. **2** a thing that serves to illustrate that a system or situation is bad and deserves to be condemned: *these rapidly escalating crime figures are an indictment of our society.*

in·dif·fer·ence /inˈdif(ə)rəns/ ▶*n.* lack of interest, concern, or sympathy: *she shrugged, feigning indifference.* ■ unimportance.

in·dif·fer·ent /inˈdif(ə)rənt/ ▶*adj.* **1** having no particular interest or sympathy; unconcerned: *most workers were indifferent to foreign affairs.* **2** neither good nor bad; mediocre: *attempts to distinguish between good,* *bad, and indifferent work.* ■ not especially good; fairly bad. —**in·dif·fer·ent·ly** *adv.*

in·dig·e·nous /inˈdijənəs/ ▶*adj.* originating or occurring naturally in a particular place; native: *the indigenous peoples of Siberia.* —**in·dig·e·nous·ly** *adv.* —**in·dig·e·nous·ness** *n.*

in·di·gent /ˈindijənt/ ▶*adj.* poor; needy.
▶*n.* a needy person. —**in·di·gence** *n.*

in·di·gest·i·ble /ˌindiˈjestəbəl/ ▶*adj.* (of food) difficult or impossible to digest. ■ *fig.* too complex or awkward to read or understand easily. —**in·di·gest·i·bil·i·ty** /-ˌjestəˈbilitē/ *n.* —**in·di·gest·i·bly** /-blē/ *adv.*

in·di·ges·tion /ˌindiˈjesCHən; -dī-/ ▶*n.* pain or discomfort in the stomach associated with difficulty in digesting food. —**in·di·ges·tive** /-tiv/ *adj.*

in·dig·nant /inˈdignənt/ ▶*adj.* feeling or showing anger or annoyance at what is perceived as unfair treatment. —**in·dig·nant·ly** *adv.*

in·dig·na·tion /ˌindigˈnāSHən/ ▶*n.* anger or annoyance provoked by what is perceived as unfair treatment: *the letter filled Lucy with indignation.*

in·dig·ni·ty /inˈdignitē/ ▶*n.* (*pl.* **-ties**) treatment or circumstances that cause one to feel shame or to lose one's dignity: *the indignity of needing financial help | he was subjected to all manner of indignities.*

in·di·go /ˈindiˌgō/ ▶*n.* (*pl.* **-os** or **-oes**) **1** a tropical plant (genus *Indigofera*) of the pea family, which was formerly widely cultivated as a source of dark blue dye. **2** the dark blue dye obtained from this plant. ■ a color between blue and violet in the spectrum.

in·di·rect /ˌindəˈrekt/ ▶*adj.* **1** not directly caused by or resulting from something: *full employment would have an indirect effect on wage levels.* ■ not done directly; conducted through intermediaries: *the nature of the threat can be pieced together only from indirect evidence.* ■ (of costs) deriving from overhead charges or subsidiary work. ■ (of taxation) levied on goods and services rather than income or profits. **2** (of a route) not straight; not following the shortest way. ■ (of lighting) from a concealed source and diffusely reflected. ■ *Soccer* denoting a free kick from which a goal may not be scored directly. **3** avoiding direct mention or exposition of a subject: *an indirect attack on the Senator.* —**in·di·rect·ly** *adv.* —**in·di·rect·ness** *n.*

in·di·rect ob·ject ▶*n. Gram.* a noun phrase referring to someone or something that is affected by the action of a transitive verb (typically as a recipient), but is not the primary object (e.g., *him* in *give him the book*). Compare with DIRECT OBJECT.

in·dis·creet /ˌindiˈskrēt/ ▶*adj.* having, showing, or proceeding from too great a readiness to reveal things that should remain secret or private: *they have been embarrassed by indiscreet friends.* —**in·dis·creet·ly** *adv.*

in·dis·cre·tion /ˌindiˈskreSHən/ ▶*n.* behavior or speech that is indiscreet or displays a lack of good judgment.

in·dis·crim·i·nate /ˌindiˈskrimənit/ ▶*adj.* done at random or without careful judgment: *terrorist gunmen engaged in indiscriminate killing.* ■ (of a person) not using or exercising discrimination: *she was indiscriminate with her affections.* —**in·dis·crim·i·nate·ly** *adv.* —**in·dis·crim·i·nate·ness** *n.* —**in·dis·crim·i·na·tion** /-ˌskrimiˈnāSHən/ *n.*

in·dis·pen·sa·ble /ˌindiˈspensəbəl/ ▶*adj.* absolutely necessary: *he made himself indispensable to the parish priest.* —**in·dis·pen·sa·bil·i·ty** /-ˌspensə-ˈbilitē/ *n.* —**in·dis·pen·sa·ble·ness** *n.* —**in·dis·pen·sa·bly** /-blē/ *adv.*

in·dis·posed /ˌindiˈspōzd/ ▶*adj.* **1** slightly unwell: *my mother is indisposed.* **2** averse; unwilling: *the potential audience seemed indisposed to attend.* —**in·dis·po·si·tion** /ˌindispəˈziSHən/ *n.*

in·dis·sol·u·ble /ˌindiˈsälyəbəl/ ▶*adj.* unable to be destroyed; lasting. —**in·dis·sol·u·bil·i·ty** /-ˌsälyəˈbilitē/ *n.* —**in·dis·sol·u·bly** /-blē/ *adv.*

in·di·um /ˈindēəm/ ▶*n.* the chemical element of atomic number 49, a soft, silvery-white metal. (Symbol: **In**)

in·di·vid·u·al /ˌindəˈvijəwəl/ ▶*adj.* **1** single; separate: *individual tiny flowers.* **2** of or for a particular person: *the individual needs of the children.* ■ designed for use by one person: *individual serving dishes.* ■ characteristic of a particular person or thing: *individual style.* ■ having a striking or unusual character; original: *she creates highly individual landscapes.*
▶*n.* a single human being as distinct from a group, class, or family: *boat trips for parties and individuals.* ■ a single member of a class: *they live in a group or as individuals.* ■ *inf.* a person of a specified kind: *the most selfish, egotistical individual I have ever met.* ■ a distinctive or original person.

in·di·vid·u·al·ism /ˌindəˈvijōōəˌlizəm/ ▶*n.* **1** the habit or principle of being independent and self-reliant. ■ self-centered feeling or conduct; egoism. **2** a social theory favoring freedom of action for individuals over collective or state control. —**in·di·vid·u·al·ist** *n.* & *adj.* —**in·di·vid·u·al·is·tic** /-,vijŌŌə'listik/ *adj.* —**in·di·vid·u·al·is·ti·cal·ly** *adv.*

in·di·vid·u·al·i·ty /,ində,vijə'walitē/ ▶*n.* **1** the quality or character of a particular person or thing that distinguishes them from others of the same kind, esp. when strongly marked: *clothes with real style and individuality.* ■ (**individualities**) individual characteristics. **2** separate existence: *anything but individuality, anything but aloneness.*

in·di·vid·u·al·ize /,ində'vijŌŌə,līz/ ▶*v.* [*tr.*] give an individual character to: *have your shirt individualized with your own club name.* ■ tailor (something) to suit the individual. —**in·di·vid·u·al·i·za·tion** /-,vijŌŌələ'zāshən/ *n.*

in·di·vid·u·al·ly /,ində'vijəwəlē/ ▶*adv.* **1** one by one; singly; separately: *individually wrapped cheeses.* ■ in a distinctive manner: *each sign is individually designed and crafted.* **2** personally; in an individual capacity.

in·doc·tri·nate /in'däktrə,nāt/ ▶*v.* [*tr.*] teach (a person or group) to accept a set of beliefs uncritically. ■ *archaic* teach or instruct (someone). —**in·doc·tri·na·tion** /-,däktrə'nāshən/ *n.* —**in·doc·tri·na·tor** /-,nātər/ *n.* —**in·doc·tri·na·to·ry** /-nə,tôrē/ *adj.*

In·do-Eu·ro·pe·an ▶*adj.* of or relating to the family of languages spoken over the greater part of Europe and Asia as far east as northern India.
▶*n.* **1** the ancestral Proto-Indo-European language. ■ the Indo-European family of languages. **2** a speaker of an Indo-European language, esp. Proto-Indo-European.

in·do·lent /'indələnt/ ▶*adj.* wanting to avoid activity or exertion; lazy. ▷mid 17th cent.: from late Latin *indolent-*, from *in-* 'not' + *dolere* 'suffer or give pain.' The sense 'idle' arose in the early 18th cent. —**in·do·lence** *n.* —**in·do·lent·ly** *adv.*

in·dom·i·ta·ble /in'dämitəbəl/ ▶*adj.* impossible to subdue or defeat: *a woman of indomitable spirit.* —**in·dom·i·ta·bil·i·ty** /-,dämitə'bilitē/ *n.* —**in·dom·i·ta·ble·ness** *n.* —**in·dom·i·ta·bly** /-blē/ *adv.*

In·do·ne·sian /,ində'nēzhən/ ▶*adj.* of or relating to Indonesia, Indonesians, or their languages.
▶*n.* **1** a native or national of Indonesia, or a person of Indonesian descent. **2** the group of Austronesian languages, closely related to Malay, that are spoken in Indonesia and neighboring islands.

in·door /'in,dôr/ ▶*adj.* situated, conducted, or used within a building or under cover: *indoor sports.* ■ of or relating to sports played indoors: *the national indoor champion.*

in·doors /in'dôrz/ ▶*adv.* into or within a building.
▶*n.* the area or space inside a building.

in·drawn /'in,drôn/ ▶*adj.* **1** [*attrib.*] (of breath) taken in. **2** (of a person) shy and introspective.

in·du·bi·ta·ble /in'd(y)ŌŌbitəbəl/ ▶*adj.* impossible to doubt; unquestionable: *an indubitable truth.* —**in·du·bi·ta·bly** /-blē/ *adv.*

in·duce /in'd(y)ŌŌs/ ▶*v.* [*tr.*] **1** succeed in persuading or influencing (someone) to do something: *the pickets induced many workers to stay away.* **2** bring about or give rise to: *none of these measures induced a change of policy.* ■ produce (an electric charge or current or a magnetic state) by induction. ■ [usu. as *adj.*] (**induced**) *Physics* cause (radioactivity) by bombardment with radiation. **3** *Med.* bring on (childbirth or abortion) artificially, typically by the use of drugs. ■ bring on childbirth in (a pregnant woman) in this way. ■ bring on the birth of (a baby) in this way. **4** *Logic* derive by inductive reasoning. —**in·duc·er** *n.* —**in·duc·i·ble** *adj.*

in·duce·ment /in'd(y)ŌŌsmənt/ ▶*n.* a thing that persuades or influences someone to do something: *companies were prepared to build only in return for massive inducements.* ■ a bribe.

in·duct /in'dəkt/ ▶*v.* [*tr.*] admit (someone) formally to a position or organization: *each worker, if formally inducted into the Mafia, is known as a "soldier."* ■ enlist (someone) for military service. ■ (**induct someone in/into**) introduce someone to (a difficult or obscure subject). —**in·duc·tee** /,indək'tē/ *n.*

in·duc·tance /in'dəktəns/ ▶*n.* *Physics* the property of an electric conductor or circuit that causes an electromotive force to be generated by a change in the current flowing.

in·duc·tion /in'dəkshən/ ▶*n.* **1** the action or process of inducting someone to a position or organization: *the league's induction into the Baseball Hall of Fame.* ■ a formal introduction to a new job or position. ■ enlistment into military service. **2** the process or action of bringing about or giving rise to something: *isolation, starvation, and other forms of stress induction.* ■ *Med.* the process of bringing on childbirth or abortion by artificial means, typically by the use of drugs. **3** *Logic* the inference of a general law from particular instances. Often contrasted with DE-DUCTION. ■ (**induction of**) the production of (facts) to prove a general statement. ■ *Math.* a means of proving a theorem by showing that if it is true of any particular case, it is true of the next case in a series, and

then showing that it is indeed true in one particular case. **4** *Physics* the production of an electric or magnetic state by the proximity (without contact) of an electrified or magnetized body. ■ the production of an electric current in a conductor by varying the magnetic field applied to the conductor. **5** the stage of the working cycle of an internal combustion engine in which the fuel mixture is drawn into the cylinders.

in·duc·tive /in'dəktiv/ ▶*adj.* characterized by the inference of general laws from particular instances: *instinct rather than inductive reasoning.* —**in·duc·tive·ly** *adv.* —**in·duc·tive·ness** *n.*

in·dulge /in'dəlj/ ▶*v.* [*intr.*] (**indulge in**) allow oneself to enjoy the pleasure of: *we indulged in some hot fudge sundaes.* ■ become involved in (an activity, typically one that is undesirable or disapproved of): *I don't indulge in idle gossip.* ■ *inf.* allow oneself to enjoy a particular pleasure, esp. that of alcohol: *I only indulge on special occasions.* ■ [*tr.*] satisfy or yield freely to (a desire or interest). ■ [*tr.*] allow (someone) to enjoy a desired pleasure: *I spent time indulging myself with secret feasts.* —**in·dulg·er** *n.*

in·dul·gence /in'dəljəns/ ▶*n.* **1** the action or fact of indulging: *indulgence in self-pity.* ■ the state or attitude of being indulgent or tolerant: *she regarded his affairs with a casual, slightly amused indulgence.* ■ a thing that is indulged in; a luxury: *Claire collects shoes—it is her indulgence.* **2** *chiefly hist.* (in the Roman Catholic Church) a grant by the pope of remission of the temporal punishment in purgatory still due for sins after absolution. **3** an extension of the time in which a bill or debt has to be paid.

in·dul·gent /in'dəljənt/ ▶*adj.* having or indicating a readiness or over-readiness to be generous to or lenient with someone. ■ self-indulgent: *a slightly adolescent, indulgent account of a love affair.* —**in·dul·gent·ly** *adv.*

in·dus·tri·al /in'dəstrēəl/ ▶*adj.* of, relating to, or characterized by industry: *a small industrial town.* ■ having highly developed industries: *the major industrial nations.* ■ designed or suitable for use in industry: *industrial heating oil.* ■ (of a disease or injury) contracted or sustained in the course of employment, esp. in a factory. ■ relating to or denoting a type of harsh, uncompromising rock music incorporating sounds resembling those produced by industrial machinery.
▶*n.* (**industrials**) shares in industrial companies. —**in·dus·tri·al·ly** *adv.*

in·dus·tri·al·ism /in'dəstrēə,lizəm/ ▶*n.* a social or economic system built on manufacturing industries.

in·dus·tri·al·ist /in'dəstrēəlist/ ▶*n.* a person involved in the ownership and management of industry.

in·dus·tri·al·ize /in'dəstrēə,līz/ ▶*v.* [*tr.*] develop industries in (a country or region) on a wide scale: *the industrialized nations.* ■ [*intr.*] (of a country or region) build up a system of industries: *the country needs to industrialize to create both exports and jobs.* —**in·dus·tri·al·i·za·tion** /in,dəstrēəli-'zāshən/ *n.*

in·dus·tri·al park ▶*n.* an area of land developed as a site for factories and other industrial businesses.

In·dus·tri·al Rev·o·lu·tion ▶*n.* the rapid development of industry that occurred in Britain in the late 18th and 19th centuries, brought about by the introduction of machinery.

in·dus·tri·ous /in'dəstrēəs/ ▶*adj.* diligent and hard-working. —**in·dus·tri·ous·ly** *adv.* —**in·dus·tri·ous·ness** *n.*

in·dus·try /'indəstrē/ ▶*n.* (*pl.* -tries) **1** economic activity concerned with the processing of raw materials and manufacture of goods in factories: *the competitiveness of American industry.* ■ a particular form or branch of economic or commercial activity: *the car industry.* ■ *inf.* an activity or domain in which a great deal of time or effort is expended: *the Shakespeare industry.* **2** hard work: *the kitchen became a hive of industry.*

in·e·bri·ant /i'nēbrēənt/ ▶*adj.* (of a substance) intoxicating.
▶*n.* an inebriating substance or agent; an intoxicant.

in·e·bri·ate *formal or humorous* ▶*v.* /i'nēbrē,āt/ [*tr.*] make drunk; intoxicate.
▶*n.* /-brē-it/ a drunkard.
▶*adj.* /-brē-it/ drunk; intoxicated. —**in·e·bri·a·tion** /i,nēbrē'āshən/ *n.* —**in·e·bri·e·ty** /,ini'brī-itē/ *n.*

in·ef·fa·ble /in'efəbəl/ ▶*adj.* too great or extreme to be expressed or described in words: *the ineffable natural beauty of the Everglades.* ■ not to be uttered: *the ineffable Hebrew name that gentiles write as Jehovah.* —**in·ef·fa·bil·i·ty** /-efə'bilitē/ *n.* —**in·ef·fa·bly** /-blē/ *adv.*

in·ef·fec·tu·al /,ini'fekchŌŌəl/ ▶*adj.* not producing any or the desired effect: *an ineffectual campaign.* ■ (of a person) lacking the ability or qualities to cope with a role or situation. —**in·ef·fec·tu·al·i·ty** /-fekchŌŌ'alitē/ *n.* —**in·ef·fec·tu·al·ly** *adv.* —**in·ef·fec·tu·al·ness** *n.*

in·ef·fi·cient /,ini'fishənt/ ▶*adj.* not achieving maximum productivity;

wasting or failing to make the best use of time or resources: *an old, inefficient factory.* —**in·ef·fi·cien·cy** *n.* —**in·ef·fi·cient·ly** *adv.*

in·el·e·gant /in'eligənt/ ▶ *adj.* having or showing a lack of physical grace, elegance, or refinement. ■ unappealing through being unnecessarily complicated: *an inelegant and complex piece of legislation.* —**in·el·e·gance** *n.* —**in·el·e·gant·ly** *adv.*

in·e·luc·ta·ble /ˌini'ləktəbəl/ ▶ *adj.* unable to be resisted or avoided; inescapable: *the ineluctable facts of history.* —**in·e·luc·ta·bil·i·ty** /-ˌləktə'bilitē/ *n.* —**in·e·luc·ta·bly** /-blē/ *adv.*

in·ept /i'nept/ ▶ *adj.* having or showing no skill; clumsy. —**in·ep·ti·tude** /-ti,t(y)ood/ *n.* —**in·ept·ly** *adv.* —**in·ept·ness** *n.*

in·e·qual·i·ty /ˌini'kwälitē/ ▶ *n.* (pl. **-ties**) difference in size, degree, circumstances, etc.; lack of equality: *social inequality.* ■ *Math.* the relation between two expressions that are not equal, employing a sign such as ≠ "not equal to," > "greater than," or < "less than." ■ *Math.* a symbolic expression of the fact that two quantities are not equal.

in·eq·ui·ta·ble /in'ekwitəbəl/ ▶ *adj.* unfair; unjust: *the present taxes are inequitable.* —**in·eq·ui·ta·bly** /-blē/ *adv.*

in·eq·ui·ty /in'ekwitē/ ▶ *n.* (pl. **-ties**) lack of fairness or justice: *policies aimed at redressing racial inequity* | *inequities in school financing.*

in·ert /i'nərt/ ▶ *adj.* lacking the ability or strength to move: *she lay inert in her bed.* ■ lacking vigor: *an inert political system.* ■ chemically inactive. ▷mid 17th cent.: from Latin *iners, inert-* 'unskilled, inactive,' from *in-* (expressing negation) + *ars, art-* 'skill, art.' —**in·ert·ly** *adv.* —**in·ert·ness** *n.*

in·ert gas ▶ *n.* another term for NOBLE GAS.

in·er·tia /i'nərSHə/ ▶ *n.* **1** a tendency to do nothing or to remain unchanged: *the bureaucratic inertia of government.* **2** *Physics* a property of matter by which it continues in its existing state of rest or uniform motion in a straight line, unless that state is changed by an external force. ■ resistance to change in some other physical property: *the thermal inertia of the oceans will delay the full rise in temperature for a few decades.* —**in·er·tia·less** *adj.*

in·es·cap·a·ble /ˌini'skāpəbəl/ ▶ *adj.* unable to be avoided or denied. —**in·es·cap·a·bil·i·ty** /-ˌskāpə'bilitē/ *n.* —**in·es·cap·a·bly** /-blē/ *adv.*

in·es·sen·tial /ˌini'senCHəl/ ▶ *adj.* not absolutely necessary. ▶ *n.* (usu. **inessentials**) a thing that is not absolutely necessary.

in·es·ti·ma·ble /in'estəməbəl/ ▶ *adj.* too great to calculate: *a treasure of inestimable value.* —**in·es·ti·ma·bly** /-blē/ *adv.*

in·ev·i·ta·ble /in'evitəbəl/ ▶ *adj.* certain to happen; unavoidable: *war was inevitable.* ■ *inf.* so frequently experienced or seen that it is completely predictable: *the inevitable letter from the bank.* ▶ *n.* (**the inevitable**) a situation that is unavoidable. —**in·ev·i·ta·bil·i·ty** /-ˌevitə'bilitē/ *n.* —**in·ev·i·ta·bly** /-blē/ *adv.*

in·ex·cus·a·ble /ˌinik'skyoozəbəl/ ▶ *adj.* too bad to be justified or tolerated: *Matt's behavior was inexcusable.* —**in·ex·cus·a·bly** /-blē/ *adv.*

in·ex·haust·i·ble /ˌinig'zôstəbəl/ ▶ *adj.* (of an amount or supply of something) unable to be used up because existing in abundance. —**in·ex·haust·i·bil·i·ty** /-ˌzôstə'bilitē/ *n.* —**in·ex·haust·i·bly** /-blē/ *adv.*

in·ex·o·ra·ble /in'eksərəbəl/ ▶ *adj.* impossible to stop or prevent: *the seemingly inexorable march of new technology.* ■ (of a person) impossible to persuade by request or entreaty: *an inexorable opponent.* —**in·ex·o·ra·bil·i·ty** /-ˌeksərə'bilitē/ *n.* —**in·ex·o·ra·bly** /-blē/ *adv.*

in·ex·pe·ri·ence /ˌinik'spi(ə)rēəns/ ▶ *n.* lack of experience, knowledge, or skill. —**in·ex·pe·ri·enced** *adj.*

in·ex·pert /in'ekspərt/ ▶ *adj.* having or showing a lack of experience, skill, or knowledge. —**in·ex·pert·ly** *adv.*

in·ex·pli·ca·ble /ˌinek'splikəbəl; in'eksplikəbəl/ ▶ *adj.* unable to be explained or accounted for: *for some inexplicable reason her mind went blank.* —**in·ex·pli·ca·bil·i·ty** /'inek,splikə'bilitē/ *n.* —**in·ex·pli·ca·bly** /-blē/ *adv.*

in·ex·press·i·ble /ˌinik'spresəbəl/ ▶ *adj.* (of a feeling) too strong to be described or conveyed in words. —**in·ex·press·i·bly** /-blē/ *adv.*

in ex·tre·mis /ˌin ek'strāmēs; ik'strēmis/ ▶ *adv.* in an extremely difficult situation: *they suddenly find themselves in extremis 20 miles out to sea.* ■ at the point of death.

in·ex·tri·ca·ble /ˌinik'strikəbəl; in'ekstri-/ ▶ *adj.* impossible to disentangle or separate. ■ impossible to escape from: *an inextricable situation.* —**in·ex·tri·ca·bil·i·ty** /ˌinik,strikə'bilitē/ *n.* —**in·ex·tri·ca·bly** /-blē/ *adv.*

in·fal·li·bil·i·ty /inˌfalə'bilitē/ ▶ *n.* the quality of being infallible; the inability to be wrong. ■ (also **papal infallibility**) (in the Roman Catholic Church) the doctrine that in specified circumstances the pope is incapable of error in pronouncing dogma.

in·fal·li·ble /in'faləbəl/ ▶ *adj.* incapable of making mistakes or being wrong. ■ never failing; always effective: *infallible cures.* ■ (in the Roman Catholic Church) credited with papal infallibility: *for an encyclical to be infallible the pope must speak ex cathedra.* —**in·fal·li·bly** /-blē/ *adv.*

in·fa·mous /'infəməs/ ▶ *adj.* well known for some bad quality or deed. ■ wicked; abominable. —**in·fa·mous·ly** *adv.* —**in·fa·my** /-mē/ *n.* (pl. **-mies**)

in·fan·cy /'infənsē/ ▶ *n.* the state or period of early childhood or babyhood: *a son who died in infancy.* ■ the early stage in the development or growth of something: *opinion polls were in their infancy.* ■ *Law* the condition of being a minor.

in·fant /'infənt/ ▶ *n.* a very young child or baby. ■ [as *adj.*] denoting something in an early stage of its development: *the infant science of genotypic medicine.* ■ *Law* a person who has not attained legal majority.

in·fan·ti·cide /in'fanti,sīd/ ▶ *n.* **1** the crime of killing a child within a year of birth. ■ the practice in some societies of killing unwanted children soon after birth. **2** a person who kills an infant, esp. their own child. —**in·fan·ti·cid·al** /-ˌfanti'sīdl/ *adj.*

in·fan·tile /'infən,tīl; 'infənt-il/ ▶ *adj.* of or occurring among babies or very young children: *infantile colic.* ■ *derog.* childish: *infantile jokes.* —**in·fan·til·i·ty** /ˌinfən'tilitē/ *n.* (pl. **-ties**).

in·fan·tile pa·ral·y·sis ▶ *n.* dated poliomyelitis.

in·fan·try /'infəntrē/ ▶ *n.* soldiers marching or fighting on foot; foot soldiers collectively. —**in·fan·try·man** *n.*

in·farct /'in,färkt/ ▶ *n. Med.* a small localized area of dead tissue resulting from failure of blood supply. —**in·farc·tion** *n.*

in·fat·u·ate /in'faCHoo,āt/ ▶ *v.* (**be infatuated with**) be inspired with an intense but short-lived passion or admiration for: *she is infatuated with a handsome police chief.* —**in·fat·u·a·tion** /-ˌfaCHoo'āsHən/ *n.*

in·fect /in'fekt/ ▶ *v.* [tr.] affect (a person, organism, cell, etc.) with a disease-causing organism: *there is no evidence that the virus can infect humans.* ■ contaminate (air, water, etc.) with harmful organisms. ■ *Comput.* affect with a virus. ■ *fig.* (of a negative feeling or idea) take hold of or be communicated to (someone): *the panic in his voice infected her.* —**in·fec·tive** *adj* —**in·fec·tor** /-'fektər/ *n.*

in·fec·tion /in'fekSHən/ ▶ *n.* the process of infecting or the state of being infected: *strict hygiene will limit the risk of infection.* ■ an infectious disease: *a chest infection.* ■ *Comput.* the presence of a virus in, or its introduction into, a computer system.

in·fec·tious /in'fekSHəs/ ▶ *adj.* (of a disease or disease-causing organism) likely to be transmitted to people, organisms, etc., through the environment. ■ likely to spread infection: *the dogs may still be infectious.* ■ likely to spread or influence others in a rapid manner: *her enthusiasm is infectious.* —**in·fec·tious·ly** *adv.* —**in·fec·tious·ness** *n.*

in·fec·tious mon·o·nu·cle·o·sis ▶ *n.* an infectious viral disease characterized by swelling of the lymph glands and prolonged lassitude. Also called MONO, GLANDULAR FEVER.

in·fe·lic·i·tous /ˌinfə'lisitəs/ ▶ *adj.* unfortunate; inappropriate: *his illustration is singularly infelicitous.* —**in·fe·lic·i·tous·ly** *adv.*

in·fe·lic·i·ty /ˌinfə'lisitē/ ▶ *n.* (pl. **-ties**) a thing that is inappropriate, esp. a remark or expression. ■ *archaic* unhappiness; misfortune.

in·fer /in'fər/ ▶ *v.* (**-ferred, -fer·ring**) [tr.] deduce or conclude (information) from evidence and reasoning rather than from explicit statements: *from these facts we can infer that crime has been increasing.* —**in·fer·a·ble** (also **in·fer·ra·ble**) *adj.*

in·fer·ence /'inf(ə)rəns/ ▶ *n.* a conclusion reached on the basis of evidence and reasoning. ■ the process of reaching such a conclusion. —**in·fer·en·tial** /ˌinfə'renCHəl/ *adj.* —**in·fer·en·tial·ly** /ˌinfə'renCHəlē/ *adv.*

in·fe·ri·or /in'fi(ə)rēər/ ▶ *adj.* **1** lower in rank, status, or quality. ■ of low standard or quality: *inferior goods.* ■ *Law* (of a court or tribunal) able to have its decisions overturned by a higher court. ■ *Econ.* denoting goods or services that are in greater demand during a recession than in a boom, e.g., secondhand clothes. **2** chiefly *Anat.* low or lower in position: *the inferior and posterior wall of the duodenum.* ■ (of a letter, figure, or symbol) written or printed below the line. ▶ *n.* **1** a person lower than another in rank, status, or ability: *her social and intellectual inferiors.* **2** *Printing* an inferior letter, figure, or symbol. —**in·fe·ri·or·ly** *adv.*

in·fe·ri·or·i·ty /inˌfi(ə)rē'ôritē; -'äritē/ ▶ *n.* the condition of being lower in status or quality than another or others.

in·fe·ri·or·i·ty com·plex ▶ *n.* an unrealistic feeling of general inadequacy caused by actual or supposed inferiority in one sphere, sometimes marked by aggressive behavior in compensation.

in·fer·nal /ɪnˈfərnl/ ▸*adj.* **1** of, relating to, or characteristic of hell or the underworld. **2** *inf.* irritating and tiresome (used for emphasis): *you're an infernal nuisance.* ▷late Middle English: from Old French, from Christian Latin *infernalis*, from Latin *infernus* 'below, underground,' used by Christians to mean 'hell,' on the pattern of *inferni* (masculine plural) 'the shades' and *inferna* (neuter plural) 'the lower regions.' —**in·fer·nal·ly** *adv.*

in·fer·no /ɪnˈfərnō/ ▸*n.* (*pl.* **-nos**) **1** a large fire that is out of control. **2** (usu. **In·fer·no**) hell (with reference to Dante's *Divine Comedy*).

in·fest /ɪnˈfest/ ▸*v.* [*tr.*] (of insects or animals) be present (in a place or site) in large numbers, typically so as to cause damage or disease: *the house is infested with cockroaches.* —**in·fes·ta·tion** /ˌinfeˈstāSHən/ *n.*

in·fi·del /ˈinfədl; -ˌdel/ ▸*n. chiefly archaic* a person who does not believe in religion or who adheres to a religion other than one's own: [as *pl. n.*] (**the infidel**) *they wanted to secure the Holy Places from the infidel.* ▸*adj.* adhering to a religion other than one's own. ▷late 15th cent.: from French *infidèle* or Latin *infidelis*, from *in-* 'not' + *fidelis* 'faithful' (from *fides* 'faith,' related to *fidere* 'to trust'). The word originally denoted a person of a religion other than one's own, specifically a Muslim (to a Christian), a Christian (to a Muslim), or a Gentile (to a Jew).

in·fi·del·i·ty /ˌinfiˈdelitē/ ▸*n.* (*pl.* **-ties**) **1** the action or state of being unfaithful to a spouse or other sexual partner. **2** unbelief in a particular religion, esp. Christianity.

in·field /ˈinˌfēld/ ▸*n.* the inner part of the field of play in various sports, in particular: ■ *Baseball* the area within and near the four bases. ■ the players stationed in the infield, collectively. ▸*adv.* into or toward the inner part of the field of play. —**in·field·er** *n.*

in·fight·ing /ˈinˌfītiNG/ ▸*n.* hidden conflict or competitiveness within an organization. ■ boxing closer to an opponent than at arm's length. —**in·fight·er** *n.*

in·fil·trate /ˈinfilˌtrāt; inˈfil-/ ▸*v.* [*tr.*] **1** enter or gain access to (an organization, place, etc.) surreptitiously and gradually, esp. in order to acquire secret information: *other areas of the establishment were infiltrated by fascists.* ■ *fig.* permeate or become a part of (something) in this way: *computing has infiltrated most professions now.* ■ *Med.* (of a tumor, cells, etc.) spread into or invade (a tissue or organ). **2** (of a liquid) permeate (something) by filtration. ■ introduce (a liquid) into something in this way: *stains caused by materials infiltrated into the wood.* —**in·fil·tra·tion** /ˌinfilˈtrāSHən/ *n.* —**in·fil·tra·tor** /-ˌtrātər/ *n.*

in·fi·nite /ˈinfənit/ ▸*adj.* limitless or endless in space, extent, or size; impossible to measure or calculate: *the infinite mercy of God.* ■ very great in amount or degree: *he bathed the wound with infinite care.* ■ *Math.* greater than any assignable quantity or countable number. ■ *Math.* (of a series) able to be continued indefinitely. ▸*n.* (**the infinite**) a space or quantity that is infinite. ■ (**the Infinite**) God. —**in·fi·nite·ly** *adv. the pay is infinitely better.* —**in·fi·nite·ness** *n.*

in·fin·i·tes·i·mal /ˌinfiniˈtes(ə)məl/ ▸*adj.* extremely small. ▸*n. Math.* an indefinitely small quantity; a value approaching zero. —**in·fin·i·tes·i·mal·ly** *adv.*

in·fin·i·tive /inˈfinitiv/ ▸*n.* the basic form of a verb, without an inflection binding it to a particular subject or tense (e.g., *see* in *we came to see, let him see*). ▸*adj.* having or involving such a form. —**in·fin·i·ti·val** /-finiˈtīvəl/ *adj.* —**in·fin·i·ti·val·ly** /-finiˈtīvəlē/ *adv.*

in·fin·i·ty /inˈfinitē/ ▸*n.* (*pl.* **-ties**) the state or quality of being infinite: *the infinity of space.* ■ an infinite or very great number or amount. ■ *Math.* a number greater than any assignable quantity or countable number (symbol ∞). ■ a point in space or time that is or seems infinitely distant.

in·firm /inˈfərm/ ▸*adj.* not physically or mentally strong, esp. through age or illness. —**in·firm·i·ty** *n.* —**in·firm·ly** *adv.*

in·fir·ma·ry /inˈfərm(ə)rē/ ▸*n.* (*pl.* **-ries**) a place in a large institution for the care of those who are ill: *the prison infirmary.*

in·fix ▸*n.* /ˈinˌfiks/ *Grammar* a formative element inserted in a word.

in fla·gran·te de·lic·to /ˌin flə̇ˈgräntā dəˈliktō; flāˈgrantē/ (also *inf.* **in fla·gran·te**) ▸*adv.* in the very act of wrongdoing, esp. in an act of sexual misconduct: *he had been caught in flagrante with the wife of the treasurer.*

in·flame /inˈflām/ ▸*v.* [*tr.*] **1** provoke or intensify (strong feelings, esp. anger) in someone. ■ provoke (someone) to strong feelings: *her sister was inflamed with jealousy.* ■ make (a situation) worse. **2** cause inflammation in (a part of the body): *the finger joints were inflamed with rheumatoid arthritis.* **3** *poetic/lit.* light up with or as if with flames. —**in·flam·er** *n.*

in·flam·ma·ble /inˈflaməbəl/ ▸*adj.* easily set on fire. ■ *fig.* likely to provoke strong feelings. —**in·flam·ma·bil·i·ty** /-ˌflaməˈbilitē/ *n.* —**in·flam·ma·ble·ness** *n.* —**in·flam·ma·bly** /-blē/ *adv.*

in·flam·ma·tion /ˌinfləˈmāSHən/ ▸*n.* a localized physical condition in which part of the body becomes reddened, swollen, hot, and often painful, esp. as a reaction to injury or infection.

in·flam·ma·to·ry /inˈflaməˌtôrē/ ▸*adj.* **1** relating to or causing inflammation of a part of the body. **2** (esp. of speech or writing) arousing or intended to arouse angry or violent feelings: *inflammatory slogans.*

in·flat·a·ble /inˈflātəbəl/ ▸*adj.* capable of being filled with air. ▸*n.* a plastic or rubber object that must be filled with air before use.

in·flate /inˈflāt/ ▸*v.* [*tr.*] **1** fill (a balloon, tire, or other expandable structure) with air or gas so that it becomes distended. ■ [*intr.*] become distended in this way. **2** increase (something) by a large or excessive amount: *objectives should be clearly set out so as not to duplicate work and inflate costs.* ■ exaggerate. ■ bring about inflation of (a currency) or in (an economy). —**in·flat·ed·ly** *adv.* —**in·fla·tor** /-ˈflātər/ (also **in·flat·er**) *n.*

in·fla·tion /inˈflāSHən/ ▸*n.* **1** the action of inflating something or the condition of being inflated. ■ *Astron.* (in some theories of cosmology) a very brief exponential expansion of the universe postulated to have interrupted the standard linear expansion shortly after the big bang. **2** *Econ.* a general increase in prices and fall in the purchasing value of money: *policies aimed at controlling inflation* | [as *adj.*] *high inflation rates.* —**in·fla·tion·ar·y** /-SHəˌnerē/ *adj.* —**in·fla·tion·ism** /-ˌnizəm/ *n.* —**in·fla·tion·ist** /-nist/ *n. & adj.*

in·flect /inˈflekt/ ▸*v.* [*tr.*] (often **be inflected**) **1** *Gram.* change the form of (a word) to express a particular grammatical function or attribute, typically tense, mood, person, number, case, and gender. ■ [*intr.*] (of a word or a language containing such words) undergo such change. **2** vary the intonation or pitch of (the voice), esp. to express mood or feeling. ■ influence or color (music or writing) in tone or style. ■ vary the pitch of (a musical note). —**in·flec·tive** /-tiv/ *adj.*

in·flec·tion /inˈflekSHən/ (*chiefly Brit.* also **in·flex·ion**) ▸*n.* **1** *Gram.* a change in the form of a word (typically the ending) to express a grammatical function or attribute such as tense, mood, person, number, case, and gender. ■ the process or practice of inflecting words. **2** the modulation of intonation or pitch in the voice: *she spoke slowly and without inflection* | *the variety of his vocal inflections.* ■ the variation of the pitch of a musical note. **3** *chiefly Math.* a change of curvature from convex to concave at a particular point on a curve. —**in·flec·tion·al** /-SHənl/ *adj.* —**in·flec·tion·al·ly** /-SHənl-ē/ *adv.* —**in·flec·tion·less** *adj.*

in·flex·i·ble /inˈfleksəbəl/ ▸*adj.* **1** unwilling to change or compromise. ■ not able to be changed or adapted to particular circumstances: *inflexible rules.* **2** not able to be bent; stiff: *the heavy inflexible armor of the beetles.* —**in·flex·i·bil·i·ty** /-ˌfleksəˈbilitē/ *n.* —**in·flex·i·bly** /-blē/ *adv.*

in·flict /inˈflikt/ ▸*v.* [*tr.*] cause (something unpleasant or painful) to be suffered by someone or something. ■ (**inflict something on**) impose something unwelcome on: *she is wrong to inflict her beliefs on everyone else.* ▷mid 16th cent. (in the sense 'afflict, trouble'): from Latin *inflict-* 'struck against,' from the verb *infligere*, from *in-* 'into' + *fligere* 'to strike.' —**in·flict·a·ble** *adj.* —**in·flict·er** *n.* —**in·flic·tion** *n.*

in-flight /ˈinˌflīt/ ▸*adj.* occurring or provided during an aircraft flight: *in-flight entertainment.*

in·flo·res·cence /ˌinflôˈresəns; -flə-/ ▸*n. Bot.* the complete flowerhead of a plant including stems, stalks, bracts, and flowers. ■ the arrangement of the flowers on a plant.

in·flow /ˈinˌflō/ ▸*n.* a large amount of money, people, or water, that moves or is transferred into a place: *some enclosed seas are subject to large inflows of fresh water* | *the firm experienced two years of cash inflow.* —**in·flow·ing** *n. & adj.*

in·flu·ence /ˈinflo͞oəns/ ▸*n.* the capacity to have an effect on the character, development, or behavior of someone or something, or the effect itself: *the influence of television violence* | *their friends are having a bad influence on them.* ■ the power to shape policy or ensure favorable treatment from someone, esp. through status, contacts, or wealth: *the institute has considerable influence with teachers.* ■ a person or thing with such a capacity or power: *Frank was a good influence on her.* ▸*v.* [*tr.*] have an influence on. ▷late Middle English: from Old French, or from medieval Latin *influentia* 'inflow,' from Latin *influere*, from *in-* 'into' + *fluere* 'to flow.' The word originally had the general sense 'an influx, flowing matter,' also specifically (in astrology) 'the flowing in of ethereal fluid (affecting human destiny).' The sense 'imperceptible or indirect action exerted to cause changes' was established in Scholastic Latin by the 13th cent., but not recorded in English until the late 16th cent. —**in·flu·ence·a·ble** *adj.* —**in·flu·enc·er** *n.*
▸ □ **under the influence** *inf.* affected by alcoholic drink; drunk.

in·flu·en·tial /ˌinflo͞oˈenCHəl/ ▸*adj.* having great influence on someone or something: *her work is influential in feminist psychology.* ▸*n.* (usu. **influentials**) an influential person. —**in·flu·en·tial·ly** *adv.*

in·flu·en·za /ˌinflo͞oˈenzə/ ▶n. a highly contagious viral infection of the respiratory passages causing fever, severe aching, and catarrh, and often occurring in epidemics. Also called FLU. —**in·flu·en·zal** adj.

in·flux /ˈinˌfləks/ ▶n. **1** an arrival or entry of large numbers of people or things: a massive influx of refugees from front-line areas. **2** an inflow of water into a river, lake, or the sea.

in·fo /ˈinfō/ ▶n. inf. information.

in·fo·hol·ic /ˌinfəˈhôlik; -ˈhäl-/ ▶n. a person who feels compelled to search out news and information, especially online.

in·fo·mer·cial /ˈinfōˌmərSHəl/ ▶n. a television program that promotes a product in an informative and supposedly objective way.

in·form /inˈfôrm/ ▶v. **1** give (someone) facts or information; tell: [tr.] he wrote to her, informing her of the situation | [tr.] they were informed that no risk was involved | [intr.] the role of television is to inform and entertain. ■ [intr.] give incriminating information about someone to the police or other authority: surrendered terrorists began to **inform on** their former comrades. **2** [tr.] give an essential or formative principle or quality to: the relationship of the citizen to the state is informed by the democratic ideal. —**in·form·ant** /-ˈfôrmənt/ n.

in·for·mal /inˈfôrməl/ ▶adj. having a relaxed, friendly, or unofficial style, manner, or nature: an informal atmosphere | an informal agreement between the two companies. ■ of or denoting a style of writing or conversational speech characterized by simple grammatical structures, familiar vocabulary, and use of idioms, e.g., tu in French. ■ (of dress) casual; suitable for everyday wear. —**in·for·mal·i·ty** /ˌinfôrˈmalitē/ n. —**in·for·mal·ly** adv.

in·for·mat·ics /ˌinfərˈmatiks/ ▶pl. n. [treated as sing.] Comput. the science of processing data for storage and retrieval; information science.

in·for·ma·tion /ˌinfərˈmāSHən/ ▶n. **1** facts provided or learned about something or someone: a vital piece of information. ■ Law a formal criminal charge lodged with a court or magistrate by a prosecutor without the aid of a grand jury: the tenant may lay an information against his landlord. **2** what is conveyed or represented by a particular arrangement or sequence of things: genetically transmitted information. ■ Comput. data as processed, stored, or transmitted by a computer. ■ (in information theory) a mathematical quantity expressing the probability of occurrence of a particular sequence of symbols, impulses, etc., as contrasted with that of alternative sequences. —**in·for·ma·tion·al** /-SHənl/ adj. —**in·for·ma·tion·al·ly** /-SHənl-ē/ adv.

in·for·ma·tion sci·ence ▶n. Comput. the study of processes for storing and retrieving information, esp. scientific or technical information.

in·for·ma·tive /inˈfôrmətiv/ ▶adj. providing useful or interesting information. —**in·for·ma·tive·ly** adv. —**in·for·ma·tive·ness** n.

in·formed /inˈfôrmd/ ▶adj. having or showing knowledge of a particular subject or situation: an informed readership. ■ (of a decision or judgment) based on an understanding of the facts of the situation: twenty-six young adults participated after giving informed consent. —**in·form·ed·ly** /-m(i)dlē/ adv. —**in·form·ed·ness** /-m(i)dnis/ n.

in·form·er /inˈfôrmər/ ▶n. a person who informs on another person to the police or other authority.

in·fo·tain·ment /ˌinfōˈtānmənt/ ▶n. broadcast material that is intended both to entertain and to inform.

in·fo·war /ˈinfōˌwôr/ ▶n. **1** hostile actions against an enemy's information infrastructure: an infowar against NATO's computer network. **2** a propaganda war waged via electronic media.

in·fra /ˈinfrə/ ▶adv. (in a written document) below; further on: see note, infra.

in·frac·tion /inˈfrakSHən/ ▶n. a violation or infringement of a law, agreement, or set of rules. —**in·frac·tor** /-tər/ n.

in·fra dig ▶adj. inf. beneath one; demeaning: it was somewhat infra dig for a man in his position to be found drinking.

in·fra·or·der /ˈinfrəˌôrdər/ ▶n. Biol. a taxonomic category that ranks below a suborder.

in·fra·red /ˌinfrəˈred/ ▶adj. (of electromagnetic radiation) having a wavelength just greater than that of the red end of the visible light spectrum but less than that of microwaves. Infrared radiation has a wavelength from about 800 nm to 1 mm, and is emitted particularly by heated objects. ■ (of equipment or techniques) using or concerned with this radiation: infrared cameras.
▶n. the infrared region of the spectrum; infrared radiation.

in·fra·struc·ture /ˈinfrəˌstrəkCHər/ ▶n. the basic physical and organizational structures and facilities (e.g., buildings, roads, and power supplies) needed for the operation of a society or enterprise. —**in·fra·struc·tur·al** /ˌinfrəˈstrəkCHərəl/ adj.

in·fre·quent /inˈfrēkwənt/ ▶adj. not occurring often; rare: her visits were so infrequent. —**in·fre·quen·cy** n. —**in·fre·quent·ly** adv.

in·fringe /inˈfrinj/ ▶v. [tr.] actively break the terms of (a law, agreement, etc.): making an unauthorized copy would infringe copyright. ■ act so as to limit or undermine (something); encroach on: his legal rights were being infringed | [intr.] I wouldn't **infringe on** his privacy. —**in·fringe·ment** n. —**in·fring·er** n.

in·fu·ri·ate /inˈfyo͝orēˌāt/ ▶v. [tr.] make (someone) extremely angry and impatient. —**in·fu·ri·at·ing·ly** adv.

in·fuse /inˈfyo͞oz/ ▶v. [tr.] **1** fill; pervade: her work is infused with an anger born of pain. ■ instill (a quality) in someone or something: he did his best to infuse good humor into his voice. ■ Med. allow (a liquid) to flow into a patient, vein, etc.: saline was infused into the aorta. **2** soak (tea, herbs, etc.) in liquid to extract the flavor or healing properties. —**in·fus·er** n.

in·fu·sion /inˈfyo͞oZHən/ ▶n. **1** a drink, remedy, or extract prepared by soaking the leaves of a plant or herb in liquid. ■ the process of preparing such a drink, remedy, or extract. **2** the introduction of a new element or quality into something: the infusion of $6.3 million for improvements. ■ Med. the slow injection of a substance into a vein or tissue.

in·ge·nious /inˈjēnyəs/ ▶adj. (of a person) clever, original, and inventive. ■ (of a machine or idea) cleverly and originally devised and well suited to its purpose. —**in·ge·nious·ly** adv. —**in·ge·nious·ness** n.

in·gé·nue /ˈanjəˌno͞o; ˈänZH-/ ▶n. an innocent or unsophisticated young woman. ■ a part of this type in a play. ■ an actress who plays such a part.

in·ge·nu·i·ty /ˌinjəˈn(y)o͞oitē/ ▶n. the quality of being clever, original, and inventive.

in·gen·u·ous /inˈjenyo͞oəs/ ▶adj. (of a person or action) innocent and unsuspecting. ▷late 16th cent.: from Latin ingenuus, literally 'native, inborn,' from in- 'into' + an element related to gignere 'beget.' The original sense was 'noble, generous,' giving rise to 'honorably straightforward, frank,' hence 'innocently frank' (late 17th cent.). —**in·gen·u·ous·ly** adv. —**in·gen·u·ous·ness** n.

in·gest /inˈjest/ ▶v. [tr.] take (food, drink, or another substance) into the body by swallowing or absorbing it. ■ fig. absorb (information). —**in·ges·tion** /-ˈjesCHən/ n. —**in·ges·tive** /-ˈjestiv/ adj.

in·glo·ri·ous /inˈglôrēəs/ ▶adj. (of an action or situation) causing shame or a loss of honor. ■ not famous or renowned. —**in·glo·ri·ous·ly** adv. —**in·glo·ri·ous·ness** n.

in·got /ˈiNGgət/ ▶n. a block of steel, gold, silver, or other metal, typically oblong in shape.

in·grain ▶v. /inˈgrān/ [tr.] firmly fix or establish (a habit, belief, or attitude) in a person.
▶adj. /ˈinˌgrān/ (of a textile) composed of fibers that have been dyed different colors before being woven.

in·grained /inˈgrānd/ ▶adj. **1** (of a habit, belief, or attitude) firmly fixed or established; difficult to change: his deeply ingrained Catholic convictions. **2** (of dirt or a stain) deeply embedded and thus difficult to remove: the ingrained dirt on the flaking paintwork.

in·gra·ti·ate /inˈgrāSHēˌāt/ ▶v. (**ingratiate oneself**) bring oneself into favor with someone by flattering or trying to please them: a social climber who had tried to **ingratiate herself with** the city gentry. —**in·gra·ti·at·ing** adj. —**in·gra·ti·at·ing·ly** adv. —**in·gra·ti·a·tion** /-ˌgrāSHēˈāSHən/ n.

in·grat·i·tude /inˈgrati,t(y)o͞od/ ▶n. a discreditable lack of gratitude: she returned her daughter's care with ingratitude and unkindness.

in·gre·di·ent /inˈgrēdēənt; iNG-/ ▶n. any of the foods or substances that are combined to make a particular dish: pork is an important ingredient in many stir-fried dishes. ■ a component part or element of something.

in·gress /ˈinˌgres/ ▶n. a place or means of access; an entrance. ■ the action or fact of going in or entering. ■ the capacity or right of entrance. —**in·gres·sion** /-ˈgreSHən/ n.

in-group ▶n. an exclusive, typically small, group of people with a shared interest or identity.

in·grown /ˈinˌgrōn/ ▶adj. growing or having grown within a thing; innate: as Greek instinct and ingrown habit would have dictated. ■ (of a toenail) having grown abnormally so as to press into the flesh.

in·gui·nal /ˈiNGgwənəl/ ▶adj. Anat. of the groin: inguinal lymph nodes. —**in·gui·nal·ly** adv.

in·hab·it /inˈhabit/ ▶v. (**-hab·it·ed, -hab·it·ing**) [tr.] (of a person, animal, or group) live in or occupy (a place or environment): a bird that inhabits

North America. —**in·hab·it·a·bil·i·ty** /-ˌhabitəˈbilitē/ n. —**in·hab·it·a·ble** adj. —**in·hab·it·ant** /-itnt/ n. —**in·hab·i·ta·tion** /-ˌhabiˈtāsʜən/ n.

in·hal·ant /inˈhālənt/ ▶n. a medicinal preparation for inhaling. ■ a solvent or other material producing vapor inhaled by drug abusers.
▶adj. chiefly Zool. serving for inhalation: inhalant canals.

in·hale /inˈhāl/ ▶v. breathe in (air, gas, smoke, etc.): [tr.] they were taken to the hospital after inhaling fumes | [intr.] she inhaled deeply on another cigarette. ■ [tr.] inf. eat (food) greedily or rapidly. —**in·ha·la·tion** /ˌinhəˈlāsʜən/ n.

in·hal·er /inˈhālər/ ▶n. a portable device for administering a drug that is to be breathed in, used for relieving asthma and other bronchial or nasal congestion.

in·here /inˈhi(ə)r/ ▶v. [intr.] (**inhere in/within**) formal exist essentially or permanently in: the potential for change that inheres within the adult education world. ■ Law (of rights, powers, etc.) be vested in a person or group or attached to the ownership of a property: the rights inhering in the property they owned.

in·her·ent /inˈhi(ə)rənt; -ˈher-/ ▶adj. existing in something as a permanent, essential, or characteristic attribute: the symbolism inherent in all folk tales. ■ Law vested in (someone) as a right or privilege: the president's inherent foreign affairs power. —**in·her·ence** n. —**in·her·ent·ly** adv.

in·her·it /inˈherit/ ▶v. (**-her·it·ed, -her·it·ing**) [tr.] receive (money, property, or a title) as an heir at the death of the previous holder. ■ derive (a quality, characteristic, or predisposition) genetically from one's parents or ancestors. ■ receive or be left with (a situation, object, etc.) from a predecessor or former owner: spending commitments inherited from previous administrations. ■ come into possession of (belongings) from someone else. —**in·her·i·tor** /-ˈheritər/ n.

in·her·it·a·ble /inˈheritəbəl/ ▶adj. capable of being inherited: these characteristics are inheritable. —**in·her·it·a·bil·i·ty** /-ˌheritəˈbilitē/ n.

in·her·it·ance /inˈheritəns/ ▶n. a thing that is inherited: he came into a comfortable inheritance. ■ the action of inheriting: the inheritance of traits.

in·hib·it /inˈhibit/ ▶v. (**-hib·it·ed, -hib·it·ing**) [tr.] hinder, restrain, or prevent (an action or process): cold inhibits plant growth. ■ prevent or prohibit someone from doing something: the earnings rule **inhibited** some retired people from working. ■ Psychol. voluntarily or involuntarily restrain the direct expression of (an instinctive impulse). ■ make (someone) self-conscious and unable to act in a relaxed and natural way: his mother's strictures would always inhibit him. ■ chiefly Physiol. Biochem. (chiefly of a drug or other substance) slow down or prevent (a process, reaction, or function) or reduce the activity of (an enzyme or other agent). —**in·hib·i·tive** /-tiv/ adj. —**in·hib·i·tor** /-itər/ n. —**in·hib·i·to·ry** /-ˌtôrē/ adj.

in·hi·bi·tion /ˌin(h)iˈbisʜən/ ▶n. a feeling that makes one self-conscious and unable to act in a relaxed and natural way: the children, at first shy, soon lost their inhibitions. ■ Psychol. a voluntary or involuntary restraint on the direct expression of an instinct. ■ the action of inhibiting, restricting, or hindering a process. ■ the slowing or prevention of a process, reaction, or function by a particular substance.

in·hos·pi·ta·ble /ˌinhäˈspitəbəl; inˈhäs-/ ▶adj. (of an environment) harsh and difficult to live in. ■ (of a person) unfriendly and unwelcoming toward people. —**in·hos·pi·ta·ble·ness** n. —**in·hos·pi·ta·bly** /-blē/ adv. —**in·hos·pi·tal·i·ty** /inˌhäspiˈtalitē/ ˌinhäs-/ n.

in-house ▶adj. done or existing within an organization: in-house publications.
▶adv. without assistance from outside an organization; internally.

in·hu·man /inˈ(h)yoōmən/ ▶adj. **1** lacking human qualities of compassion and mercy; cruel and barbaric. **2** not human in nature or character: the inhuman scale of the dinosaurs. —**in·hu·man·ly** adv.

in·hu·man·i·ty /ˌin(h)yoōˈmanitē/ ▶n. (pl. **-ties**) extremely cruel and brutal behavior: a justification for further cruelty and inhumanity.

in·im·i·cal /iˈnimikəl/ ▶adj. tending to obstruct or harm: actions **inimical** to our interests. ■ unfriendly; hostile. —**in·im·i·cal·ly** /-ik(ə)lē/ adv.

in·im·i·ta·ble /iˈnimitəbəl/ ▶adj. so good or unusual as to be impossible to copy; unique: the inimitable ambience of Hawaii. —**in·im·i·ta·bil·i·ty** /iˌnimitəˈbilitē/ n. —**in·im·i·ta·bly** /-blē/ adv.

in·iq·ui·ty /iˈnikwitē/ ▶n. (pl. **-ties**) immoral or grossly unfair behavior: a den of iniquity. —**in·iq·ui·tous** /-witəs/ adj. —**in·iq·ui·tous·ly** /-witəslē/ adv. —**in·iq·ui·tous·ness** /-witəsnəs/ n.

in·i·tial /iˈnisʜəl/ ▶adj. existing or occurring at the beginning: our initial impression was favorable. ■ (of a letter) at the beginning of a word.
▶n. (usu. **initials**) the first letter of a name or word, typically a person's name or a word forming part of a phrase. —**in·i·tial·ly** adv.
▶v. (**-tialed, -tial·ing**; Brit. **-tialled, -tial·ling**) [tr.] mark or sign (a document) with one's initials, esp. in order to authorize or validate it. ■ agree to or ratify (a treaty or contract) by signing it.

in·i·tial·ize /iˈnisʜəˌlīz/ ▶v. [tr.] Comput. **1** (often **be initialized to**) set to

the value or put in the condition appropriate to the start of an operation: the counter is initialized to one. **2** format (a computer disk). —**in·i·tial·i·za·tion** /iˌnisʜəliˈzāsʜən/ n.

in·i·ti·ate ▶v. /iˈnisʜē.āt/ [tr.] **1** cause (a process or action) to begin: he proposes to initiate discussions on planning procedures. **2** admit (someone) into a secret or obscure society or group, typically with a ritual: she had been formally **initiated into** the sorority. ■ [as pl. n.] (**the initiated**) fig. a small group of people who share obscure knowledge. ■ (**initiate someone in/into**) introduce someone to a particular activity or skill, esp. a difficult or obscure one: they were initiated into the mysteries of trigonometry.
▶n. /iˈnisʜēit/ a person who has been initiated into an organization or activity, typically recently: initiates of the Shiva cult | [as adj.] the initiate Marines. —**in·i·ti·a·tion** /iˌnisʜēˈāsʜən/ n. —**in·i·ti·a·tor** /-ˌātər/ n. —**in·i·ti·a·to·ry** /-əˌtôrē/ adj.

in·i·ti·a·tive /iˈnisʜ(ē)ətiv/ ▶n. **1** the ability to assess and initiate things independently: use your initiative, imagination, and common sense. **2** the power or opportunity to act or take charge before others do: we have lost the initiative and allowed our opponents to dictate the subject. **3** an act or strategy intended to resolve a difficulty or improve a situation; a fresh approach to something: a new initiative against car crime. ■ a proposal made by one nation to another in an attempt to improve relations: diplomatic initiatives to end the war. **4** (**the initiative**) (esp. in some U.S. states and Switzerland) the right of citizens outside the legislature to originate legislation.
▶ □ **on one's own initiative** without being prompted by others. □ **take** (or **seize**) **the initiative** be the first to take action.

in·ject /inˈjekt/ ▶v. [tr.] **1** drive or force (a liquid, esp. a drug or vaccine) into a person or animal's body with a syringe or similar device. ■ administer a drug or medicine to (a person or animal) in this way: he in**jected** himself with a drug overdose. ■ [intr.] inject oneself with a narcotic drug, esp. habitually: people who want to stop injecting. ■ introduce (something) into a passage, cavity, or solid material under pressure: inject the foam and allow it to expand. **2** introduce (a new or different element) into something, esp. as a boost or interruption: she tried to **inject** scorn **into** her tone. ■ (**inject something with**) imbue something with (a new element): he injected his voice with a confidence he didn't feel. —**in·ject·a·ble** adj. & n. —**in·jec·tor** /-ˈjektər/ n.

in·jec·tion /inˈjeksʜən/ ▶n. **1** an instance of injecting or being injected. ■ a thing that is injected: a morphine injection. ■ the action of injecting: a vaccine given by injection. **2** the entry or placing of a spacecraft or other object into an orbit or trajectory.

in·junc·tion /inˈjəNG(k)sʜən/ ▶n. an authoritative warning or order. ■ Law a judicial order that restrains a person from beginning or continuing an action threatening or invading the legal right of another, or that compels a person to carry out a certain act, e.g., to make restitution to an injured party. —**in·junc·tive** /-ˈjəNG(k)tiv/ adj.

in·jure /ˈinjər/ ▶v. [tr.] do physical harm or damage to (someone). ■ suffer physical harm or damage to (a part of one's body). ■ harm or impair (something): a libel calculated to injure the company's reputation. ■ archaic do injustice or wrong to (someone). —**in·jur·er** n.

in·jured /ˈinjərd/ ▶adj. **1** harmed, damaged, or impaired: a road accident left him severely injured. **2** offended: his injured pride.

in·ju·ri·ous /inˈjoŏrēəs/ ▶adj. causing or likely to cause damage or harm: high temperature is **injurious to** mangoes. ■ (of language) maliciously insulting; libelous. —**in·ju·ri·ous·ly** adv. —**in·ju·ri·ous·ness** n.

in·ju·ry /ˈinjərē/ ▶n. (pl. **-ries**) an instance of being injured: she suffered an injury to her back | an ankle injury. ■ the fact of being injured; harm or damage: all escaped without serious injury. ■ (**injury to**) offense to: the possible injury to the feelings of others. ▷late Middle English: from Anglo-Norman French injurie, from Latin injuria 'a wrong,' from in- (expressing negation) + jus, jur- 'right.'

in·jus·tice /inˈjəstis/ ▶n. lack of fairness or justice: the injustice of the death penalty. ■ an unjust act or occurrence: brooding over life's injustices.
▶ □ **do someone an injustice** judge a person unfairly.

ink /iNGk/ ▶n. a colored fluid used for writing, drawing, printing, or duplicating. ■ inf. publicity: cases in which prosecutors seek the death penalty are likely to be those that get lots of ink. ■ Zool. a black liquid ejected by a cuttlefish, octopus, or squid to confuse a predator.
▶v. **1** [tr.] mark (words or a design) with ink: the cork has the name of the château inked onto the side. ■ cover (type or a stamp) with ink before printing. ■ (**ink something in**) fill in writing or a design with ink: she inked in a cloud of dust. ■ (**ink something out**) obliterate something, esp. writing, with ink: he carefully inked out each word. **2** inf. sign (a contract): she's just inked a deal to host her own talk show. —**ink·er** n.

ink-jet print·er (also **ink·jet**) ▶n. a printer in which the characters are formed by minute jets of ink.

ink·ling /'ɪNGkliNG/ ▸*n.* a slight knowledge or suspicion; a hint: *the records give us an inkling of how people saw the world.*

ink pad ▸*n.* an ink-soaked pad in a shallow box, used for inking a rubber stamp or taking fingerprints.

ink·well /'ɪNGk,wel/ ▸*n.* a container for ink typically housed in a hole in a desk.

ink·y /'ɪNGkē/ ▸*adj.* (**ink·i·er, ink·i·est**) **1** as dark as ink: *the cold inky blackness of a Mexican cave.* **2** stained with ink. —**ink·i·ness** *n.*

in·laid /'ɪn,lād/ ▸ past and past participle of **INLAY**.

in·land /'ɪn,land; -lənd/ ▸*adj.* situated in the interior of a country rather than on the coast: *the deserts of inland Australia.* ▪ *chiefly Brit.* carried on within the limits of a country; domestic: *waterways allowed inland trade.* ▸*adv.* in or toward the interior of a country: *the path turned inland.* ▸*n.* (**the inland**) the parts of a country remote from the sea or borders; the interior. —**in·land·er** *n.*

in-law ▸*n.* a relative by marriage.

in·lay ▸*v.* /,ɪn'lā/ (*past* and *past part.* **-laid**) [*tr.*] ornament (an object) by embedding pieces of a different material in it, flush with its surface: *mahogany paneling inlaid with rosewood.* ▪ embed (something) in an object in this way: *a small silver crown was inlaid in the wood.* ▪ insert (a page, an illustration, etc.) in a space cut in a larger thicker page. ▸*n.* /'ɪn,lā/ **1** a design, pattern, or piece of material inlaid in something: *ivory inlays that decorated wooden furnishings.* ▪ a material or substance that is inlaid. ▪ inlaid work. ▪ the technique of inlaying material. **2** a filling shaped to fit a tooth cavity. —**in·lay·er** *n.*

in·let /'ɪn,let; -lit/ ▸*n.* **1** a small arm of the sea, a lake, or a river. **2** a place or means of entry: *an air inlet.*

in-line ▸*adj.* **1** having parts arranged in a line: *a 24-valve in-line 6-cylinder engine.* **2** constituting an integral part of a continuous sequence of operations or machines: *a two-stream in-line fuel-oil blender.* ▪ constituting an integral part of a computer program: *the parameters can be set up as in-line code.*

in-line skate ▸ *n.* a roller skate in which the wheels are fixed in a single line along the sole of the boot. —**in-line skat·er** *n.* —**in-line skat·ing** *n.*

in lo·co pa·ren·tis /ɪn ,lōkō pə'rentis/ ▸*adv.* & *adj.* (of a teacher or other adult responsible for children) in the place of a parent: [as *adv.*] *he was used to acting in loco parentis* | [as *adj.*] *they adhered to an in loco parentis approach when dealing with students.*

in-line skate

in·mate /'ɪn,māt/ ▸*n.* a person confined to an institution such as a prison or hospital. ▪ *archaic* one of several occupants of a house.

in me·mo·ri·am /,ɪn mə'môrēəm/ ▸*n.* [often as *adj.*] an article written in memory of a dead person; an obituary: *in memoriam notices in the paper.* ▸*prep.* in memory of (a dead person): *an openly revolutionary work in memoriam Che Guevara.*

in·most /'ɪn,mōst/ ▸*adj. poetic/lit.* innermost.

inn /ɪn/ ▸*n.* an establishment providing accommodations, food, and drink, esp. for travelers. ▪ [usu. in *names*] a restaurant or bar, typically one in the country, in some cases providing accommodations. ▷Old English (in the sense 'dwelling place, lodging'): of Germanic origin; related to *in*. In Middle English the word was used to translate Latin *hospitium*, denoting a house of residence for students: this sense is preserved in the names of some buildings formerly used for this purpose, notably *Gray's Inn* and *Lincoln's Inn*, two of the *Inns of Court*, legal societies that admit people to the English bar. The current sense dates from late Middle English.

in·nards /'ɪnərdz/ ▸*pl. n. inf.* entrails. ▪ internal workings (of a device or machine).

in·nate /ɪ'nāt/ ▸*adj.* inborn; natural: *her innate capacity for organization.* ▪ *Philos.* originating in the mind. —**in·nate·ly** *adv.* —**in·nate·ness** *n.*

in·ner /'ɪnər/ ▸*adj.* **1** situated inside or further in; internal: *an inner courtyard* | *the inner thigh.* ▪ close to the center: *the inner solar system.* ▪ close to the center of power: *the inner cabinet.* **2** mental or spiritual: *a test of inner strength.* ▪ (of thoughts or feelings) private and not expressed or discernible. ▸*n.* the inner part of something. ▪ (in archery and shooting) a division of the target next to the bull's-eye. ▪ a shot that strikes this. —**in·ner·ly** *adv.* (*poetic/lit.*). —**in·ner·ness** *n.* (*poetic/lit.*).

in·ner cit·y ▸*n.* the area near the center of a city, esp. when associated with social and economic problems: [as *adj.*] *inner-city schools.*

in·ner ear ▸*n.* the semicircular canals and cochlea, which form the organs of balance and hearing and are embedded in the temporal bone.

in·ner·most /'ɪnər,mōst/ ▸*adj.* [*attrib.*] **1** (of thoughts or feelings) most private and deeply felt: *innermost beliefs and convictions.* **2** furthest in; closest to the center: *the innermost layer.*

in·ner tube ▸*n.* a separate inflatable tube inside a pneumatic tire. ▪ such a tube inflated and used for recreational purposes.

in·ning /'ɪnɪNG/ ▸*n. Baseball* a division of a game during which the two teams alternate as offense and defense and during which each team is allowed three outs while batting. ▪ a single turn at bat for a team until three outs are made. ▪ a similar division of play in other games, such as horseshoes. ▪ a period during which a person or group can achieve something: *she thought that now her inning had come.*

inn·keep·er /'ɪn,kēpər/ ▸*n.* a person who runs an inn.

in·no·cent /'ɪnəsənt/ ▸*adj.* **1** not guilty of a crime or offense. ▪ (**innocent of**) without; lacking: *a street quite innocent of bookstores.* ▪ (**innocent of**) without experience or knowledge of: *a man innocent of war's cruelties.* **2** not responsible for or directly involved in an event yet suffering its consequences: *an innocent bystander.* **3** free from moral wrong; not corrupted. ▪ simple; naive. **4** not intended to cause harm or offense; harmless: *an innocent mistake.* ▸*n.* an innocent person, in particular: ▪ a pure, guileless, or naive person. ▪ a person involved by chance in a situation, esp. a victim of crime or war. ▪ (**the Innocents**) the young children killed by Herod after the birth of Jesus. —**in·no·cence** *n.* —**in·no·cent·ly** *adv.*

in·noc·u·ous /ɪ'näkyōōəs/ ▸*adj.* not harmful or offensive: *it was an innocuous question.* —**in·noc·u·ous·ly** *adv.* —**in·noc·u·ous·ness** *n.*

in·no·vate /'ɪnə,vāt/ ▸*v.* [*intr.*] make changes in something established, esp. by introducing new methods, ideas, or products: *the company's failure to diversify and innovate competitively.* ▪ [*tr.*] introduce (something new, esp. a product). —**in·no·va·tion** /,ɪnə'vāSHən/ *n.* —**in·no·va·tive** *adj.* —**in·no·va·tor** /-,vātər/ *n.*

in·nu·en·do /,ɪnyōō'endō/ ▸*n.* (*pl.* **-does** or **-dos**) an allusive or oblique remark or hint, typically a suggestive or disparaging one: *she's always making sly innuendoes.*

in·nu·mer·a·ble /ɪ'n(y)ōōmərəbəl/ ▸*adj.* too many to be counted (often used hyperbolically): *innumerable flags of all colors.* —**in·nu·mer·a·bil·i·ty** /ɪ,n(y)ōōmərə'bilitē/ *n.* —**in·nu·mer·a·bly** /-blē/ *adv.*

in·nu·mer·ate /ɪ'n(y)ōōmərit/ ▸*adj.* without a basic knowledge of mathematics and arithmetic. ▸*n.* a person lacking such knowledge. —**in·nu·mer·a·cy** /-rəsē/ *n.*

in·oc·u·late /ɪ'näkyə,lāt/ ▸*v.* [*tr.*] treat (a person or animal) with a vaccine to produce immunity against a disease: *he inoculated his tenants against smallpox.* Compare with **VACCINATE**. ▪ introduce (an infective agent) into an organism: *it can be inoculated into laboratory animals.* ▪ introduce (cells or organisms) into a culture medium. —**in·oc·u·la·ble** /-ləbəl/ *adj.* —**in·oc·u·la·tion** /ɪ,näkyə'lāSHən/ *n.* —**in·oc·u·la·tor** /-,lātər/ *n.*

in·of·fen·sive /,ɪnə'fensiv/ ▸*adj.* not objectionable or harmful: *inoffensive wallpaper.* —**in·of·fen·sive·ly** *adv.* —**in·of·fen·sive·ness** *n.*

in·op·er·a·ble /ɪn'äp(ə)rəbəl/ ▸*adj.* **1** *Med.* not able to be suitably operated on: *inoperable cancer of the pancreas.* **2** not able to be operated. **3** impractical; unworkable: *the procedures were inoperable.* —**in·op·er·a·bil·i·ty** /-,äp(ə)rə'bilitē/ *n.* —**in·op·er·a·bly** /-blē/ *adv.*

in·op·er·a·tive /ɪn'äp(ə)rətiv/ ▸*adj.* not working or taking effect.

in·or·di·nate /ɪ'nôrdn-it/ ▸*adj.* unusually or disproportionately large; excessive. ▪ *archaic* (of a person) unrestrained in feelings or behavior; disorderly. —**in·or·di·nate·ly** *adv.*

in·or·gan·ic /,ɪnôr'ganik/ ▸*adj.* not arising from natural growth. ▪ *Chem.* of, relating to, or denoting compounds that are not organic (broadly, compounds not containing carbon). Compare with **ORGANIC**. ▪ without organized physical structure. ▪ *Linguistics* not explainable by the normal processes of etymology. —**in·or·gan·i·cal·ly** /-ik(ə)lē/ *adv.*

in·pa·tient /'ɪn,pāSHənt/ ▸*n.* a patient who stays in a hospital while under treatment.

in·put /'ɪn,pŏŏt/ ▸*n.* **1** what is put in, taken in, or operated on by any process or system: *perceptions and sensory input.* ▪ a contribution of work, information, or material: *there is little input from other professional members of the team.* ▪ energy supplied to a device or system; an electrical signal: *the input is a low-frequency signal.* ▪ the action or process of putting or feeding something in: *the input of data to the system.* ▪ the information fed into a computer or computer program: *pen-based computers take input from a stylus.* **2** *Electr.* a place where, or a device through which, energy or information enters a system: *the signal being fed through the main input.*

▶ v. (**-put·ting**; past and past part. **-put** or **-put·ted**) [tr.] put (data) into a computer. —**in·put·ter** /-ˌpŏŏtər/ n.

in·quest /ˈinˌkwest; ˈING-/ ▶ n. Law a judicial inquiry to ascertain the facts relating to an incident, such as a death.

in·qui·e·tude /inˈkwiə,t(y)ōōd/ ▶ n. physical or mental restlessness or disturbance.

in·quire /inˈkwīr; ING-/ ▶ v. ask for information from someone: I inquired where he lived | [intr.] he inquired about cottages for sale. ■ [intr.] (**inquire after**) ask about the health and well-being of (someone): Annie inquired after her parents. ■ [intr.] (**inquire for**) ask to see or speak to (someone). ■ [intr.] (**inquire into**) investigate; look into: the task of political sociology is to inquire into the causes of political events. ▷Middle English enquere (later inquere), from Old French enquerre, from a variant of Latin inquirere, based on quaerere 'seek.' The spelling with in-, influenced by Latin, dates from the 15th cent. —**in·quir·er** n. —**in·quir·ing·ly** adv.

in·quir·y /inˈkwī(ə)rē; ˈin,kwī(ə)rē; ˈinkwərē; ˈING-/ ▶ n. (pl. **-quir·ies**) an act of asking for information: the deluge of phone inquiries after a crash. ■ an official investigation.

in·qui·si·tion /ˌinkwiˈziSHən; ˌING-/ ▶ n. **1** a period of prolonged and intensive questioning or investigation: she relented in her determined inquisition and offered help. ■ hist. a judicial or official inquiry. ■ the verdict or finding of an official inquiry. **2** (**the Inquisition**) an ecclesiastical tribunal established by Pope Gregory IX c.1232 for the suppression of heresy. It was active chiefly in northern Italy and southern France, becoming notorious for the use of torture. See also **SPANISH INQUISITION**. —**in·qui·si·tion·al** /-SHənl/ adj.

in·quis·i·tive /inˈkwizitiv; ING-/ ▶ adj. curious or inquiring. ■ unduly curious about the affairs of others; prying. —**in·quis·i·tive·ly** adv. —**in·quis·i·tive·ness** n.

in·quis·i·tor /inˈkwizitər/ ▶ n. a person making an inquiry, esp. one seen to be excessively harsh or searching. ■ hist. an officer of the Inquisition.

in·quis·i·to·ri·al /in,kwiziˈtôrēəl/ ▶ adj. of or like an inquisitor. ■ offensively prying. ■ Law (of a trial or legal procedure) in which the judge has an examining or inquiring role. —**in·quis·i·to·ri·al·ly** adv.

in re /,in ˈrā/ ▶ prep. in the legal case of; with regard to: In re Mancet's Estate.

in·road /ˈin,rōd/ ▶ n. **1** [usu. in pl.] progress; an advance: an important way to **make inroads in** reducing spending. ■ an instance of something being affected, encroached on, or destroyed by something else: serious inroads had been made into my cash reserves. **2** a hostile attack; a raid.

in·rush /ˈin,rəSH/ ▶ n. the sudden arrival or entry of something: a great inrush of water occurred. —**in·rush·ing** adj. & n.

INS ▶ abbr. Immigration and Naturalization Service.

ins. ▶ abbr. ■ inches. ■ insurance.

in·sane /inˈsān/ ▶ adj. in a state of mind that prevents normal perception, behavior, or social interaction; seriously mentally ill: he had gone insane. ■ (of an action or quality) characterized or caused by madness: an insane frenzy | his eyes glowing with insane fury. ■ in a state of extreme annoyance or distraction: a fly whose buzzing had been driving me insane. ■ (of an action or policy) extremely foolish; irrational or illogical. —**in·sane·ly** adv. —**in·san·i·ty** /-ˈsanitē/ n.

in·sa·tia·ble /inˈsāSHəbəl/ ▶ adj. (of an appetite or desire) impossible to satisfy: an insatiable hunger for success. ■ (of a person) having an insatiable appetite or desire for something, esp. sex. —**in·sa·tia·bil·i·ty** /-,sāSHəˈbilitē/ n. —**in·sa·tia·bly** /-blē/ adv.

in·scribe /inˈskrīb/ ▶ v. [tr.] **1** write or carve (words or symbols) on something, esp. as a formal or permanent record: his name was inscribed on the new silver trophy. ■ mark (an object) with characters: the memorial is inscribed with ten names. ■ write an informal dedication to someone in or on (a book): he inscribed the first copy "To my dearest grandmother." ■ archaic enter the name of (someone) on a list or in a book; enroll. **2** Geom. draw (a figure) within another so that their boundaries touch but do not intersect: a regular polygon inscribed in a circle. Compare with **CIRCUMSCRIBE**. —**in·scrib·a·ble** adj. —**in·scrib·er** n.

in·scrip·tion /inˈskripSHən/ ▶ n. words inscribed, as on a monument or in a book: the inscription on her headstone. ■ the action of inscribing something. —**in·scrip·tion·al** /-SHənl/ adj. —**in·scrip·tive** /-ˈskriptiv/ adj.

in·scru·ta·ble /inˈskrōōtəbəl/ ▶ adj. impossible to understand or interpret. —**in·scru·ta·bil·i·ty** /-,skrōōtəˈbilitē/ n. —**in·scru·ta·bly** /-blē/ adv.

in·sect /ˈin,sekt/ ▶ n. a small arthropod animal that has six legs and generally one or two pairs of wings. ■ inf. any small invertebrate animal, esp. one with several pairs of legs.

in·sec·ti·cide /inˈsekti,sīd/ ▶ n. a substance used for killing insects. —**in·sec·ti·cid·al** /-,sekti'sīdl/ adj.

in·sec·ti·vore /inˈsektə,vôr/ ▶ n. an insect-eating animal or plant. —**in·sec·tiv·o·rous** /,insek'tivərəs/ adj.

in·se·cure /,insi'kyŏŏr/ ▶ adj. **1** (of a person) not confident or assured; uncertain and anxious. **2** (of a thing) not firm or set; unsafe. ■ (of a job or position) from which removal or expulsion is always possible. ■ not firmly fixed; liable to give way or break: an insecure footbridge. ■ able to be broken into or illicitly accessed: an insecure computer system. —**in·se·cure·ly** adv. —**in·se·cu·ri·ty** n.

in·sem·i·nate /in'semə,nāt/ ▶ v. [tr.] introduce semen into (a woman or a female animal) by natural or artificial means. —**in·sem·i·na·tion** /-,semə'nāSHən/ n.

in·sen·sate /in'sen,sāt; -sit/ ▶ adj. lacking physical sensation. ■ lacking sympathy or compassion; unfeeling: a positively insensate hatred. ■ completely lacking sense or reason: insensate jabbering. —**in·sen·sate·ly** adv.

in·sen·si·ble /in'sensəbəl/ ▶ adj. **1** without one's mental faculties, typically a result of violence or intoxication; unconscious: they knocked each other insensible with their fists | insensible with drink. ■ (esp. of a body or bodily extremity) numb; without feeling. **2** (**insensible of/to**) unaware of; indifferent to: they slept on, insensible to the headlight beams. ■ without emotion; callous. **3** too small or gradual to be perceived; inappreciable: varying by insensible degrees. —**in·sen·si·bil·i·ty** /in-,sense'bilitē/ n. —**in·sen·si·bly** /-blē/ adv.

in·sen·si·tive /in'sensitiv/ ▶ adj. showing or feeling no concern for others' feelings: an insensitive remark. ■ not sensitive to a physical sensation: she was remarkably insensitive to pain. ■ not aware of or able to respond to something. —**in·sen·si·tive·ly** adv. —**in·sen·si·tive·ness** n. —**in·sen·si·tiv·i·ty** /-,sensi'tivitē/ n.

in·sen·ti·ent /in'senSH(ē)ənt/ ▶ adj. incapable of feeling or understanding things; inanimate. —**in·sen·ti·ence** n.

in·sep·a·ra·ble /in'sep(ə)rəbəl/ ▶ adj. unable to be separated or treated separately: research and higher education seem inseparable. ■ (of one or more people) unwilling to be separated; usually seen together: they met 18 months ago and have been inseparable ever since. ■ Gram. (of a prefix) not used as a separate word or (in German) not separated from the base verb when inflected.

▶ n. a person or thing inseparable from another. —**in·sep·a·ra·bil·i·ty** /-,sep(ə)rə'bilitē/ n. —**in·sep·a·ra·bly** /-blē/ adv.

in·sert ▶ v. /in'sərt/ [tr.] **1** place, fit, or thrust (something) into another thing, esp. with care: a steel rod was inserted into the small hole. ■ add (text) to a piece of writing. ■ place (a spacecraft or satellite) into an orbit or trajectory. ■ Biol. incorporate (a piece of genetic material) into a chromosome. **2** (**be inserted**) Anat. Zool. (of a muscle or other organ) be attached to a part, esp. that which is moved: the muscle that raises the wing is inserted on the dorsal surface of the humerus.

▶ n. /'in,sərt/ a thing that has been inserted, in particular: ■ a loose page or section, typically one carrying an advertisement, in a magazine or other publication. ■ a shot inserted into a movie or video. —**in·sert·a·ble** adj. —**in·sert·er** n.

in·ser·tion /in'sərSHən/ ▶ n. **1** the action of inserting something: the insertion of a line or two into the script. ■ the placing of a spacecraft or satellite into an orbit or trajectory. **2** a thing that is inserted, in particular: ■ an amendment or addition inserted in a text. ■ each appearance of an advertisement in a newspaper or periodical. ■ an ornamental section of cloth or needlework inserted into the plain material of a garment. **3** Anat. & Zool. the manner or place of attachment of an organ. ■ the manner or place of attachment of a muscle to the part that it moves. **4** Biol. the addition of extra DNA or RNA into a section of genetic material.

in·serv·ice ▶ adj. (of training) intended for those actively engaged in the profession or activity concerned: in-service training of library staff.

in·set ▶ n. /'in,set/ a thing that is put in or inserted: a pair of doors with their original stained-glass insets. ■ a small picture or map inserted within the border of a larger one. ■ a section of fabric or needlework inserted into the material of a garment: elastic insets in the waistband.

▶ v. /in'set/ (**-set·ting**; past and past part. **-set** or **-set·ted**) put in (something, esp. a small picture or map) as an inset: type in the text to be inset. ■ decorate with an inset: tables inset with ceramic tiles. —**in·set·ter** n.

in·shore /'in,SHôr/ ▶ adj. at sea but close to the shore: both mackerel and bluefish have returned to inshore waters by now. ■ used at sea but close to the shore: an inshore lifeboat.

▶ adv. toward or closer to the shore.

▶ □ **inshore of** nearer to shore than.

in·side ▶ n. /'in'sīd/ **1** the inner side or surface of a thing. ■ the side of a bend or curve where the edge or surface is shorter: the inside of the bend. ■ the side of a racetrack nearer to the center, where the lanes are shorter. **2** the inner part; the interior: these boats are built of very thin

cedar, with ribs **on the inside**. ■ (usu. **insides**) *inf.* the stomach and bowels: *my insides are out of order.* **3** (**the inside**) *inf.* a position affording private information: *will you be my spy on the inside?*
▶ *adj.* /ˌinˈsīd; ˈinˌsīd/ situated on or in, or derived from, the inside: *an inside pocket.* ■ (in some team sports) denoting positions nearer to the center of the field: *possibly the best inside linebacker in the country.* ■ (in basketball) taking place within the perimeter of the defense: *he missed three consecutive inside shots.* ■ (of a pitch in baseball) passing between the batter and the strike zone: *an inside pitch to a right-handed hitter.*
▶ *prep. & adv.* /ˌinˈsīd/ **1** situated within the confines of (something): [as *prep.*] *a radio was playing inside the apartment* | [as *adv.*] *Mr. Jackson is waiting for you inside.* ■ moving so as to end up within (something): [as *prep.*] *Anatoly reached inside his shirt and brought out a map* | [as *adv.*] *we walked inside.* ■ [*adv.*] indoors: *they sat inside all day playing cards.* ■ within (the body or mind of a person), typically with reference to sensations of self-awareness: [as *prep.*] *she felt a stirring of life inside her.* | [as *adv.*] *I was screaming inside.* ■ *inf.* in prison: *sentenced to three years inside.* ■ *Baseball* close to the batter. ■ (in basketball, soccer, and other sports) closer to the center of the field than (another player): [as *prep.*] *he went inside Graves and scored near the post* | [as *adv.*] *he does an excellent job of getting the ball inside to Randall.* **2** [*prep.*] in less than (the period of time specified): *the oven will have paid for itself inside 18 months.*
▶ □ **inside of** *inf.* within: *something inside of me wanted to believe him.* ■ in less than (the period of time specified): *rerigging a ship for a voyage inside of a week.*
in·side out ▶ *adv.* with the inner surface turned outward: *we made a very quick change, and her dress was put on inside out.*
▶ *adj.* in such a condition: *inside-out clothes.*
▶ □ **know something inside out** know something very thoroughly.
□ **turn something inside out** turn the inner surface of something outward. ■ change something utterly: *it is not so easy to turn your whole life inside out.*
in·sid·er /inˈsīdər/ ▶ *n.* a person within a group or organization, esp. someone privy to information unavailable to others: *political insiders.*
in·sid·er trad·ing (*Brit.* also **insider dealing**) ▶ *n.* the illegal practice of trading on the stock exchange to one's own advantage through having access to confidential information.
in·side track ▶ *n.* the inner, shorter track of a racecourse. ■ *fig.* a position of advantage: *he always had the inside track for the starring role.*
in·sid·i·ous /inˈsidēəs/ ▶ *adj.* proceeding in a gradual, subtle way, but with harmful effects: *sexually transmitted diseases can be insidious.* ■ treacherous; crafty. —**in·sid·i·ous·ly** *adv.* —**in·sid·i·ous·ness** *n.*
in·sight /ˈinˌsīt/ ▶ *n.* the capacity to gain an accurate and deep intuitive understanding of a person or thing: *this paper is alive with sympathetic insight into Shakespeare.* ■ an understanding of this kind: *the signals would give marine biologists new insights into the behavior of whales.* ■ *Psychiatry* new understanding by a mentally ill person of the causes of their disorder. ▷Middle English (in the sense 'inner sight, mental vision, wisdom'): probably of Scandinavian and Low German origin and related to Swedish *insikt*, Danish *indsigt*, Dutch *inzicht*, and German *Einsicht*. —**in·sight·ful** /inˈsītfəl/ *adj.* —**in·sight·ful·ly** /inˈsītfəlē/ *adv.*
in·sig·ni·a /inˈsignēə/ ▶ *n.* (*pl.* same or **-ni·as**) a badge or distinguishing mark of military rank, office, or membership of an organization; an official emblem: *a khaki uniform with colonel's insignia on the collar.* ■ *chiefly poetic/lit.* a distinguishing mark or token of something: *they left eternally inert blooms, the insignia of melancholy.*
in·sig·nif·i·cant /ˌinsigˈnifikənt/ ▶ *adj.* too small or unimportant to be worth consideration: *no detail is insignificant.* ■ (of a person) without power or influence: *meaningless.* —**in·sig·nif·i·cance** *n.* —**in·sig·nif·i·can·cy** *n.* —**in·sig·nif·i·cant·ly** *adv.*
in·sin·cere /ˌinsinˈsi(ə)r/ ▶ *adj.* not expressing genuine feelings. —**in·sin·cere·ly** *adv.* —**in·sin·cer·i·ty** /-ˈseritē/ *n.* (*pl.* **-ties**).
in·sin·u·ate /inˈsinyoōˌāt/ ▶ *v.* [*tr.*] **1** suggest or hint (something bad or reprehensible) in an indirect way: *he was insinuating that she had slept her way to the top.* **2** (**insinuate oneself into**) maneuver oneself into (a position of favor or office) by subtle manipulation: *she seemed to be taking over, insinuating herself into the family.* ■ [*tr.*] slide (oneself or a thing) slowly and smoothly into a position: *the bugs insinuate themselves between one's skin and clothes.* —**in·sin·u·at·ing·ly** *adv.* —**in·sin·u·a·tion** /inˌsinyoōˈāsHən/ *n.* —**in·sin·u·a·tor** /-ˌwātər/ *n.*
in·sip·id /inˈsipid/ ▶ *adj.* lacking flavor. ■ lacking vigor or interest. —**in·sip·id·i·ty** /ˌinsəˈpiditē/ *n.* —**in·sip·id·ly** *adv.* —**in·sip·id·ness** *n.*
in·sist /inˈsist/ ▶ *v.* [*intr.*] demand something forcefully, not accepting refusal: *she insisted on carrying her own bag.* ■ (**insist on**) demand forcefully to have something: *he insisted on answers to his allegations.* ■ (**insist on**) persist in doing something even though it is annoying or odd: *the heavy*

studded boots she insisted on wearing. ■ maintain or put forwar[d] ment positively and assertively: *the chairman insisted that a[ll] doom and gloom.*
in·sist·ent /inˈsistənt/ ▶ *adj.* insisting or demanding something; [al]lowing refusal: *Tony's soft, insistent questioning.* ■ regular and re[petitive] and demanding attention: *a telephone started ringing, loud and in[cessant].* —**in·sis·tence** *n.* —**in·sis·tent·ly** *adv.*
in si·tu /ˌin ˈsītoō; ˈsē-/ ▶ *adv. & adj.* in its original place: [as *adv.*] *m[urals] and frescoes have been left in situ* | [as *adj.*] *a collection of in situ pumpin[g en]gines.* ■ in position: [as *adv.*] *her guests were all in situ.*
in·so·far /ˌinsōˈfär/ (also **in so far**) ▶ *adv.* (**insofar as**) to the extent t[hat] *philosophy spoke of personal problems insofar as they illustrated general o[nes].*
in·sole /ˈinˌsōl/ ▶ *n.* a removable sole worn in a shoe for warmth, as a d[e]odorizer, or to improve the fit. ■ the fixed inner sole of a boot or sh[oe].
in·so·lent /ˈinsələnt/ ▶ *adj.* showing a rude and arrogant lack of respec[t]. —**in·so·lence** *n.* —**in·so·lent·ly** *adv.*
in·sol·u·ble /inˈsälyəbəl/ ▶ *adj.* **1** impossible to solve: *the problem is not in-soluble.* **2** (of a substance) incapable of being dissolved: *once dry, the paints become insoluble in water.* —**in·sol·u·bil·i·ty** /-ˌsälyəˈbilitē/ *n.* —**in·sol·u·bil·ize** /-ˌlīz/ *v.* —**in·sol·u·bly** /-blē/ *adv.*
in·sol·vent /inˈsälvənt/ ▶ *adj.* unable to pay debts owed: *the company became insolvent.* ■ relating to insolvency: *insolvent liquidation.*
▶ *n.* an insolvent person. —**in·sol·ven·cy** *n.*
in·som·ni·a /inˈsämnēə/ ▶ *n.* habitual sleeplessness; inability to sleep. —**in·som·ni·ac** /-nē,ak/ *n. & adj.*
in·sou·ci·ance /inˈsoōsēəns; ˌansoōˈsyäns/ ▶ *n.* casual lack of concern; indifference: *boyish insouciance.* —**in·sou·ci·ant** *adj.* —**in·sou·ci·ant·ly** *adv.*
in·sourc·ing /ˈinˌsôrsiNG/ ▶ *n.* the practice of using an organization's own personnel or other resources to accomplish a task: *offshore insourcing of expense reporting processing.* ■ the practice whereby an organization provides its own personnel to accomplish specialized tasks for a client, at the client's place of business. —**in·source** *v.*
in·spect /inˈspekt/ ▶ *v.* [*tr.*] look at (someone or something) closely, typically to assess their condition or to discover any shortcomings: *they were inspecting my outside paintwork for cracks and flaws.* ■ examine (someone or something) to ensure that they reach an official standard: *customs officers came aboard to inspect our documents.* —**in·spec·tion** /-ˈspeksHən/ *n.*
in·spec·tor /inˈspektər/ ▶ *n.* **1** an official employed to ensure that official regulations are obeyed, esp. in public services: *a prison inspector.* **2** a police officer ranking below a superintendent or police chief. —**in·spec·to·ri·al** /ˌinspekˈtôrēəl/ *adj.* —**in·spec·tor·ship** /-ˌsHip/ *n.*
in·spi·ra·tion /ˌinspəˈrāsHən/ ▶ *n.* **1** the process of being mentally stimulated to do or feel something, esp. to do something creative: *Helen had one of her flashes of inspiration.* ■ the quality of having been so stimulated, esp. when evident in something: *a rare moment of inspiration in an otherwise dull display.* ■ a person or thing that stimulates in this way: *he is an inspiration to everyone.* ■ a sudden brilliant, creative, or timely idea: *then I had an inspiration.* ■ the divine influence believed to have led to the writing of the Bible. **2** the drawing in of breath; inhalation. ■ an act of breathing in; an inhalation. —**in·spi·ra·tion·al** /-sHənl/ *adj.*
in·spire /inˈspīr/ ▶ *v.* [*tr.*] **1** fill (someone) with the urge or ability to do or feel something, esp. to do something creative: [*tr.*] *his passion for romantic literature inspired him to begin writing* | [as *adj.*] (**inspiring**) *so far, the scenery is not very inspiring.* ■ create (a feeling, esp. a positive one) in a person: *their past record does not inspire confidence.* ■ (**inspire someone with**) animate someone with (such a feeling): *he inspired his students with a vision of freedom.* ■ give rise to: *the movie was successful enough to inspire a sequel.* **2** breathe in (air); inhale. —**in·spir·er** *n.* —**in·spir·ing·ly** *adv.*
inst. ▶ *abbr.* ■ *dated* (in business letters) instant: *we are pleased to acknowledge receipt of your letter of 14 inst.* ■ institute; institution.
in·sta·bil·i·ty /ˌinstəˈbilitē/ ▶ *n.* (*pl.* **-ties**) lack of stability; the state of being unstable: *economic instability.* ■ tendency to unpredictable behavior or erratic changes of mood: *signs of mental instability.*
in·stall /inˈstôl/ (*Brit.* also **in·stal**) ▶ *v.* [*tr.*] **1** place or fix (equipment or machinery) in position ready for use: *we're planning to install a new shower.* **2** place (someone) in a new position of authority, esp. with ceremony: *he was installed as music director at the Cathedral of St. Barbara in Cracow.* ■ establish (someone) in a new place, condition, or role: *Ashley installed herself behind her table.* —**in·stall·er** *n.*

Pronunciation Key ə *ago, up;* ər *over, fur;* a *hat;* ā *ate;* ä *car;* CH *chin;* e *let;* ē *see;* e(ə)r *air;* i *fit;* ī *by;* i(ə)r *ear;* NG *sing;* ō *go;* ô *law, for;* oi *toy;* oō *good;* oō *goo;* ou *out;* sH *she;* TH *thin;* TH *then;* (h)w *why;* zH *vision*

in·stal·la·tion /ˌinstəˈlāsHən/ ▶n. **1** the action or process of installing someone or something, or of being installed: *the installation of a central air-conditioning system.* **2** a thing installed, in particular: ■ a large piece of equipment installed for use: *computer installations.* ■ a military or industrial establishment: *nuclear installations.* ■ an art exhibit constructed within a gallery: *a video installation.*

in·stall·ment /inˈstôlmənt/ (*chiefly Brit.* **in·stal·ment**) ▶n. **1** a sum of money due as one of several equal payments for something, spread over an agreed period of time: *the purchase price is paid* **in installments.** **2** any of several parts of something that are published, broadcast, or made public in sequence at intervals: *filming the final installment in his Vietnam trilogy.*

in·stance /ˈinstəns/ ▶n. an example or single occurrence of something: *a serious instance of corruption.* ■ a particular case: *in this instance it mattered little.*
▶v. [tr.] cite (a fact, case, etc.) as an instance or example: *here he instances in particular the work of Bach.* ▷Middle English: via Old French from Latin *instantia* 'presence, urgency,' from *instare* 'be present, press upon,' from *in-* 'upon' + *stare* 'to stand.' The original sense was 'urgency, urgent entreaty,' surviving in *at the instance of.* In the late 16th cent. the word denoted a particular case cited to disprove a general assertion, derived from medieval Latin *instantia* 'example to the contrary' (translating Greek *enstasis* 'objection'); hence the meaning 'single occurrence.'
▶ □ **at the instance of** *formal* at the request or instigation of. □ **for instance** as an example: *take Canada, for instance.* □ **in the first** (or **second,** etc.) **instance** in the first (or second, etc.) place; at the first (or second, etc.) stage of a proceeding: *a tribunal should be formed, in the first instance to document these and other charges.*

in·stant /ˈinstənt/ ▶adj. **1** happening or coming immediately: *the offense justified instant dismissal.* ■ (of food) processed to allow quick preparation: *instant coffee.* ■ (of a person) becoming a specified thing immediately or very suddenly: *become an instant millionaire.* ■ prepared quickly and with little effort: *we can't promise instant solutions.* ■ producing immediate results: *an instant lottery ticket.* **2** urgent; pressing: *an instant desire to blame others when things go wrong.* **3** *dated* (in business letters) of the current month: *your letter of the 6th instant.* **4** *archaic* of the present moment.
▶n. **1** a precise moment of time: *come here this instant!* **2** a very short space of time; a moment.

in·stan·ta·ne·ous /ˌinstənˈtānēəs/ ▶adj. **1** occurring or done in an instant or instantly. ■ operating or providing something instantly: *instantaneous communication.* **2** *Physics* existing or measured at a particular instant: *the instantaneous velocity.* —**in·stan·ta·ne·i·ty** /inˌstantnˈē-itē/ n. —**in·stan·ta·ne·ous·ly** adv. —**in·stan·ta·ne·ous·ness** n.

in·stant·ly /ˈinstəntlē/ ▶adv. **1** at once; immediately: *she fell asleep almost instantly.* **2** *archaic* urgently or persistently.

instant mes·sag·ing (abbr.: **IM**) ▶n. *Comput.* the exchange of typed messages between computer users in real time via the Internet. —**instant mes·sage** n.

in·stant re·play ▶n. an immediate playback of part of a television broadcast, typically one in slow motion showing an incident in a sports event.

in·stead /inˈsted/ ▶adv. as an alternative or substitute: *do not use lotions, but put on a clean dressing instead.* ■ (**instead of**) as a substitute or alternative to; in place of: *walk to work instead of going by car.*

in·step /ˈinˌstep/ ▶n. the part of a person's foot between the ball and the ankle. ■ the part of a shoe that fits over or under this part of a foot. ■ a thing shaped like the inner arch of a foot.

in·sti·gate /ˈinstiˌgāt/ ▶v. [tr.] bring about or initiate (an action or event): *instigating legal proceedings.* ■ (**instigate someone to do something**) incite someone to do something, esp. something bad: *instigating men to refuse allegiance to the civil powers.* —**in·sti·ga·tion** /ˌinstiˈgāsHən/ n. —**in·sti·ga·tor** /-ˌgātər/ n.

in·still /inˈstil/ (*Brit.* also **in·stil**) ▶v. [tr.] **1** gradually but firmly establish (an idea or attitude, esp. a desirable one) in a person's mind: *how do we instill a sense of rightness in today's youth?* **2** put (a substance) into something in the form of liquid drops: *she was told how to instill eye drops.* —**in·stil·la·tion** /ˌinstəˈlāsHən/ n. —**in·still·ment** n.

in·stinct ▶n. /ˈinˌstiNGkt/ an innate, typically fixed pattern of behavior in animals in response to certain stimuli: *maternal instincts.* ■ a natural or intuitive way of acting or thinking: *they retain their old authoritarian instincts.* ■ a natural propensity or skill of a specified kind: *his* **instinct** *for making the most of his chances.* ■ the fact or quality of possessing innate behavior patterns: *instinct told her not to ask the question.*
▶adj. /inˈstiNGkt/ (**instinct with**) *formal* imbued or filled with (a quality,

esp. a desirable one): *these canvases are instinct with passion.* ▷late Middle English (also in the sense 'instigation, impulse'): from Latin *instinctus* 'impulse,' from the verb *instinguere,* from *in-* 'toward' + *stinguere* 'to prick.' —**in·stinc·tu·al** /insˈtiNGkCHŌŌəl/ adj. —**in·stinc·tu·al·ly** adv.

in·stinc·tive /inˈstiNG(k)tiv/ ▶adj. relating to or prompted by instinct; apparently unconscious or automatic: *an instinctive distaste for conflict.* ■ (of a person) doing or being a specified thing apparently naturally or automatically: *an instinctive writer.* —**in·stinc·tive·ly** adv.

in·sti·tute /ˈinstiˌt(y)ōōt/ ▶n. [usu. in *names*] **1** a society or organization having a particular object or common factor, esp. a scientific, educational, or social one. **2** (usu. **institutes**) *archaic* a commentary, treatise, or summary of principles, esp. concerning law.
▶v. [tr.] **1** set in motion or establish (something, esp. a program, system, or inquiry): *the award was instituted in 1900.* ■ begin (legal proceedings) in a court. **2** appoint (someone) to a position, esp. as a cleric: *his sons were instituted to his benefice in 1986.*

in·sti·tu·tion /ˌinstiˈt(y)ōōsHən/ ▶n. **1** a society or organization founded for a religious, educational, social, or similar purpose: *a certificate from a professional institution.* ■ an organization providing residential care for people with special needs: *an institution for the handicapped.* ■ an established official organization having an important role in the life of a country, such as a bank, church, or legislature: *the institutions of democratic government.* ■ a large company or other organization involved in financial trading: *the interest rate financial institutions charge one another.* **2** an established law, practice, or custom: **the institution** *of marriage.* ■ *inf.* a well-established and familiar person, custom, or object: *he became something of a national institution.* **3** the action of instituting something.

in·sti·tu·tion·al /ˌinstiˈt(y)ōōsHənl/ ▶adj. of, in, or like an institution or institutions. ■ unappealing or unimaginative: *institutional chocolate-colored paint.* ■ expressed or organized in the form of institutions: *institutional religion.* ■ (of advertising) intended to create prestige rather than immediate sales. —**in·sti·tu·tion·al·ism** /-ˌizəm/ n. —**in·sti·tu·tion·al·ly** adv.

in·sti·tu·tion·al·ize /ˌinstiˈt(y)ōōsHənl.īz/ ▶v. [tr.] **1** establish (something, typically a practice or activity) as a convention or norm in an organization or culture: *a system that institutionalizes bad behavior.* **2** place or keep (someone) in a residential institution: *these adolescents had more contacts with the police and were charged and institutionalized more often.* —**in·sti·tu·tion·al·i·za·tion** /ˌinstiˌt(y)ōōsHənl-iˈzāsHən/ n.

in·struct /inˈstrəkt/ ▶v. **1** [tr.] direct or command someone to do something, esp. as an official order: [tr.] *she instructed him to wait* | *I instructed that she be given hot, sweet tea.* **2** teach (someone) a subject or skill: *he instructed them in the use of firearms* | *instructing electors how to record their votes.* **3** *Law* give a person direction, information, or authorization, in particular: ■ (of a judge) give information, esp. clarification of legal principles, to (a jury). ■ inform (someone) of a fact or situation: *the bank was instructed that the money from the savings account was now held by the company.*

in·struc·tion /inˈstrəksHən/ ▶n. **1** (often **instructions**) a direction or order: *he issued instructions to the sheriff* | *he was acting on my instructions.* ■ (**instructions**) *Law* directions to a lawyer or to a jury. ■ *Comput.* a code or sequence in a computer program that defines an operation and puts it into effect. **2** (**instructions**) detailed information telling how something should be done, operated, or assembled: *always study the instructions supplied.* **3** teaching; education: *the school offers personalized instruction in a variety of skills.* —**in·struc·tion·al** /-sHənl/ adj.

in·struc·tive /inˈstrəktiv/ ▶adj. useful and informative: *it is instructive to compare the two projects.* —**in·struc·tive·ly** adv. —**in·struc·tive·ness** n.

in·struc·tor /inˈstrəktər/ ▶n. a person who teaches something: *a driving instructor.* ■ a college teacher ranking below assistant professor. —**in·struc·tor·ship** /-ˌsHip/ n.

in·stru·ment /ˈinstrəmənt/ ▶n. **1** a tool or implement, esp. one for delicate or scientific work: *a surgical instrument.* ■ a thing used in pursuing an aim or policy; a means: *drama as an* **instrument** *of learning.* ■ a person who is exploited or made use of: *he was a mere instrument acting under coercion.* **2** a measuring device used to gauge the level, position, speed, etc., of something, esp. a motor vehicle or aircraft. **3** (also **musical instrument**) an object or device for producing musical sounds: *a percussion instrument.* **4** a formal document, esp. a legal one.
▶v. [tr.] equip (something) with measuring instruments.

in·stru·men·tal /ˌinstrəˈmentl/ ▶adj. **1** serving as an instrument or means in pursuing an aim or policy: *the society was* **instrumental** *in bringing about legislation.* ■ relating to something's function as an instrument or means to an end: *an instrumental view of education and how it relates to their needs.* **2** (of music) performed on instruments, not sung.

■ relating to musical instruments: *brilliance of instrumental color.* **3** of or relating to an implement or measuring device: *instrumental error.* **4** *Gram.* denoting or relating to a case of nouns and pronouns (and words in grammatical agreement with them) indicating a means or instrument.

▶*n.* **1** a piece of (usually nonclassical) music performed solely by instruments, with no vocals. **2** (**the instrumental**) *Gram.* the instrumental case. ■ a noun in the instrumental case. —**in·stru·men·tal·ist** *n.* —**in·stru·men·tal·ly** *adv.*

in·stru·men·ta·tion /ˌinstrəmənˈtāSHən; -menˈ-/ ▶*n.* **1** the particular instruments used in a piece of music; the manner in which a piece is arranged for instruments. ■ the arrangement or composition of a piece of music for particular musical instruments. **2** measuring instruments regarded collectively: *the controls and instrumentation of an aircraft.* ■ the design, provision, or use of measuring instruments.

in·stru·ment pan·el (also **instrument board**) ▶*n.* a surface in front of a driver's or pilot's seat, on which the vehicle's or aircraft's instruments are situated.

in·sub·or·di·nate /ˌinsəˈbôrdn-it/ ▶*adj.* defiant of authority; disobedient to orders: *an insubordinate attitude.* —**in·sub·or·di·nate·ly** *adv.* —**in·sub·or·di·na·tion** /-ˌbôrdnˈāSHən/ *n.*

in·sub·stan·tial /ˌinsəbˈstanCHəl/ ▶*adj.* lacking strength and solidity: *insubstantial evidence.* ■ not solid or real; imaginary. —**in·sub·stan·ti·al·i·ty** /-ˌstanCHēˈalitē/ *n.* —**in·sub·stan·tial·ly** *adv.*

in·suf·fer·a·ble /inˈsəf(ə)rəbəl/ ▶*adj.* too extreme to bear; intolerable: *the heat would be insufferable by July.* ■ having or showing unbearable arrogance or conceit. —**in·suf·fer·a·ble·ness** *n.* —**in·suf·fer·a·bly** /-blē/ *adv.*

in·su·lar /ˈins(y)ələr/ ▶*adj.* **1** ignorant of or uninterested in cultures, ideas, or peoples outside one's own experience: *a stubbornly insular farming people.* ■ lacking contact with other people: *people living restricted and sometimes insular existences.* **2** of, relating to, or from an island. —**in·su·lar·i·ty** /ˌins(y)əˈlaritē; -ˈler-/ *n.* —**in·su·lar·ly** *adv.*

in·su·late /ˈins(y)əˌlāt/ ▶*v.* [*tr.*] (often **be insulated**) protect (something) by interposing material that prevents the loss of heat or the intrusion of sound: *the room was heavily insulated against all outside noise.* ■ prevent the passage of electricity to or from (something) by covering it in nonconducting material: *the case is carefully insulated to prevent short circuits.* ■ *fig.* protect from the unpleasant effects or elements of something: *he claims that the service is complacent and insulated from outside pressures.* —**in·su·la·tion** /ˌinsəˈlāSHən/ *n.* —**in·su·la·tor** /-ˌlātər/ *n.*

in·su·lin /ˈinsələn/ ▶*n.* *Biochem.* a hormone produced in the pancreas by the islets of Langerhans that regulates the amount of glucose in the blood. The lack of insulin causes a form of diabetes. ■ an animal-derived or synthetic form of this substance used to treat diabetes.

in·sult ▶*v.* /inˈsəlt/ [*tr.*] speak to or treat with disrespect or scornful abuse: *you're insulting the woman I love* | [as *adj.*] (**insulting**) *their language is crude and insulting to women.*

▶*n.* /ˈinˌsəlt/ **1** a disrespectful or scornfully abusive remark or action: *he hurled insults at us* | *he saw the book as a deliberate insult to the Church.* ■ a thing so worthless or contemptible as to be offensive: *the present offer is an absolute insult.* **2** *Med.* an event or occurrence that causes damage to a tissue or organ. ▷mid 16th cent. (as a verb in the sense 'exult, act arrogantly'): from Latin *insultare* 'jump or trample on,' from *in-* 'on' + *saltare*, from *salire* 'to leap.' The noun (in the early 17th cent. denoting an attack) is from French *insulte* or ecclesiastical Latin *insultus*. The main current senses date from the 17th cent., the medical use dating from the early 20th cent. —**in·sult·er** *n.* —**in·sult·ing·ly** *adv.*

▶ □ **add insult to injury** act in a way that makes a bad or displeasing situation worse.

in·su·per·a·ble /inˈso͞op(ə)rəbəl/ ▶*adj.* (of a difficulty or obstacle) impossible to overcome: *insuperable financial problems.* —**in·su·per·a·bil·i·ty** /-ˌso͞op(ə)rəˈbilitē/ *n.* —**in·su·per·a·bly** /-blē/ *adv.*

in·sup·port·a·ble /ˌinsəˈpôrtəbəl/ ▶*adj.* **1** unable to be supported or justified: *he had arrived at a wholly insupportable conclusion.* **2** unable to be endured; intolerable. —**in·sup·port·a·bly** /-blē/ *adv.*

in·sur·ance /inˈSHo͝orəns/ ▶*n.* **1** a practice or arrangement by which a company or government agency provides a guarantee of compensation for specified loss, damage, illness, or death in return for payment of a premium: *many new borrowers take out insurance against unemployment.* ■ the business of providing such an arrangement: *Howard is in insurance.* ■ money paid for this: *my insurance has gone up.* ■ money paid out as compensation under such an arrangement: *when will I be able to collect the insurance?* ■ an insurance policy. **2** a thing providing protection against a possible eventuality: *seeking closer ties with other oil-supplying nations as insurance against disruption of Middle East supplies.*

in·sur·ance pol·i·cy ▶*n.* a document detailing the terms and conditions of a contract of insurance.

in·sure /inˈSHo͝or/ ▶*v.* [*tr.*] arrange for compensation in the event of damage to or loss of (property), or injury to or the death of (someone), in exchange for regular advance payments to a company or government agency: *the table should be insured for $2,500.* | [*intr.*] *businesses can insure against exchange rate fluctuations.* ■ provide insurance coverage with respect to: *subsidiaries set up to insure the risks of a group of companies.* ■ (**insure someone against**) *fig.* secure or protect someone against (a possible contingency): *by appeasing Celia they might insure themselves against further misfortune* | [*intr.*] *such changes could insure against further violence and unrest.* —**in·sur·a·bil·i·ty** /-ˌSHo͝orəˈbilitē/ *n.* —**in·sur·a·ble** *adj.*

in·sur·er /inˈSHo͝orər/ ▶*n.* a person or company that underwrites an insurance risk; the party in an insurance contract undertaking to pay compensation.

in·sur·gent /inˈsərjənt/ ▶*adj.* rising in active revolt: *alleged links with insurgent groups.* ■ of or relating to rebels: *a series of insurgent attacks.*

▶*n.* (usu. **insurgents**) a rebel or revolutionary: *an attack by armed insurgents.* —**in·sur·gence** *n.* —**in·sur·gen·cy** *n.* (*pl.* **-cies**).

in·sur·mount·a·ble /ˌinsərˈmountəbəl/ ▶*adj.* too great to be overcome: *an insurmountable problem.* —**in·sur·mount·a·bly** *adv.*

in·sur·rec·tion /ˌinsəˈrekSHən/ ▶*n.* a violent uprising against an authority or government: *opposition to the new regime led to armed insurrection.* —**in·sur·rec·tion·ary** *adj.* —**in·sur·rec·tion·ist** *n. & adj.*

int. ▶*abbr.* ■ interior. ■ internal. ■ international.

in·tact /inˈtakt/ ▶*adj.* not damaged or impaired in any way; complete: *the church was almost in ruins, but its tower remained intact.* —**in·tact·ness** *n.*

in·tact fam·i·ly ▶*n.* a nuclear family in which membership has remained constant, in the absence of divorce or other divisive factors.

in·ta·glio /inˈtalyō; -ˈtäl-/ ▶*n.* (*pl.* **-glios**) a design incised or engraved into a material: *the dies bore a design in intaglio.* ■ a gem with an incised design. ■ any printing process in which the type or design is etched or engraved, such as photogravure or dry point.

▶*v.* (**-glioes**, **-glioed**) [*tr.*] [usu. as *adj.*] (**intaglioed**) engrave or represent by an engraving: *a carved box with little intaglioed pineapples on it.*

in·take /ˈinˌtāk/ ▶*n.* **1** an amount of food, air, or another substance taken into the body: *your daily intake of calories* | *his alcohol intake.* ■ an act of taking something into the body: *she heard his sharp intake of breath.* **2** a location or structure through which something is taken in, e.g., water into a channel or pipe from a river, fuel or air into an engine or machine, commodities into a place, etc. ■ the action of taking something in: *facilities for the intake of grain by road.*

in·te·ger /ˈintijər/ ▶*n.* **1** a whole number; a number that is not a fraction. **2** a thing complete in itself.

in·te·gral /ˈintigrəl; inˈteg-/ ▶*adj.* **1** necessary to make a whole complete; essential or fundamental: *games are an integral part of the school's curriculum.* ■ included as part of the whole rather than supplied separately: *the unit comes complete with integral pump and heater.* ■ having or containing all parts that are necessary to be complete: *the first integral recording of the ten Mahler symphonies.* **2** *Math.* of or denoted by an integer. ■ involving only integers, esp. as coefficients of a function.

▶*n.* *Math.* a function of which a given function is the derivative, i.e., which yields that function when differentiated, and which may express the area under the curve of a graph of the function. ■ a function satisfying a given differential equation. —**in·te·gral·i·ty** /ˌintiˈgralitē/ *n.* —**in·te·gral·ly** *adv.*

in·te·gral cal·cu·lus ▶*n.* a branch of mathematics concerned with the determination, properties, and application of integrals.

in·te·grate /ˈintiˌgrāt/ ▶*v.* [*tr.*] **1** combine (one thing) with another so that they become a whole: *transportation planning should be integrated with energy policy.* ■ combine (two things) so that they become a whole: *the problem of integrating the two approaches.* ■ [*intr.*] (of a thing) combine with another to form a whole: *the stone will blend with the environment and integrate into the landscape.* **2** bring into equal participation in or membership of society or an institution or body: *integrating children with special needs into ordinary schools.* ■ [*intr.*] come into equal participation in or membership of society or an institution or body: *she was anxious to integrate well into her husband's family.* **3** desegregate (a school, neighborhood, etc.), esp. racially: *there was a national campaign under way to integrate the lunch counters* | [*intr.*] *cities' efforts to integrate across urban-suburban lines.* **4** *Math.* find the integral of. —**in·te·gra·bil·i·ty**

/ˌintigrəˈbilitē/ n. **—in·te·gra·ble** /-grəbəl/ adj. **—in·te·gra·tive** adj. **—in·te·gra·tor** /-ˌgrātər/ n.

in·te·grat·ed cir·cuit ▶ n. an electronic circuit formed on a small piece of semiconducting material, performing the same function as a larger circuit made from discrete components.

in·te·gra·tion /ˌintiˈgrāsHən/ ▶ n. **1** the action or process of integrating. ■ the intermixing of people or groups previously segregated. **2** Math. the finding of an integral or integrals. **3** Psychol. the coordination of processes in the nervous system, including diverse sensory information and motor impulses: sensory integration. ■ Psychoanalysis the process by which a well-balanced psyche becomes whole as the developing ego organizes the id, and the state that results or that treatment seeks to create or restore by countering the fragmenting effect of defense mechanisms. **—in·te·gra·tion·ist** /-nist/ n.

in·teg·ri·ty /inˈtegritē/ ▶ n. **1** the quality of being honest and having strong moral principles; moral uprightness: he is known to be a man of integrity. **2** the state of being whole and undivided: upholding territorial integrity and national sovereignty. ■ the condition of being unified, unimpaired, or sound in construction: the structural integrity of the novel. ■ internal consistency or lack of corruption in electronic data: [as adj.] integrity checking.

in·teg·u·ment /inˈtegyəmənt/ ▶ n. a tough outer protective layer, esp. that of an animal or plant. **—in·teg·u·men·tal** /-ˌtegyəˈmentl/ adj. **—in·teg·u·men·ta·ry** /-ˌtegyəˈmentərē/ adj.

in·tel·lect /ˈintlˌekt/ ▶ n. the faculty of reasoning and understanding objectively, esp. with regard to abstract or academic matters: he was a man of action rather than of intellect. ■ the understanding or mental powers of a particular person: his keen intellect. ■ an intelligent or intellectual person: sapping our country of some of its brightest intellects.

in·tel·lec·tu·al /ˌintlˈekCHŌŌəl/ ▶ adj. of or relating to the intellect: children need intellectual stimulation. ■ appealing to or requiring use of the intellect: the movie wasn't very intellectual, but it caught the mood of the times. ■ possessing a highly developed intellect: you are an intellectual girl. ▶ n. a person possessing a highly developed intellect. **—in·tel·lec·tu·al·i·ty** /ˌintlˌekCHŌŌˈalitē/ n. **—in·tel·lec·tu·al·ly** adv.

in·tel·lec·tu·al·ism /ˌintlˈekCHŌŌəˌlizəm/ ▶ n. the exercise of the intellect at the expense of the emotions. ■ Philos. the theory that knowledge is wholly or mainly derived from pure reason; rationalism. **—in·tel·lec·tu·al·ist** n.

in·tel·li·gence /inˈtelijəns/ ▶ n. **1** the ability to acquire and apply knowledge and skills: a man of great intelligence. ■ a person or being with this ability: extraterrestrial intelligences. **2** the collection of information of military or political value: the chief of military intelligence | [as adj.] the intelligence department. ■ people employed in this, regarded collectively: French intelligence has been able to secure numerous informers. ■ information collected in this way: the gathering of intelligence. ■ archaic information in general; news. **—in·tel·li·gen·tial** /inˌteləˈjenCHəl/ adj. (archaic).

in·tel·li·gence quo·tient (abbr.: **IQ**) ▶ n. a number representing a person's reasoning ability (measured using problem-solving tests) as compared to the statistical norm or average for their age, taken as 100.

in·tel·li·gent /inˈtelijənt/ ▶ adj. having or showing intelligence, esp. of a high level: Annabelle is intelligent and hardworking | an intelligent guess. ■ (of a device, machine, or building) able to vary its state or action in response to varying situations, varying requirements, and past experience. ■ (esp. of a computer terminal) incorporating a microprocessor and having its own processing capability. ▷ early 16th cent.: from Latin intelligent- 'understanding,' from the verb intelligere, variant of intellegere 'understand,' from inter 'between' + legere 'choose.' **—in·tel·li·gent·ly** adv.

in·tel·li·gent·si·a /inˌteliˈjentsēə/ ▶ n. (usu. **the intelligentsia**) [treated as sing. or pl.] intellectuals or highly educated people as a group, esp. when regarded as possessing culture and political influence.

in·tel·li·gi·ble /inˈtelijəbəl/ ▶ adj. able to be understood; comprehensible. **—in·tel·li·gi·bil·i·ty** /-ˌtelijəˈbilitē/ n. **—in·tel·li·gi·bly** /-blē/ adv.

in·tem·per·ate /inˈtemp(ə)rit/ ▶ adj. having or showing a lack of self-control; immoderate: given to or characterized by excessive indulgence, esp. in alcohol: an intemperate social occasion. **—in·tem·per·ance** /-rəns/ n. **—in·tem·per·ate·ly** adv. **—in·tem·per·ate·ness** n.

in·tend /inˈtend/ ▶ v. [tr.] **1** have (a course of action) as one's purpose or objective; plan: the company intends to cut about 4,500 jobs | it is intended that coverage shall be worldwide. ■ plan that (something) function in a particular way: a series of questions intended as a checklist. ■ plan that speech should have (a particular meaning): no offense was intended, I assure you. **2** design or destine (someone or something) for a particular purpose or end: pigs intended for human consumption. ■ (**be intended for**)

be meant or designed for (a particular person or group) to have or use: this benefit is intended for people incapable of work. **—in·tend·er** n.

in·tend·ed /inˈtendid/ ▶ adj. planned or meant: the intended victim. ▶ n. (**one's intended**) inf. the person one intends to marry; one's fiancé or fiancée. **—in·tend·ed·ly** adv.

in·tense /inˈtens/ ▶ adj. **1** (of a condition, quality, feeling, etc.) existing in a high degree; forceful or extreme: the heat was intense. ■ (of an action) highly concentrated: a phase of intense activity. ■ (of a color) very strong or deep. **2** (of a person) feeling, or apt to feel, strong emotion; extremely earnest or serious: an intense young woman, passionate about her art. ■ expressing or marked by strong emotion: a low, intense mutter. **—in·tense·ly** adv. **—in·tense·ness** n.

in·ten·si·fy /inˈtensəˌfī/ ▶ v. (**-fies, -fied**) **1** become or make more intense: [intr.] the dispute began to intensify | [tr.] they had intensified their military campaign. **2** [tr.] Photog. increase the opacity of (a negative) using a chemical: the negative may be intensified with bichloride. **—in·ten·si·fi·ca·tion** /-ˌtensəfiˈkāsHən/ n. **—in·ten·si·fi·er** n.

in·ten·si·ty /inˈtensitē/ ▶ n. (pl. **-ties**) **1** the quality of being intense: gazing into her face with disconcerting intensity. ■ an instance or degree of this: an intensity that frightened her. **2** chiefly Physics the measurable amount of a property, such as force, brightness, or a magnetic field: different light intensities.

in·ten·sive /inˈtensiv/ ▶ adj. **1** concentrated on a single area or subject or into a short time; very thorough or vigorous: an intensive Arabic course. ■ (of agriculture) aiming to achieve the highest possible level of production within a limited area, esp. by using chemical and technological aids. ■ [usu. in comb.] (typically in business and economics) concentrating on or making much use of a specified thing: computer-intensive methods. **2** Gram. (of an adjective, adverb, or particle) expressing intensity; giving force or emphasis. **3** denoting a property that is measured in terms of intensity (e.g., concentration) rather than of extent (e.g., volume), and so is not simply increased by addition of one thing to another. **—in·ten·sive·ly** adv. **—in·ten·sive·ness** n.

in·ten·sive care ▶ n. special medical treatment of a dangerously ill patient, with constant monitoring. ■ a unit or ward in a hospital devoted to such treatment: she sat outside intensive care.

in·tent /inˈtent/ ▶ n. intention or purpose: with alarm she realized his intent. ▶ adj. **1** (**intent on/upon**) resolved or determined to do (something): the administration was intent on achieving greater efficiency. ■ attentively occupied with: Jill was intent on her gardening magazine. **2** (esp. of a look) showing earnest and eager attention. **—in·tent·ly** adv. **—in·tent·ness** n. ▶ □ **to** (or **for**) **all intents and purposes** in all important respects: a man who was to all intents and purposes illiterate. □ **with intent** Law with the intention of committing a specified crime: arson with intent to endanger life.

in·ten·tion /inˈtenCHən/ ▶ n. **1** a thing intended; an aim or plan: she was full of good intentions. ■ the action or fact of intending: intention is just one of the factors that will be considered. ■ (**one's intentions**) a person's designs, esp. a man's, in respect to marriage: if his intentions aren't honorable, I never want to see him again. **2** Med. the healing process of a wound. **—in·ten·tioned** adj. [in comb.] a well-intentioned remark.

in·ten·tion·al /inˈtenCHənl/ ▶ adj. done on purpose; deliberate: intentional wrongdoing and harm. **—in·ten·tion·al·ly** adv.

in·ter /inˈtər/ ▶ v. (**-terred, -ter·ring**) [tr.] (usu. **be interred**) place (a corpse) in a grave or tomb, typically with funeral rites: he was interred with the military honors due to him.

inter. ▶ abbr. intermediate.

in·ter·act /ˌintərˈakt/ ▶ v. [intr.] act in such a way as to have an effect on another; act reciprocally: all the stages in the process interact | the user interacts directly with the library. **—in·ter·ac·tant** /-tənt/ adj. & n. **—in·ter·ac·tion** n.

in·ter·ac·tive /ˌintərˈaktiv/ ▶ adj. (of two people or things) influencing or having an effect on each other: fully sighted children in interactive play with others with defective vision. ■ (of a computer or other electronic device) allowing a two-way flow of information between it and a user, responding to the user's input: interactive video. **—in·ter·ac·tive·ly** adv. **—in·ter·ac·tiv·i·ty** /-akˈtivitē/ n.

in·ter a·li·a /ˈintər ˈālēə; ˈäləə/ ▶ adv. among other things: the study includes, inter alia, computers, aircraft, and pharmaceuticals.

in·ter·breed /ˌintərˈbrēd/ ▶ v. (past and past part. **-bred**) [intr.] (of an animal) breed with another of a different race or species: wolves and dogs can interbreed. ■ (of an animal) inbreed: [as n.] (**interbreeding**) their energy had been sapped by interbreeding. ■ [tr.] cause (an animal) to breed with another of a different race or species to produce a hybrid.

in·ter·ca·lar·y /inˈtərkəˌlerē; ˌintərˈkalərē/ ▶ adj. (of a day or a month) inserted in the calendar to harmonize it with the solar year, e.g.,

February 29 in leap years. ■ of the nature of an insertion: *elaborate intercalary notes and footnotes.*

in·ter·cede /ˌintərˈsēd/ [*intr.*] ▶*v.* intervene on behalf of another: *I begged him to intercede for Theresa, but he never did a thing.* —**in·ter·ced·er** *n.*

in·ter·cept /ˌintərˈsept/ ▶*v.* [*tr.*] obstruct (someone or something) so as to prevent them from continuing to a destination: *intelligence agencies intercepted a series of telephone calls.* ■ *Math.* (of a line or surface) mark or cut off (part of a space, line, or surface).

▶*n.* an act or instance of intercepting something: *he read the file of radio intercepts.* ■ *Math.* the point at which a given line cuts a coordinate axis; the value of the coordinate at that point. ■ *Football* (of a defensive player) catch a forward pass. —**in·ter·cep·tion** *n.* —**in·ter·cep·tive** /-tiv/ *adj.* —**in·ter·cep·tor** /ˈintərˌseptər/ *n.*

in·ter·ces·sion /ˌintərˈseSHən/ ▶*n.* the action of intervening on behalf of another: *through the intercession of friends, I was able to obtain her a sinecure.* ■ the action of saying a prayer on behalf of another person. —**in·ter·ces·sor** /ˈintərˌsesər/ *n.* —**in·ter·ces·so·ry** /-ˈsesərē/ *adj.*

in·ter·change ▶*v.* /ˌintərˈCHānj/ [*tr.*] (of two or more people) exchange (things) with each other: *superior and subordinates freely interchange ideas and information.* ■ put each of (two things) in the other's place: *the terms are often interchanged.* ■ [*intr.*] (of a thing) be able to be exchanged with another: *diesel units will interchange with the gasoline ones.*

▶*n.* /ˈintərˌCHānj/ **1** the action of interchanging things, esp. information. ■ an exchange of words: *listening in shock to this venomous interchange.* **2** alternation: *the interchange of woods and meadows.* **3** a road junction designed on several levels so that traffic streams do not intersect. —**in·ter·change·a·bil·i·ty** /ˌintərˌCHānjəˈbilitē/ *n.* —**in·ter·change·a·ble** *adj.* —**in·ter·change·a·ble·ness** *n.* —**in·ter·change·a·bly** /-blē/ *adv.*

in·ter·cit·y /ˈintərˌsitē/ ▶*adj.* existing or traveling between cities.

in·ter·com /ˈintərˌkäm/ ▶*n.* an electrical device allowing one-way or two-way communication.

in·ter·com·mu·ni·cate /ˌintərkəˈmyoōnəˌkāt/ ▶*v.* [*intr.*] **1** engage in two-way communication: *Dr. Haber gazed at this while intercommunicating with his receptionist.* **2** (of two rooms) have a common connecting door: *there were two apartments on the next floor, intercommunicating.* —**in·ter·com·mu·ni·ca·tion** /-ˌmyoōniˈkāSHən/ *n.*

in·ter·con·nect /ˌintərkəˈnekt/ ▶*v.* [*intr.*] connect with each other: *the way human activities interconnect with the environment* | [*tr.*] *a high-speed data service can interconnect the hundreds of thousands of host computers and workstations.*

▶*n.* a device used to connect two things together. —**in·ter·con·nec·tion** /-ˈnekSHən/ *n.*

in·ter·con·ti·nen·tal /ˌintərˌkäntnˈentl/ ▶*adj.* relating to or traveling between continents: *an intercontinental flight.* —**in·ter·con·ti·nen·tal·ly** *adv.*

in·ter·course /ˈintərˌkôrs/ ▶*n.* communication or dealings between individuals or groups: *everyday social intercourse.* ■ short for SEXUAL INTERCOURSE. ▷late Middle English (denoting communication or dealings): from Old French *entrecours* 'exchange, commerce,' from Latin *intercursus*, from *intercurrere* 'intervene,' from *inter-* 'between' + *currere* 'run.' The specifically sexual use arose in the late 18th cent.

in·ter·de·nom·i·na·tion·al /ˌintərdəˌnäməˈnāSHənl/ ▶*adj.* of or relating to more than one religious denomination: *an interdenominational Thanksgiving service.* —**in·ter·de·nom·i·na·tion·al·ly** *adv.*

in·ter·de·part·men·tal /ˌintərdiˌpärtˈmentl; -ˌdēpärt-/ ▶*adj.* of or relating to more than one department. —**in·ter·de·part·men·tal·ly** *adv.*

in·ter·de·pend·ent /ˌintərdiˈpendənt/ ▶*adj.* (of two or more people or things) dependent on each other. —**in·ter·de·pend** *v.* —**in·ter·de·pend·ence** *n.* —**in·ter·de·pend·en·cy** *n.*

in·ter·dict ▶*n.* /ˈintərˌdikt/ an authoritative prohibition: *an interdict against marriage of those of close kin.*

▶*v.* /ˌintərˈdikt/ [*tr.*] **1** prohibit or forbid (something). ■ (**interdict someone from**) prohibit someone from (doing something): *I have not been interdicted from consuming or holding alcoholic beverages.* **2** intercept and prevent the movement of (a prohibited commodity or person): *the police established roadblocks throughout the country for interdicting drugs.* ■ *Mil.* impede (an enemy force), esp. by aerial bombing of lines of communication or supply. —**in·ter·dic·tion** /ˌintərˈdikSHən/ *n.*

in·ter·dis·ci·pli·nar·y /ˌintərˈdisəpliˌnerē/ ▶*adj.* of or relating to more than one branch of knowledge: *an interdisciplinary research program.*

in·ter·est /ˈint(ə)rist/ ▶*n.* **1** the state of wanting to know or learn about something or someone: *she looked about her with interest.* ■ (**an interest in**) a feeling of wanting to know or learn about (something): *he developed an interest in art.* ■ the quality of exciting curiosity or holding the attention: *a tale full of interest.* ■ a subject about which one is concerned or enthusiastic: *my particular interest is twentieth-century poetry.* **2** money

paid regularly at a particular rate for the use of money lent, or for delaying the repayment of a debt: *the monthly rate of interest* | [as *adj.*] *interest payments.* **3** the advantage or benefit of a person or group: *the merger is not contrary to the public interest.* ■ *archaic* the selfish pursuit of one's own welfare; self-interest. **4** a stake, share, or involvement in an undertaking, esp. a financial one: *holders of voting rights must disclose their interests.* ■ a legal concern, title, or right in property: *third parties having an interest in a building.* **5** (usu. **interests**) a group or organization having a specified common concern, esp. in politics or business: *the regulation of national interests in India, Brazil, and Africa.*

▶*v.* [*tr.*] excite the curiosity or attention of (someone): *I thought the book might interest Eric.* ■ (**interest someone in**) cause someone to undertake or acquire (something): *efforts were made to interest her in a purchase.*

▶ □ **in the interests** (or **interest**) **of something** for the benefit of: *in the interests of security we are keeping the information confidential.* □ **of interest** interesting: *much of it is of interest to historians.*

in·ter·est·ing /ˈint(ə)ristiNG; ˈintəˌrestiNG/ ▶*adj.* arousing curiosity or interest; holding or catching the attention: *it will be very interesting to see what they come up with.* —**in·ter·est·ing·ly** *adv.* —**in·ter·est·ing·ness** *n.*

in·ter·face /ˈintərˌfās/ ▶*n.* **1** a point where two systems, subjects, organizations, etc., meet and interact: *the interface between accountancy and the law.* ■ *chiefly Physics* a surface forming a common boundary between two portions of matter or space, e.g., between two immiscible liquids: *the surface tension of a liquid at its air/liquid interface.* **2** *Comput.* a device or program enabling a user to communicate with a computer. ■ a device or program for connecting two items of hardware or software so that they can be operated jointly or communicate with each other.

▶*v.* [*intr.*] (**interface with**) **1** interact with (another system, person, organization, etc.): *his goal is to get people interfacing with each other.* **2** *Comput.* connect with (another computer or piece of equipment) by an interface.

in·ter·fere /ˌintərˈfi(ə)r/ ▶*v.* [*intr.*] **1** (**interfere with**) prevent (a process or activity) from continuing or being carried out properly: *a job would interfere with his studies.* ■ (of a thing) strike against (something) when working; get in the way of: *the rotors are widely separated and do not interfere with one another.* ■ handle or adjust (something) without permission, esp. so as to cause damage: *he admitted interfering with a van.* **2** take part or intervene in an activity without invitation or necessity: *she tried not to interfere in her children's lives.* **3** *Physics* (of light or other electromagnetic waveforms) mutually act upon each other and produce interference. ■ cause interference to a broadcast radio signal. —**in·ter·fer·er** *n.* —**in·ter·fer·ing·ly** *adv.*

in·ter·fer·ence /ˌintərˈfi(ə)rəns/ ▶*n.* **1** the action of interfering or the process of being interfered with: *he denied that there had been any interference in the country's internal affairs* | *an unwarranted interference with personal liberty.* ■ *Football* the action of illegally interfering with an opponent's ability to catch a passed or kicked ball. ■ *Football* the legal blocking of an opponent or opponents to clear a way for the teammate in possession of the ball. ■ *Baseball* any of various forms of hindering a player's ability to make a play, run, etc. ■ (in ice hockey and other sports) the illegal hindering of an opponent not in possession of the puck or ball. **2** *Physics* the combination of two or more electromagnetic waveforms to form a resultant wave in which the displacement is either reinforced or canceled. ■ the fading or disturbance of received radio signals caused by unwanted signals from other sources, such as unshielded electrical equipment, or broadcasts from other stations or channels. —**in·ter·fer·en·tial** /-fəˈrenCHəl/ *adj.*

in·ter·fer·on /ˌintərˈfi(ə)rˌän/ ▶*n.* *Biochem.* a protein released by animal cells, usually in response to the entry of a virus, that has the property of inhibiting virus replication.

in·ter·ga·lac·tic /ˌintərgəˈlaktik/ ▶*adj.* of, relating to, or situated between two or more galaxies. —**in·ter·ga·lac·ti·cal·ly** /-ik(ə)lē/ *adv.*

in·ter·gla·cial /ˌintərˈglāSHəl/ *Geol.* ▶*adj.* of or relating to a period of milder climate between two glacial periods. Compare with INTERSTADIAL.

▶*n.* an interglacial period.

in·ter·gov·ern·men·tal /ˌintərˌgəvər(n)ˈmentl/ ▶*adj.* of, relating to, or conducted between two or more governments: *an intergovernmental conference.* —**in·ter·gov·ern·men·tal·ly** *adv.*

in·ter·im /ˈintərəm/ ▶*n.* the intervening time: *in the interim I'll just keep my fingers crossed.*

Pronunciation Key ə *ago, up;* ər *over, fur;* a *hat;* ā *ate;* ä *car;* CH *chin;* e *let;* ē *see;* e(ə)r *air;* i *fit;* ī *by;* i(ə)r *ear;* NG *sing;* ō *go;* ô *law, for;* oi *toy;* oō *good;* ooō *goo;* ou *out;* SH *she;* TH *thin;* ṮH *then;* (h)w *why;* ZH *vision*

▸*adj.* in or for the intervening period; provisional or temporary: *an interim arrangement.* ■ *chiefly Brit.* relating to less than a full year's business activity: *an interim dividend | interim profit.*

in·te·ri·or /in'ti(ə)rēər/ ▸*adj.* **1** situated within or inside; relating to the inside; inner: *the interior lighting is not adequate.* **2** remote from the coast or frontier; inland: *the interior jungle regions.* ■ relating to internal or domestic affairs: *the Interior Department.* **3** existing or taking place in the mind or soul; mental: *an interior monologue.*
▸*n.* (usu. **the interior**) **1** the inner or indoor part of something, esp. a building; the inside. ■ an artistic representation of the inside of a building or room. **2** the inland part of a country or region: *the plains of the interior.* ■ the internal affairs of a country: *the Department of the Interior.* —**in·te·ri·or·ize** /-,rīz/ *v.* —**in·te·ri·or·ly** *adv.*

interj. ▸*abbr.* interjection.

in·ter·ject /,intər'jekt/ ▸*v.* [tr.] say (something) abruptly, esp. as an aside or interruption: *she interjected the odd question here and there* | [intr.] *Christine felt bound to interject before there was open warfare.* —**in·ter·jec·to·ry** /-t(ə)rē/ *adj.*

in·ter·jec·tion /,intər'jekshən/ ▸*n.* an abrupt remark, made esp. as an aside or interruption. ■ an exclamation, esp. as a part of speech, e.g., *ah!* or *dear me!* —**in·ter·jec·tion·al** /-shənl/ *adj.*

in·ter·lace /,intər'lās/ ▸*v.* [tr.] bind intricately together; interweave: *the trees interlaced their branches so that only tiny patches of sky were visible.* ■ (**interlace something with**) mingle or intersperse something with: *buttercups interlacing their gold with the silver of the daisies.* ■ [intr.] (of two or more things) cross each other intricately. ■ *Electr.* scan (a video image) in such a way that alternate lines form one sequence that is followed by the other lines in a second sequence. —**in·ter·lace·ment** *n.*

in·ter·lard /,intər'lärd/ ▸*v.* [tr.] (**interlard something with**) intersperse or embellish speech or writing with different material: *a compendium of advertisements and reviews, interlarded with gossip.*

in·ter·leave /,intər'lēv/ ▸*v.* [tr.] insert pages, typically blank ones, between the pages of (a book): *books of maps* **interleaved with** *tracing paper.* ■ place something between the layers of (something): *pasta interleaved with strips of zucchini and carrot.* ■ *Telecommunications* mix (two or more digital signals) by alternating between them. ■ *Comput.* divide (memory or processing power) between a number of tasks by allocating successive segments of it to each task in turn.

in·ter·li·brar·y loan /,intər'lībrerē/ ▸*n.* a system in which one library borrows a book from another library for the use of an individual.

in·ter·line[1] /,intər'līn/ ▸*v.* [tr.] insert words between the lines of (a document or other text): *the writing was overwritten and interlined by many hands.* ■ insert (words) in this way.

in·ter·line[2] ▸*v.* [tr.] put an extra lining between the ordinary lining and the fabric of (a garment, curtain, etc.), typically to provide extra strength.

in·ter·lock ▸*v.* /,intər'läk/ [intr.] (of two or more things) engage with each other by overlapping or by the fitting together of projections and recesses: *their fingers interlocked.*
▸*n.* /'intər,läk/ **1** a device or mechanism for connecting or coordinating the function of different components. **2** (also **interlock fabric**) a fabric knitted with closely interlocking stitches that allow it to stretch, typically used in underwear. —**in·ter·lock·er** *n.*

in·ter·loc·u·tor /,intər'läkyətər/ ▸*n.* *formal* a person who takes part in a dialogue or conversation. —**in·ter·lo·cu·tion** /-lə'kyōōshən/ *n.*

in·ter·loc·u·to·ry /,intər'läkyə,tôrē/ ▸*adj.* *Law* (of a decree or judgment) given provisionally during the course of a legal action.

in·ter·lop·er /'intər,lōpər; ,intər'lōpər/ ▸*n.* a person who becomes involved in a place or situation where they are not wanted or are considered not to belong. —**in·ter·lope** /'intər,lōp; ,intər'lōp/ *v.*

in·ter·lude /'intər,lōōd/ ▸*n.* **1** an intervening period of time: *enjoying a lunchtime interlude.* ■ a pause between the acts of a play. **2** something performed during a theater intermission. ■ a piece of music played between other pieces or between the verses of a hymn. ■ a temporary amusement or source of entertainment that contrasts with what goes before or after: *the romantic interlude withered once he was back in town.*
▷Middle English (originally denoting a light dramatic entertainment): from medieval Latin *interludium*, from *inter-* 'between' + *ludus* 'play.'

in·ter·mar·riage /,intər'marij/ ▸*n.* marriage between people of different races, castes, or religions. ■ marriage between close relations.

in·ter·mar·ry /,intər'marē/ ▸*v.* (**-ries, -ried**) [intr.] (of people belonging to different races, castes, or religions) become connected by marriage. ■ (of close relations) marry each other.

in·ter·me·di·ar·y /,intər'mēdē,erē/ ▸*n.* (pl. **-ar·ies**) a person who acts as a

link between people in order to try to bring about an agreement or reconciliation; a mediator.
▸*adj.* intermediate: *an intermediary stage.*

in·ter·me·di·ate /,intər'mēdē-it/ ▸*adj.* coming between two things in time, place, order, character, etc.: *an intermediate stage of development* | *a cooled liquid intermediate between liquid and solid.* ■ having more than a basic knowledge or level of skill but not yet advanced: *intermediate skiers.* ■ suitable for people of such a level: *an intermediate course.*
▸*n.* an intermediate thing. ■ a person at an intermediate level of knowledge or skill. ■ a chemical compound formed by one reaction and then taking part in another, esp. during synthesis.
▸*v.* [intr.] act as intermediary; mediate. —**in·ter·me·di·a·cy** /-əsē/ *n.* —**in·ter·me·di·ate·ly** *adv.* —**in·ter·me·di·ate·ness** *n.* —**in·ter·me·di·a·tion** /-,mēdē'āshən/ *n.* —**in·ter·me·di·a·tor** /-,ātər/ *n.*

in·ter·ment /in'tərmənt/ ▸*n.* the burial of a corpse in a grave or tomb, typically with funeral rites.

in·ter·mez·zo /,intər'metsō/ ▸*n.* (pl. **-mez·zi** /-'metsē/ or **-mez·zos**) a short connecting instrumental movement in an opera or other musical work. ■ a similar piece performed independently. ■ a short piece for a solo instrument. ■ a light dramatic, musical, or other performance inserted between the acts of a play.

in·ter·mi·na·ble /in'tərmənəbl/ ▸*adj.* endless (often used hyperbolically): *bogged down in interminable discussions.* —**in·ter·mi·na·bil·i·ty** /-,tərmənə'bilitē/ *n.* —**in·ter·mi·na·ble·ness** *n.* —**in·ter·mi·na·bly** /-blē/ *adv.*

in·ter·min·gle /,intər'minggəl/ ▸*v.* mix or mingle together: [intr.] *daisies* **intermingled with** *huge expanses of gorse and foxgloves* | [tr.] *Riesling grapes were always intermingled with other varieties.*

in·ter·mis·sion /,intər'mishən/ ▸*n.* a pause or break: *the work goes on without intermission.* ■ an interval between parts of a play, movie, or concert.

in·ter·mit·tent /,intər'mitnt/ ▸*adj.* occurring at irregular intervals; not continuous or steady: *intermittent rain.* —**in·ter·mit·tence** *n.* —**in·ter·mit·ten·cy** *n.* —**in·ter·mit·tent·ly** *adv.*

in·tern ▸*n.* /'in,tərn/ a recent medical graduate receiving supervised training in a hospital and acting as an assistant physician or surgeon. Compare with RESIDENT. ■ a student or trainee who works, sometimes without pay, at a trade or occupation in order to gain work experience.
▸*v.* /in'tərn/ **1** [tr.] confine (someone) as a prisoner, esp. for political or military reasons. **2** [intr.] serve as an intern. —**in·tern·ment** *n.* —**in·tern·ship** /-,ship/ *n.*

in·ter·nal /in'tərnl/ ▸*adj.* of or situated on the inside: *the tube had an internal diameter of 1.1 mm.* ■ inside the body: *internal bleeding.* ■ existing or occurring within an organization: *an internal telephone system.* ■ relating to affairs and activities within a country rather than with other countries; domestic: *internal flights.* ■ experienced in one's mind; inner rather than expressed: *internal feelings.* ■ of the inner nature of a thing; intrinsic: *he creates a dialogue* **internal** *to his work.*
▸*pl. n.* (**internals**) inner parts or features. —**in·ter·nal·i·ty** /,intər'nalitē/ *n.* —**in·ter·nal·ize** *v.* —**in·ter·nal·ly** *adv.*

in·ter·nal com·bus·tion en·gine ▸*n.* an engine that generates motive power by the burning of gasoline, oil, or other fuel with air inside the engine, the hot gases produced being used to drive a piston or do other work as they expand.

in·ter·nal med·i·cine ▸*n.* a branch of medicine specializing in the diagnosis and nonsurgical treatment of diseases.

in·ter·na·tion·al /,intər'nashənl/ ▸*adj.* existing, occurring, or carried on between two or more nations: *international trade.* ■ agreed on by all or many nations: *a violation of international law.* ■ used by people of many nations: *large international hotels.*
▸*n.* (**International**) any of four associations founded (1864–1936) to promote socialist or communist action. ■ a member of any of these. —**in·ter·na·tion·al·i·ty** /-,nashə'nalitē/ *n.* —**in·ter·na·tion·al·ly** *adv.*

In·ter·na·tion·al Date Line ▸*n.* an imaginary north–south line through the Pacific Ocean, adopted in 1884, to the east of which the date is a day earlier than it is to the west. It lies chiefly along the meridian furthest from Greenwich, England (i.e., longitude 180°), with diversions to pass around some island groups. Also called DATE LINE.

in·ter·na·tion·al·ism /,intər'nashənl,izəm/ ▸*n.* **1** the state or process of being international. ■ the advocacy of cooperation and understanding between nations. **2** (**Internationalism**) the principles of any of the four Internationals. —**in·ter·na·tion·al·ist** *n.*

In·ter·na·tion·al Sys·tem of U·nits ▸*n.* a system of physical units (**SI Units**) based on the meter, kilogram, second, ampere, kelvin, candela, and mole, together with a set of prefixes to indicate multiplication or division by a power of ten.

in·ter·ne·cine /ˌintərˈnesēn; -ˈnēsēn; -sin/ ▶*adj.* destructive to both sides in a conflict: *the region's history of savage internecine warfare.* ■ of or relating to conflict within a group or organization: *the party shrank from the trauma of more internecine strife.*

In·ter·net /ˈintərˌnet/ ▶an international computer network providing e-mail and information from computers in educational institutions, government agencies, and industry, accessible to the general public via modem line.

in·ter·o·ce·an·ic /ˌintərˌōshēˈanik/ ▶*adj.* between or connecting two oceans.

in·ter·per·son·al /ˌintərˈpərsənəl/ ▶*adj.* of or relating to relationships or communication between people: *you will need good interpersonal skills.* —**in·ter·per·son·al·ly** *adv.*

in·ter·phase /ˈintərˌfāz/ ▶*n. Biol.* the resting phase between successive mitotic divisions of a cell, or between the first and second divisions of meiosis.

in·ter·plan·e·tar·y /ˌintərˈplaniˌterē/ ▶*adj.* situated or traveling between planets: *interplanetary missions.*

in·ter·play /ˈintərˌplā/ ▶*n.* the way in which two or more things have an effect on each other: *the interplay between inheritance and learning.*

in·ter·po·late /inˈtərpəˌlāt/ ▶*v.* [*tr.*] insert (something) between fixed points: *illustrations were interpolated in the text.* ■ insert (words) in a book or other text, esp. in order to give a false impression as to its date. ■ make such insertions in (a book or text). ■ interject (a remark) in a conversation: *"I dare say," interpolated her employer.* ■ *Math.* insert (an intermediate value or term) into a series by estimating or calculating it from surrounding known values. —**in·ter·po·la·tion** /-ˌtərpəˈlāshən/ *n.* —**in·ter·po·la·tive** /-ˌlātiv/ *adj.* —**in·ter·po·la·tor** /-ˌlātər/ *n.*

in·ter·pose /ˌintərˈpōz/ ▶*v.* **1** [*tr.*] place or insert between one thing and another: *he interposed himself between her and the top of the stairs.* **2** [*intr.*] intervene between parties: *the legislature interposed to suppress these amusements.* ■ [*tr.*] say (words) as an interruption: *if I might interpose a personal remark here.* ■ [*tr.*] exercise or advance (a veto or objection) so as to interfere: *the memo interposes no objection to issuing a discharge.*

in·ter·pret /inˈtərprit/ ▶*v.* (**-pret·ed, -pret·ing**) [*tr.*] **1** explain the meaning of (information, words, or actions): *the evidence is difficult to interpret.* ■ [*intr.*] translate orally the words of another person speaking a different language. ■ perform (a dramatic role or piece of music) in a particular way that conveys one's understanding of the creator's ideas. **2** understand (an action, mood, or way of behaving) as having a particular meaning or significance: *her self-confidence was interpreted as brashness.* —**in·ter·pret·a·bil·i·ty** /-ˌtərpritəˈbilitē/ *n.* —**in·ter·pret·a·ble** *adj.* —**in·ter·pre·ta·tion** /inˌtərpriˈtāshən/ *n.* —**in·ter·pre·ta·tive** /-ˌtātiv/ *adj.* —**in·ter·pre·ta·tive·ly** /-ˌtātivlē/ *adv.* —**in·ter·pre·tive** /-ˈtərpritiv/ *adj.* —**in·ter·pre·tive·ly** /-ˈtərpritivlē/ *adv.*

in·ter·pret·er /inˈtərpritər/ ▶*n.* a person who interprets, esp. one who translates speech orally. ■ *Comput.* a program that can analyze and execute a program line by line.

in·ter·ra·cial /ˌintərˈrāshəl/ ▶*adj.* existing between or involving different races: *interracial conflict.* —**in·ter·ra·cial·ly** *adv.*

in·ter·reg·num /ˌintərˈregnəm/ ▶*n.* (*pl.* **-nums** or **-na** /-nə/) a period when normal government is suspended, esp. between successive reigns or regimes. ■ an interval or pause.

in·ter·re·late /ˌintərriˈlāt/ ▶*v.* relate or connect to one another: [*intr.*] *each component interrelates with all the others* | [*tr.*] *shared values and mechanisms that interrelate peoples in all corners of the world.* —**in·ter·re·lat·ed·ness** *n.* —**in·ter·re·la·tion·ship** *n.*

in·ter·ro·gate /inˈterəˌgāt/ ▶*v.* [*tr.*] ask questions of (someone, esp. a suspect or a prisoner) closely, aggressively, or formally. ■ *Comput.* obtain data from (a computer file, database, storage device, or terminal). ■ (of an electronic device) transmit a signal to (another device, esp. one on a vehicle) to obtain a response giving information about identity, condition, etc. —**in·ter·ro·ga·tor** /-ˌgātər/ *n.*

in·ter·ro·ga·tion /inˌterəˈgāshən/ ▶*n.* the action of interrogating or the process of being interrogated. —**in·ter·ro·ga·tion·al** /-shənl/ *adj.*

in·ter·rog·a·tive /ˌintəˈrägətiv/ ▶*adj.* having or conveying the force of a question: *a hard, interrogative stare.* ■ *Gram.* used in questions: *an interrogative adverb.*
▶*n.* a word used in questions, such as *how* or *what.* ■ a construction that has the force of a question. —**in·ter·rog·a·tive·ly** *adv.*

in·ter·rog·a·to·ry /ˌintəˈrägəˌtôrē/ ▶*adj.* conveying the force of a question; questioning: *the guard moves away with an interrogatory stare.*

▶*n.* (*pl.* **-ries**) *Law* a written question that is formally put to one party in a case by another party and that must be answered.

in·ter·rupt /ˌintəˈrəpt/ ▶*v.* [*tr.*] **1** stop the continuous progress of (an activity or process): *the buzzer interrupted his thoughts.* ■ stop (someone from speaking) by saying or doing something: *"Of course . . . " Shepherd began, but his son interrupted him.* **2** break the continuity of (a line or surface): *the coastal plain is interrupted by chains of large lagoons.* ■ obstruct (something, esp. a view). —**in·ter·rupt·i·ble** *adj.* —**in·ter·rup·tion** /-shən/ *n.* —**in·ter·rup·tive** /-tiv/ *adj.*

in·ter·sect /ˌintərˈsekt/ ▶*v.* [*tr.*] divide (something) by passing or lying across it: *occasionally the water table intersects the earth's surface, forming streams and lakes.* ■ [*intr.*] (of two or more things) pass or lie across each other: *lines of latitude and longitude intersect at right angles.*

in·ter·sec·tion /ˌintərˈsekshən/ ▶*n.* a point or line common to lines or surfaces that intersect: *the intersection of a plane and a cone.* ■ a point at which two or more things intersect, esp. roads: *red and green lights at the nearby intersection.* ■ an action of intersecting: *his course is on a direct intersection with ours.* —**in·ter·sec·tion·al** /-shənl/ *adj.*

in·ter·sperse /ˌintərˈspərs/ ▶*v.* [*tr.*] scatter among or between other things; place here and there: *interspersed between tragic stories are a few songs.* ■ diversify (a thing or things) with other things at intervals: *open fields interspersed with pine.* —**in·ter·sper·sion** /-ˈspərzhən/ *n.*

in·ter·sta·di·al /ˌintərˈstādēəl/ *Geol.* ▶*adj.* of or relating to a minor period of less cold climate during a glacial period. Compare with INTERGLACIAL.
▶*n.* an interstadial period.

in·ter·state /ˈintərˌstāt/ ▶*adj.* existing or carried on between states: *interstate travel.* ■ in a different state from one referred to or understood: *their interstate rivals.*
▶*n.* (also **interstate highway**) one of a system of expressways covering the 48 contiguous states: *a picnic area just off the interstate.*

in·ter·stel·lar /ˌintərˈstelər/ ▶*adj.* occurring or situated between stars.

in·ter·stice /inˈtərstis/ ▶*n.* (usu. **interstices**) an intervening space, esp. a very small one: *sunshine filtered through the interstices of the arching trees.* ▷late Middle English: from Latin *interstitium*, from *intersistere* 'stand between,' from *inter-* 'between' + *sistere* 'to stand.'

in·ter·sti·tial /ˌintərˈstishəl/ ▶*adj.* of, forming, or occupying interstices. ■ *Ecol.* (of minute animals) living in the spaces between individual sand grains in the soil or aquatic sediments. —**in·ter·sti·tial·ly** *adv.*

in·ter·twine /ˌintərˈtwīn/ ▶*v.* twist or twine together: [*tr.*] *a net made of cotton intertwined with other natural fibers* | [*intr.*] *the coils intertwine with one another like strands of spaghetti.* ■ [*tr.*] *fig.* connect or link (two or more things) closely: *Dickens has been very clever to intertwine all these aspects and ideas.* —**in·ter·twine·ment** *n.*

in·ter·val /ˈintərvəl/ ▶*n.* **1** an intervening time or space: *there was an interval of many years without any meetings.* **2** a pause; a break in activity: *an interval of mourning.* ■ *Brit.* an intermission separating parts of a theatrical or musical performance. ■ *Brit.* a break between the parts of an athletic contest: *leading 3-0 at the interval.* **3** a space between two things; a gap. ■ the difference in pitch between two musical sounds. —**in·ter·val·lic** /ˌintərˈvalik/ *adj.*
▶ □ **at intervals 1** with time between, not continuously: *the light flashed at intervals.* **2** with spaces between: *the path is marked with rocks at intervals.*

in·ter·vene /ˌintərˈvēn/ ▶*v.* [*intr.*] **1** come between so as to prevent or alter a result or course of events: *he acted outside his authority when he intervened in the dispute.* ■ (of an event or circumstance) occur as a delay or obstacle to something being done: *Christmas intervened, and the investigation was suspended.* ■ interrupt verbally. ■ *Law* interpose in a lawsuit as a third party. **2** occur in time between events. ■ be situated between things. —**in·ter·ven·er** *n.* —**in·ter·ven·ient** /-ˈvēnyənt/ *adj.* —**in·ter·ve·nor** /-ˈvēnər/ *n.*

in·ter·ven·tion /ˌintərˈvenshən/ ▶*n.* the action or process of intervening. ■ interference by a country in another's affairs: *the administration was considering military intervention.* ■ action taken to improve a situation, esp. a medical disorder: *two patients were referred for surgical intervention.* —**in·ter·ven·tion·al** /-shənl/ *adj.*

in·ter·ven·tion·ist /ˌintərˈvenshənist/ ▶*adj.* favoring intervention, esp. by a government in its domestic economy or by one country in the affairs of another.
▶*n.* a person who favors intervention of this kind. —**in·ter·ven·tion·ism** /-ˌnizəm/ *n.*

Pronunciation Key ə *ago,* up; ər *over, fur;* a *hat;* ā *ate;* ä *car;* CH *chin;* e *let;* ē *see;* e(ə)r *air;* i *fit;* ī *by;* i(ə)r *ear;* NG *sing;* ō *go;* ô *law, for;* oi *toy;* o͝o *good;* o͞o *goo;* ou *out;* SH *she;* TH *thin;* T͟H *then;* (h)w *why;* ZH *vision*

in·ter·view /'intər,vyōō/ ▶ *n.* a meeting of people face to face, esp. for consultation. ▪ a conversation between a journalist or radio or television presenter and a person of public interest, used as the basis of a broadcast or publication. ▪ an oral examination of an applicant for a job, college admission, etc.
▶ *v.* [*tr.*] hold an interview with (someone): *he arrived to be interviewed by a local TV station about the level of unemployment.* ▪ question (someone) to discover their opinions or experience: *in a survey more than half the women interviewed hated the label "housewife."* ▪ orally examine (an applicant for a job, college admission, etc.): *he came to be interviewed for a top job* | [*intr.*] *I was interviewing all last week.* ▪ [*intr.*] perform (well or badly) at an interview. —**in·ter·view·ee** /,intər,vyōō'ē/ *n.* —**in·ter·view·er** *n.*

in·ter·weave /,intər'wēv/ ▶ *v.* (*past -wove*; *past part. -wov·en*) weave or become woven together: [*tr.*] *the rugs are made by tightly interweaving the warp and weft strands* | [*intr.*] *the branches met and interwove above his head.* ▪ [*tr.*] *fig.* blend closely: *Wordsworth's political ideas are often interwoven with his philosophical and religious beliefs.*

in·tes·tate /in'testāt; -tit/ ▶ *adj.* not having made a will before one dies: *he died intestate.* ▪ of or relating to a person who dies without having made a will: *his brother's posthumous children are admissible as intestate heirs.*
▶ *n.* a person who has died without having made a will. —**in·tes·ta·cy** /-təsē/ *n.*

in·tes·tine /in'testən/ (also **in·tes·tines**) ▶ *n.* (in vertebrates) the lower part of the alimentary canal from the end of the stomach to the anus. See also **LARGE INTESTINE, SMALL INTESTINE.** ▪ (esp. in invertebrates) the whole alimentary canal from the mouth downward. —**in·tes·ti·nal** /-tənl/ *adj.*

in·ti·ma·cy /'intəməsē/ ▶ *n.* (*pl.* **-cies**) close familiarity or friendship; closeness: *the intimacy between a husband and wife.* ▪ a private cozy atmosphere: *the room had a peaceful sense of intimacy about it.* ▪ an intimate act, esp. sexual intercourse. ▪ an intimate remark: *here she was sitting swapping intimacies with a stranger.* ▪ closeness of observation or knowledge of a subject: *he acquired an intimacy with Swahili literature.*

in·ti·mate[1] /'intəmit/ ▶ *adj.* **1** closely acquainted; familiar, close: *intimate friends.* ▪ (of a place or setting) having or creating an informal friendly atmosphere: *an intimate little Italian restaurant.* ▪ used euphemistically to indicate that a couple is having a sexual relationship: *he was sickened by the thought of others having been intimate with her.* ▪ involving very close connection: *their intimate involvement with their community.* **2** private and personal: *intimate details of his sexual encounters* | *intimate correspondence.* ▪ used euphemistically to refer to a person's genitals: *touching her in the most intimate places.* **3** (of knowledge) detailed; thorough.
▶ *n.* a very close friend: *his circle of intimates.* —**in·ti·mate·ly** *adv.*

in·ti·mate[2] /'intə,māt/ ▶ *v.* [*tr.*] imply or hint: *he had already intimated that he might not be able to continue.* ▪ state or make known: *Mr. Hutchison has intimated his decision to retire.* —**in·ti·ma·tion** /,intə'māsHən/ *n.*

in·tim·i·date /in'timi,dāt/ ▶ *v.* frighten or overawe (someone), esp. in order to make them do what one wants: *he tries to intimidate his rivals.* —**in·tim·i·dat·ing·ly** *adv.* —**in·tim·i·da·tion** /-,timi'dāsHən/ *n.* —**in·tim·i·da·tor** /-,dātər/ *n.* —**in·tim·i·da·to·ry** /-də,tôrē/ *adj.*

in·to /'intōō/ ▶ *prep.* **1** expressing movement or action with the result that someone or something becomes enclosed or surrounded by something else: *cover the bowl and put it into the fridge.* **2** expressing movement or action with the result that someone or something makes physical contact with something else: *he crashed into a parked car.* **3** indicating a route by which someone or something may arrive at a particular destination: *the narrow road that led down into the village.* **4** indicating the direction toward which someone or something is turned when confronting something else: *with the wind blowing into your face.* **5** indicating an object of attention or interest: *a clearer insight into what is involved.* **6** expressing a change of state: *a peaceful protest which turned into a violent confrontation.* **7** expressing the result of an action: *they forced the club into a humiliating and expensive special general meeting.* **8** expressing division: *three into twelve equals four.* **9** *inf.* (of a person) taking a lively and active interest in (something): *he's into surfing.*

in·tol·er·a·ble /in'tälərəbəl/ ▶ *adj.* unable to be endured. —**in·tol·er·a·bil·i·ty** /-,tälərə'bilitē/ *n.* —**in·tol·er·a·ble·ness** *n.* —**in·tol·er·a·bly** /-blē/ *adv.*

in·tol·er·ant /in'tälərənt/ ▶ *adj.* not tolerant of others' views, beliefs, or behavior that differ from one's own. ▪ unable to be given (a medicine or other treatment) or to eat (a food) without adverse effects: *these patients were lactose intolerant.* ▪ (of a plant or animal) unable to survive exposure to (physical influence). —**in·tol·er·ance** *n.* —**in·tol·er·ant·ly** *adv.*

in·to·na·tion /,intə'nāsHən; -tō-/ ▶ *n.* **1** the rise and fall of the voice in speaking: *she spoke English with a German intonation.* ▪ the action of intoning or reciting in a singing voice. **2** accuracy of pitch in playing or

singing: *poor woodwind intonation at the opening.* **3** the opening phrase of a plainsong melody. —**in·to·na·tion·al** /-sHənl/ *adj.*

in·tone /in'tōn/ ▶ *v.* [*tr.*] say or recite with little rise and fall of the pitch of the voice: *he intoned a short Latin prayer.* —**in·ton·er** *n.*

in to·to /in 'tōtō/ ▶ *adv.* as a whole: *such proposals should be subjected to specific criticism rather than rejected in toto.* ▪ in all; overall: *there was, in toto, an increase in legal regulation and public surveillance.*

in·tox·i·cant /in'täksikənt/ ▶ *n.* an intoxicating substance.

in·tox·i·cate /in'täksikāt/ ▶ *v.* [*tr.*] (of alcoholic drink or a drug) cause (someone) to lose control of their faculties or behavior. ▪ poison. ▪ *fig.* excite or exhilarate: *the team was intoxicated by the prospect of another victorious season.* —**in·tox·i·ca·tion** /-,täksi'kāsHən/ *n.*

in·tox·i·cat·ing /in'täksikātiNG/ ▶ *adj.* (of alcoholic drink or a drug) liable to cause intoxication. ▪ *fig.* exhilarating or exciting: *the intoxicating touch of freedom.* —**in·tox·i·cat·ing·ly** *adv.*

intr. ▶ *abbr.* ▪ intransitive. ▪ introduce or introduced or introducing or introduction or introductory.

in·trac·ta·ble /in'traktəbəl/ ▶ *adj.* hard to control or deal with: *intractable pain.* ▪ (of a person) difficult; stubborn. —**in·trac·ta·bil·i·ty** /-,traktə'bilitē/ *n.* —**in·trac·ta·ble·ness** *n.* —**in·trac·ta·bly** /-blē/ *adv.*

in·tra·mu·ral /,intrə'myōōrəl/ ▶ *adj.* situated or done within the walls of a building. ▪ taking place within a single educational institution: *intramural games.* ▪ forming part of normal university or college studies. ▪ situated or done within a community: *an intramural social symbol within the tribe.* —**in·tra·mu·ral·ly** *adv.*

in·tran·si·gent /in'transijənt; -zi-/ ▶ *adj.* unwilling or refusing to change one's views or to agree about something.
▶ *n.* an intransigent person. —**in·tran·si·gence** *n.* —**in·tran·si·gen·cy** *n.* —**in·tran·si·gent·ly** *adv.*

in·tran·si·tive /in'transitiv; -zi-/ ▶ *adj.* (of a verb or a sense or use of a verb) not taking a direct object, e.g., *look* in *look at the sky.* The opposite of **TRANSITIVE.**
▶ *n.* an intransitive verb. —**in·tran·si·tive·ly** *adv.* —**in·tran·si·tiv·i·ty** /-,transi'tivitē; -zi-/ *n.*

in·tra·u·ter·ine de·vice (abbr.: **IUD**) ▶ *n.* a contraceptive device fitted inside the uterus and physically preventing the implantation of fertilized ova.

in·tra·ve·nous /,intrə'vēnəs/ (abbr.: **IV**) ▶ *adj.* existing or taking place within, or administered into, a vein or veins: *an intravenous drip.* —**in·tra·ve·nous·ly** *adv.*

in·trep·id /in'trepid/ ▶ *adj.* fearless; adventurous (often used for rhetorical or humorous effect): *our intrepid reporter.* —**in·tre·pid·i·ty** /,intrə'piditē/ *n.* —**in·trep·id·ly** *adv.* —**in·trep·id·ness** *n.*

in·tri·cate /'intrikit/ ▶ *adj.* very complicated or detailed: *an intricate network of canals.* ▷late Middle English: from Latin *intricat-* 'entangled,' from the verb *intricare,* from *in-* 'into' + *tricae* 'tricks, perplexities.' —**in·tri·ca·cy** /-kəsē/ *n.* —**in·tri·cate·ly** *adv.*

in·trigue ▶ *v.* /in'trēg/ (**-trigues, -trigued, -tri·guing**) **1** [*tr.*] arouse the curiosity or interest of; fascinate: *I was intrigued by your question.* **2** [*intr.*] make secret plans to do something illicit or detrimental to someone.
▶ *n.* /'in,trēg/ **1** the secret planning of something illicit or detrimental to someone: *the cabinet was a nest of intrigue* | *the intrigues of local government officials.* ▪ a secret love affair. **2** a mysterious or fascinating quality: *within the region's borders is a wealth of interest and intrigue.* —**in·tri·guer** *n.* —**in·tri·guing·ly** *adv.*

in·trin·sic /in'trinzik; -sik/ ▶ *adj.* belonging naturally; essential: *access to the arts is intrinsic to a high quality of life.* ▪ (of a muscle) contained wholly within the organ on which it acts. —**in·trin·si·cal·ly** /-ik(ə)lē/ *adv.*

in·tro /'intrō/ ▶ *n.* (*pl.* **-tros**) *inf.* an introduction.

in·tro·duce /,intrə'd(y)ōōs/ ▶ *v.* [*tr.*] **1** (often **be introduced**) bring (something, esp. a product, measure, or concept) into use or operation for the first time: *various new taxes were introduced.* ▪ (**introduce something to**) bring a subject to the attention of (someone) for the first time: *the program is a bid to introduce opera to the masses.* ▪ present (a new piece of legislation) for debate in a legislative assembly. ▪ bring (a new plant, animal, or disease) to a place and establish it there. **2** make (someone) known by name to another in person, esp. formally: *I hope to introduce Jenny to them very soon.* **3** insert or bring into something: *a device that introduces chlorine into the pool automatically.* **4** occur at the start of; open: *a longer, more lyrical opening that introduces her first solo.* ▪ (of a person) provide an opening explanation or announcement for (a television or radio program, book, etc.). —**in·tro·duc·er** *n.*

in·tro·duc·tion /,intrə'dəksHən/ ▶ *n.* **1** the bringing of a product, measure, concept, etc., into use or operation for the first time. ▪ the action of bringing a new plant, animal, or disease to a place. ▪ a thing, such as a product, measure, plant, etc., newly brought in: *these grains are valuable introductions from Sweden.* **2** (often **introductions**) a formal presentation of one person to another, in which each is told the other's name: *he returned to his desk, leaving Michael to make the introductions.* **3** a thing preliminary to something else: *your talk will need an introduction that states clearly what you are talking about and why.* ■ an explanatory section at the beginning of a book, report, etc. ■ a preliminary section in a piece of music, often thematically different from the main section. ■ a book or course of study intended to introduce a subject to a person. ■ a person's first experience of a subject or thing: *my introduction to drama was through an amateur dramatic society.*

in·tro·duc·to·ry /ˌintrəˈdəktərē/ ▶*adj.* serving as an introduction to a subject or topic; basic or preliminary: *an introductory course in Russian.* ■ intended to persuade someone to purchase something for the first time: *we are making a special introductory offer of a reduced subscription.*

in·tro·spec·tion /ˌintrəˈspekSHən/ ▶*n.* the examination or observation of one's own mental and emotional processes: *quiet introspection can be extremely valuable.* —**in·tro·spec·tive** /-ˈspektiv/ *adj.* —**in·tro·spec·tive·ly** /-ˈspektiv-lē/ *adv.* —**in·tro·spec·tive·ness** /-ˈspektivnis/ *n.*

in·tro·vert /ˈintrəˌvərt/ ▶*n.* a shy, reticent, and typically self-centered person. ■ *Psychol.* a person predominantly concerned with their own thoughts and feelings rather than with external things. Compare with EXTROVERT. —**in·tro·ver·sion** /-ˌvərzHən/ *n.* —**in·tro·ver·sive** /-ˌvərsiv/ *adj.*

in·tro·vert·ed /ˈintrəˌvərtid/ ▶*adj.* of, denoting, or typical of an introvert. ■ (of a community, company, or other group) concerned principally with its own affairs; inward-looking or parochial.

in·trude /inˈtro͞od/ ▶*v.* **1** [*intr.*] put oneself deliberately into a place or situation where one is unwelcome or uninvited: *he had no right to intrude into their lives.* ■ enter with disruptive or adverse effect: *politics quickly intrude into the booklet.* ■ [*tr.*] introduce into a situation with disruptive or adverse effect: *to intrude political criteria into military decisions risks reducing efficiency.* **2** [*tr.*] *Geol.* (of igneous rock) be forced into (preexisting rocks): *the granite may have intruded these rock layers.*

in·trud·er /inˈtro͞odər/ ▶*n.* a person who intrudes, esp. into a building with criminal intent.

in·tru·sion /inˈtro͞ozHən/ ▶*n.* **1** the action of intruding: *unacceptable intrusions of privacy.* ■ a thing that intrudes: *they oppose the excavations as an intrusion on their heritage.* **2** *Geol.* the action or process of forcing a body of igneous rock between or through existing formations, without reaching the surface. ■ a body of igneous rock that has intruded the surrounding strata.

in·tru·sive /inˈtro͞osiv/ ▶*adj.* **1** making an unwelcome manifestation with disruptive or adverse effect: *that was an intrusive question | tourist attractions that are environmentally intrusive.* ■ (of a person) disturbing another by one's uninvited or unwelcome presence: *giving people information about their health without being too intrusive.* **2** *Phonet.* (of a sound) pronounced between words or syllables to facilitate pronunciation, such as an *r* in *saw a movie*, which occurs in the speech of some eastern New Englanders and metropolitan New Yorkers. **3** *Geol.* of, relating to, or formed by intrusion. —**in·tru·sive·ly** *adv.* —**in·tru·sive·ness** *n.*

in·tu·it /inˈt(y)o͞o-it/ ▶*v.* [*tr.*] understand or work out by instinct: *I intuited his real identity.* —**in·tu·it·a·ble** *adj.*

in·tu·i·tion /ˌint(y)o͞oˈiSHən/ ▶*n.* the ability to understand something immediately, without the need for conscious reasoning: *we shall allow our intuition to guide us.* ■ a thing that one knows or considers likely from instinctive feeling rather than conscious reasoning: *your insights and intuitions as a native speaker are positively sought.* —**in·tu·i·tion·al** /-ˈiSHənl/ *adj.* —**in·tu·i·tion·al·ly** /-ˈiSHənl-ē/ *adv.*

in·tu·i·tive /inˈt(y)o͞oitiv/ ▶*adj.* using or based on what one feels to be true even without conscious reasoning; instinctive: *I had an intuitive conviction that there was something unsound in him.* ■ (chiefly of computer software) easy to use and understand. —**in·tu·i·tive·ly** *adv.* —**in·tu·i·tive·ness** *n.*

In·u·it /ˈin(y)o͞o-it/ ▶*n.* **1** (*pl.* same or **-its**) a member of an indigenous people of northern Canada and parts of Greenland and Alaska. **2** the family of languages of this people, one of the three branches of the Eskimo-Aleut language family. It is also known, esp. to its speakers, as **Inuktitut.**
▶*adj.* of or relating to the Inuit or their language.

in·un·date /ˈinənˌdāt/ ▶*v.* [*tr.*] flood: *the islands may be the first to be inundated as sea levels rise.* ■ *fig.* overwhelm (someone) with things or people to be dealt with: *we've been inundated with complaints.* —**in·un·da·tion** /ˌinənˈdāSHən/ *n.*

in·ure /iˈn(y)o͝or/ ▶*v.* **1** [*tr.*] accustom (someone) to something, esp. something unpleasant: *these children have been inured to violence.* **2** [*intr.*] (**enure for/to**) *Law* come into operation; take effect: *a release given to one of two joint contractors inures to the benefit of both.* —**in·ure·ment** *n.*

in u·ter·o /in ˈyo͞otərō/ ▶*adv.* & *adj.* in a woman's uterus; before birth: [as *adv.*] *this damage may occur in utero.*

in·vac·u·ate /inˈvakyo͞oˌāt/ ▶*v.* [*tr.*] confine (people) to a space in an emergency: *these buildings can now invacuate tenants to safe havens within the building.* —**in·vac·u·a·tion** /in,vakyo͞oˈāSHən/ *n.*

in va·cu·o /in ˈvakyəˌwō/ ▶*adv.* in a vacuum: *the hydrochloric acid was removed by evaporation in vacuo.* ■ away from or without the normal context or environment: *instead of dealing with individual aspects of lifestyle in vacuo, social factors are taken into account.*

in·vade /inˈvād/ ▶*v.* [*tr.*] (of an armed force or its commander) enter (a country or region) so as to subjugate or occupy it: *Iraq's intention to invade Kuwait |* [*intr.*] *they would invade at dawn.* ■ enter (a place, situation, or sphere of activity) in large numbers, esp. with intrusive effect. ■ (of a parasite or disease) spread into (an organism or bodily part). ■ (of a person or emotion) encroach or intrude on: *his privacy was being invaded.* —**in·vad·er** *n.*

in·va·lid¹ /ˈinvəlid/ ▶*n.* a person made weak or disabled by illness or injury: [as *adj.*] *an invalid husband.*
▶*v.* (**-lid·ed, -lid·ing**) [*tr.*] remove (someone) from active service in the armed forces because of injury or illness: *invalided out of the infantry.* ■ disable (someone) by injury or illness. —**in·va·lid·ism** /-ˌizəm/ *n.*

in·val·id² /inˈvalid/ ▶*adj.* not valid, in particular: ■ (esp. of an official document or procedure) not legally recognized and therefore void because contravening a regulation or law: *the vote was declared invalid due to a technicality.* ■ (esp. of an argument, statement, or theory) not true because based on erroneous information or unsound reasoning: *a comparison is invalid if we are not comparing like with like.* ■ (of computer instructions, data, etc.) not conforming to the correct format or specifications. —**in·val·id·ly** *adv.*

in·val·i·date /inˈvaliˌdāt/ ▶*v.* [*tr.*] **1** make (an argument, statement, or theory) unsound or erroneous. **2** deprive (an official document or procedure) of legal efficacy because of contravention of a regulation or law. —**in·val·i·da·tion** /-ˌvaliˈdāSHən/ *n.* —**in·val·i·da·tor** /-ˌdātər/ *n.*

in·val·u·a·ble /inˈvalyo͞oəbəl/ ▶*adj.* extremely useful; indispensable. —**in·val·u·a·ble·ness** *n.* —**in·val·u·a·bly** /-blē/ *adv.*

in·var·i·a·ble /inˈve(ə)rēəbəl/ ▶*adj.* never changing: *disillusion was the almost invariable result.* ■ (of a noun in an inflected language) having the same form in both the singular and the plural, e.g., *sheep.* ■ *Math.* (of a quantity) constant. —**in·var·i·a·bil·i·ty** /-ˌve(ə)rēəˈbilitē/ *n.* —**in·var·i·a·ble·ness** *n.* —**in·var·i·a·bly** *adv.*

in·va·sion /inˈvāzHən/ ▶*n.* an instance of invading a country or region with an armed force: *the Soviet invasion of Czechoslovakia.* ■ an incursion by a large number of people or things into a place or sphere of activity: *stadium guards are preparing for another invasion of fans.* ■ an unwelcome intrusion into another's domain: *an unwarranted invasion of privacy.* ■ the infestation of a body by harmful organisms: *a bacterial invasion.* —**in·va·sive** *adj.*

in·vec·tive /inˈvektiv/ ▶*n.* insulting, abusive, or highly critical language: *he let out a stream of invective.*

in·veigh /inˈvā/ ▶*v.* [*intr.*] (**inveigh against**) speak or write about (something) with great hostility: *Marx inveighed against the evils of the property-owning classes.*

in·vei·gle /inˈvāgəl/ ▶*v.* [*tr.*] persuade (someone) to do something by means of deception or flattery: *we cannot inveigle him into putting pen to paper.* ■ (**inveigle oneself** or **one's way into**) gain entrance to (a place) by using such methods. ▷late 15th cent. (in the sense 'beguile, deceive'; formerly also as *enveigle*): from Anglo-Norman French *enveigler*, alteration of Old French *aveugler* 'to blind,' from *aveugle* 'blind.' —**in·vei·gle·ment** *n.*

in·vent /inˈvent/ ▶*v.* [*tr.*] create or design (something that has not existed before); be the originator of: *he invented an improved form of the steam engine.* ■ make up (an idea, name, story, etc.), esp. so as to deceive.

in·ven·tion /inˈvenSHən/ ▶*n.* the action of inventing something, typically a process or device. ■ something, typically a process or device, that has been invented. ■ creative ability: *his powers of invention were rather limited.* ■ something fabricated or made up: *you know my story is an invention.* —**in·ven·tor** *n.*

Pronunciation Key ə *ago,* up; ər *over,* fur; a *hat;* ā *ate;* ä *car;* CH *chin;* e *let;* ē *see;* e(ə)r *air;* i *fit;* ī *by;* i(ə)r *ear;* NG *sing;* ō *go;* ô *law, for;* oi *toy;* o͞o *good;* o͞o *goo;* ou *out;* SH *she;* TH *thin;* TH *then;* (h)w *why;* zH *vision*

in·ven·tive /inˈventiv/ ▶*adj.* (of a person) having the ability to create or design new things or to think originally: *she is the most inventive painter around.* ■ (of a product, process, action, etc.) showing creativity or original thought: *methods of communication during the war were diverse and inventive.* —**in·ven·tive·ly** *adv.* —**in·ven·tive·ness** *n.*

in·ven·to·ry /ˈinvənˌtôrē/ ▶*n.* (*pl.* **-ries**) a complete list of items such as property, goods in stock, or the contents of a building. ■ a quantity of goods held in stock. ■ (in accounting) the entire stock of a business, including materials, components, work in progress, and finished products.
▶*v.* (**-ries, -ried**) [*tr.*] make a complete list of. ■ enter in a list: *about forty possible sites were inventoried.*

in·verse /ˈinvərs; inˈvərs/ ▶*adj.* opposite or contrary in position, direction, order, or effect: *the well-observed inverse relationship between disability and social contact.* ■ chiefly *Math.* produced from or related to something else by a process of inversion.
▶*n.* something that is the opposite or reverse of something else: *his approach is the inverse of most research on ethnic and racial groups.* ■ *Math.* a reciprocal quantity, mathematical expression, geometric figure, etc., that is the result of inversion. ■ *Math.* an element that, when combined with a given element in an operation, produces the identity element for that operation. —**in·verse·ly** *adv.*

in·verse pro·por·tion (also **inverse ratio**) ▶*n.* a relation between two quantities such that one increases in proportion as the other decreases.

in·ver·sion /inˈvərzhən/ ▶*n.* **1** the action of inverting something or the state of being inverted: *the inversion of the normal domestic arrangement.* ■ reversal of the normal order of words, typically for rhetorical effect but also found in the regular formation of questions in English. ■ *Mus.* the process of inverting an interval, chord, or phrase. ■ *Mus.* an inverted interval, chord, or phrase. ■ *Physics* the conversion of direct current into alternating current. **2** (also **temperature inversion** or **thermal inversion**) a reversal of the normal decrease of air temperature with altitude, or of water temperature with depth. ■ (also **inversion layer**) a layer of the atmosphere in which temperature increases with height. **3** *Math.* the process of finding a quantity, function, etc., from a given one such that the product of the two under a particular operation is the identity. ■ the interchanging of numerator and denominator of a fraction, or antecedent and consequent of a ratio. ■ the process of finding the expression that gives a given expression under a given transformation. ■ *Geom.* a transformation in which each point of a given figure is replaced by another point on the same straight line from a fixed point, esp. in such a way that the product of the distances of the two points from the center of inversion is constant. **4** (also **sexual inversion**) *dated Psychol.* the adoption of behavior typical of the opposite sex; homosexuality. —**in·ver·sive** /-ˈvərsiv/ *adj.*

in·vert ▶*v.* /inˈvərt/ [*tr.*] put upside down or in the opposite position, order, or arrangement: *invert the mousse onto a serving plate.* ■ *Mus.* modify (a phrase) by reversing the direction of pitch changes. ■ *Mus.* alter (an interval or triad) by changing the relative position of the notes in it. ■ chiefly *Math.* subject to inversion; transform into its inverse. —**in·vert·i·bil·i·ty** /inˌvərtəˈbilitē/ *n.* —**in·vert·i·ble** *adj.*

in·ver·te·brate /inˈvərtəbrit; -ˌbrāt/ ▶*n.* an animal lacking a backbone, such as an arthropod, mollusk, annelid, coelenterate, etc. The invertebrates constitute an artificial division of the animal kingdom. Compare with VERTEBRATE.
▶*adj.* of, relating to, or belonging to this division of animals. ■ *humorous* irresolute; spineless.

in·vest /inˈvest/ ▶*v.* **1** [*intr.*] expend money with the expectation of achieving a profit or material result by putting it into financial schemes, shares, or property, or by using it to develop a commercial venture: *getting workers to invest in private pension funds* | [*tr.*] *the company is to invest $12 million in its new manufacturing site.* ■ [*tr.*] devote (one's time, effort, or energy) to a particular undertaking with the expectation of a worthwhile result: *politicians who have invested so much time in the Constitution would be crestfallen.* ■ [*intr.*] (**invest in**) *inf.* buy (something) whose usefulness will repay the cost. **2** [*tr.*] (**invest someone/something with**) provide or endow someone or something with (a particular quality or attribute). ■ endow someone with (a rank or office). ■ (**invest something in**) establish a right or power in. **3** [*tr.*] *archaic* surround (a place) in order to besiege or blockade it. ▷mid 16th cent. (in the senses 'clothe,' 'clothe with the insignia of a rank,' and 'endow with authority): from French *investir* or Latin *investire*, from *in-* 'into, upon' + *vestire* 'clothe' (from *vestis* 'clothing'). Sense 1 (early 17th cent.)

is influenced by Italian *investire*. —**in·vest·a·ble** *adj.* —**in·vest·i·ble** *adj.* —**in·ves·tor** /-ˈvestər/ *n.*

in·ves·ti·gate /inˈvestiˌgāt/ ▶*v.* [*tr.*] carry out a systematic or formal inquiry to discover and examine the facts of (an incident, allegation, etc.) so as to establish the truth: *police are investigating the alleged beating.* ■ carry out research or study into (a subject, typically one in a scientific or academic field) so as to discover facts or information. ■ make inquiries as to the character, activities, or background of (someone). ■ [*intr.*] make a check to find out something: *when you didn't turn up, I thought I'd better come back to investigate.* —**in·ves·ti·ga·tor** /-ˌgātər/ *n.* —**in·ves·ti·ga·to·ry** /-gəˌtôrē/ *adj.*

in·ves·ti·ga·tion /inˌvestiˈgāshən/ ▶*n.* the action of investigating something or someone; formal or systematic examination or research: *he is under investigation for receiving illicit funds.* ■ a formal inquiry or systematic study: *an investigation has been launched into the potential impact of the oil spill.* —**in·ves·ti·ga·tion·al** /-shənl/ *adj.*

in·ves·ti·ga·tive /inˈvestiˌgātiv/ (also **in·ves·ti·ga·to·ry** /-gəˌtôrē/) ▶*adj.* of or concerned with investigating something. ■ (of journalism or a journalist) inquiring intensively into and seeking to expose malpractice, the miscarriage of justice, or other controversial issues.

in·ves·ti·ture /inˈvestiCHər; -ˌCHŏŏr/ ▶*n.* **1** the action of formally investing a person with honors or rank. ■ a ceremony at which honors or rank are formally conferred on a particular person. **2** the action of clothing or robing. ■ a thing that clothes or covers.

in·vest·ment /inˈves(t)mənt/ ▶*n.* the action or process of investing money for profit or material result. ■ a thing that is worth buying because it may be profitable or useful in the future: *a used car is rarely a good investment.* ■ an act of devoting time, effort, or energy to a particular undertaking with the expectation of a worthwhile result: *the time spent in attending a one-day seminar is an investment in our professional futures.*

in·vet·er·ate /inˈvetərit/ ▶*adj.* having a particular habit, activity, or interest that is long-established and unlikely to change: *he was an inveterate gambler.* ■ (of a feeling or habit) long-established and unlikely to change. —**in·vet·er·a·cy** /-rəsē/ *n.* —**in·vet·er·ate·ly** *adv.*

in·vid·i·ous /inˈvidēəs/ ▶*adj.* (of an action or situation) likely to arouse or incur resentment or anger in others: *she'd put herself in an invidious position.* ■ (of a comparison or distinction) unfairly discriminating; unjust. —**in·vid·i·ous·ly** *adv.* —**in·vid·i·ous·ness** *n.*

in·vig·or·ate /inˈvigəˌrāt/ ▶*v.* [*tr.*] give strength or energy to: *the shower had invigorated her.* —**in·vig·or·at·ing·ly** *adv.* —**in·vig·or·a·tion** /-ˌvigəˈrāshən/ *n.* —**in·vig·or·a·tor** /-ˌrātər/ *n.*

in·vin·ci·ble /inˈvinsəbəl/ ▶*adj.* too powerful to be defeated or overcome. —**in·vin·ci·bil·i·ty** /-ˌvinsəˈbilitē/ *n.* —**in·vin·ci·bly** /-blē/ *adv.*

in·vi·o·la·ble /inˈvīələbəl/ ▶*adj.* never to be broken, infringed, or dishonored: *an inviolable rule of chastity* | *the Polish–German border was inviolable.* —**in·vi·o·la·bil·i·ty** /-ˌvīələˈbilitē/ *n.* —**in·vi·o·la·bly** /-blē/ *adv.*

in·vi·o·late /inˈvīəlit/ ▶*adj.* free or safe from injury or violation: *an international memorial which must remain inviolate.* —**in·vi·o·la·cy** /-ləsē/ *n.* —**in·vi·o·late·ly** *adv.*

in·vis·i·ble /inˈvizəbəl/ ▶*adj.* unable to be seen; not visible to the eye. ■ concealed from sight; hidden: *he lounged in a doorway, invisible in the dark.* ■ *fig.* (of a person) treated as if unable to be seen; ignored or not taken into consideration: *before 1971, women artists were pretty well invisible.* ■ *Econ.* relating to or denoting earnings that a country makes from the sale of services or other items not constituting tangible commodities: *tourism is the most important of our invisible exports.*
▶*n.* an invisible thing, person, or being. ■ (**invisibles**) invisible exports and imports. —**in·vis·i·bil·i·ty** /-ˌvizəˈbilitē/ *n.* —**in·vis·i·bly** /-blē/ *adv.*

in·vi·ta·tion /ˌinviˈtāshən/ ▶*n.* a written or verbal request inviting someone to go somewhere or to do something: *a wedding invitation.* ■ the action of inviting someone to go somewhere or to do something: *a club with membership by invitation only.* ■ a situation or action that tempts someone to do something or makes a particular outcome likely: *tactics like those of the colonel would have been an invitation to disaster.*

in·vite ▶*v.* /inˈvīt/ [*tr.*] make a polite, formal, or friendly request to (someone) to go somewhere or to do something: *we were invited to a dinner at the embassy* | [*tr.*] *she invited Patrick to sit down.* ■ make a formal or polite request for (something, esp. an application for a job or opinions on a particular topic) from someone. ■ (of an action or situation) tend to elicit (a particular reaction or response) or to tempt (someone) to do something: *his use of the word did little but invite criticism.*
▶*n.* /ˈinˌvīt/ *inf.* an invitation. —**in·vi·tee** /ˌinvīˈtē/ *n.* —**in·vit·er** /inˈvītər/ *n.*

in·vit·ing /inˈvītiNG/ ▶*adj.* offering the promise of an attractive or enjoyable experience: *the sea down there looks so inviting.* —**in·vit·ing·ly** *adv.*

in vi·tro /in ˈvē·trō/ ▶*adj.* & *adv. Biol.* (of processes or reactions) taking place in a test tube, culture dish, or elsewhere outside a living organism: [as *adj.*] *in vitro fertilization.*

in·vi·vo /in 'vēvō/ ▶*adv. & adj. Biol.* (of processes) taking place in a living organism. The opposite of **IN VITRO**.

in·vo·ca·tion /,invə'kāSHən/ ▶*n.* the action of invoking something or someone for assistance or as an authority. ■ the summoning of a deity or the supernatural: *his invocation of the ancient mystical powers.* ■ an incantation used for this. ■ (in the Christian Church) a form of words such as "In the name of the Father" introducing a prayer, sermon, etc. —**in·voc·a·to·ry** /in'väkə,tôrē/ *adj.*

in·voice /'in,vois/ ▶*n.* a list of goods sent or services provided, with a statement of the sum due for these; a bill.
▶*v.* [*tr.*] send an invoice to (someone). ■ send an invoice for (goods or services provided).

in·voke /in'vōk/ ▶*v.* [*tr.*] cite or appeal to (someone or something) as an authority for an action or in support of an argument: *the antiquated defense of insanity is rarely invoked today.* ■ call on (a deity or spirit) in prayer, as a witness, or for inspiration. ■ call earnestly for: *she invoked his help against this attack.* ■ summon (a spirit) by charms or incantation. ■ give rise to; evoke. ■ *Comput.* cause (a procedure) to be carried out. ▷late 15th cent.: from French *invoquer*, from Latin *invocare*, from *in-* 'upon' + *vocare* 'to call.' —**in·vok·er** *n.*

in·vol·un·tar·y /in'välən,terē/ ▶*adj.* **1** done without conscious control: *she gave an involuntary shudder.* ■ (esp. of muscles or nerves) concerned in bodily processes that are not under the control of the will. ■ caused unintentionally, esp. through negligence: *involuntary homicide.* **2** done against someone's will; compulsory. —**in·vol·un·tar·i·ly** /in,välən'te(ə)rəlē; -'välən,ter-/ *adv.* —**in·vol·un·tar·i·ness** *n.*

in·volve /in'välv/ ▶*v.* [*tr.*] (of a situation or event) include (something) as a necessary part or result: *his transfer to another school would involve a lengthy assessment procedure.* ■ cause (a person or group) to experience or participate in an activity or situation: *what kind of organizations will be involved in setting up these projects?* —**in·volve·ment** *n.*

in·vul·ner·a·ble /in'vəln(ə)rəbəl/ ▶*adj.* impossible to harm or damage. —**in·vul·ner·a·bil·i·ty** /-,vəlnərə'bilitē/ *n.* —**in·vul·ner·a·bly** /-blē/ *adv.*

in·ward /'inwərd/ ▶*adj.* directed or proceeding toward the inside; coming in from outside: *the inward rush of air.* ■ existing within the mind, soul, or spirit, and often not expressed: *she felt an inward sense of release.*
▶*adv.* (also **in·wards**) toward the inside: *the door began to swing inward.* ■ into or toward the mind, spirit, or soul: *people must look inward to gain insight into their own stress.* —**in·ward·ly** *adv.*

I/O *Electr.* ▶*abbr.* input-output.

IOC ▶*abbr.* International Olympic Committee.

i·o·dine /'īə,dīn/ ▶*n.* the chemical element of atomic number 53, a nonmetallic element forming black crystals and a violet vapor. (Symbol: **I**) ■ a solution of this in alcohol, used as a mild antiseptic.

i·o·dize /'īə,dīz/ ▶*v.* treat or impregnate with iodine: *iodized salt.* —**i·o·di·za·tion** /,īədi'zāSHən/ *n.*

i·on /'īən; 'ī,än/ ▶*n.* an atom or molecule with a net electric charge due to the loss or gain of one or more electrons. See also **CATION**, **ANION**.

I·on·ic /ī'änik/ ▶*adj.* relating to or denoting a classical order of architecture characterized by a column with scroll shapes (volutes) on either side of the capital.
▶*n.* **1** the Ionic order of architecture. **2** the ancient Greek dialect used in Ionia.

i·on·ic /ī'änik/ ▶*adj.* of, relating to, or using ions. ■ (of a chemical bond) formed by the electrostatic attraction of oppositely charged ions. —**i·on·i·cal·ly** /-ik(ə)lē/ *adv.*

i·on·ize /'īə,nīz/ ▶*v.* [*tr.*] convert (an atom, molecule, or substance) into an ion or ions, typically by removing one or more electrons. ■ [*intr.*] become converted into an ion or ions in this way. —**i·on·iz·a·ble** *adj.* —**i·on·i·za·tion** /,īəni'zāSHən/ *n.*

i·on·iz·er /'īə,nīzər/ ▶*n.* a device that produces ionization, esp. one used to improve the quality of the air in a room.

i·on·o·sphere /ī'änə,sfi(ə)r/ ▶*n.* the layer of the earth's atmosphere that contains a high concentration of ions and free electrons and is able to reflect radio waves. It lies above the mesosphere and extends from about 50 to 600 miles (80 to 1,000 km) above the earth's surface. ■ a similar region above the surface of another planet. —**i·on·o·spher·ic** /ī,änə'sfi(ə)rik; -'sfer-/ *adj.*

i·o·ta /ī'ōtə/ ▶*n.* **1** the ninth letter of the Greek alphabet (Ι, ι), transliterated as 'i.' **2** an extremely small amount: *nothing she said seemed to make an iota of difference.*

IOU ▶*n.* a signed document acknowledging a debt.

IP ▶*abbr. Comput.* Internet protocol, the method by which information is sent between any two Internet computers on the Internet.

IPA ▶*abbr.* ■ International Phonetic Alphabet.

ip·e·cac /'ipikak/ (also **ip·e·ca·cu·a·nha** /,ipə,kakyə'wan(y)ə/) ▶*n.* **1** the dried rhizome of a South American shrub. ■ a drug prepared from this, used as an emetic and expectorant. **2** the shrub (*Cephaelis ipecacuanha*) of the bedstraw family that produces this rhizome, native to Brazil and cultivated elsewhere. ■ used in names of other plants with similar uses, e.g., **American ipecac** (*Gillenia trifoliata*) of the rose family.

ip·so fac·to /'ipsō 'faktō/ ▶*adv.* by that very fact or act: *the enemy of one's enemy may be ipso facto a friend.*

IQ ▶*abbr.* intelligence quotient.

IR ▶*abbr.* infrared.

iPod /'īpäd/ ▶*n. trademark* a type of personal digital audio player.

Ir ▶*symb.* the chemical element iridium.

IRA ▶*abbr.* ■ (often /'īrə/) individual retirement account. ■ Irish Republican Army.

I·ra·ni·an /i'rānēən; i'rä-/ ▶*adj.* of or relating to Iran or its people. ■ relating to or denoting the group of Indo-European languages that includes Persian (Farsi), Pashto, Avestan, and Kurdish.
▶*n.* a native or national of Iran, or a person of Iranian descent.

I·ra·qi /i'räkē; i'rakē/ ▶*adj.* of or relating to Iraq, its people, or their language.
▶*n.* (*pl.* **-qis**) **1** a native or national of Iraq, or a person of Iraqi descent. **2** the form of Arabic spoken in Iraq.

i·ras·ci·ble /i'rasəbəl/ ▶*adj.* (of a person) easily made angry. ■ characterized by or arising from anger: *their rebukes got progressively more irascible.* —**i·ras·ci·bil·i·ty** /i,rasə'bilitē/ *n.* —**i·ras·ci·bly** /-blē/ *adv.*

i·rate /ī'rāt/ ▶*adj.* feeling or characterized by great anger: *a barrage of irate letters.* —**i·rate·ly** *adv.* —**i·rate·ness** *n.*

ire /ī(ə)r/ ▶*n.* anger. —**ire·ful** /-fəl/ *adj.*

ir·i·des·cent /,iri'desənt/ ▶*adj.* showing luminous colors that seem to change when seen from different angles. —**ir·i·des·cence** *n.* —**ir·i·des·cent·ly** *adv.*

i·rid·i·um /i'rideəm/ ▶*n.* the chemical element of atomic number 77, a hard, dense silvery-white metal of the platinum group. (Symbol: **Ir**)

i·ris /'īris/ ▶*n.* **1** a flat, colored, ring-shaped membrane behind the cornea of the eye, with an adjustable circular opening (pupil) in the center. ■ (also **iris diaphragm**) an adjustable diaphragm of thin overlapping plates for regulating the size of a central hole, esp. for the admission of light to a lens. **2** a plant (genus *Iris*) with sword-shaped leaves and showy flowers. Native to both Eurasia and North America, it is widely cultivated as an ornamental. The **iris family** also includes the gladioli and crocuses. **3** a rainbow or a rainbowlike appearance.
▶*v.* [*intr.*] (of an aperture, typically that of a lens) open or close in the manner of an iris or iris diaphragm.

I·rish /'īriSH/ ▶*adj.* of or relating to Ireland, its people, or the Goidelic language traditionally and historically spoken there.
▶*n.* **1** (also **Irish Gaelic**) the Goidelic language that is the first official language of the Republic of Ireland. **2** [as *pl. n.*] (**the Irish**) the people of Ireland; Irish people collectively. —**I·rish·ness** *n.*
▶ □ **get one's Irish up** cause one to become angry: *if someone tries to make me do something I don't want to do, it gets my Irish up.*

I·rish cof·fee ▶*n.* coffee mixed with a dash of Irish whiskey and served with cream on top.

I·rish set·ter ▶*n.* a dog of a breed of setter with a long, silky dark red coat and a long feathered tail.

I·rish wolf·hound ▶*n.* a large, typically grayish hound of a rough-coated breed.

irk /ərk/ ▶*v.* [*tr.*] irritate; annoy: *it irks her to think of the runaround she received.*

irk·some /'ərksəm/ ▶*adj.* irritating; annoying. —**irk·some·ly** *adv.* —**irk·some·ness** *n.*

i·ron /'īərn/ ▶*n.* **1** a strong, hard magnetic silvery-gray metal, the chemical element of atomic number 26, much used as a material for construction and manufacturing, esp. in the form of steel. (Symbol: **Fe**) ■ compounds of this metal, esp. as a component of the diet: *serve liver as it's a good source of iron* | [as *adj.*] *how are your iron levels?* ■ used figuratively as a symbol or type of firmness, strength, or resistance: *her father had a will of iron* | [as *adj.*] *the iron grip of religion on minority cultures.* **2** a tool or implement now or originally made of iron: *a caulking iron.*

■ (**irons**) fetters or handcuffs. ■ *inf.* a handgun. **3** a hand-held implement with a flat steel base that is heated (typically with electricity) to smooth clothes, sheets, etc. **4** a golf club with a metal head (typically with a numeral indicating the degree to which the head is angled in order to loft the ball). **5** *Astron.* (also **iron meteorite**) a meteorite containing a high proportion of iron.

▶ *v.* [*trans.*] smooth (clothes, sheets, etc.) with an iron.

▶ *phrasal v.* □ **iron something out** remove creases from clothes, sheets, etc., by ironing. ■ *fig.* solve or settle difficulties or problems: *they had ironed out their differences.* —**i·ron·er** *n.* —**i·ron·like** /-ˌlīk/ *adj.*

▶ □ **have many** (or **other**) **irons in the fire** have many (or a range of) options or courses of action available or be involved in many activities or commitments at the same time.

I·ron Age ▶ **1** a period that followed the Bronze Age, when weapons and tools came to be made of iron. **2** (in Greek and Roman mythology) the last and worst age of the world, a time of wickedness and oppression.

i·ron·clad /ˈīərnˌklad/ ▶ *adj.* covered or protected with iron. ■ impossible to contradict, weaken, or change: *an ironclad guarantee.*

▶ *n. hist.* a 19th-century warship with armor plating.

i·ron cur·tain ▶ *n.* a notional barrier that prevents the passage of information or ideas between political entities, in particular: ■ (usu. **the Iron Curtain**) the notional barrier separating the former Soviet bloc and the West prior to the decline of communism.

i·ron·ic /īˈränik/ ▶ *adj.* using or characterized by irony: *his mouth curved into an ironic smile.* ■ happening in the opposite way to what is expected, and typically causing wry amusement because of this: *it was ironic that now that everybody had plenty of money for food, they couldn't obtain it because everything was rationed.* —**i·ron·i·cal·ly** *adv.*

i·ron·ing board ▶ *n.* a long, narrow board covered with soft material and having folding legs, on which clothes, sheets, etc., are ironed.

i·ron lung ▶ *n.* a rigid case fitted over a patient's body, used for administering prolonged artificial respiration by means of mechanical pumps.

i·ron·stone /ˈīərnˌstōn/ ▶ *n.* **1** sedimentary rock containing a substantial proportion of iron compounds. **2** [usu. as *adj.*] a kind of dense, opaque stoneware.

i·ron·ware /ˈīərnˌwer/ ▶ *n.* articles made of iron, typically domestic implements.

i·ron·wood /ˈīərnˌwo͝od/ ▶ *n.* any of a number of trees that produce very hard timber, esp. the North American hornbeams.

i·ron·works /ˈīərnˌwərks/ ▶ *n.* [treated as *sing.* or *pl.*] a place where iron is smelted or iron goods are made.

i·ro·ny[1] /ˈīrənē; ˈiərnē/ ▶ *n.* (*pl.* -**nies**) the expression of one's meaning by using language that normally signifies the opposite, typically for humorous or emphatic effect: *"Don't go overboard with the gratitude," he rejoined with heavy irony.* ■ a state of affairs or an event that seems deliberately contrary to what one expects and is often amusing as a result: *the irony is that I thought he could help me.* ■ (also **dramatic** or **tragic irony**) a literary technique, originally used in Greek tragedy, by which the full significance of a character's words or actions are clear to the audience or reader although unknown to the character.

i·ro·ny[2] /ˈīərnē/ ▶ *adj.* of or like iron: *an irony gray color.*

Ir·o·quoi·an /ˈirəˌkwoiən/ ▶ *n.* a language family of eastern North America, including the languages of the Five Nations, Tuscarora, Huron, Wyandot, and Cherokee. With the exception of Cherokee, all its members are extinct or nearly so.

▶ *adj.* of or relating to the Iroquois people or the Iroquoian language family.

Ir·o·quois /ˈirəˌkwoi/ ▶ *n.* (*pl.* same) **1** a member of a former confederacy of North American Indian peoples originally comprising the Cayuga, Mohawk, Oneida, Onondaga, and Seneca peoples (known as the **Five Nations**), and later including also the Tuscarora (thus forming the **Six Nations**). **2** any of the Iroquoian languages.

▶ *adj.* of or relating to the Iroquois or their languages.

ir·ra·di·ate /iˈrādēˌāt/ ▶ *v.* [*trans.*] **1** expose to radiation. ■ expose (food) to gamma rays to kill microorganisms. **2** illuminate (something) by or as if by shining light on it. —**ir·ra·di·a·tor** /-ˌātər/ *n.*

ir·ra·di·a·tion /iˌrādēˈāsHən/ ▶ *n.* the process or fact of irradiating or being irradiated.

ir·ra·tion·al /iˈrasHənl/ ▶ *adj.* **1** not logical or reasonable. ■ not endowed with the power of reason. **2** *Math.* (of a number, quantity, or expression) not expressible as a ratio of two integers, and having an infinite and nonrecurring expansion when expressed as a decimal, e.g., the number π and the square root of 2.

▶ *n. Math.* an irrational number. —**ir·ra·tion·al·i·ty** /iˌrasHəˈnalitē/ *n.* —**ir·**

ra·tion·al·ize /-ˌīz/ *v.* —**ir·ra·tion·al·ly** *adv.*

ir·rec·on·cil·a·ble /iˌrekənˈsīləbəl; iˈrekənˌsī-/ ▶ *adj.* (of ideas, facts, or statements) representing findings or points of view that are so different from each other that they cannot be made compatible: *these two views of the early medieval economy are irreconcilable.* ■ (of people) implacably hostile to each other.

▶ *n.* (usu. **irreconcilables**) any of two or more ideas, facts, or statements that cannot be made compatible. —**ir·rec·on·cil·a·bil·i·ty** /-ˌsīləˈbilitē/ *n.* —**ir·rec·on·cil·a·bly** /-blē/ *adv.*

ir·re·cov·er·a·ble /ˌiriˈkəvərəbəl/ ▶ *adj.* not able to be recovered, regained, or remedied. —**ir·re·cov·er·a·bly** /-blē/ *adv.*

ir·re·deem·a·ble /ˌiriˈdēməbəl/ ▶ *adj.* **1** not able to be saved, improved, or corrected. **2** (of paper currency) for which the issuing authority does not undertake ever to pay coin. —**ir·re·deem·a·bil·i·ty** /-ˌdēməˈbilitē/ *n.* —**ir·re·deem·a·bly** /-blē/ *adv.*

ir·re·duc·i·ble /ˌiriˈd(y)o͞osəbəl/ ▶ *adj.* not able to be reduced or simplified. ■ not able to be brought to a certain form or condition: *the imagery remains irreducible to textual structures.* —**ir·re·duc·i·bil·i·ty** /-ˌd(y)o͞osəˈbilitē/ *n.* —**ir·re·duc·i·bly** /-blē/ *adv.*

ir·ref·u·ta·ble /ˌireˈfyo͞otəbəl; iˈrefyə-/ ▶ *adj.* impossible to deny or disprove: *irrefutable evidence.* —**ir·ref·u·ta·bil·i·ty** /-ˌfyo͞otəˈbilitē; iˌrefyətə-/ *n.* —**ir·ref·u·ta·bly** /-blē/ *adv.*

ir·reg·u·lar /iˈregyələr/ ▶ *adj.* **1** not even or balanced in shape or arrangement: *her features were too irregular.* ■ occurring at uneven or varying rates or intervals: *an irregular heartbeat.* **2** contrary to the rules or to that which is normal or established: *they were questioned about their involvement in irregular financial dealings.* ■ (of troops) not belonging to regular or established army units. ■ *Gram.* (of a verb or other word) having inflections that do not conform to the usual rules.

▶ *n.* (usu. **irregulars**) **1** a member of an irregular military force. **2** an imperfect item of merchandise sold at a reduced price. —**ir·reg·u·lar·i·ty** /iˌregyəˈlaritē/ *n.* —**ir·reg·u·lar·ly** *adv.*

ir·rel·e·vant /iˈreləvənt/ ▶ *adj.* not connected with or relevant to something. —**ir·rel·e·vance** *n.* —**ir·rel·e·van·cy** *n.* (*pl.* -**cies**) —**ir·rel·e·vant·ly** *adv.*

ir·re·li·gious /ˌiriˈlijəs/ ▶ *adj.* indifferent or hostile to religion. —**ir·re·li·gion** /-ˈlijən/ *n.* —**ir·re·li·gious·ly** *adv.* —**ir·re·li·gious·ness** *n.*

ir·re·me·di·a·ble /ˌiriˈmēdēəbəl/ ▶ *adj.* impossible to cure or put right. —**ir·re·me·di·a·bly** /-blē/ *adv.*

ir·rep·a·ra·ble /iˈrep(ə)rəbəl/ ▶ *adj.* (of an injury or loss) impossible to rectify or repair: *they were doing irreparable damage to my heart and lungs.* —**ir·rep·a·ra·bil·i·ty** /iˌrep(ə)rəˈbilitē/ *n.* —**ir·rep·a·ra·bly** /-blē/ *adv.*

ir·re·place·a·ble /ˌiriˈplāsəbəl/ ▶ *adj.* impossible to replace if lost or damaged. —**ir·re·place·a·bly** /-blē/ *adv.*

ir·re·press·i·ble /ˌiriˈpresəbəl/ ▶ *adj.* not able to be controlled or restrained: *a great shout of irrepressible laughter.* —**ir·re·press·i·bil·i·ty** /-ˌpresəˈbilitē/ *n.* —**ir·re·press·i·bly** /-blē/ *adv.*

ir·re·proach·a·ble /ˌiriˈprōcHəbəl/ ▶ *adj.* beyond criticism; faultless. —**ir·re·proach·a·bil·i·ty** /-ˌprōcHəˈbilitē/ *n.* —**ir·re·proach·a·bly** /-blē/ *adv.*

ir·re·sist·i·ble /ˌiriˈzistəbəl/ ▶ *adj.* too attractive and tempting to be resisted. ■ too powerful or convincing to be resisted. —**ir·re·sist·i·bil·i·ty** /-ˌzistəˈbilitē/ *n.* —**ir·re·sist·i·bly** /-blē/ *adv.*

ir·res·o·lute /i(r)ˈrezəˌlo͞ot/ ▶ *adj.* showing or feeling hesitancy; uncertain: *she stood irresolute outside his door.* —**ir·res·o·lute·ly** *adv.* —**ir·res·o·lute·ness** *n.* —**ir·res·o·lu·tion** /-ˌrezəˈlo͞osHən/ *n.*

ir·re·spec·tive /ˌiriˈspektiv/ ▶ *adj.* (**irrespective of**) not taking (something) into account; regardless of: *child benefit is paid irrespective of income levels.* —**ir·re·spec·tive·ly** *adv.*

ir·re·spon·si·ble /ˌiriˈspänsəbəl/ ▶ *adj.* (of a person, attitude, or action) not showing a proper sense of responsibility. —**ir·re·spon·si·bil·i·ty** /-ˌspänsəˈbilitē/ *n.* —**ir·re·spon·si·bly** /-blē/ *adv.*

ir·re·triev·a·ble /ˌiriˈtrēvəbəl/ ▶ *adj.* not able to be retrieved or put right. —**ir·re·triev·a·bil·i·ty** /-ˌtrēvəˈbilitē/ *n.* —**ir·re·triev·a·bly** /-blē/ *adv.*

ir·rev·er·ent /iˈrev(ə)rənt/ ▶ *adj.* showing a lack of respect for people or things that are generally taken seriously. —**ir·rev·er·ence** *n.* —**ir·rev·er·en·tial** /iˌrevəˈrensHəl/ *adj.* —**ir·rev·er·ent·ly** *adv.*

ir·re·vers·i·ble /ˌiriˈvərsəbəl/ ▶ *adj.* not able to be undone or altered. —**ir·re·vers·i·bil·i·ty** /-ˌvərsəˈbilitē/ *n.* —**ir·re·vers·i·bly** /-blē/ *adv.*

ir·rev·o·ca·ble /iˈrevəkəbəl/ ▶ *adj.* not able to be changed, reversed, or recovered; final: *an irrevocable step.* —**ir·rev·o·ca·bil·i·ty** /iˌrevəkəˈbilitē/ *n.* —**ir·rev·o·ca·bly** /-blē/ *adv.*

ir·ri·gate /ˈiriˌgāt/ ▶ *v.* [*trans.*] supply water to (land or crops) to help growth, typically by means of channels. ■ (of a river or stream) supply (land) with water. ■ *Med.* apply a continuous flow of water or liquid medication to (an organ or wound). ▷early 17th cent.: from Latin *irri-*

gat- 'moistened,' from the verb *irrigare*, from *in-* 'into' + *rigare* 'moisten, wet.' —**ir·ri·ga·ble** /-gəbəl/ *adj.* —**ir·ri·ga·tion** /,iri'gāSHən/ *n.* —**ir·ri·ga·tor** /-,gātər/ *n.*

ir·ri·ta·ble /'iritəbəl/ ▶*adj.* having or showing a tendency to be easily annoyed or made angry. ■ *Med.* (of a bodily part or organ) abnormally sensitive. ■ *Med.* (of a condition) caused by such sensitivity. ■ *Biol.* (of a living organism) having the property of responding actively to physical stimuli. —**ir·ri·ta·bil·i·ty** /,irite'bilitē/ *n.* —**ir·ri·ta·bly** /-blē/ *adv.*

ir·ri·tant /'iritənt/ ▶*n.* a substance that causes slight inflammation or other discomfort to the body. ■ *fig.* a thing that is continually annoying or distracting.
▶*adj.* causing slight inflammation or other discomfort to the body. —**ir·ri·tan·cy** *n.*

ir·ri·tate /'iri,tāt/ ▶*v.* [*tr.*] make (someone) annoyed, impatient, or angry: *his tone irritated her* | [*intr.*] *his voice tends to irritate.* ■ cause inflammation or other discomfort in (a part of the body). ■ *Biol.* stimulate (an organism, cell, or organ) to produce an active response. —**ir·ri·tat·ed·ly** *adv.* —**ir·ri·tat·ing·ly** *adv.* —**ir·ri·ta·tion** *n.* —**ir·ri·ta·tive** /-,tātiv/ *adj.* —**ir·ri·ta·tor** /-,tātər/ *n.*

ir·rupt /i'rəpt/ ▶*v.* [*intr.*] enter forcibly or suddenly. ■ (of a bird or other animal) migrate into an area in abnormally large numbers. —**ir·rup·tion** /-SHən/ *n.* —**ir·rup·tive** /-tiv/ *adj.*

IRS ▶*abbr.* Internal Revenue Service.

is /iz/ ▶ third person singular present of BE.

Is. ▶*abbr.* ■ (also **Isa.**) *Bible* Isaiah. ■ Island(s). ■ Isle(s).

ISBN ▶*abbr.* international standard book number, a ten-digit number assigned to every book before publication, recording such details as language, provenance, and publisher.

is·chi·um /'iskēəm/ ▶*n.* (*pl.* **-chi·a** /-kēə/) the curved bone forming the base of each half of the pelvis. —**is·chi·ad·ic** /,iskē'adik/ *adj.* —**is·chi·al** /-kēəl/ *adj.*

i·sin·glass /'īzən,glas; 'īziNG-/ ▶*n.* a kind of gelatin obtained from fish, esp. sturgeon, and used in making jellies, glue, etc., and for clarifying ale. ■ mica or a similar material in thin transparent sheets.

isl. (also **Isl.**) ▶*abbr.* ■ island or isle.

Is·lam /is'läm; iz-/ ▶*n.* the religion of the Muslims, a monotheistic faith regarded as revealed through Muhammad as the Prophet of Allah. ■ the Muslim world: *the most enormous complex of fortifications in all Islam.* —**Is·lam·ic** /-ik/ *adj.* —**Is·lam·i·ci·za·tion** /is,lämisi'zāSHən; iz-/ *n.* —**Is·lam·i·cize** /is'lämi,sīz; iz-/ *v.* —**Is·lam·ism** /'islə,mizəm; 'iz-/ *n.* —**Is·lam·ist** /-ist/ *n.* —**Is·lam·i·za·tion** /is,lämi'zāSHən; iz-/ *n.* —**Is·lam·ize** /'islə,mīz; 'iz-/ *v.*

is·land /'īlənd/ ▶*n.* a piece of land surrounded by water. ■ *fig.* a thing resembling an island, esp. in being isolated, detached, or surrounded in some way: *the university is the last island of democracy in this country.* ■ a freestanding kitchen cupboard unit with a countertop, allowing access from all sides. ■ *Anat.* a detached portion of tissue or group of cells.

is·land·er /'īləndər/ ▶*n.* a native or inhabitant of an island.

isle /īl/ ▶*n. chiefly poetic/lit.* an island or peninsula, esp. a small one: *Crusoe's fabled isle.*

is·let /'īlət/ ▶*n.* **1** a small island. **2** *Anat.* a portion of tissue structurally distinct from surrounding tissues.

is·lets of Lang·er·hans /'laNGər,hanz; 'läNGər,häns/ (also **islands of Langerhans**) ▶*pl. n.* groups of pancreatic cells secreting insulin and glucagon.

ism /'izəm/ ▶*n. inf., chiefly derog.* a distinctive practice, system, or philosophy, typically a political ideology or an artistic movement: *of all the isms, fascism is the most repressive.* —**ist** *n.*

isn't /'izənt/ ▶*contr.* of is not.

ISO ▶*abbr.* International Organization for Standardization.

i·so·bar /'īsə,bär/ ▶*n.* **1** *Meteorol.* a line on a map connecting points having the same atmospheric pressure at a given time or on average over a given period. **2** *Physics* each of two or more isotopes of different elements, with the same atomic weight. —**i·so·bar·ic** /,īsə'barik; -'bär-/ *adj.*

i·so·late ▶*v.* /'īsə,lāt/ [*tr.*] cause (a person or place) to be or remain alone or apart from others: *a country that is isolated from the rest of the world.* ■ identify (something) and examine or deal with it separately: *you can't isolate stress from the management context.* ■ *Chem. & Biol.* obtain or extract (a compound, microorganism, etc.) in a pure form. ■ cut off the electrical or other connection to (something, esp. a part of a supply network). ■ place (a person or animal) in quarantine as a precaution against infectious or contagious disease.
▶*n.* /-lit/ a person or thing that has been or become isolated. ■ *Biol.* a cul-

ture of microorganisms isolated for study. —**i·so·la·ble** /-ləbəl/ *adj.* —**i·so·lat·a·ble** *adj.* —**i·so·la·tor** /-,lātər/ *n.*

i·so·lat·ed /'īsə,lātid/ ▶*adj.* far away from other places, buildings, or people; remote: *isolated farms and villages.* ■ having minimal contact or little in common with others: *he lived a very isolated existence.* ■ single; exceptional: *they were isolated incidents.*

i·so·la·tion /,īsə'lāSHən/ ▶*n.* the process or fact of isolating or being isolated. ■ an instance of isolating something, esp. a compound or microorganism. ■ [as *adj.*] denoting a hospital or ward for patients with contagious or infectious diseases.
▶ □ **in isolation** without relation to other people or things; separately: *environmental problems must not be seen in isolation from social ones.*

i·so·la·tion·ism /,īsə'lāSHə,nizəm/ ▶*n.* a policy of remaining apart from the affairs or interests of other groups, esp. the political affairs of other countries. —**i·so·la·tion·ist** *n.*

i·so·mer /'īsəmər/ ▶*n.* **1** *Chem.* each of two or more compounds with the same formula but a different arrangement of atoms in the molecule and different properties. **2** *Physics* each of two or more atomic nuclei that have the same atomic number and the same mass number but different energy states. ▷mid 19th cent.: from Greek *isomerēs* 'sharing equally,' from *isos* 'equal' + *meros* 'a share.' —**i·so·mer·ic** /,īsə'merik/ *adj.* —**i·som·er·ism** /ī'sämə,rizəm/ *n.* —**i·som·er·ize** /ī'sämə,rīz/ *v.*

i·so·met·ric /,īsə'metrik/ ▶*adj.* **1** of or having equal dimensions. **2** *Physiol.* of, relating to, or denoting muscular action in which tension is developed without contraction of the muscle. **3** (in technical or architectural drawing) incorporating a method of showing projection or perspective in which the three principal dimensions are represented by three axes 120° apart. **4** *Math.* (of a transformation) without change of shape or size. —**i·so·met·ri·cal·ly** /-ik(ə)lē/ *adv.* —**i·som·e·try** /ī'sämitrē/ *n.*

i·so·met·rics /,īsə'metriks/ ▶*pl. n.* a system of physical exercises in which muscles are caused to act against each other or against a fixed object. Also called **isometric exercise.**

i·sos·ce·les /ī'säsə,lēz/ ▶*adj.* (of a triangle) having two sides of equal length.

i·so·ton·ic /,īsə'tänik/ ▶*adj. Physiol.* **1** (of muscle action) taking place with normal contraction. **2** denoting or relating to a solution having the same osmotic pressure as some other solution, esp. one in a cell or a body fluid. ■ (of a drink) containing essential salts and minerals in the same concentration as in the body and intended to replace those lost as a result of sweating during vigorous exercise. —**i·so·ton·i·cal·ly** /-ik(ə)lē/ *adv.* —**i·so·to·nic·i·ty** /-tə'nisitē/ *n.*

i·so·tope /'īsə,tōp/ ▶*n. Chem.* each of two or more forms of the same element that contain equal numbers of protons but different numbers of neutrons in their nuclei, and hence differ in relative atomic mass but not in chemical properties; in particular, a radioactive form of an element. —**i·so·top·ic** /,īsə'täpik/ *adj.* —**i·so·top·i·cal·ly** /,īsə'täpik(ə)lē/ *adv.* —**i·sot·o·py** /'īsə,tōpē; ī'sätəpē/ *n.*

Is·rae·li /iz'rālē/ ▶*adj.* of or relating to the modern country of Israel.
▶*n.* (*pl.* **-lis**) a native or national of Israel, or a person of Israeli descent.

Is·ra·el·ite /'izrēə,līt/ ▶*n.* a member of the ancient Hebrew nation, esp. in the period from the Exodus to the Babylonian Captivity (*c.*12th to 6th centuries BC). ■ old-fashioned and sometimes offensive term for JEW.
▶*adj.* of or relating to the Israelites.

is·sue /'iSHŌŌ/ ▶*n.* **1** an important topic or problem for debate or discussion. ■ (**is·sues**) personal problems or difficulties: *a nice guy with a great sense of humor and not too many issues.* **2** the action of supplying or

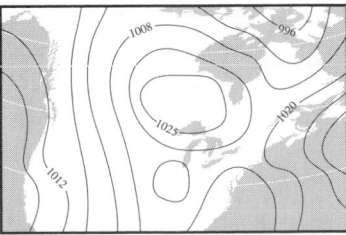

isobars

distributing an item for use, sale, or official purposes: *the issue of promissory notes.* ■ each of a regular series of publications: *the December issue.* ■ a number or set of items distributed at one time: *a share issue has been launched.* **3** *formal* or *Law* children of one's own: *he died without male issue.* **4** the action of flowing or coming out: *an issue of blood.* **5** *dated* a result or outcome of something: *the chance of carrying such a scheme to a successful issue was small.*

▶ *v.* (**is·sues, is·sued, is·su·ing**) **1** [*tr.*] supply or distribute (something): *licenses were issued indiscriminately to any company.* ■ (**issue someone with**) supply someone with (something). ■ formally send out or make known: *the minister issued a statement.* ■ put (something) on sale or into general use: *Christmas stamps to be issued in November.* **2** [*intr.*] (**issue from**) come, go, or flow out from. ■ result or be derived from. —**is·su·a·ble** *adj.* —**is·su·ance** /-əns/ *n.* —**is·sue·less** *adj.* —**is·su·er** *n.*

▶ □ **at issue** under discussion; in dispute. □ **make an issue of** treat too seriously or as a problem. □ **take issue with** disagree with; challenge.

isth·mus /'isməs/ ▶ *n.* (*pl.* **-mus·es**) a narrow strip of land with sea on either side, forming a link between two larger areas of land.

IT ▶ *abbr.* information technology.

it ▶ *pron.* [*third person sing.*] **1** used to refer to a thing previously mentioned or easily identified: *a room with two beds in it | this approach is refreshing because it breaks down barriers.* ■ referring to an animal or child of unspecified sex: *she was holding the baby, cradling it and smiling into its face.* ■ referring to a fact or situation previously mentioned, known, or happening: *stop it, you're hurting me.* **2** used to identify a person: *it's a boy!* **3** used in the normal subject position in statements about time, distance, or weather: *it was two miles to the island | it is raining.* **4** used in the normal subject or object position when a more specific subject or object is given later in the sentence: *it is impossible to assess the problem.* **5** used to emphasize a following part of a sentence: *it is the child who is the victim.* **6** the situation or circumstances; things in general: *no one can stay here—it's too dangerous now.* **7** exactly what is needed or desired: *they thought they were it.* **8** (usu. "it") *inf.* sex appeal: *he's still got "it."* ■ sexual intercourse. **9** (usu. "it") (in children's games) the player who has to catch the others.

▶ □ **that's it 1** that is the main point or difficulty: *"Is she going?" "That's just it—she can't make up her mind."* **2** that is enough or the end: *okay, that's it, you've cried long enough.* □ **this is it 1** the expected event is about to happen: *this is it—the big sale.* **2** this is enough or the end: *this is it, I'm going.* **3** this is the main point or difficulty.

It. ▶ *abbr.* ■ Italian. ■ Italy.

ital. ▶ *abbr.* italic (used as an instruction for a typesetter).

I·tal·ian /i'talyən/ ▶ *adj.* of or relating to Italy, its people, or their language.

▶ *n.* **1** a native or national of Italy, or a person of Italian descent. **2** the Romance language of Italy, also one of the official languages of Switzerland. —**I·tal·ian·ize** /-,nīz/ *v.*

I·tal·ian·ate /i'talyə,nāt/ ▶ *adj.* Italian in character or appearance.

I·tal·ic /i'talik; ī'tal-/ ▶ *adj.* relating to or denoting the branch of Indo-European languages that includes Latin, Oscan, Umbrian, and the Romance languages.

▶ *n.* the Italic group of languages.

i·tal·ic /i'talik; ī'tal-/ ▶ *adj. Printing* of the sloping kind of typeface used esp. for emphasis or distinction and in foreign words. ■ (of handwriting) modeled on 16th-century Italian handwriting, typically cursive and sloping and with elliptical or pointed letters.

▶ *n.* (also **i·tal·ics**) an italic typeface or letter: *the key words are in italics.*

i·tal·i·cize /i'tali,sīz; ī'tal-/ ▶ *v.* [*tr.*] print (text) in italics: *she italicized the title* | [*intr.*] *use this key to italicize.* —**i·tal·i·ci·za·tion** /i,talisi'zāsHən/ *n.*

itch /iCH/ ▶ *n.* an uncomfortable sensation on the skin that causes a desire to scratch. ■ *inf.* a restless or strong desire: *the itch to write.* ■ a skin disease or condition of which itching is a symptom. ■ (**the itch**) *inf.* scabies.

▶ *v.* [*intr.*] be the site of or cause an itch. ■ (of a person) experience an itch. ■ *inf.* feel a restless or strong desire to do something: *your hands itch to take the wheel.* ▷Old English *gycce, gyccan* (verb); related to Dutch *jeuk* (noun) and Dutch *jeuken,* German *jucken* (verb).

itch·y /'iCHē/ ▶ *adj.* (**itch·i·er, itch·i·est**) having or causing an itch: *dry, itchy skin | an itchy rash.* —**itch·i·ness** *n.*

it'd /'itid/ ▶ *contr. of* ■ it had. ■ it would.

i·tem /'ītəm/ ▶ *n.* an individual article or unit, esp. one that is part of a list, collection, or set: *the items on the agenda | an item of clothing.* ■ a piece of news or information. ■ an entry in an account.

▶ □ **be an item** *inf.* (of a couple) be involved in an established romantic or sexual relationship.

i·tem·ize /'ītə,mīz/ ▶ *v.* [*tr.*] present as a list of individual items. ■ break down (a whole) into its constituent parts. ■ specify (an individual item or items). —**i·tem·i·za·tion** /,ītəmi'zāsHən/ *n.* —**i·tem·iz·er** *n.*

it·er·ate /'itə,rāt/ ▶ *v.* [*tr.*] perform or utter repeatedly. ■ [*intr.*] make repeated use of a mathematical or computational procedure, applying it each time to the result of the previous application. —**it·er·a·tion** *n.*

i·tin·er·ant /ī'tinərənt; i'tin-/ ▶ *adj.* traveling from place to place.

▶ *n.* a person who travels from place to place. —**i·tin·er·a·cy** /-rəsē/ *n.* —**i·tin·er·an·cy** *n.* —**i·tin·er·ant·ly** *adv.*

i·tin·er·ar·y /ī'tinə,rerē; i'tin-/ ▶ *n.* (*pl.* **-ar·ies**) a planned route or journey. ■ a travel document recording these.

it'll /'itl/ ▶ *contr.* of it shall; it will.

its /its/ ▶ *possessive adj.* belonging to or associated with a thing previously mentioned or easily identified: *turn the camera on its side.* ■ belonging to or associated with a child or animal of unspecified sex: *a baby in its mother's womb.*

it's /its/ ▶ *contr. of* ■ it is: *it's my fault.* ■ it has: *it's been a hot day.*

it·self /it'self/ ▶ *pron.* [*third person sing.*] **1** [*reflexive*] used as the object of a verb or preposition to refer to a thing or animal previously mentioned as the subject of the clause: *his horse hurt itself.* **2** used to emphasize a particular thing or animal mentioned: *the roots are several inches long, though the plant itself is only a foot tall.* ■ used after a quality to emphasize what a perfect example of that quality someone or something is: *Mrs. Vincent was kindness itself.*

▶ □ **in itself** viewed in its essential qualities; considered separately from other things: *some would say bringing up a family was a full-time job in itself.*

it·ty-bit·ty /'itē 'bitē/ (also **it·sy-bit·sy** /'itsē 'bitsē/) ▶ *adj. inf.* very small; tiny.

IUD ▶ *abbr.* ■ intrauterine device.

IUPAC ▶ *abbr.* International Union of Pure and Applied Chemistry.

IV ▶ *abbr.* intravenous(ly).

▶ *n.* an intravenous drip feed: *they put an IV in me.*

I've /īv/ ▶ *contr. of* I have.

IVF ▶ *abbr.* in vitro fertilization.

i·vo·ry /'īv(ə)rē/ ▶ *n.* (*pl.* **-ries**) **1** a hard creamy-white substance composing the main part of the tusks of an elephant, walrus, or narwhal, often (esp. formerly) used to make ornaments and other articles. ■ an object made of ivory. ■ (**the ivories**) *inf.* the keys of a piano. ■ (**ivories**) *inf.* a person's teeth. **2** a creamy-white color. —**i·vo·ried** /-rēd/ *adj.*

i·vo·ry tow·er ▶ *n.* a state of privileged seclusion or separation from the facts and practicalities of the real world: *the ivory tower of academia.*

i·vy /'īvē/ ▶ *n.* a woody evergreen climbing plant (genus *Hedera*), typically having shiny, dark green five-pointed leaves. ■ used in names of similar climbing plants, e.g., **poison ivy, Boston ivy.**

Jj

J¹ /jā/ (also **j**) ▸ *n.* (*pl.* **Js** or **J's** /jāz/) **1** the tenth letter of the alphabet. ■ denoting the next after I (or H if I is omitted) in a set of items, categories, etc. **2** (**J**) a shape like that of a capital J.

J² ▸ *abbr.* ■ jack (used in describing play in card games). ■ *Physics* joule(s). ■ (in titles) Journal (of): *J. Biol. Chem.* ■ Judge. ■ Justice.

jab /jab/ ▸ *v.* (**jabbed**, **jab·bing**) [*tr.*] poke (someone or something) roughly or quickly, esp. with something sharp or pointed: [*intr.*] *he jabbed at the air with his finger.* ■ poke someone or something roughly or quickly with (a sharp or pointed object or a part of the body).
▸ *n.* a quick, sharp blow, esp. with the fist: *fast jabs to the face.* ■ a sharp painful sensation or feeling: *the jabs of pain up my spine* | *a jab of envy.*

jab·ber /ˈjabər/ ▸ *v.* [*intr.*] talk rapidly and excitedly but with little sense.
▸ *n.* fast, excited talk that makes little sense: *stop your jabber.*

jab·ber·wock·y /ˈjabər‚wäkē/ ▸ *n.* (*pl.* **-wock·ies**) invented or meaningless language; nonsense.

ja·bot /zнаˈbō; ja-/ ▸ *n.* an ornamental frill or ruffle on the front of a shirt or blouse, typically made of lace.

jack¹ /jak/ ▸ *n.* **1** a device for lifting heavy objects, esp. one for raising the axle of a motor vehicle off the ground. **2** a playing card bearing a representation of a soldier, page, or knave, normally ranking next below a queen. **3** a socket with two or more pairs of terminals. **4** (also **jack·stone**) a small round pebble or star-shaped piece of metal used in tossing and catching games. ■ (**jacks**) a game played by tossing and catching such pebbles or pieces of metal. **5** in lawn bowling, the small ball at which the players aim. **6** (**Jack**) *inf.* used as a form of address to a man whose name is not known. ■ *inf.* a lumberjack. **7** a small version of a national flag flown at the bow of a vessel in a harbor to indicate its nationality. **8** a device for turning a spit. **9** a marine fish that is typically laterally compressed with a row of large spiky scales along each side. The **jack family** (Carangidae) also includes the kingfishes and the pilotfish. **10** the male of some animals, esp. an ass.
▸ *phrasal v.* □ **jack something up** raise something, esp. a vehicle, with a jack. ■ *inf.* increase something by a considerable amount.

jack² /jak/ ▸ *v.* [*tr.*] *inf.* take (something) illicitly; steal. ■ rob (someone): *they jacked him for his car.*

jack·al /ˈjakəl/ ▸ *n.* a slender, long-legged wild dog (genus *Canis*) that feeds on carrion, game, and fruit and often hunts cooperatively, found in Africa and southern Asia.

jack·ass /ˈjak‚as/ ▸ *n.* **1** a stupid person. **2** a male ass or donkey.

jack·boot /ˈjak‚boōt/ ▸ *n.* a large leather military boot reaching to the knee. ■ used as a symbol of cruel or authoritarian behavior or rule: *a country under the jackboot of colonialism.* —**jack·boot·ed** *adj.*

jack·daw /ˈjak‚dô/ ▸ *n.* a small, gray-headed Eurasian crow (genus *Corvus*, esp. *C. monedula*) that typically nests in tall buildings and chimneys.

jack·et /ˈjakit/ ▸ *n.* an outer garment extending either to the waist or the hips, typically having sleeves and a fastening down the front. ■ an outer covering, esp. one placed around a tank or pipe to insulate it. ■ a metal casing for a bullet. ■ the skin of a potato: *potatoes cooked in their jackets.* ■ the dust jacket of a book. ■ a record sleeve.
▸ *v.* (**jack·et·ed**, **jack·et·ing**) [*tr.*] cover with a jacket.

Jack Frost ▸ *n.* a personification of frost: *the seedlings battled with Jack Frost.*

jack·ham·mer /ˈjak‚hamər/ ▸ *n.* a portable pneumatic hammer or drill.
▸ *v.* [*tr.*] beat or hammer heavily or loudly and repeatedly.

jack-in-the-box ▸ *n.* a toy consisting of a box containing a figure on a spring that pops up when the lid is opened.

jack-in-the-pul·pit ▸ *n.* any of several small plants of the arum family, in particular three North American species (genus *Arisaema*) with a green or purple-brown spathe.

jack·knife /ˈjak‚nīf/ ▸ *n.* (*pl.* **-knives**) **1** a knife with a folding blade. **2** a dive in which the body is first bent at the waist and then straightened.
▸ *v.* (**-knifed**, **-knif·ing**) [*tr.*] move (one's body) into a bent or doubled-up position: [*intr.*] *she jackknifed into a sitting position.* ■ [*intr.*] (of an articulated vehicle) bend into a V-shape in an uncontrolled skidding movement. ■ [*intr.*] (of a diver) perform a jackknife.

jack-o'-lan·tern /ˈjak ə ‚lantərn/ ▸ *n.* a lantern made from a hollowed-out pumpkin in which holes are cut to represent facial features, typically made at Halloween.

jack·pot /ˈjak‚pät/ ▸ *n.* a large cash prize in a game or lottery, esp. one that accumulates until it is won.
▸ □ **hit the jackpot** *inf.* **1** win a jackpot. **2** have great or unexpected success, esp. in making a lot of money quickly.

jack·rab·bit /ˈjak‚rabət/ ▸ *n.* a hare found in open country in western North America. ▷mid 19th cent.: abbreviation of *jackass-rabbit*, because of its long ears.

jack·stone /ˈjak‚stōn/ ▸ *n.* see JACK¹ (sense 4).

jack·straws /ˈjak‚strôz/ ▸ *pl. n.* [*treated as sing.*] a game played with a heap of small rods of wood, bone, or plastic, in which players try to remove one at a time without disturbing the others.

Ja·cob's lad·der ▸ *n.* **1** a plant (*Polemonium van-bruntiae*, family Polemoniaceae) of the northeastern U.S. with loose clusters of purplish-blue flowers and slender pointed leaves, rows of which are said to resemble a ladder. **2** a rope ladder with wooden rungs, esp. for access to a ship up the side.

jac·quard /ˈja‚kärd; jəˈkärd/ ▸ *n.* an apparatus with perforated cards, fitted to a loom to facilitate the weaving of figured and brocaded fabrics. ■ a fabric made on a loom with such a device, with an intricate variegated pattern.

ja·cuz·zi /jəˈkoōzē/ ▸ *n.* (*pl.* **-zis**) *trademark* a large bath with a system of underwater jets of water to massage the body. ▷1960s: named after Candido *Jacuzzi* (*c.*1903–86), Italian-born American inventor.

jade /jād/ ▸ *n.* a hard, typically green stone used for ornaments and implements. ■ an ornament made of this. ■ (also **jade green**) a light bluish-green.

jad·ed /ˈjādid/ ▸ *adj.* tired, bored, or lacking enthusiasm, typically after having had too much of something. —**jad·ed·ly** *adv.* —**jad·ed·ness** *n.*

JAG ▸ *abbr.* judge advocate general.

jag¹ /jag/ ▸ *n.* a sharp projection.
▸ *v.* (**jagged** /ˈjagd/, **jag·ging**) [*tr.*] stab, pierce, or prick. —**jag·ger** *n.*

jag² ▸ *n.* *inf.* **1** a bout of unrestrained activity or emotion, esp. drinking, crying, or laughing: *an incredible crying jag.* **2** *dial.* a bundle: *a jag of hay.*

jag·ged /ˈjagid/ ▸ *adj.* with rough, sharp points protruding: *fig. soothing her jagged nerves.* —**jag·ged·ly** *adv.* —**jag·ged·ness** *n.*

jag·gy /ˈjagē/ ▸ *adj.* (**-gi·er**, **-gi·est**) jagged.

jag·uar /ˈjag‚wär/ ▸ *n.* a large, heavily built cat (*Panthera onca*) that has a yellowish-brown coat with black spots, found mainly in the dense forests of Central and South America.

jai a·lai /ˈhī (ə)‚lī/ ▸ *n.* a game like pelota played with large, curved wicker baskets.

jail /jāl/ (*Brit.* also **gaol**) ▸ *n.* a place for the confinement of people accused or convicted of a crime: *he spent 15 years in jail.* ■ confinement in a jail: *she was sentenced to three months' jail.*
▸ *v.* [*tr.*] (usu. **be jailed**) put (someone) in jail.

jail·bait /'jāl,bāt/ ▶ n. [treated as *sing.* or *pl.*] *inf.* a young woman, or young women collectively, considered in sexual terms but under the age of consent.

jail·bird /'jāl,bərd/ ▶ n. *inf.* a person who is or has been in prison, esp. a criminal who has been jailed repeatedly.

jail·break /'jāl,brāk/ ▶ n. an escape from jail.

jail·er /'jālər/ (also Brit. **gaol·er**) ▶ n. a person in charge of a jail or of the prisoners in it.

jake /jāk/ ▶ adj. *inf.* all right; satisfactory: *everything was jake again.*

jake brake ▶ n. an engine brake for truck diesel engines that cuts off fuel flow and interrupts the transfer of mechanical energy to the drive mechanism.

ja·la·pe·ño /,hälə'pānyō; -'pē-/ (also **jalapeño pepper**) ▶ n. (pl. **-ños**) a very hot green chili pepper, used esp. in Mexican-style cooking.

ja·lop·y /jə'läpē/ ▶ n. (pl. **-lop·ies**) *inf.* an old car in a dilapidated condition.

jal·ou·sie /'jalə,sē/ ▶ n. a blind or shutter made of a row of angled slats.

jam[1] /jam/ ▶ v. (**jammed**, **jam·ming**) 1 [*tr.*] squeeze or pack (someone or something) tightly into a specified space: *four of us were jammed in one compartment.* ■ push (something) roughly and forcibly into position or a space: *he jammed his hat on.* ■ [*tr.*] crowd onto (a road) so as to block it. ■ [*intr.*] push or crowd into an area or space. 2 become or make unable to move or work due to a part seizing or becoming stuck: [*intr.*] *the photocopier jammed.* ■ [*tr.*] make (a radio transmission) unintelligible by causing interference. 3 [*intr.*] *inf.* improvise with other musicians, esp. in jazz or blues: *the opportunity to jam with Atlanta blues musicians.*
▶ n. 1 an instance of a machine or thing seizing or becoming stuck: *paper jams.* ■ *inf.* an awkward situation or predicament: *I'm in a jam.* ■ short for TRAFFIC JAM. 2 (also **jam ses·sion**) an informal gathering of musicians improvising together, esp. in jazz or blues. —**jam·mer** n.

jam[2] ▶ n. a sweet spread or preserve made from fruit and sugar boiled to a thick consistency.

jamb /jam/ ▶ n. a side post or surface of a doorway, window, or fireplace.

jam·ba·lay·a /,jəmbə'līə/ ▶ n. a Cajun dish of rice with shrimp, chicken, and vegetables.

jam·bo·ree /,jəmbə'rē/ ▶ n. a large celebration or party, typically a lavish and boisterous one. ■ a large rally of Boy Scouts or Girl Scouts.

jam-packed ▶ adj. *inf.* extremely crowded or full to capacity.

Jan. ▶ abbr. January.

jane /jān/ ▶ n. *inf.* a woman.
▶ □ **plain Jane** an unattractive girl or woman.

Jane Doe /'jān 'dō/ ▶ n. Law an anonymous female party, typically the plaintiff, in a legal action. ■ *inf.* a hypothetical average woman. See also JOHN DOE.

jan·gle /'janGgəl/ ▶ v. make or cause to make a ringing metallic sound, typically a discordant one: [*intr.*] *a bell jangled loudly* | [*tr.*] *Ryan stood on the terrace jangling his keys.* ■ [*tr.*] (with reference to nerves) set on edge.
▶ n. a ringing metallic sound: *the jangle of a telephone.* ▷Middle English (in the sense 'talk excessively or noisily, squabble'): from Old French *jangler*, of unknown origin. —**jan·gly** adj.

jan·i·tor /'janitər/ ▶ n. a person employed as a caretaker of a building; a custodian. —**jan·i·to·ri·al** /,jani'tôrēəl/ adj.

Jan·u·ar·y /'janyoo,erē/ ▶ n. (pl. **-ar·ies**) the first month of the year, in the northern hemisphere usually considered the second month of winter.

Jap /jap/ ▶ n. & adj. *inf., offens.* short for JAPANESE.

ja·pan /jə'pan/ ▶ n. a hard, dark, enamel-like varnish containing asphalt, used to give a black gloss to metal objects. ■ a kind of varnish in which pigments are ground, typically used to imitate lacquer on wood. ■ articles made in a Japanese style, esp. when decorated with lacquer or enamellike varnish.
▶ v. (**-panned**, **-pan·ning**) [*tr.*] cover (something) with a hard black varnish: [as adj.] (**japanned**) *a japanned tin tray.*

Jap·a·nese /,japə'nēz; -'nēs/ ▶ adj. of or relating to Japan or its language, culture, or people.
▶ n. (pl. same) 1 a native or national of Japan, or a person of Japanese descent. 2 the language of Japan, spoken by almost all of its population.

Jap·a·nese bee·tle ▶ n. a metallic green and copper chafer (*Popillia japonica*) that is a pest of fruit and foliage as an adult and of grass roots as a larva. It is native to Japan but has spread elsewhere.

jape /jāp/ ▶ n. a practical joke.
▶ v. [*intr.*] say or do something in jest or mockery. —**jap·er·y** /'jāp(ə)rē/ n.

ja·pon·i·ca /jə'pänikə/ ▶ n. another term for the common CAMELLIA.

jar[1] /jär/ ▶ n. a wide-mouthed, cylindrical container made of glass or pottery, esp. one used for storing food. —**jar·ful** /-,fool/ n. (pl. **-fuls**).

jar[2] ▶ v. (**jarred**, **jar·ring**) 1 [*tr.*] send a painful or damaging shock

through (something, esp. a part of the body): *he jarred his knee in training.* ■ [*intr.*] strike against something with an unpleasant vibration or jolt. 2 [*intr.*] have an unpleasant, annoying, or disturbing effect. ■ be incongruous in a striking or shocking way: [as adj.] (**jarring**) *the only jarring note was the modern appearance of the customers.*
▶ n. a physical shock or jolt. ■ archaic discord; disagreement.

jar·di·niere /,järdn'i(ə)r; ,ZHärdn'ye(ə)r/ (also **jar·di·nière**) ▶ n. 1 an ornamental pot or stand for the display of growing plants. 2 a garnish of mixed vegetables.

jar·gon[1] /'järgən/ ▶ n. special words or expressions that are used by a particular profession or group and are difficult for others to understand: *legal jargon.* —**jar·gon·is·tic** /,järgə'nistik/ adj. —**jar·gon·ize** /-,nīz/ v.

jar·gon[2] /'järgän/ (also **jar·goon** /jär'gōōn/) ▶ n. a translucent, colorless, or smoky gem variety of zircon.

jas·mine /'jazmən/ (also **jess·a·mine**) ▶ n. an Old World shrub or climbing plant (genus *Jasminum*) of the olive family that bears fragrant flowers that are used in perfumery and tea.

jas·per /'jaspər/ ▶ n. an opaque reddish-brown variety of chalcedony.

jaun·dice /'jôndis/ ▶ n. a medical condition with yellowing of the skin or whites of the eyes, arising from an excess of the pigment bilirubin and typically caused by obstruction of the bile duct, by liver disease, or by excessive breakdown of red blood cells. ■ bitterness, resentment, or envy.

jaunt /jônt/ ▶ n. a short excursion or journey for pleasure: *her little jaunt in France was over.*
▶ v. [*intr.*] make such an excursion or journey.

jaun·ty /'jôntē/ ▶ adj. (**-ti·er**, **-ti·est**) having or expressing a lively, cheerful, and self-confident manner: *there was no mistaking that jaunty walk.* —**jaun·ti·ly** /-tl-ē/ adv. —**jaun·ti·ness** n.

Ja·va /'jävə/ ▶ n. trademark a general-purpose computer programming language designed to produce programs that will run on any computer system.

Jav·a·nese /,jävə'nēz; -'nēs/ ▶ n. (pl. same) 1 a native or inhabitant of Java, or a person of Javanese descent. 2 the Indonesian language of central Java.
▶ adj. of or relating to Java, its people, or their language.

jave·lin /'jav(ə)lən/ ▶ n. a light spear thrown in a competitive sport or as a weapon. ■ (**the javelin**) the athletic event or sport of throwing the javelin: *his nearest rival in the javelin.*

jaw /jô/ ▶ n. each of the upper and lower bony structures in vertebrates forming the framework of the mouth and containing the teeth. ■ the lower movable bone of such a structure or the part of the face containing it: *she suffered a broken jaw.* ■ (**jaws**) the mouth with its bones and teeth. ■ (**jaws**) the grasping, biting, or crushing mouthparts of an invertebrate. ■ (**jaws**) used to suggest the notion of being in danger from something such as death or defeat: *victory was snatched from the jaws of defeat.* ■ (usu. **jaws**) the gripping parts of a tool or machine, such as a wrench or vise. ■ (**jaws**) an opening likened to a mouth.
▶ v. [*intr.*] *inf.* talk at length; chatter. —**jawed** adj. [in comb.] *square-jawed young men.*

jaw·bone /'jô,bōn/ ▶ n. a bone of the jaw, esp. that of the lower jaw (the mandible), or either half of this.
▶ v. [*tr.*] attempt to persuade or pressure by the force of one's position of authority: [*intr.*] *an analyst jawboning about the industry.*

jaw·break·er /'jô,brākər/ ▶ n. 1 *inf.* a word that is very long or hard to pronounce. 2 a large, hard, spherical candy.

jay /jā/ ▶ n. a bird of the crow family with boldly patterned plumage, typically having blue feathers in the wings or tail.

jay·walk /'jā,wôk/ ▶ v. [*intr.*] cross or walk in the street or road unlawfully or without regard for approaching traffic. —**jay·walk·er** n.

jazz /jaz/ ▶ n. a type of music of black American origin characterized by improvisation, syncopation, and usually a regular or forceful rhythm, emerging at the beginning of the 20th century. ■ *inf.* enthusiastic or lively talk, esp. when considered exaggerated or insincere.
▶ phrasal v. □ **jazz something up** make something more lively or cheerful: *jazz up an all-white kitchen with red tiles.*

jazz·y /'jazē/ ▶ adj. (**jazz·i·er**, **jazz·i·est**) of, resembling, or in the style of jazz: *a jazzy piano solo.* ■ bright, colorful, and showy: *jazzy ties.* —**jazz·i·ly** /'jazəlē/ adv. —**jazz·i·ness** n.

jct. ▶ abbr. junction.

jeal·ous /'jeləs/ ▶ adj. feeling or showing envy of someone or their achievements and advantages: *he grew jealous of her success.* ■ feeling or showing suspicion of someone's unfaithfulness in a relationship: *a jealous boyfriend.* ■ fiercely protective or vigilant of one's rights or possessions. —**jeal·ous·ly** adv.

jeal·ous·y /ˈjeləsē/ ▸ n. (pl. **-ous·ies**) the state or feeling of being jealous.

jean /jēn/ ▸ n. heavy twilled cotton cloth, esp. denim: [as adj.] *a jean jacket.* ■ (in commercial use) a pair of jeans: *a button-fly jean.*

jeans /jēnz/ ▸ pl. n. hard-wearing trousers made of denim or other cotton fabric, for informal wear. When blue, the typical color of jeans, they are also called BLUE JEANS.

jeep /jēp/ ▸ n. *trademark* a small, sturdy motor vehicle with four-wheel drive, esp. one used by the military. ▷World War II: from the initials GP, standing for *general purpose,* influenced by 'Eugene the Jeep,' a creature of great resourcefulness and power represented in the *Popeye* comic strip.

jee·pers /ˈjēpərz/ (also **jee·pers cree·pers**) ▸ *interj. inf.* used to express surprise or alarm: *Jeepers! Do you think she saw?*

jeer /ji(ə)r/ ▸ v. [intr.] make rude and mocking remarks, typically in a loud voice: *some of the younger men jeered at him* | [as adj.] (**jeering**) *the jeering crowds.* ■ [tr.] shout such remarks at (someone).
▸ n. a rude and mocking remark. —**jeer·ing·ly** adv.

jeez /jēz/ (also **geez**) ▸ *interj. inf.* a mild expression used to show surprise or annoyance.

je·had ▸ n. variant spelling of JIHAD.

Je·ho·vah /jəˈhōvə/ ▸ n. a form of the Hebrew name of God used in some translations of the Bible.

je·june /jiˈjōōn/ ▸ adj. **1** naive, simplistic, and superficial: *their entirely predictable and usually jejune opinions.* **2** (of ideas or writings) dry and uninteresting. —**je·june·ly** adv. —**je·june·ness** n.

je·ju·num /jiˈjōōnəm/ ▸ n. *Anat.* the part of the small intestine between the duodenum and ileum. —**je·ju·nal** /ˈjōōnl/ adj.

jell /jel/ ▸ v. [intr.] (of jelly or a similar substance) set or become firmer: *the pudding is jelling.* ■ (of a project or idea) take a definite shape; begin to work well. ■ (of people) relate well to one another.

Jell·o shot (also **jell·o shot**) ▸ n. an alcoholic beverage consisting of liquor incorporated into sweetened gelatin dessert and chilled in a small container. ▷from Jell-O, the proprietary name of a gelatin dessert.

jel·ly /ˈjelē/ ▸ n. (pl. **-lies**) a sweet, clear, semisolid, somewhat elastic spread or preserve made from fruit juice and sugar boiled to a thick consistency. ■ used figuratively and in similes to refer to sensations of fear or strong emotion: *her legs felt like jelly.* ■ a similar clear preparation made with fruit or other ingredients as a condiment: *mint jelly.* ■ a gelatinous savory preparation made by boiling meat and bones: *spermicidal jellies.* ■ *chiefly Brit.* a substance of a gelatinous consistency: *sweet, fruit-flavored gelatin dessert.*
▸ v. (**-lies, -lied**) [tr.] [usu. as adj.] (**jellied**) set (food) as or in a jelly: *jellied cranberry sauce.* —**jel·li·fi·ca·tion** /ˌjeləfiˈkāSHən/ n. —**jel·li·fy** /ˈjelə₁fī/ v. —**jel·ly·like** /-₁līk/ adj.

jel·ly bean (also **jel·ly·bean**) ▸ n. a bean-shaped candy with a jellylike center and a firm sugar coating.

jel·ly·fish /ˈjelē₁fiSH/ ▸ n. (pl. same or **-fishes**) a free-swimming marine coelenterate (classes Scyphozoa and Cubozoa) with a jellylike bell- or saucer-shaped body that is typically transparent and has stinging tentacles around the edge.

jel·ly roll ▸ n. a cylindrical cake with a spiral cross section, made from a flat sponge cake spread with a filling such as jam and rolled up.

jen·net /ˈjenit/ ▸ n. **1** a female donkey. **2** a small Spanish horse.

jen·ny /ˈjenē/ ▸ n. (pl. **-nies**) a female donkey or ass.

jeop·ard·ize /ˈjepər₁dīz/ ▸ v. [tr.] put (someone or something) into a situation in which there is a danger of loss, harm, or failure.

jeop·ard·y /ˈjepərdē/ ▸ n. danger of loss, harm, or failure: *Michael's job was not in jeopardy.* ■ *Law* danger arising from being on trial for a criminal offense.

Jer. ▸ abbr. *Bible* Jeremiah.

jer·e·mi·ad /ˌjerəˈmīəd; -ˌad/ ▸ n. a long, mournful complaint or lamentation; a list of woes.

jerk¹ /jərk/ ▸ n. **1** a quick, sharp, sudden movement: *he gave a sudden jerk of his head.* ■ a spasmodic muscular twitch. **2** *inf.* a contemptibly obnoxious person.
▸ v. [tr.] make (something) move with a jerk: *she jerked her chin up.* ■ [intr.] move with a jerk: *the van jerked forward.* ■ suddenly rouse or jolt (someone). ■ [tr.] *Weightlifting* raise (a weight) from shoulder level to above the head.
▸ phrasal v. □ **jerk someone around** *inf.* deal with someone dishonestly or unfairly.

jerk² ▸ v. [tr.] [usu. as adj.] (**jerked**) prepare (meat) by marinating it in spices and drying or barbecuing it over a wood fire: *jerked beef.*
▸ n. meat cooked in this way: *fiery Jamaican jerk* | [as adj.] *jerk chicken.*

jer·kin /ˈjərkin/ ▸ n. a sleeveless jacket.

jerk·y¹ /ˈjərkē/ ▸ adj. (**jerk·i·er, jerk·i·est**) **1** characterized by abrupt stops and starts. **2** contemptibly foolish. —**jerk·i·ly** /-kəlē/ adv. —**jerk·i·ness** n.

jerk·y² ▸ n. meat that has been cured by being cut into long, thin strips and dried: *beef jerky.*

jer·o·bo·am /ˌjerəˈbōəm/ ▸ n. a wine bottle with a capacity four times larger than that of an ordinary bottle.

jer·ry-built ▸ adj. badly or hastily built with materials of poor quality. —**jer·ry-build·er** n. —**jer·ry-build·ing** n.

jer·sey /ˈjərzē/ ▸ n. (pl. **-seys**) **1** a knitted garment with long sleeves worn over the upper body. ■ a distinctive shirt worn by a player or competitor in certain sports. ■ a soft, fine knitted fabric. **2** (**Jersey**) an animal of a breed of light brown dairy cattle from Jersey.

jerkin

Je·ru·sa·lem ar·ti·choke /ˈjəˈrōōsələm; -zə-/ ▸ n. **1** a knobby edible tuber with white flesh, eaten as a vegetable. **2** the tall North American plant, (*Helianthus tuberosus*) closely related to the sunflower, that produces this tuber.

jes·sa·mine /ˈjesəmin/ ▸ n. variant spelling of JASMINE.

jest /jest/ ▸ n. a thing said or done for amusement; a joke.
▸ v. [intr.] speak or act in a joking manner: *you jest, surely?* ▷late Middle English: from earlier *gest,* from Old French *geste,* from Latin *gesta* 'actions, exploits,' from *gerere* 'do.' The original sense was 'exploit, heroic deed,' hence 'a narrative of such deeds' (originally in verse); later the term denoted an idle tale, hence a joke (mid 16th cent.).

jest·er /ˈjestər/ ▸ n. *hist.* a professional joker or "fool" at a medieval court, typically wearing a cap with bells on it and carrying a mock scepter. ■ a person who habitually plays the fool.

Jes·u·it /ˈjezhōōit; ˈjez(y)ōō-/ ▸ n. a member of the Society of Jesus, a Roman Catholic order of priests founded by St. Ignatius Loyola, St. Francis Xavier, and others in 1534, to do missionary work.

jet¹ /jet/ ▸ n. **1** a rapid stream of liquid or gas forced out of a small opening: *a shower head with pulsating jets.* ■ a nozzle or narrow opening for sending out such a stream: *a gas jet.* **2** an aircraft powered by one or more jet engines. ■ a jet engine.
▸ v. (**jet·ted, jet·ting**) [intr.] **1** travel by jet aircraft: *the newlyweds jetted off to New York.* **2** spurt out in jets: *blood jetted from his nostrils.*

jet² ▸ n. a hard black semiprecious variety of lignite, capable of being carved and highly polished. ■ a glossy black color.

je·té /zhəˈtā/ ▸ n. *Ballet* a jump in which a dancer springs from one foot to land on the other with one leg extended outward from the body while in the air.

jet en·gine ▸ n. an engine using jet propulsion for forward thrust, mainly used for aircraft.

jet lag ▸ n. extreme tiredness and other physical effects felt by a person after a long flight across several time zones. —**jet-lagged** adj.

jet·lin·er /ˈjet₁līnər/ ▸ n. a large jet aircraft carrying passengers.

jet-pro·pelled ▸ adj. moved by jet propulsion.

jet pro·pul·sion ▸ n. propulsion by the backward ejection of a high-speed jet of gas or liquid.

jet·sam /ˈjetsəm/ ▸ n. unwanted material or goods that have been thrown overboard from a ship and washed ashore, esp. material that has been discarded to lighten the vessel. Compare with FLOTSAM.

jet set ▸ n. (**the jet set**) *inf.* wealthy and fashionable people who travel widely and frequently for pleasure: [as adj.] *the jet-set lifestyle.* —**jet-set·ter** n. —**jet-set·ting** adj.

jet stream ▸ n. **1** a narrow, variable band of very strong, predominantly westerly air currents encircling the globe several miles above the earth. **2** a flow of exhaust gases from a jet engine.

jet·ti·son /ˈjetisən; -zən/ ▸ v. [tr.] throw or drop (something) from an aircraft or ship: *six aircraft jettisoned their loads in the sea.* ■ abandon or discard (someone or something that is no longer wanted).
▸ n. the action of jettisoning something.

jet·ty /ˈjetē/ ▸ n. (pl. **-ties**) a landing stage or small pier at which boats can dock or be moored. ■ a breakwater constructed to protect or defend a harbor, stretch of coast, or riverbank.

Jew /jōō/ ▸*n.* a member of the people and cultural community whose traditional religion is Judaism and who trace their origins through the ancient Hebrew people of Israel to Abraham.

jew·el /ˈjōōəl/ ▸*n.* a precious stone, typically a single crystal or a piece of a hard lustrous or translucent mineral, cut into shape with flat facets or smoothed and polished for use as an ornament. ■ (usu. **jewels**) an ornament or piece of jewelry containing such a stone or stones. ■ a hard precious stone used as a bearing in a watch, compass, or other device. ■ a very pleasing or valued person or thing; a very fine example: *she was a jewel of a nurse.* ▷Middle English: from Old French *joel*, from *jeu* 'game, play,' from Latin *jocus* 'jest.'

jew·el box ▸*n.* (also **jewel case**) a storage box for a compact disc.

jew·eled /ˈjōōəld/ (*Brit.* **jew·elled**) ▸*adj.* adorned, set with, or made from jewels: *a jeweled dagger.*

jew·el·er /ˈjōō(ə)lər/ (*Brit.* **jew·el·ler**) ▸*n.* a person or company that makes or sells jewels or jewelry.

jew·el·ry /ˈjōō(ə)lrē/ (*Brit.* **jew·el·lery**) ▸*n.* personal ornaments, such as necklaces, rings, or bracelets, that are typically made from or contain jewels and precious metal.

Jew·ish /ˈjōō-iSH/ ▸*adj.* relating to, associated with, or denoting Jews or Judaism: *the Jewish people.* —**Jew·ish·ly** *adv.* —**Jew·ish·ness** *n.*

Jew·ry /ˈjōōrē/ ▸*n.* (*pl.* **-ries**) **1** Jews collectively. **2** *hist.* a Jewish quarter in a town or city.

Jew's harp ▸*n.* a small, lyre-shaped musical instrument held between the teeth and struck with a finger.

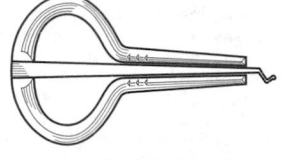

Jew's harp

jg ▸*abbr.* junior grade.

jib¹ /jib/ ▸*n.* **1** *Sailing* a triangular sail set forward of the forwardmost mast. **2** the projecting arm of a crane.

jib² ▸*v.* (**jibbed, jib·bing**) [*intr.*] (of an animal, esp. a horse) stop and refuse to go on. ■ (of a person) be unwilling to do or accept something. —**jib·ber** *n.*

jibe¹ /jīb/ ▸*n.* & *v.* variant spelling of GIBE.

jibe² *Sailing* ▸*v.* [*intr.*] change course by swinging a fore-and-aft sail across a following wind. ■ (of a sail or boom) swing or be swung across the wind: [as *adj.*] (**jibing**) *the skipper was hit by a jibing boom.*
▸*n.* an act or instance of jibing.

jibe³ ▸*v.* [*intr.*] *inf.* be in accord; agree: *the verdict does not jibe with the medical evidence.*

jig /jig/ ▸*n.* **1** a lively dance with leaping movements. ■ a piece of music for such a dance, typically in compound time. **2** a device that holds a piece of work and guides the tools operating on it. **3** *Fishing* a type of artificial bait that is jerked up and down through the water.
▸*v.* (**jigged, jig·ging**) [*intr.*] dance a jig. ■ move up and down with a quick jerky motion: *we were jigging about in our seats.* ■ fish with a jig.

jig·ger¹ /ˈjigər/ ▸*n.* **1** a machine or vehicle with a part that rocks or moves back and forth, e.g., a jigsaw. **2** a person who dances a jig. **3** a measure or small glass of spirits or wine. **4** used to refer to a thing whose name one does not know or does not wish to mention.
▸*v.* [*tr.*] *inf.* rearrange or tamper with.

jig·ger² ▸*n.* variant spelling of CHIGGER.

jig·gle /ˈjigəl/ ▸*v.* [*intr.*] move about lightly and quickly from side to side or up and down: *his head jiggles up and down as he speaks.* ■ [*tr.*] shake (something) lightly up and down or from side to side.
▸*n.* a quick light shake. —**jig·gly** /ˈjig(ə)lē/ *adj.*

jig·saw /ˈjig,sô/ ▸*n.* **1** (also **jigsaw puzzle**) a puzzle consisting of a picture printed on cardboard or wood and cut into various pieces of different shapes that have to be fitted together. **2** a machine saw with a fine blade enabling it to cut curved lines in a sheet of wood, metal, or plastic.

ji·had /jiˈhäd/ ▸*n.* a holy war undertaken by Muslims against unbelievers. ■ *inf.* a single-minded or obsessive campaign.

ji·had·i /jiˈhädē/ ▸*n.* (*pl.* **-is**) a person involved in a jihad; an Islamic militant.

ji·had·ist /jiˈhädist/ ▸*n.* a jihadi.

jil·lion /ˈjilyən/ ▸*n.* cardinal number *inf.* an extremely large number.

jilt /jilt/ ▸*v.* [*tr.*] (often **be jilted**) suddenly reject or abandon (a lover)m

Jim Crow /ˈjim ˈkrō/ ▸*n.* **1** the former practice of segregating black people. [as *adj.*] *Jim Crow laws.* ■ *offens.* a black person. **2** an implement for straightening steel bars or bending rails by screw pressure. —**Jim Crow·ism** /ˈkrō,izəm/ *n.*

jim·my /ˈjimē/ ▸*n.* (*pl.* **-mies**) a short crowbar used by a burglar to force open a window or door.
▸*v.* (**-mies, -mied**) [*tr.*] *inf.* force open (a window or door) with a jimmy.

jim·son weed /ˈjimsən/ ▸*n.* a strong-smelling poisonous plant (*Datura stramonium*) of the nightshade family, with large, trumpet-shaped white flowers and toothed leaves.

jin·gle /ˈjiNGgəl/ ▸*n.* **1** a light ringing sound such as that made by metal objects being shaken together. **2** a short slogan, verse, or tune designed to be easily remembered, esp. as used in advertising. **3** (also **jingle shell**) a bivalve mollusk of the family Anomidae, with a fragile, slightly translucent shell.
▸*v.* make or cause to make a light metallic ringing sound. —**jin·gler** *n.* —**jin·gly** /ˈjiNGg(ə)lē/ *adj.*

jin·go /ˈjiNGgō/ ▸*n.* (*pl.* **-goes**) *dated, chiefly derog.* a vociferous supporter of policy favoring war, esp. in the name of patriotism. —**jin·go·ism** *n.*

jinx /jiNGks/ ▸*n.* a person or thing that brings bad luck.
▸*v.* [*tr.*] (usu. **be jinxed**) bring bad luck to; cast an evil spell on.

jir·ga /ˈjərgə/ ▸*n.* (in Afghanistan) a tribal council.

jit·ter /ˈjitər/ *inf.* ▸*n.* **1** (**jitters**) feelings of extreme nervousness: *a bout of the jitters.* **2** slight irregular movement, variation, or unsteadiness, esp. in an electrical signal or electronic device.
▸*v.* [*intr.*] act nervously. —**jit·ter·i·ness** /-rēnis/ *n.* —**jit·ter·y** *adj.*

jit·ter·bug /ˈjitər,bəg/ ▸*n.* **1** a fast dance popular in the 1940s, performed chiefly to swing music. **2** *inf., dated* a nervous person.
▸*v.* (**-bugged, -bug·ging**) [*intr.*] dance the jitterbug.

jive /jīv/ ▸*n.* **1** a lively style of dance popular esp. in the 1940s and 1950s, performed to swing music or rock and roll. ■ swing music. **2** (also **jive talk**) a form of slang associated with black American jazz musicians. ■ *inf.* a thing, esp. talk, that is deceptive or worthless.
▸*v. inf.* **1** [*intr.*] perform the jive or a similar dance to popular music. **2** [*tr.*] taunt or sneer at. ■ [*intr.*] talk nonsense: *he wasn't jiving about that bartender.*
▸*adj. inf.* deceitful or worthless. —**jiv·er** *n.* —**jiv·ey** *adj.*

job /jäb/ ▸*n.* **1** a paid position of regular employment: *a part-time job.* **2** a task or piece of work, esp. one that is paid: *she wants to be left alone to get on with the job.* ■ a responsibility or duty: *it's our job to find things out.* ■ *inf.* a difficult task. ■ *inf.* a procedure to improve the appearance of something, esp. an operation involving plastic surgery: *she's had a nose job.* ■ *inf.* a thing of a specified nature. ■ *inf.* a crime, esp. a robbery: *a series of daring bank jobs.*
▸*v.* (**jobbed, job·bing**) **1** [*intr.*] (usu. as *adj.*) (**jobbing**) do casual or occasional work: *a jobbing builder.* **2** [*tr.*] buy and sell (stocks) as a broker-dealer, esp. on a small scale. **3** [*tr.*] *inf.* cheat; betray.
▸ □ **do the job** *inf.* achieve the required result: *a piece of board will do the job.* □ **do a job on someone** *inf.* do something that harms or defeats an opponent.

job·ber /ˈjäbər/ ▸*n.* **1** a wholesaler. **2** a person who does casual or occasional work.

job·ber·y /ˈjäbərē/ ▸*n.* the practice of using a public office or position of trust for one's own gain or advantage.

job·less /ˈjäbləs/ ▸*adj.* unemployed. —**job·less·ness** *n.*

job lot ▸*n.* a miscellaneous group of articles, esp. when sold or bought together: *a job lot of stuff I bought from a demolition firm.*

job-share ▸*v.* [*intr.*] (of two part-time employees) jointly do a full-time job, sharing the remuneration.
▸*n.* an arrangement of such a kind. —**job-shar·er** *n.*

jock¹ /jäk/ ▸*n. inf.* **1** a disc jockey. **2** an enthusiast or participant in a specified activity: *a computer jock.*

jock² ▸*n.* another term for JOCKSTRAP. ■ an enthusiastic athlete or sports fan, esp. one with few other interests. ■ a slow-witted person of large size and great physical strength. —**jock·ish** *adj.*

jock³ ▸*n. inf.* a pilot or astronaut.

jock·ey /ˈjäkē/ ▸*n.* (*pl.* **-eys**) a person who rides in horse races, esp. as a profession. ■ an enthusiast or participant in a specified activity.
▸*v.* (**-eys, -eyed**) [*intr.*] struggle by every available means to gain or achieve something: *both men will be jockeying for the two top jobs.* ■ [*tr.*] handle or manipulate (someone or something) in a skillful manner. ▷late 16th cent.: diminutive of *Jock* 'ordinary man; a rustic,' Scots form of the given name *Jack*. The word came to mean 'mounted courier,' hence the current sense (late 17th cent.). Another early use 'horse dealer' (long a byword for dishonesty) probably gave rise to the verb sense 'manipulate,' whereas the main verb sense probably relates to the behavior of jockeys maneuvering for an advantageous position during a race.

jock·strap /ˈjäk,strap/ ▸*n.* a support or protection for the male genitals, worn esp. by athletes.

joc·u·lar /ˈjäkyələr/ ▸*adj.* fond of or characterized by joking; humorous or playful: *she sounded in a jocular mood* | *his voice was jocular.* —**joc·u·lar·i·ty** /ˌjäkyəˈlaritē/ *n.* —**joc·u·lar·ly** *adv.*

joc·und /ˈjäkənd; ˈjō-/ ▸*adj. formal* cheerful and lighthearted: *a jocund wedding party.* —**jo·cun·di·ty** /jōˈkənd+ itē/ *n.* (*pl.* **-ties**) —**joc·und·ly** *adv.*

jodh·purs /ˈjädpərz/ ▸*pl. n.* full-length trousers, worn for horseback riding, that are close fitting below the knee.

Joe Blow /blō/ ▸*n. inf.* a name for a hypothetical average man.

jo·ey /ˈjō-ē/ ▸*n.* (*pl.* **-eys**) *Austral.* a young kangaroo, wallaby, or possum.

jog /jäg/ ▸*v.* (**jogged, jog·ging**) **1** [*intr.*] run at a steady gentle pace, esp. on a regular basis as a form of physical exercise. [*as n.*] (**jogging**) *try cycling or gentle jogging.* ■ (*of a horse*) move at a slow trot. ■ move in an unsteady way, typically slowly. **2** [*tr.*] nudge or knock slightly: *a hand jogged his elbow.*
▸*n.* **1** a spell of jogging: *his morning jog.* ■ a gentle running pace: *he set off along the bank at a jog.* **2** a slight push or nudge. —**jog·ger** *n.*
▸ □ **jog someone's memory** cause someone to remember something suddenly.

jog·gle[1] /ˈjägəl/ ▸*v.* move or cause to move with repeated small bobs or jerks: [*intr.*] *the car bounced and joggled on the rough road.*
▸*n.* a bobbing or jerking movement.

john /jän/ ▸*n. inf.* **1** a toilet. **2** a prostitute's client.

John Doe /dō/ ▸*n. Law* an anonymous party, typically the plaintiff, in a legal action. ■ *inf.* a hypothetical average man.

john·ny /ˈjänē/ ▸*n.* (*pl.* **-nies**) *inf.* a short gown fastened in the back, worn by hospital patients.

joie de vi·vre /ˌZHwä də ˈvēvrə/ ▸*n.* exuberant enjoyment of life.

join /join/ ▸*v.* [*tr.*] link; connect: *the tap was joined to a pipe.* ■ become linked or connected to. ■ connect (points) with a line: *join up the points in a different color.* ■ [*intr.*] unite to form one entity or group: *countries join together to abolish restrictions on trade.* ■ become a member or employee of. ■ take part in: [*intr.*] *I joined in and sang along.* ■ [*intr.*] (**join up**) become a member of the armed forces. ■ come into the company of: *after the show we were joined by Jessica's sister.* ■ support (someone) in an activity: *I am sure you will join me in wishing him every success.*
▸*n.* a place or line where two or more things are connected or fastened together. ▷*Middle English:* from Old French *joindre*, from Latin *jungere* 'to join.'
▸ □ **join forces** combine efforts.

join·der /ˈjoindər/ ▸*n. Law* the action of bringing parties together.

join·er /ˈjoinər/ ▸*n.* **1** a person who constructs the wooden components of a building, such as stairs, doors, and door and window frames. **2** *inf.* a person who readily joins groups or campaigns. —**join·er·y** *n.*

joint /joint/ ▸*n.* **1** a point at which parts of an artificial structure are joined. ■ *Geol.* a break or fracture in a mass of rock, with no relative displacement of the parts. **2** a structure in the human or animal body at which two parts of the skeleton are fitted together. ■ each of the distinct sections of a body or limb between the places at which they are connected: *the top two joints of his index finger.* ■ the part of a stem of a plant from which a leaf or branch grows. **3** *inf.* an establishment of a specified kind, esp. one where people meet for eating, drinking, or entertainment: *a burger joint.* ■ (**the joint**) prison. **4** *inf.* a marijuana cigarette.
▸*adj.* shared, held, or made by two or more people or organizations together: *the companies issued a joint statement.* ■ shared, held, or made by both houses of a bicameral legislature: *a joint session of Congress* | *a joint congressional hearing.* ■ sharing in a position, achievement, or activity: *a joint winner.* ■ *Law* applied or regarded together. —**joint·ly** *adv.*
▸ □ **out of joint** (of a joint of the body) out of position; dislocated: *he put his hip out of joint.* ■ in a state of disorder or disorientation.

Joint Chiefs of Staff ▸*n.* the chiefs of staff of the U.S. Army and Air Force, the commandant of the U.S. Marine Corps, and the chief of U.S. Naval Operations.

joint-stock com·pa·ny ▸*n. Finance* a company whose stock is owned jointly by the shareholders.

joist /joist/ ▸*n.* a length of timber or steel supporting part of the structure of a building, typically arranged in parallel series to support a floor or ceiling. —**joist·ed** *adj.*

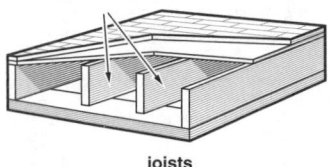

joists

jo·jo·ba /hōˈhōbə/ ▸*n.* a leathery-leaved evergreen shrub (*Simmondsia chinensis*, family Simmondsiaceae) native to the southwestern U.S., with seeds that produce an oil (**jojoba oil**) widely used in cosmetics

joke /jōk/ ▸*n.* **1** a thing that someone says to cause amusement or laughter, esp. a story with a funny punch line. ■ a trick played on someone for fun. ■ *inf.* a person or thing that is ridiculously inadequate: *the transportation system is a joke.*
▸*v.* [*intr.*] make jokes; talk humorously or flippantly. —**jok·ey** (also **jok·y**) *adj.* —**jok·i·ly** /-kəlē/ *adv.* —**jok·i·ness** *n.* —**jok·ing·ly** *adv.*
▸ □ **be no joke** *inf.* be a serious matter or difficult undertaking: *trying to shop with three children in tow is no joke.* □ **can** (or **can't**) **take a joke** be able (or unable) to receive humorous remarks or tricks in the spirit in which they are intended. □ **the joke is on someone** *inf.* someone looks foolish, esp. after trying to make someone else look so.

jok·er /ˈjōkər/ ▸*n.* **1** a person who is fond of joking. ■ *inf.* a foolish or inept person: *a bunch of jokers.* **2** a playing card, typically bearing the figure of a jester, used in some games as a wild card. **3** a clause unobtrusively inserted in a bill or document and affecting its operation in a way not immediately apparent.

jol·li·fi·ca·tion /ˌjäləfiˈkāSHən/ ▸*n.* lively celebration with others; merry-making.

jol·li·ty /ˈjälitē/ ▸*n.* (*pl.* **-ties**) lively and cheerful activity or celebration: *a night of riotous jollity.* ■ the quality of being cheerful: *full of false jollity.*

jol·ly /ˈjälē/ ▸*adj.* (**-li·er, -li·est**) happy and cheerful. ■ *inf.* or *dated* lively and entertaining: *we had a very jolly time.*
▸*v.* (**-lies, -lied**) [*tr.*] *inf.* encourage (someone) in a friendly way.
▸*adv. Brit., inf.* very; extremely: *that's a jolly good idea.* —**jol·li·ly** /ˈjäləlē/ *adv.* —**jol·li·ness** *n.*
▸ □ **get one's jollies** *inf.* have fun or find pleasure.

jolt /jōlt/ ▸*v.* [*tr.*] push or shake (someone or something) abruptly and roughly. ■ *fig.* give a surprise or shock to (someone) in order to make them act or change: *she tried to jolt him out of his depression.* ■ [*intr.*] move with sudden lurches: *the train jolted into motion.*
▸*n.* an abrupt rough or violent movement. ■ a surprise or shock, esp. of an unpleasant kind and often manifested physically. —**jolt·y** *adj.*

jon·quil /ˈjänkwəl/ ▸*n.* a widely cultivated narcissus (*Narcissus jonquilla*) with clusters of small fragrant yellow flowers and cylindrical leaves.

josh /jäSH/ *inf.* ▸*v.* [*tr.*] tease (someone) in a playful way: *he loved to josh people.* ■ [*intr.*] engage in joking or playful talk with others.
▸*n.* good-natured banter. —**josh·er** *n.*

jos·tle /ˈjäsəl/ ▸*v.* [*tr.*] push, elbow, or bump against (someone) roughly, typically in a crowd: [*intr.*] *people jostled against us.* ■ [*intr.*] (**jostle for**) struggle or compete forcefully for: *a jumble of images jostled for attention.*
▸*n.* the action of jostling.

jot /jät/ ▸*v.* (**jot·ted, jot·ting**) [*tr.*] write (something) quickly: *when you've found the answers, jot them down.*
▸*n.* a very small amount: *I have yet to see one jot of evidence.* ▷*late 15th cent.* (*as a noun*): via Latin from Greek *iōta*, the smallest letter of the Greek alphabet.

jot·ting /ˈjätiNG/ ▸*n.* (*usu.* **jottings**) a brief note.

joule /jool; joul/ ▸*n.* (*abbr.:* **J**) the SI unit of work or energy, equal to the work done by a force of one newton when its point of application moves one meter in the direction of action of the force.

jounce /jouns/ ▸*v.* jolt or bounce: [*intr.*] *the car jounced wildly.*

jour·nal /ˈjərnl/ ▸*n.* **1** a newspaper or magazine that deals with a particular subject or professional activity: *medical journals.* **2** a daily record of news and events of a personal nature; a diary. ■ (in bookkeeping) a daily record of business transactions with a statement of the accounts to which each is to be debited and credited. **3** *Mechanics* the part of a shaft or axle that rests on bearings.

jour·nal·ism /ˈjərnlˌizəm/ ▸*n.* the activity or profession of writing for newspapers or magazines or of broadcasting news on radio or television. ■ the product of such activity.

jour·nal·ist /ˈjərnl-ist/ ▸*n.* a person who writes for newspapers or magazines or prepares news to be broadcast on radio or television. —**jour·nal·is·tic** /ˌjərnlˈistik/ *adj.* —**jour·nal·is·ti·cal·ly** /ˌjərnlˈistik(ə)lē/ *adv.*

jour·ney /ˈjərnē/ ▸*n.* (*pl.* **-neys**) an act of traveling from one place to another: *she went on a long journey* | *fig. your journey through life.*
▸*v.* (**-neys, -neyed**) [*intr.*] travel somewhere: *they journeyed south.*

jour·ney·man /ˈjərnēmən/ ▸*n.* (*pl.* **-men**) a trained worker who is employed by someone else. ■ a worker or sports player who is reliable but not outstanding: [as *adj.*] *a solid journeyman professional.*

joust /joust/ ▸*v.* [*intr.*] (often as *n.*) (**jousting**) *hist.* (of a medieval knight) engage in a sports contest in which two opponents on horseback fight with lances. ■ *fig.* compete closely for superiority.
▸*n.* a medieval sports contest in which two opponents on horseback fought with lances. —**joust·er** *n.*

Jove /jōv/ ▸another name for **JUPITER**.
▸ □ **by Jove** *dated* an exclamation indicating surprise or used for emphasis: *by Jove, that's a cold wind.*

jo·vi·al /'jōvēəl/ ▸*adj.* cheerful and friendly: *she was in a jovial mood.* —**jo·vi·al·i·ty** /ˌjōvē'alitē/ *n.* —**jo·vi·al·ly** *adv.*

Jo·vi·an /'jōvēən/ ▸*adj.* **1** (in Roman mythology) of or like the god Jove (or Jupiter). **2** of or relating to the planet Jupiter or the class of giant planets to which Jupiter belongs.
▸*n.* a hypothetical or fictional inhabitant of the planet Jupiter.

jowl /joul/ ▸*n.* (often **jowls**) the lower part of a person's or animal's cheek, esp. when it is fleshy or drooping: *she had a large nose and heavy jowls.* ■ the cheek of a pig used as meat. ■ the loose fleshy part of the neck of certain animals, such as the dewlap of cattle or the wattle of birds. —**jowled** *adj.* [in *comb.*] *ruddy-jowled.* —**jowl·y** *adj.*

joy /joi/ ▸*n.* a feeling of great pleasure and happiness: *tears of joy | the joy of being alive.* ■ a thing that causes joy: *the joys of Manhattan.* —**joy·less** *adj.* —**joy·less·ly** *adv.*

joy·ful /'joifəl/ ▸*adj.* feeling, expressing, or causing great pleasure and happiness: *joyful music.* —**joy·ful·ly** *adv.* —**joy·ful·ness** *n.*

joy·ous /'joiəs/ ▸*adj.* chiefly *poetic/lit.* full of happiness and joy: *scenes of joyous celebration.* —**joy·ous·ly** *adv.* —**joy·ous·ness** *n.*

joy·ride /'joiˌrīd/ ▸*n. inf.* a fast and dangerous ride, esp. one taken in a stolen vehicle: *kids stealing cars for a Saturday night joyride.*
▸*v.* [*intr.*] go for a joyride. —**joy·rid·er** /-ˌrīdər/ *n.*

joy·stick /'joiˌstik/ ▸*n. inf.* the control column of an aircraft. ■ a lever that can be moved in several directions to control the movement of an image on a computer or similar display screen.

JP ▸*abbr.* Justice of the Peace.

Jr. ▸*abbr.* junior (in names): *John Smith Jr.*

ju·bi·lant /'jōōbələnt/ ▸*adj.* feeling or expressing great happiness and triumph. —**ju·bi·lance** *n.* —**ju·bi·lant·ly** *adv.* —**ju·bi·la·tion** /jōōbə'lāsHən/ *n.*

ju·bi·lee /'jōōbə,lē/ ; ˌjōōbə'lē/ ▸*n.* a special anniversary of an event, esp. one celebrating twenty-five or fifty years of a reign or activity: [as *adj.*] *jubilee celebrations.* ■ *Judaism* (in Jewish history) a year of emancipation and restoration, celebrated every fifty years.
▸*adj.* (of desserts) flambé: *cherries jubilee.*

Ju·da·ism /'jōōdē,izəm; -dā-/ ▸*n.* the monotheistic religion of the Jews. ■ the Jews collectively. —**Ju·da·ist** *n.*

Ju·das /'jōōdəs/ ▸*n.* (usu. **a Judas**) a person who betrays a friend or comrade.

ju·das /'jōōdəs/ (also **judas hole**) ▸*n.* a peephole in a door.

judge /jəj/ ▸*n.* a public official appointed to decide cases in a court of law. ■ a person who decides the results of a competition. ■ an official at a sports contest who watches for infractions of the rules. ■ a person able or qualified to give an opinion on something: *she was a good judge of character.*
▸*v.* [*tr.*] form an opinion or conclusion about. ■ decide (a case) in court: *other cases were judged by tribunal.* ■ [*tr.*] give a verdict on (someone) in court: *she was judged innocent of murder.* ■ decide the results of (a competition). —**judge·ship** /-ˌsHip/ *n.*

judg·ment /'jəjmənt/ (also **judge·ment**) ▸*n.* **1** the ability to make considered decisions or come to sensible conclusions. ■ an opinion or conclusion. ■ a decision of a court or judge. ■ a monetary or other obligation awarded by a court: *a lower court decision upholding the $100,000 judgment.* ■ the document recording this obligation. ■ short for **LAST JUDGMENT**. **2** a misfortune or calamity viewed as a divine punishment.
▸ □ **pass judgment** (of a court or judge) give a decision concerning a defendant or legal matter: *he passed judgment on the accused.* ■ criticize or condemn someone from a position of assumed moral superiority. □ **reserve judgment** delay the process of judging or giving one's opinion.

judg·men·tal /jəj'mentl/ (also **judge·men·tal**) ▸*adj.* of or concerning the use of judgment: *judgmental errors.* ■ having or displaying an excessively critical point of view: *to sound judgmental.* —**judg·men·tal·ly** *adv.*

Judg·ment Day ▸*n.* the time of the Last Judgment; the end of the world.

ju·di·ca·ture /'jōōdikə,CHŏŏr; -ˌkāCHər/ ▸*n.* the administration of justice. ■ (**the judicature**) judges collectively; the judiciary. —**ju·di·ca·to·ry** /-kə,tôrē/ *adj.*

ju·di·cial /jōō'disHəl/ ▸*adj.* of, by, or appropriate to a court or judge: *a judicial inquiry into the allegations | a judicial system.* —**ju·di·cial·ly** *adv.*

ju·di·ci·ar·y /jōō'disHē,erē; -'disHərē/ ▸*n.* (*pl.* **-ar·ies**) (usu. **the judiciary**) the judicial authorities of a country; judges collectively.

ju·di·cious /jōō'disHəs/ ▸*adj.* having, showing, or done with good judgment or sense: *the efficient and judicious use of pesticides.* —**ju·di·cious·ly** *adv.* —**ju·di·cious·ness** *n.*

ju·do /'jōōdō/ ▸*n.* a sport of unarmed combat derived from jujitsu and intended to train the body and mind. It involves using holds and leverage to unbalance the opponent. —**ju·do·ist** /-ist/ *n.*

jug /jəg/ ▸*n.* **1** a large container for liquids, with a narrow mouth and typically a stopper or cap. ■ the contents of such a container: *she gave us a big jug of water.* **2** (**the jug**) *inf.* prison: *three months in the jug.*
▸*v.* (**jugged, jug·ging**) [*tr.*] **1** [usu. as *adj.*] (**jugged**) stew or boil (a hare or rabbit) in a covered container: *jugged hare.* **2** *inf.* prosecute and imprison (someone). —**jug·ful** /-,fŏŏl/ *n.* (*pl.* **-fuls**).

jug·gle /'jəgəl/ ▸*v.* [*tr.*] continuously toss into the air and catch (a number of objects) so as to keep at least one in the air while handling the others, typically for the entertainment of others. ■ cope with by adroitly balancing: *she works full time, juggling her career with raising children.* ■ misrepresent (something) so as to deceive or cheat someone: *defense chiefs juggled the figures on bomb tests.*
▸*n.* an act of juggling. —**jug·gler** *n.* —**jug·gler·y** *n.*

jug·u·lar /'jəgyələr/ ▸*adj.* of the neck or throat.
▸*n.* short for **JUGULAR VEIN**.

jug·u·lar vein ▸*n.* any of several large veins in the neck, carrying blood from the head and face.

juice /jōōs/ ▸*n.* the liquid obtained from or present in fruit or vegetables. ■ a drink made from such a liquid. ■ (**juices**) fluid secreted by the body, esp. in the stomach to help digest food. ■ (**juices**) the liquid that comes from meat or other food when cooked. ■ *inf.* electrical energy: *the batteries have run out of juice.* ■ *inf.* gasoline. ■ *inf.* alcoholic drink. ■ (**juices**) a person's vitality or creative faculties: *it saps the creative juices.*
▸*v.* [*tr.*] **1** extract the juice from (fruit or vegetables): *juice one orange at a time.* **2** (**juice something up**) *inf.* liven something up. **3** [as *adj.*] (**juiced**) *inf.* drunk. ▷Middle English: via Old French from Latin *jus* 'broth, vegetable juice.'

juic·er /'jōōsər/ ▸*n.* an appliance for extracting juice from fruit and vegetables.

juic·y /'jōōsē/ ▸*adj.* (**juic·i·er, juic·i·est**) (of food) full of juice; succulent: *a juicy apple | a juicy steak.* ■ *inf.* interestingly scandalous: *juicy gossip.* ■ *inf.* temptingly appealing: *the promise of juicy returns.* —**juic·i·ly** /-səlē/ *adv.* —**juic·i·ness** *n.*

ju·jit·su /ˌjōō'jitsōō/ (also **ju·jut·su** /ˌjōō'jət-/) ▸*n.* a Japanese system of unarmed combat and physical training. Compare with **JUDO**.

ju·jube /'jōō,jōōb/ ▸*n.* **1** the edible berrylike fruit of a Eurasian plant, formerly taken as a cough cure. ■ (also) a lozenge or gumdrop. **2** (also **jujube bush**) the shrub or small tree (*Ziziphus jujuba*) of the buckthorn family that produces this fruit.

juke·box /'jōōk,bäks/ ▸*n.* a machine that automatically plays a selected musical recording when a coin is inserted.

Jul. ▸*abbr.* July.

ju·lep /'jōōləp/ ▸*n.* a sweet flavored drink made from a sugar syrup, sometimes containing alcohol. ■ short for **MINT JULEP**.

Jul·ian /'jōōlyən; -lēən/ ▸*adj.* of or associated with Julius Caesar.

Jul·ian cal·en·dar ▸*n.* a calendar introduced by the authority of Julius Caesar in 46 BC, in which the year consisted of 365 days, every fourth year having 366 days. It was superseded by the Gregorian calendar.

ju·li·enne /ˌjōōlē'en/ ▸*n.* a portion of food cut into short, thin strips.
▸*v.* [*tr.*] cut (food) into short, thin strips.

Ju·ly /jōō'lī/ ▸*n.* (*pl.* **Ju·lys**) the seventh month of the year, in the northern hemisphere usually considered the second month of summer.

jum·ble /'jəmbəl/ ▸*n.* an untidy collection or pile of things: *the books were in a chaotic jumble.* ■ *Brit.* articles collected for a jumble sale.
▸*v.* [*tr.*] mix up in a confused or untidy way: *a drawer full of letters jumbled together.*

jum·bo /'jəmbō/ *inf.* ▸*n.* (*pl.* **-bos**) a very large person or thing.
▸*adj.* very large: *a jumbo pad.*

jum·bo jet ▸*n.* a very large airliner (originally and specifically a Boeing 747).

jump /jəmp/ ▸*v.* **1** [*intr.*] push oneself off a surface and into the air by using the muscles in one's legs and feet: *the cat jumped off his lap.* ■ [*tr.*] pass over (an obstacle or barrier) in such a way. ■ (of an athlete or horse) perform in a competition involving such action: *his horse jumped well and won by five lengths.* ■ (esp. of prices or figures) rise suddenly and by a large amount: *exports jumped by 500 percent during the decade.* ■ *inf.* (of a place) be full of lively activity: *the bar is jumping on Fridays and Saturdays.* ■ [*tr.*] *inf.* (of driver or a vehicle) fail to stop at (a red traffic light). ■ [*tr.*] get on or off (a train or other vehicle) quickly, typically illegally or dangerously. ■ [*tr.*] take summary possession of (a mining concession or other piece of land) after alleged abandonment or forfeiture by the former occupant. **2** [*intr.*] (of a person) move suddenly and quickly in a specified way: *Juliet jumped to her feet | they jumped back into the car and drove off.* ■ (of a person) make a sudden involuntary movement in reaction to something that causes surprise or shock: *an owl hooted nearby, making her jump.* ■ pass quickly or abruptly from one idea, subject, or state to another: *she jumped backward and forward in her narrative.* ■ [*tr.*] omit or skip over (part of something) and pass on to a further point or stage. ■ (of a machine or device) move or jerk suddenly and abruptly: *the vibration can cause the needle to jump.* ■ (of a person) make a sudden, impulsive rush to do something: *Gordon jumped to my defense.* ■ [*tr.*] (in checkers) capture (an opponent's piece) by jumping over it. ■ [*tr.*] *inf.* attack (someone) suddenly and unexpectedly. ■ [*tr.*] *vulgar slang* have sexual intercourse with (someone). **3** [*tr.*] *inf.* start (a vehicle) using jumper cables.

▸*phrasal v.* □ **jump at** accept (an opportunity or offer) eagerly: *he jumped at the chance to start his own company.* □ **jump on** *inf.* attack or take hold of (someone) suddenly. ■ criticize (someone) suddenly and severely. ■ seize on (something) eagerly; give sudden (typically critical) attention to: *the paper jumped on the inconsistencies of his stories.* □ **jump out** have a strong visual or mental impact; be very striking: *advertising posters that really jump out at you.*

▸*n.* **1** an act of jumping from a surface by pushing upward with one's legs and feet. ■ an obstacle to be jumped, esp. by a horse and rider in an equestrian competition. ■ an act of descending from an aircraft by parachute. ■ a sudden dramatic rise in amount, price, or value: *a 51 percent jump in annual profits.* ■ a large or sudden transition or change: *the jump from mass-market to luxury goods.* ■ (in checkers) the act of capturing an opponent's piece by jumping over it. **2** a sudden involuntary movement caused by shock or surprise: *I woke up with a jump.*

▸ □ **get** (or **have**) **the jump on someone** *inf.* get (or have) an advantage over someone as a result of one's prompt action. □ **jump down someone's throat** *inf.* respond to what someone has said in a sudden and angrily critical way. □ **jump for joy** be ecstatically happy: *I'm not exactly jumping for joy at the prospect.* □ **jump in with both feet** get started enthusiastically. □ **jump out of one's skin** *inf.* be extremely startled. □ **jump ship** (of a sailor) leave the ship on which one is serving without having obtained permission to do so: *he jumped ship in Cape Town | fig. three producers jumped ship two weeks after the show's debut.* □ **jump** (or **leap**) **to conclusions** (or **the conclusion**) form an opinion hastily, before one has learned or considered all the facts. □ **one jump ahead** one step or stage ahead of someone else and so having the advantage over them: *the Americans were one jump ahead of the British in this.*

jump·er¹ /ˈjəmpər/ ▸*n.* **1** a collarless sleeveless dress, typically worn over a blouse. **2** *Brit.* a sweater.

jump·er² ▸*n.* **1** a person or animal that jumps. **2** (also **jumper wire**) a short wire used to complete an electric circuit or bypass a break in a circuit.

jump·er ca·ble ▸*n.* each of a pair of thick electric cables fitted with clips at either end, used for starting a vehicle by connecting its dead battery to the battery of another vehicle.

jump·ing bean ▸*n.* the seed from certain plants of the spurge family (esp. *Sebastiana pavoniana*) that jumps as a result of the movement of a moth larva that is developing inside it.

jump rope (also **jump·rope**) ▸*n.* a length of rope used for jumping by swinging it over the head and under the feet.

jump seat ▸*n.* an extra seat, esp. in a car or taxicab, that folds back when not in use.

jump-start ▸*v.* [*tr.*] start (a car with a dead battery) with jumper cables or by a sudden release of the clutch while it is being pushed. ■ *fig.* give an added impetus to (something that is proceeding slowly or is at a standstill): *she suggests ways to jump-start the sluggish educational system.* ▸*n. fig.* an added impetus.

jump·suit /ˈjəm(p)ˌso͞ot/ ▸*n.* a garment incorporating trousers and a top in one piece, usu. worn as a protective garment or uniform.

jump·y /ˈjəmpē/ ▸*adj.* (**jump·i·er**, **jump·i·est**) *inf.* (of a person) anxious and uneasy. ■ characterized by abrupt stops and starts or an irregular course: *a jumpy pulse.* —**jump·i·ly** /-pəlē/ *adv.* —**jump·i·ness** *n.*

Jun. ▸*abbr.* ■ June. ■ Junior (in names): *John Smith Jun.*

jun·co /ˈjəNGkō/ ▸*n.* (*pl.* **-cos**) a North American songbird (genus *Junco*) related to the buntings, with mainly gray and brown plumage.

junc·tion /ˈjəNGksHən/ ▸*n.* **1** a point where two or more things are joined: *the junction of the two rivers.* ■ a place where two or more roads or railroad lines meet. **2** *Electr.* a region of transition in a semiconductor between a part where conduction is mainly by electrons and a part where it is mainly by holes. **3** the action or fact of joining or being joined. —**junc·tion·al** /-sHənl/ *adj.*

junc·tion box ▸*n.* a box containing a junction of electric wires or cables.

junc·ture /ˈjəNGkcHər/ ▸*n.* a particular point in events or time. ■ a place where things join: *the plane crashed at the juncture of two mountains.*

June /jo͞on/ ▸*n.* the sixth month of the year, in the northern hemisphere usually considered the first month of summer.

June bug (also **June beetle**) ▸*n.* a large brown scarab beetle (genus *Phyllophaga*) that appears in late spring and early summer.

jun·gle /ˈjəNGgəl/ ▸*n.* an area of land overgrown with dense forest and tangled vegetation, typically in the tropics. ■ a wild tangled mass of vegetation or other things. ■ a situation or place of bewildering complexity or brutal competitiveness: *it's a jungle out there.* —**jun·gled** *adj.* —**jun·gly** *adj.*

▸ □ **the law of the jungle** the principle that those who are strong and apply ruthless self-interest will be most successful.

jun·gle gym ▸*n.* a structure of bars or logs for children to climb on.

jun·ior /ˈjo͞onyər/ ▸*adj.* **1** of, for, or denoting young or younger people: *junior tennis.* ■ of or for students in the third year of college or high school. ■ (often **Junior**) [in *names*] denoting the younger of two who have the same name in a family, esp. a son as distinct from his father: *John F. Kennedy Junior.* **2** low or lower in rank or status: *Virginia's junior senator | part of my function is to supervise those junior to me.*

▸*n.* **1** a person who is a specified number of years younger than someone else: *he's five years her junior.* ■ a student in the third year of college or high school. ■ (in sports) a young competitor, typically under sixteen or eighteen. ■ *inf.* used as a nickname or form of address for one's son. **2** a person with low rank or status compared with others. **3** a size of clothing for teenagers or slender women. ▷Middle English (as an adjective following a family name): from Latin, comparative of *juvenis* 'young.' —**jun·ior·i·ty** /ˌjo͞onˈyôritē, -ˈyär-/ *n.*

jun·ior col·lege ▸*n.* a college offering courses for two years beyond high school.

jun·ior high school ▸*n.* another term for **MIDDLE SCHOOL**.

ju·ni·per /ˈjo͞onəpər/ ▸*n.* an evergreen shrub or tree (genus *Juniperus*) of the cypress family that bears aromatic berrylike cones, widely distributed throughout Eurasia and North America. The **common juniper** (*J. communis*), bears berries that are used for flavoring gin.

junk¹ /jəNGk/ ▸*n.* **1** *inf.* old or discarded articles that are considered useless or of little value. ■ worthless writing, talk, or ideas: *I can't write this kind of junk.* ■ *Finance* junk bonds. **2** *inf.* heroin.

▸*v.* [*tr.*] *inf.* discard or abandon unceremoniously: *sort out what could be sold off and junk the rest.*

junk² ▸*n.* a flat-bottomed sailing vessel typical in China and the East Indies, with a prominent stem, a high stern, and lugsails.

junk

junk DNA ▸*n.* genomic DNA that does not encode proteins, and whose function, if it has one, is not well understood.

jun·ket /'jəNGkit/ ▶*n.* **1** a dish of sweetened and flavored curds of milk, often served with fruit. **2** *inf.* an extravagant trip or celebration, in particular one enjoyed by a government official at public expense.
▶*v.* (**-ket·ed, -ket·ing**) [*intr.*] [often as *n.*] (**junketing**) *inf.* attend or go on such a trip or celebration. —**jun·ke·teer** /ˌjəNGki'ti(ə)r/ *n.*

junk food ▶*n.* food that has low nutritional value, typically produced in the form of packaged snacks needing little or no preparation.

junk·ie /'jəNGkē/ (also **junk·y**) ▶*n. inf.* a drug addict. ■ a person with a compulsive habit or obsessive dependency on something: *power junkies.*

junk mail ▶*n. inf.* unsolicited advertising or promotional material received through the mail and e-mail.

junk·yard /'jəNGkˌyärd/ ▶*n.* a place where scrap is collected before being discarded, reused, or recycled.

jun·ta /'hŏŏntə; 'jəntə/ ▶*n.* **1** a military or political group that rules a country after taking power by force: *the country's ruling military junta.* **2** *hist.* a deliberative or administrative council in Spain or Portugal.

Ju·pi·ter /'jŏŏpitər/ ▶ **1** *Roman Mythol.* the chief god of the Roman state religion, originally a sky god associated with thunder and lightning. His wife was Juno. Also called **Jove**. Greek equivalent **Zeus**. **2** *Astron.* the largest planet in the solar system, a gas giant that is the fifth in order from the sun and one of the brightest objects in the night sky.

Ju·ras·sic /jə'rasik/ ▶*adj. Geol.* of, relating to, or denoting the second period of the Mesozoic era, between the Triassic and Cretaceous periods. ■ [as *n.*] (**the Jurassic**) the Jurassic period or the system of rocks deposited during it.

ju·rid·i·cal /jŏŏ'ridikəl/ ▶*adj. Law* of or relating to judicial proceedings and the administration of the law. —**ju·rid·i·cal·ly** *adv.*

ju·ris·dic·tion /ˌjŏŏris'dikSHən/ ▶*n.* the official power to make legal decisions and judgments: *federal courts had no **jurisdiction over** the case.* ■ the extent of this power: *the claim will be **within the jurisdiction** of the industrial tribunal.* ■ a system of law courts; a judicature. ■ the territory or sphere of activity over which the legal authority of a court or other institution extends. —**ju·ris·dic·tion·al** *adj.*

ju·ris·pru·dence /ˌjŏŏris'prŏŏdns/ ▶*n.* the theory or philosophy of law. ■ a legal system: *American jurisprudence.* —**ju·ris·pru·dent** *adj. & n.* —**ju·ris·pru·den·tial** /-prŏŏ'denCHəl/ *adj.*

ju·rist /'jŏŏrist/ ▶*n.* an expert in or writer on law. ■ a lawyer or a judge. —**ju·ris·tic** /jŏŏ'ristik/ *adj.*

ju·ror /'jŏŏrər; -ôr/ ▶*n.* a member of a jury.

ju·ry[1] /'jŏŏrē/ ▶*n.* (*pl.* **-ries**) a body of usu. twelve people sworn to give a verdict in a legal case on the basis of evidence submitted to them in court. ■ a body of people selected to judge a competition.
▶*v.* (**-ries, -ried**) [*tr.*] (usu. **be juried**) judge (an art or craft exhibition or exhibit): [as *adj.*] (**juried**) *the juried jewelry show.*

ju·ry[2] ▶*adj. Naut.* (of a mast or other fitting) improvised or temporary: *we need to get that jury rudder fixed.*

ju·ry-rigged ▶*adj.* (of a ship) having temporary makeshift rigging. ■ makeshift; improvised. —**ju·ry-rig** *v.*

just /jəst/ ▶*adj.* based on or behaving according to what is morally right and fair: *a just and democratic society | fighting for a just cause.* ■ (of treatment) deserved or appropriate in the circumstances: *we all get our just deserts.* ■ (of an opinion or appraisal) well founded; justifiable.
▶*adv.* **1** exactly: *that's just what I need.* ■ exactly or almost exactly at this or that moment: *we were just finishing breakfast.* **2** very recently; in the immediate past: *I've just seen the local paper.* **3** barely; by a little: *I got*

here *just after nine.* **4** simply; only; no more than: *they were just interested in making money.* ■ really; absolutely (used for emphasis): *they're just great.* ■ used as a polite formula for giving permission or making a request: *just help yourselves.* ■ possibly (used to indicate a slight chance of something happening or being true): *it might just help.* —**just·ly** *adv.* —**just·ness** *n.*
▶ □ **just about** *inf.* almost exactly; nearly: *he can do just about anything.* □ **just as well** a good or fortunate thing: *it was just as well I didn't know at the time.* □ **just in case** as a precaution. □ **just the same** nevertheless: *I put on my raincoat and big straw hat. But we got soaked just the same.* □ **just so** arranged or done very neatly and carefully: *polishing the furniture and making everything just so.*

jus·tice /'jəstis/ ▶*n.* **1** just behavior or treatment: *a concern for justice, peace, and genuine respect for people.* ■ the quality of being fair and reasonable. ■ the administration of the law or authority in maintaining this: *a tragic miscarriage of justice.* **2** a judge or magistrate, in particular a judge of the supreme court of a country or state.
▶ □ **do oneself justice** perform as well as one is able to. □ **do someone/something justice** (or **do justice to someone/something**) do, treat, or represent with due fairness or appreciation: *the brief menu does not do justice to the food.*

jus·tice of the peace ▶*n.* a magistrate appointed to hear minor cases, perform marriages, grant licenses, etc., in a local district.

jus·ti·fi·a·ble /'jəstəˌfīəbəl; ˌjəstə'fī-/ ▶*adj.* able to be shown to be right or reasonable; defensible: *it is not financially justifiable.* —**jus·ti·fi·a·bil·i·ty** /ˌjəstəˌfīə'bilitē/ *n.* —**jus·ti·fi·a·ble·ness** *n.* —**jus·ti·fi·a·bly** /-blē/ *adv.*

jus·ti·fy /'jəstəˌfī/ ▶*v.* (**-fies, -fied**) [*tr.*] **1** show or prove to be right or reasonable: *the person appointed has fully justified our confidence.* ■ be a good reason for: *the situation was grave enough to justify further investigation.* **2** *Printing* adjust (a line of type or piece of text) so that the print fills a space evenly or forms a straight edge at one or both margins. —**jus·ti·fi·ca·tion** /ˌjəstəfi'kāSHən/ *n.* —**jus·ti·fi·er** *n.*

jut /jət/ ▶*v.* (**jut·ted, jut·ting**) [*intr.*] extend out, over, or beyond the main body or line of something: *a rock jutted out from the side of the bank.* ■ [*tr.*] cause (something, such as one's chin) to protrude.
▶*n.* a point that sticks out.

Jute /jŏŏt/ ▶*n.* a member of a Germanic people invading Britain in the 5th century and settling in Kent and the Isle of Wight. —**Jut·ish** *adj.*

jute /jŏŏt/ ▶*n.* **1** rough fiber made from the stems of a tropical Old World plant, used for making twine and rope or woven into sacking or matting. **2** the herbaceous plant (genus *Corchorus*, family Tiliaceae) that is cultivated for this fiber, with edible young shoots. ■ used in names of other plants that yield fiber, e.g., **Chinese jute.**

ju·ve·nile /'jŏŏvəˌnīl; -vənl/ ▶*adj.* of, for, or relating to young people: *juvenile crime.* ■ childish; immature. ■ of or denoting a theatrical or film role representing a young person: *the romantic juvenile lead.* ■ of or relating to young birds or other animals.
▶*n.* a young person. ■ *Law* a person below the age at which ordinary criminal prosecution is possible. ■ a young bird or other animal. ■ an actor who plays juvenile roles. —**ju·ve·nil·i·ty** /ˌjŏŏvə'nilitē/ *n.*

ju·ve·nile court ▶*n.* a court of law responsible for the trial or legal supervision of children under a specified age (18 in most countries).

jux·ta·pose /'jəkstəˌpōz; ˌjəkstə'pōz/ ▶*v.* [*tr.*] place or deal with close together for contrasting effect. —**jux·ta·po·si·tion** /ˌjəkstəpə'ziSHən/ *n.* —**jux·ta·po·si·tion·al** /ˌjəkstəpə'ziSHənl/ *adj.*

JV ▶*abbr.* ■ joint venture. ■ junior varsity.

Kk

K¹ /kā/ (also **k**) ▶*n.* (*pl.* **Ks** or **K's**) the eleventh letter of the alphabet. ■ denoting the next after J in a set of items, categories, etc.

K² ▶*abbr.* ■ kelvin(s). ■ *Comput.* kilobyte(s). ■ kilometer(s). ■ kindergarten. ■ king (used esp. in describing play in card games and recording moves in chess): *declarer overruffed with* ◆*K and led another spade* | *18.Ke2.* ■ knit (as an instruction in knitting patterns): *K 42 rows.* ■ *inf.* thousand (used chiefly in expressing salaries or other sums of money). ■ *Baseball* strikeout.
▶*symb.* the chemical element potassium.

k ▶*abbr.* ■ karat. ■ [in *comb.*] (in units of measurement) kilo-: *a distance of 700 kpc.* ■ kopeck(s).
▶*symb.* a constant in a formula or equation.

Kab·ba·lah /ˈkabələ; kəˈbä-/ (also **Kab·ba·la, Ca·ba·la, Cab·ba·la**) ▶*n.* the ancient Jewish tradition of mystical interpretation of the Bible, first transmitted orally and using esoteric methods (including ciphers). It reached the height of its influence in the later Middle Ages and remains significant in Hasidism. —**Kab·ba·lism** /ˈkabəˌlizəm/ *n.* —**Kab·ba·list** /-list/ *n.* —**Kab·ba·lis·tic** /ˌkabəˈlistik/ *adj.*

ka·bob ▶*n.* variant spelling of **KEBAB**.

ka·bu·ki /kəˈbo͞okē/ ▶*n.* a form of traditional Japanese drama with highly stylized song, mime, and dance, now performed only by male actors. ▷Japanese, originally as a verb meaning 'act dissolutely,' later interpreted as if from *ka* 'song' + *bu* 'dance' + *ki* 'art.'

ka·ching /kəˈCHiNG/ ▶*n.* used to represent the sound of a cash register, especially with reference to making money.

Kad·dish /ˈkädiSH/ ▶*n.* an ancient Jewish prayer sequence regularly recited in the synagogue service, including thanksgiving and praise and concluding with a prayer for universal peace. ■ a form of this prayer sequence recited for the dead.

Kaf·fir /ˈkafər/ ▶*n. chiefly S. Afr., offens.* an insulting and contemptuous term for a black African.

kaf·fir lime /ˈkafər/ ▶*n.* a citrus tree of southeast Asia with green fruit and aromatic leaves that are used in Thai and Indonesian cooking.

Kaf·ka·esque /ˌkäfkəˈesk/ ▶*adj.* characteristic or reminiscent of the oppressive or nightmarish qualities of Franz Kafka's fictional world.

kaf·tan /ˈkaftan; -ˌtan/ (also **caf·tan**) ▶*n.* a man's long belted tunic, worn in countries of the Near East. ■ a woman's long loose dress. ■ a loose shirt or top.

kai·ser /ˈkīzər/ ▶*n. hist.* the German emperor, the emperor of Austria, or the head of the Holy Roman Empire: [as *title*] *Kaiser Wilhelm.*

kai·ser roll ▶*n.* a round, soft bread roll with a crisp crust, made by folding the corners of a square of dough into the center, resulting in a pinwheel shape when baked.

kal·an·cho·e /ˌkalənˈkō-ē; kəˈlaNGkəwē/ ▶*n.* a tropical succulent plant (genus *Kalanchoe*) of the stonecrop family, with clusters of tubular flowers, sometimes producing miniature plants along the edges of the leaves and grown as an indoor or greenhouse plant.

kale /kāl/ ▶*n.* a hardy cabbage of a variety that produces erect stems with large leaves and no compact head.

ka·lei·do·scope /kəˈlīdəˌskōp/ ▶*n.* a toy consisting of a tube containing mirrors and pieces of colored glass or paper, whose reflections produce changing patterns that are visible through an eyehole when the tube is rotated. ■ a constantly changing pattern or sequence of objects or elements: *the dancers moved in a kaleidoscope of color.* —**ka·lei·do·scop·ic** /-ˌlīdəˈskäpik/ *adj.* —**ka·lei·do·scop·i·cal·ly** /-ˌlīdəˈskäpik(ə)lē/ *adv.*

kal·ends ▶*pl. n.* variant spelling of **CALENDS**.

Ka·ma Su·tra /ˈkämə ˈso͞otrə/ ▶an ancient Sanskrit treatise on the art of love and sexual technique.

ka·mi·ka·ze /ˌkämiˈkäzē/ ▶*n.* (in World War II) a Japanese aircraft loaded with explosives and making a deliberate suicidal crash on an enemy target. ■ the pilot of such an aircraft.
▶*adj.* of or relating to such an attack or pilot. ■ reckless or potentially self-destructive: *he made a kamikaze run across three lanes of traffic.*

kan·ga·roo /ˌkaNGgəˈro͞o/ ▶*n.* a large plant-eating macropod (genus *Macropus*, family Macropodidae) with a long powerful tail and strongly developed hind limbs that enable it to travel by leaping, found only in Australia and New Guinea. ▷late 18th cent.: from an Aboriginal language.

kan·ga·roo court ▶*n.* an unofficial court held by a group of people in order to try someone regarded, esp. without good evidence, as guilty of a crime or misdemeanor.

kan·ga·roo rat ▶*n.* a seed-eating hopping rodent (genus *Dipodomys*, family Heteromyidae) with long hind legs, found from Canada to Mexico.

ka·o·lin /ˈkāəlin/ ▶*n.* a fine, soft white clay, resulting from the natural decomposition of other clays or feldspar. It is used for making porcelain and china, as a filler in paper and textiles, and in medicinal absorbents. Also called **CHINA CLAY**. —**ka·o·lin·ize** /-ˌnīz/ *v.*

ka·on /ˈkā-än/ ▶*n. Physics* a meson having a mass several times that of a pion.

ka·pok /ˈkā-päk/ ▶*n.* a fine, fibrous cottonlike substance that grows around the seeds of the ceiba tree, used as stuffing for cushions, soft toys, etc.

Ka·po·si's sar·co·ma /kəˈpōsēz särˈkōmə; ˈkapəˌsēz; ˈkäpōˌsHez/ ▶*n. Med.* a form of cancer involving multiple tumors of the lymph nodes or skin, occurring chiefly in people with depressed immune systems, e.g., as a result of AIDS.

kap·pa /ˈkapə/ ▶*n.* the tenth letter of the Greek alphabet (Κ, κ), transliterated in the traditional Latin style as 'c' (as in *Socrates* or *cyan*) or in the modern style as 'k' (as in *kyanite*).

ka·put /kəˈpo͝ot; kä-/ ▶*adj. inf.* broken and useless; no longer working or effective.

kar·a·kul /ˈkarəkəl/ (also **car·a·cul**) ▶*n.* a sheep of an Asian breed with a dark, curled fleece when young. ■ cloth or fur made from or resembling the fleece of such a sheep.

kar·a·o·ke /ˌkarēˈōkē/ ▶*n.* a form of entertainment, offered typically by bars and clubs, in which people take turns singing popular songs into a microphone over prerecorded backing tracks.

kar·at /ˈkarət/ (*chiefly Brit.* also **car·at**) ▶*n.* a measure of the purity of gold, pure gold being 24 karats.

ka·ra·te /kəˈrätē/ ▶*n.* an Asian system of unarmed combat using the hands and feet to deliver and block blows, widely practiced as a sport.

kar·ma /ˈkärmə/ ▶*n.* (in Hinduism and Buddhism) the sum of a person's actions in this and previous states of existence, viewed as deciding their fate in future existences. ■ *inf.* destiny or fate, following as effect from cause. —**kar·mic** /-mik/ *adj.* —**kar·mi·cal·ly** /-mik(ə)lē/ *adv.*

karst /kärst/ ▶*n. Geol.* landscape underlain by limestone that has been eroded by dissolution, producing ridges, towers, fissures, sinkholes, and other characteristic landforms. —**kars·tic** /ˈkärstik/ *adj.* —**kars·ti·fi·ca·tion** /ˌkärstəfiˈkāsHən/ *n.* —**kars·ti·fy** /ˈkärstəˌfī/ *v.* (**-fies, -fied**).

kas·bah /ˈkäzbä/ ▶*n.* variant spelling of **CASBAH**.

ka·ty·did /ˈkātēˌdid/ ▶*n.* a large, typically green, North American grasshopper (*Microcentrum* and other genera, family Tettigoniidae), the males of which make a sound that resembles the name.

kay·ak /'kī,ak/ ▶ *n.* a canoe of a type used originally by the Eskimo, made of a light frame with a watertight covering having a small opening in the top to sit in.
▶ *v.* (**kay·aked, kay·ak·ing**) [*intr.*] [usu. as *n.*] (**kayaking**) travel in or use a kayak. —**kay·ak·er** *n.*

kayak

kay·o /'kā'ō/ *inf. Boxing* ▶ *n.* (*pl.* **kay·os**) a knockout.
▶ *v.* (**kay·oes, kay·oed**) [*tr.*] knock (someone) out.
ka·zoo /kə'zōō/ ▶ *n.* a small, simple musical instrument consisting of a hollow pipe with a hole in it, over which is a thin covering that vibrates and produces a buzzing sound when the player sings or hums into the pipe.
kc ▶ *abbr.* kilocycle(s).
ke·a /kēə/ ▶ *n.* a New Zealand mountain parrot (*Nestor notabilis*) with a long, narrow bill and mainly olive-green plumage.
ke·bab /kə'bäb/ (also **ka·bob**) ▶ *n.* a dish of pieces of meat roasted or grilled on a skewer or spit. ■ a dish of any kind of food cooked in pieces in this way: *swordfish kebabs.*
kedge /kej/ ▶ *n.* (also **kedge anchor**) a small anchor.
keel /kēl/ ▶ *n.* the longitudinal structure along the centerline at the bottom of a vessel's hull, on which the rest of the hull is built, in some vessels extended downward as a blade or ridge to increase stability. ■ *Zool.* a ridge along the breastbone of many birds to which the flight muscles are attached; the carina.
▶ *v.* [*intr.*] (**keel over**) *inf.* (of a person or thing) fall over; collapse. —**keeled** *adj.* [in *comb.*] *a deep-keeled yacht.* —**keel·less** *adj.*
keel·haul /'kēl,hôl/ ▶ *v.* [*tr.*] *hist.* punish (someone) by dragging them through the water under the keel of a ship, either across the width or from bow to stern. ■ *often humorous* punish or reprimand severely.
keen[1] /kēn/ ▶ *adj.* **1** having or showing eagerness or enthusiasm: *keen believers in the monetary system.* ■ (**keen on**) interested in or attracted by (someone or something): *Bob makes it obvious he's keen on her.* **2** sharp or penetrating, in particular: ■ (of a sense) highly developed: *I have keen eyesight.* ■ (of mental faculties) quick to understand or function: *her keen intellect.* ■ (of the air or wind) extremely cold; biting. ■ (of the edge or point of a blade) sharp. —**keen·ly** *adv.* —**keen·ness** *n.*
keen[2] ▶ *v.* [*intr.*] wail in grief for a dead person. ■ [usu. as *n.*] (**keening**) make an eerie wailing sound: *the keening of the cold night wind.* —**keen·er** *n.*
keep /kēp/ ▶ *v.* (*past* **kept** /kept/) [*tr.*] **1** have or retain possession of: *my father would keep the best for himself.* ■ retain or reserve for use in the future: *return one copy to me, keeping the other for your files.* ■ put or store in a regular place: *the stand where her umbrella was kept.* ■ retain one's place in or on (a seat or saddle, the ground, etc.) against opposition or difficulty: *are you able to keep your saddle?* ■ delay or detain; cause to be late: *I won't keep you; I know you've got a busy evening.* **2** continue or cause to continue in a specified condition, position, course, etc.: [*intr.*] *she could have had some boyfriend she kept quiet about* | [*tr.*] *she might be kept alive artificially by machinery.* ■ [*intr.*] continue doing or do repeatedly or habitually: *he keeps going on about the murder.* ■ [*intr.*] (of a perishable commodity) remain in good condition: *fresh ginger does not keep well.* ■ [*tr.*] make (someone) do something for a period of time: *I have kept her waiting too long.* **3** provide for the sustenance of (someone): *he had to keep his large family in the manner he had chosen.* ■ provide (someone) with a regular supply of a commodity: *the money should keep him in cigarettes for a week.* ■ own and look after (an animal) for pleasure or profit. ■ own and manage (a shop or business). ■ guard; protect: *his only thought is to keep the boy from harm.* ■ support (someone, esp. a woman) financially in return for sexual favors: [as *adj.*] *a kept woman.* **4** honor or fulfill (a commitment or undertaking): *I'll keep my promise, naturally.* ■ observe (a religious occasion) in the prescribed manner: *today's consumers do not keep the Sabbath.* ■ pay due regard to (a law or custom). **5** make written entries in (a diary) on a regular basis: *the master kept a weekly journal.* ■ write down as (a record): *keep a note of the whereabouts of each item.*
▶ *phrasal v.* □ **keep to** avoid leaving (a path, road, or place). ■ adhere to (a schedule). ■ observe (a promise). ■ confine or restrict oneself to: *nothing is more irritating than people who do not keep to the point.* □ **keep up** move or progress at the same rate as someone or something else: *often they had to pause to allow him to keep up.* ■ meet a commitment to pay or do something regularly: *if you do not keep up with the payments, the loan company can make you sell your home.* □ **keep something up** maintain or preserve something in the existing state; continue a course of action: *keep up the good work.* ■ keep something in an efficient or proper state: *the new owners could not afford to keep up the grounds.* ■ make something remain at a high level: *he was whistling to keep up his spirits.*
▶ *n.* **1** food, clothes, and other essentials for living: *working overtime to earn his keep.* ■ the cost of such items. **2** the strongest or central tower of a castle, acting as a final refuge.
keep·er /'kēpər/ ▶ *n.* **1** a person who manages or looks after something or someone, in particular: ■ a guard at a prison or a museum. ■ a person who is regarded as being in charge of someone else: *I would not stop him—I'm his wife, not his keeper.* **2** a food or drink that remains in a specified condition if stored: *hazelnuts are good keepers.* **3** *inf.* a thing worth keeping: *they were deciding which drawings are questionable and which are keepers.* ■ a fish large enough to be kept when caught. **4** an object that keeps another in place, or protects something more fragile or valuable, in particular: ■ a ring worn to keep a more valuable one on the finger. ■ a bar of soft iron placed across the poles of a horseshoe magnet to maintain its strength. **5** *Football* a play in which the quarterback runs with the ball instead of handing it off or passing it. —**keep·er·ship** /-,SHip/ *n.*
keep·ing /'kēpiNG/ ▶ *n.* the action of owning, maintaining, or protecting something: *the keeping of dogs* | [in *comb.*] *careful record-keeping is needed.*
keep·sake /'kēp,sāk/ ▶ *n.* a small item kept in memory of the person who gave it or originally owned it.
kef /kef/ (also **kif**) ▶ *n.* a substance, esp. cannabis, smoked to produce a drowsy state.
ke·fir /kə'fi(ə)r/ ▶ *n.* a sour-tasting drink make from cow's milk fermented with certain bacteria.
keg /keg/ ▶ *n.* **1** a small barrel, esp. one of less than 30 gallons or (in the UK) 10 gallons. **2** a unit of weight equal to 100 lb (45 kg), used for nails.
keis·ter /'kēstər/ (also **kees·ter**) ▶ *n.* *inf.* a person's buttocks.
kelp /kelp/ ▶ *n.* a large brown seaweed (family Laminariaceae) used as a source of various salts. Some kinds form underwater "forests" that support large populations of animals. ■ the calcined ashes of seaweed.
kel·vin /'kelvən/ (abbr.: **K**) ▶ *n.* the SI base unit of thermodynamic temperature, equal in magnitude to the degree Celsius.
Kel·vin scale ▶ *n.* a scale of temperature with absolute zero as zero, and the triple point of water as exactly 273.16 degrees.
kempt /kem(p)t/ ▶ *adj. chiefly Brit.* (of a person or a place) maintained in a neat and clean condition; well cared for: *she was looking as thoroughly kempt as ever.*
ken /ken/ ▶ *n.* one's range of knowledge or sight: *such determination is beyond my ken.*
▶ *v.* (**ken·ning**; *past* and *past part.* **kenned** or **kent** /kent/) [*tr.*] *Scot. & N. English* know: *d'ye ken anyone who can boast of that?* ▷Old English *cennan* 'tell, make known,' of Germanic origin; related to Dutch and German *kennen* 'know, be acquainted with,' from an Indo-European root shared by *can* and *know.* Current senses of the verb date from Middle English; the noun from the mid 16th cent.
ken·do /'ken,dō/ ▶ *n.* a Japanese form of fencing with two-handed bamboo swords, originally developed as a safe form of sword training for samurai. —**ken·do·ist** /-dōist/ *n.*
ken·nel /'kenl/ ▶ *n.* a small shelter for a dog or cat. ■ a boarding or breeding establishment for dogs or cats. ■ *fig.* a small or sordid dwelling.
▶ *v.* (**-neled, -nel·ing**; *chiefly Brit.* **-nelled, -nel·ling**) [*tr.*] put (a dog or cat) in a kennel.
kep·i /'kāpē; 'kepē/ ▶ *n.* (*pl.* **kep·is**) a French military cap with a flat top and horizontal brim.
kept /kept/ ▶ past and past participle of **KEEP**.
ker·a·tin /'kerətin/ ▶ *n.* a fibrous protein forming the main structural constituent of hair, feathers, hoofs, claws, horns, etc. —**ke·rat·i·nized** /kə'ratn,īzd/ *adj.* —**ke·rat·i·nous** /kə'ratn-əs/ *adj.*
kerb /kərb/ ▶ *n.* British spelling of **CURB**.
ker·chief /'kərcHəf; -,chēf/ ▶ *n.* a piece of fabric used to cover the head, or worn tied around the neck. ■ a handkerchief. —**ker·chiefed** *adj.*
kerf /kərf/ ▶ *n.* a slit made by cutting, esp. with a saw. —**kerfed** *adj.*
ker·nel /'kərnl/ ▶ *n.* a softer, usually edible part of a nut, seed, or fruit stone contained within its hard shell. ■ the seed and hard husk of a cereal, esp. wheat. ■ the central or most important part of something:

this is the kernel of the argument. ■ the most basic level or core of an operating system of a computer, responsible for resource allocation, file management, and security.

ker·o·sene /ˈkerəˌsēn; ˈkar-; ˌkerəˈsēn; ˌkar-/ (also *chiefly Brit.* **ker·o·sine**) ▶n. a light fuel oil obtained by distilling petroleum, used esp. in jet engines and domestic heaters and lamps and as a cleaning solvent.

kes·trel /ˈkestrəl/ ▶n. a small falcon (genus *Falco*) that hovers with rapidly beating wings while searching for prey on the ground.

ketch /kecH/ ▶n. a two-masted, fore-and-aft-rigged sailboat with a mizzenmast stepped forward of the rudder and smaller than the foremast.

ketch·up /ˈkecHəp/ (also **cat·sup**) ▶n. a spicy sauce made chiefly from tomatoes and vinegar, used as a condiment.

ke·tone /ˈkēˌtōn/ ▶n. *Chem.* an organic compound containing a carbonyl group =C=O bonded to two alkyl groups. The simplest ketone is acetone. —**ke·ton·ic** /kēˈtänik/ *adj.*

ke·to·sis /kēˈtōsis/ ▶n. *Med.* a condition characterized by raised levels of ketone bodies in the body, associated with abnormal fat metabolism and diabetes. —**ke·tot·ic** /-ˈtätik/ *adj.*

ket·tle /ˈketl/ ▶n. a vessel, usually made of metal and with a handle, used for boiling liquids or cooking foods; a pot. ■ a teakettle. ▷Old English *cetel, cietel,* of Germanic origin, based on Latin *catillus,* diminutive of *catinus* 'deep container for cooking or serving food.' In Middle English the word's form was influenced by Old Norse *ketill.* —**ket·tle·ful** /-ˌfool/ *n.* (*pl.* **-fuls**).

ket·tle·drum /ˈketlˌdrəm/ ▶n. a large drum shaped like a bowl, with a membrane adjustable for tension (and so pitch) stretched across. Also collectively called TIMPANI. —**ket·tle·drum·mer** *n.*

keV ▶*abbr.* kiloelectronvolt(s).

Kev·lar /ˈkevˌlär/ ▶n. *trademark* a synthetic fiber of high tensile strength used esp. as a reinforcing agent in the manufacture of tires and other rubber products and protective gear such as helmets and vests.

kew·pie /ˈkyoōpē/ (also **kewpie doll**) ▶n. *trademark* a type of doll characterized by a large head, big eyes, chubby cheeks, and a curl or topknot on top of its head.

kettledrum

key¹ /kē/ ▶n. (*pl.* **keys**) **1** a small piece of shaped metal with incisions cut to fit the wards of a particular lock, and that is inserted into a lock and turned to open or close it. ■ a similar implement for operating a switch in the form of a lock, esp. one operating the ignition of a motor vehicle. ■ short for KEY CARD. ■ an instrument for grasping and turning a screw, peg, or nut, esp. one for winding a clock or turning a valve. ■ a pin, bolt, or wedge inserted between other pieces, or fitting into a hole or space designed for it, so as to lock parts together. **2** one of several buttons on a panel for operating a typewriter, word processor, or computer terminal. ■ a lever depressed by the finger in playing an instrument such as the organ, piano, flute, or concertina. ■ a lever operating a mechanical device for making or breaking an electric circuit, for example, in telegraphy. **3** a thing that provides a means of gaining access to or understanding something: *the key to Jack's behavior may lie submerged in his unhappy past.* ■ an explanatory list of symbols used in a map, table, etc. ■ a set of answers to exercises or problems. ■ a word or system for solving a cipher or code. ■ the first move in the solution of a chess problem. ■ *Comput.* a field in a record that is used to identify that record uniquely. **4** *Mus.* a group of notes based on a particular note and comprising a scale, regarded as forming the tonal basis of a piece or passage of music: *the key of E minor.* ■ the tone or pitch of someone's voice: *his voice had changed to a lower key.* **5** the dry winged fruit of an ash, maple, or sycamore maple, typically growing in bunches; a samara. **6** *Basketball* the keyhole-shaped area marked on the court near each basket, comprising the free-throw circle and the foul line.

▶*adj.* of paramount or crucial importance: *she became a key figure in the suffragette movement.*

▶*v.* (**keys, keyed** /kēd/) [*tr.*] **1** enter or operate on (data) by means of a computer keyboard: *she keyed in a series of commands* | [*intr.*] *a hacker caused considerable disruption after keying into a vital database.* **2** [*tr.*] (**be keyed**) fasten (something) in position with a pin, wedge, or bolt: *the coils may be keyed into the slots by fiber wedges.* ■ (**key something to**) make something fit in with or be linked to: *this optimism is keyed to the possibility that the U.S. might lead in the research field.* ■ (**key someone/something into/in with**) cause someone or something to be in harmony with: *to those who are keyed into his lunatic sense of humor, the*

arrival of any Bergman movie is a major comic event. **3** word (an advertisement in a particular periodical), typically by varying the form of the address given, so as to identify the publication generating particular responses. **4** *inf.* be the crucial factor in achieving: *Ewing keyed a 73–35 advantage on the boards with twenty rebounds.* **5** [*tr.*] vandalize a car by scraping the paint from it with a key: *somebody could key your car and not get punished.*

▶*phrasal v.* □ **key someone up** (usu. **be keyed up**) make someone nervous, tense, or excited, esp. before an important event. —**keyed** *adj.* —**key·er** *n.* —**key·less** *adj.*

key² ▶*n.* a low-lying island or reef, esp. in the Caribbean. Compare with CAY.

key·board /ˈkēˌbôrd/ ▶n. **1** a panel of keys that operate a computer or typewriter. **2** a set of keys on a piano or similar musical instrument. ■ an electronic musical instrument with keys arranged as on a piano: *she plays keyboard and guitar.*

▶*v.* [*tr.*] enter (data) by means of a keyboard. —**key·board·er** *n.* —**key·board·ist** /-ist/ *n.*

key card ▶*n.* a small plastic card that can be used instead of a door key, bearing magnetically encoded data that can be read and processed by an electronic device.

key·hole /ˈkēˌhōl/ ▶n. a hole in a lock into which the key is inserted. ■ a circle cut out of a garment as a decorative effect, typically at the front or back neckline of a dress.

key·note /ˈkēˌnōt/ ▶n. a prevailing tone or central theme, typically one set or introduced at the start of a conference: *individuality is the keynote of the Nineties* | [as *adj.*] *he delivered the keynote address at the launch.* —**key·not·er** *n.*

key·pad /ˈkēˌpad/ ▶n. a miniature keyboard or set of buttons for operating a portable electronic device, telephone, or other equipment.

key·pal /ˈkēˌpal/ ▶n. (especially among students) a person with whom one becomes friendly by exchanging e-mails.

key·punch /ˈkēˌpənCH/ ▶n. a device for transferring data by means of punching holes or notches on a series of cards or paper tape.

▶*v.* [*tr.*] put into the form of punched cards or paper tape by means of such a device. —**key·punch·er** *n.*

key ring ▶*n.* a metal ring onto which keys may be threaded in order to keep them together.

key sig·na·ture ▶*n.* *Mus.* any of several combinations of sharps or flats after the clef at the beginning of each stave indicating the key of a composition.

key·stone /ˈkēˌstōn/ ▶n. a central stone at the summit of an arch, locking the whole together. ■ the central principle or part of a policy, system, etc., on which all else depends: *cooperation remains the keystone of the government's security policy.*

key·stroke /ˈkēˌstrōk/ ▶n. a single depression of a key on a keyboard, esp. as a measure of work.

key·word /ˈkēˌwərd/ ▶n. a word or concept of great significance: *homes and jobs are the keywords in the campaign.* ■ a word that acts as the key to a cipher or code. ■ an informative word used in an information retrieval system to indicate the content of a document. ■ a significant word mentioned in an index.

keystone

kg ▶*abbr.* ■ keg(s). ■ kilogram(s).

KGB ▶the state security police (1954–91) of the former USSR with responsibility for external espionage, internal counterintelligence, and internal "crimes against the state."

khak·i /ˈkakē/ ▶n. (*pl.* **khak·is**) a textile fabric of a dull brownish-yellow color, in particular a strong cotton fabric used in military clothing. ■ (**khakis**) clothing of this fabric and color.

khan /kän/ ▶n. a title given to rulers and officials in central Asia, Afghanistan, and certain other Muslim countries. —**khan·ate** /ˈkänät/ *n.*

Khmer /kəˈme(ə)r; kme(ə)r/ ▶n. **1** an ancient kingdom in Southeast Asia that reached the peak of its power in the 11th century, when it ruled the entire Mekong River valley from the capital at Angkor. It was destroyed by Thai conquests in the 12th and 14th centuries. **2** a native

---

Pronunciation Key ə *ago,* up; ər *over, fur;* a *hat;* ā *ate;* ä *car;* cH *chin;* e *let;* ē *see;* e(ə)r *air;* i *fit;* ī *by;* i(ə)r *ear;* NG *sing;* ō *go;* ô *law, for;* oi *toy;* oͦo *good;* ōͦo *goo;* ou *out;* sH *she;* TH *thin;* TH *then;* (h)w *why;* ZH *vision*

or inhabitant of the ancient Khmer kingdom. **3** a native or inhabitant of Cambodia. **4** the Mon-Khmer language that is the official language of Cambodia. Also called **CAMBODIAN**.
▸*adj.* of, relating to, or denoting the Khmers or their language.

kHz ▸*abbr.* kilohertz.

kib·beh /ˈkibē/ ▸*n.* a Middle Eastern dish of ground lamb with bulgar wheat and seasonings.

kib·ble /ˈkibəl/ ▸*n.* ground meal shaped into pellets, esp. for pet food.

kib·butz /kiˈbŏŏts/ ▸*n.* (*pl.* **kib·but·zim** /ki,bŏŏtˈsēm/) a communal settlement in Israel, typically a farm.

kib·itz /ˈkibits/ ▸*v.* [*intr.*] *inf.* look on and offer unwelcome advice, esp. at a card game. ▪ speak informally; chat: *she kibitzed with friends.* —**kib·itz·er** *n.*

ki·bosh /kəˈbäsн; ˈkīˌbäsн/ ▸*n.* (in phrase **put the kibosh on**) *inf.* put an end to; dispose of decisively: *he put the kibosh on the deal.*

kick /kik/ ▸*v.* **1** [*tr.*] strike or propel forcibly with the foot: *police kicked down the door.* ▪ [*intr.*] strike out or flail with the foot or feet: *she kicked out at him* | [*tr.*] *he kicked his feet free of a vine.* ▪ [*tr.*] (**kick oneself**) be annoyed with oneself for doing something foolish or missing an opportunity. ▪ [*tr.*] (in football, rugby, etc.) score (a goal) by a kick. ▪ [*intr.*] (of a gun) recoil when fired. **2** [*tr.*] *inf.* succeed in giving up (a habit or addiction).
▸*phrasal v.* □ **kick back** *inf.* be at leisure; relax. □ **kick in** (esp. of a device or drug) become activated; come into effect. □ **kick off** (of a football game, soccer game, etc.) be started or resumed after a score by a player kicking the ball from a designated spot. ▪ (of a team or player) begin or resume a game in this way. ▪ *inf.* (of an event) begin. □ **kick something off** *inf.* begin something: *the presidential primary kicks off the political year.*
▸*n.* **1** a blow or forceful thrust with the foot: *a kick in the head.* ▪ (in sports) an instance of striking the ball with the foot: *Ball blasted the kick wide.* ▪ the recoil of a gun when discharged. ▪ a sudden forceful jolt: *the shuttle accelerated with a kick.* **2** *inf.* the sharp stimulant effect of something, esp. alcohol. ▪ a thrill of pleasurable, often reckless excitement: *rich kids turning to crime just for kicks.* ▪ a specified temporary interest or enthusiasm: *the jogging kick.* —**kick·a·ble** *adj.* —**kick·er** *n.*
▸ □ **kick someone's ass** (or **butt**) *vulgar slang* beat, dominate, or defeat someone.

Kick·a·poo /ˈkikəˌpōō/ ▸*n.* (*pl.* same or **-poos**) **1** a member of an American Indian people formerly living in Wisconsin, and now in Kansas, Oklahoma, and north central Mexico. **2** the Algonquian language of this people.
▸*adj.* of or relating to this people or their language.

kick·back /ˈkik,bak/ ▸*n.* **1** a sudden forceful recoil: *the kickback from the gun punches your shoulder.* **2** *inf.* a payment made to someone who has facilitated a transaction or appointment, esp. illicitly.

kick·off /ˈkik,ôf/ ▸*n.* the start or resumption of a football game, in which a player kicks the ball from the center of the field: *three minutes before kickoff.* ▪ *inf.* a start of an event or activity.

kick·stand /ˈkik,stand/ ▸*n.* a metal rod attached to a bicycle or motorcycle, lying horizontally when not in use, that may be kicked into a vertical position to support the vehicle when it is stationary.

kick-start ▸*v.* [*tr.*] start (an engine on a motorcycle) with a downward thrust of a pedal. ▪ *fig.* provide the initial impetus to: *they need to kick-start the economy.*
▸*n.* (also **kick start** or **kick starter**) *fig.* an impetus given to get a process or thing started or restarted: *new investment will provide the kick-start needed to escape from recession.*

kid[1] /kid/ ▸*n.* **1** *inf.* a child or young person. ▪ used as an informal form of address: *we'll be seeing ya, kid!* **2** a young goat. ▪ leather made from a young goat's skin: *white kid gloves.*

kid[2] ▸*v.* (**kid·ded**, **kid·ding**) [*tr.*] *inf.* deceive (someone) in a playful or teasing way: *you're kidding me!* | [*intr.*] *we were just kidding around.* ▪ [*tr.*] deceive or fool (someone): *he likes to kid everyone he's the big macho tough guy.* —**kid·der** *n.* —**kid·ding·ly** *adv.*

kid·die /ˈkidē/ (also **kid·dy**) ▸*n.* (*pl.* **-dies**) *inf.* a young child.

kid·do /ˈkidō/ ▸*n.* (*pl.* **-dos** or **-does**) *inf.* used as a friendly or slightly condescending form of address.

kid gloves ▸*pl. n.* gloves made of fine kid leather. ▪ (also **kid-glove**) [as *adj.*] used in reference to careful and delicate treatment of a person or situation: *the star is getting kid-glove treatment.*

kid·nap /ˈkid,nap/ ▸*v.* (**-napped**, **-nap·ping**; also **-naped**, **-nap·ing**) [*tr.*] take (someone) away illegally by force, typically to obtain a ransom.
▸*n.* the action of kidnapping someone: *they were arrested for robbery and kidnap.* —**kid·nap·per** *n.*

kid·ney /ˈkidnē/ ▸*n.* (*pl.* **-neys**) each of a pair of organs in the abdominal cavity of mammals, birds, and reptiles, excreting urine. ▪ the kidney of a sheep, ox, or pig as food. ▪ temperament, nature, or kind: *I hoped that he would not prove of similar kidney.*

kid·ney bean ▸*n.* a kidney-shaped bean, esp. a dark red variety of the common bean plant *Phaseolus vulgaris.*

kiel·ba·sa /kilˈbäsə; kēl-/ ▸*n.* a type of highly seasoned Polish sausage, typically containing garlic.

kif /kif/ ▸*n. & adj.* variant spelling of **KEF**.

kill[1] /kil/ ▸*v.* [*tr.*] **1** cause the death of (a person, animal, or other living thing): *her father was killed in a car crash* | [*intr.*] *a robber armed with a shotgun who kills in cold blood.* ▪ put an end to or cause the failure or defeat of (something): *the committee voted to kill the project.* ▪ stop (a computer program or process). ▪ *inf.* switch off (a light or engine). ▪ *inf.* delete (a line, paragraph, or file) from a document or computer. ▪ (in soccer or other ball games) make (the ball) stop. ▪ (in tennis and similar games) hit (the ball) so forcefully that it cannot be returned. ▪ neutralize or subdue (an effect or quality): *the sauce would kill the taste of the herbs.* ▪ *inf.* consume the entire contents of (a bottle containing an alcoholic drink). **2** *inf.* overwhelm (someone) with an emotion: *the suspense is killing me.* ▪ (**kill oneself**) overexert oneself: *I killed myself carrying those things home.* ▪ used hyperbolically to indicate that someone is extremely angry with another person: *my parents will kill me if they catch me out here.* ▪ cause pain or anguish to: *my feet are killing me.* **3** pass (time, or a specified amount of it), typically while waiting for a particular event: *when he reached the station, he found he actually had an hour to kill.*
▸*n.* an act of killing, esp. of one animal by another: *a lion has made a kill.* ▪ an animal or animals killed, either by a hunter or by another animal: *the vulture is able to survey the land and locate a fresh kill.* ▪ *inf.* an act of destroying or disabling an enemy aircraft, submarine, tank, etc. ▪ (in tennis and similar games) a very forceful shot that cannot be returned.

kill[2] ▸*n.* [in place names] *chiefly New York State* a stream, creek, or tributary: *Kill Van Kull.*

kill·deer /ˈkil,di(ə)r/ (also **killdeer plover**) ▸*n.* a widespread American plover (*Charadrius vociferus*) with a plaintive call that resembles its name.

kill·er /ˈkilər/ ▸*n.* a person, animal, or thing that kills: *police are still searching for the killer* | [as *adj.*] *a killer virus.* ▪ *inf.* a formidable or excellent person or thing: *that wind's a killer.* ▪ *inf.* a hilarious joke.

kill·er bee ▸*n. inf.* an Africanized honeybee. See **AFRICANIZE** (sense 2).

kill·er cell ▸*n. Physiol.* a white blood cell (a type of lymphocyte) that destroys infected or cancerous cells.

kill·er in·stinct ▸*n.* a ruthless determination to succeed or win.

kill·er whale ▸*n.* another term for **ORCA**.

kill·ing /ˈkiliNG/ ▸*n.* an act of causing death, esp. deliberately.
▸*adj.* causing death: [in comb.] *weed-killing.* ▪ *inf.* exhausting; unbearable: *the suspense will be killing.* —**kill·ing·ly** *adv.*
▸ □ **make a killing** have a great financial success: *they're a safe investment, you can make a killing overnight.*

kill·joy /ˈkil,joi/ ▸*n.* a person who deliberately spoils the enjoyment of others through resentful or overly sober behavior.

kiln /kiln; kil/ ▸*n.* a furnace or oven for burning, baking, or drying, esp. one for calcining lime or firing pottery.
▸*v.* [*tr.*] burn, bake, or dry in a kiln. ▷*Old English cylene,* from Latin *culina* 'kitchen, cooking stove.'

ki·lo /ˈkēlō/ ▸*n.* (*pl.* **ki·los**) **1** a kilogram. **2** *rare* a kilometer. **3** a code word representing the letter K, used in radio communication.

kil·o·byte /ˈkilə,bīt/ (abbr.: **Kb** or **KB**) ▸*n. Comput.* a unit of memory or data equal to 1,024 (2^{10}) bytes.

kil·o·cal·o·rie /ˈkilə,kalərē/ ▸*n.* a unit of energy of 1,000 calories (equal to 1 large calorie).

kil·o·gram /ˈkilə,gram/ (*Brit.* also **kil·o·gramme**) (abbr.: **kg**) ▸*n.* the SI unit of mass, equivalent to the international standard kept at Sèvres near Paris (approx. 2.205 lb).

kil·o·hertz /ˈkilə,hərts/ (abbr.: **kHz**) ▸*n.* a measure of frequency equivalent to 1,000 cycles per second.

kil·o·me·ter /kiˈlämitər; ˈkilə,mētər/ (*Brit.* **kil·o·me·tre**) (abbr.: **km**) ▸*n.* a metric unit of measurement equal to 1,000 meters (approx. 0.62 miles). —**kil·o·met·ric** /,kiləˈmetrik/ *adj.*

kil·o·ton /ˈkilə,tən/ ▸*n.* a unit of explosive power equivalent to 1,000 tons of TNT.

kil·o·volt /ˈkilə,vōlt/ (abbr.: **kV**) ▸*n.* 1,000 volts.

kil·o·watt /ˈkiləˌwät/ (abbr.: **kW**) ▶*n.* a measure of 1,000 watts of electrical power.

kil·o·watt-hour (abbr.: **kWh**) ▶*n.* a measure of electrical energy equivalent to a power consumption of 1,000 watts for 1 hour.

kilt /kilt/ ▶*n.* a knee-length skirt of pleated tartan cloth, traditionally worn by men as part of Scottish Highland dress and now also worn by women and girls. —**kilt·ed** *adj.*

kil·ter /ˈkiltər/ ▶*n.* (in phrase **out of kilter**) out of harmony or balance: *daylight savings throws everybody's body clock out of kilter.*

kim·ber·lite /ˈkimbərˌlīt/ ▶*n.* Geol. a rare, blue-tinged, coarse-grained intrusive igneous rock sometimes containing diamonds, found esp. in South Africa and Siberia.

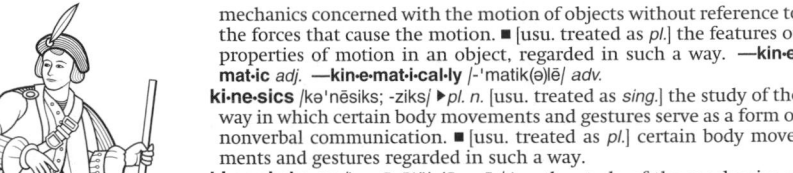

kilt

ki·mo·no /kəˈmōnō; -nə/ ▶*n.* (*pl.* **-nos**) a long, loose robe with wide sleeves and tied with a sash, originally worn as a formal garment in Japan and now also used elsewhere as a robe. —**ki·mo·noed** /-nōd; -nəd/ *adj.*

kin /kin/ ▶*n.* [treated as *pl.*] one's family and relations: *he is expected to make a payment to his wife's kin.* ■ a natural class, group, or division of people, animals, plants, etc., with shared attributes or ancestry.
▶*adj.* related: *he was **kin** to the brothers.* —**kin·less** *adj.*

kind¹ /kīnd/ ▶*n.* a group of people or things having similar characteristics: *all kinds of music.* ■ character; nature: *the trials were different **in kind** from any that preceded them.*
▶ □ **in kind** in the same way; with something similar: *if he responded positively, they would respond in kind.* ■ (of payment) in goods or services as opposed to money. □ **one of a kind** unique.

kind² ▶*adj.* having or showing a friendly, generous, and considerate nature: *she was a good, kind woman.* ■ used in a polite request: *would you be kind enough to repeat what you said?* ■ (**kind to**) (of a consumer product) gentle on (a part of the body): *look for rollers that are kind to hair.* ■ archaic affectionate; loving.

kind·a /ˈkīndə/ *inf.* ▶*contr. of* kind of: *I think it's kinda funny.*

kin·der·gar·ten /ˈkindərˌgärtn; -ˌgärdn/ ▶*n.* a school or class that prepares children for first grade. A child in kindergarten is typically 5 or 6 years old. —**kin·der·gar·ten·er** /-ˌgärtnər; -ˌgärd-/ (also **kin·der·gart·ner**) *n.*

kind·heart·ed /ˈkīndˈhärtid/ ▶*adj.* having a kind and sympathetic nature. —**kind·heart·ed·ly** *adv.* —**kind·heart·ed·ness** *n.*

kin·dle /ˈkindl/ ▶*v.* [*tr.*] light or set on fire. ■ arouse or inspire (an emotion or feeling): *a love of art was kindled in me.* ■ [*intr.*] (of an emotion) be aroused: *she hesitated, suspicion kindling within her.* ■ [*intr.*] become impassioned or excited: *the young man kindled all at once.* —**kin·dler** *n.*

kin·dling /ˈkindliNG/ ▶*n.* **1** easily combustible small sticks or twigs used for starting a fire. **2** (in neurology) a process by which a seizure or other brain event is both initiated and its recurrence made more likely.

kind·ly /ˈkīn(d)lē/ ▶*adv.* in a kind manner: *"Never mind," she said kindly.* ■ please (used in a polite request or demand, often ironically): *will you kindly sign the enclosed copy of this letter.*
▶*adj.* (**-li·er**, **-li·est**) kind; warmhearted; gentle: *he was a quiet, kindly man.* —**kind·li·ness** *n.*

kind·ness /ˈkīn(d)nis/ ▶*n.* the quality of being friendly, generous, and considerate. ■ a kind act: *it is a kindness I shall never forget.*

kin·dred /ˈkindrid/ ▶*n.* [treated as *pl.*] one's family and relations. ■ relationship by blood: *ties of kindred.*
▶*adj.* similar in kind; related: *books on kindred subjects.*

kin·e·mat·ics /ˌkinəˈmatiks/ ▶*pl. n.* [usu. treated as *sing.*] the branch of

mechanics concerned with the motion of objects without reference to the forces that cause the motion. ■ [usu. treated as *pl.*] the features or properties of motion in an object, regarded in such a way. —**kin·e·mat·ic** *adj.* —**kin·e·mat·i·cal·ly** /-'matik(ə)lē/ *adv.*

ki·ne·sics /kəˈnēsiks; -ziks/ ▶*pl. n.* [usu. treated as *sing.*] the study of the way in which certain body movements and gestures serve as a form of nonverbal communication. ■ [usu. treated as *pl.*] certain body movements and gestures regarded in such a way.

ki·ne·si·ol·o·gy /kəˌnēsēˈäləjē; -zē-/ ▶*n.* the study of the mechanics of body movements. —**ki·ne·si·o·log·i·cal** /-sēəˈläjikəl; -zēə-/ *adj.* —**ki·ne·si·ol·o·gist** /-jist/ *n.*

ki·net·ic /kəˈnetik/ ▶*adj.* of, relating to, or resulting from motion. ■ (of a work of art) depending on movement for its effect. ▷mid 19th cent.: from Greek *kinētikos,* from *kinein* 'to move.' —**ki·net·i·cal·ly** /-ik(ə)lē/ *adv.*

ki·net·ic en·er·gy ▶*n.* Physics energy that a body possesses by virtue of being in motion.

ki·net·ics /kəˈnetiks/ ▶*pl. n.* [usu. treated as *sing.*] the branch of chemistry or biochemistry concerned with measuring and studying the rates of reactions. ■ [usu. treated as *pl.*] the rates of chemical or biochemical reaction. ■ Physics the study of forces acting on mechanisms.

kin·folk /ˈkinˌfōk/ (also **kins·folk** /ˈkinz-/ or **kin·folks**) ▶*pl. n.* a person's blood relations, regarded collectively. ■ a group of people related by blood: *a set of kinfolk.*

king /kiNG/ ▶*n.* **1** the male ruler of an independent state, esp. one who inherits the position by right of birth: [as *title*] *King Henry VIII.* ■ a person or thing regarded as the finest or most important in its sphere or group: *a country where football is king.* ■ used in names of animals and plants that are particularly large, e.g., **king cobra.** **2** the most important chess piece, of which each player has one, which the opponent has to checkmate in order to win. The king can move in any direction, including diagonally, to any adjacent square that is not attacked by an opponent's piece or pawn. ■ a piece in the game of checkers with extra capacity for moving, made by crowning an ordinary piece that has reached the opponent's baseline. ■ a playing card bearing a representation of a king, normally ranking next below an ace. —**king·li·ness** *n.* —**king·ly** *adj.* —**king·ship** /-ˌSHip/ *n.*
▶ □ **live like a king** (or **queen**) live in great comfort and luxury.

king·bird /ˈkiNGˌbərd/ ▶*n.* a large American tyrant flycatcher (genus *Tyrannus,* several species), typically with a gray head and back and yellowish or white underparts.

King Charles span·iel ▶*n.* a spaniel of a small breed, typically with a white, black, and tan coat.

king co·bra ▶*n.* a cobra (*Ophiophagus hannah*), native to the Indian subcontinent, the largest of all venomous snakes. Also called **HAMADRYAD.**

king crab ▶*n.* **1** another term for HORSESHOE CRAB. **2** an edible crab (genus *Paralithodes,* family Lithodidae) of the North Pacific, resembling a spider crab.

king·dom /ˈkiNGdəm/ ▶*n.* **1** a country, state, or territory ruled by a king or queen: ■ a realm associated with or regarded as being under the control of a particular person or thing: *the kingdom of dreams.* **2** the spiritual reign or authority of God. **3** each of the three traditional divisions (animal, vegetable, and mineral) in which natural objects have conventionally been classified. ■ Biol. the highest category in taxonomic classification.

king·fish /ˈkiNGˌfiSH/ ▶*n.* (*pl.* same or **-fish·es**) **1** any of a number of large sporting fish, many of which are edible: ■ a fish of the jack family, including the **yellowtail kingfish** (*Seriola grandis*) of the South Pacific. ■ (**northern kingfish**) a fish (*Menticirrhus saxatilis*) of the drum family, of the east coast of North America. ■ a western Atlantic fish (*Scomberomorus cavalla*) of the mackerel family. **2** inf. a person regarded as an authority figure; an influential leader or boss.

king·fish·er /ˈkiNGˌfiSHər/ ▶*n.* an often brightly colored bird (family Alcedinidae) with a long sharp beak, typically diving for fish from a perch.

King James Bi·ble (also **King James Version**) ▶*n.* an English translation of the Bible made in 1611 at the order of King James I and still widely used.

king·let /ˈkiNGlit/ ▶*n.* a very small greenish bird (genus *Regulus,* family Sylviidae) with a bright orange or yellow crown.

king·pin /ˈkiNGˌpin/ ▶*n.* a main or large bolt in a central position. ■ a vertical bolt used as a pivot. ■ a person or thing that is essential to the

kimono

success of an organization or operation: *the kingpins of the television industry.*

king-sized (also **king-size**) ▶*adj.* (esp. of a commercial product) of a larger size than the standard; very large: *a king-sized bed.*

kink /kiNGk/ ▶*n.* a sharp twist or curve in something that is otherwise straight: *a kink in the road.* ■ *fig.* a flaw or obstacle in a plan, operation, etc.: *though the system is making some headway, there are still some kinks to iron out.* ■ a stiffness in the neck, back, etc.; crick: *it takes the kinks out of stiff necks.* ■ *fig.* a quirk of character or behavior. ■ *inf.* a person with unusual sexual preferences.
▶*v.* [*tr.*] form or cause to form a sharp twist or curve: *when the spine gets kinked, the muscles react with pain.*

kin·ka·jou /'kiNGkə,joō/ ▶*n.* an arboreal nocturnal fruit-eating mammal (*Potos flavus*) of the raccoon family, with a prehensile tail and a long tongue, found in the tropical forests of Central and South America.

kink·y /'kiNGkē/ ▶*adj.* (**kink·i·er, kink·i·est**) **1** *inf.,* involving or given to unusual sexual behavior. ■ (of clothing) sexually provocative in an unusual way: *kinky underwear.* **2** having kinks or twists: *long and kinky hair.* —**kink·i·ly** /-kilē/ *adv.* —**kink·i·ness** *n.*

kins·folk /'kinz,fōk/ ▶*pl. n.* another term for KINFOLK.

kin·ship /'kin,SHip/ ▶*n.* blood relationship. ■ a sharing of characteristics or origins: *they felt a kinship with architects.*

kins·man /'kinzmən/ ▶*n.* (*pl.* **-men**) one of a person's blood relations, esp. a male.

ki·osk /'kē,äsk/ ▶*n.* a small open-fronted hut or cubicle from which newspapers, refreshments, tickets, etc., are sold.

Ki·o·wa /'kīəwə/ ▶*n.* (*pl.* same or **-was**) **1** a member of an American Indian people of the southern plains of the U.S., now living mainly in Oklahoma. **2** the language of this people, related to the Tanoan group. **3** (in full **Kiowa Apache**) an Athabaskan (Apache) language of western Oklahoma and neighboring areas.
▶*adj.* of or relating to this people or these languages.

kip·per /'kipər/ ▶*n.* a kippered fish, esp. a herring.
▶*v.* [*tr.*] [usu. as *adj.*] (**kippered**) cure (a herring or other fish) by splitting it open and salting and drying it in the open air or in smoke.

Kir /ki(ə)r/ (also **kir**) ▶*n.* *trademark* a drink made from dry white wine and crème de cassis.

kirk /kərk/ ▶*n. Scot. & N. English* a church.

kirsch /ki(ə)rSH/ (also **kirsch·wa·sser** /-,väsər/) ▶*n.* brandy distilled from the fermented juice of cherries. ▷German, abbreviation of *Kirschenwasser,* from *Kirsche* 'cherry' + *Wasser* 'water.'

kis·met /'kizmit; -,met/ ▶*n.* destiny; fate: *what chance did I stand against kismet?*

kiss /kis/ ▶*v.* [*tr.*] touch with the lips as a sign of love, sexual desire, reverence, or greeting: *he kissed her on the lips* | [*tr.*] *she kissed the children good-night* | [*intr.*] *we started kissing.* ■ *Billiards* (of a ball) lightly touch (another ball) in passing.
▶*phrasal v.* ■ **kiss someone/something off** *inf.* dismiss someone rudely; end a relationship abruptly. □ **kiss up to** *inf.* behave sycophantically or obsequiously toward (someone) in order to obtain something.
▶*n.* **1** a touch with the lips in kissing. ■ *Billiards* a slight touch of a ball against another ball. ■ used to express affection at the end of a letter (conventionally represented by the letter X): *she sent lots of love and a whole line of kisses.* **2** a small cake or cookie, typically a meringue. ■ a small candy, esp. one made of chocolate. —**kiss·a·ble** *adj.*
▶ □ **kiss and tell** *chiefly derog.* recount one's sexual exploits, esp. to the media concerning a famous person: [as *adj.*] *this isn't a kiss-and-tell book.* □ **kiss something good-bye** *inf.* accept the certain loss of something: *I could kiss my career good-bye.* □ **kiss of death** an action or event that causes certain failure for an enterprise: *it would be the kiss of death for the company if it could be proved that the food was unsafe.*

kiss·er /'kisər/ ▶*n.* **1** a person who kisses someone: *he's a good kisser.* **2** *inf.* a person's mouth: *I belted him one, right on the kisser.*

kiss·ing cous·in ▶*n.* a relative known well enough to be given a kiss in greeting.

kiss·y /'kisē/ ▶*adj. inf.* characterized by or given to kissing; amorous: *Dean and I were just getting kissy.*

Ki·swa·hi·li /,kiswä'hēlē/ ▶*n.* another term for SWAHILI (sense 1).

kit¹ /kit/ ▶*n.* a set of articles or equipment needed for a specific purpose: *a first-aid kit.* ■ a set of all the parts needed to assemble something: *an aircraft kit.* ■ *Brit.* the clothing and other items belonging to a soldier or used in an activity such as a sport: *boys in football kit.*

kit² ▶*n.* the young of certain animals, such as the beaver, fox, ferret, and mink. ■ informal term for KITTEN.

kit bag (also **kit·bag**) ▶*n.* a rectangular canvas bag, used esp. for carrying a soldier's clothes and personal possessions.

kitch·en /'kiCHən/ ▶*n.* **1** a room or area where food is prepared and cooked. ■ a set of fixtures, cabinets, and appliances that are sold together and installed in such a room or area: *a complete kitchen at a bargain price.* ■ cuisine: *the dried shrimp pastes of the Thai kitchen.* **2** [as *adj.*] (of a language) in an uneducated or domestic form: *kitchen Swahili.*

kitch·en cab·i·net ▶*n.* a group of unofficial advisers to the holder of an elected office who are considered to be unduly influential.

kitch·en·ette /,kiCHə'net/ ▶*n.* a small kitchen or part of a room equipped as a kitchen.

kitch·en·ware /'kiCHən,we(ə)r/ ▶*n.* the utensils used in a kitchen.

kite /kīt/ ▶*n.* **1** a toy consisting of a light frame with thin material stretched over it, flown in the wind at the end of a long string. **2** a medium to large long-winged bird of prey (family Accipitridae) that typically has a forked tail and frequently soars on updrafts of air. **3** *inf.* a fraudulent check, bill, or receipt. ■ an illicit or surreptitious letter or note.
▶*v.* [*tr.*] *inf.* write or use (a check, bill, or receipt) fraudulently.
▶ □ (as) **high as a kite** *inf.* intoxicated with drugs or alcohol.

kite·board·ing /'kīt,bôrdiNG/ ▶*n.* another term for KITESURFING. —**kite·board·er** *n.*

kite·surf·ing /'kīt,sərfiNG/ ▶*n.* the sport or pastime of riding on a modified surfboard while holding on to a specially designed kite, using the wind for propulsion. Also called KITEBOARDING. —**kite·surf·er** *n.*

kith /kiTH/ ▶*n.* (in phrase **kith and kin** or **kith or kin**) one's friends, acquaintances, and relations: *a widow without kith or kin.*

kitsch /kiCH/ ▶*n.* art, objects, or design considered to be in poor taste because of excessive garishness or sentimentality, but sometimes appreciated in an ironic or knowing way: *the lava lamp is an example of sixties kitsch* | [as *adj.*] *kitsch decor.* —**kitsch·i·ness** *n.* —**kitsch·y** *adj.*

kit·ten /'kitn/ ▶*n.* a young cat. ■ the young of several other animals, such as the rabbit and beaver.
▶ □ **have kittens** *inf.* be extremely nervous or upset.

kit·ten·ish /'kitn-iSH/ ▶*adj.* playful, lively, or flirtatious: *her voice had that kittenish quality.* —**kit·ten·ish·ly** *adv.* —**kit·ten·ish·ness** *n.*

kit·ti·wake /'kitē,wāk/ ▶*n.* a small gull (genus *Rissa,* family Laridae) that nests in colonies on sea cliffs. Two species include the black-legged *Rissa tridactyla* of the North Atlantic and North Pacific.

kit·ty¹ /'kitē/ ▶*n.* (*pl.* **-ties**) a fund of money for communal use, made up of contributions from a group of people. ■ a pool of money in some gambling card games.

kit·ty² ▶*n.* (*pl.* **-ties**) a pet name or a child's name for a kitten or cat.

kit·ty-cor·ner ▶*adj. & adv.* another term for CATER-CORNERED.

ki·wi /'kēwē/ ▶*n.* (*pl.* **ki·wis**) **1** a flightless New Zealand bird (genus *Apteryx,* family Apterygidae) with hairlike feathers, having a long down-curved bill with sensitive nostrils at the tip. **2** (**Kiwi**) *inf.* a New Zealander, esp. a soldier or member of a national sports team.

ki·wi fruit (also **ki·wi·fruit**) ▶*n.* (*pl.* same) a fruit with a thin hairy skin, green flesh, and black seeds, obtained from the eastern Asian climbing plant *Actinidia chinensis* (family Actinidiaceae).

KKK ▶*abbr.* Ku Klux Klan.

klep·to·ma·ni·a /,kleptə'mānēə; -'mānyə/ ▶*n.* a recurrent urge to steal, typically without regard for need or profit. —**klep·to·ma·ni·ac** /-'mānē-,ak/ *n. & adj.*

kludge /kloōj/ (also **kluge**) *inf.* ▶*n.* an ill-assorted collection of parts assembled to fulfill a particular purpose. ■ *Comput.* a machine, system, or program that has been badly put together.
▶*v.* [*tr.*] use ill-assorted parts to make (something): *Hugh had to kludge something together.*

klutz /kləts/ ▶*n. inf.* a clumsy, awkward, or foolish person. —**klutz·i·ness** *n.* —**klutz·y** *adj.*

km ▶*abbr.* kilometer(s).

K-me·son ▶*n.* another term for KAON.

knack /nak/ ▶*n.* an acquired or natural skill at performing a task: *she got the knack of it in the end.* ■ a tendency to do something: *the band has a knack of warping classic soul songs.*

knack·wurst /'näk,wərst/ (also **knock·wurst**) ▶*n.* a type of short, fat, highly seasoned German sausage.

knap·sack /'nap,sak/ ▶*n.* a bag with shoulder straps, carried on the back, and typically made of canvas or other weatherproof material.

knave /nāv/ ▶*n. archaic* a dishonest or unscrupulous man. ▷Old English *cnafa* 'boy, servant'; related to German *Knabe* 'boy.' —**knav·er·y** /-vərē/ *n.* (*pl.* **-er·ies**) —**knav·ish** *adj.* —**knav·ish·ly** *adv.* —**knav·ish·ness** *n.*

knead /nēd/ ▶*v.* [*tr.*] work (moistened flour or clay) into dough or paste with the hands. ■ make (bread or pottery) by such a process. ■ massage or squeeze with the hands: *she kneaded his back.* —**knead·a·ble** *adj.* —**knead·er** *n.*

knee /nē/ ▶*n.* the joint between the thigh and the lower leg in humans. ■ the corresponding or analogous joint in other animals. ■ the upper surface of someone's thigh when sitting; a person's lap: *they were eating their supper on their knees.* ■ the part of a garment covering the knee. ■ an angled piece of wood or metal frame used to connect and support the beams and timbers of a wooden vessel; a triangular plate serving the same purpose in a modern vessel. ■ an abrupt obtuse or approximately right-angled bend in a graph between parts where the slope varies smoothly.
▶*v.* (**knees, kneed, knee·ing**) [*tr.*] hit (someone) with one's knee: *she kneed him in the groin.*
▶ □ **on one's knees** in a kneeling position. ■ *fig.* on the verge of collapse: *when they took over, the newspaper was on its knees.* □ **weak at the knees** overcome by a strong feeling, typically desire.

knee·cap /'nē,kap/ ▶*n.* the convex bone in front of the knee joint; the patella.
▶*v.* (**-capped, -cap·ping**) [*tr.*] shoot (someone) in the knee or leg as a form of punishment: [as *n.*] (**kneecapping**) *petty crimes are punished by kneecapping.*

knee-deep ▶*adj.* immersed up to the knees: *we were knee-deep in snow.* ■ having more than one needs or wants of something: *we shall soon be knee-deep in conflicting legal views.* ■ so deep as to reach the knees: *the water was knee-deep on Main Street.*
▶*adv.* so as to be immersed up to the knees: *I plodded knee-deep through the mud.*

knee·hole /'nē,hōl/ ▶*n.* a space for the knees, esp. one under a desk: [as *adj.*] *a kneehole desk.*

knee-jerk ▶*n.* a sudden involuntary reflex kick caused by a blow on the tendon just below the knee.
▶*adj.* (of a response) automatic and unthinking: *a knee-jerk reaction.* ■ (of a person) responding in this way: *knee-jerk radicals.*

kneel /nēl/ ▶*v.* (*past* and *past part.* **knelt** /nelt/ also **kneeled**) [*intr.*] (of a person) be in or assume a position in which the body is supported by a knee or the knees, typically as a sign of reverence or submission: *they knelt down and prayed.*

knell /nel/ *poetic/lit.* ▶*n.* the sound of a bell, esp. when rung solemnly for a death or funeral. ■ *fig.* used with reference to an announcement, event, or sound that is regarded as a solemn warning of the end of something: *the decision will probably toll the knell for the facility.*
▶*v.* [*intr.*] (of a bell) ring solemnly, esp. for a death or funeral.

knelt /nelt/ ▶ past and past participle of KNEEL.

knew /n(y)oo/ ▶ past of KNOW.

knick·ers /'nikərz/ ▶*pl. n.* **1** (also **knick·er·bock·ers** /-,bäkərz/) loose-fitting trousers gathered at the knee or calf. **2** *Brit.* a woman's or girl's underpants.

knick·knack /'nik,nak/ (also **knick-knack**) ▶*n.* (usu. **knickknacks**) a small worthless object, esp. a household ornament. —**knick·knack·er·y** /-,nakərē/ *n.*

knife /nīf/ ▶*n.* (*pl.* **knives** /nīvz/) a cutting instrument composed of a blade and a handle into which it is fixed, either rigidly or with a joint. ■ an instrument such as this used as a weapon. ■ a cutting blade forming part of a machine.
▶*v.* [*tr.*] stab (someone) with a knife. ■ [*intr.*] cut like a knife: *a shard of steel knifed through the mainsail.* —**knife-like** /-,līk/ *adj.* —**knif·er** *n.*

knife pleat ▶*n.* a sharp, narrow pleat on a skirt made in one direction and typically overlapping another.

knife-point /'nīf,point/ ▶*n.* the pointed end of a knife.

knight /nīt/ ▶*n.* **1** (in the Middle Ages) a man who served his sovereign or lord as a mounted soldier in armor. ■ (in the Middle Ages) a man raised by a sovereign to honorable military rank after service as a page and squire. **2** (in the UK) a man awarded a nonhereditary title by the sovereign in recognition of merit or service and entitled to use the honorific "Sir" in front of his name. **3** a chess piece, typically with its top shaped like a horse's head, that moves by jumping to the opposite corner of a rectangle two squares by three.
▶*v.* [*tr.*] (usu. **be knighted**) invest (someone) with the title of knight. —**knight·hood** *n.* —**knight·li·ness** *n.* —**knight·ly** *adj.* & (*poetic/lit.*) *adv.*

knight-er·rant (also **knight er·rant**) ▶*n.* (*pl.* **knights-er·rant**) a medieval knight wandering in search of chivalrous adventures. —**knight-er·rant·ry** *n.*

knish /k(ə)'nish/ ▶*n.* a dumpling of dough that is stuffed with a filling and baked or fried.

knit /nit/ ▶*v.* (**knit·ting**; *past* and *past part.* **knit·ted** or (esp. in sense 2) **knit**) **1** [*tr.*] make (a garment, blanket, etc.) by interlocking loops of wool or other yarn with knitting needles or on a machine. ■ make (a stitch or row of stitches) in such a way. ■ knit with a knit stitch: *knit one, purl one.* **2** [*intr.*] become united: *disparate regions had begun to knit together under the king* | [as *adj.*] (**knit**) *a closely knit family.* ■ (of parts of a broken bone) become joined during healing. ■ [*tr.*] cause to unite or combine: *he knitted together a squad of players from other clubs had disregarded.* **3** [*tr.*] tighten (one's brow or eyebrows) in a frown of concentration, disapproval, or anxiety. ■ [*intr.*] (of someone's brow or eyebrows) tighten in such a frown.
▶*adj.* denoting or relating to a knitting stitch made by putting the needle through the front of the stitch from left to right. Compare with PURL1.
▶*n.* a knitted fabric: *a machine-washable knit.* ■ a garment made of such fabric: *an array of casual knits.* ▷Old English *cnyttan*; related to German dialect *knütten*, also to KNOT1. The original sense was 'tie in or with a knot,' hence 'join, unite' (sense 2); an obsolete Middle English sense 'knot string to make a net' gave rise to sense 1. —**knit·ter** *n.*

knit·ting /'niting/ ▶*n.* the craft or action of knitting. ■ material that is in the process of being knitted: *I put down my knitting.*

knit·ting nee·dle ▶*n.* a long, thin, pointed rod used as part of a pair for knitting by hand.

knit·wear /'nit,we(ə)r/ ▶*n.* knitted garments.

knives /nīvz/ ▶ plural form of KNIFE.

knob /näb/ ▶*n.* a rounded lump or ball, esp. at the end or on the surface of something. ■ a handle on a door or drawer shaped like a ball. ■ a rounded button for adjusting or controlling a machine. ■ a small lump of a substance: *add a knob of butter or margarine.* ■ a prominent round hill. ■ *vulgar slang* a penis. —**knobbed** *adj.* —**knob·by** *adj.* —**knob·like** /-,līk/ *adj.*

knock /näk/ ▶*v.* **1** [*intr.*] strike a surface noisily to attract attention, esp. when waiting to be let in through a door: *I knocked on the kitchen door.* ■ strike or thump together or against something: *my knees were knocking and my lips quivering.* ■ (of a motor or other engine) make a regular thumping or rattling noise because of improper ignition. **2** [*tr.*] collide with (someone or something), giving them a hard blow: *he deliberately ran into her, knocking her shoulder* | [*intr.*] *he knocked into an elderly man.* ■ [*tr.*] force to move or fall with a deliberate or accidental blow or collision: *he'd knocked over a glass of water.* ■ injure or damage by striking: *she knocked her knee painfully on the table.* ■ make (a hole or a dent) in something by striking it forcefully: *he suggests we knock a hole through the wall into the broom closet.* ■ *inf.* talk disparagingly about; criticize.
▶*n.* **1** a sudden short sound caused by a blow, esp. on a door to attract attention or gain entry. ■ a continual thumping or rattling sound made by an engine because of improper ignition. **2** a blow or collision: *the casing is tough enough to withstand knocks.* ■ an injury caused by a blow or collision. ■ a discouraging experience; a setback: *the region's industries have taken a severe knock.* ■ *inf.* a critical comment.
▶ □ **knock it off** *inf.* used to tell someone to stop doing something that one finds annoying or foolish.

knock·a·bout /'näkə,bout/ ▶*adj.* **1** denoting a rough, slapstick comic performance. **2** (of clothes) suitable for rough use.
▶*n.* **1** a rough, slapstick comic performance. **2** a tramp or vagrant.

knock·down /'näk,doun/ (also **knock-down**) ▶*adj.* **1** *inf.* (of a price) very low. **2** capable of knocking down or overwhelming someone or something: *repeated knockdown blows.* ■ (of furniture) easily dismantled and reassembled.
▶*n.* *Boxing* an act of knocking an opponent down. ■ (also **knockdown pitch**) *Baseball* a pitch aimed so close to the body that the batter must drop to the ground to avoid being hit: *the catcher gave the sign for a knockdown pitch.*

knock·er /'näkər/ ▶*n.* **1** short for DOOR KNOCKER. **2** *inf.* a person who continually finds fault. **3** (**knockers**) *vulgar slang* a woman's breasts.

knock knees ▶*pl. n.* a condition in which the legs curve inward so that the feet are apart when the knees are touching. —**knock-kneed** *adj.*

knock·out /'näk,out/ ▶*n.* an act of knocking someone out, esp. in boxing: [as *adj.*] *a knockout blow.* ■ *inf.* an extremely attractive or impressive person or thing: *he must have been a knockout when he was young.*

knock·wurst /'näk,wərst/ ▶*n.* variant spelling of KNACKWURST.

knoll /nōl/ ▶*n.* a small hill or mound.

---

knot[1] /nät/ ▸ n. **1** a fastening made by tying a piece of string, rope, or something similar. ▪ a particular method of tying a knot: *you need to master two knots, the clove hitch and the sheet bend.* ▪ a tangled mass in something such as hair. ▪ a complex and intractable problem: *a complicated knot of racial politics and pride.* ▪ a tied or folded ribbon, worn as an ornament. **2** a knob, protuberance, or node in a stem, branch, or root. ▪ a hard mass formed in a tree trunk at the intersection with a branch, resulting in a round cross-grained piece in timber when cut through. ▪ a hard lump of tissue in an animal or human body. ▪ a tense constricted feeling in the body: *the knot of tension at the back of her neck.* ▪ a small tightly packed group of people: *the little knot of people clustered around the doorway.* **3** a unit of speed equivalent to one nautical mile per hour, used esp. of ships, aircraft, and winds.
▸ v. (**knot·ted, knot·ting**) [*tr.*] **1** fasten with a knot: *the scarves were knotted loosely around their throats.* ▪ make (a carpet or other decorative item) with knots. ▪ make (something, esp. hair) tangled. **2** cause (a muscle) to become tense and hard. ▪ [*intr.*] (of the stomach) tighten as a result of nervousness or tension. —**knot·less** *adj.* —**knot·ter** *n.*
▸ □ **tie the knot** *inf.* get married.

knot[2] ▸ n. (*pl.* same or **knots**) a small, relatively short-billed sandpiper (genus *Calidris*) with a reddish-brown or blackish breast in the breeding season.

knot·hole /ˈnätˌhōl/ ▸ n. a hole in a piece of timber where a knot has fallen out, or in a tree trunk where a branch has decayed.

knot·ting /ˈnätiNG/ ▸ n. the action or craft of tying knots in yarn or string to make carpets or other decorative items. ▪ the knots tied in a carpet or other item.

knot·ty /ˈnätē/ ▸ adj. (**knot·ti·er, knot·ti·est**) full of knots: *the room was paneled in knotty pine.* ▪ (of a problem or matter) extremely difficult or intricate. —**knot·ti·ly** /ˈnätəlē/ *adv.* —**knot·ti·ness** *n.*

know /nō/ ▸ v. (*past* **knew** /n(y)o͞o/; *past part.* **known** /nōn/) **1** be aware of through observation, inquiry, or information: *most people now know that CFCs can damage the ozone layer.* ▪ [*tr.*] have knowledge or information concerning: *I would write to him if I knew his address* [*intr.*] *I know of one local who shot himself.* ▪ be absolutely certain or sure about something: *I just knew it was something I wanted to do* [*tr.*] *I knew it!* **2** [*tr.*] have developed a relationship with (someone) through meeting and spending time with them; be familiar or friendly with: *he knew and respected Laura.* ▪ have a good command of (a subject or language). ▪ recognize (someone or something): *Isabel couldn't hear the words clearly, but she knew the voice.* ▪ be familiar or acquainted with (something): *a little restaurant she knew near Times Square.* ▪ have personal experience of (an emotion or situation): *a man who had known better times.* ▪ (usu. **be known as**) regard or perceive as having a specified characteristic: *he is also known as an amateur painter.* ▪ (usu. **be known as**) give (someone or something) a particular name or title: *the doctor was universally known as "Hubert."* ▷Old English *cnāwan* (earlier *gecnāwan*) 'recognize, identify,' of Germanic origin; from an Indo-European root shared by Latin (*g*)*noscere,* Greek *gignōskein.* —**know·a·ble** *adj.* —**know·er** *n.*
▸ □ **be in the know** be aware of something known only to a few people: *he had a tip from a friend in the know: the horse was a sure bet.* □ **know one's own mind** be decisive and certain. □ **know one's way around** be familiar with (an area, procedure, or subject).

know-how ▸ n. practical knowledge or skill; expertise: *technical know-how.*

know·ing /ˈnōiNG/ ▸ adj. showing or suggesting that one has knowledge or awareness that is secret or known to only a few people: *a knowing smile.* ▪ *chiefly derog.* experienced or shrewd, esp. excessively or prematurely so: *today's society is too knowing, too corrupt.* ▪ done in full awareness or consciousness: *a knowing breach of the order by the appellants.*
▸ n. the state of being aware or informed. —**know·ing·ly** *adv.* —**know·ing·ness** *n.*

know-it-all ▸ n. *inf.* a person who behaves as if they know everything.

knowl·edge /ˈnälij/ ▸ n. **1** facts, information, and skills acquired by a person through experience or education; the theoretical or practical understanding of a subject: *a thirst for knowledge.* ▪ what is known in a particular field or in total; facts and information: *the transmission of knowledge.* ▪ *Philos.* true, justified belief; certain understanding, as opposed to opinion. **2** awareness or familiarity gained by experience of a fact or situation: *the program had been developed without his knowledge.*
▸ adj. relating to organized information stored electronically or digitally: *the knowledge economy.*

knowl·edge·a·ble /ˈnälijəbəl/ (also **knowl·edg·a·ble**) ▸ adj. intelligent and well informed: *she is very knowledgeable about livestock and pedigrees.* —**know·ledge·a·bil·i·ty** /ˌnälijəˈbilitē/ *n.* —**know·ledge·a·bly** /-blē/ *adv.*

known /nōn/ ▸ past participle of **KNOW**.
▸ adj. recognized, familiar, or within the scope of knowledge: *crustaceans little known to nonprofessionals.* ▪ publicly acknowledged to be: *a known criminal.* ▪ *Math.* (of a quantity or variable) having a value that can be stated.

know-noth·ing ▸ n. **1** an ignorant person. **2** (**Know-Nothing**) *hist.* a member of a political party in the U.S., prominent from 1853 to 1856, that was antagonistic toward Roman Catholics and recent immigrants and whose members preserved its secrecy by denying its existence. —**know-noth·ing·ism** *n.*

knuck·le /ˈnəkəl/ ▸ n. a part of a finger at a joint where the bone is near the surface, esp. where the finger joins the hand: *Charlotte rapped on the window with her knuckles.* ▪ a projection of the carpal or tarsal joint of a quadruped. ▪ a cut of meat consisting of such a projection together with the adjoining parts: *a knuckle of pork.*
▸ v. [*tr.*] rub or press (something, esp. the eyes) with the knuckles.
▸ *phrasal v.* □ **knuckle down 1** apply oneself seriously to a task. **2** (also **knuckle under**) give in; submit. ▷Middle English *knokel* (originally denoting the rounded shape when a joint such as the elbow or knee is bent), from Middle Low German, Middle Dutch *knökel,* diminutive of *knoke* 'bone.' In the mid 18th cent. the verb *knuckle (down)* expressed setting the knuckles down to shoot the large marble in a game of marbles, hence the notion of applying oneself with concentration.

knuck·le·ball /ˈnəkəlˌbôl/ (also **knuck·ler**) ▸ n. Baseball a slow pitch that has virtually no spin and moves erratically, typically made by releasing the ball from between the thumb and the knuckles of the first joints of the index and middle finger. —**knuck·le·ball·er** *n.*

knuck·le·bone /ˈnəkəlˌbōn/ ▸ n. **1** a bone forming or corresponding to a knuckle. **2** (**knucklebones**) animal knucklebones used in the game of jacks. ▪ the game of jacks.

knuck·le·head /ˈnəkəlˌhed/ ▸ n. *inf.* a stupid person.

knuck·le sand·wich ▸ n. *inf.* a punch in the mouth.

knurl /nərl/ ▸ n. a small projecting knob or ridge, esp. in a series around the edge of something. —**knurled** *adj.*

KO /ˌkāˈō/ *inf.* Boxing ▸ n. a knockout in a boxing match. See also **KAYO**.
▸ v. (**KO's, KO'd, KO'ing**) [*tr.*] knock (an opponent) out in a boxing match.

ko·a /ˈkōə/ ▸ n. a large Hawaiian forest tree (*Acacia koa*) of the pea family that yields dark red timber.

ko·a·la /kōˈälə/ ▸ n. an arboreal Australian marsupial (*Phascolarctos cinereus,* family Phascolarctidae) with thick gray fur that feeds on eucalyptus leaves.

Ko·di·ak bear /ˈkōdēˌak/ ▸ n. an animal (*Ursus arctos middendorffi*) of a large race of the North American brown bear, found on islands to the south of Alaska.

kof·ta /ˈkôftə/ ▸ n. (*pl.* same or **-tas**) (in Middle Eastern and Indian cookery) a spiced meatball.

kohl /kōl/ ▸ n. a black powder, usually antimony sulfide or lead sulfide, used as eye makeup esp. in Eastern countries.

kohl·ra·bi /kōlˈräbē/ ▸ n. (*pl.* **-bies**) a cabbage of a variety with an edible turniplike swollen stem.

ko·la /ˈkōlə/ ▸ n. variant spelling of **COLA** (sense 2).

Ko·mo·do drag·on /kəˈmōdō/ ▸ n. a monitor lizard (*Varanus komodoensis*) occurring only on Komodo and neighboring Indonesian islands; the largest living lizard.

kook /ko͞ok/ ▸ n. *inf.* a crazy or eccentric person.

kook·a·bur·ra /ˈko͞okəˌbərə/ ▸ n. a very large Australasian kingfisher (genus *Dacelo*) that feeds on terrestrial prey such as reptiles and birds.

kook·y /ˈko͞okē/ ▸ adj. (**kook·i·er, kook·i·est**) *inf.* strange or eccentric: *I like kooky foreign films.* —**kook·i·ly** /-kəlē/ *adv.* —**kook·i·ness** *n.*

ko·pek /ˈkōpek/ (also **co·peck** or **ko·peck**) ▸ n. a monetary unit of Russia and some other countries of the former USSR, equal to one hundredth of a ruble.

Ko·ran /kəˈrän; kô-; ˈkôrän/ (also **Qu'ran** or **Qu·ran**) ▸ n. the Islamic sacred book, believed to be the word of God as dictated to Muhammad by the archangel Gabriel and written down in Arabic. The Koran consists of 114 units of varying lengths, known as *suras.* —**Ko·ran·ic** /-ˈranik/ *adj.*

Ko·re·an /kəˈrēən; kô-/ ▸ adj. of or relating to North or South Korea or its people or language.
▸ n. **1** a native or national of North or South Korea, or a person of Korean descent. **2** the language of Korea, which has has its own writing system and may be distantly related to Japanese.

ko·sher /ˈkōSHər/ ▸ adj. (of food, or premises in which food is sold, cooked, or eaten) satisfying the requirements of Jewish law: *a kosher*

kitchen. ■ (of a person) observing Jewish food laws. ■ (of ritual objects) fit for use according to Jewish laws. ■ *fig.* genuine and legitimate: *when he buys a record abroad, it is impossible to know whether it's kosher.*
▶*v.* [*tr.*] prepare (food) according to the requirements of Jewish law.

kow·tow /'kou'tou/ ▶*v.* [*intr.*] *hist.* kneel and touch the ground with the forehead in worship or submission as part of Chinese custom. ■ *fig.* act in an excessively subservient manner: *she didn't have to kowtow to a boss.* —**kow·tow·er** *n.*

KP ▶*abbr.* kitchen police.

kph ▶*abbr.* kilometers per hour.

KR ▶*abbr. Chess* king's rook.

Kr ▶*symb.* the chemical element krypton.

kraal /kräl/ *S. Afr.* ▶*n.* a traditional African village of huts, typically enclosed by a fence. ■ an enclosure for cattle or sheep.

kraft /kraft/ (also **kraft paper**) ▶*n.* a kind of strong, smooth brown wrapping paper.

krait /krīt/ ▶*n.* a highly venomous Asian snake (genus *Bungarus*) of the cobra family. Several species include the black and yellow **banded krait** (*B. fasciatus*).

kraut /krout/ ▶*n. inf.* sauerkraut. ■ (also **Kraut**) *inf., offens.* a German.

krem·lin /'kremlin/ ▶*n.* a citadel within a Russian town. ■ (**the Kremlin**) the citadel in Moscow. ■ the Russian or (formerly) USSR government housed within this citadel.

krill /kril/ ▶*n.* a small shrimplike planktonic crustacean (*Meganyctiphanes norvegica*, class Malacostraca) of the open seas. It is eaten by a number of larger animals, notably the baleen whales. ▷early 20th cent.: from Norwegian *kril* 'young fry of fish.'

kro·na /'krōnə/ ▶*n.* **1** (*pl.* **-nor** /-nôr/) the basic monetary unit of Sweden, equal to 100 öre. **2** (*pl.* **-nur** /-nər/) the basic monetary unit of Iceland, equal to 100 aurar.

kro·ne /'krōnə/ ▶*n.* (*pl.* **-ner** /-nər/) the basic monetary unit of Denmark and Norway, equal to 100 øre.

Kru·ger·rand /'krōōgə,rand/ (also **kru·ger·rand** or **Kru·ger**) ▶*n.* a South African gold coin with a portrait of President Kruger on the obverse.

krumm·horn /'krōōm,hôrn/ (also **crum·horn**) ▶*n.* a medieval wind instrument with an enclosed double reed and an upward-curving end, producing an even, nasal sound.

kryp·ton /'krip,tän/ ▶*n.* the chemical element of atomic number 36, a member of the noble gas series. (Symbol: **Kr**)

KS ▶*abbr.* Kaposi's sarcoma.

ku·dos /'k(y)ōō,dōs; -,dōz; -,däs/ ▶*n.* praise and honor received for an achievement.

Ku·fic /'k(y)ōōfik/ ▶*n.* an early angular form of the Arabic alphabet found chiefly in decorative inscriptions.
▶*adj.* of or in this type of script.

Ku Klux Klan /'kōō ,kləks 'klan/ (abbr.: **KKK**) ▶an extremist right-wing secret society in the U.S. —**Ku Klux·er** *n.* —**Ku Klux Klans·man** /'klanzmən/ *n.* (*pl.* **-men**).

kum·quat /'kəm,kwät/ ▶*n.* **1** an orangelike fruit with an edible sweet rind and acid pulp. **2** the eastern Asian shrub or small tree (genus *Fortunella*) of the rue family that yields this fruit and that hybridizes with citrus trees.

kung fu /'kəNG 'fōō; 'kŏŏNG/ ▶*n.* a primarily unarmed Chinese martial art resembling karate.

Kurd /kərd/ ▶*n.* a member of a mainly pastoral Islamic people living in Kurdistan.

Kurd·ish /'kərdiSH/ ▶*adj.* of or relating to the Kurds or their language.
▶*n.* the Iranian language of the Kurds.

kur·to·sis /kər'tōsis/ ▶*n. Statistics* the sharpness of the peak of a frequency-distribution curve. ▷early 20th cent.: from Greek *kurtōsis* 'a bulging,' from *kurtos* 'bulging, convex.'

kV ▶*abbr.* kilovolt(s).

kvass /k(ə)'väs; kfäs/ ▶*n.* (esp. in Russia) a fermented drink, low in alcohol, made from rye flour or bread with malt.

kvetch /k(ə)veCH; kfeCH/ *inf.* ▶*n.* a person who complains a great deal. ■ a complaint.
▶*v.* [*intr.*] complain.

kW ▶*abbr.* kilowatt(s).

kwan·za /'kwänzə/ ▶*n.* (*pl.* same or **-zas**) the basic monetary unit of Angola, equal to 100 lwei.

kWh ▶*abbr.* kilowatt-hour(s).

ky·a·nite /'kīə,nīt/ ▶*n.* a blue or green crystalline mineral consisting of aluminum silicate, used in heat-resistant ceramics. —**ky·a·nit·ic** /,kīə-'nitik/ *adj.*

L l

L¹ /el/ (also **l**) ▸*n.* (*pl.* **Ls** or **L's**) **1** the twelfth letter of the alphabet. ■ denoting the next after K in a set of items, categories, etc. **2** (**L**) a shape like that of a capital L: [in *combination*] *a four-story L-shaped building.* **3** the Roman numeral for 50. [originally a symbol identified with the letter *L*, because of coincidence of form. In ancient Roman notation, *L* with a stroke above denoted 50,000.]

L² ▸*abbr.* ■ (in tables of sports results) games lost. ■ (**L.**) Lake, Loch, or Lough (chiefly on maps): *L. Ontario.* ■ large (as a clothes size). ■ Latin. ■ Liberal. ■ (**L.**) Linnaeus (as the source of names of animal and plant species): *Swallowtail Butterfly Papilio machaon (L., 1758).* ■ lire.
▸*symb.* ■ *Chem.* Avogadro's number.

l ▸*abbr.* ■ (giving position or direction) left: *l to r: Gordon, Anthony, Jerry, and Mark.* ■ (chiefly in horse racing) length(s): *distances 5 l, 3 l.* ■ (**l.**) (in textual references) line: *l. 648.* ■ *Chem.* liquid. ■ liter(s).
▸*symb.* (in mathematical formulas) length.

£ ▸*abbr.* (preceding a numeral) pound or pounds (of money).

LA ▸*abbr.* Library Association.

La ▸*symb.* ■ the chemical element lanthanum.

la /lä/ ▸*n. Mus.* (in solmization) the sixth note of a major scale. ■ the note A in the fixed-do system.

La. ▸*abbr.* Louisiana.

Lab /lab/ ▸*abbr.* a Labrador dog.

lab /lab/ ▸*n. inf.* a laboratory: *a science lab.*

la·bel /'lābəl/ ▸*n.* a small piece of paper, fabric, plastic, or similar material attached to an object and giving information about it. ■ a company that produces recorded music: *independent labels.* ■ the name or trademark of a fashion company: *she plans to launch her own designer clothes label.* ■ a classifying phrase or name applied to a person or thing, esp. one that is inaccurate or restrictive: *my reluctance to stick a label on myself politically.* ■ (in a dictionary entry) a word or words used to specify the subject area, register, or geographical origin of the word being defined. ■ *Comput.* a string of characters used to refer to a particular instruction in a program. ■ *Biol. & Chem.* a radioactive isotope, fluorescent dye, or enzyme used to make something identifiable for study.
▸*v.* (**la·beled, la·bel·ing**; *Brit.* **la·belled, la·bel·ling**) [*tr.*] attach a label to (something): *she labeled the parcels neatly.* ■ assign to a category, esp. inaccurately or restrictively: *people who were labeled as "mentally handicapped."* ■ give a name to (something): *she labeled his new Riviera a "Star Wars" car.* ■ *Biol. & Chem.* make (a substance, molecule, or cell) identifiable or traceable by replacing an atom with one of a distinctive radioactive isotope, or by attaching a fluorescent dye, enzyme, or other molecule. —**la·bel·er** *n.*

la·bel·lum /lə'beləm/ ▸*n.* (*pl.* **-bel·la** /-'belə/) **1** *Entomol.* each of a pair of lobes at the tip of the proboscis in some insects. **2** *Bot.* a central petal at the base of an orchid flower, typically larger than the other petals and of a different shape. ▷early 19th cent.: from Latin, diminutive of *labrum* 'lip.'

la·bi·a /'lābēə/ ▸*plural n. Anat.* the inner and outer folds of the vulva, at either side of the vagina.

la·bi·al /'lābēəl/ ▸*adj.* **1** chiefly *Anat.* of or relating to the lips. ■ *Dentistry* (of the surface of a tooth) adjacent to the lips. ■ *Zool.* of, resembling, or serving as a lip, liplike part, or labium. **2** *Phonet.* (of a consonant) requiring complete or partial closure of the lips (e.g., *p, b, f, v, m, w*), or (of a vowel) requiring rounded lips (e.g., *oo* in m**oo**n).
▸*n. Phonet.* a labial sound. —**la·bi·al·ize** /-,līz/ *v.* —**la·bi·al·ly** *adv.*

la·bi·o·den·tal /,lābēō'dentl/ ▸*adj. Phonet.* (of a sound) made with the lips and teeth, for example *f* and *v.*
▸*n. Phonet.* a labiodental sound.

la·bi·um /'lābēəm/ ▸*n.* (*pl.* **-bi·a** /-bēə/) *Entomol. Anat.* a lip or liplike structure, esp. any of the four folds of skin on either side of the vulva.

la·bor /'lābər/ (*Brit.* **la·bour**) ▸*n.* **1** work, esp. hard physical work: *manual labor.* ■ workers, esp. manual workers, considered collectively: *nonunion casual labor.* ■ such workers considered as a social class or political force: [as *adj.*] *the labor movement.* ■ (**Labor**) a department of government concerned with a nation's workforce: *Secretary of Labor.* **2** the process of childbirth, esp. the period from the start of uterine contractions to delivery: *his wife is in labor.*
▸*v.* [*intr.*] work hard; make great effort: *they labored from dawn to dusk.* ■ work at an unskilled manual occupation: *he was eking out an existence by laboring.* ■ have difficulty in doing something despite working hard: *Coley labored against confident opponents.* ■ (of an engine) work noisily and with difficulty: *the wheels churned, the engine laboring.* ■ move or proceed with trouble or difficulty: *they labored up a steep, tortuous track.* ■ (of a ship) roll or pitch heavily.
▸*phrasal v.* □ **labor under 1** carry (a heavy load or object) with difficulty. **2** be deceived or misled by (a mistaken belief): *you've been laboring under a misapprehension.* ▷Middle English *labo(u)r,* from Old French *labour* (noun), *labourer* (verb), both from Latin *labor* 'toil, trouble.'
▸ □ **a labor of love** a task done for pleasure, not reward. □ **labor the point** explain or discuss something at excessive or unnecessary length.

lab·o·ra·to·ry /'labrə,tôrē/ ▸*n.* (*pl.* **-ries**) a room or building equipped for scientific experiments, research, or teaching, or for the manufacture of drugs or chemicals: *pepsin can be extracted in the laboratory* | [with *adj.*] *a film processing laboratory* | [as *adj.*] *a laboratory technician.* ■ [as *adj.*] (of an animal) bred for or used in experiments in laboratories: *studies on laboratory rats.*

la·bor camp ▸*n.* a prison camp in which a regime of hard labor is enforced.

La·bor Day ▸*n.* a public holiday or day of festivities held in honor of working people, in the U.S. and Canada on the first Monday in September, in many other countries on May 1.

la·bor·er /'lāb(ə)rər/ ▸*n.* a person doing unskilled manual work for wages: *a farm laborer.*

la·bor-in·ten·sive ▸*adj.* (of a form of work) needing a large workforce or a large amount of work in relation to output: *the labor-intensive task of tagging each item in the store.*

la·bo·ri·ous /lə'bôrēəs/ ▸*adj.* (esp. of a task, process, or journey) requiring considerable effort and time: *years of laborious training* ■ (esp. of speech or writing style) showing obvious signs of effort and lacking in fluency: *his slow, laborious style.* —**la·bo·ri·ous·ly** *adv.* —**la·bo·ri·ous·ness** *n.*

la·bor-sav·ing ▸*adj.* (of an appliance) designed to reduce the amount of work needed to complete a task.

la·bor un·ion ▸*n.* an organized association of workers, often in a trade or profession, formed to protect and further their rights and interests.

La·bour Par·ty ▸*n.* a major left-of-center British party that arose from the trade union movement at the end of the 19th century.

Lab·ra·dor (also **Labrador retriever**) ▸*n.* a retriever of a breed that predominantly has a black or yellow coat, widely used as a gun dog or as a guide for a blind person.

lab·y·rinth /'lab(ə),rinTH/ ▶n. **1** a complicated irregular network of passages or paths in which it is difficult to find one's way; a maze: *a labyrinth of passages and secret chambers.* ■ fig. an intricate and confusing arrangement: *a labyrinth of conflicting laws and regulations.* **2** *Anat.* a complex structure in the inner ear that contains the organs of hearing and balance. ■ *Zool.* an organ of intricate structure, in particular the accessory respiratory organs of certain fishes. —**lab·y·rin·thi·an** /,labə'rinTHēən/ *adj.* —**lab·y·rin·thine** /,labə'rin,THēn; -'rinTHin; -'rin,THīn/ *adj.*

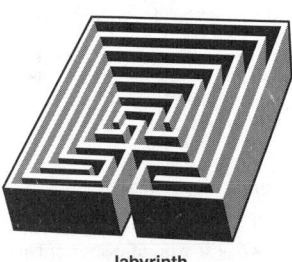

labyrinth

lace /lās/ ▶n. **1** a fine open fabric, typically one of cotton or silk, made by looping, twisting, or knitting thread in patterns and used esp. for trimming garments. ■ braid used for trimming, esp. on military dress uniforms. **2** (usu. **laces**) a cord or leather strip passed through eyelets or hooks on opposite sides of a shoe or garment and then pulled tight and fastened.
▶v. [tr.] **1** fasten or tighten (a shoe or garment) by tying its laces: *he put the shoes on and laced them up.* ■ [intr.] (of a garment or shoe) be fastened by means of laces: *is the front of the dress laced or pinned?* **2** [tr.] entwine or tangle (things, esp. fingers) together: *he laced his fingers together and sat back.* **3** (often **be laced with**) add an ingredient, esp. alcohol, to (a drink or dish) to enhance its flavor or strength: *he gave us coffee laced with brandy* | fig. *his voice was laced with derision.* ■ streak with color or something of a contrasting appearance: *her brown hair was laced with gray.* **4** hit (something, esp. a baseball) hard: *he laced a double down the first-base line.*

-laced /lāst/ ▶adj. [in *combination*] contaminated with a substance (usually harmful or toxic) present in small amounts: *dioxin-laced sludge.*

lac·er·ate /'lasə,rāt/ ▶v. [tr.] tear or deeply cut (something, esp. flesh or skin): *the point had lacerated his neck.* ■ fig. (of feelings or emotions) wound or injure: *an assertion calculated to lacerate nobody's feelings.* —**lac·er·a·tion** /,lasə'rāSHən/ *n.*

lach·es /'laCHiz/ ▶n. *Law* unreasonable delay in making an assertion or claim, such as asserting a right, claiming a privilege, or making an application for redress, which may result in refusal.

lach·ry·mal /'lakrəməl/ (also **lac·ri·mal** or **lac·ry·mal**) ▶adj. **1** formal or poetic/literary connected with weeping or tears. **2** (usu. **lacrimal**) *Physiol. & Anat.* concerned with the secretion of tears: *lacrimal cells.*
▶n. (usu. **lacrimal** or **lacrimal bone**) *Anat.* a small bone forming part of the eye socket.

lach·ry·mose /'lakrə,mōs; -,mōz/ ▶adj. formal or poetic/literary tearful or given to weeping: *she was pink-eyed and lachrymose.* ■ inducing tears; sad: *a lachrymose children's classic.* —**lach·ry·mose·ly** *adv.* —**lach·ry·mos·i·ty** /,lakrə'mäsətē/ *n.*

lac·ing /'lāsiNG/ ▶n. **1** the laced fastening of a shoe or garment. ■ lace trimming, esp. on a uniform. **2** a dash of liquor added to a drink: *coffee to which he added a liberal lacing of brandy.*

lack /lak/ ▶n. the state of being without or not having enough of something: *the case was dismissed for lack of evidence.*
▶v. [tr.] be without or deficient in: *the novel lacks imagination.*

lack·a·dai·si·cal /,lakə'dāzikəl/ ▶adj. lacking enthusiasm and determination; carelessly lazy: *a lackadaisical defense left the Spurs adrift in the second half.* —**lack·a·dai·si·cal·ly** *adv.*

lack·ey /'lakē/ ▶n. (pl. **-eys**) a servant, esp. a liveried footman or manservant. ■ derog. a person who is obsequiously willing to obey or serve another person or group of people.

lack·ing /'lakiNG/ ▶adj. [predic.] not available or in short supply: *adequate resources and funds are both sadly lacking at present.* ■ (of a quality) missing or absent: *there was something lacking in our marriage.* ■ deficient or inadequate: *the students are not lacking in intellectual ability* | *workers were asked in what way they found their managers lacking.*

lack·lus·ter /'lak,ləstər/ ▶adj. lacking in vitality, force, or conviction;

uninspired or uninspiring: *no excuses were made for the team's lackluster performance.* ■ (of the hair or the eyes) not shining; dull.

la·con·ic /lə'känik/ ▶adj. (of a person, speech, or style of writing) using very few words: *his laconic reply suggested a lack of interest in the topic.* —**la·con·i·cal·ly** /-(ə)lē/ *adv.* —**lac·o·nism** /'lakə,nizəm/ *n.*

lac·quer /'lakər/ ▶n. **1** a liquid made of shellac dissolved in alcohol, or synthetic substances, that dries to form a hard protective coating for wood, metal, etc. **2** the sap of the lacquer tree used to varnish wood or other materials. ■ decorative objects made of wood coated with lacquer: [as *adj.*] *a small lacquer box.*
▶v. [tr.] (often as *adj.* (**lacquered**)) coat with lacquer: *the lacquered Chinese table.* —**lac·quer·er** *n.*

lac·ri·mal (also **lac·ry·mal**) ▶adj. & n. variant spelling of LACHRYMAL.

la·crosse /lə'krôs; 'kräs/ ▶n. a team game, originally played by North American Indians, in which the ball is thrown, caught, and carried with a long-handled stick having a curved L-shaped or triangular frame at one end with a piece of shallow netting in the angle.

lacrosse stick

lac·tate[1] /'lak,tāt/ ▶v. [intr.] (of a female mammal) secrete milk. —**lac·ta·tion** /lak'tāSHən/ *n.*

lac·tate[2] ▶n. *Chem.* a salt or ester of lactic acid.

lac·tic /'laktik/ ▶adj. of, relating to, or obtained from milk.

lac·tic ac·id ▶n. *Biochem.* a colorless syrupy organic acid formed in sour milk, and produced in the muscle tissues during strenuous exercise.

lac·tose /'lak,tōs; -,tōz/ ▶n. *Chem.* a sugar present in milk.

la·cu·na /lə'k(y)ōōnə/ ▶n. (pl. **-nae** /-nī; -nē/ or **-nas**) an unfilled space or interval; a gap: *the journal has filled a lacuna in Middle Eastern studies.* ■ a missing portion in a book or manuscript. ▷mid 17th cent.: from Latin, 'pool,' from *lacus* 'lake.' —**la·cu·nal** /-nl/ *adj.* —**la·cu·nar** /-nər/ *adj.* —**la·cu·nar·y** /'lakyə,nerē; lə'k(y)ōōnərē/ *adj.* —**la·cu·nate** /-,nāt; -nit; 'lakyə,nāt/ *adj.* —**la·cu·nose** /'lakyə,nōs; -,nōz/ *adj.*

lac·y /'lāsē/ ▶adj. (**lac·i·er, lac·i·est**) made of, resembling, or trimmed with lace: *a lacy petticoat.* —**lac·i·ly** /-səlē/ *adv.* —**lac·i·ness** *n.*

lad /lad/ ▶n. inf. a boy or young man: *I read that book when I was a lad.*

lad·der /'ladər/ ▶n. a structure consisting of a series of bars or steps between two upright lengths of wood, metal, or rope, used for climbing up or down something. ■ fig. a series of ascending stages by which someone or something may advance or progress: *employees on their way up the career ladder.*

lad·der-back (also **ladder-back chair**) ▶n. an upright chair with a back resembling a ladder.

la·di-da /,lä dē 'dä/ (also **lah-di-dah** or **la-de-da**) inf. ▶adj. pretentious or snobbish, esp. in manner or speech: *do I really look or sound like a la-di-da society lawyer?*
▶exclam. expressing derision at someone's pretentious manner or speech: *"La-di-da!" snapped Alison, as her sister sank into a curtsy.*

la·dies /'lādēz/ ▶ plural form of LADY.

la·dies' man (also **la·dy's man**) ▶n. inf. a man who enjoys spending time and flirting with women.

la·dle /'lādl/ ▶n. a large long-handled spoon with a cup-shaped bowl, used for serving soup, stew, or sauce. ■ a vessel for transporting molten metal in a foundry.
▶v. [tr.] serve (soup, stew, or sauce) with a ladle: *she ladled out onion soup* fig. *he was ladling out his personal philosophy of life.* ■ transfer (liquid) from one receptacle to another. —**la·dle·ful** /-,fŏŏl/ *n.* (pl. **-fuls**) —**la·dler** *n.*

la·dy /'lādē/ ▶n. (pl. **-dies**) **1** a woman (used as a polite or old-fashioned form of reference): *I spoke to the lady at the travel agency* | [as *adj.*] *a lady doctor.* ■ an informal, often brusque, form of address to a woman: *I'm sorry, lady, but you have the wrong number.* **2** a woman of superior social position, esp. one of noble birth: *lords and ladies and royalty were once entertained at the house.* ■ a courteous, decorous, or genteel woman: *his wife was a real lady, with such nice manners.* ■ (**Lady**) (in the UK) a title used by peeresses, female relatives of peers, the wives and widows of knights, etc.: *Lady Caroline Lamb.* **3** (also **lady friend**) a woman with whom a man is romantically or sexually involved: *the young man bought*

Pronunciation Key ə *ago, up*; ər *over, fur*; a *hat*; ā *ate*; ä *car*; CH *chin*; e *let*; ē *see*; e(ə)r *air*; i *fit*; ī *by*; i(ə)r *ear*; NG *sing*; ō *go*; ô *law, for*; oi *toy*; ŏŏ *good*; ōō *goo*; ou *out*; SH *she*; TH *thin*; TH *then*; (h)w *why*; ZH *vision*

a rose for his lady. ▷Old English *hlǣfdīge* (denoting a woman to whom homage or obedience is due, such as the wife of a lord or the mistress of a household, also specifically the Virgin Mary), from *hlāf* 'loaf' + a Germanic base meaning 'knead,' related to *dough.*

▶ □ **Lady Luck** chance personified as a controlling power in human affairs: *it seemed Lady Luck was still smiling on them.*

la·dy·bug /ˈlādēˌbəg/ ▶*n.* a small beetle (family Coccinellidae), typically red or yellow with black spots. Both the adults and larvae are important predators of aphids.

la·dy·fin·ger /ˈlādēˌfiNGgər/ ▶*n.* a small finger-shaped sponge cake.

la·dy-in-wait·ing ▶*n.* (*pl.* **la·dies-in-wait·ing**) a woman who attends a queen or princess.

la·dy·kill·er /ˈlādēˌkilər/ ▶*n. inf.* a charming man who is very attractive to women.

la·dy·like /ˈlādēˌlīk/ ▶*adj.* behaving or dressing in a way considered appropriate or typical of a well-bred, decorous woman or girl. ■ (of an activity or occupation) considered suitable for such a woman or girl: *it wasn't ladylike to be too interested in men.* —**la·dy·like·ness** *n.*

la·dy·ship /ˈlādēˌSHip/ ▶*n.* (**Her/Your Ladyship**) a respectful form of reference or address to a woman who has a title: *the car is outside, Your Ladyship.* ■ *ironic* a form of reference or address to a woman thought to be acting in a pretentious or snobbish way: *bow everyone, Her Ladyship's actually gracing us with her presence!*

la·dy's man ▶*n.* variant spelling of **LADIES' MAN**.

la·dy's-slip·per (also **la·dy's slip·per**) ▶*n.* an orchid (genus *Cypripedium*) of north temperate regions, the flower of which has a lip that is a conspicuous slipper-shaped pouch.

lag /lag/ ▶*v.* (**lagged**, **lag·ging**) [*intr.*] fall behind in movement, progress, or development; not keep pace with another or others: *they stopped to wait for one of the children who was lagging behind.*
▶*n.* (also **time lag**) a period of time between one event or phenomenon and another: *there was a lag between the commission of the crime and its reporting to the police.* —**lag·ger** *n.*

la·ger /ˈlägər/ ▶*n.* a kind of beer, effervescent and light in color and body.

lag·gard /ˈlagərd/ ▶*n.* a person who makes slow progress and falls behind others: *there was no time for laggards.*
▶*adj.* slower than desired or expected: *a bell to summon laggard children to school.* —**lag·gard·ly** *adj. & adv.* —**lag·gard·ness** *n.*

lag·ging /ˈlagiNG/ ▶*n.* material providing heat insulation for a boiler, pipes, etc.

la·goon /ləˈgoon/ ▶*n.* a stretch of salt water separated from the sea by a low sandbank or coral reef. ■ the enclosed water of an atoll. ■ a small freshwater lake near a larger lake or river. ■ an artificial pool for the treatment of effluent or to accommodate surface water that overflows drains during heavy rain. —**la·goon·al** /-ˈgoonl/ *adj.*

laid /lād/ ▶ past and past participle of **LAY**[1].

laid-back ▶*adj. inf.* relaxed and easygoing: *a shaggy dog with an engaging, laid-back temperament.*

lain /lān/ ▶ past participle of **LIE**[1].

lair /le(ə)r/ ▶*n.* a wild animal's resting place, esp. one that is well hidden. ■ a secret or private place in which a person seeks concealment or seclusion.

lais·sez-faire /ˌlesā ˈfe(ə)r; ˌlezā/ ▶*n.* a policy or attitude of letting things take their own course, without interfering. ■ *Econ.* abstention by governments from interfering in the workings of the free market: [as *adj.*] *laissez-faire capitalism.* —**lais·sez-faire·ism** /ˈfe(ə)rˌizəm/ *n.*

la·i·ty /ˈlāətē/ ▶*n.* [usu. treated as *pl.*] (**the laity**) lay people, as distinct from the clergy. ■ ordinary people, as distinct from professionals or experts.

lake[1] /lāk/ ▶*n.* a large body of water surrounded by land. ■ a pool of liquid: *the fish was served in a bright lake of spicy carrot sauce.* —**lake·let** /-lit/ *n.*

lake[2] ▶*n.* [often with *adj.*] an insoluble pigment made by combining a soluble organic dye and an insoluble mordant. ■ a purplish-red pigment of this kind, originally one made with lac, used in dyes, inks, and paints.

lake·side /ˈlākˌsīd/ ▶*n.* the land adjacent to a lake: *this road hugs the flat land by the lakeside* | [as *adj.*] *beautiful lakeside cabins.*

lam[1] /lam/ ▶*v.* (**lammed**, **lam·ming**) [*tr.*] *inf.* hit (someone) hard: *I'll come over and lam you in the mouth in a minute.* ■ [*intr.*] (**lam into**) attack: *they surged up and down in their riot gear, lamming into anyone in their path.*

lam[2] *inf.* ▶*n.* (in phrase **on the lam**) in flight, esp. from the police: *he went on the lam and is living under a false name.*
▶*v.* (**lammed**, **lam·ming**) [*intr.*] escape; flee.

la·ma /ˈlämə/ ▶*n.* **1** an honorific title applied to a spiritual leader in Tibetan Buddhism, whether a reincarnate lama (such as the Dalai Lama) or one who has earned the title in life. **2** a Tibetan or Mongolian Buddhist monk. ▷mid 17th cent.: from Tibetan *bla-ma* (the initial *b* being silent), literally 'superior one.'

la·ma·ser·y /ˈläməˌserē/ ▶*n.* (*pl.* **-ser·ies**) a monastery of lamas.

lamb /lam/ ▶*n.* a young sheep. ■ the flesh of such young sheep as food. ■ *fig.* used as the epitome of meekness, gentleness, or innocence: *to her amazement, he accepted her decision like a lamb.* ■ used to describe or address someone regarded with affection or pity, esp. a young child: *the poor lamb is very upset.*
▶*v.* [*intr.*] (of a ewe) give birth to lambs. ■ [*tr.*] tend (ewes) at lambing time. —**lamb·er** *n.* —**lamb·kin** /-kin/ *n.* —**lamb·like** /-ˌlīk/ *adj.*
▶ □ **like a lamb to the slaughter** as a helpless victim.

lam·ba·da /lamˈbädə/ ▶*n.* a fast, erotic Brazilian dance that couples perform with their stomachs touching.

lam·baste /lamˈbāst; -ˈbast/ (also **lam·bast** /-ˈbast/) ▶*v.* [*tr.*] criticize (someone or something) harshly: *they lambasted the report as a gross distortion of the truth.*

lamb·da /ˈlamdə/ ▶*n.* the eleventh letter of the Greek alphabet (Λ, λ), transliterated as 'l.' ■ *Biol.* a type of bacteriophage virus used in genetic research: *lambda phage.*
▶*symb.* ■ (λ) wavelength.

lame /lām/ ▶*adj.* **1** (of a person or animal) unable to walk normally because of an injury or illness affecting the leg or foot: *his horse went lame.* ■ (of a leg or foot) affected in this way. **2** (of an explanation or excuse) unconvincingly feeble: *it was a lame statement and there was no excusing his behavior.* ■ (of something intended to be entertaining) uninspiring and dull. ■ (of a person) naive or inept, esp. socially: *anyone who doesn't know that is obviously lame.* ■ (of verse or metrical feet) halting; metrically defective.
▶*v.* [*tr.*] make (a person or animal) lame: *somebody lamed him with a stone.* —**lame·ly** *adv.* —**lame·ness** *n.*

la·mé /laˈmā; lä-/ ▶*n.* fabric with interwoven gold or silver threads.

lame·brain /ˈlāmˌbrān/ ▶*n. inf.* a stupid person. —**lame-brained** *adj.*

lame duck ▶*n.* an official (esp. the president) in the final period of office, after the election of a successor: *as a lame duck, the president had nothing to lose by approving the deal* | [as *adj.*] *a lame-duck governor.* ■ an ineffectual or unsuccessful person or thing.

la·ment /ləˈment/ ▶*n.* a passionate expression of grief or sorrow: *a song full of lament and sorrow.* ■ a song, piece of music, or poem expressing such emotions. ■ an expression of regret or disappointment; a complaint: *there were constant laments about the conditions of employment.*
▶*v.* [*tr.*] mourn (a person's loss or death): *he was lamenting the death of his infant daughter.* ■ [*intr.*] (**lament for/over**) express one's deep grief about. ■ express regret or disappointment over something considered unsatisfactory, unreasonable, or unfair: [*tr.*] *she lamented the lack of shops in the town.* —**lam·en·ta·tion** /ˌlamənˈtāSHən/ *n.* —**la·ment·er** *n.*

lam·en·ta·ble /ˈlaməntəbəl; ləˈmentəbəl/ ▶*adj.* **1** (of circumstances or conditions) deplorably bad or unsatisfactory: *the facilities provided were lamentable, not merely basic but squalid.* **2** *archaic* full of or expressing sorrow or grief. —**lam·en·ta·bly** /-əblē/ *adv. she was lamentably ignorant.*

lam·i·na /ˈlamənə/ ▶*n.* (*pl.* **-nae** /-ˌnē; -ˌnī/) *technical* a thin layer, plate, or scale of sedimentary rock, organic tissue, or other material. —**lam·i·nar** /-nər/ *adj.* —**lam·i·nose** /-ˌnōs; -ˌnōz/ *adj.*

lam·i·nate ▶*v.* /ˈlaməˌnāt/ [*tr.*] [often as *adj.*] (**laminated**) overlay (a flat surface, esp. paper) with a layer of plastic or some other protective material. ■ manufacture by placing layer on layer. ■ split into layers or leaves. ■ beat or roll (metal) into thin plates.
▶*n.* /-nit; -ˌnāt/ a laminated structure or material, esp. one made of layers fixed together to form a hard, flat, or flexible material.
▶*adj.* /-nit; -ˌnāt/ in the form of a lamina or laminae. —**lam·i·na·ble** /-nəbəl/ *adj.* —**lam·i·na·tion** /ˌlaməˈnāSHən/ *n.* —**lam·i·na·tor** /-ˌnātər/ *n.*

lam·i·ni·tis /ˌlaməˈnītis/ ▶*n.* inflammation of sensitive layers of tissue (laminae) inside the hoof in horses and other animals. It is particularly prevalent in ponies feeding on rich spring grass and can cause extreme lameness.

lamp /lamp/ ▶*n.* a device for giving light, either one consisting of an electric bulb together with its holder and shade or cover, or one burning gas or a liquid fuel and consisting of a wick or mantle and a glass shade: *a table lamp.* ■ an electrical device producing ultraviolet, infrared, or other radiation, used for therapeutic purposes. ■ *poetic/literary* a source of spiritual or intellectual inspiration. —**lamp·less** *adj.*

lamp·light /ˈlampˌlīt/ ▶*n.* the light cast from a lamp: *he was working in the stables by lamplight.* —**lamp·lit** /-ˌlit/ *adj.*

lamp·light·er /ˈlampˌlītər/ ▶n. hist. a person employed to light street gaslights by hand.

lam·poon /lamˈpo͞on/ ▶v. [tr.] publicly criticize (someone or something) by using ridicule, irony, or sarcasm: the senator made himself famous by lampooning dubious federal projects.
▶n. a speech or text criticizing someone or something in this way: does this sound like a lampoon of student life? —**lam·poon·er** n. —**lam·poon·ist** /-ist/ n.

lamp·post /ˈlam(p)ˌpōst/ ▶n. a tall pole with a light at the top; a street light.

lam·prey /ˈlamprē/ ▶n. (pl. **-eys**) an eellike aquatic jawless vertebrate (family Petromyzonidae) that has a sucker mouth with horny teeth and a rasping tongue. The adult is often parasitic, attaching itself to other fish and sucking their blood.

lamp·shade /ˈlampˌSHād/ ▶n. a cover for a lamp, used to soften or direct its light.

LAN /lan/ ▶abbr. local area network.

lance /lans/ ▶n. hist. a long weapon for thrusting, having a wooden shaft and a pointed steel head, used by a horseman in charging. ■ a similar weapon used in hunting fish or whales. ■ another term for LANCER (sense 1).
▶v. [tr.] Med. prick or cut open with a lancet or other sharp instrument: abscesses should not be lanced until there is a soft spot in the center | fig. the governor made it one of his priorities to lance the boil of corruption. ■ pierce with or as if with a lance: the teenager had been lanced by a wooden splinter. ■ [intr.] move suddenly and quickly: pain lanced through her. ▷Middle English: from Old French lance (noun), lancier (verb), from Latin lancea (noun).

lance·let /ˈlanslit/ ▶n. a small elongated marine invertebrate that resembles a fish but lacks jaws and obvious sense organs. Lancelets possess a notochord and are among the most primitive chordates.

lanc·er /ˈlansər/ ▶n. hist. a soldier of a cavalry regiment armed with lances.

lan·cet /ˈlansit/ ▶n. 1 a small, broad, two-edged surgical knife or blade with a sharp point. 2 a lancet arch or window. ■ [as adj.] shaped like a lancet arch: a lancet clock. —**lan·cet·ed** adj.

land /land/ ▶n. 1 the part of the earth's surface that is not covered by water, as opposed to the sea or the air: after four weeks at sea we sighted land. ■ [as adj.] living or traveling on land rather than in water or the air: a land mammal. ■ an expanse of land; an area of ground, esp. in terms of its ownership or use: the land north of the village. | (**lands**) the Indians were wiped out as gold prospectors invaded their lands. ■ (**the land**) ground or soil used as a basis for agriculture: my family had worked the land for many years. 2 a country: the valley is one of the most beautiful in the land. ■ fig. a realm or domain: you are living in a fantasy land. 3 the space between the rifling grooves in a gun.
▶v. 1 [tr.] put ashore: the lifeboat landed the survivors safely ashore. ■ [intr.] go ashore; disembark: the marines landed at a small fishing jetty. ■ unload (goods) from a ship: the fishing boats landed their catch at the port. ■ bring (a fish) to land, esp. with a net or hook: I landed a scrappy three-pound walleye. ■ inf. succeed in obtaining or achieving (something desirable), esp. in the face of strong competition: she landed the starring role in a new film. 2 [intr.] come down through the air and alight on the ground: planes landing at the rate of two a minute. ■ [tr.] bring (an aircraft or spacecraft) to the ground or the surface of water, esp. in a controlled way: the copilot landed the plane. ■ inf. (of something unpleasant or unexpected) arrive suddenly: there seemed to be more problems than ever landing on her desk this week. 3 [tr.] (**land someone in**) inf. cause someone to be in (a difficult or unwelcome situation): his exploits always landed him in trouble. ■ (**land someone with**) inflict (an unwelcome task or a difficult situation) on someone: the mistake landed the company with a massive bill. 4 [tr.] inf. inflict (a blow) on someone: I won the fight without landing a single punch. —**land·ward** /-wərd/ adj.
▶ ▢ **how the land lies** what the state of affairs is: let's keep it to ourselves until we see how the land lies. ▢ **in the land of the living** humorous alive or awake. ▢ **the land of Nod** humorous a state of sleep. ▢ **land on one's feet** have good luck or success: after some ups and downs, he has finally landed on his feet. ▢ **live off the land** live on whatever food one can obtain by hunting, gathering, or subsistence farming.

land bridge ▶n. a connection between two landmasses, esp. a prehistoric one that allowed humans and animals to colonize new territory before being cut off by the sea, as across the Bering Strait and the English Channel.

land·ed /ˈlandid/ ▶adj. owning much land, esp. through inheritance: the landed aristocracy. ■ consisting of, including, or relating to such land: the decline of landed estates.

land·fall /ˈlan(d)ˌfôl/ ▶n. 1 an arrival at land on a sea or air journey. 2 the contact of a hurricane with a landmass: Javier made landfall at 10:46 this morning. —**land·fall·ing** adj.

land·fill /ˈlan(d)ˌfil/ ▶n. a place to dispose of refuse and other waste material by burying it and covering it over with soil, esp. as a method of filling in or extending usable land. ■ waste material used to reclaim ground in this way. ■ an area filled in by this process.
▶v. [tr.] bury in a landfill: the Florida school intends to landfill its old computers.

land·form /ˈlan(d)ˌfôrm/ ▶n. a natural feature of the earth's surface.

land·hold·er /ˈlandˌhōldər/ ▶n. a person who owns land, esp. one who either makes a living from it or rents it out to others.

land·ing /ˈlandiNG/ ▶n. 1 an instance of coming or bringing something to land, either from the air or from water: we made a perfect landing at the airstrip. ■ the action or process of doing this: the landing of men on the moon. ■ (also **landing place**) a place where people and goods can be landed from a boat or ship: the ferry landing. 2 a level area at the top of a staircase or between one flight of stairs and another.

land·ing craft ▶n. a boat specially designed for putting troops and military equipment ashore on a beach.

land·ing gear ▶n. the undercarriage of an aircraft, including the wheels or pontoons on which it rests while not in the air.

land·la·dy /ˈlan(d)ˌlādē/ ▶n. (pl. **-dies**) a woman who rents land, a building, or an apartment to a tenant. ■ a woman who owns or runs a boardinghouse, inn, or similar establishment.

land·locked /ˈlan(d)ˌläkt/ ▶adj. (esp. of a country) almost or entirely surrounded by land; having no coastline or seaport: a midget state landlocked in the mountains. ■ (of a lake) enclosed by land and having no navigable route to the sea. ■ (of a fish, esp. a North American salmon) cut off from the sea in the past and now confined to fresh water.

land·lord /ˈlan(d)ˌlôrd/ ▶n. a person, esp. a man, who rents land, a building, or an apartment to a tenant. ■ a person who owns or runs a boardinghouse, inn, or similar establishment.

land·lub·ber /ˈlan(d)ˌləbər/ ▶n. inf. a person unfamiliar with the sea or sailing.

land·mark /ˈlan(d)ˌmärk/ ▶n. 1 an object or feature of a landscape or town that is easily seen and recognized from a distance, esp. one that enables one to establish their location: the spire was once a landmark for ships sailing up the river. ■ hist. the boundary of an area of land, or an object marking this. 2 an event, discovery, or change marking an important stage or turning point in something: the birth of a child is an important landmark in the lives of all concerned | [as adj.] a landmark decision.

land·mass /ˈlan(d)ˌmas/ (also **land mass**) ▶n. a continent or other large body of land.

land mine ▶n. an explosive mine laid on or just under the surface of the ground.

land·own·er /ˈlanˌdōnər/ ▶n. a person who owns land, esp. a large amount of land. —**land·own·er·ship** /-dōnərˌSHip/ n. —**land·own·ing** /-dōniNG/ adj. & n.

land·scape /ˈlan(d)ˌskāp/ ▶n. 1 all the visible features of an area of countryside or land, often considered in terms of their aesthetic appeal: the giant cacti that dominate this landscape. ■ a picture representing an area of countryside: [as adj.] a landscape painter. ■ the genre of landscape painting. ■ fig. the distinctive features of a particular situation or intellectual activity: the event transformed the political landscape. 2 [as adj.] (of a page, book, or illustration, or the manner in which it is set or printed) wider than it is high. Compare with PORTRAIT (sense 2).
▶v. [tr.] (usu. **be landscaped**) improve the aesthetic appearance of (a piece of land) by changing its contours, adding ornamental features, or planting trees and shrubs: the site has been tastefully landscaped | [as n.] (**landscaping**) the company spent $15,000 on landscaping. —**land·scap·er** n. —**land·scap·ist** /-ˌskāpist/ n.

land·scape gar·den·ing ▶n. the art and practice of laying out grounds in a way that is ornamental or that imitates natural scenery. —**land·scape gar·den·er** n.

land·slide /ˈlan(d)ˌslīd/ ▶n. 1 the sliding down of a mass of earth or rock from a mountain or cliff. 2 an overwhelming majority of votes for one party in an election: winning the election by a landslide | [as adj.] a landslide victory.

L

---

lands·man /'lan(d)zmən/ ▶*n.* **1** (*pl.* **-men**) a person unfamiliar with the sea or sailing. **2** a fellow countryman.

lane /lān/ ▶*n.* **1** a narrow road, esp. in a rural area: *she drove along the winding lane.* **2** a division of a road marked off with painted lines and intended to separate single lines of traffic according to speed or direction: *the car accelerated and moved into the outside lane.* ■ each of a number of parallel strips of track or water for runners, rowers, or swimmers in a race. ■ a path or course prescribed for or regularly followed by ships or aircraft: *the shipping lanes of the South Atlantic.* ■ (in basketball) a 12-foot-wide area extending from the free-throw line to below the basket. ■ (in bowling) a long narrow strip of floor down which the ball is bowled. ■ *Biochem.* each of a number of notional parallel strips in the gel of an electrophoresis plate, occupied by a single sample.

lan·guage /'laNGgwij/ ▶*n.* **1** the method of human communication, either spoken or written, consisting of the use of words in a structured and conventional way: [as *adj.*] *language development.* ■ any nonverbal method of expression or communication: *a language of gesture and facial expression.* **2** the system of communication used by a particular community or country: *the book was translated into twenty-five languages.* ■ *Comput.* a system of symbols and rules for writing programs or algorithms: *a new programming language.* **3** the manner or style of a piece of writing or speech: *he explained the procedure in simple, everyday language.* ■ the phraseology and vocabulary of a certain profession, domain, or group of people: *legal language.*

lan·guid /'laNGgwid/ ▶*adj.* **1** (of a person, manner, or gesture) displaying or having a disinclination for physical exertion or effort; slow and relaxed: *they turned with languid movements from back to front so as to tan evenly.* ■ (of an occasion or period of time) pleasantly lazy and peaceful: *the terrace was perfect for languid days in the Italian sun.* **2** weak or faint from illness or fatigue: *she was pale, languid, and weak.* —**lan·guid·ly** *adv.* —**lan·guid·ness** *n.*

lan·guish /'laNGgwiSH/ ▶*v.* [*intr.*] **1** (of a person or other living thing) lose or lack vitality; grow weak or feeble: *plants may appear to be languishing simply because they are dormant.* ■ fail to make progress or be successful: *many Japanese works still languish unrecognized in Europe.* ■ *archaic* pine with love or grief: *she still languished after Richard.* **2** suffer from being forced to remain in an unpleasant place or situation: *he has been languishing in a Mexican jail since 1974.* ▷Middle English (in the sense 'become faint, feeble, or ill'): from Old French *languiss*-, lengthened stem of *languir* 'languish,' from a variant of Latin *languere*, related to *laxus* 'loose, lax.' —**lan·guish·er** *n.* —**lan·guish·ing·ly** *adv.* —**lan·guish·ment** *n.* (*archaic*).

lan·guor /'laNG(g)ər/ ▶*n.* **1** the state or feeling, often pleasant, of tiredness or inertia: *he remembered the languor and warm happiness of those golden afternoons.* **2** an oppressive stillness of the air: *the afternoon was hot, quiet, and heavy with languor.* —**lan·guor·ous** /-g(ə)rəs; 'laNGgərəs/ *adj.* —**lan·guor·ous·ly** /-g(ə)rəslē; 'laNGgərəslē/ *adv.*

La Ni·ña /lä 'nēnyə/ ▶*n.* a cooling of the water in the equatorial Pacific, which occurs at irregular intervals and is associated with widespread changes in weather patterns complementary to those of El Niño, but less extensive and damaging in their effects. ▷Spanish, literally 'the girl child,' after *El Niño.*

lank /laNGk/ ▶*adj.* (of hair) long, limp, and straight. ■ (of a person) lanky. —**lank·ly** *adv.* —**lank·ness** *n.*

lank·y /'laNGkē/ ▶*adj.* (**lank·i·er, lank·i·est**) (of a person) ungracefully thin and tall. —**lank·i·ly** /-kəlē/ *adv.* —**lank·i·ness** *n.*

lan·o·lin /'lanl-in/ ▶*n.* a fatty substance found naturally on sheep's wool. It is extracted as a yellowish viscous mixture of esters and used as a base for ointments.

lan·tern /'lantərn/ ▶*n.* **1** a lamp with a transparent case protecting the flame or electric bulb, and typically having a handle by which it can be carried or hung: *a paper lantern.* ■ the light chamber at the top of a lighthouse. **2** a square, curved, or polygonal structure on the top of a dome or a room, with the sides glazed or open, so as to admit light.

lan·tha·nide /'lanTHə,nīd/ ▶*n. Chem.* any of the series of fifteen metallic elements from lanthanum to lutetium in the periodic table. See also RARE EARTH.

lan·tha·num /'lanTHənəm/ ▶*n.* the chemical element of atomic number 57, a silvery-white rare earth metal. (Symbol: **La**)

la·nu·go /lə'n(y)ōōgō/ ▶*n. Anat.* fine, soft hair, esp. that which covers the body and limbs of a human fetus or newborn.

lan·yard /'lanyərd/ ▶*n.* a cord passed around the neck, shoulder, or wrist for holding a knife, whistle, or similar object. ■ a cord attached to a breech mechanism for firing a gun.

lap[1] /lap/ ▶*n.* **1** (usu. **one's lap**) the flat area between the waist and knees of a seated person: *come and sit on my lap.* ■ the part of an item of clothing, esp. a skirt, covering the lap. **2** *archaic* a hanging flap on a garment or a saddle. ▷Old English *læppa*, of Germanic origin; related to Dutch *lap*, German *Lappen* 'piece of cloth.' The word originally denoted a fold or flap of a garment, later specifically one that could be used as a pocket or pouch, or the front of a skirt when held up to catch or carry something (Middle English), hence the area between the waist and knees as a place where a child could be nursed or an object held. —**lap·ful** /-,fŏŏl/ *n.* (*pl.* **-fuls**).

▶ □ **fall** (or **drop**) **into someone's lap** (of something unexpected) come someone's way without any effort having been made: *not many reporters are lucky enough to have stories fall into their laps.* □ **in someone's lap** as someone's responsibility: *she dumped the problem in my lap.* □ **in the lap of luxury** in conditions of great comfort and wealth.

lap[2] ▶*n.* **1** one circuit of a track or racetrack. ■ a stage in a swim consisting of two lengths of a pool. ■ a section of a journey or other undertaking: *we caught a cab for the last lap of our journey.* **2** an overlapping or projecting part.

▶*v.* (**lapped, lap·ping**) [*tr.*] **1** overtake (a competitor in a race) to become one or more laps ahead: *she lapped all of her rivals in the 3,000 meters.* ■ [*intr.*] (of a competitor or vehicle in a race) complete a lap, esp. in a specified time: *he lapped two tenths of a second faster than anyone else.* **2** [*tr.*] (**lap someone/something in**) *poetic/literary* enfold or swathe a person or thing, esp. as a part of the body, in (something soft): *he was lapped in blankets* | *fig. I was accustomed to being lapped in luxury.* **3** [*intr.*] project beyond or overlap something: *the blanket of snow lapped over the roofs of the house.*

lap[3] ▶*v.* (**lapped, lap·ping**) [*tr.*] **1** (of an animal) take up (liquid) with the tongue in order to drink: *the cat was lapping up a saucer of milk.* ■ (**lap something up**) accept something eagerly and with obvious pleasure: *she's lapping up the attention.* **2** (of water) wash against (something) with a gentle rippling sound: *the waves lapped the shore* | [*intr.*] *the sound of the river lapping against the banks.*

▶*n.* the action of water washing gently against something: *listening to the comfortable lap of the waves against the shore.* —**lap·per** *n.*

lap·a·ros·co·py /,lapə'räskəpē/ ▶*n.* (*pl.* **-pies**) a surgical procedure in which a fiber-optic instrument is inserted through the abdominal wall to view the organs in the abdomen or to permit a surgical procedure. —**lap·a·ro·scope** /'lap(ə)rə,skōp/ *n.* —**lap·a·ro·scop·ic** /,lap(ə)rə'skäpik/ *adj.* —**lap·a·ro·scop·i·cal·ly** *adv.*

lap·dog /'lap,dôg; -,däg/ (also **lap dog**) ▶*n.* a small dog kept as a pet. ■ *fig.* a person or organization that is influenced or controlled by another: *the government and its media lapdogs.*

la·pel /lə'pel/ ▶*n.* the part on each side of a coat or jacket immediately below the collar that is folded back on either side of the front opening. —**la·pelled** *adj.* [in *comb.*] *a narrow-lapelled suit.*

lap·i·dar·y /'lapə,derē/ ▶*adj.* of or relating to stone and gems and the work involved in engraving, cutting, or polishing.

▶*n.* (*pl.* **-dar·ies**) a person who cuts, polishes, or engraves gems. ■ the art of cutting, polishing, or engraving gems.

lap·is laz·u·li /'lapis 'lazyə,lī; 'lazHə,lī; 'lazyəlē/ (also **lap·is**) ▶*n.* a bright blue metamorphic rock used for decoration and in jewelry.

lap joint ▶*n.* a joint made with two pieces of metal, timber, etc., by halving the thickness of each member at the joint and fitting them together.

lapse /laps/ ▶*n.* **1** a temporary failure of concentration, memory, or judgment: *a lapse of concentration in the second set cost her the match.* ■ a weak or careless decline from previously high standards: *tracing his lapse into petty crime.* ■ *Law* the termination of a right or privilege through disuse or failure to follow appropriate procedures. **2** an interval or passage of time: *there was a considerable lapse of time between the two events.*

▶*v.* [*intr.*] **1** (of a right, privilege, or agreement) become invalid because it is not used, claimed, or renewed; expire: *my membership to the gym has lapsed.* ■ (of a state or activity) fail to be maintained; come to an end: *if your diet has lapsed it's time you revived it.* ■ (of an adherent to a particular religion or doctrine) cease to follow the rules and practices of that religion or doctrine: [as *adj.*] (**lapsed**) *a lapsed Catholic.* **2** (**lapse into**) pass gradually into (an inferior state or condition): *the country has lapsed into chaos.* ■ revert to (a previous or more familiar style of speaking or behavior): *the girls lapsed into French.*

lap·top /'lap,täp/ (also **laptop computer**) ▶*n.* a microcomputer that is portable and suitable for use while traveling.

lap·wing /'lap,wiNG/ ▶*n.* a large plover (genus *Vanellus*), typically having a black and white head and underparts and a loud call.

lar·ce·ny /'lärs(ə)nē/ ▶*n.* (*pl.* **-nies**) theft of personal property. See also

GRAND LARCENY. —**lar·ce·ner** /-nər/ n. (archaic) —**lar·ce·nist** /-nist/ n. —**lar·ce·nous** /-nəs/ adj.

larch /lärCH/ ▶n. a coniferous tree (genus *Larix*) of the pine family with bunches of deciduous bright green needles, found in cool regions of the northern hemisphere. It is grown for its tough timber and its resin (which yields turpentine).

lard /lärd/ ▶n. fat from the abdomen of a pig that is rendered and clarified for use in cooking. ▪ inf. excess human fat that is seen as unhealthy and unattractive.
▶v. [tr.] **1** insert strips of fat or bacon in (meat) before cooking. ▪ smear or cover (a foodstuff) with lard or fat, typically to prevent it from drying out during storage. **2** (usu. **be larded with**) embellish (talk or writing) with a variety of expressions: *his conversation is larded with quotations from Coleridge.* ▪ cover or fill thickly or excessively: *the pages were larded with corrections and crossings-out.* —**lard·y** adj.

lard·er /'lärdər/ ▶n. a room or large cupboard for storing food.

large /lärj/ ▶adj. **1** of considerable or relatively great size, extent, or capacity: *the concert attracted large crowds.* ▪ of greater size than the ordinary, esp. with reference to a size of clothing or to the size of a packaged commodity: *the sweater comes in small, medium, and large sizes.* **2** of wide range or scope: *we can afford to take a larger view of the situation.* **3** Sailing another term for FREE (sense 8).
▶adv. Sailing another term for FREE (sense 2). —**large·ness** n.
▶ □ **at large 1** (esp. of a criminal or dangerous animal) at liberty; escaped or not yet captured: *the fugitive was still at large.* **2** as a whole; in general: *there has been a loss of community values in society at large.* **3** in a general way; without particularizing: *the magazine's editor at large.*

large in·tes·tine ▶n. Anat. the cecum, colon, and rectum collectively.

large·ly /'lärjlē/ ▶adv. to a great extent; on the whole; mostly: *he was soon arrested, largely through the efforts of Tom Poole.*

large-scale ▶adj. **1** involving large numbers or a large area; extensive: *large-scale commercial farming.* **2** (of a map or model) made to a scale large enough to show certain features in detail.

lar·gesse /lär'jes; -'ZHes/ (also **lar·gess**) ▶n. generosity in bestowing money or gifts upon others: *dispensing his money with such largesse.* ▪ money or gifts given generously: *the distribution of largesse to the local population.*

lar·go /'lärgō/ Mus. ▶adv. & adj. (esp. as a direction) in a slow tempo and dignified in style.

lar·i·at /'lareət/ ▶n. a rope used as a lasso or for tethering.

lark[1] /lärk/ ▶n. a small ground-dwelling songbird (family Alaudidae), typically with brown streaky plumage, a crest, and elongated hind claws, and with a song that is delivered in flight.

lark[2] inf. ▶n. something done for fun, esp. something mischievous or daring; an amusing adventure or escapade: *I only went along for a lark.*
▶v. [intr.] enjoy oneself by behaving in a playful and mischievous way: *he jumped the fence to go larking the rest of the day.* —**lark·ish** adj. —**lark·y** adj.

lark·spur /'lärk,spər/ ▶n. an annual Mediterranean plant (genus *Consolida* formerly *Delphinium*) of the buttercup family that bears spikes of spurred flowers. It is closely related to the delphiniums.

lar·va /'lärvə/ ▶n. (pl. **-vae** /-vē; -,vī/) the active immature form of an insect, esp. one that differs greatly from the adult and forms the stage between egg and pupa, e.g., a caterpillar or grub. Compare with NYMPH (sense 2). ▪ an immature form of other animals that undergo some metamorphosis, e.g., a tadpole. ▷mid 17th cent. (denoting a disembodied spirit or ghost): from Latin, literally 'ghost, mask.' —**lar·val** /-vəl/ adj. —**lar·vi·cide** /-,sīd/ n.

lar·yn·gi·tis /,larən'jītis/ ▶n. inflammation of the larynx, typically resulting in huskiness or loss of the voice, harsh breathing, and a painful cough. —**lar·yn·git·ic** /-'jitik/ adj.

lar·ynx /'larinGks; 'ler-/ ▶n. (pl. **la·ryn·ges** /lə'rin,jēz/ or **lar·ynx·es**) Anat. the hollow muscular organ forming an air passage to the lungs and holding the vocal cords in humans and other mammals; the voice box.

la·sa·gna /lə'zänyə/ (also **la·sa·gne**) ▶n. pasta in the form of wide strips. ▪ a baked Italian dish consisting of this cooked and layered with meat or vegetables, cheese, and tomato sauce.

las·civ·i·ous /lə'sivēəs/ ▶adj. (of a person, manner, or gesture) feeling or revealing an overt and often offensive sexual desire: *he gave her a lascivious wink.* —**las·civ·i·ous·ly** adv. —**las·civ·i·ous·ness** n.

la·ser /'lāzər/ ▶n. a device that generates an intense beam of coherent monochromatic light (or other electromagnetic radiation) by stimulated emission of photons from excited atoms or molecules.

la·ser·disc /'lāzər,disk/ (also **laser disc**) ▶n. a disk that resembles a

compact disc and functions in a similar manner; an optical disc. It is used mainly for high-quality video and for interactive multimedia on computer.

la·ser print·er ▶n. a printer linked to a computer producing good-quality printed material by using a laser to form a pattern of electrostatically charged dots on a light-sensitive drum, which attract toner (or dry ink powder). The toner is transferred to a piece of paper and fixed by a heating process.

lash /lasH/ ▶v. [tr.] **1** strike (someone) with a whip or stick: *they lashed him repeatedly about the head.* ▪ beat forcefully against (something): *waves lashed the coast.* ▪ (**lash someone into**) drive someone into (a particular state or condition): *fear lashed him into a frenzy.* **2** [tr.] (of an animal) move (a part of the body, esp. the tail) quickly and violently: *the cat was lashing its tail back and forth.* ▪ [intr.] (of a part of the body) move in this way. **3** [tr.] fasten (something) securely with a cord or rope: *he lashed the flag to the mast.*
▶phrasal v. □ **lash out** hit or kick out at someone or something: *sticks with which to lash out and strike the prisoner.* ▪ fig. attack verbally: *he used his thank-you speech to **lash out at** critics* | *TJ lashed out, "God will hit you with a wooden spoon!"*
▶n. **1** a sharp blow or stroke with a whip or rope, typically given as a form of punishment: *he was sentenced to fifty lashes for his crime* | fig. *she felt the lash of my tongue.* ▪ the flexible leather part of a whip, used for administering such blows. ▪ (**the lash**) punishment in the form of a beating with a whip or rope: *they were living under the threat of the lash.* **2** (usu. **lashes**) an eyelash: *she fluttered her long dark lashes.* —**lashed** adj. [in comb.] *long-lashed eyes.* —**lash·er** n. —**lash·less** adj.

lash·ing /'lasHinG/ ▶n. **1** an act or instance of whipping: *I threatened to give him a good lashing!* | fig. *he was on the receiving end of a verbal lashing yesterday.* **2** (usu. **lashings**) a cord used to fasten something securely.

lass /las/ ▶n. chiefly Scot. & N. Engl. a girl or young woman: *he married a lass from Yorkshire.*

las·si·tude /'lasə,t(y)ōōd/ ▶n. a state of physical or mental weariness; lack of energy: *she was overcome by lassitude and retired to bed.*

las·so /'lasō; 'lasōō; la'sōō/ ▶n. (pl. **-sos** or **-soes**) a rope with a noose at one end, used esp. in North America for catching cattle or horses.
▶v. (**-soes, -soed**) [tr.] catch (an animal) with a lasso: *at last his father lassoed the horse.* —**las·so·er** n.

last[1] /last/ ▶adj. [attrib.] **1** coming after all others in time or order; final: *they caught the last bus.* ▪ (**the last**) the least likely or suitable: *addicts are often the last people to face up to their problems.* **2** most recent in time; latest: *last year.* ▪ immediately preceding in order; previous in a sequence: *their last album.* **3** only remaining: *it's our last hope.* **4** single; individual: *Holly was ceremoniously savoring **every last** crumb of her chocolate doughnut.*
▶adv. **1** on the last occasion before the present; previously: *he looked much older than when I'd last seen him.* **2** [in combination] after all others in order or sequence: *the two last-mentioned classes.* **3** (esp. in enumerating points) finally; in conclusion: *and last, I'd like to thank you all for coming.*
▶n. (pl. same) the last person or thing; the one occurring, mentioned, or acting after all others: *the last of their guests had gone.* ▪ (**the last of**) the only part of something that remains: *they drank the last of the wine.* ▪ last position in a race, contest, or ranking: *he came from last in a slowly run race.* ▪ (**the last**) the end or last moment, esp. death: *she did love me **to the last**.* ▪ (**the last**) the last mention or sight of someone or something: *that was **the last we saw of** her.*
▶ □ **at last** (or **at long last**) after much delay: *you've come back to me at last!* □ —— **one's last** do something for the last time: *the dying embers sparked their last.* □ **last but not least** last in order of mention or occurrence but just as important. □ **last call** (in a bar) an expression used to inform customers that closing time is approaching and that any further drinks should be purchased immediately: *the hours were 11:00 last call and drink up by 11:15.* □ **last ditch** used to denote a final, often desperate, act to achieve something in the face of difficulty: [as adj.] *a last-ditch attempt to acquire some proper qualifications.*

last[2] ▶v. [intr.] **1** (of a process, activity, or state of things) continue for a specified period of time: *the guitar solo lasted for twenty minutes.* **2** continue to function well or to be in good condition for a considerable or specified length of time: *the car is built to last* | *a lip pencil lasts longer than lipstick.* ▪ [tr.] (of provisions or resources) be adequate or sufficient for (someone), esp. for a specified length of time: *he filled the freezer with enough food to last him for three months.*

last[3] ▶*n.* a shoemaker's model for shaping or repairing a shoe or boot.

last·ing /ˈlastiNG/ ▶*adj.* enduring or able to endure over a long period of time: *they left a lasting impression.* —**last·ing·ly** *adv.* —**last·ing·ness** *n.*

Last Judg·ment ▶*n.* the judgment of humankind expected in some religious traditions to take place at the end of the world.

last·ly /ˈlastlē/ ▶*adv.* in the last place (used to introduce the last of a series of points or actions): *lastly, I would like to thank my parents.*

last rites ▶*plural n.* (in the Christian Church) rites administered to a person who is about to die.

Last Sup·per ▶the supper eaten by Jesus and his disciples on the night before the Crucifixion, as recorded in the New Testament and commemorated by Christians in the Eucharist. ■ an artistic representation based on this event.

latch /lacH/ ▶*n.* a metal bar with a catch and lever used for fastening a door or gate. ■ a spring lock for an outer door that catches when the door is closed and can only be opened from the outside with a key. ■ the part of a knitting machine needle that closes or opens to hold or release the wool.
▶*v.* [tr.] fasten (a door or gate) with a latch: *she latched the door carefully.*
▶*phrasal v.* □ **latch onto** *inf.* attach oneself to (someone) as a constant and usually unwelcome companion: *a knack for latching onto people with greater initiative and enterprise.* ■ take up (an idea or trend) enthusiastically: *the media have latched onto the snappy "Generation X" catchphrase.*

latch·key /ˈlacH,kē/ ▶*n.* (pl. **-keys**) a key of an outer door of a house.

latch·key child (also *inf.* **latchkey kid**) ▶*n.* a child who is at home without adult supervision for some part of the day, esp. after school until a parent returns from work.

late /lāt/ ▶*adj.* **1** doing something or taking place after the expected, proper, or usual time: *his late arrival.* **2** belonging or taking place near the end of a particular time or period: *they won the game with a late goal.* ■ flowering or ripening toward the end of the season: *the last late chrysanthemums.* **3** (**the/one's late**) (of a specified person) no longer alive: *the late William Jennings Bryan.* ■ no longer having the specified status; former: *a late colleague of mine.* **4** (**latest**) of recent date: *the latest news.*
▶*adv.* **1** after the expected, proper, or usual time: *she arrived late.* **2** toward the end of a period: *it happened **late in** 1984.* ■ at or until a time far into the day or night: *now I'm old enough to stay up late.* ■ (**later**) at a time in the near future; afterward: *I'll see you later.* **3** (**late of**) formerly but not now living or working in a specified place or institution: *Captain Falconer, late of the British army.*
▶*n.* (**the latest**) the most recent news or fashion: *have you heard the latest?* —**late·ness** *n.*
▶ □ **at the latest** no later than the time specified: *all new cars will be required to meet this standard by 1997 at the latest.* □ **late in the game** (or **day**) at a late stage in proceedings, esp. too late to be useful. □ **of late** recently: *she'd been drinking too much of late.*

late·com·er /ˈlāt,kəmər/ ▶*n.* a person who arrives late: *latecomers were not admitted before the intermission* | *fig. he was a **latecomer** to modernism.*

la·teen /laˈtēn; la-/ ▶*n.* (also **lateen sail**) a triangular sail on a long yard at an angle of about 45° to the mast. ■ a ship rigged with such a sail. ▷mid 16th cent.: from French (*voile*) *Latine* 'Latin (sail),' so named because it was common in the Mediterranean.

lateen

late·ly /ˈlātlē/ ▶*adv.* recently; not long ago: *she hasn't been looking too well lately.*

la·tent /ˈlātnt/ ▶*adj.* (of a quality or state) existing but not yet developed or manifest; hidden; concealed: *discovering her latent talent for diplomacy.* ■ *Biol.* (of a bud, resting stage, etc.) lying dormant or hidden until

circumstances are suitable for development or manifestation. —**la·ten·cy** /-tənsē/ *n.* —**la·tent·ly** *adv.*

lat·er·al /ˈlatərəl; ˈlatrəl/ ▶*adj.* of, at, toward, or from the side or sides: *the plant takes up water through its lateral roots.* ■ *Anat. & Zool.* situated on one side or other of the body or of an organ, esp. in the region furthest from the median plane. The opposite of **MEDIAL**. ■ *Med.* (of a disease or condition) affecting the side or sides of the body, or confined to one side of the body. ■ *Phonet.* (of a consonant, esp. *l*, or its articulation) formed by or involving partial closure of the air passage by the tongue, which is so placed as to allow the breath to flow on one or both sides of the point of contact.
▶*n.* **1** a side part of something, esp. a shoot or branch growing out from the side of a stem. **2** *Phonet.* a lateral consonant. **3** *Football* (also **lateral pass**) a pass thrown either sideways or backward from the position of the passer.
▶*v.* [tr.] throw (a football) in a sideways or backward direction: *he tried to lateral a kick return but fumbled.* ■ [intr.] throw a lateral: *he got the ball back on a handoff and then lateraled to a halfback.* —**lat·er·al·ly** *adv.*

la·tex /ˈlā,teks/ ▶*n.* (pl. **la·tex·es** or **lat·i·ces** /ˈlatə,sēz/) a milky fluid found in many plants, such as poppies and spurges, that exudes when the plant is cut and coagulates on exposure to the air. The latex of the rubber tree is the chief source of natural rubber. ■ a synthetic product resembling this consisting of a dispersion in water of polymer particles, used to make paints, coatings, and other products.

lath /laTH/ ▶*n.* (pl. **laths** /laTHZ; laTHS/) a thin flat strip of wood, esp. one of a series forming a foundation for the plaster of a wall or the tiles of a roof, or made into a trellis or fence. ■ laths collectively as a building material, esp. as a foundation for supporting plaster.
▶*v.* [tr.] cover (a wall or ceiling) with laths.

lathe /lāTH/ ▶*n.* a machine for shaping wood, metal, or other material by means of a rotating drive that turns the piece being worked on against changeable cutting tools.
▶*v.* [tr.] shape with a lathe.

lath·er /ˈlaTHər/ ▶*n.* a frothy white mass of bubbles produced by soap or a similar cleansing substance when mixed with water. ■ heavy sweat visible on a horse's coat as a white foam. ■ (**a lather**) *inf.* a state of agitation or nervous excitement: *Larry was worked into a lather and shouted at the mayor.*
▶*v.* [tr.] cause (soap) to form a frothy white mass of bubbles when mixed with water. ■ [intr.] (of soap or a similar cleansing substance) form a frothy white mass of bubbles in such a way: *soap will not lather in hard water.* ■ rub soap onto (a part of the body) until a lather is produced: *she was lathering herself languidly beneath the shower* ■ cause (a horse) to become covered with sweat: *his horse was **lathered up** by the end of the day.* ■ (**lather something with**) cover something liberally with (a substance): *she lathered a slice of toast with butter.* —**lath·er·y** *adj.*

lat·i·ces /ˈlatə,sēz/ ▶ plural form of **LATEX**.

Lat·in /ˈlatn/ ▶*n.* **1** the language of ancient Rome and its empire, widely used historically as a language of scholarship and administration. **2** a native or inhabitant of a country whose language developed from Latin, esp. a Latin American. ■ music of a kind originating in Latin America, characterized by dance rhythms and extensive use of indigenous percussive instruments.
▶*adj.* of, relating to, or in the Latin language: *Latin poetry.* ■ of or relating to the countries or peoples using languages, esp. Spanish, that developed from Latin. ■ of, relating to, or characteristic of Latin American music or dance: *snapping his fingers to a Latin beat.* ■ of or relating to the Western or Roman Catholic Church (as historically using Latin for its rites): *the Latin patriarch of Antioch.* ■ *hist.* of or relating to ancient Latium or its inhabitants. —**Lat·in·ism** /-,izəm/ *n.* —**Lat·in·ist** /-ist/ *n.*

La·ti·no /ləˈtēnō; la-/ ▶*n.* (pl. **-nos**) a Latin American inhabitant of the United States.
▶*adj.* of or relating to these inhabitants.

lat·ish /ˈlātisH/ ▶*adj. & adv.* fairly late: [as *adv.*] *Margaret came in latish.*

lat·i·tude /ˈlatə,t(y)ōōd/ ▶*n.* **1** the angular distance of a place north or south of the equator of the earth or other celestial body, usually expressed in degrees and minutes: *at a latitude of 51° N.* ■ (**latitudes**) regions, esp. with reference to their temperature and distance from the equator: *temperate latitudes.* **2** scope for freedom of action or thought: *journalists have considerable latitude in criticizing public figures.* ■ *Photog.* the range of exposures for which an emulsion or printing paper will give acceptable contrast: *a film with a latitude that is outstanding.* —**lat·i·tu·di·nal** /,latə't(y)ōōdn-əl/ *adj.* —**lat·i·tu·di·nal·ly** /,latə't(y)ōōdn-əlē/ *adv.*

la·trine /ləˈtrēn/ ▶*n.* a toilet, esp. a communal one in a camp or barracks.

lat·ter /ˈlatər/ ▶*adj.* [attrib.] **1** situated or occurring nearer to the end of something than to the beginning: *the latter half of 1989.* ■ recent: *the* *project had low cash flows in its latter years.* **2** (**the latter**) denoting the second or second mentioned of two people or things: *the Russians could advance into either Germany or Austria—they chose the latter option.*

Lat·ter-Day Saints (abbr.: **LDS**) ▶*plural n.* another name for the Mormons.

lat·ter·ly /ˈlatərlē/ ▶*adv.* recently: *latterly, his painting has shown a new freedom of expression.* ■ in the later stages of a period of time, esp. of a person's life: *he worked on the paper for fifty years, latterly as its political editor.*

lat·tice /ˈlatis/ ▶*n.* a structure consisting of strips of wood or metal crossed and fastened together with square or diamond-shaped spaces left between, used typically as a screen or fence or as a support for climbing plants. ■ an interlaced structure or pattern resembling this: *the lattice of branches above her.* ■ *Physics* a regular repeated three-dimensional arrangement of atoms, ions, or molecules in a metal or other crystalline solid. —**lat·ticed** *adj.*

lattice

lat·tice win·dow ▶*n.* a window with small panes set in diagonally crossing strips of lead.

Lat·vi·an /ˈlatvēən/ ▶*adj.* of or relating to Latvia, its people, or its language.
▶*n.* **1** a native or citizen of Latvia, or a person of Latvian descent. **2** the Baltic language of Latvia.

laud /lôd/ ▶*v.* [*tr.*] *formal* praise (a person or their achievements) highly, esp. in a public context: *the obituary lauded him as a great statesman.*
▶*n.* *archaic* praise: *all glory, laud, and honor to Thee.*

laud·a·ble /ˈlôdəbəl/ ▶*adj.* (of an action, idea, or goal) deserving praise and commendation: *laudable though the aim might be, the results have been criticized.* —**laud·a·bil·i·ty** /ˌlôdəˈbilətē/ *n.* —**laud·a·bly** /-blē/ *adv.*

lau·da·num /ˈlôdn-əm; ˈlôdnəm/ ▶*n.* an alcoholic solution containing morphine, prepared from opium and formerly used as a narcotic painkiller.

laud·a·to·ry /ˈlôdəˌtôrē/ ▶*adj.* (of speech or writing) expressing praise and commendation.

laugh /laf/ ▶*v.* [*intr.*] make the spontaneous sounds and movements of the face and body that are the instinctive expressions of lively amusement and sometimes also of contempt or derision: *she couldn't help laughing at his jokes.* ■ (**laugh at**) ridicule; scorn. ■ (**laugh something off**) dismiss something embarrassing, unfortunate, or potentially serious by treating it in a lighthearted way or making a joke of it. ■ (**be laughing**) *inf.* be in a fortunate or successful position: *if next year's model is as successful, Ford will be laughing.*
▶*n.* **1** an act of laughing: *she gave a loud, silly laugh.* **2** (**a laugh**) *inf.* a thing that causes laughter or derision: *that's a laugh, the idea of you cooking a meal!* ■ a person who is good fun or amusing company: *I like Peter—he's a good laugh.* ■ a source of fun or amusement: *she decided to play along with him for a laugh.* —**laugh·ing·ly** *adv.*
▶ □ **be laughing all the way to the bank** *inf.* be making a great deal of money very easily. □ **have the last laugh** be finally vindicated, thus confounding earlier skepticism. □ **laugh one's head off** laugh heartily or uncontrollably. □ **laugh in someone's face** show open contempt for someone by laughing rudely at them in their presence: *fig. vandals and muggers who laugh in the face of the law.* □ **the laugh is on me** (or **you**, **him**, etc.) the tables are turned and now the other person is the one who appears ridiculous: *all the critics had laughed at him—well, the laugh was on them now.* □ **laugh out of the other side of one's mouth** be discomfited after feeling satisfaction or confidence about something: *you'd be laughing out the other side of your mouth if we were sitting in jail right now.* □ **laugh someone/something out of court** dismiss with contempt as being obviously ridiculous. □ **no laughing matter** something serious that should not be joked about: *heavy snoring is no laughing matter.*

laugh·a·ble /ˈlafəbəl/ ▶*adj.* so ludicrous as to be amusing: *if it didn't make me so angry it would be laughable.* —**laugh·a·bly** /-blē/ *adv.* *his antics were laughably pretentious.*

laugh·ing gas ▶*n.* nontechnical term for **NITROUS OXIDE.**

laugh·ing·stock /ˈlafiNGˌstäk/ ▶*n.* a person subjected to general mockery or ridicule.

laugh·ter /ˈlaftər/ ▶*n.* the action or sound of laughing: *he roared with laughter.*

laugh track ▶*n.* recorded laughter added to a comedy show, esp. a television situation comedy.

launch¹ /lônCH; länCH/ ▶*v.* [*tr.*] **1** set (a boat) in motion by pushing it or allowing it to roll into the water: *the town's lifeboat was launched to rescue the fishermen.* ■ set (a newly built ship or boat) afloat for the first time, typically as part of an official ceremony: *King Gustav II Adolph of Sweden launched a huge new warship.* ■ send (a missile, satellite, or spacecraft) on its course or into orbit: *they launched two Scud missiles.* ■ [*tr.*] hurl (something) forcefully: *she launched a tortoiseshell comb.* **2** start or set in motion (an activity or enterprise): *she was launching a campaign against ugly architecture.* ■ introduce (a new product or publication) to the public for the first time: *the company has launched a software package specifically for the legal sector.*
▶*phrasal v.* □ **launch into** begin (something) energetically and enthusiastically: *he launched into a two-hour sales pitch.*
▶*n.* an act or an instance of launching something: *the launch of a new campaign against drinking and driving.* ■ an occasion at which a new product or publication is introduced to the public: *a book launch.* —**launch·er** *n.*

launch² ▶*n.* a large motorboat, used esp. for short trips. ■ *hist.* the largest boat carried on a man-of-war.

launch pad (also **launching pad**) ▶*n.* the area on which a rocket stands for launching, typically consisting of a platform with a supporting structure.

laun·der /ˈlôndər; ˈlän-/ ▶*v.* [*tr.*] wash, or wash and iron, (clothes or linens): *he wasn't used to laundering his own bed linens.* ■ conceal the origins of (money obtained illegally) by transfers involving foreign banks or legitimate businesses. ■ alter (information) to make it appear more acceptable: *we began to notice attempts to launder the data retrospectively.* ▷ Middle English (as a noun denoting a person who washes linen): contraction of *lavender*, from Old French *lavandier*, based on Latin *lavanda* 'things to be washed,' from *lavare* 'to wash.' —**laun·der·er** *n.*

laun·dress /ˈlôndrəs; ˈlän-/ ▶*n.* a woman who is employed to launder clothes and linens.

Laun·dro·mat /ˈlôndrəˌmat; ˈlän-/ (also **laun·dro·mat**) ▶*n.* *trademark* an establishment with coin-operated washing machines and dryers for public use.

laun·dry /ˌlôndrē; ˈlän-/ ▶*n.* (*pl.* **-dries**) **1** clothes and linens that need to be washed or that have been newly washed: *piles of dirty laundry.* ■ the action or process of washing such items: *I talked her into letting me help Ben with the rest of the laundry.* **2** a room in a house, hotel, or institution where clothes and linens can be washed and ironed. ■ a business that washes and irons clothes and linens commercially.

laun·dry list ▶*n.* a long or exhaustive list of people or things: *there's a laundry list of possible triggers for migraines.*

lau·re·ate /ˈlôrē-it; ˈlär-/ ▶*n.* a person who is honored with an award for outstanding creative or intellectual achievement: *a Nobel laureate.* ■ short for **POET LAUREATE.** —**lau·re·ate·ship** /-ˌSHip/ *n.*

lau·rel /ˈlôrəl; ˈlär-/ ▶*n.* **1** any of a number of shrubs and other plants with dark green glossy leaves, in particular, **BAY².** ■ short for **MOUNTAIN LAUREL.** **2** an aromatic evergreen shrub related to the bay tree (family Lauraceae), several kinds of which form forests in tropical and warm countries. **3** (usu. **laurels**) the foliage of the bay tree woven into a wreath or crown and worn on the head as an emblem of victory or mark of honor in classical times. ■ *fig.* honor: *she has rightly won laurels for this brilliantly perceptive first novel.*
▶*v.* (**-reled, -rel·ing**; *Brit.* **-relled, -rel·ling**) [*tr.*] adorn with or as if with a laurel: *they banish our anger forever when they laurel the graves of our dead.*
▶ □ **look to one's laurels** be careful not to lose one's superior position to a rival. □ **rest on one's laurels** be so satisfied with what one has already achieved that one makes no further effort.

la·va /ˈlävə; ˈlavə/ ▶*n.* hot molten or semifluid rock erupted from a volcano or fissure, or solid rock resulting from cooling of this.

la·vage /ləˈväzH; ˈlavij/ ▶*n.* *Med.* washing out of a body cavity, such as the colon or stomach, with water or a medicated solution.

lav·a·to·ry /ˈlavəˌtôrē/ ▶*n.* (*pl.* **-ries**) a room or compartment with a toilet and washbasin; a bathroom. ■ a sink or washbasin in a bathroom.

Pronunciation Key ə *ago,* up; ər *over,* fur; a *hat;* ā *ate;* ä *car;* CH *chin;* e *let;* ē *see;* e(ə)r *air;* i *fit;* ī *by;* i(ə)r *ear;* NG *sing;* ō *go;* ô *law,* for; oi *toy;* o͞o *good;* o͞o *goo;* ou *out;* SH *she;* TH *thin;* ᴛʜ *then;* (h)w *why;* ZH *vision*

lav·en·der /ˈlavəndər/ ▶n. **1** a small aromatic evergreen shrub (genus *Lavandula*) of the mint family, with narrow leaves and bluish-purple flowers. ■ the flowers and stalks of such a shrub dried and used to give a pleasant smell to clothes and bed linens. ■ (also **lavender oil**) a scented oil distilled from lavender flowers. ■ used in names of similar plants, e.g., **sea lavender**. ■ *inf.* used in reference to effeminacy or homosexuality: *he has a touch of lavender.* **2** a pale blue color with a trace of mauve.
▶v. [*tr.*] perfume with lavender.

lav·ish /ˈlaviSH/ ▶adj. sumptuously rich, elaborate, or luxurious: *a lavish banquet.* ■ (of a person) very generous or extravagant: *he was lavish with his hospitality.* ■ spent or given in profusion: *lavish praise.*
▶v. [*tr.*] (**lavish something on**) bestow something in generous or extravagant quantities upon: *the media couldn't lavish enough praise on the film.* ■ (**lavish something with**) cover something thickly or liberally with: *she lavished our son with kisses.* —**lav·ish·ly** *adv.* —**lav·ish·ness** *n.*

law /lô/ ▶n. **1** (often **the law**) the system of rules that a particular country or community recognizes as regulating the actions of its members and may enforce by the imposition of penalties: *they were taken to court for breaking the law.* | [as *adj.*] *law enforcement.* ■ an individual rule as part of such a system: *an initiative to tighten up the laws on pornography.* ■ such systems as a subject of study or as the basis of the legal profession: *he was still practicing law* | [as *adj.*] *a law firm.* ■ a thing regarded as having the binding force or effect of a formal system of rules: *what he said was law.* ■ (**the law**) *inf.* the police: *he'd never been in trouble with the law in his life.* ■ statutory law and the common law. ■ a rule defining correct procedure or behavior in a sport: *the laws of the game.* **2** a statement of fact, deduced from observation, to the effect that a particular natural or scientific phenomenon always occurs if certain conditions are present: *the second law of thermodynamics.* ■ a generalization based on a fact or event perceived to be recurrent: *the first law of American corporate life is that dead wood floats.* **3** the body of divine commandments as expressed in the Bible or other religious texts.
▶ □ **lay down the law** issue instructions to other people in an authoritative or dogmatic way. □ **take the law into one's own hands** punish someone for an offense according to one's own ideas of justice, esp. in an illegal or violent way.

law·break·er /ˈlôˌbrākər/ ▶n. a person who violates the law. —**law·break·ing** /-ˌbrākiNG/ *n.* & *adj.*

law·ful /ˈlôfəl/ ▶adj. conforming to, permitted by, or recognized by law or rules: *it is an offense to carry a weapon in public without lawful authority.* —**law·ful·ly** *adv.* —**law·ful·ness** *n.*

law·giv·er /ˈlôˌgivər/ ▶n. a person who draws up and enacts laws.

law·less /ˈlôləs/ ▶adj. not governed by or obedient to laws; characterized by a lack of civic order: *it was a lawless, anarchic city.* —**law·less·ly** *adv.* —**law·less·ness** *n.*

law·mak·er /ˈlôˌmākər/ ▶n. a legislator. —**law·mak·ing** /-ˌmākiNG/ *adj.* & *n.*

law·man /ˈlôˌmən; -ˌman/ ▶n. (pl. **-men**) a law-enforcement officer, esp. a sheriff.

lawn¹ /lôn/ ▶n. an area of short, mown grass in a yard, garden, or park. —**lawned** *adj.*

lawn² ▶n. a fine linen or cotton fabric used for making clothes. —**lawn·y** *adj.*

lawn mow·er ▶n. a machine for cutting the grass on a lawn.

law of av·er·ag·es ▶n. the principle that supposes most future events are likely to balance any past deviation from a presumed average.

law·ren·ci·um /lôˈrensēəm/ ▶n. the chemical element of atomic number 103, an artificial radioactive metal of the actinide series. (Symbol: **Lr**)

law·suit /ˈlôˌso͞ot/ ▶n. a claim or dispute brought to a court of law for adjudication: *his lawyer filed a lawsuit against Los Angeles city.*

law·yer /ˈloi-ər; ˈlôyər/ ▶n. a person who practices or studies law; an attorney or a counselor.
▶v. [*intr.*] practice law; work as a lawyer: [as *n.*] (**lawyering**) *lawyering is a craft that takes a long time to become proficient at.* ■ [*tr.*] (of a lawyer) work on the legal aspects of (a contract, lawsuit, etc.): *there is always a danger that the deal will be lawyered to death.* —**law·yer·ly** *adj.*

lax /laks/ ▶adj. **1** not sufficiently strict or severe: *lax security arrangements at the airport.* ■ careless: *why do software developers do little more than parrot their equally lax competitors?* **2** (of the limbs or muscles) relaxed. ■ (of the bowels) loose. ■ *Phonet.* (of a speech sound, esp. a vowel) pronounced with the vocal muscles relaxed. The opposite of TENSE¹. —**lax·i·ty** /ˈlaksətē/ *n.* —**lax·ly** *adv.* —**lax·ness** *n.*

lax·a·tive /ˈlaksətiv/ ▶adj. (chiefly of a drug or medicine) tending to stimulate or facilitate evacuation of the bowels.
▶n. a medicine that has such an effect. ▷late Middle English: via Old French *laxatif, -ive* or late Latin *laxativus*, from Latin *laxare* 'loosen' from *laxus* 'loose'.

lay¹ /lā/ ▶v. (*past* **laid** /lād/) **1** [*tr.*] put down, esp. gently or carefully: *she laid the baby in his crib.* ■ [*tr.*] prevent (something) from rising off the ground: *there may have been the odd light shower just to lay the dust.* **2** [*tr.*] put down and set in position for use: *it is advisable to have your carpet laid by a professional.* ■ (often **be laid with**) cover (a surface) with objects or a substance: *the floor was laid with tiles.* ■ make ready (a trap) for someone: *she wouldn't put it past him to lay a trap for her.* ■ put the material for (a fire) in place and arrange it. ■ work out (an idea or suggestion) in detail ready for use or presentation: *I'd like more time to lay my plans.* ■ (**lay something before**) present information or suggestions to be considered and acted upon by (someone): *he laid before the House proposals for the establishment of the committee.* ■ (usu. **be laid**) locate (an episode in a play, novel, etc.) in a certain place: *no one who knew the area could be in doubt where the scene was laid.* ■ [*intr.*] *Naut.* go or come: *they had to lay aloft.* **3** [*tr.*] used with an abstract noun so that the phrase formed has the same meaning as the verb related to the noun used, e.g., "lay the blame on" means 'to blame': *she laid great stress on little courtesies.* ■ (**lay something on**) require (someone) to endure or deal with a responsibility or difficulty: *this is an absurdly heavy guilt trip to lay on anyone.* **4** [*tr.*] (of a female bird, insect, reptile, or amphibian) produce (an egg) from inside the body: *flamingos lay only one egg.* **5** [*tr.*] *vulgar slang* have sexual intercourse with. ■ [*intr.*] (**get laid**) have sexual intercourse.
▶*phrasal v.* □ **lay something down 1** put something that one has been holding on the ground or another surface: *she finished her eclair and laid down her fork.* ■ give up the use or enjoyment of something: *they renounced violence and laid down their arms.* ■ sacrifice one's life in a noble cause: *he laid down his life for his country.* **2** formulate and enforce or insist on a rule or principle: *stringent criteria have been laid down.* **3** set something in position for use on the ground or a surface: *the floors were constructed by laying down precast concrete blocks.* ■ (usu. **be laid down**) build up a deposit of a substance: *these cells lay down new bone tissue.* **4** store wine in a cellar. **5** pay or wager money. **6** *inf.* record a piece of music: *he was invited to the studio to lay down some backing vocals.* □ **lay something in/up** build up a stock of something in case of need. □ **lay into** *inf.* attack violently with words or blows: *three youths laid into him.* □ **lay off** *inf.* give up: *I laid off smoking for seven years.* ■ [usu. in *imperative*] used to advise someone to stop doing something: *lay off—he's not going to tell you.* □ **lay someone off** discharge a worker, esp. because of a shortage of work. □ **lay someone out 1** prepare someone for burial after death. **2** *inf.* knock someone unconscious: *he was lucky that the punch didn't lay him out.* □ **lay something out 1** spread something out to its full extent, esp. so that it can be seen: *the police were insisting that suitcases should be opened and their contents laid out.* **2** construct or arrange according to a plan: *they proceeded to lay out a new town.* ■ explain something clearly and carefully: *we need a paper laying out our priorities.* **3** *inf.* spend a sum of money: *look at the money I had to lay out for your uniform.* □ **lay up** *Golf* hit the ball deliberately to a lesser distance than possible, typically in order to avoid a hazard. □ **lay someone up** put someone out of action through illness or injury: *he was laid up with his familiar fever.* □ **lay something up 1** see LAY SOMETHING IN above. **2** take a ship or other vehicle out of service: *our boats were laid up during the winter months.*
▶n. **1** the general appearance of an area, including the direction of streams, hills, and similar features: *the lay of the surrounding countryside.* ■ the position or direction in which something lies: *roll the carpet against the lay of the nap.* ■ the direction or amount of twist in rope strands. **2** *vulgar slang* an act of sexual intercourse. ■ [with *adj.*] a person with a particular ability or availability as a sexual partner.
▶ □ **lay something bare** bring something out of concealment; expose something: *the sad tale of failure was laid bare.* □ **lay a charge** make an accusation: *we could lay a charge of gross negligence.* □ **lay claim to something** assert that one has a right to something: *four men laid claim to the leadership.* ■ assert that one possesses a skill or quality: *she has never laid claim to medical knowledge.* □ **lay hands on 1** find and take possession of: *they huddled, trying to keep warm under anything they could lay hands on.* **2** place one's hands on or over, esp. in confirmation, ordination, or spiritual healing. □ **lay hold of** (or **on**) catch at with one's hands: *he was afraid she might vanish if he did not lay hold of her.* ■ gain possession of: *the gun was the only one he had been able to lay hold of.* □ **the lay** (*Brit.* **lie**) **of the land** the way in which the features or characteristics of an area present themselves. ■ *fig.* the current situation or state of affairs: *she was beginning to see the lay of the land with her in-laws.* □ **lay someone low** (of an illness) reduce someone to inactivity. ■ bring to an end the high position or good fortune formerly enjoyed by someone: *she reflected on how quickly fate can lay a person low.* □ **lay something on thick** (or **with a**

trowel) *inf.* grossly exaggerate or overemphasize something. □ **lay someone open to** expose someone to the risk of (something): *his position could lay him open to accusations of favoritism.* □ **lay over** break one's journey: *Steven and I will lay over in New York, then fly to London.* □ **lay someone/something to rest** bury a body in a grave. ■ soothe and dispel fear, anxiety, grief, or a similar unpleasant emotion: *suspicion will be laid to rest by fact rather than hearsay.*

lay² ▶ *adj.* [*attrib.*] **1** not ordained into or belonging to the clergy: *a lay preacher.* **2** not having professional qualifications or expert knowledge, esp. in law or medicine: *lay and professional views of medicine.*

lay³ ▶ *n.* a short lyric or narrative poem meant to be sung. ■ *poetic/literary* a song: *on his lips there died the cheery lay.*

lay⁴ ▶ past of LIE¹.

lay·a·bout /ˈlāəˌbout/ ▶ *n. derog.* a person who habitually does little or no work.

lay·a·way /ˈlāəˌwā/ ▶ *n.* (also **layaway plan**) a system of paying a deposit to secure an item for later purchase: *she picked up a coat she had on layaway.*

lay·er /ˈlāər/ ▶ *n.* **1** a sheet, quantity, or thickness of material, typically one of several, covering a surface or body: *bears depend on a layer of blubber to keep them warm in the water.* ■ a level of seniority in the hierarchy of an organization: *a managerial layer.* **2** [in *combination*] a person or thing that lays something: *the worms are prolific egg-layers.* ■ a hen that lays eggs. **3** a shoot fastened down to take root while attached to the parent plant.
▶ *v.* [*tr.*] [often as *adj.*] (**layered**) **1** arrange in a layer or layers: *the current trend for layered clothes.* ■ cut (hair) in overlapping layers: *her layered, shoulder-length hair.* **2** propagate (a plant) as a layer: *a layered shoot.*

lay·ette /lāˈet/ ▶ *n.* a set of clothing, linens, and sometimes toiletries for a newborn child.

lay·man /ˈlāmən/ ▶ *n.* (*pl.* **-men**) **1** a nonordained member of a church. **2** a person without professional or specialized knowledge in a particular subject: *the book seems well suited to the interested layman.*

lay·off /ˈlāˌôf/ ▶ *n.* **1** a discharge, esp. temporary, of a worker or workers. ■ a period when this is in force. **2** a period during which someone does not take part in a customary sport or other activity: *they needed to rehabilitate injuries or just brush up after long layoffs.*

lay·out /ˈlāˌout/ ▶ *n.* the way in which the parts of something are arranged or laid out: *changing the layout of the ground floor.* ■ the way in which text or pictures are set out on a page: *the layout is uncluttered and the illustrations are helpful.* ■ the process of setting out material on a page or in a work: *doing layout for newspapers and magazines.* ■ a thing arranged or set out in a particular way: *a model railroad layout.* ■ *Diving, Gymnastics* a position in which the body is extended, the head upright, the legs held straight and together, and the arms held out to the sides.

lay·o·ver /ˈlāˌōvər/ ▶ *n.* a period of rest or waiting before a further stage in a journey.

lay·wom·an /ˈlāˌwo͝omən/ ▶ *n.* (*pl.* **-wom·en**) a nonordained female member of a church.

laze /lāz/ ▶ *v.* [*intr.*] spend time in a relaxed, lazy manner: *she spent the day at home, reading the papers and generally lazing around.* ■ [*tr.*] (**laze something away**) pass time in such a way: *laze away a long summer day.*

la·zy /ˈlāzē/ ▶ *adj.* (**la·zi·er, la·zi·est**) **1** unwilling to work or use energy: *I'm very lazy by nature | he was too lazy to cook.* ■ characterized by lack of effort or activity: *lazy summer days.* ■ showing a lack of effort or care: *lazy writing.* ■ (of a river) slow-moving. **2** (of a livestock brand) placed on its side rather than upright: *a logo with a lazy E.* —**la·zi·ly** /-zəlē/ *adv.* —**la·zi·ness** *n.*

la·zy·bones /ˈlāzēˌbōnz/ ▶ *n.* (*pl.* same) *inf.* a lazy person (often as a form of address).

la·zy eye ▶ *n.* an eye with poor vision that is mainly caused by underuse, esp. the unused eye in strabismus.

lb. ▶ *abbr.* ■ pound(s) (in weight). [from Latin *libra*.]

LC ▶ *abbr.* ■ landing craft. ■ Library of Congress.

LCD ▶ *abbr.* ■ *Electr. & Comput.* liquid crystal display. ■ *Math.* lowest (or least) common denominator.

LCM *Math.* ▶ *abbr.* lowest (or least) common multiple.

LD ▶ *abbr.* ■ learning disabled. ■ lethal dose (of a toxic compound, drug, or pathogen). It is usually written with a following numeral indicating the percentage of a group of animals or cultured cells or microorganisms killed by such a dose, typically standardized at 50 percent (**LD₅₀**).

Ld. ▶ *abbr.* Lord: *Ld. Lothian.*

ld. ▶ *abbr.* ■ lead. ■ load.

lea /lē/ ▶ *n. poetic/literary* usually *literary* an open area of grassy or arable land: *the lowing herd winds slowly o'er the lea.*

leach /lēCH/ ▶ *v.* [*tr.*] make (a soluble chemical or mineral) drain away from soil, ash, or similar material by the action of percolating liquid, esp. rainwater: *the nutrient is quickly leached away.* ■ [*intr.*] (of a soluble chemical or mineral) drain away from soil, ash, etc., in this way: *coats of varnish prevent the dye leaching out.* ■ [*tr.*] subject (soil, ash, etc.) to this process.

lead¹ /lēd/ ▶ *v.* (*past* and *past part.* **led** /led/) [*tr.*] **1** cause (a person or animal) to go with one by holding them by the hand, a halter, a rope, etc., while moving forward: *she emerged leading a bay horse.* ■ show (someone or something) the way to a destination by going in front of or beside them: *she stood up and led her friend to the door.* ■ be a reason or motive for (someone): *nothing that I have read about the case leads me to the conclusion that anything untoward happened.* ■ [*intr.*] be a route or means of access to a particular place or in a particular direction: *a door leading to a better-lit corridor.* ■ [*intr.*] (**lead to**) culminate in (a particular event): *closing the plant will lead to the loss of 300 jobs.* **2** [*tr.*] be in charge or command of: *a military delegation was led by the Chief of Staff.* ■ set (a process) in motion: *they are waiting for an expansion of world trade to lead a recovery.* ■ be the principal player of (a group of musicians): *since the forties he has led his own big bands.* ■ [*intr.*] (**lead with**) assign the most important position to (a particular news item): *the news on the radio led with the murder.* **3** be superior to (competitors or colleagues): *there will be specific areas or skills in which other nations lead the world.* ■ have the first place in (a competition): *be ahead of (competitors): the veteran jockey was leading the field.* **4** have or experience (a particular way of life): *she's led a completely sheltered life.* **5** initiate (action in a game or contest), in particular: ■ (in card games) play (the first card) in a trick or round of play. ■ [*intr.*] (**lead with**) *Boxing* make an attack with (a particular punch or fist): *Adam led with a left.* ■ [*intr.*] *Baseball* (of a base runner) advance one or more steps from the base one occupies while the pitcher has the ball: *the runner leads from first.*
▶ *phrasal v.* □ **lead off 1** start: *the newsletter leads off with a report on tax bills.* **2** (of a door, room, or path) provide access away from a central space: *a farm track led off to the left.* □ **lead someone on** mislead or deceive someone, esp. into believing that one is in love with or attracted to them. □ **lead up to** immediately precede: *the weeks leading up to the elections.* ■ result in: *fashioning a policy appropriate to the situation entails understanding the forces that led up to it.*
▶ *n.* /lēd/ **1** the initiative in an action; an example for others to follow: *The U.S. is now taking the environmental lead.* ■ a clue to be followed in the resolution of a problem: *detectives investigating the murder are chasing new leads.* ■ (in card games) an act or right of playing first in a trick or round of play: *it's your lead.* ■ the card played first in a trick or round. **2** (**the lead**) a position of advantage in a contest; first place: *they were beaten 5-3 after twice being in the lead.* ■ an amount by which a competitor is ahead of the others: *the team held a slender one-goal lead.* ■ *Baseball* an advance of one or more steps taken by a base runner from the base they occupy while the pitcher has the ball. **3** the chief part in a play or film: *she had the lead in a new film.* ■ the person playing the chief part: *he still looked like a romantic lead.* ■ [*usu. as adj.*] the chief performer or instrument of a specified type: *that girl will be your lead dancer.* ■ [often as *adj.*] the item of news given the greatest prominence in a newspaper or magazine: *the lead story.* **4** a leash for a dog or other animal. **5** a wire that conveys electric current from a source to an appliance, or that connects two points of a circuit together. **6** a channel of open water in an ice field.
▶ □ **lead someone astray** cause someone to act or think foolishly or wrongly. □ **lead from the front** take an active role in what one is urging and directing others to do. □ **lead someone** (or **down**) **the garden path** *inf.* give someone misleading clues or signals.

lead² /led/ ▶ *n.* **1** a heavy, bluish-gray, soft, ductile metal, the chemical element of atomic number 82. (Symbol: **Pb**) **2** an item or implement made of lead, in particular: ■ *Naut.* a lead casting suspended on a line to determine the depth of water. ■ bullets. **3** graphite used as the part of a pencil that makes a mark. **4** *Printing* a blank space between lines of print. [originally with reference to the metal strip used to create this space.]
▶ □ **get the lead out** *inf.* move or work more quickly.

lead·en /ˈledn/ ▶ *adj.* dull, heavy, or slow: *his eyelids were leaden with sleep.* ■ of the color of lead; dull gray: *the snow fell from a leaden sky.* ■ *archaic* made of lead: *a leaden coffin.* —**lead·en·ly** *adv.* —**lead·en·ness** *n.*

lead·er /ˈlēdər/ ▶ *n.* **1** the person who leads or commands a group,

Pronunciation Key ə *ago, up;* ər *over, fur;* a *hat;* ā *ate;* ä *car;* CH *chin;* e *let;* ē *see;* e(ə)r *air;* i *fit;* ī *by;* i(ə)r *ear;* NG *sing;* ō *go;* ô *law, for;* oi *toy;* o͞o *good;* o͞o *goo;* ou *out;* SH *she;* TH *thin;* TH *then;* (h)w *why;* ZH *vision*

organization, or country: *the leader of a protest group.* ■ a person followed by others: *he is a leader among his classmates.* ■ an organization or company that is the most advanced or successful in a particular area: *a **leader in** the use of video conferencing.* ■ the horse placed at the front in a team or pair. **2** a conductor of a band or small musical group. **3** a short strip of nonfunctioning material at each end of a reel of film or recording tape for connection to the spool. ■ a length of filament attached to the end of a fishing line to carry the hook or fly. **4** a shoot of a plant at the apex of a stem or main branch. **5 (leaders)** *Printing* a series of dots or dashes across the page to guide the eye, esp. in tabulated material. —**lead·er·less** *adj.* —**lead·er·ship** *n.*

lead-in /ˈlēd ˌin/ ▶*n.* an introduction or preamble that allows one to move smoothly on to the next part of something: [as *adj.*] *the lead-in note.*

lead·ing[1] /ˈlēdiNG/ ▶*adj.* [attrib.] most important: *a number of leading politicians.*
▶*n.* guidance or leadership, esp. in a spiritual context. ■ an instance of such guidance: *the leadings of the Holy Spirit.*

lead·ing[2] /ˈlediNG/ ▶*n.* the amount of blank space between lines of print.

lead·ing ques·tion /ˈlēdiNG/ ▶*n.* a question that prompts or encourages the desired answer.

lead-off /ˈlēd/ ▶*adj.* (of an action) beginning a series or a process: *the album's lead-off track.* ■ **(lead-off)** *Baseball* denoting the first batter in a lineup or an inning.

lead time /lēd/ ▶*n.* the time between the initiation and completion of a production process.

leaf /lēf/ ▶*n.* (*pl.* **leaves** /lēvz/) **1** a flattened structure of a higher plant, typically green and bladelike, that is attached to a stem directly or via a stalk. ■ any of a number of similar plant structures, e.g., bracts, sepals, and petals. ■ foliage regarded collectively. ■ the state of having leaves: *the trees are still in leaf.* ■ the leaves of tobacco or tea: [as *adj.*] *leaf tea.* **2** a thing that resembles a leaf in being flat and thin, typically something that is one of two or more similar items forming a set or stack. ■ a single thickness of paper, esp. in a book with each side forming a page. ■ [with *adj.*] gold, silver, or other specified metal in the form of very thin foil. ■ the hinged part or flap of a door, shutter, or table. ■ an extra section inserted to extend a table. ■ the inner or outer part of a cavity wall or double-glazed window. ■ any of the stacked metal strips that form a leaf spring.
▶*v.* [intr.] **1** (of a plant, esp. a deciduous one in spring) put out new leaves. **2 (leaf through)** turn over (the pages of a book or the papers in a pile), reading them quickly or casually: *he leafed through the stack of notes.* ▷Old English *lēaf*, of Germanic origin; related to Dutch *loof* and German *Laub*. —**leaf·age** /ˈlēfij/ *n.* —**leaf·less** *adj.* —**leaf·like** /-ˌlīk/ *adj.*
▶ □ **shake** (or **tremble**) **like a leaf** (of a person) tremble greatly, esp. from fear.

leaf·let /ˈlēflit/ ▶*n.* **1** a printed sheet of paper, sometimes folded, containing information or advertising and usually distributed free. **2** *Bot.* each of the leaflike structures that together make up a compound leaf, such as in the ash and horse chestnut. ■ (in general use) a young leaf.
▶*v.* (**-let·ed, -let·ing**) [tr.] distribute leaflets to (people or an area): *I won't be leafleting neighborhoods.*

leaf lit·ter ▶*n.* see LITTER (sense 3).

leaf·y /ˈlēfē/ ▶*adj.* (**leaf·i·er, leaf·i·est**) (of a plant) having many leaves. ■ having or characterized by much foliage because of an abundance of trees or bushes: *a remote, leafy glade.* ■ (of a plant) producing or grown for its broad-bladed leaves: *green leafy vegetables.* ■ resembling a leaf or leaves: *a three-pointed leafy bract.* —**leaf·i·ness** *n.*

league[1] /lēg/ ▶*n.* **1** a collection of people, countries, or groups that combine for a particular purpose, typically mutual protection or cooperation: *the League of Nations.* ■ an agreement to combine in this way. **2** a group of sports clubs that play each other over a period for a championship. **3** a class or category of quality or excellence: *the two men were **not in the same league**.*
▶ □ **in league** conspiring with another or others: *he is **in league with** the devil.*

league[2] ▶*n.* a former measure of distance by land, usually about three miles.

League of Na·tions ▶an association of countries established in 1919 by the Treaty of Versailles to promote international cooperation and achieve international peace and security. It was powerless to stop Italian, German, and Japanese expansionism leading to World War II and was replaced by the United Nations in 1945.

leak /lēk/ ▶*v.* [intr.] (of a container or covering) accidentally lose or admit contents, esp. liquid or gas, through a hole or crack: *the roof leaked.* ■ (of liquid, gas, etc.) pass in or out through a hole or crack in such a way: *water kept leaking in.* ■ *fig.* (of secret information) become known: *the news leaked out.* ■ [tr.] intentionally disclose (secret information): *who had a motive to leak the story?*
▶*n.* a hole in a container or covering through which contents, esp. liquid or gas, may accidentally pass: *I checked all of the pipes for leaks.* ■ the action of leaking in such a way: *a gas leak.* ■ a similar escape of electric charge or current. ■ an intentional disclosure of secret information: *one of the employees was responsible for the leak.* —**leak·er** *n.*
▶ □ **take a leak** *inf.* urinate.

leak·age /ˈlēkij/ ▶*n.* the accidental admission or escape of a fluid or gas through a hole or crack: *we're saving water by reducing leakage.* ■ *Physics* the gradual escape of an electric charge or current, or magnetic flux. ■ deliberate disclosure of confidential information.

leak·y /ˈlēkē/ ▶*adj.* (**leak·i·er, leak·i·est**) having a leak or leaks: *a leaky roof.* —**leak·i·ness** *n.*

lean[1] /lēn/ ▶*v.* (past and past part. **leaned** /lēnd/) [intr.] be in or move into a sloping position: *he leaned back in his chair.* ■ **(lean against/on)** incline from the perpendicular and rest for support on or against (something): *a man was leaning against the wall.* ■ [tr.] **(lean something against/on)** cause something to rest on or against: *he leaned his elbows on the table.*
▶*phrasal v.* □ **lean on 1** rely on or derive support from: *they have learned to lean on each other for support.* **2** put pressure on (someone) to act in a certain way: *a determination not to allow the majority to lean on the minority.* □ **lean to/toward** incline or be partial to (a view or position): *I now lean toward sabotage as the cause of the crash.*
▶*n.* a deviation from the perpendicular; an inclination: *the vehicle has a definite lean to the left.*

lean[2] /lēn/ ▶*adj.* **1** (of a person or animal) thin, esp. healthily so; having no superfluous fat: *his lean, muscular body.* ■ (of meat) containing little fat: *lean bacon.* ■ (of an industry or company) efficient and with no waste: *he made leaner government a campaign theme.* **2** (of an activity or a period of time) offering little reward, substance, or nourishment; meager: *the lean winter months.* **3** (of a vaporized fuel mixture) having a high proportion of air: *lean air-to-fuel ratios.*
▶*n.* the lean part of meat. —**lean·ly** *adv.* —**lean·ness** *n.*

lean·ing /ˈlēniNG/ ▶*n.* (often **leanings**) a tendency or partiality of a particular kind: *his early leanings toward socialism.*

lean-to ▶*n.* (*pl.* **-tos**) a building sharing one wall with a larger building, and having a roof that leans against that wall: [as *adj.*] *a lean-to garage.* ■ a temporary shelter, either supported or freestanding.

leap /lēp/ ▶*v.* (past or past part. **leaped** /lēpt/ or **leapt** /lept/) [intr.] jump or spring a long way, to a great height, or with great force: *I leaped across the threshold* | *fig. Fabia's heart leapt excitedly.* ■ move quickly and suddenly: *Polly leapt to her feet.* ■ [tr.] jump across or over: *a coyote leaped the fence.* ■ **(leap at)** accept (an opportunity) eagerly: *they leapt at the opportunity to combine fun with fund-raising.* ■ (of a price or figure) increase dramatically: *sales leaped 40 percent during the Christmas season.* ■ **(leap out)** (esp. of writing) be conspicuous; stand out: *amid the notes, a couple of items leap out.*
▶*n.* a forceful jump or quick movement: *she came downstairs in a series of flying leaps.* ■ a dramatic increase in price, amount, etc.: *a leap of 75 percent in two years.* ■ a sudden, abrupt change or transition: *a leap of faith.* —**leap·er** *n.*
▶ □ **by** (or **in**) **leaps and bounds** with startlingly rapid progress: *productivity improved in leaps and bounds.* □ **leap to one's mind** be immediately apparent: *one dire question leaped to our minds.*

leap·frog /ˈlēpˌfrôg; -ˌfräg/ ▶*n.* a game in which players in turn vault with parted legs over the backs of others who are bending down.
▶*v.* (**-frogged, -frog·ging**) [intr.] perform such a vault: *they leapfrogged around the courtyard.* ■ (of a person or group) surpass or overtake another to move into a leading or dominant position: *she leapfrogged into a sales position.* ■ [tr.] pass over (a stage or obstacle): *attempts to leapfrog the barriers of class.*

leap year ▶*n.* a year, occurring once every four years, that has 366 days including February 29 as an intercalary day.

learn /lərn/ ▶*v.* (past learned /lərnd/) [tr.] **1** gain or acquire knowledge of or skill in (something) by study, experience, or being taught: *they'd started learning French* **2** *archaic, inf.* teach (someone): *"That'll learn you,"* he chuckled | [tr.] *we'll have to learn you to milk cows.* —**learn·a·bil·i·ty** /ˌlərnə-ˈbilətē/ *n.* —**learn·a·ble** *adj.* —**learn·er** *n.*

learn·ed /ˈlərnid/ ▶*adj.* (of a person) having much knowledge acquired by study. ■ showing, requiring, or characterized by learning; scholarly: *an article in a learned journal.* —**learn·ed·ly** /-nidlē/ *adv.* —**learn·ed·ness** /-nidnis/.

learn·ing /'lərniNG/ ▶*n.* the acquisition of knowledge or skills through experience, practice, or study, or by being taught: *these children experienced difficulties in learning.* ■ knowledge acquired in this way: *I liked to parade my learning in front of my sisters.*

learn·ing curve ▶*n.* the rate of a person's progress in gaining experience or new skills: *the latest software packages have a steep learning curve.*

learn·ing dis·a·bil·i·ty ▶*n.* a condition giving rise to difficulties in acquiring knowledge and skills to the level expected of those of the same age, esp. when not associated with a physical handicap. —**learn·ing-dis·a·bled** *adj.*

lease /lēs/ ▶*n.* a contract by which one party conveys land, property, services, etc., to another for a specified time, usually in return for a periodic payment.
▶*v.* [*tr.*] grant (property) on lease; let: *she leased the site to a local company.* ■ take (property) on lease; rent: *land was leased from the city.* ▷late Middle English: from Old French *lais, leis,* from *lesser, laissier* 'let, leave,' from Latin *laxare* 'make loose,' from *laxus* 'loose, lax.' —**leas·a·ble** *adj.*
▶ □ **a new lease on life** a substantially improved chance to lead a happy or successful life.

lease·hold /'lēs,hōld/ ▶*n.* the holding of property by lease: *a form of leasehold* | [as *adj.*] *leasehold premises.* ■ a property held by lease. —**lease·hold·er** *n.*

leash /lēsн/ ▶*n.* a strap or cord for restraining and guiding a dog or other animal. ■ *Falconry* a thong or string attached to the jesses of a hawk, used for tying it to a perch or other restraint. ■ *fig.* a restraint: *her bristling temper was kept on a leash.*
▶*v.* [*tr.*] put a leash on (a dog). ■ *fig.* restrain: *his violence was barely leashed.*

least /lēst/ ▶*adj. & pron.* (usu. **the least**) smallest in amount, extent, or significance: [as *adj.*] *he never had the least idea what to do about it* | [as *pron.*] *it's the least I can do.*
▶*adj.* used in names of very small animals and plants, e.g., **least shrew.**
▶*adv.* to the smallest extent or degree: *turning up when he was least expected.*
▶ □ **at least 1** not less than; at the minimum: *clean the windows at least once a week.* **2** if nothing else (used to add a positive comment about a generally negative situation): *the options aren't complete, but at least they're a start.* **3** anyway (used to modify something just stated): *they seldom complained—officially at least.* □ **at the least** (or **very least**) **1** (used after amounts) not less than; at the minimum: *stay ten days at the least.* **2** taking the most pessimistic or unfavorable view: *a program that is, at the very least, excellent PR for the hospital.* □ **not in the least** not in the smallest degree; not at all: *he was not in the least taken aback.* □ **not least** in particular; notably: *there is a great deal at stake, not least in relation to the environment.* □ **to say the least** used as an understatement (implying the reality is more extreme, usually worse): *his performance was disappointing to say the least.*

least com·mon mul·ti·ple ▶*n.* another term for LOWEST COMMON MULTIPLE.

leath·er /'leTHər/ ▶*n.* **1** a material made from the skin of an animal by tanning or a similar process. **2** a thing made of leather, in particular: ■ a piece of leather as a polishing cloth. ■ (**leathers**) leather clothes, esp. those worn by a motorcyclist.
▶*adj. inf.* of, relating to, or catering to people who wear leather clothing and accessories as a sign of rough masculinity, esp. homosexuals who practice sadomasochistic sex: *leather bar.*
▶*v.* [*tr.*] **1** [usu. as *adj.*] (**leathered**) cover with leather: *dancers in leathered costumes.* **2** beat or thrash (someone): *he caught me and leathered me black and blue* | [as *n.*] (**leathering**) *go, before you get a leathering.* —**leath·er·y** *adj.*

leath·er·back /'leTHər,bak/ (also **leatherback turtle**) ▶*n.* a very large black turtle (*Dermochelys coriacea,* family Dermochelyidae) with a thick leathery shell, living chiefly in tropical seas.

leath·er·ette /,leTHə'ret/ ▶*n.* imitation leather.

leath·er·neck /'leTHər,nek/ ▶*n. inf.* a U.S. marine.

leave[1] /lēv/ ▶*v.* (*past* and *past part.* **left** /left/) **1** [*tr.*] go away from: *she left New York on June 6* | *the Bruins left for Toronto on Monday.* **2** [*tr.*] allow to remain: *the parts she disliked he would alter, and the parts he didn't dislike he'd leave.* ■ (**be left**) remain to be used or dealt with: *we've even got one of the plum puddings left over from last year.* ■ abandon (a spouse or partner): *her boyfriend left her for another woman.* ■ have as (a surviving relative) after one's death: *he leaves a wife and three children.* ■ bequeath: *he left $500 to the Police Athletic League.* **3** [*tr.*] cause (someone or something) to be in a particular state or position: *I'll leave the door open.* ■ let (someone) do or deal with something without offering help or assistance: *infected people are often rejected by family and friends, leaving them to face this*

chronic condition alone. ■ cause to remain as a trace or record: *dark fruit that would leave purple stains on the table napkins.* ■ deposit or entrust to be kept, collected, or attended to: *she left a note for me.* ■ [*tr.*] (**leave something to**) entrust a decision, choice, or action to (someone else, esp. someone considered better qualified): *the choice of which link to take is generally left up to the reader.*
▶*phrasal v.* □ **leave off** discontinue (an activity): *the dog left off chasing the sheep.* □ **leave something off** omit to put on: *a bolt may have been left off the plane's forward door during production.* □ **leave someone/something out** fail to include: *it seemed unkind to leave Daisy out; so she was invited, too* | [as *adj.*] (**left out**) *Janet was feeling rather left out.* —**leav·er** *n.*
▶ □ **be left for dead** be abandoned as being almost dead or certain to die. □ **be left to oneself** be allowed to do what one wants: *women, left to themselves, would make the world a beautiful place to live in.* ■ be in the position of being alone or solitary: *left to himself, he removed his shirt and tie.* □ **leave someone be** refrain from disturbing or interfering with someone. □ **leave someone cold** fail to interest someone: *the Romantic poets left him cold.* □ **leave it at that** abstain from further comment or action: *if you are not sure of the answers, say so, and leave it at that.* □ **leave much** (or **a lot**) **to be desired** be highly unsatisfactory.

leave[2] ▶*n.* **1** (also **leave of absence**) time when one has permission to be absent from work or from duty in the armed forces: *he took a leave of absence last year.* **2** permission: *he is seeking leave to appeal the injunction.*
▶ □ **by** (or **with**) **your leave** with your permission: *with your leave, I will send him your address.* □ **take one's leave** *formal* say goodbye: *he went to take his leave of his hostess.*

leave[3] ▶*v.* put forth leaves.

leaved /lēvd/ ▶*adj.* [in *comb.*] having a leaf or leaves of a particular kind or number: *broad-leaved evergreens.*

leav·en /'levən/ ▶*n.* a substance, typically yeast, that is added to dough to make it ferment and rise. ■ dough that is reserved from an earlier batch in order to start a later one fermenting. ■ *fig.* a pervasive influence that modifies something or transforms it for the better: *they acted as an intellectual leaven to the warriors who dominated the city.*
▶*v.* [*tr.*] **1** [usu. as *adj.*] (**leavened**) cause (dough or bread) to ferment and rise by adding leaven: *leavened breads are forbidden during Passover.* **2** permeate and modify or transform (something) for the better: *the proceedings should be leavened by humor* | [as *n.*] (**leavening**) *companies of militia volunteers with a leavening of regular soldiers.*

leaves /lēvz/ ▶ plural form of LEAF.

leav·ings /'lēvingz/ ▶*plural n.* things that have been left as worthless: *she dropped her lunch leavings into the trash.*

lech·er /'lecHər/ ▶*n.* a lecherous man.

lech·er·ous /'lecH(ə)rəs/ ▶*adj.* having or showing excessive or offensive sexual desire: *she ignored his lecherous gaze.* —**lech·er·ous·ly** *adv.* —**lech·er·ous·ness** *n.*

lech·er·y /'lecH(ə)rē/ ▶*n.* excessive or offensive sexual desire; lustfulness.

lec·i·thin /'lesəthin/ ▶*n. Biochem.* a substance widely distributed in animal tissues, egg yolk, and some higher plants, consisting of phospholipids linked to choline.

lec·tern /'lektərn/ ▶*n.* a tall stand with a sloping top to hold a book or notes, and from which someone, typically a preacher or lecturer, can read while standing up.

lec·tion·ar·y /'leksHə,nerē/ ▶*n.* (*pl.* **-ar·ies**) a list or book of portions of the Bible appointed to be read at a church service.

lec·ture /'lekcHər/ ▶*n.* an educational talk to an audience, esp. to students in a university or college. ■ a long, serious speech, esp. one given as a scolding or reprimand: *the usual lecture on table manners.*
▶*v.* [*intr.*] deliver an educational lecture or lectures: *she was lecturing to her class of eighty students.* ■ [*tr.*] give a lecture to (a class or other audience): *he was lecturing future generations of health-service professionals.* ■ [*tr.*] talk seriously or reprovingly to (someone): *don't lecture me!* —**lec·tur·er** *n.*

lec·ture·ship /'lekcHər,sHip/ ▶*n.* a post as a lecturer: *a three-year lectureship in English literature.*

LED ▶*abbr.* light-emitting diode, a semiconductor diode that glows when a voltage is applied.

led /led/ ▶ past and past participle of LEAD[1].

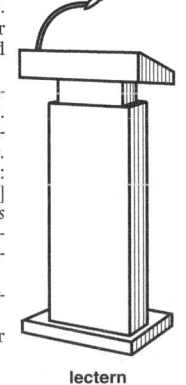

lectern

ledge /lej/ ▸ n. **1** a narrow horizontal surface projecting from a wall, cliff, or other surface: *he heaved himself up over a ledge.* **2** an underwater ridge, esp. of rocks beneath the sea near the shore. —**ledg·y** /ˈlejē/ adj.

ledg·er /ˈlejər/ ▸ n. a book or other collection of financial accounts of a particular type: *the total balance of the purchases ledger.*

ledg·er line ▸ n. Mus. a short line added for notes above or below the range of a staff.

lee /lē/ ▸ n. shelter from wind or weather given by a neighboring object, esp. nearby land: *we pitch our tents in the lee of a rock.* ■ (also **lee side**) the sheltered side; the side away from the wind: *ducks were taking shelter on the lee of the island.*

leech[1] /lēCH/ ▸ n. **1** an aquatic or terrestrial annelid (class Hirudinea) with suckers at both ends. Many species are bloodsucking parasites, esp. of vertebrates, and others are predators. **2** a person who extorts profit from or sponges on others.
▸ v. [intr.] habitually exploit or rely on: *he's leeching off the abilities of others.*

leech[2] ▸ n. archaic a doctor or healer.

leech[3] ▸ n. Sailing the after or leeward edge of a fore-and-aft sail, the leeward edge of a spinnaker, or a vertical edge of a square sail.

leek /lēk/ ▸ n. a plant (*Allium porrum*) of the lily family, closely related to the onion, with flat overlapping leaves forming an elongated cylindrical bulb that together with the leaf bases is eaten as a vegetable.

leer /li(ə)r/ ▸ v. [intr.] look or gaze in an unpleasant, malicious, or lascivious way: *bystanders were leering at the nude painting.*
▸ n. an unpleasant, malicious, or lascivious look. ▷mid 16th cent. (in the general sense 'look sideways or askance'): perhaps from obsolete *leer* 'cheek,' from Old English *hlēor*, as though the sense were 'to glance over one's cheek.' —**leer·ing·ly** adv.

leer·y /ˈli(ə)rē/ ▸ adj. (**leer·i·er, leer·i·est**) cautious or wary due to realistic suspicions: *a city leery of gang violence.* —**leer·i·ness** n.

lees /lēz/ ▸ plural n. the sediment of wine in the barrel. ■ fig. dregs; refuse: *the lees of the Venetian underworld.*

lee·ward /ˈlēwərd; ˈlo͞oərd/ ▸ adj. & adv. on or toward the side sheltered from the wind or toward which the wind is blowing; downwind: [as adj.] *the leeward side of the* | [as adv.] *we pitched our tents leeward of a hill.* Contrasted with WINDWARD.
▸ n. the side sheltered or away from the wind: *the ship was drifting to leeward.*

lee·way /ˈlēˌwā/ ▸ n. **1** the amount of freedom to move or act that is available: *the government had several months' leeway to introduce reforms.* ■ margin of safety: *there is little leeway if anything goes wrong.* **2** the sideways drift of a ship or an aircraft to leeward of the desired course: *the leeway is only about 2°.*

left[1] /left/ ▸ adj. **1** on, toward, or relating to the side of a human body or of a thing that is to the west when the person or thing is facing north: *her left eye.* ■ denoting the side of something that is in an analogous position: *the left edge of the text.* **2** of or relating to a person or group favoring liberal, socialist, or radical views: *Left politics.*
▸ adv. on or to the left side: *turn left here* | *keep left.*
▸ n. **1** (**the left**) the left-hand part, side, or direction: *a turn to the left* | (**one's left**) *the general sat to his left.* ■ (in soccer or a similar sport) the left-hand half of the field when facing the opponents' goal: *a free kick from the left.* ■ (**left**) Baseball short for LEFT FIELD: *a sacrifice fly to left.* ■ the left wing of an army: *a token attack on the Russian left.* **2** (often **the Left**) [treated as sing. or pl.] a group or party favoring liberal, socialist, or radical views: *the Left is preparing to fight presidential elections.* ■ the section of a party or group holding such views more strongly: *he is on the left of the party.* **3** a thing on the left-hand side or done with the left hand.
▸ □ **have two left feet** be clumsy or awkward.

left[2] ▸ past and past participle of LEAVE[1].

left brain ▸ n. the left-hand side of the human brain, which is believed to be associated with linear and analytical thought. —**left-brained** /ˈleft ˌbrānd/ adj.

left field ▸ n. Baseball the part of the outfield to the left of center field from the perspective of home plate: *a high fly to left field.* ■ the position of the defensive player stationed in left field: *I played left field a lot against him.* ■ fig. a position or direction that is surprising or unconventional: *seldom do so many witty touches come out of left field.* ■ fig. a position of ignorance, error, or confusion: *he's so far out in left field that even his followers are embarrassed.* —**left field·er** n.

left hand ▸ n. the hand of a person's left side. ■ the region or direction on the left side of a person or thing: *there was a vast forest on the left hand.*
▸ adj. on or toward the left side of a person or thing: *his left-hand pocket.* ■ done with or using the left hand: *an excellent left-hand catch.*

left-hand·ed ▸ adj. **1** (of a person) using the left hand more naturally than the right: *a left-handed pitcher.* ■ (of a tool or item of equipment) made to be used with the left hand: *left-handed golf clubs.* ■ made or performed with the left hand: *my left-handed scrawl.* **2** turning to the left; toward the left, in particular: ■ (of a screw) advanced by turning counterclockwise. **3** perverse: *we take a left-handed pleasure in our errors.* ■ (esp. of a compliment) ambiguous.
▸ adv. with the left hand: *a significant number play the game left-handed.* —**left-hand·ed·ly** adv. —**left-hand·ed·ness** n.

left·ist /ˈleftist/ ▸ n. a person who supports the political views or policies of the left.
▸ adj. supportive of the political views or policies of the left: *leftist radicals.* —**left·ism** /-ˌtizəm/ n.

left·most /ˈlef(t)ˌmōst/ ▸ adj. [attrib.] farthest to the left: *the leftmost edge of the screen.*

left·o·ver /ˈleftˌōvər/ ▸ n. (usu. **leftovers**) something, esp. food, remaining after the rest has been used or consumed.
▸ adj. [attrib.] remaining; surplus: *yesterday's leftover bread.*

left wing ▸ n. (**the left wing**) **1** the liberal, socialist, or radical section of a political party or system. [with reference to the National Assembly in France (1789–91), where the nobles sat to the president's right and the commons to the left.] **2** the left side of a team on the field in soccer, rugby, and field hockey: *his usual position on the left wing.* ■ the left side of an army: *the Allied left wing.*
▸ adj. liberal, socialist, or radical: *left-wing activists.* —**left-wing·er** n.

left·y /ˈleftē/ (also **left·ie**) ▸ n. (pl. **left·ies**) inf. **1** a left-handed person. **2** a leftist.

leg /leg/ ▸ n. **1** each of the limbs on which a person or animal walks and stands: *Adams broke his leg.* | [as adj.] *a leg injury.* ■ a leg of an animal or bird used as food: *a roast leg of lamb.* ■ a part of a garment covering a leg or part of a leg: *his trouser leg.* ■ (**legs**) inf. used to refer to the sustained popularity or success of a product or idea: *some books have legs; others don't.* **2** each of the supports of a chair, table, or other piece of furniture: *table legs.* ■ a long, thin support or prop: *the house was set on legs.* **3** a section or stage of a journey or process: *the return leg of his journey.* ■ Sailing a run made on a single tack. ■ (in soccer and other sports) each of two games constituting a round of a competition. ■ a section of a relay or other race done in stages: *one leg of its race around the globe.* **4** a branch of a forked object.
▸ v. (**legged, leg·ging**) [tr.] (**leg it**) inf. travel by foot; walk. ■ run away: *he legged it after someone shouted at him.* —**leg·ged** /ˈlegid/ adj. [in comb.] *a four-legged animal.* —**leg·ger** n. [in comb.] *a three-legger.* —**leg·less** adj.
▸ □ **leg up** help to mount a horse or high object: *give me a leg up over the wall.* ■ help to improve one's position: *the council is to provide a financial leg up for the club.* □ **not have a leg to stand on** have no facts or sound reasons to support one's argument or justify one's actions. □ **on one's last legs** near the end of life, usefulness, or existence: *the foundry business was on its last legs.*

leg·a·cy /ˈlegəsē/ ▸ n. (pl. **-cies**) an amount of money or property left to someone in a will. ■ a thing handed down by a predecessor: *the legacy of centuries of neglect.*
▸ adj. Comput. denoting software or hardware that has been superseded but is difficult to replace because of its wide use.

le·gal /ˈlēgəl/ ▸ adj. **1** [attrib.] of, based on, or concerned with the law: *the American legal system.* ■ Law recognized by common or statutory law, as distinct from equity. ■ (of paper) measuring 8½ by 14 inches. **2** permitted by law: *he claimed that it had all been legal.* —**le·gal·ly** adv.

le·gal age ▸ n. the age at which a person takes on the rights and responsibilities of an adult.

le·gal·ese /ˌlēgəˈlēz; -ˈlēs/ ▸ n. inf., often derog. the formal and technical language of legal documents that is often hard to understand.

le·gal·ism /ˈlēgəˌlizəm/ ▸ n. excessive adherence to law or formula. ■ Theol. dependence on moral law rather than on personal religious faith. —**le·gal·ist** n. & adj. —**le·gal·is·tic** /ˌlēgəˈlistik/ adj. —**le·gal·is·ti·cal·ly** /ˌlēgəˈlistik(ə)lē/ adv.

le·gal·i·ty /ləˈgalətē/ ▸ n. (pl. **-ties**) the quality or state of being in accordance with the law: *documentation testifying to the legality of the arms sale.* ■ (**legalities**) obligations imposed by law.

le·gal·ize /ˈlēgəˌlīz/ ▸ v. [tr.] make (something that was previously illegal) permissible by law: *a measure legalizing gambling in Deadwood.* —**le·gal·i·za·tion** /-ˌlēgələˈzāSHən; -ˌlī'zā-/ n.

le·gal ten·der ▸ n. coins or banknotes that must be accepted if offered in payment of a debt.

leg·ate /ˈlegit/ ▸ n. **1** a member of the clergy, esp. a cardinal, representing the pope. ■ archaic an ambassador or messenger. **2** a general or governor of an ancient Roman province, or their deputy: *the Roman legate of Syria.* —**leg·ate·ship** /-‚SHip/ *n.* —**leg·a·tine** /'lega‚tēn; -‚tīn/ *adj.*

leg·a·tee /‚lega'tē/ ▶*n.* a person who receives a legacy.

le·ga·tion /li'gāSHən/ ▶*n.* **1** a diplomatic minister, esp. one below the rank of ambassador, and their staff. ■ the official residence of a diplomatic minister. **2** *archaic* the position or office of legate; a legateship. ■ the sending of a legate, esp. a papal legate, on a mission.

le·ga·to /li'gäto/ ▶*adv. & adj. Mus.* in a smooth, flowing manner, without breaks between notes. Compare with **STACCATO**.
▶*n.* performance in this manner.

leg·end /'lejənd/ ▶*n.* **1** a traditional story sometimes popularly regarded as historical but unauthenticated: *the legend of King Arthur.* **2** an extremely famous or notorious person, esp. in a particular field: *the man was a living legend.* **3** an inscription, esp. on a coin or medal. ■ a caption: *a picture of a tiger with the legend "Go ahead, make my day."* ■ the wording on a map or diagram explaining the symbols used: *see legend under Fig. 1.*
▶*adj.* very well known: *his speed and ferocity in attack were legend.*

leg·end·ar·y /'lejən‚derē/ ▶*adj.* **1** of, described in, or based on legends: *a legendary British king of the 4th century.* **2** remarkable enough to be famous; very well known: *her wisdom in matters of childbirth was legendary.* —**leg·end·ar·i·ly** /-‚derəlē; ‚lejən'de(ə)r-/ *adv.*

leg·er·de·main /‚lejərdə'mān; 'lejərdə‚mān/ ▶*n.* skillful use of one's hands when performing conjuring tricks. ■ deception; trickery.

leg·gings /'legiNGz/ ▶*plural n.* tight-fitting stretch pants worn by women and children. ■ protective coverings for the legs.

leg·gy /'legē/ ▶*adj.* (**-gi·er, -gi·est**) **1** (of a woman) having attractively long legs: *a leggy redhead.* ■ long-legged: *a leggy type of collie.* **2** (of a plant) having an excessively long and straggly stem: *tulips may grow tall and leggy.* —**leg·gi·ness** *n.*

leg·i·ble /'lejəbəl/ ▶*adj.* (of handwriting or print) clear enough to read: *the original typescript is scarcely legible.* —**leg·i·bil·i·ty** /‚lejə'bilətē/ *n.* —**leg·i·bly** /-blē/ *adv.*

le·gion /'lējən/ ▶*n.* **1** a unit of 3,000–6,000 men in the ancient Roman army. ■ (**the Legion**) the Foreign Legion. ■ (**the Legion**) any of the national associations of former servicemen and servicewomen instituted after World War I, such as the American Legion. **2** (**a legion/legions of**) a vast host, multitude, or number of people or things: *legions of photographers and TV cameras.*
▶*adj.* great in number: *her fans are legion.*

le·gion·ar·y /'lējə‚nerē/ ▶*n.* (*pl.* **-ar·ies**) a soldier in a Roman legion.

le·gion·naires' dis·ease /‚lējə'nerz/ ▶*n.* a form of bacterial pneumonia first identified after an outbreak at an American Legion meeting in 1976. It is spread chiefly by water droplets through air conditioning and similar systems.

leg i·ron ▶*n.* (usu. **leg irons**) a metal band or chain placed around a prisoner's ankle as a restraint.

leg·is·late /'lejə‚slāt/ ▶*v.* [*intr.*] make or enact laws: *he didn't want to name anyone to the Court who would legislate from the bench.* ■ [*tr.*] cover, affect, or create by making or enacting laws: *Congress must legislate strong new laws.*

leg·is·la·tion /‚lejə'slāSHən/ ▶*n.* laws, considered collectively: *tax legislation.*

leg·is·la·tive /'lejə‚slātiv/ ▶*adj.* having the power to make laws: *the country's supreme legislative body.* ■ of or relating to laws or the making of them: *legislative proposals.* Often contrasted with **EXECUTIVE**. ■ of or relating to a legislature: *legislative elections.* —**leg·is·la·tive·ly** *adv.*

leg·is·la·tor /'lejə‚slātər/ ▶*n.* a person who makes laws; a member of a legislative body.

leg·is·la·ture /'lejə‚slāCHər/ ▶*n.* the legislative body of a country or state.

legit /li'jit/ ▶*adj. inf.* legal; conforming to the rules: *is this car legit?* ■ (of a person) not engaging in illegal activity or attempting to deceive; honest: *to see if he's legit, I call up the business.*
▶ □ **go legit** begin to behave honestly after a period of illegal activity.

le·git·i·mate ▶*adj.* /li'jitəmit/ conforming to the law or to rules: *his claims to legitimate authority.* ■ able to be defended with logic or justification: *a legitimate excuse for being late.* ■ (of a child) born of parents lawfully married to each other. ■ (of a sovereign) having a title based on strict hereditary right: *the last legitimate Anglo-Saxon king.* ■ constituting or relating to serious drama as distinct from musical comedy, revue, etc.: *the legitimate theater.*
▶*v.* /-‚māt/ [*tr.*] make legitimate; justify or make lawful: *the regime was not legitimated by popular support.* —**le·git·i·ma·cy** /-məsē/ *n.* —**le·git·i·mate·ly** /-mitlē/ *adv.* —**le·git·i·ma·tion** /li‚jitə'māSHən/ *n.* —**le·git·i·ma·tize** /-mə‚tīz/ *v.*

le·git·i·mize /li'jitə‚mīz/ ▶*v.* [*tr.*] make legitimate: *voters legitimize the government through the election of public officials.* —**le·git·i·mi·za·tion** /li‚jitəmə'zāSHən/ *n.*

Le·go /'legō/ ▶*n. trademark* a construction toy consisting of interlocking plastic building blocks.

leg·room /'leg‚rōōm; -‚rŏŏm/ ▶*n.* space where a seated person can put their legs.

leg·ume /'leg‚yōōm; lə'gyōōm/ ▶*n.* a leguminous plant, esp. one grown as a crop. ■ a seed, pod, or other edible part of a leguminous plant used as food. ▷mid 17th cent. (denoting the edible portion of the plant): from French *légume,* from Latin *legumen,* from *legere* 'to pick' (because the fruit may be picked by hand).

le·gu·mi·nous /li'gyōōmənəs/ ▶*adj. Bot.* of, relating to, or denoting plants of the pea family (Leguminosae). They have seeds in pods, distinctive flowers, and typically root nodules containing symbiotic bacteria able to fix nitrogen.

leg warm·ers ▶*n.* a pair of tubular knitted garments designed to cover the leg from ankle to knee or thigh, esp. worn by dancers during rehearsal.

leg·work /'leg‚wərk/ ▶*n.* work that involves much traveling to collect information, esp. when such work is difficult but boring.

lei /lā/ ▶*n.* a Polynesian garland of flowers.

leish·man·i·a /lēSH'mānēə; -'manēə/ ▶*n.* (*pl.* same or **-ma·ni·as** or **-ma·ni·ae** /-'mānē-ē; -'man-; -ē‚ī/) a single-celled parasitic protozoan that spends part of its life cycle in the gut of a sandfly and part in the blood and other tissues of a vertebrate. ▷modern Latin, from the name of William B. *Leishman* (1856–1926), British pathologist.

leish·man·i·a·sis /‚lēSHmə'nīəsəs/ ▶*n.* a tropical and subtropical disease caused by leishmania and transmitted by the bite of sandflies. It affects either the skin or the internal organs.

lei·sure /'lēZHər; 'leZHər/ ▶*n.* free time. ■ use of free time for enjoyment: *increased opportunities for leisure.* ■ (**leisure for/to do something**) opportunity afforded by free time to do something: *writers with enough leisure to practice their art.*
▶ □ **at leisure 1** not occupied; free: *the rest of the day can be spent at leisure.* **2** in an unhurried manner: *the poems were left for others to read at leisure.* □ **at one's leisure** at one's ease or convenience. □ **lady** (or **man** or **gentleman**) **of leisure** a woman or man of independent means or whose time is free from obligations to others. □ **leisure class** a social class that is independently wealthy or has much leisure.

lei·sured /'lēZHərd; 'leZHərd/ ▶*adj.* having ample leisure, esp. through being rich: *the leisured classes.* ■ leisurely: *a new, more leisured lifestyle.*

lei·sure·ly /'lēZHərlē; 'leZHər-/ ▶*adj.* acting or done at leisure; unhurried or relaxed: *a leisurely breakfast at our hotel.*
▶*adv.* without hurry: *couples strolled leisurely along.* —**lei·sure·li·ness** *n.*

leit·mo·tif /'lītmō‚tēf/ (also **leit·mo·tiv**) ▶*n.* a recurrent theme throughout a musical or literary composition, associated with a particular person, idea, or situation.

lem·ming /'lemiNG/ ▶*n.* a small, short-tailed, thickset rodent (*Lemmus, Dicrostonyx,* and other genera, family Muridae) found in the Arctic tundra. The **Norway lemming** (*L. lemmus*) is noted for its fluctuating populations and periodic mass migrations. ■ a person who unthinkingly joins a mass movement, esp. a headlong rush to destruction.

lem·on /'lemən/ ▶*n.* **1** a yellow, oval citrus fruit with thick skin and fragrant, acidic juice. ■ a drink made from or flavored with lemon juice: *a port and lemon.* **2** (also **lemon tree**) the evergreen citrus tree (*Citrus limon*) that produces this fruit, widely cultivated in warm climates. **3** a pale yellow color. **4** *inf.* a person or thing, esp. an automobile, regarded as unsatisfactory, disappointing, or feeble. —**lem·on·y** *adj.*

lem·on·ade /‚lemə'nād; 'lemə‚nād/ ▶*n.* a drink made from lemon juice and sweetened water.

le·mur /'lēmər/ ▶*n.* an arboreal primate (Lemuridae and other families) with a pointed snout and typically a long tail, found only in Madagascar.

lend /lend/ ▶*v.* (*past* and *past part.* **lent** /lent/) [*tr.*] **1** grant to (someone) the use of (something) on the understanding that it shall be returned: *Stewart asked me to lend him my car.* ■ allow (a person or organization) the use of (a sum of money) under an agreement to pay it back later, typically with interest: *no one would lend him the money* | [*intr.*] *the bank lends only to its current customers* | [as *n.*] (**lending**) *balance sheets weakened by unwise lending.* **2** contribute or add (a quality) to: *the*

Pronunciation Key ə *ago, up;* ər *over, fur;* ä *hat;* ā *ate;* ä *car;* CH *chin;* e *let;* ē *see;* e(ə)r *air;* i *fit;* ī *by;* i(ə)r *ear;* NG *sing;* ō *go;* ô *law, for;* oi *toy;* ōō *good;* ōō *goo;* ou *out;* SH *she;* TH *thin;* ŦH *then;* (h)w *why;* ZH *vision*

smile lent his face a boyish charm. **3** (**lend oneself to**) accommodate or adapt oneself to: *John stiffly lent himself to her enthusiastic embraces.* ■ (**lend itself to**) (of a thing) be suitable for: *bay windows lend themselves to blinds.* —**lend·a·ble** *adj.* —**lend·er** *n.*

▶ □ **lend an ear** (or **one's ears**) listen sympathetically or attentively: *the Samaritans lend their ears to those in crisis.* □ **lend one's name to** allow oneself to be publicly associated with: *he lent his name and prestige to the organizers of the project.*

length /leNG(k)TH; lenth/ ▶ *n.* **1** the measurement or extent of something from end to end; the greater of two or the greatest of three dimensions of a body: *the length of the airport terminal.* ■ the amount of time occupied by something: *delivery must be within a reasonable length of time.* ■ the quality of being long: *the length of the waiting list.* ■ the full distance that a thing extends for: *the muscles running the length of my spine.* ■ *Prosody & Phonet.* the metrical quantity or duration of a vowel or syllable. **2** the extent of something, esp. as a unit of measurement, in particular: ■ the length of a swimming pool as a measure of the distance swum: *fifty lengths of the pool.* ■ the length of a horse, boat, etc., as a measure of the lead in a race: *the mare won the race last year by seven lengths.* ■ (**one's length**) the full extent of one's body: *he awkwardly lowered his length into the small car.* **3** (in bridge or whist) the number of cards of a suit held in one's hand, esp. when five or more. **4** a stretch or piece of something: *a stout length of wood.* **5** a degree or extreme to which a course of action is taken: *they go to great lengths to avoid the press.*

▶ □ **at length 1** in detail; fully: *these aspects have been discussed at length.* **2** after a long time: *at length she laid down the pencil.* □ **the length and breadth of** the whole extent of: *women from the length and breadth of Russia.*

length·en /'leNG(k)THən; 'len-/ ▶ *v.* make or become longer: [*tr.*] *she lengthened her stride to catch up* | [*intr.*] *in the spring when the days are lengthening.* ■ [*tr.*] *Prosody & Phonet.* make (a vowel or syllable) long.

length·ways /'leNG(k)TH,wāz; 'lenTH-/ ▶ *adv.* lengthwise.

length·wise /'leNG(k)TH,wīz; 'lenTH-/ ▶ *adv.* in a direction parallel with a thing's length: *halve the potatoes lengthwise.*

▶ *adj.* lying or moving lengthwise: *a lengthwise crack.*

length·y /'leNG(k)THē; 'len-/ ▶ *adj.* (**length·i·er**, **length·i·est**) (esp. in reference to time) of considerable or unusual length, esp. so as to be tedious: *lengthy delays.* —**length·i·ly** /-THəlē/ *adv.* —**length·i·ness** *n.*

le·ni·ent /'lēnēənt; 'lēnyənt/ ▶ *adj.* (of punishment or a person in authority) permissive, merciful, or tolerant: *judges were far too lenient with petty criminals.* —**le·ni·ence** *n.* —**le·ni·en·cy** *n.* —**le·ni·ent·ly** *adv.*

Le·nin·ism /'lenə,nizəm/ ▶ *n.* Marxism as interpreted and applied by Lenin. —**Le·nin·ist** *n.* & *adj.* —**Le·nin·ite** /-,nīt/ *n.* & *adj.*

le·no /'lēnō/ ▶ *n.* (*pl.* -**nos**) an openwork fabric with the warp threads twisted in pairs before weaving.

lens /lenz/ ▶ *n.* a piece of glass or other transparent substance with curved sides for concentrating or dispersing light rays, used singly (as in a magnifying glass) or with other lenses (as in a telescope). ■ the light-gathering device of a camera, typically containing a group of compound lenses. ■ *Physics* an object or device that focuses or otherwise modifies the direction of movement of light, sound, electrons, etc. ■ *Anat.* the transparent elastic structure behind the iris by which light is focused onto the retina of the eye. ■ *Anat.* short for CONTACT LENS. ▷late 17th cent.: from Latin, 'lentil' (because of the similarity in shape). —**lensed** *adj.* —**lens·less** *adj.*

Lent /lent/ ▶ *n.* the period preceding Easter that in the Christian Church is devoted to fasting, abstinence, and penitence in commemoration of Christ's fasting in the wilderness. In the Western Church it runs from Ash Wednesday to Holy Saturday and so includes forty weekdays.

lent /lent/ ▶ past and past participle of LEND.

Lent·en /'lent(ə)n/ ▶ *adj.* [*attrib.*] of, in, or appropriate to Lent: *Lenten food.*

len·tic·u·lar /len'tikyələr/ ▶ *adj.* **1** shaped like a lentil, esp. by being biconvex: *lenticular lenses.* **2** of or relating to the lens of the eye.

len·ti·go /len'tīgō; -'tē-/ ▶ *n.* (*pl.* -**tig·i·nes** /-'tijə,nēz/) a condition marked by small brown patches on the skin, typically in elderly people. ▷late Middle English (denoting a freckle or pimple): from Latin, from *lens*, *lent-* 'lentil.'

len·til /'lent(ə)l/ ▶ *n.* **1** the high-protein seed of a leguminous plant that is dried and then soaked and cooked before eating. **2** the plant (*Lens culinaris*) that yields this seed, native to the Mediterranean and Africa.

len·to /'lentō/ ▶ *adv.* & *adj. Mus.* (esp. as a direction) slow or slowly.

Le·o ▶ **1** *Astron.* a large constellation (the Lion), said to represent the lion slain by Hercules. It contains the bright stars Regulus and Denebola and numerous galaxies. **2** *Astrol.* the fifth sign of the zodiac,

which the sun enters about July 23. ■ (**a Leo**) (*pl.* **Le·os**) a person born when the sun is in this sign.

Le·o·nine ▶ *adj.* **1** of or relating to one of the popes named Leo, esp. Leo IV and the part of Rome that he fortified. **2** *Prosody* (of medieval Latin verse) in hexameter or elegiac meter with internal rhyme. ■ (of English verse) with internal rhyme.

▶ *plural n.* (**Leonines**) *Prosody* verse of this type.

le·o·nine /'lēə,nīn/ ▶ *adj.* of or resembling a lion or lions: *a handsome, leonine profile.*

leop·ard /'lepərd/ ▶ *n.* a large, solitary cat (*Panthera pardus*) that has a fawn or brown coat with black spots, widespread in the forests of Africa and southern Asia. Also called PANTHER. ■ [as *adj.*] spotted like a leopard.

le·o·tard /'lēə,tärd/ ▶ *n.* a close-fitting one-piece garment, made of a stretchy fabric, which covers a person's body from the shoulders to the top of the thighs and typically the arms, worn by dancers or people exercising indoors. ■ (**leotards**) close-fitting leggings or tights, esp. those worn by dancers.

lep·er /'lepər/ ▶ *n.* a person suffering from leprosy. ■ a person who is avoided or rejected by others for moral or social reasons: *the story made her out to be a social leper.*

lep·re·chaun /'leprə,kän; -,kôn/ ▶ *n.* (in Irish folklore) a small, mischievous sprite.

lep·ro·sy /'leprəsē/ ▶ *n.* a contagious bacterial disease that affects the skin, mucous membranes, and nerves, causing discoloration and lumps on the skin and, in severe cases, disfigurement and deformities. —**lep·rous** /-rəs/ *adj.*

lep·ton ▶ *n. Physics* a subatomic particle, such as an electron, muon, or neutrino, that does not take part in the strong interaction. —**lep·ton·ic** /lep'tänik/ *adj.*

Les·bi·an /'lezbēən/ ▶ *adj.* from or relating to the island of Lesbos.

les·bi·an /'lezbēən/ ▶ *n.* a homosexual woman.

▶ *adj.* of or relating to homosexual women or to homosexuality in women: *a lesbian relationship.* —**les·bi·an·ism** /-,nizəm/ *n.*

lèse-maj·es·té /,lez 'mäjə'stā; ,lēz; 'majəstē/ ▶ *n.* the insulting of a monarch or other ruler; treason.

le·sion /'lēzhən/ ▶ *n. chiefly Med.* a region in an organ or tissue that has suffered damage through injury or disease, such as a wound, ulcer, abscess, tumor, etc.

less /les/ ▶ *adj.* & *pron.* a smaller amount of; not as much: [as *adj.*] *the less time spent there, the better* | [as *pron.*] *storage is less of a problem than it used to be.* ■ fewer in number: [as *adj.*] *short hair presented less problems than long hair* | [as *pron.*] *a population of less than 200,000.*

▶ *adj.* archaic of lower rank or importance: *James the Less.*

▶ *adv.* to a smaller extent; not so much: *he listened less to the answer than to Kate's voice.* ■ (**less than**) far from; certainly not: *Mitch looked less than happy* | *the data was less than ideal.*

▶ *prep.* before subtracting (something); minus: *$900,000 less tax.* ▷Old English *lǣssa*, of Germanic origin; related to Old Frisian *lēssa*, from an Indo-European root shared by Greek *loisthos* 'last.'

▶ □ **much** (or **still**) **less** used to introduce something as being even less likely or suitable than something else already mentioned: *what woman would consider a date with him, much less a marriage?* □ **no less** used to suggest, often ironically, that something is surprising or impressive: *Peter cooked dinner—fillet steak and champagne, no less.* ■ (**no less than**) used to emphasize a surprisingly large amount.

les·see /le'sē/ ▶ *n.* a person who holds the lease of a property; a tenant. —**les·see·ship** /-,SHip/ *n.*

less·en /'lesən/ ▶ *v.* make or become less; diminish: [*tr.*] *the years have lessened the gap in age between us* | [*intr.*] *the warmth of the afternoon lessened.*

less·er /'lesər/ ▶ *adj.* [*attrib.*] not so great or important as the other or the rest: *he was convicted of a lesser assault charge.* ■ used in names of animals and plants that are smaller than similar kinds, e.g., **lesser spotted woodpecker**, **lesser celandine**.

▶ □ **the lesser evil** (or **the lesser of two evils**) the less harmful or unpleasant of two bad choices or possibilities: *authoritarianism may seem a lesser evil than abject poverty.*

les·son /'lesən/ ▶ *n.* **1** an amount of teaching given at one time; a period of learning or teaching: *a driving lesson.* ■ a thing learned or to be learned by a student. ■ a thing learned by experience: *the tragedy is a lesson in disappointment.* **2** a passage from the Bible read aloud during a church service, esp. either of two readings at morning and evening prayer in the Anglican Church.

▶ □ **learn one's lesson** acquire a greater understanding of the world through a particular unpleasant or stressful experience. □ **teach**

someone a lesson punish or hurt someone as a deterrent: *they were teaching me a lesson for daring to complain.*

les·sor /ˈlesˌôr; leˈsôr/ ▶ *n.* a person who leases or lets a property to another; a landlord.

lest /lest/ ▶ *conj. formal* with the intention of preventing (something undesirable); to avoid the risk of: *he spent whole days in his room, headphones on lest he disturb anyone.* ■ (after a clause indicating fear) because of the possibility of something undesirable happening; in case: *she sat up late worrying lest he be held up on the way home.*

let¹ /let/ ▶ *v.* (**let·ting**; *past* **let**) **1** [*tr.*] not prevent or forbid; allow: *my boss let me leave early.* ■ [*tr.*] allow to pass in a particular direction: *a tiny window that let in hardly any light.* **2** [*tr.*] used in the imperative to formulate various expressions: ■ (**let us** or **let's**) used as a polite way of making or responding to a suggestion, giving an instruction, or introducing a remark: *let's have a drink* | *"Shall we go?" "Yes, let's."* ■ (**let me** or **let us**) used to make a polite offer of help: *"Here, let me," offered Bruce.* ■ used to express one's strong desire for something to happen or be the case: *"Dear God," Jessica prayed, "let him be all right."* ■ used as a way of expressing defiance or challenge: *if he wants to walk out, well, let him!* ■ used to express an assumption upon which a theory or calculation is to be based: *let A and B stand for X and Y, respectively.* **3** [*tr.*] allow someone to have the use of (a room or property) in return for regular payments; rent: *homeowners will be able to let rooms to lodgers without having to pay tax.* **4** [*tr.*] award (a contract for a particular project) to an applicant: *preliminary contracts were let and tunneling work started.*

▶ *phrasal v.* □ **let someone down** fail to support or help someone as they had hoped or expected. ■ (**let someone/something down**) have a detrimental effect on the overall quality or success of someone or something: *the whole machine is let down by the tacky keyboard.* □ **let something down** **1** lower something slowly or in stages: *they let down a basket on a chain.* **2** make a garment longer, esp. by lowering the hem. □ **let oneself in for** *inf.* involve oneself in (something likely to be difficult or unpleasant): *I didn't know what I was letting myself in for.* □ **let someone in on/into** allow someone to know or share something secret or confidential): *I'll let you into a secret.* □ **let someone off 1** punish someone lightly or not at all for a misdemeanor or offense: *he was let off with a warning.* **2** excuse someone from a task or obligation: *he let me off work for the day.* □ **let on** *inf.* **1** reveal or divulge information to someone: *she knows a lot more than she lets on.* **2** pretend: [*with clause*] *they all let on that they didn't hear me.* □ **let out** (of lessons at school, a meeting, or an entertainment) finish, so that those attending are able to leave: *his classes let out at noon.* □ **let someone out** release someone from obligation or suspicion: *they've started looking for motives—that lets me out.* □ **let something out 1** utter a sound or cry: *he let out a sigh of happiness.* **2** make a garment looser or larger, typically by adjusting seams. **3** reveal a piece of information: *she let out that he'd given her a ride home.* □ **let up** *inf.* (of something undesirable) become less intense or severe: *the rain's letting up—it'll be clear soon.* ■ relax one's efforts: *she was so far ahead that she could afford to let up a bit.* ■ (**let up on**) *inf.* treat or deal with in a more lenient manner: *she didn't let up on Cunningham.*

▶ □ **let alone** used to indicate that something is far less likely, possible, or suitable than something else already mentioned: *he was incapable of leading a bowling team, let alone a country.* □ **let someone/something be** stop disturbing or interfering with: *let him be—he knows what he wants.* □ **let something drop** (or **fall**) casually reveal a piece of information: *from the things he let drop, I think there was a woman in his life.* □ **let fly** attack, either physically or verbally: *the troops let fly with tear gas.* □ **let oneself go 1** act in an unrestrained or uninhibited way: *you need to unwind and let yourself go.* **2** become careless or untidy in one's habits or appearance: *he's let himself go since my mother died.* □ **let someone/something go 1** allow someone or something to escape or go free: *they let the hostages go.* ■ dismiss an employee. **2** (also **let go** or **let go of**) relinquish one's grip on someone or something: *Adam let go of the reins* | *fig. you must let the past go.* □ **let someone have it** *inf.* attack someone physically or verbally: *I really let him have it for worrying me so much.* □ **let it go** (or **pass**) choose not to react to an action or remark: *the decision worried us, but we let it go.* □ **let someone know** inform someone: *let me know what you think of him.* □ **let someone/something loose** release someone or something: *let the dog loose for a minute.* ■ allow someone freedom of action in a particular place or situation: *people are only let loose on the system once they have received sufficient training.* ■ suddenly utter a sound or remark: *he let loose a stream of abuse.* □ **let me see** (or **think**) used when one is pausing, trying to remember something, or considering one's next words: *now let me see, where did I put it?* □ **let me tell you** used to emphasize a statement: *let me tell you, I was very scared!* □ **let's face it** (or **let's be honest**) *inf.* used to convey

that one must be realistic about an unwelcome fact or situation: *let's be honest, your taste in men is famously bad.* □ **let's say** (or **let us say**) used as a way of introducing a hypothetical or possible situation: *let's say we agreed to go our separate ways.*

let² ▶ *n.* (in racket sports) a play that is nullified and has to be played again, esp. a when a served ball touches the top of the net.

▶ □ **let or hindrance** *formal* obstruction or impediment: *the passport opened frontiers to the traveler without let or hindrance.*

let·down /ˈletˌdoun/ ▶ *n.* **1** a disappointment or a feeling of disappointment: *the election was a bit of a letdown.* ■ a decrease in size, volume, force: *letdowns in sales have been frequent and widespread.* **2** the release of milk in a nursing mother or lactating animal.

le·thal /ˈlēTHəl/ ▶ *adj.* sufficient to cause death: *a lethal cocktail of alcohol and pills.* ■ harmful or destructive: *the Krakatoa eruption was the most lethal on record.* —**le·thal·i·ty** /lēˈTHalətē/ *n.* —**le·thal·ly** *adv.*

leth·ar·gy /ˈleTHərjē/ ▶ *n.* a lack of energy and enthusiasm: *periods of weakness and lethargy* | *she might have sunk into a lethargy.* ■ *Med.* a pathological state of sleepiness or deep unresponsiveness and inactivity. —**le·thar·gic** /ləˈTHärjik/ *adj.*

let's /lets/ ▶ *contr. of* let us: *let's meet for a drink sometime.*

let·ter /ˈletər/ ▶ *n.* **1** a character representing one or more of the sounds used in speech; any of the symbols of an alphabet: *a capital letter.* ■ a school or college initial as a mark of proficiency, esp. in sports: *I earned a varsity letter in tennis.* **2** a written, typed, or printed communication, esp. one sent in an envelope by mail or messenger: *he sent a letter to Mrs. Falconer.* ■ (**letters**) a legal or formal document of this kind. **3** the precise terms of a statement or requirement; the strict verbal interpretation: *we must be seen to keep the spirit of the law as well as the letter.* **4** (**letters**) literature; the world of letters. ■ *archaic* scholarly knowledge; erudition. **5** *Printing* a style of typeface.

▶ *v.* **1** [*tr.*] inscribe letters or writing on: *her name was lettered in gold.* ■ classify with letters: *he numbered and lettered the paragraphs.* **2** [*intr.*] *inf.* be given a school or college initial as a mark of proficiency in sports: *juniors who lettered in soccer, basketball or softball.*

▶ □ **to the letter** with adherence to every detail: *the method was followed to the letter.*

let·ter bomb ▶ *n.* an explosive device hidden in a small package and sent to someone with the intention of harming or killing them.

let·ter car·ri·er ▶ *n.* a mail carrier.

let·ter·head /ˈletərˌhed/ ▶ *n.* a printed heading on stationery stating a person's or organization's name and address. ■ a sheet of paper with such a heading.

let·ter·ing /ˈletəriNG/ ▶ *n.* the process of inscribing letters. ■ the letters inscribed on something, esp. decorative ones.

let·ter of cred·it ▶ *n.* a letter issued by a bank to another bank (typically in a different country) to serve as a guarantee for payments made to a specified person under specified conditions.

let·ter-per·fect ▶ *adj.* (of an actor or speaker) knowing by heart the words for one's part or speech. ■ accurate to the smallest verbal detail: *when he delivered a manuscript, it was letter-perfect.*

let·ter·press /ˈletərˌpres/ ▶ *n.* printing from a hard, raised image under pressure, using viscous ink.

let·ter-qual·i·ty ▶ *adj.* (of a printer attached to a computer) producing print of a quality suitable for business letters. ■ (of a document) printed to such a standard.

let·tuce /ˈletis/ ▶ *n.* **1** a cultivated plant (*Lactuca sativa*) of the daisy family, with edible leaves that are a usual ingredient of salads. ■ used in names of other plants with edible green leaves, e.g., **lamb's lettuce, sea lettuce. 2** *inf.* paper money; greenbacks.

let·up /ˈletˌəp/ ▶ *n. inf.* a pause or reduction in the intensity of something dangerous, difficult, or tiring: *there had been no letup in the eruption.*

leu·ke·mi·a /lo͞oˈkēmēə/ ▶ *n.* a malignant progressive disease in which the bone marrow and other blood-forming organs produce increased numbers of immature or abnormal leukocytes. —**leu·ke·mic** /-ˈkēmik/ *adj.*

leu·ko·cyte /ˈlo͞okəˌsīt/ (*Brit.* also **leu·co·cyte**) ▶ *n. Physiol.* a colorless cell that circulates in the blood and body fluids and is involved in counteracting foreign substances and disease; a white (blood) cell. —**leu·ko·cyt·ic** /ˌlo͞okəˈsitik/ *adj.*

le·va·tor /ləˈvātər/ (also **levator muscle**) ▶ *n. Anat.* a muscle whose contraction causes the raising of a part of the body.

Pronunciation Key ə *ago, up;* ər *over, fur;* a *hat;* ā *ate;* ä *car;* CH *chin;* e *let;* ē *see;* e(ə)r *air;* i *fit;* ī *by;* i(ə)r *ear;* NG *sing;* ō *go;* ô *law, for;* oi *toy;* o͝o *good;* o͞o *goo;* ou *out;* SH *she;* TH *thin;* TH͟ *then;* (h)w *why;* ZH *vision*

lev·ee[1] ▶*n.* an embankment built to prevent the overflow of a river. ■ a ridge of sediment deposited naturally alongside a river by overflowing water. ■ a ridge of earth surrounding a field to be irrigated.

lev·ee[2] /ˈlevē/ ▶*n.* a reception or assembly of people, in particular: ■ a formal reception of visitors or guests. ■ *hist.* an afternoon assembly for men held by the British monarch or their representative. ■ *archaic* a reception of visitors just after rising from bed.

lev·el /ˈlevəl/ ▶*n.* **1** a position on a real or imaginary scale of amount, quantity, extent, or quality: *a high level of unemployment.* **2** a height or distance from the ground or another stated or understood base: *storms caused river levels to rise.* **3** device consisting of a sealed glass tube partially filled with alcohol or other liquid, containing an air bubble whose position reveals whether a surface is perfectly level or plumb. ■ *Surveying* an instrument for giving a horizontal line of sight. **4** a flat tract of land: *flooded levels.*
▶*adj.* **1** having a flat and even surface without slopes or bumps: *we had reached level ground.* ■ at the same height as someone or something else: *his eyes were level with hers.* ■ having the same relative position; not in front of or behind: *the car braked suddenly, then backed rapidly until it was level with me.* ■ (of a quantity of a dry substance) with the contents not rising above the brim of the measure: *a level teaspoon of salt.* ■ unchanged; not having risen or fallen: *earnings were level at 57 cents a share.* **2** calm and steady: *"Adrian," she said in her most level voice.*
▶*v.* (**-eled, -el·ing**; also *chiefly Brit.* **-elled, -el·ling**) **1** [*tr.*] give a flat and even surface to: *contractors started leveling the ground for the new power station.* ■ *Surveying* ascertain differences in the height of (land). ■ demolish (a building or town): *bulldozers are now waiting to level their home.* **2** [*intr.*] (**level off/out**) begin to fly horizontally after climbing or diving. ■ (of a path, road, or incline) cease to slope upward or downward: *the track leveled out, and there below us was the bay.* ■ cease to fall or rise in number, amount, or quantity: *inflation has leveled out at an acceptable rate.* ■ [*tr.*] (**level something up/down**) increase or reduce the amount, number, or quantity of something in order to remove a disparity. **3** [*tr.*] aim (a weapon): *he leveled a long-barreled pistol at us.* ■ direct (a criticism or accusation): *accusations of corruption had been leveled against him.* **4** [*intr.*] (**level with**) *inf.* be frank or honest with (someone): *when are you going to level with me?* ▷Middle English (denoting an instrument to determine whether a surface is horizontal): from Old French *livel*, based on Latin *libella*, diminutive of *libra* 'scales, balance.' —**lev·el·ly** *adv.* —**lev·el·ness** *n.*
▶ ▢ **do one's level best** do one's utmost; make all possible efforts. ▢ **find one's (own) level** (of a person) reach a position or competency that seems appropriate and natural in relation to one's associates. ▢ **a level playing field** a situation in which everyone has a fair and equal chance of succeeding. ▢ **on the level** *inf.* honest; truthful: *Eddie said my story was on the level.* ▢ **on a level with** in the same horizontal plane as. ■ equal with: *they were treated as menials, on a level with cooks.*

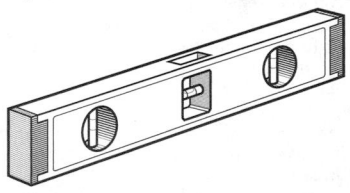

level

lev·el·head·ed /ˈlevəlˈhedid/ ▶*adj.* calm and sensible. —**lev·el·head·ed·ly** *adv.* —**lev·el·head·ed·ness** *n.*

lev·er /ˈlevər; ˈlēvər/ ▶*n.* a rigid bar resting on a pivot, used to help move a heavy or firmly fixed load with one end when pressure is applied to the other. ■ a projecting arm or handle that is moved to operate a mechanism: *she pulled a lever at the base of the cage.* ■ *fig.* a means of exerting pressure on someone to act in a particular way: *rich countries increasingly use foreign aid as a lever to promote political pluralism.*
▶*v.* [*tr.*] lift or move with a lever: *she levered the lid off the pot with a screwdriver.* ■ move (someone or something) with a concerted physical effort: *she levered herself up against the pillows.* ■ [*intr.*] use a lever: *the men got hold of the coffin and levered at it with crowbars.*

lev·er·age /ˈlev(ə)rij; ˈlēv(ə)rij/ ▶*n.* **1** the exertion of force by means of a lever or an object used in the manner of a lever: *my spade hit something solid that wouldn't respond to leverage.* ■ mechanical advantage gained in this way: *use a metal bar to increase the leverage.* ■ *fig.* the power to influence a person or situation to achieve a particular outcome: *the right wing had lost much of its political leverage in the Assembly.* **2** *Finance* the

ratio of a company's loan capital (debt) to the value of its common stock (equity).
▶*v.* [*tr.*] [usu. as *adj.*] (**leveraged**) use borrowed capital for (an investment), expecting the profits made to be greater than the interest payable: *a leveraged takeover bid.*

lev·er·aged buy·out ▶*n.* the purchase of a controlling share in a company by its management, using outside capital.

le·vi·a·than /ləˈvīəTHən/ ▶*n.* (in biblical use) a sea monster, identified in different passages with the whale and the crocodile, and with the Devil. ■ a very large aquatic creature, esp. a whale: *the great leviathans of the deep.* ■ a thing that is very large or powerful, esp. a ship. ■ an autocratic monarch or state.

lev·i·tate /ˈlevəˌtāt/ ▶*v.* [*intr.*] rise and hover in the air, esp. by means of supernatural or magical power: *he seems to levitate about three inches off the ground.* ■ [*tr.*] cause (something) to rise and hover in such a way. —**lev·i·ta·tion** /ˌlevəˈtāSHən/ *n.* —**lev·i·ta·tor** /-ˌtātər/ *n.*

lev·i·ty /ˈlevətē/ ▶*n.* humor or frivolity, esp. the treatment of a serious matter with humor or in a manner lacking due respect: *as an attempt to introduce a note of levity, the words were a disastrous flop.*

lev·y /ˈlevē/ ▶*v.* (**-vies, -vied**) [*tr.*] (often **be levied**) impose (a tax, fee, or fine): *a new tax could be levied on industry to pay for cleaning up contaminated land.* ■ [*intr.*] (**levy on/upon**) seize (property) to satisfy a legal judgment: *there were no goods to levy upon.*
▶*n.* (*pl.* **-vies**) **1** an act of levying a tax, fee, or fine: *union members were hit with a 2 percent levy on all pay.* ■ a tax so raised. ■ a sum collected for a specific purpose, esp. as a supplement to an existing subscription. ■ an item or set of items of property seized to satisfy a legal judgment. **2** *hist.* an act of enlisting troops. ■ (usu. **levies**) a body of troops that have been enlisted: *lightly armed local levies.* —**lev·i·a·ble** *adj.*

lewd /lōōd/ ▶*adj.* crude and offensive in a sexual way: *she began to gyrate to the music and sing a lewd song.* —**lewd·ly** *adv.* —**lewd·ness** *n.*

lex·eme /ˈlekˌsēm/ ▶*n.* *Linguistics* a basic lexical unit of a language, consisting of one word or several words, considered as an abstract unit, and applied to a family of words related by form or meaning.

lex·i·cal /ˈleksikəl/ ▶*adj.* of or relating to the words or vocabulary of a language: *lexical analysis.* ■ relating to or of the nature of a lexicon or dictionary: *a lexical entry.* —**lex·i·cal·ly** /-ik(ə)lē/ *adv.*

lex·i·cog·ra·phy /ˌleksəˈkägrəfē/ ▶*n.* the practice of compiling dictionaries. —**lex·i·cog·ra·pher** *n.* —**lex·i·co·graph·ic** /-kəˈgrafik/ *adj.* —**lex·i·co·graph·i·cal** /-kəˈgrafikəl/ *adj.* —**lex·i·co·graph·i·cal·ly** /-kəˈgrafik(ə)lē/ *adv.*

lex·i·col·o·gy /ˌleksəˈkäləjē/ ▶*n.* the study of the form, meaning, and use of words. —**lex·i·co·log·i·cal** /-kəˈläjikəl/ *adj.* —**lex·i·co·log·i·cal·ly** /-kəˈläjik(ə)lē/ *adv.*

lex·i·con /ˈleksiˌkän; -kən/ ▶*n.* (*pl.* **-cons** or **-ca** /-kə/) **1** the vocabulary of a person, language, or branch of knowledge: *the size of the English lexicon.* ■ a dictionary, esp. of Greek, Hebrew, Syriac, or Arabic: *a Greek–Latin lexicon.* **2** *Linguistics* the complete set of meaningful units in a language.

LF ▶*abbr.* low frequency.

LH *Biochem.* ▶*abbr.* luteinizing hormone.

LI ▶*abbr.* ■ Long Island.

Li ▶*symb.* the chemical element lithium.

li·a·bil·i·ty /ˌlīəˈbilətē/ ▶*n.* (*pl.* **-ties**) **1** the state of being responsible for something, esp. by law: *the partners accept unlimited liability for any risks they undertake.* ■ (usu. **liabilities**) a thing for which someone is responsible, esp. a debt or financial obligation: *valuing the company's liabilities and assets.* **2** a person or thing whose presence or behavior is likely to cause embarrassment or put one at a disadvantage: *he has become a political liability.*

li·a·ble /ˈlī(ə)bəl/ ▶*adj.* **1** responsible by law; legally answerable: *the supplier of goods or services can become liable for breach of contract in a variety of ways.* **2** likely to do or to be something: *patients were liable to faint if they*

fulcrum

lever

stood up too suddenly. ■ (**liable to**) likely to experience (something undesirable): *areas liable to flooding.*

li·aise /lēˈāz/ ▶*v.* [*intr.*] establish a working relationship, typically in order to cooperate on a matter of mutual concern: *she will liaise with teachers across the country.*

li·ai·son /ˈlēə,zän; lēˈā-/ ▶*n.* **1** communication or cooperation that facilitates a close working relationship between people or organizations: *the head porter works in close liaison with the reception office.* ■ a person who acts as a link to assist communication or cooperation between groups of people: *he's our liaison with a number of interested parties.* ■ a sexual relationship, esp. one that is secret and involves unfaithfulness to a partner. **2** the binding or thickening agent of a sauce, often based on egg yolks. **3** *Phonet.* (in French and other languages) the sounding of a consonant that is normally silent at the end of a word because the next word begins with a vowel. ▷mid 17th cent. (as a culinary term): from French, from *lier* 'to bind.'

li·ai·son of·fi·cer ▶*n.* a person who is employed to form a working relationship between two organizations to their mutual benefit.

li·ar /ˈlīər/ ▶*n.* a person who tells lies.

lib /lib/ ▶*n.* *inf.* (in the names of political movements) liberation: *I'm all for women's lib.*

li·ba·tion /līˈbāsHən/ ▶*n.* a drink poured out as an offering to a deity. ■ the pouring out of such a drink-offering: *gin was poured in libation.* ■ *humorous* a drink: *they steadily worked their way through free food and the occasional libation.*

li·bel /ˈlībəl/ ▶*n.* *Law* a published false statement that is damaging to a person's reputation; a written defamation. Compare with SLANDER. ■ the action or crime of publishing such a statement: *a councilor who sued two national newspapers for libel.* ■ a false and malicious statement about a person. ■ a thing or circumstance that brings undeserved discredit on a person by misrepresentation.
▶*v.* (**-beled, -bel·ing**; *Brit.* **-belled, -bel·ling**) [*tr.*] *Law* defame (someone) by publishing a libel: *she alleged the magazine had libeled her.* ■ make a false and malicious statement about. —**li·bel·er** *n.*

li·bel·ous /ˈlībələs/ (*Brit.* **li·bel·lous**) ▶*adj.* containing or constituting a libel: *a libelous newspaper story.* —**li·bel·ous·ly** *adv.*

lib·er·al /ˈlib(ə)rəl/ ▶*adj.* open to new behavior or opinions and willing to discard traditional values: *they have more liberal views toward marriage and divorce than some people.* ■ favorable to or respectful of individual rights and freedoms: *liberal citizenship laws.* ■ (in a political context) favoring maximum individual liberty in political and social reform: *a liberal democratic state.* ■ (**Liberal**) of or characteristic of Liberals or a Liberal Party. ■ *Theol.* regarding many traditional beliefs as dispensable, invalidated by modern thought, or liable to change. **2** (of education) concerned mainly with broadening a person's general knowledge and experience, rather than with technical or professional training. **3** (esp. of an interpretation of a law) broadly construed or understood; not strictly literal or exact: *they could have given the 1968 Act a more liberal interpretation.* **4** given, used, or occurring in generous amounts: *liberal amounts of wine had been consumed.* ■ (of a person) giving generously: *Sam was too liberal with the wine.*
▶*n.* a person of liberal views. ■ (**Liberal**) a supporter or member of a Liberal Party. ▷Middle English: via Old French from Latin *liberalis*, from *liber* 'free (man).' The original sense was 'suitable for a free man,' hence 'suitable for a gentleman' (one not tied to a trade), surviving in *liberal arts.* Another early sense 'generous' gave rise to an obsolete meaning 'free from restraint,' leading to sense 1 (late 18th cent.). —**lib·er·al·ism** /-,lizəm/ *n.* —**lib·er·al·ist** /-rəlist/ *n.* —**lib·er·al·is·tic** /,lib(ə)rəˈlistik/ *adj.* —**lib·er·al·ly** *adv.* —**lib·er·al·ness** *n.*

lib·er·al arts ▶*pl. n.* academic subjects such as literature, philosophy, mathematics, and social and physical sciences as distinct from professional and technical subjects.

lib·er·al·i·ty /,libəˈralətē/ ▶*n.* **1** the quality of giving or spending freely. **2** the quality of being open to new ideas and free from prejudice: *liberality toward bisexuality.*

lib·er·al·ize /ˈlib(ə)rə,līz/ ▶*v.* [*tr.*] remove or loosen restrictions on (something, typically an economic or political system): *several agreements to liberalize trade were signed.* —**lib·er·al·i·za·tion** /,lib(ə)rələˈzāsHən; -,līˈzā-/ *n.* —**lib·er·al·iz·er** *n.*

lib·er·ate /ˈlibə,rāt/ ▶*v.* [*tr.*] (often **be liberated**) set (someone) free from a situation, esp. imprisonment or slavery, in which their liberty is severely restricted: *the serfs had been liberated.* ■ free (someone) from rigid social conventions, esp. those concerned with accepted sexual roles: *ways of working politically that liberate women.* ■ *inf.* steal (something): *the drummer's wearing a beret he's liberated from Lord knows where.* ■ *Chem. & Physics* release (gas, energy, etc.) as a result of chemical reaction or

physical decomposition: *energy liberated by the annihilation of matter.* —**lib·er·a·tion** /,libəˈrāsHən/ *n.* —**lib·er·a·tion·ist** /,libəˈrāsHənist/ *n.* —**lib·er·a·tor** /-,rātər/ *n.*

lib·er·tar·i·an /,libərˈte(ə)rēən/ ▶*n.* an adherent of libertarianism: [as *adj.*] *libertarian philosophy.* ■ a person who advocates civil liberty. —**lib·er·tar·i·an·ism** *n.*

lib·er·tine /ˈlibər,tēn/ ▶*n.* **1** a person, esp. a man, who behaves without moral principles or a sense of responsibility, esp. in sexual matters. **2** a person who rejects accepted opinions in matters of religion; a free-thinker.
▶*adj.* **1** characterized by a disregard of morality, esp. in sexual matters: *his more libertine impulses.* **2** freethinking in matters of religion. —**lib·er·tin·age** /-,tēnij/ *n.* —**lib·er·tin·ism** /-,nizəm/ *n.*

lib·er·ty /ˈlibərtē/ ▶*n.* (pl. **-ties**) **1** the state of being free within society from oppressive restrictions imposed by authority on one's way of life, behavior, or political views: *compulsory retirement would interfere with individual liberty.* ■ (usu. **liberties**) an instance of this; a right or privilege, esp. a statutory one: *the Bill of Rights was intended to secure basic civil liberties.* ■ the state of not being imprisoned or enslaved: *people who have lost property or liberty without due process.* **2** the power or scope to act as one pleases: *individuals should enjoy the liberty to pursue their own interests and preferences.* ■ *Philos.* a person's freedom from control by fate or necessity. ■ *inf.* a presumptuous remark or action: *how did he know what she was thinking?—it was a liberty!* ■ *Naut.* shore leave granted to a sailor.
▶ □ **at liberty 1** not imprisoned: *he was at liberty for three months before he was recaptured.* **2** allowed or entitled to do something: *competent adults are generally at liberty to refuse medical treatment.* □ **take liberties 1** behave in an unduly familiar manner toward a person: *you've taken too many liberties with me.* **2** treat something freely, without strict faithfulness to the facts or to an original: *the scriptwriter has taken few liberties with the original narrative.* □ **take the liberty** venture to do something without first asking permission: *I have taken the liberty of submitting an idea to several of their research departments.*

li·bid·i·nous /ləˈbidn-əs/ ▶*adj.* showing excessive sexual drive; lustful. —**li·bid·i·nous·ly** *adv.* —**li·bid·i·nous·ness** *n.*

li·bi·do /ləˈbēdō/ ▶*n.* (pl. **-dos**) sexual desire: *loss of libido* | *a deficient libido.* ■ *Psychoanalysis* the energy of the sexual drive as a component of the life instinct. —**li·bid·i·nal** /-ˈbidn-əl/ *adj.* —**li·bid·i·nal·ly** /-ˈbidn-əlē/ *adv.*

Li·bra /ˈlēbrə/ ▶ **1** *Astron.* a small constellation (the Scales or Balance), said to represent the balance that is the symbol of justice. It contains no bright stars. **2** *Astrol.* the seventh sign of the zodiac, which the sun enters at the northern autumnal equinox (about September 23). ■ (**a Libra**) a person born when the sun is in this sign.

li·brar·i·an /līˈbre(ə)rēən/ ▶*n.* a person, typically with a degree in library science, who administers or assists in a library. —**li·brar·i·an·ship** /-,SHip/ *n.*

li·brar·y /ˈlī,brerē; -brərē/ ▶*n.* (pl. **-brar·ies**) a building or room containing collections of books, periodicals, and sometimes films and recorded music for people to read, borrow, or refer to. ■ a collection of books and periodicals held in such a building or room: *the Institute houses an outstanding library of 35,000 volumes on the fine arts.* ■ a collection of films, recorded music, genetic material, etc., organized systematically and kept for research or borrowing: *a record library.* ■ a series of books, recordings, etc., issued by the same company and similar in appearance. ■ a room in a private house where books are kept. ■ (also **software library**) *Comput.* a collection of programs and software packages made generally available, often loaded and stored on disk for immediate use.

li·bret·to /ləˈbretō/ ▶*n.* (pl. **-bret·ti** /-ˈbretē/ or **-bret·tos**) the text of an opera or other long vocal work. —**li·bret·tist** /-ˈbretist/ *n.*

lice /līs/ ▶ plural form of LOUSE.

li·cense /ˈlīsəns/ ▶*n.* a permit from an authority to own or use something, do a particular thing, or carry on a trade (esp. in alcoholic beverages): *a gun license.* ■ a writer's or artist's freedom to deviate from fact or from conventions such as grammar, meter, or perspective, for effect: *artistic license.* ■ freedom to behave as one wishes, esp. in a way that results in excessive or unacceptable behavior: *the government was criticized for giving the army too much license.* ■ (**a license to do something**) a reason or excuse to do something wrong or excessive: *police say that the lenient sentence is a license to assault.*
▶*v.* [*tr.*] (often **be licensed**) grant a license to (someone or something) to

---

Pronunciation Key ə *ago, up*; ər *over, fur*; a *hat*; ā *ate*; ä *car*; CH *chin*; e *let*; ē *see*; e(ə)r *air*; i *fit*; ī *by*; i(ə)r *ear*; NG *sing*; ō *go*; ô *law, for*; oi *toy*; o͝o *good*; o͞o *goo*; ou *out*; SH *she*; TH *thin*; ŦH *then*; (h)w *why*; ZH *vision*

permit the use of something or to allow an activity to take place: *brokers must be licensed to sell health-related insurance.* | [as adj.] (**licensing**) *a licensing authority.* —**li·cens·a·ble** adj. —**li·cens·er** n. —**li·cen·sor** /-sər; ˌlīsən'sôr/ n.

li·cen·see /ˌlīsən'sē/ ▸n. the holder of a license.

li·cense plate ▸n. a sign affixed to a vehicle displaying a series of letters or numbers indicating that the vehicle has been registered with the state.

li·cen·ti·ate /lī'senSH(ē)it/ ▸n. the holder of a certificate of competence to practice a certain profession. ▪ (in certain universities, esp. in Europe) a degree between that of bachelor and master or doctor. ▪ the holder of such a degree. —**li·cen·ti·ate·ship** /-ˌSHip/ n.

li·cen·tious /lī'senSHəs/ ▸adj. promiscuous and unprincipled in sexual matters. —**li·cen·tious·ly** adv. —**li·cen·tious·ness** n.

li·chee ▸n. variant spelling of LITCHI.

li·chen /'līkən/ ▸n. a simple slow-growing plant that typically forms a low crustlike, leaflike, or branching growth on rocks, walls, and trees. —**li·chened** adj. —**li·chen·ol·o·gy** /ˌlīkə'näləjē/ n.

lic·it /'lisit/ ▸adj. not forbidden; lawful: *licit and illicit drugs.* —**lic·it·ly** adv.

lick /lik/ ▸v. [tr.] **1** pass the tongue over (something), typically in order to taste, moisten, or clean it: *he licked the stamp and stuck it on the envelope.* ▪ [intr.] fig. (of a flame, wave, or breeze) move lightly and quickly like a tongue: *the flames licked around the wood.* **2** inf. defeat (someone) comprehensively: *all right Mary, I know when I'm licked.* ▪ thrash: *she stands tall and could lick any man in the place.*
▸n. **1** an act of licking something with the tongue: *Sammy gave his fingers a long lick.* ▪ fig. a movement of flame, water, etc., resembling this. **2** inf. a small amount or quick application of something, esp. paint: *all she'd need to do to the kitchen was give it a lick of paint.* **3** (often **licks**) inf. a short phrase or solo in jazz or popular music: *cool guitar licks.* **4** inf. a smart blow: *his mother gave him several licks for daring to blaspheme.* —**lick·er** n. [usu. in combination].
▸ □ **a lick and a promise** inf. a hasty performance of a task, esp. of cleaning something. □ **lick someone's boots** be excessively obsequious toward someone, esp. to gain favor from them. □ **lick one's lips** (or **chops**) look forward to something with eager anticipation. □ **lick one's wounds** retire to recover one's strength or confidence after a defeat or humiliating experience: *the political organization he worked for was licking its wounds after electoral defeat.*

lick·e·ty-split /'likətē 'split/ ▸adv. inf. as quickly as possible; immediately: *I took off lickety-split across the lawn.*

lick·ing /'likiNG/ ▸n. inf. a severe defeat or beating.

lic·o·rice /'lik(ə)riSH; -ris/ (Brit. **liqu·o·rice**) ▸n. **1** a sweet, chewy, aromatic black substance made by evaporation from the juice of a root. ▪ a candy flavored with such a substance. **2** the widely distributed plant (genus *Glycyrrhiza*) of the pea family from which this product is obtained. ▷Middle English: from Old French *licoresse*, from late Latin *liquiritia*, from Greek *glukurrhiza*, from *glukus* 'sweet' + *rhiza* 'root.'

lid /lid/ ▸n. a removable or hinged cover for the top of a container: *a large frying pan with a lid.* ▪ (usu. **lids**) an eyelid: *eyes now hooded beneath heavy lids.* ▪ inf. a hat. —**lid·ded** adj. —**lid·less** adj.
▸ □ **blow the lid off** inf. reveal unwelcome secrets about: *prosecutors have taken the lid off a multimillion-dollar payoff scandal.* □ **keep a** (or **the**) **lid on** inf. keep (an emotion or process) from going out of control: *she was no longer able to keep the lid on her simmering anger.* ▪ keep secret: *she keeps a very tight lid on her own private life.* □ **put a** (or **the**) **lid on** inf. put a stop to or be the culmination of: *it's time to put the lid on all the talk.*

lie[1] /lī/ ▸v. (**ly·ing** /'lī-iNG/; past **lay** /lā/; past part. **lain** /lān/) [intr.] **1** (of a person or animal) be in or assume a horizontal or resting position on a supporting surface: *I had to lie down for two hours because I was groggy.* ▪ (of a thing) rest flat on a surface: *a book lay open on the table.* ▪ (of a dead person) be buried in a particular place. **2** be, remain, or be kept in a specified state: *the church lies in ruins today.* ▪ (of something abstract) reside or be found: *the solution lies in a return to "traditional family values."* **3** (of a place) be situated in a specified position or direction: *the small town of Swampscott lies about ten miles north of Boston.* **4** Law (of an action, charge, or claim) be admissible or sustainable.
▸phrasal v. □ **lie ahead** be going to happen; be in store: *I'm excited by what lies ahead.* □ **lie around/about** (of an object) be left carelessly out of place: *there were pills and potions lying around in every corner of the house.* ▪ (of a person) pass the time lazily or aimlessly: *you all just lay around all day on your backsides, didn't you?* □ **lie behind** be the real, often hidden, reason for (something): *a subtle strategy lies behind such silly claims.* □ **lie with 1** (of a responsibility or problem) be attributable to (someone): *the ultimate responsibility for the violence lies with the country's president.* **2** archaic have sexual intercourse with.

▸n. (usu. **the lie**) the way, direction, or position in which something lies. ▪ Golf the position in which a golf ball comes to rest, esp. as regards the ease of the next shot. ▪ the lair or place of cover of an animal or a bird.
▸ □ **let something lie** take no action regarding a controversial or problematic matter. □ **lie in state** (of the corpse of a person of national importance) be laid in a public place of honor before burial. □ **lie in wait** conceal oneself, waiting to surprise, attack, or catch someone. □ **lie low** (esp. of a criminal) keep out of sight; avoid detection or attention: *at the time of the murder, he appears to have been lying low in a barn.* □ **take something lying down** [usu. with negative] accept an insult, setback, rebuke, etc., without reacting or protesting.

lie[2] ▸n. an intentionally false statement: *Mungo felt a pang of shame at telling Alice a lie.* ▪ used with reference to a situation involving deception or founded on a mistaken impression: *all their married life she had been living a lie.*
▸v. (**lies, lied, ly·ing** /'lī-iNG/) [intr.] tell a lie or lies: *why had Wesley lied about his visit to Philadelphia?* ▪ (of a thing) present a false impression; be deceptive: *the camera cannot lie.*
▸ □ **give the lie to** serve to show that (something seemingly apparent or previously stated or believed) is not true: *these figures give the lie to the notion that Britain is excessively strike-ridden.*

lied /lēd; lēt/ ▸n. (pl. **lie·der** /'lēdər/) a type of German song, esp. of the Romantic period, typically for solo voice with piano accompaniment.

lie de·tec·tor ▸n. an instrument for determining whether a person is telling the truth by testing for physiological changes considered to be associated with lying. Compare with POLYGRAPH.

lien /'lē(ə)n/ ▸n. Law a right to keep possession of property belonging to another person until a debt owed by that person is discharged.

lieu /loo/ ▸n. (in phrase **in lieu**) instead: *the company issued additional shares to shareholders in lieu of a cash dividend.*

Lieut. ▸abbr. lieutenant.

lieu·ten·ant /loo'tenənt/ ▸n. a deputy or substitute acting for a superior: *two of Lenin's leading lieutenants.* ▪ a naval officer of a high rank, in particular a commissioned officer in the U.S. Navy or Coast Guard ranking above lieutenant junior grade and below lieutenant commander. ▪ a police or fire department officer next in rank below captain. —**lieu·ten·an·cy** /-'tenənsē/ n. (pl. **-cies**).

lieu·ten·ant colo·nel ▸n. a commissioned officer in the U.S. Army, Air Force, or Marine Corps ranking above major and below colonel.

lieu·ten·ant com·man·der ▸n. a commissioned officer in the U.S. Navy or Coast Guard ranking above lieutenant and below commander.

lieu·ten·ant gen·er·al ▸n. a commissioned officer in the U.S. Army, Air Force, or Marine Corps ranking above major general and below general.

lieu·ten·ant gov·er·nor ▸n. the executive officer of a state who is next in rank to a governor and who takes the governor's place in case of disability or death. ▪ the executive officer of a Canadian province, appointed by the governor general. —**lieu·ten·ant gov·er·nor·ship** n.

life /līf/ ▸n. (pl. **lives** /līvz/) **1** the condition that distinguishes animals and plants from inorganic matter, including the capacity for growth, reproduction, functional activity, and continual change preceding death: *the origins of life.* ▪ living things and their activity: *some sort of life existed on Mars.* ▪ the state of being alive as a human being: *she didn't want to die; she loved life.* ▪ [with adj.] a particular type or aspect of people's existence: *an experienced teacher will help you settle into school life.* ▪ vitality, vigor, or energy: *she was beautiful and full of life.* **2** the existence of an individual human being or animal: *a disaster that claimed the lives of 266 Americans.* ▪ a biography: *a life of Shelley.* ▪ a chance to live after narrowly escaping death (esp. with reference to the nine lives traditionally attributed to cats). **3** (usu. **one's life**) the period between the birth and death of a living thing, esp. a human being: *she has lived all her life in the country.* ▪ the period during which something inanimate or abstract continues to exist, function, or be valid: *underlay helps to prolong the life of a carpet.* ▪ inf. a sentence of imprisonment for life. **4** (in art) the depiction of a subject from a real model, rather than from an artist's imagination: *the pose and clothing were sketched from life.* See also STILL LIFE.
▸ □ **bring** (or **come**) **to life** regain or cause to regain consciousness or return as if from death: *all this was of great interest to her, as if she were coming to life after a long sleep.* ▪ (with reference to a fictional character or inanimate object) cause or seem to be alive or real: *all the puppets came to life again.* ▪ make or become active, lively, or interesting: *soon, with the return of the peasants and fishermen, the village comes to life again.* □ **for dear** (or **one's**) **life** as if or in order to escape death: *I clung to the tree for dear life* | *Sue struggled free and ran for her life.* □ **get a life** [often in

imperative] *inf.* start living a fuller or more interesting existence: *if he's a jerk, then get yourself out of there and get a life.* □ **give one's life for** die for. □ **larger than life** (of a person) attracting special attention because of unusual and flamboyant appearance or behavior. ■ (of a thing) seeming disproportionately important: *your problems seem larger than life at that time of night.* □ **the life of the party** a vivacious and sociable person. □ **take one's life in one's hands** risk being killed.

life-and-death ▸*adj.* deciding whether someone lives or dies; vitally important: *life-and-death decisions.*

life·belt /'līf,belt/ ▸*n.* a life preserver in the shape of a belt.

life·blood /'līf,bləd/ ▸*n.* the blood, as being necessary to life. ■ *fig.* the indispensable factor or influence that gives something its strength and vitality: *my family was the lifeblood of the church.*

life·boat /'līf,bōt/ ▸*n.* a specially constructed boat launched from land to rescue people in distress at sea. ■ a small boat kept on a ship for use in emergency, typically one of a number on deck or suspended from davits. —**life·boat·man** /-mən/ *n.* (*pl.* **-men**).

life·bu·oy /'līf,bōō-ē; -,boi/ ▸*n.* a life preserver, esp. one in the shape of a ring.

life cy·cle ▸*n.* the series of changes in the life of an organism, including reproduction.

life ex·pec·tan·cy ▸*n.* the average period that a person may expect to live.

life force ▸*n.* the force or influence that gives something its vitality or strength: *the passionate life force of the symphony.* ■ the spirit or energy that animates living creatures; the soul.

life-giv·ing ▸*adj.* sustaining or revitalizing life: *the life-giving water of baptism.*

life·guard /'līf,gärd/ ▸*n.* an expert swimmer employed to rescue people who get into difficulty in a swimming pool or at the beach.
▸*v.* [*intr.*] work as a lifeguard.

life in·sur·ance ▸*n.* insurance that pays out a sum of money either on the death of the insured person or after a set period.

life jack·et ▸*n.* a sleeveless buoyant or inflatable jacket for keeping a person afloat in water.

life jacket

life·less /'līflis/ ▸*adj.* dead or apparently dead: *his lifeless body was taken from the river.* ■ lacking vigor, vitality, or excitement: *my hair always seems to look lifeless.* ■ devoid of living things: *the moon is lifeless.* —**life·less·ly** *adv.* —**life·less·ness** *n.*

life·like /'līf,līk/ ▸*adj.* very similar to the person or thing represented: *the artist had etched a lifelike horse.* —**life·like·ness** *n.*

life·line /'līf,līn/ ▸*n.* **1** a rope or line used for life-saving, typically one thrown to rescue someone in difficulties in water or one used by sailors to secure themselves to a boat. ■ a line used by a diver for sending signals to the surface. ■ *fig.* a thing that is essential for the continued existence of someone or something or that provides a means of escape from a difficult situation: *fertility treatment can seem like a lifeline to childless couples.* **2** (in palmistry) a line on the palm of a person's hand, regarded as indicating how long they will live.
▸ □ **throw a lifeline to** (or **throw someone a lifeline**) provide (someone) with a means of escaping from a difficult situation.

life·long /'līf,lông; -,läng/ ▸*adj.* lasting or remaining in a particular state throughout a person's life: *the two men were to remain lifelong friends.*

life pre·serv·er ▸*n.* a device made of buoyant or inflatable material, such as a life jacket or lifebelt, to keep someone afloat in water.

lif·er /'līfər/ ▸*n.* **1** *inf.* a person serving a life sentence in prison. **2** a person who spends their life in a particular career, esp. in one of the armed forces.

life raft ▸*n.* a raft, typically inflatable, for use in an emergency at sea.

life·sav·er /'līf,sāvər/ ▸*n.* **1** *inf.* a thing that saves one from serious difficulty: *a microwave oven could be a lifesaver this Christmas.* **2** a ring-shaped life preserver.

life sci·enc·es ▸*plural n.* the sciences concerned with the study of living organisms, including biology, botany, zoology, microbiology,

physiology, biochemistry, and related subjects. Often contrasted with PHYSICAL SCIENCES. —**life sci·en·tist** *n.*

life sen·tence ▸*n.* a punishment for a felon of imprisonment for life.

life-size (also **life-sized**) ▸*adj.* of the same size as the person or thing represented: *a life-size statue of a discus-thrower.*

life·skill /'līf,skil/ ▸*n.* [often *pl.*] a skill that is required to participate in everyday life: *drawing is an essential lifeskill enhancing children's powers of observation.*

life span (also **life-span**) ▸*n.* the length of time for which a person or animal lives or a thing functions: *the human life span.*

life·style /'līf,stīl/ ▸*n.* the way in which a person or group lives: *the benefits of a healthy lifestyle.*

life sup·port ▸*n. Med.* maintenance of the vital functions of a critically ill or comatose person or a person undergoing surgery. ■ *inf.* equipment in a hospital used for this: *a patient on life support.*

life·time /'līf,tīm/ ▸*n.* the duration of a person's life: *a reward for a lifetime's work.* ■ the duration of a thing's existence or usefulness: *a plan to extend the lifetime of satellites.* ■ *inf.* used to express the view that a period is very long: *five weeks was a lifetime, and anything could have happened.*
▸ □ **of a lifetime** (of a chance or experience) such as does not occur more than once in a person's life: *because of Frankie she had rejected the opportunity of a lifetime.*

life·work /'līf,wərk/ ▸*n.* the entire or principal work, labor, or task of a person's lifetime.

lift /lift/ ▸*v.* [*tr.*] **1** raise to a higher position or level: *he lifted his trophy over his head.* ■ increase the volume or pitch of (one's voice): *Willie sang boldly, lifting up his voice.* ■ transport by air: *a helicopter lifted 11 crew members to safety from the ship.* ■ hit or kick (a ball) high into the air. ■ [*intr.*] move upward; be raised: *Thomas's eyelids drowsily lifted.* ■ [*intr.*] (of a cloud, fog, etc.) move upward or away: *the factory smoke hung low, never lifted.* ■ perform cosmetic surgery on (esp. the face or breasts) to reduce sagging: *surgeons lift and remove excess skin from the face and neck.* **2** pick up and move to a different position: *he lifted her down from the pony's back.* ■ *fig.* enable (someone or something) to escape from a particular state of mind or situation, esp. an unpleasant one: *two billion barrels of oil that could lift this nation out of chronic poverty.* **3** raise (a person's spirits or confidence); encourage or cheer: *we heard inspiring talks that lifted our spirits.* ■ [*intr.*] (of a person's mood) become happier: *suddenly his heart lifted, and he could have wept with relief.* **4** formally remove or end (a legal restriction, decision, or ban): *the European Community lifted its oil embargo against South Africa.* **5** *inf.* steal (something, esp. a minor item of property): *the shirt she had lifted from a supermarket.* ■ use (a person's work or ideas) without permission or acknowledgment; plagiarize: *this is a hackneyed adventure lifted straight from a vintage Lassie episode.*
▸*phrasal v.* □ **lift off** (of an aircraft, spacecraft, or rocket) rise from the ground or a launch pad, esp. vertically.
▸*n.* **1** something that is used for lifting, in particular: ■ British term for ELEVATOR. ■ a device incorporating a moving cable for carrying people, typically skiers, up or down a mountain. ■ a built-up heel or device worn in a boot or shoe to make the wearer appear taller or to correct shortening of a leg. **2** an act of lifting: *weightlifters attempting a particularly heavy lift.* ■ an upward force that counteracts the force of gravity, produced by changing the direction and speed of a moving stream of air: *it had separate engines to provide lift and generate forward speed.* **3** a free ride in another person's vehicle: *Miss Green is giving me a lift back to school.* **4** a feeling of encouragement or increased cheerfulness: *winning this game has given everyone on the team a lift.* —**lift·a·ble** *adj.* —**lift·er** *n.*
▸ □ **lift a finger** (or **hand**) [usu. with *negative*] make the slightest effort to do something, esp. to help someone: *he never once lifted a finger to get Jimmy released from prison.*

lift·off /'lift,ôf; -,äf/ ▸*n.* takeoff, esp. the vertical takeoff of a rocket or helicopter.

lig·a·ment /'ligəmənt/ ▸*n. Anat.* a short band of tough, flexible, fibrous connective tissue that connects two bones or cartilages or holds together a joint. ■ a membranous fold that supports an organ and keeps it in position. ■ any similar connecting or binding structure. ▷late Middle English: from Latin *ligamentum* 'bond,' from *ligare* 'to bind.' —**lig·a·men·tal** /,ligə'mentl/ *adj.* —**lig·a·men·ta·ry** /,ligə'ment(ə)rē/ *adj.* —**lig·a·men·tous** /,ligə'mentəs/ *adj.*

li·gand /'ligənd; 'lī-/ ▸*n. Chem.* an ion or molecule attached to a metal atom by coordinate bonding. ■ *Biochem.* a molecule that binds to another (usually larger) molecule. ▷1950s: from Latin *ligandus* 'that can be tied,' gerundive of *ligare* 'to bind.'

li·gate /'lī,gāt/ ▶*v.* [*tr.*] (usu. **be ligated**) *Surgery* tie up or otherwise close off (an artery or vessel). —**li·ga·tion** *n.*

li·ga·ture /'ligəCHər; -,CHŏŏr/ ▶*n.* **1** a thing used for tying or binding something tightly. ■ a cord or thread used in surgery, esp. to tie up a bleeding artery. **2** *Mus.* a slur or tie. **3** *Printing* a character consisting of two or more joined letters, e.g., æ, fl. ■ a stroke that joins adjacent letters in writing or printing.
▶*v.* [*tr.*] bind or connect with a ligature.

light[1] /līt/ ▶*n.* **1** the natural agent that stimulates sight and makes things visible: *the light of the sun.* ■ a source of illumination, esp. an electric lamp: *a light came on in his room.* ■ a traffic light: *turn right at the light.* ■ an expression in someone's eyes indicating a particular emotion or mood: *a shrewd light entered his eyes.* **2** understanding of a problem or mystery; enlightenment: *she saw light dawn on the woman's face.* ■ spiritual illumination by divine truth. ■ (**lights**) a person's opinions, standards, and abilities: *leaving the police to do the job according to their lights.* **3** an area of something that is brighter or paler than its surroundings: *sunshine will brighten the natural lights in your hair.* **4** a match or lighter that produces a flame or spark. ■ the flame produced: *he asked me for a light.* **5** a window or opening in a wall to let light in. ■ any of the perpendicular divisions of a mullioned window. ■ any of the panes of glass forming the roof or side of a greenhouse or the top of a cold frame. **6** a person notable or eminent in a particular sphere of activity or place: *such lights of Liberalism as the historian Goldwin Smith.*
▶*v.* (*past* and *past part.* **lit** /lit/ or **light·ed**) [*tr.*] **1** provide with light or lighting; illuminate: *the room was lighted by a number of small lamps.* ■ switch on (an electric light): *only one of the table lamps was lit.* ■ [*intr.*] (**light up**) become illuminated: *the sign to fasten seat belts lit up.* **2** make (something) start burning; ignite: *Allen gathered sticks and lit a fire* ■ [*intr.*] begin to burn; be ignited: *the gas wouldn't light properly.* ■ (**light something up**) ignite a cigarette, cigar, or pipe and begin to smoke it: *she lit up a cigarette and puffed on it serenely.*
▶*phrasal v.* □ **light up** (or **light something up**) (with reference to a person's face or eyes) suddenly become or cause to be animated with liveliness or joy: *his eyes lit up and he smiled.*
▶*adj.* **1** having a considerable or sufficient amount of natural light; not dark: *the bedrooms are light and airy.* **2** (of a color) pale: *her eyes were light blue.* ▷Old English *lēoht*, *līht* (noun and adjective), *līhtan* (verb), of Germanic origin; related to Dutch *licht* and German *Licht*, from an Indo-European root shared by Greek *leukos* 'white' and Latin *lux* 'light.' —**light·ness** *n.*
▶ □ **bring** (or **come**) **to light** make (or become) widely known or evident: *an investigation to bring to light examples of extravagant expenditure.* □ **go out like a light** *inf.* fall asleep or lose consciousness suddenly. □ **in a —— light** in the way specified; so as to give a specified impression: *the audit portrayed the company in a very favorable light.* □ **in (the) light of** drawing knowledge or information from; taking (something) into consideration: *the exorbitant prices are explainable in the light of the facts.* □ **see the light** understand or realize something after prolonged thought or doubt. ■ undergo religious conversion. □ **shed** (or **throw** or **cast**) **light on** help to explain (something) by providing further information about it.

light[2] ▶*adj.* **1** of little weight; easy to lift: *they are very light and portable.* ■ deficient in weight, esp. by a specified amount: *the sack of potatoes is 5 pounds light.* ■ not strongly or heavily built or constructed; small of its kind: *light, impractical clothes.* ■ carrying or suitable for small loads: *light commercial vehicles.* ■ carrying only light armaments: *light infantry.* ■ (of a vehicle, ship, or aircraft) traveling unladen or with less than a full load. ■ (of food or a meal) small in quantity and easy to digest: *a light supper.* ■ (of a foodstuff) low in fat, cholesterol, sugar, or other rich ingredients: *stick to a light diet.* ■ (of drink) not too sweet or rich in flavor or strongly alcoholic: *a glass of light Hungarian wine.* ■ (of food, esp. pastry or sponge cake) fluffy or well aerated during cooking. ■ (of soil) friable, porous, and workable. ■ (of an isotope) having not more than the usual mass; (of a compound) containing such an isotope. **2** relatively low in density, amount, or intensity: *passenger traffic was light.* **3** gentle or delicate: *she planted a light kiss on his cheek | my breathing was steady and light.* ■ (of a building) having an appearance suggestive of lightness: *the building is lofty and light in its tall nave and choir.* ■ (of type) having thin strokes; not bold. **4** (of entertainment) requiring little mental effort; not profound or serious: *some light reading.* ■ not serious or solemn: *his tone was light.* ■ free from worry or unhappiness; cheerful: *I left the island with a light heart.* —**light·ly** *adv.* —**light·ness** *n.*

▶ □ **be light on** be rather short of: *light on hard news.* □ **be light on one's feet** (of a person) be quick or nimble. □ **a** (or **someone's**) **light touch** the ability to deal with something delicately, tactfully, or in an understated way: *a novel that handles its tricky subject with a light touch.* □ **make light of** treat as unimportant: *I didn't mean to make light of your problems.* □ **make light work of** accomplish (a task) quickly and easily. □ **travel light** travel with a minimum load or minimum luggage.

light[3] ▶*v.* (*past* and *past part.* **lit** /lit/ or **light·ed**) [*intr.*] **1** (**light on/upon**) come upon or discover by chance: *he lit on a possible solution.* **2** *archaic* descend: *from the horse he lit down.* ■ (**light on**) fall and settle or land on (a surface): *a feather just lighted on the ground.*
▶*phrasal v.* □ **light into** *inf.* criticize severely; attack: *he lit into him for his indiscretion.* □ **light out** *inf.* depart hurriedly.

light bulb (also **light·bulb**) ▶*n.* a glass bulb inserted into a lamp or a socket in a ceiling, that provides light by passing an electric current through a pocket of inert gas.

light-emit·ting di·ode ▶*n.* see **LED**.

light·en[1] /'lītn/ ▶*v.* make or become lighter in weight, pressure, or severity: [*tr.*] *efforts to lighten the burden of regulation.* ■ make or become more cheerful or less serious: [*tr.*] *she attempted a joke to lighten the atmosphere.*

light·en[2] ▶*v.* make or become lighter or brighter: [*intr.*] *the sky began to lighten in the east.* ■ [*tr.*] *archaic* enlighten spiritually: *now the Lord lighten thee, thou art a great fool.*

light·er[1] /'lītər/ ▶*n.* a device that produces a small flame, typically used to light cigarettes.

light-er-than-air ▶*adj.* [*attrib.*] relating to or denoting a balloon or other aircraft weighing less than the air it displaces, and so flying as a result of its own buoyancy.

light-fin·gered ▶*adj.* **1** prone to steal: *light-fingered shoplifters.* **2** having or showing delicate skill with the hands: *it is played with an irresistibly light-fingered spontaneity.*

light-foot·ed ▶*adj.* fast, nimble, or stealthy on one's feet: *a light-footed leap.* —**light-foot·ed·ly** *adv.*

light-head·ed /'līt,hedid/ ▶*adj.* dizzy and slightly faint: *I was lightheaded from fear.* —**light-head·ed·ly** *adv.* —**light-head·ed·ness** *n.*

light-heart·ed /'līt,härtid/ ▶*adj.* cheerful and carefree: *excited, lighthearted chatter.* —**light-heart·ed·ly** *adv.* —**light-heart·ed·ness** *n.*

light·house /'līt,hous/ ▶*n.* a tower or other structure containing a beacon light to warn or guide ships at sea.

light in·dus·try ▶*n.* the manufacture of small or light articles.

light·ing /'līting/ ▶*n.* equipment in a home, workplace, studio, theater, or street for producing light: *the heartless glare of strip lighting.* ■ the arrangement or effect of lights: *the lighting was very flat.*

light me·ter ▶*n.* an instrument for measuring the intensity of light, used chiefly to show the correct exposure when taking a photograph.

lighthouse

light·ning /'lītning/ ▶*n.* the occurrence of a natural electrical discharge of very short duration and high voltage between a cloud and the ground or within a cloud, accompanied by a bright flash and typically also thunder: *a tremendous flash of lightning.* ■ *poetic/literary* a flash or discharge of this kind: *the sky was a mass of black cloud out of which lightnings flashed.*
▶*v.* [*intr.*] (of the sky) emit a flash or discharge of this kind: *what's a person supposed to do when it starts to lightning?*
▶*adj.* [*attrib.*] very quick: *a lightning cure for his hangover.*
▶ □ **like** (**greased**) **lightning** very quickly.

light·ning bug ▶*n.* another term for **FIREFLY**.

light·ning rod ▶*n.* a metal rod or wire fixed to an exposed part of a building or other tall structure to divert lightning harmlessly into the ground. ■ *fig.* a person or thing that attracts a lot of criticism, esp. in order to divert attention from more serious issues or to allow a more important public figure to appear blameless.

light pen ▶*n.* **1** *Comput.* a hand-held, penlike photosensitive device held to the display screen of a computer terminal for passing information to the computer. **2** a hand-held, light-emitting device used for reading bar codes.

light·ship /'līt,SHip/ ▶*n.* a moored or anchored vessel with a beacon light to warn or guide ships at sea.

light·weight /'līt,wāt/ ▶*n.* **1** a weight in boxing and other sports intermediate between featherweight and welterweight. In the amateur boxing scale it ranges from 125 to 132 pounds (57 to 60 kg). ■ a boxer or other competitor of this weight. **2** a person or thing that is lightly built or constructed. ■ a person of little importance or influence, esp. in a particular sphere: *he was regarded as a political lightweight.* ▸*adj.* **1** of thin material or build and weighing less than average: *a lightweight gray suit.* **2** containing little serious matter: *the newspaper is lightweight and trivial.*

light year ▸*n. Astron.* a unit of astronomical distance equivalent to the distance that light travels in one year, which is 9.4607×10^{12} km (nearly 6 trillion miles). ■ (**light years**) *inf.* a long distance or great amount: *the new range puts them **light years ahead** of the competition.*

lig·ne·ous /ˈlignēəs/ ▸*adj.* made, consisting of, or resembling wood; woody.

lig·nin /ˈlignin/ ▸*n. Bot.* a complex organic polymer deposited in the cell walls of many plants, making them rigid and woody.

lig·nite /ˈligˌnīt/ ▸*n.* a soft brownish coal showing traces of plant structure, intermediate between bituminous coal and peat. —**lig·nit·ic** /ligˈnitik/ *adj.*

lik·a·ble /ˈlīkəbəl/ (also **like·a·ble**) ▸*adj.* (esp. of a person) pleasant, friendly, and easy to like. —**lik·a·bil·i·ty** /ˌlīkəˈbilətē/ *n.* —**lik·a·ble·ness** *n.* —**lik·a·bly** /-blē/ *adv.*

like[1] /līk/ ▸*prep.* **1** having the same characteristics or qualities as; similar to: *there were other suits like mine in the shop | she looked nothing like Audrey Hepburn.* ■ in a way appropriate to: *students were angry at being treated like children.* ■ such as one might expect from; characteristic of: *just like you to put a damper on people's enjoyment.* ■ used in questions to ask about the characteristics or nature of someone or something: *What is it like to be a tuna fisherman?* **2** such as; for example: *the cautionary vision of works like* Animal Farm *and* 1984. ▸*conj. inf.* **1** in the same way that; as: *people who change countries like they change clothes.* **2** as though; as if: *I felt like I'd been kicked by a camel.* ▸*n.* used with reference to a person or thing of the same kind as another: *the quotations could be arranged to put **like with like**.* ■ (**the like**) a thing or things of the same kind (often used to express surprise or for emphasis): *did you ever hear the like?* ▸*adj.* (of a person or thing) having similar qualities or characteristics to another person or thing: *I responded in like manner.* ■ (of a portrait or other image) having a faithful resemblance to the original: *"Who painted the dog's picture? It's very like."* ▸*adv.* **1** *inf.* used in speech as a meaningless filler or to signify the speaker's uncertainty about an expression just used: *there was this funny smell—sort of dusty like.* **2** *inf.* used to convey a person's reported attitude or feelings in the form of direct speech (whether or not representing an actual quotation): *so she comes into the room and she's like "Where is everybody?"* **3** (**like as/to**) *archaic* in the manner of: *like as a ship with dreadful storm long tossed.* ▸ □ **and the like** and similar things; et cetera. □ **like anything** *inf.* to a great degree: *they would probably worry like anything.* □ (**as**) **like as not** probably: *she would be in bed by now, like as not.* □ **like ——, like ——** as —— is, so is ——: *like father, like son.* □ **like so** *inf.* in this manner: *the votive candles are arranged like so.* □ **the likes of** *inf.* used of someone or something regarded as a type: *she didn't want to associate with the likes of me.* □ **more like** *inf.* nearer to (a specified number or description) than one previously given: *he believes the figure should be more like $10 million.* ■ (**more like it**) nearer to what is required or expected; more satisfactory. □ **of (a) like mind** (of a person) sharing the same opinions or tastes.

like[2] ▸*v.* [*tr.*] **1** find agreeable, enjoyable, or satisfactory: *I like all Angela Carter's stories.* **2** wish for; want: *would you like a cup of coffee?* ■ (**would like to do something**) used as a polite formula: *we would like to apologize for the late running of this service.* ■ (**not like doing/to do something**) feel reluctant to do something: *I don't like leaving her on her own too long.* ■ [in questions] feel about or regard (something): *how would you like it if it happened to you?* ▸*n.* (**likes**) the things one likes or prefers: *a wide variety of likes, dislikes, tastes, and income levels.* ▸ □ **if you like 1** if it suits or pleases you: *we could go riding if you like.* **2** used when expressing something in a new or unusual way: *it's a whole new branch of chemistry, a new science if you like.* □ **I like that!** used as an exclamation expressing affront. □ **like it or not** *inf.* used to indicate that someone has no choice in a matter: *you're celebrating with us, like it or not.* □ **not like the look** (or **sound**) **of** find worrying or alarming: *I don't like the look of that head injury.*

like·a·ble ▸*adj.* variant spelling of LIKABLE.

like·li·hood /ˈlīklēˌho͝od/ ▸*n.* the state or fact of something's being

likely; probability: *young people who can see no **likelihood of** finding employment.* ▸ □ **in all likelihood** very probably.

like·ly /ˈlīklē/ ▸*adj.* (**like·li·er, like·li·est**) **1** such as well might happen or be true; probable: *the likely effects of the drought on sugar beet yields.* **2** apparently suitable; promising: *a likely-looking spot.* ▸*adv.* probably: *we will most likely go to a bar.* —**like·li·ness** *n.* ▸ □ **a likely story** used to express disbelief in an account or excuse: *Gone running, has he? A likely story!* □ **as likely as not** probably: *I won't take their pills because as likely as not they'd poison me.* □ **not likely!** *inf.* certainly not; I refuse: *"Are you going home?" "Not likely!"*

like-mind·ed ▸*adj.* having similar tastes or opinions: *a small group of like-minded friends.* —**like-mind·ed·ness** *n.*

lik·en /ˈlīkən/ ▸*v.* [*tr.*] (**liken someone/something to**) point out the resemblance of someone or something to: *they likened the reigning emperor to a god.*

like·ness /ˈlīknis/ ▸*n.* the fact or quality of being alike; resemblance: *her likeness to him was astonishing.* ■ the semblance, guise, or outward appearance of: *humans are described as being made in God's likeness.* ■ a portrait or representation: *the only known likeness of Dorothy as a young woman.*

like·wise /ˈlīkˌwīz/ ▸*adv.* **1** in the same way; also: *the dream of young people is to grow old, and it is likewise the dream of their parents to relive youth.* ■ used to introduce a point similar or related to one just made: *you will forget the bad things that have happened in the past. Likewise, I will forget what you have done to me.* **2** in a like manner; similarly: *I stuck out my tongue and Frankie did likewise.*

lik·ing /ˈlīkiNG/ ▸*n.* a feeling of regard or fondness: *Mrs. Parsons had **a liking for** gin and tonic.* ▸ □ **for one's liking** to suit one's taste or wishes: *he is a little too showy for my liking.* □ **to one's liking** to one's taste; pleasing: *his coffee was just to his liking.*

li·lac /ˈlīˌläk, -ˌlak, -lək/ ▸*n.* a widely cultivated Eurasian shrub or small tree (genus *Syringa*) of the olive family, that has fragrant violet, pink, or white blossoms. ■ a pale pinkish-violet color. ▷early 17th cent.: from obsolete French, via Spanish and Arabic from Persian *līlak*, variant of *nīlak* 'bluish,' from *nīl* 'blue.'

lil·i·a·ceous /ˌlilēˈāSHəs/ ▸*adj. Bot.* of, relating to, or denoting plants of the lily family (Liliaceae). These have elongated leaves that grow from a corm, bulb, or rhizome.

Lil·li·pu·tian /ˌliləˈpyo͞oSHən/ ▸*adj.* trivial or very small: *America's banks no longer look Lilliputian in comparison with Japan's.* ▸*n.* a trivial or very small person or thing.

lilt /lilt/ ▸*n.* a characteristic rising and falling of the voice when speaking; a pleasant gentle accent: *he spoke with a faint but recognizable Irish lilt.* ■ a pleasant, gently swinging rhythm in a song or tune: *the lilt of the Hawaiian music.* ▸*v.* [*intr.*] [often as *adj.*] (**lilting**) speak, sing, or sound with a lilt: *a lilting Welsh accent.*

lil·y /ˈlilē/ ▸*n.* **1** a widely cultivated bulbous plant (genus *Lilium*) with large trumpet-shaped, typically fragrant, flowers on a tall, slender stem. The **lily family** (Liliaceae) includes many flowering bulbs, such as bluebells, hyacinths, and tulips. Several plants are often placed in different families, esp. Alliaceae (onions and their relatives), Aloaceae (aloes), and Amaryllidaceae (amaryllis, daffodils, jonquil). ■ short for WATER LILY. ■ used in names of other plants with similar flowers or leaves, e.g., **arum lily**. **2** a heraldic fleur-de-lis. —**lil·ied** /ˈlilēd/ *adj.*

lil·y-liv·ered ▸*adj.* weak and cowardly.

lil·y of the val·ley ▸*n.* a widely cultivated European plant (*Convallaria majalis*) of the lily family, with broad leaves and arching stems of fragrant, bell-shaped white flowers.

lil·y pad ▸*n.* a round, floating leaf of a water lily.

lil·y-white ▸*adj.* pure or ideally white. ■ without fault or corruption; totally innocent or immaculate: *they want me to conform, to be lily-white.* ■ consisting only of white people and excluding nonwhite people: *lily-white suburban communities.*

li·ma bean /ˈlīmə/ ▸*n.* **1** an edible flat whitish bean. See also BUTTER BEAN. **2** the tropical American plant (*Phaseolus lunatus*, or *P. limensis*) that yields this bean.

limb[1] /lim/ ▸*n.* an arm or leg of a person or four-legged animal, or a bird's wing. ■ a large branch of a tree. ■ a projecting section of a building. ■ a branch of a cross. ■ each half of an archery bow. —**limbed** adj. [in comb.] long-limbed. —**limb·less** adj.

▶ □ **life and limb** life and all bodily faculties: a reckless disregard for life and limb. □ **out on a limb** in or into a dangerous or uncompromising position, where one is not joined or supported by anyone else; vulnerable: she's prepared to go out on a limb and do something different.

limb[2] ▶ n. **1** Astron. the edge of the disk of a celestial object, esp. the sun or moon. **2** the graduated arc of a quadrant or other scientific instrument, used for measuring angles.

lim·ber /ˈlimbər/ ▶ adj. (of a person or body part) lithe; supple. ■ (of a thing) flexible: limber graphite fishing rods.

▶ v. [intr.] warm up in preparation for exercise or activity, esp. sports: the acrobats were limbering up for the big show. ■ [tr.] make (oneself or a body part) supple: I limbered my fingers by playing a few scales. —**lim·ber·ness** n.

lim·bo[1] /ˈlimbō/ ▶ n. **1** (also **Lim·bo**) (in some Christian beliefs) the supposed abode of the souls of unbaptized infants, and of the just who died before Christ's coming. **2** an uncertain period of awaiting a decision or resolution; an intermediate state or condition: the fate of the Contras is now in limbo. ■ a state of neglect or oblivion: children left in an emotional limbo.

lim·bo[2] ▶ n. (pl. -bos) a West Indian dance in which the dancer bends backward to pass under a horizontal bar that is progressively lowered to a position just above the ground.

▶ v. [intr.] dance in such a way.

lime[1] /līm/ ▶ n. (also **quick·lime**) a white caustic alkaline substance consisting of calcium oxide, obtained by heating limestone. ■ (also **slaked lime**) a white alkaline substance consisting of calcium hydroxide, made by adding water to quicklime. ■ (in general use) any of a number of calcium compounds, esp. calcium hydroxide, used as an additive to soil or water. ■ archaic birdlime.

▶ v. [tr.] **1** treat (soil or water) with lime to reduce acidity and improve fertility or oxygen levels. ■ [often as adj.] (**limed**) give (wood) a bleached appearance by treating it with lime: limed oak dining furniture. **2** archaic catch (a bird) with birdlime. —**lim·y** /ˈlīmē/ adj. (**lim·i·er**, **lim·i·est**).

lime[2] ▶ n. **1** a rounded citrus fruit similar to a lemon but greener, smaller, and with a distinctive acid flavor. **2** (also **lime tree**) the evergreen citrus tree (Citrus aurantifolia) that produces this fruit, widely cultivated in warm climates. **3** a bright light green color like that of a lime.

lime[3] ▶ n. another term for LINDEN, esp. the European linden (T. europaea).

lime·kiln /ˈlīmˌkil(n)/ ▶ n. a kiln in which limestone is burned or calcined to produce quicklime.

lime·light /ˈlīmˌlīt/ ▶ n. intense white light obtained by heating a cylinder of lime in an oxyhydrogen flame, formerly used in theaters. ■ (**the limelight**) the focus of public attention: the works that brought the artists into the limelight.

lim·er·ence /ˈlimərəns/ ▶ n. Psychol. the state of being infatuated or obsessed with another person, typically involuntary and characterized by a strong desire for reciprocation of one's feelings but not primarily for a sexual relationship.

lim·er·ick /ˈlim(ə)rik/ ▶ n. a humorous, frequently bawdy, verse of three long and two short lines rhyming aabba, popularized by Edward Lear.

lime·stone /ˈlīmˌstōn/ ▶ n. a sedimentary rock, composed mainly of calcium carbonate or dolomite, used as building material and in the making of cement.

lim·it /ˈlimit/ ▶ n. **1** a point or level beyond which something does not or may not extend or pass: the limits of presidential power. ■ (often **limits**) the terminal point or boundary of an area or movement: the city limits. ■ the furthest extent of one's physical or mental endurance: Mary Ann tried everyone's patience to the limit. **2** a restriction on the size or amount of something permissible or possible: an age limit. ■ (also **legal limit**) the maximum concentration of alcohol in the blood that the law allows in the driver of a motor vehicle: the risk of drinkers inadvertently going over the limit. **3** Math. a point or value that a sequence, function, or sum of a series can be made to approach progressively, until it is as close to the point or value as desired.

▶ v. (**lim·it·ed**, **lim·it·ing**) [tr.] set or serve as a limit to: try to limit the amount you drink. —**lim·i·ta·tive** /ˈliməˌtātiv/ adj.

▶ □ **be the limit** inf. be intolerably troublesome or irritating. □ **off limits** out of bounds: they declared the site off limits. □ **within limits** moderately; up to a point. □ **without limit** with no restriction.

lim·i·ta·tion /ˌliməˈtāSHən/ ▶ n. **1** (often **limitations**) a limiting rule or circumstance; a restriction: severe limitations on water use. ■ a condition of limited ability; a defect or failing: she knew her limitations better than she

knew her worth. ■ the action of limiting something: the limitation of local authorities' powers. **2** (also **limitation period**) Law a legally specified period beyond which an action may be defeated or a property right is not to continue. See also STATUTE OF LIMITATIONS.

lim·it·ed /ˈlimitid/ ▶ adj. restricted in size, amount, or extent; few, small, or short: a limited number of places are available. ■ (of a person) not great in ability or talents: I think he is a very limited man. ■ (of a train or other vehicle of public transportation) making few intermediate stops; express. ■ (**Limited**) Brit. denoting a company whose owners are legally responsible for its debts only to the extent of the amount of capital they invested (used after a company name): Times Newspapers Limited. —**lim·it·ed·ness** n.

lim·it·less /ˈlimitlis/ ▶ adj. without end, limit, or boundary: our resources are not limitless. —**lim·it·less·ly** adv. —**lim·it·less·ness** n.

lim·nol·o·gy /limˈnäləjē/ ▶ n. the study of the biological, chemical, and physical features of lakes and other bodies of fresh water. —**lim·no·log·i·cal** /ˌlimnəˈläjikəl/ adj. —**lim·nol·o·gist** /-jist/ n.

lim·o /ˈlimō/ ▶ n. (pl. **lim·os**) short for LIMOUSINE.

lim·ou·sine /ˈliməˌzēn; ˌliməˈzēn/ ▶ n. a large, luxurious automobile, esp. one driven by a chauffeur who is separated from the passengers by a partition. ■ a similar vehicle hired to take passengers to a special event or destination. ■ a passenger vehicle carrying people to and from an airport.

limp[1] /limp/ ▶ v. [intr.] walk with difficulty, typically because of a damaged or stiff leg or foot: he limped off during Saturday's game. ■ (of a damaged ship, aircraft, or vehicle) proceed with difficulty: the badly damaged aircraft limped back to Sicily.

▶ n. a tendency to limp; a gait impeded by injury or stiffness: he walked with a limp.

limp[2] ▶ adj. lacking internal strength or structure; not stiff or firm: the flags hung limp. ■ having or denoting a book cover that is not stiffened with board. ■ without energy or will: he was feeling too limp to argue. —**limp·ly** adv. —**limp·ness** n.

lim·pet /ˈlimpit/ ▶ n. a marine mollusk (Patellidae, Fissurellidae, and other families) with a shallow conical shell and a broad muscular foot, noted for the way it clings tightly to rocks.

lim·pid /ˈlimpid/ ▶ adj. (of a liquid) free of anything that darkens; completely clear. ■ (of a person's eyes) unclouded; clear. ■ (esp. of writing or music) clear and accessible or melodious: the limpid notes of a recorder. —**lim·pid·i·ty** /limˈpidətē/ n. —**lim·pid·ly** adv.

limp-wrist·ed ▶ adj. inf. **1** weak; ineffectual. **2** derog. (of a man, esp. a homosexual) effeminate.

linch·pin /ˈlinCHˌpin/ (also **lynch·pin**) ▶ n. **1** a pin passed through the end of an axle to keep a wheel in position. **2** a person or thing vital to an enterprise or organization: regular brushing is the linchpin of all good dental hygiene.

lin·den /ˈlindən/ ▶ n. a deciduous tree (genus Tilia) with heart-shaped leaves, pale soft timber and fragrant yellowish blossoms, native to north temperate regions. See also BASSWOOD.

line[1] /līn/ ▶ n. **1** a long, narrow mark or band: a row of closely spaced dots will look like a continuous line. ■ Math. a straight or curved continuous extent of length without breadth. ■ a positioning or movement of a thing or things that creates or appears to follow such a line: the ball rose in a straight line. ■ a furrow or wrinkle in the skin of the face or hands. ■ a contour or outline considered as a feature of design or composition: crisp architectural lines. ■ (on a map or graph) a curve connecting all points having a specified common property. ■ Football the line of scrimmage. ■ (**the Line**) the equator. ■ a notional limit or boundary: the issue of peace cut across class lines | television blurs the line between news and entertainment. ■ each of the very narrow horizontal sections forming a television picture. ■ Physics a narrow range of the spectrum noticeably brighter or darker than the adjacent parts. ■ (**the line**) the level of the base of most letters, such as h and x, in printing and writing. ■ Printing & Comput. denoting an illustration or graphic consisting of lines and solid areas, with no gradation of tone: line art. ■ each of (usually five) horizontal lines forming a staff in musical notation. ■ a sequence of notes or tones forming an instrumental or vocal melody: a powerful melodic line. ■ a dose of a powdered narcotic or hallucinatory drug, esp. cocaine or heroin, laid out in a line. **2** a length of cord, rope, wire, or other material serving a particular purpose: wring the clothes and hang them on the line. ■ one of a vessel's mooring ropes. ■ a telephone connection: she had a crank on the line. ■ a railroad track. ■ a branch or route of a railroad system: the Philadelphia to Baltimore line. ■ a company that provides ships, aircraft, or buses on particular routes on a regular basis: a major shipping line. **3** a horizontal row of written or printed words. ■ a part of a poem forming one such row:

each stanza has eight lines. ■ (**lines**) the words of an actor's part in a play or film. ■ a particularly noteworthy written or spoken sentence: *his speech ended with a line about the failure of justice.* **4** a row of people or things: *a line of acolytes proceeded down the aisle.* ■ a connected series of people following one another in time (used esp. of several generations of a family): *we follow the history of a family through the male line.* ■ (in football, hockey, etc.) a set of players in the forwardmost positions for offense or defense. ■ *Football* one of the positions on the line of scrimmage. ■ a series of related things: *the bill is the latest in a long line of measures to protect society from criminals.* ■ a range of commercial goods: *the company intends to hire more people and expand its product line.* ■ *inf.* a false or exaggerated account or story: *he feeds me a line about this operation.* ■ the point spread for sports events on which bets may be made. **5** an area or branch of activity: *the stresses unique to their line of work.* ■ a direction, course, or channel: *lines of communication.* ■ (**lines**) a manner of doing or thinking about something: *you can't run a business on these lines.* ■ an agreed-upon approach; a policy: *the official line is that there were no chemical attacks on allied troops.* **6** a connected series of military fieldworks or defenses facing an enemy force: *raids behind enemy lines.* ■ an arrangement of soldiers or ships in a column or line formation; a line of battle. ■ (**the line**) regular army regiments (as opposed to auxiliary forces or household troops).

▶ *v.* [tr.] **1** stand or be positioned at intervals along: *a processional route lined by people waving flags.* **2** [usu. as *adj.*] (**lined**) mark or cover with lines: *lined paper.* **3** *Baseball* hit a line drive.

▶ *phrasal v.* □ **line out** *Baseball* be put out by hitting a line drive that is caught. □ **line something out** transplant seedlings from beds into nursery lines, where they are grown before being moved to their permanent position. □ **line someone/something up** have someone or something ready or prepared: *have you got any work lined up?*

▶ □ **above the line 1** *Finance* denoting or relating to money spent on items of current expenditure. **2** *Bridge* denoting bonus points and penalty points, which do not count toward the game. □ **all** (**the way**) **down** (or **along**) **the line** at every point or stage: *the mistakes were caused by lack of care all down the line.* □ **along** (or **down**) **the line** at a further, later, or unspecified point: *I knew that somewhere down the line there would be an inquest.* □ **below the line 1** *Finance* denoting or relating to money spent on items of capital expenditure. **2** *Bridge* denoting points for tricks bid and won, which count toward the game. □ **bring someone/something into line** cause someone or something to conform: *the change in the law will bring Britain into line with Europe.* □ **come down to the line** (of a race) be closely fought right until the end. □ **come into line** conform: *Britain has come into line with other Western democracies in giving the vote to its citizens living abroad.* □ **get a line on** *inf.* learn something about. □ **in line** under control: *that threat kept a lot of people in line.* □ **in line for** likely to receive: *she might be in line for a cabinet post.* □ **in the line of duty** while one is working (used mainly of police officers firefighters, or soldiers). □ **in** (or **out of**) **line with** in (or not in) alignment or accordance with: *remuneration is in line with comparable international organizations.* □ **lay** (or **put**) **it on the line** speak frankly. □ **(draw) a line in the sand** (state that one has reached) a point beyond which one will not go. □ **line of credit** an amount of credit extended to a borrower. □ **line of fire** the expected path of gunfire or a missile: *residents within line of fire were evacuated from their homes.* □ **line of flight** the route taken through the air. □ **line of force** an imaginary line that represents the strength and direction of a magnetic, gravitational, or electric field at any point. □ **line of sight** a straight line along which an observer has unobstructed vision: *a building that obstructs our line of sight.* □ **line of vision** the straight line along which an observer looks: *Jimmy moved forward into Len's line of vision.* □ **on the line 1** at serious risk: *their careers were on the line.* **2** (of a picture in an exhibition) hung with its center about level with the spectator's eye. □ **out of line** *inf.* behaving in a way that breaks the rules or is considered disreputable or inappropriate: *he had never stepped out of line with her before.*

line[2] ▶ *v.* [tr.] cover the inside surface of (a container or garment) with a layer of different material: *a basket lined with polyethylene.* ■ form a layer on the inside surface of (an area); cover as if with a lining: *hundreds of telegrams lined the walls.*

▶ □ **line one's pockets** make money, esp. by dishonest means.

lin·e·age /ˈlinē-ij/ ▶ *n.* **1** lineal descent from an ancestor; ancestry or pedigree. ■ *Anthropol.* a social group tracing its descent from a single ancestor. **2** *Biol.* a sequence of species each of which is considered to have evolved from its predecessor: *the chimpanzee and gorilla lineages.* ■ a sequence of cells in the body that developed from a common ancestral cell: *the epithelial lineage.*

lin·e·al /ˈlinēəl/ ▶ *adj.* **1** in a direct line of descent or ancestry: *a lineal*

descendant. **2** of, relating to, or consisting of lines; linear. —**lin·e·al·ly** *adv.*

lin·e·a·ment /ˈlin(ē)əmənt/ ▶ *n.* **1** (usu. **lineaments**) *poetic/literary* a distinctive feature or characteristic, esp. of the face. **2** *Geol.* a linear feature on the earth's surface, such as a fault.

lin·e·ar /ˈlinēər/ ▶ *adj.* **1** arranged in or extending along a straight or nearly straight line: *linear movement.* ■ consisting of or predominantly formed using lines or outlines: *simple linear designs.* ■ involving one dimension only: *linear elasticity.* ■ *Math.* able to be represented by a straight line on a graph; involving or exhibiting directly proportional change in two related quantities: *linear functions.* **2** progressing from one stage to another in a single series of steps; sequential: *a linear narrative.* —**lin·e·ar·i·ty** /ˌlinēˈaretē/ *n.* —**lin·e·ar·ly** *adv.*

lin·e·ar e·qua·tion ▶ *n.* an equation between two variables that gives a straight line when plotted on a graph.

line·back·er /ˈlinˌbakər/ ▶ *n.* *Football* a defensive player normally positioned behind the line of scrimmage, but in front of the safeties.

line drive ▶ *n.* *Baseball* a powerfully hit ball that travels in the air and relatively close to and parallel with the ground.

line·man /ˈlinmən/ ▶ *n.* (*pl.* **-men**) **1** a person employed in laying and maintaining railroad track. ■ a person employed for the repair and maintenance of telephone or power lines. **2** *Football* a player normally positioned on the line of scrimmage.

lin·en /ˈlinin/ ▶ *n.* cloth woven from flax. ■ household articles and garments such as sheets made, or originally made, of linen. ▷Old English *līnen* (as an adjective in the sense 'made of flax'); related to Dutch *linnen*, German *Leinen*, also to obsolete *line* 'flax.'

line print·er ▶ *n.* a machine that prints output from a computer a line at a time rather than character by character.

lin·er[1] /ˈlinər/ ▶ *n.* **1** (also **ocean liner**) a large luxurious passenger ship of a type formerly used on a regular line. **2** a fine paintbrush used for painting thin lines and for outlining. ■ a cosmetic used for outlining or accentuating a facial feature, or a brush or pencil for applying this. **3** *inf.* another term for **LINE DRIVE**.

lin·er[2] ▶ *n.* a lining in an appliance, device, or container, esp. a removable one, in particular: ■ the lining of a garment. ■ (also **cylinder liner**) a replaceable metal sleeve placed within the cylinder of an engine, forming a durable surface to withstand wear from the piston.

lin·er note ▶ *n.* (usu. **liner notes**) the text printed on a paper insert issued as part of the packaging of a compact disc or on the sleeve of a phonograph record.

lines·man /ˈlinzmən/ ▶ *n.* (*pl.* **-men**) (in games played on a field or court) an official who assists the referee or umpire from the sideline, esp. in deciding on whether the ball is out of play.

line·up /ˈlinˌəp/ ▶ *n.* **1** a group of people or things brought together in a particular context, esp. the members of a sports team or a group of musicians or other entertainers: *a talented batting lineup.* ■ the schedule of television programs for a particular period: *NBC's Thursday lineup of hit comedies.* **2** a group of people including a suspect for a crime assembled for the purpose of having an eyewitness identify the suspect from among them. ■ a line or linelike arrangement of people or things.

lin·ger /ˈlinɡgər/ ▶ *v.* [intr.] stay in a place longer than necessary, typically because of a reluctance to leave: *she lingered in the yard, enjoying the warm sunshine.* —**lin·ger·er** *n.* —**lin·ger·ing** *adj.*

lin·ge·rie /ˌlänzhəˈrā; -jə-/ ▶ *n.* women's underwear and nightclothes.

lin·go /ˈlinɡō/ ▶ *n.* (*pl.* **-gos** or **-goes**) *inf., often humorous* or *derog.* a foreign language or local dialect: *they were unable to speak a word of the local lingo.* ■ the vocabulary or jargon of a particular subject or group of people: *fat, known in medical lingo as adipose tissue.*

lin·gua fran·ca /ˈlinɡwə ˈfranɡkə/ ▶ *n.* (*pl.* **lin·gua fran·cas**) a language that is adopted as a common language between speakers whose native languages are different. ■ *hist.* a mixture of Italian with French, Greek, Arabic, and Spanish, formerly used in the Levant.

lin·gual /ˈlinɡwəl/ ▶ *adj.* *technical* **1** of or relating to the tongue. ■ *Phonet.* (of a sound) formed by the tongue. ■ *Anat.* near or on the side toward the tongue. **2** of or relating to speech or language: *his demonstrations of lingual dexterity.* —**lin·gual·ly** *adv.*

lin·gui·ne /linɡˈgwēnē/ (also **lin·gui·ni**) ▶ *n.* pasta in the form of long, flattened strings.

Pronunciation Key ə *ago,* up; ər *over,* fur; a *hat;* ā *ate;* ä *car;* CH *chin;* e *let;* ē *see;* e(ə)r *air;* i *fit;* ī *by;* i(ə)r *ear;* NG *sing;* ō *go;* ô *law, for;* oi *toy;* oo *good;* oo *goo;* ou *out;* SH *she;* TH *thin;* TH *then;* (h)w *why;* ZH *vision*

lin·guist /ˈliNGgwist/ ▸n. **1** a person skilled in foreign languages. **2** a person who studies linguistics.

lin·guis·tic /liNGˈgwistik/ ▸adj. of or relating to language or linguistics. —**lin·guis·ti·cal·ly** /tik(ə)lē/ adv.

lin·guis·tics /liNGˈgwistiks/ ▸plural n. [treated as sing.] the scientific study of language and its structure, including the study of morphology, syntax, phonetics, and semantics. Specific branches of linguistics include sociolinguistics, dialectology, psycholinguistics, computational linguistics, historical-comparative linguistics, and applied linguistics. —**lin·guis·ti·cian** /ˌliNGgwəˈstiSHən/ n.

lin·i·ment /ˈlinəmənt/ ▸n. a liquid or lotion, esp. one made with oil, for rubbing on the body to relieve pain.

lin·ing /ˈlīniNG/ ▸n. a layer of different material covering the inside surface of something: a lining of fireproof insulation. ▪ an additional layer of different material attached to the inside of a garment or curtain to make it warmer or hang better: leather gloves with fur linings.

link /liNGk/ ▸n. **1** a relationship between two things or situations, esp. where one thing affects the other: investigating a link between pollution and forest decline. ▪ something that enables communication between people: sign language interpreters represent a vital link between the deaf and hearing communities. ▪ a means of contact by radio, telephone, or computer between two points: they set up a satellite link with Tokyo. ▪ a means of travel or transport between two places: a rail link from Newark to Baltimore. ▪ Comput. a code or instruction that connects one part of a program or an element in a list to another. **2** a ring or loop in a chain.
▸v. make, form, or suggest a connection with or between: [tr.] foreign and domestic policy are linked | [intr.] she was **linked up with** an artistic group. ▪ connect or join physically: [tr.] a network of routes linking towns and villages | [intr.] three different groups, each **linking with** the other. ▪ [tr.] clasp; intertwine: once outside he linked arms with her.

link·age /ˈliNGkij/ ▸n. the action of linking or the state of being linked. ▪ a system of links: a complex linkage of nerves. ▪ the linking of different issues in political negotiations. ▪ Genetics the tendency of groups of genes on the same chromosome to be inherited together.

links /liNGks/ ▸pl. n. (also **golf links**) [treated as sing. or pl.] a golf course.

link·up /ˈliNGk,əp/ (also **link-up**) ▸n. an instance of two or more people or things connecting or joining. ▪ a connection enabling two or more people or machines to communicate with each other: a live satellite linkup.

li·no·cut /ˈlīnō,kət/ ▸n. a design or form carved in relief on a block of linoleum. ▪ a print made from such a block. —**li·no·cut·ting** n.

li·no·le·um /ləˈnōlēəm/ ▸n. a material consisting of a canvas backing thickly coated with a preparation of linseed oil and powdered cork, used esp. as a floor covering. —**li·no·le·umed** adj.

lin·sang /ˈlin,saNG/ ▸n. a small relation of the civet, with a spotted or banded coat and a long tail, found in the forests of Southeast Asia and West Africa.

lin·seed /ˈlin,sēd/ ▸n. the seeds of the flax plant, which are the source of linseed oil and linseed cake. Also called FLAXSEED. ▪ the flax plant, esp. when grown for linseed oil.

lin·seed oil ▸n. a pale yellow oil extracted from linseed, used esp. in paint and varnish.

lint /lint/ ▸n. short, fine fibers that separate from the surface of cloth or yarn during processing. —**lint·y** adj.

lin·tel /ˈlintl/ ▸n. a horizontal support of timber, stone, concrete, or steel across the top of a door or window. —**lin·teled** (Brit. **lin·telled**) adj.

Lin·ux /ˈlinəks/ ▸n. trademark an open-source version of the UNIX operating system.

li·on /ˈlīən/ ▸n. a large tawny-colored cat (Panthera leo) that lives in prides, found in Africa and northwestern India. ▪ (**the Lion**) the zodiacal sign or constellation Leo. ▪ fig. a brave or strong person. ▪ an influential or celebrated person: a literary lion. ▪ (**Lion**) a member of a Lions Club. —**li·on·ess** n.
▸ □ **throw someone to the lions** cause someone to be in an extremely dangerous or unpleasant situation.

li·on·heart·ed /ˈlīən,härtid/ ▸adj. brave and determined.

li·on·ize /ˈlīə,nīz/ ▸v. [tr.] give a lot of public attention and approval to (someone); treat as a celebrity: modern athletes are lionized. —**li·on·i·za·tion** /ˌlīənəˈzāsHən/ n. —**li·on·iz·er** n.

li·on's share ▸n. the biggest or greatest part: William was appointed editor, which meant that he did the lion's share of the work.

lip /lip/ ▸n. **1** either of the two fleshy parts that form the upper and lower edges of the opening of the mouth: he kissed her on the lips. ▪ (**lips**) used to refer to a person's speech or to current topics of conversation: downsizing is **on everyone's lips** at the moment. **2** the edge of a hollow container or an opening: drawing her finger around the lip of the cup. ▪ a rounded, raised, or extended piece along an edge. **3** inf. impudent talk: don't give me any of your lip!
▸v. (**lipped, lip·ping**) [tr.] (of water) lap against: beaches lipped by the surf rimming the Pacific. ▪ Golf hit the rim of (a hole) but fail to go in. —**lip·less** adj. —**lip·like** /-ˌlīk/ adj. —**lipped** adj. her pale-lipped mouth.
▸ □ **bite one's lip** repress an emotion; stifle laughter or a retort: she bit her lip to stop the rush of bitter words. □ **curl one's lip** raise a corner of one's upper lip to show contempt; sneer. □ **lick** (or **smack**) **one's lips** look forward to something with relish; show one's satisfaction. □ **pass one's lips** be eaten, drunk, or spoken. □ **pay lip service to** express approval of or support for (something) without taking any significant action.

lip-gloss /ˈlip,gläs; -,glôs/ (also **lip gloss**) ▸n. a cosmetic applied to the lips to provide a glossy finish, often tinted.

lip·id /ˈlipid/ ▸n. Chem. any of a class of organic compounds that are fatty acids or their derivatives and are insoluble in water but soluble in organic solvents. They include many natural oils, waxes, and steroids.

lip·oid /ˈlip,oid; ˈlī,poid/ ▸adj. (also **lip·oid·al**) Biochem. relating to or resembling fat.
▸n. a fatlike substance; a lipid.

lip·o·pro·tein /ˌlipəˈprō,tēn; ˌlī-/ ▸n. Biochem. any of a group of soluble proteins that combine with and transport fat or other lipids in the blood plasma.

lip·o·suc·tion /ˈlipō,səksHən; ˈlī-/ ▸n. a technique in cosmetic surgery for removing excess fat from under the skin by suction.

lip·py /ˈlipē/ inf. ▸adj. (-**pi·er**, -**pi·est**) **1** insolent; impertinent. **2** having prominent lips.

lip-read /-,rēd/ (also **lip-read**) ▸v. [intr.] (of a deaf person) understand speech from observing a speaker's lip movements. —**lip-read·er** n.

lip·stick /ˈlip,stik/ ▸n. colored cosmetic applied to the lips from a small solid stick.

lip-sync /-,siNGk/ (also **lip-synch**) ▸v. [tr.] (of an actor or singer) move the lips silently in synchronization with (a recorded soundtrack).
▸n. the action of using such a technique. —**lip-sync·er** n.

liq·ue·fy /ˈlikwə,fī/ (also **liq·ui·fy**) ▸v. (-**fies**, -**fied**) make or become liquid: [tr.] the minimum pressure required to liquefy a gas —**liq·ue·fac·tion** /ˌlikwə-ˈfaksHən/ n. —**liq·ue·fac·tive** /ˌlikwəˈfaktiv/ adj. —**liq·ue·fi·a·ble** /ˌlikwə-ˈfīəbəl/ adj. —**liq·ue·fi·er** n.

li·queur /liˈkər; -ˈk(y)o͝or/ ▸n. a strong, sweet flavored alcoholic liquor, usually drunk after a meal.

liq·uid /ˈlikwid/ ▸adj. **1** having a consistency like that of water or oil, i.e., flowing freely but of constant volume. ▪ having the clear shimmer of water: looking into those liquid dark eyes. ▪ denoting a substance normally a gas that has been liquefied by cold or pressure: liquid oxygen. ▪ not fixed or stable; fluid. **2** (of a sound) clear, pure, and flowing; harmonious: the liquid song of the birds. **3** Phonet. (of a consonant) produced by allowing the airstream to flow over the sides of the tongue, typically l and r, and able to be prolonged like a vowel. **4** (of assets) held in cash or easily converted into cash. ▪ having ready cash or liquid assets. ▪ (of a market) having a high volume of activity.
▸n. **1** a liquid substance: drink plenty of liquids. **2** Phonet. a liquid consonant. —**liq·uid·ly** adv. —**liq·uid·ness** n.

liq·ui·date /ˈlikwə,dāt/ ▸v. [tr.] **1** wind up the affairs of (a company or firm) by ascertaining liabilities and apportioning assets. ▪ [intr.] (of a company) undergo such a process. ▪ convert (assets) into cash: a plan to liquidate $10,000,000 worth of property over seven years. ▪ pay off (a debt). **2** eliminate, typically by violent means; kill. —**liq·ui·da·tion** /ˌlikwə-ˈdāsHən/ n. —**liq·ui·da·tor** /-,dātər/ n.

liq·uid crys·tal ▸n. a substance that flows like a liquid but has some degree of ordering in the arrangement of its molecules.

liq·uid crys·tal dis·play ▸n. a form of visual display used in electronic devices in which a layer of a liquid crystal is sandwiched between two transparent electrodes.

liq·uid·i·ty /liˈkwidətē/ ▸n. Finance the availability of liquid assets to a market or company. ▪ liquid assets; cash. ▪ a high volume of activity in a market.

liq·uid meas·ure ▸n. a unit for measuring the volume of liquids.

liq·uor /ˈlikər/ ▸n. **1** alcoholic drink, esp. distilled spirits. **2** a liquid produced or used in a process of some kind,. ▷Middle English (denoting liquid or something to drink): from Old French lic(o)ur, from Latin liquor; related to liquare 'liquefy,' liquere 'be fluid.'
▸phrasal v. □ **liquor up** (or **liquor someone up**) inf. get (or make someone) drunk.

li·ra /ˈli(ə)rə/ ▸n. (pl. **li·re** /ˈli(ə)rā; ˈli(ə)rə/) **1** the basic monetary unit of Italy (until replaced by the euro), notionally equal to 100 centesimos. **2** the basic monetary unit of Turkey, equal to 100 kurus.

lisle /līl/ ▸n. a fine, smooth cotton thread used formerly for hosiery.

Lisp /lisp/ (also **LISP**) ▸n. a high-level computer programming language devised for list processing.

lisp /lisp/ ▸n. a speech defect in which s is pronounced like th in thick and z is pronounced like th in this.
▸v. [intr.] speak with a lisp. —**lisp·er** n. —**lisp·ing·ly** adv.

lis·some /ˈlisəm/ (also chiefly Brit. **lis·som**) ▸adj. (of a person or their body) thin, supple, and graceful. —**lis·some·ness** n.

list¹ /list/ ▸n. **1** a number of connected items or names written or printed consecutively, typically one below the other: writing a shopping list. ■ Comput. a formal structure analogous to a list by which items of data can be stored or processed in a definite order. **2** (**lists**) hist. barriers enclosing an area for a jousting tournament. ■ the scene of a contest or combat. **3** a selvage of a piece of fabric.
▸v. [tr.] make a list of: I have listed four reasons below. ■ (often **be listed**) include or enter in a list: 93 men were still listed as missing. ■ [intr.] (**list at/for**) be on a list of products at (a specified price): the bottom-of-the-line Mercedes lists for $52,050. —**list·a·ble** adj.
▸ □ **enter the lists** issue or accept a challenge.

list² ▸v. [intr.] (of a ship) lean to one side, typically because of a leak or unbalanced cargo.
▸n. an instance of a ship leaning over in such a way.

lis·ten /ˈlisən/ ▸v. [intr.] give one's attention to a sound: sit and listen to the radio. ■ take notice of and act on what someone says; respond to advice or a request: I told her over and over again, but she wouldn't listen. ■ make an effort to hear something; be alert and ready to hear something: they listened for sounds from the baby's room. ■ used to urge someone to pay attention to what one is going to say: listen, I've got an idea.
▸phrasal v. □ **listen in** listen to a private conversation, often secretly. ■ use a radio receiving set to listen to a broadcast or conversation.
▸n. an act of listening to something.

lis·ten·a·ble /ˈlisənəbəl/ ▸adj. easy or pleasant to listen to. —**lis·ten·a·bil·i·ty** /ˌlis(ə)nəˈbilitē/ n.

lis·ten·er /ˈlis(ə)nər/ ▸n. a person who listens, esp. someone who does so in an attentive manner. ■ a person listening to a radio station or program.

lis·ten·ing post ▸n. a station for intercepting electronic communications. ■ a position from which to listen or gather information. ■ a point near an enemy's lines for detecting movements by sound.

lis·te·ri·a /liˈstirēə/ ▸n. a type of bacterium that infects humans and other warm-blooded animals through contaminated food. ■ inf. food poisoning or other disease caused by infection with listeria.

list·ing /ˈlistiNG/ ▸n. a list or catalog. ■ the drawing up of a list. ■ an entry in a list or register.

list·less /ˈlis(t)lis/ ▸adj. (of a person or their manner) lacking energy or enthusiasm: bouts of listless depression. —**list·less·ly** adv. —**list·less·ness** n.

list price ▸n. the price of an article as shown in a list issued by the manufacturer or by the general body of manufacturers of the particular class of goods.

lit /lit/ ▸ past and past participle of LIGHT¹, LIGHT³.

lit ▸adj. Informal drunk.

lit·a·ny /ˈlitn-ē/ ▸n. (pl. **-nies**) a series of petitions for use in church services or processions, usually recited by the clergy and responded to in a recurring formula by the people. ■ a tedious recital or repetitive series: a litany of complaints.

li·tchi /ˈlēCHē/ (also **li·chee**) ▸n. **1** a small rounded fruit with sweet white scented flesh, a large central stone, and a thin rough skin. Also called **litchi nut** when dried. **2** the Chinese tree (Nephelium litchi, or Litchi chinensis) of the soapberry family that bears this fruit.

li·ter /ˈlētər/ (Brit. **li·tre**) (abbr.: l) ▸n. a metric unit of capacity, formerly defined as the volume of 1 kilogram of water under standard conditions, now equal to 1,000 cubic centimeters (about 1.75 pints).

lit·er·a·cy /ˈlit(ə)rəsē/ ▸n. the ability to read and write. ■ competence or knowledge in a specified area: wine literacy can't be taught in three hours.

lit·er·al /ˈlit(ə)rəl/ ▸adj. **1** taking words in their usual or most basic sense without metaphor or allegory: dreadful in its literal sense, full of dread. ■ free from exaggeration or distortion: you shouldn't take this as a literal record of events. ■ inf. absolute (used to emphasize that a strong expression is deliberately chosen to convey one's feelings: fifteen years of literal hell. **2** (of a translation) representing the exact words of the original text. ■ (of a visual representation) exactly copied; realistic as opposed to abstract or impressionistic. **3** (also **literal-minded**) (of a person or performance) lacking imagination; prosaic. **4** of, in, or expressed by a letter or the letters of the alphabet: literal mnemonics. —**lit·er·al·i·ty** /ˌlitəˈralitē/ —**lit·er·al·ize** /-ˌlīz/ v. —**lit·er·al·ness** n.

lit·er·al·ism /ˈlit(ə)rəˌlizəm/ ▸n. the interpretation of words in their usual or most basic sense, without allowing for metaphor or exaggeration: biblical literalism. ■ literal or nonidealistic representation in literature or art. —**lit·er·al·ist** n. —**lit·er·al·is·tic** /ˌlitərəˈlistik; ˌlitrə-/ adj.

lit·er·al·ly /ˈlit(ə)rəlē/ ▸adv. in a literal manner or sense; exactly: the driver took it literally when asked to go straight across the traffic circle | tiramisu, literally translated "pick me up." ■ inf. used for emphasis or to express strong feeling while not being literally true: I have received literally thousands of letters.

lit·er·ar·y /ˈlitəˌrerē/ ▸adj. **1** concerning the writing, study, or content of literature, esp. of the kind valued for quality of form: the great literary works of the nineteenth century. ■ concerned with literature as a profession: it was signed by such literary figures as Maya Angelou. **2** (of language) associated with literary works or other formal writing; having a marked style intended to create a particular emotional effect. —**lit·er·ar·i·ly** /ˌlitəˈre(ə)rəlē/ adv. —**lit·er·ar·i·ness** n.

lit·er·ate /ˈlitərit/ ▸adj. (of a person) able to read and write. ■ having or showing education or knowledge, typically in a specified area: we need people who are economically and politically literate.
▸n. a literate person. —**lit·er·ate·ly** adv.

lit·e·ra·ti /ˌlitəˈrätē/ ▸plural n. well-educated people who are interested in literature.

lit·er·a·ture /ˈlit(ə)rəCHər; -ˌCHŏŏr; -ˌt(y)ŏŏr/ ▸n. **1** written works, esp. those considered of superior or lasting artistic merit: a great work of literature. ■ books and writings published on a particular subject: the literature on environmental epidemiology. ■ the writings of a country or period: early French literature. ■ leaflets and other printed matter used to advertise products or give advice. **2** the production or profession of writing.

lithe /līTH/ (also **lithe·some** /-səm/) ▸adj. (esp. of a person's body) thin, supple, and graceful. ▷Old English līthe 'gentle, meek,' also 'mellow,' of Germanic origin; related to German lind 'soft, gentle.' —**lithe·ly** adv. —**lithe·ness** n.

lith·ic /ˈliTHik/ ▸adj. chiefly Archaeol. & Geol. of the nature of or relating to stone.

lith·i·um /ˈliTHēəm/ ▸n. the chemical element of atomic number 3, a soft silver-white metal. It is the lightest of the alkali metals. (Symbol: **Li**) ■ lithium carbonate or another lithium salt, used as a mood-stabilizing drug.

lith·o /ˈliTHō/ inf. ▸n. (pl. **-os**) short for LITHOGRAPHY or LITHOGRAPH.

lith·o·graph /ˈliTHəˌgraf/ ▸n. a lithographic print.
▸v. [tr.] print by lithography: [as adj.] (**lithographed**) a set of lithographed drawings. —**lith·o·graph·ic** /ˌliTHəˈgrafik/ adj.

li·thog·ra·phy /liˈTHägrəfē/ ▸n. the process of printing from a flat surface treated so as to repel the ink except where it is required for printing. ■ Electr. an analogous method for making printed circuits. —**li·thog·ra·pher** /-fər/ n.

li·thol·o·gy /liˈTHäləjē/ ▸n. the study of the general physical characteristics of rocks. —**lith·o·log·ic** /ˌliTHəˈläjik/ adj. —**lith·o·log·i·cal** /ˌliTHəˈläjikəl/ adj. —**lith·o·log·i·cal·ly** /ˌliTHəˈläjik(ə)lē/ adv.

lith·o·sphere /ˈliTHəˌsfi(ə)r/ ▸n. Geol. the rigid outer part of the earth, consisting of the crust and upper mantle. —**lith·o·spher·ic** /ˌliTHəˈsferik; -ˈsfi(ə)r-/ adj.

li·thot·o·my /liˈTHätəmē/ ▸n. surgical removal of a calculus (stone) from the bladder, kidney, or urinary tract. —**li·thot·o·mist** /-mist/ n.

Lith·u·a·ni·an /ˌliTHəˈwānēən/ ▸adj. of or relating to Lithuania or its people or language.
▸n. **1** a native or citizen of Lithuania, or a person of Lithuanian descent. **2** the Baltic language of Lithuania.

lit·i·gant /ˈlitəgənt/ ▸n. a person involved in a lawsuit.

lit·i·gate /ˈlitəˌgāt/ ▸v. [intr.] go to law; be a party to a lawsuit. ■ [tr.] take (a claim or a dispute) to a court of law. —**lit·i·ga·tion** /ˌlitəˈgāSHən/ —**lit·i·ga·tive** /ˈlitəˌgātiv/ adj. —**lit·i·ga·tor** /-ˌgātər/ n.

li·ti·gious /ləˈtijəs/ ▸adj. concerned with lawsuits or litigation. ■ unreasonably prone to go to law to settle disputes. ■ suitable to become the subject of a lawsuit. —**li·ti·gious·ly** adv. —**li·ti·gious·ness** n.

---

lit·mus /ˈlitməs/ ▸*n.* a dye obtained from certain lichens that is red under acid conditions and blue under alkaline conditions.

lit·mus pa·per ▸*n.* paper stained with litmus, used to indicate the acidity or alkalinity of a substance.

lit·mus test ▸*n.* a decisively indicative test: *opposition to the nomination became a litmus test for political support of candidates.*

LittD ▸*abbr.* ■ Doctor of Letters. ■ Doctor of Literature.

lit·ter /ˈlitər/ ▸*n.* **1** trash, such as paper, cans, and bottles, that is left lying in an open or public place: *fines for dropping litter.* ■ an untidy collection of things lying about: *a litter of sleeping bags on the floor.* **2** the group of young animals born to an animal at one time: *a litter of five kittens.* **3** material forming a surface-covering layer, in particular: ■ (also **cat litter**) granular absorbent material lining a tray where a cat can urinate and defecate when indoors. ■ straw or other plant matter used as bedding for animals. ■ (also **leaf litter**) decomposing but recognizable leaves and other debris forming a layer on top of the soil, esp. in forests. **4** *hist.* a vehicle containing a bed or seat enclosed by curtains and carried on men's shoulders or by animals. ■ a stretcher, for transporting the sick and wounded.
▸*v.* [*tr.*] make (a place) untidy with rubbish or a large number of objects left lying about: *clothes and newspapers littered the floor.* ■ (usu. **be littered**) leave (rubbish or a number of objects) lying untidily in a place: *there was broken glass littered about.* ■ (usu. **be littered with**) *fig.* fill (a text, history, etc.) with examples of something unpleasant: *news pages have been littered with doom and gloom about company collapses.* —**lit·ter·er** *n.*

litter

lit·té·ra·teur /ˌlitərəˈtər/ ▸*n.* a person who is interested in and knowledgeable about literature.

lit·ter·bug /ˈlitərˌbəg/ ▸*n. inf.* a person who carelessly drops litter in a public place.

lit·tle /ˈlitl/ ▸*adj.* small in size, amount, or degree (often used to convey an appealing diminutiveness or express an affectionate or condescending attitude): *the plants will grow into little bushes | he's a good little worker.* ■ (of a person) young or younger: *my little brother.* ■ denoting something, esp. a place, that is named after a similar larger one: *New York's Little Italy.*
▸*adj. & pron.* **1** (**a little**) a small amount of: [as *adj.*] *we got a little help from my sister* | [as *pron.*] *you only see a little of what he can do.* ■ [*pron.*] a short time or distance: *after a little, the rain stopped.* **2** used to emphasize how small an amount is: [as *adj.*] *I have little doubt of their identity* | [as *pron.*] *he ate and drank very little.*
▸*adv.* (**less** /les/, **least** /lēst/) **1** (**a little**) to a small extent: *he reminded me a little of my parents.* **2** hardly or not at all: *little did he know what wheels he was putting into motion.* —**lit·tle·ness** *n.*
▸ □ **little by little** by degrees; gradually: *little by little the money dried up.* □ **little or nothing** hardly anything. □ **make little of** treat as unimportant: *they made little of their royal connection.* □ **no little** considerable: *a factor of no little importance.* □ **not a little** a great deal (of); much: *not a little consternation was caused.* ■ very: *it was not a little puzzling.* □ **quite a little** a fairly large amount of: *some spoke quite a little English.* ■ a considerable: *it turned out to be quite a little bonanza.*

Lit·tle Dip·per ▸*n.* the seven bright stars of the constellation Ursa Minor.

lit·tle fin·ger ▸*n.* the smallest finger, at the outer end of the hand, farthest from the thumb.

Lit·tle League ▸*n.* youth baseball or softball under the auspices of an organization founded in 1939, for children up to age 12. —**Little Leaguer** *n.*

lit·tle peo·ple ▸*plural n.* **1** the ordinary people in a country, organization, etc., who do not have much power. **2** people of small physical stature; midgets. ■ small supernatural creatures such as fairies and leprechauns.

lit·to·ral /ˈlitərəl/ ▸*adj.* of, relating to, or situated on the shore of the sea or a lake: *the littoral states of the Indian Ocean.* ■ *Ecol.* of, relating to, or denoting the zone of the seashore between high- and low-water marks, or the zone near a lake shore with rooted vegetation: *limpets and other littoral mollusks.*
▸*n.* a region lying along a shore: *irrigated regions of the Mediterranean littoral.* ■ *Ecol.* the littoral zone.

li·tur·gi·cal /liˈtərjikəl/ ▸*adj.* of or related to liturgy or public worship. —**li·tur·gi·cal·ly** *adv.*

lit·ur·gy /ˈlitərjē/ ▸*n.* (*pl.* **-gies**) a form or formulary according to which public religious worship, esp. Christian worship, is conducted. ■ a religious service conducted according to such a form or formulary. ■ (**the Liturgy**) the Eucharistic service of the Eastern Orthodox Church. —**lit·ur·gist** *n.*

liv·a·ble /ˈlivəbəl/ (also **live·a·ble**) ▸*adj.* worth living; enjoyable: *fatherhood makes life more livable.* ■ (of an environment or climate) fit to live in: *one of the most livable cities in the world.* —**liv·a·bil·i·ty** /ˌlivəˈbilətē/ *n.*

live¹ /liv/ ▸*v.* **1** [*intr.*] remain alive: *the doctors said she had only six months to live.* ■ be alive at a specified time: *he lived four centuries ago.* ■ [*tr.*] lead (one's life) in a particular way: *he was living a life of luxury in Australia.* ■ supply oneself with the means of subsistence: *they live by hunting and fishing.* ■ survive in someone's mind; be remembered: *only the name lived on.* ■ have an exciting or fulfilling life: *he couldn't wait to get out of school and really start living.* **2** [*intr.*] make one's home in a particular place or with a particular person: *I've lived in New England all my life.*
▸*phrasal v.* □ **live something down** succeed in making others forget something embarrassing that has happened. □ **live for** regard as the purpose or most important aspect of one's life: *Tony lived for his painting.* □ **live in** (of an employee or student) reside at the place where one works or studies. □ **live off** (or **on**) depend on (someone or something) as a source of income or support: *if you think you're going to live off me for the rest of your life, you're mistaken.* ■ have (a particular amount of money) with which to buy food and other necessities. ■ subsist on (a particular type of food). □ **live something out 1** do in reality that which one has thought or dreamed about: *your wedding day is the one time that you can live out your most romantic fantasies.* **2** spend the rest of one's life in a particular place or particular circumstances: *he lived out his days as a happy family man.* □ **live through** survive (an unpleasant experience or period): *both men lived through the Depression.* □ **live together** (esp. of a couple not married to each other) share a home and have a sexual relationship. □ **live up to** fulfill (expectations). ■ fulfill (an undertaking): *the president lived up to his promise to set America swiftly on a new path.* □ **live with 1** share a home and have a sexual relationship with (someone to whom one is not married). **2** accept or tolerate (something unpleasant): *our marriage was a failure—you have to learn to live with that fact.*
▸ □ **as I live and breathe** used, esp. in spoken English, to express one's surprise at coming across someone or something: *good Lord, Jack Stone, as I live and breathe!* □ **live and breathe something** be extremely interested in or enthusiastic about a particular subject or activity and so devote a great deal of one's time to it: *they live and breathe Italy and all things Italian.* □ **live dangerously** do something risky, esp. on a habitual basis. □ **live in the past** have old-fashioned or outdated ideas and attitudes. ■ dwell on or reminisce at length about past events. □ **live it up** *inf.* spend one's time in an extremely enjoyable way, typically by spending a great deal of money or engaging in an exciting social life. □ **live out of a suitcase** live or stay somewhere on a temporary basis and with only a limited selection of one's belongings, typically because one's occupation requires a great deal of traveling. □ **live one's own life** follow one's own plans and principles independent of others. □ **live rough** live and sleep outdoors as a consequence of having no proper home. □ **live to regret something** come to wish that one had not done something: *those who put work before their family life often live to regret it.* □ **live to tell the tale** survive a dangerous experience and be able to tell others about it. □ **live with oneself** be able to retain one's self-respect as a consequence of one's actions: *taking money from children—how can you live with yourself?* □ **where one lives** *inf.* at, to, or in the right, vital, or most vulnerable spot: *it gets me where I live.* □ **you haven't lived** used, esp. in spoken English, as a way of enthusiastically recommending something to someone who has not experienced it: *you haven't lived until you've tasted their lobster ravioli.*

live² /līv/ ▸*adj.* **1** not dead or inanimate; living: *live animals.* **2** (of a musical performance) given in concert, not on a recording: *there is traditional live music played most nights.* ■ (of a broadcast) transmitted at the time of occurrence, not from a recording: *live coverage of the match.* **3** (of a wire or device) connected to a source of electric current. ■ of, containing, or using undetonated explosive: *live ammunition.* ■ (of a ball in a game) in play, esp. in contrast to being foul or out of bounds. **4** (of a question or subject) of current or continuing interest and importance: *the future organization of Europe has become a live issue.*

▸*adv.* as or at an actual event or performance: *the match will be televised live.*

▸ □ **go live** *Comput.* (of a system) become operational.

live·a·ble /'livəbəl/ ▸*adj.* variant spelling of LIVABLE.

live·bear·ing /'līv,be(ə)riNG/ ▸*adj.* (of an animal) bearing live young rather than laying eggs.

live-in /'liv ,in/ ▸*adj.* (of a domestic employee) resident in an employer's house: *a live-in housekeeper.* ■ (of a person) living with another in a sexual relationship: *a live-in lover.* ■ residential: *a live-in treatment program.*

▸*n. inf.* a person who shares another's living accommodations as a sexual partner or as an employee.

live·li·hood /'līvli,ho͝od/ ▸*n.* a means of securing the necessities of life: *people whose livelihoods depend on the rain forest.*

live load /līv/ ▸*n.* the weight of people or goods in a building or vehicle. Often contrasted with DEAD LOAD.

live·long /'liv,lôNG -,läNG/ ▸*adj. poetic/literary* (of a period of time) entire: *all this livelong day I lay in the sun.*

live·ly /'līvlē/ ▸*adj.* (**live·li·er**, **live·li·est**) full of life and energy; active and outgoing: *she joined a lively team of reporters.* ■ (of a place or atmosphere) full of activity and excitement: *Barcelona's many lively bars.* ■ intellectually stimulating or perceptive: *a lively discussion.* —**live·li·ly** /-ləlē/ *adv.* —**live·li·ness** *n.*

▸ □ **look lively** (or **alive**) [usu. in *imperative*] *inf.* move more quickly and energetically: *"Look lively, men!" Charlie shouted.*

liv·en /'līvən/ ▸*v.* make or become more lively or interesting: [*tr.*] *liven up bland foods with a touch of mustard* | [*intr.*] *the match didn't liven up until the second half.*

liv·er[1] /'livər/ ▸*n.* a large lobed glandular organ in the abdomen of vertebrates, involved in many metabolic processes. ■ a similar organ in other animals. ■ the flesh of an animal's liver as food: *slices of calf's liver.* | *chicken livers.*

liv·er[2] ▸*n.* [with *adj.*] a person who lives in a specified way: *a clean liver* | *high livers.*

liv·er spot ▸*n.* a small brown spot on the skin, esp. as caused by a skin condition such as lentigo. —**liv·er-spot·ted** *adj.*

liv·er·wort /'livər,wərt; -,wôrt/ ▸*n.* a small flowerless green plant with leaflike stems or lobed leaves, occurring in moist habitats.

liv·er·wurst /'livər,wərst/ ▸*n.* a seasoned meat paste in the form of a sausage containing cooked liver, or a mixture of liver and pork.

liv·er·y /'liv(ə)rē/ ▸*n.* (*pl.* **-er·ies**) **1** special uniform worn by a servant or official. ■ a special design and color scheme used on the vehicles, aircraft, or products of a particular company. **2** short for LIVERY STABLE. **3** (in the UK) the members of a livery company collectively. **4** *hist.* a provision of food or clothing for servants. ▷Middle English: from Old French *livree* 'delivered,' feminine past participle of *livrer*, from Latin *liberare* 'liberate' (in medieval Latin 'hand over'). The original sense was 'the dispensing of food, provisions, or clothing to servants'; hence sense 4, also 'allowance of provender for horses,' surviving in the phrase *at livery* and in *livery stable*. Sense 1 arose because medieval nobles provided matching clothes to distinguish their servants from others'. —**liv·er·ied** /'liv(ə)rēd/ *adj.*

▸ □ **at livery** (of a horse) kept for the owner and fed and cared for at a fixed charge.

liv·er·y sta·ble (also **livery yard**) ▸*n.* a stable where horses are kept at livery or let out for hire.

lives /līvz/ ▸ plural form of LIFE.

live·stock /'līv,stäk/ ▸*n.* farm animals regarded as an asset: *markets for the trading of livestock.*

live wire /līv/ ▸*n. inf.* an energetic and unpredictable person.

liv·id /'livid/ ▸*adj.* **1** *inf.* furiously angry: *he was livid at being left out.* **2** (of a color or the skin) having a dark inflamed tinge: *his face went livid, then purple.* ■ of a bluish leaden color: *livid bruises.* ▷late Middle English (in the sense 'of a bluish leaden color'): from French *livide* or Latin *lividus*, from *livere* 'be bluish.' The sense 'furiously angry' dates from the early 20th cent. —**liv·id·i·ty** /lə'videtē/ *n.* —**liv·id·ly** *adv.* —**liv·id·ness** *n.*

liv·ing /'liviNG/ ▸*n.* **1** an income sufficient to live on or the means of earning it: *she was struggling to make a living as a dancer.* ■ *Brit.* (in church use) a position as a vicar or rector with an income or property. **2** [with *adj.*] the pursuit of a lifestyle of the specified type: *the benefits of country living.*

▸*adj.* alive: *living creatures* | [as *plural n.*] (**the living**) *flowers were for the living.* ■ (of a place) used for living rather than working in: *the living*

quarters of the ship. ■ (of a language) still spoken and used. ■ *poetic/lit.* (of water) perennially flowing: *streams of living water.*

▸ □ **be (the) living proof that** (or **of**) show by one's existence and qualities that something is the case: *she is living proof that hard work need not be aging.* □ **in** (or **within**) **living memory** within or during a time that is remembered by people still alive: *the worst recession in living memory.* □ **the living image of** an exact copy or likeness of.

liv·ing death ▸*n.* a state of existence that is very difficult; a life of hopeless and unbroken misery.

liv·ing room ▸*n.* a room in a house for general and informal everyday use.

liv·ing wage ▸*n.* a wage that is high enough to maintain a normal standard of living.

liv·ing will ▸*n.* a written statement detailing a person's desires regarding their medical treatment in circumstances in which they are no longer able to express informed consent, esp. an advance directive.

liz·ard /'lizərd/ ▸*n.* a reptile that typically has a long body and tail, four legs, movable eyelids, and a rough, scaly, or spiny skin.

'll ▸*contr. of* shall; will: *I'll get the food on.*

lla·ma /'lämə/ ▸*n.* a domesticated pack animal (*Lama glama*) of the camel family found in the Andes, valued for its soft woolly fleece. ■ the wool of the llama. ■ cloth made from such wool.

lo /lō/ ▸*interj. archaic* used to draw attention to an interesting or amazing event: *and lo, the star, which they saw in the east, went before them.*

▸ □ **lo and behold** used to present a new scene, situation, or turn of events, often with the suggestion that though surprising, could in fact have been predicted: *you took me out and, lo and behold, I got home to find my house had been ransacked.*

load /lōd/ ▸*n.* **1** a heavy or bulky thing that is being carried or is about to be carried: *in addition to their own food, they must carry a load of up to eighty pounds.* ■ the total number or amount that can be carried in something, esp. a vehicle of a specified type: *a tractor-trailer load of new appliances.* **2** a weight or source of pressure borne by someone or something: *the increased load on the heart caused by a raised arterial pressure.* ■ the amount of work to be done by a person or machine: *Arthur has a light teaching load.* ■ a burden of responsibility, worry, or grief: *consumers will find it difficult to service their heavy load of debt.* **3** (**a load of**) *inf.* a lot of (often used to express one's disapproval or dislike of something): *she was talking a load of garbage.* ■ (**a load/loads**) *inf.* plenty: *she spends loads of money on clothes.* **4** the amount of power supplied by a source; the resistance of moving parts to be overcome by a motor or engine. ■ the amount of electricity supplied by a generating system at any given time. ■ *Electr.* an impedance or circuit that receives or develops the output of a transistor or other device.

▸*v.* [*tr.*] **1** put a load or large amount of something on or in (a vehicle, ship, container, etc.): *they load up their dugout canoes.* ■ [*intr.*] (of a ship or vehicle) take on a load: *when we came to the quay the ship was still loading.* **2** make (someone or something) carry or hold a large or excessive amount of heavy things: *Elaine was loaded down with bags full of shopping.* ■ (**load someone with**) *fig.* burden someone with (worries, responsibilities, etc.). ■ (usu. **be loaded**) bias toward a particular outcome: *the odds were loaded against them before the match.* **3** insert (something) into a device so that it will operate: *load the cassette into the camcorder.* ■ *Comput.* transfer (a program or data) into memory, or into the central processor from storage. ■ *Comput.* transfer programs into (a computer memory or processor). ■ add an extra charge to (an insurance premium) in the case of a poorer risk.

▸*phrasal v.* □ **load up on** consume a substantial amount of (food or beverage): *we were loading up on beer and raw oysters.* —**load·er** *n.*

▸ □ **get a load of** *inf.* used to draw attention to someone or something: *get a load of what we've just done.* □ **get** (or **have**) **a load on** *inf.* become drunk. □ **load the bases** *Baseball* (of the team at bat) fill all three bases with runners; (of a pitcher) allow all three bases to be occupied by runners. □ **load the dice against/in favor of someone** put someone at a disadvantage or advantage. □ **take a** (or **the**) **load off one's feet** sit or lie down. □ **take a load off someone's mind** bring someone relief from anxiety.

load·ed /'lōdid/ ▸*adj.* **1** carrying or bearing a load, esp. a large one: *a heavily loaded freight train.* ■ (of a firearm) charged with ammunition: *a loaded gun.* ■ (**loaded with**) containing in abundance or excess: *your average chocolate bar is loaded with fat.* ■ *inf.* having a lot of money; wealthy: *she doesn't really have to work—they're loaded.* ■ *inf.* having had

---

L

too much alcohol; drunk: *man, did I get loaded after I left his house.* ■ *inf.* (of a car) equipped with many optional extras; deluxe: *1989 Ford 250 LXT: low miles, loaded.* **2** weighted or biased toward a particular outcome: *a trick like the one with the loaded dice.* ■ (of a word, statement, or question) charged with an underlying meaning or implication: *avoid politically loaded terms like "nation".*

load·ing /'lōdɪNG/ ▸*n.* **1** the application of a mechanical load or force to something. **2** the application of an extra amount of something to balance some other factor. ■ an increase in an insurance premium due to a factor increasing the risk involved.

▸*adj.* [in *comb.*] (of a gun, machine, or truck) loaded in a specified way: *a front-loading dishwasher.*

loaf[1] /lōf/ ▸*n.* (*pl.* **loaves** /lōvz/) bread that is shaped and baked in one piece and usually sliced before being eaten: *a loaf of bread.* ■ food formed into a usu. oblong shape, and often sliced into portions.

loaf[2] ▸*v.* [*intr.*] idle one's time away, typically by aimless wandering or loitering: *don't let him see you loafing around with your hands in your pockets.*

loaf·er /'lōfər/ ▸*n.* **1** a person who idles time away. **2** *trademark* a leather shoe shaped like a moccasin, with a low flat heel.

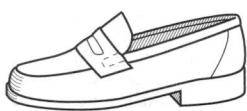

loafer

loam /lōm/ ▸*n.* a fertile soil of clay and sand containing humus. ■ *Geol.* a soil with roughly equal proportions of sand, silt, and clay. ■ a paste of clay and water with sand, chopped straw, etc., used in making bricks and plastering walls. —**loam·i·ness** *n.* —**loamy** *adj.*

loan /lōn/ ▸*n.* a thing that is borrowed, esp. a sum of money that is expected to be paid back with interest: *borrowers can take out a loan for $84,000.* ■ an act of lending something to someone: *she offered to buy him dinner in return for the loan of the car.*

▸*v.* [*tr.*] (often **be loaned**) borrow (a sum of money or item of property): *the word processor was loaned to us by the theater.* —**loan·a·ble** *adj.* —**loan·ee** /,lō'nē/ *n.* —**loan·er** *n.*

loan shark ▸*n.* *inf.*, often *derog.* a moneylender who charges extremely high rates of interest, typically under illegal conditions. —**loan·shark·ing** /'lōn,shärkɪNG/ *n.*

loan·word /'lōn,wərd/ ▸*n.* a word adopted from a foreign language with little or no modification.

loath /lōTH; lōTH/ ▸*adj.* reluctant; unwilling: *I was loath to leave.*

loathe /lōTH/ ▸*v.* [*tr.*] feel intense dislike or disgust for: *she loathed him on sight* | [as *n.*] (**loathing**) *the thought filled him with loathing.* —**loath·er** *n.*

loath·some /'lōTHsəm; 'lōTH-/ ▸*adj.* causing hatred or disgust; repulsive: *this loathsome little swine.* —**loath·some·ly** *adv.* —**loath·some·ness** *n.*

loaves /lōvz/ ▸ plural form of **LOAF**[1].

lob /läb/ ▸*v.* (**lobbed, lob·bing**) [*tr.*] throw or hit (a ball or missile) in a high arc: *he lobbed the ball over their heads.* ■ (in tennis) hit the ball over (an opponent) in such a way.

▸*n.* (chiefly in tennis) a ball hit in a high arc over an opponent.

lo·bar /'lō,bär; -bər/ ▸*adj.* chiefly *Anat.* & *Med.* of, relating to, or affecting a lobe, esp. a whole lobe of a lung: *lobar pneumonia.*

lo·bate /'lō,bāt/ ▸*adj.* *Biol.* having a lobe or lobes: *lobate oak leaves.* —**lo·ba·tion** /lō'bāSHən/ *n.*

lob·by /'läbē/ ▸*n.* (*pl.* **-bies**) **1** a room providing a space out of which one or more other rooms or corridors lead, typically one near the entrance of a public building. **2** a group of people seeking to influence politicians or public officials on a particular issue: *members of the anti-abortion lobby.* ■ an organized attempt by members of the public to influence politicians or public officials: *a recent lobby of Congress by retirees.*

▸*v.* (**-bies, -bied**) [*tr.*] seek to influence (a politician or public official) on an issue: *it is recommending that booksellers lobby their representatives* | [*intr.*] *a group lobbying for better rail services.* —**lob·by·ist** /-ist/ *n.*

lobe /lōb/ ▸*n.* a roundish and flattish part of something, typically each of two or more such parts divided by a fissure, and often projecting or hanging. See also **EARLOBE**. ■ each of the parts of the cerebrum of the brain. —**lobed** *adj.* —**lobe·less** *adj.*

lo·bel·ia /lō'bēlēə; -'bēlyə/ ▸*n.* a chiefly tropical or subtropical plant (genus *Lobelia*) of the bellflower family, in particular an annual widely grown as a bedding plant.

lo·bot·o·my /lə'bätəmē/ ▸*n.* (*pl.* **-mies**) a surgical operation involving incision into the prefrontal lobe of the brain, formerly used to treat mental illness.

lob·ster /'läbstər/ ▸*n.* a large marine crustacean (*Homarus* and other genera, class Malacostraca) with stalked eyes and the first of its five pairs of limbs modified as pincers. Several species include the **American lobster** (*H. americanus*). ■ the flesh of this animal as food. ■ any of various similar crustaceans, esp. certain crayfish whose claws are eaten as food.

▸*v.* [*intr.*] catch lobsters. ▷Old English *lopustre*, alteration of Latin *locusta* 'crustacean, locust.'

lob·ster pot (also **lobster trap**) ▸*n.* a cratelike or basketlike trap in which lobsters are caught.

lo·cal /'lōkəl/ ▸*adj.* belonging or relating to a particular area or neighborhood, typically exclusively so: *researching local history.* ■ denoting a telephone call made to a nearby place and charged at a relatively low rate. ■ denoting a train or bus serving a particular district, with frequent stops: *the town has an excellent local bus service.* Compare with **EXPRESS**[2]. ■ (in technical use) relating to a particular region or part, or to each of any number of these: *a local infection.* ■ *Comput.* denoting a variable or other entity that is only available for use in one part of a program. ■ *Comput.* denoting a device that can be accessed without the use of a network. Compare with **REMOTE**.

▸*n.* a local person or thing, in particular: ■ an inhabitant of a particular area or neighborhood: *the street was full of locals and tourists.* ■ a local train or bus service: *catch the local into New Delhi.* ■ a local branch of an organization, esp. a labor union. ■ short for **LOCAL ANESTHESIA**. ■ *Stock Exchange slang* a floor trader who trades on their own account, rather than on behalf of other investors. —**lo·cal·ly** *adv.* —**lo·cal·ness** *n.*

lo·cal an·es·the·sia ▸*n.* anesthesia that affects a restricted area of the body. Compare with **GENERAL ANESTHESIA**.

lo·cal ar·e·a net·work (abbr.: **LAN**) ▸*n.* a computer network that links devices within a building or group of adjacent buildings.

lo·cal col·or ▸*n.* **1** the customs, manner of speech, dress, or other typical features of a place or period that contribute to its particular character: *reporters in search of local color and gossip.* **2** *Art* the natural color of a thing in ordinary daylight, uninfluenced by the proximity of other colors.

lo·cale /lō'kal/ ▸*n.* a place where something happens or is set, or that has particular events associated with it: *her summers were spent in a variety of exotic locales.*

lo·cal·ism /'lōkə,lizəm/ ▸*n.* preference for a locality, particularly to one's own area or region. ■ *derog.* the limitation of ideas and interests resulting from this. ■ a characteristic of a particular locality, such as a local idiom or custom. —**lo·cal·ist** *n.* & *adj.* —**lo·cal·ize** *v.*

lo·cal·i·ty /lō'kalətē/ ▸*n.* (*pl.* **-ties**) the position or site of something: *the rock's size and locality.* ■ an area or neighborhood, esp. as regarded as a place occupied by certain people or as the scene of particular activities.

lo·cal time ▸*n.* time as reckoned in a particular region or time zone. ■ time at a particular place as measured from the sun's transit over the meridian at that place, defined as noon.

lo·cate /'lō,kāt; lō'kāt/ ▸*v.* [*tr.*] discover the exact place or position of: *engineers were working to locate the fault.* ■ (usu. **be located**) situate in a particular place: *these popular apartments are centrally located.* ■ place within a particular context: *they locate their policies in terms of wealth creation.* ▷early 16th cent.: from Latin *locat-* 'placed,' from the verb *locare*, from *locus* 'place.' The original sense was as a legal term meaning 'rent out,' later (late 16th cent.) 'assign to a particular place,' then 'establish in a place.' The sense 'discover the exact position of' dates from the late 19th cent. —**lo·cat·a·ble** /-,kātəbəl; lō'kāt-/ *adj.* —**lo·ca·tor** /-,kātər/n.

lo·ca·tion /lō'kāSHən/ ▸*n.* a particular place or position: *the property is set in a convenient location.* ■ an actual place or natural setting in which a film or broadcast is made, as distinct from a simulation in a studio: *the movie was filmed entirely on location.* ■ the action or process of placing someone or something in a particular position: *the location of new housing beyond the existing built-up areas.* ■ a position or address in computer memory. —**lo·ca·tion·al** /-SHənl; -SHnəl/ *adj.*

loc·a·tive /'läkətiv/ *Gram.* ▸*adj.* relating to or denoting a case in some languages of nouns, pronouns, and adjectives, expressing location.

▸*n.* (**the locative**) the locative case. ■ a word in the locative case.

loc. cit. ▸*abbr.* in the passage already cited.

loch /läk; läкн/ ▸*n.* *Scot.* a lake.

lo·ci /'lō,sī; -,sē; -,kē; -,kī/ ▸ plural form of **LOCUS**.

lock[1] /läk/ ▸*n.* **1** a mechanism for keeping a door, lid, etc., fastened, typically operated only by a key of a particular form: *the key turned firmly in the lock.* ■ a similar device used to prevent the operation or movement of a vehicle or other machine: *a bicycle lock.* ■ (in wrestling and martial arts) a hold that prevents an opponent from moving a limb. **2** a short confined section of a canal or other waterway used for raising and lowering vessels by varying the water level between two gates. ■ an airlock. **3** (**a lock**) *inf.* a person or thing that is certain to succeed; a certainty. **4** *archaic* a mechanism for setting off the charge of a gun.

▶*v.* **1** [*tr.*] fasten or secure (something) with a lock: *she closed and locked her desk.* ■ (**lock something up**) shut and secure something, esp. a building, by fastening its doors with locks: *the diplomatic personnel locked up their building and walked off* | [*intr.*] *you could lock up for me when you leave.* ■ enclose or shut in by locking or fastening a door, lid, etc.: *the prisoners are* **locked up** *overnight.* ■ (**lock someone up/away**) imprison someone. ■ (**lock something up/away**) invest money in something so that it is not easily accessible: *vast sums of money locked up in pension funds.* ■ (**lock someone down**) confine prisoners to their cells, esp. so as to gain control. ■ [*intr.*] (of a door, window, box, etc.) become or be able to be secured through activation of a lock: *the door will automatically lock behind you.* **2** make or become rigidly fixed or immovable: [*tr.*] *he locked his hands behind her neck* | [*intr.*] *their gaze locked for several long moments.* ■ (**lock someone/something in**) engage or entangle in (an embrace or struggle): *they were locked in a legal battle.* ■ trap or fix firmly or irrevocably: *this may tend to lock in many traders with their present holdings.* ■ (**lock someone/something into**) cause to become caught or involved in: *they were now locked into the system.* **3** [*intr.*] go through a lock on a canal: *we locked through at Moore Haven.*

▶*phrasal v.* □ **lock onto** locate (a target) by radar or similar means and then track. —**lock·a·ble** *adj.* —**lock·less** *adj.*

▶ □ **have a lock on** *inf.* have an unbreakable hold on or total control over. □ **lock horns** engage in conflict. □ **lock, stock, and barrel** including everything; completely: *the place is owned lock, stock, and barrel by an oil company.* □ **under lock and key** securely locked up.

lock² ▶*n.* a piece of a person's hair that coils or hangs together: *she pushed back* **a lock of** *hair.* ■ (**locks**) *chiefly poetic/lit.* a person's hair: *flowing locks and a long white beard.* ■ (**locks**) short for DREADLOCKS. —**locked** *adj. his curly-locked comrades.*

lock·er /ˈläkər/ ▶*n.* **1** a small lockable closet or compartment, typically as one of a number placed together for public or general use, e.g., in schools, gymnasiums, or train stations. ■ a chest or compartment on a ship or boat for clothes, stores, equipment, or ammunition. **2** a device that locks something.

lock·et /ˈläkit/ ▶*n.* a small ornamental case, typically made of gold or silver, worn around a person's neck on a chain and used to hold things of sentimental value, such as a photograph or lock of hair.

lock·jaw /ˈläkˌjô/ ▶*n.* nontechnical term for TRISMUS.

lock·nut /ˈläkˌnət/ ▶*n.* a nut screwed down on another to keep it tight. ■ a nut designed so that, once tightened, it cannot be accidentally loosened.

lock·out /ˈläkˌout/ ▶*n.* **1** the exclusion of employees by their employer from their place of work until certain terms are agreed to. **2** a device used to ensure that machines remain inoperable while repairs or adjustments are made.

lock·smith /ˈläkˌsmiTH/ ▶*n.* a person who makes and repairs locks.

lock·step /ˈläkˌstep/ ▶*n.* a way of marching with each person as close as possible to the one in front: *the trio marched* **in lockstep.** ■ *fig.* close adherence to and emulation of another's actions: *they raised prices* **in lockstep with** *those of foreign competitors* | [as *adj.*] *the party touted a lockstep unity.*

lock·up /ˈläkˌəp/ ▶*n.* **1** a jail, esp. a temporary one. **2** the locking up of premises for the night. ■ the time of doing this: *hurrying back to their dorms before lockup.* **3** the action of becoming fixed or immovable: *antilock braking helps prevent wheel lockup.* **4** an investment in assets that cannot readily be realized or sold in the short term.

lo·co¹ ▶*adj. inf.* crazy.

lo·co·mo·tion /ˌlōkəˈmōsHən/ ▶*n.* movement or the ability to move from one place to another: *the muscles that are concerned with locomotion.*

lo·co·mo·tive /ˌlōkəˈmōtiv/ ▶*n.* a powered rail vehicle used for pulling trains: *a diesel locomotive.* ▶*adj.* of, relating to, or effecting locomotion: *locomotive power.* ■ *archaic* (of a machine, vehicle, or animal) having the power of progressive motion: *locomotive bivalves have the strongest hinges.*

lo·co·mo·tor /ˌlōkəˈmōtər/ ▶*adj. chiefly Biol.* of or relating to locomotion: *locomotor organs.* —**lo·co·mo·to·ry** *adj.*

lo·co·weed /ˈlōkōˌwēd/ ▶*n.* **1** a widely distributed plant (genera *Astragalus* and *Oxytropis*) of the pea family that, if eaten by livestock, can cause a brain disorder. **2** *inf.* cannabis.

lo·cus /ˈlōkəs/ ▶*n.* (*pl.* **lo·ci** /ˈlōˌsī; -ˌsē; -ˌkē; -ˌkī/) **1** *technical* a particular position, point, or place: *it is impossible to specify the exact locus in the brain of these neural events.* ■ the effective or perceived location of something abstract: *the real locus of power is the informal council.* ■ *Genetics* the position of a gene or mutation on a chromosome. **2** *Math.* a curve or other figure formed by all the points satisfying a particular equation of the relation between coordinates, or by a point, line, or surface moving according to mathematically defined conditions.

lo·cust /ˈlōkəst/ ▶*n.* **1** a large and mainly tropical grasshopper, esp. the **migratory locust** (*Locusta migratoria*), with strong powers of flight. It is usually solitary, but from time to time there is a population explosion, and it migrates in vast swarms that cause extensive damage to crops. ■ (also **seventeen-year locust**) the periodical cicada. **2** (also **locust bean**) the large edible pod of some plants of the pea family, in particular the carob bean, which is said to resemble a locust. **3** (also **locust tree**) any of a number of pod-bearing trees of the pea family, in particular the carob tree and the black locust.

lo·cu·tion /lōˈkyōōsHən/ ▶*n.* **1** a word or phrase, esp. with regard to style or idiom. ■ a person's style of speech: *his impeccable locution.* **2** an utterance regarded in terms of its intrinsic meaning or reference, as distinct from its function or purpose in context. —**lo·cu·tion·a·ry** /-ˌnerē/ *adj.*

lode /lōd/ ▶*n.* a vein of metal ore in the earth. ■ *fig.* a rich source of something: *a rich lode of scandal and alleged crime.*

lode·star /ˈlōdˌstär/ ▶*n.* a star that is used to guide the course of a ship, esp. Polaris. ■ *fig.* a person or thing that serves as a guide: *she was his intellectual lodestar.*

lode·stone /ˈlōdˌstōn/ ▶*n.* a piece of magnetite or other naturally magnetized mineral, able to be used as a magnet. ■ a mineral of this kind; magnetite. ■ *fig.* a thing that is the focus of attention or attraction.

lodge /läj/ ▶*n.* **1** a small house at the gates of a park or in the grounds of a large house, typically occupied by a gatekeeper, gardener, or other employee. ■ a small country house occupied in season for sports such as hunting, shooting, fishing, and skiing: *a hunting lodge.* ■ an American Indian hut. ■ a beaver's den. **2** a branch or meeting place of an organization such as the Freemasons. ■ the membership of such an organization.

▶*v.* **1** [*tr.*] present (a complaint, appeal, claim, etc.) formally to the proper authorities: *he has 28 days in which to lodge an appeal.* **2** make or become firmly fixed or embedded in a particular place: [*tr.*] *they had to remove a bullet lodged near his spine* | [*intr.*] *fig. the image had lodged in her mind.* **3** [*intr.*] stay or sleep in another person's house, paying money for one's accommodations: *the man who lodged in the room next door.* ■ [*tr.*] provide (someone) with a place to sleep or stay in return for payment. **4** [*tr.*] (of wind or rain) flatten (a standing crop). ■ [*intr.*] (of a crop) be flattened in such a way.

lodge·pole pine /ˈläjˌpōl/ ▶*n.* a straight-trunked pine tree (*Pinus contorta latifolia*) that grows in the mountains of western North America, widely grown for timber and traditionally used by some American Indians in the construction of lodges.

lodg·er /ˈläjər/ ▶*n.* a roomer.

lodg·ing /ˈläjiNG/ ▶*n.* a place in which someone lives or stays temporarily: *they found a cheap lodging in a backstreet.* ■ (**lodgings**) a room or rooms rented out to someone, usually in the same residence as the owner.

lodg·ing house ▶*n.* a rooming house.

lo·ess /les; ləs; ˈlōˌes/ ▶*n. Geol.* a loosely compacted yellowish-gray deposit of windblown sediment of which extensive deposits occur, e.g., in eastern China and the American Midwest. —**lo·ess·i·al** /ˈlesēəl; ˈlə-; lōˈes-/ *adj.* —**lo·ess·ic** /ˈlesik; ˈlə-; lōˈes-/ *adj.*

loft /lôft; läft/ ▶*n.* **1** a room or space directly under the roof of a house or other building, which may be used for accommodations or storage. ■ a gallery in a church or hall: *a choir loft.* **2** *Golf* upward inclination given to the ball in a stroke. ■ backward slope of the head of a club, designed to give upward inclination to the ball. **3** the thickness of cloth or insulating matter in an object such as a sleeping bag or a padded coat.

▶*v.* [*tr.*] kick, hit, or throw (a ball or missile) high up: *he lofted the ball over the infield.* ■ (**lofted**) give backward slope to the head of (a golf club): *a lofted metal club.* ▷ late Old English, from Old Norse *lopt* 'air, sky, upper room,' of Germanic origin; related to Dutch *lucht* and German *Luft*.

loft·y /ˈlôftē; ˈläf-/ ▶*adj.* (**loft·i·er**, **loft·i·est**) **1** of imposing height: *the elegant square was shaded by lofty palms.* ■ of a noble or exalted nature: *an* *extraordinary mixture of harsh reality and lofty ideals.* ■ proud, aloof, or self-important: *lofty intellectual disdain.* **2** (of wool and other textiles) thick and resilient. —**loft·i·ly** /-təlē/ *adv.* —**loft·i·ness** *n.*

log¹ /lôg; läg/ ▶*n.* **1** a part of the trunk or a large branch of a tree that has fallen or been cut off. **2** (also **log·book**) an official record of events during the voyage of a ship or aircraft: *a ship's log.* ■ a regular or systematic record of incidents or observations: *keep a detailed log of your activities.* **3** an apparatus for determining the speed of a ship.
▶*v.* (**logged**, **log·ging**) [*tr.*] **1** enter (an incident or fact) in the log of a ship or aircraft or in another systematic record: *the red book where we log our calls.* ■ (of a ship or aircraft) achieve (a certain distance or speed): *she had logged more than 12,000 miles since she had been launched.* ■ (of an aircraft pilot) attain (a certain amount of flying time). **2** cut down (an area of forest) in order to exploit the timber commercially.
▶*phrasal v.* □ **log in** (or **on**) go through the procedures to begin use of a computer system, which includes establishing the identity of the user. □ **log off** (or **out**) go through the procedures to conclude use of a computer system.

log² ▶*n.* short for LOGARITHM: *log x.*

lo·gan·ber·ry /'lōgən,berē/ ▶*n.* **1** an edible dull-red soft fruit, considered a hybrid of a raspberry and an American dewberry. **2** the scrambling blackberrylike plant (*Rubus loganobaccus*) of the rose family that bears this fruit.

log·a·rithm /'lôgə,riᴛHəm; 'lägə-/ (abbr.: **log**) ▶*n.* a quantity representing the power to which a fixed number (the base) must be raised to produce a given number. —**log·a·rith·mic** /,lôgə'riᴛHmik/ *adj.*

log·book /'lôg,bŏŏk; 'läg-/ ▶*n.* another term for LOG¹ (sense 2).

loge /lōᴢH/ ▶*n.* a private box or enclosure in a theater. ■ the front section of the first balcony in a theater. ■ a similar section in an arena or stadium.

log·ger /'lôgər; 'lägər/ ▶*n.* **1** a person who fells trees for timber; a lumberjack. **2** a device for making a systematic recording of events, observations, or measurements.

log·ger·head /'lôgər,hed; 'lägər-/ ▶*n.* **1** (also **loggerhead turtle**) a reddish-brown turtle (*Caretta caretta*, family Cheloniidae) with a very large head, occurring chiefly in warm seas. **2** (also **loggerhead shrike**) a widespread North American shrike (*Lanius ludovicianus*), having mainly gray plumage with a black eyestripe, wings, and tail.
▶ □ **at loggerheads** in violent dispute or disagreement: *council was at loggerheads with the government.*

log·gia /'lōj(ē)ə; 'lô-/ ▶*n.* a gallery or room with one or more open sides, esp. one that forms part of a house and has one side open to the garden. ■ an open-sided extension to a house.

log·ging /'lôgɪɴɢ; 'lägɪɴɢ/ ▶*n.* the activity or business of felling trees and cutting and preparing the timber.

log·ic /'läjik/ ▶*n.* **1** reasoning conducted or assessed according to strict principles of validity: *the logic of the argument is faulty.* ■ a particular system or codification of the principles of proof and inference: *Aristotelian logic.* ■ the systematic use of symbolic and mathematical techniques to determine the forms of valid deductive argument. ■ the quality of being justifiable by reason: *there's no logic in telling her not to hit people when that's what you're doing.* **2** a system or set of principles underlying the arrangements of elements in a computer or electronic device so as to perform a specified task. ■ logical operations collectively. —**lo·gi·cian** /lə'jisHən; lō-/ *n.*

log·i·cal /'läjikəl/ ▶*adj.* of or according to the rules of logic or formal argument: *a logical impossibility.* ■ characterized by clear, sound reasoning: *the information is displayed in a simple and logical fashion.* ■ (of an action, development, decision, etc.) natural or sensible given the circumstances: *it is a logical progression from the job before.* ■ capable of clear rational thinking: *her logical mind.* —**log·i·cal·i·ty** /,läjə'kalətē/ *n.* —**log·i·cal·ly** /-ik(ə)lē/ *adv.*

lo·gis·tics /lə'jistiks; lō-/ ▶*pl. n.* [treated as *sing.* or *pl.*] the detailed coordination of a complex operation involving many people, facilities, or supplies: *the logistics and costs of a vaccination campaign.* ■ *Mil.* the organization of moving, housing, and supplying troops and equipment. ■ the commercial activity of transporting goods to customers. —**lo·gis·tic** *adj.*

log·jam /'lôg,jam; 'läg-/ ▶*n.* a crowded mass of logs blocking a river. ■ a situation that seems impossible to solve: *the president can use the power of the White House to break the logjam over this issue.* ■ a backlog: *keeping a diary may ease the logjam of work considerably.*

LOGO /'lō,gō/ ▶*n. Comput.* a high-level programming language used to teach computer programming to children.

lo·go /'lōgō/ ▶*n.* (*pl.* **-gos**) a symbol or other small design adopted by an organization to identify its products, uniform, vehicles, etc.: *the Olympic logo was emblazoned across their jackets.*

Lo·gos /'lō,gōs; -,gäs/ ▶*n. Theol.* the Word of God, or principle of divine reason and creative order, identified with the second person of the Trinity incarnate in Jesus Christ. ■ (in Jungian psychology) the principle of reason and judgment, associated with the animus.

lo·go·type /'lōgə,tīp; 'lägə-/ ▶*n. Printing* a single piece of type that prints a word or group of separate letters. ■ a single piece of type that prints a logo or emblem. ■ a logo.

log·roll·ing /'lôg,rōlɪɴɢ; 'läg-/ ▶*n.* **1** *inf.* the practice of exchanging favors, esp. in politics by reciprocal voting for each other's proposed legislation. **2** a sport in which two contestants stand on a floating log and try to knock each other off by spinning it with their feet. —**log·roll·er** /-lər/ *n.*

loin /loin/ ▶*n.* (usu. **loins**) the part of the body on both sides of the spine between the lowest (false) ribs and the hipbones. ■ (**loins**) *chiefly poetic/lit.* the region of the sexual organs, esp. when regarded as the source of erotic or procreative power: *he felt a stirring in his loins at the thought.* ■ (**loin**) a large cut of meat that includes the vertebrae of the loins: *loin of pork with potatoes.* ▷Middle English: from Old French *loigne*, based on Latin *lumbus*.

loin·cloth /'loin,klôᴛH; -,kläᴛH/ ▶*n.* a single piece of cloth wrapped round the hips, typically worn by men in some hot countries as their only garment.

loi·ter /'loitər/ ▶*v.* [*intr.*] stand or wait around idly or without apparent purpose: *she saw Mary loitering near the cloakrooms.* ■ travel indolently and with frequent pauses: *they loitered along in the sunshine, stopping at the least excuse.* —**loi·ter·er** *n.*

loll /läl/ ▶*v.* [*intr.*] sit, lie, or stand in a lazy, relaxed way: *the two girls lolled in their chairs.* ■ hang loosely; droop: *he slumped against a tree trunk, his head lolling back.* ■ [*tr.*] stick out (one's tongue) so that it hangs loosely out of the mouth: *the boy lolled out his tongue.*

lol·li·pop /'lälē,päp/ ▶*n.* a flat, rounded candy on the end of a stick.

lone /lōn/ ▶*adj.* having no companions; solitary or single: *we sheltered under a lone tree.* ■ *poetic/lit.* (of a place) unfrequented and remote: *houses in lone rural settings.*

lone·ly /'lōnlē/ ▶*adj.* (**-li·er**, **-li·est**) sad because one has no friends or company: *lonely old people whose families do not care for them.* ■ without companions; solitary: *passing long lonely hours looking onto the street.* ■ (of a place) unfrequented and remote: *a lonely stretch of country lane.* —**lone·li·ness** *n.*

lon·er /'lōnər/ ▶*n.* a person who prefers not to associate with others.

lone·some /'lōnsəm/ ▶*adj.* solitary or lonely: *she felt lonesome and out of things.* ■ remote and unfrequented: *a lonesome, unfriendly place.* —**lone·some·ness** *n.*
▶ □ **by one's lonesome** *inf.* all alone.

long¹ /lôɴɢ; läɴɢ/ ▶*adj.* (**long·er** /'lôɴɢgər; 'läɴɢ-/; **long·est** /'lôɴɢgist; 'läɴɢ-/) **1** measuring a great distance from end to end: *a long corridor.* ■ (after a measurement and in questions) measuring a specified distance from end to end: *a boat 150 feet long | how long is the leash?* ■ (of a ball in sports) traveling a great distance, or further than expected or intended: *he threw a long ball to the catcher.* ■ *inf.* (of a person) tall. **2** lasting or taking a great amount of time: *a long and distinguished career.* ■ (after a noun of duration and in questions) lasting or taking a specified amount of time: *the gardens will be 90 minutes long.* ■ seeming to last more time than is the case; lengthy or tedious: *serving long hours on the committee.* **3** relatively great in extent: *write a long report.* ■ (after a noun of extent and in questions) having a specified extent: *the statement was three pages long.* **4** *Phonet.* (of a vowel) categorized as long with regard to quality and length (e.g., in standard American English, the vowel in *food* is long, as distinct from the short vowel in *good*). ■ *Prosody* (of a vowel or syllable) having the greater of the two recognized durations. **5** (of odds or a chance) reflecting or representing a low level of probability: *winning against long odds.* **6** *Finance* (of shares, bonds, or other assets) bought in advance, with the expectation of a rise in price. ■ (of a broker or their position in the market) buying or based on long stocks. ■ (of a security) maturing at a distant date. **7** (**long on**) *inf.* well-supplied with: *an industry that seems long on ideas but short on cash.*
▶*n.* **1** a long interval or period: *see you before long.* **2** a long sound such as a long signal in Morse code or a long vowel or syllable: *two longs and a short.* **3** (**longs**) *Finance* long-dated securities, esp. gilt-edged securities. ■ assets held in a long position.
▶*adv.* (**longer**; **longest**) **1** for a long time: *we hadn't known them long.* ■ in questions about a period of time: *how long have you been working?* ■ at a time distant from a specified event or point of time: *it was abandoned*

L

long ago. ■ (after a noun of duration) throughout a specified period of time: *it rained all day long*. **2** (with reference to the ball in sports) at, to, or over a great distance, or further than expected or intended: *the quarterback dropped back and threw the ball long.* —**long·ish** *adj.*

▶ □ **as** (or **so**) **long as 1** during the whole time that: *they have been there as long as anyone can remember.* **2** provided that: *as long as you fed him, he would be cooperative.* □ **be long** take a long time to happen or arrive: *sit down, tea won't be long.* □ **in the long run** over or after a long period of time; eventually: *it saves money in the long run.* □ **the long and the short of it** all that can or need be said: *the long and short of it is that he got himself mugged.* □ **long in the tooth** rather old. □ **long time no see** *inf.* it's a long time since we last met (used as a greeting). □ **not by a long shot** by no means: *we're not there yet, not by a long shot.*

long² ▶ *v.* [*intr.*] have a strong wish or desire: *she longed for a little more excitement.*

long·board /ˈlôNGˌbôrd; ˈläNG-/ ▶ *n.* a type of long surfboard.

long·boat /ˈlôNGˌbōt; ˈläNG-/ ▶ *n.* a large boat that may be launched from a sailing ship.

long·bow /ˈlôNGˌbō; ˈläNG-/ ▶ *n.* a large bow drawn by hand and shooting a long feathered arrow. It was the chief weapon of English armies from the 14th century until the introduction of firearms.

long distance ▶ *adj.* (usu. **long-dis·tance**) traveling or operating between distant places: *a long-distance truck driver.*

▶ *adv.* between distant places: *traveling long distance.*

▶ *n.* [often as *adj.*] *Track & Field* a race distance of 6 miles or 10,000 meters (6 miles 376 yds), or longer: *a long-distance runner.*

long division ▶ *n.* arithmetical division in which the divisor has two or more figures, and a series of steps is made as successive groups of digits of the dividend are divided by the divisor, to avoid excessive mental calculation.

long-drawn (often **long-drawn-out**) ▶ *adj.* continuing for a long time, esp. for longer than is necessary: *long-drawn-out negotiations.*

lon·gev·i·ty /lônˈjevətē; län-/ ▶ *n.* long life: *the greater longevity of women compared with men.* ■ long duration of service: *her longevity in office now appeared as a handicap to the party.*

long·hand /ˈlôNGˌhand; ˈläNG-/ ▶ *n.* ordinary handwriting (as opposed to shorthand, typing, or printing): *he wrote out the reply in longhand* | [as *adj.*] *a longhand draft.*

long haul ▶ *n.* a long distance (in reference to the transport of freight or passengers). ■ a prolonged and difficult effort or task: *getting the proposal passed is likely to be a long haul.*

▶ □ **over the long haul** over an extended period of time.

long·horn /ˈlôNGˌhôrn; ˈläNG-/ ▶ *n.* **1** an animal of a breed of cattle with long horns. **2** (also **longhorn beetle**) an elongated beetle (family Cerambycidae) with long antennae, the larva of which typically bores in wood and can be a pest of timber.

long·house /ˈlôNGˌhous; ˈläNG-/ ▶ *n.* a type of dwelling housing a family and animals under one roof. ■ *hist.* the traditional dwelling of the Iroquois and other North American Indians. ■ a large communal village house in parts of Malaysia and Indonesia.

long·ing /ˈlôNGiNG/ ▶ *n.* a yearning desire: *a wistful longing for the old days.*

▶ *adj.* having or showing such desire: *her longing eyes.* —**long·ing·ly** *adv.*

lon·gi·tude /ˈlänjəˌt(y)o͞od; ˈlôn-/ ▶ *n.* the angular distance of a place east or west of the meridian at Greenwich, England, or west of the standard meridian of a celestial object, usually expressed in degrees and minutes: *at a longitude of 2° W.*

lon·gi·tu·di·nal /ˌlänjəˈt(y)o͞odn-əl; ˌlôn-; -ˈt(y)o͞odnəl/ ▶ *adj.* **1** running lengthwise rather than across: *longitudinal stripes.* ■ (of research or data) involving information about an individual or group gathered over a long period of time. **2** of or relating to longitude; measured from east to west: *longitudinal positions.* —**lon·gi·tu·di·nal·ly** *adv.*

long johns ▶ *pl. n. inf.* underwear with closely fitted legs that extend to the wearer's ankles, often with a long-sleeved top.

long jump ▶ *n.* an athletic event in which competitors jump as far as possible along the ground in one leap. —**long jump·er** *n.*

long·leaf pine /ˈlôNGˌlēf; ˈläNG-/ ▶ *n.* a large pine tree of the southeastern U.S. with very long needles and cones. It was formerly an important source of turpentine.

long-lived /livd/ ▶ *adj.* living or lasting a long time.

long-range ▶ *adj.* **1** (esp. of vehicles or missiles) able to be used or be effective over long distances: *long-range bombers.* **2** relating to a period of time that extends far into the future: *long-range plans.*

long-run·ning ▶ *adj.* continuing for a long time: *a long-running dispute* | *a long-running soap opera.*

long·shore /ˈlôNGˌSHôr; ˈläNG-/ ▶ *adj.* existing on, frequenting, or moving along the seashore: *longshore currents.*

long·shore·man /ˌlôNGˈSHôrmən; ˌläNG-/ ▶ *n.* (*pl.* **-men**) a person employed in a port to load and unload ships.

long shot ▶ *n.* a venture or guess that has only the slightest chance of succeeding or being accurate: *it's a long shot, but well worth trying.* ■ *Film* a shot including objects at a distance: *using a dummy in long shot.*

▶ □ (**not**) **by a long shot** *inf.* (not) by far or at all: *she had not told Tony everything, not by a long shot.*

long-stand·ing (also **long stand·ing**) ▶ *adj.* having existed or continued for a long time: *a long-standing tradition.*

long-suf·fer·ing ▶ *adj.* having or showing patience in spite of troubles, esp. those caused by other people: *his long-suffering wife.*

long suit ▶ *n.* (in bridge or whist) a holding of several cards of one suit in a hand, typically 5 or more out of the 13. ■ an outstanding personal quality or achievement: *tact was not his long suit.*

long-term ▶ *adj.* occurring over or relating to a long period of time: *the long-term unemployed* | *the long-term effects of smoking.*

long·time /ˈlôNGˌtīm; ˈläNG-/ (also **long-time**) ▶ *adj.* (esp. of a person) having had a specified role or identity for a long time: *his longtime friend and colleague.*

long ton ▶ *n.* see TON¹.

long un·der·wear ▶ *n.* a warm, close-fitting undergarment with ankle-length legs and often a long-sleeved top.

long week·end ▶ *n.* see WEEKEND.

long-wind·ed /ˈwindid/ ▶ *adj.* (of speech or writing) continuing at length and in a tedious way: *long wishes were long-winded but sincere.* —**long-wind·ed·ly** *adv.* —**long-wind·ed·ness** *n.*

loo·fah /ˈlo͞ofə/ (also **loo·fa**) ▶ *n.* **1** a coarse, fibrous cylindrical object used like a bath sponge for washing. It consists of the dried fibrous matter of the fluid-transport system of a marrowlike fruit. **2** the tropical Old World climbing plant (*Luffa cylindrica*) of the gourd family that produces these fruits, which are also edible.

look /lo͞ok/ ▶ *v.* [*intr.*] **1** direct one's gaze toward someone or something or in a specified direction: *people were looking at him.* ■ (of a building or room) have a view or outlook in a specified direction: *the principal rooms look out over Nahant Bay.* ■ (**look through**) ignore (someone) by pretending not to see them: *he glanced up once but looked right through me.* ■ (**look something over**) inspect something quickly with a view to establishing its merits: *they looked over a property on Ryer Avenue.* ■ (**look through**) peruse (a book or other written material): *we looked through all the books, and this was still the one we liked best.* ■ (**look around**) move around (a place or building) in order to view whatever it might contain that is of interest: *he spent the morning and afternoon looking around Cambridge.* ■ (**look at/on**) think of or regard in a specified way: *I look at tennis differently from some coaches.* ■ (**look at**) examine (a matter, esp. a problem) and consider what action to take: *a committee is looking at the financing of PBS.* ■ (**look into**) investigate: *the police looked into his business dealings.* **2** have the appearance or give the impression of being: *her father looked unhappy* | [in *comb.*] (**-looking**) *a funny-looking guy.* ■ (**look like**) *inf.* show a likelihood of: *it doesn't look like you'll be moving to Brooklyn.* ■ (**look oneself**) appear one's normal, healthy self: *he just didn't look himself at all.* **3** (**look to**) rely on to do or provide something: *she will look to you for help.* ■ hope or expect to do something: *universities are looking to expand their intakes.*

▶ *phrasal v.* □ **look after** take care of: *women who stay at home to look after children.* □ **look back 1** think of the past: *don't waste time looking back on things that have caused you distress.* **2** suffer a setback or interrupted progress: *she launched her own company in 1981 and has never looked back.* □ **look down** on regard (someone) with a feeling of superiority. □ **look forward to** await eagerly: *we look forward to seeing you.* □ **look in** make a short visit or call: *I will look in on you tomorrow.* □ **look on** watch without getting involved: *Cameron was looking on and making no move to help.* □ **look out** [usu. in *imper.*] be vigilant and take notice: *"Look out!" warned Billie, seeing a movement from the room beyond.* □ **look up** (of a situation) improve: *things seemed to be looking up at last.* □ **look someone up** *inf.* make social contact with someone. □ **look something up** search for and find a piece of information in a reference book. □ **look up to** have a great deal of respect for (someone).

▶ *n.* **1** an act of directing one's gaze in order to see someone or something: *let me get a closer look.* ■ an expression of a feeling or thought by such an act: *Brenton gave me a funny look.* ■ a scrutiny or examination: *the government should be **taking a look at** the amount of grant the council receives.* **2** the appearance of someone or something, esp. as expressing a particular quality: *the bedraggled look of the village.* ■ (**looks**) a person's facial appearance considered aesthetically: *he had charm, **good looks**, and an amusing insouciance.* ■ a style or fashion: *Italian designers unveiled their latest look.*

▸ *interj.* (also **look here!**) used to call attention to what one is going to say: *"Look, this is ridiculous."*

▸ □ **look one's age** appear to be as old as one really is. □ **look down one's nose at** another way of saying LOOK DOWN ON. □ **look someone in the eye** (or **face**) look directly at someone without showing embarrassment, fear, or shame. □ **look the other way** deliberately ignore wrongdoing by others: *they do look the other way at corrupt practices here.* □ **look sharp** be quick. □ **look to the future** consider and plan for what is in the future, rather than worrying about the past or present. □ **look someone up and down** scrutinize someone carefully.

look·a·like (also **look·a·like**) ▸ *n.* a person or thing that closely resembles another, esp. someone who looks very similar to a famous person: *an Elvis Presley look-alike.*

look·er /'lŏŏkər/ ▸ *n.* **1** a person who looks: *the percentage of lookers who actually buy is pretty low.* **2** a person with a specified appearance: *a tough looker is not necessarily a tough fighter.* ■ *inf.* a very attractive person, esp. a woman.

look·er-on ▸ *n.* (*pl.* **look·ers-on**) a person who is a spectator rather than a participant in a situation.

look·ing glass ▸ *n.* a mirror: *she stared at her reflection in the looking glass.* ■ [as *adj.*] being or involving the opposite of what is normal or expected: *looking-glass logic.*

look·out /'lŏŏk,out/ ▸ *n.* a place from which to keep watch or view landscape. ■ a person stationed to keep watch for danger or trouble: *they acted as lookouts at the post office.* ■ *archaic* a view over a landscape. ■ (**one's lookout**) *inf.* a person's own concern: *everyone's life is his own lookout.*

▸ □ **be on the lookout** (or **keep a lookout**) **for** be alert to (danger or trouble): *he told them to be on the lookout for dangerous gas.* ■ keep searching for (something that is wanted): *we kept a sharp lookout for animals.*

look-see ▸ *n. inf.* a brief look or inspection: *we are just about to take a little look-see around the hotel.*

loom¹ /lŏŏm/ ▸ *n.* an apparatus for making fabric by weaving yarn or thread.

loom² ▸ *v.* [intr.] appear as a shadowy form, esp. one that is large or threatening: *vehicles loomed out of the darkness.* ■ (of an event regarded as ominous or threatening) seem about to happen: *there is a crisis looming.*

▸ *n.* a vague and often exaggerated first appearance of an object seen in darkness or fog, esp. at sea: *the loom of the land ahead.*

loon¹ /lŏŏn/ ▸ *n. inf.* a silly or foolish person.

loon² ▸ *n.* a large diving waterbird (genus *Gavia*, family Gaviidae) with a straight pointed bill and short legs set far back under the body. Five species include the **common loon** (*G. immer*) of Canada and Eurasia.

loon·y /'lŏŏnē/ *inf.* ▸ *n.* (*pl.* **loon·ies**) a crazy or silly person: *she was working with a bunch of loonies.*

▸ *adj.* (**loon·i·er, loon·i·est**) crazy or silly: *loony drivers.* —**loon·i·ness** *n.*

loop /lŏŏp/ ▸ *n.* **1** a shape produced by a curve that bends around and crosses itself. ■ a length of thread, rope, or similar material, doubled or crossing itself, typically used as a fastening or handle. ■ (also **loop-the-loop**) a maneuver in which an aircraft describes a vertical circle in the air. ■ *Skating* a maneuver describing a curve that crosses itself, made on a single edge. **2** a structure, series, or process the end of which is connected to the beginning. ■ an endless strip of tape or film allowing continuous repetition. ■ *Comput.* a programmed sequence of instructions that is repeated until or while a particular condition is satisfied.

▸ *v.* form (something) into a loop or loops; encircle: *she looped her arms around his neck.* ■ follow a course that forms a loop or loops: *the canal loops for two miles through the city.* ■ put into or execute a loop of tape, film, or computing instructions: *the program loops back on reaching a RETURN statement.* ■ (also **loop the loop**) circle an aircraft vertically in the air.

▸ □ **in** (or **out of**) **the loop** *inf.* aware (or unaware) of information known to only a privileged few. □ **throw** (or **knock**) **someone for a loop** *inf.* surprise or astonish someone; catch someone off guard.

loop·er /'lŏŏpər/ ▸ *n. Baseball* a fly ball that becomes a hit by dropping out of the reach of the infielders.

loop·hole /'lŏŏp,hōl/ ▸ *n.* **1** an ambiguity or inadequacy in the law or a set of rules: *they exploited tax loopholes.* **2** *archaic* an arrow slit in a wall.

loop·y /'lŏŏpē/ ▸ *adj.* (**loop·i·er, loop·i·est**) **1** *inf.* crazy or silly: *the author comes across as a bit loopy.* **2** having many loops: *a big, loopy signature.* —**loop·i·ness** *n.*

loose /lŏŏs/ ▸ *adj.* **1** not firmly or tightly fixed in place: *a loose tooth.* ■ not packaged or placed in a container: *pockets bulging with loose change.* ■ (of a person or animal) free from confinement; not bound or tethered: *the bull was loose with cattle in the field.* ■ not strict or exact: *a loose interpretation.* ■ not close or compact in structure: *a loose weave* | *fig.* a loose federation of political and industrial groups. ■ typical of diarrhea: *many patients report loose bowel movements.* **2** (of a garment) not fitting tightly or closely: *she slipped into a loose T-shirt and shorts.* **3** relaxed; physically slack: *she swung back into her easy, loose stride.* ■ careless and indiscreet in what is said: *there is too much loose talk about the situation.* ■ *dated* promiscuous; immoral: *she ran the risk of being called a loose woman.* ■ (of the ball in a game) in play but not in any player's possession.

▸ *v.* [tr.] release: *he loosed his grip suddenly.* —**loose·ly** *adv.* —**loose·ness** *n.*

▸ □ **hang** (or **stay**) **loose** [often as *imper.*] *inf.* be relaxed; refrain from taking anything too seriously: *hang loose, baby!* □ **on the loose** having escaped from confinement: *a serial killer is on the loose.*

loose-leaf (also **loose-leaf**) ▸ *adj.* **1** (of a notebook or folder) having each sheet of paper separate and removable. **2** (of lettuce) having leaves that overlap each other loosely rather than forming a compact head.

loos·en /'lŏŏsən/ ▸ *v.* [tr.] make (something tied, fastened, or fixed in place) less tight or firm: *loosen your collar and tie.* ■ make more lax: *his main mistake was to loosen monetary policy* | [as *n.*] (**loosening**) *a loosening of the benefit rules.* ■ relax (one's grip or muscles): *he loosened his hold so she could pull her arms free.* ■ [intr.] become relaxed or less tight: *the stiffness in his shoulders had loosened.* ■ make (a connection or relationship) less strong: *he wanted to strengthen rather than loosen union links.*

▸ *phrasal v.* □ **loosen up** warm up in preparation for an activity: *arrive early to loosen up and hit some practice shots.* ■ make or become relaxed: *they taught me to have fun at work and loosen up.* —**loos·en·er** *n.*

▸ □ **loosen someone's tongue** make someone talk freely.

loose·strife /'lŏŏs(,)strīf/ ▸ *n.* any of various tall plants that bear upright spikes of flowers, in particular **purple loosestrife** (*Lythrum salicaria*, family Lythraceae) and the yellow-flowered **garden loosestrife** (*Lysimachia vulgaris*) of the primrose family.

loos·ey-goos·ey /'lŏŏsē 'gŏŏsē/ ▸ *adj. inf.* **1** not tense; relaxed and comfortable: *other guys can goof around, be all loosey-goosey before a game.* **2** undesirably lacking in definition, care, or precision: *a loosey-goosey interpretation of traditional doctrine.*

loot /lŏŏt/ ▸ *n.* goods, esp. private property, taken from an enemy in war. ■ stolen money or valuables: *two men wearing stocking masks, each swinging a bag of loot.* ■ *inf.* money; wealth: *the thief made off with $5 million in loot.*

▸ *v.* [tr.] steal goods from (a place), typically during a war or riot: *police confronted the rioters who were looting shops.* ■ steal (goods) in such circumstances: *tons of food aid awaiting distribution had been looted.* —**loot·er** *n.*

lop /läp/ ▸ *v.* (**lopped, lop·ping**) [tr.] cut off (a branch, limb, or other protrusion) from the main body of a tree: *they lopped off more branches to save the tree.* ■ *inf.* remove (something regarded as unnecessary or burdensome): *it lops an hour off commuting time.*

▸ *n.* branches and twigs lopped off trees.

lope /lōp/ ▸ *v.* [intr.] run or move with a long bounding stride: *the dog was loping along by his side.*

▸ *n.* a long bounding stride: *they set off at a fast lope.*

lop-eared ▸ *adj.* (of an animal) having ears that droop down by the sides of the head: *a lop-eared mule.*

lop·sid·ed /'läp,sīdid/ ▸ *adj.* with one side lower or smaller than the other: *a lopsided grin.* —**lop·sid·ed·ly** *adv.* —**lop·sid·ed·ness** *n.*

lo·qua·cious /lō'kwāsшəs/ ▸ *adj.* talkative. —**lo·qua·cious·ly** *adv.* —**lo·qua·cious·ness** *n.* —**lo·quac·i·ty** /'kwasətē/ *n.*

lord /lôrd/ ▸ *n.* someone or something having power, authority, or influence: *lord of the sea.* ■ (in the UK) a man of noble rank or high office; a peer. ■ *hist.* a feudal superior, esp. the proprietor of a manor house. ■ a master or ruler: *our lord the king.* ■ (**Lord**) a name for God or Christ: *give thanks to the Lord.*

▸ *interj.* (**Lord**) used in exclamations expressing surprise or worry, or for emphasis: *Lord, I'm cold!*

▸ *v.* **1** [tr.] *archaic* confer the title of Lord upon. **2** (**lord it over**) act in a superior and domineering manner toward (someone).

lord·ly /ˈlôrdlē/ ▸*adj.* (**lord·li·er, lord·li·est**) of, characteristic of, or suitable for a lord: *lordly titles.* —**lord·li·ness** *n.*

Lord Pro·tec·tor ▸*n.* see PROTECTOR (sense 3).

lord·ship /ˈlôrd,SHip/ ▸*n.* supreme power or rule: *his* **lordship** *over the other gods.* ■ *archaic* the authority or state of being a lord. ■ *hist.* a piece of land or territory belonging to or under the jurisdiction of a lord: *lands including the lordship of Denbigh.*

lore /lôr/ ▸*n.* a body of traditions and knowledge on a subject or held by a particular group, typically passed from person to person by word of mouth: *the otherworld of Celtic lore | baseball lore.*

lor·gnette /lôrnˈyet/ (also **lor·gnettes**) ▸*n.* a pair of glasses or opera glasses held in front of a person's eyes by a long handle at one side. ▸*early 19th cent.: from French, from lorgner* 'to squint.'

lorn /lôrn/ ▸*adj. poetic/lit.* lonely and abandoned; forlorn.

lor·ry /ˈlôrē; ˈlärē/ ▸*n.* (*pl.* **-ries**) *Brit.* a truck.

lo·ry /ˈlôrē/ ▸*n.* (*pl.* **-ies**) a small Australasian and Southeast Asian parrot (family Loridae, or Psittacidae) with a brush-tipped tongue for feeding on nectar and pollen, having mainly green plumage with patches of bright color.

lorgnette

lose /lōōz/ ▸*v.* (*past* and *past part.* **lost** /lôst; läst/) [*tr.*] **1** be deprived of or cease to have or retain (something): *I've lost my appetite.* ■ cause (someone) to fail to gain or retain (something): *you lost me my appointment at the university.* ■ (**be lost**) be destroyed or killed, esp. through accident or as a result of military action: *a fishing disaster in which 19 local men were lost.* ■ decrease in (body weight); undergo a reduction of (a specified amount of weight): *she couldn't eat and began to lose weight.* ■ waste or fail to take advantage of (time or an opportunity): *they lost every chance to score in the first inning.* ■ (of a watch or clock) become slow by (a specified amount of time): *this clock will neither gain nor lose a second.* ■ (**lose it**) *inf.* lose control of one's temper or emotions: *in the end I completely lost it—I was screaming at them.* **2** become unable to find (something or someone): *I've lost the car keys.* ■ evade or shake off (a pursuer): *he came after me waving his revolver, but I easily lost him.* ■ *inf.* get rid of (an undesirable person or thing): *lose that creep!* ■ *inf.* cause (someone) to be unable to follow an argument or explanation: *sorry, Tim, you've lost me there.* ■ (**lose oneself in/be lost in**) be or become deeply absorbed in (something): *he had been lost in thought.* **3** fail to win (a game or contest): *the Bears lost the final game of the series.* **4** earn less (money) than one is spending or has spent: *the paper is losing $500,000 a month.*
▸*phrasal v.* □ **lose out** be deprived of an opportunity to do or obtain something; be disadvantaged: *youngsters who were* **losing out on** *regular schooling.* ■ be beaten in competition or replaced by: *they were disappointed at losing out to Chicago in the playoffs.*
▸ □ **have nothing to lose** be in a situation that is so bad that even if an action or undertaking is unsuccessful, it cannot make it any worse. □ **lose face** come to be less highly respected: *he was trying to work out how he could go back home without losing face.* □ **lose heart** become discouraged. □ **lose one's mind** (or **one's marbles**) *inf.* go insane. □ **lose sleep** worry about something: *no one is losing any sleep over what he thinks of us.* □ **you can't lose** used to express the conviction that someone must inevitably profit from an action or undertaking: *we're offering them for only $5.00—you can't lose!*

los·er /ˈlōōzər/ ▸*n.* a person or thing that loses or has lost something, esp. a game or contest. ■ *inf.* a person who fails frequently or is generally unsuccessful in life: *a ragtag community of rejects and losers.* ■ *Bridge* a card that is expected to be part of a losing trick.

los·ing bat·tle ▸*n.* a struggle that seems certain to end in failure: *the police force is fighting a losing battle against a rising tide of crime.*

loss /lôs; läs/ ▸*n.* the fact or process of losing something or someone: *avoiding loss of time | loss-making industries.* ■ the state or feeling of grief when deprived of someone or something of value: *I feel a terrible sense of loss.* ■ the detriment or disadvantage resulting from losing: *his fall from power was no loss to the world.* ■ a person or thing that is badly missed when lost: *he will be a great loss to many people.*
▸ □ **at a loss** **1** puzzled or uncertain what to think, say, or do: *he was at a loss for words.* **2** making less money than is spent buying, operating, or producing something: *a railroad running at a loss.*

loss-lead·er ▸*n.* a product sold at a loss to attract customers.

lost /lôst; läst/ ▸ past and past participle of LOSE.

▸*adj.* **1** unable to find one's way; not knowing one's whereabouts: *they got lost in the fog.* ■ unable to be found: *he turned up with my lost golf clubs.* ■ (of a person) very confused or insecure or in great difficulties: *she stood there clutching a drink, feeling completely lost.* **2** denoting something that has been taken away or cannot be recovered: *if only one could recapture one's lost youth!* **3** (of a game or contest) in which a defeat has been sustained: *the lost election of 1994.*
▸ □ **all is not lost** used to suggest that there is still some chance of success or recovery. □ **be lost for words** be so surprised, confused, or upset that one cannot think what to say. □ **be lost on** fail to influence or be noticed or appreciated by (someone): *the significance of his remarks was not lost on Scott.* □ **get lost** [often in *imper.*] *inf.* go away (used as an expression of anger or impatience): *Why don't you leave me alone? Go on, get lost!* □ **give someone up for lost** stop expecting that a missing person will be found alive. □ **make up for lost time** do something faster or more often in order to compensate for not having done it quickly or often enough before.

lost cause ▸*n.* a person or thing that can no longer hope to succeed or be changed for the better.

lost gen·er·a·tion ▸*n.* the generation reaching maturity during and just after World War I, a high proportion of whose men were killed during those years. ■ an unfulfilled generation coming to maturity during a period of instability.

lot /lät/ ▸*pron.* (**a lot** or **lots**) *inf.* a large number or amount; a great deal: *there are* **a lot** *of actors in the cast.* ■ (**the lot** or **the whole lot**) the whole number or quantity that is involved or implied: *you might as well take the whole lot.*
▸*adv.* (**a lot** or **lots**) *inf.* a great deal; much: *my life is a lot better now.*
▸*n.* **1** [treated as *sing.* or *pl.*] *inf.* a particular group, collection, or set of people or things: *it's just one lot of rich people stealing from another.* **2** an article or set of articles for sale at an auction: *nineteen lots failed to sell.* **3** one of a set of objects such as straws, stones, or pieces of paper that are randomly selected as part of a decision-making process: *they* **drew lots** *to determine the order in which they asked questions.* ■ the making of a decision by such random selection: *officers were elected rather than selected* **by lot.** ■ the choice resulting from such a process: *eventually the lot fell on the king's daughter.* **4** a person's luck or condition in life, particularly as determined by fate or destiny: *plans to improve the lot of the disadvantaged.* **5** a plot of land assigned for sale or for a particular use: *a vacant lot.* ■ short for PARKING LOT. ■ an area of land near a television or movie studio where outside filming may be done. ■ the area at a car dealership where cars for sale are kept.
▸*v.* (**lot·ted, lot·ting**) [*tr.*] divide (items) into lots for sale at an auction: *the contents have been lotted up, and the auction takes place on Monday.*
▸ □ **throw in one's lot with** decide to ally oneself closely with and share the fate of (a person or group).

lo·tion /ˈlōSHən/ ▸*n.* a thick, smooth liquid preparation designed to be applied to the skin for medicinal or cosmetic purposes.

lot·ter·y /ˈlätərē/ ▸*n.* (*pl.* **-ter·ies**) a means of raising money by selling numbered tickets and giving prizes to the holders of numbers drawn at random. ■ a process or thing whose success or outcome is governed by chance: *the lottery of life.*

lot·to /ˈlätō/ ▸*n.* a lottery game similar to bingo.

lo·tus /ˈlōtəs/ ▸*n.* **1** any of a number of large water lilies of the genus *Nelumbo* in the family Nelumbonaceae, in particular: ■ (also **sacred lotus**) a water lily (*N. nucifera*) of Asia and northern Australia, typically with dark pink or white-and-pink flowers. ■ (also **American lotus**) a yellow-flowered North American water lily (*N. lutea*) with bowl-shaped leaves. **2** (in Greek mythology) a legendary plant whose fruit induces a dreamy forgetfulness and an unwillingness to depart. ■ the flower of the sacred lotus as a symbol in Asian art and religion. ■ short for LOTUS POSITION.

lo·tus po·si·tion ▸*n.* a cross-legged position for meditation, with the feet resting on the thighs.

loud /loud/ ▸*adj.* producing or capable of producing much noise; easily audible: *they were kept awake by loud music.* ■ strong or emphatic in expression: *there were loud protests from the lumber barons.* ■ vulgarly obtrusive; flashy: *a man in a loud checked suit.* ■ (of smell or flavor) powerful or offensive.
▸*adv.* with a great deal of volume: *they shouted as loud as they could.* —**loud·ly** *adv.* —**loud·ness** *n.*
▸ □ **out loud** aloud; audibly: *she laughed out loud.*

loud·mouth /ˈloud͵mouTH/ ▸*n. inf.* a person who tends to talk too much in an offensive or tactless way. —**loud·mouthed** /ˈloud͵mouTHd; -͵mouTHt/ (also **loud-mouthed**) *adj.*

loud·speak·er /ˈloud͵spēkər/ ▸*n.* an apparatus that converts electrical impulses into sound, typically as part of a public address system or stereo equipment.

lounge /lounj/ ▸*v.* [*intr.*] lie, sit, or stand in a relaxed or lazy way: *several students were lounging about reading papers.*
▸*n.* **1** a public room, as in a hotel, theater, or club, in which to sit and relax. ■ a spacious area in an airport with seats for waiting passengers: *the departure lounge.* ■ short for COCKTAIL LOUNGE. **2** a couch or sofa, esp. a backless one having a headrest at one end.

loupe /lo͞op/ ▸*n.* a small magnifying glass used by jewelers and watchmakers.

louse /lous/ ▸*n.* **1** (*pl.* **lice** /līs/) a small, wingless, parasitic insect that lives on the skin of mammals and birds. **2** (*pl.* **louses**) *inf.* a contemptible or unpleasant person.
▸*v.* /lous; louz/ [*tr.*] (**louse something up**) *inf.* spoil or ruin something.

lous·y /ˈlouzē/ ▸*adj.* (**lous·i·er, lous·i·est**) **1** *inf.* very poor or bad; disgusting: *the service is usually lousy.* ■ ill; in poor physical condition: *she felt lousy.* **2** infested with lice. ■ (**lousy with**) *inf.* teeming with (something regarded as bad or undesirable): *the town is lousy with tourists.* —**lous·i·ly** /-zəlē/ *adv.* —**lous·i·ness** *n.*

lout /lout/ ▸*n.* an uncouth or aggressive man or boy: *drunken louts.* —**lout·ish** *adj.* —**lout·ish·ly** *adv.* —**lout·ish·ness** *n.*

lou·ver /ˈlo͞ovər/ (also **lou·vre**) ▸*n.* **1** each of a set of angled slats or flat strips fixed or hung at regular intervals in a door, shutter, or screen to allow air or light to pass through. **2** a domed structure on a roof, with side openings for ventilation. —**lou·vered** *adj.*

lov·a·ble /ˈləvəbəl/ (also **love·a·ble**) ▸*adj.* inspiring or deserving love or affection. —**lov·a·bil·i·ty** /͵ləvəˈbilətē/ *n.* —**lov·a·ble·ness** *n.* —**lov·a·bly** /-blē/ *adv.*

lov·age /ˈləvij/ ▸*n.* a large, edible, white-flowered plant (esp. *Levisticum officinale*) of the parsley family.

love /ləv/ ▸*n.* **1** an intense feeling of deep affection: *babies fill parents with intense feelings of love.* ■ a deep romantic or sexual attachment to someone: *it was love at first sight.* ■ a great interest and pleasure in something: *his love for football.* ■ affectionate greetings conveyed to someone on one's behalf. **2** a person or thing that one loves: *she was the love of his life | their two great loves are tobacco and whiskey.* **3** (in tennis, squash, and some other sports) a score of zero; nil: *love fifteen | he was down two sets to love.*
▸*v.* [*tr.*] feel a deep romantic or sexual attachment to (someone): *do you love me?* ■ like very much; find pleasure in: *I'd love a cup of tea, thanks |* [as *adj.*, in *comb.*] (**-loving**) *a fun-loving girl.* —**love·less** *adj.* —**love·less·ly** *adv.* —**love·less·ness** *n.* —**love·wor·thy** /-͵wərTHē/ *adj.*
▸ □ **for love** for pleasure not profit: *he played for the love of the game.* □ **for the love of God** used to express annoyance, surprise, or urgent pleading: *for the love of God, get me out of here!* □ **make love 1** have sexual intercourse. **2** (**make love to**) *dated* pay amorous attention to (someone). □ **not for love or money** *inf.* not for any inducement or in any circumstances: *they'll not return for love or money.* □ **there's no** (or **little** or **not much**) **love lost between** there is mutual dislike between (two or more people mentioned).

love af·fair ▸*n.* a romantic or sexual relationship between two people, esp. one that is outside marriage. ■ an intense enthusiasm or liking for something: *the great American love affair with the automobile.*

love·bird /ˈləv͵bərd/ ▸*n.* **1** a very small African and Madagascan parrot (genus *Agapornis*) with mainly green plumage and typically a red or black face, noted for the affectionate behavior of mated birds. **2** (**lovebirds**) *inf.* an openly affectionate couple.

love child ▸*n.* a child born to parents who are not married to each other.

love·lorn /ˈləv͵lôrn/ ▸*adj.* unhappy because of unrequited love.

love·ly /ˈləvlē/ ▸*adj.* (**-li·er, -li·est**) exquisitely beautiful: *you have lovely eyes.* ■ *inf.* very pleasant or enjoyable; delightful: *she's a lovely person.*
▸*n.* (*pl.* **-lies**) *inf.* a glamorous woman or girl: *a bevy of rock lovelies.* —**love·li·ly** /-ləlē/ *adv.* —**love·li·ness** *n.*

love·mak·ing /ˈləv͵mākiNG/ ▸*n.* sexual activity between lovers, esp. sexual intercourse. ■ *archaic* courtship.

love nest ▸*n. inf.* a place where two lovers spend time together, esp. in secret.

lov·er /ˈləvər/ ▸*n.* a person having a sexual or romantic relationship with someone, often outside marriage. ■ a person who likes or enjoys something specified: *he was a great lover of cats.* —**lov·er·less** *adj.*

love seat ▸*n.* a small sofa for two people. ■ a small sofa for two people, designed in an S-shape so that the couple can face each other

love·sick /ˈləv͵sik/ ▸*adj.* in love, or missing the person one loves, so much that one is unable to act normally: *a lovesick teenager.* —**love·sick·ness** *n.*

love·y-dove·y /ˈləvē ˈdəvē/ ▸*adj. inf.* very affectionate or romantic, esp. excessively so: *a lovey-dovey couple.*

lov·ing /ˈləviNG/ ▸*adj.* feeling or showing love or great care: *a kind and loving father.*
▸*n.* the demonstration of love or great care. —**lov·ing·ly** *adv.* —**lov·ing·ness** *n.*

lov·ing cup ▸*n.* a large two-handled drinking vessel.

low[1] /lō/ ▸*adj.* **1** of less than average height from top to bottom or to the top from the ground: *a low table.* ■ situated not far above the ground, the horizon, or sea level: *the sun was low in the sky.* ■ located at or near the bottom of something: *low back pain | there were stunted trees low down on the ridge.* ■ *Baseball* (of a pitched ball) below a certain level, such as the batter's knees, as it comes across home plate, and thus outside the strike zone. ■ *Phonet.* (of a vowel) pronounced with the tongue held low in the mouth; open. ■ (of a sound or note) deep: *his low, husky voice.* **2** below average in amount, extent, or intensity; small: *bringing up children on a low income.* ■ (of a substance or food) containing smaller quantities than usual of a specified ingredient: *vegetables are low in calories |* [in *comb.*] *low-fat spreads.* ■ (of a sound) not loud: *they were told to keep the volume very low.* **3** ranking below other people or things in importance or class: *jobs with low status.* ■ less good than is expected or desired; inferior: *the standard of living is low.* ■ unscrupulous or dishonest: *practice a little low cunning.* ■ (of an opinion) unfavorable: *he had a low opinion of himself.* **4** depressed or lacking in energy: *I was feeling low.*
▸*n.* a low point, level or figure: *his popularity ratings are at an all-time low.* ■ a particularly bad or difficult moment: *the highs and lows of an actor's life.* ■ *inf.* a state of depression or low spirits. ■ an area of low atmospheric pressure; a depression.
▸*adv.* **1** in or into a low position or state: *she pressed on, bent low to protect her face.* **2** quietly: *we were talking low so we wouldn't wake Dean.* ■ at or to a low pitch: *the sopranos have to sing rather low.* —**low·ness** *n.*
▸ □ **the lowest of the low** the people regarded as the most immoral or socially inferior of all.

low[2] ▸*v.* [*intr.*] (of a cow) make a characteristic deep sound: [as *n.*] (**low·ing**) *the lowing of cattle.*
▸*n.* a sound made by cattle; a moo.

low·ball /ˈlō͵bôl/ ▸*adj. inf.* (of an estimate, bid, etc.) deceptively or unrealistically low.
▸*v.* [*tr.*] offer a deceptively or unrealistically low estimate, bid, etc.: *are you being lowballed by someone who hopes to make money on extras later?* —**low·ball·ing** *n.*

low beam ▸*n.* an automobile headlight providing short-range illumination, used on lit roads and when visible to oncoming traffic.

low·brow /ˈlō͵brou/ ▸*adj.* not highly intellectual or cultured: *lowbrow tabloids.*
▸*n.* a person of such a type.

low com·e·dy ▸*n.* comedy in which the subject and the treatment border on farce.

low·down /ˈlō͵doun/ *inf.* ▸*adj.* mean and unfair: *dirty lowdown tricks.*
▸*n.* (**the lowdown**) the true facts or relevant information about something: *get the lowdown on the sit-in.*

low·er[1] /ˈlōər/ ▸*adj.* **1** comparative of LOW[1]. **2** (of an animal or plant) showing relatively primitive or simple characteristics. **3** (often **Lower**) *Geol. & Archaeol.* denoting an older (and hence usually deeper) part of a stratigraphic division or archaeological deposit or the period in which it was formed or deposited: *Lower Cretaceous.* **4** [in *place names*] situated on less high land or to the south or toward the sea: *the sweatshops of the Lower East Side.*
▸*adv.* in or into a lower position: *the sun sank lower.* —**low·er·most** /-͵mōst/ *adj.*

low·er[2] /ˈlōər/ ▸*v.* [*tr.*] move (someone or something) in a downward direction: *he watched the coffin being lowered into the ground.* ■ reduce the height, pitch, or elevation of: *she lowered her voice to a whisper.* ■ make or become less in amount, extent, or value: [*tr.*] *traffic speeds must be lowered |* [*intr.*] *temperatures lowered.* ■ (**lower oneself**) behave in a way that is perceived as unworthy or debased.
▸ □ **lower the boom on** *inf.* treat or reprimand (someone) severely. ■ put a stop to (an activity): *let's lower the boom on high-level corruption.*

low·er³ /ˈlou(ə)r/ ▸v. [intr.] look angry or sullen; frown: *the lofty statue lowers at patients in the infirmary.* ■ (of the sky, weather, or landscape) look dark and threatening.
▸n. a scowl. ■ a dark and gloomy appearance of the sky, weather or landscape. —**low·er·ing·ly** adv.

low·er·case /ˈlōərˌkās/ (also **low·er case**) ▸n. small letters as opposed to capital letters (uppercase): *the name may be typed in lowercase | lowercase letters.*

low·er class /ˈlōər/ ▸n. [treated as *sing.* or *pl.*] the social group that has the lowest status; the working class.
▸adj. of, relating to, or characteristic of people belonging to such a group: *a lower-class area.*

low·er court /ˈlōər/ ▸n. Law a court whose decisions may be overruled by another court on appeal.

low·er house /ˈlōər/ ▸n. the larger of two sections of a bicameral legislature or parliament, typically with elected members and having the primary responsibility for legislation. ■ (**the Lower House**) (in the UK) the House of Commons.

low·est com·mon de·nom·i·na·tor ▸n. Math. the lowest common multiple of the denominators of several fractions. ■ figurative the broadest or most widely applicable requirement or circumstance.

low·est com·mon mul·ti·ple (abbr.: **LCM**) ▸n. Math. the lowest quantity that is a multiple of two or more given quantities (e.g., 12 is the lowest common multiple of 2, 3, and 4).

low gear ▸n. a gear that causes a wheeled vehicle to move slowly, because of a low ratio between the speed of the wheels and that of the mechanism driving them.

low-grade ▸adj. of low quality or strength: *low-grade steel.* ■ at a low level in a salary or employment structure: *low-grade clerical jobs.* ■ (of a medical condition) of a less serious kind; minor: *a low-grade fever.*

low-hang·ing fruit /ˈlō ˌhaNGiNG ˈfro͞ot/ ▸n. inf. a thing or person that can be won, obtained, or persuaded with little effort: *we know mining our own customer base is low-hanging fruit.*

low-key ▸adj. not elaborate, showy, or intensive; modest or restrained: *their wedding was a very quiet, low-key affair.* ■ Art & Photog. having a predominance of dark or muted tones.
▸v. [tr.] behave or speak with restraint: [as adj.] *a very simple, low-keyed style.*

low·land /ˈlōlənd; -ˌland/ ▸n. (also **low·lands**) low-lying country: *economic power gravitated toward the lowlands* | [as adj.] *lowland farming.* —**low·land·er** (also **Low·land·er**) n.

low-lev·el ▸adj. situated relatively near or below ground level: *low-level flying was banned.* ■ of or showing a small degree of some measurable quantity, for example radioactivity: *the dumping of low-level waste.* ■ of relatively little importance, scope, or prominence; basic: *opportunities to progress beyond low-level jobs.* ■ Comput. of or relating to programming languages or operations that are relatively close to machine code in form.

low·light /ˈlōˌlīt/ ▸n. inf. a particularly disappointing or dull event or feature.

low·ly /ˈlōlē/ ▸adj. (**low·li·er**, **low·li·est**) low in status or importance; humble: *she was too good for her lowly position.* ■ (of an organism) primitive or simple.
▸adv. to a low degree; in a low manner: *lowly paid workers.* —**low·li·ly** /ˈlōlə ˌlē/ adv. —**low·li·ness** n.

low-ly·ing ▸adj. at low altitude above sea level: *flooding problems in low-lying areas.*

low-main·te·nance /ˈlō ˈmānt(ə)nəns; ˈmāntn-əns/ ▸adj. requiring little work to keep in good condition: *low-maintenance lawns.* ■ inf. (of living and abstract things) desirably trouble-free and undemanding: *the shift toward the low-maintenance small companion dog.*

low-pitched ▸adj. **1** (of a sound or voice) deep or relatively quiet. **2** (of a roof) having only a slight slope.

low pro·file ▸n. a position of avoiding or not attracting much attention or publicity: *he's not the sort of politician to keep a low profile.*
▸adj. **1** avoiding attention or publicity: *a low-profile campaign.* **2** (of an object) lower or slimmer than is usual for objects of its type. ■ (of a motor vehicle tire) of smaller diameter and greater width than usual, for high-performance use.

low spir·its ▸pl. n. a feeling of sadness and despondency: *he was in low spirits.* —**low-spir·it·ed** adj. —**low-spir·it·ed·ness** n.

low tide ▸n. the state of the tide when at its lowest level: *islets visible at low tide.*

low wa·ter ▸n. another term for **LOW TIDE**. ■ water in a stream or river at its lowest point.

low-wa·ter mark ▸n. the lowest level reached by the sea at low tide, or by a lake or river during a drought or dry season. ■ a minimum recorded level or value: *the market was approaching its low-water mark.*

lox¹ /läks/ (also **LOX**) ▸n. liquid oxygen.

lox² ▸n. smoked salmon.

loy·al /ˈloiəl/ ▸adj. giving or showing firm and constant support or allegiance to a person or institution: *he remained loyal to the government | loyal service.* ▷mid 16th cent.: from French, via Old French *loial* from Latin *legalis* 'legal,' from *lex-, leg-* 'law.' —**loy·al·ly** adv.

loy·al·ist /ˈloiəlist/ ▸n. a person who remains loyal to the established ruler or government. ■ (**Loyalist**) a colonist of the American revolutionary period who supported the British cause. —**loy·al·ism** /-ˌlizəm/ n.

loy·al·ty /ˈloiəltē/ ▸n. (pl. **-ties**) the quality of being loyal to someone or something: *her loyalty to her husband of 34 years.* ■ (often **loyalties**) a strong feeling of support or allegiance: *fights with in-laws are distressing because they cause divided loyalties.*

loz·enge /ˈläzənj/ ▸n. a rhombus or diamond shape. ■ a small medicinal tablet taken for sore throats and dissolved in the mouth: *throat lozenges.*

LP ▸abbr. ■ long-playing (phonograph record): *two LP records | a collection of LPs.* ■ low pressure.

LSD ▸abbr. lysergic acid diethylamide, a synthetic crystalline compound that is a potent hallucinogenic drug.

Lt. ▸abbr. ■ lieutenant. ■ (also **lt**) light.

lt. ▸abbr. light.

Ltd. ▸abbr. (after a company name) Limited.

Lu ▸symb. the chemical element lutetium.

lu·bri·cant /ˈlo͞obrəkənt/ ▸n. a substance, such as oil or grease, used for minimizing friction, esp. in an engine or component.
▸adj. lubricating: *a thin lubricant film.*

lu·bri·cate /ˈlo͞obrəˌkāt/ ▸v. [tr.] apply a substance such as oil or grease to (an engine or component) to minimize friction and allow smooth movement: *remove the nut and lubricate the thread.* ■ make (something) slippery or smooth by applying an oily substance. ■ fig. make (a process) run smoothly: *the availability of credit lubricated the channels of trade.* ■ fig. make someone convivial, esp. with alcohol: *men lubricated with alcohol speak their true feelings.* —**lu·bri·ca·tion** /ˌlo͞obrəˈkāSHən/ n. —**lu·bri·ca·tor** /-ˌkātər/ n.

lu·bri·cious /lo͞oˈbriSHəs/ (also **lu·bri·cous** /ˈlo͞obrikəs/) ▸adj. **1** offensively displaying or intended to arouse sexual desire. **2** smooth and slippery with oil or a similar substance. —**lu·bri·cious·ly** adv. —**lu·bric·i·ty** /-ˈbrisitē/ n.

lu·cid /ˈlo͞osid/ ▸adj. expressed clearly; easy to understand: *a lucid account | write in a clear and lucid style.* ■ showing ability to think clearly, esp. in the intervals between periods of confusion or insanity: *he has a few lucid moments every now and then.* ■ Psychol. (of a dream) experienced with the dreamer feeling awake, aware of dreaming, and able to control events consciously. —**lu·cid·i·ty** /lo͞oˈsidətē/ n. —**lu·cid·ly** adv. —**lu·cid·ness** n.

Lu·ci·fer /ˈlo͞osəfər/ ▸n. another name for **SATAN**.

luck /lək/ ▸n. success or failure apparently brought by chance rather than through one's own actions: *it was just luck that the first kick went in.* ■ chance considered as a force that causes good or bad things to happen: *luck was with me.* ■ something regarded as bringing about or portending good or bad things: *I don't like Friday—it's bad luck.*
▸v. [intr.] (**luck into/onto**) inf. chance to find or acquire: *he lucked into a disc-jockey job.* ■ (**luck out**) achieve success or advantage by good luck: *I lucked out and found a wonderful woman.*
▸ □ **as luck would have it** used to indicate the fortuitousness of a situation: *as luck would have it, his route took him very near where they lived.* □ **be in** (or **out of**) **luck** be fortunate (or unfortunate). □ **no such luck** inf. used to express disappointment that something has not happened or is unlikely to happen.

luck·i·ly /ˈləkəlē/ ▸adv. it is fortunate that: *luckily they didn't recognize me.*

luck·less /ˈləkləs/ ▸adj. having bad luck; unfortunate. —**luck·less·ly** adv. —**luck·less·ness** n.

luck·y /ˈləkē/ ▸adj. (**luck·i·er**, **luck·i·est**) having, bringing, or resulting from good luck: *you had a very lucky escape.* —**luck·i·ness** n.
▸ □ **you, he,** etc., **should be so lucky** used to imply in an ironic or resigned way that someone's wishes or expectations are unlikely to be

fulfilled: *"Moving in?" "You should be so lucky."* □ **lucky devil** (or **lucky you**, **her**, etc.) used to express envy at someone else's good fortune.

lu·cra·tive /'lōōkrətiv/ ▶*adj.* producing a great deal of profit: *a lucrative career as a stand-up comedian.* —**lu·cra·tive·ly** *adv.* —**lu·cra·tive·ness** *n.*

lu·cre /'lōōkər/ ▶*n.* money, esp. when regarded as sordid or distasteful or gained in a dishonorable way: *officials getting their hands grubby with filthy lucre.* ▷late Middle English: from French *lucre* or Latin *lucrum*; the phrase *filthy lucre* is with biblical allusion to Titus 1:11.

Lud·dite /'ləd,īt/ ▶*n.* a member of any of the bands of English workers who destroyed machinery, esp. in cotton and woolen mills, that they believed was threatening their jobs (1811–16). ■ a person opposed to increased industrialization or new technology: *a small-minded Luddite resisting progress.* —**Lud·dism** /-,izəm/ *n.* —**Lud·dit·ism** /-,īt,izəm/ *n.*

lu·di·crous /'lōōdəkrəs/ ▶*adj.* so foolish, unreasonable, or out of place as to be amusing; ridiculous: *it's ludicrous that I have been fined.* —**lu·di·crous·ly** *adv.* —**lu·di·crous·ness** *n.*

luff /ləf/ *chiefly Sailing* ▶*n.* the edge of a fore-and-aft sail next to the mast or stay.
▶*v.* [*tr.*] steer (a sailing vessel) nearer the wind to the point at which the sails just begin to flap: *I came aft and luffed her for the open sea.*

lug[1] /ləg/ ▶*v.* (**lugged**, **lug·ging**) [*tr.*] carry or drag (a heavy or bulky object) with great effort: *she began to lug her suitcase down the stairs.* ■ *fig.* be encumbered with: *he had lugged his poor wife around for so long.*
▶*n.* a box or crate used for transporting fruit.

lug[2] ▶*n.* **1** a projection on an object by which it may be carried or fixed in place: *mount the fitting directly to the lugs at each side of the box.* **2** *inf.* an uncouth, aggressive man: *a hood who, despite his fancy clothes, remains a lug.*

luge /lōōzh/ ▶*n.* a light toboggan for one or two people, ridden in a sitting or supine position. ■ a sport in which competitors make a timed descent of a course riding such toboggans.
▶*v.* [*intr.*] ride on a luge.

lug·gage /'ləgij/ ▶*n.* suitcases or other bags in which to pack personal belongings for traveling.

lug nut ▶*n.* a large rounded nut that fits over a heavy bolt, used esp. to attach the wheel of a vehicle to its axle.

lug·sail /'ləgsəl; -,sāl/ ▶*n.* an asymmetrical four-sided sail that is hoisted on a steeply inclined yard.

lu·gu·bri·ous /lə'g(y)ōōbrēəs/ ▶*adj.* looking or sounding sad and dismal. —**lu·gu·bri·ous·ly** *adv.* —**lu·gu·bri·ous·ness** *n.*

luke·warm /'lōōk'wôrm/ ▶*adj.* (of liquid or food that should be hot) only moderately warm; tepid: *they drank bitter lukewarm coffee.* ■ (of a person, attitude, or action) unenthusiastic: *Israelis who had been lukewarm about the agreement.* —**luke·warm·ly** *adv.* —**luke·warm·ness** *n.*

lull /ləl/ ▶*v.* [*tr.*] calm or send to sleep, typically with soothing sounds or movements: *the rhythm of the boat lulled her to sleep.* ■ cause (someone) to feel deceptively secure or confident: *the rarity of earthquakes there has lulled people into a false sense of security.* ■ [*intr.*] (of noise or a storm) abate or fall quiet: *conversation lulled for an hour.*
▶*n.* a temporary interval of quiet or lack of activity: *for two days there had been a lull in the fighting.*

lull·a·by /'lələ,bī/ ▶*n.* (*pl.* **-bies**) a quiet, gentle song sung to send a child to sleep.

lum·ba·go /,ləm'bāgō/ ▶*n.* pain in the muscles and joints of the lower back.

lum·bar /'ləmbər; -,bär/ ▶*adj.* relating to the lower part of the back: *backache in the lumbar region.*

lum·ber[1] /'ləmbər/ ▶*v.* [*intr.*] move in a slow, heavy, awkward way: *a truck filled his mirror and lumbered past.*

lum·ber[2] ▶*n.* timber sawn into rough planks or otherwise partly prepared.
▶*v.* [*intr.*] [usu. as *n.*] (**lumbering**) cut and prepare forest timber for transport and sale: *the traditional resource industries of the nation, chiefly fishing and lumbering.*

lum·ber·jack /'ləmbər,jak/ ▶*n.* (a person who fells trees, cuts them into logs, or transports them to a sawmill. Also called **LUMBERMAN**.

lum·ber·man /'ləmbər,mən/ ▶*n.* (*pl.* **-men** /-mən/) another term for **LUMBERJACK**.

lum·ber·yard /'ləmbər,yärd/ ▶*n.* a place that sells lumber and other building materials, usu. outdoors.

lu·men[1] /'lōōmən/ (abbr.: **lm**) ▶*n.* *Physics* the SI unit of luminous flux, equal to the amount of light emitted per second in a unit solid angle of one steradian from a uniform source of one candela.

lu·men[2] ▶*n.* (*pl.* **-mi·na** /-mənə/) *Anat.* the central cavity of a tubular or other hollow structure in an organism or cell. —**lu·mi·nal** /-mənl/ *adj.*

lu·mi·nance /'lōōmənəns/ ▶*n.* *Physics* the intensity of light emitted from a surface per unit area in a given direction.

lu·mi·nar·y /'lōōmə,nerē/ ▶*n.* (*pl.* **-nar·ies**) **1** a person who inspires or influences others, esp. one prominent in a particular sphere: *one of the luminaries of child psychiatry.* **2** an artificial light. ■ *poetic/lit.* a natural light-giving body, esp. the sun or moon.

lu·mi·nes·cence /,lōōmə'nesəns/ ▶*n.* the emission of light by a substance that has not been heated, as in fluorescence and phosphorescence. —**lu·mi·nes·cent** *adj.*

lu·mi·nous /'lōōmənəs/ ▶*adj.* full of or shedding light; bright or shining, esp. in the dark: *the luminous dial on his watch.* ■ (of a person's complexion or eyes) glowing with health, vigor, or a particular emotion: *her eyes were luminous with joy.* —**lu·mi·nos·i·ty** /,lōōmə'nositē/ *n.* —**lu·mi·nous·ly** *adv.* —**lu·mi·nous·ness** *n.*

lum·mox /'ləməks/ ▶*n.* *inf.* a clumsy, stupid person: *watch it, you great lummox!*

lump[1] /ləmp/ ▶*n.* a compact mass of a substance, esp. one without a definite or regular shape: *there was a lump of ice floating in the milk.* ■ *inf.* a heavy, ungainly, or slow-witted person: *I wouldn't stand a chance against a big lump like you.*
▶*v.* **1** [*tr.*] put in an indiscriminate mass or group; treat as alike without regard for particulars: *Hong Kong and Bangkok tend to be lumped together in travel brochures.* ■ [*intr.*] (in taxonomy) classify plants or animals in relatively inclusive groups, disregarding minor variations. **2** [*intr.*] (**lump along**) proceed heavily or awkwardly: *I came lumping along behind him.* **3** [*intr.*] concentrate or assemble together in an irregular mass: *we're lumped in a limo, bound for a Los Angeles medical center.*
▶ □ **a lump in the throat** a feeling of tightness or dryness in the throat caused by strong emotion, esp. sadness: *there was a lump in her throat as she gazed down at her uncle's gaunt features.* □ **take** (or **get**) **one's lumps** *inf.* suffer punishment; be attacked or defeated.

lump[2] ▶*v.* [*tr.*] (**lump it**) *inf.* accept or tolerate a disagreeable situation whether one likes it or not: *you can like it or lump it but I've got to work.*

lump·ec·to·my /,ləm'pektəmē/ ▶*n.* (*pl.* **-mies**) a surgical operation in which a lump is removed from the breast, typically when cancer is present but has not spread.

lump·ish /'ləmpish/ ▶*adj.* roughly or clumsily formed or shaped: *those large and lumpish hands could produce exquisitely fine work.* ■ (of a person) stupid and lethargic. —**lump·ish·ly** *adv.* —**lump·ish·ness** *n.*

lump sum ▶*n.* a single payment made at a particular time, as opposed to a number of smaller payments or installments.

lump·y /'ləmpē/ ▶*adj.* (**lump·i·er**, **lump·i·est**) full of or covered with lumps: *he lay on the lumpy mattress.* ■ *Naut.* (of water) formed by the wind into small waves: *a large lumpy sea.* —**lump·i·ly** /-pəlē/ *adv.* —**lump·i·ness** *n.*

lu·na·cy /'lōōnəsē/ ▶*n.* (*pl.* **-cies**) the state of being a lunatic; insanity (not in technical use): *it has been suggested that originality demands a degree of lunacy.* ■ extreme folly or eccentricity: *such an economic policy would be sheer lunacy.*

lu·na moth /'lōōnə/ ▶*n.* a very large North American moth (*Actias luna*, family Saturniidae) that has pale green wings with long tails and transparent eyespots bearing crescent-shaped markings.

lu·nar /'lōōnər/ ▶*adj.* of, determined by, relating to, or resembling the moon: *a lunar landscape.*

lu·nar mod·ule (abbr.: **LM**) ▶*n.* a small craft used for traveling between the moon's surface and an orbiting spacecraft (formerly known as **lunar excursion module** or **LEM**).

lu·nar month ▶*n.* a month measured between successive new moons (roughly 29 1/2 days). ■ (in general use) a period of four weeks.

lu·nar year ▶*n.* a period of twelve lunar months (approx. 354 days).

lu·na·tic /'lōōnə,tik/ ▶*n.* a mentally ill person (not in technical use). ■ an extremely foolish or eccentric person: *this lunatic just accelerated out of the side of the road.*
▶*adj.* mentally ill (not in technical use). ■ extremely foolish, eccentric, or absurd: *he would be asked to acquiesce in some lunatic scheme.* ▷Middle English: from Old French *lunatique*, from late Latin *lunaticus*, from Latin *luna* 'moon' (from the belief that changes of the moon caused intermittent insanity).

lu·na·tic fringe ▶*n.* an extreme or eccentric minority within society or a group.

lunch /ləncн/ ▶*n.* a meal eaten in the middle of the day, typically one that is lighter or less formal than an evening meal: *a vegetarian lunch.*
▶*v.* [*intr.*] eat lunch: *he told his wife he was lunching with a client.* ■ [*tr.*] take

(someone) out for lunch: *public relations people lunch their clients there.* **—lunch·er** *n.*

▶ ☐ **do lunch** *inf.* meet for lunch. ☐ **out to lunch** *inf.* unaware of or inattentive to present conditions.

lunch·box /'lənCH,bäks/ ▶*n.* a container in which to carry a packed meal. Also called **lunch bucket**, **lunch·pail**. ■ a portable computer slightly larger than a laptop.

lunch·eon /'lənCHən/ ▶*n.* a formal lunch, or a formal word for lunch.

lunch·eon·ette /,lənCHə'net/ ▶*n.* a small, informal restaurant serving lunches.

lunch·time /'lənCH,tīm/ ▶*n.* the time in the middle of day when lunch is eaten.

lu·nette /lōō'net/ ▶*n.* something crescent-shaped, in particular: ■ an arched aperture or window, esp. one in a domed ceiling. ■ a crescent-shaped or semicircular alcove containing something such as a painting or statue.

lung /ləNG/ ▶*n.* each of the pair of organs situated within the rib cage, consisting of elastic sacs with branching passages into which air is drawn, so that oxygen can pass into the blood and carbon dioxide be removed. **—lunged** /ləNGd/ *adj.* [in *comb.*] *strong-lunged.* **—lung·ful** /-,fŏŏl/ *n.* (*pl.* **-fuls**) **—lung·less** *adj.*

lunge /lənj/ ▶*n.* a sudden forward thrust of the body, typically with an arm outstretched to attack someone or seize something: *he made a lunge at her.* ■ the basic attacking move in fencing, in which the leading foot is thrust forward with the knee bent while the back leg remains straightened. ■ an exercise or gymnastic movement resembling the lunge of a fencer.

▶*v.* (**lung·ing** or **lunge·ing**) [*intr.*] make a lunge: *the sequined guests lunged at the food.* ■ [*tr.*] make a sudden forward thrust with (a part of the body or a weapon): *Billy lunged his spear at the fish.*

lung·fish /'ləNG,fish/ ▶*n.* (*pl.* same or **-fishes**) an elongated freshwater fish (families Ceratodontidae, Lepidosirenidae, and Protopteridae) with one or two sacs that function as lungs, enabling it to breathe air. It can estivate in mud for long periods to survive drought.

lu·pine[1] /'lōōpin/ ▶*n.* a plant (genus *Lupinus*) of the pea family, with deeply divided leaves and tall, colorful, tapering spikes of flowers.

lu·pine[2] /'lōō,pīn/ ▶*adj.* of, like, or relating to a wolf or wolves.

lu·pus /'lōōpəs/ ▶*n.* any of various ulcerous skin diseases. **—lu·poid** /-,poid/ *adj.* **—lu·pous** /-pəs/ *adj.*

lurch[1] /lərCH/ ▶*n.* an abrupt uncontrolled movement, esp. an unsteady tilt or roll: *the boat gave a violent lurch, and he missed his footing.*

▶*v.* [*intr.*] make an abrupt, unsteady, uncontrolled movement or series of movements; stagger: *the car lurched forward.*

lurch[2] ▶*n.* (in phrase **leave someone in the lurch**) leave someone abruptly and without assistance or support in a difficult situation.

lure /lŏŏr/ ▶*v.* [*tr.*] tempt (a person or an animal) to do something or to go somewhere, esp. by offering some form of reward: *the child was lured into a car but managed to escape.*

▶*n.* something that tempts or is used to tempt a person or animal to do something: *the film industry always has been a glamorous lure for young girls.* ■ the strongly attractive quality of a person or thing: *the lure of the exotic East.* ■ a type of bait used in fishing or hunting. ■ *Falconry* a bunch of feathers with a weighted object attached to a long string, swung around the head of the falconer to recall a hawk.

Lur·ex /'lŏŏr,eks/ (also **lur·ex**) ▶*n. trademark* a type of yarn or fabric that incorporates a glittering metallic thread.

lu·rid /'lŏŏrid/ ▶*adj.* very vivid in color, esp. so as to create an unpleasantly harsh or unnatural effect: *lurid food colorings.* ■ (of a description) presented in vividly shocking or sensational terms, esp. giving explicit details of crimes or sexual matters: *the more lurid details of the massacre were too frightening for the children.* **—lu·rid·ly** *adv.* **—lu·rid·ness** *n.*

lurk /lərk/ ▶*v.* [*intr.*] (of a person or animal) be or remain hidden so as to wait in ambush for someone or something: *a ruthless killer still lurked in the darkness.* ■ (of an unpleasant quality) be present in a latent or barely discernible state, although still presenting a threat: *fear lurks beneath the surface.* ■ [*intr.*] read communications on an electronic network without making one's presence known.

lurk·er /'lərkər/ ▶*n.* one who lurks, in particular a user of an Internet chat room or newsgroup who does not participate.

lus·cious /'ləSHəs/ ▶*adj.* (of food or wine) having a pleasingly rich, sweet taste: *a luscious and fragrant dessert wine.* ■ richly verdant or opulent. ■ (of a woman) very sexually attractive. **—lus·cious·ly** *adv.* **—lus·cious·ness** *n.*

lush[1] /ləSH/ ▶*adj.* (of vegetation) growing luxuriantly: *lush greenery and*

cultivated fields. ■ opulent and luxurious: *a hall of gleaming marble, as lush as a Byzantine church.* **—lush·ly** *adv.* **—lush·ness** *n.*

lush[2] *inf.* ▶*n.* a heavy drinker, esp. a habitual one.

lust /ləst/ ▶*n.* very strong sexual desire: *he knew that his lust for her had returned.* ■ a passionate desire for something: *a lust for power.* ■ (usu. **lusts**) *chiefly Theol.* a sensual appetite regarded as sinful: *lusts of the flesh.*

▶*v.* [*intr.*] have a very strong sexual desire for someone: *he really lusted after me in those days.* ■ feel a strong desire for something: *pregnant women lusting for pickles and ice cream.* **—lust·ful** /-(t)fəl/ *adj.* **—lust·ful·ly** /-(t)fəlē/ *adv.* **—lust·ful·ness** /-(t)fəlnəs/ *n.*

lus·ter /'ləstər/ (*Brit.* **lus·tre**) ▶*n.* **1** a gentle sheen or soft glow, esp. that of a partly reflective surface: *the luster of the Milky Way.* ■ *fig.* glory or distinction: *a celebrity player to add luster to the lineup.* ■ the manner in which the surface of a mineral reflects light. **2** a substance imparting or having a shine or glow, in particular: ■ a thin coating containing unoxidized metal that gives an iridescent glaze to ceramics. ■ ceramics with such a glaze; lusterware. ■ a type of finish on a photographic print, less reflective than a glossy finish. **3** a prismatic glass pendant on a chandelier or other ornament. ■ a cut-glass chandelier or candelabra. **—lus·ter·less** *adj.* **—lus·trous** /-trəs/ *adj.*

lus·ter·ware /'ləstər,wer/ (*Brit.* **lus·tre·ware**) ▶*n.* ceramic articles with an iridescent metallic glaze.

lust·y /'ləstē/ ▶*adj.* (**lust·i·er**, **lust·i·est**) healthy and strong; full of vigor: *lusty singing.* **—lust·i·ly** /-təlē/ *adv.* **—lust·i·ness** *n.*

lute /lōōt/ ▶*n.* a plucked stringed instrument with a long neck bearing frets and a rounded body with a flat front.

lute

lu·te·in·iz·ing hor·mone /'lōōtēə,nīziNG; 'lōōtn,īziNG/ ▶*n. Biochem.* a hormone secreted by the anterior pituitary gland that stimulates ovulation in females and the synthesis of androgen in males.

lu·te·nist /'lōōtn-ist; 'lōōtnist/ (also **lu·ta·nist**) ▶*n.* a lute player.

lu·te·ti·um /lōō'tēSH(ē)əm/ ▶*n.* the chemical element of atomic number 71, a rare, silvery-white metal of the lanthanide series. (Symbol: **Lu**)

Lu·ther·an /'lōōTH(ə)rən/ ▶*n.* a follower of Martin Luther. ■ a member of the Lutheran Church.

▶*adj.* of or characterized by the theology of Martin Luther. ■ of or relating to the Lutheran Church. **—Lu·ther·an·ism** /-,nizəm/ *n.* **—Lu·ther·an·ize** /-,nīz/ *v.*

lutz /ləts; lŏŏts/ (also **Lutz**) ▶*n. Figure Skating* a jump with a backward takeoff from the backward outside edge of one skate to the backward outside edge of the other, with one or more full turns in the air.

lux /ləks/ (*abbr.*: **lx**) ▶*n.* (*pl.* same) the SI unit of illuminance, equal to one lumen per square meter.

luxe /ləks; lŏŏks/ ▶*n.* luxury: [as *adj.*] *the luxe life.*

lux·u·ri·ant /,ləg'zhŏŏrēənt; ,lək'shŏŏr-/ ▶*adj.* rich and profuse in growth; lush: *forests of dark, luxuriant foliage.* ■ (of hair) thick and healthy. **—lux·u·ri·ance** *n.* **—lux·u·ri·ant·ly** *adv.*

lux·u·ri·ate /,ləg'zhŏŏrē,āt; ,lək'shŏŏr-/ ▶*v.* [*intr.*] (often **luxuriate in**) enjoy oneself in a luxurious way; take self-indulgent delight: *she was luxuriating in a long bath.*

lux·u·ri·ous /,ləg'zhŏŏrēəs; ,lək'shŏŏr-/ ▶*adj.* extremely comfortable, elegant, or enjoyable, esp. in a way that involves great expense: *the bedrooms have luxurious marble bathrooms.* ■ giving self-indulgent or sensuous pleasure: *a luxurious wallow in a scented bath.* **—lux·u·ri·ous·ly** *adv.* **—lux·u·ri·ous·ness** *n.*

lux·u·ry /'ləkSH(ə)rē; 'ləgzh(ə)-/ ▶*n.* (*pl.* **-ries**) the state of great comfort

and extravagant living: *he lived a life of luxury.* ■ an inessential, desirable item that is expensive or difficult to obtain: *luxuries like raspberry vinegar and state-of-the-art CD players.*
▶*adj.* luxurious or of the nature of a luxury: *a luxury yacht | luxury goods.* ▷Middle English (denoting lechery): from Old French *luxurie, luxure,* from Latin *luxuria,* from *luxus* 'excess.' The earliest current sense dates from the mid 17th cent.

Ly·cra /ˈlīkrə/ ▶*n. trademark* an elastic polyurethane fiber or fabric used esp. for close-fitting and sports clothing.

lye /lī/ ▶*n.* a strongly alkaline solution, esp. of potassium hydroxide, used for washing or cleansing.

ly·ing[1] /ˈlī-iNG/ ▶ present participle of **LIE**[1].

ly·ing[2] ▶ present participle of **LIE**[2].
▶*adj.* not telling the truth: *he's a lying, cheating snake in the grass.* —**ly·ing·ly** *adv.*

Lyme dis·ease /līm/ ▶*n.* an inflammatory disease characterized by a rash, headache, fever, and chills, and then by possible arthritis and neurological and cardiac disorders. It is caused by a spirochete that is transmitted by ticks.

lymph /limf/ ▶*n.* **1** *Physiol.* a colorless fluid containing white blood cells, that bathes the tissues and drains through the lymphatic system into the bloodstream. ■ fluid exuding from a sore or inflamed tissue. **2** *poetic/lit.* pure water. —**lymph·ous** /-fəs/ *adj.*

lym·phat·ic /limˈfatik/ ▶*adj. Physiol.* of or relating to lymph or its secretion: *lymphatic vessels.*
▶*n. Anat.* a veinlike vessel conveying lymph in the body.

lym·phat·ic sys·tem ▶*n.* the network of vessels through which lymph drains from the tissues into the blood.

lymph node ▶*n. Physiol.* each of a number of small swellings in the lymphatic system where lymph is filtered and lymphocytes are formed.

lym·pho·cyte /ˈlimfəˌsīt/ ▶*n. Physiol.* a form of small leukocyte (white blood cell) with a single round nucleus, occurring esp. in the lymphatic system. —**lym·pho·cyt·ic** /ˌlimfəˈsitik/ *adj.*

lym·pho·ma /limˈfōmə/ ▶*n.* (*pl.* **-mas** or **-ma·ta** /-mətə/) *Med.* cancer of the lymph nodes.

lynch /linCH/ ▶*v.* [*tr.*] (of a mob) kill (someone), esp. by hanging, for an alleged offense with or without a legal trial. —**lynch·er** *n.*

lynch·pin /ˈlinCHˌpin/ ▶*n.* variant spelling of **LINCHPIN**.

lynx /liNGks/ ▶*n.* a wild cat (genus *Lynx*) with yellowish-brown fur (sometimes spotted), a short tail, and tufted ears, found chiefly in the northern latitudes of North America and Eurasia. ■ the fur of the lynx. ■ (**African lynx**) see **CARACAL**.

lynx-eyed ▶*adj.* keen-sighted.

ly·o·cell /ˈlīəˌsel/ ▶*n.* a strong synthetic fiber made from reconstituted cellulose, used in carpets and in apparel when blended with other fibers.

lyre /ˈlī(ə)r/ ▶*n.* a stringed instrument like a small U-shaped harp with strings fixed to a crossbar, used esp. in ancient Greece. Modern instruments of this type are found mainly in East Africa.

lyre·bird /ˈlī(ə)rˌbərd/ ▶*n.* a large Australian songbird (genus *Menura,* family Menuridae), the male of which has a long, lyre-shaped tail and is noted for his remarkable song and display.

lyr·ic /ˈlirik/ ▶*adj.* **1** (of poetry) expressing the writer's emotions, usually briefly and in stanzas or recognized forms. ■ (of a poet) writing in this manner. **2** (of a singing voice) using a light register: *a lyric soprano with a light, clear timbre.*

lyre

▶*n.* (usu. **lyrics**) **1** a lyric poem or verse. ■ lyric poetry as a literary genre. **2** the words of a song: *she has published both music and lyrics for a number of songs.*

lyr·i·cal /ˈlirikəl/ ▶*adj.* **1** (of literature, art, or music) expressing the writer's emotions in an imaginative and beautiful way: *the poet's combination of lyrical and descriptive power.* **2** of or relating to the words of a popular song: *the lyrical content of his songs.* —**lyr·i·cal·ly** /-ik(ə)lē/ *adv.*

lyr·i·cism /ˈlirəˌsizəm/ ▶*n.* an artist's expression of emotion in an imaginative and beautiful way; the quality of being lyrical.

lyr·i·cist /ˈlirəsist/ ▶*n.* a person who writes the words to a popular song or musical.

ly·ser·gic ac·id /līˈsərjik; li-/ ▶*n. Chem.* a crystalline compound prepared from natural ergot alkaloids or synthetically, from which the drug LSD can be made.

ly·sin /ˈlīsin/ ▶*n. Biol.* an antibody or other substance able to cause lysis of cells (esp. bacteria).

ly·sine /ˈlīˌsēn/ ▶*n. Biochem.* a basic amino acid that is a constituent of most proteins. It is an essential nutrient in the diet of vertebrates.

ly·sis /ˈlīsis/ ▶*n.* **1** *Biol.* the disintegration of a cell by rupture of the cell wall or membrane. **2** the gradual decline of disease symptoms. ▷early 19th cent.: from Latin, from Greek *lusis* 'loosening,' from *luein* 'loosen.'

ly·so·some /ˈlīsəˌsōm/ ▶*n. Biol.* an organelle in the cytoplasm of eukaryotic cells containing degradative enzymes enclosed in a membrane. —**ly·so·so·mal** /ˌlīsəˈsōməl/ *adj.*

lyt·ic /ˈlitik/ ▶*adj. Biol.* of, relating to, or causing lysis: *the lytic activity of bile acids.* —**lyt·i·cal·ly** /ik(ə)lē/ *adv.*

L

Mm

M¹ /em/ (also **m**) ▶*n.* (*pl.* **Ms** or **M's**) **1** the thirteenth letter of the alphabet. See also EM. ■ denoting the next after L in a set of items, categories, etc. **2** (**M**) a shape like that of a capital M. **3** the Roman numeral for 1,000.

M² ▶*abbr.* ■ Majesty. ■ male. ■ Marquis. ■ *Mus.* measure. ■ medicine. ■ medium (as a clothes size). ■ [in *comb.*] (in units of measurement) mega-: *8 Mbytes of memory.* ■ meridian. ■ *Chem.* (with reference to solutions) molar: *0.15 M NaCl solution.* ■ Monday. ■ Monsieur: *M Chirac.* ■ noon.

M³ ▶*symb. Physics* mutual inductance.

m ▶*abbr.* ■ mare. ■ (in Germany) mark; marks. ■ married: *m twice; two d.* ■ masculine. ■ *Physics* mass. ■ (**m-**) [in *comb.*] *Chem.* meta-: m-*xylene.* ■ meter(s). ■ middle. ■ mile(s). ■ [in *comb.*] (in units of measurement) milli-: *100 mA.* ■ million(s): *$5 m.* ■ minute(s). ■ modulus. ■ molar. ■ month. ■ moon. ■ morning. ■ mouth. ■ noon.
▶*symb. Physics* mass: *E = mc².*

'm¹ /m/ *inf.* ▶*abbr.* am: *I'm a doctor.*

'm² ▶*n. inf.* madam: *yes'm.*

MA ▶*abbr.* ■ Master of Arts: *David Jones, MA.* ■ *Psychol.* mental age. ■ Military Academy.

ma /mä/ ▶*n. inf.* one's mother: *I didn't want to make trouble for my ma.*

ma'am /mam/ ▶*n.* a term of respectful or polite address used for a woman: *excuse me, ma'am.*

Mac /mak/ ▶*n. inf.* a form of address for a man whose name is unknown to the speaker.

ma·ca·bre /məˈkäbrə; -ˈkäb/ ▶*adj.* disturbing and horrifying because of involvement with or depiction of death and injury.

mac·ad·am /məˈkadəm/ ▶*n.* broken stone used in successively compacted layers for surfacing roads and paths, and typically bound with tar or bitumen. —**mac·ad·amed** *adj.*

mac·a·da·mi·a /ˌmakəˈdämēə/ ▶*n.* an Australian tree (genus *Macadamia*, family Proteaceae) with glossy evergreen leaves and globular edible nuts. ■ (also **macadamia nut**) the edible nut of this tree.

ma·caque /məˈkäk; -ˈkak/ (also **macaque monkey**) ▶*n.* a medium-sized Old World monkey (genus *Macaca*) that has a long face and cheek pouches for holding food. Its several species include the rhesus monkey and the barbary ape.

mac·a·ro·ni /ˌmakəˈrōnē/ ▶*n.* (*pl.* **-nies**) **1** a variety of pasta formed in narrow tubes. **2** an 18th-century British dandy affecting Continental fashions. ▷late 16th cent.: from Italian *maccaroni* (now usually spelled *maccheroni*), plural of *maccarone*, from late Greek *makaria* 'food made from barley.'

mac·a·roon /ˌmakəˈrōōn/ ▶*n.* a light cookie made with egg white, sugar, and usually ground almonds or coconut.

ma·caw /məˈkô/ ▶*n.* a large long-tailed parrot (*Ara* and related genera) with brightly colored plumage, native to Central and South America.

Mace /mās/ ▶*n. trademark* an irritant chemical used in an aerosol to disable attackers.
▶*v.* (also **mace**) [*tr.*] spray (someone) with Mace.

mace¹ /mās/ ▶*n.* **1** *hist.* a heavy club, typically having a metal head and spikes. **2** a ceremonial staff of office.

mace² ▶*n.* the reddish fleshy outer covering of the nutmeg, dried as a spice.

mac·er·ate /ˈmasəˌrāt/ ▶*v.* [*tr.*] **1** soften or break up (something, esp. food) by soaking in a liquid. ■ [*intr.*] become softened or broken up by soaking. **2** *archaic* cause to grow thinner or waste away, esp. by fasting. —**mac·er·a·tion** /ˌmasəˈrāsHən/ *n.* —**mac·er·a·tor** /-ˌrātər/ *n.*

Mach (also **Mach number**) ▶*n.* the ratio of the speed of a body to the speed of sound in the surrounding medium. It is often used with a numeral (as **Mach 1**, **Mach 2**, etc.) to indicate the speed of sound, twice the speed of sound, etc.

ma·chet·e /məˈsHetē/ ▶*n.* a broad, heavy knife used as an implement or weapon, originating in Central America and the Caribbean.

machete

Mach·i·a·vel·li·an /ˌmakēəˈvelēən; ˌmäk-/ ▶*adj.* **1** cunning, scheming, and unscrupulous, esp. in politics or in advancing one's career. **2** of or relating to Niccolò Machiavelli.
▶*n.* a person who schemes in such a way. —**Mach·i·a·vel·li·an·ism** /-ˌnizəm/ *n.*

mach·i·nate /ˈmakəˌnāt; ˈmasHə-/ ▶*v.* [*intr.*] engage in plots and intrigues; scheme. —**mach·i·na·tion** /ˌmakəˈnāsHən; ˌmasHə-/ *n.* —**mach·i·na·tor** /-ˌnātər/ *n.*

ma·chine /məˈsHēn/ ▶*n.* an apparatus using or applying mechanical power and having several parts, each with a definite function and together performing a particular task. ■ a coin-operated dispenser: *a candy machine.* ■ *technical* any device that transmits a force or directs its application. ■ *fig.* an efficient and well-organized group of powerful people: *a powerful political machine.* ■ *fig.* a person who acts with the mechanical efficiency of a machine: *comedians are laugh machines.*
▶*v.* [*tr.*] (esp. in manufacturing) make or operate on with a machine: [as *adj.*] (**machined**) *a decoratively machined brass rod.*

ma·chine gun ▶*n.* an automatic gun that fires bullets in rapid succession for as long as the trigger is pressed.
▶*v.* (**ma·chine-gun**) [*tr.*] shoot with a machine gun. —**ma·chine-gun·ner** *n.*

ma·chine-read·a·ble ▶*adj.* (of data or text) in a form that a computer can process.

ma·chin·er·y /məˈsHēn(ə)rē/ ▶*n.* machines collectively: *farm machinery.* ■ the components of a machine: *the movement of the machinery.* ■ the organization or structure of something: *the machinery of democracy.* ■ the means devised or available to do something: *with the grievance machinery in place.*

ma·chine tool ▶*n.* a nonportable power tool, such as a lathe or milling machine, used for cutting or shaping metal, wood, or other material. —**ma·chine-tooled** *adj.*

ma·chin·i·ma /məˈsHēnəmə/ ▶*n.* a method of making animated film using software similar to that designed for making video and computer games. ■ the genre of films created in this way.

ma·chin·ist /məˈsHēnist/ ▶*n.* a person who operates a machine, esp. a machine tool. ■ a person who makes or repairs machinery.

ma·chis·mo /məˈcHēzmō; -ˈkēz-/ ▶*n.* strong or aggressive masculine pride. ■ *fig.* daring or bravado.

Mach num·ber ▶*n.* see MACH.

ma·cho /ˈmäcHō/ ▶*adj.* showing aggressive pride in one's masculinity: *the big macho tough guy.*
▶*n.* (*pl.* **-chos**) a man who is aggressively proud of his masculinity. ■ machismo.

mac·in·tosh ▶*n.* variant spelling of MACKINTOSH.

mack ▶*n. chiefly Brit.* short for MACKINTOSH.

mack·er·el /ˈmak(ə)rəl/ ▶*n.* (*pl.* same or **mackerels**) a migratory surface-dwelling predatory fish. The **mackerel family** (Scombridae) includes many species, in particular the **North Atlantic mackerel** (*Scomber scombrus*), commercially important as a food fish.

mack·er·el sky ▶ *n.* a sky dappled with rows of small white fleecy clouds, like the pattern on a mackerel's back.

mack·in·tosh /'makən,täsH/ (also **mac·in·tosh**) ▶ *n. chiefly Brit.* a full-length waterproof coat. ■ [usu. as *adj.*] cloth waterproofed with rubber.

mac·ra·mé /'makrə,mā/ ▶ *n.* the art of knotting cord or string in patterns to make decorative articles. ■ [usu. as *adj.*] fabric or articles made in this way.

mac·ro /'makrō/ ▶ *n.* (*pl.* **-ros**) (also **macro instruction**) *Comput.* a single instruction that expands automatically into a set of instructions to perform a particular task.
▶ *adj.* large-scale; overall: *the analysis of social events at the macro level.* Often contrasted with MICRO.

mac·ro·bi·ot·ic /,makrōbī'ätik/ ▶ *adj.* constituting, relating to, or following a diet of whole pure prepared foods that is based on Taoist principles of the balance of yin and yang.
▶ *pl. n.* (**macrobiotics**) [treated as *sing.*] the use or theory of such a diet.

mac·ro·cosm /'makrə,käzəm/ (also **mac·ro·cos·mos** /-,käzməs; -mōs/) ▶ *n.* the universe; the cosmos. ■ the whole of a complex structure, esp. as represented or epitomized in a small part of itself (a microcosm). —**mac·ro·cos·mic** /,makrə'käzmik/ *adj.* —**mac·ro·cos·mi·cal·ly** /,makrə'käzmik(ə)lē/ *adv.*

mac·ro·ec·o·nom·ics /'makrō,ekə'nämiks; -,ēkə-/ ▶ *pl. n.* [treated as *sing.*] the part of economics concerned with large-scale or general economic factors, such as interest rates and national productivity. —**mac·ro·ec·o·nom·ic** *adj.* —**mac·ro·e·con·o·mist** /-i'känəmist/ *n.*

ma·cron /'mā,krän; 'mak-; 'mākrən/ ▶ *n.* a written or printed mark (¯) used to indicate a long vowel in some languages and phonetic transcription systems, or a stressed vowel in verse.

mac·ro·phage /'makrə,fāj/ ▶ *n. Physiol.* a large phagocytic cell found in stationary form in the tissues or as a mobile white blood cell, esp. at sites of infection.

mac·ro·pod /'makrə,päd/ ▶ *n. Zool.* a plant-eating marsupial (*Macropus* and other genera) of an Australasian family (Macropodidae) that comprises the kangaroos and wallabies.

mac·ro·scop·ic /,makrə'skäpik/ ▶ *adj.* visible to the naked eye; not microscopic. ■ of or relating to large-scale or general analysis. —**mac·ro·scop·i·cal·ly** /-ik(ə)lē/ *adv.*

mad /mad/ ▶ *adj.* (**mad·der**, **mad·dest**) mentally ill; insane: *he felt as if he were going mad.* ■ (of a person, conduct, or an idea) extremely foolish or ill-advised. in a frenzied mental or physical state: *loved ones mad with anxiety about her | a mad dash to get ready.* ■ *inf.* enthusiastic about someone or something: *I wasn't mad about mountain bikes* | [in *comb.*] *a sports-mad nation.* ■ *inf.* very angry: *they were mad at each other.* ■ (of a dog) rabid. ■ *Brit., inf.* very exciting.
▶ *v.* (**mad·ded** /madəd/, **mad·ding**) [*tr.*] *archaic* make mad or insane. —**mad·ness** *n.*
▶ □ **like mad** *inf.* with great intensity, energy, or enthusiasm: *I ran like mad.* □ (**as**) **mad as a hatter** *inf.* completely crazy.

mad·am /'madəm/ ▶ *n.* used to address or refer to a woman in a polite or respectful way: *Can I help you, madam?* ■ (**Madam**) used to address a woman at the start of a formal or business letter: *Dear Madam, . . .* ■ (**Madam**) used before a title to address or refer to a female holder of that position: *Madam President.* ■ a woman who runs a brothel.

Mad·ame /mə'däm; -'dam/ ▶ *n.* (*pl.* **Mes·dames** /mā'däm; -'dam/) a title or form of address used of or to a French-speaking woman: *Madame Bovary.* ■ used as a title for women in artistic or exotic occupations, such as musicians or fortune-tellers.

mad·cap /'mad,kap/ ▶ *adj.* amusingly eccentric: *a surreal, madcap novel.* ■ done or thought up without considering the consequences; crazy or reckless: *some madcap money-making scheme.*
▶ *n.* an eccentric person.

mad cow dis·ease ▶ *n. inf.* bovine spongiform encephalopathy. See BSE.

mad·den /'madn/ ▶ *v.* [*tr.*] make (someone) extremely irritated or annoyed: *the audacity of the convicts maddened the governor.* ■ [often as *adj.*] (**maddened**) drive (someone) insane: *a maddened crowd.* —**mad·den·ing** *adj.*

mad·der /'madər/ ▶ *n.* a scrambling or prostrate Eurasian plant (genera *Rubia* and *Sherardia*) of the bedstraw family, in particular *R. tinctorum.* ■ a red dye or pigment obtained from the root of *R. tinctorum*, or a synthetic dye resembling it.

made /mād/ ▶ past and past participle of MAKE.

▶ *adj.* [usu. in *comb.*] made or formed in a particular place or by a particular process: *a Japanese-made camera | handmade chocolates.*

Ma·dei·ra (also **Madeira wine**) ▶ *n.* a fortified white wine from the island of Madeira.

Mad·e·moi·selle /,mad(ə)m(w)ə'zel; mam'zel/ ▶ *n.* (*pl.* **Mes·de·moi·selles** /,mād(ə)m(w)ə'zel(z)/) a title or form of address used of or to an unmarried French-speaking woman: ■ (**mademoiselle**) a young French-woman. ■ (**mademoiselle**) *dated* a French governess. ■ (**mademoiselle**) a female French teacher in an English-speaking school.

mad·house /'mad,hous/ ▶ *n. hist.* a mental institution. ■ *inf.* a psychiatric hospital. ■ a scene of extreme confusion or uproar: *this place is a madhouse.*

mad·ly /'madlē/ ▶ *adv.* in a manner suggesting or characteristic of insanity: *his eyes bulged madly.* ■ in a wild or uncontrolled manner. ■ *inf.* with extreme intensity: *the boys are all madly in love with you.*

mad·man /'mad,man; -mən/ ▶ *n.* (*pl.* **-men**) a man who is mentally ill. ■ an extremely foolish or reckless person: *some madman going too fast.* ■ used in similes to refer to a person who does something very fast, intensely, or violently: *I was working like a madman.*

Ma·don·na /mə'dänə/ ▶ *n.* (**the Madonna**) the Virgin Mary. ■ a picture, statue, or medallion of the Madonna, typically depicted seated and holding the infant Jesus. ■ (usu. **madonna**) an idealized virtuous and beautiful woman.

mad·ras /'madrəs; mə'dras/ ▶ *n.* a strong, fine-textured cotton fabric, typically patterned with colorful stripes or checks.

mad·ri·gal /'madrigəl/ ▶ *n.* a part-song for several voices, esp. one of the Renaissance period, typically arranged in elaborate counterpoint and without instrumental accompaniment. —**mad·ri·gal·i·an** /,madri'gālēən/ *adj.* —**mad·ri·gal·ist** /-ist/ *n.*

mad·wom·an /'mad,wŏŏmən/ ▶ *n.* (*pl.* **-wom·en**) a woman who is mentally ill. ■ used in similes to refer to a woman who does something very fast, intensely, or violently.

mael·strom /'māl,sträm; -strəm/ ▶ *n.* a powerful whirlpool in the sea or a river. ■ *fig.* a scene or state of confused and violent movement or upheaval: *a maelstrom of violence.*

maes·tro /'mīstrō/ ▶ *n.* (*pl.* **maes·tri** /'mīstrē/ or **maes·tros**) a distinguished musician, esp. a conductor of classical music. ■ a great or distinguished figure in any sphere: *a movie maestro.* ▷ early 18th cent.: Italian, 'master,' from Latin *magister.*

Ma·fi·a /'mäfēə/ ▶ *n.* (**the Mafia**) [treated as *sing.* or *pl.*] an organized international body of criminals, operating originally in Sicily and now esp. in Italy and the U.S. and having a complex and ruthless behavioral code. ■ (usu. **mafia**) any similar group using extortion and other criminal methods. ■ (usu. **mafia**) a closed group of people in a particular field, having a controlling influence: *the conservative top tennis mafia.*

Ma·fi·o·so /,mäfē'ōsō; -zō/ (also **ma·fi·o·so**) ▶ *n.* (*pl.* **-si** /-sē; -zē/) a member of the Mafia.

mag·a·zine /,magə'zēn; 'magə,zēn/ ▶ *n.* **1** a periodical publication containing articles and illustrations, typically covering a particular subject or area of interest: *a car magazine* ■ a regular television or radio program comprising a variety of topical news or entertainment items. **2** a chamber for holding a supply of cartridges to be fed automatically to the breech of a gun. ■ a similar device feeding a camera, compact disc player, etc. **3** a store for arms, ammunition, explosives, and provisions for use in military operations. ▷ late 16th cent.: from French *magasin*, from Italian *magazzino*, from Arabic *makzin*, *makzan* 'storehouse,' from *kazana* 'store up.' The term originally meant 'store' and was often used from the mid 17th cent. in the title of books providing information useful to particular groups of people, whence sense 1 (mid 18th cent.). Sense 3, a contemporary specialization of the original meaning, gave rise to sense 2 in the mid 18th cent.

ma·gen·ta /mə'jentə/ ▶ *n.* a light purplish red that is one of the primary subtractive colors, complementary to green.

mag·got /'magət/ ▶ *n.* **1** a soft-bodied legless larva, esp. that of a fly found in decaying matter. **2** *archaic* a whimsical fancy. —**mag·got·y** *adj.*

Ma·gi /'mā,jī/ (**the Magi**) ▶ the "wise men" from the East who brought gifts to the infant, said in later tradition to be kings named Caspar, Melchior, and Balthasar who brought gifts of gold, frankincense, and myrrh.

ma·gi /'mā,jī/ ▶ plural form of MAGUS.

mag·ic /'majik/ ▶ *n.* the power of apparently influencing the course of events by using mysterious or supernatural forces. ■ mysterious tricks, such as making things disappear and appear again, performed as entertainment. ■ a quality that makes something seem removed from everyday life, esp. in a way that gives delight: *enjoy the magic of the theater.* ■ *inf.* something that has such a quality: *their seaside town is pure magic.*

▶*adj.* **1** used in magic or working by magic; having or apparently having supernatural powers: *a magic wand.* ■ very effective in producing results, esp. desired ones: *confidence is the magic ingredient needed to spark recovery.* **2** *inf.* wonderful; exciting: *what a magic moment.*

▶ □ **like magic** remarkably effectively or rapidly: *it repels rain like magic.*

mag·i·cal /ˈmajikəl/ ▶*adj.* **1** relating to or using magic. ■ resembling magic; produced or working as if by magic: *he had a gentle, magical touch with the child.* **2** beautiful or delightful in such a way as to seem removed from everyday life: *it was a magical evening of pure nostalgia.* —**mag·i·cal·ly** *adv.*

ma·gi·cian /məˈjiSHən/ ▶*n.* a person with magical powers. ■ a person who performs magic tricks for entertainment. ■ *inf.* a person with exceptional skill in a particular area: *he was the magician of the fan belt.*

mag·is·te·ri·al /ˌmajəˈsti(ə)rēəl/ ▶*adj.* **1** having or showing great authority: *a magisterial pronouncement.* ■ domineering; dictatorial: *his magisterial style of questioning.* **2** relating to or conducted by a magistrate. ■ (of a person) holding the office of a magistrate. —**mag·is·te·ri·al·ly** *adv.*

mag·is·trate /ˈmajəˌstrāt/ ▶*n.* a civil officer or lay judge who administers the law, esp. one who conducts a court that deals with minor offenses and holds preliminary hearings for more serious ones. —**mag·is·tra·ture** /-ˌsträCHər; -strə,CHŎŎ(ə)r/ *n.*

mag·ma /ˈmagmə/ ▶*n.* hot fluid or semifluid material below or within the earth's crust from which igneous rock is formed by cooling. —**mag·mat·ic** /magˈmatik/ *adj.*

Mag·na Car·ta /ˌmagnə ˈkärtə/ ▶a charter of liberty and political rights obtained from King John of England by his rebellious barons at Runnymede in 1215, which came to be seen as the seminal document of English constitutional practice.

mag·nan·i·mous /magˈnanəməs/ ▶*adj.* very generous or forgiving, esp. toward a rival or someone less powerful than oneself. —**mag·na·nim·i·ty** /ˌmagnəˈnimətē/ *n.* —**mag·nan·i·mous·ly** *adv.*

mag·nate /ˈmagˌnāt; ˈmagnət/ ▶*n.* a wealthy and influential person, esp. in business: *a media magnate.*

mag·ne·sia /magˈnēZHə; -ˈnēsHə/ ▶*n.* *Chem.* magnesium oxide. ■ hydrated magnesium carbonate used as an antacid and laxative.

mag·ne·si·um /magˈnēzēəm; -ZHəm/ ▶*n.* the chemical element of atomic number 12, a silver-white metal of the alkaline earth series. It is used to make strong lightweight alloys, esp. for the aerospace industry. (Symbol: **Mg**)

mag·net /ˈmagnət/ ▶*n.* a piece of iron (or an ore, alloy, or other material) that has its component atoms so ordered that the material exhibits properties of magnetism, such as attracting other iron-containing objects or aligning itself in an external magnetic field. ■ *fig.* a person or thing that has a powerful attraction: *the beautiful stretch of white sand is a magnet for sun worshipers.*

mag·net·ic /magˈnetik/ ▶*adj.* **1** having the properties of a magnet; exhibiting magnetism. ■ capable of being attracted by or acquiring the properties of a magnet: *steel is magnetic.* ■ relating to or involving magnetism: *an airborne magnetic survey.* ■ (of a bearing in navigation) measured relative to magnetic north. **2** very attractive or alluring: *his magnetic personality.* —**mag·net·i·cal·ly** /-ik(ə)lē/ *adv.*

mag·net·ic field ▶*n.* a region around a magnetic material or a moving electric charge within which the force of magnetism acts.

mag·net·ic north ▶*n.* the direction in which the north end of a compass needle or other freely suspended magnet will point in response to the earth's magnetic field.

mag·net·ic pole ▶*n.* each of the points near the extremities of the axis of rotation of the earth or another celestial body where a magnetic needle dips vertically. ■ each of the two points or regions of an artificial or natural magnet to and from which the lines of magnetic force are directed.

mag·net·ic res·o·nance im·ag·ing (abbr.: **MRI**) ▶*n.* a form of medical imaging that measures the response of the atomic nuclei of body tissues to high-frequency radio waves when placed in a strong magnetic field, and that produces images of the internal organs.

mag·net·ic tape ▶*n.* tape used in recording sound, pictures, or computer data.

mag·net·ism /ˈmagnə,tizəm/ ▶*n.* a physical phenomenon produced by the motion of electric charge, resulting in attractive and repulsive forces between objects. ■ the property of being magnetic. ■ *fig.* the ability to attract and charm people: *personal magnetism.*

mag·net·ite /ˈmagnə,tīt/ ▶*n.* a gray-black magnetic mineral that consists of an oxide of iron and is an important form of iron ore.

mag·net·ize /ˈmagnə,tīz/ ▶*v.* [*tr.*] give magnetic properties to; make magnetic. ■ *fig.* attract strongly as if by a magnet. —**mag·net·iz·a·ble** *adj.* —**mag·net·i·za·tion** /ˌmagnətəˈzāsHən/ *n.* —**mag·net·iz·er** *n.*

mag·ne·to /magˈnētō/ ▶*n.* (*pl.* **-tos**) a small electric generator containing a permanent magnet and used to provide high-voltage pulses, esp. (formerly) in the ignition systems of internal combustion engines.

mag·net school ▶*n.* a public school offering special instruction and programs not available elsewhere, designed to attract a more diverse student body from throughout a school district.

mag·ni·fi·ca·tion /ˌmagnəfiˈkāsHən/ ▶*n.* the action or process of magnifying something or being magnified, esp. visually. ■ the degree to which something is or can be magnified. ■ the magnifying power of an instrument: *this microscope should give a magnification of about 100.* ■ a magnified reproduction of something.

mag·nif·i·cent /magˈnifəsənt/ ▶*adj.* **1** impressively beautiful, elaborate, or extravagant; striking. **2** very good; excellent: *she paid tribute to their magnificent efforts..* —**mag·nif·i·cence** *n.* —**mag·nif·i·cent·ly** *adv.*

mag·nif·i·co /magˈnifi,kō/ ▶*n.* (*pl.* **-coes**) *inf.* an eminent, powerful, or illustrious person.

mag·ni·fy /ˈmagnə,fī/ ▶*v.* (**-fies**, **-fied**) [*tr.*] **1** make (something) appear larger than it is, esp. with a lens or microscope. ■ [*intr.*] be capable of increasing the size or apparent size of something. ■ increase the volume of (a sound). ■ intensify: *the risk is magnified if there is any dirty material next to the skin.* ■ exaggerate the importance or effect of: *she tended to magnify the defects of those she disliked.* **2** *archaic* extol; glorify: *praise the Lord and magnify Him.* —**mag·ni·fi·er** /-,fīər/ *n.*

mag·ni·fy·ing glass ▶*n.* a lens that produces an enlarged image.

mag·ni·tude /ˈmagnə,tōōd/ ▶*n.* **1** the great size or extent of something: *they may feel discouraged at the magnitude of the task before them.* ■ great importance: *events of tragic magnitude.* **2** size. ■ a numerical quantity or value: *the magnitudes of all the economic variables could be determined.* **3** the degree of brightness of a star. ■ the class into which a star falls by virtue of its brightness. ■ a difference of one on a scale of brightness, treated as a unit of measurement.

mag·no·lia /magˈnōlyə/ ▶*n.* a tree or shrub (genus *Magnolia*, family Magnoliaceae) with typically creamy-pink, waxy flowers, widely grown as ornamentals.

mag·num /ˈmagnəm/ ▶*n.* (*pl.* **-nums**) a thing of a type that is larger than normal, in particular: ■ a wine bottle of twice the standard size, normally 1½ liters. ■ (often **Magnum**) [often as *adj.*] *trademark* a gun designed to fire cartridges that are more powerful than normal for its caliber: *his .357 Magnum pistol.*

mag·num o·pus /ˈmagnəm ˈōpəs/ ▶*n.* (*pl.* **mag·num o·pus·es** or **mag·na o·pe·ra** /ˈmagnə ˈōpərə; ˈäpərə/) a large and important work of art, music, or literature, esp. one regarded as the most important work of an artist or writer.

mag·pie /ˈmag,pī/ ▶*n.* **1** a long-tailed bird of the crow family with boldly marked plumage and a raucous voice. Five genera and several species include the black-and-white **black-billed magpie** (*Pica pica*) of Eurasia and North America. **2** used in similes or comparisons to refer to a person who collects things, esp. things of little value, or a person who chatters idly.

ma·gus /ˈmāgəs/ ▶*n.* (*pl.* **ma·gi** /ˈmā,jī/) a member of a priestly caste of ancient Persia. See also **Magi.** ■ a sorcerer.

Mag·yar /ˈmag,yär/ ▶*n.* **1** a member of a people who originated in the Urals and migrated westward to settle in what is now Hungary in the 9th century AD. **2** the Uralic language of this people; Hungarian.

▶*adj.* of or relating to this people or language.

ma·ha·ra·ja /ˌmähəˈräjə; -ˈräZHə/ (also **ma·ha·ra·jah**) ▶*n.* *hist.* an Indian prince.

ma·ha·ra·ni /ˌmähəˈränē/ (also **ma·ha·ra·nee**) ▶*n.* a maharaja's wife or widow.

ma·ha·ri·shi /ˌmähəˈrēsHē; məˈhärəsHē/ ▶*n.* a great Hindu sage or spiritual leader.

ma·hat·ma /məˈhätmə; -ˈhatmə/ ▶*n.* (in the Indian subcontinent) a person regarded with reverence or loving respect; a holy person or sage. ▷from Sanskrit *mahātman*, from *mahā* 'great' + *ātman* 'soul.'

Ma·hi·can /məˈhēkən/ (also **Mo·hi·can**) ▶*n.* **1** a member of an American

Indian people formerly inhabiting the Upper Hudson Valley in New York. **2** the Algonquian language of this people.
▸*adj.* of or relating to the Mahicans or their language.

ma·hi·ma·hi /ˌmähē'mähē/ ▸*n.* an edible marine fish (genus *Coryphaena*, family Coryphaenidae) of warm seas, with silver and bright blue or green coloration when alive. Also called **DOLPHIN**.

mah·jongg /mä 'zhäNG; -zHÔNG/ (also **mah-jong** or **mah·jongg** or **mah·jong**) ▸*n.* a game of Chinese origin played, usually by four people, with 136 or 144 rectangular pieces called tiles.

ma·hog·a·ny /mə'hägənē/ ▸*n.* **1** hard reddish-brown timber from a tropical tree, used for high-quality furniture. ■ a rich reddish-brown color like that of mahogany wood. **2** the tropical American tree (genus *Swietenia*) that produces this timber, widely harvested from the wild. ■ used in names of trees that yield similar timber, e.g., **Philippine mahogany**.

maid /mād/ ▸*n.* a female domestic servant. ■ *archaic* or *poetic/lit.* a girl or young woman, esp. an unmarried one. ■ *archaic* or *poetic/lit.* a virgin.

maid·en /'mādn/ ▸*n.* *archaic* or *poetic/lit.* a girl or young woman, esp. an unmarried one. ■ a virgin.
▸*adj.* **1** (of a woman, esp. an older one) unmarried: *a maiden aunt.* ■ (of a female animal) unmated. **2** being or involving the first attempt or act of its kind: *the ship's maiden voyage.* ■ denoting a horse that has never won a race. ■ (of a tree or other fruiting plant) in its first year of growth. —**maid·en·hood** /-,hŏŏd/ *n.* —**maid·en·ish** *adj.* —**maid·en·like** /-,līk/ *adj.* —**maid·en·ly** *adj.*

maid·en·hair /'mādn,her/ (also **maidenhair fern**) ▸*n.* a chiefly tropical fern (genus *Adiantum*) of delicate appearance, having slender-stalked fronds and often grown as a houseplant.

maid·en·head /'mādn,hed/ ▸*n.* virginity. ■ *dated* the hymen.

maid·en name ▸*n.* the surname that a married woman used from birth, prior to its being legally changed at marriage.

maid of hon·or ▸*n.* an unmarried woman acting as principal bridesmaid at a wedding. ■ an unmarried woman, typically of noble birth, attending a queen or princess.

maid·serv·ant /'mād,sərvənt/ ▸*n.* *dated* a female domestic servant.

mail[1] /māl/ ▸*n.* letters and packages conveyed by the postal system. ■ the postal system: ■ a single delivery or collection of mail: *the new magazine that came in the mail today.* ■ *Comput.* electronic mail. ■ *dated* a vehicle, such as a train, carrying mail. ■ *archaic* a bag of letters to be conveyed by the postal system.
▸*v.* [*tr.*] send (a letter or package) using the postal system. ■ *Comput.* send (someone) electronic mail. —**mail·a·ble** *adj.*

mail[2] ▸*n.* *hist.* armor made of metal rings or plates, joined together flexibly. ■ the protective shell or scales of certain animals.
▸*v.* [*tr.*] clothe or cover with mail: [as *adj.*] (**mailed**) *a mailed gauntlet.*

mail·box /'māl,bäks/ ▸*n.* a public box with a slot into which mail is placed for collection by the post office. ■ a private box into which mail is delivered, esp. one mounted on a post at the entrance to a person's property. ■ a computer file in which e-mail messages received by a particular user are stored.

mail car·ri·er ▸*n.* a person who is employed to deliver and collect letters and parcels.

mail·ing list ▸*n.* a list of the names and addresses of people to whom material such as advertising matter, information, or a magazine may be mailed, esp. regularly.

mail·man /'māl,man/ ▸*n.* (*pl.* **-men**) a person who is employed to deliver and collect letters and parcels.

mail or·der ▸*n.* the selling of goods to customers by mail, generally involving selection from a special catalog: *available by mail order only* | [as *adj.*] *a mail-order distributor of generic drugs.*

maim /mām/ ▸*v.* [*tr.*] wound or injure (someone) so that part of the body is permanently damaged: *100,000 soldiers were killed or maimed.*

main /mān/ ▸*adj.* chief in size or importance: *a main road* | *the main problem is one of resources.* ■ denoting the center of a network, from which other parts branch out: *I am seldom at the main office.*
▸*n.* **1** a principal pipe carrying water or gas to buildings, or taking sewage from them: *a faulty gas main.* **2** (**the main**) *archaic* or *poetic/lit.* the open ocean. **3** *Naut.* short for **MAINSAIL** or **MAINMAST**.
▸ □ **by main force** through sheer strength. □ **in the main** on the whole; chiefly.

main clause ▸*n.* *Grammar* a clause that can form a complete sentence standing alone, having a subject and a predicate.

main course ▸*n.* the most substantial course of a meal.

main drag ▸*n.* (usu. **the main drag**) *inf.* the main street of a town.

main·frame /'mān,frām/ ▸*n.* **1** a large high-speed computer, esp. one supporting numerous workstations or peripherals. **2** the central processing unit and primary memory of a computer.

main·land /'mān,land; -lənd/ ▸*n.* a large continuous extent of land that includes the greater part of a country or territory, as opposed to offshore islands and detached territories. —**main·land·er** *n.*

main line ▸*n.* a chief railroad line: [as *adj.*] *a main-line station.* ■ a principal route, course, or connection: *the main line of evolution.* ■ a chief road or street. ■ *inf.* a principal vein as a site for a drug injection.
▸*v.* (**main·line**) [*tr.*] *inf.* inject (a drug) intravenously. —**main·lin·er** *n.*

main·ly /'mānlē/ ▸*adv.* more than anything else: *he is mainly concerned with fiction.* ■ for the most part: *the west will be mainly dry.*

main·mast /'mān,mast/ ▸*n.* the principal mast of a ship, typically the second mast in a sailing ship of three or more masts.

main·sail /'mānsəl; -,sāl/ ▸*n.* the principal sail of a ship, esp. the lowest sail on the mainmast in a square-rigged vessel. ■ the sail set on the after side of the mainmast in a fore-and-aft-rigged vessel.

main se·quence ▸*n.* *Astron.* a series of star types to which most stars belong, represented on a Hertzsprung–Russell diagram as a continuous band extending from the upper left (hot, bright stars) to the lower right (cool, dim stars).

main·spring /'mān,spriNG/ ▸*n.* the principal spring in a watch, clock, or other mechanism. ■ *fig.* something that plays a principal part in motivating or maintaining a movement, process, or activity.

main·stay /'mān,stā/ ▸*n.* a stay that extends from the top of the mainmast to the foot of the foremast of a sailing ship. ■ *fig.* a thing on which something else is based or depends: *whitefish are the mainstay of the local industry.*

main·stream /'mān,strēm/ ▸*n.* (**the mainstream**) the ideas, attitudes, or activities that are regarded as normal or conventional; the dominant trend in opinion, fashion, or the arts.
▸*adj.* belonging to or characteristic of the mainstream. ■ (of a school or class) for students without special needs: *children with minor handicaps would be able to attend mainstream schools.*
▸*v.* [*tr.*] (often **be mainstreamed**) bring (something) into the mainstream: *vegetarianism has been mainstreamed.* ■ place (a student with special needs) into a mainstream class or school.

main street ▸*n.* the principal street of a town. ■ (**Main Street**) used in reference to the materialism, mediocrity, or parochialism regarded as typical of small-town life.

main·tain /mān'tān/ ▸*v.* [*tr.*] **1** cause or enable (a condition or state of affairs) to continue. ■ keep (something) at the same level or rate. ■ keep (a building, machine, or road) in good condition or in working order by checking or repairing it regularly. ■ hold (a position) in the face of attack or competition: *to maintain a competitive market position.* **2** provide with necessities for life or existence: *the basic costs of maintaining a child.* ■ keep (a military unit) supplied with equipment and other requirements. ■ *archaic* give one's support to; uphold: *the king swears he will maintain the laws of God.* **3** state something strongly to be the case; assert: [*tr.*] *he has always maintained his innocence* | *he had persistently maintained that he would not stand against his old friend* | [with *direct speech*] *"It was not an ideology at all," she maintained.* —**main·tain·a·bil·i·ty** /ˌmān,tānə'bilətē/ *n.* —**main·tain·a·ble** *adj.*

main·te·nance /'mānt(ə)nəns; 'māntn-əns/ ▸*n.* **1** the process of maintaining or preserving someone or something, or the state of being maintained. ■ the process of keeping something in good condition: *car maintenance* | [as *adj.*] *essential maintenance work.* **2** the provision of financial support for a person's living expenses, or the support so provided. ■ alimony or child support.

maî·tre d'hô·tel /ˌmātrə dō'tel; ˌmetrə/ (also **maî·tre d'** /ˌmātrə 'dē; ˌ'ātər/) ▸*n.* (*pl.* **maî·tres d'hô·tel** *pronunc.* same; also **maître d's**) the person in a restaurant who oversees the waitpersons and busboys, and who typically handles reservations. ■ the manager of a hotel.

maize /māz/ ▸*n.* technical or chiefly British term for **CORN**[1]. ▷mid 16th cent.: from Spanish *maíz*, from Taino *mahiz*.

Maj. ▸*abbr.* Major.

ma·jes·tic /mə'jestik/ ▸*adj.* having or showing impressive beauty or dignity. —**ma·jes·ti·cal·ly** /-(ə)lē/ *adv.*

maj·es·ty /'majəstē/ ▸*n.* (*pl.* **-ties**) **1** impressive stateliness, dignity, or beauty: *experience the majesty of the Rockies.* **2** royal power: *the majesty of the royal household.* ■ (**His**, **Your**, etc., **Majesty**) a title given to a sovereign or a sovereign's wife or widow: *Her Majesty the Queen.*

ma·jol·i·ca /mī'äləkə/ ▸*n.* fine earthenware with colored decoration on an opaque white tin glaze, originating in Italy during the Renaissance.

ma·jor /'mājər/ ▸*adj.* **1** important, serious, or significant: *the use of drugs is a major problem.* ■ greater or more important; main: *he got the major* *share of the spoils.* ■ (of a surgical operation) serious or life-threatening: *he had to undergo major surgery.* **2** *Mus.* (of a scale) having an interval of a semitone between the third and fourth degrees and the seventh and eighth degrees. Contrasted with MINOR. ■ (of an interval) equivalent to that between the tonic and another note of a major scale, and greater by a semitone than the corresponding minor interval. ■ (of a key) based on a major scale, tending to produce a bright or joyful effect: *Prelude in G Major.* ■ (of a triad) having a major third as the bottom interval. **3** of full legal age.

▶*n.* **1** an army officer of high rank, in particular (in the U.S. Army, Air Force, and Marine Corps) an officer ranking above captain and below lieutenant colonel. **2** *Mus.* a major key, interval, or scale. **3** a student's principal subject or course of study. ■ a student specializing in a specified subject: *a math major.* **4** (**the majors**) the major leagues. **5** a person of full legal age.

▶*v.* [*intr.*] (**major in**) specialize in (a particular subject) at a college or university: *I was trying to decide if I should major in drama or English.*

ma·jor-do·mo /ˌmājər ˈdōmō/ ▶*n.* (*pl.* **-do·mos**) the chief steward of a large household.

ma·jor gen·er·al ▶*n.* (*pl.* **ma·jor gen·er·als**) an officer in the U.S. Army, Air Force, and Marine Corps ranking above brigadier general and below lieutenant general.

ma·jor·i·ty /məˈjôrətē; -ˈjär-/ ▶*n.* (*pl.* **-ties**) **1** the greater number: *in the majority of cases all will go smoothly* | [as *adj.*] *it was a majority decision.* ■ the number by which votes for one candidate in an election are more than those for all other candidates combined. ■ *Brit.* the number by which the votes for one party or candidate exceed those of the next in rank. ■ a party or group receiving the greater number of votes. **2** the age when a person is legally considered a full adult, in most contexts either 18 or 21.

ma·jor league ▶*n.* a professional baseball league of the highest level, in the U.S. either the American League or the National League: *my dream of pitching in the major leagues* | [as *adj.*] *future major-league ballplayers.* ■ the highest-level professional league or leagues in another sport. ■ *fig.* the highest attainable level in any endeavor or activity: [as *adj.*] *major-league corporations.* —**ma·jor-lea·guer** *n.*

ma·jus·cule /ˈmajəsˌkyool/ ▶*n.* large lettering, either capital or uncial, in which all the letters are usually the same height. ■ a large letter. ▷early 18th cent.: from French, from Latin *majuscula (littera)* 'somewhat greater (letter).' —**ma·jus·cu·lar** /məˈjəskyələr/ *adj.*

make /māk/ ▶*v.* (*past* **made** /mād/) [*tr.*] **1** form (something) by putting parts together or combining substances; construct; create. ■ (**make something into**) alter something so that it forms or constitutes (something else): *buffalo's milk can be made into cheese.* ■ compose, prepare, or draw up (something written or abstract): *she made her will.* ■ prepare (a dish, drink, or meal) for consumption: *she was making lunch for Lucy and Francis* | *I'll make us both a cup of tea.* ■ arrange bedclothes tidily on (a bed) ready for use. ■ arrange and light materials for (a fire). **2** cause (something) to exist or come about; bring about: *the drips had made a pool on the floor.* ■ [*tr.*] cause to become or seem: *decorative features make brickwork more interesting* | *the best way to disarm your critics is to make them laugh.* ■ carry out, perform, or produce (a specified action, movement, or sound): *Unger made a speech of forty minutes* | *anyone can make a mistake.* ■ communicate or express (an idea, request, or requirement): *I tend to make heavy demands on people* | *make him an offer he can't refuse.* ■ undertake or agree to (an aim or purpose): *we made a deal.* ■ [*tr.*] appoint or designate (someone) to a position: *he was made a colonel in the Mexican army.* ■ [*tr.*] represent or cause to appear in a specified way: *the sale price and extended warranty make it an excellent value.* ■ cause or ensure the success or advancement of: *the work made Wordsworth's reputation.* **3** [*tr.*] compel (someone) to do something: *she bought me a brandy and made me drink it.* **4** constitute; amount to: *they made an unusual duo.* ■ serve as or become through development or adaptation: *this fern makes a good houseplant.* ■ consider to be; estimate as: *How many are there? I make it sixteen.* ■ agree or decide on (a specified arrangement), typically one concerning a time or place: *let's make it 7:30.* **5** gain or earn (money or profit): *he'd made a lot of money out of hardware.* **6** arrive at (a place) within a specified time or in time for (a train or other transport): *we've got a lot to do if you're going to make the shuttle* | *they didn't always make it on time.* ■ (**make it**) succeed in something; become successful. ■ achieve a place in: *these dogs seldom make the news* | *they made it to the semifinals.* ■ achieve the rank of: *he wasn't going to make captain.* **7** [*intr.*] go or prepare to go in a particular direction: *he made toward the car.* ■ act as if one is about to perform an action: *she made as if to leave the room.* **8** *inf.* induce (someone) to have sexual intercourse with one: *he had been trying to make Cynthia for two years now* | *his alleged quest to make it with the*

world's most attractive women. **9** (in bridge, whist, and similar games) win (a trick). ■ win a trick with (a card). ■ win the number of tricks that fulfills (a contract).

▶*phrasal v.* □ **make away** another way of saying MAKE OFF. □ **make away with** another way of saying MAKE OFF WITH. ■ kill (someone) furtively and illicitly: *for all we know she could have been made away with.* □ **make for 1** move or head toward (a place): *I made for the life raft and hung on for dear life.* **2** tend to result in or be received as (a particular thing): *job descriptions never make for exciting reading.* **3** (**be made for**) be eminently suited for (a particular function): *a man made for action.* ■ form an ideal partnership; be ideally suited: *you two were just made for each other.* □ **make something of** give or ascribe a specified amount of attention or importance to: *oddly, he makes little of America's low investment rates.* ■ understand or derive advantage from: *they stared at the stone but could make nothing of it.* ■ conclude to be the meaning or character of: *he wasn't sure what to make of Russell.* □ **make off** leave hurriedly, esp. in order to avoid duty or punishment: *they made off without paying.* □ **make off with** carry (something) away illicitly: *burglars made off with all their wedding presents.* □ **make out** *inf.* **1** make progress; fare: *how are you making out, now that the summer's over?* **2** *inf.* engage in sexual activity: *Ernie was making out with Bernice.* □ **make someone/something out 1** manage with some difficulty to see or hear something: *in the dim light it was difficult to make out the illustration.* ■ understand the character or motivation of someone: *I can't make her out—she's so inconsistent.* **2** assert; represent: *I'm not as bad as I'm made out to be.* ■ try to give a specified impression; pretend: *he made out he was leaving.* **3** draw up or write out a list or document, esp. an official one: *advice about making out a will* | *send a check made out to Trinity College.* □ **make something over 1** transfer the possession of something to someone. **2** completely transform or remodel something, esp. a person's hairstyle, makeup, or clothes. □ **make up** be reconciled after a quarrel. □ **make someone up** apply cosmetics to oneself or another. □ **make something up 1** (also **make up for**) serve or act to compensate for something lost, missed, or deficient: *I'll make up the time tomorrow.* ■ (**make it up to**) compensate someone for negligent or unfair treatment: *I'll try to make it up to you in the future.* **2** (**make up**) complete an amount or group: *he brought along a girl to make up a foursome.* **3** put together or prepare something from parts or ingredients: *make up the mortar to a consistency that can be molded in the hands* ■ get an amount or group together: *he was trying to make up a party to go dancing.* ■ prepare a bed for use with fresh bedclothes. ■ *Printing* arrange type and illustrations into pages or arrange the type and illustrations on a page. **4** concoct or invent a story, lie, or plan: *she enjoyed making up tall tales.* □ **make up to** *inf.* attempt to win the favor of (someone) by being pleasant. □ **make with** *inf.* proceed to use or supply: *make with the feet, honey—we're late.*

▶*n.* the manufacturer or trade name of a particular product: *the make, model, and year of his car.* ■ the structure or composition of something. —**mak·a·ble** /-əbəl/ (also **make·a·ble**) *adj.*

▶ □ **have** (**got**) **it made** *inf.* be in a position where success is certain: *because your dad's a manager, he's got it made.* □ **make do** manage with the limited or inadequate means available: *Dad would have to make do with an old car.* □ **make like** *inf.* pretend to be; imitate: *tell the whole group to make like a bird by putting their arms out.* □ **make or break** be the factor that decides whether (something) will succeed or fail. □ **make sail** *Sailing* spread a sail or sails. ■ start a voyage. □ **make time 1** find an occasion when time is available to do something: *the nurse should make time to talk to the patient.* **2** *inf.* make sexual advances to someone: *I couldn't make time with Marilyn because she was already a senior.* □ **make up one's mind** make a decision; decide. □ **make way** allow room for someone or something else: *the land is due to be bulldozed to make way for a parking garage.* □ **on the make** *inf.* intent on gain, typically in an unscrupulous way. ■ looking for a sexual partner. □ **put the make on** *inf.* make sexual advances to (someone).

make-be·lieve ▶*n.* the action of pretending or imagining, typically that things are better than they really are: *living in a world of make-believe.*

▶*adj.* imitating something real; pretend.

make·o·ver /ˈmākˌōvər/ ▶*n.* a complete transformation or remodeling of something, esp. a person's hairstyle, makeup, or clothes.

mak·er /ˈmākər/ ▶*n.* **1** [usu. in *comb.*] a person or thing that makes or produces something: *a cabinetmaker.* **2** (**our, the,** etc., **Maker**) God; the Creator.

▶ □ **meet one's Maker** *chiefly humorous* die.

Pronunciation Key ə *ago*, *up*; ər *over*, *fur*; a *hat*; ā *ate*; ä *car*; CH *chin*; e *let*; ē *see*; e(ə)r *air*; i *fit*; ī *by*; i(ə)r *ear*; NG *sing*; ō *go*; ô *law*, *for*; oi *toy*; ōō *good*; ōō *goo*; ou *out*; SH *she*; TH *thin*; <u>TH</u> *then*; (h)w *why*; ZH *vision*

make·shift /'māk,SHift/ ▸ *adj.* serving as a temporary substitute; sufficient for the time being: *arranging a row of chairs to form a makeshift bed.* ▸ *n.* a temporary substitute or device.

make·up /'māk,əp/ (also **make-up**) ▸ *n.* **1** cosmetics such as lipstick or powder applied to the face, used to enhance or alter the appearance. **2** the composition or constitution of something: *studying the makeup of ocean sediments.* ■ the combination of qualities that form a person's temperament: *a nastiness that had long been in his makeup.* **3** *Printing* the arrangement of type, illustrations, etc., on a printed page: *page make-up.* **4** a supplementary test or assignment given to a student who missed or failed the original one: [as *adj.*] *Tony has a makeup exam.*

mak·ing /'mākiNG/ ▸ *n.* **1** the process of making or producing something: *the making of videos* | [in *comb.*] *glassmaking.* **2** (**makings**) essential qualities or ingredients needed for something: *a film with all the makings of a cinematic success.* ▸ □ **in the making** in the process of developing or being made: *a campaign that's been two years in the making.* □ **of one's (own) making** (of a difficulty) caused by oneself.

ma·ko /'mākō; 'măkō/ (also **mako shark**) ▸ *n.* (*pl.* **-os**) a large fast-moving oceanic shark (genus *Isurus*, family Lamnidae) with a deep blue back and white underparts.

mal·a·chite /'malə,kīt/ ▸ *n.* a bright green mineral containing copper carbonate. It typically occurs in masses and fibrous aggregates and is capable of taking a high polish.

mal·a·col·o·gy /,malə'käləjē/ ▸ *n.* the branch of zoology that deals with mollusks. —**mal·a·co·log·i·cal** /-kə'läjikəl/ *adj.* —**mal·a·col·o·gist** /-jist/ *n.*

mal·ad·just·ed /,malə'jəstid/ ▸ *adj.* failing or unable to cope with the demands of a normal social environment: *maladjusted behavior.* —**mal·ad·just·ment** /-'jəstmənt/ *n.*

mal·ad·min·is·ter /,maləd'ministər/ ▸ *v.* [*tr.*] *formal* manage or administer inefficiently, badly, or dishonestly. —**mal·ad·min·is·tra·tion** /-,minə'strāSHən/ *n.*

mal·a·droit /,malə'droit/ ▸ *adj.* ineffective or bungling; clumsy. —**mal·a·droit·ly** *adv.* —**mal·a·droit·ness** *n.*

mal·a·dy /'malədē/ ▸ *n.* (*pl.* **-dies**) a disease or ailment: *an incurable malady* | *fig. the nation's maladies.*

Mal·a·gas·y /,malə'gasē/ ▸ *n.* (*pl.* same or **-gas·ies**) **1** a native or national of Madagascar. **2** the Austronesian language of Madagascar. ▸ *adj.* of or relating to Madagascar or its people or language.

ma·laise /mə'lāz; -'lez/ ▸ *n.* a general feeling of discomfort, illness, or uneasiness whose exact cause is difficult to identify.

mal·a·mute /'malə,myōōt/ (also **mal·e·mute**) ▸ *n.* see ALASKAN MALAMUTE.

mal·a·prop /'malə,präp/ (also **mal·a·prop·ism**) ▸ *n.* the mistaken use of a word in place of a similar-sounding one, often with unintentionally amusing effect, as in, for example, "dance a *flamingo*" (instead of *flamenco*).

mal·ap·ro·pos /,mal,aprə'pō/ *formal* ▸ *adv.* inopportunely; inappropriately. ▸ *adj.* inopportune; inappropriate: *these terms applied to him seem to me malapropos.* ▸ *n.* (*pl.* same) something inappropriately said or done.

ma·lar·i·a /mə'lerēə/ ▸ *n.* an intermittent and remittent fever caused by a protozoan parasite that is transmitted by mosquitoes and that invades the red blood cells. —**ma·lar·i·al** /-ēəl/ *adj.* —**ma·lar·i·an** /-ēən/ *adj.* —**ma·lar·i·ous** /-ēəs/ *adj.*

ma·lar·key /mə'lärkē/ ▸ *n. inf.* meaningless talk; nonsense: *don't give me that malarkey.*

Ma·lay /mə'lā; 'mā,lā/ ▸ *n.* **1** a member of a people inhabiting Malaysia and Indonesia. ■ a person of Malay descent. **2** the Austronesian language of the Malays, closely related to Indonesian, that is the official language of Malaysia. ▸ *adj.* of or relating to this people or language.

mal·con·tent /,malkən'tent; 'malkən,tent/ ▸ *n.* a person who is dissatisfied and rebellious. ▸ *adj.* dissatisfied and complaining or making trouble. —**mal·con·tent·ed** *adj.*

male /māl/ ▸ *adj.* of or denoting the sex that produces small, typically motile gametes, esp. spermatozoa, with which a female may be fertilized or inseminated to produce offspring. ■ relating to or characteristic of men or male animals; masculine. ■ (of a plant or flower) bearing stamens but lacking functional pistils. ■ (of parts of machinery, fittings, etc.) designed to enter, fill, or fit inside a corresponding female part. ▸ *n.* a male person, plant, or animal. —**male·ness** *n.*

mal·e·dic·tion /,malə'dikSHən/ ▸ *n.* a magical word or phrase uttered with the intention of bringing about evil or destruction; a curse. —**mal·e·dic·tive** /-'diktiv/ *adj.* —**mal·e·dic·to·ry** /-'diktərē/ *adj.*

mal·e·fac·tor /'malə,faktər/ ▸ *n. formal* a person who commits a crime or some other wrong. —**mal·e·fac·tion** /-'fakSHən/ *n.*

ma·lef·ic /mə'lefik/ ▸ *adj. poetic/lit.* causing or capable of causing harm or destruction, esp. by supernatural means. —**ma·lef·i·cence** /-'lefəsəns/ *n.* —**ma·lef·i·cent** /-'lefəsənt/ *adj.*

ma·lev·o·lent /mə'levələnt/ ▸ *adj.* having or showing a wish to do evil to others. —**ma·lev·o·lence** *n.* —**ma·lev·o·lent·ly** *adv.*

mal·fea·sance /mal'fēzəns/ ▸ *n. Law* wrongdoing, esp. by a public official. —**mal·fea·sant** /-'fēzənt/ *n.* & *adj.*

mal·for·ma·tion /,malfôr'māSHən; -fər-/ ▸ *n.* a deformity; an abnormally formed part of the body. ■ the condition of being abnormal in shape or form: *malformation of one or both ears.* —**mal·formed** /mal'fôrmd/ *adj.*

mal·func·tion /mal'fəNGkSHən/ ▸ *v.* [*intr.*] (of a piece of equipment or machinery) fail to function normally or satisfactorily: *the unit is clearly malfunctioning.* ▸ *n.* a failure to function in a normal or satisfactory manner.

mal·ice /'maləs/ ▸ *n.* the intention or desire to do evil; ill will: *I bear no malice toward anybody.* ■ *Law* wrongful intention, esp. as increasing the guilt of certain offenses.

mal·ice a·fore·thought ▸ *n. Law* the intention to kill or harm, which is held to distinguish unlawful killing from murder.

ma·li·cious /mə'lishəs/ ▸ *adj.* characterized by malice; intending or intended to do harm: *malicious destruction of property.* ▷Middle English (also in the sense 'wicked'): from Old French *malicios*, from Latin *malitiosus*, from *malitia* 'malice,' from *malus* 'bad.' —**ma·li·cious·ly** *adv.* —**ma·li·cious·ness** *n.*

ma·lign /mə'līn/ ▸ *adj.* evil in nature or effect; malevolent: *she had a strong and malign influence.* ■ *archaic* (of a disease) malignant. ▸ *v.* [*tr.*] speak about (someone) in a spitefully critical manner. —**ma·lign·er** *n.* —**ma·lig·ni·ty** /-'lignətē/ *n.* —**ma·lign·ly** *adv.*

ma·lig·nant /mə'lignənt/ ▸ *adj.* **1** (of a disease) very virulent or infectious. ■ (of a tumor) tending to invade normal tissue or to recur after removal; cancerous. Contrasted with BENIGN. **2** malevolent: *in the hands of malignant fate.* —**ma·lig·nan·cy** /-nənsē/ *n.* —**ma·lig·nant·ly** *adv.*

ma·lin·ger /mə'liNGgər/ ▸ *v.* [*intr.*] exaggerate or feign illness in order to escape duty or work. —**ma·lin·ger·er** *n.*

mall /môl/ ▸ *n.* **1** (also **shopping mall**) a large building or series of connected buildings containing a variety of retail stores and typically also restaurants. **2** a sheltered walk or promenade. ■ (also **pedestrian mall**) a section of a street, typically in the downtown area of a city, from which vehicular traffic is excluded.

mal·lard /'malərd/ ▸ *n.* (*pl.* same or **mallards**) the most common duck (*Anas platyrhynchos*) of the northern hemisphere and the ancestor of most domestic ducks, the male having a dark green head and white collar. ▷Middle English: from Old French 'wild drake,' from *masle* 'male.'

mal·le·a·ble /'malyəbəl; 'malēə-/ ▸ *adj.* (of a metal or other material) able to be hammered or pressed permanently out of shape without breaking or cracking. ■ *fig.* easily influenced; pliable: *Anna was shaken enough to be malleable.* —**mal·le·a·bil·i·ty** /,malyə'bilitē; ,malēə-/ *n.* —**mal·le·a·bly** /-blē/ *adv.*

mal·let /'malət/ ▸ *n.* a hammer with a large wooden head, used esp. for hitting a chisel. ■ a long-handled wooden stick with a head like a hammer, used for hitting a croquet or polo ball. ■ *Mus.* a wooden or plastic stick with a rounded head, used to play certain percussion instruments such as xylophone and marimba.

mal·le·us /'malēəs/ ▸ *n.* (*pl.* **mal·le·i** /'malē,ī; -ē,ē/) *Anat.* a small bone in the middle ear that transmits vibrations of the eardrum to the incus.

mal·low /'malō/ ▸ *n.* a herbaceous plant (genus *Malva*) with pink or purple flowers and disk-shaped fruit. The **mallow family** (Malvaceae) also includes the hollyhocks and hibiscus.

mal·nour·ished /mal'nərisht; -'nə-risht/ ▸ *adj.* suffering from malnutrition. —**mal·nourish·ment** /-'nərishmənt/ *n.*

mal·nu·tri·tion /,malnōō'trishən/ ▸ *n.* lack of proper nutrition, caused by not having enough to eat, not eating enough of the right things, or being unable to use the food that one does eat.

mal·oc·clu·sion /,malə'klōōzHən/ ▸ *n. Dentistry* imperfect positioning of the teeth when the jaws are closed.

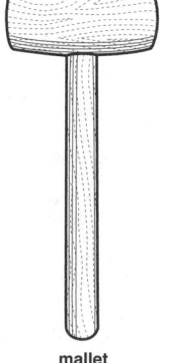

mallet

mal·o·dor·ous /mal'ōdərəs/ ▶*adj.* smelling very unpleasant.

mal·prac·tice /mal'praktəs/ ▶*n.* improper, illegal, or negligent professional activity or treatment, esp. by a medical practitioner, lawyer, or public official.

malt /môlt/ ▶*n.* barley or other grain that has been steeped, germinated, and dried, used esp. for brewing or distilling and vinegar-making. ■ *chiefly Brit.* short for MALT WHISKEY. ■ short for MALTED MILK.
▶*v.* [*tr.*] convert (grain) into malt: [as *n.*] (**malting**) *barley is grown for malting.* ■ [*intr.*] (of a seed) become malt when germination is checked by drought. —**malt·i·ness** /-tēnis/ *n.* —**malt·y** *adj.*

malt·ed milk ▶*n.* a drink combining milk, a malt preparation, and ice cream or flavoring. ■ the powdered mixture from which this drink is made.

Mal·tese¹ /môl'tēz/ ▶*n.* (*pl.* same) **1** a native or national of Malta or a person of Maltese descent. **2** the national language of Malta, a Semitic language derived from Arabic but much influenced by Italian, Spanish, and Norman French.
▶*adj.* of or relating to Malta, its people, or their language.

Mal·tese² (also **Maltese terrier**) ▶*n.* a dog of a very small long-haired breed, typically with white hair.

Mal·tese cross ▶*n.* a cross with arms of equal length that broaden from the center and have their ends indented in a shallow V-shape.

malt liq·uor ▶*n.* alcoholic liquor made from malt by fermentation rather than distillation; beer with a relatively high alcohol content.

malt·ose /'môl,tōs; -,tōz/ ▶*n.* Chem. a sugar produced by the breakdown of starch, e.g., by enzymes found in malt and saliva.

mal·treat /mal'trēt/ ▶*v.* [*tr.*] (often **be maltreated**) treat (a person or animal) cruelly or with violence. —**mal·treat·er** *n.* —**mal·treat·ment** *n.*

malt whis·key ▶*n.* whiskey made only from malted barley and not blended with grain whiskey.

ma·ma /'mämə/ (also **mam·ma**) ▶*n.* **1** one's mother (esp. as a child's term): [as *name*] *come and meet Mama.* **2** *inf.* a mature woman: *the ultimate tough blues mama.*

mam·ba /'mämbə/ ▶*n.* a large, agile, highly venomous African snake (genus *Dendroaspis*, family Elapidae).

mam·bo /'mämbō/ ▶*n.* (*pl.* **-bos**) a Latin American dance similar in rhythm to the rumba.
▶*v.* (**-boes, -boed**) [*intr.*] dance the mambo.

mam·ma¹ ▶*n.* variant spelling of MAMA.

mam·ma² /'mamə/ ▶*n.* (*pl.* **mam·mae** /'mamē; 'mam,ī/) a milk-secreting organ of female mammals (in humans, the breast). ■ a corresponding nonsecretory structure in male mammals. —**mam·mi·form** /'mamə,fôrm/ *adj.*

mam·mal /'maməl/ ▶*n.* a warm-blooded vertebrate animal of a class that is distinguished by the possession of hair or fur, the secretion of milk by females for the nourishment of the young, and (typically) the birth of live young. —**mam·ma·li·an** /mə'mālēən/ *adj.*

mam·ma·ry /'mamərē/ ▶*adj.* denoting or relating to the human female breasts or the milk-secreting organs of other mammals.
▶*n.* (*pl.* **-ries**) *inf.* a breast.

mam·mo·gram /'mamə,gram/ ▶*n.* an image obtained by mammography.

mam·mog·ra·phy /ma'mägrəfē/ ▶*n.* Med. a technique using X-rays to diagnose and locate tumors of the breasts.

mam·mon /'mamən/ (also **Mam·mon**) ▶*n.* wealth regarded as an evil influence or false object of worship and devotion.

mam·moth /'maməTH/ ▶*n.* a large extinct elephant (genus *Mammuthus*) of the Pleistocene epoch, typically hairy with a sloping back and long curved tusks.
▶*adj.* huge: *a mammoth corporation.*

man /man/ ▶*n.* (*pl.* **men** /men/) **1** an adult human male. ■ a male worker or employee: *more than 700 men were laid off.* ■ a male member of a sports team: *Johnson took the ball past three men and scored.* ■ (**men**) ordinary members of the armed forces as distinct from the officers: *he had a platoon of forty men to prepare for battle.* ■ a husband, boyfriend, or lover: *the two of them lived for a time as man and wife.* ■ a male person associated with a particular place, activity, or occupation: *I'm a union man.* ■ a male pursued or sought by another, esp. in connection with a crime: *Inspector Bull was sure they would find their man.* ■ *dated* a manservant or valet. ■ *hist.* a vassal. **2** a person: *God cares for all races and all men.* ■ (also **Man**) human beings in general; the human race: *places untouched by the ravages of man.* ■ an individual; one: *a man could buy a lot with eighteen million dollars.* ■ a person with the qualities often associated with males such as bravery, spirit, or toughness: *she was more of a man than any of them.* ■ a type of prehistoric human named after the

place where the remains were found: *Cro-Magnon man.* **3** (usu. **the Man**) *inf.* a group or person in a position of authority over others, such as a corporate employer or the police. ■ *black slang* white people collectively regarded as the controlling group in society: *he urged that black athletes boycott the Man's Rose Bowl.* **4** a figure or token used in playing a board game.
▶*v.* (**manned, man·ning**) [*tr.*] **1** (often **be manned**) provide (something, esp. a place or machine) with the personnel to run, operate, or defend it: *the firemen manned the pumps and fought the blaze.* ■ provide someone to fill (a post or office). **2** *archaic* fortify the spirits or courage of: *he manned himself with dauntless air.*
▶*interj. inf.* used, irrespective of the sex of the person addressed, to express surprise, admiration, delight, etc., or for emphasis: *man, what a show!*
▶ □ **the man in** (or **on**) **the street** an ordinary person, often with regard to their opinions, or as distinct from an expert: *it will be interesting to hear what the man in the street has to say about these latest tax cuts.* □ **man of the cloth** a clergyman. □ **man of letters** a male scholar or author. □ **man's best friend** an affectionate or approving way of referring to the dog.

man·a·cle /'manikəl/ ▶*n.* (usu. **manacles**) a metal band, chain, or shackle for fastening someone's hands or ankles.
▶*v.* [*tr.*] (usu. **be manacled**) fetter (a person or a part of the body) with manacles: *his hands were manacled behind his back.*

man·age /'manij/ ▶*v.* **1** [*tr.*] be in charge of (a company, establishment, or undertaking); administer; run. ■ administer and regulate (resources under one's control): *we manage our cash extremely well.* ■ have the position of supervising (staff) at work: *the skills needed to manage a young, dynamic team.* ■ be the manager of (a sports team or a performer): *he managed five or six bands in his career.* ■ maintain control or influence over (a person or animal): *she manages horses better than anyone I know.* ■ (often **be managed**) control the use or exploitation of (land): *the forest is managed to achieve maximum growth.* **2** [*intr.*] succeed in surviving or in attaining one's aims, esp. against heavy odds; cope: *Catherine managed on five hours' sleep a night.* ■ [*tr.*] succeed in doing, achieving, or producing (something, esp. something difficult): *she managed a brave but unconvincing smile | Beth finally managed to hail a cab* [*tr.*] succeed in dealing with or withstanding (something): *there was more stress and anxiety than he could manage.* ■ [*tr.*] be free to attend on (a certain day) or at (a certain time): *he could not manage March 24 after all.*

man·age·a·ble /'manijəbəl/ ▶*adj.* able to be managed, controlled, or accomplished without great difficulty: *the situation was manageable, if a little nerve-racking.* —**man·age·a·bil·i·ty** /,manijə'bilətē/ *n.* —**man·age·a·ble·ness** *n.* —**man·age·a·bly** /-blē/ *adv.*

man·aged care ▶*n.* a system of health care in which patients agree to visit only certain doctors and hospitals, and in which the cost of treatment is monitored by a managing company.

man·age·ment /'manijmənt/ ▶*n.* the process of dealing with or controlling things or people. ■ the responsibility for and control of a company or similar organization: *a successful career in management.* ■ [treated as *sing.* or *pl.*] the people in charge of running a company or organization, regarded collectively: *management was extremely cooperative.*

man·age·ment in·for·ma·tion sys·tem ▶(abbr. **MIS**) *n.* a computerized information-processing system designed to support the activities of company or organizational management.

man·ag·er /'manijər/ ▶*n.* a person responsible for controlling or administering all or part of a company or similar organization. ■ a person who controls the activities, business dealings, and other aspects of the career of an entertainer, athlete, group of musicians, etc.: *she left it to her manager to deal with the canceled concerts.* ■ a person in charge of the activities, tactics, and training of a sports team: *Frank Robinson became baseball's first black manager.* ■ (in a high school or college) a student who assists the coach of an athletic team. ■ *Comput.* a program or system that controls or organizes a peripheral device or process: *a file manager.* —**man·a·ge·ri·al** /,manə'jirēəl/ *adj.* —**man·ag·er·ship** /-,SHip/ *n.*

man·ag·ing /'manijiNG/ ▶*adj.* having executive or supervisory control or authority: *a managing editor | the managing director.*

ma·ña·na /mən'yänə/ ▶*adv.* in the indefinite future (used to indicate procrastination): *the exhibition will be ready mañana.*

man·a·tee /'manə,tē/ ▶*n.* an aquatic mammal (family Trichechidae, genus *Trichechus*) with a rounded tail flipper, living in shallow coastal waters of the tropical Atlantic.

Pronunciation Key ə *ago, up;* ər *over, fur;* a *hat;* ā *ate;* ä *car;* CH *chin;* e *let;* ē *see;* e(ə)r *air;* i *fit;* ī *by;* i(ə)r *ear;* NG *sing;* ō *go;* ô *law, for;* oi *toy;* oͦo *good;* oͦo *goo;* ou *out;* SH *she;* TH *thin;* T͟H *then;* (h)w *why;* ZH *vision*

man·da·la /ˈmandələ; ˈmən-/ ▶ n. a geometric figure representing the universe in Hindu and Buddhist symbolism. —**man·dal·ic** /manˈdalik; ˌmən-/ adj.

man·da·mus /manˈdāməs/ ▶ n. Law a judicial writ issued as a command to an inferior court or ordering a person to perform a public or statutory duty: a writ of mandamus.

man·da·rin¹ /ˈmandərən/ ▶ n. 1 (**Mandarin**) the standard literary and official form of Chinese based on the Beijing dialect, spoken by over 730 million people: [as adj.] Mandarin Chinese. 2 an official in any of the nine top grades of the former imperial Chinese civil service. ■ [as adj.] (esp. of clothing) characteristic or supposedly characteristic of such officials: a red-buttoned mandarin cap. ■ a powerful official or senior bureaucrat, esp. one perceived as reactionary and secretive: a civil service mandarin.

man·da·rin² (also **man·da·rine** /-rēn/, **mandarin orange**) ▶ n. 1 a small flattish citrus fruit (Citrus reticulata) with a loose skin, esp. a variety with yellow-orange skin. Compare with TANGERINE. 2 the citrus tree that yields this fruit.

man·date /ˈman,dāt/ ▶ n. 1 an official order or commission to do something. ■ Law a commission by which a party is entrusted to perform a service, esp. without payment and with indemnity against loss by that party. ■ Law an order from an appellate court to a lower court to take a specific action. ■ hist. a commission from the League of Nations to a member state to administer a territory: the British mandate in Palestine. 2 the authority to carry out a policy or course of action, regarded as given by the electorate to a candidate or party that is victorious in an election.
▶ v. [tr.] 1 give (someone) authority to act in a certain way. ■ require (something) to be done; make mandatory. 2 hist. assign (territory) under a mandate of the League of Nations.

man·da·to·ry /ˈmandəˌtôrē/ ▶ adj. required by law or rules; compulsory. ■ of or conveying a command: he did not want the guidelines to be mandatory. —**man·da·to·ri·ly** /-ˌtôrəlē/ adv.

man·di·ble /ˈmandəbəl/ ▶ n. Anat. & Zool. the jaw or a jawbone, esp. the lower jawbone in mammals and fishes. ■ either of the upper and lower parts of a bird's beak. ■ either half of the crushing organ in an arthropod's mouthparts. —**man·dib·u·lar** /manˈdibyələr/ adj. —**man·dib·u·late** /manˈdibyə,lāt/ adj.

man·do·lin /ˌmandəˈlin; ˈmandələn/ ▶ n. a musical instrument resembling a lute, having paired metal strings plucked with a plectrum. —**man·do·lin·ist** n.

man·drake /ˈman,drāk/ ▶ n. 1 a Mediterranean plant (Mandragora officinarum) of the nightshade family, with white or purple flowers and yellow berries. It has a forked root that supposedly resembles the human form and was formerly used in medicine and magic. 2 another term for MAYAPPLE.

man·drel /ˈmandrəl/ ▶ n. 1 a shaft or spindle in a lathe to which work is fixed while being turned. 2 a cylindrical rod around which metal or other material is forged or shaped.

mandolin

man·drill /ˈmandrəl/ ▶ n. a large West African baboon (Mandrillus sphinx) with a brightly colored red and blue face, the male having a blue rump.

mane /mān/ ▶ n. a growth of long hair on the neck of a horse, lion, or other animal. ■ a person's long or thick hair: he had a mane of white hair. —**maned** adj. —**mane·less** adj.

ma·nège /maˈnezh; mə-/ ▶ n. an arena or enclosed area in which horses and riders are trained. ■ the movements of a trained horse. ■ horsemanship.

ma·neu·ver /məˈnoovər/ (Brit. **ma·noeu·vre**) ▶ n. 1 a movement or series of moves requiring skill and care. ■ a carefully planned scheme or action, esp. one involving deception: shady financial maneuvers. ■ the fact or process of taking such action: the economic policy provided no room for maneuver. 2 (**maneuvers**) a large-scale military exercise of troops, warships, and other forces.
▶ v. (**-vered, -ver·ing**) 1 perform or cause to perform a movement or series of moves requiring skill and car. 2 [tr.] carefully guide or manipulate (someone or something) in order to achieve an end: they were maneuvering him into a betrayal of his countryman. ■ [intr.] carefully

manipulate a situation to achieve an end: [as n.] (**maneuvering**) two decades of political maneuvering. —**ma·neu·ver·a·ble** adj. —**ma·neu·ver·er** n.

man Fri·day ▶ n. a male helper or follower.

man·ga·nese /ˈmaNGgə,nēz; -,nēs/ ▶ n. the chemical element of atomic number 25, a hard gray metal of the transition series. Manganese is an important component of special steels and magnetic alloys. (Symbol: **Mn**)

mange /mānj/ ▶ n. a skin disease of mammals caused by parasitic mites and occasionally communicable to humans.

man·ger /ˈmānjər/ ▶ n. a long open box or trough for horses or cattle to eat from.

man·gle¹ /ˈmaNGgəl/ ▶ v. [tr.] severely mutilate, disfigure, or damage by cutting, tearing, or crushing: fig. he was mangling Bach on the piano. —**man·gler** n.

man·gle² ▶ n. a large machine for ironing sheets or other fabrics, usually when they are damp, using heated rollers. ■ chiefly Brit. a machine having two or more cylinders turned by a handle, between which wet laundry is squeezed (to remove excess moisture) and pressed.
▶ v. [tr.] press or squeeze with a mangle.

man·go /ˈmaNGgō/ ▶ n. (pl. **-oes** or **-os**) 1 a fleshy yellowish-red tropical fruit that is eaten ripe or used green for pickles or chutneys. 2 (also **mango tree**) the evergreen Indian tree (Mangifera indica) of the cashew family that bears this fruit, widely cultivated in the tropics. ▷late 16th cent.: from Portuguese manga, from a Dravidian language.

man·go·steen /ˈmaNGgə,stēn/ ▶ n. 1 a tropical fruit with sweet juicy white segments of flesh inside a thick rind. 2 the Malaysian tree (Garcinia mangostana, family Guttiferae) that bears this fruit.

man·grove /ˈman,grōv; ˈmaNG-/ ▶ n. a tree or shrub (families Rhizophoraceae and Verbenaceae or Avicenniaceae) that grows in muddy, chiefly tropical coastal swamps, typically having numerous tangled roots above ground that form dense thickets. ■ (also **mangrove swamp**) a tidal swamp that is dominated by mangroves and associated vegetation.

man·gy /ˈmānjē/ (also **man·gey**) ▶ adj. (**-gi·er, -gi·est**) having mange. ■ in poor condition; shabby: a mangy fur coat. —**man·gi·ness** /-jēnis/ n.

man·han·dle /ˈman,handl/ ▶ v. [tr.] move (a heavy object) by hand with great effort. ■ inf. handle (someone) roughly by dragging or pushing: a drunk had manhandled one of the deputies.

man·hole /ˈman,hōl/ ▶ n. a small covered opening in a floor, pavement, or other surface to allow a person to enter, esp. an opening in a city street leading to a sewer.

man·hood /ˈman,hood/ ▶ n. the state or period of being a man rather than a child. ■ men, esp. those of a country, regarded collectively: Germany had lost the best of her young manhood. ■ qualities traditionally associated with men, such as courage, strength, and sexual potency: we drank to prove our manhood. ■ archaic the condition of being human: the unity of Godhead and manhood in Christ. ■ (**one's manhood**) inf. used euphemistically to refer to a man's genitals.

man-hour ▶ n. an hour regarded in terms of the amount of work that can be done by one person within this period.

man·hunt /ˈman,hənt/ ▶ n. an organized search for a person, esp. a criminal.

ma·ni·a /ˈmānēə/ ▶ n. mental illness marked by periods of great excitement, euphoria, delusions, and overactivity. ■ an excessive enthusiasm or desire; an obsession: he had a mania for automobiles.

ma·ni·ac /ˈmānē,ak/ ▶ n. inf. a person exhibiting extreme symptoms of wild behavior, esp. when violent and dangerous: a homicidal maniac. ■ an obsessive enthusiast: a gambling maniac. ■ archaic Psychiatry a person suffering from mania. —**ma·ni·a·cal** /məˈnīəkəl/ adj. —**ma·ni·a·cal·ly** /məˈnīək(ə)lē/ adv.

man·ic /ˈmanik/ ▶ adj. showing wild and apparently deranged excitement and energy: his manic enthusiasm | a manic grin. ■ frenetically busy; frantic: the pace is utterly manic. ■ Psychiatry relating to or affected by mania: the manic interludes in depression. —**man·i·cal·ly** /-(ə)lē/ adv.

man·ic de·pres·sion ▶ n. another term, esp. formerly, for BIPOLAR DISORDER. —**man·ic-de·pres·sive** adj. & n.

man·i·cure /ˈmani,kyŏŏr/ ▶ n. a cosmetic treatment of the hands involving cutting, shaping, and often painting of the nails, removal of the cuticles, and softening of the skin.
▶ v. [tr.] give a manicure to. ■ [usu. as adj.] (**manicured**) trim neatly. —**man·i·cur·ist** n.

man·i·fest¹ /ˈmanə,fest/ ▶ adj. clear or obvious to the eye or mind: the system's manifest failings.
▶ v. [tr.] display or show (a quality or feeling) by one's acts or appearance;

demonstrate. ■ (often **be manifested in**) be evidence of; prove: *bad industrial relations are often manifested in disputes and strikes.* ■ [*intr.*] (of an ailment) become apparent through the appearance of symptoms: *a disorder that usually manifests in middle age.* ■ [*intr.*] (of a ghost or spirit) appear: *one deity manifested in the form of a bird.* —**man·i·fes·ta·tion** /ˌmanəfesˈtāsHən/ *n.* —**man·i·fest·ly** *adv.*

man·i·fest² ▶*n.* a document giving comprehensive details of a ship and its cargo and other contents, passengers, and crew for the use of customs officers. ■ a list of passengers or cargo in an aircraft. ■ a list of the cars forming a freight train.
▶*v.* [*tr.*] record in such a manifest.

Man·i·fest Des·ti·ny ▶*n.* the 19th-century doctrine or belief that the expansion of the U.S. throughout the western hemisphere was both justified and inevitable.

man·i·fes·to /ˌmanəˈfestō/ ▶*n.* (*pl.* **-tos**) a public declaration of policy and aims, esp. one issued by a political party or candidate.

man·i·fold /ˈmanəˌfōld/ ▶*adj.* many and various. ■ having many different forms or elements: *the appeal of the crusade was manifold.*
▶*n.* **1** a pipe or chamber branching into several openings: *the pipeline manifold.* ■ (in an internal combustion engine) the part conveying air and fuel from the carburetor to the cylinders or that leading from the cylinders to the exhaust pipe. **2** *technical* something with many different parts or forms, in particular: ■ *Math.* a collection of points forming a certain kind of set, such as those of a topologically closed surface or an analog of this in three or more dimensions. —**man·i·fold·ly** *adv.* —**man·i·fold·ness** *n.*

man·i·kin /ˈmanikən/ (also **man·ni·kin**) ▶*n.* **1** a person who is very small, esp. one not otherwise abnormal or deformed. **2** a jointed model of the human body, used in anatomy or as an artist's lay figure.

Ma·nil·a (also **Ma·nil·la**) ▶*n.* (also **Manila hemp**) the strong fiber of a Philippine plant, used for rope, matting, paper, etc.: [as *adj.*] *Manila rope.* ■ (also **Manila paper**) strong brown paper, originally made from Manila hemp.

man·i·oc /ˈmanēˌäk/ ▶*n.* another term for CASSAVA.

ma·nip·u·late /məˈnipyəˌlāt/ ▶*v.* [*tr.*] **1** handle or control (a tool, mechanism, etc.), typically in a skillful manner. ■ alter, edit, or move (text or data) on a computer. ■ examine or treat (a part of the body) by feeling or moving it with the hand: *a system of healing based on manipulating the ligaments of the spine.* **2** control or influence (a person or situation) cleverly, unfairly, or unscrupulously: *the masses were manipulated by a tiny group.* ■ alter (data) or present (statistics) so as to mislead. —**ma·nip·u·la·bil·i·ty** /-ˌnipyələˈbilətē/ *n.* —**ma·nip·u·la·ble** /-ləbəl/ *adj.* —**ma·nip·u·lat·a·ble** /-ˌlātəbəl/ *adj.* —**ma·nip·u·la·tion** /mə,nipyəˈlāsHən/ *n.* —**ma·nip·u·la·tor** /-ˌlātər/ *n.* —**ma·nip·u·la·to·ry** /-lə,tôrē/ *adj.*

ma·nip·u·la·tive /məˈnipyələtiv/ -ˌlātiv/ ▶*adj.* **1** characterized by unscrupulous control of a situation or person. **2** of or relating to manipulation of an object or part of the body: *a manipulative skill.* —**ma·nip·u·la·tive·ly** *adv.* —**ma·nip·u·la·tive·ness** *n.*

man·i·tou /ˈmaniˌtōō/ ▶*n.* (among certain Algonquian Indians) a good or evil spirit as an object of reverence.

man·kind /ˌmanˈkīnd; ˈman,kīnd/ ▶*n.* **1** human beings considered collectively; the human race. **2** /ˈman,kīnd/ *archaic* men, as distinct from women.

man·ly /ˈmanlē/ ▶*adj.* (**-li·er, -li·est**) having or denoting those good qualities traditionally associated with men, such as courage and strength. ■ (of an activity) befitting a man, esp. in a traditional sense: *the manly art of knife-throwing.* —**man·li·ness** /-lēnis/ *n.*

man-made ▶*adj.* made or caused by human beings (as opposed to occurring or being made naturally); artificial: *a man-made lake.*

man·na /ˈmanə/ ▶*n.* (in the Bible) the substance miraculously supplied as food to the Israelites in the wilderness. ■ an unexpected or gratuitous benefit: *the cakes were manna from heaven.*

manned /mand/ ▶*adj.* (esp. of an aircraft or spacecraft) having a human crew: *a manned mission to Mars.*

man·ne·quin /ˈmanikən/ ▶*n.* a dummy used to display clothes in a store window. ■ *chiefly hist.* a young woman or man employed to show clothes to customers.

man·ner /ˈmanər/ ▶*n.* **1** a way in which a thing is done or happens: *taking notes in an unobtrusive manner.* ■ a style in literature or art: *a dramatic poem in the manner of Goethe.* ■ (**manner of**) *chiefly poetic/lit.* a kind or sort of: *what manner of man is he?* **2** a person's outward bearing or way of behaving toward others: *his arrogance and pompous manner.* (**manners**) polite or well-bred social behavior: *didn't your mother teach you any manners?* ■ social behavior or habits: *Tim apologized for his son's bad manners.* ▷Middle English: from Old French *maniere,* based on Latin *manuarius* 'of the hand,' from *manus* 'hand.' —**man·ner·less** *adj.*

▶ □ **all manner of** many different kinds of: *they accuse me of all manner of evil things.* □ **in a manner of speaking** in some sense; so to speak. □ **to the manner born** naturally at ease in a specified job or situation. ■ destined by birth to follow a custom or way of life.

man·nered /ˈmanərd/ ▶*adj.* **1** [in *comb.*] behaving in a specified way: *pleasant-mannered.* **2** (of a writer, artist, or artistic style) marked by idiosyncratic mannerisms; artificial, stilted, and overelaborate in delivery: *inane dialogue and mannered acting.*

man·ner·ism /ˈmanə,rizəm/ ▶*n.* a habitual gesture or way of speaking or behaving.

man·ner·ly /ˈmanərlē/ ▶*adj.* well-mannered; polite. —**man·ner·li·ness** /-lēnis/ *n.*

man·ni·kin /ˈmanikən/ ▶*n.* variant spelling of MANIKIN.

man·nish /ˈmanisH/ ▶*adj.* *often derog.* (of a woman) having characteristics that are stereotypically associated with men and can be considered unbecoming in a woman. —**man·nish·ly** *adv.* —**man·nish·ness** *n.*

man-of-war (also **man-o'-war**) ▶*n.* (*pl.* **men-of-war** also **men-o'-war**) *hist.* an armed sailing ship. ■ short for PORTUGUESE MAN-OF-WAR.

ma·nom·e·ter /məˈnämətər/ ▶*n.* an instrument for measuring the pressure acting on a column of fluid, esp. one with a U-shaped tube of liquid in which a difference in the pressures acting in the two arms of the tube causes the liquid to reach different heights in the two arms. —**man·o·met·ric** /ˌmanəˈmetrik/ *adj.* —**man·o·met·ri·cal·ly** /ˌmanə-ˈmetrik(ə)lē/ *adv.* —**ma·nom·e·try** /-trē/ *n.*

man·or /ˈmanər/ ▶*n.* (also **manor house**) a large country house with lands; the principal house of a landed estate. ■ *chiefly hist.* (esp. in England and Wales) a unit of land, originally a feudal lordship, consisting of a lord's demesne and lands rented to tenants. ■ *hist.* (in North America) an estate or district leased to tenants, esp. one granted by royal charter in a British colony or by the Dutch governors of what is now New York. —**ma·no·ri·al** /məˈnôrēəl/ *adj.*

man·pow·er /ˈman,pouər/ ▶*n.* the number of people working or available for work or service: *the police had only limited manpower.*

man·sard /ˈman,särd; -sərd/ ▶*n.* (also **mansard roof**) a roof that has four sloping sides, each of which becomes steeper halfway down. ■ a story or apartment under a mansard roof.

manse /mans/ ▶*n.* the house occupied by a minister of a Presbyterian church. ■ a large stately house; a mansion.

man·serv·ant /ˈman,sərvənt/ ▶*n.* (*pl.* **men·ser·vants** /ˈmen,sərvənts/) a male servant.

man·sion /ˈmansHən/ ▶*n.* a large, impressive house. ■ a manor house (see MANOR).

man-sized (also **man-size**) ▶*adj.* of the size of a human being. ■ large enough to occupy, suit, or satisfy a man: *a man-sized breakfast.* ■ formidable: *a man-size job.*

man·slaugh·ter /ˈman,slôtər/ ▶*n.* the crime of killing a human being without malice aforethought, or otherwise in circumstances not amounting to murder: *the defendant was convicted of manslaughter.*

man·ta /ˈmantə/ ▶*n.* **1** (also **manta ray**) a devil ray (*Manta birostris,* family Mobulidae) that occurs in all tropical seas and may reach very great size. **2** a rough-textured cotton fabric made and used in Spanish America. ■ a shawl made of this fabric.

man·tel /ˈmantl/ (also **man·tle**) ▶*n.* a mantelpiece or mantelshelf.

man·tel·piece /ˈmantl,pēs/ (also **man·tle·piece**) ▶*n.* a structure of wood, marble, or stone above and around a fireplace. ■ a mantelshelf.

man·tel·shelf /ˈmantl,sHelf/ (also **man·tle·shelf**) ▶*n.* a shelf above a fireplace.

man·til·la /manˈtē(y)ə; -ˈtilə/ ▶*n.* a lace or silk scarf worn by women over the hair and shoulders, esp. in Spain.

man·tis /ˈmantis/ (also **praying mantis**) ▶*n.* (*pl.* same or **mantises**) a predatory insect (Mantidae and other families) related to the cockroach, with large spiky forelegs folded like hands in prayer.

man·tle¹ /ˈmantl/ ▶*n.* **1** a loose sleeveless cloak or shawl, worn esp. by women. ■ *fig.* a covering of a specified sort: *the houses were covered with a thick mantle of snow.* ■ (also **gas mantle**) a fragile mesh cover fixed around a gas jet, kerosene wick, etc., to give an incandescent light when heated. ■ *Zool.* an outer or enclosing layer of tissue, esp. (in mollusks and brachiopods) a fold of skin enclosing the viscera and secreting the substance that produces the shell. **2** an important role or responsibility that passes from one person to another: *the second son has now assumed his father's mantle.* **3** *Geol.* the region of the earth's interior between the crust and the core, believed to consist of hot, dense silicate rocks (mainly peridotite).

▶ *v.* [*tr.*] *poetic/lit.* clothe in or as if in a mantle; cloak or envelop: *heavy mists mantled the forested slopes.*

man·tle² ▶ *n.* variant spelling of MANTEL.

man·tra /'mantrə; 'män-/ ▶ *n.* (originally in Hinduism and Buddhism) a word or sound repeated to aid concentration in meditation. ■ a Vedic hymn. ■ a statement or slogan repeated frequently: *the environmental mantra that energy has for too long been too cheap.* —**man·tric** /-trik/ *adj.*

man·u·al /'manyə(wə)l/ ▶ *adj.* of or done with the hands. ■ (of a machine or device) worked by hand, not automatically or electronically: *a manual typewriter.* ■ using or working with the hands: *a manual laborer.*

▶ *n.* **1** a book of instructions, esp. for operating a machine or learning a subject; a handbook. ■ a small book: *a pocket-sized manual of the artist's aphorisms.* **2** a thing operated or done by hand rather than automatically or electronically. —**man·u·al·ly** *adv.*

man·u·fac·ture /,manyə'fakCHər/ ▶ *n.* the making of articles on a large scale using machinery: *the manufacture of armored vehicles.* ■ a specified branch of industry: *porcelain manufacture.* ■ the production of a natural substance by a living thing: *the genetic blueprint for the manufacture of a protein.* ■ (**manufactures**) manufactured goods or articles: *exports and imports of manufactures.*

▶ *v.* [*tr.*] **1** make (something) on a large scale using machinery. [as *adj.*] (**manufacturing**) *a manufacturing company.* ■ (of a living thing) produce (a substance) naturally. ■ make or produce (something abstract) in a merely mechanical way: [as *adj.*] (**manufactured**) *his litany of manufactured love songs.* **2** invent or fabricate (evidence or a story). —**man·u·fac·tur·a·bil·i·ty** /-,fakCHərə'bilətē/ *n.* —**man·u·fac·tur·a·ble** *adj.* —**man·u·fac·tur·er** *n.*

man·u·mit /,manyə'mit/ ▶ *v.* (**-mit·ted, -mit·ting**) [*tr.*] *hist.* release from slavery; set free. —**man·u·mis·sion** /-'misHən/ *n.* —**man·u·mit·ter** *n.*

ma·nure /mə'n(y)oor/ ▶ *n.* animal dung used for fertilizing land. ■ any compost or artificial fertilizer.

▶ *v.* [*tr.*] apply manure to (land): *the ground should be well dug and manured.*

man·u·script /'manyə,skript/ ▶ *n.* a book, document, or piece of music written by hand rather than typed or printed: *an illuminated manuscript.* ■ an author's text that has not yet been published: *preparing the final manuscript | her autobiography remained* **in manuscript**. ▷late 16th cent.: from medieval Latin *manuscriptus*, from *manu* 'by hand' + *scriptus* 'written' (past participle of *scribere*).

Manx /maNGks/ ▶ *adj.* of or relating to the Isle of Man.

▶ *n.* **1** the now extinct Goidelic language formerly spoken in the Isle of Man. **2** (**the Manx**) the Manx people collectively. —**Manx·man** /-mən/ *n.* (*pl.* **-men**). —**Manx·wom·an** /-,woomən/ *n.* (*pl.* **-wom·en**).

Manx cat ▶ *n.* a cat of a breed having no tail or an extremely short one.

man·y /'menē/ ▶ *adj. & pron.* (**more** /môr/, **most** /mōst/) a large number of: [as *adj.*] *many people arrived with her* | [as *pron.*] *the solution to* **many of** *our problems | many think it is a new craze.*

▶ *n.* [as *pl. n.*] (**the many**) the majority of people: *music for the many.*

▶ □ **as many** the same number of: *changing his mind for the third time in as many months.* □ **how many** used to ask what a particular quantity is: *how many books did you sell?*

man·y-sid·ed ▶ *adj.* having many sides or aspects: *the reasons for poor collaboration are complex and many-sided.* —**man·y-sid·ed·ness** *n.*

Mao·ism /'mou,izəm/ ▶ *n.* the communist doctrines of Mao Zedong as formerly practiced in China, having as a central idea permanent revolution and stressing the importance of the peasantry, of small-scale industry, and of abolishing the private ownership of farms. —**Mao·ist** *n. & adj.*

Ma·o·ri /'mourē/ ▶ *n.* (*pl.* same or **-ris**) **1** a member of the aboriginal people of New Zealand. **2** the Polynesian language of this people.

▶ *adj.* of or relating to the Maoris or their language.

MAP ▶ *abbr.* modified American plan (see AMERICAN PLAN).

map /map/ ▶ *n.* **1** a diagrammatic representation of an area of land or sea showing physical features, cities, roads, etc. ■ a two-dimensional representation of the positions of stars or other astronomical objects. ■ a diagram or collection of data showing the spatial arrangement or distribution of something over an area: *an electron density map.* ■ *Biol.* a representation of the sequence of genes on a chromosome or of bases in a DNA or RNA molecule. **2** *inf., dated* a person's face.

▶ *v.* (**mapped, map·ping**) [*tr.*] represent (an area) on a map; make a map of: *inaccessible parts will be mapped from the air.* ■ record in detail the spatial distribution of (something): *the project to map the human genome.* ■ *Math.* associate each element of (a set) with an element of another set.

▶ *phrasal v.* □ **map something out** plan a route or course of action in

detail: *I mapped out a route over familiar country near home.* —**map·less** *adj.* —**map·pa·ble** *adj.* —**map·per** *n.*

▶ □ **off the map** (of a place) very distant or remote. □ **put something on the map** bring something to prominence: *the exhibition put Cubism on the map.*

ma·ple /'māpəl/ ▶ *n.* a tree (genus *Acer*, family Aceraceae) with lobed leaves, winged fruits, and colorful autumn foliage, grown as an ornamental or for its timber or syrupy sap. Its many species include the North American **sugar maple** (*A. saccharum*). ■ the flavor of maple syrup or maple sugar.

ma·ple sug·ar ▶ *n.* sugar produced by evaporating the sap of certain maples, esp. the sugar maple.

ma·ple syr·up ▶ *n.* syrup produced from the sap of certain maples, esp. the sugar maple.

map pro·jec·tion ▶ *n.* see PROJECTION (sense 6).

mar /mär/ ▶ *v.* (**marred, mar·ring**) [*tr.*] impair the appearance of; disfigure: *no wrinkles marred her face.* ■ impair the quality of; spoil: *violence marred a number of New Year celebrations.*

Mar. ▶ *abbr.* March.

mar·a·bou /'marə,boo/ ▶ *n.* (also **marabou stork**) **1** a large African stork (*Leptoptilos crumeniferus*) with a massive bill and large neck pouch. ■ down from the marabou used for trimming clothing or on fishing lures. **2** raw silk that can be dyed without being separated from the gum.

ma·rac·as /mə'räkəz/ ▶ *pl. n.* a pair of hollow clublike gourd or gourd-shaped containers filled with beans, pebbles, or similar objects, shaken as a percussion instrument.

mar·a·schi·no /,marə'sHē,nō; -'skē-/ ▶ *n.* (*pl.* **-nos**) a strong, sweet liqueur made from a variety of small bitter cherries. ■ a maraschino cherry.

mar·a·schi·no cher·ry ▶ *n.* a cherry preserved in maraschino or maraschino-flavored syrup.

mar·a·thon /'marə,THän/ ▶ *n.* a long-distance running race, strictly one of 26 miles and 385 yards (42.195 km). ■ a long-lasting or difficult task or operation of a specified kind: *an interview marathon.* ■ [as *adj.*] of great duration or distance; very long. —**mar·a·thon·er** *n.*

ma·raud /mə'rôd/ ▶ *v.* [*intr.*] [often as *adj.*] (**marauding**) roam in search of things to steal or people to attack: *marauding gangs of looters.* ■ [*tr.*] raid and plunder (a place). —**ma·raud·er** *n.*

mar·ble /'märbəl/ ▶ *n.* **1** a hard crystalline metamorphic form of limestone, typically white with mottlings or streaks of color, that is capable of taking a polish and is used in sculpture and architecture. ■ used in similes and comparisons with reference to the smoothness, hardness, or color of marble: *her shoulders were as white as marble.* ■ a marble sculpture. **2** a small ball of colored glass or similar material used as a toy. ■ (**marbles**) [treated as *sing.*] a game in which such balls are rolled along the ground. **3** (**one's marbles**) *inf.* one's mental faculties: *I thought she'd* **lost her marbles**, *asking a question like that.*

▶ *v.* [*tr.*] stain or streak (something) so that it looks like variegated marble: *the low stone walls were marbled with moss and lichen.* —**mar·bler** *n.* —**mar·bly** /-blē; -bəlē/ *adj.*

mar·ble cake ▶ *n.* a cake with a streaked appearance, made of light and dark (esp. chocolate) batter.

mar·bling /'märbəliNG/ ▶ *n.* coloring or marking that resembles variegated marble. ■ streaks of fat in lean meat.

mar·ca·site /'märkə,sīt/ ▶ *n.* a semiprecious stone consisting of pyrite. ■ a bronze-yellow mineral consisting of iron disulfide but differing from pyrite in typically forming aggregates of tabular crystals. ■ a piece of polished steel or a similar metal cut as a gem.

mar·ca·to /mär'kä,tō/ ▶ *adv. & adj. Mus.* (esp. as a direction) played with emphasis.

mar·cel /mär'sel/ *dated* ▶ *n.* (also **marcel wave**) a deep artificial wave in the hair.

▶ *v.* (**-celled, -cel·ling**) [*tr.*] give such a wave to (hair).

March /märCH/ ▶ *n.* the third month of the year, in the northern hemisphere usually considered the first month of spring.

march¹ /märCH/ ▶ *v.* [*intr.*] walk in a military manner with a regular measured tread. ■ walk or proceed quickly and with determination: *without a word she marched from the room.* ■ [*tr.*] force (someone) to walk somewhere quickly: *she gripped Rachel's arm and marched her out through the doors.* ■ walk along public roads in an organized procession to protest about something: *they planned to* **march on** *Baton Rouge.* ■ *fig.* (of something abstract) proceed or advance inexorably: *time marches on.*

▶ *n.* an act or instance of marching: *the relieving force was more than a day's march away.* ■ a piece of music composed to accompany marching or

with a rhythmic character suggestive of marching. ■ a procession as a protest or demonstration: *a protest march.* ■ *fig.* the progress or continuity of something abstract that is considered to be moving inexorably onward: *Marx's theory of the inevitable march of history.*
▶ □ **on the march** marching: *the army was on the march at last.*

march² ▶*n.* (usu. **Marches**) a frontier or border area between two countries or territories, esp. between England and Wales or (formerly) England and Scotland: *the Welsh Marches.*

march·er¹ /ˈmärCHər/ ▶*n.* a person who marches, esp. one taking part in a protest march.

march·er² ▶*n. chiefly hist.* an inhabitant of a frontier or border district.

march·ing or·ders ▶*pl. n.* instructions from a superior officer for troops to depart. ■ *inf.* a dismissal or sending off: *the ref called me over and gave me my marching orders.*

Mar·di Gras /ˈmärdē ˌgrä/ ▶*n.* a carnival held in some countries on Shrove Tuesday, most famously in New Orleans.

mare¹ /me(ə)r/ ▶*n.* the female of a horse or other equine animal.

ma·re² /ˈmärā/ ▶*n.* (*pl.* **ma·ri·a** /ˈmärēə/) *Astron.* a large, level basalt plain on the surface of the moon, appearing dark by contrast with highland areas: [in names] *Mare Imbrium.*

mare's nest ▶*n.* **1** a complex and difficult situation; a muddle: *your desk is usually a mare's nest.* **2** an illusory discovery: *the mare's nest of perfect safety.*

mar·ga·rine /ˈmärjərən/ ▶*n.* a butter substitute made from vegetable oils or animal fats.

mar·ga·ri·ta /ˌmärgəˈrētə/ ▶*n.* a cocktail made with tequila and citrus fruit juice.

mar·gay /ˈmärˌgā; märˈgā/ ▶*n.* a small South American wild cat (*Felis wiedii*) with large eyes and a yellowish coat with black spots and stripes.

mar·gin /ˈmärjən/ ▶*n.* **1** the edge or border of something: *the eastern margin of the Indian Ocean* | *fig.* *they were forced to live on the margins of society.* ■ the blank border on each side of the print on a page. ■ a line ruled on paper to mark off a margin. **2** an amount by which a thing is won or falls short: *they won by a convincing 17-point margin.* ■ an amount of something included so as to be sure of success or safety: *there was no margin for error.* ■ the lower limit of possibility, success, etc.: *the lighting is considerably brighter than before but is still at the margins of acceptability.* ■ a profit margin. ■ *Finance* a sum deposited with a broker to cover the risk of loss on a transaction or account.
▶*v.* (**-gined, -gin·ing**) [*tr.*] **1** provide with an edge or border: *its leaves are margined with yellow.* **2** deposit an amount of money with a broker as security for (an account or transaction): [as *adj.*] (**margined**) *a margined transaction.*
▶ □ **margin of error** an amount (usually small) that is allowed for in case of miscalculation or change of circumstances.

mar·gin·al /ˈmärjənl/ ▶*adj.* of, relating to, or situated at the edge or margin of something. ■ of secondary or minor importance; not central: *it seems likely to make only a marginal difference.* ■ (of a decision or distinction) very narrow. ■ of or written in the margin of a page: *marginal notes.* ■ of or relating to water adjacent to the land's edge or coast: *water lilies and marginal aquatics.* ■ (chiefly of costs or benefits) relating to or resulting from small or unit changes. ■ (of taxation) relating to increases in income. ■ close to the limit of profitability, esp. through difficulty of exploitation: *marginal farmland.*
▶*n.* a plant that grows in water adjacent to the edge of land. —**mar·gin·al·i·ty** /ˌmärjəˈnalətē/ *n.* —**mar·gin·al·ly** *adv.*

mar·gi·na·li·a /ˌmärjəˈnālēə/ ▶*pl. n.* marginal notes.

mar·gin·al·ize /ˈmärjənəˌlīz/ ▶*v.* [*tr.*] treat (a person, group, or concept) as insignificant or peripheral: *attempting to marginalize those who disagree* | [as *adj.*] (**marginalized**) *members of marginalized cultural groups.* —**mar·gin·al·i·za·tion** /ˌmärjənələˈzāSHən/ *n.*

ma·ri·a /ˈmärēə/ ▶ plural form of MARE².

ma·ri·a·chi /ˌmärēˈäCHē/ ▶*n.* (*pl.* **-chis**) [as *adj.*] denoting a type of traditional Mexican folk music, typically performed by a small group of strolling musicians. ■ a musician in such a group.

mar·i·gold /ˈmariˌgōld/ ▶*n.* a plant of the daisy family, typically with yellow, orange, or copper-brown flowers, widely cultivated as an ornamental. Several general include *Tagetes* (the **French** and **African marigolds**) and *Calendula* (the **pot marigold**). ■ used in names of other plants with yellow flowers, e.g., **marsh marigold.** ▷late Middle English: from the given name *Mary* + dialect *gold* (in Old English, denoting certain types of marigold).

ma·ri·jua·na /ˌmarəˈ(h)wänə/ (also **ma·ri·hua·na**) ▶*n.* cannabis, esp. as smoked in cigarettes.

ma·rim·ba /məˈrimbə/ ▶*n.* a deep-toned xylophone of African origin.

ma·ri·na /məˈrēnə/ ▶*n.* a specially designed harbor with moorings for pleasure craft and small boats.

mar·i·nade /ˌmarəˈnād/ ▶*n.* a sauce, typically made of oil, vinegar, spices, and herbs, in which meat, fish, or other food is soaked before cooking in order to flavor or soften it. ■ a dish prepared using such a mixture: *a chicken marinade.*

ma·ri·na·ra /ˌmarəˈnärə; ˌmärəˈnärə/ ▶*n.* [usu. as *adj.*] (in Italian cooking) a sauce made from tomatoes, onions, and herbs, served esp. with pasta.

mar·i·nate /ˈmarəˌnāt/ ▶*v.* [*tr.*] soak (meat, fish, or other food) in a marinade: *the beef was marinated in red wine vinegar.* ■ [*intr.*] (of food) undergo such a process. —**mar·i·na·tion** /ˌmarəˈnāSHən/ *n.*

ma·rine /məˈrēn/ ▶*adj.* of, found in, or produced by the sea: *marine plants* | *marine biology.* ■ of or relating to shipping or naval matters: *marine insurance.* ■ (of artists or painting) depicting scenes at sea: *marine painters.*
▶*n.* a member of a body of troops trained to serve on land or at sea, in particular a member of the U.S. Marine Corps.

mar·i·ner /ˈmarənər/ ▶*n.* a sailor.

mar·i·on·ette /ˌmarēəˈnet/ ▶*n.* a puppet worked from above by strings attached to its limbs.

mar·i·tal /ˈmaritl/ ▶*adj.* of or relating to marriage or the relations between husband and wife: *marital fidelity.* —**mar·i·tal·ly** *adv.*

mar·i·time /ˈmariˌtīm/ ▶*adj.* connected with the sea, esp. in relation to seafaring commercial or military activity: *a maritime museum* | *maritime law.* ■ living or found in or near the sea. ■ bordering on the sea: *two species occur in the maritime Antarctic.* ■ denoting a climate that is moist and temperate owing to the influence of the sea.

mar·jo·ram /ˈmärjərəm/ ▶*n.* (also **sweet marjoram**) a southern European plant (*Origanum majorana*) of the mint family, used as a culinary herb. ■ (also **wild marjoram**) another term for OREGANO.

marionette

mark¹ /märk/ ▶*n.* **1** a small area on a surface having a different color from its surroundings, typically one caused by accident or damage. ■ a spot, area, or feature on a person's or animal's body by which they may be identified or recognized: *he was five feet nine, with no distinguishing marks.* **2** a line, figure, or symbol made as an indication or record of something. ■ a written symbol made on a document in place of a signature by someone who cannot write. ■ a level or stage that is considered significant: *unemployment had passed the two million mark.* ■ a sign or indication of a quality or feeling: *the flag was at half-mast as a mark of respect.* ■ a characteristic property or feature: *the mark of a civilized society.* ■ a competitor's starting point in a race. **3** a point awarded for a correct answer or for proficiency in an examination or competition. ■ a figure or letter representing the total of such points and signifying a person's score: *the highest mark was 98 percent.* ■ (esp. in track and field) a time or distance achieved by a competitor, esp. one that represents a record or personal best. **4** (followed by a numeral) a particular model or type of a vehicle, machine, or device: *a Mark 10 Jaguar.* **5** a target: *few bullets could have missed their mark.* ■ *inf.* a person who is easily deceived or taken advantage of: *they figure I'm an easy mark.*
▶*v.* [*tr.*] **1** make (a visible impression or stain) on: *he fingered the photograph gently, careful not to mark it.* ■ [*intr.*] become stained: *it is made from a sort of woven surface which doesn't mark or tear.* **2** write a word or symbol on (an object), typically for identification. ■ write (a word or figure) on an object: *she marked the date down on a card.* ■ (**mark something off**) put a line by or through something written or printed on paper to indicate that it has passed or been dealt with: *he marked off their names in a ledger.* **3** show the position of: *the top of the pass marks the border between Alaska and the Yukon.* ■ separate or delineate (a particular section or area of something): *you need to **mark out** the part of the garden where the sun lingers longest.* ■ (of a particular quality or feature) separate or distinguish (someone or something) from other people or things: *his sword **marked** him **out** as an officer.* ■ (**mark someone down as**) judge someone to be (a particular type or class of person): *she had marked him down as a liberal.* ■ acknowledge, honor, or celebrate (an

important event or occasion) with a particular action: *to mark its fifti-eth anniversary, the group held a fashion show.* ■ be an indication of (a significant occasion, stage, or development): *a series of incidents that marked a new phase in the terrorist campaign.* ■ (usu. **be marked**) characterize as having a particular quality or feature: *the reaction to these developments has been marked by a note of hysteria.* **4** (of a teacher or examiner) assess the standard of (a piece of written work) by assigning points for proficiency or correct answers: *the teachers are given adequate time to mark term papers.* ■ (**mark someone/something down**) reduce the number of marks awarded to a student, candidate, or their work: *I was marked down for having skipped the last essay question.* **5** notice or pay careful attention to: *he'll leave you, you mark my words!* **6** (of a player in a team game) stay close to (a particular opponent) in order to prevent them getting or passing the ball.

▶*phrasal v.* □ **mark something down** (of a retailer) reduce the indicated price of an item. □ **mark something up 1** (of a retailer) add a certain amount to the cost of goods to cover overhead and profit: *they mark up the price of imported wines by 66 percent.* **2** annotate or correct text for printing, keying, or typesetting.

▶ □ **be quick** (or **slow**) **off the mark** be fast (or slow) in responding to a situation or understanding something. □ **get off the mark** get started. □ **leave** (or **make**) **its** (or **one's** or **a**) **mark** have a lasting or significant effect: *she left her mark on the world of foreign policy.* □ **make one's mark** attain recognition or distinction. □ **mark time** (of troops) march on the spot without moving forward. ■ *fig.* pass one's time in routine activities until a more favorable or interesting opportunity presents itself. □ **off** (or **wide of**) **the mark** incorrect or inaccurate: *his solutions are completely off the mark.* □ **on the mark** correct; accurate. □ **on your marks** used to instruct competitors in a race to prepare themselves in the correct starting position: *on your marks, get set, go!* □ **up to the mark** of the required standard.

mark² ▶*n.* **1** the basic monetary unit of Germany (until the introduction of the euro), equal to 100 pfennigs; a Deutschmark or, formerly, an Ostmark. **2** a former English and Scottish money of account, equal to thirteen shillings and four pence in the currency of the day. ■ a denomination of weight for gold and silver, formerly used throughout western Europe and typically equal to 8 ounces (226.8 grams).

mark·down /'märk,doun/ ▶*n.* a reduction in price.

marked /märkt/ ▶*adj.* **1** having a visible mark. ■ (of playing cards) having distinctive marks on their backs to assist cheating. ■ Linguistics (of words or forms) distinguished by a particular feature. **2** clearly noticeable; evident: *a marked increase in sales.* —**mark·ed·ly** /'märkidlē/ *adv.* —**mark·ed·ness** /'märkidnis/ *n.*

mark·er /'märkər/ ▶*n.* **1** an object used to indicate a position, place, or route. ■ a thing serving as a standard of comparison or as an indication of what may be expected: *such studies may provide a unique marker in the quest to understand the brain.* ■ *inf.* a promissory note; an IOU. **2** a felt-tip pen with a broad tip.

mar·ket /'märkit/ ▶*n.* **1** a regular gathering of people for the purchase and sale of provisions, livestock, and other commodities: *farmers going to market.* ■ an open space or covered building where vendors convene to sell their goods. **2** an area or arena in which commercial dealings are conducted: *the labor market.* ■ a demand for a particular commodity or service: *there is a market for ornamental daggers.* ■ the state of trade at a particular time or in a particular context: *the bottom's fallen out of the market.* ■ the free market; the operation of supply and demand: *future development cannot simply be left to the market* | [as *adj.*] *a market economy.* ■ a stock market.

▶*v.* (**-ket·ed, -ket·ing**) [*tr.*] advertise or promote (something). ■ offer for sale: *sheep farmers are still unable to market their lambs.* ■ [*intr.*] buy or sell provisions in a market: [as *n.*] (**marketing**) *some people liked to do their marketing very early in the morning.* ▷Middle English, via Anglo-Norman French from Latin *mercatus,* from *mercari* 'buy.' —**mar·ket·er** *n.*

▶ □ **be in the market for** wish to buy. □ **on the market** available for sale: *he bought every new gadget as it came on the market.*

mar·ket·a·ble /'märkitəbəl/ ▶*adj.* able or fit to be sold or marketed. ■ in demand: *marketable skills.* —**mar·ket·a·bil·i·ty** /,märkitə'bilitē/ *n.*

mar·ket·eer /,märkə'ti(ə)r/ ▶*n.* a person who sells goods or services in a market: *a consumer-goods marketeer.* ■ a person who works in or advocates a particular type of market: *free-marketeers.*

mar·ket·ing /'märkitiNG/ ▶*n.* the action or business of promoting and selling products or services, including market research and advertising.

mar·ket·place /'märkət,plās/ ▶*n.* an open space where a market is or was formerly held in a town. ■ the arena of competitive or commercial dealings; the world of trade: *the global marketplace.*

mar·ket val·ue ▶*n.* the amount for which something can be sold on a given market. Often contrasted with BOOK VALUE.

mark·ing /'märkiNG/ ▶*n.* (usu. **markings**) an identification mark, esp. a mark or pattern of marks on an animal's fur, feathers, or skin: *the distinctive black-and-white markings on its head.* ■ *Mus.* a word or symbol on a score indicating the correct tempo, dynamic, or other aspect of performance.

marks·man /'märksmən/ ▶*n.* (*pl.* **-men**) a person skilled in shooting, esp. with a pistol or rifle: *a police marksman.* —**marks·man·ship** /-,SHip/ *n.*

mark·up /'mär,kəp/ ▶*n.* **1** the amount added to the cost price of goods to cover overhead and profit. **2** the process or result of correcting text in preparation for printing. ■ the process of making the final changes in a legislative bill: *the bill concerning acid rain is in markup.* **3** *Comput.* a set of tags assigned to elements of a text to indicate their structural or logical relation to the rest of the text.

marl /märl/ ▶*n.* an unconsolidated sedimentary rock or soil consisting of clay and lime, formerly used typically as fertilizer. —**marl·y** *adj.*

mar·lin /'märlən/ ▶*n.* a large edible billfish (genera *Makaira* and *Tetrapterus*) of warm seas.

mar·ma·lade /'märmə,lād/ ▶*n.* a preserve made from citrus fruit, esp. bitter oranges, prepared like jam.

mar·mo·set /'märmə,set; -,zet/ ▶*n.* a small Central and South American monkey (genera *Callithrix* and *Cebuella,* family Callitrichidae) with a silky coat and a long nonprehensile tail.

mar·mot /'märmət/ ▶*n.* a heavily built, gregarious, burrowing rodent (genus *Marmota*) of the squirrel family, typically living in mountainous regions of Eurasia and North America.

ma·roon¹ /mə'rōōn/ ▶*adj.* of a brownish-crimson color. ▶*n.* a brownish-crimson color.

ma·roon² /mə'rōōn/ ▶*v.* [*tr.*] (often **be marooned**) leave (someone) trapped and isolated in an inaccessible place, esp. an island.

marque /märk/ ▶*n.* a make of car, as distinct from a specific model.

mar·quee /mär'kē/ ▶*n.* **1** a rooflike projection over the entrance to a theater, hotel, or other building. ■ [as *adj.*] leading; preeminent: *a marquee player.* **2** *chiefly Brit.* a large tent used for social or commercial functions.

mar·quess /'märkwəs/ ▶*n.* a British nobleman ranking above an earl and below a duke.

mar·que·try /'märkətrē/ (also **mar·que·terie** or **mar·que·tery**) ▶*n.* inlaid work made from small pieces of variously colored wood or other materials, used chiefly for the decoration of furniture.

mar·quis /'mär,kē; 'märkwəs/ ▶*n.* (in some European countries) a nobleman ranking above a count and below a duke. ■ another term for MARQUESS.

mar·quise /mär'kēz/ ▶*n.* **1** the wife or widow of a marquis. ■ a woman holding the rank of marquis in her own right. **2** a finger ring set with a pointed oval gem or cluster of gems.

mar·riage /'marij/ ▶*n.* **1** the formal union of a man and a woman, typically recognized by law, by which they become husband and wife. ■ a similar long-term relationship between partners of the same sex. ■ a relationship between married people or the period for which it lasts: *a happy marriage* | *the children from his first marriage.* ■ *fig.* a combination or mixture of two or more elements: *a marriage of jazz, pop, blues, and gospel.* **2** (in pinochle and other card games) a combination of a king and queen of the same suit.

▶ □ **by marriage** as a result of a marriage: *a distant cousin by marriage.* □ **marriage of convenience** a marriage concluded to achieve a practical purpose.

mar·riage·a·ble /'marijəbəl/ ▶*adj.* fit, suitable, or attractive for marriage, esp. in being of the right age. —**mar·riage·a·bil·i·ty** /,marijə'bilitē/ *n.*

mar·riage por·tion ▶*n.* another term for PORTION.

mar·ried /'marēd/ ▶*adj.* (of two people) united in marriage: *a married couple.* ■ (of one person) having a husband or wife: *a happily married man.* ■ of or relating to marriage: *married life.* ■ *fig.* closely combined or linked: *in the seventeenth century, science was still married to religion.*

▶*n.* (usu. **marrieds**) a married person: *we were young marrieds.*

mar·row /'marō/ ▶*n.* **1** (also **bone marrow**) a soft fatty substance in the cavities of bones, in which blood cells are produced (often taken as typifying strength and vitality). **2** (also **vegetable marrow**) *Brit.* a white-fleshed green-skinned gourd, which is eaten as a vegetable. —**mar·row·less** *adj.* —**mar·row·y** *adj.*

▶ □ **to the marrow** to one's innermost being.

mar·row·bone /'marō,bōn/ ▶*n.* a bone containing edible marrow.

mar·ry /'marē/ ▶*v.* (**-ries, -ried**) [*tr.*] **1** join in marriage: *I was married in church* | *the priest who married us.* ■ take (someone) as one's wife or husband in marriage: *Eric asked me to marry him.* ■ [*intr.*] enter into marriage: *they had no plans to marry.* ■ [*intr.*] (**marry into**) become a member of (a family) by marriage. ■ (of a parent or guardian) give (a son or daughter) in marriage, esp. for reasons of expediency: *her parents married her to a wealthy landowner.* **2** cause to meet or fit together; combine: *the show marries poetry with art.* ■ [*intr.*] meet or blend with something: *most Chardonnays don't marry well with salmon.*

Mars /märz/ ▸*Astron.* a small, reddish planet that is the fourth in order from the sun and is periodically visible to the naked eye.

marsh /märsh/ ▸*n.* an area of low-lying land that is flooded in wet seasons or at high tide, and typically remains waterlogged at all times. ▷Old English *mer(i)sc* (perhaps influenced by late Latin *mariscus* 'marsh'), of West Germanic origin. —**marsh·i·ness** /'märshēnis/ *n.* —**marsh·y** *adj.*

mar·shal /'märshəl/ ▸*n.* **1** a federal or municipal law officer. ■ the head of a police department. ■ the head of a fire department. **2** an official responsible for supervising public events, esp. sports events or parades.
▸*v.* (**-shaled, -shal·ing**; *chiefly Brit.* **-shalled, -shal·ling**) [*tr.*] arrange or assemble (a group of people, esp. soldiers) in order: *fig. he paused for a moment, as if marshaling his thoughts.* ▷Middle English (denoting a high-ranking officer of state): from Old French *mareschal* 'blacksmith, commander,' from late Latin *mariscalcus,* from Germanic elements meaning 'horse' and 'servant.' —**mar·shal·er** *n.* —**mar·shal·ship** /-,ship/ *n.*

marsh·land /'märsh,land/ ▸*n.* (also **marshlands**) land consisting of marshes.

marsh·mal·low /'märsh,melō/ ▸*n.* a spongy confection made from a soft mixture of sugar, albumen, and gelatin.

marsh mar·i·gold ▸*n.* a plant (*Caltha palustris*) of the buttercup family that has large yellow flowers and grows in damp ground and shallow water, native to north temperate regions. Also called **COWSLIP**.

mar·su·pi·al /mär'sōōpēəl/ *Zool.* ▸*n.* a mammal of a group whose members are born incompletely developed and are typically carried and suckled in a pouch on the mother's belly. Marsupials are found mainly in Australia and New Guinea, although three families, including the opossums, live in America.
▸*adj.* of or relating to this order.

mart /märt/ ▸*n.* a trade center or market.

mar·ten /'märtn/ ▸*n.* a chiefly arboreal mammal (genus *Martes*) of the weasel family found in Eurasia and North America, hunted for its fur in many northern countries.

mar·tial /'märshəl/ ▸*adj.* of or appropriate to war; warlike: *martial bravery.* —**mar·tial·ly** *adv.*

mar·tial arts ▸*pl. n.* various sports or skills, mainly of Japanese origin, that originated as forms of self-defense or attack, such as judo, karate, and kendo. —**mar·tial art·ist** *n.*

mar·tial law ▸*n.* military government involving the suspension of ordinary law.

Mar·tian /'märshən/ ▸*adj.* of or relating to the planet Mars or its supposed inhabitants.
▸*n.* a hypothetical or fictional inhabitant of Mars.

mar·tin /'märtn/ ▸*n.* a swift-flying, insectivorous songbird of the swallow family, typically having a less strongly forked tail than a swallow.

mar·ti·net /,märtn'et/ ▸*n.* a strict disciplinarian, esp. in the armed forces. —**mar·ti·net·ish** (also **mar·ti·net·tish**) *adj.*

mar·ti·ni /mär'tēnē/ ▸*n.* a cocktail made from gin and dry vermouth.

mar·tyr /'märtər/ ▸*n.* a person who is killed because of their religious or other beliefs. ■ a person who exaggerates discomfort or distress in order to obtain sympathy or admiration: *to play the martyr.* ■ (**martyr to**) a constant sufferer from (an ailment): *I'm a martyr to migraines!*
▸*v.* [*tr.*] (usu. **be martyred**) kill (someone) because of their beliefs. —**mar·tyr·i·za·tion** /,märtərə'zāshən/ *n.* —**mar·tyr·ize** /'märtə,rīz/ *v.*

mar·tyr·dom /'märtərdəm/ ▸*n.* the death or suffering of a martyr. ■ a display of feigned or exaggerated suffering to obtain sympathy or admiration.

mar·vel /'märvəl/ ▸*v.* (**-veled, -vel·ing**; *chiefly Brit.* **-velled, -vel·ling**) [*intr.*] be filled with wonder or astonishment: *she marveled at Jeffrey's composure.*
▸*n.* a wonderful or astonishing person or thing: *the marvels of technology* | *Charlie, you're a marvel!* —**mar·vel·er** *n.*

mar·vel·ous /'märv(ə)ləs/ (*Brit.* **mar·vel·lous**) ▸*adj.* causing great wonder; extraordinary: *marvelous technological toys.* ■ extremely good or pleasing; splendid. —**mar·vel·ous·ly** *adv.* —**mar·vel·ous·ness** *n.*

Marx·ism /'märk,sizəm/ ▸*n.* the political and economic theories of Karl

Marx and Friedrich Engels, later developed by their followers to form the basis for the theory and practice of communism. —**Marx·i·an** /-sēən/ *adj.* —**Marx·ist** *n.* & *adj.*

mar·zi·pan /'märzə,pan; 'märtsə-/ ▸*n.* a sweet, yellowish paste of ground almonds, sugar, and egg whites, often colored and used to make small cakes or confections or as an icing for larger cakes. Also called **ALMOND PASTE**. ■ a confection or cake made of or based on marzipan.

mas·car·a /ma'skarə/ ▸*n.* a cosmetic for darkening and thickening the eyelashes. —**mas·car·aed** /-'skarəd/ *adj.*

mas·car·po·ne /,mäskär'pōn(ē)/ ▸*n.* a soft, mild Italian cream cheese.

mas·cot /'mas,kät; -kət/ ▸*n.* a person or thing that is supposed to bring good luck or that is used to symbolize a particular event or organization: *the squadron's mascot.* ▷late 19th cent.: from French *mascotte,* from modern Provençal *mascotto,* feminine diminutive of *masco* 'witch.'

mas·cu·line /'maskyələn/ ▸*adj.* **1** having qualities or appearance traditionally associated with men, esp. strength and aggressiveness: *he is outstandingly handsome and robust, very masculine.* ■ of or relating to men; male: *a masculine voice.* **2** *Gram.* of or denoting a gender of nouns and adjectives, conventionally regarded as male.
▸*n.* (**the masculine**) the male sex or gender. ■ *Gram.* a masculine word or form. —**mas·cu·line·ly** *adv.* —**mas·cu·lin·i·ty** /,maskyə'linitē/ *n.*

ma·ser /'māzər/ ▸*n.* a device using the stimulated emission of radiation by excited atoms to amplify or generate coherent monochromatic electromagnetic radiation in the microwave range.

MASH /mash/ ▸*abbr.* mobile army surgical hospital.

mash /mash/ ▸*n.* a uniform mass made by crushing a substance into a soft pulp, sometimes with the addition of liquid. ■ bran mixed with hot water given as a warm food to horses or other animals. ■ *Brit., inf.* mashed potatoes. ■ (in brewing) a mixture of powdered malt and hot water, which stands until the sugars dissolve to form the wort.
▸*v.* [*tr.*] reduce (a food or other substance) to a uniform mass by crushing it. ■ crush or smash (something) to a pulp. ■ *inf.* press forcefully on (something): *the worst thing you can do is mash the brake pedal.* —**mash·er** *n.*

mask /mask/ ▸*n.* **1** a covering for all or part of the face, in particular: ■ a covering worn as a disguise, or to amuse or terrify other people. ■ a covering made of fiber or gauze and fitting over the nose and mouth to protect against dust or air pollutants, or made of sterile gauze and worn to prevent infection of the wearer or (in surgery) of the patient. ■ a protective covering fitting over the whole face, worn in fencing, ice hockey, and other sports. ■ a respirator used to filter inhaled air or to supply gas for inhalation. ■ (also **masque**) a cosmetic preparation spread over the face and left for some time to cleanse and improve the skin. **2** a likeness of a person's face in clay or wax, esp. one made by taking a mold from the face. ■ a person's face regarded as having set into a characteristic expression: *his face was a mask of rage.* ■ a hollow model of a human head worn by ancient Greek and Roman actors. ■ the face or head of an animal, esp. of a fox, as a hunting trophy. **3** *fig.* a disguise or pretense: *she let her mask of moderate respectability slip.* **4** *Photog.* a piece of something, such as a card, used to cover a part of an image that is not required when exposing a print.
▸*v.* [*tr.*] cover (the face) with a mask. ■ conceal (something) from view: *the poplars masked a factory.* ■ disguise or hide (a sensation or quality): *brandy did not completely mask the bitter taste.* ■ cover (an object or surface) so as to protect it from a process, esp. painting: *mask off doors and cupboards with sheets of plastic.* —**masked** *adj.* —**mask·er** *n.*

mask·ing tape ▸*n.* adhesive tape used in painting to cover areas on which paint is not wanted.

mas·och·ism /'masə,kizəm; 'maz-/ ▸*n.* the tendency to derive pleasure, esp. sexual gratification, from one's own pain or humiliation. ■ (in general use) the enjoyment of what appears to be painful or tiresome. —**mas·och·ist** *n.* —**mas·och·is·tic** /,masə'kistik; ,maz-/ *adj.* —**mas·och·is·ti·cal·ly** /,masə'kistik(ə)lē; ,maz-/ *adv.*

ma·son /'māsən/ ▸*n.* **1** a builder and worker in stone. **2** (**Mason**) a Freemason.
▸*v.* [*tr.*] build from or strengthen with stone. ■ cut, hew, or dress (stone).

Ma·son–Dix·on line /'diksən/ (also **Ma·son–Dix·on Line**) ▸*n.* (in the U.S.) the boundary between Maryland and Pennsylvania, taken as the northern limit of the slave-owning states before the abolition of slavery.

Ma·son·ic /mə'sänik/ ▸*adj.* of or relating to Freemasons: *a Masonic lodge.*

ma·son jar (also **Ma·son jar**) ▸*n.* a wide-mouthed glass jar with an airtight screw top, used for preserving fruit and vegetables.

---

ma·son·ry /'māsənrē/ ▸n. **1** stonework. **2** (**Masonry**) Freemasonry.

masque /mask/ ▸n. **1** a form of amateur dramatic entertainment, popular among the nobility in 16th- and 17th-century England, which consisted of dancing and acting performed by masked players. ■ a masked ball. **2** variant spelling of MASK (sense 1). —**mas·quer** /'maskər/ n.

mas·quer·ade /,maskə'rād/ ▸n. a false show or pretense: *his masquerade ended when he was arrested.* ■ the wearing of disguise. ■ a masked ball.
▸v. [intr.] pretend to be someone one is not: *a journalist masquerading as a man in distress.* ■ be disguised or passed off as something else: *the idle gossip that masquerades as news in some local papers.* —**mas·quer·ad·er** n.

Mass /mas/ ▸n. the Christian Eucharist or Holy Communion, esp. in the Roman Catholic Church: *we went to Mass | the Latin Mass.* ■ a celebration of this. ■ a musical setting of parts of the liturgy used in the Mass.

mass /mas/ ▸n. **1** a coherent, typically large body of matter with no definite shape. ■ a large number of people or objects crowded together: *a mass of cyclists.* ■ a large amount of material: *a mass of conflicting evidence.* ■ (**masses**) inf. a large quantity or amount of something: *we get masses of homework.* ■ any of the main portions in a painting or drawing that each have some unity in color, lighting, or some other quality: *the masterly distribution of masses.* **2** (**the mass of**) the majority of: *the great mass of the population had little interest in the project.* ■ (**the masses**) the ordinary people. **3** *Physics* the quantity of matter that a body contains, as measured by its acceleration under a given force or by the force exerted on it by a gravitational field. ■ (in general use) weight.
▸adj. relating to, done by, or affecting large numbers of people or things: *the movie has mass appeal | a mass exodus of refugees.*
▸v. assemble or cause to assemble into a mass or as one body. —**mass·less** adj.

mas·sa·cre /'masikər/ ▸n. an indiscriminate and brutal slaughter of people: *the attack was described as a cold-blooded massacre.* ■ inf. a heavy defeat of a sports team or contestant.
▸v. [tr.] deliberately and violently kill (a large number of people). ■ inf. inflict a heavy defeat on (a sports team or contestant).

mas·sage /mə'säzн; -'säj/ ▸n. the rubbing and kneading of muscles and joints of the body with the hands, esp. to relieve tension or pain: *massage can ease tiredness and jet lag | a massage will help loosen you up.*
▸v. [tr.] **1** rub and knead (a person or part of the body) with the hands. ■ (**massage something in/into/onto**) rub a substance into (the skin or hair). ■ flatter (someone's ego). **2** manipulate (figures) to give a more acceptable result: *the accounts had been massaged and adjusted to suit the government.* —**mas·sag·er** n.

mas·sé /ma'sā/ ▸n. [usu. as adj.] *Billiards* a stroke made with an inclined cue, imparting swerve to the ball: *a massé shot.*

mas·seur /ma'sər; mə-/ ▸n. a person, esp. a man, who provides massages professionally. ▷French, from *masser* to 'massage.'

mas·seuse /ma'sōōs; mə-; ma'sœz/ ▸n. a female masseur.

mas·sive /'masiv/ ▸adj. **1** large and heavy or solid: *a massive rampart of stone.* **2** exceptionally large: *massive crowds are expected.* ■ very intense or severe. ■ inf. particularly successful or influential: *the title song became a massive hit.* **3** *Geol.* (of rocks or beds) having no discernible form or structure. ■ (of a mineral) not visibly crystalline. —**mas·sive·ly** adv. *a massively complicated network.* —**mas·sive·ness** n.

mass mar·ket ▸n. the market for goods that are produced in large quantities.
▸v. (**mass-market**) [tr.] market (a product) on a large scale.

mass me·di·a ▸pl. n. (usu. **the mass media**) [treated as *sing.* or *pl.*] the media.

mass num·ber ▸n. *Physics* the total number of protons and neutrons in a nucleus.

mass-pro·duce /prə'dōōs/ ▸v. [tr.] produce large quantities of (a standardized article) by an automated mechanical process: *cheap mass-produced goods.* —**mass-pro·duc·er** n. —**mass pro·duc·tion** n.

mast[1] /mast/ ▸n. a tall upright post, spar, or other structure on a ship or boat, in sailing vessels generally carrying a sail or sails. ■ a similar structure on land, esp. a flagpole or a television or radio transmitter.

mast[2] ▸n. the fruit of beech, oak, chestnut, and other forest trees, esp. as food for pigs and wild animals.

mas·tec·to·my /ma'stektəmē/ ▸n. (pl. **-mies**) a surgical operation to remove a breast.

mas·ter /'mastər/ ▸n. **1** chiefly hist. a man who has people working for him, esp. servants or

mast

slaves: *he acceded to his master's wishes.* ■ a person who has dominance or control of something: *he was master of the situation.* ■ a machine or device directly controlling another: [as *adj.*] *a master cylinder.* ■ dated a male head of a household: *the master of the house.* ■ the owner of a dog, horse, or other domesticated animal. **2** a skilled practitioner of a particular art or activity: *I'm a master of disguise.* ■ a great artist, esp. one belonging to the accepted canon: *the work of the great masters.* ■ a very strong chess or bridge player, esp. one who has qualified for the title at international tournaments. ■ (**Masters**) [treated as *sing.*] (in some sports) a class for competitors over the usual age for the highest level of competition. **3** a person who holds a second or further degree from a university or other academic institution (only in titles and set expressions): *a Master of Arts.* **4** a man in charge of an organization or group, in particular: ■ chiefly Brit. a male schoolteacher, esp. at a public or prep school. ■ the head of a college or school. ■ the captain of a merchant ship. **5** used as a title prefixed to the name of a boy not old enough to be called "Mr.": *Master James Williams.* **6** an original movie, recording, or document from which copies can be made: [as *adj.*] *the master tape.*
▸adj. **1** having or showing very great skill or proficiency: *a master painter.* ■ denoting a person skilled in a particular trade and able to teach others: *a master bricklayer.* **2** main; principal: *the master bedroom.*
▸v. [tr.] **1** acquire complete knowledge or skill in (an accomplishment, technique, or art): *I never mastered Latin.* **2** gain control of; overcome: *I managed to master my fears.* **3** make a master copy of (a movie or record). —**mas·ter·dom** /-dəm/ n. —**mas·ter·hood** /-,hōŏd/ n. —**mas·ter·less** adj. —**mas·ter·ship** /-,SHip/ n.

mas·ter·ful /'mastərfəl/ ▸adj. **1** powerful and able to control others. **2** performed or performing very skillfully: *a masterful assessment of the difficulties.* —**mas·ter·ful·ly** adv. —**mas·ter·ful·ness** n.

mas·ter key ▸n. a key that opens several locks, each of which also has its own key: *the custodian has the master key to all the classrooms.*

mas·ter·ly /'mastərlē/ ▸adj. performed or performing in a very skillful and accomplished way: *his masterly account of rural France.*

mas·ter·mind /'mastər,mīnd/ ▸n. a person with an outstanding intellect: *an eminent musical mastermind.* ■ someone who plans and directs an ingenious and complex scheme or enterprise.
▸v. [tr.] plan and direct (an ingenious and complex scheme or enterprise): *he was accused of masterminding a gold-smuggling racket.*

mas·ter·piece /'mastər,pēs/ ▸n. a work of outstanding artistry, skill, or workmanship. ■ an artist's or craftsman's best piece of work: *the painting is arguably Picasso's masterpiece.* ■ hist. a piece of work by a craftsman accepted as qualification for membership of a guild as an acknowledged master.

mas·ter stroke ▸n. an outstandingly skillful and opportune act; a very clever move.

mas·ter·work /'mastər,wərk/ ▸n. a masterpiece.

mas·ter·y /'mast(ə)rē/ ▸n. **1** comprehensive knowledge or skill in a subject or accomplishment: *she played with mastery.* ■ the action or process of mastering a subject or accomplishment: *a child's mastery of language.* **2** control or superiority over someone or something: *man's mastery over nature.*

mast·head /'mast,hed/ ▸n. **1** the highest part of a ship's mast or of the lower section of a mast. **2** the title of a newspaper or magazine at the head of the front or editorial page. ■ the listed details in a newspaper or magazine referring to ownership, advertising rates, etc.

mas·tic /'mastik/ ▸n. **1** an aromatic gum or resin exuded from the bark of a Mediterranean tree, used in making varnish and chewing gum and as a flavoring. **2** (also **mastic tree**) the bushy evergreen Mediterranean tree (*Pistacia lentiscus*) of the cashew family that yields mastic and has aromatic leaves and fruit, closely related to the pistachio. **3** a puttylike material used as a filler, adhesive, or sealant in building.

mas·ti·cate /'masti,kāt/ ▸v. [tr.] chew (food). —**mas·ti·ca·tion** /,masti'kāsнən/ n. —**mas·ti·ca·tor** /-,kātər/ n. —**mas·ti·ca·to·ry** /'mastikə,tôrē/ adj.

mas·tiff /'mastif/ ▸n. a dog of a large, strong breed with drooping ears and pendulous lips. ▷Middle English: obscurely representing Old French *mastin*, based on Latin *mansuetus* 'tame.'

mas·to·don /'mastə,dän/ ▸n. a large, extinct, elephantlike mammal (Mammutidae and other families, many species) of the Miocene to Pleistocene epochs, having teeth of a relatively primitive form and number.

mas·toid /'mas,toid/ ▸adj. Anat. of or relating to the mastoid process: *mastoid disease.*
▸n. Anat. the mastoid process.

mas·toid proc·ess ▸n. a conical prominence of the temporal bone behind the ear, to which neck muscles are attached, and which has air spaces linked to the middle ear.

mas·tur·bate /ˈmastərˌbāt/ ▶v. [intr.] stimulate one's own genitals for sexual pleasure. ■ [tr.] stimulate the genitals of (someone) to give them sexual pleasure. —**mas·tur·ba·tion** /ˌmastərˈbāSHən/ n. —**mas·tur·ba·tor** n. —**mas·tur·ba·to·ry** /-bəˌtôrē/ adj.

mat[1] /mat/ ▶n. **1** a piece of protective material placed on a floor, in particular: ■ a piece of coarse material placed on a floor for people to wipe their feet on. ■ a piece of resilient material for landing on in gymnastics, wrestling, or similar sports. ■ a small rug. ■ a piece of coarse material for lying on: *a beach mat.* **2** a small piece of cork, card, or similar material placed on a table or other surface to protect it from the heat or moisture of an object placed on it. **3** a thick, untidy layer of something hairy or woolly.
▶v. (**mat·ted, mat·ting**) [tr.] tangle (something, esp. hair) in a thick mass. ■ [intr.] become tangled.
▶ □ **go to the mat** inf. vigorously engage in an argument or dispute, typically on behalf of a particular person or cause. □ **on the mat** inf. being reprimanded by someone in authority.

mat[2] ▶n. short for MATRIX (sense 2).

mat[3] ▶adj., n., & v. variant spelling of MATTE[1].

mat·a·dor /ˈmatəˌdôr/ ▶n. a bullfighter whose task is to kill the bull.

match[1] /maCH/ ▶n. **1** a contest in which people or teams compete against each other in a particular sport: *a boxing match.* **2** a person or thing able to contend with another as an equal in quality or strength: *they were **no match for** mercenaries.* **3** a person or thing that resembles or corresponds to another. ■ *Comput.* a string that fulfills the specified conditions of a computer search. ■ a pair that corresponds or is very similar: *the headdresses and bouquet were a perfect match.* ■ the fact or appearance of corresponding: *stones of a perfect match and color.* **4** a person viewed in regard to eligibility for marriage, esp. as regards class or wealth: *he was an unsuitable match for any of their girls.* ■ a marriage: *a dynastic match.*
▶v. [tr.] **1** correspond or cause to correspond in some essential respect; make or be harmonious. ■ **team** (someone or something) with someone or something else appropriate or harmonious: *they **matched** suitably qualified applicants **with** institutions that had vacancies.* **2** be equal to (something) in quality or strength: *his anger matched her own.* ■ succeed in reaching or equaling (a standard or quality): *he tried to match her nonchalance.* **3** place (a person or group) in contest or competition with another: *the big names were **matched against** nobodies* | [as adj.] (**matched**) *evenly matched teams.*
▶phrasal v. □ **match up** to be as good as or equal to: *she matches up to the challenges of the job.* —**match·a·ble** adj.
▶ □ **meet one's match** encounter one's equal in strength or ability.

match[2] ▶n. a short, thin piece of wood or cardboard used to light a fire, being tipped with a composition that ignites when rubbed against a rough surface. ■ *hist.* a piece of wick or cord designed to burn at a uniform rate, used for firing a cannon or lighting gunpowder.

match·book /ˈmaCHˌbo͝ok/ ▶n. a small cardboard folder of matches with a striking surface on one side.

match·box /ˈmaCHˌbäks/ ▶n. a small box in which matches are sold. ■ [usu. as adj.] something very small, esp. a house, apartment, or room: *matchbox apartment.*

match·less /ˈmaCHləs/ ▶adj. unable to be equaled; incomparable: *the Parthenon has a matchless beauty.* —**match·less·ly** adv.

match·lock /ˈmaCHˌläk/ ▶n. hist. a type of gun with a lock in which a piece of wick or cord is used for igniting the powder.

match·mak·er /ˈmaCHˌmākər/ ▶n. a person who arranges relationships and marriages between others, either informally or, in certain cultural communities, as a formal occupation. ■ *fig.* a person or company that brings parties together for commercial purposes. —**match·mak·ing** /-ˌmākiNG/ n.

match point ▶n. (in tennis and other sports) a point that if won by one contestant will also win the match.

match·stick /ˈmaCHˌstik/ ▶n. the stem of a match, esp. a wooden one. ■ something likened to a match in being long and thin: *cut the vegetables into matchsticks* | [as adj.] *matchstick legs.*

mate[1] /māt/ ▶n. **1** each of a pair of birds or other animals. ■ *inf.* a person's husband, wife, or other sexual partner. ■ one of a matched pair: *a sock without its mate.* **2** [in *comb.*] a fellow member or joint occupant of a specified thing: *his tablemates.* ■ *Brit., inf.* used as a friendly form of address between men or boys: *"See you then, mate."* ■ *Brit., inf.* a friend or companion: *my best mate, Steve.* **3** an assistant or deputy, in particular: ■ an assistant to a skilled worker: *a plumber's mate.* ■ a deck officer on a merchant ship subordinate to the master. See also FIRST MATE.

▶v. **1** [intr.] (of animals or birds) come together for breeding; copulate: *successful males may **mate with** many females* | [as n.] (**mating**) *ovulation occurs only if mating has taken place.* ■ [tr.] bring (animals or birds) together for breeding. ■ join in marriage or sexual partnership: *people tend to **mate with** others in their own social class.* **2** [tr.] join or connect mechanically: *a four-cylinder engine **mated to** a five-speed gearbox.* ■ [intr.] be connected or joined. —**mate·less** adj.

mate[2] ▶n. & v. Chess short for CHECKMATE.

ma·té /ˈmäˌtā/ (also **yer·ba ma·té**) ▶n. **1** (also **maté tea**) a bitter, caffeine-rich infusion of the leaves of a South American shrub. ■ the leaves of this shrub. **2** the South American shrub (*Ilex paraguariensis*) of the holly family that produces these leaves.

ma·te·ri·al /məˈti(ə)rēəl/ ▶n. **1** the matter from which a thing is or can be made. ■ (usu. **materials**) things needed for an activity: *cleaning materials.* ■ a person of a specified quality or suitability: *he's not really Olympic material.* **2** facts, information, or ideas for use in creating a book or other work. ■ items, esp. songs or jokes, comprising a performer's act: *a band playing original material.* **3** cloth or fabric: *a piece of dark material* | *dress materials.*
▶adj. **1** denoting or consisting of physical objects rather than the mind or spirit: *the material world* | *moral and material support.* ■ concerned with physical needs or desires: *material living standards have risen.* ■ concerned with the matter of reasoning, not its form: *political conflict lacks mathematical or material certitude.* **2** important; essential; relevant: *the insects did not do any material damage to the crop.* ■ chiefly Law (of evidence or a fact) significant, influential, or relevant, esp. to the extent of determining a cause or affecting a judgment: *information **material to** a murder inquiry.* ▷late Middle English (in the sense 'relating to matter'): from late Latin *materialis*, adjective from Latin *materia* 'matter.'

ma·te·ri·al·ism /məˈti(ə)rēəˌlizəm/ ▶n. **1** a tendency to consider material possessions and physical comfort as more important than spiritual values. **2** *Philos.* the doctrine that nothing exists except matter and its movements and modifications. —**ma·te·ri·al·ist** n. & adj. —**ma·te·ri·al·is·tic** /məˌti(ə)rēəˈlistik/ adj. —**ma·te·ri·al·is·ti·cal·ly** adv.

ma·te·ri·al·ize /məˈti(ə)rēəˌlīz/ ▶v. [intr.] **1** (of a ghost, spirit, or similar entity) appear in bodily form. ■ [tr.] cause to appear in bodily or physical form. **2** become actual fact; happen: *the assumed savings may not materialize.* ■ appear or be present: *the train didn't materialize.* —**ma·te·ri·al·i·za·tion** /məˌti(ə)rēələˈzāSHən/ n.

ma·te·ri·al·ly /məˈti(ə)rēəlē/ ▶adv. **1** substantially; considerably: *materially different circumstances.* **2** in terms of wealth or material possessions: *a materially and culturally rich area.*

ma·te·ri·el /məˌti(ə)rēˈel/ (also **ma·té·ri·el**) ▶n. military materials and equipment.

ma·ter·nal /məˈtərnl/ ▶adj. of or relating to a mother, esp. during pregnancy or shortly after childbirth. ■ related through the mother's side of the family: *my maternal grandfather.* ■ denoting feelings associated with or typical of a mother. —**ma·ter·nal·ism** /-ˌizəm/ n. —**ma·ter·nal·ist** /-ist/ adj. —**ma·ter·nal·is·tic** /məˌtərnlˈistik/ adj. —**ma·ter·nal·ly** adv.

ma·ter·ni·ty /məˈtərnətē/ ▶n. motherhood. ■ [usu. as adj.] the period during pregnancy and shortly after childbirth: *maternity leave* | *maternity clothes.* ■ a maternity ward in a hospital.

math /maTH/ ▶n. inf. mathematics: *she teaches math and science.*

math·e·mat·i·cal /ˌmaTH(ə)ˈmatikəl/ (also **math·e·mat·ic**) ▶adj. of or relating to mathematics. ■ (of a proof or analysis) rigorously precise: *mathematical thinking.* —**math·e·mat·i·cal·ly** /-ik(ə)lē/ adv.

math·e·mat·ics /maTH(ə)ˈmatiks/ ▶pl. n. [usu. treated as *sing.*] the abstract science of number, quantity, and space. Mathematics may be studied in its own right (**pure mathematics**), or as it is applied to other disciplines such as physics and engineering (**applied mathematics**). ■ [often treated as *pl.*] the mathematical aspects of something: *the mathematics of general relativity..* —**math·e·ma·ti·cian** /-məˈtiSHən/ n.

mat·i·nee /ˌmatnˈā/ (also **mat·i·née**) ▶n. a performance in a theater or a showing of a movie that takes place in the daytime.

mat·i·nee i·dol ▶n. inf., dated a handsome actor admired chiefly by women.

mat·ins /ˈmatnz/ ▶n. a service of morning prayer in various churches, esp. the Anglican Church. ■ a service of the Western Christian Church, originally said (or chanted) at or after midnight, but historically often held with lauds on the previous evening.

ma·tri·arch /ˈmātrēˌärk/ ▶n. a woman who is the head of a family or tribe. ■ an older woman who is powerful within a family or organization: *a domineering matriarch.* —**ma·tri·ar·chal** /ˌmātrē'ärkəl/ *adj.*

ma·tri·ar·chy /'mātrēˌärkē/ ▶ *n.* (*pl.* **-chies**) a system of society or government ruled by a woman or women. ■ a form of social organization in which descent and relationship are reckoned through the female line. ■ the state of being an older, powerful woman in a family or group.

ma·tri·ces /'mātrəˌsēz/ ▶ plural form of **MATRIX**.

mat·ri·cide /'mātrəˌsīd/ 'mā-/ ▶ *n.* the killing of one's mother. ■ a person who kills their mother. —**mat·ri·cid·al** /ˌmatrə'sīdl/ ˌmā-/ *adj.*

ma·tric·u·late /mə'trikyəˌlāt/ ▶ *v.* [*intr.*] be enrolled at a college or university: *he matriculated at the University of Vermont.* ■ [*tr.*] admit (a student) to a college or university. —**ma·tric·u·la·tion** /məˌtrikyə'lāsHən/ *n.*

mat·ri·lin·e·al /ˌmatrə'linēəl/ ˌmā-/ ▶ *adj.* of or based on kinship with the mother or the female line. —**mat·ri·lin·e·al·ly** *adv.*

mat·ri·mo·ny /'mātrəˌmōnē/ ▶ *n.* the state or ceremony of being married; marriage: *a couple joined in matrimony* | *the sacrament of holy matrimony.* —**mat·ri·mo·ni·al** /ˌmatrə'mōnēəl/ *adj.*

ma·trix /'mātriks/ ▶ *n.* (*pl.* **-tri·ces** /'mātrisēz/ or **-trix·es**) 1 an environment or material in which something develops; a surrounding medium or structure. ■ a mass of fine-grained rock in which gems, crystals, or fossils are embedded. ■ *Biol.* the substance between cells or in which structures are embedded. ■ fine material: *the matrix of gravel paths is raked regularly.* 2 a mold in which something, such as printing type or a phonograph record, is cast or shaped. 3 *Math.* a rectangular array of quantities or expressions in rows and columns that is treated as a single entity and manipulated according to particular rules.

ma·tron /'mātrən/ ▶ *n.* 1 a woman in charge of domestic and medical arrangements at a boarding school or other establishment. ■ a female prison officer. 2 a married woman, esp. a dignified and sober middle-aged one. —**ma·tron·hood** /-ˌhŏŏd/ *n.*

ma·tron·ly /'mātrənlē/ ▶ *adj.* like or characteristic of a matron, esp. in being dignified and staid and typically associated with having a large or plump build: *she was beginning to look matronly.*

ma·tron of hon·or ▶ *n.* a married woman attending the bride at a wedding.

matte /mat/ (also **matt** or **mat**) ▶ *adj.* (of a color, paint, or surface) dull and flat, without a shine: *matte black.*

▶ *n.* 1 a matte color, paint, or finish: *the varnishes are available in gloss, satin, and matte.* 2 a sheet of cardboard placed on the back of a picture, either as a mount or to form a border around the picture.

▶ *v.* (**mat·ted, mat·ting**) [*tr.*] (often **be matted**) give a matte appearance to (something).

mat·ter /'matər/ ▶ *n.* 1 physical substance in general, as distinct from mind and spirit; (in physics) that which occupies space and possesses rest mass, esp. as distinct from energy: *the structure and properties of matter.* ■ a substance or material: *organic matter* | *vegetable matter.* ■ a substance in or discharged from the body: *fecal matter.* ■ written or printed material: *reading matter.* 2 an affair or situation under consideration; a topic: *a great deal of work was done on this matter.* ■ *Law* something that is to be tried or proved in court; a case. ■ (**matters**) the present situation or state of affairs: *we can do nothing to change matters.* ■ (**a matter for/of**) something that evokes a specified feeling: *it's a matter of indifference to me.* ■ (**a matter for**) something that is the concern of a specified person or agency. 3 (**the matter**) the reason for distress or a problem: *what's the matter?* | *pretend that nothing's the matter.* 4 the substance or content of a text as distinct from its manner or form. ■ *Logic* the particular content of a proposition, as distinct from its form.

▶ *v.* [*intr.*] be of importance; have significance: *it doesn't matter what the guests wear* | *what did it matter to them?* | *to him, animals mattered more than human beings.* ■ (of a person) be important or influential: *the people who matter.*

▶ ■ □ **for that matter** used to indicate that a subject or category, though mentioned second, is as relevant or important as the first: *I am not sure what value it adds to determining public, or for that matter private, policy.* □ **a matter of 1** no more than (a specified period of time): *they were shown the door in a matter of minutes.* 2 a thing that involves or depends on: *it's a matter of working out how to get something done.* □ **a matter of course** the natural or expected thing: *the reports are published as a matter of course.* □ **a matter of record** see **RECORD**. □ **no matter 1** regardless of: *no matter what the government calls them, they are cuts.* 2 it is of no importance: *"No matter, I'll go myself."*

mat·ter of fact ▶ *n.* something that belongs to the sphere of fact as distinct from opinion or conjecture: *it's a matter of fact that they had a relationship.* ■ *Law* the part of a judicial inquiry concerned with the truth of alleged facts.

▶ *adj.* (**matter-of-fact**) unemotional and practical. ■ concerned only with

factual content rather than style or expression. —**mat·ter-of-fact·ly** *adv.* —**mat·ter-of-fact·ness** *n.*

▶ ■ □ **as a matter of fact** in reality (used esp. to correct a falsehood or misunderstanding): *as a matter of fact, I was talking to him this afternoon.*

mat·ting /'matiNG/ ▶ *n.* 1 material used for mats, esp. coarse fabric woven from a natural fiber: *rush matting.* 2 the process of becoming matted.

mat·tress /'matrəs/ ▶ *n.* a fabric case filled with deformable or resilient material, used for sleeping on.

ma·ture /mə'CHŏŏr; -'t(y)ŏŏr/ ▶ *adj.* (**-tur·er, -tur·est**) 1 fully developed physically; full-grown. ■ having reached an advanced stage of mental or emotional development characteristic of an adult: *a young man mature beyond his years.* ■ (of thought or planning) careful and thorough: *on mature reflection he decided they should not go.* ■ used euphemistically to describe someone as being middle-aged or old: *Miss Walker was a mature lady when she married.* ■ (of a style) fully developed: *Van Gogh's mature work.* ■ (of certain foodstuffs or drinks) ready for consumption. 2 (of a bill) due for payment.

▶ *v.* [*intr.*] 1 (of a person or animal) become physically mature: *children mature at different ages* | *she matured into a woman.* ■ develop fully: *the trees take at least thirty years to mature.* ■ (of a person) reach an advanced stage of mental or emotional development: *men mature as they grow older.* ■ (with reference to certain foodstuffs or drinks) become or cause to become ready for consumption: [*intr.*] *leave the cheese to mature* | [*tr.*] *the Scotch is matured for a minimum of three years.* 2 (of an insurance policy, security, etc.) reach the end of its term and hence become payable. —**ma·ture·ly** *adv.*

ma·tu·ri·ty /mə'CHŏŏritē; mə't(y)ŏŏr-/ ▶ *n.* the state, fact, or period of being mature. ■ the time when an insurance policy, security, etc., matures. ■ an insurance policy, security, etc., having a fixed maturity date.

mat·zo /'mätsə/ (also **mat·zoh**) ▶ *n.* (*pl.* **-zos** or **-zoth** /-ˌsōt; -ˌsōs/) a thin, crisp unleavened bread, traditionally eaten by Jews during Passover.

maud·lin /'môdlin/ ▶ *adj.* self-pityingly or tearfully sentimental, often through drunkenness: *the drink made her maudlin* | *a maudlin ballad.*

maul /môl/ ▶ *v.* [*tr.*] (of an animal) wound (a person or animal) by scratching and tearing: *the herdsmen were mauled by lions.* ■ treat (someone or something) roughly.

▶ *n.* a tool with a heavy head and a handle, used for tasks such as splitting wood and driving wedges. ▷Middle English (in the sense 'hammer or wooden club,' also 'strike with a heavy weapon'): from Old French *mail*, from Latin *malleus* 'hammer.' —**maul·er** *n.*

maun·der /'môndər/ ▶ *v.* [*intr.*] talk in a rambling manner: *Dennis maundered on about the wine.* ■ move or act in a dreamy or idle manner: *he maunders through the bank, composing his thoughts.*

Maun·dy Thurs·day /'môndē/ ▶ *n.* the Thursday before Easter, observed in the Christian Church as a commemoration of the Last Supper.

mau·so·le·um /ˌmôzə'lēəm; ˌmôsə-/ ▶ *n.* (*pl.* **-le·a** /-'lēə/ or **-le·ums**) a building, esp. a large and stately one, housing a tomb or tombs.

mauve /mōv; môv/ ▶ *adj.* of a pale purple color.

▶ *n.* a pale purple color.

ma·ven /'māvən/ ▶ *n. inf.* an expert or connoisseur: *fashion mavens.*

mav·er·ick /'mav(ə)rik/ ▶ *n.* 1 an unorthodox or independent-minded person. ■ a person who refuses to conform to a particular party or group: *the Connecticut Republican maverick.* 2 an unbranded calf or yearling.

▶ *adj.* unorthodox: *a maverick detective.*

maw /mô/ ▶ *n.* the jaws or throat of a voracious animal: *a gigantic wolfhound with a fearful, gaping maw.* ■ *inf.* the mouth or gullet of a greedy person.

mawk·ish /'môkisH/ ▶ *adj.* sentimental in a feeble or sickly way: *a mawkish poem.* ■ *archaic* or *dial.* having a faint sickly flavor: *the mawkish smell of warm beer.* —**mawk·ish·ly** *adv.* —**mawk·ish·ness** *n.*

max·i /'maksē/ ▶ *n.* (*pl.* **max·is**) a thing that is very large of its kind, in particular: ■ a skirt or coat reaching to the ankle.

max·il·la /mak'silə/ ▶ *n.* (*pl.* **max·il·lae** /mak'silē; -'sil,ī/) *Anat.* & *Zool.* the jaw or jawbone, specifically the upper jaw in most vertebrates. In humans it also forms part of the nose and eye socket. ■ (in many arthropods) each of a pair of mouthparts used in chewing. —**max·il·lar·y** /'maksəˌlerē/ *adj.*

max·im /'maksim/ ▶ *n.* a short, pithy statement expressing a general truth or rule of conduct: *the maxim that actions speak louder than words.*

max·i·mal /'maksəməl/ ▶ *adj.* of or constituting a maximum; the highest or greatest possible: *the maximal speed.* —**max·i·mal·ly** *adv.*

max·i·mize /'maksəˌmīz/ ▶ *v.* [*tr.*] make as large or great as possible: *the*

M

company was aiming to maximize profits. ■ make the best use of: *a rider can maximize a young horse's athletic potential.* —**max·i·mi·za·tion** /ˌmaksəmə-'zāSHən/ *n.* —**max·i·miz·er** *n.*

max·i·mum /'maksəməm/ ▶ *adj.* as great, high, or intense as possible or permitted: *the vehicle's maximum speed | a maximum penalty of ten years' imprisonment.* ■ denoting the greatest or highest point or amount attained: *the maximum depth of the pool is 6 feet.*
▶ *n.* (*pl.* -**ma** /-mə/ or -**mums**) the greatest or highest amount possible or attained: *the school takes a maximum of 32 students | production levels are near their maximum.* ■ a maximum permitted prison sentence for an offense: *an offense that carries a maximum of 14 years.*
▶ *adv.* at the most: *it has a length of 4 feet maximum.*

May /mā/ ▶ *n.* the fifth month of the year, in the northern hemisphere usually considered the last month of spring. ■ (usu. **one's May**) *poetic/lit.* one's bloom or prime: *others murmured that their May was passing.*

may /mā/ ▶ *modal verb* (*3rd sing. present* **may**; *past* **might** /mīt/) **1** expressing possibility: *that may be true | he may well win.* ■ used when admitting that something is so before making another, more important point: *they may have been old-fashioned, but they were excellent teachers.* **2** expressing permission: *you may use a sling if you wish | may I ask a few questions?* **3** expressing a wish or hope: *may she rest in peace.*
▶ □ **be that as it may** despite that; nevertheless. □ **may as well** another way of saying **MIGHT AS WELL** (see **MIGHT**[1]).

Ma·ya /'mīə/ ▶ *n.* (*pl.* same or **Ma·yas**) **1** a member of an American Indian people of Yucatán and adjacent areas. **2** the Mayan language of this people.
▶ *adj.* of or relating to this people or their language. —**Ma·yan** /'mīən/ *adj.*

ma·ya /'mīə; 'māyə/ ▶ *n. Hinduism* the supernatural power wielded by gods and demons to produce illusions. ■ *Hinduism* the power by which the universe becomes manifest. ■ *Hinduism & Buddhism* the illusion or appearance of the phenomenal world.

may·ap·ple /'mā,apəl/ (also **May apple**) ▶ *n.* an American herbaceous plant (*Podophyllum peltatum*) of the barberry family with large, deeply divided leaves. It bears a yellow, egg-shaped edible fruit in May and is used medicinally. Also called **MANDRAKE**.

may·be /'mābē/ ▶ *adv.* perhaps; possibly: *maybe I won't go back | maybe she'd been wrong to accept this job.*
▶ *n.* a mere possibility or probability: *no ifs, buts, or maybes.*

May·day /'mā,dā/ (also **may·day**) ▶ *interj.* an international radio distress signal used by ships and aircraft.
▶ *n.* a distress signal using the word "Mayday": *we sent out a Mayday.*

May Day ▶ *n.* May 1, celebrated in many countries as a traditional springtime festival or as an international day honoring workers.

May·flow·er /'mā,flou(-ə)r/ ▶ the ship in which the Pilgrims sailed from England to America in 1620.

may·flow·er /'mā,flou(-ə)r/ ▶ *n.* a name given to several plants that bloom in May, esp. certain hepaticas and anemones.

may·fly /'mā,flī/ ▶ *n.* (*pl.* -**flies**) a short-lived, slender insect with delicate, transparent wings and two or three long filaments on the tail. It lives close to water, where the chiefly herbivorous aquatic larvae develop.

may·hap /'mā,hap/ ▶ *adv. archaic* perhaps; possibly.

may·hem /'mā,hem/ ▶ *n.* violent or damaging disorder; chaos: *complete mayhem broke out.* ■ *Law, chiefly hist.* the crime of maliciously injuring or maiming someone, originally so as to render the victim defenseless.

may·n't /'mā(ə)nt/ *rare* ▶ *contr. of* may not.

may·on·naise /ˌmāə'nāz; ˌmāə'nāz/ ▶ *n.* a thick, creamy dressing consisting of egg yolks beaten with oil and vinegar and seasoned.

may·or /'māər/ ▶ *n.* the elected head of a city, town, or other municipality. ■ the titular head of a municipality that is administered by a city manager. ▷Middle English: from Old French *maire*, from the Latin adjective *major* 'greater,' used as a noun in late Latin. —**may·or·al** /mā'ôrəl; 'māərəl/ *adj.* —**may·or·ship** /-,SHip/ *n.*

may·or·al·ty /'māərəltē/ ▶ *n.* (*pl.* -**ties**) the office of mayor: *the party failed to win the mayoralty.* ■ a mayor's period of office.

may·or·ess /'māərəs/ ▶ *n.* **1** the wife of a mayor. **2** a woman holding the office of mayor.

may·pole /'mā,pōl/ (also **May·pole**) ▶ *n.* a pole painted and decorated with flowers, around which people traditionally dance on May Day, holding long ribbons that are attached to the top of the pole.

mayst /māst/ ▶ *archaic* second person singular present of **MAY**[1].

maze /māz/ ▶ *n.* a network of paths and hedges designed as a puzzle through which one has to find a way. ■ a complex network of paths or passages: *they were trapped in a menacing maze of corridors.* ■ a confusing mass of information: *a maze of petty regulations.* —**maz·y** *adj.*

ma·zur·ka /mə'zərkə; -'zŏŏr-/ ▶ *n.* a lively Polish dance in triple time.

MB ▶ *abbr.* ■ (also **Mb**) *Comput.* megabyte: *a 800 MB hard disk.*

MBA ▶ *abbr.* Master of Business Administration.

MC ▶ *abbr.* ■ Master of Ceremonies. ■ (in the U.S.) Member of Congress.

Mc ▶ *abbr.* megacycle(s), a unit of frequency equal to one million cycles.

Mc·Car·thy·ism /mə'kärTHē,izəm/ ▶ *n.* a vociferous campaign against alleged communists in the U.S. government and other institutions carried out under Senator Joseph McCarthy in the period 1950–54. ■ *fig.* any similar practice that endorses the use of unfair allegations and investigations. —**Mc·Car·thy·ist** *adj.* & *n.* —**Mc·Car·thy·ite** /-THē,īt/ *adj.* & *n.*

Mc·Coy /mə'koi/ ▶ *n.* (in phrase **the real McCoy**) *inf.* the real thing; the genuine article.

MD ▶ *abbr.* Doctor of Medicine.

Md ▶ *symb.* the chemical element mendelevium.

ME ▶ *abbr.* Middle English.

me /mē/ ▶ *pron.* [*first person sing.*] **1** used by a speaker to refer to himself or herself as the object of a verb or preposition: *do you understand me? | wait for me!* Compare with I[2]. ■ used after the verb "to be" and after "than" or "as": *hi, it's me | you have more than me.* ■ *inf.* to or for myself: *I've got me a job.* **2** *inf.* used in exclamations: *dear me! | silly me!*

me·a cul·pa /ˌmāə 'kŏŏl,pə; -,pä/ ▶ *n.* an acknowledgment of one's fault or error: [as *interj.*] *"Well, whose fault was that?" "Mea culpa!" Frank said.*

mead[1] /mēd/ ▶ *n. chiefly hist.* an alcoholic drink of fermented honey and water.

mead[2] ▶ *n. poetic/lit.* a meadow.

mead·ow /'medō/ ▶ *n.* a piece of grassland, esp. one used for hay. ■ a piece of low ground near a river. —**mead·ow·y** *adj.*

mea·ger /'mēgər/ (*Brit.* **mea·gre**) ▶ *adj.* (of something provided or available) lacking in quantity or quality: *they were forced to supplement their meager earnings.* ■ (of a person or animal) lean; thin. —**mea·ger·ly** *adv.* —**mea·ger·ness** *n.*

meal[1] /mēl/ ▶ *n.* any of the regular occasions in a day when a reasonably large amount of food is eaten, such as breakfast, lunch, or dinner. ■ the food eaten on such an occasion: *a perfectly cooked meal.* ▷Old English *mǣl* (also in the sense 'measure', surviving in words such as *piecemeal* 'measure taken at one time'), of Germanic origin. The early sense of *meal* involved a notion of fixed time; compare with Dutch *maal* 'meal, (portion of) time' and German *Mal* 'time,' *Mahl* 'meal,' from an Indo-European root meaning 'to measure.'

meal[2] ▶ *n.* the edible part of any grain or seed ground to powder, such as cornmeal. ■ any powdery substance made by grinding: *herring meal.*

meal tick·et ▶ *n.* a person or thing that is used as a source of regular income: *the violin was going to be my meal ticket.*

meal·time /'mēl,tīm/ ▶ *n.* the time at which a meal is eaten.

meal·worm /'mēl,wərm/ ▶ *n.* the larva of a dark-colored nocturnal beetle (genus *Tenebrio*, family Tenebrionidae), which is widely fed to captive birds and other insectivorous animals.

meal·y /'mēlē/ ▶ *adj.* (**meal·i·er**, **meal·i·est**) of, like, or containing meal: *a mealy flavor | deep, mealy sand.* ■ (of a person's complexion, an animal's muzzle, or a bird's plumage) pale. ■ (of part of a plant or fungus) covered with granules resembling meal. —**meal·i·ness** /-lēnis/ *n.*

mean[1] /mēn/ ▶ *v.* (*past* and *past part.* **meant** /ment/) [*tr.*] **1** intend to convey, indicate, or refer to (a particular thing or notion); signify: *I don't know what you mean | he was asked what his remarks meant | I meant you, not Jones.* ■ (of a word) have (something) as its signification in the same language or its equivalent in another language: *its name means "painted rock" in Cherokee.* ■ genuinely intend to convey or express (something): *when she said that before, she meant it.* ■ (**mean something to**) be of some specified importance to (someone), esp. as a source of benefit or object of affection: *animals have always meant more to him than people.* **2** intend (something) to occur or be the case: *they mean no harm | it was meant to be a secret.* ■ (**be meant to do something**) be supposed or intended to do something: *we were meant to go yesterday.* ■ (often **be meant for**) design or destine for a particular purpose: *the jacket was meant for a much larger person.* ■ (**mean something by**) have as a motive or excuse in explanation: *what do you mean by leaving me out here in the cold?* **3** have as a consequence or result: *the proposals are likely to mean another hundred closures | heavy rain meant that the ground was waterlogged.* ■ necessarily or usually entail or involve: *coal stoves mean a lot of smoke.*

▷Old English *mænan*; related to Dutch *meenen* and German *meinen*, from an Indo-European root shared by *mind*.

▶ □ **I mean** used to clarify or correct a statement or to introduce a justification or explanation: *I mean, it's not as if I owned property.* □ **mean business** be in earnest. □ **mean to say** [usu. in *questions*] really admit or intend to say: *do you mean to say you've uncovered something new?*

mean² ▶*adj.* **1** unwilling to give or share things, esp. money; not generous: *she felt mean not giving a tip.* **2** unkind, spiteful, or unfair: *it was very mean of me* | *she is always mean to my little brother.* ■ vicious or aggressive in behavior. **3** (esp. of a place) poor in quality and appearance; shabby: *her home was mean and small.* ■ (of a person's mental capacity or understanding) inferior; poor: *it was obvious to even the meanest intelligence.* ■ *dated* of low birth or social class: *it was a hat like that worn by the meanest of people.* **4** *inf.* excellent; very skillful or effective: *he's a mean cook* | *she dances a mean Charleston.* —**mean·ly** *adv.* —**mean·ness** *n.*

▶ □ **no mean** —— denoting something very good of its kind: *it was no mean feat.*

mean³ ▶*n.* **1** the quotient of the sum of several quantities and their number; an average. ■ the term or one of the terms midway between the first and last terms of a progression. **2** a condition, quality, or course of action equally removed from two opposite (usually unsatisfactory) extremes. ▶*adj.* **1** (of a quantity) calculated as a mean; average. **2** equally far from two extremes: *hope is the mean virtue between despair and presumption.*

me·an·der /mēˈandər/ ▶*v.* [*intr.*] (of a river or road) follow a winding course: *a river that meandered gently through a meadow* | [as *adj.*] (**meandering**) *a meandering lane.* ■ (of a person) wander at random. ■ [*intr.*] (of a speaker or text) proceed aimlessly or with little purpose. ▶*n.* (usu. **meanders**) a winding curve or bend of a river or road: *the river flows in sweeping meanders.* ■ a circuitous journey, esp. an aimless one: *a leisurely meander around the twisting coastline road.* ■ an ornamental pattern of winding or interlocking lines, e.g., in a mosaic.

mean·ie /ˈmēnē/ (also **mean·y**) ▶*n.* (*pl.* **mean·ies**) *inf.* a mean or small-minded person.

mean·ing /ˈmēniNG/ ▶*n.* what is meant by a word, text, concept, or action. ■ implied or explicit significance: *he gave me a look full of meaning.* ■ important or worthwhile quality; purpose: *this can lead to new meaning in the life of older people.* ▶*adj.* intended to communicate something that is not directly expressed: *she gave Gabriel a meaning look.* —**mean·ing·ly** *adv.*

mean·ing·ful /ˈmēniNGfəl/ ▶*adj.* having meaning. ■ having a serious, important, or useful quality or purpose: *making our lives rich and meaningful.* ■ communicating something that is not directly expressed: *meaningful glances.* —**mean·ing·ful·ly** *adv.* —**mean·ing·ful·ness** *n.*

mean·ing·less /ˈmēniNGlis/ ▶*adj.* having no meaning or significance. ■ having no purpose or reason: *the Great War was an outstanding example of meaningless conflict* | *rules are meaningless to a child if they do not have a rationale.* —**mean·ing·less·ly** *adv.* —**mean·ing·less·ness** *n.*

means /mēnz/ ▶*pl. n.* **1** [usu. treated as *sing.*] (often **means of something** or **means to do something**) an action or system by which a result is brought about; a method: *these pledges are a means to avoid prosecution* | *resolving disputes by peaceful means.* **2** money; financial resources. ■ resources; capability: *every country in the world has the means to make ethanol.*

▶ □ **by all means** of course; certainly (granting a permission): *"May I make a suggestion?" "By all means."* □ **by any means** (or **by any manner of means**) (following a negative) in any way; at all: *I'm not poor by any means.* □ **by means of** with the help or agency of: *supplying water to cities by means of aqueducts.* □ **by no means** (or **by no manner of means**) not at all; certainly not: *the outcome is by no means guaranteed.* □ **a means to an end** a thing that is not valued or important in itself but is useful in achieving an aim: *a computer is merely a means to an end.*

meant /ment/ ▶ past and past participle of MEAN¹.

mean·time /ˈmēnˌtīm/ ▶*adv.* (also **in the meantime**) meanwhile.

mean·while /ˈmēn(h)wīl/ ▶*adv.* (also **in the meanwhile**) in the intervening period of time. ■ at the same time: *steam for another five minutes; meanwhile, make a white sauce.*

mea·sles /ˈmēzəlz/ ▶*pl. n.* (often **the measles**) [treated as *sing.*] an infectious viral disease causing fever and a red rash on the skin, typically occurring in childhood.

mea·sly /ˈmēzlē/ ▶*adj.* (**mea·sli·er, mea·sli·est**) *inf.* contemptibly small or few: *three measly votes.*

meas·ur·a·ble /ˈmeZH(ə)rəbəl/ ▶*adj.* able to be measured. ■ large enough to be measured; noticeable; definite: *a small but measurable improvement*

in behavior. —**meas·ur·a·bil·i·ty** /ˌmeZH(ə)rəˈbilətē/ *n.* —**meas·ur·a·bly** *adv.*

meas·ure /ˈmeZHər/ ▶*v.* [*tr.*] **1** ascertain the size, amount, or degree of (something) by using an instrument or device marked in standard units or by comparing it with an object of known size: *the amount of water collected is measured in pints.* ■ be of (a specified size or degree): *the fabric measures 45 inches wide.* ■ ascertain the size and proportions of (someone) in order to make or provide clothes for them: *he will be measured for his tuxedo next week.* ■ (**measure something out**) take an exact quantity or fixed amount of something: *she helped to measure out the ingredients.* ■ estimate or assess the extent, quality, value, or effect of (something): *it is hard to measure teaching ability.* ■ (**measure someone/something against**) judge someone or something by comparison with (a certain standard). ■ [*intr.*] (**measure up**) reach the required or expected standard; fulfill expectations: *I'm afraid we didn't measure up to the standards they set.* **2** consider (one's words or actions) carefully: *I had better measure my words so as not to embarrass anyone.*

▶*n.* **1** a plan or course of action taken to achieve a particular purpose: *cost-cutting measures* | *children were evacuated as a precautionary measure.* ■ a legislative bill: *the Senate passed the measure by a 48–30 vote.* **2** a standard unit used to express the size, amount, or degree of something: *a furlong is an obsolete measure of length* | *tables of weights and measures.* ■ a system or scale of such units: *the original dimensions were in imperial measure.* ■ a container of standard capacity used for taking fixed amounts of a substance. ■ a particular amount of something: *a measure of egg white as a binding agent.* ■ a standard official amount of an alcoholic drink. ■ a graduated rod or tape used for ascertaining the size of something. ■ *Math.* a quantity contained in another an exact number of times; a divisor. **3** a certain quantity or degree of something: *the states retain a large measure of independence.* ■ an indication or means of assessing the degree, extent, or quality of something: *it was a measure of the team's problems that they were still working after 2 a.m.* **4** the rhythm of a piece of poetry or a piece of music. ■ a particular metrical unit or group: *measures of two or three syllables.* ■ any of the sections, typically of equal time value, into which a musical composition is divided, shown on a score by vertical lines across the staff; bar. ■ *archaic* a dance, typically one that is grave or stately: *now tread we a measure!* **5** (**measures**) a group of rock strata. ▷Middle English (as a noun in the senses 'moderation,' 'instrument for measuring,' 'unit of capacity'): from Old French *mesure*, from Latin *mensura*, from *mens-* 'measured,' from the verb *metiri*.

▶ □ **beyond measure** to a very great extent. □ **for good measure** in addition to what has already been done, said, or given: *he added a couple of chili peppers for good measure.* □ **take** (or **get** or **have**) **the measure of** assess or have assessed the character, nature, or abilities of (someone or something). □ **in —— measure** to the degree specified: *his rapid promotion was due in some measure to his friendship with the CEO.*

meas·ured /ˈmeZHərd/ ▶*adj.* having a slow, regular rhythm: *he walks with confident, measured steps.* ■ (of speech or writing) carefully considered; deliberate and restrained: *his measured prose.* —**meas·ured·ly** *adv.*

meas·ure·less /ˈmeZHərlis/ ▶*adj.* having no bounds or limits; unlimited.

meas·ure·ment /ˈmeZHərmənt/ ▶*n.* the action of measuring something. ■ the size, length, or amount of something, as established by measuring: *his waist measurement.* ■ a unit or system of measuring.

meas·ur·ing cup /ˈmeZH(ə)riNG / ▶*n.* a cup marked in graded amounts, used for measuring ingredients in cooking.

meat /mēt/ ▶*n.* the flesh of an animal (esp. a mammal) as food. ■ the flesh of a person's body: *this'll put meat on your bones!* ■ the edible part of fruits or nuts. ■ (**the meat of**) the essence or chief part of something: *he did the meat of the climb on the first day.* —**meat·less** *adj.*

▶ □ **meat and potatoes** ordinary but fundamental things; basic ingredients: *the club's meat and potatoes remains blues performers.*

meat·ball /ˈmētˌbôl/ ▶*n.* a ball of ground or chopped meat, usually beef, with added seasonings. ■ *inf.* a dull, stupid, or foolish person.

meat loaf (also **meat·loaf**) ▶*n.* ground or chopped meat, usually beef, with added seasonings, molded into the shape of a loaf and baked.

meat·pack·ing /ˈmētˌpakiNG/ ▶*n.* the business of slaughtering animals and processing the meat for sale as food.

meat·y /ˈmētē/ ▶*adj.* (**meat·i·er, meat·i·est**) consisting of or full of meat. ■ fleshy; brawny. ■ full of substance or interest; satisfying: *the ballet has stayed the course because of the meaty roles it offers.* —**meat·i·ly** /ˈmētl-ē/ *adv.* —**meat·i·ness** /ˈmētēnis/ *n.*

me·chan·ic /məˈkanik/ ▶*n.* **1** a person who repairs and maintains machinery: *a car mechanic.* **2** *archaic* a manual laborer or artisan.

me·chan·i·cal /məˈkanikəl/ ▶*adj.* **1** working or produced by machines or machinery: ■ of or relating to machines or machinery: *a mechanical* *genius* | *mechanical failure.* **2** (of a person or action) not having or showing thought or spontaneity; automatic: *she stopped the mechanical brushing of her hair.* **3** relating to physical forces or motion; physical: *the smoothness was the result of mechanical abrasion.* ■ (of a theory) explaining phenomena in terms only of physical processes. ■ of or relating to mechanics as a science.

▶*n.* (**mechanicals**) the working parts of a machine, esp. a car. —**me‧chan‧i‧cal‧ly** *adv.* —**me‧chan‧i‧cal‧ness** *n.*

me‧chan‧ics /məˈkaniks/ ▶*pl. n.* **1** [treated as *sing.*] the branch of applied mathematics dealing with motion and forces producing motion. ■ machinery as a subject; engineering. **2** the machinery or working parts of something: *he looks at the mechanics of a car before the bodywork.* ■ the way in which something is done or operated; the practicalities or details of something: *the mechanics of cello playing.*

mech‧a‧nism /ˈmekəˌnizəm/ ▶*n.* **1** a system of parts working together in a machine; a piece of machinery: *the gunner injured his arm in the turret mechanism.* **2** a natural or established process by which something takes place or is brought about: *the mechanism by which genes build bodies.* ■ a contrivance in the plot of a literary work. **3** *Philos.* the doctrine that all natural phenomena, including life and thought, allow mechanical explanation by physics and chemistry.

mech‧a‧nis‧tic /ˌmekəˈnistik/ ▶*adj.* of or relating to theories that explain phenomena in purely physical or deterministic terms. ■ determined by physical processes alone: *he insisted that animals were entirely mechanistic.* —**mech‧a‧nis‧ti‧cal‧ly** /-(ə)lē/ *adv.*

mech‧a‧nize /ˈmekəˌnīz/ ▶*v.* [*tr.*] (often **be mechanized**) introduce machines or automatic devices into (a process, activity, or place). ■ equip (a military force) with modern weapons and vehicles: [as *adj.*] (**mechanized**) *the units comprised tanks and mechanized infantry.* ■ give a mechanical character to: *public virtue cannot be mechanized or formulated.* —**mech‧a‧ni‧za‧tion** /ˌmekənəˈzāSHən/ *n.* —**mech‧a‧niz‧er** *n.*

MEd ▶*abbr.* Master of Education.

med ▶*adj. inf.* medical: *med school.*

me‧da‧ka /məˈdäkə/ (also **me‧da‧ka‧fish** /məˈdäkəˌfiSH/) ▶*n.* a small Japanese freshwater fish (*Oryzias latipes*, family Adrianichthyidae) that is bred for aquariums and also extensively studied in the sciences.

med‧al /ˈmedl/ ▶*n.* a metal disk with an inscription or design, made to commemorate an event or awarded as a distinction to someone such as a soldier, athlete, or scholar.

▶*v.* (**med‧aled, med‧al‧ing**; also *chiefly Brit.* **med‧alled, med‧al‧ling**) [*intr.*] earn a medal, esp. in an athletic contest: *Norwegian athletes medaled in 12 of the 14 events.* —**me‧dal‧lic** /məˈdalik/ *adj.*

med‧al‧ist /ˈmedl-ist/ (*Brit.* **med‧al‧list**) ▶*n.* **1** an athlete or other person awarded a medal: *an Olympic gold medalist.* **2** an engraver or designer of medals.

me‧dal‧lion /məˈdalyən/ ▶*n.* a piece of jewelry in the shape of a medal, typically worn as a pendant. ■ an oval or circular painting, panel, or design used to decorate a building or textile. ■

Med‧al of Hon‧or (also **Congressional Medal of Honor**) ▶*n.* the highest U.S. military decoration, awarded by Congress to a member of the armed forces for gallantry and bravery in combat at the risk of life above and beyond the call of duty.

med‧dle /ˈmedl/ ▶*v.* [*intr.*] interfere in or busy oneself unduly with something that is not one's concern: *I don't want him meddling in our affairs* | [as *n.*] (**meddling**) *bureaucratic meddling.* ■ (**meddle with**) touch or handle (something) without permission. —**med‧dler** /ˈmedlər; ˈmedl-ər/ *n.*

med‧dle‧some /ˈmedlsəm/ ▶*adj.* fond of meddling; interfering. —**med‧dle‧some‧ly** *adv.* —**med‧dle‧some‧ness** *n.*

me‧di‧a /ˈmēdēə/ ▶*n.* **1** plural form of MEDIUM. **2** (usu. **the media**) [treated as *sing.* or *pl.*] the main means of mass communication (esp. television, radio, newspapers, and the Internet) regarded collectively.

me‧di‧ae‧val ▶*adj.* variant spelling of MEDIEVAL.

me‧di‧al /ˈmēdēəl/ ▶*adj. technical* situated in the middle, in particular: ■ *Anat. & Zool.* situated near the median plane of the body or the midline of an organ. The opposite of LATERAL. ■ *Phonet.* (of a speech sound) in the middle of a word. ■ *Phonet.* (esp. of a vowel) pronounced in the middle of the mouth; central. —**me‧di‧al‧ly** *adv.*

me‧di‧an /ˈmēdēən/ ▶*adj.* **1** denoting or relating to a value or quantity lying at the midpoint of a frequency distribution of observed values or quantities, such that there is an equal probability of falling above or below it: *the median duration of this treatment was four months.* ■ denoting the middle term of a series arranged in order of magnitude, or (if there is no middle term) the average of the middle two terms. For example, the median number of the series 55, 62, 76, 85, 93 is 76.

2 *technical, chiefly Anat.* situated in the middle, esp. of the body: *the median part of the sternum.*

▶*n.* **1** the median value of a range of values: *acreages ranged from one to fifty-two with a median of twenty-four.* **2** (also **median strip**) the strip of land between the lanes of opposing traffic on a divided highway. **3** *Geom.* a straight line drawn from any vertex of a triangle to the middle of the opposite side. —**me‧di‧an‧ly** *adv.*

me‧di‧ant /ˈmēdēənt/ ▶*n. Mus.* the third note of the diatonic scale of any key.

me‧di‧ate ▶*v.* /ˈmēdēˌāt/ **1** [*intr.*] intervene between people in a dispute in order to bring about an agreement or reconciliation: *Wilson attempted to mediate between the powers to end the war.* ■ [*tr.*] intervene in (a dispute) to bring about an agreement. ■ [*tr.*] bring about (an agreement or solution) by intervening in a dispute: *efforts to mediate a peaceful resolution of the conflict.* **2** [*tr.*] *technical* bring about (a result such as a physiological effect): *the right hemisphere plays an important role in mediating tactile perception of direction.* ■ be a means of conveying: *this important ministry of mediating the power of the word.*

▶*adj.* /ˈmēdēət/ connected indirectly through another person or thing; involving an intermediate agency: *public law institutions are a type of mediate state administration.* —**me‧di‧ate‧ly** /ˈmēdēətlē/ *adv.* —**me‧di‧a‧tion** /ˌmēdēˈāSHən/ *n.* —**me‧di‧a‧tor** /ˈmēdēˌātər/ *n.* —**me‧di‧a‧to‧ry** /ˈmēdēə‧ˌtôrē/ *adj.*

med‧ic /ˈmedik/ ▶*n. inf.* a medical practitioner or student. ■ *Mil.* a medical corpsman who dispenses first aid at combat sites.

Med‧i‧caid /ˈmediˌkād/ ▶a federal system of health insurance for those requiring financial assistance.

med‧i‧cal /ˈmedikəl/ ▶*adj.* of or relating to the science of medicine, or to the treatment of illness and injuries. ■ of or relating to conditions requiring medical but not surgical treatment: *he was transferred for further treatment to a medical ward.* —**med‧i‧cal‧ly** *adv.*

med‧i‧cal ex‧am‧in‧er ▶*n.* a person, usu. a physician, employed by a city, county, etc., to conduct autopsies and determine the cause of death.

med‧ic‧a‧ment /məˈdikəmənt; ˈmedikəˌment/ ▶*n.* a substance used for medical treatment.

Med‧i‧care /ˈmediˌke(ə)r/ ▶a federal system of health insurance for people over 65 years of age and for certain younger people with disabilities.

med‧i‧cate /ˈmediˌkāt/ ▶*v.* [*tr.*] administer medicine or a drug to (someone): *both infants were heavily medicated.* ■ treat (a condition) using medicine or a drug. ■ add a medicinal substance to (a dressing or product): [as *adj.*] (**medicated**) *medicated shampoo.* —**med‧i‧ca‧tive** /-ˌkātiv/ *adj.*

med‧i‧ca‧tion /ˌmedəˈkāSHən/ ▶*n.* a substance used for medical treatment, esp. a medicine or drug: *medication for depression* | *certain medications can cause dizziness.* ■ treatment using drugs: *chronic symptoms may require prolonged medication.*

me‧dic‧i‧nal /məˈdisənl/ ▶*adj.* (of a substance or plant) having healing properties: *medicinal herbs.* ■ relating to or involving medicines or drugs.

▶*n.* a medicinal substance. —**me‧dic‧i‧nal‧ly** *adv.*

med‧i‧cine /ˈmedisən/ ▶*n.* **1** the science or practice of the diagnosis, treatment, and prevention of disease (in technical use often taken to exclude surgery). **2** a compound or preparation used for the treatment or prevention of disease, esp. a drug or drugs taken by mouth. ■ such substances collectively: *an aid convoy loaded with food and medicine.* **3** (among North American Indians and some other peoples) a spell, charm, or fetish believed to have healing, protective, or other power: *Fleur was murdering him by use of bad medicine.* ▷Middle English: via Old French from Latin *medicina,* from *medicus* 'physician.'

▶ □ **take one's medicine** submit to something disagreeable such as punishment.

med‧i‧cine ball ▶*n.* a large, heavy solid ball thrown and caught for exercise.

med‧i‧cine man ▶*n.* (among North American Indians and some other peoples) a person believed to have magical powers of healing and of seeing into the future; a shaman.

med‧i‧co /ˈmediˌkō/ ▶*n.* (*pl.* **-cos**) *inf.* a medical practitioner or student.

me‧di‧e‧val /ˌmed(ē)ˈēvəl; ˌmēd-; ˌmid-/ (also **me‧di‧ae‧val**) ▶*adj.* of or relating to the Middle Ages: *a medieval castle.* —**me‧di‧e‧val‧ism** /-ˌizəm/ *n.* —**me‧di‧e‧val‧ist** /-ist/ *n.* —**me‧di‧e‧val‧ize** /-ˌīz/ *v.* —**me‧di‧e‧val‧ly** *adv.*

me‧di‧o‧cre /ˌmēdēˈōkər/ ▶*adj.* of only moderate quality; not very good: *a mediocre actor.* —**me‧di‧o‧cre‧ly** *adv.*

Pronunciation Key ə *ago,* up; ər *over, fur;* a *hat;* ā *ate;* ä *car;* CH *chin;* e *let;* ē *see;* e(ə)r *air;* i *fit;* ī *by;* i(ə)r *ear;* NG *sing;* ō *go;* ô *law, for;* oi *toy;* o͝o *good;* o͞o *goo;* ou *out;* SH *she;* TH *thin;* T͟H *then;* (h)w *why;* ZH *vision*

me·di·oc·ri·ty /ˌmēdēˈäkrətē/ ▶n. (pl. **-ties**) the quality or state of being mediocre: *heroes rising above the mediocrity that surrounds them.* ■ a person of mediocre ability.

med·i·tate /ˈmedəˌtāt/ ▶v. [intr.] think deeply or focus one's mind for a period of time, in silence or with the aid of chanting, for religious or spiritual purposes or as a method of relaxation. ■ (**meditate on/upon**) think deeply or carefully about (something): *he went off to meditate on the new idea.* ■ [tr.] plan mentally; consider: *they had suffered severely, and they began to meditate retreat.* —**med·i·ta·tor** /-ˌtātər/ n.

med·i·ta·tive /ˈmedəˌtātiv/ ▶adj. of, involving, or absorbed in meditation or considered thought: *meditative techniques.* —**med·i·ta·tive·ly** adv. —**med·i·ta·tive·ness** n.

Med·i·ter·ra·ne·an /ˌmedətəˈrānēən/ ▶adj. of or characteristic of the Mediterranean Sea, the countries bordering it, or their inhabitants. ■ (of a person's complexion) relatively dark, as is common in some Mediterranean countries.

me·di·um /ˈmēdēəm/ ▶n. (pl. **-di·a** /-dēə/ or **-di·ums**) **1** an agency or means of doing something: *technology as a medium for job creation* | *primitive valuables acted as a medium of exchange.* ■ a means by which something is communicated or expressed: *here the Welsh language is the medium of instruction.* **2** the intervening substance through which impressions are conveyed to the senses or a force acts on objects at a distance: *the medium between the cylinders is a vacuum.* ■ the substance in which an organism lives or is cultured: *grow bacteria in a nutrient-rich medium.* **3** a particular form of storage for digitized information, such as magnetic tape or discs. **4** a liquid (e.g., oil or water) with which pigments are mixed to make paint. ■ the material or form used by an artist, composer, or writer. **5** (pl. **-di·ums**) a person claiming to be in contact with the spirits of the dead and to communicate between the dead and the living. **6** the middle quality or state between two extremes; a reasonable balance: *you have to **strike a happy medium between** looking like royalty and looking like a housewife.*
▶adj. about halfway between two extremes of size or another quality; average: *John is of medium build* | *medium-length hair.* ■ (of cooked meat) halfway between rare and well-done. —**me·di·um·ism** /-ˌmizəm/ n. —**me·di·um·is·tic** /ˌmēdēəˈmistik/ adj. —**me·di·um·ship** /-ˌSHip/ n. .

med·ley /ˈmedlē/ ▶n. (pl. **-leys**) a varied mixture of people or things; a miscellany: *an interesting medley of flavors.* ■ a collection of songs or other musical items performed as a continuous piece. ■ a swimming race in which contestants swim sections in different strokes, either individually or in relay teams.

me·dul·la /məˈdələ/ ▶n. Anat. the inner region of an organ or tissue, esp. when it is distinguishable from the outer region or cortex (as in a kidney, an adrenal gland, or hair). ■ short for MEDULLA OBLONGATA. —**med·ul·lar·y** /məˈdələrē; ˈmejələrē/ adj.

me·dul·la ob·long·a·ta /ˌä,blôNGˈgätə/ ▶n. the continuation of the spinal cord within the skull, forming the lowest part of the brainstem and containing control centers for the heart and lungs.

Me·du·sa /məˈd(y)o͞osə; -zə/ Greek Mythol. ▶the only mortal Gorgon, whom Perseus killed by cutting off her head.

me·du·sa /məˈdo͞osə; -zə/ ▶n. (pl. **-sae** /-sē; -sī; -zē; -zī/ or **-sas**) Zool. a free-swimming sexual form of a coelenterate such as a jellyfish, typically having an umbrella-shaped body with stinging tentacles around the edge. ■ a jellyfish.

meek /mēk/ ▶adj. quiet, gentle, and easily imposed on; submissive. —**meek·ly** adv. —**meek·ness** n.

meer·kat /ˈmir,kat/ ▶n. a small southern African mongoose (*Suricata* and other genera).

meer·schaum /ˈmi(ə)r,SHôm; -SHəm/ ▶n. a soft white claylike material consisting of hydrated magnesium silicate. ■ (also **meerschaum pipe**) a tobacco pipe with the bowl made from this.

meet¹ /mēt/ ▶v. (past and past part. **met** /met/) [tr.] **1** come into the presence or company of (someone) by chance or arrangement: *a week later I met him in the street* | [intr.] *we met for lunch* | *they arranged to **meet up** that afternoon.* ■ make the acquaintance of (someone) for the first time: *she took Paul to meet her parents* | [intr.] *we met at an office party.* ■ [intr.] (of a group of people) assemble for a particular purpose: *the committee meets once a week.* ■ [intr.] (**meet with**) have a meeting with (someone). ■ go to a place and wait there for (a person or their means of transport) to arrive: *I offered to meet their train.* ■ play or oppose in a contest: *in the final match, the U.S. will meet Brazil* | [intr.] *the Twins and Mariners will not meet again until September.* ■ touch; join: *Harry's lips met hers* | [intr.] *the curtains failed to meet in the middle* | fig. *our eyes met across the table.* ■ encounter or be faced with (a particular fate, situation, attitude, or reaction): *he met his death in 1946* | [intr.] *we met with a slight setback.* ■ (**meet something with**) have (a particular reaction) to: *the*

announcement was met with widespread protests. ■ [intr.] (**meet with**) receive (a particular reaction): *I'm sorry if it doesn't meet with your approval.* **2** fulfill or satisfy (a need, requirement, or condition): *this policy is doing nothing to meet the needs of women.* ■ deal with or respond to (a problem or challenge) satisfactorily: *they failed to meet the noon deadline.* ■ pay (a financial claim or obligation): *all your household expenses will still have to be met.*
▶n. an organized event at which a number of races or other sporting contests are held: *a swim meet.*

meet² ▶adj. archaic suitable; fit; proper: *it is a theater **meet** for great events.* —**meet·ly** adv. —**meet·ness** n.

meet·ing /ˈmētiNG/ ▶n. **1** an assembly of people, esp. the members of a society or committee, for discussion or entertainment. ■ a gathering of people, esp. Quakers, for worship. **2** a coming together of two or more people, by chance or arrangement: *he intrigued her on their first meeting.*
▶ □ **a meeting of (the) minds** an understanding or agreement between people.

meet·ing·house /ˈmētiNG,hous/ (also **meeting house**) ▶n. a Quaker place of worship.

meg·a /ˈmegə/ inf. ▶adj. very large; huge: *a mega city.* ■ of great significance or importance: *it was one of the mega news stories of the century.*
▶adv. extremely: *they are mega rich.*

meg·a·byte /ˈmegə,bīt/ (abbr.: **Mb** or **MB**) ▶n. Comput. a unit of information equal to 2^{20} bytes or, loosely, one million bytes.

meg·a·hertz /ˈmegə,hərts/ (abbr.: **MHz**) ▶n. (pl. same) one million hertz, esp. as a measure of the frequency of radio transmissions or the clock speed of a computer.

meg·a·lith /ˈmegə,liTH/ ▶n. Archaeol. a large stone that forms a prehistoric monument (e.g., a menhir) or part of one (e.g., a stone circle or chamber tomb). —**meg·a·lith·ic** /ˌmegəˈliTHik/ adj.

meg·a·lo·blast /ˈmegələ,blast/ ▶n. Med. a large, abnormally developed red blood cell typical of certain forms of anemia, associated with a deficiency of folic acid or of vitamin B_{12}. —**meg·a·lo·blas·tic** /ˌmegəlō-ˈblastik/ adj.

meg·a·lo·ma·ni·a /ˌmegəlōˈmānēə/ ▶n. obsession with the exercise of power, esp. in the domination of others. ■ delusion about one's own power or importance (typically as a symptom of manic or paranoid disorder). —**meg·a·lo·man·ic** /-ˈmanik/ adj.

meg·a·lop·o·lis /ˌmegəˈläpələs/ ▶n. a very large, heavily populated city or urban complex.

meg·a·phone /ˈmegə,fōn/ ▶n. a large funnel-shaped device for amplifying and directing the voice.
▶v. utter through, or as if through, a megaphone. —**meg·a·phon·ic** /ˌmegəˈfänik/ adj.

meg·a·pix·el /ˈmegə,piksəl/ ▶n. one million pixels, used as a measure of the resolution in digital cameras: [in comb.] *a 3.2-megapixel camera*

meg·a·ton /ˈmegə,tən/ (abbr.: **MT**) ▶n. a unit of explosive power chiefly used for nuclear weapons, equivalent to one million tons of TNT: *H-bombs of fifteen megatons each.* —**meg·a·ton·nage** /ˌmegəˈtənij/ n.

megaphone

meg·a·watt /ˈmegə,wät/ (abbr.: **MW**) ▶n. a unit of power equal to one million watts, esp. as a measure of the output of a power station.

mei·o·sis /mīˈōsəs/ ▶n. (pl. **-ses** /-sēz/) Biol. a type of cell division that results in two daughter cells each with half the chromosome number of the parent cell, as in the production of gametes. Compare with MITOSIS. —**mei·ot·ic** /mīˈätik/ adj. —**mei·ot·i·cal·ly** /-ik)lē/ adv.

meit·ner·i·um /mīt'n(ə)rēəm/ ▶n. the chemical element of atomic number 109, a very unstable element made by high-energy atomic collisions. (Symbol: **Mt**)

mel·a·mine /ˈmelə,mēn/ ▶n. **1** Chem. a white crystalline compound, $(CNH_2)_3N_3$, used in making plastics. **2** (also **melamine resin**) a plastic used chiefly for laminated coatings.

mel·an·cho·li·a /ˌmelənˈkōlēə/ ▶n. deep sadness or gloom; melancholy. ■ dated a mental condition marked by persistent depression and ill-founded fears. —**mel·an·cho·li·ac** /-ˈkōlē-ak/ n. & adj.

mel·an·chol·y /ˈmelən,kälē/ ▶n. a deep, pensive, and long-lasting sadness. ■ another term for MELANCHOLIA (as a mental condition).
▶adj. sad, gloomy, or depressed. ▷Middle English: from Old French *melancolie*, via late Latin from Greek *melankholia*, from *melas, melan-* 'black' + *kholē* 'bile,' an excess of which was formerly believed to cause

depression. —**mel·an·chol·ic** /ˌmelənˈkälik/ adj. —**mel·an·chol·i·cal·ly** /ˌmelənˈkälək(ə)lē/ adv.

Mel·a·ne·sian /ˌmeləˈnēzHən/ ▶adj. of or relating to Melanesia, its peoples, or their languages.
▶n. **1** a native or inhabitant of any of the islands of Melanesia. **2** any of the languages of Melanesia, mostly Austronesian languages related to Malay.

mé·lange /māˈlänj/ (also **me·lange**) ▶n. a mixture; a medley: *a mélange of tender vegetables and herbs.*

mel·a·nin /ˈmelənin/ ▶n. a dark brown to black pigment occurring in the hair, skin, and iris of the eye in people and animals. It is responsible for tanning of skin exposed to sunlight.

mel·a·no·ma /ˌmeləˈnōmə/ ▶n. (pl. **-nomas** or **-no·ma·ta** /-ˈnōmətə/) Med. a tumor of melanin-forming cells, typically a malignant tumor associated with skin cancer: *melanomas can appear anywhere on the body.*

Mel·ba toast ▶n. very thin crisp toast.

meld[1] /meld/ ▶v. blend; combine: [tr.] *winemakers have melded modern science with traditional art* | [intr.] *the bristles shrivel and meld together.*
▶n. a thing formed by merging or blending: *a meld of many contributions.*

meld[2] ▶v. [tr.] (in rummy, canasta, and other card games) lay down or declare (a combination of cards) in order to score points.
▶n. a completed set or run of cards in any of these games.

me·lee /ˈmāˌlā; māˈlā/ (also **mê·lée**) ▶n. a confused fight, skirmish, or scuffle: *several people were hurt in the melee.* ■ a confused mass of people.

mel·i·lot /ˈmeləˌlät/ ▶n. a widespread fragrant herbaceous plant (genus *Melilotus*) of the pea family, sometimes grown as forage or green manure. Also called SWEET CLOVER.

mel·lif·lu·ous /məˈliflŏŏəs/ ▶adj. (of a voice or words) sweet or musical; pleasant to hear. —**mel·lif·lu·ous·ly** adv. —**mel·lif·lu·ous·ness** n.

mel·low /ˈmelō/ ▶adj. **1** (esp. of sound, taste, and color) pleasantly smooth or soft; free from harshness. ■ archaic (of fruit) ripe, soft, sweet, and juicy: *a dish of mellow apples.* ■ (of wine) well-matured and smooth: *delicious, mellow, ripe, fruity wines.* **2** (of a person's character) softened or matured by age or experience. ■ relaxed and good-humored: *Jean was feeling mellow.* ■ inf. relaxed and cheerful through being slightly drunk: *everybody got very mellow.* **3** (of earth) rich and loamy.
▶v. make or become mellow. —**mel·low·ly** adv. —**mel·low·ness** n.

me·lo·de·on /məˈlōdēən/ (also **me·lo·di·on**) ▶n. **1** a small accordion of German origin, played esp. by folk musicians. **2** a small organ popular in the 19th century, similar to the harmonium.

me·lod·ic /məˈlädik/ ▶adj. of, having, or producing melody: *melodic patterns.* ■ pleasant-sounding; melodious. —**me·lod·i·cal·ly** /-(ə)lē/ adv.

me·lo·di·ous /məˈlōdēəs/ ▶adj. of, producing, or having a pleasant tune; tuneful. ■ pleasant-sounding: *a melodious voice.* —**me·lo·di·ous·ly** adv. —**me·lo·di·ous·ness** n.

mel·o·dra·ma /ˈmeləˌdrämə/ ▶n. **1** a sensational dramatic piece with exaggerated characters and exciting events intended to appeal to the emotions. ■ the genre of drama of this type. ■ language, behavior, or events that resemble drama of this kind. **2** hist. a play interspersed with songs and orchestral music accompanying the action. —**mel·o·dra·mat·ic** /ˌmelədrəˈmatik/ adj. —**mel·o·dram·a·tist** /ˌmeləˈdrämətist/ n. —**mel·o·dram·a·tize** /ˌmeləˈdrämēˌtīz/ v.

mel·o·dy /ˈmelədē/ ▶n. (pl. **-dies**) a sequence of single notes that is musically satisfying. ■ such sequences of notes collectively: *his great gift was for melody.* ■ the principal part in harmonized music: *we have the melody and bass of a song composed by Strozzi.*

mel·on /ˈmelən/ ▶n. **1** the large round fruit of a plant of the gourd family, with sweet pulpy flesh and many seeds. ■ the edible flesh of such fruit: *a slice of melon.* **2** the Old World plant (*Cucumis melo melo*) that yields this fruit.

melt /melt/ ▶v. [intr.] **1** become liquefied by heat. ■ [tr.] change (something) to a liquid condition by heating it: *the hot metal melted the wax.* ■ [tr.] (**melt something down**) melt something, esp. a metal article, so that the material it is made of can be used again. ■ dissolve in liquid. **2** become more tender or loving. ■ [tr.] make (someone) more tender or loving. **3** [intr.] leave or disappear unobtrusively: *the figure melted into thin air.* ■ (of a feeling or state) disappear: *their original determination melted away.* ■ (**melt into**) change or merge imperceptibly into (another form or state): *the cheers melted into gasps of admiration.*
▶n. an act of melting: *the precipitation falls as snow and is released during the spring melt.* ■ molten metal, rock or other material. ■ an amount melted at any one time. ■ a sandwich, hamburger, or other dish containing or topped with melted cheese: *a tuna melt.* ▷Old English *meltan, mieltan*, of Germanic origin; related to Old Norse *melta* 'to malt,

digest,' from an Indo-European root shared by Greek *meldein* 'to melt,' Latin *mollis* 'soft,' also by *malt*. —**melt·a·ble** adj. —**melt·er** n. —**melt·ing·ly** adv.

melt·down /ˈmeltˌdoun/ ▶n. an accident in a nuclear reactor in which the fuel overheats and melts the reactor core or shielding. ■ fig. a disastrous event, esp. a rapid fall in share prices.

melt·ing point ▶n. the temperature at which a given solid will melt.

melt·ing pot ▶n. a pot in which metals or other materials are melted and mixed. ■ fig. a place where different peoples, styles, theories, etc., are mixed together: *a melting pot of disparate rhythms and cultures.*

melt·wa·ter /ˈmeltˌwôtər; -ˌwätər/ ▶n. (also **melt·wa·ters**) water formed by the melting of snow and ice, esp. from a glacier.

mem·ber /ˈmembər/ ▶n. **1** an individual belonging to a group such as a society or team: *a member of the drama club* | *members of the public.* ■ an animal or plant belonging to a taxonomic group: *a member of the lily family.* ■ (also **Mem·ber**) a person formally elected to take part in the proceedings of certain organizations: *members of Congress.* ■ a part or branch of a political body: [as adj.] *member countries of the Central African Customs Union.* **2** a constituent piece of a complex structure: *the main member that joins the front and rear axles.* **3** archaic a part or organ of the body, esp. a limb. ■ the penis. —**mem·bered** adj.

mem·ber·ship /ˈmembərˌSHip/ ▶n. the fact of being a member of a group. ■ the number or body of members in a group: *our membership has grown by 600,000 in the past 18 months.*

mem·brane /ˈmemˌbrān/ ▶n. Anat. & Zool. a pliable sheetlike structure acting as a boundary, lining, or partition in an organism. ■ a thin pliable sheet or skin of various kinds: *the concrete should include a membrane to prevent water seepage.* ■ Biol. a microscopic double layer of lipids and proteins that bounds cells and organelles and forms structures within cells. —**mem·bra·na·ceous** /ˌmembrəˈnāSHəs/ adj. —**mem·bra·ne·ous** /memˈbrānēəs/ adj. —**mem·bra·nous** /ˈmembrənəs; memˈbrānəs/ adj.

me·men·to /məˈmenˌtō/ ▶n. (pl. **-tos** or **-toes**) an object kept as a reminder or souvenir of a person or event.

mem·o /ˈmemō/ ▶n. (pl. **mem·os**) inf. a written message, esp. in business.

mem·oir /ˈmemˌwär; -ˌwôr/ ▶n. **1** a historical account or biography written from personal knowledge or special sources. ■ (**memoirs**) an autobiography or a written account of one's memory of certain events or people. **2** an essay on a learned subject: *an important memoir on periodic orbits.* ■ (**memoirs**) the proceedings or transactions of a learned society: *Memoirs of the Horticultural Society.* —**mem·oir·ist** /-ist/ n.

mem·o·ra·bil·i·a /ˌmem(ə)rəˈbilēə/ ▶pl. n. objects kept or collected because of their historical interest, esp. those associated with memorable people or events: *World Series memorabilia.* ■ archaic memorable or noteworthy things.

mem·o·ra·ble /ˈmem(ə)rəbəl/ ▶adj. worth remembering or easily remembered, esp. because of being special or unusual. —**mem·o·ra·bil·i·ty** /ˌmem(ə)rəˈbilətē/ n. —**mem·o·ra·bly** /-blē/ adv.

mem·o·ran·dum /ˌmeməˈrandəm/ ▶n. (pl. **-da** /-də/ or **-dums**) a note or record made for future use: *the two countries signed a memorandum of understanding on economic cooperation.* ■ a written message, esp. in business or diplomacy. ■ Law a document recording the terms of a contract or other legal details.

me·mo·ri·al /məˈmôrēəl/ ▶n. **1** something, esp. a structure, established to remind people of a person or event: *a memorial to those who fell in the Civil War.* ■ [as adj.] intended to commemorate someone or something: *a memorial service.* **2** chiefly hist. a statement of facts, esp. as the basis of a petition: *the council sent a strongly worded memorial to the chancellor.* ■ a record or chronicle.

Me·mo·ri·al Day ▶n. a day on which those who died in active military service are remembered, traditionally observed on May 30 but now officially observed on the last Monday in May. Also called (esp. formerly) DECORATION DAY.

me·mo·ri·al·ize /məˈmôrēəˌlīz/ ▶v. [tr.] preserve the memory of; commemorate: *the novel memorialized their childhood summers.* —**me·mo·ri·al·ist** /-əlist/ n. —**me·mo·ri·al·i·za·tion** /məˌmôrēələˈzāSHən/ n. —**me·mo·ri·al·iz·er** n.

mem·o·rize /ˈmeməˌrīz/ ▶v. [tr.] commit to memory; learn by heart: *he memorized thousands of verses.* —**mem·o·riz·a·ble** /-ˌrīzəbəl/ adj. —**mem·o·ri·za·tion** /ˌmeməriˈzāSHən/ n. —**mem·o·riz·er** n.

mem·o·ry /ˈmem(ə)rē/ ▶n. (pl. **-ries**) **1** a person's power to remember things: *a great memory for faces* | *my grandmother is losing her memory.*

■ the power of the mind to remember things: *the brain regions responsible for memory.* ■ the mind regarded as a store of things remembered: *he searched his memory for an answer.* ■ the capacity of a substance to return to a previous state or condition after having been altered or deformed. **2** something remembered from the past; a recollection: *one of my earliest memories is of sitting on his knee.* ■ the remembering or recollection of a dead person, esp. one who was popular or respected. ■ the length of time over which people continue to remember a person or event: *the worst slump in recent memory.* **3** the part of a computer in which data or program instructions can be stored for retrieval. ■ capacity for storing information in this way: *the module provides 16Mb of memory.*

▶ □ **from memory** without reading or referring to notes: *recite a verse from memory.* □ **in memory of** intended to remind people of, esp. to honor a dead person.

men /men/ ▶ plural form of MAN.

men·ace /'menəs/ ▶ *n.* a person or thing that is likely to cause harm; a threat or danger. ■ a threatening quality, tone, or atmosphere: *he spoke the words with a hint of menace.* ■ *often humorous* a person or thing that causes trouble or annoyance: *his kid sister, that chatty little menace.*

▶ *v.* [*tr.*] (often **be menaced**) threaten, esp. in a malignant or hostile manner. | [as *adj.*] (**menacing**) *a menacing tone of voice.* —**men·ac·er** *n.* —**men·ac·ing** *adj.* —**men·ac·ing·ly** *adv.*

mé·nage à trois /mā'näzн ä 't(r)wä; mə-/ ▶ *n.* (*pl.* **mé·nages à trois** *pronunc.* same) an arrangement in which three people share a sexual relationship, typically a domestic situation involving a married couple and the lover of one of them.

me·nag·er·ie /mə'najərē; -'nazн-/ ▶ *n.* a collection of wild animals kept in captivity for exhibition. ■ *fig.* a strange or diverse collection of people or things: *some other specimen in the television menagerie.*

men·a·qui·none /ˌmenə'kwin·ōn; -'kwī·nōn/ ▶ *n.* Biochem. one of the K vitamins, a compound produced by bacteria in the large intestine and essential for the blood-clotting process. Also called VITAMIN K₂ (see VITAMIN K.

mend /mend/ ▶ *v.* [*tr.*] repair (something that is broken or damaged): *a patch was used to mend the garment.* ■ [*intr.*] return to health; heal: *foot injuries can take months to mend.* ■ improve (an unpleasant situation, esp. a disagreement): *quarrels could be mended by talking.*

▶ *n.* a repair in a material. —**mend·a·ble** *adj.* —**mend·er** *n.*

▶ □ **mend (one's) fences** make peace with a person: *is it too late to mend fences with your ex-wife?* □ **mend one's ways** improve one's habits or behavior. □ **on the mend** improving in health or condition; recovering.

men·da·cious /men'dāsнəs/ ▶ *adj.* not telling the truth; lying: *mendacious propaganda.* —**men·da·cious·ly** *adv.* —**men·da·cious·ness** *n.* —**men·dac·i·ty** /-'dasitē/ *n.*

men·de·le·vi·um /ˌmendə'lēvēəm; -'lā-/ ▶ *n.* the chemical element of atomic number 101, an artificial radioactive metal of the actinide series. (Symbol: **Md**)

men·di·cant /'mendikənt/ ▶ *adj.* given to begging. ■ of or denoting one of the religious orders that originally relied solely on alms: *a mendicant friar.*

▶ *n.* a beggar. ■ a member of a mendicant order. —**men·di·can·cy** /-kənsē/ *n.*

mend·ing /'mending/ ▶ *n.* things to be repaired by sewing or darning.

men·folk /'men,fōk/ (also **men·folks**) ▶ *pl. n.* a group of men considered collectively, esp. the men of a particular family or community: *the menfolk of the village watch the goings-on.*

men·ha·den /men'hādn; mən-/ ▶ *n.* a large deep-bodied fish (genus *Brevoortia*) of the herring family that occurs along the east coast of North America. The oil-rich flesh is used to make fish meal and fertilizer.

men·hir /'men,hi(ə)r/ ▶ *n.* Archaeol. a tall upright stone of a kind erected in prehistoric times in western Europe.

me·ni·al /'mēnēəl/ ▶ *adj.* (of work) not requiring much skill and lacking prestige: *menial factory jobs.* ■ *dated* (of a servant) domestic.

▶ *n.* a person with a menial job. ■ *dated* a domestic servant. —**me·ni·al·ly** *adv.*

me·nin·ges /mə'ninjēz/ ▶ *plural n.* (*sing.* **me·ninx** /'mēninGks; 'meninGks/) Anatomy the three membranes (the dura mater, arachnoid, and pia mater) that line the skull and vertebral canal and enclose the brain and spinal cord. —*modern Latin, from Greek mēninx, mēning-* 'membrane.' —**me·nin·ge·al** /mə'ninjēəl/ *adj.*

men·in·gi·tis /ˌmenən'jītis/ ▶ *n.* inflammation of the meninges caused by viral or bacterial infection and marked by intense headache and fever, sensitivity to light, and muscular rigidity, leading (in severe cases) to convulsions, delirium, and death. —**men·in·git·ic** /-'jitik/ *adj.*

me·nis·cus /mə'niskəs/ ▶ *n.* (*pl.* **-ci** /-kē; -kī/ or **-cus·es**) Physics the curved upper surface of a liquid in a tube. ■ *Anat.* a thin fibrous cartilage between the surfaces of some joints, e.g., the knee.

Men·non·ite /'menə,nīt/ ▶ *n.* (chiefly in the U.S. and Canada) a member of a Protestant sect originating in Friesland in the 16th century, emphasizing adult baptism and rejecting church organization, military service, and public office. ▷from the name of its founder, *Menno Simons* (1496–1561). —**Men·no·nit·ism** /-izəm/ *n.*

men·o·pause /'menə,pôz/ ▶ *n.* the ceasing of menstruation. ■ the period in a woman's life (typically between 45 and 50 years of age) when this occurs. —**men·o·pau·sal** /ˌmenə'pôzəl/ *adj.*

me·nor·ah /mə'nôrə/ ▶ *n.* (**the Menorah**) a sacred candelabrum with seven branches used in the Temple in Jerusalem, originally that and placed in the sanctuary of the Tabernacle. ■ a candelabrum used in Jewish worship, esp. one with eight branches and a central socket used at Hanukkah.

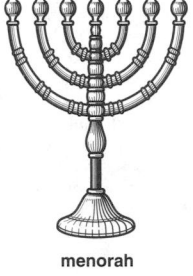

menorah

men·ses /'men,sēz/ ▶ *pl. n.* blood and other matter discharged from the uterus at menstruation. ■ [treated as *sing.*] the time of menstruation: *a late menses.*

men's room ▶ *n.* a restroom for men in a public or institutional building.

men·stru·al /'menstr(oо)əl/ ▶ *adj.* of or relating to the menses or menstruation: *menstrual blood.*

men·stru·al cy·cle ▶ *n.* the process of ovulation and menstruation in women and other female primates.

men·stru·al per·i·od ▶ *n.* see PERIOD (sense 4).

men·stru·ate /'menstrə,wāt; 'men,strāt/ ▶ *v.* [*intr.*] (of a woman) discharge blood and other material from the lining of the uterus as part of the menstrual cycle.

men·stru·a·tion /ˌmenstroо'āsнən; men'strā-/ ▶ *n.* the process in a woman of discharging blood and other materials from the lining of the uterus at intervals of about one lunar month from puberty until menopause, except during pregnancy.

mens·wear /'menz,we(ə)r/ (also **men's wear**) ▶ *n.* clothes for men.

men·tal /'mentl/ ▶ *adj.* **1** of or relating to the mind. ■ carried out by or taking place in the mind: *a quick mental calculation.* **2** of, relating to, or suffering from disorders or illnesses of the mind: *a mental hospital.* ■ *inf.* insane; crazy: *every time I'm late, they go mental.* —**men·tal·ly** *adv.*

men·tal·i·ty /men'talitē/ ▶ *n.* (*pl.* **-ties**) **1** *often derog.* the characteristic attitude of mind or way of thinking of a person or group: *the yuppie mentality of the eighties.* **2** the capacity for intelligent thought.

men·thol /'men,тнôl; -,тнäl/ ▶ *n.* a crystalline compound, $C_{10}H_{19}OH$, with a cooling minty taste and odor, found in peppermint and other natural oils. It is used as a flavoring and in decongestants and analgesics.

men·tho·lat·ed /'menтнə,lātid/ ▶ *adj.* treated with or containing menthol: *mentholated shaving creams.*

men·tion /'mencнən/ ▶ *v.* [*tr.*] refer to something briefly and without going into detail: *I haven't mentioned it to William yet* | *I mentioned that my father was meeting me later.* ■ [*tr.*] (often **be mentioned**) make a reference to (someone) as being noteworthy.

▶ *n.* a reference to someone or something. ■ a formal acknowledgment of something outstanding or noteworthy: *he received a special mention.* See also HONORABLE MENTION. —**men·tion·a·ble** *adj.*

▶ □ **not to mention** used to introduce an additional fact or point that reinforces the point being made: *I'm amazed you find the time, not to mention the energy, to do any work at all.*

men·tor /'men,tôr; -tər/ ▶ *n.* an experienced and trusted adviser. ■ an experienced person in a company, college, or school who trains and counsels new employees or students.

▶ *v.* [*tr.*] to advise or train (someone, esp. a younger colleague). —**men·tor·ship** /-,sнip/ *n.*

men·u /'menyoо/ ▶ *n.* (*pl.* **men·us**) a list of dishes available in a restaurant. ■ the food available or to be served in a restaurant or at a meal. ■ *Comput.* a list of commands or options, esp. one displayed on screen. ▷mid 19th cent.: from French, 'detailed list' (noun use of *menu* 'small, detailed'), from Latin *minutus* 'very small.'

me·ow /mē'ou/ ▶ *n.* the characteristic crying sound of a cat.

▶ *v.* [*intr.*] (of a cat) make such a sound.

me·phit·ic /mə'fitik/ ▶ *adj.* (esp. of a gas or vapor) foul-smelling; noxious.

mer·can·tile /'mərkən,tēl; -,tīl/ ▶ *adj.* of or relating to trade or commerce; commercial. ■ of or relating to mercantilism.

mer·can·til·ism /ˈmərkəntiˌlizəm; -ˌtē-; -ˌtī-/ ▶n. belief in the benefits of profitable trading; commercialism. ■ *chiefly hist.* the economic theory that trade generates wealth and is stimulated by the accumulation of profitable balances, which a government should encourage by means of protectionism. —**mer·can·til·ist** n. & adj. —**mer·can·til·is·tic** /ˌmərkəntiˈlistik; -ˌtē-; -ˌtī-/ adj.

Mer·ca·tor pro·jec·tion /mərˈkātər/ (also **Mer·ca·tor's pro·jec·tion**) ▶n. a projection of a map of the world onto a cylinder in such a way that all the parallels of latitude have the same length as the equator, used esp. for marine charts and certain climatological maps.

mer·ce·nar·y /ˈmərsəˌnerē/ ▶adj. derog. (of a person or their behavior) primarily concerned with making money at the expense of ethics. ▶n. (pl. **-ies**) a professional soldier hired to serve in a foreign army. ■ a person primarily concerned with material reward at the expense of ethics: *the sport's most infamous mercenary.* —**mer·ce·nar·i·ness** n.

mer·cer·ize /ˈmərsəˌrīz/ ▶v. [tr.] [often as adj.] (**mercerized**) treat (cotton fabric or thread) under tension with caustic alkali to increase its strength and give it a shiny, silky appearance.

mer·chan·dise ▶n. /ˈmərchənˌdīz; -ˌdīs/ goods to be bought and sold. ▶v. /ˈmərchənˌdīz/ (also **mer·chan·dize**) [tr.] promote the sale of (goods), esp. by their presentation in retail outlets. ■ advertise or publicize (an idea or person): *they are merchandising "niceness" to children.* ■ archaic trade or traffic in (something), esp. inappropriately. ■ [intr.] archaic engage in the business of a merchant. —**mer·chan·dis·er** /-ˌdīzər/ n.

mer·chant /ˈmərchənt/ ▶n. **1** a person or company involved in wholesale trade, esp. one dealing with foreign countries or supplying merchandise to a particular trade. ■ a retail trader; a store owner. ■ (esp. in historical contexts) a person involved in trade or commerce: *prosperous merchants and clothiers had established a middle class.* **2** inf., chiefly derog. a person with a partiality or aptitude for a particular activity or viewpoint: *his driver was no speed merchant | a merchant of death.* ▶adj. of or relating to merchants, trade, or commerce: *the growth of the merchant classes.* ■ (of ships, sailors, or shipping activity) involved with commerce rather than military activity: *a merchant seaman.*

mer·chant·man /ˈmərchəntmən/ ▶n. (pl. **-men**) a ship used in commerce; a vessel of the merchant marine.

mer·chant ma·rine ▶n. (often **the merchant marine**) a country's shipping that is involved in commerce and trade, as opposed to military activity.

mer·ci·ful /ˈmərsifəl/ ▶adj. showing or exercising mercy. ■ (of an event) coming as a mercy; bringing someone relief from something unpleasant: *her death was a merciful release.* —**mer·ci·ful·ness** n.

mer·ci·ful·ly /ˈmərsif(ə)lē/ ▶adv. **1** in a merciful manner. **2** to one's great relief; fortunately.

mer·ci·less /ˈmərsiləs/ ▶adj. showing no mercy or pity: *a merciless attack with | fig. the merciless summer heat.* —**mer·ci·less·ly** adv. —**mer·ci·less·ness** n.

mer·cu·ri·al /mərˈkyo͝orēəl/ ▶adj. **1** (of a person) subject to sudden or unpredictable changes of mood or mind: *his mercurial temperament.* ■ (of a person) sprightly; lively. **2** of or containing the element mercury. —**mer·cu·ri·al·i·ty** /-ˌkyo͝orēˈalitē/ n. —**mer·cu·ri·al·ly** adv.

Mer·cu·ry /ˈmərkyərē/ ▶ **1** Roman Mythol. the Roman god of eloquence, skill, trading, and thieving, herald and messenger of the gods, who was identified with Hermes. **2** Astron. a small planet that is the closest to the sun in the solar system, sometimes visible to the naked eye just after sunset. —**Mer·cu·ri·an** /mərˈkyo͝orēən/ adj.

mer·cu·ry[1] /ˈmərkyərē/ ▶n. the chemical element of atomic number 80, a heavy silvery-white metal that is liquid at ordinary temperatures. (Symbol: **Hg**) Also called QUICKSILVER. ■ the column of such metal in a thermometer or barometer, or its height as indicating atmospheric temperature or pressure: *the mercury rises and the nights swelter.* ■ hist. this metal or one of its compounds used medicinally. —**mer·cu·ric** /mərˈkyo͝orik/ adj.

mer·cu·ry[2] ▶n. a plant (genera *Mercurialis* and *Acalypha*) of the spurge family.

mer·cy /ˈmərsē/ ▶n. (pl. **-cies**) compassion or forgiveness shown toward someone whom it is within one's power to punish or harm: *the boy was begging for mercy.* ■ an event to be grateful for, esp. because its occurrence prevents something unpleasant or provides relief from suffering: *his death was in a way a mercy.* ■ [as adj.] (esp. of a journey or mission) performed out of a desire to relieve suffering; motivated by compassion. ▶interj. archaic used in expressions of surprise or fear. ▷Middle English: from Old French *merci* 'pity' or 'thanks,' from Latin *merces, merced-* 'reward,' in Christian Latin 'pity, favor, heavenly reward.'

▶ □ **at the mercy of** completely in the power or under the control of: *consumers were at the mercy of every rogue in the marketplace.*

mer·cy kill·ing ▶n. the killing of a patient suffering from an incurable and painful disease, typically by the administration of large doses of painkilling drugs. See also EUTHANASIA. ■ the killing of an animal that is suffering from an incurable and painful disease or from extreme, life-threatening injuries.

mere[1] /mi(ə)r/ ▶adj. that is solely or no more or better than what is specified: *it happened a mere decade ago | questions that cannot be answered by mere mortals.* ■ (**the merest**) the smallest or slightest: *the merest hint of makeup.* —**mere·ly** adv.

mere[2] ▶n. chiefly poetic/lit. a lake, pond, or arm of the sea.

mer·e·tri·cious /ˌmerəˈtrishəs/ ▶adj. **1** apparently attractive but having in reality no value or integrity: *meretricious souvenirs for the tourist trade.* **2** archaic of, relating to, or characteristic of a prostitute. —**mer·e·tri·cious·ly** adv. —**mer·e·tri·cious·ness** n.

mer·gan·ser /mərˈgansər/ ▶n. a fish-eating diving duck with a long, thin serrated and hooked bill.

merge /mərj/ ▶v. combine or cause to combine to form a single entity. ■ incorporate revisions to a document to supersede the original. ■ [intr.] blend or fade gradually into something else so as to become indistinguishable from it: *he crouched low and endeavored to merge into the darkness of the forest.* ■ [tr.] cause to blend or fade into something else in such a way.

merg·er /ˈmərjər/ ▶n. a combination of two things, esp. companies, into one. ■ *local companies ripe for merger or acquisition.*

me·rid·i·an /məˈridēən/ ▶n. **1** a circle of constant longitude passing through a given place on the earth's surface and the terrestrial poles. ■ (also **celestial meridian**) Astron. a circle passing through the celestial poles and the zenith of a given place on the earth's surface. **2** (in acupuncture and Chinese medicine) each of a set of pathways in the body along which vital energy is said to flow. ▶adj. relating to or situated at a meridian: *the meridian moon.* ■ poetic/lit. of noon. ■ poetic/lit. of the period of greatest splendor, vigor, etc.

me·ringue /məˈraNG/ ▶n. an item of sweet food made from a mixture of well-beaten egg whites and sugar, baked until crisp and typically used as a topping for desserts, esp. pies. Individual meringues are often filled with fruit or whipped cream.

me·ri·no /məˈrēnō/ ▶n. (pl. **-nos**) (also **merino sheep**) a sheep of a breed with long, fine wool. ■ a soft woolen or wool-and-cotton material resembling cashmere, originally of merino wool. ■ a fine woolen yarn.

mer·it /ˈmerit/ ▶n. the quality of being particularly good or worthy, esp. so as to deserve praise or reward: *composers of outstanding merit.* ■ a feature or fact that deserves praise or reward. ■ (**merits**) chiefly Law the intrinsic rights and wrongs of a case, outside of any other considerations: *a good arguable case on the merits.* ▶v. (**mer·it·ed, mer·it·ing**) [tr.] deserve or be worthy of (something, esp. reward, punishment, or attention): *the results have been encouraging enough to merit further investigation.*

mer·i·toc·ra·cy /ˌmeriˈtäkrəsē/ ▶n. (pl. **-cies**) government or the holding of power by people selected on the basis of their ability. ■ a society governed by such people or in which such people hold power. ■ a ruling or influential class of educated or skilled people. —**mer·i·to·crat·ic** /ˌmeritəˈkratik/ adj.

mer·i·to·ri·ous /ˌmeriˈtôrēəs/ ▶adj. deserving reward or praise: *meritorious conduct.* ■ Law (of an action or claim) likely to succeed on the merits of the case. —**mer·i·to·ri·ous·ly** adv. —**mer·i·to·ri·ous·ness** n.

mer·maid /ˈmərˌmād/ ▶n. a fictitious or mythical half-human sea creature with the head and trunk of a woman and the tail of a fish, conventionally depicted as beautiful and with long flowing golden hair.

mer·man /ˈmərˌman; -mən/ ▶n. (pl. **-men**) the male equivalent of a mermaid.

mer·ri·ment /ˈmerēmənt/ ▶n. gaiety and fun: *her eyes sparkled with merriment.*

mer·ry /ˈmerē/ ▶adj. (**mer·ri·er, mer·ri·est**) cheerful and lively: *merry throngs of students | a merry grin.* ■ (of an occasion or season) characterized by festivity and rejoicing: *he wished me a merry Christmas.* ■ Brit., inf. slightly and good-humored drunk: *after the third bottle of beer he began to feel quite merry.* —**mer·ri·ly** adv. —**mer·ri·ness** n. ▶ □ **make merry** enjoy oneself with others, esp. by drinking.

M

mer·ry-go-round ▶ *n.* a revolving machine with model horses or other animals on which people ride for amusement. ■ a large revolving device in a playground, for children to ride on. ■ *fig.* a continuous cycle of activities or events, esp. when perceived as having no purpose or producing no result: *the football management merry-go-round.*

mer·ry·mak·ing /ˈmerēˌmākiNG/ ▶ *n.* the process of enjoying oneself with others, esp. by dancing and drinking. —**mer·ry·mak·er** /-ˌmākər/ *n.*

me·sa /ˈmāsə/ ▶ *n.* an isolated flat-topped hill with steep sides, found in landscapes with horizontal strata.

mes·cal /meˈskal; mə-/ ▶ *n.* **1** an intoxicating liquor distilled from the sap of an agave. **2** another term for PEYOTE.

mes·ca·line /ˈmeskəlin; -ˌlēn/ ▶ *n.* a hallucinogenic and intoxicating compound present in mescal buttons from the peyote cactus.

Mes·dames /māˈdäm/ ▶ *pl. n.* **1** plural form of MADAME. **2** *formal* used as a title to refer to more than one woman simultaneously: *prizes were won by Mesdames Carter, Roseby, and Barrington.*

Mes·de·moi·selles /ˈmādəm(w)əˌzel; ˈmādˌmwäˌzel/ ▶ plural form of MADEMOISELLE.

mes·en·ceph·a·lon /ˌmezənˈsefəˌlän; ˌmes-/ ▶ *n. Anatomy* another term for MIDBRAIN.

mesh /meSH/ ▶ *n.* **1** material made of a network of wire or thread: *mesh for fishing nets.* ■ the spacing of the strands of such material: *if the mesh is too big, small rabbits can squeeze through.* **2** an interlaced structure: *cell fragments that agglutinate and form intricate meshes.* ■ *fig.* used with reference to a complex or constricting situation: *the raveled mesh of events and her own emotions.* ■ *Comput.* a set of finite elements used to represent a geometric object for modeling or analysis. ■ *Comput.* a computer network in which each computer or processor is connected to a number of others.
▶ *v.* **1** [*intr.*] (of the teeth of a gear) lock together or be engaged with another gear: *one gear meshes with the input gear.* ■ make or become entangled or entwined. ■ *fig.* be in or bring into harmony: [*intr.*] *her memory of events doesn't mesh with the world around her.* **2** [*tr.*] represent (a geometric object) as a set of finite elements for computational analysis or modeling. —**meshed** *adj.* —**mesh·y** *adj.*

mes·mer·ism /ˈmezməˌrizəm/ ▶ *n. hist.* (in general use) hypnotism. —**mes·mer·ic** /mezˈmerik/ *adj.* —**mes·mer·ist** /-ist/ *n.*

mes·mer·ize /ˈmezməˌrīz/ ▶ *v.* [*tr.*] (often **be mesmerized**) hold the attention of (someone) to the exclusion of all else or so as to transfix them. ■ *archaic* hypnotize (someone). —**mes·mer·i·za·tion** /ˌmezmərəˈzāSHən/ *n.* —**mes·mer·iz·er** *n.* —**mes·mer·iz·ing·ly** *adv.*

mes·o·derm /ˈmezəˌdərm; ˈmē-/ ▶ *n. Embryology* the middle layer of an embryo in early development, between the endoderm and ectoderm. —**mes·o·der·mal** /ˌmezəˈdərməl; mē-/ *adj.* —**mes·o·der·mic** /-ˈdərmik/ *adj.*

Mes·o·lith·ic /ˌmezəˈliTHik; ˌmē-/ ▶ *adj. Archaeol.* of, relating to, or denoting the middle part of the Stone Age, between the Paleolithic and Neolithic. ■ [as *n.*] (**the Mesolithic**) the Mesolithic period.

mes·o·morph /ˈmezəˌmôrf; ˈmē-/ ▶ *n. Physiol.* a person with a compact and muscular body build. Compare with ECTOMORPH and ENDOMORPH. —**mes·o·mor·phic** /ˌmezəˈmôrfik; ˌmē-/ *adj.*

me·son /ˈmezˌän; ˈmāˌzän; ˈmēˌzän/ ▶ *n. Physics* a subatomic particle that is intermediate in mass between an electron and a proton and transmits the strong interaction that binds nucleons together in the atomic nucleus. —**me·son·ic** /meˈzänik; mā-/ *adj.*

mes·o·sphere /ˈmezəˌsfi(ə)r; ˈmē-/ ▶ *n.* the region of the earth's atmosphere above the stratosphere and below the thermosphere, between about 30 and 50 miles (50 and 80 km) in altitude. —**mes·o·spher·ic** /ˌmezəˈsfi(ə)rik; ˌmē-/ *adj.*

mes·o·the·li·o·ma /ˌmezəˌTHēlēˈōmə; ˌmē-/ ▶ *n.* (*pl.* **-mas** or **-ma·ta**) *Med.* a cancer of mesothelial tissue, associated esp. with exposure to asbestos.

mes·o·the·li·um /ˌmezəˈTHēlēəm; ˌmē-/ ▶ *n.* (*pl.* **-the·li·a** /-ˈTHēlēə/) *Anat.* the epithelium that lines the pleurae, peritoneum, and pericardium. ■ *Embryol.* the surface layer of the embryonic mesoderm, from which this is derived. —**mes·o·the·li·al** /-ˈTHēlēəl/ *adj.*

Mes·o·zo·ic /ˌmezəˈzōik; ˌmē-/ ▶ *adj. Geol.* of, relating to, or denoting the era between the Paleozoic and Cenozoic eras, comprising the Triassic, Jurassic, and Cretaceous periods. ■ [as *n.*] (**the Mesozoic**) the Mesozoic era or the system of rocks deposited during it.

mes·quite /meˈskēt/ ▶ *n.* a spiny tree or shrub (genus *Prosopis*) of the pea family, native to arid regions of southwestern U.S. and Mexico. It yields useful timber, tanbark, medicinal products, and edible pods.The timber is used for fencing and flooring, and burned in barbecues as flavoring.

mess /mes/ ▶ *n.* **1** a dirty or untidy state of things or of a place: *she made a mess of the kitchen | my hair was a mess.* ■ a thing or collection of things causing such a state. ■ a person who is dirty or untidy. ■ a portion of semisolid or pulpy food, esp. one that looks unappetizing: *a mess of mashed black beans and rice.* ■ *fig.* a situation or state of affairs that is confused or full of difficulties: *the economy is still in a terrible mess.* ■ *fig.* a person whose life or affairs are confused or troubled: *he needs treatment of some kind—he's a real mess.* **2** a building or room in which members of the armed forces take their meals; mess hall: *the sergeants' mess.* ■ a meal taken there.
▶ *v.* **1** [*tr.*] make untidy or dirty: *you've* **messed up** *my beautiful carpet.* **2** [*intr.*] take one's meals in a particular place or with a particular person, esp. in an armed forces' mess: *they messed together.*
▶ *phrasal v.* □ **mess around/about** behave in a silly or playful way, esp. so as to cause irritation. ■ spend time doing something in a pleasantly desultory way, with no definite purpose or serious intent: *messing around in boats.* □ **mess around/about with** interfere with. ■ *inf.* engage in a sexual relationship with (someone, esp. the partner of another person). □ **mess up** *inf.* mishandle a situation. □ **mess someone up** *inf.* cause someone emotional or psychological problems: *I was unhappy and really messed up.* ■ inflict violence or injury on someone: *the wreck messed him up so much that he can't walk.* □ **mess something up** *inf.* cause something to be spoiled by inept handling: *an error like that could easily mess up an entire day's work.* □ **mess with** *inf.* meddle or interfere with so as to spoil or cause trouble. ▷Middle English: from Old French *mes* 'portion of food,' from late Latin *missum* 'something put on the table,' past participle of *mittere* 'send, put.' The original sense was 'a serving of food,' also 'a serving of liquid or pulpy food,' later 'liquid food for an animal'; this gave rise (early 19th cent.) to the senses 'unappetizing concoction' and 'predicament,' on which sense 1 is based. In late Middle English the term also denoted any of the small groups into which the company at a banquet was divided (who were served from the same dishes); hence, 'a group of people who regularly eat together' (recorded in military use from the mid 16th cent.).
▶ □ **mess with someone's head** *inf.* cause someone to feel frustrated, anxious, or upset.

mes·sage /ˈmesij/ ▶ *n.* a verbal, written, or recorded communication sent to or left for a recipient who cannot be contacted directly. ■ an official or formal communication, esp. a speech delivered by a head of state to a legislative assembly or the public: *the president's message to Congress.* ■ an item of electronic mail. ■ an electronic communication generated automatically by a computer program and displayed on a VDT: *an error message.* ■ a significant point or central theme, esp. one that has political, social, or moral importance: *a campaign to get the message about home security across.* ■ a divinely inspired communication from a prophet or preacher. ■ a television or radio commercial. ▷Middle English: from Old French, based on Latin *missus*, past participle of *mittere* 'send.'
▶ □ **get the message** *inf.* infer an implication from a remark or action. □ **send a message** make a significant statement, either implicitly or by one's actions.

mes·sage board ▶ *n. Comput.* an Internet site where people can post and read messages, usually on a specific topic or area of interest. Compare with BULLETIN BOARD.

Mes·sei·gneurs /ˌmāsānˈyər(z)/ ▶ plural form of MONSEIGNEUR.

mes·sen·ger /ˈmesənjər/ ▶ *n.* **1** a person who carries a message or is employed to carry messages. ■ *Biochem.* a substance that conveys information or a stimulus within the body. **2** *Naut.* (also **messenger line**) a light line used to haul or support a larger one.
▶ *v.* [*tr.*] send (a document or package) by messenger: *could you have it messengered over to me?*
▶ □ **shoot** (or **kill**) **the messenger** treat the bearer of bad news as if they were to blame for it.

mes·sen·ger RNA (abbr.: **mRNA**) ▶ *n.* the form of RNA in which genetic information transcribed from DNA as a sequence of bases is transferred to a ribosome.

mess hall ▶ *n.* a room or building where groups of people, esp. soldiers, eat together.

mes·si·ah /məˈsīə/ ▶ *n.* **1** (**the Messiah**) the promised deliverer of the Jewish nation prophesied in the Hebrew Bible. ■ Jesus regarded by Christians as the Messiah of the Hebrew prophecies and the savior of humankind. **2** a leader or savior of a particular group or cause. —**mes·si·ah·ship** /-ˌSHip/ *n.*

mes·si·an·ic /ˌmesēˈanik/ ▶ *adj.* (also **Mes·si·an·ic**) of or relating to the Messiah. ■ inspired by hope or belief in a messiah: *messianic expectations.* ■ fervent or passionate: *messianic zeal.* —**mes·si·a·nism** /ˈmesēəˌnizəm; məˈsīə-/ *n.*

Mes·sieurs /məsˈyœ(r)(z); mäs-; məˈsi(ə)r(z)/ ▶ plural form of MONSIEUR.

mess kit ▶ n. a set of cooking and eating utensils, as used esp. by soldiers, scouts, or campers.

Messrs. ▶ pl. n. dated or chiefly Brit. used as a title to refer formally to more than one man simultaneously, or in names of companies.

mess·y /ˈmesē/ ▶ adj. (**mes·si·er**, **mes·si·est**) **1** untidy or dirty: his messy hair. ■ generating or involving mess or untidiness: stripping wallpaper can be a messy job. **2** (of a situation) confused and difficult to deal with: a messy divorce. —**mess·i·ly** /ˈmesəlē/ adv. —**mess·i·ness** n.

mes·ti·zo /meˈstēzō/ ▶ n. (pl. **-zos**) (in Latin America) a man of mixed race, esp. the offspring of a Spaniard and an American Indian.

met /met/ ▶ past and past participle of MEET[1].

met. ▶ abbr. ■ metaphor. ■ metaphysics. ■ meteorology. ■ metropolitan.

met·a·bol·ic path·way /ˈmetəˈbälik/ ▶ n. see PATHWAY.

me·tab·o·lism /məˈtabəˌlizəm/ ▶ n. the chemical processes that occur within a living organism in order to maintain life. —**met·a·bol·ic** /ˈmetəˈbälik/ adj. —**met·a·bol·i·cal·ly** /ˌmetəˈbälik(ə)lē/ adv.

me·tab·o·lite /məˈtabəˌlīt/ ▶ n. Biochem. a substance formed in or necessary for metabolism.

me·tab·o·lize /məˈtabəˌlīz/ ▶ v. [tr.] (of a body or organ) process (a substance) by metabolism. ■ [intr.] (of a substance) undergo processing by metabolism. —**me·tab·o·liz·a·ble** adj. —**me·tab·o·liz·er** n.

met·a·car·pus /ˈmetəˌkärpəs/ ▶ n. (pl. **-pi** /-pē; -ˌpī/) the group of five bones of the hand between the wrist (carpus) and the fingers. ■ this part of the hand. ■ the equivalent group of bones in an animal's forelimb. —**met·a·car·pal** /-ˈkärpəl/ adj.

met·al /ˈmetl/ ▶ n. **1** a solid material that is typically hard, shiny, malleable, fusible, and ductile, with good electrical and thermal conductivity (e.g., iron, gold, silver, copper, and aluminum, and alloys such as brass and steel). **2** Brit. (also **road met·al**) broken stone for use in making roads. **3** molten glass before it is blown or cast. **4** heavy metal or similar rock music.
▶ v. (**met·aled**, **met·al·ing**; chiefly Brit. **met·alled**, **met·al·ling**) [tr.] [usu. as adj.] (**metaled**) make out of or coat with metal: metaled key rings.

me·tal·lic /məˈtalik/ ▶ adj. of, relating to, or resembling metal or metals. ■ (of sound) resembling that produced by metal objects striking each other; sharp and ringing: the metallic clamor of the fire-engine bell. ■ (of a person's voice); emanating or as if emanating via an electronic medium: a metallic voice rasped from a concealed speaker. ■ having the sheen or luster of metal.
▶ n. a paint, fiber, fabric, or color with a metallic sheen: dresses that shine with sequins and metallics. —**me·tal·li·cal·ly** /-ik(ə)lē/ adv.

met·al·loid /ˈmetlˌoid/ ▶ n. Chem. an element (e.g., germanium or silicon) whose properties are intermediate between those of metals and solid nonmetals. They are electrical semiconductors.

met·al·lur·gy /ˈmetlˌərjē/ ▶ n. the branch of science and technology concerned with the properties of metals and their production and purification. —**met·al·lur·gic** /ˌmetlˈərjik/ adj. —**met·al·lur·gi·cal** adj. —**met·al·lur·gi·cal·ly** adv. —**met·al·lur·gist** n.

met·al·work /ˈmetlˌwərk/ ▶ n. the art of making things out of metal. ■ metal objects collectively: a wealth of fine metalwork, including a sword. ■ the metal part of a construction: engineers spotted cracks in the metalwork. —**met·al·work·er** n. —**met·al·work·ing** n.

met·a·mor·phic /ˌmetəˈmôrfik/ ▶ adj. **1** Geol. denoting rock that has undergone transformation by heat, pressure, or other natural agencies, e.g., in deep burial or the nearby intrusion of igneous rocks. ■ of or relating to such rocks or metamorphism. **2** of or marked by metamorphosis.

met·a·mor·phose /ˌmetəˈmôrˌfōz; -ˌfōs/ ▶ v. [intr.] (of an insect or amphibian) undergo metamorphosis, esp. into the adult form. ■ change completely in nature or form: a father seeing his daughter metamorphosing from girl into woman. ■ [tr.] cause (something) to change completely. ■ [tr.] Geol. subject (rock) to metamorphism: [as adj.] (**metamorphosed**) a metamorphosed sandstone.

met·a·mor·pho·sis /ˌmetəˈmôrfəsəs/ ▶ n. (pl. **-pho·ses** /-fəˌsēz/) Zool. (in an insect or amphibian) the process of transformation from an immature form to an adult form in two or more distinct stages. ■ a change of the form or nature of a thing or person into a different one, by natural or supernatural means: his metamorphosis from presidential candidate to talk-show host.

met·a·phor /ˈmetəˌfôr; -fər/ ▶ n. a figure of speech in which a word or phrase is applied to an object or action to which it is not literally applicable: "I had fallen through a trapdoor of depression," said Mark, who was fond of theatrical metaphors. ■ a thing regarded as representative or symbolic of something else, esp. something abstract: the amounts lost by the company were enough to make it a **metaphor for** an industry that was teetering. —**met·a·phor·ic** /ˌmetəˈfôrik/ adj. —**met·a·phor·i·cal** /ˌmetəˈfôrikəl/ adj. —**met·a·phor·i·cal·ly** /ˌmetəˈfôrik(ə)lē/ adv.

met·a·phys·i·cal /ˌmetəˈfizikəl/ ▶ adj. of or relating to metaphysics. ■ based on abstract (typically, excessively abstract) reasoning. ■ transcending physical matter or the laws of nature: Good and Evil are linked in a metaphysical battle across space and time. —**met·a·phys·i·cal·ly** /-ik(ə)lē/ adv.

met·a·phys·ics /ˌmetəˈfiziks/ ▶ pl. n. [usu. treated as sing.] the branch of philosophy that deals with the first principles of things, including abstract concepts such as being, knowing, substance, cause, identity, time, and space. ■ abstract theory or talk with no basis in reality. —**met·a·phy·si·cian** /-fəˈzishən/ n.

me·tas·ta·sis /məˈtastəsəs/ ▶ n. (pl. **-ses** /-ˌsēz/) Med. the development of secondary malignant growths at a distance from a primary site of cancer. ■ a growth of this type. —**me·tas·ta·size** v. —**met·a·stat·ic** /ˌmetəˈstatik/ adj.

met·a·tar·sus /ˌmetəˈtärsəs/ ▶ n. (pl. **-si** /-ˌsē; -ˌsī/) the group of bones in the foot, between the ankle and the toes. ■ this part of the foot. ■ the equivalent group of bones in an animal's hind limb. —**met·a·tar·sal** /-ˈtärsəl/ adj.

me·tath·e·sis /məˈtaTHəsəs/ ▶ n. (pl. **-ses** /-ˌsēz/) Gram. the transposition of sounds or letters in a word. —**met·a·thet·ic** /ˌmetəˈTHetik/ adj. —**met·a·thet·i·cal** /ˌmetəˈTHetikəl/ adj.

mete[1] /mēt/ ▶ v. [tr.] (**mete something out**) dispense or allot justice, a punishment, or harsh treatment: he denounced the maltreatment meted out to minorities.

mete[2] ▶ n. (usu. **metes and bounds**) chiefly hist. a boundary or boundary stone.

me·te·or /ˈmētēər; -ˌôr/ ▶ n. a small body of matter from outer space that enters the earth's atmosphere, becoming incandescent as a result of friction and appearing as a streak of light.

me·te·or·ic /ˌmētēˈôrik/ ▶ adj. **1** fig. (of the development of something, esp. a person's career) very rapid: her meteoric rise to the top of her profession. **2** chiefly Geol. relating to or denoting water derived from the atmosphere by precipitation or condensation. —**me·te·or·i·cal·ly** /-ik(ə)lē/ adv.

me·te·or·ite /ˈmētēəˌrīt/ ▶ n. a meteor that survives its passage through the earth's atmosphere such that part of it strikes the ground. More than 90 percent of meteorites are of rock, while the remainder consist wholly or partly of iron and nickel. —**me·te·or·it·ic** /ˌmētēəˈritik/ adj.

me·te·or·oid /ˈmētēəˌroid/ ▶ n. Astron. a small body moving in the solar system that would become a meteor if it entered the earth's atmosphere. —**me·te·or·oid·al** /ˌmētēəˈroidl/ adj.

me·te·or·ol·o·gy /ˌmētēəˈräləjē/ ▶ n. the branch of science concerned with the processes and phenomena of the atmosphere, esp. as a means of forecasting the weather. ■ the climate and weather of a region. —**me·te·or·o·log·i·cal** /-rəˈläjikəl/ adj. —**me·te·or·o·log·i·cal·ly** /-rəˈläjik(ə)lē/ adv. —**me·te·or·ol·o·gist** /-rəˈläjist/ n.

me·te·or show·er ▶ n. Astron. a number of meteors that appear to radiate from one point in the sky at a particular date each year, due to the earth's regularly passing through a field of particles at that position in its orbit. Meteor showers are named after the constellation in which the radiant is situated, e.g., the Perseids.

me·ter[1] /ˈmētər/ (Brit. **me·tre**) ▶ n. the fundamental unit of length in the metric system, equal to 100 centimeters or approx. 39.37 inches. ■ (—— **meters**) a race over a specified number of meters: he placed third in the 1,000 meters. —**me·ter·age** /-ij/ n.

me·ter[2] (Brit. **me·tre**) ▶ n. the rhythm of a piece of poetry, determined by the number and length of feet in a line. ■ the basic pulse and rhythm of a piece of music.

me·ter[3] ▶ n. a device that measures and records the quantity, degree, or rate of something, esp. the amount of electricity, gas, or water used.
▶ v. [tr.] [often as adj.] (**metered**) measure by means of a meter: a metered supply of water.

meth /meTH/ ▶ n. inf. **1** (also **crystal meth**) the drug methamphetamine. **2** short for METHADONE.

meth·a·done /ˈmeTHəˌdōn/ ▶ n. a synthetic analgesic drug that is similar

---

Pronunciation Key ə ago, up; ər over, fur; a hat; ā ate; ä car; CH chin; e let; ē see; ə(ə)r air; i fit; ī by; i(ə)r ear; NG sing; ō go; ô law, for; oi toy; ठठ good; ठठ goo; ou out; SH she; TH thin; TH then; (h)w why; ZH vision

to morphine in its effects but longer acting, used as a substitute drug in the treatment of morphine and heroin addiction.

meth·am·phet·a·mine /ˌmeᴛнəmˈfetəˌmēn; -min/ ▶n. a synthetic drug used illegally as a stimulant and as a prescription drug to treat narcolepsy and maintain blood pressure.

meth·ane /ˈmeᴛн,ān/ ▶n. Chem. a colorless, odorless flammable gas, CH_4, that is the main constituent of natural gas. It is the simplest member of the alkane series of hydrocarbons.

meth·a·nol /ˈmeᴛнə,nôl; -,nōl/ ▶n. Chem. a toxic, colorless, volatile flammable liquid alcohol, CH_3OH. Also called METHYL ALCOHOL.

me·thinks /miˈᴛнiNGks/ ▶v. (past **me·thought** /miˈᴛнôt/) [intr.] archaic or humorous it seems to me: life has been rather hard on her, methinks | methought you knew all about it.

meth·od /ˈmeᴛнəd/ ▶n. (often **method for/of**) a particular form of procedure for accomplishing or approaching something, esp. a systematic or established one. ■ orderliness of thought or behavior; systematic planning or action: historical study is the rigorous combination of knowledge and method. ■ (often **Method**) short for METHOD ACTING.

meth·od act·ing ▶n. a technique of acting in which an actor aspires to complete emotional identification with a part. —**meth·od ac·tor** n.

me·thod·i·cal /məˈᴛнädikəl/ ▶adj. done according to a systematic or established form of procedure: a methodical approach to the evaluation of computer systems. ■ (of a person) orderly or systematic in thought or behavior. —**me·thod·ic** adj. —**me·thod·i·cal·ly** /-ik(ə)lē/ adv.

Meth·od·ist /ˈmeᴛнədəst/ ▶n. a member of a Christian Protestant denomination originating in the 18th-century evangelistic movement of Charles and John Wesley and George Whitefield.
▶adj. of or relating to Methodists or Methodism: a Methodist chapel. —**Meth·od·ism** /-,dizəm/ n. —**Meth·od·is·tic** /ˌmeᴛнəˈdistik/ adj. —**Meth·od·is·ti·cal** /ˌmeᴛнəˈdistikəl/ adj.

meth·od·ize /ˈmeᴛнə,dīz/ ▶v. [tr.] rare arrange in an orderly or systematic manner. —**meth·od·iz·er** n.

meth·od·ol·o·gy /ˌmeᴛнəˈdäləjē/ ▶n. (pl. **-gies**) a system of methods used in a particular area of study or activity. —**meth·od·o·log·i·cal** /-dəˈläjikəl/ adj. —**meth·od·o·log·i·cal·ly** /-dəˈläjik(ə)lē/ adv. —**meth·od·ol·o·gist** /-ˈdäləjist/ n.

me·thought /miˈᴛнôt/ ▶ past of METHINKS.

meth·yl /ˈmeᴛнəl/ ▶n. [as adj.] Chem. of or denoting the alkyl radical $-CH_3$, derived from methane and present in many organic compounds: methyl bromide.

meth·yl al·co·hol ▶n. another term for METHANOL.

meth·yl·ben·zene /ˌmeᴛнəlˈben,zēn/ ▶n. systematic chemical name for TOLUENE.

me·tic·u·lous /məˈtikyələs/ ▶adj. showing great attention to detail; very careful and precise. —**me·tic·u·lous·ly** adv. —**me·tic·u·lous·ness** n.

mé·tier /meˈtyā; ˈme,tyā/ ▶n. a trade, profession, or occupation. ■ an occupation or activity that one is good at: her real métier was grand opera. ■ an outstanding or advantageous characteristic: subtlety is not his métier.

me·ton·y·my /məˈtänəmē/ ▶n. (pl. **-mies**) the substitution of the name of an attribute or adjunct for that of the thing meant, for example suit for business executive, or the track for horse racing. ▷mid 16th cent.: via Latin from Greek metōnumia, literally 'change of name.' —**met·o·nym** /ˈmetə,nim/ n. —**met·o·nym·ic** /ˌmetəˈnimik/ adj. —**met·o·nym·i·cal** /ˌmetəˈnimikəl/ adj. —**met·o·nym·i·cal·ly** /ˌmetəˈnimik(ə)lē/ adv.

met·ric¹ /ˈmetrik/ ▶adj. **1** of or based on the meter as a unit of length; relating to the metric system. ■ using the metric system: we should have **gone metric** years ago. **2** Math. & Physics relating to or denoting a metric.
▶n. **1** technical a system or standard of measurement. **2** inf. metric units, or the metric system: it's easier to work in metric.

met·ric² ▶adj. relating to or composed in a poetic meter.
▶n. (**metrics**) [treated as sing.] the meter of a poem.

met·ri·cal /ˈmetrikəl/ ▶adj. **1** of, relating to, or composed in poetic meter. **2** of or involving measurement: a metrical analysis of male and female scapulae. —**met·ri·cal·ly** /-ik(ə)lē/ adv.

met·rics /ˈmetriks/ ▶n. [treated as sing. or pl.] a method of measuring something, or the results obtained from this: the report provides various metrics at the class and method level.

met·ric sys·tem ▶n. the decimal measuring system based on the meter, liter, and gram as units of length, capacity, and weight or mass.

met·ric ton (also **tonne**) ▶n. a unit of weight equal to 1,000 kilograms (2,204.6 lb).

met·ro /ˈmetrō/ ▶n. (pl. **-ros**) (also **Met·ro**) a subway system in a city, esp. Paris. ■ a subway train, esp. in Paris.
▶adj. metropolitan: the Detroit metro area.

met·ro·nome /ˈmetrə,nōm/ ▶n. a device used by musicians that marks time at a selected rate by giving a regular tick. —**met·ro·nom·ic** /ˌmetrəˈnämik/ adj. —**met·ro·nom·i·cal·ly** /ˌmetrəˈnämik(ə)lē/ adv.

me·trop·o·lis /məˈträp(ə)ləs/ ▶n. the capital or chief city of a country or region. ■ a very large and densely populated industrial and commercial city.

met·ro·pol·i·tan /ˌmetrəˈpälitn/ ▶adj. **1** of, relating to, or denoting a metropolis, often inclusive of its surrounding areas: the Boston metropolitan area. **2** of, relating to, or denoting the parent state of a colony or dependency: metropolitan Spain. **3** Christian Church of, relating to, or denoting a metropolitan or his see: a metropolitan bishop.

metronome

▶n. **1** Christian Church a bishop having authority over the bishops of a province, in particular (in many Orthodox Churches) one ranking above archbishop and below patriarch. **2** an inhabitant of a metropolis: the sophisticated metropolitan.

met·ro·sex·u·al /ˌmetrōˈsekshōōəl/ ▶n. a young, urban, heterosexual male with liberal political views, an interest in fashion, and a refined sense of taste. —**met·ro·sex·u·al·i·ty** /-,sekshōōˈalitē/ n.

met·tle /ˈmetl/ ▶n. a person's ability to cope well with difficulties or to face a demanding situation in a spirited and resilient way: the team showed their true mettle in the second half. —**met·tle·some** /-səm/ adj.
▶ □ **be on one's mettle** be ready or forced to prove one's ability to cope well with a demanding situation.

meu·nière /mœnˈyer/ ▶adj. [usu. postpositive] (esp. of fish) cooked or served in lightly browned butter with lemon juice and parsley: sole meunière.

mew¹ /myōō/ ▶v. [intr.] (of a cat or some kinds of bird) make a characteristic high-pitched crying noise.
▶n. the high-pitched crying noise made by a cat or bird: a kitten's mew.

mew² Falconry ▶n. (usu. **mews**) a cage or building for trained hawks, esp. while they are molting.
▶v. **1** [intr.] (esp. of a trained hawk) molt. **2** [tr.] confine (a trained hawk) to a cage or building at the time of molting.

mewl /myōōl/ ▶v. [intr.] (often as adj.) (**mewling**) (esp. of a baby) cry feebly or querulously; whimper: dozens of mewling babies. ■ (of a cat or bird) mew: the mewling cry of a hawk.

mews /myōōz/ ▶n. (pl. same) chiefly Brit. a row or street of houses or apartments that have been converted from stables or built to look like former stables. ■ a group of stables, typically with rooms above, built around a yard or along an alley.

me·zu·zah /məˈzōōzə/ (also **me·zu·za**) ▶n. (pl. **me·zu·zahs** or **me·zu·zas** or **me·zu·zot** or **me·zu·zoth** /məˈzōōzōt/) a parchment inscribed with religious texts and attached in a case to the doorpost of a Jewish house as a sign of faith.

mez·za·nine /ˈmezə,nēn; ,mezəˈnēn/ ▶n. a low story between two others in a building, typically between the ground and second floors. ■ the lowest balcony of a theater, stadium, etc., or the front rows of the balcony.

mez·zo /ˈmetsō; ˈmedzō/ ▶n. (pl. **-zos**) (also **mez·zo·so·pra·no**) a female singer with a voice pitched between soprano and contralto. ■ a singing voice of this type, or a part written for one.
▶adv. half, moderately.

mfg. ▶abbr. manufacturing.

mfr. ▶abbr. manufacture. ■ (pl. **mfrs.**) manufacturer.

Mg ▶symb. the chemical element magnesium.

mg ▶abbr. milligram(s): 100 mg acetaminophen.

mho /mō/ ▶n. (pl. **mhos**) the reciprocal of an ohm, a former unit of electrical conductance.

MHz ▶abbr. megahertz.

MI ▶abbr. Brit., hist. Military Intelligence: MI5.

mi /mē/ ▶n. Mus. (in solmization) the third note of a major scale. ■ the note E in the fixed-do system.

mi. ▶abbr. mile(s): 10 km/6 mi.

MIA ▶abbr. missing in action. ■ [as n.] a member of the armed forces who is missing in action.

mi·as·ma /mī'azmə; mē-/ ▶ *n.* (*pl.* **-mas** or **-ma·ta** /-mətə/) *poetic/lit.* a highly unpleasant or unhealthy smell or vapor. ■ *fig.* an oppressive or unpleasant atmosphere that surrounds or emanates from something: *a miasma of despair.* —**mi·as·mal** *adj.* —**mi·as·mat·ic** /ˌmīəz'matik/ *adj.* —**mi·as·mic** /-mik/ *adj.* —**miasmically** /mik(ə)lē/ *adv.*

mi·ca /'mīkə/ ▶ *n.* a shiny silicate mineral with a layered structure, commonly found in igneous and metamorphic rocks. —**mi·ca·ceous** /mī'kāsHəs/ *adj.*

mice /mīs/ ▶ plural form of MOUSE.

mi·cro /'mīkrō/ ▶ *n.* (*pl.* **-cros**) **1** short for MICROCOMPUTER. **2** short for MICROPROCESSOR.
▶ *adj.* extremely small: *a micro dining area.* ■ small-scale: *CO₂ emissions cannot be dealt with at the micro level.* Often contrasted with MACRO.

mi·cro·a·nal·y·sis /ˌmīkrōə'naləsəs/ ▶ *n.* the quantitative analysis of chemical compounds using a sample of a few milligrams. —**mi·cro·an·a·lyt·ic** /-ˌanl'itik/ *adj.* —**mi·cro·an·a·lyt·i·cal** /-ˌanl'itikəl/ *adj.*

mi·crobe /'mī,krōb/ ▶ *n.* a microorganism, esp. a bacterium causing disease or fermentation. ▷late 19th cent.: from French, from Greek *mikros* 'small' + *bios* 'life.' —**mi·cro·bi·al** /mī'krōbēəl/ *adj.* —**mi·cro·bic** /mī'krōbik/ *adj.*

mi·cro·bi·ol·o·gy /ˌmīkrō,bī'äləjē/ ▶ *n.* the branch of science that deals with microorganisms. —**mi·cro·bi·o·log·ic** /-ˌbīə'läjik/ *adj.* —**mi·cro·bi·o·log·i·cal** /-ˌbīə'läjikəl/ *adj.* —**mi·cro·bi·o·log·i·cal·ly** /-ˌbīə'läjik(ə)lē/ *adv.* —**mi·cro·bi·ol·o·gist** /-jist/ *n.*

mi·cro·brew·er·y /ˌmīkrə'brōōərē/ ▶ *n.* (*pl.* **-er·ies**) a limited-production brewery, typically producing specialty beers and often selling its products only locally.

mi·cro·brows·er /'mīkrō,brouzər/ ▶ *n.* *Comput.* a small Internet browser for use with cellular phones and other hand-held devices.

mi·cro·burst /'mīkrō,bərst/ ▶ *n.* a sudden, powerful, localized air current, esp. a downdraft.

mi·cro·chip /'mīkrō,CHip/ ▶ *n.* a tiny wafer of semiconducting material used to make an integrated circuit.

mi·cro·cir·cuit /'mīkrō,sərkət/ ▶ *n.* a minute electric circuit, esp. an integrated circuit. —**mi·cro·cir·cuit·ry** /ˌmīkrō'sərkətrē/ *n.*

mi·cro·cli·mate /'mīkrō,klīmət/ ▶ *n.* the climate of a very small or restricted area, esp. when this differs from the climate of the surrounding area. —**mi·cro·cli·mat·ic** /ˌmīkrō,klī'matik/ *adj.* —**mi·cro·cli·mat·i·cal·ly** /ˌmīkrō,klī'matik(ə)lē/ *adv.*

mi·cro·com·pu·ter /'mīkrōkəm,pyōōtər/ ▶ *n.* a small computer that contains a microprocessor as its central processor.

mi·cro·cosm /'mīkrə,käzəm/ (also **mi·cro·cos·mos** /ˌmīkrə'käzməs; -mōs/) ▶ *n.* a community, place, or situation regarded as encapsulating in miniature the characteristic qualities or features of something much larger. —**mi·cro·cos·mic** /ˌmīkrə'käzmik/ *adj.* —**mi·cro·cos·mi·cal·ly** /-'käzmik(ə)lē/ *adv.*
▶ □ in microcosm in miniature.

mi·cro·dose /'mīkrō,dōs/ ▶ *n.* a dose of as little as one milligram of a drug that is intended to produce a beneficial result while avoiding undesirable side effects.

mi·cro·dot /'mīkrə,dät/ ▶ *n.* **1** a microphotograph, esp. of a printed or written document, that is only about 0.04 inch (1 mm) across. ■ [usu. as *adj.*] denoting a pattern of very small dots. **2** a tiny tablet or capsule (of LSD): *more than 1,000 microdots of LSD.*

mi·cro·ec·o·nom·ics /ˌmīkrō,ekə'nämiks; -,ēkə-/ ▶ *pl. n.* [treated as *sing.*] the part of economics concerned with single factors and the effects of individual decisions. —**mi·cro·ec·o·nom·ic** *adj.*

mi·cro·e·lec·tron·ics /ˌmīkrōi,lek'träniks/ ▶ *pl. n.* [usu. treated as *sing.*] the design, manufacture, and use of microchips and microcircuits. —**mi·cro·e·lec·tron·ic** *adj.*

mi·cro·fiche /'mīkrə,fēsH/ ▶ *n.* (*pl.* same or **-fich·es**) a flat piece of film containing microphotographs of the pages of a newspaper, catalog, or other document.
▶ *v.* [*tr.*] make a microfiche of (a newspaper, catalog, or other document).

mi·cro·film /'mīkrə,film/ ▶ *n.* a length of film containing microphotographs of a newspaper, catalog, or other document.
▶ *v.* [*tr.*] make a microfilm of (a newspaper, catalog, or other document).

mi·cro·graph /'mīkrə,graf/ ▶ *n.* a photograph taken by means of a microscope. —**mi·cro·graph·ic** /ˌmīkrə'grafik/ *adj.* —**mi·cro·graph·ics** /ˌmīkrə'grafiks/ *n.* —**mi·crog·ra·phy** /mī'krägrəfē/ *n.*

mi·cro·man·age /ˌmīkrō'manij/ ▶ *v.* [*tr.*] control every part, however small, of (an enterprise or activity). —**mi·cro·man·age·ment** /'manijmənt/ *n.* —**mi·cro·man·ag·er** *n.*

mi·crom·e·ter¹ /mī'krämətər/ (also **micrometer caliper**) ▶ *n.* a gauge that measures small distances or thicknesses between its two faces. —**mi·crom·e·try** /-ətrē/ *n.*

mi·cro·me·ter² /'mīkrō,mētər/ (abbr.: μm) ▶ *n.* one millionth of a meter.

mi·cron /'mī,krän/ ▶ *n.* a unit of length equal to one millionth of a meter, used in many technological and scientific fields.

Mi·cro·ne·sian /ˌmīkrə'nēzHən/ ▶ *adj.* of or relating to Micronesia, its people, or their languages.
▶ *n.* **1** a native of Micronesia. **2** the group of Austronesian languages spoken in Micronesia.

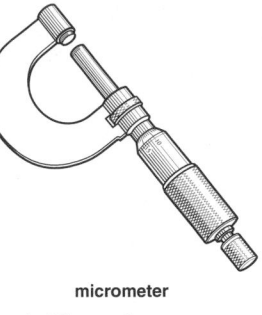

micrometer

mi·cro·or·gan·ism /ˌmīkrō'ôrgə,nizəm/ ▶ *n.* a microscopic organism, esp. a bacterium, virus, or fungus.

mi·cro·phone /'mīkrə,fōn/ ▶ *n.* an instrument for converting sound waves into electrical energy variations, which may then be amplified, transmitted, or recorded. —**mi·cro·phon·ic** /ˌmīkrə'fänik/ *adj.*

mi·cro·pho·to·graph /ˌmīkrə'fōtə,graf/ ▶ *n.* a photograph reduced to a very small size. ■ another term for PHOTOMICROGRAPH. —**mi·cro·pho·to·graph·ic** /-ˌfōtə'grafik/ *adj.* —**mi·cro·pho·tog·ra·phy** /-fə'tägrəfē/ *n.*

mi·cro·proc·es·sor /ˌmīkrə'präsesər; -'prō,sesər/ ▶ *n.* an integrated circuit that contains all the functions of a central processing unit of a computer. —**mi·cro·proc·ess·ing** *n.*

mi·cro·scope /'mīkrə,skōp/ ▶ *n.* an optical instrument used for viewing very small objects, such as mineral samples or animal or plant cells.

mi·cro·scop·ic /ˌmīkrə'skäpik/ ▶ *adj.* **1** so small as to be visible only with a microscope: *microscopic algae.* ■ *inf.* extremely small: *a microscopic skirt.* ■ concerned with minute detail: *such a vision is as microscopic as his is panoramic.* **2** of or relating to a microscope. —**mi·cro·scop·i·cal** *adj.* —**mi·cro·scop·i·cal·ly** /-ik(ə)lē/ *adv.*

mi·cro·sec·ond /'mīkrō,sekənd/ (abbr.: μs) ▶ *n.* one millionth of a second.

microscope

mi·cro·struc·ture /ˌmīkrə'strəkCHər/ ▶ *n.* the fine structure (in a metal or other material) that can be made visible and examined with a microscope.

mi·cro·sur·ger·y /ˌmīkrō'sərjərē/ ▶ *n.* intricate surgery performed using miniaturized instruments and a microscope. —**mi·cro·sur·geon** /-'sərjən/ *n.* —**mi·cro·sur·gi·cal** /-'sərjikəl/ *adj.*

mi·cro·wave /'mīkrə,wāv/ ▶ *n.* an electromagnetic wave with a wavelength in the range 0.001–0.3 m, shorter than that of a normal radio wave but longer than those of infrared radiation. ■ short for MICROWAVE OVEN.
▶ *v.* [*tr.*] cook (food) in a microwave oven. —**mi·cro·wave·a·ble** *adj.*

mi·cro·wave ov·en ▶ *n.* an oven that uses microwaves to cook or heat food.

mid¹ /mid/ ▶ *adj.* of or in the middle part or position of a range: *the mid 17th century.* ■ *Phonet.* (of a vowel) pronounced with the tongue neither high nor low: *a mid-central vowel.*

mid² ▶ *prep. poetic/lit.* in the middle of. ■ in the course of.

mid·air /'mid'e(ə)r/ (also **mid-air**) ▶ *n.* a part or section of the air above ground level or above another surface: *he caught Murray's keys in midair* | [as *adj.*] *a midair collision.*

mid·brain /'mid,brān/ ▶ *n. Anat.* a small central part of the brainstem, developing from the middle of the primitive or embryonic brain.

mid·day /'mid'dā/ ▶ *n.* the middle of the day; noon.

mid·den /'midn/ ▶ *n.* a dunghill or refuse heap.

mid·dle /'midl/ ▶ *adj.* **1** at an equal distance from the extremities of something; central. ■ (of a member of a group, series, or sequence) so placed as to have the same number of members on each side: *the woman was in her middle forties.* ■ intermediate in rank, quality, or ability. ■ (of a language) of the period between the old and modern forms:

Middle High German. **2** *Gram.* denoting a voice of verbs in some languages, such as Greek, that expresses reciprocal or reflexive action.
▶*n.* **1** the point or position at an equal distance from the sides, edges, or ends of something: *she stood alone in the middle of the street.* ■ the point at or around the center of a process or activity, period of time, etc.: *in the middle of December.* ■ *inf.* a person's waist or waist and stomach: *he had a towel around his middle.* **2** *Gram.* the form or voice of a verb expressing reflexive or reciprocal action.
▶ □ **down the middle** divided or dividing something equally into two parts. □ **in the middle of** in the process of doing something. ■ involved in something, typically something unpleasant or dangerous: *he was caught in the middle of the emotional triangle.*
mid·dle age ▶*n.* the period between early adulthood and old age, usually considered as the years from about 45 to 65. —**mid·dle-aged** (also **mid·dle-age**) *adj.*
Mid·dle Ag·es ▶*pl. n.* the period of European history from the fall of the Roman Empire in the West (5th century) to the fall of Constantinople (1453), or, more narrowly, from *c.*1100 to 1453.
Mid·dle A·mer·i·ca ▶*n.* the middle class in the U.S., esp. when regarded as a conservative political force. ■ the Midwest of the U.S. —**Mid·dle A·mer·i·can** *n.* —**Mid·dle-A·mer·i·can** *adj.*
mid·dle·brow /ˈmidlˌbrou/ *inf., chiefly derog.* ▶*adj.* (of art or literature or a system of thought) demanding or involving only a moderate degree of intellectual application, typically as a result of not deviating from convention: *middlebrow fiction.*
▶*n.* a person who is capable of or enjoys only a moderate degree of intellectual effort.
mid·dle class ▶*n.* [treated as *sing.* or *pl.*] the social group between the upper and working classes, including professional and business workers and their families.
▶*adj.* of, relating to, or characteristic of this section of society: *a middle-class suburb.* ■ attaching too much importance to convention, security, and material comfort. —**mid·dle-class·ness** *n.*
mid·dle ear ▶*n.* the air-filled central cavity of the ear, behind the eardrum.
Mid·dle Eng·lish ▶*n.* the English language from *c.*1150 to *c.*1470.
mid·dle ground ▶*n.* (usu. **the middle ground**) **1** an area of compromise or possible agreement between two extreme positions, esp. political ones. **2** the middle distance of a painting or photograph.
mid·dle·man /ˈmidlˌman/ ▶*n.* (*pl.* **-men**) a person who buys goods from producers and sells them to retailers or consumers. ■ a person who arranges business or political deals between other people.
mid·dle man·age·ment ▶*n.* the level in an organization just below that of senior administrators. ■ the managers at this level regarded collectively. —**mid·dle man·ag·er** *n.*
mid·dle name ▶*n.* a person's name (typically a personal name) placed after the first name and before the surname. ■ a quality for which a person is notable: *optimism is my middle name.*
mid·dle-of-the-road ▶*adj.* avoiding extremes; moderate. ■ (of music) tuneful but somewhat bland and unadventurous. —**mid·dle-of-the-road·er** *n.*
mid·dle school ▶*n.* a school intermediate between an elementary school and a high school.
mid·dle·weight /ˈmidlˌwāt/ ▶*n.* a weight in boxing and other sports intermediate between welterweight and light heavyweight. ■ a boxer or other competitor of this weight.
mid·dling /ˈmidliNG; ˈmidlin/ ▶*adj.* moderate or average in size, amount, or rank. ■ neither very good nor very bad: *he had a fair to middling season.* ■ *inf.* (of a person) in reasonably good but not perfect health.
▶*n.* (**middlings**) bulk goods of medium grade.
▶*adv. inf., dated* fairly or moderately. —**mid·dling·ly** *adv.*
mid·field /ˈmidˌfēld; midˈfēld/ ▶*n.* (in football, soccer, etc.) the central part of the field. ■ *Soccer* the players on a team who play in a central position between attack and defense. —**mid·field·er** *n.*
midge /mij/ ▶*n.* **1** a small two-winged fly that is often seen in swarms near water or marshy areas where it breeds. There are two families: Chironomidae (the **nonbiting midges**), and Ceratopogonidae (the **biting midges**). ■ any of a number of small flies whose larvae can be pests of plants. **2** *inf.* a small person. ▷Old English *mycg(e)*; related to German *Mücke*, from an Indo-European root shared by Latin *musca.*
mid·get /ˈmijit/ ▶*n. often offens.* an extremely or unusually small person.
▶*adj.* very small: *a midget submarine.*
MIDI /ˈmidē/ ▶*n.* [usu. as *adj.*] a widely used standard for interconnecting electronic musical instruments and computers: *a MIDI controller.*

mid·i /ˈmidē/ ▶*n.* (*pl.* **mid·is** /ˈmidēz/) short for **midiskirt**, a skirt that ends at the middle of the calf.
mid·land /ˈmidlənd; -ˌland/ ▶*n.* the middle part of a country.
▶*adj.* of or in the middle part of a country. —**mid·land·er** *n.*
mid·life /midˈlīf/ (also **mid-life**) ▶*n.* the central period of a person's life, generally considered as the years from about 45 to 55.
mid·life cri·sis ▶*n.* an emotional crisis of identity and self-confidence that can occur in early middle age.
mid·line /ˈmidˌlīn/ ▶*n.* [often as *adj.*] a median line or plane of bilateral symmetry, esp. that of the body: *the abdomen was opened by a midline incision.*
mid·most /ˈmidˌmōst/ ▶*adj.* & *adv. poetic/lit.* in the very middle or nearest the middle.
mid·night /ˈmidˌnīt/ ▶*n.* twelve o'clock at night: *I left at midnight* | [as *adj.*] *a midnight deadline.* ■ [often as *adj.*] the middle period of the night: *the midnight hours.*
mid·night sun ▶*n.* the sun when seen at midnight during the summer north of the Arctic Circle or south of the Antarctic Circle.
mid·point /ˈmidˌpoint/ ▶*n.* the exact middle point: *the midpoint of the line segment.* ■ a point somewhere in the middle: *he would have been at the midpoint in his career.*
mid·rib /ˈmidˌrib/ ▶*n.* a large strengthened vein along the midline of a leaf.
mid·riff /ˈmidˌrif/ ▶*n.* the region of the front of the body between the chest and the waist.
mid·ship /ˈmidˌSHip/ ▶*n.* [usu. as *adj.*] the middle part of a ship or boat: *its powerful midship section.*
mid·ship·man /ˈmidˌSHipmən; midˈSHip-/ ▶*n.* (*pl.* **-men**) a naval cadet in the US Navy. ■ an officer in the Royal Navy ranking below sublieutenant.
mid·ships /ˈmidˌSHips/ ▶*adv.* & *adj.* another term for AMIDSHIPS.
midst /midst; mitst/ ▶*prep. archaic* or *poetic/lit.* in the middle of.
mid·sum·mer /ˈmidˈsəmər/ ▶*n.* the middle part of summer: [as *adj.*] *the midsummer heat.* ■ another term for SUMMER SOLSTICE.
mid·town /ˈmidˌtoun/ ▶*n.* [usu. as *adj.*] the central part of a city: *a huge midtown apartment.*
mid·way /ˈmidˌwā; -ˈwā/ ▶*adv.* & *adj.* in or toward the middle of something. ■ having some of the characteristics of one thing and some of another: [as *adj.*] *a midway path between the diverging aspirations* | [as *adv.*] *the leaves have a unique smell* **midway between** *eucalyptus and mint.*
▶*n.* an area of sideshows, games of chance or skill, or other amusements at a fair or exhibition: *the kids head straight for* **the midway.**
Mid·west /midˈwest/ ▶*n.* the region of northern states of the U.S. from Ohio west to the Rocky Mountains. Formerly called FAR WEST. —**Mid·west·ern** /ˌmidˈwestərn/ *adj.*
mid·wife /ˈmidˌwīf/ ▶*n.* (*pl.* **-wives**) a person (typically a woman) trained to assist women in childbirth. ■ *fig.* a person or thing that helps to bring something into being or assists its development.
▶*v.* [*tr.*] assist (a woman) during childbirth. ■ *fig.* bring into being: *revolutions midwifed by new technologies.* —**mid·wife·ry** /midˈwīf(ə)rē; -ˈwīf(ə)rē/ *n.*
mid·win·ter /ˈmidˈwintər/ ▶*n.* the middle part of winter: [as *adj.*] *the midwinter full moon.* ■ another term for WINTER SOLSTICE.
mien /mēn/ ▶*n. poetic/lit.* a person's look or manner, esp. one of a particular kind indicating their character or mood: *he has a cautious, academic mien.*
miff /mif/ ▶*v.* [*tr.*] (usu. **be miffed**) *inf.* annoy: *she was miffed at not being invited.*
▶*n. archaic* a petty quarrel or fit of pique.
might[1] /mīt/ ▶*modal verb* (*3rd sing. present* **might**) **1** past of MAY[1], used esp.: ■ in reported speech, expressing possibility or permission: *he said he might be late.* ■ expressing a possibility based on a condition not fulfilled: *we might have won if we'd played better.* ■ expressing annoyance about something that someone has not done: *you might have told me!* ■ expressing purpose: *he avoided social engagements so that he might work.* **2** used in questions and requests: ■ tentatively asking permission: *might I ask one question?* ■ expressing a polite request: *you might just call me Jane, if you don't mind.* ■ asking for information, esp. condescendingly: *and who might you be?* **3** expressing possibility: *this might be true.* ■ making a suggestion: *you might try nonprescription pain relievers.*
▶ □ **might as well 1** used to make an unenthusiastic suggestion: *I might as well begin.* **2** used to indicate that a situation is the same as if the hypothetical thing stated were true: *for readers seeking illumination, this book might as well have been written in Serbo-Croatian.* □ **might have known** (or **guessed**) used to express one's lack of surprise about something: *I might have known it was you.*

might[2] ▸*n.* great and impressive power or strength, esp. of a nation, large organization, or natural force: *a convincing display of military might.*

might·n't /ˈmītnt/ ▸*contr. of* might not.

might·y /ˈmītē/ ▸*adj.* (**might·i·er**, **might·i·est**) possessing great and impressive power or strength, esp. on account of size. ■ (of an action) performed with or requiring great strength: *a mighty heave* | *fig. a mighty blow against racism.* ■ *inf.* very large: *she gave a mighty hiccup.* ▸*adv. inf.* extremely: *this is mighty early to be planning a presidential campaign.* —**might·i·ly** /ˈmītl-ē/ *adv.* —**might·i·ness** *n.*

mi·graine /ˈmīˌgrān/ (also **migraine headache**) ▸*n.* a recurrent throbbing headache that typically affects one side of the head and is often accompanied by nausea and disturbed vision. ▷late Middle English: from French, via late Latin from Greek *hēmikrania,* from *hēmi-* 'half' + *kranion* 'skull.' —**mi·grain·ous** /-ˌgrānəs/ *adj.*

mi·grant /ˈmīgrənt/ ▸*n.* an animal that migrates. ■ (also **migrant worker**) a worker who moves from place to place to do seasonal work. ▸*adj.* tending to migrate or having migrated: *migrant birds.*

mi·grate /ˈmīˌgrāt/ ▸*v.* [*intr.*] (of an animal, typically a bird or fish) move from one region or habitat to another, esp. regularly according to the seasons. ■ (of a person) move from one area or country to settle in another, esp. in search of work. ■ move from one specific part of something to another: *cells that can form pigment migrate beneath the skin.* ■ *Comput.* change or cause to change from using one system to another. ■ [*tr.*] *Comput.* transfer (programs or hardware) from one system to another. —**mi·gra·tion** /mīˈgrāSHən/ *n.* —**mi·gra·tion·al** /mīˈgrāSHənl/ *adj.* —**mi·gra·tor** /-ˌgrātər/ *n.* —**mi·gra·to·ry** /ˈmīgrəˌtôrē/ *adj.*

mi·ka·do /miˈkädō/ ▸*n. hist.* a title given to the emperor of Japan.

mike *inf.* ▸*n.* a microphone. ▸*v.* [*tr.*] place a microphone close to (someone or something) or in (a place).

mil[1] /mil/ *inf.* ▸*abbr.* ■ millimeters. ■ milliliters. ■ (used in sums of money) millions: *the insurance company coughed up five mil.*

mil[2] ▸*n.* one thousandth of an inch.

mi·la·dy /məˈlādē; mī-/ ▸*n.* (*pl.* **-dies**) *hist.* or *humorous* used to address or refer to an English noblewoman or great lady: *I went off to milady's boudoir.*

milch /milk; milCH/ ▸*adj.* denoting a cow or other domestic mammal giving or kept for milk.

mild /mīld/ ▸*adj.* gentle and not easily provoked: *she was implacable, despite her mild exterior.* ■ (of a rule or punishment) of only moderate severity: *he received a mild sentence.* ■ not keenly felt or seriously intended: *she looked at him in mild surprise.* ■ (of an illness or pain) not serious or dangerous. ■ (of weather) moderately warm, esp. less cold than expected: *it is still mild enough to work outdoors.* ■ (of a medicine or cosmetic) acting gently and without causing harm. ■ (of food, drink, or tobacco) not sharp or strong in flavor: *a mild Italian cheese.* —**mild·ish** *adj.* —**mild·ness** *n.*

mil·dew /ˈmilˌd(y)oo/ ▸*n.* a thin whitish coating consisting of minute fungal filaments, growing on plants or damp organic material such as paper or leather. ▸*v.* affect or be affected with mildew. —**mil·dew·y** *adj.*

mild·ly /ˈmīldlē/ ▸*adv.* in a mild manner, in particular without anger or severity. ■ not seriously or dangerously: *he had suffered mildly from the illness since he was 23.* ■ to a slight extent.

mile /mīl/ ▸*n.* (also **statute mile**) a unit of linear measure equal to 5,280 feet, or 1,760 yards (approx. 1.609 kilometers). ■ (usu. **miles**) *inf.* a very long way or a very great amount: *vistas that stretch for miles.* ■ a race extending over a mile.

mile·age /ˈmīlij/ ▸*n.* **1** a number of miles traveled or covered: *the car is in good condition, considering its mileage.* ■ [usu. *as adj.*] traveling expenses paid according to the number of miles traveled: *the mileage rate will be 34 cents.* **2** *inf.* the contribution made by something to one's aims or interests: *he was getting a lot of mileage out of the mix-up.*

mile·post /ˈmīlˌpōst/ ▸*n.* a marker set up to indicate how distant a particular place is. ■ another term for MILESTONE.

mil·er /ˈmīlər/ ▸*n. inf.* a person or horse trained specially to run a mile. —**mil·ing** /ˈmīliNG/ *n.*

mile·stone /ˈmīlˌstōn/ ▸*n.* a stone set up beside a road to mark the distance in miles to a particular place. ■ *fig.* an action or event marking a significant change or stage in development: *the speech is being hailed as a milestone in race relations.*

mi·lieu /milˈyoo; -ˈyə(r)/ ▸*n.* (*pl.* **mi·lieux** *pronunc.* same, or **mi·lieus**) a person's social environment: *he grew up in a military milieu.*

mil·i·tant /ˈmilətənt/ ▸*adj.* combative and aggressive in support of a political or social cause, and typically favoring extreme, violent, or confrontational methods: *an uprising by militant Islamic fundamentalists.* ▸*n.* a person who is active in this way. —**mil·i·tan·cy** /-tənsē/ *n.* —**mil·i·tant·ly** *adv.*

mil·i·ta·rism /ˈmilətəˌrizəm/ ▸*n. chiefly derog.* the belief or desire of a government or people that a country should maintain a strong military capability and be prepared to use it aggressively to defend or promote national interests. —**mil·i·ta·rist** *n.* & *adj.* —**mil·i·ta·ris·tic** /ˌmilətəˈristik/ *adj.*

mil·i·ta·rize /ˈmilətəˌrīz/ ▸*v.* [*tr.*] [often *as adj.*] (**militarized**) give (something, esp. an organization) a military character or style. ■ equip or supply (a place) with soldiers and other military resources: *a militarized security zone.* —**mil·i·ta·ri·za·tion** /ˌmilətərəˈzāSHən/ *n.*

mil·i·tar·y /ˈmiləˌterē/ ▸*adj.* of, relating to, or characteristic of soldiers or armed forces. ▸*n.* (**the military**) the armed forces of a country. —**mil·i·tar·i·ly** /ˌmiləˈte(ə)rəlē/ *adv.*

mil·i·tar·y po·lice ▸*n.* [treated as *pl.*] the corps responsible for police and disciplinary duties in an army. —**mil·i·tar·y po·lice·man** *n.* —**mil·i·tar·y po·lice·wom·an** *n.*

mil·i·tate /ˈmiləˌtāt/ ▸*v.* [*intr.*] (**militate against**) (of a fact or circumstance) be a powerful or conclusive factor in preventing: *these fundamental differences will militate against the two communities coming together.*

mi·li·tia /məˈliSHə/ ▸*n.* a military force that is raised from the civil population to supplement a regular army in an emergency. ■ a military force that engages in rebel or terrorist activities, typically in opposition to a regular army. ■ all able-bodied civilians eligible by law for military service.

mi·li·tia·man /məˈliSHəmən/ ▸*n.* (*pl.* **-men**) a member of a militia.

milk /milk/ ▸*n.* an opaque white fluid rich in fat and protein, secreted by female mammals for the nourishment of their young. ■ the milk of cows (or occasionally goats or ewes) as food for humans: *a glass of milk.* ■ the white juice of certain plants: *coconut milk.* ■ a creamy-textured liquid with a particular ingredient or use: *cleansing milk.* ▸*v.* [*tr.*] draw milk from (a cow or other animal), either by hand or mechanically. ■ [*intr.*] (of an animal, esp. a cow) produce or yield milk: *the breed does seem to milk better in harder conditions.* ■ extract sap, venom, or other substances from. ■ *fig.* exploit or defraud (someone), typically by taking regular small amounts of money over a period of time: *he had milked his grandmother dry of all her money.* ■ *fig.* get all possible advantage from (a situation): *the newspapers were milking the story.* ■ *fig.* elicit a favorable reaction from (an audience) and prolong it for as long as possible: *he milked the crowd for every last drop of applause.* —**milk·er** *n.*

milk·ing par·lor ▸*n.* see PARLOR (sense 3).

milk·maid /ˈmilkˌmād/ ▸*n. chiefly archaic* a girl or woman who milks cows or does other work in a dairy.

milk·man /ˈmilkmən; -ˌman/ ▸*n.* (*pl.* **-men**) a person who delivers and sells milk.

milk of mag·ne·sia ▸*n.* a white suspension of hydrated magnesium carbonate in water, used as an antacid or laxative.

milk run ▸*n.* a routine, uneventful journey, esp. by plane.

milk shake (also **milk·shake**) ▸*n.* a cold drink made of milk, a sweet flavoring such as fruit or chocolate, and typically ice cream, whisked until it is frothy.

milk·sop /ˈmilkˌsäp/ ▸*n.* a person who is indecisive and lacks courage.

milk tooth ▸*n.* any of a set of early, temporary (deciduous) teeth in children or young mammals that fall out as the permanent teeth erupt (in children, between the ages of about 6 and 12).

milk·weed /ˈmilkˌwēd/ ▸*n.* a herbaceous American plant (genus *Asclepias,* family Asclepiadaceae) with milky sap. The large, showy pods contain flossy downlike tufts.

milk·y /ˈmilkē/ ▸*adj.* (**milk·i·er**, **milk·i·est**) containing or mixed with a large amount of milk: *a cup of sweet milky coffee.* ■ (of a cow) producing a lot of milk. ■ resembling milk, esp. in color: *not a blemish marred her milky skin.* ■ (of something that is usually clear) cloudy: *the old man's milky, uncomprehending eyes.* —**milk·i·ly** /-əlē/ *adv.* —**milk·i·ness** *n.*

Milk·y Way ▸a faint band of light crossing the sky, made up of vast numbers of faint stars. It corresponds to the plane of our Galaxy, in which most of its stars are located. ■ the galaxy in which our sun is located.

mill[1] /mil/ ▸*n.* **1** a building equipped with machinery for grinding grain

into flour. ■ a piece of machinery of this type. ■ a domestic device for grinding a solid substance to powder or pulp: *a coffee mill.* ■ a building fitted with machinery for a manufacturing process: *a steel mill.* ■ a piece of manufacturing machinery. ■ a place that processes things or people in a mechanical way: *a correspondence school that was just a diploma mill.* **2** *inf.* dated a boxing match or a fistfight.
▶ *v.* **1** [*tr.*] grind or crush (something) in a mill: *hard wheats are easily milled into white flour.* ■ cut or shape (metal) with a rotating tool: [as *adj.*] (**milling**) *lathes and milling machines.* ■ [usu. as *adj.*] (**milled**) produce regular ribbed markings on the edge of (a coin) as a protection against illegal clipping. **2** [*intr.*] (**mill about/around**) (of people or animals) move around in a confused mass: *people milled about the room, shaking hands.* —**mill·a·ble** *adj.*
▶ □ **go** (or **put someone**) **through the mill** undergo (or cause someone to undergo) an unpleasant experience.
mill² ▶ *n.* a monetary unit used only in calculations, worth one thousandth of a dollar.
mill·dam /'mil,dam/ ▶ *n.* a dam built across a stream to raise the level of the water so that it will turn the wheel of a water mill.
mil·le·nar·y /'milə,nerē/ ▶ *n.* (*pl.* **-nar·ies**) a period of a thousand years. ■ a thousandth anniversary.
▶ *adj.* consisting of a thousand people, years, etc.
mil·len·ni·um /mə'lenēəm/ ▶ *n.* (*pl.* **-len·ni·a** /-'lenēə/ or **-len·ni·ums**) a period of a thousand years, esp. when calculated from the traditional date of the birth of Jesus Christ. ■ an anniversary of a thousand years: *the millennium of the Russian Orthodox Church.* ■ (**the millennium**) the point at which one period of a thousand years ends and another begins. ■ (**the millennium**) *Christian Theol.* the prophesied thousand-year reign of Christ at the end of the age. ■ (**the millennium**) *fig.* a utopian period of good government, great happiness, and prosperity. —**mil·len·ni·al** /-ēəl/ *adj.*
mil·le·pede /'milə,pēd/ ▶ *n.* variant spelling of MILLIPEDE.
mill·er /'milər/ ▶ *n.* a person who owns or works in a grain mill.
mil·les·i·mal /mə'lesəməl/ ▶ *adj.* consisting of thousandth parts; thousandth.
▶ *n.* a thousandth part. —**mil·les·i·mal·ly** *adv.*
mil·let /'milit/ ▶ *n.* a fast-growing cereal plant that is widely grown in warm countries and regions with poor soils.
mil·liard /'mil,yärd; -yərd/ ▶ *n. Brit.* one thousand million (a term now largely superseded by billion).
mil·li·bar /'milə,bär/ ▶ *n.* one thousandth of a bar, the cgs unit of atmospheric pressure equivalent to 100 pascals.
mil·li·gram /'milə,gram/ (*Brit.* also **mil·li·gramme**) (abbr.: **mg**) ▶ *n.* one thousandth of a gram.
mil·li·li·ter /'milə,lētər/ (*Brit.* **mil·li·li·tre**) (abbr.: **ml**) ▶ *n.* one thousandth of a liter (0.002 pint).
mil·li·me·ter /'milə,mētər/ (*Brit.* **mil·li·me·tre**) (abbr.: **mm**) ▶ *n.* one thousandth of a meter (0.039 in.).
mil·li·ner /'milənər/ ▶ *n.* a person who makes or sells women's hats. —**mil·li·ner·y** /-,nerē/ *n.*
mil·lion /'milyən/ ▶ *cardinal number* (*pl.* **-lions** or (with numeral or quantifying word) same) (**a/one million**) the number equivalent to the product of a thousand and a thousand; 1,000,000 or 10⁶. ■ (**millions**) the numbers from a million to a billion. ■ (**millions**) several million things or people: *millions of TV viewers.* ■ *inf.* an unspecified but very large number or amount of something. ■ (**the millions**) the bulk of the population: *movies for the millions.* ■ a million dollars: *the author is set to make millions.* ▷late Middle English: from Old French, probably from Italian *milione,* from *mille* 'thousand' + the augmentative suffix *-one.* —**mil·lion·fold** /-,fōld/ *adj. & adv.* —**mil·lionth** /-yənтн/ *ordinal number* .
mil·lion·aire /,milyə'ne(ə)r; 'milyə,ner/ ▶ *n.* a person whose assets are worth one million dollars or more.
mil·li·pede /'milə,pēd/ (also **mil·le·pede**) ▶ *n.* a myriapod invertebrate (class Diplopoda) with an elongated body composed of many segments, most of which bear two pairs of legs.
mil·li·sec·ond /'milə,sekənd/ ▶ *n.* one thousandth of a second.
mill·pond /'mil,pänd/ (also **mill pond**) ▶ *n.* the pool that is created by a milldam and provides the head of water that powers a water mill.
mill·race /'mil,rās/ ▶ *n.* the channel carrying the swift current of water that drives a mill wheel.
mill·stone /'mil,stōn/ ▶ *n.* each of two circular stones used for grinding grain. ■ *fig.* a heavy and inescapable responsibility: *she threatened to become a millstone around his neck.*
mill·wright /'mil,rīt/ ▶ *n.* a person who designs or builds mills or who maintains mill machinery.

milt /milt/ ▶ *n.* the semen of a male fish. ■ a sperm-filled reproductive gland of a male fish.
MIME /mīm; 'em 'ī 'em 'ē/ ▶ *n. Comput.* a standard for formatting files of different types, such as text, graphics, or audio, so they can be sent over the Internet and seen or played by a Web browser or e-mail application.
mime /mīm/ ▶ *n.* **1** the theatrical technique of suggesting action, character, or emotion without words, using only gesture, expression, and movement. ■ a theatrical performance or part of a performance using such a technique. ■ an action or set of actions intended to convey the idea of another action or an idea or feeling: *he performed a brief mime of someone fencing.* ■ a practitioner of mime or a performer in a mime. **2** (in ancient Greece and Rome) a simple farcical drama including mimicry.
▶ *v.* [*tr.*] use gesture and movement without words in the acting of (a play or role). ■ convey an impression of (an idea or feeling) by gesture and movement, without using words; mimic (an action or set of actions) in this way: *he stands up and mimes throwing a spear.* —**mim·er** *n.*
mim·e·o·graph /'mimēə,graf/ ▶ *n.* a duplicating machine that produces copies from a stencil, now superseded by the photocopier. ■ a copy produced on such a machine.
▶ *v.* [*tr.*] make a copy of (a document) with such a machine.
mi·me·sis /mə'mēsis; mī-/ ▶ *n. formal* or *technical* imitation, in particular: ■ representation or imitation of the real world in art and literature. ■ the deliberate imitation of the behavior of one group of people by another as a factor in social change. ■ *Zool.* another term for MIMICRY.
mi·met·ic /mə'metik/ ▶ *adj. formal* or *technical* relating to, constituting, or habitually practicing mimesis. —**mi·met·i·cal·ly** /-ik(ə)lē/ *adv.*
mim·ic /'mimik/ ▶ *v.* (**mim·icked, mim·ick·ing**) [*tr.*] imitate (someone or their actions or words), typically in order to entertain or ridicule: *she mimicked Eileen's voice.* ■ (of an animal or plant) resemble or imitate (another animal or plant), esp. to deter predators or for camouflage. ■ (of a drug) replicate the physiological effects of (another substance). ■ (of a disease) exhibit symptoms that bear a deceptive resemblance to those of (another disease).
▶ *n.* a person skilled in imitating the voice, mannerisms, or movements of others in an entertaining way. ■ an animal or plant that exhibits mimicry.
▶ *adj.* imitative of something, esp. for amusement: *they were waging mimic war.* —**mim·ick·er** *n.*
mim·ic·ry /'mimikrē/ ▶ *n.* (*pl.* **-ries**) the action or art of imitating someone or something, typically in order to entertain or ridicule: *the word was spoken with gently teasing mimicry | a playful mimicry of the techniques of realist writers.* ■ *Biol.* the close external resemblance of an animal or plant (or part of one) to another animal, plant, or inanimate object.
mi·mo·sa /mə'mōsə; -zə; mī-/ ▶ *n.* **1** an Australian acacia tree (*Acacia dealbata*) with delicate fernlike leaves and yellow flowers that are used by florists. **2** a pea-family plant of a genus (*Mimosa*) that includes the sensitive plant. **3** a drink of champagne and orange juice.
min·a·ret /,minə'ret/ ▶ *n.* a tall slender tower, typically part of a mosque, with a balcony from which a muezzin calls Muslims to prayer. —**min·a·ret·ed** *adj.*
min·a·to·ry /'minə,tôrē; 'mī-/ ▶ *adj. formal* expressing or conveying a threat: *he is unlikely to be deterred by minatory finger-wagging.*
mince /mins/ ▶ *v.* [*tr.*] **1** [often as *adj.*] (**minced**) cut up or grind (food, esp. meat) into very small pieces, typically in a machine with revolving blades: *minced beef.* **2** [*intr.*] walk with an affected delicacy or fastidiousness, typically with short quick steps: *secretaries mincing about.*
▶ *n.* something minced, esp. mincemeat. —**minc·er** *n.* —**minc·ing·ly** *adv.*
▶ □ **not mince words** (or **one's words**) speak directly, esp. when criticizing someone or something.

minaret

mince·meat /'mins,mēt/ ▶ *n.* **1** a mixture of currants, raisins, sugar, apples, candied citrus peel, spices, and suet, typically baked in a pie. **2** minced meat.
▶ □ **make mincemeat of** *inf.* defeat decisively or easily in a fight, contest, or argument.

mind /mīnd/ ▸n. **1** the element of a person that enables them to be aware of the world and their experiences, to think, and to feel; the faculty of consciousness and thought. ■ a person's mental processes contrasted with physical action: *I wrote a letter in my mind.* **2** a person's intellect: *his keen mind.* ■ the state of normal mental functioning in a person: *the strain has affected his mind.* ■ a person's memory: *the name slips my mind.* ■ a person identified with their intellectual faculties: *one of the greatest minds of his time.* **3** a person's attention: *I expect my employees to keep their minds on the job.* ■ the will or determination to achieve something: *anyone can lose weight if they set their mind to it.*
▸v. [*tr.*] **1** be distressed, annoyed, or worried by: *I don't mind the rain.* ■ have an objection to: *what does that mean, if you don't mind my asking?* ■ (**mind doing something**) be reluctant to do something (often used in polite requests): *I don't mind admitting I was worried.* ■ (**would not mind something**) *inf.* used to express one's enthusiasm for something: *I wouldn't mind some coaching from him!* **2** regard as important and worthy of attention: *never mind the opinion polls.* ■ [*intr.*] feel concern: *why should she mind about snubs from people she didn't care for?* ■ [in *imper.*] *dated* used to urge someone to remember or take care to bring about something: *mind you look after the children.* ■ [*intr.*] (also **mind you**) used to introduce a qualification to a previous statement: *we've got some decorations up—not a lot, mind you.* ■ be obedient to. **3** take care of temporarily: *we left our husbands to mind the children while we went out.* ■ [in *imper.*] used to warn someone to avoid injury or damage from a hazard: *mind your head!* ■ [in *imper.*] be careful about the quality or nature of: *mind your manners!* ▷Old English *gemynd* 'memory, thought,' of Germanic origin, from an Indo-European root meaning 'revolve in the mind, think,' shared by Sanskrit *manas* and Latin *mens* 'mind.'
▸ ☐ **be of two minds** be unable to decide between alternatives. ☐ **be of one mind** share the same opinion. ☐ **bear** (or **keep**) **in mind** take into account: *you need to bear in mind that the figures vary from place to place.* ☐ **come** (or **spring**) **to mind** (of a thought or idea) occur to someone. ☐ **have someone or something in mind** be thinking of. ■ intend: *I had it in mind to ask you to work for me.* ☐ **never mind 1** used to urge someone not to feel anxiety or distress: *never mind—it's all right now.* ■ used to suggest that a problem or objection is not important: *that's getting off the subject, but never mind.* **2** (also **never you mind**) used in refusing to answer a question: *never mind where I'm going.* **3** used to indicate that what has been said of one thing applies even more to another: *he was so tired that he found it hard to think, never mind talk.* ☐ **on someone's mind** preoccupying someone, esp. in a disquieting way: *new parents have many worries on their minds.* ☐ **out of one's mind** having lost control of one's mental faculties. ■ *inf.* suffering from a particular condition to a very high degree: *she was bored out of her mind.* ☐ **put someone in mind of** resemble and so cause someone to think of or remember: *he was a small, well-dressed man who put her in mind of a jockey.* ☐ **put** (or **set**) **one's mind to** direct all one's attention to (achieving something). ☐ **to my mind** in my opinion: *this story is, to my mind, a masterpiece.*
mind-bend·ing ▸*adj. inf.* (chiefly of a hallucinogenic drug) influencing or altering one's state of mind. —**mind-bend·er** *n.* —**mind-bend·ing·ly** *adv.*
mind-blow·ing ▸*adj. inf.* overwhelmingly impressive: *Chicago was mind-blowing.* ■ (of a drug) inducing hallucinations. —**mind-blow·ing·ly** *adv.*
mind-bog·gling ▸*adj. inf.* overwhelming; startling: *a chip that processes data at mind-boggling speed.* —**mind-bog·gling·ly** *adv.*
mind·ed /ˈmīndid/ ▸*adj.* [in *comb.*] inclined to think in a particular way: *liberal-minded scholars* | *I'm not scientifically minded.* ■ [in *comb.*] interested in or enthusiastic about the thing specified: *conservation-minded citizens.*
mind·ful /ˈmīndfəl/ ▸*adj.* conscious or aware of something. —**mind·ful·ly** *adv.* —**mind·ful·ness** *n.*
mind·less /ˈmīn(d)lis/ ▸*adj.* (of a person) acting without concern for the consequences: *mindless vandals.* ■ (esp. of harmful or evil behavior) done for no particular reason: *mindless violence.* ■ (**mindless of**) not thinking of or concerned about: *mindless of the fact she was in her nightgown, she rushed to the door.* ■ (of an activity) so simple or repetitive as to be performed automatically without thought or skill. —**mind·less·ly** *adv.* —**mind·less·ness** *n.*
mind read·er (also **mind-read·er** or **mind·read·er**) ▸*n.* a person who can supposedly discern what another person is thinking. —**mind-read** /ˈmīnd ˌred/ *v.* —**mind-read·ing** *n.*
mind-set (also **mind·set**) ▸*n.* the established set of attitudes held by someone.
mine[1] /mīn/ ▸*possessive pron.* used to refer to a thing or things belonging to or associated with the speaker.
▸*possessive adj. archaic* (used before a vowel) my: *tears did fill mine eyes.*
mine[2] ▸*n.* **1** an excavation in the earth for extracting coal or other

minerals: *a copper mine.* ■ an abundant source of something: *the book contains a mine of information.* **2** a type of bomb placed on or just below the surface of the ground or in the water that detonates when disturbed by a person, vehicle, or ship.
▸v. [*tr.*] (often **be mined**) **1** obtain (coal or other minerals) from a mine. ■ dig in (the earth) for coal or other minerals. ■ dig or burrow in (the earth). ■ *fig.* delve into (an abundant source) to extract something of value, esp. information or skill: *to mine such a rich vein of talent.* **2** lay explosive mines on or just below the surface of (the ground or water): *the area was heavily mined.* —**mine·a·ble** /ˈmīnəbəl/ (also **min·a·ble**) *adj.* —**min·ing** *n.*
mine·field /ˈmīnˌfēld/ (also **mine field**) ▸*n.* an area planted with explosive mines. ■ *fig.* a subject or situation presenting unseen hazards: *a minefield of technical regulations.*
mine·lay·er /ˈmīnˌlāər/ ▸*n.* a warship, aircraft, or land vehicle from which explosive mines are laid. —**mine·lay·ing** /-ˌlāiNG/ *n.*
min·er /ˈmīnər/ ▸*n.* a person who works in a mine. ■ a device used to mine ores, etc.
min·er·al /ˈmin(ə)rəl/ ▸*n.* **1** a solid inorganic substance of natural occurrence. ■ such a substance having a definite chemical composition and usually a fixed crystal form. ■ a substance obtained by mining. ■ an inorganic substance needed by the human body for good health. **2** (**minerals**) *Brit.* (in commercial use) effervescent soft drinks.
▸*adj.* of or denoting a mineral: *mineral ingredients such as zinc oxide.*
min·er·al·o·gy /ˌminəˈrälejē, -ˈral-/ ▸*n.* the scientific study of minerals. —**min·er·al·og·i·cal** /ˌmin(ə)rəˈläjikəl/ *adj.* —**min·er·al·og·i·cal·ly** /ˌmin(ə)rəˈläjik(ə)lē/ *adv.* —**min·er·al·o·gist** /-jist/ *n.*
min·er·al oil ▸*n.* a distillation product of petroleum, esp. one used as a lubricant, moisturizer, or laxative.
min·er·al wa·ter ▸*n.* water found in nature with some dissolved salts present. ■ *chiefly Brit.* an artificial imitation of this, esp. soda water.
min·e·stro·ne /ˌminəˈstrōnē/ ▸*n.* a thick soup containing vegetables and pasta.
mine·sweep·er /ˈmīnˌswēpər/ ▸*n.* a warship equipped for detecting and removing or destroying tethered explosive mines. —**mine·sweep·ing** /-ˌswēpiNG/ *n.*
Ming /miNG/ ▸*n.* the dynasty ruling China 1368–1644. ■ [usu. as *adj.*] Chinese porcelain made during the rule of the Ming dynasty, characterized by elaborate designs and vivid colors: *a priceless Ming vase.*
min·gle /ˈmiNGgəl/ ▸*v.* mix or cause to mix together: ■ [*intr.*] move freely around a place or at a social function, associating with others: *a chance to mingle with friends old and new.*
min·i /ˈminē/ ▸*adj.* denoting a miniature version of something: *a bouquet of mini carnations.*
▸*n.* (*pl.* **min·is**) **1** short for MINISKIRT. **2** short for MINICOMPUTER.
min·i·a·ture /ˈmin(ē)əcHər; -ˌcHŏŏr/ ▸*adj.* (esp. of a replica of something) of a much smaller size than normal; very small: *children dressed as miniature adults.*
▸*n.* a thing that is much smaller than normal, esp. a small replica or model. ■ a plant or animal that is a smaller version of an existing variety or breed. ■ a very small and highly detailed portrait or other painting. ■ a picture or decorated letter in an illuminated manuscript.
▸*v.* [*tr.*] *rare* represent on a smaller scale; reduce to miniature dimensions.
▸ ☐ **in miniature** on a small scale, but otherwise a replica.
min·i·a·tur·ize /ˈmin(ē)əcHəˌrīz/ ▸*v.* [*tr.*] [usu. as *adj.*] (**miniaturized**) make on a smaller or miniature scale: *miniaturized computers.* —**min·i·a·tur·ist** *n.* —**min·i·a·tur·i·za·tion** /ˌmin(ē)əcHərəˈzāsHən/ *n.*
min·i·cam /ˈminēˌkam/ ▸*n.* a hand-held video camera.
min·i·com·pu·ter /ˈminēkəmˌpyōōtər/ ▸*n.* a computer of medium power, more than a microcomputer but less than a mainframe.
min·im /ˈminim/ ▸*n.* one sixtieth of a fluid dram, about one drop of liquid.
min·i·ma /ˈminəmə/ ▸ plural form of MINIMUM.
min·i·mal /ˈminəməl/ ▸*adj.* **1** of a minimum amount, quantity, or degree; negligible. **2** *Art* characterized by the use of simple or primary forms or structures, esp. geometric or massive ones. ■ *Mus.* characterized by the repetition and gradual alteration of short phrases. —**min·i·mal·ly** *adv.*
min·i·mal·ism /ˈminəməˌlizəm/ ▸*n.* **1** a trend in sculpture and painting that arose in the 1950s and used simple, typically massive, forms.

2 an avant-garde movement in music characterized by the repetition of very short phrases that change gradually, producing a hypnotic effect. —**min·i·mal·ist** *n.*

min·i·mize /'minəˌmīz/ ▶*v.* [*tr.*] reduce (something, esp. something unwanted or unpleasant) to the smallest possible amount or degree: *the aim is to minimize costs.* ■ represent or estimate at less than the true value or importance: *they may minimize the importance of such beliefs.* —**min·i·mi·za·tion** /ˌminəməˈzāSHən/ *n.* —**min·i·miz·er** *n.*

min·i·mum /'minəməm/ ▶*n.* (*pl.* -**ma** /-mə/ or -**mums**) the least or smallest amount or quantity possible, attainable, or required: *technical difficulties have been* **kept to a minimum** | *they checked passports with the minimum of fuss.* ■ the lowest or smallest value of a varying quantity (e.g., temperature) allowed, attained, or recorded: *clients with a minimum of $500,000 to invest.* ■ *Math.* a point at which a continuously varying quantity ceases to decrease and begins to increase; the value of a quantity at such a point.
▶*adj.* smallest or lowest.

min·i·mum wage ▶*n.* the lowest wage permitted by law or by a special agreement (such as one with a labor union).

min·ion /'minyən/ ▶*n.* a follower or underling of a powerful person, esp. a servile or unimportant one.

min·i·se·ries /'minēˌsi(ə)rēz/ ▶*n.* (*pl.* same) a television drama shown in a number of episodes.

min·i·skirt /'minēˌskərt/ ▶*n.* a very short skirt.

min·is·ter /'minəstər/ ▶*n.* **1** (also **minister of religion**) a member of the clergy, esp. in Protestant churches. **2** (in certain countries) a head of a government department: *Britain's defense minister.* ■ a diplomatic agent, usually ranking below an ambassador, representing a state or sovereign in a foreign country. **3** *archaic* a person or thing used to achieve or convey something: *the Angels are ministers of the Divine Will.*
▶*v.* [*intr.*] **1** (**minister to**) attend to the needs of (someone): *ministering to the injured.* **2** act as a minister of religion. —**min·is·ter·ship** /-ˌSHip/ *n.*

min·is·te·ri·al /ˌminəˈsti(ə)rēəl/ ▶*adj.* **1** of or relating to a minister of religion. **2** of or relating to a government minister or ministers. —**min·is·te·ri·al·ly** *adv.*

min·is·tra·tion /ˌminəˈstrāSHən/ ▶*n.* (usu. **ministrations**) *chiefly formal* or *humorous* the provision of assistance or care: *a kitchen made spotless by the ministrations of a cleaning lady.* —**min·is·trant** /'minəstrənt/ *n.*

min·is·try /'minəstrē/ ▶*n.* (*pl.* -**tries**) **1** the work or vocation of a minister of religion: *he is training for the ministry.* ■ the period of tenure of a minister of religion. ■ the spiritual work or service of any Christian or a group of Christians, esp. evangelism: *a ministry of Christian healing.* **2** (in certain countries) a government department headed by a minister of state: *the Ministry of Agriculture.* **3** (in certain countries) a period of government under one prime minister: *Gladstone's first ministry was outstanding.*

min·i·van /'minēˌvan/ ▶*n.* a small van, typically one fitted with seats in the back for passengers.

mink /miNGk/ ▶*n.* (*pl.* same or **minks**) a small, semiaquatic carnivore (genus *Mustela*) of the weasel family, native to North America and Eurasia. ■ the thick brown fur of the mink. ■ a coat made of this.

min·now /'minō/ ▶*n.* any fish of the **minnow family** (Cyprinidae), the largest family of fishes, which includes carps, shiners, chubs, and daces. ■ a person or organization of relatvely small size, power, or influence. [in reference to the characteristic diminutive size of several fish in the minnow family.]

Mi·no·an /məˈnōən; mī-/ ▶*adj.* of, relating to, or denoting a Bronze Age civilization centered on Crete (*c.*3000–1050 BC), its people, or its language.
▶*n.* **1** an inhabitant of Minoan Crete or member of the Minoan people. **2** the language or scripts associated with the Minoans.

mi·nor /'mīnər/ ▶*adj.* **1** lesser in importance, seriousness, or significance. **2** *Mus.* (of a scale) having intervals of a semitone between the second and third degrees, and (usually) the fifth and sixth, and the seventh and eighth. Contrasted with MAJOR. ■ (of an interval) characteristic of a minor scale and less by a semitone than the equivalent major interval. ■ (of a key or mode) based on a minor scale, tending to produce a sad or pensive effect.
▶*n.* **1** a person under the age of full legal responsibility. **2** *Mus.* a minor key, interval, or scale. **3** (**the minors**) the minor leagues in a particular professional sport, esp. baseball. **4** a college student's subsidiary subject or area of concentration: *a minor in American Indian studies.*
▶*phrasal v.* □ **minor in** study or qualify in as a subsidiary subject in college.

mi·nor·i·ty /məˈnôrətē/ ▶*n.* (*pl.* -**ties**) **1** the smaller number or part, esp. a number that is less than half the whole number: *harsher measures for*

the minority of serious offenders | [as *adj.*] *a minority party.* ■ the number of votes cast for or by the smaller party in a legislative assembly: *a minority of 23 votes.* ■ a relatively small group of people, esp. one commonly discriminated against in a community, society, or nation, differing from others in race, religion, language, or political persuasion: *ethnic minorities* | [as *adj.*] *minority rights.* **2** the state or period of being under the age of full legal responsibility.

mi·nor·i·ty lead·er ▶*n.* the head of the minority party in a legislative body, esp. the U.S. Senate or House of Representatives.

mi·nor league ▶*n.* a league below the level of the major league in a particular professional sport, esp. baseball: *a minor-league outfielder.* ■ [as *adj.*] *fig.* of lesser power or significance. —**mi·nor-lea·guer** *n.*

Min·o·taur /'minəˌtôr; 'mī-/ *Greek Mythol.* ▶a creature who was half man and half bull, confined in a labyrinth in Crete.

min·ox·i·dil /məˈnäksəˌdil/ ▶*n. Med.* a synthetic drug that is used as a vasodilator in the treatment of hypertension, and is also used in lotions to promote hair growth.

min·strel /'minstrəl/ ▶*n.* a medieval singer or musician, esp. one who sang or recited lyric or heroic poetry to a musical accompaniment for the nobility. ■ a member of a band of entertainers with blackened faces who perform songs and music ostensibly of black American origin. —**min·strel·sy** /-sē/ *n.*

mint¹ /mint/ ▶*n.* **1** an aromatic plant (genus *Mentha*) native to temperate regions of the Old World, several kinds of which are used as culinary herbs. The **mint family** (Labiatae, or Lamiaceae) includes such herbs as lavender, rosemary, sage, and thyme. **2** a mint-flavored candy. —**mint·y** *adj.* (**mint·i·er, mint·i·est**) .

mint² ▶*n.* a place where money is coined, esp. under state authority. ■ (**a mint**) *inf.* a vast sum of money: *the car doesn't cost a mint.*
▶*adj.* (of an object) in pristine condition; as new: *a pair of speakers including stands, mint, $160.*
▶*v.* [*tr.*] (often **be minted**) make (a coin) by stamping metal. ■ [usu. as *adj.*] (**minted**) produce for the first time: *an example of newly minted technology.* —**mint·er** *n.*
▶ □ **in mint condition** (of an object) new or as if new.

mint ju·lep ▶*n.* a drink consisting of bourbon, crushed ice, sugar, and fresh mint, typically served in a tall frosted glass.

min·u·end /'minyəˌwend/ ▶*n. Math.* a quantity or number from which another is to be subtracted.

min·u·et /ˌminyoōˈet/ ▶*n.* a slow, stately ballroom dance for two in triple time, popular esp. in the 18th century. ■ a piece of music in triple time in the style of such a dance, typically as a movement in a suite, sonata, or symphony and frequently coupled with a trio.
▶*v.* (-**et·ed, -et·ing**) [*intr.*] dance a minuet.

mi·nus /'mīnəs/ ▶*prep.* **1** with the subtraction of: *what's ninety-three minus seven?* ■ *inf.* lacking; deprived of: *he was minus a finger on each hand.* **2** (of temperature) below zero: *minus 10° Fahrenheit.*
▶*adj.* **1** (before a number) below zero; negative: *minus five.* **2** (after a grade) slightly worse than: *a B minus.* **3** having a negative electric charge.
▶*n.* **1** short for MINUS SIGN. **2** a disadvantage: *for every plus with this equipment there can be a minus.*

mi·nus·cule /'minəˌskyoōl; min'əsˌkyoōl/ ▶*adj.* **1** extremely small; tiny. ■ *inf.* so small as to be negligible or insufficient: *the risk of infection was minuscule.* **2** of or in lowercase letters, as distinct from capitals or uncials. ■ of or in a small cursive script of the Roman alphabet developed in the 7th century AD.
▶*n.* minuscule script. ■ a small or lowercase letter. —**mi·nus·cu·lar** /məˈnəskyələr/ *adj.*

mi·nus sign ▶*n.* the symbol −, indicating subtraction or a negative value.

mi·nute¹ /'minit/ ▶*n.* **1** a period of time equal to sixty seconds or a sixtieth of an hour. ■ the distance covered in this length of time by someone driving or walking: *the hotel is situated just ten* **minutes** *from the center of the resort.* ■ *inf.* a very short time: *come and sit down* **for a minute.** ■ an instant or a point of time: *she had been laughing one minute and crying the next.* **2** (also **arc minute** or **minute of arc**) a sixtieth of a degree of angular measurement (symbol: ′). ▷late Middle English: via Old French from late Latin *minuta*, feminine (used as a noun) of *minutus* 'made small.' The senses 'period of sixty seconds' and 'sixtieth of a degree' derive from medieval Latin *pars minuta prima* 'first minute part.'
▶ □ **any minute** (or **at any minute**) very soon. □ **the minute** (or **the minute that**) as soon as: *let me know the minute he returns.* □ **this minute** (or **this very minute**) *inf.* at once; immediately: *pull yourself together this minute.*

mi·nute² /mī'n(y)oōt; mə-/ ▶*adj.* (-**nut·est**) extremely small. ■ so small as to verge on insignificance. ∎ (of an inquiry or investigation, or an account of one) taking the smallest points into consideration; precise and meticulous. —**mi·nute·ly** adv. —**mi·nute·ness** n.

mi·nute³ /'minit/ ▸n. (**minutes**) a summarized record of the proceedings at a meeting. ∎ an official memorandum authorizing or recommending a course of action.
▸v. [tr.] record or note (the proceedings of a meeting or a specified item among such proceedings).

min·ute hand ▸n. the hand on a watch or clock that indicates minutes.

min·ute·man /'minət,man/ ▸n. (pl. -**men**) hist. (in the period preceding and during the American Revolution) a member of a class of American militiamen who volunteered to be ready for service at a minute's notice.

mi·nu·ti·ae /mə'n(y)ōōsHē,ē; -sHē,ī/ (also **mi·nu·ti·a** /-sHē,ə; -sHə/) ▸pl. n. small, precise, or trivial details: the minutiae of everyday life.

minx /minGks/ ▸n. humorous or derog. an impudent, cunning, or boldly flirtatious girl or young woman. —**minx·ish** adj.

Mi·o·cene /'mīə,sēn/ ▸adj. Geol. of, relating to, or denoting the fourth epoch of the Tertiary period, between the Oligocene and Pliocene epochs. ∎ [as n.] (**the Miocene**) the Miocene epoch or the system of rocks deposited during it.

mir·a·cle /'mirikəl/ ▸n. a surprising and welcome event that is not explicable by natural or scientific laws and is therefore considered to be the work of a divine agency: the miracle of rising from the grave. ∎ a highly improbable or extraordinary event, development, or accomplishment that brings very welcome consequences: it was a miracle that more people hadn't been killed. ∎ an amazing product or achievement, or an outstanding example of something: a miracle of design.

mi·rac·u·lous /mə'rakyələs/ ▸adj. occurring through divine or supernatural intervention, or manifesting such power: a miraculous cure. ∎ highly improbable and extraordinary and bringing very welcome consequences: I felt grateful for our miraculous escape. —**mi·rac·u·lous·ly** adv. —**mi·rac·u·lous·ness** n.

mi·rage /mə'räzH/ ▸n. an optical illusion caused by atmospheric conditions, esp. the appearance of a sheet of water in a desert or on a hot road caused by the refraction of light from the sky by heated air. ∎ something that appears real or possible but is not in fact so.

mire /mīr/ ▸n. a stretch of swampy or boggy ground. ∎ soft and slushy mud or dirt.
▸v. [tr.] (usu. **be mired**) cause to become stuck in mud: sometimes a heavy truck gets mired down. ∎ cover or spatter with mud. ∎ (**mire someone/something in**) fig. involve someone or something in (difficulties).

mirk ▸n. & adj. archaic spelling of MURK.

mirk·y ▸adj. archaic spelling of MURKY.

mir·ror /'mirər/ ▸n. a reflective surface, now typically of glass coated with a metal amalgam, that reflects a clear image. ∎ fig. something regarded as accurately representing something else: the stage is supposed to be the mirror of life. ∎ (also **mirror site**) Comput. a site on a network that stores some or all of the contents from another site.
▸v. [tr.] (of a reflective surface) show a reflection of: the clear water mirrored the sky. ∎ fig. correspond to: gradations that mirror differences in social background. ∎ Comput. keep a copy of some or all of the contents of (a network site) at another site, typically in order to improve accessibility or to protect the data. —**mir·rored** adj.

mirth /mərtH/ ▸n. amusement, esp. as expressed in laughter: his six-foot frame shook with mirth. —**mirth·ful** /-fəl/ adj. —**mirth·ful·ly** /-fəlē/ adv. —**mirth·less** adj.

MIRV /mərv/ ▸n. a type of intercontinental nuclear missile carrying several independent warheads.

MIS Comput. ▸abbr. management information system.

mis·ad·ven·ture /,misəd'vencHər/ ▸n. an unfortunate incident; a mishap. ▷Middle English: from Old French mesaventure, from mesavenir 'turn out badly.'

mis·a·ligned /,misə'līnd/ ▸adj. having an incorrect position or alignment: misaligned headlights.. —**mis·a·lign·ment** n.

mis·al·li·ance /,misə'līəns/ ▸n. an unsuitable, unhappy, or unworkable alliance or marriage.

mis·an·thrope /'misən,THrōp; 'miz/ (also **mis·an·thro·pist** /mi-'sanTHrəpist; -'zan-/) ▸n. a person who dislikes humankind and avoids human society. —**mis·an·throp·ic** /,misən'THräpik/ adj. —**mis·an·throp·i·cal** /,misən'THräpikəl/ adj. —**mis·an·throp·i·cal·ly** /,misən'THräpik(ə)lē/ adv. —**mis·an·thro·py** /mi'santHrəpē/ n.

mis·ap·ply /,misə'plī/ ▸v. (-**plies, -plied**) [tr.] (usu. **be misapplied**) use (something) for the wrong purpose or in the wrong way. —**mis·ap·pli·ca·tion** /-,aplə'kāsHən/ n.

mis·ap·pre·hend /,mis,apri'hend/ ▸v. [tr.] misunderstand (words, a person, a situation, etc.). —**mis·ap·pre·hen·sion** n.

mis·ap·pro·pri·ate /,misə'prōprē,āt/ ▸v. [tr.] (of a person) dishonestly or unfairly take (something, esp. money, belonging to another) for one's own use: department officials had misappropriated funds. —**mis·ap·pro·pri·a·tion** /-,prōprē'āsHən/ n.

mis·be·got·ten /,misbə'gätn/ ▸adj. badly conceived, designed, or planned: a misbegotten journey to Indianapolis.

mis·be·have /,misbi'hāv/ ▸v. [intr.] (of a person, esp. a child) fail to conduct oneself in a way that is acceptable to others; behave badly. —**mis·be·hav·ior** /-'hāvyər/ n.

misc. ▸abbr. miscellaneous.

mis·cal·cu·late /mis'kalkyə,lāt/ ▸v. [tr.] calculate (an amount, distance, or measurement) wrongly. ∎ assess (a situation) wrongly. —**mis·cal·cu·la·tion** /,mis,kalkyə'lāsHən/ n.

mis·call /mis'kôl/ ▸v. [tr.] call (something) by a wrong or inappropriate name: it is amazing how many different trees have been miscalled by this name.

mis·car·riage /mis'karij; 'mis,karij/ ▸n. **1** the expulsion of a fetus from the womb before it is able to survive independently, esp. spontaneously or as the result of accident: his wife had a miscarriage. **2** an unsuccessful outcome of something planned.

mis·car·ry /mis'karē; 'mis,karē/ ▸v. (-**ries, -ried**) [intr.] **1** also 'mis,karē (of a pregnant woman) have a miscarriage: Wendy conceived, but she miscarried after five weeks | [tr.] she had miscarried her baby. **2** (of something planned) fail to attain an intended or expected outcome. ∎ dated (of a letter) fail to reach its intended destination.

mis·cast /mis'kast/ ▸v. (past and past part. -**cast**) [tr.] (usu. **be miscast**) allot an unsuitable role to (a particular actor): he is badly miscast in the romantic lead. ∎ allot the roles in (a play, movie, television show, etc.) to unsuitable actors.

mis·ceg·e·na·tion /mi,sejə'nāsHən; ,misəjə-/ ▸n. the interbreeding of people considered to be of different racial types.

mis·cel·la·ne·ous /,misə'lānēəs/ ▸adj. (of items or people gathered or considered together) of various types or from different sources: he picked up the miscellaneous papers. ∎ (of a collection or group) composed of members or elements of different kinds. —**mis·cel·la·ne·ous·ly** adv. —**mis·cel·la·ne·ous·ness** n.

mis·cel·la·ny /'misə,lānē; mi'selənē/ ▸n. (pl. -**nies**) a group or collection of different items; a mixture. ∎ a book containing a collection of pieces of writing by different authors.

mis·chance /mis'cHans/ ▸n. bad luck: by pure mischance, the secret was revealed. ∎ an unlucky occurrence: innumerable mischances might ruin the enterprise.

mis·chief /'miscHif/ ▸n. playful misbehavior or troublemaking, esp. in children. ∎ playfulness that is intended to tease, mock, or create trouble: her eyes twinkled with irrepressible mischief. ∎ harm or trouble caused by someone or something: she was bent on making mischief. ∎ archaic a person responsible for harm or annoyance.

mis·chie·vous /'miscHivəs/ ▸adj. (of a person, animal, or their behavior) causing or showing a fondness for causing trouble in a playful way. ∎ (of an action or thing) causing or intended to cause harm or trouble: a mischievous allegation for which there is not a shred of evidence. ▷Middle English: from Anglo-Norman French meschevous, from Old French meschever 'come to an unfortunate end,' from mes- 'adversely' + chever 'come to an end' (from chef 'head'). The early sense was 'unfortunate or calamitous,' later 'having harmful effects'; the sense 'playfully troublesome' dates from the late 17th cent. —**mis·chie·vous·ly** adv. —**mis·chie·vous·ness** n.

mis·ci·ble /'misəbəl/ ▸adj. (of liquids) forming a homogeneous mixture when added together: ethanol has two carbon atoms and is miscible with water. —**mis·ci·bil·i·ty** /,misə'bilətē/ n.

mis·con·ceive /,miskən'sēv/ ▸v. [tr.] fail to understand correctly. ∎ (usu. **be misconceived**) judge or plan badly, typically on the basis of faulty understanding: criticism of the trade surplus is misconceived | [as adj.] (**misconceived**) misconceived notions about gypsies. —**mis·con·ceiv·er** n.

mis·con·cep·tion /,miskən'sepsHən/ ▸n. a view or opinion that is incorrect because it is based on faulty thinking or understanding: public misconceptions about AIDS remain high.

mis·con·duct ▸n. /mis'kän,dəkt/ **1** unacceptable or improper behavior, esp. by an employee or professional person: she was found guilty of professional misconduct. ∎ Ice Hockey a penalty assessed against a player for unsportsmanlike conduct. **2** mismanagement, esp. culpable neglect of duties.

▸*v.* /ˌmiskənˈdəkt/ **1** (**misconduct oneself**) behave in an improper or unprofessional manner. **2** [*tr.*] mismanage (duties or a project).

mis·con·strue /ˌmiskənˈstrōō/ ▸*v.* (**-strues, -strued, -stru·ing**) [*tr.*] interpret (something, esp. a person's words or actions) wrongly: *my advice was deliberately misconstrued.* **—mis·con·struc·tion** /-ˈstrəkSHən/ *n.*

mis·count ▸*v.* /misˈkount/ [*tr.*] count (something) incorrectly.

▸*n.* /ˈmisˌkount/ an incorrect reckoning of the total number of something: *a miscount necessitates a recount.*

mis·cre·ant /ˈmiskrēənt/ ▸*n.* a person who behaves badly or in a way that breaks the law.

▸*adj.* (of a person) behaving badly or in a way that breaks a law or rule: *her miscreant husband.*

mis·cue /misˈkyōō/ ▸*n.* (in billiards) a shot in which the player fails to strike the ball properly with the cue. ■ (in other sports) a faulty strike, kick, or catch. ■ *fig.* a miscalculated action; a mistake.

▸*v.* (**-cues, -cued, -cue·ing** or **-cu·ing**) [*tr.*] (in billiards and other games) fail to strike (the ball or a shot) properly.

mis·date /misˈdāt/ ▸*v.* [*tr.*] assign an incorrect date to (a document, event, or work of art).

mis·deal /misˈdēl/ ▸*v.* (*past* and *past part.* **-dealt**) [*intr.*] make a mistake when dealing cards.

▸*n.* a hand dealt wrongly.

mis·deed /misˈdēd/ ▸*n.* a wicked or illegal act.

mis·de·mean·or /ˈmisdiˌmēnər/ (*Brit.* **mis·de·mean·our**) ▸*n.* a minor wrongdoing. ■ *Law* a nonindictable offense, regarded in the U.S. (and formerly in the UK) as less serious than a felony.

mis·di·ag·nose /misˈdī-igˌnōs; -ˌnōz/ ▸*v.* [*tr.*] make an incorrect diagnosis of (a particular illness). ■ make an incorrect diagnosis of the illness from which (someone) is suffering: *the consultant misdiagnosed her as having cancer.* **—mis·di·ag·no·sis** /ˌmisˌdī-igˈnōsəs/ *n.*

mis·di·rect /ˌmisdəˈrekt; -dī-/ ▸*v.* [*tr.*] (often **be misdirected**) send (someone or something) to the wrong place or in the wrong direction. ■ aim (something) in the wrong direction. ■ use or apply (something) wrongly or inappropriately: *their efforts have been largely misdirected.* **—mis·di·rec·tion** /-ˈrekSHən/ *n.*

mise en scène /ˌmēz ˌän ˈsen/ ▸*n.* the arrangement of scenery and stage properties in a play. ■ the setting or surroundings of an event or action.

mi·ser /ˈmīzər/ ▸*n.* a person who hoards wealth and spends as little money as possible. **—mi·ser·ly** *adj.*

mis·er·a·ble /ˈmiz(ə)rəbəl/ ▸*adj.* **1** (of a person) wretchedly unhappy or uncomfortable. ■ (of a situation or environment) causing someone to feel wretchedly unhappy or uncomfortable. ■ (of a person) habitually morose. **2** pitiably small or inadequate: *all they pay me is a miserable $10,000 a year.* ■ contemptible (used as a term of abuse or for emphasis): *you miserable creep!* **—mis·er·a·ble·ness** *n.* **—mis·er·a·bly** /-blē/ *adv.*

mis·er·y /ˈmiz(ə)rē/ ▸*n.* (*pl.* **-er·ies**) a state or feeling of great distress or discomfort of mind or body. ■ (usu. **miseries**) a cause or source of great distress or discomfort: *the miseries of war.*

▸ □ **put someone/something out of their misery** end the suffering of a person or animal in pain by killing them. ■ *inf.* release someone from suspense or anxiety by telling them something they are anxious to know.

mis·fire ▸*v.* /misˈfīr/ [*intr.*] (of a gun or missile) fail to discharge or fire properly. ■ (of an internal combustion engine) undergo failure of the fuel to ignite correctly or at all. ■ (esp. of a plan) fail to produce the intended result.

▸*n.* /ˈmisˌfīr/ a failure of a gun or missile to fire correctly or of fuel in an internal combustion engine to ignite.

mis·fit /ˈmisˌfit/ ▸*n.* a person whose behavior or attitude sets them apart from others in an uncomfortably conspicuous way: *a motley collection of social misfits.* ■ *archaic* something that does not fit or that fits badly.

mis·for·tune /misˈfôrCHən/ ▸*n.* bad luck. ■ an unfortunate condition or event: *never laugh at other people's misfortunes.*

mis·giv·ing /misˈgiviNG/ ▸*n.* (usu. **misgivings**) a feeling of doubt or apprehension about the outcome or consequences of something: *we have misgivings about the way the campaign is being run | I felt a sense of misgiving at the prospect of retirement.*

mis·gov·ern /misˈgəvərn/ ▸*v.* [*tr.*] govern (a state or country) unfairly or inefficiently. **—mis·gov·ern·ment** /-ˈgəvər(n)mənt/ *n.*

mis·guide /misˈgīd/ ▸*v.* [*tr.*] *rare* mislead: *a long survey that can only baffle and misguide the general reader.* **—mis·guid·ance** /-gīdns/ *n.*

mis·han·dle /misˈhandəl/ ▸*v.* [*tr.*] **1** manage or deal with (something)

wrongly or ineffectively. **2** manipulate roughly or carelessly: *the equipment could be dangerous if mishandled.*

mis·hap /ˈmisˌhap/ ▸*n.* an unlucky accident.

mis·hit /ˌmisˈhit/ ▸*v.* (**-hit·ting**; *past* and *past part.* **-hit**) [*tr.*] (in various sports) hit or kick (a ball) badly or in the wrong direction.

▸*n.* an instance of hitting or kicking a ball in such a way.

mish·mash /ˈmiSHˌmaSH; -ˌmäSH/ ▸*n.* a confused mixture: *a mishmash of outmoded ideas.*

mis·in·form /ˌmisinˈfôrm/ ▸*v.* [*tr.*] (often **be misinformed**) give (someone) false or inaccurate information. **—mis·in·for·ma·tion** /ˌmisinfərˈmāSHən/ *n.*

mis·in·ter·pret /ˌmisinˈtərprət/ ▸*v.* (**-pret·ed, -pret·ing**) [*tr.*] interpret (something or someone) wrongly. **—mis·in·ter·pre·ta·tion** /-inˌtərprəˈtāSHən/ *n.* **—mis·in·ter·pret·er** *n.*

mis·judge /ˌmisˈjəj/ ▸*v.* [*tr.*] form a wrong opinion or conclusion about. ■ make an incorrect estimation or assessment of. **—mis·judg·ment** (also **mis·judge·ment**) *n.*

mis·lay /misˈlā/ ▸*v.* (*past* and *past part.* **-laid**) [*tr.*] unintentionally put (an object) where it cannot readily be found and so lose it temporarily: *I seem to have mislaid my car keys.*

mis·lead /misˈlēd/ ▸*v.* (*past* and *past part.* **-led**) [*tr.*] cause (someone) to have a wrong idea or impression about someone or something: *the government misled the public about the environmental impact.* **—mis·lead·er** *n.* **—mis·lead·ing** *adj.* **—mis·lead·ing·ly** *adv.*

mis·man·age /misˈmanij/ ▸*v.* [*tr.*] manage (something) badly or wrongly. **—mis·man·age·ment** *n.*

mis·match ▸*n.* /ˈmisˌmaCH/ a failure to correspond or match; a discrepancy: *a huge mismatch between supply and demand.*

▸*v.* /ˌmisˈmaCH/ [*tr.*] [usu. as *adj.*] (**mismatched**) match (people or things) unsuitably or incorrectly: *funky mismatched chairs and tables.*

mis·no·mer /misˈnōmər/ ▸*n.* a wrong or inaccurate name or designation: *"king crab" is a misnomer—these creatures are not crustaceans at all.* ■ a wrong or inaccurate use of a name or term: *to call this "neighborhood policing" would be a misnomer.*

mi·so /ˈmēsō/ ▸*n.* paste made from fermented soybeans and barley or rice malt, used in Japanese cooking.

mi·sog·a·my /məˈsägəmē/ ▸*n.* *rare* the hatred of marriage. **—mi·sog·a·mist** /-mist/ *n.*

mi·sog·y·ny /məˈsäjənē/ ▸*n.* the hatred of women by men: *she felt she was struggling against thinly disguised misogyny.* **—mi·sog·y·nist** *n.* **—mi·sog·y·nous** /-nəs/ *adj.*

mis·place /misˈplās/ ▸*v.* [*tr.*] (usu. **be misplaced**) put in the wrong place and lose temporarily because of this; mislay: *I'm sure the jewelry has just been misplaced, and not stolen.* **—mis·place·ment** *n.*

mis·play ▸*v.* /misˈplā/ play (a ball or card) wrongly, badly, or in contravention of the rules.

▸*n.* /ˈmisˌplā/ an instance of playing a ball or card in such a way.

mis·print ▸*n.* /ˈmisˌprint/ an error in printed text.

▸*v.* /ˈmisˌprint/ [*tr.*] print (something) incorrectly.

mis·pro·nounce /ˌmisprəˈnouns/ ▸*v.* [*tr.*] pronounce (a word) incorrectly. **—mis·pro·nun·ci·a·tion** /-prəˌnənsēˈāSHən/ *n.*

mis·quote /misˈkwōt/ ▸*v.* [*tr.*] quote (a person or a piece of written or spoken text) inaccurately: *the foreign secretary had misquoted Qian.*

▸*n.* a passage or remark quoted inaccurately: *a misquote from a poem by Robert Burns.* **—mis·quo·ta·tion** /ˌmiskwōˈtāSHən/ *n.*

mis·read /misˈrēd/ ▸*v.* (*past* and *past part.* **-read** /-ˈred/) [*tr.*] read (a piece of text) wrongly. ■ judge or interpret (a situation or a person's manner or behavior) incorrectly: *had she been completely misreading his intentions?*

mis·rep·re·sent /ˌmisˌrepriˈzent/ ▸*v.* [*tr.*] give a false or misleading account of the nature of. **—mis·rep·re·sen·ta·tion** /-ˌzenˈtāSHən; -zən-/ *n.* **—mis·rep·re·sen·ta·tive** /-ˈzentətiv/ *adj.*

mis·rep·re·sen·ta·tion /ˌmisˌreprəzenˈtāSHən/ ▸*n.* *Law* a false or misleading statement. ■ the legal action to provide a remedy for a false or misleading statement.

miss¹ /mis/ ▸*v.* [*tr.*] **1** fail to hit, reach, or come into contact with (something aimed at): *a laser-guided bomb had missed its target* | [*intr.*] *he was given two free throws, but missed both times.* ■ pass by without touching; chance not to hit: *a piece of shrapnel missed him by inches.* ■ fail to catch (something thrown or dropped). ■ be too late to catch (a passenger vehicle, etc.): *we'll miss the train.* ■ fail to notice, hear, or understand: *the villa is impossible to miss—it's right by the road.* ■ fail to attend, participate in, or watch (something one is expected to or habitually does): *students who missed class.* ■ fail to see or have a meeting with (someone): *"Potter's been here this morning?" "You've just missed him."* ■ not be able to experience or fail to take advantage of (an opportunity or chance):

don't miss the chance to visit the breathtaking Dolomites. ■ avoid; escape: *smart Christmas shoppers go out early to miss the crowds.* ■ fail to include (someone or something); omit: *if we miss a few things in the first draft, we can add them later.* ■ [*intr.*] (of an engine or motor vehicle) undergo failure of ignition in one or more cylinders. **2** notice the loss or absence of: *she slipped away when she thought she wouldn't be missed.* ■ feel regret or sadness at no longer being able to enjoy the presence of.

▶ *n.* a failure to hit, catch, or reach something. ■ a failure, esp. an unsuccessful movie, television show, recording, etc.: *audiences will decide whether Brando's latest flick is a hit or a miss.* —**miss·a·ble** /ˈmisəbəl/ *adj.*

▶ □ **miss a beat 1** (of the heart) temporarily fail or appear to fail to beat. **2** *inf.* hesitate or falter, esp. in demanding circumstances or when making a transition from one activity to another: *his speech segued to nuclear disarmament, without missing a beat.* □ **miss the boat** (or **bus**) *inf.* be too slow to take advantage of an opportunity.

miss² ▶ *n.* **1** (**Miss**) a title prefixed to the name of an unmarried woman or girl, or to that of a married woman retaining her maiden name for professional purposes: *Miss Hazel Armstrong.* ■ used in the title of the winner in a beauty contest: *Miss World.* ■ used as a polite form of address to a young woman or to a waitress, etc. **2** *often derog.* or *humorous* a girl or young woman. **3** (**misses**) a range of standard sizes, usually 8 to 20, in women's clothing.

mis·sal /ˈmisəl/ ▶ *n.* a book containing the texts used in the Catholic Mass throughout the year.

mis·shap·en /misˈSHāpən/ ▶ *adj.* not having the normal or natural shape or form: *misshapen fruit.* —**mis·shap·en·ly** *adv.* —**mis·shap·en·ness** *n.*

mis·sile /ˈmisəl/ ▶ *n.* an object that is forcibly propelled at a target, either by hand or from a mechanical weapon. ■ a weapon that is self-propelled or directed by remote control, carrying a conventional or nuclear explosive. —**mis·sile·ry** /-rē/ *n.*

miss·ing /ˈmisiNG/ ▶ *adj.* (of a thing) not able to be found because it is not in its expected place. ■ not present or included when expected or supposed to be. ■ (of a person) absent from a place, esp. home, and of unknown whereabouts. ■ (of a person) not yet traced or confirmed as alive, but not known to be dead, after an accident or during wartime: *missing in action.*

miss·ing link ▶ *n.* a thing that is needed in order to complete a series, provide continuity, or gain complete knowledge. ■ a hypothetical fossil form intermediate between two living forms, esp. between humans and apes.

mis·sion /ˈmisHən/ ▶ *n.* an important assignment carried out for political, religious, or commercial purposes, typically involving travel: *a fact-finding mission to China.* ■ [treated as *sing.* or *pl.*] a group of people taking part in such an assignment: *the mission had journeyed more than 3,500 miles.* ■ an organization or institution involved in a long-term assignment in a foreign country: *the West German mission* | [as *adj.*] *the mission school.* ■ the vocation or calling of a religious organization, esp. a Christian one, to go out into the world and spread its faith. ■ a strongly felt aim, ambition, or calling: *his main mission in life has been to cut unemployment.* ■ an operation carried out by military aircraft at a time of conflict.

mis·sion·ar·y /ˈmisHəˌnerē/ ▶ *n.* (*pl.* **-ar·ies**) a person sent on a religious mission, esp. one sent to promote Christianity in a foreign country.

▶ *adj.* of, relating to, or characteristic of a missionary or a religious mission.

mis·sis ▶ *n.* variant spelling of MISSUS.

mis·sive /ˈmisiv/ ▶ *n.* a letter, esp. a long or official one.

mis·spell /misˈspel/ ▶ *v.* (*past* and *past part.* **-spelled** or **-spelt**) [*tr.*] spell (a word) incorrectly.

mis·state /misˈstāt/ ▶ *v.* [*tr.*] make wrong or inaccurate statements about. —**mis·state·ment** *n.*

mis·sus /ˈmisəz; -əs/ (also **mis·sis**) ▶ *n.* *inf.* or *humorous* a man's wife: *I promised the missus I'd be home by eleven.*

miss·y /ˈmisē/ ▶ *n.* (*pl.* **miss·ies**) used as an affectionate or disparaging form of address to a young girl: *"Don't tell lies, missy,"* he said sternly.

▶ *adj.* of or relating to the misses range of garment sizes: *available in missy and petite sizes.*

mist /mist/ ▶ *n.* a cloud of tiny water droplets suspended in the atmosphere at or near the earth's surface limiting visibility, but to a lesser extent than fog. ■ a condensed vapor settling in fine droplets on a surface: *the mist of perspiration that had dampened her temples.* ■ a haze or film over the eyes, esp. caused by tears, and resulting in blurred vision. ■ used in reference to something that blurs one's perceptions or memory: *Sardinia's origins are lost in the mists of time.*

▶ *v.* cover or become covered with mist. ■ [*intr.*] (of a person's eyes) become covered with a film of tears causing blurred vision: *her eyes misted*

at this heroic image. ■ [*tr.*] spray (something, esp. a plant) with a fine cloud of water droplets. ▷Old English, of Germanic origin; from an Indo-European root shared by Greek *omikhlē* 'mist, fog.'

mis·take /məˈstāk/ ▶ *n.* an action or judgment that is misguided or wrong: *coming here was a mistake* | *she made the mistake of thinking they were important.* ■ something, esp. a word, figure, or fact, that is not correct; an inaccuracy: *spelling mistakes.*

▶ *v.* (*past* **-took**; *past part.* **-tak·en**) [*tr.*] be wrong about. ■ (**mistake someone/something for**) wrongly identify someone or something as: *she thought he'd mistaken her for someone else.* —**mis·tak·a·ble** *adj.* —**mis·tak·a·bly** /-əblē/ *adv.*

mis·tak·en /məˈstākən/ ▶ *adj.* wrong in one's opinion or judgment. ■ (esp. of a belief) based on or resulting from a misunderstanding or faulty judgment: *an unfortunate case of mistaken identity.* —**mis·tak·en·ly** *adv.* —**mis·tak·en·ness** *n.*

mis·ter /ˈmistər/ ▶ *n.* variant form of MR., often used humorously or with offensive emphasis: *don't sass me, mister!* ■ *inf.* used as a form of address to a man whose name is not known: *thanks, mister.* ■ *dial.* a woman's husband: *my thanks to you and the mister.*

mis·ter² ▶ *n.* a device, such as a bottle, with a nozzle for spraying a mist of water, esp. on houseplants.

mis·time /misˈtīm/ ▶ *v.* [*tr.*] choose a bad or inappropriate moment to do or say (something): *he lost $800 million by mistimimg his withdrawal from the market.* —**mis·timed** *adj.*

mis·tle·toe /ˈmisəlˌtō/ ▶ *n.* a leathery-leaved parasitic plant that grows on a variety of trees and bears white glutinous berries in winter. Its several species include the American *Phoradendron serotinum* (family Loranthaceae).

mis·took /misˈtŏŏk/ ▶ past of MISTAKE.

mis·tral /ˈmistrəl; miˈsträl/ ▶ *n.* a strong, cold northwesterly wind that blows through the Rhône valley and southern France into the Mediterranean, mainly in winter.

mis·treat /misˈtrēt/ ▶ *v.* [*tr.*] treat (a person or animal) badly, cruelly, or unfairly. —**mis·treat·ment** *n.*

mis·tress /ˈmistris/ ▶ *n.* **1** a woman in a position of authority or control: *she is always mistress of the situation.* ■ a woman who is skilled in a particular subject or activity: *a mistress of the sound bite, she is famed for the acidity of her tongue.* ■ the female owner of a dog, cat, or other domesticated animal. ■ *chiefly Brit.* a female schoolteacher who teaches a particular subject: *a Geography mistress.* ■ *archaic* a female head of a household: *he asked for the mistress of the house.* **2** a woman having an extramarital sexual relationship, esp. with a married man: *Elsie knew her husband had a mistress tucked away somewhere.* ■ *archaic* or *poetic/lit.* a woman loved and courted by a man. **3** (**Mistress**) *archaic* or *dial.* used as a title prefixed to the name of a married woman; Mrs.

mis·tri·al /ˈmisˌtrī(ə)l/ ▶ *n.* a trial rendered invalid through an error in the proceedings. ■ an inconclusive trial, such as one in which the jury cannot agree on a verdict.

mis·trust /misˈtrəst/ ▶ *v.* [*tr.*] be suspicious of; have no confidence in: *she had no cause to mistrust him.*

▶ *n.* lack of trust: suspicion: *the public mistrust of government.*

mis·trust·ful /ˌmisˈtrəstfəl/ ▶ *adj.* lacking in trust; suspicious: *he had been unduly mistrustful of her.* —**mis·trust·ful·ly** *adv.* —**mis·trust·ful·ness** *n.*

mist·y /ˈmistē/ ▶ *adj.* (**mist·i·er, mist·i·est**) full of, covered with, or accompanied by mist. ■ (of a person's eyes) full of tears so as to blur the vision. ■ indistinct or dim in outline: *a misty silhouette* | *fig.* a few misty memories. ■ (of a color) not bright; soft: *a misty pink.* —**mist·i·ly** /ˈmistəlē/ *adv.* —**mist·i·ness** *n.*

mis·un·der·stand /ˌmisˌəndərˈstand/ ▶ *v.* (*past* and *past part.* **-stood**) [*tr.*] fail to interpret or understand (something) correctly: *he had misunderstood the policeman's hand signals* | [*intr.*] *I must have misunderstood—I thought you were anxious to leave.* ■ fail to interpret or understand the words or actions of (someone) correctly.

mis·un·der·stand·ing /ˌmisˌəndərˈstandiNG/ ▶ *n.* a failure to understand something correctly. ■ a disagreement or quarrel.

mis·use ▶ *v.* /misˈyōōz; ˈmisˌyōōz/ [*tr.*] use (something) in the wrong way or for the wrong purpose: *he was found guilty of misusing public funds.* ■ treat (someone or something) badly or unfairly.

▶ *n.* /ˌmisˈyōōs; ˈmisˌyōōs/ the wrong or improper use of something: *drugs of such potency that their misuse can have dire consequences* | *a misuse of power.* —**mis·us·er** /-ˈyōōzər/ *n.*

mite[1] /mīt/ ▶*n.* a minute arachnid (order or subclass Acari) that has four pairs of legs when adult, related to the ticks. Many kinds live in the soil and a number are parasitic on plants or animals.

mite[2] ▶*n.* **1** a small child or animal, esp. when regarded as an object of sympathy: *the poor little mite looks half-starved.* **2** a very small amount: *his teacher thought he needed **a mite of** discipline.* ■ *hist.* a small coin, in particular a small Flemish copper coin of very low face value.
▶*adv.* (**a mite**) *inf.* a little; slightly: *all evening he's seemed a mite awkward.*

mi·ter /'mītər/ (*Brit.* **mi·tre**) ▶*n.* **1** a tall headdress worn by bishops and senior abbots as a symbol of office, tapering to a point at front and back with a deep cleft between. **2** (also **miter joint**) a joint made between two pieces of wood or other material at an angle of 90°, such that the line of junction bisects this angle.
▶*v.* [*tr.*] join by means of a miter. —**mi·tered** *adj.*

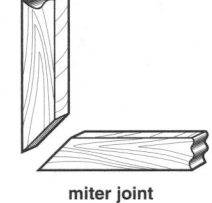

miter joint

mi·ter box ▶*n.* a guide to enable a saw to cut miter joints at the desired angle.

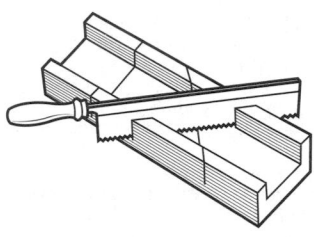

miter box

mit·i·gate /'mitə,gāt/ ▶*v.* [*tr.*] make less severe, serious, or painful: *he wanted to mitigate misery in the world.* ■ lessen the gravity of (an offense or mistake): [as *adj.*] (**mitigating**) *he would have faced a prison sentence but for **mitigating circumstances**.* ▷late Middle English: from Latin *mitigat-* 'softened, alleviated,' from the verb *mitigare*, from *mitis* 'mild.' —**mit·i·ga·ble** /-gibəl/ *adj.* —**mit·i·ga·tion** /,mitə'gāSHən/ *n.* —**mit·i·ga·tor** /-,gātər/ *n.* —**mit·i·ga·to·ry** /-gə,tôrē/ *adj.*

mi·to·chon·dri·on /,mītə'kändrēən/ ▶*n.* (*pl.* **-dri·a** /-drēə/) *Biol.* an organelle found in large numbers in most cells, in which the biochemical processes of respiration and energy production occur.. —**mi·to·chon·dri·al** /-drēəl/ *adj.*

mi·to·sis /mī'tōsəs/ ▶*n.* (*pl.* **-ses** /-sēz/) *Biol.* a type of cell division that results in two daughter cells each having the same number and kind of chromosomes as the parent nucleus, typical of ordinary tissue growth. Compare with MEIOSIS. —**mi·tot·ic** /mī'tätik/ *adj.*

mi·tral /'mītrəl/ ▶*adj.* denoting or relating to the mitral valve.

mi·tral valve ▶*n. Anat.* the valve between the left atrium and the left ventricle of the heart, consisting of two tapered cusps.

mitt /mit/ ▶*n.* (usu. **mitts**) a mitten: *oven mitts.* ■ *Baseball* a mittenlike glove, worn by the catcher and first baseman. ■ a glove leaving the fingers and thumb-tip exposed. ■ *inf.* a person's hand.

mit·ten /'mitn/ ▶*n.* (usu. **mittens**) a glove with two sections, one for the thumb and the other for all four fingers. —**mit·tened** *adj.*

mitz·vah /'mitsvə/ ▶*n.* (*pl.* **mitz·voth** /'mits,vōt; -,vōs/) *Judaism* a precept or commandment. ■ a good deed done from religious duty.

mix /miks/ ▶*v.* [*tr.*] combine or put together to form one substance or mass. ■ [*intr.*] (of different substances) be able to be combined in this way: *oil and water don't mix.* ■ make or prepare by combining various ingredients: *mixing concrete is hard physical work.* ■ (esp. in sound recording) combine (two or more signals or soundtracks) into one. ■ produce (a sound signal or recording) by combining a number of separate signals or recorded soundtracks. ■ juxtapose or put together to form a whole whose constituent parts are still distinct: *he continues to **mix** an offhand sense of humor with a sharp insight.* ■ [*intr.*] (of a person) associate with others socially: *the people he **mixed with** were nothing to do with show business.* ■ (**mix it** or **mix it up**) *inf.* be belligerent verbally or physically, esp. with one's fists.
▶*phrasal v.* □ **mix something up** spoil the order or arrangement of a collection of things: *disconnect all the cables, mix them up, then try to reconnect them.* **mix someone/something up** confuse someone or something with another person or thing: *I'd got her **mixed up with** her sister.*
▶*n.* two or more different qualities, things, or people placed,

combined, or considered together: *the decor is a mix of antique and modern.* ■ a group of people of different types within a particular society or community: *the school has a good social mix.* ■ a commercially prepared mixture of ingredients for making a particular type of food or a product such as concrete: *cake mixes have made cooking easier.* ■ the proportion of different people or other constituents that make up a mixture: *arriving at the correct mix of full-time to part-time staff.* ■ an image or sound produced by the combination of two separate images or sounds. —**mix·a·ble** *adj.*

▶ □ **be** (or **get**) **mixed up in** be (or become) involved in (something regarded as dubious or dishonest): *Steve was mixed up in an insurance swindle.* □ **be** (or **get**) **mixed up with** be (or become) associated with (someone unsuitable or unreliable).

mixed /mikst/ ▶*adj.* consisting of different qualities or elements. ■ (of an assessment of, reaction to, or feeling about something) containing a mixture of both favorable and negative elements: *the movie opened last Friday to mixed reviews* | *I had **mixed feelings** about seeing Laura again.* ■ composed of different varieties of the same thing: *crab on a bed of mixed greens.* ■ involving or showing a mixture of races or social classes: *people of mixed race.* ■ (esp. of an educational establishment or a sports team or competition) of or for members of both sexes.

mixed bag ▶*n.* a diverse assortment of things or people: *a mixed bag of applause and catcalls.*

mixed bless·ing ▶*n.* a situation or thing that has disadvantages as well as advantages: *having children so early in their marriage was a mixed blessing.*

mixed dou·bles ▶*pl. n.* [treated as *sing.*] (esp. in tennis and badminton) a game or competition involving teams, each consisting of a man and a woman.

mixed mar·riage ▶*n.* a marriage between people of different races or religions.

mixed met·a·phor ▶*n.* a combination of two or more incompatible metaphors, which produces a ridiculous effect (e.g., *this tower of strength will forge ahead*).

mixed-up ▶*adj. inf.* (of a person) suffering from psychological or emotional problems: *a lonely, mixed-up teenager.*

mix·er /'miksər/ ▶*n.* **1** a machine or device for mixing things. esp. an electrical appliance for mixing foods. **2** a person considered in terms of their ability to mix socially with others: *media people need to be good mixers.* **3** a social gathering where people can make new acquaintances. **4** a soft drink that can be mixed with alcohol. **5** (in sound recording and cinematography) a device for merging input signals to produce a combined output in the form of sound or pictures. ■ a person who operates such a device: *a sound mixer.*

mix·ture /'miksCHər/ ▶*n.* a substance made by mixing other substances together. ■ the process of mixing or being mixed. ■ (**a mixture of**) a combination of different qualities, things, or emotions in which the component elements are individually distinct: *the old town is a mixture of narrow medieval streets and 18th-century architecture.* ■ a person regarded as a combination of qualities and attributes: *he was a curious mixture, an unpredictable man.* ■ *Chem.* the product of the random distribution of one substance through another without any chemical reaction, as distinct from a compound. ■ the charge of gas or vapor mixed with air that is admitted to the cylinder of an internal combustion engine, esp. as regards the ratio of fuel to air:

mix-up (also **mix·up**) ▶*n. inf.* a confusion of one thing with another, or a misunderstanding or mistake that results in confusion: *there's been a mix-up over the tickets.*

miz·zen /'mizən/ (also **miz·en**) ▶*n.* **1** (also **miz·zen·mast** /-,mast/) the mast aft of the main mast of a ship's mainmast. **2** (also **miz·zen·sail** /,sāl/) the lowest sail on a mizzenmast.

ml ▶*abbr.* ■ milliliter(s).

Mlle (*pl.* **Mlles**) ▶*abbr.* Mademoiselle.

MLS ▶*abbr.* ■ Master of Library Science. ■ Multiple Listing Service, an organization that holds computerized listings of U.S. real estate offered for sale. ■ Major League Soccer.

mm ▶*abbr.* millimeter(s).

Mme (*pl.* **Mmes**) ▶*abbr.* Madame.

Mn ▶*symb.* the chemical element manganese.

mne·mon·ic /nə'mänik/ ▶*n.* a device such as a pattern of letters, ideas, or associations that assists in remembering something.
▶*adj.* aiding or designed to aid the memory. ■ of or relating to the power of memory. —**mne·mon·i·cal·ly** /-ik(ə)lē/ *adv.*

mne·mon·ics /nə'mäniks/ ▶*pl. n.* [usu. treated as *sing.*] the study and development of systems for improving and assisting the memory.

MO ▶*abbr.* ■ Medical Officer. ■ modus operandi. ■ money order.

Mo ▸*symb.* the chemical element molybdenum.

mo /mō/ ▸*n. inf., chiefly Brit.* a moment: *hang on a mo!*

mo. ▸*abbr.* month.

-mo ▸*suffix* forming nouns denoting a book size by the number of leaves into which a sheet of paper has been folded: *twelvemo.*

mo·a /'mōə/ ▸*n.* a large, extinct, flightless bird (family Dinornithidae) resembling the emu, formerly found in New Zealand.

moan /mōn/ ▸*n.* a long, low sound made by a person expressing physical or mental suffering or sexual pleasure: *she gave a low moan of despair.* ■ a sound resembling this, esp. one made by the wind. ■ *inf.* a complaint that is perceived as trivial and not taken seriously by others.
▸*v.* [*intr.*] make a long, low sound expressing physical or mental suffering or sexual pleasure. ■ (of a thing) make a sound resembling this: *the foghorn moaned at intervals.* ■ *inf.* complain or grumble, typically about something trivial. ■ *poetic/lit.* lament. —**moan·er** *n.* —**moan·ful** /-fəl/ *adj.*

moat /mōt/ ▸*n.* a deep, wide ditch surrounding a castle, fort, or town, typically filled with water and intended as a defense against attack.
▸*v.* [*tr.*] [often as *adj.*] (**moated**) surround (a place) with a moat: *a moated castle.*

mob /mäb/ ▸*n.* a large crowd of people, esp. one that is disorderly and intent on causing trouble or violence: *a mob of protesters.* ■ (usu. **the Mob**) the Mafia or a similar criminal organization. ■ (**the mob**) the ordinary people: *the age-old fear that the mob may organize to destroy the last vestiges of civilized life.*
▸*v.* (**mobbed, mob·bing**) [*tr.*] (often **be mobbed**) crowd around (someone) in an unruly and excitable way in order to admire or attack them: *he was mobbed by autograph hunters.* ■ crowd into (a building or place): *an unruly crowd mobbed the White House.* —**mob·ber** *n.*

mob·cap /'mäb,kap/ ▸*n.* a large soft hat covering all of the hair and typically having a decorative frill, worn indoors by women in the 18th and early 19th centuries.

mo·bile ▸*adj.* /'mōbəl; -,bēl; -,bīl/ able to move or be moved freely or easily. ■ (of the face or its features) indicating feelings with fluid and expressive movements. ■ (of a store, library, or other service) accommodated in a vehicle so as to travel around and serve various places. ■ (of a military or police unit) equipped and prepared to move quickly to any place it is needed. ■ able or willing to move easily or freely between occupations, places of residence, or social classes: *an increasingly mobile and polarized society.*
▸*n.* /'mō,bēl/ a decorative structure that is suspended so as to turn freely in the air. —**mo·bil·i·ty** /mō'bilitē/ *n.*

mobile home ▸*n.* a large house trailer that is parked in one particular place and used as a permanent living accommodation.

mo·bi·lize /'mōbə,līz/ ▸*v.* [*tr.*] **1** (of a country or its government) prepare and organize (troops) for active service. [*intr.*] *Russia is in no position to mobilize any time soon.* ■ organize and encourage (people) to act in a concerted way: *he used the press to mobilize support for his party.* ■ bring (resources) into use in order to achieve a particular goal. **2** make (something) movable or capable of movement: *doing yoga stretches to mobilize compacted joints.* ■ make (a substance) able to be transported by or as a liquid: *acid rain mobilizes the aluminum in forest soils.* —**mo·bi·liz·a·ble** *adj.* —**mo·bi·li·za·tion** /,mōbələ'zāSHən/ *n.* —**mo·bi·liz·er** *n.*

Mö·bi·us strip /'mōbēəs/ ▸*n.* a surface with one continuous side formed by joining the ends of a rectangular strip after twisting one end through 180°.

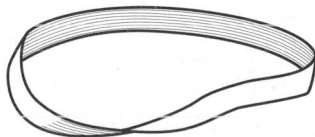

Möbius strip

mo·blog /'mō,bläg/ ▸*n.* a weblog whose content originates from cell phones and other portable wireless devices.

mob·ster /'mäbstər/ ▸*n. inf.* a member of a group of violent criminals; a gangster.

moc·ca·sin /'mäkəsən/ ▸*n.* **1** a soft leather slipper or shoe, without a separate heel, having the sole turned up on all sides and sewn to the upper in a simple gathered seam, in a style originating among North American Indians. **2** an American pit viper (genus *Agkistrodon*). Its several species include the **water moccasin** (see COTTONMOUTH) and the **highland moccasin** (see COPPERHEAD) .

mo·cha /'mōkə/ ▸*n.* **1** a fine-quality coffee. ■ a drink or flavoring made with or in imitation of this, typically with chocolate added. ■ a dark brown color. **2** a soft kind of leather made from sheepskin.

mock /mäk/ ▸*v.* [*tr.*] tease or laugh at in a scornful or contemptuous manner. ■ make (something) seem laughably unreal or impossible: *at Christmas, arguments and friction mock our pretense of peace.* ■ mimic (someone or something) scornfully or contemptuously.
▸*adj.* not authentic or real, but without the intention to deceive: *a mock-Georgian red brick house* | *Jim threw up his hands in mock horror.* ■ (of an examination, battle, etc.) arranged for training or practice, or performed as a demonstration.
▸*n. dated* an object of derision: *he has become the mock of all his contemporaries.* —**mock·a·ble** *adj.* —**mock·er** *n.* —**mock·ing·ly** *adv.*

mock·er·y /'mäk(ə)rē/ ▸*n.* (*pl.* **-er·ies**) derision; ridicule. ■ an absurd misrepresentation or imitation of something: *after a mockery of a trial in London, he was executed.* ■ *archaic* ludicrously futile action: *in her bitterness she felt that all rejoicing was mockery.*

mock·ing·bird /'mäkiNG,bərd/ ▸*n.* a long-tailed thrushlike songbird (*Mimus* and other genera) with grayish plumage, noted for its mimicry of the calls and songs of other birds. The **mockingbird family** (Mimidae) also includes the catbirds and thrashers.

mock or·ange ▸*n.* a bushy shrub (genus *Philadelphus*) of the hydrangea family of north temperate regions that is cultivated for its strongly scented white flowers whose perfume resembles orange blossom.

mock-up (also **mock·up**) ▸*n.* a model or replica of a machine or structure, used for instructional or experimental purposes. ■ an arrangement of text and pictures to be printed.

mod /mäd/ ▸*adj. inf.* modern.
▸*n. Brit.* (esp. in the early 1960s) a young person of a subculture characterized by stylish dress and a liking for soul music.

mod·al /'mōdl/ ▸*adj.* **1** of or relating to mode or form as opposed to substance. **2** *Gram.* of or denoting the mood of a verb. **3** *Statistics* of or relating to a mode; occurring most frequently in a sample or population. **4** *Mus.* of or denoting music using melodies or harmonies based on modes other than the ordinary major and minor scales.
▸*n. Gram.* a modal word or construction. —**mod·al·ly** /'mōdl-ē/ *adv.*

mo·dal·i·ty /mō'dalitē/ ▸*n.* (*pl.* **-ties**) **1** modal quality: *the harmony had a touch of modality.* **2** a particular mode in which something exists or is experienced or expressed. ■ a particular method or procedure: *questions concerning the modalities of Soviet troop withdrawals.* ■ a particular form of sensory perception: *the visual and auditory modalities.*

mode /mōd/ ▸*n.* **1** a way or manner in which something occurs or is experienced, expressed, or done: *his preferred mode of travel was a kayak* | *differences between language modes, namely speech and writing.* ■ an option allowing a change in the method of operation of a device, esp. a camera: *a camcorder in automatic mode.* ■ *Comput.* a way of operating or using a system: *some computers provide several so-called processor modes.* ■ *Physics* any of the distinct kinds or patterns of vibration of an oscillating system. **2** a fashion or style in clothes, art, literature, etc. **3** *Statistics* the value that occurs most frequently in a given set of data. **4** *Mus.* a set of musical notes forming a scale and from which melodies and harmonies are constructed.

mod·el /'mädl/ ▸*n.* **1** a three-dimensional representation of a person or thing or of a proposed structure, typically on a smaller scale than the original. ■ (in sculpture) a figure or object made in clay or wax, to be reproduced in another more durable material. **2** a system or thing used as an example to follow or imitate: *a model for dozens of laws banning nondegradable plastic products* | [as *adj.*] *a model farm.* ■ a simplified description, esp. a mathematical one, of a system or process, to assist calculations and predictions: *a statistical model.* ■ (**model of**) a person or thing regarded as an excellent example of a specified quality: *as she grew older, she became a model of self-control* | [as *adj.*] *he was a model husband and father.* ■ (**model for**) an actual person or place on which a specified fictional character or location is based: *the author denied that Marilyn was the model for his tragic heroine.* **3** a person, typically a woman, employed to display clothes by wearing them: *a fashion model.* ■ a person employed to pose for an artist, photographer, or sculptor. **4** a particular design or version of a product: *trading your car in for a newer model.*
▸*v.* (**-eled, -el·ing**; *Brit.* **-elled, -el·ling**) [*tr.*] **1** fashion or shape (a three-dimensional figure or object) in a malleable material such as clay or wax. ■ (in drawing or painting) represent so as to appear

three-dimensional: *the body of the woman to the right is modeled in softer, riper forms.* ■ (**model something on/after**) use (esp. a system or procedure) as an example to follow or imitate: *the research method will be modeled on previous work.* ■ (**model oneself on**) take (someone admired or respected) as an example to copy: *he models himself on Elvis Presley.* ■ devise a representation, esp. a mathematical one, of (a phenomenon or system): *a computer program that can model how smoke behaves.* **2** display (clothes) by wearing them. ■ [*intr.*] work as a model by displaying clothes or posing for an artist, photographer, or sculptor. —**mod·el·er** /ˈmädl-ər/ *n.*

mo·dem /ˈmōdəm; ˈmōˌdem/ ▶*n.* a combined device for modulation and demodulation, for example, between the digital data of a computer and the analog signal of a telephone line.
▶*v.* [*tr.*] send (data) by modem.

mod·er·ate ▶*adj.* /ˈmäd(ə)rət/ average in amount, intensity, quality, or degree: *we walked at a moderate pace.* ■ (of a person, party, or policy); not radical or excessively right- or left-wing: *a moderate reform program.*
▶*n.* /ˈmäd(ə)rət/ a person who holds moderate views, esp. in politics.
▶*v.* /ˈmädəˌrāt/ **1** make or become less extreme, intense, rigorous, or violent. **2** [*tr.*] (in academic and ecclesiastical contexts) preside over (a deliberative body) or at (a debate): *a panel moderated by a Harvard University law professor.* ■ [*intr.*] preside; act as a moderator. **3** [*tr.*] *Physics* retard (neutrons) with a moderator. —**mod·er·ate·ly** *adv.* —**mod·er·at·ism** /-ˌtizəm/ *n.*

mod·er·a·tion /ˌmädəˈrāSHən/ ▶*n.* the avoidance of excess or extremes, esp. in one's behavior or political opinions: *he urged the police to show moderation.* ■ the action of making something less extreme, intense, or violent: *the union's approach was based on increased dialogue and the moderation of demands.*
▶ □ **in moderation** within reasonable limits; not to excess: *nuts can be eaten in moderation.*

mod·e·ra·to /ˌmädəˈrätō/ *Mus.* ▶*adv.* & *adj.* (esp. as a direction after a tempo marking) at a moderate pace: *allegro moderato.*

mod·er·a·tor /ˈmädəˌrātər/ ▶*n.* **1** an arbitrator or mediator: *Egypt managed to assert its role as a regional moderator.* **2** *Physics* a substance used in a nuclear reactor to retard neutrons. —**mod·er·a·tor·ship** /-ˌSHip/ *n.*

mod·ern /ˈmädərn/ ▶*adj.* of or relating to the present or recent times as opposed to the remote past. ■ characterized by or using the most up-to-date techniques, ideas, or equipment: *they do not have modern weapons.* ■ denoting the form of a language that is currently used, as opposed to any earlier form: *modern German.* ■ denoting a current or recent style or trend in art, architecture, or other cultural activity marked by a significant departure from traditional styles and values.
▶*n.* (usu. **moderns**) a person who advocates or practices a departure from traditional styles or values. —**mod·ern·ist** *n.* —**mod·ern·is·tic** /ˌmädərˈnistik/ *adj.* —**mo·der·ni·ty** /mäˈdərnitē; mə-; -ˈder-/ *n.* —**mod·ern·ly** *adv.* —**mod·ern·ness** *n.*

mod·ern Eng·lish ▶*n.* the English language as it has been since about 1500.

mod·ern·ism /ˈmädərˌnizəm/ ▶*n.* modern character or quality of thought, expression, or technique. ■ a style or movement in the arts that aims to break with classical and traditional forms.

mod·ern·ize /ˈmädərˌnīz/ ▶*v.* [*tr.*] adapt (something) to modern needs or habits, typically by installing modern equipment or adopting modern ideas or methods: *a five-year plan to modernize Algerian agriculture.* —**mod·ern·i·za·tion** /ˌmädərnəˈzāSHən/ *n.* —**mod·ern·iz·er** *n.*

mod·est /ˈmädəst/ ▶*adj.* **1** unassuming or moderate in the estimation of one's abilities or achievements. **2** (of an amount, rate, or level of something) relatively moderate, limited, or small: *drink modest amounts of alcohol* | *employment growth was relatively modest.* ■ (of a place in which one lives, eats, or stays) not excessively large, elaborate, or expensive: *we had bought a modest house.* **3** (of a woman) dressing or behaving so as to avoid impropriety or indecency, esp. to avoid attracting sexual attention. ■ (of clothing) not revealing or emphasizing the figure. —**mod·est·ly** *adv.*

mod·es·ty /ˈmädəstē/ ▶*n.* the quality or state of being unassuming or moderate in the estimation of one's abilities. ■ the quality of being relatively moderate, limited, or small in amount, rate, or level: *the modesty of his aspirations.* ■ behavior, manner, or appearance intended to avoid impropriety or indecency.

mod·i·cum /ˈmädikəm; ˈmōd-/ ▶*n.* a small quantity of a particular thing, esp. something considered desirable or valuable: *his statement had more than a modicum of truth.*

mod·i·fi·ca·tion /ˌmädəfəˈkāSHən/ ▶*n.* the action of modifying something: *the parts supplied should fit with little or no modification.* ■ a change made: *there will be a number of modifications to the engines.*

mod·i·fi·er /ˈmädəˌfīər/ ▶*n.* a person or thing that makes partial or minor changes to something. ■ *Gram.* a word, esp. an adjective or noun used attributively, that restricts or adds to the sense of a head noun (e.g., *good* and *family* in *a good family house*). ■ *Genetics* a gene that modifies the phenotypic expression of a gene at another locus.

mod·i·fy /ˈmädəˌfī/ ▶*v.* (**-fies, -fied**) [*tr.*] make partial or minor changes to (something), typically so as to improve it or to make it less extreme: *she may be prepared to modify her views* | [as *adj.*] (**modified**) *a modified version of the aircraft.* ■ *Biol.* transform (a structure) from its original anatomical form during development or evolution. ■ *Gram.* (esp. of an adjective) restrict or add to the sense of (a noun): *the target noun is modified by a 'direction' word.* —**mod·i·fi·a·ble** *adj.* —**mod·i·fi·ca·to·ry** /ˈmädəfəkəˌtôrē; ˌmädəˈfikəˌtôrē/ *adj.*

mod·ish /ˈmōdiSH/ ▶*adj.* often derog. conforming to or following what is currently popular and fashionable: *it seems sad that a scholar should feel compelled to use this modish jargon.* —**mod·ish·ly** *adv.* —**mod·ish·ness** *n.*

mod·u·lar /ˈmäjələr/ ▶*adj.* employing or involving a module or modules as the basis of design or construction: *modular housing units.* —**mod·u·lar·i·ty** /ˌmäjəˈle(ə)ritē/ *n.*

mod·u·late /ˈmäjəˌlāt/ ▶*v.* [*tr.*] exert a modifying or controlling influence on: *the state attempts to modulate private business's cash flow.* ■ vary the strength, tone, or pitch of (one's voice): *we all modulate our voice by hearing it.* ■ alter the amplitude or frequency of (an electromagnetic wave or other oscillation) in accordance with the variations of a second signal, typically one of a lower frequency: *radio waves are modulated to carry the analog information of the voice.* ■ [*intr.*] *Mus.* change from one key to another: *the first half of the melody, modulating from E minor to G.* ■ [*intr.*] (**modulate into**) change from one form or condition into (another). —**mod·u·la·tion** /ˌmäjəˈlāSHən/ *n.* —**mod·u·la·tor** /-ˌlātər/ *n.*

mod·ule /ˈmäjo͞ol/ ▶*n.* each of a set of standardized parts or independent units that can be used to construct a more complex structure, such as an item of furniture or a building. ■ an independent self-contained unit of a spacecraft. ■ *Comput.* any of a number of distinct but inter-related units from which a program may be built up or into which a complex activity may be analyzed.

mod·u·lus /ˈmäjələs/ *Math.* ▶*n.* (*pl.* **-li** /-ˌlī; -ˌlē/) **1** another term for AB-SOLUTE VALUE. ■ the positive square root of the sum of the squares of the real and imaginary parts of a complex number. **2** a constant factor or ratio. ■ a constant indicating the relation between a physical effect and the force producing it. **3** a number used as a divisor for considering numbers in sets, numbers being considered congruent when giving the same remainder when divided by a particular modulus.

mo·dus op·e·ran·di /ˈmōdəs ˌäpəˈrandē; -ˌdī/ ▶*n.* (*pl.* **mo·di op·e·ran·di** /ˈmōdē; ˈmōdī/) (also **M.O.**) a particular way or method of doing something, esp. one that is characteristic or well-established. ■ the way something operates or works.

mo·dus vi·ven·di /ˈmōdəs vəˈvendē; -ˌdī/ ▶*n.* (*pl.* **mo·di vi·ven·di** /ˈmōdē; ˈmōdī/) an arrangement or agreement allowing conflicting parties to coexist peacefully, either indefinitely or until a final settlement is reached. ■ a way of living.

Mo·gul /ˈmōgəl/ (also **Mo·ghul**) ▶*n.* a member of the Muslim dynasty of Mongol origin founded by the successors of Tamerlane, which ruled much of India from the 16th to the 19th century: [as *adj.*] *Mogul architecture.*

mo·gul[1] /ˈmōgəl/ ▶*n. inf.* an important or powerful person, esp. in the motion picture or media industry.

mo·gul[2] ▶*n.* a bump on a ski slope formed by the repeated turns of skiers over the same path.

mo·hair /ˈmōˌhe(ə)r/ ▶*n.* the long, silky hair of the angora goat. ■ a yarn or fabric made from this, typically mixed with wool.

Mo·ham·me·dan /mōˈhamid(ə)n; mə-/ ▶*n.* & *adj.* variant spelling of MUHAMMADAN.

Mo·hawk /ˈmōˌhôk/ ▶*n.* (*pl.* same or **-hawks**) **1** a member of an American Indian people, one of the Five Nations, originally inhabiting parts of eastern New York. **2** the Iroquoian language of this people. **3** a hairstyle with the head shaved except for a strip of hair from the middle of the forehead to the back of the neck, typically stiffened to stand erect or in spikes.
▶*adj.* of or relating to the Mohawks or their language. ▷from Narragansett *mohowawog*, literally 'man-eaters.'

Mo·he·gan /mōˈhēgən/ (also **Mo·hi·can** /-ˈhēkən/) ▶*n.* **1** a member of an American Indian people formerly inhabiting eastern Connecticut. Compare with MAHICAN. **2** the Algonquian language of this people, closely related to Pequot.
▶*adj.* of or relating to the Mohegans or their language.

Mo·hi·can /mōˈhēkən/ ▶*adj. & n.* old-fashioned variant spelling of **MAHI-CAN** or **MOHEGAN**.

moi·e·ty /ˈmoiətē/ ▶*n.* (pl. **-ties**) *formal* or *technical* each of two parts into which a thing is or can be divided. ■ *Anthropol.* each of two social or ritual groups into which a people is divided. ■ a part or portion, esp. a lesser share. ■ *Chem.* a distinct part of a large molecule: *the enzyme removes the sulfate moiety.*

moi·re /mōˈrā; mwä-; mwär/ (also **moi·ré** /mwäˈrā; mô-/) ▶*n.* silk fabric that has been subjected to heat and pressure rollers after weaving to give it a rippled appearance.
▶*adj.* (of silk) having a rippled, lustrous finish. ■ denoting or showing a pattern of irregular wavy lines like that of such silk.

moist /moist/ ▶*adj.* slightly wet; damp or humid: *the air was moist and heavy.* ■ (of the eyes) wet with tears: *her brother's eyes became moist.* ■ (of a climate) rainy. ■ *Med.* marked by a fluid discharge. —**moist·ly** *adv.* —**moist·ness** *n.*

mois·ten /ˈmoisən/ ▶*v.* [*tr.*] wet slightly: *she moistened her lips with the tip of her tongue.* ■ [*intr.*] (of the eyes) fill with tears: *her eyes moistened.*

mois·ture /ˈmoischər/ ▶*n.* water or other liquid diffused in a small quantity as vapor, within a solid, or condensed on a surface. —**mois·ture·less** *adj.*

mois·tur·ize /ˈmoischəˌrīz/ ▶*v.* [*tr.*] make (something, esp. the skin) less dry. —**mois·tur·iz·er** *n.*

mol /mōl/ *Chem.* ▶*abbr.* **MOLE**⁴.

mo·lar¹ /ˈmōlər/ ▶*n.* a grinding tooth at the back of a mammal's mouth.

mo·lar² ▶*adj.* of or relating to mass; acting on or by means of large masses or units.

mo·lar³ ▶*adj. Chem.* of or relating to one mole of a substance. ■ (of a solution) containing one mole of solute per liter of solvent. —**mo·lar·i·ty** /mōˈler(ə)itē/ *n.*

mo·las·ses /məˈlasəz/ ▶*n.* thick, dark brown, uncrystallized juice obtained from raw sugar during the refining process. ■ a paler, sweeter version of this used as a table syrup and in baking.

mold¹ /mōld/ (*Brit.* **mould**) ▶*n.* a hollow container used to give shape to molten or hot liquid material (such as wax or metal) when it cools and hardens. ■ something made in this way, esp. a gelatin dessert or a mousse. ■ *fig.* a distinctive and typical style, form, or character: *a roving reporter in the mold of his hero* | *the latest policy document is still stuck in the old mold.*
▶*v.* [*tr.*] form (an object with a particular shape) out of easily manipulated material. ■ give a shape to (a malleable substance). ■ influence the formation or development of: *the professionals helping to mold U.S. policy.* ■ shape (clothing) to fit a particular part of the body: [as *adj.*] (**molded**) *a shoe with molded insole.* ■ [often as *adj.*] (**molded**) shape (a column, ceiling, or other part of a building) to a particular design, esp. a decorative molding: *a corridor with a lovely molded cornice.* —**mold·a·ble** *adj.* —**mold·er** *n.*

mold² (*Brit.* **mould**) ▶*n.* a furry growth of minute fungal hyphae (subdivision Deuteromycotina, or Ascomycotina) occurring typically in moist conditions, esp. on food or other organic matter.

mold³ (*Brit.* **mould**) ▶*n.* soft loose earth. ■ the upper soil of cultivated land, esp. when rich in organic matter.

mold·er /ˈmōldər/ (*Brit.* **mould·er**) ▶*v.* [*intr.*] [often as *adj.*] (**moldering**) slowly decay or disintegrate, esp. because of neglect.| *fig.* *I couldn't permit someone of your abilities to molder away in a backwater.*

mold·ing /ˈmōldiNG/ (*Brit.* **mould·ing**) ▶*n.* an ornamentally shaped outline as an architectural feature, esp. in a cornice. ■ material such as wood, plastic, or stone shaped for use as a decorative or architectural feature.

mold·y /ˈmōldē/ (*Brit.* **mould·y**) ▶*adj.* (**mold·i·er, mold·i·est**) covered with a fungal growth that causes decay, due to age or damp conditions: *moldy bread.* ■ tediously old-fashioned: *moldy conventions.* —**mold·i·ness** *n.*

mole¹ /mōl/ ▶*n.* **1** a small burrowing insectivorous mammal (family Talpidae) with dark velvety fur, a long muzzle, and very small eyes. **2** a spy who achieves over a long period an important position within the security defenses of a country. ■ someone within an organization who anonymously betrays confidential information.

mole² /mōl/ ▶*n.* a small, often slightly raised blemish on the skin made dark by a high concentration of melanin.

mole³ /mōl/ ▶*n.* a large solid structure on a shore serving as a pier, breakwater, or causeway.

mole⁴ /mōl/ ▶*n. Chem.* the SI unit of amount of substance, equal to the quantity containing as many elementary units as there are atoms in 0.012 kg of carbon-12.

mo·le⁵ /ˈmōlā/ ▶*n.* a highly spiced Mexican sauce made chiefly from chili peppers and flavored with chocolate, served with meat.

mo·lec·u·lar /məˈlekyələr/ ▶*adj.* of, relating to, or consisting of molecules. —**mo·lec·u·lar·i·ty** /məˌlekyəˈle(ə)ritē/ *n.* —**mo·lec·u·lar·ly** *adv.*

mol·e·cule /ˈmäləˌkyōōl/ ▶*n. Chem.* a group of atoms bonded together, representing the smallest fundamental unit of a chemical compound that can take part in a chemical reaction.

mole·hill /ˈmōlˌhil/ ▶*n.* a small mound of earth thrown up by a mole burrowing near the surface.
▶ □ **make a mountain out of a molehill** exaggerate the importance of something trivial.

mole·skin /ˈmōlˌskin/ ▶*n.* **1** the skin of a mole used as fur. **2** a thick, strong cotton fabric with a shaved pile surface: [as *adj.*] *a moleskin coat.* ■ (**moleskins**) clothes, esp. trousers, made of such a fabric. ■ a soft fabric with adhesive backing used as a foot bandage.

mo·lest /məˈlest/ ▶*v.* [*tr.*] pester or harass (someone), typically in an aggressive or persistent manner: *the crowd was molesting the two police officers.* ■ assault or abuse (a person, esp. a woman or child) sexually. —**mo·les·ta·tion** /ˌmō·le-; ˌmōlə'stāSHən/ *n.* —**mo·lest·er** *n.*

moll /mäl/ ▶*n. inf.* **1** (also **gun moll**) a gangster's female companion. **2** a prostitute.

mol·li·fy /ˈmäləˌfī/ ▶*v.* (**-fies, -fied**) [*tr.*] appease the anger or anxiety of (someone): *nature reserves were set up around the power stations to mollify local conservationists.* ■ *rare* reduce the severity of (something); soften. —**mol·li·fi·ca·tion** /ˌmäləfəˈkāSHən/ *n.* —**mol·li·fi·er** *n.*

mol·lusk /ˈmäləsk/ (*chiefly Brit.* also **mollusc**) ▶*n.* an invertebrate of a large phylum (Mollusca) that includes snails, slugs, mussels, and octopuses. They have a soft, unsegmented body and live in aquatic or damp habitats, and most kinds have an external calcareous shell. —**mol·lus·kan** /məˈləsˌkən/ (or **mol·lus·can**) *adj.*

mol·ly·cod·dle /ˈmäléˌkädl/ ▶*v.* [*tr.*] treat (someone) very indulgently or protectively.
▶*n.* an effeminate or ineffectual man or boy; a milksop.

Mo·lo·tov cock·tail ▶*n.* a crude incendiary device typically consisting of a bottle filled with flammable liquid and with a means of ignition.

molt /mōlt/ (*Brit.* **moult**) ▶*v.* [*intr.*] (of an animal) shed old feathers, hair, or skin, or an old shell, to make way for new growth: *the adult birds were already molting into their winter shades of gray* | [*tr.*] *the snake molts its skin.* ■ (of hair or feathers) fall out to make way for new growth: *the last of his juvenile plumage had molted.*
▶*n.* a loss of plumage, skin, or hair, esp. as a regular feature of an animal's life cycle.

mol·ten /ˈmōltn/ ▶*adj.* (esp. of materials with a high melting point, such as metal and glass) liquefied by heat.

mol·to /ˈmōl,tō; 'môl-/ ▶*adv. Mus.* (in directions) very: *molto adagio.*

mo·lyb·de·num /məˈlibdənəm/ ▶*n.* the chemical element of atomic number 42, a brittle silver-gray metal of the transition series, used in some alloy steels. (Symbol: **Mo**)

mom /mäm/ ▶*n. inf.* one's mother.

mom-and-pop ▶*adj. inf.* denoting a small store or business of a type often run by a married couple.

mo·ment /ˈmōmənt/ ▶*n.* **1** a very brief period of time. ■ an exact point in time: *she would always remember the moment they met.* ■ an appropriate time for doing something; an opportunity: *I was waiting for the right moment.* ■ a particular stage in something's development or in a course of events: *one of the great moments in aviation history.* **2** *formal* importance: *the issues were of little moment to the electorate.* **3** *Physics* a turning effect produced by a force acting at a distance on an object. **4** *Statistics* a quantity that expresses the average or expected value of the first, second, third, or fourth power of the deviation of each component of a frequency distribution from some given value, typically mean or zero. The **first moment** is the mean, the **second moment** the variance, the **third moment** the skew, and the **fourth moment** the kurtosis.
▶ □ **any moment** (or **at any moment**) very soon. □ **at the** (or **this**) **moment** at the present time; now. □ **for the moment** for now. □ **in a moment 1** very soon: *I'll be back in a moment.* **2** instantly. □ **moment of truth** a time when a person or thing is tested, a decision has to be made, or a crisis has to be faced. □ **not for a** (or **one**) **moment** not at all; never. □ **of the moment** currently popular, famous, or important: *the buzzword of the moment.*

mo·men·tar·i·ly /ˌmōmənˈte(ə)rəlē/ ▶*adv.* **1** for a very short time: *as he*

passed Jenny's door, he paused momentarily. **2** at any moment; very soon: *my husband will be here to pick me up momentarily.*

mo·men·tar·y /'mōmən,terē/ ▶*adj.* lasting for a very short time; brief: *a momentary lapse of concentration.* —**mo·men·tar·i·ness** *n.*

mo·men·tous /mō'men(t)əs; mə'-/ ▶*adj.* (of a decision, event, or change) of great importance or significance, esp. in its bearing on the future. —**mo·men·tous·ly** *adv.* —**mo·men·tous·ness** *n.*

mo·men·tum /mō'mentəm; mə-/ ▶*n.* (*pl.* **-ta** /-tə/ or **-tums**) **1** *Physics* the quantity of motion of a moving body, measured as a product of its mass and velocity. **2** the impetus gained by a moving object: *the vehicle gained momentum as the road dipped.* ■ the impetus and driving force gained by the development of a process or course of events: *the investigation gathered momentum in the spring.* ▷late 17th cent.: from Latin, from *movimentum*, from *movere* 'to move.'

mom·ma ▶*n.* variant spelling of MAMA.

mom·my /'mämē/ ▶*n.* (*pl.* **-mies**) *inf.* one's mother (chiefly as a child's term).

Mon /mōn/ ▶*n.* (*pl.* same or **Mons**) **1** a member of a people now inhabiting parts of southeastern Myanmar (Burma) and western Thailand but having their ancient capital at Pegu in southern Myanmar. **2** the language of this people, related to Khmer (Cambodian). ▶*adj.* of or relating to this people or their language.

mon·ad /'mō,nad/ ▶*n.* *technical* a single unit; the number one. ■ *dated Biol.* a single-celled organism, esp. a flagellate protozoan, or a single cell. —**mo·nad·ic** /mō'nadik; mə-/ *adj.* —**mon·ad·ism** /-,izəm/ *n.* (*Philos.*).

mon·arch /'mänərk; 'män,ärk/ ▶*n.* **1** a sovereign head of state, esp. a king, queen, or emperor. **2** see MONARCH BUTTERFLY. —**mo·nar·chal** /mə'närkəl/ *adj.* —**mo·nar·chi·al** /mə'närkēəl/ *adj.* —**mo·nar·chic** /mə'närkik/ *adj.* —**mo·nar·chi·cal** /mə'närkikəl/ *adj.* —**mo·nar·chi·cal·ly** /mə'närkik(ə)lē/ *adv.*

mon·arch but·ter·fly (also **monarch**) ▶*n.* a large migratory orange and black butterfly (*Danaus plexippus*, family Nymphalidae) that occurs mainly in North America and whose caterpillar feeds on milkweed.

mon·ar·chism /'mänər,kizəm; 'män,är-/ ▶*n.* support for the principle of having monarchs. —**mon·ar·chist** *n.* & *adj.*

mon·ar·chy /'mänərkē; 'män,är-/ ▶*n.* (*pl.* **-chies**) a form of government with a monarch at the head. ■ a state that has a monarch. ■ (**the monarchy**) the monarch and royal family of a country.

mon·as·ter·y /'mänə,sterē/ ▶*n.* (*pl.* **-ter·ies**) a community of persons, esp. monks or nuns, living under religious vows. ■ the place of residence occupied by such persons.

mo·nas·tic /mə'nastik/ ▶*adj.* of or relating to monks, nuns, or others living under religious vows, or the buildings in which they live: *a monastic order.* ■ resembling or suggestive of monks or their way of life, esp. in being austere, solitary, or celibate: *a monastic student bedroom.* ▶*n.* a monk or other follower of a monastic rule. —**mo·nas·ti·cal·ly** /-ik(ə)lē/ *adv.* —**mo·nas·ti·cism** /-tə,sizəm/ *n.*

mon·a·tom·ic /,mänə'tämik/ ▶*adj.* *Chem.* consisting of one atom.

Mon·day /'məndā; -dē/ ▶*n.* the day of the week before Tuesday and following Sunday. ▶*adv.* on Monday: *I'll call you Monday.* ■ (**Mondays**) on Mondays; each Monday: *the restaurant is closed Mondays.*

mon·e·ta·rism /'mänitə,rizəm; 'mən-/ ▶*n.* the theory or practice of controlling the supply of money as the chief method of stabilizing the economy. —**mon·e·ta·rist** *n.* & *adj.*

mon·e·tar·y /'mänə,terē; 'mən-/ ▶*adj.* of or relating to money or currency. —**mon·e·tar·i·ly** /-,te(ə)rəlē/ *adv.*

mon·ey /'mənē/ ▶*n.* a current medium of exchange in the form of coins and banknotes; coins and banknotes collectively: *I counted the money before putting it in my wallet.* ■ (**moneys** or **monies**) *formal* sums of money: *a statement of all moneys paid into and out of the account.* ■ the assets, property, and resources owned by someone or something; wealth. ■ payment for work; wages: *she accepted the job at the public school since the money was better.* ■ a wealthy person or group: *her aunt had married money.* —**mon·ey·less** *adj.*
▶ □ **be in the money** *inf.* have or win a lot of money. □ **for my money** in my opinion or judgment: *for my money, they're one of the best bands around.* □ **on the money** accurate; correct: *every criticism she made was right on the money.* □ **put money** (or **put one's money**) **on 1** place a bet on. **2** used to express one's confidence in the truth or success of something: *she won't have him back—I'd put money on it.*

mon·ey·bags /'mänē,bagz/ ▶*pl. n.* [usu. treated as *sing.*] *inf.* a wealthy person.

mon·eyed /'mänēd/ ▶*adj.* having much money; affluent. ■ characterized by affluence: *a moneyed lifestyle.*

mon·ey-grub·bing ▶*adj.* *inf.* overeager to make money; grasping: *money-grubbing speculators.* —**mon·ey-grub·ber** /-,grəbər/ *n.*

mon·ey-lend·er /'mänē,lendər/ (also **mon·ey-lend·er**) ▶*n.* a person whose business is lending money to others who pay interest. —**mon·ey-lend·ing** /-,lendiNG/ *n.* & *adj.*

mon·ey-mak·er /'mänē,mākər/ (also **mon·ey-mak·er**) ▶*n.* a person or thing that earns a lot of money: *the movie became one of the year's top moneymakers.* —**mon·ey-mak·ing** /-,mākiNG/ *n.* & *adj.*

mon·ey mar·ket ▶*n.* the trade in short-term loans between banks and other financial institutions.

mon·ey or·der ▶*n.* a printed order for payment of a specified sum, issued by a bank or post office.

Mon·gol /'mäNGgəl/ ▶*adj.* of or relating to the people of Mongolia or their language. ▶*n.* **1** a native or national of Mongolia; a Mongolian. **2** the language of this people; Mongolian.

Mon·go·li·an /män'gōlēən; mäNG-/ ▶*adj.* of or relating to Mongolia, its people, or their language. ▶*n.* **1** a native or national of Mongolia. **2** the Altaic language of Mongolia, written in an unusual vertical cursive script; related forms are spoken in northern China.

mon·gol·ism /'mäNGgə,lizəm/ ▶*n. offens.* another term for DOWN SYNDROME.

Mon·gol·oid /'mäNGgə,loid/ ▶*adj.* **1** *sometimes offens.* of or relating to the broad division of humankind including the indigenous peoples of eastern Asia, Southeast Asia, and the Arctic region of North America. **2** (**mongoloid**) *often offens.* affected with Down syndrome. ▶*n.* **1** *sometimes offens.* a person of a Mongoloid physical type. **2** *offens.* a person with Down syndrome.

mon·goose /'män,gōōs; 'mäNG-/ ▶*n.* (*pl.* **mongooses** /'mäNG,gōōsəz/) a small carnivorous mammal (*Herpestes*, *Mungos*, and other genera) of the civet family, with a long body and tail and a grizzled or banded coat, native to Africa and Asia. Its many species include the **banded mongoose** (*M. mungo*).

mon·grel /'mäNGgrəl; 'məNG-/ ▶*n.* a dog of no definable type or breed. ■ any other animal resulting from the crossing of different breeds or types. ■ *offens.* a person of mixed descent. —**mon·grel·ism** /-grə,lizəm/ *n.*

'mongst /'məNGst/ ▶*prep. poetic/lit.* short for AMONGST (see AMONG).

mon·ies /'mənēz/ ▶ plural form of MONEY, as used in financial contexts.

mon·i·ker /'mänikər/ (also **mon·ick·er**) ▶*n. inf.* a name, esp. a nickname: *Martha's been answering to the moniker "Ant Pant" for many years now.* —**mon·i·kered** *adj.*

mon·i·tor /'mänətər/ ▶*n.* **1** an instrument or device used for observing, checking, or keeping a continuous record of a process or quantity: *a heart monitor.* ■ a person operating such an instrument or device. ■ a person who observes a process or activity to check that it is carried out fairly or correctly, esp. in an official capacity. **2** a student with disciplinary or other special duties during school hours: *show the hall monitor your pass.* **3** a television receiver used in a studio to select or verify the picture being broadcast from a particular camera. ■ a television that displays an image generated by a computer. ■ a loudspeaker, esp. one used by performers on stage to hear themselves or in the studio to hear what has been recorded. **4** (also **monitor lizard**) a large tropical Old World lizard (genus *Varanus*, family Varanidae) with a long neck, narrow head, forked tongue, strong claws, and a short body. **5** *hist.* a shallow-draft armored warship mounting one or two heavy guns for bombardment.
▶*v.* [*tr.*] observe and check the progress or quality of (something) over a period of time; keep under systematic review: *equipment was installed to monitor air quality.* ■ maintain regular surveillance over: *it was easy for the enemy to monitor his movements.* ■ listen to and report on (a foreign radio broadcast or a telephone conversation). ■ check or regulate the technical quality of (a radio transmission or television signal). —**mon·i·to·ri·al** /,mänə'tôrēəl/ *adj.* —**mon·i·tor·ship** /-,SHip/ *n.*

monk /məNGk/ ▶*n.* a member of a religious community of men typically living under vows of poverty, chastity, and obedience. —**monk·ish** *adj.* —**monk·ish·ly** *adv.* —**monk·ish·ness** *n.*

mon·key /'məNGkē/ ▶*n.* (*pl.* **-eys**) a small to medium-sized primate that typically has a long tail, most kinds of which live in trees in tropical countries. The **New World monkeys** (families Cebidae and Callitrichidae, or Callithricidae) have prehensile tails; the **Old World monkeys** (family Cercopithecidae) do not. ■ (in general use) any primate. ■ a mischievous person, esp. a child: *you little monkey!* ■ *fig.* a person who is dominated or controlled by another (with reference to the monkey traditionally kept by an organ grinder).

▶*v.* (**-keys, -keyed**) [*intr.*] (**monkey around/about**) behave in a silly or playful way. ■ (**monkey with**) tamper with. ■ [*tr.*] *archaic* ape; mimic.
▶ □ **make a monkey of** (or **out of**) **someone** humiliate someone by making them appear ridiculous. □ **a monkey on one's back** *inf.* a burdensome problem. ■ a dependence on drugs.

mon·key busi·ness ▶*n. inf.* mischievous or deceitful behavior.

mon·key·shines /ˈməNGkē,SHīnz/ ▶*pl. n. inf.* mischievous behavior.

mon·key suit ▶*n. inf.* a man's evening dress or formal suit.

mon·key wrench ▶*n.* an adjustable wrench with large jaws that has its adjusting screw contained in the handle.

monk·fish /ˈməNGk,fiSH/ ▶*n.* (*pl.* same or **-fishes**) a bottom-dwelling anglerfish (*Lophius piscatorius*, family Lophiidae) of European waters.

monks·hood /ˈməNGks,hŏŏd/ ▶*n.* an aconite with blue or purple flowers. The upper sepal of the flower covers the topmost petals, giving a hoodlike appearance.

mon·o /ˈmänō/ ▶*adj.* **1** monophonic. **2** monochrome.
▶*n.* (*pl.* **-os**) **1** a monophonic recording. ■ monophonic reproduction. **2** short for INFECTIOUS MONONUCLEOSIS.

mon·o·chro·mat·ic /ˌmänəkrōˈmatik/ ▶*adj.* containing or using only one color: *monochromatic light.* ■ *Physics* (of light or other radiation) of a single wavelength or frequency. ■ lacking in variety; monotonous: *her monochromatic acting style.* —**mon·o·chro·mat·i·cal·ly** /-ik(ə)lē/ *adv.*

mon·o·chrome /ˈmänə,krōm/ ▶*n.* a photograph or picture developed or executed in black and white or in varying tones of only one color. ■ representation or reproduction in black and white or in varying tones of only one color.
▶*adj.* **1** (of a photograph or picture, or a television screen) consisting of or displaying images in black and white or in varying tones of only one color. **2** lacking variety and interest; insipid: *monochrome Broadway productions.* —**mon·o·chrom·ic** /ˌmänəˈkrōmik/ *adj.*

mon·o·cle /ˈmänikəl/ ▶*n.* a single eyeglass, kept in position by the muscles around the eye. —**mon·o·cled** /-kəld/ *adj.*

mon·o·clin·ic /ˌmänəˈklinik/ ▶*adj.* of or denoting a crystal system or three-dimensional geometric arrangement having three unequal axes of which one is at right angles to the other two.

mon·o·clo·nal /ˌmänəˈklōnl/ ▶*adj.* *Biol.* forming a clone that is derived asexually from a single individual or cell.

mon·o·cot /ˈmänə,kät/ ▶*n. Bot.* short for MONOCOTYLEDON.

mon·o·cot·y·le·don /ˌmänə,kätl̍ˈēdn/ ▶*n. Bot.* a flowering plant (class Monocotyledoneae or Liliopsida) with an embryo that bears a single cotyledon (seed leaf). Monocotyledons constitute the smaller of the two great divisions of flowering plants, and typically have elongated stalkless leaves with parallel veins (e.g., grasses, lilies, palms). —**mon·o·cot·y·le·don·ous** /-ˈēdn-əs/ *adj.*

mon·o·crop /ˈmänə,kräp/ ▶*n.* a cultivated crop that does not rotate with other crops in a particular field or area: [as *adj.*] *bananas grown in a monocrop system for commercial production.*

mo·noc·u·lar /məˈnäkyələr; mä-/ ▶*adj.* with, for, or in one eye: *he had only monocular vision.*
▶*n.* an optical instrument for viewing distant objects with one eye, like one half of a pair of binoculars. —**mo·noc·u·lar·ly** *adv.*

mon·o·cyte /ˈmänə,sīt/ ▶*n. Physiol.* a large phagocytic white blood cell with a simple oval nucleus and clear, grayish cytoplasm.

mon·o·fil·a·ment /ˌmänəˈfiləmənt/ (also **mon·o·fil** /ˈmänə,fil/) ▶*n.* a single strand of synthetic fiber.

mo·nog·a·my /məˈnägəmē/ ▶*n.* the practice or state of being married to one person at a time. ■ the practice or state of having a sexual relationship with only one partner. ■ *Zool.* the habit of having only one mate at a time. —**mo·nog·a·mist** /-mist/ *n.* —**mo·nog·a·mous** /-məs/ *adj.* —**mo·nog·a·mous·ly** /-məslē/ *adv.*

mon·o·gen·e·sis /ˌmänəˈjenəsəs/ ▶*n.* the theory that humans are all descended from a single pair of ancestors. —**mon·o·ge·net·ic** /-jəˈnetik/ *adj.*

mon·o·glot /ˈmänə,glät/ ▶*adj.* using or speaking only one language: *the moment when the monoglot heroine suddenly finds she can understand French.*
▶*n.* a person who speaks only one language.

mon·o·gram /ˈmänə,gram/ ▶*n.* a motif of two or more letters, typically a person's initials, usually interwoven or otherwise combined in a decorative design, used as a logo or to identify a personal possession.
▶*v.* [*tr.*] decorate with a monogram: [as *adj.*] (**monogrammed**) *monogrammed sheets.* —**mon·o·gram·mat·ic** /ˌmänəgrəˈmatik/ *adj.*

mon·o·graph /ˈmänə,graf/ ▶*n.* a detailed written study of a single specialized subject or an aspect of it: *a series of monographs on music in late medieval and Renaissance cities.*
▶*v.* [*tr.*] write a monograph on; treat in a monograph. —**mo·nog·ra·pher**
/məˈnägrəfər/ *n.* —**mon·o·graph·ic** /ˌmänəˈgrafik/ *adj.* —**mo·nog·ra·phist** /məˈnägrəfist/ *n.*

mon·o·line /ˈmänə,līn/ ▶*n.* a company specializing in a single type of financial service, such as consumer credit, home mortgages, or a sole class of insurance.

mon·o·lin·gual /ˌmänəˈliNGg(yə)wəl/ ▶*adj.* (of a person or society) speaking only one language: *monolingual families.* ■ (of a text, conversation, etc.) written or conducted in only one language: *monolingual and bilingual editions.*
▶*n.* a person who speaks only one language. —**mon·o·lin·gual·ism** /-,lizəm/ *n.*

mon·o·lith /ˈmänl-ith/ ▶*n.* **1** a large single upright block of stone, esp. one shaped into or serving as a pillar or monument. ■ a very large and characterless building: *the 72-story monolith overlooking the waterfront.* **2** a large and impersonal political, corporate, or social structure regarded as intractably indivisible and uniform. —**mon·o·lith·ic** /ˌmänəˈliTHik/ *adj.*

mon·o·logue /ˈmänl,ôg; -,äg/ ▶*n.* a long speech by one actor in a play or movie, or as part of a theatrical or broadcast program. ■ the form or style of such speeches: *the play oscillates between third-person narration and monologue.* ■ a long and typically tedious speech by one person during a conversation: *Fred carried on with his monologue as if I hadn't spoken.* —**mon·o·log·ic** /ˌmänl̍ˈäjik/ *adj.* —**mon·o·log·i·cal** /ˌmänl̍ˈäjikəl/ *adj.* —**mon·o·log·ist** /məˈnäləjist/ (also **mon·o·logu·ist**) *n.* —**mon·o·log·ize** /məˈnälə,jīz/ *v.*

mon·o·ma·ni·a /ˌmänəˈmänēə/ ▶*n.* exaggerated or obsessive enthusiasm for or preoccupation with one thing. —**mon·o·ma·ni·ac** /-ˈmänē-,ak/ *n. & adj.* —**mon·o·ma·ni·a·cal** /-məˈnīəkəl/ *adj.*

mon·o·mer /ˈmänəmər/ ▶*n. Chem.* a molecule that can be bonded to other identical molecules to form a polymer. —**mon·o·mer·ic** /ˌmänə-ˈmerik/ *adj.*

mon·o·nu·cle·o·sis /ˌmänə,n(y)ōōklēˈōsəs/ ▶*n. Med.* an abnormally high proportion of monocytes in the blood. ■ short for INFECTIOUS MONONUCLEOSIS. Also called MONO, GLANDULAR FEVER.

mon·o·phon·ic /ˌmänəˈfänik/ ▶*adj.* **1** *Mus.* consisting of a single musical line, without accompaniment: *the style of monophonic singing known as Gregorian chant.* **2** (of sound reproduction) using only one channel of transmission. —**mon·o·phon·i·cal·ly** /-ik(ə)lē/ *adv.* —**mo·noph·o·ny** /mə-ˈnäfənē/ *n.*

mo·nop·o·lize /məˈnäpə,līz/ ▶*v.* [*tr.*] (of an organization or group) obtain exclusive possession or control of (a trade, commodity, or service). —**mo·nop·o·li·za·tion** /mə,näpələˈzāsHən/ *n.* —**mo·nop·o·liz·er** *n.*

mo·nop·o·ly /məˈnäpəlē/ ▶*n.* (*pl.* **-lies**) the exclusive possession or control of the supply or trade in a commodity or service: *his regional monopoly on furs.* ■ the exclusive possession, control, or exercise of something: *men don't have a monopoly on unrequited love.* ■ a company or group having exclusive control over a commodity or service: *areas where cable companies operate as monopolies.* ■ a commodity or service controlled in this way: *electricity, gas, and water were considered to be natural monopolies.* ▷mid 16th cent.: via Latin from Greek *monopōlion,* from *monos* 'single' + *pōlein* 'sell.' —**mo·nop·o·lis·tic** /mə,näpəˈlistik/ *adj.*

mon·o·rail /ˈmänə,rāl/ ▶*n.* a railroad in which the track consists of a single rail, typically elevated, with the trains suspended from it or balancing on it.

mon·o·sac·cha·ride /ˌmänəˈsakə,rīd/ ▶*n. Chem.* any of the class of sugars (e.g., glucose) that cannot be hydrolyzed to give a simpler sugar.

mon·o·so·di·um glu·ta·mate /ˌmänə,sōdēəm ˈglōōtə,māt/ (abbr.: **MSG**) ▶*n.* a compound that occurs naturally as a breakdown product of proteins and is used as a flavor enhancer in food.

mon·o·syl·lab·ic /ˌmänəsəˈlabik/ ▶*adj.* (of a word or utterance) consisting of one syllable. ■ (of a person) using brief words to signify reluctance to engage in conversation: *the nearer they came to Rome, the more monosyllabic Paul seemed to become.* —**mon·o·syl·lab·i·cal·ly** /-ik(ə)lē/ *adv.*

mon·o·syl·la·ble /ˌmänəˈsiləbəl; ˈmänə,sil-/ ▶*n.* a word consisting of only one syllable. ■ (**monosyllables**) brief words, signifying reluctance to engage in conversation: *if she spoke at all it was in monosyllables.*

mon·o·the·ism /ˈmänə,THēˌizəm/ ▶*n.* the doctrine or belief that there is only one God. —**mon·o·the·ist** *n. & adj.* —**mon·o·the·is·tic** /ˌmänəTHē-ˈistik/ *adj.* —**mon·o·the·is·ti·cal·ly** /ˌmänəTHēˈistik(ə)lē/ *adv.*

mon·o·tone /ˈmänə,tōn/ ▶*n.* a continuing sound, esp. of someone's voice, that is unchanging in pitch and without intonation.

▸*adj.* (of a voice or other sound) unchanging in pitch; without intonation or expressiveness: *his monotone reading of the two-hour report.* ■ *fig.* without vividness or variety; dull: *monotone housing developments.* ■ of a single color.

mo·not·o·nous /mə'nätn-əs/ ▸*adj.* dull, tedious, and repetitious; lacking in variety and interest. ■ (of a sound or utterance) lacking in variation in tone or pitch. —**mo·not·o·nous·ly** *adv.*

mo·not·o·ny /mə'nätn-ē/ ▸*n.* lack of variety and interest; tedious repetition and routine. ■ sameness of pitch or tone in a sound or utterance: *depression flattens the voice almost to monotony.*

mon·o·treme /'mänə,trēm/ ▸*n.* Zool. a primitive mammal that lays large yolky eggs and has a common opening for the urogenital and digestive systems. Monotremes are now restricted to Australia and New Guinea, and comprise the platypus and the echidnas.

mon·o·va·lent /,mänə'vālənt/ ▸*adj.* Chem. having a valence of one.

mon·ox·ide /mə'näk,sīd/ ▸*n.* Chem. an oxide containing one atom of oxygen in its molecule or empirical formula.

Mon·roe Doc·trine /mən'rō/ ▸a principle of U.S. policy, originated by President James Monroe in 1823, that any intervention by external powers in the politics of the Americas is a potentially hostile act against the U.S.

Mon·sei·gneur /,mōNsān'yər/ ▸*n.* (pl. **Mes·sei·gneurs** /,māsān'yər(z)/) a title or form of address used of or to a French-speaking prince, cardinal, archbishop, or bishop.

Mon·sieur /mə'syœ(r); mə'syər/ ▸*n.* (pl. **Mes·sieurs** /mə'syœ(r)(z); mā-; mə'syər(z)/) a title or form of address used of or to a French-speaking man, corresponding to *Mr.* or *sir*: *Monsieur Hulot | you are right, Monsieur.*

Mon·si·gnor /män'sēnyər; mən-/ ▸*n.* (pl. **Mon·si·gno·ri** /,mänsēn'yôrē/) the title of various senior Roman Catholic positions, such as a prelate or an officer of the papal court.

mon·soon /män'sōōn; 'män,sōōn/ ▸*n.* a seasonal prevailing wind in the region of the Indian subcontinent and Southeast Asia, blowing from the southwest between May and September and bringing rain (the **wet monsoon**), or from the northeast between October and April (the **dry monsoon**). ■ the rainy season accompanying the wet monsoon. —**mon·soon·al** /män'sōōnl/ *adj.*

mons pu·bis /'mänz 'pyōōbis/ ▸*n.* (pl. **mon·tes p·ubis** /'mäntēz/) the rounded mass of fatty tissue lying over the joint of the pubic bones, in women typically more prominent and also called the **mons ven·e·ris** /'venəris/ .

mon·ster /'mänstər/ ▸*n.* an imaginary creature that is typically large, ugly, and frightening. ■ an inhumanly cruel or wicked person. ■ *often humorous* a person, typically a child, who is rude or badly behaved: *Christopher is already a **little monster**.* ■ a thing or animal that is excessively or dauntingly large: *this is a **monster of** a book.* ■ a congenitally malformed or mutant animal or plant.
▸*adj. inf.* of an extraordinary and daunting size or extent.

mon·stros·i·ty /män'sträsətē/ ▸*n.* (pl. **-ties**) **1** something, esp. a building, that is very large and is considered unsightly. ■ something that is outrageously or offensively wrong. ■ a grossly malformed animal, plant, or person. **2** the state or fact of being monstrous.

mon·strous /'mänstrəs/ ▸*adj.* having the ugly or frightening appearance of a monster. ■ (of a person or an action) inhumanly or outrageously evil or wrong: *it is a monstrous waste of money.* ■ extremely and dauntingly large: *the monstrous tidal wave swamped the countryside.* —**mon·strous·ly** *adv.* —**mon·strous·ness** *n.*

mon·tage /män'täzh; mōn-; mōn-/ ▸*n.* the process or technique of selecting, editing, and piecing together separate sections of film to form a continuous whole. ■ a sequence of film resulting from this: *a dazzling montage of the banquet scene.* ■ the technique of producing a new composite whole from fragments of pictures, text, or music.

mon·tane /män'tān; 'män,tān/ ▸*adj.* of or inhabiting mountainous country: *montane grasslands.*

month /mənTH/ ▸*n.* (also **calendar month**) each of the twelve named periods into which a year is divided. ■ a period of time between the same dates in successive calendar months: *the president's rule was extended for six more months from March 3.* ■ a period of 28 days or four weeks: *the fourth month of pregnancy.* ■ a lunar month.
▸ □ **a month of Sundays** *inf.* a very long, seemingly endless period of time.

month·ly /'mənTHlē/ ▸*adj.* done, produced, or occurring once a month: *the council held monthly meetings.*
▸*adv.* once a month; every month; from month to month: *most of us get paid monthly.*

▸*n.* (pl. **-lies**) **1** a magazine that is published once a month. **2** (**month-lies**) *inf.* a menstrual period.

mon·u·ment /'mänyəmənt/ ▸*n.* a statue, building, or other structure erected to commemorate a famous or notable person or event. ■ a statue or other structure placed by or over a grave in memory of the dead. ■ a building, structure, or site that is of historical importance or interest: *the amphitheater is one of the many Greek monuments in Sicily.* ■ *fig.* an outstanding, enduring, and memorable example of something: *recordings that are a **monument to** the art of playing the piano.* ■ a marker, typically of concrete or stone, placed at the boundary of a piece of property. ▷Middle English (denoting a burial place): via French from Latin *monumentum*, from *monere* 'remind.'

mon·u·men·tal /,mänyə'mentl/ ▸*adj.* great in importance, extent, or size: *a monumental effort.* ■ (of a work of art) great in ambition and scope. ■ of or serving as a monument: *additional details are found in monumental inscriptions.* —**mon·u·men·tal·ism** *n.* —**mon·u·men·tal·i·ty** /,mänyə,men'talətē/ *n.* —**mon·u·men·tal·ly** /-'mentl-ē/ *adv.*

-mony ▸*suffix* forming nouns often denoting an action, state, or quality: *ceremony | harmony.*

moo /mōō/ ▸*v.* (**moos**, **mooed**) [*intr.*] make the characteristic deep vocal sound of a cow.
▸*n.* (pl. **moos**) a sound of this kind.

mooch /mōōCH/ ▸*v. inf.* **1** [*tr.*] ask for or obtain (something) without paying for it: *a bunch of your friends, mooching food* | [*intr.*] *I'm mooching off you all the time.* **2** [*intr.*] (**mooch around/about**) loiter in a bored or listless manner.
▸*n.* (also **mooch·er**) a beggar or scrounger.

mood¹ /mōōd/ ▸*n.* a temporary state of mind or feeling: *he appeared to be in a very good mood about something.* ■ an angry, irritable, or sullen state of mind: *he was obviously **in a mood**.* ■ the atmosphere or pervading tone of something, esp. a work of art: *Monet's "Mornings on the Seine" series, with their hushed and delicate mood.*
▸*adj.* (esp. of music) inducing or suggestive of a particular feeling or state of mind: *mood music | a Chekhov mood piece.*

mood² ▸*n.* Gram. a category of verb use, typically expressing fact (indicative mood), command (imperative mood), question (interrogative mood), wish (optative mood), or conditionality (subjunctive mood). ■ a form or set of forms of a verb in an inflected language such as French, Latin, or Greek, serving to indicate whether it expresses fact, command, wish, or conditionality.

mood swing ▸*n.* an abrupt and apparently unaccountable change of mood.

mood·y /'mōōdē/ ▸*adj.* (**mood·i·er**, **mood·i·est**) (of a person) given to unpredictable changes of mood, esp. sudden bouts of gloominess or sullenness. ■ giving an impression of melancholy or mystery: *grainy film that gives a soft, moody effect.* —**mood·i·ly** /'mōōdl-ē/ *adv.* —**mood·i·ness** *n.*

moon /mōōn/ ▸*n.* (also **Moon**) the natural satellite of the earth, visible (chiefly at night) by reflected light from the sun. ■ a natural satellite of any planet. ■ (**the moon**) *fig.* anything that one could desire: *you must know he'd give any of us the moon.* ■ a month, esp. a lunar month.
▸*v.* **1** [*intr.*] behave or move in a listless and aimless manner. ■ act in a dreamily infatuated manner: *Timothy's **mooning over** her like a schoolboy.* **2** [*tr.*] *inf.* expose one's buttocks to (someone) in order to insult or amuse them: *Dan bent over and mooned the crowd.* —**moon·less** *adj.* —**moon·like** /-,līk/ *adj.*

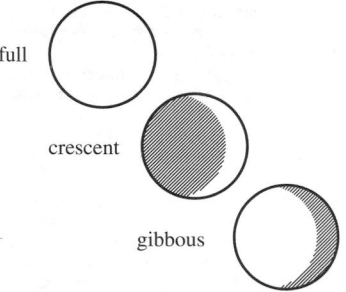

full

crescent

gibbous

phases of the moon

moon·beam /'mōōn,bēm/ ▸*n.* a ray of moonlight.
moon-faced ▸*adj.* having a round face.

moon·light /ˈmo͞onˌlīt/ ▸*n.* the light of the moon: *I wanted you to see the courtyard by moonlight.*
▸*adj.* illuminated or happening by the light of the moon: *a moonlight stroll.*
▸*v.* (*past* and *past part.* **-light·ed**) [*intr.*] *inf.* have a second job in addition to one's regular employment: *many instructors moonlight as professional consultants.* —**moon·light·er** *n.*

moon·lit /ˈmo͞onˌlit/ ▸*adj.* lit by the moon.

moon·rat /ˈmo͞onˌrat/ ▸*n.* a shy insectivorous mammal (several genera and species, in particular *Echinosorex gymnurus*) of the hedgehog family, with a long snout and ratlike appearance, native to Southeast Asia and China.

moon·scape /ˈmo͞onˌskāp/ ▸*n.* a landscape having features characteristic of the surface of the moon, esp. in being rocky and barren: *the once-barren moonscape around Mount St. Helens.*

moon·set /ˈmo͞onˌset/ ▸*n.* the setting of the moon below the horizon. ■ the time of this: *we left before moonset in the morning.*

moon·shine /ˈmo͞onˌSHīn/ ▸*n.* **1** *inf.* illicitly distilled or smuggled liquor. **2** foolish talk or ideas. **3** another term for MOONLIGHT.

moon·shin·er /ˈmo͞onˌSHīnər/ ▸*n.* *inf.* an illicit distiller or smuggler of liquor.

moon shot (also **moon·shot**) ▸*n.* the launching of a spacecraft to the moon.

moon·stone /ˈmo͞onˌstōn/ ▸*n.* a pearly white semiprecious stone consisting of alkali feldspar.

moon·struck /ˈmo͞onˌstrək/ ▸*adj.* unable to think or act normally, esp. because of being in love.

moon·y /ˈmo͞onē/ ▸*adj.* (**moon·i·er**, **moon·i·est**) **1** dreamy and unaware of one's surroundings, for example because one is in love: *she's not drunk, but still smiling in the same moony way* | *little girls go moony over horses.* **2** of or like the moon.

Moor /mo͝or/ ▸*n.* a member of a northwestern African Muslim people of mixed Berber and Arab descent. In the 8th century they conquered the Iberian peninsula, but were driven out at the end of the 15th century. —**Moor·ish** *adj.*

moor[1] /mo͝or/ ▸*n.* a tract of open uncultivated upland; a heath. ■ a tract of such land preserved for shooting: *a grouse moor.* ■ a fen. —**moor·ish** *adj.* —**moor·y** *adj.*

moor[2] ▸*v.* [*tr.*] (often **be moored**) make fast (a vessel) to the shore or to an anchor. —**moor·age** /ˈmo͝orij/ *n.*

moor·hen /ˈmo͝orˌhen/ ▸*n.* a small aquatic rail with mainly blackish plumage, esp. *Gallinula chloropus*, which has a distinctive red and yellow bill.

moor·ing /ˈmo͝oriNG/ ▸*n.* (often **moorings**) a place where a boat or ship is moored: *the boat had been at its usual moorings.* ■ the ropes, chains, or anchors by or to which a boat, ship, or buoy is moored: *the great ship slipped its moorings and slid out into the Atlantic.* ■ *fig.* the ideas, beliefs, or habits to which one is accustomed and from which one gains security or stability: *we can lose our spiritual moorings and drift into uncertain waters.*

moor·land /ˈmo͝o(ə)rlənd; -ˌland/ ▸*n.* (also **moorlands**) an extensive area of moor.

moose /mo͞os/ ▸*n.* (*pl.* same) a large deer (*Alces alces*) with palmate antlers, a sloping back, and a growth of skin hanging from the neck. It is native to northern Eurasia and northern North America.

moot /mo͞ot/ ▸*adj.* subject to debate, dispute, or uncertainty, and typically not admitting of a final decision: *whether the temperature rise was mainly due to the greenhouse effect was a moot point.* ■ having no practical significance, typically because the subject is too uncertain to allow a decision: *it is moot whether this phrase should be treated as metaphor or not.*
▸*v.* [*tr.*] (usu. **be mooted**) raise (a question or topic) for discussion; suggest (an idea or possibility): *a trip to Ireland had been mooted.*
▸*n.* *Law* a mock trial set up to examine a hypothetical case as an academic exercise.

mop /mäp/ ▸*n.* an implement consisting of a sponge or a bundle of thick loose strings attached to a handle, used for wiping floors or other surfaces. ■ a thick mass of disordered hair. ■ an act of wiping something clean, esp. a floor: *the kitchen needed a quick mop.*
▸*v.* (**mopped**, **mop·ping**) [*tr.*] clean or soak up (something) by wiping. ■ [*tr.*] wipe (something) away from a surface: *a barmaid rushed forward to mop up the spilled beer.* ■ wipe sweat or tears from (one's face or eyes): *he pulled a handkerchief from his pocket to mop his brow.*

mope /mōp/ ▸*v.* [*intr.*] be dejected and apathetic: *no use moping—things could be worse.* ■ (**mope around/about**) wander around listlessly and aimlessly because of unhappiness or boredom: *moping around at home won't get you anywhere.*
▸*n.* a person given to prolonged spells of low spirits. ■ (**mopes**) *dated* low spirits; depression. ▷mid 16th cent. (the early noun sense being 'fool or simpleton'): perhaps of Scandinavian origin; compare with Swedish *mopa* 'to sulk.' —**mop·er** *n.* —**mop·ey** (also **mop·y**) *adj.* —**mop·i·ly** /ˈmōpəlē/ *adv.* —**mop·i·ness** /ˈmōpēnis/ *n.* —**mop·ish** *adj.*

mo·ped /ˈmōˌped/ ▸*n.* a low-power, lightweight motorized bicycle.

mop·pet /ˈmäpət/ ▸*n.* *inf.* a small endearingly sweet child.

mo·raine /məˈrān/ ▸*n.* *Geol.* a mass of rocks and sediment carried down and deposited by a glacier, typically as ridges at its edges or extremity. —**mo·rain·al** /-ˈrānl/ *adj.* —**mo·rain·ic** /-ˈrānik/ *adj.*

mor·al /ˈmôrəl; ˈmär-/ ▸*adj.* concerned with the principles of right and wrong behavior and the goodness or badness of human character. ■ concerned with or adhering to the code of interpersonal behavior that is considered right or acceptable in a particular society: *an individual's ambitions may get out of step with the general moral code.* ■ holding or manifesting high principles for proper conduct: *he is a caring, efficient, moral man.* ■ derived from or based on ethical principles or a sense of these: *the moral obligation of society to do something about the inner city's problems.* ■ examining the nature of ethics and the foundations of good and bad character and conduct: *moral philosophers.*
▸*n.* **1** a lesson, esp. one concerning what is right or prudent, that can be derived from a story, a piece of information, or an experience. **2** (**morals**) a person's standards of behavior or beliefs concerning what is and is not acceptable for them to do. ■ standards of behavior that are considered good or acceptable. ▷late Middle English: from Latin *moralis*, from *mos, mor-* 'custom,' (plural) *mores* 'morals.' As a noun the word was first used to translate Latin *Moralia*, the title of St. Gregory the Great's moral exposition of the Book of Job, and was subsequently applied to the works of various classical writers. —**mor·al·ly** *adv.*

mo·rale /məˈral/ ▸*n.* the confidence, enthusiasm, and discipline of a person or group at a particular time: *their morale was high.*

mor·al·ism /ˈmôrəˌlizəm; ˈmär-/ ▸*n.* the practice of moralizing, esp. showing a tendency to make judgments about others' morality.

mor·al·ist /ˈmôrəlist/ ▸*n.* a person who teaches or promotes morality. ■ a person given to moralizing. ■ a person who behaves in a morally commendable way. —**mor·al·is·tic** /ˌmôrəˈlistik/ *adj.* —**mor·al·is·ti·cal·ly** /ˌmôrəˈlistik(ə)lē/ *adv.*

mo·ral·i·ty /məˈralətē; mô-/ ▸*n.* (*pl.* **-ties**) principles concerning the distinction between right and wrong or good and bad behavior. ■ behavior as it is affected by the observation of these principles. ■ a particular system of values and principles of conduct, esp. one held by a specified person or society: *a bourgeois morality.* ■ the extent to which an action is right or wrong: *the issue of the morality of the possession of nuclear weapons.* ■ behavior or qualities judged to be good.

mo·ral·i·ty play ▸*n.* a kind of drama with personified abstract qualities as the main characters and presenting a lesson about good conduct and character, popular in the 15th and early 16th centuries.

mor·al·ize /ˈmôrəˌlīz; ˈmär-/ ▸*v.* [*intr.*] [often *as n.*] (**moralizing**) comment on issues of right and wrong, typically with an unfounded air of superiority: *self-righteous moralizing.* ■ [*tr.*] interpret or explain as giving lessons on good and bad character and conduct. ■ [*tr.*] reform the character and conduct of: *he endeavored to moralize an immoral society.* —**mor·al·i·za·tion** /ˌmôrələˈzāSHən; ˌmär-/ *n.* —**mor·al·iz·er** *n.* —**mor·al·iz·ing·ly** *adv.*

mo·rass /məˈras; mô-/ ▸*n.* an area of muddy or boggy ground. ■ *fig.* a complicated or confused situation: *a morass of lies and explanations.*

mor·a·to·ri·um /ˌmôrəˈtôrēəm; ˌmär-/ ▸*n.* (*pl.* **-to·ri·ums** or **-to·ri·a** /-ˈtôrēə/) a temporary prohibition of an activity: *an indefinite moratorium on the use of drift nets.* ■ *Law* a legal authorization to debtors to postpone payment. ■ *Law* the period of this postponement.

Mo·ra·vi·an /məˈrāvēən/ ▸*n.* a native of Moravia. ■ a member of a Protestant Church founded in Saxony by emigrants from Moravia holding views derived from the Hussites and accepting the Bible as the only source of faith.
▸*adj.* of or relating to Moravia or its people. ■ of or relating to the Moravian Church.

mo·ray /ˈmôrˌā; məˈrā/ (also **moray eel**) ▸*n.* a mainly nocturnal eellike predatory fish (family Muraenidae) of warm seas that typically hides in crevices with just the head protruding.

mor·bid /ˈmôrbəd/ ▸*adj.* **1** characterized by or appealing to an abnormal and unhealthy interest in disturbing and unpleasant subjects, esp. death and disease: *a morbid fascination with the horrors of warfare.* **2** *Med.* of the nature of or indicative of disease: *the treatment of morbid obesity.* —**mor·bid·i·ty** /môrˈbidətē/ *n.* —**mor·bid·ly** *adv.* —**mor·bid·ness** *n.*

mor·dant /ˈmôrdnt/ ▸*adj.* (esp. of humor) having or showing a sharp or critical quality; biting: *a mordant sense of humor.*
▸*n.* a substance, typically an inorganic oxide, that combines with a dye or stain and thereby fixes it in a material. ■ a corrosive liquid used to etch the lines on a printing plate.
▸*v.* [*tr.*] impregnate or treat (a fabric) with a mordant. —**mor·dan·cy** /-dnsē/ *n.* —**mor·dant·ly** *adv.*

mor·dent /ˈmôrdnt/ ▸*n.* *Mus.* an ornament consisting of one rapid alternation of a written note with the note immediately below or above it in the scale.

more /môr/ ▸*adj. & pron.* **1** comparative of MANY, MUCH. **2** a greater or additional amount or degree: [as *adj.*] *I poured myself more coffee* | [as *pron.*] *tell me more* | *they proved more of a hindrance than a help.*
▸*adv.* **1** comparative of MUCH. **2** forming the comparative of adjectives and adverbs, esp. those of more than one syllable: *for them, enthusiasm is more important than talent.* **3** to a greater extent: *I like chicken more than turkey.* ■ (**more than**) extremely (used before an adjective conveying a positive feeling or attitude): *she is more than happy to oblige.* **4** again: repeat *once more.* **5** moreover: *he was rich, and more, he was handsome.*
▸ □ **more or less** speaking imprecisely; to a certain extent: *they are more or less a waste of time.* ■ approximately: *more or less symmetrical.* □ **no more 1** nothing further: *there was no more to be said about it.* **2** no further: *you must have some soup, but no more wine.* **3** (**be no more**) exist no longer. **4** never again: *mention his name no more to me.*

mo·rel /məˈrel; môˈ-/ ▸*n.* a widely distributed edible fungus (genus *Morchella*) that has a brown oval or pointed fruiting body with an irregular honeycombed surface bearing the spores.

more·o·ver /môrˈōvər/ ▸*adv.* as a further matter; besides: *moreover, glass is electrically insulating.*

mo·res /ˈmôrˌāz/ ▸*pl. n.* the essential or characteristic customs and conventions of a community: *an offense against social mores.*

morgue /môrg/ ▸*n.* **1** a place where bodies are kept, esp. to be identified or claimed. ■ used metaphorically to refer to a place that is quiet, gloomy, or cold: *that drafty morgue of a sitting room.* **2** *inf.* in a newspaper office, a collection of old cuttings, photographs, and information.

mor·i·bund /ˈmôrəˌbənd; ˈmär-/ ▸*adj.* (of a person) at the point of death. ■ (of a thing) in terminal decline; lacking vitality or vigor: *the moribund commercial property market.* —**mor·i·bun·di·ty** /ˌmôrəˈbəndətē; ˌmär-/ *n.*

Mor·mon /ˈmôrmən/ ▸*n.* a member of the Church of Jesus Christ of Latter-Day Saints, a religion founded in the U.S. in 1830 by Joseph Smith.
▸*adj.* of or relating to the Church of Jesus Christ of Latter-Day Saints: *the leader of a Mormon congregation.* —**Mor·mon·ism** /-ˌnizəm/ *n.*

morn /môrn/ ▸*n.* *poetic/lit.* term for MORNING.

mor·nay /môrˈnā/ (also **Mor·nay**) ▸*adj.* denoting or served in a cheese-flavored white sauce: *mornay sauce* | *cauliflower mornay.*

morn·ing /ˈmôrniNG/ ▸*n.* the period of time between midnight and noon, esp. from sunrise to noon: *I toiled in the fields from morning till night* | *it was a little after eight in the morning.* ■ this time on a particular day, characterized by a specified type of activity or particular weather conditions: *it was a beautiful sunny morning.* ■ sunrise: *a hint of steely light showed that morning was on its way.*
▸*adv.* (**mornings**) *inf.* every morning: *mornings, she'd sleep late.*
▸ □ **morning, noon, and night** all the time.

morn·ing glo·ry ▸*n.* a climbing plant (genus *Ipomoea*, family Convolvulaceae) often cultivated for its showy trumpet-shaped flowers, which typically open in the early morning and wither by midday.

morn·ing sick·ness ▸*n.* nausea in pregnancy, typically occurring in the first few months at any time of day.

morn·ing star ▸*n.* (**the morning star**) a bright planet, esp. Venus, when visible in the east before sunrise.

mo·roc·co /məˈräkō/ ▸*n.* (*pl.* **-cos**) fine flexible leather made (originally in Morocco) from goatskin tanned with sumac, used esp. for book covers and shoes: *a volume bound in red morocco.*

mo·rose /məˈrōs; môˈ-/ ▸*adj.* sullen and ill-tempered. —**mo·rose·ly** *adv.* —**mo·rose·ness** *n.*

mor·pheme /ˈmôrˌfēm/ ▸*n.* *Linguistics* a meaningful morphological unit of a language that cannot be further divided (e.g., *in, come, -ing,*

forming *incoming*). —**mor·phe·mic** /môrˈfēmik/ *adj.* —**mor·phe·mi·cal·ly** /môrˈfēmik(ə)lē/ *adv.*

mor·phine /ˈmôrˌfēn/ ▸*n.* an analgesic and narcotic drug, $C_{17}H_{19}NO_3$, obtained from opium and used medicinally to relieve pain.

mor·phol·o·gy /môrˈfäləjē/ ▸*n.* (*pl.* **-gies**) the study of the forms of things, in particular: ■ *Biol.* the branch of biology that deals with the form of living organisms, and with relationships between their structures. ■ *Linguistics* the study of the forms of words. —**mor·pho·log·ic** /ˌmôrfəˈläjik/ *adj.* —**mor·pho·log·i·cal** /ˌmôrfəˈläjikəl/ *adj.* —**mor·pho·log·i·cal·ly** /ˌmôrfəˈläjik(ə)lē/ *adv.* —**mor·phol·o·gist** /-jist/ *n.*

mor·row /ˈmôrō; ˈmärō/ ▸*n.* (**the morrow**) *archaic* or *poetic/lit.* the following day: *on the morrow, they attacked the city.* ■ the time following an event: *in the morrow of great victory.* ■ the near future: *the religious enthusiast who takes no thought for the morrow.*

Morse code /môrs/ ▸*n.* an alphabet or code in which letters are represented by combinations of long and short signals of light or sound.
▸*v.* [*tr.*] signal (something) using Morse code.

mor·sel /ˈmôrsəl/ ▸*n.* a small piece or amount of food; a mouthful. ■ a small piece or amount: *reporters do their best to ferret out every morsel of information.* ▷Middle English: from Old French, diminutive of *mors* 'a bite,' from Latin *mors-* 'bitten,' from the verb *mordere*.

mor·tal /ˈmôrtl/ ▸*adj.* **1** (of a living human being, often in contrast to a divine being) subject to death: *all men are mortal.* ■ of or relating to humanity as subject to death: *the coffin held the mortal remains of her uncle.* ■ *inf.* conceivable or imaginable: *punishment out of all mortal proportion to the offense.* **2** causing or liable to cause death; fatal: *a mortal disease* | *fig. the scandal appeared to have struck a mortal blow to the government.* ■ (of a battle) fought to the death: *the screams of men in mortal combat.* ■ (of an enemy or a state of hostility) admitting or allowing no reconciliation until death. ■ *Christian Theol.* denoting a grave sin that is regarded as depriving the soul of divine grace. Often contrasted with VENIAL. ■ (of a feeling, esp. fear) very intense: *parents live in mortal fear of children's diseases.* ■ *inf., dated* long and tedious: *for three mortal days it rained.*
▸*n.* a human being subject to death, often contrasted with a divine being. ■ *humorous* a person contrasted with others regarded as being of higher status or ability: *an ambassador had to live in a style that was not expected of lesser mortals.* —**mor·tal·ly** *adv.*

mor·tal·i·ty /môrˈtalətē/ ▸*n.* (*pl.* **-ties**) **1** the state of being subject to death. **2** death, esp. on a large scale: *the causes of mortality among young children.* ■ (also **mortality rate**) the number of deaths in a given area or period, or from a particular cause.

mor·tar¹ /ˈmôrtər/ ▸*n.* **1** a cup-shaped receptacle made of hard material, in which ingredients are crushed or ground, used esp. in cooking or pharmacy: *a mortar and pestle.* **2** a short, smoothbore gun for firing shells (technically called bombs) at high angles. ■ a similar device used for firing a lifeline or firework.
▸*v.* [*tr.*] attack or bombard with shells fired from a mortar.

mortar and pestle

mor·tar² ▸*n.* a mixture of lime with cement, sand, and water, used in building to bond bricks or stones.
▸*v.* [*tr.*] fix or join using mortar: *the pipe can be mortared in place.* —**mor·tar·less** *adj.* —**mor·tar·y** *adj.*

mor·tar·board /ˈmôrtərˌbôrd/ ▸*n.* **1** an academic cap with a stiff, flat, square top and a tassel. **2** a small square board with a handle on the underside, used by bricklayers for holding mortar.

mort·gage /ˈmôrgij/ ▸*n.* the charging of real (or personal) property by a debtor to a creditor as security for a debt (esp. one incurred by the purchase of the property), on the condition that it shall be returned on payment of the debt within a certain period. ■ a deed effecting such a transaction. ■ a loan obtained through the conveyance of property as security: *I put down a hundred thousand in cash and took out a mortgage for the rest.*
▸*v.* [*tr.*] (often **be mortgaged**) convey (a property) to a creditor as security on a loan. ■ *fig.* expose to future risk or constraint for the sake of

mortarboard

immediate advantage: *some people worry that selling off federal assets mortgages the country's future.* —**mort·gage·a·ble** *adj.*

mort·ga·gee /ˌmôrgəˈjē/ ▶ *n.* the lender in a mortgage, typically a bank.

mort·ga·gor /ˌmôrgiˈjôr; ˈmôrgijər/ ▶ *n.* the borrower in a mortgage, typically a homeowner.

mor·tice /ˈmôrtəs/ ▶ *n.* & *v.* variant spelling of MORTISE.

mor·ti·cian /môrˈtishən/ ▶ *n.* an undertaker.

mor·ti·fy /ˈmôrtəˌfī/ ▶ *v.* (**-fies, -fied**) **1** (often **be mortified**) cause (someone) to feel embarrassed, ashamed, or humiliated: [*tr.*] *she was mortified to see her wrinkles in the mirror.* **2** subdue (the body or its needs and desires) by self-denial or discipline: *return to heaven by mortifying the flesh.* —**mor·ti·fi·ca·tion** /ˌmôrtəfəˈkāshən/ *n.* —**mor·ti·fy·ing·ly** *adv.*

mor·tise /ˈmôrtis/ (also **mor·tice**) ▶ *n.* a hole or recess cut into a part, designed to receive a corresponding projection (a tenon) on another part so as to join or lock the parts together.
▶ *v.* [*tr.*] join securely by using a mortise and tenon. ■ [*tr.*] [often as *adj.*] (**mortised**) cut a mortise in or through. —**mor·tis·er** *n.*

mor·tise lock ▶ *n.* a lock that is set within the body of a door in a recess or mortise, as opposed to one attached to the door surface.

mor·tu·ar·y /ˈmôrcHˌʊerē/ ▶ *n.* (*pl.* **-ar·ies**) a funeral home or morgue.
▶ *adj.* of or relating to burial or tombs: *a mortuary temple.*

Mo·sa·ic /mōˈzāik/ ▶ *adj.* of or associated with Moses.

mo·sa·ic /mōˈzāik/ ▶ *n.* **1** a picture or pattern produced by arranging together small colored pieces of hard material, such as stone, tile, or glass. ■ decorative work of this kind: *the walls and vaults are decorated by marble and mosaic.* ■ a colorful and variegated pattern. ■ a combination of diverse elements forming a more or less coherent whole: *a mosaic of competing interests.* ■ an arrangement of photosensitive elements in a television camera. **2** *Biol.* an individual (esp. an animal) composed of cells of two genetically different types. **3** (also **mosaic disease**) a viral disease that results in leaf variegation in tobacco, corn, sugar cane, and other plants.
▶ *v.* (**-sa·icked, -sa·ick·ing**) [*tr.*] decorate with a mosaic: [as *adj.*] (**mosaicked**) *the mosaicked swimming pool.* ■ combine (distinct or disparate elements) to form a picture or pattern. —**mo·sa·i·cist** /mōˈzāəsist/ *n.*

mo·sey /ˈmōzē/ *inf.* ▶ *v.* (**-seys, -seyed**) [*intr.*] walk or move in a leisurely manner: *we decided to mosey on up to Montgomery.*
▶ *n. chiefly Brit.* a leisurely walk or drive.

Mos·lem /ˈmäzləm; ˈmäs-/ ▶ *n.* & *adj.* variant spelling of MUSLIM.

mosque /mäsk/ ▶ *n.* a Muslim place of worship.

mos·qui·to /məˈskētō/ ▶ *n.* (*pl.* **-toes** or **-tos**) a slender long-legged fly (*Culex, Anopheles,* and other genera, family Culicidae) with aquatic larvae. The bite of the bloodsucking female can transmit a number of serious diseases including malaria and encephalitis. —**mos·qui·to·ey** /məˈskētəwē/ *adj.*

moss /môs/ ▶ *n.* a small flowerless green plant that lacks true roots, growing in low carpets or rounded cushions in damp habitats and reproducing by means of spores released from stalked capsules: *the trees are overgrown with vines and moss* | *the bog is home to rare mosses.* ■ used in names of algae, lichens, and higher plants resembling moss, e.g., **reindeer moss, Ceylon moss, Spanish moss.**
▶ *v.* [usu. as *adj.*] (**mossed**) cover with moss. —**moss·like** /-ˌlīk/ *adj.*

moss·y /ˈmôsē/ ▶ *adj.* (**moss·i·er, moss·i·est**) covered in or resembling moss: *mossy tree trunks.* ■ *inf.* old-fashioned or extremely conservative. —**moss·i·ness** *n.*

most /mōst/ ▶ *adj.* & *pron.* **1** superlative of MANY, MUCH. **2** greatest in amount or degree: [as *adj.*] *they've had the most success* | [as *pron.*] *they had the most to lose.* ■ the majority of; nearly all of: [as *adj.*] *most oranges are sweeter than these.* | [as *pron.*] *I spent most of the winter on the coast.*
▶ *adv.* **1** superlative of MUCH. **2** to the greatest extent: *the things he most enjoyed* | *what she wanted most of all.* ■ forming the superlative of adjectives and adverbs, esp. those of more than one syllable: *the most important event of my life* | *plains where fire tends to spread most quickly.* **3** extremely; very: *it was most kind of you.* **4** *inf.* almost: *most everyone understood.*
▶ □ **at (the) most** not more than: *the walk took four minutes at the most.* □ **be the most** *inf.* be the best of all; be the ultimate. □ **for the most part** in most cases; usually: *the older members, for the most part, shun him.* □ **make the most of** use to the best advantage: *he was eager to make the most of his visit.* ■ represent at its best: *how to make the most of your features.*

-most ▶ *suffix* forming superlative adjectives and adverbs from prepositions and other words indicating relative position: *innermost* | *uppermost.*

most·ly /ˈmōstlē/ ▶ *adv.* as regards the greater part or number: *I grow mostly annuals.* ■ usually: *weekends spent mostly alone.*

mot /mō/ ▶ *n.* (*pl.* **mots** /mō(z)/) short for BON MOT.

mote /mōt/ ▶ *n.* a tiny piece of a substance: *the tiniest mote of dust.*

mo·tel /mōˈtel/ ▶ *n.* a roadside hotel designed primarily for motorists, typically having the rooms arranged in a low building with parking directly outside.

mo·tet /mōˈtet/ ▶ *n.* a short piece of sacred choral music, typically polyphonic and unaccompanied.

moth /môTH/ ▶ *n.* (*pl.* **moths** /môTHz; môTHs/) a chiefly nocturnal insect related to the butterflies. It lacks the clubbed antennae of butterflies and typically has a stout body, drab coloration, and wings that fold flat when resting. ■ *inf.* short for CLOTHES MOTH.

moth·ball /ˈmôTH,bôl/ ▶ *n.* (usu. **mothballs**) a small pellet of a pungent substance, typically naphthalene, put among stored clothes to keep away moths.
▶ *v.* [*tr.*] store (clothes) among or in mothballs. ■ stop using (a piece of equipment or a building) but keep it in good condition so that it can readily be used again. ■ cancel or postpone work on (a plan or project): *plans to invest in four superstores have been mothballed.*

moth-eat·en /ˈmôTH ˌētn/ ▶ *adj.* damaged or destroyed by moths. ■ old-fashioned and no longer appropriate or useful.

moth·er /ˈməTHər/ ▶ *n.* a woman in relation to a child or children to whom she has given birth. ■ a person who provides the care and affection normally associated with a female parent: *my adoptive mother.* ■ a female animal in relation to its offspring: [as *adj.*] *a mother penguin.* ■ *archaic* (esp. as a form of address) an elderly woman. ■ (**Mother, Mother Superior,** or **Reverend Mother**) (esp. as a title or form of address) the head of a female religious community. ■ [as *adj.*] denoting an institution or organization from which more recently founded institutions of the same type derive: *the mother church.* ■ *fig.* something that is the origin of or stimulus for something else: *the wish was the mother of the deed.* ■ *inf.* an extreme example or very large specimen of something: *I got stuck in the mother of all traffic jams.*
▶ *v.* [*tr.*] [often as *n.*] (**mothering**) bring up (a child) with care and affection: *the art of mothering.* ■ look after kindly and protectively, sometimes excessively so: *she felt mothered by her older sister.* ▷Old English *mōdor,* of Germanic origin; related to Dutch *moeder* and German *Mutter,* from an Indo-European root shared by Latin *mater* and Greek *mētēr.* —**moth·er·hood** /-ˌho͝od/ *n.* —**moth·er·less** *adj.* —**moth·er·like** /-ˌlīk/ *adj.* & *adv.*

moth·er·board /ˈməTHər,bôrd/ ▶ *n. Comput.* a printed circuit board containing the principal components of a microcomputer or other device, with connectors into which other circuit boards can be slotted.

moth·er coun·try ▶ *n.* (also **the mother country**) a country in relation to its colonies: *the bicentennial of our separation from the mother country.*

Moth·er Goose ▶ *n.* the fictitious creator of a collection of nursery rhymes that was first published in London in the 1760s.

moth·er-in-law ▶ *n.* (*pl.* **moth·ers-in-law**) the mother of one's husband or wife.

moth·er·land /ˈməTHər,land/ ▶ *n.* (often **the motherland**) one's native country.

moth·er lode ▶ *n. Mining* a principal vein of an ore or mineral. ■ *fig.* a rich source of something: *a mother lode of opportunities.*

moth·er·ly /ˈməTHərlē/ ▶ *adj.* of, resembling, or characteristic of a mother, esp. in being caring, protective, and kind: *she held both her arms wide in a gesture of motherly love.* —**moth·er·li·ness** *n.*

Moth·er Na·ture ▶ *nature* personified as a creative and controlling force: *Mother Nature has 80 percent control in putting out fires like this.*

moth·er-of-pearl ▶ *n.* a smooth shining iridescent substance forming the inner layer of the shell of some mollusks, esp. oysters and abalones, used in ornamentation.

Moth·er's Day ▶ *n.* a day of the year (in the U.S., the second Sunday in May) on which mothers are particularly honored by their children.

Moth·er Su·pe·ri·or (also **mother superior**) ▶ *n.* the head of a female religious community.

moth·er tongue ▶ *n.* the language that a person has grown up speaking from early childhood.

moth·proof /ˈmôTH,pro͞of/ ▶ *adj.* (of clothes or fabrics) treated with a substance that repels moths.
▶ *v.* [*tr.*] treat with a substance that repels moths.

mo·tif /mōˈtēf/ ▶ *n.* a decorative design or pattern. ■ a distinctive feature or dominant idea in an artistic or literary composition: *the nautical*

motif of his latest novel. ■ *Mus.* a short succession of notes producing a single impression; a brief melodic or rhythmic formula out of which longer passages are developed.

mo·tile /'mōtl; 'mō,tīl/ ▸*adj. Zool.* & *Bot.* (of cells, gametes, and single-celled organisms) capable of motion. —**mo·til·i·ty** /mō'tilətē/ *n.*

mo·tion /'mōsHən/ ▸*n.* **1** the action or process of moving or being moved. ■ a gesture: *she made a motion with her free hand.* ■ a piece of moving mechanism. **2** a formal proposal put to a legislature or committee: *the head of our commission made a motion that we rewrite the constitution.* ■ *Law* an application for a rule or order of court. **3** *Mus.* the movement of a melodic line between successive pitches.
▸*v.* [*tr.*] **1** direct or command (someone) with a movement of the hand or head: *he motioned Dennis to a plush chair* | [*tr.*] *he motioned the young officer to sit down.* **2** make a proposal in a deliberative or legislative body: [with *clause*] *she recognized the majority leader, who motioned that the body adjourn.* —**mo·tion·al** /-SHənl/ *adj.* —**mo·tion·less** *adj.* —**mo·tion·less·ly** *adv.*
▸ □ **go through the motions** do something perfunctorily, without any enthusiasm or commitment. ■ simulate an action: *a child goes through the motions of washing up.*

mo·tion pic·ture ▸*n.* another term for MOVIE: [as *adj.*] *the motion-picture industry.*

mo·ti·vate /'mōtə,vāt/ ▸*v.* [*tr.*] provide (someone) with a motive for doing something: *he was primarily motivated by the desire for profit.* ■ stimulate (someone's) interest in or enthusiasm for doing something: *I'm going to motivate kids to study civics.* —**mo·ti·va·tion** *n.* —**mo·ti·va·tor** /-,vātər/ *n.*

mo·tive /'mōtiv/ ▸*n.* **1** a reason for doing something, esp. one that is hidden or not obvious. **2** (in art, literature, or music) a motif: *the entire work grows organically from the opening horn motive.*
▸*adj.* **1** producing physical or mechanical motion: *the charge of gas is the motive force for every piston stroke.* **2** causing or being the reason for something: *the motive principle of a writer's work.* —**mo·tive·less** *adj.* —**mo·tive·less·ly** *adv.* —**mo·tive·less·ness** *n.*

mot·ley /'mätlē/ ▸*adj.* (**mot·li·er, mot·li·est**) incongruously varied in appearance or character; disparate: *a motley crew.*
▸*n.* **1** an incongruous mixture: *a motley of interacting interest groups.* **2** *hist.* the particolored costume of a jester.

mo·to·cross /'mōtō,krôs; -,kräs/ ▸*n.* cross-country racing on motorcycles. —**mo·to·cross·er** *n.*

mo·tor /'mōtər/ ▸*n.* a machine, esp. one powered by electricity or internal combustion, that supplies motive power for a vehicle or for some other device with moving parts. ■ a source of power, energy, or motive force: *hormones are the motor of the sexual functions.*
▸*adj.* **1** giving, imparting, or producing motion or action: *demand is the principle motor force governing economic activity.* ■ *Physiol.* relating to muscular movement or the nerves activating it: *the motor functions of each hand.* **2** *chiefly Brit.* driven by a motor. ■ of or relating to motor vehicles: *the world of motor sports.*
▸*v.* [*intr.*] *inf.* travel in a motor vehicle, typically a car or a boat. ■ *inf.* run or move as fast as possible. ▷late Middle English (denoting a person who imparts motion): from Latin, literally 'mover,' based on *movere* 'to move.' The current sense of the noun dates from the mid 19th cent.

mo·tor·bike /'mōtər,bīk/ ▸*n.* a lightweight motorcycle. ■ a motorized bicycle.

mo·tor·boat /'mōtər,bōt/ ▸*n.* a boat powered by a motor, esp. a recreational boat.

mo·tor·cade /'mōtər,kād/ ▸*n.* a procession of motor vehicles, typically carrying and escorting a prominent person.

mo·tor·car /'mōtər,kär/ ▸*n. dated* or *Brit.* an automobile.

mo·tor·cy·cle /'mōtər,sīkəl/ ▸*n.* a two-wheeled vehicle that is powered by a motor and has no pedals. —**mo·tor·cy·cling** /-,sīk(ə)liNG/ *n.* —**mo·tor·cy·clist** /-,sīk(ə)list/ *n.*

motorcycle

mo·tor home ▸*n.* a motor vehicle equipped like a trailer for living in, with kitchen facilities, beds, etc.

mo·tor·ist /'mōtərist/ ▸*n.* the driver of an automobile.

mo·tor·ize /'mōtə,rīz/ ▸*v.* [*tr.*] [usu. as *adj.*] (**motorized**) equip (a vehicle or device) with a motor to operate or propel it: *a motorized wheelchair.* ■ equip (troops) with motor transportation: *three motorized divisions.* —**mo·tor·i·za·tion** /,mōtərə'zāsHən/ *n.*

mo·tor·mouth /'mōtər,mouTH/ (also **mo·tor-mouth**) ▸*n. inf.* a person who talks quickly and incessantly. —**mo·tor·mouthed** /-,mouTHd; -,mouTHt/ (also **mo·tor-mouthed**) *adj.*

mo·tor pool ▸*n.* a group of vehicles maintained by a government agency, military installation, etc., for use by personnel as needed.

mo·tor scoot·er ▸*n.* see SCOOTER.

mo·tor ve·hi·cle ▸*n.* a road vehicle powered by an internal combustion engine; an automobile.

Mo·town /'mō,toun/ ▸*n.* music released on or reminiscent of the U.S. record label Motown, important in popularizing soul music.

mot·tle /'mätl/ ▸*v.* [*tr.*] (usu. **be mottled**) mark with spots or smears of color: *the cow's coat was light red mottled with white* | [as *adj.*] (**mottled**) *a bird with mottled brown plumage.*
▸*n.* an irregular arrangement of spots or patches of color: *the ship was a mottle of khaki and black.* ■ (also **mottling**) a spot or patch forming part of such an arrangement: *white marble with mottlings of black and gray.*

mot·to /'mätō/ ▸*n.* (pl. **-toes** or **-tos**) a short sentence or phrase chosen as encapsulating the beliefs or ideals guiding an individual, family, or institution. ■ *Mus.* a phrase that recurs throughout a musical work and has some symbolic significance.

moue /mōō/ ▸*n.* a pouting expression used to convey annoyance or distaste.

mould /mōld/ ▸*n.* & *v.* British spelling of MOLD[1], MOLD[2], and MOLD[3].

mound /mound/ ▸*n.* a rounded mass projecting above a surface. ■ a raised mass of earth or other compacted material, sometimes created for purposes of defense or burial. ■ a small hill. ■ (**a mound of/mounds of**) a large pile or quantity of something: *mounds of cash.* ■ *Baseball* (in full **pitcher's mound**) the elevated area from which the pitcher delivers the ball.
▸*v.* [*tr.*] heap up into a rounded pile.

mount[1] /mount/ ▸*v.* [*tr.*] **1** climb up (stairs, a hill, or other rising surface). ■ climb or move up on to (a raised surface): *the master of ceremonies mounted the platform.* ■ get up on (an animal or bicycle) in order to ride it. ■ (often **be mounted**) set (someone) on horseback; provide with a horse: *she was mounted on a white horse.* ■ (of a male mammal or bird) get on (a female) for the purpose of copulation. ■ [*intr.*] (of the blood or its color) rise into the cheeks: *feeling the blush mount in her cheeks.* **2** organize and initiate (a campaign or other significant course of action): *the company mounted takeover bids.* ■ establish; set up: *security forces mounted checkpoints.* ■ produce (a play, exhibition, or other artistic event); present for public view or display. **3** [*intr.*] grow larger or more numerous: *the costs mount up when you buy a home.* ■ (of a feeling) become stronger or more intense: *his anxiety mounted.* **4** [*tr.*] place or fix (an object) on an elevated support: *fluorescent lights are mounted on the ceiling.* ■ fix (an object) in position: *the engine is mounted behind the rear seats.* ■ [*tr.*] place (a gun) on a fixed mounting. ■ [*tr.*] set in or attach to a backing or setting: *the photographs will be mounted and framed.* ■ [*tr.*] fix (an object for viewing) on a microscope slide.
▸*n.* **1** a backing or setting on which a photograph, gem, or work of art is set for display. ■ a glass microscope slide for securing a specimen to be viewed. ■ *Philately* a clear plastic or paper sleeve used to display a postage stamp. **2** a support for a gun, camera, or similar piece of equipment. **3** a horse being ridden or that is available for riding. ■ an opportunity to ride a horse, esp. as a jockey. —**mount·a·ble** *adj.* —**mount·er** *n.*

mount[2] ▸*n.* a mountain or hill (archaic except in place names): *Mount Everest.*

moun·tain /'mountn/ ▸*n.* a large natural elevation of the earth's surface rising abruptly from the surrounding level; a large steep hill. ■ (**mountains**) a region where there are many such features, characterized by remoteness and inaccessibility: *they sought refuge in the mountains* | [as *adj.*] (**mountain**) *his attempt to picture the mountain folk in ridiculous attire.* ■ (**a mountain/mountains of**) a large pile or quantity of something: *a mountain of paperwork.* —**moun·tain·y** *adj.*
▸ □ **move mountains 1** achieve spectacular and apparently impossible results. **2** make every possible effort: *his fans move mountains to catch as many of his performances as possible.*

moun·tain ash ▸*n.* a small deciduous tree (genus *Sorbus*) of the rose family, with compound leaves, white flowers, and red berries. Also called ROWAN.

moun·tain bike ▸*n.* a bicycle with a light sturdy frame, broad deep-treaded tires, and multiple gears, originally designed for riding on mountainous terrain. —**moun·tain bik·er** *n.* —**moun·tain bik·ing** *n.*

moun·tain·eer /ˌmountnˈi(ə)r/ ▸*n.* a person who takes part in mountaineering. ■ *rare* a person living in a mountainous area. —**moun·tain·eer·ing** *n.*

moun·tain goat ▸*n.* (also **Rocky Mountain goat**) a goat-antelope (*Oreamnos americanus*) with shaggy white hair and backward curving horns, living in the Rocky Mountains.

moun·tain lau·rel ▸*n.* a North American evergreen leathery-leaved shrub (*Kalmia latifolia*) of the heath family, bearing clusters of white or pink flowers.

moun·tain li·on ▸*n.* another term for COUGAR.

moun·tain·ous /ˈmountn-əs/ ▸*adj.* (of a region) having many mountains. ■ huge: *struggling under mountainous debts.*

moun·tain range ▸*n.* a line of mountains connected by high ground.

moun·tain·side /ˈmountnˌsīd/ ▸*n.* the sloping surface of a mountain.

Moun·tain time ▸the standard time in a zone including parts of the U.S. and Canada in or near the Rocky Mountains, specifically: ■ (**Mountain Standard Time** abbrev.: **MST**) standard time based on the mean solar time at the meridian 105° W., seven hours behind GMT. ■ (**Mountain Daylight Time** abbrev.: **MDT**) Mountain time during daylight saving time, eight hours behind GMT.

moun·te·bank /ˈmountiˌbaNGk/ ▸*n.* a person who deceives others, esp. in order to trick them out of their money; a charlatan. ■ *hist.* a person who sold patent medicines in public places. —**moun·te·bank·er·y** /-ˌbaNGkərē/ *n.*

Moun·tie /ˈmountē/ ▸*n.* *inf.* a member of the Royal Canadian Mounted Police.

mount·ing /ˈmountiNG/ ▸*n.* **1** a backing, setting, or support for something: *he pulled the curtain rod from its mounting.* **2** the action of mounting something: *the mounting of rapid-fire guns.*

mourn /môrn/ ▸*v.* [*tr.*] feel or show deep sorrow or regret for (someone or their death). ■ feel regret or sadness about (the loss or disappearance of something): *publishers mourned declining sales.*

mourn·er /ˈmôrnər/ ▸*n.* a person who attends a funeral as a relative or friend of the dead person. ■ *chiefly hist.* a person hired to attend a funeral.

mourn·ful /ˈmôrnfəl/ ▸*adj.* feeling or expressing sadness, regret, or grief. ■ suggestive of or inducing sadness, regret, or unhappiness: *his voice on one track, mournful piano on another.* —**mourn·ful·ly** *adv.* —**mourn·ful·ness** *n.*

mourn·ing /ˈmôrniNG/ ▸*n.* the expression of deep sorrow for someone who has died. ■ black clothes worn as an expression of grief when someone dies.

mourn·ing dove ▸*n.* a North and Central American dove (*Zenaida macroura*) with a long tail, a gray-brown back, and a plaintive call.

mouse ▸*n.* /mous/ (*pl.* **mice** /mīs/) **1** a small rodent (family Muridae) that typically has a pointed snout, relatively large ears and eyes, and a long tail. ■ (in general use) any similar small mammal, such as a shrew or vole. ■ a shy, timid, and quiet person. **2** (*pl.* usu. **mouses**) *Comput.* a small hand-held device that is dragged across a flat surface to move the cursor on a computer screen, typically having buttons that are pressed to control computer functions. **3** *inf.* a lump or bruise, esp. one on or near the eye.
▸*v.* /mouz/ [*intr.*] **1** (of a cat or an owl) hunt for or catch mice. ■ prowl around as if searching. **2** *Comput., inf.* use a mouse to move a cursor on a computer screen. ▷Old English *mūs*, (plural) *mȳs*; related to German *Maus*, Latin and Greek *mus.* —**mous·er** /ˈmousər/, -zər/ *n.*

mouse pad (also **mouse-pad**) ▸*n.* a piece of rigid or slightly resilient material on which a computer mouse is moved.

mouse·trap /ˈmousˌtrap/ ▸*n.* a trap for catching and usually killing mice, esp. one with a spring bar that snaps down onto the mouse when it touches bait attached to the mechanism.
▸*v.* (**-trapped, -trap·ping**) [*tr.*] *inf.* induce (someone) to do something by means of a trick: *the editor mousetrapped her into giving him an article.*

mous·sa·ka /mooˈsäkə; ˌmoosəˈkä/ ▸*n.* a Greek dish made of ground lamb, eggplant, and tomatoes, with cheese on top.

mousse /moos/ ▸*n.* a sweet or savory dish made as a smooth light mass with whipped cream and beaten egg white: *dark chocolate mousse.* ■ a soft, light, or aerated gel such as a soap preparation: *shower mousse.* ■ a frothy preparation that is applied to the hair, enabling it to be styled more easily.
▸*v.* [*tr.*] style (hair) using mousse.

mous·tache ▸*n.* variant spelling of MUSTACHE.

mous·y /ˈmousē; -zē/ (also **mous·ey**) ▸*adj.* (**mous·i·er, mous·i·est**) of or like a mouse. ■ (of hair) of a dull light brown color. ■ (of a person) nervous, shy, or timid; lacking in presence or charisma. —**mous·i·ness** *n.*

mouth ▸*n.* /mouTH/ (*pl.* **mouths** /mouTHz; mouTHs/) **1** the opening in the lower part of the human face, surrounded by the lips, through which food is taken in and from which speech and other sounds are emitted. ■ the cavity behind this, containing the teeth and tongue. ■ the corresponding opening through which an animal takes in food, or the cavity behind this. ■ *inf.* talkativeness; impudence: *you've got more mouth on you than anyone I've ever known.* **2** an opening or entrance to a structure that is hollow, concave, or almost completely enclosed: *standing before the mouth of a cave.* ■ the opening for filling or emptying something used as a container: *the mouth of the bottle.* ■ the muzzle of a gun. ■ the opening or entrance to a harbor or bay. ■ the place where a river enters the sea.
▸*v.* /mouTH; mouTH/ [*tr.*] **1** say (something dull or unoriginal), esp. in a pompous or affected way: *this clergyman mouths platitudes.* ■ utter very clearly and distinctly: *she would carefully mouth the right pronunciation.* ■ move the lips as if saying (something) or in a grimace: *she mouthed a silent farewell.* **2** take in or touch with the mouth: *puppies may mouth each other's collars during play.*
▸*phrasal v.* □ **mouth off** *inf.* talk in an unpleasantly loud and boastful or opinionated way. ■ (**mouth off at**) loudly criticize or abuse. —**mouthed** /mouTHd; mouTHt/ *adj.* —**mouth·er** /ˈmouTHər/ *n.* —**mouth·less** /ˈmouTHləs/ *adj.*

mouth·breed·er /ˈmouTHˌbrēdər/ ▸*n.* a freshwater cichlid (*Sarotherodon* and other genera) that protects its eggs (and in some cases its young) by carrying them in its mouth. Also called **mouth·brood·er.**

mouth·feel /ˈmouTHˌfēl/ ▸*n.* the physical sensations in the mouth produced by a particular food.

mouth·ful /ˈmouTHˌfool/ ▸*n.* (*pl.* **-fuls**) **1** a quantity of food or drink that fills or can be put into the mouth. **2** a long or complicated word or phrase that is difficult to say: *"Galinsoga" was too much of a mouthful for most nonbotanists.*

mouth or·gan ▸*n.* another term for HARMONICA.

mouth·part /ˈmouTHˌpärt/ ▸*n.* (usu. **mouthparts**) *Zool.* any of the appendages, typically found in pairs, surrounding the mouth of an insect or other arthropod and adapted for feeding.

mouth·piece /ˈmouTHˌpēs/ ▸*n.* **1** a thing designed to be put in or against the mouth: *the snorkel's mouthpiece.* ■ a part of a musical instrument placed between or against the lips. ■ the part of a telephone for speaking into. ■ the part of a tobacco pipe placed between the lips. **2** *chiefly derog.* a person or organization that speaks on behalf of another person or organization: *they become nothing more than a mouthpiece for the company.* ■ *inf.* a lawyer.

mouth-to-mouth ▸*adj.* denoting a method of artificial respiration in which a person breathes into an unconscious patient's lungs through the mouth: *mouth-to-mouth resuscitation.*
▸*n.* respiration of this kind.

mouth·wash /ˈmouTHˌwôsh; -ˌwäsh/ ▸*n.* a liquid used for rinsing the mouth or gargling with, typically containing an antiseptic.

mouth·wa·ter·ing /ˈmouTHˌwôtəriNG; -ˌwätəriNG/ ▸*adj.* smelling, looking, or sounding delicious: *a small but mouthwatering collection of recipes.* ■ highly attractive or tempting: *investors expected mouthwatering deals.*

mov·a·ble /ˈmoovəbəl/ (also **move·a·ble**) ▸*adj.* **1** capable of being moved: *they stripped the town of all movable objects and fled.* ■ (of a feast or festival) variable in date from year to year. **2** *Law* (of property) of the nature of a chattel, as distinct from land or buildings.
▸*n.* (usu. **movables**) property or possessions not including land or buildings. ■ an article of furniture that may be removed from a house, as distinct from a fixture. —**mov·a·bil·i·ty** /ˌmoovəˈbilətē/ *n.* —**mov·a·bly** /-blē/ *adv.*

move /moov/ ▸*v.* **1** [*intr.*] go in a specified direction or manner; change position: *she moved to the door* | *he let his eyes move across the rows of faces.* ■ [*tr. often*] change the place or position of: *she moved the tray to a side table.* ■ change one's place of residence or work: *his family moved to London.* ■ [*tr.*] change the date or time of (an event). ■ (of a player) change the position of a piece in a board game. **2** change or cause to change from one state, opinion, sphere, or activity to another: [*intr.*] *the school moved over to the new course in 1987* | [*tr.*] *she deftly moved the conversation to safer territory.* ■ [*tr.*] influence or prompt (someone) to do something: *his deep love of music moved him to take lessons with Dr. Hill.* ■ [*intr.*] take action:

hard-liners may yet **move against** him. ■ [tr.] (usu. **be moved**) provoke a strong feeling, esp. of sorrow or sympathy, in: *he was moved to tears by a get-well message from the president.* ■ [tr.] *archaic* stir up (an emotion) in someone. **3** [intr.] make progress; develop in a particular manner or direction: *aircraft design had moved forward* | *legislators are anxious to get things moving.* ■ [intr.] *inf.* depart; start off: *let's move—it's time we started shopping.* ■ [in *imper.*] (**move it**) *inf.* used to urge or command someone to hurry up. ■ [intr.] *inf.* go quickly: *Kenny was really moving when he flipped over.* ■ [intr.] (of merchandise) be sold: *despite the high prices, goods are moving.* ■ [tr.] sell (merchandise). **4** [intr.] (**move in/within**) spend one's time or be socially active in (a particular sphere) or among (a particular group of people): *they moved in different circles.* **5** [tr.] propose for discussion and resolution at a meeting or legislative assembly: ■ make a formal request or application to (a court or assembly) for something: *his family moved the court for adequate "maintenance expenses".* **6** [tr.] empty (one's bowels). ■ [intr.] (of the bowels) be emptied.
▶*phrasal v.* □ **move in** **1** take possession of a new house or business premises. ■ (**move in with**) start to share accommodations with (an existing resident). **2** intervene, esp. so as to take control of a situation. □ **move in on** approach, esp. so as to take action: *the police moved in on him.* □ **move on** progress: b ˮ t has moved on, leaving Russia behind. ■ (**move on**) progress: *ballet ha͞ noved on, leaving Russia behind.* □ **move over** (or **aside**) adjust one's position to make room for someone else.
▶*n.* a change of place or position: *his eyes followed her every move.* ■ a change of house or business premises. ■ a change of job, career, or business direction: *a career move.* ■ a change of state or opinion: *the country's move to independence.* ■ an action that initiates or advances a process or plan: *my next move is to talk to Matthew.* ■ a maneuver in a sport or game. ■ a change of position of a piece in a board game. ■ a player's turn to make such a change: *it's your move.*
▶ □ **get a move on** [often in *imper.*] *inf.* hurry up. □ **get moving** [often in *imper.*] *inf.* make a prompt start (on a journey or an undertaking): *you're here to work, so get moving.* □ **make a move** take action. □ **on the move** in the process of moving from one place or job to another: *it's difficult to contact her because she's always on the move.* ■ making progress: *the economy appeared to be on the move.*

move·a·ble /'mo͞ovəbəl/ ▶*adj. & n.* variant spelling of MOVABLE.
move·ment /'mo͞ovmənt/ ▶*n.* **1** an act of changing physical location or position or of having this changed. ■ (also **bowel movement**) an act of defecation. ■ (**movements**) the activities and whereabouts of someone, esp. during a particular period of time: *your movements and telephone conversations are recorded.* ■ the general activity or bustle of people or things in a particular place: *the scene was almost devoid of movement.* ■ the quality of suggesting motion in a work of art: *the painting was a busy landscape, full of detail and movement.* ■ the progressive development of a poem or story: *the novel shows minimal concern for narrative movement.* ■ a change or development in something: *movements in the underlying financial markets.* **2** a group of people working together to advance their shared political, social, or artistic ideas: *the labor movement.* ■ a campaign undertaken by such a group. ■ a change in policy or general attitudes seen as positive: *the movement toward greater sexual equality.* **3** *Mus.* a principal division of a longer musical work, self-sufficient in terms of key, tempo, and structure: *the slow movement of his violin concerto.* **4** the moving parts of a mechanism, esp. a clock or watch.
mov·er /'mo͞ovər/ ▶*n.* **1** a person or thing in motion, esp. an animal. ■ a person whose job is to remove and transport furniture from one building, esp. a house, to another. **2** a person who makes a formal proposal at a meeting or in an assembly: *movers and seconders rise and give speeches.* ■ a person who instigates or organizes something: *she was a key mover in making this successful conference happen.*
▶ □ **mover and shaker** a powerful person who initiates events and influences people.
mov·ie /'mo͞ove͞/ ▶*n.* a story or event recorded by a camera as a set of moving images and shown in a theater or on television; a motion picture. ■ (**the movies**) a movie theater: *we decided to go to the movies.* ■ motion pictures generally or the motion-picture industry.
mov·ing /'mo͞oviNG/ ▶*adj.* **1** in motion: *a fast-moving river.* **2** producing strong emotion, esp. sadness or sympathy: *an unforgettable and moving book.* **3** relating to the process of changing one's residence: *moving expenses.* **4** involving a moving vehicle: *tickets for moving violations.* —**mov·ing·ly** *adv.*
mow[1] /mo͞/ ▶*v.* (*past part.* **mowed** or **mown** /mo͞n/) [tr.] cut down (an area of grass) with a machine: *Roger mowed the lawn* | [as *adj.*] (**mown**) *the smell of newly mown grass.* ■ *chiefly hist.* cut down (grass or a cereal crop) with a scythe or a sickle.
▶*phrasal v.* □ **mow someone down** kill someone with a fusillade of

bullets or other missiles. ■ recklessly knock someone down with a car or other vehicle. —**mow·er** *n.*
mow[2] /mou/ ▶*n.* a stack of hay, grain, or other similar crop: *the hay mow.* ■ a place in a barn where such a stack is put.
mox·ie /'mäkse͞/ ▶*n.* *inf.* force of character, determination, or nerve.
moz·za·rel·la /ˌmätsə'relə/ ▶*n.* a mild, semisoft white Italian cheese, often used in Italian cooking as a melted topping, esp. on pizzas.
MP ▶*abbr.* ■ Member of Parliament: *Robert Brown, MP.* ■ military police. ■ military policeman.
mpg ▶*abbr.* miles per gallon (a measurement of a vehicle's rate of fuel consumption).
Mr. /'mistər/ ▶*abbr.* a title used before a surname or full name to address or refer to a man without a higher or honorific or professional title: *Mr. Robert Smith.* ■ used before the name of an office to address a man who holds it: *yes, Mr. President.* ■ *humorous* used before an invented surname to imply that someone has a particular characteristic: *Mr. Big-Shot.* ■ (often as **Mister**) used in the armed forces to address a senior warrant officer, officer cadet, or junior naval officer.
MRI ▶*abbr.* magnetic resonance imaging.
mRNA *Biol.* ▶*abbr.* messenger RNA.
Mrs. /'misəz/ 'miz-; -əs/ ▶*n.* a title used before a surname or full name to address or refer to a married woman, or a woman who has been married, without a higher or honorific or professional title: *Mrs. Sally Jones.*
MS ▶*abbr.* ■ (also **ms**) manuscript. ■ Master of Science. ■ motor ship. ■ multiple sclerosis.
Ms. /miz/ ▶*n.* a title used before the surname or full name of any woman regardless of her marital status (a neutral alternative to **Mrs.** or **Miss**): *Ms. Sarah Brown.* ■ *humorous* used before an invented surname to imply that someone has a particular characteristic: *Ms. Do-Right.*
MS-DOS /ˌem ˌes 'däs; dôs/ *trademark Comput.* ▶*abbr.* Microsoft disk operating system.
MSG ▶*abbr.* monosodium glutamate.
Msgr ▶*abbr.* ■ Monseigneur. ■ Monsignor.
MSS (also **mss**) ▶*abbr.* manuscripts.
MST ▶*abbr.* Mountain Standard Time (see MOUNTAIN TIME).
MT ▶*abbr.* ■ megaton. ■ (also **m.t.**) metric ton.
Mt ▶*abbr.* ■ the Gospel of Matthew (in biblical references). ■ [in *place names*] (also **Mt.**) Mount: *Mt. Everest.*
▶*symb.* the chemical element meitnerium.
mu /m(y)o͞o/ ▶*n.* the twelfth letter of the Greek alphabet (**M**, **μ**), transliterated as 'm.' ■ [as *adj.*] *Physics* relating to muons: *mu particle.*
▶*symb.* ■ (μ) micron. ■ (μ) [in *comb.*] "micro-" in symbols for units: *the recommended daily amount is 750 μg.*
much /məCH/ ▶*adj. & pron.* (**more** /môr/, **most** /mōst/) a large amount: [as *adj.*] *I did not get much sleep* | *I did so much shopping* | [as *pron.*] *he does not eat much* | *they must bear much of the blame.* ■ [as *pron.*] used to refer to someone or something as being a poor specimen: *I'm not much of a gardener.*
▶*adv.* to a great extent; a great deal: *did it hurt much?* | *thanks very much* | *they did not mind, much to my surprise* ■ for a large part of one's time; often: *I'm not there much.* —**much·ly** *adv.* (*humorous*).
▶ □ **as much** the same: *I am sure she would do as much for me.* □ (**as**) **much as** even though: *much as I had enjoyed my adventure, it was good to be back.*
mu·ci·lage /'myo͞os(ə)lij/ ▶*n.* a polysaccharide substance extracted as a viscous or gelatinous solution from plant roots, seeds, etc., and used in medicines and adhesives. ■ an adhesive solution; gum or glue. —**mu·ci·lag·i·nous** /ˌmyo͞osə'lajənəs/ *adj.*
muck /mək/ ▶*n.* dirt, rubbish, or waste matter. ■ farmyard manure, widely used as fertilizer. ■ *inf.* something regarded as worthless, sordid, or corrupt.
▶*v.* [tr.] **1** (**muck up**) *inf.* mishandle (a job or situation); spoil (something): *she had mucked up her first few weeks at college.* **2** *rare* spread manure on (land).
▶*phrasal v.* □ **muck about/around** *chiefly Brit., inf.* behave in a silly or aimless way: *he spent his summers mucking about in boats.* ■ (**muck about/around with**) spoil (something) by interfering with it: *they did not want designers mucking about with their newspapers.* ▷Middle English *muk*, probably of Scandinavian origin: compare with Old Norse *myki* 'dung,' from a Germanic base meaning 'soft,' shared by *meek*.
muck·rak·ing /'mək,rākiNG/ ▶*n.* the action of searching out and publicizing scandalous information about famous people in an underhanded way, esp. with the political aim of exposing corruption. —**muck·rake** /-,rāk/ *v.* —**muck·rak·er** /-,rākər/ *n.*

muck·y /'məkē/ ▶*adj.* (**muck·i·er, muck·i·est**) covered with or consisting of dirt or filth. —**muck·i·ness** *n.*

mu·co·sa /myōō'kōzə/ ▶*n.* (*pl.* **-sae** /-zē; -,zī/) a mucous membrane: *the intestinal mucosa.* —**mu·co·sal** *adj.*

mu·cous /'myōōkəs/ ▶*adj.* relating to, producing, covered with, or of the nature of mucus. —**mu·cos·i·ty** /,myōō'käsətē/ *n.*

mu·cus /'myōōkəs/ ▶*n.* a slimy substance, typically not miscible with water, secreted by mucous membranes and glands for lubrication, protection, etc.

mud /məd/ ▶*n.* soft, sticky matter resulting from the mixing of earth and water. ■ *fig.* information or allegations regarded as damaging, typically concerned with corruption: *they are trying to **sling mud** at me to cover up their defeat.*

mud·bank /'məd,baNGk/ ▶*n.* a bank of mud on the bed of a river or the bottom of the sea.

mud·dle /'mədl/ ▶*v.* [*tr.*] bring into a disordered or confusing state. ■ confuse (a person or their thoughts): *I do not wish to muddle him by making him read more books.* ■ [*intr.*] busy oneself in a confused and ineffective way: *he was muddling about in the kitchen.* ■ mix (a drink) or stir (an ingredient) into a drink.
▶*phrasal v.* □ **muddle through** cope more or less satisfactorily despite lack of expertise, planning, or equipment: *we don't have an ultimate ambition; we just muddle through.*
▶*n.* an untidy and disorganized state or collection: *a muddle of French, English, Ojibwa, and Gaelic* | *the finances were **in a muddle*** | *she cut through the confusion and muddle.* ■ a mistake arising from or resulting in confusion: *a bureaucratic muddle.* ▷late Middle English (in the sense 'wallow in mud'): perhaps from Middle Dutch *moddelen,* frequentative of *modden* 'dabble in mud.' The sense 'confuse' was initially associated with alcoholic drink (late 17th cent.), giving rise to 'busy oneself in a confused way' and 'jumble up' (mid 19th cent.). —**mud·dling·ly** /'mədliNGlē; 'mədl-iNGlē/ *adv.* —**mud·dly** /'mədlē; 'mədl-ē/ *adj.*

mud·dle-head·ed (also **mud·dle·head·ed**) ▶*adj.* mentally disorganized or confused. —**mud·dle-head·ed·ness** (also **mud·dle·head·ed·ness**) *n.*

mud·dy /'mədē/ ▶*adj.* (**-di·er, -di·est**) covered in or full of mud. ■ (of a liquid) discolored and made cloudy by mud. ■ (of a color) dull and dirty-looking. ■ (of a sound, esp. in music) not clearly defined: *an awful muddy sound that renders his vocal incoherent.* ■ confused, vague, or illogical: *some sentences are so muddy that their meaning can only be guessed.*
▶*v.* (**-dies, -died**) [*tr.*] cause to become covered in or full of mud. ■ make (something) hard to perceive or understand: *the first year's results muddy rather than clarify the situation.* —**mud·di·ly** /'mədl-ē/ *adv.* —**mud·di·ness** *n.*

mud flap (also **mud·flap**) ▶*n.* a flap that hangs behind the wheel of a vehicle and is designed to prevent water, mud, and stones thrown up from the road from hitting the bodywork of the vehicle or any following vehicles.

mud·guard /'məd,gärd/ ▶*n.* a curved strip or cover over a wheel of a vehicle, esp. a bicycle or motorcycle, designed to the protect the vehicle and rider from water and dirt thrown up from the road.

mud·pup·py ▶*n.* a large aquatic salamander (*Necturus maculosus,* family Proteidae) of the eastern US, reaching sexual maturity while retaining an immature body form with feathery external gills.

mud·slide /'məd,slīd/ ▶*n.* a mass of mud and other earthy material that is falling or has fallen down a hillside or other slope.

mues·li /'m(y)ōōzlē/ ▶*n.* (*pl.* **mues·lis**) a mixture of cereals (esp. rolled oats), dried fruit, and nuts, typically eaten with milk at breakfast.

mu·ez·zin /m(y)ōō'ezən; 'mōōəzən/ ▶*n.* a man who calls Muslims to prayer from the minaret of a mosque.

muff¹ /məf/ ▶*n.* a tube made of fur or other warm material into which the hands are placed for warmth. ■ a warm or protective covering for other parts of the body.

muff² *inf.* ▶*v.* [*tr.*] handle (a situation, task, or opportunity) clumsily or badly: *the administration muffed several of its biggest projects.* ■ fail to catch or receive (a ball) or to hit (a shot or a target): *the catcher muffed a perfect throw home.* ■ speak (lines from a theatrical part) badly.
▶*n.* a mistake or failure, esp. a failure to catch or receive a ball cleanly.

muf·fin /'məfən/ ▶*n.* a small domed cake or quick bread made from batter or dough: *blueberry muffins.* ■ short for **ENGLISH MUFFIN.**

muf·fle /'məfəl/ ▶*v.* [*tr.*] (often **be muffled**) wrap or cover for warmth: *muffled in an absurd overcoat.* ■ cover or wrap up (a source of sound) to reduce its loudness: [as *adj.*] (**muffled**) *a muffled drum.* ■ make (a sound) quieter or less distinct: *his voice was muffled.*

muf·fler /'məf(ə)lər/ ▶*n.* **1** a scarf or wrap worn around the neck and face for warmth. **2** a part of a motor vehicle's exhaust system, serving to muffle the sound of the vehicle. ■ a device used to deaden the sound of a drum, bell, piano, or other instrument.

muf·ti¹ /'məftē/ ▶*n.* (*pl.* **muf·tis**) a Muslim legal expert who is empowered to give rulings on religious matters.

muf·ti² ▶*n.* plain clothes worn by a person who wears a uniform for their job, such as a soldier or police officer: *I was a flying officer in mufti.*

mug /məg/ ▶*n.* **1** a large cup, typically cylindrical and with a handle and used without a saucer: ■ the contents of such a cup: *a large mug of tea vanished in a single gulp.* **2** *inf.* a person's face. **3** *inf.* a hoodlum or thug. **4** *Brit., inf.* a stupid or gullible person.
▶*v.* (**mugged, mug·ging**) *inf.* **1** [*tr.*] (often **be mugged**) attack and rob (someone) in a public place: *he was mugged by three men who stole his bike* | [as *n.*] (**mugging**) *a brutal mugging.* ■ *dated* fight or hit (someone). **2** [*intr.*] make faces, esp. silly or exaggerated ones, before an audience or a camera: *he mugged for the camera.* —**mug·ful** /'məg,fōōl/ *n.* (*pl.* **-fuls**). —**mug·ger** *n.*

mug·gy /'məgē/ ▶*adj.* (**-gi·er, -gi·est**) (of the weather) unpleasantly warm and humid. —**mug·gi·ness** *n.*

mug shot (also **mug·shot**) ▶*n.* a photograph of a person's face made for an official purpose, esp. police records.

mug·wort /'məg,wərt; -,wôrt/ ▶*n.* a plant (genus *Artemisia*) of the daisy family, with aromatic divided leaves that are dark green above and whitish below, native to north temperate regions.

mug·wump /'məg,wəmp/ ▶*n.* a person who remains aloof or independent, esp. from party politics. ■ a Republican who in 1884 refused to support James G. Blaine, the Republican nominee for president.

Mu·ham·mad·an /mōō'hämədən; mə-; 'ham-/ (also **Mo·ham·med·an**) ▶*n.* & *adj.* archaic term for **MUSLIM** (not favored by Muslims). —**Mu·ham·mad·an·ism** *n.*

mu·lat·to /m(y)ōō'lätō; -'latō/ *dated* ▶*n.* (*pl.* **-toes** or **-tos**) a person of mixed white and black ancestry, esp. a person with one white and one black parent.
▶*adj.* relating to or denoting a mulatto or mulattoes.

mul·ber·ry /'məl,berē/ ▶*n.* **1** (also **mulberry tree** or **bush**) a small deciduous tree (genus *Morus,* family Moraceae) with broad leaves, native to the Far East and long cultivated elsewhere. ■ the dark red or white loganberrylike fruit of this tree. **2** a dark red or purple color.

mulch /məlCH/ ▶*n.* a material (such as decaying leaves, bark, or compost) spread around or over a plant to enrich or insulate the soil.
▶*v.* [*intr.*] apply a mulch. ■ [*tr.*] treat or cover with mulch.

mulct /məlkt/ *formal* ▶*v.* [*tr.*] extract money from (someone) by fine or taxation. ■ (**mulct someone of**) deprive someone of (money or possessions) by fraudulent means: *he mulcted Shelly of $75,000.*
▶*n.* a fine or compulsory payment.

mule¹ /myōōl/ ▶*n.* **1** the offspring of a donkey and a horse (strictly, a male donkey and a female horse), typically sterile and used as a beast of burden. ■ a person compared to a mule, esp. in being stubborn or obstinate. ■ *inf.* a courier for illegal drugs. ■ a small tractor or locomotive, typically one that is electrically powered. **2** a hybrid plant or animal, esp. a sterile one. **3** (also **spinning mule**) a kind of spinning machine producing yarn on spindles, invented by Samuel Crompton (1753–1827) in 1779. **4** a coin with the obverse and reverse of designs not originally intended to be used together.

mule² ▶*n.* a slipper or light shoe without a back.

mul·ish /'myōōlisH/ ▶*adj.* resembling or likened to a mule in being stubborn. —**mul·ish·ly** *adv.* —**mul·ish·ness** *n.*

mull¹ /məl/ ▶*v.* [*tr.*] think about (a fact, proposal, or request) deeply and at length: *she began to **mull** over the various possibilities.*

mull² ▶*v.* [*tr.*] [usu. as *adj.*] (**mulled**) warm (a beverage, esp. wine, beer, or cider) and add spices and sweetening to it: *a tankard of mulled ale.*

mull³ ▶*n.* thin, soft, plain muslin, used in bookbinding for joining the spine of a book to its cover.

mul·lah /'mōōlə; 'mōōlə/ (also **mul·la**) ▶*n.* a Muslim learned in Islamic theology and sacred law. ▷early 17th cent.: from Persian, Turkish, and Urdu *mullā,* from Arabic *mawlā.*

mul·lein /'mələn/ ▶*n.* a herbaceous Eurasian plant (genus *Verbascum*) of the figwort family, with woolly leaves and tall spikes of yellow flowers.

mul·let /'mələt/ ▶*n.* a chiefly marine fish (families Mullidae and Mugilidae) that is widely caught for food.

mul·li·ga·taw·ny /ˌməligəˈtônē; -ˈtänē/ (also **mulligatawny soup**) ▶n. a spicy meat or chicken soup originally made in India.

mul·lion /ˈməlyən/ ▶n. a vertical bar between the panes of glass in a window. Compare with TRANSOM. —**mul·lioned** adj.

mul·ti·cel·lu·lar /ˌməltiˈselyələr; ˌməltī-/ ▶adj. Biol. (of an organism or part) having or consisting of many cells. —**mul·ti·cel·lu·lar·i·ty** /-ˌselyəˈle(ə)rətē/ n.

mul·ti·col·ored /ˌməltiˈkələrd; ˌməlˌtī-/ (also **mul·ti·col·or**) ▶adj. having many colors.

mul·ti·cul·tur·al /ˌməltēˈkəlCH(ə)rəl; ˌməlˌtī-/ ▶adj. of, relating to, or constituting several cultural or ethnic groups within a society: *multicultural education.* —**mul·ti·cul·tur·al·ism** n. —**mul·ti·cul·tur·al·ist** n. & adj. —**mul·ti·cul·tur·al·ly** adv.

mul·ti·di·men·sion·al /ˌməltidəˈmenCHənəl; ˌməlˌtī-/ ▶adj. of or involving several dimensions or aspects: *multidimensional space | a reading that lends itself to multidimensional readings.* —**mul·ti·di·men·sion·al·i·ty** /-dəˌmenCHəˈnalətē/ n. —**mul·ti·di·men·sion·al·ly** /-dəˈmenCHənl-ē/ adv.

mul·ti·di·rec·tion·al /ˌməltidəˈrekSHənl/ ▶adj. of, involving, or operating in several directions: *a multidirectional antenna.*

mul·ti·far·i·ous /ˌməlt(ə)ˈfe(ə)rēəs/ ▶adj. many and of various types: *multifarious activities.* ■ having many varied parts or aspects: *a vast multifarious organization.* —**mul·ti·far·i·ous·ly** adv. —**mul·ti·far·i·ous·ness** n.

mul·ti·lat·er·al /ˌməltiˈlatərəl/ ▶adj. agreed upon or participated in by three or more parties, esp. the governments of different countries. ■ having members or contributors from several groups, esp. several different countries: *multilateral aid agencies.* —**mul·ti·lat·er·al·ism** /-ˌlizəm/ n. —**mul·ti·lat·er·al·ist** /-list/ adj. & n. —**mul·ti·lat·er·al·ly** adv.

mul·ti·lin·gual /ˌməltēˈliNGɡ(yə)wəl; ˌməlˌtī-/ ▶adj. in or using several languages: *a multilingual dictionary.* —**mul·ti·lin·gual·ism** /-ˌlizəm/ n. —**mul·ti·lin·gual·ly** adv.

mul·ti·me·di·a /ˌməltiˈmēdēə; ˌməlˌtī-/ ▶adj. (of art, education, etc.) using more than one medium of expression or communication.

mul·ti·na·tion·al /ˌməltiˈnaSHənl; ˌməlˌtī-/ ▶adj. including or involving several countries or individuals of several nationalities: *1,500 troops were sent to join the multinational force.* ■ (of a business organization) operating in several countries: *multinational corporations.* ▶n. a company operating in several countries. —**mul·ti·na·tion·al·ly** adv.

mul·ti·ple /ˈməltəpəl/ ▶adj. having or involving several parts, elements, or members. ■ numerous and often varied: *words with multiple meanings.* ■ (of a disease, injury, or disability) complex in its nature or effects, or affecting several parts of the body: *a multiple fracture of the femur | multiple births.* ▶n. a number that can be divided by another number without a remainder: *15, 20, or any other multiple of five.*

mul·ti·ple-choice ▶adj. (of a question on a test) accompanied by several possible answers from which the candidate must try to choose the correct one.

mul·ti·ple per·son·al·i·ty ▶n. [often as adj.] Psychol. a rare dissociative disorder in which two or more personalities with distinct memories and behavior patterns apparently exist in one individual: *multiple-personality disorder.* Also called SPLIT PERSONALITY.

mul·ti·ple scle·ro·sis ▶n. a chronic, typically progressive disease involving damage to the sheaths of nerve cells in the brain and spinal cord, whose symptoms may include numbness, impairment of speech and of muscular coordination, blurred vision, and severe fatigue.

mul·ti·plex /ˈməlti,pleks/ ▶adj. consisting of many elements in a complex relationship. ■ involving simultaneous transmission of several messages along a single channel of communication. ■ (of a movie theater) having several separate screens within one building. ▶n. **1** a system or signal involving simultaneous transmission of several messages along a single channel of communication. Compare with DUPLEX, SIMPLEX. **2** a movie theater with several separate screens. —**mul·ti·plex·er** (also **mul·ti·plex·or**) n.

mul·ti·pli·cand /ˌməltəpliˈkand/ ▶n. a quantity that is to be multiplied by another (the multiplier).

mul·ti·pli·ca·tion /ˌməltəpliˈkāSHən/ ▶n. the process or skill of multiplying. ■ Math. the process of combining matrices, vectors, or other quantities under specific rules to obtain their product.

mul·ti·pli·ca·tion sign ▶n. a sign, esp. ×, used to indicate that one quantity is to be multiplied by another, as in $2 \times 3 = 6$.

mul·ti·pli·ca·tion ta·ble ▶n. a table of the products of two factors, esp. the integers 1 to 12.

mul·ti·plic·i·ty /ˌməltəˈplisətē/ ▶n. (pl. **-ties**) a large number. ■ a large variety: *the rain forests and the multiplicity of species that they harbor.*

mul·ti·pli·er /ˈməltə,plīər/ ▶n. a person or thing that multiplies. ■ a

quantity by which a given number (the multiplicand) is to be multiplied. ■ *Econ.* a factor by which an increment of income exceeds the resulting increment of savings or investment.

mul·ti·ply[1] /ˈməltə,plī/ ▶v. (**-plies, -plied**) [tr.] obtain from (a number) another that contains the first number a specified number of times: *I asked you to multiply fourteen by nineteen | [intr.] we all know how to multiply by ten.* ■ increase or cause to increase greatly in number or quantity: [intr.] *ever since I became a landlord my troubles have multiplied tenfold | [tr.] cigarette smoking combines with other factors to multiply the risks of atherosclerosis.* ■ [intr.] (of an animal or other organism) increase in number by reproducing. ■ propagate (plants).

mul·ti·ply[2] /ˈməltəplē/ ▶adv. in several different ways or respects: *multiply injured patients.*

mul·ti·po·lar /ˌməltiˈpōlər; ˌməlˌtī-/ ▶adj. **1** having many poles or extremities. **2** polarized in several ways or directions. —**mul·ti·po·lar·i·ty** /-pōˈlaritē; -pə-/ n. —**mul·ti·pole** /ˈməlti,pōl; ˈməlˌtī-/ n.

mul·ti·proc·ess·ing /ˌməltiˈpräs,esiNG; ˌməlˌtī-; -ˈprä,sesiNG/ ▶n. Comput. the running of two or more programs or sequences of instructions simultaneously by a computer with more than one central processor.

mul·ti·pur·pose /ˌməltēˈpərpəs; ˌməlˌtī-/ ▶adj. having several purposes or functions: *a multipurpose civic center.*

mul·ti·ra·cial /ˌməltiˈrāSHəl; ˌməlˌtī-/ ▶adj. made up of or relating to people of several or many races: *multiracial education.* —**mul·ti·ra·cial·ism** /-ˌlizəm/ n. —**mul·ti·ra·cial·ist** /-list/ adj. & n. —**mul·ti·ra·cial·ly** adv.

mul·ti·sto·ry /ˈməlti,stôrē; ˈməlˌtī-/ (also **mul·ti·sto·ried**) ▶adj. (of a building) having several stories.

mul·ti·task·ing /ˌməltiˈtaskiNG; ˌməlˌtī-/ ▶n. **1** Comput. the simultaneous execution of more than one program or task by a single computer processor. **2** the handling of more than one task at the same time by a single person. —**mul·ti·task** /ˈməlti,task; ˈməlˌtī-/ v.

mul·ti·tude /ˈməltə,t(y)ōōd/ ▶n. a large number. ■ (**the multitudes**) large numbers of people: *the multitudes using the roads.* ■ (**the multitude**) a large gathering of people: *Father Peter addressed the multitude.* ■ (**the multitude**) the mass of ordinary people without power or influence. ■ *archaic* the state of being numerous: *they would swarm over the river in their multitude.* ▷Middle English: via Old French from Latin *multitudo*, from *multus* 'many.'

mul·ti·tu·di·nous /ˌməltəˈt(y)ōōdn-əs/ ▶adj. very numerous. ■ consisting of or containing many individuals or elements: *the multitudinous array of chemical substances that exist in the natural world.* —**mul·ti·tu·di·nous·ly** adv. —**mul·ti·tu·di·nous·ness** n.

mul·ti·us·er /ˈməltē,yōōzər; ˈməlˌtī-/ ▶adj. (of a computer system) able to be used by a number of people simultaneously. ■ denoting a computer game in which several players interact simultaneously using the Internet or other communications.

mum[1] /məm/ ▶adj. silent. ▶ □ **keep mum** inf. remain silent, esp. so as not to reveal a secret.

mum[2] ▶v. (**mummed, mum·ming**) [intr.] act in a traditional masked mime or a mummers' play.

mum[3] ▶n. inf. a cultivated chrysanthemum.

mum·ble /ˈməmbəl/ ▶v. **1** say something indistinctly and quietly, making it difficult for others to hear: [tr.] *he mumbled something she didn't catch | [with direct speech] "Sorry," she mumbled.* **2** [tr.] bite or chew with toothless gums or eat without making much use of the teeth. ▶n. a quiet and indistinct utterance: *Rosie replied in a mumble.* —**mum·bler** /ˈməmb(ə)lər/ n. —**mum·bling·ly** /ˈməmb(ə)liNGlē/ adv.

mum·bo-jum·bo /ˈməmbō ˈjəmbō/ (also **mum·bo- jum·bo**) ▶n. inf. language or ritual causing or intended to cause confusion or bewilderment: *a maze of legal mumbo jumbo.*

mum·mer /ˈməmər/ ▶n. an actor in a traditional masked mime, esp. of a type associated with Christmas and popular in England in the 18th and early 19th centuries. ■ a pantomimist. ■ *archaic or derog.* an actor in the theater.

mum·mer·y /ˈməmərē/ ▶n. (pl. **-mer·ies**) a performance by mummers. ■ ridiculous ceremonial, esp. of a religious nature.

mum·mi·fy /ˈməmə,fī/ ▶v. (**-fies, -fied**) [tr.] [usu. as adj.] (**mummified**) (esp. in ancient Egypt) preserve (a body) by embalming it and wrapping it in cloth: *the mummified bodies in the pyramids.* ■ shrivel or dry up (a body or a thing), thus preserving it: *the wind must have dehydrated and mummified the body.* —**mum·mi·fi·ca·tion** /ˌməməfiˈkāSHən/ n.

mum·my[1] /ˈməmē/ ▶n. (pl. **-mies**) **1** (esp. in ancient Egypt) a body of a human being or animal that has been ceremonially preserved by removal of the internal organs, treatment with mineral salt and resin, and wrapping in bandages. **2** a well-preserved, desiccated body.

mum·my[2] ▶n. (pl. **-mies**) British term for MOMMY.

mumps /məmps/ ▸pl. n. [treated as *sing.*] a contagious and infectious viral disease causing swelling of the salivary glands in the face, and a risk of sterility in adult males.

munch /mənCH/ ▸v. [*tr.*] eat (something) with a continuous and often audible action of the jaws: *he munched a chicken wing* | [*intr.*] *popcorn to munch on while watching the movie.* —**munch·er** n.

munch·ie /'mənCHē/ ▸n. (pl. **munch·ies**) (usu. **munchies**) *inf.* a snack or small item of food. ■ (**the munchies**) a sudden strong desire for food.

mun·dane /ˌmənˈdān/ ▸adj. **1** lacking interest or excitement; dull. **2** of this earthly world rather than a heavenly or spiritual one: *according to the Shinto doctrine, spirits of the dead can act upon the mundane world.* —**mun·dane·ly** adv. —**mun·dane·ness** n. —**mun·dan·i·ty** /-ˈdānətē/ n. (pl. **-ties**) .

mung /məNG/ (also **mung bean**) ▸n. **1** a small round green bean. **2** the tropical Old World plant (*Vigna radiata*, or *Phaseolus aureus*) that yields these beans, commonly grown as a source of bean sprouts.

mu·nic·i·pal /myŏŏˈnisəpəl; myə-/ ▸adj. of or relating to a city or town or its governing body. —**mu·nic·i·pal·ly** adv.

mu·nic·i·pal·i·ty /myŏŏˌnisəˈpalətē; myə-/ ▸n. (pl. **-ties**) an urban unit of government that has corporate status. ■ the governing body of such an area.

mu·nif·i·cent /myŏŏˈnifəsənt; myə-/ ▸adj. (of a gift or sum of money) larger or more generous than is usual. ■ (of a person) very generous. —**mu·nif·i·cence** n. —**mu·nif·i·cent·ly** adv.

mu·ni·tion /myŏŏˈnishən; myə-/ ▸pl. n. (**munitions**) military weapons, ammunition, equipment, and stores: *reserves of nuclear, chemical, and conventional munitions*

mu·on /'myŏŏˌän/ ▸n. Physics an unstable subatomic ·particle of the same class as an electron (a lepton), but with a mass around 200 times greater. Muons make up much of the cosmic radiation reaching the earth's surface. —**mu·on·ic** /myŏŏˈänik/ adj.

mu·ral /'myŏŏrəl/ ▸n. a painting or other work of art executed directly on a wall.
▸adj. of, like, or relating to a wall: *a mural escarpment.* —**mu·ral·ist** n.

mur·der /'mərdər/ ▸n. the unlawful premeditated killing of one human being by another. ■ *inf.* a very difficult or unpleasant task or experience: *my job at the mill was murder.* ■ *inf.* something causing great discomfort to a part of the body: *that exercise is **murder** on the lumbar regions.*
▸v. [*tr.*] kill (someone) unlawfully and with premeditation. ■ *inf.* punish severely or be very angry with: *my father will murder me if I'm home late.* ■ *inf.* conclusively defeat (an opponent) in a game or sport. ■ spoil by lack of skill or knowledge: *the only thing he had murdered was the English language.* ▷Old English *morthor*, of Germanic origin; related to Dutch *moord* and German *Mord*, from an Indo-European root shared by Sanskrit *mará* 'death' and Latin *mors*; reinforced in Middle English by Old French *murdre*. —**mur·der·er** n. —**mur·der·ess** /'mərdərəs/ n.

mur·der·ous /'mərdərəs/ ▸adj. capable of or intending to murder; dangerously violent. ■ (of an action, event, or plan) involving murder or extreme violence: *murderous acts of terrorism.* ■ *inf.* extremely arduous or unpleasant: *a murderous schedule of four games in ten days.* ■ *inf.* (of a person or their expression) extremely angry: *Mary emerged from the locker room, looking murderous.* —**mur·der·ous·ly** adv. —**mur·der·ous·ness** n.

murk /mərk/ ▸n. darkness or thick mist that makes it difficult to see: *my eyes were straining to see through the murk.*
▸adj. archaic murky; gloomy.

murk·y /'mərkē/ ▸adj. (**murk·i·er**, **murk·i·est**) dark and gloomy, esp. due to thick mist. ■ (of liquid) dark and dirty; not clear: *the murky silt of a pond.* ■ not fully explained or understood, esp. with concealed dishonesty or immorality. —**murk·i·ly** adv. —**murk·i·ness** n.

mur·mur /'mərmər/ ▸n. a soft, indistinct sound made by a person or group of people speaking quietly or at a distance. ■ a softly spoken or almost inaudible utterance: *she accepted his offer with a quiet murmur of thanks.* ■ the quiet or subdued expression of a particular feeling by a group of people: *there was a murmur of approval from the crowd.* ■ a rumor. ■ a low continuous sound: *the murmur of bees.* ■ Med. a recurring sound heard in the heart through a stethoscope that is usually a sign of disease or damage. ■ *inf.* a condition in which the heart produces or is apt to produce such a sound: *she had been born with a heart murmur.*
▸v. say something in a low, soft, or indistinct voice: ■ [*intr.*] make a low continuous sound: *the wind was murmuring through the trees.* ■ say something cautiously and discreetly: [*intr.*] *they began to murmur of an uprising.* ■ [*intr.*] (**murmur against**) archaic express one's discontent about (someone or something) in a subdued manner. —**mur·mur·er** n. —**mur·mur·ous** /-mərəs/ adj.

Mur·phy's Law /'mərfēz/ ▸a supposed law of nature, expressed in various humorous popular sayings, to the effect that anything that can go wrong will go wrong.

mus·cat /'məsˌkat; -kət/ ▸n. [often as *adj.*] a variety of white, red, or black grape with a musky scent, grown in warm climates for wine or raisins or as table grapes. ■ a wine made from a muscat grape, esp. a sweet or fortified white wine.

mus·ca·tel /ˌməskəˈtel/ (also **mus·ca·del** /-ˈdel/) ▸n. a muscat grape, esp. as grown for drying to make raisins. ■ a raisin made from such a grape. ■ a wine made from such a grape.

mus·cle /'məsəl/ ▸n. **1** a band or bundle of fibrous tissue in a human or animal body that has the ability to contract, producing movement in or maintaining the position of parts of the body. ■ such a band or bundle of tissue when well developed or prominently visible under the skin: *showing off our muscles.* **2** physical power; strength: *he had muscle but no brains.* ■ *inf.* a person or persons exhibiting such power or strength: *an ex-marine who'd been brought along as muscle.* ■ power or influence, esp. in a commercial or political context: *he had enough muscle and resources to hold his position on the council.*
▸v. [*tr.*] *inf.* move (an object) in a particular direction by using one's physical strength: *muscling baggage into the hold.* ■ *inf.* coerce by violence or by economic or political pressure: *he was eventually muscled out of business.*
▸phrasal v. □ **muscle in/into** *inf.* force one's way into (something): *he was determined to muscle in on the union's affairs.* —**mus·cled** /'məsəld/ adj. [in comb.] hard-muscled. —**mus·cle·less** adj. —**mus·cly** /'məs(ə)lē/ adj.

mus·cle-bound ▸adj. having well-developed or overdeveloped muscles: *the muscle-bound bartender.*

mus·cle·man /'məsəlˌman/ ▸n. (pl. **-men**) a large, strong man, esp. one employed to protect someone or to intimidate people.

mus·cle tone ▸n. see TONE (sense 6).

Mus·co·vite /'məskəˌvīt/ ▸n. a native or citizen of Moscow. ■ archaic a Russian.
▸adj. of or relating to Moscow. ■ archaic of or relating to Russia.

mus·co·vite /'məskəˌvīt/ ▸n. a silver-gray form of mica.

Mus·co·vy duck /'məskəvē; -ˌkōvē/ ▸n. a large tropical American tree-nesting duck (*Cairina moschata*), having glossy greenish-black plumage in the wild but bred in a variety of colors as a domestic bird.

mus·cu·lar /'məskyələr/ ▸adj. of or affecting the muscles. ■ having well-developed muscles: *her legs were strong and muscular.* ■ fig. vigorously robust: *a muscular economy.* —**mus·cu·lar·i·ty** /ˌməskyəˈle(ə)ritē/ n. —**mus·cu·lar·ly** adv.

mus·cu·lar dys·tro·phy ▸n. a hereditary condition marked by progressive weakening and wasting of the muscles.

mus·cu·la·ture /'məskyələchər; -ˌchŏŏr/ ▸n. the system or arrangement of muscles in a body, a part of the body, or an organ.

mus·cu·lo·skel·e·tal /ˌməskyəlōˈskelətl/ ▸adj. relating to or denoting the musculature and skeleton together.

Muse /myŏŏz/ ▸n. (in Greek and Roman mythology) each of nine goddesses, the daughters of Zeus and Mnemosyne, who preside over the arts and sciences. ■ (**muse**) a woman, or a force personified as a woman, who is the source of inspiration for a creative artist.

muse /myŏŏz/ ▸v. [*intr.*] be absorbed in thought: *he was **musing** on the problems he faced.* ■ [with *direct speech*] say to oneself in a thoughtful manner: *"I think I've seen him somewhere before," mused Rachel.* ■ (**muse on**) gaze thoughtfully at.
▸n. dated an instance or period of reflection. —**mus·ing·ly** adv.

mu·se·um /myŏŏˈzē·əm/ ▸n. a building in which objects of historical, scientific, artistic, or cultural interest are stored and exhibited.

mush¹ /məsh/ ▸n. **1** a soft, wet, pulpy mass: *she trudged through the mush of fallen leaves.* ■ fig. feeble or cloying sentimentality: *romantic mush.* **2** thick porridge, esp. made of cornmeal.
▸v. [*tr.*] reduce (a substance) to a soft, wet, pulpy mass: *simmer until the apples and potatoes are tender but not mushed.* —**mush·y** adj.

mush² ▸v. [*intr.*] go on a journey across snow with a dogsled: *by the end of winter he will have snowshoed up to 700 miles and mushed about the same.* ■ [*tr.*] urge on (the dogs) during such a journey.
▸interj. a command urging on dogs during such a journey.
▸n. a journey across snow with a dogsled: *a twelve-day mush.*

mush·room /'məshˌrŏŏm; -ˌrŏŏm/ ▸n. a fungal growth that typically takes the form of a domed cap on a stalk, often with gills on the underside of the cap. ■ a thing resembling a mushroom in shape: *a mushroom of smoke and flames.* ■ fig. a person or thing that appears or develops suddenly or is ephemeral: *one of those showbiz mushrooms who spring up overnight.*

▸*v.* [*intr.*] **1** increase, spread, or develop rapidly: *environmental concern mushroomed in the 1960s.* **2** (of the smoke, fire, or flames produced by an explosion) spread into the air in a shape resembling that of a mushroom. **3** [usu. as *n.*] (**mushrooming**) (of a person) gather mushrooms. —**mush·room·y** *adj.*

mush·room cloud ▸*n.* a mushroom-shaped cloud of dust and debris formed after a nuclear explosion.

mu·sic /ˈmyoozik/ ▸*n.* **1** the art or science of combining vocal or instrumental sounds (or both) to produce beauty of form, harmony, and expression of emotion. ■ the vocal or instrumental sound produced in this way: *couples were dancing to the music.* ■ a sound perceived as pleasingly harmonious: *the background music of lapping water.* **2** the written or printed signs representing such sound: *Tony learned to **read music**.* ■ the score or scores of a musical composition or compositions: *the music was open on a stand.* ▷Middle English: from Old French *musique*, via Latin from Greek *mousikē (tekhnē)* '(art) of the Muses,' from *mousa* 'muse.'

mu·si·cal /ˈmyoozikəl/ ▸*adj.* **1** of or relating to music. ■ set to or accompanied by music: *an evening of musical entertainment.* ■ fond of or skilled in music: *Henry was very musical.* **2** having a pleasant sound; melodious; tuneful: *rich, musical laughter.*

▸*n.* a play or movie in which singing and dancing play an essential part. —**mu·si·cal·i·ty** /ˌmyoozəˈkalitē/ *n.* —**mu·si·cal·ly** /-ik(ə)lē/ *adv.*

mu·si·cal chairs ▸*n.* a party game in which players compete for a decreasing number of chairs, the losers in successive rounds being those unable to find a chair to sit on when the accompanying music is abruptly stopped. ■ a series of changes or exchanges of position, esp. in a political or commercial organization.

mu·sic box ▸*n.* a small box that plays a tune, typically when the lid is opened.

mu·si·cian /myooˈzishən/ ▸*n.* a person who is talented or skilled in music. ■ a person who plays a musical instrument, esp. professionally. —**mu·si·cian·ly** *adj.* —**mu·si·cian·ship** /-ˌship/ *n.*

mu·si·col·o·gy /ˌmyoozəˈkäləjē/ ▸*n.* the study of music as an academic subject, as distinct from training in performance or composition; scholarly research into music. —**mu·si·co·log·i·cal** /-kəˈläjikəl/ *adj.* —**mu·si·col·o·gist** /-jist/ *n.*

musk /məsk/ ▸*n.* **1** a strong-smelling substance that is secreted by the male musk deer for scent-marking and is an important ingredient in perfumery. ■ a similar secretion of another animal, such as a civet. **2** (also **musk plant** or **musk flower**) a plant (genus *Mimulus*) of the figwort family that was formerly cultivated for its musky perfume. —**musk·y** *adj.*

musk deer ▸*n.* a small solitary deerlike eastern Asian mammal (genus *Moschus*, family Moschidae) without antlers, the male having long protruding upper canine teeth. Musk is produced in a sac on the abdomen of the male.

mus·kel·lunge /ˈməskəˌlenj/ ▸*n.* a large pike (*Esox masquinongy*) that occurs only in the Great Lakes region.

mus·ket /ˈməskit/ ▸*n. hist.* an infantryman's light gun with a long barrel, typically smooth-bored, muzzleloading, and fired from the shoulder.

mus·ket·eer /ˌməskəˈtir/ ▸*n. hist.* a soldier armed with a musket.

musk·mel·on /ˈməskˌmelən/ ▸*n.* an edible melon of a type that has a raised network of markings on the skin. Its many varieties include those with orange, yellow, green, or white juicy flesh.

musk·ox /ˈməskˌäks/ (also **musk ox**) ▸*n.* (*pl.* **-oxen** /-ˈäksən/) a large heavily built goat-antelope (*Ovibos moschatus*) with a thick shaggy coat and large curved horns, native to the tundra of North America and Greenland.

musk·rat /ˈməˌskrat/ ▸*n.* a large semiaquatic North American rodent (*Ondatra zibethicus*, family Muridae) with a musky smell, valued for its fur. ■ the fur of the muskrat.

Mus·lim /ˈməzləm; ˈmooz-/ (also **Mos·lem** /ˈmäzləm; ˈmäs-/) ▸*n.* a follower of the religion of Islam.

▸*adj.* of or relating to the Muslims or their religion.

mus·lin /ˈməzlən/ ▸*n.* lightweight cotton cloth in a plain weave: [as *adj.*] *a white muslin dress.* —**mus·lined** /ˈməzlənd/ *adj.*

muss /məs/ *inf.* ▸*v.* [*tr.*] make (someone's) hair or clothes untidy or messy: *she sat down carefully so she wouldn't muss her clothes.*

▸*n.* a state of disorder. —**muss·y** /ˈməsē/ *adj.* (*dated*).

mus·sel /ˈməsəl/ ▸*n.* any of a number of bivalve mollusks with a brown or purplish-black shell, in particular: ■ a marine bivalve, including the

edible mussel (*Mytilus edulis*). ■ a freshwater bivalve (family Unionidae) that typically lies on the bed of a river.

must¹ /məst/ ▸*modal verb* (*past* **had to** or in reported speech **must**) **1** be obliged to; should (expressing necessity): *you must show your ID card* | *it must not be over 2,000 words.* ■ expressing insistence: *you must try some of this fish.* ■ used in ironic questions expressing irritation: *must you look so utterly suburban?* **2** expressing an opinion about something that is logically very likely: *there must be something wrong.*

▸*n. inf.* something that should not be overlooked or missed: *this video is a must for parents.*

must² ▸*n.* grape juice before or during fermentation.

must³ ▸*n.* mustiness, dampness, or mold: *a pervasive smell of must.*

mus·tache /ˈməsˌtash; məˈstash/ (also **mous·tache**) ▸*n.* a strip of hair left to grow above the upper lip. ■ (**mustaches**) a long mustache. ■ a similar growth, or a marking that resembles it, around the mouth of some animals. ▷late 16th cent.: from French, from Italian *mostaccio*, from Greek *mustax, mustak-.* —**mus·tached** *adj.*

mus·tang /ˈməsˌtang/ ▸*n.* an American feral horse, typically small and lightly built.

mus·tard /ˈməstərd/ ▸*n.* **1** a pungent-tasting yellow or brown paste made from the crushed seeds of certain plants, typically eaten with meat or used as a cooking ingredient. **2** the yellow-flowered Eurasian plant (genera *Brassica* and *Sinapis*) of the cabbage family whose seeds are used to make this paste. —**mus·tard·y** *adj.*

mus·tard gas ▸*n.* a colorless oily liquid ($Cl_2C_4H_8S$) whose vapor is a powerful irritant and blistering agent, used in chemical weapons.

mus·te·lid /ˈməstəlid/ ▸*n. Zool.* a mammal of the weasel family, distinguished by having a long body, short legs, and musky scent glands under the tail.

mus·ter /ˈməstər/ ▸*v.* [*tr.*] **1** assemble (troops), esp. for inspection or in preparation for battle. ■ [*intr.*] (of troops) come together in this way: *the cavalrymen mustered beside the other regiments.* ■ [*intr.*] (of a group of people) gather together: *reporters mustered outside her house.* **2** collect or assemble (a number or amount): *he could fail to muster a majority.* ■ summon up (a particular feeling, attitude, or response): *he replied with as much dignity as he could muster.*

▸*phrasal v.* □ **muster someone in** (or **out**) enroll someone into (or discharge someone from) military service.

▸*n.* a formal gathering of troops, esp. for inspection, display, or exercise.

▸ □ **pass muster** be accepted as adequate or satisfactory: *a treaty that might pass muster with the voters.*

must·n't /ˈməsənt/ ▸*contr.* of must not.

mus·ty /ˈməstē/ ▸*adj.* (**mus·ti·er**, **mus·ti·est**) having a stale, moldy, or damp smell. ■ having a stale taste. ■ *fig.* lacking originality or interest: *when I read it again, the play seemed musty.* —**mus·ti·ly** /-təlē/ *adv.* —**mus·ti·ness** *n.*

mu·ta·ble /ˈmyootəbəl/ ▸*adj.* liable to change: *the mutable nature of fashion.* ■ *poetic/lit.* inconstant in one's affections: *youth is said to be fickle and mutable.* —**mu·ta·bil·i·ty** /ˌmyootəˈbilətē/ *n.*

mu·ta·gen /ˈmyootəjən/ ▸*n.* an agent, such as radiation or a chemical substance, that causes genetic mutation. —**mu·ta·gen·e·sis** /ˌmyootəˈjenəsəs/ *n.* —**mu·ta·gen·ic** /ˌmyootəˈjenik/ *adj.*

mu·tant /ˈmyootnt/ ▸*adj.* resulting from or showing the effect of mutation: *a mutant gene.*

▸*n.* a mutant form.

mu·tate /ˈmyooˌtāt/ ▸*v.* change or cause to change in form or nature. ■ *Biol.* (with reference to a cell, DNA molecule, etc.) undergo or cause to undergo change in a gene or genes. —**mu·ta·tor** /-ˌtātər/ *n.*

mu·ta·tion /myooˈtāshən/ ▸*n.* **1** the action or process of mutating: *the mutation of ethnic politics into nationalist politics* | *his first novel went through several mutations.* **2** the changing of the structure of a gene, resulting in a variant form that may be transmitted to subsequent generations. ■ a distinct form resulting from such a change. **3** *Linguistics* regular change of a sound when it occurs adjacent to another. —**mu·ta·tion·al** /-shənl/ *adj.* —**mu·ta·tion·al·ly** /-shənl-ē/ *adv.* —**mu·ta·tive** /ˈmyootətiv/ *adj.*

mute /myoot/ ▸*adj.* **1** refraining from speech or temporarily speechless: *Irene, the talkative one, was now mute.* ■ not expressed in speech: *she gazed at him in mute appeal.* ■ (of a person) without the power of speech. **2** (of a letter) not pronounced: *mute e is generally dropped before suffixes beginning with a vowel.*

▸*n.* **1** *dated, usu. offens.* a person without the power of speech. **2** a device that softens the sound (and typically alters the tone) of a musical instrument, in particular: ■ a clamp placed over the bridge of a stringed instrument to deaden its resonance. ■ a pad or cone placed in the opening of a brass or other wind instrument. **3** a device on a television, telephone, or other appliance that temporarily turns off the sound: *she put the remote on mute.*

▶*v.* [*tr.*] **1** (often **be muted**) deaden, muffle, or soften the sound of: *her footsteps were muted by the thick carpet.* ■ muffle the sound of (a musical instrument), esp. by the use of a mute. ■ *fig.* reduce the strength or intensity of: *his professional contentment was muted by personal sadness.* **2** turn off (the sound on a television, telephone, or other appliance) by activating the mute. —**mute·ly** *adv.* —**mute·ness** *n.*

mute swan ▶*n.* the most common Eurasian swan (*Cygnus olor*), having white plumage and an orange-red bill with a black knob at the base.

mu·ti·late /ˈmyo͞otlˌāt/ ▶*v.* [*tr.*] (usu. **be mutilated**) inflict a violent and disfiguring injury on. ■ inflict serious damage on: *the 14th-century church had been mutilated.* —**mu·ti·la·tion** /ˌmyo͞otlˈāSHən/ *n.* —**mu·ti·la·tor** /-ˌātər/ *n.*

mu·ti·neer /ˌmyo͞otnˈi(ə)r/ ▶*n.* a person, esp. a soldier or sailor, who rebels or refuses to obey the orders of a person in authority.

mu·ti·nous /ˈmyo͞otn-əs/ ▶*adj.* (of a soldier or sailor) refusing to obey the orders of a person in authority. ■ willful or disobedient. —**mu·ti·nous·ly** *adv.*

mu·ti·ny /ˈmyo͞otn-ē/ ▶*n.* (*pl.* **-nies**) an open rebellion against the proper authorities, esp. by soldiers or sailors against their officers.

▶*v.* (**-nies, -nied**) [*intr.*] refuse to obey the orders of a person or persons in authority.

mutt /mət/ ▶*n.* *inf.* **1** *humorous* or *derog.* a dog, esp. a mongrel. **2** a person regarded as stupid or incompetent.

mut·ter /ˈmətər/ ▶*v.* say something in a low or barely audible voice, esp. in dissatisfaction or irritation: ■ [*intr.*] speak privately or unofficially about someone or something; spread rumors: *when he disappeared, people began to mutter.*

▶*n.* a barely audible utterance, esp. a dissatisfied or irritated one: *a little mutter of disgust.* —**mut·ter·er** *n.* —**mut·ter·ing·ly** *adv.*

mut·ton /ˈmətn/ ▶*n.* the flesh of sheep, esp. mature sheep, used as food: *roast mutton.* —**mut·ton·y** *adj.*

mut·ton·chops /ˈmətnˌCHäps/ (also **mut·ton·chop whiskers**) ▶*n.* the whiskers on a man's cheek when shaped like a meat chop, narrow at the top and broad and rounded at the bottom.

mu·tu·al /ˈmyo͞oCHo͞oəl/ ▶*adj.* **1** (of a feeling or action) experienced or done by each of two or more parties toward the other or others: *mutual respect and understanding.* ■ (of two or more people) having the same specified relationship to each other: *they were mutual beneficiaries of the settlement.* **2** held in common by two or more parties: *we were introduced by a mutual friend.* ■ denoting an insurance company or other corporate organization owned by its members and dividing some or all of its profits between them. —**mu·tu·al·ly** *adv.*

mu·tu·al fund ▶*n.* an investment program funded by shareholders that trades in diversified holdings and is professionally managed.

mu·tu·al·ism /ˈmyo͞oCHo͞oəˌlizəm/ ▶*n.* the doctrine that mutual dependence is necessary to social well-being. ■ *Biol.* symbiosis that is beneficial to both organisms involved. —**mu·tu·al·ist** *n.* & *adj.* —**mu·tu·al·is·tic** /ˌmyo͞oCHo͞oəˈlistik/ *adj.* —**mu·tu·al·is·ti·cal·ly** /ˌmyo͞oCHo͞oəˈlistik(ə)lē/ *adv.*

muu·muu /ˈmo͞oˌmo͞o/ ▶*n.* a woman's loose, brightly colored dress, esp. one traditionally worn in Hawaii.

Mu·zak /ˈmyo͞oˌzak/ ▶*n. trademark* recorded light background music played through speakers in public places.

muz·zle /ˈməzəl/ ▶*n.* **1** the projecting part of the face, including the nose and mouth, of an animal. ■ a guard, typically made of straps or wire, fitted over this part of an animal's face to stop it from biting or feeding. ■ *fig.* any restraint on free speech: *the muzzle put on foreign journalists.* **2** the open end of the barrel of a firearm.

▶*v.* [*tr.*] put a muzzle on (an animal). ■ *fig.* prevent (a person or an institution, esp. the press) from expressing opinions freely.

muz·zle·load·er /ˈməzəlˌlōdər/ (also **muz·zle-load·er**) ▶*n. hist.* a gun that is loaded through its muzzle. —**muz·zle·load·ing** /-ˌlōdiNG/ (also **muz·zle-load·ing**) *adj.*

muz·zy /ˈməzē/ ▶*adj.* (**muz·zi·er, muz·zi·est**) unable to think clearly; confused: *muzzy from sleep.* ■ not thought out clearly; vague: *society's muzzy notion of tolerance.* —**muz·zi·ly** /ˈməzəlē/ *adv.* —**muz·zi·ness** *n.*

MVP ▶*abbr.* most valuable player (an award given in various sports to the best player on a team or in a league).

MW ▶*abbr.* megawatt(s).

mW ▶*abbr.* milliwatt(s).

my /mī/ ▶*possessive adj.* **1** belonging to or associated with the speaker: *my name is John* | *my friend.* ■ *inf.* used with a name to refer to a member of the speaker's family: *my Francine won top honors in the science fair.*

■ used with forms of address in affectionate, sympathetic, humorous, or patronizing contexts: *my dear boy* | *my poor baby.* **2** used in various expressions of surprise: *my goodness!* | *oh my!*

my·al·gi·a /mīˈalj(ē)ə/ ▶*n.* pain in a muscle or group of muscles. —**my·al·gic** /-jik/ *adj.*

my·as·the·ni·a /ˌmīəsˈTHēnēə/ ▶*n.* a condition causing abnormal weakness of certain muscles. ■ (in full **myasthenia gravis** /ˈgravis/) a rare chronic autoimmune disease marked by muscular weakness without atrophy.

my·ce·li·um /mīˈsēlēəm/ ▶*n.* (*pl.* **-li·a** /-lēə/) *Bot.* the vegetative part of a fungus, consisting of a network of fine white filaments (hyphae). —**my·ce·li·al** /-lēəl/ *adj.*

my·col·o·gy /mīˈkäləjē/ ▶*n.* the scientific study of fungi. —**my·co·log·i·cal** /ˌmīkəˈläjikəl/ *adj.* —**my·co·log·i·cal·ly** /ˌmīkəˈläjik(ə)lē/ *adv.* —**my·col·o·gist** /-jist/ *n.*

my·co·sis /mīˈkōsəs/ ▶*n.* (*pl.* **-ses** /-sēz/) a disease caused by infection with a fungus, such as ringworm or thrush. —**my·cot·ic** /-ˈkätik/ *adj.*

my·e·lin /ˈmīələn/ ▶*n. Anat.* & *Physiol.* a mixture of proteins and phospholipids forming a whitish insulating sheath around many nerve fibers, increasing the speed at which impulses are conducted. —**my·e·li·nat·ed** /-ləˌnātəd/ *adj.* —**my·e·li·na·tion** /ˌmīələˈnāSHən/ *n.*

my·e·li·tis /ˌmīəˈlītəs/ ▶*n. Med.* inflammation of the spinal cord.

my·e·lo·ma /ˌmīəˈlōmə/ ▶*n.* (*pl.* **-mas** or **-ma·ta** /-mətə/) *Med.* a malignant tumor of the bone marrow.

My·lar /ˈmīˌlär/ ▶*n. trademark* a form of polyester resin used to make heat-resistant plastic films and sheets.

my·nah /ˈmīnə/ (also **my·na** or **mynah bird**) ▶*n.* an Asian and Australasian starling that typically has dark plumage, gregarious behavior, and a loud call; in particular the **hill mynah** (*Gracula religiosa*).

my·o·car·di·al in·farc·tion /ˌmīəˈkärdēəl/ ▶*n.* another term for HEART ATTACK.

my·o·car·di·um /ˌmīəˈkärdēəm/ ▶*n. Anat.* the muscular tissue of the heart. —**my·o·car·di·al** /-dēəl/ *adj.*

my·ol·o·gy /mīˈäləjē/ ▶*n.* the study of the structure, arrangement, and action of muscles. —**my·o·log·i·cal** /ˌmīəˈläjikəl/ *adj.* —**my·ol·o·gist** /-jist/ *n.*

my·o·pi·a /mīˈōpēə/ ▶*n.* nearsightedness. ■ lack of imagination, foresight, or intellectual insight. —**my·op·ic** /mīˈäpik/ *adj.* —**my·op·i·cal·ly** /mīˈäpik(ə)lē/ *adv.*

myr·i·ad /ˈmirēəd/ *poetic/lit.* ▶*n.* **1** a countless or extremely great number: *networks connecting a myriad of computers.* **2** (chiefly in classical history) a unit of ten thousand.

▶*adj.* countless or extremely great in number. ■ having countless or very many elements or aspects: *the myriad political scene.*

myr·i·a·pod /ˈmirēəˌpäd/ ▶*n. Zool.* an arthropod of a group that includes the centipedes, millipedes, and related animals. Myriapods have elongated bodies with numerous leg-bearing segments.

▶*adj.* (also **myriapodous**) of or belonging to the myriapods.

myrrh /mər/ ▶*n.* a fragrant gum resin obtained from certain trees (genus *Commiphora*, family Burseraceae) and used, esp. in the Near East, in perfumery, medicines, and incense. —**myrrh·y** *adj.*

myr·tle /ˈmərtl/ ▶*n.* **1** an evergreen shrub (*Myrtus communis*) that has glossy aromatic foliage and white flowers followed by purple-black oval berries. The **myrtle family** (Myrtaceae) also includes several aromatic plants (e.g., clove, allspice) and trees (e.g., eucalyptus). **2** the lesser periwinkle (*Vinca minor*). ▷late Middle English: from medieval Latin *myrtilla, myrtillus*, diminutive of Latin *myrta, myrtus*, from Greek *murtos*.

my·self /mīˈself; mə-/ ▶*pron.* [*first person sing.*] **1** [*reflexive*] used by a speaker to refer to himself or herself as the object of a verb or preposition when he or she is the subject of the clause: *I hurt myself by accident* | *I strolled around, muttering to myself.* **2** I or me personally (used to emphasize the speaker): *I myself am unsure how this problem should be handled* | *I wrote it myself.* **3** poetic/literary term for I[2] : *myself presented to him a bronze sword.*

mys·te·ri·ous /məˈsti(ə)rēəs/ ▶*adj.* **1** difficult or impossible to understand, explain, or identify. ■ (of a location) having an atmosphere of strangeness or secrecy: *a mysterious, windowless building.* **2** (of a person) deliberately enigmatic: *she was mysterious about herself.* —**mys·te·ri·ous·ly** *adv.* —**mys·te·ri·ous·ness** *n.*

mys·ter·y[1] /ˈmist(ə)rē/ ▶*n.* (*pl.* **-ter·ies**) **1** something that is difficult or impossible to understand or explain. ■ the condition or quality of being secret, strange, or difficult to explain: *much of her past is shrouded in mystery.* ■ a person or thing whose identity or nature is puzzling or unknown: *"He's a bit of a mystery," said Nina.* **2** a novel, play, or movie dealing with a puzzling crime, esp. a murder. **3** (**mysteries**) the secret rites of Greek and Roman pagan religion, or of any ancient or tribal religion, to which only initiates are admitted. ■ the practices, skills, or lore peculiar to a particular trade or activity and regarded as baffling to those without specialized knowledge **4** *chiefly Christian Theol.* a religious belief based on divine revelation, esp. one regarded as beyond human understanding: *the mystery of Christ.*

mys·ter·y² ▶*n.* (*pl.* **-ter·ies**) *archaic* a handicraft or trade.

mys·tic /ˈmistik/ ▶*n.* a person who seeks by contemplation and self-surrender to obtain unity with or absorption into the Deity or the absolute, or who believes in the spiritual apprehension of truths that are beyond the intellect.
▶*adj.* another term for MYSTICAL. ▷Middle English (in the sense 'mystical meaning'): from Old French *mystique*, or via Latin from Greek *mustikos*, from *mustēs* 'initiated person,' from *muein* 'close the eyes or lips,' also 'initiate.' The current sense of the noun dates from the late 17th cent.

mys·ti·cal /ˈmistikəl/ ▶*adj.* **1** of or relating to mystics or religious mysticism: *the mystical experience.* ■ spiritually allegorical or symbolic; transcending human understanding: *the mystical body of Christ.* ■ of or relating to ancient religious mysteries or other occult or esoteric rites: *the mystical practices of the Pythagoreans.* ■ of hidden or esoteric meaning: *a geometric figure of mystical significance.* **2** inspiring a sense of spiritual mystery, awe, and fascination: *the mystical forces of nature.* ■ concerned

with the soul or the spirit, rather than with material things. —**mys·ti·cal·ly** /-ik(ə)lē/ *adv.* —**mys·ti·cism** /-ˌsizəm/ *n.*

mys·ti·fy /ˈmistəˌfī/ ▶*v.* (**-fies**, **-fied**) [*tr.*] utterly bewilder or perplex (someone): ■ *dated* take advantage of the credulity of; hoax: *he took a childlike delight in mystifying his officials.* ■ make obscure or mysterious: *lawyers who mystify the legal system.* —**mys·ti·fi·ca·tion** /ˌmistəfiˈkāSHən/ *n.* —**mys·ti·fi·er** *n.* —**mys·ti·fy·ing·ly** *adv.*

mys·tique /misˈtēk/ ▶*n.* a fascinating aura of mystery, awe, and power surrounding someone or something. ■ an air of secrecy surrounding a particular activity or subject that makes it impressive or baffling to those without specialized knowledge: *the mystique associated with computers.*

myth /miTH/ ▶*n.* **1** a traditional story, esp. one concerning the early history of a people or explaining some natural or social phenomenon, and typically involving supernatural beings or events. ■ such stories collectively: *the heroes of Greek myth.* **2** a widely held but false belief or idea: *the myth that sea kayaking is too risky.* ■ a misrepresentation of the truth: *irresponsible myths about privatization.* ■ a fictitious or imaginary person or thing. ■ an exaggerated or idealized conception of a person or thing: *the Churchill myth.* —**myth·ic** *adj.* —**myth·i·cal** *adj.*

my·thol·o·gy /məˈTHäləjē/ ▶*n.* (*pl.* **-gies**) **1** a collection of myths, esp. one belonging to a particular religious or cultural tradition. ■ a set of stories or beliefs about a particular person, institution, or situation, esp. when exaggerated or fictitious: *in popular mythology, truckers are kings of the road.* **2** the study of myths. —**myth·o·log·ic** /ˌmiTHəˈläjik/ *adj.* —**myth·o·log·i·cal** /ˌmiTHəˈläjikəl/ *adj.* —**myth·o·log·i·cal·ly** /ˌmiTHəˈläjik(ə)lē/ *adv.* —**my·thol·o·gist** /-jist/ *n.*

M

Nn

N¹ /en/ (also **n**) ▶*n.* (*pl.* **Ns** or **N's**) the fourteenth letter of the alphabet. See also **EN**. ■ denoting the next after M in a set of items, categories, etc.

N² ▶*abbr.* ■ (used in recording moves in chess) knight: *17.Na4?* ■ Nationalist. ■ (on a gear lever) neutral. ■ (chiefly in place names) New: *N Zealand*. ■ Physics newton(s). ■ Noon. ■ *Chem.* (with reference to solutions) normal: *the pH was adjusted to 7.0 with 1 N HCl*. ■ Norse. ■ North or Northern: *78° N | N Ireland*. ■ *Finance* note. ■ nuclear: *the N bomb*.
▶*symb.* the chemical element nitrogen.

n ▶*abbr.* ■ [in *comb.*] (in units of measurement) nano- (10^{-9}): *the plates were coated with 500 ng of protein in sodium carbonate buffer*. ■ born. ■ nephew. ■ net. ■ *Gram.* neuter. ■ new. ■ nominative. ■ noon. ■ (**n-**) [in *comb.*] *Chem.* normal (denoting straight-chain hydrocarbons): *n-hexane*. ■ north or northern. ■ note (used in a book's index to refer to a footnote): *450n.* ■ *Finance* note. ■ *Gram.* noun. ■ number.
▶*symb.* an unspecified or variable number: *at the limit where n equals infinity*. See also **NTH**.

'n' /ən/ ▶*contr.* of and (conventionally used in informal contexts to coordinate two closely connected elements): *rock 'n' roll*.

Na ▶*symb.* the chemical element sodium.

NAACP /'en dəbəl ā sē 'pē/ ▶*abbr.* National Association for the Advancement of Colored People.

nab /nab/ ▶*v.* (**nabbed**, **nab·bing**) [*tr.*] *inf.* catch (someone) doing something wrong: *Olympic drug tests nabbed another athlete yesterday*. ■ take or grab (something): *Dan nabbed the seat next to mine*. ■ steal.

na·bob /'nābäb/ ▶*n. hist.* a Muslim official or governor under the Mogul empire. ■ a person of conspicuous wealth or high status. ■ *chiefly hist.* a person who returned from India to Europe with a fortune. ▷from Portuguese *nababo* or Spanish *nabab*, from Urdu.

na·cho /'nächō/ ▶*n.* (*pl.* **-chos**) a small crisp piece of a tortilla, typically topped with melted cheese and spices.

na·dir /'nādər; 'nādi(ə)r/ ▶*n.* the lowest point in the fortunes of a person or organization: *they had reached the nadir of their sufferings*. ■ *Astron.* the point on the celestial sphere directly below an observer. The opposite of **ZENITH**.

NAFTA /'naftə/ (also **Nafta**) ▶*abbr.* North American Free Trade Agreement.

nag¹ /nag/ ▶*v.* (**nagged**, **nag·ging**) [*tr.*] annoy or irritate (a person) with persistent fault-finding or continuous urging: *she constantly nags her daughter about getting married*. ■ [often as *adj.*] (**nagging**) be persistently painful, troublesome, or worrying to: *there was a nagging pain in his chest* | [*intr.*] *something nagged at the back of his mind*.
▶*n.* a person who nags someone. ■ a persistent feeling of anxiety: *he felt that little nag of doubt*. —**nag·ger** *n.* —**nag·ging·ly** *adv.* —**nag·gy** *adj.*

nag² ▶*n. inf., often derog.* a horse, esp. one that is old or in poor health. ■ *archaic* a horse suitable for riding as opposed to a draft animal.

Na·hua·tl /'nä,wätl/ ▶*n.* (*pl.* same) **1** a member of a group of peoples native to southern Mexico and Central America, including the Aztecs. **2** the Uto-Aztecan language of these peoples.
▶*adj.* of or relating to these peoples or their language.

nai·ad /'nāad; -əd; nī-/ ▶*n.* (*pl.* **naiads** or **naiades** /-ə,dēz/) **1** (also **Nai·ad**) (in classical mythology) a water nymph said to inhabit a river, spring, or waterfall. **2** the aquatic larva or nymph of a dragonfly or mayfly. **3** a submerged aquatic plant (genus *Najas*, family Najadaceae) with narrow leaves and minute flowers.

nail /nāl/ ▶*n.* **1** a small metal spike with a broadened flat head, driven typically into wood with a hammer to join things together or to serve as a peg or hook. **2** a horny covering on the upper surface of the tip of the finger and toe in humans and other primates. ■ an animal's claw.
▶*v.* [*tr.*] **1** [*tr.*] fasten to a surface or to something else with a nail or nails: *nail the edge framing to the wall.* **2** *inf.* expose (someone) as deceitful or criminal; catch or arrest: *have you nailed the killer?* **3** *inf.* (of a player) secure (esp. a victory) conclusively: *there's no doubt I had chances to nail it in the last set.*
▶*phrasal v.* □ **nail someone down** elicit a firm promise or commitment from someone: *I can't nail her down to a specific date.* □ **nail something down 1** fasten something securely with nails. **2** identify something precisely: *something seems unexpected—I can't nail it down, but it makes me uneasy.* **3** secure something, esp. an agreement: *the company has finally nailed down the agreement with its distributors.* —**nailed** *adj.* [in *comb.*] *dirty-nailed fingers.* —**nail·less** *adj.*
▶ □ **hard as nails** (of a person) very tough; completely callous or unfeeling. □ **a nail in the coffin** an action or event regarded as likely to have a detrimental or destructive effect on a situation, enterprise, or person: *this was going to put the final nail in the coffin of his career.*

nail·head /'nāl,hed/ ▶*n.* the rounded head of a nail. ■ an ornament like the head of a nail, used chiefly in architecture and on clothing.

nail wrap ▶*n.* a type of beauty treatment, in which a nail strengthener, usu. containing fibers, is either brushed on or applied with adhesive.

na·ive /nī'ēv/ (also **na·ïve**) ▶*adj.* (of a person or action) showing a lack of experience, wisdom, or judgment: *the rather naive young man had been totally misled.* ■ (of a person) natural and unaffected; innocent: *Andy had a sweet, naive look when he smiled.* ■ of or denoting art produced in a straightforward style that deliberately rejects sophisticated artistic techniques and has a bold directness resembling a child's work, typically in bright colors with little or no perspective. —**na·ive·ly** *adv.* —**na·ive·ness** *n.*

na·ive·té /,nī,ēv(ə)'tā; nī'ēv(ə),tā/ (also **na·ïve·té**, *Brit.* **na·ive·ty**) ▶*n.* lack of experience, wisdom, or judgment: *the administration's naiveté and inexperience in foreign policy.* ■ innocence or unsophistication: *they took advantage of his naiveté and deep pockets.*

na·ked /'nākid/ ▶*adj.* (of a person or part of the body) without clothes: *he'd never seen a naked woman before.* ■ (of an object) without the usual covering or protection: *her room was lit by a single naked bulb.* ■ (of a tree, plant, or animal) without leaves, hairs, scales, shell, etc.: *the twisted trunks and naked branches of the trees.* ■ *fig.* exposed to harm; unprotected or vulnerable: *John looked naked and defenseless without his glasses.* ■ (of something such as feelings or behavior) undisguised; blatant: *the naked truth.* ▷Old English *nacod*, of Germanic origin; related to Dutch *naakt* and German *nackt*, from an Indo-European root shared by Latin *nudus* and Sanskrit *nagna*. —**na·ked·ly** *adv.* —**na·ked·ness** *n.*

na·ked eye ▶*n.* (usu. **the naked eye**) unassisted vision, without a telescope, microscope, or other device.

nam·by-pam·by /'nambē 'pambē/ ▶*adj. derog.* lacking energy, strength, or courage; feeble or effeminate in behavior or expression: *these weren't namby-pamby fights, but brutal affairs where heads hit the sidewalk.*
▶*n.* (*pl.* **-bies**) a feeble or effeminate person.

name /nām/ ▶*n.* **1** a word or set of words by which a person, animal, place, or thing is known, addressed, or referred to: *my name is Parsons, John Parsons.* ■ a famous person: *as usual, the big race will lure the top names.* ■ a reputation, esp. a good one: *he set up a school that gained a name for excellence.*
▶*v.* [*tr.*] give a name to: *hundreds of diseases had not yet been isolated or named.*

■ identify by name; give the correct name for: *the dead man has been named as John Mackintosh.* ■ give a particular title or epithet to: *she was named "Artist of the Decade."* ■ appoint (someone) to a particular position or task: *he was named to head a joint UN–OAS diplomatic effort.*

▶ *phrasal v.* □ **name someone/something after** (also **for**) call someone or something by the same name as: *Nathaniel was named after his maternal grandfather.*

▶ *adj.* (of a person or commercial product) having a name that is widely known: *countless specialized name brands geared to niche markets.* —**name·a·ble** /'nāməbəl/ *adj.* —**nam·er** *n.*

▶ □ **by the name of** called: *a woman by the name of Smith.* □ **call someone names** insult someone verbally. □ **give one's name to** invent, discover, found, or be closely associated with something that then becomes known by one's name: *Lou Gehrig gave his name to the disease that claimed his life.* □ **something has someone's name on it** a person is destined or particularly suited to receive or experience a specified thing: *he feared the next bullet would have his name on it.* □ **have to one's name** have in one's possession: *I had a child on the way and hardly a penny to my name.* □ **in all but name** existing in a particular state but not formally recognized as such: *these new punks are hippies in all but name.* □ **in the name of** bearing or using the name of a specified person or organization.■ for the sake of: *he withdrew his candidacy in the name of party unity.* ■ by the authority of: *crimes committed in the name of religion.* ■ **(in the name of Christ/God/Allah/heaven,** etc.) used for emphasis: *what in the name of God do you think you're doing?* □ **in name only** by description but not in reality: *a college in name only.* □ **make a name for oneself** become well known: *by the time he was thirty-five, he had made a name for himself as a contractor.* □ **name names** mention specific names, esp. of people involved in something wrong or illegal: *if you're convinced my staff is part of this operation, then name names.* □ **the name of the game** *inf.* the main purpose or most important aspect of a situation: *the name of the game is short-term gain.* □ **put a name to** remember or report what someone or something is called: *viewers were asked if they could put a name to the voice of the kidnapper.* □ **you name it** *inf.* whatever you can think of (used to express the extent or variety of something): *easy-to-assemble kits of trains, cars, trucks, ships . . . you name it.*

name-call·ing ▶*n.* abusive language or insults. —**name-call·er** *n.*

name-drop·ping ▶*n.* the practice of casually mentioning the names of famous people one knows or claims to know in order to impress others. —**name-drop** *v.* —**name-drop·per** *n.*

name·less /'nāmlis/ ▶*adj.* **1** having no name or no known name. ■ deliberately not identified; anonymous: *the director of a voluntary organization which shall remain nameless.* ■ *archaic* (of a child) illegitimate. **2** (esp. of an emotion) not easy to describe; indefinable: *a nameless yearning for transcendence.* ■ too loathsome or horrific to be described: *the myths talk about nameless horrors infesting our universe.* —**name·less·ly** *adv.* —**name·less·ness** *n.*

name·ly /'nāmlē/ ▶*adv.* that is to say; to be specific (used to introduce detailed information or a specific example): *to me there is only one kind of rock, namely, loud rock.*

name·sake /'nām,sāk/ ▶*n.* a person or thing that has the same name as another: *Hugh Capet paved the way for his son and namesake to be crowned king of France.*

nan·ny /'nanē/ ▶*n.* (*pl.* **-nies**) **1** a person, typically a woman, employed to care for a child in its own home. ■ *fig.* a person or institution regarded as interfering and overprotective: [as *adj.*] *a precarious path between freedom and the nanny state.* **2** (in full **nanny goat**) a female goat.

na·no /'nanō/ ▶*n. inf.* short for NANOTECHNOLOGY.

nan·o·me·ter /'nanə,mētər/ (*Brit.* **nan·o·me·tre**) (abbr.: **nm**) ▶*n.* one billionth of a meter.

nan·o·ro·bot /'nanə,rōbät; -bət; 'nä-/ ▶*n.* a machine made from individual atoms or molecules that is designed to perform a small and specific job.

nan·o·scale /'nanə,skāl, 'nä-/ ▶*adj.* of a size measurable in nanometers or microns: *the use of viruses as nanoscale building tools.*

nan·o·sec·ond /'nanə,sekənd/ (abbr.: **ns**) ▶*n.* one billionth of a second.

nan·o·struc·ture /'nanə,strəkchər; 'nä-/ ▶*n.* a nanoscale object: *tightly bound nanostructures.*

nan·o·tech·nol·o·gy /,nanə,tek'näləjē; ,nanō-/ ▶*n.* the branch of technology that deals with dimensions and tolerances of less than 100 nanometers, esp. the manipulation of individual atoms and molecules. —**nan·o·tech·no·log·i·cal** *adj.* —**nan·o·tech·nol·o·gist** *n.*

nan·o·wire /'nanə,wī(ə)r; 'nä-/ ▶*n.* a nanoscale rod made of semiconducting material, used in miniature transistors and some laser applications.

nap[1] /nap/ ▶*v.* (**napped, nap·ping**) [*intr.*] sleep lightly or briefly, esp. during the day.

▶*n.* a short sleep, esp. during the day: *excuse me, I'll just take a little nap.*
■ □ **catch someone napping** *inf.* (of a person, action, or event) find someone off guard and unprepared to respond: *he caught the runner napping off second base and tagged him out.*

nap[2] ▶*n.* the raised hairs, threads, or similar small projections on the surface of fabric or suede (used esp. with reference to the direction in which they naturally lie). —**nap·less** *adj.*

na·palm /'nāpä(l)m/ ▶*n.* a highly flammable sticky jelly used in incendiary bombs and flamethrowers, consisting of gasoline thickened with special soaps.

▶*v.* [*tr.*] attack with bombs containing napalm.

nape /nāp/ ▶*n.* (also **nape of the neck**) the back of a person's neck.

naph·tha /'naftнə; 'nap-/ ▶*n. Chem.* a flammable oil containing various hydrocarbons.

naph·tha·lene /'naftнə,lēn; 'nap-/ ▶*n. Chem.* a volatile white crystalline compound, $C_{10}H_8$, produced by the distillation of coal tar, used in mothballs and as a raw material for chemical manufacture. —**naph·thal·ic** /naf'тнalik; nap-/ *adj.*

nap·kin /'napkin/ ▶*n.* **1** (also **table napkin**) a square piece of cloth or paper used at a meal to wipe the fingers or lips and to protect garments, or to serve food on. **2** another term for SANITARY NAPKIN.

nap·kin ring ▶*n.* a ring used to hold (and distinguish) a person's table napkin when not in use.

narc /närk/ (also **nark**) ▶*n. inf.* a federal agent or police officer who enforces the laws regarding illicit sale or use of drugs and narcotics.

nar·cis·sism /'närsə,sizəm/ ▶*n.* excessive or erotic interest in oneself and one's physical appearance. ■ *Psychol.* extreme selfishness, with a grandiose view of one's own talents and a craving for admiration, as characterizing a personality type. ■ *Psychoanalysis* self-centeredness arising from failure to distinguish the self from external objects, either in very young babies or as a feature of mental disorder. —**nar·cis·sist** /'närsəsəst/ *n.* —**nar·cis·sis·tic** /,närsə'sistik/ *adj.* —**nar·cis·sis·ti·cal·ly** /,närsə'sistik(ə)lē/ *adv.*

nar·cis·sus /när'sisəs/ ▶*n.* (*pl.* same, **-cis·si** /-'sisī; -sē/, or **-cissuses**) a bulbous Eurasian plant (genus *Narcissus*) of the lily family. Various species include the daffodil, esp. one with flowers that have white or pale outer petals and a shallow orange or yellow cup in the center.

nar·co·lep·sy /'närkə,lepsē/ ▶*n. Med.* a condition characterized by an extreme tendency to fall asleep whenever in relaxing surroundings. —**nar·co·lep·tic** /,närkə'leptik/ *adj. & n.*

nar·co·sis /när'kōsis/ ▶*n. Med.* a state of stupor, drowsiness, or unconsciousness produced by drugs.

nar·cot·ic /när'kätik/ ▶*n.* a drug or other substance affecting mood or behavior and sold for nonmedical purposes, esp. an illegal one. ■ *Med.* a drug that relieves pain and induces drowsiness, stupor, or insensibility.

▶*adj.* relating to or denoting narcotics or their effects or use: *the substance has a mild narcotic effect.* ▷late Middle English: from Old French *narcotique*, via medieval Latin from Greek *narkōtikos*, from *narkoun* 'make numb.' —**nar·cot·i·cal·ly** /-tik(ə)lē/ *adv.* —**nar·co·tism** /'närkə,tizəm/ *n.*

nar·rate /'nar,āt/ ▶*v.* [*tr.*] (often **be narrated**) give a spoken or written account of: *the voyages, festivities, and intrigues are narrated with gusto.* ■ provide a spoken commentary to accompany (a movie, broadcast, piece of music, etc.). —**nar·rat·a·ble** *adj.* —**nar·ra·tion** /na'rāsнən/ *n.*

nar·ra·tive /'narətiv/ ▶*n.* a spoken or written account of connected events; a story: *the hero of his modest narrative.* ■ the narrated part or parts of a literary work, as distinct from dialogue.

▶*adj.* in the form of or concerned with narration: *a narrative poem* | *narrative technique.* —**nar·ra·tive·ly** *adv.*

nar·ra·tor /'narātər/ ▶*n.* a person who narrates something, esp. a character who recounts the events of a novel or narrative poem. ■ a person who delivers a commentary accompanying a movie, broadcast, piece of music, etc. —**nar·ra·to·ri·al** /,narə'tôrēəl/ *adj.*

nar·row /'narō/ ▶*adj.* (**-row·er, -row·est**) **1** (esp. of something that is considerably longer or higher than it is wide) of small width: *he made his way down the narrow road.* **2** limited in extent, amount, or scope; restricted: *his ability to get good results within narrow constraints of money and manpower.* ■ (of a phonetic transcription) showing fine details of accent. ■ *Phonet.* denoting a vowel pronounced with the root of the tongue drawn back so as to narrow the pharynx. **3** (esp. of a victory, defeat, or escape) with only a small margin; barely achieved.

▶*v.* **1** become or make less wide: [*intr.*] *the road narrowed and crossed an old bridge* | [*tr.*] *the embankment was built to narrow the river.* ■ [*intr.*] (of a person's eyes) almost closed so as to focus on something or someone, or to indicate anger, suspicion, or other emotion: *Jake's eyes had narrowed to pinpoints.* ■ [*tr.*] (of a person) cause (one's eyes) to do this: *she narrowed her eyes at him suspiciously.* **2** become or make more limited or restricted in extent or scope: [*intr.*] *their trade surplus narrowed to $70 million.*

▸*phrasal v.* □ **narrow something down** reduce the number of possibilities or options of something: *the company has narrowed down the candidates for the job to two.*

▸*n.* (**narrows**) a narrow channel connecting two larger areas of water: *a basaltic fang rising from the narrows of the Upper Missouri.* —**nar·row·ly** *adv.* —**nar·row·ness** *n.*

nar·row-mind·ed ▸*adj.* not willing to listen to or tolerate other people's views; prejudiced. —**nar·row-mind·ed·ly** *adv.* —**nar·row-mind·ed·ness** *n.*

nar·thex /'närтнeks/ ▸*n.* an antechamber or distinct area at the western entrance of some early Christian churches, separated off by a railing. ■ an antechamber or vestibule in a modern church.

nar·whal /'närwəl/ ▸*n.* a small Arctic whale (*Monodon monoceros*, family Monodontidae), the male of which has a long spirally twisted tusk developed from one of its teeth.

nar·y /'ne(ə)rē/ ▸*adj.* informal or dialect form of **NOT**: *nary a complaint.*

NASA /'nasə/ ▸*abbr.* National Aeronautics and Space Administration.

na·sal /'nāzəl/ ▸*adj.* **1** of, for, or relating to the nose: *the nasal passages | a nasal spray.* **2** (of a speech sound) pronounced by the voice resonating in the nose, e.g., *m, n, ng.* ■ (of the voice or speech) produced or characterized by resonating in the nose as well as the mouth.

▸*n.* a nasal speech sound. —**na·sal·i·ty** /nā'zalitē/ *n.* —**na·sal·ly** *adv.*

nas·cent /'nāsent; 'nasənt/ ▸*adj.* (esp. of a process or organization) just coming into existence and beginning to display signs of future potential: *the nascent space industry.* —**nas·cence** *n.* —**nas·cen·cy** *n.*

NASDAQ /'nazdak/ ▸*abbr.* National Association of Securities Dealers Automated Quotations, a computerized system for trading in securities.

nas·tur·tium /nə'stərsʜəm; nə-/ ▸*n.* a South American trailing plant (*Tropaeolum majus*, family Tropaeolaceae) with round leaves and bright orange, yellow, or red flowers that is widely grown as an ornamental.

nas·ty /'nastē/ ▸*adj.* (**-ti·er, -ti·est**) **1** highly unpleasant, to the senses; physically nauseating: *plastic bags burn with a nasty, acrid smell.* ■ (of the weather) unpleasantly cold or wet: *a cold, nasty day.* ■ repugnant to the mind; morally bad: *her stories are very nasty, full of murder and violence.* **2** (of a person or animal) behaving in an unpleasant or spiteful way: *Harry was a nasty, foul-mouthed old devil.*

▸*n.* (*pl.* **-ties**) (often **nasties**) *inf.* an unpleasant or harmful person or thing: *bacteria and other nasties.* —**nas·ti·ly** /-təlē/ *adv.* —**nas·ti·ness** *n.*

nat. ▸*abbr.* ■ national. ■ nationalist. ■ native. ■ natural.

na·tal /'nātl/ ▸*adj.* of or relating to the place or time of one's birth: *after puberty a Hindu girl does not stay long in her natal home.*

na·tion /'nāsʜən/ ▸*n.* a large aggregate of people united by common descent, history, culture, or language, inhabiting a particular country or territory: *leading industrialized nations.* ■ a North American Indian people or confederation of peoples. —**na·tion·hood** /-,hŏŏd/ *n.*

na·tion·al /'nasʜənəl/ ▸*adj.* of or relating to a nation; common to or characteristic of a whole nation: *a national newspaper.* ■ owned, controlled, or financially supported by the federal government: *plans for a national art library.*

▸*n.* **1** a citizen of a particular country, typically entitled to hold that country's passport: *a German national.* **2** (usu. **nationals**) a nationwide competition or tournament: *she finished 16th at the nationals that year.* —**na·tion·al·ly** *adv.* nationally, *there has been a 2.5% drop in car crime.*

na·tion·al debt ▸*n.* the total amount of money that a country's government has borrowed, by various means.

Na·tion·al Guard ▸*n.* (in the U.S.) the primary reserve military force, partly maintained by the states but also available for federal use. ■ the primary military force of some other countries. —**Na·tion·al Guards·man** *n.*

na·tion·al·ism /'nasʜənə,lizəm/ ▸*n.* patriotic feeling, principles, or efforts. ■ an extreme form of this, esp. marked by a feeling of superiority over other countries. ■ advocacy of political independence for a particular country: *Palestinian nationalism.* —**na·tion·al·ist** *n. & adj.* —**na·tion·al·is·tic** *adj.*

na·tion·al·i·ty /,nasʜə'nalitē/ ▸*n.* (*pl.* **-ties**) **1** the status of belonging to a particular nation: *they changed their nationality and became Lebanese.* ■ distinctive national or ethnic character: *the change of a name does not discard nationality.* ■ patriotic sentiment; nationalism. **2** an ethnic group forming a part of one or more political nations: *all the main nationalities of Ethiopia.*

na·tion·al·ize /'nasʜənə,līz/ ▸*v.* [*tr.*] **1** transfer (a major branch of industry or commerce) from private to state ownership or control. **2** make distinctively national; give a national character to: *in the 13th and 14th centuries church designs were further nationalized.* **3** [usu. as *adj.*] (**nationalized**) naturalize (a foreigner): *he is now a nationalized Frenchman.* —**na·tion·al·i·za·tion** /,nasʜənəli'zāsʜən/ *n.* —**na·tion·al·iz·er** *n.*

na·tion·al park ▸*n.* a scenic or historically important area of countryside protected by a national government for the enjoyment of the general public or the preservation of wildlife.

Na·tion of Is·lam ▸an exclusively black Islamic sect proposing a separate black nation, founded in Detroit *c.*1930. It was led from 1934 by Elijah Muhammad (1897–1975) and came to prominence under the influence of Malcolm X. Its current leader is Louis Farrakhan.

na·tion·wide /'nāsʜən'wīd/ ▸*adj.* extending or reaching throughout the whole nation: *a nationwide hunt.*

▸*adv.* throughout a whole nation: *it employs 6,000 people nationwide.*

na·tive /'nātiv/ ▸*n.* a person born in a specified place or associated with a place by birth, whether subsequently resident there or not: *a native of Montreal.* ■ a local inhabitant: *New York in the summer was too hot even for the natives.* ■ *dated, often offens.* one of the original inhabitants of a country, esp. a nonwhite as regarded by European colonists or travelers. ■ an animal or plant indigenous to a place: *the marigold is a native of southern Europe.*

▸*adj.* **1** associated with the country, region, or circumstances of a person's birth: *he's a native New Yorker.* ■ of the indigenous inhabitants of a place: *a ceremonial native dance from Fiji.* **2** (of a plant or animal) of indigenous origin or growth: *pigs are native to China.* **3** (of a quality) belonging to a person's character from birth rather than acquired; innate: *a jealousy and rage native to him.* ■ *Comput.* designed for or built into a given system, esp. denoting the language associated with a given processor, computer, or compiler, and programs written in it. **4** (of a metal or other mineral) found in a pure or uncombined state. —**na·tive·ly** *adv.* —**na·tive·ness** *n.*

▸ □ **go native** *humorous* or *derog.* (of a person living away from their own country or region) abandon one's own culture, customs, or way of life and adopt those of the country or region one is living in.

Na·tive A·mer·i·can ▸*n.* a member of any of the indigenous peoples of the Americas.

▸*adj.* of or relating to these peoples.

na·tiv·i·ty /nə'tivitē; nā-/ ▸*n.* (*pl.* **-ties**) the occasion of a person's birth: *the place of my nativity.* ■ (usu. **the Nativity**) the birth of Jesus Christ. ■ a picture, carving, or model representing Jesus Christ's birth. ■ the Christian festival of Christ's birth; Christmas.

NATO /'nātō/ ▸*abbr.* North Atlantic Treaty Organization.

nat·ty /'natē/ ▸*adj.* (**-ti·er, -ti·est**) *inf.* (esp. of a person or an article of clothing) smart and fashionable: *a natty blue blazer and designer jeans.* —**nat·ti·ly** /-təlē/ *adv.* —**nat·ti·ness** *n.*

nat·u·ral /'nacʜərəl/ ▸*adj.* **1** existing in or caused by nature; not made or caused by humankind: *natural disasters such as earthquakes.* **2** born with a particular skill, quality, or ability: *he was a natural entertainer.* ■ (of a skill, quality, or ability) coming instinctively to a person; innate: *writing appears to demand muscular movements that are not natural to children.* ■ (of a person or their behavior) relaxed and unaffected; spontaneous: *he replied with too much nonchalance to sound natural.* ■ occurring as a matter of course and without debate; inevitable: *Ken was a natural choice for coach.* ■ *Bridge* (of a bid) straightforwardly reflecting one's holding of cards. **3** (of a parent or child) related by blood: *such adopted children always knew who their natural parents were.* ■ *chiefly archaic* illegitimate: *the Baron left a natural son by his mistress.* **4** *Mus.* (of a note) not sharped or flatted: *the bassoon plays G-natural instead of A-flat.* ■ (of a brass instrument) having no valves and able to play only the notes of the harmonic series above a fundamental note. ■ of or relating to the notes and intervals of the harmonic series. **5** *Christian Theol.* relating to earthly or unredeemed human or physical nature as distinct from the spiritual or supernatural realm.

▸*n.* **1** a person regarded as having an innate gift or talent for a particular task or activity: *she was a natural for the sort of television work required of her.* ■ a thing that is particularly suited for something: *perky musical accompaniment would seem a natural for this series.* **2** *Mus.* a sign (♮) denoting a natural note when a previous sign or the key signature would otherwise demand a sharp or a flat. ■ a natural note. ■ any of the longer keys on a keyboard instrument that are normally white.

▶*adv. inf.* or *dial.* naturally: *keep walking—just act natural.* —**nat·u·ral·ness** *n.*

nat·u·ral child·birth ▶*n.* childbirth with minimal medical or technological intervention, usually involving special breathing and relaxation techniques.

nat·u·ral gas ▶*n.* flammable gas, consisting largely of methane and other hydrocarbons, occurring naturally underground (often in association with petroleum) and used as fuel.

nat·u·ral his·to·ry ▶*n.* the scientific study of animals or plants, esp. as concerned with observation rather than experiment, and presented in popular rather than academic form. ■ the study of the whole natural world, including the earth sciences. —**nat·u·ral his·to·ri·an** *n.*

nat·u·ral·ism /ˈnaCHərəˌlizəm/ ▶*n.* **1** (in art and literature) a style and theory of representation based on the accurate depiction of detail. **2** a philosophical viewpoint according to which everything arises from natural properties and causes, and supernatural or spiritual explanations are excluded or discounted.

nat·u·ral·ist /ˈnaCHərəlist/ ▶*n.* **1** an expert in or student of natural history. **2** a person who practices naturalism in art or literature. ■ a person who adopts philosophical naturalism.
▶*adj.* another term for NATURALISTIC.

nat·u·ral·is·tic /ˌnaCHərəˈlistik/ ▶*adj.* **1** derived from real life or nature, or imitating it very closely: *verbatim records of children's speech in naturalistic settings.* **2** based on the theory of naturalism in art or literature: *naturalistic paintings of the city.* ■ of or according to the philosophy of naturalism: *phenomena once considered supernatural have yielded to naturalistic explanation.* —**nat·u·ral·is·ti·cal·ly** *adv.*

nat·u·ral·ize /ˈnaCHərəˌlīz/ ▶*v.* [*tr.*] **1** (often **be/become naturalized**) admit (a foreigner) to the citizenship of a country: *he was born in a foreign country and had never been naturalized.* ■ [*intr.*] (of a foreigner) be admitted to the citizenship of a country: *the opportunity to naturalize as American.* ■ alter (an adopted foreign word) so that it conforms more closely to the phonology or orthography of the adopting language: *the stoccafisso of Liguria was naturalized in Nice as* stocofocada. **2** [usu. as *adj.*] (**naturalized**) *Biol.* establish (a plant or animal) so that it lives wild in a region where it is not indigenous: *native and naturalized species.* ■ establish (a cultivated plant) in a natural situation: *this species of crocus naturalizes itself very easily.* ■ [*intr.*] (of a cultivated plant) become established in a natural situation: *these perennials should be planted where they can naturalize.* —**nat·u·ral·i·za·tion** /ˌnaCHərələˈzāSHən/ *n.*

nat·u·ral law ▶*n.* **1** a body of unchanging moral principles regarded as a basis for all human conduct. **2** an observable law relating to natural phenomena: *the natural laws of perspective.*

nat·u·ral·ly /ˈnaCHərəlē/ ▶*adv.* **1** in a natural manner, in particular: ■ in a normal manner; without distortion or exaggeration: *act naturally.* ■ as a natural result: *one leads naturally into the other.* ■ without special help or intervention: *naturally curly hair.* **2** as may be expected; of course: *naturally, I hoped for the best.*

nat·u·ral num·bers ▶*pl. n.* the positive integers (whole numbers) 1, 2, 3, etc., and sometimes zero as well.

nat·u·ral re·sources ▶*pl. n.* materials or substances such as minerals, forests, water, and fertile land that occur in nature and can be used for economic gain.

nat·u·ral sci·ence ▶*n.* (usu. **natural sciences**) a branch of science that deals with the physical world, e.g., physics, chemistry, geology, and biology. ■ the branch of knowledge that deals with the study of the physical world. —**nat·u·ral sci·en·tist** *n.*

nat·u·ral se·lec·tion ▶*n. Biol.* the process whereby organisms better adapted to their environment tend to survive and produce more offspring. Compare with SURVIVAL OF THE FITTEST (see SURVIVAL).

na·ture /ˈnāCHər/ ▶*n.* **1** the phenomena of the physical world collectively, including plants, animals, the landscape, and other features and products of the earth, as opposed to humans or human creations: *the breathtaking beauty of nature.* ■ the physical force regarded as causing and regulating these phenomena: *it is impossible to change the laws of nature.* See also MOTHER NATURE. ■ the countryside, esp. when picturesque. **2** the basic or inherent features of something, esp. when seen as characteristic of it: *helping them to realize the nature of their problems.* ■ inborn or hereditary characteristics as an influence on or determinant of personality. Often contrasted with NURTURE. ▷Middle English (denoting the physical power of a person): from Old French, from Latin *natura* 'birth, nature, quality,' from *nat-* 'born,' from the verb *nasci.*

na·tured /ˈnāCHərd/ ▶*adj.* [in *comb.*] having a nature or disposition of a specified kind: *a good-natured man.*

naught /nôt/ ▶*n.* the digit 0; zero.

naugh·ty /ˈnôtē/ ▶*adj.* (**-ti·er, -ti·est**) **1** (esp. of children) disobedient; badly behaved: *you've been a really naughty boy.* **2** *inf.* mildly rude or indecent, typically because related to sex: *naughty drawings.* **3** *archaic* wicked. —**naugh·ti·ly** /-təlē/ *adv.* —**naugh·ti·ness** *n.*

nau·se·a /ˈnôzēə; -ZHə/ ▶*n.* a feeling of sickness with an inclination to vomit. ■ loathing; revulsion: *intended to induce a feeling of nostalgia, it only induces in me a feeling of nausea.*

nau·se·ate /ˈnôzēˌāt; - ZHēˌāt/ ▶*v.* [*tr.*] make (someone) feel sick; affect with nausea: *the thought of food nauseated her.* ■ fill (someone) with revulsion; disgust: *I was nauseated by the vicious comment.* —**nau·se·at·ing·ly** *adv.*

nau·seous /ˈnôSHəs; -ZHəs; -ēəs/ ▶*adj.* **1** affected with nausea; inclined to vomit: *a rancid, cloying odor that made him nauseous.* **2** causing nausea; offensive to the taste or smell: *the smell was nauseous.* ■ disgusting, repellent, or offensive: *this nauseous account of a court case.* —**nau·seous·ly** *adv.* —**nau·seous·ness** *n.*

nau·ti·cal /ˈnôtikəl/ ▶*adj.* of or concerning sailors or navigation; maritime: *nautical charts.* —**nau·ti·cal·ly** /-ik(ə)lē/ *adv.*

nau·ti·cal mile ▶*n.* a unit used in measuring distances at sea, equal to approx. 2,025 yards (1,852 m).

Nau·ti·lus /ˈnôtl-əs/ ▶the first nuclear-powered submarine, launched in 1954 for the U.S. Navy. ■ *trademark* an exercise machine that matches resistance with output of force.

nau·ti·lus /ˈnôtl-əs/ ▶*n.* (*pl.* **nau·ti·lus·es** or **nau·ti·li** /ˈnôtl-ī/) **1** a cephalopod (genus *Nautilus*, subclass Nautiloidea) with a light external spiral shell and numerous short tentacles around the mouth. Its several species include the common **chambered nautilus** (*Nautilus pompilius*) of the Indo-Pacific, with a shell that is white with brownish bands on the outside and lined with mother-of-pearl on the inside. **2** (also **paper nautilus**) another term for ARGONAUT.

Nav·a·jo /ˈnavəˌhō; ˈnä-/ (also **Nav·a·ho**) ▶*n.* (*pl.* same or **-jos**) **1** a member of an American Indian people of New Mexico and Arizona. **2** the Athabaskan language of this people.
▶*adj.* of or relating to this people or their language.

na·val /ˈnāvəl/ ▶*adj.* of, in, or relating to a navy or navies: *a naval officer.*

nave /nāv/ ▶*n.* the central part of a church building, intended to accommodate most of the congregation. In traditional Western churches it is rectangular, separated from the chancel by a step or rail, and from adjacent aisles by pillars.

na·vel /ˈnāvəl/ ▶*n.* a rounded, knotty depression in the center of a person's belly caused by the detachment of the umbilical cord after birth; the umbilicus. ■ *fig.* the central point of a place: *the Incas saw Cuzco as the navel of the world.* ▷Old English *nafela,* of Germanic origin; related to Dutch *navel* and German *Nabel,* from an Indo-European root shared by Latin *umbo* 'boss of a shield,' *umbilicus* 'navel,' and Greek *omphalos* 'boss, navel.'

na·vel or·ange ▶*n.* a large, seedless orange that has a navel-like depression at the top and contains a small secondary fruit embedded underneath it.

na·vic·u·lar /nəˈvikyələr/ ▶*n.* **1** (also **navicular bone**) a boat-shaped bone in the ankle or wrist, esp. that in the ankle between the talus and the cuneiform bones. **2** (also **navicular disease** or **navicular syndrome**) a chronic disorder of the navicular bone in horses, causing lameness in the front feet.

nav·i·ga·ble /ˈnavigəbəl/ ▶*adj.* (of a waterway or sea) able to be sailed on by ships or boats. ■ (of a track or road) suitable for transportation; passable: *those minor roads would be navigable in emergencies.* ■ (esp. of a Web site) easy to get around in; maneuverable: *a navigable Web browser.* —**nav·i·ga·bil·i·ty** /ˌnavəgəˈbilitē/ *n.*

nav·i·gate /ˈnaviˌgāt/ ▶*v.* **1** [*intr.*] plan and direct the route or course of a ship, aircraft, or other form of transportation, esp. by using instruments or maps: *they navigated by the stars.* ■ (of a passenger in a vehicle) assist the driver by reading the map and planning a route: *we'll go in my car—you can navigate.* **2** [*tr.*] sail or travel over (a stretch of water or terrain), esp. carefully or with difficulty: *ships had been lost while navigating the narrows.* ■ guide (a vessel or vehicle) over a specified route or terrain: *she navigated the car safely through the traffic.* ■ *Comput.* [*intr.*] move from one accessible page, section, or view of a file or Web site to another: *the new layout makes it easier to navigate through their atlas of world maps.*

nav·i·ga·tion /ˌnaviˈgāSHən/ ▶*n.* **1** the process or activity of accurately ascertaining one's position and planning and following a route. **2** the passage of ships: *bridges to span rivers without hindering navigation.* —**nav·i·ga·tion·al** /-nəl/ *adj.*

nav·i·ga·tor /ˈnaviˌgātər/ ▶*n.* a person who directs the route or course of a ship, aircraft, or other form of transportation, esp. by using

N

instruments and maps. ■ an instrument or device that assists in directing the course of a vessel or aircraft. ■ *Comput.* a browser program for retrieving data on the World Wide Web or another information system. ■ *hist.* a person who explores by sea.

na·vy /ˈnāvē/ ▶ *n.* (*pl.* **-vies**) **1** (often **the navy** or **the Navy**) the branch of a nation's armed services that conducts military operations at sea. ■ the ships of a navy: *a 600-ship navy.* ■ *poetic/lit.* a fleet of ships. **2** (also **navy blue**) a dark blue color: [as *adj.*] *a navy-blue suit.*

na·vy bean ▶ *n.* a small white type of kidney bean.

na·vy yard ▶ *n.* a shipyard for the construction, repair, and equipping of naval vessels.

nay /nā/ ▶ *adv.* **1** or rather; and more than that (used to emphasize a more appropriate word than one just used): *it will take months, nay years.* **2** *archaic* or *dial.* no: *nay, I must not think thus.*
▶ *n.* a negative answer or vote: *the cabinet sits to give the final yea or nay to policies.*

nay·say /ˈnāˌsā/ ▶ *v.* (*past* and *past part.* **-said**) [*tr.*] say no to; deny or oppose: *I'm not going to naysay anything he does.* —**nay·say·er** *n.*

Naz·a·rene /ˈnazəˌrēn/ ▶ *n.* a native or inhabitant of Nazareth. ■ (**the Nazarene**) Jesus Christ. ■ (chiefly in Jewish or Muslim use) a Christian. ■ a member of the Church of the Nazarene, a Christian Protestant denomination.
▶ *adj.* of or relating to Nazareth or Nazarenes.

Na·zi /ˈnätsē/ ▶ *n.* (*pl.* **Na·zis**) *hist.* a member of the National Socialist German Workers' Party. ■ a member of an organization with similar ideology. ■ *derog.* a person who holds and acts brutally in accordance with extreme racist or authoritarian views.
▶ *adj.* of or concerning the Nazis or Nazism. —**Na·zi·fy** /ˈnätsiˌfī/ *v.* (**-fies**, **-fied**). —**Na·zi·ism** /-ˌizəm/ *n.* —**Na·zism** /ˈnätˌsizəm/ *n.*

NB ▶ *abbr.* ■ New Brunswick (in official postal use). ■ nota bene; take special note (used to precede a written note).

Nb ▶ *symb.* the chemical element niobium.

NBC ▶ *abbr.* ■ (in the U.S.) National Broadcasting Company. ■ (of weapons or warfare) nuclear, biological, and chemical.

NC ▶ *abbr.* network computer, a personal computer with reduced functionality intended to be used to access services on a network.

NC-17 ▶ *symb.* no one 17 and under admitted, a rating in the Voluntary Movie Rating System forbidding admission to children 17 years old and under. ▷representing *no children (under) 17.*

NCO ▶ *abbr.* noncommissioned officer.

Nd ▶ *symb.* the chemical element neodymium.

NE ▶ *abbr.* northeast or northeastern.

Ne ▶ *symb.* the chemical element neon.

NEA ▶ *abbr.* ■ National Education Association. ■ National Endowment for the Arts.

Ne·an·der·thal /nēˈandərˌtôl/ ▶ *n.* (also **Neanderthal man**) an extinct species of human (*Homo neanderthalensis*) that was widely distributed in ice-age Europe between *c.*120,000 and 35,000 years ago, with a receding forehead and prominent brow ridges. ■ *fig.* an uncivilized, unintelligent, or uncouth person, esp. a man.
▶ *adj.* of or relating to this extinct human species. ■ *fig.* (esp. of a man) uncivilized, unintelligent, or uncouth.

neap /nēp/ ▶ *n.* (usu. **neap tide**) a tide just after the first or third quarters of the moon when there is the least difference between high and low water. Compare with SPRING TIDE.

Ne·a·pol·i·tan /ˌnēəˈpälitn/ ▶ *n.* a native or citizen of Naples.
▶ *adj.* of or relating to Naples.

Ne·a·pol·i·tan ice cream ▶ *n.* ice cream made in layers of different colors, typically including chocolate, vanilla, and strawberry.

near /ni(ə)r/ ▶ *adv.* **1** at or to a short distance away; nearby: *a bomb exploding somewhere near* | [*comparative*] *she took a step nearer.* **2** a short time away in the future: *the time for his retirement was drawing near.* **3** almost: *a near perfect fit.*
▶ *prep.* (also **near to**) **1** at or to a short distance away from (a place): *the parking lot near the sawmill* | [*superlative*] *the table nearest the door.* **2** a short period of time from: *near the end of the war.* **3** close to (a state); verging on: *she was near death.* ■ (used before an amount) a small amount below; approaching: *temperatures near 2 million degrees K.* **4** similar to: *a shape near to the original.*
▶ *adj.* **1** located a short distance away: *a big house in the near distance* | [*superlative*] *I was fifteen miles from the nearest town.* **2** only a short time ahead: *the conflict is unlikely to be resolved in the near future.* **3** similar: [*superlative*] *walking in these shoes is the nearest thing to floating on air.* ■ close to being (the thing mentioned): *a near disaster.* ■ having a close family connection: *the loss of a child or other near relative.* **4** located on the side

of a vehicle that is normally closest to the curb: *the near right-hand end window of the trailer.*
▶ *v.* [*tr.*] come near to (someone or something); approach: *soon the cab would be nearing State Street* | [*intr.*] *lunchtime neared.* ▷Middle English: from Old Norse *nær* 'nearer,' comparative of *ná*, corresponding to Old English *nēah* 'nigh.' —**near·ness** *n.*
▶ □ **one's nearest and dearest** one's close friends and relatives. □ **so near and yet so far** a rueful comment on someone's narrow failure to achieve an aim.

near·by ▶ *adj.* /ˈni(ə)rˌbī/ close at hand; not far away: *he slung his jacket over a nearby chair.*
▶ *adv.* /ˌni(ə)rˈbī/ (*Brit.* also **near by**) close by; very near: *his four sisters live nearby.*

near·ly /ˈni(ə)rlē/ ▶ *adv.* **1** very close to; almost: *David was nearly asleep.* **2** closely: *in the absence of anyone more nearly related, I had been designated next of kin.*
▶ □ **not nearly** nothing like; far from: *you're not nearly as clever as you think you are.*

near miss ▶ *n.* **1** a narrowly avoided collision, esp. between two aircraft. ■ something narrowly avoided; a lucky escape: *she had a near miss when her horse was nearly sucked into a dike.* **2** a bomb or shot that just misses its target. ■ something almost achieved: *a victory in Houston and a near miss in the semifinals of the French Open.*

near·sight·ed /ˈnirˌsītid/ ▶ *adj.* unable to see things clearly unless they are relatively close to the eyes, owing to the focusing of rays of light by the eye at a point in front of the retina; myopic. —**near·sight·ed·ly** *adv.* —**near·sight·ed·ness** *n.*

neat /nēt/ ▶ *adj.* **1** (of a place or thing) arranged in an orderly, tidy way: *the books had been stacked up in neat piles.* ■ (of a person) habitually tidy, well groomed, or well organized: *her daughter was always neat and clean.* ■ *inf.* very good or pleasant; excellent: *I've been taking lessons in tracking from this really neat Indian guide.* **2** done with or demonstrating skill or efficiency: *Howard's neat, precise tackling.* ■ tending to disregard specifics for the sake of convenience; slick or facile: *this neat division does not take into account a host of associated factors.* **3** (of liquid, esp. liquor) not diluted or mixed with anything else: *he drank neat Scotch.* —**neat·ly** *adv.* —**neat·ness** *n.*

neat·en /ˈnētn/ ▶ *v.* [*tr.*] make neat; arrange in an orderly, tidy way: *she made an attempt to neaten her hair.*

'neath /nēTH/ (also **neath**) ▶ *prep. chiefly poetic/lit.* beneath: *'neath the trees.*

neb·u·la /ˈnebyələ/ ▶ *n.* (*pl.* **-lae** /-lē/ or **-las**) *Astron.* a cloud of gas and dust in outer space, visible in the night sky either as an indistinct bright patch or as a dark silhouette against other luminous matter. ■ (in general use) any indistinct bright area in the night sky, for example, a distant galaxy. —**neb·u·lar** /-lər/ *adj.*

neb·u·lous /ˈnebyələs/ ▶ *adj.* in the form of a cloud or haze; hazy: *a giant nebulous glow.* ■ (of a concept or idea) unclear, vague, or ill-defined: *nebulous concepts like quality of life.* —**neb·u·los·i·ty** /ˌnebyəˈläsitē/ *n.* —**neb·u·lous·ly** *adv.* —**neb·u·lous·ness** *n.*

nec·es·sar·i·ly /ˌnesəˈse(ə)rəlē/ ▶ *adv.* as a necessary result; inevitably: *the prognosis can necessarily be only an educated guess.*
▶ □ **not necessarily** (as a response) what has been said or suggested may not be true or unavoidable.

nec·es·sar·y /ˈnesəˌserē/ ▶ *adj.* **1** required to be done, achieved, or present; needed; essential: *members are admitted only after they have gained the necessary experience.* **2** determined, existing, or happening by natural laws or predestination; inevitable: *a necessary consequence.*
▶ *n.* (usu. **necessaries**) (also **necessaries of life**) the basic requirements of life, such as food and warmth. ■ small items required for a particular journey or purpose: *I hastily threw a few necessaries into a kit bag.*
▶ □ **a necessary evil** something that is undesirable but must be accepted.

ne·ces·si·tate /nəˈsesəˌtāt/ ▶ *v.* [*tr.*] make (something) necessary as a result or consequence: *the severe arthritis eventually necessitated a total hip replacement.*

ne·ces·si·ty /nəˈsesitē/ ▶ *n.* (*pl.* **-ties**) **1** the fact of being required or indispensable: *the necessity for law and order.* ■ unavoidability: *the necessity of growing old.* ■ a state of things or circumstances enforcing a certain course: *created more by necessity than design.* **2** an indispensable thing: *a good book is a necessity when traveling.*

Pronunciation Key ə *ago*, *up*; ər *over*, *fur*; a *hat*; ā *ate*; ä *car*; CH *chin*; e *let*; ē *see*; e(ə)r *air*; i *fit*; ī *by*; i(ə)r *ear*; NG *sing*; ō *go*; ô *law*, *for*; oi *toy*; o͝o *good*; o͞o *goo*; ou *out*; SH *she*; TH *thin*; <u>TH</u> *then*; (h)w *why*; ZH *vision*

N

▶ □ **of necessity** unavoidably: *to alleviate labor shortages employers will, of necessity, offer better deals for part-timers.*

neck /nek/ ▶ *n.* **1** the part of a person's or animal's body connecting the head to the rest of the body: *she is wearing a silk scarf around her neck.* ■ the part of a shirt, dress, or other garment that is around or close to the neck: *her dress had three buttons at the neck undone.* ■ *fig.* a person's neck regarded as bearing a burden of responsibility or guilt for something: *he'll be stuck with a loan around his neck.* **2** a narrow part of something, resembling a neck in shape or position: ■ the part of a bottle or other container near the mouth. ■ a narrow piece of terrain or sea, such as an isthmus, channel, or pass. ■ *Anat.* a narrow part near one end of an organ such as the uterus. ■ the part of a violin, guitar, or other similar instrument that bears the fingerboard. ■ (often **volcanic neck**) *Geol.* a column of solidified lava or igneous rock formed in a volcanic vent, esp. when exposed by erosion. **3** the length of a horse's head and neck as a measure of its lead in a race: *the colt won the 122nd running of the Midsummer Derby by a neck.*

▶ *v.* **1** [*intr.*] *inf.* (of two people) kiss and caress amorously: *we started necking on the sofa.* **2** [*intr.*] form a narrowed part at a particular point when subjected to tension: *the nylon filament **necks down** to a fraction of its original diameter.* —**necked** *adj.* [in *comb.*] *an open-necked shirt.* —**neck·less** *adj.*

▶ □ **break one's neck** *inf.* exert oneself to the utmost (to achieve something). □ **neck and neck** even in a race, competition, or comparison: *we have six contestants who are neck and neck.* □ **neck of the woods** *inf.* a particular area or locality: *imagine seeing her in this neck of the woods.* □ **up to one's neck** *inf.* heavily burdened by or busily involved in: *they were up to their necks in debt* | *I'm up to my neck in rearranging the tournament.*

neck·band /'nek,band/ ▶ *n.* a strip of material around the neck of a garment.

neck·er·chief /'nekər,CHif; -,CHēf/ ▶ *n.* a square of cloth worn around the neck.

neck·lace /'neklis/ ▶ *n.* **1** an ornamental chain or string of beads, jewels, or links worn around the neck. **2** (chiefly in South Africa) a tire doused or filled with gasoline, placed around a victim's neck, and set on fire.

▶ *v.* [*tr.*] (chiefly in South Africa) kill (someone) with a tire necklace.

neck·line /'nek,līn/ ▶ *n.* the edge of a woman's garment at or below the neck, used with reference to its height or shape: *a sundress with a square neckline.*

neck·tie /'nek,tī/ ▶ *n.* another term for TIE (sense 2).

neck·wear /'nek,we(ə)r/ ▶ *n.* items worn around the neck, such as ties or scarves, collectively.

nec·ro·man·cy /'nekrə,mansē/ ▶ *n.* the supposed practice of communicating with the dead, esp. in order to predict the future. ■ witchcraft, sorcery, or black magic in general. —**nec·ro·man·cer** /-sər/ *n.* —**nec·ro·man·tic** /,nekrə'mantik/ *adj.*

nec·ro·phil·i·a /,nekrə'filēə/ ▶ *n.* a morbid and esp. erotic attraction toward corpses. ■ sexual intercourse with a corpse. —**nec·ro·phile** /'nekrə,fīl/ *n.* —**nec·ro·phil·i·ac** /-'filē,ak/ *n.* —**nec·ro·phil·ic** /-'filik/ *adj.* —**nec·roph·i·lism** /ne'kräfə,lizəm/ *n.* —**nec·roph·i·list** /ne'kräfəlist/ *n.*

ne·crop·o·lis /ne'kräpəlis/ ▶ *n.* a cemetery, esp. a large one belonging to an ancient city.

ne·cro·sis /ne'krōsis/ ▶ *n. Med.* the death of most or all of the cells in an organ or tissue due to disease, injury, or failure of the blood supply. —**ne·crot·ic** /-'krätik/ *adj.*

nec·tar /'nektər/ ▶ *n.* **1** a sugary fluid secreted by plants, esp. within flowers to encourage pollination by insects and other animals. It is collected by bees to make into honey. **2** (in Greek and Roman mythology) the drink of the gods. ■ a delicious drink: *the cold beer at the pub was nectar.* ■ a thick fruit juice: *peach nectar.* —**nec·tar·e·an** /nek'te(ə)rēən/ *adj.* —**nec·tar·e·ous** /nek'te(ə)rēəs/ *adj.* —**nec·tar·ous** /-əs/ *adj.*

nec·tar·ine /,nektə'rēn/ ▶ *n.* a peach of a variety with smooth, thin, brightly colored skin and rich firm flesh. ■ the tree bearing this fruit.

née /nā/ ▶ *adj.* originally called; born (used esp. in adding a woman's maiden name after her married name): *Mary Toogood, née Johnson.*

need /nēd/ ▶ *v.* [*tr.*] **1** require (something) because it is essential or very important: *I need help now.* ■ (**not need something**) not want to be subjected to something: *I don't need your sarcasm.* **2** expressing necessity or obligation: *need I say more?*

▶ *n.* **1** circumstances in which something is necessary, or that require some course of action; necessity: *the basic human need for food.* **2** (often **needs**) a thing that is wanted or required: *his day-to-day needs.* **3** the state of lacking basic necessities such as food or money: *a family whose need was particularly pressing.* ■ the state of requiring help or support: *help us in our hour of need.*

▶ □ **if need be** if necessary. □ **in need** requiring help: *children in need.* ■ **in need of** requiring or needing (something): *he was in desperate need of medical care.*

need·ful /'nēdfəl/ ▶ *adj.* **1** *formal* necessary; requisite: *a further word was needful.* **2** needy: *she gave her money away to needful people.* —**need·ful·ly** *adv.* —**need·ful·ness** *n.*

nee·dle /'nēdl/ ▶ *n.* **1** a very fine slender piece of polished metal with a point at one end and a hole or eye for thread at the other, used in sewing. **2** something resembling a sewing needle in use, shape, or appearance: ■ such an instrument used in crafts such as crochet, knitting, and lacemaking. ■ the pointed hollow end of a hypodermic syringe. ■ a long, thin, narrow crystal. ■ a thin, typically metal pointer on a dial, compass, or other instrument. ■ the sharp, stiff, slender leaf of a fir or pine tree. ■ a pointed rock or peak. ■ a stylus used to play phonograph records.

▶ *v.* [*tr.*] **1** prick or pierce (something) with or as if with a needle. **2** *inf.* provoke or annoy (someone), esp. by continual criticism or questioning: *I just said that to Charlie to needle him.* ▷Old English *nǣdl*, of Germanic origin; related to Dutch *naald* and German *Nadel*, from an Indo-European root shared by Latin *nere* 'to spin' and Greek *nēma* 'thread.'

▶ □ **the eye of a needle** a tiny aperture or opening through which it would seem impossible to pass. □ **give someone the needle** *inf.* provoke or annoy someone: *Lady gives him the needle because she knows it isn't true.* □ **a needle in a haystack** something that is almost impossible to find because it is hidden among so many other things.

nee·dle·point /'nēdl,point/ ▶ *n.* **1** embroidery worked over canvas, typically in diagonal stitches covering the entire surface of the fabric. **2** (also **needlepoint lace**) lace made by hand using a needle rather than bobbins.

▶ *v.* [*tr.*] embroider in needlepoint.

need·less /'nēdlis/ ▶ *adj.* (of something bad) unnecessary; avoidable: *I deplore needless waste.* —**need·less·ly** *adv.* —**need·less·ness** *n.*

▶ □ **needless to say** of course.

nee·dle·work /'nēdl,wərk/ ▶ *n.* the art or practice of sewing or embroidery: *Mrs. Zurndorfer specializes in needlework.* ■ sewn or embroidered items collectively: *exhibits include European and Eastern needlework.* —**nee·dle·work·er** *n.*

need·y /'nēdē/ ▶ *adj.* (**need·i·er**, **need·i·est**) (of a person) lacking the necessities of life; very poor: *needy and elderly people.* ■ (of circumstances) characterized by poverty: *those from needy backgrounds.* —**need·i·ness** *n.*

ne'er /ne(ə)r/ ▶ *poetic/lit.* or *dial.* contr. of never.

ne'er-do-well /'ne(ə)r doo ,wel/ ▶ *n.* a person who is lazy and irresponsible.

▶ *adj.* lazy and irresponsible.

ne·far·i·ous /ni'fe(ə)rēəs/ ▶ *adj.* (typically of an action or activity) wicked or criminal: *the nefarious activities of the organized-crime syndicates.* —**ne·far·i·ous·ly** *adv.* —**ne·far·i·ous·ness** *n.*

neg /neg/ ▶ *n. inf.* a photographic negative.

ne·gate /nə'gāt/ ▶ *v.* [*tr.*] **1** nullify; make ineffective: *alcohol negates the effects of the drug.* **2** . *Logic* & *Gram.* make (a clause, sentence, or proposition) negative in meaning. **3** deny the existence of (something): *negating the political nature of education.* —**ne·ga·tor** /-'gātər/ *n.*

ne·ga·tion /nə'gāsHən/ ▶ *n.* **1** the contradiction or denial of something: *there should be confirmation—or negation—of the findings.* ■ *Gram.* denial of the truth of a clause or sentence, typically involving the use of a negative word (e.g., *not, no, never*) or a word or affix with negative force (e.g., *nothing, non-*). ■ *Math.* inversion: *these formulae and their negations.* **2** the absence or opposite of something actual or positive: *evil is not merely the negation of goodness.* —**neg·a·to·ry** /'negə,tôrē/ *adj.*

neg·a·tive /'negətiv/ ▶ *adj.* **1** consisting in or characterized by the absence rather than the presence of distinguishing features. ■ (of a statement or decision) expressing or implying denial, disagreement, or refusal: *that, I take it, was a negative answer.* ■ (of the results of a test or experiment) indicating that a certain substance is not present or a certain condition does not exist: *so far all the patients have tested negative for TB.* ■ (of a person, attitude, or situation) not optimistic; harmful or unwelcome: *not all the news is negative.* ■ *inf.* denoting a complete lack of something: *they were described as having negative vulnerability to water entry.* ■ *Gram.* & *Logic* (of a word, clause, or proposition) expressing denial, negation, or refutation; stating or asserting that something is not the case. Contrasted with AFFIRMATIVE and INTERROGATIVE. **2** (of a quantity) less than zero; to be subtracted from others or from zero. ■ denoting a direction of decrease or reversal: *the industry suffered negative growth in 1992.* **3** of, containing, producing, or denoting the kind

of electric charge carried by electrons. **4** (of a photographic image) showing light and shade or colors reversed from those of the original.
▸*n.* **1** a word or statement that expresses denial, disagreement, or refusal: *she replied* **in the negative.** ■ (often **the negative**) a bad, unwelcome, or unpleasant quality, characteristic, or aspect of a situation or person: *confidence will not be instilled by harping solely on the negative.* ■ *Gram.* a word, affix, or phrase expressing negation. **2** a photographic image made on film or specially prepared glass that shows the light and shade or color values reversed from the original, and from which positive prints can be made. **3** a result of a test or experiment indicating that a certain substance is not present or a certain condition does not exist: *the percentage of false negatives generated by a cancer test was of great concern.* **4** the part of an electric circuit that is at a lower electrical potential than another part designated as having zero electrical potential. **5** a number less than zero.
▸*interj.* no (usually used in a military context): *"Any snags, Captain?" "Negative, she's running like clockwork."* —**neg·a·tive·ly** *adv.* —**neg·a·tive·ness** *n.* —**neg·a·tiv·i·ty** /ˌnegəˈtivitē/ *n.*
neg·a·tiv·ism /ˈnegətivˌizəm/ ▸*n.* the practice of being or tendency to be negative or skeptical in attitude while failing to offer positive suggestions. —**neg·a·tiv·ist** *n. & adj.* —**neg·a·tiv·is·tic** /ˌnegətivˈistik/ *adj.*
ne·glect /niˈglekt/ ▸*v.* [*tr.*] fail to care for properly: *the old churchyard has been sadly neglected.* ■ not pay proper attention to; disregard: *you neglect our advice at your peril.* ■ fail to do something: *he neglected to write to her.*
▸*n.* the state or fact of being uncared for: *animals dying through disease or neglect.* ■ the action of not taking proper care of someone or something: *she was accused of child neglect.* ■ failure to do something: *he was reported for* **neglect** *of duty.* —**ne·glect·ful** /-fəl/ *adj.* —**ne·glect·ful·ly** /-fəlē/ *adv.* —**ne·glect·ful·ness** /-fəlnəs/ *n.*
neg·li·gee /ˈneglə͵ZHā/ ▸*n.* a woman's light dressing gown, typically made of a filmy, soft fabric.
neg·li·gence /ˈneglajəns/ ▸*n.* failure to take proper care in doing something: *some of these accidents are due to negligence.* ■ *Law* failure to use reasonable care, resulting in damage or injury to another.
neg·li·gent /ˈneglajənt/ ▸*adj.* failing to take proper care in doing something: *directors have been negligent in the performance of their duties.* ▷late Middle English: from Old French, or from Latin *negligent-* 'disregarding,' from the verb *negligere* (variant of *neglegere* 'disregard, slight,' from *neg-* 'not' + *legere* 'choose, pick up'). —**neg·li·gent·ly** *adv.*
neg·li·gi·ble /ˈneglijəbəl/ ▸*adj.* so small or unimportant as to be not worth considering; insignificant: *sound could at last be recorded with incredible ease and at negligible cost.* —**neg·li·gi·bil·i·ty** /ˌnegləjəˈbilitē/ *n.* —**neg·li·gi·bly** /-blē/ *adv.*
ne·go·ti·a·ble /nəˈgōSHəbəl/ ▸*adj.* open to discussion or modification: *the price was not negotiable.* ■ (of a document) able to be transferred or assigned to the legal ownership of another person. ■ (of an obstacle or pathway) able to be traversed; passable: *such walkways must be accessible and negotiable for all users.* —**ne·go·ti·a·bil·i·ty** /nəˌgōSHəˈbilitē/ *n.*
ne·go·ti·ate /nəˈgōSHē͵āt/ ▸*v.* **1** [*intr.*] try to reach an agreement or compromise by discussion with others: *his government's willingness to negotiate.* ■ [*tr.*] obtain or bring about by negotiating: *he negotiated a new contract with the sellers.* **2** [*tr.*] find a way over or through (an obstacle or difficult path): *Tim negotiated his way through a field of angry cattle.* **3** [*tr.*] transfer (a check, bill, or other document) to the legal ownership of another person. ■ convert (a check) into cash. —**ne·go·ti·ant** /-SH(ē)ənt/ *n.* (*archaic*). —**ne·go·ti·a·tion** /nəˌgōSHēˈāSHən/ *n.* —**ne·go·ti·a·tor** /-ˌātər/ *n.*
Ne·gro /ˈnēgrō/ ▸*n.* (*pl.* **-groes**) *dated, often offens.* a member of a dark-skinned group of peoples originally native to Africa south of the Sahara.
▸*adj.* dated, often offens. of or relating to such people.
Ne·groid /ˈnēgroid/ ▸*adj.* often offens. of or relating to the division of humankind represented by the indigenous peoples of central and southern Africa.
Ne·gro spir·it·u·al ▸*n.* see SPIRITUAL.
neigh /nā/ ▸*n.* a characteristic high-pitched sound uttered by a horse.
▸*v.* [*intr.*] (of a horse) make such a sound; utter a neigh. ■ (of a person) make a similar sound: *they neighed dutifully at dull jokes.*
neigh·bor /ˈnābər/ (*Brit.* **neigh·bour**) ▸*n.* a person living near or next door to the speaker or person referred to: *our garden was the envy of the neighbors.* ■ a person or place in relation to others near or next to it: *I chatted with my neighbor on the flight to New York.*
▸*v.* [*tr.*] (of a place or thing) be situated near to or very near (another): *the square neighbors the old quarter of the town.* —**neigh·bor·less** *adj.*
neigh·bor·hood /ˈnābər͵ho͝od/ (*Brit.* **neigh·bour·hood**) ▸*n.* a district, esp. one forming a community within a town or city: *she lived in a wealthy neighborhood of Boston.* ■ the people of such a district: *the party disturbed*

the whole neighborhood. ■ neighborly feeling or conduct: *the importance of neighborhood to old people.* ■ the area surrounding a particular place, person, or object: *he was reluctant to leave the neighborhood of Butte.* ■ *Math.* the set of points whose distance from a given point is less than (or less than or equal to) some value.
▸ □ **in the neighborhood of** approximately; about: *the cost would be in the neighborhood of three billion.*
neigh·bor·ly /ˈnābərlē/ (*Brit.* **neigh·bour·ly**) ▸*adj.* characteristic of a good neighbor, esp. helpful, friendly, or kind. —**neigh·bor·li·ness** *n.*
nei·ther /ˈnēTHər, ˈnī-/ ▸*adj. & pron.* not the one nor the other of two people or things; not either: [as *adj.*] *neither side of the brain is dominant over the other* | [as *pron.*] *neither of us believes it.*
▸*adv.* **1** used before the first of two (or occasionally more) alternatives that are being specified (the others being introduced by "nor") to indicate that they are each untrue or each do not happen: *I am neither a liberal nor a conservative.* **2** used to introduce a further negative statement: *he didn't remember, and neither did I.*
nel·son /ˈnelsən/ ▸*n.* a wrestling hold in which one arm is passed under the opponent's arm from behind and the hand is applied to the neck (**half nelson**), or both arms and hands are applied (**full nelson**).
nem·a·tode /ˈnemə͵tōd/ ▸*n.* any worm of the group including roundworms and threadworms, with a slender unsegmented cylindrical body.
nem·e·sis /ˈneməsis/ ▸*n.* (*pl.* **-ses** /-ˌsēz/) (usu. **one's nemesis**) the inescapable or implacable agent of someone's or something's downfall: *the balance beam was the team's nemesis, as two gymnasts fell from it.* ■ a downfall caused by such an agent: *one risks nemesis by uttering such words.* ■ (often **Nemesis**) retributive justice: *nemesis is notoriously slow.*
ne·o·clas·si·cal /ˌnēōˈklasikəl/ (also **ne·o·clas·sic** /-ˈklasik/) ▸*adj.* of or relating to neoclassicism.
ne·o·clas·si·cism /ˌnēōˈklasi͵sizəm/ ▸*n.* the revival of a classical style or treatment in art, literature, architecture, or music. —**ne·o·clas·si·cist** *n. & adj.*
ne·o·co·lo·ni·al·ism /ˌnēōkəˈlōnēə͵lizəm/ ▸*n.* the use of economic, political, cultural, or other pressures to control or influence other countries, esp. former dependencies. —**ne·o·co·lo·ni·al** *adj.* —**ne·o·co·lo·ni·al·ist** *n. & adj.*
ne·o·con /ˌnēōˈkän/ ▸*adj.* neoconservative, esp. in advocating democratic capitalism.
▸*n.* a neoconservative.
ne·o·con·ser·va·tive /ˌnēōkənˈsərvətiv/ ▸*adj.* of or relating to an approach to politics, literary criticism, theology, history, or any other branch of thought, that represents a return to a modified form of a traditional viewpoint, in contrast to more radical or liberal schools of thought.
▸*n.* a person with neoconservative views. —**ne·o·con·ser·va·tism** /-tizəm/ *n.*
ne·o·dym·i·um /ˌnēōˈdimēəm/ ▸*n.* the chemical element of atomic number 60, a silvery-white metal of the lanthanide series. (Symbol: **Nd**)
Ne·o·lith·ic /ˌnēəˈliTHik/ ▸*adj. Archaeol.* of, relating to, or denoting the later part of the Stone Age, when ground or polished stone weapons and implements prevailed. ■ [as *n.*] (**the Neolithic**) the Neolithic period.
ne·ol·o·gism /nēˈälə͵jizəm/ ▸*n.* a newly coined word or expression. ■ the coining or use of new words. —**ne·ol·o·gist** /-jist/ *n.* —**ne·ol·o·gize** /-͵jīz/ *v.*
ne·on /ˈnēän/ ▸*n.* the chemical element of atomic number 10, an inert gaseous element of the noble gas group. It is obtained by the distillation of liquid air and is used in fluorescent lamps and advertising signs. (Symbol: **Ne**) ■ fluorescent lighting or signs (whether containing neon or some other gas): *the lobby of the hotel was bright with neon.* ■ a small lamp containing neon. ■ a very bright or fluorescent color: *a denim cap outlined in neon.*
ne·o·nate /ˈnēə͵nāt/ ▸*n.* a newborn child or mammal. ■ *Med.* an infant less than four weeks old. —**ne·o·na·tal** /ˌnēōˈnātl/ *adj.*
ne·o·Na·zi /ˈnēō-/ ▸*n.* (*pl.* **ne·o-Na·zis**) a member of an organization similar to the German Nazi Party. ■ a person of extreme racist or nationalist views.
▸*adj.* of or relating to neo-Nazis or neo-Nazism. —**ne·o·Na·zism** *n.*
ne·on tet·ra ▸*n.* a small Amazonian freshwater fish (*Paracheirodon innesi*, family Characidae) with a shining blue-green stripe along each side and a red band near the tail, popular in aquariums.

Pronunciation Key ə *ago,* up; ər *over, fur;* a *hat;* ā *ate;* ä *car;* CH *chin;* e *let;* ē *see;* e(ə)r *air;* i *fit;* ī *by;* i(ə)r *ear;* NG *sing;* ō *go;* ô *law, for;* oi *toy;* o͝o *good;* o͞o *goo;* ou *out;* SH *she;* TH *thin;* T͟H *then;* (h)w *why;* ZH *vision*

ne·o·pa·gan·ism /ˌnēōˈpāgāˌnizəm; -gə-/ ▶n. a modern religious movement that seeks to incorporate beliefs or ritual practices from traditions outside the main world religions, esp. those of pre-Christian Europe and North America. —**ne·o·pa·gan** n. & adj.

ne·o·phyte /ˈnēəˌfīt/ ▶n. a person who is new to a subject, skill, or belief: *four-day cooking classes are offered to neophytes and experts.* ■ a new convert to a religion. ■ a novice in a religious order, or a newly ordained priest.

ne·o·plasm /ˈnēəˌplazəm/ ▶n. a new and abnormal growth of tissue in some part of the body, esp. as a characteristic of cancer. —**ne·o·plas·tic** /ˌnēəˈplastik/ adj.

ne·o·prene /ˈnēəˌprēn/ ▶n. a synthetic polymer resembling rubber, resistant to oil, heat, and weathering.

neph·ew /ˈnefyōō/ ▶n. a son of one's brother or sister, or of one's brother-in-law or sister-in-law. ▷Middle English: from Old French *neveu,* from Latin *nepos* 'grandson, nephew,' from an Indo-European root shared by Dutch *neef* and German *Neffe.*

ne·phrid·i·um /nəˈfridēəm/ ▶n. (pl. **-phrid·i·a** /-ˈfridēə/) *Zool.* (in many invertebrate animals) a tubule open to the exterior that acts as an organ of excretion or osmoregulation. It typically has ciliated or flagellated cells and absorptive walls. —**ne·phrid·i·al** /-ēəl/ adj.

ne·phrit·ic /nəˈfritik/ ▶adj. of or in the kidneys; renal. ■ of or relating to nephritis.

ne·phri·tis /nəˈfrītis/ ▶n. *Med.* inflammation of the kidneys. Also called **BRIGHT'S DISEASE.**

ne plus ul·tra /ˈnē ˌpləs ˈəltrə; ˈnā ˌplōōs ˈōōltrə/ ▶n. the perfect or most extreme example of its kind; the ultimate: *he became **the ne plus ultra** of bebop trombonists.*

nep·o·tism /ˈnepəˌtizəm/ ▶n. the practice among those with power or influence of favoring relatives or friends, esp. by giving them jobs. —**nep·o·tist** n. —**nep·o·tis·tic** /ˌnepəˈtistik/ adj.

Nep·tune /ˈnept(y)ōōn/ ▶*Astron.* a planet of the solar system, eighth in order from the sun, discovered in 1846.

nep·tu·ni·um /nepˈt(y)ōōnēəm/ ▶n. the chemical element of atomic number 93, a radioactive metal of the actinide series. It occurs only in trace amounts in nature. (Symbol: **Np**)

nerd /nərd/ ▶n. *inf.* a foolish or contemptible person who lacks social skills or is boringly studious: *one of those nerds who never asked a girl to dance.* ■ an intelligent, single-minded expert in a particular technical discipline or profession: *he single-handedly changed the Zero image of the computer nerd into one of savvy Hero.* —**nerd·ish** adj. —**nerd·ish·ness** n. —**nerd·y** adj.

nerve /nərv/ ▶n. **1** (in the body) a whitish fiber or bundle of fibers that transmits impulses of sensation to the brain or spinal cord, and impulses from these to the muscles and organs: *the optic nerve.* **2** (**nerves**) a person's mental state, in particular the extent to which they are agitated or worried: *an amazing journey that tested her nerves to the full.* **3** (often **one's nerve**) a person's steadiness, courage, and sense of purpose when facing a demanding situation: *the army's commanders were beginning to **lose their nerve**.* ■ *inf.* impudence or audacity: *he had the nerve to insult my cooking.*
▶v. (**nerve oneself**) brace oneself mentally to face a demanding situation: *she nerved herself to enter the room.* —**nerved** adj. [usu. in comb.] *she was still raw-nerved from reliving the past.*
▶ □ **a bundle of nerves** *inf.* someone who is extremely timid or tense. □ **get on someone's nerves** *inf.* irritate or annoy someone. □ **have nerves of steel** not be easily upset or frightened. □ **strain every nerve** make every possible effort. □ **touch** (or **hit** or **strike**) **a nerve** (or **a raw nerve**) provoke a reaction by referring to a sensitive topic: *there are signs that some comments strike a raw nerve.*

nerve cell ▶n. a neuron.

nerve cen·ter ▶n. a group of closely connected nerve cells that perform a particular function in the body; a ganglion. ■ the control center of an organization or operation: *Frankfurt is the economic nerve center of Germany.*

nerve gas ▶n. a poisonous vapor that rapidly disables or kills by disrupting the transmission of nerve impulses.

nerve·less /ˈnərvlis/ ▶adj. **1** inert; lacking vigor or feeling: *the knife dropped from Grant's nerveless fingers.* ■ (of literary or artistic style) diffuse or insipid: *Wilde and his art are described as "nerveless and effeminate."* **2** confident; not nervous: *with nerveless panache.* —**nerve·less·ly** adv. —**nerve·less·ness** n.

nerve-rack·ing (also **nerve-wrack·ing**) ▶adj. causing stress or anxiety: *his driving test was a nerve-racking ordeal.*

nerv·ous /ˈnərvəs/ ▶adj. **1** easily agitated or alarmed; tending to be anxious; highly strung: *a sensitive, nervous person.* ■ anxious or apprehensive: *staying in the house on her own made her nervous.* ■ (of a feeling or reaction) resulting from anxiety or anticipation: *nervous energy.* **2** relating to or affecting the nerves: *a nervous disorder.* —**nerv·ous·ly** adv. —**nerv·ous·ness** n.

nerv·ous break·down ▶n. a period of mental illness resulting from severe depression, stress, or anxiety.

nerv·ous sys·tem ▶n. the network of nerve cells and fibers that transmits nerve impulses between parts of the body. See also **CENTRAL NERVOUS SYSTEM, PERIPHERAL NERVOUS SYSTEM.**

nerv·ous wreck ▶n. *inf.* a person suffering from stress or emotional exhaustion: *by the end of the day I was a nervous wreck.*

nerv·y /ˈnərvē/ ▶adj. (**nerv·i·er, nerv·i·est**) *inf.* bold or impudent: *it was kind of nervy for Billy to be telling him how to play.* —**nerv·i·ly** /ˈnərvəlē/ adv. —**nerv·i·ness** n.

nest /nest/ ▶n. **1** a structure or place made or chosen by a bird for laying eggs and sheltering its young. ■ a place where an animal or insect breeds or shelters: *an ants' nest.* ■ a person's snug or secluded retreat or shelter. ■ a bowl-shaped object likened to a bird's nest: *arrange in nests of lettuce leaves.* ■ a place filled with or frequented by undesirable people or things: *a nest of spies.* **2** a set of similar objects of graduated sizes, made so that each smaller one fits into the next in size for storage: *a nest of tables.*
▶v. **1** [intr.] (of a bird or other animal) use or build a nest: *the owls often nest in barns.* **2** [tr.] (often **be nested**) fit (an object or objects) inside a larger one: *the town is nested inside a large crater on the flanks of a volcano.* ■ [intr.] (of a set of objects) fit inside one another: *Russian dolls that nest inside one another.* ■ (esp. in computing and linguistics) place (an object or element) in a hierarchical arrangement, typically in a subordinate position: [as adj.] (**nested**) *organisms classified in a series of nested sets.* —**nest·ful** /-ˌfōōl/ n. (pl. **-fuls**) . —**nest·like** /-ˌlīk/ adj.

nest egg ▶n. **1** a sum of money saved for the future: *I worked hard to build up a nice little nest egg.* **2** a real or artificial egg left in a nest to induce hens to lay eggs there.

nes·tle /ˈnesəl/ ▶v. [intr.] settle or lie comfortably within or against something: *the baby deer nestled in her arms.* ■ (of a place) lie or be situated in a half-hidden or obscured position: *picturesque villages nestle in the wooded hills* | (**be nestled**) *the hotel is nestled between two headlands.*

nest·ling /ˈnes(t)liNG/ ▶n. a bird that is too young to leave its nest.

net¹ /net/ ▶n. **1** a length of open-meshed material made of twine, cord, rope, or something similar, used typically for catching fish or other animals. ■ a piece of such material supported by a frame at the end of a handle, used typically for catching fish or other aquatic animals or insects. ■ a length of such material supported on a frame and forming part of the goal in various games such as soccer and hockey: *he turned Wilson's cross into the net.* ■ a length of such material supported on a cord between two posts to divide the playing area in various games such as tennis, badminton, and volleyball. **2** a fine fabric with a very open weave: [as adj.] *net curtains.* **3** *fig.* a system or procedure for catching or entrapping someone; a trap: *the search was delayed, allowing the murderers to escape the net.* ■ a system or procedure for selecting or recruiting someone: *he spread his net far and wide in his search for success.* **4** a network, in particular: ■ a communications or broadcasting network: *the radio net was brought to life with a mayday.* ■ a network of interconnected computers: *a computer news net.* ■ (**the Net**) the Internet.
▶v. (**net·ted, net·ting**) [tr.] **1** catch or land (a fish or other animal) with a net. ■ fish with nets in (a river): *he has netted the creeks and found them clogged with fish.* ■ *fig.* acquire or obtain as if with a net: *customs officials have netted large caches of drugs.* **2** cover with a net: *we fenced off a rabbit-proof area for vegetables and netted the top.* —**net·ful** /-ˌfōōl/ n. (pl. **-fuls**). —**net·like** /-ˌlīk/ adj.

net² ▶adj. **1** (of an amount, value, or price) remaining after a deduction, such as tax or a discount, has been made: *net earnings per share rose* | *the net worth of the business.* Often contrasted with **GROSS** (sense 2). ■ (of a price) to be paid in full; not reducible. ■ (of a weight) excluding that of the packaging or container. **2** (of an effect or result) final or overall: *the net result is the same.*
▶v. (**net·ted, net·ting**) [tr.] acquire or obtain (a sum of money) as clear profit: *they sold their 20% stake, netting a huge profit in the process.* ■ get; obtain: *the Bills netted 5,276 yards of offense.*

neth·er /ˈneT͟Hər/ ▶adj. lower in position: *the ballast is suspended from its nether end.* —**neth·er·most** /-ˌmōst/ adj.

neth·er re·gions ▶pl. n. the lowest or furthest parts of a place, esp. with allusion to hell or the underworld: *rumors of strange creatures haunting the lake's bottomless nether regions.* ■ (**one's nether regions**) used euphemistically to refer to a person's genitals and buttocks.

net·ting /ˈnetiNG/ ▸*n.* open-meshed material made by knotting together twine, wire, rope, or thread.

net·tle /ˈnetl/ ▸*n.* a herbaceous plant (genus *Urtica*, family Urticaceae) that has jagged leaves covered with stinging hairs. Its several species include the Eurasian **stinging nettle** (*U. dioica*). ■ used in names of other plants of a similar appearance or properties, e.g., **dead-nettle**.
▸*v.* [*tr.*] irritate or annoy (someone): *I was nettled by her tone.*

net·work /ˈnetˌwərk/ ▸*n.* **1** an arrangement of intersecting horizontal and vertical lines. ■ a complex system of roads, railroads, or other transportation routes: *a network of railroads.* **2** a group or system of interconnected people or things: *a trade network.* ■ a group of broadcasting stations that connect for the simultaneous broadcast of a program: *the introduction of a second TV network.* ■ a number of interconnected computers, machines, or operations: *specialized computers that manage multiple outside connections to a network | a local cellular phone network.* ■ a system of connected electrical conductors.
▸*v.* [*tr.*] connect as or operate with a network: *the stock exchanges have proven to be resourceful in networking these deals.* ■ link (machines, esp. computers) to operate interactively. ■ [*intr.*] [often as *n.*] (**networking**) interact with other people to exchange information and develop contacts, esp. to further one's career: *the skills of networking, bargaining, and negotiation.* —**net·work·a·ble** *adj.*

neu·ral /ˈn(y)o͝orəl/ ▸*adj.* of or relating to a nerve or the nervous system: *patterns of neural activity.* —**neu·ral·ly** *adv.*

neu·ral·gia /n(y)o͝oˈraljə/ ▸*n.* intense, typically intermittent pain along the course of a nerve, esp. in the head or face. —**neu·ral·gic** /-jik/ *adj.*

neu·ral net·work (also **neural net**) ▸*n.* a computer system modeled on the human brain and nervous system.

neur·as·the·ni·a /ˌn(y)o͝orəsˈTHēnēə/ ▸*n.* an ill-defined medical condition characterized by lassitude, fatigue, headache, and irritability, associated chiefly with emotional disturbance. —**neur·as·then·ic** /-ˈTHenik/ *adj.* & *n.*

neu·ri·tis /n(y)o͝oˈrītis/ ▸*n. Med.* inflammation of a peripheral nerve or nerves, usually causing pain and loss of function. ■ (in general use) neuropathy. —**neu·rit·ic** /-ˈritik/ *adj.*

neu·rol·o·gy /n(y)o͝oˈräləjē/ ▸*n.* the branch of medicine or biology that deals with the anatomy, functions, and organic disorders of nerves and the nervous system. —**neu·rolog·i·cal** /-rəˈläjikəl/ *adj.* —**neu·ro·log·i·cal·ly** *adv.* —**neu·rol·o·gist** *n.*

neu·ron /ˈn(y)o͝oˌrän/ ▸*n.* a specialized cell transmitting nerve impulses; a nerve cell. ▷late 19th cent.: from Greek *neuron*, special use of the literal sense 'sinew, tendon.' —**neu·ron·al** /ˈn(y)o͝orənl; n(y)o͝oˈrōnl/ *adj.* —**neu·ron·ic** /n(y)o͝oˈränik/ *adj.*

neu·rop·a·thy /n(y)o͝oˈräpəTHē/ ▸*n. Med.* disease or dysfunction of one or more peripheral nerves, typically causing numbness or weakness. —**neu·ro·path·ic** /ˌn(y)o͝orəˈpaTHik/ *adj.*

neu·ro·sis /n(y)o͝oˈrōsis/ ▸*n.* (*pl.* **-ses** /-ˌsēz/) *Med.* a relatively mild mental illness that is not caused by organic disease, involving symptoms of stress (depression, anxiety, obsessive behavior, hypochondria) but not a radical loss of touch with reality. Compare with PSYCHOSIS. ■ (in nontechnical use) excessive and irrational anxiety or obsession: *apprehension over mounting debt has created a collective neurosis in the business world.*

neu·ro·sur·ger·y /ˌn(y)o͝orōˈsərjərē/ ▸*n.* surgery performed on the nervous system, esp. the brain and spinal cord. —**neu·ro·sur·geon** /ˈn(y)ərō,sərjən/ *n.* —**neu·ro·sur·gi·cal** /-jikəl/ *adj.*

neu·rot·ic /n(y)o͝oˈrätik/ ▸*adj. Med.* suffering from, caused by, or relating to neurosis. ■ abnormally sensitive, obsessive, or tense and anxious: *everyone was neurotic about burglars.*
▸*n.* a neurotic person. —**neu·rot·i·cal·ly** *adv.* —**neu·rot·i·cism** /-ˈrätəˌsizəm/ *n.*

neu·ro·trans·mit·ter /ˌn(y)o͝orōˈtranzmitər/ ▸*n. Physiol.* a chemical substance that is released at the end of an axon by the arrival of a nerve impulse and, by diffusing across the synapse or junction, causes the transfer of the impulse, esp. to another axon or a muscle fiber.

neu·ter /ˈn(y)o͝otər/ ▸*adj.* **1** of or denoting a gender of nouns in some languages, typically contrasting with masculine and feminine or common: *it is a neuter word in Greek.* **2** (of an animal) lacking developed sexual organs, or having had them removed. ■ (of a person) apparently having no sexual characteristics; asexual.
▸*n.* **1** *Gram.* a neuter word. ■ (**the neuter**) the neuter gender. **2** a nonfertile caste of social insect, esp. a worker bee or ant. ■ a castrated or spayed domestic animal. ■ a person who appears to lack sexual characteristics.
▸*v.* [*tr.*] castrate or spay (a domestic animal). ■ render ineffective;

deprive of vigor or force: *disarmament negotiations that will neuter their military power.*

neu·tral /ˈn(y)o͝otrəl/ ▸*adj.* **1** not helping or supporting either of two opposing sides, esp. countries at war; impartial: *during the Second World War Portugal was neutral.* ■ unbiased; disinterested: *neutral, expert scientific advice.* **2** having no strongly marked or positive characteristics or features: *the tone was neutral, devoid of sentiment.* ■ *Chem.* neither acid nor alkaline; having a pH of about 7. ■ electrically neither positive nor negative.
▸*n.* **1** an impartial and uninvolved country or person: *Sweden and its fellow neutrals.* ■ an unbiased person. **2** a neutral color or shade, esp. light gray or beige. **3** a disengaged position of gears in which the engine is disconnected from the driven parts. **4** an electrically neutral point, terminal, conductor, or wire. —**neu·tral·i·ty** /n(y)o͝oˈtralitē/ *n.* —**neu·tral·ly** *adv.*

neu·tral·ism /ˈn(y)o͝otrəˌlizəm/ ▸*n.* a policy of political neutrality. —**neu·tral·ist** *n.*

neu·tral·ize /ˈn(y)o͝otrəˌlīz/ ▸*v.* [*tr.*] render (something) ineffective or harmless by applying an opposite force or effect: *impatience at his frailty began to neutralize her fear.* ■ make (an acidic or alkaline substance) chemically neutral. ■ disarm (a bomb or similar weapon). ■ a euphemistic way of saying kill or destroy, esp. in a covert or military operation. —**neu·tral·i·za·tion** /ˌn(y)o͝otrəliˈzāSHən/ *n.* —**neu·tral·iz·er** *n.*

neu·tri·no /n(y)o͝oˈtrēnō/ ▸*n.* (*pl.* **-nos**) a neutral subatomic particle with a mass close to zero and half-integral spin, rarely reacting with normal matter.

neu·tron /ˈn(y)o͝oˌträn/ ▸*n.* a subatomic particle of about the same mass as a proton but without an electric charge, present in all atomic nuclei except those of ordinary hydrogen.

neu·tron bomb ▸*n.* a nuclear weapon that produces large numbers of neutrons rather than heat or blast like conventional nuclear weapons.

nev·er /ˈnevər/ ▸*adv.* **1** at no time in the past or future; on no occasion; not ever: *they had never been camping in their lives | I will **never** ever forget it.* **2** not at all: *he never turned up.*

nev·er·more /ˌnevərˈmôr/ ▸*adv. poetic/lit.* at no future time; never again: *I order you gone, nevermore to return.*

nev·er-nev·er land ▸*n.* an imaginary utopian place or situation: *a never-never land of unreal prices and easy bank loans.*

nev·er·the·less /ˌnevərTHəˈles/ ▸*adv.* in spite of that; notwithstanding; all the same: *statements which, although literally true, are nevertheless misleading.*

ne·vus /ˈnēvəs/ ▸*n.* (*pl.* **-vi** /-ˌvī/) a birthmark or a mole on the skin, esp. a birthmark in the form of a raised red patch.

new /n(y)o͝o/ ▸*adj.* **1** not existing before; made, introduced, or discovered recently or now for the first time: *new crop varieties | [as n.]* (**the new**) *a fascinating mix of the old and the new.* ■ in original condition; not worn or used: *check that the wiring is new and in good condition.* ■ not previously used or owned: *a secondhand bus cost a fraction of a new one.* ■ of recent origin or arrival: *a new baby.* **2** already existing but seen, experienced, or acquired recently or now for the first time: *her new bike.* ■ different from a recent previous one: *I have a new assistant.* ■ in addition to another or others already existing: *recruiting new pilots overseas.* **3** just beginning and regarded as better than what went before: *starting a new life.* ■ (of a person) reinvigorated or restored: *a bottle of pills would make him a new man.* ■ reviving another or others of the same kind: *the New Bohemians.*
▸*adv.* [usu. in *comb.*] newly; recently: *new-mown hay.* ▷Old English *nīwe, nēowe*, of Germanic origin; related to Dutch *nieuw* and German *neu*, from an Indo-European root shared by Sanskrit *nava*, Latin *novus*, and Greek *neos* 'new.' —**new·ness** *n.*
▸ □ **a new one** *inf.* an account, idea, or joke not previously encountered by someone: *I've heard of lazy, but somebody being too lazy to talk—that's a new one on me.* □ **what's new? 1** (said on greeting someone) what's going on? how are you? **2** (also **what else is new?**) that is the usual situation: *she and I squabbled—so what's new?*

New Age ▸*n.* a broad movement characterized by alternative approaches to traditional Western culture, with an interest in spirituality, mysticism, holism, and environmentalism: [as *adj.*] *the New Age movement.* —**New Ag·er** *n.* —**New Ag·ey** *adj.*

new·born /ˈn(y)o͝oˌbôrn/ ▸*adj.* (of a child or animal) recently or just born: *newborn babies | fig. a newborn star.*
▸*n.* a recently born child or animal.

Pronunciation Key ə *ago, up;* ər *over, fur;* a *hat;* ā *ate;* ä *car;* CH *chin;* e *let;* ē *see;* e(ə)r *air;* i *fit;* ī *by;* i(ə)r *ear;* NG *sing;* ō *go;* ô *law, for;* oi *toy;* o͝o *good;* o͞o *goo;* ou *out;* SH *she;* TH *thin;* ᴛʜ *then;* (h)w *why;* ZH *vision*

new·com·er /'n(y)ōō,kəmər/ ▸n. a person or thing that has recently arrived in a place or joined a group. ■ a novice in a particular activity or situation.

new·el /'n(y)ōōwəl/ ▸n. the central supporting pillar of a spiral or winding staircase. ■ (also **newel post**) a post at the head or foot of a flight of stairs, supporting a handrail.

newel post

newel post

new·fan·gled /'n(y)ōō'faNGgəld; -,faNG-/ (also **new-fan-gled**) ▸adj. derog. different from what one is used to; objectionably new: *I've no time for such newfangled nonsense.*

new·ly /'n(y)ōōlē/ ▸adv. **1** recently: *a newly acquired skill.* **2** again; afresh: *social confidence for the newly single.* ■ in a new or different manner: *we have to make ourselves newly aware of each text.*

new·ly·wed /'n(y)ōōlē,wed/ ▸n. (usu. **newlyweds**) a recently married person.

new moon ▸n. the phase of the moon when it is in conjunction with the sun and invisible from earth, or shortly thereafter when it appears as a slender crescent. ■ the time when this occurs.

news /n(y)ōōz/ ▸n. newly received or noteworthy information, esp. about recent or important events: *I've got some good news for you.* ■ (**the news**) a broadcast or published report of news: *he was back in the news again.* ■ (**news to**) *inf.* information not previously known to someone: *this was hardly news to her.* ■ a person or thing considered interesting enough to be reported in the news: *Chanel became the hottest news in fashion.*
▸ □ **make news** become a story in the news: *stolen babies make news.*

news·cast /'n(y)ōōz,kast/ ▸n. a radio or television broadcast of news reports. —**news·cast·er** *n.*

news·feed /'n(y)ōōz,fēd/ ▸n. an electronic transmission of news, as from a broadcaster or an Internet newsgroup.

news flash ▸n. a single item of important news that is broadcast separately and often interrupts other programs.

news·group /'n(y)ōōz,grōōp/ ▸n. a group of Internet users who exchange e-mail messages on a topic of mutual interest.

news·let·ter /'n(y)ōōz,letər/ ▸n. a bulletin issued periodically to the members of a society, business, or organization.

news·pa·per /'n(y)ōōz,pāpər/ ▸n. a printed publication (usually issued daily or weekly) consisting of folded unstapled sheets and containing news, feature articles, advertisements, and correspondence. ■ the organization responsible for producing a particular newspaper. ■ another term for NEWSPRINT.

new·speak /'n(y)ōō,spēk/ ▸n. ambiguous euphemistic language used chiefly in political propaganda.

news·print /'n(y)ōōz,print/ ▸n. cheap, low-quality, absorbent printing paper made from coarse wood pulp and used chiefly for newspapers.

news·reel /'n(y)ōōz,rēl/ ▸n. a short film of news and current affairs, formerly made for showing as part of the program in a movie theater.

news·room /'n(y)ōōz,rōōm; -,rŏŏm/ ▸n. the area in a newspaper or broadcasting office where news is written and edited.

news·serv·er /n(y)ōōz,sərvər/ ▸n. an Internet-connected server that receives and disseminates messages for a newsgroup.

news·stand /'n(y)ōōz,stand/ ▸n. a stand or stall for the sale of newspapers.

news·wor·thy /'n(y)ōōz,wərTHē/ ▸adj. noteworthy as news; topical: *you had to cover a lot of ground to find anything newsworthy.* —**news·wor·thi·ness** *n.*

news·y /'n(y)ōōzē/ ▸adj. (**news·i·er**, **news·i·est**) *inf.* full of news, esp. of a personal kind: *short, newsy letters.*

newt /n(y)ōōt/ ▸n. a small, slender-bodied amphibian (*Notophthalmus, Taricha,* and other genera, family Salamandridae) with lungs and a well-developed tail, typically spending its adult life on land and returning to water to breed.

New Tes·ta·ment ▸n. the second part of the Christian Bible, written originally in Greek and recording the life and teachings of Jesus and his earliest followers. It includes the four Gospels, the Acts of the Apostles, twenty-one epistles by St. Paul and others, and the book of Revelation.

new·ton /'n(y)ōōtn/ (abbr.: **N**) ▸n. *Physics* the SI unit of force. It is equal to the force that would give a mass of one kilogram an acceleration of one meter per second per second, and is equivalent to 100,000 dynes.

New·to·ni·an /n(y)ōō'tōnēən/ ▸adj. relating to or arising from the work of Sir Isaac Newton. ■ formulated or behaving according to the principles of classical physics.

new wave ▸n. **1** another term for NOUVELLE VAGUE. **2** a style of rock music popular in the 1970s and 1980s, deriving from punk but generally more pop in sound and less aggressive in performance.

New World ▸North and South America regarded collectively in relation to Europe, esp. after the early voyages of European explorers. Compare with OLD WORLD.

New Year's Day ▸n. the first day of the year; in the modern Western calendar, January 1.

New Year's Eve ▸n. the last day of the year; in the modern Western calendar, December 31. ■ the evening of this day, typically marked with a celebration.

next /nekst/ ▸adj. **1** (of a time or season) coming immediately after the time of writing or speaking: *we'll go next year.* ■ (of a day of the week) nearest (or the nearest but one) after the present: *not this Wednesday, next Wednesday.* **2** coming immediately after the present one in order or space: *the woman in the next room | the next chapter | who's next?* ■ coming immediately after the present one in rank: *building materials were next in importance.*
▸adv. on the first or soonest occasion after the present; immediately afterward: *wondering what would happen next.* ■ following in the specified order: *Joe was the next oldest after Martin.*
▸n. the next person or thing: *the week after next.*
▸prep. archaic next to: *he plodded along next him.*
▸ □ **next in line** immediately below the present holder of a position in order of succession: *he is next in line to the throne.* □ **next to 1** in or into a position immediately to one side of; beside: *we sat next to each other.* **2** following in order or importance: *next to buying a whole new wardrobe, nothing lifts the spirits quite like a new hairdo!* **3** almost: *Charles knew next to nothing about farming.* **4** in comparison with: *next to her I felt like a fraud.* □ **the next world** (according to some religious beliefs) the place where one goes after death. □ **what next** an expression of surprise or amazement.

next best ▸adj. second in order of preference; to be preferred if one's first choice is not available: *the next best thing to flying is gliding.*

next door ▸adv. in or to the next house or room: *the caretaker lives next door.*
▸adj. (**next-door**) living or situated next door: *next-door neighbors.*
▸n. the building, room, or people next door: *a bleary-eyed man emerged from next door.*

next of kin ▸n. [treated as *sing.* or *pl.*] a person's closest living relative or relatives.

nex·us /'neksəs/ ▸n. (*pl.* same or **-us·es**) a connection or series of connections linking two or more things: *the nexus between industry and political power.* ■ a connected group or series: *a nexus of ideas.* ■ the central and most important point or place: *the nexus of all this activity was the disco.* ▷mid 17th cent.: from Latin, 'a binding together,' from *nex-* 'bound,' from the verb *nectere.*

Nez Per·cé /,nez 'pərz; pər'sā/ ▸n. (*pl.* same or **Nez Per·cés**) **1** a member of an American Indian people of central Idaho, northeastern Oregon, and southeastern Washington. **2** the Sahaptian language of this people.
▸adj. of or relating to this people or their language.

NFL ▸abbr. National Football League.

Ni ▸symb. the chemical element nickel.

ni·a·cin /'nīəsin/ ▸n. another term for NICOTINIC ACID.

nib /nib/ ▸n. **1** the pointed end part of a pen, which distributes the ink on the writing surface. ■ a pointed or projecting part of an object. **2** (**nibs**) shelled and crushed coffee or cocoa beans. ■ small pieces of caramel, licorice, or other sweets.

nib·ble /'nibəl/ ▸v. take small bites out of: [tr.] *he sat nibbling a cookie* | [intr.] *she nibbled at her food.* ■ [intr.] eat in small amounts, esp. between meals. ■ gently bite at (a part of the body), esp. amorously or nervously: [tr.] *Tamar nibbled her bottom lip.* ■ *fig.* gradually erode or eat away: [intr.] *inflation was nibbling away at spending power.* ■ [intr.] *fig.* show cautious interest in a project or proposal: *there's a New York agent nibbling.*
▸n. an instance of nibbling something. ■ a small piece of food bitten off. ■ (**nibbles**) *inf.* small savory snacks, typically eaten before a meal or with drinks. ■ an expression of cautious interest in a project or proposal: *now and then she gets a nibble, but no one will commit to an interview.* —**nib·bler** *n.*

N

ni·Cad /ˈnīˌkad/ (also *trademark* **Ni·cad**) ▸*n.* [usu. as *adj.*] a battery or cell with a nickel anode, a cadmium cathode, and a potassium hydroxide electrolyte. NiCads are used chiefly as a rechargeable power source for portable equipment.

nice /nīs/ ▸*adj.* **1** pleasant; agreeable; satisfactory: *we had a nice time.* **2** fine or subtle: *a nice distinction.* ■ requiring careful thought or attention: *a nice point.* **3** *archaic* fastidious; scrupulous. —**nice·ly** *adv.* —**nice·ness** *n.*

▸ □ **make nice** *inf.* be pleasant or polite to someone, typically in a hypocritical way: *the seat next to him was empty, so he wasn't required to make nice with a stranger.* □ **nice and —** satisfactorily or adequately in terms of the quality described: *it's nice and warm in here.* □ **nice one** *inf.* expressing approval or commendation. ■ used sarcastically to comment on an inept act: *oh, nice one, she put her finger up to her eye and tugged at the skin.* □ **nice to meet you** a polite formula used on being introduced to someone. □ **nice work if you can get it** *inf.* used to express envy of what is perceived to be another person's more favorable situation, esp. if they seem to have reached it with little effort.

ni·ce·ty /ˈnīsitē/ ▸*n.* (*pl.* **-ties**) (usu. **niceties**) a fine detail or distinction, esp. one regarded as intricate and fussy: *she was never interested in the niceties of Greek and Latin.* ■ accuracy or precision: *she prided herself on her nicety of pronunciation.* ■ a minor aspect of polite social behavior; a detail of etiquette: *we were brought up to observe the niceties.*

▸ □ **to a nicety** precisely.

niche /nicH/ ▸*n.* a shallow recess, esp. one in a wall to display a statue or other ornament. ■ (**one's niche**) a comfortable or suitable position in life or employment: *he is now a partner at a leading law firm and feels he has found his niche.* ■ a specialized but profitable corner of the market: [as *adj.*] *important new niche markets.* ■ *Ecol.* a position or role taken by a kind of organism within its community.
▸*v.* [*tr.*] place or position (something) in a niche.

nick /nik/ ▸*n.* a small cut or notch.
▸*v.* [*tr.*] **1** make a nick or nicks in: *he had nicked himself while shaving.* **2** (**nick someone for**) *inf.* cheat someone of (something, typically a sum of money): *he nicked me for fifteen hundred dollars.* **3** *Brit., inf.* steal: *he'd had his car nicked by joyriders.* ■ arrest or apprehend (someone): *I got nicked for burglary.*
▸ □ **in the nick of time** only just in time.

nick·el /ˈnikəl/ ▸*n.* **1** a silvery-white metal, the chemical element of atomic number 28. (Symbol: **Ni**) **2** *inf.* a five-cent coin; five cents.

nick·el-and-dime ▸*v.* [*tr.*] put a financial strain on (someone) by charging small amounts for many minor services: *we don't nickel-and-dime our customers like some vendors that charge extra for every little utility.*
▸*adj.* of little importance; petty: *the only games this weekend are nickel-and-dime stuff.*

nick·el·o·de·on /ˌnikəˈlōdēən/ ▸*n.* **1** *inf., dated* a jukebox, originally one operated by the insertion of a nickel coin. **2** *hist.* a movie theater with an admission fee of one nickel.

nick·name /ˈnikˌnām/ ▸*n.* a familiar or humorous name given to a person or thing instead of or as well as the real name.
▸*v.* [*tr.*] give a nickname to; call by a nickname: *his fraternity brothers nicknamed him "The Bird" because of his skydiving skills.*

nic·o·tine /ˈnikəˌtēn/ ▸*n.* a toxic colorless or yellowish oily liquid, $C_{10}H_{14}N_2$, that is the chief active constituent of tobacco. In small doses, it acts as a stimulant.

nic·o·tin·ic ac·id /ˌnikəˈtinik; -ˈtēnik/ ▸*n.* *Biochem.* a vitamin of the B complex that is widely distributed in foods such as milk, wheat germ, and meat, and can be synthesized in the body from tryptophan. Its deficiency causes pellagra. —**nic·o·tin·ate** /-ˈtēˌnāt/ *n.*

niece /nēs/ ▸*n.* a daughter of one's brother or sister, or of one's brother-in-law or sister-in-law. ▷Middle English: from Old French, based on Latin *neptis* 'granddaughter,' feminine of *nepos* 'nephew, grandson,' from an Indo-European root shared by Dutch *nicht*, German *Nichte*.

nif·ty /ˈniftē/ ▸*adj.* (**-ti·er, -ti·est**) *inf.* particularly good, skillful, or effective: *nifty footwork.* —**nif·ti·ly** /-təlē/ *adv.* —**nif·ti·ness** *n.*

nig·gard /ˈnigərd/ ▸*n. often offens.* a stingy or ungenerous person. —**nig·gard·ly** *adj.*

nig·ger /ˈnigər/ ▸*n. offens.* a contemptuous term for a black or dark-skinned person.

nig·gle /ˈnigəl/ ▸*v.* [*intr.*] cause slight but persistent annoyance, discomfort, or anxiety: *a suspicion niggled at the back of her mind* | [as *adj.*] (**niggling**) *niggling aches and pains.* ■ [*tr.*] find fault with (someone) in a petty way: *colleagues say he loved to niggle and criticize people.*
▸*n.* a trifling complaint, dispute, or criticism. —**nig·gling·ly** *adv.*

nigh /nī/ ▸*adv., prep.,* & *adj.* near: [as *adj.*] *departure time was drawing nigh*

| [as *adv.*] *they drew nigh unto the city.* ■ almost: [as *adv.*] *a car weighing nigh on two tons.*

night /nīt/ ▸*n.* **1** the period of darkness in each twenty-four hours; the time from sunset to sunrise: *a moonless night.* ■ this as the interval between two days: *a two-bedroom cabin costs $90 per night.* ■ the darkness of night: *the thief vanished into the night.* **2** the period of time between afternoon and bedtime; an evening: *he was not allowed to go out on weekday nights.* ■ an evening appointed for some activity, or spent or regarded in a certain way: *wasn't it a great night out?*
▸ □ **night and day** all the time; constantly: *she studied night and day.*

night blind·ness ▸*n.* less technical term for **NYCTALOPIA**.

night·cap /ˈnītˌkap/ ▸*n.* **1** *hist.* a cap worn in bed. **2** an alcoholic or hot drink taken at the end of the day or before going to bed. **3** *Baseball* the second game of a doubleheader: *he pitched a four-hit shutout in the nightcap.*

night·clothes /ˈnītˌklō(TH)z/ ▸*pl. n.* clothes worn to bed.

night·club /ˈnītˌkləb/ ▸*n.* an establishment for nighttime entertainment, typically serving drinks and offering music, dancing, etc. —**night·club·ber** *n.* —**night·club·bing** *n.*

night·fall /ˈnītˌfôl/ ▸*n.* the onset of night; dusk.

night·gown /ˈnītˌgoun/ ▸*n.* **1** a light, loose garment worn by a woman or child in bed. **2** *hist.* a dressing gown.

night·ie /ˈnītē/ ▸*n. inf.* a nightgown.

night·in·gale /ˈnītnˌgāl; ˈnītiNG-/ ▸*n.* a small European thrush (*Luscinia megarhynchos*) with drab brownish plumage, noted for the rich melodious song of the male, heard esp. at night in breeding season.

night·life /ˈnītˌlīf/ ▸*n.* social activities or entertainment available at night in a town or city.

night·light /ˈnītˌlīt/ (also **night-light** or **night light**) ▸*n.* a small lamp, typically attached directly to an electrical outlet, providing a dim light during the night.

night·ly /ˈnītlē/ ▸*adj.* **1** happening or done every night: *his prime-time, nightly TV talk show.* **2** happening, done, or existing in the night.
▸*adv.* every night: *the hotel features live music nightly.*

night·mare /ˈnītˌme(ə)r/ ▸*n.* a frightening or unpleasant dream: *I had nightmares after watching the horror movie.* ■ a terrifying or very unpleasant experience or prospect: *the nightmare of racial hatred.* —**night·mar·ish** *adj.* —**night·mar·ish·ly** *adv.*

night owl ▸*n. inf.* a person who is habitually active or wakeful at night.

night school ▸*n.* an institution providing evening classes for those working during the day.

night·shade /ˈnītˌSHād/ ▸*n.* a plant (*Solanum* and other genera), typically having poisonous black or red berries. The **nightshade family** (Solanaceae) includes many commercially important plants (e.g., potato, tomato, tobacco) as well as several highly poisonous ones (e.g., jimson weed).

night shift ▸*n.* the period of time scheduled for work at night, as in a factory or other institution. ■ the group of people working during this period.

night·shirt /ˈnītˌSHərt/ ▸*n.* a long, loose shirt worn to bed.

night·spot /ˈnītˌspät/ ▸*n. inf.* a nightclub.

night·stick /ˈnītˌstik/ ▸*n.* a police officer's club or billy.

night·time /ˈnītˌtīm/ ▸*n.* the time between evening and morning; the time of darkness: *slipping away over the river in the nighttime* | [as *adj.*] *the government imposed a nighttime curfew.*

NIH ▸*abbr.* National Institutes of Health.

ni·hil·ism /ˈnīəˌlizəm; ˈnē-/ ▸*n.* the rejection of all religious and moral principles, often in the belief that life is meaningless. ■ *Philos.* extreme skepticism maintaining that nothing in the world has a real existence. —**ni·hil·ist** *n.* —**ni·hil·is·tic** /ˌnīəˈlistik; ˌnēə-/ *adj.*

nil /nil/ ▸*n.* zero, esp. as a score in certain games: *they beat us three-nil.*
▸*adj.* nonexistent: *his chances for survival were slim, almost nil.*

nim·ble /ˈnimbəl/ ▸*adj.* (**-bler, -blest**) quick and light in movement or action; agile: *with a deft motion of her nimble fingers.* ■ (of the mind) quick to comprehend: *she is well-read and intellectually nimble.* —**nim·ble·ness** *n.* —**nim·bly** /-blē/ *adv.*

nim·bo·stra·tus /ˌnimbōˈstrātəs; -ˈsträ-/ ▸*n.* a type of cloud forming a thick uniform gray layer at low altitude, from which rain or snow often falls (without any lightning or thunder).

nim·bus /ˈnimbəs/ ▸*n.* (*pl.* **-bi** /-ˌbī/ or **-bus·es**) **1** a luminous cloud or a halo surrounding a supernatural being or a saint. ■ a light, aura, color, etc., that surrounds someone or something. **2** a large gray rain cloud: [as adj.] *nimbus clouds.* ▷early 17th cent.: from Latin, literally 'cloud, aureole.'

NIMBY /'nimbē/ (also **Nimby**) ▶*n.* (*pl.* **NIMBYs**) acronym for *not in my backyard,* referring to those who object to the siting of something perceived as unpleasant or potentially dangerous in their own neighborhood, such as a landfill or hazardous waste facility. —**Nim·by·ism** /-izəm/ *n.*

nin·com·poop /'ninkəm,poōp; 'niNG-/ ▶*n.* a foolish or stupid person.

nine /nīn/ ▶*cardinal number* equivalent to the product of three and three; one more than eight, or one less than ten; 9. (Roman numeral: **ix** or **IX.**) ■ a group or unit of nine individuals. ■ nine years old: *I was only nine.* ■ nine o'clock: *it's ten to nine.* ■ a size of garment or other merchandise denoted by nine. ■ a playing card with nine pips. ■ (**the Nine**) *Greek Mythol.* the nine Muses.

nine·fold /'nīn,fōld/ ▶*adj.* nine times as great or as numerous: *a ninefold increase in the amount of traffic.* ■ having nine parts or elements.

▶*adv.* by nine times; to nine times the number or amount: *consumption increased ninefold.*

nine·teen /nīn'tēn; 'nīn,tēn/ ▶*cardinal number* one more than eighteen; nine more than ten; 19. (Roman numeral: **xix** or **XIX.**) ■ nineteen years old: *she married at nineteen.* —**nine·teenth** /nīn'tēnTH; 'nīn,tēnTH/ *ordinal number.*

nine·ty /'nīntē/ ▶*n.* (*pl.* **-ties**) equivalent to the product of nine and ten; ten less than one hundred; 90. (Roman numeral: **xc** or **XC.**) ■ (**nineties**) the numbers from 90 to 99, esp. the years of a century or of a person's life: *art in the nineties.* ■ ninety years old: *she is nearly ninety.* ■ ninety miles an hour: *we passed the junction doing about ninety.* —**nine·ti·eth** /-tēiTH/ *ordinal number.* —**nine·ty·fold** /-,fōld/ *adj. & adv.*

nin·ja /'ninjə/ ▶*n.* a person skilled in ninjutsu.

nin·jut·su /nin'joōtsoō/ ▶*n.* the traditional Japanese technique of espionage, characterized by stealthy movement and camouflage. It was developed in feudal times for military purposes and subsequently used in the training of samurai.

nin·ny /'ninē/ ▶*n.* (*pl.* **-nies**) *inf.* a foolish person.

ninth /nīnTH/ ▶*ordinal number* constituting number nine in a sequence; 9th. ■ (**a ninth/one ninth**) each of nine equal parts into which something is or may be divided. ■ *Mus.* an interval spanning nine consecutive notes in a diatonic scale. ■ *Mus.* the note that is higher by this interval than the tonic of a diatonic scale or root of a chord. ■ *Mus.* a chord in which the ninth note above the root forms an important component. —**ninth·ly** *adv.*

ni·o·bi·um /nī'ōbēəm/ ▶*n.* the chemical element of atomic number 41, a silver-gray metal of the transition series, used in superconducting alloys. (Symbol: **Nb**)

Nip /nip/ ▶*n.* *inf., offens.* a Japanese person.

nip¹ /nip/ ▶*v.* (**nipped**, **nip·ping**) [*tr.*] pinch, squeeze, or bite sharply: *the dog nipped him on the leg.* ■ (of the cold or frost) cause sharp pain or harm to: *the vegetable garden, nipped now by frost.*

▶*n.* a sharp pinch, squeeze, or bite. ■ a feeling of biting cold: *there was a real winter nip in the air.*

▶ □ **nip something in the bud** suppress or destroy something at an early stage: *the idea has been nipped in the bud at the local level.*

nip² ▶*n.* a small quantity or sip of liquor.

▶*v.* (**nipped**, **nip·ping**) [*intr.*] take a sip or sips of liquor: *the men nipped from the bottle.*

nip·per /'nipər/ ▶*n.* **1** *inf.* a child, esp. a small boy. **2** (**nippers**) pliers, pincers, forceps, or a similar tool for gripping or cutting. **3** (usu. **nippers**) the grasping claw of a crab or lobster.

nip·ple /'nipəl/ ▶*n.* **1** the small projection of a woman's or girl's breast in which the mammary ducts terminate and from which milk can be secreted. ■ the corresponding vestigial structure in a male. ■ the teat of a female animal. ■ the flexible tip of a baby's pacifier or feeding bottle. **2** a small projection on a device or machine, esp. one from which oil, grease, or other fluid is dispensed in small amounts. ■ a short section of pipe threaded at each end.

▶*v.* [*tr.*] (usu. **be nippled**) provide (something) with a projection like a nipple: *rocks nippled with limpets.*

nip·py /'nipē/ ▶*adj.* (**-pi·er**, **-pi·est**) *inf.* **1** (of the weather) rather cold; chilly: *it's a bit nippy this morning.* **2** inclined to nip or bite: *macaws can sometimes be nippy and unpredictable.* —**nip·pi·ly** /'nipəlē/ *adv.*

nir·va·na /nər'vänə; nir-/ ▶*n.* *Buddhism* a transcendent state in which there is neither suffering, desire, nor sense of self, and the subject is released from the effects of karma and samsara. It represents the final goal of Buddhism. ■ *Hinduism* liberation of the soul from the

effects of karma and from bodily existence. ■ a state of perfect happiness; an ideal or idyllic place: *Hollywood's dearest dream of small-town nirvana.*

ni·sei /nē'sā; 'nēsā/ (also **Ni·sei**) ▶*n.* (*pl.* same or **-seis**) a person born in the U.S. or Canada whose parents were immigrants from Japan.

nit /nit/ ▶*n.* the egg or young form of a louse or other parasitic insect, esp. the egg of a head louse attached to a human hair. —**nit·ty** *adj.*

▶ □ **pick nits** look for and criticize small or insignificant faults or errors; nitpick.

ni·ter /'nītər/ ▶*n.* another term for POTASSIUM NITRATE.

nit·pick·ing /'nit,pikiNG/ *inf.* ▶*adj.* looking for small or unimportant errors or faults, esp. in order to criticize unnecessarily: *a nitpicking legalistic exercise.*

▶*n.* such fault-finding: *nitpicking over tiny details.* —**nit·pick** *v.* —**nit·pick·er** /-,pikər/ *n.*

ni·trate /'nītrāt/ ▶*n.* *Chem.* a salt or ester of nitric acid, containing the anion NO_3^- or the group $-NO_3$. ■ sodium nitrate, potassium nitrate, or ammonium nitrate, used as fertilizer: *the fertilizer is usually a basic nitrate.*

▶*v.* [*tr.*] treat (a substance) with nitric acid (typically a concentrated mixture of nitric and sulfuric acids), esp. so as to introduce nitro groups. —**ni·tra·tion** /nī'trāSHən/ *n.*

ni·tric /'nītrik/ ▶*adj.* *Chem.* of or containing nitrogen with a higher valence, often five.

ni·tric ac·id ▶*n.* *Chem.* a colorless or pale yellow liquid acid, HNO_3, that is corrosive and poisonous and has strong oxidizing properties.

ni·tri·fy /'nītrə,fī/ ▶*v.* **1** (**-fies**, **-fied**) [*tr.*] *Chem.* convert (ammonia or another nitrogen compound) into nitrites or nitrates. **2** impregnate with nitrogen or nitrogen compounds. —**ni·tri·fi·ca·tion** /,nītrəfi'kāSHən/ *n.*

ni·trite /'nītrīt/ ▶*n.* *Chem.* a salt or ester of nitrous acid, containing the anion NO_2^- or the group $-NO_2$.

ni·tro /'nītrō/ ▶*n.* short for NITROGLYCERIN.

ni·tro·ben·zene /,nītrō'benzēn/ ▶*n.* *Chem.* a yellow oily liquid, $C_6H_5NO_2$, used in chemical synthesis.

ni·tro·cel·lu·lose /,nītrō'selyə,lōs/ ▶*n.* *Chem.* a highly flammable material made by treating cellulose with concentrated nitric acid, used to make explosives and celluloid.

ni·tro·gen /'nītrəjən/ ▶*n.* the chemical element of atomic number 7, a colorless, odorless unreactive gas that forms about 78 percent of the earth's atmosphere. Liquid nitrogen boils at −195.8°C and is used as a coolant. (Symbol: **N**). —**ni·trog·e·nous** /nī'träjənəs/ *adj.*

ni·tro·glyc·er·in /,nītrō'glisərin/ (also **ni·tro·glyc·er·ine**) ▶*n.* *Chem.* an explosive yellow liquid used in explosives such as dynamite. It is also used in medicine as a vasodilator in the treatment of angina.

ni·trous /'nītrəs/ ▶*adj.* **1** *Chem.* of or containing nitrogen with a lower valence, often three. **2** of nitrogen; nitrogenous: *the effect of nitrous emissions on acid rain.*

ni·trous ox·ide ▶*n.* *Chem.* a colorless gas, N_2O, with a sweetish odor, prepared by heating ammonium nitrate. It produces exhilaration or anesthesia when inhaled and is used as an anesthetic and as an aerosol propellant. Also called LAUGHING GAS.

nit·ty-grit·ty /'nitē 'gritē/ ▶*n.* (**the nitty-gritty**) *inf.* the most important aspects or practical details of a subject or situation: *let's get down to the nitty-gritty of finding a job.*

nit·wit /'nit,wit/ ▶*n.* *inf.* a silly or foolish person (often as a general term of abuse). —**nit·wit·ted** *adj.* —**nit·wit·ted·ness** *n.*

nix¹ /niks/ *inf.* ▶*n.* nothing: *apart from that, nix.*

▶*interj.* expressing denial or refusal: *"I owe you some money." "Nix, nix."*

▶*v.* [*tr.*] put an end to; cancel: *he nixed the deal just before it was to be signed.*

nix² ▶*n.* (*fem.* **nix·ie** /'niksē/) (in Germanic mythology) a water sprite.

nm ▶*abbr.* ■ nanometer. ■ nautical mile.

NMR *Physics* ▶*abbr.* nuclear magnetic resonance.

No ▶*symb.* the chemical element nobelium.

no /nō/ ▶*adj.* **1** not any: *there is no excuse.* **2** used to indicate that something is quite the opposite of what is being specified: *Toby is no fool.* **3** hardly any: *you'll be back in no time.*

▶*interj.* used to give a negative response: *"Is anything wrong?" "No."* ■ expressing disagreement or contradiction: *"This is boring." "No, it's not!"* ■ expressing agreement with or affirmation of a negative statement: *they would never cause a fuss, oh no.* ■ expressing shock or disappointment at something one has heard or discovered: *oh no, look at this!*

▶*adv.* not at all; to no extent: *they were no more able to perform the task than I was.*

▶*n.* (*pl.* **noes**) a negative answer or decision, as in voting: *he was unable to change his automatic yes to a no.*

▶ □ **no can do** *inf.* I am unable to do it. □ **the noes have it** the negative votes are in the majority. □ **no longer** not now as formerly: *they no longer live here.* □ **not take no for an answer** persist in spite of refusals. □ **no two ways about it** used to convey that there can be no doubt about something. □ **no way** *inf.* under no circumstances; not at all: *You think she's alone? No way.* □ **or no** or not: *she'd have ridden there, winter or no.* □ —— **or no** —— regardless of the specified thing: *recession or no recession there is always going to be a shortage of good people.*

No. ▶*abbr.* ■ North. ■ (also **no.**) number: *No. 27.*

no-ac·count *inf.* ▶*adj.* of little or no importance, value, or use; worthless: *a series of no-account boyfriends.*

▶*n.* such a person: *I do not intend to let some no-account get his hands on my money.*

No·ah's ark ▶*n.* the ship in which Noah, his family, and the animals were saved from the Flood, according to the biblical account.

no·bel·i·um /nōˈbelēəm/ ▶*n.* the chemical element of atomic number 102, an artificial radioactive metal of the actinide series. (Symbol: **No**)

No·bel Prize /ˈnōbel/ ▶*n.* any of six international prizes awarded annually for outstanding work in physics, chemistry, physiology or medicine, literature, economics (since 1969), and the promotion of peace. The Nobel Prizes were established by the will of Alfred Nobel. —**No·bel Prize win·ner** *n.*

no·bil·i·ty /nōˈbilitē/ ▶*n.* (*pl.* **-ties**) **1** the quality of being noble in character, mind, birth, or rank. **2** (usu. **the nobility**) the group of people belonging to the noble class in a country, esp. those with a hereditary or honorary title: *a member of the English nobility.*

no·ble /ˈnōbəl/ ▶*adj.* (**-bler, -blest**) **1** belonging to a hereditary class with high social or political status; aristocratic: *the Duchess of Kent and other noble ladies.* **2** having or showing fine personal qualities or high moral principles and ideals: *the promotion of human rights was a noble aspiration.* ■ of imposing or magnificent size or appearance: *entering the building with its noble arches and massive granite columns.* ■ of excellent or superior quality.

▶*n.* **1** (esp. in former times) a person of noble rank or birth. **2** *hist.* a former English gold coin. —**no·ble·ness** *n.* —**no·bly** /-blē/ *adv.*

no·ble gas ▶*n.* Chem. any of the gaseous elements helium, neon, argon, krypton, xenon, and radon, occupying Group 0 (or 18) of the periodic table. They are mostly unreactive chemically.

no·ble·man /ˈnōbəlmən/ ▶*n.* (*pl.* **-men**) a man who belongs to the noble class.

no·ble·wom·an /ˈnōbəlˌwo͝omən/ ▶*n.* (*pl.* **-wom·en**) a woman who belongs to the noble class.

no·bod·y /ˈnōˌbädē; -bədē/ ▶*pron.* no person; no one: *nobody was at home.*

▶*n.* (*pl.* **-bod·ies**) a person of no importance or authority: *they went from nobodies to superstars.*

no-brain·er ▶*n. inf.* something that requires or involves little or no mental effort.

nock /näk/ ▶*n.* Archery a notch at either end of a bow for holding the string. ■ a notch at the back end of an arrow into which the bowstring fits.

▶*v.* [*tr.*] fit (an arrow) to the bowstring to ready it for shooting.

noc·tur·nal /näkˈtərnl/ ▶*adj.* done, occurring, or active at night: *most owls are nocturnal.* —**noc·tur·nal·ly** *adv.*

noc·turne /ˈnäkˌtərn/ ▶*n.* **1** *Mus.* a short composition of a romantic or dreamy character suggestive of night, typically for piano. **2** *Art* a picture of a night scene.

nod /näd/ ▶*v.* (**nod·ded, nod·ding**) **1** [*intr.*] lower and raise one's head slightly and briefly, esp. in greeting, assent, or understanding, or to give someone a signal: *he nodded to Monica to unlock the door.* ■ [*tr.*] signify or express (greeting, assent, or understanding) in this way: *he nodded his consent.* ■ [*intr.*] draw or direct attention to someone or something by moving one's head: *he nodded toward the corner of the room.* ■ move one's head up and down repeatedly: *he shut his eyes, nodding to the beat* | *fig. foxgloves nodding by the path.* **2** [*intr.*] have one's head fall forward when drowsy or asleep: *Anna nodded over her book.*

▶*phrasal v.* □ **nod off** *inf.* fall asleep, esp. briefly or unintentionally: *some of the congregation nodded off during the sermon.*

▶*n.* an act of nodding the head: *at a nod from his father, he left the room.* ■ *fig.* a gesture of acknowledgment or concession: *a feel-good musical with a nod to pantomime.*

▶ □ **a nodding acquaintance** a slight acquaintance with a person or cursory knowledge of a subject: *students will need a nodding acquaintance with three other languages.* □ **get the nod 1** be selected or approved. **2** receive a signal or information. □ **give someone/some-**

thing **the nod 1** select or approve someone or something: *they banned one book but gave the other the nod.* **2** give someone a signal.

node /nōd/ ▶*n.* **1** a point at which lines or pathways intersect or branch; a central or connecting point. ■ *Comput.* a piece of equipment, such as a PC or peripheral, attached to a network. ■ *Math.* a point at which a curve intersects itself. ■ (in generative grammar) a vertex or endpoint in a tree diagram. **2** *Bot.* the part of a plant stem from which one or more leaves emerge, often forming a slight swelling or knob. **3** *Anat.* a lymph node or other structure consisting of a small mass of differentiated tissue. **4** *Physics* & *Math.* a point at which the amplitude of vibration in a standing wave system is zero. ▷late Middle English (denoting a knotty swelling or a protuberance): from Latin *nodus* 'knot'. —**nod·al** /ˈnōdl/ *adj.*

nod·ule /ˈnäjo͞ol/ ▶*n.* **1** a small swelling or aggregation of cells in the body, esp. an abnormal one. ■ (usu. **root nodule**) a swelling on a root of a leguminous plant, containing nitrogen-fixing bacteria. **2** a small rounded lump of matter distinct from its surroundings, for example, of flint in chalk, carbon in cast iron, or a mineral on the seabed. —**nod·u·lar** /-jələr/ *adj.* —**nod·u·lat·ed** /-jəˌlātid/ *adj.* —**nod·u·la·tion** /ˌnäjəˈlāSHən/ *n.* —**nod·u·lose** /-jəlōs/ *adj.* —**nod·u·lous** /-jələs/ *adj.*

No·el /nōˈel/ ▶*n.* Christmas, esp. as a refrain in carols and on Christmas cards.

no-fault ▶*adj.* not assigning fault or blame, in particular: ■ denoting an insurance policy that is valid regardless of whether the policyholder was at fault: *no-fault automobile insurance.* ■ denoting an insurance or compensation plan (esp. one covering medical or industrial accidents) whereby a claimant need not legally prove negligence against any party. ■ of or denoting a form of divorce granted without requiring one party to prove that the other is to blame for the breakdown of the marriage.

no-fly ▶*adj.* designating a list, person, or category of persons prevented from flying for security reasons.

no-frills ▶*adj.* without unnecessary extras, esp. ones for decoration or additional comfort: *cheap fast food in no-frills surroundings.*

nog·gin /ˈnägin/ ▶*n. inf.* **1** a person's head. **2** a small quantity of liquor, typically a quarter of a pint.

no-go ▶*adj. inf.* not ready or not functioning properly. ■ impossible, hopeless, or forbidden: *no-go zones for cars.*

▶*n.* a negative response; no.

no-good ▶*adj. inf.* (of a person) contemptible; worthless: *a no-good layabout.*

▶*n.* a worthless or contemptible person.

Noh /nō/ (also **No** or **Nō**) ▶*n.* traditional Japanese masked drama with dance and song, evolved from Shinto rites.

no-hit·ter ▶*n.* Baseball a complete game in which a pitcher yields no hits to the opposing team.

no·how /ˈnōˌho͝o/ ▶*adv.* **1** used, esp. in jocular or dialectal speech, to emphasize a negative: *the records simply don't exist—never, nowhere, and nohow.* **2** *archaic* not attractive, well, or in good order.

noise /noiz/ ▶*n.* **1** a sound, esp. one that is loud or unpleasant or that causes disturbance: *what's that rustling noise outside the door?* ■ a series or combination of loud, confused sounds, esp. when causing disturbance: *vibration and noise from traffic.* ■ (**noises**) conventional remarks or other sounds that suggest some emotion or quality: *Clarissa made encouraging noises.* **2** *technical* irregular fluctuations that accompany a transmitted electrical signal but are not part of it and tend to obscure it. ■ random fluctuations that obscure or do not contain meaningful data or other information: *over half the magnitude of the differences came from noise in the data.*

noise·less /ˈnoizlis/ ▶*adj.* silent; quiet: *the bicycle is a benign form of transportation, being noiseless and nonpolluting.* ■ *technical* accompanied by or introducing no random fluctuations that would obscure the real signal or data. —**noise·less·ly** *adv.* —**noise·less·ness** *n.*

noise pol·lu·tion ▶*n.* harmful or annoying levels of noise, as from airplanes, industry, etc.

noi·some /ˈnoisəm/ ▶*adj.* poetic/lit. having an extremely offensive smell: *noisome vapors from the smoldering waste.* ■ disagreeable; unpleasant: *involved in noisome scandals.* ■ harmful, noxious. —**noi·some·ness** *n.*

nois·y /ˈnoizē/ ▶*adj.* (**nois·i·er, nois·i·est**) **1** making or given to making a lot of noise: *diesel cars can be very noisy.* ■ (of a person or group of people) stridently seeking to attract attention to their views. **2** full of or characterized by noise: *the bar was crowded and noisy.* ■ *technical*

Pronunciation Key ə *ago,* up; ər *over,* fur; a *hat;* ā *ate;* ä *car;* CH *chin;* e *let;* ē *see;* e(ə)r *air;* i *fit;* ī *by;* i(ə)r *ear;* NG *sing;* ō *go;* ô *law, for;* oi *toy;* o͝o *good;* o͞o *goo;* ou *out;* SH *she;* TH *thin;* TH *then;* (h)w *why;* ZH *vision*

N

accompanied by or introducing random fluctuations that obscure the real signal or data. **—nois·i·ly** /-əlē/ *adv.* **—nois·i·ness** *n.*

no·lo con·ten·de·re /ˌnōlō kənˈtendərē/ ▸*n.* (also **no·lo**) *Law* a plea by which a defendant in a criminal prosecution accepts conviction as though a guilty plea had been entered but does not admit guilt. ▷Latin, 'I do not wish to contend.'

no·mad /ˈnōˌmad/ ▸*n.* a member of a people having no permanent abode, and who travel from place to place to find fresh pasture for their livestock. ■ a person who does not stay long in the same place; a wanderer.

▸*adj.* relating to or characteristic of nomads. **—no·mad·ic** /nōˈmadik/ *adj.* **—no·mad·i·cal·ly** /nōˈmadiklē/ *adv.* **—no·mad·ism** /ˈnōmaˌdizəm/ *n.*

no man's land ▸*n.* disputed ground, as between the front lines or trenches of two opposing armies: *enemy soldiers facing you across no man's land* | *fig. an unmapped no man's land between the traditional command economy and the market.* ■ land or area that is unowned, uninhabited, or undesirable.

nom de guerre /ˌnäm də ˈger/ ▸*n.* (*pl.* **noms de guerre** *pronunc.* same) an assumed name under which a person engages in combat or some other activity or enterprise.

nom de plume /ˌnäm də ˈplo͞om/ ▸*n.* (*pl.* **noms de plume** *pronunc.* same) a pen name.

no·men·cla·ture /ˈnōmənˌklāCHər/ ▸*n.* the devising or choosing of names for things, esp. in a science or other discipline. ■ the body or system of such names in a particular field: *the nomenclature of chemical compounds.* ■ *formal* the term or terms applied to someone or something: *"customers" was preferred to the original nomenclature "passengers."* **—no·men·cla·tur·al** /ˌnōmənˈklāCHərəl/ *adj.*

nom·i·nal /ˈnäminəl/ ▸*adj.* **1** (of a role or status) existing in name only: *Thailand retained nominal independence under Japanese military occupation.* ■ of, relating to, or consisting of names. ■ *Gram.* relating to, headed by, or having the function of a noun. **2** (of a price or amount of money) very small; far below the real value or cost: *some firms charge only a nominal fee for the service.* **3** (of a quantity or dimension, esp. of manufactured articles) stated or expressed but not necessarily corresponding exactly to the real value: *legislation allowed variation around the nominal weight (that printed on each packet).* ■ *Econ.* (of a rate or other figure) expressed in terms of a certain amount, without making allowance for changes in real value over time: *the nominal exchange rate.* **4** *inf.* (chiefly in the context of space travel) functioning normally or acceptably. **—nom·i·nal·ly** *adv.*

nom·i·nal val·ue ▸*n. Econ.* the value that is stated on currency; face value. ■ the price of a share, bond, or security when it was issued, rather than its current market value.

nom·i·nate /ˈnäməˌnāt/ ▸*v.* [*tr.*] **1** propose or formally enter as a candidate for election or for an honor or award: *the film was nominated for several Oscars.* ■ appoint to a job or position: *the company nominated her as a delegate to the convention.* **2** specify (something) formally, typically the date or place for an event: *a day was nominated for the exchange of contracts.* ▷late Middle English (as an adjective in the sense 'named'): from Latin *nominat-* 'named,' from the verb *nominare,* from *nomen, nomin-* 'a name.' The verb senses are first found in English in the 16th cent. **—nom·i·na·tor** /-ˌnātər/ *n.*

nom·i·na·tion /ˌnäməˈnāSHən/ ▸*n.* the action of nominating or state of being nominated: *women's groups opposed the nomination of the judge.* ■ a person or thing nominated: *send your nominations in by November 30th.*

nom·i·na·tive /ˈnämənətiv/ ▸*adj.* **1** *Gram.* relating to or denoting a case of nouns, pronouns, and adjectives (as in Latin and other inflected languages) used for the subject of a verb. **2** /-ˌnātiv/ of or appointed by nomination as distinct from election.

▸*n. Gram.* a word in the nominative case. ■ (**the nominative**) the nominative case.

nom·i·nee /ˌnäməˈnē/ ▸*n.* **1** a person who is proposed or formally entered as a candidate for an office or as the recipient of a grant or award: *the party's presidential nominee.* **2** a person or company whose name is given as having title to a stock, real estate, etc., but who is not the actual owner.

non- ▸*prefix* **1** not doing; not involved with: *nonaggression.* **2** not of the kind or class described: *nonbeliever* | *nonconformist.* ■ also forming nouns used attributively (such as *nonunion* in *nonunion miners*). **3** not of the importance implied: *nonissue.* **4** a lack of: *nonsense.* **5** (added to adverbs) not in the way described: *nonuniformly.* **6** (added to verbs to form adjectives) not causing or requiring: *nonskid* | *noniron.* **7** expressing a neutral negative sense when a corresponding form beginning with *in-* or *un-* has a special connotation (such as *nonhuman* compared with *inhuman*).

non·a·ge·nar·i·an /ˌnänəjəˈne(ə)rēən; ˌnōnə-/ ▸*n.* a person who is from 90 to 99 years old.

non·ag·gres·sion /ˌnänəˈgreSHən/ ▸*n.* absence of the desire or intention to be aggressive, esp. on the part of nations or governments: *a treaty of nonaggression and friendship.*

non·a·ligned /ˌnänəˈlīnd/ ▸*adj.* not aligned with something else. ■ (of countries) not aligned with a major power, esp. the former USSR or the U.S. **—non·a·lign·ment** /-ˈlīnmənt/ *n.*

---

non·a·bra·sive *adj.*	**non·con·struc·tive** *adj.*	**non·liq·uid** *n. & adj.*	**non·re·cip·ro·cal** *adj. & n.*
non·ab·sor·bent *adj.*	**non·con·ta·gious** *adj.*	**non·lit·er·ar·y** *adj.*	**non·re·cur·ring** *adj.*
non·a·bu·sive *adj.*	**non·con·ten·tious** *adj.*	**non·mag·net·ic** *adj.*	**non·re·deem·a·ble** *adj.*
non·ac·cep·tance *n.*	**non·con·tro·ver·sial** *adj.*	**non·ma·lig·nant** *adj.*	**non·re·fill·a·ble** *adj.*
non·a·chiev·er *n.*	**non·crys·tal·line** *adj.*	**non·med·i·cal** *adj.*	**non·re·new·a·ble** *adj.*
non·ac·tion *n.*	**non·de·duct·i·ble** *adj.*	**non·met·al** *n.*	**non·rep·re·sen·ta·tion·al** *adj.*
non·ac·tive *adj.*	**non·de·grad·a·ble** *adj.*	**non·met·al·lic** *adj.*	**non·re·sis·tant** *adj.*
non·ad·dic·tive *adj.*	**non·dis·clo·sure** *n.*	**non·mil·i·tant** *adj.*	**non·rhyth·mic** *adj.*
non·ad·he·sive *adj.*	**non·dry·ing** *adj.*	**non·mil·i·tary** *adj.*	**non·sal·a·ried** *adj.*
non·ad·just·a·ble *adj.*	**non·earn·ing** *adj.*	**non·nar·cot·ic** *adj. & n.*	**non·sci·en·tif·ic** *adj.*
non·al·ler·gen·ic *adj.*	**non·ef·fec·tive** *adj.*	**non·ob·lig·a·to·ry** *adj.*	**non·sci·en·tist** *n.*
non·al·ler·gic *adj.*	**non-Eu·ro·pe·an** *adj. & n.*	**non·ob·serv·ance** *n.*	**non·sea·son·al** *adj.*
non·am·big·u·ous *adj.*	**non·ex·ec·u·tive** *adj. & n.*	**non·ob·serv·ant** *adj.*	**non·smok·er** *n.*
non-A·mer·i·can *adj. & n.*	**non·ex·ist·ence** *n.*	**non·oc·cur·rence** *n.*	**non·sol·u·ble** *adj.*
non·at·tached *adj.*	**non·ex·ist·ent** *adj.*	**non·of·fi·cial** *adj.*	**non·speak·ing** *adj.*
non·at·trib·ut·a·ble *adj.*	**non·fat·ten·ing** *adj.*	**non·op·er·a·tion·al** *adj.*	**non·spe·cial·ist** *n.*
non·bel·lig·er·ence *n.*	**non·gas·eous** *adj.*	**non·pay·ing** *adj.*	**non·spe·cif·ic** *adj.*
non·bel·lig·er·ent *adj. & n.*	**non·greas·y** *adj.*	**non·per·ish·a·ble** *adj.*	**non·stain·ing** *adj.*
non·bi·o·de·grad·a·ble *adj.*	**non·haz·ard·ous** *adj.*	**non·per·son·al** *adj.*	**non·swim·mer** *n.*
non·break·a·ble *adj.*	**non·he·red·i·tary** *adj.*	**non·phy·si·cal** *adj.*	**non·tar·nish·ing** *adj.*
non·ca·lor·ic *adj.*	**non·his·tor·i·cal** *adj.*	**non·play·ing** *adj.*	**non·tax·a·ble** *adj.*
non·can·cer·ous *adj.*	**non·i·den·ti·cal** *adj.*	**non·poi·son·ous** *adj.*	**non·think·ing** *adj.*
non-Cath·o·lic *adj. & n.*	**non·in·clu·sive** *adj.*	**non·po·lit·i·cal** *adj.*	**non·threat·en·ing** *adj.*
non-Chris·tian *adj.*	**non·in·dus·tri·al** *adj.*	**non·pol·lut·ing** *adj.*	**non·tra·di·tion·al** *adj.*
non·cler·i·cal *adj. & n.*	**non·in·fec·tious** *adj.*	**non·po·rous** *adj.*	**non·trans·fer·a·ble** *adj.*
non·clin·i·cal *adj.*	**non·in·flam·ma·to·ry** *adj.*	**non·prac·tic·ing** *adj.*	**non·u·ni·form** *adj.*
non·col·le·giate *adj.*	**non·in·fla·tion·ar·y** *adj.*	**non·pre·hen·sile** *adj.*	**non·ven·om·ous** *adj.*
non·com·bus·ti·ble *adj.*	**non·in·flect·ed** *adj.*	**non·pre·scrip·tion** *adj.*	**non·vi·a·ble** *adj.*
non·com·mu·ni·cat·ing *adj.*	**non·in·te·grat·ed** *adj.*	**non·prof·it·a·ble** *adj.*	**non·vir·u·lent** *adj.*
non·com·mu·nist *adj. & n.* (also	**non·in·ter·fer·ence** *n.*	**non·pub·lic** *adj.*	**non·vo·cal** *adj.*
non-Com·mu·nist)	**non·in·tox·i·cat·ing** *adj.*	**non·ran·dom** *adj.*	**non·vot·er** *n.*
non·com·pet·i·tive *adj.*	**non·ir·ri·tat·ing** *adj.*	**non·ra·tion·al** *adj.*	**non·vot·ing** *adj.*
non·con·fi·den·tial *adj.*	**non-Jew·ish** *adj.*	**non·re·ac·tive** *adj.*	**non·work·ing** *adj.*

non·be·liev·er /ˌnänbəˈlēvər/ ▶ n. a person who does not believe in something, esp. one who has no religious faith.

non·bi·o·log·i·cal /ˌnänbīəˈläjikəl/ ▶ adj. not involving, relating to, or derived from biology or living organisms. ■ (of a detergent) not containing enzymes.

nonce /näns/ ▶ adj. (of a word or expression) coined for or used on one occasion: *a nonce usage.*

▶ □ **for the nonce** for the present; temporarily: *the room had been converted for the nonce into a nursery.*

non·cha·lant /ˌnänshəˈlänt/ ▶ adj. (of a person or manner) feeling or appearing casually calm and relaxed; not displaying anxiety, interest, or enthusiasm: *she gave a nonchalant shrug.* —**non·cha·lance** n. —**non·cha·lant·ly** adv.

non·com /ˈnänˌkäm/ ▶ n. inf. Mil. a noncommissioned officer.

non·com·bat·ant /ˌnänkəmˈbatnt/ ▶ n. a person who is not engaged in fighting during a war, esp. a civilian, chaplain, or medical practitioner.

non·com·mis·sioned /ˌnänkəˈmishənd/ ▶ adj. Mil. (of an officer in the armed forces) ranking below warrant officer, as sergeant or petty officer.

non·com·mit·tal /ˌnänkəˈmitl/ ▶ adj. (of a person or a person's behavior or manner) not expressing or revealing commitment to a definite opinion or course of action: *her tone was noncommittal, and her face gave nothing away.* —**non·com·mit·tal·ly** adv.

non·com·pli·ance /ˌnänkəmˈplīəns/ ▶ n. failure to act in accordance with a wish or command.

non com·pos men·tis /ˌnän ˈkämpəs ˈmentis/ (also **non com·pos**) ▶ adj. not sane or in one's right mind.

non·con·duc·tor /ˌnänkənˈdəktər/ ▶ n. a substance that does not conduct heat or electricity. —**non·con·duct·ing** /-ˈdəktiNG/ adj.

non·con·form·ist /ˌnänkənˈfôrmist/ ▶ n. a person whose behavior or views do not conform to prevailing ideas or practices.

▶ adj. of or characterized by behavior or views that do not conform to prevailing ideas or practices. —**non·con·form·ism** /-ˌmizəm/ n.

non·con·form·i·ty /ˌnänkənˈfôrmitē/ ▶ n. failure or refusal to conform to a prevailing rule or practice. ■ lack of similarity in form or type.

non·con·trib·u·to·ry /ˌnänkənˈtribyəˌtôrē/ ▶ adj. **1** not playing a part in bringing something about. **2** (of a pension or pension plan) funded by regular payments by the employer, not the employee.

non·de·nom·i·na·tion·al /ˌnändəˌnäməˈnāshənəl/ ▶ adj. open or acceptable to people of any Christian denomination.

non·de·script /ˌnändəˈskript/ ▶ adj. lacking distinctive or interesting features or characteristics: *she lived in a nondescript suburban apartment block.*

▶ n. a nondescript person or thing. —**non·de·script·ly** adv. —**non·de·script·ness** /-ˈskrip(t)nis/ n.

non·dig·i·tal /nänˈdijitl/ ▶ adj. **1** not represented by numbers, especially binary codes; not digitized: *nondigital items have only their location information (catalog records) in the digital library.* **2** not using the Internet or computers: *nondigital submissions will be accepted only until February 1st.*

none[1] /nən/ ▶ pron. not any: *none of you want to work.* ■ no person; no one: *none could match her looks.*

▶ adv. (**none the**) by no amount; not at all: *it is made none the easier by the differences in approach.*

▶ □ **none other than** used to emphasize the surprising identity of a person or thing: *her first customer was none other than Henry du Pont.* □ **want** (or **will have**) **none of** (esp. with reference to behavior) refuse to accept (something): *Danny offered to wait below, but Peter would have none of it.*

none[2] (also **nones**) ▶ n. a service forming part of the Divine Office of the Western Christian Church, traditionally said (or chanted) at the ninth hour of the day (3 p.m.).

non·en·ti·ty /nänˈentitē/ ▶ n. (pl. **-ties**) **1** a person or thing with no special or interesting qualities; an unimportant person or thing: *a political nonentity.* **2** nonexistence: *asserting the nonentity of evil.* ▷late 16th cent.: from medieval Latin *nonentitas* 'nonexistence.'

none·such /ˈnənˌsəCH/ ▶ n. a person or thing that is regarded as perfect or excellent.

none·the·less /ˌnənTHəˈles/ (also **none the less**) ▶ adv. in spite of that; nevertheless: *it was the barest of welcomes, but it was a welcome nonetheless.*

non-Eu·clid·e·an /ˌnän yooˈklidēən/ ▶ adj. Geom. denying or going beyond Euclidean principles in geometry, esp. in contravening the postulate that only one line through a given point can be parallel to a given line.

non·e·vent /ˌnänēˈvent/ ▶ n. a disappointing or insignificant event or occasion, esp. one that was expected or intended to be exciting or interesting. ■ a scheduled event that did not happen.

non·fer·rous /nänˈferəs/ ▶ adj. relating to or denoting a metal other than iron or steel.

non·fic·tion /nänˈfikSHən/ ▶ n. prose writing that is based on facts, real events, and real people, such as biography or history. —**non·fic·tion·al** /-nəl/ adj.

non·flam·ma·ble /nänˈflaməbəl/ ▶ adj. not catching fire easily; not flammable.

non·hu·man /nänˈ(h)yoōmən/ ▶ adj. of, relating to, or characteristic of a creature or thing that is not a human being: *ascribing human characteristics to nonhuman animals.*

▶ n. a creature that is not a human being.

non·in·ter·ven·tion /ˌnäninter·ˈvensHən/ ▶ n. the principle or practice of not becoming involved in the affairs of others. ■ such a policy adopted by a country in its international relations. —**non·in·ter·ven·tion·ism** /-ˌnizəm/ n. —**non·in·ter·ven·tion·ist** /-nist/ adj. & n.

non·ju·di·cial /ˌnänjoōˈdiSHəl/ ▶ adj. **1** not resulting from a court ruling or judgment: *nonjudicial punishment.* **2** not involving courts or judges: *nonjudicial appointments.*

non·lin·e·ar /nänˈlinēər/ ▶ adj. not denoting, involving, or arranged in a straight line. ■ Math. designating or involving an equation whose terms are not of the first degree. ■ Physics involving a lack of linearity between two related qualities such as input and output. ■ Math. involving measurement in more than one dimension. ■ not linear, sequential, or straightforward; random: *Joyce's stream-of-consciousness, nonlinear narrative.* —**non·lin·e·ar·i·ty** /ˌnänlinēˈaritē/ n. —**non·lin·e·ar·ly** adv.

non·mem·ber /ˈnänˌmembər/ ▶ n. a person, body, or country that is not a member of a particular organization. —**non·mem·ber·ship** /nänˈmembərˌSHip/ n.

non·nat·u·ral /nänˈnaCHərəl/ ▶ adj. not involving or manifesting natural means or processes.

non·ne·go·ti·a·ble /ˌnä(n)nəˈgōSHəbəl/ ▶ adj. not open to discussion or modification. ■ (of a document) not able to be transferred or assigned to the legal ownership of another person.

non·nu·cle·ar /nänˈn(y)ooklēər/ ▶ adj. **1** not involving or relating to nuclear energy or nuclear weapons. ■ (of a country) not possessing nuclear weapons. **2** Physics not involving, relating to, or forming part of a nucleus or nuclei.

no-no ▶ n. (pl. **-nos**) inf. a thing that is not possible or acceptable: *perming highlighted hair used to be a definite no-no, but it's now possible.*

non·non·sense ▶ adj. simple and straightforward; sensible.

non·or·gan·ic /ˌnänôrˈganik/ ▶ adj. not organic, in particular: ■ not relating to or derived from living matter: *nonorganic archaeological finds.* ■ (esp. of food or farming methods) not using or relating to production by organic methods: *nonorganic pesticides.*

non·pa·reil /ˌnänpəˈrel/ ▶ adj. having no match or equal; unrivaled: *he is a nonpareil storyteller.*

▶ n. **1** an unrivaled or matchless person or thing. **2** a flat round candy made of chocolate covered with white sugar sprinkles. **3** Printing an old type size equal to six points (larger than ruby or agate, smaller than emerald or minion).

non·pay·ment ▶ n. failure to pay an amount of money that is owed: *homes repossessed for nonpayment of mortgages.*

non·per·son /ˌnänˈpərsən/ ▶ n. a person regarded as nonexistent or unimportant, or as having no rights; an ignored or forgotten person: *these players were famous within their own communities, but nonpersons outside them.*

non·plus /nänˈpləs/ ▶ v. (**-plussed, -plus·sing**) [tr.] (usu. **be nonplussed**) surprise and confuse (someone) so much that they are unsure how to react: *Diane was nonplussed by such an odd question.*

▶ n. a state of being surprised and confused in this way.

non·point source /nänˈpoint/ ▶ n. a source of pollution that issues from widely distributed or pervasive environmental elements: *cattle are the leading nonpoint source of pollution in Canada today.*

non·pro·duc·tive /ˌnänprəˈdəktiv/ ▶ adj. not producing or able to produce goods, crops, or economic benefit (tending to be less forceful in meaning than **unproductive**). ■ achieving little. —**non·pro·duc·tive·ly** adv.

non·pro·fes·sion·al /ˌnänprəˈfeSHənəl/ ▶ adj. relating to or engaged in a paid occupation that does not require advanced education or training:

N

nonprofessional grades of staff. ■ relating to or engaged in an activity (esp. an interest or hobby) that is not a person's main paid occupation: *nonprofessional actors.*

▶*n.* a nonprofessional person.

non·prof·it /ˈnänˈpräfit/ ▶*adj.* not making or conducted primarily to make a profit: *charities and other nonprofit organizations.*

non·pro·lif·er·a·tion /ˌnänprəˌlifəˈrāSHən/ ▶*n.* the prevention of an increase or spread of something, esp. the number of countries possessing nuclear weapons: [as *adj.*] *a nuclear nonproliferation treaty.*

non·res·i·dent /nänˈrezidənt/ ▶*adj.* not living in a particular place, esp. a country or a place of work: *the building had a nonresident, part-time caretaker.* ■ (of a job or program of study) not requiring the holder or participant to reside at the place of work or instruction. ■ *Comput.* (of software) not kept permanently in memory but available to be loaded from secondary storage or external device: *if you want to use a nonresident font, you can manually download it.*

▶*n.* a person not living in a particular place: *parking permits are available for Richmond residents and nonresidents.* —**non·res·i·dence** *n.* —**non·res·i·den·tial** /ˌnänreziˈdenCHəl/ *adj.*

non·re·sis·tance /ˌnänriˈzistəns/ ▶*n.* the practice or principle of not resisting authority, even when it is unjustly exercised.

non·re·turn·a·ble /ˌnänriˈtərnəbəl/ ▶*adj.* (esp. of a deposit paid) not repayable in any circumstances. ■ (of bottles or other containers) not intended to be returned empty to the suppliers.

non·sense /ˈnänˌsens/ ▶*n.* **1** spoken or written words that have no meaning or make no sense: *he was talking absolute nonsense.* ■ [as *interj.*] used to show strong disagreement: *"Nonsense! No one can do that."* ■ [as *adj.*] denoting verse or other writing intended to be amusing by virtue of its absurd or whimsical language: *nonsense poetry.* **2** foolish or unacceptable behavior: *put a stop to that nonsense, will you?* ■ something that one disagrees with or disapproves of: *the idea that the gut is full of toxins that have to be flushed away is dismissed as nonsense by gastroenterologists.* —**non·sen·si·cal** /nänˈsensikəl/ *adj.* —**non·sen·si·cal·i·ty** /ˌnänsensəˈkalitē/ *n.* —**non·sen·si·cal·ly** /nänˈsensik(ə)lē/ *adv.*

non se·qui·tur /ˌnän ˈsekwitər/ ▶*n.* a conclusion or statement that does not logically follow from the previous argument or statement.

non·skid /ˌnänˈskid/ ▶*adj.* designed to prevent sliding or skidding: *nonskid tires.*

non·slip ▶*adj.* designed to prevent slipping: *a nonslip bath mat.*

non·stand·ard /ˈnänˈstandərd/ ▶*adj.* not average, normal, or usual. ■ (of language) not of the accepted standard.

non·start·er /ˈnänˈstärtər/ ▶*n.* a person or animal that fails to take part in a race. ■ *inf.* a person, plan, or idea that has no chance of succeeding or being effective.

non·stick /ˈnänˈstik/ ▶*adj.* (of a pan or surface) covered with a substance that prevents food from sticking to it during cooking: *a nonstick frying pan.*

non·stop /ˈnänˈstäp/ ▶*adj.* continuing without stopping or pausing: *we had two days of almost nonstop rain.* ■ (of a passenger vehicle or journey) not having or making stops at intermediate places on the way to its destination: *a nonstop flight to Los Angeles.* ■ oppressively constant; relentless: *the show was axed after nonstop criticism.*

▶*adv.* without stopping or pausing: *Stephen had been working nonstop.*

▶*n.* a nonstop flight or train: *seven nonstops to New York every business day.*

non·tech·ni·cal /ˈnänˈteknikəl/ ▶*adj.* not relating to or involving science or technology: *a simple, nontechnical procedure.* ■ without specialized or technical knowledge: *a nontechnical background.* ■ not using technical terms or requiring specialized knowledge.

non·un·ion /nänˈyōōnyən/ ▶*adj.* not belonging or relating to a labor union: *nonunion farm workers | nonunion agreements.* ■ (of a company) not having labor union members: *a high proportion of newly established firms are nonunion.* ■ not done or produced by members of a labor union: *he sells nonunion doughnuts.*

non·ver·bal /nänˈvərbəl/ ▶*adj.* not involving or using words or speech: *forms of nonverbal communication.* —**non·ver·bal·ly** *adv.*

non·vi·o·lence /nänˈvīələns/ ▶*n.* the use of peaceful means, not force, to bring about political or social change. —**non·vi·o·lent** *adj.*

noo·dle[1] /ˈnōōdl/ ▶*n.* (usu. **noodles**) a strip, ring, or tube of pasta or a similar dough, typically made with egg and usually eaten with a sauce or in a soup.

noo·dle[2] ▶*n. inf.* a stupid or silly person. ■ a person's head.

noo·dle[3] /ˈnōōdl/ ▶*v.* [*intr.*] *inf.* improvise or play casually on a musical instrument: *tapes of him noodling on his guitar.*

noog·ie /ˈnōōgē/ ▶*n.* a hard poke or grind with the knuckles, esp. on a

person's head: *maybe he would just grab the little guy and plant a friendly noogie on his head.*

nook /nōōk/ ▶*n.* a corner or recess, esp. one offering seclusion or security: *the nook beside the fire.*

▶ □ **every nook and cranny** every part or aspect of something: *the party reached into every nook and cranny of people's lives.*

nook·y /ˈnōōkē/ (also **nook·ie**) ▶*n. vulgar slang* sexual activity or intercourse.

noon /nōōn/ ▶*n.* twelve o'clock in the day; midday: *his classes let out at noon | the service starts at twelve noon.*

noon·day /ˈnōōnˌdā/ ▶*n.* the middle of the day: [as *adj.*] *the blinds were lowered to keep out the noonday sun.*

no one ▶*pron.* no person; not a single person: *no one came.*

noon·tide /ˈnōōnˌtīd/ (also **noon·time** /-ˌtīm/) ▶*n. poetic/lit.* noon.

noose /nōōs/ ▶*n.* a loop with a running knot, tightening as the rope or wire is pulled and typically used to hang people or trap animals. ■ (**the noose**) death by hanging. ■ (**the noose**) *fig.* a difficult situation regarded as a restraint or bond: *the West is exploring ways to tighten the economic noose.*

▶*v.* [*tr.*] put a noose on (someone): *she was noosed and hooded, then strangled by the executioner.* ■ catch (an animal) with a noose. ■ form (a rope) into a noose. ▷late Middle English: probably via Old French *no(u)s* from Latin *nodus* 'knot.'

▶ □ **put one's head in a noose** bring about one's own downfall.

nope /nōp/ ▶*interj. informal* variant of **no**.

nor /nôr/ ▶*conj. & adv.* **1** used before the second or further of two or more alternatives (the first being introduced by a negative such as "neither" or "not") to indicate that they are each untrue or each do not happen: *they were neither cheap nor convenient.* ■ [as *adv.*] poetic/literary term for **neither**: *nor God nor demon can undo the done.* **2** used to introduce a further negative statement: *the struggle did not end, nor was it any less diminished.*

▶*n.* (usu. **NOR**) *Electr.* a Boolean operator that gives the value one if and only if all operands have a value of zero and otherwise has a value of zero. ■ (also **NOR gate**) a circuit that produces an output signal only when there are no signals on any of the input connections.

nor' /nôr/ ▶*abbr.* (esp. in compounds) north: *seek shelter from a raging nor'easter.*

nor·a·dren·a·line /ˌnôrəˈdrenəlin/ (also **nor·a·dren·a·lin**) ▶*n.* another term for **norepinephrine**.

Nor·dic /ˈnôrdik/ ▶*adj.* of or relating to Scandinavia, Finland, Iceland, and the Faroe Islands. ■ relating to or denoting a physical type of northern European peoples characterized by tall stature, a bony frame, light coloring, and a relatively long skull. ■ *Skiing* relating to or denoting the disciplines of cross-country skiing or ski jumping.

▶*n.* a native of Scandinavia, Finland, or Iceland.

nor'·east·er /ˌnôrˈēstər/ ▶*n.* another term for **northeaster**.

nor·ep·i·neph·rine /ˌnôrepəˈnefrin/ ▶*n. Biochem.* a hormone, $(HO)_2C_6H_3CHOHCH_2NH_2$, that is released by the adrenal medulla and by the sympathetic nerves and functions as a neurotransmitter. It is also used as a drug to raise blood pressure. Also called **noradrenaline**.

norm /nôrm/ ▶*n.* **1** (**the norm**) something that is usual, typical, or standard: *this system has been the norm in Germany for decades.* ■ (usu. **norms**) a standard or pattern, esp. of social behavior, that is typical or expected of a group: *the norms of good behavior in the civil service.* ■ a required standard; a level to be complied with or reached: *the 7% pay norm had been breached again.* **2** *Math.* the product of a complex number and its conjugate, equal to the sum of the squares of its real and imaginary components, or the positive square root of this sum. ■ an analogous quantity used to represent the magnitude of a vector.

nor·mal /ˈnôrməl/ ▶*adj.* **1** conforming to a standard; usual, typical, or expected: *it's quite normal for puppies to bolt their food.* ■ (of a person) free from physical or mental disorders. **2** *technical* (of a line, ray, or other linear feature) intersecting a given line or surface at right angles. **3** *Med.* (of a salt solution) containing the same salt concentration as the blood. **4** *Geol.* denoting a fault or faulting in which a relative downward movement occurred in the strata situated on the upper side of the fault plane.

▶*n.* **1** the usual, average, or typical state or condition: *her temperature was above normal | the service will be back to normal next week.* ■ a person who is physically or mentally healthy. **2** *technical* a line at right angles to a given line or surface. —**nor·mal·cy** /-məlsē/ *n.* —**nor·mal·i·ty** /nôrˈmalitē/ *n.*

nor·mal dis·tri·bu·tion ▶*n. Statistics* a function that represents the distribution of many random variables as a symmetrical bell-shaped graph.

nor·mal·ize /'nôrmə,līz/ ▸v. **1** [tr.] bring or return to a normal condition or state: *Vietnam and China agreed to normalize diplomatic relations in 1991* | [intr.] *the situation had normalized.* **2** [tr.] (often **be normalized**) *Math.* multiply (a series, function, or item of data) by a factor that makes the norm or some associated quantity such as an integral equal to a desired value (usually 1). ■ *Comput.* (in floating-point representation) express (a number) in the standard form with regard to the position of the radix point, usually immediately preceding the first nonzero digit. —**nor·mal·i·za·tion** /,nôrmələ'zāsHən/ *n.* —**nor·mal·iz·er** *n.*

nor·mal·ly /'nôrməlē/ ▸adv. **1** under normal or usual conditions; as a rule: *normally, it takes three or four years to complete the training.* **2** in a normal manner; in the usual way: *try to breathe normally.* **3** *technical* at right angles to a given line or surface.

Nor·man ▸n. **1** a member of a people of mixed Frankish and Scandinavian origin who settled in Normandy from about AD 912 and became a dominant military power in western Europe and the Mediterranean in the 11th century. ■ in particular, any of the Normans who conquered England in 1066 or their descendants. ■ a native or inhabitant of modern Normandy. ■ any of the English kings from William I to Stephen. **2** the form of French spoken by the Normans. ▸adj. of, relating to, or denoting the Normans. ■ denoting, relating to, or built in the style of Romanesque architecture used in Britain under the Normans. ■ of or relating to modern Normandy. —**Nor·man·esque** /,nôrmə'nesk/ *adj.* —**Nor·man·ism** /-,nizəm/ *n.* —**Nor·man·ize** /-,nīz/ *v.*

Nor·man Con·quest ▸the conquest of England by William of Normandy (William the Conqueror) after the Battle of Hastings in 1066.

nor·ma·tive /'nôrmətiv/ ▸adj. *formal* establishing, relating to, or deriving from a standard or norm, esp. of behavior: *negative sanctions to enforce normative behavior.* —**nor·ma·tive·ly** *adv.* —**nor·ma·tive·ness** *n.*

no·ro·vi·rus /'nôrə,vīrəs/ ▸n. any of various single-stranded RNA nonenveloped viruses that can cause acute gastroenteritis in humans.

Norse /nôrs/ ▸n. **1** the Norwegian language, esp. in its medieval form. ■ the Scandinavian language group. **2** [treated as *pl.*] Norwegians or Scandinavians, esp. in medieval times. ▸adj. of or relating to medieval Norway or Scandinavia, or their inhabitants or language. —**Norse·man** /'nôrsmən/ *n.* (*pl.* -**men**) .

north /nôrTH/ ▸n. (usu. **the north**) **1** the direction in which a compass needle normally points, toward the horizon on the left side of a person facing east, or the part of the horizon lying in this direction: *a bitter wind blew from the north.* ■ the compass point corresponding to this. ■ a direction in space parallel to the earth's axis of rotation and toward the point on the celestial sphere around which the stars appear to turn counterclockwise. **2** the northern part of the world or of a specified country, region, or town: *cuisine from the north of Spain.* **3** (**North**) *Bridge* the player occupying a designated position at the table, sitting opposite and partnering South. ▸adj. lying toward, near, or facing the north: *the north door.* ■ (of a wind) blowing from the north. ▸adv. to or toward the north: *a north-facing wall.* ▸ □ **north by east** (or **west**) between north and north-northeast (or north-northwest). □ **up north** *inf.* to or in the north of a country: *he's taken a teaching job up north.*

North A·mer·i·can ▸adj. of or relating to North America. ▸n. a native or inhabitant of North America, esp. a citizen of the U.S. or Canada.

north·bound /'nôrTH,bound/ ▸adj. traveling or leading toward the north: *northbound traffic.*

north·east /,nôrTH'ēst/ ▸n. **1** (usu. **the northeast**) the point of the horizon midway between north and east: *I pointed to the northeast.* ■ the compass point corresponding to this. ■ the direction in which this lies: *the entrance was through a small door to the northeast.* **2** the northeastern part of a country, region, or town: *the northeast of Brazil.* ▸adj. **1** lying toward, near, or facing the northeast. ■ (of a wind) coming from the northeast. **2** of or denoting the northeastern part of a specified country, region, or town, or its inhabitants: *northeast Baltimore.* ▸adv. to or toward the northeast: *the ship sailed northeast.* —**north·east·er·ly** *adj. & adv.* —**north·east·ern** /-'ēstərn/ *adj.*

north·east·er /,nôrTH'ēstər/ (also **nor'east·er** /,nôr'ēstər/) ▸n. a wind or storm from the northeast.

north·er·ly /'nôrTHərlē/ ▸adj. & adv. in a northward position or direction: [as adj.] *he set off in a northerly direction.* ■ (of wind) blowing from the north: [as adj.] *it will feel cold in the fresh northerly wind* | [as adv.] *the wind was gusting northerly.* ▸n. (often **northerlies**) a wind blowing from the north.

north·ern /'nôrTHərn/ ▸adj. **1** situated in the north, or directed toward

or facing the north: *the northern slopes.* **2** living in or originating from the north: *northern breeds of cattle.* ■ of, relating to, or characteristic of the north or its inhabitants: *an unmistakable northern accent.* —**north·ern·most** /-,mōst/ *adj.*

North·ern·er /,nôrTHərnər/ (also **north·ern·er**) ▸n. a native or inhabitant of the north, esp. of the northern U.S.

north·ern lights ▸another name for the aurora borealis. See AURORA.

north-north·east ▸n. the compass point or direction midway between north and northeast.

north-north·west ▸n. the compass point or direction midway between north and northwest.

North Pole ▸n. see POLE[2].

North Star *Astron.* ▸another term for POLARIS.

north·ward /'nôrTHwərd/ ▸adj. in a northerly direction. ▸adv. (also **northwards**) toward the north. ▸n. (**the northward**) the direction or region to the north. —**north·ward·ly** *adj. & adv.*

north·west /,nôrTH'west/ ▸n. (usu. **the northwest**) **1** the point of the horizon midway between north and west: *he pointed to the northwest.* ■ the compass point corresponding to this. ■ the direction in which this lies. **2** the northwestern part of a country, region, or town: *they had originally come from someplace in the northwest of Mexico.* ▸adj. **1** lying toward, near, or facing the northwest: *the northwest corner of the square.* ■ (of a wind) blowing from the northwest. **2** of or denoting the northwestern part of a country, region, or town, or its inhabitants: *northwest Europe.* ▸adv. to or toward the northwest: *he turned onto the highway and headed northwest.* —**north·west·er·ly** *adj. & adv.* —**north·west·ern** /-'western/ *adj.*

north·west·er /,nôrTH'westər/ ▸n. a wind or storm blowing from the northwest.

Nor·we·gian /nôr'wējən/ ▸adj. of or relating to Norway or its people or language. ▸n. **1** a native or national of Norway, or a person of Norwegian descent. **2** the North Germanic language of Norway.

nos ▸abbr. numbers.

nose /nōz/ ▸n. **1** the part projecting above the mouth on the face of a person or animal, containing the nostrils and used for breathing and smelling. ■ the sense of smell, esp. a dog's ability to track something by its scent: *a dog with a keen nose.* ■ *fig.* an instinctive talent for detecting something: *he has a nose for a good script.* ■ the aroma of a particular substance, esp. wine. **2** the front end of an aircraft, car, or other vehicle. ■ a projecting part of something: *the nose of the saddle.* **3** a look, esp. out of curiosity: *she wanted a good nose around the house.* ■ *inf.* a police informer. ▸v. **1** [intr.] (of an animal) thrust its nose against or into something, esp. in order to smell it: *the pony nosed at the straw.* ■ [tr.] smell or sniff (something). **2** [intr.] investigate or pry into something: *she's always nosing into my business.* ■ [tr.] detect in such a way. **3** [intr.] (of a vehicle or its driver) make one's way cautiously forward: *he turned left and nosed into an empty parking space.* ■ (of a competitor) manage to achieve a winning or leading position, esp. by a small margin: *they nosed ahead by one point.* ▷Old English *nosu;* related to Dutch *neus,* and more remotely to German *Nase,* Latin *nasus,* and Sanskrit *nāsā.* —**nosed** *adj.* [in comb.] *snub-nosed.* —**nose·less** *adj.*

▸ □ **by a nose** (of a victory) by a very narrow margin. ■ **count noses** count people, typically in order to determine the numbers in a vote. □ **cut off one's nose to spite one's face** hurt oneself in the course of trying to hurt another. □ **give someone a bloody nose** inflict a resounding defeat on someone. □ **keep one's nose clean** *inf.* stay out of trouble. □ **keep one's nose out of** refrain from interfering in (someone else's affairs). □ **not see further than one's** (or **the end of one's**) **nose** be unwilling or fail to consider different possibilities or to foresee the consequences of one's actions. □ **on the nose 1** *inf.* precisely: *at ten on the nose the van pulled up.* **2** *inf.* (of betting) on a horse to win (as opposed to being placed). □ **put someone's nose out of joint** *inf.* upset or annoy someone. □ **speak through one's nose** pronounce words with a nasal twang. □ **turn one's nose up at something** *inf.* show distaste or contempt for something: *he turned his nose up at the job.* □ **under someone's nose** *inf.* directly in front of someone: *he thrust the paper under the inspector's nose.* ■ (of an action) committed openly and boldly, but without someone noticing or noticing in time to prevent it. □ **with**

Pronunciation Key ə *ago,* up; ər *over, fur;* a *hat;* ā *ate;* ä *car;* CH *chin;* e *let;* ē *see;* e(ə)r *air;* i *fit;* ī *by;* i(ə)r *ear;* NG *sing;* ō *go;* ô *law, for;* oi *toy;* o͝o *good;* o͞o *goo;* ou *out;* SH *she;* TH *thin;* TH *then;* (h)w *why;* ZH *vision*

N

one's nose in the air haughtily: *she walked past the cars with her nose in the air.*

nose·bleed /'nōz,blēd/ ▶*n.* an instance of bleeding from the nose. ■ [as *adj.*] *inf.* denoting cheap seating located in an extremely high position in a sports stadium, large theater, or concert hall: *he declined an offer of $2,200 for his game ticket in the nosebleed section.*

nose cone ▶*n.* the cone-shaped nose of a rocket or aircraft.

nose·dive /'nōz,dīv/ ▶*n.* a steep downward plunge by an aircraft. ■ *fig.* a sudden dramatic deterioration: *the player's fortunes took a nosedive.*

no-see-um /nō 'sē ,əm/ ▶*n.* a minute bloodsucking insect, esp. a biting midge.

nose·gay /'nōz,gā/ ▶*n.* a small bunch of flowers, typically one that is sweet-scented.

nose job ▶*n. inf.* an operation involving rhinoplasty or cosmetic surgery on a person's nose.

nose·piece /'nōz,pēs/ ▶*n.* the part of a helmet or headdress that protects a person's nose. ■ another term for **NOSEBAND**. ■ the central part of a pair of glasses that fits over the bridge of the nose.

nosh /näSH/ *inf.* ▶*n.* food: *filling the freezer with all kinds of nosh.* ■ a small item of food: *have plenty of noshes and nibbles conveniently placed.* ■ a light meal; a snack: *in between noshes we explored the city.*
▶*v.* [*intr.*] eat food enthusiastically or greedily: *there are several restaurants, so you can nosh to your heart's content* | [*tr.*] *there I sat, noshing my favorite food.* ■ eat between meals: *today's grazing is different from what we used to call noshing or snacking.*

no-show ▶*n.* a person who has made a reservation, booking, or appointment but neither keeps nor cancels it.

nos·tal·gia /nä'staljə; nə-/ ▶*n.* a sentimental longing or wistful affection for the past, typically for a period or place with happy personal associations: *I was overcome with acute nostalgia for my days in college.* ■ the evocation of these feelings or tendencies, esp. in commercialized form: *an evening of TV nostalgia.* —**nos·tal·gic** /-jik/ *adj.*. —**nos·tal·gi·cal·ly** *adv.* —**nos·tal·gist** /-jist/ *n.*

nos·tril /'nästrəl/ ▶*n.* either of two external openings of the nasal cavity in vertebrates that admit air to the lungs and odors to the olfactory nerves. —**nos·trilled** *adj.* [in *comb.*].

nos·trum /'nästrəm/ ▶*n.* a medicine, esp. one that is not considered effective, prepared by an unqualified person. ■ a pet scheme or favorite remedy, esp. one for bringing about some social or political reform or improvement.

nos·y /'nōzē/ (also **nos·ey**) *inf.* ▶*adj.* (**nos·i·er**, **nos·i·est**) (of a person or their behavior) showing too much curiosity about other people's affairs: *he had to whisper to avoid being overheard by their nosy neighbors.* —**nos·i·ly** /-zəlē/ *adv.* —**nos·i·ness** *n.*

not /nät/ ▶*adv.* **1** (also **n't** joined to a preceding verb) used with an auxiliary verb or "be" to form the negative: *he would not say.* ■ used in some constructions with other verbs: *he has been warned not to touch.* **2** used as a short substitute for a negative clause: *maybe I'll regret it, but I hope not.* **3** used to express the negative of other words: *not a single attempt was made.* ■ used with a quantifier to exclude a person or part of a group: *not all the poems are serious.* ■ less than (used to indicate a surprisingly small quantity): *the brakes went on not ten feet from him.* **4** used in understatements to suggest that the opposite of a following word or phrase is true: *the not too distant future.* ■ *inf.* humorous following and emphatically negating a statement: *that sounds like quality entertainment—not.*
▶*n.* (often **NOT**) *Electr.* a Boolean operator with only one variable that has the value one when the variable is zero and vice versa. ■ (also **not gate**) a circuit that produces an output signal only when there is not a signal on its input.
▶*adj.* (often **Not**) *Art* (of paper) not hot-pressed, and having a slightly textured surface.
▶ □ **not at all 1** used as a polite response to thanks. **2** definitely not: *"You don't mind?" "Not at all."* □ **not but what** *archaic* nevertheless: *not but what the picture has its darker side.* □ **not that** it is not to be inferred that: *I'll never be allowed back—not that I'd want to go back.* □ **not a thing** nothing at all.

no·ta be·ne /'nōtə 'benē/ (abbr.**n.b.** or **N.B.**) ▶*v.* [in *imper.*] *formal* observe carefully or take special notice (used in written text to draw attention to what follows).

no·ta·ble /'nōtəbəl/ ▶*adj.* worthy of attention or notice; remarkable: *the gardens are notable for their collection of magnolias and camellias.*
▶*n.* (usu. **notables**) a famous or important person: *businessmen and local notables.* —**no·ta·bly** *adv.*

no·ta·rize /'nōtə,rīz/ ▶*v.* [*tr.*] have (a document) legalized by a notary.

no·ta·ry /'nōtərē/ (in full **notary public**) ▶*n.* (*pl.* **-ries**) a person authorized to perform certain legal formalities, esp. to draw up or certify contracts, deeds, and other documents for use in other jurisdictions. —**no·tar·i·al** /nō'terēəl/ *adj.*

no·tate /'nō,tāt/ ▶*v.* [*tr.*] write (something, typically music) in notation. —**no·ta·tor** /-,tātər/ *n.*

no·ta·tion /nō'tāSHən/ ▶*n.* **1** a series or system of written symbols used to represent numbers, amounts, or elements in something such as music or mathematics: *algebraic notation.* **2** a note or annotation: *he noticed the notations in the margin.* —**no·ta·tion·al** /-nəl/ *adj.*

notch /näCH/ ▶*n.* **1** an indentation or incision on an edge or surface: *there was a notch in the end of the arrow for the bowstring.* ■ each of a series of holes for the tongue of a buckle: *he tightened his belt an extra notch.* ■ a point or degree in a scale: *her opinion of Nicole dropped a few notches.* **2** a deep, narrow mountain pass.
▶*v.* [*tr.*] **1** make notches in: [as *adj.*] (**notched**) *notched bamboo sticks.* ■ secure or insert by means of notches: *she notched her belt tighter.* **2** score or achieve (something): *she notched her second major championship.* —**notch·er** *n.* —**notch·y** *adj.*

note /nōt/ ▶*n.* **1** a brief record of facts, topics, or thoughts, written down as an aid to memory: *I'll make a note in my diary.* ■ a short comment on or explanation of a word or passage in a book or article; an annotation: *see note iv above.* **2** a short informal letter or written message: *I left her a note explaining where I was going.* ■ an official letter sent from the representative of one government to another. **3** *Brit.* a banknote: *a ten-pound note.* **4** a single tone of definite pitch made by a musical instrument or the human voice: *the last notes of the symphony died away.* ■ a written sign representing the pitch and duration of such a sound. ■ a key of a piano or similar instrument: *black notes | white notes.* ■ a bird's song or call, or a single tone in this: *the tawny owl has a harsh flight note.* **5** a particular quality or tone that reflects or expresses a mood or attitude: *there was a note of scorn in her voice.* ■ any of the basic components of fragrance or flavor: *the fresh note of bergamot.*
▶*v.* [*tr.*] **1** notice or pay particular attention to (something): *noting his mother's unusual gaiety.* ■ remark upon (something), typically in order to draw someone's attention to it: *we noted earlier the difficulties inherent in this strategy.* **2** record (something) in writing: *he noted down her address on a piece of paper.* —**not·ed** *adj.*
▶ □ **hit** (or **strike**) **the right** (or **wrong**) **note** say or do something in exactly the right (or wrong) way. □ **of note 1** worth paying attention to: *many of his comments are worthy of note.* **2** important; distinguished: *Roman historians of note include Livy, Tacitus, and Sallust.* □ **strike a false note** appear insincere or inappropriate: *she greeted him gushingly, and that struck a false note.* □ **strike** (or **sound**) **a note of** express (a particular feeling or view) about something: *he sounded a note of caution about the trend toward health foods.* □ **take note** pay attention: *employers should take note of the needs of disabled people.*

note·book /'nōt,boŏk/ ▶*n.* a small book with blank or ruled pages for writing notes in. ■ a portable computer that is smaller than a laptop.

note·pad /'nōt,pad/ ▶*n.* a pad of blank or ruled pages for writing notes on. ■ (also **notepad computer**) a pocket-sized personal computer that has a stylus with which the user writes on the screen to input text.

note-per·fect ▶*adj.* (of music) performed with technical perfection: *they sounded like the other time I saw them: not incredibly exciting, but note-perfect.*

note·wor·thy /'nōt,wərTHē/ ▶*adj.* interesting, significant, or unusual: *it is noteworthy that no one at the bank has accepted responsibility for the failure.* —**note·wor·thi·ness** *n.*

noth·ing /'nəTHiNG/ ▶*pron.* not anything; no single thing: *I said nothing.* ■ something of no importance or concern: *"What are you laughing at?" "Oh, nothing, sir."* | [as *n.*] *no longer could we be treated as nothings.* ■ (in calculations) no amount; zero.
▶*adv.* not at all: *she cares nothing for others.* ■ *inf.* used to contradict something emphatically: *"This is a surprise." "Surprise nothing."*
▶ □ **for nothing 1** at no cost; without payment: *working for nothing.* **2** to no purpose: *he died anyway; so it had all been for nothing.* □ **no nothing** *inf.* (concluding a list of negatives) nothing at all: *how could you solve it with no clues, no witnesses, no nothing?* □ **not for nothing** for a very good reason: *not for nothing have I got a brother-in-law who cooks professionally.* □ **nothing doing** *inf.* **1** there is no prospect of success or agreement: *He wants to marry her. Nothing doing!* **2** nothing is happening: *there's nothing doing, and I've been waiting for weeks.* □ **nothing** (or **nothing else**) **for it** *Brit.* no alternative: *there was nothing for it but to follow.* □ **nothing less than** used to emphasize how extreme something is: *it was nothing less than sexual harassment.* □ **nothing much** not a great amount; nothing of importance. □ **there is nothing to it** there is no difficulty involved.

□ **sweet nothings** words of affection exchanged by lovers: *whispering sweet nothings in her ear.* □ **think nothing of it** do not apologize or feel bound to show gratitude (used as a polite response). □ **you ain't seen nothing yet** *inf.* used to indicate that although something may be considered extreme or impressive, there is something even more extreme or impressive in store: *if you think that was muddy, you ain't seen nothing yet.*

noth·ing·ness /'nəTHiNGnis/ ▸*n.* the absence or cessation of life or existence: *the fear of the total nothingness of death.* ■ worthlessness; insignificance; unimportance: *the nothingness of it all overwhelmed him.*

no·tice /'nōtis/ ▸*n.* **1** attention; observation: *their silence did not escape my notice.* **2** notification or warning of something, esp. to allow preparations to be made: *interest rates are subject to fluctuation without notice.* ■ a formal declaration of one's intention to end an agreement, typically one concerning employment or tenancy, at a specified time: *she handed in her notice.* **3** a displayed sheet or placard giving news or information: *the jobs were advertised in a notice posted in the common room.* ■ a small advertisement or announcement in a newspaper or magazine: *an obituary notice.* ■ (usu. **notices**) a short published review or comment about a new film, play, or book: *she had good notices in her first film.*
▸*v.* [*tr.*] become aware of: *he noticed the youths behaving suspiciously.* ■ (usu. **be noticed**) treat (someone) with some degree of attention or recognition: *it was only last year that the singer really began to be noticed.*
▸ □ **at short** (or **a moment's**) **notice** with little warning or time for preparation: *tours may be canceled at short notice.* □ **put someone on notice** (or **serve notice**) warn someone of something about or likely to occur, esp. in a formal or threatening manner: *we're going to put foreign governments on notice that we want a change of trade policy.* □ **take no notice** pay no attention to someone or something. □ **take notice** pay attention; show signs of interest.

no·tice·a·ble /'nōtisəbəl/ ▸*adj.* easily seen or noticed; clear or apparent: *a noticeable increase in staff motivation.* ■ noteworthy: *a noticeable new phenomenon.* —**no·tice·a·bly** /-blē/ *adv.*

no·ti·fi·a·ble /ˌnōtə'fīəbəl/ ▸*adj.* denoting something, typically a serious infectious disease, that must be reported to the appropriate authorities.

no·ti·fy /'nōtəˌfī/ ▸*v.* (**-fies, -fied**) [*tr.*] inform (someone) of something, typically in a formal or official manner: *you will be notified of our decision as soon as possible.* —**no·ti·fi·ca·tion** /ˌnōtəfi'kāSHən/ *n.*

no·tion /'nōSHən/ ▸*n.* **1** a conception of or belief about something: *children have different notions about the roles of their parents.* ■ a vague awareness or understanding of the nature of something: *I had no notion of what her words meant.* **2** an impulse or desire, esp. one of a whimsical kind: *she had a notion to call her friend at work.* **3** (**notions**) items used in sewing, such as buttons, pins, and hooks.

no·tion·al /'nōSHənəl/ ▸*adj.* **1** existing only in theory or as a suggestion or idea: *notional budgets for hospital and community health services.* ■ existing only in the imagination: *Lizzie seemed to vanish into thin air, as if her presence were merely notional.* **2** *Linguistics* denoting or relating to an approach to grammar that is dependent on the definition of terminology (e.g., "a verb is an action word") as opposed to identification of structures and processes. **3** (in language teaching) denoting or relating to a syllabus that aims to develop communicative competence. —**no·tion·al·ly** *adv.*

no·to·chord /'nōtəˌkôrd/ ▸*n.* *Zool.* a cartilaginous skeletal rod supporting the body in all embryonic and some adult chordate animals.

no·to·ri·ous /nə'tôrēəs; nō-/ ▸*adj.* famous or well known, typically for some bad quality or deed: *Los Angeles is notorious for its smog* | *he was a notorious womanizer.* —**no·to·ri·e·ty** /ˌnōtə'rīətē/ *n.* —**no·to·ri·ous·ly** *adv.*

not·with·stand·ing /ˌnätwiTH'standiNG; -wiTH-/ ▸*prep.* in spite of: *notwithstanding the evidence, the consensus is that the jury will not reach a verdict* | *this small contretemps notwithstanding, they both had a good time.*
▸*adv.* nevertheless; in spite of this: *she tells us she is an intellectual; notwithstanding, she faces the future as unprovided for as a beauty queen.*
▸*conj.* although; in spite of the fact that: *notwithstanding that the hall was packed with bullies, our champion played on steadily and patiently.*

nou·gat /'nōōgit/ ▸*n.* a candy made from sugar or honey, nuts, and egg white.

nought ▸*n. & pron.* variant spelling of **NAUGHT**.

noun /noun/ ▸*n.* *Gram.* a word (other than a pronoun) used to identify any of a class of people, places, or things (**common noun**), or to name a particular one of these (**proper noun**) . ▷late Middle English: from Anglo-Norman French, from Latin *nomen* 'name.' —**noun·al** /'nounəl/ *adj.*

nour·ish /'nəriSH; 'nə-riSH/ ▸*v.* [*tr.*] **1** provide with the food or other substances necessary for growth, health, and good condition: *I was doing everything I could to nourish and protect the baby* | *fig. spiritual resources that nourished her in her darkest hours.* **2** keep (a feeling or belief) in one's mind, typically for a long time: *he has long nourished an ambition to bring the show to Broadway.* —**nour·ish·er** *n.*

nour·ish·ing /'nəriSHiNG; 'nə-ri-/ ▸*adj.* (of food) containing substances necessary for growth, health, and good condition: *a simple but nourishing meal.* —**nour·ish·ing·ly** *adv.*

nour·ish·ment /'nəriSHmənt; 'nə-riSH-/ ▸*n.* the substances necessary for growth, health, and good condition: *tubers from which plants obtain nourishment.* ■ food: *they often go days with little or no nourishment.* ■ the action of nourishing someone or something: *they suck out the sap and eliminate from it a sweet liquid for the nourishment of their young.*

nou·veau riche /ˌnōōvō 'rēSH/ ▸*n.* [treated as *pl.*] (usu. **the nouveau riche**) people who have recently acquired wealth, typically those perceived as ostentatious or lacking in good taste.
▸*adj.* of, relating to, or characteristic of such people: *nouveau-riche social climbers.*

nou·velle cui·sine /nōō'vel kwi'zēn/ ▸*n.* a modern style of cooking that avoids rich, heavy foods and emphasizes the freshness of the ingredients and the presentation of the dishes.

nou·velle vague /nōō'vel ˌväg/ ▸*n.* a grouping of French movie directors in the late 1950s and 1960s who reacted against established French cinema and sought to make more innovative films. ▷French, literally 'new wave.'

Nov. ▸*abbr.* November.

no·va /'nōvə/ ▸*n.* (*pl.* **-vae** /-vē; -ˌvī/ or **-vas**) *Astron.* a star showing a sudden large increase in brightness and then slowly returning to its original state over a few months. See also **SUPERNOVA**.

nov·el¹ /'nävəl/ ▸*n.* a fictitious prose narrative of book length, typically representing character and action with some degree of realism: *the novels of Jane Austen.* ■ a book containing such a narrative: *she was reading a paperback novel.* ■ (**the novel**) the literary genre represented or exemplified by such works: *the novel is the most adaptable of all literary forms.* ▷mid 16th cent.: from Italian *novella (storia)* 'new (story),' feminine of *novello* 'new,' from Latin *novellus,* from *novus* 'new.'

nov·el² ▸*adj.* new or unusual in an interesting way: *he hit on a novel idea to solve his financial problems.* —**nov·el·ly** *adv.*

nov·el·ist /'nävəlist/ ▸*n.* a writer of novels. —**nov·el·is·tic** /ˌnävə'listik/ *adj.*

no·vel·la /nō'velə/ ▸*n.* a short novel or long short story.

nov·el·ty /'nävəltē/ ▸*n.* (*pl.* **-ties**) **1** the quality of being new, original, or unusual: *the novelty of being a married woman wore off.* ■ a new or unfamiliar thing or experience: *in 1914 air travel was still a novelty.* ■ [as *adj.*] denoting something intended to be amusing as a result of its new or unusual quality: *a novelty teapot.* **2** a small and inexpensive toy or ornament: *he bought chocolate novelties to decorate the Christmas tree.*

No·vem·ber /nō'vembər; nə-/ ▸*n.* **1** the eleventh month of the year, in the northern hemisphere usually considered the last month of autumn. **2** a code word representing the letter N, used in radio communication.

no·ve·na /nō'vēnə/ ▸*n.* (in the Roman Catholic Church) a form of worship consisting of special prayers or services on nine successive days.

nov·ice /'nävəs/ ▸*n.* a person new to or inexperienced in a field or situation: *he was a complete novice in foreign affairs.* ■ a person who has entered a religious order and is under probation, before taking vows. ■ an animal, esp. a racehorse, that has not yet won a major prize or reached a level of performance to qualify for important events.

no·vi·ti·ate /nō'viSH(ē)ət; nə-/ ▸*n.* the period or state of being a novice, esp. in a religious order. ■ a place housing religious novices. ■ a novice, esp. in a religious order.

no·vo·caine /'nōvəˌkān/ (also *trademark* **No·vo·cain**) ▸*n.* another term for **PROCAINE**.

NOW ▸*abbr.* National Organization for Women.

now /nou/ ▸*adv.* **1** at the present time or moment: *where are you living now?* ■ at the time directly following the present moment; immediately: *if we leave now, we can be home by ten.* ■ under the present circumstances; as a result of something that has recently happened: *it is now clear that we should not pursue this policy.* ■ on this further occasion, typically as the latest in a series of annoying situations or events: *what do you want now?* ■ used to emphasize a particular length of time: *they've*

N

been married four years now. ■ (in a narrative or account of past events) at the time spoken of or referred to: *it had happened three times now.* **2** used, esp. in conversation, to draw attention to a particular statement or point in a narrative: *now, my first impulse was to run away.* **3** used in or as a request, instruction, or question, typically to give a slight emphasis to one's words: *now, if you'll excuse me?* ■ used when pausing or considering one's next words: *let me see now; oh yes, I remember.* **4** used at the end of an ironic question echoing a previous statement: *"Mom says for you to give me some of your stamps." "Does she now?"*

▶*conj.* as a consequence of the fact: *they spent a lot of time together now that he had retired.*

▶*adj. inf.* fashionable; up to date: *seventies disco dancing—very now.*

▶ □ **for now** until a later time: *that's all the news there is for now.* □ **now and again** (or **then**) from time to time. □ **now now** used as an expression of mild remonstrance: *now now, that's not the way to behave.* □ **now ——, now ——** at one moment ——, at the next ——: *a wind whipped about the house, now this way, now that.* □ **now or never** used to convey urgency: *it was now or never—I had to move fast.* □ **now then** used to get someone's attention or to invite a response: *now then, who's for a coffee?* □ **now you're talking** used to express one's enthusiastic agreement with or approval of a statement or suggestion: *The Beatles! Now you're talking.*

now·a·days /ˈnouə,dāz/ ▶*adv.* at the present time, in contrast with the past: *the sort of clothes worn by almost all young people nowadays.*

no·where /ˈnō,(h)we(ə)r/ ▶*adv.* not in or to any place; not anywhere: *plants and animals found nowhere else in the world.*

▶*pron.* **1** no place: *there was nowhere for her to sit.* **2** a place that is remote, uninteresting, or nondescript: *a stretch of road between nowhere and nowhere* | [as *n.*] *the town is a particularly American nowhere.*

▶*adj. inf.* having no prospect of progress or success: *she's involved in a nowhere affair with a married executive.*

▶ □ **from** (or **out of**) **nowhere** appearing or happening suddenly and unexpectedly: *he materialized a taxi out of nowhere.* □ **get** (or **go**) **nowhere** make no progress: *I'm getting nowhere—maybe I should give up* | *the project was going nowhere fast.* □ **get someone nowhere** be of no use or benefit to someone: *being angry would get her nowhere.* □ **nowhere near** not nearly: *he's nowhere near as popular as he used to be.* □ **a road to nowhere** a situation or course of action offering no prospects of progress or advancement.

no-win ▶*adj.* of or denoting a situation in which success or a favorable outcome is impossible.

nox·ious /ˈnäkSHəs/ ▶*adj.* harmful, poisonous, or very unpleasant: *they were overcome by the noxious fumes.* —**nox·ious·ly** *adv.* —**nox·ious·ness** *n.*

noz·zle /ˈnäzəl/ ▶*n.* a cylindrical or round spout at the end of a pipe, hose, or tube, used to control a jet of gas or liquid.

NP ▶*abbr.* notary public.

Np ▶*symb.* the chemical element neptunium.

NRA ▶*abbr.* ■ National Rifle Association.

NRC ▶*abbr.* ■ National Research Council. ■ National Response Center. ■ Nuclear Regulatory Commission.

NS ▶*abbr.* ■ New Style. ■ Nova Scotia (in official postal use).

ns ▶*abbr.* nanosecond.

NSF ▶*abbr.* National Science Foundation.

NT ▶*abbr.* ■ New Testament. ■ *Bridge* no-trump.

n't ▶*contr.* of not, used with auxiliary verbs (e.g., *can't, won't, didn't,* and *isn't*).

nth /enTH/ ▶*adj. Math.* denoting an unspecified member of a series of numbers or enumerated items: *systematic sampling by taking every nth name from the list.* ■ (in general use) denoting an unspecified item or instance in a series, typically the last or latest in a long series: *for the nth time that day they were forced to relate the whole story.*

▶ □ **to the nth degree** to the utmost: *the gullibility of the electorate was tested to the nth degree by such promises.*

nu /n(y)ōō/ ▶*n.* the thirteenth letter of the Greek alphabet (Ν, ν), transliterated as 'n.'

▶*symb.* (ν) frequency.

nu·ance /ˈn(y)ōō,äns/ ▶*n.* a subtle difference in or shade of meaning, expression, or sound: *the nuances of facial expression and body language.*

▶*v.* [*tr.*] (usu. **be nuanced**) give nuances to: *the effect of the music is nuanced by the social situation of listeners.* ▷late 18th cent.: from French, 'shade, subtlety,' from *nuer* 'to shade,' based on Latin *nubes* 'cloud.'

nub /nəb/ ▶*n.* **1** (**the nub**) the crux or central point of a matter: *the nub of the problem lies elsewhere.* **2** a small lump or protuberance: *he pressed*

down on the two nubs on top of the phone. ■ a small chunk or nugget of metal or rock: *a nub of gold.* —**nub·by** *adj.*

nu·bile /ˈn(y)ōō,bīl; -bəl/ ▶*adj.* (of a girl or young woman) sexually mature; suitable for marriage. ■ (of a girl or young woman) sexually attractive: *he employed a procession of nubile young secretaries.* —**nu·bil·i·ty** /n(y)ōōˈbilitē/ *n.*

nu·cle·ar /ˈn(y)ōōklēər; -klī(ə)r/ ▶*adj.* **1** of or relating to the nucleus of an atom. ■ denoting, relating to, or powered by the energy released in nuclear fission or fusion: *nuclear energy.* ■ denoting, possessing, or involving weapons using this energy: *a nuclear bomb.* **2** *Biol.* of or relating to the nucleus of a cell: *nuclear DNA.*

nu·cle·ar fam·i·ly ▶*n.* a couple and their dependent children, regarded as a basic social unit.

nu·cle·ar fis·sion ▶*n.* a nuclear reaction in which a heavy nucleus splits spontaneously or on impact with another particle, with the release of energy.

nu·cle·ar fu·sion ▶*n.* a nuclear reaction in which atomic nuclei of low atomic number fuse to form a heavier nucleus with the release of energy.

nu·cle·ar mag·net·ic res·o·nance (abbr.: **NMR**) ▶*n.* the absorption of electromagnetic radiation by a nucleus having a magnetic moment when in an external magnetic field, used mainly as an analytical technique and in diagnostic body imaging.

nu·cle·ar med·i·cine ▶*n.* the branch of medicine that deals with the use of radioactive substances in research, diagnosis, and treatment.

nu·cle·ar phys·ics ▶*pl. n.* [treated as *sing.*] the physics of atomic nuclei and their interactions, esp. in the generation of nuclear energy.

nu·cle·ar pow·er ▶*n.* **1** electric or motive power generated by a nuclear reactor. **2** a country that has nuclear weapons. —**nu·cle·ar-pow·ered** *adj.*

nu·cle·ar re·ac·tor ▶*n.* see REACTOR.

nu·cle·ar waste ▶*n.* radioactive waste material, for example from the use or reprocessing of nuclear fuel.

nu·cle·ate ▶*adj.* /ˈn(y)ōōklēət; -,āt/ *chiefly Biol.* having a nucleus.

▶*v.* /ˈn(y)ōōklē,āt/ [*intr.*] [usu. as *adj.*] (**nucleated**) form a nucleus. ■ form around a central area: *a nucleated village.* —**nu·cle·a·tion** /,n(y)ōōklē-ˈāsHən/ *n.*

nu·cle·i /ˈn(y)ōōklē,ī/ ▶ plural form of NUCLEUS.

nu·cle·ic ac·id /n(y)ōōˈklē-ik/ ▶*n. Biochem.* a complex organic substance present in living cells, esp. DNA or RNA, whose molecules consist of many nucleotides linked in a long chain.

nu·cle·o·lus /n(y)ōōˈklēələs/ ▶*n.* (*pl.* **-li** /-,lī; -,lē/) *Biol.* a small dense spherical structure in the nucleus of a cell during interphase. —**nu·cle·o·lar** /-lər/ *adj.*

nu·cle·on /ˈn(y)ōōklē,än/ ▶*n. Physics* a proton or neutron.

nu·cle·o·pro·tein /,n(y)ōōklē-ōˈprō,tēn/ ▶*n. Biochem.* a complex consisting of a nucleic acid bonded to a protein.

nu·cle·o·side /ˈn(y)ōōklēə,sīd/ ▶*n. Biochem.* a compound (e.g., adenosine) commonly found in DNA or RNA, consisting of a purine or pyrimidine base linked to a sugar.

nu·cle·o·tide /ˈn(y)ōōklēə,tīd/ ▶*n. Biochem.* a compound consisting of a nucleoside linked to a phosphate group. Nucleotides form the basic structural unit of nucleic acids such as DNA.

nu·cle·us /ˈn(y)ōōklēəs/ ▶*n.* (*pl.* **-cle·i** /-klē,ī/) the central and most important part of an object, movement, or group, forming the basis for its activity and growth: *the nucleus of a film-producing industry.* ■ *Physics* the positively charged central core of an atom, containing most of its mass. ■ *Biol.* a dense organelle present in most eukaryotic cells, typically a single rounded structure bounded by a double membrane, containing the genetic material. ■ *Astron.* the solid part of the head of a comet. ■ *Anat.* a discrete mass of gray matter in the central nervous system.

nu·clide /ˈn(y)ōō,klīd/ ▶*n. Physics* a distinct kind of atom or nucleus characterized by a specific number of protons and neutrons. —**nu·clid·ic** /n(y)ōōˈklidik/ *adj.*

nude /n(y)ōōd/ ▶*adj.* wearing no clothes; naked: *a painting of a nude model.* ■ depicting or performed by naked people: *he was asked to act in a frank nude scene.* ■ (esp. of hosiery) flesh-colored: *black shoes with beige or nude stockings.*

▶*n.* a naked human figure, typically as the subject of a painting, sculpture, or photograph: *a study of a kneeling nude.* ■ (**the nude**) the representation of the naked human figure as a genre in art: *the nude was regarded as the ultimate test of artistic skill.* ■ flesh color.

▶ □ **in the nude** in an unclothed state: *I like to swim in the nude.*

nudge /nəj/ ▶*v.* [*tr.*] prod (someone) gently, typically with one's elbow, in order to draw their attention to something: *people were nudging each other and pointing at me.* ■ touch or push (something) gently or gradually: *the canoe nudged a bank of reeds.* ■ *fig.* coax or gently encourage (someone) to do something: *we have to nudge the politicians in the right direction.* ■ approach (an age, figure, or level) very closely: *both men were nudging fifty.*

▶ *n.* a light touch or push: *he gave her shoulder a nudge* | *fig. she appreciated the nudge to her memory.* —**nudg·er** *n.*

nud·ist /'n(y) o͞odist/ ▶ *n.* a person who engages in the practice of going naked wherever possible: *a mission to encourage more public places to allow nudists.* —**nud·ism** /-,dizəm/ *n.*

nu·di·ty /'n(y) o͞odətē/ ▶ *n.* the state or fact of being naked: *scenes of full frontal nudity.*

nug·get /'nəgət/ ▶ *n.* a small lump of gold or other precious metal found ready-formed in the earth. ■ a small chunk or lump of another substance: *tiny nuggets of chicken and shrimp.* ■ a valuable idea or fact: *nuggets of information.* —**nug·get·y** *adj.*

nui·sance /'n(y) o͞osəns/ ▶ *n.* a person, thing, or circumstance causing inconvenience or annoyance: *an unreasonable landlord could become a nuisance.* ■ *Law* an unlawful interference with the use and enjoyment of a person's land. ■ *Law* see **PUBLIC NUISANCE.**

nuke /n(y) o͞ok/ *inf.* ▶ *n.* a nuclear weapon. ■ a nuclear power station. ■ a nuclear-powered vessel.

▶ *v.* [*tr.*] attack or destroy with nuclear weapons. ■ destroy; get rid of: *I fertilized the lawn and nuked the weeds.* ■ cook or heat up (food) in a microwave oven: *I nuked a quick burger.*

null /nəl/ ▶ *adj.* **1** having no legal or binding force; invalid: *the establishment of a new interim government was declared null and void.* **2** having or associated with the value zero. ■ *Math.* (of a set or matrix) having no elements, or only zeros as elements. ■ lacking distinctive qualities; having no positive substance or content: *his curiously null life.*

▶ *n. poetic/lit.* a zero. ■ a dummy letter in a cipher. ■ *Electr.* a condition of no signal. ■ a direction in which no electromagnetic radiation is detected or emitted.

nul·li·fy /'nələ,fī/ ▶ *v.* (**-fies, -fied**) [*tr.*] make legally null and void; invalidate: *judges were unwilling to nullify government decisions.* ■ make of no use or value; cancel out: *insulin can block the release of the hormone and thereby nullify the effects of training.* —**nul·li·fi·ca·tion** /,nələfə'kāSHən/ *n.* —**nul·li·fi·er** *n.*

numb /nəm/ ▶ *adj.* deprived of the power of sensation: *my feet were numb with cold* | *fig. the tragic events left us shocked and numb.*

▶ *v.* [*tr.*] deprive of feeling or responsiveness: *the cold had numbed her senses.* ■ cause (a sensation) to be felt less intensely; deaden: *vodka might numb the pain in my hand.* —**numb·ly** *adv.* —**numb·ness** *n.*

num·ber /'nəmbər/ ▶ *n.* **1** an arithmetical value, expressed by a word, symbol, or figure, representing a particular quantity and used in counting and making calculations and for showing order in a series or for identification: *she dialed the number carefully.* **2** a quantity or amount: *the exhibition attracted vast numbers of visitors.* ■ (**a number of**) several: *we have discussed the matter on a number of occasions.* ■ a group or company of people: *there were some distinguished names among our number.* **3** a single issue of a magazine: *the October number of "Travel."* ■ a song, dance, piece of music, etc., esp. one of several in a performance: *they go from one melodious number to another.* ■ *inf.* a thing, typically an item of clothing, of a particular type, regarded with approval or admiration: *Yvonne was wearing a little black number.* **4** *Gram.* a distinction of word form denoting reference to one person or thing or to more than one. See also **SINGULAR** (sense 2), **PLURAL.** ■ a particular form so classified.

▶ *v.* [*tr.*] **1** amount to (a specified figure or quantity); comprise: *the demonstrators numbered more than 5,000.* ■ include or classify as a member of a group: *the orchestra numbers Brahms among its past conductors.* **2** (often **be numbered**) mark with a number or assign a number to, typically to indicate position in a series: *each document was numbered consecutively.* ■ count: *strategies like ours can be numbered on the fingers of one hand.* ■ assess or estimate the size or quantity of (something) to be a specified figure: *he numbers the fleet at a thousand.*

▶ □ **any number of** any particular whole quantity of: *the game can involve any number of players.* ■ a large and unlimited quantity or amount of: *the results can be read any number of ways.* □ **by numbers** following simple instructions identified by numbers or as if identified: *painting by numbers.* □ **by the numbers** following standard operating procedure. □ **someone's/something's days are numbered** someone or something will not survive or remain in a position of power or advantage for much longer: *my days as director were numbered.* □ **do a number on** *inf.* treat someone badly, typically by deceiving, humiliating, or criticizing

them in a calculated and thorough way. □ **have someone's number** *inf.* understand a person's real motives or character and thereby gain some advantage. □ **have someone's number on it** *inf.* (of a bomb, bullet, or other missile) destined to find a specified person as its target. □ **someone's number is up** *inf.* the time has come when someone is doomed to die or suffer some other disaster or setback. □ **without number** too many to count: *they forgot the message times without number.*

num·ber crunch·er (also **num·ber-crunch·er**) ▶ *n. inf.* **1** a computer or software capable of performing rapid calculations with large amounts of data. **2** *often derog.* a statistician, accountant, or other person whose job involves dealing with large amounts of numerical data. —**num·ber crunch·ing** *n.*

num·ber one *inf.* ▶ *n.* **1** oneself: *you must look after number one.* **2** a person or thing that is the best or the most important in an activity or area: *businesses that were number one in their markets.* **3** used euphemistically to refer to urine, esp. in reference to children.

▶ *adj.* most important or prevalent: *a number-one priority.* ■ best selling: *a number-one album.*

numb·skull /'nəm,skəl/ (also **num·skull**) ▶ *n. inf.* a stupid or foolish person.

nu·mer·al /'n(y) o͞om(ə)rəl/ ▶ *n.* a figure, symbol, or group of these denoting a number. ■ a word expressing a number.

▶ *adj.* of or denoting a number.

nu·mer·ate /'n(y) o͞om(ə)rət/ ▶ *adj.* having a good basic knowledge of arithmetic; able to understand and work with numbers. —**nu·mer·a·cy** /-əsē/ *adj.*

nu·mer·a·tion /,n(y) o͞omə'rāSHən/ ▶ *n.* the action or process of calculating or assigning a number to something. ■ a method or process of numbering, counting, or computing.

nu·mer·a·tor /'n(y) o͞omə,rātər/ ▶ *n.* the number above the line in a common fraction showing how many of the parts indicated by the denominator are taken, for example, 2 in $2/3$.

nu·mer·i·cal /n(y) o͞o'merikəl/ (also **nu·mer·ic**) ▶ *adj.* of, relating to, or expressed as a number or numbers: *the lists are in numerical order.* —**nu·mer·i·cal·ly** *adv.*

nu·mer·ol·o·gy /,n(y) o͞omə'räləjē/ ▶ *n.* the branch of knowledge that deals with the occult significance of numbers. —**nu·mer·o·log·i·cal** /-rə'läjikəl/ *adj.* —**nu·mer·ol·o·gist** /-jist/ *n.*

nu·mer·ous /'n(y) o͞om(ə)rəs/ ▶ *adj.* great in number; many: *he has attended numerous meetings and social events.* ■ consisting of many members: *the orchestra and chorus were numerous.* —**nu·mer·ous·ly** *adv.* —**nu·mer·ous·ness** *n.*

nu·mi·nous /'n(y) o͞omənəs/ ▶ *adj.* having a strong religious or spiritual quality; indicating or suggesting the presence of a divinity: *the strange, numinous beauty of this ancient landmark.*

nu·mis·mat·ic /,n(y) o͞oməz'matik; -məs-/ ▶ *adj.* of, relating to, or consisting of coins, paper currency, and medals. —**nu·mis·mat·i·cal·ly** /-ik(ə)lē/ *adv.*

nu·mis·mat·ics /,n(y) o͞oməz'matiks; -məs-/ ▶ *pl. n.* [usu. treated as *sing.*] the study or collection of coins, paper currency, and medals. —**nu·mis·ma·tist** /n(y) o͞o'mizmətist; -'mis-/ *n.*

nun /nən/ ▶ *n.* a member of a religious community of women, esp. a cloistered one, living under vows of poverty, chastity, and obedience. —**nun·like** /-,līk/ *adj.* —**nun·nish** *adj.*

nun·ci·o /'nənsē,ō; 'no͞on-/ ▶ *n.* (*pl.* **-os**) (in the Roman Catholic Church) a papal ambassador to a foreign court or government.

nun·ner·y /'nən(ə)rē/ ▶ *n.* (*pl.* **-ner·ies**) a building or group of buildings in which nuns live as a religious community; a convent.

nup·tial /'nəpSHəl; -CHəl/ ▶ *adj.* of or relating to marriage or weddings: *moments of nuptial bliss.* ■ *Zool.* denoting the characteristic breeding behavior, coloration, or structures of some animals: *nuptial plumage.*

▶ *n.* (usu. **nuptials**) a wedding: *the forthcoming nuptials between Richard and Jocelyn.*

nurse /nərs/ ▶ *n.* a person trained to care for the sick or infirm, esp. in a hospital. ■ *dated* a person employed or trained to take charge of young children: *her mother's old nurse.* ■ *archaic* a wet nurse. ■ [often as *adj.*] *Forestry* a tree or crop planted as a shelter to others. ■ *Entomol.* a worker bee, ant, or other social insect, caring for a young brood.

▶ *v.* [*tr.*] **1** give medical and other attention to (a sick person): *she nursed the girl through a dangerous illness.* ■ [*intr.*] care for the sick and infirm, esp. as a profession: *she nursed at the hospital for thirty years.* ■ try to cure or alleviate (an injury, injured part, or illness) by treating it carefully and protectively: *he has been nursing a cold* | *fig. he nursed his hurt pride.* ■ hold closely and carefully or caressingly: *he nursed his small case on his lap.* ■ hold (a cup or glass) in one's hands, drinking from it occasionally: *I nursed a double brandy.* ■ harbor (a belief or feeling), esp. for a long time: *I still nurse anger and resentment.* ■ *Billiards* try to play strokes that keep (the balls) close together. **2** feed (a baby) at the breast: *lionesses who were nursing their own cubs.* ■ [*intr.*] be fed at the breast: *the baby wiggled as he nursed.* ▷late Middle English: contraction of earlier *nourice*, from Old French, from late Latin *nutricia*, feminine of Latin *nutricius* '(person) that nourishes,' from *nutrix, nutric-* 'nurse,' from *nutrire* 'nourish.' The verb was originally a contraction of *nourish*, altered under the influence of the noun.

nurse·maid /ˈnərsˌmād/ ▶*n.* a woman or girl employed to look after a young child or children.
▶*v.* [*tr.*] look after or be overprotective toward: *I haven't got time to nursemaid you through these blips.*

nurse prac·ti·tion·er (also **nurse-prac·ti·tion·er**) ▶*n.* a registered nurse who has been specially trained to treat routine or minor ailments, and to perform many tasks ordinarily performed by a doctor.

nurs·er·y /ˈnərs(ə)rē/ ▶*n.* (*pl.* **-er·ies**) a room in a house for the special use of young children. ■ a place where young children are cared for during the working day; a nursery school. ■ a place where young plants and trees are grown for sale or for planting elsewhere. ■ a place or natural habitat that breeds or supports animals: *this estuary provides a vast nursery for fish.* ■ an institution or environment in which certain types of people or qualities are fostered or bred: *that nursery of traitors.*

nurs·er·y·man /ˈnərs(ə)rēmən/ ▶*n.* (*pl.* **-men**) a worker in or owner of a plant or tree nursery.

nurs·er·y rhyme ▶*n.* a simple traditional song or poem for children.

nurs·er·y school ▶*n.* a school for young children, mainly between the ages of three and five.

nurs·ing /ˈnərsiNG/ ▶*n.* the profession or practice of providing care for the sick and infirm.

nur·ture /ˈnərCHər/ ▶*v.* [*tr.*] care for and encourage the growth or development of: *fig. my father nurtured my love of art.* ■ cherish (a hope, belief, or ambition): *for a long time she had nurtured the dream of buying a shop.*
▶*n.* the process of caring for and encouraging the growth or development of someone or something: *the nurture of ethics and integrity.* ■ upbringing, education, and environment, contrasted with inborn characteristics as an influence on or determinant of personality. Often contrasted with NATURE. —**nur·tur·er** *n.*

nut /nət/ ▶*n.* **1** a fruit consisting of a hard or tough shell around an edible kernel. ■ the hard kernel of such a fruit. ■ *inf.* a person's head. ■ (usu. **nuts**) *vulgar slang* testicles. **2** a small flat piece of metal or other material, typically square or hexagonal, with a threaded hole through it for screwing onto a bolt as a fastener. ■ *Mus.* the part at the lower end of the bow of a violin or similar instrument, with a screw for adjusting tension. **3** *inf.* a crazy or eccentric person. ■ a person who is excessively interested in or enthusiastic about a specified thing: *a football nut.* **4** the fixed ridge on the neck of a stringed instrument over which the strings pass. —**nut·like** /-ˌlīk/ *adj.*
▶ □ **nuts and bolts** *inf.* the basic practical details: *the nuts and bolts of public policy.* □ **a tough** (or **hard**) **nut to crack** *inf.* a difficult problem or an opponent hard to beat.

nut case (also **nut·case**) ▶*n. inf.* a crazy or foolish person.

nut·crack·er /ˈnətˌkrakər/ ▶*n.* a device for cracking nuts.

nut·hatch /ˈnətˌhaCH/ ▶*n.* a small songbird (genus *Sitta*, family Sittidae) with a long strong bill, a stiffened square-cut tail, and the habit of climbing down tree trunks head first.

nut·meg /ˈnətˌmeg/ ▶*n.* **1** the hard, aromatic, almost spherical seed of a tropical tree. ■ this seed grated and used as a spice. **2** the evergreen tree (*Myristica fragrans*, family Myristicaceae) that bears these seeds, native to the Moluccas.

nu·tra·ceu·ti·cal /ˌn(y)ōōtrəˈsōōtikəl/ ▶*n.* a food containing health-giving additives and having medicinal benefit. ▷1990s: from Latin *nutrire* 'nourish' + *pharmaceutical.*

nu·tri·a /ˈn(y)ōōtrēə/ ▶*n.* a large semiaquatic beaverlike rodent (*Myocastor coypus*, family Myocastoridae) native to South America. It is kept in captivity for its fur and has become naturalized in many other areas. ■ the pelt of this animal.

nu·tri·ent /ˈn(y)ōōtrēənt/ ▶*n.* a substance that provides nourishment essential for growth and the maintenance of life: *fish is a source of many important nutrients, including protein, vitamins, and minerals.*

nu·tri·tion /n(y)ōōˈtriSHən/ ▶*n.* the process of providing or obtaining the food necessary for health and growth: *a guide to good nutrition.* ■ food; nourishment: *a feeding tube gives her nutrition and water.* ■ the branch of science that deals with nutrients and nutrition, particularly in humans: *she took a short course in nutrition.* —**nu·tri·tion·al** /-SHənl/ *adj.* —**nu·tri·tion·al·ly** /-SHənl-ē/ *adv.*

nu·tri·tion·ist /n(y)ōōˈtriSH(ə)nist/ ▶*n.* a person who studies or is an expert in nutrition.

nu·tri·tious /n(y)ōōˈtriSHəs/ ▶*adj.* nourishing; efficient as food: *like all spinach, it is very nutritious and best when young.* —**nu·tri·tious·ly** *adv.* —**nu·tri·tious·ness** *n.*

nu·tri·tive /ˈn(y)ōōtrətiv/ ▶*adj.* of or relating to nutrition: *the food was low in nutritive value.* ■ providing nourishment; nutritious: *nutritive food.*

nuts /nəts/ ▶*adj. inf.* insane: *the way he turns on the television as soon as he walks in drives me nuts.*
▶*interj. inf.* an expression of contempt or derision: *keep up the good work, and nuts to everyone who doesn't like it.*
▶ □ **be nuts about** *inf.* like very much: *I was nuts about him.*

nut·shell /ˈnətˌSHel/ ▶*n.* the hard woody covering around the kernel of a nut.
▶ □ **in a nutshell** in the fewest possible words: *she put the matter in a nutshell.*

nut·ty /ˈnətē/ ▶*adj.* (**nut·ti·er, nut·ti·est**) **1** tasting like nuts: *wild rice has a very nutty flavor.* ■ containing a lot of nuts: *a nutty vegetable bake.* **2** *inf.* peculiar; insane: *he came up with a few nutty proposals.* —**nut·ti·ness** *n.*
▶ □ **be nutty about** *inf.* like very much: *he is nutty about boats.* □ (**as**) **nutty as a fruitcake** *inf.* completely insane.

nuz·zle /ˈnəzəl/ ▶*v.* [*tr.*] rub or push against gently with the nose and mouth: *he nuzzled her hair* | [*intr.*] *the foal nuzzled at its mother.* ■ [*intr.*] (**nuzzle up to/against**) lean or snuggle against: *the dog nuzzled up against me.*

NW ▶*abbr.* ■ northwest. ■ northwestern.

N-word ▶*n. inf.* used instead of or in reference to the word "nigger" because of its taboo nature: *I can't believe he used the N-word in front of her.*

nyc·ta·lo·pi·a /ˌniktəˈlōpēə/ ▶*n. Med.* the inability to see in dim light or at night. Also called NIGHT BLINDNESS.

ny·lon /ˈnīˌlän/ ▶*n.* a tough, lightweight, elastic synthetic polymer with a proteinlike chemical structure, able to be produced as filaments, sheets, or molded objects. ■ fabric or yarn made from nylon fibers. ■ (**nylons**) stockings or hose made of nylon.

nymph /nimf/ ▶*n.* **1** a mythological spirit of nature imagined as a beautiful maiden inhabiting rivers, woods, or other locations. ■ *chiefly poetic/lit.* a beautiful young woman. **2** an immature form of an insect that does not change greatly as it grows, e.g., a dragonfly, mayfly, or locust. Compare with LARVA. ■ an artificial fly made to resemble the aquatic nymph of an insect, used in fishing. **3** a mainly brown butterfly (subfamily Satyrinae, family Nymphalidae) that frequents woods and forest glades. ▷late Middle English: from Old French *nimphe*, from Latin *nympha*, from Greek *numphē* 'nymph, bride.' —**nymph·al** /ˈnimfəl/ *adj.* —**nym·phe·an** /ˈnimfēən/ *adj.* —**nymph·like** /-ˌlīk/ *adj.*

nym·pho /ˈnimˌfō/ ▶*n. inf.* a nymphomaniac.

nym·pho·ma·ni·a /ˌnimfəˈmānēə/ ▶*n.* uncontrollable or excessive sexual desire in a woman. —**nym·pho·ma·ni·ac** /-ˈmānē,ak/ *n. & adj.* —**nym·pho·ma·ni·a·cal** /-məˈnīəkəl/ *adj.*

NYSE ▶*abbr.* New York Stock Exchange.

Oo

O[1] /ō/ (also **o**) ▸*n.* (*pl.* **Os** or **O's** /ōz/) **1** the fifteenth letter of the alphabet. ▪ denoting the next after N in a set of items, categories, etc. ▪ a human blood type (in the ABO system) lacking both the A and B antigens. In blood transfusion, a person with blood of this group is a potential universal donor. **2** (also **oh**) zero (in a sequence of numerals, esp. when spoken). **3** a shape like that of a capital O; a circle.

O[2] ▸*abbr.* ▪ Ocean. ▪ (in prescriptions) a pint. ▪ octavo. ▪ October. ▪ Ohio. ▪ old. ▪ Ontario. ▪ Oregon.
▸*symb.* the chemical element oxygen.

O[3] ▸*interj.* **1** archaic spelling of **OH**[1]. **2** archaic used before a name in direct address, as in prayers and poetry: *give peace in our time, O Lord.*

O' ▸*prefix* in Irish patronymic names such as *O'Neill.*

o ▸*abbr.* ▪ pint. ▪ octavo. ▪ off. ▪ old. ▪ only. ▪ order. ▪ *Baseball* out; outs.

o' /ə; ō/ ▸*prep.* short for **OF**, used to represent an informal pronunciation: *a cup o' coffee.*

oaf /ōf/ ▸*n.* a stupid, uncultured, or clumsy person. —**oaf·ish** *adj.* —**oaf·ish·ly** *adv.* —**oaf·ish·ness** *n.*

oak /ōk/ ▸*n.* (also **oak tree**) a tree (genus *Quercus*) of the beech family that bears acorns as fruit, and typically has lobed deciduous leaves. Oaks are common in many north temperate forests. —**oak·en** /'ōkən/ *adj.*

oa·kum /'ōkəm/ ▸*n. chiefly hist.* loose fiber obtained by untwisting old rope, used esp. in caulking wooden ships.

oar /ôr/ ▸*n.* a pole with a flat blade, pivoting in an oar lock, used to row or steer a boat through the water. ▪ a rower.
▸*v.* [*tr.*] row; propel with or as with oars: *oaring the sea like madmen* | [*intr.*] *oaring through the weeds.* —**oar·less** *adj.*

oar·lock /'ôr,läk/ ▸*n.* a fitting on the gunwale of a boat that serves as a fulcrum for an oar and keeps it in place.

oars·man /'ôrzmən/ ▸*n.* (*pl.* **-men**) a rower, esp. as a member of a racing team.

OAS ▸*abbr.* Organization of American States.

o·a·sis /ō'āsis/ ▸*n.* (*pl.* **-ses** /ō'āsēz/) **1** a fertile spot in a desert where water is found. ▪ *fig.* a pleasant or peaceful area or period in the midst of a difficult, troubled, or hectic place or situation: *an oasis of calm in the center of the city.* **2** (**Oasis**) *trademark* a type of rigid foam into which the stems of flowers can be secured in flower arranging. ▷early 17th cent.: via late Latin from Greek, apparently of Egyptian origin.

oat /ōt/ ▸*n.* a cereal plant (*Avena sativa*) cultivated chiefly in cool climates and widely used for animal feed as well as human consumption. ▪ (**oats**) the grain yielded by this, used as food. ▪ used in names of wild grasses related to the cultivated oat, e.g., **wild oat.** —**oat·y** *adj.*
▸ □ **feel one's oats** *inf.* feel lively and energetic. □ **sow one's wild oats** go through a period of wild or promiscuous behavior while young.

oath /ōth/ ▸*n.* (*pl.* **oaths** /ōths; ōthz/) **1** a solemn promise, often invoking a divine witness, regarding one's future action or behavior: *they took an oath of allegiance to the king.* ▪ a sworn declaration that one will tell the truth, esp. in a court of law. **2** a profane or offensive expression used to express anger or other strong emotions.
▸ □ **under oath** having sworn to tell the truth, esp. in a court of law.

oat·meal /'ōt,mēl/ ▸*n.* **1** meal made from ground oats, used in breakfast cereals or other food. **2** a grayish-beige color flecked with brown: [as *adj.*] *an oatmeal jacket.*

ob. ▸*abbr.* he or she died: *ob. 1867.*

ob·bli·ga·to /,äblə'gätō/ (also **ob·li·ga·to** /-'gätē/) ▸*n.* (*pl.* **-ga·tos** or **-ga·ti** /-'gätē/) an instrumental part, typically distinctive in effect, that is integral to a piece of music and should not be omitted in performance.

ob·du·rate /'äbd(y)ərit/ ▸*adj.* stubbornly refusing to change one's opinion or course of action. —**ob·du·ra·cy** /-rəsē/ *n.* —**ob·du·rate·ly** *adv.* —**ob·du·rate·ness** *n.*

o·be·di·ence /ō'bēdēəns/ ▸*n.* compliance with someone's wishes or orders or acknowledgment of their authority: *unquestioning obedience to the commander in chief.* ▪ submission to a law or rule: *obedience to moral standards.* ▪ observance of a monastic rule: *vows of poverty, chastity, and obedience.*

o·be·di·ent /ō'bēdēənt/ ▸*adj.* complying or willing to comply with orders or requests; submissive to another's will: *she was totally obedient to him.* —**o·be·di·ent·ly** *adv.*

o·bei·sance /ō'bāsəns; ō'bē-/ ▸*n.* deferential respect: *they paid obeisance to the prince.* ▪ a gesture expressing deferential respect, such as a bow or curtsy: *she made a deep obeisance.* —**o·bei·sant** /ō'bāsənt/ *adj.*

ob·e·lisk /'äbə,lisk/ ▸*n.* a stone pillar, typically having a square or rectangular cross section and a pyramidal top, set up as a monument or landmark. ▪ a mountain, tree, or other natural object of similar shape.

ob·e·lus /'äbələs/ ▸*n.* (*pl.* **-li** /-,lī/) a symbol (†) used as a reference mark in printed matter, or to indicate that a person is deceased. Also called **DAGGER.**

o·bese /ō'bēs/ ▸*adj.* grossly fat or overweight. —**o·be·si·ty** /-sitē/ *n.*

o·bey /ō'bā/ ▸*v.* [*tr.*] comply with the command, direction, or request of (a person or a law); submit to the authority of: *I always obey my father.* ▪ carry out (a command or instruction): *the officer was convicted for refusing to obey orders* | [*intr.*] *when the order was repeated, he refused to obey.* ▪ behave in accordance with (a general principle, natural law, etc.): *the universe was complex but it obeyed certain rules.* ▷Middle English: from Old French *obeir*, from Latin *oboedire*, from *ob-* 'in the direction of' + *audire* 'hear.' —**o·bey·er** *n.*

obelisk

ob·fus·cate /'äbfə,skāt/ ▸*v.* [*tr.*] render obscure, unclear, or unintelligible: *the spelling changes will deform some familiar words and obfuscate their etymological origins.* ▪ bewilder (someone): *it is more likely to obfuscate people than enlighten them.* —**ob·fus·ca·tion** /,äbfə'skāSHən/ *n.* —**ob·fus·ca·to·ry** /äb'fəskə,tôrē/ *adj.*

ob-gyn /'ō'bē 'jē,wī'en/ ▸*abbr.* obstetrics and gynecology.

o·bit /'ōbit; ō'bit/ ▸*n. inf.* an obituary.

ob·i·ter dic·tum /'ōbitər 'diktəm/ ▸*n.* (*pl.* **dic·ta** /'diktə/) *Law* a judge's incidental expression of opinion, not essential to the decision and not establishing precedent. ▪ an incidental remark. ▷Latin *obiter* 'in passing' + *dictum* 'something that is said.'

o·bit·u·ar·y /ō'bichoo,erē/ ▸*n.* (*pl.* **-ar·ies**) a notice of a death, esp. in a newspaper, typically including a brief biography of the deceased person: *the obituary of a friend.* —**o·bit·u·ar·ist** /-ərist/ *n.*

ob·ject ▸*n.* /'äbjəkt/ **1** a material thing that can be seen and touched: *he was dragging a large object.* **2** a person or thing to which a specified action or feeling is directed: *disease became the object of investigation.* ▪ a goal or purpose: *the institute was opened with the object of promoting scientific study.* ▪ *Gram.* a noun or noun phrase governed by an active transitive verb. ▪ *Comput.* a data construct that provides a description of something that may be used by a computer (such as a processor, a peripheral, a document, or a data set) and defines its status, its method of operation, and how it interacts with other objects.

▶*v.* /əb'jekt/ say something to express one's disapproval of or disagreement with something: [*intr.*] *residents* **object to** *the volume of traffic* | *the boy's father objected that the police had arrested him unlawfully.* —**ob·ject·less** /'äbjektləs/ *adj.* —**ob·jec·tor** /əb'jektər/ *n.*

ob·jec·ti·fy /əb'jektə,fī/ ▶*v.* (**-fies, -fied**) [*trans.*] express (something abstract) in a concrete form: *good poetry objectifies feeling.* ■ degrade to the status of a mere object: *a deeply sexist attitude that objectifies women.* —**ob·jec·ti·fi·ca·tion** /əb,jektəfi'kāSHən/ *n.*

ob·jec·tion /əb'jeksHən/ ▶*n.* an expression or feeling of disapproval or opposition; a reason for disagreeing: *they have raised no objections to the latest plans.* ■ the action of challenging or disagreeing with something: *his view is open to objection.*

ob·jec·tion·a·ble /əb'jeksHənəbəl/ ▶*adj.* arousing distaste or opposition; unpleasant or offensive: *I find his theory objectionable in its racist undertones.* —**ob·jec·tion·a·ble·ness** *n.* —**ob·jec·tion·a·bly** /-blē/ *adv.*

ob·jec·tive /əb'jektiv/ ▶*adj.* **1** (of a person or their judgment) not influenced by personal feelings or opinions in considering and representing facts: *historians try to be objective and impartial.* Contrasted with **SUBJECTIVE.** ■ not dependent on the mind for existence; actual: *a matter of objective fact.* **2** *Gram.* of, relating to, or denoting a case of nouns and pronouns used as the object of a transitive verb.

▶*n.* **1** a thing aimed at or sought; a goal: *the system has achieved its objective.* **2** (also **objective lens**) the lens in a telescope or microscope nearest to the object observed. —**ob·jec·tive·ly** *adv.* —**ob·jec·tive·ness** *n.* —**ob·jec·tiv·i·ty** /,äbjek'tivitē/ *n.* —**ob·jec·ti·vi·za·tion** /əb,jektəvi'zāSHən/ *n.* —**ob·jec·tiv·ize** /-,vīz/ *v.*

ob·ject les·son ▶*n.* a striking practical example of some principle or ideal: *they responded to emergencies in a way that was an object lesson to us all.*

ob·jet d'art /,ôbzHä 'där/ ▶*n.* (*pl.* **ob·jets d'art** *pronunc.* same) a small decorative or artistic object, typically when regarded as a collectible item.

ob·la·tion /ə'blāSHən/ ▶*n.* a thing presented or offered to God or a god. —**ob·la·tion·al** /-SHənl; -SHnəl/ *adj.*

ob·li·gate ▶*v.* /'äbli,gāt/ **1** bind or compel (someone), esp. legally or morally: *the medical establishment is obligated to take action in the best interest of the public.* **2** [*trans.*] commit (assets) as security: *the money must be obligated within thirty days.*

▶*adj.* /'äbligit/ *Biol.* restricted to a particular function or mode of life: *an obligate intracellular parasite.* —**ob·li·ga·tor** /-,gātər/ *n.*

ob·li·ga·tion /,äbli'gāSHən/ ▶*n.* an act or course of action to which a person is morally or legally bound; a duty or commitment: *he has enough cash to meet his present obligations.* ■ the condition of being morally or legally bound to do something: *they are* **under no obligation** *to stick to the scheme.* ■ a debt of gratitude for a service or favor: *she didn't want to be under an obligation to him.* ■ *Law* a binding agreement committing a person to a payment or other action. ■ *Law* a document containing a binding agreement; a written contract or bond. —**ob·li·ga·tion·al** /-SHənl; -SHnəl/ *adj.*

o·blig·a·to·ry /ə'bligə,tôrē/ ▶*adj.* required by a legal, moral, or other rule; compulsory: *use of seat belts in cars is now obligatory.* ■ so customary or routine as to be expected of everyone or on every occasion: *after the obligatory preamble on the weather he got down to business.* ■ (of a ruling) having binding force: *a sovereign whose laws are obligatory.* —**ob·lig·a·to·ri·ly** /-,tôrəlē/ *adv.*

o·blige /ə'blīj/ ▶*v.* [*trans.*] make (someone) legally or morally bound to an action or course of action: *doctors are obliged by law to keep patients alive while there is a chance of recovery.* ■ [*trans.*] do as (someone) asks or desires in order to help or please them: *oblige me by not being sorry for yourself* | [*intr.*] *tell me what you want to know and I'll see if I can oblige.* ■ (**be obliged**) be indebted or grateful: *if you can give me a few minutes of your time I'll be much obliged.* —**o·blig·er** *n.*

o·blig·ing /ə'blījiNG/ ▶*adj.* willing to do a service or kindness; helpful. —**o·blig·ing·ly** *adv.* —**o·blig·ing·ness** *n.*

o·blique /ə'blēk; ō'blēk/ ▶*adj.* **1** neither parallel nor at a right angle to a specified or implied line; slanting: *we sat on the settee oblique to the fireplace.* ■ not explicit or direct in addressing a point: *he issued an oblique attack on the president.* ■ *Geom.* (of a line, plane figure, or surface) inclined at other than a right angle. ■ *Geom.* (of an angle) acute or obtuse. ■ *Geom.* (of a cone, cylinder, etc.) with an axis not perpendicular to the plane of its base. ■ *Anat.* (esp. of a muscle) neither parallel nor perpendicular to the long axis of a body or limb. **2** *Gram.* denoting any case other than the nominative or vocative. —**o·blique·ly** *adv.* —**o·blique·ness** *n.* —**o·bliq·ui·ty** /ə'blikwətē/ *n.*

ob·lit·er·ate /ə'blitə,rāt/ ▶*v.* [*trans.*] destroy utterly; wipe out: *fig. the memory*

was so painful that he obliterated it from his mind. ■ cause to become invisible or indistinct; blot out: *clouds were darkening, obliterating the sun.* —**ob·lit·er·a·tion** /ə,blitə'rāSHən/ *n.* —**ob·lit·er·a·tive** /-,rātiv/ *adj.* —**o·blit·er·a·tor** /-,rātər/ *n.*

ob·liv·i·on /ə'blivēən/ ▶*n.* the state of being unaware or unconscious of what is happening: *they drank themselves into oblivion.* ■ the state of being forgotten, esp. by the public: *his name will fade into oblivion.* ■ *fig.* extinction: *only our armed forces stood between us and oblivion.*

ob·liv·i·ous /ə'blivēəs/ ▶*adj.* not aware of or not concerned about what is happening around one: *she became absorbed,* **oblivious to** *the passage of time* | *the women were oblivious of his presence.* —**ob·liv·i·ous·ly** *adv.* —**ob·liv·i·ous·ness** *n.*

ob·long /'äb,lôNG; -,läNG/ ▶*adj.* having an elongated shape, as a rectangle or an oval.

▶*n.* an object or flat figure in this shape.

ob·lo·quy /'äbləkwē/ ▶*n.* strong public criticism or verbal abuse: *he endured years of contempt and obloquy.* ■ disgrace, esp. that brought about by public abuse: *conduct to which no more obloquy could reasonably attach.* —**ob·lo·qui·al** /äb'lōkwēəl/ *adj.* —**ob·lo·qui·ous** /äb'lōkwēəs/ *adj.*

ob·nox·ious /əb'näkSHəs/ ▶*adj.* extremely unpleasant. —**ob·nox·ious·ly** *adv.* —**ob·nox·ious·ness** *n.*

o·boe /'ōbō/ ▶*n.* a woodwind instrument with a slender, tubular body, played with a double-reed mouthpiece. —**o·bo·ist** *n.*

ob·scene /əb'sēn/ ▶*adj.* (of the portrayal or description of sexual matters) offensive or disgusting by accepted standards of morality and decency: *obscene literature.* ■ offensive to moral principles; repugnant: *using animals' skins for fur coats is obscene.* —**ob·scene·ly** *adv.*

ob·scen·i·ty /əb'senitē/ ▶*n.* (*pl.* **-ties**) the state or quality of being obscene; obscene behavior, language, or images: *the book was banned for obscenity.* ■ an extremely offensive word or expression: *the men scowled and muttered obscenities.*

oboe

ob·scure /əb'skyoor/ ▶*adj.* (**-scur·er, -scur·est**) not discovered or known about; uncertain: *his origins and parentage are obscure.* ■ not clearly expressed or easily understood: *obscure references to Proust.* ■ not important or well known: *an obscure religious sect.* ■ hard to make out or define; vague: *fig. I feel an obscure resentment.* ■ (of a color) not sharply defined; dim or dingy.

▶*v.* [*trans.*] keep from being seen; conceal: *gray clouds obscure the sun.* ■ make unclear and difficult to understand: *the debate has become obscured by conflicting ideological perspectives.* ■ overshadow: *none of this should obscure the skill, experience, and perseverance of the workers.* ▷late Middle English: from Old French *obscur,* from Latin *obscurus* 'dark,' from an Indo-European root meaning 'cover.' —**ob·scu·ra·tion** /,äbskyə'rāSHən/ *n.* —**ob·scure·ly** *adv.*

ob·scu·ri·ty /əb'skyoŏritē/ ▶*n.* (*pl.* **-ties**) the state of being unknown, inconspicuous, or unimportant: *he is too good a player to slide into obscurity.* ■ the quality of being difficult to understand: *poems of impenetrable obscurity.* ■ a thing that is unclear or difficult to understand: *the obscurities in his poems and plays.*

ob·se·quies /'äbsəkwēz/ ▶*pl. n.* funeral rites.

ob·se·qui·ous /əb'sēkwēəs/ ▶*adj.* obedient or attentive to an excessive or servile degree: *they were served by obsequious waiters.* —**ob·se·qui·ous·ly** *adv.* —**ob·se·qui·ous·ness** *n.*

ob·serv·ance /əb'zərvəns/ ▶*n.* **1** the action or practice of fulfilling or respecting the requirements of law, morality, or ritual: *strict observance of the rules.* ■ (usu. **observances**) an act performed for religious or ceremonial reasons: *official anniversary observances.* ■ a rule to be followed by a religious order: *he drew up a body of monastic observances.* **2** the action of watching or noticing something: *the baby's motionless observance of me.*

ob·serv·ant /əb'zərvənt/ ▶*adj.* **1** quick to notice things: *her observant eye took in every detail.* **2** adhering strictly to the rules of a particular religion, esp. Judaism.

ob·ser·va·tion /,äbzər'vāSHən/ ▶*n.* **1** the action or process of observing something or someone carefully or in order to gain information: *she was brought into the hospital for observation.* ■ the ability to notice things, esp. significant details: *his powers of observation.* ■ the taking of the altitude of the sun or another celestial body for navigational purposes. **2** a remark, statement, or comment based on something one has seen, heard, or noticed: *he made a telling observation about Hugh.* —**ob·ser·va·tion·al** /-SHənl/ *adj.* —**ob·ser·va·tion·al·ly** /-SHənl-ē/ *adv.*

ob·serv·a·to·ry /əb′zərvə,tôrē/ ▶*n.* (*pl.* **-ries**) a room or building housing an astronomical telescope or other scientific equipment for the study of natural phenomena. ■ a position or building affording an extensive view.

ob·serve /əb′zərv/ ▶*v.* [*tr.*] **1** notice or perceive (something) and register it as being significant: *young people observe that decisions are made by others.* ■ watch (someone or something) carefully and attentively: *Rob stood in the hallway, where he could observe the happenings on the street.* ■ take note of or detect (something) in the course of a scientific study: *the behavior observed in groups of chimpanzees.* ■ make a remark or comment: [with *direct speech*] *"It's chilly," she observed.* **2** fulfill or comply with (a social, legal, ethical, or religious obligation): *a tribunal must observe the principles of natural justice.* ■ (usu. **be observed**) maintain (silence) in compliance with a rule or custom, or temporarily as a mark of respect: *a minute's silence will be observed.* ■ perform or take part in (a rite or ceremony): *relations gather to observe the funeral rites.* ■ celebrate or acknowledge (an anniversary): *many observed the one-year anniversary of the flood.* —**ob·serv·a·ble** *adj.* —**ob·serv·a·bly** /-blē/ *adv.*

ob·serv·er /əb′zərvər/ ▶*n.* a person who watches or notices something: *to a casual observer, he was at peace.* ■ a person who follows events, esp. political ones, closely and comments publicly on them: *some observers expect interest rates to rise.* ■ a person posted to an area in an official capacity to monitor political or military events: *elections scrutinized by international observers.* ■ a person who attends a conference, inquiry, etc., to note the proceedings without participating in them. ■ (in science or art) a real or hypothetical person whose observation is regarded as having a particular viewpoint or effect.

ob·sess /əb′ses/ ▶*v.* [*tr.*] (usu. **be obsessed**) preoccupy or fill the mind of (someone) continually, intrusively, and to a troubling extent: *he was obsessed with thoughts of suicide.* ■ [*intr.*] (of a person) be preoccupied in this way: *her husband, who is obsessing about the wrong she has done him.* —**ob·ses·sive** /-′sesiv/ *adj.* & *n.* —**ob·ses·sive·ly** /-′sesivlē/ *adv.* —**ob·ses·sive·ness** /-′sesivnis/ *n.*

ob·ses·sion /əb′seSHən/ ▶*n.* the state of being obsessed with someone or something: *she cared for him with a devotion bordering on obsession.* ■ an idea or thought that continually preoccupies or intrudes on a person's mind: *he was in the grip of an obsession he was powerless to resist.* —**ob·ses·sion·al** /-SHənl/ *adj.* —**ob·ses·sion·al·ly** /-SHənl-ē/ *adv.*

ob·sid·i·an /əb′sidēən/ ▶*n.* a hard, dark, glassy volcanic rock.

ob·so·les·cent /,äbsə′lesənt/ ▶*adj.* becoming obsolete: *the custom is now obsolescent.* —**ob·so·lesce** *v.* existing systems begin to obsolesce. —**ob·so·les·cence** *n.*

ob·so·lete /,äbsə′lēt/ ▶*adj.* **1** no longer produced or used; out of date: *the disposal of old and obsolete machinery.* **2** *Biol.* (of a part or characteristic of an organism) less developed than formerly or in a related species; rudimentary; vestigial. ▶*v.* [*tr.*] cause (a product or idea) to be or become obsolete by replacing it with something new: *we're trying to stimulate the business by obsoleting last year's designs.* —**ob·so·lete·ly** *adv.* —**ob·so·lete·ness** *n.* —**ob·so·let·ism** /-′lē,tizəm/ *n.*

ob·sta·cle /′äbstəkəl/ ▶*n.* a thing that blocks one's way or prevents or hinders progress: *the major **obstacle to** achieving that goal is money.*

ob·stet·rics /əb′stetriks; äb-/ ▶*pl. n.* [usu. treated as *sing.*] the branch of medicine and surgery concerned with childbirth and the care of women giving birth. —**ob·stet·ric** *adj.* —**ob·stet·ri·cal** *adj.* —**ob·ste·tri·cian** /,äbstə′triSHən/ *n.*

ob·sti·nate /′äbstənit/ ▶*adj.* stubbornly refusing to change one's opinion or chosen course of action, despite attempts to persuade one to do so. ■ (of an unwelcome phenomenon or situation) very difficult to change or overcome: *the obstinate problem of unemployment.* —**ob·sti·na·cy** /-nəsē/ *n.* —**ob·sti·nate·ly** *adv.*

ob·strep·er·ous /əb′strepərəs; äb-/ ▶*adj.* noisy and difficult to control: *the boy is cocky and obstreperous.* —**ob·strep·er·ous·ly** *adv.* —**ob·strep·er·ous·ness** *n.*

ob·struct /əb′strəkt; äb-/ ▶*v.* [*tr.*] block (an opening, path, road, etc.); be or get in the way of: *she was obstructing the entrance.* ■ prevent or hinder (movement or someone or something in motion): *they had to alter the course of the stream and obstruct the natural flow of the water.* ■ block (someone's view): *the view of the driver had been obstructed by the bend in the road.* ■ *fig.* put difficulties in the way of: *fears that the regime would obstruct the distribution of food.* ■ *Law* commit the offense of

intentionally hindering (a legal process). ■ (in various sports) impede (a player on the opposing team) in a manner that constitutes an offense. —**ob·struc·tive** *adj.* —**ob·struc·tor** /-tər/ *n.*

ob·struc·tion /əb′strəkSHən; äb-/ ▶*n.* the action of obstructing or the state of being obstructed: *they faced obstruction in carrying out their research.* ■ a thing that impedes or prevents passage or progress; an obstacle or blockage: *the tractor hit an obstruction.* ■ (in various sports) the action of unlawfully obstructing a player on the opposing team. ■ *Med.* blockage of a bodily passageway, as the intestines. ■ *Law* the action of deliberately hindering a legal process.

ob·tain /əb′tān; äb-/ ▶*v.* **1** [*tr.*] get, acquire, or secure (something): *an opportunity to obtain advanced degrees.* **2** [*intr.*] *formal* be prevalent, customary, or established: *the price of silver fell to that obtaining elsewhere in the ancient world.* —**ob·tain·a·bil·i·ty** /-nə′bilətē/ *n.* —**ob·tain·a·ble** *adj.* —**ob·tain·er** *n.* —**ob·tain·ment** *n.* —**ob·ten·tion** /-′tenCHən/ *n.*

ob·trude /əb′trood/ ▶*v.* [*intr.*] become noticeable in an unwelcome or intrusive way: *a sound from the reception hall obtruded into his thoughts.* ■ [*tr.*] impose or force (something) on someone in such a way: *I felt unable to obtrude my private sorrow upon anyone.* —**ob·trud·er** *n.* —**ob·tru·sion** /-′trooZHən/ *n.*

ob·tru·sive /əb′troosiv; äb-/ ▶*adj.* noticeable or prominent in an unwelcome or intrusive way: *high-powered satellites can reach smaller and less obtrusive antennas.* —**ob·tru·sive·ly** *adv.* —**ob·tru·sive·ness** *n.*

ob·tuse /əb′t(y)oos; äb-/ ▶*adj.* **1** annoyingly insensitive or slow to understand: *he wondered if the account was being deliberately obtuse.* ■ difficult to understand: *some of the lyrics are a bit obtuse.* **2** (of an angle) more than 90° and less than 180°. ■ not sharp-pointed or sharp-edged; blunt. —**ob·tuse·ly** *adv.* —**ob·tuse·ness** *n.* —**ob·tu·si·ty** /-sitē/ *n.*

ob·verse ▶*n.* /′äb,vərs/ the side of a coin or medal bearing the head or principal design. ■ the design or inscription on this side. **2** the opposite or counterpart of a fact or truth: *true solitude is the obverse of true society.* ▶*adj.* /əb′vərs; äb-/ **1** of or denoting the obverse of a coin or medal. **2** corresponding to something else as its opposite or counterpart. —**ob·verse·ly** /əb′vərslē; äb-/ *adv.*

ob·vi·ate /′äbvē,āt/ ▶*v.* [*tr.*] remove (a need or difficulty): *the Venetian blinds obviated the need for curtains.* ■ avoid; prevent: *a parachute can be used to obviate disaster.* —**ob·vi·a·tion** /äbvē′āsHən/ *n.* —**ob·vi·a·tor** /-,ātər/ *n.*

ob·vi·ous /′äbvēəs/ ▶*adj.* easily perceived or understood; clear, self-evident, or apparent: *unemployment has been the most obvious cost of the recession.* ■ *derog.* predictable and lacking in subtlety: *it was an obvious remark to make.* —**ob·vi·ous·ly** *adv.* —**ob·vi·ous·ness** *n.*

oc·a·ri·na /,äkə′rēnə/ ▶*n.* a small egg-shaped wind instrument with a mouthpiece and holes for the fingers.

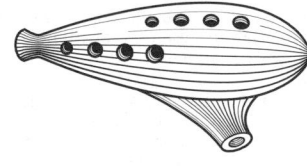

ocarina

oc·ca·sion /ə′kāZHən/ ▶*n.* **1** a particular time or instance of an event: *on one occasion I stayed up until two in the morning.* ■ a special or noteworthy event, ceremony, or celebration: *she was presented with a gold watch to mark the occasion.* | ■ a suitable or opportune time for doing something: *elections are an occasion for registering protest votes.* **2** *formal* reason; cause: *it's the first time that I've had occasion to complain.* ▶*v.* [*tr.*] *formal* cause (something): *something vital must have occasioned this visit* | *his death occasioned her much grief.* ▶ □ **on occasion** occasionally; from time to time: *on occasion, the state was asked to intervene.*

oc·ca·sion·al /ə′kāZHənl/ ▶*adj.* occurring, appearing, or done infrequently and irregularly: *the occasional car went by but no taxis.* ■ (of furniture) made or adapted for use on a particular occasion or for irregular use: *an occasional table.* ■ (of a literary composition, speech, religious service, etc.) produced on or intended for a special occasion: *he wrote occasional verse for patrons.* —**oc·ca·sion·al·ly** /-ZHənl-ē/ *adv*

Oc·ci·dent /′äksidənt; -,dent/ ▶*n.* (**the Occident**) *formal* or *poetic/lit.* the

---

Pronunciation Key ə *ago,* up; ər *over, fur;* a *hat;* ā *ate;* ä *car;* CH *chin;* e *let;* ē *see;* e(ə)r *air;* i *fit;* ī *by;* i(ə)r *ear;* NG *sing;* ō *go;* ô *law, for;* oi *toy;* oo *good;* oo *goo;* ou *out;* SH *she;* TH *thin;* TH *then;* (h)w *why;* ZH *vision*

countries of the West, esp. Europe and the Americas (contrasted with ORIENT). —**oc·ci·den·tal** /ˈäksiˈdentl/ adj.

oc·ci·put /ˈäksəpət/ ▶n. (pl. **oc·ci·puts** or **oc·cip·i·ta** /äkˈsipitə/) Anat. the back of the head or skull. —**oc·cip·i·tal** /äkˈsipitl/ adj.

oc·clude /əˈklōōd/ ▶v. formal or technical **1** [tr.] stop, close up, or obstruct (an opening, orifice, or passage): thick makeup can occlude the pores. ■ shut (something) in: they were occluding the waterfront with a wall of buildings. ■ Chem. (of a solid) absorb and retain (a gas or impurity). **2** [intr.] (of a tooth) close on or come into contact with another tooth in the opposite jaw.

oc·clu·sion /əˈklōōZHən/ ▶n. **1** Med. the blockage or closing of a blood vessel or hollow organ. **2** Meteorol. a process in which the cold front of a rotating low pressure system overtakes the warm front, forcing the warm air upward above a wedge of cold air. ■ an occluded front. **3** Dentistry the position of the teeth when the jaws are closed. —**oc·clu·sive** /-siv/ adj.

oc·cult /əˈkəlt/ ▶n. (**the occult**) supernatural, mystical, or magical beliefs, practices, or phenomena: a secret society to study alchemy and the occult.
▶adj. **1** of, involving, or relating to supernatural, mystical, or magical powers or phenomena: a follower of occult practices similar to voodoo. ■ beyond the range of ordinary knowledge or experience; mysterious: a weird occult sensation of having experienced the identical situation before. ■ communicated only to the initiated; esoteric: the typically occult language of the time. **2** Med. (of a disease or process) not accompanied by readily discernible signs or symptoms. ■ (of blood) abnormally present, e.g., in feces, but detectable only chemically or microscopically.
▶v. [tr.] cut off from view by interposing something: a wooden screen designed to occult the competitors. —**oc·cul·ta·tion** /ˌäkəlˈtāSHən/ n. —**oc·cult·ism** /-ˌtizəm/ n. —**oc·cult·ist** /-tist/ n. —**oc·cult·ly** adv. —**oc·cult·ness** n.

oc·cu·pant /ˈäkyəpənt/ ▶n. a person who resides or is present in a house, vehicle, seat, place, etc., at a given time. ■ the holder of a position or office: the first occupant of the Oval Office. ■ Law a person holding property, esp. land, in actual possession. —**oc·cu·pan·cy** n.

oc·cu·pa·tion /ˌäkyəˈpāSHən/ ▶n. **1** a job or profession: his prime occupation was as editor. ■ a way of spending time: a game of cards is a pretty harmless occupation. **2** the action, state, or period of occupying or being occupied by military force: the Roman occupation of Britain. ■ the action of entering and taking control of a building: the workers remained in occupation until October 16. **3** the action or fact of living in or using a building or other place: a property suitable for occupation by older people.

oc·cu·pa·tion·al /ˌäkyəˈpāSHənl/ ▶adj. of or relating to a job or profession: hepatitis B may be an occupational disease for some health-care workers. —**oc·cu·pa·tion·al·ly** adv.

oc·cu·pa·tion·al ther·a·py ▶n. a form of therapy for those recuperating from physical or mental illness that encourages rehabilitation through the performance of activities required in daily life. —**oc·cu·pa·tion·al ther·a·pist** n.

oc·cu·py /ˈäkyəˌpī/ ▶v. (**-pies, -pied**) [tr.] **1** reside or have one's place of business in (a building): the apartment she occupies in Manhattan. ■ fill or take up (a space or time): two long windows occupied almost the whole wall. ■ be situated in or at (a place or position in a system or hierarchy): on the corporate ladder, they occupy the lowest rungs. ■ hold (a position or job). **2** (often **be occupied with/in**) fill or preoccupy (the mind or thoughts): her mind was occupied with alarming questions. ■ keep (someone) busy and active: Sarah occupied herself taking the coffee cups over to the sink. **3** take control of (a place, esp. a country) by military conquest or settlement: Syria was occupied by France under a League of Nations mandate. ■ enter, take control of, and stay in (a building) illegally and often forcibly, esp. as a form of protest: the workers occupied the factory. ▷Middle English: formed irregularly from Old French occuper, from Latin occupare 'seize.' —**oc·cu·pi·er** /-ˌpīər/ n.

oc·cur /əˈkər/ ▶v. (**-curred, -cur·ring**) [intr.] happen; take place: the accident occurred at about 3:30 p.m. ■ exist or be found to be present in a place or under a particular set of conditions: radon occurs naturally in rocks such as granite. ■ (**occur to**) (of a thought or idea) come into the mind of (someone): it occurred to him that he hadn't eaten.

oc·cur·rence /əˈkərəns/ ▶n. an incident or event: vandalism used to be a rare occurrence. ■ the fact or frequency of something happening: the occurrence of cancer increases with age. ■ the fact of something existing or being found in a place or under a particular set of conditions: the occurrence of natural gas fields.

o·cean /ˈōSHən/ ▶n. a very large expanse of sea, in particular, each of the main areas into which the sea is divided geographically: the

Atlantic Ocean. ■ (usu. **the ocean**) the sea: [as adj.] the ocean floor. ■ (**an ocean of/oceans of**) fig. a very large expanse or quantity: she had oceans of energy. —**o·ce·an·ic** /ˌōSHēˈanik/ adj. —**o·cean·ward** /-wərd/ (also **o·cean·wards**) adv. & adj.

o·cea·nar·i·um /ˌōSHəˈne(ə)rēəm/ ▶n. (pl. **-nar·i·ums** or **-nar·i·a** /-ˈne(ə)rēə/) a large seawater aquarium in which marine animals are kept for study and public exhibit.

o·cea·nog·ra·phy /ˌōSHəˈnägrəfē/ ▶n. the branch of science that deals with the physical and biological properties and phenomena of the sea. —**o·cea·nog·ra·pher** /-fər/ n. —**o·cea·no·graph·ic** /-nəˈgrafik/ adj. —**o·cea·no·graph·i·cal** /-nəˈgrafəkəl/ adj.

oc·e·lot /ˈäsəˌlät/ ˈōsə-/ ▶n. a medium-sized wild cat (Felis pardalis, family Felidae) that has a tawny yellow coat marked with black blotches and spots. It ranges from southern Texas through South America.

o·cher /ˈōkər/ (chiefly Brit. also **o·chre**) ▶n. an earthy pigment containing ferric oxide, typically with clay, varying from light yellow to brown or red. ■ a pale brownish yellow color.

o'clock /əˈkläk/ ▶adv. used to specify the hour in telling time: the gates will open at eight o'clock. ■ used following a numeral to indicate direction or bearing with reference to an imaginary clock face, 12 o'clock being thought of as directly in front or overhead, or at the top of a circular target, etc.: "I think we've got some action at 11 o'clock," he said, gesturing toward the eastern plains.

OCR ▶abbr. optical character recognition.

Oct. ▶abbr. October.

oct. ▶abbr. octavo.

oc·ta·gon /ˈäktəˌgän; -gən/ ▶n. a plane figure with eight straight sides and eight angles. ■ an object or building with a plan or cross section of this shape. —**oc·tag·o·nal** /äkˈtagənl/ adj. —**oc·tag·o·nal·ly** /äkˈtagənəlē/ adv.

oc·ta·he·dron /ˌäktəˈhēdrən/ ▶n. (pl. **-drons** or **-dra** /-drə/) a three-dimensional shape having eight plane faces, esp. a regular solid figure with eight equal triangular faces. ■ a body, esp. a crystal, in the form of a regular octahedron. —**oc·ta·he·dral** /-drəl/ adj.

oc·tane /ˈäktān/ ▶n. Chem. a colorless flammable liquid hydrocarbon of the alkane series, C_8H_{18}, obtained in petroleum refining. ■ another term for OCTANE NUMBER.

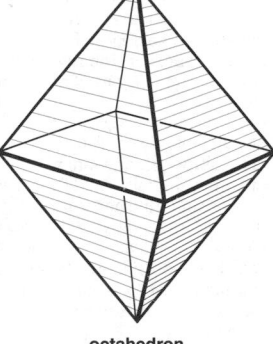

octahedron

oc·tane num·ber (also **octane rat·ing**) ▶n. a number indicating the tendency of gasoline to knock, higher numbers meaning less knocking.

oc·tave /ˈäktəv; ˈäkˌtāv/ ▶n. **1** Mus. a series of eight notes occupying the interval between (and including) two notes, one having twice or half the frequency of vibration of the other. ■ the interval between these two notes. ■ each of the two notes at the extremes of this interval. ■ these two notes sounding together. **2** a poem or stanza of eight lines; an octet.

oc·ta·vo /äkˈtāvō/ (abbr.: **8vo**) ▶n. (pl. **-vos**) a size of book page that results from the folding of each printed sheet into eight leaves (sixteen pages). ■ a book of this size.

oc·tet /äkˈtet/ (also **oc·tette**) ▶n. a group of eight people or things, in particular: ■ a group of eight musicians. ■ a musical composition for eight voices or instruments. ■ the first eight lines of a sonnet. ■ Chem. a stable group of eight electrons occupying a single shell in an atom.

Oc·to·ber /äkˈtōbər/ ▶n. the tenth month of the year, in the northern hemisphere usually considered the second month of autumn.

oc·to·ge·nar·i·an /ˌäktōjəˈne(ə)rēən/ ▶n. a person who is from 80 to 89 years old: [as adj.] the octogenarian leaders of China.

oc·to·pod /ˈäktəˌpäd/ ▶n. any mollusk with eight arms, of the group comprising the octopuses.

oc·to·pus /ˈäktəpəs/ ▶n. (pl. **octopuses**) **1** a cephalopod (Octopus and other genera, order Octopoda) with eight sucker-bearing arms, a soft saclike body, strong beaklike jaws, and no internal shell. **2** fig. an organization or system perceived to have far-reaching and typically harmful effects. —**oc·to·poid** adj. /-ˌpoid/

oc·tu·ple /ˈäktəpəl; -ˈt(y)ōōpəl/ ▶adj. consisting of eight parts or things. ■ eight times as many or as much.
▶v. make or become eight times as numerous or as large.

oc·u·lar /'äkyələr/ ▶adj. Med. of or connected with the eyes or vision: *ocular trauma.*
▶n. another term for EYEPIECE. —**oc·u·lar·ly** adv.

oc·u·list /'äkyəlist/ ▶n. dated a person who specializes in the medical treatment of diseases or defects of the eye; an ophthalmologist. ■ an optometrist.

OD inf. ▶v. (**OD's, OD'd, OD'ing**) [intr.] take an overdose of a drug: *Spike had OD'd on barbiturates.* ■ humorous have too much of something: *I almost OD'd on mushroom salad.*
▶n. an overdose of a narcotic drug.

od /äd/ ▶n. hist. a hypothetical power once thought to pervade nature and account for various phenomena, such as magnetism.

odd /äd/ ▶adj. **1** different from what is usual or expected; strange: *the neighbors thought him very odd.* **2** (of whole numbers such as 3 and 5) having one left over as a remainder when divided by two. ■ (of things numbered consecutively) represented or indicated by such a number: *he has come to us every odd year since 1981.* ■ [in comb.] in the region of or somewhat more than a particular number or quantity: *she looked younger than her fifty-odd years.* **3** happening or occurring infrequently and irregularly; occasional: *neither did she want a secret affair, snatching odd moments together.* ■ spare; unoccupied: *when you've got an odd five minutes, could I have a word?* **4** separated from a usual pair or set and therefore out of place or mismatched: *he's wearing odd socks.* —**odd·ish** adj. —**odd·ly** adv. oddly enough, I didn't feel nervous | *she felt oddly guilty.* —**odd·ness** n.

odd·ball /'äd,bôl/ inf. ▶n. a strange or eccentric person.
▶adj. strange; bizarre: *oddball training methods.*

odd·i·ty /'äditē/ ▶n. (pl. **-ties**) a strange or peculiar person, thing, or trait: *she was regarded as a bit of an oddity.* ■ the quality of being strange or peculiar: *realizing the oddity of the remark, he retracted it.*

odd·ment /'ädmənt/ ▶n. (usu. **oddments**) a remnant or part of something, typically left over from a larger piece or set: *a quilt made from oddments of silk.*

odds /ädz/ ▶pl. n. the ratio between the amounts staked by the parties to a bet, based on the expected probability either way: *the bookies are offering odds of 8-1.* ■ (usu. **the odds**) the chances or likelihood of something happening or being the case: *the odds are that he is no longer alive.* ■ (usu. **the odds**) superiority in strength, power, or resources; advantage: *the odds were overwhelmingly in favor of the banks rather than the customer.*
▶ □ **at odds** in conflict or at variance: *his behavior is at odds with the interests of the company.*

odds and ends ▶pl. n. miscellaneous articles or remnants.

odds-on ▶adj. (esp. of a horse) rated as most likely to win: *the odds-on favorite.*

ode /ōd/ ▶n. a lyric poem in the form of an address to a particular subject, often elevated in style or manner and written in varied or irregular meter. ■ hist. a poem meant to be sung. —**od·ic** /'ōdik/ adj.

O·din /'ōdin/ Scandinavian Mythol. ▶the supreme god and creator, god of victory and the dead. Wednesday is named after him.

o·di·ous /'ōdēəs/ ▶adj. extremely unpleasant; repulsive. —**o·di·ous·ly** adv. —**o·di·ous·ness** n.

o·di·um /'ōdēəm/ ▶n. general or widespread hatred or disgust directed toward someone as a result of their actions: *his job had made him the target of public hostility and odium.* ■ disgrace over something hated or shameful; opprobrium. ▷early 17th cent.: from Latin, 'hatred,' from the verb stem od- 'hate.'

o·dom·e·ter /ō'dämitər/ ▶n. an instrument for measuring the distance traveled by a vehicle.

o·dor /'ōdər/ (Brit. **o·dour**) ▶n. a distinctive smell, esp. an unpleasant or distinctive one: *the odor of cigarette smoke.* ■ fig. a lingering quality, impression, or feeling attaching to something: *an odor of suspicion.* ■ fig. the state of being held in a specified regard: *a decade of bad odor between Britain and the European Community.* —**o·dor·less** adj.

o·dor·if·er·ous /,ōdə'rifərəs/ ▶adj. having or giving off a smell, esp. an unpleasant or distinctive one: *spicily concocted with odoriferous herbs.* —**o·dor·if·er·ous·ly** adv.

o·dor·ous /'ōdərəs/ ▶adj. having or giving off a smell.

Od·ys·sey /'ädəsē/ ▶a Greek epic poem traditionally ascribed to Homer, describing the travels of Odysseus during his ten years of wandering after the fall of Troy. —**Od·ys·se·an** /ädə'sēən/ adj.

od·ys·sey ▶n. (pl. **-seys**) a long and eventful or adventurous journey: *fig. his odyssey from military man to politician.* —**od·ys·se·an** adj.

OED ▶abbr. Oxford English Dictionary.

Oed·i·pus com·plex ▶n. Psychoanalysis (in Freudian theory) the complex of emotions aroused in a young child, typically around the age of four, by an unconscious sexual desire for the parent of the opposite sex and a wish to exclude the parent of the same sex. (The term was originally applied to boys, the equivalent in girls being called the **Electra complex**.) —**Oed·i·pal** /-pəl/ adj.

o'er /ôr/ ▶adv. & prep. archaic or poetic/lit. contraction for OVER.

oeu·vre /'œvrə/ ▶n. the works of a painter, composer, or author regarded collectively: *the complete oeuvre of Mozart.* ■ a work of art, music, or literature: *an early oeuvre.*

OF ▶abbr. Old French.

of /əv/ ▶prep. **1** expressing the relationship between a part and a whole: *the sleeve of his coat.* **2** expressing the relationship between a scale or measure and a value: *an increase of 5 percent.* ■ expressing an age: *a boy of fifteen.* **3** indicating an association between two entities, typically one of belonging: *the son of a friend.* ■ expressing the relationship between an author, artist, or composer and their works collectively: *the plays of Shakespeare.* **4** expressing the relationship between a direction and a point of reference: *north of Chicago.* **5** expressing the relationship between a general category and the thing being specified which belongs to such a category: *the city of Prague | the idea of a just society.* ■ governed by a noun expressing the fact that a category is vague: *this type of book.* **6** indicating the relationship between a verb and an indirect object: ■ with a verb expressing a mental state: *they must be persuaded of the severity of the problem.* ■ expressing a cause: *he died of cancer.* **7** indicating the material or substance constituting something: *the house was built of bricks.* **8** expressing time in relation to the following hour: *it would be just a quarter of three in New York.*

off /ôf; äf/ ▶adv. **1** away from the place in question; to or at a distance: *the man ran off.* ■ away from the main route: *turning off for Ripon.* **2** so as to be removed or separated: *he whipped off his coat.* ■ absent; away from work: *take a day off.* **3** starting a journey or race; leaving: *they're off!* ■ so as to bring to an end or be discontinued: *the Christmas party rounded off a hugely successful year.* ■ canceled: *tell them the wedding's off.* **5** (of an electrical appliance or power supply) not functioning or so as to cease to function: *switch the TV off.*
▶prep. **1** moving away and often down from: *he rolled off the bed.* **2** situated or leading in a direction away from (a main route or intersection): *single wires leading off the main lines.* ■ out at sea from (a place on the coast): *anchoring off Blue Bay.* **3** so as to be removed or separated from: *threatening to tear it off its hinges.* ■ absent from: *I took a couple of days off work.* ■ inf. abstaining from: *he managed to stay off alcohol.*
▶adj. **1** characterized by someone performing or feeling worse than usual; unsatisfactory or inadequate: *even the greatest athletes have off days.* **2** (of food) no longer fresh: *the fish was a bit off.* **3** located on the side of a vehicle that is normally furthest from the curb; offside.
▶v. inf. [tr.] kill; murder: *she might off a cop, but she wouldn't shoot her boyfriend.*
▶ □ **off and on** intermittently; now and then.

Off. ▶abbr. ■ Office. ■ Officer.

of·fal /'ôfəl; 'äfəl/ ▶n. the entrails and internal organs of an animal used as food. ■ refuse or waste material.

off·beat /'ôf,bēt; 'äf-/ ▶adj. **1** Mus. not coinciding with the beat. **2** inf. unconventional; unusual: *she's a little offbeat but she's a wonderful actress.*
▶n. Mus. any of the normally unaccented beats in a bar.

off-col·or (also **off col·or**) ▶adj. **1** somewhat indecent or in poor taste: *off-color jokes.* **2** of the wrong or an inferior color: *the new paint doesn't match, it's off-color.* ■ (of a diamond) neither white nor any definite color.

of·fend /ə'fend/ ▶v. **1** [tr.] (often **be offended**) cause to feel upset, annoyed, or resentful: *viewers said they had been offended by bad language.* ■ be displeasing to: *he didn't smoke and the smell of ash offended him.* **2** [intr.] commit an illegal act: *a small hard core of young criminals who offend again and again.* ■ break a commonly accepted rule or principle: *those activities which offend against public order and decency.* —**of·fend·ed·ly** adv. —**of·fend·er** n.

of·fense /ə'fens/ (Brit. **of·fence**) ▶n. **1** a breach of a law or rule; an illegal act: *neither offense violates any federal law.* ■ a thing that constitutes a violation of what is judged to be right or natural: *the outcome is an offense to basic justice.* **2** annoyance or resentment brought about by a perceived insult to or disregard for oneself or one's standards or principles: *he went out, making it clear he'd taken offense.* **3** /'ôfens; 'äf-/ the action of attacking: [as adj.] *reductions in strategic offense arsenals.* ■ (in sports) the team or players who are attempting to score or advance the ball. ■ (in sports) the condition of possessing the ball or being on the team attempting to score. ▷late Middle English: from Old French *offens* 'misdeed,' from Latin *offensus* 'annoyance,' reinforced by French *offense*, from Latin *offensa* 'a striking against, a hurt, or displeasure'; based on Latin *offendere* 'strike against.'

of·fen·sive ▶*adj.* **1** /əˈfensiv/ causing someone to feel deeply hurt, upset, or angry: *the allegations made are deeply offensive to us.* ■ (of a sight or smell) disgusting; repulsive: *an offensive odor.* **2** /ˈäfensiv/ actively aggressive; attacking: *offensive operations against the insurgents.* ■ (of a weapon) meant for use in attack. ■ (in a game) of or relating to the team or player who is seeking to score.

▶*n.* /əˈfensiv/ an attacking military campaign: *an impending military offensive against the guerrillas.* ■ an organized and forceful campaign to achieve something, typically a political or social end: *the need to launch an offensive against crime.* **—of·fen·sive·ly** *adv.* **—of·fen·sive·ness** *n.*

of·fer /ˈôfər; ˈäfər/ ▶*v.* present or proffer (something) for (someone) to accept or reject as so desired: *may I offer you a drink?* ■ express readiness or the intention to do something for or on behalf of someone: *he offered to fix the gate* | [with *direct speech*] *"Can I help you, dear?" a kindly voice offered.* ■ [*tr.*] (usu. **be offered**) make available for sale: *the product is offered at a very competitive price.* ■ [*tr.*] provide (something): *the highway offers easy access to the public beaches.* ■ [*tr.*] present (something, esp. an opportunity) for consideration and possible exploitation: *a good understanding of what a particular career can offer.* ■ [*tr.*] present (a prayer or sacrifice) to a deity: *villagers have gone to offer prayers for the souls of the sailors.* ■ [*tr.*] make an attempt at or show one's readiness for (violence or resistance): *he had to offer some resistance to her tirade.*

▶*n.* an expression of readiness to do or give something if desired: *he had accepted Mallory's offer to buy him a drink a job offer.* ■ an amount of money that someone is willing to pay for something: *the prospective purchaser who made the highest offer.* ■ a specially reduced price or terms for something on sale: *the offer runs right up until Christmas Eve.* ■ a proposal of marriage. **—of·fer·er** (or **of·fer·or**) *n.*

of·fer·ing /ˈôf(ə)riNG; ˈäf-/ ▶*n.* a thing offered, esp. as a gift or contribution: *animals as sacrificial offerings.* ■ a thing produced or manufactured for entertainment or sale: *Hollywood's latest offerings for the European market.* ■ a contribution, esp. of money, to a church. ■ a thing offered as a religious sacrifice or token of devotion.

of·fer·to·ry /ˈôfər,tôrē; ˈäfər-/ ▶*n.* (*pl.* **-ries**) *Christian Church* **1** the offering of the bread and wine at the Eucharist. ■ prayers or music accompanying this. **2** an offering or collection of money made at a religious service. ■ prayers or music accompanying this.

off·hand /ˈôfˈhand; ˈäf-/ ▶*adj.* (also **off·hand·ed**) ungraciously or offensively nonchalant or cool in manner: *his offhand way of talking.*

▶*adv.* without previous thought or consideration: *I can't think of a better answer offhand.* **—off·hand·ed·ly** *adv.* **—off·hand·ed·ness** *n.*

of·fice /ˈôfis; ˈäf-/ ▶*n.* **1** a room, set of rooms, or building used as a place for commercial, professional, or bureaucratic work: *computers first appeared in offices in the late 1970s.* ■ the local center of a large business: *a company that has four U.S. and four European offices.* ■ a room, department, or building used to provide a particular service: *a ticket office.* ■ the consulting room of a professional person. **2** a position of authority, trust, or service, typically one of a public nature: *the office of attorney general.* ■ tenure of an official position, esp. a government position: *a year ago, when the president took office.* ■ (**Office**) *Brit.* the quarters, staff, or collective authority of a particular government department or agency: *the Foreign Office.* **3** (usu. **offices**) a service or kindness done for another person or group of people. ■ *dated* a duty attaching to one's position; a task or function: *his family had escaped to Canada through the good offices of a Jewish agency in 1923.* **4** (also **Divine Office**) *Christian Church* the series of services of prayers and psalms said (or chanted) daily by Roman Catholic priests, members of religious orders, and other clergy. ▷Middle English: via Old French from Latin *officium* 'performance of a task' (in medieval Latin also 'office, divine service'), based on *opus* 'work' + *facere* 'do.'

of·fi·cer /ˈôfisər; ˈäf-/ ▶*n.* **1** a person holding a position of command or authority in the armed services, in the merchant marine, or on a passenger ship. ■ a policeman or policewoman. ■ a bailiff. **2** a holder of a public, civil, or ecclesiastical office: *a probation officer.* ■ a holder of a post in a society, company, or other organization, esp. one who is involved at a senior level in its management: *a chief executive officer.* **3** a member of a certain grade in some honorary orders.

▶*v.* [*tr.*] provide with military officers: *the aristocracy continued to wield considerable political power, officering the army.* ■ act as the commander of (a unit): *foreign mercenaries were hired to officer new regiments.*

of·fi·cial /əˈfiSHəl/ ▶*adj.* of or relating to an authority or public body and

its duties, actions, and responsibilities: *the governor's official engagements.* ■ having the approval or authorization of such a body: *French is the official language of Quebec.* ■ employed by such a body in a position of authority or trust: *an official spokesman.* ■ emanating from or attributable to a person in office; properly authorized: *official statistics.* ■ *often derog.* perceived as characteristic of officials and bureaucracy; officious: *he sat up straight and became official.*

▶*n.* a person holding public office or having official duties, esp. as a representative of an organization or government department: *a union official.* **—of·fi·cial·dom** *n.* **—of·fi·cial·ism** *n.* **—of·fi·cial·ize** *v.* **—of·fi·cial·ly** *adv.*

of·fi·ci·ate /əˈfiSHē,āt/ ▶*v.* act as an official in charge of something, as a sporting event: *the first woman to officiate a men's basketball game.* ■ perform a religious service or ceremony: *he baptized children and officiated at weddings.* **—of·fi·ci·a·tion** /ə,fiSHēˈāSHən/ *n.* **—of·fi·ci·a·tor** /-,ātər/ *n.*

of·fi·cious /əˈfiSHəs/ ▶*adj.* assertive of authority in an annoyingly domineering way, esp. with regard to petty or trivial matters: *a policeman came to move them on, an officious, spiteful man.* ■ intrusively enthusiastic in offering help or advice; interfering: *an officious bystander.* **—of·fi·cious·ly** *adv.* **—of·fi·cious·ness** *n.*

off·ing /ˈôfiNG; ˈäf-/ ▶*n.* the more distant part of the sea in view.

▶ □ **in the offing** likely to happen or appear soon: *there are several initiatives in the offing.*

off-key ▶*adj.* & *adv.* (of music or singing) not having the correct tone or pitch; out of tune. ■ not in accordance with what is appropriate or correct in the circumstances: [as *adv.*] *some of the cinematic effects are distractingly off-key.*

off-la·bel ▶*adj.* (of a drug) prescribed in a way or for a condition not covered by the original FDA approval: *this drug has been found useful in several off-label treatments.*

off-lim·its ▶*adj.* not to be entered or used; out of bounds: *the place was off-limits to Americans.* ■ not to be mentioned or discussed: *no subject is off-limits.*

off·line /ˈôfˈlīn; ˈäf-/ (also **off-line**) *Comput.* ▶*adj.* not controlled by or directly connected to a computer or external network.

▶*adv.* (also **off line**) while not directly controlled by or connected to a computer or external network. ■ with a delay between the production of data and its processing.

off·load /ˈôf,lōd; ˈäf-/ (also **off-load**) ▶*v.* [*tr.*] unload (a cargo): *men were offloading bags of salt.* ■ rid oneself of (something) by selling or passing it on to someone else: *a dealer offloaded 5,000 of these shares on a client.* ■ relieve oneself of (a problem or worry) by talking to someone else: *it would be nice to have been able to offload your worries onto someone.* ■ *Comput.* move (data or a task) from one processor to another in order to free the first processor for other tasks: *a system designed to offload the text on to a host computer.*

off-peak ▶*adj.* & *adv.* at a time when demand is less: [as *adj.*] *off-peak travel.*

off·print /ˈôf,print; ˈäf-/ ▶*n.* a printed copy of an article or chapter that originally appeared as part of a larger publication.

off-put·ting ▶*adj.* unpleasant, disconcerting, or repellent: *his scar is somewhat off-putting.* **—off-put·ting·ly** *adv.*

off-road ▶*adj.* away from a smooth road; on rough terrain. ■ (of a vehicle or bicycle) designed for use on rough terrain.

off-screen (also **off screen** or **off-screen**) ▶*adj.* not appearing on a movie or television screen: *he drawls to an off-screen interrogator.* ■ happening in real life rather than fictionally on-screen: *they were off-screen lovers.*

▶*adv.* outside what can be seen on a movie or television screen: *the girl is looking off-screen to the right.* ■ in real life rather than fictionally in a movie or on television: *happy endings rarely happen off-screen.*

off-sea·son (also **off-sea·son** or **off sea·son**) ▶*n.* a time of year when a particular activity, typically a sport, is not engaged in: *during baseball's winter off-season.* ■ a time of year when business in a particular sphere is slack: [as *adj.*] *off-season rates.*

▶*adv.* in or during the off-season: *he never trains off-season.*

off·set ▶*n.* /ˈôf,set; ˈäf-/ **1** a consideration or amount that diminishes or balances the effect of a contrary one: *an offset against taxable profits.* **2** the amount or distance by which something is out of line: *these wheels have an offset of four inches.* **3** *Archit.* a sloping ledge in a wall or other feature where the thickness of the part above is diminished. **4** [often as *adj.*] a method of printing in which ink is transferred from a plate or stone to a uniform rubber surface and from that to the paper.

▶*v.* /ˈôf'set; ˌäf-/ (**-set·ting**; *past* and *past part.* **-set**) **1** [*tr.*] (often **be offset**) counteract (something) by having an opposing force or effect: *the* *deficit has been more than offset by capital inflows.* **2** [*tr.*] place out of line: *several places where the ridge was offset at right angles to its length.*

off·shoot /'ôf,sHŌōt; 'äf-/ ▸ *n.* a side shoot or branch on a plant. ■ a thing that originated or developed from something else: *commercial offshoots of universities.*

off·shore /'ôf'sHôr; 'äf-/ ▸ *adj. & adv.* **1** situated at sea some distance from the shore: [as *adj.*] *this huge stretch of coastline is dominated by offshore barrier islands* | [as *adv.*] *we dropped anchor offshore.* ■ (of the wind) blowing toward the sea from the land. ■ of or relating to the business of extracting oil or gas from the seabed: *offshore drilling.* **2** made, situated, or conducting business abroad, esp. in order to take advantage of lower costs or less stringent regulation: [as *adj.*] *deposits in offshore accounts.* ■ of, relating to, or derived from a foreign country: [as *adj.*] *offshore politics.*
▸ *v.* [*trans.*] relocate (a business or department) to a foreign country to take advantage of lower costs: *firms had offshored some activities by early 2004.*

off·side /'ôf'sīd; 'äf-/ ▸ *adj. & adv.* (of a player in certain sports) occupying an illegal position on the field, in particular: ■ *Ice Hockey* moving into the attacking zone ahead of the puck. ■ (usu. **offsides**) *Football* over the scrimmage line or otherwise ahead of the ball before the play has begun. ■ *Soccer* in the attacking half ahead of the ball and having fewer than two defenders nearer the goal line at the moment the ball is played. ■ *Field Hockey* in the attacking half of the field when there are fewer than three defenders nearer the goal line at the moment the ball is played.
▸ *n.* (also **off·sides**) the fact or an instance of being offside.

off·spring /'ôf,sprING; 'äf-/ ▸ *n.* (*pl.* same) a person's child or children: *the offspring of middle-class parents.* ■ an animal's young. ■ *fig.* the product or result of something: *German nationalism was the offspring of military ambition.*

off·stage /'ôf'stāj; 'äf-/ (also **off-stage**) ▸ *adj. & adv.* (in a theater) not on the stage and so not visible to the audience.

off-white ▸ *n.* a white color with a gray or yellowish tinge: [as *adj.*] *a frilly off-white blouse.*

oft /ôft; äft/ ▸ *adv.* archaic, poetic/lit., or jocular form of OFTEN: [in *comb.*] *an oft-quoted tenet.*

of·ten /'ôf(t)ən; 'äf-/ ▸ *adv.* (**of·ten·er, of·ten·est**) frequently; many times: *how often do you have your hair cut?* ■ in many instances: *vocabulary often reflects social standing.*

o·gee /ō'jē/ *Archit.* ▸ *adj.* having a double continuous S-shaped curve.
▸ *n.* an S-shaped line or molding. —**o·geed** *adj.*

o·gle /'ōgəl/ ▸ *v.* [*tr.*] stare at in a lecherous manner: *he was ogling her breasts* | [*intr.*] *men who had turned up to ogle.*
▸ *n.* a lecherous look. —**o·gler** /'ōg(ə)lər/ *n.*

o·gre /'ōgər/ ▸ *n.* (in folklore) a man-eating giant. ■ a cruel or terrifying person. —**o·gre·ish** /'ōg(ə)risH/ (also **o·grish**) *adj.*

oh[1] /ō/ ▸ *interj.* used to express a range of emotions including surprise, anger, disappointment, or joy, or when reacting to something that has just been said: *"Oh no," said Daisy, appalled.*

oh[2] ▸ *n.* variant spelling of O[1] (sense 2).

ohm /ōm/ ▸ *n.* the SI unit of electrical resistance, expressing the resistance in a circuit transmitting a current of one ampere when subjected to a potential difference of one volt. (Symbol: Ω) —**ohm·ic** /'ōmik/ *adj.* —**ohm·i·cal·ly** /'ōmik(ə)lē/ *adv.*

o·ho /ō'hō/ ▸ *interj.* used to express pleased surprise or recognition.

oil /oil/ ▸ *n.* **1** a viscous liquid derived from petroleum, esp. for use as a fuel or lubricant. ■ petroleum. ■ any of various thick, viscous, typically flammable liquids that are insoluble in water but soluble in organic solvents and are obtained from animals or plants: *potatoes fried in vegetable oil.* ■ a liquid preparation used on the hair or skin as a cosmetic: *suntan oil.* ■ *Chem.* any of a group of natural esters of glycerol and various fatty acids that are liquid at room temperature. **2** (often **oils**) oil paint: *a portrait in oils.*
▸ *v.* [*tr.*] (often as *adj.*) (**oiled**) lubricate or coat (something) with oil: *a lightly oiled baking tray.* ■ impregnate or treat (something) with oil: *her hair was heavily oiled.* ▷Middle English: from Old Northern French *olie*, Old French *oile*, from Latin *oleum* '(olive) oil.' —**oil·less** *adj.*

oil·can /'oil,kan/ ▸ *n.* a can containing lubricating oil, esp. one with a long nozzle.

oil·cloth /'oil,klôTH/ ▸ *n.* a canvas coated with linseed or other oil and used to cover a table or floor.

oil·er /'oilər/ ▸ *n.* a thing that holds or supplies oil, in particular: ■ an oil tanker. ■ an oilcan. ■ a person who oils machinery. ■ an unskilled member of a ship's engine-room crew. ■ *inf.* an oil well.

oil of win·ter·green ▸ *n.* see WINTERGREEN (sense 1).

oil paint ▸ *n.* a paste made with ground pigment and a drying oil such as linseed oil, used chiefly by artists.

oil paint·ing ▸ *n.* the art of painting with oil paints. ■ a picture painted with oil paints.

oil plat·form ▸ *n.* a structure designed to stand on the seabed to provide a stable base above water for drilling and servicing oil wells.

oil rig ▸ *n.* a structure with equipment for drilling and servicing an oil well.

oil·seed /'oil,sēd/ ▸ *n.* any of several seeds from cultivated crops yielding oil, e.g., rape, peanut, soybean, or cotton.

oil·skin /'oil,skin/ ▸ *n. dated* heavy cotton cloth waterproofed with oil. ■ (also **oil·skins**) a raincoat or set of garments made of such cloth.

oil slick ▸ *n.* a film or layer of oil floating on an expanse of water, esp. one that has leaked or been discharged from a ship.

oil·stone /'oil,stōn/ ▸ *n.* a fine-grained flat stone used with oil for sharpening cutting edges.

oil well ▸ *n.* a well or shaft drilled through rock, from which petroleum is drawn.

oil·y /'oilē/ ▸ *adj.* (**oil·i·er, oil·i·est**) **1** containing oil: *oily fish such as mackerel and sardines.* ■ covered or soaked with oil: *an oily rag.* ■ resembling oil in appearance or behavior: *the oily swell of the river.* **2** *fig.* (of a person or their behavior) unpleasantly smooth and ingratiating: *his oily smile.* —**oil·i·ness** *n.*

oink /oiNGk/ ▸ *n.* the characteristic grunting sound of a pig.
▸ *v.* [*intr.*] make such a sound.

oint·ment /'ointmənt/ ▸ *n.* a smooth oily preparation that is rubbed on the skin for medicinal purposes or as a cosmetic.

O·jib·wa /ō'jib,wä; -wə/ (also **O·jib·way** /-,wā/) ▸ *n.* (*pl.* same or **-was** or **-ways**) **1** a member of a North American Indian people native to the region around Lake Superior. Also called CHIPPEWA. **2** the Algonquian language of this people.
▸ *adj.* of or relating to this people or their language.

OK (also **o·kay** /'ō'kā/) *inf.* ▸ *interj.* used to express assent, agreement, or acceptance: *OK, I'll pass on your message.* ■ used to introduce an utterance: *"OK, let's go."*
▸ *adj.* satisfactory but not exceptionally or especially good: *the flight was OK.* ■ (of a person) in a satisfactory physical or mental state: *are you OK, Ben?* ■ permissible; allowable: *I'm not sure if it's OK to say that to a teacher.*
▸ *adv.* in a satisfactory manner or to a satisfactory extent: *the computer continues to work OK.*
▸ *n.* an authorization or approval: *do you know how long it takes for those pen-pushers to give us the OK?*
▸ *v.* (**OK's, OK'd, OK'ing**) [*tr.*] sanction or give approval to: *the governor recently OK'd the execution of a man who had committed murder.* ▷mid 19th cent.: probably an abbreviation of *orl korrect*, humorous form of *all correct*, popularized as a slogan during President Van Buren's reelection campaign of 1840; his nickname *Old Kinderhook* (derived from his birthplace) provided the initials.

o·kay /'ō'kā/ ▸ *interj., adj., adv., n., & v.* variant spelling of OK[1].

o·key-doke /'ōkē 'dōk/ (also **o·key-do·key** /'dōkē/) ▸ *interj., adj., & adv.* variant form of OK[1].

o·kra /'ōkrə/ ▸ *n.* a plant (*Abelmoschus esculentus*) of the mallow family with long ridged seedpods, native to the Old World tropics. ■ the immature seedpods of this plant eaten as a vegetable and also used to thicken soups and stews.

old /ōld/ ▸ *adj.* (**old·er, old·est**) See also ELDER[1], ELDEST. **1** having lived for a long time; no longer young: *the old man lay propped up on cushions.* ■ made or built long ago: *the old quarter of the town.* ■ possessed or used for a long time: *he gave his old clothes away.* ■ having the characteristics or showing the signs of age: *marble now so old that it has turned gray and chipped.* **2** belonging only or chiefly to the past; former or previous: *valuation under the old rating system was inexact.* ■ used to refer to the first of two or more similar things: *I was going to try to get my old job back.* ■ dating from far back; long-established or known: *we greet each other like old friends.* ■ (of a form of a language) as used in former or earliest times. **3** [in *comb.*] of a specified age: *he was fourteen years old.* ■ [as *n.*] [in *comb.*] a person or animal of the age specified: *a nineteen-year-old.*

---

4 *inf.* used to express affection, familiarity, or contempt: *it gets the old adrenaline going.* —**old·ish** *adj.* —**old·ness** *n.*

old age ▶*n.* the later part of normal life: *loneliness affects many people in old age.* ■ the state of being old: *old age itself is not a disease.*

old-boy net·work (also **old boy net·work**) ▶*n.* an informal system of support and friendship through which men use their positions of influence to help others who went to the same school or college as they did or who share a similar social background.

old coun·try ▶*n.* (**the old country**) the native country of a person who has gone to live abroad.

olde ▶*adj.* [*attrib.*] pseudoarchaic variant spelling of **OLD**, intended to be quaint: *Ye Olde Tea Shoppe.*

old·en /'ōldən/ ▶*adj.* archaic or jocular of or relating to former times: *the olden days.*

Old Eng·lish ▶*n.* the language of the Anglo-Saxons (up to about 1150), a highly inflected language with a largely Germanic vocabulary, very different from modern English. Also called **ANGLO-SAXON**.

old-fash·ioned ▶*adj.* in or according to styles or types no longer current or common; not modern: *an old-fashioned kitchen range.* ■ (of a person or their views) favoring traditional and usually restrictive styles, ideas, or customs: *she's stuffy and old-fashioned.*
▶*n.* a cocktail consisting chiefly of whiskey, bitters, water, and sugar. —**old-fash·ioned·ness** *n.*

Old Glo·ry ▶an informal name for the U.S. national flag.

old guard (also **Old Guard**) ▶*n.* (usu. **the old guard**) the original or long-standing members of a group or party, esp. ones who are unwilling to accept change or new ideas: *the aging right-wing old guard.* —**old guard·ism** *n.* —**old guards·man** *n.* (*pl.* -**men**)

old hat ▶*n.* *inf.* used to refer to something considered uninteresting, predictable, tritely familiar, or old-fashioned.

old·ie /'ōldē/ ▶*n.* *inf.* an old song, film, or television program that is still well known or popular.

old la·dy ▶*n.* *inf., often derog.* one's mother, wife, or girlfriend.

old maid ▶*n.* **1** *derog.* a single woman regarded as too old for marriage. ■ a prim and fussy person: *he said James was an old maid.* **2** a card game in which players collect pairs and try not to be left with an odd penalty card, typically a black queen. —**old-maid·ish** *adj.*

old man ▶*n.* *inf., often derog.* or *humorous* one's father, husband, or boyfriend. ■ (**the old man**) a man in authority over others, esp. an employer or commanding officer: *the old man wants a progress report.* ■ used with a surname instead of "Mr.": *old man Roberts.*

old mas·ter ▶*n.* a great artist of former times, esp. of the 13th–17th century in Europe. ■ a painting by such a painter: *he formed a large collection of old masters.*

old school ▶*n.* (often **of/from the old school**) used, usually approvingly, to refer to someone or something that is old-fashioned or traditional: *amenities that my parents, being of the old school, still take for granted.*

old·ster /'ōl(d)stər/ ▶*n.* *inf.* an older person.

Old Tes·ta·ment ▶*n.* the first part of the Christian Bible, comprising thirty-nine books and corresponding approximately to the Hebrew Bible. Most of the books were originally written in Hebrew, some in Aramaic, between about 1200 and 100 BC. They comprise the chief texts of the law, history, prophecy, and wisdom literature of the ancient people of Israel.

old-time ▶*adj.* used to refer to something old-fashioned in an approving or nostalgic way: *old-time dancing.* ■ denoting traditional or folk styles of American popular music, such as gospel or bluegrass.

old-tim·er ▶*n.* *inf.* a person who has had the same job, membership, or residence, etc., for a long time. ■ *derog.* an old person.

old wives' tale ▶*n.* a superstition or traditional belief that is regarded as unscientific or incorrect.

Old World ▶Europe, Asia, and Africa, regarded collectively as the part of the world known before the discovery of the Americas. Compare with **NEW WORLD**.

o·le·ag·i·nous /ˌōlē'ajənəs/ ▶*adj.* rich in, covered with, or producing oil; oily or greasy. ■ *fig.* exaggeratedly and distastefully complimentary; obsequious: *candidates made the usual oleaginous speeches in the debate.*

o·le·an·der /'ōlē,andər/ ▶*n.* a poisonous evergreen Old World shrub (*Nerium oleander*, family Apocynaceae) that is widely grown in warm countries for its clusters of white, pink, and red flowers.

o·le·fin /'ōləfin/ ▶*n.* Chem. another term for **ALKENE**. —**o·le·fin·ic** /ˌōlə'finik/ *adj.*

o·le·o /'ōlēō/ ▶*n.* another term for **MARGARINE**.

o·le·o·mar·ga·rine /ˌōlēō'märjərən/ ▶*n.* another term for **MARGARINE**.

o·le·o·res·in /ˌōlē-ō'rezən/ ▶*n.* a natural or artificial mixture of essential oils and a resin, e.g., balsam. —**o·le·o·res·in·ous** /-nəs/ *adj.*

ol·fac·tion /äl'faksнən; ōl-/ ▶*n.* technical the action or capacity of smelling; the sense of smell. —**ol·fac·tive** /-tiv/ *adj.*

ol·fac·to·ry /äl'fakt(ə)rē; ōl-/ ▶*adj.* of or relating to the sense of smell: *the olfactory organs.*

ol·i·garch /'äli,gärk; 'ōl-/ ▶*n.* a ruler in an oligarchy.

ol·i·gar·chy /'äli,gärkē; 'ōli-/ ▶*n.* (*pl.* -**chies**) a small group of people having control of a country, organization, or institution: *the ruling oligarchy of military men around the president.* ■ a state governed by such a group: *the English aristocratic oligarchy of the 19th century.* ■ government by such a group. —**ol·i·gar·chic** /ˌäli'gärkik; ˌōli-/ *adj.* —**ol·i·gar·chi·cal** /ˌäli'gärkikəl; ˌōli-/ *adj.* —**ol·i·gar·chi·cal·ly** /ˌäli'gärkik(ə)lē; ˌōli-/ *adv.*

Ol·i·go·cene /'äligō,sēn/ ▶*adj.* Geol. of, relating to, or denoting the third epoch of the Tertiary period, between the Eocene and Miocene epochs. The Oligocene epoch lasted from 35.4 million to 23.3 million years ago. It was a time of falling temperatures, with evidence of the first primates. ■ [as n.] (**the Oligocene**) the Oligocene epoch or the system of rocks deposited during it.

ol·ive /'äləv/ ▶*n.* **1** a small oval fruit with a hard pit and bitter flesh, green when unripe and brownish black when ripe, used as food and as a source of oil. **2** (also **olive tree**) the widely cultivated evergreen tree (*Olea europaea*) that yields this fruit, native to warm regions of the Old World. The **olive family** (Oleaceae) also includes the ash, lilac, and jasmine. **3** (also **olive green**) a grayish-green color like that of an unripe olive.
▶*adj.* grayish-green, like an unripe olive. ■ (of the complexion) yellowish brown; sallow. ▷Middle English: via Old French from Latin *oliva*, from Greek *elaia*, from *elaion* 'oil.'

ol·ive branch ▶*n.* the branch of an olive tree, traditionally regarded as a symbol of peace (in allusion to the biblical story of Noah, in which a dove returns with an olive branch after the Flood). ■ an offer of reconciliation: *the government is **holding out an olive branch** to the demonstrators.*

ol·ive drab ▶*n.* a dull olive-green color, used in some military uniforms.

ol·ive oil ▶*n.* an oil pressed from ripe olives, used in cooking, medicines, soap, etc.

ol·i·vine /'älə,vēn/ ▶*n.* an olive-green, gray-green, or brown mineral occurring widely in basalt and other basic igneous rocks. It is a silicate containing varying proportions of magnesium, iron, and other elements.

O·lym·pi·ad /ō'limpē,ad; ə'lim-/ ▶*n.* a celebration of the ancient or modern Olympic Games. ■ a period of four years between Olympic Games, used by the ancient Greeks in dating events. ■ a major national or international contest in some activity, notably chess or bridge.

O·lym·pi·an /ə'limpēən; ō'lim-/ ▶*adj.* **1** associated with Mount Olympus in northeastern Greece, or with the Greek gods whose home was traditionally held to be there. ■ resembling or appropriate to a god, esp. in superiority and aloofness: *the court is capable of an Olympian detachment.* **2** relating to the ancient or modern Olympic Games.
▶*n.* **1** any of the twelve Greek gods regarded as living on Olympus. ■ a person of great attainments or exalted position. **2** a competitor in the Olympic Games.

O·lym·pic /ə'limpik; ō'lim-/ ▶*adj.* of or relating to the ancient city of Olympia or the Olympic Games: *an Olympic champion.*
▶*n.* (**the Olympics**) the Olympic Games.

O·lym·pic Games (also **the O·lym·pics**) ▶a modern sports festival held traditionally every four years in different venues beginning in 1896. ■ an ancient Greek festival with athletic, literary, and musical competitions, held at Olympia every four years traditionally from 776 BC until abolished by the Roman emperor Theodosius I in AD 393.

O·ma·ha ▶*n.* (*pl.* same or -**has**) **1** a member of an American Indian people of northeastern Nebraska. **2** the Siouan language of this people.
▶*adj.* of or relating to this people or their language.

OMB ▶*abbr.* (in the federal government) Office of Management and Budget.

om·buds·man /'ämbədzmən; -,bŏŏdz-/ ▶*n.* (*pl.* -**men**) an official appointed to investigate individuals' complaints against maladministration, esp. that of public authorities.

o·me·ga /ō'māgə; ō'mē-/ ▶*n.* the twenty-fourth, and last, letter of the Greek alphabet (Ω, ω), transliterated as 'o' or 'ō.' ■ the last of a series; the final development: [as adj.] *the omega point.*
▶*symb.* ■ (Ω) ohm(s): *a 100Ω resistor.*

om·e·let /ˈäm(ə)lit/ (also **om·e·lette**) ▶ *n.* a dish of beaten eggs cooked in a frying pan until firm, often with a filling added while cooking, and usually served folded over.

o·men /ˈōmən/ ▶ *n.* an event regarded as a portent of good or evil: *the ghost's appearance was an ill omen | a rise in imports might be an omen of recovery.* ■ prophetic significance: *the raven seemed a bird of evil omen.*

o·men·tum /ōˈmentəm/ ▶ *n.* (*pl.* **-ta** /-tə/) *Anat.* a fold of peritoneum connecting the stomach with other abdominal organs. —**o·men·tal** /ōˈmentl/ *adj.*

om·i·cron /ˈämi,krän; ˈōm-/ ▶ *n.* the fifteenth letter of the Greek alphabet (Ο, ο), transliterated as 'o.'

om·i·nous /ˈämənəs/ ▶ *adj.* giving the impression that something bad or unpleasant is going to happen; threatening; inauspicious: *there were ominous dark clouds gathering overhead.* —**om·i·nous·ly** *adv.* —**om·i·nous·ness** *n.*

o·mis·sion /ōˈmiSHən/ ▶ *n.* someone or something that has been left out or excluded: *there are glaring omissions in the report.* ■ the action of excluding or leaving out someone or something: *the omission of recent publications from his bibliography.* ■ a failure to do something, esp. something that one has a moral or legal obligation to do: *to pay compensation for a wrongful act or omission.* —**o·mis·sive** /ōˈmisiv/ *adj.*

o·mit /ōˈmit/ ▶ *v.* (**o·mit·ted, o·mit·ting**) [*tr.*] (often **be omitted**) leave out or exclude (someone or something), either intentionally or forgetfully: *a significant detail was omitted from your story.* ■ fail or neglect to do (something); leave undone: *the final rinse is omitted.* —**o·mis·si·ble** /ōˈmisəbəl/ *adj.*

om·ni·bus /ˈämnə,bəs/ ▶ *n.* a volume containing several novels or other items previously published separately: *an omnibus of her first trilogy.*
▶ *adj.* comprising several items: *Congress passed an omnibus anticrime package.* ▷early 19th cent.: via French from Latin, literally 'for all,' dative plural of *omnis.*

om·nip·o·tent /ämˈnipətənt/ ▶ *adj.* (of a deity) having unlimited power; able to do anything. ■ having ultimate power and influence: *an omnipotent sovereign.*
▶ *n.* (**the Omnipotent**) God. —**om·nip·o·tence** *n.* —**om·nip·o·tent·ly** *adv.*

om·ni·pres·ent /,ämnəˈpreznt/ ▶ *adj.* (of God) present everywhere at the same time. ■ widely or constantly encountered; common or widespread: *the omnipresent threat of natural disasters.* —**om·ni·pres·ence** *n.*

om·nis·cient /ämˈniSHənt/ ▶ *adj.* knowing everything: *the story is told by an omniscient narrator.* —**om·nis·cience** *n.* —**om·nis·cient·ly** *adv.*

om·niv·o·rous /ämˈniv(ə)rəs/ ▶ *adj.* (of an animal or person) feeding on food of both plant and animal origin. ■ taking in or using whatever is available: *an omnivorous reader.* —**om·ni·vore** /ˈämnə,vôr/ *n.* —**om·niv·o·rous·ly** *adv.* —**om·niv·o·rous·ness** *n.*

ON ▶ *abbr.* Old Norse.

on /än; ôn/ ▶ *prep.* **1** physically in contact with and supported by (a surface): *she was lying on the floor.* ■ located somewhere in the general surface area of (a place): *an internment camp on the island | the house on the corner.* ■ as a result of accidental physical contact with: *he banged his head on a beam.* ■ supported by (a part of the body): *he was lying on his back.* ■ so as to be supported or held by: *put it on the table.* ■ in the possession of (the person referred to): *she only had a few dollars on her.* **2** forming a distinctive or marked part of (the surface of something): *a smile on her face.* **3** having (the thing mentioned) as a topic: *essays on a wide range of issues.* ■ having (the thing mentioned) as a basis: *modeled on the Mayflower Compact.* **4** as a member of (a committee, jury, or other body): *they would be allowed to serve on committees.* **5** having (the place or thing mentioned) as a target: *five air raids on the city.* ■ having (the thing mentioned) as a target for visual focus: *her eyes were fixed on his dark profile.* **6** having (the thing mentioned) as a medium for transmitting or storing information: *put your ideas down on paper.* ■ being broadcast by (a radio or television channel): *a new TV series on Channel 4.* **7** in the course of (a journey): *he was on his way to see his mother.* ■ while traveling in (a public conveyance): *John got some sleep on the plane.* ■ on to (a public conveyance) with the intention of traveling in it: *we got on the train.* **8** indicating the day or part of a day during which an event takes place: *on a very hot evening in July.* ■ at the time of: *she was booed on arriving home.* **9** engaged in: *his attendant was out on errands.* **10** regularly taking (a drug or medicine): *he is on morphine to relieve the pain.* **11** paid for by: *the drinks are on me.* **12** added to: *a few cents on the electric bill is nothing compared with your security.*
▶ *adv.* **1** physically in contact with and supported by a surface: *make sure the lid is on.* ■ (of clothing) being worn by a person: *sitting with her coat on | get your shoes on.* **2** indicating continuation of a movement or action: *she burbled on.* ■ further forward; in an advanced state: *later on.* **3** (of an entertainment or other event) taking place or being

presented: *there's a good film on this afternoon.* ■ due to take place as planned: *the reorganization is still on.* **4** (of an electrical appliance or power supply) functioning: *they always left the lights on.* ■ (of a performer, etc.) broadcasting or acting. ■ (of an employee) working.
▶ □ **on and off** intermittently: *it rained on and off most of the afternoon.* □ **on and on** continually; at tedious length: *he went on and on about his grandad's trombone.*

on·a·ger /ˈänəjər/ ▶ *n.* an animal of a race of the Asian wild ass (*Equus hemionus onager*) native to northern Iran.

o·nan·ism /ˈōnə,nizəm/ ▶ *n.* *formal* **1** masturbation. **2** coitus interruptus. —**o·nan·ist** *n.* —**o·nan·is·tic** /,ōnəˈnistik/ *adj.*

once /wəns/ ▶ *adv.* **1** on one occasion or for one time only: *they deliver once a week.* ■ at all; on even one occasion (used for emphasis): *he never once complained.* **2** at some time in the past; formerly: *He had once been an Army officer.*
▶ *conj.* as soon as; when: *once the grapes were pressed, the juice was put into barrels.*

once-o·ver ▶ *n.* *inf.* a rapid inspection or search: *some doctor came and gave us all a once-over.* ■ a piece of work that is done quickly: *a quick once-over with a broom.*

on·co·gene /ˈäNGkə,jēn/ ▶ *n.* *Med.* a gene that in certain circumstances can transform a cell into a tumor cell. —**on·co·gen·ic** /,äNGkəˈjenik/ *adj.*

on·col·o·gy /änˈkäləjē; äNG-/ ▶ *n.* *Med.* the study and treatment of tumors. —**on·co·log·ic** /,äNGkəˈläjik; ,äNG-/ *adj.* —**on·co·log·i·cal** /-kə-ˈläjikəl/ *adj.* —**on·col·o·gist** /-ˈkäləjist/ *n.*

on·com·ing /ˈän,kəmiNG; ˈôn-/ ▶ *adj.* approaching; moving toward: *she walked into the path of an oncoming car.* ■ *fig.* due to happen or occur in the near future: *the oncoming Antarctic winter.*

on·co·pro·tein /,äNGkəˈprōtē(ə)n/ ▶ *n.* a protein encoded by an oncogene that, if introduced into a cell, can transform it into a tumor cell.

one /wən/ ▶ *cardinal number* the lowest cardinal number; half of two; 1: *there's only room for one person.* (Roman numeral: **i, I**) ■ a single person or thing, viewed as taking the place of a group: *they would straggle home in ones and twos.* ■ single; just one as opposed to any more or to none at all (used for emphasis): *her one concern is to save her daughter.* ■ denoting a particular item of a pair or number of items: *electronics is one of his hobbies.* ■ denoting a particular but unspecified occasion or period: *one afternoon in late October.* ■ used before a name to denote a person who is not familiar or has not been previously mentioned; a certain: *he worked as a clerk for one Mr. Ming.* ■ *inf.* a noteworthy example of (used for emphasis): *the actor was one smart-mouthed troublemaker.* ■ identical; the same: *all types of training meet one common standard.* ■ identical and united; forming a unity: *the two things are one and the same.* ■ one year old. ■ one o'clock: *it's half past one.* ■ *inf.* a one-dollar bill. ■ *inf.* an alcoholic drink: *a cool one after a day on the water.* ■ *inf.* a joke or story: *the one about the chicken farmer and the spaceship.* ■ a size of garment or other merchandise denoted by one. ■ a domino or dice with one spot.
▶ *pron.* **1** referring to a person or thing previously mentioned: *her mood changed from one of moroseness to one of joy.* ■ used as the object of a verb or preposition to refer to any example of a noun previously mentioned or easily identified: *do you want one?* **2** a person of a specified kind: *Eleanor was never one to be trifled with.* ■ a person who is remarkable or extraordinary in some way: *you never saw such a one for figures.* **3** [*third person sing.*] used to refer to any person as representing people in general: *one must admire him for his willingness.* ■ referring to the speaker as representing people in general: *one gets the impression that he is ahead.*
▶ □ **at one** in agreement or harmony: *they were completely at one with their environment.*

one-armed ban·dit ▶ *n.* *inf.* a slot machine operated by pulling a long handle at the side.

one-horse ▶ *adj.* drawn by or using a single horse. ■ *inf.* small and insignificant: *a one-horse town.*

O·nei·da /ōˈnīdə/ ▶ *n.* (*pl.* same or **-das**) **1** a member of an American Indian people formerly inhabiting upper New York state, one of the Five Nations. **2** the Iroquoian language of this people.
▶ *adj.* of or relating to this people or their language.

one-lin·er ▶ *n.* *inf.* a short joke or witty remark.

one·ness /ˈwən(n)is/ ▶ *n.* **1** the fact or state of being unified or whole, though comprised of two or more parts: *the oneness of man and nature.* ■ identity or harmony with someone or something: *a strong sense of* *oneness is felt with all things.* **2** the fact or state of being one in number: *belief in the oneness of God.*

one-night stand ▶ *n.* **1** *inf.* (also **one-night·er**) a sexual relationship lasting only one night. ■ a person with whom one has such a relationship. **2** a single performance of a play or show in a particular place.

one-piece ▶ *adj.* (esp. of an article of clothing) made or consisting of a single piece.
▶ *n.* an article of clothing made or consisting of a single piece: *I was wearing a tight black one-piece.*

on·er·ous /'ōnərəs; 'änərəs/ ▶ *adj.* (of a task, duty, or responsibility) involving an amount of effort and difficulty that is oppressively burdensome: *he found his duties increasingly onerous.* ■ *Law* involving heavy obligations: *an onerous lease.* ▷late Middle English: from Old French *onereus*, from Latin *onerosus*, from *onus, oner-* 'burden.' —**on·er·ous·ly** *adv.* —**on·er·ous·ness** *n.*

one·self /wən'self/ (also **one's self**) ▶ *pron.* [third person sing.] **1** [reflexive] a person's own self: *it is difficult to wrest oneself away.* **2** used to emphasize that one does something individually or unaided: *the idea of publishing a book oneself.* **3** in one's normal and individual state of body or mind; not influenced by others: *freedom to be oneself.*

one-sid·ed ▶ *adj.* unfairly giving or dealing with only one side of a contentious issue or question; biased or partial: *the press was accused of being one-sided, of not giving a balanced picture.* ■ (of a contest or conflict) having a gross inequality of strength or ability between the opponents. ■ (of a relationship or conversation) having all the effort or activity coming from one participant. ■ having or occurring on one side of something only: *printing one-sided documents.* —**one-sid·ed·ly** *adv.* —**one-sid·ed·ness** *n.*

one-time (also **one·time**) ▶ *adj.* **1** former: *a one-time football player.* **2** of or relating to a single occasion: *a one-time charge.*

one-on-one ▶ *n. inf.* a face-to-face encounter.

one-track mind ▶ *n.* used in reference to a person whose thoughts are preoccupied with one subject or interest.

one-up·man·ship /wən 'əpmən,ship/ (also **one-ups·man·ship** /'əps-/) ▶ *n. inf.* the technique or practice of gaining a feeling of superiority over another person.

one-way ▶ *adj.* moving or allowing movement in one direction only: *a one-way valve.* ■ (of a road or system of roads) along which traffic may pass in one direction only. ■ (of a ticket) allowing a person to travel to a place but not back again. ■ (of glass or a mirror) seen as a mirror from one side but transparent from the other. ■ denoting a relationship in which all the action or contribution of a particular kind comes from only one member: *interaction between the organism and the environment is not a one-way process.*

on·go·ing /'än,gōiNG; 'ôn-/ ▶ *adj.* continuing; still in progress: *ongoing negotiations.* —**on·go·ing·ness** *n.*

on·ion /'ənyən/ ▶ *n.* **1** an edible bulb with a pungent taste and smell, composed of several concentric layers, used in cooking. **2** the plant (*Allium cepa*) of the lily family that produces this bulb, with long rolled or straplike leaves and spherical heads of greenish-white flowers. —**on·ion·y** *adj.*

on·line /'än,līn; 'ôn-/ (also **on-line**) *Comput.* ▶ *adj.* controlled by or connected to another computer or to a network. ■ connected to the Internet or World Wide Web: *the ease and convenience of online shopping.*
▶ *adv.* (also **on line**) **1** while so connected or under computer control. ■ with processing of data carried out simultaneously with its production. **2** in or into operation or existence: *the town's new high-tech power plant is expected to go online this month.*

on·look·er /'än,lŏŏkər; 'ôn-/ ▶ *n.* a nonparticipating observer; a spectator: *a crowd of fascinated onlookers.* —**on·look·ing** /-,lŏŏkiNG/ *adj.*

on·ly /'ōnlē/ ▶ *adv.* **1** and no one or nothing more besides; solely or exclusively: *there was only a limited number of tickets available.* ■ no more than (implying that more was hoped for or expected); merely: *she was still only in her mid-thirties.* ■ no longer ago than: *genes that were discovered only last year.* ■ not until: *a final report reached him only on January 15.* **2** with the negative or unfortunate result that: *she turned into the parking car, only to find her way blocked.* ■ inevitably, although unfortunate or undesirable: *if banks canceled the debts, these countries would only borrow more.*
▶ *adj.* alone of its or their kind; single or solitary: *the only medal we had ever won.* ■ alone deserving consideration: *it's simply the only place to be seen these days.*
▶ *conj. inf.* except that; but for the fact that: *he is still a young man, only he seems older because of his careworn expression.*

on·o·mas·tics /,änə'mastiks/ ▶ *pl. n.* [usu. treated as *sing.*] the study of the history and origin of proper names, esp. personal names.

on·o·mat·o·poe·ia /,änə,matə'pēə; -,mätə-/ ▶ *n.* the formation of a word from a sound associated with what is named (e.g., *cuckoo, sizzle*). ■ the use of such words for rhetorical effect. —**on·o·mat·o·poe·ic** /-'pē-ik/ or **on·o·mat·o·po·et·ic** /-pō'etik/ *adj.* —**on·o·mat·o·poe·i·cal·ly** /-'pē-ik(ə)lē/ or **on·o·mat·o·po·et·i·cal·ly** /-'pō'etik(ə)lē/ *adv.*

On·on·da·ga /,änən'dôgə; ,ōnən-; -'dägə/ ▶ *n.* (*pl.* same or **-gas**) **1** a member of an Iroquois people, one of the Five Nations, formerly inhabiting an area near Syracuse, New York. **2** the Iroquoian language of this people.
▶ *adj.* of or relating to this people or their language.

on·rush /'än,rəsh; 'ôn-/ ▶ *n.* a surging rush forward: *the mesmerizing onrush of the sea.*
▶ *v.* [intr.] [usu. as *adj.*] (**onrushing**) move forward in a surging rush: *the walls of onrushing whitewater.*

on-screen (also **on screen** or **on-screen**) ▶ *adj. & adv.* shown or appearing in a movie or television program: [as *adj.*] *on-screen violence.* ■ making use of or performed with the aid of a video screen: [as *adj.*] *on-screen editing facilities.*

on·set /'än,set; 'ôn-/ ▶ *n.* the beginning of something, esp. something unpleasant: *the onset of winter.*

on·shore /'än'shôr; 'ôn-/ ▶ *adj. & adv.* situated or occurring on land: [as *adj.*] *an onshore oil field.* ■ (esp. of the direction of the wind) from the sea toward the land.

on·side /'än'sīd; 'ôn-/ ▶ *adj. & adv.* (of a player, esp. in soccer or hockey) occupying a position on the field where playing the ball or puck is allowed; not offside.

on·slaught /'än,slôt; 'ôn-/ ▶ *n.* a fierce or destructive attack: *a series of onslaughts on the citadel.* ■ a large quantity of people or things that is difficult to cope with: *an onslaught of electronic mail.*

on·stage /'än'stāj; 'ôn-/ (also **on-stage**) ▶ *adj. & adv.* (in a theater) on the stage and so visible to the audience.

on·to /'än,tŏŏ; 'ôn-/ ▶ *prep.* **1** moving to a location on (the surface of something): *they went up onto the ridge.* **2** moving aboard (a public conveyance) with the intention of traveling in it: *we got onto the train.*
▶ □ **be onto someone** *inf.* be close to discovering the truth about an illegal or undesirable activity that someone is engaging in. □ **be onto something** *inf.* have an idea or information that is likely to lead to an important discovery.

on·to·gen·e·sis /,äntə'jenəsis/ ▶ *n. Biol.* the development of an individual organism or anatomical or behavioral feature from the earliest stage to maturity. —**on·to·ge·net·ic** /-jə'netik/ *adj.* —**on·to·ge·net·i·cal·ly** /-jə'netik(ə)lē/ *adv.*

on·tog·e·ny /än'täjənē/ ▶ *n.* the branch of biology that deals with ontogenesis. ■ another term for ONTOGENESIS. —**on·to·gen·ic** /,äntə'jenik/ *adj.* —**on·to·gen·i·cal·ly** /,äntə'jenik(ə)lē/ *adv.*

on·tol·o·gy /än'täləjē/ ▶ *n.* the branch of metaphysics dealing with the nature of being. —**on·to·log·i·cal** /,äntə'läjikəl/ *adj.* —**on·to·log·i·cal·ly** /,äntə'läjik(ə)lē/ *adv.* —**on·tol·o·gist** /-jist/ *n.*

o·nus /'ōnəs/ ▶ *n.* (usu. as **the onus**) one's duty or responsibility; burden: *the onus is on you to show that you have suffered loss.*

on·ward /'änwərd; 'ôn-/ ▶ *adv.* (also **on·wards**) in a continuing forward direction; ahead: *she stumbled onward.* ■ forward in time: *the period from 1969 onward.* ■ *fig.* so as to make progress or become more successful: *the business moved onward and upward.*
▶ *adj.* going further rather than coming to an end or halt; moving forward: *oil was pumped to a port for onward shipment.*

on·yx /'äniks/ ▶ *n.* a semiprecious variety of agate with different colors in layers.

oo·dles /'ŏŏdlz/ ▶ *pl. n. inf.* a very great number or amount of something: *if only I had oodles of cash.*

oom·pah /'ŏŏm,pä; 'ŏŏm-/ (also **oom-pah-pah**) *inf.* ▶ *n.* used to refer to the rhythmical sound of deep-toned brass instruments in a band.
▶ *v.* (**-pahed, -pah·ing**) [intr.] make such a sound.

oomph /ŏŏmf; ŏŏmf/ ▶ *n. inf.* the quality of being exciting, energetic, or sexually attractive: *he showed entrepreneurial oomph.*

oops /(w)ŏŏps; ŏŏps/ ▶ *interj. inf.* used to show recognition of a mistake or minor accident, often as part of an apology: *"Oops! I'm sorry. I just made you miss your bus."*

ooze¹ /ŏŏz/ ▶ *v.* [intr.] (of a fluid) slowly trickle or seep out of something; flow in a very gradual way: *blood was oozing from a wound in his scalp.* ■ [intr.] slowly exude or discharge a viscous fluid: *her mosquito bites were oozing and itching like mad.* ■ [tr.] *fig.* give a powerful impression of (a quality): *he oozed charm and poise.*
▶ *n.* the sluggish flow of a fluid. —**ooz·y** /'ŏŏzē/ *adj.*

ooze² ▶ *n.* wet mud or slime, esp. that found at the bottom of a river, lake, or sea. ■ *Geol.* a deposit of white or gray calcareous matter covering extensive areas of the ocean floor. —**ooz·y** *adj.*

o·pac·i·ty /ō'pasitē/ ▸*n.* the condition of lacking transparency or translucence; opaqueness: *thinner paints need black added to increase opacity.* ■ *fig.* obscurity of meaning: *the difficulty and opacity in Barthes' texts.*

o·pal /'ōpəl/ ▸*n.* a gemstone consisting of hydrated silica, typically semi-transparent and showing varying colors against a pale or dark ground. ▷late 16th cent.: from French *opale* or Latin *opalus*, probably based on Sanskrit *upala* 'precious stone' (having been first brought from India).

o·pal·es·cent /,ōpə'lesənt/ ▸*adj.* showing varying colors as an opal does. —**o·pal·es·cence** *n.*

o·paque /ō'pāk/ ▸*adj.* (**o·paqu·er**, **o·paqu·est**) not able to be seen through; not transparent: *the windows were opaque with steam.* ■ *fig.* (esp. of language) hard or impossible to understand; unfathomable: *technical jargon that was opaque to her.*
▸*n.* an opaque thing or substance. ■ *Photog.* a substance for producing opaque areas on negatives. —**o·paque·ly** *adv.* —**o·paque·ness** *n.*

op art (also **optical art**) ▸*n.* a form of abstract art that gives the illusion of movement by the precise use of pattern and color, or in which conflicting patterns emerge and overlap.

op. cit. /'äp ,sit/ ▸*adv.* in the work already cited.

OPEC /'ōpek/ ▸*abbr.* Organization of the Petroleum Exporting Countries.

o·pen /'ōpən/ ▸*adj.* **1** allowing access, passage, or a view through an empty space; not closed or blocked up: *it was a warm evening and the window was open.* ■ (of a container) not fastened or sealed; in a position or with the lid or other covering in a position allowing access to the inside part or the contents: *the case burst open and its contents flew all over the place.* ■ (of a garment or its fasteners) not buttoned or fastened: *his tie was knotted below the open collar of his shirt.* ■ (of the mouth or eyes) with lips or lids parted: *his eyes were open but he could see nothing.* ■ free from obstructions: *the pass is kept open all year by snowplows.* ■ *inf.* (of a car or house) unlocked. ■ *Phonet.* (of a vowel) produced with a relatively wide opening of the mouth and the tongue kept low. ■ *Phonet.* (of a syllable) ending in a vowel. ■ (of a game or style of play) characterized by action that is spread out over the field. **2** exposed to the air or to view; not covered: *an open fire burned in the grate.* ■ (of an area of land) not covered with buildings or trees: *increasing numbers of new houses in open countryside.* ■ having spaces or gaps between elements: *air circulates more readily through an open tree.* ■ (of a fabric) loosely knitted or woven. ■ (of a team member in a game) unguarded and therefore able to receive a pass: *the trick is spreading the defense so that at least one receiver gets open.* ■ (of a goal or other object of attack in a game) unprotected; vulnerable. ■ (of a boat) without a deck: *days without food and water in an open boat.* ■ (**open to**) likely to suffer from or be affected by; vulnerable or subject to: *the system is open to abuse.* ■ with the outer edges or sides drawn away from each other; unfolded: *the trees had buds and a few open flowers.* ■ (of a book or file) with the covers parted or the contents in view, allowing it to be read: *she was copying verses from an open Bible | fig. her mind was an open book to him.* ■ (of a hand) not clenched into a fist. ■ damaged or injured by a deep cut in the surface: *he had his arm slashed open.* **3** (of a store, place of entertainment, etc.) officially admitting customers or visitors; available for business: *the store stays open until 9 p.m.* ■ (of a bank account) available for transactions: *the minimum required to keep the account open.* ■ (of a telephone line) ready to take calls: *our free advice line is open from 8:30 to 5:30.* ■ (of a choice, offer, or opportunity) still available; such that people can take advantage of it: *the offer is open while supplies last.* **4** (of a person) frank and communicative; not given to deception or concealment: *she was open and naive.* ■ not concealed; manifest: *his eyes showed open admiration.* ■ (of conflict) fully developed and unconcealed: *the dispute erupted into open war.* ■ involving no concealment, restraint, or deception; welcoming discussion, criticism, and inquiry: *the conclusions were reached in open discussion.* **5** (of a question, case, or decision) not finally settled; still admitting of debate: *students' choice of major can be kept open until the second year.* ■ (of the mind) accessible to new ideas; unprejudiced: *I'm keeping an open mind about my future.* ■ (**open to**) receptive to: *the union was open to suggestions for improvements.* ■ (**open to**) admitting of; making possible: *the message is open to different interpretations.* ■ freely available or accessible; offered without restriction: *the service is open to all students at the university.* ■ with no restrictions on those allowed to attend or participate: *an open audition was announced.* ■ (also **Open**) (of an award or the competition for it) unrestricted as to who may qualify to compete: *each horse had won two open races.* ■ (of a ticket) not restricted as to day of travel. **6** *Mus.* (of a string) allowed to vibrate along its whole length. ■ (of a pipe) unstopped at each end. ■ (of a note) sounded from an open string

or pipe. **7** (of an electrical circuit) having a break in the conducting path. **8** *Math.* (of a set) not containing any of its limit points.
▸*v.* [*tr.*] **1** move or adjust (a door or window) so as to leave a space allowing access and view: *she opened the door and went in | [intr.] "Open up!" he said.* ■ [*intr.*] (of a door or window) be moved or adjusted to leave a space allowing access and view: *the door opened and a man came out.* ■ undo or remove the lid, cover, or fastener of (a container) to get access to the contents: *he opened a bottle inexpertly, spilling some of the wine.* ■ remove the covers or wrapping from: *can we open the presents now?* ■ part the lips or lids of (a mouth or eye): *she opened her mouth to argue.* ■ [*intr.*] (of the mouth or eyes) have the lips or lids parted in this way: *her eyes slowly opened.* ■ (of a wound) lose or lack its protective covering: *old wounds opened and I bled a little bit.* ■ improve or make possible access to or passage through: *the president announced that his government would open the border.* ■ [*intr.*] (**open onto/into**) (of a room, door, or window) give access to: *beautiful French doors that opened onto a balcony.* ■ [*intr.*] (of a panorama) come into view; spread out before someone: *stop to marvel at the views that open out below.* **2** spread out; unfold: *the eagle opened its wings and circled up into the air.* ■ [*intr.*] be unfolded; spread out to the full extent: *the flowers never opened beyond narrow points.* ■ increase the spaces or gaps between elements of (something): *spacing the scaffolds opens up the tree so light can penetrate.* ■ part the covers or display the contents of (a book or file) to read it: *she opened her book at the prologue.* **3** allow public access to: *one woman raised $731 by opening her home and selling coffee and tea.* ■ make available: *the new plan proposed to open up opportunities to immigrants.* ■ make more widely known; reveal: *the move may force the company to open up its plans for the future.* ■ [*intr.*] (**open up**) become more communicative or confiding: *neither one of them had opened up to me about their troubles.* ■ make (one's mind or heart) more receptive or sympathetic: *open your mind to what is going on around you.* ■ (**open someone (up) to**) make someone vulnerable to: *the process is going to open them to a legal threat.* **4** establish (a new business, movement, or enterprise): *they have opened a new restaurant across the street.* ■ [*intr.*] (of an enterprise, esp. a commercial one) be established: *two new restaurants open this week.* ■ [*intr.*] (of a store, place of entertainment, etc.) be officially ready to receive customers or visitors; become ready for business: *the mall didn't open until 10.* ■ take the action required to make ready for use: *they have the $10 necessary to open a savings account.* ■ [*intr.*] (of a meeting or a sporting or artistic event) formally begin: *the incident occurred just before the Olympic Games were due to open.* ■ [*intr.*] (of a piece of writing or music) begin: *the chapter opens with a discussion of Anglo-American relations.* ■ (**open up**) [*intr.*] (of a process) start to develop: *a new and dramatic phase was opening up.* ■ officially or ceremonially declare (a building, road, etc.) to be completed and ready for use: *we will have to wait until a new bypass is opened before we can tackle the problem of congestion.* ■ (of a counsel in a court of law) make a preliminary statement in (a case) before calling witnesses. ■ [*tr.*] *Bridge* make (the first bid) in the auction. **5** break the conducting path of (an electrical circuit): *the switch opens the motor circuit.* ■ [*intr.*] (of an electrical circuit or device) suffer a break in its conducting path.
▸*n.* (**Open**) a championship or competition with no restrictions on who may qualify to compete: *the venue for the British Open.* —**o·pen·a·ble** *adj.* —**o·pen·ness** *n.*
▸ □ **in** (or **into**) **the open** out of doors; not under cover. ■ not subject to concealment or obfuscation; made public: *we have never let our dislike for him come into the open.* □ **open-and-shut** (of a case or argument) admitting no doubt or dispute; straightforward.

o·pen air ▸*n.* a free or unenclosed space outdoors: *getting out in the open air.*
▸*adj.* positioned or taking place out of doors: *an open-air swimming pool.*

o·pen book ▸*n.* a person or thing that is easily understood or interpreted: *my life's an open book.*

o·pen-end·ed (also **o·pen-end**) ▸*adj.* having no determined limit or boundary: *the return invitation was open-ended.* ■ (of a question or set of questions) allowing the formulation of any answer, rather than a selection from a set of possible answers: *the interview includes both open-ended and multiple-choice questions.* —**o·pen-end·ed·ness** *n.*

o·pen en·roll·ment ▸*n.* **1** the unrestricted enrollment of students at schools, colleges, or universities of their choice. **2** a period during which a health insurance company or HMO is statutorily required to accept applicants without regard to health history. ■ such a period

---

Pronunciation Key ə *ago*, *up*; ər *over*, *fur*; a *hat*; ā *ate*; ä *car*; CH *chin*; e *let*; ē *see*; e(ə)r *air*; i *fit*; ī *by*; i(ə)r *ear*; NG *sing*; ō *go*; ô *law*, *for*; oi *toy*; o͞o *good*; o͞o *goo*; ou *out*; SH *she*; TH *thin*; T͟H *then*; (h)w *why*; ZH *vision*

when employees can change insurance plans offered by their employer, without proof of insurability.

o·pen·er /'ōp(ə)nər/ ▶n. **1** a device for opening something, esp. a container: *a bottle opener.*| **2** the first of a series of games, cultural events, etc.: *the league opener is three weeks away.* ■ the first point or points scored in a sports event. ■ a remark used as an excuse to initiate a conversation: *we blurted out the obvious opener.* ■ Poker (**openers**) a hand of sufficient value to allow the opening of betting.

o·pen-heart·ed (also **o·pen·heart·ed**) ▶adj. expressing or displaying one's warm and kindly feelings without concealment: *Betty's open-hearted goodwill.* —**o·pen-heart·ed·ness** n.

o·pen-heart sur·ger·y ▶n. surgery in which the heart is exposed and the blood made to bypass it.

o·pen house ▶n. a place or situation in which all visitors are welcome: *they kept open house, entertaining a wide variety of artists and writers.* ■ a day when members of the public are invited to visit a place or institution, esp. one to which they do not normally have access: *the president spent all morning greeting thousands of visitors to a White House open house.* ■ an informal reception or party during which one's home is open to visitors: *on New Year's Day they had an open house.* ■ a time when real estate offered for sale is open to prospective buyers.

o·pen·ing /'ōp(ə)niNG/ ▶n. **1** an aperture or gap, esp. one allowing access: *she peered through one of the smaller openings.* ■ fig. an opportunity to achieve something: *they seem to have exploited fully the openings offered.* ■ an available job or position: *an opening for a professional engineer in the public works department.* **2** a beginning; an initial part: *Maya started tapping out the opening of her story.* ■ a formal or official beginning: *the official opening of the tourist season.* ■ the occasion of the first performance of a play, movie, etc., or the start of an exhibition, marked by a celebratory gathering. ■ the occasion of a public building being officially ready for use, marked by a ceremony. ■ Chess a recognized sequence of moves at the beginning of a game. ■ an open piece of ground in a wooded area; a clearing: *I reached an opening in the forest.*
▶adj. coming at the beginning of something; initial: *she stole the show with her opening remark.*

o·pen jaw ▶n. a two-flight itinerary in which the second flight destination is not a return, but in the same general direction as the first flight's origin: [as adj.] *an open-jaw ticket for Washington-Chicago-Philly.*

o·pen·ly /'ōpənlē/ ▶adv. without concealment, deception, or prevarication, esp. where these might be expected; frankly or honestly: *he could no longer speak openly of his problems.*

o·pen-mind·ed ▶adj. willing to consider new ideas; unprejudiced. —**o·pen-mind·ed·ly** adv. —**o·pen-mind·ed·ness** n.

o·pen ques·tion ▶n. a matter on which differences of opinion are possible; a matter not yet decided.

o·pen sea·son ▶n. a period when restrictions on the hunting of certain types of wildlife are lifted. ■ a period when all restrictions on a particular activity or product are abandoned or ignored: *an hour before departure, it's open season on all remaining seats.*

o·pen·work /'ōpən,wərk/ ▶n. [usu. as adj.] ornamental work in cloth, metal, leather, or other material with regular patterns of openings and holes.

o·pe·ra[1] /'äp(ə)rə/ ▶n. a dramatic work in one or more acts, set to music for singers and instrumentalists. ■ such works as a genre of classical music. ■ a building for the performance of opera.

o·pe·ra[2] ▶ plural form of OPUS.

op·er·a·ble /'äp(ə)rəbəl/ ▶adj. **1** able to be used: *the storm left only one operable voice channel.* **2** able to be treated by means of a surgical operation: *operable breast cancer.* —**op·er·a·bil·i·ty** /,äp(ə)rə'bilitē/ n.

op·er·a glass·es (or **op·er·a glass**) ▶pl. n. small binoculars for use at the opera or theater.

op·er·and /'äpə,rand/ ▶n. Math. the quantity on which an operation is to be done.

op·er·ate /'äpə,rāt/ ▶v. **1** [tr.] (of a person) control the functioning of (a machine, process, or system): *a shortage of workers to operate new machines.* ■ [intr.] (of a machine, process, or system) function in a specified manner: *market forces were allowed to operate freely.* ■ [intr.] be in effect: *there is a powerful law that operates in politics.* ■ (of a person or organization) manage and run (a business): *many foreign companies operate factories in the U.S.* ■ [intr.] (of an organization) be managed and run in a specified way: *neither company had operated within the terms of its charter.* ■ [intr.] (of an armed force) conduct military activities in a specified area or from a specified base: *the mountain bases from which the guerrillas were operating.* **2** [intr.] perform a surgical operation: *the surgeons refused to operate* | *my brother had to be **operated on** last week.* **3** [intr.] function; work: *we have as yet no conclusive evidence on how these cells operate.*

op·er·at·ic /,äpə'ratik/ ▶adj. of, relating to, or characteristic of opera: *operatic arias.* ■ extravagantly theatrical; overly dramatic: *she wrung her hands in operatic despair.* —**op·er·at·i·cal·ly** /-ik(ə)lē/ adv.

op·er·at·ing room (abbr.: **OR**) (Brit. **operating theatre**) ▶n. a room in a hospital specially equipped for surgical operations.

op·er·at·ing sys·tem ▶n. the software that supports a computer's basic functions, such as scheduling tasks, executing applications, and controlling peripherals.

op·er·a·tion /,äpə'rāSHən/ ▶n. **1** the fact or condition of functioning or being active: *the construction and operation of power stations.* ■ an active process; a discharge of a function: *the operations of the mind.* ■ a business organization; a company: *he reopened his operation under a different name.* ■ an activity in which such an organization is involved: *the company is selling most of its commercial banking operations.* **2** an act of surgery performed on a patient. **3** a piece of organized and concerted activity involving a number of people, esp. members of the armed forces or the police: *a rescue operation.* ■ (**Operation**) preceding a code name for such an activity: *Operation Desert Storm.* **4** Math. a process in which a number, quantity, expression, etc., is altered or manipulated according to formal rules, such as those of addition, multiplication, and differentiation.

op·er·a·tion·al /,äpə'rāSHənl/ ▶adj. in or ready for use: *the new laboratory is fully operational.* ■ of or relating to the routine functioning and activities of a business or organization: *the coffee bar's initial operational costs.* ■ engaged in or relating to active operations of the armed forces, police, or emergency services: *an operational fighter squadron.* —**op·er·a·tion·al·ly** adv.

op·er·a·tive /'äp(ə)ritiv; 'äpə,rātiv/ ▶adj. **1** functioning; having effect: *the transmitter is operative.* ■ (of a word) having the most relevance or significance in a phrase or sentence: *a young man, and the operative word is young, should go into the armed services at around seventeen.* **2** of or relating to surgery: *they had wounds needing operative treatment.*
▶n. a worker, esp. a skilled one in a manufacturing industry. ■ a private detective or secret agent. —**op·er·a·tive·ly** adv. —**op·er·a·tive·ness** n.

op·er·a·tor /'äpə,rātər/ ▶n. **1** a person who operates equipment or a machine: *a radio operator.* ■ (usu. **the operator**) a person who works for a telephone company assisting users, or who works at a telephone switchboard. **2** a person or company that engages in or runs a business or enterprise: *a tour operator.* **3** inf. a person who acts in a specified, esp. a manipulative, way: *her reputation as a cool, clever operator.* **4** Math. a symbol or function denoting an operation (e.g., ×, +).

op·er·et·ta /,äpə'retə/ ▶n. a short opera, usually on a light or humorous theme and typically having spoken dialogue.

oph·thal·mic /äf'THalmik; äp-/ ▶adj. of or relating to the eye and its diseases.

oph·thal·mol·o·gy /,äfTHə(l)'mäləjē; ,äp-/ ▶n. the branch of medicine concerned with the study and treatment of disorders and diseases of the eye. —**oph·thal·mo·log·i·cal** /-mə'läjikəl/ adj. —**oph·thal·mol·o·gist** /-jist/ n.

oph·thal·mo·scope /äf'THalmə,skōp; äp-/ ▶n. an instrument for inspecting the retina and other parts of the eye. —**oph·thal·mo·scop·ic** /,äfTHalmə'skäpik; ,äp-/ adj. —**oph·thal·mos·co·py** /,äfTHəl'mäskəpē; ,äp-/ n.

o·pi·ate ▶adj. /'ōpē-it; -,āt/ relating to, resembling, or containing opium: *the use of opiate drugs.*
▶n. /'ōpē-it; -,āt/ a drug with morphinelike effects, derived from opium. ■ fig. a thing that soothes or stupefies.

o·pine /ō'pīn/ ▶v. formal hold and state as one's opinion: [with direct speech] *"The man is a genius," he opined.*

o·pin·ion /ə'pinyən/ ▶n. a view or judgment formed about something, not necessarily based on fact or knowledge: *I'm writing to voice my opinion on an issue of great importance.* ■ the beliefs or views of a large number or majority of people about a particular thing: *the changing climate of opinion.* ■ (**opinion of**) an estimation of the quality or worth of someone or something: *I had a higher opinion of myself than I deserved.* ■ a formal statement of advice by an expert on a professional matter: *seeking a second opinion from a specialist.* ■ Law a formal statement of reasons for a judgment given. ■ Law a lawyer's advice on the merits of a case.

o·pin·ion·at·ed /ə'pinyə,nātid/ ▶adj. conceitedly assertive and dogmatic in one's opinions: *an arrogant and opinionated man.*

o·pi·um /'ōpēəm/ ▶n. a reddish-brown heavy-scented addictive drug prepared from the juice of the opium poppy, used as a narcotic and in medicine as an analgesic. ▷late Middle English: via Latin from Greek *opion* 'poppy juice,' from *opos* 'juice,' from an Indo-European root meaning 'water.'

o·pos·sum /(ə)'päsəm/ ▶ *n.* an American marsupial (family Didelphidae) that has a ratlike prehensile tail and hind feet with opposable thumbs.

opp. ▶ *abbr.* opposite.

op·po·nent /ə'pōnənt/ ▶ *n.* someone who competes against or fights another in a contest, game, or argument; a rival or adversary: *he beat his opponent by a landslide margin.* ■ a person who disagrees with or resists a proposal or practice: *an opponent of the economic reforms.*

op·por·tune /ˌäpər't(y)ōōn/ ▶ *adj.* (of a time) well-chosen or particularly favorable or appropriate: *he couldn't have arrived at a less opportune moment.* ■ done or occurring at a favorable or useful time; well-timed: *the opportune use of humor to lower tension.* —**op·por·tune·ly** *adv.* —**op·por·tune·ness** *n.*

op·por·tun·ist /ˌäpər't(y)ōōnist/ ▶ *n.* a person who exploits circumstances to gain immediate advantage rather than being guided by consistent principles or plans: *most burglaries are committed by casual opportunists.*
▶ *adj.* opportunistic: *the calculating and opportunist politician.* —**op·por·tun·ism** /-ˌnizəm/ *n.* —**op·por·tun·is·tic** /ˌäpərt(y)ōō'nistik/ *adj.* —**op·por·tun·is·ti·cal·ly** *adv.*

op·por·tu·ni·ty /ˌäpər't(y)ōōnitē/ ▶ *n.* (*pl.* **-ties**) a set of circumstances that makes it possible to do something: *we may see increased opportunities for export.* ■ a chance for employment or promotion: *career opportunities in our New York headquarters.*

op·pos·a·ble /ə'pōzəbəl/ ▶ *adj. Zool.* (of the thumb of a primate) capable of moving toward and touching the other digits on the same hand.

op·pose /ə'pōz/ ▶ *v.* [*tr.*] disapprove of and attempt to prevent, esp. by argument: *those of you who oppose capital punishment.* ■ actively resist or refuse to comply with (a person or a system): *off-roaders adamantly opposed new trail restrictions.* ■ compete against (someone) in a contest: *a candidate to oppose the leader in the presidential contest.* —**op·pos·er** *n.*

op·po·site /'äpəzit/ ▶ *adj.* **1** having a position on the other or further side of something; facing something, esp. something of the same type: *a crowd gathered on the opposite side of the street.* ■ facing the speaker or a specified person or thing: *he went into the store opposite.* ■ *Bot.* (of leaves or shoots) arising in opposed pairs, one on each side of the stem. **2** diametrically different; of a contrary kind: *a word that is opposite in meaning to another.* ■ being the other of a contrasted pair: *the opposite ends of the price range.*
▶ *n.* a person or thing that is totally different from or the reverse of someone or something else: *we were opposites in temperament.*
▶ *adv.* in a position facing a specified or implied subject: *she was sitting almost opposite.*
▶ *prep.* in a position on the other side of a specific area from; facing: *they sat opposite one another.* ■ *fig.* (of someone taking a leading part in a play or movie) in a complementary role to (another performer). —**op·po·site·ly** *adv.* —**op·po·site·ness** *n.*

op·po·site num·ber ▶ *n.* (**someone's opposite number**) a person whose position or rank in another group, organization, or country is equivalent to that held by someone already mentioned.

op·po·site sex ▶ *n.* women in relation to men or vice versa.

op·po·si·tion /ˌäpə'zisHən/ ▶ *n.* resistance or dissent, expressed in action or argument: *there was considerable opposition to the proposal.* ■ (often **the opposition**) a group of adversaries or competitors, esp. a rival political party or athletic team. ■ (**the opposition**) the principal political party opposed to the one in office. ■ a contrast or antithesis: *a nature-culture opposition.* ■ *Astron.* & *Astrol.* the apparent position of two celestial objects that are directly opposite each other in the sky, esp. when a superior planet is opposite the sun. —**op·po·si·tion·al** /-sHənl/ *adj.*

op·press /ə'pres/ ▶ *v.* [*tr.*] (often **be oppressed**) keep (someone) in subservience and hardship, esp. by the unjust exercise of authority: *a system that oppressed working people.* ■ cause (someone) to feel distressed, anxious, or uncomfortable: *he was oppressed by some secret worry.* —**op·pres·sor** /ə'presər/ *n.*

op·pres·sion /ə'presHən/ ▶ *n.* prolonged cruel or unjust treatment or control: *a region shattered by oppression and killing.* ■ the state of being subject to such treatment or control. ■ mental pressure or distress: *her mood had initially been alarm and a sense of oppression.*

op·pres·sive /ə'presiv/ ▶ *adj.* unjustly inflicting hardship and constraint, esp. on a minority or other subordinate group: *an oppressive dictatorship.* ■ weighing heavily on the mind or spirits; causing depression or discomfort: *a profound loneliness, an oppressive emptiness.* ■ (of weather) excessively hot and humid. —**op·pres·sive·ly** *adv.* —**op·pres·sive·ness** *n.*

op·pro·bri·ous /ə'prōbrēəs/ ▶ *adj.* (of language) expressing opprobrium:

■ disgraceful; shameful: *their opprobrious conduct.* —**op·pro·bri·ous·ly** *adv.*

op·pro·bri·um /ə'prōbrēəm/ ▶ *n.* harsh criticism or censure: *his films and the critical opprobrium they have generated.* ■ the public disgrace arising from someone's shameful conduct: *the opprobrium of being closely associated with thugs and gangsters.*

opt /äpt/ ▶ *v.* [*intr.*] make a choice from a range of possibilities: *consumers will opt for low-priced goods.*
▶ *phrasal v.* □ **opt out** choose not to participate in or carry on with something: *they had both opted out of the medical plan.*

op·ta·tive /'äptətiv/ *Gram.* ▶ *adj.* relating to or denoting a mood of verbs in Greek and other languages, expressing a wish, equivalent to English expressions *if only.*
▶ *n.* a verb in the optative mood. ■ (**the optative**) the optative mood. —**op·ta·tive·ly** *adv.*

op·tic /'äptik/ ▶ *adj.* of or relating to the eye or vision.
▶ *n.* a lens or other optical component in an optical instrument. ▷late Middle English: from French *optique* or medieval Latin *opticus*, from Greek *optikos*, from *optos* 'seen.'

op·ti·cal /'äptikəl/ ▶ *adj.* **1** of or relating to sight, esp. in relation to the physical action of light: *optical illusions.* ■ constructed to assist sight. ■ devised on the principles of optics. **2** *Physics* operating in or employing the visible part of the electromagnetic spectrum: *optical telescopes.* ■ *Electr.* (of a device) requiring electromagnetic radiation for its operation: *integrated optical circuits.* —**op·ti·cal·ly** /-ik(ə)lē/ *adv.*

op·ti·cal art ▶ *n.* another term for OP ART.

op·ti·cal char·ac·ter rec·og·ni·tion (abbr.: **OCR**) ▶ *n.* the identification of printed characters using photoelectric devices and computer software.

op·ti·cal fi·ber ▶ *n.* a thin glass fiber through which light can be transmitted.

op·ti·cal il·lu·sion ▶ *n.* an experience of seeming to see something that does not exist or that is other than it appears. ■ something that deceives one's eyes and causes such an experience.

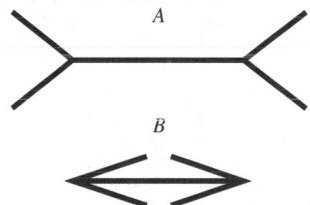

horizontal line *A* appears to be longer
than horizontal line *B*, but in fact,
they are of equal length

optical illusion

op·ti·cian /äp'tisHən/ ▶ *n.* a person qualified to make and supply eyeglasses and contact lenses for correction of vision.

op·tic nerve ▶ *n. Anat.* each of the second pair of cranial nerves, transmitting impulses to the brain from the retina at the back of the eye.

op·tics /'äptiks/ ▶ *pl. n.* [usu. treated as *sing.*] the scientific study of sight and the behavior of light, or the properties of transmission and deflection of other forms of radiation.

op·ti·mal /'äptəməl/ ▶ *adj.* best or most favorable; optimum: *seeking the optimal solution.* —**op·ti·mal·i·ty** /ˌäptə'malitē/ *n.* —**op·ti·mal·ly** /-(ə)lē/ *adv.*

op·ti·mism /'äptəˌmizəm/ ▶ *n.* hopefulness and confidence about the future or the successful outcome of something: *the talks had been amicable, and there were grounds for optimism.* —**op·ti·mist** *n.*

op·ti·mis·tic /ˌäptə'mistik/ ▶ *adj.* hopeful and confident about the future: *the optimistic mood of the sixties* | *he was optimistic about the deal.* ■ involving an overestimate: *previous estimates may be wildly optimistic.* —**op·ti·mis·ti·cal·ly** /-ik(ə)lē/ *adv.*

op·ti·mize /'äptəˌmīz/ ▶ *v.* [*tr.*] make the best or most effective use of (a situation, opportunity, or resource): *to optimize viewing conditions the microscope should be correctly adjusted.* ■ *Comput.* rearrange or rewrite data

---

Pronunciation Key ə *ago,* up; ər *over,* fur; a *hat;* ā *ate;* ä *car;* CH *chin;* e *let;* ē *see;* ə(ə)r *air;* i *fit;* ī *by;* i(ə)r *ear;* NG *sing;* ō *go;* ô *law, for;* oi *toy;* ōō *good;* ōō *goo;* ou *out;* SH *she;* TH *thin;* T͟H *then;* (h)w *why;* ZH *vision*

to improve efficiency of retrieval or processing. **—op·ti·mi·za·tion** /ˌäptəˌmīˈzāSHən/ n. **—op·ti·miz·er** n.

op·ti·mum /ˈäptəməm/ ▶adj. most conducive to a favorable outcome; best: *the optimum childbearing age.*

▶n. (pl. **-ma** /-mə/ or **-mums**) the most favorable conditions or level for growth, reproduction, or success.

op·tion /ˈäpSHən/ ▶n. **1** a thing that is or may be chosen: *choose the cheapest options for supplying energy.* ■ the freedom, power, or right to choose something: *she was given the option of resigning or being dismissed.* ■ a right to buy or sell a particular thing at a specified price within a set time: *Columbia Pictures has an option on the script.* **2** *Football* an offensive play in which the ball carrier has the option to run, pass, hand off, or lateral.

▶v. [tr.] buy or sell an option on (something): *his second script will have been optioned by the time you read this.* ■ *Sports* transfer a player (to a minor league team) with an option to recall him.

op·tion·al /ˈäpSHənl/ ▶adj. available to be chosen but not obligatory: *a wide range of optional excursions is offered.* **—op·tion·al·i·ty** /ˌäpSHəˈnalitē/ n. **—op·tion·al·ly** adv.

op·tion·ee /ˌäpSHəˈnē/ ▶n. a recipient or holder of stock options.

op·tom·e·try /äpˈtämitrē/ ▶n. the practice or profession of examining the eyes for visual defects and prescribing corrective lenses. **—op·to·met·ric** /ˌäptəˈmetrik/ adj. **—op·tom·e·trist** n.

op·u·lent /ˈäpyələnt/ ▶adj. ostentatiously rich and luxurious or lavish: *the opulent comfort of a limousine.* ■ wealthy: *his more opulent tenants.* **—op·u·lence** n. **—op·u·lent·ly** adv.

o·pus /ˈōpəs/ ▶n. (pl. **o·pus·es** or **o·pe·ra** /ˈäp(ə)rə/) **1** *Mus.* a separate composition or set of compositions by a particular composer, usually ordered by date of publication: *The Gambler was Prokofiev's sixth opera, despite its early **opus** number.* **2** any artistic work, esp. one on a large scale: *he was writing an opus on Mexico.*

OR ▶abbr. operational research.

or /ôr/ ▶conj. **1** used to link alternatives: *a cup of tea or coffee.* **2** introducing a synonym or explanation of a preceding word or phrase: *the espionage novel, or, as it is known in the trade, the thriller.* **3** otherwise (used to introduce the consequences of something not being done or not being the case): *hurry up, or you'll miss it all.* **4** introducing an afterthought, usually in the form of a question: *John's indifference—or was it?—left her unsettled.*

▶n. (often **OR**) *Electr.* a Boolean operator that gives the value one if at least one operand (or input) has a value of one, and otherwise has a value of zero. ■ (also **OR gate**) a circuit that gives an output signal if there is a signal on any of its inputs.

or·a·cle /ˈôrəkəl/ ▶n. **1** a priest or priestess acting as a medium through whom advice or prophecy was sought from the gods in classical antiquity. ■ a place at which such advice or prophecy was sought. ■ a person or thing regarded as an infallible authority or guide on something: *casting the attorney general as the oracle for and guardian of the public interest is simply impossible.* **2** a response or message given by an oracle, typically one that is ambiguous or obscure. **—or·ac·u·lar** /ôˈrakyələr/ adj.

o·ral /ˈôrəl/ ▶adj. **1** by word of mouth; spoken rather than written: *they had reached an oral agreement.* ■ relating to the transmission of information or literature by word of mouth rather than in writing: *oral literature.* ■ (of a society) not having reached the stage of literacy. **2** of or relating to the mouth: *oral hygiene.* ■ done or taken by the mouth: *oral contraceptives.* ■ *Phonet.* pronounced by the voice resonating in the mouth, as the vowels in English. ■ *Psychoanalysis* (in Freudian theory) relating to or denoting a stage of infantile psychosexual development in which the mouth is the main source of pleasure and the center of experience.

▶n. (often **orals**) a spoken examination or test: *he was preparing for his orals.* **—o·ral·ly** adv.

or·ange /ˈôrənj; ˈär-/ ▶n. **1** a round juicy citrus fruit with a tough bright reddish-yellow rind. ■ a drink made from or flavored with orange: *a vodka and orange.* **2** (also **orange tree**) the leathery-leaved evergreen tree (genus *Citrus*) that bears this fruit, native to warm regions of south and Southeast Asia. ■ used in names of other plants with similar fruit or flowers, e.g., **mock orange**. **3** a bright reddish-yellow color like that of the skin of a ripe orange.

▶adj. **1** reddish yellow, like a ripe orange in color: *an orange glow in the sky.* **2** made from or flavored with oranges, or having an orangelike flavoring. **—or·ang·ey** (also **or·ang·y**) adj. **—or·ang·ish** (also **or·ange·ish**) adj.

or·ange·ade /ˌôrənjˈād; ˌär-/ ▶n. a drink made with orange juice, sweetener, and water, sometimes carbonated.

o·rang·u·tan /əˈraNG(g)əˌtan/ (also **o·rang·u·tang, o·rang·ou·tang** /-ˌtaNG/, **orang-utan**) ▶n. a large mainly solitary arboreal ape (*Pongo pygmaeus*, family Pongidae) with long reddish hair, long arms, and hooked hands and feet, native to Borneo and Sumatra.

o·rate /ôˈrāt; ˈôrˌāt/ ▶v. [intr.] make a speech, esp. pompously or at length.

o·ra·tion /ôˈrāSHən/ ▶n. a formal speech, esp. one given on a ceremonial occasion. ■ the style or manner in which such a speech is given: *there is nothing quite like his messianic oration.*

or·a·tor /ˈôrətər; ˈär-/ ▶n. a public speaker, esp. one who is eloquent or skilled. **—or·a·to·ri·al** /ˌôrəˈtôrēəl/ adj.

or·a·to·ri·o /ˌôrəˈtôrēˌō; ˌär-/ ▶n. (pl. **-os**) a large-scale musical work for orchestra and voices, typically a narrative on a religious theme, performed without the use of costumes, scenery, or action.Well-known examples include Bach's *Christmas Oratorio*, Handel's *Messiah*, and Haydn's *The Creation*.

or·a·to·ry¹ /ˈôrəˌtôrē; ˈär-/ ▶n. (pl. **-ries**) a small chapel, esp. for private worship.

or·a·to·ry² ▶n. the art or practice of formal speaking in public. ■ exaggerated, eloquent, or highly colored language: *learned discussions degenerated into pompous oratory.* **—or·a·tor·i·cal** /ˌôrəˈtôrikəl/ adj.

orb /ôrb/ ▶n. a spherical body; a globe. ■ a golden globe surmounted by a cross, forming part of the regalia of a monarch. ■ *poetic/lit.* a celestial body.

or·bit /ˈôrbit/ ▶n. **1** the closed curved path of a celestial object or spacecraft around a star, planet, or moon, esp. a periodic elliptical revolution. ■ one complete circuit around an orbited body. ■ the state of being on or moving in such a course: *the earth is in orbit around the sun.* ■ the path of an electron around an atomic nucleus. **2** a sphere of activity, interest, or application: *he moved into the orbit of two great anticommunist socialists of the 1940s and 1950s.* **3** *Anat.* the cavity in the skull of a vertebrate that contains the eye; the eye socket.

▶v. (**-bit·ed, -bit·ing**) [tr.] (of a celestial object or spacecraft) move in orbit around (a star, planet, or moon): *Mercury orbits the Sun.* ■ [intr.] fly or move around in a circle: *the mobile's disks spun and orbited slowly.* ■ put (a satellite) into orbit.

▶ □ **into orbit** inf. into a state of heightened performance, activity, anger, or excitement: *his goal sent the fans into orbit.*

or·bit·al /ˈôrbitl/ ▶adj. of or relating to an orbit or orbits.

▶n. *Physics* each of the actual or potential patterns of electron density that may be formed in an atom or molecule by one or more electrons.

or·bit·al sand·er ▶n. a sander in which the sanding surface moves in a very tight orbital motion, driven at high speed by an electric motor.

or·ca /ˈôrkə/ ▶n. a large toothed whale (*Orcinus orca*, family Delphinidae) with distinctive black-and-white markings and a prominent dorsal fin. It lives in groups that cooperatively hunt fish, seals, and penguins. Also called **KILLER WHALE**.

or·chard /ˈôrCHərd/ ▶n. a piece of land planted with fruit trees. **—or·chard·ist** /-ist/ n.

or·ches·tra /ˈôrkistrə; -ˌkestrə/ ▶n. **1** a group of instrumentalists, esp. one combining string, woodwind, brass, and percussion sections and playing classical music. **2** (also **orchestra pit**) the part of a theater where the orchestra plays, typically in front of the stage and on a lower level than the audience. ■ the seats on the ground floor in a theater. **3** the semicircular space in front of an ancient Greek theater stage where the chorus danced and sang. ▷early 17th cent.: via Latin from Greek *orkhēstra*, from *orkheisthai* 'to dance.' **—or·ches·tral** /ôrˈkestrəl/ adj.

or·ches·trate /ˈôrkiˌstrāt/ ▶v. [tr.] **1** arrange or score (music) for orchestral performance. **2** arrange or direct the elements of (a situation) to produce a desired effect, esp. surreptitiously: *the developers were able to orchestrate a favorable media campaign.* **—or·ches·tra·tion** /ˌôrkəˈstrāSHən/ n. **—or·ches·tra·tor** /-ˌstrātər/ n.

or·chid /ˈôrkid/ ▶n. a plant (numerous genera, family Orchidaceae) with complex flowers that are typically showy or bizarrely shaped, having a large specialized lip (labellum) and frequently a spur. Orchids occur worldwide, esp. as epiphytes in tropical forests, and are valuable hothouse plants. **—or·chid·ist** /-ist/ n.

or·dain /ôrˈdān/ ▶v. [tr.] **1** make (someone) a priest or minister; confer holy orders on. **2** order or decree (something) officially: *equal punishment was ordained for the two crimes.* ■ (esp. of God or fate) prescribe; determine (something): *the path ordained by God.* **—or·dain·er** n. **—or·dain·ment** n.

or·deal /ôrˈdēl/ ▶n. **1** a painful or horrific experience, esp. a protracted one: *the ordeal of having to give evidence.* **2** *hist.* an ancient test of guilt or innocence by subjection of the accused to severe pain, survival of which was taken as divine proof of innocence.

or·der /'ôrdər/ ▶n. **1** the arrangement or disposition of people or things in relation to each other according to a particular sequence, pattern, or method: *I filed the cards in alphabetical order.* ■ a state in which everything is in its correct or appropriate place: *she tried to put her shattered thoughts into some semblance of order.* ■ a state in which the laws and rules regulating the public behavior of members of a community are observed and authority is obeyed: *the army was deployed to keep order.* ■ the overall state or condition of something: *the house had just been vacated and was in good order.* ■ a particular social, political, or economic system: *if only the peasantry would rise up against the established order.* ■ the prescribed or established procedure followed by a meeting, legislative assembly, debate, or court of law: *the meeting was called to order.* **2** an authoritative command, direction, or instruction: *he was not going to take orders from a mere administrator.* ■ an oral or written request for something to be made, supplied, or served: *the company has won an order for six tankers.* ■ a thing made, supplied, or served as a result of such a request: *orders will be delivered the next business day.* ■ a written direction of a court or judge: *a judge's order forbidding the reporting of evidence.* ■ a written direction to pay money or deliver property. **3** (often **orders**) a social class: *the upper social orders.* ■ *Biol.* a principal taxonomic category that ranks below class and above family. ■ a grade or rank in the Christian ministry, esp. that of bishop, priest, or deacon. ■ (**orders**) the rank or position of a member of the clergy or an ordained minister of a church: *he took priest's orders.* **4** (also **Order**) a society of monks, priests, nuns, etc., living according to certain religious and social regulations and discipline and at least some of whose members take solemn vows: *the Franciscan Order.* ■ an institution founded by a monarch for the purpose of conferring an honor or honors for merit on those appointed to it. ■ a Masonic or similar fraternal organization. **5** used to describe the quality, nature, or importance of something: *with musical talent of this order, von Karajan would have been a phenomenon in any age.* **6** any of the five classical styles of architecture (Doric, Ionic, Corinthian, Tuscan, and Composite) based on the proportions of columns, amount of decoration, etc. ■ any style or mode of architecture subject to uniform established proportions. **7** *Mil.* equipment or uniform for a specified purpose or of a specified type: *drill order.* **8** *Math.* the degree of complexity of an equation, expression, etc., as denoted by an ordinal number. ■ the number of differentiations required to reach the highest derivative in a differential equation. ■ the number of elements in a finite group. ■ the number of rows or columns in a square matrix.
▶v. **1** give an authoritative direction or instruction to do something: [tr.] *she ordered me to leave.* ■ [tr.] (**order someone around/about**) continually tell someone in an overbearing way what to do. ■ command (something) to be done or (someone) to be treated in a particular way: *he ordered the anchor dropped.* **2** [tr.] request (something) to be made, supplied, or served: *my friend ordered the tickets last week* | [intr.] *Are you ready to order, sir?* **3** [tr.] arrange (something) in a methodical or appropriate way: *all entries are ordered by date* | [as adj. in comb.] (**-ordered**) *her normally well-ordered life.*
▶ □ **in order to** as a means to: *he slouched into his seat in order to avoid drawing attention to himself.* □ **of the order of 1** approximately: *sales increases are of the order of 20%.* **2** *Math.* having the order of magnitude specified by. □ **out of order 1** (of an electrical or mechanical device) not working properly or at all. **2** not in the correct sequence. **3** not according to the rules of a meeting, legislative assembly, etc. ■ *inf.* (of a person or their behavior) unacceptable or wrong: *he's getting away with things that are out of order.*

or·der·ly /'ôrdərlē/ ▶adj. neatly and methodically arranged: *an orderly arrangement of objects.* ■ (of a person or group) well behaved; disciplined.
▶n. (pl. **-lies**) **1** an attendant in a hospital responsible for the nonmedical care of patients and the maintenance of order and cleanliness. **2** a soldier who carries out orders or performs minor tasks for an officer. —**or·der·li·ness** n.

Or·der of the Gar·ter ▶the highest order of English knighthood, founded by Edward III c.1344.

or·di·nal /'ôrdn-əl/ ▶n. short for ORDINAL NUMBER.
▶adj. of or relating to a thing's position in a series: *ordinal position of birth.* ■ of or relating to an ordinal number. ■ *Biol.* of or relating to a taxonomic order.

or·di·nal num·ber ▶n. a number defining a thing's position in a series, such as "first," "second," or "third." Ordinal numbers are used as adjectives, nouns, and pronouns. Compare with CARDINAL NUMBER.

or·di·nance /'ôrdn-əns/ ▶n. **1** a piece of legislation enacted by a municipal authority: *a city ordinance banned smoking in nearly all types of* restaurants. **2** an authoritative order; a decree. **3** a prescribed religious rite: *Talmudic ordinances.*

or·di·nar·y /'ôrdn,erē/ ▶adj. with no special or distinctive features; normal: *he sets out to depict ordinary people.* ■ uninteresting; commonplace: *ordinary items of everyday wear.*
▶n. (pl. **-nar·ies**) what is commonplace or standard: *their clichés were vested with enough emotion to elevate them above the ordinary.* —**or·di·nar·i·ly** /,ôrdn'erilē/ adv. —**or·di·nar·i·ness** n.

or·di·nate /'ôrdnit; -,āt/ ▶n. Math. (in a system of Cartesian coordinates) the y-coordinate, representing the distance from a point to the horizontal or x-axis measured parallel to the vertical or y-axis.

or·di·na·tion /,ôrdn'āsHən/ ▶n. **1** the action of ordaining or conferring holy orders on someone. ■ a ceremony in which someone is ordained. **2** *chiefly Ecol.* a statistical technique in which data from a large number of sites or populations are represented as points in a two- or three-dimensional coordinate frame.

ord·nance /'ôrdnəns/ ▶n. **1** mounted guns; artillery. ■ military weapons, ammunition, and equipment used in connection with them. **2** a branch of the armed forces dealing with the supply and storage of weapons, ammunition, and related equipment.

Or·do·vi·cian /,ôrdə'visHən/ ▶adj. Geol. of, relating to, or denoting the second period of the Paleozoic era, between the Cambrian and Silurian periods. ■ [as n.] (**the Ordovician**) the Ordovician period or the system of rocks deposited during it.

or·dure /'ôrjər/ ▶n. excrement; dung. ■ something regarded as vile or abhorrent.

ore /ôr/ ▶n. a naturally occurring solid material from which a metal or valuable mineral can be profitably extracted.

o·reg·a·no /ə'regə,nō/ ▶n. an aromatic plant (*Origanum vulgare*) of the mint family, related to marjoram, with leaves that are used fresh or dried as a culinary herb.

o·rex·in ▶n. either of two hormones produced by the mammalian hypothalamus and functional in the regulation of appetite and sleep.

or·gan /'ôrgən/ ▶n. **1** (also **pipe organ**) a large musical instrument having rows of tuned pipes sounded by compressed air, and played using one or more keyboards. ■ a smaller instrument without pipes, producing similar sounds electronically. **2** *Biol.* a part of an organism that is typically self-contained and has a specific vital function, such as the heart or liver in humans. ■ a department or organization that performs a specified function: *the central organs of administration and business.* ■ a medium of communication, esp. a newspaper or periodical that serves a particular organization, political party, etc.: *the People's Daily, the official organ of the Chinese Communist Party.* ■ (used euphemistically) the penis.

or·gan·dy /'ôrgəndē/ (also **or·gan·die**) ▶n. (pl. **-dies**) a fine translucent cotton or silk fabric that is usually stiffened and is used for women's clothing.

or·gan·elle /,ôrgə'nel/ ▶n. Biol. any of a number of organized or specialized structures within a living cell, such as a nucleus, chloroplast or mitochondrion.

or·gan grind·er ▶n. a street musician who plays a barrel organ.

or·gan·ic /ôr'ganik/ ▶adj. **1** of, relating to, or derived from living matter: *organic soils.* ■ *Chem.* of, relating to, or denoting compounds containing carbon (other than simple binary compounds and salts) and chiefly or ultimately of biological origin. Compare with INORGANIC. ■ (of food or farming methods) produced or involving production without the use of chemical fertilizers, pesticides, or other artificial agents. **2** *Physiol.* of or relating to a bodily organ or organs. **3** denoting a relation between elements of something such that they fit together harmoniously as necessary parts of a whole: *the organic unity of the integral work of art.* ■ characterized by continuous or natural development: *companies expand as much by acquisition as by organic growth.* —**or·gan·i·cal·ly** /-ik(ə)lē/ adv.

or·gan·ic chem·is·try ▶n. the chemistry of carbon compounds (other than simple salts such as carbonates, oxides, and carbides).

or·gan·ism /'ôrgə,nizəm/ ▶n. an individual animal, plant, or single-celled life form. ■ the material structure of such an individual: *the heart's contribution to the maintenance of the human organism.* ■ a whole with interdependent parts, likened to a living being: *the upper strata of the American social organism.* —**or·gan·is·mal** /,ôrgə'nizməl/ adj. —**or·gan·is·mic** /,ôrgə'nizmik/ adj.

or·gan·ist /'ôrgənist/ ▶n. a person who plays the organ.

---

or·gan·i·za·tion /ˌôrgəniˈzāSHən/ ▸n. **1** the action of organizing something: *the organization of conferences and seminars.* ■ the structure or arrangement of related or connected items: *the spatial organization of the cells.* ■ an efficient and orderly approach to tasks: *apparent disorder and lack of organization.* **2** an organized body of people with a particular purpose, esp. a business, society, association, etc.: *a research organization.* —**or·gan·i·za·tion·al** /-SHənl/ *adj.* —**or·gan·i·za·tion·al·ly** /-SHən-lē/ *adv.*

or·gan·ize /ˈôrgəˌnīz/ ▸v. [tr.] **1** arrange into a structured whole; order: *organize lessons in a planned way.* ■ coordinate the activities of (a person or group of people) efficiently: *organize and lead a group of people.* ■ form (a number of people) into a labor union, political group, etc.: *an attempt to organize unskilled workers* | [intr.] *campaigns brought women together to organize.* ■ form (a labor union, political group, etc.). **2** make arrangements or preparations for (an event or activity); coordinate: *the union organized a 24-hour general strike.* ■ take responsibility for providing or arranging: *he is sometimes asked to stay behind, organizing transportation.* —**or·gan·iz·a·ble** *adj.* —**or·gan·iz·er** *n.*

or·ga·no·phos·pho·rus /ˌôrgənəˈfäsf(ə)rəs; ôrˌganōˈ-/ ▸adj. [attrib.] denoting synthetic organic compounds containing phosphorus, esp. pesticides and nerve gases of this kind. —**or·ga·no·phos·phate** /-ˈfäsˌfāt/ *n.*

or·gan·za /ôrˈganzə/ ▸n. a thin, stiff, transparent fabric made of silk or a synthetic yarn.

or·gasm /ˈôrˌgazəm/ ▸n. a climax of sexual excitement, characterized by feelings of pleasure centered in the genitals and (in men) experienced as an accompaniment to ejaculation.

▸v. [intr.] experience an orgasm. —**or·gas·mic** /ôrˈgazmik/ *adj.*

or·gi·as·tic /ˌôrjēˈastik/ ▸adj. of or resembling an orgy. —**or·gi·as·ti·cal·ly** /-ik(ə)lē/ *adv.*

or·gy /ˈôrjē/ ▸n. (pl. **-gies**) a wild party, esp. one involving excessive drinking and unrestrained sexual activity: *he had a reputation for drunken orgies.* ■ excessive indulgence in a specified activity: *an orgy of buying.* ▷early 16th cent.: originally plural, from French *orgies*, via Latin from Greek *orgia* 'secret rites or revels.'

o·ri·el /ˈôrēəl/ ▸n. a projection from the wall of a building, typically supported from the ground or by corbels. ■ (also **oriel window**) a window in such a structure. ■ a projecting window, often on an upper story; a bay window.

oriel

o·ri·ent /ˈôrēˌənt/ ▸n. **1** (**the Orient**) *poetic/lit.* the countries of Asia, esp. eastern Asia. **2** the special luster of a pearl of the finest quality. ■ a pearl with such a luster.

▸v. /ˈôrēˌent/ **1** [tr.] (often **be oriented**) align or position (something) relative to the points of a compass or other specified positions: *the fires are oriented in direct line with the midsummer sunset.* ■ adjust or tailor (something) to specified circumstances or needs: *magazines oriented to the business community* | [as adj., in comb.] (**-oriented**) *market-oriented economic reforms.* ■ guide (someone) physically in a specified direction. **2** (**orient oneself**) find one's position in relation to new and strange surroundings: *there are no street names that would enable Martha to orient herself.*

o·ri·en·tal /ˌôrēˈentl/ ▸adj. (also **O·ri·en·tal**) of, from, or characteristic of the Far East: *oriental countries.* ■ (**Oriental**) *Zool.* of, relating to, or denoting a zoogeographical region comprising Asia south of the Himalayas and Indonesia west of Wallace's line. Distinctive animals include pandas, gibbons, tree shrews, tarsiers, and moonrats.

▸n. (**Oriental**) *dated, often offens.* a person of Far Eastern descent.

o·ri·en·ta·tion /ˌôrēənˈtāSHən/ ▸n. the determination of the relative position of something or someone (esp. oneself): *the child's surroundings provide clues to help in orientation.* ■ the relative physical position or direction of something: *two complex shapes, presented in different orientations.* ■ *Zool.* an animal's change of position in response to an external stimulus, esp. with respect to compass directions. ■ familiarization with something: *their training and orientation comes out of magazine and newspaper distribution.* ■ a program of introduction for students new to a school or college: *she attended freshman orientation.* ■ the direction of someone's interest or attitude, esp. political or sexual: *a common age of consent regardless of gender or sexual orientation.* —**o·ri·en·ta·tion·al** *adj.*

o·ri·en·teer·ing /ˌôrēənˈti(ə)riNG/ ▸n. a competitive sport in which participants find their way to various checkpoints across rough country with the aid of a map and compass, the winner being the one with the lowest elapsed time. —**o·ri·en·teer** *n. & v.*

or·i·fice /ˈôrəfis/ ▸n. an opening, as of a pipe or tube, or one in the body, such as a nostril or the anus.

o·ri·ga·mi /ˌôrəˈgämē/ ▸n. the Japanese art of folding paper into decorative shapes and figures.

or·i·gin /ˈôrəjən/ ▸n. **1** the beginning of something's existence: *a novel theory about the origin of oil.* ■ a person's social background or ancestry: *they will be asked about their ethnic origin.* ■ the place or situation from which something comes: *an indication of the country of origin.* **2** *Anat.* the place or point where a muscle, nerve, or other body part arises, in particular: ■ the more fixed end or attachment of a muscle. ■ a place where a nerve or blood vessel begins or branches from a main nerve or blood vessel. **3** *Math.* a fixed point from which coordinates are measured, as where axes intersect.

o·rig·i·nal /əˈrijənl/ ▸adj. **1** used or produced at the creation or earliest stage of something: *costumes made from the original designs.* ■ present or existing at the beginning of a series or process; first: *the original owner of the house.* **2** created directly and personally by a particular artist; not a copy or imitation: *original Rembrandts.* **3** not dependent on other people's ideas; inventive and unusual: *a subtle and original thinker.*

▸n. **1** something serving as a model or basis for imitations or copies: *the portrait may be a copy of the original.* ■ (**the original**) the form or language in which something was first produced or created: *the study of Russian texts in the original.* ■ (**the original of**) a person or place on which a character or location in a literary work is based: *the paper where the original of the play's Walter Burns worked.* ■ a song, picture, etc., produced by a performer or artist personally: *a mix of traditional tunes and originals.* ■ a book or recording that has not been previously made available in a different form: *paperback originals.* ■ a garment made to order from a design specially prepared for a fashion collection. **2** an eccentric or unusual person: *he was one of the true originals.* —**o·rig·i·nal·ly** *adv.*

o·rig·i·nal·i·ty /əˌrijəˈnalitē/ ▸n. the ability to think independently and creatively: *a writer of great originality.* ■ the quality of being novel or unusual: *he congratulated her on the originality of her costume.*

o·rig·i·nal sin ▸n. *Christian Theol.* the tendency to sin innate in all human beings, held to be inherited from Adam in consequence of the Fall.

o·rig·i·nate /əˈrijəˌnāt/ ▸v. [intr.] have a specified beginning: *the word originated as a marketing term.* ■ [tr.] create or initiate (something): *he is responsible for originating this particular cliché.* —**o·rig·i·na·tion** /əˌrijəˈnāSHən/ *n.* —**o·rig·i·na·tive** /-ˌnātiv/ *adj.* —**o·rig·i·na·tor** /-ˌnātər/ *n.*

O-ring ▸n. a gasket in the form of a ring with a circular cross section, typically made of pliable material such as neoprene, used to seal connections in pipes, tubes, etc.

o·ri·ole /ˈôrēˌōl/ ▸n. **1** an Old World bird (genus *Oriolus*, family Oriolidae) related to the starlings that feeds on fruit and insects, the male typically having bright yellow and black plumage. **2** a New World bird (genus *Icterus*) of the American blackbird family, with black and orange or yellow plumage, including the **Baltimore oriole** (*I. galbula*).

O·ri·on /əˈrīən/ ▸ **1** *Greek Mythol.* a giant and hunter who was changed into a constellation at his death. **2** *Astron.* a conspicuous constellation (the Hunter), said to represent a hunter holding a club and shield. It lies on the celestial equator and contains many bright stars, including Rigel, Betelgeuse, and a line of three that form **Orion's belt**.

or·mo·lu /ˈôrməˌloō/ ▸n. a gold-colored alloy of copper, zinc, and sometimes tin, cast into desired shapes and often gilded, used esp. in the 18th century for decorating furniture and making ornaments.

or·na·ment ▸n. /ˈôrnəmənt/ a thing used to adorn something but usually having no practical purpose, esp. a small object such as a figurine. ■ a quality or person adding grace, beauty, or honor to something: *the design would be a great ornament to the metropolis.* ■ decoration added to embellish something, esp. a building: *it served more for ornament than for protection.* ■ (**ornaments**) *Mus.* embellishments and decorations, such as trills or grace notes, added to a melody.

▸v. /ˈôrnəˌment/ [tr.] adorn; beautify: *the men and women in the Stone Age ornamented their caves.* —**or·na·men·ta·tion** /ˌôrnəmenˈtāSHən/ *n.*

or·na·men·tal /ˌôrnəˈmentl/ ▸adj. serving or intended as an ornament; decorative: *an ornamental fountain.*

▸n. a plant or tree grown for its attractive appearance. —**or·na·men·tal·ism** /-ˌizəm/ *n.* —**or·na·men·tal·ist** /-ist/ *n.* —**or·na·men·tal·ly** *adv.*

or·nate /ôrˈnāt/ ▸adj. made in an intricate shape or decorated with complex patterns: *an ornate wrought-iron railing.* ■ (of literary style) using unusual words and complex constructions: *peculiarly ornate and metaphorical language.* ■ (of musical composition or performance) using many ornaments such as grace notes and trills. —**or·nate·ly** *adv.* —**or·nate·ness** *n.*

or·ner·y /ˈôrn(ə)rē/ ▸adj. *inf.* bad-tempered and combative: *some hogs are just mean and ornery.* ■ stubborn: *taking the singer's ornery radicalism in a* *different direction.* ▷early 19th cent.: variant of *ordinary*, representing a dialect pronunciation. **—or·ner·i·ness** *n.*

or·ni·thol·o·gy /ˌôrnəˈTHäləjē/ ▶*n.* the scientific study of birds. **—or·ni·tho·log·i·cal** /ˌôrniTHəˈläjikəl/ *adj.* **—or·ni·tho·log·i·cal·ly** /ˌôrniTHəˈläjik(ə)lē/ *adv.* **—or·ni·thol·o·gist** /-jist/ *n.*

o·rog·e·ny /ôˈräjənē/ ▶*n. Geol.* a process in which a section of the earth's crust is folded and deformed by lateral compression to form a mountain range. **—or·o·gen·e·sis** /ˌôrōˈjenəsis/ *n.* **—or·o·gen·ic** /ˌôrōˈjenik/ *adj.*

o·ro·tund /ˈôrəˌtənd/ ▶*adj.* (of the voice or phrasing) full, round, and imposing. ■ (of writing, style, or expression) pompous; pretentious. **—o·ro·tun·di·ty** /ˌôrəˈtənditē/ *n.*

or·phan /ˈôrfən/ ▶*n.* **1** a child whose parents are dead. ■ a person or thing bereft of protection, position, etc.: *radioactive wastes are the main orphan of the nuclear era.* **2** *Printing* the first line of a paragraph set as the last line of a page or column, considered undesirable.
▶*v.* [*tr.*] (usu. **be orphaned**) make (a person or animal) an orphan: *John was orphaned at 12.*
▶*adj.* denoting, of, or for an orphan or orphans. ■ bereft of protection, position, etc.: *orphan garbage barges aimlessly wandering the oceans.* **—or·phan·hood** /-ˌho͝od/ *n.*

or·phan·age /ˈôrfənij/ ▶*n.* a residential institution for the care and education of orphans. ■ *archaic* the state or condition of being an orphan.

or·rer·y /ˈôrərē/ ▶*n.* (*pl.* **-rer·ies**) a mechanical model of the solar system, or of just the sun, earth, and moon, used to represent their relative positions and motions.

or·tho·don·tics /ˌôrTHəˈdäntiks/ (also **or·tho·don·tia** /-ˈdänsH(ē)ə/) ▶*pl. n.* [treated as *sing.*] the treatment of irregularities in the teeth (esp. of alignment and occlusion) and jaws, including the use of braces. **—or·tho·don·tic** *adj.* **—or·tho·don·ti·cal·ly** /-tik(ə)lē/ *adv.* **—or·tho·don·tist** /-tist/ *n.*

or·tho·dox /ˈôrTHəˌdäks/ ▶*adj.* **1** (of a person or their views, esp. religious or political ones, or other beliefs or practices) conforming to what is generally or traditionally accepted as right or true; established and approved: *the orthodox economics of today.* ■ (of a person) not independent-minded; conventional and unoriginal: *a relatively orthodox artist.* **2** (of a thing) of the ordinary or usual type; normal: *they avoided orthodox jazz venues.* **3** (usu. **Orthodox**) (of the Jews or Judaism) strictly keeping to traditional doctrine and ritual. **4** (usu. **Orthodox**) of or relating to the Orthodox Church. **—or·tho·dox·ly** *adv.*

Or·tho·dox Church ▶a Christian church or federation of churches originating in the Greek-speaking church of the Byzantine Empire, not accepting the authority of the pope, and using ancient forms of service.

or·tho·dox·y /ˈôrTHəˌdäksē/ ▶*n.* (*pl.* **-dox·ies**) **1** authorized or generally accepted theory, doctrine, or practice: *monetarist orthodoxy.* ■ the quality of conforming to such theories, doctrines, or practices: *writings of unimpeachable orthodoxy.* **2** the whole community of Orthodox Jews or Orthodox Christians.

or·thog·ra·phy /ôrˈTHägrəfē/ ▶*n.* (*pl.* **-phies**) the conventional spelling system of a language. ■ the study of spelling and how letters combine to represent sounds and form words. **—or·thog·ra·pher** /-fər/ *n.* **—or·tho·graph·ic** /ˌôrTHəˈgrafik/ *adj.* **—or·tho·graph·i·cal** /ˌôrTHəˈgrafikəl/ *adj.* **—or·tho·graph·i·cal·ly** /ˌôrTHəˈgrafik(ə)lē/ *adv.*

or·tho·ker·a·tol·o·gy /ˌôrTHōˌkerəˈtäləjē/ ▶*n.* the temporary reshaping of the cornea (usually overnight) with specially made rigid contact lenses, in order to correct myopia.

or·tho·pe·dics /ˌôrTHəˈpēdiks/ (*Brit.* **or·tho·pae·dics**) ▶*pl. n.* [treated as *sing.*] the branch of medicine dealing with the correction of deformities of bones or muscles. **—or·tho·pe·dic** *adj.* **—or·tho·pe·di·cal·ly** /-ik(ə)lē/ *adv.* **—or·tho·pe·dist** /-dist/ *n.*

or·tho·pox·vi·rus /ˈôrTHōˌpäksˌvīrəs/ ▶*n.* any of a group of viruses pathological in humans and animals that includes the cowpox, smallpox, and monkeypox viruses.

OS ▶*abbr.* ■ (in calculating dates) Old Style. ■ *Comput.* operating system. ■ Ordinary Seaman. ■ (in the UK) Ordnance Survey. ■ (as a size of clothing) outsize. ■ out of stock.

Os ▶*symb.* the chemical element osmium.

O·sage /ˈōˌsāj/ ▶*n.* (*pl.* same or **O·sages**) **1** a member of an American Indian people formerly inhabiting Missouri. **2** the Siouan language of this people.
▶*adj.* of or relating to this people or their language.

Os·car[1] /ˈäskər/ ▶*n. trademark* the nickname for one of the golden statuettes given as an Academy Award. ■ (**the Oscars**) the annual presentation of the Academy Awards.

Os·car[2] ▶*n.* a code word representing the letter O, used in radio communication.

os·car /ˈäskər/ (also **oscar cichlid**) ▶*n.* a South American cichlid (*Astronotus ocellatus*, family Cichlidae) with velvety brown young and multicolored adults, popular in aquariums.

os·cil·late /ˈäsəˌlāt/ ▶*v.* [*intr.*] **1** move or swing back and forth at a regular speed: *a pendulum oscillates about its lowest point.* ■ *fig.* waver between extremes of opinion, action, or quality: *he was oscillating between fear and bravery.* **2** *Physics* vary in magnitude or position in a regular manner around a central point. **—os·cil·la·tion** /ˌäsəˈlāsHən/ *n.* **—os·cil·la·tor** /-tər/ *n.* **—os·cil·la·to·ry** /əˈsiləˌtôrē/ *adj.*

os·cil·lo·scope /əˈsiləˌskōp/ ▶*n.* a device for viewing oscillations, as of electrical voltage or current, by a display on the screen of a cathode-ray tube. **—os·cil·lo·scop·ic** /əˌsiləˈskäpik/ *adj.*

OSHA /ˈōsHə/ ▶*abbr.* (in the U.S.) Occupational Safety and Health Administration.

o·sier /ˈōzHər/ ▶*n.* **1** a small Eurasian willow (*Salix viminalis*) that grows mostly in wet habitats and is a major source of the long flexible shoots used in basketwork. **2** *n.* any of several North American dogwoods.

os·mi·um /ˈäzmēəm/ ▶*n.* the chemical element of atomic number 76, a hard, dense, silvery-white metal of the transition series. (Symbol: **Os**)

os·mo·sis /äzˈmōsis; äs-/ ▶*n. Biol. & Chem.* a process by which molecules of a solvent tend to pass through a semipermeable membrane from a less concentrated solution into a more concentrated one, thus equalizing the concentrations of solute on each side of the membrane. ■ *fig.* the process of gradual or unconscious assimilation of ideas, knowledge, etc.: *what she knows of the blue-blood set she learned not through birthright, not even through wealth, but through osmosis.* **—os·mot·ic** /-mätik/ *adj.* **—os·mot·i·cal·ly** /-ˈmädik(ə)lē/ *adv.*

os·prey /ˈäsprā; -prē/ ▶*n.* (*pl.* **-eys**) a large fish-eating bird of prey (*Pandion haliaetus*, family Pandionidae) with long narrow wings and a white underside and crown, found throughout the world. Also called **FISH HAWK**.

OSS ▶*abbr.* Office of Strategic Services, a U.S. intelligence organization during World War II.

os·si·fy /ˈäsəˌfī/ ▶*v.* (**-fies, -fied**) [*intr.*] turn into bone or bony tissue: *these tracheal cartilages may ossify.* ■ [often as *adj.*] (**ossified**) *fig.* cease developing; be stagnant or rigid: *ossified political institutions.* **—os·si·fi·ca·tion** /ˌäsəfiˈkāsHən/ *n.*

os·so buc·co /ˈäsō ˈbo͞okō/ ▶*n.* an Italian dish made with veal shank containing marrowbone, stewed in wine with vegetables and seasonings.

os·su·ar·y /ˈäsHo͞oˌerē; ˈäs(y)o͞o-/ ▶*n.* (*pl.* **-ar·ies**) a container or room into which the bones of dead people are placed.

os·ten·si·ble /äˈstensəbəl; əˈsten-/ ▶*adj.* stated or appearing to be true, but not necessarily so: *the delay may have a deeper cause than the ostensible reason.* **—os·ten·si·bil·i·ty** /-ˌstensəˈbilitē/ *n.* **—os·ten·si·bly** *adv.*

os·ten·sive /äˈstensiv/ ▶*adj.* directly or clearly demonstrative. **—os·ten·sive·ly** *adv.* **—os·ten·sive·ness** *n.*

os·ten·ta·tion /ˌästənˈtāsHən/ ▶*n.* pretentious and vulgar display, esp. of wealth and luxury, intended to impress or attract notice: *the office was spacious, but without any trace of ostentation.*

os·ten·ta·tious /ˌästənˈtāsHəs/ ▶*adj.* characterized by vulgar or pretentious display; designed to impress or attract notice: *books that people buy and display ostentatiously but never actually finish.* **—os·ten·ta·tious·ly** *adv.* **—os·ten·ta·tious·ness** *n.*

os·te·o·ar·thri·tis /ˌästēōˌärˈTHrītis/ ▶*n. Med.* degeneration of joint cartilage and the underlying bone, most common from middle age onward. It causes pain and stiffness, esp. in the hip, knee, and thumb joints. Compare with **RHEUMATOID ARTHRITIS**. **—os·te·o·ar·thrit·ic** /-ˈTHritik/ *adj.*

os·te·ol·o·gy /ˌästēˈäləjē/ ▶*n.* the study of the structure and function of the skeleton and bony structures. **—os·te·o·log·i·cal** /ˌästēəˈläjikəl/ *adj.* **—os·te·o·log·i·cal·ly** /ˌästēəˈläjik(ə)lē/ *adv.* **—os·te·ol·o·gist** /-jist/ *n.*

os·te·o·my·e·li·tis /ˌästēōˌmīəˈlītis/ ▶*n. Med.* inflammation of bone or bone marrow, usually due to infection.

os·te·op·a·thy /ˌästēˈäpəTHē/ ▶*n.* a branch of medical practice that emphasizes the treatment of medical disorders through the manipulation and massage of the bones, joints, and muscles. **—os·te·o·path** /ˈästēəˌpaTH/ *n.* **—os·te·o·path·ic** /ˌästēəˈpaTHik/ *adj.* **—os·te·o·path·i·cal·ly** /ˌästēəˈpaTHik(ə)lē/ *adv.*

Pronunciation Key ə *ago, up;* ər *over, fur;* a *hat;* ā *ate;* ä *car;* CH *chin;* e *let;* ē *see;* e(ə) *air;* i *fit;* ī *by;* i(ə)r *ear;* NG *sing;* ō *go;* ô *law, for;* oi *toy;* o͞o *good;* o͞o *goo;* ou *out;* SH *she;* TH *thin;* TH *then;* (h)w *why;* ZH *vision*

os·te·o·pe·ni·a /ˌästēō'pēnēə/ ▶n. reduced bone mass of lesser severity than osteoporosis.

os·te·o·po·ro·sis /ˌästēōpə'rōsis/ ▶n. a medical condition in which the bones become brittle and fragile from loss of tissue, typically as a result of hormonal changes, or deficiency of calcium or vitamin D. —**os·te·o·po·rot·ic** /-'rätik/ adj.

os·ti·na·to /ˌästi'nätō/ ▶n. (pl. -tos or -ti /-tē/) a continually repeated musical phrase or rhythm.

ost·ler /'äslər/ ▶n. variant spelling of HOSTLER.

os·tra·cize /'ästrə,sīz/ ▶v. [tr.] exclude (someone) from a society or group: a group of people who have been ridiculed, ostracized, and persecuted for centuries. —**os·tra·cism** /-,sizəm/ n.

os·trich /'ästrich/ ▶n. 1 a flightless swift-running African bird (Struthio camelus, family Struthionidae) with a long neck, long legs, and two toes on each foot. It is the largest living bird. 2 a person who refuses to face reality or accept facts.

OT ▶abbr. ■ occupational therapist. ■ occupational therapy. ■ Old Testament. ■ overnight telegram. ■ overtime.

oth·er /'əTHər/ ▶adj. & pron. 1 used to refer to a person or thing that is different or distinct from one already mentioned or known about: [as adj.] stick the camera on a tripod or some other means of support other people found her difficult | [as pron.] a language unrelated to any other. ■ the alternative of two: [as adj.] the other side of the page | [as pron.] flinging up first one arm and then the other. ■ those remaining in a group; those not already mentioned: [as adj.] they took the other three away in an ambulance | [as pron.] Fred set off and the others followed. 2 further; additional: [as adj.] one other word of advice | [as pron.] reporting three stories and rewriting three others. ▷Old English ōther, of Germanic origin; related to Dutch and German ander, from an Indo-European root meaning 'different.'

oth·er·ness /'əTHərnis/ ▶n. the quality or fact of being different: the developed world has been celebrating African music while altogether denying its otherness.

oth·er·wise /'əTHər,wīz/ ▶adv. 1 in circumstances different from those present or considered: the collection brings visitors who might not come to the college otherwise. ■ or else: I'm not motivated by money, otherwise I would have quit. 2 in other respects; apart from that: an otherwise totally black cat with a single white whisker. 3 in a different way: he means mischief—it's no good pretending otherwise. ■ as an alternative: pre-Renaissance mathematician Leonardo Pisano, otherwise known as Fibonacci. ▶adj. in a different state or situation: if it were otherwise, we would be unable to acquire knowledge.

oth·er·world·ly /ˌəTHər'wərldlē/ ▶adj. of or relating to an imaginary or spiritual world: music of almost otherworldly beauty. ■ unworldly: celibate clerics with a very otherworldly outlook. —**oth·er·world·li·ness** n.

o·ti·ose /'ōshē,ōs; 'ōtē,ōs/ ▶adj. serving no practical purpose or result: he did fuss, uttering otiose explanations. —**o·ti·ose·ly** adv.

o·ti·tis /ō'tītis/ ▶n. Med. inflammation of the ear.

o·to·scope /'ōtə,skōp/ ▶n. an instrument designed for visual examination of the eardrum and the passage of the outer ear, typically having a light and a set of lenses. —**o·to·scop·ic** /ˌōtə'skäpik/ adj. —**o·to·scop·i·cal·ly** /ˌōtə'skäpik(ə)lē/ adv.

ot·ter /'ätər/ ▶n. a fish-eating mammal (Lutra and other genera) of the weasel family, typically semiaquatic, with an elongated body, dense fur, and webbed feet. Its several species include the **river otter** (L. canadensis). See also SEA OTTER.

Ot·to·man /'ätəmən/ ▶adj. hist. 1 of or relating to the Turkish dynasty of Osman I. ■ of or relating to the branch of the Turks to which he belonged. ■ of or relating to the Ottoman Empire ruled by his successors. 2 Turkish. ▶n. (pl. -mans) a Turk, esp. of the period of the Ottoman Empire.

ot·to·man /'ätəmən/ ▶n. (pl. -mans) a low upholstered seat, or footstool, without a back or arms that typically serves also as a box, with the seat hinged to form a lid.

ouch /ouch/ ▶interj. used to express pain.

ought¹ /ôt/ ▶modal verb (3rd sing. present and past **ought**) 1 used to indicate duty or correctness, typically when criticizing someone's actions: they ought to respect the law | it ought not to be allowed. ■ used to indicate a desirable or expected state: he ought to be able to take the initiative. ■ used to give or ask advice: you ought to go. 2 used to indicate something that is probable: five minutes ought to be enough time.

ought² ▶n. archaic term for AUGHT².

ought³ ▶pron. variant spelling of AUGHT¹.

ought·n't /'ôtnt/ ▶contr. of ought not.

Oui·ja board /'wēja; -jē/ ▶n. trademark a board printed with letters, numbers, and other signs, to which a planchette or movable indicator points, supposedly in answer to questions from people at a seance.

ounce¹ /ouns/ ▶n. 1 (abbr.: **oz**) a unit of weight of one sixteenth of a pound avoirdupois (approx. 28 grams). ■ a unit of one twelfth of a pound troy or apothecaries' measure, equal to 480 grains (approx. 31 grams). 2 a very small amount of something: Robin summoned up every ounce of strength. 3 short for FLUID OUNCE.

ounce² ▶n. another term for SNOW LEOPARD.

our /ou(ə)r; är/ ▶possessive adj. 1 belonging to or associated with the speaker and one or more other people previously mentioned or easily identified: Jo and I had our hair cut. ■ belonging to or associated with people in general: when we hear a sound, our brains identify the source quickly. 2 used by a writer, editor, or monarch to refer to something belonging to or associated with himself or herself: we want to know what you, our readers, think.

ours /'ou(ə)rz; ärz/ ▶possessive pron. used to refer to a thing or things belonging to or associated with the speaker and one or more other people previously mentioned or easily identified: ours was the ugliest house on the block.

our·selves /ou(ə)r'selvz; är-/ ▶pron. [first person pl.] 1 [reflexive] used as the object of a verb or preposition when this is the same as the subject of the clause and the subject is the speaker and one or more other people considered together: for this we can only blame ourselves. 2 we or us personally (used to emphasize the speaker and one or more other people considered together): we invented it ourselves.

oust /oust/ ▶v. [tr.] drive out or expel (someone) from a position or place: he ousted a long-term incumbent by only 500 votes.

oust·er /'oustər/ ▶n. dismissal or expulsion from a position: a showdown that may lead to his ouster as leader of the party.

out /out/ ▶adv. 1 moving or appearing to move away from a particular place, esp. one that is enclosed or hidden: he walked out into the street. ■ situated or operating in the open air, not in buildings: the search-and-rescue team have been out looking for you. ■ no longer detained in custody or in jail: they would be out on bail in no time. 2 away from one's usual base or residence: the team had put on a marvelous display out in Georgia. ■ in a public place for purposes of pleasure or entertainment: an evening out at a restaurant. 3 to sea, away from the land: the fleet put out from Cyprus. ■ (of the tide) falling or at its lowest level: the tide was going out. 4 indicating a specified distance away from the goal line or finishing line: he scored from 70 meters out. 5 so as to be revealed or known: find out what you can. ■ aloud; so as to be heard: Miss Beard cried out in horror. 6 at or to an end: the romance fizzled out. ■ so as to be finished or complete: I'll leave them to fight it out | I typed out the poem. ■ (to add a sense of completeness to another word or phrase): the crowd had thinned out | he crossed out a word. 7 (of a light or fire) so as to be extinguished or no longer burning: at ten o'clock the lights went out. ■ (of a stain or mark) no longer visible; removed: try to get the stain out. 8 (of a party, politician, etc.) not in office. 9 (of a jury) considering its verdict in secrecy.

▶prep. through to the outside: he ran out the door.

▶adj. 1 not at home or at one's place of work: if he called, she'd pretend to be out. 2 revealed or made public: the secret was soon out. ■ (of a flower) in bloom; open. ■ published: the book should be out before the end of the month. ■ inf. in existence or in use: it works as well as any system that's out. ■ not concealing one's homosexuality: I had been out since I was seventeen. 3 no longer alight; extinguished: the fire was nearly out. 4 at an end: school was out for the summer. ■ inf. no longer in fashion: life in the fast lane is out. 5 not possible or worth considering: a trip to the seaside is out. 6 in a state of unconsciousness. ■ Boxing unable to rise before the count of ten. 7 mistaken; in error: he was slightly out in his calculations. 8 (of the ball in tennis and similar games) outside the designated playing area. 9 Baseball & Cricket no longer batting or on base, having had one's turn ended by the team in the field: the Yankees are out in the ninth | Johnson was out at second.

▶n. 1 inf. a way of escaping from a problem or dilemma: he was desperately looking for an out. 2 Baseball an act of putting a player out. 3 (**the outs**) the political party or politicians not in office.

▶v. 1 [intr.] come or go out; emerge: the truth will out. 2 [tr.] inf. reveal the homosexuality of (a prominent person). ▷Old English ūt (adverb), ūtian (verb), of Germanic origin; related to Dutch uit and German aus.

out·age /'outij/ ▶n. a period when a power supply or other service is not available or when equipment is closed down.

out-and-out ▶adj. in every respect; absolute; without question: an out-and-out crook.

out·back /'out,bak/ ▶n. (**the outback**) the remote and often uninhabited inland regions of Australia. ■ any remote or sparsely populated region. **—out·back·er** n.

out·bal·ance /ˌout'baləns/ ▶v. [tr.] be more valuable, important, or influential than; make up for: *their high capacity outbalances this defect.*

out·bid /ˌout'bid/ ▶v. (**-bid·ding**; *past* and *past part.* **-bid**) [tr.] offer to pay a higher price for something (than another person): *residential builders could always outbid any farmer for the land.*

out·board /'out,bô(ə)rd/ ▶adj. & adv. on, toward, or near the outside, esp. of a ship or vehicle: [as adj.] *the outboard rear seats* | [as adv.] *the chart table faces outboard.* ■ [as adj.] (of a motor) portable and usually mounted on the outside of the stern of a boat. ▶n. an outboard motor. ■ a boat with such a motor.

out·bound /'out'bound/ ▶adj. & adv. traveling away from a particular place, esp. on the first leg of a round trip: [as adj.] *an outbound flight.*

out·break /'out,brāk/ ▶n. the sudden or violent start of something unwelcome, such as war, disease, etc.: *the outbreak of World War II.*

out·build·ing /'out,bildiNG/ ▶n. a building, such as a shed, barn, or garage, on the same property but separate from a more important one, such as a house.

out·burst /'out,bərst/ ▶n. a sudden release of strong emotion: *"she screamed at him about it one day," said one source who witnessed the outburst.* ■ a sudden outbreak of a particular activity: *a wild outburst of applause.* ■ *Physics* a sudden emission of energy or particles: *a very dramatic outburst of neutrons.*

out·cast /'out,kast/ ▶n. a person who has been rejected by society or a social group. ▶adj. rejected or cast out: *made to feel outcast and inadequate.*

out·class /ˌout'klas/ ▶v. [tr.] be far superior to: *they totally outclassed us in the first half.*

out·come /'out,kəm/ ▶n. the way a thing turns out; a consequence: *it is the outcome of the vote that counts.*

out·crop /'out,kräp/ ▶n. bedrock exposed at the surface: *dramatic limestone outcrops.* ■ *fig.* a noticeable manifestation or occurrence. ▶v. (**-cropped, -crop·ping**) [intr.] [often as n.] (**outcropping**) appear as an outcrop: *jumbled outcroppings of bedrock.*

out·cry /'out,krī/ ▶n. (pl. **-cries**) an exclamation or shout: *an outcry of spontaneous passion.* ■ a strong expression of public disapproval or anger: *the public outcry over the bombing.*

out·dat·ed /ˌout'dātid/ ▶adj. out of date; obsolete. **—out·dat·ed·ness** n.

out·dis·tance /ˌout'distəns/ ▶v. [tr.] leave (a competitor or pursuer) far behind: *she could maintain a fast enough pace to outdistance any pursuers.*

out·do /ˌout'dōō/ ▶v. (**-does, -doing**; *past* **-did**; *past part.* **-done**) [tr.] be more successful than: *the men tried to outdo each other in their generosity* | *not to be outdone, Vicky and Laura reached the same standard.*

out·door /'out'dôr/ ▶adj. done, situated, or used out of doors: *a huge outdoor concert.* ■ (of a person) fond of the open air or open-air activities: *a rugged, outdoor type.*

out·doors /ˌout'dôrz/ ▶adv. in or into the open air; outside a building or shelter: *it was warm enough to eat outdoors.* ▶n. (usu. **the outdoors**) any area outside buildings or shelter, typically far away from human habitation: *a lover of the great outdoors.*

out·doors·man /ˌout'dôrzmən/ ▶n. (pl. **-men**; fem. **out·doors·wom·an** /-,wŏomən/ pl. **-wom·en**) a person who spends a lot of time outdoors or doing outdoor activities.

out·er /'outər/ ▶adj. outside; external: *the outer door.* ■ further from the center or inside: *the outer hall at the museum's main entrance.* ■ (esp. in place names) more remote: *Outer Mongolia.*

out·er·most /'outər,mōst/ ▶adj. farthest from the center: *the outermost layer of the earth.* ▶pron. the one that is farthest from the center: *the orbit of the outermost of these eight planets.*

out·er space ▶n. the physical universe beyond the earth's atmosphere.

out·er·wear /'outər,we(ə)r/ ▶n. clothing worn over other clothes, esp. for the outdoors.

out·field /'out,fēld/ ▶n. the outer part of the field of play in various sports, in particular: ■ *Baseball* the grassy area beyond the infield. ■ [treated as sing. or pl.] the players stationed in the outfield, collectively. **—out·field·er** n.

out·fight /ˌout'fīt/ ▶v. (*past* and *past part.* **-fought**) [tr.] fight better than and beat (an opponent).

out·fit /'out,fit/ ▶n. a set of clothes worn together, typically for a particular occasion or purpose: *a riding outfit.* ■ *inf.* a group of people undertaking a particular activity together, as a group of musicians, a military unit, or a business concern: *Tom was the brains of the outfit.* ■ a

complete set of equipment or articles needed for a particular purpose: *a repair outfit.*
▶v. (**-fit·ted, -fit·ting**) [tr.] (usu. **be outfitted**) provide (someone) with a set of clothes: *an auction of dolls outfitted by world-famous designers.* ■ provide with equipment: *planes outfitted with sophisticated electronic gear.*

out·fit·ter /'out,fitər/ (also **out·fit·ters**) ▶n. an establishment that sells clothing, equipment, and services, esp. for outdoor activities: *an outfitter that provides professional guides.*

out·flank /ˌout'flaNGk/ ▶v. [tr.] move around the side of (an enemy) so as to outmaneuver them: *the Germans had sought to outflank them from the northeast.* ■ *fig.* outwit: *an attempt to outflank the opposition.*

out·flow /'out,flō/ ▶n. a large amount of money, liquid, or people that moves or is transferred out of a place: *an outflow of foreign currency.* ■ the flowing out of a liquid from a container or cavity: *the combination of arterial inflow and venous outflow.* ■ *Meteorol.* the outward flow of air from a weather system, associated with wind shift and temperature drop.

out·fox /ˌout'fäks/ ▶v. [tr.] *inf.* defeat or deceive (someone) by being more clever or cunning than they are; outwit.

out·go·ing /'out,gōiNG/ ▶adj. **1** friendly and socially confident: *she's an extremely affable, jovial, outgoing type of person.* **2** leaving an office or position, esp. after an election defeat or completed term of office: *the outgoing governor.* ■ going out or away from a particular place: *incoming and outgoing calls.*

out·grow /ˌout'grō/ ▶v. (*past* **-grew**; *past part.* **-grown**) [tr.] grow too big for (something): *babies outgrow their first car seat at six to nine months.* ■ leave behind as one matures: *is it a permanent injury, or will the colt outgrow it?* ■ grow faster or taller than: *the more vigorous plants outgrow their weaker neighbors.*

out·growth /'out,grōTH/ ▶n. something that grows out of something else: *outgrowths at the base of the leaf.* ■ a natural development or result of something: *the book is an imaginative outgrowth of practical criticism.* ■ the process of growing out: *with further outgrowth the radius and ulna develop.*

out·gun /ˌout'gən/ ▶v. (**-gunned, -gun·ning**) [tr.] [often as adj.] (**outgunned**) have better or more weaponry than: *offensives that overwhelmed the outgunned and outmanned armies.*

out·house /'out,hous/ ▶n. an outbuilding containing a toilet, typically with no plumbing. ■ any outbuilding.

out·ing /'outiNG/ ▶n. **1** a trip taken for pleasure, esp. one lasting a day or less: *they would go on family outings to the movies.* ■ a brief journey from home: *her daily outing to the stores.* ■ *inf.* an appearance in something, as an athletic event or show: *her first screen outing in three years.* **2** the act or practice of revealing the homosexuality of a person.

out·land·ish /out'landiSH/ ▶adj. looking or sounding bizarre or unfamiliar: *outlandish brightly colored clothes* | *the most outlandish ideas.* **—out·land·ish·ly** adv. **—out·land·ish·ness** n.

out·last /ˌout'last/ ▶v. [tr.] outlive; last longer than: *the kind of beauty that will outlast youth.* ■ endure longer so as to overcome (an opponent or challenge).

out·law /'out,lô/ ▶n. a person who has broken the law, esp. one who remains at large or is a fugitive. ■ an intractable horse or other animal. ■ *hist.* a person deprived of the benefit and protection of the law. ▶v. [tr.] ban; make illegal: *Maryland outlawed cheap small-caliber pistols.* **—out·law·ry** /-,lôrē/ n.

out·lay /'out,lā/ ▶n. an amount of money spent on something.

out·let /'out,let/ ▶n. a means by which something escapes, passes, or is released, in particular: ■ a pipe or hole through which water or gas may escape. ■ the mouth of a river. ■ a point in an electrical circuit from which current may be drawn. ■ a place from which goods are sold or distributed: *a fast-food outlet.* ■ a retail store that sells the goods of a specific manufacturer or brand: [as adj.] *an outlet store.* ■ a retail store offering discounted merchandise, esp. overstocked or irregular items. ■ a market for goods: *the indoor markets in Moscow were an outlet for surplus collective-farm produce.* ■ *fig.* a means of expressing one's talents, energy, or emotions: *writing became the main outlet for his energies.*

out·line /'out,līn/ ▶n. **1** a line or set of lines enclosing or indicating the shape of an object in a sketch or diagram: *fill in the outlines with color.* ■ a line or set of lines of this type, perceived as defining the contours or bounds of an object: *the outlines of her face.* **2** a general plan giving the essential features but not the detail: *an outline of the theory of evolution* | *a course outline.* ■ a draft of a diagram, plan, proposal, etc.,

---

Pronunciation Key ə *ago,* up; ər *over, fur;* a *hat;* ā *ate;* ä *car;* CH *chin;* e *let;* ē *see;* e(ə)r *air;* i *fit;* ī *by;* i(ə)r *ear;* NG *sing;* ō *go;* ô *law, for;* oi *toy;* ŏŏ *good;* ōō *goo;* ou *out;* SH *she;* TH *thin;* TH *then;* (h)w *why;* ZH *vision*

summarizing the main points: *draw up an outline for the essay.* ■ the main features or general principles of something: *the main outlines of Elizabeth's career.*

▶*v.* [*tr.*] **1** draw, trace, or define the outer edge or shape of (something): *her large eyes were darkly outlined with eyeliner.* **2** give a summary of (something): *she outlined the case briefly.*

out·live /ˌoutˈliv/ ▶*v.* [*tr.*] (of a person) live longer than (another person): *women generally outlive men.* ■ survive or last beyond (a specified period or expected life span): *the organization had largely* **outlived its usefulness.** ■ *archaic* live through (an experience): *the world has outlived much.*

out·look /ˈoutˌlo͝ok/ ▶*n.* a person's point of view or general attitude to life: *broaden your* **outlook on life.** ■ a view: *the pleasant outlook from the lodge window.* ■ a place from which a view is possible: *emerging onto a cliffy outlook over a river.* ■ the prospect for the future: *the deteriorating economic outlook.* ■ the weather as forecast for the near future.

out·ly·ing /ˈoutˌlī-iNG/ ▶*adj.* situated far from a center; remote: *an outlying village.*

out·man /ˌoutˈman/ ▶*v.* (**-manned, -man·ning**) [*tr.*] [usu. as *adj.*] (**out-manned**) outnumber: *the rebels are outmanned and outmatched in armaments.* ■ overpower with skill or physical strength: *Mexico controlled the game and ran circles around the outmanned Guatemalan team.*

out·ma·neu·ver /ˌoutməˈno͞ovər/ ▶*v.* [*tr.*] evade (an opponent) by moving faster or with greater agility: *the YF-22 can outmaneuver any fighter flying today.* ■ use skill and cunning to secure an advantage over (someone): *he would be able to outmaneuver his critics.*

out·mod·ed /ˌoutˈmōdid/ ▶*adj.* old-fashioned. **—out·mod·ed·ness** *n.*

out·num·ber /ˌoutˈnəmbər/ ▶*v.* [*tr.*] be more numerous than: *women outnumbered men by three to one.*

out of date ▶*adj.* old-fashioned: *an out-of-date kitchen.* ■ no longer valid or relevant: *your passport is out of date.*

out·pace /ˌoutˈpās/ ▶*v.* [*tr.*] go faster than: *he took the pass and outpaced the defense to score in the corner.* ■ be more than; surpass: *salsa sales now outpace those for ketchup.*

out·par·cel /ˈoutˌpärsəl/ ▶*n.* a building lot separated or separable from a commercial development, the selling of which provides liquidity for the developer.

out·pa·tient /ˈoutˌpāSHənt/ ▶*n.* a patient who receives medical treatment without being admitted to a hospital.

out·per·form /ˌoutpərˈfôrm/ ▶*v.* [*tr.*] perform better than: *an experienced employee will outperform the novice.* ■ (of an investment) be more profitable than: *silver has outperformed the stock market.* **—out·per·for·mance** /-ˈfôrməns/ *n.*

out·place·ment /ˈoutˌplāsmənt/ ▶*n.* the provision of assistance to laid-off employees in finding new employment, either as a benefit provided by the employer directly, or through a specialist service.

out·post /ˈoutˌpōst/ ▶*n.* a small military camp or position at some distance from the main force, used esp. as a guard against surprise attack. ■ a remote part of a country or empire. ■ *fig.* something regarded as an isolated or remote branch of something: *the community is the last outpost of civilization in the far north.*

out·pour·ing /ˈoutˌpôriNG/ ▶*n.* something that streams out rapidly: *a massive outpouring of high-energy gamma rays.* ■ (often **outpourings**) an outburst of strong emotion: *spontaneous outpourings of affection and support.*

out·put /ˈoutˌpo͝ot/ ▶*n.* **1** the amount of something produced by a person, machine, or industry: *the diverse range of Liszt's output.* ■ the action or process of producing something: *the output of epinephrine.* ■ the power, energy, or other results supplied by a device or system: *the quality of the output from the printer is very good.* **2** *Electr.* a place where power or information leaves a system.

▶*v.* (**-put·ting**; *past* and *past part.* **-put** or **-put·ted**) [*tr.*] produce, deliver, or supply (data) using a computer or other device: *you can output the image directly to a video recording system.*

out·rage /ˈoutˌrāj/ ▶*n.* an extremely strong reaction of anger, shock, or indignation: *her voice trembled with outrage.* ■ an action or event causing such a reaction: *the decision was an outrage.*

▶*v.* [*tr.*] (usu. **be outraged**) arouse fierce anger, shock, or indignation in (someone): *he was outraged at this attempt to take his victory away from him.*

out·ra·geous /outˈrājəs/ ▶*adj.* **1** shockingly bad or excessive: *an outrageous act of bribery.* ■ wildly exaggerated or improbable: *the outrageous claims made by the previous administration.* **2** very bold, unusual, and startling: *her outrageous leotards and sexy routines.* **—out·ra·geous·ly** *adv.* **—out·ra·geous·ness** *n.*

out·rank /ˌoutˈraNGk/ ▶*v.* [*tr.*] have a higher rank than (someone else): *a father figure to many of the junior officers theoretically outranking him.* ■ be

better, more important, or more significant than: *fishing provided the chief employment, outranking both clothing and canning.*

ou·tré /o͞oˈtrā/ ▶*adj.* unusual and startling: *in 1975 the suggestion was considered outré—today it is orthodox.*

out·reach ▶*n.* /ˈoutˌrēCH/ the extent or length of reaching out. ■ an organization's involvement with or activity in the community, esp. in the context of social welfare: *her goal is to increase educational outreach.*

out·rid·er /ˈoutˌrīdər/ ▶*n.* a person in a motor vehicle or on horseback who goes in front of or beside a vehicle as an escort or guard: *an escort of police outriders.* ■ a person or thing that accompanies or precedes another, esp. as a precursor: *gray-white cumulus clouds—outriders of the storm.* ■ a mounted official who escorts racehorses to the starting post. **—out·rid·ing** /ˌoutˈrīdiNG/ *n.*

out·rig·ger /ˈoutˌrigər/ ▶*n.* a beam, spar, or framework projecting from or over the side of a ship or boat. ■ a float or secondary hull fixed parallel to a canoe or other boat to stabilize it. ■ a boat fitted with such a structure. ■ a similar projecting support in another structure or vehicle. **—out·rigged** /-ˌrigd/ *adj.*

outrigger

out·right ▶*adv.* /ˈoutˌrīt/ **1** altogether; completely: *logging has been banned outright.* ■ without reservation; openly: *she couldn't ask him outright.* **2** immediately: *the impact killed four horses outright.* ■ not by degrees or installments: *they decided to buy the company outright.*

▶*adj.* open and direct; not concealed: *an outright refusal.* ■ total; complete: *the outright abolition of the death penalty.* ■ undisputed; clear: *an outright victory.*

out·run /ˌoutˈrən/ ▶*v.* (**-run·ning**; *past* **-ran**; *past part.* **-run**) [*tr.*] run or travel faster or farther than. ■ escape from: *it's harder than anyone imagines to outrun destiny.* ■ go beyond; exceed: *his courage outran his prudence.*

out·sell /ˌoutˈsel/ ▶*v.* (*past* and *past part.* **-sold**) [*tr.*] be sold in greater quantities than: *his first foray into the assassin/thriller area could well outsell his other books.* ■ (of a person) sell more of something than (someone else): *Garth Brooks is outselling Michael Jackson.*

out·set /ˈoutˌset/ ▶*n.* the start or beginning of something: *a field of which he had known nothing at the outset and learned on the job.*

out·shine /ˌoutˈSHīn/ ▶*v.* (*past* and *past part.* **-shone**) [*tr.*] shine more brightly than. ■ be much better than (someone) in a particular area: *it is a shame when a mother outshines a daughter.*

out·shoot /ˌoutˈSHo͞ot/ ▶*v.* (*past* and *past part.* **-shot**) [*tr.*] shoot better than (someone else). ■ *Sports* make or take more shots than (another player or team).

out·side /ˈoutˌsīd/ ▶*n.* the external side or surface of something: *record the date on the outside of the file.* ■ the side of a bend or curve where the edge or surface is longer in extent. ■ the side of a racetrack farther from the center, where the lanes are longer. ■ the external appearance of someone or something: *was he as straight as he appeared* **on the outside**? ■ (in basketball) the area beyond the perimeter of the defense: *he often set up the Lakers' plays from the outside.*

▶*adj.* **1** situated on or near the exterior or external surface of something: *put the outside lights on.* ■ *Baseball* (of a pitch) passing home plate on the side of the plate away from the batter, not in the strike zone. ■ (in soccer and other sports) denoting positions nearer to the sides of the field. ■ (in basketball) taking place beyond the perimeter of the defense: *he needs work on his outside shot.* **2** not belonging to or coming from within a particular group: *I have some outside help.* ■ beyond one's own immediate personal concerns: *I was able to face the outside world again.* **3** (of an estimate) the greatest or highest possible: *new monthly charges that, according to outside estimates, may total $8 per line.*

▶*prep.* & *adv.* **1** situated or moving beyond the boundaries of (a room, building, or other enclosed space): [as *prep.*] *there was a boy outside the door* | [as *adv.*] *the dog was still barking outside.* ■ situated beyond the boundaries of (a particular location): [as *prep.*] *Vincennes, just outside Paris* | [as *adv.*] *those in the occupied territories and those outside.* ■ not being a member of (a particular group): [as *prep.*] *those of us outside the university.* ■ (in football, soccer, and other sports) closer to the side of the field than (another player): [as *prep.*] *Swift appeared outside him with Andrews on his left.* **2** [*prep.*] beyond the limits or scope of: *the high cost of shipping has put it outside their price range.*

out·sid·er /ˌoutˈsīdər/ ▶*n.* **1** a person who does not belong to a particular group. ■ a person who is not accepted by or who is isolated from society. **2** a competitor, applicant, etc., thought to have little chance of success: *he started as a rank outsider for the title.*

out·size /ˈoutˌsīz/ ▶*adj.* (also **out·sized**) exceptionally large.
▶*n.* an exceptionally large person or thing, esp. a garment made to measurements larger than the standard.

out·skirts /ˈoutˌskərts/ ▶*pl. n.* the outer parts of a town or city: *the park was built on the outskirts of New York in 1857.* ■ the fringes of something: *he likes to be on the outskirts of a discussion.*

out·smart /ˌoutˈsmärt/ ▶*v.* [*tr.*] *inf.* defeat or get the better of (someone) by being clever or cunning: *content with the illusion that they can outsmart the market.*

out·spend /ˌoutˈspend/ ▶*v.* [*trans.*] (*past* and *past part.* **-spent**) **1** spend more than (another person, agency, etc.): *Pashayan outspent Gene three dollars to one.* **2** exceed (one's resources) in spending: *by July, he had outspent his inheritance.*

out·spo·ken /ˌoutˈspōkən/ ▶*adj.* frank in stating one's opinions, esp. if they are critical or controversial: *he has been outspoken in his criticism.* **—out·spok·en·ly** *adv.* **—out·spok·en·ness** *n.*

out·spread /ˌoutˈspred/ ▶*adj.* fully extended or expanded: *outspread arms.*

out·stand·ing /ˌoutˈstandiNG, ˈout-/ ▶*adj.* **1** exceptionally good: *the team's outstanding performance.* ■ clearly noticeable: *works of outstanding banality.* **2** remaining to be done or dealt with: *how much work is still outstanding?* ■ (of a debt) remaining to be paid or dealt with: *there was a small charge outstanding.* **—out·stand·ing·ly** *adv.*

out·stay /ˌoutˈstā/ ▶*v.* [*tr.*] stay beyond the limit of (one's expected or permitted time): *employees who had outstayed their coffee break.*

out·step /ˌoutˈstep/ ▶*v.* (**-stepped**, **-step·ping**) [*tr.*] *rare* exceed.

out·stretch /ˌoutˈstreCH/ ▶*v.* [*tr.*] [usu. as *adj.*] (**outstretched**) extend or stretch out (something, esp. a hand or arm): *I walked with my arms outstretched.* ■ go beyond the limit of: *their good intentions far outstretched their capacity to offer help.*

out·strip /ˌoutˈstrip/ ▶*v.* (**-stripped**, **-strip·ping**) [*tr.*] move faster than and overtake (someone else). ■ exceed: *supply far outstripped demand.*

out·take /ˈouˌtāk/ ▶*n.* a scene or sequence filmed or recorded for a movie or program but not included in the final version.

out·vote /ˌoutˈvōt/ ▶*v.* [*tr.*] defeat by tallying a greater number of votes.

out·ward /ˈoutwərd/ ▶*adj.* **1** of, on, or from the outside: *the vehicle's outward and interior appearance.* ■ relating to the external appearance of something rather than its true nature or substance: *an outward display of friendliness.* **2** going out or away from a place: *the outward voyage.*
▶*adv.* away from the center or a particular point; toward the outside: *a window that opens outward.* **—out·ward·ly** *adv.* **—out·ward·ness** *n.*

out·wash /ˈoutˌwôSH, -ˌwäSH/ ▶*n.* material carried away from a glacier by meltwater and deposited beyond the moraine.

out·weigh /ˌoutˈwā/ ▶*v.* [*tr.*] be heavier than: *Bob outweighed him by more than twenty-five pounds.* ■ be greater or more significant than: *the advantages greatly outweigh the disadvantages.*

out·wit /ˌoutˈwit/ ▶*v.* (**-wit·ted**, **-wit·ting**) [*tr.*] deceive or defeat by greater ingenuity: *Ray had outwitted many an opponent.*

ou·zo /ˈo͞ozō/ ▶*n.* a Greek anise-flavored liqueur.

o·va /ˈōvə/ ▶ plural form of **OVUM**.

o·val /ˈōvəl/ ▶*adj.* having a rounded and slightly elongated outline or shape, like that of an egg: *her smooth oval face.*
▶*n.* a body, object, or design with such a shape or outline: *cut out two small ovals from the felt.* ■ an oval playing field or racing track. **—o·val·i·ty** /ōˈvalitē/ *n.* **—o·val·ness** *n.*

O·val Of·fice ▶the office of the president of the U.S., in the White House. ■ *fig.* this office regarded as representing the power of the executive branch of the U.S. government: *on orders from the Oval Office.*

o·va·ry /ˈōv(ə)rē/ ▶*n.* (*pl.* **-ries**) a female reproductive organ in which ova or eggs are produced, present in humans and other vertebrates as a pair. ■ *Bot.* the hollow base of the carpel of a flower, containing one or more ovules. **—o·var·i·an** /ōˈve(ə)rēən/ *adj.*

o·vate /ˈōˌvāt/ ▶*adj.* *chiefly Biol.* having an oval outline or ovoid shape, like an egg.

o·va·tion /ōˈvāSHən/ ▶*n.* a sustained and enthusiastic show of appreciation from an audience, esp. by means of applause: *the performance received a thundering ovation.*

ov·en /ˈəvən/ ▶*n.* an enclosed compartment, as in a kitchen range, for cooking and heating food. ■ a small furnace or kiln. ■ a cremation chamber in a Nazi concentration camp.

ov·en·proof /ˈəvənˌpro͞of/ ▶*adj.* (of cookware) suitable for use in an oven; heat-resistant.

ov·en·ware /ˈəvənˌwer/ ▶*n.* dishes that can be used for cooking food in an oven.

o·ver /ˈōvər/ ▶*prep.* **1** extending directly upward from: *I saw flames over Berlin.* ■ above so as to cover or protect: *an oxygen tent over the bed.* ■ extending above (a general area) from a vantage point: *views over Hyde Park.* ■ at the other side of; beyond: *over the hill is a small village.* **2** expressing passage or trajectory across: *she trudged over the lawn.* ■ beyond and falling or hanging from: *it toppled over the cliff.* ■ expressing duration: *she told me over coffee.* ■ by means of; by the medium of: *over the loudspeaker.* **3** at a higher level or layer than: *watching a television hanging over the bar.* ■ higher in grade or rank than: *over him is the financial director.* ■ expressing authority or control: *editorial control over what is included.* ■ expressing preference: *I'd choose the well-known brand over that one.* ■ expressing greater number: *the predominance of Asian over African managers in the sample.* ■ higher in volume or pitch than: *he shouted over the noise of the taxis.* **4** higher than or more than (a specified number or quantity): *over 40 degrees C.* **5** on the subject of: *a heated debate over unemployment.*
▶*adv.* **1** expressing passage or trajectory across an area: *he leaned over and tapped me on the hand.* ■ beyond and falling or hanging from a point: *listing over at an acute angle.* **2** in or to the place mentioned or indicated: *over here.* **3** used to express action and result: *hand the money over.* ■ finished: *the match is over* | *message understood, **over and out.*** **4** used to express repetition of a process: *twice over* | *the sums will have to be done over again.*
▶*n. Cricket* a sequence of six balls bowled by a bowler from one end of the pitch. ▷Old English *ofer*, of Germanic origin; related to Dutch *over* and German *über*, from an Indo-European word (originally a comparative of the element represented by *-ove* in *above*) which is also the base of Latin *super* and Greek *huper*.
▶ □ **be over** no longer be affected by: *we were over the worst.* □ **get something over with** do or undergo something unpleasant or difficult, so as to be rid of it. □ **over and over** again and again.

over- ▶*prefix* **1** excessively; to an unwanted degree: *overambitious* | *overcareful.* ■ completely; utterly: *overawe* | *overjoyed.* **2** upper; outer; extra: *overcoat* | *overtime.* ■ overhead; above: *overcast* | *overhang.*

---

o·ver·a·bun·dance *n.*	**o·ver·de·pend·ent** *adj.*	**o·ver·fa·mil·iar** *adj.*	**o·ver·re·fine** *v.*
o·ver·a·bundant *adj.*	**o·ver·dra·mat·ic** *adj.*	**o·ver·feed** *v.*; **-fed**	**o·ver·re·fine·ment** *n.*
o·ver·ac·tive *adj.*	**o·ver·ea·ger** *adj.*	**o·ver·fine** *adj.*	**o·ver·re·stric·tive** *adj.*
o·ver·am·bi·tious *adj.*	**o·ver·rea·ger·ly** *adv.*	**o·ver·fond** *adj.*	**o·ver·scru·pu·lous** *adj.*
o·ver·am·bi·tion *n.*	**o·ver·eat** *v.*; **-ate, -eat·en**	**o·ver·full** *adj.*	**o·ver·sen·si·tive** *adj.*
o·ver·anx·ious *adj.*	**o·ver·eat·er** *n.*	**o·ver·gar·ment** *n.*	**o·ver·sen·si·tiv·i·ty** *n.*
o·ver·bold *adj.*	**o·ver·e·lab·o·rate** *adj. & v.*	**o·ver·gen·er·ous** *adj.*	**o·ver·sen·ti·men·tal** *adj.*
o·ver·bold·ly *adv.*	**o·ver·em·bel·lished** *adj.*	**o·ver·hast·y** *adj.*	**o·ver·staff** *v.*
o·ver·bus·y *adj.*	**o·ver·e·mo·tion·al** *adj.*	**o·ver·im·ag·i·na·tive** *adj.*	**o·ver·stress** *v. & n.*
o·ver·care·ful *adj.*	**o·ver·em·pha·sis** *n.*	**o·ver·large** *adj.*	**o·ver·stretch** *v.*
o·ver·cau·tion *n.*	**o·ver·em·pha·size** *v.*	**o·ver·op·ti·mism** *n.*	**o·ver·stretched** *adj.*
o·ver·cau·tious *adj.*	**o·ver·en·thu·si·as·tic** *adj.*	**o·ver·op·ti·mis·tic** *adj.*	**o·ver·sus·cep·ti·ble** *adj.*
o·ver·cau·tious·ly *adv.*	**o·ver·ex·cite** *v.*	**o·ver·pre·cise** *adj.*	**o·ver·zeal·ous** *adj.*
o·ver·cook *v.*	**o·ver·ex·er·cise** *v.*		
o·ver·cu·ri·ous *adj.*	**o·ver·ex·ert** *v.*		
o·ver·del·i·cate *adj.*	**o·ver·ex·er·tion** *n.*		
o·ver·de·pend·ence *n.*	**o·ver·ex·pan·sion** *n.*		

Pronunciation Key ə *ago, up*; ər *over, fur*; a *hat*; ā *ate*; ä *car*; CH *chin*; e *let*; ē *see*; eər *air*; i *fit*; ī *by*; i(ə)r *ear*; NG *sing*; ō *go*; ô *law, for*; oi *toy*; o͝o *good*; o͞o *goo*; ou *out*; SH *she*; TH *thin*; T͟H *then*; (h)w *why*; ZH *vision*

o·ver·a·chieve /ˌōvərəˈCHēv/ ▶ v. [intr.] do better than is expected, esp. in academic work: *David continued to overachieve all through high school.* ■ be excessively dedicated to the achievement of success in one's work. —**o·ver·a·chieve·ment** n. —**o·ver·a·chiev·er** n.

o·ver·act /ˌōvərˈakt/ ▶ v. [intr.] (of an actor) act a role in an exaggerated manner: *a weepy actress with a strong tendency to overact* | [as n.] (**overacting**) *there was a certain amount of overacting.*

o·ver·all ▶ adj. /ˈōvəˌrôl/ total: *an overall cut of 30 percent.* ■ taking everything into account: *the overall effect is impressive.*
▶ adv. /ˈōvəˈrôl/ in all parts; taken as a whole: *overall, 10,000 jobs will go.*
▶ n. /ˈōvəˌrôl/ (**overalls**) a garment consisting of trousers with a front flap over the chest held up by straps over the shoulders, made of sturdy material and worn esp. as casual or working clothes. —**o·ver·alled** /ˈōvəˌrôld/ adj.

o·ver·arch /ˌōvərˈärCH/ ▶ v. [tr.] form an arch over: *an old dirt road, overarched by forest.*

o·ver·arch·ing /ˌōvərˈärCHiNG/ ▶ adj. forming an arch over something: *the overarching mangroves.* ■ comprehensive; all-embracing: *a single overarching principle.*

o·ver·arm /ˈōvərˌärm/ ▶ adj. & adv. done with the arm moving above the level of the shoulder.

o·ver·awe /ˌōvərˈô/ ▶ v. [tr.] (usu. **be overawed**) impress (someone) so much that they become silent or inhibited: *he used firepower to overawe the hostile tribes.*

o·ver·bal·ance /ˌōvərˈbaləns/ ▶ v. [tr.] outweigh: *I fault the university for many things, but all are overbalanced by its unparalleled resources.* ■ fall or cause to fall over from loss of balance: [intr.] *the ladder overbalanced on top of her.*

o·ver·bear /ˌōvərˈber/ ▶ v. (past **-bore**; past part. **-borne**) [tr.] overcome by emotional pressure or physical force: *his will had not been overborne by another's influence* | *he overbore the others who still favored a bold policy.*

o·ver·bear·ing /ˌōvərˈbe(ə)riNG/ ▶ adj. unpleasantly or arrogantly domineering: *his overbearing, sometimes ruthless desire to succeed.* —**o·ver·bear·ing·ly** adv. —**o·ver·bear·ing·ness** n.

o·ver·bid ▶ v. /ˌōvərˈbid/ (**-bid·ding**; past and past part. **-bid**) [intr.] **1** (in an auction) make a higher bid than a previous bid. **2** (in competitive bidding, the auction in bridge, etc.) bid more than is warranted or manageable.
▶ n. /ˈōvərˌbid/ a bid that is higher than is justified. —**o·ver·bid·der** n.

o·ver·bite /ˈōvərˌbīt/ ▶ n. Dentistry the overlapping of the lower teeth by the upper.

o·ver·blouse /ˈōvərˌblous; -ˌblouz/ ▶ n. a blouse designed to be worn without being tucked in at the waist.

o·ver·blown /ˌōvərˈblōn/ ▶ adj. **1** excessively inflated or pretentious: *overblown dreams of glory and success.* **2** (of a flower) past its prime: *an overblown rose.*

o·ver·board /ˈōvərˌbôrd/ ▶ adv. from a ship into the water: *the severe storm washed a man overboard.*
▶ □ **go overboard 1** be very enthusiastic: *Gary went overboard for you.* **2** react in an immoderate way: *Chris has a bit of a temper and can sometimes go overboard.*

o·ver·bur·den ▶ v. /ˌōvərˈbərdn/ [tr.] (often **be overburdened**) load (someone) with too many things to carry: *they were overburdened with luggage.* ■ give (someone) more work or pressure than they can deal with: *the courts became overburdened with large numbers of relatively trivial offenses.*
▶ n. /ˈōvərˌbərdn/ rock or soil overlying a mineral deposit, archaeological site, or other underground feature. ■ an excessive burden: *an overburden of costs.* —**o·ver·bur·den·some** /-səm/ adj.

o·ver·came /ˌōvərˈkām/ ▶ past of OVERCOME.

o·ver·cast ▶ adj. /ˈōvərˌkast; ˌōvərˈkast/ **1** (of the sky or weather) marked by a covering of gray clouds; dull: *a chilly overcast day.* **2** (in sewing) edged with stitching to prevent fraying.
▶ n. /ˈōvərˌkast/ clouds covering a large part of the sky: *the sky was leaden with overcast.*
▶ v. /ˌōvərˈkast/ (past and past part. **-cast**) [tr.] **1** cover with clouds or shade: *the pebbled beach, overcast with the shadows of the high cliffs.* **2** stitch over (an unfinished edge) to prevent fraying.

o·ver·charge ▶ v. /ˌōvərˈCHärj/ [tr.] **1** charge (someone) too high a price for goods or a service: *that makes it easy for wheeler-dealers to overcharge customers.* ■ charge someone (a sum) beyond the correct amount: *the company overcharged the government $3 million.* **2** put too much electric charge into (a battery). ■ put exaggerated or excessive detail into a text or work of art: *the scenes are overcharged.*
▶ n. /ˈōvərˌCHärj/ an excessive charge for goods or a service.

o·ver·coat /ˈōvərˌkōt/ ▶ n. **1** a long warm coat worn over other clothing. **2** a top, final layer of paint or a similar covering.

o·ver·come /ˌōvərˈkəm/ ▶ v. (past **-came**; past part. **-come**) [tr.] succeed in dealing with (a problem or difficulty): *she worked hard to overcome her paralyzing shyness.* ■ defeat (an opponent); prevail: *without firing a shot they overcame the guards* | [intr.] *we shall overcome.* ■ (usu. **be overcome**) (of an emotion) overpower or overwhelm: *she was obviously overcome with excitement.*

o·ver·com·pen·sate /ˌōvərˈkämpənˌsāt/ ▶ v. [intr.] take excessive measures in attempting to correct or make amends for an error, weakness, or problem: *he was overcompensating for fears about the future.* —**o·ver·com·pen·sat·ing·ly** /ˈōvərˌkämpənˈsātiNGlē/ adv. —**o·ver·com·pen·sa·tion** /ˈōvərˌkämpənˈsāSHən/ n. —**o·ver·com·pen·sa·to·ry** /ˈōvərkəmˈpensəˌtôrē/ adj.

o·ver·con·fi·dent /ˌōvərˈkänfidənt/ ▶ adj. excessively or unreasonably confident: *mistakes made through being overconfident.* —**o·ver·con·fi·dence** n. —**o·ver·con·fi·dent·ly** adv.

o·ver·crowd /ˌōvərˈkroud/ ▶ v. [tr.] fill (accommodations or a space) beyond what is usual or comfortable: [as adj.] (**overcrowded**) *overcrowded dormitories* | [as n.] (**overcrowding**) *trying to eliminate overcrowding in the downtown area.* ■ house (people or animals) in accommodations that are too confined.

o·ver·do /ˌōvərˈdoo/ ▶ v. (**-does**; past **-did**; past part. **-done**) [tr.] carry to excess; exaggerate: *dramatic yet never overdone.* ■ use too much of (something): *I'd overdone the garlic in the curry.* ■ (**overdo it/things**) exhaust oneself by overwork or overexertion: *I'd simply overdone it in the gym.* ■ [often as adj.] (**overdone**) overcook (food): *chewing his overdone steak.*

o·ver·dose ▶ n. /ˈōvərˌdōs/ an excessive and dangerous dose of a drug: *she took an overdose the day her husband left.*
▶ v. /ˈōvərˌdōs; ˌōvərˈdōs/ [intr.] take an overdose of a drug: *he was admitted to the hospital after overdosing on cocaine.* ■ [tr.] give an overdose to. —**o·ver·dos·age** /-ˈdōsij/ n.

o·ver·draft /ˈōvərˌdraft/ ▶ n. a deficit in a bank account caused by drawing more money than the account holds.

o·ver·draw /ˌōvərˈdrô/ ▶ v. (past **-drew**; past part. **-drawn**) [tr.] **1** (usu. **be overdrawn**) draw money from (one's bank account) in excess of what the account holds: *you only pay interest if your account is overdrawn.* ■ (**be overdrawn**) (of a person) have taken money out of an account in excess of what it holds: *I'm already overdrawn this month.* **2** exaggerate in describing or depicting (someone or something): *some of the characters were overdrawn.* **3** draw (a bow) too far.

o·ver·drive /ˈōvərˌdrīv/ ▶ n. a gear in a motor vehicle providing a gear ratio higher than that of the drive gear or top gear, so that engine speed and fuel consumption are reduced in highway travel. ■ a state of high or excessive activity: *the city's worried public relations arm went into overdrive.* ■ a mechanism that permits a higher than normal operating level in a piece of equipment, such as the amplifier of an electric guitar.

o·ver·due /ˌōvərˈd(y)oo/ ▶ adj. not yet having arrived, happened, or been done, though after the expected time: *reform is now overdue.* ■ (of a payment) not having been made, though required: *the rent was nearly three months overdue.* ■ (of a woman) having gone beyond the expected time for a menstrual period. ■ (of a baby) not having been born, though beyond full gestation: *our daughter was six days overdue.* ■ having deserved or needed something for some time: *she was overdue for some leave.* ■ (of a library book) retained longer than the period allowed.

o·ver·es·ti·mate ▶ v. /ˌōvərˈestəˌmāt/ [tr.] estimate (something) to be better, larger, or more important than it really is: *his influence cannot be overestimated.*
▶ n. /-mit/ an excessively high estimate. —**o·ver·es·ti·ma·tion** /ˈōvərˌestəˈmāSHən/ n.

o·ver·ex·pose /ˌōvərikˈspōz/ ▶ v. [tr.] expose too much, esp. to the public eye or to risk: *anybody in the public eye has situations that make them feel overexposed.* ■ Photog. expose (film or a part of an image) for too long a time or for extra time: *the sunlit background is overexposed.* —**o·ver·ex·po·sure** /-ikˈspōZHər/ n.

o·ver·ex·tend /ˌōvərikˈstend/ ▶ v. [tr.] (usu. **be overextended**) **1** make too long: *at nine minutes plus the song is somewhat overextended.* **2** impose on (someone) an excessive burden of work or commitments: *he should not overextend himself on the mortgage.* —**o·ver·ex·ten·sion** /-ˈstenSHən/ n.

o·ver·fill /ˌōvərˈfil/ ▶ v. [tr.] put more into (a container) than it either should or can contain.

o·ver·flow ▶ v. /ˌōvərˈflō/ [intr.] (esp. of a liquid) flow over the brim of a receptacle: *chemicals overflowed from a storage tank* | [tr.] *the river overflowed its banks.* ■ (of a container) be so full that the contents go over or extend above the sides: *a bath had overflowed upstairs.* ■ (of a space) be so crowded that people cannot fit inside: *the waiting area was overflowing.* ■ [*tr.*] flood or flow over (a surface or area): *her hair overflowed her shoulders.* ■ (**overflow with**) *fig.* be very full of (an emotion or quality): *her heart overflowed with joy.*

▶ *n.* /ˈōvərˌflō/ **1** the excess or surplus not able to be accommodated by an available space: *to accommodate the overflow, five more offices have been built.* ■ the flowing over of a liquid: *there was some overflow after heavy rainfall.* **2** (also **overflow pipe**) (in a bathtub or sink) an outlet for excess water. **3** *Comput.* the generation of a number or some other data item that is too large for an assigned location or memory space.

o·ver·fly /ˌōvərˈflī/ ▶ *v.* (**-flies**; *past* **-flew**; *past part.* **-flown**) [*tr.*] fly over (a place or territory): *there was a delay in obtaining clearance to overfly Israel.* ■ fly beyond (a place or thing): *overfly the radio beacon by approximately fifteen seconds.* —**o·ver·flight** /ˈōvərˌflīt/ *n.*

o·ver·gen·er·al·ize /ˌōvərˈjen(ə)rəˌlīz/ ▶ *v.* [*tr.*] draw a conclusion or make a statement about (something) that is more general than is justified by the available evidence. —**o·ver·gen·er·al·i·za·tion** /-ˌjen(ə)rəliˈzāsHən/ *n.*

o·ver·ground /ˈōvərˌground/ ▶ *adv. & adj.* on or above the ground: [as *adv.*] *subway lines that go overground.* ■ legitimate; not underground: *overground political processes.*

o·ver·grow /ˌōvərˈgrō/ ▶ *v.* (*past* **-grew**; *past part.* **-grown**) [*tr.*] grow or spread over (something), esp. so as to choke or stifle it: *the mussels overgrow and smother whatever is underneath.* —**o·ver·growth** /ˈōvərˌgrōtH/ *n.*

o·ver·hand /ˈōvərˌhand/ ▶ *adj. & adv.* (chiefly of a throw or a stroke with a racket) made with the hand or arm passing above the level of the shoulder: *pitch overhand.* ■ with the palm of the hand over what it grasps: [as *adj.*] *an overhand grip.* ■ *Boxing* (of a punch) passing over the other hand: *caught him with an overhand right.*

o·ver·hang ▶ *v.* /ˌōvərˈhang/ (*past* and *past part.* **-hung**) [*tr.*] hang or extend outward over: *a concrete path overhung by trees* | [as *adj.*] (**overhanging**) *overhanging branches.* ■ *fig.* loom over: *the film's mood is overhung with impending death.*

▶ *n.* /ˈōvərˌhang/ a part of something that sticks out or hangs over another thing: *he crouched beneath an overhang of bushes.*

o·ver·haul ▶ *v.* /ˌōvərˈhôl/ [*tr.*] take apart (a piece of machinery or equipment) in order to examine it and repair it if necessary: *a company that overhauls and repairs aircraft engines.*

▶ *n.* /ˈōvərˌhôl/ a thorough examination of machinery or a system, with repairs or changes made if necessary: *a major overhaul of environmental policies.*

o·ver·head ▶ *adv.* /ˈōvərˈhed/ above the level of the head; in the sky: *a helicopter buzzed overhead.*

▶ *adj.* /ˈōvərˌhed/ **1** situated above the level of the head: *the sun was directly overhead* | *overhead power cables.* **2** (of a driving mechanism) above the object driven: *an overhead cam four-cylinder engine.* **3** (of a cost or expense) incurred in the general upkeep or running of a plant, premises, or business, and not attributable to specific products or items.

▶ *n.* /ˈōvərˌhed/ **1** overhead cost or expense: *research conducted in space requires more overhead.* **2** a transparency designed for use with an overhead projector. **3** an overhead compartment: *fits in most airline overheads.* **4** *Tennis* a shot directed sharply downward, hit while the ball is over the head; a smash.

o·ver·head pro·jec·tor ▶ *n.* a device that projects an enlarged image of a transparency placed on it onto a wall or screen by means of an overhead mirror.

o·ver·hear /ˌōvərˈhir/ ▶ *v.* (*past* and *past part.* **-heard**) [*tr.*] hear (someone or something) without meaning to or without the knowledge of the speaker: *I couldn't help overhearing your conversation.*

o·ver·heat /ˌōvərˈhēt/ ▶ *v.* make or become too hot: [*intr.*] *her car started to overheat* | [*tr.*] *it's vital not to overheat the liquid.* ■ make too excited: [as *adj.*] (**overheated**) *his overheated imagination.* ■ *Econ.* (of a country's economy) show marked inflation when increased demand results in rising prices rather than increased output: [*intr.*] *lending rates could soar as the economy overheats* | [*tr.*] *credit expansion helped overheat the economy.*

o·ver·in·dulge /ˌōvərənˈdəlj/ ▶ *v.* [*intr.*] have too much of something enjoyable, esp. food or drink: *it is easy to* **overindulge in** *these kinds of foods.* ■ [*tr.*] gratify the wishes of (someone) to an excessive extent: *his mother had overindulged him.* —**o·ver·in·dul·gence** /-ˈdəljəns/ *n.* —**o·ver·in·dul·gent** /-ˈdəljənt/ *adj.*

o·ver·in·sured /ˌōvərənˈsHo͝ord/ ▶ *adj.* having insurance coverage beyond what is necessary. —**o·ver·in·sur·ance** /-ˈsHo͝orəns/ *n.*

o·ver·joyed /ˌōvərˈjoid/ ▶ *adj.* extremely happy: *Joanna will be overjoyed to see you.*

o·ver·kill /ˈōvərˌkil/ ▶ *n.* the amount by which destruction or the capacity for destruction exceeds what is necessary: *the existing nuclear overkill.* ■ excessive use, treatment, or action; too much of something: *animators now face a dilemma of technology overkill.*

o·ver·land /ˈōvərˌland/ ▶ *adj. & adv.* by land: [as *adj.*] *an overland trade route* | [as *adv.*] *she journeyed overland.*

o·ver·lap ▶ *v.* /ˌōvərˈlap/ (**-lapped**, **-lap·ping**) [*tr.*] extend over so as to cover partly: *the canopy overlaps the house roof at one end* | [*intr.*] *the curtains overlap at the center when closed.* ■ [*intr.*] cover part of the same area of interest, responsibility, etc.: *their duties sometimes overlapped.* ■ [*intr.*] partly coincide in time: *two new series overlapped.*

▶ *n.* /ˈōvərˌlap/ a part or amount that overlaps: *an overlap of about half an inch.* ■ a common area of interest, responsibility, etc.: *there are many overlaps between the approaches* | *there is some overlap in requirements.* ■ a period of time in which two events or activities happen together.

o·ver·lay[1] ▶ *v.* /ˌōvərˈlā/ (*past* and *past part.* **-laid**) [*tr.*] (often **be overlaid with**) cover the surface of (a thing) with a coating: *their fingernails were overlaid with silver or gold.* ■ lie on top of: *a third screen which will overlay the others.* ■ *fig.* (of a quality or feeling) become more prominent than (a previous quality or feeling): *his openness had been overlaid by his new self-confidence.*

▶ *n.* /ˈōvərˌlā/ **1** something laid as a covering over something else: *a durable, cost-effective floor overlay.* ■ a transparency placed over artwork or something such as a map, marked with additional information or detail. ■ a graphical computer display that can be superimposed on another. **2** *Comput.* the process of transferring a block of program code or other data into internal memory, replacing what is already stored. ■ a block of code or other data transferred in such a way.

o·ver·lay[2] /ˈōvərˌlā/ ▶ *past of* **OVERLIE**.

o·ver·leaf /ˈōvərˌlēf/ ▶ *adv.* on the other side of the page: *an information sheet is printed overleaf.*

o·ver·lie /ˌōvərˈlī/ ▶ *v.* (**-ly·ing**; *past* **-lay**; *past part.* **-lain**) [*tr.*] lie on top of: *soft clays overlie the basalt.*

o·ver·load ▶ *v.* /ˌōvərˈlōd/ load with too great a burden or cargo: [as *adj.*] (**overloaded**) *overloaded vehicles are dangerous.* ■ give too much of something, typically something undesirable, to (someone): *the staff is heavily overloaded with casework.* ■ put too great a demand on (an electrical system): *the wiring had been overloaded.*

▶ *n.* /ˈōvərˌlōd/ an excessive load or amount: *an overload of stress* | *momentary surges and overloads in the circuit.*

o·ver·look ▶ *v.* /ˌōvərˈlo͝ok/ **1** fail to notice (something): *he seems to have overlooked one important fact.* ■ ignore or disregard (something, esp. a fault or offense): *she was more than ready to overlook his faults.* ■ pass over (someone) in favor of another: *he was overlooked by the Nobel committee.* **2** have a view of from above: *the chateau overlooks fields of corn and olive trees.*

▶ *n.* /ˈōvərˌlo͝ok/ a commanding position or view: *he veered off the highway onto an overlook.*

o·ver·lord /ˈōvərˌlôrd/ ▶ *n.* a ruler, esp. a feudal lord. ■ a person of great power or authority: *the undisputed overlord of the crime family.* —**o·ver·lord·ship** /-ˌsHip/ *n.*

o·ver·ly /ˈōvərlē/ ▶ *adv.* excessively: *she was a jealous and overly possessive woman.*

o·ver·much /ˈōvərˈməCH/ ▶ *adv., adj., & pron.* too much: [as *adv.*] *I would not worry myself overmuch* | [as *adj.*] *the police may have overmuch regard for public order considerations.*

o·ver·night /ˈōvərˈnīt/ ▶ *adv.* for the duration of a night: *they refused to stay overnight.* ■ during the course of a night: *you can recharge the battery overnight.* ■ very quickly; suddenly: *attitudes will not change overnight.*

▶ *adj.* /ˈōvərˌnīt/ for use overnight: *an overnight bag.* ■ done or happening overnight: *an overnight stay.* ■ sudden, rapid, or instant: *Tom became an overnight celebrity.*

▶ *v.* /ˌōvərˈnīt/ [*intr.*] stay for the night in a particular place: *I overnighted at the Beverly Wilshire.* ■ [*tr.*] ship for delivery the next day: *Forster overnighted the sample to headquarters by courier.*

▶ *n.* /ˈōvərˌnīt/ a stop or stay lasting one night: *overnights can be arranged in Kathmandu.*

o·ver·night·er /ˌōvərˈnītər/ ▶ *n.* a person who stops at a place overnight. ■ an overnight bag. ■ an overnight trip or stay.

o·ver·pass ▶ *n.* /ˈōvərˌpas/ a bridge by which a road or railroad passes over another.

o·ver·pay /ˌōvərˈpā/ ▶ *v.* (*past* and *past part.* **-paid**) [*tr.*] pay (someone) too highly: *many fans think our top players are overpaid.* ■ pay (money) in excess of what is due: *to overpay taxes.* —**o·ver·pay·ment** *n.*

---

o·ver·play /ˌōvərˈplā/ ▶v. [tr.] give undue importance to; overemphasize: *he thinks the idea of a special relationship between sitter and artist is much overplayed.* ■ exaggerate the performance of (a dramatic role): *the uncontrollable urge of ham actors to overplay their parts.*
▶ □ **overplay one's hand** spoil one's chance of success through excessive confidence in one's position.

o·ver·pop·u·late /ˌōvərˈpäpyəˌlāt/ ▶v. [tr.] populate (an area) in too large numbers: *the country was overpopulated.* ■ [intr.] (of an animal) breed too rapidly: *without natural predators, deer would overpopulate.* —**o·ver·pop·u·la·tion** /ˈōvərˌpäpyəˈlāSHən/ n.

o·ver·pow·er /ˌōvərˈpou(-ə)r/ ▶v. [tr.] defeat or overcome with superior strength. ■ be too intense for; overwhelm: *they were overpowered by the fumes.* —**o·ver·pow·er·ing·ly** adv.

o·ver·price /ˌōvərˈprīs/ ▶v. [tr.] [often as adj.] (**overpriced**) charge too high a price for: *overpriced hotels.*

o·ver·print ▶v. /ˌōvərˈprint/ [tr.] **1** print additional matter on (a stamp or other surface already bearing print): *menus will be* **overprinted with** *company logos.* ■ **2** print too many copies or too much of: [as n.] (**overprinting**) *the overprinting of paper money.* **3** Photog. make (a print or other positive) darker than intended.
▶n. /ˈōvərˌprint/ words or other matter printed onto something already bearing print. ■ an overprinted postage stamp.

o·ver·pro·duce /ˌōvərprəˈd(y)o͞os/ ▶v. [tr.] **1** produce more of (a product or commodity) than is wanted or needed: *our unplanned manufacturing system continually overproduces consumer products.* **2** [often as adj.] (**overproduced**) record or produce (a song or film) in an elaborate or overdone way: *a series of overproduced albums.* —**o·ver·pro·duc·tion** /-ˈdəkSHən/ n.

o·ver·pro·tec·tive /ˌōvərprəˈtektiv/ ▶adj. having a tendency to protect someone, esp. a child, excessively. —**o·ver·pro·tect** v. —**o·ver·pro·tec·tion** /-ˈtekSHən/ n. —**o·ver·pro·tec·tive·ness** n.

o·ver·qual·i·fied /ˌōvərˈkwôləˌfīd/ ▶adj. having qualifications that exceed the requirements of a particular job.

o·ver·rate /ˌōvərˈrāt/ ▶v. [tr.] [often as adj.] (**overrated**) have a higher opinion of (someone or something) than is deserved: *dismissing the work as pompous and overrated.*

o·ver·reach /ˌōvərˈrēCH/ ▶v. [intr.] reach too far: *never lean sideways from a ladder or overreach.* ■ (**overreach oneself**) defeat one's own purpose by trying to do more than is possible: *he was an arrogant egotist who overreached himself.* ■ (of a horse, dog, or other quadruped) bring the hind feet so far forward that they fall alongside or strike the forefeet: *the horse overreached jumping the first hurdle.*

o·ver·re·act /ˌōvərrēˈakt/ ▶v. [intr.] respond more emotionally or forcibly than is justified: *they are urging people not to* **overreact to** *the problem.* —**o·ver·re·ac·tion** /-rēˈakSHən/ n.

o·ver·ride ▶v. /ˌōvərˈrīd/ (past **-rode**; past part. **-rid·den**) [tr.] **1** use one's authority to reject or cancel (a decision, view, etc.): *the legislature's insistence on overriding his budget vetoes.* ■ interrupt the action of (an automatic device), typically in order to take manual control: *you can override the cutout by releasing the switch.* ■ be more important than: *this commitment should override all other considerations.* **2** technical extend over; overlap: *the external rendering should not override the vapor barrier.* **3** travel or move over (a place or thing): *part of the deposit was overridden and covered by the advancing ice.*
▶n. /ˈōvərˌrīd/ **1** a device for suspending an automatic function on a machine. ■ the action or process of suspending an automatic function. **2** an excess or increase on a budget, salary, or cost. ■ a commission paid to a manager on sales made by a subordinate or representative. **3** a cancellation of a decision by exertion of authority or winning of votes: *the House vote in favor of the bill was ten votes short of the requisite majority for an override.*

o·ver·ripe /ˌōvərˈrīp/ ▶adj. too ripe; past its best: *overripe tomatoes.* ■ fig. decadent: *overripe civilizations wavering on the brink of decay.*

o·ver·rule /ˌōvərˈro͞ol/ ▶v. [tr.] reject or disallow by exercising one's superior authority: *the Supreme Court overruled the lower court.* ■ reject the decision or argument of (someone): *he was overruled by his senior managers.*

o·ver·run ▶v. /ˌōvərˈrən/ (**-run·ning**; past **-ran**; past part. **-run**) [tr.] **1** spread over or occupy (a place) in large numbers: *the Mediterranean has been overrun by tourists.* ■ conquer or occupy (territory) by force: *the northern frontier was overrun by invaders.* ■ move or extend over or beyond: *let the text overrun the right-hand margin.* ■ run over or beyond (a thing or place): *she overran third base.* **2** continue beyond or above (an expected or allowed time or cost): *he mustn't overrun his budget.*
▶n. /ˈōvərˌrən/ **1** an instance of something exceeding an expected or allowed time or cost: *an unexpectedly large cost overrun in the program.* ■ the amount by which this happens: *a $2.7 billion overrun on development and*

production. ■ a surplus in manufacturing: *production overruns by some OPEC members.* **2** the movement or extension of something beyond an allotted or particular position or space: *the system acts as a brake to prevent cable overrun.* ■ a clear area beyond the end of an airport runway.

o·ver·seas /ˈōvərˈsēz/ ▶adv. in or to a foreign country, esp. one across the sea: *he spent quite a lot of time working overseas.*
▶adj. from, to, or relating to a foreign country, esp. one across the sea: *overseas trips.*

o·ver·see /ˌōvərˈsē/ ▶v. (**-sees**; past **-saw**; past part. **-seen**) [tr.] supervise (a person or work), esp. in an official capacity: *a trustee appointed to oversee Corrie's finances.* —**o·ver·se·er** /ˈōvərˌsēər/ n.

o·ver·sexed /ˌōvərˈsekst/ ▶adj. having unusually strong sexual desires.

o·ver·shad·ow /ˌōvərˈSHadō/ ▶v. [tr.] tower above and cast a shadow over: *an enormous oak tree stood overshadowing the cottage.* ■ fig. cast a gloom over: *it is easy to let this feeling of tragedy overshadow his story.* ■ appear much more prominent or important than: *his competitive nature often overshadows the other qualities.* ■ (often **be overshadowed**) be more impressive or successful than (another person): *he was always overshadowed by his brilliant elder brother.*

o·ver·shoe /ˈōvərˌSHo͞o/ ▶n. a shoe worn over a normal shoe, typically either of waterproof material to protect the normal shoe in wet weather or of fabric to protect a floor surface.

o·ver·shoot ▶v. /ˌōvərˈSHo͞ot/ (past and past part. **-shot**) [tr.] go past (a point) unintentionally, esp. through traveling too fast or being unable to stop: *they overshot their intended destination* | [intr.] *he had overshot by fifty yards but backed up to the junction.* ■ (of an aircraft) fly beyond or taxi too far along (the runway) when landing or taking off: *he has overshot the landing strip again.* ■ exceed (a target or limit): *the department may overshoot its cash limit.*
▶n. /ˈōvərˌSHo͞ot/ an act of going past or beyond a point, target, or limit. ■ an amount or distance by which a target is passed.

o·ver·sight /ˈōvərˌsīt/ ▶n. **1** an unintentional failure to notice or do something: *he said his failure to pay for the tickets was an oversight.* **2** the action of overseeing something: *effective oversight of the financial reporting process.*

o·ver·sim·pli·fy /ˌōvərˈsimpləˌfī/ ▶v. (**-fies, -fied**) [tr.] [often as adj.] (**oversimplified**) simplify (something) so much that a distorted impression of it is given: *a false and oversimplified view of human personality.* —**o·ver·sim·pli·fi·ca·tion** /ˈōvərˌsimpləfəˈkāSHən/ n.

o·ver·sized /ˌōvərˈsīzd/ (also **o·ver·size** /-ˈsīz/) ▶adj. bigger than the usual size: *an oversized T-shirt.*

o·ver·sleep /ˌōvərˈslēp/ ▶v. (past and past part. **-slept**) [intr.] sleep longer or later than one intended: *we talked until the early hours and consequently I overslept.*

o·ver·spend /ˌōvərˈspend/ ▶v. (past and past part. **-spent**) [intr.] spend too much: *she overspent on her husband's funeral.* ■ [tr.] spend more than (a specified amount): *the department can see that it is going to overspend its budget.*

o·ver·state /ˌōvərˈstāt/ ▶v. [tr.] express or state too strongly; exaggerate: *I may have overstated my case to make my point.* —**o·ver·state·ment** n.

o·ver·stay /ˌōvərˈstā/ ▶v. [tr.] stay longer than the time, limits, or duration of: *he was arrested for overstaying his visa.* —**o·ver·stay·er** /ˈōvərˌstāər/ n.

o·ver·steer ▶v. /ˌōvərˈstir/ [intr.] (of a motor vehicle) have a tendency to turn more sharply than was intended.

o·ver·step /ˌōvərˈstep/ ▶v. (**-stepped, -step·ping**) pass beyond (a limit): *you must not overstep your borrowing limit.* ■ violate (a rule or standard of behavior): *he has overstepped the bounds of acceptable discipline.*

o·ver·stock ▶v. /ˌōvərˈstäk/ [tr.] supply with more of something than is necessary or required: *do not overstock the kitchen with food.*
▶n. /ˈōvərˌstäk/ (esp. in a manufacturing or retailing context) a supply or quantity in excess of demand or requirements: *factory overstock.*

o·ver·stuff /ˌōvərˈstəf/ ▶v. [tr.] [usu. as adj.] (**overstuffed**) **1** force too much into (a container): *an overstuffed briefcase.* **2** cover (furniture) completely with padded upholstery: *an overstuffed armchair.*

o·ver·sub·scribed /ˌōvərsəbˈskrībd/ ▶adj. applied for in greater quantities than are available or expected: *those bonds were said to be twelve to fourteen times oversubscribed.* ■ (of a course, etc.) having more applications than available places.

o·ver·sup·ply ▶n. /ˈōvərsəˌplī/ an excessive supply: *an oversupply of music teachers.*
▶v. /ˌōvərsəˈplī/ (**-plies, -plied**) [tr.] [usu. **be oversupplied**) supply with too much or too many: *the country was oversupplied with lawyers.*

o·vert /ōˈvərt; ˈōvərt/ ▶adj. done or shown openly; plainly or readily apparent, not secret or hidden: *an overt act of aggression.* ▷Middle English:

from Old French, past participle of *ovrir* 'to open,' from Latin *aperire*. —**o·vert·ly** *adv.* —**o·vert·ness** *n.*

o·ver·take /ˌōvərˈtāk/ ▶*v.* (*past* **-took**; *past part.* **-tak·en**) [*tr.*] **1** catch up with and pass while traveling in the same direction: *the driver overtook a line of vehicles.* ■ become greater or more successful than: *Germany rapidly overtook Britain in industrial output.* **2** (esp. of misfortune) come suddenly or unexpectedly upon: *the pattern of economic ruin overtook them.* ■ (of a feeling) affect (someone) suddenly and powerfully: *weariness overtook him and he retired to bed.*

o·ver·tax /ˌōvərˈtaks/ ▶*v.* [*tr.*] **1** require to pay too much tax: *if you're overtaxed, we want you in our party.* **2** make excessive demands on (a person's strength, abilities, etc.): *do athletes overtax their hearts?* —**o·ver·tax·a·tion** /-takˈsāSHən/ *n.*

o·ver·throw ▶*v.* /ˌōvərˈTHrō/ (*past* **-threw**; *past part.* **-thrown**) [*tr.*] **1** remove forcibly from power: *military coups which had attempted to overthrow the king.* ■ put an end to (something), typically by the use of force or violence: *their subversive activities are calculated to overthrow parliamentary democracy.* **2** throw (a ball) further or harder than intended: *he grips the ball too tight and overthrows it.* ■ throw a ball beyond (a receiving player): *he overthrew a receiver in the end zone.*
▶*n.* /ˈōvərˌTHrō/ **1** a removal from power; a defeat or downfall: *plotting the overthrow of the government.* **2** (in baseball and other games) a throw that sends a ball past its intended recipient or target. **3** a panel of decorated wrought-iron work above an arch or gateway.

o·ver·time /ˈōvərˌtīm/ ▶*n.* time in addition to what is normal, as time worked beyond one's scheduled working hours: *fewer opportunities for overtime.* ■ payment for such extra work. ■ extra time played at the end of a game that is tied at the end of the regulation time: *they lost in overtime.*
▶*adv.* in addition to normal working hours: *they were working overtime to fulfill a big order.*

o·ver·tire /ˌōvərˈtīr/ ▶*v.* [*tr.*] exhaust (someone): *walk at a pace that does not overtire you.*

o·ver·tone /ˈōvərˌtōn/ ▶*n.* **1** a musical tone that is a part of the harmonic series above a fundamental note and may be heard with it. **2** (often **overtones**) a subtle or subsidiary quality, implication, or connotation: *the decision may have political overtones.*

o·ver·train /ˌōvərˈtrān/ ▶*v.* [*intr.*] (esp. of an athlete) train too hard or for too long. ■ [*tr.*] subject to excessive training: *the team overtrained their young players.*

o·ver·ture /ˈōvərCHər, -ˌCHo͝or/ ▶*n.* **1** an introduction to something more substantial: *the talks were no more than an overture to a long debate.* ■ (usu. **overtures**) an approach or proposal made to someone with the aim of opening negotiations or establishing a relationship: *Coleen listened to his overtures of love.* **2** *Mus.* an orchestral piece at the beginning of an opera, suite, play, oratorio, or other extended composition. ■ an independent orchestral composition in one movement.

o·ver·turn ▶*v.* /ˌōvərˈtərn/ [*tr.*] **1** tip (something) over so that it is on its side or upside down: *the crowd proceeded to overturn cars and set them on fire.* ■ [*intr.*] turn over and come to rest upside down, typically as the result of an accident: *a large tractor-trailer overturned in the middle of the road.* **2** abolish, invalidate, or turn around (an established fact, system, etc.): *the results overturned previous findings.* ■ reverse (a legal decision): *he fought for eight years to overturn a conviction for armed robbery.*
▶*n.* /ˈōvərˌtərn/ *rare* an act of turning over or upsetting something; a revolution, subversion, or reversal. ■ *Ecol.* the occasional (typically twice yearly) mixing of the water of a thermally stratified lake.

o·ver·use ▶*v.* /ˌōvərˈyo͞oz/ [*tr.*] use too much: *young children sometimes overuse "and" in their writing.*
▶*n.* /ˈōvərˈyo͞os/ excessive use: *overuse of natural resources.*

o·ver·val·ue /ˌōvərˈvalyo͞o/ ▶*v.* (**-val·ues**, **-val·ued**, **-val·uing**) [*tr.*] overestimate the importance of: *intelligence can be overvalued.* ■ fix the value of (something, esp. a currency) at too high a level: *sterling was overvalued against the dollar.* —**o·ver·val·u·a·tion** /ˈōvərəˌvalyo͞oˈāSHən/ *n.*

o·ver·view /ˈōvərˌvyo͞o/ ▶*n.* a general review or summary of a subject: *a critical overview of the scientific issues of our time.*
▶*v.* [*tr.*] give a general review or summary of: *the report overviews the needs of the community.*

o·ver·ween·ing /ˈōvərˈwēniNG/ ▶*adj.* showing excessive confidence or pride: *overweening ambition.* —**o·ver·ween·ing·ly** *adv.*

o·ver·weight ▶*adj.* /ˈōvərˈwāt/ above a weight considered normal or desirable: *he's forty pounds overweight.* ■ above legal weight: *an overweight truck.*
▶*n.* /ˈōvərˌwāt/ excessive or extra weight.
▶*v.* /ˌōvərˈwāt/ [*tr.*] [usu. as *adj.*] (**overweighted**) *Finance* invest in (a mar-

ket sector, industry, etc.) to a greater than normal degree: *we were overweighted in technology last year.*

o·ver·whelm /ˌōvər(h)welm/ ▶*v.* [*tr.*] bury or drown beneath a huge mass: *the water flowed through to overwhelm the whole dam and the village beneath.* ■ defeat completely: *his teams overwhelmed their opponents.* ■ (often **be overwhelmed**) give too much of a thing to (someone); inundate: *they were overwhelmed by farewell messages.* ■ (usu. **be overwhelmed**) have a strong emotional effect on: *I was overwhelmed with guilt.* ■ be too strong for; overpower: *the wine doesn't overwhelm the flavor of the trout.*

o·ver·whelm·ing /ˌōvər(h)welmiNG/ ▶*adj.* very great in amount: *he was elected president by an overwhelming majority.* ■ (esp. of an emotion) very strong: *an overwhelming feeling of gratitude.* —**o·ver·whelm·ing·ly** *adv.* —**o·ver·whelm·ing·ness** *n.*

o·ver·win·ter /ˈōvərˈwin(t)ər/ ▶*v.* [*intr.*] **1** spend the winter: *many birds overwinter in equatorial regions.* **2** (of an insect, plant, etc.) live through the winter: *the germinated seeds will overwinter.*

o·ver·work /ˈōvərˈwərk/ ▶*v.* [*tr.*] exhaust with too much work: *executives who are overworked and worried* | [as *adj.*] (**overworked**) *tired, overworked, demoralized staff.* ■ [*intr.*] (of a person) work too hard: *the doctor advised a complete rest because he had been overworking.* ■ [usu. as *adj.*] (**overworked**) make excessive use of: *the city's overworked sewer system.* ■ [usu. as *adj.*] (**overworked**) use (a word or idea) too much and so make it weaker in meaning or effect: *"Breathtaking" is an overworked brochure cliché.*
▶*n.* excessive work: *his health broke down under the strain of overwork.*

o·ver·write /ˌōvərˈrīt/ ▶*v.* (*past* **-wrote**; *past part.* **-writ·ten**) [*tr.*] **1** *Comput.* destroy (data) or the data in (a file) by entering new data in its place: *an entry stating who is allowed to overwrite the file.* **2** write too elaborately or ornately: *there is a tendency to overwrite their parts and fall into cliché.*

o·ver·wrought /ˈōvəˈrôt/ ▶*adj.* **1** in a state of nervous excitement or anxiety: *she was too overwrought to listen to reason.* **2** (of a piece of writing or a work of art) too elaborate or complicated in design or construction.

o·vi·duct /ˈōviˌdəkt/ ▶*n.* *Anat.* & *Zool.* the tube through which an ovum passes from an ovary. —**o·vi·du·cal** /ˌōvēˈdo͞okəl/ *adj.* —**o·vi·duc·tal** /ˌōvēˈdəktəl/ *adj.*

o·vi·form /ˈōvəˌfôrm/ ▶*adj.* egg-shaped.

o·vine /ˈōˌvīn/ ▶*adj.* of, relating to, or resembling sheep.

o·vip·a·rous /ōˈvipərəs/ ▶*adj.* *Zool.* (of a bird, etc.) producing young by means of eggs that are hatched after they have been laid by the parent. —**o·vi·par·i·ty** /-ˈparitē/ *n.*

o·void /ˈōˌvoid/ ▶*adj.* (of a solid or a three-dimensional surface) egg-shaped. ■ (of a plane figure) oval, esp. with one end more pointed than the other.
▶*n.* an ovoid body or surface.

ov·u·late /ˈōvyəˌlāt; ˈäv-/ ▶*v.* [*intr.*] discharge ova or ovules from the ovary. —**ov·u·la·tion** /ˌōvyəˈlāSHən; -ˈläSHən/ *n.* —**ov·u·la·to·ry** /-ləˌtôrē/ *adj.*

ov·ule /ˈōvyo͞ol; ˈäv-/ ▶*n.* a small or immature ovum. ■ *Bot.* the part of the ovary of seed plants that contains the female germ cell and after fertilization becomes the seed. —**ov·u·lar** /-lər/ *adj.*

o·vum /ˈōvəm/ ▶*n.* (*pl.* **o·va** /ˈōvə/) *Biol.* a mature female reproductive cell, esp. of a human or other animal, that can divide to give rise to an embryo usually only after fertilization by a male cell. ▷early 18th cent.: from Latin, literally 'egg.'

ow /ou/ ▶*interj.* used to express sudden pain: *Ow! You're hurting me!*

owe /ō/ ▶*v.* [*tr.*] have an obligation to pay or repay (something, esp. money) in return for something received: *they have denied they owe money to the company.* ■ owe something, esp. money, to (someone): *I owe you for the taxi.* ■ be under a moral obligation to give someone (gratitude, respect, etc.): *I owe it to him to explain what's happened* | *I owe you an apology.* ■ (**owe something to**) have something because of (someone or something): *he owed his success not to chance but to insight.* ■ be indebted to someone or something for (something): *I owe my life to you.*

ow·ing /ˈō-iNG/ ▶*adj.* (of money) yet to be paid: *no rent was owing.*
▶ □ **owing to** because of or on account of: *his reading was hesitant owing to a stammer.*

owl /oul/ ▶*n.* a nocturnal bird of prey with large forward-facing eyes surrounded by facial disks, a hooked beak, and typically a loud call. Two families: Strigidae (**typical owls**, such as saw-whet owls and the snowy owl) and Tytonidae (**barn owls** and their relatives). —**owl·ish** *adj.*

Pronunciation Key ə *ago, up*; ər *over, fur*; a *hat*; ā *ate*; ä *car*; CH *chin*; e *let*; ē *see*; e(ə)r *air*; i *fit*; ī *by*; i(ə)r *ear*; NG *sing*; ō *go*; ô *law, for*; oi *toy*; o͞o *good*; o͞o *goo*; ou *out*; SH *she*; TH *thin*; T͟H *then*; (h)w *why*; ZH *vision*

owl·et /'oulit/ ▶*n.* a small owl (genera *Glaucidium* and *Athene*, family Strigidae) found chiefly in Asia and Africa. ■ a young owl of any kind.

own /ōn/ ▶*adj. & pron.* used with a possessive to emphasize that someone or something belongs or relates to the person mentioned: [as *adj.*] *they can't handle their own children* | *I was an outcast among my own kind* | [as *pron.*] *the Church would look after its own.* ■ done or produced by and for the person specified: [as *adj.*] *I used to design all my own clothes* | [as *pron.*] *they claimed the work as their own.* ■ particular to the person or thing mentioned; individual: [as *adj.*] *the style had its own charm* | [as *pron.*] *the film had a quality all its own.*

▶*v.* **1** [*tr.*] have (something) as one's own; possess: *his father owns a restaurant* | [as *adj.*, in *comb.*] (**-owned**) *state-owned property.* **2** [*intr.*] *formal* admit or acknowledge that something is the case or that one feels a certain way: *she owned to a feeling of profound jealousy.*

▶*phrasal v.* □ **own up** admit or confess to having done something wrong or embarrassing: *he owns up to few mistakes.*

▶ □ **hold one's own** retain a position of strength in a challenging situation: *I can hold my own in a fight.*

own·er /'ōnər/ ▶*n.* a person who owns something: *the proud owner of a huge Dalmatian.* —**own·er·less** *adj.* —**own·er·ship** *n.*

ox /äks/ ▶*n.* (*pl.* **ox·en** /'äksən/) a domesticated bovine animal kept for milk or meat; a cow or bull. See CATTLE (sense 1). ■ a castrated male of this, formerly much used as a draft animal: [as *adj.*] *an ox cart.* ■ an animal of a group related to the domestic ox. See CATTLE (sense 2).

ox·bow /'äks,bō/ ▶*n.* **1** a U-shaped bend in the course of a river. **2** a U-shaped collar of an ox yoke.

ox·bow lake ▶*n.* a curved lake formed at a former oxbow where the main stream of the river has cut across the narrow end and no longer flows around the loop of the bend.

ox·en /'äksən/ ▶ plural form of **ox.**

ox·eye /'äks,ī/ ▶*n.* a yellow-flowered North American plant (*Heliopsis helianthoides*) of the daisy family.

ox·ford /'äksfərd/ ▶*n.* **1** (also **oxford shoe**) a type of lace-up shoe with a low heel. **2** (also **oxford cloth**) a heavy cotton cloth chiefly used to make shirts.

ox·i·dant /'äksidənt/ ▶*n.* an oxidizing agent.

ox·i·da·tion /,äksi'dāsHən/ ▶*n. Chem.* the process or result of oxidizing or being oxidized. —**ox·i·da·tion·al** /-sHənl/ *adj.* —**ox·i·da·tive** /'äksi,dātiv/ *adj.*

ox·ide /'äk,sīd/ ▶*n. Chem.* a binary compound of oxygen with another element or group.

ox·i·dize /'äksi,dīz/ ▶*v.* combine or become combined chemically with oxygen: [*tr.*] *when coal is burned any sulfur is oxidized to sulfur dioxide* | [*intr.*] *the fats in the food will oxidize, turning it rancid.* ■ *Chem.* undergo or cause to undergo a reaction in which electrons are lost to another species. —**ox·i·diz·a·ble** *adj.* —**ox·i·di·za·tion** /,äksidi'zāsHən/ *n.* —**ox·i·diz·er** *n.*

ox·tail /'äks,tāl/ ▶*n.* the tail of a cow. ■ meat from this, used esp. for making soup.

ox·y·a·cet·y·lene /,äksēə'setl-in; -,ēn/ ▶*adj.* of or denoting welding or cutting techniques using a very hot flame produced by mixing acetylene and oxygen.

Ox·y·Con·tin /,äksē'käntin/ ▶*n. trademark* a synthetic analgesic drug that is similar to morphine in its effects and subject to abuse and addiction.

ox·y·gen /'äksəjən/ ▶*n.* a colorless, odorless reactive gas, the chemical element of atomic number 8 and the life-supporting component of the air. (Symbol: **O**) —**ox·yg·e·nous** /äk'sijənəs/ *adj.*

ox·y·gen·ate /'äksəjə,nāt/ ▶*v.* [*tr.*] supply, treat, charge, or enrich with oxygen: [as *adj.*] (**oxygenated**) *a good supply of oxygenated blood.* —**ox·y·gen·a·tion** /,äksəjə'nāsHən/ *n.*

ox·y·gen mask ▶*n.* a mask placed over the nose and mouth and connected to a supply of oxygen, used when the body is not able to gain enough oxygen by breathing air.

ox·y·gen tent ▶*n.* a tentlike enclosure within which the air supply can be enriched with oxygen to aid a patient's breathing.

ox·y·mo·ron /,äksə'môr,än/ ▶*n.* a figure of speech in which apparently contradictory terms appear in conjunction (e.g., *faith unfaithful kept him falsely true*). —**ox·y·mo·ron·ic** /-mə'ränik/ *adj.*

ox·y·to·cin /,äksə'tōsən/ ▶*n. Biochem.* a hormone released by the pituitary gland that causes increased contraction of the uterus during labor and stimulates the ejection of milk into the ducts of the breasts.

oys·ter /'oistər/ ▶*n.* **1** any of a number of bivalve mollusks with rough irregular shells. Several kinds are eaten (esp. raw) as a delicacy and may be farmed for food or pearls, in particular: ■ a true oyster (family Ostreidae), including the edible **American oyster** (*Crassostrea virginica*). ■ a similar bivalve of another family, esp. the **thorny oysters** (Spondylidae), **wing oysters** (Pteriidae), and **saddle oysters** (Anomiidae). **2** an oyster-shaped morsel of meat on each side of the backbone in poultry. **3** (also **oyster white**) a shade of grayish white.

▶*v.* [*intr.*] raise, dredge, or gather oysters.

▶*adj.* of the color oyster white. ▷Middle English: from Old French *oistre*, via Latin from Greek *ostreon*; related to *osteon* 'bone' and *ostrakon* 'shell or tile.'

Oz /äz/ *Austral., inf.* ▶*adj.* Australian.

▶*n.* Australia. ■ a person from Australia.

o·zone /'ō,zōn/ ▶*n.* a colorless unstable toxic gas, O_3, with a pungent odor and powerful oxidizing properties, formed from oxygen by electrical discharges or ultraviolet light. —**o·zon·ic** /ō'zänik/ *adj.*

o·zone hole ▶*n.* a region of marked thinning of the ozone layer in high latitudes, chiefly in winter, attributed to the chemical action of chlorofluorocarbons and other atmospheric pollutants.

o·zone lay·er ▶*n.* a layer in the earth's stratosphere at an altitude of about 10 km (6.2 miles) containing a high concentration of ozone, which absorbs most of the ultraviolet radiation reaching the earth from the sun.

Pp

P[1] /pē/ (also **p**) ▶*n.* (*pl.* **Ps** or **P's** /pēz/) the sixteenth letter of the alphabet. ■ denoting the next after O (or N if O is omitted) in a set of items, categories, etc.

P[2] ▶*abbr.* ■ pastor. ■ father. ■ (on an automatic gearshift) park. ■ (on road signs and street plans) parking. ■ peseta. ■ peso. ■ [in *comb.*] (in units of measurement) peta- (10¹⁵): *27 PBq of radioactive material.* ■ post. ■ president. ■ pressure. ■ priest. ■ prince. ■ proprietary. ■ progressive. ▶*symb.* ■ the chemical element phosphorus.

p ▶*abbr.* ■ page. ■ (*p-*) [in *comb.*] *Chem.* para-: *p-xylene.* ■ *Brit.* penny or pence. ■ *Mus.* piano (softly). ■ [in *comb.*] (in units of measurement) pico- (10⁻¹²): *a 220 pf capacitor.* ■ *Chem.* denoting electrons and orbitals possessing one unit of angular momentum. ▶*symb.* ■ *Physics* pressure. ■ *Statistics* probability.

PA ▶*abbr.* ■ Press Association. ■ public address.

Pa ▶*abbr.* ■ pascal; pascals. ■ Pennsylvania. ▶*symb.* the chemical element protactinium.

pa /pä/ ▶*n. inf.* father.

pab·lum /'pabləm/ ▶*n.* (also **pab·u·lum** /'pabyələm/) bland or insipid intellectual fare, entertainment, etc.; pap. ■ (**Pablum**) *trademark* a soft breakfast cereal for infants.

PAC /pak/ ▶*abbr.* ■ Pan-Africanist Congress. ■ political action committee.

pace[1] /pās/ ▶*n.* **1** a single step taken when walking or running. ■ a unit of length representing the distance between two successive steps in walking. ■ a gait of a horse or other animal, esp. one of the recognized trained gaits of a horse. ■ *poetic/lit.* a person's manner of walking or running: *I steal with quiet pace.* **2** consistent and continuous speed in walking, running, or moving: *traffic moved at the pace of the riverboat* | *walking at a fast pace.* ■ the speed or rate at which something happens, changes, or develops: *the children work separately at their own pace.* ▶*v.* [*intr.*] walk at a steady and consistent speed, esp. back and forth and as an expression of one's anxiety or annoyance: *we paced up and down in exasperation* | [*tr.*] *she had been pacing the room.* ■ [*tr.*] measure (a distance) by walking it and counting the number of steps taken. ■ [*tr.*] lead (another runner in a race) in order to establish a competitive speed. ■ (**pace oneself**) do something at a slow and steady rate or speed in order to avoid overexerting oneself. ■ [*tr.*] move or develop (something) at a particular rate or speed: *the action is paced to the beat of a march* | [as *adj.* in *comb.*] (**-paced**) *our fast-paced lives.* ■ [*intr.*] (of a horse) move in a distinctive lateral gait in which both legs on the same side are lifted together, seen mostly in specially bred or trained horses. —**pac·er** *n.*

▶ □ **change of pace** a change from what one is used to. □ **keep pace with** move, develop, or progress at the same speed as. □ **put someone (or something) through their (or its) paces** make someone (or something) demonstrate their (or its) qualities or abilities. □ **set the pace** be the fastest runner in the early part of a race. ■ lead the way in doing or achieving something.

pace[2] /'pā,sē; 'pä,CHā/ ▶*prep.* with due respect to (someone or their opinion), used to express polite disagreement or contradiction: *narrative history, pace some theorists, is by no means dead.*

pace·mak·er /'pās,mākər/ ▶*n.* **1** an artificial device for stimulating the heart muscle and regulating its contractions. ■ the part of the heart muscle (the sinoatrial node) that normally performs this role. ■ the part of an organ or of the body that controls any other rhythmic physiological activity. **2** another term for PACESETTER. —**pace·mak·ing** /-,mākiNG/ *adj.* & *n.*

pace·set·ter /'pās,setər/ ▶*n.* a runner or competitor who sets the pace at the beginning of a race or competition, sometimes in order to help another runner break a record. ■ a person or organization viewed as taking the lead or setting standards of achievement for others. —**pace·set·ting** *adj.* & *n.*

pach·y·derm /'pakə,dərm/ ▶*n.* a very large mammal with thick skin, esp. an elephant, rhinoceros, or hippopotamus. ▷mid 19th cent.: from French *pachyderme*, from Greek *pakhudermos*, from *pakhus* 'thick' + *derma* 'skin.' —**pach·y·der·mal** /,pakə'dərməl/ *adj.* —**pach·y·der·ma·tous** /,pakə'dərmətəs/ *adj.* —**pach·y·der·mic** /,pakə'dərmik/ *adj.*

pa·cif·ic /pə'sifik/ ▶*adj.* peaceful in character or intent: *a pacific gesture.* —**pa·cif·i·cal·ly** /-(ə)lē/ *adv.*

Pa·cif·ic time ▶the standard time in a zone including the Pacific coastal region of the U.S. and Canada, specifically: ■ (**Pacific Standard Time**, abbrev.: **PST**) standard time based on the mean solar time at longitude 120° W, eight hours behind GMT. ■ (**Pacific Daylight Time**, abbrev.: **PDT**) Pacific time during daylight saving time, nine hours behind GMT.

pac·i·fi·er /'pasə,fīər/ ▶*n.* a person or thing that pacifies. ■ a rubber or plastic nipple for a baby to suck on.

pac·i·fism /'pasə,fizəm/ ▶*n.* the belief that any violence, including war, is unjustifiable under any circumstances, and that all disputes should be settled by peaceful means. ■ the refusal to participate in war or military service because of such a belief. —**pac·i·fist** *n.* & *adj.* —**pac·i·fis·tic** /,pasə'fistik/ *adj.*

pac·i·fy /'pasə,fī/ ▶*v.* (**-fies, -fied**) [*tr.*] quell the anger, agitation, or excitement of: *to pacify angry spectators.* ■ bring peace to (a country or warring factions), esp. by the use or threatened use of military force. —**pa·cif·i·ca·tion** /,pasifi'kāSHən/ *n.* —**pa·cif·i·ca·to·ry** /pə'sifikə,tôrē/ *adj.*

pack[1] /pak/ ▶*n.* **1** a small cardboard or paper container and the items contained within it: *a pack of cigarettes.* ■ a set of playing cards. ■ a knapsack or backpack. ■ a collection of related documents, esp. one kept in a folder: *an information pack.* ■ (often **the pack**) a quantity of food packed or canned in a particular season or year. **2** a group of wild animals, esp. wolves, living and hunting together. ■ a group of hounds kept and used for hunting, esp. fox hunting. ■ an organized group of Cub Scouts. ■ (**the pack**) the main body of competitors following the leader or leaders in a competition: *fig. the company was demonstrating the kind of innovations needed to keep it ahead of the pack.* ■ *chiefly derog.* a group or set of similar things or people: *the reports were a pack of lies.* **3** a hot or cold pad of absorbent material, esp. as used for treating an injury. ■ a cosmetic mask.

▶*v.* [*tr.*] fill (a suitcase or bag), esp. with clothes and other items needed when away from home: *I packed a bag with a few clothes* | [*intr.*] *she had packed and checked out of the hotel.* ■ place (something) in a container, esp. for transportation or storage. ■ [*intr.*] be capable of being folded up for transportation or storage: *these silver foil blankets pack into a small area.* ■ (**pack something in**) store something perishable in (a specified substance) in order to preserve it. ■ *inf.* carry (a gun). ■ cram a large number of things into (a container or space). ■ (of a large number of people) crowd into and fill (a room, building, or place): *the waiting room was packed.* ■ cover, surround, or fill (something): *he packed the wounds with ice.*

▶*phrasal v.* □ **pack someone off** *inf.* send someone somewhere without much warning or notice: *they packed me off to the academy in Baltimore.* —**pack·a·ble** *adj.*

▶ □ **pack it in** *inf.* stop what one is doing. □ **send someone packing** *inf.* make someone leave in an abrupt or peremptory way.

pack² ▶ *v.* [*tr.*] fill (a jury, committee, etc.) with people likely to support a particular verdict or decision.

pack·age /'pakij/ ▶ *n.* an object or group of objects wrapped in paper or plastic, or packed in a box. ■ the box or bag in which things are packed. ■ a packet: *a package of peanuts.* ■ (also **package deal**) a set of proposals, products, etc., offered or agreed to as a whole.
▶ *v.* [*tr.*] (usu. **be packaged**) put into a box or wrapping, esp. for sale. ■ present (someone or something) in a particular way, esp. to make them more attractive. ■ combine (various products) for sale as one unit: *films would be packaged with the pictures of a production company.* ■ commission and produce (a book, typically a highly illustrated one) to sell as a complete product to publishers. —**pack·ag·er** *n.*

pack·age store ▶ *n.* a store that sells alcoholic beverages in sealed containers for consumption elsewhere; a liquor store.

pack·ag·ing /'pakijiNG/ ▶ *n.* materials used to wrap or protect goods. ■ the business or process of packing goods. ■ the presentation of a person, product, or action in a particular way.

pack an·i·mal ▶ *n.* **1** an animal used to carry heavy loads. **2** an animal that lives and hunts in a pack.

pack·er /'pakər/ ▶ *n.* a person or machine that packs something, esp. someone who prepares and packs food for transportation and sale.

pack·et /'pakit/ ▶ *n.* **1** a paper or cardboard container, typically one in which goods are packed to be sold: *a packet of cigarettes.* ■ the contents of such a container. ■ a block of data transmitted across a network. **2** (also **packet boat**) *dated* a ship traveling at regular intervals between two ports, originally for the conveyance of mail.
▶ *v.* (**-et·ed**, **-et·ing**) [*tr.*] make up into or wrap up in a packet.

pack·horse /'pak,hôrs/ ▶ *n.* a horse used to carry loads.

pack ice ▶ *n.* an expanse of large pieces of floating ice driven together into a nearly continuous mass, as occurs in polar seas.

pack·ing /'pakiNG/ ▶ *n.* the action or process of packing something. ■ material used to protect fragile goods, esp. in transit. ■ material used to seal a joint or assist in lubricating an axle or shaft.

pack rat ▶ *n.* a ratlike rodent (*Neotoma* and other genera, family Muridae) that accumulates a mound of sticks and debris in the nest hole, native to North and Central America. ■ a person who saves unnecessary objects or hoards things.

pact /pakt/ ▶ *n.* a formal agreement between individuals or parties. ▷late Middle English: from Old French, from Latin *pactum* 'something agreed upon,' neuter past participle (used as a noun) of *paciscere* 'agree.'

pad¹ /pad/ ▶ *n.* **1** a thick piece of soft material used to reduce friction or jarring, enlarge or change the shape of something, or hold or absorb liquid: *sterile gauze pads.* ■ short for INK PAD. ■ the fleshy underpart of an animal's foot or of a human finger. ■ a protective guard worn by a sports player to protect a part of the body from blows. **2** a number of sheets of blank paper fastened together at one edge, used for writing or drawing on. **3** a flat-topped structure or area used for helicopter takeoff and landing or for rocket launching. **4** *inf.* a person's home.
▶ *v.* (**pad·ded**, **pad·ding**) [*tr.*] fill or cover (something) with a soft material in order to give it a particular shape, protect it or its contents, or make it more comfortable. ■ add false items to (an expense report or bill) in order to receive unjustified payment.

pad² ▶ *v.* (**pad·ded**, **pad·ding**) [*intr.*] walk with steady steps making a soft dull sound: *she padded along the corridor.* ■ [*tr.*] travel along (a road or route) on foot: *he was padding the streets.*
▶ *n.* the soft dull sound of steady steps: *he heard the pad of feet.*

pad·ding /'padiNG/ ▶ *n.* soft material such as foam or cloth used to pad or stuff something. ■ superfluous material in a book, speech, etc., introduced in order to make it reach a desired length.

pad·dle¹ /'padl/ ▶ *n.* a short pole with a broad blade at one or both ends, used without an oarlock to move a small boat or canoe through the water. ■ an act of using a paddle in a boat. ■ a short-handled bat used in various ball games, esp. table tennis. ■ a paddle-shaped instrument used for mixing food or for stirring or mixing in industrial processes. ■ another term for PEEL². ■ *inf.* a paddle-shaped instrument used for administering corporal punishment. ■ each of the boards fitted around the circumference of a paddle wheel or mill wheel. ■ *Med.* a plastic-covered electrode used in cardiac stimulation.
▶ *v.* **1** [*intr.*] move through the water in a boat using a paddle or paddles. ■ [*tr.*] propel (a small boat or canoe) with a paddle or paddles. ■ (of a bird or other animal) swim with short fast strokes. **2** [*tr.*] *inf.* beat (someone) with a paddle as a punishment. —**pad·dler** *n.*

pad·dle² ▶ *v.* [*intr.*] walk with bare feet in shallow water. ■ dabble the feet or hands in water.
▶ *n.* an act of walking with bare feet in shallow water. —**pad·dler** *n.*

pad·dle-boat /'padl,bōt/ ▶ *n.* a small pleasure boat driven by pedals that in turn drive a paddle wheel.

pad·dle wheel ▶ *n.* a large wheel, usually steam-driven, with boards around its circumference, situated at the stern or side of a ship so as to propel the ship through the water by its rotation.

paddle wheel

paddle wheel

pad·dock /'padək/ ▶ *n.* a small field or enclosure where horses are kept or exercised. ■ an enclosure adjoining a racetrack where horses are gathered and displayed before a race.
▶ *v.* [*tr.*] (usu. **be paddocked**) keep or enclose (a horse) in a paddock.

Pad·dy /'padē/ ▶ *n.* (*pl.* **-dies**) *inf., often offens.* an Irishman (often as a form of address).

pad·dy /'padē/ ▶ *n.* (*pl.* **-dies**) (also **rice paddy**) a field where rice is grown. ■ rice before threshing or in the husk.

pad·dy wag·on ▶ *n.* *inf.* a police van.

pad·lock /'pad,läk/ ▶ *n.* a detachable lock hanging by a pivoted hook on the object fastened.
▶ *v.* [*tr.*] [usu. as *adj.*] (**padlocked**) secure with such a lock: *a padlocked door.*

pa·dre /'pädrā/ ▶ *n.* father; the title of a priest or chaplain in some regions. ■ *inf.* a chaplain (typically a Roman Catholic chaplain) in any of the armed services.

pae·an /'pēən/ ▶ *n.* a song of praise or triumph. ■ a thing that expresses enthusiastic praise: *his books are paeans to combat.*

pa·el·la /pä'āyä; pī'elə/ ▶ *n.* a Spanish dish of rice, saffron, chicken, seafood, etc., cooked and served in a large shallow pan.

pae·on /'pēən/ ▶ *n.* *Prosody* a metrical foot of one long syllable and three short syllables in any order. —**pae·on·ic** /pē'änik/ *adj.*

pa·gan /'pāgən/ ▶ *n.* a person holding religious beliefs other than those of the main world religions. ■ *dated, derog.* a non-Christian. ■ an adherent of neopaganism.
▶ *adj.* of or relating to such people or beliefs: *a pagan god.* —**pa·gan·ish** *adj.* —**pa·gan·ism** /-,nizəm/ *n.* —**pa·gan·ize** /-,nīz/ *v.*

page¹ /pāj/ ▶ *n.* one side of a sheet of paper in a collection of sheets bound together, esp. as a book, magazine, or newspaper. ■ the material written or printed on such a sheet of paper: *she silently read several pages.* ■ a sheet of paper of such a kind considered as a whole, comprising both sides. ■ a page of a newspaper or magazine set aside for a particular topic: *the editorial page.* ■ *Printing* the type set for the printing of a page. ■ *Comput.* a section of stored data, esp. that which can be displayed on a screen at one time. ■ a significant episode or period considered as a part of a longer history: *this transaction has no parallel on any page of our political history.*
▶ *v.* [*intr.*] (**page through**) leaf through (a book, magazine, or newspaper). ■ *Comput.* move through and display (text) one page at a time. ■ [usu. as *n.*] (**paging**) *Comput.* divide (a piece of software or data) into sections, keeping the most frequently accessed in main memory and storing the rest in virtual memory. ■ [*tr.*] assign numbers to the pages in (a book or periodical); paginate. ■ [as *adj.*, in *comb.*] (**-paged**) having pages of a particular kind or number: *a many-paged volume.*
▶ □ **on the same page** (of two or more people) in agreement.

page² ▶ *n.* a young person, usually in uniform, employed in a hotel or other establishment to run errands, open doors, etc. ■ a young boy attending a bride at a wedding. ■ *hist.* a boy in training for knighthood, ranking next below a squire in the personal service of a knight. ■ *hist.* a man or boy employed as the personal attendant of a person of rank.
▶ *v.* [*tr.*] summon (an individual) by name, typically over a public address system, so as to pass on a message. ■ [often as *n.*] (**paging**) contact (someone) by means of a pager: *many systems have paging as a standard feature.*

pag·eant /'pajənt/ ▸ n. a public entertainment consisting of a procession of people in elaborate, colorful costumes, or an outdoor performance of a historical scene. ■ (also **beauty pageant**) a beauty contest. ■ a thing that looks impressive or grand, but is actually shallow and empty. ■ *hist.* a scene erected on a fixed stage or moving vehicle as a public show.

pag·eant·ry /'pajəntrē/ ▸ n. elaborate display or ceremony.

page·boy /'pāj,boi/ ▸ n. 1 a woman's hairstyle consisting of a shoulder-length bob with the ends rolled under. 2 a male page, esp. in a hotel or attending a bride at a wedding.

pag·er /'pājər/ ▸ n. an electronic device, usually worn on one's person, that receives messages and signals the user by beeping or vibrating.

pag·i·na·tion /,pajə'nāsHən/ ▸ n. the sequence of numbers assigned to pages in a book or periodical. —**pag·i·nate** /'pajə,nāt/ v.

pa·go·da /pə'gōdə/ ▸ n. a Hindu or Buddhist temple or sacred building, typically a many-tiered tower, in India and the Far East. ■ an ornamental imitation of this.

paid /pād/ ▸ past and past participle of **PAY**. ▸ adj. (of work or leave) for or during which one receives pay: *a one-month paid vacation.* ■ (of a person in a specified occupation) in receipt of pay: *a paid, anonymous informer.*

pail /pāl/ ▸ n. a bucket. —**pail·ful** /-,fŏŏl/ n. (pl. -fuls)

pain /pān/ ▸ n. 1 physical suffering or discomfort caused by illness or injury. ■ a feeling of marked discomfort in a particular part of the body: *chest pains.* ■ mental suffering or distress: *the pain of loss.* ■ (also **pain in the neck** or *vulgar slang* **pain in the ass**) *inf.* an annoying or tedious person or thing. 2 (**pains**) careful effort; great care or trouble: *she took pains to see that everyone ate well.*

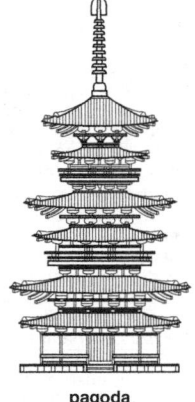

pagoda

▸ v. [tr.] cause mental or physical pain to. ■ [intr.] (of a part of the body) hurt. ▷ Middle English (in the sense 'suffering inflicted as punishment for an offense'): from Old French *peine,* from Latin *poena* 'penalty,' later 'pain.'

▸ □ **on** (or **under**) **pain of** the penalty for disobedience or shortcoming being: *all persons are commanded to keep silent on pain of imprisonment.*

pain·ful /'pānfəl/ ▸ adj. (of part of the body) affected with pain: *her ankle was painful.* ■ causing physical pain: *a painful knock.* ■ causing distress or trouble: *change is inevitably slow and painful.* —**pain·ful·ly** adv. —**pain·ful·ness** n.

pain·kil·ler /'pān,kilər/ ▸ n. a drug or medicine for relieving pain. —**pain·kill·ing** /-,kiliNG/ adj.

pain·less /'pānləs/ ▸ adj. not causing or suffering physical pain. ■ involving little effort or stress. —**pain·less·ly** adv. —**pain·less·ness** n.

pains·tak·ing /'pānz,tākiNG; 'pān,stākiNG/ ▸ adj. done with or employing great care and thoroughness: *painstaking attention to detail | he is a gentle, painstaking man.* —**pains·tak·ing·ly** adv. —**pains·tak·ing·ness** n.

paint /pānt/ ▸ n. 1 a colored substance that is spread over a surface and dries to leave a thin decorative or protective coating. ■ an act of covering something with paint. ■ *inf.* cosmetic makeup. ■ *Basketball* the rectangular area marked near the basket at each end of the court; the foul lane. 2 a piebald horse: [as adj.] *a paint mare.*

▸ v. [tr.] 1 (often **be painted**) cover the surface of (something) with paint, as decoration or protection. ■ apply cosmetics to (the face or skin). ■ apply (a liquid) to a surface with a brush. ■ *Comput.* create (a graphic or screen display) using a paint program. ■ display a mark representing (an aircraft or vehicle) on a radar screen. 2 depict (an object, person, or scene) with paint. ■ produce (a picture) in such a way: *a self-taught artist who paints portraits | [intr.] she paints and makes sculptures.* ■ give a description of (someone or something): *I'm painted as some nut case living in the woods.* —**paint·a·ble** adj. —**paint·y** adj. (**paint·i·er**, **paint·i·est**)

▸ □ **paint the town (red)** *inf.* go out and enjoy oneself flamboyantly.

paint·box /'pānt,bäks/ ▸ n. a box holding dry paints for painting pictures. ■ (**Paintbox**) *trademark* an electronic system used to create video graphics by storing filmed material on disk and manipulating it using a graphics tablet.

paint·brush /'pānt,brəsH/ ▸ n. 1 a brush for applying paint. 2 a North American plant (genus *Castilleja*) of the figwort family that bears brightly colored flowering spikes with a brushlike appearance. Its several species include the **Indian paintbrush** (*C. coccinea*).

paint·ed la·dy ▸ n. 1 a migratory butterfly (genus *Cynthia,* family Nymphalidae) with predominantly orange-brown wings and darker markings. 2 (also **Painted Lady**) a Victorian house, the exterior of which is painted in three or more colors, effectively highlighting the architecture.

paint·er[1] /'pāntər/ ▸ n. 1 an artist who paints pictures. 2 a person who paints buildings, walls, ceilings, and woodwork, esp. as a job.

paint·er[2] ▸ n. a rope attached to the bow of a boat for making it fast.

paint·ing /'pāntiNG/ ▸ n. the process or art of using paint, in a picture, as a protective coating, or as decoration. ■ a painted picture.

paint job ▸ n. the decorative or finishing application of paint to an object. ■ *derog.* a cosmetic treatment that does not address underlying problems: *this administration will settle for a paint job to try to hide the fact that it lives in a La-La Land of its own construction.*

paint·work /'pānt,wərk/ ▸ n. painted surfaces in a building or vehicle.

pair /pe(ə)r/ ▸ n. a set of two things used together or regarded as a unit: *a pair of gloves.* ■ an article or object consisting of two joined or corresponding parts not used separately: *a pair of jeans.* ■ two playing cards of the same denomination: *I have a pair of jacks.* ■ two people related in some way or considered together: *a pair of brothers.* ■ the second member of a pair in relation to the first: *each course member tries to persuade his pair of the merits of his model.* ■ a mated couple of animals: *nine breeding pairs of birds.* ■ two horses harnessed side by side. ■ either or both of two members of a legislative assembly on opposite sides who absent themselves from voting by mutual arrangement, leaving the relative position of the parties unaffected.

▸ v. [tr.] (often **be paired**) join or connect to form a pair: *a cardigan paired with a matching skirt.* ■ [intr.] (of animals) mate. ■ [intr.] (**pair off/up**) form a couple. ■ give (a member of a legislative assembly) another member as a pair, to allow both to absent themselves from a vote without affecting the result.

pais·ley /'pāzlē/ ▸ n. [usu. as adj.] a distinctive intricate pattern of curved, feather-shaped figures based on a design from India: *a paisley silk tie.*

Pai·ute /'pī(y)ŏŏt; pī'(y)ŏŏt/ ▸ n. (pl. same or -utes) 1 a member of either of two culturally similar but geographically separate and linguistically distinct American Indian peoples, the **Southern Paiute** of the southwestern U.S. and the **Northern Paiute** of Oregon and Nevada. 2 either of the Uto-Aztecan languages of these peoples.

▸ adj. of or relating to the Paiute or their languages.

pa·ja·mas /pə'jäməz; -'jaməz/ (*Brit.* **py·ja·mas**) ▸ pl. n. a suit of loose pants and jacket or shirt for sleeping in: *a pair of pajamas | [as adj.]* (**pajama**) *pajama bottoms.* ■ a pair of loose pants tied by a drawstring around the waist, worn in some Asian countries.

pal /pal/ *inf.* ▸ n. a friend: *we're best pals.* ■ used as a form of address, esp. to indicate anger or aggression: *back off, pal.*

▸ v. (**palled**, **pal·ling**) [intr.] (**pal around**) spend time with a friend.

pal·ace /'palis/ ▸ n. the official residence of a sovereign, archbishop, bishop, or other exalted person. ■ *inf.* a large, splendid house.

pal·at·a·ble /'palətəbəl/ ▸ adj. (of food or drink) pleasant to taste: *a very palatable local red wine.* ■ (of an action or proposal) acceptable or satisfactory: *a device that made increased taxation more palatable.* —**pal·at·a·bil·i·ty** /,palətə'bilətē/ n. —**pal·at·a·bly** /-blē/ adv.

pal·ate /'palit/ ▸ n. 1 the roof of the mouth, separating the cavities of the nose and the mouth in vertebrates. 2 a person's appreciation of taste and flavor, esp. when discriminating: *a drink for sophisticated palates.* ■ a person's taste or liking: *the suggestions may not suit everyone's palate.* ■ taste or flavor of wine or beer: *a wine with a zingy, peachy palate.*

pa·la·tial /pə'lāsHəl/ ▸ adj. resembling a palace in being spacious and splendid: *her palatial apartment in Chicago.* —**pa·la·tial·ly** adv.

pal·a·tine[1] /'palə,tīn/ ▸ adj. *chiefly hist.* (of an official or feudal lord) having local authority that elsewhere belongs only to a sovereign. ■ (of a territory) subject to this authority.

pal·a·tine[2] *chiefly Anat.* ▸ adj. of or relating to the palate or esp. the palatine bone.

▸ n. (also **palatine bone**) each of two bones within the skull forming parts of the eye socket, the nasal cavity, and the hard palate.

pa·la·ver /pə'lavər; -'läv-/ ▸ n. prolonged and idle discussion. ■ *dated* a parley or improvised conference between two sides.

▸ v. [intr.] talk unnecessarily at length: *it's too hot for palavering.*

pale[1] /pāl/ ▸ adj. light in color or having little color. ■ (of a person's face

---

or complexion) having less color than usual, typically as a result of shock, fear, or ill health. ■ *fig.* feeble and unimpressive: *unconvincing rock that came across as a pale imitation of Bruce Springsteen.*
▶ *v.* [*intr.*] **1** become pale in one's face from shock or fear. **2** seem less impressive or important: *all else pales by comparison.* —**pale·ly** *adv.* —**pale·ness** *n.* —**pal·ish** *adj.*

pale[2] ▶ *n.* **1** a wooden stake or post used as an upright along with others to form a fence. ■ *fig.* a boundary: *within the pale of decency.* ■ *archaic* or *hist.* an area within determined bounds, or subject to a particular jurisdiction. **2** *Heraldry* a broad vertical stripe down the middle of a shield.
▶ □ **beyond the pale** outside the bounds of acceptable behavior.

pale·face /'pāl,fās/ ▶ *n.* a name supposedly used by North American Indians for a white person.

Pa·le·o·cene /'pālēə,sēn/ ▶ *adj. Geol.* of, relating to, or denoting the earliest epoch of the Tertiary period, between the Cretaceous period and the Eocene epoch. ■ [as *n.*] (**the Paleocene**) the Paleocene epoch or the system of rocks deposited during it, which lasted from 65 million to 56.5 million years ago.

Pa·le·o·gene /'pālēəjēn/ ▶ *adj. Geol.* of, relating to, or denoting the earlier division of the Tertiary period, comprising the Paleocene, Eocene, and Oligocene epochs. ■ [as *n.*] (**the Paleogene**) the Paleogene subperiod or the system of rocks deposited during it. It lasted from about 65 million to 23 million years ago.

pa·le·og·ra·phy /,pālē'ägrəfē/ (*Brit.* **pa·lae·og·ra·phy**) ▶ *n.* the study of ancient writing systems and the deciphering and dating of historical manuscripts. —**pa·le·og·ra·pher** /-fər/ *n.* —**pa·le·o·graph·ic** /,pālēə'grafik/ *adj.* —**pa·le·o·graph·i·cal** /,pālēə'grafikəl/ *adj.* —**pa·le·o·graph·i·cal·ly** /,pālēə'grafik(ə)lē/ *adv.*

Pa·le·o·lith·ic /,pālēə'liтHik/ ▶ *adj. Archaeol.* of, relating to, or denoting the early phase of the Stone Age, lasting about 2.5 million years, when primitive stone implements were used. ■ [as *n.*] (**the Paleolithic**) the Paleolithic period.

pa·le·on·tol·o·gy /,pālē,än'täləjē/ ▶ *n.* the branch of science concerned with fossil animals and plants. —**pa·le·on·to·log·i·cal** /,pālē,äntə'läjikəl/ *adj.* —**pa·le·on·tol·o·gist** /-jist/ *n.*

Pa·le·o·zo·ic /,pālēə'zōik/ ▶ *adj. Geol.* of, relating to, or denoting the era between the Precambrian eon and the Mesozoic era. Formerly called PRIMARY. ■ [as *n.*] (**the Paleozoic**) the Paleozoic era or the system of rocks deposited during it.

Pal·es·tin·i·an /,palə'stinēən/ ▶ *adj.* of or relating to Palestine or its peoples.
▶ *n.* a member of the native Arab population of the region of Palestine (including the modern state of Israel).

pal·ette /'palit/ ▶ *n.* a thin board or slab on which an artist lays and mixes colors. ■ the range of colors used by a particular artist or in a particular picture. ■ (in computer graphics) the range of colors or shapes available to the user. ▷late 18th cent.: from French, diminutive of *pale* 'shovel,' from Latin *pala* 'spade.'

pal·i·mo·ny /'palə,mōnē/ ▶ *n. inf.* compensation made by one member of an unmarried couple to the other after separation.

pal·imp·sest /'palimp,sest/ ▶ *n.* a manuscript or piece of writing material on which the original writing has been effaced to make room for later writing but of which traces remain. ■ *fig.* something reused or altered but still bearing visible traces of its earlier form. —**pal·imp·ses·tic** /,palimp'sestik/ *adj.*

pal·in·drome /'palin,drōm/ ▶ *n.* a word, phrase, or sequence that reads the same backward as forward, e.g., *madam* or *nurses run.* —**pal·in·drom·ic** /,palin'drämik/ *adj.* —**pa·lin·dro·mist** /pə'lindrəmist/ *n.*

pal·ing /'pāliNG/ ▶ *n.* a fence made from pointed wooden or metal stakes. ■ a stake used in such a fence.

pal·i·sade /,palə'sād/ ▶ *n.* a fence of wooden stakes or iron railings fixed in the ground, forming an enclosure or defense. ■ (**palisades**) a line of high cliffs.
▶ *v.* [*tr.*] [usu. as *adj.*] (**palisaded**) enclose or provide (a building or place) with a palisade.

pall[1] /pôl/ ▶ *n.* a cloth spread over a coffin, hearse, or tomb. ■ *fig.* a dark cloud or covering of smoke, dust, or similar matter. ■ *fig.* something regarded as enveloping a situation with an air of gloom, heaviness, or fear: *torture and murder have cast a pall of terror over the villages.*

pall[2] ▶ *v.* [*intr.*] become less appealing or interesting through familiarity.

pal·la·di·um[1] /pə'lādēəm/ ▶ *n.* the chemical element of atomic number 46, a rare silvery-white metal resembling platinum. (Symbol: **Pd**)

pal·la·di·um[2] ▶ *n.* (*pl.* **-di·a** /-dēə/) *archaic* a safeguard or source of protection.

pall·bear·er /'pôl,be(ə)rər/ ▶ *n.* a person helping to carry or officially escorting a coffin at a funeral.

pal·let[1] /'palit/ ▶ *n.* a straw mattress. ■ a crude or makeshift bed.

pal·let[2] ▶ *n.* **1** a portable platform on which goods can be moved, stacked, and stored, esp. with the aid of a forklift. **2** a flat wooden blade with a handle, used to shape clay or plaster. **3** an artist's palette.

pal·liasse /,pal'yas; 'pal,yas/ ▶ *n.* a straw mattress.

pal·li·ate /'palē,āt/ ▶ *v.* [*tr.*] make (a disease or its symptoms) less severe or unpleasant without removing the cause. ■ allay or moderate (fears or suspicions). ■ disguise the seriousness or gravity of (an offense). —**pal·li·a·tion** /,palē'āsHən/ *n.* —**pal·li·a·tor** /-,ātər/ *n.*

pal·li·a·tive /'palē,ātiv; 'palēətiv/ ▶ *adj.* (of a treatment or medicine) relieving pain or alleviating a problem without dealing with the underlying cause: *short-term, palliative measures had been taken.*
▶ *n.* a remedy, medicine, etc., of such a kind. —**pal·li·a·tive·ly** *adv.*

pal·lid /'palid/ ▶ *adj.* (of a person's face) pale, typically because of poor health. ■ feeble or insipid. —**pal·lid·ly** *adv.* —**pal·lid·ness** *n.*

pal·lor /'palər/ ▶ *n.* an unhealthy pale appearance.

palm[1] /pä(l)m/ ▶ *n.* (also **palm tree**) an unbranched evergreen tree (numerous genera, family Palmae, or Arecaceae) with a crown of long feathered or fan-shaped leaves. Palms grow in tropical and warm regions, and many are of great commercial importance, esp. the **oil palm**, **date palm**, and coconut. ■ a leaf of such a tree awarded as a prize or viewed as a symbol of victory or triumph.

palm[2] ▶ *n.* the inner surface of the hand between the wrist and fingers. ■ a part of a glove that covers this part of the hand. ■ the palmate part of an antler.
▶ *v.* **1** [*tr.*] conceal (a card or other small object) in the hand, esp. as part of a trick or theft. **2** [*tr.*] hit (something) with the palm of the hand. ■ *Basketball* illegally grip (the ball) with the hand while dribbling.
▶ *phrasal v.* □ **palm someone off** *inf.* persuade someone to accept something by deception. □ **palm something off** sell or dispose of something by misrepresentation or fraud. —**pal·mar** /'palmər; 'pä(l)mər/ *adj.* —**palmed** *adj.* [in *comb.*] *sweaty-palmed.* —**palm·ful** /-fəl/ *n.*
▶ □ **have** (or **hold**) **someone in the palm of one's hand** have someone under one's control or influence.

pal·mate /'pal,māt; 'pä(l)-/ ▶ *adj.* **1** *Bot.* (of a leaf) having several lobes (typically 5–7) whose midribs all radiate from one point. **2** *Zool.* (of an antler) in which the angles between the tines are partly filled in to form a broad flat surface, as in fallow deer and moose. ■ web-footed. —**pal·mat·ed** *adj.*

pal·met·to /pä(l)'metō; pal-/ ▶ *n.* (*pl.* **-os**) a fan palm (*Sabal* and other genera), esp. one of a number occurring from the southern U.S. to northern South America.

palm·is·try /'pä(l)məstrē/ ▶ *n.* the art or practice of supposedly interpreting a person's character or predicting their future by examining the lines and other features of the hand, esp. the palm and fingers. —**palm·ist** /'pä(l)mist/ *n.*

Palm Pi·lot ▶ *n. trademark* a brand of PDA.

Palm Sun·day ▶ *n.* the Sunday before Easter, when the triumphal entry of Jesus into Jerusalem is celebrated in many Christian churches by processions in which palm fronds are carried.

pal·o·mi·no /,palə'mēnō/ ▶ *n.* (*pl.* **-nos**) a pale golden or tan-colored horse with a white mane and tail, originally bred in the southwestern U.S.

pal·pa·ble /'palpəbəl/ ▶ *adj.* able to be touched or felt: *the palpable bump at the bridge of the nose.* ■ (of a feeling or atmosphere) so intense as to be almost touched or felt: *a palpable sense of loss.* ■ clear to the mind or plain to see: *to talk of dawn raids in the circumstances is palpable nonsense.* ▷late Middle English: from late Latin *palpabilis*, from Latin *palpare* 'feel, touch gently.' —**pal·pa·bil·i·ty** /,palpə'bilitē/ *n.* —**pal·pa·bly** /-blē/ *adv.*

pal·pate /'pal,pāt/ ▶ *v.* [*tr.*] examine (a part of the body) by touch, esp. for medical purposes. —**pal·pa·tion** /pal'pāsHən/ *n.*

pal·pi·tate /'palpi,tāt/ ▶ *v.* [*intr.*] [often as *adj.*] (**palpitating**) (of the heart) beat rapidly, strongly, or irregularly: *it wakened him in the night with a palpitating heart.* ■ shake; tremble: *she was palpitating with terror.*

pal·pi·ta·tion /,palpi'tāsHən/ ▶ *n.* (usu. **palpitations**) a noticeably rapid, strong, or irregular heartbeat due to agitation, exertion, or illness.

pal·sy /'pôlzē/ ▶ *n.* (*pl.* **-sies**) *dated* paralysis, esp. that which is accompanied by involuntary tremors: *a kind of palsy had seized him.*
▶ *v.* (**-sies, -sied**) [*tr.*] (often **be palsied**) affect with paralysis and involuntary tremors.

pal·try /'pôltrē/ ▶ *adj.* (**pal·tri·er, pal·tri·est**) (of an amount) small or meager: *she would earn a paltry $33 more each month.* ■ petty; trivial: *naval glory struck him as paltry.* —**pal·tri·ness** *n.*

pam·pas /ˈpampəz; -pəs/ ▶n. [treated as sing. or pl.] extensive, treeless plains in South America.

pam·pas grass /ˈpampəs/ ▶n. a tall South American grass (*Cortaderia selloana*) with silky flowering plumes, widely cultivated as an ornamental plant.

pam·per /ˈpampər/ ▶v. [tr.] indulge with every attention, comfort, and kindness; spoil: *famous people just love being pampered.*

pam·phlet /ˈpamflit/ ▶n. a small booklet or leaflet containing information or arguments about a single subject.
▶v. (**-phlet·ed, -phlet·ing**) [tr.] distribute pamphlets to.

pam·phlet·eer /ˌpamfliˈti(ə)r/ ▶n. a writer of pamphlets, esp. ones of a political and controversial nature.
▶v. [intr.] [usu. as n.] (**pamphleteering**) write and issue such pamphlets.

Pan /pan/ *Greek Mythol.* ▶a god of flocks and herds, typically represented with the horns, ears, and legs of a goat on a man's body.

pan[1] /pan/ ▶n. **1** a container made of metal and used for cooking food in. ■ an amount of something contained in such a container: *a pan of hot water.* ■ a large container used in a technical or manufacturing process for subjecting a material to heat or a mechanical or chemical process. ■ a bowl fitted at either end of a balance, in which items to be weighed are set. ■ another term for STEEL DRUM. ■ a shallow bowl in which gold is separated from gravel and mud by agitation and washing. ■ a hollow in the ground in which water may collect or in which a deposit of salt remains after water has evaporated. ■ a small ice floe. ■ a part of the lock that held the priming powder in old types of guns. **2** *inf.* a face. **3** a hard stratum of compacted soil.
▶v. (**panned, pan·ning**) [tr.] **1** (often **be panned**) *inf.* criticize (someone or something) severely. **2** wash gravel in a pan to separate out (gold): *the old-timers panned gold* | [intr.] *prospectors panned for gold in the Yukon.*
▶*phrasal v.* □ **pan out** (of gravel) yield gold. ■ turn out well: *Harold's idea had been a good one even if it hadn't panned out.* ■ end up; conclude: *he's happy with the way the deal panned out.* —**pan·ful** /-ˌfoŏol/ n. (pl. **-fuls**)

pan[2] ▶v. (**panned, pan·ning**) [tr.] swing (a video or movie camera) in a horizontal or vertical plane, typically to give a panoramic effect or follow a subject. ■ [intr.] (of a camera) be swung in such a way: *the camera panned to the dead dictator.*
▶n. a panning movement: *that slow pan over Los Angeles.*

pan·a·ce·a /ˌpanəˈsēə/ ▶n. a solution or remedy for all difficulties or diseases: *the panacea for all corporate ills.* —**pan·a·ce·an** /-ˈsēən/ adj.

pa·nache /pəˈnaSH; -ˈnäSH/ ▶n. **1** flamboyant confidence of style or manner: *he entertained Palm Springs society with great panache.* **2** *hist.* a tuft or plume of feathers, esp. as a headdress or on a helmet.

pan·a·ma /ˈpanəˌmä/ (also **panama hat**) ▶n. a wide-brimmed hat of strawlike material, originally made from the leaves of a particular tropical palm tree, worn chiefly by men.

pan·a·tel·a /ˌpanəˈtelə/ ▶n. a long thin cigar.

pan·cake /ˈpanˌkāk/ ▶n. a thin, flat cake of batter, usually fried in a pan. ■ (also **pancake makeup**) makeup consisting of a flat solid layer of compressed powder, widely used in the theater.
▶v. **1** [intr.] (of an aircraft) make a pancake landing. ■ [tr.] (of a pilot) cause (an aircraft) to make such a landing. **2** *inf.* flatten or become flattened: [intr.] *the hotel had pancaked into a heap of concrete.*
▶ □ (**as**) **flat as a pancake** completely flat.

pan·cake land·ing ▶n. an emergency landing in which an aircraft levels out close to the ground and drops vertically with its undercarriage still retracted.

pan·chro·mat·ic /ˌpankrōˈmatik/ ▶adj. *Photog.* (of photographic film) sensitive to all visible colors of the spectrum.

pan·cre·as /ˈpaNGkrēəs; ˈpankrēəs/ ▶n. (pl. **-cre·as·es**) a large gland behind the stomach that secretes digestive enzymes into the duodenum. Embedded in the pancreas are the islets of Langerhans. —**pan·cre·at·ic** /-krēˈatik/ adj.

pan·da /ˈpandə/ ▶n. a large bearlike mammal (*Ailuropoda melanoleuca*) with black and white markings, native to China. It feeds almost entirely on bamboo and has become increasingly rare. It is now usually placed in the bear family.

pan·dem·ic /panˈdemik/ ▶adj. (of a disease) prevalent over a whole country or the world.
▶n. an outbreak of such a disease.

pan·de·mo·ni·um /ˌpandəˈmōnēəm/ ▶n. wild and noisy disorder or confusion; uproar: *pandemonium broke out.*

pan·der /ˈpandər/ ▶v. [intr.] (**pander to**) gratify or indulge (an immoral or distasteful motive, need, or habit or a person with such a desire, etc.).
▶n. *dated* a pimp. ■ *archaic* a person who assists the baser urges or evil designs of others: *the lowest panders of a venal press.*

pan·dit /ˈpəndit; ˈpan-/ (also **pun·dit**) ▶n. a Hindu scholar learned in Sanskrit and Hindu philosophy and religion, typically also a practicing priest. ■ *Indian* a wise man or teacher. ■ *Indian* a talented musician (used as a respectful title or form of address).

Pan·do·ra's box ▶n. a process that generates many complicated problems as the result of unwise interference in something.

pane /pān/ ▶n. a single sheet of glass in a window or door. ■ *Comput.* a separate defined area within a window for the display of, or interaction with, a part of that window's application or output. ■ a sheet or page of postage stamps. ▷late Middle English (originally denoting a section or piece of something, such as a fence or strip of cloth): from Old French *pan*, from Latin *pannus* 'piece of cloth.'

pan·e·gyr·ic /ˌpanəˈjirik/ ▶n. a public speech or published text in praise of someone or something: *Vera's panegyric on friendship.* —**pan·e·gyr·i·cal** /-ˈjirikəl/ adj. —**pan·e·gyr·i·cal·ly** adv.

pan·el /ˈpanl/ ▶n. **1** a thin, typically rectangular piece of wood or glass forming or set into the surface of a door, wall, or ceiling. ■ a thin piece of metal forming part of the outer shell of a vehicle. ■ a flat board on which instruments or controls are fixed: *a control panel.* ■ a decorated area within a larger design containing a separate subject: *the central panel depicts the Crucifixion.* ■ one of several drawings making up a comic strip. ■ a piece of material forming part of a garment. **2** a small group of people brought together to discuss, investigate, or decide on a particular matter, esp. in the context of business or government: *a panel of experts.* ■ a list of available jurors or a jury.
▶v. (**-eled, -el·ing**; *Brit.* **-elled, -el·ling**) [tr.] [usu. as adj.] (**paneled**) cover (a wall or other surface) with panels: *an elegant paneled dining room.* ▷Middle English: from Old French, literally 'piece of cloth,' based on Latin *pannus* '(piece of) cloth.' The early sense 'piece of parchment' was extended to mean 'list,' whence the notion 'advisory group.' Sense 1 derives from the late Middle English sense 'distinct (usually framed) section of a surface.'

pan·el·ing /ˈpanəliNG/ (*Brit.* **pan·el·ling**) ▶n. panels collectively, when used to decorate a wall.

pan·el·ist /ˈpanəlist/ (*Brit.* **pan·el·list**) ▶n. a member of a panel, esp. in a formal public discussion.

pan·el truck ▶n. a small enclosed delivery truck.

pang /paNG/ ▶n. a sudden sharp pain or painful emotion: *Lindsey experienced a sharp pang of guilt* | *the snack bar will keep those hunger pangs at bay.*

pan·go·lin /ˈpaNGgəlin; paNGˈgōlin/ ▶n. a mammal (family Manidae) of Asia (genus *Manis*) and Africa (genus *Phataginus*) that has a body covered with horny overlapping scales, an elongated snout, and long sticky tongue for catching ants and termites.

pan·gram /ˈpanˌgram/ ▶n. a sentence or verse that contains all the letters of the alphabet.

pan·han·dle /ˈpanˌhandl/ ▶n. a narrow strip of territory projecting from the main territory of one state into another state.
▶v. [intr.] *inf.* beg in the street. —**pan·han·dler** n.

pan·ic[1] /ˈpanik/ ▶n. sudden uncontrollable fear or anxiety, often causing wildly unthinking behavior: *she hit him in panic* | *he ran to the library in a blind panic.* ■ widespread financial or commercial apprehension provoking hasty action. ■ *inf.* a frenzied hurry to do something: *a workload of constant panics and rush jobs.*
▶v. (**-icked, -ick·ing**) [intr.] be affected by panic. ■ [tr.] cause to feel panic. —**pan·ick·y** adj.

pan·ic[2] (also **panic grass**) ▶n. any of a number of cereal and fodder grasses (*Panicum* and related genera) related to millet.

pan·ic but·ton ▶n. a button for summoning help in an emergency: *personal attack circuits are operated by panic buttons.*
▶ □ **press** (or **push** or **hit**) **the panic button** *inf.* respond to a situation by panicking or taking emergency measures.

pan·i·cle /ˈpanikəl/ ▶n. *Bot.* a loose, branching cluster of flowers, as in oats. —**pan·i·cled** adj.

panic room ▶another term for a SAFE ROOM.

pan·ic-strick·en (also **pan·ic-struck**) ▶adj. affected with panic; very frightened: *the panic-stricken victims rushed out of their blazing homes.*

pa·nir /pəˈni(ə)r/ (also **pa·neer**) ▶n. a type of curd cheese used in Indian, Iranian, and Afghan cooking.

pan·nier /ˈpanyər; ˈpanēər/ ▶n. **1** a basket, esp. one of a pair carried by a beast of burden. ■ each of a pair of bags or boxes fitted on either side

par·a·le·gal /ˌparəˈlēgəl/ ▶n. a person trained in subsidiary legal matters but not fully qualified as a lawyer.
▶adj. of or relating to auxiliary aspects of the law.

par·al·lax /ˈparəˌlaks/ ▶n. the effect whereby the position or direction of an object appears to differ when viewed from different positions, e.g., through the viewfinder and the lens of a camera. ■ the angular amount of this in a particular case, esp. that of a star viewed from different points in the earth's orbit. —**par·al·lac·tic** /ˌparəˈlaktik/ adj.

par·al·lel /ˈparəˌlel; -ləl/ ▶adj. (of lines, planes, surfaces, or objects) side by side and having the same distance continuously between them. ■ occurring or existing at the same time or in a similar way; corresponding: they shared an apartment while establishing parallel careers. ■ Comput. involving the simultaneous performance of operations. ■ of or denoting electrical components or circuits connected to common points at each end, rather than one to another in sequence. The opposite of SERIES. ■ Mus. containing or denoting successive intervals of the same size in otherwise independent voices: an answering phrase in parallel thirds. ■ Gram. characterized by parallelism.
▶n. **1** a person or thing that is similar or analogous to another. ■ a similarity. ■ a comparison. **2** (also **parallel of latitude**) each of the imaginary parallel circles of constant latitude on the earth's surface. ■ a corresponding line on a map. **3** Printing two parallel lines (‖) as a reference mark.
▶v. (**-leled, -lel·ing**) [tr.] (of something extending in a line) be side by side with (something extending in a line), always keeping the same distance: a big concrete gutter that paralleled the road. ■ be similar or corresponding to (something): U.S. naval and air superiority was paralleled by Soviet superiority in land-based missile systems.
▶ □ **in parallel** occurring at the same time and having some connection. ■ (of electrical components or circuits) connected to common points at each end; not in series.

par·al·lel bars ▶pl. n. a pair of parallel rails mounted on posts, used in gymnastics.

par·al·lel·ism /ˈparəlelˌizəm/ ▶n. the state of being parallel or corresponding in some way. ■ the use of successive verbal constructions in poetry or prose that correspond in grammatical structure, sound, meter, meaning, etc. ■ the use of parallel processing in computer systems. —**par·al·lel·is·tic** /ˌparəlelˈistik/ adj.

par·al·lel·o·gram /ˌparəˈleləˌgram/ ▶n. a four-sided plane rectilinear figure with opposite sides parallel.

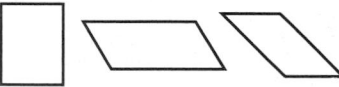

parallelograms

pa·ral·y·sis /pəˈraləsis/ ▶n. (pl. **-ses** /-sēz/) the loss of the ability to move (and sometimes to feel anything) in part or most of the body, typically as a result of illness, poison, or injury. ■ inability to act or function in a person, organization, or place: the paralysis gripping the country.

par·a·lyt·ic /ˌparəˈlitik/ ▶adj. of or relating to paralysis.
▶n. a person affected by paralysis. —**par·a·lyt·i·cal·ly** adv.

par·a·lyze /ˈparəˌlīz/ (Brit. **par·a·lyse**) ▶v. [tr.] (often **be paralyzed**) cause (a person or part of the body) to become partly or wholly incapable of movement. ■ render (someone) unable to think or act normally, esp. through panic or fear: some people are paralyzed by the thought of failure. ■ bring (a system, place, or organization) to a standstill by causing disruption or chaos: the regional capital was paralyzed by a general strike. —**par·a·lyz·ing·ly** /-ˌlīziNGlē/ adv.

par·a·me·ci·um /ˌparəˈmēsēəm/ ▶n. Zool. a single-celled freshwater animal (genus Paramecium, phylum Ciliophora) that has a characteristic slipperlike shape and is covered with cilia.

par·a·med·ic /ˌparəˈmedik/ ▶n. a person who is trained to do medical work, esp. emergency first aid, but is not usually a fully qualified physician.

par·a·med·i·cal /ˌparəˈmedikəl/ ▶adj. of or relating to services and professions that supplement and support medical work but do not require a fully qualified physician (such as nursing).

pa·ram·e·ter /pəˈramitər/ ▶n. technical a numerical or other measurable factor forming one of a set that defines a system or sets the conditions of its operation: the transmission will not let you downshift unless your speed is within the lower gear's parameters. ■ Math. a quantity whose value is selected for the particular circumstances and in relation to which other variable quantities may be expressed. ■ Statistics a numerical

characteristic of a population, as distinct from a statistic of a sample. ■ (in general use) a limit or boundary that defines the scope of a particular process or activity: they set the parameters of the debate. —**par·a·met·ric** /ˌparəˈmetrik/ adj.

par·a·mil·i·tar·y /ˌparəˈmiliˌterē/ ▶adj. (of an unofficial force) organized similarly to a military force.
▶n. (pl. **-tar·ies**) a member of an unofficial paramilitary organization.

par·a·mount /ˈparəˌmount/ ▶adj. more important than anything else; supreme: the interests of the child are of paramount importance. ■ having supreme power. —**par·a·mount·cy** /-sē/ n. —**par·a·mount·ly** adv.

par·a·mour /ˈparəˌmŏŏr/ ▶n. a lover, esp. the illicit partner of a married person.

par·a·noi·a /ˌparəˈnoiə/ ▶n. a mental condition characterized by delusions of persecution, unwarranted jealousy, or exaggerated self-importance, typically elaborated into an organized system. ■ suspicion and mistrust of people or their actions without evidence or justification. ▷early 19th cent.: modern Latin, from Greek, from paranoos 'distracted,' from para 'irregular' + noos 'mind.' —**par·a·noi·ac** /-ˈnoi-ak; -ˈnoi-ik/ adj. & n. —**par·a·no·ic** /-ˈnoi-ik/ adj. —**par·a·no·i·cal·ly** adv. —**par·a·noid** /ˈparəˌnoid/ adj.

par·a·nor·mal /ˌparəˈnôrməl/ ▶adj. denoting events or phenomena such as telekinesis or clairvoyance that are beyond the scope of normal scientific understanding: [as n.] (**the paranormal**) an investigator of the paranormal. —**par·a·nor·mal·ly** adv.

par·a·pet /ˈparəpit/ ▶n. a low, protective wall along the edge of a roof, bridge, or balcony. ■ a protective wall or earth defense along the top of a trench or other place of concealment for troops. —**par·a·pet·ed** adj.

par·a·pher·na·lia /ˌparəfə(r)ˈnālyə/ ▶n. [treated as sing. or pl.] miscellaneous articles, esp. the equipment needed for a particular activity: drugs and drug paraphernalia that had been discovered on the premises. ■ trappings associated with a particular institution or activity that are regarded as superfluous: the rituals and paraphernalia of government.

par·a·phrase /ˈparəˌfrāz/ ▶v. [tr.] express the meaning of (the writer or speaker or something written or spoken) using different words, esp. to achieve clarity.
▶n. a rewording of something written or spoken by someone else. —**par·a·phras·a·ble** adj. —**par·a·phras·tic** /ˌparəˈfrastik/ adj.

par·a·ple·gi·a /ˌparəˈplēj(ē)ə/ ▶n. paralysis of the legs and lower body. —**par·a·ple·gic** /-jik/ adj. & n.

par·a·psy·chol·o·gy /ˌparəsīˈkäləjē/ ▶n. the study of mental phenomena that are excluded from or inexplicable by orthodox scientific psychology (such as hypnosis, telepathy, etc.). —**par·a·psy·cho·log·i·cal** /-ˌsīkəˈläjikəl/ adj. —**par·a·psy·chol·o·gist** /-jist/ n.

par·a·pto·sis /ˌparə(p)ˈtōsis/ ▶n. a system of programmed cell death in which empty spaces form in the cell cytoplasm and the mitochondria swells, causing the cell to lose its vitality. —**par·a·ptot·ic** /ˌparə(p)ˈtätik; -ˈtōtik/ adj.

par·a·quat /ˈparəˌkwät/ ▶n. a fast-acting herbicide, toxic to humans, that becomes deactivated in the soil.

par·a·site /ˈparəˌsīt/ ▶n. an organism that lives in or on another organism (its host) and benefits by deriving nutrients at the host's expense. ■ derog. a person who habitually relies on or exploits others and gives nothing in return. —**par·a·sit·ic** /ˌparəˈsitik/ adj.

par·a·sol /ˈparəˌsôl; -ˌsäl/ ▶n. a light umbrella used to give shade from the sun.

par·a·sym·pa·thet·ic /ˌparəˌsimpəˈTHetik/ ▶adj. Physiol. of or relating to the part of the automatic nervous system that counterbalances the action of the sympathetic nerves.

par·a·thy·roid /ˌparəˈTHīˌroid/ ▶n. Anat. a gland next to the thyroid that secretes a hormone (**parathyroid hormone**) that regulates calcium levels in a person's body.

par·a·troop·er /ˈparəˌtrŏŏpər/ ▶n. a member of a paratroop regiment or airborne unit.

par·a·troops /ˈparəˌtrŏŏps/ ▶pl. n. troops equipped to be dropped by parachute from aircraft: [as adj.] (usu. **paratroop**) a paratroop regiment.

par·boil /ˈpärˌboil/ ▶v. [tr.] partly cook (food) by boiling.

par·cel /ˈpärsəl/ ▶n. **1** a thing or collection of things wrapped in paper in order to be carried or sent by mail. **2** a quantity or amount of something, in particular: ■ a piece of land, esp. one considered as part of an estate. ■ a quantity dealt with in one commercial transaction: a parcel of shares. ■ technical a portion of a larger body of air or other fluid considered as a discrete element.
▶v. (**-celed, -cel·ing**; Brit. **-celled, -cel·ling**) [tr.] make (something) into a

parcel by wrapping it. ■ (**parcel something out**) divide into portions and then distribute.

par·cel post ▶*n.* mail consisting of parcels.

parch /pärCH/ ▶*v.* make or become dry through intense heat: [*tr.*] *a piece of grassland parched by the sun* | [*intr.*] *his crops parched during the last two summers.* ■ [*tr.*] roast (corn, peas, etc.) lightly.

parched /pärCHt/ ▶*adj.* dried out with heat: *the parched earth.* ■ *inf.* extremely thirsty. ■ lightly roasted: *parched corn.*

parch·ment /'pärCHmənt/ ▶*n.* a stiff, flat, thin material made from the prepared skin of an animal and used as a durable writing surface in ancient and medieval times. ■ a manuscript written on this material. ■ (also **parchment paper**) a type of stiff translucent paper treated to resemble parchment and used for lampshades, as a writing surface, and in baking. ■ *inf.* a diploma or other formal document.

pard·ner /'pärdnər/ ▶*n. dated* or *humorous* variant spelling of **PARTNER**, used to represent U.S. dialect speech.

par·don /'pärdn/ ▶*n.* the action of forgiving or being forgiven for an error or offense. ■ a remission of the legal consequences of an offense or conviction: *he offered a full pardon to five convicted men.* ■ *hist. Christian Church* an indulgence, as widely sold in medieval Europe.
▶*v.* [*tr.*] forgive or excuse (a person, error, or offense). ■ release (an offender) from the legal consequences of an offense or conviction, and often implicitly from blame. ■ (usu. **be pardoned**) used to indicate that the actions or thoughts of someone are justified or understandable given the circumstances: *one can be pardoned the suspicion that some of his errors were deliberate.*
▶*interj.* a request to a speaker to repeat something because one did not hear or understand it: *"Pardon?" I said, cupping a hand to my ear.* —**par·don·a·ble** *adj.* —**par·don·a·bly** /-əblē/ *adv.*
▶ □ **beg someone's pardon** express polite apology: *I beg your pardon for intruding.* □ **pardon me** (or **I beg your pardon**) used to indicate that one has not heard or understood something. ■ used to express one's anger or indignation at what someone has just said.

pare /pe(ə)r/ ▶*v.* [*tr.*] trim (something) by cutting away its outer edges: *Carlo pared his thumbnails with his knife.* ■ cut off the outer skin of (something): *pare off the rind using a peeler.* ■ reduce (something) in size, extent, quantity, or number, usually in a number of small successive stages: *union leaders publicly pared down their demands.* —**par·er** *n.*

par·e·gor·ic /,parə'gôrik/ ▶*n.* a medicine consisting of opium flavored with camphor, aniseed, and benzoic acid, formerly used to treat diarrhea and coughing in children.

par·ent /'pe(ə)rənt; 'par-/ ▶*n.* a father or mother. ■ *archaic* a forefather or ancestor. ■ an animal or plant from which younger ones are derived. ■ a source or origin of a smaller or less important part. ■ [often as *adj.*] an organization or company that owns or controls a number of subsidiary organizations or companies: *policy was determined largely by the parent institution.*
▶*v.* [*tr.*] [often as *n.*] (**parenting**) be or act as a mother or father to (someone): *the warmth and attention that are the hallmarks of good parenting.* —**pa·ren·tal** /pə'rentl/ *adj.* —**pa·ren·tal·ly** /pə'rentl-ē/ *adv.* —**parent·hood** /-,hŏŏd/ *n.*

par·ent·age /'pe(ə)rəntij; 'par-/ ▶*n.* the identity and origins of one's parents: *a boy of Jamaican parentage.*

pa·ren·the·sis /pə'renTHəsis/ ▶*n.* (*pl.* -**ses** /-,sēz/) a word, clause, or sentence inserted as an explanation or afterthought into a passage that is grammatically complete without it, in writing usually marked off by curved brackets, dashes, or commas. ■ (usu. **parentheses**) one or both of a pair of marks () used to include such a word, clause, or sentence. ■ an interlude or interval. ▷mid 16th cent.: via late Latin from Greek, from *parentithenai* 'put in beside.'

par·en·thet·i·cal /,parən'THetikəl/ ▶*adj.* of, relating to, or inserted as a parenthesis: *ignore the parenthetical remarks that pockmark every page.* —**par·en·thet·ic** /-'THetik/ *adj.* —**par·en·thet·i·cal·ly** *adv.*

pa·reve /'pärəve/ (also **par·ve** 'pärvə) ▶*adj. Judaism* prepared without meat, milk, or their derivatives and therefore permissible to be eaten with both meat and dairy dishes according to dietary laws.

par ex·cel·lence /,pär ,eksə'läns/ ▶*adj.* better or more than all others of the same kind: *he has won a reputation for being a designer par excellence.*

par·fait /pär'fā/ ▶*n.* **1** a dessert consisting of layers of ice cream, fruit, etc., served in a tall glass. **2** a rich cold dessert made with whipped cream, eggs, and often fruit.

pa·ri·ah /pə'rīə/ ▶*n.* **1** an outcast: *they were treated as social pariahs.* **2** *hist.* a member of a low caste or of no caste in southern India.

pa·ri·e·tal /pə'rīətl/ ▶*adj.* **1** *Anat. Biol.* of, relating to, attached to, or denoting the wall of the body or of a body cavity or hollow structure. ■ of the parietal lobe: *the parietal cortex.* **2** relating to residence in a college

or university dormitory and esp. to visits from members of the opposite sex: *parietal rules.*
▶*n.* **1** *Anat. & Zool.* a parietal structure. ■ short for **PARIETAL BONE**. **2** (**parietals**) *inf.* dormitory rules governing visits from members of the opposite sex.

pa·ri·e·tal bone ▶*n.* a bone forming the central side and upper back part of each side of the skull.

par·i·mu·tu·el /,parə 'myŏŏCHŏŏəl/ (also **par·i·mu·tu·el**) ▶*n.* [often as *adj.*] a form of betting in which those backing the first three places divide the losers' stakes (less the operator's commission): *pari-mutuel betting.* ■ a booth for placing bets under such a system.

par·ings /'pe(ə)riNGZ/ ▶*pl. n.* thin strips that have been pared off from something: *fingernail parings.*

par·ish /'pariSH/ ▶*n.* (in the Christian Church) a small administrative district typically having its own church and a priest or pastor: [as *adj.*] *a parish church.* ■ (in Louisiana) a territorial division corresponding to a county in other states.

par·ish·ion·er /pə'riSHənər/ ▶*n.* an inhabitant of a parish, esp. one who belongs to or attends a particular church.

Pa·ri·sian /pə'rēzHən/ ▶*adj.* of or relating to Paris.
▶*n.* a native or inhabitant of Paris.

par·i·ty /'paritē/ ▶*n.* **1** the state or condition of being equal, esp. regarding status or pay. ■ the value of one currency in terms of another at an established exchange rate. ■ a system of providing farmers with consistent purchasing power by regulating prices of farm products, usually with government price supports. **2** *Math.* (of a number) the fact of being even or odd. ■ *Comput.* a function whose being even (or odd) provides a check on a set of binary values.

park /pärk/ ▶*n.* **1** a large public green area in a town, used for recreation. ■ a large area of land kept in its natural state for public recreational use. ■ (also **wildlife park**) a large enclosed area of land used to accommodate wild animals in captivity. ■ a stadium or enclosed area used for sports. ■ a large enclosed piece of ground, typically with woodland and pasture, attached to a large country house. ■ (in the western U.S.) a broad, flat, mostly open area in a mountainous region. **2** an area devoted to a specified purpose: *an industrial park.* ■ *chiefly Brit.* a parking lot or garage: *a coach park.* **3** (in a car with automatic transmission) the position of the gear selector in which the gears are locked, preventing the vehicle's movement.
▶*v.* [*tr.*] bring (a vehicle that one is driving) to a halt and leave it temporarily, typically in a parking lot or by the side of the road: *he parked his car outside her house* | [*intr.*] *he couldn't find anywhere to park.* ■ [*tr.*] *inf.* deposit and leave in a convenient place until required: *park your bag by the door.* ■ (**park oneself in/on**) *inf.* sit down on or in.

par·ka /'pärkə/ ▶*n.* a large windproof jacket with a hood, designed to be worn in cold weather. ■ a hooded jacket made of animal skin, worn by Eskimos.

park·ing lot ▶*n.* an area where cars or other vehicles may be left temporarily.

park·ing me·ter ▶*n.* a machine next to a parking space in a street, into which the driver puts money so as to be authorized to park the vehicle for a particular length of time.

Par·kin·son's dis·ease /'pärkinsənz/ ▶*n.* a progressive disease of the nervous system marked by tremor, muscular rigidity, and slow, imprecise movement, chiefly affecting middle-aged and elderly people.

Par·kin·son's law ▶*n.* the notion that work expands to fill the time available for its completion.

park·land /'pärk,land/ ▶*n.* (also **parklands**) open land consisting of fields and scattered groups of trees. ■ land reserved for a public park.

park·way /'pärk,wā/ ▶*n.* an open landscaped highway.

par·lance /'pärləns/ ▶*n.* a particular way of speaking or using words, esp. a way common to those with a particular job or interest: *dated terms that were once in common parlance* | *medical parlance.*

par·lay /'pär,lā; -lē/ ▶*v.* [*tr.*] (**parlay something into**) turn an initial stake or winnings from a previous bet into (a greater amount) by gambling: *it involved parlaying a small bankroll into big winnings.* ■ *inf.* transform into (something greater or more valuable): *a banker who parlayed a sizable inheritance into a financial empire.*
▶*n.* a cumulative series of bets in which winnings accruing from each transaction are used as a stake for a further bet.

Pronunciation Key ə *ago,* up; ər *over, fur;* a *hat;* ā *ate;* ä *car;* CH *chin;* e *let;* ē *see;* e(ə)r *air;* i *fit;* ī *by;* i(ə)r *ear;* NG *sing;* ō *go;* ô *law, for;* oi *toy;* ŏŏ *good;* ōō *goo;* ou *out;* SH *she;* TH *thin;* TH *then;* (h)w *why;* ZH *vision*

par·ley /ˈpärlē/ ▸ n. (pl. **-leys**) a conference between opposing sides in a dispute, esp. a discussion of terms for an armistice.
▸ v. (**-leys, -leyed**) [intr.] hold a conference with the opposing side to discuss terms: *they disagreed over whether to **parley** with the enemy*.

par·lia·ment /ˈpärləmənt/ ▸ n. (**Parliament**) (in the UK) the highest legislature, consisting of the sovereign, the House of Lords, and the House of Commons. ■ the members of this legislature for a particular period, esp. between one dissolution and the next. ■ a similar legislature in other nations and states.

par·lia·men·tar·i·an /ˌpärləmɛnˈte(ə)rēən/ ▸ n. **1** a member of a parliament, esp. one well versed in parliamentary procedure and experienced in debate. **2** *hist.* a supporter of Parliament in the English Civil War; a Roundhead.
▸ adj. **1** of or relating to Parliament or its members: *parliamentarian committees*. **2** *hist.* of or relating to the Roundheads. **—par·lia·men·tar·i·an·ism** /-ˌnizəm/ n.

par·lia·men·ta·ry /ˌpärləˈmentərē/ ▸ adj. relating to, enacted by, or suitable for a parliament: *parliamentary legislation*.

par·lor /ˈpärlər/ (*Brit.* **par·lour**) ▸ n. **1** *dated* a sitting room in a private house. ■ a room in a public building for receiving guests. **2** a shop or business providing specified goods or services: *an ice-cream parlor*. **3** (also **milking parlor**) a room or building equipped for milking cows.
▸ adj. *dated, derog.* denoting a person who professes but does not actively give support to a specified (esp. radical) political view: *the new "parlor communists."* ▷Middle English: from Anglo-Norman French *parlur* 'place for speaking,' from Latin *parlare* 'speak.'

Par·me·san /ˈpärməˌzän/ ▸ n. a hard, dry cheese used in grated form, esp. on Italian dishes.

pa·ro·chi·al /pəˈrōkēəl/ ▸ adj. of or relating to a church parish. ■ having a limited or narrow outlook or scope: *this worldview seems parochial*. **—pa·ro·chi·al·ism** /-ˌizəm/ n. **—pa·ro·chi·al·i·ty** /-ˌrōkēˈalitē/ n. **—pa·ro·chi·al·ly** adv.

pa·ro·chi·al school ▸ n. a private school supported by a particular church or parish.

par·o·dy /ˈparədē/ ▸ n. (pl. **-dies**) an imitation of the style of a particular writer, artist, or genre with deliberate exaggeration for comic effect: *the movie is a parody of the horror genre*. ■ an imitation or a version of something that falls far short of the real thing; a travesty.
▸ v. (**-dies, -died**) [tr.] produce a humorously exaggerated imitation of (a writer, artist, or genre): *his specialty was parodying schoolgirl fiction*. ■ mimic humorously. **—pa·rod·ic** /pəˈrädik/ adj. **—par·o·dist** /-dist/ n.

pa·role /pəˈrōl/ ▸ n. **1** the release of a prisoner temporarily (for a special purpose) or permanently before the completion of a sentence, on the promise of good behavior: *he committed a burglary while on parole*. ■ *hist.* a promise or undertaking given by a prisoner of war not to escape or, if released, not to engage in hostilities, or to return to custody under stated conditions. **2** *Linguistics* the actual linguistic behavior or performance of individuals, in contrast to the linguistic system of a community.
▸ v. [tr.] (usu. **be paroled**) release (a prisoner) on parole. **—pa·rol·ee** /-ˌrōˈlē/ n.

par·ox·ysm /ˈparəkˌsizəm/ ▸ n. a sudden attack or violent expression of a particular emotion or activity: *a paroxysm of weeping*. ■ *Med.* a sudden recurrence or attack of a disease; a sudden worsening of symptoms. **—par·ox·ys·mal** /ˌparəkˈsizməl/ adj.

par·quet /pärˈkā/ ▸ n. **1** (also **parquet flooring**) flooring composed of wooden blocks arranged in a geometric pattern. **2** the ground floor of a theater or auditorium.

par·quet·ry /ˈpärkitrē/ ▸ n. inlaid work of blocks of various woods arranged in a geometric pattern, esp. for flooring or furniture.

parr /pär/ ▸ n. (pl. same) a young salmon or trout between the stages of fry and smolt, distinguished by dark rounded patches evenly spaced along its sides.

par·ri·cide /ˈparəˌsīd/ ▸ n. the killing of a parent or other near relative. ■ a person who commits parricide. **—par·ri·cid·al** /ˌparəˈsīdl/ adj.

par·rot /ˈperət; ˈpærət/ ▸ n. a bird (family Psittacidae), often vividly colored, with a hooked bill and grasping feet, found esp. in the tropics. Some are able to mimic the human voice. The **parrot order** (Psittaciformes) also contains the cockatoos, lories, lovebirds, macaws, and budgerigars.
▸ v. (**parroted, parroting**) [tr.] repeat mechanically.

par·rot·fish /ˈperətˌfish; ˈpar-/ ▸ n. (pl. same or **-fishes**) **1** any of a number of brightly colored marine fish with a parrotlike beak, which they use to scrape food from coral and other hard surfaces, in particular: ■ a widespread fish (*Scarus* and other genera, family Scaridae) of warm seas that can secrete a mucous cocoon to deter predators. ■ an edible fish of the southern Indian ocean (*Oplegnathus conwayi*, family

Oplegnathidae). **2** *Austral.* a brightly colored marine fish, esp. one of the wrasse family.

par·ry /ˈparē/ ▸ v. (**-ries, -ried**) [tr.] ward off (a weapon or attack), esp. with a countermove. ■ answer (a question or accusation) evasively.
▸ n. (pl. **-ries**) an act of warding off a blow. ■ *Fencing* block or turn aside (an opponent's blade). ■ an evasive reply.

parse /pärs/ ▸ v. [tr.] analyze (a sentence) into its parts and describe their syntactic roles. ■ *Comput.* analyze (a string or text) into logical syntactic components, typically in order to test conformability to a logical grammar. ■ examine or analyze minutely.
▸ n. *Comput.* an act of or the result obtained by parsing a string or a text. **—pars·er** n.

par·sec /ˈpärˌsek/ (abbr.: **pc**) ▸ n. a unit of distance used in astronomy, equal to about 3.25 light years (3.08×10^{16} meters).

par·si·mo·ny /ˈpärsəˌmōnē/ ▸ n. extreme unwillingness to spend money or use resources. **—par·si·mo·ni·ous** /ˌpärsəˈmōnēəs/ adj.
▸ □ **principle** (or **law**) **of parsimony** the scientific principle that things are usually connected or behave in the simplest or most economical way, esp. with reference to alternative evolutionary pathways.

pars·ley /ˈpärslē/ ▸ n. a biennial plant (*Petroselinum crispum*) with white flowers and aromatic leaves that are either crinkly or flat and used as a culinary herb and for garnishing food. Members of the **parsley family** (Umbelliferae) have their flowers arranged in umbels. Typical members include Queen Anne's lace as well as many food plants and herbs (e.g., carrot, celery, anise).

pars·nip /ˈpärsnip/ ▸ n. **1** a long tapering cream-colored root with a sweet flavor. **2** the widely cultivated Eurasian plant (*Pastinaca sativa*) of the parsley family that yields this root.

par·son /ˈpärsən/ ▸ n. a beneficed member of the clergy; a rector or a vicar. ■ *inf.* any member of the clergy, esp. a Protestant one. **—par·son·ic** /pärˈsänik/ adj. **—par·son·i·cal** /pärˈsänikəl/ adj.

par·son·age /ˈpärsənij/ ▸ n. a church house provided for a member of the clergy.

part /pärt/ ▸ n. **1** a piece or segment of something such as an object, activity, or period of time, which combined with other pieces makes up the whole. ■ an element or constituent that belongs to something and is essential to its nature: *I was part of the family*. ■ a component of a machine. ■ a measure allowing comparison between the amounts of different ingredients used in a mixture: *repot plants in a mixture of three parts soil, one part sand*. ■ a specified fraction of a whole: *they paid a twentieth part of the cost*. ■ each of two or more equal portions into which a book treated as a unit. ■ the amount of a serial that is published or broadcast at one time. **2** some but not all of something: *the painting tells only part of the story*. ■ a point on or area of something: *hold the furthest part of your leg that you can reach*. ■ (**parts**) *inf.* a region, esp. one not clearly specified or delimited: *they wanted to know why he was loitering in these parts*. **3** a character as represented in a play or movie; a role played by an actor or actress. ■ the words and directions to be learned and performed by an actor in such a role. ■ *Mus.* a melody or other constituent of harmony assigned to a particular voice or instrument in a musical work: *the percussion part*. ■ the contribution made by someone or something to an action or situation: *he played a key part in ending the revolt*. ■ the behavior appropriate to or expected of a person in a particular role or situation; a person's duty: *his part is to make good*. ■ the chance to be involved in something: *a future they had no part in*. **4** (**parts**) *archaic* abilities. **5** a line of scalp revealed in a person's hair by combing the hair away in opposite directions on either side.
▸ v. [intr.] (of two things) move away from each other. ■ divide to leave a central space: *at that moment the mist parted*. ■ [tr.] cause to divide or move apart, leaving a central space: *she parted the ferns and looked between them*. ■ leave someone's company. ■ (**be parted**) leave the company of someone: *she can't bear to be parted from her daughter again*. ■ (**part with**) give up possession of; hand over. ■ [tr.] separate (the hair of the head on either side of the part) with a comb.
▸ adv. to some extent; partly (often used to contrast different parts of something): *the city is now part slum, part consumer paradise*.
▸ □ **for my** (or **his, her,** etc.) **part** used to focus attention on one person or group and distinguish them from others involved in a situation: *for my part I was glad when the end of September came*. □ **in part** to some extent though not entirely. □ **on the part of** (or **on my, their,** etc., **part**) used to ascribe responsibility for something to someone: *there was a series of errors on my part*. □ **part company** (of two or more people) cease to be together; go in different directions. ■ (of two or more parties) cease to associate with each other, esp. as the result of a disagreement. □ **take part** join in an activity; be involved.

par·take /pärˈtāk/ ▸ v. (*past* **-took** /-ˈto͝ok/; *past part.* **-tak·en** /-ˈtākən/) [intr.]

(**partake in**) *formal* join in (an activity): *visitors can partake in clay pigeon shooting.* ▪ (**partake of**) be characterized by (a quality): *an event that partook of the mythic.* ▪ (**partake of**) eat or drink (something): *she had partaken of a cheese sandwich and a cup of coffee.* —**par·tak·er** *n.*

par·the·no·gen·e·sis /ˌpärπHənō'jenəsis/ ▶*n. Biol.* reproduction from an ovum without fertilization, esp. as a normal process in some invertebrates and lower plants. —**par·the·no·ge·net·ic** /-jə'netik/ *adj.* —**par·the·no·ge·net·i·cal·ly** /-jə'netik(ə)lē/ *adv.*

par·tial /'pärSHəl/ ▶*adj.* **1** existing only in part; incomplete: *a question to which we have only partial answers.* **2** favoring one side in a dispute above the other; biased. ▪ (**partial to**) having a liking for: *you know I'm partial to bacon and eggs.*
▶*n. Mus.* a component of a musical sound; an overtone or harmonic: *the upper partials of the string.* —**par·tial·ly** *adv.* —**par·tial·ness** *n.*

par·tial-birth a·bor·tion ▶*n.* a late-term abortion of a fetus that has already died, or is killed before being completely removed from the mother. The term **partial-birth abortion** is used primarily in legislation and pro-life writing about this procedure. Pro-choice, scientific, and medical writing uses the term *D&X*, for *dilation and extraction.*

par·ti·al·i·ty /ˌpärSHē'alitē/ ▶*n.* unfair bias in favor of one thing or person compared with another; favoritism. ▪ a particular liking or fondness for something: *she spoke openly, not concealing her **partiality** for him.*

par·tic·i·pant /pär'tisəpənt/ ▶*n.* a person who takes part in something: *firsthand **participants in** an archaeological exploration.*

par·tic·i·pate /pär'tisə͵pāt/ ▶*v.* [*intr.*] **1** take part: *thousands **participated in** a nationwide strike.* **2** (**participate of**) *archaic* have or possess (a particular quality): *both members participate of harmony.* —**par·tic·i·pa·tion** /pär͵tisə'pāSHən/ *n.* —**par·tic·i·pa·tive** /-͵pātiv; -pətiv/ *adj.* —**par·tic·i·pa·tor** /-͵pātər/ *n.* —**par·tic·i·pa·to·ry** /-pə͵tôrē/ *adj.*

par·ti·ci·ple /'pärtə͵sipəl/ ▶*n. Gram.* a word formed from a verb (e.g., *going, gone, being, been*) and used as an adjective (e.g., *working woman, burned toast*) or a noun (e.g., *good breeding*). In English, participles are also used to make compound verb forms (e.g., *is going, has been*). Compare with GERUND. —**par·ti·cip·i·al** /ˌpärtə'sipēəl/ *adj.* —**par·ti·cip·i·al·ly** /ˌpärtə'sipēəlē/ *adv.*

par·ti·cle /'pärtikəl/ ▶*n.* **1** a minute portion of matter: *tiny **particles** of dust.* ▪ the least possible amount: *he agrees without hearing the least particle of evidence.* ▪ *Physics* another term for ELEMENTARY PARTICLE. ▪ *Physics* another term for SUBATOMIC PARTICLE. ▪ *Math.* a hypothetical object having mass but no physical size. **2** *Gram.* a minor function word that has comparatively little meaning and does not inflect, in particular: ▪ (in English) any of the class of words such as *in, up, off, over*, used with verbs to make phrasal verbs. ▪ (in ancient Greek) any of the class of words such as *de* and *ge*, used for contrast and emphasis.

par·ti·cle·board /'pärtikəl͵bôrd/ ▶*n.* material made in rigid sheets or panels from compressed wood chips and resin, often coated or veneered, and used in furniture, buildings, etc.

par·ti-col·ored /'pärtē ͵kələrd/ (also **par·ti-col·ored**) ▶*adj.* having or consisting of two or more different colors: *parti-colored light effects.*

par·tic·u·lar /pə(r)'tikyələr/ ▶*adj.* **1** used to single out an individual member of a specified group or class: *to discriminate against a particular group of companies.* **2** esp. great or intense: *the cashier should exercise particular care.* **3** insisting that something should be correct or suitable in every detail; fastidious: *she is very **particular about** cleanliness.*
▶*n.* a detail: *he is wrong **in every particular**.* ▪ (**particulars**) detailed information about someone or something.
▶ □ **in particular** especially (used to show that a statement applies to one person or thing more than any other): *he socialized with the other young people, one boy in particular.*

par·tic·u·lar·ism /pə(r)'tikyələ͵rizəm/ ▶*n.* exclusive attachment to one's own group, party, or nation. ▪ the principle of leaving each state in an empire or federation free to govern itself and promote its own interests, without reference to those of the whole. —**par·tic·u·lar·ist** *n.* & *adj.* —**par·tic·u·lar·is·tic** /-͵tikyələ'ristik/ *adj.*

par·tic·u·lar·i·ty /pə(r)͵tikyə'laritē/ ▶*n.* (*pl.* **-ties**) the quality of being individual. ▪ fullness or minuteness of detail in the treatment of something: *parties must present their case with some degree of accuracy and particularity.* ▪ (**particularities**) small details.

par·tic·u·lar·ize /pə(r)'tikyələ͵rīz/ ▶*v.* [*tr.*] *formal* mention or describe particularly; treat individually or in detail: *he was the first to particularize the theme of the mother in Palestinian poetry.* —**par·tic·u·lar·i·za·tion** /-͵tikyələri'zāSHən; pə(r)͵tikyələ͵rī'zāSHən/ *n.*

par·tic·u·lar·ly /pə(r)'tikyələrlē/ ▶*adv.* **1** to a higher degree than is usual or average: *I don't particularly want to be reminded | particularly able students.* ▪ used to single out a subject to which a statement is especially

applicable: *the team's defense is excellent, particularly their two center backs.* **2** so as to give special emphasis to a point; specifically: *he particularly asked for you.*

par·tic·u·late /pär'tikyəlit; -͵lāt/ ▶*adj.* of, relating to, or in the form of minute separate particles: *particulate pollution.*
▶*n.* (**particulates**) matter in such a form.

part·ing /'pärting/ ▶*n.* **1** the action of leaving or being separated from someone: *they exchanged a few words on parting.* ▪ a leave-taking or departure: *anguished partings at railroad stations.* **2** the action of dividing something into parts.
▶ □ **a** (or **the**) **parting of the ways** a point at which two people must separate or at which a decision must be taken.

par·ti·san /'pärtəzən/ ▶*n.* **1** a strong supporter of a party, cause, or person. **2** a member of an armed group formed to fight secretly against an occupying force, in particular one operating in enemy-occupied Yugoslavia, Italy, and parts of eastern Europe in World War II.
▶*adj.* prejudiced in favor of a particular cause. —**par·ti·san·ship** /-͵SHip/ *n.*

par·tite /'pär͵tīt/ ▶*adj.* [usu. in *comb.*] divided into parts.

par·ti·tion /pär'tiSHən; pər-/ ▶*n.* (esp. with reference to a country with separate areas of government) the action or state of dividing or being divided into parts. ▪ a structure dividing a space into two parts, esp. a light interior wall. ▪ *Chem.* the distribution of a solute between two immiscible or slightly miscible solvents in contact with one another, in accordance with its differing solubility in each. ▪ *Comput.* each of a number of portions into which some operating systems divide memory or storage.
▶*v.* [*tr.*] divide into parts. ▪ divide (a room) into smaller rooms or areas by erecting partitions. ▪ (**partition something off**) separate a part of a room from the rest by erecting a partition. —**par·ti·tion·er** *n.* —**par·ti·tion·ist** /-ist/ *n.*

part·ly /'pärtlē/ ▶*adv.* to some extent; not completely.

part·ner /'pärtnər/ ▶*n.* a person who takes part in an undertaking with another or others, esp. in a business or company with shared risks and profits. ▪ either of two people dancing together or playing a game or sport on the same side. ▪ either member of a married couple or of an established unmarried couple. ▪ a person with whom one has sex; a lover. ▪ *dated* or *dial.* a friendly form of address by one man to another.
▶*v.* [*tr.*] be the partner of. ▪ [*intr.*] associate as partners: *I never expected to partner with a man like you.* —**part·ner·less** *adj.*

part·ner·ship /'pärtnər͵SHip/ ▶*n.* the state of being a partner or partners. ▪ an association of two or more people as partners. ▪ a business or firm owned and run by two or more partners. ▪ a position as one of the partners in a business or firm.

part of speech ▶*n.* a category to which a word is assigned in accordance with its syntactic functions. In English the main parts of speech are noun, pronoun, adjective, determiner, verb, adverb, preposition, conjunction, and interjection.

par·took /pär'tŏŏk/ ▶ past of PARTAKE.

par·tridge /'pärtrij/ ▶*n.* (*pl.* same or **partridges**) a short-tailed Eurasian game bird of the grouse family, with mainly brown plumage. ▪ *inf.* any of a number of birds, such as the bobwhite or quail, that resemble the partridge. ▷*Middle English* partrich, *from Old French* pertriz, perdriz, *from Latin* perdix.

part song ▶*n.* an unaccompanied secular song with three or more voice parts, typically homophonic rather than contrapuntal in style.

part-time ▶*adj.* & *adv.* for only part of the usual working day or week: [as *adj.*] *part-time jobs | a part-time teacher* | [as *adv.*] *he only worked part-time.* —**part-tim·er** *n.*

par·tu·ri·tion /ˌpärchŏŏ'riSHən/ ▶*n. formal* or *technical* the action of giving birth to young; childbirth: *the weeks following parturition.*

par·ty /'pärtē/ ▶*n.* (*pl.* **-ties**) **1** a social gathering of invited guests, typically involving eating, drinking, and entertainment. **2** a formally constituted political group, typically operating on a national basis, that contests elections and attempts to form or take part in a government. ▪ a group of people taking part in a particular activity or trip, esp. one for which they have been chosen: *the fishing party.* **3** a person or people forming one side in an agreement or dispute. ▪ *inf.* a person, esp. one with specified characteristics: *will you help the party on line 2?*

▶ *v.* (**-ties, -tied**) [*intr.*] *inf.* enjoy oneself at a party or other lively gathering, typically with drinking and music: *put on your glad rags and party!*
▶ □ **be (a) party to** be involved in.

par·ty line ▶*n.* **1** a policy, or the policies collectively, officially adopted by a political party: [as *adj.*] *a party-line voter.* **2** *dated* a telephone line or circuit shared by two or more subscribers.

par·ty poop·er ▶*n. inf.* a person who throws gloom over social enjoyment. —**par·ty-poop·ing** *n.*

par·ve /'pärvə/ ▶*n.* variant spelling of PAREVE.

par·ve·nu /'pärvə,n(y) o͞o/ *often derog.* ▶*n.* a person of obscure origin who has gained wealth, influence, or celebrity.
▶*adj.* having recently achieved, or associated with someone who has recently achieved wealth, influence, or celebrity despite obscure origins: *he concealed the details of his parvenu lifestyle.*

pas /pä/ ▶*n.* (*pl.* same) a step in dancing, esp. in classical ballet.

pas·cal /'pä'skäl/ ▶*n.* the SI unit of pressure, equal to one newton per square meter (approx. 0.000145 pounds per square inch, or 9.9×10^{-6} atmospheres).

pas·chal /'paskəl/ ▶*adj. formal* **1** of or relating to Easter. **2** of or relating to the Jewish Passover.

pas de deux /,pä də 'do͞o/ ▶*n.* (*pl.* same) a dance for two people, typically a man and a woman.

pa·sha /'päSHə; 'paSHə; pə'SHä/ ▶*n. hist.* the title of a Turkish officer of high rank.

Pash·to /'pəSHto͞o/ ▶*n.* the Iranian language of the Pathans, also spoken in northern areas of Pakistan, that is an official language of Afghanistan.
▶*adj.* of or relating to this language.

pasque·flow·er /'pask,flou(-ə)r/ ▶*n.* a spring-flowering plant (genera *Anemone* and *Pulsatilla*) of the buttercup family, with purple or white flowers.

pass[1] /pas/ ▶*v.* **1** [*intr.*] move in a specified direction: *he passed through towns and villages.* ■ [*tr.*] cause (something) to move or lie in a specified direction or position: *he passed a weary hand across his forehead.* ■ change from one state or condition to another: *homes that have passed from public to private ownership.* ■ [*intr.*] die (used euphemistically): *she passed away peacefully in her sleep.* **2** [*tr.*] go past or across; leave behind or on one side in proceeding: *she passed a rest area with a pay phone* | [*intr.*] *we will not let you pass.* ■ go beyond the limits of; surpass; exceed: *this item has passed its sell-by date.* ■ *Tennis* hit a winning shot past (an opponent). **3** [*intr.*] (of time or a point in time) elapse; go by: *the day and night passed slowly.* ■ happen; be done or said: *not another word passed between them.* ■ [*tr.*] spend or use up (a period of time). ■ come to an end: *the danger had passed.* **4** [*tr.*] transfer (something) to someone, esp. by handing or bequeathing it to the next person in a series: *your letter has been passed to Mr. Rich for action.* ■ [*intr.*] be transferred from one person or place to another, esp. by inheritance: *infections can pass from mother to child at birth.* ■ (in football, soccer, hockey, and other games) throw, kick, or hit (the ball or puck) to another player on one's own team. ■ put (something, esp. money) into circulation: *persons who have passed bad checks.* ■ [*intr.*] (esp. of money) circulate; be current. **5** [*tr.*] (of a candidate) be successful in (an examination, test, or course). ■ judge the performance or standard of (someone or something) to be satisfactory: [*tr.*] *he was passed fit by army doctors.* ■ [*intr.*] be accepted as adequate; go uncensored: *she couldn't agree, but let it pass.* ■ [*intr.*] (**pass as/for**) be accepted as or taken for. **6** [*tr.*] (of a legislative or other official body) approve or put into effect (a proposal or law) by voting on it. ■ (of a proposal or law) be examined and approved by (a legislative body or process). ■ [*intr.*] (of a proposal) be approved: *the bill passed by 164 votes to 107.* **7** [*tr.*] pronounce (a judgment or judicial sentence). ■ utter (something, esp. criticism). ■ [*intr.*] (**pass on/upon**) *archaic* adjudicate or give a judgment on. **8** [*tr.*] discharge (something, esp. urine or feces) from the body. **9** [*intr.*] forgo one's turn in a game or an offered opportunity: *we pass on dessert and have coffee.* ■ [as *interj.*] said when one does not know the answer to a question, for example in a quizzing game. ■ [*tr.*] (of a company) not declare or pay (a dividend). ■ *Bridge* make no bid when it is one's turn during an auction. ■ [*tr.*] *Bridge* make no bid in response to (one's partner's bid).
▶*phrasal v.* □ **pass someone by** happen without being noticed or fully experienced by someone. □ **pass something off 1** evade or lightly dismiss an awkward remark: *he made a light joke and passed it off.* **2** *Basketball* throw the ball to a teammate who is unguarded: *he scored eight times and passed off six assists.* □ **pass someone/something off as** falsely represent a person or thing as (something else): *the drink was packaged in champagne bottles and was being passed off as the real stuff.* □ **pass out 1** become unconscious. **2** (of bridge players) not play a hand

because all players have passed. □ **pass someone over** ignore the claims of someone to promotion or advancement. □ **pass something over** avoid mentioning or considering something. □ **pass something up** refrain from taking up an opportunity.
▶*n.* **1** an act or instance of moving past or through something. ■ *inf.* an amorous or sexual advance made to someone: *she made a pass at Stephen.* ■ an act of passing the hands over anything, as in conjuring or hypnotism. ■ a thrust in fencing. ■ a juggling trick. ■ *Bridge* an act of refraining from bidding during the auction. ■ *Comput.* a single scan through a set of data or a program. **2** a successful completion of an examination or course, usually without honors: [as *adj.*] *a 100 percent pass rate.* ■ the grade indicating this. ■ *Brit.* an achievement of a university degree without honors: [as *adj.*] *a pass degree.* **3** a card, ticket, or permit giving authorization for the holder to enter or have access to a place, form of transportation, or event. **4** (in football, soccer, hockey, and other games) an act of throwing, kicking, or hitting the ball or puck to another player on the same team. **5** a state or situation of a specified, usually bad or difficult, nature: *this is a sad pass for a fixture that used to crackle with excitement.* —**pass·er** *n.*
▶ □ **pass the baton** see BATON. □ **pass the buck** see BUCK[3]. □ **pass one's eye over** read (a document) cursorily. □ **pass the hat** see HAT. □ **pass one's lips** see LIP. □ **pass muster** see MUSTER. □ **pass the parcel** see PARCEL. □ **pass the time of day** see TIME. □ **pass water** urinate.

pass[2] ▶*n.* a route over or through mountains. ■ a passage for fish over or past a weir or dam. ■ a navigable channel, esp. at the mouth of a river.
▶ □ **head** (or **cut**) **someone/something off at the pass** forestall someone or something: *the doctor's aim to head the infection off at the pass.*

pass·a·ble /'pasəbəl/ ▶*adj.* **1** just good enough to be acceptable; satisfactory: *he spoke passable English.* **2** (of a route or road) clear of obstacles and able to be traveled along or on. —**pass·a·bly** /-əblē/ *adv.*

pas·sage /'pasij/ ▶*n.* **1** the act or process of moving through, under, over, or past something on the way from one place to another. ■ the act or process of moving forward: *the passage of time.* ■ the right to pass through somewhere: *a permit for safe passage from the embassy.* ■ a journey or ticket for a journey by sea or air: *he booked passage home aboard a Spanish warship.* ■ *Ornithol.* (of a migrating bird) the action of passing through a place en route to its final destination: *the species occurs regularly on passage* | [as *adj.*] *a passage migrant.* **2** a passageway. ■ a duct, vessel, or other channel in the body. **3** the process of transition from one state to another. ■ the passing of a bill into law. **4** a short extract from a book or other printed material. ■ a section of a piece of music. ■ an episode in a longer activity such as a sporting event.
▶ □ **passage of** (or **at**) **arms** a fight or dispute. □ **work one's passage** work in return for a free place on a voyage: *he worked his passage home as a steward.*

pas·sage·way /'pasij,wā/ ▶*n.* a long, narrow way, typically having walls on either side, that allows access between buildings or to different rooms within a building.

pass·book /'pas,bo͝ok/ ▶*n.* a booklet issued by a bank to an account holder for recording sums deposited and withdrawn.

pas·sé /pa'sā/ ▶*adj.* no longer fashionable; out of date: *miniskirts are passé.* ■ *archaic* (esp. of a woman) past one's prime.

pas·sen·ger /'pasinjər/ ▶*n.* a traveler on a public or private conveyance other than the driver, pilot, or crew.

pas·sen·ger pi·geon ▶*n.* an extinct long-tailed North American pigeon (*Ectopistes migratorius*), noted for its long migrations in huge flocks.

pass·er·by /'pasər,bī/ (also **pass·er-by**) ▶*n.* (*pl.* **pass·ers·by**) a person who happens to be going past something, esp. on foot.

pas·ser·ine /'pasərin; -,rīn/ *Ornithol.* ▶*adj.* of, relating to, or denoting birds of a large order distinguished by feet that are adapted for perching, including all songbirds.
▶*n.* a passerine bird; a perching bird.

pas·sim /'pasim/ ▶*adv.* (of allusions or references in a published work) to be found at various places throughout the text. ▷Latin, from *passus* 'scattered,' from the verb *pandere.*

pass·ing /'pasiNG/ ▶*adj.* **1** going past: *passing cars.* **2** (of a period of time) going by: *she detested him more with every passing second.* ■ carried out quickly and lightly: *a passing glance.* **3** meeting or surpassing the requirements of a course or examination: *a passing grade.*
▶*n.* [in *sing.*] **1** the passage of something, esp. time: *with the passing of the years she had become a little eccentric.* ■ the action of throwing, kicking, or hitting a ball or puck to another team member during a sports match. **2** used euphemistically to refer to a person's death: *her passing*

will be felt deeply by many people. ■ the end of something: *the passing of the Cold War.* —**pass·ing·ly** *adv.*

▶ □ **in passing** briefly and casually.

pas·sion /ˈpashən/ ▶ *n.* **1** strong and barely controllable emotion. ■ a state or outburst of such emotion: *oratory in which he gradually works himself up into a passion.* ■ intense sexual love. ■ an intense desire or enthusiasm for something: *the English have a passion for gardens.* ■ a thing arousing enthusiasm: *modern furniture is a particular passion of Bill's.* **2** (**the Passion**) the suffering and death of Jesus. ■ a narrative of this from any of the Gospels. ■ a musical setting of any of these narratives. —**pas·sion·less** *adj.*

pas·sion·ate /ˈpashənit/ ▶ *adj.* showing or caused by strong feelings or a strong belief. ■ showing or caused by intense feelings of sexual love. ■ dominated by or easily affected by intense emotion. —**pas·sion·ate·ly** *adv.* —**pas·sion·ate·ness** *n.*

pas·sion·flow·er /ˈpashən,flou(-ə)r/ (also **passion flower**) ▶ *n.* an evergreen climbing plant (genus *Passiflora,* family Passifloraceae) of warm regions that bears distinctive flowers with parts that supposedly resemble instruments of the Crucifixion.

pas·sion play ▶ *n.* a dramatic performance representing Christ's Passion from the Last Supper to the Crucifixion.

pas·sive /ˈpasiv/ ▶ *adj.* **1** accepting or allowing what happens or what others do, without active response or resistance: *the women were portrayed as passive victims.* ■ *Chem.* (of a metal) made unreactive by a thin inert surface layer of oxide. ■ (of a circuit or device) containing no source of electromotive force. ■ (of radar or a satellite) receiving or reflecting radiation from a transmitter or target rather than generating its own signal. ■ relating to or denoting heating systems that make use of incident sunlight as an energy source. **2** *Gram.* denoting or relating to a voice of verbs in which the subject undergoes the action of the verb (e.g., *they were killed* as opposed to *he killed them*). The opposite of ACTIVE.

▶ *n. Gram.* a passive form of a verb. ■ (**the passive**) the passive voice. —**pas·sive·ly** *adv.* —**pas·sive·ness** *n.* —**pas·siv·i·ty** /paˈsivitē/ *n.*

pas·sive re·sist·ance ▶ *n.* nonviolent opposition to authority, esp. a refusal to cooperate with legal requirements.

pas·sive smok·ing ▶ *n.* the involuntary inhaling of smoke from other people's cigarettes, cigars, or pipes.

pass·key /ˈpas,kē/ ▶ *n.* **1** a key to the door of a restricted area, given only to those who are officially allowed access. **2** a master key.

Pass·o·ver /ˈpas,ōvər/ ▶ *n.* the major Jewish spring festival that commemorates the liberation of the Israelites from Egyptian bondage, lasting seven or eight days from the 15th day of Nisan.

pass·port /ˈpas,pôrt/ ▶ *n.* an official document issued by a government, certifying the holder's identity and citizenship and entitling them to travel under its protection to and from foreign countries. ■ a thing that ensures admission to or the achievement of something.

pass·word /ˈpas,wərd/ ▶ *n.* a secret word or phrase that must be used to gain admission to something. ■ a string of characters that allows someone access to a computer system.

past /past/ ▶ *adj.* gone by in time and no longer existing: *the danger is now past.* ■ belonging to a former time: *past attempts had failed.* ■ (of a specified period of time) occurring before and leading up to the time of speaking or writing: *the past twelve months.* ■ *Gram.* (of a tense) expressing an action that has happened or a state that previously existed.

▶ *n.* **1** (usu. **the past**) the time or a period of time before the moment of speaking or writing. ■ the events of an earlier time: *a reminder of the past.* ■ the history of a person, country, or institution: *the country's colorful past.* ■ a part of a person's history that is considered to be shameful: *the heroine was a lady with a past.* **2** *Gram.* a past tense or form of a verb: *a simple past of the first conjugation.*

▶ *prep.* to or on the further side of: *he rode on past the crossroads.* ■ in front of or from one side to the other of: *to drive past the houses.* ■ beyond in time; later than: *by this time it was past 3:30.* ■ no longer capable of: *he is past giving advice.* ■ beyond the scope of: *my hair was past praying for.*

▶ *adv.* **1** so as to pass from one side of something to the other: *angelfish swim slowly past.* ■ used to indicate the lapse of time: *a week went past.* **2** at a time later by a specified amount than a particular known hour: *we're having speeches in the dining room at half past.*

▶ □ **not put it past someone** believe someone to be capable of doing something wrong or rash.

pas·ta /ˈpästə/ ▶ *n.* a dish originally from Italy consisting of dough made from durum wheat and water, extruded or stamped into various shapes and typically cooked in boiling water.

paste /pāst/ ▶ *n.* a thick, soft, moist substance, usually produced by mixing dry ingredients with a liquid. ■ a substance such as this that is

used as an adhesive, esp. for sticking paper and other light materials: *wallpaper paste.* ■ a mixture consisting mainly of clay and water that is used in making ceramic ware, esp. a mixture of low plasticity based on kaolin for making porcelain. ■ a hard vitreous composition used in making imitation gems: [as *adj.*] *paste brooches.*

▶ *v.* [*tr.*] **1** coat with paste. ■ [*tr.*] fasten or stick (something) onto something with paste: *ads are pasted on the walls.* ■ *Comput.* insert (text) into a document. **2** *inf.* beat or defeat severely.

paste·board /ˈpās(t),bôrd/ ▶ *n.* a type of thin board made by pasting together sheets of paper.

pas·tel /paˈstel/ ▶ *n.* **1** a crayon made of powdered pigments bound with gum or resin. ■ a work of art created using such crayons. **2** a soft and delicate shade of a color.

▶ *adj.* of a soft and delicate shade or color: *pastel blue curtains.* —**pas·tel·ist** /-ist/ (also **pas·tel·list**) *n.*

pas·tern /ˈpastərn/ ▶ *n.* the sloping part of a horse's foot between the fetlock and the hoof. ■ a corresponding part in some other domestic animals.

pas·teur·ize /ˈpaschə,rīz/ ▶ *v.* [*tr.*] subject (milk, wine, or other products) to a process of partial sterilization, esp. one involving heat treatment or irradiation, thus making the product safe and improving its keeping quality. —**pas·teur·i·za·tion** /,paschəri'zāshən/ *n.* —**pas·teur·iz·er** *n.*

pas·tiche /paˈstēsh; pä-/ ▶ *n.* an artistic work in a style that imitates that of another work, artist, or period. ■ an artistic work consisting of a medley of pieces taken from various sources. ■ a confused mixture or jumble.

▶ *v.* [*tr.*] imitate the style of (an artist or work).

pas·tille /paˈstēl/ ▶ *n.* a small candy or lozenge. ■ a small pellet of aromatic paste burned as a perfume or deodorizer.

pas·time /ˈpas,tīm/ ▶ *n.* an activity that someone does regularly for enjoyment rather than work; a hobby.

past mas·ter ▶ *n.* **1** a person who is particularly skilled at a specified activity or art: *he's a past master at keeping his whereabouts secret.* **2** a person who has held the position of master in an organization.

pas·tor /ˈpastər/ ▶ *n.* a minister in charge of a Christian church or congregation.

▶ *v.* [*tr.*] be pastor of (a church or a congregation): *he pastored Peninsula Bible Church in Palo Alto* | [*intr.*] *he continued to study law while pastoring in Chicago.* ▷late Middle English: from Anglo-Norman French *pastour,* from Latin *pastor* 'shepherd,' from *past-* 'fed, grazed,' from the verb *pascere.* —**pas·tor·ship** /-,ship/ *n.*

pas·to·ral /ˈpastərəl; pasˈtôrəl/ ▶ *adj.* **1** (esp. of land or a farm) used for or related to the keeping or grazing of sheep or cattle. ■ associated with country life: *the view was pastoral, with rolling fields and grazing sheep.* ■ (of a work of art) portraying or evoking country life, typically in a romanticized or idealized form. **2** (in the Christian Church) concerning or appropriate to the giving of spiritual guidance: *clergy doing pastoral work.*

▶ *n.* a work of literature portraying an idealized version of country life. —**pas·to·ral·ism** /ˈpastərə,lizəm/ *n.* —**pas·to·ral·ly** *adv.*

pas·to·rale /,pastəˈräl; -ˈral/ ▶ *n.* (pl. **-rales** or **-ra·li** /-ˈrälē/) **1** a slow instrumental composition in compound time, usually with drone notes in the bass. **2** a simple musical play with a rural subject.

past per·fect ▶ *adj. Gram.* (of a tense) denoting an action completed prior to some past point of time specified or implied, formed in English by *had* and the past participle, as in *he had gone by then.*

▶ *n.* the past perfect tense.

pas·tra·mi /pəˈsträmē/ ▶ *n.* highly seasoned smoked beef, typically served in thin slices.

pas·try /ˈpāstrē/ ▶ *n.* (pl. **-tries**) a dough of flour, shortening, and water, used as a base and covering in baked dishes such as pies. ■ an item of food consisting of sweet pastry with a cream, jam, or fruit filling.

pas·tur·age /ˈpaschərij/ ▶ *n.* land used for pasture. ■ the occupation or process of pasturing cattle, sheep, or other grazing animals.

pas·ture /ˈpaschər/ ▶ *n.* land covered with grass and other low plants suitable for grazing animals, esp. cattle or sheep. ■ the grass and other low plants growing on such land. ■ *fig.* a place or activity regarded as offering new opportunities: *he has departed for the greener pastures of a corner office.*

▶ *v.* [*tr.*] put (animals) in a pasture to graze. ■ [*intr.*] (of animals) graze.

▶ □ **put someone out to pasture** force someone to retire.

Pronunciation Key ə *ago,* up; ər *over, fur;* a *hat;* ā *ate;* ä *car;* CH *chin;* e *let;* ē *see;* e(ə)r *air;* i *fit;* ī *by;* i(ə)r *ear;* NG *sing;* ō *go;* ô *law, for;* oi *toy;* o͝o *good;* o͞o *goo;* ou *out;* SH *she;* TH *thin;* T͟H *then;* (h)w *why;* ZH *vision*

past·y[1] /ˈpāstē/ (also **past·ie**) ▶*n.* (*pl.* **past·ies**) *chiefly Brit.* a folded pastry case filled with seasoned meat and vegetables.

past·y[2] /ˈpāstē/ ▶*adj.* (**past·i·er**, **past·i·est**) **1** (of a person's face) unhealthily pale: *a pasty complexion.* **2** of or like paste: *a pasty mixture.* —**past·i·ness** /-stēnis/ *n.*

pat[1] /pat/ ▶*v.* (**pat·ted**, **pat·ting**) [*tr.*] touch quickly and gently with the flat of the hand: *he patted him consolingly on the shoulder.* ■ draw attention to (something) by tapping it gently: *he patted the bench beside him and I sat down.* ■ mold into shape or put in position with gentle taps: *she patted down the earth in each pot.*
▶*n.* **1** a light stroke with the hand: *a friendly pat on the arm.* **2** a compact mass of soft material: *a pat of butter.*
▶ □ **a pat on the back** an expression of approval or congratulation: *they deserve a pat on the back for a job well done.* □ **pat someone on the back** express approval of or admiration for someone.

pat[2] ▶*adj.* simple and somewhat glib or unconvincing.
▶*adv.* at exactly the right moment or in the right way; conveniently or opportunely: *the ending came rather pat.* —**pat·ly** *adv.* —**pat·ness** *n.*
▶ □ **stand pat** stick stubbornly to one's opinion or decision: *many ranchers stood pat with the old strains of cattle.* ■ (in poker and blackjack) retain one's hand as dealt, without drawing other cards.

Pat·a·go·ni·an tooth·fish /ˌpataˈgōnēan ˈtooth,fish/ ▶*n.* a food fish (*Dissostichus eleginoides*, family Nototheniidae) of Antarctic waters, marketed as Chilean sea bass and recently overfished.

patch /pacH/ ▶*n.* **1** a piece of cloth or other material used to mend or strengthen a torn or weak point. ■ a pad or shield worn over a sightless or injured eye or an eye socket. ■ a piece of cloth sewn onto clothing as a badge or distinguishing mark. ■ *Comput.* a small piece of code inserted into a program to improve its functioning or to correct an error. ■ an adhesive piece of drug-impregnated material worn on the skin so that the drug can be absorbed gradually over a period of time. ■ (on an animal or bird) an area of hair or plumage different in color from that on most of the rest of the body. ■ a part of something marked out from the rest by a particular characteristic: *hair combed forward to hide a bald patch.* ■ a small area or amount of something: *patches of bluebells in the grass.* ■ *hist.* a small disk of black silk attached to the face, esp. as worn by women in the 17th and 18th centuries for adornment. **2** a small piece of ground, esp. one used for gardening: *their vegetable patch.* ■ *Brit., inf.* an area for which someone is responsible or in which they operate: *we didn't want any secret organizations on our patch.* **3** *inf.* a period of time seen as a distinct unit with a characteristic quality: *he was going through a bad patch.* **4** a temporary electrical or telephone connection. ■ a preset configuration or sound-data file in an electronic musical instrument, esp. a synthesizer.
▶*v.* [*tr.*] **1** mend or strengthen (fabric or an item of clothing) by putting a piece of material over a hole or weak point in it: *her jeans were neatly patched.* ■ *Comput.* correct, enhance, or modify (a routine or program) by inserting a patch. ■ **be patched** (usu. **be patched**) cover small areas of (a surface) with something different, causing it to appear variegated. ■ (**patch someone/something up**) *inf.* treat someone's injuries or repair the damage to something, esp. hastily: *they did their best to patch up the gaping wounds.* ■ (**patch something together**) construct something hastily from unsuitable components: *lean-tos patched together from aluminum siding and planks* | *fig. they were trying to patch together an arrangement for cooperation.* ■ (**patch something up**) *inf.* restore peaceful or friendly relations after a quarrel or dispute: *any ill feeling could be patched up with a phone call.* **2** [*tr.*] connect by a temporary electrical, radio, or telephonic connection: *Ralph had patched her through to the meeting by walkie-talkie.* ■ [*intr.*] become connected in this way: *stay on the open line and we'll patch in on you.* ▷*late Middle English:* perhaps from a variant of Old French *pieche*, dialect variant of *piece* 'piece.' —**patch·er** *n.*

patch·ou·li /pəˈchoolē/ ▶*n.* **1** an aromatic oil obtained from a Southeast Asian shrub and used in perfumery, insecticides, and medicine. **2** the strongly scented shrub (*Pogostemon cablin*) of the mint family from which this oil is made.

patch·work /ˈpacH,wərk/ ▶*n.* needlework in which small pieces of cloth in different designs, colors, or textures are sewn together: *a quilt of patchwork* ■ the craft of sewing in this way. ■ a thing composed of many different elements so as to appear variegated.

patch·y /ˈpacHē/ ▶*adj.* (**patch·i·er**, **patch·i·est**) existing or happening in small, isolated areas: *patchy fog.* ■ not of the same quality throughout; inconsistent. ■ incomplete: *my knowledge of Egyptology is patchy.* —**patch·i·ly** /ˈpacHəlē/ *adv.* —**patch·i·ness** /ˈpacHēnis/ *n.*

pate /pāt/ ▶*n. archaic* or *humorous* a person's head: *his balding pate.*

pâte /pät/ ▶*n.* the paste of which porcelain is made.

pâ·té /päˈtā/ ▶*n.* a rich, savory paste made from finely minced or mashed ingredients, typically seasoned meat or fish.

pâ·té de foie gras /päˈtā də ˌfwä ˈgrä/ ▶*n.* a smooth rich paste made from fattened goose liver.

pa·tel·la /pəˈtelə/ ▶*n.* (*pl.* **-lae** /-lē/) *Anat.* the kneecap. —**pa·tel·lar** /-ˈtelər/ *adj.* —**pa·tel·late** /-ˈtelit; -ˌlāt/ *adj.*

pat·ent ▶*n.* /ˈpatnt/ **1** a government authority to an individual or organization conferring a right or title, esp. the sole right to make, use, or sell some invention: *he took out a patent for an improved steam hammer.* **2** short for PATENT LEATHER.
▶*adj.* **1** /ˈpātnt; ˈpat-/ easily recognizable; obvious: *she was smiling with patent insincerity.* **2** *Med.* /ˈpātnt; ˈpat-/ showing detectable parasites in the tissues or feces. **3** /ˈpatnt/ made and marketed under a patent; proprietary: *patent milk powder.*
▶*v.* /ˈpatnt/ [*tr.*] obtain a patent for (an invention). —**pat·en·cy** *n.* —**pat·ent·a·ble** *adj.* —**pat·ent·ly** /ˈpatntlē; ˈpā-/ *adv.*

pat·ent leath·er ▶*n.* leather with a glossy varnished surface, used chiefly for shoes, belts, and purses.

pat·ent med·i·cine ▶*n.* a proprietary medicine made and marketed under a patent and available without prescription.

pat·er·a /ˈpatərə/ ▶*n.* (*pl.* **-er·ae** /-ərē/) a broad shallow dish used in ancient Rome for pouring libations. ■ *Archit.* a flat, round ornament resembling a shallow dish.

pa·ter·nal /pəˈtərnl/ ▶*adj.* of or appropriate to a father: *he reasserted his paternal authority.* ■ showing a kindness and care associated with a father; fatherly: *my elders in the newsroom kept a paternal eye on me.* ■ related through the father: *his paternal grandfather.* —**pa·ter·nal·ly** *adv.*

pa·ter·nal·ism /pəˈtərnl,izəm/ ▶*n.* the policy or practice on the part of people in positions of authority of restricting the freedom and responsibilities of those subordinate to them in the subordinates' supposed best interest. —**pa·ter·nal·ist** *n.* & *adj.* —**pa·ter·nal·is·tic** /-ˌtərnlˈistik/ *adj.* —**pa·ter·nal·is·ti·cal·ly** /-ˌtərnlˈistik(ə)lē/ *adv.*

pa·ter·ni·ty /pəˈtərnitē/ ▶*n.* **1** (esp. in legal contexts) the state of being someone's father. **2** paternal origin.

path /paTH/ ▶*n.* (*pl.* **paths** /paTHz; paTHs/) a way or track laid down for walking or made by continual treading. ■ such a way or track designed for a particular purpose: *a nature path.* ■ the course or direction in which a person or thing is moving: *the missile traced a fiery path* | *fig. a career path.* ■ a course of action or conduct. ■ *Comput.* a definition of the order in which an operating system or program searches for a file or executable program. —**path·less** *adj.*
▶ □ **the path of least resistance** see RESISTANCE.

path. ▶*abbr.* ■ pathological. ■ pathology.

pa·thet·ic /pəˈTHetik/ ▶*adj.* **1** arousing pity, esp. through vulnerability or sadness. ■ *inf.* miserably inadequate: *his test scores in Chemistry were pathetic.* **2** *archaic* relating to the emotions. —**pa·thet·i·cal·ly** /-(ə)lē/ *adv.*

Path·find·er /ˈpaTH,fīndər/ (in full **Mars Pathfinder**) ▶*an* unmanned American spacecraft that landed on Mars in 1997, deploying a small robotic rover (*Sojourner*) to explore the surface and examine the rocks.

path·find·er /ˈpaTH,fīndər/ ▶*n.* a person who goes ahead and discovers or shows others a path or way. ■ an aircraft or its pilot sent ahead to locate and mark the target area for bombing. ■ [usu. as *adj.*] an experimental plan or forecast: *a pathfinder prospectus.*

path·o·gen /ˈpaTHəjən; -ˌjen/ ▶*n.* *Med.* a bacterium, virus, or other microorganism that can cause disease. —**path·o·gen·ic** /ˌpaTHəˈjenik/ *adj.* —**path·o·ge·nic·i·ty** /ˌpaTHəjəˌnisitē/ *n.* —**pa·thog·e·nous** /pəˈTHäjənəs/ *adj.*

path·o·log·i·cal /ˌpaTHəˈläjikəl/ (also **path·o·log·ic**) ▶*adj.* of or relating to pathology. ■ involving, caused by, or of the nature of a physical or mental disease: *pathological changes associated with senile dementia.* ■ *inf.* compulsive; obsessive: *a pathological gambler.* —**path·o·log·i·cal·ly** *adv.*

pa·thol·o·gy /pəˈTHäləjē/ ▶*n.* the science of the causes and effects of diseases, esp. the branch of medicine that deals with the laboratory examination of samples of body tissue for diagnostic or forensic purposes. ■ *Med.* pathological features considered collectively; the typical behavior of a disease. ■ *Med.* a pathological condition. ■ mental, social, or linguistic abnormality or malfunction: *the pathology of a burgeoning underclass.* —**pa·thol·o·gist** /-jist/ *n.*

pa·thos /ˈpā,THäs; -,THôs/ ▶*n.* a quality that evokes pity or sadness: *the actor injects his customary humor and pathos into the role.*

path·way /ˈpaTH,wā/ ▶*n.* a way that constitutes or serves as a path. ■ *Physiol.* a route, formed by a chain of nerve cells, along which impulses of a particular kind usually travel. ■ (also **metabolic pathway**) *Biochem.* a sequence of chemical reactions undergone by a compound or class of compounds in a living organism.

pa·tience /ˈpāSHəns/ ▶n. **1** the capacity to accept or tolerate delay, trouble, or suffering without getting angry or upset. **2** chiefly British term for SOLITAIRE (sense 1).
▶ □ **lose patience** (or **lose one's patience**) become unable to keep one's temper: *even Lawrence finally lost patience with him.*

pa·tient /ˈpāSHənt/ ▶adj. able to wait without becoming annoyed or anxious. ▪ slow to lose one's temper with irritating people or situations.
▶n. **1** a person receiving or registered to receive medical treatment. **2** *Linguistics* the semantic role of a noun phrase denoting something that is affected or acted upon by the action of a verb. —**pa·tient·ly** adv.

pat·i·na /pəˈtēnə/ ▶n. a green or brown film on the surface of bronze or similar metals, produced by oxidation over a long period. ▪ a gloss or sheen on wooden furniture produced by age and polishing. ▪ an acquired change in the appearance of a surface: *plankton added a golden patina to the shallow, slowly moving water.* ▪ *fig.* an impression or appearance of something: *he carries the patina of old money and good breeding.* —**pat·i·nat·ed** /ˈpatnˌātid/ adj. —**pat·i·na·tion** /ˌpatnˈāSHən/ n.

pa·ti·o /ˈpatēˌō/ ▶n. (pl. -os) a paved outdoor area adjoining a house. ▪ a roofless inner courtyard in a Spanish or Spanish-American house.

pa·tis·se·rie /pəˈtisərē/ ▶n. a shop where French pastries and cakes are sold. ▪ French pastries and cakes collectively.

pat·ois /ˈpaˌtwä; ˈpä-/ ▶n. (pl. same) the dialect of the common people of a region, differing in various respects from the standard language of the rest of the country. ▪ the jargon or informal speech used by a particular social group.

pa·tri·arch /ˈpātrēˌärk/ ▶n. **1** the male head of a family or tribe. ▪ a man who is the oldest or most venerable of a group. ▪ a man who behaves in a commanding manner. ▪ a person or thing that is regarded as the founder of something. **2** any of those biblical figures regarded as fathers of the human race. **3** the title of a most senior Orthodox or Catholic bishop, in particular: ▪ a bishop of one of the most ancient Christian sees (Alexandria, Antioch, Constantinople, Jerusalem, and formerly Rome). ▪ the head of an independent Orthodox church. —**pa·tri·arch·al** /ˌpātrēˈärkəl/ adj.

pa·tri·arch·ate /ˈpātrēˌärkit/ ▶n. the office, see, or residence of an ecclesiastical patriarch.

pa·tri·arch·y /ˈpātrēˌärkē/ ▶n. (pl. -arch·ies) a system of society or government in which the father or eldest male is head of the family and descent is traced through the male line. ▪ a system of society or government in which men hold the power and women are largely excluded from it. ▪ a society or community organized in this way.

pa·tri·cian /pəˈtriSHən/ ▶n. an aristocrat or nobleman. ▪ a member of a long-established wealthy family. ▪ a member of a noble family or class in ancient Rome.
▶adj. belonging to or characteristic of the aristocracy: *a proud, patrician face.* ▪ belonging to or characteristic of a long-established and wealthy family. ▪ belonging to the nobility of ancient Rome.

pat·ri·cide /ˈpatrəˌsīd/ ▶n. the killing of one's father. ▪ a person who kills their father. —**pat·ri·cid·al** /ˌpatrəˈsīdl/ adj.

pat·ri·lin·e·al /ˌpatrəˈlinēəl/ ▶adj. of, relating to, or based on relationship to the father or descent through the male line.

pat·ri·mo·ny /ˈpatrəˌmōnē/ ▶n. (pl. -nies) property inherited from one's father or male ancestor. ▪ heritage. —**pat·ri·mo·ni·al** /ˌpatrəˈmōnēəl/ adj.

pa·tri·ot /ˈpātrēət/ ▶n. **1** a person who vigorously supports their country and is prepared to defend it against enemies or detractors. **2** (**Patriot**) *trademark* an automated surface-to-air missile designed for early detection and interception of missiles or aircraft. —**pa·tri·ot·ic** /ˌpātrēˈätik/ adj. —**pa·tri·ot·ism** /-ˌtizəm/ n.

pa·trol /pəˈtrōl/ ▶n. a person or group of people sent to keep watch over an area, esp. a detachment of guards or police. ▪ the action of keeping watch over an area by walking or driving around it at regular intervals: *the policemen were on patrol.* ▪ an expedition to carry out reconnaissance: *we were ordered to investigate on a night patrol.* ▪ a detachment of troops sent out to reconnoiter: *you couldn't go through the country without meeting an enemy patrol.* ▪ a routine operational voyage of a ship or aircraft: *a submarine patrol.* ▪ a unit of six to eight Girl Scouts or Boy Scouts forming part of a troop.
▶v. (-trolled, -trol·ling) [tr.] keep watch over (an area) by regularly walking or traveling around or through it: *the garrison had to patrol the streets to maintain order* | [intr.] *pairs of men were patrolling on each side of the thoroughfare.* —**pa·trol·ler** n.

pa·trol·man /pəˈtrōlmən/ ▶n. (pl. -men) a patrolling police officer.

pa·tron /ˈpātrən/ ▶n. **1** a person who gives financial or other support to a person, organization, cause, or activity: *a celebrated patron of the arts.*

2 a customer, esp. a regular one, of a store, restaurant, or theater. **3** short for PATRON SAINT.

pa·tron·age /ˈpatrənij; ˈpā-/ ▶n. **1** the support given by a patron. **2** the power to control appointments to office or the right to privileges: *recruits are selected on merit, not through political patronage.* **3** a patronizing or condescending manner. **4** the regular business given to a store, restaurant, or public service by a person or group. **5** (in ancient Rome) the rights and duties or the position of a patron.

pa·tron·ize /ˈpātrəˌnīz; ˈpa-/ ▶v. **1** treat with an apparent kindness that betrays a feeling of superiority: *she was determined not to be put down or patronized.* **2** frequent (a store, theater, restaurant, or other establishment) as a customer. ▪ give encouragement and financial support to (a person, esp. an artist, or a cause). —**pa·tron·i·za·tion** /ˌpātrəni-ˈzāSHən; ˌpa-/ n. —**pa·tron·iz·er** n. —**pa·tron·iz·ing·ly** /-ˌnīziNGlē/ adv.

pa·tron saint ▶n. the protecting or guiding saint of a person or place.

pat·ro·nym·ic /ˌpatrəˈnimik/ ▶n. a name derived from the name of a father or ancestor, typically by the addition of a prefix or suffix, e.g., *Johnson, O'Brien, Ivanovich.*

pa·troon /pəˈtrōōn/ ▶n. *hist.* a person given land and granted certain manorial privileges under the former Dutch governments of New York and New Jersey.

pat·sy /ˈpatsē/ ▶n. (pl. -sies) *inf.* a person who is easily taken advantage of, esp. by being cheated or blamed for something.

pat·ter¹ /ˈpatər/ ▶v. [intr.] make a repeated light tapping sound: *a flurry of rain pattered against the window.* ▪ run with quick light steps.
▶n. [in sing.] a repeated light tapping.

pat·ter² ▶n. rapid or smooth-flowing continuous talk, such as that used by a comedian or salesman. ▪ rapid speech included in a song, esp. for comic effect: [as adj.] *a patter song of invective.* ▪ the special language or jargon of a profession or other group.
▶v. [intr.] talk at length without saying anything significant.

pat·tern /ˈpatərn/ ▶n. **1** a repeated decorative design. ▪ an arrangement or sequence regularly found in comparable objects or events. ▪ a regular and intelligible form or sequence discernible in certain actions or situations: *the change in working patterns.* **2** a model or design used as a guide in needlework and other crafts. ▪ a set of instructions to be followed in making a sewn or knitted item. ▪ a wooden or metal model from which a mold is made for a casting. ▪ an example for others to follow. ▪ a sample of cloth or wallpaper.
▶v. [tr.] **1** [usu. as adj.] (**patterned**) decorate with a recurring design. **2** give a regular or intelligible form to: *the brain not only receives information, but interprets and patterns it.* ▪ (**pattern something on/after**) give something a form based on that of (something else): *the clothing is patterned on athletes' wear.*

pat·ty /ˈpatē/ ▶n. (pl. -ties) a small flat cake of minced or finely chopped food, esp. meat. ▪ a small, round, flat chocolate-covered peppermint candy.

pat·ty·pan /ˈpatēˌpan/ (also **pattypan squash**) ▶n. a squash of a saucer-shaped variety with a scalloped rim and creamy white flesh.

pau·ci·ty /ˈpôsitē/ ▶n. [in sing.] the presence of something only in small or insufficient quantities or amounts; scarcity: *a paucity of information.* ▷late Middle English: from Old French *paucite* or Latin *paucitas*, from *paucus* 'few.'

paunch /pônCH; pänCH/ ▶n. a large or protruding abdomen or stomach. —**paunch·i·ness** /ˈpônCHēnis/ n. —**paunch·y** adj.

pau·per /ˈpôpər/ ▶n. a very poor person. ▪ *hist.* a recipient of government relief or public charity. —**pau·per·dom** /-dəm/ n. —**pau·per·ism** /-ˌrizəm/ n. —**pau·per·i·za·tion** /ˌpôpəriˈzāSHən/ n. —**pau·per·ize** /-ˌrīz/ v.

pause /pôz/ ▶n. a temporary stop in action or speech. ▪ (also **pause button**) a control allowing the temporary interruption of an electronic (or mechanical) process, esp. video or audio recording or reproduction.
▶v. [intr.] interrupt action or speech briefly: *she paused, at a loss for words.* ▪ [tr.] temporarily interrupt the operation of (a videotape, audiotape, or computer program): *she had paused a tape on the VCR.*
▶ □ **give someone pause** cause someone to think carefully or hesitate before doing something: *public outrage has given him pause.*

pave /pāv/ ▶v. [tr.] (often **be paved with**) cover (a piece of ground) with concrete, asphalt, stones, or bricks; lay paving over: *the yard at the front was paved with flagstones* | *fig. the streets of the big city are not paved with gold.* —**pav·er** n.
▶ □ **pave the way for** create the circumstances to enable (something) to happen or be done.

P

pave·ment /ˈpāvmənt/ ▶n. any paved area or surface. ■ the hard surface of a road or street.

pa·vil·ion /pəˈvilyən/ ▶n. **1** a building or similar structure used for a specific purpose, in particular: ■ a summerhouse or other decorative building used as a shelter in a park or large garden. ■ a detached or semidetached block at a hospital or other building complex. ■ a large tent with a peak and crenellated decorations, used esp. at a show or fair. ■ a temporary building, stand, or other structure in which items are displayed by a dealer or exhibitor at a trade exhibition. **2** a usually highly decorated projecting subdivision of a building. **3** the part of a cut gemstone below the girdle.

Pav·lov·i·an /pavˈlōvēən; -ˈläv-/ ▶adj. of or relating to a learning process described by I. P. Pavlov that occurs when two stimuli are repeatedly paired: a response that is at first elicited by the second stimulus is eventually elicited by the first stimulus alone.

paw /pô/ ▶n. an animal's foot having claws and pads. ■ *chiefly derog.* a person's hand: *don't touch her with your filthy paws.*
▶v. [tr.] (of an animal) feel or scrape with a paw or hoof: *the horse rose on its haunches, its forelegs pawing the air* | [intr.] *young dogs may **paw** at the floor and whine.* ■ *inf.* (of a person) touch or handle awkwardly or roughly. ■ (of a person) touch (someone) in a lascivious and offensive way.

pawl /pôl/ ▶n. a pivoted curved bar or lever whose free end engages with the teeth of a cogwheel or ratchet so that the wheel or ratchet can only turn or move one way.

pawn[1] /pôn/ ▶n. a chess piece of the smallest size and value. ■ a person used by others for their own purposes.

pawn[2] ▶v. [tr.] deposit (an object) with a pawnbroker as security for money lent: *I pawned the necklace to cover the loan.*
▶phrasal v. □ **pawn someone/something off** pass off someone or something unwanted.
▶n. *archaic* an object left as security for money lent.
▶ □ **in pawn** (of an object) held as security by a pawnbroker.

pawn·brok·er /ˈpônˌbrōkər/ ▶n. a person who lends money at interest on the security of an article pawned. —**pawn·brok·ing** /-kiNG/ n.

Paw·nee /pôˈnē/ ▶n. (pl. same or **-nees**) **1** a member of an American Indian confederacy formerly in Nebraska, and now mainly in Oklahoma. **2** the Caddoan language of these peoples.
▶adj. of or relating to these people or their language.

pawn·shop /ˈpônˌSHäp/ ▶n. a pawnbroker's shop, esp. one where unredeemed items are sold to the public.

paw·paw /ˈpôpô/ (also **pa·paw** /pəˈpô; ˈpôpô/) ▶n. **1** another term for PAPAYA. **2** (also **pawpaw tree**) a North American tree (*Asimina triloba*, family Annonaceae), with purple flowers and edible oblong yellow fruit with sweet pulp. ■ the fruit of this tree.

pay /pā/ ▶v. (past **paid**) **1** [tr.] give (someone) money that is due for work done, goods received, or a debt incurred: [tr.] *he paid the locals to pick his coffee beans* | [intr.] *TV licenses can be **paid for** by direct debit.* ■ give (a sum of money) in exchange for goods or work done or in discharge of a debt: *he paid $1,000 to have it built in 1977* | *a museum paid him a four-figure sum for it.* ■ hand over or transfer the amount due of (a debt, wages, etc.) to (someone). ■ (of work, an investment, etc.) yield or provide someone with (a specified sum of money): *jobs that pay $5 an hour.* ■ [intr.] (of a business or undertaking, or an attitude) be profitable or advantageous to someone: *it pays to choose varieties carefully.* **2** [intr.] suffer a loss or other misfortune as a consequence of an action: *the destroyer responsible for these atrocities would have to **pay with** his life.* ■ [tr.] give what is due or deserved to (someone); reward or punish. **3** [tr.] give or bestow (attention, respect, or a compliment) on (someone): *no one paid them any attention.* ■ make (a visit or a call) to (someone).
▶phrasal v. □ **pay someone back** repay a loan to someone. ■ *fig.* take revenge on someone. ■ reward someone for something done earlier. □ **pay something back** repay a loan to someone. □ **pay off** *inf.* (of a course of action) yield good results; succeed. □ **pay someone off** dismiss someone with a final payment. □ **pay something off** pay a debt in full. □ **pay something out** (or **pay out**) **1** pay a large sum of money from funds under one's control. **2** let out (a rope) by slackening it. □ **pay up** (or **pay something up**) pay a debt in full.
▶n. the money paid to someone for regular work. —**pay·ee** /pāˈē/ n. —**pay·er** n.
▶ □ **pay dearly** obtain something at a high cost or great effort. ■ suffer for an error or failure. □ **pay for itself** (of an object or system) earn or save enough money to cover the cost of its purchase. □ **pay its** (or **one's**) **way** (of an enterprise or person) earn enough to cover its (or one's) costs. □ **pay one's last respects** show respect toward a dead person by attending their funeral. □ **pay one's respects** make a polite visit to someone. □ **pay through the nose** *inf.* pay much more than a fair price.

pay·a·ble /ˈpāəbəl/ ▶adj. **1** (of money) required to be paid; due: *interest is payable on the money owing* | *send a check, payable to the ASPCA.* **2** able to be paid: *it costs just $195, payable in five monthly installments.*
▶n. (**payables**) debts owed by a business; liabilities.

pay·back /ˈpāˌbak/ ▶n. **1** financial return or reward, esp. profit equal to the initial outlay of an investment. **2** an act of revenge or retaliation: *the drive-by shootings are mainly paybacks.*

pay·check /ˈpāˌCHek/ ▶n. a check for salary or wages made out to an employee. ■ *fig.* salary or income: *socking away money for the time when he wouldn't have a steady paycheck.*

pay·day /ˈpāˌdā/ ▶n. a day on which someone is paid or expects to be paid their wages. ■ *inf.* money or success won or earned.

pay dirt ▶n. *Mining* ground containing ore in sufficient quantity to be profitably extracted. ■ profit; reward: *the gig pays three hundred bucks a week—looks like I just **hit pay dirt**.*

pay·load /ˈpāˌlōd/ ▶n. the part of a vehicle's load, esp. an aircraft's, from which revenue is derived; passengers and cargo. ■ the total load of bombs carried by a bomber. ■ an explosive warhead carried by a missile. ■ equipment, personnel, or satellites carried by a spacecraft.

pay·mas·ter /ˈpāˌmastər/ ▶n. an official who pays troops or workers.

pay·ment /ˈpāmənt/ ▶n. **1** the action or process of paying someone or something, or of being paid. **2** an amount paid or payable: *an interim compensation payment of $2500.* ■ *fig.* something given as a reward or in recompense for something done: *a suit with a velvet collar that I got as payment for being in the show.*

pay·off /ˈpāˌôf/ ▶n. *inf.* a payment made to someone, esp. as a bribe or reward, or on leaving a job. ■ the return on an investment or a bet. ■ a final outcome; a conclusion.

pay·o·la /pāˈōlə/ ▶n. the practice of bribing someone to use their influence or position to promote a particular product or interest.

pay·roll /ˈpāˌrōl/ ▶n. a list of a company's employees and the amount of money they are to be paid. ■ the total amount of wages and salaries paid by a company to its employees: *a payroll of less than $45,000.*

PB ▶abbr. ■ British Pharmacopoeia. ■ Prayer Book. ■ petabyte.

Pb ▶symb. the chemical element lead.

pb ▶abbr. paperback: hb $18.99, pb $6.99.

PBS ▶abbr. Public Broadcasting Service.

PC ▶abbr. ■ Past Commander. ■ personal computer. ■ (also **pc**) politically correct; political correctness: *PC language* | *the cult of PC.* ■ Post Commander. ■ *Brit.* Prince Consort. ■ *Brit.* Privy Council. ■ professional corporation.

pc ▶abbr. parsec.

PCB ▶abbr. ■ *Electr.* printed circuit board. ■ *Chem.* polychlorinated biphenyl.

PCP ▶abbr. ■ phencyclidine. ■ primary care physician. ■ (in Canada) Progressive-Conservative Party.

pct. ▶abbr. percent.

PD ▶abbr. ■ Police Department: *the Chicago PD.* ■ public domain: *PD software.*

Pd ▶symb. the chemical element palladium.

pd ▶abbr. paid.

p.d. ▶abbr. ■ per diem. ■ potential difference.

PDA ▶n. a pocket-sized computer used to store information such as addresses and telephone numbers, and for simple computing tasks. ▷late 20th cent.: abbreviation of *personal digital assistant.*

p.d.q. *inf.* ▶abbr. pretty damn quick.

PDT ▶abbr. Pacific Daylight Time (see **PACIFIC TIME**).

PE ▶abbr. ■ physical education. ■ Prince Edward Island (in official postal use).

pea /pē/ ▶n. **1** a spherical green seed that is widely eaten as a vegetable. ■ any of a number of edible spherical seeds of the pea family, e.g., **chickpea** and **black-eyed pea**. **2** the widely cultivated Eurasian climbing plant (*Pisum sativum*) that yields pods containing these seeds. The **pea family** (Leguminosae, or Fabaceae) also includes beans, clovers, mimosas, acacias, cassia, and carob.
▶ □ **like peas** (or **two peas**) **in a pod** so similar as to be indistinguishable or nearly so.

peace /pēs/ ▶n. **1** freedom from disturbance; quiet and tranquility. ■ mental calm; serenity: *the **peace of mind** this insurance gives you.* **2** freedom from or the cessation of war or violence: *the Straits were to be open to warships in time of peace.* ■ [in sing.] a period of this: *the peace didn't last.* ■ [in sing.] a treaty agreeing to the cessation of war between warring states: *support for a negotiated peace.* ■ freedom from civil disorder: *police* *action to restore peace.* ■ freedom from dispute or dissension between individuals or groups: *the 8.8 percent offer that promises peace with the board.* **3** (**the peace**) a ceremonial handshake or kiss exchanged during a service in some churches, symbolizing Christian love and unity.

▶*interj.* **1** used as a greeting. **2** used as an order to remain silent.

▶ □ **at peace 1** free from anxiety or distress. ■ dead (used to suggest that someone has escaped from the difficulties of life). **2** in a state of friendliness: *a man at peace with the world.* □ **hold one's peace** remain silent about something. □ **keep the peace** refrain or prevent others from disturbing civil order. □ **make peace** (or **one's peace**) reestablish friendly relations; become reconciled.

peace·a·ble /'pēsəbəl/ ▶*adj.* inclined to avoid argument or violent conflict. ■ free from argument or conflict; peaceful. ▷Middle English: from Old French *peisible,* alteration of *plaisible,* from late Latin *placibilis* 'pleasing,' from Latin *placere* 'to please.' —**peace·a·ble·ness** *n.* —**peace·a·bly** /-blē/ *adv.*

Peace Corps /'pēs ,kôr/ ▶an organization sponsored by the U.S. government that sends young people to work as volunteers in developing countries.

peace·ful /'pēsfəl/ ▶*adj.* **1** free from disturbance; tranquil. **2** not involving war or violence. ■ (of a person) inclined to avoid conflict; not aggressive. —**peace·ful·ly** *adv.* —**peace·ful·ness** *n.*

peace·mak·er /'pēs,mākər/ ▶*n.* a person who brings about peace, esp. by reconciling adversaries. —**peace·mak·ing** /-,mākiNG/ *n. & adj.*

peace of·fer·ing ▶*n.* a propitiatory or conciliatory gift.

peace pipe ▶*n.* a tobacco pipe offered and smoked as a token of peace among North American Indians.

peace·time /'pēs,tīm/ ▶*n.* a period when a country is not at war.

peach¹ /pēCH/ ▶*n.* **1** a round stone fruit with juicy yellow flesh and downy pinkish-yellow skin. ■ a pinkish-yellow color like that of a peach. ■ *inf.* an exceptionally good or attractive person or thing: *what a peach of a shot!* **2** (also **peach tree**) the tree (*Prunus persica*) of the rose family that bears this fruit. —**peach·y** *adj.*

peach² ▶*v.* [*intr.*] (**peach on**) *inf.* inform on.

pea·cock /'pē,käk/ ▶*n.* a male peafowl, which has very long tail feathers that have eyelike markings and that can be erected and expanded in display like a fan. ■ an ostentatious strutting person.

▶*v.* [*intr.*] display oneself ostentatiously; strut like a peacock.

pea·fowl /'pē,foul/ ▶*n.* a large crested pheasant native to Asia, esp the widely introduced **common peafowl** (*Pavo cristatus*).

pea·hen /'pē,hen/ ▶*n.* a female peafowl, having drabber colors and a shorter tail than the male.

peak¹ /pēk/ ▶*n.* the pointed top of a mountain. ■ a mountain, esp. one with a pointed top. ■ a projecting pointed part or shape: *whisk 2 egg whites to stiff peaks.* ■ a point in a curve or on a graph, or a value of a physical quantity, higher than those around it. ■ the point of highest activity, quality, or achievement: *anyone who saw Jones at his peak looked upon genius.* ■ *chiefly Brit.* a stiff brim at the front of a cap. ■ the narrow part of a ship's hull at the bow or stern.

▶*v.* [*intr.*] reach a highest point, either of a specified value or at a specified time: *its popularity peaked in the 1940s.*

▶*adj.* greatest; maximum: *he did not expect to be anywhere near peak fitness until Christmas.* ■ characterized by maximum activity or demand: *at peak hours, traffic speeds are reduced considerably.* —**peak·y** *adj.* —**peak·i·ness** /-kēnis/ *n.*

peak² ▶*v.* [*intr.*] *archaic* decline in health and spirits; waste away.

peal /pēl/ ▶*n.* **1** a loud ringing of a bell or bells. ■ *Bell-ringing* a series of unique changes rung on a set of bells. ■ a set of bells. **2** a loud repeated or reverberating sound of thunder or laughter: *Ross burst into peals of laughter.*

▶*v.* [*intr.*] (of a bell or bells) ring loudly or in a peal. ■ (of laughter or thunder) sound in a peal. ■ [*tr.*] convey or give out by the ringing of bells: *the carillon pealed out the news to the waiting city.*

pea·nut /'pēnət/ ▶*n.* **1** the oval seed of a South American plant, widely roasted and salted and eaten as a snack. ■ (**peanuts**) *inf.* a paltry thing or amount, esp. a very small amount of money. ■ a small person (often used as a term of endearment). ■ (**peanuts**) small pieces of styrofoam used for packing material. **2** the plant (*Arachis hypogaea*) of the pea family that bears these seeds. It is widely cultivated, esp. in the southern U.S., and large quantities are used to make oil or animal feed.

pea·nut but·ter ▶*n.* a paste of ground roasted peanuts, usually eaten spread on bread.

pear /per/ ▶*n.* **1** a yellowish- or brownish-green edible fruit that is typically narrow at the stalk and wider toward the tip, with sweet,

slightly gritty flesh. **2** (also **pear tree**) the tree (genus *Pyrus*) of the rose family that bears this fruit.

pearl /pərl/ ▶*n.* a hard, lustrous spherical mass, typically white or bluish-gray, formed within the shell of a pearl oyster or other bivalve mollusk and highly prized as a gem. ■ an artificial imitation of this. ■ (**pearls**) a necklace of pearls. ■ something resembling a pearl in appearance: *the sweat stood in pearls along his forehead.* ■ short for MOTHER-OF-PEARL. ■ *fig.* a precious thing; the finest example of something: *the nation's media were assembled to hear his pearls of wisdom.* ■ a very pale bluish gray or white like the color of a pearl.

▶*v.* [*intr.*] **1** *poetic/lit.* form pearl-like drops. ■ [*tr.*] make bluish-gray like a pearl. **2** [usu. as *n.*] (**pearling**) dive or fish for pearl oysters.

▶ □ **pearls before swine** valuable things offered or given to people who do not appreciate them.

pearl bar·ley ▶*n.* barley reduced to small round grains by grinding.

pearl·es·cent /pər'lesənt/ ▶*adj.* having a luster resembling that of mother-of-pearl: *pearlescent colors.*

pearl on·ion ▶*n.* a very small onion used esp. for pickling.

pearl oys·ter ▶*n.* a tropical marine bivalve mollusk (genus *Pinctada,* family Pteriidae) that has a ridged scaly shell and produces pearls.

pearl·y /'pərlē/ ▶*adj.* (**pearl·i·er, pearl·i·est**) resembling a pearl in luster or color: *the pearly light of a clear, still dawn.* ■ containing or adorned with pearls or mother-of-pearl. —**pearl·i·ness** /-lēnis/ *n.*

▶ □ **pearly whites** *inf.* a person's teeth.

peas·ant /'pezənt/ ▶*n.* a poor farmer of low social status who owns or rents a small piece of land for cultivation (chiefly in historical use or with reference to subsistence farming in poorer countries). ■ *inf.* an ignorant, rude, or unsophisticated person; a person of low social status. —**peas·ant·ry** /-trē/ *n.* —**peas·ant·y** *adj.*

pease /pēz/ ▶*pl. n. archaic* peas.

pea·shoot·er /'pē,SHŌŌtər/ ▶*n.* a toy weapon consisting of a small tube that is blown through in order to shoot out dried peas.

peat /pēt/ ▶*n.* a brown, soil-like material characteristic of boggy, acid ground, consisting of partly decomposed vegetable matter. It is widely cut and dried for use in gardening and as fuel: [as *adj.*] *most of Lewis is acid peat bog.* —**peat·y** *adj.*

peat moss ▶*n.* **1** a large absorbent moss (genus *Sphagnum,* family Sphagnaceae) that grows in dense masses on boggy ground, where the lower parts decay slowly to form peat deposits. Peat moss is widely used in horticulture. **2** a lowland peat bog.

peb·ble /'pebəl/ ▶*n.* a small stone made smooth and round by the action of water or sand.

▶*adj. inf.* (of an eyeglass lens) very thick and convex: *pebble glasses.* —**peb·bled** *adj.* —**peb·bly** /-(ə)lē/ *adj.*

pec /pek/ ▶*n.* (usu. **pecs**) *inf.* a pectoral muscle (esp. with reference to the development of these muscles in bodybuilding).

pe·can /pə'kän; 'pē,kan/ ▶*n.* a smooth brown nut with an edible kernel similar to a walnut, obtained from the hickory tree *Carya illinoensis,* native to the southern U.S. ▷late 18th cent.: from French *pacane,* from Illinois (an American Indian language).

pec·ca·dil·lo /,pekə'dilō/ ▶*n.* (*pl.* **-loes** or **-los**) a small, relatively unimportant offense or sin.

pec·ca·ry /'pekərē/ ▶*n.* (*pl.* **-ies**) a gregarious piglike mammal (family Tayassuidae) that is found from the southwestern US to Paraguay.

peck¹ /pek/ ▶*v.* [*intr.*] (of a bird) strike or bite something with its beak: *two geese were pecking at some grain* | [*tr.*] *beaks may be cut off to stop the hens pecking each other.* ■ [*tr.*] make (a hole) by striking with the beak. ■ [*tr.*] remove or pluck out by biting with the beak: *vultures swooping down to peck out the calf's eyes.* ■ [*tr.*] kiss (someone) lightly or perfunctorily: *she pecked him on the cheek.* ■ (**peck at**) *inf.* (of a person) eat (food) listlessly or daintily: *don't peck at your food, eat a whole mouthful.* ■ (**peck at**) criticize or nag. ■ [*tr.*] type (something) slowly and laboriously: *his son Paul was pecking out letters with two fingers on his typewriter.* ■ *inf.* (of a horse) pitch forward or stumble as a result of striking the ground with the front rather than the flat of the hoof. ■ [*tr.*] *archaic* strike with a pick or other tool.

▶*n.* **1** a stroke or bite by a bird with its beak. ■ a light or perfunctory kiss: *a fatherly peck on the cheek.* **2** *archaic* food.

peck² ▶*n.* a measure of capacity for dry goods, equal to a quarter of a bushel (8 U.S. quarts = 8.81 liters, or 2 imperial gallons = 9.092 liters). ■ *archaic* a large number or amount of something: *a peck of dirt.*

peck·er /ˈpekər/ ▶n. vulgar slang a penis.

peck·ing or·der (also **peck order**) ▶n. a hierarchy of status seen among members of a group of people or animals, originally as observed among hens.

peck·ish /ˈpekiSH/ ▶adj. inf., chiefly Brit. hungry.

pec·o·ri·no /pekəˈrēnō/ ▶n. (pl. **-nos**) an Italian cheese made from ewes' milk.

pec·tin /ˈpektin/ ▶n. a soluble gelatinous polysaccharide that is present in ripe fruits and is extracted for use as a setting agent in jams and jellies. —**pec·tic** /ˈpektik/ adj.

pec·to·ral /ˈpektərəl/ ▶adj. of or relating to the breast or chest: pectoral development. ■ worn on the chest: a pectoral shield.
▶n. (usu. **pectorals**) a pectoral muscle. ■ a pectoral fin.

pec·u·late /ˈpekyəˌlāt/ ▶v. [tr.] formal embezzle or steal (money, esp. public funds). —**pec·u·la·tion** /pekyəˈlāSHən/ n. —**pec·u·la·tor** /-ˌlātər/ n.

pe·cu·liar /pəˈkyo͞olyər/ ▶adj. **1** strange or odd; unusual. ■ inf. slightly and indefinably unwell; faint or dizzy. **2** (**peculiar to**) belonging exclusively to: the air hung with an antiseptic aroma peculiar to hospitals. ■ formal particular; special: any attempt to explicate the theme is bound to run into peculiar difficulties. ▷late Middle English (in the sense 'particular, special'): from Latin peculiaris 'of private property,' from peculium 'property,' from pecu 'cattle' (cattle being private property). The sense 'odd' dates from the early 17th cent.

pe·cu·li·ar·i·ty /pəˌkyo͞olēˈaritē/ ▶n. (pl. **-ties**) an odd or unusual feature or habit. ■ a characteristic or quality that is distinctive of a particular person or place: his essays characterized decency as a British peculiarity. ■ the quality or state of being peculiar: the peculiarity of their upbringing.

pe·cu·liar·ly /pəˈkyo͞olyərlē/ ▶adv. **1** more than usually; especially: some patients were peculiarly difficult to cure. **2** oddly: the town is peculiarly built. **3** used to emphasize restriction to an individual or group: a manner peculiarly his own.

pe·cu·ni·ar·y /piˈkyo͞onēˌerē/ ▶adj. formal of, relating to, or consisting of money. —**pe·cu·ni·ar·i·ly** /pəˌkyo͞onēˈe(ə)rəlē/ adv.

ped·a·gogue /ˈpedəˌgäg/ ▶n. a teacher, esp. a strict or pedantic one.

ped·a·go·gy /ˈpedəˌgäjē; -ˌgōjē/ ▶n. (pl. **-gies**) the method and practice of teaching, esp. as an academic subject or theoretical concept. —**ped·a·go·gic** /ˌpedəˈgäjik/ adj. —**ped·a·gog·ics** /ˌpedəˈgäjiks/ n.

ped·al[1] /ˈpedl/ ▶n. a foot-operated lever or control for a vehicle, musical instrument, or other mechanism, in particular: ■ each of a pair of cranks used for powering a bicycle or other vehicle propelled by leg power. ■ a foot-operated throttle, brake, or clutch control in a motor vehicle. ■ each of a set of two or three levers on a piano, particularly (also **sustaining pedal**) one that, when depressed by the foot, prevents the dampers from stopping the sound when the keys are released. The second is the **soft pedal**; a third, if present, produces either selective sustaining or complete muffling of the tone. ■ Mus. (usu. **pedals**) each key of an organ keyboard that is played with the feet.
▶v. (**ped·aled, ped·al·ing;** Brit. **ped·alled, ped·al·ling**) [intr.] move by working the pedals of a bicycle. ■ [tr.] move (a bicycle) by working its pedals. ■ [intr.] work the pedals of a bicycle. ■ [intr.] use the pedals of a piano, esp. in a particular style: [as n.] (**pedaling**) Chopin gave no indications of pedaling in his manuscript. —**ped·al·er** (Brit. **ped·al·ler**) n.

ped·al[2] /ˈpedl/ ▶adj. chiefly Med. Zool. of or relating to the foot or feet.

ped·ant /ˈpednt/ ▶n. a person who is excessively concerned with minor details and rules or with displaying academic learning. —**pe·dan·tic** /pəˈdantik/ adj. —**ped·ant·ry** /-trē/ n.

ped·dle /ˈpedl/ ▶v. [tr.] try to sell (something, esp. small goods) by going from house to house or place to place. ■ sell (an illegal drug or stolen item): [as n.] (**peddling**) certain youths who were involved in theft and drug peddling. ■ derog. promote (an idea or view) persistently or widely.

ped·dler /ˈpedlər; ˈpedl-ər/ (also **ped·lar**) ▶n. a person who goes from place to place selling small goods. ■ a person who sells illegal drugs or stolen goods: a drug peddler. ■ a person who promotes an idea or view persistently or widely: peddlers of dangerous Utopianism.

ped·er·as·ty /ˈpedəˌrastē/ ▶n. sexual activity involving a man and a boy. —**ped·er·ast** n. —**ped·er·as·tic** /ˌpedəˈrastik/ adj.

ped·es·tal /ˈpedəstl/ ▶n. the base or support on which a statue, obelisk, or column is mounted. ■ fig. a position in which one is greatly or uncritically admired: the heroes they have created and **placed on pedestals**. ■ each of the two supports of a kneehole desk or table, typically containing drawers. ■ the supporting column or base of a washbasin or toilet bowl.

pe·des·tri·an /pəˈdestrēən/ ▶n. a person walking along a road or in a developed area.
▶adj. lacking inspiration or excitement; dull. —**pe·des·tri·an·ly** adv.

pe·des·tri·an mall ▶n. see MALL sense 2.

pe·di·at·rics /ˌpēdēˈatriks/ (Brit. **pae·di·at·rics**) ▶pl. n. [treated as sing.] the branch of medicine dealing with children and their diseases. —**pe·di·at·ric** /-ˈatrik/ adj. —**pe·di·a·tri·cian** /ˌpēdēəˈtriSHən/ n.

ped·i·cab /ˈpedikab/ ▶n. a small pedal-operated vehicle, serving as a taxi in some countries.

ped·i·cure /ˈpediˌkyo͝or/ ▶n. a cosmetic treatment of the feet and toenails.
▶v. [tr.] [usu. as adj.] (**pedicured**) give such a cosmetic treatment to (the feet).

ped·i·gree /ˈpedəˌgrē/ ▶n. **1** the record of descent of an animal, showing it to be purebred. ■ inf. a purebred animal. **2** the recorded ancestry, esp. upper-class ancestry, of a person or family. ■ the background or history of a person or thing, esp. as conferring distinction or quality. ■ a genealogical table. ▷late Middle English: from Anglo-Norman French pé de grue 'crane's foot,' a mark used to denote succession in pedigrees. —**ped·i·greed** adj.

ped·i·ment /ˈpedəmənt/ ▶n. the triangular upper part of the front of a building in classical style, typically surmounting a portico of columns. ■ a similar feature surmounting a door, window, front, or other part of a building in another style. ■ Geol. a broad, gently sloping expanse of rock debris extending outward from the foot of a mountain slope, esp. in a desert. —**ped·i·men·tal** /ˌpedəˈmentl/ adj. —**ped·i·ment·ed** adj.

pediment

pe·dom·e·ter /pəˈdämitər/ ▶n. an instrument for estimating the distance traveled on foot by recording the number of steps taken.

pe·do·phile /ˈpedəˌfīl/ (Brit. **pae·do·phile**) ▶n. a person who is sexually attracted to children.

pe·do·phil·i·a /ˌpedəˈfilēə; ˌpēdə-/ (Brit. **pae·do·phil·i·a**) ▶n. sexual feelings directed toward children. —**pe·do·phil·i·ac** /-ˈfilēˌak/ n. & adj.

pe·dun·cle /ˈpēˌdeNGkəl; pəˈdeNGkəl/ ▶n. Bot. the stalk bearing a flower or fruit, or the main stalk of an inflorescence. ■ Zool. a stalklike part by which an organ is attached to an animal's body, or by which a barnacle or other sedentary animal is attached to a substrate. ■ Anat. any of several bundles of nerve fibers connecting two parts of the brain. —**pe·dun·cu·lar** /pəˈdeNGkyələr/ adj.

pee /pē/ inf. ▶v. (**pees, peed, pee·ing**) [intr.] urinate: the puppy was peeing on the carpet. ■ [tr.] (**pee in one's pants**) wet one's underpants by urinating involuntarily (often used to suggest the notion of losing control of oneself through fear or hilarity).
▶n. an act of urinating: I really need to **take a pee**. ■ urine.

peek /pēk/ ▶v. [intr.] look quickly, typically in a furtive manner: faces peeked from behind the curtains. ■ fig. protrude slightly so as to be just visible: his socks were so full of holes his toes peeked through.
▶n. **1** a quick and typically furtive look. **2** (usu. **PEEK**) Comput. a statement or function in BASIC for reading the contents of a specified memory location.

peek·a·boo /ˈpēkəˌbo͞o/ (also **peek·a·boo**) ▶n. a game played with a young child, which involves hiding behind something and suddenly reappearing, saying "peekaboo."
▶adj. (of a garment) revealing glimpses of the skin or body. ■ (of a hairstyle) concealing one eye with a fringe or wave of hair.

peel[1] /pēl/ ▶v. **1** [tr.] remove the outer covering or skin from (a fruit, vegetable, or shrimp). ■ remove (the outer covering or skin) from a fruit or vegetable. ■ [intr.] (of a fruit or vegetable) have a skin that can be removed. ■ (**peel something away/off**) remove or separate a thin covering or part from the outside or surface of something: carefully peel away the wax paper. ■ remove (an article of clothing): Suzy peeled off her white pullover. **2** [intr.] (of a surface or object) lose parts of its outer layer or covering in small strips or pieces: the walls are peeling. ■ (of an outer layer or covering) come off, esp. in strips or small pieces.
▶phrasal v. □ **peel off** (of a member of a formation, esp. a flying

formation) leave the formation by veering away to one side. □ **peel out** *inf.* leave quickly: *he peeled out down the street.*

▶*n.* the outer covering or rind of a fruit or vegetable. —**peel·er** *n.*

peel² ▶*n.* a flat, shovel-like implement, esp. one used by baker for carrying loaves, pies, etc., into or out of an oven: *a wooden pizza peel.*

peel³ (also **peel tower**) ▶*n.* a small square defensive tower of a kind built in the 16th century in the border counties of England and Scotland.

peel·ings /'pēliNGZ/ ▶*pl. n.* strips of the outer skin of a vegetable or fruit: *potato peelings.*

peen /pēn/ ▶*n.* the end of a hammer head opposite the face, typically wedge-shaped, curved, or spherical.

▶*v.* [*tr.*] strike with a hammer or the peen of a hammer.

peep¹ /pēp/ ▶*v.* [*intr.*] look quickly and furtively at something, esp. through a narrow opening: *the door was ajar and she couldn't resist peeping in.* ■ (**peep out**) be just visible; appear slowly or partly or through a small opening: *a wad of money that was peeping out of his pocket.*

▶*n.* a quick or furtive look: *Jonathan took a peep at his watch.* ■ a momentary or partial view of something.

peep² ▶*n.* a high-pitched feeble sound made by a young bird or mammal. ■ a slight sound, utterance, or complaint: *not a peep out of them since shortly after eight.* ■ (usu. **peeps**) *inf.* a small sandpiper or similar wading bird.

▶*v.* [*intr.*] make a cheeping or beeping sound.

peep·er¹ /'pēpər/ ▶*n.* a person who peeps at someone or something, esp. in a voyeuristic way. ■ (**peepers**) *inf.* a person's eyes.

peep·er² (also **spring peeper**) ▶*n.* a small North American tree frog (*Hyla crucifer*) that has brownish-gray skin with a dark cross on the back, the males of which sing in early spring.

peep·hole /'pēp,hōl/ ▶*n.* a small hole that may be looked through, esp. one in a door through which visitors may be identified.

peep·ing Tom ▶*n.* a person who gets sexual pleasure from secretly watching people undressing or engaging in sexual activity.

peep show ▶*n.* a sequence of pictures viewed through a lens or hole set into a box, traditionally offered as a public entertainment. ■ an erotic or pornographic film or show viewed from a coin-operated booth.

peer¹ /pi(ə)r/ ▶*v.* [*intr.*] look keenly or with difficulty at someone or something: *trying to peer through the fog.* ■ be just visible: *the two towers peer over the roofs.* ■ [*intr.*] *archaic* come into view; appear.

peer² ▶*n.* **1** a member of the nobility in Britain or Ireland, comprising the ranks of duke, marquess, earl, viscount, and baron. **2** a person of the same age, status, or ability as another specified person.

▶*v.* *archaic* make or become equal with or of the same rank. —**peer·less** *adj.*

▶ □ **without peer** unequaled; unrivaled: *he is a goalkeeper without peer.*

peer·age /'pi(ə)rij/ ▶*n.* the title and rank of peer or peeress: *on his retirement as cabinet secretary, he was given a peerage.* ■ (**the peerage**) peers as a class; those holding a hereditary or honorary title. ■ a book containing a list of peers and peeresses, with their genealogy and history.

peer·ess /'pi(ə)ris/ ▶*n.* a woman holding the rank of a peer in her own right. ■ the wife or widow of a peer.

peer group ▶*n.* a group of people of approximately the same age, status, and interests.

peeve /pēv/ *inf.* ▶*v.* [*tr.*] (usu. **be peeved**) annoy; irritate.

▶*n.* a cause of annoyance: *his pet peeve is not having answers for questions from players.*

peev·ish /'pēvish/ ▶*adj.* easily irritated, esp. by unimportant things: *all this makes Steve fretful and peevish.* ■ querulous: *a peevish, whining voice.* —**peev·ish·ly** *adv.* —**peev·ish·ness** *n.*

PEG ▶*abbr.* polyethylene glycol.

peg /peg/ ▶*n.* **1** a short cylindrical piece of wood, metal, or plastic, typically tapered at one end, that is used for holding things together, hanging things on, or marking a position. ■ such an object attached to a wall on which to hang garments. ■ (also **tent peg**) such an object driven into the ground to hold one of the ropes or corners of a tent. ■ such an object in the neck of a stringed musical instrument around which the strings are wound, and which are turned to adjust their tension and so tune the instrument. ■ a bung for stoppering a cask. ■ *inf.* a person's leg. ■ a point or limit on a scale, esp. of exchange rates. **2** *chiefly Indian* a measure of liquor. **3** *inf.* a strong throw, esp. in baseball.

▶*v.* (**pegged, peg·ging**) **1** [*tr.*] fix or make fast with a peg or pegs: *drape individual plants with nets, **pegging down** the edges.* ■ [*tr.*] mark (the score) with pegs on a cribbage board. **2** [*tr.*] fix (a price, rate, or amount) at a particular level. ■ *inf.* form a fixed opinion of; categorize: *the officer*

probably *has us pegged as anarchists.* **3** *inf.* throw (a ball) hard and low, esp. in baseball: *the catcher pegs the ball to the first baseman.*

▶ □ **a square peg in a round hole** a person in a situation unsuited to their abilities or character. □ **take someone down a peg or two** make someone realize that they are less talented or important than they think are.

peg·board /'peg,bôrd/ ▶*n.* a board having a regular pattern of small holes for pegs, used chiefly for games or the display of information.

peg leg ▶*n.* *inf.* an artificial leg, esp. a wooden one. ■ a person with such an artificial leg.

peign·oir /,pān'wär/ ▶*n.* a woman's light dressing gown or negligee.

pe·jo·ra·tive /pə'jôrətiv; 'pejə,rātiv/ ▶*adj.* expressing contempt or disapproval: *permissiveness is used almost universally as a pejorative term.*

▶*n.* a word expressing contempt or disapproval. ▷late 19th cent.: from French *péjoratif, -ive,* from late Latin *pejorare* 'make worse,' from Latin *pejor* 'worse.' —**pe·jo·ra·tive·ly** *adv.*

peke /pēk/ ▶*n.* *inf.* a Pekingese dog.

Pe·king·ese (also **Pe·kin·ese**) ▶*n.* /'pēkə,nēz; -,nēs/ (*pl.* same) a lapdog of a short-legged breed with long hair and a snub nose, originally brought to Europe from the Summer Palace at Beijing (Peking).

▶*adj.* /,pēkiNG'ēz; -'ēs/ of or relating to Beijing, its citizens, or their culture or cuisine.

pe·koe /'pē,kō/ ▶*n.* a high-quality black tea made from young leaves.

pe·lag·ic /pə'lajik/ ▶*adj. technical* of or relating to the open sea. ■ (chiefly of fish) inhabiting the upper layers of the open sea.

pel·ar·go·ni·um /,pelär'gōnēəm/ ▶*n.* a tender shrubby plant (genus *Pelargonium,* family Geraniaceae) that is widely cultivated for its red, pink, or white flowers. Some kinds have fragrant leaves that yield an essential oil. See also GERANIUM.

pelf /pelf/ ▶*n.* money, esp. when gained in a dishonest or dishonorable way.

pel·i·can /'pelikən/ ▶*n.* a large gregarious waterbird (genus *Pelecanus,* family Pelecanidae) with a long bill, an extensible throat pouch for scooping up fish, and mainly white or gray plumage.

pel·la·gra /pə'lagrə; -'lāgrə; -'lägrə/ ▶*n.* a deficiency disease caused by a lack of nicotinic acid or its precursor tryptophan in the diet. It is characterized by dermatitis, diarrhea, and mental disturbance. —**pel·la·grous** /-grəs/ *adj.*

pel·let /'pelit/ ▶*n.* a small, rounded, compressed mass of a substance: *fish food pellets.* ■ a piece of small shot or other lightweight bullet. ■ *Ornithol.* a small mass of bones and feathers regurgitated by a bird of prey or other bird. ■ a small round piece of animal feces, esp. from a rabbit or rodent.

▶*v.* (**-let·ed, -let·ing**) [*tr.*] **1** form or shape (a substance, esp. animal food) into pellets. **2** hit with or as though with pellets: *the last drops of rain were pelleting the windshield.*

pell-mell /'pel 'mel/ ▶*adv.* in a confused, rushed, or disorderly manner: *the contents of the sacks were thrown pell-mell to the ground.*

▶*adj.* recklessly hasty or disorganized; headlong.

▶*n.* a state of affairs or collection of things characterized by haste or confusion: *the pell-mell of ascending gables and roof tiles.*

pel·lu·cid /pə'lōōsid/ ▶*adj.* translucently clear. ■ lucid in style or meaning; easily understood. ■ (of music or other sound) clear and pure in tone. —**pel·lu·cid·ly** *adv.*

pe·lo·ta /pə'lōtə/ ▶*n.* a Basque or Spanish game played in a walled court with a ball and basketlike rackets attached to the hand. ■ the ball used in such a game.

pelt¹ /pelt/ ▶*v.* [*tr.*] attack (someone) by repeatedly hurling things at them. ■ hurl (something) at someone or something in this way: *four boys pelting stones at ducks.* ■ [*intr.*] (**pelt down**) (of rain, hail, or snow) fall quickly and very heavily. ■ [*intr.*] *inf.* run somewhere very quickly: *I pelted across the road.*

▶*n.* *archaic* an act of hurling something at someone.

pelt² ▶*n.* the skin of an animal with the fur, wool, or hair still on it. ■ an animal's coat of fur or hair. ■ the raw skin of a sheep or goat, stripped and ready for tanning.

pel·vic /'pelvik/ ▶*adj.* of, relating to, or situated within the bony pelvis. ■ of or relating to the renal pelvis.

pel·vis /'pelvis/ ▶*n.* (*pl.* **-vis·es** or **-ves** /-vēz/) **1** the large bony structure near the base of the spine to which the hind limbs or legs are attached in humans and many other vertebrates. ■ the part of the abdomen including or enclosed by the pelvis. **2** (also **renal pelvis**) the broadened top part of the ureter into which the kidney tubules drain.

PEN ▶*abbr.* International Association of Poets, Playwrights, Editors, Essayists, and Novelists.

pen[1] /pen/ ▶*n.* **1** an instrument for writing or drawing with ink, typically consisting of a metal nib or ball, or a nylon tip, fitted into a metal or plastic holder. ■ (**the pen**) the occupation or practice of writing. ■ an electronic penlike device used in conjunction with a writing surface to enter commands or data into a computer. **2** *Zool.* the tapering cartilaginous internal shell of a squid.
▶*v.* (**penned**, **pen·ning**) [*tr.*] write or compose: *she penned "The Spoon" at age six.*
▶ □ **put** (or **set**) **pen to paper** write or begin to write something.

pen[2] ▶*n.* a small enclosure in which sheep, pigs, cattle, or other domestic animals are kept. ■ a number of animals in or sufficient to fill such an enclosure: *a pen of young horses.* ■ any small enclosure in which someone or something can be confined. ■ a covered dock for a submarine or other warship.
▶*v.* (**penned**, **pen·ning**) [*tr.*] put or keep (an animal) in a pen. ■ (**pen someone up/in**) confine someone in a restricted space.

pen[3] ▶*n.* a female swan.

pen[4] ▶*n. inf.* short for PENITENTIARY (sense 1).

pe·nal /ˈpēnəl/ ▶*adj.* of, relating to, or prescribing the punishment of offenders under the legal system: *the campaign for penal reform.* ■ used or designated as a place of punishment: *a former penal colony.* ■ (of an act or offense) punishable by law. —**pe·nal·ly** *adv.*

pe·nal·ize /ˈpēnəˌlīz; ˈpē-/ ▶*v.* [*tr.*] (often **be penalized**) subject to some form of punishment. ■ (in various sports) punish (a player or team) for a breach of the rules by awarding an advantage to the opposition. ■ put in an unfavorable position or at an unfair disadvantage. ■ *Law* make or declare (an act or offense) legally punishable. —**pe·nal·i·za·tion** /ˌpēnəliˈzāSHən; ˌpē-/ *n.*

pen·al·ty /ˈpenltē/ ▶*n.* (*pl.* **-ties**) **1** a punishment imposed for breaking a law, rule, or contract. ■ a disadvantage or unpleasant experience suffered as the result of an action or circumstance: *the cold never leaves my bones these days—one of the penalties of age.* **2** (in sports and games) a disadvantage or handicap imposed on a player or team, typically for infringement of rules. ■ a kick or shot awarded to a team because of a serious infringement of the rules by an opponent. ■ *Bridge* points won by the defenders when a declarer fails to make the contract.
▶ □ **under** (or **on**) **penalty of** under the threat of.

pen·al·ty box ▶*n.* Ice Hockey an enclosure alongside the rink where players who have been assessed penalties must remain while they serve out their penalties.

pen·ance /ˈpenəns/ ▶*n.* **1** voluntary self-punishment inflicted as an outward expression of repentance for having done wrong: *he had done public penance for those hasty words.* **2** a Christian sacrament in which a member of the Church confesses sins to a priest and is given absolution. See SACRAMENT OF RECONCILIATION. ■ a religious observance or other duty required of a person by a priest as part of this sacrament to indicate repentance.

pence /pens/ ▶ plural form of PENNY.

pen·chant /ˈpenCHənt/ ▶*n.* a strong or habitual liking for something or tendency to do something.

pen·cil /ˈpensəl/ ▶*n.* an instrument for writing or drawing, consisting of a thin stick of graphite or a similar substance enclosed in a long thin piece of wood or fixed in a case. ■ used to refer to the composition, skill, or style of a drawing: *her pencil had captured the dark brooding atmosphere of the place.* ■ graphite or a similar substance used in such a way as a medium for writing or drawing: *words scribbled in pencil.* ■ a cosmetic in a long thin stick, designed to be applied to a particular part of the face: *an eyebrow pencil.* ■ something with the shape of a pencil: *a pencil of light* | [as *adj.*] *a long pencil beam.* ■ *Physics & Geom.* a set of light rays, lines, etc., converging to or diverging narrowly from a single point.
▶*v.* (**-ciled**, **-cil·ing**; *Brit.* **-cilled**, **-cil·ling**) [*tr.*] write, draw, or color (something) with a pencil.
▶*phrasal v.* □ **pencil something in 1** fill in an area or shape with pencil strokes. **2** arrange, forecast, or note down something provisionally or tentatively: *May 15 was penciled in as the date for the meeting.* ■ (**pencil someone in**) make a provisional or tentative arrangement with or for someone. —**pen·cil·er** *n.*

pen·cil push·er ▶*n. inf.* a person with a clerical job involving a lot of tedious and repetitive paperwork.

pend·ant /ˈpendənt/ ▶*n.* **1** a piece of jewelry that hangs from a chain worn around the neck. ■ a necklace with such a piece of jewelry. ■ a

light designed to hang from the ceiling. ■ the part of a pocket watch by which it is suspended. **2** an artistic, literary, or musical composition intended to match or complement another.
▶*adj.* hanging downward; pendent: *pendant flowers on frail stems.*

pend·ent /ˈpendənt/ ▶*adj.* **1** hanging down or overhanging: *pendent lichens.* **2** undecided; pending. **3** *Gram.* (esp. of a sentence) incomplete; not having a finite verb. —**pen·den·cy** *n.*

pend·ing /ˈpendiNG/ ▶*adj.* awaiting decision or settlement: *nine cases were still pending.* ■ about to happen; imminent: *with a presidential election pending, it would be wrong to force the changes through now.*
▶*prep.* until (something) happens or takes place: *they were released on bail pending an appeal.*

pen·du·lous /ˈpenjələs; ˈpendyə-/ ▶*adj.* hanging down loosely: *pendulous branches.* —**pen·du·lous·ly** *adv.*

pen·du·lum /ˈpenjələm; ˈpendyə-/ ▶*n.* a weight hung from a fixed point so that it can swing freely backward and forward, esp. a rod with a weight at the end that regulates the mechanism of a clock. ■ *fig.* used to refer to the tendency of a situation or state of affairs to oscillate regularly between one extreme and another: *the pendulum of fashion.* —**pen·du·lar** /-lər/ *adj.*

pen·e·trate /ˈpeniˌtrāt/ ▶*v.* [*tr.*] succeed in forcing a way into or through (a thing): *the shrapnel had penetrated his head and chest* | [*intr.*] *tunnels that penetrate deep into the earth's core.* ■ (of a man) insert the penis into the vagina or anus of (a sexual partner). ■ infiltrate (an enemy group or rival organization) in order to spy on it. ■ (of a company) begin to sell its products in (a particular market or area). ■ succeed in understanding or gaining insight into (something complex or mysterious). ■ [*intr.*] be fully understood or realized by someone: *as his words penetrated, she saw a mental picture of him with Dawn.* ▷mid 16th cent.: from Latin *penetrat-* 'placed or gone into,' from the verb *penetrare*; related to *penitus* 'inner.' —**pen·e·tra·bil·i·ty** /ˌpenitrəˈbilitē/ *n.* —**pen·e·tra·ble** /-trəbəl/ *adj.* —**pen·e·trant** /-trənt/ *n.* —**pen·e·tra·tion** /ˌpeniˈtrāSHən/ *n.* —**pen·e·tra·tive** *adj.*

pendulum

pen·guin /ˈpeNGgwin; ˈpeNGgwin/ ▶*n.* a large flightless seabird (family Spheniscidae) of the southern hemisphere, with black upper parts and white underparts and wings developed into flippers.

pen·i·cil·lin /ˌpenəˈsilən/ ▶*n.* **1** an antibiotic or group of antibiotics produced naturally by certain blue molds, now usually prepared synthetically. **2** a blue mold of a type that produces these antibiotics.

pe·nile /ˈpēnəl; -nīl/ ▶*adj. chiefly technical* of, relating to, or affecting the penis.

pen·in·su·la /pəˈninsələ/ ▶*n.* a piece of land almost surrounded by water or projecting out into a body of water. —**pen·in·su·lar** /-lər/ *adj.*

pe·nis /ˈpēnis/ ▶*n.* (*pl.* **-nis·es** or **-nes** /-nēz/) the male genital organ of higher vertebrates, carrying the duct for the transfer of sperm during copulation. In humans and most other mammals, it consists largely of erectile tissue and serves also for the elimination of urine. ■ *Zool.* a type of male copulatory organ present in some invertebrates, such as gastropod mollusks.

pen·i·tent /ˈpenitnt/ ▶*adj.* feeling or showing sorrow and regret for having done wrong; repentant: *a penitent expression.*
▶*n.* a person who repents their sins or wrongdoings and (in the Christian Church) seeks forgiveness from God. ■ (in the Roman Catholic Church) a person who confesses their sins to a priest and submits to the penance that he imposes. —**pen·i·tence** *n.* —**pen·i·tent·ly** *adv.*

pen·i·ten·tial /ˌpeniˈtenSHəl/ ▶*adj.* relating to or expressing penitence or penance: *penitential tears.* —**pen·i·ten·tial·ly** *adv.* (*archaic*)

pen·i·ten·tia·ry /ˌpeniˈtenSHərē/ ▶*n.* (*pl.* **-ries**) a prison for people convicted of serious crimes.

pen·knife /ˈpenˌnīf/ ▶*n.* (*pl.* **-knives** /-ˌnīvz/) a small pocketknife with a blade that folds into the handle.

pen·light /ˈpenˌlīt/ ▶*n.* a small flashlight shaped like a fountain pen.

pen name ▶*n.* an assumed name used by a writer instead of their real name.

pen·nant /ˈpenənt/ ▶*n.* **1** a flag denoting a sports championship or other achievement. **2** a tapering flag on a ship, esp. one flown at the masthead of a vessel in commission. Also called PENNON. **3** *Mil.* another term for PENNON (sense 1).

pen·ni·less /ˈpenēlis/ ▶*adj.* (of a person) having no money; very poor. —**pen·ni·less·ness** *n.*

pen·non /ˈpenən/ ▶n. **1** a long triangular or swallow-tailed flag, esp. as the military ensign of lancer regiments. Also called PENNANT. **2** another term for PENNANT (sense 2). —**pen·noned** adj.

Penn·syl·va·nia Dutch (also **Pennsylvania German**) ▶n. **1** a dialect of High German spoken in parts of Pennsylvania. **2** [as pl. n.] (**the Pennsylvania Dutch** or **Germans**) the German-speaking inhabitants of Pennsylvania, descendants of 17th- and 18th-century Protestant immigrants from the Rhineland.

Penn·syl·va·nian /ˌpensəlˈvānyən; -ˈvānēən/ ▶adj. **1** of or relating to the state of Pennsylvania. **2** Geol. of, relating to, or denoting the later part of the Carboniferous period in North America, corresponding to the Upper Carboniferous of Europe. This period lasted from about 323 to 290 million years ago.
▶n. (**the Pennsylvanian**) Geol. the Pennsylvanian period or the system of rocks deposited during it.

pen·ny /ˈpenē/ ▶n. **1** a one-cent coin equal to one hundredth of a dollar. ■ (pl. for separate coins **pen·nies**, for a sum of money **pence** /pens/) (abbr.: **p.**) a British bronze coin and monetary unit equal to one hundredth of a pound. ■ (abbr.: **d.**) a former British coin and monetary unit equal to one twelfth of a shilling and one 240th of a pound. ■ (**pennies**) a small sum of money: *any chance to save a few pennies is welcome.* **2** (**a penny**) used for emphasis to denote no money at all: *we didn't get paid a penny.*
▶ □ **pinch** (or **count** or **watch**) (**one's**) **pennies** be careful about how much one spends. □ **a pretty penny** a considerable amount of money.

pen·ny-pinch·ing ▶adj. unwilling to spend or share money; miserly.
▶n. unwillingness to spend or share money. —**pen·ny-pinch·er** n.

pen·ny·roy·al /ˈpenēˌroiəl/ ▶n. either of two small-leaved plants of the mint family, used in herbal medicine: a creeping Eurasian plant (*Mentha pulegium*), and **American pennyroyal** (*Hedeoma pulegioides*).

pen·ny·weight /ˈpenēˌwāt/ ▶n. a unit of weight, 24 grains or one twentieth of an ounce troy.

pen·ny·wort /ˈpenēˌwərt; -ˌwôrt/ ▶n. any of a number of plants with rounded leaves, in particular a creeping perennial of the parsley family belonging to the genus *Hydrocotyle*.

Pe·nob·scot /pəˈnäbskət; -ˌskät/ ▶n. (pl. same) **1** a member of an American Indian people of the Penobscot River valley in Maine. **2** the Algonquian language of this people, a dialect of Eastern Abnaki.
▶adj. of or relating to this people or their language.

pe·nol·o·gy /pēˈnäləjē/ ▶n. the study of the punishment of crime and of prison management. —**pe·no·log·i·cal** /ˌpēnəˈläjikəl/ adj. —**pe·nol·o·gist** /-jist/ n.

pen pal ▶n. a person with whom one becomes friendly by exchanging letters, esp. someone in a foreign country whom one has never met.

pen·sion[1] /ˈpenSHən/ ▶n. a regular payment made during a person's retirement from an investment fund to which that person or their employer has contributed during their working life. ■ a regular payment made by the government to people of or above the official retirement age and to some widows and disabled people. ■ chiefly hist. a regular payment made to a royal favorite or to an artist or scholar to enable them to carry on work that is of public interest or value.
▶v. [tr.] (**pension someone off**) dismiss someone from employment because of age or ill health, and pay them a pension. —**pen·sion·less** adj.

pen·sion[2] /pänsēˈôn/ ▶n. a boardinghouse in France and other European countries, providing full or partial board at a fixed rate.

pen·sive /ˈpensiv/ ▶adj. engaged in, involving, or reflecting deep or serious thought: *a pensive mood.* —**pen·sive·ly** adv. —**pen·sive·ness** n.

pent /pent/ ▶adj. chiefly poetic/lit. another term for PENT-UP.

pen·ta·chlo·ro·phe·nol /ˌpentəˌklôrəˈfēnäl/ ▶n. Chem. a colorless, crystalline, synthetic compound, C_6Cl_5OH, used in insecticides, fungicides, weed killers, and wood preservatives.

pen·ta·cle /ˈpentəkəl/ ▶n. a talisman or magical object, typically disk-shaped and inscribed with a pentagram or other figure, and used as a symbol of the element of earth.

pen·ta·gon /ˈpentəˌgän/ ▶n. **1** a plane figure with five straight sides and five angles. **2** (**the Pentagon**) the pentagonal building serving as the headquarters of the U.S. Department of Defense, near Washington, DC. ■ the U.S. Department of Defense. —**pen·tag·o·nal** /penˈtagənəl/ adj.

pen·ta·gram /ˈpentəˌgram/ ▶n. a five-pointed star that is formed by drawing a continuous line in five straight segments, often used as a mystic and magical symbol.

pen·tam·e·ter /penˈtamitər/ ▶n. Prosody a line of verse consisting of five metrical feet, or (in Greek and Latin verse) of two halves each of two feet and a long syllable.

pen·tan·gle /ˈpenˌtaNGgəl/ ▶n. another term for PENTAGRAM.

Pen·ta·teuch /ˈpentəˌt(y)ook/ ▶the first five books of the Hebrew Bible (Genesis, Exodus, Leviticus, Numbers, and Deuteronomy). Jewish name TORAH. —**Pen·ta·teuch·al** /-ˌt(y)ookəl/ adj.

pen·tath·lon /penˈtaTH(ə)län/ ▶n. an athletic event comprising five different events for each competitor, in particular (also **modern pentathlon**) a men's event involving fencing, shooting, swimming, riding, and cross-country running. —**pen·tath·lete** /-ˈtaTHlēt/ n.

Pen·te·cost /ˈpentəˌkôst; -ˌkäst/ ▶n. **1** the Christian festival celebrating the descent of the Holy Spirit on the disciples of Jesus after his Ascension, held on the seventh Sunday after Easter. ■ the day on which this festival is held. Also called WHITSUNDAY. **2** the Jewish festival of Shavuoth.

Pen·te·cos·tal /ˌpentəˈkôstl; -ˈkästl/ ▶adj. **1** of or relating to Pentecost. **2** of, relating to, or denoting any of a number of Christian sects and individuals emphasizing baptism in the Holy Spirit, evidenced by speaking in tongues, prophecy, healing, and exorcism.
▶n. a member of a Pentecostal sect. —**Pen·te·cos·tal·ism** /-ˌizəm/ n. —**Pen·te·cos·tal·ist** /-ist/ adj. & n.

pent·house /ˈpentˌhous/ ▶n. an apartment on the top floor of a tall building, typically luxuriously fitted. ■ a structure on the roof of a building housing machinery or equipment.

Pen·to·thal /ˈpentəˌTHôl; -ˌTHäl/ ▶n. trademark for THIOPENTAL.

pent-up ▶adj. closely confined or held back: *pent-up frustrations.*

pen·tyl /ˈpentəl/ ▶n. [as adj.] Chem. of or denoting an alkyl radical $-C_5H_{11}$.

pe·nul·ti·mate /pəˈnəltəmit/ ▶adj. last but one in a series of things; second to the last: *the penultimate chapter.* ▷late 17th cent.: from Latin *paenultimus*, from *paene* 'almost' + *ultimus* 'last,' on the pattern of *ultimate.*

pe·num·bra /pəˈnəmbrə/ ▶n. (pl. **-brae** /-brē; -brī/ or **-bras**) the partially shaded outer region of the shadow cast by an opaque object. ■ Astron. the shadow cast by the earth or moon over an area experiencing a partial eclipse. Compare with UMBRA. ■ any area of partial shade. —**pe·num·bral** /-brəl/ adj.

pe·nu·ri·ous /pəˈn(y)oorēəs/ ▶adj. formal **1** extremely poor; poverty-stricken: *a penurious old tramp.* ■ characterized by poverty or need: *penurious years.* **2** parsimonious; mean. —**pe·nu·ri·ous·ly** adv. —**pe·nu·ri·ous·ness** n.

pen·u·ry /ˈpenyərē/ ▶n. extreme poverty; destitution.

pe·on /ˈpēˌän; ˈpēən/ ▶n. **1** a Spanish-American day laborer or unskilled farm worker. ■ hist. a debtor held in servitude by a creditor, esp. in the southern U.S. and Mexico. ■ a person who does menial work; a drudge. **2** (in the Indian subcontinent and Southeast Asia) someone of low rank. ■ a foot soldier. ■ an attendant or messenger. ■ a person who does minor jobs in an office. —**pe·on·age** /ˈpēənij/ n.

pe·o·ny /ˈpēənē/ ▶n. a herbaceous or shrubby plant (genus *Paeonia*, family Paeoniaceae) of north temperate regions, which has long been cultivated for its showy flowers.

peo·ple /ˈpēpəl/ ▶pl. n. **1** human beings in general or considered collectively: *the earthquake killed 30,000 people.* ■ (**the people**) the citizens of a country, esp. when considered in relation to those who govern them: *the support of the people.* ■ (**the people**) those without special rank or position in society; the populace: *he is a man of the people.* ■ (**one's people**) a person's parents or relatives: *my people live in West Virginia.* ■ (**one's people**) the supporters or employees of a person in a position of power or authority: *I've had my people watching the house.* **2** (pl. **peoples**) [treated as sing. or pl.] the men, women, and children of a particular nation, community, or ethnic group: *the native peoples of Canada.*
▶v. [tr.] (usu. **be peopled**) (of a particular group of people) inhabit (an area or place): *an arid mountain region peopled by warring clans.* ■ fill or be present in (a place, environment, or domain): *the street is peopled with hippies.* ■ fill (an area or place) with a particular group of inhabitants.

pep /pep/ inf. ▶n. energy and high spirits; liveliness.
▶v. (**pepped**, **pep·ping**) [tr.] (**pep someone/something up**) add liveliness or vigor to someone or something: *measures to pep up the economy.*

pentagram

pep·er·o·ni ▶n. variant spelling of PEPPERONI.

pep·lum /'pepləm/ ▶n. a short flared, gathered, or pleated strip of fabric attached at the waist of a woman's jacket, dress, or blouse to create a hanging frill or flounce. ■ (in ancient Greece) a woman's loose outer tunic or shawl.

pep·per /'pepər/ ▶n. **1** a pungent, hot-tasting powder prepared from dried and ground peppercorns, used as a spice or condiment. ■ a reddish and typically hot-tasting spice prepared from various forms of capsicum. See also CAYENNE. ■ a capsicum, esp. a sweet pepper. **2** a climbing vine (*Piper nigrum*, family Piperaceae) with berries that are dried as black or white peppercorns. ■ used in names of other plants that are related to this, have hot-tasting leaves, or have fruits used as a pungent spice. **3** *Baseball* a practice game in which fielders throw at close range to a batter who hits to the fielders.
▶v. [tr.] sprinkle or season (food) with pepper. ■ (usu. **be peppered with**) cover or fill with a liberal amount of scattered items. ■ hit repeatedly with small missiles or gunshot. ▷Old English *piper*, *pipor*, of West Germanic origin, via Latin from Greek *peperi*, from Sanskrit *pippalī* 'berry, peppercorn.'

pep·per·corn /'pepər,kôrn/ ▶n. the dried berry of a climbing vine, used whole as a spice or crushed or ground to make pepper. See PEPPER (sense 2).

pep·per mill ▶n. a device for grinding peppercorns by hand to make pepper.

pep·per·mint /'pepər,mint/ ▶n. **1** the aromatic leaves of a plant of the mint family, or an essential oil obtained from them, used as a flavoring in food. ■ a candy flavored with such oil. **2** the cultivated Old World plant (*Mentha × piperita*) that yields these leaves or oil. —**pep·per·mint·y** adj.

pep·per·o·ni /,pepə'rōnē/ ▶n. beef and pork sausage seasoned with pepper.

pep·per·y /'pepərē/ ▶adj. strongly flavored with pepper or other hot spices. ■ having a flavor or scent like that of pepper. ■ (of a person) irritable and sharp-tongued. —**pep·per·i·ness** /-rēnis/ n.

pep pill ▶n. *inf.* a pill containing a stimulant drug.

pep·py /'pepē/ ▶adj. (**pep·pi·er**, **pep·pi·est**) *inf.* lively and high-spirited. —**pep·pi·ly** /'pepəlē/ adv. —**pep·pi·ness** /-ēnis/ n.

pep·sin /'pepsin/ ▶n. *Biochem.* the chief digestive enzyme in the stomach, which breaks down proteins into polypeptides.

pep talk ▶n. *inf.* a talk intended to make someone feel more courageous or enthusiastic.

pep·tic /'peptik/ ▶adj. of or relating to digestion, esp. that in which pepsin is concerned.

pep·tic ul·cer ▶n. a lesion in the lining (mucosa) of the digestive tract, typically in the stomach or duodenum, caused by the digestive action of pepsin and stomach acid.

pep·tide /'peptīd/ ▶n. *Biochem.* a compound consisting of two or more amino acids linked in a chain, the carboxyl group of each acid being joined to the amino group of the next by a bond of the type $-OC-NH-$.

Pe·quot /'pē,kwät/ ▶n. (*pl.* same or **-quots**) **1** a member of an American Indian people of southern New England. **2** the Algonquian language of this people, closely related to Mohegan.
▶adj. of or relating to this people or their language.

per /pər/ ▶prep. **1** for each (used with units to express a rate): *a gas station that charges $1.29 per gallon.* **2** *archaic* by means of: *send it per express.* **3** (**as per**) in accordance with: *made as per instructions.*

per. ▶abbr. ■ percentile. ■ period. ■ person.

per·ad·ven·ture /,pərəd'venCHər; ,per-/ ▶adv. or *humorous* perhaps: *peradventure I'm not as wealthy as he is.*
▶n. *archaic* or *humorous* uncertainty or doubt as to whether something is the case: *that shows beyond peradventure the strength of the economy.*

per·am·bu·late /pə'rambyə,lāt/ ▶v. [tr.] *formal* walk or travel through or around (a place or area), esp. for pleasure and in a leisurely way. ■ [intr.] walk from place to place; walk about. —**per·am·bu·la·tion** /pə,rambyə-'lāSHən/ n. —**per·am·bu·la·to·ry** /-lə,tôrē/ adj.

per·am·bu·la·tor /pə'rambyə,lātər/ ▶n. **1** a person who perambulates; a pedestrian. **2** *Brit.* a baby carriage.

per an·num /pər 'anəm/ ▶adv. for each year (used in financial contexts): *an average growth rate of around 2 percent per annum.*

per·cale /pər'kāl; -'kal/ ▶n. a closely woven fine cotton or polyester fabric used esp. for sheets.

per cap·i·ta /pər 'kapitə/ ▶adv. & adj. for each person; in relation to people taken individually: [as adv.] *the state had fewer banks per capita than elsewhere* | [as adj.] *per capita spending.*

per·ceive /pər'sēv/ ▶v. [tr.] **1** become aware or conscious of (something); come to realize or understand: *his mouth fell open as he perceived the truth.* ■ become aware of (something) by the use of one of the senses, esp. that of sight: *he perceived the faintest of flushes creeping up her neck.* **2** interpret or look on (someone or something) in a particular way; regard as: *if Guy does not perceive himself as disabled, nobody else should.* ▷Middle English: from a variant of Old French *perçoivre*, from Latin *percipere* 'seize, understand,' from *per-* 'entirely' + *capere* 'take.' —**per·ceiv·a·ble** adj. —**per·ceiv·er** n.

per·cent /pər'sent/ (also *chiefly Brit.* **per cent**) ▶adv. by a specified amount in or for every hundred: *new car sales may be down 5 percent.*
▶n. one part in every hundred: *a reduction of half a percent or so in price.* ■ the rate, number, or amount in each hundred; percentage.

per·cent·age /pər'sentij/ ▶n. a rate, number, or amount in each hundred: *the percentage of cesareans at the hospital was three percent higher than the national average* | [as adj.] *a large percentage increase in the population over 85.* ■ an amount, such as an allowance or commission, that is a proportion of a larger sum of money: *I hope to be on a percentage.* ■ any proportion or share in relation to a whole: *only a small percentage of black Americans have Caribbean roots.* ■ *inf.* personal benefit or advantage: *you explain to me* **the percentage in** *looking like a hoodlum.*
▶ □ **play the percentages** (or **the percentage game**) *inf.* choose a safe and methodical course of action when calculating the odds in favor of success.

per·cen·tile /pər'sen,tīl/ ▶n. *Statistics* each of the 100 equal groups into which a population can be divided according to the distribution of values of a particular variable. ■ each of the 99 intermediate values of a random variable that divide a frequency distribution into 100 such groups: *the tenth percentile for weight.*

per·cept /'pərsept/ ▶n. *Philos.* an object of perception; something that is perceived. ■ a mental concept that is developed as a consequence of the process of perception.

per·cep·ti·ble /pər'septəbəl/ ▶adj. (esp. of a slight movement or change of state) able to be seen or noticed: *a perceptible decline in confidence.* —**per·cep·ti·bil·i·ty** /pər,septə'bilitē/ n. —**per·cep·ti·bly** /-blē/ adv.

per·cep·tion /pər'sepSHən/ ▶n. the ability to see, hear, or become aware of something through the senses. ■ the state of being or process of becoming aware of something in such a way. ■ a way of regarding, understanding, or interpreting something; a mental impression: *Hollywood's perception of the tastes of the American public.* ■ intuitive understanding and insight: *"He wouldn't have accepted," said my mother with unusual perception.* ■ *Psychol.* & *Zool.* the neurophysiological processes, including memory, by which an organism becomes aware of and interprets external stimuli. —**per·cep·tion·al** /-SHənl; -SHnəl/ adj.

per·cep·tive /pər'septiv/ ▶adj. having or showing sensitive insight: *an extraordinarily perceptive account of their relationship.* —**per·cep·tive·ly** adv. —**per·cep·tive·ness** n. —**per·cep·tiv·i·ty** /,pərsep'tivitē/ n.

per·cep·tu·al /pər'sepCHōōəl/ ▶adj. of or relating to the ability to interpret or become aware of something through the senses: *a patient with perceptual problems who cannot judge distances.* —**per·cep·tu·al·ly** adv.

perch[1] /pərCH/ ▶n. a thing on which a bird alights or roosts, typically a branch or a horizontal rod or bar in a birdcage. ■ a place where someone or something rests or sits, esp. a place that is high or precarious.
▶v. [intr.] (of a bird) alight or rest on something. ■ (of a person) sit somewhere, esp. on something high or narrow: *Eve perched on the side of the armchair.* ■ (**be perched**) (of a building) be situated above or on the edge of something: *the fortress is perched on a crag in the mountains.* ■ [tr.] (**perch someone/something on**) set or balance someone or something on (something).
▶ □ **knock someone off their perch** *inf.* cause someone to lose a position of superiority or preeminence.

perch[2] ▶n. (*pl.* same or **perches**) an edible freshwater fish (genus *Perca*) with a high spiny dorsal fin, dark vertical bars on the body, and orange lower fins. The **perch family** (Percidae) also includes the pikeperches. ■ used in names of other freshwater and marine fishes resembling or related to this, e.g., **climbing perch**.

per·chance /pər'CHans/ ▶adv. *archaic* or *poetic/lit.* by some chance; perhaps: *we dare not go ashore lest perchance we should fall into some snare.*

per·co·late /'pərkə,lāt/ ▶v. **1** [intr.] (of a liquid or gas) filter gradually through a porous surface or substance: *the water percolating through the soil may leach out minerals.* ■ *fig.* (of information or an idea or feeling) spread gradually through an area or group of people. **2** [intr.] (of coffee) be prepared in a percolator. ■ [tr.] prepare (coffee) in a percolator. ■ *fig.* be or become full of lively activity or excitement: *the night was percolating with an expectant energy.* —**per·co·la·tion** /,pərkə'lāSHən/ n.

per·co·la·tor /'pərkə,lātər/ ▶n. a machine for making coffee, consisting of a pot in which boiling water is circulated through a small chamber that holds the ground beans.

per·cus·sion /pərˈkəsHən/ ▶ n. **1** musical instruments played by striking with the hand or with a hand-held or pedal-operated stick or beater, or by shaking, including drums, cymbals, xylophones, gongs, bells, and rattles: [as adj.] *the percussion section.* **2** the striking of one solid object with or against another with some degree of force. ■ *Med.* the action of tapping a part of the body as part of a diagnosis. —**per·cus·sion·ist** /-ist/ n. —**per·cus·sive** /-ˈkəsiv/ adj. —**per·cus·sive·ly** /-ˈkəsivlē/ adv. —**per·cus·sive·ness** /-ˈkəsivnis/ n.

per·cus·sion cap ▶ n. a small amount of explosive powder contained in metal or paper and exploded by striking. Percussion caps are used chiefly in toy guns and formerly in some firearms.

per di·em /pər ˈdēəm/ ▶ adv. & adj. for each day (used in financial contexts): [as adv.] *he agreed to pay at certain specified rates per diem* | [as adj.] *they are now demanding a per diem rate.*
▶ n. an allowance or payment made for each day.

per·di·tion /pərˈdisHən/ ▶ n. (in Christian theology) a state of eternal punishment and damnation into which a sinful and unpenitent person passes after death.

per·e·gri·nate /ˈperigrəˌnāt/ ▶ v. [intr.] archaic or humorous travel or wander around from place to place. —**per·e·gri·na·tion** /ˌperigrəˈnāsHən/ n. —**per·e·gri·na·tor** /-ˌnātər/ n.

per·e·grine /ˈperəgrin/ ▶ n. (also **peregrine falcon**) a powerful falcon (*Falco peregrinus*) found on most continents, much used for falconry.
▶ adj. archaic coming from another country; foreign or outlandish: *peregrine species of grass.* ▷ late Middle English: from Latin *peregrinus* 'foreign,' from *peregre* 'abroad,' from *per-* 'through' + *ager* 'field.'

per·emp·to·ry /pəˈremptərē/ ▶ adj. (esp. of a person's manner or actions) insisting on immediate attention or obedience, esp. in a brusquely imperious way: *"Just do it!" came the peremptory reply.* ■ *Law* not open to appeal or challenge; final: *a peremptory order of the court.* —**per·emp·to·ri·ly** /-tərəlē/ adv. —**per·emp·to·ri·ness** /-rēnis/ n.

per·en·ni·al /pəˈrenēəl/ ▶ adj. lasting or existing for a long or apparently infinite time; enduring. ■ (of a plant) living for several years: *tarragon is perennial.* Compare with **ANNUAL**, **BIENNIAL**. ■ (esp. of a problem or difficult situation) continually occurring. ■ (of a person) apparently permanently engaged in a specified role or way of life. ■ (of a stream or spring) flowing throughout the year.
▶ n. a perennial plant. —**per·en·ni·al·ly** adv.

pe·re·stroi·ka /ˌperəˈstroikə/ ▶ n. (in the former Soviet Union) the policy or practice of restructuring or reforming the economic and political system. Perestroika was first proposed by Leonid Brezhnev in 1979 and actively promoted by Mikhail Gorbachev.

per·fect ▶ adj. /ˈpərfikt/ **1** having all the required or desirable elements, qualities, or characteristics; as good as it is possible to be. ■ free from any flaw or defect in condition or quality; faultless. ■ precisely accurate; exact: *a perfect circle.* ■ highly suitable for someone or something; exactly right: *Gary was perfect for her—ten years older and with his own career.* ■ *Printing* denoting a way of binding books in which pages are glued to the spine rather than sewn together. ■ *dated* thoroughly trained in or conversant with: *she was perfect in French.* **2** absolute; complete (used for emphasis): *a perfect stranger.* **3** *Math.* (of a number) equal to the sum of its positive divisors, e.g., the number 6, whose divisors (1, 2, 3) also add up to 6. **4** *Gram.* (of a tense) denoting a completed action or a state or habitual action that began in the past. The perfect tense is formed in English with *have* or *has* and the past participle, as in *they have eaten* and *they have been eating* (since dawn) (**present perfect**), *they had eaten* (**past perfect**), and *they will have eaten* (**future perfect**). **5** *Bot.* (of a flower) having both stamens and carpels present and functional. ■ *Entomol.* (of an insect) fully adult and (typically) winged.
▶ v. /pərˈfekt/ [tr.] make (something) completely free from faults or defects, or as close to such a condition as possible.
▶ n. /ˈpərfikt/ (**the perfect**) *Gram.* the perfect tense. ▷ Middle English: from Old French *perfet*, from Latin *perfectus* 'completed,' from the verb *perficere*, from *per-* 'through, completely' + *facere* 'do.' —**per·fect·er** /pərˈfektər/ n. —**per·fect·i·bil·i·ty** /pərˌfektəˈbilitē/ n. —**per·fect·i·ble** /pərˈfektəbəl/ adj. —**per·fect·ness** /ˈpərfək(t)nəs/ n.

per·fec·tion /pərˈfeksHən/ ▶ n. the condition, state, or quality of being free or as free as possible from all flaws or defects. ■ a person or thing perceived as the embodiment of such a condition, state, or quality. ■ the action or process of improving something until it is faultless or as faultless as possible.
▶ □ **to perfection** in a manner or way that could not be better.

per·fec·tion·ism /pərˈfeksHəˌnizəm/ ▶ n. refusal to accept any standard short of perfection. —**per·fec·tion·ist** n. & adj. —**per·fec·tion·is·tic** /-ˌfeksHənˈistik/ adj.

per·fec·tive /pərˈfektiv/ *Gram.* ▶ adj. denoting or relating to an aspect of verbs, esp. in Slavic languages that expresses completed action.
▶ n. a perfective form of a verb. ■ (**the perfective**) the perfective aspect.

per·fect·ly /ˈpərfik(t)lē/ ▶ adv. in a manner or way that could not be better. ■ used for emphasis, esp. in order to assert something that has been challenged or doubted: *you know perfectly well I can't stay.*

per·fec·to /pərˈfektō/ ▶ n. (pl. **-tos**) a type of cigar that is thick in the center and tapered at each end.

perfect pitch ▶ n. the ability to recognize the pitch of a note or to produce any given note; a sense of absolute pitch.

per·fi·dy /ˈpərfidē/ ▶ n. poetic/lit. deceitfulness; untrustworthiness. —**per·fid·i·ous** /pərˈfidēəs/ adj.

per·fo·rate ▶ v. /ˈpərfəˌrāt/ [tr.] pierce and make a hole or holes in: [as adj.] (**perforated**) *a perforated appendix.* ■ make a row of small holes in (paper) so that a part may be torn off easily. —**per·fo·ra·tion** /ˌpərfəˈrāsHən/ n. —**per·fo·ra·tor** /-ˌrātər/ n.

per·force /pərˈfôrs/ ▶ adv. formal used to express necessity or inevitability: *amateurs, perforce, have to settle for less expensive solutions.*

per·form /pərˈfôrm/ ▶ v. [tr.] **1** carry out, accomplish, or fulfill (an action, task, or function). ■ [intr.] work, function, or do something to a specified standard: *the car performs well at low speeds.* ■ [intr.] (of an investment) yield a profitable return. ■ [intr.] *inf.* have successful or satisfactory sexual intercourse with someone. **2** present (a form of entertainment) to an audience. ■ [intr.] entertain an audience, typically by acting, singing, or dancing on stage. —**per·form·a·bil·i·ty** /-ˌfôrmə-ˈbilitē/ n. —**per·form·a·ble** adj. —**per·form·er** n.

per·for·mance /pərˈfôrməns/ ▶ n. **1** an act of staging or presenting a play, concert, or other form of entertainment. ■ a person's rendering of a dramatic role, song, or piece of music. ■ *inf.* a display of exaggerated behavior or a process involving a great deal of unnecessary time and effort; a fuss: *he stopped to tie his shoe and seemed to be making quite a performance of it.* **2** the action or process of carrying out or accomplishing an action, task, or function. ■ an action, task, or operation, seen in terms of how successfully it was performed: *pay increases are now being linked more closely to performance.* ■ the capabilities of a machine or product, esp. when observed under particular conditions. ■ a vehicle's capacity to gain speed rapidly and move efficiently and safely at high speed. ■ the extent to which an investment is profitable, esp. in relation to other investments. ■ *Linguistics* an individual's use of a language, i.e., what a speaker actually says, including hesitations, false starts, and errors.

per·form·ing arts ▶ pl. n. forms of creative activity that are performed in front of an audience, such as drama, music, and dance.

per·fume /ˈpərˌfyoōm; ˌpərˈfyoōm/ ▶ n. a fragrant liquid typically made from essential oils extracted from flowers and spices, used to impart a pleasant smell to one's body or clothes. ■ a pleasant smell.
▶ v. [tr.] impart a pleasant smell to. ■ impregnate (something) with perfume or a sweet-smelling ingredient. ■ apply perfume to (someone or something). —**per·fum·y** /-mē/ adj.

per·fum·er /pərˈfyoōmər/ ▶ n. a producer or seller of perfumes. —**per·fum·er·y** n.

per·func·to·ry /pərˈfəNGktərē/ ▶ adj. (of an action or gesture) carried out with a minimum of effort or reflection: *he gave a perfunctory nod.* —**per·func·to·ri·ly** /-ˈfəNGktərəlē/ adv. —**per·func·to·ri·ness** /-rēnis/ n.

per·go·la /ˈpərgələ/ ▶ n. an archway in a garden or park consisting of a framework covered with trained climbing or trailing plants.

per·haps /pərˈ(h)aps/ ▶ adv. used to express uncertainty or possibility: *perhaps I should have been frank.* ■ used when one does not wish to be too definite or assertive in the expression of an opinion: *perhaps not surprisingly, he was cautious about committing himself.* ■ used when making a polite request, offer, or suggestion: *would you perhaps consent to be our guide?* ■ used to express reluctant or qualified agreement or acceptance: *"She understood him better than his wife did." "Perhaps so, but . . ."*

pe·ri /ˈpi(ə)rē/ ▶ n. (pl. **pe·ris**) (in Persian mythology) a mythical superhuman being, originally represented as evil but subsequently as a good or graceful genie or fairy.

per·i·anth /ˈperēˌanTH/ ▶ n. *Bot.* the outer part of a flower, consisting of the calyx (sepals) and corolla (petals).

per·i·car·di·um /ˌperiˈkärdēəm/ ▶ n. (pl. **-car·di·a** /-ˈkärdēə/) *Anat.* the membrane enclosing the heart, consisting of an outer fibrous layer and an inner double layer of serous membrane. —**per·i·car·di·al** /-'kärdēəl/ adj. —**per·i·car·di·tis** /ˌperikär'dītis/ n.

per·i·carp /'periˌkärp/ ▶n. Bot. the part of a fruit formed from the wall of the ripened ovary.

per·i·derm /'periˌdərm/ ▶n. Bot. the corky outer layer of a plant stem formed in secondary thickening or as a response to injury or infection. —**per·i·der·mal** /ˌperi'dərməl/ adj.

per·i·dot /'periˌdät/ ▶n. a green semiprecious variety of olivine.

per·i·do·tite /'peridəˌtīt; ˌperi'dəˌtīt/ ▶n. Geol. a dense, coarse-grained plutonic rock containing a large amount of olivine, believed to be the main constituent of the earth's mantle. —**per·i·do·tit·ic** /ˌperidə'titik; pəˌridə-/ adj.

per·i·gee /'perəˌjē/ ▶n. Astron. the point in the orbit of the moon or a satellite at which it is nearest to the earth. The opposite of APOGEE.

per·i·he·li·on /ˌperə'hēlyən; -'hēlēən/ ▶n. (pl. **-he·li·a** /-'hēlyə; -'hēlēə/ or **-he·li·ons**) Astron. the point in the orbit of a planet, asteroid, or comet at which it is closest to the sun. The opposite of APHELION.

per·il /'perəl/ ▶n. serious and immediate danger: *his family was in peril.* ■ (**perils**) the dangers or difficulties that arise from a particular situation or activity.
▶v. (**per·iled, per·il·ing**; Brit. **per·illed, per·il·ling**) [tr.] archaic expose to danger; threaten: *Jonathon periled his life for love of David.*
▶ □ **at one's peril** at one's own risk (used esp. in warnings): *neglect our advice at your peril.*

per·il·ous /'perələs/ ▶adj. full of danger or risk. ■ exposed to imminent risk of disaster or ruin. —**per·il·ous·ly** adv. —**per·il·ous·ness** n.

pe·rim·e·ter /pə'rimitər/ ▶n. the continuous line forming the boundary of a closed geometric figure: *the perimeter of a rectangle.* ■ the length of such a line: *the rectangle has a perimeter of 30 cm.* ■ the outermost parts or boundary of an area or object: *the perimeter of the garden.* ■ a defended boundary of a military position or base. ■ Basketball an area away from the basket, beyond the reach of the defensive team. —**per·i·met·ric** /ˌperə'metrik/ adj.

per·i·ne·um /ˌperə'nēəm/ ▶n. Anat. the area between the anus and the scrotum or vulva. —**per·i·ne·al** /-'nēəl/ adj.

pe·ri·od /'pi(ə)rēəd/ ▶n. **1** a length or portion of time. ■ a portion of time in the life of a person, nation, or civilization characterized by the same prevalent features or conditions: *the medieval period.* ■ one of the set divisions of the day in a school allocated to a lesson or other activity. ■ a set period of time during which a particular activity takes place: *the training period.* ■ each of the intervals into which the playing time of a sporting event is divided. ■ a major division of geological time that is a subdivision of an era and is itself subdivided into epochs. **2** a punctuation mark (.) used at the end of a sentence or an abbreviation. ■ inf. added to the end of a statement to indicate that no further discussion is possible or desirable: *he is the sole owner of the trademark, period.* **3** Physics the interval of time between successive occurrences of the same state in an oscillatory or cyclic phenomenon, such as a mechanical vibration, an alternating current, a variable star, or an electromagnetic wave. ■ Astron. the time taken by a celestial object to rotate around its axis, or to make one circuit of its orbit. ■ Math. the interval between successive equal values of a periodic function. **4** (also **menstrual period**) a flow of blood and other material from the lining of the uterus, lasting for several days and occurring in sexually mature women (who are not pregnant) at intervals of about one lunar month. **5** Chem. a set of elements occupying an entire horizontal row in the periodic table. **6** Rhetoric a complex sentence, esp. one consisting of several clauses, constructed as part of a formal speech or oration.
▶adj. belonging to or characteristic of a past historical time, esp. in style or design: *a splendid selection of period furniture.* ▷late Middle English (denoting the time during which something, esp. a disease, runs its course): from Old French periode, via Latin from Greek periodos 'orbit, recurrence, course,' from peri- 'around' + hodos 'way, course.' The sense 'portion of time' dates from the early 17th cent.

pe·ri·od·ic /ˌpi(ə)rē'ädik/ ▶adj. **1** appearing or occurring at intervals: *the periodic visits she made to her father.* **2** Chem. relating to the periodic table of the elements or the pattern of chemical properties that underlies it. **3** of or relating to a rhetorical period. See PERIOD (sense 6).

pe·ri·od·i·cal /ˌpi(ə)rē'ädikəl/ ▶n. a magazine or newspaper published at regular intervals.
▶adj. occurring or appearing at intervals; occasional. ■ (of a magazine or newspaper) published at regular intervals. —**pe·ri·od·i·cal·ly** adv.

pe·ri·od·i·cal ci·ca·da ▶n. an American cicada (genus Magicicada) whose nymphs emerge from the soil in large numbers periodically. The mature nymphs of the northern species (**seventeen-year locust**) emerge

every seventeen years; those of the southern species emerge every thirteen years.

pe·ri·od·ic ta·ble ▶n. Chem. a table of the chemical elements arranged in order of atomic number, usually in rows, so that elements with similar atomic structure (and hence similar chemical properties) appear in vertical columns.

per·i·o·don·tics /ˌperēə'däntiks/ (also **per·i·o·don·tia** /-'dänsHə/) ▶pl. n. [treated as sing.] the branch of dentistry concerned with the structures surrounding and supporting the teeth. —**per·i·o·don·tal** /-'däntl/ adj. —**per·i·o·don·tist** /-'däntist/ n.

per·i·o·don·ti·tis /ˌperēədän'tītis/ ▶n. Med. inflammation of the tissue around the teeth, often causing shrinkage of the gums and loosening of the teeth. Also called PYORRHEA.

pe·ri·od piece ▶n. an object or work that is set in or strongly reminiscent of an earlier historical period.

per·i·pa·tet·ic /ˌperipə'tetik/ ▶adj. traveling from place to place, esp. working or based in various places for relatively short periods: *the peripatetic nature of military life.*
▶n. a person who travels from place to place. —**per·i·pa·tet·i·cal·ly** /-ik(ə)lē/ adv. —**per·i·pa·tet·i·cism** /-'tetəˌsizəm/ n.

pe·riph·er·al /pə'rifərəl/ ▶adj. of, relating to, or situated on the edge or periphery of something: *the peripheral areas of Europe.* ■ of secondary or minor importance; marginal: *she will see their problems as* **peripheral to** *her own.* ■ (of a device) able to be attached to and used with a computer, although not an integral part of it. ■ Anat. near the surface of the body, with special reference to the circulation and nervous system: *lymphocytes from peripheral blood.*
▶n. Comput. a peripheral device. —**pe·riph·er·al·i·ty** /-ˌrifə'ralitē/ n. —**pe·riph·er·al·i·za·tion** /pəˌrifərəli'zāsHən/ n. —**pe·riph·er·al·ize** /-ˌīz/ v. —**pe·riph·er·al·ly** adv.

pe·riph·er·al nerv·ous sys·tem ▶n. Anat. the nervous system outside the brain and spinal cord.

pe·riph·er·al vi·sion ▶n. side vision; what is seen on the side by the eye when looking straight ahead.

pe·riph·er·y /pə'rifərē/ ▶n. (pl. **-er·ies**) the outer limits or edge of an area or object: *new buildings on the periphery of the hospital site.* ■ a marginal or secondary position in, or part or aspect of, a group, subject, or sphere of activity: *a shift in power from the center to the periphery.*

pe·riph·ra·sis /pə'rifrəsis/ ▶n. (pl. **-ses** /-ˌsēz/) the use of indirect and circumlocutory speech or writing. ■ an indirect and circumlocutory phrase. ■ Gram. the use of separate words to express a grammatical relationship that is otherwise expressed by inflection, e.g., *did go* as opposed to *went* and *more intelligent* as opposed to *smarter.* —**per·i·phras·tic** /ˌperə'frastik/ adj.

per·i·scope /'perəˌskōp/ ▶n. an apparatus consisting of a tube attached to a set of mirrors or prisms, by which an observer (typically in a submerged submarine) can see things that are otherwise out of sight. —**per·i·scop·ic** /ˌperə'skäpik/ adj.

per·ish /'perisH/ ▶v. [intr.] suffer death, typically in a violent, sudden, or untimely way. ■ suffer complete ruin or destruction: *the old regime had to perish.* ■ (of rubber, a foodstuff, or other organic substance) lose its normal qualities; rot or decay. ▷Middle English: from Old French periss-, lengthened stem of perir, from Latin perire 'pass away,' from per- 'through, completely' + ire 'go.'
▶ □ **perish the thought** inf. used, often ironically, to show that one finds a suggestion or idea completely ridiculous or unwelcome: *he wasn't out to get drunk—perish the thought!*

per·ish·a·ble /'perisHəbəl/ ▶adj. (esp. of food) likely to decay or go bad quickly. ■ (of something abstract) having a brief life or significance.
▶n. (**perishables**) things, esp. foodstuffs, likely to decay or go bad quickly. —**per·ish·a·bil·i·ty** /ˌperisHə'bilitē/ n.

pe·ris·so·dac·tyl /pəˌrisə'daktəl/ ▶n. any ungulate with either one or three toes on each hind foot, including horses, asses, zebras, tapirs, and rhinoceroses.
▶adj. of or relating to perissodactyls.

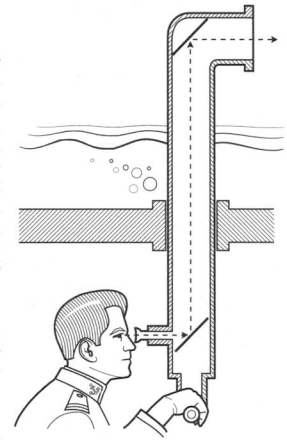

periscope

per·i·to·ne·um /ˌperitnˈēəm/ ▸n. (pl. **-ne·ums** or **-ne·a** /-ˈnēə/) *Anat.* the serous membrane lining the cavity of the abdomen and covering the abdominal organs. —**per·i·to·ne·al** /-ˈēəl/ adj.

per·i·to·ni·tis /ˌperitnˈītis/ ▸n. *Med.* inflammation of the peritoneum, typically caused by bacterial infection either via the blood or after rupture of an abdominal organ.

per·i·wig /ˈperiˌwig/ ▸n. a highly styled wig worn formerly as a fashionable headdress by both women and men. ■ archaic term for WIG[1]. —**per·i·wigged** adj.

per·i·win·kle[1] /ˈperiˌwiNGkəl/ ▸n. a plant (genera *Vinca* and *Catharanthus*, family Apocynaceae) with flat, five-petaled flowers and glossy leaves.

per·i·win·kle[2] ▸n. another term for WINKLE.

per·jure /ˈpərjər/ ▸v. (**perjure oneself**) *Law* willfully tell an untruth when giving evidence to a court; commit perjury. —**per·jur·er** n.

per·ju·ry /ˈpərjərē/ ▸n. (pl. **-ries**) *Law* the offense of willfully telling an untruth in a court after having taken an oath or affirmation. —**per·ju·ri·ous** /pərˈjŏŏrēəs/ adj.

perk[1] /pərk/ ▸v. [intr.] (**perk up**) become more cheerful, lively, or interesting. ■ [tr.] (**perk someone/something up**) make someone or something more cheerful, lively, or interesting.
▸adj. dial. perky; pert.

perk[2] ▸n. (usu. **perks**) inf. money, goods, or other benefit to which one is entitled as an employee or as a shareholder of a company. ■ an advantage or benefit following from a job or situation.

perk[3] inf. ▸v. [intr.] (of coffee) percolate: *while the coffee perks, head out for the morning paper.* ■ [tr.] percolate (coffee).

perk·y /ˈpərkē/ ▸adj. (**perk·i·er, perk·i·est**) cheerful and lively. —**perk·i·ly** /-kəlē/ adv. —**perk·i·ness** /-kēnis/ n.

per·lite /ˈpərlīt/ ▸n. a form of obsidian characterized by spherulites formed by cracking of the volcanic glass during cooling, used as insulation or in plant growth media.

per·lo·cu·tion /ˌpərləˈkyŏŏSHən/ ▸n. *Philos. & Linguistics* an act of speaking or writing that has an action as its aim but that in itself does not effect or constitute the action, for example persuading or convincing. —**per·lo·cu·tion·ar·y** /-ˌnerē/ adj.

perm /pərm/ ▸n. (also **permanent wave**) a method of setting the hair in waves or curls and then treating it with chemicals so that the style lasts for several months.
▸v. [tr.] (often **be permed**) treat (the hair) in such a way.

per·ma·frost /ˈpərməˌfrôst; -ˌfräst/ ▸n. a thick subsurface layer of soil that remains frozen throughout the year, occurring chiefly in polar regions.

per·ma·lanc·er /ˈpərməˌlansər/ ▸n. a long-term freelance, part-time, or temporary worker who does not have employee benefits: *the permalancers always have to park in the temporary spaces.* Also called PER·MATEMP. ▷blend of *permanent* and *freelancer.*

per·ma·nent /ˈpərmənənt/ ▸adj. lasting or intended to last or remain unchanged indefinitely. ■ lasting or continuing without interruption.
▸n. a perm for the hair. —**per·ma·nence** n. —**per·ma·nent·ly** adv.

per·ma·nent wave ▸n. see PERM.

per·man·ga·nate /pərˈmaNGgəˌnāt/ ▸n. *Chem.* a salt containing the anion MnO_4^-, typically deep purplish-red and with strong oxidizing properties.

per·ma·temp /ˈpərməˌtemp/ ▸ another term for PERMALANCER.

per·me·a·bil·i·ty /ˌpərmēəˈbilitē/ ▸n. the state or quality of a material or membrane that causes it to allow liquids or gases to pass through it.

per·me·a·ble /ˈpərmēəbəl/ ▸adj. (of a material or membrane) allowing liquids or gases to pass through it: *a frog's skin is permeable to water.*

per·me·ate /ˈpərmēˌāt/ ▸v. [tr.] spread throughout (something); pervade: *the aroma of soup permeated the air* | [intr.] *his personality has begun to permeate through the whole organization.* —**per·me·a·tion** /ˌpərmēˈāSHən/ n.

per·mis·si·ble /pərˈmisəbəl/ ▸adj. permitted; allowed. —**per·mis·si·bil·i·ty** /-ˌmisəˈbilitē/ n. —**per·mis·si·bly** /-blē/ adv.

per·mis·sion /pərˈmiSHən/ ▸n. consent; authorization. ■ an official document giving authorization: *permissions to reproduce copyright material.*

per·mis·sive /pərˈmisiv/ ▸adj. **1** allowing or characterized by great or excessive freedom of behavior. **2** *Law* allowed but not obligatory; optional. **3** *Biol.* allowing a biological or biochemical process to occur: *the mutants grow well at the permissive temperature.* ■ allowing the infection and replication of viruses. —**per·mis·sive·ly** adv. —**per·mis·sive·ness** n.

per·mit[1] ▸v. /pərˈmit/ (**-mit·ted, -mit·ting**) [tr.] give authorization or consent to (someone) to do something. ■ [tr.] authorize or give permission for (something): *the country is not ready to permit any imports.* ■ [tr.] (of a thing, circumstance, or condition) provide an opportunity or scope for

(something) to take place; make possible: *some properties are too small to permit mechanized farming* | [intr.] *when weather permits, lunches are served outside.* ■ [intr.] (**permit of**) dated allow for; admit of.
▸n. /ˈpərmit/ an official document giving someone authorization to do something: *he is in Britain on a work permit.* ■ official or formal permission to do something: *parking on University grounds is by permit only.* —**per·mit·tee** /ˌpərmiˈtē/ n. —**per·mit·ter** /pərˈmitər/ n.
▸ □—— **permitting** if the specified thing does not prevent one from doing something: *weather permitting, guests can dine outside on the veranda.*

per·mit[2] /ˈpərmit/ ▸n. a deep-bodied fish (*Trachinotus falcatus*) of the jack family, found in warm waters of the western Atlantic and Caribbean and caught for food and sport.

per·mu·tate /ˈpərmyŏŏˌtāt/ ▸v. [tr.] change the order or arrangement of.

per·mu·ta·tion /ˌpərmyŏŏˈtāSHən/ ▸n. a way, esp. one of several possible variations, in which a set or number of things can be ordered or arranged. ■ *Math.* the action of changing the arrangement, esp. the linear order, of a set of items. —**per·mu·ta·tion·al** /-ˈtāSHənəl/ adj.

per·mute /pərˈmyŏŏt/ ▸v. [tr.] technical submit to a process of alteration, rearrangement, or permutation: *we wish to permute the order of the bytes.*

per·ni·cious /pərˈniSHəs/ ▸adj. having a harmful effect, esp. in a gradual or subtle way: *the pernicious influences of the mass media.* ▷late Middle English: from Latin *perniciosus* 'destructive,' from *pernicies* 'ruin,' based on *nex, nec-* 'death.' —**per·ni·cious·ly** adv. —**per·ni·cious·ness** n.

per·ni·cious a·ne·mi·a ▸n. a deficiency in the production of red blood cells through a lack of vitamin B[12].

per·o·ra·tion /ˌperəˈrāSHən/ ▸n. the concluding part of a speech, typically intended to inspire enthusiasm in the audience.

per·ox·ide /pəˈräksīd/ ▸n. *Chem.* a compound containing two oxygen atoms bonded together in its molecule or as the anion O_2^{2-}. ■ hydrogen peroxide, esp. as used as a bleach for the hair: [as adj.] *a peroxide blonde.*
▸v. [tr.] bleach (hair) with peroxide.

per·pen·dic·u·lar /ˌpərpənˈdikyələr/ ▸adj. **1** at an angle of 90° to a given line, plane, or surface. ■ at an angle of 90° to the ground; vertical: *the perpendicular cliff.* ■ (of something with a slope) so steep as to be almost vertical. **2** (**Per·pen·dic·u·lar**) denoting the latest stage of English Gothic church architecture, prevalent from the late 14th to mid 16th centuries and characterized by broad arches, elaborate fan vaulting, and large windows with vertical tracery.
▸n. a straight line at an angle of 90° to a given line, plane, or surface. ■ (usu. **the perpendicular**) perpendicular position or direction. ■ an instrument for indicating the vertical line from any point, as a spirit level or plumb line. —**per·pen·dic·u·lar·i·ty** /-ˌdikyəˈlaritē/ n. —**per·pen·dic·u·lar·ly** adv.

per·pe·trate /ˈpərpəˌtrāt/ ▸v. [tr.] carry out or commit (a harmful, illegal, or immoral action). ▷mid 16th cent.: from Latin *perpetrat-* 'performed,' from the verb *perpetrare*, from *per-* 'to completion' + *patrare* 'bring about.' In Latin the act perpetrated might be good or bad; in English the verb was first used in the statutes referring to crime, hence the negative association. —**per·pe·tra·tion** /ˌpərpəˈtrāSHən/ n. —**per·pe·tra·tor** /-ˌtrātər/ n.

per·pet·u·al /pərˈpeCHŏŏəl/ ▸adj. **1** never ending or changing: *deep caves in perpetual darkness.* ■ denoting a position, job, or trophy held for life rather than a limited period, or the person holding it: *a perpetual secretary of the society.* ■ (of an investment) having no fixed maturity. **2** occurring repeatedly; so frequent as to seem endless and uninterrupted. ■ (of a plant) blooming or fruiting several times in one season.
▸n. a perpetual plant, esp. a hybrid rose. —**per·pet·u·al·ly** adv.

per·pet·u·al mo·tion ▸n. a state in which movement or action is or appears to be continuous and unceasing. ■ the motion of a hypothetical machine that, once activated, would run forever unless subject to an external force or to wear.

per·pet·u·ate /pərˈpeCHŏŏˌāt/ ▸v. [tr.] make (something, typically an undesirable situation or an unfounded belief) continue indefinitely. ■ preserve (something valued) from oblivion or extinction. —**per·pet·u·ance** /-ŏŏəns/ n. —**per·pet·u·a·tion** /pərˌpeCHŏŏˈāSHən/ n. —**per·pet·u·a·tor** n.

per·pe·tu·i·ty /ˌpərpiˈt(y)ŏŏitē/ ▸n. (pl. **-ties**) **1** a thing that lasts forever or for an indefinite period, in particular: ■ a bond or other security with no fixed maturity. **2** the state or quality of lasting forever.
▸ □ **in** (or **for**) **perpetuity** forever.

per·plex /pər'pleks/ ▶v. [tr.] (often **be perplexed**) (of something complicated or unaccountable) cause (someone) to feel completely baffled: *she was perplexed by her husband's moodiness.* ■ *dated* complicate or confuse (a matter). —**per·plex·ed·ly** /-'pleksidlē/ *adv.* —**per·plex·ing·ly** *adv.*

per·plex·i·ty /pər'pleksitē/ ▶n. (pl. **-ties**) **1** inability to deal with or understand something complicated or unaccountable. ■ (usu. **per·plexities**) a complicated or baffling situation or thing. **2** *archaic* an entangled state.

per·qui·site /'pərkwəzit/ ▶n. *formal* another term for PERK². ■ a thing regarded as a special right or privilege enjoyed as a result of one's position. ■ *hist.* a thing that has served its primary use and is then given to a subordinate or employee as a customary right.

per se /pər 'sā/ ▶adv. by or in itself or themselves; intrinsically: *it is not these facts per se that are important.*

per·se·cute /'pərsə,kyōōt/ ▶v. [tr.] (often **be persecuted**) subject (someone) to hostility and ill-treatment, esp. because of their race or political or religious beliefs. ■ harass or annoy (someone) persistently. —**per·se·cu·tion** /,pərsə'kyōōshən/ *n.* —**per·se·cu·tor** /-,kyōōtər/ *n.* —**per·se·cu·to·ry** /-kyōō,tôrē/ *adj.*

per·se·ver·ance /,pərsə'vi(ə)rəns/ ▶n. steadfastness in doing something despite difficulty or delay in achieving success.

per·se·vere /,pərsə'vi(ə)r/ ▶v. [intr.] continue in a course of action even in the face of difficulty or with little or no prospect of success. —**per·se·ver·ance** /-'vi(ə)rəns/ *n.* —**per·se·ver·ing·ly** *adv.*

Per·sian /'pərzhən/ ▶n. **1** a native or national of ancient or modern Persia (or Iran), or a person of Persian descent. ■ (also **Persian cat**) a long-haired domestic cat of a breed originating in Persia, having a broad round head, stocky body, and short thick legs. **2** the Iranian language of modern Iran, written in Arabic script. Also called FARSI. ■ an earlier form of this language spoken in ancient or medieval Persia.

▶adj. of or relating to ancient Persia or modern Iran or its people or language.

per·si·flage /'pərsə,fläzh/ ▶n. *formal* light and slightly contemptuous mockery or banter.

per·sim·mon /pər'simən/ ▶n. **1** an edible fruit that resembles a large tomato and has sweet flesh. **2** the tree (genus *Diospyros*, family Ebenaceae), related to ebony, that yields this fruit.

per·sist /pər'sist/ ▶v. [intr.] continue firmly or obstinately in an opinion or a course of action in spite of difficulty, opposition, or failure: *the minority of drivers who* **persist** *in drinking.* ■ continue to exist; be prolonged: *if the symptoms persist for more than a few days, contact your doctor.*

per·sis·tent /pər'sistənt/ ▶adj. **1** continuing firmly or obstinately in a course of action in spite of difficulty or opposition. ■ characterized by a specified habitual behavior pattern, esp. a dishonest or undesirable one: *they accused officials of persistent discrimination.* **2** continuing to exist or endure over a prolonged period: *persistent rain.* ■ occurring repeatedly over a prolonged period: *persistent reports of human rights abuses.* ■ (of a chemical or radioactivity) remaining within the environment for a long time after its introduction. **3** *Bot. & Zool.* (of a part of an animal or plant, such as a horn, leaf, etc.) remaining attached instead of falling off in the normal manner. —**per·sis·tence** *n.* —**per·sis·tent·ly** *adv.*

per·sis·tent veg·e·ta·tive state ▶n. a condition in which a medical patient is completely unresponsive to psychological and physical stimuli and displays no sign of higher brain function, being kept alive only by medical intervention.

per·snick·et·y /pər'snikətē/ ▶adj. *inf.* placing too much emphasis on trivial or minor details; fussy. ■ requiring a particularly precise or careful approach.

per·son /'pərsən/ ▶n. (pl. **peo·ple** /'pēpəl/ or **per·sons**) **1** a human being regarded as an individual. ■ used in legal or formal contexts to refer to an unspecified individual: *the entrance fee is $10.00 per person.* ■ an individual characterized by a preference or liking for a specified thing: *she's not a cat person.* ■ an individual's body: *I have publicity photographs* **on my person** *at all times.* ■ a character in a play or story: *his previous roles in the person of a fallible cop.* **2** *Gram.* a category used in the classification of pronouns, possessive determiners, and verb forms, according to whether they indicate the speaker (**first person**), the addressee (**second person**), or a third party (**third person**) . ▷Middle English: from Old French *persone*, from Latin *persona* 'actor's mask, character in a play,' later 'human being.'

▶ □ **be one's own person** do or be what one wishes or in accordance with one's own character rather than as influenced by others. □ **in person** with the personal presence or action of the individual specified: *he had to pick up his welfare check in person.*

per·so·na /pər'sōnə/ ▶n. (pl. **-so·nas** or **-so·nae** /-'sōnē/) the aspect of someone's character that is presented to or perceived by others: *her public persona.* In psychology, often contrasted with ANIMA. ■ a role or character adopted by an author or an actor.

per·son·a·ble /'pərsənəbəl/ ▶adj. (of a person) having a pleasant appearance and manner. —**per·son·a·ble·ness** *n.* —**per·son·a·bly** /-blē/ *adv.*

per·son·age /'pərsənij/ ▶n. a person (often used to express their significance, importance, or elevated status): *it was no less a personage than the bishop.* ■ a character in a play or other work.

per·son·al /'pərsənəl/ ▶adj. **1** of, affecting, or belonging to a particular person rather than to anyone else. ■ done or made by a particular person; involving the actual presence or action of a particular individual: *the president made personal appearances for the reelection of the governor.* ■ done, intended, or made for a particular person: *a personal loan.* **2** of or concerning one's private life, relationships, and emotions rather than matters connected with one's public or professional career. ■ referring to an individual's character, appearance, or private life, esp. in a hostile or critical way: *you look like a drowned rat—nothing personal.* **3** of or relating to a person's body. **4** *Gram.* of or denoting one of the three persons. See PERSON (sense 2). **5** existing as a self-aware entity, not as an abstraction or an impersonal force: *Jews, Christians, and Muslims believe in a personal God.*

▶n. an advertisement or message in the personal column of a newspaper; personal ad. ■ (**personals**) another term for PERSONAL COLUMN.

per·son·al col·umn ▶n. (usu. **personal columns**) a section of a newspaper devoted to personal ads.

per·son·al com·pu·ter ▶n. a microcomputer designed for use by one person at a time.

per·son·al i·den·ti·fi·ca·tion num·ber (abbr.: **PIN**) ▶n. a number allocated to an individual and used to validate electronic transactions.

per·son·al·i·ty /,pərsə'nalitē/ ▶n. (pl. **-ties**) **1** the combination of characteristics or qualities that form an individual's distinctive character: *she had a sunny personality* | *fig. each brand of gin has its own personality.* ■ qualities that make someone interesting or popular: *she's always had loads of personality.* **2** a famous person, esp. in entertainment or sports. **3** *archaic* the quality or fact of being a person as distinct from a thing or animal. **4** (**personalities**) *archaic* disparaging remarks about an individual.

per·son·al·ize /'pərsənəl,īz/ ▶v. [tr.] **1** (usu. **be personalized**) design or produce (something) to meet someone's individual requirements: *the wedding invitations will be personalized to your requirements.* ■ make (something) identifiable as belonging to a particular person, esp. by marking it with their name or initials. **2** cause (something, esp. an issue, argument, or debate) to become concerned with personalities or feelings rather than with general or abstract matters: *the media's tendency to personalize politics.* **3** (often **be personalized**) personify (something, esp. a deity or spirit). —**per·son·al·i·za·tion** /,pərsənəli·'zāshən/ *n.*

per·son·al·ly /'pərsənəlē/ ▶adv. **1** with the personal presence or action of the individual specified; in person: *she stayed to thank O'Brien personally.* ■ used to indicate that a specified person and no other is involved in something: *he held her* **personally responsible** *for this betrayal.* ■ used to indicate that one knows or has contact with someone in person rather than indirectly through their work, reputation, or a third party: *they had made conclusions without getting to know me personally.* **2** from someone's personal standpoint or according to their particular nature; in a subjective rather than an objective way: *he had spoken personally and emotionally.* ■ used to emphasize that one is expressing one's personal opinion: *personally, I think he made a very sensible move.* ■ with regard to one's personal and private rather than public or professional capacity: *nothing had gone well personally or politically.*

▶ □ **take something personally** interpret a remark or action as directed against oneself and be upset or offended by it.

per·son·al pro·noun ▶n. each of the pronouns in English (*I, you, he, she, it, we, they, me, him, her, us,* and *them*) comprising a set that shows contrasts of person, gender, number, and case.

per·son·al prop·er·ty ▶n. *Law* movable property; belongings exclusive of land and buildings. Used in contrast to REAL PROPERTY.

per·son·al·ty /'pərsənəltē/ ▶n. *Law* personal, movable property. Used in contrast to REALTY.

per·so·na non gra·ta /pər'sōnə nän 'grätə/ ▶n. (pl. **per·so·nae non gra·tae** /pər'sōnē nän 'grätē/) an unacceptable or unwelcome person: *from now on, these yellow journalists can consider themselves personae non grata.*

per·son·i·fi·ca·tion /pər,sänəfi'kāshən/ ▶n. the attribution of a personal nature or human characteristics to something nonhuman, or the representation of an abstract quality in human form. ■ a figure intended to represent an abstract quality: *the design on the franc shows Marianne, the personification of the French republic.* ■ a person, animal, or object regarded as representing or embodying a quality, concept, or thing: *he was the very personification of British pluck and diplomacy.*

per·son·i·fy /pərˈsänəˌfī/ ▶ v. (**-fies, -fied**) [*tr.*] represent (a quality or concept) by a figure in human form. ■ (usu. **be personified**) attribute a personal nature or human characteristics to (something nonhuman). ■ represent or embody (a quality, concept, or thing) in a physical form. **—per·son·i·fi·er** /-ˌfī(ə)r/ *n.*

per·son·nel /ˌpərsəˈnel/ ▶ pl. *n.* people employed in an organization or engaged in an organized undertaking such as military service: *sales personnel.* ■ short for **PERSONNEL DEPARTMENT**.

per·son·nel de·part·ment ▶ n. the part of an organization concerned with the appointment, training, and welfare of employees.

per·spec·tive /pərˈspektiv/ ▶ n. **1** the art of drawing solid objects on a two-dimensional surface so as to give the right impression of their height, width, depth, and position in relation to each other when viewed from a particular point: [as *adj.*] *a perspective drawing.* ■ a picture drawn in such a way, esp. one appearing to enlarge or extend the actual space. ■ a view or prospect. ■ *Geom.* the relation of two figures in the same plane, such that pairs of corresponding points lie on concurrent lines, and corresponding lines meet in collinear points. **2** particular attitude toward or way of regarding something; a point of view: *it is written from the editor's perspective.* ■ true understanding of the relative importance of things; a sense of proportion: *we must keep a sense of perspective about what he's done.* **3** an apparent spatial distribution in perceived sound. **—per·spec·tiv·al** /-tivəl/ *adj.*

▶ □ **in** (or **out of**) **perspective** showing the right (or wrong) relationship between visible objects. ■ correctly (or incorrectly) regarded in terms of relative importance: *these expenses may seem high, but they need to be put into perspective.*

per·spi·ca·cious /ˌpərspiˈkāSHəs/ ▶ adj. having a ready insight into and understanding of things. **—per·spi·ca·cious·ly** adv. **—per·spi·cac·i·ty** /-ˈkasitē/ n.

per·spic·u·ous /pərˈspikyo͞oəs/ ▶ adj. formal (of an account or representation) clearly expressed and easily understood; lucid. ■ (of a person) able to give an account or express an idea clearly. **—per·spi·cu·i·ty** /ˌpərspiˈkyo͞oitē/ n. **—per·spic·u·ous·ly** adv.

per·spi·ra·tion /ˌpərspəˈrāSHən/ ▶ n. the process of sweating: *it causes perspiration and a rapid heartbeat.* ■ sweat: *perspiration ran down his forehead.* **—per·spir·a·to·ry** /pərˈspīrəˌtôrē/ adj.

per·spire /pərˈspīr/ ▶ v. [*intr.*] give out sweat through the pores of the skin as the result of heat, physical exertion, or stress.

per·suade /pərˈswād/ ▶ v. [*tr.*] cause (someone) to do something through reasoning or argument. ■ [*tr.*] cause (someone) to believe something, esp. after a sustained effort; convince: *they must be persuaded of the potential severity of their drinking problems.* ■ (of a situation or event) provide a sound reason for (someone) to do something: *the cost of the manor's restoration persuaded them to take in guests.* **—per·suad·a·bil·i·ty** /-ˌswādəˈbilitē/ n. **—per·suad·a·ble** /-ˈswādəbəl/ adj. **—per·sua·si·ble** /-ˈswāzəbəl/ adj.

per·sua·sion /pərˈswāZHən/ ▶ n. **1** the action or fact of persuading someone or of being persuaded to do or believe something. ■ a means of persuading someone to do or believe something; an argument or inducement: *he gave way to the persuasions of his half-brother.* **2** a belief or set of beliefs, esp. religious or political ones: *writers of all political persuasions.* ■ a group or sect holding a particular religious belief: *two chapels for those of the Methodist persuasion.* ■ *humorous* any group or type of person or thing linked by a specified characteristic, quality, or attribute: *an ancient gas oven of the enamel persuasion.*

per·sua·sive /pərˈswāsiv; -ziv/ ▶ adj. good at persuading someone to do or believe something through reasoning or the use of temptation. **—per·sua·sive·ly** adv. **—per·sua·sive·ness** n.

pert /pərt/ ▶ adj. (of a girl or young woman) sexually attractive because lively or saucy. ■ (of a bodily feature or garment) attractive because neat and jaunty: *she had a pert nose.* ■ (of a young person or their speech or behavior) impudent. **—pert·ly** adv. **—pert·ness** n.

pert. ▶ abbr. pertaining.

per·tain /pərˈtān/ ▶ v. [*intr.*] be appropriate, related, or applicable: *matters pertaining to government.* ■ *chiefly Law* belong to something as a part, appendage, or accessory: *assets pertaining to the business.* ■ be in effect or existence in a specified place or at a specified time: *circumstances vastly different from those which pertained in their land of origin.*

per·ti·na·cious /ˌpərtnˈāSHəs/ ▶ adj. formal holding firmly to an opinion or a course of action. **—per·ti·na·cious·ly** adv. **—per·ti·na·cious·ness** n. **—per·ti·nac·i·ty** /-ˈasitē/ n.

per·ti·nent /ˈpərtn-ənt/ ▶ adj. relevant or applicable to a particular matter; apposite: *the unreleased section of tape was pertinent to the investigation.* **—per·ti·nence** n. **—per·ti·nen·cy** n. **—per·ti·nent·ly** adv.

per·turb /pərˈtərb/ ▶ v. [*tr.*] **1** (often **be perturbed**) make (someone) anxious or unsettled: *they were perturbed by her capricious behavior.* **2** subject (a system, moving object, or process) to an influence tending to alter its normal or regular state or path: *nuclear weapons could be used to perturb the orbit of an asteroid.* **—per·turb·a·ble** adj. **—per·tur·ba·tion** /ˌpərtərˈbāSHən/ n. **—per·tur·ba·tive** /ˈpərtərˌbātiv; pərˈtərbətiv/ adj. **—per·turb·ing·ly** adv.

per·tus·sis /pərˈtəsis/ ▶ n. medical term for **WHOOPING COUGH**.

pe·ruse /pəˈro͞oz/ ▶ v. [*tr.*] formal read thoroughly or carefully. ■ examine carefully or at length. **—pe·rus·al** /-ˈro͞ozəl/ n. **—pe·rus·er** n.

per·vade /pərˈvād/ ▶ v. [*tr.*] (esp. of a smell) spread through and be perceived in every part of: *a smell of stale cabbage pervaded the air.* ■ (of an influence, feeling, or quality) be present and apparent throughout. ▷ mid 17th cent. (also in the sense 'traverse'): from Latin *pervadere,* from *per-* 'throughout' + *vadere* 'go.' **—per·va·sion** /pərˈvāZHən/ n.

per·va·sive /pərˈvāsiv/ ▶ adj. (esp. of an unwelcome influence or physical effect) spreading widely throughout an area or a group of people. **—per·va·sive·ly** adv. **—per·va·sive·ness** n.

per·verse /pərˈvərs/ ▶ adj. (of a person or their actions) showing a deliberate and obstinate desire to behave in a way that is unreasonable or unacceptable, often in spite of the consequences. ■ contrary to the accepted or expected standard or practice: *in two general elections the outcome was quite perverse.* ■ sexually perverted. **—per·verse·ly** adv. **—per·verse·ness** n. **—per·ver·si·ty** /-ˈvərsitē/ n. (pl. **-ties**) .

per·ver·sion /pərˈvərZHən/ ▶ n. the alteration of something from its original course, meaning, or state to a distortion or corruption of what was first intended: *a scandalous perversion of the law.* ■ sexual behavior or desire that is considered abnormal or unacceptable.

per·vert ▶ v. /pərˈvərt/ [*tr.*] alter (something) from its original course, meaning, or state to a distortion or corruption of what was first intended: *he was charged with conspiring to pervert the course of justice.* ■ lead (someone) away from what is considered right, natural, or acceptable. ▶ n. /ˈpərvərt/ a person whose sexual behavior is regarded as abnormal and unacceptable. **—per·vert·er** n.

per·vi·ous /ˈpərvēəs/ ▶ adj. (of a substance) allowing water to pass through; permeable: *pervious rocks.* **—per·vi·ous·ness** n.

pe·se·ta /pəˈsātə/ ▶ n. the basic monetary unit of Spain (until replaced by the euro), equal to 100 centimos. ■ *hist.* a silver coin.

pes·ky /ˈpeskē/ ▶ adj. (**-ki·er, -ki·est**) *inf.* causing trouble; annoying: *pesky mosquitoes.* **—pesk·i·ly** /-kələ/ adv. **—pesk·i·ness** /-kēnis/ n.

pe·so /ˈpāsō/ ▶ n. (pl. **-sos**) the basic monetary unit of Mexico, several other Latin American countries, and the Philippines, equal to 100 centésimos in Uruguay and 100 centavos elsewhere.

pes·sa·ry /ˈpesərē/ ▶ n. (pl. **-ries**) a small soluble block that is inserted into the vagina to treat infection or as a contraceptive. ■ an elastic or rigid device that is inserted into the vagina to support the uterus.

pes·si·mism /ˈpesəˌmizəm/ ▶ n. a tendency to see the worst aspect of things or believe that the worst will happen; a lack of hope or confidence in the future. **—pes·si·mist** n. **—pes·si·mis·tic** /ˌpesəˈmistik/ adj.

pest /pest/ ▶ n. a destructive insect or other animal that attacks crops, food, livestock, etc. ■ *inf.* an annoying person or thing; a nuisance. ■ (**the pest**) *archaic* bubonic plague.

pes·ter /ˈpestər/ ▶ v. trouble or annoy (someone) with frequent or persistent requests or interruptions. **—pes·ter·er** n.

pes·ti·cide /ˈpestəˌsīd/ ▶ n. a substance used for destroying insects or other organisms harmful to cultivated plants or to animals. **—pes·ti·cid·al** /ˌpestəˈsīdl/ adj.

pes·ti·lence /ˈpestələns/ ▶ n. *archaic* a fatal epidemic disease, esp. bubonic plague.

pes·ti·lent /ˈpestələnt/ ▶ adj. destructive to life; deadly: *pestilent diseases.* ■ *inf., dated* causing annoyance; troublesome. ■ *archaic, fig.* harmful or dangerous to morals or public order; pernicious. **—pes·ti·lent·ly** adv.

pes·ti·len·tial /ˌpestəˈlenSHəl/ ▶ adj. harmful or destructive to crops or livestock. ■ *dated* of, relating to, or tending to cause infectious diseases. ■ *inf.* annoying. **—pes·ti·len·tial·ly** adv.

pes·tle /ˈpestl; ˈpesəl/ ▶ n. a heavy tool with a rounded end, used for crushing and grinding substances such as spices or drugs, usually in a mortar. ■ a mechanical device for grinding, pounding, or stamping something.

▶ *v.* [*tr.*] crush or grind (a substance) with a pestle.

pes·to /ˈpestō/ ▶ *n.* a sauce of crushed basil leaves, pine nuts, garlic, Parmesan cheese, and olive oil, typically served with pasta.

PET /pet/ ▶ *abbr.* ■ polyethylene terephthalate. ■ positron emission tomography, used esp. for brain scans.

pet¹ /pet/ ▶ *n.* a domestic or tamed animal or bird kept for companionship or pleasure and treated with care and affection. ■ a person treated with special favor, esp. in a way that others regard as unfair: *Liz was teacher's pet.* ■ used as an affectionate form of address.

▶ *adj.* (of an animal or bird) kept as a pet. ■ of or relating to pet animals. ■ denoting a thing that one devotes special attention to or feels particularly strongly about: *another of her pet projects was the arts center.* ■ denoting a person or establishment that one regards with particular favor or affection: *his pet performer was Hollander.*

▶ *v.* (**pet·ted, pet·ting**) [*tr.*] stroke or pat (an animal) affectionately. ■ treat (someone) with affection or favoritism; pamper. ■ [*intr.*] engage in sexually stimulating caressing and touching: *couples necking and petting in the cars.* —**pet·ter** *n.*

pet² ▶ *n.* a fit of sulking or ill humor: *Mother's in a pet.*

PETA /ˈpetə/ ▶ *abbr.* People for the Ethical Treatment of Animals.

pe·ta·byte /ˈpetəˌbīt/ (abbr: **PB**) ▶ *n.* 2⁵⁰ bytes; 1024 terabytes, or a million gigabytes: *research projects that generate tens of petabytes of data*

pet·al /ˈpetl/ ▶ *n.* each of the segments of the corolla of a flower, which are modified leaves and are typically colored. —**pet·al·ine** /ˈpetlˌīn; -in/ *adj.* —**pet·aled** *adj.* [in *comb.*] *pink-petaled trailing phlox.* —**pet·al·like** /-ˌlīk/ *adj.* —**pet·al·oid** /-ˌoid/ *adj.*

pe·tard /piˈtärd/ ▶ *n. hist.* a small bomb made of a metal or wooden box filled with powder, used to blast down a door or to make a hole in a wall. ■ a kind of firework that explodes with a sharp report.

▶ □ **hoist with** (or **by**) **one's own petard** have one's plans to cause trouble for others backfire on one.

Pe·ter /ˈpētər/ ▶ *n.* either of two books of the New Testament, epistles ascribed to St. Peter.

pe·ter¹ /ˈpētər/ ▶ *v.* [*intr.*] decrease or fade gradually before coming to an end: *the storm had petered out.*

pe·ter² ▶ *n. inf.* a man's penis.

Pe·ter Prin·ci·ple ▶ the principle that members of a hierarchy are promoted until they reach the level at which they are no longer competent.

pet·i·ole /ˈpetēˌōl/ ▶ *n. Bot.* the stalk that joins a leaf to a stem. —**pet·i·o·lar** /ˌpetēˈōlər/ *adj.* —**pet·i·o·late** /ˈpetēˌlāt/ *adj.*

pet·it /ˈpetē/ ▶ *adj. Law* (of a crime) petty: *petit larceny.*

pet·it bour·geois /ˈpetē bŏŏrˈzhwä; pəˈtē/ ▶ *adj.* of or characteristic of the lower middle class, esp. with reference to a perceived conventionalism and conservatism.

▶ *n.* (*pl.* **pet·its bour·geois** *pronunc.* same) a member of the lower middle class, esp. when perceived as conventional and conservative.

pe·tite /pəˈtēt/ ▶ *adj.* (of a woman) having a small and attractively dainty build. ■ (of a size of women's clothing) smaller than standard.

pe·tite bour·geoi·sie /pəˈtēt ˌbŏŏrzhwäˈzē/ (also **pe·tit bourgeoisie**) ▶ *n.* (**the petite bourgeoisie**) [treated as *sing.* or *pl.*] the lower middle class.

pe·tit four /ˈpetē ˈfôr/ ▶ *n.* (*pl.* **pe·tits fours** /ˈpetē ˈfôrz/ or **pe·tit fours** /ˈpetē ˈfôrz/) a very small fancy cake, cookie, or confection, typically made with marzipan and traditionally served after a meal.

pe·ti·tion /pəˈtishən/ ▶ *n.* a formal written request, typically one signed by many people, appealing to authority with respect to a particular cause. ■ an appeal or request, esp. a solemn or humble one to a deity or a superior. ■ *Law* an application to a court for a writ, judicial action in a suit, etc.

▶ *v.* [*tr.*] make or present a formal request to (an authority) with respect to a particular cause. ■ make a solemn or humble appeal to (a figure of authority). ■ *Law* make a formal application to (a court) for a writ, judicial action in a suit, etc.: *the custodial parent petitioned the court for payment of the arrears* | [*intr.*] *the process allows both spouses to jointly petition for divorce.* —**pe·ti·tion·ar·y** /-ˌnerē/ *adj.* —**pe·ti·tion·er** *n.*

pe·tit ju·ry /ˈpetē/ ▶ *n.* a jury of twelve persons who listen to the evidence and pronounce a verdict in civil and criminal cases. Compare with GRAND JURY.

pe·tit mal /ˈpetē ˈmäl/ ▶ *n.* a mild form of epilepsy characterized by brief spells of unconsciousness without loss of posture. Compare with GRAND MAL. ■ an epileptic fit of this kind.

pe·tit point /ˈpetē ˌpoint/ ▶ *n.* a type of embroidery on canvas, consisting of small, diagonal, adjacent stitches.

pet peeve ▶ *n. informal* a particular or recurring source of irritation: *limited service is a pet peeve among cell-phone users.*

pet·rel /ˈpetrəl/ ▶ *n.* a seabird (order Procellariiformes, esp. families Procellariidae and Hydrobatidae) related to the shearwaters, typically flying far from land.

pe·tri dish /ˈpētrē/ ▶ *n.* a shallow, circular, transparent dish with a flat lid, used for the culture of microorganisms.

pet·ri·fy /ˈpetrəˌfī/ ▶ *v.* (**-fies, -fied**) [*tr.*] **1** make (someone) so frightened that they are unable to move or think. **2** change (organic matter) into a stony concretion by encrusting or replacing its original substance with a calcareous, siliceous, or other mineral deposit. ■ [*intr.*] (of organic matter) become converted into stone or a stony substance in such a way. ■ *fig.* deprive or become deprived of vitality or the capacity for change: [*tr.*] *death merely petrifies things for those who go on living* | [*intr.*] *the inner life of the communist parties petrified.*

pet·ro·chem·i·cal /ˌpetrōˈkemikəl/ ▶ *adj.* relating to or denoting substances obtained by the refining and processing of petroleum or natural gas. ■ of or relating to petrochemistry.

▶ *n.* (usu. **petrochemicals**) a chemical obtained from petroleum and natural gas. —**pet·ro·chem·is·try** /-əstrē/ *n.*

pet·ro·dol·lar /ˈpetrōˌdälər/ ▶ *n.* a notional unit of currency earned by a country from the export of petroleum.

pet·ro·glyph /ˈpetrəˌglif/ ▶ *n.* a rock carving, esp. a prehistoric one.

pe·trog·ra·phy /pəˈträgrəfē/ ▶ *n.* the branch of science concerned with the description and classification of rocks, esp. by microscopic study. Compare with PETROLOGY. —**pe·trog·ra·pher** *n.* —**pet·ro·graph·ic** /ˌpetrəˈgrafik/ *adj.* —**pet·ro·graph·i·cal** *adj.*

pet·rol /ˈpetrəl/ ▶ *n.* British term for GASOLINE.

pe·tro·le·um /pəˈtrōlēəm/ ▶ *n.* a liquid mixture of hydrocarbons that is present in certain rock strata and can be extracted and refined to produce fuels including gasoline, kerosene, and diesel oil; oil.

pe·tro·le·um jel·ly ▶ *n.* a translucent jelly consisting of a mixture of hydrocarbons, used as a lubricant and ointment.

pe·trol·o·gy /pəˈträləjē/ ▶ *n.* the branch of science concerned with the origin, small-scale structure, and composition of rocks. Compare with LITHOLOGY, PETROGRAPHY. —**pet·ro·log·ic** /ˌpetrəˈläjik/ *adj.* —**pet·ro·log·i·cal** /ˌpetrəˈläjikəl/ *adj.* —**pe·trol·o·gist** /-jist/ *n.*

pet·ti·coat /ˈpetēˌkōt/ ▶ *n.* a woman's light, loose undergarment hanging from the shoulders or the waist, worn under a skirt or dress. ■ [as *adj.*] *inf., often derog.* used to denote female control of something regarded as more commonly dominated by men: *he was in danger of succumbing to the petticoat government of Mary and Sarah.* —**pet·ti·coat·ed** *adj.*

pet·ti·fog /ˈpetēˌfôg; ˈpetēˌfäg/ ▶ *v.* (**-fogged, -fog·ging**) [*intr.*] *rare* quibble about petty points. ■ *archaic* practice legal deception or trickery. —**pet·ti·fog·ger·y** /-ˌfôgərē; -ˈfäg-/ *n.*

pet·ti·fog·ger /ˈpetēˌfôgər; -ˌfäg-/ ▶ *n. archaic* an inferior legal practitioner, esp. one who deals with petty cases or employs dubious practices.

pet·tish /ˈpetisH/ ▶ *adj.* (of a person or their behavior) childishly bad-tempered and petulant. —**pet·tish·ly** *adv.* —**pet·tish·ness** *n.*

pet·ty /ˈpetē/ ▶ *adj.* (**pet·ti·er, pet·ti·est**) **1** of little importance; trivial: *the petty divisions of party politics.* ■ (of behavior) characterized by an undue concern for trivial matters, esp. in a small-minded or spiteful way. **2** of secondary or lesser importance, rank, or scale; minor: *a petty official.* ■ *Law* (of a crime) of lesser importance: *petty theft.* Compare with GRAND. —**pet·ti·ly** /ˈpetəlē/ *adv.* —**pet·ti·ness** /ˈpetēnəs/ *n.*

pet·ty bour·geois ▶ *n.* another term for PETIT BOURGEOIS.

pet·ty bour·geoi·sie ▶ *n.* another term for PETITE BOURGEOISIE.

pet·ty cash ▶ *n.* an accessible store of money kept by an organization for expenditure on small items.

pet·ty of·fi·cer ▶ *n.* a noncommissioned officer in a navy, in particular an NCO in the U.S. Navy or Coast Guard ranking above seaman and below chief petty officer.

pet·u·lant /ˈpeCHələnt/ ▶ *adj.* (of a person or their manner) childishly sulky or bad-tempered. —**pet·u·lance** *n.* —**pet·u·lant·ly** *adv.*

pe·tu·nia /pəˈt(y)ōōnyə/ ▶ *n.* a plant (Petunia × hybrida) of the nightshade family with brightly colored funnel-shaped flowers. Native to tropical America, it has been widely developed as an ornamental hybrid.

pew /pyōō/ ▶ *n.* a long bench with a back, placed in rows in the main part of some churches to seat the congregation. ■ an enclosure or compartment containing a number of seats, used in some churches to seat a particular worshiper or group of worshipers.

pew·ter /ˈpyōōtər/ ▶ *n.* a gray alloy of tin with copper and antimony (formerly, tin and lead). ■ utensils made of this: *the kitchen pewter.* ■ a shade of bluish or silver gray. —**pew·ter·er** *n.*

pe·yo·te /pāˈyōtē/ ▶ *n.* a small, soft, blue-green, spineless cactus

(*Lophophora williamsii*), native to Mexico and the southern U.S. Also called **MESCAL**. ■ a hallucinogenic drug prepared from this cactus, containing mescaline.

PFC (also **Pfc.**) ▶*abbr.* Private First Class.

PG ▶*abbr.* ■ parental guidance suggested, a rating in the Voluntary Movie Rating System indicating that some material may not be suitable for children. ■ paying guest.

pg. ▶*abbr.* page.

PG-13 ▶*symb.* parents strongly cautioned, a rating in the Voluntary Movie Rating System indicating that some material may be inappropriate for children under 13.

PGA ▶*abbr.* Professional Golfers' Association (of America).

PH (also **P.H.**) ▶*abbr.* ■ Public Health. ■ Purple Heart.

pH ▶*n. Chem.* a figure expressing the acidity or alkalinity of a solution on a logarithmic scale on which 7 is neutral, lower values are more acid, and higher values more alkaline. The pH is equal to $-\log_{10} c$, where *c* is the hydrogen ion concentration in moles per liter.

pha·e·ton /ˈfā-itn/ ▶*n. hist.* a light, open, four-wheeled horse-drawn carriage. ■ a vintage touring car.

phage /fāj/ ▶*n.* short for **BACTERIOPHAGE**.

phag·o·cyte /ˈfagəˌsīt/ ▶*n. Physiol.* a type of cell within the body capable of engulfing and absorbing bacteria and other small cells and particles. —**phag·o·cyt·ic** /ˌfagəˈsitik/ *adj.*

pha·lanx /ˈfālaNGks; ˈfal-/ ▶*n.* **1** (*pl.* **pha·lanx·es**) a group of people or things of a similar type forming a compact body or brought together for a common purpose. ■ a body of troops or police officers, standing or moving in close formation. ■ (in ancient Greece) a body of Macedonian infantry with long spears, drawn up in close order with shields overlapping. **2** (*pl.* **pha·lan·ges** /fəˈlanjēz; fāˈlanjēz/) *Anat.* a bone of the finger or toe.

phal·li /ˈfalī/ ▶ plural form of **PHALLUS**.

phal·lic /ˈfalik/ ▶*adj.* of, relating to, or resembling a phallus or erect penis: *a phallic symbol.* ■ *Psychoanalysis* of or denoting the genital phase of psychosexual development, esp. in males. —**phal·li·cal·ly** /-(ə)lē/ *adv.*

phal·lus /ˈfaləs/ ▶*n.* (*pl.* **phal·li** /ˈfalī/ or **phal·lus·es**) a penis, esp. when erect (typically used with reference to male potency or dominance). ■ an image or representation of an erect penis, typically symbolizing fertility or potency. —**phal·li·cism** /-ˌsizəm/ *n.* —**phal·lism** /ˈfalizəm/ *n.*

Phan·er·o·zo·ic /ˌfanərəˈzōik/ ▶*adj. Geol.* of, relating to, or denoting the eon covering the whole of time since the beginning of the Cambrian period, and comprising the Paleozoic, Mesozoic, and Cenozoic eras. ■ [as *n.*] (**the Phanerozoic**) the Phanerozoic eon or the system of rocks deposited during it.

phan·tasm /ˈfantazəm/ ▶*n. poetic/lit.* a figment of the imagination; an illusion or apparition. ■ *archaic* an illusory likeness of something: *every phantasm of a hope was quickly nullified.* —**phan·tas·mal** /fanˈtazməl/ *adj.* —**phan·tas·mic** /fanˈtazmik/ *adj.*

phan·tas·ma·go·ri·a /fanˌtazməˈɡôrēə/ ▶*n.* a sequence of real or imaginary images like that seen in a dream. —**phan·tas·ma·gor·ic** /-ˈɡôrik/ *adj.* —**phan·tas·ma·gor·i·cal** /ˈɡôrikəl/ *adj.*

phan·tom /ˈfantəm/ ▶*n.* a ghost: *a phantom who haunts lonely roads* | *fig. the centrist and conservative parties were mere phantoms in 1943* | [as *adj.*] *a phantom ship.* ■ a figment of the imagination: *he tried to clear the phantoms from his head and grasp reality* | [as *adj.*] *the women suffered from phantom pain.* ■ [as *adj.*] denoting a financial arrangement or transaction that has been invented for fraudulent purposes but that does not really exist: *he diverted an estimated $1,500,000 into "phantom" bank accounts.*

Phar·aoh /ˈfarˌō; ˈfe(ə)rˌō; ˈfāˌrō/ (also **phar·aoh**) ▶*n.* a ruler in ancient Egypt. —**phar·a·on·ic** /ˌfarāˈnik; ˌfe(ə)r-/ *adj.*

Phar·i·see /ˈfarəsē/ ▶*n.* a member of an ancient Jewish sect, distinguished by strict observance of the traditional and written law. ■ a self-righteous person; a hypocrite.

phar·ma·ceu·ti·cal /ˌfärməˈso͞otikəl/ ▶*adj.* of or relating to medicinal drugs, or their preparation, use, or sale.
▶*n.* (usu. **pharmaceuticals**) a compound manufactured for use as a medicinal drug. ■ (**pharmaceuticals**) companies manufacturing drugs. —**phar·ma·ceu·ti·cal·ly** /-(ə)lē/ *adv.* —**phar·ma·ceu·tics** /-so͞otiks/ *n.*

phar·ma·cist /ˈfärməsist/ ▶*n.* a person who is professionally qualified to prepare and dispense medicinal drugs.

phar·ma·col·o·gy /ˌfärməˈkäləjē/ ▶*n.* the branch of medicine concerned with the uses, effects, and modes of action of drugs. —**phar·ma·co·log·ic** /ˌfärməkəˈläjik/ *adj.* —**phar·ma·co·log·i·cal** /-ˈläjikəl/ *adj.* —**phar·ma·co·log·i·cal·ly** *adv.* —**phar·ma·col·o·gist** /-ˈkäləjist/ *n.*

phar·ma·co·pe·ia /ˌfärməkəˈpēə/ (also *chiefly Brit.* **phar·ma·co·poe·ia**) ▶*n.* a book, esp. an official publication, containing a list of medicinal drugs with their effects and directions for their use. ■ a stock of medicinal drugs.

phar·ma·cy /ˈfärməsē/ ▶*n.* (*pl.* **-cies**) a store where medicinal drugs are dispensed and sold. ■ the science or practice of the preparation and dispensing of medicinal drugs.

phar·ynx /ˈfariNGks/ ▶*n.* (*pl.* **pha·ryn·ges** /fəˈrinjēz/ or **phar·ynx·es**) *Anat. & Zool.* the membrane-lined cavity behind the nose and mouth, connecting them to the esophagus. —**pha·ryn·ge·al** /fəˈrinjēəl/ *adj.*

phase /fāz/ ▶*n.* **1** a distinct period or stage in a process of change or forming part of something's development: *the final phases of the war* | [as *adj.*] *phase two of the development is in progress.* ■ a stage in a person's psychological development, esp. a period of temporary unhappiness or difficulty during adolescence or a particular stage during childhood: *you are going through a phase.* ■ each of the aspects of the moon or a planet, according to the amount of its illumination, esp. the new moon, the first quarter, the full moon, and the last quarter. **2** *Zool.* a genetic or seasonal variety of an animal's coloration. ■ a stage in the life cycle or annual cycle of an animal. **3** *Chem.* a distinct and homogeneous form of matter (i.e., a particular solid, liquid, or gas) separated by its surface from other forms. **4** *Physics* the relationship in time between the successive states or cycles of an oscillating or repeating system (such as an alternating electric current or a sound wave) and either a fixed reference point or the states or cycles of another system with which it may or may not be in synchrony.
▶*v.* [*tr.*] (usu. **be phased**) carry out (something) in gradual stages: *the work is being phased over a number of years.* ■ (**phase something in/out**) introduce into (or withdraw from) use in gradual stages: *our armed forces policy was to be phased in over 10 years.* ▷early 19th cent. (denoting each aspect of the moon): from French *phase*, based on Greek *phasis* 'appearance,' from the base of *phainein* 'to show.'
▶ □ **in** (or **out of**) **phase** being or happening in (or out of) synchrony or harmony: *the cabling work should be carried out in phase with the building work.*

PhD ▶*abbr.* Doctor of Philosophy.

pheas·ant /ˈfezənt/ ▶*n.* a large long-tailed game bird (family Phasianidae) native to Asia, the male of which typically has very showy plumage. Its several species include the widely introduced **ring-necked pheasant** (*Phasianus colchicus*).

phen·cy·cli·dine /fenˈsīkliˌdēn; -ˈsik-/ (abbr.: **PCP**) ▶*n.* a synthetic compound used as a veterinary anesthetic and in hallucinogenic drugs such as angel dust.

phe·no·bar·bi·tal /ˌfēnōˈbärbiˌtôl/ ▶*n. Med.* a narcotic and sedative barbiturate drug used chiefly to treat epilepsy.

phe·nol /ˈfēˌnôl; -ˌnäl/ ▶*n. Chem.* a mildly acidic toxic white crystalline solid, C_6H_5OH, used in chemical manufacture. ■ any compound with a hydroxyl group linked directly to a benzene ring. —**phe·no·lic** /fiˈnälik/ *adj.*

phe·nom·e·na /fəˈnämənə/ ▶ plural form of **PHENOMENON**.

phe·nom·e·nal /fəˈnämənəl/ ▶*adj.* **1** very remarkable; extraordinary. **2** perceptible by the senses or through immediate experience. —**phe·nom·e·nal·ize** /-ˌīz/ *v.* —**phe·nom·e·nal·ly** *adv.*

phe·nom·e·non /fəˈnäməˌnän; -nən/ ▶*n.* (*pl.* **-na** /-nə/) **1** a fact or situation that is observed to exist or happen, esp. one whose cause or explanation is in question: *glaciers are unique and interesting natural phenomena.* ■ a remarkable person, thing, or event. **2** *Philos.* the object of a person's perception; what the senses or the mind notice.

phe·no·type /ˈfēnəˌtīp/ ▶*n. Biol.* the set of observable characteristics of an individual resulting from the interaction of its genotype with the environment. —**phe·no·typ·ic** /ˌfēnəˈtipik/ *adj.* —**phe·no·typ·i·cal** /ˌfēnəˈtipikəl/ *adj.* —**phe·no·typ·i·cal·ly** /ˌfēnəˈtipik(ə)lē/ *adv.*

phen·ter·mine /ˈfentərˌmēn/ ▶*n. Med.* a prescription appetite-suppressant drug that is one of the pair of drugs known as fen-phen.

phen·yl /ˈfenəl; ˈfē-/ ▶*n.* [as *adj.*] *Chem.* of or denoting the radical $-C_6H_5$: *a phenyl group.*

phen·yl·al·a·nine /ˌfenəlˈaləˌnēn; ˌfēnəl-/ ▶*n. Biochem.* an amino acid widely distributed in plant proteins. It is an essential nutrient in the diet of vertebrates.

phen·yl·ke·to·nu·ri·a /ˌfenlˌkētōˈn(y)o͝orēə; ˌfēnl-/ (abbr.: **PKU**) ▶*n. Med.* an inherited inability to metabolize phenylalanine that causes brain and nerve damage if untreated.

pher·o·mone /ˈferəˌmōn/ ▶*n. Zool.* a chemical substance produced and released into the environment by an animal, esp. a mammal or an insect, affecting the behavior or physiology of others of its species. —**pher·o·mo·nal** /ferə'mōnl/ adj.

phew /fyōō/ ▶interj. inf. expressing a strong reaction of relief: *phew, what a year!*

phi /fī/ ▶n. the twenty-first letter of the Greek alphabet (Φ, φ), transliterated as 'ph.'
▶symb. ■ (φ) a plane angle. ■ (φ) a polar coordinate.

phi·al /'fīəl/ ▶n. another term for VIAL.

Phil. ▶abbr. ■ *Bible* Philippians. ■ *Bible* Philemon. ■ Philharmonic. ■ Philippine.

Phil·a·del·phi·a cheese·steak (also **Phil·ly cheesesteak** /'filē/) ▶n. see CHEESE STEAK.

phi·lan·der /fə'landər/ ▶v. [intr.] (of a man) readily or frequently enter into casual sexual relationships with women. —**phi·lan·der·er** n.

phil·an·thrope /'filən,THrōp/ ▶n. archaic term for PHILANTHROPIST.

phil·an·throp·ic /,filən'THrăpik/ ▶adj. (of a person or organization) seeking to promote the welfare of others, esp. by donating money to good causes; generous and benevolent. —**phil·an·throp·i·cal·ly** /-(ə)lē/ adv.

phi·lan·thro·pist /fə'lanTHrəpist/ ▶n. a person who seeks to promote the welfare of others, esp. by the generous donation of money to good causes.

phi·lan·thro·py /fə'lanTHrəpē/ ▶n. the desire to promote the welfare of others, expressed esp. by the generous donation of money to good causes. ■ a philanthropic institution; a charity. —**phi·lan·thro·pism** /-pizəm/ n. —**phi·lan·thro·pize** /-pīz/ v.

phi·lat·e·ly /fə'latl-ē/ ▶n. the collection and study of postage stamps. —**phil·a·tel·ic** /,filə'telik/ adj. —**phil·a·tel·i·cal·ly** /,filə'telik(ə)lē/ adv. —**phi·lat·e·list** /-ist/ n.

phil·har·mon·ic /,filər'mänik; ,filhär-/ ▶adj. devoted to music (chiefly used in the names of orchestras): *the Vienna Philharmonic Orchestra.*
▶n. a philharmonic orchestra or the society that sponsors it (chiefly used in names): *the tireless musicians of the Philharmonic.*

phi·lip·pic /fə'lipik/ ▶n. poetic/lit. a bitter attack or denunciation, esp. a verbal one.

Phil·ip·pine /'filə,pēn/ ▶adj. of or relating to the Philippines. See also FILIPINO.

Phil·is·tine /'filə,stēn; -,stīn/ ▶n. **1** a member of a non-Semitic (perhaps originally Anatolian) people of southern Palestine in ancient times, who came into conflict with the Israelites during the 12th and 11th centuries BC. **2** (usu. **philistine**) a person who is hostile or indifferent to culture and the arts, or who has no understanding of them: [as adj.] *a philistine government.* —**phil·is·tin·ism** /'filəstē,nizəm; fə'listə-/ n.

Phil·lips /'filəps/ ▶adj. trademark denoting a screw with a cross-shaped slot for turning, the head of such a screw, or a corresponding screwdriver.

phil·o·den·dron /,filə'dendrən/ ▶n. (pl. **philodendrons** or **philodendra** /-drə/) a tropical American climbing plant (genus *Philodendron*) of the arum family that is widely grown as a greenhouse or indoor plant.

phi·lol·o·gy /fə'läləjē/ ▶n. the branch of knowledge that deals with the structure, historical development, and relationships of a language or languages. ■ literary or classical scholarship. —**phil·o·lo·gi·an** /,filə'lōjēən/ n. —**phil·o·log·i·cal** /,filə'läjikəl/ adj. —**phil·o·log·i·cal·ly** /,filə'läjik(ə)lē/ adv. —**phil·ol·o·gist** /-jist/ n.

phi·los·o·pher /fə'läsəfər/ ▶n. a person engaged or learned in philosophy, esp. as an academic discipline.

phil·o·soph·i·cal /,filə'säfikəl/ ▶adj. **1** of or relating to the study of the fundamental nature of knowledge, reality, and existence. ■ devoted to the study of such issues: *American Philosophical Society.* **2** having or showing a calm attitude toward disappointments or difficulties. —**phil·o·soph·ic** /-'säfik/ adj. —**phil·o·soph·i·cal·ly** /-ik(ə)lē/ adv.

phi·los·o·phize /fə'läsə,fīz/ ▶v. [intr.] speculate or theorize about fundamental or serious issues, esp. in a tedious or pompous way. ■ [tr.] explain or argue (a point or idea) in terms of one's philosophical theories. —**phi·los·o·phiz·er** n.

phi·los·o·phy /fə'läsəfē/ ▶n. (pl. **-phies**) the study of the fundamental nature of knowledge, reality, and existence, esp. when considered as an academic discipline. ■ a set of views and theories of a particular philosopher concerning such study or an aspect of it: *rival socialist philosophies.* ■ the study of the theoretical basis of a particular branch of knowledge or experience: *the philosophy of science.* ■ a theory or attitude held by a person or organization that acts as a guiding principle for behavior. ▷Middle English: from Old French *philosophie*, via Latin from Greek *philosophia* 'love of wisdom.'

phil·ter /'filtər/ (*Brit.* **phil·tre**) ▶n. a drink supposed to excite sexual love in the drinker.

phish·ing /'fiSHiNG/ ▶n. the activity of defrauding an online account holder of financial information by posing as a legitimate company: [as adj.] *phishing exercises in which criminals create replicas of commercial Web sites.* —**phish** v.

phiz /fiz/ ▶n. *Brit., inf.* a person's face or expression.

phle·bi·tis /flə'bītis/ ▶n. *Med.* inflammation of the walls of a vein. —**phle·bit·ic** /-'bitik/ adj.

phle·bot·o·my /flə'bätəmē/ ▶n. (pl. **-mies**) the surgical opening or puncture of a vein in order to withdraw blood or introduce a fluid. —**phle·bot·o·mist** n. —**phle·bot·o·mize** /-'bätə,mīz/ v. (archaic).

phlegm /flem/ ▶n. the thick viscous substance secreted by the mucous membranes of the respiratory passages, esp. when produced in excessive or abnormal quantities, e.g., when someone is suffering from a cold. ■ (in medieval science and medicine) one of the four bodily humors, believed to be associated with a calm, stolid, or apathetic temperament. ■ calmness of temperament. ▷Middle English *fleem, fleume*, from Old French *fleume*, from late Latin *phlegma* 'clammy moisture (of the body),' from Greek *phlegma* 'inflammation,' from *phlegein* 'to burn.' The spelling change in the 16th cent. was due to association with the Latin and Greek. —**phlegm·y** adj.

phleg·mat·ic /fleg'matik/ ▶adj. (of a person) having an unemotional and stolidly calm disposition. —**phleg·mat·i·cal·ly** /-ik(ə)lē/ adv.

phlo·em /'flō,em/ ▶n. *Bot.* the vascular tissue in plants that conducts sugars and other metabolic products downward from the leaves.

phlo·gis·ton /flō'jistän; -tən/ ▶n. a substance supposed by 18th-century chemists to exist in all combustible bodies, and to be released in combustion.

phlox /fläks/ ▶n. a North American plant (genus *Phlox*, family Polemoniaceae) that typically has dense clusters of colorful scented flowers, widely grown as a rock-garden or border plant.

pho·bi·a /'fōbēə/ ▶n. an extreme or irrational fear of or aversion to something. —**pho·bic** /'fōbik/ adj. & n.

phoe·be /'fēbē/ ▶n. an American tyrant flycatcher (*Sayornis*) with mainly gray-brown or blackish plumage.

Phoe·ni·cian /fə'nēSHən/ ▶n. **1** a member of a Semitic people inhabiting ancient Phoenicia and its colonies. **2** the Semitic language of this people, written in an alphabet that was the ancestor of the Greek and Roman alphabets.
▶adj. of or relating to Phoenicia or its colonies, or its people, language, or alphabet.

phoe·nix /'fēniks/ ▶n. (in classical mythology) a bird that lived for five or six centuries in the Arabian desert, after this time burning itself on a funeral pyre and rising from the ashes with renewed youth. ■ a person or thing regarded as uniquely remarkable in some respect.
▶ □ **rise like a phoenix from the ashes** emerge renewed after apparent disaster or destruction.

phone¹ /fōn/ ▶n. short for TELEPHONE. ■ (**phones**) *inf.* headphones or earphones.
▶v. short for TELEPHONE.

phone² ▶n. *Phonet.* a speech sound; the smallest discrete segment of sound in a stream of speech.

phone book ▶n. a telephone directory.

pho·neme /'fōnēm/ ▶n. *Phonet.* any of the perceptually distinct units of sound in a specified language that distinguish one word from another, for example *p, b, d,* and *t* in the English words *pad, pat, bad,* and *bat.* —**pho·ne·mic** /fə'nēmik; fō-/ adj. —**pho·ne·mics** /fə'nēmiks; fō-/ n.

pho·net·ic /fə'netik/ ▶adj. *Phonet.* of or relating to speech sounds. ■ (of a system of writing) having a direct correspondence between symbols and sounds. ■ of or relating to phonetics. —**pho·net·i·cal·ly** /-ik(ə)lē/ adv. —**pho·net·i·cism** /-'neti,sizəm/ n. —**pho·net·i·cist** /-'netisist/ n.

pho·net·ics /fə'netiks/ ▶pl. n. [treated as *sing.*] the study and classification of speech sounds. —**pho·ne·ti·cian** /,fōnə'tiSHən/ n.

phon·ic /'fänik/ ▶adj. of or relating to speech sounds. ■ of or relating to phonics. —**phon·i·cal·ly** /ik(ə)lē/ adv.

phon·ics /'fäniks/ ▶pl. n. [treated as *sing.*] a method of teaching people to read by correlating sounds with letters or groups of letters in an alphabetic writing system.

pho·no /'fōnō/ ▶n. short for PHONOGRAPH.
▶adj. denoting a type of plug, and the corresponding socket, used with audio and video equipment, in which one conductor is cylindrical and the other is a central prong that extends beyond it.

pho·no·gram /'fōnə,gram/ ▶n. *Phonet.* a symbol representing a vocal sound.

pho·no·graph /'fōnə,graf/ ▶n. a record player. ■ *chiefly hist.* an early sound-reproducing machine that used cylinders to record as well as reproduce sound. —**pho·no·graph·ic** /ˌfōnə'grafik/ adj.

pho·nol·o·gy /fə'näləjē; fō-/ ▸n. the branch of linguistics that deals with systems of sounds, esp. in a particular language. ■ the system of relationships among the speech sounds that constitute the fundamental components of a language. —**pho·no·log·i·cal** /ˌfōnə'läjikəl/ adj. —**pho·no·log·i·cal·ly** /ˌfōnə'läjik(ə)lē/ adv. —**pho·nol·o·gist** /-jist/ n.

pho·ny /'fōnē/ (also **pho·ney**) inf. ▸adj. (**-ni·er, -ni·est**) not genuine; fraudulent: I thought your accent was a bit phony.
▸n. (pl. **-nies**) a fraudulent person or thing. ▷late 19th cent.: of unknown origin. —**pho·ni·ly** /'fōnilē/ adv. —**pho·ni·ness** n.

phoo·ey /'fōōē/ inf. ▸interj. used to express disdain or disbelief: I say phooey to all their money and fine clothes.
▸n. nonsense: those excuses are a lot of phooey.

phos·gene /'fäsjēn/ ▸n. Chem. a colorless poisonous gas, $COCl_2$, made by the reaction of chlorine and carbon dioxide. It was used as a poison gas, notably in World War I.

phos·phate /'fäsfāt/ ▸n. **1** Chem. a salt or ester of phosphoric acid, containing PO_4^{3-} or a related anion or a group such as $-OPO(OH)_2$. **2** a soft drink containing phosphoric acid, soda water, and flavoring.

phos·pho·lip·id /ˌfäsfō'lipid/ ▸n. Biochem. a lipid containing a phosphate group in its molecule, e.g., lecithin.

phos·phor /'fäsfər/ ▸n. a synthetic fluorescent or phosphorescent substance, esp. any of those used to coat the screens of cathode-ray tubes.

phos·pho·rat·ed /'fäsfəˌrātid/ ▸adj. combined or impregnated with phosphorus.

phos·pho·res·cence /ˌfäsfə'resəns/ ▸n. light emitted by a substance without combustion or perceptible heat. ■ the emission of radiation in a similar manner to fluorescence but on a longer timescale, so that emission continues after excitation ceases. —**phos·pho·resce** v. —**phos·pho·res·cent** adj.

phos·pho·rus /'fäsfərəs/ ▸n. the chemical element of atomic number 15, a poisonous, combustible nonmetal. (Symbol: **P**). —**phos·phor·ic** /fäs'fôrik/ adj. —**phos·phor·ous** /-fərəs/ adj.

pho·to /'fōtō/ ▸n. (pl. **-tos**) a photograph. ■ inf. a photo finish.

pho·to·cell /'fōtōˌsel/ ▸n. short for PHOTOELECTRIC CELL.

pho·to·chem·is·try /ˌfōtō'keməstrē/ ▸n. the branch of chemistry concerned with the chemical effects of light. —**pho·to·chem·i·cal** /-ikəl/ adj

pho·to·com·po·si·tion /ˌfōtōˌkämpə'zishən/ ▸n. Printing the setting of material to be printed by projecting it onto photographic film from which the printing surface is prepared.

pho·to·con·duc·tiv·i·ty /ˌfōtōˌkändak'tivitē/ ▸n. increased electrical conductivity caused by the presence of light. —**pho·to·con·duc·tive** /-kən'dəktiv/ adj. —**pho·to·con·duc·tor** /-kən'dəktər/ n.

pho·to·cop·i·er /'fōtəˌkäpēər/ ▸n. a machine for making photocopies.

pho·to·cop·y /'fōtəˌkäpē/ ▸n. (pl. **-cop·ies**) a photographic copy of printed or written material produced by a process involving the action of light on a specially prepared surface.
▸v. (**-cop·ies, -cop·ied**) [tr.] make a photocopy of. —**pho·to·cop·i·a·ble** /-ˌkäpēəbəl/ adj.

pho·to·e·lec·tric /ˌfōtōi'lektrik/ ▸adj. characterized by or involving the emission of electrons from a surface by the action of light. —**pho·to·e·lec·tric·i·ty** /ˌfōtōiˌlek'trisitē/ n.

pho·to·e·lec·tric cell ▸n. a device that generates an electric current or voltage dependent on the degree of illumination.

pho·to fin·ish ▸n. a close finish of a race in which the winner is identifiable only from a photograph taken at the finish line.

pho·to·gen·ic /ˌfōtō'jenik/ ▸adj. **1** (esp. of a person) looking attractive in photographs or on film: a photogenic child. **2** Biol. (of an organism or tissue) producing or emitting light. —**pho·to·gen·i·cal·ly** /-(ə)lē/ adv.

pho·to·graph /'fōtəˌgraf/ ▸n. a picture made using a camera, in which an image is focused onto film or other light-sensitive material and then made visible and permanent by chemical treatment.
▸v. [tr.] take a photograph of. ■ [intr.] appear in a particular way when in a photograph: that cityscape photographs well. —**pho·to·graph·a·ble** adj. —**pho·tog·ra·pher** /fə'tägrəfər/ n. —**pho·to·graph·ic** /ˌfōtə'grafik/ adj. —**pho·to·graph·i·cal·ly** /ˌfōtə'grafik(ə)lē/ adv.

pho·tog·ra·phy /fə'tägrəfē/ ▸n. the art or practice of taking and processing photographs.

pho·to·gra·vure /ˌfōtəgrə'vyo͝or/ ▸n. an image produced from a photographic negative transferred to a metal plate and etched in. ■ the production of images in this way.

pho·to·jour·nal·ism /ˌfōtō'jərnəˌlizəm/ ▸n. the art or practice of

communicating news by photographs, esp. in magazines. —**pho·to·jour·nal·ist** n.

pho·ton /'fōtän/ ▸n. Physics a particle representing a quantum of light or other electromagnetic radiation. A photon carries energy proportional to the radiation frequency but has zero rest mass.

pho·to·sen·si·tive /ˌfōtə'sensitiv/ ▸adj. having a chemical, electrical, or other response to light: photosensitive cells | photosensitive drugs. —**pho·to·sen·si·tiv·i·ty** /-ˌsensə'tivitē/ n.

pho·to·sphere /'fōtəˌsfi(ə)r/ ▸n. Astron. the luminous envelope of a star from which its light and heat radiate. —**pho·to·spher·ic** /ˌfōtə'sfi(ə)rik; 'sferik/ adj.

pho·to·stat /'fōtōˌstat/ (also **Pho·to·stat**) ▸n. trademark a type of machine for making photocopies on special paper. ■ a copy made by this means.
▸v. (**-stat·ed, -stat·ing**) [tr.] make a copy of (a document) using a photostat machine. —**pho·to·stat·ic** /ˌfōtō'statik/ adj.

pho·to·syn·the·sis /ˌfōtō'sinThəsis/ ▸n. the process by which green plants and some other organisms use sunlight to synthesize organic compounds from carbon dioxide and water. Photosynthesis generates oxygen as a byproduct. —**pho·to·syn·the·size** v. —**pho·to·syn·thet·ic** /-ˌsin'Thetik/ adj. —**pho·to·syn·thet·i·cal·ly** /-ˌsin'Thetik(ə)lē/ adv.

pho·to·vol·ta·ic /ˌfōtəvōl'tāik; ˌfōtōväl-/ ▸adj. relating to the production of electric current at the junction of two substances exposed to light.

phras·al /'frāzəl/ ▸adj. Gram. consisting of a phrase or phrases: the text fragments itself into phrasal units. —**phras·al·ly** adv.

phras·al verb ▸n. Gram. an idiomatic phrase consisting of a verb and another element, typically either an adverb, as in break down, or a preposition, for example see to.

phrase /frāz/ ▸n. a small group of words standing together as a conceptual unit. ■ an idiomatic or pithy expression. ■ Mus. a group of notes forming a distinct unit within a longer passage. ■ Ballet a group of steps within a longer sequence or dance.
▸v. [tr.] put into a particular form of words. ■ divide (music) into phrases in a particular way, esp. in performance: [as n.] (**phrasing**) original phrasing brought out unexpected aspects of the music. ▷mid 16th cent. (in the sense 'style or manner of expression'): via late Latin from Greek phrasis, from phrazein 'declare, tell.'

phrase·ol·o·gy /ˌfrāzē'äləjē/ ▸n. (pl. **-gies**) a mode of expression, esp. one characteristic of a particular speaker or writer: legal phraseology. —**phra·se·o·log·i·cal** /-zēə'läjikəl/ adj.

phre·nol·o·gy /fre'näləjē/ ▸n. chiefly hist. the detailed study of the shape and size of the cranium as a supposed indication of character and mental abilities. —**phre·no·log·i·cal** /ˌfrenə'läjikəl/ adj. —**phre·nol·o·gist** /-jist/ n.

phy·la /'fīlə/ ▸ plural form of PHYLUM.

phy·lac·ter·y /fī'laktərē/ ▸n. (pl. **-ter·ies**) a small leather box containing Hebrew texts on vellum, worn by Jewish men at morning prayer.

phyl·lo·qui·none /ˌfilō'kwinōn; -kwi'nōn/ ▸n. Biochem. one of the K vitamins, found in cabbage, spinach, and other leafy green vegetables, and essential for the blood-clotting process. Also called VITAMIN K_1 (see VITAMIN K).

phy·lum /'fīləm/ ▸n. (pl. **-la** /-lə/) Zool. a principal taxonomic category that ranks above class and below kingdom. ■ Linguistics a group of languages related to each other less closely than those forming a family, esp. one in which the relationships are disputed or unclear.

phys·ic /'fizik/ archaic ▸n. medicine, esp. a cathartic.

phys·i·cal /'fizikəl/ ▸adj. **1** of or relating to the body as opposed to the mind. ■ involving bodily contact or activity: verbal or physical abuse. ■ sexual: a physical relationship. **2** of or relating to things perceived through the senses as opposed to the mind; tangible or concrete: physical assets such as houses. ■ of or relating to physics or the operation of natural forces generally: physical laws.
▸n. (also **physical examination**) a medical examination to determine a person's bodily fitness. —**phys·i·cal·i·ty** /ˌfizi'kalitē/ n. —**phys·i·cal·ly** /-ik(ə)lē/ adv. —**phys·i·cal·ness** n.
▸ □ **get physical** inf. become aggressive or violent. ■ become sexually intimate with someone.

phys·i·cal ed·u·ca·tion ▸n. instruction in physical exercise and games, esp. in schools.

phys·i·cal sci·enc·es ▸pl. n. the sciences concerned with the study of inanimate natural objects, including physics, chemistry, astronomy, and related subjects. Often contrasted with LIFE SCIENCES.

Pronunciation Key ə ago, up; ər over, fur; a hat; ā ate; ä car; CH chin; e let; ē see; e(ə)r air; i fit; ī by; i(ə)r ear; NG sing; ō go; ô law, for; oi toy; o͞o good; o͞o goo; ou out; SH she; TH thin; T͟H then; (h)w why; ZH vision

phys·i·cal ther·a·py ▶*n.* the treatment of disease, injury, or deformity by physical methods such as massage, heat treatment, and exercise rather than by drugs or surgery. —**phys·i·cal ther·a·pist** *n.*

phy·si·cian /fɪˈzɪsHən/ ▶*n.* a person qualified to practice medicine. ■ a healer: *physicians of the soul.*

phys·i·cist /ˈfɪzəsist/ ▶*n.* an expert in or student of physics.

phys·ics /ˈfɪziks/ ▶*pl. n.* [treated as *sing.*] the branch of science concerned with the nature and properties of matter and energy. The subject matter of physics includes mechanics, heat and other radiation, sound, electricity, magnetism, and the structure of atoms. ■ the physical properties and phenomena of something.

phys·i·og·no·my /ˌfɪzēˈä(g)nəmē/ ▶*n.* (*pl.* **-mies**) a person's facial features or expression, esp. when regarded as indicative of character or ethnic origin. ■ the supposed art of judging character from facial characteristics. ■ the general form or appearance of something: *the physiognomy of the landscape.* —**phys·i·og·nom·ic** /ˌfɪzēəˈnämik/ *adj.* —**phys·i·og·nom·i·cal** /ˌfɪzēəˈnämikəl/ *adj.* —**phys·i·og·nom·i·cal·ly** /ˌfɪzēə-ˈnämik(ə)lē/ *adv.* —**phys·i·og·no·mist** *n.*

phys·i·ol·o·gy /ˌfɪzēˈäləjē/ ▶*n.* the branch of biology that deals with the normal functions of living organisms and their parts. ■ the way in which a living organism or bodily part functions. —**phys·i·o·log·ic** /ˌfɪzēəˈläjik/ *adj.* —**phys·i·o·log·i·cal** /ˌfɪzēəˈläjikəl/ *adj.* —**phys·i·o·log·i·cal·ly** /ˌfɪzēəˈläjik(ə)lē/ *adv.* —**phys·i·ol·o·gist** /-jist/ *n.*

phy·sique /fɪˈzēk/ ▶*n.* the form, size, and development of a person's body: *a sturdy, muscular physique | they were much alike in physique.*

phy·to·es·tro·gen /ˌfɪtōˈestrəjən/ ▶*n.* an estrogen occurring naturally in legumes, considered beneficial in some diets.

phy·to·ge·og·ra·phy /ˌfɪtōjēˈägrəfē/ ▶*n.* the branch of botany that deals with the geographical distribution of plants. —**phy·to·ge·o·graph·ic** *adj.* —**phy·to·ge·o·graph·i·cal** *adj.*

phy·to·nu·tri·ent /ˌfɪtōˈnoōtrēənt/ ▶*n.* a substance of plant origin that has nutritional value. ■ a nutritional supplement based on such a substance; a nutraceutical.

phy·to·plank·ton /ˌfɪtōˈplaNGktən/ ▶*n.* Biol. plankton consisting of microscopic plants.

phy·to·san·i·tar·y /ˌfɪtōˈsaniterē/ ▶*adj.* (of agricultural goods crossing borders) sanitary with regard to pests and pathogens: *a point-of-origin phytosanitary certificate.*

PI ▶*abbr.* private investigator.

pi /pī/ ▶*n.* the sixteenth letter of the Greek alphabet (Π, π), transliterated as 'p.' ■ the numerical value of the ratio of the circumference of a circle to its diameter (approx. 3.14159). ■ Chem. & Physics relating to or denoting an electron or orbital with one unit of angular momentum about an internuclear axis. ▶*symb.* ■ (π) the numerical value of pi. ■ (Π) osmotic pressure. ■ (Π) mathematical product.

pi·a ma·ter /ˈpīə ˈmātər; ˈpēə ˈmätər/ ▶*n.* Anat. the delicate innermost membrane enveloping the brain and spinal cord.

pi·a·nis·si·mo /ˌpēəˈnisiˌmō/ Mus. ▶*adv.* & *adj.* (esp. as a direction) very soft or softly.

pi·an·ist /ˈpēənist; pēˈanist/ ▶*n.* a person who plays the piano, esp. professionally.

pi·an·o¹ /pēˈanō/ ▶*n.* (*pl.* **-os**) a large keyboard musical instrument with a wooden case enclosing a soundboard and metal strings, which are struck by hammers when the keys are depressed.

pi·a·no² /pēˈänō; pēˈanō/ Mus. ▶*adv.* & *adj.* (esp. as a direction) soft or softly.

pi·an·o·forte /pēˌanōˈfôrtā; pēˈanōˌfôrt/ ▶*n.* formal term for PIANO¹.

pi·as·ter /pēˈastər/ (also **pi·as·tre**) ▶*n.* a monetary unit of several Middle Eastern countries, equal to one hundredth of a pound.

pi·az·za /pēˈätsə; pēˈazə/ ▶*n.* **1** /pēˈätsə/ a public square or marketplace, esp. in an Italian town. **2** /pēˈazə/ the veranda of a house.

pic /pik/ ▶*n.* (*pl.* **pics** or **pix** /piks/) inf. a photograph or movie; a picture.

pi·ca¹ /ˈpīkə/ ▶*n.* Printing a unit of type size and line length equal to 12 points (about 1/6 inch or 4.2 mm). ■ a size of letter in typewriting, with 10 characters to the inch (about 3.9 to the centimeter).

pi·ca² ▶*n.* Med. a tendency or craving to eat substances other than normal food (such as clay, plaster, or ashes), occurring during childhood or pregnancy, or as a symptom of disease.

pi·ca·dor /ˈpikəˌdôr/ ▶*n.* a bullfighter on horseback who pricks the bull with a lance to weaken it and goad it.

pic·a·resque /ˌpikəˈresk/ ▶*adj.* of or relating to a style of fiction dealing with the adventures of a roguish but appealing hero.

pic·a·yune /ˌpikiˈyoōn/ ▶*adj.* inf. petty; worthless. ▶*n.* a small coin of little value, esp. a 5-cent piece. ■ inf. an insignificant person or thing.

pic·ca·lil·li /ˈpikəˌlilē/ ▶*n.* (*pl.* **-lies** or **-lis**) a relish of chopped vegetables, mustard, and hot spices.

pic·co·lo /ˈpikəˌlō/ ▶*n.* (*pl.* **-los**) a small flute sounding an octave higher than the ordinary one.

pick¹ /pik/ ▶*v.* **1** [*tr.*] take hold of and remove (a flower, fruit, or vegetable) from where it is growing. ■ [*tr.*] take hold of and lift or move: *picking her up, he carried her into the next room.* ■ [*intr.*] (**pick up**) Golf lift up one's ball, esp. when conceding a hole. **2** [*tr.*] choose (someone or something) from a number of alternatives, typically after careful thought: *she left Jed to pick out some toys* | [*intr.*] *this time, I get to pick.* ■ (**pick one's way**) walk slowly and carefully, selecting the best or safest places to put one's feet. **3** [*intr.*] repeatedly pull at something with one's fingers: *the old woman was picking at the sheet.* ■ [*tr.*] make (a hole) in fabric by doing this. ■ eat food or a meal in small amounts or without much appetite: *she picked at her breakfast.* ■ criticize someone in a niggling way: *now, please don't start picking at Ruth.* ■ [*tr.*] remove unwanted matter from (one's nose or teeth) by using one's finger or a pointed instrument. ■ [*tr.*] pluck the strings of (a guitar or banjo). ■ [*tr.*] (**pick something out**) play a tune on such an instrument slowly or with difficulty.

▶*phrasal v.* ■ **pick someone/something off** shoot a member of a group of people or things, aiming carefully from a distance. □ **pick on** repeatedly single (someone) out for blame, criticism, or unkind treatment. □ **pick someone/something out** distinguish someone or something among a group of people or things. □ **pick something over** (or **pick through**) examine or sort through a number of items carefully: *they picked through the charred remains of their home.* □ **pick up** become better; improve. ■ become stronger; increase: *the wind has picked up.* □ **pick oneself up** stand up again after a fall. □ **pick someone up** go somewhere to collect someone, typically in one's car. ■ stop for someone and take them into one's vehicle or vessel. ■ inf. arrest someone. ■ inf. casually strike up a relationship with someone one has never met before, as a sexual overture. □ **pick something up 1** collect something that has been left elsewhere. ■ inf. pay the bill for something, esp. when others have contributed to the expense. ■ tidy a room or building. **2** obtain, acquire, or learn something, esp. without formal arrangements or instruction. ■ catch an illness or infection. **3** detect or receive a signal or sound, esp. by means of electronic apparatus. ■ (also **pick up on**) become aware of or sensitive to something: *she is very quick to pick up emotional atmospheres.* ■ find and take a particular road or route. **4** (also **pick up**) resume something. ■ (also **pick up on**) refer to or develop a point or topic mentioned earlier. □ **pick up after** tidy up things left strewn around by (someone).

▶*n.* **1** an act or the right of selecting something from among a group of alternatives. ■ (**the pick of**) inf. the person or thing perceived as the best in a particular group: *he was the pick of the bunch.* ■ someone or something that has been selected: *the club made him their first pick.* **2** Basketball an act of blocking or screening a defensive player from the ball handler, allowing an open shot. —**pick·a·ble** /ˈpikəbəl/ *adj.*

▶ □ **pick and choose** select only the best or most desirable from among a number of alternatives. □ **pick someone's brains** (or **brain**) inf. obtain information by questioning someone who is better informed. □ **pick a fight** (or **quarrel**) talk or behave in such a way as to provoke an argument or fight. □ **pick holes in** find fault with. □ **pick a lock** open a lock with an instrument other than the proper key. □ **pick someone's pockets** steal something from another person's pocket. □ **pick someone/something to pieces** (or **apart**) criticize someone or something severely and in detail. □ **pick up the pieces** restore one's life or a situation to a more normal state, typically after a shock or disaster. □ **pick up speed** (or **steam**) (of a vehicle) go faster; accelerate.

pick² ▶*n.* **1** a tool consisting of a long handle set at right angles in the middle of a curved iron or steel bar with a point at one end and a chisel edge or point at the other, used for breaking up hard ground or rock. **2** an instrument for picking: *an ebony hair pick.* ■ inf. a plectrum: *a pink guitar pick.*

pick·ax /ˈpikˌaks/ (also **pick·axe**) ▶*n.* another term for PICK² (sense 1). ▶*v.* [*tr.*] break or strike with a pickax.

pick·er /ˈpikər/ ▶*n.* a person or machine that gathers or collects something: *a tomato picker.* ■ a person who plays a plucked instrument, esp. a guitar, banjo, or mandolin: *a capable singer, writer, and picker.*

grand piano

pick·er·el /ˈpik(ə)rəl/ ▸n. (pl. same or **pickerels**) a small North American pike (genus *Esox*). ■ a young pike.

pick·et /ˈpikit/ ▸n. **1** a person or group of people standing outside a place of work or other venue, protesting or trying to persuade others not to enter during a strike. ■ a blockade of a workplace or other venue staged by such a person or group. **2** *chiefly hist.* a small body of troops or a single soldier sent out to watch for the enemy. **3** [usu. as *adj.*] a pointed wooden stake driven into the ground, typically to form a fence or palisade or to tether a horse: *a cedar-picket stockade.*
▸v. (**-et·ed**, **-et·ing**) [tr.] **1** act as a picket outside (a place of work or other venue): *strikers picketed the newspaper's main building* | [intr.] *18,000 people turned up to picket.* **2** tether (an animal). —**pick·et·er** n.

pick·et line ▸n. a boundary established by workers on strike, esp. at the entrance to the place of work, that others are asked not to cross.

pick·ings /ˈpikiNGz/ ▸pl. n. **1** profits or gains that are made effortlessly or dishonestly, as by picking: *he found, as strays often do,* **slim pickings.** **2** remaining scraps or leftovers.

pick·le /ˈpikəl/ ▸n. **1** a small cucumber preserved in vinegar, brine, or a similar solution. ■ any relish preserved in this way. ■ the liquid used to preserve food or other perishable items. ■ an acid solution for cleaning metal objects. **2** *inf.* a difficult or messy situation: *in a pickle.*
▸v. [tr.] preserve (food or other items) in vinegar, brine, or a similar solution. ■ immerse (a metal object) in an acid solution for cleaning.

pick·lock /ˈpikˌläk/ ▸n. a person who picks locks. ■ an instrument for picking locks.

pick-me-up ▸n. *inf.* a thing that makes one feel more energetic or cheerful. ■ an alcoholic drink.

pick·pock·et /ˈpikˌpäkət/ ▸n. a person who steals from other people's pockets.
▸v. [tr.] steal from the pockets of (someone). ■ [intr.] steal from other people's pockets.

pick·up /ˈpikˌəp/ ▸n. **1** (also **pickup truck**) a small truck with an enclosed cab and open back. **2** an act of collecting a person or goods, esp. in a vehicle: *curbside pickup* | [as *adj.*] *travel by bus from your local pickup point to your hotel.* **3** the reception of signals, esp. interference or noise, by electrical apparatus. **4** *inf.* a casual encounter with someone, with a view to having a sexual relationship. ■ a person met in such an encounter. **5** an improvement in an economic indicator. **6** a device that produces an electrical signal in response to some other kind of signal or change, in particular: ■ the cartridge of a record player, carrying the stylus. ■ a device on a musical instrument, particularly an electric guitar, that converts sound vibrations into electrical signals for amplification. **7** *Mus.* a note or series of introductory notes leading into the opening part of a tune. **8** *Fishing* a semicircular loop of metal for guiding the line back onto the spool as it is reeled in.
▸adj. informal and spontaneous: *a full-court pickup basketball game.*

pick·y /ˈpikē/ ▸adj. (**pick·i·er**, **pick·i·est**) *inf.* fastidious, esp. excessively so: *she had been a picky eater as a child.* —**pick·i·ness** /-ēnis/ n.

pic·nic /ˈpikˌnik/ ▸n. an outing or occasion that involves taking a packed meal to be eaten outdoors. ■ a meal eaten outdoors on such an occasion.
▸v. (**-nicked**, **-nick·ing**) [intr.] have or take part in a picnic. —**pic·nick·er** n.
▸ □ **no picnic** *inf.* used of something difficult or unpleasant.

pi·cot /ˈpēkō/ ▸n. a small loop or series of small loops of thread, typically on the border of a fabric.

pic·quet /piˈkāt/ ▸n. variant spelling of PIQUET.

pic·to·graph /ˈpiktəˌgraf/ (also **pic·to·gram** /-ˌgram/) ▸n. a pictorial symbol for a word or phrase. Pictographs were used as the earliest known form of writing. ■ a pictorial representation of statistics on a chart, graph, or computer screen. —**pic·to·graph·ic** /ˌpiktəˈgrafik/ adj. —**pic·tog·ra·phy** /pikˈtägrəfē/ n.

pic·to·ri·al /pikˈtôrēəl/ ▸adj. of or expressed in pictures; illustrated. ■ suggestive of pictures.
▸n. a newspaper or periodical with pictures as a main feature. —**pic·to·ri·al·ly** adv.

pic·ture /ˈpikCHər/ ▸n. a painting or drawing. ■ a photograph. ■ a portrait. ■ *archaic* a person or thing resembling another closely: *she is the picture of her mother.* ■ *fig.* an impression of something formed from an account or description: *a full picture of the disaster.* ■ an image on a television screen. ■ a movie. ■ (**the pictures**) the movies.
▸v. [tr.] (often **be pictured**) represent (someone or something) in a photograph or picture. ■ describe (someone or something) in a certain way. ■ form a mental image of.
▸ □ **get the picture** *inf.* understand a situation. □ **in the picture** fully informed about something. □ **out of the picture** no longer involved;

irrelevant. □ **the** (or **a**) **picture of** —— the embodiment of a specified state or emotion: *she looked the picture of forbearance.* □ (**as**) **pretty as a picture** very pretty.

pic·tur·esque /ˌpikCHəˈresk/ ▸adj. visually attractive, esp. in a quaint or pretty style. ■ (of language) unusual and vivid. —**pic·tur·esque·ly** adv. —**pic·tur·esque·ness** n.

pic·ture tube ▸n. *Electr.* the cathode-ray tube of a television set designed for the reproduction of television pictures.

pic·ture win·dow ▸n. a large window consisting of one pane of glass, typically in a living room.

pid·dle /ˈpidl/ *inf.* ▸v. [intr.] urinate.
▸phrasal v. □ **piddle around** (or **about**) spend time in trifling activities: *I piddled around the house all day.*
▸n. an act of urinating. ■ urine. —**pid·dler** n.

pidg·in /ˈpijən/ ▸n. [often as *adj.*] a grammatically simplified form of a language, used for communication between people not sharing a common language. Pidgins have a limited vocabulary, some elements of which are taken from local languages. ▷late 19th cent.: Chinese alteration of English *business.*

pidg·in Eng·lish ▸n. a pidgin based on English, esp. as used originally by the Chinese for commerce.

pie¹ /pī/ ▸n. a baked dish of fruit, or meat and vegetables, typically with a top and base of pastry. ■ a pizza.
▸ □ (**as**) **easy as pie** *inf.* very easy. □ **a piece** (or **slice**) **of the pie** a share of an amount of money or business available to be claimed or distributed. □ **pie in the sky** *inf.* used to describe or refer to something that is pleasant to contemplate but is very unlikely to be realized.

pie² ▸n. short for MAGPIE.

pie·bald /ˈpīˌbôld/ ▸adj. (of a horse) having irregular patches of two colors, typically black and white.
▸n. a piebald horse or other animal.

piece /pēs/ ▸n. a portion of an object or of material, produced by cutting, tearing, or breaking the whole. ■ one of the items that were put together to make something and into which it naturally divides: *take a car to pieces.* ■ an item of a particular type, esp. one forming one of a set: *a piece of luggage.* ■ an instance or example: *a crucial piece of evidence.* ■ a financial share. ■ a written, musical, or artistic creation or composition. ■ a coin of specified value: *a 10-cent piece.* ■ a figure or token used to make moves in a board game. ■ *Chess* a king, queen, bishop, knight, or rook, as opposed to a pawn. ■ *inf.* a firearm. ■ *inf., offens.* a woman.
▸v. [tr.] **1** (**piece something together**) assemble something from individual parts. ■ slowly make sense of something from separate facts and pieces of evidence. **2** (**piece something out**) *archaic* extend. **3** *archaic* patch.
▸ □ **a piece of ass** (or **tail**) *vulgar slang* a person, usually a woman, regarded as a sexual partner. □ **a piece of the action** *inf.* a share in the excitement of something. ■ a share in the profits accruing from something. □ **go to pieces** become so nervous or upset that one is unable to behave or perform normally. □ **in one piece** unharmed or undamaged, esp. after a dangerous experience. □ **say one's piece** give one's opinion or make a prepared statement. □ **tear** (or **rip**) **someone/something to pieces** criticize someone or something harshly.

pièce de ré·sis·tance /pēˈes də ˌrəziˈstäns; -räziˈstäns/ ▸n. (esp. with reference to creative work or a meal) the most important or remarkable feature: *the pièce de résistance of the meal was flaming ice cream.*

piece·meal /ˈpēsˌmēl/ ▸adj. & adv. characterized by unsystematic partial measures taken over a period of time: [as *adj.*] *piecemeal development* | [as *adv.*] *some can be installed piecemeal.*

piece of eight ▸n. *hist.* a Spanish dollar, equivalent to 8 reals.

piece·work /ˈpēsˌwərk/ ▸n. work paid for according to the amount produced. —**piece·work·er** n.

pie chart ▸n. a type of graph in which a circle is divided into sectors that each represent a proportion of the whole.

pied /pīd/ ▸adj. having two or more different colors.

pied-à-terre /pēˌyäd ə ˈter/ ▸n. (pl. **pieds-à-terre** pronunc. same) a small apartment, house, or room kept for occasional use.

pied·mont /ˈpēdˌmänt/ ▸n. a gentle slope leading from the base of mountains to a region of flat land.

Pied Pip·er /ˈpīd ˈpīpər/ ▸the hero of *The Pied Piper of Hamelin,* a poem by

Robert Browning (1842). The piper rid the town of Hamelin of rats by enticing them away with his music, and when refused payment he lured away the children of the citizens. ■ [as n.] (**a Pied Piper**) a person who entices people to follow them, esp. to their doom.

pier /pi(ə)r/ ▸n. **1** a structure leading out from the shore into a body of water, in particular: ■ a platform supported on pillars or girders, used as a landing for boats. ■ a similar structure leading out to sea and used as an entertainment area. ■ a breakwater or mole. **2** a solid support designed to sustain vertical pressure, in particular: ■ a pillar supporting an arch or a bridge. ■ a section of a wall between windows or other adjacent openings.

pierce /pi(ə)rs/ ▸v. [tr.] (of a sharp pointed object) go into or through (something). ■ prick (something) with a sharp instrument. ■ make (a hole) with a sharp instrument. ■ make a hole in (the ears, nose, or other part of the body) so as to wear jewelry in them. ■ (usu. **be pierced**) bore a hole or tunnel through: *the dividing wall is pierced by arches and piers.* ■ force or cut a way through: *a shrill voice pierced the air.* —**pierc·er** n.

pie·ro·gi ▸n. variant spelling of PIROGI.

pie·tà /ˌpēäˈtä/ (often **Pie·tà**) ▸n. a picture or sculpture of the Virgin Mary holding the dead body of Jesus Christ on her lap or in her arms.

pi·e·tism /ˈpī-iˌtizəm/ ▸n. pious sentiment, esp. of an exaggerated or affected nature.

pi·e·ty /ˈpīətē/ ▸n. (pl. **-ties**) the quality of being religious or reverent: *acts of piety.* ■ the quality of being dutiful: *filial piety.* ■ a belief or point of view that is accepted with unthinking conventional reverence.

pif·fle /ˈpifəl/ ▸n. & interj. inf. nonsense.

pif·fling /ˈpiflɪNG/ ▸adj. inf. trivial; unimportant.

pig /pig/ ▸n. **1** an omnivorous domesticated hoofed mammal (numerous varieties of *Sus domesticus*) with sparse bristly hair and a flat snout, kept for its meat. The **pig family** (Suidae) also includes the boar and warthog. ■ a wild animal of this family. ■ a young pig; a piglet. ■ the flesh of a pig, esp. a young one, as food. ■ inf. derog. a greedy, dirty, or unpleasant person. ■ inf. derog. a police officer. **2** an oblong mass of iron or lead from a smelting furnace. See also PIG IRON. ■ a device that fits snugly inside an oil or gas pipeline and is sent through it to clean or test the inside, or to act as a barrier.

▸v. (**pigged**, **pigging**) [intr.] **1** inf. gorge oneself with food: *don't pig out on chips.* **2** inf. crowd together with other people in disorderly or dirty conditions. **3** (of a sow) give birth to piglets; farrow. —**pig·gish** adj.

▸ □ **bleed like a pig** bleed copiously. □ **in a pig's eye** inf. expressing scornful disbelief at a statement. □ **a pig in a poke** something that is bought or accepted without knowing its value or seeing it first.

pi·geon[1] /ˈpijən/ ▸n. **1** a stout seed- or fruit-eating bird (family Columbidae) with a small head, short legs, and a cooing voice, typically having gray and white plumage. ■ a pigeon descended from the wild rock dove, kept for racing, showing, and carrying messages, and common as a feral bird in towns. **2** inf. a gullible person, esp. someone swindled in gambling or the victim of a confidence game. **3** *military slang* an aircraft flown on its own side.

pi·geon[2] ▸n. archaic spelling of PIDGIN.

pi·geon·hole /ˈpijənˌhōl/ ▸n. a small recess for a domestic pigeon to nest in. ■ a small compartment, open at the front and forming part of a set, where letters or messages may be left for someone. ■ a similar compartment built into a desk for keeping documents in. ■ fig. a category to which someone or something is assigned.

▸v. [tr.] deposit (a document) into a pigeonhole. ■ assign to a particular category or class, esp. in a manner that is too rigid or exclusive: *a tendency to pigeonhole him as a photographer and neglect his work in painting.* ■ put aside for future consideration: *she pigeonholed her worry about him.*

pi·geon-toed ▸adj. having the toes or feet turned inward.

pig·ger·y /ˈpigərē/ ▸n. (pl. **-er·ies**) **1** a farm where pigs are bred or kept. ■ a pigpen. **2** behavior regarded as characteristic of pigs in greed or unpleasantness.

pig·gy /ˈpigē/ ▸n. (pl. **-gies**) (used by or when talking to children) a pig or piglet.

▸adj. resembling a pig, esp. in features or appetite.

pig·gy·back /ˈpigēˌbak/ ▸n. a ride on someone's back and shoulders.

▸adv. on the back and shoulders of another person. ■ on top of something else: *Dave headed back with the car riding piggyback on his truck.*

▸v. [tr.] carry by or as if by piggyback. ■ mount on or attach to (an existing object or system). ■ [intr.] use existing work or an existing product as a basis or support: *we were piggybacking on their training program.*

▸adj. on the back and shoulders of another person: *enjoying a piggyback ride.* ■ attached to or riding on a larger object: *a telescope with fittings for*

piggyback cameras | fig. a piggyback income tax, under which taxpayers would pay the state 21 percent of whatever they paid the federal government.

pig·gy bank ▸n. a container for saving money in, esp. one shaped like a pig, with a slit through which coins are dropped. ■ fig. savings.

pig·head·ed /ˈpigˌhedid/ ▸adj. stupidly obstinate. —**pig·head·ed·ly** adv. —**pig·head·ed·ness** n.

pig i·ron ▸n. crude iron as first obtained from a smelting furnace, in the form of oblong blocks.

pig Lat·in ▸n. a made-up language formed from English by transferring the initial consonant or consonant cluster of each word to the end of the word and adding a syllable (usually /ā/): so *chicken soup* would be translated to *ickenchay oupsay.*

pig·let /ˈpiglit/ ▸n. a young pig.

pig·ment /ˈpigmənt/ ▸n. the natural coloring matter of animal or plant tissue. ■ a substance used for coloring or painting, esp. a dry powder that, when mixed with oil, water, or another medium, constitutes a paint or ink.

▸v. [tr.] color (something) with or as if with pigment. —**pig·men·tar·y** /-ˌterē/ adj.

pig·men·ta·tion /ˌpigmənˈtāSHən/ ▸n. the natural coloring of animal or plant tissue. ■ the coloring of a person's skin, esp. when abnormal or distinctive.

pig·my ▸n. variant spelling of PYGMY.

pi·gno·li /pinˈyōlē/ ▸pl. n. pine nuts.

pig·pen /ˈpigˌpen/ ▸n. a pen or enclosure for a pig or pigs. ■ a very dirty or untidy house or room.

pig·skin /ˈpigˌskin/ ▸n. **1** the hide of a domestic pig. ■ leather made from this. **2** inf. a football.

pig·sty /ˈpigˌstī/ ▸n. (pl. **-sties**) a pigpen.

pig·tail /ˈpigˌtāl/ ▸n. **1** a braid or gathered hank of hair hanging from the back of the head, or either of a pair at the sides. **2** a short length of flexible braided wire connecting a stationary part to a moving part in an electrical device. **3** a thin twist of tobacco. —**pig·tailed** adj.

pike[1] /pīk/ ▸n. (pl. same) a long-bodied predatory freshwater fish (genus *Esox*, family Esocidae) with a pointed snout and large teeth, of North America and Eurasia. ■ any fish with similar characteristics, such as the walleye.

pike[2] ▸n. hist. an infantry weapon with a pointed steel or iron head on a long wooden shaft.

pike[3] ▸n. short for TURNPIKE.

▸ □ **come down the pike** appear on the scene; come to notice.

pike[4] (also **pike position**) ▸n. [often as adj.] a position in diving or gymnastics in which the body is bent at the waist but the legs remain straight.

pike-perch /ˈpīkˌpərCH/ ▸n. (pl. same) a predatory pikelike freshwater fish (genus *Stizostedion*) of the perch family, esp. the walleye.

pik·er /ˈpīkər/ ▸n. inf. **1** a gambler who makes only small bets. ■ a stingy or cautious person. **2** Austral./NZ a person who withdraws from a commitment.

pi·laf /piˈläf; ˈpēläf/ (also **pi·laff** or **pi·lau** /piˈlou/) ▸n. a Middle Eastern or Indian dish of rice or wheat, with vegetables and spices, typically having added meat or fish.

pi·las·ter /pəˈlastər/ ▸n. a rectangular column, esp. one projecting from a wall. —**pi·las·tered** adj.

pil·chard /ˈpilCHərd/ ▸n. a small, edible, commercially valuable marine fish (*Sardinops* and other genera) of the herring family.

pile[1] /pīl/ ▸n. a heap of things laid or lying one on top of another. ■ inf. a large amount of something. ■ inf. a lot of money. ■ a large imposing building or group of buildings.

▸v. **1** [tr.] place (things) one on top of another. ■ (**be piled with**) be stacked or loaded with. ■ (**pile up**) [intr.] increase in quantity. ■ (**pile something up**) cause to increase in quantity: *the debts he piled up.* ■ (**pile something on**) inf. intensify or exaggerate something for effect: *you can pile on the guilt, but my heart has turned to stone.* **2** [intr.] (**pile in/out**) (of a group of people) get into or out of a vehicle in a disorganized manner. ■ (**pile into**) (of a vehicle) crash into.

▸ □ **pile it on** inf. exaggerate the seriousness of a situation or of someone's behavior to increase guilt or distress.

pile[2] ▸n. a heavy beam or post driven vertically into the bed of a river, soft ground, etc., to support the foundations of a structure.

pile[3] ▸n. the soft projecting surface of a carpet or of a fabric such as velvet, consisting of many small threads.

▸v. [tr.] [usu. in comb.] (**-piled**) furnish with a pile: *a thick-piled carpet.*

pi·le·at·ed wood·peck·er /ˈpīlēˌātid; ˈpil-/ ▸n. a large North American woodpecker (*Dryocopus pileatus*) with mainly black plumage and a red cap and crest.

pile driv·er (also **pile-driv·er**) ▶*n.* a machine for driving piles into the ground. —**pile-driv·ing** *n.* & *adj.*

piles /pīlz/ ▶*pl. n.* hemorrhoids.

pile·up /'pīl,əp/ (also **pile-up**) ▶*n. inf.* **1** a crash involving several vehicles. ■ a confused mass of people fallen on top of one another, esp. in a team game. **2** an accumulation of a specified thing.

pil·fer /'pilfər/ ▶*v.* [*tr.*] steal (typically things of relatively little value). —**pil·fer·age** /-rij/ *n.* —**pil·fer·er** *n.*

pil·grim /'pilgrəm/ ▶*n.* a person who journeys to a sacred place for religious reasons. ■ (usu. **Pilgrim**) a member of a group of English Puritans fleeing religious persecution who founded the colony of Plymouth, Massachusetts, in 1620. ■ a person who travels on long journeys. ▷Middle English: from Provençal *pelegrin*, from Latin *peregrinus* 'foreign.'

pil·grim·age /'pilgrəmij/ ▶*n.* a pilgrim's journey. ■ a journey to a place associated with someone or something well known or respected. ■ life viewed as a journey: *life's pilgrimage.*
▶*v.* [*intr.*] go on a pilgrimage.

Pil·i·pi·no /,pilə'pēnō/ ▶*n.* & *adj.* variant of **Filipino**.

pill[1] /pil/ ▶*n.* a small round mass of solid medicine to be swallowed whole. ■ (**the pill** or **the Pill**) a contraceptive pill: *she is on the pill.* ■ *inf.* a tedious or unpleasant person. ■ *inf.* (in some sports) a humorous term for a ball. —**pil·u·lar** /'pilyələr/ *adj.*
▶ □ **a bitter pill** (**to swallow**) an unpleasant or painful necessity (to accept).

pill[2] ▶*v.* [*intr.*] (of knitted fabric) form small balls of fluff on its surface.

pil·lage /'pilij/ ▶*v.* [*tr.*] rob (a place) using violence, esp. in wartime. ■ steal (something) using violence, esp. in wartime.
▶*n.* the action of pillaging a place or property, esp. in wartime. —**pil·lag·er** *n.*

pil·lar /'pilər/ ▶*n.* a tall vertical structure of stone, wood, or metal, used as a support for a building, or as an ornament or monument. ■ something shaped like such a structure: *a pillar of smoke.* ■ a person or thing regarded as reliably providing essential support for something: *he was a pillar of his local community.* —**pil·lared** *adj.*
▶ □ **from pillar to post** from one place to another in an unceremonious or fruitless manner.

pill·box /'pil,bäks/ ▶*n.* a small shallow cylindrical box for holding pills. ■ (usu. **pillbox hat**) a hat of a similar shape. ■ a small, enclosed, partly underground concrete fort used as an outpost.

pil·lo·ry /'pilərē/ *hist.* ▶*n.* (*pl.* **-ries**) a wooden framework with holes for the head and hands, in which an offender was imprisoned and exposed to public abuse.
▶*v.* (**-ries**, **-ried**) [*tr.*] put (someone) in the pillory. ■ *fig.* attack or ridicule publicly: *he found himself pilloried by members of his own party.*

pil·low /'pilō/ ▶*n.* a rectangular cloth bag stuffed with feathers, foam rubber, or other soft materials, used to support the head when lying down. ■ a piece of wood or metal used as a support.
▶*v.* [*tr.*] rest (one's head) as if on a pillow. ■ *poetic/lit.* serve as a pillow for: *her shoulder pillowed his weary head.* —**pil·low·y** *adj.*

pil·low·case /'pilō,kās/ ▶*n.* a removable cloth cover for a pillow.

pil·low sham ▶*n.* a decorative pillowcase for covering a pillow when it is not in use.

pil·low talk ▶*n.* intimate conversation in bed.

pill push·er ▶*n. inf.* a person, specifically a doctor, who resorts too readily to advocating the use of medication to cure illness rather than considering other treatments. ■ any seller of drugs for profit, such as a pharmaceutical company or a drug dealer. —**pill-push·ing** *n.* & *adj.*

pi·lot /'pīlət/ ▶*n.* **1** a person who operates the flying controls of an aircraft. ■ a person with expert local knowledge qualified to take charge of a ship entering or leaving confined waters; a helmsman. ■ *archaic* a guide or leader. ■ [often as *adj.*] *Telecommunications* an unmodulated reference signal transmitted with another signal for the purposes of control or synchronization. **2** a television program made to test audience reaction with a view to the production of a series. **3** short for **PILOT LIGHT** (sense 1).
▶*adj.* **1** done as an experiment or test before introducing something more widely: *a pilot study.* **2** leading or guiding.
▶*v.* (**-lot·ed**, **-lot·ing**) [*tr.*] **1** act as a pilot of (an aircraft or ship). ■ [*tr.*] guide; steer. **2** test (a plan, project, etc.) before introducing it more widely. —**pi·lot·age** /'pīlətij/ *n.* —**pi·lot·less** *adj.*

pi·lot boat ▶*n.* a boat used to transport pilots to and from ships.

pi·lot·fish /'pīlət,fish/ ▶*n.* (*pl.* same or **-fishes**) a fish (*Naucrates ductor*) of the jack family, often seen swimming close to sharks.

pi·lot·house /'pīlət,hous/ ▶*n.* another term for **WHEELHOUSE**.

pi·lot light ▶*n.* **1** a small gas burner kept continuously burning to light a larger burner when needed, esp. on a gas stove or water heater. **2** an electric indicator light or control light.

Pil·sner /'pilznər/ (also **pil·sner**, **Pil·sen·er**, or **pil·sen·er**) ▶*n.* a lager beer with a strong hop flavor, originally brewed at Pilsen (Plzeň;) in the Czech Republic, and traditionally served in a tall tapered glass.

Pi·ma /'pēmə/ ▶*n.* (*pl.* same or **Pi·mas**) **1** a member of either of two American Indian peoples, the (**Upper**) **Pima** living chiefly along the Gila and Salt rivers of southern Arizona, and the **Lower Pima** of central Sonora. **2** the Uto-Aztecan languages of these peoples. See **PAPAGO**.
▶*adj.* of or relating to this people or their language.

pi·men·to /pə'mentō/ ▶*n.* (*pl.* **-tos**) **1** variant spelling of **PIMIENTO**. **2** *chiefly W. Indian* another term for **ALLSPICE** (sense 2).

pi me·son /'pī 'māsän; -,zän/ ▶*n.* another term for **PION**.

pi·mien·to /pə'm(y)entō/ (also **pi·men·to**) ▶*n.* (*pl.* **-tos**) a red sweet pepper. ■ a piece of pimiento used as a garnish, esp. stuffed inside a pitted green olive.

pimp /pimp/ ▶*n.* a man who controls prostitutes and arranges clients for them, taking part of their earnings in return.
▶*v.* [*intr.*] (often as *n.*) (**pimping**) act as a pimp. ■ [*tr.*] provide (someone) as a prostitute.

pim·per·nel /'pimpər,nel; -pərnəl/ ▶*n.* a small plant (genera *Anagallis* and *Lysimachia*) of the primrose family, with creeping stems and flat five-petaled flowers.

pim·ple /'pimpəl/ ▶*n.* a small hard inflamed spot on the skin. —**pim·pled** *adj.* —**pim·ply** *adj.*

PIN /pin/ (also **PIN number**) ▶*abbr.* personal identification number.

pin /pin/ ▶*n.* **1** a small piece of metal or wood for fastening or attaching things, in particular: ■ a thin piece of metal with a sharp point at one end and a round head at the other, used esp. for fastening pieces of cloth. ■ a small brooch or badge. ■ *Med.* a steel rod used to join the ends of fractured bones while they heal. ■ a metal peg that holds down the activating lever of a hand grenade, preventing its explosion. ■ short for **HAIRPIN**. ■ *Mus.* a peg around which one string of a musical instrument is fastened. **2** a short piece of wood or metal for various purposes, in particular: ■ (in bowling) one of a set of bottle-shaped wooden pieces that are arranged in an upright position at the end of a lane in order to be toppled by a rolling ball. ■ a metal projection from a plug or an integrated circuit that makes an electrical connection with a socket or another part of a circuit. ■ *Golf* a stick with a flag placed in a hole to mark the hole's position. **3** (**pins**) *inf.* legs.
▶*v.* (**pinned**, **pin·ning**) [*tr.*] attach with a pin or pins. ■ fasten (something) with a pin or pins in a specified position: *her hair was pinned back.* ■ (**pin something on**) fix blame or responsibility for something on (someone). ■ hold someone firmly in a specified position so they are unable to move: *she was pinned against the door.* ■ [*tr.*] transfix (something) with a pin or other pointed instrument. ■ [*tr.*] *Chess* hinder or prevent (a piece or pawn) from moving because of the danger to a more valuable piece standing behind it along the line of an attack.
▶*phrasal v.* □ **pin someone down** force someone to be specific and make their intentions clear. □ **pin something down** define something precisely.
▶ □ (**as**) **neat** (or **clean**) **as a pin** extremely neat or clean. □ **hear a pin drop** used to describe absolute silence. □ **on pins and needles** in an agitated state of suspense. □ **pin one's hopes** (or **faith**) **on** rely heavily on.

pi·ña co·la·da /'pēnyə kə'lädə/ ▶*n.* a cocktail made with rum, pineapple juice, and coconut.

pin·a·fore /'pinə,fôr/ ▶*n.* a sleeveless apronlike garment worn over a child's dress. ■ a collarless sleeveless dress, tied or buttoned in the back and typically worn as a jumper, over a blouse or sweater. ■ *Brit.* a woman's loose sleeveless garment, typically full length and worn over clothes to keep them clean.

pinafore

pi·ña·ta /pēn'yätə/ ▶*n.* (esp. in Spanish-speaking communities) a brightly decorated figure of an animal, usually made of papier mâché, containing toys and candy, and hung in the air so that blindfolded children, taking turns swinging sticks and bats, can smash the figure and share the scattered contents as part of a celebration.

pin·ball /'pin,bôl/ ▶n. a game in which small metal balls are shot across a sloping board and score points by striking various targets.

pince-nez /'pans,nā; 'pins/ ▶n. [treated as *sing.* or *pl.*] a pair of eyeglasses with a nose clip instead of earpieces.

pince-nez

pin·cer /'pinsər/ ▶n. (usu. **pincers**) (also **pin·cers**) a tool made of two pieces of metal bearing blunt concave jaws that are arranged like the blades of scissors, used for gripping and pulling things. ■ a front claw of a lobster, crab, or similar crustacean.

pinch /pinCH/ ▶v. [tr.] **1** grip (the skin of someone's body) tightly and sharply between finger and thumb. ■ grip the skin of a part of the body of (someone) in such a way. ■ (of a shoe) hurt (a foot) by being too tight. ■ compress (the lips), esp. with worry or tension. ■ remove (a bud, leaves, etc.) to encourage bushy growth. **2** [intr.] live in a frugal way: *if I pinch and scrape, I might manage.* **3** *inf.* arrest (someone). ■ *inf.* steal.
▶n. **1** an act of gripping the skin of someone's body between finger and thumb. ■ an amount of an ingredient that can be held between fingers and thumb: *add a pinch of salt.* **2** *inf.* an arrest. ■ an act of theft. —**pinch·er** n.
▶ □ **in a pinch** in a critical situation; if absolutely necessary. □ **feel the pinch** experience hardship, esp. financial.

pinch-hit ▶v. [intr.] *Baseball* bat in place of another player, typically at a critical point in the game: *he pinch-hit for O'Brien and hit a grounder.* ■ (of a team manager or coach) assign a player to pinch-hit in place of another. ■ *inf.* act as a substitute for someone, esp. in an emergency: *last year I briefly pinch-hit for a movie critic on leave.* —**pinch hit·ter** n.

pinch·pen·ny /'pinCH,penē/ ▶n. (pl. **-nies**) [usu. as *adj.*] a miserly person.

pin·cush·ion /'pin,kŏŏSHən/ ▶n. a small cushion into which pins are stuck for convenient storage.

pine¹ /pīn/ ▶n. (also **pine tree**) an evergreen coniferous tree (genus *Pinus*, family Pinaceae) that has clusters of long needle-shaped leaves. Many kinds are grown for their soft timber. ■ used in names of coniferous trees of other families, e.g., **Norfolk Island pine.** ■ used in names of unrelated plants that resemble the pines in some way, e.g., **ground pine.** ■ [as *adj.*] having the scent of pine needles.

pine² ▶v. [intr.] suffer a mental and physical decline, esp. because of a broken heart: *she thinks I am pining away from love.* ■ (**pine for**) miss and long for the return of: *I was pining for my boyfriend.*

pin·e·al /'pinēəl; 'pī-/ (also **pineal gland**, **pineal body**) ▶n. a pea-sized conical mass of tissue behind the third ventricle of the brain, secreting a hormonelike substance in some mammals.
▶adj. of, denoting, or relating to the pineal.

pine·ap·ple /'pī,napəl/ ▶n. **1** a large juicy tropical fruit consisting of aromatic edible yellow flesh surrounded by a tough segmented skin and topped with a tuft of stiff leaves. **2** the widely cultivated tropical American bromeliad (*Ananas comosus*) that bears this fruit. **3** *inf.* a hand grenade.

pine cone ▶n. the conical or rounded woody fruit of a pine tree, with scales that open to release the seeds.

pine mar·ten ▶n. a marten with a dark brown coat, a yellowish throat, and a bushy tail. Two species: *Martes martes* of northern Eurasia, and *M. americana* of North America, esp. Canada and Alaska.

pine nut ▶n. the edible seed of various pine trees.

pine·y /'pīnē/ (also **pin·y**) ▶adj. of, like, or full of pines.

ping /piNG/ ▶n. **1** a short high-pitched ringing sound, as of a tap on a crystal glass. ■ a percussive knocking sound, esp. in an internal combustion engine. **2** Packet Internet Gopher, a utility that is used to query another computer on a TCP/IP network to determine whether there is a connection to it.
▶v. [intr.] **1** make such a sound. ■ [tr.] cause (something) to make such a sound. **2** to query another computer on a TCP/IP network to determine whether there is a connection to it. ■ contact a person briefly (esp. electronically) for a brief purpose: *he just pinged me, pointing to a breaking news story.*

Ping-Pong /'piNG ,pôNG; -,päNG/ ▶n. *trademark* another term for TABLE TENNIS.

pin·head /'pin,hed/ ▶n. **1** the flattened head of a pin. ■ [often as *adj.*] a very small rounded object: *pinhead dots.* **2** *inf.* a stupid or foolish person.

pin·head·ed /'pin,hedəd/ ▶adj. *inf.* stupid; foolish. —**pin·head·ed·ness** n.

pin·hole /'pin,hōl/ ▶n. a very small hole.

pin·hole cam·er·a ▶n. a camera with a pinhole aperture and no lens.

pin·ion¹ /'pinyən/ ▶n. the outer part of a bird's wing including the flight feathers. ■ *poetic/lit.* a bird's wing as used in flight.
▶v. [tr.] tie or hold the arms or legs of (someone): *he pinioned his opponent.* ■ bind (the arms or legs) of someone. **2** cut off the pinion of (a wing or bird) to prevent flight.

pin·ion² ▶n. a small gear or spindle engaging with a large gear.

pink¹ /piNGk/ ▶adj. **1** of a color intermediate between red and white, as of coral or salmon. ■ (of wine) rosé. **2** *inf., often derog.* having or showing left-wing tendencies. **3** of or associated with homosexuals.
▶n. **1** pink color or pigment. ■ pink clothes or material: *she looks good in pink.* ■ the red clothing or material worn by fox hunters. **2** a pink thing, such as a rosé wine. **3** the best condition or degree: *the economy is not in the pink of health.* **4** *inf., often derog.* a person with left-wing tendencies.
▶v. [tr.] blush, as from embarrassment. —**pink·ish** adj. —**pink·ly** adv. —**pink·ness** n. —**pink·y** adj.
▶ □ **in the pink** *inf.* in very good health and spirits.

pink² ▶n. a herbaceous Eurasian plant (genus *Dianthus*) with sweet-smelling pink or white flowers and slender, typically gray-green leaves. The **pink family** (Caryophyllaceae) includes the campions, stitchworts, and cultivated carnations.

pink³ ▶v. [tr.] **1** cut a scalloped or zigzag edge on. ■ pierce or nick (someone) slightly with a weapon or missile. **2** *archaic* decorate: *April pinked the earth with flowers.*

pink⁴ ▶n. *dated* a yellowish lake pigment made by combining vegetable coloring matter with a white base.

pink·eye /'piNGk,ī/ ▶n. **1** conjunctivitis in humans and some livestock. **2** a viral disease of horses, symptoms of which include fever, spontaneous abortion, and redness of the eyes.

pink·ie /'piNGkē/ (also **pink·y**) ▶n. *inf.* the little finger.

pink·ing shears ▶pl. n. shears with a serrated blade, used to cut a zigzag edge in fabric to prevent it from fraying.

pink slip *inf.* ▶n. a notice of dismissal from employment.
▶v. (**pink-slip**) [tr.] dismiss (someone) from employment.

pin mon·ey ▶n. a small sum of money for spending on inessentials. ■ *hist.* an allowance to a woman from her husband for clothing and other personal expenses.

pin·na /'pinə/ ▶n. (pl. **pin·nae** /'pinē/) *Zool.* any of a number of animal structures resembling fins or wings.

pinking shears

pin·na·cle /'pinəkəl/ ▶n. a high, pointed piece of rock. ■ a small pointed turret built as an ornament on a roof. ■ the most successful point.
▶v. [tr.] *poetic/lit.* set on or as if on a pinnacle. ■ form the culminating point or example of. —**pin·na·cled** adj.

pin·nae /'pinē/ ▶ plural form of PINNA.

pin·nate /'pināt; -it/ ▶adj. *Bot.* (of a compound leaf) having leaflets arranged on either side of the stem, typically in pairs opposite each other. ■ *Zool.* (esp. of an invertebrate animal) having branches, tentacles, etc., on each side of an axis, like the vanes of a feather. —**pin·nat·ed** adj. —**pin·nate·ly** adv. —**pin·na·tion** /pi'nāSHən/ n.

pin·ni·ped /'pinə,ped/ ▶n. any carnivorous aquatic mammal with flipperlike limbs, including seals, sea lions, and walruses.
▶adj. of or relating to pinnipeds.

pin·nule /'pin,yŏŏl/ ▶n. *Bot.* a secondary division of a pinnate leaf, esp. of a fern.

pi·noch·le /'pēnəkəl/ ▶n. a card game for two or more players using a 48-card deck consisting of two of each card from nine to ace, the object being to score points for various combinations and to win tricks. ■ the combination of queen of spades and jack of diamonds in this game.

pi·ñon /ˈpinyən; ˌpinˈyōn/ (also **pinyon** or **piñon pine**) ▶ *n.* a small pine tree (*Pinus cembroides*) with edible seeds, native to Mexico and the southwestern U.S. ■ (also **piñon nut**) a pine nut obtained from this tree.

pin·point /ˈpinˌpoint/ ▶ *n.* a tiny dot or point.
▶ *adj.* absolutely precise; to the finest degree: *this weapon fired shells with pinpoint accuracy.* ■ tiny: *a pinpoint laser beam.*
▶ *v.* [*tr.*] find or locate exactly: *one flare had pinpointed the target* | *fig.* *it is difficult to pinpoint the source of his life's inspiration.*

pin·prick /ˈpinˌprik/ ▶ *n.* a prick caused by a pin. ■ a cause of minor irritation.

pins and nee·dles ▶ *pl. n.* a tingling sensation in a limb recovering from numbness.

pin·stripe /ˈpinˌstrīp/ ▶ *n.* a very narrow stripe in cloth, esp. of the type used for formal suits. ■ a pinstripe suit. —**pin·striped** *adj.*

pint /pint/ (abbr.: **pt**) ▶ *n.* a unit of liquid or dry capacity equal to one half of a quart. ■ *Brit., inf.* a pint of beer.

pin·tail /ˈpinˌtāl/ ▶ *n.* a mainly migratory duck (genus *Anas*) with a pointed tail, in particular the **common pintail** (*A. acuta*) of North America and Eurasia, the male of which has boldly marked plumage and two long tail streamers. ■ *inf.* any of a number of other birds with long pointed tails, esp. a grouse.

pin·to /ˈpintō/ ▶ *adj.* piebald.
▶ *n.* (*pl.* **-tos**) a piebald horse.

pin·to bean ▶ *n.* a medium-sized speckled variety of kidney bean.

pint-sized (also **pint-size**) ▶ *adj. inf.* very small.

pin·up /ˈpinˌəp/ ▶ *n.* a poster showing a famous person or sex symbol, designed to be displayed on a wall. ■ a person shown in such a poster.

pin·wheel /ˈpin,(h)wēl/ ▶ *n.* a child's toy consisting of a stick with colored vanes that twirl in the wind. ■ a fireworks device that whirls and emits colored fire. ■ something shaped or rotating like a pinwheel.
▶ *v.* [*intr.*] spin or rotate like a pinwheel.

pin·worm /ˈpinˌwərm/ ▶ *n.* a small nematode (family Oxyuridae, class Phasmida) that is an internal parasite of vertebrates.

pin·y /ˈpīnē/ ▶ *adj.* variant spelling of PINEY.

Pin·yin /ˈpinˈyin/ (also **pin·yin**) ▶ *n.* the standard system of romanized spelling for transliterating Chinese.

pi·on /ˈpīˌän/ ▶ *n. Physics* a meson having a mass approximately 270 times that of an electron. Also called **PI MESON.** —**pi·on·ic** /pīˈänik/ *adj.*

Pi·o·neer /ˌpīəˈnir/ ▶ a series of American space probes launched between 1958 and 1973, two of which provided the first clear pictures of Jupiter and Saturn (1973–79).

pi·o·neer /ˌpīəˈnir/ ▶ *n.* a person who is among the first to explore or settle a new country or area. ■ a person who is among the first to research and develop a new area of knowledge or activity. ■ (in the former USSR and other communist countries) a member of a movement for children below the age of sixteen that aimed to foster communist ideals. ■ a member of an infantry group preparing roads or terrain for the main body of troops. ■ (also **pioneer species**) a plant or animal that establishes itself in an unoccupied area.
▶ *v.* [*tr.*] develop or be the first to use or apply (a new method, area of knowledge, or activity).

pi·ous /ˈpīəs/ ▶ *adj.* devoutly religious. ■ making a hypocritical display of virtue. ■ (of a hope) sincere but unlikely to be fulfilled. ■ (of a deception) with good or religious intentions, whether professed or real. ▷late Middle English: from Latin *pius* 'dutiful, pious.' —**pi·ous·ly** *adv.* —**pi·ous·ness** *n.*

pip[1] /pip/ ▶ *n.* a small hard seed in a fruit. —**pip·less** /ˈpipləs/ *adj.*

pip[2] ▶ *n.* a small shape or symbol, in particular: ■ any of the spots on playing cards, dice, or dominoes. ■ a single blossom of a clustered head of flowers. ■ a diamond-shaped segment of the surface of a pineapple. ■ an image of an object on a radar screen; blip.

pip[3] ▶ *n.* a disease of poultry or other birds causing thick mucus in the throat and white scale on the tongue.

pip[4] ▶ *v.* (**pipped**, **pip·ping**) [*tr.*] (of a young bird) crack (the shell of the egg) when hatching.

pip[5] *Brit., inf.* ▶ *v.* (**pipped**, **pip·ping**) [*tr.*] (usu. **be pipped**) defeat by a small margin or at the last moment. ■ *dated* hit or wound (someone) with a gunshot.

pipe /pīp/ ▶ *n.* **1** a tube of metal, plastic, or other material used to convey water, gas, oil, or other fluid substances. ■ a cylindrical vein of ore or rock, esp. one in which diamonds are found. ■ *inf.* a duct, vessel, or tubular structure in the body, or in an animal or plant. **2** a narrow tube made from wood, clay, etc., with a bowl at one end for containing burning tobacco, the smoke from which is drawn into the mouth. ■ a quantity of tobacco held by this. **3** a wind instrument consisting of a single tube with holes along its length that are covered by the fingers to produce different notes. ■ (usu. **pipes**) bagpipes. ■ (**pipes**) a set of pipes joined together, as in panpipes. ■ a tube by which sound is produced in an organ. ■ a high-pitched cry or song, esp. of a bird. ■ a boatswain's whistle. **4** *Comput.* a command that causes the output from one routine to be the input for another. **5** *Comput.* a connection to the Internet or to a Web site. **6** a cask for wine, esp. as a measure equal to two hogsheads, usually equivalent to 105 gallons (about 477 liters).
▶ *v.* **1** [*tr.*] convey (water, gas, oil, or other fluid substances) through a pipe or pipes. ■ transmit (music, a radio or television program, signals, etc.) by wire or cable. **2** [*tr.*] play (a tune) on a pipe or pipes. ■ [*intr.*] (of a bird) sing in a high or shrill voice. ■ [*tr.*] say (something) in a high, shrill voice. ■ [*tr.*] use a boatswain's whistle to summon (the crew) to work or a meal. **3** [*tr.*] decorate (clothing or soft furnishings) with a thin cord covered in fabric. ■ put (a decorative line or pattern) on a cake or similar dish using icing, whipped cream, etc.
▶ *phrasal v.* □ **pipe down** [often in *imper.*] *inf.* stop talking; be less noisy. □ **pipe up** say something suddenly. —**pipe·ful** /ˈpipˌfŏŏl/ *n.* (*pl.* **-fuls**) —**pipe·less** *adj.* —**pip·y** /ˈpīpē/ *adj.* (**pip·i·er**, **pip·i·est**)

pipe bomb ▶ *n.* a homemade bomb, the components of which are contained in a pipe.

pipe clean·er ▶ *n.* a piece of wire covered with tufted fiber, used to clean a tobacco pipe and for a variety of handicrafts.

pipe dream ▶ *n.* an unattainable or fanciful hope or scheme.

pipe·fish /ˈpīpˌfiSH/ ▶ *n.* (*pl.* same or **-fishes**) a narrow, elongated, chiefly marine fish (*Syngnathus* and other genera, family Syngnathidae) with segmented bony armor beneath the skin and a long tubular snout.

pipe·fit·ting /ˈpīpˌfitiNG/ ▶ *n.* the work of installing and repairing pipes in residential, commercial, and industrial facilities. ■ a connector in a pipe system. —**pipe·fit·ter** *n.*

pipe·line /ˈpīpˌlīn/ ▶ *n.* a long pipe for conveying oil, gas, etc., over long distances. ■ *fig.* a channel supplying goods or information. ■ (in surfing) the hollow formed by the breaking of a large wave. ■ *Comput.* a linear sequence of specialized modules used for pipelining.
▶ *v.* [*tr.*] convey (a substance) by a pipeline. ■ [*tr.*] [often as *adj.*] (**pipelined**) *Comput.* design or execute (a computer or instruction) using the technique of pipelining.
▶ □ **in the pipeline** awaiting completion or processing.

pipe or·gan ▶ *n. Mus.* see ORGAN (sense 1).

pip·er /ˈpīpər/ ▶ *n.* **1** a bagpipe player. **2** a person who plays a pipe, esp. an itinerant musician.
▶ □ **pay the piper** bear the consequences of an action or activity that one has enjoyed.

pipe stem (also **pipe·stem**) ▶ *n.* the shaft of a tobacco pipe. ■ [as *adj.*] used to describe anything resembling this, such as a very narrow pants leg.

pi·pette /pīˈpet/ (also **pi·pet**) ▶ *n.* a slender tube attached to or incorporating a bulb, for transferring or measuring out small quantities of liquid, esp. in a laboratory.
▶ *v.* [*tr.*] pour, convey, or draw off using a pipette.

pip·ing /ˈpīpiNG/ ▶ *n.* **1** lengths of pipe, or a network of pipes, made of metal, plastic, or other materials. **2** ornamentation on food consisting of lines of icing, whipped cream, etc. ■ thin cord covered in fabric, used to decorate clothing or soft furnishings and reinforce seams. **3** the action or art of playing a pipe or pipes.
▶ *adj.* **1** (of a voice or sound) high-pitched. **2** (of a time) peaceful; characterized by the playing of pipes.
▶ □ **piping hot** (of food or water) very hot.

pip·i·strelle /ˌpipəˈstrel; ˈpipəˌstrel/ ▶ *n.* a small insectivorous Old World bat (genus *Pipistrellus*, family Vespertilionidae) with jerky, erratic flight.

pip·it /ˈpipit/ ▶ *n.* a mainly ground-dwelling songbird (*Anthus* and other genera, family Motacillidae) of open country, typically having brown streaky plumage.

pip·pin /ˈpipin/ ▶ *n.* a red and yellow dessert apple. ■ *inf.* an excellent person or thing.

pip·squeak /ˈpipˌskwēk/ ▶ *n. inf.* a person considered to be insignificant, esp. because they are small or young.

Pronunciation Key ə *ago*, *up*; ər *over*, *fur*; a *hat*; ā *ate*; ä *car*; CH *chin*; e *let*; ē *see*; e(ə)r *air*; i *fit*; ī *by*; i(ə)r *ear*; NG *sing*; ō *go*; ô *law*, *for*; oi *toy*; ŏŏ *good*; ōō *goo*; ou *out*; SH *she*; TH *thin*; TH *then*; (h)w *why*; ZH *vision*

pi·quant /'pēkənt; -känt/ ▶*adj.* having a pleasantly sharp taste or appetizing flavor. ■ pleasantly stimulating or exciting to the mind. —**pi·quan·cy** /-kənsē/ *n.* —**pi·quant·ly** *adv.*

pique /pēk/ ▶*n.* a feeling of irritation or resentment resulting from a slight, esp. to one's pride: *he left in a fit of pique.*
▶*v.* (**piques** /pēks/, **piqued** /pēkt/, **piqu·ing** /'pēkiNG/) **1** [*tr.*] stimulate (interest or curiosity). **2** (**be piqued**) feel irritated or resentful. **3** (**pique oneself**) *archaic* pride oneself.

pi·qué /pē'kā; pi-/ ▶*n.* stiff fabric, typically cotton, woven in a strongly ribbed or raised pattern.

pi·quet /pi'kā; 'ket/ ▶*n.* a trick-taking card game for two players, using a 32-card deck consisting of cards from the seven to the ace.

pi·ra·cy /'pīrəsē/ ▶*n.* the practice of attacking and robbing ships at sea. ■ a similar practice in other contexts, esp. hijacking: *air piracy.* ■ the unauthorized use or reproduction of another's work: *software piracy.*

pi·ra·nha /pə'ränə/ ▶*n.* (*pl.* same or **piranhas**) a deep-bodied South American freshwater fish (*Serrasalmus* and other genera, family Characidae) that typically lives in shoals and has very sharp teeth that are used to tear flesh from prey. It has a reputation as a fearsome predator.

pi·rate /'pīrət/ ▶*n.* a person who attacks and robs ships at sea. ■ a person who appropriates or reproduces the work of another for profit without permission, usually in contravention of patent or copyright: *software pirates.* ■ a person or organization that broadcasts radio or television programs without official authorization.
▶*v.* [*tr.*] use or reproduce (another's work) for profit without permission, usually in contravention of patent or copyright. —**pi·rat·ic** /pī'ratik; pi-/ *adj.* —**pi·rat·i·cal** /pī'ratikəl/ *adj.* —**pi·rat·i·cal·ly** /pī'ratiklē/ *adv.*

pi·ro·gi /pi'rōgē/ (also **pie·ro·gi**) ▶*n.* (*pl.* same or **-gies**) a dough dumpling stuffed with a filling such as potato or cheese, typically served with onions or sour cream.

pir·ou·ette /,pirŏō'et/ ▶*n.* chiefly *Ballet* an act of spinning on one foot, typically with the raised foot touching the knee of the supporting leg.
▶*v.* [*intr.*] perform a pirouette.

pis·ca·to·ri·al /,piskə'tôrēəl/ ▶*adj. formal* of or concerning fishermen or fishing.

pis·ca·to·ry /'piskə,tôrē/ ▶*adj.* another term for **PISCATORIAL**.

Pis·ces /'pīsēz/ ▶ **1** *Astron.* a large constellation (the Fish or Fishes), said to represent a pair of fish tied together by their tails. **2** *Astrol.* the twelfth sign of the zodiac, which the sun enters about February 20. ■ (**a Pisces**) (*pl.* same) a person born when the sun is in this sign.

pis·cine /'pīsēn; 'pisīn/ ▶*adj.* of or concerning fish.

pish /pisH/ ▶*interj. dated* used to express annoyance, impatience, or disgust.

piss /pis/ *vulgar slang* ▶*v.* [*intr.*] urinate. ■ [*tr.*] wet with urine. ■ [*tr.*] discharge (something, esp. blood) when urinating.
▶*phrasal v.* □ **piss something away** waste something, esp. money or time. □ **piss off** [usu. in *imper.*] go away (usually used to angrily dismiss someone). □ **piss someone off** annoy someone.
▶*n.* urine. ■ an act of urinating.

pis·tach·i·o /pə'stasHē,ō/ ▶*n.* (*pl.* **-os**) **1** (also **pistachio nut**) the edible pale green seed of an Asian tree. ■ a pale green color. **2** the evergreen tree (*Pistacia vera*) of the cashew family that produces this nut. ▷late Middle English *pistace*, based on Greek *pistakion*, from Old Persian.

piste /pēst/ ▶*n.* **1** a ski run of compacted snow. **2** the specially marked-out rectangular playing area in fencing.

pis·til /'pistl/ ▶*n. Bot.* the female organs of a flower, comprising the stigma, style, and ovary.

pis·tol /'pistl/ ▶*n.* a small firearm designed to be held in one hand.
▶*v.* (**-toled, -tol·ing**; *Brit.* **-tolled, -tol·ling**) [*tr.*] *dated* shoot (someone) with a pistol. ▷mid 16th cent.: from obsolete French *pistole*, from German *Pistole*, from Czech *píšt'ala*, of which the original meaning was 'whistle,' hence 'a firearm' by the resemblance in shape.

pis·tol-whip ▶*v.* [*tr.*] hit or beat (someone) with a pistol.

pis·ton /'pistn/ ▶*n.* a disk or short cylinder fitting closely within a tube in which it moves up and down against a liquid or gas, used in an internal combustion engine to derive motion, or in a pump to impart motion.

pis·ton ring ▶*n.* a ring on a piston sealing the gap between the piston and the cylinder wall.

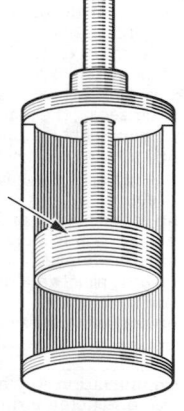

piston

pis·ton rod ▶*n.* a rod or crankshaft attached to a piston to drive a wheel or to impart motion.

pit[1] /pit/ ▶*n.* **1** a large hole in the ground. ■ a large deep hole from which stones or minerals are dug. ■ a coal mine. ■ a sunken enclosure in which certain animals are kept in captivity. ■ short for **ORCHESTRA PIT** (see **ORCHESTRA**). ■ a sunken area in a workshop floor allowing access to a car's underside. ■ *fig.* a low or wretched psychological state. ■ (**the pit**) *poetic/lit.* hell. **2** an area reserved or enclosed for a specific activity, in particular: ■ (usu. **pits**) an area at the side of a track where race cars are serviced and refueled. ■ a part of the floor of an exchange in which a particular stock or commodity is traded. ■ *chiefly hist.* an enclosure in which animals are made to fight. **3** a hollow or indentation in a surface. ■ a small indentation left on the skin after smallpox, acne, or other diseases; a pockmark.
▶*v.* (**pit·ted, pit·ting**) [*tr.*] **1** (**pit someone/something against**) set someone or something in conflict or competition with. ■ *hist.* set an animal to fight against (another animal) for sport. **2** make a hollow or indentation in the surface of. ■ [*intr.*] sink in or contract so as to form a pit or hollow. **3** [*intr.*] drive a race car into the pits for fuel or maintenance.
▶ □ **be the pits** *inf.* be extremely bad or the worst of its kind. □ **the pit of one's** (or **the**) **stomach** an ill-defined region of the lower abdomen regarded as the seat of strong feelings, esp. anxiety.

pit[2] ▶*n.* the stone of a fruit.
▶*v.* (**pit·ted, pit·ting**) [*tr.*] remove the pit from (fruit).

pi·ta /'pētə/ (also **pita bread**) ▶*n.* flat hollow unleavened bread that can be split open to hold a filling.

pit-a-pat /'pit ə ,pat/ (also **pit·a·pat**) ▶*adv.* with a sound like quick light steps or taps: *my heart goes pit-a-pat.*
▶*n.* a sound of this kind.

pit bull (in full **pit bull terrier**) ▶*n.* a dog of an American variety of bull terrier, noted for its muscular build and associated with ferocity.

pitch[1] /picH/ ▶*n.* **1** the quality of a sound governed by the rate of vibrations producing it; the degree of highness or lowness of a tone. ■ a standard degree of highness or lowness used in performance. See also **CONCERT PITCH**. **2** the steepness of a slope, esp. of a roof. ■ *Climbing* a section of a climb, esp. a steep one. ■ the height to which a hawk soars before swooping on its prey. **3** the level of intensity of something: *he brought the machine to a high pitch of development.* ■ (**a pitch of**) a very high degree of: *rousing herself to a pitch of indignation.* **4** *Baseball* a legal delivery of the ball by the pitcher. ■ (also **pitch shot**) *Golf* a high approach shot onto the green. **5** *Brit.* a playing field. ■ *Cricket* the strip of ground between the two sets of stumps. **6** a form of words used when trying to persuade someone to buy or accept something: *a good sales pitch.* **7** a swaying or oscillation of a ship, aircraft, or vehicle around a horizontal axis perpendicular to the direction of motion. ■ the degree of slope or angle, as of a roof. **8** *technical* the distance between successive corresponding points or lines, e.g., between the teeth of a cogwheel. ■ a measure of the angle of the blades of a screw propeller, equal to the distance forward a blade would move in one revolution if it exerted no thrust on the medium. ■ the density of typed or printed characters on a line, typically expressed as numbers of characters per inch.
▶*v.* **1** [*tr.*] *Baseball* throw (the ball) for the batter to try to hit. ■ *Baseball* assign (a player) to pitch. ■ [*intr.*] be a pitcher: *she pitched in a minor-league game* | [*tr.*] *he pitched the entire game.* ■ *Golf* hit (the ball) onto the green with a pitch shot. ■ [*intr.*] *Golf* (of the ball) strike the ground in a particular spot. **2** [*tr.*] throw or fling roughly or casually. ■ [*intr.*] fall heavily, esp. headlong. **3** [*tr.*] express at a particular level of difficulty: *he should pitch his talk at a suitable level for the age group.* ■ aim (a product) at a particular section of the market. **4** [*intr.*] make a bid to obtain a contract or other business. **5** [*tr.*] set up and fix in a definite position: *we pitched camp for the night.* **6** [*intr.*] (of a moving ship, aircraft, or vehicle) rock or oscillate around a lateral axis, so that the front and back move up and down. ■ (of a vehicle) move with a vigorous jogging motion. **7** [*tr.*] cause (a roof) to slope downward from the ridge. ■ [*intr.*] slope downward.
▶*phrasal v.* □ **pitch in** *inf.* vigorously join in to help with a task or activity. □ **pitch into** *inf.* vigorously tackle or begin to deal with. ■ forcefully assault.
▶ □ **make a pitch** make a bid to obtain a contract or other business.

pitch[2] ▶*n.* a sticky black or dark brown substance that is semiliquid when hot, hard when cold. It is obtained by distilling tar or petroleum and is used for waterproofing. ■ any of various similar substances, such as asphalt or bitumen. ■ a sticky resinous sap from a conifer.
▶*v.* [*tr.*] cover, coat, or smear with pitch.

pitch-black ▸*adj.* completely dark; as black as pitch. —**pitch-black·ness** *n.*

pitch·blende /ˈpɪCH,blend/ ▸*n.* a form of uranium ore occurring in brown or black pitchlike masses.

pitched bat·tle /pɪCHt ˈbatl/ ▸*n.* a planned military encounter on a pre-arranged battleground. ■ a violent or vigorous confrontation involving large numbers of people.

pitch·er[1] /ˈpɪCHər/ ▸*n.* a large container, typically earthenware, glass, or plastic, with a handle and a lip, used for holding and pouring liquids. ■ the contents of such a container: *a pitcher of water.* —**pitch·er·ful** /-ˌfo͝ol/ *n.* (*pl.* **-fuls**).

pitch·er[2] ▸*n.* *Baseball* the player who delivers the ball to the batter.

pitch·er plant ▸*n.* a plant (families Nepenthaceae, Sarraceniaceae, and Droseraceae) with a pitcher-shaped pouch that contains fluid into which insects are trapped.

pitch·fork /ˈpɪCH,fôrk/ ▸*n.* a farm tool with a long handle and sharp metal prongs, used esp. for lifting hay. ▸*v.* [*tr.*] lift with a pitchfork. ■ *fig.* thrust (someone) suddenly into an unexpected and difficult situation.

pitch·man /ˈpɪCHmən/ ▸*n.* (*pl.* **-men**) *inf.* a person delivering a sales pitch.

pitch-per·fect ▸*adj.* exactly right in tone, mood, or pitch: *a pitch-perfect, hilarious sendup of a Ken Burns style documentary.*

pitch pine ▸*n.* a pine tree that is a source of pitch or turpentine, and typically yielding hard timber that is used in building, esp. the longleaf *Pinus rigida* of the Appalachians and northeastern U.S.

pitch pipe ▸*n.* *Mus.* a small reed pipe or set of pipes blown to set the pitch for singing or tuning an instrument.

pit·e·ous /ˈpɪtēəs/ ▸*adj.* deserving or arousing pity. —**pit·e·ous·ly** *adv.* —**pit·e·ous·ness** *n.*

pit·fall /ˈpit,fôl/ ▸*n.* a hidden or unsuspected danger or difficulty. ■ a covered pit used as a trap.

pith /pɪtH/ ▸*n.* **1** soft or spongy tissue in plants or animals, in particular: ■ spongy white tissue lining the rind of an orange, lemon, and other citrus fruits. ■ *Bot.* the spongy cellular tissue in the stems and branches of many higher plants. **2** *fig.* the essence of something. **3** *fig.* forceful and concise expression. ▸*v.* [*tr.*] **1** *dated, chiefly fig.* remove the pith from. **2** *rare* pierce or sever the spinal cord of (an animal) so as to kill or immobilize it. —**pith·less** *adj.*

pith·y /ˈpɪtHē/ ▸*adj.* (**pith·i·er**, **pith·i·est**) **1** (of language or style) concise and forcefully expressive. **2** (of a fruit or plant) containing much pith. —**pith·i·ly** /ˈpɪtHəlē/ *adv.* —**pith·i·ness** *n.*

pit·i·a·ble /ˈpɪtēəbəl/ ▸*adj.* deserving or arousing pity. ■ contemptibly poor or small. —**pit·i·a·ble·ness** *n.* —**pit·i·a·bly** /-əblē/ *adv.*

pit·i·ful /ˈpɪtifəl/ ▸*adj.* deserving or arousing pity. ■ very small or poor; inadequate. ■ *archaic* compassionate. —**pit·i·ful·ly** *adv.* —**pit·i·ful·ness** *n.*

pit·i·less /ˈpɪtēlɪs/ ▸*adj.* showing no pity; cruel. —**pit·i·less·ly** *adv.* —**pit·i·less·ness** *n.*

pi·ton /ˈpētän/ ▸*n.* a peg or spike driven into a rock or crack to support a climber or a rope.

pit stop ▸*n.* *Auto Racing* a stop in the pits for servicing and refueling, esp. during a race. ■ a brief rest, esp. during a journey. ■ *inf.* a place where one takes such a rest.

pit·ta[1] /ˈpɪtə/ ▸*n.* variant spelling of **PITA**.

pit·ta[2] ▸*n.* a small ground-dwelling thrushlike bird (genus *Pitta*, family Pittidae) with brightly colored plumage and a very short tail, found in the Old World tropics.

pit·tance /ˈpɪtns/ ▸*n.* a very small or inadequate amount of money paid to someone as an allowance or wage. ▷Middle English: from Old French *pitance*, from medieval Latin *pitantia*, from Latin *pietas* 'pity.'

pit·ter-pat·ter /ˈpɪtər ˈpatər/ ▸*n.* a sound as of quick light steps or taps. ▸*adv.* with this sound: *footsteps that go pitter-patter.*

pi·tu·i·tar·y /pəˈt(y)o͞oəˌterē/ ▸*n.* (*pl.* **-tar·ies**) (in full **pituitary gland** or **pituitary body**) the major endocrine gland. a pea-sized body attached to the base of the brain, the pituitary is important in controlling growth and development and the functioning of the other endocrine glands. ▸*adj.* of or relating to this gland.   **piton**

pit vi·per ▸*n.* a viper of a group distinguished by visible sensory pits on the head that can detect prey by heat.

pit·y /ˈpɪtē/ ▸*n.* (*pl.* **pit·ies**) **1** the feeling of sorrow and compassion caused by the suffering and misfortunes of others. **2** a cause for regret or disappointment: *what a pity we can't be friends.* ▸*v.* (**pit·ies**, **pit·ied**) [*tr.*] feel sorrow for the misfortunes of. —**pit·y·ing·ly** *adv.* ▸ □ **take** (or **have**) **pity** show compassion: *they took pity on him and gave him food.*

piv·ot /ˈpɪvət/ ▸*n.* the central point, pin, or shaft on which a mechanism turns or oscillates. ■ a person or thing that plays a central part in an activity or organization. ■ the person or people about whom a body of troops wheels. ■ (also **piv·ot·man**) a player in a central position in a team sport. ■ *Basketball* a movement in which the player holding the ball may move in any direction with one foot, while keeping the other (the **pivot foot**) in contact with the floor. ▸*v.* (**piv·ot·ed**, **piv·ot·ing**) [*intr.*] turn on or as if on a pivot: *the sail pivots around the axis of a virtually static mast* | *he swung around, pivoting on his heel.* ■ (**pivot on**) *fig.* depend on: *your escape pivots on my disappearing with you.* ■ [*tr.*] provide (a mechanism) with a pivot; fix (a mechanism) on a pivot: [as *adj.*] (**pivoted**) *a pivoted bracket.* —**piv·ot·a·bil·i·ty** /ˌpɪvətəˈbilitē/ *n.* —**piv·ot·a·ble** *adj.* —**piv·ot·al** /-ətl/ *adj.*

pix /pɪks/ ▸*pl. n.* *inf.* pictures, esp. photographs.

pix·el /ˈpɪksəl/ ▸*n.* *Electr.* a minute area of illumination on a display screen, one of many of which an image is composed.

pix·ie /ˈpɪksē/ (also **pix·y**) ▸*n.* (*pl.* **pix·ies**) a supernatural being in folklore and children's stories, typically portrayed as small and humanlike in form and mischievous in character. —**pix·ie·ish** *adj.*

pix·il·at·ed /ˈpɪksəˌlātid/ (*Brit.* also **pix·il·lat·ed**) ▸*adj.* crazy; confused.

piz·za /ˈpētsə/ ▸*n.* a dish of Italian origin consisting of a flat, round base of dough baked with a topping of tomato sauce and cheese, typically with added meat or vegetables.

piz·zazz /pəˈzaz/ (also **pi·zazz**) ▸*n.* *inf.* an attractive combination of vitality and glamour.

piz·ze·ri·a /ˌpētsəˈrēə/ ▸*n.* a place where pizzas are made or sold.

piz·zi·ca·to /ˌpitsiˈkätō/ *Mus.* ▸*adv.* (often as a direction) plucking the strings of a violin or other stringed instrument with one's finger. ▸*adj.* performed in this way. ▸*n.* (*pl.* **-tos** or **-ti** /-tē/) this technique of playing.

pkg. ▸*abbr.* (*pl.* **pkgs.**) package.

PKU ▸*abbr.* phenylketonuria.

PL ▸*abbr.* ■ *Comput.* programming language. ■ *Mil.* patrol leader.

plac·a·ble /ˈplakəbəl/ ▸*adj.* *archaic* easily calmed; gentle and forgiving. —**plac·a·bil·i·ty** /ˌplakəˈbilitē/ *n.* —**plac·a·bly** /-əblē/ *adv.*

plac·ard /ˈplakärd; -ərd/ ▸*n.* a poster or sign for public display, either fixed to a wall or carried during a demonstration. ▸*v.* [*tr.*] cover with placards: *they were placarding the town with posters.*

pla·cate /ˈplākāt/ ▸*v.* [*tr.*] make (someone) less angry or hostile. —**pla·cat·er** *n.* —**pla·cat·ing·ly** /pləˈkātɪNG-lē/ *adv.* —**pla·ca·tion** /plāˈkāSHən/ *n.* —**pla·ca·to·ry** /-kəˌtôrē; ˈplakə-/ *adj.*

place /plās/ ▸*n.* **1** a particular position or point in space. ■ used to refer to an area already identified (giving an impression of informality): *we head to a disco—the place is pandemonium.* ■ a particular point on a larger surface or in a larger object or area: *he cut the policeman's hand in three places.* ■ a building or area used for a specified purpose or activity: *excellent eating places.* ■ *inf.* a person's home. ■ a point in a book or other text reached by a reader at a particular time. **2** a portion of space occupied by someone. ■ a portion of space available or designated for someone. ■ a vacancy or available position. ■ the regular or proper position of something: *lay each slab in place.* ■ somewhere where it is appropriate or prudent for someone to be or for something to occur: *that street was no place for a lady.* ■ a chance to be accepted or to be of use: *the policy left no place for individual initiative.* ■ a person's rank or status. ■ a right or privilege resulting from someone's role or position: *I'm sure she has a story to tell, but it's not my place to ask.* ■ the role played by or importance attached to someone or something in a particular context. **3** a position in a sequence, in particular: ■ a position in a contest: *in ninth place.* ■ the second position, esp. in a horse race. ■ *Brit.* any of the first three or sometimes four positions in a race (used esp. of the second, third, or fourth positions). ■ the degree of priority given to something: *accurate reportage takes second place to lurid detail.* ■ the position of a figure in a series indicated in decimal or similar notation, esp. one after the decimal point. **4** [in *place names*] a square or a short street. ■ a country house with its grounds.

▶*v.* [*tr.*] **1** [*tr.*] put in a particular position. ■ cause to be in a particular situation. ■ used to express the attitude someone has toward someone or something: *I am not able to place any trust in you.* ■ (**be placed**) used to indicate the degree of advantage or convenience enjoyed by someone or something as a result of their position or circumstances: *the company is well placed to seize the opportunity.* **2** [*tr.*] find a home or employment for. ■ dispose of (something, esp. shares) by selling to a customer. ■ arrange for the recognition and implementation of (an order, bet, etc.). ■ order or obtain a connection for (a telephone call) through an operator. **3** [*tr.*] identify or classify as being of a specified type or as holding a specified position in a sequence or hierarchy. ■ [*tr.*] remember where one has seen or how one comes to recognize (someone or something): *she eventually said she couldn't place him.* ■ (**be placed**) *Brit.* achieve a specified position in a race. ■ [*intr.*] be among the first three in a race (or the first three or four in the UK). —**place·less** *adj.* —**place·ment** *n.*

▶ □ **go places** *inf.* visit places; travel. ■ be increasingly successful. □ **in place 1** working or ready to work; established. **2** not traveling any distance: *running in place.* □ **in place of** instead of. □ **out of place** not in the proper position; disarranged. ■ in a setting where one is or feels inappropriate or incongruous. □ **put someone in his** (or **her**) **place** deflate or humiliate someone regarded as being presumptuous. □ **take place** occur. □ **take the place of** replace.

pla·ce·bo /pləˈsēbō/ ▶*n.* (*pl.* **-bos**) a harmless pill, medicine, or procedure prescribed more for the psychological benefit to the patient than for any physiological effect. ■ a substance that has no therapeutic effect, used as a control in testing new drugs. ■ *fig.* a measure designed merely to calm or please someone.

place card ▶*n.* a card bearing a person's name and used to mark their place at a dining or meeting table.

place-kick /ˈplāsˌkik/ *Football* ▶*n.* a kick made with the ball held on the ground or on a tee.
▶*v.* [*intr.*] [often as *n.*] (**placekicking**) take such a kick: *our placekicking struggled at times last season.* —**place·kick·er** *n.*

place mat (also **place·mat**) ▶*n.* a small mat beneath a place setting at a dining table.

place name ▶*n.* the name of a geographical location, such as a town, lake, or range of hills.

pla·cen·ta /pləˈsentə/ ▶*n.* (*pl.* **-tae** /-tē/ or **-tas**) a flattened circular organ in the uterus of pregnant mammals, nourishing and maintaining the fetus through the umbilical cord. —**pla·cen·tal** *adj.*

plac·er[1] /ˈplāsər/ ▶*n.* a deposit of sand or gravel formed in the bed of a river or lake, containing particles of valuable minerals.

plac·er[2] ▶*n.* **1** a person or animal gaining a specified position in a competition or race: *last year's fifth placer.* **2** a person who positions, sets, or arranges something: *he was a shrewd placer of the ball.*

place set·ting ▶*n.* a complete set of dishes and cutlery provided for one person at a meal.

plac·id /ˈplasid/ ▶*adj.* (of a person or animal) not easily upset or excited. ■ (esp. of a place or stretch of water) calm and peaceful, with little movement or activity. —**pla·cid·i·ty** /pləˈsiditē/ *n.* —**plac·id·ly** *adv.*

pla·gia·rism /ˈplājəˌrizəm/ ▶*n.* the practice of taking someone else's work or ideas and passing them off as one's own. —**pla·gia·rist** *n.* —**pla·gia·ris·tic** /ˌplājəˈristik/ *adj.*

pla·gia·rize /ˈplājəˌrīz/ ▶*v.* [*tr.*] take (the work or an idea of someone else) and pass it off as one's own. ■ copy from (someone) in such a way. —**pla·gia·riz·er** *n.*

plague /plāg/ ▶*n.* a contagious bacterial disease characterized by fever and delirium, typically with the formation of buboes (see **BUBONIC PLAGUE**) and sometimes infection of the lungs (**pneumonic plague**). ■ a contagious disease that spreads rapidly and kills many people. ■ an unusually large number of insects or animals infesting a place and causing damage. ■ a thing causing trouble or irritation: *staff theft is usually the plague of restaurants.* ■ a widespread affliction regarded as divine punishment: *the plagues of Egypt.* ■ *archaic* used as a curse or an expression of despair or disgust: *a plague on all their houses!*
▶*v.* (**plagues, plagued, pla·guing**) [*tr.*] cause continual trouble or distress to. ■ pester or harass (someone) continually. ▷late Middle English: Latin *plaga* 'stroke, wound,' probably from Greek (Doric dialect) *plaga*, from a base meaning 'strike.'

plaice /plās/ ▶*n.* (*pl.* same) a North Atlantic flatfish (family Pleuronectidae) that is a commercially important food fish.

plaid /plad/ ▶*n.* checkered or tartan twilled cloth, typically made of wool. ■ a long piece of plaid worn over the shoulder as part of Scottish Highland dress. —**plaid·ed** *adj.*

plain[1] /plān/ ▶*adj.* **1** not decorated or elaborate; simple or ordinary in character. ■ without a pattern; in only one color. ■ bearing no indication as to source, contents, or affiliation: *donations can be put in a plain envelope.* ■ (of a person) having no pretensions; not remarkable or special. ■ (of a person) without a special title or status: *for years he was just plain Bill.* **2** easy to perceive or understand; clear. ■ (of written or spoken usage) clearly expressed, without the use of technical or abstruse terms. ■ not using concealment or deception; frank. **3** (of a person) not beautiful or attractive. **4** sheer; simple (used for emphasis): *the main problem is just plain exhaustion.*
▶*adv. inf.* clearly; unequivocally (used for emphasis): *just plain stupid.*
▶*n.* a large area of flat land with few trees. —**plain·ly** *adj.* —**plain·ness** *n.*
▶ □ **as plain as the nose on one's face** *inf.* very obvious. □ **plain and simple** *inf.* used to emphasize the statement preceding or following: *she was a genius, plain and simple.* □ **plain as day** *inf.* very clearly.

plain[2] ▶*v.* [*intr.*] *archaic* mourn; lament. ■ complain. ■ emit a mournful or plaintive sound.

plain-clothes-man /ˌplānˈklō(TH)zmən/ ▶*n.* (*pl.* **-men**) a police officer, esp. a detective, who wears ordinary clothes while on duty.

plains-man /ˈplānzmən/ ▶*n.* (*pl.* **-men**) a person who lives on a plain, esp. a frontiersman who lived on the Great Plains of North America.

plain-song /ˈplānˌsôNG, -säNG/ ▶*n.* unaccompanied church music sung in unison in medieval modes and in free rhythm corresponding to the accentuation of the words, which are taken from the liturgy. Compare with **GREGORIAN CHANT**.

plain-spo-ken (also **plain·spo·ken**) ▶*adj.* outspoken; blunt. —**plain·spok·en·ness** *n.*

plaint /plānt/ ▶*n. Brit. Law* an accusation; a charge. ■ *chiefly poetic/lit.* a complaint; a lamentation.

plain·tiff /ˈplāntif/ ▶*n. Law* a person who brings a case against another in a court of law. Compare with **DEFENDANT**.

plain·tive /ˈplāntiv/ ▶*adj.* sounding sad and mournful: *a plaintive cry.* —**plain·tive·ly** *adv.* —**plain·tive·ness** *n.*

plait /plāt; plat/ ▶*n.* a single length of hair or other flexible material made up of three or more interlaced strands; a braid. ■ archaic term for **PLEAT**.
▶*v.* [*tr.*] form (hair or other material) into a plait or plaits. ■ make (something) by forming material into a plait or plaits.

plan /plan/ ▶*n.* **1** a detailed proposal for doing or achieving something. ■ a scheme for the regular payment of contributions toward a pension, savings account, or insurance policy: *a pension plan.* **2** (usu. **plans**) an intention or decision about what one is going to do. **3** a detailed diagram, drawing, or program, in particular: ■ a fairly large-scale map of a town or district. ■ a drawing or diagram made by projection on a horizontal plane, esp. one showing the layout of a building or one floor of a building. ■ a diagram showing how something will be arranged: *the seating plan.*
▶*v.* (**planned, pla·nning**) [*tr.*] **1** decide on and arrange in advance: *they were planning a trip to Egypt* | [*intr.*] *we plan on getting married.* ■ [*intr.*] make preparations for an anticipated event or time: *to plan for the future.* **2** design or make a plan of (something to be made or built).
▶ □ **someone's** (or **the**) **best plan** a person's (or the) most sensible course of action. □ **go according to plan** happen as one arranged or intended. □ **plan of action** (or **attack**) an organized program of measures to be taken in order to achieve a goal.

pla·nar·i·an /pləˈne(ə)rēən/ ▶*n.* a free-living flatworm (*Planaria* and other genera) that has a three-branched intestine and a tubular pharynx, typically located halfway down the body.

plan·chette /planˈSHet/ ▶*n.* a small board supported on casters, typically heart-shaped and fitted with a vertical pencil, used for automatic writing and in seances.

plane[1] /plān/ ▶*n.* **1** a flat surface on which a straight line joining any two points on it would wholly lie. ■ an imaginary flat surface through or joining material objects: *the planets orbit the sun in roughly the same plane.* ■ a flat or level surface of a material object. ■ a flat surface producing lift by the action of air or water over and under it. **2** a level of existence, thought, or development: *on the spiritual plane.*
▶*adj.* completely level or flat. ■ of or relating to only two-dimensional surfaces or magnitudes: *plane and solid geometry.*
▶*v.* [*intr.*] (of a bird or an airborne object) soar without moving the wings; glide. ■ [*intr.*] (of a boat, surfboard, etc.) skim over the surface of water as a result of lift produced hydrodynamically. —**plan·ar** /ˈplānər/ *adj.*

plane[2] ▶*n.* an airplane.
▶*v.* [*intr.*] *rare* travel in an airplane.

plane[3] ▶*n.* a tool consisting of a block with a projecting steel blade, used to smooth a wooden or other surface by paring shavings from it.

▶*v.* [*tr.*] smooth (wood or other material) with a plane. ■ [*tr.*] reduce or remove (redundant material) with a plane. ■ *archaic* make smooth or level.

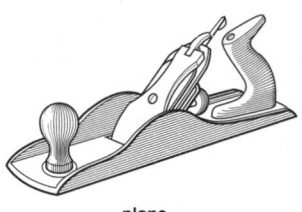

plane

plane[4] (also **plane tree**) ▶*n.* a tall spreading tree (genus *Platanus*, family Platanaceae) of the northern hemisphere, with maplelike leaves and bark that peels in uneven patches. See also SYCAMORE.

plan·et /'planit/ ▶*n.* a celestial body moving in an elliptical orbit around a star. ■ (**the planet**) the earth. ■ *chiefly Astrol., hist.* a celestial body distinguished from the fixed stars by having an apparent motion of its own (including the moon and sun), esp. with reference to its supposed influence on people and events. —**plan·e·tol·o·gy** /,plani'tälǝjē/ *n.*

plan·e·tar·i·um /,plani'te(ǝ)rēǝm/ ▶*n.* (*pl.* **-tar·i·ums** or **-tar·i·a** /-'te(ǝ)rēǝ/) **1** a building in which images of stars, planets, and constellations are projected on the inside of a dome for entertainment or education. ■ a device used to project such images. **2** another term for ORRERY.

plan·e·tar·y /'plani,terē/ ▶*adj.* of, relating to, or belonging to a planet or planets: *planetary motion.* ■ of or relating to the earth as a planet.

plan·et·oid /'plani,toid/ ▶*n.* another term for ASTEROID.

plan·gent /'planjǝnt/ ▶*adj. chiefly poetic/lit.* (of a sound) loud, reverberating, and often melancholy. —**plan·gen·cy** *n.* —**plan·gent·ly** *adv.*

plank /plaNGk/ ▶*n.* **1** a thin, flat piece of timber, used in building and flooring. **2** a fundamental point of a political or other program. ▶*v.* [*tr.*] **1** make, provide, or cover with planks. **2** *inf.* another term for PLUNK (sense 3). **3** cook and serve (meat or fish) on a plank.
▶ □ **walk the plank** (formerly) be forced by pirates to walk blindfold along a plank over the side of a ship to one's death in the sea.

plank·ing /'planGkiNG/ ▶*n.* planks collectively, esp. when used for flooring or as part of a boat. ■ the act or process of laying planks.

plank·ton /'planGktǝn/ ▶*n.* the small and microscopic organisms drifting or floating in the sea or fresh water, consisting chiefly of diatoms, protozoans, small crustaceans, and the eggs and larval stages of larger animals. —**plank·tic** /-tik/ *adj.* —**plank·ton·ic** /-'tänik/ *adj.*

plan·ner /'planǝr/ ▶*n.* **1** a person who makes plans. ■ a person who controls or plans urban development: *city planners.* **2** a list or chart with information that is an aid to planning: *my day planner.*

plan·o·gram /'planǝ,gram/ ▶*n.* a diagram or model that indicates the placement of retail products on shelves in order to maximize sales.

plant /plant/ ▶*n.* **1** a living organism of the kind exemplified by trees, shrubs, herbs, grasses, ferns, and mosses absorbing water and inorganic substances through its roots, and synthesizing nutrients in its leaves by photosynthesis. ■ a small organism of this kind, as distinct from a shrub or tree. **2** a place where an industrial or manufacturing process takes place. ■ machinery used in an industrial or manufacturing process: *investment in new plant.* ■ any system that is analyzed and controlled, e.g., the dynamic equations of an aircraft or the equations governing chemical processes. **3** a person placed in a group as a spy or informer. ■ a thing put among someone's belongings to incriminate or compromise them. ▶*v.* [*tr.*] **1** place (a seed, bulb, or plant) in the ground so that it can grow. ■ place a seed, bulb, or plant in (a place) to grow. ■ *inf.* bury (someone). **2** [*tr.*] place or fix in a specified position. ■ (**plant oneself**) position oneself. ■ establish (an idea) in someone's mind. ■ secretly place (a bomb that is set to go off at a later time). ■ put or hide (something) among someone's belongings to compromise or incriminate the owner. ■ send (someone) to join a group or organization to act as a spy or informer. ■ found or establish (a colony, city, or community). ■ deposit (young fish, spawn, oysters, etc.) in a river or lake. —**plant·a·ble** *adj.* —**plant·let** /-lit/ *n.* —**plant·like** /-,līk/ *adj.*
▶ □ **have** (or **keep**) **one's feet firmly planted on the ground** be (or remain) level-headed and sensible.

plan·tain[1] /'plantǝn/ ▶*n.* a low-growing plant (genus *Plantago*, family Plantaginaceae) that typically has a rosette of leaves and a slender green flower spike, widely growing as a weed of lawns.

plan·tain[2] ▶*n.* **1** a banana (*Musa × paradisiaca*) containing high levels of starch and little sugar, harvested green and widely used as a cooked vegetable in the tropics. **2** the plant that bears this fruit.

plan·tar /'plantǝr/ ▶*adj. Anat.* of or relating to the sole of the foot.

plan·ta·tion /plan'tāshǝn/ ▶*n.* an estate on which crops such as coffee and tobacco are cultivated by resident labor. ■ an area in which trees have been planted, esp. for commercial purposes. ■ *hist.* a colony.

plant·er /'plantǝr/ ▶*n.* **1** a manager or owner of a plantation: *sugar planters.* **2** a decorative container in which plants are grown. **3** a machine or person that plants seeds, bulbs, etc.

plan·ti·grade /'planti,grād/ ▶*adj.* (of a mammal) walking on the soles of the feet, like a human or a bear.

plaque /plak/ ▶*n.* **1** an ornamental tablet, typically of metal, porcelain, or wood, that is fixed to a wall or other surface in commemoration of a person or event. **2** a sticky deposit on teeth in which bacteria proliferate. **3** *Med.* a small, distinct, typically raised patch or region resulting from local damage or deposition of material, such as a fatty deposit on an artery wall. ■ *Microbiology* a clear area in a cell culture caused by the inhibition of growth or destruction of cells by an agent such as a virus.

plas·ma /'plazmǝ/ (also **plasm** /'plazǝm/) ▶*n.* **1** the colorless fluid part of blood, lymph, or milk, in which corpuscles or fat globules are suspended. ■ this substance taken from donors or donated blood for administering in transfusions. **2** an ionized gas consisting of positive ions and free electrons in proportions resulting in more or less no overall electric charge, typically at low pressures or at very high temperatures. ■ an analogous substance consisting of mobile charged particles (such as a molten salt or the electrons within a metal). **3** a dark green, translucent variety of quartz used in mosaic and for other decorative purposes. **4** another term for CYTOPLASM or PROTOPLASM. ▷early 18th cent. (in the sense 'mold, shape'): from late Latin, literally 'mold,' from Greek *plasma*, from *plassein* 'to shape.' —**plas·mat·ic** /plaz'matik/ *adj.* —**plas·mic** /-mik/ *adj.*

plas·mid /'plazmid/ ▶*n. Biol.* a genetic structure in a cell that can replicate independently of the chromosomes, typically a small circular DNA strand in the cytoplasm of a bacterium or protozoan. Plasmids are much used in the laboratory manipulation of genes.

plas·mo·di·um /plaz'mōdēǝm/ ▶*n.* (*pl.* **plasmodia** /plaz'mōdēǝ/) **1** a parasitic protozoan of a genus (*Plasmodium*) that includes those causing malaria. **2** *Biol.* a form within the life cycle of some simple organisms such as slime molds, typically consisting of a mass of naked protoplasm containing many nuclei. —**plas·mo·di·al** /-mōdēǝl/ *adj.*

plas·ter /'plastǝr/ ▶*n.* a soft mixture of lime with sand or cement and water for spreading on walls, ceilings, or other structures to form a smooth hard surface when dried. ■ (also **plaster of Paris**) a hard white substance made by the addition of water to powdered and partly dehydrated gypsum, used for holding broken bones in place and making sculptures and casts. ■ the powder from which such a substance is made. ▶*v.* [*tr.*] cover (a wall, ceiling, or other structure) with plaster. ■ (**plaster something with/in**) coat or cover something with (a substance), esp. to an extent considered excessive. ■ [*tr.*] make (hair) lie flat by applying a liquid to it. ■ apply a plaster cast or medical plaster to (a part of the body). ■ (**plaster something with**) cover a surface with (large numbers of pictures or posters). ■ (**plaster something over**) present a story or picture conspicuously and sensationally in (a newspaper or magazine). ■ *inf., dated* bomb or shell (a target) heavily. —**plas·ter·er** *n.* —**plas·ter·y** *adj.*

plas·ter·board /'plastǝr,bôrd/ ▶*n.* a type of drywall made of plaster between two sheets of heavy paper.

plas·tic /'plastik/ ▶*n.* a synthetic material made from a wide range of organic polymers such as polyethylene, nylon, etc., that can be molded while soft and then set into a rigid or slightly elastic form. ■ *inf.* credit cards or other types of plastic card that can be used as money. ▶*adj.* **1** made of plastic. ■ looking or tasting artificial. **2** (of substances or materials) easily shaped or molded. ■ (in art) of or relating to molding or modeling in three dimensions, or producing three-dimensional effects. ■ (in science and technology) of or relating to the permanent deformation of a solid without fracture by the temporary application of force. ■ offering scope for creativity: *words as a plastic medium.* ■ *Biol.* exhibiting adaptability to change or variety in the environment. —**plas·ti·cal·ly** /-(ǝ)lē/ *adv.* —**plas·tic·i·ty** /plas'tisitē/ *n.* —**plas·ti·cize** /-tǝ'sēz/ *v.* —**plas·ti·ciz·er** *n.*

plas·tic sur·ger·y ▸*n.* the process of reconstructing or repairing parts of the body, esp. by the transfer of tissue, either in the treatment of injury or for cosmetic reasons. —**plas·tic sur·geon** *n.*

plas·tid /ˈplastid/ ▸*n. Bot.* any of a class of small organelles, such as chloroplasts, in the cytoplasm of plant cells, containing pigment or food.

plas·ti·na·tion /ˌplastəˈnāSHən/ ▸*n.* the preservation of body parts through a process that replaces water and fat with various enduring plastics. —**plas·ti·nate** *v.*

plat du jour /ˌplä də ˈZHŏŏr/ ▸*n. (pl.* **plats du jour** *pronunc.* same) a dish specially prepared by a restaurant on a particular day.

plate /plāt/ ▸*n.* **1** a flat dish, typically circular and made of china, from which food is eaten or served. ■ an amount of food on such a dish: *a plate of* spaghetti. ■ a flat dish passed around a church congregation to collect donations of money. ■ a course of a meal, served on one plate: *I'll have the salad plate.* ■ an individual meal, with reference to its cost: *a $1,000-a-plate dinner.* ■ *Biol.* a shallow glass dish on which a culture of cells or microorganisms may be grown. ■ dishes, bowls, cups, and other utensils made of gold, silver, or other metal. ■ a silver or gold dish or trophy awarded as a prize in a race or competition. **2** a thin, flat sheet or strip of metal or other material, typically one used to join or strengthen things or forming part of a machine. ■ a small, flat piece of metal or other material bearing a name or inscription and attached to a door or other object. ■ (usu. **plates**) short for **LICENSE PLATE.** ■ *Bot. & Zool.* a thin, flat organic structure or formation. ■ *Geol.* each of the several rigid pieces of the earth's lithosphere that together make up the earth's surface. (See also **PLATE TECTONICS.**) ■ *Baseball* short for **HOME PLATE.** ■ a piece of lumber laid horizontally along the top of a wall to support the ends of joists or rafters. ■ a light horseshoe for a racehorse. **3** a sheet of metal, plastic, or some other material bearing an image of type or illustrations from which multiple copies are printed. ■ a printed photograph, picture, or illustration, esp. one on superior-quality paper in a book. ■ a thin sheet of metal, glass, or other substance coated with a light-sensitive film on which an image is formed, used in larger or older types of cameras. **4** a thin piece of plastic molded to the shape of a person's mouth and gums, to which artificial teeth or another orthodontic appliance are attached. **5** a thin piece of metal that acts as an electrode in a capacitor, battery, or cell. ■ the anode of a thermionic tube.

▸*v. [tr.]* **1** cover (a metal object) with a thin coating or film of a different metal: [as *adj.*, in *comb.*] (**-plated**) *the cylinder is nickel-plated.* ■ cover (an object) with plates of metal for decoration, protection, or strength. **2** serve or arrange (food) on a plate or plates before a meal. **3** *Baseball* score (a run or runs); cause (someone) to score. **4** *Biol.* inoculate (cells or infective material) onto a culture plate, esp. with the object of isolating a particular strain of microorganisms or estimating viable cell numbers. ▷Middle English (denoting a flat, thin sheet, usually of metal): from Old French, from medieval Latin *plata* 'plate armor,' based on Greek *platus* 'flat.' Sense 1 represents Old French *plat* 'platter, large dish,' also 'dish of meat,' noun use of Old French *plat* 'flat.' —**plate·ful** /-ˌfŏŏl/ *n. (pl.* **-fuls**) —**plate·less** *adj.* —**plat·er** /ˈplātər/ *n.*

▸ ▫ **on one's plate** occupying one's time or energy.

pla·teau /plaˈtō/ ▸*n. (pl.* **-teaus** or **-teaux** /-ˈtōz/) an area of relatively level high ground. ■ *fig.* a state of little or no change following a period of activity or progress. ■ [as *adj.*] denoting a group of American Indian peoples of the plateau country of western Canada and the U.S., including the Nez Percé.

▸*v. (*-teaus, -teaued, -teau·ing*)* [*intr.*] reach a state of little or no change after a time of activity or progress.

plate glass ▸*n.* [often as *adj.*] (**plate-glass**) thick fine-quality glass, typically used for doors and store windows and originally cast in plates.

plate·let /ˈplāt-lit/ ▸*n. Physiol.* a small colorless disk-shaped cell fragment without a nucleus, found in large numbers in blood and involved in clotting. Also called **THROMBOCYTE.**

plat·en /ˈplatn/ ▸*n.* **1** the plate in a small letterpress printing press that presses the paper against the type. **2** the cylindrical roller in a typewriter against which the paper is held.

plate tec·ton·ics ▸*pl. n.* [treated as *sing.*] a theory explaining the structure of the earth's crust and many associated phenomena as resulting from the interaction of rigid lithospheric plates that move slowly over the underlying mantle. —**plate-tec·ton·ic** *adj.*

plat·form /ˈplatfôrm/ ▸*n.* **1** a raised level surface on which people or things can stand. ■ a raised floor or stage used by public speakers or performers so that they can be seen by their audience. ■ a raised structure along the side of a railroad track where passengers get on and off

trains at a station. ■ a raised structure standing in the sea from which oil or gas wells can be drilled or regulated. ■ a raised structure or orbiting satellite from which rockets or missiles may be launched. ■ *Comput.* a standard for the hardware of a computer system, determining what kinds of software it can run. **2** the declared policy of a political party or group. ■ an opportunity to voice one's views or initiate action. **3** (**platforms**) shoes with very thick soles: [as *adj.*] *yellow platform shoes.*

plat·ing /ˈplātiNG/ ▸*n.* **1** a thin coating of gold, silver, or other metal. ■ the process of applying such a layer. **2** an outer covering of broad, flattish sections, typically of metal.

plat·i·num /ˈplatn-əm/ ▸*n.* a precious silvery-white metal, the chemical element of atomic number 78. (Symbol: **Pt**) ■ the grayish-white or silvery color of platinum.

▸*adj.* **1** of a platinum color: *a platinum wig.* **2** (of a recording) having sold enough copies to merit a platinum disk.

▸ ▫ **go platinum** (of a recording) achieve sales meriting a platinum disk.

plat·i·num blonde ▸*n.* a woman with silvery-blond hair.

▸*adj.* (of a woman's hair) silvery blond.

plat·i·tude /ˈplati,t(y)ōōd/ ▸*n.* a remark or statement, esp. one with a moral content, that has been used too often to be interesting or thoughtful. ■ the quality of being dull, ordinary, or trite. —**plat·i·tu·di·nize** /ˌplati't(y)ōōdn,īz/ *v.* —**plat·i·tu·di·nous** /ˌplati't(y)ōōdn-əs/ *adj.*

Pla·ton·ic /pləˈtänik/ ▸*adj.* of or associated with the Greek philosopher Plato or his ideas. ■ (**platonic**) (of love or friendship) intimate and affectionate but not sexual. ■ (**platonic**) confined to words, theories, or ideals, and not leading to practical action. —**pla·ton·i·cal·ly** /-(ə)lē/ *adv.*

Pla·to·nism /ˈplātn,izəm/ ▸*n.* the philosophy of Plato or his followers. —**Pla·to·nist** *n.*

pla·toon /pləˈtōōn/ ▸*n.* a subdivision of a company of soldiers, usually forming a tactical unit that is commanded by a lieutenant and divided into several sections. ■ a group of people acting together. ■ (in baseball and other sports) a pairing of two or more teammates who play the same position at different times.

▸*v. [tr.]* (in baseball and other sports) have (an athlete) play in rotation with one or more teammates at the same position. ■ [*intr.*] play a sport in this way.

plat·ter /ˈplatər/ ▸*n.* **1** a large flat dish or plate, typically oval or circular in shape, used for serving food. ■ a quantity of food served on such a dish: *huge platters of cold cuts.* ■ a meal or selection of food placed on a platter, esp. one served in a restaurant: *I'll have the seafood platter.* **2** something shaped like such a dish or plate, esp. of a circular shape, in particular: ■ *inf., dated* a phonograph record. ■ the rotating metal disk forming the turntable of a record player. ■ *Comput.* a rigid rotating disk on which data is stored in a disk drive; a hard disk (considered as a physical object).

▸ ▫ **on a (silver) platter** *inf.* used to indicate that someone receives or achieves something with little or no effort.

plat·y·pus /ˈplatəpəs; -,pōōs/ ▸*n. (pl.* **platypuses**) a semiaquatic egg-laying mammal (*Ornithorhynchus anatinus*, family Ornithorhynchidae) of eastern Australia. It has a sensitive pliable bill shaped like that of a duck and webbed feet with venomous spurs. ▷late 18th cent.: modern Latin, from Greek *platupous* 'flatfooted,' from *platus* 'flat' + *pous* 'foot.'

plau·dits /ˈplôdits/ ▸*pl. n.* praise. ■ the applause of an audience.

plau·si·ble /ˈplôzəbəl/ ▸*adj.* (of an argument or statement) seeming reasonable or probable. ■ (of a person) skilled at producing persuasive arguments, esp. ones intended to deceive. —**plau·si·bil·i·ty** /ˌplôzə'bilitē/ *n.* —**plau·si·bly** /-əblē/ *adv.*

play /plā/ ▸*v.* **1** [*intr.*] engage in activity for enjoyment and recreation rather than a serious or practical purpose: *her friends were **playing with** their dolls.* ■ [*tr.*] engage in (a game or activity) for enjoyment. ■ amuse oneself by engaging in imaginative pretense: *the boys were playing cops and robbers.* ■ (**play at**) engage in without proper seriousness or understanding: *you cannot play at being a Christian.* ■ (**play with**) treat inconsiderately for one's own amusement. ■ (**play with**) handle without skill so as to damage or prevent from working. **2** [*tr.*] take part in (a sport) on a regular basis. ■ participate in (an athletic match or contest). ■ compete against (another player or team) in an athletic match or contest. ■ [*intr.*] *fig.* be cooperative: *he needs financial backing, but the bank won't play.* ■ [*intr.*] be part of a team, esp. in a specified position, in a game: *he played shortstop.* ■ strike (a ball) or execute (a stroke) in a game. ■ assign to take part in an athletic contest, esp. in a specified position: *the manager will want to play the right-handed Curtis.* ■ move (a piece) or display (a playing card) in one's turn in a game. ■ bet or gamble at or on: *he didn't play the ponies.* **3** [*tr.*] represent (a character) in a

theatrical performance or on film. ■ [*intr.*] perform in a theatrical production or on film. ■ put on or take part in (a theatrical performance or concert). ■ give a dramatic performance at (a particular theater or place). ■ behave as though one were (a specified type of person). ■ (**play someone for**) treat someone as being of (a specified type): *don't imagine you can play me for a fool.* ■ (**play a trick/joke on**) behave in a deceptive or teasing way toward. **4** [*tr.*] perform on (a musical instrument): *someone playing a harmonica* | [*intr.*] *a pianist who will play for us.* ■ possess the skill of performing upon (a musical instrument). ■ produce (notes) from a musical instrument; perform (a piece of music). ■ make (an audiotape, CD, radio, etc.) produce sounds. ■ [*intr.*] (of a musical instrument, audiotape, CD, radio, etc.) produce sounds. **5** [*intr.*] move lightly and quickly, so as to appear and disappear; flicker: *a smile played about her lips.* ■ (of a fountain or similar source of water) emit a stream of gently moving water. **6** [*tr.*] allow (a fish) to exhaust itself pulling against a line before reeling it in.
▸*phrasal v.* □ **play around** (or **about**) behave in a casual, foolish, or irresponsible way. ■ *inf.* (of a married person) have a love affair. □ **play along** pretend to cooperate. □ **play something back** play sounds that one has recently recorded, esp. to monitor recording quality. □ **play something down** represent something as being less important than it in fact is. □ **play someone off** bring people into conflict or competition for one's own advantage: *China can no longer play one superpower off against the other.* □ **play off** (of two teams or competitors) play an extra game or match to decide a draw or tie. □ **play on** exploit (a weak or vulnerable point in someone). □ **play someone out** (usu. **be played out**) drain someone of strength or life. □ **play something out** act the whole of a drama; enact a scene or role. □ **play something up** emphasize the extent or importance of something. □ **play up to** humor or flatter, esp. to win favor.
▸*n.* **1** activity engaged in for enjoyment and recreation, esp. by children. ■ behavior or speech that is not intended seriously: *I flinched, but only in play.* ■ [as *adj.*] designed to be used in games of pretense; not real: *play houses.* **2** the conducting of an athletic match or contest. ■ the action or manner of engaging in a sport or game: *he maintained the same rhythm of play throughout the game.* ■ the status of the ball in a game as being available to be played according to the rules: *the ball was put in play.* ■ *fig.* the state of being active, operative, or effective: *luck comes into play.* ■ a move or maneuver in a sport or game. **3** a dramatic work for the stage or to be broadcast. **4** the space in or through which a mechanism can or does move: *the steering rack was loose, and there was a little play.* ■ *fig.* scope or freedom to act or operate: *our policy allows the market to have freer play.* ■ light and constantly changing movement: *the artist exploits the play of light across the surface.* —**play·a·bil·i·ty** /ˌplāəˈbilitē/ *n.* —**play·a·ble** *adj.*
▸ ■ **make a play for** *inf.* attempt to attract or attain. □ **play both ends against the middle** keep one's options open by supporting or favoring opposing sides. □ **play something by ear** perform music without having to read from a score. ■ (**play it by ear**) *inf.* proceed instinctively according to results and circumstances rather than according to rules or a plan. □ **play by the rules** follow what is generally held to be the correct line of behavior. □ **play fair** observe principles of justice; avoid cheating. □ **play fast and loose** behave irresponsibly or immorally. □ **play favorites** show favoritism toward someone or something. □ **play for time** use specious excuses or unnecessary maneuvers to gain time. □ **play into someone's hands** act in such a way as unintentionally to give someone an advantage. □ **play it cool** *inf.* make an effort to be or appear to be calm and unemotional. □ **play the market** speculate in stocks. □ **a play on words** a pun. □ **play** (or **play it**) **safe** take precautions; avoid risks. □ **play with fire** take foolish risks.
play·act /ˈplāˌakt/ ▸*v.* [*intr.*] act in a play. ■ [*tr.*] act (a scene, role, etc.). ■ [usu. as *n.*] (**playacting**) engage in histrionic pretense: *the defender indulged in some playacting after tumbling to the ground.* —**play·ac·tor** *n.*
play·back /ˈplāˌbak/ ▸*n.* the reproduction of previously recorded sounds or moving images.
play·bill /ˈplāˌbil/ ▸*n.* a poster announcing a theatrical performance. ■ a theater program.
play·boy /ˈplāˌboi/ ▸*n.* a wealthy man who spends his time enjoying himself, esp. one who behaves irresponsibly or is promiscuous.
play-by-play ▸*n.* a detailed running commentary on an athletic contest: [as *adj.*] *the play-by-play announcer.*
play·er /ˈplāər/ ▸*n.* **1** a person taking part in a sport or game. ■ a person or body that is involved and influential in an area or activity: *the country's isolationism made it a secondary player in world political events.* **2** a person who plays a musical instrument: *a guitar player.* ■ a device for playing compact discs, audiocassettes, etc. **3** an actor.

play·er pi·an·o ▸*n.* a piano fitted with an apparatus enabling it to be played automatically.
play·ful /ˈplāfəl/ ▸*adj.* fond of games and amusement; lighthearted. ■ intended for one's own or others' amusement rather than seriously: *a playful punch on the arm.* ■ giving or expressing pleasure and amusement: *the playful use of movement.* —**play·ful·ly** *adv.* —**play·ful·ness** *n.*
play·go·er /ˈplāˌgōər/ ▸*n.* a person who goes to the theater, esp. regularly.
play·ground /ˈplāˌground/ ▸*n.* an outdoor area provided for children to play on, esp. at a school or public park. ■ a place where a particular group of people choose to enjoy themselves.
play·house /ˈplāˌhous/ ▸*n.* **1** a theater. **2** a toy house for children to play in.
play·ing card ▸*n.* each of a set of rectangular cards with an identical pattern on one side and different numbers and symbols on the other, used to play various games, some involving gambling. A standard deck contains 52 cards divided into four suits.
play·mate /ˈplāˌmāt/ ▸*n.* **1** a friend with whom a child plays. **2** used euphemistically to refer to a person's lover.
play·off /ˈplāˌôf/ ▸*n.* an additional game or period of play that decides the outcome of a tied contest. ■ (**playoffs**) a series of contests played to determine the winner of a championship, as between the leading teams in different divisions or leagues.
play·pen /ˈplāˌpen/ ▸*n.* a small portable enclosure in which a baby or small child can play safely.
play·thing /ˈplāˌTHiNG/ ▸*n.* a toy. ■ *fig.* a person treated as amusing but unimportant by someone else.
play·wright /ˈplāˌrīt/ ▸*n.* a person who writes plays.
pla·za /ˈplazə; ˈpläzə/ ▸*n.* **1** a public square, marketplace, or similar open space in a built-up area. **2** a shopping center. ■ a service area on a highway, typically with a gas station and restaurants.
plea /plē/ ▸*n.* **1** a request made in an urgent and emotional manner. ■ a claim that a circumstance means that one should not be blamed for or should not be forced to do something. **2** *Law* a formal statement by or on behalf of a defendant or prisoner, stating guilt or innocence in response to a charge, offering an allegation of fact, or claiming that a point of law should apply.
plea bar·gain·ing ▸*n. Law* an arrangement between a prosecutor and a defendant whereby the defendant pleads guilty to a lesser charge in the expectation of leniency. —**plea-bar·gain** *v.* —**plea bar·gain** *n.*
plead /plēd/ ▸*v.* (*past* **plead·ed** or **pled** /pled/) **1** [*intr.*] make an emotional appeal: *they pleaded with Carol to come home again.* **2** [*tr.*] present and argue for (a position), esp. in court or in another public context: *using cheap melodrama to plead the case for three prisoners.* ■ [*intr.*] *Law* address a court as an advocate on behalf of a party. ■ [*intr.*] *Law* state formally in court whether one is guilty or not guilty of the offense with which one is charged: *he pleaded guilty.* ■ *Law* invoke (a reason or a point of law) as an accusation or defense. ■ offer or present as an excuse for doing or not doing something: *he pleaded family commitments as a reason for not attending.* —**plead·er** *n.* —**plead·ing·ly** *adv.*
plead·ing /ˈplēdiNG/ ▸*n.* **1** the action of making an emotional or earnest appeal to someone: *he ignored her pleading.* **2** (usu. **pleadings**) *Law* a formal statement of the cause of an action or defense.
pleas·ant /ˈplezənt/ ▸*adj.* (**pleas·ant·er**, **pleas·ant·est**) giving a sense of happy satisfaction or enjoyment. ■ (of a person or their manner) friendly and considerate; likable. —**pleas·ant·ly** *adv.* —**pleas·ant·ness** *n.*
pleas·ant·ry /ˈplezntrē/ ▸*n.* (*pl.* **-ries**) (usu. **pleasantries**) an inconsequential remark made as part of a polite conversation. ■ a mild joke.
please /plēz/ ▸*v.* [*tr.*] **1** cause to feel happy and satisfied: *he arranged a fishing trip to please his son.* ■ [*intr.*] give satisfaction: *she was quiet and eager to please.* ■ satisfy aesthetically: [as *adj.*] (**pleasing**) *the pleasing austerity of the surroundings.* **2** (**please oneself**) take only one's own wishes into consideration in deciding how to act or proceed: *this is the first time in ages that I can just please myself.* ■ [*intr.*] wish or desire to do something: *feel free to wander around as you please.* ■ (**it pleases, pleased,** etc., **someone to do something**) *dated* it is someone's choice to do something: *it pleased him to go off hunting.*
▸*adv.* used in polite requests or questions: *please address letters to the Editor.* ■ used to add urgency and emotion to a request: *please come home!* ■ used to agree politely to a request: *"May I call you at home?" "Please do."*

Pronunciation Key ə *ago, up;* ər *over, fur;* a *hat;* ā *ate;* ä *car;* CH *chin;* e *let;* ē *see;* e(ə)r *air;* i *fit;* ī *by;* i(ə)r *ear;* NG *sing;* ō *go;* ô *law, for;* oi *toy;* o͝o *good;* o͞o *goo;* ou *out;* SH *she;* TH *thin;* TH *then;* (h)w *why;* ZH *vision*

■ used in polite or emphatic acceptance of an offer: *"Would you like a drink?" "Yes, please."* ■ used to ask someone to stop doing something of which the speaker disapproves: *Rita, please—people are looking.* ■ used to express incredulity or irritation: *You cleaned out the barn in two hours? Oh, please!* —**pleas·er** *n.* —**pleas·ing·ly** /'plēziNGlē/ *adv.*

▶ □ **if you please 1** used in polite requests: *follow me, if you please.* **2** used to express indignation at something perceived as unreasonable: *she wants me to make fifty cakes, if you please!*

pleas·ur·a·ble /'plezHərəbəl/ ▶ *adj.* pleasing; enjoyable. —**pleas·ur·a·ble·ness** *n.* —**pleas·ur·a·bly** /-blē/ *adv.*

pleas·ure /'plezHər/ ▶ *n.* a feeling of happy satisfaction and enjoyment. ■ enjoyment and entertainment, contrasted with things done out of necessity: *travel for pleasure.* ■ an event or activity from which one derives enjoyment. ■ sensual gratification.

▶ *adj.* used or intended for entertainment rather than business: *pleasure boats.*

▶ *v.* [*tr.*] give sexual enjoyment or satisfaction to. ■ [*intr.*] (**pleasure in**) derive enjoyment from.

▶ □ **at someone's pleasure** as and when someone wishes. □ **have the pleasure of something** used in formal requests and descriptions. □ **my pleasure** used as a polite reply to thanks. □ **take pleasure in** derive happiness or enjoyment from. □ **what's your pleasure?** what would you like? (used esp. when offering someone a choice). □ **with pleasure** gladly (used to express polite agreement or acceptance).

pleat /plēt/ ▶ *n.* a double or multiple fold in a garment or other item made of cloth, held by stitching the top or side.

▶ *v.* [*tr.*] fold into pleats: [as *adj.*] (**pleated**) *a short pleated skirt.* —**pleat·er** *n.*

pleb /pleb/ ▶ *n.* (usu. **plebs**) *derog.* an ordinary person, esp. one from the lower social classes. —**pleb·by** /'plebē/ *adj.*

plebe /plēb/ ▶ *n. inf.* a newly entered cadet or freshman, esp. at a military academy.

ple·be·ian /pli'bēən/ ▶ *n.* (in ancient Rome) a commoner. ■ a member of the lower social classes.

▶ *adj.* of or belonging to the commoners of ancient Rome. ■ of or belonging to the lower social classes. ■ lacking in refinement.

pleb·i·scite /'plebə,sīt/ ▶ *n.* the direct vote of all the members of an electorate on an important public question such as a change in the constitution. ■ *Roman Hist.* a law enacted by the plebeians' assembly. —**ple·bis·ci·tar·y** /plə'bisi,terē/ *adj.*

plec·trum /'plektrəm/ ▶ *n.* (*pl.* **-trums** or **-tra** /-trə/) a thin flat piece of plastic, tortoiseshell, or other slightly flexible material held by or worn on the fingers and used to pluck the strings of a musical instrument such as a guitar. ■ the corresponding mechanical part that plucks the strings of an instrument such as a harpsichord.

pled /pled/ ▶ past and past participle of PLEAD.

pledge /plej/ ▶ *n.* **1** a solemn promise or undertaking. ■ a promise of a donation to charity. ■ (**the pledge**) a solemn undertaking to abstain from alcohol: *she persuaded Arthur to **take the pledge**.* **2** *Law* a thing that is given as security for the fulfillment of a contract or the payment of a debt and is liable to forfeiture in the event of failure. ■ a thing given as a token of love, favor, or loyalty. **3** a person who has promised to join a fraternity or sorority. **4** *archaic* the drinking to a person's health; a toast.

▶ *v.* **1** [*tr.*] commit (a person or organization) by a solemn promise. ■ formally declare or promise that something is or will be the case. ■ [*intr.*] solemnly undertake to do something: *they pledged to continue the campaign.* ■ [*tr.*] undertake formally to give: *Japan pledged $100 million in aid.* **2** [*tr.*] *Law* give as security on a loan: *the creditor to whom the land is pledged.* **3** [*tr.*] promise to join (a fraternity or sorority). **4** [*tr.*] *archaic* drink to the health of. —**pledg·er** *n.* —**pledg·or** /'plejər/ *n.* (*Law*).

Ple·ia·des /'plēədēz/ ▶ **1** *Greek Mythol.* the seven daughters of the Titan Atlas and the Oceanid Pleione. They were pursued by the hunter Orion until Zeus changed them into a cluster of stars. **2** *Astron.* a well-known open cluster of stars in the constellation Taurus. Also called SEVEN SISTERS.

Pleis·to·cene /'plīstə,sēn/ ▶ *adj.* *Geol.* of, relating to, or denoting the first epoch of the Quaternary period, between the Pliocene and Holocene epochs. ■ [as *n.*] (**the Pleistocene**) the Pleistocene epoch or the system of deposits laid down during it.

ple·na·ry /'plenərē/ ▶ *adj.* **1** unqualified; absolute: *a plenary indulgence by the pope.* **2** (of a meeting) to be attended by all participants at a conference or assembly, who otherwise meet in smaller groups.

▶ *n.* a meeting or session of this type.

plen·i·po·ten·ti·a·ry /,plenəpə'tensHē,erē; -'tensHərē/ ▶ *n.* (*pl.* **-ar·ies**) a person, esp. a diplomat, invested with the full power of independent action on behalf of their government, typically in a foreign country.

▶ *adj.* having full power to take independent action. ■ (of power) absolute.

plen·i·tude /'pleni,t(y)ōōd/ ▶ *n.* an abundance: *the farm boasts a plenitude of animals and birds.* ■ the condition of being full or complete.

plen·te·ous /'plentēəs/ ▶ *adj. poetic/lit.* plentiful. —**plen·te·ous·ly** *adv.* —**plen·te·ous·ness** *n.*

plen·ti·ful /'plentəfəl/ ▶ *adj.* existing in or yielding great quantities; abundant. —**plen·ti·ful·ly** *adv.* —**plen·ti·ful·ness** *n.*

plen·ty /'plentē/ ▶ *pron.* a large or sufficient amount or quantity; more than enough: *I would have **plenty of** time to get home* | [as *adj.*] *inf.* or *dial.* *there was plenty room.*

▶ *n.* a situation in which food and other necessities are available in sufficiently large quantities: *such natural phenomena as famine and plenty.*

▶ *adv. inf.* used to emphasize the degree of something: *she has **plenty** more ideas.* ▷Middle English (in the sense 'fullness, perfection'): from Old French *plente*, from Latin *plenitas*, from *plenus* 'full.'

ple·num /'plenəm; 'plēnəm/ ▶ *n.* **1** an assembly of all the members of a group or committee. **2** an enclosed chamber where a treated substance collects for distribution, as heated or conditioned air through a ventilation system.

ple·o·nasm /'plēə,nazəm/ ▶ *n.* the use of more words than are necessary to convey meaning (e.g., *see with one's eyes*), either as a fault of style or for emphasis. —**ple·o·nas·tic** /,plēə'nastik/ *adj.* —**ple·o·nas·ti·cal·ly** /,plēə'nastik(ə)lē/ *adv.*

pleth·o·ra /'plethərə/ ▶ *n.* (**a plethora of**) an excess of (something). —**ple·thor·ic** /'plethərik; plə'THôrik/ *adj.* (*archaic* or *Med.*).

pleu·ra[1] /'plŏŏrə/ ▶ *n.* (*pl.* **pleu·rae** /'plŏŏrē/) **1** each of a pair of serous membranes lining the thorax and enveloping the lungs in humans and other mammals. **2** *Zool.* a lateral part in an animal body or structure. —**pleu·ral** *adj.*

pleu·ra[2] ▶ *plural form of* PLEURON.

pleu·ri·sy /'plŏŏrəsē/ ▶ *n. Med.* inflammation of the pleurae, which impairs their lubricating function and causes pain when breathing. It is caused by pneumonia and other diseases of the chest or abdomen. —**pleu·rit·ic** /plŏŏ'ritik/ *adj.*

Plex·i·glas /'pleksi,glas/ (also **plex·i·glas** or **plex·i·glass**) ▶ *n. trademark* a solid transparent plastic.

plex·us /'pleksəs/ ▶ *n.* (*pl.* same or **plex·us·es**) *Anat.* a network of nerves or vessels in the body. ■ an intricate network or weblike formation. —**plex·i·form** /'pleksə,fôrm/ *adj.*

pli·a·ble /'plīəbəl/ ▶ *adj.* easily bent; flexible. ■ *fig.* easily influenced: *pliable teenage minds.* —**pli·a·bil·i·ty** /,plīə'bilitē/ *n.* —**pli·a·bly** /-əblē/ *adv.*

pli·ant /'plīənt/ ▶ *adj.* pliable. —**pli·an·cy** /'plīənsē/ *n.* —**pli·ant·ly** *adv.*

pli·é /plē'ā/ *Ballet* ▶ *n.* a movement in which a dancer bends the knees and straightens them again, usually with the feet turned out and heels firmly on the ground.

▶ *v.* [*intr.*] perform a plié.

pli·ers /'plīərz/ ▶ *pl. n.* pincers with parallel, flat, and typically serrated surfaces, used chiefly for gripping small objects or bending wire.

plight[1] /plīt/ ▶ *n.* a dangerous, difficult, or otherwise unfortunate situation: *relieving the plight of children living in poverty.*

plight[2] ▶ *v.* [*tr.*] *archaic* pledge or promise solemnly (one's faith or loyalty). ■ (**be plighted to**) be engaged to be married to.

pliers

plim·soll /'plimsəl; -sōl/ ▶ *n. Brit.* a light rubber-soled canvas shoe, worn esp. for sports.

plinth /plinTH/ ▶ *n.* a heavy base supporting a statue or vase. ■ *Archit.* the lower square slab at the base of a column.

Pli·o·cene /'plīə,sēn/ ▶ *adj. Geol.* of, relating to, or denoting the last epoch of the Tertiary period, between the Miocene and Pleistocene epochs. ■ [as *n.*] (**the Pliocene**) the Pliocene epoch or the system of rocks deposited during it.

PLO ▶ *abbr.* Palestine Liberation Organization.

plod /pläd/ ▶ *v.* (**plod·ded**, **plod·ding**) [*intr.*] walk doggedly and slowly with heavy steps: *we plodded up the hill fig. talks have plodded on.* ■ work slowly and perseveringly at a dull task: *we were plodding through a textbook.*

▶ *n.* a slow, heavy walk. ■ the sound of a heavy, dull tread. —**plod·der** *n.*

plop /pläp/ ▶ *n.* a short sound as of a small, solid object dropping into water without a splash.

▸ *v.* (**plopped**, **plop·ping**) fall or cause to fall with such a sound: [*intr.*] *the stone plopped into the pond* | [*tr.*] *she plopped a sugar cube into the cup.* ■ (**plop oneself down**) sit or lie down gently but clumsily.

plo·sion /ˈplōzhən/ ▸ *n. Phonet.* the sudden release of air in the pronunciation of a plosive consonant.

plo·sive /ˈplōsiv/ *Phonet.* ▸ *adj.* denoting a consonant that is produced by stopping the airflow using the lips, teeth, or palate, followed by a sudden release of air.
▸ *n.* a plosive speech sound. The basic plosives in English are *t, k,* and *p* (voiceless) and *d, g,* and *b* (voiced).

plot /plät/ ▸ *n.* **1** a plan made in secret by a group of people to do something illegal or harmful. **2** the main events of a play, novel, movie, or similar work, devised and presented by the writer as an interrelated sequence. **3** a small piece of ground marked out for a purpose such as building or gardening: *a vegetable plot.* **4** a graph showing the relation between two variables. ■ a diagram, chart, or map.
▸ *v.* (**plot·ted**, **plot·ting**) [*tr.*] **1** secretly make plans to carry out (an illegal or harmful action): *the two men are plotting a bomb campaign* | [*intr.*] *Erica has been* **plotting against** *me.* **2** devise the sequence of events in (a play, novel, movie, or similar work). **3** mark (a route or position) on a chart. ■ mark out or allocate (points) on a graph. ■ make (a curve) by marking out a number of such points. ■ illustrate by use of a graph. —**plot·less** *adj.* —**plot·ter** /ˈplätər/ *n.*

plough /plou/ ▸ *n. & v.* British spelling of **PLOW**.

plov·er /ˈpləvər; ˈplō-/ ▸ *n.* a short-billed gregarious wading bird, typically found by water but sometimes frequenting grassland, tundra, and mountains. The **plover family** (Charadriidae) includes several genera, esp. *Charadrius* (ringed plovers), *Pluvialis* (golden plovers), and *Vanellus* (lapwings). ▷ Middle English: from Anglo-Norman French, based on Latin *pluvia* 'rain.'

plow /plou/ (*Brit.* **plough**) ▸ *n.* a large farming implement with one or more blades fixed in a frame, used for cutting furrows in the soil and turning it over, esp. to prepare for sowing. ■ a snowplow.
▸ *v.* [*tr.*] **1** turn up the earth of (an area of land) with a plow, esp. before sowing. ■ cut (a furrow or line) with or as if with a plow. ■ (of a ship or boat) travel through (an area of water). **2** [*intr.*] (esp. of a vehicle) move in a fast and uncontrolled manner: *the car* **plowed into** *the side of a van.* ■ advance or progress laboriously or forcibly: *they plowed their way through deep snow* | *the students are* **plowing through** *a set of grammar exercises.* ■ (**plow on**) continue steadily despite difficulties or warnings to stop. **3** clear snow from (a road) using a snowplow.
▸ *phrasal v.* □ **plow something in/back** plow grass or other material into the soil to enrich it. ■ invest money in a business or reinvest profits in the enterprise producing them. □ **plow under** bury in the soil by plowing. □ **plow up** till (soil) completely or thoroughly. ■ uncover by plowing. —**plow·a·ble** *adj.* —**plow·er** *n.*
▸ □ **plow a lonely** (or **one's own**) **furrow** follow a course of action in which one is isolated or in which one can act independently. □ **put** (or **set**) **one's hand to the plow** embark on a task.

plow·share /ˈplouˌSHe(ə)r/ (*Brit.* **plough·share**) ▸ *n.* the main cutting blade of a plow.

ploy /ploi/ ▸ *n.* a cunning plan or action designed to turn a situation to one's own advantage.

pluck /plək/ ▸ *v.* [*tr.*] take hold of (something) and quickly remove it from its place; pick: *she plucked a blade of grass.* ■ catch hold of and pull quickly: *she plucked his sleeve* | [*intr.*] *brambles* **plucked at** *her jeans.* ■ quickly or suddenly remove (someone) from a dangerous or unpleasant situation. ■ pull the feathers from (a bird's carcass) to prepare it for cooking. ■ pull some of the hairs from (one's eyebrows) to make them look neater. ■ sound (a musical instrument or its strings) with one's finger or a plectrum. ■ select for a move to a new job or position.
▸ *n.* spirited and determined courage; guts. ■ the heart, liver, and lungs of an animal as food. —**pluck·er** *n.* [usu. in *comb.*] *a goose-plucker.*

pluck·y /ˈpləkē/ ▸ *adj.* (**pluck·i·er**, **pluck·i·est**) having or showing determined courage in the face of difficulties. —**pluck·i·ly** /ˈpləkəlē/ *adv.* —**pluck·i·ness** *n.*

plug /pləg/ ▸ *n.* **1** an obstruction blocking a hole, pipe, etc. ■ a circular piece of metal, rubber, or plastic used to stop the drain of a bathtub or basin and keep the water in it. ■ *inf.* a baby's pacifier. ■ a mass of solidified lava filling the neck of an old volcano. ■ (in gardening) a young plant or clump of grass with a small mass of soil protecting its roots, for planting in the ground. **2** a device for making an electrical connection, esp. between an appliance and a power supply, consisting of an insulated casing with metal pins that fit into holes in an outlet. ■ short for **SPARK PLUG**. **3** *inf.* a piece of publicity promoting a product, event, or establishment. **4** a piece of tobacco cut from a larger cake

for chewing. ■ (also **plug tobacco**) tobacco in large cakes designed to be cut for chewing. **5** *Fishing* a lure with one or more hooks attached. **6** short for **FIREPLUG**. **7** *inf.* a tired or old horse.
▸ *v.* (**plugged**, **plug·ging**) [*tr.*] **1** block or fill in (a hole or cavity): *fig. the sanctions are meant to plug the gaps in the trade embargo.* ■ insert (something) into an opening so as to fill it. **2** *inf.* mention (a product, event, or establishment) publicly in order to promote it. **3** *inf.* shoot or hit (someone or something). **4** [*intr.*] proceed steadily and laboriously with a journey or task: *he* **plugged away** *at his writing.*
▸ *phrasal v.* □ **plug something in** connect an electrical appliance to a power supply by inserting a plug into an outlet. □ **plug into** (of an electrical appliance) be connected to another appliance by a plug inserted in an outlet. ■ gain or have access to a system of computerized information: *we plug into the research facilities available at the institute.* ■ *fig.* become knowledgeable about and involved with: *the good thing about this job is that I'm plugged into what's going on.* —**plug·ger** *n.*

plum /pləm/ ▸ *n.* **1** an oval fleshy fruit that is purple, reddish, or yellow when ripe and contains a flattish pointed pit. **2** (also **plum tree**) the tree (genus *Prunus*) of the rose family that bears this fruit. **3** a reddish-purple color: [as *adj.*] *a plum blazer.* **4** [usu. as *adj.*] *inf.* a thing, typically a job, considered to be highly desirable: *a plum assignment.*
▸ *adv.* variant spelling of **PLUMB**[1].

plum·age /ˈplo͞omij/ ▸ *n.* a bird's feathers collectively. —**plum·aged** *adj.* [usu. in *comb.*] *a gray-plumaged bird.*

plumb[1] /pləm/ ▸ *v.* [*tr.*] **1** measure (the depth of a body of water). ■ [*intr.*] (of water) be of a specified depth: *at its deepest, the lake scarcely seven feet.* ■ explore or experience fully or to extremes: *she had* **plumbed the depths** *of depravity.* **2** test (an upright surface) to determine the vertical.
▸ *n.* a plumb bob.
▸ *adv.* **1** *inf.* exactly: *seats plumb in the middle of the front row.* ■ to a very high degree; extremely: *plumb crazy.* ■ completely: *the transmission was plumb worn out.* **2** *archaic* vertically: *drapery fell from their human forms plumb down.*
▸ *adj.* vertical: *ensure that the baseboard is straight and plumb.*
▸ □ **out of plumb** not exactly vertical.

plumb[2] ▸ *v.* [*tr.*] install and connect water and drainage pipes in (a building or room): *the house could not be plumbed at all.*

plumb·er /ˈpləmər/ ▸ *n.* a person who installs and repairs the pipes and fittings of water supply, sanitation, or heating systems.

plumber's snake ▸ *n.* see **SNAKE**.

plumb·ing /ˈpləmiNG/ ▸ *n.* the system of pipes, tanks, fittings, and other apparatus for the water supply, heating, and sanitation in a building. ■ the work of installing and maintaining such a system. ■ *inf.* used as a humorous euphemism for the excretory tracts and urinary system.

plume /plo͞om/ ▸ *n.* a long, soft feather or arrangement of feathers used by a bird for display or worn by a person for ornament. ■ *Zool.* a part of an animal's body that resembles a feather: *the antennae are divided into feathery plumes.* ■ a long cloud of smoke or vapor resembling a feather as it spreads from its point of origin. ■ a mass of material, typically a pollutant, spreading from a source: *a radioactive plume.* ■ *Geol.* a localized column of hot magma rising by convection in the mantle, believed to cause volcanic activity in hot spots, such as the Hawaiian Islands, away from plate margins.
▸ *v.* [*intr.*] spread out in a shape resembling a feather: *smoke plumed from the chimneys.* ■ [*tr.*] decorate with or as if with feathers. —**plume·less** *adj.* —**plume·like** /-ˌlīk/ *adj.* —**plum·er·y** /-mərē/ *n.*

plum·met /ˈpləmit/ ▸ *v.* (**-met·ed**, **-met·ing**) [*intr.*] fall or drop straight down at high speed. ■ decrease rapidly in value or amount.
▸ *n.* **1** a steep and rapid fall or drop. **2** a plumb or plumb line.

plu·mose /ˈplo͞oˌmōs/ ▸ *adj.* chiefly *Biol.* having many fine filaments or branches that give a feathery appearance.

plump[1] /pləmp/ ▸ *adj.* having a full rounded shape. ■ slightly fat.
▸ *v.* [*tr.*] shake or pat (a cushion or pillow) to adjust its stuffing and make it rounded and soft. ■ [*intr.*] (**plump up**) become rounder and fatter. —**plump·ish** *adj.* —**plump·ly** *adv.* —**plump·ness** *n.* —**plump·y** *adj.*

plump[2] ▸ *v.* **1** [*tr.*] set down heavily or unceremoniously: *she plumped her bag on the table.* ■ (**plump oneself**) sit down in this way: *she plumped herself down in the nearest seat* | [*intr.*] *he plumped down on the bench beside me.* **2** [*intr.*] (**plump for**) decide definitely in favor of (one of two or more possibilities): *offered a choice of drinks, he plumped for brandy.*
▸ *n. archaic* an abrupt plunge; a heavy fall.

▸*adv. inf.* **1** with a sudden or heavy fall: *she sat down plump on the bed.* **2** *dated* directly and bluntly: *he must tell her plump and plain.*

plu·mule /ˈploomyool/ ▸*n.* **1** *Bot.* the rudimentary shoot or stem of an embryo plant. **2** *Ornithol.* a bird's down feather, numbers of which form an insulating layer under the outer feathers.

plun·der /ˈpləndər/ ▸*v.* [*tr.*] steal goods from (a place or person), typically using force and in a time of war or civil disorder: *looters moved into the disaster area to plunder stores* | [*intr.*] *the invaders were ready to plunder.* ■ steal (goods) in such a way. ■ take material from (artistic or academic work) for one's own purposes.
▸*n.* the violent and dishonest acquisition of property. ■ property acquired illegally and violently. —**plun·der·er** *n.*

plunge /plənj/ ▸*v.* **1** [*intr.*] jump or dive quickly and energetically. ■ fall suddenly and uncontrollably: *a car plunged into a ravine.* ■ embark impetuously on a speech or course of action: *overconfident researchers who plunge ahead.* ■ suffer a rapid decrease in value. **2** [*tr.*] push or thrust quickly: *he plunged his hands into his pockets.* ■ put (something) in liquid so as to immerse it completely. ■ (often **be plunged into**) suddenly bring into a specified condition or state: *for a moment the scene was illuminated, then it was plunged back into darkness.* ■ [*tr.*] sink (a plant or a pot containing a plant) in the ground.
▸*n.* an act of jumping or diving into water. ■ a swift and drastic fall in value or amount.
▸ □ **take the plunge** *inf.* commit oneself to a course of action about which one is nervous.

plung·er /ˈplənjər/ ▸*n.* **1** a device consisting of a rubber cup on a long handle, used to clear blocked pipes by means of water pressure. ■ a part of a device or mechanism that works with a plunging or thrusting movement. **2** *inf.* a person who gambles or spends money recklessly.

plunk /pləNGk/ *inf.* ▸*v.* **1** [*intr.*] play a keyboard or plucked stringed instrument, esp. in an unexpressive or unskilled way. **2** [*tr.*] hit (someone) abruptly. **3** (also **plank**) [*tr.*] put or set (something) down heavily or abruptly. ■ pay (money) on the spot or abruptly: *I gladly plunked down my ten dollars.* ■ (**plunk oneself down**) sit down in a hurried or undignified way.
▸*n.* **1** the sound made by abruptly plucking a string of a stringed instrument. **2** a heavy blow. **3** an act of setting something down heavily. —**plunk·er** *n.*

plu·per·fect /ˌploo'pərfikt/ ▸*adj. & n.* another term for **PAST PERFECT.** ■ [as *adj.*] more than perfect.

plu·ral /ˈploorəl/ ▸*adj.* more than one in number: *the meanings of the text are plural.* ■ *Gram.* (of a word or form) denoting more than one, or (in languages with dual number) more than two: *the first person plural.*
▸*n. Gram.* a plural word or form. ■ the plural number: *the verb is in the plural.* ▷late Middle English: from Old French *plurel* or Latin *pluralis,* from *plus, plur-* 'more.' —**plu·ral·ly** *adv.*

plu·ral·ism /ˈploorəˌlizəm/ ▸*n.* a condition or system in which two or more states, groups, principles, sources of authority, etc., coexist. ■ a form of society in which the members of minority groups maintain their independent cultural traditions. ■ a political theory or system of power-sharing among a number of political parties. ■ a theory or system of devolution and autonomy for individual bodies in preference to monolithic state control. —**plu·ral·ist** *n. & adj.* —**plu·ral·is·tic** /-ˈlistik/ *adj.* —**plu·ral·is·ti·cal·ly** /-ˈlistək(ə)lē/ *adv.*

plu·ral·i·ty /plooˈralitē/ ▸*n.* (*pl.* **-ties**) **1** the fact or state of being plural. ■ a large number of people or things: *a plurality of critical approaches.* **2** the number of votes cast for a candidate who receives more than any other but does not receive an absolute majority. ■ the number by which this exceeds the number of votes cast for the candidate who placed second.

plu·ral·ize /ˈploorəˌlīz/ ▸*v.* [*tr.*] **1** cause to become more numerous. ■ cause to be made up of several different elements. **2** give a plural form to (a word). —**plu·ral·i·za·tion** /ˌploorəliˈzāSHən/ *n.*

plus /pləs/ ▸*prep.* with the addition of: *two plus four is six.* ■ *inf.* together with: *all apartments have a small kitchen plus private bathroom.*
▸*adj.* **1** (after a number or amount) at least: *companies put losses at $500,000 plus.* ■ (after a grade) better than: *B plus.* **2** (before a number) above zero; positive: *plus 60 degrees centigrade.* **3** having a positive electric charge.
▸*n.* **1** short for **PLUS SIGN.** ■ a mathematical operation of addition. **2** an advantage: *knowing the language is a decided plus* | [as *adj.*] **on the plus side,** *the employees are enthusiastic and good-natured.*
▸*conj. inf.* furthermore; also: *it's packed full of medical advice, plus it keeps you informed about the latest research.*
▸ □ **plus or minus** used to define the margin of error of an estimate or calculation: *it is estimated to be 840 years old, plus or minus 40 years.*

plus fours /pləs ˈfôrz/ ▸*pl. n. dated* baggy knickers reaching below the knee, worn esp. by men for playing golf.

plush /pləSH/ ▸*n.* a rich fabric of silk, cotton, wool, or synthetic fiber, with a long, soft nap: [as *adj.*] *deep-buttoned plush upholstery.*
▸*adj. inf.* richly luxurious and expensive: *the plush chrome and leather office.* —**plush·ly** *adv.* —**plush·ness** *n.* —**plush·y** (**plush·i·er, plush·i·est**) *adj.*

plus sign ▸*n.* the symbol +, indicating addition or a positive value.

Plu·to /ˈplootō/ ▸ **1** *Greek Mythol.* the god of the underworld. Also called **HADES. 2** *Astron.* the most remote known planet of the solar system, usually ninth in order from the sun.

plu·toc·ra·cy /plooˈtäkrəsē/ ▸*n.* (*pl.* **-cies**) government by the wealthy. ■ a country or society governed in this way. ■ an elite or ruling class of people whose power derives from their wealth. —**plu·to·crat·ic** /ˌplootəˈkratik/ *adj.* —**plu·to·crat·i·cal·ly** /ˌplootəˈkratiklē/ *adv.*

plu·to·crat /ˈplootəˌkrat/ ▸*n. often derog.* a person whose power derives from their wealth.

plu·to·ni·um /plooˈtōnēəm/ ▸*n.* the chemical element of atomic number 94, a dense silvery radioactive metal of the actinide series, used as a fuel in nuclear reactors and as an explosive in nuclear fission weapons. Plutonium only occurs in trace amounts in nature but is manufactured in nuclear reactors from uranium-238. (Symbol: **Pu**)

plu·vi·al /ˈploovēəl/ *chiefly Geol.* ▸*adj.* relating to or characterized by rainfall.
▸*n.* a period marked by increased rainfall.

ply[1] /plī/ ▸*n.* (*pl.* **plies**) **1** a thickness or layer of a folded or laminated material. ■ [usu. in *comb.*] a strand of yarn or rope: [as *adj.*] *four-ply yarn.* ■ the number of layers or strands of which something is made: *the yarn can be any ply from two to eight.* ■ [usu. in *comb.*] a reinforcing layer of fabric in a tire: [as *adj.*] *a six-ply whitewall tire.* **2** (in game theory) the number of levels at which branching occurs in a tree of possible outcomes, typically corresponding to the number of moves ahead (in chess strictly half-moves ahead) considered by a computer program. ■ a half-move (i.e., one player's move) in computer chess.

ply[2] ▸*v.* (**plies, plied**) [*tr.*] **1** work with (a tool, esp. one requiring steady, rhythmic movements): *a tailor delicately plying his needle.* ■ work steadily at (one's business or trade); conduct. **2** [*intr.*] (of a vessel or vehicle) travel regularly over a route, typically for commercial purposes. ■ [*tr.*] travel over (a route) in this way. **3** (**ply someone with**) provide someone with (food or drink) in a continuous or insistent way. ■ direct (numerous questions) at someone.

ply·wood /ˈplīˌwood/ ▸*n.* a type of strong thin wooden board consisting of two or more layers glued and pressed together.

PM ▸*abbr.* ■ Past Master. ■ Paymaster. ■ Postmaster. ■ postmortem. ■ Prime Minister. ■ Provost Marshal.

Pm ▸*symb.* the chemical element promethium.

p.m. ▸*abbr.* after noon, used after times of day between noon and midnight: *at 3:30 p.m.*

PMS ▸*abbr.* premenstrual syndrome.

pneu·mat·ic /n(y)ooˈmatik/ ▸*adj.* containing or operated by air or gas under pressure. ■ *inf.* (of certain body parts, esp. a woman's breasts) large, as if inflated. ■ *inf.* (of a woman) having large breasts. —**pneu·mat·i·cal·ly** /n(y)ooˈmadək(ə)lē/ *adv.* —**pneu·ma·tic·i·ty** /ˌn(y)oomə-ˈtisədē/ *n.*

pneumatic drill ▸*n.* a large, heavy mechanical drill driven by compressed air, used for drilling into hard materials such as rock or concrete.

pneu·mo·co·ni·o·sis /ˌn(y)oomōˌkōnēˈōsəs/ ▸*n. Med.* a disease of the lungs due to inhalation of dust, characterized by inflammation, coughing, and fibrosis.

pneu·mo·nia /n(y)ooˈmōnēə; -ˈmōnyə/ ▸*n.* lung inflammation caused by bacterial or viral infection, in which the air sacs fill with pus and may become solid. —**pneu·mon·ic** /n(y)ooˈmänik/ *adj.*

PO ▸*abbr.* ■ Petty Officer. ■ postal order. ■ Post Office. ■ purchase order.

Po[2] ▸*symb.* the chemical element polonium.

poach[1] /pōCH/ ▸*v.* [*tr.*] cook (an egg), without its shell, in or over boiling water. ■ cook by simmering in a small amount of liquid.

poach[2] ▸*v.* [*tr.*] **1** illegally hunt or catch (game or fish) on land that is not one's own, or in contravention of official protection. ■ take or acquire in an unfair or clandestine way. ■ [*intr.*] (in ball games) take a shot that a partner or teammate would have expected to take. **2** (of an animal) trample or cut up (turf) with its hoofs. ■ [*intr.*] (of land) become sodden by being trampled. —**poach·er** *n.*

pock /päk/ ▸*n.* a pockmark. —**pocked** *adj.* —**pock·y** *adj.* (*archaic*).

pock·et /ˈpäkət/ ▸*n.* **1** a small bag sewn into or on clothing so as to form part of it, used for carrying small articles. ■ a pouchlike com-

partment providing separate storage space, for example in a suitcase. ■ *inf.* (often **pockets**) a person or organization's financial resources. ■ *Baseball* the hollow in the center of a baseball glove or mitt where the ball can best be caught. ■ an opening at the corner or on the side of a billiard table into which balls are struck. **2** a small patch of something: *the gardens still had pockets of dirty snow in them.* ■ a small, isolated group or area. ■ *Football* the protected area behind the offensive line from which the quarterback throws passes. ■ (in bowling) the space between the head pin and the pin immediately behind it on the left or right. ■ a cavity in a rock or stratum filled with ore or other distinctive component. ■ *Aeron.* an air pocket.
▶*adj.* of a suitable size for carrying in a pocket: *a pocket dictionary.* ■ on a small scale: *a 6,000-acre pocket paradise.*
▶*v.* (**pock·et·ed, pock·et·ing**) [*tr.*] put into one's pocket. ■ take or receive (money or other valuables) for oneself, esp. dishonestly. ■ *Billiards* drive (a ball) into a pocket. ■ enclose as though in a pocket: *the fillings can be pocketed in a pita bread.* ■ suppress (one's feelings) and proceed despite them. ■ block passage of (a bill) by a pocket veto. —**pock·et·a·ble** *adj.* —**pock·et·ful** /-ˌfŏŏl/ (*pl.* **-fuls**) *n.* —**pock·et·less** *adj.*
▶ □ **out of pocket** having lost money in a transaction. ■ (**out-of-pocket**) [as *adj.*] (of an expense or cost) paid for directly rather than being put on account or charged to some other person or organization.

pock·et·book /ˈpäkətˌbŏŏk/ ▶*n.* **1** a woman's handbag. ■ one's financial resources: *packages for every pocketbook.* **2** (**pocket book**) a paperback or other small or cheap edition of a book. **3** *Brit.* a notebook.

pock·et·knife /ˈpäkətˌnīf/ ▶*n.* (*pl.* **pocketknives**) a knife with a folding blade or blades, suitable for carrying in a pocket.

pock·et ve·to ▶*n.* an indirect veto of a legislative bill by the president or a governor by retaining the bill unsigned until it is too late for it to be dealt with during the legislative session.

pock·et watch ▶*n.* a watch on a chain, intended to be carried in the pocket of a jacket or vest.

pock·mark /ˈpäkˌmärk/ ▶*n.* a pitted scar or mark on the skin left by a pustule or pimple. ■ a scar, mark, or pitted area disfiguring a surface.
▶*v.* [*tr.*] (usu. **be pockmarked**) cover or disfigure with such marks: *the area is pockmarked by gravel pits* | [as *adj.*] (**pockmarked**) *a pockmarked face.*

pod¹ /päd/ ▶*n.* **1** an elongated seed vessel of a leguminous plant such as the pea, splitting open on both sides when ripe. ■ the egg case of a locust. **2** a detachable or self-contained unit on an aircraft, spacecraft, vehicle, or vessel, having a particular function.
▶*v.* (**pod·ded, pod·ding**) **1** [*intr.*] (of a plant) bear or form pods: *the peas have failed to pod.* **2** [*tr.*] remove (peas or beans) from their pods prior to cooking. —**pod·like** /-ˌlīk/ *adj.*

pod² ▶*n.* a small herd or school of marine animals, esp. whales.

p.o.'d (also **PO'd, po'd**) ▶*abbr. inf.* pissed off: *what was he p.o'd about?*

pod·cast /ˈpädˌkast/ ▶*n.* a digital recording of a radio broadcast or similar program, made available on the Internet for downloading to a personal audio player. ▷*early 21st century: from iPod,* a trademark for a personal digital audio player. —**pod·cast·ing** *n.*

po·di·a·try /pəˈdīətrē/ ▶*n.* the treatment of the feet and their ailments. —**po·di·a·trist** /-trəst/ *n.*

po·di·um /ˈpōdēəm/ ▶*n.* (*pl.* **-di·ums** or **-di·a** /-dēə/) a small platform on which a person may stand to be seen by an audience, as when making a speech or conducting an orchestra. ■ a lectern. ■ a continuous projecting base or pedestal under a building. ■ a raised platform surrounding the arena in an ancient amphitheater.

po·em /ˈpōəm; ˈpōim; pōm/ ▶*n.* a piece of writing that partakes of the nature of speech and song that is usually metaphorical and often exhibits such formal elements as meter, rhyme, and stanzaic structure. ■ something that arouses strong emotions because of its beauty.

po·e·sy /ˈpōəzē; -sē/ ▶*n. archaic* or *poetic/lit.* poetry. ■ the art or composition of poetry.

po·et /ˈpōət; ˈpōit/ ▶*n.* a person who writes poems. ■ a person possessing special powers of imagination or expression. ▷*Middle English:* from Old French *poete,* via Latin from Greek *poētēs,* variant of *poiētēs* 'maker, poet,' from *poiein* 'create.'

po·et·ic /pōˈetik/ ▶*adj.* of, relating to, or used in poetry. ■ written in verse rather than prose. ■ having an imaginative or sensitively emotional style of expression. —**po·et·i·cal** /pōˈetikəl/ *adj.* —**po·et·i·cal·ly** /-ik(ə)lē/ *adv.*

po·et·ic jus·tice ▶*n.* the fact of experiencing a fitting or deserved retribution for one's actions.

po·et·ic li·cense ▶*n.* the freedom to depart from the facts of a matter or from the conventional rules of language when speaking or writing in order to create an effect.

po·et·ics /pōˈetiks; ▶*pl. n.* [treated as *sing.*] the art of writing poetry. ■ writing that deals with the art of poetry or presents a theory of poetry or literary discourse.

po·et lau·re·ate /ˈlôrēət/ ▶*n.* (*pl.* **po·ets lau·re·ate**) an eminent poet appointed for life as a member of the British royal household. ■ a poet appointed to, or regarded unofficially as holding, an honorary representative position in a particular country, region, or group.

po·et·ry /ˈpōətrē; ˈpōitrē/ ▶*n.* literary work in which special intensity is given to the expression of feelings and ideas by the use of distinctive style and rhythm; poems collectively or as a genre of literature. ■ a quality of beauty and intensity of emotion regarded as characteristic of poems. ■ something regarded as comparable to poetry in its beauty: *a building that is pure poetry.*

po·go stick /ˈpōgō/ ▶*n.* a toy for jumping around on, consisting of a long, spring-loaded pole with a handle at the top and rests for a person's feet near the bottom.

po·grom /ˈpōgrəm; pəˈgräm/ ▶*n.* an organized massacre of a particular ethnic group, in particular that of Jews in Russia or eastern Europe.

poign·ant /ˈpoinyənt/ ▶*adj.* evoking a keen sense of sadness or regret. ■ keenly felt. ■ *archaic* sharp or pungent in taste or smell. —**poign·ance** *n.* —**poign·an·cy** /-yənsē/ *n.* —**poign·ant·ly** /-yəntlē/ *adv.*

poi·ki·lo·therm /poiˈkēlə,THərm; -kil-/ ▶*n. Zool.* an organism that cannot regulate its body temperature except by behavioral means such as basking or burrowing. —**poi·ki·lo·ther·mal** /ˌpoi,kēlə'THərməl; -,kil-/ *adj.* —**poi·ki·lo·ther·mic** /ˌpoi,kēlə'THərmik; -,kilə-/ *adj.* —**poi·ki·lo·ther·my** *n.*

poin·set·ti·a /poin'set(ē)ə/ ▶*n.* a small Mexican shrub (*Euphorbia pulcherrima,* formerly *Poinsettia pulcherrima*) of the spurge family, with large showy scarlet bracts surrounding the small yellow flowers, popular as a Christmas houseplant.

point /point/ ▶*n.* **1** the tapered, sharp end of a tool, weapon, or other object. ■ *Archaeol.* a pointed flake or blade, esp. one that has been worked. ■ see GLAZIER'S POINT. ■ *Ballet* another term for POINTE. ■ *Boxing* the tip of a person's chin as a spot for a blow. ■ the prong of a deer's antler. **2** a dot or other punctuation mark, in particular a period. ■ a decimal point: *fifty-five point nine.* ■ a dot or small stroke used in the alphabets of Semitic languages to indicate vowels or distinguish particular consonants. ■ a very small dot or mark on a surface: *points of light.* **3** a particular spot, place, or position in an area or on a map, object, or surface: *at the western point of the rock.* ■ a particular moment in time or stage in a process: *from this point onward, the teacher was won over.* ■ (usu. **the point**) the critical or decisive moment. ■ (**the point of**) the verge or brink of (doing or being something): *she was on the point of leaving.* ■ a stage or level at which a change of state occurs: *it is packed to the bursting point.* ■ any of the twenty-four triangles on a backgammon board. ■ (in geometry) something having position but not spatial extent, magnitude, dimension, or direction, for example the intersection of two lines. **4** a single item or detail in an extended discussion, list, or text. ■ an argument or idea put forward by a person in discussion: *he does have a point.* ■ an interesting or convincing idea: *he does have a point.* ■ (usu. **the point**) the significant or essential element of what is intended or being discussed: *it took her a long time to* **come to the point.** ■ advantage or purpose that can be gained from doing something: *there was* **no point in** *denying the truth.* ■ relevance or effectiveness. ■ a distinctive feature or characteristic, typically a good one, of a person or thing: *he has his good points.* **5** (in sports and games) a mark or unit of scoring. ■ (in craps) the combination total of the two thrown dice (4, 5, 6, 8, 9, or 10) that permits a shooter to keep throwing until the shooter throws the same number again and wins. ■ a unit used in measuring value, achievement, or extent: *the shares index was down seven points.* ■ an advantage or success in an argument or discussion: *she had* **won her point.** ■ a unit of credit toward an award or benefit. ■ a percentage of the profits from a movie or recording offered to certain people involved in its production. ■ a punishment awarded by the courts for a driving offense and recorded cumulatively on a person's driver's license. ■ a unit of weight (one hundredth of a carat, or 2 mg) for diamonds. ■ a unit of varying value, used in quoting the price of stocks, bonds, or futures. ■ *Bridge* a value assigned to certain cards by a player in assessing the strength of a hand. ■ (**point of**) (in piquet) the longest suit in a player's hand, containing a specified number of up to eight cards. **6** each of thirty-two directions marked at equal distances around a compass. ■ the angular interval between two successive points of a compass, i.e., one eighth of a right angle (11° 15′). ■ (**points ——**) unspecified places considered in

---

terms of their direction from a specified place: *to Philadelphia and points south.* **7** a narrow piece of land jutting out into a lake or ocean. **8** *Printing* a unit of measurement for type sizes and spacing, which in the U.S. and UK is one twelfth of a pica, or 0.013835 inch (0.351 mm). **9** *Basketball* a frontcourt position, usually manned by the guard who sets up the team's defense. ■ *Ice Hockey* either of two areas in each attacking zone, just inside the blue line where it meets the boards. **10** (usu. **points**) each of a set of electrical contacts in the distributor of a motor vehicle. **11** a small leading party of an advanced guard of troops. ■ the position at the head of a column or wedge of troops: *another marine said he would walk point.* ■ short for POINT MAN. **12** (usu. **points**) the extremities of an animal, typically a horse or cat, such as the face, paws, and tail of a Siamese cat. **13** (usu. **points**) *hist.* a tagged piece of ribbon or cord used for lacing a garment or attaching breeches to a doublet. **14** a short piece of cord for tying up a reef in a sail. **15** the action or position of a dog in pointing: *a bird dog on point.* **16** *Mus.* an important phrase or subject, esp. in a contrapuntal composition. Compare with COUNTERPOINT.

▶*v.* **1** [*intr.*] direct someone's attention to the position or direction of something, typically by extending one's finger: *he gripped her arm and pointed to the seat* | *it's rude to point.* ■ indicate a particular time, direction, or reading: *a sign pointing left.* ■ [*tr.*] direct or aim (something) at someone or something. ■ face or be turned in a particular direction: *two of its toes point forward.* ■ cite or put forward a fact or situation as evidence of something: *he points to several factors supporting this conclusion.* ■ (**point to**) (of a situation) be evidence or an indication that (something) is likely to happen or be the case: *everything pointed to an eastern attack.* ■ [*tr.*] (of a dog) indicate the presence of (game) by acting as pointer. ■ [*tr.*] chiefly *Ballet* extend (the toes or feet) by tensing the foot and ankle so as to form a point. **2** [*tr.*] give force or emphasis to (words or actions). ■ (**point something up**) reveal the true nature or importance of something: *he did so much to point up their plight.* **3** [*tr.*] fill in or repair the joints of (brickwork, a brick structure, or tiling) with smoothly finished mortar or cement. **4** [*tr.*] give a sharp, tapered point to. **5** [*tr.*] insert points in (written Hebrew). ■ mark (Psalms) with signs for chanting. **6** [*intr.*] *Naut.* (of a sailing vessel) sail close to the wind.

▶*phrasal v.* □ **point something out** direct someone's gaze or attention toward something, esp. by extending one's finger. ■ say something to make someone aware of a fact or circumstance. ▷Middle English: the noun partly from Old French *point*, from Latin *punctum* 'something that is pricked,' giving rise to the senses 'unit, mark, point in space or time'; partly from Old French *pointe*, from Latin *puncta* 'pricking,' giving rise to the senses 'sharp tip, promontory.' The verb is from Old French *pointer*, and in some senses from the English noun.

▶ □ **beside the point** irrelevant. □ **case in point** an instance or example that illustrates what is being discussed: *the "green revolution" in agriculture is a good case in point.* □ **get the point** understand or accept the validity of someone's idea or argument. □ **make one's point** put across a proposition clearly and convincingly. □ **make a point of** make a special and noticeable effort to do (a specified thing). □ **the point of no return** the point in a journey or enterprise at which it becomes essential or more practical to continue instead of returning to the point of departure. □ **score points** deliberately make oneself appear superior to someone else by making clever remarks. □ **to the point** relevant. □ **up to a point** to some extent but not completely.

point-blank ▶*adj. & adv.* (of a shot, bullet, or other missile) fired from very close to its target. ■ [as *adj.*] (of the range of a shot, bullet, or other missile) so close as to allow no possibility of missing: *the weapon was inaccurate beyond point-blank range.* ■ (of a statement or question) blunt and direct; without explanation or qualification: [as *adj.*] *this point-blank refusal* | [as *adv.*] *he refuses point-blank to be photographed.*

pointe /point; pwANt/ ▶*n.* (*pl.* pronunc. same) *Ballet* the tips of the toes. ■ (also **pointe work**) dance performed on the tips of the toes. ▷French, literally 'tip.'

▶ □ **on** (or **en**) **pointe** /än; än; ôn/ on the tips of the toes.

point-ed /'pointid/ ▶*adj.* **1** having a sharpened or tapered tip or end. **2** (of a remark or look) expressing criticism in a direct and unambiguous way. —**point·ed·ly** *adv.* —**point·ed·ness** *n.*

point·er /'pointər/ ▶*n.* **1** a long thin piece of metal on a scale or dial that moves to indicate a figure or position. ■ a rod used for pointing to features on a map or chart. ■ a hint as to what might happen in the future: *the figures were a pointer to economic recovery.* ■ a small piece of advice; a tip. ■ *Comput.* another term for CURSOR. ■ *Comput.* a variable whose value is the address of another variable; a link. **2** a dog of a breed that on scenting game stands rigid looking toward it.

poin·til·lism /'pwANtē,yizəm; 'pointl,izəm/ ▶*n.* a technique of neo-

Impressionist painting using tiny dots of various pure colors, which become blended in the viewer's eye. It was developed by Seurat. —**poin·til·list** /,pwANtē'yēst; 'pointl-ist/ *n. & adj.* —**poin·til·list·ic** /,pwANtē'yistik; ,pointl'istik/ *adj.*

point·ing /'pointiNG/ ▶*n.* cement or mortar used to fill the joints of brickwork, esp. when added externally to a wall to improve its appearance and weatherproofing. ■ the process of adding such cement or mortar.

point·less /'pointlis/ ▶*adj.* **1** having little or no sense, use, or purpose. **2** (of a contest or competitor) without a point scored. —**point·less·ly** *adv.* —**point·less·ness** *n.*

point man ▶*n.* the soldier at the head of a patrol. ■ (esp. in a political context) a person at the forefront of an activity or endeavor.

point of de·par·ture ▶*n.* the starting point of a line of thought or course of action; an initial assumption. ■ *Naut.* the precise location of a vessel at the outset of a voyage.

point of or·der ▶*n.* a query in a formal debate or meeting as to whether correct procedure is being followed.

point of view ▶*n.* a particular attitude or way of considering a matter: *I'm trying to get Matthew to change his point of view.* ■ (in fictional writing) the narrator's position in relation to the story being told. ■ the position from which something or someone is observed.

point spread ▶*n.* a forecast of the number of points by which a stronger team is expected to defeat a weaker one, used for betting purposes.

point·y /'pointē/ ▶*adj.* (**point·i·er, point·i·est**) *inf.* having a pointed tip or end: *a pointy goatee.*

poise[1] /poiz/ ▶*n.* **1** graceful and elegant bearing in a person. ■ composure and dignity of manner. **2** *archaic* balance; equilibrium.

▶*v.* be or cause to be balanced or suspended: [*intr.*] *he poised motionless on his toes* | [*tr.*] *fig. the world was poised between peace and war.* ■ (**be poised**) (of a person or organization) be ready to do something: *teachers are poised to resume their attack on government school tests.*

poise[2] ▶*n. Physics* a unit of dynamic viscosity.

poised /poizd/ ▶*adj.* having a composed and self-assured manner. ■ having a graceful and elegant bearing.

poi·son /'poizən/ ▶*n.* a substance that, when introduced into or absorbed by a living organism, causes death or injury, esp. one that kills by rapid action even in a small quantity. ■ *Chem.* a substance that reduces the activity of a catalyst. ■ *Physics* an additive or impurity in a nuclear reactor that slows a reaction by absorbing neutrons. ■ a person, idea, action, or situation that is considered to have a destructive or corrupting effect or influence.

▶*v.* [*tr.*] administer poison to (a person or animal), either deliberately or accidentally. ■ adulterate or contaminate (food or drink) with poison. ■ [usu. as *adj.*] (**poisoned**) treat (a weapon or missile) with poison in order to augment its lethal effect. ■ (of a dangerous substance) kill or cause to become very ill. ■ contaminate or pollute (an area, the air, or water). ■ *fig.* prove harmful or destructive to. ■ *Chem.* (of a substance) reduce the activity of (a catalyst). Compare with PROMOTER. ▷Middle English (denoting a harmful medicinal drink): from Old French *poison* 'magic potion,' from Latin *potio(n-)* 'potion,' related to *potare* 'to drink.' —**poi·son·er** /'poizənər/ *n.* —**poi·son·ous** *adj.*

▶ □ **what's your poison?** *inf.* used to ask someone what they would like to drink.

poi·son i·vy ▶*n.* a North American climbing plant (*Rhus radicans*) of the cashew family that secretes an irritant oil from its leaves, which can cause dermatitis.

poi·son pill a·mend·ment ▶*n.* an amendment to a legislative bill that considerably weakens the bill's intended effect, or ruins the bill's chances of passing.

poke[1] /pōk/ ▶*v.* **1** [*tr.*] jab or prod (someone or something), esp. with one's finger: *he poked Benny in the ribs* | [*intr.*] *they sniffed and poked at everything they bought.* ■ [*tr.*] jab (one's finger) at someone or into something. ■ prod and stir (a fire) with a poker to make it burn more fiercely. ■ make (a hole) in something by prodding or jabbing at it. ■ [*tr.*] thrust (something) in a particular direction. ■ [*intr.*] protrude and be or become visible: *wisps of hair poking out from under her bonnet.* ■ *vulgar slang* (of a man) have sexual intercourse with (another person). **2** [*intr.*] move slowly; dawdle: *I was poking along, my vision blocked by that curtain of sleet.*

▶*phrasal v.* □ **poke around/about** look around a place, typically in search of something.

▶*n.* **1** an act of poking someone or something: *she gave the fire a poke.* ■ (**a poke around**) *inf.* a look or search around a place. ■ *vulgar slang* an act of sexual intercourse. **2** (also **poke bonnet**) a woman's bonnet with a projecting brim or front, popular esp. in the early 19th century.

3 (usu. **POKE**) *Comput.* a statement or function in BASIC for altering the contents of a specified memory location.
▶ □ **poke fun at** tease or make fun of. □ **poke one's nose into** *inf.* take an intrusive interest in. □ **take a poke at someone** *inf.* hit or punch someone. ■ criticize someone.
poke[2] ▶ *n. dial.* a bag or small sack. ■ *inf.* a purse or wallet.
poke[3] ▶ *n.* **1** another term for **POKEWEED**. **2** (**Indian poke**) another term for **FALSE HELLEBORE**.
Po·ke·mon /'pōki,män/ ▶ *n. trademark* a video game, card game, or other toy featuring certain Japanese cartoon characters. ■ a colorful toy model of such a character.
pok·er[1] /'pōkər/ ▶ *n.* a metal rod with a handle, used for prodding and stirring an open fire.
pok·er[2] ▶ *n.* a card game played by two or more people who bet on the value of the hands dealt to them. A player wins the pool either by having the highest combination at the showdown or by forcing all opponents to concede without a showing of the hand.
pok·er face ▶ *n.* an impassive expression that hides one's true feelings. ■ a person with such an expression. —**pok·er-faced** *adj.*
poke·weed /'pōk,wēd/ ▶ *n.* a North American plant (*Phytolacca americana*, family Phytolaccaceae) with red stems, spikes of cream flowers, and purple berries.
pok·ey /'pōkē/ ▶ *n.* (usu. **the pokey**) *inf.* prison: *25 years in the pokey.*
pok·y /'pōkē/ (also **pok·ey**) ▶ *adj.* (**pok·i·er**, **pok·i·est**) **1** annoyingly slow or dull. **2** (of a room or building) uncomfortably small and cramped. —**pok·i·ly** /-kəlē/ *adv.* —**pok·i·ness** *n.*
po·lar /'pōlər/ ▶ *adj.* **1** of or relating to the North or South Pole: *the polar regions.* ■ (of an animal or plant) living in the north or south polar region. ■ *Astron.* of or relating to the poles of a celestial body. ■ *Geom.* of or relating to the poles of a sphere. See **POLE**[2]. ■ *Biol.* of or relating to the poles of a cell, organ, or part. **2** *Physics & Chem.* having electrical or magnetic polarity. ■ (of a liquid, esp. a solvent) consisting of molecules with a dipole moment. ■ (of a solid) ionic. **3** directly opposite in character or tendency.
▶ *n. Geom.* the straight line joining the two points at which tangents from a fixed point touch a conic section.
po·lar bear ▶ *n.* a large white arctic bear (*Thalarctos maritimus*) that lives mainly on the pack ice. It is a powerful swimmer.
Po·lar·is /pə'le(ə)rəs; -'lärəs/ ▶ **1** *Astron.* a fairly bright star located within one degree of the north celestial pole, in the constellation Ursa Minor. Also called **NORTH STAR**, **POLESTAR**. **2** a type of submarine-launched ballistic missile.
po·lar·i·ty /pō'laritē; pə-/ ▶ *n.* (*pl.* **-ties**) the property of having poles or being polar. ■ the relative orientation of poles; the direction of a magnetic or electric field. ■ the state of having two opposite or contradictory tendencies, opinions, or aspects: *the polarity between male and female.* ■ *Biol.* the tendency of living organisms or parts to develop with distinct anterior and posterior (or uppermost and lowermost) ends, or to grow or orient in a particular direction.
po·lar·ize /'pōlə,rīz/ ▶ *v.* **1** [tr.] *Physics* restrict the vibrations of (a transverse wave, esp. light) wholly or partially to one direction. **2** [tr.] *Physics* cause (something) to acquire polarity. **3** divide or cause to divide into two sharply contrasting groups or sets of opinions or beliefs: [intr.] *the cultural sphere has polarized into two competing ideological positions* | [tr.] *Vietnam polarized political opinion.* —**po·lar·iz·a·bil·i·ty** /ˌpōlə,rīzə'bilətē/ *n.* —**po·lar·iz·a·ble** *adj.* —**po·lar·i·za·tion** /ˌpōlərə'zāsHən/ *n.* —**po·lar·iz·er** *n.*
Po·lar·oid /'pōlə,roid/ ▶ *n. trademark* **1** material in thin plastic sheets that produces a high degree of plane polarization in light passing through it. ■ (**Polaroids**) sunglasses with lenses made from such material. **2** a photograph taken with a Polaroid camera.
▶ *adj. Photog.* denoting a type of camera with internal processing that produces a finished print rapidly after each exposure. ■ denoting film for or a photograph taken with such a camera: *a Polaroid snapshot.*
Pole /pōl/ ▶ *n.* a native or national of Poland, or a person of Polish descent.
pole[1] /pōl/ ▶ *n.* a long, slender, rounded piece of wood or metal, typically used with one end placed in the ground as a support for something: *a tent pole.* ■ *Track & Field* a long, slender, flexible rod of wood or fiberglass used by a competitor in pole-vaulting. ■ short for **SKI POLE**. ■ a wooden shaft fitted to the front of a cart or carriage drawn by animals and attached to their yokes or collars. ■ a simple fishing rod.
▶ *v.* [tr.] propel (a boat) by pushing a pole against the bottom of a river, canal, or lake.
pole[2] ▶ *n.* either of the two locations (**North Pole** or **South Pole**) on the

surface of the earth (or of a celestial object) that are the northern and southern ends of the axis of rotation. See also **MAGNETIC POLE**. ■ *Geom.* either of the two points at which the axis of a sphere intersects its surface. ■ *Geom.* a fixed point to which other points or lines are referred, e.g., the origin of polar coordinates or the point of which a line or curve is a polar. ■ *Biol.* an extremity of the main axis of a cell, organ, or part. ■ each of the two points on the surface of a magnet at which magnetic forces are strongest and opposite. ■ *fig.* one of two opposed or contradictory principles or ideas. —**pole·ward** /-wərd/ *adj.* —**pole·wards** /-wərdz/ *adj. & adv.*
▶ □ **be poles apart** have nothing in common.
pole·ax /'pōl,aks/ (also **pole·axe**) ▶ *n.* a short-handled ax with a spike at the back, formerly used in naval warfare for boarding, resisting boarders, and cutting ropes. ■ a butcher's ax with a hammerhead at the back, used to slaughter animals.
▶ *v.* [tr.] hit, kill, or knock down with or as if with a poleax. ■ (often **be poleaxed**) cause great shock to (someone).
pole build·ing ▶ *n.* a quickly constructed building in which vertical poles are secured in the ground to serve as the framework.
pole·cat /'pōl,kat/ ▶ *n.* a weasel-like Eurasian mammal (genus *Mustela*, family Mustelidae) with mainly dark brown fur and a darker mask across the eyes, noted for ejecting a fetid fluid when threatened. ■ another term for **SKUNK**.
po·lem·ic /pə'lemik/ ▶ *n.* a strong verbal or written attack on someone or something: *a writer of feminist polemic.* ■ (usu. **polemics**) the art or practice of engaging in controversial debate or dispute.
▶ *adj.* another term for **POLEMICAL**. ▷ mid 17th cent.: via medieval Latin from Greek *polemikos*, from *polemos* 'war.' —**po·lem·i·cist** /pə'leməsist/ *n.* —**po·lem·i·cize** /pə'lemə,sīz/ *v.*
po·len·ta /pō'lentə/ ▶ *n.* cornmeal as used in Italian cooking. ■ a paste or dough made from cornmeal, which is boiled and typically then fried or baked.
pole·star /'pōl,stär/ ▶ *n. Astron.* (also **Pole Star**) another term for **POLARIS**. ■ *fig.* a thing or principle that guides or attracts people.
pole vault ▶ *n.* (**the pole vault**) an athletic event in which competitors attempt to vault over a high bar with the end of an extremely long flexible pole held in the hands. ■ a vault performed in this way.
▶ *v.* (**pole-vault**) [intr.] perform a pole vault. —**pole-vault·er** *n.* —**pole-vault·ing** *n.*
po·lice /pə'lēs/ ▶ *n.* [treated as *pl.*] (usu. **the police**) the civil force of a national or local government, responsible for the prevention and detection of crime and the maintenance of public order. ■ members of a police force: *there are fewer women police than men.* ■ an organization engaged in the enforcement of official regulations in a specified domain: *transit police fig., humorous the fashion police.*
▶ *v.* [tr.] (often as *n.*) (**policing**) (of a police force) have the duty of maintaining law and order in or for (an area or event). ■ enforce regulations or an agreement in (a particular area or domain). ■ enforce the provisions of (a law, agreement, or treaty). ■ maintain order and neatness in (an area, as a military camp).
po·lice·man /pə'lēsmən/ ▶ *n.* (*pl.* **-men**) a member of a police force.
po·lice of·fi·cer ▶ *n.* a policeman or policewoman.
po·lice state ▶ *n.* a totalitarian state controlled by a political police force that secretly supervises the citizens' activities.
po·lice sta·tion ▶ *n.* the office or headquarters of a local police force.
po·lice·wom·an /pə'lēs,wŏŏmən/ ▶ *n.* (*pl.* **-wom·en**) a female member of a police force.
pol·i·cy[1] /'päləsē/ ▶ *n.* (*pl.* **-cies**) a course or principle of action adopted or proposed by a government, party, business, or individual. ■ *archaic* prudent or expedient conduct or action: *a course of policy and wisdom.*
pol·i·cy[2] ▶ *n.* (*pl.* **-cies**) **1** a contract of insurance: *they took out a joint policy.* **2** an illegal lottery or numbers game.
pol·i·cy·hold·er /'päləsē,hōldər/ ▶ *n.* a person or group in whose name an insurance policy is held.
po·li·o /'pōlē,ō/ ▶ *n.* short for **POLIOMYELITIS**.
po·li·o·my·e·li·tis /ˌpōlēō,mīə'lītis/ ▶ *n. Med.* an infectious viral disease that affects the central nervous system and can cause temporary or permanent paralysis.
Pol·ish /'pōlisH/ ▶ *adj.* of or relating to Poland, its inhabitants, or their language.
▶ *n.* the West Slavic language of Poland.

Pronunciation Key ə *ago, up;* ər *over, fur;* a *hat;* ā *ate;* ä *car;* CH *chin;* e *let;* ē *see;* e(ə)r *air;* i *fit;* ī *by;* i(ə)r *ear;* NG *sing;* ō *go;* ô *law, for;* oi *toy;* ŏŏ *good;* ōō *goo;* ou *out;* SH *she;* TH *thin;* ṮH *then;* (h)w *why;* ZH *vision*

pol·ish /'pälisH/ ▶v. [tr.] make the surface of (something) smooth and shiny by rubbing it. ■ improve, refine, or add the finishing touches to: *he's got to **polish up** his French for his job.*
▶phrasal v. □ **polish something off** finish or consume something quickly: *they polished off most of the sausages.*
▶n. a substance used to give something a smooth and shiny surface when rubbed in: *furniture polish.* ■ an act of rubbing something to give it a shiny surface: *I could give the cabinet a polish.* ■ smoothness or glossiness produced by rubbing or friction. ■ refinement or elegance in a person or thing: *his poetry has clarity and polish.* —**pol·ish·a·ble** *adj.* —**pol·ish·er** *n.*

po·lit·bu·ro /'pälət,byo͝oro͝o; 'pō-/ ▶n. (pl. **-ros**) the principal policymaking committee of a Communist Party. ■ (**Politburo**) this committee in the former Soviet Union, founded in 1917. Also called (1952–66) the PRESIDIUM.

po·lite /pə'līt/ ▶adj. (**-lit·er**, **-lit·est**) having or showing behavior that is respectful and considerate of other people. ■ of or relating to people who regard themselves as more cultured and refined than others: *the picture outraged polite society.* —**po·lite·ly** *adv.* —**po·lite·ness** *n.*

pol·i·tic /'pälə,tik/ ▶adj. (of an action) seeming sensible and judicious under the circumstances: *I did not think it politic to express my reservations.* ■ (also **pol·i·tick**) archaic (of a person) prudent and sagacious.
▶v. (**-ticked**, **-ticking**) [intr.] [often as n.] (**politicking**) often derog. engage in political activity: *news of this unseemly politicking invariably leaks into the press.* —**pol·i·tic·ly** *adv.* (rare).

po·lit·i·cal /pə'litikəl/ ▶adj. of or relating to the government or the public affairs of a country. ■ of or relating to the ideas or strategies of a particular party or group in politics. ■ interested in or active in politics. ■ motivated or caused by a person's beliefs or actions concerning politics: *a political crime.* ■ chiefly derog. relating to, affecting, or acting according to the interests of status or authority within an organization rather than matters of principle. —**po·lit·i·cal·ly** /-ik(ə)lē/ *adv.*

po·lit·i·cal ac·tion com·mit·tee (abbr.: **PAC**) ▶n. an organization that raises money privately and employs lobbyists to influence legislation, particularly at the federal level.

po·lit·i·cal a·sy·lum ▶n. see ASYLUM.

po·lit·i·cal cor·rect·ness ▶n. the avoidance, often considered as taken to extremes, of forms of expression or action that are perceived to exclude, marginalize, or insult groups of people who are socially disadvantaged or discriminated against.

po·lit·i·cal·ly cor·rect /pə'litik(ə)lē/ (or **in·correct**) ▶adj. exhibiting (or failing to exhibit) political correctness: *it is not politically correct to laugh at speech impediments.*

po·lit·i·cal pris·on·er ▶n. a person imprisoned for their political beliefs or actions.

po·lit·i·cal sci·ence ▶n. the branch of knowledge that deals with systems of government; the analysis of political activity and behavior. —**po·lit·i·cal sci·en·tist** *n.*

po·li·ti·cian /,pälə'tishən/ ▶n. a person who is professionally involved in politics, esp. as a holder of or a candidate for an elected office. ■ a person who acts in a manipulative and devious way, typically to gain advancement within an organization.

po·lit·i·cize /pə'litə,sīz/ ▶v. [tr.] cause (an activity or event) to become political in character: *art was becoming politicized.* ■ make (someone) politically aware, esp. by persuading them of the truth of views considered radical. ■ [intr.] engage in or talk about politics. —**po·lit·i·ci·za·tion** /pə,litəsi'zāsHən/ *n.*

po·lit·i·co /pə'litikō/ ▶n. (pl. **-cos**) informal term for POLITICIAN.

pol·i·tics /'pälə,tiks/ ▶pl. n. [usu. treated as *sing.*] the activities associated with the governance of a country or other area, esp. the debate or conflict among individuals or parties having or hoping to achieve power. ■ the activities of governments concerning the political relations between countries: *in the conduct of global politics, economic status must be backed by military capacity.* ■ the academic study of government and the state: [as adj.] *a politics lecturer.* ■ activities within an organization that are aimed at improving someone's status or position and are typically considered to be devious or divisive. ■ a particular set of political beliefs or principles. ■ (often **the politics of**) the assumptions or principles relating to or inherent in a sphere, theory, or thing, esp. when concerned with power and status in a society: *the politics of gender.*
▶ □ **play politics** act for political or personal gain rather than from principle.

pol·i·ty /'pälətē/ ▶n. (pl. **-ties**) a form or process of civil government or constitution. ■ an organized society; a state as a political entity.

pol·ka /'pō(l)kə/ ▶n. a lively dance of Bohemian origin in duple time. ■ a piece of music for this dance or in its rhythm.
▶v. (**pol·kas**, **pol·kaed** or **pol·ka'd**, **pol·ka·ing**) [intr.] dance the polka.

pol·ka dot ▶n. one of a number of round dots repeated to form a regular pattern on fabric: [as adj.] *a red and white polka-dot shirt.* —**pol·ka-dot·ted** *adj.*

poll /pōl/ ▶n. **1** (often **the polls**) the process of voting in an election: *the country went to the polls on March 10.* ■ a record of the number of votes cast in an election. ■ (**the polls**) the places where votes are cast in an election. **2** *dial.* a person's head. ■ the part of the head on which hair grows; the scalp.
▶v. [tr.] **1** (often **be polled**) record the opinion or vote of. ■ [intr.] (of a candidate in an election) receive a specified number of votes. ■ *Telecommunications & Comput.* check the status of (a measuring device, part of a computer, or a node in a network), esp. as part of a repeated cycle. **2** cut the horns off (an animal, esp. a young cow). ■ *archaic* cut off the top of (a tree or plant), typically to encourage further growth; pollard.

pol·lack /'pälək/ (also **pol·lock**) ▶n. (pl. same or **-lacks**) an edible greenish-brown fish (*Pollachius pollachius*) of the cod family. Found in the northeastern Atlantic, it is popular with anglers.

pol·lard /'pälərd/ ▶v. [tr.] [often as adj.] (**pollarded**) cut off the top and branches of (a tree) to encourage new growth at the top.
▶n. **1** a tree whose top and branches have been cut off for this reason. **2** *archaic* an animal, e.g., a sheep or deer, that has lost its horns or cast its antlers.

pol·len /'pälən/ ▶n. a fine powdery substance, typically yellow, consisting of microscopic grains discharged from the male part of a flower or from a male cone. Each grain contains a male gamete that can fertilize the female ovule, to which pollen is transported by the wind, insects, or other animals.

pol·li·nate /'pälə,nāt/ ▶v. [tr.] convey pollen to or deposit pollen on (a stigma, ovule, flower, or plant) and so allow fertilization. —**pol·li·na·tion** /,pälə'nāsHən/ *n.* —**pol·li·na·tor** /-,nātər/ *n.*

poll·ing booth ▶n. British and Canadian term for VOTING BOOTH.

pol·li·wog /'pälē,wäg; -,wôg/ (also **pol·ly·wog**) ▶n. a tadpole.

pol·lute /pə'lo͞ot/ ▶v. [tr.] contaminate (water, air, or a place) with harmful or poisonous substances. ■ *fig.* defile; corrupt: *a society polluted by racism.* ▷late Middle English: from Latin *pollut-* 'soiled, defiled,' from the verb *polluere*, based on the root of *lutum* 'mud.' —**pol·lu·tant** /-'lo͞otnt/ *adj.* & *n.* —**pol·lut·er** *n.* —**pol·lu·tion** *n.*

Pol·ly·an·na /,pälē'anə/ ▶n. an excessively cheerful or optimistic person. —**Pol·ly·an·na·ish** /-isH/ *adj.* —**Pol·ly·an·na·ism** /-,izəm/ *n.*

po·lo /'pōlō/ ▶n. a game of Eastern origin resembling field hockey, played on horseback with a long-handled mallet.

pol·o·naise /,pälə'nāz; ,pō-/ ▶n. **1** a slow dance of Polish origin in triple time, consisting chiefly of an intricate march or procession. ■ a piece of music for this dance or in its rhythm. **2** *hist.* a woman's dress with a tight bodice and a skirt open from the waist downward, looped up to show a decorative underskirt.
▶adj. (of a dish, esp. a vegetable dish) garnished with chopped hard-boiled egg yolk, breadcrumbs, and parsley.

po·lo·ni·um /pə'lōnēəm/ ▶n. the chemical element of atomic number 84, a radioactive metal occurring in nature only as a product of radioactive decay of uranium. (Symbol: **Po**)

po·lo shirt ▶n. a casual short-sleeved cotton shirt with a collar and several buttons at the neck.

pol·ter·geist /'pōltər,gīst/ ▶n. a ghost or other supernatural being supposedly responsible for physical disturbances such as loud noises and objects thrown around.

pol·troon /päl'tro͞on/ ▶n. archaic or poetic/lit. an utter coward. —**pol·troon·er·y** /-'tro͞onərē/ *n.*

pol·y /'pälē/ ▶n. (pl. **polys**) *inf.* short for: ■ polyester. ■ polytechnic. ■ polyethylene.

pol·y·an·dry /'pälē,andrē/ ▶n. polygamy in which a woman has more than one husband. ■ *Zool.* a pattern of mating in which a female animal has more than one male mate. —**pol·y·an·drous** /,pälē'andrəs/ *adj.*

pol·y·chlo·rin·at·ed bi·phen·yl /,pälē'klôrə,nātid bī'fenəl/ (abbr.: **PCB**) ▶n. *Chem.* any of a class of toxic aromatic compounds, often formed as waste in industrial processes, whose molecules contain two benzene rings in which hydrogen atoms have been replaced by chlorine atoms.

pol·y·chro·mat·ic /,pälikrō'matik/ ▶adj. of two or more colors; multicolored. ■ *Physics* (of light or other radiation) of a number of wavelengths or frequencies. —**pol·y·chro·ma·tism** /-'krōmə,tizəm/ *n.*

pol·y·chrome /'päli,krōm/ ▸adj. painted, printed, or decorated in several colors.
▸n. varied coloring. ■ a work of art in several colors, esp. a statue.
▸v. [tr.] execute or decorate (a work of art) in several colors. —**pol·y·chrom·y** n.

pol·y·es·ter /'päle,estər/ ▸n. a synthetic resin in which the polymer units are linked by ester groups, used chiefly to make synthetic textile fibers. ■ a fabric made from polyester fiber.

pol·y·eth·yl·ene /,päle'eтнəlēn/ ▸n. a tough, light, flexible synthetic resin made by polymerizing ethylene, chiefly used for plastic bags, food containers, and other packaging.

po·lyg·a·mous /pə'ligəməs/ ▸adj. practicing, relating to, or involving polygamy: *polygamous societies.* ■ *Zool.* (of an animal) typically having more than one mate. —**po·lyg·a·mous·ly** adv.

po·lyg·a·my /pə'ligəmē/ ▸n. **1** the practice or custom of having more than one wife or husband at the same time. ■ *Zool.* a pattern of mating in which an animal has more than one mate. **2** *Bot.* the condition of bearing some male, some female, and sometimes some perfect flowers on the same plant. —**po·lyg·a·mist** /-mist/ n.

pol·y·glot /'päli,glät/ ▸adj. knowing or using several languages. ■ (of a book) having the text translated into several languages.
▸n. a person who knows and is able to use several languages. —**pol·y·glot·ism** /-,glät,izəm/ n.

pol·y·gon /'päli,gän/ ▸n. *Geom.* a plane figure with at least three straight sides and angles, and typically five or more. —**po·lyg·o·nal** /pə'ligənl/ adj. —**po·lyg·o·nal·ly** adv.

pol·y·graph /'päli,graf/ ▸n. a machine designed to detect and record changes in physiological characteristics, such as a person's pulse and breathing rates, used esp. as a lie detector. ■ a lie-detector test carried out with a machine of this type. —**pol·y·graph·ic** /,päli'grafik/ adj.

pol·y·he·dron /,päli'hēdrən/ ▸n. (pl. **-he·drons** or **-he·dra** /-'hēdrə/) *Geom.* a solid figure with many plane faces, typically more than six. —**pol·y·he·dral** /-'hēdrəl/ adj. —**pol·y·he·dric** /-'hēdrik/ adj.

pol·y·math /'päli,maтн/ ▸n. a person of wide-ranging knowledge or learning. —**pol·y·math·ic** /,päli'maтнik/ adj. —**po·lym·a·thy** /pə'liməтнē; 'päli,maтнē/ n.

pol·y·mer /'päləmər/ ▸n. *Chem.* a substance that has a molecular structure consisting chiefly or entirely of a large number of similar units bonded together, e.g., many synthetic organic materials used as plastics and resins. Compare with **MONOMER**. —**pol·y·mer·ic** /,päle'merik/ adj. —**pol·y·mer·i·za·tion** /,päləmərə'zāshən/ n. —**pol·y·mer·ize** v.

Pol·y·ne·sian /,päle'nēzhən/ ▸adj. of or relating to Polynesia, its people, or their languages.
▸n. **1** a native or inhabitant of Polynesia, or a person of Polynesian descent. **2** a group of Austronesian languages spoken in Polynesia, including Maori, Hawaiian, and Samoan.

pol·y·no·mi·al /,päle'nōmēəl/ ▸adj. consisting of several terms. ■ *Math.* of, relating to, or denoting a polynomial or polynomials.
▸n. *Math.* an expression of more than two algebraic terms, esp. the sum of several terms that contain different powers of the same variable(s). ■ *Biol.* a Latin name with more than two parts.

pol·y·nos·ic /päli'näsik/ ▸n. a long-fiber rayon-and-polyester blend with a soft finish, used mainly in clothing.

pol·y·nu·cle·o·tide /,päli'n(y)ōōklēə,tīd/ ▸n. *Biochem.* a linear polymer whose molecule is composed of many nucleotide units, constituting a section of a nucleic acid molecule.

pol·yp /'päləp/ ▸n. **1** *Zool.* a solitary or colonial sedentary form of a coelenterate such as a sea anemone, typically having a columnar body with the mouth uppermost surrounded by a ring of tentacles. **2** *Med.* a small growth, typically benign and with a stalk, protruding from a mucous membrane. —**pol·yp·ous** /'päləpəs/ adj.

pol·y·pep·tide /,päli'pep,tīd/ ▸n. *Biochem.* a linear organic polymer consisting of a large number of amino-acid residues bonded together in a chain, forming part of (or the whole of) a protein molecule.

pol·y·phar·ma·cy /,päle'färməsē/ ▸n. (pl. **-cies**) the simultaneous use of multiple drugs to treat a single ailment or condition. ■ the simultaneous use of multiple drugs by a single patient, for one or more conditions.

pol·y·phon·ic /,päli'fänik/ ▸adj. producing many sounds simultaneously; many voiced. ■ *Mus.* (esp. of vocal music) in two or more parts, each having a melody of its own; contrapuntal. Compare with **HOMOPHONIC**. ■ *Mus.* (of an instrument) capable of producing more than one note at a time. —**pol·y·phon·i·cal·ly** /-ik(ə)lē/ adv.

po·lyph·o·ny /pə'lifənē/ ▸n. (pl. **-nies**) *Mus.* the style of simultaneously combining a number of parts, each forming an individual melody and

harmonizing with each other. ■ a composition written, played, or sung in this style. ■ (on an electronic keyboard or synthesizer) the number of notes or voices that can be played simultaneously without loss. —**pol·y·pho·nist** /-fənist/ n. —**pol·y·pho·nous** /-fənəs/ adj.

pol·y·pill /'päle,pil/ ▸n. a pill containing a number of medicines that all treat the same condition.

pol·y·pro·pyl·ene /,päli'prōpə,lēn/ ▸n. a synthetic resin that is a polymer of propylene, used esp. for ropes, fabrics, and molded objects.

pol·y·sac·cha·ride /,päli'sakə,rīd/ ▸n. *Biochem.* a carbohydrate (e.g., starch, cellulose, or glycogen) whose molecules consist of a number of sugar molecules bonded together.

pol·y·sty·rene /,päli'stīrēn/ ▸n. a synthetic resin that is a polymer of styrene, used chiefly as lightweight rigid foams and films.

pol·y·syl·lab·ic /,pälisə'labik/ ▸adj. (of a word) having more than one syllable. ■ using or characterized by words of many syllables: *polysyllabic jargon.* —**pol·y·syl·lab·i·cal·ly** /-sə'labək(ə)lē/ adv.

pol·y·tech·nic /,päli'teknik/ ▸n. an institution of higher education offering courses in many subjects, esp. vocational or technical subjects.
▸adj. dealing with or devoted to vocational or technical subjects.

pol·y·tet·ra·fluor·o·eth·yl·ene /,päli,tetrə,flŏōrō'eтнə,lēn/ ▸n. a tough translucent synthetic resin made by polymerizing tetrafluoroethylene, chiefly used to make seals and bearings and to coat nonstick cooking utensils.

pol·y·the·ism /'päliтнē,izəm/ ▸n. the belief in or worship of more than one god. —**pol·y·the·ist** /-,тнēist/ n. —**pol·y·the·is·tic** /,päliтнē'istik/ adj.

pol·y·un·sat·u·rat·ed /,päleən'sachə,rātid/ ▸adj. *Chem.* (of an organic compound, esp. a fat or oil molecule) containing several double or triple bonds between carbon atoms.

pol·y·u·re·thane /,päli'yŏŏrə,тнān/ ▸n. a synthetic resin in which the polymer units are linked by urethane groups, used chiefly as constituents of paints, varnishes, adhesives, and foams.
▸v. [tr.] coat or protect with paint or varnish of this kind.

pol·y·vi·nyl /,päli'vīnl/ ▸adj. [attrib.] denoting materials or objects made from polymers of vinyl compounds.

pol·y·vi·nyl chlo·ride (abbr.: **PVC**) ▸n. a tough, chemically resistant synthetic resin made by polymerizing vinyl chloride and used for a wide variety of products including pipes, flooring, and sheeting.

po·made /pə'mād; -'mäd/ *dated* ▸n. a scented ointment applied to the hair or scalp.
▸v. [tr.] (**pomaded**) apply pomade to. ▷mid 16th cent.: from French *pommade*, based on Latin *pomum* 'apple' (from which it was originally made).

po·man·der /pō'mandər; 'pō,mandər/ ▸n. a ball or perforated container of sweet-smelling herbs and spices, placed in a closet, drawer, or room to perfume the air or (formerly) carried as a supposed protection against infection. ■ a piece of fruit, typically an orange or apple, studded with cloves and hung in a closet for a similar purpose.

pome·gran·ate /'päm(ə),granət; 'pəm,granət/ ▸n. **1** an orange-sized fruit with a tough reddish outer skin and sweet red gelatinous flesh containing many seeds. **2** the widely cultivated tree (*Punica granatum*, family Punicaceae) that bears this fruit, which is native to North Africa and western Asia.

Pom·er·a·ni·an /,pämə'rānēən/ ▸n. a small dog of a breed with long silky hair, a pointed muzzle, and pricked ears.

pom·mel ▸n. /'päməl; 'pəməl/ **1** a rounded knob on the end of the handle of a sword, dagger, or old-fashioned gun. **2** the upward curving or projecting part of a saddle in front of the rider.
▸v. /'pəməl; 'pāməl/ (**-meled, -mel·ing**; *Brit.* **-melled, -mel·ling**) another term for **PUMMEL**.

pom·mel horse ▸n. a vaulting horse fitted with a pair of curved handgrips, used for a gymnastic exercise consisting of swings of the legs and body. ■ the set of exercises performed on such a piece of equipment.

pomp /pämp/ ▸n. ceremony and splendid display, esp. at a public event. ■ (**pomps**) *archaic* ostentatious boastfulness or vanity.

pom-pom /'päm ,päm/ (also **pom-pom** or **pom·pon** /-,pän/) ▸n. a small woolen ball attached to a garment, esp. a hat, for decoration. ■ a cluster of brightly colored strands of yarn or plastic, waved in pairs by cheerleaders. ■ a dahlia, chrysanthemum, or aster with small tightly clustered petals: [as adj.] *miniature, pompom, and border dahlias.*

pomp·ous /'pämpəs/ ▸adj. affectedly and irritatingly grand, solemn, or self-important. ■ *archaic* characterized by pomp or splendor. —**pom·pos·i·ty** /ˌpämˈpäsətē/ *n.* —**pomp·ous·ly** *adv.* —**pomp·ous·ness** *n.*

pon·cho /ˈpänCHō/ ▶*n.* (*pl.* **-chos**) a garment of a type originally worn in South America, made of a thick piece of woolen cloth with a slit in the middle for the head. ■ a garment in this style, esp. a waterproof one worn as a raincoat.

pond /pänd/ ▶*n.* a small body of still water formed naturally or by hollowing or embanking. ■ (**the pond**) *inf.* the Atlantic ocean.
▶*v.* [*tr.*] hold back or dam up (flowing water or another liquid) to form a small lake. ■ [*intr.*] (of flowing water or other liquids) form such a lake: [as *n.*] (**ponding**) *where a path goes down into a dip, you'll have to ensure that ponding doesn't occur.*

pon·der /ˈpändər/ ▶*v.* [*tr.*] think about (something) carefully, esp. before making a decision or reaching a conclusion: *I pondered the question of what clothes to wear* [*intr.*] *she sat pondering over her problem.* —**pon·der·a·tion** /ˌpändəˈrāSHən/ *n.* (*rare*).

pon·der·o·sa /ˌpändəˈrōsə/ (also **ponderosa pine**) ▶*n.* a tall slender pine tree (*Pinus ponderosa*), the most widespread conifer of western North America.

pon·der·ous /ˈpändərəs/ ▶*adj.* slow and clumsy because of great weight. ■ dull, laborious, or excessively solemn. —**pon·der·os·i·ty** /ˌpändəˈräsətē/ *n.* —**pon·der·ous·ly** *adv.* —**pon·der·ous·ness** *n.*

pone /pōn/ ▶*n.* (also **corn pone** or **pone bread**) unleavened cornbread in the form of flat oval cakes or loaves, originally as prepared with water by North American Indians and cooked in hot ashes.

pon·gid /ˈpänjəd; -gəd/ ▶*n. Zool.* a primate of a family (Pongidae) that comprises the great apes.

pons /pänz/ (in full **pons Va·ro·li·i** /vəˈrōlēˌī/) ▶*n.* (*pl.* **pon·tes** /ˈpänˌtēz/) *Anat.* the part of the brainstem that links the medulla oblongata and the thalamus.

pon·tiff /ˈpäntəf/ ▶*n.* the pope.

pon·tif·i·cal /pänˈtifikəl/ ▶*adj.* **1** (in the Roman Catholic Church) of or relating to the pope: *a pontifical commission.* **2** characterized by a pompous and superior air of infallibility. —**pon·tif·i·cal·ly** /-ik(ə)lē/ *adv.*

pon·tif·i·cate ▶*v.* /pänˈtifiˌkāt/ [*intr.*] **1** (in the Roman Catholic Church) officiate as bishop, esp. at Mass. **2** express one's opinions in a way considered annoyingly pompous and dogmatic.
▶*n.* /-kət/ (also **Pon·tif·i·cate**) (in the Roman Catholic Church) the office of pope or bishop. ■ the period of such an office: *Pope Gregory VIII enjoyed only a ten-week pontificate.* —**pon·tif·i·ca·tor** /-ˌkātər/ *n.*

pon·toon /ˌpänˈtoōn/ ▶*n.* a flat-bottomed boat or hollow metal cylinder used with others to support a temporary bridge or floating landing stage. ■ a bridge or landing stage supported by pontoons. ■ a large flat-bottomed barge or lighter equipped with cranes. ■ either of the floats fitted to an aircraft to enable it to land on water.

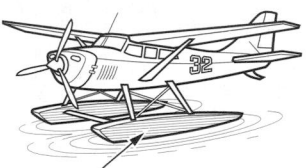

pontoons

po·ny /ˈpōnē/ ▶*n.* (*pl.* **-nies**) **1** a horse of a small breed, esp. one whose height at the withers is below 14 hands 2 inches (58 inches). ■ (**the ponies**) *inf.* racehorses: *he had been playing the ponies on the side.* **2** *inf.* a small drinking glass or the drink contained in it: *a pony of vodka.* **3** a literal translation of a foreign-language text, used illicitly by students; a trot. **4** *Brit., inf.* twenty-five pounds sterling.
▶*v.* (**-nies, -nied**) [*intr.*] (**pony up**) *inf.* pay (money), esp. as a contribution or an unavoidable expense.

Po·ny Ex·press ▶ a system of mail delivery operating from 1860 to 1861 over a distance of 1,800 miles (2,900 km) between St. Joseph, Missouri, and Sacramento, California, using continuous relays of horse riders.

po·ny·tail /ˈpōnēˌtāl/ ▶*n.* a hairstyle in which the hair is drawn back and tied at the back of the head, causing it to hang down like a pony's tail. —**po·ny·tailed** *adj.*

pooch¹ /poōCH/ ▶*n. inf.* a dog.

pooch² ▶*v. inf.* protrude or cause to protrude: [*intr.*] *a dress that made her stomach pooch out even more than usual.*

poo·dle /ˈpoōdl/ ▶*n.* a dog of a breed with a curly coat that is usually clipped. The numerous varieties of poodle include standard, miniature, and toy.

pooh /poō; poŏ/ (also **poo**) *inf.* ▶*interj.* used to express disgust at an unpleasant smell. ■ used to express impatience or contempt: *Oh pooh! Don't be such a spoilsport.*
▶*n.* excrement. ■ an act of defecating.
▶*v.* [*intr.*] defecate.

pooh-pooh /ˈpoō ˌpoō; poō ˈpoō/ ▶*v.* [*tr.*] *inf.* dismiss (an idea or suggestion) as being foolish or impractical.

pool¹ /poōl/ ▶*n.* **1** a small area of still water, typically one formed naturally. ■ a small, shallow patch of liquid lying on a surface: *a pool of blood* | *fig. the lamps cast pools of light on the wet streets.* ■ a swimming pool. ■ a deep place in a river.
▶*v.* [*intr.*] (of water or another liquid) form a pool on the ground or another surface: *the oil pooled behind the quay walls, escaping slowly into the river.* ■ (of blood) accumulate in parts of the venous system.

pool² ▶*n.* **1** a supply of vehicles or goods available for use when needed: *the oldest vehicle in the motor pool.* ■ a group of people available for work when required: *the typing pool.* ■ a group of people considered as a resource: *a pool of promising high-school students.* ■ an arrangement, illegal in many countries, between competing parties to fix prices or rates and share business in order to eliminate competition. ■ a common fund into which all contributors pay and from which financial backing is provided. ■ a source of common funding for speculative operations on financial markets. ■ a group of contestants who compete against each other in a tournament for the right to advance to the next round. ■ the collective amount of players' stakes in gambling or sweepstakes; a kitty. **2** *Billiards* a game played on a table using fifteen colored and numbered balls and a white cue ball.
▶*v.* [*tr.*] (of two or more people or organizations) put (money or other assets) into a common fund. ■ share (things) for the benefit of all those involved: [as *n.*] (**pooling**) *a pooling of ideas.* —**pool·er** *n.*

pool·room /ˈpoōlˌroōm; -ˌroōm/ ▶*n.* (also **pool hall**) a commercial establishment where pool or billiard games are played.

poop¹ /poōp/ ▶*n.* (also **poop deck**) the aftermost and highest deck of a ship, esp. in a sailing ship where it typically forms the roof of a cabin in the stern.

poop² ▶*v.* [*tr.*] (usu. **be pooped**) *inf.* exhaust.
▶*phrasal v.* □ **poop out** stop functioning.

poop³ *inf.* ▶*n.* excrement.
▶*v.* [*intr.*] defecate.

poop⁴ ▶*n. inf.* up-to-date or inside information: *what's the latest poop?*

poop⁵ ▶*n. inf.* a stupid or ineffectual person. —**poop·y** *adj.*

poor /poŏr; pôr/ ▶*adj.* **1** lacking sufficient money to live at a standard considered comfortable or normal in a society: [as *n.*] (**the poor**) *the gap between the rich and the poor has widened.* ■ (of a place) inhabited by people without sufficient money. **2** worse than is usual, expected, or desirable; of a low or inferior standard or quality. ■ (**poor in**) deficient or lacking in. ■ *dated* used ironically to deprecate something belonging to or offered by oneself: *he is, in my poor opinion, a more handsome young man.* **3** (of a person) considered to be deserving of pity or sympathy: *they inquired after poor Dorothy's broken hip.* ▷Middle English: from Old French *poure*, from Latin *pauper*.
▶ □ (**as**) **poor as a church mouse** (or **as church mice**) extremely poor. □ **poor little rich boy** (or **girl**) a wealthy young person whose money brings them no contentment (often used as an expression of mock sympathy). □ **the poor man's ——** an inferior or cheaper substitute for the thing specified: *corduroy has always been the poor man's velvet.* □ **poor relation** a person or thing that is considered inferior or subordinate to others of the same type or group: *for many years radio has been the poor relation of the media.* □ **take a poor view of** regard with disfavor or disapproval.

poor·house /ˈpoŏrˌhous; ˈpôr-/ ▶*n. hist.* an institution where paupers were maintained with public funds.

poo·ri /ˈpoŏrē/ ▶*n.* see PURI.

poor·ly /ˈpoŏrlē; ˈpôr-/ ▶*adv.* in a way or at a level that is considered inadequate: *schools that were performing poorly.* ■ with insufficient money or resources: *he lived as poorly as his peasant parishioners.*
▶*adj.* unwell: *she looked poorly.*

poor·ness /ˈpoŏrnəs; ˈpôr-/ ▶*n.* the state of lacking or being deficient in some desirable quality or constituent: *the poorness of the food.*

POP /päp/ (also **PoP**) ▶*abbr.* (in computing) point of presence, denoting equipment that acts as access to the Internet. ■ point of purchase, denoting products or promotions located adjacent to a retail checkout or cashier.

pop¹ /päp/ ▶*v.* (**popped, pop·ping**) **1** [*intr.*] make a sudden, sharp, explosive sound. ■ [*tr.*] cause (something) to burst, making such a sound: *they were popping balloons with darts.* ■ (of a person's ears) make a small

popping sound within the head as pressure is equalized, typically because of a change of altitude. ■ [*tr.*] heat (popcorn or another foodstuff) until it bursts open, making such a sound. ■ [*intr.*] (of popcorn or another foodstuff) burst open in such a way. ■ (of a person's eyes) bulge or appear to bulge when opened wide, esp. as an indication of surprise. ■ [*tr.*] shoot (a gun). ■ [*tr.*] shoot (something) with a gun. **2** [*intr.*] go somewhere, typically for a short time and often without notice: *she popped in to see if she could help.* ■ [*tr.*] put or move (something) somewhere quickly: *he popped his head around the door.* **3** [*intr.*] *Baseball* (of a batter) hit a pop fly. ■ [*tr.*] (of a pitcher) cause (a batter) to pop up. **4** [*tr.*] *inf.* take or inject (a drug).
▸*phrasal v.* □ **pop off** *inf.* **1** die. **2** speak spontaneously and at length, typically angrily. □ **pop out** make an out in a baseball game by hitting a pop fly that is caught. □ **pop up 1** appear or occur suddenly and unexpectedly. **2** hit a baseball high into the air but not deep, providing an easy catch.
▸*n.* **1** a sudden sharp explosive sound. **2** *inf.* short for SODA POP (see SODA). **3** (also **pop fly** or **pop-up**) *Baseball* a ball hit high in the air but not deep, providing an easy catch. **4** an attempt: *he grabs with a paw and hooks about two hundred berries at a pop.*
▸*adv.* with a sudden explosive sound: *the champagne went pop.*
▸*adj.* sudden or unexpected: *a pop quiz on the capitals of South America.*
▸ □ —— **a pop** *inf.* costing a specified amount per item: *those swimsuits she wears are $50 a pop.* □ **pop the question** *inf.* propose marriage.
pop² ▸*adj.* **1** of or relating to commercial popular music: *a pop star* | *a pop group.* ■ of, denoting, or relating to pop art. **2** *often derog.* (esp. of a technical, scientific, or academic subject) made accessible to the general public; popularized: *pop psychology.*
▸*n.* (also **pop music**) commercial popular music, in particular accessible, tuneful music of a kind popular since the 1950s and sometimes contrasted with rock, soul, or other forms of popular music. ■ *dated* a pop record or song.
pop³ (also **pops**) ▸*n.* informal term for FATHER.
POP3 /ˈpäp ˈTHrē/ ▸*n.* *Comput.* a protocol for receiving e-mail by downloading it to a computer from a mailbox on the server of an Internet service provider.
pop art ▸*n.* art based on modern popular culture and the mass media, esp. as a critical or ironic comment on traditional fine art values.
pop·corn /ˈpäpˌkôrn/ ▸*n.* corn of a variety with hard kernels that swell up and burst open with a pop when heated. ■ these kernels when popped, typically buttered and salted and eaten as a snack.
pop cul·ture ▸*n.* commercial culture based on popular taste.
pope /pōp/ ▸*n.* (usu. **the pope** or **the Pope**) the bishop of Rome as head of the Roman Catholic Church. ■ the head of the Coptic Church, the bishop or patriarch of Alexandria. —**pope·dom** /-dəm/ *n.*
pop·in·jay /ˈpäpənˌjā/ ▸*n.* **1** *dated* a vain or conceited person, esp. one who dresses or behaves extravagantly. **2** *archaic* a parrot.
pop·lar /ˈpäplər/ ▸*n.* **1** a tall, fast-growing tree (genus *Populus*) of the willow family, widely grown in shelter belts and for timber and pulp. **2** (**yellow poplar**) another term for TULIP TREE.
pop·lin /ˈpäplən/ ▸*n.* a plain-woven ribbed fabric, typically a lightweight cotton.
pop·o·ver /ˈpäpˌōvər/ ▸*n.* a light muffin made from a thin batter, which rises to form a hollow shell when baked.
pop·pa /ˈpäpə/ ▸*n.* informal term for FATHER.
pop·ple /ˈpäpəl/ ▸*n.* *dial.* any of various poplar trees, especially of northern forests.
pop·py /ˈpäpē/ ▸*n.* a herbaceous plant (*Papaver*, *Eschscholzia*, and other genera, family Papaveraceae) with showy flowers, milky sap, and rounded seed capsules. Many poppies contain alkaloids and are a source of drugs such as morphine and codeine.
pop·py·cock /ˈpäpēˌkäk/ ▸*n.* *inf.* nonsense.
Pop·si·cle /ˈpäpˌsikəl/ ▸*n.* *trademark* a piece of flavored ice or ice cream on a stick.
pop·u·lace /ˈpäpyələs/ ▸*n.* [treated as *sing.* or *pl.*] the people living in a particular country or area: *the party misjudged the mood of the populace.*
pop·u·lar /ˈpäpyələr/ ▸*adj.* **1** liked, admired, or enjoyed by many people or by a particular person or group. **2** (of cultural activities or products) intended for or suited to the taste, understanding, or means of the general public rather than specialists or intellectuals: *the popular press.* ■ (of a belief or attitude) held by the majority of the general public. **3** (of political activity) of or carried on by the people as a whole rather than restricted to politicians or political parties: *a popular revolt against colonial rule.* —**pop·u·lar·ism** /-ˌrizəm/ *n.* —**pop·u·lar·i·ty** /ˌpäpyəˈlaritē/ *n.* —**pop·u·lar·ly** *adv.*

pop·u·lar front ▸*n.* a party or coalition representing left-wing elements, in particular (**the Popular Front**) an alliance of communist, radical, and socialist elements formed and gaining some power in countries such as France and Spain in the 1930s.
pop·u·lar·ize /ˈpäpyələˌrīz/ ▸*v.* [*tr.*] cause (something) to become generally liked. ■ make (something technical, scientific, or academic) accessible or interesting to the general public by presenting it in a readily understandable form. —**pop·u·lar·i·za·tion** /ˌpäpyələrəˈzāSHən/ *n.* —**pop·u·lar·iz·er** *n.*
pop·u·lar mu·sic ▸*n.* music appealing to the popular taste, including rock and pop and also soul, country, reggae, rap, and dance music.
pop·u·late /ˈpäpyəˌlāt/ ▸*v.* [*tr.*] (usu. **be populated**) form the population of (a town, area, or country): *the island is populated by scarcely 40,000 people.* ■ *fig.* fill or be present in (a place, environment, or domain): *the spirit of the book and the characters who populate its pages.* ■ cause people to settle in (an area or place). ■ fill something in, such as a table of values.
pop·u·la·tion /ˌpäpyəˈlāSHən/ ▸*n.* all the inhabitants of a particular town, area, or country. ■ a particular section, group, or type of people or animals living in an area or country: *the immigrant population.* ■ the specified extent or degree to which an area is populated: *areas of sparse population.* ■ the action of populating an area. ■ *Biol.* a community of animals, plants, or humans among whose members interbreeding occurs. ■ *Statistics* a finite or infinite collection of items under consideration. ■ *Astron.* each of three groups (designated I, II, and III) into which stars can be approximately divided on the basis of their manner of formation.
pop·u·list /ˈpäpyələst/ ▸*n.* a member or adherent of a political party seeking to represent the interests of ordinary people. ■ a person who holds, or who is concerned with, the views of ordinary people. ■ (**Populist**) a member of the Populist Party, a U.S. political party formed in 1891 that advocated the interests of labor and farmers.
▸*adj.* of or relating to a populist or populists: *a populist leader.* —**pop·u·lism** /-ˌlizəm/ *n.* —**pop·u·lis·tic** /ˌpäpyəˈlistik/ *adj.*
pop·u·lous /ˈpäpyələs/ ▸*adj.* having a large population; densely populated. —**pop·u·lous·ly** *adv.* —**pop·u·lous·ness** *n.*
pop-up ▸*adj.* (of a book or greeting card) containing folded cut-out pictures that rise up to form a three-dimensional scene or figure when the page is turned. ■ (of an electric toaster) operating so as to push up a piece of toast quickly when it is ready. ■ *Comput.* (of a menu or other utility) able to be superimposed on the screen being worked on and suppressed rapidly.
▸*n.* **1** a pop-up picture in a book. ■ a book containing such pictures. **2** *Baseball* see POP¹ (sense 3). **3** *Comput.* a pop-up menu or other utility.
por·ce·lain /ˈpôrs(ə)lən/ ▸*n.* a white vitrified translucent ceramic; china. ■ (usu. **porcelains**) articles made of this. ■ such articles collectively: *Chinese porcelain.* —**por·ce·la·ne·ous** /ˌpôrsəˈlānēəs/ *adj.* —**por·cel·la·nous** /-əs/ *adj.*
porch /pôrCH/ ▸*n.* a covered shelter projecting in front of the entrance of a building. ■ a veranda. ▷Middle English: from Old French *porche*, from Latin *porticus* 'colonnade,' from *porta* 'passage.' —**porched** *adj.* —**porch·less** *adj.*
por·cine /ˈpôrˌsīn/ ▸*adj.* of, affecting, or resembling a pig or pigs.
por·cu·pine /ˈpôrkyəˌpīn/ ▸*n.* a large rodent (Old World family Hystricidae and New World family Erethizontidae) with defensive spines or quills on the body and tail. The common North American species is *Erethizon dorsatum.*
pore¹ /pôr/ ▸*n.* chiefly *Biol.* a minute opening in a surface, esp. the skin or integument of an organism, through which gases, liquids, or microscopic particles can pass.
pore² ▸*v.* [*intr.*] (**pore over/through**) be absorbed in the reading or study of: *Heather spent hours poring over cookbooks.* ■ *archaic* think intently; ponder: *when he has thought and pored on it.*
por·gy /ˈpôrgē/ ▸*n.* (*pl.* same or **-ies**) a deep-bodied fish (*Calamus* and other genera) of the sea bream family, typically silvery but sometimes changing to a blotched pattern.
pork /pôrk/ ▸*n.* **1** the flesh of a pig used as food, esp. when uncured. **2** short for PORK BARREL.
▸*v.* **1** [*tr.*] *vulgar slang* (of a man) have sexual intercourse with. **2** [*intr.*] *inf.* stuff oneself with food; overeat: *I porked out on the roast pig.*
pork bar·rel ▸*n.* *inf.* the use of government funds for projects designed to please voters or legislators and win votes: *political pork barrel for the*

benefit of their respective sponsors | [as *adj.*] *wasteful, pork-barrel spending.* **—pork·bar·rel·ing** *n.*

pork·er /'pôrkər/ ▶*n.* a pig raised for food. ■ *inf., derog.* a fat person.

pork·pie hat /'pôrk,pī/ ▶*n.* a hat with a flat crown and a brim turned up all around.

pork·y[1] /'pôrkē/ ▶*adj.* (**pork·i·er, pork·i·est**) **1** *inf.* (of a person or part of their body) fleshy or fat. **2** of or resembling pork.

pork·y[2] ▶*n.* (*pl.* **pork·ies**) *inf.* a porcupine.

porn /pôrn/ (also **porn·o** /'pôrnō/) *inf.* ▶*n.* **1** pornography. **2** television programs, books, etc., regarded as catering to a voyeuristic or obsessive interest in a specified subject: *weather porn of the highest order.*
▶*adj.* pornographic: *a porn video.*

por·nog·ra·phy /pôr'nägrəfē/ ▶*n.* printed or visual material containing the explicit description or display of sexual organs or activity, intended to stimulate erotic rather than aesthetic or emotional feelings. **—por·nog·ra·pher** /-fər/ *n.* **—por·no·graph·ic** /,pôrnə'grafik/ *adj.* **—por·no·graph·i·cal·ly** /,pôrnə'grafik(ə)lē/ *adv.*

po·rous /'pôrəs/ ▶*adj.* (of a rock or other material) having spaces or holes through which liquid or air may pass. ■ *fig.* not retentive or secure: *he ran through a porous defense to score easily.* **—po·ros·i·ty** /pə-'räsətē; pôr'äs-/ *n.* **—po·rous·ness** *n.*

por·phy·ry /'pôrfərē/ ▶*n.* (*pl.* **-ries**) a hard igneous rock containing crystals, usually of feldspar, in a fine-grained, typically reddish groundmass. **—por·phy·rit·ic** /,pôrfə'ritik/ *adj.*

por·poise /'pôrpəs/ ▶*n.* a small toothed whale with a low triangular dorsal fin and a blunt rounded snout. Its several species include the **harbor** (or **common**) **porpoise** (*Phocoena phocoena*) of the North Atlantic and North Pacific.
▶*v.* [*intr.*] move through the water like a porpoise, alternately rising above it and submerging.

por·ridge /'pôrij/ ▶*n.* a dish consisting of oatmeal or another meal or cereal boiled in water or milk. **—por·ridg·y** *adj.*

por·rin·ger /'pôrənjər/ ▶*n. hist.* a small bowl, typically with a handle, used for soup, stew, or similar dishes.

port[1] /pôrt/ ▶*n.* a town or city with a harbor where ships load or unload, esp. one where customs officers are stationed. ■ a harbor: *the port has miles of docks.* ■ (also **inland port**) an inland town or city whose connection to the coast by a river or other body of water enables it to act as a port.
▶ □ **port of entry** a harbor or airport by which people and goods may enter a country.

port[2] (also **port wine**) ▶*n.* a strong, sweet, typically dark red fortified wine, originally from Portugal, typically drunk as a dessert wine.

port[3] ▶*n.* the side of a ship or aircraft that is on the left when one is facing forward: *the ferry was listing to port.* The opposite of STARBOARD.

port[4] ▶*n.* an aperture or opening, in particular: ■ a socket in a computer or network into which a device can be plugged. ■ an opening for the passage of steam, liquid, or gas. ■ an opening in the side of a ship for boarding or loading.

port[5] ▶*v.* **1** [*tr.*] *Comput.* transfer (software) from one system or machine to another: *the software can be ported to an IBM RS/6000.* **2** [*tr.*] [often in *imper.*] *Mil.* carry (a rifle or other weapon) diagonally across and close to the body with the barrel or blade near the left shoulder: *Detail! For inspection—port arms!*
▶*n.* **1** *poetic/lit.* a person's carriage or bearing. **2** *Comput.* a transfer of software from one system or machine to another.

port·a·ble /'pôrtəbəl/ ▶*adj.* able to be easily carried or moved, esp. because of being a lighter and smaller version than usual: *a portable television.* ■ *Comput.* (of software) able to be transferred from one machine or system to another.
▶*n.* a version of something, such as a small lightweight television or computer, that can be easily carried. ■ a small transportable building used as a classroom. **—port·a·bil·i·ty** /,pôrtə'bilətē/ *n.* **—port·a·bly** /-blē/ *adv.*

por·tage /'pôrtij/ ▶*n.* the carrying of a boat or its cargo between two navigable waters. ■ a place at which this is necessary: *a portage over the dam.*
▶*v.* [*tr.*] carry (a boat or its cargo) between navigable waters: *they are incapable of portaging a canoe* | [*intr.*] *they would only run the rapid if they couldn't portage.*

por·tal[1] /'pôrtl/ ▶*n.* **1** a doorway, gate, or other entrance, esp. a large and elaborate one. **2** *Comput.* an Internet site providing access or links to other sites.

por·tal[2] ▶*adj. Anat.* of or relating to an opening in an organ through

which major blood vessels pass, esp. the transverse fissure of the liver.

por·ta·men·to /,pôrtə'men,tō/ ▶*n.* (*pl.* **-tos** or **-ti** /-tē/) *Mus.* **1** a slide from one note to another, esp. in singing or playing a bowed string instrument. **2** piano playing in a manner intermediate between legato and staccato: [as *adj.*] *a portamento style.*

port block·ing ▶*n.* the selective prevention of traffic from certain Internet addresses or domains, typically as a means of censorship and of preventing spam and cyberattacks, or as a malicious attempt to impede commerce: *an extra layer of security to protect the perimeter of the network from port blocking.*

port·cul·lis /pôrt'kələs/ ▶*n.* a strong, heavy grating sliding up and down in vertical grooves, lowered to block a gateway to a fortress or town. **—port·cul·lised** *adj.*

por·tend /pôr'tend/ ▶*v.* [*tr.*] be a sign or warning that (something, esp. something momentous or calamitous) is likely to happen. ■ be a signal of.

por·tent /'pôr,tent/ ▶*n.* **1** a sign or warning that something, esp. something momentous or calamitous, is likely to happen. ■ future significance. **2** *archaic* an exceptional or wonderful person or thing.

portcullis

por·ten·tous /pôr'tentəs/ ▶*adj.* of or like a portent. ■ done in a pompously or overly solemn manner so as to impress: *the author's portentous moralizings.* **—por·ten·tous·ly** *adv.* **—por·ten·tous·ness** *n.*

por·ter[1] /'pôrtər/ ▶*n.* **1** a person employed to carry luggage and other loads, esp. in a railroad station, airport, or hotel. ■ a person employed to carry supplies on a mountaineering expedition. ■ an attendant in a railroad sleeping car or parlor car. **2** dark brown bitter beer brewed from malt partly charred or browned by drying at a high temperature.

por·ter[2] ▶*n.* an employee in charge of the entrance of a hotel, apartment complex, or other large building.

por·ter·house steak ▶*n.* a choice steak cut from the thick end of a sirloin.

port·fo·li·o /pôrt'fōlē,ō/ ▶*n.* (*pl.* **-os**) **1** a large, thin, flat case for loose sheets of paper such as drawings or maps. ■ a set of pieces of creative work collected by someone to display their skills, esp. to a potential employer. ■ a varied set of photographs of a model or actor intended to be shown to a potential employer. **2** a range of investments held by a person or organization. ■ a range of products or services offered by an organization, esp. when considered as a business asset: *an unrivaled portfolio of quality brands.* **3** the position and duties of a minister of state or a member of a cabinet: *he took on the Foreign Affairs portfolio.*
▶*adj.* relating to, denoting, or engaged in an employment pattern that involves a succession of short-term contracts and part-time work: *portfolio careers allow women to balance work with family.*

port·hole /'pôrt,hōl/ ▶*n.* a small exterior window in a ship or aircraft.

por·ti·co /'pôrti,kō/ ▶*n.* (*pl.* **-coes** or **-cos**) a structure consisting of a roof supported by columns at regular intervals, typically attached as a porch to a building.

por·tion /'pôrSHən/ ▶*n.* a part of a whole; an amount, section, or piece of something. ■ a part of something divided between two or more people; a share: *her portion of the allowance.* ■ an amount of food suitable for or served to one person: *a portion of ice cream.* ■ *Law* the part or share of an estate given or

portico

descending by law to an heir. ■ *archaic* a person's future as allotted by fate; one's destiny or lot: *what will be my portion?* ■ (also **marriage portion**) *archaic* a dowry given to a bride at her marriage.
▶*v.* [*tr.*] (usu. **be portioned**) divide (something) into shares to be distributed among two or more people: *the fish are **portioned out** to the different families.* ■ [usu. as *adj.*] (**portioned**) serve (food) in an amount suitable for one person: *generously portioned lunches.* ■ *archaic* give a dowry to (a bride at her marriage). ▷Middle English: from Old French *porcion,* from Latin *portio(n-),* from the phrase *pro portione* 'in proportion.'

port·ly /'pôrtlē/ ▸adj. (**-li·er, -li·est**) **1** (esp. of a man) having a stout body; somewhat fat. **2** archaic of a stately or dignified appearance and manner: *he was a man of portly presence.* —**port·li·ness** n.

port·man·teau /pôrt'mantō/ ▸n. (pl. **-teaus** /-tōz/ or **-teaux** /-tōz/) a large trunk or suitcase, typically made of stiff leather and opening into two equal parts. ■ [as adj.] consisting of or combining two or more separable aspects or qualities: *a portmanteau movie composed of excerpts from his most famous films.*

port·man·teau word ▸n. a word blending the sounds and combining the meanings of two others, for example *motel* (from 'motor' and 'hotel') or *brunch* (from 'breakfast' and 'lunch').

port of call ▸n. a place where a ship stops on a voyage. ■ any of a number of places that a person visits in succession.

por·trait /'pôrtrət; -,trāt/ ▸n. **1** a painting, drawing, photograph, or engraving of a person, esp. one depicting only the face or head and shoulders. ■ a representation or impression of someone or something in language or on film. **2** [as adj.] (of a page, book, or illustration, or the manner in which it is set or printed) higher than it is wide: *you can print landscape and portrait pages in the same document.* Compare with LANDSCAPE (sense 2). —**por·trait·ist** /'pôrtrətist; -,trātist/ n.

por·trai·ture /'pôrtrɪCHər; -,CHŏŏr/ ▸n. the art of creating portraits. ■ graphic and detailed description, esp. of a person: *it's part murder mystery and part portraiture through poetry.* ■ formal a portrait.

por·tray /pôr'trā/ ▸v. [tr.] depict (someone or something) in a work of art or literature. ■ (of an actor) represent or play the part of (someone) on film or stage. ■ [tr.] describe (someone or something) in a particular way. —**por·tray·a·ble** adj. —**por·tray·al** /-'trā(ə)l/ n. —**por·tray·er** n.

Por·tu·guese /'pôrCHə,gēz/ ▸adj. of or relating to Portugal or its people or language.
▸n. (pl. same) **1** a native or national of Portugal, or a person of Portuguese descent. **2** the Romance language of Portugal and Brazil.

Por·tu·guese man-of-war ▸n. a floating colonial coelenterate (*Physalia physalis*, order Siphonophora, class Hydrozoa) that bears long tentacles that are able to inflict painful stings.

pose¹ /pōz/ ▸v. **1** [tr.] present or constitute (a problem, danger, or difficulty). ■ raise (a question or matter for consideration). **2** [intr.] assume a particular attitude or position in order to be photographed, painted, or drawn: *she posed for TV cameramen.* ■ [tr.] place (someone) in a particular attitude or position in order to be photographed, painted, or drawn: *he posed her on the sofa.* ■ (**pose as**) set oneself up as or pretend to be (someone or something): *a detective posing as a customer* | *fig. whitewashed chicken coops that posed as villas.* ■ behave affectedly in order to impress others: *some people like to drive these cars, but most just like to pose in them.*
▸n. a particular way of standing or sitting, usually adopted for effect or in order to be photographed, painted, or drawn. ■ a particular way of behaving adopted in order to give others a false impression or to impress others: *the man dropped his pose of amiability.*

pose² ▸v. [tr.] archaic puzzle or perplex (someone) with a question or problem: *we have thus posed the mathematician and the historian.*

pos·er¹ /'pōzər/ ▸n. a person who acts in an affected manner in order to impress others.

pos·er² ▸n. a difficult or perplexing question or problem.

po·seur /pō'zər/ ▸n. another term for POSER¹.

posh /päSH/ inf. ▸adj. elegant or stylishly luxurious: *a posh Munich hotel.* ■ chiefly Brit. typical of or belonging to the upper class of society.
▸adv. Brit. in an upper-class way: *trying to talk posh.* ▷early 20th cent.: perhaps from slang *posh*, denoting a dandy. There is no evidence to support the folk etymology that *posh* is formed from the initials of *port out starboard home* (referring to the practice of using the more comfortable accommodations, out of the heat of the sun, on ships between England and India). —**posh·ly** adv. —**posh·ness** n.

pos·it /'päzit/ ▸v. (**pos·it·ed, pos·it·ing**) **1** [tr.] assume as a fact; put forward as a basis of argument. ■ (**posit something on**) base something on the truth of (a particular assumption). **2** [tr.] put in position; place.

po·si·tion /pə'ziSHən/ ▸n. **1** a place where someone or something is located or has been put: *the distress call had given the ship's position.* ■ the location where someone or something should be; the correct place: *make sure that no slates have slipped out of position.* ■ (often **positions**) a place where part of a military force is posted for strategic purposes. **2** a particular way in which someone or something is placed or arranged: *he moved himself into a reclining position.* ■ in a game of chess, the configuration of the pieces and pawns on the board at any point. ■ Mus. a particular location of the hand on the fingerboard of a stringed instrument. ■ Mus. a particular location of the slide of a

trombone. ■ Mus. the arrangement of the constituent notes of a chord. **3** a situation or set of circumstances, esp. one that affects one's power to act: *the company's financial position is grim.* ■ a job. ■ the state of being placed where one has an advantage over one's rivals in a competitive situation: *his successors were jockeying for position.* ■ a person's place or rank in relation to others, esp. in a competitive situation: *finished in second position.* ■ high rank or social standing: *a woman of supposed wealth and position.* ■ (in team games) a set of functions considered as the responsibility of a particular player based on the location in which they play: *a chance to play every fielding position.* **4** a person's particular point of view or attitude toward something: *the official U.S. position on Palestine.* **5** an investor's net holdings in one or more markets at a particular time; the status of an individual or institutional trader's open contracts: *traders were covering short positions.* **6** Logic a proposition laid down or asserted; a tenet or assertion.
▸v. [tr.] put or arrange (someone or something) in a particular place or way: *he pulled out a chair and positioned it between them.* ■ promote (a product, service, or business) within a particular sector of a market, or as the fulfillment of that sector's specific requirements: *a development plan that will position the city as a major economic force.* ■ [tr.] fig. portray or regard (someone) as a particular type of person. —**po·si·tion·al** /-ənl/ adj.

pos·i·tive /'päzətiv; 'päztiv/ ▸adj. **1** consisting in or characterized by the presence or possession of features or qualities rather than their absence. ■ (of a statement or decision) expressing or implying affirmation, agreement, or permission. ■ (of the results of a test or experiment) indicating the presence of something: *players who tested positive for cocaine use.* ■ constructive in intention or attitude: *a positive approach to youthful offenders.* ■ showing optimism and confidence. ■ showing pleasing progress, gain, or improvement. **2** with no possibility of doubt; clear and definite: *he made a positive identification of a glossy ibis.* ■ convinced or confident in one's opinion; certain: *I am positive that he is not coming back.* ■ inf. downright; complete (used for emphasis): *it's a positive delight to see you.* **3** of, containing, producing, or denoting an electric charge opposite to that carried by electrons. **4** (of a photographic image) showing lights and shades or colors true to the original. **5** Gram. (of an adjective or adverb) expressing a quality in its basic, primary degree. **6** (of a quantity) greater than zero.
▸n. **1** a good, affirmative, or constructive quality or attribute. **2** a photographic image showing lights and shades or colors true to the original, esp. one printed from a negative. **3** a result of a test or experiment indicating the presence of something. **4** the part of an electric circuit that is at a higher electrical potential than another point designated as having zero electrical potential. **5** Gram. an adjective or adverb in the positive degree. **6** Mus. another term for POSITIF. **7** a number greater than zero. ▷late Middle English: from Old French *positif, -ive* or Latin *positivus*, from *posit-* 'placed,' from the verb *ponere.* The original sense referred to laws as being formally 'laid down,' which gave rise to the sense 'explicitly laid down and admitting no question,' hence 'very sure, convinced.' —**pos·i·tive·ly** adv. —**pos·i·tive·ness** n. —**pos·i·tiv·i·ty** /,päzə'tivətē/ n.

pos·i·tive feed·back ▸n. chiefly Biol. the enhancement or amplification of an effect by its own influence on the process that gives rise to it. ■ Electr. the return of part of an output signal to the input, which is in phase with it, so that the amplifier gain is increased and the output is often distorted.

pos·i·tiv·ism /'päzətiv,izəm; 'päztiv-/ ▸n. the state or quality of being positive. —**pos·i·tiv·ist** n. & adj. —**pos·i·tiv·is·tic** /,päzətə'vistik/ adj. —**pos·i·tiv·is·ti·cal·ly** /,päzətə'vistə(ə)lē/ adv.

pos·i·tron /'päzə,trän/ ▸n. Physics a subatomic particle with the same mass as an electron and a numerically equal but positive charge.

poss /päs/ ▸abbr. possible.

pos·se /'päsē/ ▸n. hist. a body of men, typically armed, summoned by a sheriff to enforce the law. ■ (also **pos·se com·i·ta·tus** /,kämi'tātəs; -tātəs/) hist. the body of men in a county whom the sheriff could summon to enforce the law. ■ inf. a group of people who have a common characteristic, occupation, or purpose: *a posse of medical students.* ■ inf. a gang of youths involved in (usually drug-related) crime. ■ inf. a group of people who socialize together, esp. to go to clubs or raves. ▷mid 17th cent.: from medieval Latin, literally 'power,' from Latin *posse* 'be able.'

pos·sess /pə'zes/ ▸v. [tr.] **1** have as belonging to one; own. ■ Law have possession of as distinct from ownership: *a two-year suspended sentence*

Pronunciation Key ə *ago, up;* ər *over, fur;* a *hat;* ā *ate;* ä *car;* CH *chin;* e *let;* ē *see;* e(ə) *air;* i *fit;* ī *by;* i(ə) *ear;* NG *sing;* ō *go;* ô *law, for;* oi *toy;* o͝o *good;* o͞o *goo;* ou *out;* SH *she;* TH *thin;* T͟H *then;* (h)w *why;* ZH *vision*

for possessing cocaine. ■ have as an ability, quality, or characteristic: *he did not possess a sense of humor* | (**be possessed of**) *a fading blonde possessed of a powerful soprano.* ■ (**possess oneself of**) *archaic* take for one's own. **2** (usu. **be possessed**) (of a demon or spirit, esp. an evil one) have complete power over (someone) and be manifested through their speech or actions: *she was possessed by the Devil.* ■ (of an emotion, idea, etc.) dominate the mind of; have an overpowering influence on: *I was possessed by a desire to tell her everything.* **3** *chiefly poetic/lit.* have sexual intercourse with (a woman). —**pos·ses·sor** /-zesər/ *n.*

▶ □ **what possessed you?** used to express surprise at an action regarded as extremely unwise: *what possessed you to come here?*

pos·ses·sion /pəˈzeSHən/ ▶*n.* **1** the state of having, owning, or controlling something. ■ *Law* visible power or control over something, as distinct from lawful ownership; holding or occupancy: *they were imprisoned for possession of explosives.* ■ *inf.* the state of possessing an illegal drug: *they're charged with possession.* ■ (in football, basketball, and other ball games) temporary control of the ball by a particular player or team. **2** (usu. **possessions**) an item of property; something belonging to one. ■ a territory or country controlled or governed by another: *France's former colonial possessions.* **3** the state of being controlled by a demon or spirit. ■ the state of being completely under the influence of an idea or emotion: *fear took possession of my soul.* —**pos·ses·sion·less** *adj.*

pos·ses·sive /pəˈzesiv/ ▶*adj.* **1** demanding someone's total attention and love: *she was possessive of our eldest son.* ■ showing a desire to own things and an unwillingness to share what one already owns. **2** *Gram.* relating to or denoting the case of nouns and pronouns expressing possession.

▶*n. Gram.* a possessive word or form. ■ (**the possessive**) the possessive case. —**pos·ses·sive·ly** *adv.* —**pos·ses·sive·ness** *n.*

pos·ses·sive pro·noun ▶*n. Gram.* a pronoun indicating possession, for example *mine, yours, hers, theirs.*

pos·si·bil·i·ty /ˌpäsəˈbilətē/ ▶*n.* (*pl.* **-ties**) a thing that may happen or be the case. ■ the state or fact of being likely or possible; likelihood: *there was no possibility of recompense for him.* ■ a thing that may be chosen or done out of several possible alternatives. ■ (**possibilities**) unspecified qualities of a promising nature; potential: *the house was old but it had possibilities.*

pos·si·ble /ˈpäsəbəl/ ▶*adj.* able to be done; within the power or capacity of someone or something: *what are the possible alternatives?* | *contact me as soon as possible.* ■ able to happen although not certain to; denoting a fact, event, or situation that may or may not occur or be so: *a theory about the possible cause of the plane crash.* ■ able to be or become; potential: *he was a possible future customer.* ■ having as much or as little of a specified quality as can be achieved. *the shortest possible route.* ■ (of a number or score) as high as is achievable in a test, competition, or game: *he scored 723 points out of a possible 900.*

▶*n.* a person or thing that has the potential to become or do something, esp. a potential candidate for a job or membership on a team. ■ (**the possible**) that which is likely or achievable.

pos·si·bly /ˈpäsəblē/ ▶*adv.* **1** perhaps (used to indicate doubt or hesitancy): *he found himself alone, possibly the only survivor.* ■ used in polite requests: *could you possibly pour me another cup of coffee?* **2** in accordance with what is likely or achievable, in particular: ■ used to emphasize that something is difficult, surprising, or bewildering: *what can you possibly mean?* ■ used to emphasize that someone has or will put all their effort into something: *be as noisy as you possibly can.*

pos·sum /ˈpäsəm/ ▶*n.* **1** *inf.* an opossum. **2** a tree-dwelling Australasian marsupial (Petauridae and other families) that typically has a prehensile tail.

▶ □ **play possum 1** pretend to be asleep or unconscious when threatened (in imitation of an opossum's behavior). **2** feign ignorance.

post[1] /pōst/ ▶*n.* **1** a long, sturdy piece of timber or metal set upright in the ground or on a ship's deck and used to support something or as a marker. ■ a goalpost. ■ (**the post**) a starting post or winning post.

▶*v.* [tr.] (often **be posted**) display (a notice) in a public place. ■ announce or publish (something, esp. a financial result): *the company posted a $460,000 loss.* ■ (of a player or team) achieve or record (a particular score or result). ■ *Comput.* make (information) available on the Internet. ■ put notices on or in: *we have posted all the bars.*

post[2] ▶*n.* **1** *chiefly Brit.* the official service or system that delivers letters and parcels. ■ letters and parcels delivered. ■ a single collection or delivery of letters or parcels: *entries must be received no later than first post on Friday, June 14th.* ■ used in names of newspapers: *the Washington Post.* **2** *hist.* one of a series of couriers who carried mail on horseback between fixed stages. ■ *archaic* a person or vehicle that carries mail.

▶*v.* **1** [tr.] *chiefly Brit.* send (a letter or parcel) via the postal system. **2** [tr.] (in bookkeeping) enter (an item) in a ledger: *post the transaction in the second column.* ■ complete (a ledger) in this way. **3** [intr.] *hist.* travel with relays of horses. ■ *archaic* travel with haste; hurry: *he comes posting up the street.*

▶*adv. archaic* with haste: *come now, come post.*

▶ □ **keep someone posted** keep someone informed of the latest developments or news.

post[3] ▶*n.* **1** a position of paid employment; a job. **2** a place where someone is on duty or where a particular activity is carried out: *a customs post.* ■ a place where a soldier, guard, or police officer is stationed or which they patrol. ■ a force stationed at a permanent position or camp; a garrison. ■ a local group in an organization of military veterans. **3** *Brit., hist.* the status or rank of full-grade captain in the Royal Navy.

▶*v.* [tr.] (usu. **be posted**) send (someone) to a particular place to take up an appointment. ■ station (someone, esp. a soldier, guard, or police officer) in a particular place.

post·age /ˈpōstij/ ▶*n.* the sending or conveying of letters and parcels by mail. ■ the amount required to send a letter or parcel by mail.

post·age me·ter ▶*n.* a machine that prints an official mark or signature on a letter or parcel to indicate that postage has been paid or does not need to be paid.

post·age stamp ▶*n.* a small adhesive piece of paper of specified value issued by a postal authority to be affixed to a letter or parcel to indicate the amount of postage paid.

post·al /ˈpōstəl/ ▶*adj.* of or relating to the post office or the mail: *increased postal rates.* ■ *chiefly Brit.* done through the mail: *a postal ballot.*

▶*n.* (in full **postal card**) another term for POSTCARD. —**post·al·ly** *adv.*

▶ □ **go postal** become crazed and violent, esp. as the result of stress.

post·al code ▶*n. Brit.* another term for POSTCODE. ■ *Can.* a mailing code similar to the U.S. zip code.

post·card /ˈpōstˌkärd/ ▶*n.* a card for sending a message by mail without an envelope, typically having a picture on one side.

post·date /pōstˈdāt/ ▶*v.* [tr.] **1** [usu. as *adj.*] (**postdated**) affix or assign a date later than the actual one to (a document or event): *a postdated check.* **2** occur or come at a later date than.

post·doc·tor·al /pōstˈdäktərəl/ ▶*adj.* of, relating to, or denoting research undertaken after the completion of doctoral research: *a postdoctoral fellowship.*

post·er /ˈpōstər/ ▶*n.* **1** a large printed picture used for decoration. ■ a large printed picture, notice, or advertisement displayed in a public place: [as *adj.*] *a poster campaign.* **2** *Comput.* someone who sends a message to a newsgroup.

pos·te·ri·or /päˈsti(ə)rēər; pō-/ ▶*adj.* **1** *chiefly Anat., technical* further back in position; of or nearer the rear or hind end, esp. of the body or a part of it. **2** the opposite of ANTERIOR. *a basal body situated just posterior to the nucleus.* ■ *Med.* relating to or denoting presentation of a fetus in which the rear or caudal end is nearest the cervix and emerges first at birth: *a posterior labor.* **3** *formal* coming after in time or order; later: *a date posterior to the first Reform Bill.*

▶*n. humorous* a person's buttocks. —**pos·te·ri·or·i·ty** /pä,sti(ə)rēˈôritē; pō-/ *n.* —**pos·te·ri·or·ly** *adv.*

pos·ter·i·ty /päˈsteritē/ ▶*n.* all future generations of people: *the victims' names are recorded for posterity.* ■ *archaic* the descendants of a person: *God offered Abraham a posterity like the stars of heaven.*

post·grad·u·ate /pōstˈgrajōōit/ ▶*adj.* of, relating to, or denoting a course of study undertaken after completing a first degree: *a postgraduate degree.*

▶*n.* a student engaged in such a course of study.

post·haste /ˈpōstˈhāst/ ▶*adv.* with great speed or immediacy: *she would go posthaste to England.*

post hoc /ˈpōst ˈhäk/ ▶*adj. & adv.* occurring or done after the event: *a post hoc justification for the changes.*

▶ □ **post hoc, ergo propter hoc** after this, therefore resulting from it. Used to indicate that a causal relationship has erroneously been assumed from a merely sequential one.

post·hu·mous /ˈpäsCHəməs; päst'(h)yōōməs/ ▶*adj.* occurring, awarded, or appearing after the death of the originator. ■ (of a child) born after the death of its father. —**post·hu·mous·ly** *adv.*

post-Im·pres·sion·ism (also **Post-Im·pres·sion·ism**) ▶*n.* the work or style of a varied group of late 19th-century and early 20th-century artists including Van Gogh, Gauguin, and Cézanne. They reacted against the naturalism of the Impressionists. —**post-Im·pres·sion·ist** *n. & adj.* —**post-Im·pres·sion·is·tic** *adj.*

post·in·dus·tri·al /ˌpōstinˈdəstrēəl/ ▶adj. of or relating to an economy that no longer relies on heavy industry: *a postindustrial society.* —**post·in·dus·tri·al·ism** /-ˌlizəm/ n.

post·ing /ˈpōstiNG/ ▶n. **1** *chiefly Brit.* an appointment to a job, esp. one abroad or in the armed forces: *he requested a posting to Japan.* ■ the location of such an appointment: *Norway was an attractive posting.* **2** *Comput.* a message sent to an Internet bulletin board or newsgroup. ■ the sending of a message to an Internet bulletin board or newsgroup.

post·lude /ˈpōsˌlo͞od/ ▶n. *Mus.* a concluding piece of music, esp. an organ piece played at the end of a religious service. ■ a written or spoken epilogue; an afterword.

post·man /ˈpōstmən/ ▶n. (pl. **-men**) a mail carrier.

post·mark /ˈpōstˌmärk/ ▶n. an official mark stamped on a letter or other postal package, giving the place, date, and time of posting, and serving to cancel the postage stamp: *an envelope with a London postmark.*
▶v. [tr.] (usu. **be postmarked**) stamp (a letter or other postal package) officially with such a mark: *the letter was postmarked New York.*

post·mas·ter /ˈpōstˌmastər/ ▶n. a person in charge of a post office.

post·mod·ern·ism /pōstˈmädərˌnizəm/ ▶n. a late 20th-century style and concept in the arts, architecture, and criticism that represents a departure from modernism and has at its heart a general distrust of grand theories and ideologies as well as a problematical relationship with any notion of "art." —**post·mod·ern** adj. —**post·mod·ern·ist** n. & adj. —**post·mod·er·ni·ty** /ˌpōstməˈdərnətē/ n.

post·mor·tem /pōstˈmôrtəm/ ▶n. (also **postmortem examination**) an examination of a dead body to determine the cause of death. ■ an analysis or discussion of an event held soon after it has occurred, esp. in order to determine why it was a failure.
▶adj. of or relating to a postmortem: *a postmortem report.* ■ happening after death: *postmortem changes in his body.*

post·na·tal /pōstˈnātl/ ▶adj. of, relating to, characteristic of, or denoting the period after childbirth: *postnatal care.* —**post·na·tal·ly** adv.

post·nup·tial /pōstˈnəpsHəl/; -CHəl/ ▶adj. occurring or relating to the period after marriage. ■ *Zool.* occurring in or relating to the period after the mating season of an animal.

post of·fice ▶n. **1** the public department or corporation responsible for postal services and (in some countries) telecommunications. ■ a building where postal business is carried on. **2** a game, played esp. by children, in which imaginary letters are delivered in exchange for kisses.

post·paid /pōstˈpād/ ▶adj. & adv. (with reference to a letter or parcel) on which postage has already been paid: [as adj.] *a postpaid envelope.*

post·pone /pōstˈpōn/ ▶v. [tr.] cause or arrange for (something) to take place at a time later than that first scheduled. —**post·pon·a·ble** adj. —**post·pone·ment** n. —**post·pon·er** n.

PostScript /ˈpōstˌskript/ ▶n. *trademark Comput.* a page description language that is an industry standard for outputting high-resolution text and graphics: *PostScript files.*

post·script /ˈpōs(t)ˌskript/ ▶n. an additional remark at the end of a letter, after the signature and introduced by "P.S.": *he added a postscript: "Leaving tomorrow."* ■ an additional statement or action that provides further information on or a sequel to something: *as a postscript to this, Paul did finally marry.*

post-tax /pōst tax/ ▶adj. *Finance* (of income or profits) remaining after the deduction of taxes.

pos·tu·lant /ˈpäscHələnt/ ▶n. a candidate, esp. one seeking admission into a religious order.

pos·tu·late ▶v. /ˈpäscHəˌlāt/ [tr.] suggest or assume the existence, fact, or truth of (something) as a basis for reasoning, discussion, or belief.
▶n. /ˈpäscHələt/ *formal* a thing suggested or assumed as true as the basis for reasoning, discussion, or belief. ■ *Math.* an assumption used as a basis for mathematical reasoning. —**pos·tu·la·tion** /ˌpäscHəˈlāsHən/ n. —**pos·tu·la·tor** /-ˌlātər/ n.

pos·ture /ˈpäscHər/ ▶n. a position of a person's body when standing or sitting. ■ *Zool.* a particular pose adopted by a bird or other animal, interpreted as a signal of a specific pattern of behavior. ■ *fig.* a particular way of dealing with or considering something; an approach or attitude: *labor unions adopted a more militant posture in wage negotiations.* ■ *fig.* a particular way of behaving that is intended to convey a false impression; a pose.
▶v. **1** [intr.] [often as n.] (**posturing**) behave in a way that is intended to impress or mislead others: *a masking of fear with macho posturing.* ■ [tr.] adopt (a certain attitude) so as to impress or mislead. **2** [tr.] *archaic* place (someone) in a particular attitude or pose. —**pos·tur·al** adj. —**pos·tur·er** n.

post·war /ˈpōstˌwär/ ▶adj. occurring or existing after a war (esp. World War II): *postwar Britain | postwar reconstruction.*

po·sy /ˈpōzē/ ▶n. (pl. **-sies**) **1** a small bunch of flowers. **2** *archaic* a short motto or line of verse inscribed inside a ring.

po·sy ▶adj. variant spelling of POSEY.

pot¹ /pät/ ▶n. **1** a container, typically rounded or cylindrical and of ceramic ware or metal, used for storage or cooking. ■ short for TEAPOT, FLOWERPOT, LOBSTER POT, etc. ■ (**the pot**) a toilet. ■ a container for holding drink, esp. beer. ■ the contents of any of such containers: *a pot of coffee.* **2** (**the pot**) the total sum of the bets made on a round in poker and other card games: *Jim raked in the pot.* ■ all the money contributed by a group of people for a particular purpose. **3** *inf.* a potbelly.
▶v. (**pot·ted, pot·ting**) [tr.] **1** plant in a flowerpot. **2** *chiefly Brit.* preserve (food, esp. meat or fish) in a sealed pot or jar. **3** *Brit., Billiards* another term for POCKET. **4** *inf.* hit or kill (someone or something) by shooting. —**pot·ful** /-ˌfo͝ol/ n. (pl. **-fuls**).
▶ □ **go to pot** *inf.* deteriorate through neglect: *the foundry was allowed to go to pot in the seventies.*

pot² ▶n. *inf.* cannabis.

po·ta·ble /ˈpōtəbəl/ ▶adj. *formal* safe to drink; drinkable: *there is no supply of potable water available.* —**po·ta·bil·i·ty** /ˌpōtəˈbilətē/ n.

po·tage /pôˈtäzH/ ▶n. thick soup.

pot·ash /ˈpätˌasH/ ▶n. an alkaline potassium compound, esp. potassium carbonate or hydroxide.

po·tas·si·um /pəˈtasēəm/ ▶n. the chemical element of atomic number 19, a soft, silvery-white reactive metal of the alkali metal group. (Symbol: **K**) —**po·tas·sic** /-ˈtasik/ adj. (*Mineralogy*).

po·tas·si·um ni·trate ▶n. a white crystalline salt, KNO_3, occurring naturally and produced synthetically, used in fertilizer, as a meat preservative, and as a constituent of gunpowder. Also called SALTPETER and NITER.

po·ta·tion /pōˈtāsHən/ ▶n. *archaic* or *humorous* a drink. ■ the action of drinking something, esp. alcohol. ■ (often **potations**) a drinking bout.

po·ta·to /pəˈtātō/ ▶n. (pl. **-oes**) **1** a starchy plant tuber that is one of the most important food crops, cooked and eaten as a vegetable. ■ see SWEET POTATO. **2** the plant (*Solanum tuberosum*) of the nightshade family that produces these tubers on underground runners. ▷mid 16th cent.: from Spanish *patata*, variant of Taino *batata* 'sweet potato.'

pot·bel·ly /ˈpätˌbelē/ (also **pot belly**) ▶n. a large, protruding, rotund stomach. —**pot·bel·lied** adj.

pot·boil·er /ˈpätˌboilər/ ▶n. *inf.* a book, painting, or recording produced merely to make the writer or artist a living by catering to popular taste.

po·tent /ˈpōtnt/ ▶adj. **1** having great power, influence, or effect: *thrones were potent symbols of authority.* **2** (of a male) able to achieve an erection or to reach an orgasm. —**po·tence** n. —**po·ten·cy** n. —**po·tent·ly** adv.

po·ten·tate /ˈpōtnˌtāt/ ▶n. a monarch or ruler, esp. an autocratic one.

po·ten·tial /pəˈtenCHəl/ ▶adj. having or showing the capacity to become or develop into something in the future: *a two-pronged campaign to woo potential customers.*
▶n. **1** latent qualities or abilities that may be developed and lead to future success or usefulness: *a young broadcaster with great potential.* ■ (often **potential for/to do something**) the possibility of something happening or of someone doing something in the future: *pesticides with the potential to cause cancer.* **2** *Physics* the quantity representing the energy of mass in a gravitational field or of charge in an electric field. —**po·ten·ti·al·i·ty** /pəˌtenCHēˈalətē/ n. —**po·ten·tial·ize** /-ˌlīz/ v. —**po·ten·tial·ly** adv.

po·ten·ti·ate /pəˈtenCHēˌāt/ ▶v. [tr.] *technical* increase the power, effect, or likelihood of (something, esp. a drug or physiological reaction).

pot·head /ˈpätˌhed/ ▶n. *inf.* a person who smokes marijuana, esp. habitually.

poth·er /ˈpäTHər/ ▶n. *poetic/lit.* a commotion or fuss.

pot·hole /ˈpätˌhōl/ ▶n. a deep natural underground cavity formed by the erosion of rock, esp. by the action of water. ■ a deep circular hole in a riverbed formed by the erosion of the rock by the rotation of stones in an eddy. ■ a depression or hollow in a road surface caused by wear or subsidence. ■ (also **pothole lake**) a pond in a natural hollow in the ground. —**pot·holed** adj.

po·tion /ˈpōsHən/ ▶n. a liquid with healing, magical, or poisonous properties: *a love potion.*

Pronunciation Key ə *ago, up;* ər *over, fur;* a *hat;* ā *ate;* ä *car;* CH *chin;* e *let;* ē *see;* e(ə)r *air;* i *fit;* ī *by;* i(ə)r *ear;* NG *sing;* ō *go;* ô *law, for;* oi *toy;* o͞o *good;* o͞o *goo;* ou *out;* sH *she;* TH *thin;* TH *then;* (h)w *why;* zH *vision*

pot·luck /ˈpätˈlək/ ▸n. used in reference to a situation in which one must take a chance that whatever is available will prove to be good or acceptable: *he could take potluck in a town not noted for its hotels.* ■ a meal or party to which each of the guests contributes a dish: [as adj.] *a potluck supper.*

pot pie ▸n. **1** a meat and vegetable pie baked in a deep dish, often with a top crust only. **2** a stew with dumplings.

pot·pour·ri /ˌpōpəˈrē; pōpŏŏˈrē/ ▸n. (pl. **-ris**) a mixture of dried petals and spices placed in a bowl or small sack to perfume clothing or a room. ■ a mixture of things, esp. a musical or literary medley.

pot roast ▸n. a piece of meat cooked slowly in a covered dish.
▸v. (**pot-roast**) [tr.] cook (a piece of meat) slowly in a covered dish.

pot·sherd /ˈpätˌSHərd/ ▸n. a broken piece of ceramic material, esp. one found on an archaeological site.

pot·shot /ˈpätˌSHät/ ▸n. a shot aimed unexpectedly or at random at someone or something with no chance of self-defense. ■ fig. a criticism, esp. a random or unfounded one. ■ a shot at a game bird or other animal purely to kill it for food, without regard to the rules of the sport.

pot·ter[1] /ˈpätər/ ▸v. British term for **PUTTER**[3].

pot·ter[2] ▸n. a person who makes pottery.

pot·ter's field ▸n. hist. a burial place for paupers and strangers.

pot·ter's wheel ▸n. a horizontal revolving disk on which wet clay is shaped into pots or other round ceramic objects.

pot·ter·y /ˈpätərē/ ▸n. (pl. **-er·ies**) pots, dishes, and other articles made of earthenware or baked clay. Pottery can be broadly divided into earthenware, porcelain, and stoneware. ■ the craft or profession of making such ware. ■ a factory or workshop where such ware is made.

pot·ting shed ▸n. a shed that is used for potting plants and in which plants and garden tools and supplies are stored.

pot·ty[1] /ˈpätē/ ▸n. (pl. **-ties**) inf. a bowl used by small children as a toilet. ■ inf. a toilet.

potter's wheel

pot·ty[2] ▸adj. (**pot·ti·er**, **pot·ti·est**) inf., chiefly Brit. **1** foolish; crazy. ■ extremely enthusiastic about or fond of someone or something. **2** insignificant or feeble: *that potty little mower.* **—pot·ti·ness** n.

pouch /pouCH/ ▸n. **1** a small bag or other flexible receptacle, typically carried in a pocket or attached to a belt: *a tobacco pouch.* ■ a lockable bag for mail or dispatches. **2** a pocketlike abdominal receptacle in which marsupials carry their young during lactation. ■ any of a number of similar animal structures, such as those in the cheeks of rodents.
▸v. [tr.] **1** put into a pouch. **2** make (part of a garment) hang like a pouch: *the muslin is lightly pouched over the belt.* **—pouched** adj. **—pouch·y** adj.

poul·tice /ˈpōltəs/ ▸n. a soft, moist mass of material, typically of plant material or flour, applied to the body to relieve soreness and inflammation and kept in place with a cloth.
▸v. [tr.] apply a poultice to: *he poulticed the wound.*

poul·try /ˈpōltrē/ ▸n. domestic fowl, such as chickens, turkeys, ducks, and geese.

pounce[1] /pouns/ ▸v. [intr.] (of an animal or bird of prey) spring or swoop suddenly so as to catch prey: *the wolf pounced on the rat.* ■ (of a person) spring forward suddenly so as to attack or seize someone or something: *the gang pounced on him.* ■ fig. take sudden decisive action so as to grasp an opportunity. ■ fig. notice and take swift and eager advantage of a mistake, remark, or sign of weakness: *eager to pounce on a gaffe.*
▸n. a sudden swoop or spring. **—pounc·er** n.

pounce[2] ▸n. a fine resinous powder formerly used to prevent ink from spreading on unglazed paper or to prepare parchment to receive writing. ■ powdered charcoal or other fine powder dusted over a perforated pattern to transfer the design to the object beneath.
▸v. [tr.] **1** smooth down by rubbing with pounce or pumice. **2** transfer (a design) by the use of pounce. **—pounc·er** n.

pound[1] /pound/ ▸n. **1** (abbr.: **lb**) a unit of weight in general use equal to 16 oz. avoirdupois (0.4536 kg). ■ a unit of weight equal to 12 oz. troy (0.3732 kg) used for precious metals. **2** (also **pound sterling**) the basic monetary unit of the UK, equal to 100 pence. ■ another term for **PUNT**[4]. ■ the basic monetary unit of several Middle Eastern countries, equal to 100 piastres. ■ the basic monetary unit of Cyprus, equal to

100 cents. ■ a monetary unit of the Sudan, equal to one tenth of a dinar.
▸ □ **one's pound of flesh** something that one is strictly or legally entitled to, but that it is ruthless or inhuman to demand.

pound[2] ▸v. [tr.] strike or hit heavily and repeatedly: *U.S. gunships pounded the capital* | [intr.] *pounding on the door, she shouted at the top of her voice.* ■ crush or grind (something) into a powder or paste by beating it with an instrument such as a pestle. ■ [intr.] beat, throb, or vibrate with a strong regular rhythm: *her heart was pounding.* ■ [intr.] walk or run with heavy steps. ■ inf. defeat (an opponent) in a resounding way.
▸phrasal v. □ **pound something out** type something with heavy keystrokes. ■ produce music by striking an instrument heavily and repeatedly. **—pound·er** n.
▸ □ **pound the pavement** walk the streets in an effort to accomplish something. ■ search diligently for something, typically for a job.

pound[3] ▸n. a place where stray animals, esp. dogs, may be officially taken and kept until claimed by their owners or otherwise disposed of. ■ a place where illegally parked motor vehicles removed by the police are kept until their owners pay a fine in order to reclaim them. ■ archaic a place of confinement; a trap or prison.
▸v. [tr.] archaic shut (an animal) in a pound.

pound·age /ˈpoundij/ ▸n. weight, esp. when regarded as excessive: *reduce excess poundage without risking overexertion.*

pound cake ▸n. a rich cake containing a pound, or equal weights, of each chief ingredient, typically flour, butter, and sugar.

pound·er /ˈpoundər/ ▸n. [usu. in comb.] **1** a person or thing weighing a specified number of pounds: *Sloan set a blue-shark record with a 184-pounder.* ■ a gun designed to fire a projectile weighing a specified number of pounds. **2** a person or thing that pounds something: *he's direct, but not abrasive, not a desk-pounder.*

pound sign ▸n. **1** the sign (#), representing a pound as a unit of weight or mass. ■ used to refer to this sign, esp. as represented on a telephone keypad or a computer keyboard. **2** the sign (£), representing a British pound sterling.

pour /pôr/ ▸v. [intr.] (esp. of a liquid) flow rapidly in a steady stream: *water poured off the roof* | fig. *words poured from his mouth.* ■ [tr.] cause (a liquid) to flow from a container in a steady stream by holding the container at an angle. ■ [tr.] serve (a drink) in this way: *she poured out a cup of tea* | *Harry poured her a drink.* ■ [intr.] (of rain) fall heavily: *the storm clouds gathered and the rain poured down* [tr.] *it's pouring rain.* ■ (of people or things) come or go in a steady stream and in large numbers: *letters poured in.* ■ [tr.] (**pour something into**) donate something, esp. money, to (a particular enterprise or project) in large amounts. ■ [tr.] (**pour something out**) express one's feelings or thoughts in a full and unrestrained way: *in his letters, Edward poured out his hopes.* **—pour·a·ble** adj. **—pour·er** n.

pout /pout/ ▸v. [intr.] push one's lips or one's bottom lip forward as an expression of petulant annoyance or in order to make oneself look sexually attractive: *she lounged on the steps, pouting* | [tr.] *he shrugged and pouted his lips.* ■ (of a person's lips) be pushed forward in such a way.
▸n. a pouting expression. **—pout·er** n. **—pout·ing·ly** adv. **—pout·y** adj.

pov·er·ty /ˈpävərtē/ ▸n. the state of being extremely poor: *thousands of families are living in abject poverty.* ■ the state of being inferior in quality or insufficient in amount: *the poverty of her imagination.* ▷Middle English: from Old French *poverte*, from Latin *paupertas*, from *pauper* 'poor.'

pov·er·ty-strick·en ▸adj. extremely poor: *thousands of poverty-stricken people.*

POW ▸abbr. prisoner of war.

pow /pou/ ▸interj. expressing the sound of a blow or explosion: *Pow! Bombs went off on six beaches at once.*

pow·der /ˈpoudər/ ▸n. fine dry particles produced by the grinding, crushing, or disintegration of a solid substance: *when the powder is mixed with water, it becomes a creamy white paste* | *cocoa powder* | *crush the poppy seeds to a powder.* ■ (also **face powder**) a cosmetic in this form designed to be applied to a person's face with a brush or soft pad. ■ (also **powder snow**) light, dry, newly fallen snow: [as adj.] *powder skiing.* ■ short for **GUNPOWDER** (sense 1).
▸v. [tr.] **1** apply powder to (the face or body). ■ sprinkle or cover (a surface) with powder or a powdery substance: *broken glass powdered the floor* | fig. *high cheekbones powdered with freckles.* **2** reduce (a substance) to a powder by drying or crushing it: [as adj.] (**powdered**) *powdered milk.* **—pow·der·y** adj.
▸ □ **keep one's powder dry** remain cautious and ready for a possible emergency. □ **take a powder** inf. depart quickly, esp. in order to avoid a difficult situation.

pow·der blue ▸n. a soft, pale blue: [as adj.] *a powder-blue jumpsuit.*

pow·der keg ▶*n.* a barrel of gunpowder. ■ *fig.* a dangerous or volatile situation: *the place had been a powder keg since the uprising.*

pow·der puff (also **pow·der-puff**) ▶*n.* a soft pad for applying powder to the skin, esp. the face.
▶*adj.* **1** (of sports) played by women or girls only: *a fifth grade powder-puff football game.* **2** *inf.* (of a person or thing) ineffectual.

pow·der room ▶*n.* used euphemistically to refer to a women's toilet in a public building.

pow·er /'pou(-ə)r/ ▶*n.* **1** the ability to do something or act in a particular way, esp. as a faculty or quality: *the power of speech* | (**powers**) *his powers of concentration.* **2** the capacity or ability to direct or influence the behavior of others or the course of events: *she had me under her power.* ■ political or social authority or control, esp. that exercised by a government: [as *adj.*] *a power struggle.* ■ a right or authority that is given or delegated to a person or body: *police do not have the power to stop and search.* ■ the military strength of a state: *the sea power of Venice.* ■ a state or country, esp. one viewed in terms of its international influence and military strength. ■ a person or organization that is strong or influential within a particular context: *he was a power in the university.* ■ a supernatural being, deity, or force: *the powers of darkness.* ■ [as *adj.*] *inf.* denoting something associated with people who hold authority and influence, esp. in the context of business or politics: *a red power tie.* ■ used in the names of movements aiming to enhance the status of a specified group: *gay power.* **3** physical strength and force exerted by something or someone: *the power of the storm.* ■ capacity or performance of an engine or other device: *he applied full power.* ■ the capacity of something to affect the emotions or intellect strongly: *the lyrical power of his prose.* ■ [as *adj.*] denoting a sports player, team, or style of play that makes use of power rather than finesse: *a power pitcher.* ■ the magnifying capacity of a lens or set of lenses. **4** energy that is produced by mechanical, electrical, or other means and used to operate a device: [as *adj.*] *power cables.* ■ electrical energy supplied to an area, building, etc.: *the power went off.* ■ [as *adj.*] driven by such energy: *a power drill.* ■ [as *adj.*] power-assisted: *power brakes.* ■ *Physics* the time-rate of doing work, measured in watts or less frequently horsepower. **5** *Math.* the number of times a certain number is to be multiplied by itself: *2 to the power of 4 equals 16.*
▶*v.* **1** [*tr.*] supply (a device) with mechanical or electrical energy: [as *adj.*] in *comb.*] (**-powered**) *a nuclear-powered submarine.* ■ (**power something up/down**) switch a device on or off: *the officer powered up the fighter's radar.* **2** [*intr.*] move or travel with great speed or force: *they powered past the dock toward the mouth of the creek.* ■ [*tr.*] direct (something, esp. a ball) with great force: *Nicholas powered a header into the net.*
▶ □ **the powers that be** the authorities.

pow·er·boat /'pou(-ə)r,bōt/ ▶*n.* a motorboat designed for racing or recreation.

pow·er·ful /'pou(-ə)rfəl/ ▶*adj.* having great power or strength. ■ (of a person, organization, or country) having control and influence over people and events. ■ having a strong effect on people's feelings or thoughts.
▶*adv.* chiefly *dial.* very: *walking in this weather is powerful hot work.* —**pow·er·ful·ly** /-f(ə)lē/ *adv.* —**pow·er·ful·ness** *n.*

pow·er·head /'pou(-ə)r,hed/ ▶*n.* **1** *inf.* a powerful egomaniac. **2** any of various mechanical or electrical devices, including: ■ a submersible pump for an aquarium that creates current in a tank. ■ a vacuum-cleaner attachment that houses an independent motor that drives a carpet-beating rotating brush. ■ the internal combustion engine of an outboard motor. ■ the power unit of an automatic garage door opener.

pow·er·house /'pou(-ə)r,hous/ ▶*n.* a person or thing of great energy, strength, or power.

pow·er·less /'pou(-ə)rləs/ ▶*adj.* without ability, influence, or power. —**pow·er·less·ly** *adv.* —**pow·er·less·ness** *n.*

pow·er of at·tor·ney ▶*n. Law* the authority to act for another person in specified or all legal or financial matters. ■ a legal document giving such authority to someone.

pow·er plant ▶*n.* an installation where electrical power is generated for distribution. ■ an engine or other apparatus that provides power for a machine, building, etc.

pow·er play ▶*n.* **1** tactics exhibiting or intended to increase a person's power or influence. ■ the use of physical strength to defeat one's opponent in a sport through sheer force. **2** tactics in a team sport involving the concentration of players at a particular point. ■ *Ice Hockey* a situation in which a team has a numerical advantage over its opponents while one or more players is serving a penalty.

pow·er pole ▶*n.* a pole, mast, or tower that carries electric wires.

pow·er rat·ing ▶*n.* **1** the amount of electrical power required for a particular device: *a continuous power rating of 150 watts.* **2** a numerical representation of a sports team's strength for betting purposes: *a 99 power rating and a home field edge of four points.*

pow·er-shar·ing ▶*n.* a policy agreed between political parties or within a coalition to share responsibility for decision-making and political action.

pow·wow /'pou,wou/ ▶*n.* a North American Indian ceremony involving feasting, singing, and dancing. ■ a conference or meeting for discussion, esp. among friends or colleagues.
▶*v.* [*intr.*] *inf.* hold a powwow; confer. ▷early 17th cent.: from Narragansett *powáw* 'magician' (literally 'he dreams').

pox /päks/ ▶*n.* any of several viral diseases producing a rash of pimples that become pus-filled and leave pockmarks on healing. ■ (**the pox**) *inf.* syphilis. ■ (**the pox**) *hist.* smallpox. ■ a plant disease that causes pock-like spots.
▶ □ **a pox on** *archaic* used to express anger or intense irritation with someone or something: *a pox on both their houses!*

pp ▶*abbr.* ■ pages: *pp 71—73.* ■ parcel post. ■ past participle. ■ per person. ■ per procurationem (used when signing a letter on someone else's behalf). ■ *Mus.* pianissimo. ■ postpaid. ■ privately printed.

ppb (also **p.p.b.**) ▶*abbr.* ■ (in publishing) paper, printing, and binding. ■ parts per billion.

ppd. ▶*abbr.* ■ postpaid. ■ prepaid.

ppm ▶*abbr.* ■ part(s) per million: *water containing 1 ppm fluoride.* ■ *Comput.* page(s) per minute, a measure of the speed of printers.

PPS ▶*abbr.* ■ additional postscript: *PS Those photos are awful! PPS Can I have your other address?*

PR ▶*abbr.* ■ parliamentary report. ■ press release. ■ prize ring. ■ proportional representation. ■ public relations.

Pr ▶*abbr.* ■ preferred (stock). ■ Priest. ■ Prince. ■ Provençal.
▶*symb.* the chemical element praseodymium.

pr ▶*abbr.* ■ pair: *patterned gloves, $17.95/pr.* ■ *archaic* per: *$6 pr day.*

prac·ti·ca·ble /'praktikəbəl/ ▶*adj.* able to be done or put into practice successfully. ■ able to be used; useful. —**prac·ti·ca·bil·i·ty** /,praktikə'bilətē/ *n.* —**prac·ti·ca·bly** /-blē/ *adv.*

prac·ti·cal /'praktikəl/ ▶*adj.* **1** of or concerned with the actual doing or use of something rather than with theory and ideas. ■ (of an idea, plan, or method) likely to succeed or be effective in real circumstances; feasible. ■ suitable for a particular purpose: *a practical, stylish kitchen.* ■ (of a person) sensible and realistic in their approach to a situation or problem. ■ (of a person) skilled at manual tasks. **2** so nearly the case that it can be regarded as so; virtual: *it was a practical certainty that he would try to raise more money.* —**prac·ti·cal·i·ty** /,prakti'kalitē/ *n.*
▶ □ **for all practical purposes** virtually, or essentially.

prac·ti·cal joke ▶*n.* a trick played on someone in order to make them look foolish and to amuse others. —**prac·ti·cal jok·er** *n.*

prac·ti·cal·ly /'praktik(ə)lē/ ▶*adv.* **1** virtually; almost: *the risk of default was practically zero* | *the place was practically empty.* **2** in a practical manner. ■ in practical terms: *the law isn't practically inconvenient.*

prac·ti·cal nurse ▶*n.* a nurse who has completed a training course of a lower standard than a registered nurse, esp. one who is licensed by the state to perform certain duties (a **licensed practical nurse**).

prac·tice /'praktəs/ ▶*n.* **1** the actual application or use of an idea, belief, or method as opposed to theories about such application or use: *he **put** his self-defense training **into** practice by helping police arrest the robber.* ■ the customary, habitual, or expected procedure of something: *modern child-rearing practices.* ■ the carrying out or exercise of a profession, esp. that of a doctor or lawyer: *he abandoned medical practice.* ■ the business or premises of a doctor or lawyer: *Dr. Weiss has a practice in Essex.* ■ an established method of legal procedure. **2** repeated exercise in or performance of an activity or skill so as to acquire or maintain proficiency in it. ■ a period of time spent doing this: *daily choir practices.*
▶*v.* [*tr.*] (*Brit.* **prac·tise**) **1** perform (an activity) or exercise (a skill) repeatedly or regularly in order to improve or maintain one's proficiency: *I need to practice my French* | [*intr.*] *they were practicing for the Olympics.* **2** carry out or perform (a particular activity, method, or custom) habitually or regularly. ■ actively pursue or be engaged in (a particular profession or occupation): *he began to practice law* | [*intr.*] *he practiced as an attorney.* ■ observe the teaching and rules of (a particular religion): [as *adj.*] (**practicing**) *a practicing Roman Catholic.* ■ [*intr.*] *archaic* scheme or plot for an evil purpose. —**prac·tic·er** *n.*

▸ □ **in practice** in reality (used to refer to what actually happens as opposed to what is meant or believed to happen). ■ currently proficient in a particular activity or skill as a result of repeated exercise or performance of it. □ **out of practice** not currently proficient in a particular activity or skill due to not having exercised or performed it for some time.

prac·ti·tion·er /prak'tishənər/ ▸n. a person actively engaged in an art, discipline, or profession, esp. medicine.

prae·sid·i·um /pri'sidēəm; prī-/ ▸n. Brit. variant spelling of PRESIDIUM.

prae·tor /'prētər/ (also **pre·tor**) ▸n. Roman Hist. each of two ancient Roman magistrates ranking below consul. —**prae·to·ri·al** /prē'tôrēəl/ adj. —**prae·tor·ship** /'prētər, SHip/ n.

prae·to·ri·an /prē'tôrēən/ (also **pre·to·ri·an**) ▸adj. Roman Hist. of or having the powers of a praetor.
▸n. a man of praetorian rank.

prae·to·ri·an guard ▸n. Roman Hist. the bodyguard of the Roman emperor.

prag·mat·ic /prag'matik/ ▸adj. dealing with things sensibly and realistically in a way that is based on practical rather than theoretical considerations. ■ relating to philosophical or political pragmatism. ■ Linguistics of or relating to pragmatics. —**prag·mat·i·cal·ly** /-ik(ə)lē/ adv.

prag·mat·ics /prag'matiks/ ▸pl. n. [usu. treated as sing.] the branch of linguistics dealing with language in use and the contexts in which it is used, including such matters as taking turns in conversation, text organization, presupposition, and implicature.

prag·ma·tism /'pragmə,tizəm/ ▸n. **1** a pragmatic attitude or policy. **2** Philos. an approach that assesses the truth of meaning of theories or beliefs in terms of the success of their practical application. —**prag·ma·tist** n. —**prag·ma·tis·tic** /,pragmə'tistik/ adj.

prai·rie /'pre(ə)rē/ ▸n. a large open area of grassland, esp. in the Mississippi River valley.

prai·rie dog ▸n. a gregarious ground squirrel (genus Cynomys) that lives in interconnected burrows that may cover many acres. It is native to the grasslands of North America.

prai·rie schoon·er ▸n. a covered wagon used by the 19th-century pioneers in crossing the North American prairies.

praise /prāz/ ▸v. [tr.] express warm approval or admiration of. ■ express one's respect and gratitude toward (a deity), esp. in song.
▸n. the expression of approval or admiration for someone or something. ■ the expression of respect and gratitude as an act of worship: give praise to God. —**praise·ful** /-fəl/ adj.
▸ □ **praise be** archaic used as an expression of relief, joy, or gratitude. □ **sing the praises of** express enthusiastic approval or admiration of (someone or something): Uncle Felix never stopped singing her praises.

praise·wor·thy /'prāz,wərTHē/ ▸adj. deserving approval and admiration. —**praise·wor·thi·ly** /-,wərTHəlē/ adv. —**praise·wor·thi·ness** n.

pra·line /'prā,lēn/ ▸n. a smooth, sweet substance made by boiling nuts in sugar and grinding the mixture, used esp. as a filling for chocolates. ■ a crisp or semicrisp candy made by a similar process and typically consisting of butter, brown sugar, and pecans.

pram¹ /pram/ ▸n. short for PERAMBULATOR.

pram² /präm; pram/ ▸n. a flat-bottomed sailboat. ■ a small, flat-bottomed rowboat for fishing.

prance /prans/ ▸v. [intr.] (of a horse) move with high springy steps. ■ (of a person) walk or move around with ostentatious, exaggerated movements: she pranced around the lounge impersonating her favorite pop stars.
▸n. an act or instance of prancing. —**pranc·er** n.

pran·di·al /'prandēəl/ ▸adj. formal, often humorous during or relating to dinner or lunch. ■ Med. during or relating to the eating of food.

prang /praNG/ chiefly Brit., inf. ▸v. [tr.] crash (a motor vehicle or aircraft).
▸n. a crash involving a motor vehicle or aircraft. ■ dated a bombing raid.

prank /praNGk/ ▸n. a practical joke or mischievous act. —**prank·ish** adj. —**prank·ish·ness** n.

prank·ster /'praNGkstər/ ▸n. a person fond of playing pranks.

pra·se·o·dym·i·um /,prāzēō'dimēəm/ ▸n. the chemical element of atomic number 59, a soft silvery-white metal of the lanthanide series. (Symbol: **Pr**)

prate /prāt/ ▸v. [intr.] talk foolishly or tediously about something. —**prat·er** n. (rare)

prat·fall /'prat,fôl/ ▸n. inf. a fall onto one's buttocks: he took a pratfall into the sand. ■ a stupid and humiliating action.

prat·tle /'pratl/ ▸v. [intr.] talk at length in a foolish or inconsequential way: she began to prattle on about her visit to the dentist.
▸n. foolish or inconsequential talk. —**prat·tler** /'pratlər; 'pratl-ər/ n.

prawn /prôn/ ▸n. a marine crustacean (Leander and other genera, class Malacostraca) that resembles a large shrimp.

pray /prā/ ▸v. [intr.] address a solemn request or expression of thanks to a deity or other object of worship: the whole family is praying for Michael | [tr.] pray God this is true. ■ wish or hope strongly for a particular outcome or situation: after several days of rain, we were praying for sun | [tr.] I prayed that James wouldn't notice.

prayer /pre(ə)r/ ▸n. a solemn request for help or expression of thanks addressed to God or an object of worship. ■ (**prayers**) a religious service, esp. a regular one, at which people gather in order to pray together. ■ an earnest hope or wish.
▸ □ **not have a prayer** inf. have no chance at all of succeeding.

prayer·ful /'pre(ə)rfəl/ ▸adj. (of an action or event) characterized by or expressive of prayer: prayerful self-examination. ■ (of a person) given to praying; devout. —**prayer·ful·ly** adv. —**prayer·ful·ness** n.

pray·ing man·tis ▸n. see MANTIS.

preach /prēCH/ ▸v. [intr.] deliver a sermon or religious address to an assembled group of people, typically in church: he preached to a large congregation | [tr.] our pastor will preach the sermon. ■ [tr.] publicly proclaim or teach (a religious message or belief). ■ [tr.] earnestly advocate (a belief or course of action). ■ give moral advice to someone in an annoying or pompously self-righteous way: viewers want to be entertained, not preached at. ▷Middle English: from Old French prechier, from Latin praedicare 'proclaim,' in ecclesiastical Latin 'preach,' from prae 'before' + dicare 'declare.'
▸ □ **preach to the choir** (or **the converted**) advocate something to people who already share one's convictions about its merits or importance.

preach·er /'prēCHər/ ▸n. a person who preaches, esp. a minister of religion.

preach·i·fy /'prēCHi,fī/ ▸v. (-fies, -fied) [intr.] inf. preach or moralize tediously.

preach·y /'prēCHē/ ▸adj. (preach·i·er, preach·i·est) inf. having or revealing a tendency to give moral advice in a tedious or self-righteous way: some were put off by the preachy tone of these stories. —**preach·i·ness** n.

pre·am·ble /'prē,ambəl/ ▸n. a preliminary or preparatory statement; an introduction. ■ Law the introductory part of a statute or deed, stating its purpose, aims, and justification. —**pre·am·bu·lar** /prē'ambyələr/ adj. (formal).

pre·amp /'prē,amp/ ▸n. short for PREAMPLIFIER.

pre·am·pli·fi·er /prē'amplə,fīər/ ▸n. an electronic device that amplifies a very weak signal, for example from a microphone or pickup, and transmits it to a main amplifier.

pre·ar·range /,prēə'rānj/ ▸v. [tr.] [usu. as adj.] (**prearranged**) arrange or agree upon (something) in advance: did she have a prearranged meeting? —**pre·ar·range·ment** n.

pre·a·tom·ic /,prēə'tämik/ ▸adj. existing or occurring before the use of atomic weapons or energy.

pre-Böt·zing·er com·plex /prē 'bœtsiNGər/ ▸n. a structure in the mammalian brain stem that controls respiration.

Pre·cam·bri·an /prē'kambrēən; -kām-/ ▸adj. Geol. of, relating to, or denoting the earliest eon, preceding the Cambrian period and the Phanerozoic eon. ■ [as n.] (**the Precambrian**) the Precambrian eon or the system of rocks deposited during it.

pre·can·cer·ous /prē'kansərəs/ ▸adj. Med. (of a cell or medical condition) likely to develop into cancer if untreated: precancerous skin lesions.

pre·car·i·ous /pri'ke(ə)rēəs/ ▸adj. **1** not securely held or in position; dangerously likely to fall or collapse: a precarious ladder. **2** dependent on chance; uncertain. —**pre·car·i·ous·ly** adv. —**pre·car·i·ous·ness** n.

pre·cast /'prē'kast/ ▸v. (past and past part. **pre·cast**) [tr.] [usu. as adj.] (**pre·cast**) cast (an object or material, typically concrete) in its final shape before positioning: precast concrete beams.

prec·a·to·ry /'prekə,tôrē/ ▸adj. formal of, relating to, or expressing a wish or request.

pre·cau·tion /pri'kôSHən/ ▸n. a measure taken in advance to prevent something dangerous, unpleasant, or inconvenient from happening. —**pre·cau·tion·ar·y** /-,nerē/ adj.

pre·cau·tion·ar·y prin·ci·ple ▸n. the principle that the introduction of a new product or process whose ultimate effects are disputed or unknown should be resisted. It has mainly been used to prohibit the importation of genetically modified organisms and food.

pre·cede /pri'sēd/ ▸v. [tr.] come before (something) in time. ■ come before in order or position. ■ go in front or ahead of. ■ (**precede something with**) preface or introduce something with: he preceded the book with a collection of poems.

prec·e·dence /ˈpresədəns; priˈsēdns/ ▶ *n.* the condition of being considered more important than someone or something else; priority in importance, order, or rank: *his desire for power soon **took precedence over** any other consideration.* ■ the order to be ceremonially observed by people of different rank, according to an acknowledged or legally determined system: *quarrels over precedence among the Bonaparte family.*

prec·e·dent ▶ *n.* /ˈpresid(ə)nt/ an earlier event or action that is regarded as an example or guide to be considered in subsequent similar circumstances: *breaking with precedent.* ■ *Law* a previous case or legal decision that may be or (**binding precedent**) must be followed in subsequent similar cases: *the decision set a precedent for others to be sent to trial.*
▶ *adj.* /priˈsēd(ə)nt/ preceding in time, order, or importance.

pre·cept /ˈprēˌsept/ ▶ *n.* **1** a general rule intended to regulate behavior or thought: *moral precepts.* **2** a writ or warrant: *precepts requiring the companies to provide information.* —**pre·cep·tive** /priˈseptiv/ *adj.*

pre·cep·tor /ˈprēˌseptər; priˈseptər/ ▶ *n.* a teacher or instructor. —**pre·cep·to·ri·al** /ˌprēˌsepˈtôrēəl; ˌprē-/ *adj.* —**pre·cep·tor·ship** /-ˌSHip/ *n.*

pre·ces·sion /prəˈseSHən/ ▶ *n.* *Physics* the slow movement of the axis of a spinning body around another axis due to a torque (such as gravitational influence) acting to change the direction of the first axis. —**pre·cess** /prēˈses; ˈprēˌses/ *v.* —**pre·ces·sion·al** /priˈseSHənl/ *adj.*

pre·cinct /ˈprēˌsiNGkt/ ▶ *n.* **1** a district of a city or town as defined for police purposes. ■ the police station situated in such a subdivision. ■ an electoral district of a city or town served by a single polling place. **2** (usu. **precincts**) the area within the walls or perceived boundaries of a particular building or place: *all strata of society live within these precincts.* ■ an enclosed or clearly defined area of ground around a cathedral, church, or college. **3** *Brit.* an area in a town designated for specific or restricted use, esp. one that is closed to traffic: *a pedestrian precinct.*

pre·cious /ˈpreSHəs/ ▶ *adj.* **1** (of an object, substance, or resource) of great value; not to be wasted or treated carelessly. ■ greatly loved or treasured by someone. ■ *inf.* used to express the speaker's contempt for someone or something greatly valued by another person: *you and your precious schedule—you've got to lighten up!* ■ *inf.* used for emphasis, often in an ironic context: *a precious lot you know about dogs!* **2** *derog.* affectedly concerned with elegant or refined behavior, language, or manners.
▶ *n.* used as a term of address to a beloved person: *don't be frightened, my precious.* —**pre·cious·ly** *adv.* —**pre·cious·ness** *n.*
▶ □ **precious little/few** extremely little or few (used for emphasis): *police still know precious little about the dead man.*

precious met·als ▶ *pl. n.* gold, silver, and platinum.

prec·i·pice /ˈpresəpəs/ ▶ *n.* a very steep rock face or cliff, typically a tall one: *the edge of the precipice* | *fig. the country was teetering on the precipice of political anarchy.*

pre·cip·i·tant /priˈsipətənt/ ▶ *n.* a cause of a particular action or event. ■ *chiefly Psychol.* a cause or stimulus that precipitates a particular condition. ■ *Chem.* a substance that causes the precipitation of a specified substance: *a protein precipitant.* —**pre·cip·i·tance** *n.* —**pre·cip·i·tan·cy** *n.*

pre·cip·i·tate ▶ *v.* /priˈsipəˌtāt/ [*tr.*] **1** cause (an event or situation, typically one that is bad or undesirable) to happen suddenly, unexpectedly, or prematurely. ■ [*tr.*] cause to move suddenly and with force. ■ (**precipitate someone/something into**) send someone or something suddenly into a particular state or condition: *they were precipitated into a conflict for which they were quite unprepared.* **2** (usu. **be precipitated**) *Chem.* cause (a substance) to be deposited in solid form from a solution. ■ cause (drops of moisture or particles of dust) to be deposited from the atmosphere or from a vapor or suspension.
▶ *adj.* /priˈsipətət/ done, made, or acting suddenly or without careful consideration. ■ (of an event or situation) occurring suddenly or abruptly: *a precipitate decline in cultural literacy.*
▶ *n.* /priˈsipətət; -ˌtāt/ *Chem.* a substance precipitated from a solution. —**pre·cip·i·ta·ble** /priˈsipətəbəl/ *adj.* —**pre·cip·i·tate·ly** /priˈsipətətlē/ *adv.* —**pre·cip·i·tate·ness** /priˈsipətətnəs/ *n.* —**pre·cip·i·ta·tor** /-ˌtātər/ *n.*

pre·cip·i·ta·tion /priˌsipəˈtāSHən/ ▶ *n.* **1** *Chem.* the action or process of precipitating a substance from a solution. **2** rain, snow, sleet, or hail that falls to the ground. **3** *archaic* the fact or quality of acting suddenly and rashly: *Cora was already regretting her precipitation.*

pre·cip·i·tous /priˈsipətəs/ ▶ *adj.* **1** dangerously high or steep. ■ (of a change to a worse situation or condition) sudden and dramatic: *a precipitous decline in exports.* **2** (of an action) done suddenly and without careful consideration. —**pre·cip·i·tous·ly** *adv.* —**pre·cip·i·tous·ness** *n.*

pré·cis /prāˈsē; ˈprāsē/ ▶ *n.* (*pl.* same) a summary or abstract of a text or speech.
▶ *v.* (**pré·cis·es** /prāˈsēz; ˈprāsēz/, **pré·cised**, **pré·cis·ing**) [*tr.*] make a précis of (a text or speech).

pre·cise /priˈsīs/ ▶ *adj.* marked by exactness and accuracy of expression or detail. ■ (of a person) exact, accurate, and careful about details. ■ used to emphasize that one is referring to an exact and particular thing: *at that precise moment the car stopped.* —**pre·cise·ness** *n.*
▶ □ **to be precise** used to indicate that one is now giving more exact or detailed information: *there were not many—five, to be precise.*

pre·cise·ly /priˈsīslē/ ▶ *adv.* in exact terms; without vagueness. ■ exactly (used to emphasize the complete accuracy or truth of a statement): *at 2:00 precisely, the phone rang.* ■ used as a reply to assert emphatic agreement with or confirmation of a statement: *"You mean it was a conspiracy?" "Precisely."*

pre·ci·sion /priˈsiZHən/ ▶ *n.* the quality, condition, or fact of being exact and accurate. ■ [as *adj.*] marked by or adapted for accuracy and exactness: *a precision instrument.* ■ *technical* refinement in a measurement, calculation, or specification, esp. as represented by the number of digits given. *a precision of six decimal figures.*

pre·clin·i·cal /prēˈklinikəl/ ▶ *adj.* *Med.* relating to or denoting the stage in a disease prior to the appearance of symptoms that make a diagnosis possible.

pre·clude /priˈklo͞od/ ▶ *v.* [*tr.*] prevent from happening; make impossible: *the secret nature of his work precluded official recognition.* ■ (**preclude someone from**) (of a situation or condition) prevent someone from doing something. ▷late 15th cent. (in the sense 'bar (a route or passage)': from Latin *praecludere,* from *prae* 'before' + *claudere* 'to shut.' —**pre·clu·sion** /-ˈklo͞oZHən/ *n.* —**pre·clu·sive** /-ˈklo͞osiv; -ziv/ *adj.*

pre·co·cious /priˈkōSHəs/ ▶ *adj.* (of a child) having developed certain abilities or proclivities at an earlier age than usual. ■ (of behavior or ability) indicative of such development: *a precocious talent for computing.* ■ (of a plant) flowering or fruiting earlier than usual. —**pre·co·cious·ly** *adv.* —**pre·co·cious·ness** *n.* —**pre·coc·i·ty** /priˈkäsətē/ *n.*

pre·cog·ni·tion /ˌprēkägˈniSHən/ ▶ *n.* foreknowledge of an event, esp. foreknowledge of a paranormal kind. —**pre·cog·ni·tive** /prēˈkägnətiv/ *adj.*

pre-Co·lum·bi·an /kəˈləmbēən/ ▶ *adj.* of or relating to the history and cultures of the Americas before the arrival of Columbus in 1492.

pre·con·ceived /ˌprēkənˈsēvd/ ▶ *adj.* (of an idea or opinion) formed before having the evidence for its truth or usefulness.

pre·con·cep·tion /ˌprēkənˈsepSHən/ ▶ *n.* a preconceived idea or prejudice.

pre·con·di·tion /ˌprēkənˈdiSHən/ ▶ *n.* a condition that must be fulfilled before other things can happen or be done: *a precondition for peace.*
▶ *v.* [*tr.*] **1** (usu. **be preconditioned**) condition (an action) to happen in a certain way: *inquiries are always preconditioned by cultural assumptions.* ■ condition or influence (a person or animal) by exposing them to stimuli or information prior to the relevant behavioral situation: [*tr.*] *the anthropologist is not preconditioned to interact with those he studies* | [as *n.*] (**preconditioning**) *the protective effect of preconditioning.* **2** bring (something) into the desired state for use: [as *adj.*] (**preconditioned**) *preconditioned paper.*

pre·cur·sor /ˈprēˌkərsər; priˈkər-/ ▶ *n.* a person or thing that comes before another of the same kind; a forerunner: [as *adj.*] *precursor cells.* ■ *Biochem.* a substance from which another is formed, esp. by metabolic reaction.

pre·cur·so·ry /priˈkərsərē/ ▶ *adj.* preceding something in time, development, or position; preliminary: *precursory seismic activity.*

pre·da·cious /priˈdāSHəs/ (also **pre·da·ceous**) ▶ *adj.* (of an animal) predatory. —**pre·da·cious·ness** *n.* —**pre·dac·i·ty** /priˈdasətē/ *n.*

pre·date /prēˈdāt/ ▶ *v.* [*tr.*] exist or occur at a date earlier than (something): *this letter predates her illness.*

pre·da·tion /priˈdāSHən/ ▶ *n.* *Zool.* the preying of one animal on others.

pred·a·tor /ˈpredətər/ ▶ *n.* an animal that naturally preys on others. ■ *fig.* a rapacious, exploitative person or group: *her wealth made her vulnerable to predators.* ■ *fig.* a company that tries to take over another.

pred·a·to·ry /ˈpredəˌtôrē/ ▶ *adj.* relating to or denoting an animal or animals preying naturally on others: *predatory birds.* ■ *fig.* seeking to exploit or oppress others: *a life destroyed by predatory biographers and yellow journalists.* —**pred·a·to·ri·ly** /ˌpredəˈtôrəlē/ *adv.* —**pred·a·to·ri·ness** *n.*

pre·de·cease /ˌprēdiˈsēs/ *formal* ▶ *v.* [*tr.*] die before (another person, typically someone related by blood or marriage).

Pronunciation Key ə *ago,* up; ər *over, fur;* a *hat;* ā *ate;* ä *car;* CH *chin;* e *let;* ē *see;* e(ə)r *air;* i *fit;* ī *by;* i(ə)r *ear;* NG *sing;* ō *go;* ô *law, for;* oi *toy;* o͝o *good;* o͞o *goo;* ou *out;* SH *she;* TH *thin;* T͟H *then;* (h)w *why;* ZH *vision*

P

pred·e·ces·sor /ˈpredəˌsesər; ˈprē-/ ▸n. a person who held a job or office before the current holder: *the new president's foreign policy is very similar to that of his predecessor.* ■ a thing that has been followed or replaced by another: *the chapel was built in 1864 on the site of its predecessor.*

pre·des·ti·na·tion /prēˌdestəˈnāSHən/ ▸n. (as a doctrine in Christian theology) the divine foreordaining of all that will happen, esp. with regard to the salvation of some and not others. It has been particularly associated with the teachings of St. Augustine of Hippo and of Calvin.

pre·des·tine /prēˈdestin/ ▸v. [usu. **be predestined**] (of God) destine (someone) for a particular fate or purpose. ■ determine (an outcome or course of events) in advance by divine will or fate: *she was certain that fate was with her and everything was predestined.*

pre·de·ter·mine /ˌprēdiˈtərmən/ ▸v. [tr.] establish or decide in advance. ■ (usu. **be predetermined**) predestine (an outcome or course of events). —**pre·de·ter·min·a·ble** *adj.* —**pre·de·ter·mi·nate** /-ˈtərmənit/ *adj.* —**pre·de·ter·mi·na·tion** /-ˌtərməˈnāSHən/ *n.*

pred·i·ca·ble /ˈpredikəbəl/ ▸*adj.* that may be predicated or affirmed. ▸n. a thing that is predicable. —**pred·i·ca·bil·i·ty** /ˌpredikəˈbilətē/ *n.*

pre·dic·a·ment /priˈdikəmənt/ ▸n. a difficult, unpleasant, or embarrassing situation: *the club's financial predicament.*

pred·i·cate ▸n. /ˈprediket/ *Gram.* the part of a sentence or clause containing a verb and stating something about the subject (e.g., *went home* in *John went home*): [as *adj.*] *predicate adjective.* ■ *Logic* something that is affirmed or denied concerning an argument of a proposition.
▸v. /ˈprediˌkāt/ [tr.] **1** *Gram.* & *Logic* state, affirm, or assert (something) about the subject of a sentence or an argument of proposition. **2** (**predicate something on/upon**) found or base something on: *the theory of structure on which later chemistry was predicated.* —**pred·i·ca·tion** /ˌprediˈkāSHən/ *n.*

pred·i·ca·tive /ˈpredəˌkātiv; -ikətiv/ ▸*adj.* **1** *Gram.* (of an adjective or noun) forming or contained in the predicate, as *old* in *the dog is old* (but not in *the old dog*) and *house* in *there is a large house*. Contrasted with **ATTRIBUTIVE**. ■ denoting a use of the verb *to be* to assert something about the subject. **2** *Logic* acting as a predicate. —**pred·i·ca·tive·ly** *adv.*

pre·dict /priˈdikt/ ▸v. [tr.] say or estimate that (a specified thing) will happen in the future or will be a consequence of something: *to predict a result* | [as *adj.*] (**predicted**) *predicted growth is 47 percent.* —**pre·dic·tive** *adj.* —**pre·dic·tor** /-tər/ *n.*

pre·dict·a·ble /priˈdiktəbəl/ ▸*adj.* able to be predicted. ■ *chiefly derog.* behaving or occurring in a way that is expected. —**pre·dict·a·bil·i·ty** /-ˌdiktəˈbilətē/ *n.* —**pre·dict·a·bly** /-blē/ *adv.*

pre·dic·tion /priˈdikSHən/ ▸n. a thing predicted; a forecast. ■ the action of predicting something.

pre·di·lec·tion /ˌpredlˈekSHən; ˌprēdl-/ ▸n. a preference or special liking for something; a bias in favor of something: *my predilection for Asian food.*

pre·dis·pose /ˌprēdiˈspōz/ ▸v. [tr.] (**predispose someone to/to do something**) make someone liable or inclined to a specified attitude, action, or condition: *lack of exercise may predispose you to high blood pressure.* —**pre·dis·po·si·tion** /ˌprēdispəˈziSHən/ *n.*

pre·dom·i·nant /priˈdämənənt/ ▸*adj.* present as the strongest or main element. ■ having or exerting control or power. —**pre·dom·i·nance** *n.* —**pre·dom·i·nant·ly** *adv.*

pre·dom·i·nate /priˈdäməˌnāt/ ▸v. [intr.] be the strongest or main element; be greater in number or amount. ■ have or exert control or power: *private interest was not allowed to* **predominate** *over the public good.*

pre·e·clamp·si·a /ˌprē-iˈklampsēə/ ▸n. a condition in pregnancy characterized by high blood pressure, sometimes with fluid retention and potentially dangerous quantities of protein in the urine. —**pre·e·clamp·tic** /-ˈklamptik/ *adj.* & *n.*

pree·mie /ˈprēmē/ ▸n. (*pl.* **-mies**) *inf.* a baby born prematurely.

pre·em·i·nent /prēˈemənənt/ ▸*adj.* surpassing all others; very distinguished in some way. —**pre·em·i·nence** *n.*

pre·empt /prēˈempt/ ▸v. [tr.] **1** take action in order to prevent (an anticipated event) from happening; forestall. ■ act in advance of (someone) in order to prevent them from doing something. ■ (of a broadcast) interrupt or replace (a scheduled program). **2** acquire or appropriate (something) in advance. ■ take (something, esp. public land) for oneself so as to have the right of preemption. **3** [intr.] *Bridge* make a preemptive bid.
▸n. *Bridge* a preemptive bid. —**pre·emp·tor** /-tər/ *n.*

pre·emp·tion /prēˈempSHən/ ▸n. **1** the purchase of goods or shares by one person or party before the opportunity is offered to others: *the commission had the right of preemption.* ■ *hist.* the right to purchase public land in this way. **2** the action of preempting or forestalling, esp. of

making a preemptive attack. ■ the interruption or replacement of a scheduled radio or television program.

pre·emp·tive /prēˈemptiv/ ▸*adj.* serving or intended to preempt or forestall something, esp. to prevent attack by disabling the enemy: *preemptive action.* ■ relating to the purchase of goods or shares by one person or party before the opportunity is offered to others: *preemptive rights.* ■ *Bridge* denoting a bid, typically an opening bid, intended to be so high that it prevents or interferes with effective bidding by the opponents.

preen /prēn/ ▸v. [intr.] (of a bird) straighten and clean its feathers with its beak: *robins preened at the pool's edge* | [tr.] *the pigeon preened her feathers.* ■ (of a person) devote effort to making oneself look attractive and then admire one's appearance: *adolescents preening in their mirrors.* ■ (**preen oneself**) congratulate or pride oneself. —**preen·er** *n.*

pre·ex·ist /ˌprē-igˈzist/ ▸v. [intr.] [usu. as *adj.*] (**preexisting**) exist at or from an earlier time: *a preexisting contractual obligation.* ■ [tr.] exist at or from an earlier time than (something): *demons who preexisted the Great Flood.* —**pre·ex·ist·ence** /-ˈzistəns/ *n.* —**pre·ex·ist·ent** /-ˈzistənt/ *adj.*

pre·fab /ˈprēˌfab; ˈprēˌfab/ *inf.* ▸n. a prefabricated building.
▸*adj.* prefabricated: *prefab walls.*

pre·fab·ri·cate /prēˈfabriˌkāt/ ▸v. [tr.] [usu. as *adj.*] (**prefabricated**) manufacture sections of (esp. a building or piece of furniture) to enable quick or easy assembly on site. —**pre·fab·ri·ca·tion** /-ˌfabrəˈkāSHən/ *n.*

pref·ace /ˈprefəs/ ▸n. an introduction to a book, typically stating its subject, scope, or aims. ■ the introduction or preliminary part of a speech or event.
▸v. [tr.] provide (a book) with a preface. ■ (**preface something with/by**) introduce or begin (a speech or event) with or by doing something: *to preface the debate with a general comment.* —**pref·a·to·ry** /ˈprefəˌtôrē/ *adj.*

pre·fect /ˈprēˌfekt/ ▸n. a chief officer, magistrate, or regional governor in certain countries: *the prefect of police.* ■ a senior magistrate or governor in the ancient Roman world: *Avitus was prefect of Gaul from AD 439.* —**pre·fec·tor·al** /prēˈfektərəl/ *adj.* —**pre·fec·to·ri·al** /ˌprēˌfekˈtôrēəl/ *adj.*

pre·fec·ture /ˈprēˌfekCHər/ ▸n. a district under the government of a prefect. ■ a prefect's office or tenure. ■ the official residence or headquarters of a prefect. —**pre·fec·tur·al** /prēˈfekCHərəl/ *adj.*

pre·fer /priˈfər/ ▸v. (**pre·ferred**, **pre·fer·ring**) [tr.] **1** like (one thing or person) better than another or others; tend to choose: *I prefer Venice* **to** *Rome* | *I would prefer to discuss the matter in private.* **2** *formal* submit (a charge or a piece of information) for consideration: *the police will prefer charges.* **3** *archaic* promote or advance (someone) to a prestigious position: *he was preferred to the post.*

pref·er·a·ble /ˈpref(ə)rəbəl/ ▸*adj.* more desirable or suitable: *lower interest rates were preferable to higher ones.* —**pref·er·a·bil·i·ty** /ˌpref(ə)rəˈbilətē/ *n.* —**pref·er·a·bly** *adv.*

pref·er·ence /ˈpref(ə)rəns/ ▸n. **1** a greater liking for one alternative over another or others: *a preference for long walks and tennis over jogging.* ■ a thing preferred: *my musical preferences are blues and swing.* ■ favor shown to one person or thing over another or others: *preference is given to those who make a donation.* **2** *Law* a prior right or precedence, esp. in connection with the payment of debts.

pref·er·en·tial /ˌprefəˈrenCHəl/ ▸*adj.* of or involving preference or partiality; constituting a favor or privilege: *preferential interest rates may be offered to employees.* ■ (of regulations or rates) favoring particular countries: *preferential trade terms.* ■ (of a union shop) giving employment preference to union members. ■ (of voting or an election) in which the voter puts candidates in order of preference. ■ (of a creditor) having a claim on the receipt of payment from a debtor that will be met before those of other creditors. —**pref·er·en·tial·ly** *adv.*

pre·fer·ment /priˈfərmənt/ ▸n. promotion or appointment to a position or office: *after ordination, preferment was fast.*

pre·ferred stock ▸n. stock that entitles the holder to a fixed dividend, whose payment takes priority over that of common-stock dividends.

pre·fig·ure /prēˈfigyər/ ▸v. [tr.] **1** be an early indication or version of (something): *the Hussite movement prefigured the Reformation.* **2** *archaic* imagine beforehand: *she had prefigured her small pilgrimage as made in solitude.* —**pre·fig·u·ra·tion** /prēˌfigyəˈrāSHən/ *n.* —**pre·fig·ur·a·tive** /prēˈfigyərətiv/ *adj.* —**pre·fig·ure·ment** *n.*

pre·fix /ˈprēˌfiks/ ▸n. a word, letter, or number placed before another: *add the prefix 83 to the extension number.* ■ an element placed at the beginning of a word to adjust or qualify its meaning, e.g., *ex-, non-, re-* or (in some languages) as an inflection. ■ a title placed before a name, e.g., *Mr.*
▸v. [tr.] add (something) at the beginning as a prefix or introduction: *a preface is prefixed to the book.* ■ add a prefix or introduction to

(something): *all three-digit numbers will now be prefixed by 580.* —**pre·fix·a·tion** /ˌprēfik'sāsHən/ *n.*

pre·fron·tal /prē'frəntl/ ▶ *adj.* **1** *Anat.* in or relating to the foremost part of the frontal lobe of the brain: *the prefrontal cortex.* **2** *Zool.* relating to or denoting a bone in front of the eye socket in some lower vertebrates.
▶ *n. Zool.* a prefrontal bone.

preg·nan·cy /'pregnənsē/ ▶ *n.* (*pl.* **-cies**) the condition or period of being pregnant. ■ a case or situation of being pregnant: *an easy pregnancy.*

preg·nant /'pregnənt/ ▶ *adj.* **1** (of a woman or female animal) having a child or young developing in the uterus. ■ having been in such a condition for a specified time: *she was six months pregnant.* **2** full of meaning; significant or suggestive: *a pregnant pause.* ▷late Middle English: from Latin *praegnant-*, probably from *prae* 'before' + the base of *gnasci* 'be born.' —**preg·nant·ly** *adv.*

pre·hen·sile /prē'hensəl; -ˌsīl/ ▶ *adj.* (chiefly of an animal's limb or tail) capable of grasping. —**pre·hen·sil·i·ty** /ˌprē,hen'silətē/ *n.*

pre·his·tor·ic /ˌprē(h)i'stôrik/ ▶ *adj.* of, relating to, or denoting the period before written records: *prehistoric man.* ■ *inf.* very old, primitive, or out of date: *my dad's electric typewriter was a prehistoric machine.* —**pre·his·to·ri·an** /-'stôrēən/ *n.* —**pre·his·tor·i·cal·ly** /-ik(ə)lē/ *adv.* —**pre·his·to·ry** /ˌprē'histərē/ *n.*

pre·judge /prē'jəj/ ▶ *v.* [*tr.*] form a judgment on (an issue or person) prematurely and without having adequate information. —**pre·judg·ment** (also **pre·judge·ment**) *n.*

prej·u·dice /'prejədəs/ ▶ *n.* **1** preconceived opinion that is not based on reason or actual experience: *English* **prejudice against** *foreigners* | *anti-Jewish prejudices.* ■ dislike, hostility, or unjust behavior formed on such a basis: *accusations of racial prejudice.* **2** *chiefly Law* harm or injury that results or may result from some action or judgment.
▶ *v.* [*tr.*] **1** give rise to prejudice in (someone); make biased. **2** *chiefly Law* cause harm to (a state of affairs): *delay is likely to prejudice the child's welfare.*
▶ □ **without prejudice** *Law* without detriment to any existing right or claim: *the payment was made* **without** *any* **prejudice to** *her rights.*

prej·u·di·cial /ˌprejə'disHəl/ ▶ *adj.* harmful to someone or something; detrimental: *the behavior is* **prejudicial to** *good order and discipline.* —**prej·u·di·cial·ly** *adv.*

pre·kin·der·gar·ten /prē'kindərˌgärtn; -ˌgärdn/ (abbr: **pre-K**) ▶ *n.* day care with some educational content for children younger than five, provided by elementary schools or preschools.

prel·ate /'prelət/ ▶ *n. formal or hist.* a bishop or other high ecclesiastical dignitary. —**pre·lat·ic** /pri'latik/ *adj.* —**pre·lat·i·cal** /pri'latikəl/ *adj.*

pre·life /prē'līf/ ▶ *adj.* **1** prior to the appearance of life forms on earth: *prelife molecules.* **2** (often in religious contexts) prior to a particular life or stage of life.

pre·lim·i·nar·y /pri'limə,nerē/ ▶ *adj.* denoting an action or event preceding or done in preparation for something fuller or more important: *preliminary talks* | *the discussions were seen as* **preliminary to** *the policy paper.*
▶ *n.* (*pl.* **-nar·ies**) an action or event preceding or preparing for something fuller or more important: *the bombardment was* **a preliminary to** *an infantry attack.* ■ (**preliminaries**) business or talk, esp. of a formulaic or polite nature, taking place before an action or event. ■ a preliminary round in a sporting competition. —**pre·lim·i·nar·i·ly** /-ˌlimə'nerəlē/ *adv.*
▶ □ **preliminary to** preparatory to; in advance of.

pre·lit·er·ate /prē'litərit/ ▶ *adj.* of, relating to, or denoting a society or culture that has not developed the use of writing.

prel·ude /'prel,(y)ōōd; 'prā,l(y)ōōd/ ▶ *n.* **1** an action or event serving as an introduction to something more important: *education cannot simply be* **a prelude to** *a career.* **2** an introductory piece of music, most commonly an orchestral opening to an act of an opera, the first movement of a suite, or a piece preceding a fugue. ■ a short piece of music of a similar style, esp. for the piano. ■ the introductory part of a poem or other literary work.
▶ *v.* [*tr.*] serve as a prelude or introduction to: *the bombardment preluded an all-out final attack.* —**pre·lu·di·al** /pri'lōōdēəl; prā-/ *adj.*

pre·mar·i·tal /prē'maritl/ ▶ *adj.* occurring or existing before marriage: *premarital sex.* —**pre·mar·i·tal·ly** *adv.*

pre·ma·ture /ˌprēmə'cHŏŏr; -'t(y)ŏŏr/ ▶ *adj.* occurring or done before the usual or proper time; too early: *the sun can cause premature aging* | *it would be premature to do so at this stage.* ■ (of a baby) born before the end of the full term of gestation, esp. three or more weeks before. —**pre·ma·ture·ly** *adv.* —**pre·ma·tu·ri·ty** /-'cHŏŏritē; -'t(y)ŏŏr-/ *n.*

pre·med /'prē'med/ ▶ *n.* **1** a program of premedical studies. ■ a student in such a program. **2** short for PREMEDICATION.
▶ *adj.* short for PREMEDICAL.

pre·med·i·cal /prē'medikəl/ ▶ *adj.* of, relating to, or engaged in study in preparation for medical school.

pre·med·i·ca·tion /ˌprē,medə'kāsHən/ ▶ *n.* medication that is given in preparation for an operation or other treatment.

pre·med·i·tate /pri'medə,tāt; prē-/ ▶ *v.* [*tr.*] [usu. as *adj.*] (**premeditated**) think out or plan (an action, esp. a crime) beforehand: *premeditated murder.* —**pre·med·i·ta·tion** /-,medə'tāsHən/ *n.*

pre·men·stru·al /prē'menstr(ōō)əl/ ▶ *adj.* of, occurring, or experienced before menstruation: *premenstrual tension.* —**pre·men·stru·al·ly** *adv.*

pre·men·stru·al syn·drome (abbr.: **PMS**) ▶ *n.* any of a complex of symptoms (including emotional tension and fluid retention) experienced by some women in the days immediately before menstruation.

pre·mier /prē'm(y)i(ə)r; 'prēmēər; 'prē,mi(ə)r/ ▶ *adj.* first in importance, order, or position; leading: *Germany's premier rock band.* ■ of earliest creation: *the premier issue of the quarterly.*
▶ *n.* a Prime Minister or other head of government. ■ (in Australia and Canada) the chief minister of a government of a state or province. —**pre·mier·ship** *n.*

pre·miere /prē'myer; -'mi(ə)r/ ▶ *n.* the first performance of a musical or theatrical work or the first showing of a movie.
▶ *v.* [*tr.*] give the first performance of: *his first stage play was premiered at the Birmingham Repertory Theatre.* ■ [*intr.*] (of a musical or theatrical work or a film) have its first performance: *the show premiered in New York.*

prem·ise /'preməs/ ▶ *n.* *Logic* a previous statement or proposition from which another is inferred or follows as a conclusion: *if the premise is true, then the conclusion must be true.* ■ an assertion or proposition which forms the basis for a work or theory.
▶ *v.* [*tr.*] (**premise something on/upon**) base an argument, theory, or undertaking on: *the reforms were premised on our findings.* ■ state or presuppose (something) as a premise: *one school of thought premised that the cosmos is indestructible.*

pre·mi·um /'prēmēəm/ ▶ *n.* (*pl.* **-ums**) **1** an amount to be paid for an insurance policy. **2** a sum added to an ordinary price or charge: *to pay a premium for organic fruit.* ■ a sum added to interest or wages; a bonus. ■ [as *adj.*] relating to or denoting a commodity or product of superior quality and therefore a higher price: *premium beers.* ■ *Stock Market* the amount by which the price of a share or other security exceeds its issue price, its nominal value, or the value of the assets it represents: *the fund has traded at a premium of 12%.* **3** something given as a reward, prize, or incentive.
▶ □ **at a premium** **1** scarce and in demand. **2** above the usual or nominal price. □ **put** (or **place**) **a premium on** regard or treat as particularly valuable or important.

pre·mo·lar /prē'mōlər/ ▶ *n.* a tooth situated between the canine and the molar teeth. An adult human normally has eight, two in each jaw on each side.

pre·mo·ni·tion /ˌprēmə'nisHən; ˌprem-/ ▶ *n.* a strong feeling that something is about to happen, esp. something unpleasant: *he had a* **premonition** *of imminent disaster.* —**pre·mon·i·to·ry** /prē'mänə,tôrē/ *adj.*

pre·na·tal /prē'nātl/ ▶ *adj.* before birth; during or relating to pregnancy: *prenatal development.* —**pre·na·tal·ly** /-'nātl-ē/ *adv.*

pren·tice /'prentis/ ▶ *n.* & *v.* archaic term for APPRENTICE. —**pren·tice·ship** /-,sHip/ *n.*

pre·nup·tial /prē'nəpsHəl; -cHəl/ ▶ *adj.* existing or occurring before marriage: *prenuptial pregnancy.* ■ *Zool.* existing or occurring before mating.

pre·nup·tial a·gree·ment ▶ *n.* an agreement made by a couple before they marry concerning the ownership of their respective assets should the marriage fail.

pre·oc·cu·pa·tion /ˌprē,äkyə'pāsHən/ ▶ *n.* the state or condition of being preoccupied or engrossed with something: *his* **preoccupation with** *politics.* ■ a subject or matter that engrosses someone.

pre·oc·cu·py /prē'äkyə,pī/ ▶ *v.* (**-pies, -pied**) [*tr.*] (of a matter or subject) dominate or engross the mind of (someone) to the exclusion of other thoughts: *his mother was* **preoccupied with** *paying the bills.*

pre·op /'prē,äp/ *inf.* ▶ *adj.* short for PREOPERATIVE.

pre·op·er·a·tive /prē'äp(ə)rətiv/ ▶ *adj.* denoting, administered in, or occurring in the period before a surgical operation. —**pre·op·er·a·tive·ly** *adv.*

Pronunciation Key ə *ago, up;* ər *over, fur;* a *hat;* ā *ate;* ä *car;* cH *chin;* e *let;* ē *see;* e(ə)r *air;* i *fit;* ī *by;* i(ə)r *ear;* NG *sing;* ō *go;* ô *law, for;* oi *toy;* ŏŏ *good;* ōō *goo;* ou *out;* sH *she;* TH *thin;* ŦH *then;* (h)w *why;* zH *vision*

pre·or·dain /ˌprēôrˈdān/ ▶v. [tr.] (usu. **be preordained**) decide or determine (an outcome or course of action) beforehand.

prep[1] /prep/ ▶n. inf. a student or graduate of a preparatory school.

prep[2] inf. ▶v. (**prepped, prep·ping**) [tr.] prepare (something); make ready: *scores of volunteers help prep the food.* ■ [intr.] prepare oneself for an event.
▶n. preparation: *I do the prep* | [as adj.] *I had virtually no prep time.*

pre·pack·age /prēˈpakij/ ▶v. [tr.] [usu. as adj.] (**prepackaged**) pack or wrap (goods, esp. food) on the site of production or before sale.

pre·paid /prēˈpād/ ▶ past and past participle of PREPAY.

prep·a·ra·tion /ˌprepəˈrāSHən/ ▶n. the action or process of making ready or being made ready for use or consideration. ■ (usu. **preparations**) something done to get ready for an event or undertaking: *she continued her preparations for the party.* ■ a substance that is specially made up and usually sold, esp. a medicine or food. ■ a specimen that has been prepared for scientific or medical examination: *a microscope preparation.* ■ *Mus.* (in conventional harmony) the sounding of the discordant note in a chord in the preceding chord where it is not discordant, lessening the effect of the discord.

pre·par·a·tive /prēˈpe(ə)rətiv; -ˈpar-/ ▶adj. preparatory.
▶n. a thing that acts as a preparation. —**pre·par·a·tive·ly** adv.

pre·par·a·to·ry /prīˈpe(ə)rəˌtôrē; -ˈparə-; ˈprep(ə)rə-/ ▶adj. serving as or carrying out preparation for a task or undertaking: *more preparatory work is needed.* ■ *Brit.* relating to education in a preparatory school: *preparatory schooling.*
▶ □ **preparatory to** as a preparation for.

pre·par·a·to·ry school ▶n. **1** a private school that prepares students for college. **2** *Brit.* a private school for students between the ages of seven and thirteen.

pre·pare /prīˈpe(ə)r/ ▶v. [tr.] **1** make (something) ready for use or consideration. ■ make (food or a meal) ready for cooking or eating. ■ make (someone) ready or able to do or deal with something. ■ [intr.] make oneself ready to do or deal with something: *she took time off to prepare for her exams.* ■ (**be prepared to do something**) be willing to do something: *I wasn't prepared to go along with that.* ■ make (a chemical product) by a reaction or series of reactions. **2** *Mus.* (in conventional harmony) lead up to (a discord) by means of preparation. ▷late Middle English: from French *préparer* or Latin *praeparare,* from *prae* 'before' + *parare* 'make ready.' —**pre·par·er** n.

pre·par·ed·ness /prəˈpe(ə)r(ə)dnis/ ▶n. a state of readiness, esp. for war.

pre·pay /prēˈpā/ ▶v. (past and past part. **prepaid**) [tr.] [usu. as adj.] (**prepaid**) pay for in advance: *prepaid health plans.* —**pre·pay·a·ble** adj. —**pre·pay·ment** n.

pre·pon·der·ant /prīˈpändərənt/ ▶adj. predominant in influence, number, or importance. —**pre·pon·der·ance** n. —**pre·pon·der·ant·ly** adv.

pre·pon·der·ate /prīˈpändəˌrāt/ ▶v. [intr.] be greater in number, influence, or importance.

prep·o·si·tion /ˌprepəˈziSHən/ ▶n. *Gram.* a word governing, and usually preceding, a noun or pronoun and expressing a relation to another word or element in the clause, as in "the man *on* the platform," "she arrived *after* dinner," "what did you do it *for?*" —**prep·o·si·tion·al** /-SHənl/ adj. —**prep·o·si·tion·al·ly** /-SHənl-ē/ adv.

pre·pos·sess·ing /ˌprēpəˈzesiNG/ ▶adj. attractive or appealing in appearance: *he was not a prepossessing sight.* —**pre·pos·ses·sion** /-ˈzeSHən/ n.

pre·pos·ter·ous /prīˈpäst(ə)rəs/ ▶adj. contrary to reason or common sense; utterly absurd or ridiculous: *a preposterous suggestion.* —**pre·pos·ter·ous·ly** adv. —**pre·pos·ter·ous·ness** n.

prep·py /ˈprepē/ (also **prep·pie**) inf. ▶n. (pl. **-pies**) a student or graduate of an expensive preparatory school or a person resembling such a student in dress or appearance.
▶adj. (**-pi·er, -pi·est**) of or typical of such a person, esp. with reference to their style of dress: *the preppy look.*

pre·proc·es·sor /prēˈpräsˌesər; -ˈprōsˌesər; -əsər/ ▶n. a computer program that modifies data to conform with the input requirements of another program.

prep school ▶n. another term for PREPARATORY SCHOOL.

pre·pu·bes·cent /ˌprēpyōōˈbesənt/ ▶adj. relating to or in the period preceding puberty: *a prepubescent girl.*
▶n. a prepubescent boy or girl. —**pre·pu·bes·cence** n.

pre·pub·li·ca·tion /ˌprēpəbliˈkāSHən/ ▶adj. issued or occurring before publication: *prepublication censorship.*
▶n. publication in advance.

pre·puce /ˈprēˌpyōōs/ ▶n. *Anat.* **1** technical term for FORESKIN. **2** the fold of skin surrounding the clitoris. —**pre·pu·tial** /prēˈpyōōSHəl/ adj.

pre·quel /ˈprēkwəl; -kwil/ ▶n. a story or movie containing events that precede those of an existing work.

pre·req·ui·site /prēˈrekwəzət/ ▶n. a thing that is required as a prior condition for something else to happen or exist.
▶adj. required as a prior condition.

pre·rog·a·tive /prīˈrägətiv; pəˈräg-/ ▶n. a right or privilege exclusive to a particular individual or class. ■ a faculty or property distinguishing a person or class: *it's not a female prerogative to feel insecure.*

Pres. ▶abbr. President.

pres·age /ˈpresij/ ▶v. [tr.] (of an event) be a sign or warning that (something, typically something bad) will happen. ■ *archaic* (of a person) predict: *lands he could measure, terms and tides presage.*
▶n. a sign or warning that something, typically something bad, will happen; an omen or portent. ■ *archaic* a feeling of presentiment or foreboding. —**pres·ag·er** n. (*archaic*)

pres·by·ter /ˈprezbitər; ˈpres-/ ▶n. *hist.* an elder or minister of the Christian Church. ■ *formal* (in Presbyterian churches) an elder. ■ *formal* (in Episcopal churches) a minister of the second order, under the authority of a bishop; a priest. —**pres·byt·er·al** /prezˈbitərəl; pres-/ adj. —**pres·byt·er·ate** /prezˈbitəˌrāt; pres-/ n. —**pres·by·te·ri·al** /ˌprezbiˈti(ə)rēəl; ˌpres-/ adj. —**pres·by·ter·ship** /-ˌSHip/ n.

Pres·by·te·ri·an /ˌprezbəˈti(ə)rēən; ˌpres-/ ▶adj. of, relating to, or denoting a Christian Church or denomination governed by elders according to the principles of Presbyterianism.
▶n. a member of a Presbyterian Church. ■ an advocate of the Presbyterian system. —**Pres·by·te·ri·an·ism** n.

pres·by·ter·y /ˈprezbəˌterē; ˈpres-; -bətrē/ ▶n. (pl. **-ter·ies**) **1** [treated as *sing.* or *pl.*] a body of church elders and ministers, esp. (in Presbyterian churches) an administrative body (court) representing all the local congregations of a district. ■ a district represented by such a body of elders and ministers. **2** the house of a Roman Catholic parish priest.

pre·school ▶adj. /ˈprēˈskōōl/ of or relating to the time before a child is old enough to go to elementary school: *a preschool play group.* ■ (of a child) under the age at which compulsory schooling begins.
▶n. /ˈprēˌskōōl/ a nursery school: *she goes to preschool.* —**pre·school·er** n.

pre·scient /ˈpreSH(ē)ənt; ˈprē-/ ▶adj. having or showing knowledge of events before they take place: *a prescient warning.* —**pre·science** /-əns/ n. —**pre·scient·ly** adv.

pre·scind /prīˈsind/ ▶v. [intr.] (**prescind from**) *formal* leave out of consideration. ■ [tr.] cut off or separate from something.

pre·scribe /prīˈskrīb/ ▶v. [tr.] (of a medical practitioner) advise and authorize the use of (a medicine or treatment) for someone, esp. in writing. ■ recommend (a substance or action) as something beneficial: *marriage is often prescribed as a universal remedy.* ■ state authoritatively or as a rule that (an action or procedure) should be carried out. | [as adj.] (**prescribed**) *doing things in the prescribed manner.* —**pre·scrib·er** n.

pre·scrip·tion /prīˈskripSHən/ ▶n. **1** an instruction written by a medical practitioner that authorizes a patient to be provided a medicine or treatment: [as adj.] *prescription drugs.* ■ the action of prescribing a medicine or treatment: *the unnecessary prescription of antibiotics.* ■ a medicine or remedy that is prescribed: *I've got to pick up my prescription.* **2** a recommendation that is authoritatively put forward. ■ the authoritative recommendation of an action or procedure: *rather than prescription there would be guidance.* **3** *Law* the establishment of a claim founded on the basis of a long or indefinite period of uninterrupted use or of long-standing custom.

pre·scrip·tive /prīˈskriptiv/ ▶adj. **1** of or relating to the imposition or enforcement of a rule or method: *these guidelines are not intended to be prescriptive.* ■ *Linguistics* attempting to impose rules of correct usage on the users of a language: *a prescriptive grammar book.* Often contrasted with DESCRIPTIVE. **2** (of a right, title, or institution) having become legally established or accepted by long usage or the passage of time. ■ *archaic* established by long-standing custom or usage. —**pre·scrip·tive·ly** adv. —**pre·scrip·tive·ness** n. —**pre·scrip·tiv·ism** /-ˈskriptəˌvizəm/ n. —**pre·scrip·tiv·ist** /-vist/ n. & adj.

pres·ence /ˈprezəns/ ▶n. the state or fact of existing, occurring, or being present in a place or thing. ■ a person or thing that exists or is present in a place but is not seen: *the monks became aware of a strange presence.* ■ a group of people, esp. soldiers or police, stationed in a particular place: *the USA would maintain a presence in the region.* ■ the impressive manner or appearance of a person: *Richard was not a big man, but his presence was overwhelming* | *he has a real physical presence.*
▶ □ **make one's presence felt** have a strong and obvious effect or influence on others or on a situation. □ **presence of mind** the ability to remain calm and take quick, sensible action.

pres·ent[1] /ˈprezənt/ ▶adj. **1** (of a person) in a particular place: *the speech* *caused embarrassment to all those present.* ■ (often **present in**) (of a thing) existing or occurring in a place or thing: *organic molecules are present in comets.* **2** existing or occurring now: *in her present situation.* ■ now being considered or discussed: *the present article cannot answer every question.* ■ *Gram.* (of a tense or participle) expressing an action now going on or habitually performed or a condition now existing.

▶*n.* (usu. **the present**) the period of time now occurring: *to think beyond the present.* ■ *Gram.* a present tense: *the verbs are all in the present.*

▶ □ **at present** now: *membership at present stands at about 5,000.* □ **for the present** for now; temporarily. □ **present company excepted** excluding those who are here now. □ **these presents** *formal Law* this document: *the premises outlined in red on the Plan annexed to these presents.*

pre·sent[2] /pri'zent/ ▶*v.* [tr.] **1** (**present something to**) give something to (someone) formally or ceremonially. ■ (**present someone with**) give someone (something) in such a way. ■ show or offer (something) for others to scrutinize or consider: *he stopped and presented his passport.* ■ formally introduce (someone) to someone else: *may I present my wife?* ■ proffer (compliments or good wishes) in a formal manner. ■ formally deliver (a check or bill) for acceptance or payment. ■ *Law* bring (a complaint, petition, or evidence) formally to the notice of a court. ■ (of a company or producer) put (a show or exhibition) before the public. **2** bring about or be the cause of (a problem or difficulty). ■ exhibit (a particular state or appearance) to others: *the EC presented a united front over the crisis.* ■ represent (someone) to others in a particular way, typically one that is false or exaggerated: *he presented himself as a hardworking man.* ■ (**present oneself**) come forward into the presence of another or others, esp. for a formal occasion; appear. ■ (**present itself**) (of an opportunity or idea) occur and be available for use or exploitation. ■ [*intr.*] (**present with**) *Med.* (of a patient) come forward for or undergo initial medical examination for a particular condition or symptom. ■ [*intr.*] *Med.* (of a part of a fetus) be directed toward the cervix during labor. ■ [*intr.*] *Med.* (of an illness) manifest itself. **3** hold out or aim (a firearm) at something so as to be ready to fire. —**pre·sent·er** *n.*

▶ □ **present arms** (usually as a command) hold a rifle vertically in front of the body as a salute.

pres·ent[3] /'prezənt/ ▶*n.* a thing given to someone as a gift.

▶ □ **make a present of** give as a gift.

pre·sent·a·ble /pri'zentəbəl/ ▶*adj.* clean, well dressed, or decent enough to be seen in public: *I did my best to make myself look presentable.* —**pre·sent·a·bil·i·ty** /-,zentə'bilətē/ *n.* —**pre·sent·a·bly** /-blē/ *adv.*

pres·en·ta·tion /,prē,zen'tāSHən; ,prezən-; ,prēzən-/ ▶*n.* **1** the proffering or giving of something to someone, esp. as part of a formal ceremony. ■ the manner or style in which something is given, offered, or displayed: *the presentation of foods is designed to stimulate your appetite.* ■ a formal introduction of someone, esp. at court. ■ the official submission of something for consideration in a law court. ■ *chiefly hist.* the action or right of formally proposing a candidate for a church benefice or other position: *the Earl of Pembroke offered Herbert the presentation of the living of Bremerton.* ■ a demonstration or display of a product or idea: *a sales presentation.* ■ an exhibition or theatrical performance. **2** *Med.* the position of a fetus in relation to the cervix at the time of delivery: *breech presentation.* ■ the coming forward of a patient for initial examination and diagnosis: *all patients in this group were symptomatic at initial presentation.* —**pres·en·ta·tion·al** /-SHənl/ *adj.* —**pres·en·ta·tion·al·ly** /-SHənl-ē/ *adv.*

pres·ent-day ▶*adj.* of or relating to the current period of time: *present-day technological developments.*

pre·sen·tient /prē'senCHənt/ ▶*adj. rare* having a presentiment.

pre·sen·ti·ment /pri'zentəmənt/ ▶*n.* an intuitive feeling about the future, esp. one of foreboding: *a presentiment of disaster.*

pres·ent·ly /'prezəntlē/ ▶*adv.* **1** after a short time; soon: *this will be examined in more detail presently.* **2** at the present time; now: *there are presently 1,128 people on the waiting list.*

pre·sent·ment /pri'zentmənt/ ▶*n. Law, chiefly hist.* a formal presentation of information to a court, esp. by a sworn jury regarding an offense or other matter.

pres·er·va·tion /,prezər'vāSHən/ ▶*n.* the action of preserving something. ■ the state of being preserved, esp. to a specified degree.

pres·er·va·tion·ist /,prezər'vāSHənəst/ ▶*n.* a supporter or advocate of the preservation of something, esp. of historic buildings and artifacts.

pre·serv·a·tive /pri'zərvətiv/ ▶*n.* a substance used to preserve foodstuffs, wood, or other materials against decay.

▶*adj.* acting to preserve something: *the preservative effects of freezing.*

pre·serve /pri'zərv/ ▶*v.* [tr.] maintain (something) in its original or existing state: *all records of the past were zealously preserved.* ■ retain (a

condition or state of affairs): *a fight to preserve local democracy.* ■ maintain or keep alive (a memory or quality): *the film has preserved all the qualities of the novel.* ■ keep safe from harm or injury: *a place for preserving endangered species.* ■ treat or refrigerate (food) to prevent its decomposition or fermentation. ■ prepare (fruit) for long-term storage by boiling it with sugar. ■ keep (game or an area where game is found) undisturbed to allow private hunting or shooting.

▶*n.* **1** (usu. **preserves**) food made with fruit preserved in sugar, such as jam or marmalade. **2** a sphere of activity regarded as being reserved for a particular person or group: *the civil service became the preserve of the educated middle class.* **3** a place where game is protected and kept for private hunting or shooting. —**pre·serv·a·ble** *adj.* —**pre·serv·er** *n.*

pre·set /prē'set/ ▶*v.* (**-set·ting**; *past* and *past part.* **-set**) [tr.] [usu. as *adj.*] (**preset**) set or adjust (a value that controls the operation of a device) in advance of its use: *the water is heated quickly at a preset temperature.*

▶*n.* a control on electronic equipment or on software that is set or adjusted beforehand to facilitate use.

pre·shrunk /prē'SHrəNGk/ ▶*adj.* (of a fabric or garment) having undergone a shrinking process during manufacture to prevent further shrinking in use. —**pre·shrink** /-'SHriNGk/ *v.*

pre·side /pri'zīd/ ▶*v.* [intr.] **1** be in the position of authority in a meeting or gathering: *Bishop Herbener presided at the meeting.* ■ (**preside over**) be in charge of (a place or situation): *he presided over a period of great budgetary recklessness.* **2** (**preside at**) play (a musical instrument, esp. a keyboard instrument) at a public gathering. ▶*early 17th cent.:* from French *présider,* from Latin *praesidere,* from *prae* 'before' + *sedere* 'sit.'

pres·i·den·cy /'prez(ə)dənsē; 'prezə,densē/ ▶*n.* (*pl.* **-cies**) the office of president: *the presidency of the U.S.* ■ the period of this: *during Carter's presidency.*

pres·i·dent /'prez(ə)dənt; 'prezə,dent/ ▶*n.* the elected head of a republican state. ■ the head of a society, council, or other organization. ■ the head of a college or university. ■ the head of a company. —**pres·i·den·tial** /,prezə'denCHəl/ *adj.* —**pres·i·den·tial·ly** /,prezə'denCHəlē/ *adv.* —**pres·i·dent·ship** /-,SHip/ *n.* (*archaic*).

pre·sid·i·um /pri'sidēəm; -'zid-/ (also **prae·sid·i·um**) ▶*n.* a standing executive committee in a communist country. ■ (**Presidium**) the committee of this type in the former USSR, which functioned as the legislative authority when the Supreme Soviet was not sitting.

press[1] /pres/ ▶*v.* **1** move or cause to move into a position of contact with something by exerting continuous physical force: [tr.] *he pressed his face to the glass* | [intr.] *her body pressed against his.* ■ [tr.] exert continuous physical force on (something), typically in order to operate a device or machine: *he pressed a button and the doors slid open.* ■ [tr.] squeeze (someone's arm or hand) as a sign of affection. ■ [intr.] move in a specified direction by pushing: *the mob was still pressing forward.* ■ *fig.* (of an enemy or opponent) attack persistently and fiercely: [intr.] *their enemies pressed in on all sides* | [tr.] *two assailants were pressing Agrippa.* ■ [intr.] (**press on/ahead**) *fig.* continue in one's action. ■ [tr.] *Weightlifting* raise (a specified weight) by first lifting it to shoulder height and then gradually pushing it upward above the head. **2** [tr.] apply pressure to (something) to flatten, shape, or smooth it, typically by ironing. ■ apply pressure to (a flower or leaf) between sheets of paper in order to dry and preserve it. ■ extract (juice or oil) by crushing or squeezing fruit, vegetables, etc. ■ squeeze or crush (fruit, vegetables, etc.) to extract the juice or oil. ■ manufacture (something, esp. a phonograph record) by molding under pressure. **3** [tr.] forcefully put forward (an opinion, claim, or course of action). ■ make strong efforts to persuade or force (someone) to do or provide something: *when I pressed him for precise figures, he evaded the subject* | [intr.] *they continued to press for changes in legislation.* ■ (**press something on/upon**) insist that (someone) accept an offer or gift. ■ [intr.] (of something, esp. time) be in short supply and so demand immediate action. ■ (**be pressed**) have barely enough of something, esp. time: *I'm very pressed for time.* ■ (**be pressed to do something**) have difficulty doing or achieving something: *they may be hard pressed to keep their promise.*

▶*n.* **1** a device for applying pressure to something in order to flatten or shape it or to extract juice or oil: *a flower press* | *a wine press.* ■ a machine that applies pressure to a workpiece by means of a tool, in order to punch shapes. **2** a printing press. ■ [often in *names*] a business that prints or publishes books: *the Clarendon Press.* ■ the process of printing: *the book is ready to go to press.* **3** (**the press**) [treated as *sing.* or *pl.*] newspapers or journalists viewed collectively: *the press was notified* | [as *adj.*]

Pronunciation Key ə *ago, up;* ər *over, fur;* a *hat;* ā *ate;* ä *car;* CH *chin;* e *let;* ē *see;* e(ə)r *air;* i *fit;* ī *by;* i(ə)r *ear;* NG *sing;* ō *go;* ô *law, for;* oi *toy;* oo͝ *good;* oo͞ *goo;* ou *out;* SH *she;* TH *thin;* T͟H *then;* (h)w *why;* ZH *vision*

press coverage. ■ coverage in newspapers and magazines: *there's no point in demonstrating if you don't get any press | the mayor has had a bad press.* **4** an act of pressing something. ■ a closely packed crowd or mass of people or things: *the press of cars.* ■ *Weightlifting* an act of raising a weight to shoulder height and then gradually pushing it above the head. ■ *Basketball* any of various forms of close guarding by the defending team.

▶ □ **press (the) flesh** *inf.* (of a celebrity or politician) greet people by shaking hands.

press² ▶ *v.* [tr.] (**press someone/something into**) put (someone or something) to a specified use, esp. as a temporary or makeshift measure: *the high school gym was pressed into service as a first-aid station.*

press a·gent ▶ *n.* a person employed to organize advertising and publicity in the press on behalf of an organization or well-known person.

press box ▶ *n.* an area reserved for journalists at a sports event.

press con·fer·ence ▶ *n.* an interview given to journalists by a prominent person in order to make an announcement or answer questions.

press gang ▶ *n. hist.* a body of men employed to enlist men forcibly into service in the army or navy.

press·ing /ˈpresiNG/ ▶ *adj.* (of a problem, need, or situation) requiring quick or immediate action or attention. ■ (of an engagement or activity) important and requiring one's attendance or presence: *he had pressing business in Albany.* ■ (of an invitation) strongly expressed.

▶ *n.* a thing made by the application of force or weight, esp. a phonograph record. ■ a series of such things made at one time: *the first pressing of the live album.* ■ an act or instance of applying force or weight to something: *pure-grade olive oil is the product of the second or third pressings.* —**press·ing·ly** *adv.*

pres·sure /ˈpreSHər/ ▶ *n.* **1** the continuous physical force exerted on or against an object by something in contact with it. ■ the force exerted per unit area: *gas can be fed to the turbines at a pressure of around 250 psi.* **2** the use of persuasion, influence, or intimidation to make someone do something: *the proposals put pressure on Britain to drop its demand.* ■ the influence or effect of someone or something: *oil prices came under some downward pressure.* ■ the feeling of stressful urgency caused by the necessity of doing or achieving something, esp. with limited time: *you need to be able to work under pressure and not get flustered.*

▶ *v.* [tr.] attempt to persuade or coerce (someone) into doing something.

pres·sure cook·er ▶ *n.* an airtight pot in which food can be cooked quickly under steam pressure. ■ *fig.* a highly stressful situation or assignment. —**pres·sure-cook** *v.*

pres·sure group ▶ *n.* a group that tries to influence public policy in the interest of a particular cause: *an environmental pressure group.*

pres·sure point ▶ *n.* a point on the surface of the body sensitive to pressure. ■ a point where an artery can be pressed against a bone to inhibit bleeding.

pres·sur·ize /ˈpreSHəˌrīz/ ▶ *v.* [tr.] **1** produce or maintain raised pressure artificially in (a gas or its container). ■ maintain an adequate air pressure in (an aircraft cabin) at a high altitude. **2** [tr.] attempt to persuade or coerce (someone) into doing something. —**pres·sur·i·za·tion** /ˌpreSHərəˈzāSHən/ *n.*

pres·ti·dig·i·ta·tion /ˌprestəˌdijəˈtāSHən/ ▶ *n. formal* magic tricks performed as entertainment. —**pres·ti·dig·i·ta·tor** /-ˈdijəˌtātər/ *n.*

pres·tige /preˈstēZH; -ˈtēj/ ▶ *n.* widespread respect and admiration felt for someone or something on the basis of a perception of their achievements or quality. ■ [as *adj.*] denoting something that arouses such respect or admiration: *prestige wines.* ▷mid 17th cent. (in the sense 'illusion, conjuring trick'): from French, literally 'illusion, glamour,' from late Latin *praestigium* 'illusion,' from Latin *praestigiae* (plural) 'conjuring tricks.' The transference of meaning occurred by way of the sense 'dazzling influence, glamour,' at first depreciatory.

pres·tig·ious /preˈstijəs; -ˈstē-/ ▶ *adj.* inspiring respect and admiration; having high status. —**pres·tig·i·ous·ly** *adv.* —**pres·tig·i·ous·ness** *n.*

pres·tis·si·mo /preˈstisəˌmō/ *Mus.* ▶ *adv.* & *adj.* (esp. as a direction) in a very quick tempo.

pres·to /ˈprestō/ ▶ *adv.* & *adj. Mus.* (esp. as a direction) in a quick tempo. ▶ *interj.* a phrase announcing the successful completion of a trick, or suggesting that something has been done so easily that it seems to be magic: *just one quick squeeze and presto! A stir fry in seconds.*

pre·sum·a·bly /priˈzōōməblē/ ▶ *adv.* used to convey that what is asserted is very likely though not known for certain: *the Yakima Indians presumably came from Asia by way of the Bering Strait.*

pre·sume /priˈzōōm/ ▶ *v.* **1** [tr.] suppose that something is the case on the basis of probability: *I presumed that the man had been escorted from the building.* ■ take for granted that something exists or is the case: | *the*

task demands skills which cannot be presumed and therefore require proper training. **2** [intr.] be audacious enough to do something: *kindly don't presume to issue me orders.* ■ [intr.] make unjustified demands; take liberties: *forgive me if I have presumed.* ■ [intr.] (**presume on/upon**) unjustifiably regard (something) as entitling one to privileges: *she knew he regarded her as his protégée, but was determined not to presume on that.* ▷late Middle English: from Old French *presumer*, from Latin *praesumere* 'anticipate' (in late Latin 'take for granted'), from *prae* 'before' + *sumere* 'take.' —**pre·sum·a·ble** *adj.*

pre·sum·ing /priˈzōōmiNG/ ▶ *adj. archaic* presumptuous. —**pre·sum·ing·ly** *adv.*

pre·sump·tion /priˈzəmpSHən/ ▶ *n.* **1** an act or instance of taking something to be true or adopting a particular attitude toward something, esp. at the start of a chain of argument or action. ■ an idea that is taken to be true, and often used as the basis for other ideas, although it is not known for certain. ■ *chiefly Law* an attitude adopted in law or as a matter of policy toward an action or proposal in the absence of acceptable reasons to the contrary: *a general presumption in favor of development.* **2** behavior perceived as arrogant, disrespectful, and transgressing the limits of what is permitted or appropriate.

pre·sump·tive /priˈzəmptiv/ ▶ *adj.* of the nature of a presumption; presumed in the absence of further information. ■ *Law* giving grounds for the inference of a fact or of the appropriate interpretation of the law. ■ another term for PRESUMPTUOUS. —**pre·sump·tive·ly** *adv.*

pre·sump·tu·ous /priˈzəmpCH(ōō)əs/ ▶ *adj.* (of a person or their behavior) failing to observe the limits of what is permitted or appropriate. —**pre·sump·tu·ous·ly** *adv.* —**pre·sump·tu·ous·ness** *n.*

pre·sup·pose /ˌprēsəˈpōz/ ▶ *v.* [tr.] (of an action, process, or argument) require as a precondition of possibility or coherence: *his relationships did not permit the degree of self-revelation that true intimacy presupposes.* ■ tacitly assume at the beginning of a line of argument or course of action that something is the case: *your argument presupposes that it does not matter who is in power.* —**pre·sup·po·si·tion** /ˌprē,səpəˈziSHən/ *n.*

pre·tax /ˈprēˈtaks/ ▶ *adj.* (of income or profits) considered or calculated before the deduction of taxes: *pretax profits rose 23 percent.*

pre·teen /ˈprēˈtēn/ ▶ *adj.* of or relating to a child just under the age of thirteen.

▶ *n.* a child of such an age.

pre·tend /priˈtend/ ▶ *v.* **1** [tr.] speak and act so as to make it appear that something is the case when in fact it is not: *she turned the pages and pretended to read.* ■ engage in a game or fantasy that involves supposing something that is not the case to be so: [intr.] *children like to pretend.* ■ [tr.] give the appearance of feeling or possessing (an emotion or quality); simulate: *she pretended a greater surprise than she felt.* **2** [intr.] (**pretend to**) lay claim to (a quality or title): *he cannot pretend to sophistication.*

▶ *adj. inf.* not really what it is represented as being; used in a game or deception: *the children are pouring out pretend tea for the dolls.*

pre·tend·er /priˈtendər/ ▶ *n.* a person who claims or aspires to a title or position: *the pretender to the throne.*

pre·tense /ˈprēˌtens; priˈtens/ (*Brit.* **pre·tence**) ▶ *n.* **1** an attempt to make something that is not the case appear true: *his anger is masked by a pretense that all is well.* ■ a false display of feelings, attitudes, or intentions: *he asked me questions without any pretense at politeness.* ■ the practice of inventing imaginary situations in play. ■ affected and ostentatious speech and behavior. **2** (**pretense to**) a claim, esp. a false or ambitious one: *he was quick to disclaim any pretense to superiority.*

pre·ten·sion¹ /priˈtenCHən/ ▶ *n.* **1** (**pretension to**) a claim or the assertion of a claim to something: *their pretensions to culture.* ■ (often **pretensions**) an aspiration or claim to a certain status or quality: *another aging rocker with literary pretensions.* **2** the use of affectation to impress; ostentatiousness: *he spoke simply, without pretension.*

pre·ten·sion² /ˈprēˈtenCHən/ ▶ *v.* [tr.] apply tension to (an object) before some other process or event: *the safety system pretensions the seat belts.* ■ strengthen (reinforced concrete) by applying tension to the reinforcing rods before the concrete has set.

pre·ten·tious /priˈtenCHəs/ ▶ *adj.* attempting to impress by affecting greater importance, talent, culture, etc., than is actually possessed: *a pretentious literary device.* —**pre·ten·tious·ly** *adv.* —**pre·ten·tious·ness** *n.*

pre·term /ˈprēˈtərm/ *Med.* ▶ *adj.* born or occurring after a pregnancy significantly shorter than normal, esp. after no more than 37 weeks of pregnancy: *babies born during preterm labor.*

pre·ter·nat·u·ral /ˌprētərˈnaCH(ə)rəl/ ▶ *adj.* beyond what is normal or natural: *autumn had arrived with preternatural speed.* —**pre·ter·nat·u·ral·ism** /-ˈnaCH(ə)rəˌlizəm/ *n.* —**pre·ter·nat·u·ral·ly** *adv.*

pre·text /ˈprēˌtekst/ ▶ *n.* a reason given in justification of a course of action that is not the real reason.

▸ □ **on** (or **under**) **the pretext** giving the specified reason as one's justification: *the police raided Grand River* **on the pretext of** *looking for moonshiners.*

pre·tor /ˈprētər/ ▸ *n.* variant spelling of PRAETOR.

pre·to·ri·an /priˈtôrēən/ ▸ *adj.* & *n.* variant spelling of PRAETORIAN.

pret·ti·fy /ˈpritəˌfī/ ▸ *v.* (**-fies, -fied**) [*tr.*] make (someone or something) appear superficially pretty or attractive: *nothing has been done to prettify the site.* —**pret·ti·fi·ca·tion** /ˌpritəfəˈkāSHən/ *n.* —**pret·ti·fi·er** *n.*

pret·ty /ˈpritē/ ▸ *adj.* (**-ti·er, -ti·est**) attractive in a delicate way without being truly beautiful or handsome: *a pretty little girl with an engaging grin.* ■ *inf.* used ironically in expressions of annoyance or disgust: *it is a pretty state of affairs.*
▸ *adv. inf.* to a moderately high degree; fairly: *he was pretty fit for his age.*
▸ *n.* (*pl.* **-ties**) *inf.* an attractive thing, typically a pleasing but unnecessary accessory. ■ used to refer in a condescending way to an attractive person, usually a girl or a woman: *six pretties in sequined leotards.*
▸ *v.* (**-ties, -tied**) [*tr.*] make pretty or attractive: *she'll be all* **prettied up** *and ready to go in an hour.* ▷Old English *prættig*; related to Middle Dutch *pertich* 'brisk, clever,' obsolete Dutch *prettig* 'humorous, sporty,' from a West Germanic base meaning 'trick.' The sense development 'deceitful, cunning, clever, skillful, admirable, pleasing, nice' has parallels in adjectives such as *canny, fine, nice,* etc. —**pret·ti·ly** /ˈpritl-ē/ *adv.* —**pret·ti·ness** *n.* —**pret·ty·ish** *adj.*
▸ □ **pretty much** (or **nearly** or **well**) *inf.* very nearly: *the case is pretty well over.* □ **a pretty penny** *inf.* a large sum of money. □ **pretty please** used as an emphatic or wheedling form of request. □ **be sitting pretty** *inf.* be in an advantageous position or situation.

pret·zel /ˈpretsəl/ ▸ *n.* a crisp biscuit baked in the form of a knot or stick and flavored with salt.
▸ *v.* (**-zeled, -zel·ing**) [*tr.*] twist, bend, or contort.

pre·vail /priˈvāl/ ▸ *v.* [*intr.*] prove more powerful than opposing forces; be victorious: *it is hard for logic to* **prevail over** *emotion.* ■ be widespread in a particular area at a particular time; be current: *an atmosphere of crisis prevails.* ■ (**prevail on/upon**) persuade (someone) to do something: *she was prevailed upon to give an account of her work.* —**pre·vail·ing·ly** *adv.*

pre·vail·ing wind ▸ *n.* a wind from the direction that is predominant at a particular place or season.

prev·a·lent /ˈprevələnt/ ▸ *adj.* widespread in a particular area at a particular time: *the social ills prevalent in society today.* ■ *archaic* predominant; powerful. —**prev·a·lence** *n.* —**prev·a·lent·ly** *adv.*

pre·var·i·cate /priˈvariˌkāt/ ▸ *v.* [*intr.*] speak or act in an evasive way. —**pre·var·i·ca·tion** /priˌvariˈkāSHən/ *n.* —**pre·var·i·ca·tor** /-ˌkātər/ *n.*

pre·vent /priˈvent/ ▸ *v.* [*tr.*] **1** keep (something) from happening or arising. ■ make (someone or something) unable to do something: *window locks won't* **prevent** *a determined burglar* **from** *getting in.* **2** *archaic* (of God) go before (someone) with spiritual guidance and help. —**pre·vent·a·bil·i·ty** /priˌventəˈbilətē/ *n.* —**pre·vent·a·ble** (also **pre·vent·i·ble**) *adj.* —**pre·vent·er** *n.* —**pre·ven·tion** *n.*

pre·ven·ta·tive /prēˈventətiv/ ▸ *adj.* & *n.* another term for PREVENTIVE. —**pre·ven·ta·tive·ly** *adv.*

pre·ven·tive /priˈventiv/ ▸ *adj.* designed to keep something undesirable such as illness, harm, or accidents from occurring: *preventive medicine.*
▸ *n.* a medicine or other treatment designed to stop disease or ill health from occurring. —**pre·ven·tive·ly** *adv.*

pre·view /ˈprēˌvyoo/ ▸ *n.* an inspection or viewing of something before it is bought or becomes generally known and available: *a* **sneak preview** *of the pictures on sale.* ■ a showing of a movie, play, exhibition, etc., before its official opening. ■ a short extract shown in a movie theater as publicity for a forthcoming film. ■ a commentary on or appraisal of a forthcoming film, play, book, etc., based on an advance viewing. ■ *Comput.* a facility for inspecting the appearance of a document prepared in a word-processing or other program before it is printed.
▸ *v.* [*tr.*] display (a product, movie, play, etc.) before it officially goes on sale or opens to the public. ■ see or inspect (something) before it is used or becomes generally available. ■ comment on or appraise (a forthcoming event) in advance: *next week we'll be previewing the new season.*

pre·vi·ous /ˈprēvēəs/ ▸ *adj.* **1** existing or occurring before in time or order: *tickets will be sold on the same basis as in previous years.* **2** *inf.* overly hasty in acting or in drawing a conclusion. —**pre·vi·ous·ly** *adv.*
▸ □ **previous to** before: *the month previous to publication.*

pre·vue /ˈprēˌvyoo/ ▸ *n.* variant spelling of PREVIEW.

pre·war /ˈprēˈwôr/ ▸ *adj.* existing, occurring, or built before a war.

prey /prā/ ▸ *n.* an animal that is hunted and killed by another for food. ■ a person or thing easily injured or taken advantage of: *he was easy*

prey for the two con men. ■ a person who is vulnerable to distressing emotions or beliefs: *the settlers become* **prey to** *nameless fears.*
▸ *v.* [*intr.*] (**prey on/upon**) hunt and kill for food. ■ take advantage of; exploit or injure. ■ cause constant trouble and distress to: *the problem had begun to* **prey on my mind.**
▸ □ **fall prey to** be hunted and killed by. ■ be vulnerable to or overcome by: *he would often fall prey to melancholy.*

price /prīs/ ▸ *n.* the amount of money expected, required, or given in payment for something. ■ *fig.* an unwelcome experience, event, or action involved as a condition of achieving a desired end: *the price of their success was an entire day spent in discussion.* ■ the odds in betting. ■ *archaic* value; worth: *a pearl of great price.*
▸ *v.* [*tr.*] (often **be priced**) decide the amount required as payment for (something offered for sale).
▸ □ **at any price** no matter what expense, sacrifice, or difficulty is involved: *they wanted peace at any price.* □ **at a price** requiring great expense or involving unwelcome consequences: *his generosity comes at a price.* □ **beyond** (or **without**) **price** so valuable that no price can be stated. □ **a price on someone's head** a reward offered for someone's capture or death. □ **put a price on** determine the value of: *you can't put a price on what she has to offer.*

price-fix·ing (also **price fix·ing**) ▸ *n.* the maintaining of prices at a certain level by agreement between competing sellers.

price·less /ˈprīsləs/ ▸ *adj.* so precious that its value cannot be determined: *priceless works of art.* ■ *inf.* used to express great and usually affectionate amusement: *darling, you're priceless!* —**price·less·ly** *adv.* —**price·less·ness** *n.*

price tag ▸ *n.* the label on an item for sale, showing its price. ■ *fig.* the cost of a company, enterprise, or undertaking: *a $400 billion price tag was put on the venture.*

price war ▸ *n.* a fierce competition in which retailers cut prices in an attempt to increase their share of the market.

pric·ey /ˈprīsē/ (also **pric·y**) ▸ *adj.* (**pric·i·er, pric·i·est**) *inf.* expensive: *boutiques selling pricey clothes.* —**pric·i·ness** *n.*

prick /prik/ ▸ *v.* [*tr.*] **1** make a small hole in (something) with a sharp point; pierce slightly. ■ [*intr.*] feel a sensation as though a sharp point were sticking into one: *she felt her scalp prick and her palms were damp.* ■ (of tears) cause the sensation of imminent weeping in (a person's eyes): *tears of disappointment were pricking her eyelids.* ■ [*intr.*] (of a person's eyes) experience such a sensation. ■ cause mental or emotional discomfort to: *her conscience pricked her as she told the lie.* ■ arouse or provoke to action. **2** (usu. **be pricked**) (esp. of a horse or dog) make (the ears) stand erect when on the alert.
▸ *n.* an act of piercing something with a fine, sharp point: *the pin prick.* ■ a small hole or mark made by piercing something with a fine, sharp point. ■ a sharp pain caused by being pierced with a fine point. ■ a sudden feeling of distress, anxiety, or some other unpleasant emotion: *she felt a prick of resentment.* ■ *archaic* a goad for oxen. **2** *vulgar slang* a penis. ■ a man regarded as stupid, unpleasant, or contemptible.
▸ □ **prick up one's ears** (esp. of a horse or dog) make the ears stand erect when on the alert. ■ (of a person) become suddenly attentive.

prick·le /ˈprikəl/ ▸ *n.* a short, slender, sharp-pointed outgrowth on the bark or epidermis of a plant; a small thorn. ■ a small spine or pointed outgrowth on the skin of certain animals. ■ a tingling sensation on someone's skin, typically caused by strong emotion: *a prickle of excitement.*
▸ *v.* [*intr.*] (of a person's skin or a part of the body) experience a tingling sensation, esp. as a result of strong emotion: *the sound made her skin prickle with horror.* ■ [*tr.*] cause a tingling or mildly painful sensation in: *I hate the way the fibers prickle your skin.* ■ (of a person) react defensively or angrily to something: *she prickled at the implication that she had led a soft and protected life.*

prick·ly /ˈprik(ə)lē/ ▸ *adj.* (**-li·er, -li·est**) **1** covered in prickles. ■ resembling or feeling like prickles: *his hair was prickly and short.* ■ having or causing a tingling or itching sensation: *a dress that was prickly around the neck.* **2** (of a person) ready to take offense. ■ liable to cause someone to take offense. —**prick·li·ness** *n.*

prick·ly heat ▸ *n.* an itchy inflammation of the skin, typically with a rash of small vesicles, common in hot moist weather.

prick·ly pear ▸ *n.* a cactus (genus *Opuntia*) with jointed stems and oval flattened segments, having barbed bristles and large pear-shaped, prickly fruits. ■ the edible orange or red fruit of this plant.

Pronunciation Key ə *ago,* up; ər *over, fur;* a *hat;* ā *ate;* ä *car;* CH *chin;* e *let;* ē *see;* e(ə)r *air;* i *fit;* ī *by;* i(ə)r *ear;* NG *sing;* ō *go;* ô *law, for;* oi *toy;* ōō *good;* ōō *goo;* ou *out;* SH *she;* TH *thin;* ᴛʜ *then;* (h)w *why;* ZH *vision*

pric·y /ˈprīsē/ ▸*adj.* variant spelling of PRICEY.

pride /prīd/ ▸*n.* **1** a feeling or deep pleasure or satisfaction derived from one's own achievements, the achievements of those with whom one is closely associated, or from qualities or possessions that are widely admired: *a woman who takes great pride in her appearance.* ■ the consciousness of one's own dignity: *he swallowed his pride and asked for help.* ■ the quality of having an excessively high opinion of oneself or one's importance. ■ a person or thing that is the object or source of a feeling or deep pleasure or satisfaction: *the swimming pool is the pride of the community.* ■ *poetic/lit.* the best state or condition of something; the prime: *in the pride of youth.* **2** a group of lions forming a social unit.
▸*v.* (**pride oneself on/upon**) be especially proud of a particular quality or skill: *she'd always prided herself on her ability to deal with a crisis.* —**pride·ful** /-fəl/ *adj.* —**pride·ful·ly** /-fəlē/ *adv.*
▸ □ **one's pride and joy** a person or thing of which one is very proud and which is a source of great pleasure. □ **pride of place** the most prominent or important position among a group of things.

prie-dieu /prē ˈdyə(r); -ˈdyœ/ ▸*n.* (*pl.* **prie-dieux** /ˈdyə(r)(z); -ˈdyœ(z)/) a piece of furniture for use during prayer, consisting of a kneeling surface and a narrow upright front with a rest for the elbows or for books.

priest /prēst/ ▸*n.* an ordained minister of the Catholic, Orthodox, or Anglican Church having the authority to perform certain rites and administer certain sacraments. ■ a person who performs religious ceremonies and duties in a non-Christian religion.
▸*v.* [*tr.*] (usu. **be priested**) *formal* ordain to the priesthood. —**priest·like** /-ˌlīk/ *adj.*

priest·ess /ˈprēstis/ ▸*n.* a female priest of a non-Christian religion.

priest·hood /ˈprēst,hŏŏd; ˈprē,stŏŏd/ ▸*n.* (often **the priesthood**) the office or position of a priest. ■ priests in general.

priest·ly /ˈprēstlē/ ▸*adj.* of, relating to, or befitting a priest or priests: *performing priestly duties.* —**priest·li·ness** *n.*

prig /prig/ ▸*n.* a self-righteously moralistic person who behaves as if superior to others. —**prig·ger·y** /ˈprigərē/ *n.* —**prig·gish** *adj.* —**prig·gish·ly** *adv.* —**prig·gish·ness** *n.*

prim /prim/ ▸*adj.* (**prim·mer, prim·mest**) stiffly formal and respectable; feeling or showing disapproval of anything regarded as improper.
▸*v.* (**primmed, prim·ming**) [*tr.*] purse (the mouth or lips) into a prim expression: *Larry primmed up his mouth.* ▷late 17th cent. (as a verb): probably ultimately from Old French *prin*, Provençal *prim* 'excellent, delicate,' from Latin *primus* 'first.' —**prim·ly** *adv.* —**prim·ness** *n.*

pri·ma bal·le·ri·na /ˈprēmə/ ▸*n.* the chief female dancer in a ballet or ballet company.

pri·ma·cy /ˈprīməsē/ ▸*n.* **1** the fact of being primary, preeminent, or more important: *the primacy of air power in the modern war.* **2** the office, period of office, or authority of a primate of the Church.

pri·ma don·na /ˌprimə ˈdänə; ˌprēmə/ ▸*n.* the chief female singer in an opera company. ■ a very temperamental person with an inflated view of their own talent or importance. —**pri·ma don·na-ish** *adj.*

pri·ma fa·ci·e /ˌprimə ˈfāsHə; ˈfāsHē; ˈfāsHē,ē/ ▸*adj. & adv. Law* based on the first impression; accepted as correct until proved otherwise: [as *adj.*] *a prima facie case of professional misconduct* | [as *adv.*] *the original lessee prima facie remains liable for the payment of the rent.*

pri·mal /ˈprīməl/ ▸*adj.* essential; fundamental: *for me, writing is a primal urge.* ■ relating to an early stage in evolutionary development; primeval: *primal hunting societies.* ■ *Psychol.* of, relating to, or denoting the needs, fears, or behavior that are postulated (esp. in Freudian theory) to form the origins of emotional life. —**pri·mal·ly** *adv.*

pri·ma·ri·ly /prīˈme(ə)rəlē/ ▸*adv.* for the most part; mainly: *around 80 percent of personal computers are used primarily for word processing.*

pri·ma·ry /ˈprī,merē; ˈprīm(ə)rē/ ▸*adj.* **1** of chief importance; principal. **2** earliest in time or order of development. ■ not derived from, caused by, or based on anything else: *the research involved the use of primary source materials in national and local archives.* **3** of or relating to education for children between the ages of about five and ten: *a primary school.* **4** *Biol. & Med.* belonging to or directly derived from the first stage of development or growth: *a primary bone tumor.* **5** relating to or denoting the input side of a device using electromagnetic induction, esp. in a transformer.
▸*n.* (*pl.* **-ries**) **1** (also **primary election**) a preliminary election to appoint delegates to a party conference or to select the candidates for a principal, esp. presidential, election. **2** short for: ■ a primary color. ■ *Ornithol.* a primary feather. ■ a primary coil or winding in an electrical transformer. **3** *Astron.* the body orbited by a smaller satellite or companion.

pri·mate¹ /ˈprī,māt; ˈprīmət/ ▸*n. Christian Church* the chief bishop or archbishop of a province. —**pri·ma·tial** /prīˈmāsHəl/ *adj.*

pri·mate² /ˈprī,māt/ ▸*n. Zool.* a mammal of an order (Primates) that includes the lemurs, bush babies, tarsiers, marmosets, monkeys, apes, and humans. They are distinguished by having hands, handlike feet, and forward-facing eyes.

pri·ma·ve·ra /ˌprēmə'verə/ ▸*adj.* (of a pasta dish) made with lightly sautéed spring vegetables: *linguine primavera.*

prime¹ /prīm/ ▸*adj.* **1** of first importance; main. ■ from which another thing may derive or proceed: *Diogenes' conclusion that air is the prime matter.* **2** of the best possible quality; excellent: *prime cuts of meat.* ■ having all the expected or typical characteristics of something: *the novel is a prime example of the genre.* ■ most suitable or likely: *the prime contender for best comedy.* **3** *Math.* (of a number) evenly divisible only by itself and one (e.g., 2, 3, 5, 7, 11). ■ (of two or more numbers in relation to each other) having no common factor but one.
▸*n.* **1** a state or time of greatest strength, vigor, or success in a person's life: *you're in the prime of life.* **2** *Christian Church* a service forming part of the Divine Office, traditionally said (or chanted) at the first hour of the day (i.e., 6 a.m.), but now little used. **3** a prime number. **4** *Printing* a symbol (ʹ) written after a letter or symbol as a distinguishing mark or after a figure as a symbol for minutes or feet. **5** short for PRIME RATE. —**prime·ness** *n.*

prime² ▸*v.* [*tr.*] **1** make (something) ready for use or action, in particular: ■ prepare (a firearm or explosive device) for firing or detonation. ■ cover (wood, canvas, or metal) with a preparatory coat of paint in order to prevent the absorption of subsequent layers of paint. ■ pour or spray liquid into (a pump) before starting in order to seal the moving parts and facilitate its operation. ■ inject extra fuel into (the cylinder or carburetor of an internal combustion engine) in order to facilitate starting. **2** prepare (someone) for a situation or task, typically by supplying them with relevant information.
▸ □ **prime the pump** stimulate or support the growth or success of something by supplying it with money.

prime con·tract ▸*n.* a contract whose requirements are partly fulfilled by the awarding of subcontracts. —**prime con·trac·tor** *n.*

prime min·is·ter ▸*n.* the head of an elected government; the principal minister of a sovereign or state. —**prime min·is·ter·ship** *n.*

prime mov·er ▸*n.* a person or establishment that is chiefly responsible for the creation or execution of a plan or project. ■ an initial natural or mechanical source of motive power.

prim·er¹ /ˈprīmər/ ▸*n.* a substance used as a preparatory coat on previously unpainted wood, metal, or canvas, esp. to prevent the absorption of subsequent layers of paint or the development of rust. ■ a cap or cylinder containing a compound that responds to friction or an electrical impulse and ignites the charge in a cartridge or explosive. ■ a small pump for pumping fuel to prime an internal combustion engine, esp. in an aircraft. ■ *Biochem.* a molecule that serves as a starting material for a polymerization process.

prim·er² /ˈprimər/ ▸*n.* an elementary textbook that serves as an introduction to a subject of study or is used for teaching children to read.

prime rate ▸*n.* the lowest rate of interest at which money may be borrowed commercially.

prime time ▸*n.* the regularly occurring time at which a television or radio audience is expected to be greatest, generally regarded in the television industry as the hours between 8 and 11 p.m.

pri·me·val /prīˈmēvəl/ (*Brit.* also **pri·mae·val**) ▸*adj.* of or resembling the earliest ages in the history of the world: *mile after mile of primeval forest.* —**pri·me·val·ly** *adv.*

prim·i·tive /ˈprimətiv/ ▸*adj.* **1** relating to, denoting, or preserving the character of an early stage in the evolutionary or historical development of something. ■ relating to or denoting a preliterate, nonindustrial society or culture characterized by simple social and economic organization. ■ having a quality or style that offers an extremely basic level of comfort, convenience, or efficiency. ■ (of behavior, thought, or emotion) apparently originating in unconscious needs or desires and unaffected by objective reasoning. ■ of or denoting a simple, direct style of art that deliberately rejects sophisticated artistic techniques. **2** not developed or derived from anything else. **3** *Biol.* (of a part or structure) in the first or early stage of formation or growth; rudimentary.
▸*n.* **1** a person belonging to a preliterate, nonindustrial society or culture. **2** a pre-Renaissance painter. ■ a modern painter who imitates the pre-Renaissance style. ■ an artist employing a simple, naive style that rejects subtlety or conventional techniques. ■ a painting by a primitive artist, or an object in a primitive style. **3** *Linguistics* a word, base, or root from which another is historically derived. ■ *Linguistics* an irreducible form. ■ *Math.* an algebraic or geometric expression

from which another is derived; a curve of which another is the polar or reciprocal. ■ *Comput.* a simple operation or procedure of a limited set from which complex operations or procedures may be constructed, esp. a simple geometric shape that may be generated in computer graphics by such an operation or procedure. —**prim·i·tive·ly** *adv.* —**prim·i·tive·ness** *n.* —**prim·i·tiv·i·ty** /ˌprimə'tivətē/ *n.*

prim·i·tiv·ism /'primətivˌizəm/ ▸*n.* **1** a belief in the value of what is simple and unsophisticated, expressed as a philosophy of life or through art or literature. **2** unsophisticated behavior that is unaffected by objective reasoning. —**prim·i·tiv·ist** *n. & adj.*

pri·mo /'prēmō/ ▸*n. (pl.* -**mos**) *Mus.* the leading or upper part in a duet. ▸*adj. inf.* of top quality or importance: *the primo team in the land.*

pri·mo·gen·i·tor /ˌprīmō'jenətər/ ▸*n.* an ancestor, esp. the earliest ancestor of a people; a progenitor.

pri·mo·gen·i·ture /ˌprīmō'jeni,CHƏr; -,CHŏŏr/ ▸*n.* the state of being the firstborn child. ■ the right of succession belonging to the firstborn child, esp. the feudal rule by which the whole real estate of an intestate passed to the eldest son. —**pri·mo·gen·i·tal** /-'jenitl/ *adj.* —**pri·mo·gen·i·tar·y** /-'jeni,terē/ *adj.*

pri·mor·di·al /prī'môrdēəl/ ▸*adj.* existing at or from the beginning of time; primeval. ■ (esp. of a state or quality) basic and fundamental. ■ *Biol.* (of a cell, part, or tissue) in the earliest stage of development. —**pri·mor·di·al·i·ty** /ˌprī,môrdē'alətē/ *n.* —**pri·mor·di·al·ly** *adv.*

primp /primp/ ▸*v.* [*tr.*] spend time making minor adjustments to (one's hair, makeup, or clothes): *they primped his hair* | [*intr.*] *the girls who were primping in front of the mirror.*

prim·rose /'prim,rōz/ ▸*n.* a cultivated plant (*Primula vulgaris*) of European woodlands that produces pale yellow flowers in the early spring. The **primrose family** (Primulaceae) also includes the cowslips, pimpernels, and cyclamens. ■ (also **primrose yellow**) a pale yellow color. ▸ □ **primrose path** the pursuit of pleasure, esp. when it is seen to bring disastrous consequences.

prim·u·la /'primyələ/ ▸*n.* a plant (genus *Primula*) of the primrose family.

prince /prins/ ▸*n.* the son of a monarch. ■ a close male relative of a monarch, esp. a son's son. ■ a male royal ruler of a small state, actually, nominally, or originally subject to a king or emperor. ■ (in France, Germany and other European countries) a nobleman, usually ranking next below a duke. ■ (**prince of/among**) a man regarded as outstanding in a particular group. —**prince·dom** /dəm/ *n.*

Prince Charm·ing (also **prince charm·ing**) ▸an ideal male lover who is both handsome and of admirable character.

prince·ly /'prinslē/ ▸*adj.* of or held by a prince. ■ sumptuous and splendid. ■ (of a sum of money) large or generous (often used ironically): *she's paying a princely sum.* —**prince·li·ness** *n.*

Prince of Wales ▸*n.* a title traditionally granted to the heir apparent to the British throne (usually the eldest son of the sovereign) since Edward I of England gave the title to his son in 1301 after the conquest of Wales.

prin·cess /'prinsəs; 'prin,ses; prin'ses/ ▸*n.* the daughter of a monarch. ■ a close female relative of monarch, esp. a son's daughter. ■ the wife or widow of a prince. ■ the female ruler of a small state, actually, nominally, or originally subject to a king or emperor. ■ *inf.* a spoiled or arrogant young woman.

prin·ci·pal /'prinsəpəl/ ▸*adj.* **1** first in order of importance; main. **2** (of money) denoting an original sum invested or lent. ▸*n.* **1** the person with the highest authority or most important position in an organization, institution, or group. ■ the head of a school, college, or other educational institution. ■ the leading performer in a concert, play, ballet, or opera. ■ *Mus.* the leading player in each section of an orchestra. **2** a sum of money lent or invested on which interest is paid. **3** a person for whom another acts as an agent or representative. ■ *Law* the person directly responsible for a crime. ■ *hist.* each of the combatants in a duel. —**prin·ci·pal·ship** /-,SHip/ *n.*

prin·ci·pal·i·ty /ˌprinsə'palətē/ ▸*n. (pl.* -**ties**) a state ruled by a prince.

prin·ci·pal·ly /'prinsəp(ə)lē/ ▸*adv.* for the most part; chiefly.

prin·ci·ple /'prinsəpəl/ ▸*n.* **1** a fundamental truth or proposition that serves as the foundation for a system of belief or behavior or for a chain of reasoning. ■ (usu. **principles**) a rule or belief governing one's personal behavior. ■ morally correct behavior and attitudes: *a man of principle.* ■ a general scientific theorem or law that has numerous special applications across a wide field. ■ a natural law forming the basis for the construction or working of a machine: *these machines all operate on the same principle.* **2** a fundamental source or basis of something: *the first principle of all things was water.* ■ a fundamental quality or attribute determining the nature of something; an essence: *the combination of male and female principles.* ■ *Chem.* an active or characteristic

constituent of a substance, obtained by simple analysis or separation: *the active principle in the medulla is epinephrine.*

▸ □ **in principle** as a general idea or plan, although the details are not yet established or clear. ■ used to indicate that although something is theoretically possible, it may not actually happen. □ **on principle** because of or in order to demonstrate one's adherence to a particular belief.

prin·ci·pled /'prinsəpəld/ ▸*adj.* **1** (of a person or their behavior) acting in accordance with morality and showing recognition of right and wrong. **2** (of a system or method) based on a given set of rules.

print /print/ ▸*v.* [*tr.*] (often **be printed**) **1** produce (books, newspapers, magazines, etc.) by a mechanical process involving the transfer of text, images, or designs to paper. ■ produce (text or a picture) in such a way: *the words had been printed in blue type.* ■ (of a newspaper or magazine) publish (a piece of writing) within its pages: *the article was printed in the first edition.* ■ (of a publisher or printer) arrange for (a book, manuscript, etc.) to be reproduced in large quantities. ■ produce a paper copy of (information stored on a computer): *the results of a search can be printed out.* ■ send (a computer file) to a printer or to another, temporary file. ■ produce (a photographic print) from a negative. ■ write (text) clearly without joining the letters: *print your name and address on the back of the check* | [*intr.*] *it will be easier to read if I print.* **2** mark (a surface, typically a textile or a garment) with a colored design or pattern. ■ make (a mark or indentation) on a surface or in a soft substance by pressing something onto it. ■ mark or indent (the surface of a soft substance) in such a way: *we printed the butter with carved wooden butter molds.* ■ *fig.* fix (something) firmly or indelibly in someone's mind: *his face was printed on her memory.*

▸*n.* **1** the text appearing in a book, newspaper, or other printed publication, esp. with reference to its size, form, or style. ■ the state of being available in published form: *the news will never get into print.* ■ a newspaper or magazine: [as *adj.*] *the print media.* ■ [as *adj.*] of or relating to the printing industry or the printed media: *the print unions.* **2** an indentation or mark left on a surface or soft substance by pressure, esp. that of a foot or hand: *there were paw prints everywhere.* ■ (**prints**) fingerprints. **3** a picture or design printed from a block or plate or copied from a painting by photography. ■ a photograph printed on paper from a negative or transparency. ■ a copy of a motion picture on film, esp. a particular version of it. **4** a piece of fabric or clothing with a decorative colored pattern or design printed on it. ■ such a pattern or design. —**print·a·bil·i·ty** *n.* —**print·a·ble** *adj.*

▸ □ **in print 1** (of a book) available from the publisher. **2** in printed or published form. □ **out of print** (of a book) no longer available from the publisher.

print·er /'printər/ ▸*n.* a person whose job or business is commercial printing. ■ a machine for printing text or pictures onto paper, esp. one linked to a computer.

print·ing /'printiNG/ ▸*n.* the production of books, newspapers, or other printed material. ■ a single impression of a book: *the second printing.* ■ handwriting in which the letters are written separately rather than being joined together.

print·ing press ▸*n.* a machine for printing text or pictures from type or plates.

print·mak·er /'print,mākər/ ▸*n.* a person who makes pictures or designs by printing them from specially prepared plates or blocks. —**print·mak·ing** /-kiNG/ *n.*

print·out /'print,out/ ▸*n. Comput.* a page or set of pages of printed material produced by a computer's printer.

pri·or[1] /'prīər/ ▸*adj.* existing or coming before in time, order, or importance: *he has a prior engagement this evening.* ▸*n. inf.* a previous criminal conviction: *he had no juvenile record, no priors.* ▸ □ **prior to** before a particular time or event.

pri·or[2] ▸*n.* a man who is head of a house or group of houses of certain religious orders. —**pri·or·ate** /'prīərət/ *n.* —**pri·or·ship** /-,SHip/ *n.*

pri·or·ess /'prīərəs/ ▸*n.* a woman who is head of a house of certain orders of nuns. ■ the woman next in rank below an abbess.

pri·or·i·ty /prī'ôrətē/ ▸*n. (pl.* -**ties**) a thing that is regarded as more important than another. ■ the fact or condition of being regarded or treated as more important: *the safety of the country takes priority over any other matter.* ■ the right to take precedence or to proceed before others. —**pri·or·i·tize** *v.*

Pronunciation Key ə *ago, up;* ər *over, fur;* a *hat;* ā *ate;* ä *car;* CH *chin;* e *let;* ē *see;* e(ə)r *air;* i *fit;* ī *by;* i(ə)r *ear;* NG *sing;* ō *go;* ô *law, for;* oi *toy;* ŏŏ *good;* ōō *goo;* ou *out;* SH *she;* TH *thin;* TH *then;* (h)w *why;* ZH *vision*

pri·or re·straint ▶*n. Law* judicial suppression of material that would be published or broadcast, on the grounds that it is libelous or harmful.

pri·o·ry /'prīərē/ ▶*n.* (*pl.* **-ries**) a small monastery or nunnery that is governed by a prior or prioress.

prism /'prizəm/ ▶*n. Geom.* a solid geometric figure whose two end faces are similar, equal, and parallel rectilinear figures, and whose sides are parallelograms. ■ *Optics* a glass or other transparent object in this form, esp. one that is triangular with refracting surfaces at an acute angle with each other and that separates white light into a spectrum of colors. ■ used figuratively with reference to the clarification or distortion afforded by a particular viewpoint: *they were forced to imagine the disaster through the prism of television.* ▷late 16th cent.: via late Latin from Greek *prisma* 'thing sawn,' from *prizein* 'to saw.'

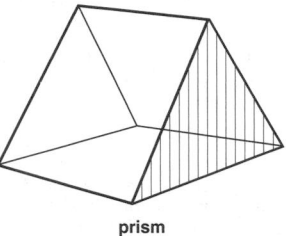

prism

pris·mat·ic /priz'matik/ ▶*adj.* of, relating to, or having the form of a prism or prisms. ■ (of colors) formed, separated, or distributed by an optical prism or something acting as one. ■ (of colors) varied and brilliant. ■ (of an instrument) incorporating a prism or prisms. —**pris·mat·i·cal·ly** /-ik(ə)lē/ *adv.*

pris·on /'prizən/ ▶*n.* a building (or vessel) to which people are legally committed as a punishment for crimes they have committed or while awaiting trial. ■ confinement in such a building.

▶*v.* (**-oned, -on·ing**) [*tr.*] *poetic/lit.* imprison.

pris·on camp ▶*n.* a camp where prisoners of war or political prisoners are kept under guard. ■ a minimum-security prison, typically where prisoners have outdoor work assignments.

pris·on·er /'priz(ə)nər/ ▶*n.* a person legally committed to prison as a punishment for crimes committed or while awaiting trial. ■ a person captured and kept confined by an enemy, opponent, or criminal. ■ *fig.* a person who is or feels confined or trapped by a situation or set of circumstances: *he's become a prisoner of the publicity he's generated.*

▶ □ **take no prisoners** be ruthlessly aggressive or uncompromising in the pursuit of one's objectives.

pris·on·er of con·science ▶*n.* a person who has been imprisoned for holding political or religious views that are not tolerated by their own government.

pris·sy /'prisē/ ▶*adj.* (**-si·er, -si·est**) (of a person or their manner) fussily and excessively respectable: *her prissy mother.* ■ (of clothes) overadorned with details such as ruffles and bows: *prissy little dresses.* —**pris·si·ly** /'prisəlē/ *adv.* —**pris·si·ness** *n.*

pris·tine /'pris,tēn; pri'stēn/ ▶*adj.* in its original condition; unspoiled. ■ clean and fresh as if new; spotless. —**pris·tine·ly** *adv.*

prith·ee /'priTHē/ ▶*interj. archaic* please (used to convey a polite request): *prithee, Jack, answer me honestly.*

pri·va·cy /'prīvəsē/ ▶*n.* the state or condition of being free from being observed or disturbed by other people: *she returned to the privacy of her own home.* ■ the state of being free from public attention.

pri·vate /'prīvit/ ▶*adj.* **1** belonging to or for the use of one particular person or group of people only. ■ (of a situation, activity, or gathering) affecting or involving only a particular person or group of people. ■ (of thoughts and feelings) not to be shared with or revealed to others. ■ (of a person) not choosing to share thoughts and feelings with others. ■ (of a meeting or discussion) involving only a small number of people and dealing with matters that are not to be disclosed to others. ■ (of a place) quiet and free from people who can interrupt. **2** (of a person) having no official or public role or position: *the paintings were sold to a private collector.* ■ not connected with one's work or official position: *the president was visiting China in a private capacity.* **3** (of a service or industry) provided or owned by an individual or an independent, commercial company rather than by the government. ■ of or relating to a system of education or medical treatment conducted outside the system of government and charging fees to the individuals who make use of it. ■ of, relating to, or denoting a transaction between individuals and not involving commercial organizations: *it was a private sale— no agent's commission.*

▶*n.* **1** a soldier of the lowest rank, in particular an enlisted person in the U.S. Army or Marine Corps ranking below private first class. **2** (**privates**) *inf.* short for PRIVATE PARTS. —**pri·vate·ly** *adj.*

▶ □ **in private** with no one else present: *I've got to talk to you in private.*

pri·vate de·tec·tive ▶*n.* another term for PRIVATE INVESTIGATOR.

pri·vate en·ter·prise ▶*n.* business or industry that is managed by independent companies or private individuals rather than by the state.

pri·va·teer /ˌprīvə'tir/ ▶*n. chiefly hist.* an armed ship owned and officered by private individuals holding a government commission and authorized for use in war, esp. in the capture of enemy merchant shipping. ■ (also **privateersman**) a commander or crew member of such a ship, often regarded as a pirate.

▶*v.* [*intr.*] engage in the activities of a privateer. —**pri·va·teer·ing** *n.*

pri·vate eye ▶*n. inf.* a private investigator.

pri·vate in·ves·ti·ga·tor (also **private detective**) ▶*n.* a freelance detective who carries out covert investigations on behalf of private clients.

pri·vate parts ▶*pl. n.* used euphemistically to refer to a person's genitals.

pri·vate prac·tice ▶*n.* the work of a professional practitioner, such as a doctor or lawyer, who is self-employed.

pri·vate school ▶*n.* **1** a school supported by a private organization or private individuals rather than by the government. **2** *Brit.* a school supported wholly by the payment of fees.

pri·vate sec·tor ▶*n.* the part of the national economy that is not under direct government control.

pri·va·tion /prī'vāsHən/ ▶*n.* a state in which things that are essential for human well-being are scarce or lacking. ■ *formal* the loss or absence of a quality or attribute that is normally present.

pri·va·tize /'prīvə,tīz/ ▶*v.* [*tr.*] transfer (a business, industry, or service) from public to private ownership and control: *a plan for privatizing education.* —**pri·va·ti·za·tion** /ˌprīvəti'zāsHən/ *n.* —**pri·va·tiz·er** *n.*

priv·et /'privit/ ▶*n.* a shrub (genus *Ligustrum*) of the olive family, with small white, heavily scented flowers and poisonous black berries. Its several species include the semievergreen **common privet** (*L. vulgare*), often grown as a hedge.

priv·i·lege /'priv(ə)lij/ ▶*n.* a special right, advantage, or immunity granted or available only to a particular person or group of people. ■ something regarded as a rare opportunity and bringing particular pleasure. ■ (in a parliamentary context) the right to say or write something without the risk of incurring punishment or legal action for defamation. ■ the right of a lawyer or official to refuse to divulge confidential information. ■ *chiefly hist.* a grant to an individual, corporation, or place of special rights or immunities, esp. in the form of a franchise or monopoly.

▶*v.* [*tr.*] *formal* grant a privilege or privileges to: *English inheritance law privileged the eldest son.* ■ (usu. **be privileged from**) exempt (someone) from a liability or obligation to which others are subject.

priv·i·leged /'priv(ə)lijd/ ▶*adj.* having special rights, advantages, or immunities. ■ having the rare opportunity to do something that brings particular pleasure: *I felt I had been privileged to compete in such a race.* ■ (of information) legally protected from being made public.

priv·y /'privē/ ▶*adj.* (**privy to**) sharing in the knowledge of (something secret or private): *he was no longer privy to her innermost thoughts.* ■ *archaic* hidden; secret: *a privy place.*

▶*n.* (*pl.* **priv·ies**) **1** a toilet located in a small shed outside a house or other building; outhouse. **2** *Law* a person having a part or interest in any action, matter, or thing. —**priv·i·ly** /'privəlē/ *adv.*

prize[1] /prīz/ ▶*n.* a thing given as a reward to the winner of a competition or race or in recognition of another outstanding achievement. ■ a thing, esp. an amount of money or a valuable object, that can be won in a lottery or other game of chance. ■ something of great value that is worth struggling to achieve. ■ *chiefly hist.* an enemy ship captured during the course of naval warfare.

▶*adj.* (esp. of something entered in a competition) having been or likely to be awarded a prize: *prize onions.* ■ denoting something for which a prize is awarded: *a prize crossword.* ■ excellent of its kind; outstanding. ■ complete; utter: *you must think I'm a prize idiot.*

▶*v.* [*tr.*] (often **be prized**) value extremely highly: *the berries were prized for their healing properties.*

prize[2] (also **prise**) ▶*v.* another term for PRY[2].

prize·fight /'prīz,fīt/ (also **prize fight**) ▶*n.* a boxing match fought for prize money. —**prize·fight·er** *n.* —**prize·fight·ing** *n.*

PRO ▶*abbr.* ■ public relations officer. ■ *Brit.* Public Record Office.

pro[1] /prō/ ▶*n.* (*pl.* **pros**) *inf.* a professional, esp. in sports: *a tennis pro.*

▶*adj.* (of a person or an event) professional: *a pro golfer.*

pro[2] ▶*n.* (*pl.* **pros**) (usu. **pros**) an advantage of something or an argument in favor of a course of action: *the pros and cons of joint ownership.*

▶*prep. & adv.* in favor of: [as *prep.*] *they were pro the virtues of individualism.*

pro·ac·tive /prō'aktiv/ ▶*adj.* (of a person, policy, or action) creating or controlling a situation by causing something to happen rather than

responding to it after it has happened. —**pro·ac·tion** /prō'akSHən/ *n.* —**pro·ac·tive·ly** *adv.* —**pro·ac·tiv·i·ty** /,prō,ak'tivətē/ *n.*
pro-am /'prō 'am/ ▶ *adj.* (of a sports event) involving both professionals and amateurs: *a pro-am golf tournament.*
▶ *n.* an event of this type.
prob /präb/ ▶ *n. inf.* problem: *there's no prob.*
prob·a·bi·lis·tic /,präbəbə'listik/ ▶ *adj.* based on or adapted to a theory of probability; subject to or involving chance variation. —**prob·a·bi·lism** /'präbəbə,lizəm/ *n.*
prob·a·bil·i·ty /,präbə'bilətē/ ▶ *n.* (*pl.* **-ties**) the extent to which something is probable; the likelihood of something happening or being the case. ■ a probable event. ■ the most probable thing: *the probability is that it will be phased in over a number of years.* ■ *Math.* the extent to which an event is likely to occur, measured by the ratio of the favorable cases to the whole number of cases possible.
▶ □ **in all probability** used to convey that something is very likely.
prob·a·ble /'präbəbəl/ ▶ *adj.* likely to be the case or to happen: *it is probable that the economic situation will deteriorate further.*
▶ *n.* a person who is likely to become or do something, esp. one who is likely to be chosen for a team: *Merson and Wright are probables.*
prob·a·bly /'präbəblē; 'präblē/ ▶ *adv.* almost certainly; as far as one knows or can tell: *she would probably never see him again | "Would you recognize them?" "Probably."*
pro·bate /'prō,bāt/ ▶ *n.* the official proving of a will: *the will was in probate | [as adj.] a probate court.* ■ a verified copy of a will with a certificate as handed to the executors.
▶ *v.* [*tr.*] establish the validity of (a will).
pro·ba·tion /prō'bāSHən/ ▶ *n. Law* the release of an offender from detention, subject to a period of good behavior under supervision. ■ the process or period of testing or observing the character or abilities of a person in a certain role, for example, a new employee. —**pro·ba·tion·ar·y** /-,nerē/ *adj.*
pro·ba·tion·er /prō'bāSHənər/ ▶ *n.* a person who is serving a probationary or trial period in a job or position to which they are newly appointed. ■ an offender on probation.
pro·ba·tion of·fi·cer ▶ *n.* a person appointed to supervise offenders who are on probation.
probe /prōb/ ▶ *n.* a blunt-ended surgical instrument used for exploring a wound or part of the body. ■ a small device, esp. an electrode, used for measuring, testing, or obtaining information. ■ (also **space probe**) an unmanned exploratory spacecraft designed to transmit information about its environment. ■ an investigation into a crime or other matter: *a probe into the maritime industry by the FBI.*
▶ *v.* [*tr.*] physically explore or examine (something) with the hands or an instrument. ■ [*intr.*] seek to uncover information about someone or something: *he began to probe into Donald's whereabouts | [tr.] police are probing another murder.* —**prob·er** *n.* —**prob·ing·ly** *adv.*
pro·bi·ty /'prōbitē/ ▶ *n. formal* the quality of having strong moral principles; honesty and decency: *financial probity.*
prob·lem /'präbləm/ ▶ *n.* **1** a matter or situation regarded as unwelcome or harmful and needing to be dealt with and overcome:| [as adj.] *city planners consider it a problem district.* ■ a thing that is difficult to achieve or accomplish: *motivation of staff can also be a problem.* **2** *Physics & Math.* an inquiry starting from given conditions to investigate or demonstrate a fact, result, or law. ■ *Geom.* a proposition in which something has to be constructed. ■ (in various games, esp. chess) an arrangement of pieces in which the solver has to achieve a specified result.
▶ □ **have a problem with** disagree with or have an objection to. □ **no problem** used to express one's agreement or acquiescence: *"Can you help?" "No problem."*
prob·lem·at·ic /,präblə'matik/ ▶ *adj.* constituting or presenting a problem or difficulty. ■ doubtful or questionable.
▶ *n.* a thing that constitutes a problem or difficulty. —**prob·lem·at·i·cal** *adj.* —**prob·lem·at·i·cal·ly** /-ik(ə)lē/ *adv.*
pro bo·no pu·bli·co /,prō 'bōnō 'pōōbli,kō; 'bōnō 'pəbli,kō/ ▶ *adv. & adj.* for the public good: [as adv.] *the burden they carried pro bono publico.* ■ (usu. **pro bono**) denoting work undertaken for the public good without charge, esp. legal work for a client with a low income: [as adv.] *the attorneys are representing him pro bono | [as adj.] pro bono legal services.*
pro·bos·cis /prə'bäsəs; -'bäskəs/ ▶ *n.* (*pl.* **-bos·cis·es**, **-bos·ci·des** /-'bäsə,dēz/, or **-bos·ces** /-'bäsēz/) the nose of a mammal, esp. when it is long and mobile, such as the trunk of an elephant or the snout of a tapir. ■ *Entomol.* (in many insects) an elongated sucking mouthpart that is typically tubular and flexible.
pro·caine /'prō,kān/ ▶ *n.* a synthetic compound derived from benzoic

acid, used as a local anesthetic, esp. in dentistry. ▷early 20th cent.: from *pro-* (denoting substitution) + *-caine* (from *cocaine*).
pro·car·y·ote ▶ *n.* variant spelling of PROKARYOTE.
pro·ce·dure /prə'sējər/ ▶ *n.* an established or official way of doing something. ■ a series of actions conducted in a certain order or manner. ■ a surgical operation. ■ *Comput.* another term for SUBROUTINE. —**pro·ce·dur·al** *adj.* —**pro·ce·dur·al·ly** *adv.*
pro·ceed /prə'sēd; prō-/ ▶ *v.* [*intr.*] begin or continue a course of action. ■ [*intr.*] move forward, esp. after reaching a certain point. ■ do something as a natural or seemingly inevitable next step: *opposite the door was a staircase, which I proceeded to climb.* ■ *Law* start a lawsuit against someone: *he may be able to proceed against the contractor under the common law negligence rules.* ■ (of an action) be started. ■ (of an action) be carried on or continued. ■ originate from: *his claim that all power proceeded from God.* ▷late Middle English: from Old French *proceder*, from Latin *procedere*, from *pro-* 'forward' + *cedere* 'go.'
pro·ceed·ings /prə'sēdiNGz; prō-/ ▶ *pl. n.* an event or a series of activities involving a formal or set procedure. ■ *Law* action taken in a court to settle a dispute: *criminal proceedings were brought against him.* ■ a published report of a set of meetings or a conference.
pro·ceeds /'prō,sēdz/ ▶ *pl. n.* money obtained from an event or activity: *proceeds will help purchase new equipment.*
proc·ess[1] /'prä,ses; 'präsəs; 'prō-/ ▶ *n.* **1** a series of actions or steps taken in order to achieve a particular end. ■ a natural or involuntary series of changes: *the aging process.* ■ a systematic series of mechanized or chemical operations that are performed in order to produce or manufacture something. ■ [as adj.] *Printing* relating to or denoting printing using ink in three colors (cyan, magenta, and yellow) and black to produce a complete range of color. **2** *Law* a summons or writ requiring a person to appear in court. **3** *Biol. Anat.* a natural appendage or outgrowth on or in an organism, such as a protuberance on a bone.
▶ *v.* perform a series of mechanical or chemical operations on (something) in order to change or preserve it. ■ *Comput.* operate on (data) by means of a program. ■ deal with (someone) using an official and established procedure. ■ another term for CONK[3]. —**proc·ess·a·ble** *adj.*
▶ □ **be in the process of doing something** be continuing with an action already started. □ **in the process** as an unintended part of a course of action. □ **in process of time** as time goes on.
pro·cess[2] /prə'ses/ ▶ *v.* [*intr.*] walk or march in procession: *they processed down the aisle.*
pro·ces·sion /prə'seSHən/ ▶ *n.* a number of people or vehicles moving forward in an orderly fashion, esp. as part of a ceremony or festival. ■ the action of moving forward in such a way. ■ *fig.* a relentless succession of people or things.
pro·ces·sion·al /prə'seSHənl/ ▶ *adj.* of, for, or used in a religious or ceremonial procession: *a processional cross.*
▶ *n.* a book containing litanies and hymns for use in religious processions, esp. at the beginning of a religious service. ■ a hymn or other musical composition sung or played during a procession.
proc·es·sor /'präs,esər; 'präsəsər; 'prō-/ ▶ *n.* a machine that processes something: *the processor overexposed the film.* ■ *Comput.* another term for CENTRAL PROCESSING UNIT. ■ short for FOOD PROCESSOR.
pro-choice /prō'CHois/ (also **pro·choice**) ▶ *adj.* advocating legalized abortion. Compare with PRO-LIFE. —**pro-choic·er** *n.*
pro·claim /prə'klām; prō-/ ▶ *v.* [*tr.*] announce officially or publicly. ■ declare something one considers important with due emphasis: *he proclaimed the car to be in sound condition.* ■ declare officially or publicly to be: *he proclaimed James III as King of England.* ■ demonstrate or indicate clearly: *the decor proclaimed a family history of taste and tradition.* —**pro·claim·er** *n.* —**proc·la·ma·tion** /,präklə'māSHən/ *n.* —**pro·clam·a·to·ry** /-'klamə,tôrē/ *adj.*
pro·cliv·i·ty /prō'klivitē; prə-/ ▶ *n.* (*pl.* **-ties**) a tendency to choose or do something regularly; an inclination or predisposition toward a particular thing: *a proclivity for hard work.*
Pro·con·sul /prō'känsəl/ ▶ *n.* a fossil hominoid (genus *Proconsul*, family Pongidae) primate found in Lower Miocene deposits in East Africa, one of the last common ancestors of both humans and the great apes.
pro·con·sul /prō'känsəl/ ▶ *n.* **1** a governor of a province in ancient Rome, having much of the authority of a consul. **2** a governor or deputy consul of a modern colony. —**pro·con·su·lar** /-'käns(y)ələr/ *adj.* —**pro·con·su·late** /-'käns(y)ələt/ *n.* —**pro·con·sul·ship** /-SHip/ *n.*

pro·cras·ti·nate /prəˈkrastəˌnāt; prō-/ ▶v. [intr.] delay or postpone action; put off doing something. —**pro·cras·ti·na·tion** /prəˌkrastəˈnāSHən; prō-/ n. —**pro·cras·ti·na·tor** /-ˌnātər/ n. —**pro·cras·ti·na·to·ry** /-nəˌtôrē/ adj.

pro·cre·ate /ˈprōkrēˌāt/ ▶v. [intr.] (of people or animals) produce young; reproduce. —**pro·cre·ant** /-krēənt/ adj. (archaic). —**pro·cre·a·tion** /ˌprōkrēˈāSHən/ n. —**pro·cre·a·tive** /-krēˌātiv/ adj. —**pro·cre·a·tor** /-ˌātər/ n.

proc·tol·o·gy /präkˈtäləjē/ ▶n. the branch of medicine concerned with the anus and rectum. —**proc·to·log·i·cal** /ˌpräktəˈläjikəl/ adj. —**proc·tol·o·gist** /-jist/ n.

proc·tor /ˈpräktər/ ▶n. 1 a person who monitors students during an examination. 2 Brit. an officer (usually one of two) at certain universities, appointed annually and having mainly disciplinary functions.
▶v. serve as a proctor. —**proc·to·ri·al** /präkˈtôrēəl/ adj. —**proc·tor·ship** /-ˌSHip/ n.

pro·cum·bent /prōˈkəmbənt/ ▶adj. Bot. (of a plant or stem) growing along the ground without setting forth roots. ■ archaic (of a person) lying face down; prone; prostrate.

proc·u·ra·tor /ˈpräkyəˌrātər/ ▶n. Law an agent representing others in a court of law in countries retaining Roman civil law. ■ hist. a treasury officer in a province of the Roman Empire. —**proc·u·ra·to·ri·al** /ˌpräkyərəˈtôrēəl/ adj. —**proc·u·ra·tor·ship** n.

pro·cure /prəˈkyŏor; prō-/ ▶v. [tr.] 1 obtain (something), esp. with care or effort: food procured for the rebels. ■ obtain (someone) as a prostitute for another person: he was charged with procuring a minor. 2 [tr.] Law persuade or cause (someone) to do something. —**pro·cur·a·ble** adj. —**pro·cure·ment** n.

pro·cur·er /prəˈkyŏorər; prō-/ ▶n. a person who obtains a woman as a prostitute for another person.

prod /präd/ ▶v. (**prod·ded, prod·ding**) [tr.] poke (someone) with a finger, foot, or pointed object: he prodded her in the ribs to stop her snoring | [intr.] a woman prods at a tiger with a stick. ■ stimulate or persuade (someone who is reluctant or slow) to do something.
▶n. 1 a poke with a finger, foot, or pointed object. ■ an act of stimulating or reminding someone to do something. 2 a pointed implement, typically one discharging an electric current and used as a goad: a cattle prod. —**prod·der** n.

prod·i·gal /ˈprädigəl/ ▶adj. 1 spending money or resources freely and recklessly; wastefully extravagant. 2 having or giving something on a lavish scale.
▶n. a person who spends money in a recklessly extravagant way. ■ (also **prodigal son** or **daughter**) a person who leaves home and behaves in such a way, but later makes a repentant return. —**prod·i·gal·i·ty** /ˌprädəˈgalətē/ n. —**prod·i·gal·ly** /-g(ə)lē/ adv.

pro·di·gious /prəˈdijəs/ ▶adj. 1 remarkably or impressively great in extent, size, or degree. 2 archaic unnatural or abnormal. —**pro·di·gious·ly** adv. —**pro·di·gious·ness** n.

prod·i·gy /ˈprädəjē/ ▶n. (pl. -**gies**) a person, esp. a young one, endowed with exceptional qualities or abilities: a Russian pianist who was a child prodigy. ■ an impressive or outstanding example of a particular quality: Germany seemed a prodigy of industrial discipline. ■ an amazing or unusual thing, esp. one out of the ordinary course of nature.

pro·duce ▶v. /prəˈd(y)ōōs; prō-/ [tr.] 1 make or manufacture from components or raw materials. ■ (of a region, country, or process) yield, grow, or supply. ■ create or form (something) as part of a physical, biological, or chemical process. ■ make (something) using creative or mental skills. 2 cause (a particular result or situation) to happen or come into existence: no conventional drugs had produced any significant change. 3 show or provide (something) for consideration, inspection, or use: he produced a sheet of paper from his pocket. 4 administer the financial and managerial aspects of (a movie or broadcast) or the staging of (a play, opera, etc.). ■ supervise the making of a (musical recording), esp. by determining the overall sound.
▶n. /ˈpräd(y)ōōs; ˈprō-/ things that have been produced or grown, esp. by farming: dairy produce. —**pro·duc·i·bil·i·ty** /prəˌd(y)ōōsəˈbilətē; prō-/ n. —**pro·duc·i·ble** adj.

pro·duc·er /prəˈd(y)ōōsər; prō-/ ▶n. 1 a person, company, or country that makes, grows, or supplies goods or commodities for sale: an oil producer. ■ a person or thing that makes or causes something. 2 a person responsible for the financial and managerial aspects of making of a movie or broadcast or for staging a play, opera, etc. ■ a person who supervises the making of a musical recording.

prod·uct /ˈprädəkt/ ▶n. 1 an article or substance that is manufactured or refined for sale. ■ a substance produced during a natural, chemical, or manufacturing process: waste products. ■ a thing or person that is

the result of an action or process: his daughter, the product of his first marriage. ■ a person whose character and identity have been formed by a particular period or situation: an aging academic who is a product of the 1960s. ■ commercially manufactured articles, esp. recordings, viewed collectively. 2 Math. a quantity obtained by multiplying quantities together, or from an analogous algebraic operation.

pro·duc·tion /prəˈdəkSHən; prō-/ ▶n. 1 the action of making or manufacturing from components or raw materials, or the process of being so manufactured. ■ the harvesting or refinement of something natural. ■ the total amount of something that is manufactured, harvested, or refined. ■ the creation or formation of something as part of a physical, biological, or chemical process: excess production of collagen by the liver. ■ [as adj.] denoting a car or other vehicle that has been manufactured in large numbers. 2 the process of or financial and administrative management involved in making a movie, play, or record: the movie was still **in production** | [as adj.] a production company. ■ a movie, play, or record, esp. when viewed in terms of its making or staging. ■ the overall sound of a musical recording; the way a record is produced.
▶ □ **make a production of** do (something) in an unnecessarily elaborate or complicated way.

pro·duc·tive /prəˈdəktiv; prō-/ ▶adj. producing or able to produce large amounts of goods, crops, or other commodities. ■ relating to or engaged in the production of goods, crops, or other commodities. ■ achieving or producing a significant amount or result: a long and productive career. ■ (**productive of**) producing or giving rise to. ■ Linguistics (of a morpheme or other linguistic unit) currently used in forming new words or expressions: many suffixes are common and productive. ■ Med. (of a cough) that raises mucus from the respiratory tract. —**pro·duc·tive·ly** adv. —**pro·duc·tive·ness** n.

pro·duc·tiv·i·ty /ˌprōˌdəkˈtivətē; ˌprädək-; prəˌdək-/ ▶n. the state or quality of producing something, esp. crops. ■ the effectiveness of productive effort, esp. in industry, as measured in terms of the rate of output per unit of input: workers have boosted productivity by 30 percent. ■ Ecol. the rate of production of new biomass by an individual, population, or community; the fertility or capacity of a given habitat or area.

pro·em /ˈprōˌem; -əm/ ▶n. formal a preface or preamble to a book or speech. —**pro·e·mi·al** /prōˈēmēəl/ adj.

prof /präf/ ▶n. inf. a professor.

pro·fane /prəˈfān; prō-/ ▶adj. 1 relating or devoted to that which is not sacred or biblical; secular rather than religious. 2 (of a person or their behavior) not respectful of orthodox religious practice; irreverent. ■ (of language) blasphemous or obscene.
▶v. [tr.] treat (something sacred) with irreverence or disrespect. ▷late Middle English (in the sense 'heathen'): from Old French prophane, from Latin profanus 'outside the temple, not sacred,' from pro- (from pro 'before') + fanum 'temple.' —**prof·a·na·tion** /ˌpräfəˈnāSHən; ˌprō-/ n. —**pro·fane·ly** adv. —**pro·fane·ness** n. —**pro·fan·er** n.

pro·fan·i·ty /prəˈfanətē; prō-/ ▶n. (pl. -**ties**) blasphemous or obscene language. ■ a swear word; an oath. ■ irreligious or irreverent behavior.

pro·fess /prəˈfes; prō-/ ▶v. [tr.] 1 claim openly but often falsely that one has (a quality or feeling): he had professed his love for her | (**profess oneself**) he professed himself amazed at the boy's ability. 2 affirm one's faith in or allegiance to (a religion or set of beliefs).

pro·fessed /prəˈfest; prō-/ ▶adj. 1 (of a quality, feeling, or belief) claimed or asserted openly but often falsely. 2 (of a person) self-acknowledged or openly declared to be. —**pro·fess·ed·ly** /-ˈfesidlē/ adv.

pro·fes·sion /prəˈfeSHən/ ▶n. 1 a paid occupation, esp. one that involves prolonged training and a formal qualification: a lawyer by profession. ■ [treated as sing. or pl.] a body of people engaged in a particular profession: the profession is divided on the issue. 2 an open but often false declaration or claim. ■ a declaration of belief in a religion. ▷Middle English (denoting the vow made on entering a religious order): via Old French from Latin professio(n-), from profiteri 'declare publicly' derives from the notion of an occupation that one "professes" to be skilled in.
▶ □ **the oldest profession** humorous the practice of working as a prostitute.

pro·fes·sion·al /prəˈfeSHənl/ ▶adj. 1 of, relating to, or connected with a profession. 2 (of a person) engaged in a specified activity as one's main paid occupation rather than as a pastime. ■ having or showing the skill appropriate to a professional person; competent or skillful. ■ worthy of or appropriate to a professional person. ■ inf., derog. denoting a person who persistently makes a feature of a particular activity or attribute: a professional naysayer.
▶n. a person engaged or qualified in a profession. ■ a person engaged in

a specified activity, esp. a sport or branch of the performing arts, as a main paid occupation rather than as a pastime. ■ a person competent or skilled in a particular activity. —**pro·fes·sion·al·ly** /-sHənl-ē/ adv.

pro·fes·sion·al·ism /prə'feSHənl,izəm/ ▶n. the competence or skill expected of a professional. ■ the practicing of an activity, esp. a sport, by professional players: *the trend toward professionalism.*

pro·fes·sor /prə'fesər/ ▶n. a teacher of the highest rank in a college or university. ■ an associate professor or an assistant professor. ■ *inf.* any instructor, esp. in a specialized field. —**pro·fes·sor·ate** /-rət/ n. —**pro·fes·so·ri·al** /,präfə'sôrēəl/ adj. —**pro·fes·so·ri·al·ly** /,präfə'sôrēəlē/ adv. —**pro·fes·so·ri·ate** /,präfə'sôrēət/ n. —**pro·fes·sor·ship** /-,SHip/ n.

prof·fer /'präfər/ ▶v. [tr.] hold out (something) to someone for acceptance; offer: *he proffered his resignation.*
▶n. *poetic/lit.* an offer or proposal.

pro·fi·cient /prə'fiSHənt/ ▶adj. competent or skilled in doing or using something: *I was proficient at my job.*
▶n. *rare* a person who is proficient. —**pro·fi·cien·cy** n. —**pro·fi·cient·ly** adv.

pro·file /'prō,fīl/ ▶n. **1** an outline of something, esp. a person's face, as seen from one side. ■ a drawing or other representation of such an outline. ■ a vertical cross section of a structure: *vessels with an S-shaped profile.* ■ *Geog.* an outline of part of the earth's surface, e.g., the course of a river, as seen in a vertical section. ■ *Theater* a flat piece of scenery or stage property that has been cut so as to form an outline or silhouette of an object. ■ a graphical or other representation of information relating to particular characteristics of something, recorded in quantified form: *the blood profiles of cancer patients.* ■ a short article giving a description of a person or organization, esp. a public figure. **2** the extent to which a person or organization attracts public notice or comment: *raising the profile of women in industry.*
▶v. [tr.] **1** describe (a person or organization, esp. a public figure) in a short article. **2** (usu. **be profiled**) represent in outline from one side. ■ (**be profiled**) have a specified shape or appearance in outline. ■ shape (something), esp. by means of a tool guided by a template. —**pro·fil·er** n.
▶ □ **in profile** (in reference to someone's face) as seen from one side.

prof·it /'präfit/ ▶n. a financial gain, esp. the difference between the amount earned and the amount spent in buying, operating, or producing something. ■ advantage; benefit.
▶v. (**-it·ed, -it·ing**) [intr.] obtain a financial advantage or benefit, esp. from an investment: *the only people to profit from the episode were the lawyers.* ■ obtain an advantage or benefit. ■ [tr.] be beneficial to: *it would profit us to change our plans.* —**prof·it·less** adj.
▶ □ **at a profit** making more money than is spent buying, operating, or producing something: *fixing up houses and selling them at a profit.*

prof·it·a·ble /'präfitəbəl/ ▶adj. **1** (of a business or activity) yielding profit or financial gain. **2** beneficial; useful: *he'd had a profitable day.* —**prof·it·a·bil·i·ty** /,präfitə'bilətē/ n. —**prof·it·a·bly** /-blē/ adv.

prof·it and loss ac·count (abbr.: **P & L**) ▶n. *Finance* an account in the books of an organization to which incomes and gains are credited and expenses and losses debited, so as to show the net profit or loss over a given period. ■ a financial statement showing a company's net profit or loss in a given period.

prof·it·eer /,präfə'ti(ə)r/ ▶v. [intr.] make or seek to make an excessive or unfair profit, esp. illegally or in a black market: [as n.] (**profiteering**) *the profiteering of tabloid journalists.*
▶n. a person who profiteers: *a war profiteer.*

pro·fit·er·ole /prə'fitə,rōl/ ▶n. a small hollow pastry typically filled with cream and covered with chocolate sauce.

prof·it mar·gin ▶n. the amount by which revenue from sales exceeds costs in a business.

prof·li·gate /'präfligət; -lə,gāt/ ▶adj. recklessly extravagant or wasteful in the use of resources. ■ licentious; dissolute.
▶n. a licentious, dissolute person. —**prof·li·ga·cy** /'präfligəsē/ n. —**prof·li·gate·ly** adv.

pro for·ma /prō 'fôrmə/ ▶adv. as a matter of form or politeness.
▶adj. done or produced as a matter of form: *pro forma reports.* ■ denoting a standard document or form, esp. an invoice sent in advance of or with goods supplied. ■ (of a financial statement) showing potential or expected income, costs, assets, or liabilities, esp. in relation to some planned or expected act or situation.
▶n. a standard document or form or financial statement of such a type.

pro·found /prə'found; prō-/ ▶adj. (**-found·er, -found·est**) **1** (of a state, quality, or emotion) very great or intense. ■ (of a disease or disability) very severe; deep-seated. **2** (of a person or statement) having or showing great knowledge or insight. ■ (of a subject or thought) demanding

deep study or thought: *expressing profound truths.* **3** *archaic* at, from, or extending to a great depth; very deep.
▶n. (**the profound**) *poetic/lit.* the vast depth of the ocean or of the mind. —**pro·found·ly** adv. —**pro·found·ness** n. —**pro·fun·di·ty** /-'fəndītē/ n.

pro·fuse /prə'fyoōs; prō-/ ▶adj. (esp. of something offered or discharged) exuberantly plentiful; abundant. ■ *archaic* (of a person) lavish; extravagant. —**pro·fuse·ly** adv. —**pro·fuse·ness** n. —**pro·fu·sion** /-'fyoōzHən/ n.

pro·gen·i·tive /prə'jenətiv; prō-/ ▶adj. *formal* having the quality of producing offspring; having reproductive power.

pro·gen·i·tor /prə'jenətər; prō-/ ▶n. a person or thing from which a person, animal, or plant is descended or originates; an ancestor or parent. ■ a person who originates an artistic, political, or intellectual movement. —**pro·gen·i·to·ri·al** /-,jenə'tôrēəl/ adj.

prog·e·ny /'präjənē/ ▶n. [treated as *sing.* or *pl.*] a descendant or the descendants of a person, animal, or plant; offspring.

pro·ges·ter·one /prō'jestə,rōn; prə-/ ▶n. *Biochem.* a steroid hormone released by the corpus luteum that stimulates the uterus to prepare for pregnancy.

pro·ges·to·gen /prō'jestəjən/ ▶n. *Biochem.* another term for PROGESTIN.

prog·na·thous /'prägnəTHəs; präg'nā-/ ▶adj. (esp. of a person) having a projecting lower jaw or chin. ■ (of a jaw or chin) projecting. ■ (of an insect) having projecting mouthparts. —**prog·nath·ic** /präg'naTHik/ adj. —**prog·na·thism** /-,THizəm/ n.

prog·no·sis /präg'nōsəs/ ▶n. (*pl.* **-ses** /-,sēz/) the likely course of a disease or ailment. ■ a forecast of the likely course of a disease or ailment. ■ a forecast of the likely outcome of a situation.

prog·nos·tic /präg'nästik/ ▶adj. serving to predict the likely outcome of a disease or ailment; of or relating to a medical prognosis.
▶n. *archaic* an advance indication or portent of a future event. —**prog·nos·ti·cal·ly** /-ik(ə)lē/ adv.

prog·nos·ti·cate /präg'nästə,kāt/ ▶v. [tr.] foretell or prophesy (an event in the future). —**prog·nos·ti·ca·tion** /-,nästi'kāSHən/ n. —**prog·nos·ti·ca·tor** /-,kātər/ n. —**prog·nos·ti·ca·to·ry** /-kə,tôrē/ adj.

pro·gram /'prō,gram; -grəm/ (*Brit.* **pro·gramme**) ▶n. **1** a planned series of future events, items, or performances. ■ a set of related measures, events, or activities with a particular long-term aim. **2** a sheet or booklet giving details of items or performers at an event or performance. **3** a presentation or item on radio or television, esp. one broadcast regularly between stated times. ■ *dated* a radio or television service or station providing a regular succession of programs on a particular frequency; a channel. **4** (**program**) a series of coded software instructions to control the operation of a computer or other machine.
▶v. (**-grammed, -gram·ming;** or **-gramed, -gram·ing**) [tr.] **1** (**program**) provide (a computer or other machine) with coded instructions for the automatic performance of a particular task. ■ input (instructions for the automatic performance of a task) into a computer or other machine: *simply program in your desired volume level.* ■ (often **be programmed**) *fig.* cause (a person or animal) to behave in a predetermined way: *all members of a particular species are programmed to build nests in the same way.* **2** arrange according to a plan or schedule: *we learn how to program our own lives consciously.* ■ schedule (an item) within a framework. ■ broadcast (an item). —**pro·gram·ma·bil·i·ty** /-ə'bilətē/ n. —**pro·gram·ma·ble** /'prō,graməbəl; prō'gram-/ adj. —**pro·gram·mat·ic** /,prōgrə'matik/ adj. —**pro·gram·mer** n.

pro·gress ▶n. /'prägrəs; 'präg,res; 'prō,gres/ forward or onward movement toward a destination. ■ advance or development toward a better, more complete, or more modern condition.
▶v. /prə'gres/ [intr.] move forward or onward in space or time. ■ advance or develop toward a better, more complete, or more modern state.
▶ □ **in progress** in the course of being done or carried out.

pro·gres·sion /prə'greSHən/ ▶n. a movement or development toward a destination or a more advanced state, esp. gradually or in stages. ■ a succession; a series: *counting the twenty-four hours in a single progression from midnight.* ■ *Mus.* a passage or movement from one note or chord to another: *a blues progression.* ■ *Math.* short for ARITHMETIC PROGRESSION, GEOMETRIC PROGRESSION, or HARMONIC PROGRESSION. —**pro·gres·sion·al** /-SHənl/ adj.

pro·gres·sive /prə'gresiv/ ▶adj. **1** happening or developing gradually or in stages; proceeding step by step. ■ (of a disease or ailment) increasing in severity or extent. ■ (of taxation or a tax) increasing as a proportion of the sum taxed as that sum increases. ■ (of a card game

or dance) involving a series of sections for which participants successively change place or relative position. ■ *archaic* engaging in or constituting forward motion. **2** (of a group, person, or idea) favoring or implementing social reform or new, liberal ideas. ■ favoring or promoting change or innovation. ■ relating to or denoting a style of rock music popular esp. in the 1980s and characterized by classical influences, the use of keyboard instruments, and lengthy compositions. **3** *Gram.* denoting an aspect or tense of a verb that expresses an action in progress, e.g., *am writing, was writing.* Also called CONTINUOUS.
▶*n.* **1** a person advocating or implementing social reform or new, liberal ideas. **2** *Gram.* a progressive tense or aspect: *the present progressive.* **3** (also **progressive proof**) (usu. **progressives**) *Printing* each of a set of proofs of color work, showing all the colors separately and the cumulative effect of overprinting them. —**pro·gres·sive·ly** *adv.* —**pro·gres·sive·ness** *n.* —**pro·gres·siv·ism** /-'grəsə,vizəm/ *n.* —**pro·gres·siv·ist** /-'grəsəvist/ *n. & adj.*

pro·hib·it /prə'hibit; prō-/ ▶*v.* (**-hib·it·ed, -hib·it·ing**) [*tr.*] formally forbid (something) by law, rule, or other authority. ■ (**prohibit someone/something from doing something**) formally forbid a person or group from doing something. ■ (of a fact or situation) prevent (something); make impossible: *the budget agreement had prohibited any tax cuts.* ▷late Middle English: from Latin *prohibit-* 'kept in check,' from the verb *prohibere*, from *pro-* 'in front' + *habere* 'to hold.' —**pro·hib·it·er** *n.* —**pro·hib·i·tor** /-ər/ *n.* —**pro·hib·i·to·ry** /-,tôrē/ *adj.*
pro·hi·bi·tion /,prō(h)ə'bishən/ ▶*n.* **1** the action of forbidding something, esp. by law. ■ a law or regulation forbidding something. **2** (**Prohibition**) the prevention by law of the manufacture and sale of alcohol, esp. in the U.S. between 1920 and 1933. —**pro·hi·bi·tion·ar·y** /-,nerē/ *adj.* —**Pro·hi·bi·tion·ist** /-nist/ *n.*
pro·hib·i·tive /prə'hibitiv; prō-/ ▶*adj.* **1** (of a price or charge) excessively high; difficult or impossible to pay. **2** (esp. of a law or rule) forbidding or restricting something. ■ (of a condition or situation) preventing someone from doing something. —**pro·hib·i·tive·ly** *adv.* —**pro·hib·i·tive·ness** *n.*
pro·ject ▶*n.* /'präj,ekt; -ikt/ **1** an individual or collaborative enterprise that is carefully planned and designed to achieve a particular aim. ■ a school assignment undertaken by a student or group of students, typically as a long-term task that requires independent research. ■ a proposed or planned undertaking. **2** a government-subsidized housing development with relatively low rents: *her family still lives in the projects.*
▶*v.* /prə'jekt; prō'jekt/ [*tr.*] **1** (usu. **be projected**) estimate or forecast (something) on the basis of present trends. ■ plan (a scheme or undertaking). **2** [*intr.*] extend outward beyond something else; protrude: *I noticed a slip of paper projecting from the book.* **3** [*tr.*] throw or cause to move forward or outward: *seeds are projected from the tree.* ■ cause (light, shadow, or an image) to fall on a surface. ■ cause (a sound, esp. the voice) to be heard at a distance. ■ imagine (oneself, a situation, etc.) as having moved to a different place or time: *people may be projecting the present into the past.* **4** present or promote (a particular view or image). ■ present (someone or something) in a way intended to create a favorable impression: *she liked to project herself more as a friend than a doctor.* ■ display (an emotion or quality) in one's behavior. ■ (**project something onto**) transfer or attribute one's own emotion or desire to (another person), esp. unconsciously: *men may sometimes project their own fears onto women.* **5** *Geom.* draw straight lines from a center of or parallel lines through every point of (a given figure) to produce a corresponding figure on a surface or a line by intersecting the surface. ■ draw (such lines). ■ produce (such a corresponding figure). **6** make a projection of (the earth, sky, etc.) on a plane surface. ▷late Middle English (in the sense 'preliminary design, tabulated statement'): from Latin *projectum* 'something prominent,' neuter past participle of *proicere* 'throw forth,' from *pro-* 'forth' + *jacere* 'to throw.' Early senses of the verb were 'plan, devise' and 'cause to move forward.' —**pro·ject·a·ble** /prə'jektəbəl/ *adj.*
pro·jec·tile /prə'jektl; -,tīl/ ▶*n.* a missile designed to be fired from a rocket or gun. ■ an object propelled through the air, esp. one thrown as a weapon.
▶*adj.* of or relating to such a missile or object: *a projectile weapon.* ■ propelled with great force: *projectile vomiting.*
pro·jec·tion /prə'jekshən/ ▶*n.* **1** an estimate or forecast of a future situation or trend based on a study of present ones. **2** the presentation of an image on a surface, esp. a movie screen. ■ an image projected in such a way. ■ the ability to make a sound, esp. the voice, heard at a distance. **3** the presentation or promotion of someone or something in a particular way: *the legal profession's projection of an image of altruism.* ■ a mental image viewed as reality: *monsters can be understood as mental*

projections of mankind's fears. ■ the unconscious transfer of one's own desires or emotions to another person: *we protect the self by a number of defense mechanisms, including repression and projection.* **4** a thing that extends outward from something else. **5** *Geom.* the action of projecting a figure. **6** the representation on a plane surface of any part of the surface of the earth or a celestial sphere. ■ (also **map projection**) a method by which such representation may be done. —**pro·jec·tion·ist** /-ist/ *n.*
pro·jec·tive /prə'jektiv/ ▶*adj. Geom.* relating to or derived by projection. ■ (of a property of a figure) unchanged by projection. —**pro·jec·tive·ly** *adv.* —**pro·jec·tiv·i·ty** /,prō,jek'tivətē; ,präj,ek-/ *n.*
pro·jec·tor /prə'jektər/ ▶*n.* **1** an object that is used to project rays of light, esp. an apparatus with a system of lenses for projecting slides or film onto a screen. **2** *archaic* a person who plans and sets up a project or enterprise. ■ a promoter of a dubious or fraudulent enterprise.
pro·kar·y·ote /prō'karē,ōt/ (also **pro·car·y·ote**) ▶*n. Biol.* a single-celled organism, including the bacteria and cyanobacteria, that has neither a distinct nucleus with a membrane nor other specialized organelles. —**pro·kar·y·ot·ic** /prō,karē'ätik/ *adj.*
pro·lapse ▶*n.* /prō'laps; 'prō,laps/ a slipping forward or down of one of the parts or organs of the body: *a rectal prolapse.* ■ a prolapsed part or organ, esp. a uterus or rectum.
▶*v.* /prō'laps/ [*intr.*] (usu. as *adj.*) (**prolapsed**) (of a part or organ of the body) slip forward or down: *a prolapsed uterus.*
prole /prōl/ *inf., derog.* ▶*n.* a member of the working class; a worker.
▶*adj.* working-class: *prole soldiers.*
pro·le·tar·i·an /,prōli'te(ə)rēən/ ▶*adj.* of or relating to the proletariat.
▶*n.* a member of the proletariat. —**pro·le·tar·i·an·ism** /-,nizəm/ *n.* —**pro·le·tar·i·an·i·za·tion** /-,terēənə'zāshən/ *n.* —**pro·le·tar·i·an·ize** /-,nīz/ *v.*
pro·le·tar·i·at /,prōli'te(ə)rēət/ ▶*n.* [treated as *sing.* or *pl.*] workers or working-class people, regarded collectively (often used with reference to Marxism): *the growth of the industrial proletariat.* ■ the lowest class of citizens in ancient Rome.
pro-life /prō'līf/ ▶*adj.* opposing abortion and euthanasia: *she is a pro-life activist.* Compare with PRO-CHOICE. —**pro-lif·er** *n.*
pro·lif·er·ate /prə'lifə,rāt/ ▶*v.* [*intr.*] increase rapidly in numbers; multiply. ■ (of a cell, structure, or organism) reproduce rapidly. ■ [*tr.*] cause (cells, tissue, structures, etc.) to reproduce rapidly. ■ [*tr.*] produce (something) in large or increasing quantities. —**pro·lif·er·a·tive** /-,rātiv/ *adj.* —**pro·lif·er·a·tion** /prə,lifə'rāshən/ *n.* —**pro·lif·er·a·tor** /-,rātər/ *n.*
pro·lif·ic /prə'lifik/ ▶*adj.* **1** (of a plant, animal, or person) producing much fruit or foliage or many offspring. ■ (of an artist, author, or composer) producing many works. **2** present in large numbers or quantities; plentiful. ■ (of a river, area, or season of the year) characterized by plentiful wildlife or produce. —**pro·lif·i·ca·cy** /-ikəsē/ *n.* —**pro·lif·i·cal·ly** /-ik(ə)lē/ *adv.* —**pro·lif·ic·ness** *n.*
pro·lix /prō'liks/ ▶*adj.* (of speech or writing) using or containing too many words; tediously lengthy. —**pro·lix·i·ty** /-'liksətē/ *n.* —**pro·lix·ly** *adv.*
pro·logue /'prō,lôg; -,läg/ ▶*n.* a separate introductory section of a literary or musical work. ■ an event or action that leads to another event or situation: *civil unrest in a few villages became the prologue to widespread rebellion.* ■ the actor who delivers the prologue in a play.
pro·long /prə'lông; -'läng/ (also **pro·lon·gate** /-'lônggāt; -'läng-/) ▶*v.* [*tr.*] extend the duration of. ■ (usu. **be prolonged**) *rare* extend in spatial length: *the line of his lips was prolonged in a short red scar.* —**pro·lon·ga·tion** /prō,lông'gāshən; prə-/ *n.* —**pro·long·er** *n.*
PROM /präm/ ▶*n. Comput.* a memory chip that can be programmed only once by the manufacturer or user.
prom /präm/ ▶*n. inf.* a formal dance, esp. one held by a class in high school or college at the end of a year.
prom·e·nade /,prämə'nād; -'näd/ ▶*n.* **1** a paved public walk, typically one along a waterfront at a resort. ■ a leisurely walk, or sometimes a ride or drive, typically one taken in a public place so as to meet or be seen by others. ■ (in country dancing) a movement in which couples follow one another in a given direction, each couple having both hands joined. **2** archaic term for PROM (sense 1).
▶*v.* [*intr.*] take a leisurely walk, ride, or drive in public, esp. to meet or be seen by others. ■ [*tr.*] take such a walk through (a place). ■ [*tr.*] *dated* escort (someone) about a place, esp. so as to be seen by others. —**prom·e·nad·er** *n.*
prom·e·nade deck ▶*n.* an upper deck on a passenger ship for the use of passengers who wish to enjoy the open air.
Pro·me·the·an /prə'mēᴛʜēən/ ▶*adj.* daring or defiant, esp. in a creative or inventive way: *a Promethean man who awed his allies and terrified his*

enemies. ▷an allusion to Prometheus, a demigod from Greek mythology who used trickery to steal fire and return it to earth after Zeus had hidden it from humankind.

pro·me·thi·um /prōˈmēTHēəm/ ▸*n.* the chemical element of atomic number 61, a radioactive metal of the lanthanide series. (Symbol: **Pm**)

prom·i·nence /ˈprämənəns/ ▸*n.* **1** the state of being important or famous. **2** the fact or condition of standing out from something by physically projecting or being particularly noticeable. ■ a thing that projects from something, esp. a projecting feature of the landscape or a protuberance on a part of the body: *the rocky prominence resembled a snow-capped mountain.* ■ *Astron.* a stream of incandescent gas projecting above the sun's chromosphere.

prom·i·nent /ˈprämənənt/ ▸*adj.* **1** important; famous. **2** projecting from something; protuberant: *a man with big, prominent eyes like a lobster's.* ■ situated so as to catch the attention; noticeable. —**prom·i·nen·cy** *n.* —**prom·i·nent·ly** *adv.*

pro·mis·cu·ous /prəˈmiskyōōəs/ ▸*adj.* **1** *derog.* (of a person) having many sexual relationships, esp. transient ones. ■ (of sexual behavior or a society) characterized by such relationships. **2** demonstrating or implying an undiscriminating or unselective approach; indiscriminate or casual: *the city fathers were promiscuous with their honors.* ■ consisting of a wide range of different things. —**prom·is·cu·i·ty** /ˌpräməˈskyōōətē; prəˌmisˈkyōō-/ *n.* —**prom·is·cu·ous·ly** *adv.* —**prom·is·cu·ous·ness** *n.*

prom·ise /ˈpräməs/ ▸*n.* a declaration or assurance that one will do a particular thing or that guarantees that a particular thing will happen. ■ the quality of potential excellence: *he showed great promise even as a junior officer.* ■ an indication that something specified is expected or likely to occur: *the promise of peace.*
▸*v.* **1** [*tr.*] assure someone that one will definitely do, give, or arrange something; undertake or declare that something will happen: *he promised to forward my mail.* ■ [*tr.*] (usu. **be promised**) *archaic* pledge (someone, esp. a woman) to marry someone else; betroth: *I've been promised to him for years.* **2** [*tr.*] give good grounds for expecting (a particular occurrence or situation): *forthcoming concerts promise a feast of music from around the world.* ■ (of a person, publication, institution, etc.) announce (something) as being expected to happen: *China yesterday promised a record grain harvest.* ■ (**promise oneself**) contemplate the pleasant expectation of. —**prom·i·see** /präməˈsē/ *n.* —**prom·is·er** *n.* —**prom·i·sor** /-əsər/ *n.*
▸ □ **I promise** (or **I promise you**) *inf.* used for emphasis, esp. so as to reassure, encourage, or threaten someone.

prom·is·ing /ˈpräməsiNG/ ▸*adj.* showing signs of future success: *a promising actor | a promising start to the season.* —**prom·is·ing·ly** *adv.*

prom·is·so·ry note ▸*n.* a signed document containing a written promise to pay a stated sum to a specified person or the bearer at a specified date or on demand.

pro·mo /ˈprōmō/ *inf.* ▸*n.* (*pl.* **-mos**) a piece of publicity or advertising, esp. in the form of a short film or video: [as *adj.*] *a promo video.*

prom·on·to·ry /ˈprämənˌtôrē/ ▸*n.* (*pl.* **-ries**) a point of high land that juts out into a large body of water; a headland.

pro·mote /prəˈmōt/ ▸*v.* [*tr.*] **1** further the progress of (something, esp. a cause, venture, or aim); support or actively encourage. ■ give publicity to (a product, organization, or venture) so as to increase sales or public awareness. **2** (often **be promoted**) advance or raise (someone) to a higher position or rank. ■ *Chess* exchange (a pawn) for a more powerful piece of the same color, typically a queen, as part of the move in which it reaches the opponent's end of the board. ▷late Middle English: from Latin *promot-* 'moved forward,' from the verb *promovere,* from *pro-* 'forward, onward' + *movere* 'to move.' —**pro·mot·a·bil·i·ty** /prəˌmōtəˈbilətē/ *n.* —**pro·mot·a·ble** *adj.* —**pro·mo·tion** *n.* —**pro·mo·tion·al** /-SHənl/ *adj.* —**pro·mo·tive** /-tiv/ *adj.*

pro·mot·er /prəˈmōtər/ ▸*n.* a person or thing that promotes something, in particular: ■ a person or company that finances or organizes a sporting event or theatrical production. ■ a person involved in setting up and funding a new company. ■ a supporter of a cause or aim. ■ (also **pro·mo·tor**) *Chem.* an additive that increases the activity of a catalyst. Compare with **POISON.** ■ *Biol.* a region of a DNA molecule that forms the site at which transcription of a gene starts.

prompt /prämpt/ ▸*v.* [*tr.*] **1** (of an event or fact) cause or bring about (an action or feeling): *his death has prompted an industry-wide investigation of safety violations.* ■ cause (someone) to take a course of action. **2** assist or encourage (a hesitating speaker) to say something. ■ supply a forgotten word or line to (an actor) during the performance of a play. ■ *Comput.* (of a computer) request input from (a user).
▸*n.* **1** an act of assisting or encouraging a hesitating speaker. ■ the

word or phrase spoken as a reminder to an actor of a forgotten word or line. ■ *Comput.* a message or symbol on a monitor to show that the system is waiting for input. ■ another term for **PROMPTER. 2** the time limit for the payment of an account, as stated on a prompt note.
▸*adj.* done without delay; immediate. ■ (of a person) acting without delay. ■ (of goods) for immediate delivery and payment. —**promp·ti·tude** /ˈprämptəˌt(y)ōōd/ *n.* —**prompt·ly** *adv.* —**prompt·ness** *n.*

prompt·er /ˈprämptər/ ▸*n.* a person seated out of sight of the audience who supplies a forgotten word or line to an actor during the performance of a play.

prom·ul·gate /ˈpräməlˌgāt; prōˈməl-/ ▸*v.* [*tr.*] promote or make widely known (an idea or cause). ■ put (a law or decree) into effect by official proclamation. —**prom·ul·ga·tion** /ˌpräməlˈgāSHən; ˌprōməl-/ *n.* —**prom·ul·ga·tor** /-ˌgātər/ *n.*

pro·nate /ˈprōˌnāt/ ▸*v.* [*tr.*] *technical* **1** put or hold (a hand, foot, or limb) with the palm or sole turned downward. Compare with **SUPINATE. 2** walk or run with most of the weight on the outside of the feet. —**pro·na·tion** /prōˈnāSHən/ *n.*

pro·na·tor /ˈprōˌnātər/ ▸*n. Anat.* **1** a muscle whose contraction produces or assists in the pronation of a limb or part of a limb. ■ any of several specific muscles in the forearm. **2** one who pronates when walking or running.

prone /prōn/ ▸*adj.* **1** (**prone to/prone to do something**) likely to or liable to suffer from, do, or experience something, typically something regrettable or unwelcome: *years of logging had left the mountains prone to mudslides.* **2** lying flat, esp. face downward: *I was lying prone on a foam mattress.* ■ *technical* denoting the position of the forearm with the palm of the hand facing downward. **3** *archaic* with a downward slope or direction. —**prone·ness** *n.*

prong /prôNG/ ▸*n.* each of two or more projecting pointed parts at the end of a fork. ■ a projecting part on various other devices. ■ *fig.* each of the separate parts of an attack or operation.
▸*v.* [*tr.*] pierce or stab with a fork. —**pronged** /prôNGd/ *adj.* [in *comb.*] *a three-pronged attack.*

prong·horn /ˈprôNGˌhôrn/ (also **pronghorn antelope**) ▸*n.* a deerlike North American mammal (*Antilocapra americana*) with a stocky body, long slim legs, and black horns that are shed and regrown annually.

pro·noun /ˈprōˌnoun/ ▸*n.* a word that can function by itself as a noun phrase and that refers either to the participants in the discourse (e.g., *I, you*) or to someone or something mentioned elsewhere in the discourse (e.g., *she, it, this*).

pro·nounce /prəˈnouns/ ▸*v.* [*tr.*] **1** make the sound of (a word or part of a word), typically in the correct or a particular way. **2** declare or announce, typically formally or solemnly: *the doctors pronounced that he would never improve.* ■ [*intr.*] (**pronounce on**) pass judgment or make a decision on: *the secretary of state will shortly pronounce on alternative measures.* —**pro·nounce·a·bil·i·ty** /prəˌnounsəˈbilətē/ *n.* —**pro·nounce·a·ble** *adj.* —**pro·nounce·ment** *n.* —**pro·nounc·er** *n.*

pro·nounced /prəˈnounst/ ▸*adj.* very noticeable or marked; conspicuous. —**pro·nounc·ed·ly** /-ˈnounsədlē; -ˈnounstlē/ *adv.*

pron·to /ˈpräntō/ ▸*adv. inf.* promptly; quickly: *put it in the refrigerator, pronto.*

pro·nun·ci·a·tion /prəˌnənsēˈāSHən/ ▸*n.* the way in which a word is pronounced: *spelling does not determine pronunciation.*

proof /prōōf/ ▸*n.* **1** evidence or argument establishing or helping to establish a fact or the truth of a statement. ■ *Law* the spoken or written evidence in a trial. ■ the action or process of establishing the truth of a statement: *it shifts the onus of proof in convictions from the police to the public.* ■ *archaic* a test or trial. ■ a series of stages in the resolution of a mathematical or philosophical problem. **2** a trial print of something, in particular: ■ *Printing* a trial impression of a page, taken from type or film and used for making corrections before final printing. ■ a trial photographic print made for initial selection. ■ each of a number of impressions from an engraved plate, esp. (in commercial printing) of a limited number before the ordinary issue is printed and before an inscription or signature is added. ■ any of various preliminary impressions of coins struck as specimens. **3** the strength of distilled alcoholic liquor, relative to proof spirit taken as a standard of 100: [in *comb.*] *powerful 132-proof rum.*
▸*adj.* **1** able to withstand something damaging; resistant: *the marine battle armor was **proof against** most weapons* | [in *comb.*] *the system comes with*

---

idiot-proof instructions. **2** denoting a trial impression of a page or printed work: *a proof copy is sent up for checking.*

▶*v.* [*tr.*] **1** make (fabric) waterproof: [as *adj.*] (**proofed**) *the tent is made from proofed nylon.* **2** make a proof of (a printed work, engraving, etc.): [as *n.*] (**proofing**) *proofing could be done on a low-cost printer.* ■ proofread (a text). **3** activate (yeast) by the addition of liquid. ■ knead (dough) until light and smooth. ■ [*intr.*] (of dough) prove.

proof·read /ˈpro͞ofˌrēd/ (also **proof-read**) ▶*v.* (*past* and *past part.* **-read** /-ˌred/) [*tr.*] read (printer's proofs or other written or printed material) and mark any errors. —**proof·read·er** *n.*

prop[1] /präp/ ▶*n.* a pole or beam used as a support or to keep something in position, typically one that is not an integral part of the thing supported. ■ *fig.* a person or thing that is a major source of support or assistance: *the second institutional prop of conservative Spain was the army.* ■ *Gram.* a word used to fill a syntactic role without any specific meaning of its own, for example *one* in *it's a nice one* and *it* in *it is raining.*

▶*v.* (**propped, prop·ping**) [*tr.*] position something underneath (someone or something) for support. ■ position (something or someone) more or less upright by leaning it against something else: *a jug of milk with a note propped against it.* ■ use an object to keep (something) in position: *he found that the door to the office was propped open.*

▶*phrasal v.* □ **prop someone/something up** provide support or assistance for someone or something that would otherwise fail or decline.

prop[2] ▶*n.* (usu. **props**) a portable object other than furniture or costumes used on the set of a play or movie.

prop[3] ▶*n.* *inf.* an aircraft propeller.

prop. ▶*abbr.* ■ proposition. ■ proprietor.

prop·a·gan·da /ˌpräpəˈgandə/ ▶*n.* *chiefly derog.* information, esp. of a biased or misleading nature, used to promote or publicize a particular political cause or point of view. ■ the dissemination of such information as a political strategy. —**prop·a·gan·dize** *v.*

prop·a·gan·dist /ˌpräpəˈgandist/ *chiefly derog.* ▶*n.* a person who promotes or publicizes a particular organization or cause.

▶*adj.* consisting of or spreading propaganda: *propagandist films.* —**prop·a·gan·dism** /-ˌdizəm/ *n.* —**prop·a·gan·dis·tic** /-ˌganˈdistik/ *adj.* —**prop·a·gan·dis·ti·cal·ly** /-ˌganˈdistik(ə)lē/ *adv.*

prop·a·gate /ˈpräpəˌgāt/ ▶*v.* [*tr.*] **1** breed specimens of (a plant, animal, etc.) by natural processes from the parent stock. ■ [*intr.*] (of a plant, animal, etc.) reproduce in such a way. ■ cause (something) to increase in number or amount. **2** spread and promote (an idea, theory, knowledge, etc.) widely. **3** [*tr.*] transmit (motion, light, sound, etc.) in a particular direction or through a medium: *electromagnetic effects can be propagated at a finite velocity only through material substances.* ■ [*intr.*] (of motion, light, sound, etc.) be transmitted or travel in such a way. —**prop·a·ga·tion** /ˌpräpəˈgāSHən/ *n.* —**prop·a·ga·tive** /-ˌgātiv/ *adj.* —**prop·a·ga·tor** /-ˌgātər/ *n.*

pro·pane /ˈprōˌpān/ ▶*n.* *Chem.* a flammable hydrocarbon gas, C_3H_8, of the alkane series, present in natural gas and used as bottled fuel.

pro·pel /prəˈpel/ ▶*v.* (**-pelled, -pel·ling**) [*tr.*] drive, push, or cause to move in a particular direction, typically forward: [as *adj.* in *comb.*] (**-propelled**) *a rocket-propelled grenade launcher.* ■ [*tr.*] *fig.* spur or drive into a particular situation: *fear propelled her out of her stillness.*

pro·pel·lant /prəˈpelənt/ ▶*n.* a thing or substance that causes something to move or be driven forward or outward, in particular: ■ an inert fluid, liquefied under pressure, in which the active contents of an aerosol are dispersed. ■ an explosive that fires bullets from a firearm. ■ a substance used as a reagent in a rocket engine to provide thrust.

▶*adj.* another term for PROPELLENT.

pro·pel·lent /prəˈpelənt/ ▶*adj.* capable of driving, pushing, or moving something in a particular direction: *propellent gases.*

pro·pel·ler /prəˈpelər/ ▶*n.* a mechanical device for propelling a boat or aircraft, consisting of a revolving shaft with two or more broad, angled blades attached to it.

pro·pene /ˈprōˌpēn/ ▶*n.* *Chem.* another term for PROPYLENE.

pro·pen·si·ty /prəˈpensətē/ ▶*n.* (*pl.* **-ties**) an inclination or natural tendency to behave in a particular way: *a propensity for violence.*

prop·er /ˈpräpər/ ▶*adj.* **1** truly what something is said or regarded to be; genuine: *she's never had a proper job.* ■ strictly so called; in its true form: *some of the dos and don'ts in espionage proper.* ■ *inf. chiefly Brit.* used as an intensifier, often in derogatory contexts: *she looked like a proper harlot.* **2** of the required type; suitable or appropriate: *an artist needs the proper tools.* ■ according to what is correct or prescribed for a particular situation or thing: *they had not followed the proper procedures.* ■ according to or respecting recognized social standards or conventions; respectable, esp. excessively so: *a very prim and proper lady.* **3** (**proper to**) belonging or relating exclusively or distinctively to; particular to: *the two elephant*

types proper to Africa and to southern Asia. **4** *Heraldry* in the natural colors. **5** *Math.* denoting a subset or subgroup that does not constitute the entire set or group, esp. one that has more than one element.

▶*n.* the part of a church service that varies with the season or festival. —**prop·er·ness** *n.*

prop·er frac·tion ▶*n.* a fraction that is less than one, with the numerator less than the denominator.

prop·er·ly /ˈpräpərlē/ ▶*adv.* correctly or satisfactorily. ■ appropriately for the circumstances; suitably; respectably. ■ in the strict sense; exactly: *algebra is, properly speaking, the analysis of equations.*

prop·er noun (also **proper name**) ▶*n.* a name used for an individual person, place, or organization, spelled with initial capital letters, e.g., *Larry, Mexico,* and *Boston Red Sox.* Often contrasted with COMMON NOUN.

prop·er·ty /ˈpräpərtē/ ▶*n.* (*pl.* **-ties**) **1** a thing or things belonging to someone; possessions collectively. ■ a building or buildings and the land belonging to it or them: *the renovation of commercial properties.* ■ *Law* the right to the possession, use, or disposal of something; ownership: *rights of property.* ■ old-fashioned term for PROP[2]. **2** an attribute, quality, or characteristic of something.

proph·e·cy /ˈpräfəsē/ ▶*n.* (*pl.* **-cies**) a prediction: *a bleak prophecy of war and ruin.* ■ the faculty, function, or practice of prophesying.

proph·e·sy /ˈpräfəˌsī/ ▶*v.* (**-sies, -sied**) [*tr.*] say that (a specified thing) will happen in the future: *the papers prophesied that he would resign after the weekend.* ■ [*intr.*] speak or write by divine inspiration; act as a prophet. —**proph·e·si·er** /-ˌsīər/ *n.*

proph·et /ˈpräfit/ ▶*n.* **1** a person regarded as an inspired teacher or proclaimer of the will of God: *the Old Testament prophet Jeremiah.* ■ (**the Prophet**) (among Muslims) Muhammad. ■ (**the Prophet**) (among Mormons) Joseph Smith or one of his successors. ■ a person who advocates or speaks in a visionary way about a new belief, cause, or theory: *he was a prophet of revolutionary socialism.* ■ a person who makes or claims to be able to make predictions: *the anti-technology prophets of doom.* **2** (**the Prophets**) the prophetic writings of the Old Testament or Hebrew scriptures, in particular: ■ (in Christian use) the books of Isaiah, Jeremiah, Ezekiel, Daniel, and the twelve minor prophets. ■ (in Jewish use) one of the three canonical divisions of the Hebrew Bible, distinguished from the Law and the Hagiographa, and comprising the books of Joshua, Judges, Samuel, Kings, Jeremiah, Ezekiel, Isaiah, and the twelve minor prophets.

pro·phet·ic /prəˈfetik/ ▶*adj.* **1** accurately describing or predicting what will happen in the future. **2** of, relating to, or characteristic of a prophet or prophecy. —**pro·phet·i·cal** *adj.* —**pro·phet·i·cal·ly** /-ik(ə)lē/ *adv.*

pro·phy·lac·tic /ˌprōfəˈlaktik/ ▶*adj.* intended to prevent disease.

▶*n.* a medicine or course of action used to prevent disease: *I took malaria prophylactics.* ■ a condom. ▷late 16th cent.: from French *prophylactique,* from Greek *prophulaktikos,* from *pro* 'before' + *phulassein* 'to guard.' —**pro·phy·lac·ti·cal·ly** /-ik(ə)lē/ *adv.*

pro·phy·lax·is /ˌprōfəˈlaksəs/ ▶*n.* action taken to prevent disease, esp. by specified means or against a specified disease.

pro·pin·qui·ty /prəˈpiNGkwətē/ ▶*n.* **1** the state of being close to someone or something; proximity. **2** *technical* close kinship.

pro·pi·ti·ate /prəˈpiSHēˌāt/ ▶*v.* [*tr.*] win or regain the favor of (a god, spirit, or person) by doing something that pleases them. —**pro·pi·ti·a·tion** /-ˌpiSHēˈāSHən/ *n.* —**pro·pi·ti·a·tor** /-ˌātər/ *n.* —**pro·pi·ti·a·to·ry** /-ˈpiSHēəˌtôrē/ *adj.*

pro·pi·tious /prəˈpiSHəs/ ▶*adj.* giving or indicating a good chance of success; favorable. ■ *archaic* favorably disposed toward someone: *there were points on which they did not agree, moments in which she did not seem propitious.* —**pro·pi·tious·ly** *adv.* —**pro·pi·tious·ness** *n.*

prop jet ▶*n.* a turboprop aircraft or engine.

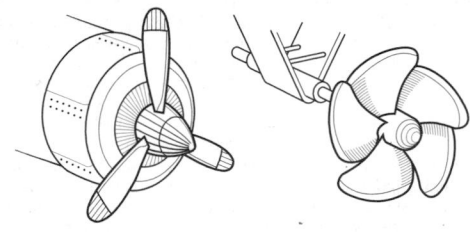

aircraft   marine

propellers

pro·po·nent /prəˈpōnənt/ ▶ n. a person who advocates a theory, proposal, or project.

pro·por·tion /prəˈpôrSHən/ ▶ n. a part, share, or number considered in comparative relation to a whole: *the proportion of greenhouse gases in the atmosphere is rising.* ■ the relationship of one thing to another in terms of quantity, size, or number; the ratio: *the proportion of exams to schoolwork.* ■ (**proportions**) the comparative measurements or size of different parts of a whole: *perfect bodily proportions.* ■ (**proportions**) dimensions; size: *the room, despite its ample proportions, seemed too small for him.* ■ the correct, attractive, or ideal relationship in size or shape between one thing and another or between the parts of a whole.
▶ v. [tr.] *formal* adjust or regulate (something) so that it has a particular or suitable relationship to something else: *a life after death in which happiness can be proportioned to virtue.* —**pro·por·tion·less** *adj.*
▶ □ **in proportion** according to a particular relationship in size, amount, or degree: *each region was represented in proportion to its population.* ■ in comparison with; in relation to: *the cuckoo's eggs are unusually small in proportion to its size.* ■ in the correct or appropriate relation to the size, shape, or position of other things: *her figure was in proportion.* ■ correctly or realistically regarded in terms of relative importance or seriousness: *the problem has to be kept in proportion.* □ **out of proportion** in the wrong relation to the size, shape, or position of other things: *the sculpture seemed out of proportion to its surroundings.* ■ greater or more serious than is necessary or appropriate: *the award was out of all proportion to the alleged libel.* ■ wrongly or unrealistically regarded in terms of relative importance or seriousness. □ **sense of proportion** the ability to judge the relative importance or seriousness of things.

pro·por·tion·al /prəˈpôrSHənl/ ▶ *adj.* corresponding in size or amount to something else. ■ *Math.* (of a variable quantity) having a constant ratio to another quantity. —**pro·por·tion·al·i·ty** /prə,pôrSHəˈnalətē; pər-,pôrSHəˈnalədē/ *n.* —**pro·por·tion·al·ly** /-SHənl-ē/ *adv.*

pro·por·tion·ate /prəˈpôrSHənət/ ▶ *adj.* another term for PROPORTIONAL. —**pro·por·tion·ate·ly** *adv.*

pro·pos·al /prəˈpōzəl/ ▶ *n.* **1** a plan or suggestion, esp. a formal or written one, put forward for consideration or discussion by others. ■ the action of putting forward such a plan or suggestion. **2** an offer of marriage.

pro·pose /prəˈpōz/ ▶ v. **1** [tr.] put forward (an idea or plan) for consideration or discussion by others. ■ nominate (someone) for an elected office or as a member of a society. ■ put forward (a motion) to a legislature or committee. **2** [intr.] make an offer of marriage to someone. —**pro·pos·er** *n.*
▶ □ **propose marriage** make an offer of marriage to someone. □ **propose a toast** ask a group of people at a social occasion to drink to the health and happiness of a specified person: *I hereby propose a toast to the bride and groom.*

prop·o·si·tion /,präpəˈziSHən/ ▶ *n.* **1** a statement or assertion that expresses a judgment or opinion. ■ *Logic* a statement that expresses a concept that can be true or false. ■ *Math.* a formal statement of a theorem or problem, typically including the demonstration. **2** a suggested scheme or plan of action, esp. in a business context. ■ (in the U.S.) a constitutional proposal; a bill. ■ *inf.* an offer of sexual intercourse made to a person with whom one is not sexually involved, esp. one that is made in an unsubtle or offensive way. **3** a project, task, or idea considered in terms of its likely success or difficulty, esp. in a commercial context: *a paper that has lost half its readers is unlikely to be an attractive proposition.* ■ a person considered in terms of the likely success or difficulty of one's dealings with them: *as a potential manager, Sandy is a better proposition than Dave.*
▶ v. [tr.] *inf.* make a suggestion of sexual intercourse to (someone with whom one is not sexually involved), esp. in an unsubtle or offensive way. ■ make an offer or suggestion to (someone). —**prop·o·si·tion·al** /-SHənl/ *adj.* (*chiefly Logic*).

pro·pound /prəˈpound/ ▶ v. [tr.] put forward (an idea, theory, or point of view) for consideration by others. —**pro·pound·er** *n.*

pro·pri·e·tar·y /p(r)əˈprī-i,terē/ ▶ *adj.* of or relating to an owner or ownership: *the company has a proprietary right to the property.* ■ (of a product) marketed under and protected by a registered trade name: *proprietary brands of insecticide.* ■ behaving as if one were the owner of someone or something: *he looked about him with a proprietary air.*
▶ *n.* an owner; proprietor. ■ *hist.* esp. in North America, a grantee or owner of a colony who has been granted, as an individual or as part of a group, the full rights of self-government.

pro·pri·e·tar·y name ▶ *n.* a name of a product or service registered by its owner as a trademark and not usable by others without permission.

pro·pri·e·tor /p(r)əˈprīətər/ ▶ *n.* the owner of a business. ■ a holder of property. —**pro·pri·e·to·ri·al** /p(r)ə,prīəˈtôrēəl/ *adj.* —**pro·pri·e·to·ri·al·ly** /p(r)ə,prīəˈtôrēəlē/ *adv.* —**pro·pri·e·tor·ship** /-,SHip/ *n.*

pro·pri·e·ty /p(r)əˈprīətē/ ▶ *n.* (*pl.* **-ties**) the state or quality of conforming to conventionally accepted standards of behavior or morals. ■ (**proprieties**) the details or rules of behavior conventionally considered to be correct. ■ the condition of being right, appropriate, or fitting: *they questioned the propriety of certain investments made by the council.*

pro·pul·sion /prəˈpəlSHən/ ▶ *n.* the action of driving or pushing forward: *they use their wings for propulsion under water.* —**pro·pul·sive** /-siv/ *adj.*

pro·pyl /ˈprōpəl/ ▶ *n.* [as *adj.*] *Chem.* of or denoting the alkyl radical $-C_3H_7$, derived notionally from propane.

pro·pyl·ene /ˈprōpə,lēn/ ▶ *n.* *Chem.* a gaseous hydrocarbon of the alkene series, C_3H_6, made by cracking alkanes. Also called PROPENE.

pro ra·ta /prō ˈrātə; ˈrätə; ˈratə/ ▶ *adj.* proportional: *as the dollar has fallen, costs have risen on a pro rata basis* | *pro-rata ownership.*
▶ *adv.* proportionally: *their fees will rise pro rata with salaries.*

pro·rate /prōˈrāt; ˈprō,rāt/ ▶ v. [tr.] (usu. **be prorated**) allocate, distribute, or assess pro rata: *bonuses are prorated over the life of a player's contract.* —**pro·ra·tion** /prōˈrāSHən/ *n.*

pro·rogue /prəˈrōg/ ▶ v. (**-rogues, -rogued, -rogu·ing**) [tr.] discontinue a session of (a parliament or other legislative assembly) without dissolving it. ■ [intr.] (of such an assembly) be discontinued in this way. —**pro·ro·ga·tion** /,prōrəˈgāSHən/ *n.*

pro·sa·ic /prōˈzāik/ ▶ *adj.* having the style or diction of prose; lacking poetic beauty. ■ commonplace; unromantic. —**pro·sa·i·cal·ly** /-ik(ə)lē/ *adv.* —**pro·sa·ic·ness** *n.*

pro·sce·ni·um /prəˈsēnēəm; prō-/ ▶ *n.* (*pl.* **-ni·ums** or **-ni·a** /-nēə/) the part of a theater stage in front of the curtain.

pro·sciut·to /prəˈSHo͞otō/ ▶ *n.* Italian ham cured by drying and typically served in very thin slices.

pro·scribe /prōˈskrīb/ ▶ v. [tr.] forbid, esp. by law. ■ denounce or condemn. ■ *hist.* outlaw (someone). —**pro·scrip·tion** /-ˈskripSHən/ *n.* —**pro·scrip·tive** /-ˈskriptiv/ *adj.*

prose /prōz/ ▶ *n.* written or spoken language in its ordinary form, without metrical structure. ■ *fig.* plain or dull writing, discourse, or expression.

pros·e·cute /ˈpräsi,kyo͞ot/ ▶ v. [tr.] **1** institute legal proceedings against (a person or organization). ■ institute legal proceedings in respect of (a claim or offense): *this was a case worth prosecuting* | [intr.] *the company didn't prosecute because of his age.* ■ [intr.] (of a lawyer) conduct the case against the party being accused or sued in a lawsuit. **2** continue with (a course of action) with a view to its completion. ■ *archaic* carry on (a trade or pursuit). —**pros·e·cut·a·ble** *adj.*

pros·e·cu·tion /,präsiˈkyo͞oSHən/ ▶ *n.* **1** the institution and conducting of legal proceedings against someone in respect of a criminal charge. ■ (**the prosecution**) [treated as *sing.* or *pl.*] the party instituting or conducting legal proceedings against someone in a lawsuit: *the main witness for the prosecution.* **2** the continuation of a course of action with a view to its completion: *the network's prosecution of its commercial ends.*

pros·e·cu·tor /ˈpräsi,kyo͞otər/ ▶ *n.* a person, esp. a public official, who institutes legal proceedings against someone. ■ a lawyer who conducts the case against a defendant in a criminal court. Also called **prosecuting attorney.** —**pros·e·cu·to·ri·al** /,präsikyəˈtôrēəl/ *adj.*

pros·e·lyte /ˈpräsə,līt/ ▶ *n.* a person who has converted from one opinion, religion, or party to another, esp. recently. ■ a Gentile who has converted to Judaism.
▶ v. another term for PROSELYTIZE. —**pros·e·lyt·ism** /-lə,tizəm/ *n.*

pros·e·lyt·ize /ˈpräsələ,tīz/ ▶ v. [tr.] convert or attempt to convert (someone) from one religion, belief, or opinion to another: *the program did have a tremendous evangelical effect, proselytizing many* | [intr.] *proselytizing for converts* | [as *n.*] (**proselytizing**) *no amount of proselytizing was going to change their minds.* ■ advocate or promote (a belief or course of action). —**pros·e·lyt·iz·er** *n.*

pro·sim·i·an /prōˈsimēən/ *Zool.* ▶ *n.* a primitive primate of a group (suborder Prosimii) that includes the lemurs, bush babies, and tarsiers.
▶ *adj.* of or relating to the prosimians.

pros·o·dy /ˈpräsədē/ ▶ *n.* the patterns of rhythm and sound used in poetry. ■ the theory or study of these patterns, or the rules governing them. ■ the patterns of stress and intonation in a language.

—**pro·sod·ic** /prəˈsädik; -zädik/ or **pro·sod·i·cal** /prəˈsädikəl; -ˈzäd-/ adj. —**pros·o·dist** /ˈpräsədist; ˈpräz-/ n.

pros·pect /ˈpräsˌpekt/ ▶n. **1** the possibility or likelihood of some future event occurring: *there was no prospect of a reconciliation.* ■ a mental picture of a future or anticipated event: *this presents a disturbing prospect of one-party government.* ■ (usu. **prospects**) chances or opportunities for success or wealth. **2** a person regarded as a potential customer or subscriber to something. ■ a person regarded as likely to succeed, esp. in a sporting event. ■ a place likely to yield mineral deposits. ■ a place being explored for mineral deposits. **3** an extensive view of landscape.
▶v. [intr.] search for mineral deposits in a place, esp. by means of experimental drilling and excavation: *the company is also* **prospecting for** *gold.* ■ (**prospect for**) *fig.* look out for; search for: *the responsibilities of salespeople to prospect for customers.* ▷late Middle English (as a noun denoting the action of looking toward a distant object): from Latin *prospectus* 'view,' from *prospicere* 'look forward,' from *pro-* 'forward' + *specere* 'to look.' Early use, referring to a view of landscape, gave rise to the meaning 'mental picture' (mid 16th cent.), whence 'anticipated event.' —**pros·pec·tor** n.

pro·spec·tive /prəˈspektiv/ ▶adj. (of a person) expected or expecting to be something particular in the future: *she showed a prospective buyer around the house.* ■ likely to happen at a future date; concerned with or applying to the future: *to discuss prospective changes in government legislation.* —**pro·spec·tive·ly** adv. —**pro·spec·tive·ness** n.

pro·spec·tus /prəˈspektəs/ ▶n. (pl. **-tus·es**) a printed document that advertises or describes a school, commercial enterprise, forthcoming book, etc., in order to attract or inform clients, members, buyers, or investors.

pros·per /ˈpräspər/ ▶v. [intr.] succeed in material terms; be financially successful: *his business prospered* | *the nation plans to prosper from free trade with the U.S.* ■ flourish physically; grow strong and healthy. ■ [tr.] archaic make successful: *God has wonderfully prospered this nation.*

pros·per·i·ty /präˈsperitē/ ▶n. the state of being prosperous.

pros·per·ous /ˈpräspərəs/ ▶adj. successful in material terms; flourishing financially: *prosperous middle-class professionals.* ■ bringing wealth and success: *we wish you a prosperous New Year.* —**pros·per·ous·ly** adv. —**pros·per·ous·ness** n.

pros·tate /ˈpräsˌtāt/ (also **prostate gland**) ▶n. a gland surrounding the neck of the bladder in male mammals and releasing prostatic fluid. —**pros·tat·ic** /präˈstatik/ adj.

pros·the·sis /präsˈTHēsis/ ▶n. (pl. **-ses** /-sēz/) **1** an artificial body part, such as a leg, a heart, or a breast implant: *his upper jaw was removed and a prosthesis was fitted.* **2** (also **prothesis**) the addition of a letter or syllable at the beginning of a word, as in Spanish *escribo* derived from Latin *scribo.* —**pros·thet·ic** /-ˈTHetik/ adj. —**pros·thet·i·cal·ly** /-ˈTHetik(ə)lē/ adv.

pros·thet·ics /präsˈTHetiks/ ▶pl. n. artificial body parts; prostheses. ■ pieces of flexible material applied to actors' faces to transform their appearance. ■ [treated as sing.] the making and fitting of artificial body parts.

pros·ti·tute /ˈprästəˌt(y)o͞ot/ ▶n. a person, typically a woman, who engages in sexual activity for payment. ■ *fig.* a person who misuses their talents or who sacrifices their self-respect for the sake of personal or financial gain: *careerist political prostitutes.*
▶v. [tr.] offer (someone, typically a woman) for sexual activity in exchange for payment: *although she was paid $15 to join a man at his table, she never* **prostituted** *herself.* ■ *fig.* put (oneself or one's talents) to an unworthy or corrupt use or purpose for the sake of personal or financial gain. —**pros·ti·tu·tion** /ˌprästiˈto͞oSHən/ n. —**pros·ti·tu·tor** /-ˌt(y)o͞otər/ n.

pros·trate ▶adj. /ˈpräsˌtrāt/ lying stretched out on the ground with one's face downward. ■ *fig.* completely overcome or helpless, esp. with illness, distress, or exhaustion: *his wife was* **prostrate** *with shock.* ■ *Bot.* growing along the ground.
▶v. [tr.] (**prostrate oneself**) lay oneself flat on the ground face downward, esp. in reverence or submission. ■ (often **be prostrated**) (of distress, exhaustion, or illness) reduce (someone) to extreme physical weakness: *she was prostrated by a migraine.* ▷Middle English: from Latin *prostratus* 'thrown down,' past participle of *prosternere*, from *pro-* 'before' + *sternere* 'lay flat.' —**pros·tra·tion** /präˈstrāSHən/ n.

pros·y /ˈprōzē/ ▶adj. (**pros·i·er**, **pros·i·est**) (esp. of speech or writing) showing no imagination; commonplace or dull. —**pros·i·ly** /-əlē/ adv. —**pros·i·ness** n.

prot·ac·tin·i·um /ˌprōˌtakˈtinēəm/ ▶n. the chemical element of atomic number 91, a radioactive metal of the actinide series, occurring in small amounts as a product of the natural decay of uranium. (Symbol: **Pa**)

pro·tag·o·nist /prōˈtagənist; prō-/ ▶n. the leading character or one of the major characters in a drama, movie, novel, or other fictional text. ■ the main figure or one of the most prominent figures in a real situation. ■ an advocate or champion of a particular cause or idea.

pro·te·an /ˈprōtēən; prōˈtēən/ ▶adj. tending or able to change frequently or easily: *it is difficult to comprehend the whole of this protean subject.* ■ able to do many different things; versatile. —**pro·te·an·ism** /-ˌnizəm/ n.

pro·te·ase /ˈprōtēˌāz; -ˌās/ ▶n. Biochem. an enzyme that breaks down proteins and peptides.

pro·tect /prəˈtekt/ ▶v. [tr.] keep safe from harm or injury: *he tried to protect Kelly from the attack* | [intr.] *certain vitamins may* **protect against** *heart disease.* ■ aim to preserve (a threatened plant or animal species) by legislating against collecting or hunting. ■ restrict by law access to or development of (land) so as to preserve its natural state. ■ (often **be protected**) (of an insurance policy) promise to pay (someone) an agreed amount in the event of loss, injury, fire, theft, or other misfortune: *in the event of your death, your family will be protected against any financial problems that may arise.* ■ *Econ.* shield (a domestic industry) from competition by imposing import duties on foreign goods. ■ *Comput.* restrict access to or use of (data or a memory location): *security products are designed to* **protect** *information* **from** *unauthorized access.* ■ provide funds to meet (a bill of exchange or commercial draft). —**pro·tect·a·ble** adj.

pro·tec·tion /prəˈtekSHən/ ▶n. the action of protecting someone or something, or the state of being protected: *the B vitamins give protection against infection.* ■ a person or thing that prevents someone or something from suffering harm or injury: *the castle was built as protection against the Saxons.* ■ the cover provided by an insurance policy. ■ (usu. **protections**) a legal or other formal measure intended to preserve civil liberties and rights. ■ a document guaranteeing immunity from harm to the person specified in it. ■ the practice of paying money to criminals so as to prevent them from attacking oneself or one's property: [as adj.] *a protection racket.* ■ (also **protection money**) the money so paid to criminals, esp. on a regular basis. ■ *archaic* used euphemistically to refer to the keeping of a mistress by her lover in a separate establishment: *she was living* **under his lordship's protection** *at Gloucester Gate.*

pro·tec·tive /prəˈtektiv/ ▶adj. capable of or intended to protect someone or something: *protective gloves.* ■ having or showing a strong wish to keep someone or something safe from harm. ■ *Econ.* of or relating to the protection of domestic industries from foreign competition: *protective tariffs.* —**pro·tec·tive·ly** adv. —**pro·tec·tive·ness** n.

pro·tec·tive or·der ▶n. a court order instructing a person to desist from abusing or harassing the petitioner (usu. a related person) for a fixed period: *a protective order against the man accused of setting his wife on fire.*

pro·tec·tor /prəˈtektər/ ▶n. **1** a person who protects or defends someone or something: *a passionate protector of animal rights.* **2** a thing that protects someone or something from injury: *ear protectors.* **3** (chiefly **Protector**) *hist.* a regent in charge of a kingdom during the minority, absence, or incapacity of the sovereign. ■ (also **Lord Protector**) the title of the head of state in England during the later period of the Commonwealth between 1653 and 1659, first Oliver Cromwell (1653–58), then his son Richard (1658–59). —**pro·tec·tor·al** /-rəl/ adj. —**pro·tec·tor·ship** /-ˌSHip/ n.

pro·tec·tor·ate /prəˈtektərət/ ▶n. **1** a state that is controlled and protected by another. ■ the relationship between a state of this kind and the one that controls it: *a French protectorate had been established over Tunis.* **2** (usu. **Protectorate**) *hist.* the position or office of a Protector, esp. that in England of Oliver and Richard Cromwell.

pro·té·gé /ˈprōtəˌZHā; ˌprōtəˈZHā/ (also **pro·te·ge**) ▶n. a person who is guided and supported by an older and more experienced or influential person: *he was an aide and protégé of the former Tennessee senator.*

pro·tein /ˈprōˌtē(ə)n/ ▶n. any of a class of nitrogenous organic compounds that consist of large molecules composed of one or more long chains of amino acids and are an essential part of all living organisms, esp. as structural components of body tissues such as muscle, hair, collagen, etc., and as enzymes and antibodies. ■ such substances collectively, esp. as a dietary component: *a diet high in protein.* —**pro·tein·a·ceous** /ˌprōˌtē(ə)ˈnāSHəs; ˌprōtnˈā-/ adj.

pro tem /prō ˈtem/ ▶adv. & adj. for the time being: [as adv.] *a printer that Marisa could use pro tem* | [as adj.] *a pro tem committee.* ▷abbreviation of Latin *pro tempore.*

pro·test ▶n. /ˈprōˌtest/ a statement or action expressing disapproval of or objection to something: *the Hungarian team lodged an official protest* | *two senior scientists resigned* **in protest.** ■ an organized public demonstration expressing strong objection to a policy or course of action adopted by those in authority: [as *adj.*] *a protest march.*

▶*v.* /prəˈtest; prōˈtest; ˈprōˌtest/ **1** [*intr.*] express an objection to what someone has said or done. ■ publicly demonstrate strong objection to a policy or course of action adopted by those in authority: *doctors and patients* **protested against** *plans to cut services at the hospital.* ■ [*tr.*] publicly demonstrate such objection to (a policy or course of action). **2** [*tr.*] declare (something) firmly and emphatically in the face of stated or implied doubt or in response to an accusation: *she has always protested her innocence.* ▷late Middle English (as a verb in the sense 'make a solemn declaration'): from Old French *protester,* from Latin *protestari,* from *pro-* 'forth, publicly' + *testari* 'assert' (from *testis* 'witness'). —**pro·test·er** /ˈprō,testər; prəˈtes-/ *n.* —**pro·test·ing·ly** *adv.* —**pro·tes·tor** /ˈprō,testər; prəˈtes-/ *n.*

▶ □ **under protest** after expressing one's objection or reluctance; unwillingly: *"I'm only here under protest," Jenna said shortly.*

Prot·es·tant /ˈprätəstənt/ ▶*n.* a member or follower of any of the Western Christian churches that are separate from the Roman Catholic Church and follow the principles of the Reformation, including the Baptist, Presbyterian, and Lutheran churches. —**Prot·es·tant·ism** *n.*
▶*adj.* of, relating to, or belonging to any of the Protestant churches.

prot·es·ta·tion /ˌprätəˈstāSHən; ˌprō,tesˈtā-/ ▶*n.* an emphatic declaration that something is or is not the case. ■ an objection or protest.

pro·ti·um /ˈprōtēəm; ˈprōSH(ē)əm/ ▶*n. Chem.* the common, stable isotope of hydrogen, as distinct from deuterium and tritium.

pro·to·col /ˈprōtə,kôl; -,käl/ ▶*n.* **1** the official procedure or system of rules governing affairs of state or diplomatic occasions. ■ the accepted or established code of procedure or behavior in any group, organization, or situation: *what is the protocol at a conference if one's neighbor dozes off during the speeches?* ■ *Comput.* a set of rules governing the exchange or transmission of data electronically between devices. **2** the original draft of a diplomatic document, esp. of the terms of a treaty agreed to in conference and signed by the parties. ■ an amendment or addition to a treaty or convention. **3** a formal or official record of scientific experimental observations. ■ a procedure for carrying out a scientific experiment or a course of medical treatment. ▷late Middle English (denoting the original record of an agreement, forming the legal authority for future dealings relating to it): from Old French *prothocole,* via medieval Latin from Greek *prōtokollon* 'first page, flyleaf,' from *prōtos* 'first' + *kolla* 'glue.' Sense 1 derives from French *protocole,* the collection of set forms of etiquette to be observed by the French head of state, and the name of the government department responsible for this (in the 19th cent.).

pro·to·lan·guage /ˈprōtō,laNG(g)wij/ ▶*n.* a hypothetical undocumented parent language from which actual languages are derived.

pro·ton /ˈprō,tän/ ▶*n. Physics* a stable subatomic particle occurring in all atomic nuclei, with a positive electric charge equal in magnitude to that of an electron, but of opposite sign. —**pro·ton·ic** /prōˈtänik/ *adj.*

pro·to·plasm /ˈprōtə,plazəm/ ▶*n. Biol.* the colorless material comprising the living part of a cell, including the cytoplasm, nucleus, and other organelles. —**pro·to·plas·mic** /ˌprōtəˈplazmik/ *adj.*

pro·to·plast /ˈprōtə,plast/ ▶*n. chiefly Bot.* the protoplasm of a living plant or bacterial cell whose cell wall has been removed. —**pro·to·plas·tic** /ˌprōtəˈplastik/ *adj.*

pro·to·type /ˈprōtə,tīp/ ▶*n.* a first or preliminary model of something, esp. a machine, from which other forms are developed or copied. ■ a typical example of something: *the prototype of all careerists is Judas.* ■ the archetypal example of a class of living organisms, astronomical objects, or other items: *these objects are the prototypes of a category of rapidly spinning neutron stars.* ■ a building, vehicle, or other object that acts as a pattern for a full-scale model.

▶*v.* [*tr.*] make a prototype of (a product). —**pro·to·typ·al** /ˌprōtəˈtīpəl/ *adj.* —**pro·to·typ·ic** /ˌprōtəˈtipik/ *adj.* —**pro·to·typ·i·cal** /ˌprōtəˈtipikəl/ *adj.* —**pro·to·typ·i·cal·ly** /ˌprōtəˈtipik(ə)lē/ *adv.*

pro·to·zo·an /ˌprōtəˈzōən/ ▶*n.* (*pl.* **-zo·a, -zo·ans**) any single-celled microscopic animal of the group including amebas and ciliates.
▶*adj.* of or relating to the protozoa.

pro·tract /prəˈtrakt; prō-/ ▶*v.* [*tr.*] **1** prolong. **2** extend a part of the body. **3** draw (a plan, etc.) to scale. —**pro·trac·tion** /-ˈtrakSHən/ *n.*

pro·trac·tor /ˈprō,traktər/ ▶*n.* **1** an instrument for measuring angles, typically in the form of a flat semicircle marked with degrees along the curved edge. **2** (also **protractor muscle**) *chiefly Zool.* a muscle serving to extend a part of the body.

pro·trude /prəˈtrōōd; prō-/ ▶*v.* [*intr.*] extend beyond or above a surface: *a fin protruded from the water.* ■ [*tr.*] (of an animal) cause (a body part) to do this. —**pro·tru·sion** /-ˈtrōōzHən/ *n.* —**pro·tru·sive** /-ˈtrōōsiv; -ziv/ *adj.*

pro·tu·ber·ant /prəˈt(y)ōōb(ə)rənt; prō-/ ▶*adj.* protruding; bulging. —**pro·tu·ber·ance** *n.*

proud /proud/ ▶*adj.* feeling deep pleasure or satisfaction as a result of one's own achievements, qualities, or possessions or those of someone with whom one is closely associated. ■ (of an event, achievement, etc.) causing someone to feel this way: *we have a proud history of innovation.* ■ having or showing a consciousness of one's own dignity: *I was too proud to go home.* ■ having or showing a high or excessively high opinion of oneself or one's importance. ■ imposing; splendid. —**proud·ly** *adv.* —**proud·ness** *n.*

▶ □ **do someone proud** *inf.* act in a way that gives someone cause to feel pleased or satisfied.

Prov. ▶*abbr.* ■ Bible Proverbs. ■ *chiefly Can.* Province or Provincial. ■ Provost.

prove /prōōv/ ▶*v.* (*past part.* **proved** or **prov·en** /ˈprōōvən/) **1** [*tr.*] demonstrate the truth or existence of (something) by evidence or argument. ■ [*tr.*] demonstrate by evidence or argument (someone or something) to be: *innocent until proven guilty.* ■ *Law* establish the genuineness and validity of (a will). ■ [*intr.*] be seen or found to be: *the plan has proved a great success.* ■ (**prove oneself**) demonstrate one's abilities or courage. ■ subject (a gun or other item) to a testing process. **2** [*intr.*] (of bread dough) become aerated by the action of yeast; rise. —**prov·a·bil·i·ty** /ˌprōōvəˈbilətē/ *n.* —**prov·a·ble** *adj.* —**prov·a·bly** /-blē/ *adv.* —**prov·er** *n.*

prov·e·nance /ˈprävənəns/ ▶*n.* the place of origin or earliest known history of something: *an orange rug of Iranian provenance.* ■ the beginning of something's existence; something's origin: *they try to understand the whole universe, its provenance and fate.* ■ a record of ownership of a work of art or an antique, used as a guide to authenticity or quality.

Pro·ven·çal /ˌprävənˈsäl; ˌprōvən-; ˌprō,vän-/ ▶*adj.* of, relating to, or denoting Provence or its people or language.
▶*n.* **1** a native or inhabitant of Provence. **2** the Romance language of Provence.

prov·en·der /ˈprävəndər/ ▶*n. often humorous* food.

pro·verb /ˈpräv,ərb/ ▶*n.* a short pithy saying in general use, stating a general truth or piece of advice.

pro·ver·bi·al /prəˈvərbēəl/ ▶*adj.* (of a word or phrase) referred to in a proverb or idiom: *I'm going to stick out like the proverbial sore thumb.* ■ well known, esp. so as to be stereotypical: *the Welsh people, whose hospitality is proverbial.* —**pro·ver·bi·al·i·ty** /-,vərbēˈalətē/ *n.* —**pro·ver·bi·al·ly** *adv.*

pro·vide /prəˈvīd/ ▶*v.* **1** [*tr.*] make available for use; supply. ■ (**provide someone with**) equip or supply someone with (something useful or necessary). ■ present or yield (something useful). **2** [*intr.*] (**provide for**) make adequate preparation for (a possible event): *new qualifications must provide for changes in technology.* ■ supply sufficient money to ensure the maintenance of (someone). ■ (of a law) enable or allow (something to be done). **3** [*tr.*] stipulate in a will or other legal document: *the order should be varied to provide that there would be no contact with the father.*

pro·vid·ed /prəˈvīdid/ ▶*conj.* on the condition or understanding that: *cutting corners was acceptable, provided that you could get away with it.*

prov·i·dence /ˈprävədəns; -,dens/ ▶*n.* the protective care of God or of nature as a spiritual power: *their trust in divine providence.* ■ (**Providence**) God or nature as providing such care. ■ timely preparation for future eventualities: *it was considered a duty to encourage providence.*

prov·i·dent /ˈprävədənt; -,dent/ ▶*adj.* making or indicative of timely preparation for the future. —**prov·i·dent·ly** *adv.*

prov·i·den·tial /ˌprävəˈdenCHəl/ ▶*adj.* **1** occurring at a favorable time; opportune: *thanks to that providential snowstorm, the attack had been*

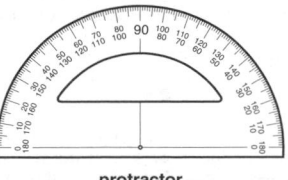

protractor

---

repulsed. **2** involving divine foresight or intervention: *God's providential care for each of us.* —**prov·i·den·tial·ly** *adv.*

pro·vid·er /prə'vīdər/ ▸*n.* a person or thing that provides something: *a leading provider of personal financial services.* ■ a breadwinner.

pro·vid·ing /prə'vīdiNG/ ▸*conj.* on the condition or understanding that: *we can win the championship, providing we avoid bad injuries.*

prov·ince /'prävins/ ▸*n.* **1** a principal administrative division of certain countries or empires: *Chengdu, capital of Sichuan province.* ■ (**the provinces**) the whole of a country outside the capital, esp. when regarded as lacking in sophistication or culture. ■ an area of the world with respect to its flora, fauna, or physical characteristics: *the inaccessibility of underwater igneous provinces.* **2** (**one's province**) an area of special knowledge, interest, or responsibility.

pro·vin·cial /prə'vinSHəl/ ▸*adj.* **1** of or concerning a province of a country or empire. ■ of or pertaining to a style of architecture or furniture in fashion in the provinces of various European countries: *French Provincial furnishing.* **2** of or concerning the regions outside the capital city of a country. ■ unsophisticated or narrow-minded, esp. when considered as typical of such regions.
▸*n.* **1** an inhabitant of a province of a country or empire. **2** an inhabitant of the regions outside the capital city of a country, esp. when regarded as unsophisticated or narrow-minded. —**pro·vin·ci·al·i·ty** /prə,vinSHē'alətē/ *n.* —**pro·vin·cial·i·za·tion** /prə,vinSHələ'zāSHən/ *n.* —**pro·vin·cial·ly** *adv.*

pro·vin·cial·ism /prə'vinCHə,lizəm/ ▸*n.* **1** the way of life or mode of thought characteristic of the regions outside the capital city of a country, esp. when regarded as unsophisticated or narrow-minded. ■ narrow-mindedness, insularity, or lack of sophistication. **2** concern for one's own area or region at the expense of national or supranational unity. **3** a word or phrase peculiar to a local area. **4** the degree to which plant or animal communities are restricted to particular areas. —**pro·vin·cial·ist** *n.* & *adj.*

prov·ing ground ▸*n.* an environment that serves to demonstrate whether something, such as a theory or product, really works. ■ a military facility for the testing of materiel and equipment.

pro·vi·sion /prə'viZHən/ ▸*n.* **1** the action of providing or supplying something for use. ■ (**provision for/against**) financial or other arrangements for future eventualities or requirements: *farmers have been slow to* **make provision for** *their retirement.* ■ an amount set aside out of profits in the accounts of an organization for a known liability, esp. a bad debt or the diminution in value of an asset. **2** an amount or thing supplied or provided: *low levels of social provision.* ■ (**provisions**) supplies of food, drink, or equipment, esp. for a journey. **3** a condition or requirement in a legal document: *a key provision in civil rights law.* **4** *hist.* Christian Church an appointment to a benefice, esp. directly by the pope rather than by the patron, and originally before it became vacant.
▸*v.* **1** [*tr.*] supply with food, drink, or equipment, esp. for a journey. **2** [*intr.*] set aside an amount in an organization's accounts for a known liability: *financial institutions have to* **provision against** *loan losses.* —**pro·vi·sion·er** *n.*

pro·vi·sion·al /prə'viZHənl/ ▸*adj.* **1** arranged or existing for the present, possibly to be changed later: *a provisional government.* ■ (of a postage stamp) put into circulation temporarily, usually owing to the unavailability of the definitive issue. **2** (**Provisional**) of or relating to the unofficial wings of the Irish Republican Army and Sinn Fein established in 1969 and advocating terrorism.
▸*n.* **1** a provisional postage stamp. **2** (**Provisional**) a member of the Provisional wings of the Irish Republican Army or Sinn Fein. —**pro·vi·sion·al·i·ty** /prə,viZHə'nalətē/ *n.* —**pro·vi·sion·al·ly** /-ZHənl-ē/ *adv.*

pro·vi·so /prə'vīzō/ ▸*n.* (pl. **-sos**) a condition attached to an agreement: *he left his unborn grandchild a trust fund* **with the proviso that** *he be named after the old man.*

pro·vi·so·ry /prə'vīzərē/ ▸*adj.* **1** *rare* subject to a proviso; conditional. **2** another term for **PROVISIONAL** (sense 1).

prov·o·ca·tion /,prävə'kāSHən/ ▸*n.* **1** action or speech that makes someone annoyed or angry, esp. deliberately: *you should remain calm and not respond to provocation.* **2** *Med.* testing to elicit a particular response or reflex.

pro·voc·a·tive /prə'väkətiv/ ▸*adj.* causing annoyance, anger, or another strong reaction, esp. deliberately. ■ arousing sexual desire or interest, esp. deliberately. —**pro·voc·a·tive·ly** *adv.* —**pro·voc·a·tive·ness** *n.*

pro·voke /prə'vōk/ ▸*v.* [*tr.*] stimulate or give rise to (a reaction or emotion, typically a strong or unwelcome one) in someone: [as *adj.*, in *comb.*] (*-provoking*) *anxiety-provoking situations.* ■ stimulate or incite (someone) to do or feel something, esp. by arousing anger in them: *a*

teacher can **provoke** *you* **into** *working harder.* ■ deliberately make (someone) annoyed or angry. —**pro·vok·a·ble** *adj.* —**pro·vok·er** *n.* —**pro·vok·ing·ly** *adv.*

pro·vo·lo·ne /,prōvə'lōnē/ ▸*n.* an Italian soft smoked cheese made from cow's milk and having a mellow flavor.

pro·vost /'prō,vōst/ ▸*n.* **1** a senior administrative officer in certain colleges and universities. ■ *Brit.* the head of certain university colleges, esp. at Oxford or Cambridge, and public schools. **2** the head of a chapter in a cathedral. **3** short for **PROVOST MARSHAL**. **4** Scottish term for **MAYOR**. —**pro·vost·ship** /-,SHip/ *n.*

pro·vost mar·shal ▸*n.* the head of military police in camp or on active service.

prow /prou/ ▸*n.* the portion of a ship's bow above water. ■ the pointed or projecting front part of something such as a car or building.

prow·ess /'prou-əs; 'prōəs/ ▸*n.* **1** skill or expertise in a particular activity or field: *his prowess as a fisherman.* **2** bravery in battle.

prowl /proul/ ▸*v.* [*tr.*] (of a person or animal) move around (a place) in search of or as if in search of prey: *black bears prowl the canyons.* ■ [*intr.*] (of a person or animal) move stealthily or restlessly as or like a hunter: *committee members prowling around the offices at night with flashlights.*
▸*n.* an act of prowling. —**prowl·er** *n.*
▸ □ **on the prowl** (of a person or animal) moving around in search or as if in search of prey.

prox·i·mal /'präksəməl/ ▸*adj.* *Anat.* situated nearer to the center of the body or the point of attachment. The opposite of **DISTAL**. —**prox·i·mal·ly** *adv.*

prox·im·i·ty /präk'simətē/ ▸*n.* nearness in space, time, or relationship.

prox·y /'präksē/ ▸*n.* (pl. **prox·ies**) **1** the authority to represent someone else, esp. in voting: *they may register to vote* **by proxy**. ■ a person authorized to act on behalf of another. ■ a document authorizing a person to vote on another's behalf. **2** a figure that can be used to represent the value of something in a calculation: *the use of a U.S. wealth measure as a proxy for the true worldwide measure.*

prude /prŌŌd/ ▸*n.* a person who is or claims to be easily shocked by matters relating to sex or nudity. ▷early 18th cent.: from French, back-formation from *prudefemme*, feminine of *prud'homme* 'good man and true,' from *prou* 'worthy.' —**prud·er·y** /'prŌŌdərē/ *n.* —**prud·ish** *adj.* —**prud·ish·ly** *adv.* —**prud·ish·ness** *n.*

pru·dent /'prŌŌdnt/ ▸*adj.* acting with or showing care and thought for the future: *a prudent money manager.* —**pru·dence** *n.* —**pru·dent·ly** *adv.*

pru·den·tial /prŌŌ'denCHəl/ ▸*adj.* involving or showing care and forethought, typically in business. —**pru·den·tial·ly** *adv.*

prune[1] /prŌŌn/ ▸*n.* a plum preserved by drying, having a black, wrinkled appearance. ■ *inf.* an unpleasant or disagreeable person.

prune[2] ▸*v.* [*tr.*] trim (a tree, shrub, or bush) by cutting away dead or overgrown branches or stems, esp. to increase fruitfulness and growth. ■ cut away (a branch or stem) in this way: *prune back the branches.* ■ reduce the extent of (something) by removing superfluous or unwanted parts: *reduction achieved by pruning costs.* ■ remove (superfluous or unwanted parts) from something. —**prun·er** *n.*

pru·ri·ent /'prŌŌrēənt/ ▸*adj.* having or encouraging an excessive interest in sexual matters. —**pru·ri·ence** *n.* —**pru·ri·en·cy** *n.* —**pru·ri·ent·ly** *adv.*

pry[1] /prī/ ▸*v.* (**pries**, **pried**) [*intr.*] inquire too closely into a person's private affairs: *I'm sick of you* **prying into** *my personal life* | [as *adj.*] (**prying**) *no place where she could escape from the prying eyes.* —**pry·ing·ly** *adv.*

pry[2] ▸*v.* (**pries**, **pried**) [*tr.*] use force in order to move or open (something) or to separate (something) from something else: *using a screwdriver, he pried open the window.* ■ (**pry something out of/from**) obtain something from (someone) with effort or difficulty.

PS ▸*abbr.* ■ passenger steamer. ■ permanent secretary. ■ police sergeant. ■ postscript. ■ private secretary. ■ Privy Seal. ■ *Theater* prompt side. ■ Public School.

Ps. (pl. **Pss.**) ▸*abbr.* Bible Psalm or Psalms.

psalm /sä(l)m/ (also **Psalm**) ▸*n.* a sacred song or hymn, in particular any of those contained in the biblical Book of Psalms and used in Christian and Jewish worship. ■ (**the Psalms**) a book of the Bible comprising a collection of religious verses, sung or recited in both Jewish and Christian worship. —**psalm·ic** /'sä(l)mik/ *adj.*

psalm·ist /'sä(l)mist/ ▸*n.* the author or composer of a psalm, esp. any of the biblical Psalms.

psal·ter /'sôltər/ ▸*n.* (**the psalter** or **the Psalter**) the Book of Psalms. ■ a copy of the biblical Psalms, esp. for liturgical use.

psal·ter·y /'sôltərē/ ▸*n.* (pl. **-ter·ies**) an ancient and medieval musical instrument like a dulcimer but played by plucking the strings with the fingers or a plectrum.

PSAT ▸*abbr.* Preliminary Scholastic Aptitude Test.

pseud /sōōd/ *inf.* ▸*adj.* intellectually or socially pretentious.
▸*n.* a pretentious person; a poseur.

pseud. ▸*abbr.* pseudonym.

pseu·do /'sōōdō/ ▸*adj.* not genuine; sham.

pseu·do·nym /'sōōdn-im/ ▸*n.* a fictitious name, esp. one used by an author. —**pseu·do·nym·i·ty** /,sōōdn'imətē/ *n.*

pseu·don·y·mous /sōō'dänəməs/ ▸*adj.* writing or written under a false name. —**pseu·don·y·mous·ly** *adv.*

psf ▸*abbr.* pounds per square foot.

psi /(p)sī/ ▸*n.* **1** the twenty-third letter of the Greek alphabet (Ψ, ψ), transliterated as 'ps.' **2** supposed parapsychological or psychic faculties or phenomena.

p.s.i. ▸*abbr.* pounds per square inch.

psit·ta·co·sis /,sitə'kōsəs/ ▸*n.* a contagious disease of birds, caused by chlamydiae and transmissible (esp. from parrots) to human beings as a form of pneumonia.

pso·ri·a·sis /sə'rīəsəs/ ▸*n. Med.* a skin disease marked by red, itchy, scaly patches. ▷late 17th cent.: modern Latin, from Greek *psōriasis*, from *psōrian* 'have an itch,' from *psōra* 'itch.' —**pso·ri·at·ic** /,sôrē'atik/ *adj.*

PST ▸*abbr.* Pacific Standard Time (see **PACIFIC TIME**).

psych /sīk/ (also **psyche**) ▸*v.* **1** [*tr.*] *inf.* mentally prepare (someone) for a testing task or occasion: *we had to psych ourselves up for the race.* **2** (usu. **psyche**) [*intr.*] *Bridge* make a psychic bid.
▸*phrasal v.* □ **psych someone out** *inf.* intimidate an opponent or rival by appearing confident or aggressive.
▸*n. inf.* short for **PSYCHOLOGY**. ■

psy·che[1] /'sīkē/ ▸*n.* the human soul, mind, or spirit.

psy·che[2] /sīk/ ▸*v., n.,* & *adj.* variant spelling of **PSYCH**.

psych·e·de·lia /,sīkə'dēlyə/ ▸*n.* music, culture, or art based on the experiences produced by psychedelic drugs.

psy·che·del·ic /,sīkə'delik/ ▸*adj.* relating to or denoting drugs (esp. LSD) that produce hallucinations and apparent expansion of consciousness. ■ relating to or denoting a style of rock music originating in the mid-1960s, characterized by musical experimentation and drug-related lyrics. ■ denoting or having an intense, vivid color or a swirling abstract pattern: *a psychedelic T-shirt.*
▸*n.* a psychedelic drug. —**psy·che·del·i·cal·ly** /-ik(ə)lē/ *adv.*

psy·chi·a·try /sə'kīətrē; sī-/ ▸*n.* the study and treatment of mental illness, emotional disturbance, and abnormal behavior. —**psy·chi·at·ric** /-sīkē'atrik/ *adj.* —**psy·chi·a·trist** *n.*

psy·chic /'sīkik/ ▸*adj.* **1** relating to or denoting faculties or phenomena that are apparently inexplicable by natural laws, esp. involving telepathy or clairvoyance. ■ (of a person) appearing or considered to have powers of telepathy or clairvoyance. **2** of or relating to the soul or mind: *his psychic pain.* **3** *Bridge* denoting a bid that deliberately misrepresents the bidder's hand, in order to mislead the opponents.
▸*n.* a person considered or claiming to have psychic powers; a medium. ■ (**psychics**) [treated as *sing.* or *pl.*] the study of psychic phenomena. —**psy·chi·cal** /'sīkikəl/ *adj.* —**psy·chi·cal·ly** /'sīkik(ə)lē/ *adv.* —**psy·chism** /'sī,kizəm/ *n.*

psy·cho /'sīkō/ *inf.* ▸*n.* (*pl.* **-chos**) a psychopath.
▸*adj.* psychopathic.

psy·cho·ac·tive /,sīkō'aktiv/ ▸*adj.* (chiefly of a drug) affecting the mind.

psy·cho·a·nal·y·sis /,sīkōə'naləsəs/ ▸*n.* a system of psychological theory and therapy that aims to treat mental disorders by investigating the interaction of conscious and unconscious elements in the mind and bringing repressed fears and conflicts into the conscious mind. —**psy·cho·an·a·lyze** /,sīkō'anl,īz/ (*Brit.* **psy·cho·an·a·lyse**) *v.* —**psy·cho·an·a·lyt·ic** /,sīkō,anl'itik/ *adj.* —**psy·cho·an·a·lyt·i·cal** /,sīkō,anl'itikəl/ *adj.* —**psy·cho·an·a·lyt·i·cal·ly** /,sīkō,anl'itik(ə)lē/ *adv.*

psy·cho·an·a·lyst /,sīkō'anl-əst/ ▸*n.* a person who practices psychoanalysis.

psy·cho·bab·ble /'sīkō,babəl/ ▸*n. inf., derog.* jargon used in popular psychology.

psy·cho·dra·ma /sīkō'drämə; -'dramə/ ▸*n.* **1** a form of psychotherapy in which patients act out events from their past. **2** a play, movie, or novel in which psychological elements are the main interest. ■ the genre to which such works belong. —**psy·cho·dra·mat·ic** /-drə'matik/ *adj.*

psy·cho·ki·ne·sis /,sīkōkə'nēsis/ ▸*n.* the supposed ability to move objects by mental effort alone. —**psy·cho·ki·net·ic** /-'netik/ *adj.*

psy·cho·lin·guis·tics /,sīkōliNG'gwistiks/ ▸*pl. n.* [treated as *sing.*] the study of the relationships between linguistic behavior and

psychological processes, including the process of language acquisition. —**psy·cho·lin·guist** /-'liNGgwist/ *n.* —**psy·cho·lin·guis·tic** *adj.*

psy·cho·log·i·cal /,sīkə'läjəkəl/ ▸*adj.* of, affecting, or arising in the mind; related to the mental and emotional state of a person. ■ of or relating to psychology: *psychological research.* ■ (of an ailment or problem) having a mental rather than a physical cause. —**psy·cho·log·i·cal·ly** /-ik(ə)lē/ *adv.*

psy·cho·log·i·cal war·fare ▸*n.* actions intended to reduce an opponent's morale.

psy·chol·o·gy /sī'käləjē/ ▸*n.* the scientific study of the human mind and its functions, esp. those affecting behavior in a given context. ■ the mental characteristics or attitude of a person or group: *the psychology of Americans in the 1920s.* ■ the mental and emotional factors governing a situation or activity: *the psychology of interpersonal relationships.* —**psy·chol·o·gist** *n.* —**psy·chol·o·gize** /-,jīz/ *v.*

psy·cho·met·rics /,sīkə'metriks/ ▸*pl. n.* [treated as *sing.*] the science of measuring mental capacities and processes. —**psy·chom·e·tri·cian** /-mə'trishən/ *n.*

psy·chom·e·try /sī'kämətrē/ ▸*n.* **1** the supposed ability to discover facts about an event or person by touching inanimate objects associated with them. **2** another term for **PSYCHOMETRICS**. —**psy·chom·e·trist** /-trist/ *n.*

psy·cho·path /'sīkə,paTH/ ▸*n.* a person suffering from chronic mental disorder with abnormal or violent social behavior. —**psy·cho·path·ic** /,sīkə'paTHik/ *adj.* —**psy·cho·path·i·cal·ly** /,sīkə'paTHik(ə)lē/ *adv.*

psy·cho·pa·thol·o·gy /,sīkōpə'THäləjē; -paTH'äl-/ ▸*n.* the scientific study of mental disorders. ■ features of people's mental health considered collectively: *ageism, family discord and psychopathology all play their part in abuse.* ■ mental or behavioral disorder. —**psy·cho·path·o·log·i·cal** /-paTHō'läjikəl/ *adj.* —**psy·cho·pa·thol·o·gist** /-THäləjist/ *n.*

psy·chop·a·thy /sī'käpəTHē/ ▸*n.* mental illness or disorder.

psy·cho·sex·u·al /,sīkō'seksHōōəl/ ▸*adj.* of or involving the psychological aspects of the sexual impulse. —**psy·cho·sex·u·al·ly** *adv.*

psy·cho·sis /sī'kōsəs/ ▸*n.* (*pl.* **-ses** /-,sēz/) a severe mental disorder in which thought and emotions are so impaired that contact is lost with external reality.

psy·cho·so·mat·ic /,sīkōsə'matik/ ▸*adj.* (of a physical illness or other condition) caused or aggravated by a mental factor such as internal conflict or stress. ■ of or relating to the interaction of mind and body. —**psy·cho·so·mat·i·cal·ly** /-ik(ə)lē/ *adv.*

psy·cho·ther·a·py /,sīkō'THerəpē/ ▸*n.* the treatment of mental disorder by psychological rather than medical means. —**psy·cho·ther·a·peu·tic** /-,THerə'pyōōtik/ *adj.* —**psy·cho·ther·a·pist** /-'THerəpist/ *n.*

psy·chot·ic /sī'kätik/ ▸*adj.* of, denoting, or suffering from a psychosis.
▸*n.* a person suffering from a psychosis. —**psy·chot·i·cal·ly** /-ik(ə)lē/ *adv.*

psy·cho·tro·pic /,sīkə'trōpik; -'träpik/ ▸*adj.* relating to or denoting drugs that affect a person's mental state.
▸*n.* a drug of this kind.

PT ▸*abbr.* ■ Pacific Time. ■ physical therapy. ■ physical training. ■ postal telegraph. ■ post town. ■ *Brit.* pupil teacher.

Pt ▸*symb.* the chemical element platinum.

p.t. ▸*abbr.* ■ past tense. ■ pro tempore.

PTA ▸*abbr.* parent–teacher association.

ptar·mi·gan /'tärməgən/ ▸*n.* (*pl.* same or **ptarmigans**) a northern grouse, esp. the **rock ptarmigan** (*Lagopus mutus*) of Eurasia and North America, with splumage that typically changes to white in winter.

PT boat ▸*n.* a motorboat equipped with torpedoes and used by the military, esp. during World War II.

pter·o·dac·tyl /,terə'daktəl/ ▸*n.* a pterosaur (*Pterodactylus* and other genera, family Pterodactylidae) of the late Jurassic period, with a long slender head and neck and a very short tail. ■ (in general use) any pterosaur.

pter·o·saur /'terə,sôr/ ▸*n.* an extinct warm-blooded flying reptile (order Pterosauria) of the Jurassic and Cretaceous periods, with membranous wings supported by a greatly lengthened fourth finger, and probably covered with fur. Its several families include the pterodactyls.

PTO ▸*abbr.* ■ please turn over (written at the foot of a page to indicate that the text continues on the reverse). ■ (also **pto**) (in a tractor or other vehicle) power takeoff. ■ Parent-Teacher Organization.

Ptol·e·ma·ic /,tälə'mā-ik/ ▸*adj.* **1** of or relating to the Greek astronomer Ptolemy or his theories. **2** of or relating to the Ptolemies of Egypt.

Pronunciation Key ə *ago,* up; ər *over, fur;* a *hat;* ā *ate;* ä *car;* CH *chin;* e *let;* ē *see;* e(ə)r *air;* i *fit;* ī *by;* i(ə)r *ear;* NG *sing;* ō *go;* ô *law, for;* oi *toy;* ŏŏ *good;* ōō *goo;* ou *out;* SH *she;* TH *thin;* <u>TH</u> *then;* (h)w *why;* ZH *vision*

Ptol·e·ma·ic sys·tem (also **Ptolemaic theory**) ▶*n. hist. Astron.* the theory that the earth is the stationary center of the universe, with the planets moving in epicyclic orbits within surrounding concentric spheres. Compare with COPERNICAN SYSTEM.

pto·maine /'tō,mān; tō'mān/ ▶*n. dated Chem.* any of a group of amine compounds of unpleasant taste and odor formed in putrefying animal and vegetable matter and formerly thought to cause food poisoning.

Pu ▶*symb.* the chemical element plutonium.

pub /pəb/ *Brit.* ▶*n.* a tavern or bar. ■ *Austral.* a hotel.
▶*v.* [*intr.*] [usu. as *n.*] (**pubbing**) *inf.* spend time in pubs.

pub. ▶*abbr.* ■ publication(s). ■ published. ■ publisher.

pu·ber·ty /'pyoōbərtē/ ▶*n.* the period during which adolescents reach sexual maturity and become capable of reproduction. —**pu·ber·tal** /-bərtl/ *adj.*

pu·bes /'pyoōbēz/ ▶*n.* **1** (*pl.* same) the lower part of the abdomen at the front of the pelvis, covered with hair from puberty. **2** plural form of PUBIS.

pu·bes·cence /pyoō'besəns/ ▶*n. Bot. & Zool.* soft down or fine short hairs on the leaves and stems of plants or on various parts of animals, esp. insects. —**pu·bes·cent** *adj.*

pu·bic /'pyoōbik/ ▶*adj.* of or relating to the pubes or pubis: *pubic hair.*

pu·bis /'pyoōbəs/ ▶*n.* (*pl.* **-bes** /-bēz/) either of a pair of bones forming the two sides of the pelvis.

pub·lic /'pəblik/ ▶*adj.* **1** of or concerning the people as a whole: *public concern.* ■ open to or shared by all the people of an area or country: *a public library.* ■ of or provided by the government rather than an independent, commercial company: *public spending.* ■ of or involved in the affairs of the community, esp. in government: *his public career.* ■ known to many people; famous: *a public figure.* **2** done, perceived, or existing in open view: *he wanted a public apology.* **3** *Brit.* of, for, or acting for a university: *public examination results.*
▶*n.* (**the public**) [treated as *sing.* or *pl.*] ordinary people in general; the community: *the library is open to the public.* ■ a section of the community having a particular interest or connection: *the reading public.* ■ (**one's public**) the people who watch or are interested in an artist, writer, or performer. ▷late Middle English: from Old French, from Latin *publicus*, blend of *poplicus* 'of the people' (from *populus* 'people') and *pubes* 'adult.' —**pub·lic·ly** *adv.*
▶ □ **go public 1** become a public company. **2** reveal details about a previously private concern. □ **in public** in view of other people; when others are present. □ **the public eye** the state of being known or of interest to people in general, esp. through the media: *the pressures of being constantly in the public eye.*

pub·lic-ad·dress sys·tem ▶*n.* a system of microphones, amplifiers, and loudspeakers used to amplify speech or music in a large building or at an outdoor gathering.

pub·li·can /'pəblikən/ ▶*n.* **1** *Brit.* a person who owns or manages a pub. **2** (in ancient Roman and biblical times) a collector of taxes.

pub·li·ca·tion /,pəbli'kāSHən/ ▶*n.* the preparation and issuing of a book, journal, piece of music, or other work for public sale. ■ a book, journal, etc. issued for public sale: *scientific publications.* ■ the action of making something generally known.

pub·lic de·fend·er ▶*n. Law* a lawyer employed at public expense in a criminal trial to represent a defendant who is unable to afford legal assistance.

pub·lic en·e·my ▶*n.* a notorious wanted criminal. ■ *fig.* a person or thing regarded as the greatest threat to a group or community: *he identified inflation as public enemy number one.*

pub·li·cist /'pəbləsist/ ▶*n.* **1** a person responsible for publicizing a product, person, or company. **2** *dated* a journalist, esp. one concerned with current affairs. —**pub·li·cis·tic** /,pəblə'sistik/ *adj.*

pub·lic·i·ty /pə'blisətē/ ▶*n.* the notice or attention given to someone or something by the media. ■ public exposure; notoriety. ■ the giving out of information about a product, person, or company for advertising or promotional purposes: *head of publicity and marketing* | [as *adj.*] *publicity photographs.* ■ material or information used for such a purpose.

pub·lic·i·ty a·gent ▶*n.* another term for PUBLICIST (sense 1).

pub·li·cize /'pəblə,sīz/ ▶*v.* [*tr.*] make (something) widely known: *to publicize human rights abuses.* ■ give out publicity about (a product, person, or company) for advertising or promotional purposes.

pub·lic nui·sance ▶*n.* an act, condition, or thing that is illegal because it interferes with the rights of the public generally. ■ *inf.* an obnoxious or dangerous person or group of people.

pub·lic o·pin·ion ▶*n.* views prevalent among the general public.

pub·lic re·la·tions ▶*pl. n.* [also treated as *sing.*] the professional maintenance of a favorable public image by a company or other organization or a famous person. ■ the state of the relationship between the public and a company or other organization or a famous person.

pub·lic school ▶*n.* **1** (chiefly in North America) a school supported by public funds. **2** (in the UK) a private for-fee secondary school.

pub·lic sec·tor ▶*n.* the part of an economy that is controlled by the government.

pub·lic serv·ant ▶*n.* a government official.

pub·lic u·til·i·ty ▶*n.* an organization supplying a community with electricity, gas, water, or sewerage.

pub·lish /'pəbliSH/ ▶*v.* [*tr.*] **1** (of an author or company) prepare and issue (a book, journal, piece of music, or other work) for public sale: *we publish reference books* | [*intr.*] *the pressures on researchers to publish.* ■ print (something) in a book or journal so as to make it generally known. ■ [usu. as *adj.*] (**published**) prepare and issue the works of (a particular writer). ■ formally announce or read (an edict or marriage banns). **2** *Law* communicate (a libel) to a third party. —**pub·lish·a·ble** *adj.*

pub·lish·er /'pəbliSHər/ ▶*n.* (also **publishers**) a person or company that prepares and issues books, journals, music, or other works for sale. ■ a newspaper proprietor.

puce /pyoōs/ ▶*adj.* of a dark red or purple-brown color.
▶*n.* a dark red or purple-brown color.

puck[1] /pək/ ▶*n.* a mischievous or evil sprite. —**puck·ish** *adj.* —**puck·like** /-,līk/ *adj.*

puck[2] /pək/ ▶*n.* **1** a black disk made of hard rubber, the focus of play in ice hockey. **2** *Comput.* an input device similar to a mouse that is dragged across a sensitive surface, which notes the puck's position to move the cursor on the screen.

puck·er /'pəkər/ ▶*v.* [*intr.*] (esp. of a person's face or a facial feature) tightly gather or contract into wrinkles or small folds: *her brows puckered in a frown.* ■ [*tr.*] cause to do this: *the baby stirred,* **puckering up** *its tiny face.*
▶*n.* a tightly gathered wrinkle or small fold, esp. on a person's face: *a pucker between his eyebrows.* —**puck·er·y** /'pəkərē/ *adj.*
▶ □ **pucker up** contract one's lips as in preparation for a kiss.

pud·ding /'poōdiNG/ ▶*n.* **1** a dessert with a creamy consistency. ■ *chiefly Brit.* any dessert. ■ *chiefly Brit.* the dessert course of a meal: *what's for pudding?* **2** a sweet or savory steamed dish made with flour: *Yorkshire pudding.* ■ the intestines of a pig or sheep stuffed with oatmeal, spices, and meat and boiled. ■ *inf.* a fat, dumpy, or stupid person. —**pud·ding·y** *adj.*

pud·dle /'pədl/ ▶*n.* **1** a small pool of liquid, esp. of rainwater on the ground: *fig. a little puddle of light.* **2** clay and sand mixed with water and used as a watertight covering for embankments.
▶*v.* [*tr.*] wet or cover (a surface) with water, esp. rainwater. ■ [*intr.*] (of liquid) form a small pool. —**pud·dly** /'pədlē; 'pədl-ē/ *adj.*

pu·den·dum /pyoō'dendəm/ ▶*n.* (*pl.* **-den·da** /-'dendə/) (often **pudenda**) a person's external genitals, esp. a woman's. —**pu·den·dal** /-'dendəl/ *adj.* —**pu·dic** /'pyoōdik/ *adj.*

pudg·y /'pəjē/ ▶*adj.* (**pudg·i·er, pudg·i·est**) *inf.* (of a person or part of their body) slightly fat: *his pudgy fingers.* —**pudge** *n.* —**pudg·i·ly** /'pəjəlē/ *adv.* —**pudg·i·ness** *n.*

pueb·lo /'pweblō; pōō'eb-/ ▶*n.* (*pl.* **-los**) **1** an American Indian settlement of the southwestern U.S., esp. one consisting of multistoried adobe houses built by the Pueblo people. ■ (in Spanish-speaking regions) a town or village. **2** (**Pueblo**) (*pl.* same or **-los**) a member of any of various American Indian peoples, including the Hopi, occupying pueblo settlements chiefly in New Mexico and Arizona.
▶*adj.* (**Pueblo**) of, relating to, or denoting the Pueblos or their culture.

pu·er·ile /'pyoō(ə)rəl; 'pyoōr,īl/ ▶*adj.* childishly silly and trivial. —**pu·er·ile·ly** *adv.* —**pu·er·il·i·ty** /pyoō(ə)'rilətē/ *n.* (*pl.* **-ties**)

puff /pəf/ ▶*n.* **1** a short, explosive burst of breath or wind. ■ the sound of air or vapor escaping suddenly: *the whistle and puff of steam.* ■ a small quantity of vapor or smoke, emitted in one blast: *the fire breathed out a puff of blue smoke.* ■ an act of drawing quickly on a pipe, cigarette, or cigar. **2** a light pastry case, typically one made of puff pastry, containing a sweet or savory filling: *a cream puff.* ■ a gathered mass of material in a dress or other garment. ■ a rolled protuberant mass of hair. ■ a powder puff. ■ a soft quilt. **3** *inf.* a review of a work of art, book, or theatrical production, esp. an excessively complimentary one.
▶*v.* **1** [*intr.*] breathe in repeated short gasps. ■ (of a person, engine, etc.) move with short, noisy breaths or bursts of air or steam: *the train came*

puffing in. ■ smoke a pipe, cigarette, or cigar: *he **puffed on** his pipe contentedly.* ■ [tr.] blow (dust, smoke, or a light object) in a specified direction with a quick breath or blast of air. ■ move through the air in short bursts: *his breath puffed out like white smoke.* **2** (**puff something out/up** or **puff out/up**) cause to swell or become swollen: [tr.] *he puffed his chest out* | [intr.] *when he was in a temper, his cheeks puffed up.* ■ [tr.] (usu. **be puffed up**) fig. cause to become conceited. **3** [tr.] advertise with exaggerated or false praise.

puff ad·der ▶n. a large, sluggish, mainly nocturnal African viper (*Bitis arietans*) that inflates the upper part of its body and hisses loudly in threat.

puff·ball /ˈpəf,bôl/ ▶n. **1** a fungus (*Lycoperdon* and other genera, family Lycoperdaceae) that produces a spherical or pear-shaped fruiting body that ruptures when ripe to release a cloud of spores. **2** anything round and fluffy, such as a powder puff.

puff·er /ˈpəfər/ ▶n. **1** inf. a person or thing that puffs, in particular, a person who smokes. **2** short for PUFFERFISH.

puff·er·fish /ˈpəfər,fiSH/ (also **puffer fish**) ▶n. (pl. same or **-fishes**) a stout-bodied marine or freshwater fish (family Tetraodontidae) that typically has spiny skin and inflates itself like a balloon when threatened. It is sometimes used as food, but some parts are highly toxic.

puf·fin /ˈpəfən/ ▶n. a hole-nesting auk (genera *Fratercula* and *Lunda*) of northern and Arctic waters, with a large head and a massive brightly colored triangular bill, in particular the **Atlantic puffin** (*F. arctica*).

puff·y /ˈpəfē/ ▶adj. (**puff·i·er**, **puff·i·est**) **1** (esp. of part of the body) unusually swollen and soft. ■ soft, rounded, and light: *small puffy clouds.* ■ (of a garment or part of a garment) padded or gathered to give a rounded shape. ■ fig. (of a piece of writing) overembellished and pompous. **2** (of wind or breath) coming in short bursts. —**puff·i·ly** /ˈpəfəlē/ adv. —**puff·i·ness** n.

pug¹ /pəg/ ▶n. (also **pug dog**) a dog of a dwarf breed like a bulldog with a broad flat nose and deeply wrinkled face. —**pug·gish** adj. —**pug·gy** /ˈpəgē/ adj.

pug² ▶n. loam or clay mixed and worked into a soft, plastic condition without air pockets for making bricks or pottery.
▶v. (**pugged**, **pug·ging**) [tr.] **1** prepare (clay) in this way, typically in a machine with rotating blades. **2** [usu. as n.] (**pugging**) pack (a space, typically the space under a floor) with pug, sawdust, or other material in order to deaden sound.

pug³ ▶n. inf. a boxer.

pug⁴ ▶n. the footprint of an animal: [as adj.] *I saw the pug marks of the tigress in the soft earth.*
▶v. (**pugged**, **pug·ging**) [tr.] track (an animal) by its footprints.

pu·gi·list /ˈpyoōjəlist/ ▶n. dated or humorous a boxer, esp. a professional one. —**pu·gi·lism** /-,lizəm/ n. —**pu·gi·lis·tic** /,pyoōjəˈlistik/ adj.

pug·na·cious /pəgˈnāSHəs/ ▶adj. eager or quick to argue, quarrel, or fight. ■ having the appearance of a willing fighter: *the set of her pugnacious jaw.* —**pug·na·cious·ly** adv. —**pug·nac·i·ty** /,pəgˈnasətē/ n.

pug nose ▶n. a short nose with an upturned tip. —**pug-nosed** adj.

pu·is·sant /ˈpwisənt; ˈpwēsənt; ˈpyoōəsənt/ ▶adj. archaic or poetic/lit. having great power or influence. —**pu·is·sance** n. —**pu·is·sant·ly** adv.

puke /pyook/ inf. ▶v. vomit: [intr.] *I had eaten to the point of puking* | [tr.] *he puked up his pizza.*
▶n. vomit. —**puk·ey** adj.

pul·chri·tude /ˈpəlkrə,t(y)oōd/ ▶n. poetic/lit. beauty. —**pul·chri·tu·di·nous** /,pəlkrəˈt(y)oōdn-əs/ adj.

pule /pyoōl/ ▶v. [intr.] poetic/lit. cry querulously or weakly.

Pu·litz·er Prize ▶n. an award for an achievement in American journalism, literature, or music. There are thirteen made each year.

pull /pool/ ▶v. [tr.] **1** exert force on (someone or something), typically by taking hold of them, in order to move or try to move them toward oneself or the origin of the force: *he pulled the car door handle and began to get out* | [intr.] *the little boy **pulled at** her skirt.* ■ (of an animal or vehicle) be attached to the front and be the source of forward movement of (a vehicle): *the carriage was pulled by four horses.* ■ [tr.] take hold of and exert force on (something) so as to move it from a specified position or in a specified direction: *she pulled a handkerchief out of her pocket.* ■ inf. bring out (a weapon) to attack or threaten someone. ■ [intr.] (**pull at/on**) inhale deeply while smoking (a pipe or cigar). ■ damage (a muscle, ligament, etc.) by abnormal strain. ■ print (a proof). ■ Comput. retrieve (an item of data) from the top of a stack. **2** [intr.] (of a vehicle or person) move steadily in a specified direction or to reach a specified point: *the bus was about to pull away.* ■ (**pull oneself**) move in a specified direction with effort, esp. by taking hold of something and exerting force on it: *he pulled himself into the saddle.* ■ [intr.] move one's

body in a specified direction, esp. against resistance: *she tried to pull away from him.* ■ [intr.] (of an engine) exert propulsive force; deliver power. ■ [intr.] work oars to cause a boat to move: *he pulled at the oars, and the boat moved swiftly.* **3** cause (someone) to patronize, buy, or show interest in something; attract: *tourist attractions that **pull in** millions of foreign visitors.* ■ influence in favor of a particular course of action: *they are pulled in incompatible directions by external factors.* ■ inf. carry out or achieve (something requiring skill, luck, or planning): *the magazine pulled its trick of producing the right issue at the right time.* **4** inf. cancel or withdraw (an entertainment or advertisement). ■ withdraw (a player) from a game. ■ check the speed of (a horse), esp. so as to make it lose a race. **5** chiefly Baseball Golf strike (a ball) in the direction of one's follow-through so that it travels to the left (or, with a left-handed player, to the right. **6** [intr.] Football (of a lineman) withdraw from position and cross parallel to and behind the line of scrimmage to block opposing players for a runner.
▶phrasal v. □ **pull back** (or **pull someone/something back**) retreat or cause troops to retreat from an area. ■ (**pull back**) withdraw from an undertaking. □ **pull something down 1** demolish a building. **2** inf. earn a sum of money: *he was pulling down sixty grand.* □ **pull in 1** (of a vehicle or its driver) move to the side of or off the road. **2** (of a bus or train) arrive to take passengers. □ **pull someone/something in 1** succeed in securing or obtaining something: *the Reform Party pulled in 10% of the vote.* ■ inf. earn a sum of money: *you could pull in $100,000.* **2** inf. arrest someone. **3** use reins to check a horse. □ **pull something off** inf. succeed in achieving or winning something difficult. □ **pull out 1** withdraw from an undertaking. ■ retreat or cause to retreat from an area: *the army pulled out, leaving the city in ruins* | (**pull someone out**) *the CIA had pulled its operatives out of Tripoli.* **2** (of a bus or train) leave with its passengers. **3** (of a vehicle or its driver) move out from the side of the road, or from its normal position in order to pass: *a police car pulled out in front of him.* □ **pull over** (of a vehicle or its driver) move to the side of or off the road. □ **pull someone over** cause a driver to move to the side of the road to be charged for a traffic offense. □ **pull through** (or **pull someone/something through**) get through or enable someone or something to get through an illness or other dangerous or difficult situation. □ **pull up 1** (of a vehicle or its driver) come to a halt. **2** increase the altitude of an aircraft.
▶n. **1** an act of taking hold of something and exerting force to draw it toward one. ■ a handle to hold while performing such an action. ■ a deep draft of a drink. ■ an act of sucking at a cigar or pipe. ■ an injury to a muscle or ligament caused by abnormal strain. ■ a printer's proof. **2** a force drawing someone or something in a particular direction: *the pull of the water.* ■ a powerful influence or compulsion: *the pull of her hometown was a strong one.* ■ something exerting an influence or attraction: *one of the pulls of urban life is the opportunity of finding work.* ■ the condition of being able to exercise influence: *the political pull of the mayor's office.* —**pull·er** n.
▶ □ **like pulling teeth** inf. extremely difficult to do. □ **pull someone's leg** deceive someone playfully. □ **pull the plug 1** inf. prevent something from happening or continuing: *the company pulled the plug on the deal.* **2** inf. remove (a patient) from life support. □ **pull (one's) punches** be less forceful, severe, or violent than one could be: *a smooth-tongued critic who doesn't pull his punches.* □ **pull strings** make use of one's influence and contacts to gain an advantage unofficially or unfairly. □ **pull the strings** be in control of events or of other people's actions. □ **pull together** cooperate in a task or undertaking. □ **pull oneself together** recover control of one's emotions. □ **pull one's weight** do one's fair share of work.

pull-down ▶adj. designed to be worked or made operable by being pulled down: *pull-down beds.* ■ Comput. (of a menu) appearing below a menu title only while selected.
▶n. Comput. a pull-down menu.

pul·let /ˈpoolət/ ▶n. a young hen, esp. one less than one year old.

pul·ley /ˈpoolē/ ▶n. (pl. **-leys**) (also **pulley wheel**) a wheel with a grooved rim around which a cord passes. It acts to change the direction of a force applied to the cord and is chiefly used (typically in combination) to raise heavy weights. ■ (on a bicycle) a wheel with a toothed rim

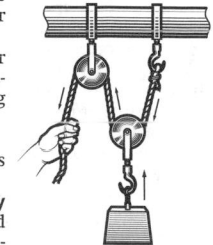

pulley

around which the chain passes. ■ a wheel or drum fixed on a shaft and turned by a belt, used esp. to increase speed or power.
▸ *v.* (**-leys, -leyed**) [*tr.*] hoist with a pulley.

Pull·man ▸ *n.* (*pl.* **-mans**) [usu. as *adj.*] a railroad car affording special comfort, esp. one with sleeping berths: *a train of Pullman cars.* ■ a train consisting of such cars. ■ (**pullman**) a large suitcase designed to fit under the seat in a Pullman car.

pull·o·ver /'pŏŏl,ōvər/ ▸ *n.* a garment, esp. a sweater or jacket, put on over the head and covering the top half of the body.
▸ *adj.* (of a sweater, jacket, or shirt) designed to be put on by pulling over the head.

pull-up ▸ *n.* **1** an exercise involving raising oneself with one's arms by pulling up against a horizontal bar fixed above one's head. **2** an act of pulling up; a sudden stop.

pul·mo·nar·y /'pŏŏlmə,nerē; 'pəl-/ ▸ *adj.* of or relating to the lungs.

pul·mon·ic /pŏŏl'mänik; pəl-/ ▸ *adj.* another term for PULMONARY.

pulp /pəlp/ ▸ *n.* a soft, wet, shapeless mass of material: *boiling with soda will reduce your peas to pulp.* ■ the soft fleshy part of a fruit. ■ a soft wet mass of fibers derived from rags or wood, used in papermaking. ■ vascular tissue filling the interior cavity and root canals of a tooth. ■ *Mining* pulverized ore mixed with water. ■ [usu. as *adj.*] *fig.* popular or sensational writing that is generally regarded as being of poor quality: *pulp fiction.*
▸ *v.* [*tr.*] crush into a soft, shapeless mass. —**pulp·er** *n.* —**pulp·i·ness** *n.* —**pulp·y** *adj.*
▸ □ **beat** (or **smash**) **someone to a pulp** beat someone severely.

pul·pit /'pŏŏl,pit; 'pəl-; -pət/ ▸ *n.* a raised platform or lectern in a church or chapel from which the preacher delivers a sermon. ■ (**the pulpit**) religious teaching as expressed in sermons; preachers collectively. ■ a raised platform in the bow of a fishing boat or whaler. ■ a guard rail enclosing a small area at the bow of a yacht. ▷Middle English: from Latin *pulpitum* 'scaffold, platform,' in medieval Latin 'pulpit.'

pulp·wood /'pəlp,wŏŏd/ ▸ *n.* wood suitable for making into pulp for making paper.

pul·sar /'pəl,sär/ ▸ *n. Astron.* a celestial object, thought to be a rapidly rotating neutron star, that emits regular pulses of radio waves and other electromagnetic radiation at rates of up to one thousand pulses per second.

pul·sate /'pəl,sāt/ ▸ *v.* [*intr.*] expand and contract with strong regular movements: *blood vessels throb and pulsate.* ■ produce a regular throbbing sensation or sound. —**pul·sa·tion** /,pəl'sāSHən/ *n.* —**pul·sa·tor** /-,sātər/ *n.* —**pul·sa·to·ry** /-sə,tôrē/ *adj.*

pulse¹ /pəls/ ▸ *n.* a rhythmical throbbing of the arteries as blood is propelled through them, typically as felt in the wrists or neck. ■ the rate of this throbbing, used to ascertain the rate of someone's heartbeat and so their state of health or emotions: *the idea was enough to set my pulse racing.* ■ (usu. **pulses**) each successive throb of the arteries or heart. ■ a single vibration or short burst of sound, electric current, light, or other wave: *radio pulses* | [as *adj.*] *a pulse generator.* ■ a musical beat or other regular rhythm. ■ *fig.* the central point of energy and organization in an area or activity: *those close to the financial pulse maintain that there have been fundamental changes.*
▸ *v.* [*intr.*] throb rhythmically; pulsate: *a knot of muscles at the side of his jaw pulsed.* ■ [*tr.*] transmit in rhythmical beats: *the sun pulsed fire into her eyes.* —**pulse·less** *adj.* —**puls·er** *n.*
▸ □ **take** (or **feel**) **the pulse of** determine the heart rate of (someone) by feeling and timing the pulsation of an artery. ■ *fig.* ascertain the general mood or opinion of: *he hopped around the country to visit stores and take the pulse of consumers.*

pulse² ▸ *n.* (usu. **pulses**) the edible seeds of various leguminous plants, for example chickpeas, lentils, and beans. ■ the plant or plants producing such seeds.

pul·ver·ize /'pəlvə,rīz/ ▸ *v.* [*tr.*] reduce to fine particles: *the brick of the villages was pulverized by the bombardment.* ■ *inf.* defeat utterly. —**pul·ver·iz·a·ble** *adj.* —**pul·ver·i·za·tion** /,pəlvərə'zāSHən/ *n.* —**pul·ver·iz·er** *n.*

pu·ma /'p(y)ōōmə/ ▸ *n.* another term for COUGAR.

pum·ice /'pəməs/ ▸ *n.* a very light and porous volcanic rock formed when a gas-rich froth of glassy lava solidifies rapidly. ■ (also **pumice stone**) a piece of such rock or a similar substance used as an abrasive, esp. for removing hard skin.
▸ *v.* [*tr.*] rub with pumice to smooth or clean. —**pu·mi·ceous** /pyōō'miSHəs; pəm'iSH-/ *adj.*

pum·mel /'pəməl/ ▸ *v.* (**-meled, -mel·ing;** *Brit.* **-mel·led, -mel·ling**) [*tr.*] strike repeatedly, typically with the fists. ■ *inf.* criticize adversely.

pump¹ /pəmp/ ▸ *n.* a mechanical device using suction or pressure to raise or move liquids, compress gases, or force air into inflatable objects such as tires: *a gas pump.* ■ an instance of moving something or being moved by or as if by such a machine. ■ *Physiol.* an active transport mechanism in living cells by which specific ions are moved through the cell membrane against a concentration gradient: *the bacterium's sodium pump.* ■ a pump-action shotgun.
▸ *v.* **1** [*tr.*] force (liquid, gas, etc.) to move in a specified direction by or as if by means of a pump: *the blood is pumped around the body* | [*intr.*] *if we pump long enough, we should bring the level up.* ■ [*intr.*] move in spurts as though driven by a pump: *blood was pumping from a wound.* ■ fill with something: *my veins had been pumped full of glucose.* ■ shoot (bullets) into a target. ■ (**pump something in/into**) *inf.* invest a large amount of money in (something). ■ [*tr.*] *inf.* try to elicit information from (someone) by persistent questioning. **2** [*tr.*] move (something) vigorously up and down. ■ [*intr.*] move vigorously up and down or back and forth: *that's superb running—look at his legs pumping.* ■ apply and release (a brake pedal or lever) several times in quick succession, typically to prevent skidding. ■ move one's arm as if throwing a ball held in the hand, but without releasing the ball: [in *comb.*] *behind the plate Howard double-pumped then threw to second.*
▸ *phrasal v.* □ **pump out** produce or emit (something) in large quantities or amounts. □ **pump up** inflate (a tire, balloon, etc.) ■ *inf.* increase. ■ *inf.* turn up the volume of (music). ■ *inf.* give inappropriate support and encouragement to.
▸ □ **pump iron** *inf.* exercise with weights.

pump² ▸ *n.* a light shoe, in particular: ■ a woman's plain, lightweight shoe that has a low-cut upper, no fastening, and typically a medium heel. ■ a man's slip-on patent leather shoe for formal wear.

pump-ac·tion ▸ *adj.* [*attrib.*] **1** denoting a repeating firearm, typically a shotgun, in which a new round is brought from the magazine into the breech by a slide action in line with the barrel. **2** denoting a spray dispenser for a liquid such as deodorant or cooking oil that is worked by finger action.

pum·per·nick·el /'pəmpər,nikəl/ ▸ *n.* dark, dense German bread made from coarsely ground whole-grain rye.

pump·kin /'pəm(p)kən; 'pəNGkən/ ▸ *n.* **1** a large rounded orange-yellow fruit with a thick rind, edible flesh, and many seeds. ■ the flesh of this fruit, esp. used as food. ■ *inf.* used as an affectionate term of address, esp. to a child. **2** the plant (genus *Cucurbita*) of the gourd family that produces this fruit, having tendrils and large lobed leaves and native to warm regions of America. ■ *Brit.* another term for SQUASH².

pun /pən/ ▸ *n.* a joke exploiting the different possible meanings of a word or the fact that there are words that sound alike but have different meanings: *the pigs were a squeal (if you'll forgive the pun).*
▸ *v.* (**punned, pun·ning**) [*intr.*] make a joke exploiting the different possible meanings of a word: *his first puzzle punned on composers, with answers like "Handel with care."* —**pun·ning·ly** *adv.* —**pun·ster** /'pənstər/ *n.*

Punch /pənCH/ ▸ *n.* a grotesque, hook-nosed, humpbacked buffoon, the chief male character of Punch and Judy, a traditional English puppet show. Punch is derived ultimately from Italian *commedia dell'arte.* Also called **Pun·chi·nel·lo** /,pənCHə'nelō/.
▸ □ **pleased as Punch** feeling great delight or pride.

punch¹ /pənCH/ ▸ *v.* [*tr.*] **1** strike with the fist. ■ drive with a blow from the fist: *he punched the ball into his own goal.* **2** press (a button or key on a machine). ■ (**punch something in/into**) enter information by this action. **3** drive (cattle) by prodding them with a stick.
▸ *phrasal v.* □ **punch in** (or **out**) register one's arrival at (or departure from) work, esp. by means of a time clock.
▸ *n.* a blow with the fist. ■ *inf.* the strength needed to deliver such a blow. ■ *inf.* the power to impress or startle: *photos give their arguments an extra visual punch.* —**punch·er** *n.*
▸ □ **beat someone to the punch** *inf.* anticipate or forestall someone's actions. □ **punch the (time) clock** (of an employee) punch in or out. ■ be employed in a conventional job with regular hours. □ **punch something up 1** use a computer keyboard to call something to the screen: *to punch up Andy Warhol and get text, photographs, and video on the Pop Art period.* **2** enliven.

punch² ▸ *n.* **1** a device or machine for making holes in materials such as paper, leather, metal, and plaster. **2** a tool or machine for impressing a design or stamping a die on a material.
▸ *v.* [*tr.*] pierce a hole in (metal, paper, leather, etc.) with or as though with a punch. ■ pierce (a hole) with or as though with a punch.

punch³ ▸ *n.* a drink made with fruit juices, soda, spices, and sometimes liquor, typically served in small cups from a large bowl.

punch-drunk ▶*adj.* stupefied by or as if by a series of heavy blows.

pun·cheon /ˈpənCHən/ ▶*n.* a rough board or other length of wood, usually with one flattened side, used for construction.

punch·ing bag ▶*n.* a stuffed or inflated bag, typically cylindrical or pear-shaped, suspended so it can be punched for exercise or training, esp. by boxers. ▪ a person on whom another person vents their anger.

punch line ▶*n.* the final phrase or sentence of a joke or story, providing the humor or some other crucial element.

punch·y /ˈpənCHē/ ▶*adj.* (**punch·i·er, punch·i·est**) **1** having an immediate impact; forceful: *his style is journalistic, with short punchy sentences.* **2** another term for PUNCH-DRUNK. —**punch·i·ly** /ˈpənCHəlē/ *adv.* —**punch·i·ness** *n.*

punc·til·i·ous /ˌpəNGkˈtilēəs/ ▶*adj.* showing great attention to detail or correct behavior. —**punc·til·i·ous·ly** *adv.* —**punc·til·i·ous·ness** *n.*

punc·tu·al /ˈpəNGkCHo͞oəl/ ▶*adj.* happening or doing something at the agreed or proper time; on time. ▪ *Gram.* denoting or relating to an action that takes place at a particular point in time. —**punc·tu·al·i·ty** /ˌpəNGkCHo͞oˈalitē/ *n.* —**punc·tu·al·ly** *adv.*

punc·tu·ate /ˈpəNGkCHo͞oˌāt/ ▶*v.* [*tr.*] **1** (often **be punctuated**) occur at intervals throughout (a continuing event or a place): *the country's history has been punctuated by coups.* ▪ (**punctuate something with**) interrupt or intersperse (an activity) with: *she punctuates her conversation with snatches of song.* **2** insert punctuation marks in (text). **3** accentuate; emphasize.

punc·tu·a·tion /ˌpəNGkCHo͞oˈāSHən/ ▶*n.* **1** the marks, such as period, comma, and parentheses, used in writing to separate sentences and their elements and to clarify meaning. **2** *Biol.* rapid or sudden speciation, as posited by the theory of punctuated equilibrium. —**punc·tu·a·tion·al** /-SHənl/ *adj.*

punc·tu·a·tion mark ▶*n.* a comma, period, apostrophe, or other symbol inserted into written or printed matter that aids the sense of the text by indicating such attributes as pauses, stops, possessives, queries, and dialogue.

punc·ture /ˈpəNGkCHər/ ▶*n.* a small hole in a tire resulting in an escape of air. ▪ a small hole in something such as the skin, caused by a sharp object: [as *adj.*] *a puncture wound.*
▶*v.* [*tr.*] make such a hole in (something). ▪ [*intr.*] sustain such a small hole. ▪ *fig.* bring about a dramatic reversal in (mood or behavior) resembling a sudden deflation or collapse: *the earlier mood of optimism was punctured.* ▷late Middle English: from Latin *punctura*, from *punct-* 'pricked,' from the verb *pungere.* The verb dates from the late 17th cent.

pun·dit /ˈpəndit/ ▶*n.* **1** an expert in a particular subject or field who is frequently called on to give opinions about it to the public. **2** variant spelling of PANDIT. —**pun·dit·ry** /-trē/ *n.*

pun·gent /ˈpənjənt/ ▶*adj.* having a sharply strong taste or smell. ▪ (of comment, criticism, or humor) having a sharp and caustic quality. —**pun·gen·cy** /ˈpənjənsē/ *n.* —**pun·gent·ly** *adv.*

pun·ish /ˈpəniSH/ ▶*v.* [*tr.*] inflict a penalty or sanction on (someone) as retribution for an offense, esp. a transgression of a legal or moral code. ▪ inflict a penalty or sanction on someone for (such an offense). ▪ treat (someone) in an unfairly harsh way: *a rise in prescription charges would punish the poor.* ▪ subject (someone or something) to severe and debilitating treatment. —**pun·ish·a·ble** *adj.* —**pun·ish·er** *n.* —**pun·ish·ing·ly** *adv.*

pun·ish·ment /ˈpəniSHmənt/ ▶*n.* the infliction or imposition of a penalty as retribution for an offense. ▪ the penalty inflicted: *she assisted her husband to escape punishment for the crime.* ▪ *inf.* rough treatment or handling inflicted on or suffered by a person or thing: *your machine can take a fair amount of punishment before falling to pieces.*

pu·ni·tive /ˈpyo͞onətiv/ ▶*adj.* inflicting or intended as punishment: *he called for punitive measures against the Eastern bloc.* ▪ (of a tax or other charge) extremely high. —**pu·ni·tive·ly** *adv.* —**pu·ni·tive·ness** *n.*

punk /pəNGk/ ▶*n.* **1** *inf.* a worthless person (often used as a general term of abuse). ▪ a criminal or hoodlum. ▪ *derog.* (in prison slang) a passive male homosexual. ▪ an inexperienced young person. **2** (also **punk rock**) a loud, fast-moving, and aggressive form of rock music, popular in the late 1970s and early 1980s. ▪ (also **punk rocker**) an admirer or player of such music, typically characterized by colored spiked hair and clothing decorated with safety pins or zippers. **3** soft, crumbly wood that has been attacked by fungus, sometimes used as tinder.
▶*adj.* **1** *inf.* in poor or bad condition. **2** of or relating to punk rock and its associated subculture: *a punk haircut.* —**punk·ish** *adj.* —**punk·y** *adj.*

punt¹ /pənt/ ▶*n.* a long, narrow, flat-bottomed boat, square at both ends and propelled with a long pole, used on inland waters chiefly for recreation.

punt² ▶*v.* **1** [*tr.*] *Football* kick (the ball) after it is dropped from the hands and before it reaches the ground. ▪ [*intr.*] (of an offensive team) turn possession over to the defensive team by punting the ball after failing to make a first down. **2** [*intr.*] delay in answering or taking action; equivocate: *he would continue to punt on questions of Medicare.* —**punt·er** *n.*
▶*n.* a kick of this kind.

punt³ ▶*v.* [*intr.*] (in some gambling card games) place a bet against the bank. ▪ *Brit., inf.* bet or speculate on something: *investors are punting on a takeover.*
▶*n.* *inf., chiefly Brit.* a bet: *those taking a punt on the company's success.*

punt⁴ ▶*n.* the basic monetary unit of the Republic of Ireland (until replaced by the euro), equal to 100 Irish pence.

pu·ny /ˈpyo͞onē/ ▶*adj.* (**-ni·er, -ni·est**) small and weak: *skeletal, white-faced, puny children.* ▪ poor in quality, amount, or size: *the army was reduced to a puny 100,000 men.* —**pu·ni·ly** /ˈpyo͞onl-ē/ *adv.* —**pu·ni·ness** *n.*

pup /pəp/ ▶*n.* a young dog. ▪ a young wolf, seal, rat, or other mammal. ▪ *dated chiefly Brit.* a cheeky or arrogant boy or young man.
▶*v.* (**pupped, pup·ping**) [*intr.*] (of female dogs and certain other animals) give birth to young.

pu·pa /ˈpyo͞opə/ ▶*n.* (*pl.* **-pae** /-ˌpē; -ˌpī/) an insect in its inactive immature form between larva and adult, e.g., a chrysalis. —**pu·pal** *adj.*

pu·pate /ˈpyo͞oˌpāt/ ▶*v.* [*intr.*] (of a larva) become a pupa. —**pu·pa·tion** /pyo͞oˈpāSHən/ *n.*

pu·pil¹ /ˈpyo͞opəl/ ▶*n.* a student in school.

pu·pil² ▶*n.* the dark circular opening in the center of the iris of the eye, varying in size to regulate the amount of light reaching the retina. —**pu·pil·lar·y** /ˈpyo͞opə,lerē/ (also **pu·pil·ar·y**) *adj.*

pup·pet /ˈpəpət/ ▶*n.* a model of a person or animal that is used in entertainment and is typically moved either by strings controlled from above or by a hand inside it. ▪ *fig.* a person, party, or state under the control of another person, group, or power. —**pup·pet·ry** /-trē/ *n.*

pup·pet·eer /ˌpəpəˈtir/ ▶*n.* a person who works puppets. —**pup·pet·eer·ing** *n.*

pup·py /ˈpəpē/ ▶*n.* (*pl.* **-pies**) a young dog. ▪ *inf., dated* a conceited or arrogant young man. —**pup·py·hood** /-ˌho͝od/ *n.* —**pup·py·ish** *adj.*

pup·py love ▶*n.* an intense but relatively shallow romantic attachment, typically associated with adolescents.

pup tent ▶*n.* a small triangular tent, esp. one with a pole at either end and room for one or two people.

pur·blind /ˈpərˌblīnd/ ▶*adj.* having impaired or defective vision. ▪ *fig.* slow or unable to understand; dim-witted. —**pur·blind·ness** *n.*

pur·chase /ˈpərCHəs/ ▶*v.* [*tr.*] acquire (something) by paying for it; buy.
▶*n.* **1** the action of buying something. ▪ a thing that has been bought. ▪ *Law* the acquisition of property by means other than inheritance. **2** a hold or position on something for applying power advantageously, or the advantage gained by such application: *the horse's hooves fought for purchase on the slippery pavement* | *an attempt to gain a purchase on the soft earth.* ▪ a block and tackle. —**pur·chas·a·ble** *adj.* —**pur·chas·er** *n.*

pure /pyo͝or/ ▶*adj.* not mixed or adulterated with any other substance or material. ▪ without any extraneous and unnecessary elements: *pure art devoid of social responsibility.* ▪ free of any contamination: *the pure, clear waters of Montana.* ▪ wholesome and untainted by immorality, esp. that of a sexual nature. ▪ (of a sound) perfectly in tune and with a clear tone. ▪ (of an animal or plant) of unmixed origin or descent. ▪ (of a subject of study) dealing with abstract concepts and not practical application: *a theoretical discipline such as pure physics.* Compare with APPLIED. ▪ *Phonet.* (of a vowel) not joined with another to form a diphthong. ▪ involving or containing nothing else but; sheer (used for emphasis): *an outcome that may be a matter of pure chance.* —**pure·ness** *n.*
▶ □ **pure and simple** and nothing else (used for emphasis): *it was revenge, pure and simple.*

pure·bred /ˈpyo͝orˌbred/ ▶*adj.* (of an animal) bred from parents of the same breed or variety.
▶*n.* an animal of this kind.

pu·rée /pyo͝oˈrā; -ˈrē/ ▶*n.* a smooth, creamy substance made of liquidized or crushed fruit or vegetables: *stir in the tomato purée.*

▶*v.* (**pu·rées, pu·réed, pu·rée·ing**) [*tr.*] make a purée of (fruit or vegetables).

pure·ly /'pyŏŏrlē/ ▶*adv.* in a pure manner: *act nobly, speak purely, and think charitably.* ■ entirely; exclusively: *the purpose was purely to inform.*

pur·ga·tive /'pərgətiv/ ▶*adj.* strongly laxative in effect. ■ *fig.* having the effect of ridding someone of unwanted feelings or memories.
▶*n.* a laxative. ■ *fig.* a thing that rids someone of unwanted feelings or memories: *confrontation would be a purgative.*

pur·ga·to·ry /'pərgə,tôrē/ ▶*n.* (*pl.* **-ries**) (in Roman Catholic doctrine) a place or state of suffering inhabited by the souls of sinners who are expiating their sins before going to heaven. ■ mental anguish or suffering: *this was purgatory, worse than anything she'd faced in her life.* —**pur·ga·to·ri·al** /,pərgə'tôrēəl/ *adj.*

purge /pərj/ ▶*v.* [*tr.*] rid (someone) of an unwanted feeling, memory, or condition, typically giving a sense of cathartic release. ■ remove (an unwanted feeling, memory, or condition) in such a way. ■ remove (a group of people considered undesirable) from an organization or place, typically in an abrupt or violent manner. ■ remove someone from (an organization or place) in such a way. ■ physically remove (something) completely: *a cold air blower purges residual solvents from the body.* ■ [*intr.*] [often as *n.*] (**purging**) evacuate one's bowels, esp. as a result of taking a laxative.
▶*n.* an abrupt or violent removal of a group of people from an organization or place. *the Stalinist purges.* ■ *dated* a laxative. —**purg·er** *n.*

pu·ri /'pŏŏrē/ (also **poo·ri**) ▶*n.* (*pl.* **pu·ris**) (in Indian cooking) a small, round, flat piece of bread made of unleavened wheat flour, deep-fried and served with meat or vegetables.

pu·ri·fy /'pyŏŏrə,fī/ ▶*v.* (**-fies, -fied**) [*tr.*] remove contaminants from: *the filtration plant is able to purify 70 tons of water a day.* ■ make ceremonially clean: *a ritual bath to purify the soul.* ■ rid (something) of an unwanted element: *Mao's campaign to purify the Communist Party hierarchy.* ■ (**purify something from**) extract something from: *genomic DNA was purified from whole blood.* —**pu·ri·fi·ca·tion** /,pyŏŏrəfi'kāSHən/ *n.* —**pu·rif·i·ca·to·ry** /pyŏŏ'rifikə,tôrē/ *adj.* —**pu·ri·fi·er** *n.*

Pu·rim /'pŏŏrim; pŏŏ'rēm/ ▶*n.* a lesser Jewish festival held in spring (on the 14th or 15th day of Adar) to commemorate the defeat of Haman's plot to massacre the Jews as recorded in the book of Esther.

pu·rine /'pyŏŏr,ēn/ ▶*n. Chem.* a colorless crystalline compound, $C_5H_4N_4$, with basic properties, forming uric acid on oxidation. ■ (also **purine base**) a substituted derivative of this, esp. the bases adenine and guanine present in DNA and RNA.

pur·ism /'pyŏŏr,izəm/ ▶*n.* **1** scupulous or exaggerated observance of or insistence on traditional rules or structures, esp. in language or style. **2** (**Purism**) an early 20th-century artistic style and movement emphasizing purity of geometric form. It arose out of rejection of cubism and was characterized by a return to the representation of recognizable objects.

pur·ist /'pyŏŏrist/ ▶*n.* **1** a person who insists on absolute adherence to traditional rules or structures, esp. in language or style. **2** (**Purist**) an adherent of Purism. —**pu·ris·tic** /pyŏŏr'istik/ *adj.*

Pu·ri·tan /'pyŏŏritn/ ▶*n.* a member of a group of English Protestants of the late 16th and 17th centuries who regarded the Reformation of the Church of England under Elizabeth as incomplete and sought to simplify and regulate forms of worship. ■ (**puritan**) a person with censorious moral beliefs, esp. about pleasure and sex.
▶*adj.* of or relating to the Puritans. ■ (**puritan**) having or displaying censorious moral beliefs, esp. about pleasure and sex. —**Pu·ri·tan·ism** (also **pu·ri·tan·ism**) *n.*

pu·ri·tan·i·cal /,pyŏŏri'tanikəl/ ▶*adj. often derog.* practicing or affecting strict religious or moral behavior. —**pu·ri·tan·i·cal·ly** *adv.*

pu·ri·ty /'pyŏŏritē/ ▶*n.* freedom from adulteration or contamination. ■ freedom from immorality, esp. of a sexual nature.

purl[1] /pərl/ ▶*adj.* denoting or relating to a knitting stitch made by putting the needle through the front of the stitch from right to left. Compare with **KNIT**.
▶*n.* a purl stitch.
▶*v.* [*tr.*] knit with a purl stitch: *knit one, purl one.*

purl[2] ▶*v.* [*intr.*] (of a stream or river) flow with a swirling motion and babbling sound.
▶*n.* a motion or sound of this kind.

pur·lieu /'pərl(y)ŏŏ/ ▶*n.* (*pl.* **-lieus** or **-lieux** /-l(y)ŏŏ(z)/) the area near or surrounding a place: *the photogenic purlieus of Princeton.* ■ *fig.* a person's usual haunts.

pur·loin /pər'loin/ ▶*v.* [*tr.*] steal (something). —**pur·loin·er** *n.*

pur·ple /'pərpəl/ ▶*n.* a color intermediate between red and blue. ■

purple clothing or material. ■ (**the purple**) (in ancient Rome) a position of rank, authority, or privilege.
▶*adj.* of a color intermediate between red and blue: *a faded purple T-shirt.*
▶*v.* become or make purple in color: [*intr.*] *Ed's cheeks purpled.* | [*tr.*] *the neon was purpling the horizon above the highway.* —**pur·ple·ness** *n.* —**pur·plish** /'pərp(ə)lisH/ *adj.* —**pur·ply** /'pərp(ə)lē/ *adj.*
▶ ▢ **born in** (or **to**) **the purple** born into a reigning family or privileged class.

Pur·ple Heart ▶*n.* (in the US) a military decoration for those wounded or killed in action, established in 1782 and reestablished in 1932.

pur·ple pas·sage ▶*n.* an elaborate or excessively ornate passage in a literary composition.

pur·port ▶*v.* /pər'pôrt/ appear or claim to be or do something, esp. falsely; profess: *she is not the person she purports to be.*
▶*n.* /'pər,pôrt/ the meaning or substance of something, typically a document or speech: *I do not understand the purport of your remarks.* ■ the purpose of a person or thing. —**pur·port·ed·ly** *adv.*

pur·pose /'pərpəs/ ▶*n.* the reason for which something is done or created or for which something exists. ■ a person's sense of resolve or determination: *there was a new **sense of purpose** in her step as she set off.* ■ (usu. **purposes**) a particular requirement or consideration, typically one that is temporary or restricted in scope or extent: *pensions are considered as earned income for tax purposes.*
▶*v.* [*tr.*] *formal* have as one's intention or objective.
▶ ▢ **on purpose** intentionally. ▢ **to no purpose** with no result or effect; pointlessly.

pur·pose·ful /'pərpəsfəl/ ▶*adj.* having or showing determination or resolve: *the purposeful stride of a great lawyer.* ■ having a useful purpose: *purposeful activities.* ■ intentional: *if his sudden death was not accidental, it must have been purposeful.* —**pur·pose·ful·ly** *adv.* —**pur·pose·ful·ness** *n.*

pur·pose·less /'pərpəslis/ ▶*adj.* done or made with no discernible point or purpose: *purposeless vandalism.* ■ having no aim or plan: *his purposeless life.* —**pur·pose·less·ly** *adv.* —**pur·pose·less·ness** *n.*

pur·pose·ly /'pərpəslē/ ▶*adv.* on purpose; intentionally.

pur·pos·ive /'pərpəsiv; pər'pō-/ ▶*adj.* having, serving, or done with a purpose. —**pur·pos·ive·ly** *adv.* —**pur·pos·ive·ness** *n.*

pur·pu·ra /'pərp(y)ərə/ ▶*n. Med.* a rash of purple spots on the skin caused by internal bleeding from small blood vessels. ■ any of a number of diseases characterized by such a rash. —**pur·pu·ric** /pər'pyŏŏrik/ *adj.*

purr /pər/ ▶*v.* [*intr.*] (of a cat) make a low continuous vibratory sound usually expressing contentment. ■ (of a vehicle or machine) make such a sound when running smoothly at low speed. ■ [*intr.*] (of a vehicle or engine) move smoothly while making such a sound. ■ speak in a low soft voice, esp. when expressing contentment or acting seductively: *"Would you like coffee?" she purred* | [*tr.*] *she purred her lines seductively.*
▶*n.* a low continuous vibratory sound, typically that made by a cat or vehicle.

purse /pərs/ ▶*n.* a small bag used esp. by a woman to carry everyday personal items. ■ a small pouch of leather or plastic used for carrying money, typically by a woman. ■ the money possessed or available to a person or country. ■ a sum of money given as a prize in a sporting contest, esp. a boxing match.
▶*v.* (with reference to the lips) pucker or contract, typically to express disapproval or irritation: [*tr.*] *Marianne took a glance at her reflection and pursed her lips disgustedly* | [*intr.*] *under stress his lips would purse slightly.* ▷late Old English, alteration of late Latin *bursa* 'purse,' from Greek *bursa* 'hide, leather.' The current verb sense (from the notion of drawing purse strings) dates from the early 17th cent.
▶ ▢ **hold the purse strings** have control of expenditure. ▢ **tighten** (or **loosen**) **the purse strings** restrict (or increase) the amount of money available to be spent.

purs·er /'pərsər/ ▶*n.* an officer on a ship who keeps the accounts, esp. the head steward on a passenger vessel.

purs·lane /'pərslən; -,slān/ ▶*n.* any of a number of small, typically fleshy-leaved plants (family Portulacaceae) that grow in damp habitats or waste places, in particular *Portulaca oleracea*, a prostrate North American plant with tiny yellow flowers.

pur·su·ance /pər'sŏŏəns/ ▶*n. formal* the carrying out of a plan or action: *you have a right to use public areas in the **pursuance** of your lawful hobby.* ■ the action of trying to achieve something: *they are considering a walk-out in pursuance of a better deal.*

pur·su·ant /pər'sŏŏənt/ ▶*adv.* (**pursuant to**) *formal* in accordance with (a law or a legal document or resolution).
▶*adj. archaic* following; going in pursuit. —**pur·su·ant·ly** *adv.*

pur·sue /pər'sŏŏ/ ▶*v.* (**-sues, -sued, -su·ing**) [*tr.*] **1** follow (someone or something) in order to catch or attack them: *the officer pursued the van* | *fig. a businessman was being pursued by creditors.* ■ seek to form a sexual relationship with (someone) in a persistent way. ■ seek to attain or accomplish (a goal), esp. over a long period. ■ *archaic* or *poetic/lit.* (of something unpleasant) persistently afflict (someone). **2** (of a person or way) continue or proceed along (a path or route): *the road pursued a straight course over the mountain.* ■ engage in (an activity or course of action): *the council decided not to pursue an appeal.* ■ continue to investigate, explore, or discuss (a topic, idea, or argument). —**pur·su·a·ble** *adj.* —**pur·su·er** *n.*

pur·suit /pərˈsoot/ ▶*n.* **1** the action of following or pursuing someone or something: *the cat crouched in the grass **in pursuit of** a bird.* ■ a bicycle race in which competitors start from different parts of a track and attempt to overtake one another. ■ *Physiol.* the action of the eye in following a moving object. **2** (often **pursuits**) an activity of a specified kind, esp. a recreational or athletic one: *a range of leisure pursuits.*
▶ □ **give pursuit** (of a person, animal, or vehicle) start to chase another.

pu·ru·lent /ˈpyŏor(y)ələnt/ ▶*adj. Med.* consisting of, containing, or discharging pus.

pur·vey /pərˈvā/ ▶*v.* [*tr.*] provide or supply (food, drink, or other goods) as one's business: *shops purveying cooked food* | *fig. this magazine feels like a concerted effort to purvey gloom and doom.* —**pur·vey·ance** *n.* —**pur·vey·or** /-ˈvāər/ *n.*

pur·view /ˈpərˌvyoo/ ▶*n.* the scope of the influence or concerns of something: *such a case might be within the purview of the legislation.* ■ a range of experience or thought: *social taboos meant that little information was likely to come within the purview of women generally.*

pus /pəs/ ▶*n.* a thick yellowish or greenish opaque liquid produced in infected tissue, consisting of dead white blood cells and bacteria with tissue debris and serum.

push /pŏosh/ ▶*v.* **1** [*tr.*] exert force on (someone or something), typically with one's hand, in order to move them away from oneself or the origin of the force: *she pushed her glass toward him* | [*intr.*] *he **pushed at** the skylight, but it wouldn't budge.* ■ [*tr.*] hold and exert force on (something) so as to cause it to move along in front of one: *a woman was pushing a stroller.* ■ move one's body or a part of it into a specified position, esp. forcefully or with effort: *she pushed her hands into her pockets.* ■ [*tr.*] press (a part of a machine or other device). ■ *fig.* affect (something) so that it reaches a specified level or state: *they expect that the huge crop will push down prices.* **2** [*intr.*] move forward by using force to pass people or cause them to move aside: *he pushed past an old woman in his haste.* ■ (of an army) advance over territory: *the guerrillas have pushed south.* ■ exert oneself to attain something or surpass others. ■ (**push for**) demand persistently. ■ [*tr.*] compel or urge (someone) to do something, esp. to work hard. ■ (**be pushed**) *inf.* have very little of something, esp. time: *I'm a bit pushed for time at the moment.* ■ (**be pushing**) *inf.* be nearly (a particular age): *she must be pushing forty.* **3** [*tr.*] *inf.* promote the use, sale, or acceptance of. ■ put forward (an argument or demand) with undue force or in too extreme a form. ■ sell (a narcotic drug) illegally. ■ *Comput.* prepare (a stack) to receive a piece of data on the top. ■ transfer (data) to the top of a stack. **5** [*tr.*] *Photog.* develop (film) so as to compensate for deliberate underexposure.
▶*phrasal v.* □ **push ahead** proceed with or continue a course of action or policy. □ **push someone around** *inf.* treat someone roughly or inconsiderately. □ **push off** use an oar, pole, etc., to exert pressure so as to move a boat out from shore or away from another vessel. □ **push on** continue on a journey. □ **push something through** get a proposed measure completed or accepted quickly.
▶*n.* **1** an act of exerting force on someone or something in order to move them away from oneself. ■ an act of pressing a part of a machine or device: *the door locks at the push of a button.* ■ *fig.* something that encourages or assists something else: *the fall in prices was given a push by official policy.* **2** a vigorous effort to do or obtain something: *the fund-raising push.* ■ a military attack in force: *a push against guerrilla strongholds.* ■ forcefulness and enterprise.
▶ □ **push someone's buttons** see BUTTON. □ **pushing up daisies** see DAISY. □ **push one's luck** *inf.* take a risk on the assumption that one will continue to be successful or in favor. □ **when push comes to shove** *inf.* when one must commit oneself to an action or decision.

push but·ton ▶*n.* a button that is pushed to operate an electrical device: [as *adj.*] *a push-button telephone.*

push·cart /ˈpŏoshˌkärt/ ▶*n.* a small handcart or barrow.

push·er /ˈpŏoshər/ ▶*n.* **1** *inf.* a person who sells illegal drugs. **2** a person or thing that pushes something. ■ *inf.* a forceful or pushy person.

push·o·ver /ˈpŏoshˌōvər/ ▶*n. inf.* a person who is easy to overcome or

influence: *Colonel Moore was no pushover.* ■ a thing that is very easily done.

push-start ▶*v.* [*tr.*] start (a motor vehicle) by pushing it and putting it in gear in order to make the engine turn.
▶*n.* an act of starting a motor vehicle in this way.

push·up /ˈpŏoshˌəp/ (also **push-up**) ▶*n.* an exercise in which a person lies facing the floor and, keeping their back straight, raises their body by pressing down on their hands.
▶*adj.* (**push-up**) denoting a padded or underwired bra or similar garment that gives uplift to the breasts.

push·y /ˈpŏoshē/ ▶*adj.* (**push·i·er, push·i·est**) excessively or unpleasantly self-assertive or ambitious. —**push·i·ly** /ˈpŏoshəlē/ *adv.* —**push·i·ness** *n.*

pu·sil·lan·i·mous /ˌpyoosəˈlanəməs/ ▶*adj.* showing a lack of courage or determination; timid. —**pu·sil·la·nim·i·ty** /-ləˈnimətē/ *n.* —**pu·sil·lan·i·mous·ly** *adv.*

puss[1] /pŏos/ ▶*n. inf.* a cat (esp. as a form of address): *You naughty little puss!* ■ a playful or coquettish girl or young woman: *you old snuggle puss.*

puss[2] ▶*n. inf.* a person's face or mouth.

pus·sy /ˈpŏosē/ ▶*n.* (*pl.* **-sies**) **1** (also **pus·sy·cat**) *inf.* a cat. **2** *vulgar slang* a woman's genitals. ■ *offens.* women in general, considered sexually. ■ *offens.* sexual intercourse with a woman. ■ *inf.* a weak, cowardly, or effeminate man.

pus·sy·foot /ˈpŏosēˌfŏot/ ▶*v.* [*intr.*] act in a cautious or noncommittal way: *I realized I could no longer **pussyfoot around**.* ■ move stealthily or warily: *they make a great show of pussyfooting through the greenery.* —**pus·sy·foot·er** /-ˌfŏotər/ *n.*

pus·sy wil·low ▶*n.* a willow with soft fluffy silvery or yellow catkins that appear before the leaves, esp. the North American *Salix discolor.*

pus·tule /ˈpəschŏol; ˈpəst(y)ŏol/ ▶*n. Med.* a small blister or pimple on the skin containing pus. ■ *Biol.* a small raised spot or rounded swelling, esp. one on a plant resulting from fungal infection. —**pus·tu·lar** /ˈpəschələr; ˈpəstyə-/ *adj.*

put /pŏot/ ▶*v.* (**put·ting**; *past* **put**) [*tr.*] **1** move to or place in a particular position: *Harry put down his cup.* ■ cause (someone or something) to go to a particular place and remain there for a time: *India has put three experimental satellites into space.* ■ [*intr.*] (of a ship or the people on it) proceed in a particular direction: *the boat **put out to sea**.* ■ write or print (something) in a particular place: *they put my name on the cover page.* ■ [*intr.*] *archaic* (of a river) flow in a particular direction. **2** bring into a particular state or condition: *they tried to put me at ease.* ■ (**put oneself in**) imagine oneself in (a particular situation): *it was no use trying to put herself in his place.* ■ express (a thought or comment) in a particular way, form, or language: *to put it bluntly, he was not really divorced.* **3** (**put something on/on to**) cause (someone or something) to carry or be subject to something: *commentators put some of the blame on Congress.* ■ assign a particular value, figure, or limit to: *it is very difficult to put a figure on the size of the budget.* ■ (**put something at**) estimate something to be (a particular amount): *estimates put the war's cost at $1,000,000 a day.* **4** throw (a shot or weight) in a pushing motion from the shoulder, as an athletic sport: *she set a women's record by putting the shot 56′ 7″.*
▶*phrasal v.* □ **put something across** (or **over**) communicate something effectively. □ **put something aside 1** save money for future use. **2** forget or disregard something, typically a feeling or a past difference. □ **put someone away** (often **be put away**) *inf.* confine someone in a prison or psychiatric hospital. □ **put something away 1** save money for future use. **2** *inf.* consume food or drink in large quantities. **3** *inf.* (in sports) dispatch or deal with a goal or shot. □ **put something back** reschedule a planned event to a later time or date. ■ delay something. □ **put something by** another way of saying PUT SOMETHING ASIDE (sense 1 above). □ **put someone down 1** *inf.* lower someone's self-esteem by criticizing them in front of others. **2** lay a baby down to sleep. □ **put something down 1** record something in writing. **2** suppress a rebellion, riot, or other disturbance by force. **3** (usu. **be put down**) kill an animal because it is sick, injured, or old. **4** pay a specified sum as a deposit. **5** preserve or store food or wine for future use. **6** (also **put down**) land an aircraft. □ **put someone down as** consider or judge someone or something to be. □ **put something down to** attribute something to. □ **put something forward** submit a plan, proposal, or theory for consideration. □ **put in at/into** (of a ship) enter (a port or harbor). □ **put someone in** appoint someone to fulfill a particular role or job. ■ (in team sports) send a player out to participate

---

Pronunciation Key ə *ago,* up; ər *over, fur;* a *hat;* ā *ate;* ä *car;* CH *chin;* e *let;* ē *see;* e(ə)r *air;* i *fit;* ī *by;* i(ə)r *ear;* NG *sing;* ō *go;* ô *law, for;* oi *toy;* ŏo *good;* ŏo *goo;* ou *out;* SH *she;* TH *thin;* TH *then;* (h)w *why;* ZH *vision*

into a game. □ **put something in/into 1** present or submit something formally. ■ **(put in for)** apply formally for. **2** devote time or effort to something. **3** invest money or resources in. □ **put someone off 1** cancel or postpone an appointment with someone. **2** cause someone to lose interest or enthusiasm: *she wanted to be a nurse, but the thought of night shifts put her off.* ■ cause someone to feel dislike or distrust: *she had a coldness that just put me off.* **3** distract someone. □ **put something off** postpone something. □ **put someone on** *inf.* deceive or hoax someone. □ **put something on 1** place a garment, glasses, or jewelry on part of one's body. ■ attach or apply something. **2** cause a device to operate. ■ start cooking something. ■ play recorded music or a video. **3** organize or present a play, exhibition, or event. **4** add a specified amount to (the cost of something): *the news put 12 cents on the share price.* ■ increase in body weight; become heavier by a specified amount. **5** assume a particular expression, accent, etc. ■ behave deceptively: *she doesn't feel she has to put on an act.* **6** bet a specified amount of money on: *he put $1,000 on the horse to win.* □ **put someone on to** draw someone's attention to (someone or something useful, notable, or interesting). □ **put out** *vulgar slang* be willing to have sexual intercourse. □ **put someone out 1** cause someone trouble or inconvenience. ■ (often **be put out**) upset or annoy someone. **2** (in sports) defeat a player or team and so cause them to be out of a competition. **3** make someone unconscious, typically by means of drugs or an anesthetic. □ **put something out 1** extinguish something that is burning. ■ turn off a light. **2** lay something out ready for use. **3** issue or broadcast something. **4** dislocate a joint. **5** (of an engine or motor) produce a particular amount of power. □ **put something over** another way of saying **PUT SOMETHING ACROSS** above. □ **put someone through 1** connect someone by telephone to another person or place: *put me through to the mayor, please.* **2** subject someone to an unpleasant or demanding experience: *I hate Brian for what he put me through.* **3** pay for someone to attend school or college. □ **put something through** initiate something and see it through to a successful conclusion: *he put through a reform program.* □ **put someone to** cause inconvenience or difficulty to someone: *I don't want to put you to any trouble.* □ **put something together** make something by assembling different parts or people: *he can take a clock apart and put it back together again.* ■ assemble things or people to make something: *a carpenter puts together shaped pieces of wood to make a table.* □ **put someone under** another way of saying **PUT SOMEONE OUT** (sense 3 above). □ **put up 1** offer or show (a particular degree of resistance, effort, or skill) in a fight or competitive situation. **2** stay temporarily in lodgings other than one's own home: *we put up at a hotel in the city center.* □ **put someone up 1** accommodate someone temporarily. **2** propose someone for election or adoption: *they should have put themselves up for election.* □ **put something up 1** construct or erect something: *I put up the tent and cooked a meal.* **2** raise one's hand to signal that one wishes to answer or ask a question. **3** display a notice, sign, or poster. ■ present a proposal, theory, or argument for discussion or consideration. **4** provide money as backing for an enterprise: *the sponsors are putting up $5,000 for the event.* **5** (often **be put up for**) offer something for sale or auction. **6** *archaic* return a sword to its sheath. □ **put upon** [often as *adj.*] **(put-upon)** *inf.* take advantage of (someone) by exploiting their good nature: *a put-upon drudge who slaved for her employer.* □ **put someone up to** *inf.* encourage someone to do (something wrong or unwise): *Who else would play a trick like that on me? I expect Rose put him up to it.* □ **put up with** tolerate; endure.
▸*n.* a throw of the shot or weight.
▸ □ **put something behind one** get over a bad experience by distancing oneself from it. □ **put one's hands up** raise one's hands in surrender. □ **put it to** make a statement or allegation to (someone) and challenge them to deny it: *I put it to him that he was just a political groupie.* □ **put one over on** *inf.* deceive (someone) into accepting something false.

pu·ta·tive /'pyo͞otətiv/ ▸*adj.* generally considered or reputed to be: *the putative father of a boy of two.* —**pu·ta·tive·ly** *adv.*

put-down ▸*n. inf.* a remark intended to humiliate or criticize someone.

put-on ▸*n. inf.* a deception; a hoax.

pu·tre·fy /'pyo͞otrə,fī/ ▸*v.* (**-fies, -fied**) [*intr.*] (of a body or other organic matter) decay or rot and produce a fetid smell. —**pu·tre·fac·tion** /,pyo͞otrə'fakSHən/ *n.* —**pu·tre·fac·tive** /-,faktiv/ *adj.*

pu·tres·cent /pyo͞o'tresənt/ ▸*adj.* undergoing the process of decay; rotting: *the odor of putrescent flesh.* —**pu·tres·cence** *n.*

pu·trid /'pyo͞otrid/ ▸*adj.* (of organic matter) decaying or rotting and emitting a fetid smell. ■ of or characteristic of rotting matter: *the putrid smells from the slaughterhouses.* ■ *inf.* very unpleasant; repulsive. —**pu·trid·i·ty** /pyo͞o'tridətē/ *n.* —**pu·trid·ly** *adv.* —**pu·trid·ness** *n.*

putsch /po͝oCH/ ▸*n.* a violent attempt to overthrow a government.

putt /pət/ ▸*v.* (**put·ted, put·ting**) [*intr.*] try to hit a golf ball into a hole by striking it gently so that it rolls across the green: *Nicklaus putted for eagle on 11 of the 16 par 5s* | [*tr.*] *putt the balls into the hole.*
▸*n.* a stroke of this kind made in an attempt to hole the ball.

put·tee /,pə'tē/ ▸*n.* a long strip of cloth wound spirally around the leg from ankle to knee for protection and support. ■ a leather legging.

put·ter[1] /'pətər/ ▸*n.* **1** a golf club designed for use in putting, typically with a flat-faced malletlike head. **2** a golfer considered in terms of putting ability: *you'll need to be a good putter to break par.*

put·ter[2] ▸*n. & v.* another term for **PUTT-PUTT**.

put·ter[3] (*Brit.* **pot·ter**) ▸*v.* [*intr.*] occupy oneself in a desultory but pleasant manner, doing a number of small tasks or not concentrating on anything particular. ■ move or go in a casual, unhurried way. —**put·ter·er** *n.*

putt-putt (also **put-put**) ▸*n.* the rapid intermittent sound of a small gasoline engine: *she heard the putt-putt of a boat coming toward them.*
▸*v.* [*intr.*] make such a sound. ■ [*intr.*] move under the power of an engine that makes such a sound: *the car at last putt-putted down the hill.*

put·ty /'pətē/ ▸*n.* **1** a soft, malleable paste that hardens after a few hours and is used chiefly for sealing glass panes in wooden window frames. ■ any of a number of similar malleable substances, e.g., **plumber's putty,** or used for modeling or casting. **2** a polishing powder, usually made from tin oxide, used in jewelry work.
▸*v.* (**-ties, -tied**) [*tr.*] seal or cover (something) with putty. ▷mid 17th cent.: from French *potée*, literally 'potful,' from *pot* 'pot.'

putz /pəts; po͝ots/ *inf.* ▸*n.* **1** a stupid or worthless person. **2** *vulgar slang* a penis.
▸*v.* [*intr.*] engage in inconsequential or unproductive activity: *too much putzing around up there would ruin them.*

puz·zle /'pəzəl/ ▸*v.* [*tr.*] cause (someone) to feel confused because they cannot understand or make sense of something. ■ [*intr.*] think hard about something difficult to understand or explain: *she was still puzzling over this problem when she reached the office.* ■ **(puzzle something out)** solve or understand something by thinking hard.
▸*n.* a game, toy, or problem designed to test ingenuity or knowledge. ■ short for **JIGSAW PUZZLE** (see **JIGSAW**). ■ a person or thing that is difficult to understand or explain: *the meaning of the poem has always been a puzzle.* —**puz·zle·ment** *n.* —**puz·zling·ly** /'pəz(ə)liNGlē/ *adv.*

puz·zler /'pəz(ə)lər/ ▸*n.* a difficult question or problem. ■ a person who solves puzzles as a pastime. ■ *inf.* a computer game in which the player must solve puzzles.

PVC ▸*abbr.* polyvinyl chloride.

Pvt. (also **PVT**) ▸*abbr.* ■ (in the U.S. Army) private. ■ (in company names) private.

PX ▸*abbr.* ■ post exchange.

Pyg·my /'pigmē/ (also **Pig·my**) ▸*n.* (*pl.* **-mies**) a member of certain peoples of very short stature in equatorial Africa and parts of Southeast Asia. ■ **(pygmy)** *chiefly derog.* a very small person, animal, or thing. ■ **(pygmy)** an insignificant person, esp. one who is deficient in a particular respect: *he regarded them as intellectual pigmies.*
▸*adj.* of, relating to, or denoting the Pygmies: *centuries-old Pygmy chants from central Africa.* ■ **(pygmy)** (of a person or thing) very small. ■ **(pygmy)** used in names of animals and plants that are much smaller than more typical kinds, e.g., **pygmy hippopotamus, pygmy water lily.** —**pyg·me·an** /'pigmēən; pig'mēən/ *adj.* (*archaic*).

py·lon /'pī,län; -lən/ ▸*n.* an upright structure that is used for support or for navigational guidance, in particular: ■ a tower used for carrying power lines high above the ground. ■ a pillarlike structure on the wing of an aircraft used for carrying an engine, weapon, fuel tank, or other load. ■ a tower or post marking a path for light aircraft, cars, or other vehicles, esp. in racing. ■ a monumental gateway to an ancient Egyptian temple formed by two truncated pyramidal towers.

py·lo·rus /pī'lôrəs; pə-/ ▸*n.* (*pl.* **-lo·ri** /-'lôr,ī; -'lôrē/) *Anat.* the opening from the stomach into the duodenum.

py·or·rhe·a /,pīə'rēə/ ▸*n.* another term for **PERIODONTITIS**.

pyr·a·mid /'pirə,mid/ ▸*n.* **1** a monumental structure with a square or triangular base and sloping sides that meet in a point at the top, esp. one built of stone as a royal tomb in ancient Egypt. **2** a thing, shape, or graph with such a form. ■ *Geom.* a polyhedron of which one face is a polygon of any number of sides, and the other faces are triangles with a common vertex. ■ a pile of things with such a form. ■ *Anat.* a structure of more or less pyramidal form, esp. in the brain or the renal medulla. ■ an organization or system that is structured with fewer people or things at each level as one approaches the top: *the lowest*

strata of the social pyramid. ◾ a system of financial growth achieved by a small initial investment, with subsequent investments being funded by using unrealized profits as collateral.
▸ *v.* [*tr.*] heap or stack in the shape of a pyramid. ◾ achieve a substantial return on (money or property) after making a small initial investment. —**py·ram·i·dal** /pi'ramidl/ *adj.* —**py·ram·i·dal·ly** *adv.* —**pyr·a·mid·i·cal** /ˌpirə'midikəl/ *adj.* —**pyr·a·mid·i·cal·ly** *adv.*

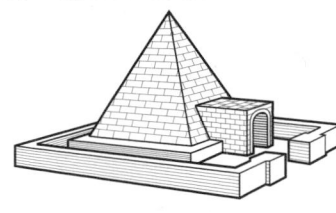

pyramid

pyre /pīr/ ▸*n.* a heap of combustible material, esp. one for burning a corpse as part of a funeral ceremony. ▷mid 17th cent.: via Latin from Greek *pura*, from *pur* 'fire.'

py·re·thrum /pī'rēтнrəm; -'reтнrəm/ ▸*n.* an aromatic plant (genus *Tanacetum*, formerly *Chrysanthemum* or *Pyrethrum*) of the daisy family, typically having feathery foliage and brightly colored flowers. ◾ an insecticide made from the dried flowers of these plants.

Py·rex /'pī,reks/ ▸*n.* [usu. as *adj.*] *trademark* a hard, heat-resistant type of glass, typically used for ovenware: *a set of Pyrex dishes.*

pyr·i·dox·ine /ˌpirə'däk,sēn/ ▸*n.* *Biochem.* a colorless weakly basic solid present chiefly in cereals, liver oils, and yeast, and important in the metabolism of unsaturated fatty acids. Also called **VITAMIN B₆** (see **VITAMIN B**).

py·rim·i·dine /pə'rimə,dēn; pī-/ ▸*n.* *Chem.* a colorless crystalline compound, $C_4H_4N_2$, with basic properties. ◾ (also **pyrimidine base**) a substituted derivative of this, esp. the bases thymine and cytosine present in DNA.

py·rite /'pī,rīt/ (also **py·rites** /pə'rītēz; pī-/) ▸*n.* a shiny yellow mineral consisting of iron disulfide and typically occurring as intersecting cubic crystals. Also called **FOOL'S GOLD.** —**py·rit·ic** /pī'ritik; pə-/ *adj.*

—**py·rit·i·za·tion** /pə,rītə'zāsʜən; pī-/ *n.* —**py·ri·tize** /'pīrīt,īz/ *v.* —**py·ri·tous** /pə'rītəs; pī-/ *adj.*

py·ro·e·lec·tric /ˌpirō-i'lektrik/ ▸*adj.* having the property of becoming electrically charged when heated. ◾ of, relating to, or utilizing this property: *a pyroelectric detector.* —**py·ro·e·lec·tric·i·ty** /-i,lek'trisitē/ *n.*

py·ro·gen·ic /ˌpirō'jenik/ ▸*adj.* *Med.* inducing fever. ◾ caused or produced by combustion or the application of heat. —**py·ro·ge·nic·i·ty** /ˌpirōjə'nisitē/ *n.*

py·ro·ma·ni·a /ˌpirō'mānēə/ ▸*n.* an obsessive desire to set fire to things. —**py·ro·ma·ni·ac** /-'mānē,ak/ *n.* —**py·ro·ma·ni·a·cal** /-mə'nīəkəl/ *adj.* —**py·ro·man·ic** /-'manik/ *adj.*

py·rom·e·ter /pī'rämitər/ ▸*n.* an instrument for measuring high temperatures, esp. in furnaces and kilns. —**py·ro·met·ric** /ˌpirō'metrik/ *adj.* —**py·ro·met·ri·cal·ly** /ˌpirō'metrik(ə)lē/ *adv.* —**py·rom·e·try** /-trē/ *n.*

py·ro·tech·nic /ˌpirə'teknik/ ▸*adj.* of or relating to fireworks. ◾ brilliant or sensational. —**py·ro·tech·ni·cal** *adj.* —**py·ro·tech·nist** /-nist/ *n.* —**py·ro·tech·ny** /'pīrə,teknē/ *n.*

py·ro·tech·nics /ˌpirə'tekniks/ ▸*pl. n.* a fireworks display. ◾ a brilliant performance or display, esp. of a specified skill: *he thrilled his audience with vocal pyrotechnics.* ◾ [treated as *sing.*] the art of making or displaying fireworks.

py·rox·ene /pī'räk,sēn; pə-/ ▸*n.* any of a large class of rock-forming silicate minerals, generally containing calcium, magnesium, and iron and typically occurring as prismatic crystals.

Pyr·rhic /'pirik/ (also **pyr·rhic**) ▸*adj.* (of a victory) won at too great a cost to have been worthwhile for the victor.

pyr·rhic /'pirik/ ▸*n.* a metrical foot of two short or unaccented syllables. ▸*adj.* written in or based on such a measure.

Py·thag·o·re·an the·o·rem /pə,тнagə'rēən; pī-/ ▸a theorem attributed to Pythagoras that the square of the hypotenuse of a right triangle is equal to the sum of the squares of the other two sides.

py·thon /'pī,тнän; 'pīтнən/ ▸*n.* a large heavy-bodied nonvenomous snake (genera *Python*, *Morelia*, and *Aspidites*, family Pythonidae) occurring throughout the Old World tropics, killing prey by constriction and asphyxiation. —**py·thon·ic** /pī'тнänik/ *adj.*

pyx /piks/ ▸*n.* **1** *Christian Church* the container in which the consecrated bread of the Eucharist is kept. **2** (in the UK) a box at the Royal Mint in which specimen gold and silver coins are deposited to be tested annually at the trial of the pyx.

Qq

Q¹ /kyōō/ (also **q**) ▸*n.* (*pl.* **Qs** or **Q's**) the seventeenth letter of the alphabet. ■ denoting the next after P in a set of items, categories, etc.

Q² ▸*abbr.* ■ quarter (used to refer to a specified quarter of the fiscal year). ■ queen (used esp. in describing card games and recording moves in chess): *17.Qb4.* ■ question.

q ▸*symb. Physics* electric charge.

QB ▸*abbr.* ■ *Football* quarterback.

QED ▸*abbr.* ■ quod erat demonstrandum (Latin 'which was to be demonstrated'), used to convey that a fact or situation demonstrates the truth of one's theory or claim, esp. to mark the conclusion of a formal proof.

QT (also **q.t.**) ▸*n.* (in phrase **on the QT**) *inf.* secretly; stealthily.

qt. ▸*abbr.* quart(s).

qty. ▸*abbr.* quantity.

quack¹ /kwak/ ▸*n.* the characteristic harsh sound made by a duck. ▸*v.* [*intr.*] (of a duck) make this sound. ■ *inf.* talk loudly and foolishly.

quack² ▸*n.* a person who dishonestly claims to have special knowledge and skill in some field, typically in medicine: [as *adj.*] *quack cures.* —**quack·er·y** /'kwakərē/ *n.* —**quack·ish** *adj.*

quad /kwäd/ ▸*n.* **1** *inf.* short for: ■ a quadrangle. ■ QUADRUPLET (sense 1). ■ a quadriceps. ■ quadraphonic sound. ■ a quadriplegic. **2** a radio antenna in the form of a square or rectangle broken in the middle of one side. **3** a traditional roller skate. **4** a metal block in various sizes, lower than type height, used in letterpress printing for filling up short lines.
▸*adj. inf.* short for: ■ quadruple. ■ quadrophonic.

quad. ▸*abbr.* ■ quadrangle. ■ quadrant.

quad·ran·gle /'kwä,draNGgəl/ ▸*n. Geom.* a four-sided plane figure, esp. a square or rectangle. ■ a square or rectangular space or courtyard enclosed by buildings. ■ the area shown on a standard topographic map sheet of the U.S. Geological Survey. —**quad·ran·gu·lar** /kwä-'draNGgyələr/ *adj.*

quad·rant /'kwädrənt/ ▸*n. technical* each of four quarters of a circle. ■ each of four parts of a plane, sphere, space, or body divided by two lines or planes at right angles. ■ *hist.* an instrument used for taking angular measurements of altitude in astronomy and navigation. ■ a panel with slots through which a lever is moved to orient or otherwise control a mechanism. ▷late Middle English (denoting the astronomical instrument): from Latin *quadrans, quadrant-* 'quarter,' from *quattuor* four. —**quad·ran·tal** /kwä'dran(t)l/ *adj.*

quad·ra·phon·ic /ˌkwädrə'fänik/ (also **quad·ro·phon·ic**) ▸*adj.* (of sound reproduction) transmitted through four channels. —**quad·ra·phon·i·cal·ly** /-ik(ə)lē/ *adv.* —**quad·ra·phon·ics** *pl. n.* —**qua·draph·o·ny** /kwä-'dräfənē/ *n.*

quad·rat·ic /kwä'dratik/ ▸*adj. Math.* involving the second and no higher power of an unknown quantity or variable: *a quadratic equation.* ▸*n.* a quadratic equation.

quad·ren·ni·al /kwä'dreNēəl/ ▸*adj.* recurring every four years. ■ lasting for or relating to a period of four years. —**quad·ren·ni·al·ly** *adv.*

quad·ri·ceps /'kwädrə,seps/ ▸*n.* (*pl.* same) *Anat.* the large muscle at the front of the thigh that acts to extend the leg.

quad·ri·lat·er·al /ˌkwädrə'latərəl/ ▸*n.* a four-sided figure.
▸*adj.* having four straight sides.

quad·rille¹ /kwä'dril; k(w)ə-/ ▸*n.* a square dance performed typically by four couples and containing five figures, each of which is a complete dance in itself.

quad·rille² ▸*n.* a trick-taking card game for four players using a deck of forty cards (i.e., one lacking eights, nines, and tens), fashionable in the 18th century.

quad·rille³ ▸*n.* a ruled grid of small squares, esp. on paper.

quad·ril·lion /kwä'drilyən/ ▸*cardinal number* (*pl.* **-lions** or (with numeral or quantifying word) same) a thousand raised to the power of five (10¹⁵). —**quad·ril·lionth** /-'drilyənTH/ *ordinal number.*

quad·ri·ple·gi·a /ˌkwädrə'plēj(ē)ə/ ▸*n. Med.* paralysis of all four limbs; tetraplegia. —**quad·ri·ple·gic** /-'plējik/ *adj. & n.*

quad·roon /kwä'drōōn/ ▸*n.* a person whose parents are a mulatto and a white person and who is therefore one-quarter black by descent.

quad·ro·phon·ic /ˌkwädrə'fänik/ ▸*adj.* variant spelling of QUADRAPHONIC.

quad·ru·ped /'kwädrə,ped/ ▸*n.* an animal that has four feet. —**quad·ru·pe·dal** /ˌkwädrə'pedl; kwä'drōōpədl/ *adj.*

quad·ru·ple /kwä'drōōpəl/ ▸*adj.* consisting of four parts or elements: *a quadruple murder.* ■ consisting of four times as much or as many as usual. ■ (of time in music) having four beats in a bar.
▸*v.* increase or be increased fourfold: [*intr.*] *oil prices quadrupled.*
▸*n.* a quadruple thing, number, or amount. —**quad·ru·ply** /-p(ə)lē/ *adv.*

quad·ru·plet /kwä'drōōplit/ ▸*n.* **1** (usu. **quadruplets**) each of four children born at one birth. **2** *Mus.* a group of four notes to be performed in the time of three.

quad·ru·pli·cate ▸*adj.* /kwä'drōōpləkit/ consisting of four parts or elements: ■ of which four copies are made. —**quad·ru·pli·ca·tion** /kwä-ˌdrōōplə'kāshən/ *n.*

quaff /kwäf/ ▸*v.* [*tr.*] drink (something, esp. an alcoholic drink) heartily.
▸*n. inf., dated* an alcoholic drink. —**quaff·a·ble** *adj.* —**quaff·er** *n.*

quag·ga /'kwagə/ ▸*n.* an extinct South African zebra (*Equus quagga*) that had a yellowish-brown coat with darker stripes, exterminated in 1883.

quag·mire /'kwag,mīr/ ▸*n.* a soft boggy area of land that gives way underfoot. ■ an awkward, complex, or hazardous situation: *a legal quagmire.*

qua·hog /'kwô,hôg; -,häg; 'kwō-; 'kō-/ (also **qua·haug**) ▸*n.* a large, rounded edible clam (*Venus mercenaria*, family Veneridae) of the Atlantic coast of North America.

quail¹ /kwāl/ ▸*n.* (*pl.* same or **quails**) **1** a small, short-tailed Old World game bird (family Phasianidae) resembling a tiny partridge, typically having brown camouflaged plumage. Three genera, in particular *Coturnix*, and several species include the **common quail** (*C. coturnix*). **2** a small or medium-sized New World game bird (family Phasianidae or Odontophoridae) the male of which has distinctive facial markings. Several genera and many species include the bobwhite.

quail² ▸*v.* [*intr.*] feel or show fear or apprehension.

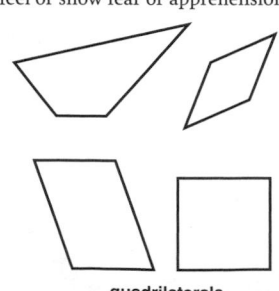

quadrilaterals

quaint /kwānt/ ▸*adj.* attractively unusual or old-fashioned. ▷Middle English: from Old French *cointe*, from Latin *cognitus* 'ascertained,' past participle of *cognoscere.* The original sense was 'wise, clever,' also 'ingenious, cunningly devised,' hence 'out of the ordinary' and the current sense (late 18th cent.). —**quaint·ly** *adv.* —**quaint·ness** *n.*

quake /kwāk/ ▸*v.* [intr.] (esp. of the earth) shake or tremble: *the rumbling vibrations set the whole valley quaking.* ■ (of a person) shake or shudder with fear: *those words should have them quaking in their boots.*
▸*n. inf.* an earthquake. ■ an act of shaking or quaking. —**quak·y** *adj.* (**quak·i·er, quak·i·est**).

Quak·er /'kwākər/ ▸*n.* a member of the Religious Society of Friends, a Christian movement founded by George Fox *c.*1650 and devoted to peaceful principles. Central to the Quakers' belief is the rejection of both formal ministry and all set forms of worship. —**Quak·er·ish** *adj.* —**Quak·er·ism** /-izəm/ *n.*

quak·ing grass ▸*n.* a slender-stalked grass (genus *Briza*) with oval or heart-shaped flowerheads that tremble in the wind.

qual·i·fi·ca·tion /ˌkwäləfə'kāSHən/ ▸*n.* **1** a quality or accomplishment that makes someone suitable for a particular job or activity. ■ the action or fact of becoming qualified as a practitioner of a particular profession or activity. ■ a condition that must be fulfilled before a right can be acquired; an official requirement: *the five-year residency qualification for presidential candidates.* **2** the action or fact of qualifying or being eligible for something: *they need to beat Poland to ensure qualification for the World Cup finals.* **3** a statement or assertion that makes another less absolute: *this important qualification needs to be remembered when interpreting the results.* **4** *Gram.* the attribution of a quality to a word, esp. a noun. —**qual·i·fi·ca·to·ry** /'kwäləfikəˌtôrē/ *adj.*

qual·i·fy /'kwäləˌfī/ ▸*v.* (**-fies, -fied**) **1** [intr.] be entitled to a particular benefit or privilege by fulfilling a necessary condition: *they do not qualify for compensation payments.* ■ become eligible for a competition or its final rounds, by reaching a certain standard or defeating a competitor: *he failed to qualify for the Olympic team.* ■ be or make properly entitled to be classed in a particular way: [intr.] *he qualifies as a genuine political refugee.* **2** [intr.] become officially recognized as a practitioner of a particular profession or activity by satisfying the relevant conditions or requirements, typically by undertaking a course of study and passing examinations: *after the war he qualified as a lawyer.* ■ [tr.] officially recognize or establish (someone) as a practitioner of a particular profession or activity: *the courses qualify you as an instructor of the sport.* ■ [tr.] make (someone) competent or knowledgeable enough to do something: *I'm not qualified to write on the subject.* **3** [tr.] make (a statement or assertion) less absolute; add reservations to: *she felt obliged to qualify her first short answer.* ■ archaic make (something extreme or undesirable) less severe or extreme. ■ archaic alter the strength or flavor of (something, esp. a liquid). ■ (**qualify something as**) archaic attribute a specified quality to something; describe something as. ■ [tr.] *Gram.* (of a word or phrase) attribute a quality to (another word, esp. a preceding noun). —**qual·i·fi·a·ble** *adj.* —**qual·i·fi·er** *n.*

qual·i·ta·tive /'kwäliˌtātiv/ ▸*adj.* relating to, measuring, or measured by the quality of something rather than its quantity: *a qualitative change in the undergraduate curriculum.* Often contrasted with QUANTITATIVE. ■ *Gram.* (of an adjective) describing the quality of something in size, appearance, value, etc. Such adjectives can be submodified by words such as *very* and have comparative and superlative forms. —**qual·i·ta·tive·ly** *adv.*

qual·i·ty /'kwälitē/ ▸*n.* (*pl.* -ties) **1** the standard of something as measured against other things of a similar kind; the degree of excellence of something. ■ general excellence of standard or level: *a masterpiece for connoisseurs of quality* | [as *adj.*] *a choice of quality beers.* ■ archaic high social standing: *people of quality.* ■ [treated as *pl.*] archaic people of high social standing: *he's dazed at being called on to speak before quality.* **2** a distinctive attribute or characteristic possessed by someone or something: *strong leadership qualities* ■ *Phonet.* the distinguishing characteristic or characteristics of a speech sound. ■ *Mus.* another term for TIMBRE. ▷Middle English (in the senses 'character, disposition' and 'particular property or feature'): from Old French *qualite,* from Latin *qualitas* (translating Greek *poiotēs*), from *qualis* 'of what kind, of such a kind.'

qual·i·ty con·trol ▸*n.* a system of maintaining standards in manufactured products by testing a sample of the output against the specification. —**qual·i·ty con·trol·ler** *n.*

qualm /kwä(l)m; kwô(l)m/ ▸*n.* an uneasy feeling of doubt, worry, or fear, esp. about one's own conduct; a misgiving: *military regimes generally have no qualms about controlling the press.* ■ a momentary faint or sick feeling. —**qualm·ish** *adj.*

quan·da·ry /'kwänd(ə)rē/ ▸*n.* (*pl.* -ries) a state of perplexity or uncertainty over what to do in a difficult situation: *Kate is in a quandary.* ■ a difficult situation; a practical dilemma: *a legal quandary.*

quan·ti·fi·er /'kwäntəˌfīər/ ▸*n.* *Logic* expression (e.g., *all, some*) that indicates the scope of a term to which it is attached. ■ *Gram.* a determiner or pronoun indicative of quantity (e.g., *all, both*).

quan·ti·fy /'kwäntəˌfī/ ▸*v.* (**-fies, -fied**) [tr.] express or measure the quantity of: *it's very hard to quantify the cost.* —**quan·ti·fi·a·bil·i·ty** /ˌkwäntəˌfīə'bilətē/ *n.* —**quan·ti·fi·a·ble** /'kwäntəˌfīəbəl/ *adj.* —**quan·ti·fi·ca·tion** /ˌkwäntəfi'kāSHən/ *n.*

quan·ti·ta·tive /'kwäntəˌtātiv/ ▸*adj.* relating to, measuring, or measured by the quantity of something rather than its quality: *quantitative analysis.* Often contrasted with QUALITATIVE. ■ denoting or relating to verse whose meter is based on the length of syllables, as in Latin, as opposed to the stress, as in English. —**quan·ti·ta·tive·ly** *adv.*

quan·ti·tive /'kwäntətiv/ ▸*adj.* another term for QUANTITATIVE. —**quan·ti·tive·ly** *adv.*

quan·ti·ty /'kwäntətē/ ▸*n.* (*pl.* -ties) **1** the amount or number of a material or immaterial thing not usually estimated by spatial measurement. ■ a certain, usually specified, amount or number of something: *a small quantity of food.* ■ (often **quantities**) a considerable number or amount of something: *she was able to drink quantities of beer.* **2** *Phonet.* the perceived length of a vowel sound or syllable. **3** *Math. & Physics* a value or component that may be expressed in numbers. ■ the figure or symbol representing this.

quan·tize /'kwänˌtīz/ ▸*v.* [tr.] *Physics* apply quantum theory to, in particular restrict the number of possible values of (a quantity) or states of (a system). —**quan·ti·za·tion** /ˌkwäntə'zāSHən/ *n.*

quan·tum /'kwäntəm/ ▸*n.* (*pl.* -ta /-tə/) **1** *Physics* a discrete quantity of energy proportional in magnitude to the frequency of the radiation it represents. ■ an analogous discrete amount of any other physical quantity, such as momentum or electric charge. ■ *Physiol.* the unit quantity of acetylcholine released at a neuromuscular junction by a single synaptic vesicle, contributing a discrete small voltage to the measured end-plate potential. **2** a required or allowed amount. ■ a share or portion.

quan·tum jump ▸*n.* *Physics* an abrupt transition of an electron, atom, or molecule from one quantum state to another, with the absorption or emission of a quantum. ■ (also **quantum leap**) *fig.* a huge, often sudden, increase or change in something.

quan·tum me·chan·ics ▸*pl. n.* [treated as *sing.*] *Physics* the branch of mechanics that deals with the mathematical description of the motion and interaction of subatomic particles, incorporating the concepts of quantization of energy, wave-particle duality, the uncertainty principle, and the correspondence principle. —**quan·tum·me·chan·i·cal** *adj.*

quan·tum med·i·cine ▸*n.* a branch of complementary medicine that uses low-dosage electromagnetic radiation in the treatment, diagnosis, and prevention of disease.

quan·tum state ▸*n.* *Physics* a state of a quantized system that is described by a set of quantum numbers.

quar·an·tine /'kwôrənˌtēn/ ▸*n.* a state, period, or place of isolation in which people or animals that have arrived from elsewhere or been exposed to infectious or contagious disease are placed.
▸*v.* [tr.] impose such isolation on (a person, animal, or place); put in quarantine.

quark¹ /kwärk/ ▸*n.* *Physics* any of a number of subatomic particles carrying a fractional electric charge, postulated as building blocks of the hadrons.

quark² ▸*n.* a type of low-fat curd cheese.

quar·rel¹ /'kwôrəl; 'kwä-/ ▸*n.* an angry argument or disagreement, typically between people who are usually on good terms. ■ a reason for disagreement with a person, group, or principle: *we have no quarrel with the people of the country, only with the dictator.*
▸*v.* (**-reled, -rel·ing**; *Brit.* **-relled, -rel·ling**) [intr.] have an angry argument or disagreement. ■ (**quarrel with**) take exception to or disagree with (something): *some people quarrel with this approach.* —**quar·rel·er** *n.*

quar·rel² ▸*n.* **1** *hist.* a short, heavy, square-headed arrow or bolt used in a crossbow. **2** another term for QUARRY³.

quar·rel·some /'kwôrəlsəm; 'kwä-/ ▸*adj.* given to or characterized by quarreling. —**quar·rel·some·ly** *adv.* —**quar·rel·some·ness** *n.*

Pronunciation Key ə *ago,* up; ər *over, fur;* a *hat;* ā *ate;* ä *car;* CH *chin;* e *let;* ē *see;* e(ə)r *air;* i *fit;* ī *by;* i(ə)r *ear;* NG *sing;* ō *go;* ô *law, for;* oi *toy;* ōō *good;* o͞o *goo;* ou *out;* SH *she;* TH *thin;* TH *then;* (h)w *why;* ZH *vision*

quar·ry[1] /'kwôrē; 'kwä-/ ▶n. (pl. **-ries**) a place, typically a large, deep pit, from which stone or other materials are or have been extracted.
▶v. (**-ries, -ried**) [tr.] extract (stone or other materials) from a quarry. ■ cut into (rock or ground) to obtain stone or other materials.

quar·ry[2] ▶n. (pl. **-ries**) an animal pursued by a hunter, hound, predatory mammal, or bird of prey. ■ a thing or person that is chased or sought: *the security police crossed the border in pursuit of their quarry.*

quar·ry[3] ▶n. (pl. **-ries**) (also **quarry tile**) an unglazed floor tile.

quart /kwôrt/ ▶n. a unit of liquid capacity equal to a quarter of a gallon or two pints, equivalent in the U.S. to approx. 0.94 liter and in Britain to approx. 1.13 liters. ■ a unit of dry capacity equivalent to approx. 1.10 liters.

quar·ter /'kwôrtər/ ▶n. **1** each of four equal or corresponding parts into which something is or can be divided: *she cut each apple into quarters* ■ a period of three months regarded as one fourth of a year, used esp. in reference to financial transactions such as the payment of bills or a company's earnings. ■ a period of fifteen minutes or a point of time marking the transition from one fifteen-minute period to the next: *the baby was born at a quarter past nine.* ■ a coin representing 25 cents, one fourth of a U.S. or Canadian dollar. ■ each of the four parts into which an animal's or bird's carcass may be divided, each including a leg or wing. ■ (**quarters**) the haunches or hindquarters of a horse. ■ one fourth of a lunar month. ■ (in various sports) each of four equal periods into which a game is divided. ■ one of four terms into which a school or college year may be divided. **2** a part of a town or city having a specific character or use: *a city with a fascinating medieval quarter.* **3** the direction of one of the points of the compass, esp. as a direction from which the wind blows. ■ a particular but unspecified person, group of people, or area: *help from an unexpected quarter.* ■ either side of a ship aft of the beam: *he trained his glasses over the starboard quarter.* **4** (**quarters**) rooms or lodgings, esp. those allocated to servicemen or to staff in domestic service: *the servants' quarters.* **5** pity or mercy shown toward an enemy or opponent who is in one's power: *the riot squad gave no quarter.*
▶v. [tr.] **1** divide into four equal or corresponding parts. ■ *hist.* cut (the body of an executed person) into four parts. ■ cut (a log) into quarters, and these into planks so as to show the grain well. **2** (**be quartered**) be stationed or lodged in a specified place. **3** range over or traverse (an area) in every direction. ■ [intr.] move at an angle; go in a diagonal or zigzag direction: *his young dog quartered back and forth in quick turns.*

quar·ter·back /'kwôrtər,bak/ ▶n. *Football* a player positioned behind the center who directs a team's offensive play. ■ *fig.* a person who directs or coordinates an operation or project.
▶v. [tr.] *Football* play as a quarterback for (a particular team). ■ *fig.* direct or coordinate (an operation or project).

quar·ter·deck /'kwôrtər,dek/ ▶n. the part of a ship's upper deck near the stern, traditionally reserved for officers. ■ the officers of a ship or the navy.

quar·ter·fi·nal /'kwôrtər,fīnl/ ▶n. a match or round of a tournament that precedes the semifinal.

quar·ter·ing /'kwôrtəriNG/ ▶n. **1** the provision of accommodations or lodgings, esp. for troops. **2** the action of dividing something into four parts.

quar·ter·ly /'kwôrtərlē/ ▶adj. done, produced, or occurring once every quarter of a year: *a quarterly newsletter is distributed to members.*
▶adv. once every quarter of a year: *interest is paid quarterly.*
▶n. (pl. **-lies**) a magazine or journal that is published four times a year.

quar·ter·mas·ter /'kwôrtər,mastər/ ▶n. **1** a military officer responsible for providing quarters, rations, clothing, and other supplies. **2** a naval petty officer with particular responsibility for steering and signals.

quarter note ▶n. *Mus.* a musical note having the time value of a quarter of a whole note or half a half note, represented by a large solid dot with a plain stem.

quar·tet /kwôr'tet/ ▶n. a group of four people playing music or singing together. ■ a composition for such a group. ■ a set of four people or things.

quar·to /'kwôrtō/ (abbr.: **4to**) ▶n. (pl. **-tos**) *Printing* a size of book page resulting from folding each printed sheet into four leaves (eight pages). ■ a book of this size. ■ a size of writing paper, 10 in. × 8 in. (254 × 203 mm).

quartz /kwôrts/ ▶n. a common hard white or colorless rock-forming mineral consisting of silicon dioxide. It is often colored by impurities (as in amethyst). ▷mid 18th cent.: from German *Quarz*, from Polish dialect *kwardy*, corresponding to standard Polish *twardy* 'hard.'

qua·sar /'kwā,zär/ ▶n. *Astron.* a massive and extremely remote celestial object, emitting exceptionally large amounts of energy, and typically having a starlike image in a telescope.

quash /kwôsh; kwäsh/ ▶v. [tr.] reject or void, esp. by legal procedure: *his conviction was quashed on appeal.* ■ put an end to; suppress.

quat·er·cen·ten·ar·y /,kwätərsen'tenərē; -'sentn,erē/ ▶n. (pl. **-ar·ies**) the four-hundredth anniversary of a significant event.
▶adj. of or relating to such an anniversary.

quat·er·nar·y /'kwätər,nerē/ ▶adj. **1** fourth in order or rank; belonging to the fourth order. **2** (**Quaternary**) *Geol.* of, relating to, or denoting the most recent period in the Cenozoic era, following the Tertiary period and comprising the Pleistocene and Holocene epochs (and thus including the present).
▶n. (**the Quaternary**) *Geol.* the Quaternary period or the system of deposits laid down during it.

quat·rain /'kwä,trān/ ▶n. a stanza of four lines, esp. one having alternate rhymes.

quat·re·foil /'katər,foil; 'katrə-/ ▶n. an ornamental design of four lobes or leaves as used in architectural tracery, resembling a flower or four-leaf clover.

quat·tro·cen·to /,kwätrō'CHentō/ ▶n. (**the quattrocento**) the 15th century as a period of Italian art or architecture.

qua·ver /'kwāvər/ ▶v. [intr.] (of a person's voice) shake or tremble in speaking, typically through nervousness or emotion.
▶n. **1** a shake or tremble in a person's voice. **2** *Mus., chiefly Brit.* another term for EIGHTH NOTE. —**qua·ver·ing·ly** adv. —**qua·ver·y** adj.

quay /kē; k(w)ā/ ▶n. a concrete, stone, or metal platform lying alongside or projecting into water for loading and unloading ships. —**quay·age** /'kēij; 'k(w)āij/ n.

quay·side /'kē,sīd; 'k(w)ā-/ ▶n. a quay and the area around it.

quea·sy /'kwēzē/ ▶adj. (**queas·i·er, queas·i·est**) nauseated; feeling sick. ■ inducing a feeling of nausea. ■ *fig.* slightly nervous or worried about something. —**quea·si·ly** /-zəlē/ adv. —**quea·si·ness** n.

Quech·ua /'keCHwə/ (also **Quech·a** /'keCHə/) ▶n. (pl. same or **Quech·uas**) **1** a member of an American Indian people of Peru and parts of Bolivia, Chile, Colombia, and Ecuador. **2** the language or group of languages of this people.
▶adj. of or relating to this people or their language. —**Quech·uan** /-wən/ (also **Quech·an** /'keCHən/) adj. & n.

queen /kwēn/ ▶n. **1** the female ruler of an independent state, esp. one who inherits the position by right of birth. ■ (also **queen consort**) a king's wife. ■ a woman or thing regarded as excellent or outstanding of its kind: *the queen of romance novelists.* ■ a woman or girl chosen to hold the most important position in a festival or event: *football stars and homecoming queens.* ■ (**the Queen**) *dated* (in the UK) the national anthem when there is a female sovereign. ■ *inf.* a man's wife or girlfriend. **2** the most powerful chess piece that each player has, able to move any number of unobstructed squares in any direction along a rank, file, or diagonal on which it stands. **3** a playing card bearing a representation of a queen, normally ranking next below a king and above a jack. **4** *Entomol.* a reproductive female in a colony of social ants, bees, wasps, etc. **5** *inf., offens.* a male homosexual, typically one regarded as ostentatiously effeminate. ■ a man with a particular obsession or fetish: *a leather queen.*
▶v. [tr.] **1** (**queen it over**) (of a woman) behave in an unpleasant and superior way toward. **2** *Chess* convert (a pawn) into a queen when it reaches the opponent's back rank on the board. —**queen·dom** /-dəm/ n. —**queen·like** /-,līk/ adj. —**queen·ship** /-,SHip/ n.

Queen Anne's lace ▶n. the uncultivated form of the carrot (*Daucus carota*), with broad round heads of tiny white flowers that resemble lace.

queen bee ▶n. the single reproductive female in a hive or colony of honeybees. ■ *inf.* a woman who has a dominant or controlling position in a particular group or sphere.

queen·ly /'kwēnlē/ ▶adj. (**-li·er, -li·est**) fit for or appropriate to a queen. —**queen·li·ness** /-lēnis/ n.

queen-sized (also **queen-size**) ▶adj. (esp. of a commercial product) of a larger size than the standard but smaller than something that is king-sized: *a queen-sized comforter.*

queer /kwi(ə)r/ ▶adj. **1** strange; odd: *a queer feeling.* ■ *dated* slightly ill. **2** *inf., usu. offens.* (esp. of a man) homosexual.
▶n. *inf., usu. offens.* a homosexual man.
▶v. [tr.] *inf.* spoil or ruin (an agreement, event, or situation). —**queer·ish** adj. —**queer·ly** adv. —**queer·ness** n.

quell /kwel/ ▶v. [tr.] put an end to (a rebellion or other disorder), typically by the use of force. ■ subdue or silence (someone): *Connor quelled him* *with a look.* ■ suppress (a feeling, esp. an unpleasant one): *he spoke up again to quell any panic among the assembled youngsters.* —**quell·er** *n.*

quench /kwenCH/ ▶ *v.* [tr.] **1** satisfy (one's thirst) by drinking. ■ satisfy (a desire). **2** extinguish (a fire). ■ stifle or suppress (a feeling). ■ rapidly cool (red-hot metal or other material), esp. in cold water or oil.
▶ *n.* an act of quenching something very hot. —**quench·a·ble** *adj.* —**quench·er** *n.* (*chiefly Physics Metallurgy*) —**quench·less** *adj.* (*poetic/lit.*)

quer·u·lous /ˈkwer(y)ələs/ ▶ *adj.* complaining in a petulant or whining manner. —**quer·u·lous·ly** *adv.* —**quer·u·lous·ness** *n.*

que·ry /ˈkwi(ə)rē/ ▶ *n.* (*pl.* **-ries**) a question, esp. one addressed to an official or organization. ■ used in writing or speaking to question the accuracy of a following statement or to introduce a question.
▶ *v.* (**-ries, -ried**) [tr.] ask a question about (something), esp. in order to express one's doubts about it or to check its validity or accuracy: *he queried the medical database.* ■ [tr.] put a question or questions to (someone).

que·so fres·co /ˈkāsō ˈfreskō/ ▶ *n.* a semisoft fresh Mexican cheese, white in color, typically served shredded over hot foods.

quest /kwest/ ▶ *n.* a long or arduous search for something. ■ (in medieval romance) an expedition made by a knight to accomplish a prescribed task.
▶ *v.* [intr.] search for something: *he was a real scientist, questing after truth.* ■ [tr.] *poetic/lit.* search for; seek out. —**quest·er** (also **ques·tor**) *n.* —**quest·ing·ly** *adv.*

ques·tion /ˈkwesCHən/ ▶ *n.* a sentence worded or expressed so as to elicit information. ■ a doubt about the truth or validity of something: *there is no question that America faces the threat of Balkanization.* ■ the raising of a doubt about or objection to something: *her loyalty is really beyond question.* ■ a matter forming the basis of a problem requiring resolution: *the question of political authority.* ■ a matter or concern depending on or involving a specified condition or thing: *it was not simply a question of age.*
▶ *v.* [tr.] ask questions of (someone), esp. in an official context: *four men were being questioned about the killings* | [as *n.*] (**questioning**) *the young lieutenant escorted us to the barracks for questioning.* ■ feel or express doubt about; raise objections to: *members had questioned the cost of the scheme.* —**ques·tion·er** *n.* —**ques·tion·ing·ly** *adv.*
▶ □ **be** (just or only) **a question of time** be certain to happen sooner or later. □ **bring something into question** raise an issue for further consideration or discussion. □ **in question 1** being considered or discussed. **2** in doubt. □ **out of the question** too impracticable or unlikely to merit discussion.

ques·tion·a·ble /ˈkwesCHənəbəl/ ▶ *adj.* doubtful as regards truth or quality: *it is questionable whether any of these exceptions is genuine.* ■ not clearly honest, honorable, or wise. —**ques·tion·a·bil·i·ty** /ˌkwesCHənəˈbilətē/ *n.* —**ques·tion·a·ble·ness** *n.* —**ques·tion·a·bly** /-əblē/ *adv.*

ques·tion mark ▶ *n.* a punctuation mark (?) indicating a question. ■ *fig.* used to express doubt or uncertainty about something: *there's a question mark over his future.*

ques·tion·naire /ˌkwesCHəˈne(ə)r/ ▶ *n.* a set of printed or written questions with a choice of answers, devised for the purposes of a survey or statistical study.

quet·zal /ketˈsäl/ ▶ *n.* **1** a bird (genus *Pharomachrus*, family Trogonidae) with iridescent green plumage and typically red underparts, found in the forests of tropical America. The male **resplendent quetzal** (*P. mocinno*) has very long tail coverts and was venerated by the Aztecs. **2** the basic monetary unit of Guatemala, equal to 100 centavos.

queue /kyo͞o/ ▶ *n.* **1** *chiefly Brit.* a line or sequence of people or vehicles awaiting their turn to be attended to or to proceed. **2** *Comput.* a list of data items, commands, etc., stored so as to be retrievable in a definite order, usually the order of insertion. **3** *archaic* a braid of hair worn at the back.
▶ *v.* (**queues, queued, queu·ing** or **queue·ing**) [intr.] *chiefly Brit.* **1** take one's place in a queue: *they had queued for food* | *fig. companies are queuing up to move to the bay.* **2** [tr.] *Comput.* arrange in a queue.

quib·ble /ˈkwibəl/ ▶ *n.* **1** a slight objection or criticism: *the only quibble about this book is the price.* **2** *archaic* a play on words; a pun.
▶ *v.* [intr.] argue or raise objections about a trivial matter. —**quib·bler** *n.* —**quib·bling·ly** *adv.*

Qui·ché /kēˈCHā/ ▶ *n.* (*pl.* same or **-chés**) **1** a member of a people inhabiting the western highlands of Guatemala. **2** the Mayan language of this people.
▶ *adj.* of or relating to this people or their language. ▷ the name in Quiché.

quick /kwik/ ▶ *adj.* **1** moving fast or doing something in a short time. ■ lasting or taking a short time: *she took a quick look through the drawers.*

■ happening with little or no delay: prompt: *children like to see quick results from their efforts.* **2** (of a person) prompt to understand, think, or learn; intelligent: *it was quick of him to spot the mistake.* ■ (of a person's eye or ear) keenly perceptive; alert. ■ (of a person's temper) easily roused.
▶ *adv. inf.* at a fast rate; quickly: *he'll find some place where he can make money quicker* | [as *interj.*] *Get out, quick!*
▶ *n.* **1** (**the quick**) the soft, tender flesh below the growing part of a fingernail or toenail. ■ *fig.* the central or most sensitive part of someone or something. **2** [as *pl. n.*] (**the quick**) *archaic* those who are living: *the quick and the dead.* ▷Old English *cwic, cwicu* 'alive, animated, alert,' of Germanic origin; related to Dutch *kwiek* 'sprightly' and German *keck* 'saucy,' from an Indo-European root shared by Latin *vivus* 'alive' and Greek *bios, zōē* 'life.' —**quick·ly** *adv.* —**quick·ness** *n.*
▶ □ **cut someone to the quick** cause someone deep distress by a hurtful remark or action.

quick·en /ˈkwikən/ ▶ *v.* **1** make or become faster or quicker: [tr.] *she quickened her pace, desperate to escape* | [intr.] *I felt my pulse quicken.* **2** [intr.] spring to life; become animated: *her interest quickened.* ■ [tr.] stimulate: *the coroner's words suddenly quickened his own memories.* ■ [tr.] give or restore life to: *on the third day after his death the human body of Jesus was quickened by the Spirit.* ■ [tr.] *archaic* make (a fire) burn brighter.

quick·ie /ˈkwikē/ *inf.* ▶ *n.* a thing done or made quickly or hastily, in particular: ■ a rapidly consumed alcoholic drink. ■ a brief act of sexual intercourse.
▶ *adj.* done or made quickly: *his wife cooperated with a quickie divorce.*

quick·lime /ˈkwikˌlīm/ ▶ *n.* see LIME¹.

quick·sand /ˈkwikˌsand/ ▶ *n.* (also **quicksands**) loose wet sand that yields easily to pressure and in which things easily sink: *fig. John found himself sinking fast in financial quicksand.*

quick·sil·ver /ˈkwikˌsilvər/ ▶ *n.* the liquid metal mercury. ■ used in similes and metaphors to describe something that moves or changes very quickly, or that is difficult to hold or contain.

quick·step /ˈkwikˌstep/ ▶ *n.* a dance that combines the movements of the waltz and the Charleston. ■ a piece of music written for such a dance, much like a fast foxtrot. ■ a step used when marching in quick time.
▶ *v.* (**-stepped, -step·ping**) [intr.] dance the quickstep.

quick-tem·pered ▶ *adj.* quick to lose one's temper; irascible.

quick-wit·ted ▶ *adj.* showing or characterized by an ability to think or respond quickly or effectively. —**quick-wit·ted·ness** *n.*

quid¹ /kwid/ ▶ *n.* (*pl.* same) *Brit., inf.* one pound sterling.

quid² ▶ *n.* a lump of tobacco for chewing.

quid pro quo /ˈkwid ˌprō ˈkwō/ ▶ *n.* (*pl.* **quos**) a favor or advantage granted or expected in return for something: *the pardon was a quid pro quo for their help in releasing hostages.*

qui·es·cent /kwēˈesnt; kwī-/ ▶ *adj.* in a state or period of inactivity or dormancy. —**qui·es·cence** *n.* —**qui·es·cent·ly** *adv.*

qui·et /ˈkwīət/ ▶ *adj.* (**qui·et·er, qui·et·est**) **1** making little or no noise. ■ (of a place, period of time, or situation) without much activity, disturbance, or excitement: *the street below was quiet, little traffic braving the snow.* ■ without being disturbed or interrupted: *all he wanted was a quiet drink.* **2** carried out discreetly, secretly, or with moderation: *we wanted a quiet wedding.* ■ (of a person) tranquil and reserved by nature; not brash or forceful. ■ expressed in a restrained or understated way: *Molly spoke with quiet confidence.* ■ (of a color or garment) unobtrusive; not bright or showy.
▶ *n.* absence of noise or bustle; silence; calm: *the ringing of the telephone shattered the morning quiet.* ■ freedom from disturbance or interruption by others: *her wish for peace and quiet.* ■ a peaceful or settled state of affairs in social or political life: *a period of comparative quiet.*
▶ *v.* make or become silent, calm, or still: [tr.] *there are ways of quieting kids down* | [intr.] *the journalists quieted down as Judy stepped on to the dais.* —**qui·et·ly** *adv.* —**qui·et·ness** *n.*
▶ □ **keep quiet** (or **keep someone quiet**) refrain or prevent someone from speaking or from disclosing something secret. □ **keep something quiet** (or **keep quiet about something**) refrain from disclosing information about something; keep something secret. □ (**as**) **quiet as a mouse** (of a person or animal) extremely quiet or docile.

qui·e·tude /ˈkwīəˌt(y)o͞od/ ▶ *n.* a state of stillness, calmness, and quiet in a person or place.

qui·e·tus /kwīˈētəs/ ▶ *n.* (*pl.* **qui·e·tus·es**) death or something that causes

---

Pronunciation Key ə *ago, up*; ər *over, fur*; a *hat*; ā *ate*; ä *car*; CH *chin*; e *let*; ē *see*; e(ə)r *air*; i *fit*; ī *by*; i(ə)r *ear*; NG *sing*; ō *go*; ô *law, for*; oi *toy*; o͝o *good*; o͞o *goo*; ou *out*; SH *she*; TH *thin*; T͟H *then*; (h)w *why*; ZH *vision*

death, regarded as a release from life. ■ *archaic* something that has a calming or soothing effect.

quill /kwil/ ▶*n.* **1** (also **quill feather**) any of the main wing or tail feathers of a bird. ■ the hollow shaft of a feather, esp. the lower part that lacks barbs. ■ (also **quill pen**) a pen made from a main wing or tail feather of a large bird by pointing and slitting the end of the shaft. **2** an object in the form of a thin tube, in particular: ■ the hollow sharp spines of a porcupine, hedgehog, or other spiny mammal. ■ (**quills**) *inf., dated* panpipes. ■ a weaver's spindle.
▶*v.* [*tr.*] **1** form (fabric) into small cylindrical folds. **2** pierce or cover (fabric or bark) with quills.

quilt /kwilt/ ▶*n.* a warm bed covering made of padding enclosed between layers of fabric and kept in place by lines of stitching, typically applied in a decorative design. ■ a knitted or fabric bedspread with decorative stitching. ■ a layer of padding used for insulation.
▶*v.* [*tr.*] join together (layers of fabric or padding) with lines of stitching to form a bed covering or a warm garment, or for decorative effect. —**quilt·er** *n.* —**quilt·ing** *n.*

qui·na·ry /'kwīnərē/ ▶*adj.* of or relating to the number five, in particular: ■ of the fifth order or rank.

quince /kwins/ ▶*n.* **1** a hard, acid, pear-shaped fruit used in preserves or as flavoring. **2** the shrub or small tree (*Cydonia oblonga*) of the rose family that bears this fruit, native to western Asia.

quin·cen·ten·ar·y /ˌkwinsən'tenərē; kwin'sentəˌnerē/ ▶*n.* & *adj.* another term for QUINCENTENNIAL.

quin·cen·ten·ni·al /ˌkwinsən'tenēəl/ ▶*n.* the five-hundredth anniversary of a significant event.
▶*adj.* of or relating to such an anniversary.

qui·nine /'kwīˌnīn/ ▶*n.* a bitter crystalline compound, $C_{20}H_{24}N_2O_2$, present in cinchona bark, used as a tonic and formerly as an antimalarial drug.

quin·o·lone /'kwinəˌlōn; 'kwinlˌōn/ ▶*n.* any of a class of antibiotics used in treating a variety of infections, and thought to be responsible for antibiotic resistance in some microbes.

quin·sy /'kwinzē/ ▶*n.* inflammation of the throat, esp. an abscess in the region of the tonsils.

quint /kwint/ ▶*n.* **1** (in piquet) a sequence of five cards of the same suit. A run of ace, king, queen, jack, and ten is a **quint major** and one of jack, ten, nine, eight, and seven a **quint minor**. **2** short for QUINTUPLET.

quin·tal /'kwintl/ ▶*n.* a unit of weight equal to a hundredweight (112 lb) or formerly, 100 lb. ■ a unit of weight equal to 100 kg.

quin·tes·sence /kwin'tesəns/ ▶*n.* the most perfect or typical example of a quality or class. ■ the aspect of something regarded as the intrinsic and central constituent of its character: *advertising is the quintessence of marketing.* ■ a refined essence or extract of a substance. ■ (in classical and medieval philosophy) a fifth substance in addition to the four elements, thought to compose the heavenly bodies and to be latent in all things. —**quin·tes·sen·tial** /ˌkwintə'senSHəl/ *adj.*

quin·tet /kwin'tet/ ▶*n.* a group of five people playing music or singing together. ■ a musical composition for such a group. ■ any group of five people or things: *a novel about a quintet of interrelated lovers.*

quin·til·lion /kwin'tilyən/ ▶*cardinal number* (*pl.* **-lions** or (with numeral) same) a thousand raised to the power of six (10^{18}). —**quin·til·lionth** /-yənTH/ *ordinal number* .

quin·tu·ple /kwin't(y)ŌŌpəl; -'təpəl/ ▶*adj.* consisting of five parts or things. ■ five times as much or as many. ■ (of time in music) having five beats in a bar.
▶*v.* increase or cause to increase fivefold.
▶*n.* a fivefold number or amount; a set of five. —**quin·tu·ply** /-(ə)lē/ *adv.*

quin·tu·plet /kwin'təplət; -'t(y)ŌŌplət/ ▶*n.* **1** (usu. **quintuplets**) each of five children born to the same mother at one birth. **2** *Mus.* a group of five notes to be performed in the time of three or four.

quip /kwip/ ▶*n.* a witty remark. ■ *archaic* a verbal equivocation.
▶*v.* (**quipped, quip·ping**) [*intr.*] make a witty remark. —**quip·ster** /-stər/ *n.*

quire /kwīr/ ▶*n.* four sheets of paper or parchment folded to form eight leaves, as in medieval manuscripts. ■ any collection of leaves one within another in a manuscript or book. ■ 25 (formerly 24) sheets of paper; one twentieth of a ream.

quirk /kwərk/ ▶*n.* **1** a peculiar behavioral habit: *his distaste for travel is an endearing quirk.* ■ a strange chance occurrence: *a strange quirk of fate had led her to working for Nathan.* ■ a sudden twist, turn, or curve. **2** *Archit.* an acute hollow between convex or other moldings.
▶*v.* [*intr.*] (of a person's mouth or eyebrow) move or twist suddenly, esp. to express surprise or amusement. ■ [*tr.*] move or twist (one's mouth or eyebrow) in such a way. ▷early 16th cent. (as a verb): of unknown

origin. The early sense of the noun was 'subtle verbal twist, quibble,' later 'unexpected twist.' —**quirk·ish** *adj.* —**quirk·y** *adj.*

quirt /kwərt/ ▶*n.* a short-handled riding whip with a braided leather lash.
▶*v.* [*tr.*] hit with a whip of this kind.

quis·ling /'kwizliNG/ ▶*n.* a traitor who collaborates with an enemy force occupying their country.

quit[1] /kwit/ ▶*v.* (**quit·ting**; *past* and *past part.* **quit·ted** or **quit**) **1** [*tr.*] leave (a place), usually permanently. ■ *inf.* resign from (a job): *she quit her job in a pizza restaurant* | [*intr.*] *he quit as manager.* ■ *inf.* stop or discontinue (an action or activity): *quit moaning!* | *I want to quit smoking.* **2** (**quit oneself**) *archaic* behave in a specified way: *quit yourselves like men, and fight.*
▶*adj.* (**quit of**) rid of: *I want to be quit of him.*

quit[2] ▶*n.* [in comb.] used in names of various small songbirds found in the Caribbean area, e.g., **bananaquit, grassquit.**

quite /kwīt/ ▶*adv.* **1** to the utmost or most absolute extent or degree; absolutely; completely: *are you quite certain about this?* ■ very; really (used as an intensifier): *"You've no intention of coming back?" "I'm quite sorry, but no, I have not."* **2** to a certain or fairly significant extent or degree; fairly: *it's quite warm outside.*
▶*interj.* (also **quite so**) *Brit.* expressing agreement with or understanding of a remark or statement: *"I don't want to talk about that now." "Quite."*
▶ □ **not quite** not completely or entirely: *my hair's not quite dry.* □ **quite a —** (also *often ironic* **quite the —**) used to indicate that the specified person or thing is perceived as particularly notable, remarkable, or impressive: *quite a party, isn't it?* □ **quite a lot** (or **a bit**) a considerable number or amount of something: *he's quite a bit older than she is.* □ **quite some** a considerable amount of: *she hasn't been seen for quite some time.* □ **quite the thing** *dated* socially acceptable: *she was quite the thing in heels and stockings and lipstick.*

quits /kwits/ ▶*adj.* (of two people) on even terms, esp. because a debt or score has been settled: *I think we're just about quits now, don't you?*
▶ □ **call it quits** agree or acknowledge that terms are now equal, esp. on the settlement of a debt. ■ decide to abandon an activity or venture.

quit·ter /'kwitər/ ▶*n.* *inf.* a person who gives up easily or does not have the courage or determination to finish a task.

quiv·er[1] /'kwivər/ ▶*v.* [*intr.*] tremble or shake with a slight rapid motion. ■ (of a person, a part of their body, or their voice) tremble with sudden strong emotion. ■ [*tr.*] cause (something) to make a slight rapid motion.
▶*n.* a slight trembling movement or sound, esp. one caused by a sudden strong emotion. —**quiv·er·ing·ly** *adv.* —**quiv·er·y** *adj.*

quiv·er[2] ▶*n.* an archer's portable case for holding arrows.

quiver

quix·ot·ic /kwik'sätik/ ▶*adj.* exceedingly idealistic; unrealistic and impractical: *a vast and perhaps quixotic project.* —**quix·ot·i·cal·ly** /-ik(ə)lē/ *adv.* —**quix·o·tism** /'kwiksəˌtizəm/ *n.* —**quix·o·try** /'kwiksətrē/ *n.*

quiz[1] /kwiz/ ▶*n.* (*pl.* **quiz·zes**) a test of knowledge, esp. a brief, informal test given to students.
▶*v.* (**quiz·zes, quizzed, quiz·zing**) [*tr.*] (often **be quizzed**) ask (someone) questions. ■ give (a student or class) an informal test or examination.

quiz[2] *archaic* ▶*v.* (**quiz·zes, quizzed, quiz·zing**) [*tr.*] **1** look curiously or intently at (someone) through or as if through an eyeglass. **2** make fun of.
▶*n.* (*pl.* **quiz·zes**) **1** a practical joke or hoax; a piece of banter or ridicule. ■ a person who ridicules another; a hoaxer or practical joker. **2** a person who is odd or eccentric in character or appearance. —**quiz·zer** *n.*

quiz·zi·cal /'kwizəkəl/ ▶*adj.* (of a person's expression or behavior) indicating mild or amused puzzlement. ■ *rare* causing mild amusement because of its oddness or strangeness. —**quiz·zi·cal·i·ty** /ˌkwizi'kalətē/ *n.* —**quiz·zi·cal·ly** *adv.* —**quiz·zi·cal·ness** *n.*

quoin /k(w)oin/ ▶*n.* **1** an external angle of a wall or building. ■ (also **quoin stone**) any of the stones or bricks forming such an angle; a cornerstone. **2** a wedge for raising the level of a cannon barrel or for keeping it from rolling.

quoit /k(w)oit/ ▶*n.* **1** a ring of iron, rope, or rubber thrown in a game to encircle or land as near as possible to an upright peg. ■ (**quoits**) [treated as *sing.*] a game consisting of aiming and throwing such rings. **2** the flat covering stone of a dolmen. ■ the dolmen itself.
▶*v.* [*tr.*] *archaic* throw or propel like a quoit.

quon·dam /'kwändəm; -,dam/ ▶*adj. formal* that once was; former: *quondam dissidents joined the establishment* | *its quondam popularity.*

Quon·set /'kwänsət/ (usu. **Quonset hut**) ▶*n. trademark* a building made of corrugated metal and having a semicircular cross section.

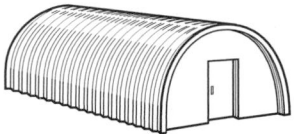

Quonset hut

quo·rum /'kwôrəm/ ▶*n.* (*pl.* **quo·rums**) the minimum number of members of an assembly or society that must be present at any of its meetings to make the proceedings of that meeting valid.

quo·ta /'kwōtə/ ▶*n.* a limited or fixed number or amount of people or things, in particular: ■ a limited quantity of a particular product that under official controls can be produced, exported, or imported. ■ a fixed share of something that a person or group is entitled to receive from a total: *the Faeroe Islands' commercial salmon quota.* ■ a person's share of something that must be done: *they were arrested to help fill the quota of arrests the security police had to make.* ■ a fixed minimum or maximum number of a particular group of people allowed to do something, as immigrants to enter a country, workers to undertake a job, or students to enroll for a course. ■ (in a system of proportional representation) the minimum number of votes required to elect a candidate. ■ *fig.* a person's share of a particular thing, quality, or attribute: *an Irishman with a treble quota of charm.*

quot·a·ble /'kwōtəbəl/ ▶*adj.* (of a person or remark) suitable for or worth quoting. —**quot·a·bil·i·ty** /,kwōtə'bilətē/ *n.*

quo·ta·tion /,kwō'tāsHən/ ▶*n.* **1** a group of words taken from a text or speech and repeated by someone other than the original author or speaker. ■ a short musical passage or visual image taken from one piece of music or work of art and used in another. ■ the action of quoting from a text, speech, piece of music, or work of art. **2** a formal statement setting out the estimated cost for a particular job or service. ■ *Stock Market* a price offered by a broker for the sale or purchase of a stock or other security. ■ *Stock Market* a registration granted to a company enabling their shares to be officially listed and traded.

quo·ta·tion mark ▶*n.* each of a set of punctuation marks, single (' ') or double (" "), used either to mark the beginning and end of a title or quoted passage or to indicate that a word or phrase is regarded as slang or jargon or is being discussed rather than used within the sentence.

quote /kwōt/ ▶*v.* [*tr.*] **1** repeat or copy out (a group of words from a text or speech), typically with an indication that one is not the original author or speaker: *he quoted a passage from the Psalms* | [*intr.*] *when we told her this she said, and I quote, "Phooey!"* ■ repeat a passage from (a work or author) or statement by (someone): *he quoted Shakespeare, Goethe, and other poets.* ■ mention or refer to (someone or something) to provide evidence or authority for a statement, argument, or opinion: *they won't be here at all in three years—you can quote me on that.* **2** give someone (the estimated price of a job or service). ■ (usu. **be quoted**) *Stock Market* give (a company) a quotation or listing on a stock exchange.
▶*n.* **1** a quotation from a text or speech. **2** a quotation giving the estimated cost for a particular job or service. ■ *Stock Market* a price offered by a broker for the sale or purchase of a stock or other security. ■ *Stock Market* a quotation or listing of a company on a stock exchange. **3** (**quotes**) quotation marks.
▶ □ **quote —— unquote** *inf.* used parenthetically when speaking to suggest quotation marks, to indicate the beginning and end of a statement or passage that one is reciting or repeating, in particular: ■ used to indicate the speaker's verbatim recitation of written words: *the second sentence says, quote, There has never been a better time to invest, unquote.* ■ used to repeat a spoken passage, esp. to emphasize the speaker's detachment from or disagreement with the original: *this is exactly what they told me: quote, You cannot bring a wheelchair into this restaurant, unquote.* □ **quote, unquote** *inf.* **1** used parenthetically when speaking to suggest quotation marks, to precede a statement or passage that one is reciting or repeating, in particular: ■ used to indicate the speaker's verbatim recitation of written words: *the brochure describes the view as, quote, unquote, unforgettably breathtaking.* **2** used parenthetically when speaking to suggest quotation marks, to precede a word or phrase that is meant to be sarcastic, mocking, or disapproving in its context: *she shows up with her quote, unquote sophisticated friends.*

quoth /kwōTH/ ▶*v.* [*tr.*] *archaic* or *humorous* said (used only in first and third person singular before the subject): *"Well, the tide is going out" quoth the sailor.*

quo·tid·i·an /kwō'tidēən/ ▶*adj.* of or occurring every day; daily: *the car sped noisily off through the quotidian traffic.* ■ ordinary or everyday, esp. when mundane: *his story is an achingly human one, mired in quotidian details.*

quo·tient /'kwōsHənt/ ▶*n.* **1** *Math.* a result obtained by dividing one quantity by another. **2** a degree or amount of a specified quality or characteristic: *Washington's cynicism quotient.*

Qu·r'an /kə'rän; -'ran/ (also **Qu·ran**) ▶*n.* variant spelling of **Koran**.

q.v. ▶*abbr.* used to direct a reader to another part of a book or article for further information.

qwerty /'kwərtē/ ▶*adj.* denoting the standard layout on English-language typewriters and keyboards, having *q, w, e, r, t,* and *y* as the first keys from the left on the top row of letters.

Rr

R[1] /är/ (also **r**) ▸*n.* (*pl.* **Rs** or **R's**) the eighteenth letter of the alphabet. ■ denoting the next after Q in a set of items, categories, etc.
▸ □ **the three Rs** reading, writing, and arithmetic, regarded as the fundamentals of learning.

R[2] ▸*abbr.* ■ rand: *a farm worth nearly R1,3-million.* ■ Réaumur: *198.6 °R.* ■ Regina or Rex: *Elizabeth R.* ■ (also ®) registered as a trademark. ■ (in the U.S.) Republican: *congressman Henry Hyde (R-Illinois).* ■ restricted, a rating in the Voluntary Movie Rating System that children under 17 require an accompanying parent or adult guardian for admission. ■ (on a gearshift) reverse. ■ (**R.**) River (chiefly on maps): *R. Cherwell.* ■ roentgen(s). ■ rook (in recording moves in chess): *21.Rh4.*
▸*symb.* ■ *Chem.* an unspecified alkyl or other organic radical or group. ■ electrical resistance. ■ *Chem.* the gas constant.

r ▸*abbr.* ■ recto. ■ (giving position or direction) right: *l to r: Evan, Nick, and David.* ■ *Law* rule: *under r 7.4 (6) the court may hear an application immediately.*
▸*symb.* ■ radius: $2\pi r$. ■ *Statistics* correlation coefficient.

RA ▸*abbr. Astron.* right ascension.

Ra[2] ▸*symb.* the chemical element radium.

rab·bet /'rabit/ ▸*n.* a step-shaped recess cut along the edge or in the face of a piece of wood, typically forming a match to the edge or tongue of another piece: [as adj.] *a rabbet joint.*

rab·bi /'rab,ī/ ▸*n.* (*pl.* -**bis**) a Jewish scholar or teacher, esp. one who studies or teaches Jewish law. ■ a person appointed as a Jewish religious leader. —**rab·bin·ate** /'rabənət; -,nāt/ *n.* —**rab·bin·i·cal** /rə'binikəl/ *adj.*

rab·bit /'rabit/ ▸*n.* a burrowing, gregarious, plant-eating mammal (family Leporidae) with long ears, long hind legs, and a short tail. ■ the fur of the rabbit. ■ another term for HARE. ■ a runner who acts as pacesetter in the first laps of a race. ▷late Middle English: apparently from Old French (compare French dialect *rabotte* 'young rabbit'), perhaps of Dutch origin (compare Flemish *robbe*).
▸ □ **pull a rabbit out of the hat** used to describe an action that is fortuitous, and may involve sleight of hand or deception.

rab·bit ears ▸*pl. n.* an indoor television antenna consisting of two movable telescoping rods, usu. on top of the television set.

rab·bit fe·ver ▸*n.* informal term for TULAREMIA.

rab·bit punch ▸*n.* a sharp chop with the edge of the hand to the back of the neck.

rab·ble /'rabəl/ ▸*n.* a disorderly crowd; a mob: *he was met by a rabble of noisy, angry youths.* ■ (**the rabble**) ordinary people, esp. when regarded as socially inferior or uncouth.

rab·ble-rous·er ▸*n.* a person who speaks with the intention of inflaming the emotions of a crowd of people, typically for political reasons. —**rab·ble-rous·ing** *adj. & n.*

rab·id /'rabəd; 'rā-/ ▸*adj.* **1** having or proceeding from an extreme or fanatical support of or belief in something: *a rabid feminist.* **2** (of an animal) affected with rabies. ■ of or connected with rabies. —**rab·id·i·ty** /rə'bidətē; ra-; rā-/ *n.* —**rab·id·ly** *adv.* —**rab·id·ness** *n.*

ra·bies /'rābēz/ ▸*n.* a contagious and fatal viral disease of dogs and other mammals, transmissible through the saliva to humans. Also called HYDROPHOBIA.

rac·coon /ra'kōōn; rə-/ (also **ra·coon**) ▸*n.* a grayish-brown American mammal (esp. the **common raccoon**, *Procyon lotor*) that has a foxlike face with a black mask, a ringed tail, and the habit of washing its food in water. The **raccoon family** (Procyonidae) also includes the coati and kinkajou.

race[1] /rās/ ▸*n.* **1** a competition between runners, horses, vehicles, boats, etc., to see which is the fastest in covering a set course: *I won the first 50-lap race.* ■ (**the races**) a series of such competitions for horses or dogs, held at a fixed time on a set course. ■ a situation in which individuals or groups compete to be first to achieve a particular objective: *the race for nuclear power.* **2** a strong or rapid current flowing through a narrow channel in the sea or a river: *angling for tuna in turbulent tidal races.*
▸*v.* **1** [intr.] compete with another or others to see who is fastest at covering a set course or achieving an objective: *the vet took blood samples from the horses before they raced.* ■ compete regularly in races as a sport or leisure activity: *the next year, he raced again for the team.* ■ [tr.] prepare and enter (an animal or vehicle) in races as a sport or leisure activity: *he raced his three horses simply for the fun of it.* **2** [intr.] move or progress swiftly or at full speed: *I raced into the house* | *fig. she spoke automatically, while her mind raced ahead.* ■ (of an engine or other machinery) operate at excessive speed. ■ (of a person's heart or pulse) beat faster than usual because of fear or excitement.
▸ □ **a race against time** a situation in which something must be done before a particular point in time: *it was a race against time to reach shore before the dinghy sank.*

race[2] ▸*n.* each of the major divisions of humankind, having distinct physical characteristics: *people of all races, colors, and creeds.* ■ a group of people sharing the same culture, history, language, etc.; an ethnic group: *we Scots were a bloodthirsty race then.* ■ a group or set of people or things with a common feature or features: *some male firefighters still regarded women as a race apart.* ■ *Biol.* a population within a species that is distinct in some way, esp. a subspecies: *people have killed so many tigers that two races are probably extinct.* ■ (in nontechnical use) each of the major divisions of living creatures: *a member of the human race* | *the race of birds.*

race·horse /'rās,hôrs/ ▸*n.* a horse bred, trained, and kept for racing.

ra·ceme /rā'sēm; rə-/ ▸*n. Bot.* a flower cluster with the separate flowers attached by short equal stalks at equal distances along a central stem. The flowers at the base of the central stem develop first.

race·track /'rās,trak/ ▸*n.* a ground or track for horse or dog racing. ■ a track for auto racing.

race·way /'rās,wā/ ▸*n.* **1** a track or channel along which something runs, in particular: ■ a water channel, esp. an artificial one of running water in which fish are reared. ■ a groove or race in which bearings run. ■ a pipe or tubing enclosing electric wires. **2** a track for trotting, pacing, or harness racing. ■ a track for auto racing.

ra·cial /'rāSHəl/ ▸*adj.* of or relating to race: *a racial minority.* ■ on the grounds of or connected with difference in race: *racial hatred.* —**ra·cial·ly** *adv.*

rac·ism /'rā,sizəm/ ▸*n.* the belief that all members of each race possess characteristics or abilities specific to that race, esp. so as to distinguish it as inferior or superior to another race or races. ■ prejudice, discrimination, or antagonism directed against someone of a different race based on such a belief: *a program to combat racism.* —**rac·ist** *n. & adj.*

rack[1] /rak/ ▸*n.* **1** a framework, typically with rails, bars, hooks, or pegs, for holding or storing things: *a magazine rack.* ■ an overhead shelf on a bus, train, or plane for stowing luggage. ■ a vertically barred frame or wagon for holding animal fodder: *a hay rack.* ■ a lift used for elevating and repairing motor vehicles. ■ a set of antlers. **2** a cogged or toothed bar or rail engaging with a wheel or pinion, or using pegs to adjust the position of something: *a steering rack.* **3** (**the rack**) *hist.* an instrument of torture consisting of a frame on which the victim was stretched by

turning rollers to which the wrists and ankles were tied. **4** a triangular structure for positioning the balls in pool. ■ the triangular arrangement of balls set up for the beginning of a game of pool. **5** a digital effects unit for a guitar or other instrument, typically giving many different sounds.
▶ *v.* [*tr.*] **1** (also **wrack**) (often **be racked**) cause extreme physical or mental pain to; subject to extreme stress: *he was racked with guilt.* **2** [*tr.*] place in or on a rack: *the shoes were racked neatly beneath the dresses.* ■ [*tr.*] put (pool balls) in a rack.
▶ *phrasal v.* □ **rack something up** accumulate or achieve something, typically a score or amount: *Japan is racking up record trade surpluses with the U.S.*
▶ □ **go to rack** (or **wrack**) **and ruin** gradually deteriorate in condition because of neglect: *fall into disrepair.* □ **rack** (or **wrack**) **one's brains** (or **brain**) make a great effort to think of or remember something.
rack² ▶ *n.* a large cut of meat, typically lamb, that includes the front ribs.
rack·et¹ /'rakit/ (also **rac·quet**) ▶ *n.* a type of bat with a round or oval frame strung with catgut, nylon, etc., used esp. in tennis, badminton, and squash. ■ a snowshoe resembling such a bat.
rack·et² ▶ *n.* **1** a loud unpleasant noise; a din: *the kids were making a racket.* **2** *inf.* an illegal or dishonest scheme for obtaining money: *a protection racket.* ■ a person's line of business or way of life: *I'm in the insurance racket.* —**rack·et·y** *adj.*
rack·et·eer /ˌrakiˈti(ə)r/ ▶ *n.* a person who engages in dishonest and fraudulent business dealings. —**rack·et·eer·ing** *n.*
rac·on·teur /ˌrak,änˈtər, -ən-/ ▶ *n.* a person who tells anecdotes in a skillful and amusing way.
rac·quet /'rakit/ ▶ *n.* variant spelling of RACKET¹.
rac·quet·ball /'rakit,bôl/ ▶ *n.* a game played with a small hard ball and a short-handled racket in a four-walled handball court.
rac·y /'rāsē/ ▶ *adj.* (**rac·i·er, rac·i·est**) (of speech, writing, or behavior) lively, entertaining, and typically mildly titillating sexually: *the novel was considered rather racy at the time.* ■ (of a person or thing) showing vigor or spirit: *a racy fiddle.* ■ (of a wine, flavor, etc.) having a characteristic quality in a high degree. ■ (of a vehicle or animal) designed or bred to be suitable for racing: *the yacht is fast and racy.* —**rac·i·ly** /-səlē/ *adv.* —**rac·i·ness** *n.*
rad /rad/ ▶ *adj. inf.* excellent; impressive: *a really rad game.*
ra·dar /'rā,där/ ▶ *n.* a system for detecting the presence, direction, distance, and speed of aircraft, ships, and other objects, by sending out pulses of high-frequency electromagnetic waves that are reflected off the object back to the source. ■ an apparatus used for this. ▷1940s: from ra(dio) d(etection) a(nd) r(anging).
ra·di·al /'rādēəl/ ▶ *adj.* **1** of or arranged like rays or the radii of a circle; diverging in lines from a common center. ■ (or a road or route) running directly from a town or city center to an outlying district. ■ denoting a tire in which the layers of fabric have their cords running at right angles to the circumference of the tire and the tread is strengthened by further layers around the circumference. ■ denoting an internal combustion engine with its cylinders fixed like the spokes of a wheel around a rotating crankshaft (a type used chiefly in aircraft). **2** *Anat. & Zool.* of or relating to the radius.
▶ *n.* **1** a radial tire. **2** a radial road. —**ra·di·al·ly** *adv.*
ra·di·an /'rādēən/ ▶ *n. Geom.* a unit of angle, equal to an angle at the center of a circle whose arc is equal in length to the radius.
ra·di·ant /'rādēənt/ ▶ *adj.* **1** sending out light; shining or glowing brightly: *a bird with radiant green and red plumage.* ■ (of a person or their expression) clearly emanating great joy, love, or health: *she gave him a radiant smile.* ■ (of an emotion or quality) emanating powerfully from someone or something; very intense or conspicuous: *he praised her radiant self-confidence.* **2** (of heat) transmitted by radiation, rather than conduction or convection. —**ra·di·ance** *n.* —**ra·di·ant·ly** *adv.*
ra·di·ate ▶ *v.* /'rādē,āt/ **1** [*tr.*] emit (energy, esp. light or heat) in the form of rays or waves: *the hot stars radiate energy.* ■ [*intr.*] (of light, heat, or other energy) be emitted in such a way: *the continual stream of energy that radiates from the sun.* ■ (of a person) clearly emanate (a strong feeling or quality) through their expression or bearing: *she lifted her chin, radiating defiance.* ■ (**radiate from**) (of a feeling or quality) emanate clearly from: *leadership and confidence radiate from her.* **2** [*intr.*] diverge or spread from or as if from a central point: *he ran down one of the passages that radiated from the room.* ■ *Biol.* (of an animal or plant group) evolve into a variety of forms adapted to new situations or ways of life. —**ra·di·a·tive** /-,ātiv/ *adj.*
ra·di·a·tion /ˌrādēˈāSHən/ ▶ *n.* **1** *Physics* the emission of energy as electromagnetic waves or as moving subatomic particles, esp. high-

energy particles that cause ionization. ■ the energy transmitted in this way, as heat, light, electricity, etc. **2** *chiefly Biol.* divergence out from a central point, in particular evolution from an ancestral animal or plant group into a variety of new forms. —**ra·di·a·tion·al** /-'āSHənl/ *adj.* —**ra·di·a·tion·al·ly** /-'āSHənl-ē/ *adv.*
ra·di·a·tion sick·ness ▶ *n.* illness caused by exposure of the body to ionizing radiation, characterized by nausea, hair loss, diarrhea, bleeding, and damage to the bone marrow and central nervous system.
ra·di·a·tion ther·a·py (also **radiation treatment**) ▶ *n.* the treatment of disease, esp. cancer, using X-rays or similar forms of radiation.
ra·di·a·tor /'rādē,ātər/ ▶ *n.* **1** a thing that radiates or emits light, heat, or sound. ■ a device for heating a room consisting of a metal case connected by pipes through which hot water is pumped by a central heating system. ■ a portable heater resembling such a device. **2** an engine-cooling device in a motor vehicle or aircraft consisting of a bank of thin tubes in which circulating fluid is cooled by the surrounding air.
rad·i·cal /'radikəl/ ▶ *adj.* **1** (esp. of change or action) relating to or affecting the fundamental nature of something; far-reaching or thorough: *a radical overhaul of the existing regulatory framework.* ■ forming an inherent or fundamental part of the nature of someone or something: *the assumption of radical differences between the mental attributes of literate and nonliterate peoples.* ■ (of surgery or medical treatment) thorough and intended to be completely curative. **2** advocating thorough or complete political or social reform; representing or supporting an extreme section of a political party: *a radical American activist.* ■ (of a measure or policy) following or based on such principles. **3** of or relating to the root of something, in particular: ■ *Math.* of the root of a number or quantity. **4** [usu. as *interj.*] *inf.* very good; excellent: *Okay, then. Seven o'clock. Radical!*
▶ *n.* **1** a person who advocates thorough or complete political or social reform; a member of a political party or part of a party pursuing such aims. **2** *Chem.* a group of atoms behaving as a unit in a number of compounds. See also FREE RADICAL. **3** *Math.* a quantity forming or expressed as the root of another. ■ a radical sign. —**rad·i·cal·ism** /-,lizəm/ *n.* —**rad·i·cal·ize** *v.* —**rad·i·cal·ly** /-ik(ə)lē/ *adv. a radically different approach.* —**rad·i·cal·ness** *n.*
rad·ic·chi·o /raˈdēkē,ō; rə-/ ▶ *n.* (*pl.* **-os**) chicory of a variety that has dark red leaves.
rad·i·cle /'radikəl/ ▶ *n. Bot. Anat.* a rootlike subdivision of a nerve or vein. —**ra·dic·u·lar** /rəˈdikyələr/ *adj.* (*Anat.*).
ra·di·i /'rādē,ī/ ▶ plural form of RADIUS.
ra·di·o /'rādē,ō/ ▶ *n.* (*pl.* **-os**) the transmission and reception of electromagnetic waves of radio frequency, esp. those carrying sound messages: *cellular phones are linked by radio rather than wires.* ■ the activity or industry of broadcasting sound programs to the public: *she has written much material for radio* | [as *adj.*] *a radio station.* ■ radio programs: *we used to listen to a lot of radio.* ■ an apparatus for receiving such programs: *she turned on the radio.* ■ an apparatus capable of both receiving and transmitting radio messages between individuals, ships, planes, etc.: *a ship-to-shore radio.* ■ [in *names*] a broadcasting station or channel: *Monitor Radio.*
▶ *v.* (**-oes, -oed**) [*intr.*] communicate or send a message by radio: *the pilot radioed for help.* ■ [*tr.*] communicate with (a person or place) by radio: *we'll radio Athens right away.*
ra·di·o·ac·tive /ˌrādēōˈaktiv/ ▶ *adj.* emitting or relating to the emission of ionizing radiation or particles: *radioactive decay* | *the water was radioactive.* —**ra·di·o·ac·tive·ly** *adv.*
ra·di·o·ac·tiv·i·ty /ˌrādēōakˈtivətē/ ▶ *n.* the emission of ionizing radiation or particles caused by the spontaneous disintegration of atomic nuclei. ■ radioactive substances, or the radiation emitted by these.
ra·di·o as·tron·o·my ▶ *n.* the branch of astronomy concerned with radio emissions from celestial objects.
ra·di·o·car·bon /ˌrādēōˈkärbən/ ▶ *n. Chem.* a radioactive isotope of carbon.
ra·di·o·car·bon dat·ing ▶ *n.* another term for CARBON DATING.
ra·di·o·gen·ic /ˌrādēōˈjenik/ ▶ *adj.* produced by radioactivity: *a radiogenic isotope.* —**ra·di·o·gen·i·cal·ly** /-ik(ə)lē/ *adv.*
ra·di·o·i·so·tope /ˌrādēōˈīsə,tōp/ ▶ *n. Chem.* a radioactive isotope. —**ra·di·o·i·so·top·ic** /-,īsəˈtäpik/ *adj.*
ra·di·ol·o·gy /ˌrādēˈäləjē/ ▶ *n.* the science dealing with X-rays and other high-energy radiation, esp. the use of such radiation for the diagnosis

and treatment of disease. **—ra·di·o·log·ic** /ˌrādēə'läjik/ *adj.* **—ra·di·o·log·i·cal** /ˌrādēə'läjikəl/ *adj.* **—ra·di·o·log·i·cal·ly** /ˌrādēə'läjik(ə)lē/ *adv.* **—ra·di·ol·o·gist** /-jist/ *n.*

ra·di·om·e·ter /ˌrādē'ämitər/ ▶*n.* an instrument for detecting or measuring the intensity or force of radiation. **—ra·di·o·met·ric** /-dēə'metrik/ *adj.* **—ra·di·o·met·ri·cal·ly** /-dēə'metrik(ə)lē/ *adv.* **—ra·di·om·e·try** /-trē/ *n.*

ra·di·o·tel·e·phone /ˌrādēō'telə.fōn/ ▶*n.* a telephone that uses radio transmission. **—ra·di·o·te·leph·o·ny** /-tə'lefənē/ *n.* **—ra·di·o·tel·e·phon·ic** /-ˌteləˈfänik/ *adj.*

ra·di·o tel·e·scope ▶*n. Astron.* an instrument used to detect radio emissions from the sky, whether from natural celestial objects or from artificial satellites.

rad·ish /'radiSH/ ▶*n.* **1** a pungent-tasting edible root, esp. a variety that is small, spherical, and red. **2** the plant (*Raphanus sativus*) of the cabbage family that yields this root.

ra·di·um /'rādēəm/ ▶*n.* the chemical element of atomic number 88, a rare radioactive metal of the alkaline earth series. (Symbol: **Ra**)

ra·di·us /'rādēəs/ ▶*n.* (pl. **ra·di·i** /'rādē.ī/ or **ra·di·us·es**) **1** a straight line from the center to the circumference of a circle or sphere. ■ a radial line from the focus to any point of a curve. ■ the length of the radius of a circle or sphere. ■ a specified distance from a center in all directions: *there are plenty of local pubs within a two-mile radius.* **2** *Anat.* the thicker and shorter of the two bones in the human forearm. Compare with ULNA. ■ *Zool.* the corresponding bone in a vertebrate's foreleg or a bird's wing. ■ *Zool.* (in an echinoderm or coelenterate) any of the primary axes of radial symmetry.

ra·dix /'rādiks/ 'rad-/ ▶*n.* (pl. **ra·di·ces** /'radə.sēz/ 'rā-/) **1** *Math.* the base of a system of numeration. See also BASE¹ (sense 8). **2** *formal* a source or origin of something: *Judaism is the radix of Christianity.*

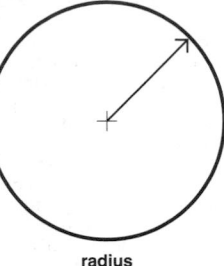

radius

ra·don /'rā.dän/ ▶*n.* the chemical element of atomic number 86, a rare radioactive gas belonging to the noble gas series. (Symbol: **Rn**)

RAF *inf.* ▶*abbr.* (in the UK) Royal Air Force.

raf·fi·a /'rafēə/ ▶*n.* a palm tree (*Raphia ruffia*) native to tropical Africa and Madagascar, with a short trunk and leaves that may be up to 60 feet (18 m) long. ■ the fiber from these leaves, used for making items such as hats, baskets, and mats.

raf·fle /'rafəl/ ▶*n.* a means of raising money by selling numbered tickets, one or some of which are subsequently drawn at random, the holder or holders of such tickets winning a prize.
▶*v.* [*tr.*] (usu. **be raffled**) offer (something) as a prize in such a lottery: *a work that will be raffled off for a fine arts scholarship.*

raft¹ /raft/ ▶*n.* a flat buoyant structure of timber or other materials fastened together, used as a boat or floating platform. ■ a small, inflatable rubber or plastic boat, esp. one for use in emergencies. ■ a floating mass of fallen trees, vegetation, ice, or other material. ■ a dense flock of swimming birds or mammals: *great rafts of cormorants, often 5,000 strong.*
▶*v.* **1** [*intr.*] travel on or as if on a raft: *I have rafted along the Rio Grande.* ■ [*tr.*] transport on or as a raft: *the stores were rafted ashore* | *I rafted 400 logs to my mill.* ■ [*tr.*] transport (logs) on water in the form of a raft. **2** [*tr.*] bring or fasten together (a number of boats or other objects) side by side.

raft² ▶*n.* a large amount of something: *a raft of government initiatives.*

raft·er /'raftər/ ▶*n.* one of several internal beams extending from the eaves to the peak of a roof and constituting its framework.

rag¹ /rag/ ▶*n.* **1** a piece of old cloth, esp. one torn from a larger piece, used typically for cleaning things: *he wiped his hands on an oily rag* | *a piece of rag.* ■ (**rags**) old or tattered clothes. ■ (**rags**) *fig.* the remnants of something: *she clung to the rags of her self-control.* ■ *archaic* the smallest scrap of cloth or clothing: *not a rag of clothing has arrived to us this winter.* **2** *inf.* a newspaper, typically one regarded as being of low quality: *the local rag.*

rag² ▶*v.* (**ragged** /ragd/, **rag·ging**) [*tr.*] **1** make fun of (someone) in a loud, boisterous manner. **2** rebuke severely.
▶*phrasal v.* □ **rag on** *inf.* **1** complain about or criticize continually. **2** make fun of; tease constantly.

ra·ga /'rägə/ ▶*n.* (in Indian music) a pattern of notes having characteristic intervals, rhythms, and embellishments, used as a basis for improvisation. ■ a piece using a particular raga.

rag·a·muf·fin /'ragə,məfən/ ▶*n.* a person, typically a child, in ragged, dirty clothes.

rag doll ▶*n.* a soft doll made from pieces of cloth.

rage /rāj/ ▶*n.* violent, uncontrollable anger: *her face was distorted with rage* | *she flew into a rage.* ■ *fig.* the violent action of a natural agency: *the rising rage of the sea.* ■ a vehement desire or passion: *a rage for absolute honesty informs much western art.* ■ an instance of aggressive behavior or violent anger caused by a stressful or frustrating situation: *desk rage* | *sports rage* | *PC rage.* ■ (**the rage**) a widespread temporary enthusiasm or fashion: *video and computer games are all the rage.*
▶*v.* [*intr.*] feel or express violent uncontrollable anger: *he raged at the futility of it all* | [with *direct speech*] *"That's unfair!" Maggie raged.* ■ (of a natural agency or a conflict) continue violently or with great force: *the argument raged for days.* ■ (of an illness) spread very rapidly or uncontrollably: *the great cholera epidemic that raged across Europe in 1831.* ■ (of an emotion) have or reach a high degree of intensity: *she couldn't hide the fear that raged within her.* ▷Middle English (also in the sense 'madness'): from Old French *rage* (noun), *rager* (verb), from a variant of Latin *rabies* 'rage,' from *rabere* 'rave.'

rag·ged /'ragid/ ▶*adj.* **1** (of cloth or clothes) old and torn. ■ (of a person) wearing such clothes: *a ragged child.* **2** having a rough, irregular, or uneven surface, edge, or outline: *a ragged coastline.* ■ lacking finish, smoothness, or refinement: *the ragged discipline of the players.* ■ (of a sound) rough or uneven: *his breathing became ragged.* ■ (of an animal) having a rough, shaggy coat: *a pair of ragged ponies.* ■ *Printing* (esp. of a right margin) uneven because the lines are unjustified. **3** suffering from exhaustion or stress: *he looked a little ragged, a little shadowy beneath the eyes.* **—rag·ged·ly** *adv.* **—rag·ged·ness** *n.* **—rag·ged·y** *adj.*
▶ □ **run someone ragged** exhaust someone by making them undertake a lot of physical activity.

rag·lan /'raglən/ ▶*adj.* (of a sleeve) continuing in one piece up to the neck of a garment, without a shoulder seam. ■ (of a garment) having sleeves of this type.
▶*n.* an overcoat with sleeves of this type.

ra·gout /ra'gōō/ ▶*n.* a highly seasoned dish of meat cut into small pieces and stewed with vegetables.

rag·tag /'rag.tag/ ▶*adj.* untidy, disorganized, or incongruously varied in character: *a ragtag group of idealists.*
▶*n.* (also **rag·tag and bob·tail** /'bäb.tāl/) a group of people perceived as disreputable or undesirable.

rag·time /'rag.tīm/ ▶*n.* music characterized by a syncopated melodic line and regularly accented accompaniment, evolved by black American musicians in the 1890s and played esp. on the piano.

rag·weed /'rag.wēd/ ▶*n.* a North American plant (*Ambrosia artemisia*) of the daisy family. Its tiny green flowers produce copious amounts of pollen, making it a major causative agent of hay fever.

rah /rä/ ▶*interj. inf.* a cheer of encouragement or approval.

RAID /rād/ ▶*abbr.* redundant array of independent (or inexpensive) disks, a system for providing greater capacity, faster access, and security against data corruption by spreading the data across several disk drives.

raid /rād/ ▶*n.* a sudden attack on an enemy by troops, aircraft, or other armed forces in warfare: *a bombing raid.* ■ a surprise attack to commit a crime, esp. to steal from business premises: *an early morning raid on a bank.* ■ a surprise visit by police to arrest suspected people or seize illicit goods. ■ *Stock Market* a hostile attempt to buy a major or controlling interest in the shares of a company.
▶*v.* [*tr.*] conduct a raid on: *officers raided thirty homes yesterday.* ■ quickly and illicitly take something from (a place): *she crept down the stairs to raid the larder.* **—raid·er** *n.*

rail¹ /rāl/ ▶*n.* **1** a bar or series of bars, typically fixed on upright supports, serving as part of a fence or barrier or used to hang things on. **2** a steel bar or continuous line of bars laid on the ground as one of a pair forming a railroad track: *trolley rails.* ■ [often as *adj.*] railroads as a means of transportation: *rail fares.* **3** *Electr.* a conductor that is maintained at a fixed potential and to which other parts of a circuit are connected. **—rail·less** *adj.*
▶ □ **go off the rails** *inf.* begin behaving in a strange, abnormal, or wildly uncontrolled way.

rail² ▶*v.* [*intr.*] (**rail against/at/about**) complain or protest strongly and persistently about: *he railed at human fickleness.* **—rail·er** *n.*

rail³ ▶*n.* a secretive bird (*Rallus* and other genera) with drab gray and brown plumage, typically having a long bill and found in dense waterside vegetation. The **rail family** (Rallidae) also includes the moorhens and coots.

rail car ▶*n.* any railroad car or wagon.

rail·ing /'rāliNG/ ▶n. (usu. **railings**) a fence or barrier made of rails.

rail·road /'rāl,rōd/ ▶n. **1** a track or set of tracks made of steel rails along which passenger and freight trains run: [as adj.] a railroad line. ■ a set of tracks for other vehicles. **2** a system of such tracks with the trains, organization, and personnel required for its working: [in names] the Union Pacific Railroad.
▶v. **1** [tr.] inf. press (someone) into doing something by rushing or co-ercing them: she hesitated, unwilling to be **railroaded** into a decision. ■ cause (a measure) to be passed or approved quickly by applying pressure: the Bill had been **railroaded** through the House. ■ send (someone) to prison without a fair trial or by means of false evidence. **2** [intr.] [usu. as n.] (**railroading**) travel or work on the railroads.

rai·ment /'rāmənt/ ▶n. archaic or poetic/lit. clothing: ladies clothed in raiment bedecked with jewels.

rain /rān/ ▶n. moisture condensed from the atmosphere that falls visibly in separate drops: it's pouring rain. ■ (**rains**) falls of rain: the plants were washed away by some unusually heavy rains. ■ a large or overwhelming quantity of things that fall or descend: he fell under the **rain of** blows.
▶v. [intr.] (**it rains, it is raining,** etc.) rain falls: it was beginning to rain. ■ poetic/lit. (of the sky, the clouds, etc.) send down rain. ■ (of objects) fall in large or overwhelming quantities: bombs rained down. ■ [tr.] (**it rains ——, it is raining ——,** etc.) used to convey that a specified thing is falling in large or overwhelming quantities: it was just raining glass. ■ [tr.] send down in large or overwhelming quantities: she rained blows onto him.
▶phrasal v. □ **rain something out** (usu. **be rained out**) cause an event to be terminated or canceled because of rain: the tournament was rained out. ▷Old English regn (noun), regnian (verb), of Germanic origin; related to Dutch regen and German Regen. —**rain·less** adj.
▶ □ **rain cats and dogs** rain very hard. ■ (**come**) **rain or shine** whether it rains or not: he runs six miles every morning, rain or shine.

rain·bow /'rān,bō/ ▶n. an arch of colors formed in the sky, caused by the refraction and dispersion of the sun's light by rain or other water droplets in the atmosphere. ■ any display of the colors of the spectrum produced by dispersion of light. ■ a wide range or variety of related and typically colorful things: a rainbow of medals decorated his chest. ■ [as adj.] many-colored: a big rainbow packet of felt pens.

rain·bow trout ▶n. a large, partly migratory trout (Salmo gairdneri) native to the Pacific seaboard of North America.

rain check /'rān,CHek/ (also **rain-check**) ▶n. a ticket given for later use when a sports event or other outdoor event is interrupted or postponed by rain. ■ a coupon issued to a customer by a store, guaranteeing that a sale item that is out of stock may be purchased by that customer at a later date at the same reduced price.
▶ □ **take a rain check** said when politely refusing an offer, with the implication that one may accept it at a later date: I can't make it tonight, but I'd like to take a rain check.

rain·coat /'rān,kōt/ ▶n. a long coat made from waterproofed or water-resistant fabric.

rain date ▶n. an alternative date for an event in case of inclement weather. ■ Baseball the day to which a rained-out game is postponed.

rain·drop /'rān,dräp/ ▶n. a single drop of rain.

rain·fall /'rān,fôl/ ▶n. the fall of rain. ■ the quantity of rain falling within a given area in a given time: low rainfall.

rain for·est (also **rain·for·est**) ▶n. a luxuriant, dense forest rich in biodiversity, found typically in tropical areas with consistently heavy rainfall.

rain gauge ▶n. a device for collecting and measuring the amount of rain that falls.

rain·proof /'rān,prōof/ ▶adj. (esp. of a building or garment) impervious to rain: a rainproof coat.

rain·storm /'rān,stôrm/ ▶n. a storm with heavy rain.

rain·wa·ter /'rān,wôtər; -,wätər/ ▶n. water that has fallen as or been obtained from rain.

rain·y /'rānē/ ▶adj. (**rain·i·er, rain·i·est**) (of weather, a period of time, or an area) having a great deal of rainfall: a rainy afternoon. —**rain·i·ness** n.
▶ □ **a rainy day** used in reference to a possible time in the future when something, esp. money, will be needed: invest and save for a rainy day.

raise /rāz/ ▶v. [tr.] **1** lift or move to a higher position or level: his flag was raised over the city. ■ lift or move to a vertical position; set upright: Melody managed to raise him to his feet. ■ construct or build (a structure): a fence was being raised around the property. ■ cause to rise or form: the galloping horse raised a cloud of dust. **2** increase the amount, level, or strength of: the bank raised interest rates | the aim was to raise awareness of the plight of the homeless. ■ promote (someone) to a higher rank: the king

raised him to the title of Count Torre Bella. ■ (**raise something to**) Math. multiply a quantity by itself to (a specified power): 3 raised to the 7th power is 2,187. ■ (in poker or brag) bet (a specified amount) more than (another player): I'll raise you another hundred dollars. ■ [tr.] increase (a bid) in this way. **3** cause to be heard, considered, or discussed: the alarm was raised when he failed to return home. ■ cause to occur, appear, or be felt: recent sightings have raised hopes that otters are making a return. **4** collect, levy, or bring together (money or resources): she was attempting to raise $20,000. **5** bring up (a child): he was born and raised in San Francisco. ■ breed or grow (animals or plants): they raised pigs and kept a pony. **6** bring (someone) back from death: God **raised** Jesus **from the dead.**
▶n. an increase in salary: he wants a raise and some perks. —**rais·a·ble** adj. —**rais·er** n.
▶ □ **raise hell** inf. make a noisy disturbance. ■ complain vociferously: he raised hell with real estate developers and polluters. □ **raise the roof** make or cause someone else to make a great deal of noise, esp. through cheering: when I finally scored, the fans raised the roof. □ **raise one's voice** speak more loudly. ■ begin to speak or sing.

rai·sin /'rāzən/ ▶n. a partially dried grape. —**rai·sin·y** adj.

rai·son d'ê·tre /rā'zôN 'detr(ə)/ ▶n. (pl. **rai·sons d'ê·tre** /rā'zôN(z)/) the most important reason or purpose for someone or something's existence: an institution whose raison d'être is public service broadcasting.

ra·jah /'räjə; 'räzHə/ (also **ra·ja**) ▶n. hist. an Indian king or prince. ■ a title extended to petty dignitaries and nobles in India during the British Raj. ■ a title extended by the British to a Malay or Javanese ruler or chief.

rake[1] /rāk/ ▶n. an implement consisting of a pole with a crossbar toothed like a comb at the end, or with several tines held together by a crosspiece, used esp. for drawing together cut grass or smoothing loose soil or gravel. ■ a wheeled implement used for the same purposes. ■ a similar implement used for other purposes, e.g., by a croupier drawing in money at a gaming table.
▶v. [tr.] collect, gather, or move with a rake or similar implement: they started **raking up** hay. ■ make (a stretch of ground) tidy or smooth with a rake: the infield dirt is meticulously raked. ■ scratch or scrape (something, esp. a person's flesh) with a long sweeping movement: her fingers raked Bill's face. ■ [tr.] draw or drag (something) with a long sweeping movement: she raked a comb through her hair.
▶phrasal v. □ **rake in something** inf. make a lot of money, typically very easily: he was now raking in $250 million a year. —**rak·er** n.

rake[2] ▶n. a fashionable or wealthy man of dissolute or promiscuous habits.

rak·ish[1] /'rākiSH/ ▶adj. having or displaying a dashing, jaunty, or slightly disreputable quality or appearance: he had a rakish, debonair look. —**rak·ish·ly** adv. —**rak·ish·ness** n.

rak·ish[2] ▶adj. (esp. of a car) trim and fast-looking, with streamlined angles and curves.

rale /räl; ral/ ▶n. (usu. **rales**) Med. an abnormal rattling sound heard when examining unhealthy lungs with a stethoscope.

ral·len·tan·do /,rälən'tändō; ,ralən'tandō/ Mus. ▶adv., adj., & n. (pl. **-dos** or **-di** /-dē/) Mus. another term for RITARDANDO.

ral·ly /'ralē/ ▶v. (**-lies, -lied**) [intr.] **1** (of troops) come together again in order to continue fighting after a defeat or dispersion: De Montfort's troops rallied and drove back the king's infantry. ■ [tr.] bring together (forces) again in order to continue fighting: the king escaped to Perth to rally his own forces. ■ assemble in a mass meeting: up to 50,000 people rallied in the city center. ■ come together in order to support a person or cause or for concerted action: conservatives in the GOP **rallied behind** Goldwater. ■ [tr.] bring together (forces or support) in such a way: a series of meetings to rally support for the union. ■ Sports come from behind in scoring: the Edmeston Panthers rallied in overtime to win the championship. ■ (of a person) recover their health, spirits, or poise: she floundered for a moment, then rallied again. ■ [tr.] revive (a person or their health or spirits): they rallied her with a drink. ■ (of share, currency, or commodity prices) increase after a fall: prices of metals such as aluminum and copper have rallied. **2** drive in a rally. ■ (in tennis and other racket sports) engage in a rally.
▶n. (pl. **-lies**) **1** a mass meeting of people making a political protest or showing support for a cause: a rally attended by around 100,000 people. ■ an open-air event for people who own a particular kind of vehicle: a traction engine rally. **2** (also **rallye**) a competition for motor vehicles

---

Pronunciation Key ə *ago,* up; ər *over, fur;* a *hat;* ā *ate;* ä *car;* CH *chin;* e *let;* ē *see;* ə(ə)r *air;* i *fit;* ī *by;* i(ə)r *ear;* NG *sing;* ō *go;* ô *law, for;* oi *toy;* oŏ *good;* oō *goo;* ou *out;* SH *she;* TH *thin;* TH *then;* (h)w *why;* ZH *vision*

in which they are driven a long distance over public roads or rough terrain, typically in stages and through checkpoints: [as adj.] *a rally driver.* **3** a quick or marked recovery after a reverse or a period of weakness: *the market staged a late rally.* ■ (in baseball and football) a renewed or sustained offensive, usually by the losing team, that ties or wins the game. **4** (in tennis and other racket sports) an extended exchange of strokes between players. ■ hitting the ball back and forth to warm up before a match begins. —**ral·li·er** *n.* —**ral·ly·ist** *n.*

RAM /ram/ ▶*abbr. Comput.* random-access memory.

ram /ram/ ▶*n.* **1** an uncastrated male sheep. ■ (**the Ram**) the zodiacal sign or constellation Aries. **2** a hydraulic water-raising or lifting machine. ■ the piston of a hydraulic press. ■ the plunger of a force pump.
▶*v.* (**rammed, ram·ming**) [*tr.*] roughly force (something) into place: *he rammed his stick into the ground.* ■ (of a vehicle or vessel) be driven violently into (something, typically another vehicle or vessel) in an attempt to stop or damage it: *their boat was rammed by a Japanese warship.* ■ [*intr.*] crash violently against something: *the stolen car rammed into the front of the house.* ■ [*tr.*] [often as adj.] (**rammed**) beat (earth or the ground) with a heavy implement to make it hard and firm: *portions of the Great Wall of China are made of rammed earth.* ■ (**ram through**) [*tr.*] force (something) to be accepted: *Sunday's referendum to ram through a new constitution.* —**ram·mer** *n.*

Ram·a·dan /'räma,dän, 'rama,dan/ ▶*n.* the ninth month of the Muslim year, during which strict fasting is observed from sunrise to sunset.

ram·ble /'rambəl/ ▶*v.* [*intr.*] **1** walk for pleasure, typically without a definite route. ■ (of a plant) put out long shoots and grow over walls or other plants. **2** talk or write at length in a confused or inconsequential way: *he rambled on about his acting career.*
▶*n.* a walk taken for pleasure, esp. in the countryside.

ram·bler /'ramb(ə)lər/ ▶*n.* **1** a person who walks for pleasure, esp. in the countryside. **2** a straggling or climbing rose. **3** another term for RANCH HOUSE (SEE RANCH).

ram·bling /'ramb(ə)liNG/ ▶*adj.* **1** (of writing or speech) lengthy and confused or inconsequential. **2** (of a plant) putting out long shoots and growing over walls or other plants; climbing: *rambling roses.* ■ (of a building or path) spreading or winding irregularly in various directions: *a big old rambling house.* ■ (of a person) traveling from place to place; wandering. —**ram·bling·ly** *adv.*

ram·bunc·tious /ram'bəNGkSHəs/ ▶*adj. inf.* uncontrollably exuberant; boisterous. —**ram·bunc·tious·ly** *adv.* —**ram·bunc·tious·ness** *n.*

ram·e·kin /'ramikən/ (also **ramekin dish**) ▶*n.* a small dish for baking and serving an individual portion of food.

ram·i·fi·ca·tion /,raməfə'kāSHən/ ▶*n.* (usu. **ramifications**) a consequence of an action or event, esp. when complex or unwelcome: *any change is bound to have serious ramifications.* ■ a subdivision of a complex structure or process perceived as comparable to a tree's branches: *an extended family with its ramifications of neighboring in-laws.* ■ *formal* or *technical* the action or state of ramifying or being ramified.

ram·i·fy /'ramə,fī/ ▶*v.* (**-fies, -fied**) [*intr.*] *formal, technical* form branches or offshoots; spread or branch out: *an elaborate system of canals was built, ramifying throughout Britain.* ■ [*tr.*] [often as adj.] (**ramified**) cause to branch or spread out: *a ramified genealogical network.*

ram·jet /'ram,jet/ ▶*n.* a type of jet engine in which the air drawn in for combustion is compressed solely by the forward motion of the aircraft.

ra·mose /'rāmōs/ ▶*adj.* branched; branching: *the leaves are borne on a ramose stalk.*

ramp /ramp/ ▶*n.* **1** a slope or inclined plane for joining two different levels, as at the entrance or between floors of a building: *a wheelchair ramp.* ■ a movable set of steps for entering or leaving an aircraft. ■ an inclined road leading onto or off a main road or highway: *an exit ramp.* **2** an upward bend in a stair rail.
▶*phrasal v.* □ **ramp something up** (or **ramp up**) (esp. in reference to the production of goods) increase or cause to increase in amount: *they ramped up production to meet booming demand.*

ram·page ▶*v.* /'ram,pāj/ [*intr.*] (esp. of a large group of people) rush around in a violent and uncontrollable manner: *several thousand demonstrators rampaged through the city.*
▶*n.* /'ram,pāj/ a period of violent and uncontrollable behavior, typically involving a large group of people: *thugs went on a rampage and wrecked a classroom.* —**ram·pag·er** /'ram,pājər/ *n.*

ramp·ant /'rampənt/ ▶*adj.* (esp. of something unwelcome or unpleasant) flourishing or spreading unchecked: *political violence was rampant.* ■ (of a person or activity) violent or unrestrained in action or performance: *rampant sex.* ■ (of a plant) lush in growth; luxuriant: *a rich soil*

soon becomes home to rampant weeds. —**ramp·an·cy** /-pənsē/ *n.* —**ramp·ant·ly** *adv.*

ram·part /'ram,pärt/ ▶*n.* (usu. **ramparts**) a defensive wall of a castle or walled city, having a broad top with a walkway and typically a stone parapet. ■ a defensive or protective barrier.

ram·rod /'ram,räd/ ▶*n.* a rod for ramming down the charge of a muzzleloading firearm. ■ used in similes and metaphors to describe someone's erect or rigid posture: *he held himself ramrod straight.* ■ a person, esp. one in a position of leadership, who is strict and uncompromising.
▶*v.* (**-rod·ded, -rod·ding**) [*tr.*] (**ramrod something through**) force a proposed measure to be accepted or completed quickly: *they ramrodded through legislation voiding the court injunctions.*

ram·shack·le /'ram,SHakəl/ ▶*adj.* (esp. of a house or vehicle) in a state of severe disrepair: *a ramshackle cottage.*

ran /ran/ ▶ past of RUN.

ranch /ranCH/ ▶*n.* a large farm, esp. in the western U.S. and Canada, where cattle or other animals are bred and raised. ■ (also **ranch house**) a single-story house, typically with a low-pitched roof. ■ short for RANCH DRESSING.
▶*v.* [*intr.*] [often as *n.*] (**ranching**) run a ranch: *cattle ranching.* ■ [*tr.*] [often as *adj.*] (**ranched**) breed (animals) on a ranch. ■ [*tr.*] use (land) as a ranch. ▷early 19th cent.: from Spanish *rancho* 'group of persons eating together.'

ranch dress·ing ▶*n.* a type of thick white salad dressing made with sour cream or buttermilk.

ranch·er /'ranCHər/ ▶*n.* a person who owns or runs a ranch.

ran·che·ro /ran'CHerō/ ▶*n.* (*pl.* **-ros**) a person who farms or works on a ranch, esp. in the southwestern U.S. and Mexico.

ran·cid /'ransid/ ▶*adj.* (of foods containing fat or oil) smelling or tasting unpleasant as a result of being old and stale. —**ran·cid·i·ty** /ran'sidətē/ *n.*

ran·cor /'raNGkər/ (*Brit.* **ran·cour**) ▶*n.* bitterness or resentfulness, esp. when long-standing: *he spoke without rancor.* —**ran·cor·ous** /-rəs/ *adj.* —**ran·cor·ous·ly** /-k(ə)rəslē/ *adv.*

rand /rand; ränd; ränt/ ▶*n.* the basic monetary unit of South Africa, equal to 100 cents.

R & B ▶*abbr.* rhythm and blues.

R & D ▶*abbr.* research and development.

ran·dom /'randəm/ ▶*adj.* made, done, happening, or chosen without method or conscious decision: *a random sample of 100 households.* ■ *Statistics* governed by or involving equal chances for each item. —**ran·dom·ly** *adv.* —**ran·dom·ness** *n.*
▶ □ **at random** without method or conscious decision: *he opened the book at random.*

ran·dom ac·cess *Comput.* ▶*n.* the process of transferring information to or from memory in which every memory location can be accessed directly rather than being accessed in a fixed sequence: [as adj.] *random-access programming.*

R & R ▶*abbr.* ■ *inf.* rest and recreation. ■ *Med.* rescue and resuscitation. ■ (also **R'n'R**) rock and roll.

rang /raNG/ ▶ past of RING[2].

range /rānj/ ▶*n.* **1** the area of variation between upper and lower limits on a particular scale: *it's outside my price range.* ■ a set of different things of the same general type: *the area offers a wide range of activities for the tourist.* ■ the scope of a person's knowledge or abilities: *he gave some indication of his range.* ■ the area or extent covered by or included in something: *an introductory guide to the range of debate this issue has generated.* ■ *Math.* the set of values that a given function can take as its argument varies. **2** the distance within which something can be reached or perceived: *something lurked just beyond her range of vision.* **3** a line or series of mountains or hills: *the coastal ranges of the northwest.* **4** a large area of open land for grazing or hunting. ■ an area of land or sea used as a testing ground for military equipment. ■ an open or enclosed area with targets for shooting practice. ■ the area over which a thing, esp. a plant or animal, is distributed. **5** an electric or gas stove with several burners and one or more ovens. **6** *Building* a course of masonry extending from end to end at one height. ■ a row of buildings.
▶*v.* **1** [*intr.*] vary or extend between specified limits: *patients whose ages ranged from 13 to 25 years.* **2** [*tr.*] (usu. **be ranged**) place or arrange in a row or rows or in a specified order or manner: *a table with half a dozen chairs ranged around it.* ■ [*intr.*] run or extend in a line in a particular direction: *he regularly came to the benches that ranged along the path.* **3** [*intr.*] (of a person or animal) travel or wander over a wide area: *patrols ranged thousands of miles deep into enemy territory* | [*tr.*] *nomadic tribesmen who*

ranged the windswept lands of the steppe. ■ (of a person's eyes) pass from one person or thing to another: *his eyes ranged over them.* ■ (of something written or spoken) cover or embrace a wide number of different topics: *tutorials ranged over a variety of subjects.*

range·find·er /ˈrānjˌfīndər/ ▶ *n.* an instrument for estimating the distance of an object, esp. for use with a camera or gun.

rang·er /ˈrānjər/ ▶ *n.* **1** a keeper of a park, forest, or area of countryside. **2** a member of a body of armed men, in particular: ■ a commando or highly trained infantryman.

rang·y /ˈrānjē/ ▶ *adj.* (**rang·i·er, rang·i·est**) **1** (of a person or animal) tall and slim with long, slender limbs. **2** (of land) having a large, open range: *the rangy, hard, scruffy frontier.*

ra·ni /rä′nē/ (also **ra·nee**) ▶ *n.* (*pl.* **ra·nis**) *hist.* a Hindu queen, either by marriage to a raja or in her own right.

rank[1] /raNGk/ ▶ *n.* **1** a position in the hierarchy of the armed forces: *an army officer of fairly high rank.* ■ a position within the hierarchy of an organization or society: *only two cabinet members had held ministerial rank before.* ■ high social position: *persons of rank and breeding.* ■ *Statistics* a number specifying position in a numerically ordered series. **2** a single line of soldiers or police officers drawn up abreast. ■ (**the ranks**) common soldiers as opposed to officers: *he was fined and reduced to the ranks.* ■ (**ranks**) the people belonging to or constituting a group or class: *the ranks of the unemployed.* ■ *Chess* each of the eight rows of eight squares running from side to side across a chessboard.

▶ *v.* [*tr.*] **1** give (someone or something) a rank or place within a grading system: *rank them in order of preference.* ■ [*intr.*] have a specified rank or place within a grading system: *he ranks with Newman as one of the outstanding English theologians.* ■ [*tr.*] take precedence over (someone) in respect to rank; outrank: *the Secretary of State ranks all the other members of the cabinet.* **2** arrange in a rank or ranks: *the tents were ranked in orderly rows.*

▶ □ **break rank** (or **ranks**) (of soldiers or police officers) fail to remain in line. ■ *fig.* fail to maintain solidarity: *the government is prepared to break ranks with the Allied states.* □ **close ranks** (of soldiers or police officers) come closer together in a line. ■ *fig.* unite in order to defend common interests: *the family had always closed ranks in times of crisis.* □ **pull rank** take unfair advantage of one's seniority or privileged position.

rank[2] ▶ *adj.* **1** (of vegetation) growing too thickly and coarsely. **2** (esp. of air or water) having a foul or offensive smell. **3** (esp. of something bad or deficient) complete and utter (used for emphasis): *rank stupidity* | *rank amateurs* | *a rank outsider.* **—rank·ly** *adv.* **—rank·ness** *n.*

rank and file ▶ *n.* [treated as *pl.*] (**the rank and file**) the ordinary members of an organization as opposed to its leaders: *the rank and file of the Labor party are dissatisfied* | [as *adj.*] *rank-and-file members.*

rank·ing ▶ *n.* /ˈraNGkiNG/ a position in a scale of achievement or status; a classification: *his number-one world ranking.* ■ the action or process of giving a specified rank or place within a grading system: *the ranking of students.*

▶ *adj.* /raNGkiNG/ [in *comb.*] having a specified position in a scale of achievement or status: *high-ranking army officers.* ■ having a high position in such a scale: *two ranking PLO figures.*

ran·kle /ˈraNGkəl/ ▶ *v.* [*intr.*] (of a comment, event, or fact) cause annoyance or resentment that persists: *the casual manner of his dismissal still rankles.* ■ [*tr.*] annoy or irritate (someone): *Lisa was rankled by his assertion.*

ran·sack /ˈranˌsak; ranˈsak/ ▶ *v.* [*tr.*] go hurriedly through (a place) stealing things and causing damage: *burglars ransacked her home.* ■ search through (a place or receptacle) to find something, esp. in such a way as to cause disorder and damage: *Hollywood ransacks the New York stage for actors.* **—ran·sack·er** /ˈranˌsakər/ *n.*

ran·som /ˈransəm/ ▶ *n.* a sum of money or other payment demanded or paid for the release of a prisoner. ■ the holding or freeing of a prisoner in return for payment of such money: *the capture and ransom of the king.*

▶ *v.* [*tr.*] obtain the release of (a prisoner) by making a payment demanded: *the lord was captured in war and had to be ransomed.* ■ hold (a prisoner) and demand payment for their release: *mercenaries burned the village and ransomed the inhabitants.* ■ release (a prisoner) after receiving payment.

▶ □ **hold someone/something at** (or **for**) **ransom** hold someone prisoner and demand payment for their release. ■ demand concessions from a person or organization by threatening damaging action. □ **a king's ransom** a huge amount of money; a fortune.

rant /rant/ ▶ *v.* [*intr.*] speak or shout at length in a wild, impassioned way: *she was still ranting on about the unfairness of it all.*

▶ *n.* a spell of ranting; a tirade: *his rants against organized religion.* **—rant·er** *n.* **—rant·ing·ly** *adv.*

▶ □ **rant and rave** shout and complain angrily and at length.

rap /rap/ ▶ *v.* (**rapped, rap·ping**) **1** [*tr.*] strike (a hard surface) with a series of rapid audible blows, esp. in order to attract attention: *he stood up and rapped the table* | [*intr.*] *she rapped angrily on the window.* ■ strike (something) against a hard surface in such a way: *she rapped her stick on the floor.* ■ strike (someone or something) sharply with stick or similar implement: *she rapped my fingers with a ruler.* ■ *inf.* rebuke or criticize sharply: *executives rapped the U.S. for having too little competition in international phone service.* ■ say sharply or suddenly: *the ambassador rapped out an order.* **2** [*intr.*] *inf.* talk or chat in an easy and familiar manner: *we could be here all night rapping about the finer points of spiritualism.* **3** [*intr.*] perform rap music.

▶ *n.* a quick, sharp knock or blow: *there was a confident rap at the door.* **2** a type of popular music of U.S. black origin in which words are recited rapidly and rhythmically over a prerecorded, typically electronic instrumental backing. ■ a piece of music performed in this style, or the words themselves. **3** *inf.* a talk or discussion, esp. a lengthy or impromptu one: *dropping in after work for a rap over a beer* | [as *adj.*] *a rap session.* **4** *inf.* a criminal charge, esp. of a specified kind: *acquitted on a murder rap.* ■ a person or thing's reputation, typically a bad one: *there's no reason why drag queens should get a bad rap.* **—rap·per** *n.*

▶ □ **beat the rap** *inf.* escape punishment for or be acquitted of a crime. □ **take the rap** *inf.* be punished or blamed, esp. for something that is not one's fault or for which others are equally responsible.

ra·pa·cious /rəˈpāSHəs/ ▶ *adj.* aggressively greedy or grasping: *rapacious landlords.* **—ra·pa·cious·ly** *adv.* **—ra·pa·cious·ness** *n.* **—ra·pac·i·ty** /rəˈpasətē/ *n.*

rape[1] /rāp/ ▶ *n.* the crime, committed by a man, of forcing another person to have sexual intercourse with him without their consent and against their will, esp. by the threat or use of violence against them: *he denied two charges of attempted rape.* ■ *fig.* the wanton destruction or spoiling of a place or area: *the rape of the Russian countryside.*

▶ *v.* [*tr.*] (of a man) force (another person) to have sexual intercourse with him without their consent and against their will, esp. by the threat or use of violence against them: *the woman was raped at knifepoint.* ■ *fig.* spoil or destroy (a place): *the timber industry is raping the land.* **—rap·er** *n.*

rape[2] ▶ *n.* a plant (genus *Brassica*) of the cabbage family with bright yellow, heavily scented flowers, esp. a variety (**oilseed rape**) grown for its oil-rich seed and as stockfeed.

rap·id /ˈrapid/ ▶ *adj.* happening in a short time or at a fast pace: *the country's rapid economic decline* | *he was disposing of wives in rapid succession.* ■ (of movement or activity) characterized by great speed: *his breathing was rapid and jerky.*

▶ *n.* (usu. **rapids**) a fast-flowing and turbulent part of the course of a river. ▷mid 17th cent.: from Latin *rapidus,* from *rapere* 'take by force.' **—ra·pid·i·ty** /rəˈpidətē/ *n.* **—rap·id·ly** *adv.* **—rap·id·ness** *n.*

rap·id eye move·ment ▶ *n.* a jerky motion of a person's eyes occurring in REM sleep.

rap·id-fire ▶ *adj.* (esp. of something said in dialogue or done in a sequence) unhesitating and rapid: *a rapid-fire exchange of questions and answers.* ■ (of a gun) able to fire shots in rapid succession.

ra·pi·er /ˈrāpēər/ ▶ *n.* a thin, light, sharp-pointed sword used for thrusting. ■ [as *adj.*] (esp. of speech or intelligence) quick and incisive: *rapier wit.*

rapier

rap·ist /ˈrāpist/ ▶ *n.* a man who commits rape.

rap·pel /raˈpel/ ▶ *v.* (**-pelled, -pel·ling**) [*intr.*] descend a rock face or other near-vertical surface by using a doubled rope coiled around the body and fixed at a higher point: *they had to rappel down a long steep ice face.* ▶ *n.* a descent made by rappeling: *they were careful in setting up the rappel.*

rap·port /raˈpôr; rə-/ ▶ *n.* a close and harmonious relationship in which the people or groups concerned understand each other's feelings or ideas and communicate well: *she was able to establish a good rapport with the children.*

Pronunciation Key ə *ago,* up; ər *over, fur;* a *hat;* ā *ate;* ä *car;* cH *chin;* e *let;* ē *see;* e(ə)r *air;* i *fit;* ī *by;* i(ə)r *ear;* NG *sing;* ō *go;* ô *law, for;* oi *toy;* o͞o *good;* o͞o *goo;* ou *out;* sH *she;* ᴛH *thin;* ᴛH *then;* (h)w *why;* zH *vision*

rap·proche·ment /ˌrap͟ˌrōSHˈmän; -ˌrōSH-/ ▶n. (esp. in international relations) an establishment or resumption of harmonious relations: *there were signs of a growing rapprochement between the two countries.*

rapt /rapt/ ▶adj. completely fascinated by what one is seeing or hearing: *Andrew looked at her, rapt.* ■ indicating or characterized by such a state of fascination: *they listened with rapt attention.* ■ filled with an intense and pleasurable emotion; enraptured: *she shut her eyes and seemed rapt with desire.* —**rapt·ly** *adv.* —**rapt·ness** *n.*

rap·tor /ˈraptər/ ▶n. a bird of prey, e.g., an eagle, hawk, falcon, or owl. ■ *inf.* a velociraptor, utahraptor, or related dinosaur. —**rap·tor·i·al** /rapˈtôrēəl/ *adj.*

rap·ture /ˈrapCHər/ ▶n. **1** a feeling of intense pleasure or joy: *Leonora listened with rapture.* ■ **(raptures)** expressions of intense pleasure or enthusiasm about something: *the tabloids went into raptures about her.* **2 (the Rapture)** (according to some millenarian teaching) the transporting of believers to heaven at the second coming of Christ.
▶v. [tr.] (usu. **be raptured**) (according to some millenarian teaching) transport (a believer) from earth to heaven at the second coming of Christ. —**rap·tur·ous** *adj.*

rare[1] /re(ə)r/ ▶adj. (**rar·er**, **rar·est**) (of an event, situation, or condition) not occurring very often: *a rare genetic disorder.* ■ (of a thing) not found in large numbers and consequently of interest or value: *the jellyfish tree, one of the rarest plants on earth.* ■ unusually good or remarkable: *he plays with rare strength and sensitivity.* —**rare·ness** *n.*

rare[2] ▶adj. (**rar·er**, **rar·est**) (of meat, esp. beef) lightly cooked, so that the inside is still red.

rare·bit /ˈre(ə)rbit/ (also **Welsh rare·bit**) ▶n. a dish of melted and seasoned cheese on toast, sometimes with other ingredients.

rare earth (also **rare earth element** or **rare earth metal**) ▶n. *Chem.* any of a group of chemically similar metallic elements comprising the lanthanide series and (usually) scandium and yttrium. They are not esp. rare, but they tend to occur together in nature and are difficult to separate from one another.

rar·e·fac·tion /ˌre(ə)rəˈfakSHən/ (also **rar·i·fac·tion**) ▶n. diminution in the density of something, esp. air or a gas. ■ *Med.* the lessening of density of tissue, esp. of nervous tissue or bone. [early 17th cent.: from medieval Latin *rarefactio(n-)*, from the verb *rarefacere* 'grow thin, become rare.']

rar·e·fied /ˈrerəˌfīd/ (also **rar·i·fied**) ▶adj. (of air, esp. that at high altitudes) containing less oxygen than usual. ■ *fig.* esoterically distant from the lives and concerns of ordinary people: *debates about the nature of knowledge can seem very rarefied.*

rare·ly /ˈre(ə)rlē/ ▶adv. not often; seldom: *I rarely drive above 60 mph.*

rar·ing /ˈre(ə)riNG/ ▶adj. *inf.* very enthusiastic and eager to do something: *she was raring to get back to her work.*

rar·i·ty /ˈre(ə)ritē/ ▶n. (pl. **-ties**) the state or quality of being rare: *the rarity of the condition.* ■ a thing that is rare, esp. one having particular value as a result of this: *to take the morning off was a rarity.*

ras·cal /ˈraskəl/ ▶n. a mischievous or cheeky person or child (typically used in an affectionate way). ■ a dishonest person. —**ras·cal·i·ty** /rasˈkalətē/ *n.* (pl. **-ties**) —**ras·cal·ly** *adj.*

rash[1] /raSH/ ▶adj. displaying or proceeding from a lack of careful consideration of the possible consequences of an action: *a rash decision.* —**rash·ly** *adv.* —**rash·ness** *n.*

rash[2] ▶n. an area of reddening of a person's skin, sometimes with raised spots, appearing esp. as a result of allergy or illness. ■ a series of things of the same type, esp. when unpleasant or undesirable, occurring or appearing one after the other within a short space of time: *a rash of auto accidents.*

rash·er /ˈraSHər/ ▶n. a thin slice of bacon. ■ a serving of several such slices.

rasp /rasp/ ▶n. **1** a coarse file or similar metal tool with a roughened surface for scraping, filing, or rubbing down objects of metal, wood, or other hard material. **2** a harsh, grating noise: *the rasp of the engine.*
▶v. **1** [tr.] scrape (something) with a rasp in order to make it smoother. ■ (of a rough surface or object) scrape (something, esp. someone's skin) in a painful or unpleasant way. ■ (**rasp something away/off**) remove something by scraping it off. **2** [intr.] make a harsh, grating noise: *my breath rasped in my throat.* ■ [with direct speech] say in a harsh, grating voice: *"Stay where you are!" he rasped.* —**rasp·er** *n.* —**rasp·ing·ly** *adv.* —**rasp·y** *adj.*

rasp·ber·ry /ˈrazˌberē; -b(ə)rē/ ▶n. **1** an edible soft fruit related to the blackberry, consisting of a cluster of reddish-pink drupelets. **2** the plant (*Rubus idaeus*) of the rose family that yields this fruit, forming tall, stiff, prickly stems (canes). **3** a deep reddish-pink color like that of a ripe raspberry. **4** *inf.* a sound made with the tongue and lips in order to express derision or contempt.

Ras·ta·far·i·an /ˌrastəˈfe(ə)rēən; -ˈfärēən/ ▶adj. of or relating to a religious movement of Jamaican origin holding that blacks are the chosen people, that Emperor Haile Selassie of Ethiopia was the Messiah, and that black people will eventually return to their Africa.
▶n. a member of the Rastafarian religious movement. Rastafarians have distinctive codes of behavior and dress, including the wearing of dreadlocks, the smoking of cannabis, the rejection of Western medicine, and adherence to a diet that excludes pork, shellfish, and milk. —**Ras·ta·far·i·an·ism** *n.*

rat /rat/ ▶n. **1** a rodent (*Rattus* and other genera, family Muridae) that resembles a large mouse, typically having a pointed snout and a long, sparsely haired tail. **2** *inf.* a person regarded as despicable, esp. a man who has been deceitful or disloyal. ■ an informer. **3** a person who is associated with or frequents a specified place: *mall rats.*
▶interj. (**rats**) *inf.* used to express mild annoyance or irritation.
▶v. (**ratted, ratting**) [intr.] *inf.* (**rat on**) report the misdeeds of (someone) to the authorities.

ra·ta·touille /ˌratəˈtōō-ē; ˌrä,tä-/ ▶n. a vegetable dish consisting of onions, zucchini, tomatoes, eggplant, and peppers, stewed in oil and sometimes served cold.

ratch·et /ˈraCHit/ ▶n. a device consisting of a bar or wheel with a set of angled teeth in which a pawl, cog, or tooth engages, allowing motion in one direction only. ■ a bar or wheel that has such a set of teeth.
▶v. (**ratch·et·ed, ratch·et·ing**) [tr.] operate by means of a ratchet. ■ (**ratchet something up/down**) *fig.* cause something to rise (or fall) as a step in what is perceived as a steady and irreversible process: *the Bank of Japan ratcheted up interest rates again.* ■ [intr.] make a sound like a ratchet.

rate /rāt/ ▶n. **1** a measure, quantity, or frequency, typically one measured against some other quantity or measure: *the crime rate rose by 26 percent.* ■ the speed with which something moves, happens, or changes: *your heart rate.* **2** a fixed price paid or charged for something, esp. goods or services: *the basic rate of pay.* ■ the amount of a charge or payment expressed as a percentage of some other amount, or as a basis of calculation: *you'll find our current interest rate very competitive.*
▶v. **1** [tr.] assign a standard or value to (something) according to a particular scale: *they were asked to rate their ability at different driving maneuvers.* **2** consider to be of a certain quality, standard, or rank: *he rates the company's stock a "buy."* ■ be regarded in a specified way: *Jeff still rates as one of the nicest people I have ever met.* ■ be worthy of; merit: *the ambassador rated a bulletproof car and a police escort.*
▶ □ **at any rate** whatever happens or may have happened: *for the moment, at any rate, he was safe.* ■ used to indicate that one is correcting or clarifying a previous statement or emphasizing a following one: *the story, or at any rate, a public version of it, was known and remembered.*

rate of ex·change ▶n. another term for EXCHANGE RATE.

rat·fink /ˈratˌfiNGk/ ▶n. another term for FINK.

rath·er /ˈraT͟Hər; ˈräT͟Hər; ˈrəT͟Hər/ ▶adv. **1** (**would rather**) used to indicate one's preference in a particular matter: *I'd rather you not tell him.* **2** to a certain or significant extent or degree: *she's been behaving rather strangely | he's rather an unpleasant man.* ■ used before verbs as a way of making the expression of a feeling or opinion less assertive: *I rather think he wants me to marry him.* **3** on the contrary (used to suggest that the opposite of what has just been implied or stated is the case): *There is no shortage of basic skills in the workplace. Rather, the problem is poor management.* ■ more precisely (used to modify or clarify something previously stated): *I walked, or rather limped, the two miles home.*

rat·i·fy /ˈratəˌfī/ ▶v. (**-fies, -fied**) [tr.] sign or give formal consent to (a treaty, contract, or agreement), making it officially valid. —**rat·i·fi·a·ble** /ˈratəˌfīəbəl/ *adj.* —**rat·i·fi·ca·tion** /ˌratəfəˈkāSHən/ *n.* —**rat·i·fi·er** *n.*

rat·ing /ˈrātiNG/ ▶n. a classification or ranking of someone or something based on a comparative assessment of their quality, standard, or performance: *the hotel regained its five-star rating.* ■ an enlisted specialist in the navy. ■ (**ratings**) the estimated audience size of a particular television or radio program: *the soap's ratings have recently picked up.*

ra·tio /ˈrāSHō; ˈrāSHēˌō/ ▶n. (pl. **-tios**) the quantitative relation between two amounts showing the number of times one value contains or is contained within the other: *the ratio of men's jobs to women's is 8 to 1.*

ra·tion /ˈraSHən; ˈrā-/ ▶n. a fixed amount of a commodity officially allowed to each person during a time of shortage, as in wartime: *1918 saw the bread ration reduced on two occasions.* ■ (usu. **rations**) an amount of food supplied on a regular basis, esp. to members of the armed forces during a war. ■ (**rations**) food; provisions: *their emergency rations ran out.* ■ *fig.* a fixed amount of a particular thing: *their daily **ration of** fresh air.*

▶ *v.* [*tr.*] (usu. **be rationed**) allow each person to have only a fixed amount of (a particular commodity): *shoes were rationed from 1943.* ■ (**ration someone to**) allow someone to have only (a fixed amount of a certain commodity): *they were requested to ration themselves to one glass of wine each.*

ra·tion·al /ˈrasHənl; ˈrasHnəl/ ▶ *adj.* **1** based on or in accordance with reason or logic: *I'm sure there's a perfectly rational explanation.* ■ (of a person) able to think clearly, sensibly, and logically: *Andrea's upset—she's not being very rational.* ■ endowed with the capacity to reason: *man is a rational being.* **2** *Math.* (of a number, quantity, or expression) expressible, or containing quantities that are expressible, as a ratio of whole numbers. When expressed as a decimal, a rational number has a finite or recurring expansion. —**ra·tion·al·i·ty** /ˌrasHəˈnalətē/ *n.* —**ra·tion·al·ly** /ˈrasHənl-ē; ˈrasHnəlē/ *adv.*

ra·tion·ale /ˌrasHəˈnal/ ▶ *n.* a set of reasons or a logical basis for a course of action or a particular belief: *he explained the rationale behind the change.*

ra·tion·al·ism /ˈrasHnlˌizəm; ˈrasHnəˌlizəm/ ▶ *n.* a belief or theory that opinions and actions should be based on reason and knowledge rather than on religious belief or emotional response: *scientific rationalism.* —**ra·tion·al·ist** *n.* —**ra·tion·al·is·tic** /ˌrasHnlˈistik; ˌrasHnəˈlistik/ *adj.* —**ra·tion·al·is·ti·cal·ly** /ˌrasHnlˈistik(ə)lē; ˌrasHnəˈlistik(ə)lē/ *adv.*

ra·tion·al·ize /ˈrasHnlˌīz; ˈrasHnəˌlīz/ ▶ *v.* [*tr.*] **1** attempt to explain or justify (one's own or another's behavior or attitude) with logical, plausible reasons, even if these are not true or appropriate: *she couldn't rationalize her urge to return to the cottage.* **2** make (a company, process, or industry) more efficient by reorganizing it in such a way as to dispense with unnecessary personnel or equipment: *his success was due primarily to his ability to rationalize production.* **3** *Math.* convert (a function or expression) to a rational form. —**ra·tion·al·i·za·tion** /ˌrasHnl-ə-ˈzāsHən; ˌrasHnələ-/ *n.* —**ra·tion·al·iz·er** *n.*

rat race ▶ *n. inf.* a way of life in which people are caught up in a fiercely competitive struggle for wealth or power. ■ an exhausting, usually competitive routine.

rat·tan /raˈtan; rə-/ ▶ *n.* **1** the thin pliable stems of a palm, used to make furniture. ■ a length of such a stem used as a walking stick. **2** the tropical Old World climbing palm (genus *Calamus*) that yields this product, with long, spiny, jointed stems.

rat·tle /ˈratl/ ▶ *v.* **1** [*intr.*] make a rapid succession of short, sharp knocking sounds, typically as a result of being shaken and striking repeatedly against a hard surface or object: *there was a sound of bottles rattling as he stacked the crates.* ■ [*tr.*] cause (something) to make such sounds: *he rattled some change in his pocket.* ■ (of a vehicle or its driver or passengers) move or travel somewhere while making such sounds: *trains rattled past at frequent intervals.* ■ (**rattle around in**) *fig.* be in or occupy (an unnecessarily or undesirably spacious room or building). **2** [*tr.*] (often **be rattled**) *inf.* cause (someone) to feel nervous, worried, or irritated: *she turned quickly, rattled by his presence.*
▶ *phrasal v.* □ **rattle something off** say, perform, or produce something quickly and effortlessly: *he rattled off some instructions.*
▶ *n.* **1** a rapid succession of short, sharp, hard sounds: *the rattle of teacups on the tray.* ■ a gurgling sound in the throat of a dying person. **2** a thing used to make a rapid succession of short, sharp sounds, in particular: ■ a baby's toy consisting of a container filled with small pellets that makes a noise when shaken. ■ the set of horny rings at the end of a rattlesnake's tail, shaken with a dry buzzing sound as a warning. —**rat·tly** /ˈratl-ē; ˈratlē/ *adj.*

rat·tler /ˈratl-ər; ˈratlər/ ▶ *n. inf.* a rattlesnake.

rat·tle·snake /ˈratlˌsnāk/ ▶ *n.* a heavy-bodied American pit viper (genera *Crotalus* and *Sistrurus*) with a series of horny rings on the tail that, when vibrated, produce a characteristic rattling sound as a warning.

rat·tle·trap /ˈratlˌtrap/ ▶ *n. inf.* an old or rickety vehicle.

rat·ty /ˈratē/ ▶ *adj.* (**-ti·er, -ti·est**) resembling or characteristic of a rat: *his ratty eyes glittered.* ■ (of a place) infested with rats. ■ *inf.* shabby, untidy or in bad condition: *a ratty old armchair.* —**rat·ti·ly** /ˈratl-ē/ *adv.* —**rat·ti·ness** *n.*

rau·cous /ˈrôkəs/ ▶ *adj.* making or constituting a disturbingly harsh and loud noise: *raucous youths.* —**rau·cous·ly** *adv.* —**rau·cous·ness** *n.*

raun·chy /ˈrônCHē; ˈrän-/ ▶ *adj.* (**-chi·er, -chi·est**) *inf.* **1** earthy, vulgar, and often sexually explicit: *a raunchy new novel.* **2** (esp. of a person or place) slovenly; grubby: *the restaurant's style is raunchy and the sanitation chancy.* —**raunch·i·ly** /-CHəlē/ *adv.* —**raunch·i·ness** *n.*

rav·age /ˈravij/ ▶ *v.* [*tr.*] cause severe and extensive damage to: *fears that a war could ravage their country.*
▶ *n.* (**ravages**) the severely damaging or destructive effects of some-

thing: *his face had withstood the ravages of time.* ■ acts of destruction: *the ravages committed by man.* —**rav·ag·er** *n.*

rave /rāv/ ▶ *v.* [*intr.*] **1** talk wildly or incoherently, as if one were delirious or insane: *Nancy's having hysterics and raving about a black ghost.* ■ address someone in an angry, uncontrolled way: [with *direct speech*] *"Never mind how he feels!" Melissa raved.* **2** speak or write about someone or something with great enthusiasm or admiration: *New York's theater critics raved about the acting.* **3** *inf.* attend or take part in a rave (party).
▶ *n.* **1** *inf.* an extremely enthusiastic recommendation or appraisal of someone or something: *the film has won raves from American reviewers* | [as *adj.*] *their recent tour received rave reviews.* **2** *inf.* a party or event attended by large numbers of young people, involving drug use and dancing to fast, electronic music. ■ dance music of the kind played at such events.

rav·el /ˈravəl/ ▶ *v.* (**rav·eled, rav·el·ing**; *Brit.* **rav·el·led, rav·el·ling**) [*tr.*] **1** (**ravel something out**) untangle or unravel something: *Davy had finished raveling out his herring net* | *fig. sleep raveled out the tangles of his mind.* **2** confuse or complicate (a question or situation).

rav·en /ˈrāvən/ ▶ *n.* a large heavily built crow, esp. the all-black **common raven** (*Corvus corax*), feeding chiefly on carrion.
▶ *adj.* (esp. of hair) of a glossy black color.

rav·en·ous /ˈravənəs/ ▶ *adj.* extremely hungry. ■ (of hunger or need) very great; voracious: *a ravenous appetite.* —**rav·en·ous·ly** *adv.* —**rav·en·ous·ness** *n.*

ra·vine /rəˈvēn/ ▶ *n.* a deep, narrow gorge with steep sides. —**ra·vined** *adj.*

rav·ing /ˈrāviNG/ ▶ *n.* (usu. **ravings**) wild, irrational, or incoherent talk: *the ravings of a madwoman.*
▶ *adj. inf.* used to emphasize the bad or extreme quality of someone or something: *she'd never been a raving beauty.*

ra·vi·o·li /ˌravēˈōlē/ ▶ *n.* small pasta envelopes containing ground meat, cheese, or vegetables.

rav·ish /ˈraviSH/ ▶ *v.* [*tr.*] **1** *archaic* seize and carry off (someone) by force. ■ *dated* (of a man) force (a woman or girl) to have sexual intercourse against her will; rape. **2** (often **be ravished**) *poetic/lit.* fill (someone) with intense delight; enrapture: *ravished by a sunny afternoon, she had agreed without even thinking.* ▷Middle English: from Old French *raviss-*, lengthened stem of *ravir*, from an alteration of Latin *rapere* 'seize.' —**rav·ish·er** *n.* —**rav·ish·ment** *n.*

rav·ish·ing /ˈraviSHiNG/ ▶ *adj.* delightful; entrancing: *the keyboardist for Day's Reason is ravishing.* —**rav·ish·ing·ly** *adv.*

raw /rô/ ▶ *adj.* **1** (of food) uncooked: *raw eggs.* ■ (of a material or substance) in its natural state; not yet processed or purified: *raw sewage.* ■ (of information) not analyzed, evaluated, or processed for use: *there were a number of errors in the raw data.* ■ (of the edge of a piece of cloth) not having a hem or selvage. ■ (of a person) new to an activity or job and therefore lacking experience or skill: *they were replaced by raw recruits.* **2** (of a part of the body) red and painful, esp. as the result of skin abrasion: *he scrubbed his hands until they were raw* | *fig. Fran's nerves were raw.* **3** (of the weather) bleak, cold, and damp: *a raw February night.* **4** (of an emotion or quality) strong and undisguised: *he exuded an air of raw, vibrant masculinity.* —**raw·ly** *adv.* —**raw·ness** *n.*
▶ □ **in the raw 1** in its true state; not made to seem better or more palatable than it actually is: *he didn't much care for nature in the raw.* **2** *inf.* (of a person) naked: *I slept in the raw.*

raw deal ▶ *n.* harsh or unfair treatment: *educators tell us that inner-city kids are getting a raw deal.*

raw·hide /ˈrôˌhīd/ ▶ *n.* stiff untanned leather. ■ a whip or rope made of such leather.

raw ma·te·ri·al ▶ *n.* the basic material from which a product is made.

ray¹ /rā/ ▶ *n.* **1** each of the lines in which light (and heat) may seem to stream from the sun or any luminous body, or pass through a small opening: *a ray of sunlight came through the window.* ■ (**rays**) a specified form of nonluminous radiation: *water reflects and intensifies UV rays.* ■ *Math.* any of a set of straight lines passing through one point. ■ (**rays**) *inf.* sunlight considered in the context of sunbathing: *Sarah's catching some rays on a beach in Cruz Bay.* ■ *fig.* an initial or slight indication of a positive or welcome quality in a time of difficulty or trouble: *if only I could see some ray of hope.* **2** a thing that is arranged radially, in particular: ■ *Bot.* (in a composite flowerhead of the daisy family) an array of ray florets arranged radially around the central disc, forming the white part of the flowerhead of a daisy.

Pronunciation Key ə *ago*, *up*; ər *over*, *fur*; a *hat*; ā *ate*; ä *car*; CH *chin*; e *let*; ē *see*; e(ə)r *air*; i *fit*; ī *by*; i(ə)r *ear*; NG *sing*; ō *go*; ô *law*, *for*; oi *toy*; o͝o *good*; o͞o *goo*; ou *out*; SH *she*; TH *thin*; ŦH *then*; (h)w *why*; ZH *vision*

▶ *v.* [*intr.*] spread from or as if from a central point: *delicate lines rayed out at each corner of her eyes.* **—ray·ed** *adj.* **—ray·less** *adj.* (*chiefly Bot.*).

ray² ▶ *n.* a broad, flat marine or freshwater fish (Rajidae and other families) with a cartilaginous skeleton, winglike pectoral fins, and a long slender tail.

Ray·naud's dis·ease /rā'nōz/ (also **Raynaud's syndrome**) ▶ *n.* a disease characterized by spasm of the arteries in the extremities, esp. the fingers.

ray·on /'rā,än/ ▶ *n.* a textile fiber made from viscose. ■ fabric or cloth made from this fiber.

raze /rāz/ ▶ *v.* [*tr.*] (usu. **be razed**) completely destroy (a building, town, or other site): *villages were razed to the ground.*

ra·zor /'rāzər/ ▶ *n.* an instrument with a sharp blade or combination of blades, used to remove unwanted hair from the face or body.
▶ *v.* [*tr.*] cut with a razor.

ra·zor·back /'rāzər,bak/ ▶ *n.* **1** (also **razorback hog**) a pig of a half-wild breed common in the southern U.S., with the back formed into a high, narrow ridge. **2** (also **razorback ridge**) a steep-sided, narrow ridge of land.

ra·zor clam ▶ *n.* a burrowing bivalve mollusk (*Ensis* and other genera) with a long, slender shell that resembles the handle of a straight razor.

ra·zor edge (also **ra·zor's edge**) ▶ *n.* a sharp edge of a knife, ax, or similar implement. ■ *fig.* a state of sharp incisiveness: *he had honed his mind to a razor edge.* ■ **(the razor edge)** *fig.* the most advanced stage in the development of something; the cutting edge: *in 1960 jet planes were the razor edge of chic.* **—ra·zor-edged** *adj.*

ra·zor wire ▶ *n.* a metal wire or ribbon with sharp edges or studded with small sharp blades, used as a barrier.

raz·zle-daz·zle /,razəl 'dazəl/ ▶ *n. inf.* noisy, showy, and exciting activity and display designed to attract and impress: *myth, legend, and razzle-dazzle all rolled into one show* | [as *adj.*] *hyped-up, razzle-dazzle gimmicks of quick-sell advertising.*

razz·ma·tazz /'razmə,taz/ ▶ *n.* another term for RAZZLE-DAZZLE.

Rb ▶ *symb.* the chemical element rubidium.

RC ▶ *abbr.* ■ Red Cross. ■ Roman Catholic.

Rd ▶ *abbr.* Road (used in street names).

RDA ▶ *abbr.* recommended daily (or dietary) allowance, the quantity of a particular nutrient which should be consumed daily in order to maintain good health.

Re ▶ *symb.* the chemical element rhenium.

re- ▶ *prefix* **1** once more; afresh; anew: *reactivate.* ■ with return to a previous state: *revert.* **2** (also **red-**) in return; mutually: *resemble.* ■ in opposition: *resistance.* **3** behind or after: *remain.* ■ in a withdrawn state: *reticent.* ■ back and away; down: *relegation.* **4** with frequentative or intensive force: *resound.* **5** with negative force: *recant.*

re /rā/ ▶ *n. Mus.* (in solmization) the second note of a major scale. ■ the note D in the fixed-do system.

reach /rēCH/ ▶ *v.* **1** [*intr.*] stretch out an arm in a specified direction in order to touch or grasp something: *he reached over and turned off his bedside light.* ■ hand (something) to (someone): *reach me those glasses.* ■ [*intr.*] be able to touch something with an outstretched arm or leg: *I had to stand on tiptoe and even then I could hardly reach.* ■ **(reach out)** extend help, understanding, or influence: *he felt such an urge to reach out to his fellow sufferer.* **2** [*tr.*] arrive at; get as far as: *"Goodbye," she said as they reached the door* | *the show is due to reach our screens early next year.* ■ make contact or communicate with (someone) by telephone or other means: *I've been trying to reach you all morning.* ■ succeed in influencing or having an effect on: *their fresh sound and message reach people who may never set foot in a church.*
▶ *n.* **1** an act of reaching out with one's arm: *she made a reach for him.* ■ the distance to which someone can stretch out their hand (used esp. of a boxer): *a giant, over six feet seven with a reach of over 81 inches.* ■ the extent or range of application, effect, or influence: *the diameter and the reach of the spark plug varies from engine to engine.* **2** (often **reaches**) a continuous extent of land or water, esp. a stretch of river between two bends, or the part of a canal between locks: *the upper reaches of the Nile.* **—reach·a·ble** *adj.*

re·act /rē'akt/ ▶ *v.* [*intr.*] respond or behave in a particular way in response to something: *Iraq reacted angrily to Jordan's shift in policy.* ■ **(react against)** respond with hostility, opposition, or a contrary course of action to: *they reacted against the elite art music of their time.* ■ (of a person) suffer from adverse physiological effects after ingesting, breathing, or touching a substance: *many babies react to soy-based formulas.* ■ *Chem. & Physics* interact and undergo a chemical or physical change: *the sulfur in the coal reacts with the limestone during combustion.* ■ *Stock Market* (of stock prices) fall or rise in reaction to events, developments, etc.

re·ac·tance /rē'aktəns/ ▶ *n. Physics* the nonresistive component of impedance in an AC circuit, arising from the effect of inductance or capacitance or both and causing the current to be out of phase with the electromotive force causing it.

re·ac·tant /rē'aktənt/ ▶ *n. Chem.* a substance that takes part in and undergoes change during a reaction.

re·ac·tion /rē'akshən/ ▶ *n.* an action performed or a feeling experienced in response to a situation or event: *Carrie's immediate reaction was one of relief.* ■ **(reactions)** a person's ability to respond physically and mentally to external stimuli: *a skilled driver with quick reactions.* ■ an adverse physiological response to a substance that has been breathed in, ingested, or touched: *such allergic reactions as hay fever and asthma.* ■ a chemical process in which two or more substances act mutually on each other and are changed into different substances, or one substance changes into two or more other substances. ■ *Physics* an analogous transformation of atomic nuclei or other particles. ■ a mode of thinking or behaving that is deliberately different from previous modes of thought and behavior: *the work of these painters was a reaction*

re·ab·sorb *v.*	**re·con·firm** *v.*	**re·e·val·u·a·tion** *n.*	**re·roof** *v.*
re·ab·sorp·tion *n.*	**re·con·fir·ma·tion** *n.*	**re·fi·nance** *v.*	**re·seal** *v.*
re·ac·cept *v.*	**re·con·quer** *v.*	**re·for·mu·late** *v.*	**re·seal·a·ble** *adj.*
re·ac·cept·ance *n.*	**re·con·quest** *n.*	**re·for·mu·la·tion** *n.*	**re·se·lect** *v.*
re·ac·cus·tom *v.*	**re·con·se·crate** *v.*	**re·freeze** *v.*; **-froze, -fro·zen**	**re·shape** *v.*
re·ac·quire *v.*	**re·con·se·cra·tion** *n.*	**re·gild** *v.*	**re·shoot** *v.*
re·ac·ti·vate *v.*	**re·con·sol·i·date** *v.*	**re·grow** *v.*; **-grew, -grown**	**re·spray** *v.*
re·a·dapt *v.*	**re·con·sol·i·da·tion** *n.*	**re·growth** *n.*	**re·stage** *v.*
re·ad·mis·sion *n.*	**re·crys·tal·lize** *v.*	**re·meas·ure** *v.*	**re·start** *v. & n.*
re·ad·mit *v.*	**re·ded·i·cate** *v.*	**re·meas·ure·ment** *n.*	**re·stud·y** *v. & n.*; **-ied**
re·a·dopt *v.*	**re·ded·i·ca·tion** *n.*	**re·mod·i·fy** *v.*; **-fied**	**re·sup·ply** *v.*; **-plied**
re·a·dop·tion *n.*	**re·dis·solve** *v.*	**re·na·tion·al·ize** *v.*	**re·tag** *v.*; **-tagged, -tag·ging**
re·ad·ver·tise *v.*	**re·em·bark** *v.*	**re·nom·i·nate** *v.*	**re·take** *v. & n.*
re·ad·ver·tise·ment *n.*	**re·em·bar·ka·tion** *n.*	**re·nom·i·na·tion** *n.*	**re·teach** *v.*; **-taught**
re·al·lot *v.*	**re·em·pha·sis** *n.*	**re·num·ber** *v.*	**re·tell** *v.*; **-told**
re·al·lot·ment *n.*	**re·em·pha·size** *v.*	**re·oc·cu·pa·tion** *n.*	**re·tie** *v.*; **-tied, -ty·ing**
re·ap·pear *v.*	**re·em·ploy** *v.*	**re·oc·cu·py** *v.*; **-pied**	**re·ti·tle** *v.*
re·ap·pear·ance *n.*	**re·em·ploy·ment** *n.*	**re·oc·cur** *v.*; **-curred, -cur·ring**	**re·type** *v.*
re·ar·rest *v. & n.*	**re·en·ter** *v.*	**re·oc·cur·rence** *n.*	**re·u·til·ize** *v.*
re·as·sert *v.*	**re·en·trance** *v.*	**re·o·pen** *v.*	**re·vac·ci·nate** *v.*
re·as·ser·tion *n.*	**re·e·quip** *v.*; **-e·quipped, -e·quip·ping**	**re·pack** *v.*	**re·vac·ci·na·tion** *n.*
re·at·tain·ment *n.*	**re·e·rect** *v.*	**re·pag·i·nate** *v.*	**re·var·nish** *v.*
re·at·tempt *v.*	**re·e·rec·tion** *n.*	**re·pag·i·na·tion** *n.*	**re·wash** *v.*
re·bur·y *v.*	**re·es·tab·lish** *v.*	**re·paint** *v. & n.*	**re·weigh** *v.*
re·cir·cu·late *v.*	**re·es·tab·lish·ment** *n.*	**re·pol·ish** *v.*	**re·wire** *v.*
re·cir·cu·la·tion *n.*	**re·e·val·u·ate** *v.*	**re·pro·gram** *v.*; **-grammed, -gram·ming**	**re·wrap** *v.*; **-wrapped, -wrap·ping**
re·com·mence *v.*			

against fauvism. ■ opposition to political or social progress or reform: *the institution is under threat from the forces of reaction.* ■ *Physics* repulsion or resistance exerted in opposition to the impact or pressure of another body; a force equal and opposite to the force giving rise to it. —**re·ac·tion·ist** /-nist/ *n. & adj.*

re·ac·tion·ar·y /rēˈakshəˌnerē/ ▶*adj.* (of a person or a set of views) opposing political or social liberalization or reform.
▶*n.* (*pl.* **-ar·ies**) a person who holds such views.

re·ac·tive /rēˈaktiv/ ▶*adj.* showing a response to a stimulus: *pupils are reactive to light.* ■ acting in response to a situation rather than creating or controlling it: *a proactive rather than a reactive approach.* ■ having a tendency to react chemically: *nitrogen dioxide is a highly reactive gas.* ■ *Physiol.* showing an immune response to a specific antigen. ■ (of a disease or illness) caused by a reaction to something: *reactive depression.* —**re·ac·tiv·i·ty** /ˌrēakˈtivitē/ *n.*

re·ac·tor /rēˈaktər/ ▶*n.* **1** (also **nuclear reactor**) an apparatus or structure in which fissile material can be made to undergo a controlled, self-sustaining nuclear reaction with the consequent release of energy. ■ a container or apparatus in which substances are made to react chemically, esp. one in an industrial plant. **2** *Physics* a coil or other component that provides reactance in a circuit.

read /rēd/ ▶*v.* (*past* **read** /red/) [*tr.*] **1** look at and comprehend the meaning of (written or printed matter) by mentally interpreting the characters or symbols of which it is composed: *it's the best novel I've ever read.* ■ speak (the written or printed matter that one is reading) aloud, typically to another person: *the charges against him were read out.* ■ [*intr.*] have the ability to look at and comprehend the meaning of written or printed matter: *only three of the girls could read and none could write.* ■ habitually read (a particular newspaper or journal). ■ discover (information) by reading it in a written or printed source: *he was arrested yesterday—I read it in the paper.* ■ [as *adj.*] (**read**) (of a person) knowledgeable and informed as a result of extensive reading: *Ada was well read in French and German literature.* ■ understand or interpret the nature or significance of: *he didn't dare look away, in case this was read as a sign of weakness.* ■ [*intr.*] (of a piece of writing) convey a specified impression to the reader: *the brief note read like a cry for help.* ■ [*intr.*] (of a passage, text, or sign) contain or consist of specified words; have a certain wording: *the placard read "We want justice."* ■ [*intr.*] (**read for**) (of an actor) audition for (a part in a play or film). ■ (of a device) obtain data from (light or other input). **2** inspect and record the figure indicated on (a measuring instrument): *I've come to read the gas meter.* ■ [*intr.*] (of such an instrument) indicate a specified measurement or figure: *the thermometer read 0° C.* **3** (of a computer) copy or transfer (data). ■ [*tr.*] enter or extract (data) in an electronic storage device: *the commonest way of reading a file into the system.* **4** hear and understand the words of (someone speaking on a radio transmitter): *"Do you read me? Over."* ■ interpret the words formed by (a speaking person's lips) by watching rather than listening.
▶*phrasal v.* □ **read something into** attribute a meaning or significance to (something) that it may not in fact possess: *was I reading too much into his behavior?* □ **read up on something** acquire information about a particular subject by studying it intensively or systematically: *she spent the time reading up on antenatal care.*
▶*n.* a person's interpretation of something: *their read on the national situation may be correct.* ■ *inf.* a book considered in terms of its readability: *the book is a thoroughly entertaining read.* ▷Old English *rǣdan,* of Germanic origin; related to Dutch *raden* and German *raten* 'advise, guess.' Early senses included 'advise' and 'interpret (a riddle or dream)'
▶ □ **read between the lines** look for or discover a meaning that is hidden or implied rather than explicitly stated. □ **read someone's mind** (or **thoughts**) discern what someone is thinking. □ **read my lips** *inf.* listen carefully (used to emphasize the importance of the speaker's words or the earnestness of their intent).

read·a·ble /ˈrēdəbəl/ ▶*adj.* (of a text, script, or code) able to be read or deciphered; legible. ■ easy or enjoyable to read: *a marvelously readable book.* —**read·a·bil·i·ty** /ˌrēdəˈbilitē/ *n.* —**read·a·bly** /-blē/ *adv.*

re·ad·dress /ˌrēəˈdres/ ▶*v.* [*tr.*] **1** change the address written or printed on (a letter or parcel). **2** look at or attend to (an issue or problem) once again.

read·er /ˈrēdər/ ▶*n.* **1** a person who reads or who is fond of reading: *the books of Roald Dahl appeal to young readers | she's an avid reader.* ■ a person who reads and reports to a publisher or producer on the merits of manuscripts submitted for publication or production, or who provides critical comments on the text prior to publication. ■ a person who reads and grades examinations and papers for a professor. ■ a person who interprets the significance of tarot cards, horoscopes, lines in the palm of a hand, etc., so as to predict the future: *a tarot read-*

er. **2** a person who inspects and records the figure indicated on a measuring instrument: *a meter reader.* **3** a book containing extracts of a particular author's work or passages of text designed to give learners of a language practice in reading. **4** a machine for producing on a screen a magnified, readable image of any desired part of a microfiche or microfilm. ■ *Comput.* a device or piece of software used for reading or obtaining data stored on tape, cards, or other media.

read·er·ship /ˈrēdərˌship/ ▶*n.* [treated as *sing.* or *pl.*] the readers of a newspaper, magazine, or book regarded collectively: *it has a readership of 100 million.*

read·i·ly /ˈredl-ē/ ▶*adv.* without hesitation or reluctance; willingly: *he readily admits that the new car surpasses its predecessors.* ■ without delay or difficulty; easily: *illegal fireworks are readily available.*

read·ing /ˈrēdiNG/ ▶*n.* **1** the action or skill of reading written or printed matter silently or aloud: *suggestions for further reading.* ■ written or printed matter that can be read: *his main reading was detective stories.* ■ knowledge of literature: *a man of wide reading.* ■ an occasion at which poetry or other pieces of literature are read aloud to an audience. ■ a piece of literature or passage of scripture read aloud to a group of people: *readings from the Bible.* **2** an interpretation: *feminist readings of Goethe | his reading of the situation was justified.* **3** a figure or amount shown by a meter or other measuring instrument: *radiation readings were taken every hour.*

re·ad·just /ˌrēəˈjəst/ ▶*v.* [*tr.*] set or adjust (something) again: *I readjusted the rear-view mirror.* ■ [*intr.*] adjust or adapt to a changed environment or situation: [as *adj.*] (**readjusted**) *she wondered if she could ever become readjusted to this sort of life.* —**re·ad·just·ment** *n.*

read-on·ly mem·o·ry /rēd/ (abbr.: **ROM**) ▶*n. Comput.* memory read at high speed but not capable of being changed by program instructions.

read·out /ˈrēdˌout/ (also **read-out**) ▶*n.* a visual record or display of the output from a computer or scientific instrument. ■ the process of transferring or displaying such data.

read-write /ˈrēd ˈrīt/ ▶*adj. Comput.* capable of reading existing data and accepting further input.

read·y /ˈredē/ ▶*adj.* (**read·i·er, read·i·est**) **1** in a suitable state for an activity, action, or situation; fully prepared: *are you ready, Carrie? | I began to get ready for bed | she was about ready to leave.* ■ (of a thing) made suitable and available for immediate use: *dinner's ready! | could you have the list ready by this afternoon?* ■ (**ready with**) keen or quick to give: *I'm always ready with a wisecrack.* ■ (**ready for**) in need of or having a desire for: *I expect you're ready for a drink.* ■ eager, inclined, or willing to do something: *she is ready to die for her political convictions.* ■ in such a condition as to be likely to do something: *by the time he arrived he was ready to drop.* **2** easily available or obtained; within reach: *there was a ready supply of drink.*
▶*v.* (**read·ies, read·ied**) [*tr.*] prepare (someone or something) for an activity or purpose: *the spare transformer was readied for shipment* | [*tr.*] *she had readied herself to speak first.* —**read·i·ness** *n.*
▶ □ **at the ready** prepared or available for immediate use: *the men walk with their guns at the ready.* □ **make ready** prepare: *they were told to make ready for the journey home.* □ **ready and waiting** used to emphasize that someone or something is fully prepared or immediately available: *the apartment was all ready and waiting for them.*

read·y-made ▶*adj.* (esp. of products such as clothes and curtains) made to a standard size or specification rather than to order. ■ available straight away; not needing to be specially created or devised: *we have no ready-made answers.* ■ (of food) ready to be served without further preparation: *a ready-made Christmas cake.*
▶*n.* (usu. **ready-mades**) a ready-made article: *on the top shelf of ready-mades is Stromboli.* ■ a mass-produced article selected by an artist and displayed as a work of art.

read·y mon·ey (also **ready cash**) ▶*n.* money in the form of cash that is immediately available.

read·y-to-wear ▶*adj.* (of clothes) made for the general market and sold through stores rather than made to order for an individual customer; off the rack.

re·af·firm /ˌrēəˈfərm/ ▶*v.* state again as a fact; assert again strongly: *the prime minister reaffirmed his commitment to the agreement.* ■ [*tr.*] confirm the validity or correctness of (something previously established): *the election reaffirmed his position as leader.* —**re·af·fir·ma·tion** /ˌrē,afərˈmāshən/ *n.*

re·a·gent /rēˈājənt/ ▶*n.* a substance or mixture for use in chemical analysis or other reactions: *this compound is a very sensitive reagent for copper.*

R

re·al¹ /ˈrē(ə)l/ ▸*adj.* **1** actually existing as a thing or occurring in fact; not imagined or supposed: *a story drawing on real events* | *her many illnesses, real and imaginary.* **2** (of a substance or thing) not imitation or artificial; genuine: *the earring was presumably real gold.* ■ true or actual: *his real name is James* | *this isn't my real reason for coming.* ■ (of a person or thing) rightly so called; proper: *he's my idea of a real man* | *Jamie is my only real friend.* **3** *inf.* complete; utter (used for emphasis): *the tour turned out to be a real disaster.* **4** adjusted for changes in the value of money; assessed by purchasing power: *real incomes had fallen by 30 percent.* **5** *Law* of fixed property (i.e., land and buildings), as distinct from personal property: *he lost nearly all of his real holdings.* **6** *Math.* (of a number or quantity) having no imaginary part. See IMAGINARY.
▸*adv. inf.* really; very: *my head hurts real bad.* —**real·ness** *n.*
▸ □ **for real** *inf.* used to assert that something is genuine or is actually the case: *I'm not playing games—this is for real!* ■ used in questions to express surprise or to question the truth or seriousness of what one has seen or heard: *are these guys for real?* □ **get real!** *inf.* used to convey that an idea or statement is foolish or overly idealistic: *You want teens to have committed sexual relationships? Get real!*

re·al² /rāˈäl/ ▸*n.* (*pl.* **re·als** or **reis** /rāsʜ; räs/) the basic monetary unit of Brazil since 1994, equal to 100 centavos. ■ (*pl.* **re·a·les** /rāˈäles/ or **re·als**) a former coin and monetary unit of various Spanish-speaking countries.

real es·tate ▸*n.* the more commonly used term for REAL PROPERTY: *most of her real estate is in New Mexico.* ■ the business of selling real property, esp. in the capacity of an agent to either the buyer or the seller: *Bryce has been in real estate for 11 years.*

re·a·lign /ˌrēəˈlīn/ ▸*v.* [*tr.*] change or restore to a different or former position or state: *they worked to relieve his shoulder pain and realign the joint.* —**re·a·lign·ment** *n.*

re·al·ism /ˈrēəˌlizəm/ ▸*n.* **1** the attitude or practice of accepting a situation as it is and being prepared to deal with it accordingly: *the summit was marked by a new mood of realism.* ■ the view that the subject matter of politics is political power, not matters of principle: *political realism is the oldest approach to global politics.* **2** the quality or fact of representing a person, thing, or situation accurately or in a way that is true to life: *the earthy realism of Raimu's characters.* ■ (in art and literature) the movement or style of representing familiar things as they actually are. Often contrasted with IDEALISM (sense 1). —**re·al·ist** /ˈrēəlist/ *n.*

re·al·is·tic /ˌrēəˈlistik/ ▸*adj.* **1** having or showing a sensible and practical idea of what can be achieved or expected: *jobs are scarce at the moment, so you've got to be realistic.* **2** representing familiar things in a way that is accurate or true to life: *a realistic human drama.* —**re·al·is·ti·cal·ly** /-ik(ə)lē/ *adv.* *realistically, there was little prospect of any improvement.*

re·al·i·ty /rēˈalətē/ ▸*n.* (*pl.* **-ties**) **1** the world or the state of things as they actually exist, as opposed to an idealistic or notional idea of them: *he refuses to face reality.* ■ a thing that is actually experienced or seen, esp. when this is grim or problematic: *the harsh realities of life in a farming community.* ■ the quality of being lifelike or resembling an original: *the reality of Marryat's detail.* **2** the state or quality of having existence or substance: *youth, when death has no reality.*
▸ □ **in reality** in fact (used to contrast a false idea of what is true or possible with one that is more accurate): *she had believed she could control these feelings, but in reality that was not so easy.*

re·al·ize /ˈrē(ə)ˌlīz/ ▸*v.* [*tr.*] **1** become fully aware of (something) as a fact; understand clearly: *he realized his mistake at once.* **2** cause (something desired or anticipated) to happen: *his worst fears have been realized.* ■ fulfill: *it is only now that she is beginning to realize her potential.* **3** (usu. **be realized**) give actual or physical form to: *the stage designs have been beautifully realized.* ■ use (a linguistic feature) in a particular spoken or written form. **4** make (money or a profit) from a transaction: *she realized a profit of $100,000.* ■ convert (an asset) into cash: *he realized all the assets in her trust fund.* —**re·al·iz·a·ble** *adj.* —**re·al·i·za·tion** *n.* —**re·al·iz·er** *n.*

real life ▸*n.* life as it is lived in reality, involving unwelcome as well as welcome experiences, as distinct from a fictional world: [as *adj.*] *real-life situations.*

re·al·ly /ˈrē(ə)lē/ ▸*adv.* **1** in actual fact, as opposed to what is said or imagined to be true or possible: *so what really happened?.* ■ used to add strength, sincerity, or seriousness to a statement or opinion: *I really want to go.* ■ seriously (used in questions and exclamations with an implied negative answer): *do you really expect me to believe that?* **2** very; thoroughly: *a really cold day.*
▸*interj.* used to express interest, surprise, or doubt: *"I've been working hard." "Really?"* ■ used to express mild protest: *really, Marjorie, you do jump to conclusions!* ■ used to express agreement: *"It's a nightmare finding somewhere to live in this town." "Yeah, really."*

realm /relm/ ▸*n. archaic, poetic/lit.,* or *Law* a kingdom: *the peers of the realm* | *the defense of the realm.* ■ a field or domain of activity or interest: *the realm of applied chemistry.* ■ *Zool.* a primary biogeographical division of the earth's surface.

real prop·er·ty ▸*n. Law* fixed property, principally land and buildings. Used in contrast to PERSONAL PROPERTY.

real time ▸*n.* the actual time during which a process or event occurs: *information updated in real time.* ■ [as *adj.*] (**real-time**) *Comput.* of or relating to a system in which input data is processed within milliseconds so that it is available virtually immediately as feedback, e.g., in a missile guidance or airline booking system: *real-time signal processing.* ■ *inf.* a two-way conversation, as opposed to the delay of written correspondence: *a place where two people can talk to one another* **in real time.**

re·al·tor /ˈrē(ə)ltər; -ˌtôr; ˈrē(ə)lətər/ ▸*n. trademark* a person who acts as an agent for the sale and purchase of buildings and land; a real estate agent.

re·al·ty /ˈrē(ə)ltē/ ▸*n. Law* real, fixed property. Used in contrast to PERSONALTY.

ream¹ /rēm/ ▸*n.* 500 (formerly 480) sheets of paper. ■ a large quantity of something, typically paper or writing on paper: *reams of paper have been used to debate these questions.*

ream² ▸*v.* [*tr.*] widen (a bore or hole) with a special tool. ■ clear out or remove (material) from something. ■ *inf.* rebuke someone fiercely: *the agent was reaming him out for walking away from the deal.* —**ream·er** *n.*

reap /rēp/ ▸*v.* [*tr.*] cut or gather (a crop or harvest): *large numbers of men were employed to reap the harvest* | *fig. in terms of science, the Apollo program reaped a meager harvest.* ■ *fig.* receive (a reward or benefit) as a consequence of one's own or other people's actions: *the company is poised to reap the benefits of this investment.*

re·ap·ply /ˌrēəˈplī/ ▸*v.* (**-plies, -plied**) **1** [*intr.*] make another application or request: *he was ordered to take a driving test before reapplying for a license.* **2** [*tr.*] apply (an existing rule or principle) in a different context. **3** [*tr.*] spread (a substance) on a surface again: *reapply the sunscreen hourly.* —**re·ap·pli·ca·tion** /ˌrē,apləˈkāsʜən/ *n.*

rear¹ /ri(ə)r/ ▸*n.* the back part of something, esp. a building or vehicle: *the kitchen door at the rear of the house.* ■ the space or position at the back of something or someone: *the field at the rear of the church.* ■ the hindmost part of an army, fleet, or line of people: *two blue policemen at the rear fell out of the formation.* ■ (also **rear end**) *inf.* a person's buttocks.
▸*adj.* at the back: *the car's rear window.*
▸ □ **bring up the rear** be at the very end of a line of people. ■ come last in a race or other contest.

rear² ▸*v.* **1** [*tr.*] (usu. **be reared**) bring up and care for (a child) until they are fully grown, esp. in a particular manner or place: *a generation reared on video.* ■ (of an animal) care for (its young) until they are fully grown. ■ breed and raise (animals): *the calves are reared for beef.* **2** [*intr.*] (of a horse or other animal) raise itself upright on its hind legs: *the horse reared in terror.* ■ (of a building, mountain, etc.) extend or appear to extend to a great height: *houses reared up on either side.*
▸*phrasal v.* □ **rear up** (of a person) show anger or irritation; go on the attack: *the press reared up in the wake of the bombings.* —**rear·er** *n.*
▸ □ **rear one's head** raise one's head. ■ (**rear its head**) (of an unpleasant matter) emerge; present itself: *elitism is* **rearing its ugly head** *again.*

rear ad·mi·ral ▸*n.* an officer in the U.S. Navy or Coast Guard ranking above commodore and below vice admiral.

rear·guard /ˈri(ə)r,gärd/ ▸*n.* the soldiers positioned at the rear of a body of troops, esp. those protecting an army when it is in retreat. ■ a defensive or conservative element in an organization or community.

rear·guard ac·tion ▸*n.* a defensive action carried out by a retreating army.

re·arm /rēˈärm/ ▸*v.* provide with or acquire a new supply of weapons: *his plan to rearm Germany.* —**re·arm·a·ment** /rēˈärməmənt/ *n.*

rear·most /ˈri(ə)r,mōst/ ▸*adj.* furthest back: *the rearmost door.*

re·ar·range /ˌrēəˈrānj/ ▸*v.* [*tr.*] move (something) into a more acceptable position or state: *she rearranged her skirt as she sat back in her chair.* ■ change (the position, time, or order of something): *he had rearranged his schedule.* —**re·ar·range·ment** *n.*

rear·view mir·ror /ˈri(ə)r,vyo͞o/ (also **rear-view mir·ror**) ▸*n.* a small angled mirror fixed inside the windshield of a motor vehicle, enabling the driver to see the vehicle or road behind.

rear·ward /ˈri(ə)rwərd/ ▸*adj.* directed toward the back: *a slight rearward movement.*
▸*adv.* (also *chiefly Brit.* **rear·wards**) toward the back: *the engine nozzles point rearward.*

rea·son /ˈrēzən/ ▸*n.* **1** a cause, explanation, or justification for an action or event: *it is hard to know for the simple reason that few records survive.*

■ good or obvious cause to do something: *we have reason to celebrate.* **2** the power of the mind to think, understand, and form judgments by a process of logic: *there is a close connection between reason and emotion.* ■ what is right, practical, or possible; common sense: *people are willing, within reason, to pay for schooling.* ■ (**one's reason**) one's sanity: *she is in danger of losing her reason.*

▶ *v.* [*intr.*] think, understand, and form judgments by a process of logic: *humans do not reason entirely from facts* | [as *n.*] (**reasoning**) *the present chapter will outline the reasoning behind the review.* ■ [*tr.*] (**reason something out**) find an answer to a problem by considering various possible solutions. ■ (**reason with**) persuade (someone) with rational argument: *I tried to reason with her, but without success.* ▷Middle English: from Old French *reisun* (noun), *raisoner* (verb), from a variant of Latin *ratio(n-)*, from the verb *reri* 'consider.' —**rea·son·er** /ˈrēz(ə)nər/ *n.* —**rea·son·less** *adj.* (*archaic*).

▶ □ **listen to reason** be persuaded to act sensibly: *the child is usually too emotionally overwrought to listen to reason.* □ (**it**) **stands to reason** it is obvious or logical: *it stands to reason that if you can eradicate the fear, the nervousness will subside.*

rea·son·a·ble /ˈrēz(ə)nəbəl/ ▶*adj.* **1** (of a person) having sound judgment; fair and sensible: *no reasonable person could have objected.* ■ based on good sense: *it seems a reasonable enough request.* **2** as much as is appropriate or fair; moderate: *a police officer may use reasonable force to gain entry.* ■ fairly good; average: *the carpet is in reasonable condition.* ■ (of a price or product) not too expensive: *a restaurant serving excellent food at reasonable prices* | *they are lovely shoes and very reasonable.* —**rea·son·a·ble·ness** *n.* —**rea·son·a·bly** *adv.*

re·as·sure /ˌrēəˈSHo͝or/ ▶*v.* [*tr.*] say or do something to remove the doubts and fears of someone: *he understood her feelings and tried to reassure her* | [*tr.*] *Joachim reassured him that he was needed* | [as *adj.*] (**reassuring**) *Gina gave her a reassuring smile.* —**re·as·sur·ance** *n.* —**re·as·sur·ing·ly** *adv.*

Ré·au·mur /ˌrāōˈmyo͝or/ (abbr.: **Ré**) ▶*adj.* of or denoting a scale of temperature on which water freezes at 0° and boils at 80° under standard conditions.

▶*n.* (also **Réaumur scale**) this scale of temperature. ▷1730s: named after René-Antoine Ferchault de *Réaumur* (1683–1757), French physicist.

re·bate ▶*n.* /ˈrēˌbāt/ a partial refund to someone who has paid too much money for tax, rent, or a utility. ■ a deduction or discount on a sum of money due.

▶*v.* /ˈrēˌbāt; riˈbāt/ [*tr.*] pay back (such a sum of money). —**re·bat·a·ble** /ˈrēˌbātəbəl; riˈbāt-/ *adj.*

reb·el ▶*n.* /ˈrebəl/ a person who rises in opposition or armed resistance against an established government or ruler: *Tory rebels* | [as *adj.*] *rebel forces.* ■ a person who resists authority, control, or convention.

▶*v.* /riˈbel/ (**-elled, -el·ling**) [*intr.*] rise in opposition or armed resistance to an established government or ruler: *the Earl of Pembroke subsequently rebelled against Henry III.* ■ (of a person) resist authority, control, or convention: *respect did not prevent children from rebelling against their parents.* ■ show or feel repugnance for or resistance to something: *as I came over the hill my legs rebelled—I could walk no further.*

re·bel·lion /riˈbelyən/ ▶*n.* an act of violent or open resistance to an established government or ruler: *the authorities put down a rebellion by landless colonials.* ■ the action or process of resisting authority, control, or convention: *an act of teenage rebellion.*

re·bel·lious /riˈbelyəs/ ▶*adj.* showing a desire to resist authority, control, or convention: *young people with a rebellious streak.* ■ (of a person, city, or state) engaged in opposition or armed resistance to an established government or ruler: *the rebellious republics.* ■ (of a thing) not easily handled or kept in place: *he smoothed back a rebellious lock of hair.* —**re·bel·lious·ly** *adv.* —**re·bel·lious·ness** *n.*

re·birth /rēˈbərTH; ˈrēˌbərTH/ ▶*n.* the process of being reincarnated or born again: *the endless cycle of birth, death, and rebirth.* ■ the action of reappearing or starting to flourish or increase after a decline; revival: *the rebirth of a defeated nation.* —**re·born** /rēˈbôrn/ *adj.*

re·boot /rēˈbo͞ot/ ▶*v.* [*tr.*] boot (a computer system) again. ■ [*intr.*] (of a computer system) be booted again.

▶*n.* an act or instance of booting a computer system again.

re·born /rēˈbôrn/ ▶*adj.* brought back to life or activity: *the grand concourse stands reborn as a four-star restaurant.* ■ having experienced a complete spiritual change: *a reborn Catholic.*

re·bound ▶*v.* /riˈbound; ˈrēˌbound/ [*intr.*] bounce back through the air after hitting a hard surface or object: *his shot hammered into the post and rebounded across the goal.* ■ [*intr.*] recover in value, amount, or strength after a previous decrease or decline: *NASDAQ rebounded to show a twenty-point gain.* ■ [*intr.*] (**rebound on/upon**) (of an event or situation) have an unexpected adverse consequence for (someone, esp. the per-

son responsible for it): *Nicholas's tricks are rebounding on him.* ■ [*intr.*] *Basketball* gain possession of a missed shot after it bounces off the backboard or basket rim.

▶*n.* /ˈrēˌbound/ (in sporting contexts) a ball or shot that bounces back after striking a hard surface: *he blasted the rebound into the net.* ■ *Basketball* a recovery of possession of a missed shot. ■ an instance of increasing in value, amount, or strength after a previous decline: *they revealed a big rebound in profits for last year.* ■ [usu. as *adj.*] the recurrence of a medical condition, esp. after withdrawal of medication: *rebound hypertension.*

▶ □ **on the rebound** in the process of bouncing back after striking a hard surface. ■ still affected by the emotional distress caused by the ending of a romantic or sexual relationship: *I was on the rebound when I met Jack.*

re·buff /riˈbəf/ ▶*v.* [*tr.*] reject (someone or something) in an abrupt or ungracious manner: *I asked her to be my wife, and was rebuffed in no uncertain terms.*

▶*n.* an abrupt or ungracious refusal or rejection of an offer, request, or friendly gesture: *any attempt to win her friendship was met with rebuffs.*

re·build /rēˈbild/ ▶*v.* (*past* and *past part.* **-built** /-ˈbilt/) [*tr.*] build (something) again after it has been damaged or destroyed: *he rebuilt the cathedral church* | *fig.* *we try to help them rebuild their lives.*

▶*n.* /ˈrēˌbild/ an instance or rebuilding something, esp. a vehicle or other machine. ■ a thing that has been rebuilt, esp. a part of a motor vehicle, e.g., a motor or an alternator. —**re·build·a·ble** *adj.* —**re·build·er** *n.*

re·buke /riˈbyo͞ok/ ▶*v.* [*tr.*] express sharp disapproval or criticism of (someone) because of their behavior or actions: *she had rebuked him for drinking too much.*

▶*n.* an expression of sharp disapproval or criticism: *he hadn't meant it as a rebuke, but Neil flinched.* —**re·buk·er** *n.* —**re·buk·ing·ly** *adv.*

re·bus /ˈrēbəs/ ▶*n.* (*pl.* **-bus·es**) a puzzle in which words are represented by combinations of pictures and individual letters; for instance, *apex* might be represented by a picture of an ape followed by a letter X.

re·but /riˈbət/ ▶*v.* (**-but·ted, -but·ting**) [*tr.*] claim or prove that (evidence or an accusation) is false: *he had to rebut charges of acting for the convenience of his political friends.* —**re·but·ta·ble** *adj.* —**re·but·tal** /-ˈbətl/ *n.*

re·cal·ci·trant /riˈkalsətrənt/ ▶*adj.* having an obstinately uncooperative attitude toward authority or discipline: *a class of recalcitrant fifteen-year-olds.*

▶*n.* a person with such an attitude. ▷mid 19th cent.: from Latin *recalcitrant-* 'kicking out with the heels,' from the verb *recalcitrare*, based on *calx, calc-* 'heel.' —**re·cal·ci·trance** *n.* —**re·cal·ci·trant·ly** *adv.*

re·call ▶*v.* /riˈkôl/ [*tr.*] **1** bring (a fact, event, or situation) back into one's mind, esp. so as to recount it to others; remember: *I can still vaguely recall being taken to the hospital* | *"He was awfully fond of teasing people," she recalled.* ■ cause one to remember or think of: *the film's analysis of contemporary concerns recalls The Big Chill.* ■ (**recall someone/something to**) bring the memory or thought of someone or something to (a person or their mind): *the smell of a black-currant bush has ever since recalled to me that evening.* ■ call up (stored computer data) for processing or display. **2** officially order (someone) to return to a place: *the Panamanian ambassador was recalled from Peru.* ■ select (a sports player) as a member of a team from which they have previously been dropped: *the Fulham defender has been recalled to the Welsh squad for the World Cup.* ■ (of a manufacturer) request all the purchasers of (a certain product) to return it, as the result of the discovery of a fault. ■ bring (someone) out of a state of inattention or reverie: *her action recalled him to the present.*

▶*n.* /ˈrēˌkôl; riˈkôl; rēˈkôl/ **1** an act or instance of officially recalling someone or something: *a recall of Parliament.* ■ a request for the return of a faulty product, issued by a manufacturer to all those who have purchased it. ■ the removal of an elected government official from office by a petition followed by voting. **2** the action or faculty of remembering something learned or experienced: *he has amazing recall* | *people's understanding and subsequent recall of stories or events.* ■ the proportion of the number of relevant documents retrieved from a database in response to an inquiry. —**re·call·a·ble** *adj.*

▶ □ **beyond recall** in such a way that restoration is impossible: *shopping developments have already blighted other parts of the city beyond recall.*

re·cant /riˈkant/ ▶*v.* [*intr.*] say that one no longer holds an opinion or belief, esp. one considered heretical: *heretics were burned if they would not recant.* —**re·can·ta·tion** /ˌrēˌkanˈtāSHən/ *n.* —**re·cant·er** *n.*

re·cap inf. ▶v. /rē'kap/ (-capped, -cap·ping) [tr.] state again as a summary; recapitulate: *a way of recapping the story so far.*
▶n. /'rē,kap/ a summary of what has been said; a recapitulation: *a quick recap of the idea and its main advantages.*

re·cap·i·tal·ize /rē'kapətl,īz/ ▶v. [tr.] provide (a business) with more capital, esp. by replacing debt with stock. —**re·cap·i·tal·i·za·tion** /rē,kapətl-ə'zāSHən/ n.

re·ca·pit·u·late /,rēkə'piCHə,lāt/ ▶v. [tr.] summarize and state again the main points of: *he began to recapitulate his argument with care.* ■ *Biol.* repeat (an evolutionary or other process) during development and growth. —**re·ca·pit·u·la·to·ry** /-lə,tôrē/ adj.

re·ca·pit·u·la·tion /,rēkə,piCHə'lāSHən/ ▶n. an act or instance of summarizing and restating the main points of something: *his recapitulation of the argument.* ■ *Biol.* the repetition of an evolutionary or other process during development or growth. ■ *Mus.* a part of a movement (esp. one in sonata form) in which themes from the exposition are restated.

re·cap·ture /rē'kapCHər/ ▶v. [tr.] capture (a person or animal that has escaped): *armed police have recaptured a prisoner who's been on the run for five days.* ■ recover (something previously captured by an enemy): *Edward I recaptured the castle.* ■ regain (something that has been lost): *Democrats might recapture both the House and the Senate.* ■ recreate or experience again (a past time, event, or feeling): *the programs give viewers a chance to recapture their own childhoods.*
▶n. an act of recapturing.

re·cast /rē'kast/ ▶v. (*past* and *past part.* -cast) [tr.] **1** give (a metal object) a different form by melting it down and reshaping it. ■ present or organize in a different form or style: *his doctoral thesis has been recast for the general reader.* **2** allocate the parts in (a play or film) to different actors: *there are moves to recast the play.*

re·cede /ri'sēd/ ▶v. [intr.] go or move back or further away from a previous position: *the flood waters had receded.* ■ (of a quality, feeling, or possibility) gradually diminish: *the prospects of an early end to the war receded.* ■ (of a man's hair) cease to grow at the temples and above the forehead: *his dark hair was was receding a little* | [as adj.] (**receding**) *a receding hairline.* ■ (of a man) begin to go bald in such a way: *Fred was receding a bit.* ■ [usu. as adj.] (**receding**) (of a facial feature) slope backward: *a slightly receding chin.*

re·ceipt /ri'sēt/ ▶n. the action of receiving something or the fact of its being received: *I would be grateful if you would acknowledge receipt of this letter.* ■ a written or printed statement acknowledging that something has been paid for or that goods have been received. ■ (**receipts**) an amount of money received during a particular period by an organization or business: *box-office receipts.*
▶v. [tr.] [usu. as adj.] (**receipted**) mark (a bill) as paid: *the receipted hotel bill.* ■ write a receipt for (goods or money): *all fish shall be receipted at time of purchase.*

re·ceive /ri'sēv/ ▶v. [tr.] **1** be given, presented with, or paid (something): *she received her prize from the manager.* ■ detect or pick up (broadcast signals): *Turkish television began to be received in Tashkent.* ■ form (an idea or impression) as a result of perception or experience: *the impression she received was one of unhurried leisure.* ■ (in tennis and similar games) be the player to whom the server serves (the ball). ■ (in Christian services) eat or drink (the Eucharistic bread or wine): *he received Communion and left.* ■ serve as a receptacle for: *the basin that receives your blood.* **2** suffer, experience, or be subject to (specified treatment): *the event received wide press coverage* | *she received only cuts and bruises.* ■ [tr.] (usu. be **received**) respond to (something) in a specified way: *her first poem was not well received.* ■ [as adj.] (**received**) widely accepted as authoritative or true: *the myths and received wisdom about the country's past.* **3** greet or welcome (a visitor) formally: *representatives of the club will be received by the Mayor.* ■ admit as a member: *hundreds of converts were received into the Church.* —**re·ceiv·a·ble** adj.

re·ceiv·er /ri'sēvər/ ▶n. **1** the part of a telephone apparatus contained in the earpiece, in which electrical signals are converted into sounds. ■ a complete telephone handset: *he picked up the receiver.* ■ a piece of radio or television apparatus that detects broadcast signals and converts them into visible or audible form: *a satellite receiver.* **2** a person who gets or accepts something that has been sent or given to them: *the receiver of a gift.* ■ (in tennis and similar games) the player to whom the ball is served to begin play. ■ *Football* a player who catches a pass or a kick. **3** a person or company appointed by a court to manage the financial affairs of a business or person that has gone bankrupt: *the company is in the hands of the receivers.* **4** *Chem.* a container for collecting the products of distillation, chromatography, or other process. **5** the part of a firearm that houses the action and to which the barrel and other parts are attached.

re·ceiv·er·ship /ri'sēvər,SHip/ ▶n. the state of being dealt with by an official receiver: *the company went into receivership last week.*

re·cent /'rēsənt/ ▶adj. **1** having happened, begun, or been done not long ago or not long before; belonging to a past period of time comparatively close to the present: *a recent edition of the newspaper.* **2** (**Re·cent**) *Geol.* another term for **HOLOCENE**. —**re·cen·cy** n. —**re·cent·ly** adv. —**re·cent·ness** n.

re·cep·ta·cle /ri'septikəl/ ▶n. an object or space used to contain something: *trash receptacles.* ■ *chiefly Zool.* an organ or structure that receives a secretion, eggs, sperm, etc. ■ an electrical outlet into which the plug of an electrical device may be inserted.

re·cep·tion /ri'sepSHən/ ▶n. **1** the action or process of receiving something sent, given, or inflicted: *the reception of impulses from other neurons.* ■ the way in which a person or group of people reacts to someone or something: *the proposal continued to get a lukewarm reception on Wall Street.* ■ the receiving of broadcast signals: *poor reception* | *a microchip that will allow parents to block reception of violent programs.* ■ *Football* an act of catching the ball. **2** a formal social occasion held to welcome someone or to celebrate a particular event: *a wedding reception.* **3** the area in a hotel, office, or other establishment where guests and visitors are greeted and dealt with: [as adj.] *the reception desk.*

re·cep·tion·ist /ri'sepSHənist/ ▶n. a person employed in an office or other establishment to answer the telephone, deal with clients, and greet visitors.

re·cep·tive /ri'septiv/ ▶adj. able or willing to receive something, esp. signals or stimuli. ■ willing to consider or accept new suggestions and ideas: *a receptive audience.* ■ (of a female animal) ready to mate. —**re·cep·tive·ly** adv. —**re·cep·tive·ness** n. —**re·cep·tiv·i·ty** /,rē,sep'tivətē/ n.

re·cep·tor /ri'septər/ ▶n. *Physiol.* an organ or cell able to respond to light, heat, or other external stimulus and transmit a signal to a sensory nerve. ■ a region of tissue, or a molecule in a cell membrane, that responds specifically to a particular neurotransmitter, hormone, antigen, or other substance.

re·cess /'rē,ses; ri'ses/ ▶n. **1** a small space created by building part of a wall further back from the rest: *a table set into a recess.* ■ a hollow space inside something: *the concrete block has a recess in its base.* ■ (usu. **recesses**) a remote, secluded, or secret place: *the recesses of the silent pine forest.* **2** a period of time when the proceedings of a parliament, committee, court of law, or other official body are temporarily suspended: *talks resumed after a month's recess.* ■ a break between school classes: *the mid-morning recess.*
▶v. **1** [tr.] (often as adj.) (**recessed**) attach (a fixture) by setting it back into the wall or surface to which it is fixed: *recessed ceiling lights.* **2** [intr.] (of formal proceedings) be temporarily suspended: *the talks recessed at 2:15.* ■ [tr.] suspend (such proceedings) temporarily.

re·ces·sion /ri'seSHən/ ▶n. **1** a period of temporary economic decline during which trade and industrial activity are reduced, generally identified by a fall in GDP in two successive quarters. **2** *chiefly Astron.* the action of receding; motion away from an observer. —**re·ces·sion·ar·y** /-,nerē/ adj.

re·ces·sion·al /ri'seSHənl; ri'seSHnəl/ ▶adj. of or relating to an economic recession: *recessional times.* ■ *chiefly Astron.* relating to or denoting motion away from the observer. ■ *Geol.* (of a moraine or other deposit) left during a pause in the retreat of a glacier or ice sheet.
▶n. a hymn sung while the clergy and choir process out of church at the end of a service. Compare with **PROCESSIONAL**.

re·ces·sive /ri'sesiv/ ▶adj. **1** *Genetics* relating to or denoting heritable characteristics controlled by genes that are expressed in offspring only when inherited from both parents, i.e., when not masked by a dominant characteristic inherited from one parent. Often contrasted with **DOMINANT**. **2** undergoing an economic recession: *the recessive housing market.* **3** *Phonet.* (of the stress on a word or phrase) tending to fall on the first syllable.
▶n. *Genetics* a recessive trait or gene. —**re·ces·sive·ly** adv. —**re·ces·sive·ness** n. —**re·ces·siv·i·ty** /,rē,ses'ivətē/ n.

re·charge ▶v. /rē'CHärj/ [tr.] restore an electric charge to (a battery or a battery-operated device) by connecting it to a device that draws power from another source of electricity: *he plugged his razor in to recharge it.* ■ [intr.] (of a battery or battery-operated device) be refilled with electrical power in such a way: *the drill takes about three hours to recharge.* ■ refill (a container, lake, or aquifer) with water. ■ [intr.] be refilled: *the rate at which the aquifer recharges naturally.* ■ [intr.] fig. (of a person) return to a normal state of mind or strength after a period of physical or mental exertion: *she needs a bit of time to recharge after giving so much of herself this morning.*

▶*n.* /'rēCHärj/ the replenishment of an aquifer by the absorption of water. —**re·charge·a·ble** *adj.* —**re·charg·er** *n.*
▶ □ **recharge one's batteries** regain one's strength and energy by resting and relaxing for a time.

re·cid·i·vist /ri'sidəvist/ ▶*n.* a convicted criminal who reoffends, esp. repeatedly. —**re·cid·i·vism** /-,vizəm/ *n.* —**re·cid·i·vis·tic** /ri,sidə'vistik/ *adj.*

rec·i·pe /'resə,pē/ ▶*n.* a set of instructions for preparing a particular dish, including a list of the ingredients required: *a traditional Indonesian recipe.* ■ *fig.* something which is likely to lead to a particular outcome: *sky-high interest rates are a recipe for disaster.*

re·cip·i·ent /ri'sipēənt/ ▶*n.* a person or thing that receives or is awarded something: *the recipient of the Nobel Peace Prize.*
▶*adj.* receiving or capable or receiving something: *a recipient country.* —**re·cip·i·en·cy** *n.*

re·cip·ro·cal /ri'siprəkəl/ ▶*adj.* **1** given, felt, or done in return: *she was hoping for some reciprocal comment or gesture.* **2** (of an agreement or obligation) bearing on or binding each of two parties equally: *the treaty is a bilateral commitment with reciprocal rights and duties.* ■ *Gram.* (of a pronoun or verb) expressing mutual action or relationship. **3** (of a course or bearing) differing from a given course or bearing by 180 degrees. **4** *Math.* (of a quantity or function) related to another so that their product is one.
▶*n.* **1** *technical* a mathematical expression or function so related to another that their product is one; the quantity obtained by dividing the number one by a given quantity. **2** *Gram.* a pronoun or verb expressing mutual action or relationship, e.g., *each other, fight.* —**re·cip·ro·cal·i·ty** /ri,siprə'kalətē/ *n.* —**re·cip·ro·cal·ly** /-ək(ə)lē/ *adv.*

re·cip·ro·cate /ri'siprə,kāt/ ▶*v.* **1** [*tr.*] respond to (a gesture or action) by making a corresponding one: *the favor was reciprocated.* ■ experience the same (love, liking, or affection) for someone as that person does for oneself: *her passion for him was not reciprocated.* **2** [*intr.*] [usu. as *adj.*] (**reciprocating**) (of a part of a machine) move backward and forward in a straight line: *a reciprocating blade.* —**re·cip·ro·ca·tion** /ri,siprə'kāSHən/ *n.* —**re·cip·ro·ca·tor** /-,kātər/ *n.*

rec·i·proc·i·ty /,resə'präsətē/ ▶*n.* the practice of exchanging things with others for mutual benefit, esp. privileges granted by one country or organization to another.

re·cit·al /ri'sītl/ ▶*n.* **1** the performance of a program of music by a solo instrumentalist or singer or by a small group: *a piano recital.* **2** an enumeration or listing of connected names, facts, or elements; *a recital of their misfortunes.* —**re·cit·al·ist** /-ist/ *n.*

rec·i·ta·tive /,resə'tə'tēv/ ▶*n.* musical declamation of the kind usual in the narrative and dialogue parts of opera and oratorio, sung in the rhythm of ordinary speech with many words on the same note: *singing in recitative.*

re·cite /ri'sīt/ ▶*v.* [*tr.*] repeat aloud or declaim (a poem or passage) from memory before an audience: *we provided our own entertainment by singing and reciting poetry.* ■ state (names, facts, etc.) in order: *she recited the dates and names of kings and queens.* —**rec·i·ta·tion** /,resi'tāSHən/ *n.* —**re·cit·er** *n.*

reck·less /'rekləs/ ▶*adj.* (of a person or their actions) without thinking or caring about the consequences of an action: *reckless driving.* —**reck·less·ly** *adv.* —**reck·less·ness** *n.*

reck·on /'rekən/ ▶*v.* **1** [*tr.*] establish by counting or calculation; calculate: *his debts were reckoned at $300,000.* ■ (**reckon someone/something among**) include in (a class or group): *in high school and college he was always reckoned among the brainiest.* **2** *inf.* conclude after calculation; be of the opinion: *he reckons that the army should pull out entirely.* ■ [*tr.*] (often **be reckoned**) consider or regard in a specified way: *it was generally reckoned a failure.* **3** [*intr.*] (**reckon on**) rely on or be sure of doing, having, or dealing with: *they had reckoned on a day or two more of privacy.* ■ *inf.* expect to do a particular thing: *I reckon to get away by two-thirty.* ▷Old English *(ge)recenian* 'recount, relate'; related to Dutch *rekenen* and German *rechnen* 'to count (up).' Early senses included 'give an account of items received' and 'mention things in order,' which gave rise to the notion of 'calculation' and hence of 'coming to a conclusion.'
▶ □ **a —— to be reckoned with** (or **to reckon with**) a thing or person of considerable importance or ability that is not to be ignored or underestimated: *the trade unions were a political force to be reckoned with.*

reck·on·ing /'rekəniNG/ ▶*n.* the action or process of calculating or estimating something: *last year was not, by any reckoning, a particularly good one.* ■ a person's view, opinion, or judgment: *by ancient reckoning, bacteria are plants.* ■ *archaic* a bill or account, or its settlement. ■ the avenging or punishing of past mistakes or misdeeds: *the fear of being brought to reckoning | there will be a terrible reckoning.*

re·claim /ri'klām/ ▶*v.* [*tr.*] **1** retrieve or recover (something previously

lost, given, or paid); obtain the return of: *he returned three years later to reclaim his title as director of advertising.* ■ redeem (someone) from a state of vice; reform: *societies for reclaiming beggars and prostitutes.* **2** bring (waste land or land formerly under water) under cultivation: *little money is available to reclaim and cultivate the desert | [as adj.] (reclaimed) reclaimed land.* ■ recover (material) for reuse; recycle: *a sufficient weight of plastic could easily be reclaimed.*
▶*n.* the action or process of reclaiming or being reclaimed: *beyond reclaim.* —**re·claim·a·ble** *adj.* —**re·claim·er** *n.* —**rec·la·ma·tion** /,reklə'māSHən/ *n.*

re·cline /ri'klīn/ ▶*v.* [*intr.*] lean or lie back in a relaxed position with the back supported: *she was reclining in a deck chair | [as adj.] (reclining) a reclining figure.* —**re·clin·a·ble** *adj.*

re·clin·er /ri'klīnər/ ▶*n.* an upholstered armchair that can be tilted backward, esp. one with a footrest that simultaneously extends from the front.

re·cluse /'rek,lōōs; ri'klōōs; 'rek,lōōz/ ▶*n.* a person who lives a solitary life and tends to avoid other people. —**re·clu·sion** /ri'klōōZHən/ *n.* —**re·clu·sive** /ri'klōōsiv/ *adj.*

rec·og·ni·tion /,rekig'niSHən/ ▶*n.* the action or process of recognizing or being recognized, in particular: ■ identification of a thing or person from having encountered them before; knowledge: *she saw him pass by without a sign of recognition.* ■ acknowledgment of something's existence, validity, or legality: *the unions must receive proper recognition.* ■ formal acknowledgment by a country that another political entity fulfills the conditions of statehood and is eligible to be dealt with as a member of the international community. —**re·cog·ni·to·ry** /ri'kägnə,tôrē/ *adj.* (*rare*).

re·cog·ni·zance /ri'kägnəzəns; -'känəzəns/ ▶*n.* *Law* a bond by which a person undertakes before a court or magistrate to observe some condition, esp. to appear when summoned: *he was released on his own recognizance.*

rec·og·nize /'rekig,nīz; 'rekə(g),nīz/ ▶*v.* [*tr.*] **1** identify (someone or something) from having encountered them before; know again: *I recognized her when her wig fell off | Julia hardly recognized Jill when they met.* ■ identify from knowledge of appearance or character: *Pat is very good at recognizing wildflowers.* ■ (of a computer or other machine) automatically identify and respond correctly to (a sound, printed character, etc.). **2** acknowledge the existence, validity, or legality of: *the defense is recognized in Mexican law.* ■ officially regard (a qualification) as valid or proper: *these qualifications are recognized by the Department of Education | [as adj.] (recognized) courses that lead to recognized qualifications.* ■ grant diplomatic recognition to (a country or government): *they were refusing to recognize the puppet regime.* ■ show official appreciation of; reward formally: *his work was recognized by an honorary degree from Georgetown University.* ■ (of a person presiding at a meeting or debate) call on (someone) to speak. —**rec·og·niz·a·bil·i·ty** *n.* —**rec·og·niz·a·ble** *adj.* —**rec·og·niz·a·bly** *adv.* —**rec·og·niz·er** *n.*

re·coil ▶*v.* /ri'koil/ [*intr.*] suddenly spring or flinch back in fear, horror, or disgust: *he recoiled in horror.* ■ feel fear, horror, or disgust at the thought or prospect of something; shrink mentally: *Renee felt herself recoil at the very thought.* ■ (of a gun) move abruptly backward as a reaction on firing a bullet, shell, or other missile. ■ rebound or spring back through force of impact or elasticity: *the muscle has the ability to recoil.* ■ (**recoil on/upon**) (of an action) have an adverse reactive effect on (the originator): *the soothsayers agreed that all the dangers would recoil on the heads of those who were in possession of the entrails.*
▶*n.* /'rē,koil; ri'koil/ the action of recoiling: *his body jerked with the recoil of the rifle.*

rec·ol·lect /,rekə'lekt/ ▶*v.* [*tr.*] remember (something); call to mind: *he could not quite recollect the reason.*

re-col·lect /,rēkə'lekt/ ▶*v.* [*tr.*] collect or gather again: *after re-collecting our apples for the second time, Bruno brought us a couple of nice sturdy sacks.*

rec·ol·lec·tion /,rekə'lekSHən/ ▶*n.* the action or faculty of remembering something: *to the best of my recollection no one ever had a bad word to say about him.* ■ a thing recollected; a memory: *a biography based on his wife's recollections.* —**rec·ol·lec·tive** /-tiv/ *adj.*

re·com·bi·na·tion /rē,kämbə'nāSHən/ ▶*n.* the process of recombining things. ■ *Genetics* the rearrangement of genetic material, esp. by crossing over in chromosomes or by the artificial joining of segments of DNA from different organisms.

re·com·bine /ˌrēkəmˈbīn/ ▶ v. combine or cause to combine again or differently: [intr.] *carbohydrates can recombine with oxygen.*

rec·om·mend /ˌrekəˈmend/ ▶ v. [tr.] **1** put forward (someone or something) with approval as being suitable for a particular purpose or role: *George had recommended some local architects.* ■ advise or suggest (something) as a course of action: *some doctors recommend putting a board under the mattress* ■ make (someone or something) appealing or desirable: *the house had much to recommend it.* **2** (**recommend someone/something to**) *archaic* commend or entrust someone or something to (someone): *I devoutly recommended my spirit to its maker.* —**rec·om·mend·a·ble** *adj.* —**rec·om·men·da·tion** /ˌrekəmənˈdāSHən; -ˌmen-/ *n.* —**rec·om·mend·a·to·ry** /-ˈmendəˌtôrē/ *adj.* —**rec·om·mend·er** *n.*

rec·om·pense /ˈrekəmˌpens/ ▶ v. [tr.] make amends to (someone) for loss or harm suffered; compensate: *offenders should recompense their victims.* ■ pay or reward (someone) for effort or work: *he was handsomely recompensed.*
▶ *n.* compensation or reward given for loss or harm suffered or effort made: *substantial damages were paid in recompense.*

rec·on·cile /ˈrekənˌsīl/ ▶ v. [tr.] (often **be reconciled**) restore friendly relations between: *she wanted to be reconciled with her father.* ■ cause to coexist in harmony; make or show to be compatible: *a landscape in which inner and outer vision were reconciled.* ■ make (one account) consistent with another, esp. by allowing for transactions begun but not yet completed: *it is not necessary to reconcile the cost accounts to the financial accounts.* ■ settle (a disagreement): *advice on how to reconcile the conflict.* ■ (**reconcile someone to**) make someone accept (a disagreeable or unwelcome thing): *he could not reconcile himself to the thought of his mother stocking shelves.* —**rec·on·cil·a·bil·i·ty** /ˌrekənˌsīləˈbilətē/ *n.* —**rec·on·cil·a·ble** /ˌrekənˈsīləbəl/ *adj.* —**rec·on·cile·ment** *n.* —**rec·on·cil·er** *n.* —**rec·on·cil·i·a·tion** /ˌrekənˌsilēˈāSHən/ *n.* —**rec·on·cil·i·a·to·ry** /ˌrekənˈsilēəˌtôrē/ *adj.*

re·con·di·tion /ˌrēkənˈdiSHən/ ▶ v. [tr.] condition again. ■ overhaul or renovate (a vehicle engine or piece of equipment): *a ship was being reconditioned* | [as *adj.*] (**reconditioned**) *a reconditioned engine.*

re·con·fig·ure /ˌrēkənˈfigyər/ ▶ v. [tr.] configure (something) differently: *you don't have to reconfigure the modem each time you make a connection.* —**re·con·fig·ur·a·ble** *adj.* —**re·con·fig·u·ra·tion** /ˌrēkənˌfigyəˈrāSHən/ *n.*

re·con·nais·sance /riˈkänəzəns; -səns/ ▶ *n.* military observation of a region to locate an enemy or ascertain strategic features: *an excellent aircraft for low-level reconnaissance.* ■ preliminary surveying or research: *conducting client reconnaissance.*

re·con·nect /ˌrēkəˈnekt/ ▶ v. [tr.] connect back together: *surgeons had to reconnect tendons, nerves, and veins.* ■ [intr.] reestablish a bond of communication or emotion: *in order to keep your marriage healthy, it is important to reconnect as mature individuals.* —**re·con·nec·tion** /ˌrēkəˈnekSHən/ *n.*

re·con·noi·ter /ˌrēkəˈnoitər; ˌrek-/ (*Brit.* **re·con·noi·tre**) ▶ v. [tr.] make a military observation of (a region): *they reconnoitered the beach some weeks before the landing.*

re·con·sid·er /ˌrēkənˈsidər/ ▶ v. [tr.] consider (something) again, esp. for a possible change of decision regarding it: *they called on the government to reconsider its policy* | [intr.] *I beg you to reconsider.* —**re·con·sid·er·a·tion** /ˌrēkənˌsidəˈrāSHən/ *n.*

re·con·sti·tute /rēˈkänstəˌt(y)o͞ot/ ▶ v. [tr.] build up again from parts; reconstruct. ■ change the form and organization of (an institution): *he reconstituted his cabinet.* ■ restore (something dried, esp. food) to its original state by adding water to it: [as *adj.*] (**reconstituted**) *reconstituted milk.* —**re·con·sti·tu·tion** /ˌrē,känstəˈt(y)o͞oSHən/ *n.*

re·con·struct /ˌrēkənˈstrəkt/ ▶ v. [tr.] build or form (something) again after it has been damaged or destroyed: *a small area of painted Roman plaster has been reconstructed.* ■ reorganize (something): *later emperors reconstructed the army.* ■ form an impression, model, or reenactment of (a past event or thing) from the available evidence: *from copies of correspondence it is possible to reconstruct the broad sequence of events.* ■ reenact (a crime or other incident) with the aim of discovering the culprit or cause: *reconstructing the last walk of murdered Tracey.* —**re·con·struct·a·ble** (also **re·con·struct·i·ble**) *adj.* —**re·con·struc·tive** /-tiv/ *adj.* —**re·con·struc·tor** /-tər/ *n.*

re·con·struc·tion /ˌrēkənˈstrəkSHən/ ▶ *n.* the action or process of reconstructing or being reconstructed: *the economic reconstruction of Russia* | [as *adj.*] *reconstruction work.* ■ a thing that has been rebuilt after being damaged or destroyed: *comparison between the original and the reconstruction.* ■ an impression, model, or reenactment of a past event formed from the available evidence: *a reconstruction of the accident would be staged to try to discover the cause of the tragedy.* ■ (**Reconstruction**) the period 1865–77 following the Civil War, during which the states of the Confederacy were controlled by federal government and social legislation, including the granting of new rights to African-Americans, was introduced.

rec·ord ▶ *n.* /ˈrekərd/ **1** a thing constituting a piece of evidence about the past, esp. an account of an act or occurrence kept in writing or some other permanent form: *identification was made through dental records.* ■ (also **court record**) *Law* an official report of the proceedings and judgment in a court. ■ *Comput.* a number of related items of information that are handled as a unit. **2** the sum of the past achievements or actions of a person or organization; a person or thing's previous conduct or performance: *the safety record at the airport.* ■ short for CRIMINAL RECORD. **3** (esp. in sports) the best performance or most remarkable event of its kind that has been officially measured and noted: *he held the world record for over a decade.* **4** a thin plastic disk carrying recorded sound, esp. music, in grooves on each surface, for reproduction by a record player. ■ a piece or collection of music reproduced on such a disk or on another medium, such as compact disc: *my favorite record.*
▶ *v.* (**re·cord**) /riˈkôrd/ [tr.] **1** set down in writing or some other permanent form for later reference, esp. officially: *they were asked to keep a diary and record everything they ate or drank.* ■ state or express publicly or officially; make an official record of: *the coroner recorded a verdict of accidental death.* ■ (of an instrument or observer) show or register (a measurement or result): *the temperature was the lowest recorded since 1926.* ■ achieve (a certain score or result): *they recorded their first win of the season.* **2** convert (sound or a broadcast) into permanent form for later reproduction: *they were recording a guitar recital.* ▷Middle English: from Old French *record* 'remembrance,' from *recorder* 'bring to remembrance,' from Latin *recordari* 'remember,' based on *cor, cord-* 'heart.' The noun was earliest used in law to denote the fact of being written down as evidence. The verb originally meant 'narrate orally or in writing,' also 'repeat so as to commit to memory.' —**re·cord·a·ble** /rəˈkôrdəbəl; rē-/ *adj.*
▶ □ **for the record** so that the true facts are recorded or known: *for the record, I have never been to the apartment.* □ **a matter of record** a thing that is established as a fact through being officially recorded. □ **off the record** not made as an official or attributable statement. □ **on the record 1** used in reference to the making of an official or public statement: *he seems shadowy because he rarely speaks on the record.* **2** officially measured and noted: *it proved to be one of the warmest Decembers on record.* □ **set** (or **put**) **the record straight** give the true version of events that have been reported incorrectly; correct a misapprehension.

re·cord·er /riˈkôrdər/ ▶ *n.* **1** an apparatus for recording sound, pictures, or data, esp. a tape recorder. **2** a person who keeps records: *a poet and recorder of rural and industrial life.* **3** a simple woodwind instrument with finger holes and no keys, held vertically and played by blowing air through a shaped mouthpiece against a sharp edge.

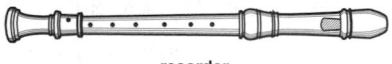

recorder

re·cord·ing /riˈkôrdiNG/ ▶ *n.* a recorded sound or picture. ■ a tape or disc on which sounds or visual images have been recorded.

re·cord·ist /riˈkôrdist/ ▶ *n.* a person who makes recordings, esp. of sound: *a sound recordist.*

rec·ord play·er ▶ *n.* an apparatus for reproducing sound from phonograph records, comprising a turntable that spins the record at a constant speed and a stylus that slides along in the groove and picks up the sound, together with an amplifier and a loudspeaker.

rec·ord·set /ˈrekərdˌset/ ▶ *n.* *Comput.* a set of records in a database that share an identifiable or isolatable characteristic.

re·count¹ /riˈkount/ ▶ v. tell someone about something; give an account of an event or experience: *I recounted the tale to Steve.*
▶ *n.* an act or instance of giving an account of an event or experience: *one woman's recount of a prolonged battle with "huge centipedes."*

re·count² ▶ v. /rēˈkount; ˈrē-/ [tr.] count again.
▶ *n.* /ˈrēˌkount/ an act of counting something again, esp. votes in an election.

re·coup /riˈko͞op/ ▶ v. [tr.] regain (something lost): *rains have helped recoup water levels.* ■ regain (money spent or lost), esp. through subsequent profits: *oil companies are keen to recoup their investment.* ■ *Law* deduct or keep back (part of a sum due). ■ regain (lost physical or mental resources): *sleep was what she needed to recoup her strength.* ▷early 17th cent. (as a legal term): from French *recouper* 'retrench, cut back,' from *re-* 'back' + *couper* 'to cut.' —**re·coup·a·ble** *adj.* —**re·coup·ment** *n.*

re·course /ˈrēˌkôrs; riˈkôrs/ ▶ *n.* a source of help in a difficult situation: *surgery may be the only recourse.* ■ (**recourse to**) the use of someone or something as a source of help in a difficult situation: *a means of solving disputes without recourse to courts of law.* ■ the legal right to demand compensation or payment: *the bank has recourse against the exporter for losses incurred.*

re·cov·er /ri'kəvər/ ▸v. **1** [intr.] return to a normal state of health, mind, or strength: *Neil is still recovering from shock.* ■ (**be recovered**) (of a person) be well again: *you'll be fully recovered before you know it.* **2** [tr.] find or regain possession of. ■ regain or secure (compensation) by means of a legal process or subsequent profits: *many companies recovered their costs within six months.* ■ remove or extract (an energy source or industrial chemical) for use, reuse, or waste treatment.
▸n. (**the recover**) a defined position of a firearm forming part of a military drill: *bring the musket to the recover.* —**re·cov·er·a·ble** *adj.* —**re·cov·er·er** *n.*

re·cov·er /rē'kəvər; 'rē-/ ▸v. [tr.] put a new cover or covering on: *the cost of re-covering the armchair.*

re·cov·er·y /ri'kəvərē/ ▸n. (*pl.* **-er·ies**) **1** a return to a normal state of health, mind, or strength: *signs of recovery in the housing market.* **2** the action or process of regaining possession or control of something stolen or lost: *a team of salvage experts to ensure the recovery of family possessions.* ■ the action of regaining or securing compensation or money lost or spent by means of a legal process or subsequent profits: *debt recovery.* ■ an object or amount of money recovered: *the recoveries included gold jewelry.* ■ the process of removing or extracting an energy source or industrial chemical for use, reuse, or waste treatment. ■ (also **recovery shot**) *Golf* a stroke bringing the ball from the rough or from a hazard back on to the fairway or the green. ■ *Football* an act of taking possession of a fumbled ball. ■ (in rowing, cycling, or swimming) the action of returning the paddle, leg, or arm to its initial position ready to make a new stroke.
▸ □ **in recovery** in the process of recovering from mental illness, drug addiction, or past abuse: *support groups for parents whose children are in recovery.*

re·cre·ate /,rēkrē'āt/ (also **re-cre·ate**) ▸v. [tr.] create again: *the door was now open to recreate a single German state.* ■ reproduce; reenact: *he recreated Mallory's 1942 climb for TV.*

rec·re·a·tion[1] /,rekrē'āSHən/ ▸n. activity done for enjoyment when one is not working: *areas used for recreation such as hiking or biking.* —**rec·re·a·tion·al** /-SHənl/ *adj.*

re·cre·a·tion[2] /,rēkrē'āSHən/ (also **re-cre·a·tion**) ▸n. the action or process of creating something again: *the periodic destruction and recreation of the universe.* ■ a reenactment or simulation of something.

re·crim·i·na·tion /ri,krimə'nāSHən/ ▸n. [usu. **recriminations**] an accusation in response to one from someone else: *there are no tears, no recriminations.*

re·cruit /ri'kroōt/ ▸v. [tr.] enlist (someone) in the armed forces: *they recruit their toughest soldiers from the desert tribes.* ■ form (an army or other force) by enlisting new people: *a basis for recruiting an army.* ■ enroll (someone) as a member or worker in an organization or as a supporter of a cause: *there are plans to recruit more staff later this year.*
▸n. a person newly enlisted in the armed forces and not yet fully trained: *3,000 army recruits at Ft. Benjamin.* ■ a new member of an organization or a new supporter of a cause: *after agreeing on a salary, the new recruit failed to turn up on Monday morning.* —**re·cruit·a·ble** *adj.* —**re·cruit·er** *n.* —**re·cruit·ment** *n.*

rec·tal /'rektəl/ ▸*adj.* of, relating to, or affecting the rectum: *rectal cancer.* —**rec·tal·ly** *adv.*

rec·tan·gle /'rek,taNGgəl/ ▸n. a plane figure with four straight sides and four right angles, esp. one with unequal adjacent sides, in contrast to a square. —**rec·tan·gu·lar** /rek'taNGgyələr/ *adj.*

rec·ti·fy /'rektə,fī/ ▸v. (**-fies, -fied**) [tr.] **1** put (something) right; correct: *mistakes made now cannot be rectified later.* ■ [usu. as *adj.*] (**rectified**) purify or refine (a substance), esp. by repeated distillation: *add 10 cc of rectified alcohol.* **2** convert (alternating current) to direct current: *rectified AC power systems.* —**rec·ti·fi·a·ble** *adj.* —**rec·ti·fi·ca·tion** /,rektəfi'kāSHən/ *n.*

rec·ti·lin·e·ar /,rektə'linēər/ (also **rec·ti·lin·e·al** /-ēəl/) ▸*adj.* contained by, consisting of, or moving in a straight line or lines: *a rectilinear waveform.* ■ *Photog.* of or relating to a straight line or lines: *rectilinear distortion.* ■ *Photog.* (of a wide-angle lens) corrected as much as possible, so that straight lines in the subject appear straight in the image. —**rec·ti·lin·e·ar·i·ty** /-,linē'aritē/ *n.* —**rec·ti·lin·e·ar·ly** *adv.*

rec·ti·tude /'rektə,t(y)ood/ ▸n. *formal* morally correct behavior or thinking; righteousness: *Maddie is a model of rectitude.*

rec·to /'rektō/ ▸n. (*pl.* **-tos**) a right-hand page of an open book, or the front of a loose document. Contrasted with **VERSO**.

rec·tor /'rektər/ ▸n. **1** (in the Episcopal Church) a member of the clergy who has charge of a parish. ■ (in the Roman Catholic Church) a priest

in charge of a church or of a religious institution. **2** the head of certain universities, colleges, and schools.

rec·to·ry /'rektərē/ ▸n. (*pl.* **-ries**) a rector's house.

rec·tum /'rektəm/ ▸n. (*pl.* **-tums** or **-ta** /-tə/) the final section of the large intestine, terminating at the anus.

rec·tus /'rektəs/ ▸n. (*pl.* **-ti** /-tī/) *Anat.* any of several straight structures, in particular: ■ (also **rec·tus ab·dom·i·nis** /ab'dämənis/) each of a pair of long flat muscles at the front of the abdomen, joining the sternum to the pubis and acting to bend the whole body forward or sideways. ■ any of a number of muscles controlling the movement of the eyeball.

re·cum·bent /ri'kəmbənt/ ▸*adj.* (esp. of a person or human figure) lying down: *recumbent statues.* ■ (of a bicycle) designed to be ridden lying almost flat on one's back or sitting up with the legs stretched out in front. ■ (of a plant) growing close to the ground: *recumbent shrubs.*
▸n. a recumbent bicycle. —**re·cum·ben·cy** *n.* —**re·cum·bent·ly** *adv.*

re·cu·per·ate /ri'koōpə,rāt/ ▸v. **1** [intr.] recover from illness or exertion: *she has been recuperating from a shoulder wound.* **2** [tr.] recover or regain (something lost or taken): *they will seek to recuperate the returns that go with investment.* —**re·cu·per·a·ble** /-pərəbəl/ *adj.* —**re·cu·per·a·tion** /ri,koōpə'rāSHən/ *n.* —**re·cu·per·a·tive** /-pə,rātiv/ *adj.*

re·cur /ri'kər/ ▸v. (**-curred, -cur·ring**) [intr.] occur again, periodically, or repeatedly: *when the symptoms recurred, the doctor diagnosed something different* | [as *adj.*] (**recurring**) *a recurring theme.* ■ (of a thought, image, or memory) come back to one's mind: *Steve's words kept recurring to him.* ■ (**recur to**) go back to (something) in thought or speech: *the book remained a favorite and she constantly recurred to it.* —**re·cur·rence** /ri'kərəns; -'kə-rəns/ *n.*

re·cur·rent /ri'kərənt; -'kə-rənt/ ▸*adj.* **1** occurring often or repeatedly: *she had a recurrent dream about falling.* ■ (of a disease or symptom) recurring after apparent cure or remission: *recurrent fever.* **2** *Anat.* (of a nerve or blood vessel) turning back so as to reverse direction. —**re·cur·rent·ly** *adv.*

re·cur·sion /ri'kərzHən/ ▸n. *Math. & Linguistics* the repeated application of a recursive procedure or definition. ■ a recursive definition.

re·cur·sive /ri'kərsiv/ ▸*adj.* characterized by recurrence or repetition, in particular: ■ *Math. & Linguistics* relating to or involving the repeated application of a rule, definition, or procedure to successive results. ■ *Comput.* relating to or involving a program or routine of which a part requires the application of the whole, so that its explicit interpretation requires in general many successive executions. —**re·cur·sive·ly** *adv.*

re·cy·cle /rē'sīkəl/ ▸v. [tr.] convert (waste) into reusable material: *car hulks were recycled into new steel* | [as *n.*] (**recycling**) *a call for the recycling of all paper.* ■ return (material) to a previous stage in a cyclic process. ■ use again: *he reserves the right to recycle his own text.* —**re·cy·cla·ble** *adj.* —**re·cy·cler** /-k(ə)lər/ *n.*

red /red/ ▸*adj.* (**red·der, red·dest**) **1** of a color at the end of the spectrum next to orange and opposite violet, as of blood, fire, or rubies: *her red lips.* ■ of or denoting the suits hearts and diamonds in a deck of cards. ■ (of wine) made from dark grapes and colored by their skins. ■ used to denote something forbidden, dangerous, or urgent: *the force went on red alert.* ■ (of a ski run) of the second highest level of difficulty, as indicated by colored markers. **2** (**Red**) *inf., chiefly derog.* communist or socialist (used esp. during the Cold War with reference to the Soviet Union): *the Red Menace.* **3** stained or covered with blood: *the red hands and sharp knives of the fishermen.*
▸n. **1** red color or pigment: *colors range from yellow to deep red.* ■ red clothes or material: *she could not wear red.* **2** a red thing or person, in particular: ■ a red wine. ■ a red light. **3** (also **Red**) *inf., chiefly derog.* a communist or socialist. **4** (**the red**) the situation of owing money or showing a debit: *the company was $4,000,000 in the red.* ▷Old English *rēad*, of Germanic origin; related to Dutch *rood* and German *rot*, from an Indo-European root shared by Latin *rufus, ruber*, Greek *eruthros*, and Sanskrit *rudhira-* 'red.' —**red·dish** *adj.* —**red·ness** *n.*
▸ □ **the red planet** a name for Mars. □ **the red, white, and blue** *inf.* the U.S. national flag: *learning respect for the red, white, and blue.* □ **see red** *inf.* become very angry suddenly: *the mere thought of Peter with Nicole made her see red.*

red. ▸*abbr.* reduction.

red-blood·ed ▸*adj.* (of a man) vigorous or virile, esp. in having strong heterosexual appetites: *he was attracted to her, as any red-blooded male would be.* —**red-blood·ed·ness** *n.*

red car·pet ▸n. a long, narrow red carpet laid on the ground for a

R

Pronunciation Key ə *ago,* up; ər *over, fur;* a *hat;* ā *ate;* ä *car;* CH *chin;* e *let;* ē *see;* e(ə)r *air;* i *fit;* ī *by;* i(ə)r *ear;* NG *sing;* ō *go;* ô *law, for;* oi *toy;* oō *good;* oō *goo;* ou *out;* SH *she;* TH *thin;* TH *then;* (h)w *why;* zH *vision*

distinguished visitor to walk on when arriving. ■ (**the red carpet**) privileged treatment of a distinguished visitor: *they rolled out the red carpet for two special guests.*

red cell ▸*n.* less technical term for ERYTHROCYTE.

red cent ▸*n.* a one-cent coin; a penny. ■ the smallest amount of money: *some of the people don't deserve a single red cent.*

red·coat /'red,kōt/ ▸*n. hist.* a British soldier.

Red Cross ▸the International Movement of the Red Cross and the Red Crescent, an international humanitarian organization that provides relief to victims of war or natural disaster. The Red Cross was set up in 1864 at the instigation of the Swiss philanthropist Henri Dunant (1828–1910) according to the Geneva Convention, and its headquarters are in Geneva.

red·den /'redn/ ▸*v.* make or become red: [*tr.*] *bare arms reddened by sun and wind.* ■ [*intr.*] (of a person) blush: *Lynn reddened at the description of herself.* ■ [*intr.*] (of the eyes) become pink at the rims as a result of crying.

re·deem /ri'dēm/ ▸*v.* [*tr.*] **1** compensate for the faults or bad aspects of (something): *a disappointing debate redeemed only by an outstanding speech* | [as *adj.*] (**redeeming**) *the splendid views are the one redeeming feature of the center.* ■ (**redeem oneself**) do something that compensates for poor past performance or behavior: *they redeemed themselves in the playoffs by pushing the Detroit Red Wings to a seventh and deciding game.* ■ (of a person) atone or make amends for (error or evil): *the thief on the cross who by a single act redeemed a life of evil.* ■ save (someone) from sin, error, or evil: *he was a sinner, redeemed by the grace of God.* **2** gain or regain possession of (something) in exchange for payment: *his best suit had been redeemed from the pawnbrokers.* ■ *Finance* repay (a stock, bond, or other instrument) at the maturity date. ■ exchange (a coupon, voucher, or trading stamp) for merchandise, a discount, or money. ■ pay the necessary money to clear (a debt): *owners were unable to redeem their mortgages.* ■ exchange (paper money) for gold or silver. ■ fulfill or carry out (a pledge or promise): *the party prepared to redeem the pledges of the past three years.* ■ *archaic* buy the freedom of. —**re·deem·a·ble** *adj.*

re·deem·er /ri'dēmər/ ▸*n.* a person who redeems someone or something. ■ (often **the Redeemer**) Christ.

re·demp·tion /ri'dempSHən/ ▸*n.* **1** the action of saving or being saved from sin, error, or evil: *God's plans for the redemption of his world.* ■ *fig.* a thing that saves someone from error or evil: *his marginalization from the Hollywood jungle proved to be his redemption.* **2** the action of regaining or gaining possession of something in exchange for payment, or clearing a debt. ■ *archaic* the action of buying one's freedom. —**re·demp·tive** *adj.*
▸ □ **beyond** (or **past**) **redemption** (of a person or thing) too bad to be improved or saved.

re·de·vel·op /,rēdi'veləp/ ▸*v.* [*tr.*] develop (something) again or differently. ■ erect new buildings in (an urban area), typically after demolishing the existing buildings: *the site that the city planned to redevelop with family attractions.* —**re·de·vel·op·er** *n.* —**re·de·vel·op·ment** *n.*

red-eye ▸*n.* **1** the undesirable effect in flash photography of people appearing to have red eyes, caused by a reflection from the retina when the flashgun is too near the camera lens. **2** (also **red-eye flight**) *inf.* an overnight or late-night flight on a commercial airline: *she caught the red-eye back to New York.* **3** a freshwater fish with red eyes, in particular a rock bass. **4** *inf.* cheap whiskey.

red-faced ▸*adj.* (of a person) having a red face, esp. as a result of exertion, embarrassment, or shame: *Steve was left red-faced when a fan tried to rip his pants off.*

red flag ▸*n.* a red flag as a warning of danger or a problem: *fig. they had overlooked the red flags that should have alerted them to the county's disastrous investment strategy.* ■ a red flag as the symbol of socialist revolution.

red gi·ant ▸*n. Astron.* a very large star of high luminosity and low surface temperature. Red giants are thought to be in a late stage of evolution when no hydrogen remains in the core to fuel nuclear fusion.

red-hand·ed ▸*adj.* (of a person) having been discovered in or just after the act of doing something wrong or illegal: *I caught him red-handed, stealing a wallet.*

red·head /'red,hed/ ▸*n.* a person with reddish hair.

red·head·ed ▸*adj.* (of a person) having reddish-brown hair: *a red-headed man.* ■ used in names of birds, insects, and other animals with red heads.

red her·ring ▸*n.* something, esp. a clue, that is or is intended to be misleading or distracting: *the book is fast-paced, exciting, and full of red herrings.*

red-hot ▸*adj.* **1** (of a substance) so hot as to glow red: *red-hot coals.* ■ very hot, esp. too hot to touch: *the red-hot handle burned his hand.* **2** extremely exciting or popular: *red-hot jazz.* ■ very passionate: *a red-hot lover.*

re·di·al ▸*v.* /rē'dīl/ (**-di·aled, -di·al·ing;** *Brit.* **-di·alled, -di·al·ling**) [*tr.*] dial (a telephone number) again, esp. automatically.
▸*n.* /-'rē,dī/ the facility on a telephone by which the number just dialed may be automatically redialed by pressing a single button.

re·dis·tri·bute /,rēdə'strib,yōōt/ ▸*v.* [*tr.*] distribute (something) differently or again, typically to achieve greater social equality: *their primary concern was to redistribute income from rich to poor.* —**re·dis·tri·bu·tion** /,rē,distrə'byōōSHən/ *n.* —**re·dis·trib·u·tive** /-'stribyətiv/ *adj.*

red-let·ter day ▸*n.* a day that is pleasantly noteworthy or memorable.

red light ▸*n.* a red traffic light or similar signal that instructs moving vehicles to stop. ■ *fig.* a refusal, or an order to stop an action: *some subsidies would get a red light and be prohibited.* ■ a red light used as a signal of warning, danger, or, on a machine, operation: *the winking red light of a video camera.*

red-light dis·trict ▸*n.* an area of a town or city containing many brothels, strip clubs, and other sex businesses.

red·neck /'red,nek/ ▸*n. inf., derog.* a working-class white person, esp. a politically reactionary one from a rural area: *rednecks in the high, cheap seats stomped their feet and hooted.* —**red-necked** *adj.*

re-do ▸*v.* /rē'dōō/ (**re·does** /rē'dəz/; *past* **re·did** /rē'did/; *past part.* **re·done** /rē'dən/) [*tr.*] do (something) again or differently: *a whole day's work has to be redone.* ■ redecorate (a room or building): *the house is being redone exactly to suit his taste.*
▸*n.* /'rē,dōō/ a redecoration of a room or building: *a total redo of the second floor shopping concourse.*

red·o·lent /'redl-ənt/ ▸*adj.* (**redolent of/with**) strongly reminiscent or suggestive of (something): *names redolent of history and tradition.* ■ *poetic/lit.* strongly smelling of something: *the church was old, dark, and redolent of incense.* —**red·o·lence** *n.* —**red·o·lent·ly** *adv.*

re·dou·ble /rē'dəbəl/ ▸*v.* [*tr.*] make much greater, more intense, or more numerous: *we will redouble our efforts to reform agricultural policy.* ■ [*intr.*] become greater or more intense or numerous: *pressure to solve the problem has redoubled.* ■ [*intr.*] *Bridge* double a bid already doubled by an opponent.
▸*n. Bridge* a call that doubles a bid already doubled by an opponent.

re·doubt /ri'dout/ ▸*n. Mil.* a temporary or supplementary fortification, typically square or polygonal and without flanking defenses. ■ an entrenched stronghold or refuge.

re·doubt·a·ble /ri'doutəbəl/ ▸*adj. often humorous* (of a person) formidable, esp. as an opponent: *he was a redoubtable debater.* —**re·doubt·a·bly** /-blē/ *adv.*

re·dound /ri'dound/ ▸*v.* [*intr.*] **1** (**redound to**) *formal* contribute greatly to (a person's credit or honor): *his latest diplomatic effort will redound to his credit.* **2** (**redound upon**) *archaic* come back upon; rebound on: *may his sin redound upon his head!* ▷*late Middle English* (in the sense 'surge up, overflow'): from Old French *redonder,* from Latin *redundare* 'surge,' from *re(d)-* 'again' + *unda* 'a wave.'

red pep·per ▸*n.* the ripe red fruit of a sweet pepper. ■ another term for CAYENNE.

re·dress /ri'dres; 'rē,dres/ ▸*v.* [*tr.*] remedy or set right (an undesirable or unfair situation): *the power to redress the grievances of our citizens.*
▸*n.* remedy or compensation for a wrong or grievance: *those seeking redress for an infringement of public law rights.* —**re·dress·a·ble** *adj.* —**re·dress·al** /-əl/ *n.* —**re·dress·er** *n.*

red·shift /'red,SHift/ (also **red shift**) ▸*n. Astron.* the displacement of spectral lines toward longer wavelengths (the red end of the spectrum) in radiation from distant galaxies and celestial objects. This is interpreted as a Doppler shift that is proportional to the velocity of recession and thus to distance.

red·skin /'red,skin/ ▸*n. dated, offens.* an American Indian.

red squir·rel ▸*n.* a small tree squirrel with a reddish coat, in particular the North American *Tamiasciurus hudsonicus.*

red tape ▸*n.* excessive bureaucracy or adherence to rules and formalities, esp. in public business: *this law will just create more red tape.*

re·duce /ri'd(y)ōōs/ ▸*v.* [*tr.*] **1** make smaller or less in amount, degree, or size: *the need for businesses to reduce costs.* ■ [*intr.*] become smaller or less in size, amount, or degree: *the number of priority homeless cases has reduced slightly.* ■ boil (a sauce or other liquid) in cooking so that it becomes thicker and more concentrated. ■ [*intr.*] (of a person) lose weight, typically by dieting: *by May she had reduced to 125 pounds.* ■ *Phonet.* articulate (a speech sound) in a way requiring less muscular effort. In vowels, this gives rise to a more central articulatory position. **2** (**reduce someone/something to**) bring someone or something to (a lower or weaker state, condition, or role): *she has been reduced to near poverty.* ■ (**be reduced to doing something**) (of a person) be forced by difficult circumstances into doing something desperate: *ordinary soldiers are reduced to begging.* ■ make someone helpless with (an expression of emotion, esp. with hurt, shock, or amusement): *Olga was reduced to stunned silence.* ■ force into (obedience or submission): *he succeeds in reducing his grandees to due obedience.* **3 (reduce something to)** change a substance to (a different or more basic form): *it is difficult to understand how lava could have been reduced to dust.* ■ present a problem or subject in (a simplified form): *he reduces unimaginable statistics to manageable proportions.* ■ convert a fraction to (the form with the lowest terms). **4** *Chem.* cause to combine chemically with hydrogen. ■ undergo or cause to undergo a reaction in which electrons are gained by one atom from another. **5** restore (a dislocated part) to its proper position by manipulation or surgery. ▷late Middle English: from Latin *reducere,* from *re-* 'back, again' + *ducere* 'bring, lead.' The original sense was 'bring back' (hence 'restore,' now surviving in sense 5); this led to 'bring to a different state,' then 'bring to a simpler or lower state' (hence sense 3); and finally 'diminish in size or amount' (sense 1, dating from the late 18th cent.). **—re·duc·er** *n.* **re·duc·i·ble** *adj.*

re·duc·tion /rɪ'dəkʃən/ ▶*n.* **1** the action or fact of making a specified thing smaller or less in amount, degree, or size: *talks on arms reduction.* ■ the amount by which something is made smaller, less, or lower in price: *special reductions on knitwear.* ■ the simplification of a subject or problem to a particular form in presentation or analysis: *the reduction of classical genetics to molecular biology.* ■ *Math.* the process of converting an amount from one denomination to a smaller one, or of bringing down a fraction to its lowest terms. ■ *Biol.* the halving of the number of chromosomes per cell that occurs during meiosis. **2** a thing that is made smaller or less in size or amount, in particular: ■ an arrangement of an orchestral score for piano or for a smaller group of performers. ■ a thick and concentrated liquid or sauce made by boiling. ■ a copy of a picture or photograph made on a smaller scale than the original. **3** the action of remedying a dislocation or fracture by returning the affected part of the body to its normal position. **4** *Chem.* the process or result of reducing or being reduced. **5** *Phonet.* substitution of a sound that requires less muscular effort to articulate: *the process of vowel reduction.*

re·dun·dant /rɪ'dəndənt/ ▶*adj.* no longer needed or useful; superfluous: *an appropriate use of a redundant church* | *many of the old skills had become redundant.* ■ (of words or data) able to be omitted without loss of meaning or function. ■ *Engineering* (of a component) not strictly necessary to functioning but included in case of failure in another component. **—re·dun·dan·cy** *n.* **re·dun·dant·ly** *adv.*

re·du·pli·cate /rɪ'd(y)oopli,kāt; 'rē-/ ▶*v.* [*tr.*] repeat or copy so as to form another of the same kind: *the upper parts of the harmony may be reduplicated at the octave above.* ■ repeat (a syllable or other linguistic element) exactly or with a slight change, e.g., *hurly-burly, see-saw.* **—re·du·pli·ca·tion** /rɪ,d(y)oopli'kāshən; ,rē-/ *n.* **re·du·pli·ca·tive** /-,kātiv/ *adj.*

red·wing /'red,wiNG/ ▶*n.* any of a number of red-winged birds, esp. the American red-winged blackbird (*Agelaius phoeniceus,* family Icteridae).

red·wood /'red,wood/ ▶*n.* a giant conifer (family Taxodiaceae) with thick fibrous bark, native to California and Oregon. Two species: the **California** (or **coast**) **redwood** (*Sequoia sempervirens*), and the **giant redwood** (*Sequoiadendron giganteum*). Growing to heights as great as 325 feet (110 m), they are the world's tallest trees.

ree·bok /'rēbäk/ ▶*n.* a small South African antelope (*Pelea capreolus*) with a long slender neck and short straight horns.

reed /rēd/ ▶*n.* **1** a tall, slender-leaved plant (genera *Phragmites* and *Arundo*) of the grass family that grows in water or on marshy ground. ■ used in names of similar plants growing in wet habitats, e.g., **bur reed.** ■ a tall, thin, straight stalk of such a plant, used esp. as material for thatching. **2** a thing or person resembling or likened to such plants, in particular: ■ a weak or impressionable person: *the jurors were mere reeds in the wind.* ■ a weaver's comblike implement for separating the threads of the warp and correctly positioning the weft. ■ (**reeds**) semicylindrical adjacent moldings grouped like reeds laid together. **3** a piece of thin cane or metal, sometimes doubled, that vibrates in a current of air to produce the sound of various musical instruments, as in the mouthpiece of a clarinet or oboe, at the base of some organ pipes, and as part of a set in the accordion and harmonica. ■ a wind instrument played with a reed. **4** an electrical contact used in a magnetically operated switch or relay. **—reed·like** /-,līk/ *adj.*

re·ed·u·cate /rē'ejə,kāt/ ▶*v.* [*tr.*] educate or train (someone) in order to change their beliefs or behavior: *criminals are to be reeducated.* **—re·ed·u·ca·tion** /,rē,ejə'kāshən/ *n.*

reed·y /'rēdē/ ▶*adj.* (**reed·i·er, reed·i·est**) **1** (of a voice, sound, or instrument) high and thin in tone: *Frank's reedy voice.* **2** (of water or land) full of or edged with reeds: *they swam in the reedy lake.* **3** (of a person) tall and thin: *a reedy twelve-year-old.* **—reed·i·ness** *n.*

reef[1] /rēf/ ▶*n.* a ridge of rock, coral, or sand just above or below the surface of the sea.

reef[2] *Sailing* ▶*n.* each of the several strips across a sail that can be taken in or rolled up to reduce the area exposed to the wind.

▶*v.* [*tr.*] take in one or more reefs of (a sail): *reefing the mainsail in strong winds.*

reef·er[1] /'rēfər/ ▶*n. inf.* a marijuana cigarette. ■ marijuana.

reef·er[2] ▶*n. inf.* a refrigerated truck, railroad car, or ship.

reek /rēk/ ▶*v.* [*intr.*] smell strongly and unpleasantly; stink: *the yard reeked of wet straw and stale horse manure.* ■ *fig.* be suggestive of something unpleasant or disapproved of: *the speeches reeked of anti-Semitism.*

▶*n.* a foul smell: *the reek of cattle dung.* **—reek·y** *adj.*

reel /rēl/ ▶*n.* **1** a cylinder on which film, wire, thread, or other flexible materials can be wound. ■ a length of something wound on to such a device: *a reel of copper wire.* ■ a part of a movie: *in the final reel he is transformed from unhinged sociopath into local hero.* ■ a device for winding and unwinding a line as required, in particular a fishing reel. **2** a lively Scottish or Irish folk dance. ■ a piece of music for such a dance, typically in simple or duple time. ■ short for **VIRGINIA REEL.**

▶*v.* **1** [*tr.*] (**reel something in**) wind a line on to a reel by turning the reel. ■ bring something attached to a line, esp. a fish, toward one by turning a reel and winding in the line: *he struck, and reeled in a good perch.* **2** [*intr.*] lose one's balance and stagger or lurch violently: *she reeled back against the van.* ■ feel very giddy, disoriented, or bewildered, typically as a result of an unexpected setback: *the unaccustomed intake of alcohol made my head reel.* ■ walk in a staggering or lurching manner, esp. while drunk: *the two reeled out of the bar arm in arm.* **3** [*intr.*] dance a reel.

▶*phrasal v.* □ **reel (something) off** say or recite something rapidly and without apparent effort: *she proceeded to reel off in rapid Italian the various dishes of the day.* ▷Old English *hrēol,* denoting a rotatory device on which spun thread is wound; of unknown origin. **—reel·er** *n.*

re·en·act /,rēə'nakt/ ▶*v.* [*tr.*] **1** act out (a past event): *bombers were gathered together to reenact the historic first air attack.* **2** bring (a law) into effect again when the original statute has been repealed. **—re·en·act·ment** *n.*

re·en·list /,rēən'list/ ▶*v.* [*intr.*] enlist again in the armed forces.

re·en·try /rē 'entrē/ ▶*n.* (*pl.* **-tries**) **1** the action or process of reentering something: *programs designed to prepare you for re-entry to the profession.* ■ the return of a spacecraft or missile into the earth's atmosphere. **2** *Law* the action of retaking or repossession. **3** a visible duplication of part of the design for a postage stamp due to an inaccurate first impression. ■ a stamp displaying such a duplication.

re·ex·am·ine /,rē-ig'zamən/ ▶*v.* [*tr.*] examine again or further: *I will have the body reexamined.* ■ *Law* examine (a witness) again, after cross-examination by the opposing counsel. **—re·ex·am·i·na·tion** /-,zamə-'nāshən/ *n.*

ref /ref/ ▶*n. inf.* (in sports) a referee.

re·face /rē'fās/ ▶*v.* [*tr.*] put a new facing on (a building): *part of the tower was refaced with brick.*

re·fec·to·ry /rɪ'fekt(ə)rē/ ▶*n.* (*pl.* **-ries**) a room used for communal meals, esp. in an educational or religious institution.

re·fer /rɪ'fər/ ▶*v.* (**-ferred, -fer·ring**) **1** [*intr.*] (**refer to**) mention or allude to: *the reports of the commission are often referred to in the media.* ■ [*tr.*] (**refer someone to**) direct the attention of someone to: *I refer my colleague to the reply that I gave some moments ago.* ■ (**refer to**) (of a word or phrase) describe or denote; have as a referent: *the term "rhetoric" almost invariably refers to persuasion.* **2** [*tr.*] (**refer something to**) pass a matter to (another body) for a decision: *disagreement arose and the issue was referred back to the Executive Committee.* ■ [*intr.*] (**refer to**) read or otherwise use (a source of information) in order to ascertain something; consult: *I always refer to a dictionary when I come across a new word.* **—re·fer·a·ble** /'ref(ə)rəbəl; rɪ'fər-/ *adj.* **—re·fer·rer** *n.*

ref·er·ee /,refə'rē/ ▶*n.* **1** an official who watches a game or match closely to ensure that the rules are adhered to and (in some sports) to arbitrate on matters arising from the play. **2** a person whose opinion or judgment is sought in some connection, or who is referred to for a decision in a dispute. ■ a person willing to testify in writing about the character or ability of someone, esp. an applicant for a job. ■ a person appointed to examine and assess for publication a scientific or other academic work.

▶*v.* (**-ees, -eed, -ee·ing**) **1** [*tr.*] officiate as referee at (a game or match): *the man who refereed the World Cup final.* **2** act as referee: [*tr.*] *to*

Pronunciation Key ə *ago,* up; ər *over, fur;* a *hat;* ā *ate;* ä *car;* cH *chin;* e *let;* ē *see;* e(ə)r *air;* i *fit;* ī *by;* i(ə)r *ear;* NG *sing;* ō *go;* ô *law, for;* oi *toy;* oo *good;* oo *goo;* ou *out;* sH *she;* TH *thin;* ṮH *then;* (h)w *why;* zH *vision*

referee a split between deficit hawks and doves | [as adj.] (**refereed**) the only journal that publishes refereed articles.

ref·er·ence /ˈref(ə)rəns/ ▶ n. **1** the action of mentioning or alluding to something: he **made reference to** the enormous power of the mass media. ■ a mention or citation of a source of information in a book or article. ■ a book or passage cited in such a way. **2** use of a source of information in order to ascertain something: popular works of reference. ■ the sending of a matter for decision or consideration to some authority: demanded the immediate reference of the whole dispute to the United Nations. **3** a letter from a previous employer testifying to someone's ability or reliability, used when applying for a new job. ■ a person giving this.
▶ v. [tr.] provide (a book or article) with citations of authorities: each chapter is referenced, citing literature up to 1990.
▶ adj. of, denoting, or pertaining to a reference library: most reference departments house magazine rooms. —**ref·er·en·tial** /ˌrefəˈrensHəl/ adj.
▶ □ **for future reference** for use at a later date: she lodged this idea in the back of her mind for future reference. □ **with** (or **in**) **reference to** in relation to; as regards: war can only be explained with reference to complex social factors.

ref·er·ence book ▶ n. a book intended to be consulted for information on specific matters rather than read from beginning to end: a beat-up old grade-school dictionary was the only reference book we ever had in our house.

ref·er·ence frame ▶ n. see FRAME OF REFERENCE.

ref·er·en·dum /ˌrefəˈrendəm/ ▶ n. (pl. **-dums** or **-da** /-də/) a general vote by the electorate on a single political question that has been referred to them for a direct decision. ■ the process of referring a political question to the electorate for this purpose.

ref·er·ent /ˈref(ə)rənt/ ▶ n. Linguistics the thing that a word or phrase denotes or stands for: "the Morning Star" and "the Evening Star" have the same referent (the planet Venus).

re·fer·ral /rɪˈfərəl/ ▶ n. an act of referring someone or something for consultation, review, or further action. ■ the directing of a patient to a medical specialist by a primary care physician. ■ a person whose case has been referred to a specialist doctor or a professional body.

re·ferred pain ▶ n. Med. pain felt in a part of the body other than its actual source.

re·fi /rēˈfī/ ▶ v. (**-fies, -fied, -fy·ing**) [tr.] refinance (a mortgage):
▶ adj. relating to refinancing and the refinancing market: the refi boom is over.

re·fill ▶ v. /rēˈfil/ [tr.] fill (a container) again: she paused and refilled her glass with wine before going on. ■ replenish the supply of (medicine called for in a prescription): there's nothing he can do but refill his Valium prescription.
▶ n. /ˈrēˌfil/ an act of filling a container again: he proffered his glass for a refill. ■ a container, esp. a glass, that is so filled: the waitress appeared with refills. ■ a replenished supply of medicine called for in a prescription: an oral contraceptive refill was dispensed. —**re·fill·a·ble** adj.

re·fine /rɪˈfīn/ ▶ v. [tr.] remove impurities or unwanted elements from (a substance), typically as part of an industrial process: sugar was refined by boiling it in huge iron vats. ■ improve (something) by making small changes, in particular make (an idea, theory, or method) more subtle and accurate: ease of access to computers has refined analysis and presentation of data. —**re·fin·er** n.

re·fined /rɪˈfīnd/ ▶ adj. with impurities or unwanted elements having been removed by processing. ■ elegant and cultured in appearance, manner, or taste: her voice was very low and refined. ■ precise; subtle: a more refined timetable for continental drift.

re·fine·ment /rɪˈfīnmənt/ ▶ n. the process of removing impurities or unwanted elements from a substance: the refinement of uranium. ■ the improvement or clarification of something by the making of small changes: this gross figure needs considerable refinement. ■ cultured elegance in behavior or manner: her carefully cultivated veneer of refinement. ■ sophisticated and superior good taste: the refinement of Hellenistic art.

re·fin·er·y /rɪˈfīnərē/ ▶ n. (pl. **-er·ies**) an industrial installation where a substance is refined: an oil refinery.

re·fit ▶ v. /rēˈfit/ (**-fit·ted, -fit·ting**) [tr.] replace or repair machinery, equipment, and fittings in (a ship, building, etc.): a lucrative contract to refit a submarine fleet.
▶ n. /ˈrēˌfit; rēˈfit/ a restoration or repair of machinery, equipment, or fittings.

re·flect /rɪˈflekt/ ▶ v. **1** [tr.] (of a surface or body) throw back (heat, light, or sound) without absorbing it: when the sun's rays hit the earth a lot of the heat is reflected back into space. ■ (of a mirror or shiny surface) show an image of: he could see himself reflected in Keith's mirrored glasses. ■ embody or represent (something) in a faithful or appropriate way: stocks are priced at a level that reflects a company's prospects. ■ (of an action or situation) bring (credit or discredit) to the relevant parties: the main contract

is progressing well, which reflects great credit on those involved. ■ [intr.] (**reflect well/badly on**) bring about a good or bad impression of: the incident reflects badly on the operating practices of the airlines. **2** [intr.] (**reflect on/upon**) think deeply or carefully about: he reflected with sadness on the unhappiness of his marriage. ■ archaic make disparaging remarks about.

re·flec·tion /rɪˈfleksHən/ ▶ n. **1** the throwing back by a body or surface of light, heat, or sound without absorbing it: the reflection of light. ■ an amount of light, heat, or sound that is thrown back in such a way: the reflections from the streetlights gave us just enough light. ■ an image seen in a mirror or shiny surface: Marianne surveyed her reflection in the mirror. ■ a thing that is a consequence of or arises from something else: a healthy skin is a reflection of good health in general. ■ a thing bringing discredit to someone or something: it was a sad **reflection on** society that because of his affliction he was picked on. ■ Math. the conceptual operation of inverting a system or event with respect to a plane, each element being transferred perpendicularly through the plane to a point the same distance the other side of it. **2** serious thought or consideration: he doesn't get much time for reflection. ■ an idea about something, esp. one that is written down or expressed: reflections on human destiny and art.

re·flec·tive /rɪˈflektiv/ ▶ adj. **1** providing a reflection; capable of reflecting light or other radiation: reflective glass. ■ produced by reflection: a colorful reflective glow. **2** relating to or characterized by deep thought; thoughtful: a quiet, reflective, astute man. —**re·flec·tive·ly** adv. —**re·flec·tive·ness** n.

re·flec·tor /rɪˈflektər/ ▶ n. a piece of glass, metal, or other material for reflecting light in a required direction, e.g., a red one on the back of a motor vehicle or bicycle. ■ an object or device that reflects radio waves, seismic vibrations, sound, or other waves. ■ a reflecting telescope.

re·flex /ˈrēˌfleks/ ▶ n. **1** an action that is performed as a response to a stimulus and without conscious thought: a newborn baby is equipped with basic reflexes. ■ (**reflexes**) a person's ability to perform such actions, esp. quickly: he was saved by his superb reflexes. ■ (in reflexology) a response in a part of the body to stimulation of a corresponding point on the feet, hands, or head: [as adj.] reflex points. **2** a thing that is determined by and reproduces the essential features or qualities of something else: politics was no more than a reflex of economics. ■ a word formed by development from an earlier stage of a language.
▶ adj. **1** (of an action) performed without conscious thought as an automatic response to a stimulus: sneezing is a reflex action. **2** (of an angle) exceeding 180°. ■ (also **re·flexed**) (esp. of flower petals) bent or turned backward. —**re·flex·ly** /ˈrēˌflekslē; rɪˈflekslē/ adv.

re·flex cam·er·a ▶ n. a camera with a ground glass focusing screen on which the image is formed by a combination of lens and mirror, enabling the scene to be correctly composed and focused.

re·flex·i·ble /rɪˈfleksəbəl/ ▶ adj. chiefly technical capable of being reflected. —**re·flex·i·bil·i·ty** /rɪˌfleksəˈbilətē/ n.

re·flex·ive /rɪˈfleksiv/ ▶ adj. **1** Gram. denoting a pronoun that refers back to the subject of the clause in which it is used, e.g., myself, themselves. ■ (of a verb or clause) having a reflexive pronoun as its object, e.g., wash oneself. **2** (of an action) performed as a reflex, without conscious thought: at concerts like this one, standing ovations have become reflexive. **3** (of a method or theory in the social sciences) taking account of itself or of the effect of the personality or presence of the researcher on what is being investigated.
▶ n. a reflexive word or form, esp. a pronoun. —**re·flex·ive·ly** adv. —**re·flex·ive·ness** n. —**re·flex·iv·i·ty** /rɪˌflekˈsivətē; ˌrēˌflek/ n.

re·flex·ol·o·gy /ˌrēˌflekˈsäləjē/ ▶ n. **1** a system of massage used to relieve tension and treat illness, based on the theory that there are reflex points on the feet, hands, and head linked to every part of the body. **2** Psychol. the scientific study of reflex action as it affects behavior. —**re·flex·ol·o·gist** /-jist/ n.

re·flux /ˈrēˌfləks/ ▶ n. Chem. the process of boiling a liquid in such a way that any vapor is liquefied and returned to the stock. ■ technical the flowing back of a liquid, esp. that of a fluid in the body.
▶ v. Chem. boil or cause to boil in circumstances such that the vapor returns to the stock of liquid after condensing. ■ [intr.] technical (of a liquid, esp. a bodily fluid) flow back.

re·fo·cus /rēˈfōkəs/ ▶ v. (**-fo·cused, -fo·cus·ing** or **-fo·cussed, -fo·cus·sing**) [tr.] adjust the focus of (a lens or one's eyes). ■ focus (attention or resources) on something new or different: refocus attention on yourself through repeating your main points.

re·for·est /rēˈfôrəst; -ˈfärəst/ ▶ v. [tr.] replant with trees; cover again with forest: a project to reforest the country's coastal areas. —**re·for·est·a·tion** /rēˌfôrəˈstāsHən; -ˈfärə-/ n.

re·form /rɪˈfôrm/ ▶ v. [tr.] **1** make changes in (something, typically a social, political, or economic institution or practice) in order to improve it: *an opportunity to reform and restructure an antiquated schooling model.* ■ bring about a change in (someone) so that they no longer behave in an immoral, criminal, or self-destructive manner: *the state has a duty to reform criminals.* ■ [*intr.*] (of a person) change oneself in such a way: *it was only when his drunken behavior led to blows that he started to reform.* **2** *Chem.* subject (hydrocarbons) to a catalytic process in which straight-chain molecules are converted to branched forms for use in gasoline to improve its antiknock properties.

▶*n.* the action or process of reforming an institution or practice: *the reform of the divorce laws.*

▶*adj.* (**Reform**) of, denoting, or pertaining to Reform Judaism: *a Reform rabbi.* —**re·form·a·ble** *adj.* —**re·form·a·tive** /-mətiv/ *adj.* —**re·form·er** *n.* —**re·form·ist** *n.*

re-form /ˈrēˈfôrm/ ▶*v.* form or cause to form again: [*intr.*] *the clouds reformed over the sun.*

re·for·mat /rēˈfôrˌmat/ ▶*v.* (**-mat·ted, -mat·ting**) [*tr.*] *chiefly Comput.* give a new format to; revise or represent in another format.

ref·or·ma·tion /ˌrefərˈmāsHən/ ▶*n.* **1** the action or process of reforming an institution or practice: *the reformation of the Senate.* **2** (**the Reformation**) a 16th-century movement for the reform of abuses in the Roman Catholic Church ending in the establishment of the Reformed and Protestant Churches. —**ref·or·ma·tion·al** /-sHənl/ *adj.*

re·form·a·to·ry /riˈfôrməˌtôrē/ ▶*n.* (*pl.* **-ries**) an institution to which youthful offenders are sent as an alternative to prison; a reform school.

▶*adj.* tending or intended to produce reform.

re·form·ist /riˈfôrmist/ ▶*adj.* supporting or advancing gradual reform rather than abolition or revolution.

▶*n.* a person who advocates gradual reform rather than abolition or revolution. —**re·form·ism** /-ˌmizəm/ *n.*

re·form school ▶*n.* an institution to which youthful offenders are sent as an alternative to prison.

re·fract /riˈfrakt/ ▶*v.* [*tr.*] (usu. **be refracted**) (of water, air, or glass) make (a ray of light) change direction when it enters at an angle: *the rays of light are refracted by the material of the lens.* ■ measure the focusing characteristics of (an eye) or of the eyes of (someone). ▷*early 17th cent.:* from Latin *refract-* 'broken up,' from the verb *refringere,* from *re-* 'back' + *frangere* 'to break.' —**re·frac·tion** *n.* —**re·frac·tive** *adj.*

re·frac·tor /riˈfraktər/ ▶*n.* a lens or other object that causes refraction. ■ a refracting telescope.

re·frac·to·ry /riˈfraktərē/ ▶*adj.* *formal* **1** stubborn or unmanageable: *his refractory pony.* **2** resistant to a process or stimulus: *some granules are refractory to secretory stimuli.* ■ *Med.* (of a person, illness, or diseased tissue) not yielding to treatment: *healing of previously refractory ulcers.* ■ *technical* (of a substance) resistant to heat; hard to melt or fuse.

▶*n.* (*pl.* **-ries**) *technical* a substance that is resistant to heat. —**re·frac·to·ri·ness** *n.*

re·frain¹ /riˈfrān/ ▶*v.* [*intr.*] stop oneself from doing something: *she refrained from comment.*

re·frain² ▶*n.* a repeated line or number of lines in a poem or song, typically at the end of each verse. ■ a comment or complaint that is often repeated: *"Poor Tom" had become the constant refrain of his friends.*

re·fresh /riˈfresH/ ▶*v.* [*tr.*] give new strength or energy to; reinvigorate: *the shower had refreshed her.* ■ stimulate or jog (someone's memory) by checking or going over previous information: *he was able to refresh her memory on many points.* ■ revise or update (skills or knowledge): *short-term courses give nurses an opportunity to refresh their skills.* ■ *Comput.* update the display on (a screen). ■ pour more (drink) for someone or refill (a container) with drink: *the tea is cold and the pot needs refreshing.* ■ place or keep (food) in cold water so as to cool or maintain freshness.

▶*n.* *Comput.* an act or function of updating the display on a screen.

re·fresh·er /riˈfresHər/ ▶*n.* a thing that refreshes, in particular: ■ [usu. as *adj.*] an activity that revises or updates one's skills or knowledge: *candidates take some refresher training before coming back.*

re·fresh·er course ▶*n.* a short course reviewing or updating previous studies or training connected with one's profession.

re·fresh·ing /riˈfresHiNG/ ▶*adj.* serving to refresh or reinvigorate someone: *a refreshing drink.* ■ welcome or stimulating because new or different: *her directness is refreshing.* —**re·fresh·ing·ly** *adv.* *a refreshingly different concept.*

re·fresh·ment /riˈfresHmənt/ ▶*n.* **1** (usu. **refreshments**) a light snack or drink, esp. one provided in a public place or at a public event: *light refreshments are available.* **2** the giving of fresh mental or physical strength or energy: *hobbies and vacations are for refreshment and recreation.*

re·frig·er·ant /riˈfrijərənt/ ▶*n.* a substance used for refrigeration.

▶*adj.* causing cooling or refrigeration.

re·frig·er·ate /riˈfrijəˌrāt/ ▶*v.* [*tr.*] subject (food or drink) to cold in order to chill or preserve it, typically by placing it in a refrigerator: *refrigerate the dough for one hour.* —**re·frig·er·a·tion** /riˌfrijəˈrāsHən/ *n.* —**re·frig·er·a·to·ry** /riˈfrijərəˌtôrē/ *adj.*

re·frig·er·a·tor /riˈfrijəˌrātər/ ▶*n.* an appliance or compartment that is artificially kept cool and used to store food and drink. Modern refrigerators generally make use of the cooling effect produced when a volatile liquid is forced to evaporate in a sealed system in which it can be condensed back to liquid outside the refrigerator.

ref·uge /ˈrefˌyōōj; -ˌyōōzH/ ▶*n.* a condition of being safe or sheltered from pursuit, danger, or trouble: *he was forced to **take refuge in** the French embassy.* ■ something providing such shelter: *the family came to be seen as a refuge from a harsh world.* ■ an institution providing safe accommodations for women who have suffered violence from a husband or partner.

ref·u·gee /ˌrefyōōˈjē; ˈrefyōōˌjē/ ▶*n.* a person who has been forced to leave their country in order to escape war, persecution, or natural disaster: *refugees from Nazi persecution.*

re·fund¹ ▶*v.* /riˈfənd; ˈrēˌfənd/ [*tr.*] pay back (money), typically to a customer who is not satisfied with goods or services bought: *if you're not delighted with your purchase, we guarantee to refund your money in full.* ■ pay back money to (someone): *I'll refund you for the apples and any other damage.*

▶*n.* /ˈrēˌfənd/ a repayment of a sum of money, typically to a dissatisfied customer: *you are entitled to reject it and insist on a refund.* —**re·fund·a·ble** *adj.*

re·fund² /rēˈfənd; ˈrē-/ ▶*v.* fund (a debt, etc.) again.

re·fur·bish /riˈfərbisH/ ▶*v.* [*tr.*] (usu. **be refurbished**) renovate and redecorate (something, esp. a building): *the premises have been completely refurbished in our corporate style.* —**re·fur·bish·ment** *n.*

re·fus·al /riˈfyōōzəl/ ▶*n.* an act or an instance of refusing; the state of being refused.

re·fuse¹ /riˈfyōōz/ ▶*v.* [*intr.*] indicate or show that one is not willing to do something: *I refused to answer.* ■ *inf.* (of a thing) fail to perform a required action: *the car refused to start.* ■ [*tr.*] decline to accept an offer of marriage from (someone): *he's so conceited he'd never believe anyone would refuse him.* —**re·fus·er** *n.*

re·fuse² /ˈrefˌyōōs; -ˌyōōz/ ▶*n.* matter thrown away or rejected as worthless; trash: *heaps of refuse.*

re·fuse·nik /riˈfyōōznik/ ▶*n.* **1** a person in the former Soviet Union who was refused permission to emigrate, in particular, a Jew forbidden to emigrate to Israel. **2** a person who refuses to follow orders or obey the law, esp. as a protest.

re·fute /riˈfyōōt/ ▶*v.* [*tr.*] prove (a statement or theory) to be wrong or false; disprove: *these claims have not been convincingly refuted.* ■ prove that (someone) is wrong. ■ deny or contradict (a statement or accusation): *a spokesman totally refuted the allegation of bias.* —**re·fut·a·ble** *adj.* —**re·fut·al** /-ˈfyōōtl/ *n.* (*rare*) —**ref·u·ta·tion** /ˌrefyōōˈtāsHən/ *n.* —**re·fut·er** *n.*

reg /reg/ ▶*n. inf.* regulation: *we're fed up with all the rules and regs.*

re·gain /riˈgān/ ▶*v.* [*tr.*] obtain possession or use of (something) again after losing it: *she died without regaining consciousness.* ■ reach (a place, position, or thing) again; get back to: *they were unable to regain their boats.*

re·gal /ˈrēgəl/ ▶*adj.* of, resembling, or fit for a monarch, esp. in being magnificent or dignified: *regal authority.* —**re·gal·i·ty** /riˈgalitē/ *n.* —**re·gal·ly** *adv.*

re·gale /riˈgāl/ ▶*v.* [*tr.*] entertain or amuse (someone) with talk: *he regaled her with a colorful account of that afternoon's meeting.* ■ lavishly supply (someone) with food or drink: *he was regaled with excellent home cooking.* —**re·gale·ment** *n.* (*rare*).

re·ga·li·a /riˈgālyə/ ▶*pl. n.* [treated as *sing.* or *pl.*] the emblems or insignia of royalty, esp. the crown, scepter, and other ornaments used at a coronation. ■ the distinctive clothing worn and ornaments carried at formal occasions as an indication of status: *the Bishop of Florence in full regalia.* ■ distinctive, elaborate clothing: *young men, a few in gang regalia.*

re·gard /riˈgärd/ ▶*v.* [*tr.*] consider or think of (someone or something) in a specified way: *she regarded Omaha as her base.* ■ gaze at steadily in a specified fashion: *Professor Ryker regarded him with a faint smile.* ■ (of a thing) have relation to or connection with; concern: *if these things regarded only myself, I could stand it with composure.*

▶*n.* **1** attention to or concern for something: *the court must have **regard** to the principle of welfare.* ■ high opinion; liking and respect; esteem: *she had a particular **regard** for Eliot.* ■ a gaze; a steady or significant look: *he* *shifted uneasily before their clear regard.* **2** (**regards**) best wishes (used to express friendliness in greetings, esp. at the end of letters): *give her my regards.*

▶ □ **as regards** concerning; with respect to: *as regards content, the program will cover important current issues.* □ **in this** (or **that**) **regard** in connection with the point previously mentioned: *there was little incentive for them to be active in this regard.* □ **with** (or **in**) **regard to** as concerns; with respect to: *he made inquiries with regard to Beth.*

re·gard·ing /ri'gärdiNG/ ▶*prep.* with respect to; concerning: *your recent letter regarding the above proposal.*

re·gard·less /ri'gärdləs/ ▶*adv.* without paying attention to the present situation; despite the prevailing circumstances: *they were determined to carry on regardless.* —**re·gard·less·ly** *adv.* —**re·gard·less·ness** *n.*

▶ □ **regardless of** without regard or consideration for: *the allowance is paid regardless of age or income.*

re·gat·ta /ri'gätə; ri'gatə/ ▶*n.* a sporting event consisting of a series of boat or yacht races.

re·gen·cy /'rējənsē/ ▶*n.* (pl. **-cies**) the office or period of government by a regent. ■ a commission acting as regent. ■ (**the Regency**) the particular period of a regency, esp. (in Britain) from 1811 to 1820 and (in France) from 1715 to 1723.

▶*adj.* (**Regency**) relating to or denoting British architecture, clothing, and furniture of the Regency or, more widely, of the late 18th and early 19th centuries. Regency style was contemporary with the Empire style and shares many of its features: elaborate and ornate, it is generally neoclassical, with a generous borrowing of Greek and Egyptian motifs.

re·gen·er·ate ▶*v.* /ri'jenə,rāt/ [*tr.*] (of a living organism) regrow (new tissue) to replace lost or injured tissue: *a crab in the process of regenerating a claw.* ■ [*intr.*] (of an organ or tissue) regrow: *once destroyed, brain cells do not regenerate.* ■ bring into renewed existence; generate again: *the issue was regenerated last month.* ■ bring new and more vigorous life to (an area or institution), esp. in economic terms: *regenerating the inner cities.* ■ (esp. in Christian use) give a new and higher spiritual nature to.

▶*adj.* /ri'jenərət/ reformed or reborn, esp. in a spiritual or moral sense. —**re·gen·er·a·tion** /ri,jenə'rāSHən/ *n.* —**re·gen·er·a·tive** /-ərətiv; -ə,rātiv/ *adj.* —**re·gen·er·a·tor** /-,rātər/ *n.*

re·gent /'rējənt/ ▶*n.* **1** a person appointed to administer a country because the monarch is a minor or is absent or incapacitated. **2** a member of the governing body of a university or other academic institution.

▶*adj.* acting as regent for a monarch: *the queen regent of Portugal.*

reg·gae /'regā; 'rāgā/ ▶*n.* a style of popular music with a strongly accented subsidiary beat, originating in Jamaica. Reggae evolved in the late 1960s from ska and other local variations on calypso and rhythm and blues, and became widely known in the 1970s through the work of Bob Marley; its lyrics are much influenced by Rastafarian ideas.

reg·i·cide /'rejə,sīd/ ▶*n.* the action of killing a king. ■ a person who kills or takes part in killing a king. —**reg·i·cid·al** /,rejə'sīdl/ *adj.*

re·gime /ri'ZHēm/ (also **ré·gime**) ▶*n.* **1** a government, esp. an authoritarian one. **2** a system or planned way of doing things, esp. one imposed from above: *detention centers with a very tough physical regime.* ■ a coordinated program for the promotion or restoration of health; a regimen: *a low-calorie, low-fat regime.* ■ the conditions under which a scientific or industrial process occurs.

reg·i·men /'rejəmən; 'reZH-/ ▶*n.* a prescribed course of medical treatment, way of life, or diet for the promotion or restoration of health: *a treatment regimen.*

reg·i·ment ▶*n.* /'rejəmənt/ a permanent unit of an army typically commanded by a colonel and divided into several companies, squadrons, or batteries and often into two battalions: *two or three miles inland a highly experienced artillery regiment had established a defensive position.* ■ a large array or number of people or things: *a neat regiment of jars and bottles.*

▶*v.* /'rejə,ment/ [*tr.*] (usu. **be regimented**) organize according to a strict, sometimes oppressive system or pattern: *every aspect of their life is strictly regimented.* —**reg·i·men·ta·tion** /,rejəmən'tāSHən; -,men-/ *n.*

reg·i·men·tal /,rejə'mentl/ ▶*adj.* of or relating to a regiment: *regimental colors.* —**reg·i·men·tal·ly** /-'mentl-ē/ *adv.*

re·gion /'rējən/ ▶*n.* an area or division, esp. part of a country or the world having definable characteristics but not always fixed boundaries: *one of the region's major employers.* ■ an administrative district of a city or country. ■ a part of the body, esp. around or near an organ: *an unexpected clenching sensation in the region of her heart.* ■ *fig.* the sphere or realm of something: *his work takes needlework into the region of folk art.* ▷Middle English: from Old French, from Latin *regio(n-)* 'direction, district,' from *regere* 'to rule, direct.' —**re·gion·al** *adj.*

reg·is·ter /'rejəstər/ ▶*n.* **1** an official list or record. **2** a particular part of the range of a voice or instrument: *his voice moved up a register.* ■ a

sliding device controlling a set of organ pipes that share a tonal quality. ■ a set of organ pipes so controlled. **3** *Linguistics* a variety of a language or a level of usage, as determined by degree of formality and choice of vocabulary, pronunciation, and syntax, according to the communicative purpose, social context, and social status of the user. **4** *Printing & Photog.* the exact correspondence of the position of color components in a printed positive. ■ *Printing* the exact correspondence of the position of printed matter on the two sides of a page. **5** (in electronic devices) a location in a store of data, used for a specific purpose and with quick access time. **6** an adjustable plate for widening or narrowing an opening and regulating a draft, esp. in a fire grate. **7** short for CASH REGISTER. **8** *Art* one of a number of bands or sections into which a design is divided.

▶*v.* [*tr.*] **1** enter or record in an official list as being in a particular category, having a particular eligibility or entitlement, or in keeping with a requirement: *the vessel is registered as Liberian.* ■ [*intr.*] put one's name on an official list under such terms: *34,500 registered to vote.* ■ entrust (a letter or parcel) to a post office for transmission by registered mail: [as *adj.*] (**registered**) *a registered letter.* ■ express (an opinion or emotion): *I wish to register an objection.* **2** (of an instrument) detect and show (a reading) automatically: *the electroscope was too insensitive to register the tiny changes.* ■ (of an event) give rise to a specified reading on an instrument: *the blast registered 5.4 on the Richter scale.* ■ properly notice or become aware of (something): *he had not even registered her presence.* ■ (of an emotion) show in a person's face or gestures: *nothing registered on their faces.* **3** *Printing & Photog.* correspond or cause to correspond exactly in position: *they are adjusted until the impressions register.* —**reg·is·tra·ble** /-st(ə)rəbəl/ *adj.*

reg·is·tered mail ▶*n.* prepaid first class mail that is recorded by the post office before being sent and at each point along its route to safeguard against loss, theft, or damage.

reg·is·tered nurse (abbr.: **RN**) ▶*n.* a nurse who has graduated from a college's nursing program or from a school of nursing and has passed a national licensing exam. Compare with PRACTICAL NURSE.

reg·is·trar /'rejə,strär/ ▶*n.* an official responsible for keeping a register or official records: *the registrar of births and deaths.* ■ an official in a college or university who is responsible for keeping student records. —**reg·is·trar·ship** /-,SHip/ *n.*

reg·is·tra·tion /,rejə'strāSHən/ ▶*n.* the action or process of registering or of being registered: *the registration of births, marriages, and deaths.* ■ a certificate that attests to the registering of (a person, automobile, etc.). ■ *Mus.* a combination of stops used when playing the organ.

reg·is·try /'rejəstrē/ ▶*n.* (pl. **-tries**) **1** a place or office where registers or records are kept. **2** an official list or register: *a recognized purebred dog registry.* **3** registration. **4** the nationality of a merchant ship: *converted trawlers of local registry.*

re·gress ▶*v.* /ri'gres/ **1** return to a former or less developed state: *art has been regressing toward adolescence for more than a generation now.* ■ return mentally to a former stage of life or a supposed previous life, esp. through hypnosis or mental illness: *she claims to be able to regress to the Roman era.* **2** *Statistics* calculate the coefficient or coefficients of regression of (a variable) against or on another variable.

▶*n.* /'rē,gres/ the action of returning to a former or less developed state.

re·gres·sion /ri'greSHən/ ▶*n.* **1** a return to a former or less developed state. ■ a return to an earlier stage of life or a supposed previous life, esp. through hypnosis or mental illness, or as a means of escaping present anxieties: [as *adj.*] *regression therapy.* ■ a lessening of the severity of a disease or its symptoms: *he seemed able to produce a regression in this disease.* **2** *Statistics* a measure of the relation between the mean value of one variable (e.g., output) and corresponding values of other variables (e.g., time and cost).

re·gres·sive /ri'gresiv/ ▶*adj.* **1** becoming less advanced; returning to a former or less developed state: *the regressive, infantile wish for the perfect parent of early childhood.* ■ of, relating to, or marked by psychological regression. **2** (of a tax) taking a proportionally greater amount from those on lower incomes. —**re·gres·sive·ly** *adv.* —**re·gres·sive·ness** *n.*

re·gret /ri'gret/ ▶*v.* (**-gret·ted**, **-gret·ting**) [*tr.*] feel sad, repentant, or disappointed over (something that has happened or been done, esp. a loss or missed opportunity): *she immediately regretted her words.* ■ used in polite formulas to express apology for or sadness over something unfortunate or unpleasant: *any inconvenience to readers is regretted.* ■ *archaic* feel sorrow for the loss or absence of (something pleasant): *my home, when shall I cease to regret you!*

▶*n.* a feeling of sadness, repentance, or disappointment over something that has happened or been done: *she expressed her regret at Virginia's death.* ■ (often **regrets**) an instance or cause of such a feeling: *she had* *few regrets in leaving the house.* ■ (often **one's regrets**) used in polite formulas to express apology for or sadness at an occurrence or an inability to accept an invitation: *please give your grandmother my regrets.*

re·gret·ful /ri'gretfəl/ ▸ *adj.* feeling or showing regret: *he sounded regretful but pointed out that he had committed himself.* —**re·gret·ful·ly** *adv.* —**re·gret·ful·ness** *n.*

re·gret·ta·ble /ri'gretəbəl/ ▸ *adj.* (of conduct or an event) giving rise to regret; undesirable; unwelcome: *the loss of this number of jobs is regrettable.* —**re·gret·ta·bly** *adv.*

re·group /rē'grōōp/ ▸ *v.* [*intr.*] (of troops) reassemble into organized groups, typically after being attacked or defeated: *their heroic resistance gave American forces time to regroup.* ■ [*tr.*] cause to reassemble in this way: *he regrouped his fighters in the hills.* ■ [*tr.*] rearrange (something) into a new group or groups: *she was regrouping the numeric data.* —**re·group·ment** *n.*

reg·u·lar /'regyələr/, 'reg(ə)lər/ ▸ *adj.* **1** arranged in or constituting a constant or definite pattern, esp. with the same space between individual instances: *place the flags at regular intervals.* ■ (of a person) doing the same thing or going to the same place with the same time between individual instances: *regular worshipers.* ■ (of a structure or arrangement) arranged in or constituting a symmetrical or harmonious pattern: *beautifully regular, heart-shaped leaves.* ■ (of a person) defecating or menstruating at predictable times. **2** done or happening frequently: *regular border clashes.* **3** conforming to or governed by an accepted standard of procedure or convention: *policies carried on by his deputies through regular channels.* ■ of or belonging to the permanent professional armed forces of a country: *a regular soldier.* ■ *inf.* rightly so called; complete; absolute (used for emphasis): *this place is a regular fisherman's paradise.* **4** used, done, or happening on a habitual basis; usual; customary: *our regular suppliers.* ■ of a normal or ordinary kind; not special: *it's richer than regular pasta.* ■ (chiefly in commercial use) denoting merchandise, esp. food or clothing, of average, medium, or standard size: *a shake and regular fries.* ■ (of a person) not pretentious or arrogant; ordinary and friendly: *advertising agencies who try to portray their candidates as **regular guys.*** **5** *Gram.* (of a word) following the normal pattern of inflection: *a regular verb.* **6** *Geom.* (of a figure) having all sides and all angles equal: *a regular polygon.* ■ (of a solid) bounded by a number of equal figures.
▸ *n.* a regular customer or member, for example of a bar, store, or team: *attracting a richer clientele as its regulars.* ■ a regular member of the armed forces. ■ a member of a political party who is faithful to that party: *he plans to sell tickets to the big-money party regulars.* —**reg·u·lar·i·ty** /,regyə'laritē/ *n.* —**reg·u·lar·ize** *v.* —**reg·u·lar·ly** *adv.*

reg·u·late /'regyə,lāt/ ▸ *v.* [*tr.*] control or maintain the rate or speed of (a machine or process) so that it operates properly: *a hormone that regulates metabolism and organ function.* ■ control or supervise (something, esp. a company or business activity) by means of rules and regulations: *the organization that regulates fishing in the region.* ■ set (a clock or other apparatus) according to an external standard. —**reg·u·la·tive** /-,lātiv/ *adj.* —**reg·u·la·tor** /-,lātər/ *n.* —**reg·u·la·to·ry** /-lə,tôrē/ *adj.*

reg·u·la·tion /,reg(y)ə'lāSHən/ ▸ *n.* **1** a rule or directive made and maintained by an authority: *planning regulations.* ■ [as *adj.*] in accordance with regulations; of the correct type: *regulation army footwear.* ■ [as *adj.*] *inf.* of a familiar or predictable type; formulaic; standardized: *a regulation Western parody.* **2** the action or process of regulating or being regulated: *the regulation of financial markets.*

re·gur·gi·tate /ri'gərjə,tāt/ ▸ *v.* [*tr.*] bring (swallowed food) up again to the mouth: *gulls regurgitate food for the chicks.* ■ *fig.* repeat (information) without analyzing or comprehending it: *facts that can then be regurgitated at examinations.* —**re·gur·gi·ta·tion** /ri,gərjə'tāSHən/ *n.*

re·hab /'rē,hab/ *inf.* ▸ *n.* **1** rehabilitation, in particular: ■ a course of treatment for drug or alcohol addiction, typically at a facility in which the patient is compelled to reside for a period of several weeks or months: *the success of rehab is entirely dependent on the patient's commitment to the process.* ■ a course of treatment, largely physical therapy, designed to reverse the debilitating effects of an injury: *their best hitter has been in rehab since August, after his collision with the left-field wall.* **2** a thing, esp. a building, that has been rehabilitated or restored.
▸ *v.* (**-habbed, -hab·bing**) [*tr.*] rehabilitate or restore: *they don't rehab you at all in jail* | [as *adj.*] (**rehabbed**) *newly rehabbed apartments for rent.* —**re·hab·ber** *n.*

re·ha·bil·i·tate /,rē(h)ə'bilə,tāt/ ▸ *v.* [*tr.*] restore (someone) to health or normal life by training and therapy after imprisonment, addiction, or illness: *helping to rehabilitate former criminals.* ■ restore (someone) to former privileges or reputation after a period of critical or official disfavor: *with the fall of the government many former dissidents were rehabilitated.* ■ return (something, esp. an environmental feature) to its former con-

dition. —**re·ha·bil·i·ta·tion** /-,bilə'tāSHən/ *n.* —**re·ha·bil·i·ta·tive** /-,tātiv/ *adj.*

re·hash ▸ *v.* /rē'hasH/ [*tr.*] put (old ideas or material) into a new form without significant change or improvement: *he contented himself with occasional articles in journals, rehashing his own work.* ■ consider or discuss (something) at length after it has happened: *is it really necessary to rehash that trauma all over again?*
▸ *n.* /'rē,hasH/ a reuse of old ideas or material without significant change or improvement: *the spring show was a rehash of the summer show from the previous year.*

re·hears·al /ri'hərsəl/ ▸ *n.* a practice or trial performance of a play or other work for later public performance: *rehearsals for the opera season.* ■ the action or process of rehearsing: *I've had two weeks in rehearsal.*

re·hearse /ri'hərs/ ▸ *v.* [*tr.*] practice (a play, piece of music, or other work) for later public performance: *we were rehearsing a play.* ■ mentally prepare or recite (words one intends to say): *he had rehearsed a thousand fine phrases.* ■ state (a list of points, esp. those that have been made many times before); enumerate: *criticisms of factory farming have been rehearsed often enough.* —**re·hears·er** *n.*

re·heat ▸ *v.* /rē'hēt/ [*tr.*] heat (something, esp. cooked food) again. —**re·heat·er** *n.*

re·hy·drate /rē'hī,drāt/ ▸ *v.* absorb or cause to absorb moisture after dehydration: [*tr.*] *the slides were rehydrated in water.* —**re·hy·drat·a·ble** *adj.* —**re·hy·dra·tion** /,rē,hī'drāSHən/ *n.*

Reich /rīk; rīкн/ ▸ the former German state, most often used to refer to the Third Reich, the Nazi regime from 1933 to 1945.

reign /rān/ ▸ *v.* [*intr.*] hold royal office; rule as king or queen: *Queen Elizabeth reigns over the UK* | *fig. the Nashville sound will reign supreme once again.* ■ [usu. as *adj.*] (**reigning**) (of an athlete or team) currently hold a particular title: *the reigning world champion.* ■ (of a quality or condition) prevail; predominate: *confusion reigned.*
▸ *n.* the period during which a sovereign rules: *the original chapel was built in the reign of Charles I.* ■ the period of prevalence or domination of a specified thing: *these historic seconds inaugurated the reign of negative political advertising.*

reign of ter·ror ▸ *n.* a period of remorseless repression or bloodshed, in particular (**Reign of Terror**), the period of the Terror during the French Revolution.

re·im·burse /,rē·im'bərs/ ▸ *v.* [*tr.*] (often **be reimbursed**) repay (a person who has spent or lost money): *the investors should be reimbursed for their losses.* ■ repay (a sum of money that has been spent or lost): *they spend thousands of dollars that are not reimbursed by insurance.* —**re·im·burs·a·ble** *adj.* —**re·im·burse·ment** *n.*

rein /rān/ ▸ *n.* (usu. **reins**) a long, narrow strap attached at one end to a horse's bit, typically used in pairs to guide or check a horse while riding or driving. ■ *fig.* the power to direct and control: *management is criticized for its unwillingness to let go of the reins of an organization and delegate routine tasks.*
▸ *v.* [*tr.*] cause (a horse) to stop or slow down by pulling on its reins: *he reined in his horse and waited for her.* ■ cause (a horse) to change direction by pulling on its reins: *he reined the mare's head about and rode off.* ■ keep under control; restrain: *with an effort, she reined back her impatience.*
▹ Middle English: from Old French *rene*, based on Latin *retinere* 'retain.'
▸ □ (a) **free rein** freedom of action or expression: *he was given free rein to work out his designs.* □ **keep a tight rein on** exercise strict control over; allow little freedom to: *her only chance of survival was to keep a tight rein on her feelings and words.*

re·in·car·nate ▸ *v.* /,rē·in'kär,nāt/ [*tr.*] (often **be reincarnated**) cause (someone) to undergo rebirth in another body: *a man may be reincarnated in animal form* | [as *adj.*] (**reincarnated**) *a reincarnated soul.* ■ [*intr.*] (of a person) be reborn in this way: *they were afraid she would reincarnate as a vampire.*
▸ *adj.* /-nit/ [usu. *postpositive*] reborn in another body: *he claims that the girl is his dead daughter reincarnate.*

re·in·car·na·tion /,rē·inkär'nāSHən/ ▸ *n.* the rebirth of a soul in a new body. ■ a person or animal in whom a particular soul is believed to have been reborn: *he is said to be **a reincarnation of** the Hindu god Vishnu.* ■ *fig.* the newest version or closest match of something from the past: *the latest reincarnation of the hippie look.*

re·in·cor·po·rate /,rē·in'kôrpə,rāt/ ▸ *v.* [*tr.*] make (something) a part of something else once more: *a campaign to reincorporate the visual arts into religious devotion.* —**re·in·cor·po·ra·tion** /,rē·in,kôrpə'rāSHən/ *n.*

Pronunciation Key ə *ago,* up; ər *over, fur;* a *hat;* ā *ate;* ä *car;* CH *chin;* e *let;* ē *see;* e(ə)r *air;* i *fit;* ī *by;* i(ə)r *ear;* NG *sing;* ō *go;* ô *law, for;* oi *toy;* ŌŌ *good;* ōō *goo;* ou *out;* SH *she;* TH *thin;* TH *then;* (h)w *why;* ZH *vision*

rein·deer /ˈrānˌdir/ ▶*n.* (*pl.* same or **reindeers**) a deer (genus *Rangifer*) of the tundra and subarctic regions of Eurasia and North America, both sexes of which have large branching antlers. Most Eurasian reindeer are domesticated and used for drawing sleds and as a source of milk, flesh, and hide.

re·in·force /ˌrē-inˈfôrs/ ▶*v.* [*tr.*] strengthen or support, esp. with additional personnel or material: *paratroopers were sent to reinforce the troops already in the area.* ■ strengthen (an existing feeling, idea, or habit): *various actions of the leaders so reinforced fears and suspicions that war became unavoidable.* —**re·in·forc·er** *n.*

re·in·forced con·crete ▶*n.* concrete in which wire mesh or steel bars are embedded to increase its tensile strength.

re·in·force·ment /ˌrē-inˈfôrsmənt/ ▶*n.* the action or process of reinforcing or strengthening. ■ the process of encouraging or establishing a belief or pattern of behavior, esp. by encouragement or reward. ■ (**reinforcements**) extra personnel sent to increase the strength of an army or similar force: *a small force would hold the position until reinforcements could be sent.* ■ the strengthening structure or material employed in reinforced concrete or plastic.

re·in·state /ˌrē-inˈstāt/ ▶*v.* [*tr.*] (often **be reinstated**) restore (someone or something) to their former position or condition: *the union is fighting to reinstate the fired journalists.* —**re·in·state·ment** *n.*

re·in·sure /ˌrē-inˈSHo͝or/ ▶*v.* [*tr.*] (of an insurer) transfer (all or part of a risk) to another insurer to provide protection against the risk of the first insurance. —**re·in·sur·ance** /-ˈSHo͝orəns/ *n.* —**re·in·sur·er** *n.*

re·in·te·grate /rēˈintəˌgrāt/ ▶*v.* [*tr.*] restore (elements regarded as disparate) to unity. ■ restore to a position as a part fitting easily into a larger whole: *it can be difficult for an offender to be reintegrated into the community.* —**re·in·te·gra·tion** /ˌrē,intəˈgrāSHən/ *n.*

re·in·ter·pret /ˌrē-inˈtərprət/ ▶*v.* (**-pret·ed, -pret·ing**) [*tr.*] (often **be reinterpreted**) interpret (something) in a new or different way. —**re·in·ter·pre·ta·tion** /ˌrē-in,tərprəˈtāSHən/ *n.*

re·it·er·ate /rēˈitəˌrāt/ ▶*v.* say something again or a number or times, typically for emphasis or clarity: *she reiterated that the administration would remain steadfast in its support.* —**re·it·er·a·tion** /rē,itəˈrāSHən/ *n.* —**re·it·er·a·tive** /-ˌrātiv; -rətiv/ *adj.*

re·ject ▶*v.* /riˈjekt/ [*tr.*] dismiss as inadequate, inappropriate, or not to one's taste: *union negotiators rejected a 1.5 percent pay increase.* ■ refuse to agree to (a request): *an application to hold a pop concert at the club was rejected.* ■ fail to show due affection or concern for (someone); rebuff: *she didn't want him to feel he had been rejected after his sister was born.* ■ *Med.* show an immune response to (a transplanted organ or tissue) so that it fails to survive.
▶*n.* /ˈrēˌjekt/ a person or thing dismissed as failing to meet standards or satisfy tastes: *some of the team's rejects have gone on to prove themselves in championships.* —**re·ject·ee** /riˌjekˈtē; ˌrē-/ *n.* —**re·jec·tion** /riˈjekSHən/ *n.* —**re·jec·tive** /riˈjektiv/ *adj.* (*rare*). —**re·jec·tor** /-tər/ *n.*

re·joice /riˈjois/ ▶*v.* [*intr.*] feel or show great joy or delight: *he rejoiced when he saw his family alive* | [as *n.*] (**rejoicing**) *an occasion for rejoicing.* —**re·joic·er** *n.* —**re·joic·ing·ly** *adv.*

re·join¹ /rēˈjoin; ˈrē-/ ▶*v.* [*tr.*] join together again; reunite: *the stone had been cracked and crudely rejoined.* ■ return to (a companion, organization, or route that one has left): *the soldiers were returning from leave to rejoin their unit.*

re·join² /riˈjoin/ ▶*v.* say something in answer to a remark, typically rudely or in a discouraging manner: *Harry said that he longed for a bath and soft towels, to which his father rejoined that he was a gross materialist.*

re·join·der /riˈjoindər/ ▶*n.* a reply, esp. a sharp or witty one: *she would have made some cutting rejoinder but none came to mind.* ■ *dated Law* a defendant's answer to the plaintiff's reply or replication.

re·ju·ve·nate /riˈjo͞ovəˌnāt/ ▶*v.* [*tr.*] make (someone or something) look or feel younger, fresher, or more lively: *a bid to rejuvenate the town center* | [as *adj.*] (**rejuvenating**) *the rejuvenating effects of therapeutic clay.* —**re·ju·ve·na·tion** /ri,jo͞ovəˈnāSHən/ *n.* —**re·ju·ve·na·tor** /-,nātər/ *n.*

re·kin·dle /rēˈkindəl/ ▶*v.* [*tr.*] relight (a fire). ■ revive (something that has been lost): *he tried to rekindle their friendship.*

rel. ▶*abbr.* ■ relating to. ■ relative. ■ relatively. ■ released. ■ religion. ■ religious.

re·lapse ▶*v.* /riˈlaps; ˈrēˌlaps/ [*intr.*] (of someone suffering from a disease) suffer deterioration after a period of improvement. ■ (**relapse into**) return to (a less active or a worse state): *he relapsed into silence.*
▶*n.* /ˈrēˌlaps/ a deterioration in someone's state of health after a temporary improvement: *he suffered a relapse of schizophrenia after a car crash.* —**re·laps·er** *n.*

re·late /riˈlāt/ ▶*v.* [*tr.*] **1** give an account of (a sequence of events); narrate: *various versions of the chilling story have been related by the locals.* **2** (**be related**) be connected by blood or marriage: *he was related to my mother.* ■ be causally connected: *high unemployment is related to high crime rates.* ■ (**relate something to**) discuss something in such a way as to indicate its connections with (something else): *the study examines social change within the city and relates it to wider developments in the country as a whole.* ■ [*intr.*] (**relate to**) have reference to; concern: *the new legislation related to corporate activities.* ■ [*intr.*] (**relate to**) feel sympathy with; identify with: *kids related to him because he was so anti-establishment.* —**re·lat·a·ble** *adj.*

re·lat·ed /riˈlātid/ ▶*adj.* belonging to the same family, group, or type; connected: *sleeping sickness and related diseases.* ■ [in *comb.*] associated with the specified item or process, esp. causally: *income-related benefits.* —**re·lat·ed·ness** *n.*

re·la·tion /riˈlāSHən/ ▶*n.* **1** the way in which two or more concepts, objects, or people are connected; a thing's effect on or relevance to another: *questions about the relation between writing and reality.* ■ (**relations**) the way in which two or more people, countries, or organizations feel about and behave toward each other: *the improvement in relations between the two countries* | *the meetings helped cement Anglo-American relations.* ■ (**relations**) *chiefly formal* sexual intercourse: *he wanted an excuse to abandon sexual relations with her.* **2** a person who is connected by blood or marriage; a kinsman or kinswoman: *she was no relation at all, but he called her Aunt Nora.* **3** the action of telling a story.

re·la·tion·al /riˈlāSHənl/ ▶*adj.* concerning the way in which two or more people or things are connected: *power is a relational concept that can only be understood in terms of interactions between individuals and groups.* —**re·la·tion·al·ly** *adv.*

re·la·tion·ship /riˈlāSHənˌSHip/ ▶*n.* the way in which two or more concepts, objects, or people are connected, or the state of being connected: *the study will assess the relationship between unemployment and political attitudes.* ■ the state of being connected by blood or marriage: *they can trace their relationship to a common ancestor.* ■ the way in which two or more people or organizations regard and behave toward each other: *the landlord–tenant relationship.* ■ an emotional and sexual association between two people: *she has a daughter from a previous relationship.*

rel·a·tive /ˈrelətiv/ ▶*adj.* **1** considered in relation to or in proportion to something else: *the relative effectiveness of the various mechanisms is not known.* ■ existing or possessing a specified characteristic only in comparison to something else; not absolute: *she went down the steps into the relative darkness of the dining room.* **2** *Gram.* denoting a pronoun, determiner, or adverb that refers to an expressed or implied antecedent and attaches a subordinate clause to it, e.g., *which, who.* ■ (of a clause) attached to an antecedent by a relative word. **3** *Mus.* (of major and minor keys) having the same key signature.
▶*n.* **1** a person connected by blood or marriage: *much of my time is spent visiting relatives.* ■ a species related to another by common origin: *the plant is a relative of ivy.* **2** *Gram.* a relative pronoun, determiner, or adverb. —**rel·a·tive·ly** *adj.*
▶ □ **relative to 1** in comparison with: *the figures suggest that girls are underachieving relative to boys.* **2** in connection with; concerning: *if you have any questions relative to payment, please contact us.*

rel·a·tive hu·mid·i·ty ▶*n.* the amount of water vapor present in air expressed as a percentage of the amount needed for saturation at the same temperature.

rel·a·tiv·ism /ˈrelətəˌvizəm/ ▶*n.* the doctrine that knowledge, truth, and morality exist in relation to culture, society, or historical context, and are not absolute. —**rel·a·tiv·ist** *n.*

rel·a·tiv·is·tic /ˌrelətəˈvistik/ ▶*adj.* **1** *Physics* accurately described only by the theory of relativity. **2** of or relating to the doctrine of relativism. —**rel·a·tiv·is·ti·cal·ly** /-ik(ə)lē/ *adv.*

rel·a·tiv·i·ty /ˌreləˈtivətē/ ▶*n.* **1** the absence of standards of absolute and universal application: *moral relativity.* **2** *Physics* the dependence of various physical phenomena on relative motion of the observer and the observed objects, esp. regarding the nature and behavior of light, space, time, and gravity.

re·lax /riˈlaks/ ▶*v.* make or become less tense or anxious: [*intr.*] *he relaxed and smiled confidently.* ■ [*intr.*] rest or engage in an enjoyable activity so as to become less tired or anxious: *the team relaxes with a lot of skiing.* ■ [*tr.*] cause (a limb or muscle) to become less rigid: *relax the leg by bringing the knee toward the chest.* ■ make (something) less firm or tight: *Cicely relaxed her hold.* ■ [*tr.*] make (a rule or restriction) less strict while not abolishing it: *they persuaded the local authorities concerned to relax their restrictions.* —**re·lax·er** *n.*

re·lax·ant /rəˈlaksənt/ ▶*n.* a drug used to promote relaxation or reduce

tension: *a muscle relaxant.* ■ a thing having a relaxing effect: *sex can be a great relaxant.*
▶*adj.* causing relaxation.

re·lax·a·tion /ˌrilakˈsāSHən; rē-/ ▶*n.* **1** the state of being free from tension and anxiety. ■ recreation or rest, esp. after a period of work: *his favorite form of relaxation was reading detective novels.* ■ the loss of tension in a part of the body, esp. in a muscle when it ceases to contract. ■ the action of making a rule or restriction less strict: *relaxation of censorship rules.* **2** *Physics* the restoration of equilibrium following disturbance.

re·lay[1] ▶*n.* /ˈrēˌlā/ **1** a group of people or animals engaged in a task or activity for a fixed period of time and then replaced by a similar group: *the wagons were pulled by relays of horses.* ■ [usu. as *adj.*] a race between teams usually of sprinters or swimmers, each team member in turn covering part of the total distance: *a 550-meter relay race.* **2** an electrical device, typically incorporating an electromagnet, that is activated by a current or signal in one circuit to open or close another circuit. **3** a device to receive, reinforce, and retransmit a broadcast or program. ■ a message or program transmitted by such a device: *a relay of a performance live from the concert hall.*
▶*v.* /ˈrēˌlā; ˈrēˌlā/ [*tr.*] receive and pass on (information or a message): *she intended to relay everything she had learned.* ■ broadcast (something) by passing signals received from elsewhere through a transmitting station: *the speech was relayed live from the White House.*

re·lay[2] /rēˈlā/ ▶*v.* (*past* and *past part.* **-laid**) [*tr.*] lay again or differently: *they plan to re-lay about half a mile of the track.*

re·lease /riˈlēs/ ▶*v.* [*tr.*] **1** allow or enable to escape from confinement; set free: *the government announced that the prisoners would be released.* ■ remove restrictions or obligations from (someone or something) so that they become available for other activity: *the strategy would release forces for service in other areas.* ■ allow (information) to be generally available: *no details about the contents of the talks were released.* ■ make (a movie or recording) available for general viewing or purchase: *nine singles and one album had been released.* ■ remove (part of a machine or appliance) from a fixed position, allowing something else to move or function: *he released the handbrake.* ■ allow (something) to return to its resting position by ceasing to put pressure on it: *press the cap down and release.* **2** *Law* surrender (a right). ■ make over (property or money) to another person or entity.
▶*n.* **1** the action or process of releasing or being released: *a campaign by the prisoner's mother resulted in his release.* ■ the action of making a movie, recording, or other product available for general viewing or purchase: *the film was withheld for two years before its release.* ■ a movie or other product issued for viewing or purchase: *his current album release has topped the charts for six months.* ■ a press release. ■ a handle or catch that releases part of a mechanism. **2** *Law* the action of releasing property, money, or a right to another. ■ a document effecting this. —**re·leas·a·ble** *adj.* —**re·leas·ee** /riˌlēˈsē/ *n.* (*Law*). —**re·leas·er** /riˈlēsər/ *n.* —**re·leas·or** /riˈlēsər/ *n.* (*Law*).

rel·e·gate /ˈreləˌgāt/ ▶*v.* [*tr.*] consign or dismiss to an inferior rank or position: *they aim to prevent women from being **relegated to** a secondary role.* —**rel·e·ga·tion** /ˌreləˈgāSHən/ *n.*

re·lent /riˈlent/ ▶*v.* [*intr.*] abandon or mitigate a harsh intention or cruel treatment: *she was going to refuse his request, but relented.* ■ (esp. of bad weather) become less severe or intense: *by evening the rain relented.*

re·lent·less /riˈlentləs/ ▶*adj.* oppressively constant; incessant: *the relentless heat of the desert.* —**re·lent·less·ly** *adv.* —**re·lent·less·ness** *n.*

rel·e·vant /ˈreləvənt/ ▶*adj.* closely connected or appropriate to the matter at hand: *the candidate's experience is **relevant to** the job.* —**rel·e·vance** *n.* —**rel·e·van·cy** /-vənsē/ *n.* —**rel·e·vant·ly** *adv.*

re·li·a·ble /riˈlīəbəl/ ▶*adj.* consistently good in quality or performance; able to be trusted: *a reliable source of information.*
▶*n.* a person or thing with such trustworthy qualities: *the supporting cast includes old reliables like Mitchell.* —**re·li·a·bil·i·ty** /riˌlīəˈbilətē/ *n.* —**re·li·a·ble·ness** *n.* —**re·li·a·bly** /-blē/ *adv.*

re·li·ance /riˈlīəns/ ▶*n.* dependence on or trust in someone or something: *the farmer's **reliance on** pesticides.* —**re·li·ant** /-ənt/ *adj.*

rel·ic /ˈrelik/ ▶*n.* an object surviving from an earlier time, esp. one of historical or sentimental interest. ■ a part of a deceased holy person's body or belongings kept as an object of reverence. ■ an object, custom, or belief that has survived from an earlier time but is now outmoded: *individualized computer programming and time-sharing would become expensive relics.* ■ (**relics**) all that is left of something: *relics of a lost civilization.*

rel·ict /ˈrelikt/ ▶*n.* a thing that has survived from an earlier period or in a primitive form. ■ an animal or plant that has survived while others of its group have become extinct, e.g., the coelacanth. ■ a species of

community that formerly had a wider distribution but now survives in only a few localities.

re·lief /riˈlēf/ ▶*n.* **1** a feeling of reassurance and relaxation following release from anxiety or distress: *much to her relief, she saw the door open.* ■ the alleviation of pain, discomfort, or distress: *tablets for the relief of pain.* ■ a temporary break in a generally tense or tedious situation: *the comic characters aren't part of the plot but just light relief.* **2** assistance, esp. in the form of food, clothing, or money, given to those in special need or difficulty: *raising money for famine relief.* ■ a remission of tax normally due: *people who donate money to charity will receive tax relief.* ■ *chiefly Law* the redress of a hardship or grievance. **3** a person or group of people replacing others who have been on duty: [as *adj.*] *the relief nurse was late.* **4** the state of being clearly visible or obvious due to being accentuated in some way: *the setting sun threw the snow-covered peaks **into** relief.* ■ a method of molding, carving, or stamping in which the design stands out from the surface, to a greater (**high relief**) or lesser (**bas-relief**) extent. ■ a piece of sculpture in relief. ■ *Geog.* difference in height from the surrounding terrain; the amount of variation in elevation and slope in a particular area. ▷late Middle English: from Old French, from *relever* 'raise up, relieve,' from Latin *relevare* 'raise again, alleviate.'
▶ □ **in relief 1** *Art* carved, molded, or stamped so as to stand out from the surface. **2** *Baseball* acting as a replacement pitcher. □ **on relief** receiving government assistance because of need.

re·lief map ▶*n.* a map indicating hills and valleys by shading rather than by contour lines alone. ■ a map model with elevations and depressions representing hills and valleys, typically on an exaggerated relative scale.

re·lieve /riˈlēv/ ▶*v.* [*tr.*] **1** cause (pain, distress, or difficulty) to become less severe or serious: *the drug was used to promote sleep and to relieve pain.* ■ make less tedious or monotonous by the introduction of variety or of something striking or pleasing: *the bird's body is black, relieved only by white under the tail.* **2** release (someone) from duty by taking their place: *another signalman relieved him at 5:30.* ■ *Baseball* (of a relief pitcher) take the place of (another pitcher) during a game. **3** (**relieve someone of**) take (a burden) from someone: *he relieved her of her baggage.* ■ used euphemistically to indicate that someone has been deprived of something: *he was relieved of his world title.* **4** (**relieve oneself**) urinate or defecate (used euphemistically). —**re·liev·a·ble** *adj.* —**re·liev·ed·ly** /riˈlēvədlē/ *adv.* —**re·liev·er** *n.*

re·li·gion /riˈlijən/ ▶*n.* the belief in and worship of a superhuman controlling power, esp. a personal God or gods: *ideas about the relationship between science and religion.* ■ details of belief as taught or discussed: *when the school first opened they taught only religion, Italian, and mathematics.* ■ a particular system of faith and worship: *the world's great religions.* ■ a pursuit or interest to which someone ascribes supreme importance: *consumerism is the new religion.* —**re·li·gion·less** *adj.*

re·li·gi·os·i·ty /riˌlijēˈäsətē/ ▶*n.* excessively religious behavior.

re·li·gious /riˈlijəs/ ▶*adj.* believing in and worshiping a superhuman controlling power or powers, esp. a personal God or gods: *both men were deeply religious, intelligent, and moralistic.* ■ (of a belief or practice) forming part of someone's thought about or worship of a divine being: *he has strong religious convictions.* ■ of or relating to the worship of or a doctrine concerning a divine being or beings: *religious music.* ■ belonging or relating to a monastic order or other group of people who are united by their practice of religion: *religious houses were built on ancient pagan sites.* ■ treated or regarded with a devotion and scrupulousness appropriate to worship: *I have a religious aversion to reading manuals.*
▶*n.* (*pl.* same) a person bound by monastic vows. —**re·li·gious·ly** *adv.* —**re·li·gious·ness** *n.*

Re·li·gious So·ci·e·ty of Friends ▶official name for the Quakers (see QUAKER).

re·lin·quish /riˈliNGkwiSH/ ▶*v.* [*tr.*] voluntarily cease to keep or claim; give up: *he relinquished his managerial role to become chief executive.* —**re·lin·quish·ment** *n.*

rel·i·quar·y /ˈreləˌkwerē/ ▶*n.* (*pl.* **-quar·ies**) a container for holy relics.

rel·ish /ˈreliSH/ ▶*n.* **1** great enjoyment: *she swigged a mouthful of wine with relish.* ■ liking for or pleasurable anticipation of something: *I was appointed to a position for which I had little relish.* **2** a condiment eaten with plain food to add flavor: *use salsa as a relish with grilled meat or fish.*
▶*v.* [*tr.*] enjoy greatly: *he was relishing his moment of glory.* ▷Middle English: alteration of obsolete *reles*, from Old French, 'remainder,' from *relaisser* 'to release.' The early noun sense was 'odor, taste,' giving rise to

---

'appetizing flavor, piquant taste' (mid 17th cent.), and hence sense 2 (late 18th cent.). —**re·lish·a·ble** *adj.*

re·live /rēˈliv; ˈrē-/ ▶*v.* [*tr.*] live through (an experience or feeling, esp. an unpleasant one) again in one's imagination or memory: *he broke down sobbing as he relived the attack.*

re·lo·cate /rēˈlōˌkāt; ˌrēlōˈkāt/ ▶*v.* [*intr.*] move to a new place and establish one's home or business there: *if you are relocating here from another state* | [*tr.*] *distribution staff will be relocated to Holland.* —**re·lo·ca·tion** /ˌrēlōˈkāSHən/ *n.*

re·luc·tant /riˈləktənt/ ▶*adj.* unwilling and hesitant; disinclined: *she seemed reluctant to discuss the matter.* —**re·luc·tance** *n.* —**re·luc·tant·ly** *adv.*

re·ly /riˈlī/ ▶*v.* (**-lies, -lied**) [*intr.*] (**rely on/upon**) depend on with full trust or confidence: *I know I can rely on your discretion.* ■ be dependent on: *the charity has to rely entirely on public donations.*

REM ▶*abbr.* rapid eye movement.

rem /rem/ ▶*n.* (*pl.* same) a unit of effective absorbed dose of ionizing radiation in human tissue, equivalent to one roentgen of X-rays.

re·main /riˈmān/ ▶*v.* [*intr.*] continue to exist, esp. after other similar or related people or things have ceased to exist: *a cloister is all that remains of the monastery.* ■ stay in the place that one has been occupying: *her husband remained at the beach condo.* ■ continue to possess a particular quality or fulfill a particular role: *he had remained alert the whole time.*
▶ □ **remain to be seen** used to express the notion that something is not yet known or certain: *she has broken her leg, but it remains to be seen how badly.*

re·main·der /riˈmāndər/ ▶*n.* **1** a part, number, or quantity that is left over: *leave a few mushrooms for garnish and slice the remainder.* ■ the number that is left over in a division in which one quantity does not exactly divide another: *23 divided by 3 is 7, remainder 2.* ■ a copy of a book left unsold when demand has fallen. **2** *Law* an interest in an estate that becomes effective in possession only when a prior interest (devised at the same time) ends.
▶*v.* [*tr.*] (often **be remaindered**) dispose of (a book left unsold) at a reduced price: *titles are being remaindered increasingly quickly to save on overheads.*

re·mains /riˈmānz/ ▶*pl. n.* the parts left over after other parts have been removed, used, or destroyed: *the remains of a sandwich lunch were on the table.* ■ historical or archaeological relics: *Roman remains.* ■ a person's body after death.

re·make ▶*v.* /rēˈmāk; ˈrē-/ (*past* and *past part.* **-made**) [*tr.*] make (something) again or differently: *the bed would be more comfortable if it were remade.*
▶*n.* /ˈrēˌmāk/ a movie or piece of music that has been filmed or recorded again and rereleased.

re·mand /riˈmand/ *Law* ▶*v.* [*tr.*] place (a defendant) on bail or in custody, esp. when a trial is adjourned: *I had a seventeen-year-old son remanded to a drug-addiction program.* ■ return (a case) to a lower court for reconsideration: *the Supreme Court summarily vacated the opinion and remanded the matter back to the California Court of Appeal.*
▶*n.* a committal to custody.

re·mark /riˈmärk/ ▶*v.* **1** say something as a comment; mention: [with direct speech] *"Tom's looking peaked," she remarked.* **2** [*tr.*] regard with attention; notice: *he remarked the man's inflamed eyelids.*
▶*n.* a written or spoken comment: *I decided to ignore his rude remarks.* ■ notice or comment: *the landscape was not worthy of remark.*

re·mark·a·ble /riˈmärkəbəl/ ▶*adj.* worthy of attention; striking: *a remarkable coincidence.* —**re·mark·a·ble·ness** *n.* —**re·mark·a·bly** /-blē/ *adv.*

re·mas·ter /rēˈmastər/ ▶*v.* [*tr.*] make a new master of (a recording), typically in order to improve the sound quality: *all the tracks have been remastered from the original tapes.*

re·match /ˈrēˌmaCH/ ▶*n.* a second match or game between two teams or players.

re·me·di·al /riˈmēdēəl/ ▶*adj.* giving or intended as a remedy or cure: *remedial surgery.* ■ provided or intended for students who are experiencing learning difficulties: *remedial education.* —**re·me·di·al·ly** *adv.*

rem·e·dy /ˈremədē/ ▶*n.* (*pl.* **-dies**) a medicine or treatment for a disease or injury: *herbal remedies for aches and pains.* ■ a means of counteracting or eliminating something undesirable: *shopping became a remedy for personal problems.* ■ a means of legal reparation: *the doctrine took away their only remedy against merchants who refused to honor their contracts.*
▶*v.* (**-dies, -died**) [*tr.*] set right (an undesirable situation): *by the time a problem becomes patently obvious, it may be almost too late to remedy it.* —**re·me·di·a·ble** /riˈmēdēəbəl/ *adj.* —**rem·e·di·less** *adj.*

re·mem·ber /riˈmembər/ ▶*v.* [*tr.*] have in or be able to bring to one's mind

an awareness of (someone or something that one has seen, known, or experienced in the past): *no one remembered his name.* ■ do something that one has undertaken to do or that is necessary or advisable: *did you remember to mail the letters?* ■ used to emphasize the importance of what is asserted: *you must remember that this is a secret.* ■ (**remember someone to**) convey greetings from one person to another: *remember me to Charlie.* ■ (**remember oneself**) recover one's manners after a lapse. —**re·mem·ber·er** *n.*

re·mem·brance /riˈmembrəns/ ▶*n.* the action of remembering something: *a flash of understanding or remembrance passed between them.* ■ a memory or recollection: *the remembrance of her visit came back with startling clarity.* ■ a thing kept or given as a reminder or in commemoration of someone.

re·mind /riˈmīnd/ ▶*v.* [*tr.*] cause (someone) to remember someone or something: *he would have forgotten the boy's birthday if you hadn't reminded him.* ■ (**remind someone of**) cause someone to think of (something) because of a resemblance or likeness: *his impassive, fierce stare reminded her of an owl.* ■ bring something, esp. a commitment or necessary course of action, to the attention of (someone): [*tr.*] *the bartender reminded them that singing was not permitted.*

re·mind·er /riˈmīndər/ ▶*n.* a thing that causes someone to remember something: *the watchtower is a reminder of the days when an enemy might appear at any moment.* ■ a message or communication designed to ensure that someone remembers something.

rem·i·nisce /ˌreməˈnis/ ▶*v.* [*intr.*] indulge in enjoyable recollection of past events: *they reminisced about their summers abroad.* —**rem·i·nis·cer** *n.*

rem·i·nis·cence /ˌreməˈnisəns/ ▶*n.* a story told about a past event remembered by the narrator: *his reminiscences of his early days in Washington.* ■ the enjoyable recollection of past events: *his story made me smile in reminiscence.* ■ (**reminiscences**) a collection in literary form of incidents and experiences that someone remembers. ■ a characteristic of one thing reminding or suggestive of another: *his first works are too full of reminiscences of earlier poetry.* —**rem·i·nis·cen·tial** /ˌre/mənisˈenCHəl/ *adj.* (archaic).

rem·i·nis·cent /ˌreməˈnisənt/ ▶*adj.* tending to remind one of something: *the sights were reminiscent of my childhood.* ■ suggesting something by resemblance: *her suit was vaguely reminiscent of military dress.* ■ (of a person or their manner) absorbed in or suggesting absorption in memories: *her expression was wistful and reminiscent.* —**rem·i·nis·cent·ly** *adv.*

re·miss /riˈmis/ ▶*adj.* lacking care or attention to duty; negligent: *the writer was remiss to have overlooked the group.* —**re·miss·ly** *adv.* —**re·miss·ness** *n.*

re·mis·sion /riˈmiSHən/ ▶*n.* the cancellation of a debt, charge, or penalty: *the plan allows for the partial remission of tuition fees.* ■ a diminution of the seriousness or intensity of disease or pain; a temporary recovery: *ten out of twenty patients remained in remission.* ■ *formal* forgiveness of sins.

re·mit ▶*v.* /riˈmit/ (**-mit·ted, -mit·ting**) [*tr.*] **1** cancel or refrain from exacting or inflicting (a debt or punishment): *the excess of the sentence over 12 months was remitted.* ■ *Theol.* pardon (a sin). **2** send (money) in payment or as a gift: *the income they remitted to their families.* **3** refer (a matter for decision) to some authority: *the request for an investigation was remitted to a special committee.* ■ *Law* send (someone) from one tribunal to another for a trial or hearing.
▶*n.* /riˈmit; ˈrēˌmit/ **1** the task or area of activity officially assigned to an individual or organization: *the committee was becoming caught up in issues that did not fall within its remit.* **2** an item referred to someone for consideration. ▷late Middle English: from Latin *remittere* 'send back, restore,' from *re-* 'back' + *mittere* 'send.' The noun dates from the early 20th cent. —**re·mit·ta·ble** *adj.* —**re·mit·tal** /-ˈmitl/ *n.* —**re·mit·ter** *n.*

re·mit·tance /riˈmitns/ ▶*n.* a sum of money sent, esp. by mail, in payment for goods or services or as a gift. ■ the action of sending money in such a way.

re·mix ▶*v.* /rēˈmiks; ˈrē-/ [*tr.*] mix (something) again. ■ produce a different version of (a musical recording) by altering the balance of the separate tracks.
▶*n.* /ˈrēˌmiks/ a different version of a musical recording produced in such a way. —**re·mix·er** *n.*

rem·nant /ˈremnənt/ ▶*n.* a small remaining quantity of something. ■ a piece of cloth or carpeting left when the greater part has been used or sold. ■ a surviving trace: *a remnant of the past.*
▶*adj.* remaining: *remnant strands of hair.*

re·mod·el /rēˈmädl/ ▶*v.* (**-mod·eled, -mod·el·ing**; *Brit.* **-mod·elled, -mod·el·ling**) [*tr.*] change the structure or form of (something, esp. a building, policy, or procedure): *the station was remodeled and enlarged in 1927.*

■ fashion or shape (a figure or object) again or differently: *she remodeled the head with careful fingers.*

re·mon·strance /ri'mänstrəns/ ▶*n.* a forcefully reproachful protest: *angry remonstrances in the Senate | he shut his ears to any remonstrance.*

re·mon·strate /ri'män,strāt; 'remən-/ ▶*v.* [*intr.*] make a forcefully reproachful protest: *he turned angrily to remonstrate with Tommy* | [with direct speech] *"You don't mean that," she remonstrated.* —**re·mon·stra·tion** /,ri,män'strāSHən/ ,remən-/ *n.* —**re·mon·stra·tive** /-strətiv/ *adj.* —**re·mon·stra·tor** /-,strātər/ *n.*

re·morse /ri'môrs/ ▶*n.* deep regret or guilt for a wrong committed: *they were filled with remorse and shame.* —**re·morse·ful** /-fəl/ *adj.* —**re·morse·ful·ly** /-fəlē/ *adv.*

re·morse·less /ri'môrsləs/ ▶*adj.* without regret or guilt: *a remorseless killer.* ■ (of something unpleasant) never ending or improving; relentless: *remorseless poverty.* —**re·morse·less·ly** *adv.* —**re·morse·less·ness** *n.*

re·mort·gage /rē'môrgij/ ▶*v.* take out another or a different kind of mortgage on (a property).

re·mote /ri'mōt/ ▶*adj.* (**-mot·er, -mot·est**) **1** (of a place) far away; distant: *I'd chosen a spot that looked as remote from any road as possible.* ■ (of an electronic device) operating or operated by means of radio or infrared signals. ■ distant in time: *a golden age in the remote past.* ■ distantly related: *a remote cousin.* ■ having very little connection with or relationship to: *the theory seems rather intellectual and remote from everyday experience.* ■ (of a person) aloof and unfriendly in manner: *this morning Maria again seemed remote and patronizing.* ■ *Comput.* denoting a device that can only be accessed by means of a network. **2** (of a chance or possibility) unlikely to occur: *chances of a genuine and lasting peace become even more remote.*
▶*n.* a remote control device. —**re·mote·ly** *adv.* —**re·mote·ness** *n.*

re·mote con·trol ▶*n.* control of a machine or apparatus from a distance by means of signals transmitted from a radio or electronic device. ■ a device that controls an apparatus, esp. a television or VCR, in such a way. —**re·mote-con·trolled** *adj.*

re·mount /rē'mount; 'rē-/ ▶*v.* [*tr.*] mount (something) again, in particular: ■ get on (something) in order to ride it again: *she went to remount her horse.* ■ attach to a new frame or setting: *remount the best photos in glass-fronted mounts.* ■ produce (a play or exhibition) again. ■ organize and embark on (a significant course of action) again: *the raid was remounted in August.*

re·mov·al /ri'mōōvəl/ ▶*n.* the action of removing someone or something.

re·move /ri'mōōv/ ▶*v.* [*tr.*] take away (something unwanted or unnecessary) from the position it occupies: *she sat down to remove her makeup.* ■ take (something) from a place in order to take it to another location: *customs officials also removed documents from the premises.* ■ take off (clothing): *he sat down on the ground and quickly removed his shoes and socks.* ■ dismiss from a job or office: *a judge was removed from office in 1988 for a number of lapses from proper judicial standards.* ■ (**be removed**) be very different from: *an explanation that is far removed from the truth.* ■ [as *adj.*] (**removed**) separated by a particular number of steps of descent: *his second cousin once removed.*
▶*n.* a degree of remoteness or separation: *at this remove, the whole incident seems insane.* —**re·mov·a·bil·i·ty** /ri,mōōvə'bilətē/ *n.* —**re·mov·a·ble** *adj.* —**re·mov·er** *n.*

re·mu·ner·ate /ri'myōōnə,rāt/ ▶*v.* [*tr.*] pay (someone) for services rendered or work done: *they should be remunerated fairly for their work.* —**re·mu·ner·a·tion** /ri,myōōnə'rāSHən/ *n.* —**re·mu·ner·a·tive** /-rətiv/ -,rātiv/ *adj.*

Ren·ais·sance /'renə,säns; -,zäns/ ▶*the revival of art and literature under the influence of classical models in the 14th–16th centuries.* ■ the culture and style of art and architecture developed during this era. ■ [as *n.*] (**a renaissance**) a revival of or renewed interest in something: *rail travel is enjoying a renaissance.*

re·nal /'rēnl/ ▶*adj. technical* of or relating to the kidneys: *renal failure.*

re·nal pel·vis ▶*n.* see PELVIS (sense 2).

re·nas·cence /ri'nasəns; -'nāsəns/ ▶*n. formal* the revival of something that has been dormant: *the renascence of poetry as an oral art.* ■ another term for RENAISSANCE.

re·nas·cent /ri'nasənt; -'nāsənt/ ▶*adj.* becoming active or popular again: *renascent fascism.*

rend /rend/ ▶*v.* (*past* **rent** /rent/) [*tr.*] tear (something) into two or more pieces: *snapping teeth that would rend human flesh to shreds* | *fig. the speculation and confusion that was rending the civilized world.* ■ *poetic/lit.* cause great emotional pain to (a person or their heart).

ren·der /'rendər/ ▶*v.* [*tr.*] **1** provide: *money serves as a reward for services rendered.* ■ submit or present for inspection or consideration: *he would*

render income tax returns at the end of the year. ■ deliver (a verdict or judgment): *the jury's finding amounted to the clearest verdict yet rendered upon the scandal.* **2** [*tr.*] cause to be or become; make: *the rains rendered his escape impossible.* **3** represent or depict artistically: *the eyes and the cheeks are exceptionally well rendered.* ■ translate: *the phrase was rendered into English.* ■ *Mus.* perform (a piece): *a soprano solo reverently rendered by Linda Howie.* ■ *Comput.* process (an outline image) using color and shading in order to make it appear solid and three-dimensional. **4** melt down (fat): *the fat was being cut up and rendered for lard.* ■ process (the carcass of an animal) in order to extract proteins, fats, and other usable parts: [as *adj.*] (**rendered**) *the rendered down remains of sheep.* —**ren·der·er** *n.*

ren·der·ing /'rendərinG/ ▶*n.* a performance of a piece of music or drama: *her fine rendering of "Che farò senza Eurydice" was enough to win her strong commendation.* ■ a translation: *a literal rendering of an idiom.* ■ a work of visual art, esp. a detailed architectural drawing: *a consummately lifelike three-dimensional rendering of a building interior.* ■ *Comput.* the processing of an outline image using color and shading to make it appear solid and three-dimensional.

ren·dez·vous /'rändi,vōō; -dā-/ ▶*n.* (*pl.* same) a meeting at an agreed time and place, typically between two people. ■ a place used for such a meeting.
▶*v.* (**-vouses** /-,vōōz/, **-voused** /-,vōōd/, **-vous·ing** /-,vōōinG/) [*intr.*] meet at an agreed time and place: *I rendezvoused with Bea as planned.* ▷late 16th cent.: from French *rendez-vous!* 'present yourselves!,' imperative of *se rendre.*

ren·di·tion /ren'diSHən/ ▶*n.* a performance or interpretation, esp. of a dramatic role or piece of music: *a wonderful rendition of "Nessun Dorma."* ■ a visual representation or reproduction: *a pen-and-ink rendition of Mars with his sword drawn.* ■ a translation or transliteration.

ren·e·gade /'reni,gād/ ▶*n.* a person who deserts and betrays an organization, country, or set of principles. ■ a person who behaves in a rebelliously unconventional manner.
▶*adj.* having treacherously changed allegiance: *a renegade bodyguard.*

re·nege /ri'neg; -'nig/ ▶*v.* [*intr.*] go back on a promise, undertaking, or contract: *the administration had reneged on its election promises.* ■ another term for REVOKE (sense 2). —**re·neg·er** *n.*

re·new /ri'n(y)ōō/ ▶*v.* [*tr.*] resume (an activity) after an interruption: *the parents renewed their campaign to save the school.* ■ repeat (an action or statement): *detectives renewed their appeal for those in the area at the time to contact them.* ■ give fresh life or strength to: [as *adj.*] (**renewed**) *she would face the future with renewed determination.* ■ extend for a further period the validity of (a license, subscription, or contract): *her contract had not been renewed.* ■ replace (something that is broken or worn out): *check the joints—they may need renewing.* —**re·new·a·ble** *adj.* —**re·new·al** /-əl/ *n.* —**re·new·er** *n.*

ren·net /'renit/ ▶*n.* curdled milk from the stomach of an unweaned calf, containing rennin and used in curdling milk for cheese.

ren·nin /'renin/ ▶*n.* an enzyme secreted into the stomach of unweaned mammals, and produced in some lower animals and plants, causing the curdling of milk.

re·nounce /ri'nouns/ ▶*v.* [*tr.*] formally declare one's abandonment of (a claim, right, or possession): *Isabella offered to renounce her son's claim to the French crown.* ■ refuse to recognize or abide by any longer: *these agreements were renounced after the fall of the czarist regime.* ■ declare that one will no longer engage in or support: *they renounced the armed struggle.* ■ reject and stop using or consuming: *he renounced drugs and alcohol completely.* ■ [*intr.*] *Law* refuse or resign a right or position, esp. one as an heir or trustee: *there will be forms enabling the allottee to renounce.* —**re·nounce·a·ble** *adj.* —**re·nounce·ment** *n.* —**re·nounc·er** *n.*
▶ □ **renounce the world** completely withdraw from society or material affairs in order to lead a life considered to be more spiritually fulfilling.

ren·o·vate /'renə,vāt/ ▶*v.* [*tr.*] restore (something old, esp. a building) to a good state of repair: *the old school has been tastefully renovated as a private house.* —**ren·o·va·tion** /,renə'vāSHən/ *n.* —**ren·o·va·tor** /-,vātər/ *n.*

re·nown /ri'noun/ ▶*n.* the condition of being known or talked about by many people; fame: *authors of great renown.*

re·nowned /ri'nound/ ▶*adj.* known or talked about by many people; famous: *a restaurant renowned for its Peking duck.*

rent¹ /rent/ ▶*n.* a tenant's regular payment to a landlord for the use of property or land. ■ a sum paid for the hire of equipment.
▶*v.* [*tr.*] pay someone for the use of (something, typically property, land,

R

or a car): *they rented a house together in Spain* | [as *adj.*] (**rented**) *a rented apartment.* ■ (of an owner) let someone use (something) in return for payment: *he purchased a large tract of land and* **rented out** *most of it to local farmers.* ■ [*intr.*] be let or hired out at a specified rate: *skis or snowboards* **rent** *for $60–80 for six days.*

▶ □ **for rent** available to be rented.

rent² ▶ *n.* a large tear in a piece of fabric. ■ an opening or gap resembling such a tear: *they stared at the rents in the clouds.*

rent³ ▶ past and past participle of REND.

ren·tal /ˈrentl/ ▶ *n.* an amount paid or received as rent. ■ the action of renting something: *the office was* **on** *weekly* **rental.** ■ a rented house or car.
▶ *adj.* of, relating to, or available for rent: *rental properties.*

rent·er /ˈrentər/ ▶ *n.* **1** a person who rents an apartment, a car, or other object. **2** a rented car or videocassette.

re·nun·ci·a·tion /riˌnənsēˈāSHən/ ▶ *n.* the formal rejection of something, typically a belief, claim, or course of action: *entry into the priesthood requires renunciation of marriage.* —**re·nun·ci·ant** /riˈnənsēənt/ *n.* & *adj.*

re·o·ri·ent /rēˈôrē,ent/ ▶ *v.* [*tr.*] change the focus or direction of: *the will is dislodged from false values and reoriented toward God.* ■ (**reorient oneself**) find one's position again in relation to one's surroundings: *slowly they advanced, stopping every so often and then reorienting themselves.* —**re·o·ri·en·tate** /-ēən,tāt/ *v.* —**re·o·ri·en·ta·tion** /,rē,ôrēən'tāSHən/ *n.*

rep¹ /rep/ *inf.* ▶ *n.* a representative: *a union rep.* ■ a sales representative.
▶ *v.* (**repped, rep·ping**) [*intr.*] act as a sales representative for a company or product: *at eighteen she was working for her dad, repping on the road.*

rep² ▶ *n. inf.* repertory: *once, when I was in rep, I learned the part of Iago in three days.* ■ a repertory theater or company.

rep³ ▶ *n. inf.* short for REPUTATION: *I don't know why caffeine's suddenly got such a bad rep.*

rep⁴ ▶ *n.* (in bodybuilding) a repetition of a set of exercises.

re·paid /rēˈpād/ ▶ past and past participle of REPAY.

re·pair¹ /riˈpe(ə)r/ ▶ *v.* [*tr.*] fix or mend (a thing suffering from damage or a fault): *faulty electrical appliances should be repaired by an electrician.*
▶ *n.* the action of fixing or mending something: *the abandoned house they bought needs repairs.* ■ a result of such fixing or mending: *a coat of French polish was brushed over the repair.* ■ the relative physical condition of an object: *the existing hospital is in a bad* **state of repair.** —**re·pair·a·ble** *adj.* —**re·pair·er** *n.*

re·pair² ▶ *v.* [*intr.*] (**repair to**) *formal* or *humorous* go to (a place), esp. in company: *we repaired to the tranquility of a nearby café.*

rep·a·ra·ble /ˈrep(ə)rəbəl/ ▶ *adj.* (esp. of an injury or loss) possible to rectify or repair.

rep·a·ra·tion /,repəˈrāSHən/ ▶ *n.* the making of amends for a wrong one has done, by paying money to or otherwise helping those who have been wronged: *the courts required a convicted offender to* **make** *financial* **reparation** *to his victim.* ■ (**reparations**) the compensation for war damage paid by a defeated state. —**re·par·a·tive** /riˈparətiv/ *adj.*

rep·ar·tee /,repərˈtē; ,rep,ärˈtē; -ˈtā/ ▶ *n.* conversation or speech characterized by quick, witty comments or replies.

re·past /riˈpast; ˈrē,past/ ▶ *n. formal* a meal: *a sumptuous repast.*

re·pa·tri·ate /rēˈpātrē,āt; rēˈpa-/ ▶ *v.* [*tr.*] send (someone) back to their own country: *the government sought to repatriate thousands of Albanian refugees.* ■ send or bring (money) back to one's own country: *foreign firms would be permitted to repatriate all profits.*
▶ *n.* a person who has been repatriated. —**re·pa·tri·a·tion** /,rē,pātrē-ˈāSHən; ,rē,pa-/ *n.*

re·pay /rēˈpā/ ▶ *v.* (*past* and *past part.* **-paid** /rēˈpād/) [*tr.*] pay back (a loan, debt, or sum of money): *the loans were to be repaid over a 20-year period.* —**re·pay·a·ble** *adj.* —**re·pay·ment** *n.*

re·peal /riˈpēl/ ▶ *v.* [*tr.*] revoke or annul (a law or congressional act): *the legislation was repealed five months later.*
▶ *n.* the action of revoking or annulling a law or congressional act: *the House voted in favor of repeal.* —**re·peal·a·ble** *adj.*

re·peat /riˈpēt/ ▶ *v.* **1** say again something one has already said: *"Are you hurt?" he repeated.* ■ (**repeat oneself**) say or do the same thing again. ■ used for emphasis: *force was not—repeat, not—to be used.* **2** [*tr.*] do (something) again, either once or a number of times: *earlier experiments were to be repeated on a far larger scale* | [as *adj.*] (**repeated**) *there were repeated attempts to negotiate.* ■ (**repeat itself**) occur again in the same way or form: *I don't intend to let history repeat itself.* **3** [*intr.*] (of food) be tasted intermittently for some time after being swallowed as a result of belching or indigestion: *it sat rather uncomfortably on my stomach and re- peated on me for hours.*
▶ *n.* an action, event, or other thing that occurs or is done again: *the final*

will be a repeat of last year. ■ [as *adj.*] occurring, done, or used more than once: *a repeat prescription.* ■ *Mus.* a passage intended to be repeated. ■ a mark indicating this. —**re·peat·a·bil·i·ty** /ri,pētəˈbilətē/ *n.* —**re·peat·a·ble** *adj.* —**re·peat·ed·ly** *adv.*

re·peat·ing dec·i·mal ▶ *n.* a decimal fraction in which a figure or group of figures is repeated indefinitely, as in *0.666 …* or as in *1.851851851 … .*

re·pel /riˈpel/ ▶ *v.* (**-pelled, -pel·ling**) [*tr.*] **1** drive or force back or away: *government units sought to repel the rebels.* **2** be repulsive or distasteful to: *she was repelled by the permanent smell of drink on his breath.* **3** *formal* refuse to accept (something, esp. an argument or theory): *the alleged right of lien led by the bankrupt's attorney was repelled.* —**re·pel·ler** *n.*

re·pel·lent /riˈpelənt/ (also **re·pel·lant**) ▶ *adj.* **1** [often in *comb.*] able to repel a particular thing; impervious to a particular substance: *water- repellent nylon.* **2** causing disgust or distaste: *the idea was slightly repel- lent to her.*
▶ *n.* **1** a substance that dissuades particular insects or other pests from approaching or settling: *a flea repellent.* **2** a substance used to treat something, esp. fabric or stone, so as to make it impervious to water: *treat brick with a silicone water repellent.* —**re·pel·lence** *n.* —**re·pel·len·cy** *n.* —**re·pel·lent·ly** *adv.*

re·pent /riˈpent/ ▶ *v.* [*intr.*] feel or express sincere regret or remorse about one's wrongdoing or sin: *the priest urged his listeners to repent* | *he repent- ed of his action.* ■ [*tr.*] view or think of (an action or omission) with deep regret or remorse: *Marian came to repent her hasty judgment.* —**re·pent- ance** /riˈpentns/ *n.* —**re·pent·ant** /riˈpentnt/ *adj.* —**re·pent·er** *n.*

re·per·cus·sion /,rēpərˈkəSHən; ,rep-/ ▶ *n.* (usu. **repercussions**) an unin- tended consequence occurring some time after an event or action, esp. an unwelcome one: *the move would have grave repercussions for the en- tire region.* —**re·per·cus·sive** /-ˈkəsiv/ *adj.*

rep·er·toire /ˈrepə(r),twär/ ▶ *n.* a stock of plays, dances, or pieces that a company or a performer knows or is prepared to perform. ■ the whole body of items that are regularly performed: *the mainstream concert repertoire.* ■ a stock of skills or types of behavior that a person habitu- ally uses: *his repertoire of threats, stares, and denigratory gestures.*

rep·er·to·ry /ˈrepə(r),tôrē/ ▶ *n.* (*pl.* **-ries**) **1** the performance of various plays, operas, or ballets by a company at regular short intervals: [as *adj.*] *a repertory actor.* ■ repertory theaters regarded collectively. ■ a repertory company. **2** another term for REPERTOIRE. ■ a repository or collection, esp. of information or retrievable examples. —**rep·er·to·ri- al** /,repə(r)ˈtôrēəl/ *adj.*

rep·e·ti·tion /,repəˈtiSHən/ ▶ *n.* the action of repeating something that has already been said or written: *her comments are worthy of repetition.* ■ a thing repeated: *the geometric repetitions of Islamic art.* ■ a training ex- ercise that is repeated, esp. a series of repeated raisings and lowerings of the weight in weight training. —**rep·e·ti·tion·al** /-SHənl/ *adj.*

rep·e·ti·tious /,repəˈtiSHəs/ ▶ *adj.* another term for REPETITIVE. —**rep·e- ti·tious·ly** *adv.* —**rep·e·ti·tious·ness** *n.*

re·pet·i·tive /riˈpetətiv/ ▶ *adj.* containing or characterized by repetition, esp. when unnecessary or tiresome: *a repetitive task.* —**re·pet·i·tive·ly** *adv.* —**re·pet·i·tive·ness** *n.*

re·place /riˈplās/ ▶ *v.* [*tr.*] **1** take the place of: *Ian's smile was replaced by a frown.* ■ provide or find a substitute for (something that is broken, old, or inoperative): *the light bulb needs replacing.* **2** put (something) back in a previous place or position: *he drained his glass and replaced it on the bar.* —**re·place·a·ble** *adj.* —**re·plac·er** *n.*

re·place·ment /riˈplāsmənt/ ▶ *n.* the action or process of replacing some- one or something: *a hip replacement.* ■ a person or thing that takes the place of another.

re·play ▶ *v.* /rēˈplā; ˈrē-/ [*tr.*] **1** play back (a recording on tape, video, or film): *he could stop the tape and replay it whenever he wished.* ■ *fig.* repeat (something, esp. an event or sequence of events): *she replayed in her mind every detail of the night before.* **2** play (a match or contest) again to decide a winner after the original encounter ended in a draw or con- tentious result.
▶ *n.* /ˈrē,plā/ **1** the playing again of a section of a recording, esp. so as to be able to watch an incident more closely: *clouds can be studied in speeded-up replay* | *the umpire studied TV replays.* ■ *fig.* an occurrence that closely follows the pattern of a previous event: *a replay of last summer's civil disturbance.* **2** a replayed match.

re·plen·ish /riˈpleniSH/ ▶ *v.* [*tr.*] fill (something) up again: *he replenished Justin's glass with mineral water.* ■ restore (a stock or supply of some- thing) to the former level or condition: *all creatures need sleep to replen- ish their energies.* —**re·plen·ish·er** *n.* —**re·plen·ish·ment** *n.*

re·plete /riˈplēt/ ▶ *adj.* filled or well-supplied with something: *sensational popular fiction,* **replete with** *adultery and sudden death.* ■ very full of or sated by food: *I went out into the sun-drenched streets again, replete and relaxed.* —**re·ple·tion** /ri'plēsHən/ *n.*

rep·li·ca /'replikə/ ▶*n.* an exact copy or model of something, esp. one on a smaller scale: *a replica of the Empire State Building.* ■ a duplicate of an original artistic work. ▷mid 18th cent. (as a musical term in the sense 'a repeat'): from Italian, from *replicare* 'to reply.'

rep·li·cate ▶*v.* /'repli,kāt/ [*tr.*] make an exact copy of; reproduce: *it might be impractical to replicate eastern culture in the west.* ■ (**replicate itself**) (of genetic material or a living organism) reproduce or give rise to a copy of itself: *interleukin-16 prevents the virus from replicating itself.* ■ repeat (a scientific experiment or trial) to obtain a consistent result: *these findings have been replicated by Atwood and Jackson.*
▶*adj.* /-kit/ of the nature of a copy: *a replicate Earth.* ■ of the nature of a repetition of a scientific experiment or trial: *the variation of replicate measurements.*
▶*n.* /-kit/ **1** a close or exact copy; a replica. ■ a repetition of an experimental test or procedure. **2** *Mus.* a tone one or more octaves above or below the given tone. —**rep·li·ca·bil·i·ty** /,replikə'bilətē/ *n.* —**rep·li·ca·ble** /'replikəbəl/ *adj.* —**rep·li·ca·tive** /-,kātiv/ *adj.*

rep·li·ca·tion /,repli'kāsHən/ ▶*n.* **1** the action of copying or reproducing something. ■ a copy: *a twentieth-century building would be cheaper than a replication of what was there before.* ■ the repetition of a scientific experiment or trial to obtain a consistent result. ■ the process by which genetic material or a living organism gives rise to a copy of itself: *HIV replication.* **2** *dated Law* a plaintiff's reply to the defendant's plea.

re·ply /ri'plī/ ▶*v.* (**-plies**, **-plied**) say something in response to something someone has said: [*intr.*] *he was gone before we could* **reply to** *his last remark.* ■ [*intr.*] respond by a similar action or gesture: *they* **replied to** *the shelling with a heavy mortar attack on the area.*
▶*n.* (*pl.* **-plies**) a verbal or written answer: *I received a reply from the firm's managing director.* ■ a response in the form of a gesture, action, or expression: *we scored the first goal and they hit a late reply.* ■ *Law* a plaintiff's response to the defendant's plea. —**re·pli·er** *n.*

re·port /ri'pôrt/ ▶*v.* **1** give a spoken or written account of something that one has observed, heard, done, or investigated: *the representative reported a decline in milk and meat production.* ■ (**be reported**) used to indicate that something has been stated, although one cannot confirm its accuracy: *these hoaxers are reported to be hacking into airline frequencies to impersonate air traffic controllers* | [as *adj.*] (**reported**) *a reported $50,000 in debt.* ■ make a formal statement or complaint about (someone or something) to the necessary authority: *undisclosed illegalities are* **reported to** *the company's directors.* **2** [*intr.*] present oneself formally as having arrived at a particular place or as ready to do something: *he was given three days to say goodbye to his family and* **report for** *active duty.* **3** [*intr.*] (**report to**) be responsible to (a superior or supervisor): *the officers now report to the Russian president, not the Politburo.*
▶*phrasal v.* □ **report back** (or **report something back**) **1** deliver a spoken or written account of something one has been asked to do or investigate: *the deadpan voice of a police officer* **reporting back** *to his superior.* **2** return to work or duty after a period of absence. □ **report a bill out** (of a committee of Congress) return a bill to the legislative body for action.
▶*n.* **1** an account given of a particular matter, esp. in the form of an official document, after thorough investigation or consideration by an appointed person or body: *the chairman's annual report.* ■ a spoken or written description of an event or situation, esp. one intended for publication or broadcast in the media: *press reports suggested that the government was still using secret police to help maintain public order.* ■ a teacher's written assessment of a student's work, progress, and conduct, issued at the end of a term or academic year. ■ *Law* a detailed formal account of a case heard in a court, giving the main points in the judgment, esp. as prepared for publication. **2** a sudden loud noise of or like an explosion or gunfire. ▷late Middle English: from Old French *reporter* (verb), *report* (noun), from Latin *reportare* 'bring back,' from *re-* 'back' + *portare* 'carry.' The sense 'give an account' gave rise to 'submit a formal report,' hence 'inform an authority of one's presence' (sense 2, mid 19th cent.) and 'be accountable (to a superior)' (sense 3, late 19th cent.). —**re·port·a·ble** *adj.* —**re·port·ed·ly** *adj.*

re·port·age /rə'pôrtij; ,repôr'täzH/ ▶*n.* the reporting of news, for the press and the broadcast media: *extensive reportage of elections.* ■ factual presentation in a book or other text, esp. when this adopts a journalistic style.

re·port card ▶*n.* a teacher's written assessment of a student's work, progress, and conduct, sent home to a parent or guardian. ■ an evaluation of performance: *Democrat legislators fared poorly in a recent report card.*

re·port·er /ri'pôrtər/ ▶*n.* a person who reports, esp. one employed to report news or conduct interviews for newspapers or broadcasts.

re·por·to·ri·al /,repə(r)'tôrēəl; ,rē-/ ▶*adj.* of or characteristic of newspaper reporters: *reportorial ambition and curiosity.* —**re·por·to·ri·al·ly** *adv.*

re·pose[1] /ri'pōz/ ▶*n.* temporary rest from activity, excitement, or exertion. ■ sleep or the rest given by sleep: *in repose her face looked relaxed.* ■ a state of peace: *the repose of the soul of the dead man.* ■ composure: *he had lost none of his grace or his repose.* ■ *Art* harmonious arrangement of colors and forms, providing a restful visual effect.
▶*v.* [*intr.*] be lying, situated, or kept in a particular place: *the diamond now reposes in the Louvre.* —**re·pose·ful** /-fəl/ *adj.* —**re·pose·ful·ly** /-fəlē/ *adv.*

re·pose[2] ▶*v.* [*tr.*] (**repose something in**) place something, esp. one's confidence or trust, in: *we have never betrayed the trust that you have reposed in us.*

re·pos·i·to·ry /ri'päzə,tôrē/ ▶*n.* (*pl.* **-ries**) a place, building, or receptacle where things are or may be stored: *a deep repository for nuclear waste.* ■ a place in which something, esp. a natural resource, has accumulated or where it is found in significant quantities: *accessible repositories of water.* ■ a person or thing regarded as a store of information or in which something abstract is held to exist or be found: *his mind was a rich repository of the past.*

re·pos·sess /,rēpə'zes/ ▶*v.* [*tr.*] retake possession of (something) when a buyer defaults on payments: *565 homes were repossessed for nonpayment of mortgages.* —**re·pos·ses·sion** /-'zesHən/ *n.*

rep·re·hen·si·ble /,repri'hensəbəl/ ▶*adj.* deserving censure or condemnation: *his complacency and reprehensible laxity.* —**rep·re·hen·si·bil·i·ty** /-,hensə'bilətē/ *n.* —**rep·re·hen·si·bly** /-blē/ *adv.*

rep·re·sent /,repri'zent/ ▶*v.* [*tr.*] **1** be entitled or appointed to act or speak for (someone), esp. in an official capacity: *for purposes of litigation, an infant can and must be represented by an adult.* ■ (usu. **be represented**) act as a substitute for (someone), esp. on an official or ceremonial occasion: *the president was represented by the secretary of state.* **2** constitute; amount to: *this figure represents eleven percent of the company's total sales.* ■ be a specimen or example of; typify: *twenty parents, picked to represent a cross section of rural life.* ■ (**be represented**) (of a group or type of person or thing) be present or found in something, esp. to a particular degree: *abstraction is well represented in this exhibition.* **3** depict (a particular subject) in a picture or other work of art: *small wooden figures representing saints.* ■ [*tr.*] describe or depict (someone or something) as being of a certain nature; portray in a particular way: *the young were consistently represented as being in need of protection.* ■ (of a sign or symbol) have a particular signification; stand for: *the numbers 1–10 represent the letters A–Z.* **4** *formal* allege; claim: *the vendors have represented that such information is accurate.* —**rep·re·sent·a·bil·i·ty** /,repri,zentə'bilətē/ *n.* —**rep·re·sent·a·ble** *adj.*

rep·re·sen·ta·tion /,repri,zen'tāsHən; -zən-/ ▶*n.* **1** the action of speaking or acting on behalf of someone or the state of being so represented: *asylum-seekers should be guaranteed good legal advice and representation.* **2** the description or portrayal of someone or something in a particular way or as being of a certain nature: *the representation of women in newspapers.* **3** (**representations**) formal statements made to a higher authority, esp. so as to communicate an opinion or register a protest: *certain church groups are making strong representations to our government.* ■ a statement or allegation: *any buyer was relying on a representation that the tapes were genuine.* —**rep·re·sen·ta·tion·al** /-sHənl/ *adj.*

rep·re·sen·ta·tive /,repri'zentətiv/ ▶*adj.* **1** typical of a class, group, or body of opinion: *these courses are representative of those taken by most Harvard undergraduates.* **2** (of a legislative or deliberative assembly) consisting of people chosen to act and speak on behalf of a wider group. **3** serving as a portrayal or symbol of something: *the show should be more representative of how women really are.* ■ (of art) representational: *the bust involves a high degree of representative abstraction.*
▶*n.* **1** a person chosen or appointed to act or speak for another or others. **2** an example of a class or group: *fossil representatives of lampreys and hagfishes.* —**rep·re·sent·a·tive·ly** *adv.* —**rep·re·sent·a·tive·ness** *n.*

re·press /ri'pres/ ▶*v.* [*tr.*] subdue (someone or something) by force: *the uprisings were repressed.* ■ restrain or prevent (the expression of a feeling): *Isabel couldn't repress a sharp cry of fear.* ■ inhibit the natural development or self-expression of (someone or something): *too much bureaucracy represses creativity.* ■ *Biol.* prevent the transcription of (a gene). —**re·press·er** *n.* —**re·press·i·ble** /-əbəl/ *adj.* —**re·pres·sion** /ri'presHən/ *n.* —**re·pres·sive** *adj.*

re·prieve /ri'prēv/ ▸v. [tr.] cancel or postpone the punishment of (someone, esp. someone condemned to death): *under the new regime, prisoners under sentence of death were reprieved.*
▸n. a cancellation or postponement of a punishment. ■ a temporary escape from an undesirable fate or unpleasant situation: *a mother who faced eviction has been given a reprieve.* ▷late 15th cent. (as the past participle *repryed*): from Anglo-Norman French *repris*, past participle of *reprendre*, from Latin *re-* 'back' + *prehendere* 'seize.' The insertion of *-v-* (16th cent.) remains unexplained. Sense development has undergone a reversal, from the early meaning 'send back to prison,' via 'postpone (a legal process),' to the current sense 'rescue from impending punishment.'

rep·ri·mand /'reprə,mand/ ▸n. a rebuke, esp. an official one.
▸v. [tr.] rebuke (someone), esp. officially: *officials were dismissed or reprimanded for poor work.*

re·print ▸n. /'rē,print/ a copy of a book or other material that has been reprinted.

re·pris·al /ri'prīzəl/ ▸n. an act of retaliation: *three youths died in the reprisals that followed.* ■ *hist.* the forcible seizure of a foreign subject or their goods as an act of retaliation.

re·prise /ri'prēz/ ▸n. a repeated passage in music. ■ a repetition or further performance of something: *many Syrians fear a reprise of the showdown 12 years ago.*
▸v. [tr.] repeat (a piece of music or a performance).

re·pro /'rē,prō/ ▸n. (pl. **-pros**) [usu. as *adj.*] *inf.* **1** a reproduction or copy, particularly of a piece of furniture: *a Georgian repro cabinet.* **2** the action or process of copying a document or image: *a repro house.*

re·proach /ri'prōCH/ ▸v. [tr.] address (someone) in such a way as to express disapproval or disappointment: *critics of the administration reproached the president for his failure to tackle the deficiency.* ■ (**reproach someone with**) accuse someone of: *his wife reproached him with cowardice.*
▸n. the expression of disapproval or disappointment: *he gave her a look of reproach.* ■ (**a reproach to**) a thing that makes the failings of someone or something else more apparent: *his elegance is a living reproach to our slovenly habits.* —**re·proach·a·ble** *adj.* —**re·proach·er** *n.* —**re·proach·ing·ly** *adv.*
▸ □ **above** (or **beyond**) **reproach** such that no criticism can be made; perfect.

re·proach·ful /ri'prōCHfəl/ ▸*adj.* expressing disapproval or disappointment: *she gave him a reproachful look.* —**re·proach·ful·ly** *adv.* —**re·proach·ful·ness** *n.*

rep·ro·bate /'reprə,bāt/ ▸n. an unprincipled person (often used humorously or affectionately). —**rep·ro·ba·tion** /,reprə'bāSHən/ *n.*

re·proc·ess /rē'präs,es; -'präsəs; -'prō-/ ▸v. [tr.] process (something, esp. spent nuclear fuel) again or differently, typically in order to reuse it: *the costs of reprocessing radioactive waste.*

re·pro·duce /,rēprə'd(y)ōōs/ ▸v. [tr.] produce again: *a concert performance cannot reproduce all the subtleties of a recording.* ■ produce a copy or representation of: *his works are reproduced on postcards and posters.* ■ create something very similar to (something else), esp. in a different medium or context: *the problems are difficult to reproduce in the laboratory.* ■ (of an organism) produce offspring by a sexual or asexual process: *bacteria normally divide and reproduce themselves every twenty minutes.* —**re·pro·duc·er** *n.* —**re·pro·duc·i·bil·i·ty** /-,d(y)ōōsə'bilətē/ *n.* —**re·pro·duc·i·ble** *adj.* —**re·pro·duc·i·bly** /-əblē/ *adv.*

re·pro·duc·tion /,rēprə'dəkSHən/ ▸n. the action or process of making a copy of something: *the cost of color reproduction in publication is high.* ■ the production of offspring by a sexual or asexual process. ■ a copy of a work of art, esp. a print or photograph of a painting. ■ [as *adj.*] made to imitate the style of an earlier period or of a particular artist or craftsman: *reproduction French classical beds.* —**re·pro·duc·tive** /-'dəktiv/ *adj.* —**re·pro·duc·tive·ly** /-'dəktivlē/ *adv.* —**re·pro·duc·tive·ness** /-'dəktivnis/ *n.*

re·proof /ri'prōōf/ ▸n. blame: *a glance of reproof.* ■ an expression of criticism; rebuke.

re·prove /ri'prōōv/ ▸v. [tr.] reprimand or censure someone: *he was reproved for obscenity* | [as *adj.*] (**reproving**) *a reproving glance.* —**re·prov·a·ble** *adj.* —**re·prov·er** *n.* —**re·prov·ing·ly** *adv.*

rep·tile /'reptəl; 'rep,tīl/ ▸n. **1** a cold-blooded vertebrate animal of a class (Reptilia) that includes snakes, lizards, crocodiles, turtles, and tortoises. They are distinguished by having a dry scaly skin, and typically laying soft-shelled eggs on land. **2** *inf.* a person regarded with loathing and contempt.
▸*adj.* belonging to a reptile or to the class of reptiles. ▷late Middle English: from late Latin, neuter of *reptilis*, from Latin *rept-* 'crawled,' from the verb *repere.* —**rep·til·i·an** /rep'tilēən; -'tilyən/ *adj. & n.*

re·pub·lic /ri'pəblik/ ▸n. a state in which supreme power is held by the people and their elected representatives, and which has an elected or nominated president rather than a monarch.

re·pub·li·can /ri'pəblikən/ ▸*adj.* (of a form of government, constitution, etc.) belonging to, or characteristic of a republic. ■ advocating or supporting republican government: *the republican movement.*
▸n. **1** a person advocating or supporting republican government. **2** (**Republican**) a member or supporter of the Republican Party. —**re·pub·li·can·ism** /-,nizəm/ *n.*

Re·pub·li·can Par·ty ▸one of the two main U.S. political parties (the other being the Democratic Party), favoring a conservative stance, limited central government, and a strong national defense.

re·pu·di·ate /ri'pyōōdē,āt/ ▸v. [tr.] refuse to accept or be associated with: *she has repudiated policies associated with previous party leaders.* ■ deny the truth or validity of: *the minister repudiated allegations of human rights abuses.* ■ *chiefly Law* refuse to fulfill or discharge (an agreement, obligation, or debt): *breach of a condition gives the other party the right to repudiate a contract.* —**re·pu·di·a·tion** /ri,pyōōdē'āSHən/ *n.* —**re·pu·di·a·tor** /-,ātər/ *n.*

re·pug·nance /ri'pəgnəns/ ▸n. intense disgust: *our growing repugnance at the bleeding carcasses.*

re·pug·nant /ri'pəgnənt/ ▸*adj.* **1** extremely distasteful; unacceptable: *the thought of going back into the fog was repugnant to him.* **1** (**repugnant to**) in conflict with; incompatible with: *a bylaw must not be repugnant to the general law of the country.* —**re·pug·nant·ly** *adv.*

re·pulse /ri'pəls/ ▸v. [tr.] **1** drive back (an attack or attacking enemy) by force: *rioters tried to storm ministry buildings but were repulsed by police.* ■ fail to welcome (friendly advances or the person making them); rebuff: *she left, feeling hurt because she had been repulsed.* ■ refuse to accept (an offer): *his bid for the company was repulsed.* **2** (usu. **be repulsed**) cause (someone) to feel intense distaste and aversion: *audiences at early screenings of the film were repulsed by its brutality.*
▸n. the action of driving back an attacking force or of being driven back: *the repulse of the invaders.* ■ a discouraging response to friendly advances: *his evasion of her plan had been another repulse.*

re·pul·sion /ri'pəlSHən/ ▸n. **1** a feeling of intense distaste or disgust: *people talk about the case with a mixture of fascination and repulsion.* **2** *Physics* a force under the influence of which objects tend to move away from each other, e.g., through having the same magnetic polarity or electric charge.

re·pul·sive /ri'pəlsiv/ ▸*adj.* arousing intense distaste or disgust: *a repulsive smell.* ■ *archaic* lacking friendliness or sympathy. —**re·pul·sive·ly** *adv.* —**re·pul·sive·ness** *n.*

rep·u·ta·ble /'repyətəbəl/ ▸*adj.* having a good reputation: *a reputable company.* —**rep·u·ta·bly** /-blē/ *adv.*

rep·u·ta·tion /,repyə'tāSHən/ ▸n. the beliefs or opinions that are generally held about someone or something: *his reputation was tarnished by allegations that he had taken bribes.*

re·pute /ri'pyōōt/ ▸n. the opinion generally held of someone or something; the state of being generally regarded in a particular way: *pollution could bring the authority's name into bad repute.*
▸v. (**be reputed**) be generally said or believed to do something or to have particular characteristics: *he was reputed to have a fabulous house.* ■ [usu. as *adj.*] (**reputed**) be generally said or believed to exist or be of a particular type, despite not being so: *this area gave the lie to the reputed flatness of the country.* ■ [usu. as *adj.*] (**reputed**) be widely known and well thought of: *intensive training with reputed coaches.* —**re·put·ed·ly** *adv.*

re·quest /ri'kwest/ ▸n. an act of asking politely or formally for something: *a request for information.* ■ a thing that is asked for: *to have our ideas taken seriously is surely a reasonable request.* ■ an instruction to a computer to provide information or perform another function.
▸v. [tr.] politely or formally ask for: *he received the information he had requested.* ■ politely ask (someone) to do something: *the letter requested him to report to New York immediately.* —**re·quest·er** *n.*

req·ui·em /'rekwēəm; 'rā-/ ▸n. (also **requiem mass**) (esp. in the Roman Catholic Church) a Mass for the repose of the souls of the dead. ■ a musical composition setting parts of such a Mass, or of a similar character. ■ an act or token of remembrance: *he designed the epic as a requiem for his wife.*

re·quire /ri'kwīr/ ▸v. [tr.] need for a particular purpose; depend on for success or survival: *three patients required operations.* ■ cause to be necessary: *it would have required much research to produce a comprehensive list.* ■ [tr.] (of someone in authority) instruct or expect (someone) to do something: *you will be required to attend for cross-examination.* ■ (**require something of**) regard an action, ability, or quality as due from (someone) by virtue of their position: *the care and diligence required of him as a trustee.* —**re·quire·ment** *n.* —**re·quir·er** *n.*

req·ui·site /'rekwəzət/ ▸*adj.* made necessary by particular circumstances or regulations: *the application will not be processed until the requisite fee is paid.*

▶*n.* a thing that is necessary for the achievement of a specified end: *she believed privacy to be a requisite for a peaceful life.* —**req·ui·site·ly** *adv.*

req·ui·si·tion /ˌrekwəˈzishən/ ▶*n.* an official order laying claim to the use of property or materials: *I had to make various requisitions for staff and accommodations.* ■ a formal written demand that some duty should be performed or something be put into operation. ■ the appropriation of goods, esp. for military or public use.

▶*v.* [*tr.*] demand the use or supply of, esp. by official order and for military or public use: *the government had assumed powers to requisition cereal products at fixed prices.*

re·quite /riˈkwīt/ ▶*v.* [*tr.*] *formal* make appropriate return for (a favor or service); reward: *they are quick to requite a kindness.* ■ avenge or retaliate for (an injury or wrong). ■ return a favor to (someone): *to win enough to requite my friends.* ■ respond to (love or affection); return: *she did not requite his love.* —**re·quit·al** /-ˈkwītl/ *n.*

rere·dos /ˈrerəˌdäs; ˈri(ə)rə-/ ▶*n.* (*pl.* same) *Christian Church* an ornamental screen covering the wall at the back of an altar.

re·run ▶*v.* /rēˈrən/ (**-run·ning**; *past* **-ran**; *past part.* **-run**) [*tr.*] show or perform (something, esp. a television program) again.

▶*n.* /ˈrēˌrən/ a program, event, or competition that occurs or is run again: *a rerun of the Mideast crisis | watching reruns on TV.*

re·scind /riˈsind/ ▶*v.* [*tr.*] revoke, cancel, or repeal (a law, order, or agreement): *the government eventually rescinded the directive.* —**re·scind·a·ble** *adj.* —**re·scis·sion** /-ˈsizhən/ *n.*

res·cue /ˈreskyoo/ ▶*v.* (**-cues, -cued, -cu·ing**) [*tr.*] save (someone) from a dangerous or distressing situation: *firemen were called out to rescue a man trapped in the river.* ■ *inf.* keep from being lost or abandoned; retrieve: *he got out of his chair to rescue his cup of coffee.*

▶*n.* an act of saving or being saved from danger or distress: *he came to our rescue with a loan of $100.* —**res·cu·a·ble** *adj.* —**res·cu·er** *n.*

re·search /ˈrēˌsərch; riˈsərch/ ▶*n.* the systematic investigation into and study of materials and sources in order to establish facts and reach new conclusions: *we are fighting meningitis by raising money for medical research.* ■ (**researches**) acts or periods of such investigation: *his pathological researches were included in official reports.* ■ [as *adj.*] engaged in or intended for use in such investigation and discovery: *a research paper.*

▶*v.* [*tr.*] investigate systematically: *the biographer spent 25 years researching Stalin's life.* ■ discover facts by investigation for use in (a book, program, etc.): [as *adj.*] (**researched**) *this is a well-researched and readable account.* —**re·search·a·ble** *adj.* —**re·search·er** *n.*

re·search and de·vel·op·ment ▶*n.* (in industry) work directed toward the innovation, introduction, and improvement of products and processes.

re·seat /rēˈsēt/ ▶*v.* [*tr.*] cause (someone) to sit down again after they have risen: *he reseated himself in his armchair.* ■ cause to sit in a new position: *we reseated the orchestra for each variation.* ■ realign or repair (a tap, valve, or other object) in order to fit it into its correct position.

re·sem·blance /riˈzembləns/ ▶*n.* the state of resembling or being alike: *they bear some resemblance to Italian figurines.* ■ a way in which two or more things are alike: *the physical resemblances between humans and apes.*

re·sem·ble /riˈzembəl/ ▶*v.* [*tr.*] have qualities or features, esp. those of appearance, in common with (someone or something); look or seem like: *they seemed to resemble each other closely.* ▷Middle English: from Old French *resembler*, based on Latin *similare* (from *similis* 'like'). —**re·sem·bler** /-blər/ *n.* (*rare*).

re·sent /riˈzent/ ▶*v.* [*tr.*] feel bitterness or indignation at (a circumstance, action, or person): *she resented the fact that I had children.* —**re·sent·ful** *adj.* —**re·sent·ful·ly** *adv.* —**re·sent·ful·ness** *n.*

re·sent·ment /riˈzentmənt/ ▶*n.* bitter indignation at having been treated unfairly: *his resentment at being demoted.*

res·er·va·tion /ˌrezərˈvāshən/ ▶*n.* **1** the action of reserving something: *the reservation of positions for non-Americans.* ■ an area of land set aside for occupation by North American Indians or Australian Aboriginals. **2** a qualification to an expression of agreement or approval; a doubt: *some generals voiced reservations about making air strikes.*

re·serve /riˈzərv/ ▶*v.* [*tr.*] refrain from using or disposing of (something); retain for future use: *roll out half the dough and reserve the other half.* ■ arrange for (a room, seat, ticket, etc.) to be kept for the use of a particular person and not given to anyone else: *a place was reserved for her in the front row.* ■ retain or hold (an entitlement to something), esp. by formal or legal stipulation: [*tr.*] *the editor reserves the right to edit letters.* ■ refrain from delivering (a judgment or decision) immediately or without due consideration or evidence: *I'll reserve my views on his ability until he's played again.* ■ (**reserve something for**) use or engage in some-

thing only in or at (a particular circumstance or time): *Japanese food has been presented as expensive and reserved for special occasions.*

▶*n.* **1** (often **reserves**) a supply of a commodity not needed for immediate use but available if required: *Australia has major coal, gas, and uranium reserves.* ■ a force or body of troops kept back from action to reinforce or protect others, or additional to the regular forces and available in an emergency. ■ an extra player who is a possible substitute in a team. ■ (**the reserves**) the second-string team. ■ funds kept available by a bank, company, or government: *the foreign exchange reserves.* ■ a part of a company's profits added to capital rather than paid as a dividend. **2** a place set aside for special use, in particular: ■ an area designated as a habitat for a native people. ■ a protected area for wildlife. **3** a lack of warmth or openness in manner or expression: *she smiled and some of her natural reserve melted.* ■ qualification or doubt attached to some statement or claim: *she trusted him **without reserve.*** **4** short for RESERVE PRICE. —**re·serv·a·ble** *adj.* —**re·serv·er** *n.*

▶ □ **in reserve** unused and available if required: *the platoon that had been kept in reserve.*

re·served /riˈzərvd/ ▶*adj.* **1** slow to reveal emotion or opinions: *he is a reserved, almost taciturn man.* **2** kept specially for a particular purpose or person: *a reserved seat.* —**re·serv·ed·ly** /riˈzərvədlē/ *adv.* —**re·serv·ed·ness** /riˈzərvədnəs/ *n.*

re·serve price ▶*n.* the price stipulated as the lowest acceptable by the seller for an item sold at auction.

re·serv·ist /riˈzərvist/ ▶*n.* a member of the military reserve forces.

res·er·voir /ˈrezə(r)ˌvwär; -ˌv(w)ôr/ ▶*n.* a large natural or artificial lake used as a source of water supply. ■ a supply or source of something: *tapping into a universal reservoir of information.* ■ a place where fluid collects, esp. in rock strata or in the body. ■ a receptacle or part of a machine designed to hold fluid. ■ *Med.* a population, tissue, etc., that is chronically infested with the causative agent of a disease and can act as a source of further infection.

re·set /rēˈset/ ▶*v.* (**-set·ting**; *past* and *past part.* **-set**) [*tr.*] set again or differently: *I must reset the alarm.* ■ *Electr.* cause (a binary device) to enter the state representing the numeral 0. —**re·set·ta·bil·i·ty** /ˌrē,setəˈbilətē/ *n.* —**re·set·ta·ble** *adj.*

re·side /riˈzīd/ ▶*v.* [*intr.*] have one's permanent home in a particular place: *people who work in the city actually reside in neighboring towns.* ■ be situated: *the paintings now reside on the walls of a restaurant.* ■ be present or inherent in something: *the meaning of an utterance does not wholly reside in the semantic meaning.*

res·i·dence /ˈrez(ə)dəns; ˈrezəˌdens/ ▶*n.* a person's home; the place where someone lives. ■ the official house of a government minister or other public and official figure. ■ the fact of living in a particular place: *Rome was his main place of residence.*

▶ □ **in residence** living in or occupying a particular place: *the guests in residence at the hotel.* ■ (**—— in residence**) a person with a particular occupation (esp. an artist or writer) paid to work in a college or other institution. □ **take up residence** start living in a particular place.

res·i·den·cy /ˈrez(ə)dənsē; ˈrezəˌdensē/ ▶*n.* (*pl.* **-cies**) **1** the fact of living in a place: *a government ruling confirmed the returning refugees' right to residency.* ■ a residential post held by a writer, musician, or artist, typically for teaching purposes. **2** a period of specialized medical training in a hospital; the position of a resident.

res·i·dent /ˈrez(ə)dənt; ˈrezəˌdent/ ▶*n.* **1** a person who lives somewhere permanently or on a long-term basis. ■ a bird, butterfly, or other animal of a species that does not migrate. ■ a person who boards at a boarding school. **2** a medical graduate engaged in specialized practice under supervision in a hospital.

▶*adj.* living somewhere on a long-term basis: *he has been **resident in** Brazil for a long time.* ■ having quarters on the premises of one's work: *resident farm workers.* ■ attached to and working regularly for a particular institution: *the film studio needed a resident historian.* ■ (of a bird, butterfly, or other animal) nonmigratory; remaining in an area throughout the year. ■ (of a computer program, file, etc.) immediately available in computer memory, rather than having to be loaded from elsewhere. —**res·i·dent·ship** /-ˌSHip/ *n.* (*hist.*).

res·i·den·tial /ˌrezəˈdenCHəl/ ▶*adj.* designed for people to live in: *private residential and nursing homes.* ■ providing accommodations in addition to other services: *a residential college.* ■ occupied by private houses: *quieter traffic in residential areas.* ■ concerning or relating to residence: *land has been diverted from residential use.* —**res·i·den·tial·ly** *adv.*

Pronunciation Key ə *ago*, *up*; ər *over*, *fur*; a *hat*; ā *ate*; ä *car*; CH *chin*; e *let*; ē *see*; e(ə)r *air*; i *fit*; ī *by*; i(ə)r *ear*; NG *sing*; ō *go*; ô *law*, *for*; oi *toy*; oo *good*; oo *goo*; ou *out*; SH *she*; TH *thin*; TH *then*; (h)w *why*; ZH *vision*

re·sid·u·al /ri'zijo͞oəl/ ▶ *adj.* remaining after the greater part or quantity has gone: *the withdrawal of residual occupying forces.* ■ (of an experimental or arithmetical error) not accounted for or eliminated. ■ (of a soil or other deposit) formed in situ by weathering.
▶ *n.* a quantity remaining after other things have been subtracted or allowed for. ■ a difference between a value measured in a scientific experiment and the theoretical or true value. ■ a royalty paid to a performer, writer, etc., for a repeat of a play, television show, etc. ■ the resale value of a new car or other item at a specified time after purchase, expressed as a percentage of its purchase price. —**re·sid·u·al·ly** *adv.*

res·i·due /'rezə,d(y)o͞o/ ▶ *n.* a small amount of something that remains after the main part has gone or been taken or used. ■ *Law* the part of an estate that is left after the payment of charges, debts, and bequests. ■ a substance that remains after a process such as combustion or evaporation.

re·sign /ri'zīn/ ▶ *v.* **1** [*intr.*] voluntarily leave a job or other position: *he resigned from the government in protest at the policy.* ■ [*tr.*] give up (an office, power, privilege, etc.): *four deputies resigned their seats.* **2** (**be resigned**) accept that something undesirable cannot be avoided: *he seems resigned to a shortened career.* ■ *archaic* surrender oneself to another's guidance: *he vows to resign himself to her direction.* —**re·sign·ed·ly** /ri'zīnədlē/ *adv.* —**re·sign·ed·ness** /ri'zīnədnəs/ *n.* —**re·sign·er** *n.*

res·ig·na·tion /,rezig'nāSHən/ ▶ *n.* **1** an act of retiring or giving up a position: *he announced his resignation.* ■ a document conveying someone's intention of retiring: *I'm thinking of handing in my resignation.* **2** the acceptance of something undesirable but inevitable: *a shrug of resignation.*

re·sil·ient /ri'zilyənt/ ▶ *adj.* (of a substance or object) able to recoil or spring back into shape after bending, stretching, or being compressed. ■ (of a person or animal) able to withstand or recover quickly from difficult conditions: *the fish are resilient to most infections.* —**re·sil·ience** *n.* —**re·sil·ien·cy** *n.* —**re·sil·ient·ly** *adv.*

res·in /'rezən/ ▶ *n.* a sticky flammable organic substance, insoluble in water, exuded by some trees and other plants (notably fir and pine). Compare with GUM¹ (sense 1). ■ (also **synthetic resin**) a solid or liquid synthetic organic polymer used as the basis of plastics, adhesives, varnishes, or other products.
▶ *v.* (**res·ined, res·in·ing**) [*tr.*] [usu. as *adj.*] (**resined**) rub or treat with resin: *resined canvas.* —**res·in·ous** /'rezənəs/ *adj.*

re·sist /ri'zist/ ▶ *v.* [*tr.*] withstand the action or effect of: *antibodies help us to resist infection.* ■ try to prevent by action or argument: *we will continue to resist changes to the treaty.* ■ succeed in ignoring the attraction of (something wrong or unwise): *she resisted his advances | I couldn't resist buying the blouse.* ■ [*intr.*] struggle against someone or something: *without giving her time to resist, he dragged her off her feet.*
▶ *n.* a resistant substance applied as a coating to protect a surface during some process, for example to prevent dye or glaze adhering. —**re·sist·er** *n.* —**re·sist·i·ble** *adj.* —**re·sist·i·bil·i·ty** /ri,zistə'bilətē/ *n.*

re·sist·ance /ri'zistəns/ ▶ *n.* **1** the refusal to accept or comply with something; the attempt to prevent something by action or argument: *she put up no resistance to being led away.* ■ armed or violent opposition: *government forces were unable to crush guerrilla-style resistance.* ■ (also **resistance movement**) a secret organization resisting authority, esp. in an occupied country. ■ (**the Resistance**) the underground movement formed in France during World War II to fight the German occupying forces and the Vichy government. ■ the impeding, slowing, or stopping effect exerted by one material thing on another: *air resistance would need to be reduced by streamlining.* **2** the ability not to be affected by something, esp. adversely: *some of us have a lower resistance to cold than others.* ■ *Med. & Biol.* lack of sensitivity to a drug, insecticide, etc., esp. as a result of continued exposure or genetic change. **3** the degree to which a substance or device opposes the passage of an electric current, causing energy dissipation. ■ a resistor or other circuit component that opposes the passage of an electric current.
▶ □ **the line** (or **path**) **of least resistance** an option avoiding difficulty or unpleasantness; the easiest course of action.

re·sist·ant /ri'zistənt/ ▶ *adj.* offering resistance to something or someone: *some of the old churches are resistant to change | [in comb.] a water-resistant adhesive.*

re·sis·tiv·i·ty /ri,zis'tivətē/ ▶ *n.* *Physics* a measure of the resisting power of a specified material to the flow of an electric current.

re·sis·tor /ri'zistər/ ▶ *n.* *Physics* a device having a designed resistance to the passage of an electric current.

res·o·lute /'rezə,lo͞ot, -lət/ ▶ *adj.* admirably purposeful, determined, and unwavering: *she was resolute and unswerving.* —**res·o·lute·ly** *adv.* —**res·o·lute·ness** *n.*

res·o·lu·tion /,rezə'lo͞oSHən/ ▶ *n.* **1** a firm decision to do or not to do something: *she kept her resolution not to see Anne any more.* ■ a formal expression of opinion or intention agreed on by a legislative body, committee, or other formal meeting, typically after taking a vote: *the conference passed two resolutions.* ■ the quality of being determined or resolute: *he handled the last French actions of the war with resolution.* **2** the action of solving a problem, dispute, or contentious matter: *the peaceful resolution of all disputes.* ■ *Mus.* the passing of a discord into a concord during the course of changing harmony. ■ *Med.* the disappearance of inflammation, or of any other symptom or condition. **3** *Physics* the replacing of a single force or other vector quantity by two or more jointly equivalent to it. ■ the conversion of something abstract into another form. **4** the smallest interval measurable by a scientific (esp. optical) instrument; the resolving power. ■ the degree of detail visible in a photographic or television image.

re·solve /ri'zälv; -'zôlv/ ▶ *v.* **1** [*tr.*] settle or find a solution to (a problem, dispute, or contentious matter): *the firm aims to resolve problems within 30 days.* ■ [*tr.*] *Med.* cause (a symptom or condition) to disperse, subside, or heal: *endoscopic biliary drainage can rapidly resolve jaundice.* ■ [*intr.*] (of a symptom or condition) disperse, subside, or heal: *symptoms resolved after a median of four weeks.* ■ [*tr.*] *Mus.* (of a discord) lead into a concord during the course of harmonic change. ■ [*tr.*] *Mus.* cause (a discord) to pass into a concord. **2** [*intr.*] decide firmly on a course of action: *she resolved to call Dana as soon as she got home.* **3** *chiefly Chem.* separate or cause to be separated into components. ■ [*intr.*] (of something seen at a distance) turn into a different form when seen more clearly: *the orange glow resolved itself into four lanterns.* ■ [*tr.*] (of optical or photographic equipment) separate or distinguish between (closely adjacent objects): *Hubble was able to resolve six variable stars in M31.* ■ [*tr.*] separately distinguish (peaks in a graph or spectrum). ■ [*tr.*] *Physics* analyze (a force or velocity) into components acting in particular directions.
▶ *n.* firm determination to do something: *she received information that strengthened her resolve.* —**re·solv·a·bil·i·ty** /ri,zälvə'bilətē; -'zôlvə-/ *n.* —**re·solv·a·ble** *adj.* —**re·solv·er** *n.*

res·o·nance /'rezənəns/ ▶ *n.* the quality in a sound of being deep, full, and reverberating: *the resonance of his voice.* ■ *fig.* the ability to evoke or suggest images, memories, and emotions: *the concepts lose their emotional resonance.* ■ *Physics* the reinforcement or prolongation of sound by reflection from a surface or by the synchronous vibration of a neighboring object. ■ *Mechanics* the condition in which an object or system is subjected to an oscillating force having a frequency close to its own natural frequency.

res·o·nant /'rezənənt/ ▶ *adj.* (of sound) deep, clear, and continuing to sound or ring: *a full-throated and resonant guffaw.* ■ (of a room, a musical instrument, or a hollow body) tending to reinforce or prolong sounds, esp. by synchronous vibration. ■ (of a color) enhancing or enriching another color or colors by contrast. ■ (**resonant with**) (of a place) filled or resounding with the sound of something: *alpine valleys resonant with the sound of church bells.* —**res·o·nant·ly** *adv.*

res·o·nate /'rezn,āt/ ▶ *v.* [*intr.*] produce or be filled with a deep, full, reverberating sound: *the sound of the siren resonated across the harbor.* ■ *fig.* evoke or suggest images, memories, and emotions: *the words resonate with so many different meanings.* ■ (of an idea or action) meet with someone's agreement: *the judge's ruling resonated among many of the women.* ■ *technical* produce electrical or mechanical resonance: *the crystal resonates at 16 MHz.* —**res·o·na·tor** /-,nātər/ *n.*

re·sort /ri'zôrt/ ▶ *n.* **1** a place that is a popular destination for vacations or recreation, or which is frequented for a particular purpose: *a seaside resort | a health resort.* ■ *archaic* the tendency of a place to be frequented by many people: *places of public resort.* **2** the action of turning to and adopting a strategy or course of action, esp. a disagreeable or undesirable one, so as to resolve a difficult situation: *Germany and Italy tried to resolve their economic and social failures by resort to fascism.* ■ a strategy or course of action that may be adopted in a difficult situation: *her only resort is surgery.*
▶ *v.* [*intr.*] (**resort to**) **1** turn to and adopt (a strategy or course of action, esp. a disagreeable or undesirable one) so as to resolve a difficult situation: *the duke was prepared to resort to force if negotiation failed.* **2** *formal* go often or in large numbers to: *local authorities have a duty to provide adequate sites for gypsies "residing in or resorting to" their areas.*
▶ □ **as a first** (or **last** or **final**) **resort** before anything else is attempted (or when all else has failed). □ **in the last resort** ultimately: *in the last resort what really moves us is our personal convictions.*

re·sound /ri'zound/ ▶ *v.* [*intr.*] (of a sound, voice, etc.) fill a place with sound; be loud enough to echo: *another scream resounded through the school.* ■ (of a place) be filled or echo with a particular sound or sounds: *the office resounds with the metronomic clicking of keyboards.* ■ *fig.* (of fame, a person's reputation, etc.) be much talked of: *whatever they do in the nineties will not resound in the way that their earlier achievements did.*

re·sound·ing /ri'zoundɪNG/ ▶*adj.* **1** (of a sound) loud enough to reverberate: *a resounding smack across the face.* **2** unmistakable; emphatic: *the evening was a resounding success.* —**re·sound·ing·ly** *adv.*

re·source /'rē,sôrs; 'rē'zôrs; ri·sôrs; ri'zôrs/ ▶*n.* **1** (usu. **resources**) a stock or supply of money, materials, staff, and other assets that can be drawn on by a person or organization in order to function effectively: *local authorities complained that they lacked resources.* **2** an action or strategy that may be adopted in adverse circumstances: *sometimes anger is the only resource left in a situation like this.* ■ (**resources**) one's personal attributes and capabilities regarded as able to help or sustain one in adverse circumstances: *we had been left very much to our own resources.* ■ the ability to find quick and clever ways to overcome difficulties: *a man of resource.* ■ a teaching aid.

▶*v.* [*tr.*] provide (a person or organization) with materials, money, staff, and other assets necessary for effective operation: *ensuring that primary health care workers are adequately resourced.* —**re·source·ful** *adj.* —**re·source·ful·ness** *n.* —**re·source·less** *adj.* —**re·source·less·ness** *n.*

re·spect /ri'spekt/ ▶*n.* **1** a feeling of deep admiration for someone or something elicited by their abilities, qualities, or achievements: *the director had a lot of **respect for** Douglas as an actor.* ■ due regard for the feelings, wishes, rights, or traditions of others: ***respect for** human rights.* ■ (**respects**) a person's polite greetings: *give my respects to your parents.* **2** a particular aspect, point, or detail: *the government's record **in this respect** is a mixed one.*

▶*v.* [*tr.*] admire (someone or something) deeply, as a result of their abilities, qualities, or achievements: *she was respected by everyone she worked with* | [as *adj.*] (**respected**) *a respected academic.* ■ have due regard for the feelings, wishes, rights, or traditions of: *I respected his views.* ■ avoid harming or interfering with: *it is incumbent upon all boaters to respect the environment.* ▷late Middle English: from Latin *respectus*, from the verb *respicere* 'look back at, regard,' from *re-* 'back' + *specere* 'look at.' —**re·spec·ter** *n.*

re·spect·a·ble /ri'spektəbəl/ ▶*adj.* **1** regarded by society to be good, proper, or correct: *they thought the stage no life for a respectable lady.* ■ (of a person's appearance, clothes, or behavior) decent or presentable: *a perfectly respectable pair of pajamas!* **2** of some merit or importance: *a respectable botanical text.* ■ adequate or acceptable in number, size, or amount: *America's GDP grew by a respectable 2.6 percent.* —**re·spec·ta·bil·i·ty** /ri,spektə'bilitē/ *n.* —**re·spec·ta·bly** /-blē/ *adv. an architecture of respectably high standards.*

re·spect·ful /ri'spektfəl/ ▶*adj.* feeling or showing deference and respect: *they sit in respectful silence.* —**re·spect·ful·ly** *adv.* —**re·spect·ful·ness** *n.*

re·spect·ing /ri'spektɪNG/ ▶*prep. dated* or *formal* with reference or regard to: *he began to have serious worries respecting his car.*

re·spec·tive /ri'spektiv/ ▶*adj.* belonging or relating separately to each of two or more people or things: *they chatted about their respective childhoods.* —**re·spec·tive·ly** *adv.*

res·pi·ra·tion /,respə'rāSHən/ ▶*n.* the action of breathing: *opiates affect respiration.* ■ *chiefly Med.* a single breath. ■ *Biol.* a process in living organisms involving the production of energy, typically with the intake of oxygen and the release of carbon dioxide from the oxidation of complex organic substances. —**res·pi·ra·to·ry** /'respərə,tôrē/ *adj.*

res·pi·ra·tor /'respə,rātər/ ▶*n.* an apparatus worn over the mouth and nose or the entire face to prevent the inhalation of dust, smoke, or other noxious substances. ■ an apparatus used to induce artificial respiration.

res·pite /'respət; ri'spīt/ ▶*n.* a short period of rest or relief from something difficult or unpleasant: *the refugee encampments will provide some **respite from** the suffering.*

re·splend·ent /ri'splendənt/ ▶*adj.* attractive and impressive through being richly colorful or sumptuous: *she was **resplendent in** a sea-green dress.* —**re·splend·ence** *n.* —**re·splend·en·cy** *n.* —**re·splend·ent·ly** *adv.*

re·spond /ri'spänd/ ▶*v.* say something in reply: [*intr.*] *she could not get Robert to **respond to** her words.* ■ (of a congregation) say or sing the response in reply to a priest. ■ [*intr.*] (of a person) act or behave in reaction to someone or something: *she turned her head, **responding to** his grin with a smile.* ■ react quickly or positively to a stimulus or treatment: *his back injury has failed to respond to treatment.* —**re·spond·er** *n.*

re·spond·ent /ri'spändənt/ ▶*n.* **1** a defendant in a lawsuit, esp. one in an appeals or divorce case. **2** a person who replies to something, esp. one supplying information for a survey or questionnaire or responding to an advertisement.

▶*adj.* **1** replying to something, esp. a survey or questionnaire: *the*

respondent firms in the survey. **2** *Psychol.* involving or denoting a response, esp. a conditioned reflex, to a specific stimulus.

re·sponse /ri'späns/ ▶*n.* a verbal or written answer: *without waiting for a response, she returned to her newspaper.* ■ a reaction to something: *an extended, jazzy piano solo drew the biggest **response from** the crowd.* ■ *Psychol. & Physiol.* an excitation of a nerve impulse caused by a change or event; a physical reaction to a specific stimulus or situation. ■ the way in which a mechanical or electrical device responds to an input or a range of inputs. ■ (usu. **responses**) a part of a religious liturgy said or sung by a congregation in answer to a minister or cantor.

re·spon·si·bil·i·ty /ri,spänsə'bilitē/ ▶*n.* (*pl.* **-ties**) the state or fact of having a duty to deal with something or of having control over someone: *women bear children and **take responsibility for** child care.* ■ the opportunity or ability to act independently and make decisions without authorization: *we would expect individuals lower down the organization to take on more responsibility.* ■ (often **responsibilities**) a thing that one is required to do as part of a job, role, or legal obligation: *he will take over the responsibilities of overseas director.* ■ (**responsibility to/toward**) a moral obligation to behave correctly toward or in respect of: *individuals have a responsibility to control personal behavior.*

re·spon·si·ble /ri'spänsəbəl/ ▶*adj.* having an obligation to do something, or having control over or care for someone, as part of one's job or role: *the department **responsible for** education.* ■ being the primary cause of something and so able to be blamed or credited for it: *the gene was **responsible for** a rare type of eye cancer.* ■ (of a job or position) involving important duties, independent decision-making, or control over others. ■ (**responsible to**) having to report to (a superior or someone in authority) and be answerable to them for one's actions: *the team manager is responsible to the league president.* ■ capable of being trusted: *a responsible adult.* ■ morally accountable for one's behavior: *the progressive emergence of the child as a responsible being.* —**re·spon·si·ble·ness** *n.* —**re·spon·si·bly** /-blē/ *adv.*

re·spon·sive /ri'spänsiv/ ▶*adj.* **1** reacting quickly and positively: *a flexible service that is **responsive to** changing social and economic patterns.* **2** answering: *I'm distracted by a nibble on my line: I jig it several times, but there is no responsive tug.* —**re·spon·sive·ly** *adv.* —**re·spon·sive·ness** *n.*

rest¹ /rest/ ▶*v.* [*intr.*] **1** cease work or movement in order to relax, refresh oneself, or recover strength: *he needed to rest after the feverish activity.* ■ (of a dead person or body) lie buried: *the king's body rested in his tomb.* ■ (of a problem or subject) be left without further investigation, discussion, or treatment: *the council has urged the planning committee not to allow the matter to rest.* **2** [*intr.*] be placed or supported so as to stay in a specified position: *her elbow was resting on the arm of the sofa.* ■ [*tr.*] place (something) so that it is supported in a specified position: *he rested a hand on her shoulder.* ■ (**rest on/upon**) (of a look) alight or be steadily directed on: *his eyes rested briefly on the boy.* ■ (**rest on/upon**) be based on or grounded in; depend on: *the country's security rested on its alliances.* ■ [*tr.*] (**rest something in/on**) place hope, trust, or confidence on or in: *she rested her hopes in her attorney.* ■ belong or be located at a specified place or with a specified person: *ultimate control rested with the founders.*

▶*n.* **1** an instance or period of relaxing or ceasing to engage in strenuous or stressful activity: *you look as though you need a rest.* ■ refreshment through sleep: *she curled up in a corner to get some rest.* ■ a motionless state: *the car accelerates rapidly from rest.* ■ *Mus.* an interval of silence of a specified duration. ■ *Mus.* the sign denoting such an interval. ■ [in *place names*] a place where people can stay: *we spent the night at Riverview Rest.* **2** [in *comb.*] an object that is used to support something: *a shoulder-rest.*

▶ □ **at rest** not moving or exerting oneself. ■ not agitated or troubled; tranquil: *he felt at rest, the tension gone.* □ **give it a rest** *inf.* used to ask someone to stop doing something or talking about something that the speaker finds irritating or tedious. □ **rest one's case** conclude one's presentation of evidence and arguments in a lawsuit. ■ *humorous* said to show that one believes one has presented sufficient evidence for one's views.

rest² ▶*n.* the remaining part of something: *what do you want to do for the rest of your life?* | *I'll tell you the rest tomorrow night.* ■ [treated as *pl.*] the remaining people or things; the others: *the rest of us were experienced skiers.*

▶*v.* [*intr.*] remain or be left in a specified condition: *you can rest assured she will do everything she can to help her.*

re·state /rē'stāt/ ▶*v.* [*tr.*] state (something) again or differently, esp. in order to correct or to make more clear or convincing: *he restated his op-position to abortion* | [as adj.] *restated earnings.* **—re·state·ment** *n.*

res·tau·rant /'rest(ə)rənt; 'restə,ränt; 'res,tränt/ ▶*n.* a place where people pay to sit and eat meals that are cooked and served on the premises.

res·tau·ra·teur /,restərə'tər/ ▶*n.* a person who owns and manages a restaurant.

rest·ful /'restfəl/ ▶*adj.* having a quiet and soothing quality: *the rooms were cool and restful.* **—rest·ful·ly** *adv.* **—rest·ful·ness** *n.*

rest home ▶*n.* a residential institution where old or frail people are cared for.

res·ti·tu·tion /,restə't(y)o͞oSHən/ ▶*n.* **1** the restoration of something lost or stolen to its proper owner: *seeking the restitution of land taken from blacks under apartheid.* **2** recompense for injury or loss: *he was ordered to pay $6,000 in restitution.* **3** the restoration of something to its original state: *restitution of the damaged mucosa.* **—res·ti·tu·tive** /'restə,t(y)o͞otiv/ *adj.*

res·tive /'restiv/ ▶*adj.* unable to keep still or silent and becoming increasingly difficult to control, esp. because of impatience, dissatisfaction, or boredom. **—res·tive·ly** *adv.* **—res·tive·ness** *n.*

rest·less /'restləs/ ▶*adj.* (of a person or animal) unable to rest or relax as a result of anxiety or boredom: *the audience grew restless and inattentive.* ■ offering no physical or emotional rest; involving constant activity or motion: *a restless night.* **—rest·less·ly** *adv.* **—rest·less·ness** *n.*

res·to·ra·tion /,restə'rāSHən/ ▶*n.* **1** the action of returning something to a former owner, place, or condition: *the restoration of Andrew's sight.* ■ the process of repairing or renovating a building, work of art, vehicle, etc., so as to restore it to its original condition: *the altar paintings seem in need of restoration.* ■ the reinstatement of a previous practice, right, custom, or situation: *the restoration of capital punishment.* ■ *Dentistry* a structure provided to replace or repair dental tissue so as to restore its form and function, such as a filling, crown, or bridge. **2** the return of a hereditary monarch to a throne, a head of state to government, or a regime to power. ■ (**the Restoration**) the reestablishment of Charles II as King of England in 1660. ■ (**Restoration**) [usu. as *adj.*] the period following this, esp. with regard to its literature or architecture: *Restoration drama.*

re·stor·a·tive /ri'stôrətiv/ ▶*adj.* having the ability to restore health, strength, or a feeling of well-being: *the restorative power of long walks.* ■ *Surgery & Dentistry* relating to or concerned with the restoration of form or function to a damaged tooth or other part of the body.
▶*n.* something, esp. a medicine or drink, that restores health, strength, or well-being. **—re·stor·a·tive·ly** *adv.*

re·store /ri'stôr/ ▶*v.* [*tr.*] bring back (a previous right, practice, custom, or situation); reinstate: *the government restored confidence in the housing market.* ■ return (someone or something) to a former condition, place, or position: *the effort to **restore** him **to** office isn't working.* ■ repair or renovate (a building, work of art, vehicle, etc.) so as to return it to its original condition: *the building has been lovingly restored.* **—re·stor·a·ble** *adj.* **—re·stor·er** *n.*

re·strain /ri'strān/ ▶*v.* [*tr.*] prevent (someone or something) from doing something; keep under control or within limits: *he had to be **restrained** from walking out of the meeting* | [as adj.] (**restraining**) *Cara put a restraining hand on his arm.* ▷Middle English: from Old French *restreign-*, stem of *restreindre*, from Latin *restringere*, from *re-* 'back' + *stringere* 'to tie, pull tight.' **—re·strain·a·ble** *adj.* **—re·strain·er** *n.*

re·strained /ri'strānd/ ▶*adj.* characterized by reserve or moderation; unemotional or dispassionate: *he had restrained manners.* ■ (of color, clothes, decoration, etc.) understated and subtle; not excessively showy or ornate: *kept under control; prevented from freedom of movement or action: *a patch of land turned into a restrained wilderness.* **—re·strain·ed·ly** /ri'strānidlē/ *adv.*

re·straint /ri'strānt/ ▶*n.* **1** (often **restraints**) a measure or condition that keeps someone or something under control or within limits: *decisions are made within the financial restraints of the budget.* ■ the action of keeping someone or something under control. ■ deprivation or restriction of personal liberty or freedom of movement: *he remained aggressive and required physical restraint.* ■ a device that limits or prevents freedom of movement: *car safety restraints.* **2** unemotional, dispassionate, or moderate behavior; self-control: *he urged the protesters to exercise restraint.* ■ understatement, esp. of artistic expression: *with strings and piano, all restraint vanished.*

re·strict /ri'strikt/ ▶*v.* [*tr.*] put a limit on; keep under control: *some roads may have to be closed at peak times to restrict the number of visitors.* ■ deprive (someone or something) of freedom of movement or action: *cities can **restrict** groups of protesters **from** gathering on a residential street.*
■ (**restrict someone to**) limit someone to only doing or having (a par-

ticular thing) or staying in (a particular place): *I shall restrict myself to a single example.* ■ (**restrict something to**) limit something, esp. an activity, to (a particular place, time, or category of people): *the zoological gardens were at first restricted to members and their guests.*

re·stric·tion /ri'strikSHən/ ▶*n.* (often **restrictions**) a limiting condition or measure, esp. a legal one: *planning restrictions on commercial development.* ■ the limitation or control of someone or something, or the state of being limited or restricted: *the restriction of local government power.* **—re·stric·tion·ism** /-,nizəm/ *n.* **—re·stric·tion·ist** /-nist/ *adj. & n.*

re·stric·tive /ri'striktiv/ ▶*adj.* **1** imposing restrictions or limitations on someone's activities or freedom: *a web of restrictive regulations.* **2** *Gram.* (of a relative clause or descriptive phrase) serving to specify the particular instance or instances being mentioned. **—re·stric·tive·ly** *adv.* **—re·stric·tive·ness** *n.*

rest·room /'rest,ro͞om; -,ro͝om/ (also **rest room**) ▶*n.* a bathroom in a public building.

re·struc·ture /rē'strəkCHər/ ▶*v.* [*tr.*] organize differently: *a plan to strengthen and restructure the department* | [as *n.*] (**restructuring**) *the restructuring of this wing of the Louvre.* ■ *Finance* convert (the debt of a business in difficulty) into another kind of debt, typically one that is repayable at a later time.

re·struc·tur·ing /rē'strəkCHəriNG/ ▶*n.* *Commerce* a reorganization of a company with a view to achieving greater efficiency and profit, or to adapt to a changing market.

re·style ▶*v.* /rē'stīl/ [*tr.*] **1** rearrange or remake in a new shape or layout: *Nick restyled Rebecca's hair.* **2** give a new designation to: [*tr.*] *the division has restyled the branch the Lovejoy Line.*
▶*n.* /'rēstīl/ an instance of reshaping or rearranging something. ■ a new shape or arrangement.

re·sult /ri'zəlt/ ▶*n.* a consequence, effect, or outcome of something: *the tower collapsed **as a result of** safety violations.* ■ an item of information obtained by experiment or some other scientific method; a quantity or formula obtained by calculation. ■ (often **results**) a final score, mark, or placing in a sporting event or examination.
▶*v.* [*intr.*] occur or follow as the consequence of something: *government unpopularity **resulting from** the state of the economy* | [as *adj.*] (**resulting**) *talk of a general election and the resulting political uncertainty.* ■ (**result in**) have (a specified end or outcome): *talks in July had resulted in stalemate.*
▶ □ **without result** in vain: *Danny had inquired about getting work, without result.*

re·sult·ant /ri'zəltnt/ ▶*adj.* occurring or produced as a result or consequence of something: *restructuring and the resultant cost savings.*
▶*n.* *technical* a force, velocity, or other vector quantity that is equivalent to the combined effect of two or more component vectors acting at the same point.

re·sume /ri'zo͞om/ ▶*v.* [*tr.*] begin to do or pursue (something) again after a pause or interruption: *a day later normal service was resumed.* ■ [*intr.*] begin to be done, pursued, or used again after a pause or interruption: *hostilities had ceased and normal life had resumed.* ■ take, pick up, or put on again; return to the use of: *the judge resumed his seat.*
▶*n.* variant spelling of RÉSUMÉ. **—re·sum·a·ble** *adj.* **—re·sump·tion** /ri'zəmpSHən/ *n.*

ré·su·mé /'rezə,mā; ,rezə'mā/ (also **re·su·mé** or **re·su·me**) ▶*n.* **1** a curriculum vitae. **2** a summary: *I gave him a quick résumé of events.*

re·sur·face /rē'sərfəs/ ▶*v.* **1** [*tr.*] put a new coating on or reform (a surface such as a road, a floor, or ice). **2** [*intr.*] come back up to the surface: *he resurfaced beside the boat.* ■ arise or become evident again: *serious concerns about the welfare of animals eventually resurfaced.*

re·sur·gent /ri'sərjənt/ ▶*adj.* increasing or reviving after a period of little activity, popularity, or occurrence: *resurgent nationalism.* **—re·sur·gence** *n.*

res·ur·rect /,rezə'rekt/ ▶*v.* [*tr.*] restore (a dead person) to life: *he queried whether Jesus was indeed resurrected.* ■ revive the practice, use, or memory of (something); bring new vigor to: *the deal collapsed and has yet to be resurrected.*

res·ur·rec·tion /,rezə'rekSHən/ ▶*n.* the action or fact of resurrecting or being resurrected: *the story of the resurrection of Osiris.* ■ (**the Resurrection**) (in Christian belief) Christ's rising from the dead. ■ (**the Resurrection**) (in Christian belief) the rising of the dead at the Last Judgment. ■ the revitalization or revival of something: *the resurrection of the country under a charismatic leader.*

re·sus·ci·tate /ri'səsə,tāt/ ▶*v.* [*tr.*] revive (someone) from unconsciousness or apparent death: *an ambulance crew tried to resuscitate him.* ■ *fig.* make (something such as an idea or enterprise) active or vigorous again: *measures to resuscitate the ailing Japanese economy.* **—re·sus·ci·ta·**

tion /ri,səsə'tāsHən/ *n.* —**re·sus·ci·ta·tive** /-,tātiv/ *adj.* —**re·sus·ci·ta·tor** /-,tātər/ *n.*

re·tail /'rē,tāl/ ▶*n.* the sale of goods to the public in relatively small quantities for use or consumption rather than for resale: [as *adj.*] *the product's retail price.*
▶*adv.* being sold in such a way: *it is not yet available retail.*
▶*v.* [*tr.*] **1** /'rē,tāl/ sell (goods) to the public in such a way: *the difficulties in retailing the new products.* ■ [*intr.*] (**retail at/for**) (of goods) be sold in this way for (a specified price): *the product retails for around $20.* **2** /'rē,tāl; ri-'tāl/ recount or relate details of (a story or event) to others: *his inimitable way of retailing a diverting anecdote.* —**re·tail·er** *n.*

re·tain /ri'tān/ ▶*v.* continue to have (something); keep possession of: *built in 1830, the house retains many of its original features.* ■ absorb and continue to hold (a substance): *limestone is known to retain water.* ■ [often as *adj.*] (**retaining**) keep (something) in place; hold fixed: *remove the retaining bar.* ■ keep (someone) engaged in one's service: *he has been retained as a freelance.* ■ secure the services of (a person, esp. an attorney) with a preliminary payment: *retain an attorney to handle the client's business.* —**re·tain·a·bil·i·ty** /ri,tānə'bilətē/ *n.* —**re·tain·a·ble** *adj.* —**re·tain·ment** *n.*

re·tain·er /ri'tānər/ ▶*n.* **1** a thing that holds something in place: *a guitar string retainer.* ■ an appliance for keeping a loose tooth, an orthodontic prosthesis, or orthodontically aligned teeth in place. **2** a fee paid in advance to someone, esp. an attorney, in order to secure or keep their services when required. **3** a servant or follower of a noble or wealthy person, esp. one that has worked for a person or family for a long time.

re·take ▶*v.* /rē'tāk; 'rē-/ (*past* **-took**; *past part.* **-taken**) [*tr.*] take again, in particular: ■ take (a test or examination) again after a failure or irregularity: *Dan had to retake his driving test.* ■ recapture: *in 799, the Moors retook Barcelona.* ■ regain possession of (something left or lost): *he retook the world driver's championship.* ■ reshoot a movie sequence or a photograph, or re-record a piece of music.
▶*n.* /'rē,tāk/ a thing that is retaken, esp. a test or examination. ■ an instance of filming a scene, taking a photograph, or recording a piece of music again.

re·tal·i·ate /ri'talē,āt/ ▶*v.* [*intr.*] make an attack or assault in return for a similar attack: *the blow stung and she retaliated immediately.* —**re·tal·i·a·tion** /ri,talē'āsHən/ *n.* —**re·tal·i·a·tive** /ri'talē,ātiv; -ēətiv/ *adj.* —**re·tal·i·a·tor** /-,ātər/ *n.* —**re·tal·i·a·to·ry** /ri'talēə,tôrē/ *adj.*

re·tard ▶*v.* /ri'tärd/ [*tr.*] delay or hold back in terms of progress, development, or accomplishment: *his progress was retarded by his limp.*
▶*n.* /'rē,tärd/ *offens.* a mentally handicapped person (often used as a general term of abuse). —**re·tar·dant** /-'tärdnt/ *n.* —**re·tar·da·tion** /,rē,tär-'dāsHən; ri-/ *n.* —**re·tard·er** *n.* —**re·tard·ment** *n.* (*rare*).

re·tard·ed /ri'tärdid/ ▶*adj.* less advanced in mental, physical, or social development than is usual for one's age.

retch /rECH/ ▶*v.* [*intr.*] make the sound and movement of vomiting. ■ vomit.

re·ten·tion /ri'tenCHən/ ▶*n.* the continued possession, use, or control of something: *the retention of direct control by central government.* ■ the action of absorbing and continuing to hold a substance: *the soil's retention of moisture.*

re·ten·tive /ri'tentiv/ ▶*adj.* **1** (of a person's memory) having the ability to remember facts and impressions easily. **2** (of a substance) able to absorb and hold moisture. —**re·ten·tive·ly** *adv.* —**re·ten·tive·ness** *n.*

re·think ▶*v.* /rē'THiNGk/ (*past* and *past part.* **-thought**) [*tr.*] think again about (something such as a policy or course of action), esp. in order to make changes to it: *the government was forced to rethink its plans* | [*intr.*] *I've had to rethink.*
▶*n.* /'rē,THiNGk/ a reassessment of something, esp. one that results in changes being made: *a last-minute rethink of their tactics.*

ret·i·cent /'retəsənt/ ▶*adj.* not revealing one's thoughts or feelings readily: *she was extremely reticent about her personal affairs.* —**ret·i·cence** *n.* —**ret·i·cent·ly** *adv.*

re·tic·u·lum /ri'tikyələm/ ▶*n.* (*pl.* **-la** /-lə/) **1** a fine network or netlike structure. **2** *Zool.* the second stomach of a ruminant, having a honeycomblike structure, receiving food from the rumen and passing it to the omasum. —**re·tic·u·lar** /-lər/ *adj.* —**re·tic·u·la·tion** /ri,tikyə'lāsHən/ *n.*

ret·i·na /'retn-ə/ ▶*n.* (*pl.* **ret·i·nas** or **ret·i·nae** /'retn,ē; 'retn,ī/) a layer at the back of the eyeball containing cells that are sensitive to light and that trigger nerve impulses that pass via the optic nerve to the brain, where a visual image is formed. —**ret·i·nal** /'retn-əl/ *adj.*

ret·i·nal scan·ner ▶*n.* a device that scans a person's or animal's retina in infrared for identification purposes.

ret·i·nol /'retn,ôl; -,ōl/ ▶*n.* *Biochem.* a yellow compound found in green and yellow vegetables, egg yolk, and fish-liver oil. It is essential for growth and vision in dim light. Also called **VITAMIN A**.

ret·i·nue /'retn,(y)ō͞o/ ▶*n.* a group of advisers, assistants, or others accompanying an important person.

re·tire /ri'tī(ə)r/ ▶*v.* **1** [*intr.*] leave one's job and cease to work, typically upon reaching the normal age for leaving employment: *he retired from the navy in 1966.* ■ [*tr.*] compel (an employee) to leave their job, esp. before they have reached such an age: *the home office retired him.* ■ (of an athlete) withdraw from a race or match, typically as a result of accident or injury: *he was forced to retire to the bench.* ■ [*tr.*] *Baseball* put out (a batter); cause (a side) to end a turn at bat: *the pitcher retired twelve batters in a row.* ■ [*tr.*] *Econ.* withdraw (a bill or note) from circulation or currency. ■ *Finance* pay off or cancel (a debt): *the debt is to be retired from state gaming-tax receipts.* **2** withdraw to or from a particular place: *she retired into the bathroom with her toothbrush.* ■ go to bed: *everyone retired early that night.* —**re·tir·ee** /ri,tī'rē/ *n.* —**re·tir·er** *n.*

re·tired /ri'tīrd/ ▶*adj.* **1** having left one's job and ceased to work: *a retired teacher.* **2** (of a person's way of life) quiet and involving little contact with other people. —**re·tired·ness** *n.* (*archaic*).

re·tire·ment /ri'tīrmənt/ ▶*n.* **1** the action or fact of leaving one's job and ceasing to work: *a man nearing retirement.* ■ the period of one's life after leaving one's job and ceasing to work: *he spent much of his retirement traveling in Europe.* **2** the withdrawal of a jury from the courtroom to decide their verdict. ■ the period of time during which a jury decides their verdict: *a three-hour retirement.* **3** seclusion: *he lived in retirement in Miami.*

re·tir·ing /ri'tīriNG/ ▶*adj.* shy and fond of being on one's own: *a retiring, acquiescent woman.* —**re·tir·ing·ly** *adv.*

re·tool /rē'tōōl/ ▶*v.* [*tr.*] equip (a factory) with new or adapted tools. ■ adapt or alter (someone or something) to make them more useful or suitable: *he likes to retool the old stories to make them relevant for today's kids.* ■ [*intr.*] adapt or prepare oneself for something: *perhaps one can even retool for the afterlife.*

re·tort[1] /ri'tôrt/ ▶*v.* say something in answer to a remark or accusation, typically in a sharp, angry, or wittily incisive manner: [with *direct speech*] *"No need to be rude," retorted Isabel.*
▶*n.* a sharp, angry, or wittily incisive reply to a remark: *she opened her mouth to make a suitably cutting retort.*

re·tort[2] ▶*n.* a container or furnace for carrying out a chemical process on a large or industrial scale.

re·touch /rē'təCH/ ▶*v.* [*tr.*] improve or repair (a painting, a photograph, makeup, etc.) by making slight additions or alterations. —**re·touch·er** *n.*

re·trace /rē'trās/ ▶*v.* [*tr.*] go back over (the same route that one has just taken): *he began to retrace his steps to the parking lot.* ■ discover and follow (a route or course taken by someone else): *I've tried to retrace some of her movements.* ■ trace (something) back to its source or beginning: *I wanted to retrace a particular evolutionary pathway.*

re·tract /ri'trakt/ ▶*v.* [*tr.*] draw or pull (something) back or back in: *she retracted her hand as if she'd been burned.* ■ withdraw (a statement or accusation) as untrue or unjustified: *he retracted his allegations.* ■ withdraw or go back on (an undertaking or promise): *the parish council was forced to retract a previous resolution.* ■ [*intr.*] be drawn back into something: *the tentacle retracted quickly.* —**re·tract·a·ble** *adj.* —**re·trac·tion** /ri'traksHən/ *n.* —**re·trac·tive** /-'tiv/ *adj.*

re·trac·tor /ri'traktər/ ▶*n.* a device for retracting something: *seat belts with automatic retractors.* ■ (also **retractor muscle**) *chiefly Zool.* a muscle serving to retract a part of the body.

re·trans·mit /,rētrans'mit; -tranz-/ ▶*v.* (**-mit·ted**, **-mit·ting**) [*tr.*] transmit (data, a radio signal, or a broadcast program) again or on to another receiver. —**re·trans·mis·sion** /-'misHən/ *n.*

re·tread ▶*v.* /rē'tred/ **1** (*past* **-trod**; *past part.* **-trod·den**) [*tr.*] go back over (a path or one's steps): *they never retread the same ground.* **2** (*past* and *past part.* **-tread·ed**) [*tr.*] put a new tread on (a worn tire).
▶*n.* /'rē,tred/ a tire that has been given a new tread. ■ *inf.* a person retrained for new work or recalled for service. ■ *inf.* a superficially altered version of an original: *a retread of the 30s romantic comedy.*

re·treat /ri'trēt/ ▶*v.* [*intr.*] (of an army) withdraw from enemy forces as a result of their superior power or after a defeat: *the French retreated in disarray.* ■ move back or withdraw, esp. so as to remove oneself from a difficult or uncomfortable situation: *it becomes so hot that the lizards retreat into the shade* | [as *adj.*] (**retreating**) *the sound of retreating footsteps.* ■ (of an expanse of ice or water) become smaller in size or extent: *a series of trenches which filled with water when the ice retreated.* ■ change one's

Pronunciation Key ə *ago,* up; ər *over,* fur; a *hat;* ā *ate;* ä *car;* CH *chin;* e *let;* ē *see;* e(ə)r *air;* i *fit;* ī *by;* i(ə)r *ear;* NG *sing;* ō *go;* ô *law, for;* oi *toy;* ō͞o *good;* ō͞o *goo;* ou *out;* SH *she;* TH *thin;* TH *then;* (h)w *why;* ZH *vision*

decisions, plans, or attitude, as a result of criticism from others: *his proposals were clearly unreasonable and he was soon forced to retreat.*
▶ *n.* **1** an act of moving back or withdrawing: *a speedy retreat.* ■ an act of changing one's decisions, plans, or attitude, esp. as a result of criticism from others: *the unions made a retreat from their earlier position.* **2** a signal for a military force to withdraw: *the bugle sounded a retreat.* ■ a military musical ceremony carried out at sunset. **3** a quiet or secluded place in which one can rest and relax: *their mountain retreat in New Hampshire.* ■ a period of seclusion for the purposes of prayer and meditation: *the bishop is away on his annual retreat.*

re·trench /rɪˈtrɛnCH/ ▶ *v.* [*intr.*] (of a company, government, or individual) reduce costs or spending in response to economic difficulty: *as a result of the recession the company retrenched* | [*tr.*] *if people are forced to retrench their expenditure trade will suffer.* ■ [*tr.*] *formal* reduce or diminish (something) in extent or quantity: *fortune had retrenched her once abundant gifts.* —**re·trench·ment** *n.*

ret·ri·bu·tion /ˌretrəˈbyo͞oSHən/ ▶ *n.* punishment that is considered to be morally right and fully deserved: *settlers drove the Navajo out of Arizona in retribution for their raids.* —**re·trib·u·tive** /rɪˈtribyətiv/ *adj.* —**re·trib·u·to·ry** /rɪˈtribyə,tôrē/ *adj.*

re·trieve /rɪˈtrēv/ ▶ *v.* [*tr.*] get (something) back; regain possession of: *I was sent to retrieve the balls from his garden.* ■ bring (something) back into one's mind: *the hope hope to encourage him to retrieve forgotten memories.* ■ find or extract (information stored in a computer). ■ put right or improve (an unwelcome situation): *he made one last desperate attempt to retrieve the situation.* —**re·triev·a·bil·i·ty** /rɪ,trēvəˈbilətē/ *n.* —**re·triev·a·ble** *adj.* —**re·triev·al** /-ˈtrēvəl/ *n.*

re·triev·er /rɪˈtrēvər/ ▶ *n.* **1** a dog of a breed used for retrieving game. **2** a person or thing that retrieves something.

ret·ro[1] /ˈretrō/ ▶ *adj.* imitative of a style, fashion, or design from the recent past: *retro 60s fashions.*
▶ *n.* clothes or music whose style or design is imitative of those of the recent past: *a look that mixes Italian casual wear and American retro.*

ret·ro[2] ▶ *n.* (*pl.* **-tros**) short for RETROROCKET.

ret·ro·ac·tive /ˌretrōˈaktiv/ ▶ *adj.* (esp. of legislation) taking effect from a date in the past: *a big retroactive tax increase.* —**ret·ro·ac·tion** /-ˈakSHən/ *n.* —**ret·ro·ac·tive·ly** *adv.* —**ret·ro·ac·tiv·i·ty** /-,akˈtivətē/ *n.*

re·trod /rēˈträd/ ▶ past of RETREAD (sense 1).

re·trod·den /rēˈträdn/ ▶ past participle of RETREAD (sense 1).

ret·ro·fit /ˌretrōˈfit/ ▶ *v.* (**-fit·ted, -fit·ting**) [*tr.*] add (a component or accessory) to something that did not have it when manufactured: *drivers who retrofit catalysts to older cars.* ■ provide (something) with a component or accessory not fitted to it during manufacture: *buses have been retrofitted with easy-access features.*
▶ *n.* an act of adding a component or accessory to something that did not have it when manufactured. ■ a component or accessory added to something after manufacture.

ret·ro·flex /ˈretrəˌfleks/ (also **ret·ro·flexed**) ▶ *adj. Anat. & Med.* turned backward: *a retroflex fibers.* ■ *Phonet.* pronounced with the tip of the tongue curled up toward the hard palate: *the retroflex /r/.* —**ret·ro·flex·ion** /ˌretrəˈflekSHən/ *n.*

ret·ro·gra·da·tion /ˌretrōgrāˈdāSHən/ ▶ *n. Astron. & Astrol.* the apparent temporary reverse motion of a planet (from east to west), resulting from the relative orbital progress of the earth and the planet. ■ the orbiting or rotation of a planet or planetary satellite in a reverse direction from that normal in the solar system.

ret·ro·grade /ˈretrəˌgrād/ ▶ *adj.* directed or moving backward: *a retrograde flow.* ■ reverting to an earlier and inferior condition: *to go back on the progress that has been made would be a retrograde step.* ■ (of the order of something) reversed; inverse: *the retrograde form of these inscriptions.* ■ (of amnesia) involving the period immediately preceding the causal event. ■ *Geol.* (of a metamorphic change) resulting from a decrease in temperature or pressure. ■ *Astron. & Astrol.* (of the apparent motion of a planet) in a reverse direction from normal (from east to west), resulting from the relative orbital progress of the earth and the planet. ■ *Astron.* (of the orbit or rotation of a planet or planetary satellite) in a reverse direction from that normal in the solar system.
▶ *v.* [*intr.*] **1** *archaic* go back in position or time: *our history must retrograde for the space of a few pages.* ■ revert to an earlier and usually inferior condition: *people cannot habitually trample on law and justice without retrograding toward barbarism.* **2** *Astron.* show retrogradation: *all the planets will at some time appear to retrograde.* —**ret·ro·grade·ly** *adv.* (*rare*).

ret·ro·gress /ˌretrəˈgres/ ▶ *v.* [*intr.*] go back to an earlier state, typically a worse one: *she retrogressed to the starting point of her rehabilitation.* —**ret·ro·gres·sion** *n.*

ret·ro·rock·et /ˈretrōˌräkit/ ▶ *n.* a small auxiliary rocket on a spacecraft or missile, fired in the direction of travel to slow the craft down, for example, when landing on the surface of a planet.

ret·ro·spect /ˈretrəˌspekt/ ▶ *n.* a survey or review of a past course of events or period of time.
▶ □ **in retrospect** when looking back on a past event or situation; with hindsight: *perhaps, in retrospect, I shouldn't have gone.*

ret·ro·spec·tion /ˌretrəˈspekSHən/ ▶ *n.* the action of looking back on or reviewing past events or situations, esp. those in one's own life: *he was disinclined to indulge in retrospection.*

ret·ro·spec·tive /ˌretrəˈspektiv/ ▶ *adj.* looking back on or dealing with past events or situations: *our survey was retrospective.* ■ (of an exhibition or compilation) showing the development of an artist's work over a period of time. ■ (of a statute or legal decision) taking effect from a date in the past: *retrospective pay awards.*
▶ *n.* an exhibition or compilation showing the development of the work of a particular artist over a period of time: *a Georgia O'Keeffe retrospective.* —**ret·ro·spec·tive·ly** *adv.*

ret·ro·vi·rus /ˌretrōˈvīrəs; ˈretrō,vīrəs/ ▶ *n. Biol.* any of a group of RNA viruses that insert a DNA copy of their genome into the host cell in order to replicate, e.g., HIV.

re·turn /rɪˈtərn/ ▶ *v.* **1** [*intr.*] come or go back to a place or person: *he returned to Canada in the fall.* ■ (**return to**) go back to (a particular state or activity): *Ollie had returned to full health.* **2** [*tr.*] give, put, or send (something) back to a place or person: *complete the application form and return it to this address.* ■ feel, say, or do (the same feeling, action, etc.) in response: *she returned his kiss.* **3** [*tr.*] yield or make (a profit): *the company returned a profit of 4.3 million dollars.* **4** [*tr.*] (of an electorate) elect (a person or party) to office: *the Democrat was returned in the third district.*
▶ *n.* **1** an act of coming or going back to a place or activity: *he celebrated his safe return from the war.* ■ an act of going back to an earlier state or condition: *the designer advocated a return to elegance.* ■ the action of giving, sending, or putting something back: *we demand the return of our books and papers.* ■ *Football* a play in which the ball is caught after a kick or pass interception and is advanced by running; an advance of this kind. ■ (in tennis and other sports) a stroke played in response to a serve or other stroke by one's opponent. ■ a thing that has been given or sent back, esp. an unwanted ticket for a sports event or play. ■ (also **return ticket**) *chiefly Brit.* a ticket that allows someone to travel to a place and back again; a round trip ticket. **2** (often **returns**) a profit from an investment: *product areas are being developed to produce maximum returns.* ■ a good rate of return. **3** an official report or statement submitted in response to a formal demand: *census returns.* ■ *Law* an endorsement or report by a court officer or sheriff on a writ. **4** election to office: *we campaigned for the return of Young and Elkins.* ■ an official report of the results of an election: *falsification of the election return.* **5** a key pressed to move the carriage of an electric typewriter back to a fixed position. ■ (also **return key**) a key pressed on a computer keyboard to simulate a carriage return in a word-processing program, or to indicate the end of a command or data string. —**re·turn·a·ble** *adj.* —**re·turn·er** *n.*
▶ □ **in return** as a response, exchange, or reward for something: *he leaves the house to his sister in return for her kindness.*

re·turn·ee /rɪ,tərˈnē/ ▶ *n.* a person who returns, esp. after a prolonged absence, in particular: ■ a member of the armed forces returning from overseas duty. ■ a traveler returning home. ■ a refugee returning from abroad.

re·u·ni·fy /rēˈyo͞onə,fī/ ▶ *v.* (**-fies, -fied**) [*tr.*] restore political unity to (a place or group, esp. a divided territory): *communist insurgents had effectively reunified the country.* —**re·u·ni·fi·ca·tion** /,rē,yo͞onəfiˈkāSHən/ *n.*

re·un·ion /rēˈyo͞onyən/ ▶ *n.* an instance of two of more people coming together again after a period of separation. ■ a social gathering attended by members of a certain group of people who have not seen each other for some time: *a school reunion.* ■ the act of process of being brought together again as a unified whole: *the reunion of East and West Germany.*

re·u·nite /,rēyo͞oˈnīt/ ▶ *v.* come together or cause to come together again after a period of separation or disunity: [*intr.*] *the three friends reunited in 1959* | [*tr.*] *Stephanie was reunited with her parents.*

re·use ▶ *v.* /rēˈyo͞oz/ [*tr.*] use again or more than once: *the tape could be magnetically erased and reused.*
▶ *n.* /rēˈyo͞os/ the action of using something again: *the ballast was cleaned and ready for reuse.* —**re·us·a·ble** /rēˈyo͞ozəbəl/ *adj.*

rev /rev/ *inf.* ▶ *n.* (usu. **revs**) a revolution of an engine per minute: *an engine speed of 1,750 revs.* ■ an act of increasing the speed of revolution of a vehicle's engine by pressing the accelerator, esp. while the clutch is disengaged.
▶ *v.* (**revved, rev·ving**) [*tr.*] increase the running speed of (an engine) or

the engine speed of (a vehicle) by pressing the accelerator, esp. while the clutch is disengaged: *he got into the car, **revved up** the engine and drove off* | [*intr.*] *I **revved up** enthusiastically.* ■ [*intr.*] (of an engine or vehicle) operate with increasing speed when the accelerator is pressed, esp. while the clutch is disengaged: *he could hear the sound of an engine revving nearby.*

Rev. ▶*abbr.* ■ *Bible* the book of Revelation. ■ (as the title of a priest) Reverend.

re·val·ue /rēˈvalyoō/ ▶*v.* (**-val·ues, -val·ued, -val·u·ing**) [*tr.*] assess the value of (something) again. ■ *Econ.* adjust the value of (a currency) in relation to other currencies. —**re·val·u·a·tion** /rē,valyoōˈāSHən/ *n.*

re·vamp /rēˈvamp/ ▶*v.* [*tr.*] give new and improved form, structure, or appearance to: *an attempt to revamp the museum's image* | [as *adj.*] (**re·vamped**) *a revamped magazine.*
▶*n.* an act of improving the form, structure, or appearance of something. ■ a new and improved version: *the show was a revamp of an old idea.*

re·veal¹ /riˈvēl/ ▶*v.* [*tr.*] make (previously unknown or secret information) known to others: *Brenda was forced to reveal Robbie's whereabouts.* ■ cause or allow (something) to be seen: *the clouds were breaking up to reveal a clear blue sky.* —**re·veal·a·ble** *adj.* —**re·veal·er** *n.*

re·veal² ▶*n.* either side surface of an aperture in a wall for a door or window.

rev·eil·le /ˈrevəlē/ ▶*n.* a signal sounded esp. on a bugle or drum to wake personnel in the armed forces.

rev·el /ˈrevəl/ ▶*v.* (**rev·eled, rev·el·ing**; *chiefly Brit.* **rev·elled, rev·el·ling**) [*intr.*] engage in lively and noisy festivities, esp. those which involve drinking and dancing: [as *n.*] (**reveling**) *a night of drunken reveling.* ■ (**revel in**) get great pleasure from (a situation or experience): *Bill said he was secretly reveling in his new-found fame.*
▶*n.* (**revels**) lively and noisy festivities, esp. those which involve drinking and dancing. ▷*late Middle English:* from Old French *reveler* 'rise up in rebellion,' from Latin *rebellare* 'to rebel.' —**rev·el·er** or **rev·el·ler** *n.* —**rev·el·ry** *n.*

rev·e·la·tion /,revəˈlāSHən/ ▶*n.* **1** a surprising and previously unknown fact, esp. one that is made known in a dramatic way: *revelations about his personal life.* ■ the making known of something that was previously secret or unknown: *the revelation of an alleged plot to assassinate the king.* ■ used to emphasize the surprising or remarkable quality of someone or something: *seeing them play at international level was a revelation.* **2** the divine or supernatural disclosure to humans of something relating to human existence or the world: *a divine revelation.* ■ (**Revelation** or *inf.* **Revelations**) (in full **the Revelation of St. John the Divine**) the last book of the New Testament, recounting a divine revelation of the future to St. John. —**rev·e·la·tion·al** /-SHənl/ *adj.*

re·vel·a·to·ry /ˈrevələ,tôrē; riˈvel-/ ▶*adj.* revealing something hitherto unknown: *an invigorating and revelatory performance.*

re·venge /riˈvenj/ ▶*n.* the action of inflicting hurt or harm on someone for an injury or wrong suffered at their hands: *other spurned wives have taken public **revenge** on their husbands.* ■ the desire to inflict such retribution: *it was difficult not to be overwhelmed with feelings of hate and revenge.*
▶*v.* (**revenge oneself** or **be revenged**) *chiefly archaic poetic/lit.* inflict hurt or harm on someone for an injury or wrong done to oneself: *I'll be **revenged on** the whole pack of you.* ■ [*tr.*] inflict such retribution on behalf of (someone else): *it's a pity he chose that way to revenge his sister.* ■ inflict retribution for (a wrong or injury done to oneself or another): *her brother was slain, and she revenged his death.* —**re·veng·er** *n.* (*poetic/lit.*).

re·venge·ful /riˈvenjfəl/ ▶*adj.* eager for revenge. —**re·venge·ful·ly** *adv.* —**re·venge·ful·ness** *n.*

rev·e·nue /ˈrevə,n(y)oō/ ▶*n.* income, esp. when of a company or organization and of a substantial nature. ■ (**revenues**) items or amounts constituting such income: *the government's tax revenues.* ■ the government department collecting such income.

re·verb /ˈrē,vərb; riˈvərb/ ▶*n.* an effect whereby the sound produced by an amplifier or an amplified musical instrument is made to reverberate slightly. ■ a device for producing such an effect.

re·ver·ber·ate /riˈvərbə,rāt/ ▶*v.* [*intr.*] (of a loud noise) be repeated several times as an echo: *her deep booming laugh reverberated around the room.* ■ (of a place) appear to vibrate or be disturbed because of a loud noise: *the hall reverberated with gaiety and laughter.* ■ have continuing and serious effects: *the statements by the professor reverberated through the capitol.* —**re·ver·ber·ant** /-rənt/ *adj.* —**re·ver·ber·ant·ly** /-rəntlē/ *adv.* —**re·ver·ber·a·tion** /ri,vərbəˈrāSHən/ *n.* —**re·ver·ber·a·tive** /-rətiv/ *adj.* —**re·ver·ber·a·tor** /-,rātər/ *n.* —**re·ver·ber·a·to·ry** /-rə,tôrē/ *adj.*

re·vere /riˈvi(ə)r/ ▶*v.* [*tr.*] (often **be revered**) feel deep respect or admiration for (something): *Cézanne's still lifes were revered by his contemporaries.*

rev·er·ence /ˈrev(ə)rəns/ ▶*n.* deep respect for someone or something: *rituals showed honor and reverence for the dead.* ■ (**His/Your Reverence**) a title given to a member of the clergy, or used in addressing them.
▶*v.* [*tr.*] regard or treat with deep respect: *the many divine beings reverenced by Hindu tradition.*

rev·er·end /ˈrev(ə)rənd; ˈrevərnd/ ▶*adj.* (usu. **Reverend**) used as a title or form of address to members of the clergy: *the Reverend Jesse Jackson.*
▶*n. inf.* a member of the clergy.

rev·er·ent /ˈrev(ə)rənt; ˈrevərnt/ ▶*adj.* feeling or showing deep and solemn respect: *a reverent silence.* —**rev·er·ent·ly** *adv.*

rev·er·en·tial /,revəˈrenCHəl/ ▶*adj.* of the nature of, due to, or characterized by reverence: *their names are always mentioned in reverential tones.* —**rev·er·en·tial·ly** *adv.*

rev·er·ie /ˈrevərē/ ▶*n.* a state of being pleasantly lost in one's thoughts; a daydream: *a knock on the door broke her reverie.* ■ *Mus.* an instrumental piece suggesting a dreamy or musing state.

re·ver·sal /riˈvərsəl/ ▶*n.* a change to an opposite direction, position, or course of action: *a dramatic reversal in population decline in the Alps* | *the reversal of tidal currents.* ■ *Law* an annulment of a judgment, sentence, or decree made by a lower court or authority: *the Court has upheld the appellate justices in their reversal of the trial court judgment.* ■ an adverse change of fortune: *the league champions suffered a reversal at the finals last month.* ■ *Photog.* direct production of a positive image from an exposed film or plate; direct reproduction of a positive or negative image.

re·verse /riˈvərs/ ▶*v.* [*intr.*] move backward: *the truck reversed into the back of a bus.* ■ [*tr.*] cause (a vehicle) to move backward: *I got in the car, reversed it and drove it up the driveway.* ■ [*tr.*] turn (something) the other way around or up or inside out: [as *adj.*] (**reversed**) *a reversed S-shape.* ■ [*tr.*] make (something) the opposite of what it was: *the damage done to the ozone layer may be reversed.* ■ [*tr.*] exchange (the position or function) of two people or things: *the experimenter and the subject reversed roles and the experiment was repeated.* ■ [*tr.*] *Law* revoke or annul (a judgment, sentence, or decree made by a lower court or authority): *the court reversed his conviction.* ■ (of an engine) work in a contrary direction: *the ship's engines reversed and cut out altogether.*
▶*adj.* going in or turned toward the direction opposite to that previously stated: *the trend appears to be going in the reverse direction.* ■ operating, behaving, or ordered in a way contrary or opposite to that which is usual or expected: *here are the results in reverse order.* ■ *Geol.* denoting a fault or faulting in which a relative downward movement occurred in the strata situated on the underside of the fault plane.
▶*n.* **1** a complete change of direction or action: *the growth actuates a reverse of photosynthesis.* ■ reverse gear on a motor vehicle; the position of a gear lever or selector corresponding to this. ■ (**the reverse**) the opposite or contrary to that previously stated: *he didn't feel homesick—quite the reverse.* ■ an adverse change of fortune; a setback or defeat: *the team suffered its heaviest reverse of the season.* **2** the opposite side or face to the observer: *the address is given on the reverse of this leaflet.* ■ a left-hand page of an open book, or the back of a loose document. ■ the side of a coin or medal bearing the value or secondary design. ■ the design or inscription on this side. See also OBVERSE (sense 1). —**re·verse·ly** *adv.* —**re·vers·er** *n.* —**re·vers·i·ble** *adj.* —**re·vers·i·bly** *adv.*
▶ □ **reverse the charges** make the recipient of a telephone call responsible for payment.

re·ver·sion /riˈvərzHən/ ▶*n.* **1** a return to a previous state, practice, or belief: *there was some reversion to polytheism* | *a **reversion to** the two-party system.* ■ *Biol.* the action of reverting to a former or ancestral type. **2** *Law* the right, esp. of the original owner or their heirs, to possess or succeed to property on the death of the present possessor or at the end of a lease: *the reversion of property.* ■ a property to which someone has such a right. ■ the right of succession to an office or post after the death or retirement of the holder: *he was given a promise of **the reversion** of Boraston's job.* —**re·ver·sion·ar·y** /-,nerē/ *adj.*

re·vert /riˈvərt/ ▶*v.* [*intr.*] (**revert to**) return to (a previous state, condition, practice, etc.): *he reverted to his native language.* ■ *Biol.* return to (a former or ancestral type): *it is impossible that a fishlike mammal will actually revert to being a true fish.* ■ *Law* (of property) return or pass to (the original owner) by reversion. —**re·vert·er** *n.* (*Law*).

re·vet·ment /riˈvetmənt/ ▶*n.* (esp. in fortification) a retaining wall or facing of masonry or other material, supporting or protecting a rampart, wall, etc. ■ a barricade of earth or sandbags set up to provide protection from blast or to prevent planes from overrunning when landing.

re·view /riˈvyoō/ ▶*n.* **1** a formal assessment or examination of something with the possibility or intention of instituting change if necessary: *a comprehensive review of defense policy.* ■ a critical appraisal of a book, play, movie, exhibition, etc., published in a newspaper or magazine. ■ [often in *names*] a periodical publication with critical articles on current events, the arts, etc. ■ *Law* a reconsideration of a judgment, sentence, etc., by a higher court or authority: *a review of her sentence.* ■ a survey or evaluation of a particular subject: *a review of recent developments in multicultural education.* **2** a ceremonial display and formal inspection of military or naval forces, typically by a sovereign, commander in chief, or high-ranking visitor.

▶ *v.* [*tr.*] **1** examine or assess (something) formally with the possibility or intention of instituting change if necessary: *the company's safety procedures are being reviewed.* ■ write a critical appraisal of (a book, play, movie, etc.) for publication in a newspaper or magazine: *I reviewed his first novel.* ■ survey or evaluate (a particular subject): *in the next chapter we review a number of recent empirical studies.* **2** (of a sovereign, commander in chief, or high-ranking visitor) make a ceremonial and formal inspection of (military or naval forces). **3** view or inspect visually for a second time or again: *all slides were then reviewed by one pathologist.* ▷late Middle English (as a noun denoting a formal inspection of military or naval forces): from obsolete French *reveue*, from *revoir* 'see again.' —**re·view·a·ble** *adj.* —**re·view·al** /-'vyoōəl/ *n.* —**re·view·er** *n.*

re·vile /ri'vīl/ ▶ *v.* [*tr.*] (usu. **be reviled**) criticize in an abusive or angrily insulting manner: *he was now reviled by the party that he had helped to lead.* —**re·vile·ment** *n.* —**re·vil·er** *n.*

re·vise /ri'vīz/ ▶ *v.* [*tr.*] reconsider and alter (something) in the light of further evidence: *he had cause to revise his opinion a moment after expressing it.* ■ reexamine and make alterations to (written or printed matter): *the book was published in 1960 and revised in 1968* | [as *adj.*] (**revised**) *a revised edition.* ■ alter so as to make more efficient or realistic: [as *adj.*] (**revised**) *the revised finance and administrative groups.* ▶ *n. Printing* a proof including corrections made in an earlier proof. —**re·vis·a·ble** *adj.* —**re·vis·al** /-'vīzəl/ *n.* —**re·vis·er** *n.* —**re·vi·so·ry** /-'vīzərē/ *adj.*

re·vi·sion /ri'vizhən/ ▶ *n.* the action of revising: *the plan needs drastic revision.* ■ a revised edition or form of something. —**re·vi·sion·ar·y** /-,nerē/ *adj.*

re·vi·sion·ism /ri'vizhə,nizəm/ ▶ *n. often derog.* a policy of revision or modification, esp. of Marxism on evolutionary socialist (rather than revolutionary) or pluralist principles. ■ the theory or practice of revising one's attitude to a previously accepted situation or point of view. —**re·vi·sion·ist** *n.* & *adj.*

re·vis·it /rē'vizit/ ▶ *v.* (**-vis·it·ed, -vis·it·ing**) [*tr.*] come back to or visit again: *he'll revisit old friends* | [as *adj.*] (**revisited**) *the battle of Midway revisited.*

re·vi·tal·ize /rē'vītl,īz/ ▶ *v.* [*tr.*] imbue (something) with new life and vitality: *a package of spending cuts to revitalize the economy.* —**re·vi·tal·i·za·tion** /rē,vītl-ə'zāshən/ *n.*

re·viv·al /ri'vīvəl/ ▶ *n.* an improvement in the condition or strength of something: *an economic revival.* ■ an instance of something becoming popular, active, or important again: *cross-country skiing is enjoying a revival.* ■ a new production of an old play or similar work. ■ a reawakening of religious fervor, esp. by means of a series of evangelistic meetings: *the revivals of the nineteenth century.* ■ such a meeting or series of meetings: *an usher for the revival had the job of helping the sick who went up to seek healing.*

re·viv·al·ism /ri'vīvə,lizəm/ ▶ *n.* belief in or the promotion of a revival of religious fervor. ■ a tendency or desire to revive a former custom or practice: *French rococo revivalism.* —**re·viv·al·ist** *n.* & *adj.* —**re·viv·al·is·tic** /-,vīvə'listik/ *adj.*

re·vive /ri'vīv/ ▶ *v.* [*tr.*] restore to life or consciousness: *both men collapsed, but were revived.* ■ [*intr.*] regain life, consciousness, or strength: *she was beginning to revive from her faint.* ■ give new strength or energy to: *the cool, refreshing water revived us all.* ■ improve the position or condition of: *the paper made panicky attempts to revive falling sales.* —**re·viv·a·ble** *adj.* —**re·viv·er** *n.*

re·voke /ri'vōk/ ▶ *v.* [*tr.*] put an end to the validity or operation of (a decree, decision, or promise): *the men appealed and the sentence was revoked.* —**re·voc·a·ble** *adj.* —**rev·o·ca·tion** /,revə'kāshən; ri,vō-/ *n.* —**re·vo·ca·to·ry** /'revəkə,tôrē; ri'vōkə-/ *adj.* —**re·vok·er** *n.*

re·volt /ri'vōlt/ ▶ *v.* **1** [*intr.*] rise in rebellion: *the insurgents revolted and had to be suppressed.* ■ refuse to acknowledge someone or something as having authority: *voters may revolt when they realize the cost of the measures.* **2** [often **be revolted**] cause to feel disgust: *he was revolted by the stench that greeted him* | [as *adj.*] (**revolting**) *revolting green scum.* ▶ *n.* an attempt to put an end to the authority of a person or body by rebelling: *a countrywide revolt against the central government.* ■ a refusal to

continue to obey or conform: *a revolt over tax increases.* —**re·volt·ing·ly** *adv.*

rev·o·lu·tion /,revə'loōshən/ ▶ *n.* **1** a forcible overthrow of a government or social order in favor of a new system. ■ (**the Revolution**) the American Revolution. ■ (often **the Revolution**) (in Marxism) the class struggle that is expected to lead to political change and the triumph of communism. ■ a dramatic and wide-reaching change in the way something works or is organized or in people's ideas about it: *marketing underwent a revolution.* **2** an instance of revolving: *one revolution a second.* ■ motion in orbit or a circular course or around an axis or center. ■ the single completion of an orbit or rotation. —**rev·o·lu·tion·ism** /-,nizəm/ *n.* —**rev·o·lu·tion·ist** /-nist/ *n.*

rev·o·lu·tion·ar·y /,revə'loōshə,nerē/ ▶ *adj.* engaged in or promoting political revolution: *the revolutionary army.* ■ (**Revolutionary**) of or relating to the American Revolution. ■ involving or causing a complete or dramatic change: *a revolutionary new drug.* ▶ *n.* (*pl.* **-ar·ies**) a person who works for or engages in political revolution.

rev·o·lu·tion·ize /,revə'loōshə,nīz/ ▶ *v.* [*tr.*] change (something) radically or fundamentally: *this fabulous new theory will revolutionize the whole of science.*

re·volve /ri'välv; ri'vôlv/ ▶ *v.* [*intr.*] move in a circle on a central axis: *overhead, the fan revolved slowly.* ■ (**revolve around/about**) move in a circular orbit around: *the earth revolves around the sun.* ■ (**revolve around**) treat as the most important point or element: *her life revolved around her husband.* ■ [*tr.*] consider (something) repeatedly and from different angles: *her mind revolved the possibilities.*

re·volv·er /ri'välvər; -'vôl-/ ▶ *n.* a pistol with revolving chambers enabling several shots to be fired without reloading.

revolver

re·volv·ing door ▶ *n.* an entrance to a large building in which four partitions turn about a central axis. ■ used to refer to a situation in which the same events or problems recur in a continuous cycle: *many patients are trapped in a revolving door of admission, discharge, and readmission.* ■ [usu. as *adj.*] a place or organization that people tend to enter and leave very quickly: *the newsroom became a revolving-door workplace.* ■ used to refer to a situation in which someone moves from an influential government position to a position in a private company, or vice versa.

re·vue /ri'vyoō/ ▶ *n.* a light theatrical entertainment consisting of a series of short sketches, songs, and dances, typically dealing satirically with topical issues.

re·vul·sion /ri'vəlshən/ ▶ *n.* a sense of disgust and loathing: *news of the attack will be met with sorrow and revulsion.*

re·ward /ri'wôrd/ ▶ *n.* a thing given in recognition of service, effort, or achievement: *the holiday was a reward for 40 years' service with the company.* ■ a fair return for good or bad behavior: *a slap on the face was his reward for his impudence.* ■ a sum offered for the detection of a criminal, the restoration of lost property, or the giving of information. ▶ *v.* [*tr.*] make a gift of something to (someone) in recognition of their services, efforts, or achievements: *the engineer who supervised the work was rewarded with a bonus.* ■ (**be rewarded**) receive what one deserves: *their hard work was rewarded by the winning of a five-year contract.* —**re·ward·less** *adj.*

re·ward·ing /ri'wôrdiNG/ ▶ *adj.* providing satisfaction; gratifying: *skiing can be hugely rewarding.* —**re·ward·ing·ly** *adv.*

re·wind ▶ *v.* /rē'wīnd/ (*past* and *past part.* **-wound** /-'wound/) [*tr.*] wind (a tape or film) back to the beginning. ■ [*intr.*] (of a tape or film) wind back to the beginning. ▶ *n.* /'rē,wīnd/ a mechanism for rewinding a tape or film. —**re·wind·er** /rē'wīndər/ *n.*

re·word /rē'wərd/ ▶ *v.* put (something) into different words: *there is a sound reason for rewording that clause.*

re·work /rē'wərk/ ▶ *v.* [*tr.*] (often **be reworked**) make changes to something, esp. in order to make it more up to date: *he reworked the orchestral score for two pianos* | [as *n.*] (**reworking**) *a reworking of the Sherwood Forest legend.*

re·wound /rē'wound/ ▶ past and past participle of REWIND.

re·write ▶ *v.* /rē'rīt/ (*past* **-wrote**; *past part.* **-writ·ten**) [*tr.*] write (something) again so as to alter or improve it: *the songs may have to be rewritten* | [*intr.*] *he began rewriting, adding more and more layers.*

▶ *n.* /ˈrē,rīt/ an instance of writing something again so as to alter or improve it. ■ a piece of text that has been altered or improved in such a way. —**re·writ·a·ble** *adj.*

▶ □ **rewrite history** select or interpret events from the past in a way that suits one's own particular purposes. □ **rewrite the record books** (of an athlete) break a record or several records.

Reye's syn·drome /rīz; rāz/ ▶ *n.* a life-threatening metabolic disorder in young children, of uncertain cause but sometimes precipitated by aspirin and resulting in encephalitis and liver failure.

Rf ▶ *symb.* the chemical element rutherfordium.

RFD (also **R.F.D.**) ▶ *abbr.* rural free delivery.

Rh ▶ *abbr.* Rhesus (factor).

▶ *symb.* the chemical element rhodium.

r.h. ▶ *abbr.* right hand.

rhap·so·dize /ˈrapsə,dīz/ ▶ *v.* [*intr.*] speak or write about someone or something with great enthusiasm and delight: *he began to rhapsodize about Gaby's beauty and charm.*

rhap·so·dy /ˈrapsədē/ ▶ *n.* (*pl.* **-dies**) an effusively enthusiastic or ecstatic expression of feeling: *rhapsodies of praise.* ■ *Mus.* a free instrumental composition in one extended movement, typically one that is emotional or exuberant in character. —**rhap·sod·ic** /rapˈsädik/ *adj.* —**rhap·so·dist** *n.*

rhe·a /ˈrēə/ ▶ *n.* a large flightless bird of either of two species (*Rhea americana* and *Pterocnemia pennata*, family Rheidae) of South American grasslands, resembling a small ostrich.

rhe·ni·um /ˈrēnēəm/ ▶ *n.* the chemical element of atomic number 75, a rare silvery-white metal. (Symbol: **Re**)

rhe·o·stat /ˈrēə,stat/ ▶ *n.* an electrical instrument used to control a current by varying the resistance. —**rhe·o·stat·ic** /ˌrēəˈstatik/ *adj.*

Rhe·sus fac·tor /ˈrēsəs/ (abbr.: **Rh fac·tor**) ▶ *n.* an antigen occurring on the red blood cells of many humans (around 85 percent) and some other primates.

rhe·sus mon·key (also **rhesus macaque**) ▶ *n.* a small brown macaque (*Macaca mulatta*) with red skin on the face and rump, native to southern Asia. It is often kept in captivity and is widely used in medical research.

rhet·o·ric /ˈretərik/ ▶ *n.* the art of effective or persuasive speaking or writing, esp. the use of figures of speech and other compositional techniques. ■ language designed to have a persuasive or impressive effect on its audience, but is often regarded as lacking in sincerity or meaningful content: *all we have from the opposition is empty rhetoric.*

rhe·tor·i·cal /rəˈtôrikəl/ ▶ *adj.* of, relating to, or concerned with the art of rhetoric: *repetition is a common rhetorical device.* ■ expressed in terms intended to persuade or impress: *the rhetorical commitment of the government to give priority to primary education.* ■ (of a question) asked in order to produce an effect or to make a statement rather than to elicit information. —**rhe·tor·i·cal·ly** /-ik(ə)lē/ *adv.*

rhet·o·ri·cian /ˌretəˈrishən/ ▶ *n.* an expert in formal rhetoric. ■ a speaker whose words are primarily intended to impress or persuade.

rheu·mat·ic /ro͞oˈmatik/ ▶ *adj.* of, relating to, or caused by rheumatism: *rheumatic pains.* ■ (of a person or part of the body) suffering from or affected by rheumatism.

▶ *n.* a person suffering from rheumatism. —**rheu·mat·i·cal·ly** /-ik(ə)lē/ *adv.* —**rheu·mat·ick·y** /ro͞oˈmatikē; ˈro͞omə,tikē/ *adj.* (*inf.*).

rheu·mat·ic fe·ver ▶ *n.* a noncontagious acute fever marked by inflammation and pain in the joints. It chiefly affects young people and is caused by a streptococcal infection.

rheu·ma·tism /ˈro͞omə,tizəm/ ▶ *n.* any disease marked by inflammation and pain in the joints, muscles, or fibrous tissue, esp. rheumatoid arthritis.

rheu·ma·toid /ˈro͞omə,toid/ ▶ *adj. Med.* relating to, affected by, or resembling rheumatism.

rheu·ma·toid ar·thri·tis ▶ *n.* a chronic progressive disease causing inflammation in the joints and resulting in painful deformity and immobility, esp. in the fingers, wrists, feet, and ankles. Compare with OSTEOARTHRITIS.

rheu·ma·tol·o·gy /ˌro͞omə'täləjē/ ▶ *n. Med.* the study of rheumatism, arthritis, and other disorders of the joints, muscles, and ligaments. —**rheu·ma·to·log·i·cal** /ˌro͞omətl'äjikəl/ *adj.* —**rheu·ma·tol·o·gist** /-jist/ *n.*

rhine·stone /ˈrīn,stōn/ ▶ *n.* an imitation diamond used in costume jewelry and to decorate clothes.

rhi·ni·tis /rīˈnītis/ ▶ *n. Med.* inflammation of the mucous membrane of the nose, caused by a virus infection (e.g., the common cold) or by an allergic reaction (e.g., hay fever).

rhi·no /ˈrīnō/ ▶ *n.* (*pl.* same or **-nos**) *inf.* a rhinoceros.

rhi·noc·er·os /rīˈnäs(ə)rəs/ ▶ *n.* (*pl.* same or **rhinoceroses**) a large, heavily built plant-eating endangered mammal (family Rhinocerotidae) with one or two horns on the nose and thick folded skin, native to Africa and South Asia. All kinds have become endangered through hunting.

rhi·no·plas·ty /ˈrīnō,plastē/ ▶ *n.* (*pl.* **-ties**) plastic surgery performed on the nose. —**rhi·no·plas·tic** /ˌrīnō'plastik/ *adj.*

rhi·zome /ˈrī,zōm/ ▶ *n. Bot.* a continuously growing horizontal underground stem that puts out lateral shoots and adventitious roots at intervals. Compare with BULB (sense 1), CORM.

rho /rō/ ▶ *n.* the seventeenth letter of the Greek alphabet (Ρ, ρ), transliterated as 'r' or (when written with a rough breathing) 'rh.'

rho·di·um /ˈrōdēəm/ ▶ *n.* the chemical element of atomic number 45, a hard silvery-white metal of the transition series, typically occurring in association with platinum. (Symbol: **Rh**)

rho·do·den·dron /ˌrōdə'dendrən/ ▶ *n.* a shrub or small tree (genus *Rhododendron*) of the heath family, with large clusters of bell-shaped flowers and typically with large evergreen leaves, widely grown as an ornamental.

rhom·bi /ˈräm,bī; -,bē/ ▶ plural form of RHOMBUS.

rhom·bo·he·dron /ˌrämbō'hēdrən/ ▶ *n.* (*pl.* **-drons** or **-dra** /-drə/) a solid figure whose faces are six equal rhombuses. —**rhom·bo·he·dral** /-hēdrəl/ *adj.*

rhom·boid /ˈräm,boid/ ▶ *adj.* having or resembling the shape of a rhombus.

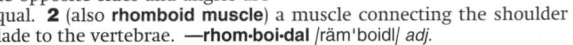

rhomboid

▶ *n.* **1** a quadrilateral of which only the opposite sides and angles are equal. **2** (also **rhomboid muscle**) a muscle connecting the shoulder blade to the vertebrae. —**rhom·boi·dal** /räm'boidl/ *adj.*

rhom·bus /ˈrämbəs/ ▶ *n.* (*pl.* **-bus·es** or **-bi** /-,bī; -,bē/) a parallelogram with opposite equal acute angles, opposite equal obtuse angles, and four equal sides. ■ any parallelogram with equal sides, including a square.

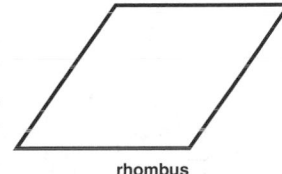

rhombus

rhu·barb /ˈro͞o,bärb/ ▶ *n.* **1** the thick leaf stalks of a cultivated plant of the dock family, which are reddish or green and eaten as a fruit after cooking. **2** the large-leaved Eurasian plant (*Rheum rhaponticum*) that produces these stems. **3** *chiefly Brit. inf.* the noise made by a group of actors to give the impression of indistinct background conversation or to represent the noise of a crowd, esp. by the random repetition of the word "rhubarb" with different intonations. ■ nonsense. ■ a heated dispute.

rhum·ba ▶ *n.* variant spelling of RUMBA.

rhyme /rīm/ ▶ *n.* correspondence of sound between words or the endings of words, esp. when these are used at the ends of lines of poetry. ■ a short poem in which the sound of the word or syllable at the end of each line corresponds with that at the end of another. ■ poetry or verse marked by such correspondence of sound: *the clues were written in rhyme.* ■ a word that has the same sound as another.

▶ *v.* [*intr.*] (of a word, syllable, or line) have or end with a sound that corresponds to another: *balloon rhymes with moon* | [as *adj.*] (**rhyming**) *rhyming couplets.* ■ (of a poem or song) be composed of lines that end in words or syllables with sounds that correspond with those at the ends of other lines: *the poem would have been better if it had rhymed.* ■ [*tr.*] (**rhyme something with**) put a word together with (another word that has a corresponding sound), as when writing poetry: *I'm not sure about rhyming perestroika with balalaika.* —**rhym·er** *n.* —**rhym·ist** /-ist/ *n.* (*archaic*).

▶ □ **rhyme or reason** logical explanation or reason: *without rhyme or reason his mood changed.*

rhythm /ˈriT͟Həm/ ▶ *n.* a strong, regular, repeated pattern of movement or sound: *Ruth listened to the rhythm of his breathing.* ■ the systematic arrangement of musical sounds, principally according to duration and periodic stress. ■ a particular type of pattern formed by such arrangement: *guitar melodies with deep African rhythms.* ■ a person's natural feeling for such arrangement: *they've got no rhythm.* ■ the measured flow of words and phrases in verse or prose as determined by the relation of long and short or stressed and unstressed syllables. ■ a regularly recurring sequence of events, actions, or processes: *the twice daily rhythms of the tides.* ■ *Art* a harmonious sequence or correlation of colors or elements. —**rhythm·less** *adj.*

rhythm and blues (abbr.: **R & B**) ▶ *n.* a form of popular music of African-American origin that arose during the 1940s from blues, with the addition of driving rhythms taken from jazz. It was an immediate precursor of rock and roll.

rhyth·mic /'riᴛʜmik/ ▶ *adj.* having or relating to rhythm: *a rhythmic dance.* ■ occurring regularly: *there are rhythmic changes in our bodies.* —**rhyth·mi·cal** *adj.* —**rhyth·mi·cal·ly** /-ik(ə)lē/ *adv.* —**rhyth·mic·i·ty** /riᴛʜ'misitē/ *n.*

rhythm meth·od ▶ *n.* a method of avoiding conception by which sexual intercourse is restricted to the times of a woman's menstrual cycle when ovulation is least likely to occur.

ri·a /'rēə/ ▶ *n. Geog.* a long narrow inlet formed by the partial submergence of a river valley.

rib /rib/ ▶ *n.* **1** each of a series of slender curved bones articulated in pairs to the spine (twelve pairs in humans), protecting the thoracic cavity and its organs. ■ a rib of an animal with meat adhering to it used as food; a joint or cut from the ribs of an animal. **2** a long raised piece of stronger or thicker material across a surface or through a structure, and typically serving to support or strengthen it, in particular: ■ *Archit.* a curved member supporting a vault or defining its form. ■ any of the curved transverse pieces of metal or timber in a ship, extending up from the keel and forming part of the framework of the hull. ■ each of the curved pieces of wood forming the body of a lute or the sides of a violin. ■ each of the hinged rods supporting the fabric of an umbrella. ■ a vein of a leaf (esp. the midrib) or an insect's wing. ■ *Knitting* a combination of alternate knit (plain) and purl stitches producing a ridged, slightly elastic fabric, used esp. for the cuffs and bottom edges of sweaters.

▶ *v.* (**ribbed, rib·bing**) [*tr.*] **1** (usu. **be ribbed**) mark with or form into raised bands or ridges: *the road ahead was ribbed with furrows of slush.* **2** *inf.* tease good-naturedly: *the first time I appeared in the outfit I was ribbed mercilessly.* —**rib·less** *adj.*

rib·ald /'ribəld; 'rib,ôld; 'rī,bôld/ ▶ *adj.* referring to sexual matters in an amusingly rude or irreverent way: *a ribald comment.*

rib·ald·ry /'ribəldrē; 'rī-/ ▶ *n.* ribald talk or behavior.

ribbed /ribd/ ▶ *adj.* (esp. of a fabric or garment) having a pattern of raised bands: *a ribbed cashmere sweater.* ■ *Archit.* (of a vault or other structure) strengthened with ribs.

rib·bing /'ribiNG/ ▶ *n.* **1** a riblike structure or pattern, esp. a band of knitting in rib. **2** *inf.* good-natured teasing.

rib·bon /'ribən/ ▶ *n.* a long, narrow strip of fabric, used esp. for tying something or for decoration: *the tiny pink ribbons in her hair.* ■ a strip of fabric of a special color or design awarded as a prize or worn to indicate the holding of an honor, esp. a small multicolored piece of ribbon worn in place of the medal it represents: *old horse show ribbons and rosettes.* ■ a long, narrow strip of something: *slice the peppers into ribbons lengthwise.* ■ a narrow band of inked material wound on a spool and forming the inking agent in some typewriters and computer printers.

▶ *v.* [*intr.*] extend or move in a long narrow strip like a ribbon: *miles of concrete ribboned behind the bus.* —**rib·boned** *adj.* —**rib·bon·like** /-,līk/ *adj.*

▶ □ **cut a** (or **the**) **ribbon** perform an opening ceremony, typically by formally cutting a ribbon across the entrance to somewhere. □ **cut** (or **tear**) **something to ribbons** cut (or tear) something so badly that only ragged strips remain. ■ *fig.* damage something severely: *the country has seen its economy torn to ribbons by recession.*

rib cage ▶ *n.* the bony frame formed by the ribs.

ri·bo·fla·vin /,rībə'flāvin; 'rībə,flā-/ ▶ *n. Biochem.* a yellow vitamin of the B complex that is essential for metabolic energy production. It is present in many foods, esp. milk, liver, eggs, and green vegetables, and is also synthesized by the intestinal flora. Also called **VITAMIN B₂** (see **VIT-AMIN B**).

ri·bo·nu·cle·ic ac·id /,rībōn(y)ŏŏ'klē-ik; -'klā-ik/ ▶ *n.* see **RNA**.

ri·bose /'rī,bōs; -,bōz/ ▶ *n. Chem.* a sugar of the pentose class that occurs widely in nature as a constituent of nucleosides and several vitamins and enzymes.

ri·bo·some /'rībə,sōm/ ▶ *n. Biochem.* a minute particle consisting of RNA and associated proteins, found in large numbers in the cytoplasm of living cells. They make messenger RNA and transfer RNA to synthesize polypeptides and proteins. —**ri·bo·so·mal** /,rībə'sōməl/ *adj.*

rice /rīs/ ▶ *n.* a swamp grass (*Oryza sativa*) that is widely cultivated as a source of food, esp. in Asia. ■ the grains of this cereal used as food.

▶ *v.* [*tr.*] force (cooked potatoes or other foods) through a sieve or ricer.

rice pad·dy ▶ *n.* see **PADDY**.

ric·er /'rīsər/ ▶ *n.* a utensil with small holes through which boiled potatoes or other soft food can be pushed to form particles of a similar size to grains of rice.

rich /riCH/ ▶ *adj.* **1** having a great deal of money or assets; wealthy: *most of these artists are already quite rich* | [as *pl. n.*] (**the rich**) *every day the gap between the rich and the poor widens.* ■ (of a country or region) having valuable natural resources or a successful economy. ■ of expensive materials or workmanship; demonstrating wealth: *rich mahogany furniture.* ■ generating wealth; valuable: *not all football players enjoy rich rewards from the game.* **2** plentiful; abundant: *China's rich and diverse mammalian fauna.* ■ having (a particular thing) in large amounts: *many vegetables and fruits are **rich in** antioxidant vitamins* | [in *comb.*] *a protein-rich diet.* ■ (of food) containing a large amount of fat, spices, sugar, etc.: *dishes with wonderfully rich sauces.* ■ (of drink) full-bodied: *a rich, hoppy beer.* ■ (of the fuel-air mixture in an internal combustion engine) containing a high proportion of fuel. ■ (of a color or sound) pleasantly deep and strong: *his rich bass voice.* ■ (of a smell or taste) pleasantly smooth and mellow: *Basmati rice has a rich aroma.* ■ *fig.* interesting because full of diversity or complexity: *what a full, rich life you lead!* **3** producing a large quantity of something: *novels have always been a rich source of material for the film industry.* ■ (of soil or a piece of land) having the properties necessary to produce fertile growth. ■ (of a mine or mineral deposit) yielding a large quantity or proportion of precious metal. **4** *inf.* (of a remark) causing ironic amusement or indignation: *these comments are **a bit rich** coming from a woman with no money worries.* —**rich·ness** *n.*

rich·es /'riCHiz/ ▶ *pl. n.* material wealth: *riches beyond their wildest dreams.* ■ valuable natural resources: *the riches of the world's waters.*

rich·ly /'riCHlē/ ▶ *adv.* in an elaborate, generous, or plentiful way: *she was richly dressed in the height of fashion.* ■ fully (used esp. to indicate that someone or something merits a particular thing): *give your family a richly deserved vacation.*

Rich·ter scale /'riktər/ ▶ *n. Geol.* a numerical scale for expressing the magnitude of an earthquake on the basis of seismograph oscillations. The more destructive earthquakes typically have magnitudes between about 5.5 and 8.9.

rick /rik/ ▶ *n.* a stack of hay, corn, straw, or similar material, esp. one built into a regular shape and thatched. ■ a pile of firewood somewhat smaller than a cord.

▶ *v.* [*tr.*] form into rick or ricks; stack: *the nine cords of good spruce wood ricked up in the back yard.*

rick·ets /'rikits/ ▶ *n.* [treated as *sing.* or *pl.*] *Med.* a disease of children caused by vitamin D deficiency, characterized by imperfect calcification, softening, and distortion of the bones typically resulting in bow legs.

rick·ett·si·a /ri'ketsēə/ ▶ *n.* (*pl.* **-si·ae** /-sē,ē; -sē,ī/ or **-si·as**) any of a group of very small bacteria (genus *Rickettsia*) that includes the causative agents of typhus and various other febrile diseases in humans. Like viruses, many of them can grow only inside living cells. —**rick·ett·si·al** *adj.* ▷ modern Latin, named after Howard Taylor *Ricketts* (1871–1910), American pathologist.

rick·et·y /'rikitē/ ▶ *adj.* (of a structure or piece of equipment) poorly made and likely to collapse: *we went carefully up the rickety stairs* | *fig. a rickety banking system.* —**rick·et·i·ness** *n.*

rick·rack /'rik,rak/ ▶ *n.* braided trimming in a zigzag pattern, used esp. as decoration on clothes.

rick·sha /'rik,SHô/ (also **rick·shaw**) ▶ *n.* a light two-wheeled hooded vehicle drawn by one or more people, used chiefly in Asian countries. ■ a similar vehicle like a three-wheeled bicycle, having a seat for passengers behind the driver.

ricksha

ri·co·chet /'rikə,SHā; -,SHet/ ▶ *n.* a shot or hit that rebounds one or more times off a surface. ■ the action or movement of a bullet, shell, or other projectile when rebounding in such a way.

▶ *v.* (**-cheted** /-,SHäd/, **-chet·ing** /-,SHä-iNG/ or **-chet·ted** /-,SHetid/, **-chet·ting** /-,SHetiNG/) [*intr.*] (of a bullet, shell, or other projectile) rebound one or more times off a surface: *a bullet ricocheted off a nearby wall.* ■ [*tr.*] cause to rebound in such a way: *they fired off a couple of rounds, ricocheting the bullets against a wall.* ■ *fig.* move or appear to move with a series of such rebounds: *the sound ricocheted around the hall.*

ri·cot·ta /ri'kätə/ ▶ *n.* a soft white unsalted Italian cheese.

rid /rid/ ▶ *v.* (**rid·ding**; *past* and *past part.* **rid** or *archaic* **rid·ded**) [*tr.*] (**rid someone/something of**) make someone or something free of (a troublesome or unwanted person or thing): *we now have the greatest chance ever to rid the world of nuclear weapons.* ■ (**be rid of**) be freed or relieved from: *she couldn't wait to be rid of us.*
▶ □ **be well rid of** be in a better state for having removed or disposed of (a troublesome or unwanted person or thing). □ **get rid of** take action so as to be free of (a troublesome or unwanted person or thing).

rid·dance /'ridns/ ▶ *n.* the action of getting rid of a troublesome or unwanted person or thing.
▶ □ **good riddance** said to express relief at being free of a troublesome or unwanted person or thing.

rid·den /'ridn/ ▶ past participle of RIDE.

rid·dle¹ /'ridl/ ▶ *n.* a question or statement intentionally phrased so as to require ingenuity in ascertaining its answer or meaning, typically presented as a game. ■ a person, event, or fact that is difficult to understand or explain: *the riddle of her death.*
▶ *v.* [*intr.*] *archaic* speak in or pose riddles: *he who knows not how to riddle.* ■ solve or explain (a riddle) to (someone): *riddle me this then.* —**rid·dler** /'ridlər; 'ridl-ər/ *n.*
▶ □ **talk** (or **speak**) **in riddles** express oneself in an ambiguous or puzzling manner.

rid·dle² ▶ *v.* [*tr.*] (usu. **be riddled**) make many holes in (someone or something), esp. with gunshot: *his car was riddled by sniper fire.* ■ fill or permeate (someone or something), esp. with something unpleasant or undesirable: *the existing law is riddled with loopholes.*

ride /rid/ ▶ *v.* (*past* **rode** /rōd/; *past part.* **rid·den** /'ridn/) [*tr.*] **1** sit on and control the movement of (an animal, esp. a horse), typically as a recreation or sport: *Diana went to watch him ride his horse.* ■ travel on a horse or other animal: *we rode on horseback.* ■ sit on and control (a bicycle or motorcycle) for recreation or as a means of transport: *he rode a Harley Davidson across the U.S.* ■ (**ride in/on**) travel in or on (a vehicle) as a passenger: *I started riding on the buses.* ■ (of a vehicle, animal, racetrack, etc.) be of a particular character for riding on or in: *the van rode as well as some cars of twice the price.* ■ *inf.* transport (someone) in a vehicle: *the taxi driver who rode Kelly into the airport not long ago.* **2** be carried or supported by (something with a great deal of momentum): *a stream of young surfers fighting the elements to ride the waves.* ■ [*intr.*] project or overlap: *when two lithospheric plates collide, one tends to ride over the other.* ■ [*intr.*] (of a vessel) sail or float: *a large cedar barque rode at anchor.* ■ [*intr.*] float or seem to float: *the moon was riding high in the sky.* ■ yield to (a blow) so as to reduce its impact: *Harrison drew back his jaw as if riding the blow.* ■ *vulgar slang* have sexual intercourse with. ■ (of a supernatural being) take spiritual possession of (someone). ■ annoy, pester, or tease: *if you don't give all the kids a chance to play, the parents ride you.* **3** (**be ridden**) be full of or dominated by: *you must not think him ridden with angst* | [as *adj.* in *comb.*] (**-ridden**) *the crime-ridden streets.*
▶ *phrasal v.* □ **ride on** depend on: *there is a great deal of money riding on the results of these studies.* □ **ride something out** come safely through something, esp. a storm or a period of danger or difficulty: *the fleet had ridden out the storm.*
▶ *n.* **1** a journey made on horseback, on a bicycle or motorcycle, or in a vehicle: *did you enjoy your ride?* ■ a person giving someone a lift in their vehicle: *their ride into town had dropped them off near the bridge.* ■ *inf.* a motor vehicle: *that green Chevy over there, that's my ride.* ■ the quality of comfort or smoothness offered by a vehicle while it is being driven, as perceived by the driver or passenger: *the ride is comfortable, though there is a slight roll when cornering.* **2** a roller coaster, merry-go-round, or other amusement ridden at a fair or amusement park. **3** *vulgar slang* an act of sexual intercourse. —**ride·a·ble** (also **rid·a·ble**) *adj.*
▶ □ **be riding for a fall** *inf.* be acting in a reckless or arrogant way that invites defeat or failure. □ **for the ride** for pleasure or interest, rather than any serious purpose: *I don't need anything at the mall, but I'm happy to go along for the ride.* □ **let something ride** take no immediate action over something. □ **ride herd on** keep watch over: *a man to ride herd on this frenetically paced enterprise.* □ **ride roughshod over** carry out one's own plans or wishes with arrogant disregard for (others or their wishes): *he rode roughshod over everyone else's opinions.*

rid·er /'rīdər/ ▶ *n.* **1** a person who is riding or who can ride something,

esp. a horse, bicycle, motorcycle, or snowboard. **2** a condition or proviso added to something already said or decreed: *one rider to the deal—if the hurricane heads north, we run for shelter.* ■ an addition or amendment to a document, esp. a piece of legislation: *the rules of Congress make it difficult to attach a rider to an appropriations bill* | *a rider to an eligible life insurance policy.* —**rid·er·less** *adj.*

ridge /rij/ ▶ *n.* a long narrow hilltop, mountain range, or watershed: *the northeast ridge of Everest.* ■ the line or edge formed where the two sloping sides of a roof meet at the top. ■ *Meteorol.* an elongated region of high atmospheric pressure. ■ a narrow raised band running along or across a surface: *buff your nails in order to smooth ridges.* —**ridg·y** *adj.*

ridge·pole /'rij,pōl/ ▶ *n.* **1** a horizontal beam along the ridge of a roof, into which the rafters are fastened. **2** the horizontal pole of a tent.

rid·i·cule /'ridi,kyōōl/ ▶ *n.* the subjection of someone or something to mockery and derision: *he is held up as an object of ridicule.*
▶ *v.* [*tr.*] subject (someone or something) to mockery and derision: *his theory was ridiculed and dismissed.*

ri·dic·u·lous /ri'dikyələs/ ▶ *adj.* deserving or inviting derision or mockery; absurd: *when you realize how ridiculous these scenarios are, you will have to laugh.* —**ri·dic·u·lous·ly** *adv.* —**ri·dic·u·lous·ness** *n.*

rid·ing¹ /'rīdiNG/ ▶ *n.* the sport or activity of riding horses.
▶ *adj.* **1** designed for or associated with the sport of riding: *smartly tailored riding clothes.* **2** (of a machine or device) designed to be operated while riding on it: *a riding mower.*

rid·ing² ▶ *n.* an electoral district of Canada.

rid·ing crop ▶ *n.* a short flexible whip with a loop for the hand, used in riding horses.

rife /rīf/ ▶ *adj.* (esp. of something undesirable or harmful) of common occurrence; widespread: *male chauvinism was rife in medicine in those days.* ■ (**rife with**) full of: *the streets were rife with rumor and fear.*
▶ *adv.* in an unchecked or widespread manner: *speculation ran rife that he was an arms dealer.* —**rife·ness** *n.*

riff /rif/ ▶ *n.* (in popular music and jazz) a short repeated phrase, frequently played over changing chords or harmonies or used as a background to a solo improvisation: *a brilliant guitar riff.*
▶ *v.* [*intr.*] play such phrases: *the other horns would be riffing behind him.*

rif·fle /'rifəl/ ▶ *v.* turn over something, esp. the pages of a book, quickly and casually: *he riffled through the pages* | *she opened a book with her thumbnail and riffled the pages.* ■ disturb the surface of; ruffle: *there was a slight breeze that riffled her hair.* ■ shuffle (playing cards) by flicking up and releasing the corners or sides of two piles of cards so that they intermingle and may be slid together to form a single pile.
▶ *n.* **1** a quick or casual leaf or search through something. ■ the rustle of paper being leafed through in such a way. ■ a shuffle performed by riffling playing cards. **2** a rocky or shallow part of a stream or river with rough water. ■ a patch of waves or ripples.

riff·raff /'rif,raf/ ▶ *n.* disreputable or undesirable people: *I don't think they talk to riffraff off the street.*

ri·fle¹ /'rifəl/ ▶ *n.* a gun, esp. one fired from shoulder level, having a long barrel spirally grooved on the inside in order to make a bullet spin and thereby have greater accuracy over a long distance.
▶ *v.* **1** [usu. as *adj.*] (**rifled**) make spiral grooves in (a gun or its barrel or bore) to make a bullet spin and thereby have greater accuracy over a long distance: *a line of replacement rifled barrels.* **2** [*tr.*] hit, throw, or kick (a ball or puck) hard and straight: *he rifled a hard, rising shot from just inside the blue line.*

rifle

ri·fle² ▶ *v.* [*intr.*] search through something in a hurried way in order to find or steal something: *she rifled through the cassette tapes* | [*tr.*] *they rifled the house for money.* ■ [*tr.*] steal: *the lieutenant's servant rifled the dead man's possessions.*

ri·fle range ▶ *n.* a place for practicing shooting with rifles.

ri·fling /'rīf(ə)liNG/ ▶ *n.* the arrangement of spiral grooves on the inside of a rifle barrel.

rift /rift/ ▶ *n.* a crack, split, or break in something: *the wind had torn open a rift in the clouds.* ■ *Geol.* a major fault separating blocks of the earth's

surface; a rift valley. ■ *fig.* a serious break in friendly relations: *their demise caused a rift between the city's town and gown.*
▶ *v. [intr.] chiefly Geol.* form fissures, cracks, or breaks, esp. through large-scale faulting; move apart: *a fragment of continental crust that rifted away from eastern Australia* | [as n.] (**rifting**) *active rifting in southwestern Mexico.* ■ [tr.] [usu. as adj.] (**rifted**) tear or force (something) apart: *the nascent rifted margins of the Red Sea.*

rig[1] /rig/ ▶ *v.* (**rigged, rig·ging**) [tr.] make (a sailing ship or boat) ready for sailing by providing it with sails and rigging: *the catamaran will be rigged as a ketch* | [as adj., in comb.] (**-rigged**) *a gaff-rigged cutter.* ■ assemble and adjust (the equipment of a sailboat, aircraft, etc.) to make it ready for operation: *most sails are kept ready rigged.* ■ set up (equipment or a device or structure), typically hastily or in makeshift fashion: *he had rigged up a sort of tent.* ■ provide (someone) with clothes of a particular style or type: *a cavalry regiment rigged out in green and gold.*
▶ *n.* **1** the particular way in which a sailboat's masts, sails, and rigging are arranged: *the yacht will emerge from the yard with her original rig.* ■ the sail, mast, and boom of a sailboard. **2** an apparatus, device, or piece of equipment designed for a particular purpose: *a lighting rig.* ■ an oil rig or drilling rig. ■ (in CB and shortwave radio) a transmitter and receiver. **3** a tractor-trailer. ■ another type of vehicle, such as a horse-drawn carriage.
▶ □ (**in**) **full rig** *inf.* (wearing) fancy or ceremonial clothes.

rig[2] ▶ *v.* (**rigged, rig·ging**) [tr.] manage or conduct (something) fraudulently so as to produce a result or situation that is advantageous to a particular person: *the results of the elections had been rigged* | [as n., in comb.] (**-rigging**) *charges of vote-rigging.* ■ cause an artificial rise or fall in prices in (a market, esp. the stock market) with a view to personal profit: *he accused games manufacturers of rigging the market.*

rig·ging /ˈrigiNG/ ▶ *n.* **1** the system of ropes, cables, and chains employed to support a ship's masts (**standing rigging**) and to control or set the yards and sails (**running rigging**). **2** the ropes and wires supporting the structure of an airship, biplane, hang glider, or parachute. ■ the system of cables and fittings controlling the flight surfaces and engines of an aircraft. ■ the action of assembling and adjusting such rigging.

right /rīt/ ▶ *adj.* **1** morally good, justified, or acceptable: *I hope we're doing the right thing.* **2** true or correct as a fact: *her theories were proved right.* ■ correct in one's opinion or judgment: *she was right about Tom having no money.* ■ used as an interrogative at the end of a statement as a way of inviting agreement, approval, or confirmation: *you went to see Angie on Monday, right?* ■ the best or most suitable of a number of possible choices for a particular purpose or occasion: *he was clearly the right man for the job.* ■ in a satisfactory, sound, or normal state or condition: *that sausage doesn't smell right* | *if only I could have helped put matters right.* **3** denoting or worn on the side of a person's body which is toward the east when they are facing north: *her right shoe.* ■ denoting the corresponding side of any other object: *the right edge of the field.* ■ on this side from the point of view of a spectator. **4** of or relating to a person or political party or grouping favoring conservative views: *are you politically right, left, or center?*
▶ *adv.* **1** to the furthest or most complete extent or degree (used for emphasis): *the car spun right off the track.* ■ exactly; directly (used to emphasize the precise location or time of something): *Harriet was standing right behind her.* ■ *inf.* immediately; without delaying or hesitating: *I'll be right back.* **2** correctly: *he had guessed right.* ■ in the required or necessary way; properly; satisfactorily: *nothing's going right for me this season.* **3** on or to the right side: *turn right at Main Street.*
▶ *n.* **1** that which is morally correct, just, or honorable: *she doesn't understand the difference between right and wrong.* **2** a moral or legal entitlement to have or obtain something or to act in a certain way: *she had every right to be angry.* ■ (**rights**) the authority to perform, publish, film, or televise a particular work, event, etc.: *they sold the paperback rights.* **3** (**the right**) the right-hand part, side, or direction: *take the first turning on the right* | (**one's right**) *she seated me on her right.* ■ a right turn: *he made a right in Dorchester Avenue.* ■ a road or entrance on the right: *take the first right over the stream.* **4** (often **the Right**) [treated as *sing.* or *pl.*] a grouping or political party favoring conservative views and supporting capitalist economic principles. ■ the section of a group or political party adhering particularly strongly to such views.
▶ *v.* [tr.] restore to a normal or upright position: *we righted the capsized dinghy.* ■ restore to a normal or correct condition or situation: *righting the economy demanded major cuts in defense spending.* ■ redress or rectify (a wrong or mistaken action): *she was determined to right the wrongs done to her father.*
▶ *interj. inf.* used to indicate one's agreement with a suggestion or to acknowledge a statement or order: *"Barry's here." "Oh, right."* ■ used as a

filler in speech or as a way of confirming that someone is listening to or understanding what one is saying: *and I didn't think any more of it, right, but Mom said I should take him to a doctor.* ■ used to introduce an utterance, exhortation, or suggestion: *right, let's have a drink.* ▷Old English *riht* (adjective and noun), *rihtan* (verb), *rihte* (adverb), of Germanic origin; related to Latin *rectus* 'ruled,' from an Indo-European root denoting movement in a straight line. —**right·a·ble** *adj.* —**right·ness** *n.*
▶ □ **be in the right** be morally or legally justified in one's views, actions, or decisions. □ **in one's own right** as a result of one's own claims, qualifications, or efforts, rather than an association with someone else: *he was already established as a poet in his own right.* □ (**not**) **in one's right mind** (not) sane. □ **put** (or **set**) **something to rights** restore something to its correct or normal state or condition. □ **right on** *inf.* used an expression of strong support, approval, or encouragement.

right an·gle ▶ *n.* an angle of 90°, as in a corner of a square or, more generally, at the intersection of two perpendicular straight lines. —**right-an·gled** *adj.*

right-click ▶ *v.* [intr.] *Comput.* depress the right-hand button on a mouse. ■ [tr.] click on a link or other screen object in this way: *right-click a graphic and choose 'Resize.'*

right·eous /ˈrīcHəs/ ▶ *adj.* **1** (of a person or conduct) morally right or justifiable; virtuous: *feelings of righteous indignation about pay and conditions.* **2** *inf.* perfectly wonderful; fine and genuine: *righteous bread pudding.* —**right·eous·ly** *adv.* —**right·eous·ness** *n.*

right field (also **right**) ▶ *n. Baseball* the part of the outfield to the right of center field from the perspective of home plate. ■ the position of the defensive player stationed there. —**right field·er** *n.*

right·ful /ˈrītfəl/ ▶ *adj.* having a legitimate right to property, position, or status: *the rightful owner of the jewels.* ■ legitimately claimed; fitting: *they are determined to take their rightful place in a new South Africa.* —**right·ful·ly** *adv.* —**right·ful·ness** *n.*

right hand ▶ *n.* the hand of a person's right side. ■ the region or direction on the right side of a person or thing: *a great wall loomed above the street on the right hand.* ■ the most important position next to someone: *the place of honor at his host's right hand.* ■ an efficient or indispensable assistant: *she could have helped him, been her father's right hand.*
▶ *adj.* on or toward the right side of a person or thing: *the top right-hand corner.* ■ done with or using the right hand: *wild right-hand punches.*

right-hand·ed ▶ *adj.* **1** (of a person) using the right hand more naturally than the left: *the slant of the stab wounds suggested that the assailant was right-handed.* ■ (of a tool or item of equipment) made to be used with the right hand or by right-handed people: *a right-handed guitar.* ■ made or done with the right hand, or in a manner natural to right-handed people: *right-handed batting.* **2** going toward or turning to the right, in particular: ■ (of a screw) advanced by turning clockwise.
▶ *adv.* with the right hand, or in a manner natural to right-handed people: *Jackson bats right-handed.* —**right-hand·ed·ly** *adv.* —**right-hand·ed·ness** *n.*

right·ist /ˈrītist/ ▶ *n.* a person who supports the political views or policies of the right.
▶ *adj.* supportive of the political views or policies of the right: *rightist doctrine.* —**right·ism** /-ˌizəm/ *n.*

right·ly /ˈrītlē/ ▶ *adv.* correctly: *if I remember rightly, she never gives interviews.* ■ with good reason: *the delicious cuisine for which her country was rightly famous.* ■ in accordance with justice or what is morally right: *the key rightly belonged to Craig.*

right-mind·ed ▶ *adj.* having sound views and principles. —**right-mind·ed·ness** *n.*

right of way (also **right-of-way**) ▶ *n.* **1** the legal right, established by usage or grant, to pass along a specific route through grounds or property belonging to another. ■ a path or thoroughfare subject to such a right. **2** the legal right of a pedestrian, rider, or driver to proceed with precedence over other road users at a particular point: *he waves on other drivers, even when it's not their right of way.* ■ the right of a ship, boat, or aircraft to proceed with precedence over others in a particular situation. **3** the land on which a railroad line, road, or utility is built.

right-to-die ▶ *adj.* pertaining to, expressing, or advocating the right to refuse extraordinary measures intended to prolong someone's life when they are terminally ill or comatose.

right-to-life ▶ *adj.* another term for PRO-LIFE. —**right-to-lif·er** /ˈlīfər/ *n.*

right whale ▶ *n.* a baleen whale (family Balaenidae) with a large head and a deeply curved jaw, of Arctic and temperate waters.

right wing ▶ *n.* (**the right wing**) **1** the conservative or reactionary section of a political party or system. **2** the right side of a team on the field in soccer, rugby, and field hockey. ■ the right side of an army.

▶*adj.* conservative or reactionary: *a right-wing Republican senator.* —**right-wing·er** *n.*

rig·id /ˈrijid/ ▶*adj.* unable to bend or be forced out of shape; not flexible: *a seat of rigid orange plastic* | *rigid ships are the dirigibles in which the bag is built around a metallic framework.* ■ (of a person or part of the body) stiff and unmoving, esp. as a result of shock or fear: *his face grew rigid with fear.* ■ *fig.* not able to be changed or adapted: *teachers are being asked to unlearn rigid rules for labeling children.* —**ri·gid·i·fy** /rəˈjidə‚fī/ *v.* —**ri·gid·i·ty** /rəˈjidətē/ *n.* —**rig·id·ly** *adv.* —**rig·id·ness** *n.*

rig·ma·role /ˈrig(ə)mə‚rōl/ ▶*n.* a lengthy and complicated procedure: *he went through the rigmarole of securing the front door.* ■ a long, rambling story or statement.

rig·or /ˈrigər/ ▶*n.* **1** the quality of being extremely thorough, exhaustive, or accurate: *his analysis is lacking in rigor.* ■ severity or strictness: *the full rigor of the law.* ■ (**rigors**) demanding, difficult, or extreme conditions: *the rigors of a harsh winter.* **2** *Med.* a sudden feeling of cold with shivering accompanied by a rise in temperature, often with copious sweating, esp. at the onset or height of a fever. ■ short for RIGOR MORTIS.

rig·or mor·tis /‚rigər ˈmôrtəs/ ▶*n.* *Med.* stiffening of the joints and muscles of a body a few hours after death, usually lasting from one to four days.

rig·or·ous /ˈrigərəs/ ▶*adj.* extremely thorough, exhaustive, or accurate: *the rigorous testing of consumer products.* ■ (of a rule, system, etc.) strictly applied or adhered to: *rigorous controls on mergers.* ■ (of a person) adhering strictly or inflexibly to a belief, opinion, or way of doing something: *a rigorous teetotaler.* ■ (of an activity) physically demanding: *my exercise regime is a little more rigorous than most.* ■ (of the weather or climate) harsh: *the rigorous climate in the regions of perpetual snow high in the Himalayas.* —**rig·or·ous·ly** *adv.* —**rig·or·ous·ness** *n.*

rile /rīl/ ▶*v.* [*tr.*] **1** *inf.* make (someone) annoyed or irritated: *it was his air of knowing all the answers that riled her* | *he's getting you all riled up.* **2** make (water) turbulent or muddy.

rill /ril/ ▶*n.* a small stream. ■ a shallow channel cut in the ground by running water.

▶*v.* [*intr.*] (of water) flow in or as in a rill: *the water rilled over our cold hands.* ■ [as *adj.*] (**rilled**) indented with small grooves: *blocks of butter pounded into artful shapes with rilled paddles.*

rim /rim/ ▶*n.* the upper or outer edge of an object, typically something circular or approximately circular: *a china egg cup with a gold rim.* ■ the outer edge of a wheel, on which the tire is fitted. ■ the metal hoop from which a basketball net is suspended. ■ (often **rims**) the part of a glasses frame surrounding the lenses.

▶*v.* (**rimmed**, **rim·ming**) [*tr.*] form or act as an outer edge or rim for: *a huge lake rimmed by glaciers* | [as *adj.*, in *comb.*] (**-rimmed**) *steel-rimmed glasses.* ■ (usu. **be rimmed**) mark with an encircling stain or deposit: *his collar was rimmed with dirt.* —**rim·less** *adj.*

rime /rīm/ ▶*n.* (also **rime ice**) frost formed on cold objects by the rapid freezing of water vapor in cloud or fog. ■ *poetic/lit.* hoarfrost.

▶*v.* [*tr.*] *poetic/lit.* cover (an object) with hoarfrost: *he does not brush away the frost that rimes his beard.* —**rim·y** *adj.*

rind /rīnd/ ▶*n.* the tough outer layer of something, in particular: ■ the tough outer skin of certain fruit, esp. citrus fruit. ■ the hard outer edge of cheese or bacon, usually removed before eating. ■ the bark of a tree or plant. ■ the hard outer layer of a rhizomorph or other part of a fungus.

▶*v.* [*tr.*] strip the bark from (a tree). —**rind·ed** *adj.* [in *comb.*] *yellow-rinded lemons.* —**rind·less** *adj.*

ring¹ /riNG/ ▶*n.* **1** a small circular band, typically of precious metal and often set with one or more gemstones, worn on a finger as an ornament or a token of marriage, engagement, or authority. ■ a circular band of any material: *fried onion rings.* ■ *Astron.* a thin band or disk of rock and ice particles around a planet. ■ a circular marking or pattern: *black rings around her eyes.* ■ short for TREE RING. ■ [usu. as *adj.*] *Archaeol.* a circular prehistoric earthwork, typically consisting of a bank and ditch: *a ring ditch.* **2** an enclosed space, typically surrounded by seating for spectators, in which a sport, performance, or show takes place: *a circus ring.* ■ (**the ring**) the profession, sport, or institution of boxing. **3** a group of people or things arranged in a circle: *he pointed to the ring of trees.* ■ a group of people drawn together due to a shared interest or goal, esp. one involving illegal or unscrupulous activity: *the police had been investigating the drug ring.* ■ *Chem.* another term for CLOSED CHAIN. **4** *Math.* a set of elements with two binary operations, addition and multiplication, the second being distributive over the first and associative.

▶*v.* [*tr.*] (often **be ringed**) surround (someone or something), esp. for protection or containment: *the courthouse was ringed with police.* ■ form a

line around the edge of (something circular): *dark shadows ringed his eyes.* ■ draw a circle around (something), esp. to focus attention on it: *an area of Tribeca had been ringed in red.* —**ringed** *adj.* [in *comb.*] *the five-ringed Olympic emblem.* —**ring·less** *adj.*

▶ □ **run rings around someone** *inf.* outclass or outwit someone very easily.

ring² ▶*v.* (past **rang** /raNG/; past part. **rung** /rəNG/) [*intr.*] make a clear resonant or vibrating sound: *a bell rang loudly* | [as *n.*] (**ringing**) *the ringing of fire alarms.* ■ [*tr.*] cause (a bell or alarm) to make such a sound: *he walked up to the door and rang the bell.* ■ (of a telephone) produce a series of resonant or vibrating sounds to signal an incoming call: *the phone rang again as I replaced it.* ■ call for service or attention by sounding a bell: *Ruth, will you ring for some tea?* ■ (of a person's ears) be filled with a continuous buzzing or humming sound, esp. as the aftereffect of a blow or loud noise: *he yelled so loudly that my eardrums rang.* ■ (**ring with/to**) (of a place) resound or reverberate with (a sound or sounds): *the room rang with laughter.* ■ (**ring with**) *fig.* be filled or permeated with (a particular quality): *those whose names ring with ethnicity.* ■ [*intr.*] convey a specified impression or quality: *the author's honesty rings true.* ■ [*tr.*] sound (the hour, a peal, etc.) on a bell or bells: *a bell ringing the hour.*

▶*phrasal v.* □ **ring something up** record an amount on a cash register. ■ *fig.* make, spend, or announce a particular amount in sales, profits, or losses.

▶*n.* an act of causing a bell to sound, or the resonant sound caused by this: *there was a ring at the door.* ■ each of a series of resonant or vibrating sounds signaling an incoming telephone call. ■ *inf.* a telephone call: *I'd better give her a ring tomorrow.* ■ a loud clear sound or tone: *the ring of sledgehammers on metal.* ■ a particular quality conveyed by something heard or expressed: *the song had a curious ring of nostalgia to it.* ■ a set of bells, esp. church bells.

ring bind·er ▶*n.* a loose-leaf binder with ring-shaped clasps that can be opened to pass through holes in the paper.

ring·er /ˈriNGər/ ▶*n.* **1** *inf.* an athlete or horse fraudulently substituted for another in a competition or event. ■ a person's or thing's double, esp. an impostor: *he's a ringer for the French actor Fernandel.* ■ a person who is highly proficient at a particular skill or sport and is brought in to supplement a team or group of people: *league eligibility rules had grown flexible to accommodate new teams, and ringers began suiting up.* **2** a person who rings something, esp. a bell-ringer. ■ a device for ringing a bell or producing a similar tone, esp. on a telephone.

ring fin·ger ▶*n.* the finger next to the little finger, esp. of the left hand, on which the wedding band is worn.

ring·lead·er /ˈriNG‚lēdər/ ▶*n.* a person who initiates or leads an illicit or illegal activity.

ring·let /ˈriNGlit/ ▶*n.* a lock of hair hanging in a corkscrew-shaped curl. —**ring·let·ed** *adj.* —**ring·let·y** *adj.*

ring·mas·ter /ˈriNG‚mastər/ ▶*n.* the person directing a circus performance.

ring·side /ˈriNG‚sīd/ ▶*n.* [often as *adj.*] the area immediately beside a boxing ring or circus ring: *a ringside judge.* ■ *fig.* an advantageous position from which to observe or monitor something: *having a ringside seat at the healthcare committee hearings.* —**ring·sid·er** *n.*

ring·worm /ˈriNG‚wərm/ ▶*n.* a contagious itching skin disease (e.g., athlete's foot), occurring in small circular patches, caused by various fungi and affecting chiefly the scalp or the feet.

rink /riNGk/ ▶*n.* (also **ice rink**) an enclosed area of ice for skating, ice hockey, or curling, esp. one artificially prepared. ■ (also **roller rink**) a smooth enclosed floor for roller skating. ■ a building containing either of these. ■ a team in curling. ▷late Middle English (originally Scots in the sense 'jousting ground'): perhaps originally from Old French *renc* 'rank.'

rinse /rins/ ▶*v.* [*tr.*] wash (something) with clean water to remove soap, detergent, dirt, or impurities: *always rinse your hair thoroughly.* ■ wash (something) quickly, esp. without soap: *Rose rinsed out a tumbler.*

▶*n.* **1** an act of rinsing something: *I gave my hands a quick rinse.* **2** an antiseptic solution for cleansing the mouth. **3** a preparation for conditioning or temporarily tinting the hair. —**rins·er** *n.*

ri·ot /ˈrīət/ ▶*n.* **1** a violent disturbance of the peace by a crowd: *riots broke out in the capital.* ■ [as *adj.*] concerned with or used in the suppression of such disturbances: *riot police.* ■ *fig.* an uproar: *the film's sex scenes caused a riot in Cannes.* ■ *fig.* an outburst of uncontrolled feelings: *a riot of emotions raged through Frances.* **2** an impressively large or varied display of something: *the garden was a riot of color.* **3** *inf.* a highly amusing or entertaining person or thing: *everyone thought she was a riot.*

▸*v.* [*intr.*] take part in a violent public disturbance: *students rioted in Paris* | [as *n.*] (**rioting**) *a night of rioting.* ■ *fig.* behave in an unrestrained way: *another set of emotions rioted through him.* —**ri·ot·er** *n.*

▸ □ **run riot** behave in a violent and unrestrained way. ■ (of a mental faculty or emotion) function or be expressed without restraint: *her imagination ran riot.* ■ proliferate or spread uncontrollably: *traditional prejudices were allowed to run riot.*

ri·ot·ous /ˈrīətəs/ ▸*adj.* marked by or involving public disorder: *a riotous crowd.* ■ characterized by wild and uncontrolled behavior: *a riotous party.* ■ having a vivid, varied appearance: *a riotous display of bright red, green, and yellow vegetables.* ■ hilariously funny: *a riotous account of the making of the movie.* —**ri·ot·ous·ly** *adv.* —**ri·ot·ous·ness** *n.*

RIP ▸*abbr.* rest in peace (used on grave markers).

rip[1] /rip/ ▸*v.* (**ripped, rip·ping**) **1** [*tr.*] tear or pull (something) quickly or forcibly away from something or someone: *a fan tried to rip his pants off during a show* | *fig. countries ripped apart by fighting.* ■ make (a hole) by force: *the truck was struck by lightning and had a hole ripped out of its roof.* ■ [*intr.*] come violently apart; tear: *he heard something rip.* ■ cut (wood) in the direction of the grain. **2** [*intr.*] move forcefully and rapidly: *fire ripped through her bungalow.* **3** use a program to copy (a sound sequence on a compact disc) on to a computer's hard drive: *every Beatles song ever made, ripped from my boxed set of CDs.*

▸*phrasal v.* □ **rip someone off** *inf.* cheat someone, esp. financially. □ **rip something off** *inf.* steal: *they have ripped off $6.7 billion.* ■ copy; plagiarize: *the film is a shameless collection of ideas ripped off from other movies.*

▸*n.* **1** a long tear or cut. ■ an act of tearing something forcibly. **2** a fraud or swindle; a rip-off.

▸ □ **let something rip** *inf.* allow something, esp. a vehicle, to go at full speed. ■ allow something to happen forcefully or without interference: *once she started a tirade, it was best to let it rip.* ■ utter or express something forcefully and noisily: *when I passed the exam I let rip a "yippee."*

rip[2] ▸*n.* a stretch of fast-flowing and rough water in the sea or in a river, caused by the meeting of currents. ■ short for RIP CURRENT.

ri·par·i·an /riˈpe(ə)rēən, rī-/ ▸*adj.* chiefly *Law* of, relating to, or situated on the banks of a river: *all the riparian states must sign an agreement.* ■ *Ecol.* of or relating to wetlands adjacent to rivers and streams.

rip·cord /ˈrip,kôrd/ ▸*n.* a cord that is pulled to open a parachute.

rip cur·rent ▸*n.* a relatively strong, narrow current flowing outward from the beach through the surf zone and presenting a hazard to swimmers. Also called UNDERTOW. Compare with RIP TIDE.

ripe /rīp/ ▸*adj.* (of fruit or grain) developed to the point of readiness for harvesting and eating. ■ (of a cheese or wine) fully matured: *a ripe Brie.* ■ (of a smell or flavor) rich, intense, or pungent: *rich, ripe flavors emanate from this wine.* ■ (**ripe for**) arrived at the fitting stage or time for (a particular action or purpose): *land ripe for development.* ■ (**ripe with**) full of: *a population ripe with discontent.* ■ (of a person's age) advanced: *she lived to a ripe old age.* ■ *inf.* (of a person's language) beyond the bounds of propriety; coarse. —**ripe·ly** *adv.* —**ripe·ness** *n.*

▸ □ **the time is ripe** a suitable time has arrived: *the time was ripe to talk about peace.*

rip·en /ˈrīpən/ ▸*v.* become or make ripe: [*intr.*] *honeydew melons ripen slowly.*

rip-off ▸*n. inf.* a fraud or swindle, esp. something that is grossly overpriced: *designer label clothes are just expensive rip-offs.* ■ an inferior imitation of something: *rip-offs of all the latest styles.*

ri·poste /riˈpōst/ ▸*n.* **1** a quick clever reply to an insult or criticism. **2** *Fencing* a quick return thrust following a parry.

▸*v.* **1** [with *direct speech*] make a quick clever reply to an insult or criticism: *"You've got a strange sense of humor," Grant riposted.* **2** [*intr.*] make a quick return thrust in fencing.

rip·ple /ˈripəl/ ▸*n.* a small wave or series of waves on the surface of water, esp. as caused by an object dropping into it or a slight breeze. ■ a thing resembling such a wave or series of waves in appearance or movement: *the sand undulated and was ridged with ripples.* ■ a gentle rising and falling sound, esp. of laughter or conversation, that spreads through a group of people: *a ripple of laughter ran around the room.* ■ a particular feeling or effect that spreads through or to someone or something: *his words set off a ripple of excitement within her.*

▸*v.* [*intr.*] (of water) form or flow with small waves on the surface: *the Mediterranean rippled and sparkled* | [as *adj.*] (**rippling**) *the rippling waters.* ■ [*tr.*] cause (the surface of water) to form small waves: *a cool wind rippled the surface of the estuary.* ■ move or cause to move in a way resembling such waves: [*intr.*] *fields of grain rippling in the wind.* ■ [*intr.*] (of a

sound or feeling) spread through a person, group, or place: *applause rippled around the tables.* ■ [as *adj.*] (**rippled**) having the appearance of small waves: *a broad noodle, rippled on both sides, wider than fettuccine.* —**rip·plet** /ˈriplit/ *n.* —**rip·ply** /ˈrip(ə)lē/ *adj.*

rip·rap /ˈrip,rap/ ▸*n.* loose stone used to form a foundation for a breakwater or other structure.

rip-roar·ing ▸*adj.* full of energy and vigor: *a rip-roaring rodeo.* —**rip-roar·ing·ly** *adv.*

rip·saw /ˈrip,sô/ ▸*n.* a coarse-toothed saw for cutting wood along the grain.

rip-snort·ing /ˈrip'snôrting/ ▸*adj. inf.* showing great vigor or intensity: *a ripsnorting editorial.* —**rip-snort·er** /-'snôrtər/ *n.* —**rip-snort·ing·ly** *adv.*

rip tide ▸*n.* a strong current caused by tidal flow in confined areas such as inlets and presenting a hazard to swimmers and boaters. ■ another term for RIP CURRENT.

rise /rīz/ ▸*v.* (*past* **rose** /rōz/; *past part.* **ris·en** /ˈrizən/) [*intr.*] **1** move from a lower position to a higher one; come up or go up: *the tiny aircraft rose from the ground.* ■ (of a voice) become higher in pitch: *my voice rose an octave or two as I screamed.* ■ reach a higher position in society or one's profession: *the officer was a man of great courage who had risen from the ranks.* ■ (**rise above**) succeed in not being limited or constrained by (a restrictive environment or situation): *he struggled to rise above his humble background.* **2** get up from lying, sitting, or kneeling: *she pushed back her chair and rose.* ■ get out of bed, esp. in the morning: *I rose and got dressed.* ■ be restored to life: *your sister has risen from the dead.* ■ (of a wind) start to blow or to blow more strongly: *the wind continued to rise.* ■ (of a river) have its source: *the Euphrates rises in Turkey.* ■ cease to be submissive, obedient, or peaceful: *the activists urged militant factions to rise up.* ■ (**rise to**) (of a person) react with annoyance or argument to (provocation): *he didn't rise to my teasing.* ■ (**rise to**) find the strength or ability to respond adequately to (a challenging situation): *many participants in the race had never sailed before, but they rose to the challenge.* **3** increase in number, size, amount, or quality: *land prices had risen.* ■ (of a person's mood) become more cheerful: *her spirits rose as they left the ugly city behind.* **4** (**rising**) approaching (a specified age): *she was thirty-nine rising forty* | *Polly shall have a young mare rising three years old.*

▸*n.* **1** an upward movement; an instance of becoming higher: *the bird has a display flight of steep flapping rises.* ■ an increase in sound or pitch: *the rise and fall of his voice.* ■ an instance of social, commercial, or political advancement: *few models have had such a meteoric rise.* ■ an upward slope or hill. ■ the vertical height of a step, arch, or incline. **2** an increase in amount, extent, size, or number: *local people are worried by the rise in crime.*

▸ □ **get a rise out of** *inf.* provoke an angry or irritated response from (someone), esp. by teasing.

ris·er /ˈrīzər/ ▸*n.* **1** a person who habitually gets out of bed at a particular time of the morning: *late risers always exasperate early risers.* **2** a vertical section between the treads of a staircase. **3** a vertical pipe for the upward flow of liquid or gas. **4** a low platform on a stage or in an auditorium, used to give greater prominence to a speaker or performer.

ris·i·ble /ˈrizəbəl/ ▸*adj.* such as to provoke laughter: *a risible scene of lovemaking in a tent.* —**ris·i·bil·i·ty** /,rizəˈbilətē/ *n.* —**ris·i·bly** /-blē/ *adv.*

ris·ing /ˈrīziNG/ ▸*adj.* going up; getting higher: *the rising temperature.* ■ increasing. ■ advancing to maturity or high standing: *the rising generation of American writers.*

▸*n.* an armed protest against authority; a revolt.

risk /risk/ ▸*n.* a situation involving exposure to danger: *flouting the law was too much of a risk.* ■ the possibility that something unpleasant or unwelcome will happen: *reduce the risk of heart disease* | [as *adj.*] *a high consumption of caffeine was suggested as a risk factor for loss of bone mass.* ■ a person or thing regarded as likely to turn out well or badly, as specified, in a particular context or respect: *Western banks regarded Romania as a good risk.* ■ a person or thing regarded as a threat to something in need of protection: *she's a security risk.* ■ (usu. **risks**) a possibility of harm or damage against which something is insured.

▸*v.* [*tr.*] expose (someone or something valued) to danger, harm, or loss: *he risked his life to save his dog.* ■ act or fail to act in such a way as to bring about the possibility of (an unpleasant or unwelcome event): *unless you're dealing with pure alcohol you're risking contamination from benzene.* ▷mid 17th cent.: from French *risque* (noun), *risquer* (verb), from Italian *risco* 'danger' and *rischiare* 'run into danger.'

risk·y /ˈriskē/ ▸*adj.* (**risk·i·er, risk·i·est**) full of the possibility of danger, failure, or loss: *it was much too risky to try to disarm him.* —**risk·i·ly** /-kəlē/ *adv.* —**risk·i·ness** *n.*

ri·sot·to /riˈzôtō; -'sôtō/ ▸*n.* (*pl.* **-tos**) an Italian dish of rice cooked in stock with other ingredients such as meat and vegetables.

ris·qué /ri'skā/ ▸*adj.* slightly indecent or liable to shock, esp. by being sexually suggestive: *his risqué humor.*

Ris·so's dol·phin /'risōz/ ▸*n.* a gray dolphin (*Grampus griseus*) that has long black flippers and a rounded snout with no beak, living mainly in temperate seas. Also called GRAMPUS.

ri·tar·dan·do /ri,tär'dändō/ (also **ri·tard** /ri'tärd/) ▸*adv. & adj.* (esp. as a musical direction) with a gradual decrease of speed.
▸*n.* (*pl.* **-dos** or **-di** /-dē/) a gradual decrease in speed.

rite /rīt/ ▸*n.* a religious or other solemn ceremony or act: *the rite of communion* | *fertility rites.* ■ a body of customary observances characteristic of a church or a part of it: *the Byzantine rite.* ■ a social custom, practice, or conventional act: *the family Christmas rite.*
▸ □ **rite of passage** a ceremony or event marking an important stage in someone's life, esp. birth, puberty, marriage, and death: *a novel that depicts the state of adolescence and the rites of passage that lead to adulthood.*

rit·u·al /'richŌŌəl/ ▸*n.* a religious or solemn ceremony consisting of a series of actions performed according to a prescribed order: *the ancient rituals of Christian worship* | *the role of ritual in religion.* ■ a prescribed order of performing such a ceremony, esp. one characteristic of a particular religion or church. ■ a series of actions or type of behavior regularly and invariably followed by someone: *her visits to Joy became a ritual.*
▸*adj.* of, relating to, or done as a religious or solemn rite: *ritual burial.* ■ (of an action) arising from convention or habit: *the players gathered for the ritual pregame huddle.* —**rit·u·al·ly** *adv.* —**rit·u·al·i·za·tion** *n.* —**rit·u·al·ize** *adv.*

rit·u·al·ism /'richŌŌə,lizəm/ ▸*n.* the regular observance or practice of ritual, esp. when excessive or without regard to its function. —**rit·u·al·ist** *n.* —**rit·u·al·is·tic** /,richŌŌə'listik/ *adj.* —**rit·u·al·is·ti·cal·ly** *adv.*

ritz·y /'ritsē/ ▸*adj.* (**ritz·i·er, ritz·i·est**) *inf.* expensively stylish: *the ritzy Plaza Hotel.* —**ritz·i·ly** /'ritsilē/ *adv.* —**ritz·i·ness** *n.*

ri·val /'rīvəl/ ▸*n.* a person or thing competing with another for the same objective or for superiority in the same field of activity: *he has no serious rival for the job* | [as *adj.*] *gun battles between rival gangs.* ■ a person or thing that equals another in quality: *she has no rivals as a female rock singer.*
▸*v.* (**-valed, -val·ing**; *Brit.* **-valled, -val·ling**) [*tr.*] compete for superiority with; be or seem to be equal or comparable to: *the efficiency of the Bavarians rivals that of the Viennese.*

ri·val·ry /'rīvəlrē/ ▸*n.* (*pl.* **-ries**) competition for the same objective or for superiority in the same field: *commercial rivalry* | *ethnic rivalries.*

riv·er /'rivər/ ▸*n.* a large natural stream of water flowing in a channel to the sea, a lake, or another such stream. ■ a large quantity of a flowing substance: *great rivers of molten lava* | *fig. the trickle of disclosures has grown into a river of revelations.* —**riv·ered** *adj.*
▸ □ **sell someone down the river** *inf.* betray someone, esp. so as to benefit oneself. □ **up the river** *inf.* to or in prison.

riv·er·bed /'rivər,bed/ ▸*n.* the bed or channel in which a river flows. ■ the bottom of a river.

riv·er·boat /'rivər,bōt/ ▸*n.* a boat with a shallow draft, designed for use on rivers.

riv·er·side /'rivər,sīd/ ▸*n.* [often as *adj.*] the ground along a riverbank: *dinner in one of the better riverside hotels.*

riv·et /'rivit/ ▸*n.* a short metal pin or bolt for holding together two plates of metal, its headless end being beaten out or pressed down when in place. ■ a similar device for holding seams of clothing together.
▸*v.* (**riv·et·ed, riv·et·ing**) [*tr.*] join or fasten (plates of metal or other material) with a rivet or rivets: *the linings are bonded, not riveted, to the brake shoes for longer wear.* ■ hold (someone or something) fast so as to make them incapable of movement: *the grip on her arm was firm enough to rivet her to the spot.* ■ attract and completely engross (someone): *he was riveted by the reports shown on television* | [as *adj.*] (**riveting**) *a riveting story.* ■ (usu. **be riveted**) direct (one's eyes or attention) intently: *all eyes were riveted on him.* —**riv·et·er** *n.* —**riv·et·ing·ly** *adv.*

rivet

ri·vi·er·a /,rivē'e(ə)rə; ri'vye(ə)rə/ ▸*n.* a coastal region with a subtropical climate and vegetation.

riv·u·let /'riv(y)ələt/ ▸*n.* a very small stream: *sweat ran in rivulets down his back.*

RN ▸*abbr.* ■ (chiefly in North America) Registered Nurse. ■ (in the UK) Royal Navy.

Rn ▸*symb.* the chemical element radon.

RNA ▸*n. Biochem.* ribonucleic acid, a nucleic acid present in all living cells. Its principal role is to act as a messenger carrying instructions from DNA for controlling the synthesis of proteins.

roach /rōch/ ▸*n. inf.* **1** a cockroach. **2** the butt of a marijuana cigarette.

road /rōd/ ▸*n.* **1** a wide way leading from one place to another, esp. one with a specially prepared surface that vehicles can use. ■ the part of such a way intended for vehicles, esp. in contrast to a shoulder or sidewalk. ■ *hist.* a regular trade route for a particular commodity: *the Silk Road across Asia to the West.* ■ a railroad. **2** *fig.* a series of events or a course of action that will lead to a particular outcome: *he's well on the road to recovery.* ■ a particular course or direction taken or followed: *the low road of apathy and alienation.*
▸ □ **one for the road** *inf.* a final drink, esp. an alcoholic one, before leaving for home. □ **on the road** on a long journey or series of journeys, esp. as part of one's job as a sales representative or a performer. ■ (of a person) without a permanent home and moving from place to place.

road·bed /'rōd,bed/ ▸*n.* the material laid down to form a road. ■ the part of a road on which vehicles travel. ■ the foundation structure on which railroad tracks are laid.

road·block /'rōd,bläk/ ▸*n.* a barrier or barricade on a road, esp. one set up by the authorities to stop and examine traffic. ■ *fig.* any hindrance: *the tax has become a roadblock against investment incentives.*

road hog ▸*n. inf.* a motorist who drives recklessly or inconsiderately, making it difficult for others to proceed safely or at a normal speed.

road·house /'rōd,hous/ ▸*n.* a tavern, inn, or club on a country road.

road·ie /'rōdē/ *inf.* ▸*n.* a person employed by a touring band of musicians to set up and maintain equipment.

road·map /'rōd,map/ ▸*v.* (**-mapped, -map·ping**) [*tr.*] schedule as part of a lengthy or complex program: *originally roadmapped for an early Q4 release, the next generation of the processor will ship in the last few days of the year.*

road met·al ▸*n.* see METAL (sense 2).

road·run·ner /'rōd,rənər/ ▸*n.* a slender fast-running bird (genus *Geococcyx*) of the cuckoo family, found chiefly in arid country from the southern US to Central America.

road show (also **road·show**) ▸*n.* a touring show of performers, esp. pop musicians. ■ a touring political or promotional campaign. ■ a radio or television program broadcast on location, esp. each of a series done from different venues.

road·side /'rōd,sīd/ ▸*n.* the strip of land beside a road: *trash left on the roadside* | [as *adj.*] *roadside cafés.*

road·ster /'rōdstər/ ▸*n.* an open-top automobile with two seats. ■ *hist.* a horse for use on the road.

road test ▸*n.* a test of the performance of a vehicle or engine on the road. ■ *fig.* a test of equipment carried out in working conditions: *he hopes to present a road test of whiskeys and to debate the various aromas and tastes.* ■ a test of a person's competence in driving a motor vehicle that must be passed in order to get a driver's license.
▸*v.* (**road-test**) [*tr.*] test (a vehicle or engine) on the road. ■ *fig.* try out (something) in working conditions for review or prior to purchase or release: *we road-tested a new laptop computer.*

road·way /'rōd,wā/ ▸*n.* a road. ■ the part of a road intended for vehicles, in contrast to a sidewalk or median. ■ the part of a bridge or railroad used by traffic.

road·work /'rōd,wərk/ ▸*n.* **1** work done in building or repairing roads. **2** athletic exercise or training involving running on roads. ■ time spent traveling while working or on tour.

roam /rōm/ ▸*v.* [*intr.*] move about or travel aimlessly or unsystematically, esp. over a wide area: *tigers once roamed over most of Asia* | [as *adj.*] (**roaming**) *roaming elephants.* ■ (of a person's eyes or hands) pass lightly over something without stopping: *her eyes roamed over the chattering women.* ■ [*intr.*] (of a person's mind or thoughts) drift along without dwelling on anything in particular: *he let his mind roam as he walked.* ■ [*tr.*] move from site to site on (the Internet); browse.
▸*n.* an aimless walk. —**roam·er** *n.*

roam·ing /'rōmiNG/ ▸*n.* the use of a cellular phone outside of its local area: *the roaming charges were too high.*

roan /rōn/ ▸*adj.* denoting an animal, esp. a horse or cow, having a coat of a main color thickly interspersed with hairs of another color, typically bay, chestnut, or black mixed with white.
▸*n.* an animal with such a coat: *the roan on the right is a stallion.*

roar /rôr/ ▸*n.* a full, deep, prolonged cry uttered by a lion or other large wild animal. ■ a loud and deep sound uttered by a person or crowd, generally as an expression of pain, anger, or approval: *he gave a roar of rage.* ■ a loud outburst of laughter. ■ a loud, prolonged sound made by

---

Pronunciation Key ə *ago*, *up*; ər *over*, *fur*; a *hat*; ā *ate*; ä *car*; CH *chin*; e *let*; ē *see*; e(ə)r *air*; i *fit*; ī *by*; i(ə)r *ear*; NG *sing*; ō *go*; ô *law*, *for*; oi *toy*; ŌŌ *good*; ŌŌ *goo*; ou *out*; SH *she*; TH *thin*; <u>TH</u> *then*; (h)w *why*; ZH *vision*

something inanimate, such as a natural force, an engine, or traffic: *the roar of the sea.*
▶ *v.* **1** [*intr.*] (of a lion or other large wild animal) utter a full, deep, prolonged cry. ■ (of something inanimate) make a loud, deep, prolonged sound: *a huge fire roared in the grate.* ■ (of a person or crowd) utter a loud, deep, prolonged sound, typically because of anger, pain, or excitement: *Manny roared with rage.* **2** [*intr.*] (esp. of a vehicle) move at high speed making a loud prolonged sound: *a car roared past.* ■ proceed, act, or happen fast and decisively or conspicuously: *the Clippers came roaring back to take lead.* ▷Old English *rārian* (verb), imitative of a deep prolonged cry; related to German *röhren.* The noun dates from late Middle English. —**roar·er** *n.*

roar·ing /'rôriNG/ ▶ *adj.* **1** (of a person, crowd, or animal) making a loud and deep sound, esp. as an expression of pain, anger, or approval: *he was greeted everywhere with roaring crowds.* ■ (of something inanimate, esp. a natural phenomenon) making a loud, deep, or harsh prolonged sound: *a swollen, roaring river.* ■ (of a fire) burning fiercely and noisily. ■ (of business) lively; brisk: *cafés that do a roaring trade.* **2** *inf.* obviously or unequivocally the thing mentioned (used for emphasis): *the final week of Hamlet was a roaring success* | *two roaring drunk firemen.* —**roar·ing·ly** *adv.*

Roar·ing Twen·ties ▶ *pl. n.* the decade of the 1920s, characterized by the optimism, buoyancy, and extravagance that followed the somber years of World War I.

roast /rōst/ ▶ *v.* [*tr.*] **1** cook (food, esp. meat) by prolonged exposure to heat in an oven or over a fire: *she was going to roast a leg of lamb for Sunday dinner* | [as *adj.*] (**roasted**) *roasted chestnuts.* ■ [*intr.*] (of food) be cooked in such a way: *she checked the meat roasting in the oven.* ■ process (a foodstuff, metal ore, etc.) by subjecting it to intense heat: *coffee beans are roasted and ground.* ■ make (someone or something) very warm, esp. by exposure to the heat of the sun or a fire: *the fire was hot enough to roast anyone who stood close to it.* ■ [*intr.*] become very hot: *Jessica could feel her face begin to roast.* **2** criticize or reprimand severely: *if you waste his time he'll roast you.* ■ offer a mocking tribute to (someone) at a roast.
▶ *adj.* (of food) having been cooked in an oven or over an open fire: *a plate of cold roast beef.*
▶ *n.* **1** a cut of meat that has been roasted or that is intended for roasting: *carving the Sunday roast.* ■ a dish or meal of roasted food. ■ the process of roasting something, esp. coffee, or the result of this. ■ a particular type of roasted coffee: *continental roasts.* ■ an outdoor party at which meat, esp. of a particular type, is roasted: *Harold put on a terrific pig roast.* **2** a banquet to honor a person at which the honoree is subjected to good-natured ridicule. —**roast·er** *n.*

roast·ing /'rōstiNG/ ▶ *adj.* (of a container) used for roasting food: *a roasting pan.* ■ (of a foodstuff) particularly suitable for roasting: *a roasting chicken.* ■ (of food) undergoing roasting: *the aroma of a roasting pig.* ■ *inf.* very hot and dry: *a roasting day in Miami.*
▶ *n.* the action of cooking something in an oven or over an open fire. ■ *inf.* a severe criticism or reprimand: *I was in for a roasting at the next meeting.*

rob /räb/ ▶ *v.* (**robbed**, **rob·bing**) [*tr.*] take property unlawfully from (a person or place) by force or threat of force: *he tried, with three others, to rob a bank* | *she robbed her of her handbag* | [*intr.*] *he was convicted of assault with intent to rob.* ■ (usu. **be robbed**) *inf.* overcharge (someone) for something: *Bob thinks my suit cost $100, and even then he thinks I was robbed.* ■ *inf.* or *dial.* steal: *he accused her of robbing the cream out of his chocolate eclair.* ■ deprive (someone or something) of something needed, deserved, or significant: *poor health has robbed her of a normal social life.*
▶ □ **rob Peter to pay Paul** take something away from one person to pay another, leaving the former at a disadvantage; discharge one debt only to incur another.

rob·ber /'räbər/ ▶ *n.* a person who commits robbery.

rob·ber·y /'räb(ə)rē/ ▶ *n.* (*pl.* **-ber·ies**) the action of robbing a person or place: *an armed robbery.* ■ *Law* the felonious taking of personal property from someone using force or the threat of force. ■ *inf.* unashamed swindling or overcharging.

robe /rōb/ ▶ *n.* a long, loose outer garment. ■ (often **robes**) such a garment worn, esp. on formal or ceremonial occasions, as an indication of the wearer's rank, office, or profession. ■ a dressing gown or bathrobe.
▶ *v.* [*tr.*] [usu. as *adj.*] (**robed**) clothe in a long, loose outer garment: *a circle of robed figures* | [in *comb.*] *a white-robed Bedouin.* ■ [*intr.*] put on robes, esp. for a formal or ceremonial occasion: *I went into the vestry and robed for the Mass.*

rob·in /'räbən/ ▶ *n.* a large New World thrush (genus *Turdus*) that typically has a reddish breast.

Rob·in Hood /'räbən ˌhŏŏd/ ▶a semilegendary English medieval outlaw, reputed to have robbed the rich and helped the poor. ■ [as *n.*] (**a Robin Hood**) a person considered to be taking from the wealthy and giving to the poor.

ro·bot /'rō,bät; 'rōbət/ ▶ *n.* a machine capable of carrying out a complex series of actions automatically, esp. one programmable by a computer. ■ (esp. in science fiction) a machine resembling a human being and able to replicate certain human movements and functions automatically. ■ used to refer to a person who behaves in a mechanical or unemotional manner: *terminally bored tour guides chattering like robots.*

ro·bot·ics /rō'bätiks/ ▶ *pl. n.* [treated as *sing.*] the branch of technology that deals with the design, construction, operation, and application of robots. —**ro·bot·ic** *adj.* —**ro·bot·i·cist** /-'bätəsist/ *n.*

ro·bust /rō'bəst; 'rō,bəst/ ▶ *adj.* (**-bust·er**, **-bust·est**) (of a person, animal, or plant) strong and healthy; vigorous: *the Caplans are a robust, healthy lot.* ■ (of an object) sturdy in construction: *a robust metal cabinet.* ■ (of a process or system, esp. an economic one) able to withstand or overcome adverse conditions: *California's robust property market.* ■ (of action) involving physical force or energy: *a robust game of rugby.* ■ (of wine or food) strong and rich in flavor or smell. ▷mid 16th cent.: from Latin *robustus* 'firm and hard,' from *robus,* earlier form of *robur* 'oak, strength.' —**ro·bust·ly** *adv.* —**ro·bust·ness** *n.*

rock¹ /räk/ ▶ *n.* **1** the solid mineral material forming part of the surface of the earth and other similar planets, exposed on the surface or underlying the soil or oceans. ■ a mass of such material projecting above the earth's surface or out of the sea: *there are dangerous rocks around the island.* ■ *Geol.* any natural material, hard or soft (e.g., clay, but excluding soil), having a distinctive mineral composition. **2** a large piece of such material that has become detached from a cliff or mountain; a boulder: *the stream flowed through a jumble of rocks.* ■ a stone of any size, esp. one small enough to be picked up and used as a projectile. ■ *inf.* a precious stone, esp. a diamond. ■ *inf.* a small piece of crack cocaine. ■ (**rocks**) *vulgar slang* testicles. **3** used in similes and metaphors to refer to someone or something that is extremely strong, reliable, or hard: *imagining himself as the last rock of civilization being swept over by a wave of barbarism.* ■ (usu. **rocks**) (esp. with allusion to shipwrecks) a source of danger or destruction: *the new system is heading for the rocks.* **4** (**rocks**) *inf., dated* money.
▶ □ **between a rock and a hard place** *inf.* in a situation where one is faced with two equally difficult alternatives. □ **on the rocks** *inf.* **1** (of a relationship or enterprise) experiencing difficulties and likely to fail. **2** (of a drink) served undiluted and with ice cubes.

rock² ▶ *v.* **1** cause (someone or something) to move gently to and fro or from side to side: *she rocked the baby in her arms.* ■ move in such a way: *the vase rocked back and forth on its base* | [as *adj.*] (**rocking**) *the rocking movement of the boat.* ■ (with reference to a building or region) shake or cause to shake or vibrate, esp. because of an impact, earthquake, or explosion: *a terrorist blast rocked a Tube station* | *the building began to rock on its foundations.* ■ cause great shock or distress to (someone or something), esp. so as to weaken or destabilize them or it: *diplomatic upheavals that rocked the British Empire.* **2** [*intr.*] *inf.* dance to or play rock music. ■ *fig.* (of a place) have an atmosphere of excitement or much social activity: *the new town really rocks* | [as *adj.*] (**rocking**) *a rocking resort.*
▶ *n.* **1** rock music: [as *adj.*] *a rock star.* ■ rock and roll. **2** a gentle movement to and fro or from side to side: *she placed the baby in the cradle and gave it a rock.*

rock·a·bil·ly /'räkə,bilē/ ▶ *n.* a type of popular music, originating in the southeastern U.S. in the 1950s, combining elements of rock and roll and country music.

rock and roll (also **rock 'n' roll**) ▶ *n.* a type of popular dance music originating in the 1950s, characterized by a heavy beat and simple melodies. —**rock and roll·er** *n.*

rock-bot·tom ▶ *adj.* at the lowest possible level: *rock-bottom prices.* ■ fundamental: *a pure, rock-bottom kind of realism.*
▶ *n.* (**rock bot·tom**) the lowest possible level: *morale is at rock bottom.*

rock-bound ▶ *adj.* (of a coast or shore) rocky and inaccessible.

rock climb·ing ▶ *n.* the sport or pastime of climbing rock faces, esp. with the aid of ropes and special equipment. —**rock climb** *n.* —**rock climb·er** *n.*

rock crys·tal ▶ *n.* transparent quartz, typically in the form of colorless hexagonal crystals.

rock·er /'räkər/ ▶ *n.* **1** a person who performs, dances to, or enjoys rock music, esp. of a particular type: *a punk rocker.* ■ a rock song. **2** a thing that rocks, in particular: ■ a rocking chair. ■ a rocking device forming part of a mechanism, esp. one for controlling the positions of brushes in a generator. **3** a curved bar or similar support on which some-

thing such as a chair or cradle can rock. **4** any of the curved stripes below the chevron of a noncommissioned officer above the rank of sergeant. ■ the curved strip above the chevron of a chief petty officer.
▶ □ **off one's rocker** *inf.* insane.
rock·er·y /ˈräkərē/ ▶*n.* (*pl.* **-er·ies**) a heaped arrangement of rough stones with soil between them, planted with rock plants, esp. alpines.
rock·et[1] /ˈräkit/ ▶*n.* a cylindrical projectile that can be propelled to a great height or distance by the combustion of its contents, used typically as a firework or signal. ■ (also **rocket engine** or **rocket motor**) an engine operating on the same principle, providing thrust as in a jet engine but without depending on the intake of air for combustion, an oxidizer being carried on board along with the fuel. ■ an elongated rocket-propelled missile or spacecraft. ■ used, esp. in similes and comparisons, to refer to a person or thing that moves very fast or to an action that is done with great force: *she shot out of her chair like a rocket.*
▶*v.* (**rock·et·ed, rock·et·ing**) **1** increase, move, or progress very rapidly: *the cab rocketed down a ramp* **2** [*tr.*] attack with rocket-propelled missiles: *the city was rocketed and bombed from the air.* —**rock·et·like** /-ˌlīk/ *adj.*
rock·et[2] ▶*n.* an edible Mediterranean plant (*Eruca vesicaria sativa*) of the cabbage family, sometimes eaten in salads.
rock·et·ry /ˈräkətrē/ ▶*n.* the branch of science that deals with rockets and rocket propulsion. ■ the use of rockets.
rock gar·den ▶*n.* an artificial mound or bank built of earth and stones and planted with rock plants. ■ a garden in which rockeries are the chief feature.
rock·ing chair ▶*n.* a chair mounted on rockers or springs, so as to rock back and forth.
rock·ing horse ▶*n.* a model of a horse mounted on rockers or springs for a child to sit on and rock back and forth.

rocking horse

rock 'n' roll ▶*n.* variant spelling of ROCK AND ROLL.
rock salt ▶*n.* common salt occurring naturally as a mineral; halite.
rock·y[1] /ˈräkē/ ▶*adj.* (**rock·i·er, rock·i·est**) consisting or formed of rock, esp. when exposed to view: *a rocky crag above the village.* ■ full of rocks: *hillsides of dry, rocky soil.* ■ *fig.* difficult; full of obstacles: *a long, rocky road to pop celebrity.* —**rock·i·ness** *n.*
rock·y[2] ▶*adj.* (**rock·i·er, rock·i·est**) tending to rock or shake; unsteady. ■ *fig.* not stable or firm; full of problems: *the marriage seemingly got off to a rocky start.* —**rock·i·ly** /ˈräkəlē/ *adv.* —**rock·i·ness** *n.*
Rock·y Moun·tain goat ▶*n.* see MOUNTAIN GOAT.
ro·co·co /rəˈkōkō; ˌrōkəˈkō/ ▶*adj.* (of furniture or architecture) of or characterized by an elaborately ornamental late baroque style of decoration prevalent in 18th-century Continental Europe, with asymmetrical patterns involving motifs and scrollwork. ■ extravagantly or excessively ornate, esp. (of music or literature) highly ornamented and florid.
▶*n.* the rococo style of art, decoration, or architecture.
rod /räd/ ▶*n.* **1** a thin straight bar, esp. of wood or metal. ■ a wand or staff as a symbol of office, authority, or power. ■ (**the rod**) the use of such a stick as punishment: *if you'd been my daughter, you'd have felt the rod.* ■ *vulgar slang* a penis. **2** a fishing rod. **3** *hist.* a linear measure, esp. for land, equal to $5\frac{1}{2}$ yards (approx. 5.03 m). **4** *inf.* a pistol or revolver. **5** *Anat.* a light-sensitive cell of one of the two types present in large numbers in the retina of the eye, responsible mainly for monochrome vision in poor light. —**rod·less** *adj.* —**rod·let** /-lət/ *n.* —**rod·like** /-ˌlīk/ *adj.*
rode /rōd/ ▶ past of RIDE.
ro·dent /ˈrōdnt/ ▶*n.* a gnawing mammal of a group that includes rats, mice, squirrels, hamsters, porcupines, and their relatives, distinguished by strong constantly growing incisors and no canine teeth.
ro·de·o /ˈrōdēˌō; rəˈdāō/ ▶*n.* (*pl.* **-de·os**) **1** an exhibition or contest in which cowboys show their skill at riding broncos, roping calves, wrestling steers, etc. ■ a similar exhibition or contest demonstrating other skills, such as motorcycle riding or canoeing. **2** a roundup of

cattle on a ranch for branding, counting, etc. ■ an enclosure for such a roundup.
▶*v.* (**-de·oed, -de·o·ing**) [*intr.*] compete in a rodeo. ▷mid 19th cent.: from Spanish, from *rodear* 'go around,' based on Latin *rotare* 'rotate.'
roe[1] /rō/ ▶*n.* the mass of eggs contained in the ovaries of a female fish or shellfish, typically including the ovaries themselves, esp. when ripe and used as food. ■ the ripe testes of a male fish, esp. when used as food.
roe[2] (also **roe deer**) ▶*n.* (*pl.* same or **roes**) a small Eurasian deer (genus *Capreolus*) that lacks a visible tail and has a reddish summer coat.
roe·buck /ˈrōˌbək/ ▶*n.* a male roe deer.
roent·gen /ˈrentgən; ˈrənt-; -jən/ (abbr.: **R**) ▶*n.* a unit of ionizing radiation, the amount producing one electrostatic unit of positive or negative ionic charge in one cubic centimeter of air under standard conditions.
rog·er /ˈräjər/ ▶*interj.* your message has been received and understood (used in radio communication): *"Roger; we'll be with you in about ten minutes."* ■ *inf.* used to express assent or understanding: *"Go light the stove." "Roger, Mister Bossman,"* Frank replied.
rogue /rōg/ ▶*n.* **1** a dishonest or unprincipled man: *you are a rogue and an embezzler.* ■ a person whose behavior one disapproves of but who is nonetheless likable or attractive (often used as a playful term of reproof): *Cenzo, you old rogue!* **2** [usu. as *adj.*] an elephant or other large wild animal driven away or living apart from the herd and having savage or destructive tendencies: *a rogue elephant.* ■ a person or thing that behaves in an aberrant, faulty, or unpredictable way: *he hacked into data and ran rogue programs.* ■ an inferior or defective specimen among many satisfactory ones, esp. a seedling or plant deviating from the standard variety.
▶*v.* [*tr.*] remove inferior or defective plants or seedlings from (a crop).
ro·guish /ˈrōgiSH/ ▶*adj.* characteristic of a dishonest or unprincipled person: *he led a roguish and uncertain existence.* ■ playfully mischievous, esp. in a way that is sexually attractive: *he gave her a roguish smile.* —**ro·guish·ly** *adv.* —**ro·guish·ness** *n.*
roist·er /ˈroistər/ ▶*v.* [*intr.*] enjoy oneself or celebrate in a noisy or boisterous way: *workers from the refinery roistered in the bars.* —**roist·er·er** *n.* —**roist·er·ous** /ˈroist(ə)rəs/ *adj.*
role /rōl/ ▶*n.* an actor's part in a play, movie, etc.: *Dietrich's role as a wife in war-torn Paris.* ■ the function assumed or part played by a person or thing in a particular situation: *religion plays a vital role in society.*
role mod·el ▶*n.* a person looked to by others as an example to be imitated.
role-play·ing (also **role-play**) ▶*n.* **1** *chiefly Psychol.* the acting out or performance of a particular role, either consciously (as a technique in psychotherapy or training) or unconsciously, in accordance with the perceived expectations of society with regard to a person's behavior in a particular context. **2** participation in a role-playing game. —**role-play** *v.* —**role-play·er** *n.*
roll /rōl/ ▶*v.* **1** move or cause to move in a particular direction by turning over and over on an axis: *the car rolled down into a ditch | she rolled the ball across the floor.* ■ turn (one's eyes) upward, typically to show surprise or disapproval: *Sarah rolled her eyes.* ■ (of a moving ship, aircraft, or vehicle) rock or oscillate around an axis parallel to the direction of motion: *the ship pitched and rolled.* ■ move along or from side to side unsteadily or uncontrollably: *they were rolling about with laughter.* ■ *inf.* overturn (a vehicle): *he rolled his Mercedes in a 100 mph crash.* ■ throw (a die or dice). ■ obtain (a particular score) by doing this: *roll a 2, 3, or 12.* **2** (of a vehicle) move or run on wheels: *the van was rolling along the highway.* ■ move or push (a wheeled object): *Pat rolled the cart back and forth.* ■ (**roll something up/down**) make a car window or a window blind move up or down. ■ (of time) elapse steadily: *the years rolled by.* ■ (of a drop of liquid) flow: *huge tears rolled down her cheeks.* ■ [usu. as *adj.*] (**rolling**) (of land) extend in gentle undulations: *the rolling countryside.* ■ (of a machine, esp. a camera) operate or begin operating: *the cameras started to roll.* ■ cause (a machine, esp. a camera) to begin operating: *roll the camera.* **3** turn (something flexible) over and over on itself to form a cylinder, tube, or ball: *she started to roll up her sleeping bag.* ■ (of a person or animal) curl up tightly: *the shock made the armadillo roll into a ball.* **4** flatten (something) by passing a roller over it or by passing it between rollers: *roll out the dough on a floured surface.* **5** (of a loud, deep sound such as that of thunder or drums) reverberate: *the first peals of thunder rolled across the sky.* ■ pronounce (a consonant, typically an r)

---

with a trill: *when he wanted to emphasize a point he rolled his rrrs.* **6** *inf.* rob (someone, typically when they are intoxicated or asleep): *if you don't get drunk, you don't get rolled.*

▸ *phrasal v.* ▢ **roll something back** reverse the progress or reduce the power or importance of something: *the strategy to roll back communism.* ▢ **roll something out** officially launch or unveil a new product or service: *the firm rolled out its newest generation of supercomputers.* ▢ **roll something over** *Finance* contrive or extend a particular financial arrangement: *this is not a good time for rolling over corporate debt.*

▸ *n.* **1** a cylinder formed by winding flexible material around a tube or by turning it over and over on itself without folding: *a roll of carpet.* ■ a cylindrical mass of something or a number of items arranged in a cylindrical shape: *a roll of mints.* ■ an item of food that is made by wrapping a flat sheet of pastry, cake, meat, or fish around a sweet or savory filling: *salmon and rice rolls.* ■ a roller for flattening something, esp. one used to shape metal in a rolling mill. **2** a movement in which someone or something turns or is turned over on itself: *a roll of the dice.* **3** a prolonged, deep, reverberating sound, typically made by thunder or a drum: *thunder exploded, roll after roll.* ■ *Mus.* one of the basic patterns (rudiments) of drumming, consisting of a sustained, rapid alternation of single or double strokes of each stick. **4** a very small loaf of bread, typically eaten with butter or a filling: *a sausage roll.* **5** an official list or register of names. ■ the total numbers on such a list: *a review of secondary schools to assess the effects of falling rolls.* ■ a document, typically an official record, in scroll form. ▷Middle English: from Old French *rolle* (noun), *roller* (verb), from Latin *rotulus* 'a roll,' variant of *rotula* 'little wheel,' diminutive of *rota.* —**roll·a·ble** *adj.*

▸ ▢ **a roll in the hay** (or **the sack**) *inf.* an act of sexual intercourse. ▢ **on a roll** *inf.* experiencing a prolonged spell of success or good luck: *the organization is on a roll.* ▢ **rolling in the aisles** *inf.* (of an audience) laughing uncontrollably. ▢ **roll up one's sleeves** prepare to fight or work. ▢ **roll with the punches** (of a boxer) move one's body away from an opponent's blows so as to lessen the impact. ■ *fig.* adapt oneself to adverse circumstances.

roll bar ▸ *n.* a metal bar running up the sides and across the top of a vehicle, esp. one used in motor sports, strengthening its frame and protecting the occupants should the vehicle overturn.

roll bar

roll call ▸ *n.* the process of calling out a list of names to establish who is present. ■ *fig.* a list or group of people or things that are notable in some specified way: *the roll call of nations that lack full religious rights.*

roll·er /'rōlər/ ▸ *n.* a cylinder that rotates around a central axis and is used in various machines and devices to move, flatten, or spread something. ■ a long swelling wave that appears to roll steadily toward the shore. ■ [as *adj.*] of, relating to, or involving roller skates.

roll·er bear·ing ▸ *n.* a bearing similar to a ball bearing but using small cylindrical rollers instead of balls.

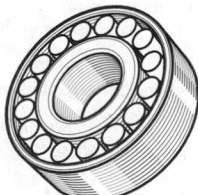
roller bearing

Roll·er·blade /'rōlər,blād/ ▸ *n.* trademark an in-line skate.

▸ *v.* [*intr.*] skate using Rollerblades: *the muscular actor loves to Rollerblade.* —**roll·er·blad·er** *n.*

roll·er coast·er ▸ *n.* an amusement park attraction that consists of a light railroad track with many tight turns and steep slopes, on which people ride in small fast open cars. ■ *fig.* a thing that contains or goes through wild and unpredictable changes: *a terrific roller coaster of a book.*

▸ *v.* (**roll·er-coast·er**) (also **roll·er-coast**) [*intr.*] move, change, or occur in

the dramatically changeable manner of a roller coaster: *the twentieth century fades behind us and history roller-coasters on.*

roll·er rink ▸ *n.* see RINK.

roll·ing pin ▸ *n.* a cylinder rolled over pastry or dough to flatten or shape it.

roll·ing stone ▸ *n.* a person who is unwilling to settle for long in one place.

roll·o·ver /'rōl,ōvər/ ▸ *n.* **1** *Finance* the extension or transfer of a debt or other financial arrangement. ■ (in a lottery) the unwon prize money carried over to the following drawing. **2** *inf.* the overturning of a vehicle.

roll·top desk /'rōl,täp/ ▸ *n.* a writing desk with a flexible cover sliding in curved grooves.

ro·ly-po·ly /'rōlē 'pōlē/ ▸ *adj.* (of a person) having a round, plump appearance: *a roly-poly young boy.*

ROM /räm/ ▸ *abbr.* *Comput.* read-only memory.

Rom /räm/ ▸ *n.* (pl. **Ro·ma** /'rōmə/) a gypsy, esp. a man.

ro·maine /rō'mān/ ▸ *n.* a lettuce of a variety with crisp narrow leaves that form a tall head.

Ro·man /'rōmən/ ▸ *adj.* **1** of or relating to ancient Rome or its empire or people: *an old Roman road.* ■ of or relating to medieval or modern Rome: *the Roman and Pisan lines of popes.* **2** denoting the alphabet (or any of the letters in it) used for writing Latin, English, and most European languages, developed in ancient Rome. ■ (**roman**) (of printing type) of a plain upright kind used in ordinary print, esp. as distinguished from italic.

▸ *n.* **1** a citizen or soldier of the ancient Roman Republic or Empire. ■ a citizen of modern Rome. **2** (**roman**) roman type.

ro·man à clef /rō,män ä 'klā/ ▸ *n.* (pl. **ro·mans à clef** *pronunc.* same) a novel in which real people or events appear with invented names.

Ro·man Cath·o·lic ▸ *adj.* of or relating to the Roman Catholic Church: *a Roman Catholic bishop.*

▸ *n.* a member of this church. —**Ro·man Ca·thol·i·cism** *n.*

Ro·mance /rō'mans; 'rō,mans/ ▸ *n.* the group of Indo-European languages descended from Latin, principally French, Spanish, Portuguese, Italian, Catalan, Occitan, and Romanian.

▸ *adj.* of, relating to, or denoting this group of languages: *the Romance languages.*

ro·mance /rō'mans; 'rō,mans/ ▸ *n.* **1** a feeling of excitement and mystery associated with love: *in search of romance.* ■ love, esp. when sentimental or idealized: *he asked her for a date and romance blossomed.* ■ a book or movie dealing with love in a sentimental or idealized way: *light historical romances.* ■ a genre of fiction dealing with love in such a way: *wartime passion from the master of romance.* **2** a quality or feeling of mystery, excitement, and remoteness from everyday life: *the beauty and romance of the night.* ■ wild exaggeration; picturesque falsehood: *she slammed the claims as "pure romance, complete fiction."* ■ a work of fiction dealing with events remote from real life. **3** a medieval tale dealing with a hero of chivalry, of the kind common in the Romance languages: *the Arthurian romances.* ■ the literary genre of such works. **4** *Mus.* a short informal piece.

▸ *v.* [*tr.*] **1** court; woo: *the wealthy estate owner romanced her.* ■ *inf.* seek the attention or patronage of (someone), esp. by use of flattery: *he is being romanced by the big boys in New York.* ■ [*intr.*] engage in a love affair: *we start romancing.* **2** another term for ROMANTICIZE: *to a certain degree I am romancing the past.*

Ro·man Em·pire ▸ the empire established by Augustus in 27 BC and divided in AD 395 into the Western or Latin and Eastern or Greek Empire.

Ro·man·esque /,rōmə'nesk/ ▸ *adj.* of or relating to a style of architecture that prevailed in Europe c.900–1200, although sometimes dated back to the end of the Roman Empire (5th century).

▸ *n.* Romanesque architecture.

Ro·ma·ni·an /rō'mānēən; rōō-/ (also **Ru·ma·ni·an**) ▸ *adj.* of or relating to Romania or its people or language.

▸ *n.* **1** a native or national of Romania, or a person of Romanian descent. **2** the language of Romania, a Romance language influenced by the neighboring Slavic languages, also spoken by the majority of the population of Moldova.

Ro·man·ist /'rōmənist/ ▸ *n.* an expert in or student of Roman antiquities or law, or of the Romance languages.

ro·man·ize /'rōmə,nīz/ (also **Ro·man·ize**) ▸ *v.* [*tr.*] **1** *hist.* bring (something, esp. a region or people) under Roman influence or authority: *though not himself a Roman, he was fully Romanized, spoke Latin, and lived in a Roman-style villa.* **2** make Roman Catholic in character: *he has Roman-*

ized the services of his church. **3** put (text) into the Roman alphabet or into roman type: *Atatürk's decision to romanize the written language.* —**ro·man·i·za·tion** /ˌrōmənəˈzāsHən/ *n.*

Ro·man num·er·al ▸*n.* any of the letters representing numbers in the Roman numerical system: I = 1, V = 5, X = 10, L = 50, C = 100, D = 500, M = 1,000. In this system, a letter placed after another of greater value adds (thus XVI or xvi is 16), whereas a letter placed before another of greater value subtracts (thus XC or xc is 90).

Ro·ma·no /rəˈmänō/ ▸*n.* a strong-tasting hard cheese, originally made in Italy .

ro·man·tic /rōˈmantik; rə-/ ▸*adj.* **1** inclined toward or suggestive of the feeling of excitement and mystery associated with love: *a romantic dinner by the fire.* ■ relating to love, esp. in a sentimental or idealized way: *a romantic comedy.* **2** . of, characterized by, or suggestive of an idealized view of reality: *a romantic attitude toward the past | some romantic dream of country peace.* **3** (usu. **Romantic**) of, relating to, or denoting the artistic and literary movement of Romanticism: *the Romantic tradition.*
▸*n.* a person with romantic beliefs or attitudes: *I am an incurable romantic.* ■ (usu. **Romantic**) a writer or artist of the Romantic movement. —**ro·man·ti·cal·ly** /-ik(ə)lē/ *adv.*

ro·man·ti·cism /rōˈmantəˌsizəm; rə-/ ▸*n.* **1** (often **Romanticism**) a movement in the arts and literature that originated in the late 18th century, emphasizing inspiration, subjectivity, and the primacy of the individual. **2** the state or quality of being romantic: *a quality of romanticism about women that leads to the creation of a pipe-dream fantasy.*

ro·man·ti·cist /rōˈmantəsist; rə-/ ▸*n.* a writer, artist, or musician of the Romantic movement. ■ a person who subscribes to the artistic movement or ideas of Romanticism.

ro·man·ti·cize /rōˈmantəˌsīz; rə-/ ▸*v.* [*tr.*] deal with or describe in an idealized or unrealistic fashion; make (something) seem better or more appealing than it really is: *the tendency to romanticize nonindustrial societies* | [*intr.*] *she was romanticizing about the past.* —**ro·man·ti·ci·za·tion** /rōˌmantəsəˈzāsHən; rə-/ *n.*

Rom·a·ny /ˈrämənē; ˈrō-/ (also **Rom·a·ni**) ▸*n.* (*pl.* **-nies**) **1** the Indic language of the gypsies, spoken in many dialects. **2** a gypsy.
▸*adj.* of or relating to gypsies or their language.

romp /rämp; rômp/ ▸*v.* [*intr.*] (esp. of a child or animal) play roughly and energetically: *the noisy pack of children romped around the garden.* ■ *inf.* proceed without effort to achieve something: *the Vikings romped to victory.* ■ *inf.* engage in sexual activity, esp. illicitly: *a colleague stumbled on the couple romping in an office.*
▸*n.* a spell of rough, energetic play: *a romp in the snow.* ■ a lighthearted movie or other work: *an enjoyably gross sci-fi romp.* ■ *inf.* an easy victory: *the 45–28 romp over the Owls yesterday at Alumni Stadium.* ■ *inf.* a spell of sexual activity, esp. an illicit one: *three-in-a-bed sex romps.*

romp·er /ˈrämpər; ˈrôm-/ ▸*n.* **1** (also **romper suit** or **romp·ers**) a young child's one-piece outer garment. ■ a similar item of clothing for adults, typically worn as overalls or as sports clothing. **2** a person who romps.

ron·do /ˈrändō; ränˈdō/ ▸*n.* (*pl.* **-dos**) a musical form with a recurring leading theme, often found in the final movement of a sonata or concerto.

rood /rōōd/ ▸*n.* a crucifix, esp. one positioned above the rood screen of a church or on a beam over the entrance to the chancel.

rood screen ▸*n.* a screen, typically of richly carved wood or stone, separating the nave from the chancel of a church.

roof /rōōf; rōof/ ▸*n.* (*pl.* **roofs**) the structure forming the upper covering of a building or vehicle. ■ the top inner surface of a covered area or space; the ceiling: *the roof of the cave fell in.* ■ used to signify a house or other building, esp. in the context of hospitality or shelter: *helping those without a roof over their heads.* ■ (**roof of the mouth**) the palate.
▸*v.* [*tr.*] (usu. **be roofed**) cover with a roof: *the yard had been roughly roofed over with corrugated iron.* ■ function as the roof of: *fan vaults roof these magnificent buildings.* ▷Old English *hrōf*, of Germanic origin; related to Old Norse *hróf* 'boat shed,' Dutch *roef* 'deckhouse.' English alone has the general sense 'covering of a house'; other Germanic languages use forms related to *thatch*. —**roof·less** *adj.*
▸ □ **go through the roof** *inf.* (of prices or figures) reach extreme or unexpected heights. □ **hit the roof** *inf.* suddenly become very angry.

roof·er /ˈrōōfər; ˈrōof-/ ▸*n.* a person who constructs or repairs roofs.

roof·ing /ˈrōōfiNG; ˈrōof-/ ▸*n.* material for constructing a building's roof: *a house with corrugated tin roofing.* ■ the process of constructing a roof or roofs: *jobs such as roofing.*

roof·line /ˈrōōf,līn; ˈrōof-/ ▸*n.* the design or proportions of the roof of a building or vehicle.

roof rack ▸*n.* a framework for carrying luggage or equipment on the roof of a vehicle.

roof·top /ˈrōōf,täp; ˈrōof-/ ▸*n.* the outer surface of a building's roof.

rook[1] /rōōk/ ▸*v.* [*tr.*] *inf.* take money from (someone) by cheating, defrauding, or overcharging them.

rook[2] ▸*n.* a chess piece, typically with its top in the shape of a battlement, that can move in any direction along a rank or file on which it stands. Each player starts the game with two rooks at opposite ends of the first rank. See also CASTLE.

rook·ie /ˈrōōkē/ ▸*n. inf.* a new recruit, esp. in the army or police: [as *adj.*] *a rookie cop.* ■ a member of an athletic team in his or her first full season in that sport.

room /rōōm; rōom/ ▸*n.* **1** space that can be occupied or where something can be done, esp. viewed in terms of whether there is enough: *there's only room for a single bed in there.* ■ *fig.* opportunity or scope for something to happen or be done, esp. without causing trouble or damage: *there is plenty of room for disagreement in this controversial area.* **2** a part or division of a building enclosed by walls, floor, and ceiling: *he wandered from room to room.* ■ (**rooms**) a set of rooms, typically rented, in which a person, couple, or family live: *my rooms at Mrs. Jenks's house.* ■ the people present in a room: *the whole room burst into an uproar of approval.*
▸*v.* [*intr.*] share a room or house or flat, esp. a rented one at a college or similar institution: *I was rooming with my cousin.* ■ [*tr.*] provide with a shared room or lodging: *they roomed us together.* —**roomed** *adj.* [in comb.] *a four-roomed house.* —**room·ful** /-,fōol/ *n.* (*pl.* **-fuls**).
▸ □ **make room** move aside or move something aside to allow someone to enter or pass or to clear space for something: *the secretary entered with the coffee tray and made room for it on the desk.*

room·er /ˈrōōmər; ˈrōom-/ ▸*n.* a renter of a room in another person's house.

room·ie /ˈrōōmē; ˈrōomē/ ▸*n. inf.* a roommate.

room·ing house ▸*n.* a private house in which rooms are rented for living or staying temporarily.

room·mate /ˈrōōm,māt; ˈrōom-/ ▸*n.* a person occupying the same room as another. ■ a person occupying the same apartment or house as another.

room serv·ice ▸*n.* service provided in a hotel allowing guests to order food and drink to be brought to their rooms.

room·y /ˈrōōmē; ˈrōomē/ ▸*adj.* (**room·i·er**, **room·i·est**) (esp. of accommodations) having plenty of room; spacious. —**room·i·ly** /-məlē/ *adv.* —**room·i·ness** *n.*

roost /rōōst/ ▸*n.* a place where birds regularly settle or congregate to rest at night, or where bats congregate to rest in the day.
▸*v.* [*intr.*] (of a bird or bat) settle or congregate for rest or sleep: *migrating martins and swallows were settling to roost.*
▸ □ **come home to roost** (of a scheme, etc.) recoil unfavorably upon the originator: *ensuring that the liability does not come home to roost.* □ **rule the roost** see RULE.

roost·er /ˈrōōstər; ˈrōostər/ ▸*n.* a male domestic fowl; a cock.

root[1] /rōōt; rōot/ ▸*n.* **1** the part of a plant that attaches it to the ground or to a support, typically underground, conveying water and nourishment to the rest of the plant via numerous branches and fibers: *a tree root.* ■ the embedded part of a bodily organ or structure such as a hair, tooth, or nail: *her hair was fairer at the roots.* ■ the part of a thing attaching it to a greater or more fundamental whole; the end or base: *a little lever near the root of the barrel.* **2** the basic cause, source, or origin of something: *love of money is the root of all evil.* ■ the essential substance or nature of something: *matters at the heart and root of existence.* ■ (**roots**) family, ethnic, or cultural origins, esp. as the reasons for one's longstanding emotional attachment to a place or community: *it's always nice to return to my roots.* ■ [as *adj.*] (**roots**) denoting or relating to something, esp. music, from a particular ethnic or cultural origin, esp. a non-Western one: *roots music.* ■ *Linguistics* a morpheme, not necessarily surviving as a word in itself, from which words have been made by the addition of prefixes or suffixes or by other modification: *many European words stem from this linguistic root.* ■ *Mus.* the fundamental note of a chord. **3** *Math.* a number or quantity that when multiplied by itself, typically a specified number of times, gives a specified number or quantity: *find the cube root of the result.* ■ short for SQUARE ROOT. ■ a value of an unknown quantity satisfying a given equation: *the roots of the equation differ by an integer.*

Pronunciation Key ə *ago,* *up;* ər *over, fur;* a *hat;* ā *ate;* ä *car;* CH *chin;* e *let;* ē *see;* e(ə)r *air;* i *fit;* ī *by;* i(ə)r *ear;* NG *sing;* ō *go;* ô *law, for;* oi *toy;* ŏŏ *good;* ōō *goo;* ou *out;* SH *she;* TH *thin;* ŦH *then;* (h)w *why;* ZH *vision*

▸*v.* [*tr.*] **1** cause (a plant or cutting) to grow roots: *root your own cuttings from stock plants.* ■ [*intr.*] (of a plant or cutting) establish roots: *large trees had rooted in the canal bank.* **2** (usu. **be rooted**) establish deeply and firmly: *vegetarianism is rooted in Indian culture.* ■ (**be rooted in**) have as an origin or cause: *the Latin* dubitare *is rooted in an Indo-European word.* ■ [*tr.*] [often as *adj.*] (**rooted**) cause (someone) to stand immobile through fear or amazement: *she found herself rooted to the spot in disbelief.*
▸*phrasal v.* □ **root something out** (also **root something up**) dig or pull up a plant by the roots. ■ find and get rid of someone or something regarded as pernicious or dangerous: *a campaign to root out corruption.* —**root·ed·ness** *n* —**root·less** *adj.* —**root·let** /-lət/ *n.* —**root·like** /-,līk/ *adj.*
root² ▸*v.* [*intr.*] (of an animal) turn up the ground with its snout in search of food: *stray dogs rooting around for bones and scraps.* ■ search unsystematically through an untidy mass or area; rummage: *she was rooting through a pile of papers.* ■ [*tr.*] (**root something out**) find or extract something by rummaging: *he managed to root out the cleaning kit.*
▸*phrasal v.* □ **root for** *inf.* support or hope for the success of (a person or group entering a contest or undertaking a challenge): *the whole of this club is rooting for him.*
▸*n.* an act of rooting: *I have a root through the open drawers.* —**root·er** *n.*
root beer ▸*n.* an effervescent drink made from an extract of the roots and bark of certain plants.
root ca·nal ▸*n.* the pulp-filled cavity in the root of a tooth. ■ a procedure to replace infected pulp in a root canal with an inert material.
root·stock /'rŏot,stäk; 'rŏŏt-/ ▸*n.* a rhizome. ■ a plant onto which another variety is grafted. ■ a primary form or source from which offshoots have arisen.
rope /rōp/ ▸*n.* **1** a length of strong cord made by twisting together strands of natural fibers such as hemp or artificial fibers such as polypropylene. ■ a lasso. ■ (**the rope**) used in reference to execution by hanging: *executions by the rope continued well into the twentieth century.* ■ (**the ropes**) the ropes enclosing a boxing or wrestling ring. **2** (**the ropes**) *inf.* the established procedures in an organization or area of activity: *I want you to show her the ropes.*
▸*v.* [*tr.*] catch, fasten, or secure with rope: *the climbers were all roped together.* ■ (**rope someone in/into**) persuade someone to take part in (an activity): *anyone who could play an instrument or sing in tune was roped in.* ■ (**rope something off**) enclose or separate an area with a rope or tape: *police roped off the area of the find.* —**rop·er** *n.*
▸ □ **on the ropes** *Boxing* forced against the ropes by the opponent's attack. ■ in state of near collapse or defeat: *behind the apparent success the company was on the ropes.*
rop·y /'rōpē/ (also **rop·ey**) ▸*adj.* (**rop·i·er**, **rop·i·est**) resembling a rope in being long, strong, and fibrous: *the ropy roots of the old tree.* ■ (of a liquid) resembling a rope in forming viscous or gelatinous threads: *his spit was thick and ropey as he spat.* —**rop·i·ly** /'rōpəlē/ *adv.* —**rop·i·ness** *n.*
Roque·fort /'rōkfərt/ ▸*n. trademark* a soft blue cheese made from ewes' milk. It is ripened in limestone caves and has a strong flavor.
Ror·schach test /'rôr,SHäk/ ▸*n. Psychol.* a type of projective test used in psychoanalysis, in which a standard set of symmetrical ink blots of different shapes and colors is presented one by one to the subject, who is asked to describe what they suggest or resemble.
ro·sa·ceous /rō'zāSHəs/ ▸*adj. Bot.* of, relating to, or denoting plants of the rose family (Rosaceae).
ro·sa·ry /'rōzərē/ ▸*n.* (*pl.* **-ries**) (in the Roman Catholic Church) a form of devotion in which five (or fifteen) decades of Hail Marys are repeated, each decade preceded by an Our Father and followed by a Glory Be: *the congregation said the rosary.* ■ a string of beads for keeping count in such a devotion or in the devotions of some other religions, in Roman Catholic use 55 or 165 in number. ■ a book containing such a devotion.
rose¹ /rōz/ ▸*n.* **1** a prickly bush or shrub (genus *Rosa*) that typically bears red, pink, yellow, or white fragrant flowers, native to north temperate regions. Numerous hybrids and cultivars are grown as ornamentals. The **rose family** (Rosaceae) also includes most temperate fruits (e.g., apple, plum, cherry, strawberry), as well as the hawthorns and rowans. ■ the flower of such a plant: [as *adj.*] *a rose garden.* ■ used in names of other plants whose flowers resemble roses, e.g., **rose of Sharon.** ■ used in similes and comparisons in reference to the rose flower's beauty or its typical rich red color. **2** a thing representing or resembling the flower, in particular: ■ a stylized representation of the flower in heraldry or decoration, typically with five petals (esp. as a national emblem of England): *the Tudor rose.* **3** a warm pink or light crimson color. ■ (usu. **roses**) used in reference to a rosy complexion: *the fresh air will soon put the roses back in her cheeks.*
rose² ▸ past of **RISE**.
ro·sé /rōzā/ ▸*n.* any light pink wine, colored by only brief contact with red grape skins. ▷French, literally 'pink.'

ro·se·ate /'rōzēət; -,āt/ ▸*adj.* **1** rose-colored: *the early, roseate light.* ■ used in names of birds with partly pink plumage, e.g., **roseate tern, roseate spoonbill. 2** optimistic; promising good fortune: *his letters home give a very good, although somewhat too roseate, idea of how he lived.*
rose·bud /'rōz,bəd/ ▸*n.* an unopened flower of a rose.
rose-col·ored ▸*adj.* of a warm pink color: *rose-colored silks.* ■ used in reference to a naively optimistic or unrealistic viewpoint: *you are still seeing the profession through rose-colored glasses.*
rose hip ▸*n.* see **HIP²**.
rose·mar·y /'rōz,merē/ ▸*n.* an evergreen aromatic shrub (*Rosmarinus officinalis*) of the mint family, native to southern Europe. The narrow leaves are used as a culinary herb, in perfumery, and as an emblem of remembrance.
ro·se·o·la /,rōzē'ōlə; rō'zēələ/ ▸*n. Med.* a rose-colored rash occurring in measles, typhoid fever, syphilis, and some other diseases. ■ (in full **roseola infantum** /in'fantəm/) a disease of young children in which a fever is followed by a rash, caused by a herpes virus.
ro·sette /rō'zet/ ▸*n.* **1** a rose-shaped decoration, typically made of ribbon and awarded to winners of a competition. **2** a design, arrangement, or growth resembling a rose, in particular: ■ *Archit.* a carved or molded ornament resembling or representing a rose. ■ a roselike cluster of parts, esp. a radiating arrangement of horizontally spreading leaves at the base of a low-growing plant. ■ a rose diamond. —**ro·set·ted** /rō'zetəd/ *adj.*
rose win·dow ▸*n.* a circular window with mullions or tracery radiating in a form suggestive of a rose.
rose·wood /'rōz,wŏod/ ▸*n.* **1** fragrant close-grained tropical timber with a distinctive fragrance, used particularly for making furniture and musical instruments. **2** the tree (genus *Dalbergia*) of the pea family that produces this timber.
Rosh Ha·sha·nah /,rôSH (h)ə'SHōnə; ,räSH; -'SHänə/ (also **Rosh Ha·sha·na**) ▸*n.* the Jewish New Year festival, held on the first (also sometimes the second) day of Tishri (in September).
ros·in /'räzən/ ▸*n.* resin, esp. the solid amber residue obtained after the distillation of crude turpentine oleoresin.
▸*v.* (**ros·ined, ros·in·ing**) [*tr.*] rub (something, esp. the bow of a stringed instrument) with rosin. —**ros·in·y** *adj.*
ros·ter /'rästər; 'rô-/ ▸*n.* a list or plan showing turns of duty or leave for individuals or groups in an organization: *next week's duty roster.* ■ a list of members of a team or organization, in particular of athletes available for team selection.
ros·tra /'rästrə; 'rô-/ ▸ plural form of **ROSTRUM**.
ros·trum /'rästrəm; 'rô-/ ▸*n.* (*pl.* **ros·tra** /'rästrə; 'rô-/ or **ros·trums**) a raised platform on which a person stands to make a public speech, receive an award or medal, play music, or conduct an orchestra. ■ a similar platform for supporting a movie or television camera. ▷mid 16th cent.: from Latin, literally 'beak' (from *rodere* 'gnaw'). The word was originally used (at first in the plural *rostra*) to denote part of the Forum in Rome, which was decorated with the beaks of captured galleys, and was used as a platform for public speakers.
ros·y /'rōzē/ ▸*adj.* (**ros·i·er, ros·i·est**) **1** (esp. of a person's skin) colored like a pink or red rose, typically as an indication of health, youth, or embarrassment: *the memory had the power to make her cheeks turn rosy.* **2** promising or suggesting good fortune or happiness; hopeful: *the strategy has produced results beyond the most rosy forecasts.* ■ easy and pleasant: *life could never be rosy for them.* —**ros·i·ly** /'rōzəlē/ *adv.* —**ros·i·ness** *n.*
rot /rät/ ▸*v.* (**rot·ted, rot·ting**) [*intr.*] (chiefly of animal or vegetable matter) decompose by the action of bacteria and fungi; decay: *the chalets were neglected and their woodwork was rotting away.* ■ [*tr.*] cause to decay: *caries sets in at a weak point and spreads to rot the whole tooth.* ■ *fig.* gradually deteriorate through lack of attention or opportunity: *he cannot understand the way the education system has been allowed to rot.*
▸*n.* **1** the process of decaying: *the leaves were turning black with rot.* ■ rotten or decayed matter: *she was busy cutting the rot from the potatoes.* ■ any of a number of fungal or bacterial diseases that cause tissue deterioration, esp. in plants. **2** *inf.* nonsense; rubbish: *don't talk rot.*
ro·ta·ry /'rōtərē/ ▸*adj.* (of motion) revolving around a center or axis; rotational: *a rotary motion.* ■ (of a thing) acting by means of rotation, esp. (of a machine) operating through the rotation of some part: *a rotary mower.*
▸*n.* (*pl.* **-ries**) a traffic circle.
ro·tate¹ /'rō,tāt/ ▸*v.* [*intr.*] move in a circle around an axis or center: *the wheel continued to rotate* | [as *adj.*] (**rotating**) *a rotating drum.* ■ [*tr.*] cause to move around an axis or in a circle: *the small directional side rockets rotated the craft.* ■ pass to each member of a group in a regularly recurring order: *the job of chairing the meeting rotates.* ▷late 17th cent.: from Latin *rotat-* 'turned in a circle,' from the verb *rotare*, from *rota* 'wheel.' —**ro·**

tat·a·ble /'rō,tātəbəl; rō'tāt-/ *adj.* —**ro·ta·tive** /'rō,tātiv/ *adj.* —**ro·ta·to·ry** /'rōtə,tôrē/ *adj.*

ro·tate² ▸*adj.* shaped like a wheel, as the corolla of some flowers.

ro·ta·tion /rō'tāSHən/ ▸*n.* the action of rotating around an axis or center: *the moon moves in the same direction as the earth's rotation.* ■ (also **crop rotation**) the action or system of rotating crops. ■ *Forestry* the cycle of planting, felling, and replanting. ■ the passing of a privilege or responsibility from one member of a group to another in a regularly recurring succession: *it has become common for senior academics to act as heads of department in rotation.* ■ a tour of duty, esp. by a medical practitioner in training: *she was completing a rotation in trauma surgery.* ■ *Math.* the conceptual operation of turning a system around an axis. —**ro·ta·tion·al** /-SHənl/ *adj.* —**ro·ta·tion·al·ly** /-SHənl-ē/ *adv.*

ROTC /'är ,ō 'tē 'sē; 'rätsē/ ▸*abbr.* (in the U.S.) Reserve Officers' Training Corps.

rote /rōt/ ▸*n.* mechanical or habitual repetition of something to be learned: *a poem learned by rote in childhood.*

rot·gut /'rät,gət/ ▸*n. inf.* poor-quality and potentially toxic alcoholic liquor.

ro·ti·fer /'rōtəfər/ ▸*n.* any minute multicellular aquatic animal that has wheellike ciliated organs used in swimming and feeding.

ro·tis·ser·ie /rō'tisərē/ ▸*n.* **1** a cooking appliance with a rotating spit for roasting and barbecuing meat. **2** a restaurant specializing in roasted or barbecued meat.

ro·to·gra·vure /,rōtəgrə'vyŏŏr/ ▸*n.* a printing system using a rotary press with intaglio cylinders, typically running at high speed. ■ a sheet or magazine printed with this system, esp. the color magazine of a Sunday newspaper.

ro·tor /'rōtər/ ▸*n.* a rotary part of a machine or vehicle, in particular: ■ a hub with a number of radiating airfoils that is rotated in an approximately horizontal plane to provide the lift for a helicopter or autogiro. ■ the rotating assembly in a turbine, esp. a wind turbine. ■ the armature of an electric motor. ■ the rotating part of the distributor of an internal combustion engine that successively makes and breaks electrical contacts so that each spark plug fires in turn. ■ the rotating container in a centrifuge.

ro·to·till·er /'rōtə,tilər/ ▸*n. trademark* a motor-driven machine with rotating blades for breaking up or tilling the soil. —**ro·to·till** *v.*

rot·ten /'rätn/ ▸*adj.* (**-ten·er, -ten·est**) suffering from decay: *the supporting beams were rotten.* ■ morally, socially, or politically corrupt: *he believed that the whole art business was rotten.* ■ *inf.* very bad: *she was a rotten cook.*
▸*adv. inf.* to an extreme degree; very much: *your mother said that I spoiled you rotten.* —**rot·ten·ly** *adv.* —**rot·ten·ness** *n.*

Rott·wei·ler /'rät,wīlər; 'rôt,vīlər/ ▸*n.* a large powerful dog of a tall black-and-tan breed.

ro·tund /rō'tənd; 'rō,tənd/ ▸*adj.* (of a person) plump. ■ round or spherical: *huge stoves held great rotund cauldrons.* ■ *fig.* (of speech or literary style) indulging in grandiloquent expression. —**ro·tun·di·ty** /-'təndətē/ *n.* —**ro·tund·ly** *adv.*

ro·tun·da /rō'təndə/ ▸*n.* a round building or room, esp. one with a dome.

rou·é /rōō'ā/ ▸*n.* a debauched man, esp. an elderly one.

rouge /rōōzH/ ▸*n.* a red powder or cream used as a cosmetic for coloring the cheeks or lips.
▸*v.* [*tr.*] [often as *adj.*] (**rouged**) color with rouge: *her brightly rouged cheeks.*

rough /rəf/ ▸*adj.* **1** having an uneven or irregular surface; not smooth or level: *take a square of sandpaper, rough side out.* ■ (of a voice) coming out with difficulty so as to sound harsh and rasping: *his voice was rough with barely suppressed fury.* ■ (of wine or another alcoholic drink) sharp or harsh in taste. **2** (of a person or their behavior) not gentle; violent or boisterous: *strollers should be capable of withstanding rough treatment.* ■ (of an area or occasion) characterized by or notorious for the occurrence of violent behavior: *the workmen hate going to the rough areas of town.* ■ *inf.* difficult and unpleasant; hard; severe: *the teachers gave me a rough time because my image didn't fit..* ■ *inf.* unwell: *the altitude had hit her and she was feeling rough.* ■ *inf.* depressed and anxious: *when he's feeling rough, he comes and talks things over to calm him down.* **3** not finished tidily or decoratively; plain and basic: *the customers sat at rough wooden tables.* ■ lacking sophistication or refinement: *she took care of him in her rough, kindly way.* ■ not worked out or correct in every detail: *he had a rough draft of his new novel.*
▸*adv. inf.* in a manner that lacks gentleness; harshly or violently: *treat 'em rough but treat 'em fair.*
▸*n.* (on a golf course) longer grass around the fairway and the green: *his second shot was in the rough on the left.*
▸*v.* [*tr.*] **1** work or shape (something) in a rough, preliminary fashion: *flat surfaces of wood are roughed down.* ■ (**rough something out**) produce

a preliminary and unfinished sketch or version of something: *the engineer roughed out a diagram on his notepad.* ■ make uneven or ruffled: *rough up the icing with a palette knife | the water was roughed by the wind.* **2** (**rough it**) live in discomfort with only basic necessities: *she had had to rough it alone in a dive.*
▸*phrasal v.* □ **rough someone up** *inf.* beat someone up. —**rough·ish** *adj.* —**rough·ness** *n.*
▸ □ **in the rough 1** in a natural state; without decoration or other treatment: *a diamond in the rough.* **2** in difficulties: *even before the recession hit, the project was in the rough.* □ **rough and ready** crude but effective: *a rough-and-ready estimating method.* ■ (of a person or place) unsophisticated or unrefined. □ **rough around the edges** having a few imperfections: *until we clean up and lay down the new carpet, it's going to look a little rough around the edges.* ■ not refined: *Donnie is a bit rough around the edges, but she loves him.* □ **rough edges** small imperfections in someone or something that is basically satisfactory.

rough·age /'rəfij/ ▸*n.* fibrous indigestible material in vegetable foodstuffs that aids the passage of food and waste products through the gut. ■ *Farming* coarse, fibrous fodder.

rough and tum·ble (also **rough-and-tum·ble**) ▸*n.* a situation without rules or organization; a free-for-all: *the rough and tumble of political life | [as adj.] the rough-and-tumble atmosphere of the dealing room.*

rough·en /'rəfən/ ▸*v.* make or become rough: [*tr.*] *the wind was roughening the surface of the river | [intr.] his voice roughened.*

rough·house *inf.* ▸*v.* /'rəf,hous; -,houz/ [*intr.*] act in a boisterous, violent manner: *in front of the stage hundreds of teens and young adults roughhouse, flinging themselves into each other.* ■ [*tr.*] handle (someone) roughly or violently: *the police department grabbed Danny as a suspect and roughhoused him.*
▸*n.* /-,hous/ a violent disturbance or an instance of boisterous play.

rough·ly /'rəflē/ ▸*adv.* **1** in a manner lacking gentleness; harshly or violently: *the man picked me up roughly.* **2** in a manner lacking refinement and precision: *people were crouching over roughly built brick fireplaces.* ■ approximately: *this is a walk of roughly 13 miles | the narrative is, roughly speaking, contemporary with the earliest of the gospels.*

rough·neck /'rəf,nek/ ▸*n.* **1** *inf.* a rough and uncouth person. **2** an oil rig worker.
▸*v.* [*intr.*] [usu. as *n.*] (**roughnecking**) work on an oil rig: *his savings from roughnecking are gone.*

rough·shod /'rəf,SHäd/ ▸*adj. archaic* (of a horse) having shoes with nail-heads projecting to prevent slipping.

rough·y /'rəfē/ ▸*n.* (*pl.* **rough·ies**) *Austral.* a marine fish with a deep laterally compressed body and large rough-edged scales that become spiny on the belly.

rou·lette /rōō'let/ ▸*n.* a gambling game in which a ball is dropped onto a revolving wheel (**rou·lette wheel**) with numbered compartments, the players betting on the number at which the ball will come to rest.
▸*v.* [*tr.*] make slit-shaped perforations in (paper, esp. sheets of postage stamps): *the pages are rouletted next to the binding.* ▷mid 18th cent.: from French, diminutive of *rouelle* 'wheel,' from late Latin *rotella*, diminutive of Latin *rota* 'wheel.'

round /round/ ▸*adj.* **1** shaped like or approximately like a circle or cylinder: *she was seated at a small, round table.* ■ having a curved shape like part of the circumference of a circle: *round arches.* **2** shaped like or approximately like a sphere: *a round glass ball.* ■ having a curved surface with no sharp or jagged projections: *the boulders look round and smooth.* ■ *fig.* (of a voice) rich and mellow; not harsh. **3** (of a number) altered for convenience of expression or calculation, for example to the nearest whole number or multiple of ten or five: *the size of the fleet is given in round numbers.*
▸*n.* **1** a circular piece of a particular substance: *cut the pastry into rounds.* ■ a thick disk of beef cut from the haunch as a joint. **2** an act of visiting each of a number of people or places: *she did the rounds of her family to say goodbye.* **3** one of a sequence of sessions or groups of related actions or events, typically such that development or progress can be seen between one group and another: *the two sides held three rounds of talks.* ■ an act of playing all the holes in a golf course once: *Eileen enjoys the occasional round of golf.* **4** a regularly recurring sequence of activities or functions: *their lives were a daily round of housework and laundry.* ■ *Mus.* a song for three or more unaccompanied voices or parts, each singing the same theme but starting one after another, at the same pitch or in octaves; a simple canon. ■ a set of drinks bought for all the

---

Pronunciation Key ə *ago,* up; ər *over, fur;* a *hat;* ā *ate;* ä *car;* CH *chin;* e *let;* ē *see;* e(ə)r *air;* i *fit;* ī *by;* i(ə)r *ear;* NG *sing;* ō *go;* ô *law, for;* oi *toy;* ōō *good;* ōō *goo;* ou *out;* SH *she;* TH *thin;* T͟H *then;* (h)w *why;* ZH *vision*

members of a group, typically as part of a sequence in which each member in turn buys such a set: *it's my round.* **5** a measured quantity or number of something, in particular: ■ the amount of ammunition needed to fire one shot. ■ *Archery* a fixed number of arrows shot from a fixed distance.

▶*adv. chiefly Brit.* variant of **AROUND**.

▶*prep. chiefly Brit.* variant of **AROUND**.

▶*v.* [*tr.*] **1** pass and go around (something) so as to move on in a changed direction: *the ship rounded the cape and sailed north.* **2** alter (a number) to one less exact but more convenient for calculations: *we'll round the weight up to the nearest pound.* **3** give a round shape to: *a lathe that rounded chair legs.* ■ [*intr.*] become circular in shape: *her eyes rounded in dismay.*

▶*phrasal v.* □ **round something off** make the edges or corners of something smooth: *round off the spars with a soft plastic fitting.* ■ complete something in a satisfying or suitable way: *I rounded off my visit to Ganu by purchasing a number of exquisite masks.* □ **round someone/something up** drive or collect a number of people or animals together for a particular purpose: *in the afternoon the cows are rounded up for milking.* ■ arrest a number of people. —**round·ish** *adj.* —**round·ness** *n.*

▶ □ **in the round** (of a theatrical performance) with the audience placed on at least three sides of the stage. □ **make** (or **go**) **the rounds** (of a story or joke) be passed on from person to person.

round·a·bout /ˈraʊndəˌbaʊt/ ▶*adj.* not following a short direct route; circuitous: *we need to take a roundabout route to throw off any pursuit.* ■ not saying what is meant clearly and directly; circumlocutory: *in a roundabout way, he was fishing for information.*

Round·head /ˈraʊndˌhed/ ▶*n. hist.* a member or supporter of the Parliamentary party in the English Civil War. ▷so named because of the short-cropped hairstyle of the Puritans, who formed an important element in the party.

round·house /ˈraʊndˌhaʊs/ ▶*n.* **1** a locomotive maintenance shed built around a turntable. **2** *inf.* a blow given with a wide sweep of the arm.

round·ly /ˈraʊndlē/ ▶*adv.* **1** in a vehement or emphatic manner: *the latest attacks have been roundly condemned by campaigners for peace.* **2** so as to form a circular or roughly circular shape: *he was a middle-aged, roundly built man.*

round rob·in ▶*n.* **1** [often as *adj.*] a tournament in which each competitor plays in turn against every other: *a round-robin competition.* **2** a petition, esp. one with signatures written in a circle to conceal the order of writing. ■ a letter written by several people in turn, each person adding text before passing the letter on to someone else: [as *adj.*] *a round-robin letter.* **3** a series or sequence: *an inconclusive round robin of talks in Cairo, Washington, and New York.*

Round Ta·ble ▶*n.* **1** the table at which King Arthur and his knights sat so that none should have precedence. **2** an international charitable association that holds discussions and undertakes community service. **3** (**round table**) an assembly for discussion, esp. at a conference: *art historians fly around the world to attend colloquia and round tables.*

round trip ▶*n.* a journey to one or more places and back again.

round·up /ˈraʊndˌəp/ ▶*n.* a systematic gathering together of people or things: *mass police roundups and detentions.* ■ a summary of facts or events: *a news roundup every fifteen minutes.*

round·worm /ˈraʊndˌwərm/ ▶*n.* a nematode worm (class Phasmida), esp. a parasitic one found in the intestines of mammals.

rouse /raʊz/ ▶*v.* [*tr.*] bring out of sleep; awaken: *she was roused from a deep sleep by a hand on her shoulder.* ■ [*intr.*] cease to sleep or to be inactive; wake up: *she roused and opened her eyes.* ■ startle out of inactivity; cause to become active: *once the enemy camp was roused, they would move on the castle.* ■ cause or give rise to (an emotion or feeling): *his evasiveness roused my curiosity.* —**rous·a·ble** *adj.* —**rous·er** *n.*

rous·ing /ˈraʊzɪŋ/ ▶*adj.* exciting; stirring: *a rousing speech.* —**rous·ing·ly** *adv.*

roust /raʊst/ ▶*v.* [*tr.*] cause to get up or start moving; rouse: *I rousted him out of his bed with a cup of coffee.* ■ *inf.* treat roughly; harass: *the detectives who had rousted him the night of the murder.*

roust·a·bout /ˈraʊstəˌbaʊt/ ▶*n.* an unskilled or casual laborer. ■ a laborer on an oil rig. ■ a dock laborer or deckhand. ■ a circus laborer.

rout[1] /raʊt/ ▶*n.* a disorderly retreat of defeated troops: *the retreat degenerated into a rout.* ■ a decisive defeat: *the party lost more than half their seats in the rout.*

▶*v.* [*tr.*] defeat and cause to retreat in disorder: *in a matter of minutes the attackers were routed.*

▶ □ **put to rout** put to flight; defeat utterly: *I once put a gang to rout.*

rout[2] ▶*v.* **1** cut a groove, or any pattern not extending to the edges, in (a wooden or metal surface): *you routed each plank all along its length.*

2 another term for **ROOT**[2]. ■ find (someone or something), or force them from a place: *Simon routed him from the stable.*

route /raʊt; ruːt/ ▶*n.* a way or course taken in getting from a starting point to a destination: *our route was via the Jerusalem road.* ■ the line of a road, path, railroad, etc. ■ a circuit traveled in delivering, selling, or collecting goods. ■ a method or process leading to a specified result: *the many routes to a healthier diet will be described.*

▶*v.* (**rout·ing**; *Brit.* also **route·ing**) [*tr.*] send or direct along a specified course: *all lines of communication were routed through Atlanta.* ▷Middle English: from Old French *rute* 'road,' from Latin *rupta (via)* 'broken (way),' feminine past participle of *rumpere.*

rout·er[1] /ˈraʊtər/ ▶*n.* a power tool with a shaped cutter, used in carpentry for making grooves for joints, decorative moldings, etc.

rout·er[2] /ˈruːtər; ˈraʊtər/ ▶*n.* a device that forwards data packets to the appropriate parts of a computer network.

rou·tine /ruːˈtēn/ ▶*n.* a sequence of actions regularly followed; a fixed program: *I settled down into a routine of work and sleep.* ■ a set sequence in a performance such as a dance or comedy act: *he was trying to persuade her to have a tap routine in the play.* ■ *Comput.* a sequence of instructions for performing a task that forms a program or a distinct part of one.

▶*adj.* performed as part of a regular procedure rather than for a special reason: *the principal insisted that this was just a routine annual drill.* ■ monotonous or tedious: *we are set in our dull routine existence.* —**rou·tine·ly** *adv.*

rout·ing code ▶*n.* any of various codes used to direct data, documents, or merchandise, including: ■ the magnetically encoded numbers on a check. ■ a numeric code that directs telephone calls or Internet traffic.

rou·tin·ize /ruːˈtēˌnīz; ˈruːtnˌīz/ ▶*v.* [*tr.*] (usu. **be routinized**) make (something) into a matter of routine; subject to a routine: *communication was routinized to ensure consistency of information.* —**rou·tin·i·za·tion** /-ˌtēnə-ˈzāSHən; ˌruːtn-ə-/ *n.*

roux /ruː/ ▶*n.* (*pl.* same) *Cooking* a mixture of fat (esp. butter) and flour used in making sauces.

rove /rōv/ ▶*v.* [*intr.*] travel constantly without a fixed destination; wander: *a quarter of a million refugees roved around the country.* ■ [*tr.*] wander over or through (a place) in such a way: *children roving the streets.* ■ [usu. as *adj.*] (**roving**) travel for one's work, having no fixed base: *he trained as a roving reporter.* ■ (of eyes) look in changing directions in order to see something thoroughly: *the policeman's eyes roved around the bar.*

rov·er /ˈrōvər/ ▶*n.* **1** a person who spends their time wandering: *they became rovers who departed further and further from civilization.* **2** (in various sports) a player not restricted to a particular position on the field. **3** a vehicle for driving over rough terrain. ■ a vehicle driven by remote control over extraterrestrial terrain.

rov·ing eye ▶*n.* a tendency to flirt or be constantly looking to start a new sexual relationship: *if his wife wasn't around, he had a roving eye.*

row[1] /rō/ ▶*n.* a number of people or things in a more or less straight line: *her villa stood in a row of similar ones.* ■ a street with a continuous line of houses along one or both of its sides, esp. when specifying houses of a particular type or function: *fraternity row.* ■ a horizontal line of entries in a table.

▶ □ **a hard** (or **tough**) **row to hoe** a difficult task. □ **in a row** forming a line: *four chairs were set in a row.* ■ *inf.* in succession: *we get six days off in a row.*

row[2] /rō/ ▶*v.* [*tr.*] propel (a boat) with oars: *out in the bay a small figure was rowing a rubber dinghy.* ■ [*intr.*] travel by propelling a boat in this way: *we rowed down the river all day.* ■ convey (a passenger) in a boat by propelling it with oars: *her father was rowing her across the lake.* ■ [*intr.*] engage in the sport of rowing, esp. competitively: *he rowed for Yale.*

▶*n.* a period of rowing. —**row·er** *n.*

row[3] /raʊ/ *inf.* ▶*n.* a noisy acrimonious quarrel: *they had a row and she stormed out of the house.* ■ a serious dispute: *the director is at the center of a row over policy decisions.* ■ a loud noise or uproar: *if he's at home he must have heard that row.*

▶*v.* [*intr.*] have a quarrel: *they rowed about who would receive the money from the sale.*

row·an /ˈraʊən; ˈrōən/ (also **rowan tree**) ▶*n.* a mountain ash, in particular the European *Sorbus aucuparia.*

row·boat /ˈrōˌbōt/ ▶*n.* a small boat propelled by oars.

row·dy /ˈraʊdē/ ▶*adj.* (**-di·er**, **-di·est**) noisy and disorderly: *it was a rowdy but good-natured crowd.*

▶*n.* (*pl.* **-dies**) a noisy and disorderly person. —**row·di·ly** /ˈraʊdl-ē/ *adv.* —**row·di·ness** *n.* —**row·dy·ism** /-ˌizəm/ *n.*

row·ing ma·chine ▶*n.* an exercise machine with a sliding seat, used to strengthen the muscles used in rowing.

roy·al /ˈroiəl/ ▸*adj.* having the status of a king or queen or a member of their family: *contributors included members of the royal family.* ■ belonging to or carried out or exercised by a king or queen: *the royal palace.* ■ in the service or under the patronage of a king or queen: *a royal maid.* ■ of a quality or size suitable for a king or queen; splendid: *a royal fortune.* ■ *inf.* unmitigated; extreme: *he might turn out to be a royal pain.*
▸*n. inf.* a member of a royal family, esp. in England. —**roy·al·ly** *adv.*

roy·al blue ▸*n.* a deep, vivid blue.

roy·al·ist /ˈroiəlist/ ▸*n.* a person who supports the principle of monarchy or a particular monarchy. ■ a supporter of the king against Parliament in the English Civil War. ■ a supporter of the British during the American Revolution; a Tory.
▸*adj.* giving support to the monarchy: *the paper claims to be royalist.* ■ (in the English Civil War) supporting the king against Parliament: *the royalist army.* —**roy·al·ism** /-ˌizəm/ *n.*

roy·al·ty /ˈroiəltē/ ▸*n.* (*pl.* **-ties**) **1** people of royal blood or status: *diplomats, heads of state, and royalty shared tables at the banquet.* ■ the status or power of a king or queen: *the brilliance of her clothes, her jewels, all revealed her royalty.* **2** a sum of money paid to a patentee for the use of a patent or to an author or composer for each copy of a book sold or for each public performance of a work. **3** a royal right (now esp. over minerals) granted by a sovereign to an individual or corporation. ■ a payment made by a producer of minerals, oil, or natural gas to the owner of the site or of the mineral rights over it. ▷late Middle English: from Old French *roialte*, from *roial* 'royal,' from Latin *regalis* 'regal.' The sense 'royal right (esp. over minerals)' (late 15th cent.) developed into the sense 'payment made by a mineral producer to the site owner' (mid 19th cent.), which was then transferred to payments for the use of patents and published materials.

rpm ▸*abbr.* ■ resale price maintenance. ■ revolutions per minute.

RR ▸*abbr.* ■ railroad. ■ rural route.

RSS ▸*n.* any of various XML file formats suitable for disseminating real-time information via the Internet on a subscription basis.

RSVP ▸*abbr.* répondez s'il vous plaît, or please reply (used at the end of invitations to request a response).

rte. ▸*abbr.* route.

Ru ▸*symb.* the chemical element ruthenium.

rub /rəb/ ▸*v.* (**rubbed, rub·bing**) [*tr.*] move one's hand or a cloth repeatedly to and fro on the surface of (something) with firm pressure: *she rubbed her arm, where she had a large bruise* | *he rubbed at the dirt on his jeans.* ■ cause (two things) to move to and fro against each other with a certain amount of pressure and friction: *many insects make noises by rubbing parts of their bodies together.* ■ move to and fro over something while pressing or grinding against it: *the ice breaks into small floes that rub against each other.* ■ (**rub something in/into/through**) work an ingredient into (a mixture) by breaking and blending it with firm movements of one's fingers: *sift the flour into a bowl and rub in the fat.* ■ reproduce the design of (a gravestone, memorial tablet, etc.) by laying paper on it and rubbing the paper with charcoal, colored chalk, etc.
▸*phrasal v.* □ **rub something down** dry, smooth, or clean something by rubbing. ■ rub the sweat from a horse or one's own body after exercise. □ **rub off** be transferred by contact or association: *when parents are having a hard time, their tension can easily rub off on the kids.*
▸*n.* **1** an act of rubbing: *she pulled out a towel and gave her head a quick rub.* ■ an ointment designed to be rubbed on the skin to ease pain: *a muscle rub.* **2** (usu. **the rub**) a difficulty, esp. one of central importance in a situation: *that was the rub—she had not cared enough.*
▸ □ **rub elbows** (or **shoulders**) associate or come into contact (with another person): *he rubbed elbows with TV stars at the party.* □ **rub it in** (or **rub someone's nose in something**) *inf.* emphatically draw someone's attention to an embarrassing or painful fact: *they don't just beat you, they rub it in.* □ **rub someone the wrong way** irritate or repel someone as by stroking a cat against the lie of its fur.

rub·ber[1] /ˈrəbər/ ▸*n.* a tough elastic polymeric substance made from the latex of a tropical plant or synthetically. ■ (**rubbers**) rubber boots; galoshes. ■ *Baseball* an oblong piece of rubber or similar material embedded in the pitcher's mound, on which the pitcher must keep one foot while delivering the ball. ■ *inf.* a condom. —**rub·ber·i·ness** *n.* —**rub·ber·y** *adj.*

rub·ber[2] ▸*n.* a contest consisting of a series of successive matches (typically three or five) between the same sides or people in tennis, cricket, and other games. ■ (usu. **rubber match** or **rubber game**) a game played to determine the winner of a series: *Clemens will pitch in the rubber game of this tied-up series.* ■ *Bridge* a unit of play in which one side scores bonus points for winning the best of three games.

rub·ber band ▸*n.* a loop of stretchy rubber for holding things together.

rub·ber·ize /ˈrəbəˌrīz/ ▸*v.* [*tr.*] [usu. as *adj.*] (**rubberized**) treat or coat (something) with rubber.

rub·ber·neck /ˈrəbərˌnek/ *inf.* ▸*n.* a person who turns their head to stare at something in a foolish manner, esp. while driving a car.
▸*v.* [*intr.*] stare in such a way: *a passerby rubbernecking at the accident scene.* —**rub·ber·neck·er** *n.*

rub·ber plant ▸*n.* an evergreen tree (*Ficus elastica*) of the mulberry family that has large dark green shiny leaves and is widely cultivated as a houseplant.

rub·ber stamp ▸*n.* a hand-held device for inking and imprinting a message or design on a surface. ■ *fig.* a person or organization that approves the decisions of others, not having the power or ability to reject or alter them: *I hope we never get to the day judges dictate to juries so they become rubber stamps.* ■ an indication of such an approval.
▸*v.* (**rub·ber-stamp**) [*tr.*] approve automatically without proper consideration: *the college would not rubber-stamp its athletes for graduation.*

rub·bing /ˈrəbiNG/ ▸*n.* **1** the action of rubbing something: *dab at the stain—vigorous rubbing could damage the carpet.* **2** an impression of a design on brass or stone, made by rubbing on paper laid over it with colored wax, pencil, chalk, etc.

rub·bing al·co·hol ▸*n.* denatured alcohol, typically perfumed, used as an antiseptic or in massage.

rub·bish /ˈrəbiSH/ ▸*n.* waste material; refuse or litter: *an alley full of rubbish.* ■ material that is considered unimportant or valueless: *she had to sift through the rubbish in every drawer.* ■ absurd, nonsensical, or worthless talk or ideas: *I suppose you believe that rubbish about vampires.* —**rub·bish·y** *adj.*

rub·ble /ˈrəbəl/ ▸*n.* waste or rough fragments of stone, brick, concrete, etc., esp. as the debris from the demolition of buildings: *two buildings collapsed, trapping scores of people in the rubble.* ■ pieces of rough or undressed stone used in building walls, esp. as filling for cavities. —**rub·bly** /ˈrəb(ə)lē/ *adj.*

rube /rōōb/ ▸*n. inf., often derog.* a country bumpkin.

Rube Gold·berg /ˈgōldˌbərg/ ▸*adj.* unnecessarily or comically complex in design. ▷an allusion to the humorously complicated, impracticable, or ingenious devices dreamed up and illustrated by U.S. artist Reuben ('Rube') Lucius *Goldberg* (1883–1970).

ru·bel·la /rōōˈbelə/ ▸*n.* a contagious viral disease, with symptoms like mild measles. It can cause fetal malformation if contracted in early pregnancy. Also called **GERMAN MEASLES**. ▷late 19th cent.: modern Latin, neuter plural of Latin *rubellus* 'reddish.'

ru·be·o·la /ˌrōōbēˈōlə/ ▸*n.* medical term for **MEASLES**.

Ru·bi·con /ˈrōōbəˌkän/ ▸a point of no return: *on the way to political union we are now crossing the Rubicon.*

ru·bid·i·um /rōōˈbidēəm/ ▸*n.* the chemical element of atomic number 37, a rare soft silvery reactive metal of the alkali metal group. (Symbol: **Rb**)

ru·ble /ˈrōōbəl/ (also **rou·ble**) ▸*n.* the basic monetary unit of Russia and some other former republics of the USSR, equal to 100 kopeks.

ru·bric /ˈrōōbrik/ ▸*n.* a heading on a document. ■ a direction in a liturgical book as to how a church service should be conducted. ■ a statement of purpose or function: *art of a purpose, not for its own sake, was his rubric.* ■ a category: *party policies on matters falling under the rubric of law and order.* ▷late Middle English *rubrish* (originally referring to a heading, section of text, etc., written in red for distinctiveness), from Old French *rubriche*, from Latin *rubrica (terra)* 'red (earth or ocher as writing material),' from the base of *ruber* 'red'; the later spelling is influenced by the Latin form. —**ru·bri·cal** *adj.*

ru·by /ˈrōōbē/ ▸*n.* (*pl.* **-bies**) a precious stone consisting of corundum in color varieties varying from deep crimson or purple to pale rose. ■ an intense purplish-red color.

ruck·sack /ˈrək,sak, ˈrŏŏk-/ ▸*n.* a bag with shoulder straps that allow it to be carried on someone's back, typically made of a strong, waterproof material and widely used by hikers; a backpack.

ruck·us /ˈrəkəs/ ▸*n.* a disturbance or commotion: *a child is raising a ruckus in class.*

ruc·tion /ˈrəkSHən/ ▸*n. inf.* a disturbance or quarrel. ■ (**ructions**) unpleasant reactions to or complaints about something: *If Mrs. Salt catches her there'll be ructions.*

Pronunciation Key ə *ago, up*; ər *over, fur*; a *hat*; ā *ate*; ä *car*; CH *chin*; e *let*; ē *see*; e(ə)r *air*; i *fit*; ī *by*; i(ə)r *ear*; NG *sing*; ō *go*; ô *law, for*; oi *toy*; ŏŏ *good*; ōō *goo*; ou *out*; SH *she*; TH *thin*; TH *then*; (h)w *why*; ZH *vision*

rud·der /ˈrədər/ ▸*n.* a flat piece, usu. of wood, metal, or plastic, hinged vertically near the stern of a boat or ship for steering. ■ a vertical airfoil pivoted from the horizontal stabilizer of an aircraft, for controlling movement around the vertical axis. ■ application of a rudder in steering a boat, ship, or aircraft: *a small amount of extra rudder.* —**rud·der·less** *adj.*

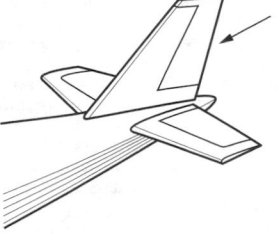

aircraft rudder

rud·dy /ˈrədē/ ▸*adj.* (**-di·er, -di·est**) (of a person's face) having a healthy red color: *a cheerful pipe-smoking man of ruddy complexion.* ■ having a reddish color: *the ruddy evening light.* —**rud·di·ly** /ˈrədl-ē/ *adv.* (*rare*) —**rud·di·ness** *n.*

rude /rood/ ▸*adj.* **1** offensively impolite or ill-mannered: *she had been rude to her boss.* ■ referring to a taboo subject such as sex in a way considered improper and offensive: *he made a rude gesture.* ■ having a startling abruptness: *the war came as a very rude awakening.* **2** roughly made or done; lacking subtlety or sophistication: *a rude coffin.* ■ *archaic* ignorant and uneducated: *the new religion was first promulgated by rude men.* —**rude·ly** *adv.* —**rude·ness** *n.* —**ru·der·y** /-ərē/ *n.*

ru·di·ment /ˈroodəmənt/ ▸*n.* **1** (**the rudiments of**) the first principles of a subject: *she taught the girls the rudiments of reading and writing.* ■ an elementary or primitive form of something: *the rudiments of a hot-water system.* **2** *Biol.* an undeveloped or immature part or organ, esp. a structure in an embryo or larva that will develop into an organ, limb, etc.: *the fetal lung rudiment.* **3** *Mus.* a basic pattern used by drummers.

ru·di·men·ta·ry /ˌroodəˈment(ə)rē/ ▸*adj.* involving or limited to basic principles: *he received a rudimentary education.* ■ of or relating to an immature, undeveloped, or basic form: *a rudimentary stage of evolution.* —**ru·di·men·ta·ri·ly** /-menˈte(ə)rəlē; -ˈment(ə)rəlē/ *adv.* —**ru·di·men·ta·ri·ness** *n.*

rue[1] /roo/ ▸*v.* (**rues, rued, ru·ing** or **rue·ing**) [*tr.*] bitterly regret (something one has done or allowed to happen): *Ferguson will rue the day he turned down that offer.*
▸*n. archaic* repentance; regret: *with rue my heart is laden.* ■ compassion; pity: *tears of pitying rue.*

rue[2] ▸*n.* a perennial evergreen shrub (*Ruta graveolens*, family Rutaceae) with bitter strong-scented lobed leaves that are used in herbal medicine. ■ used in names of other plants that resemble rue, esp. in leaf shape, e.g., **goat's-rue**.

rue·ful /ˈrooful/ ▸*adj.* expressing sorrow or regret, esp. when in a slightly humorous way: *she gave a rueful grin.* —**rue·ful·ly** *adv.* —**rue·ful·ness** *n.*

ruff[1] /rəf/ ▸*n.* **1** a projecting starched frill worn around the neck. **2** a projecting or conspicuously colored ring of feathers or hair around the neck of a bird or mammal. —**ruffed** *adj.*

ruff[2] ▸*n. Mus.* one of the basic patterns (rudiments) of drumming, consisting of a single note preceded by either two grace notes played with the other stick (**double-stroke ruff** or **drag**) or three grace notes played with alternating sticks (**four-stroke ruff**).

ruf·fi·an /ˈrəfēən/ ▸*n.* a violent person, esp. one involved in crime. —**ruf·fi·an·ism** /-ˌnizəm/ *n.* —**ruf·fi·an·ly** *adv.*

ruf·fle /ˈrəfəl/ ▸*v.* [*tr.*] **1** disorder or disarrange (someone's hair), typically by running one's hands through it: *he ruffled her hair affectionately.* ■ (of a bird) erect (its feathers) in anger or display: *on his departure to the high wires, the starling ruffled his feathers and flirted his wings.* ■ disturb the smoothness or tranquility of: *the evening breeze ruffled the surface of the pond in the yard.* ■ disconcert or upset the composure of (someone): *Brian had been ruffled by her questions.* **2** [usu. as *adj.*] (**ruffled**) ornament with or gather into a frill: *a blouse with a high ruffled neck.*
▸*n.* **1** an ornamental gathered or goffered frill of lace or other cloth on a garment, esp. around the wrist or neck. **2** a vibrating drumbeat.
▸ □ **ruffle someone's feathers** cause someone to become annoyed or upset: *tampering with the traditional approach would ruffle a few feathers.*

rug /rəg/ ▸*n.* a floor covering of shaggy or woven material, typically not extending over the entire floor. ■ *inf.* a toupee or wig.
▸ □ **pull the rug (out) from under someone** abruptly withdraw support (from someone): *the rug was pulled right out from beneath our feet.*

rug·by /ˈrəgbē/ (also **rugby football**) ▸*n.* a team game played with an oval ball that may be kicked, carried, and passed from hand to hand.

rug·ged /ˈrəgid/ ▸*adj.* (of ground or terrain) having a broken, rocky, and uneven surface: *a rugged coastline.* ■ (of a machine or other manufactured object) strongly made and capable of withstanding rough han-

dling: *the binoculars are compact, lightweight, and rugged.* ■ having or requiring toughness and determination: *a week of rugged, demanding adventure at an outdoor training center.* ■ (of a man's face or looks) having attractively strong, rough-hewn features: *he was known for his rugged good looks.* —**rug·ged·ly** *adv.* —**rug·ged·ness** *n.*

ru·in /ˈrooin/ ▸*n.* the physical destruction or disintegration of something or the state of disintegrating or being destroyed: *a large white house falling into gentle ruin.* ■ the remains of a building, typically an old one, that has suffered much damage or disintegration: *the ruins of the castle.* ■ the disastrous disintegration of someone's life: *the ruin and heartbreak wrought by alcohol, divorce, and violence.* ■ the cause of such disintegration: *they don't know how to say no, and that's been their ruin.* ■ the complete loss of one's money and other assets: *the financial cost could mean ruin.*
▸*v.* [*tr.*] reduce (a building or place) to a state of decay, collapse, or disintegration: [as *adj.*] (**ruined**) *a ruined castle.* ■ cause great and usually irreparable damage or harm to; have a disastrous effect on: *a noisy freeway has ruined village life.* ■ reduce to a state of poverty: *they were ruined by the highest interest rates this century.* ▷Middle English (in the sense 'collapse of a building'): from Old French *ruine*, from Latin *ruina*, from *ruere* 'to fall.'

ru·in·a·tion /ˌrooəˈnāSHən/ ▸*n.* the action or fact of ruining someone or something or of being ruined: *commercial malpractice causes the ruination of thousands of people.* ■ the state of being ruined: *the headquarters fell into ruination.*

ru·in·ous /ˈrooənəs/ ▸*adj.* **1** disastrous or destructive: *a ruinous effect on the environment.* **2** in ruins; dilapidated: *the castle is ruinous.* —**ru·in·ous·ly** *adv.* —**ru·in·ous·ness** *n.*

rule /rool/ ▸*n.* **1** one of a set of explicit or understood regulations or principles governing conduct within a particular activity or sphere: *the rules of the game were understood.* ■ a code of practice and discipline for a religious order or community: *the Rule of St. Benedict.* ■ control of or dominion over an area or people: *the revolution brought an end to British rule.* ■ (**the rule**) the normal or customary state of things: *such accidents are the exception rather than the rule.* **2** a strip of wood or other rigid material used for measuring length or marking straight lines; a ruler. ■ a thin printed line or dash, generally used to separate headings, columns, or sections of text.
▸*v.* **1** exercise ultimate power or authority over (an area and its people): *Latin America today is ruled by elected politicians | the period in which Spain ruled over Portugal.* ■ be a dominant or powerful factor or force: *the black market rules supreme.* ■ pronounce authoritatively and legally to be the case: *a federal court ruled that he was unfairly dismissed from his job.* **2** [*tr.*] make parallel lines across (paper): *a sheet of ruled paper.* ■ make (a straight line) on paper with a ruler.
▸*phrasal v.* □ **rule something out** (or **in**) exclude (or include) something as a possibility: *the doctor ruled out appendicitis.* —**rule·less** *adj.*
▸ □ **as a rule** usually, but not always. □ **rule of law** the restriction of the arbitrary exercise of power by subordinating it to well-defined and established laws. □ **rule of thumb** a broadly accurate guide or principle, based on experience or practice rather than theory. □ **rule the roost** be in complete control.

rul·er /ˈroolər/ ▸*n.* **1** a person exercising government or dominion. **2** a straight strip or cylinder of plastic, wood, or other rigid material, typically marked at regular intervals, to draw straight lines or measure distances. —**rul·er·ship** /-ˌSHip/ *n.*

rul·ing /ˈrooliNG/ ▸*n.* an authoritative decision or pronouncement, esp. one made by a judge.
▸*adj.* currently exercising authority or influence: *the ruling coalition.*

rum /rəm/ ▸*n.* an alcoholic liquor distilled from sugar-cane residues or molasses. ■ intoxicating liquor.

Ru·ma·ni·an /rooˈmānēən; -nyən/ ▸*adj. & n.* variant spelling of **ROMANIAN**.

rum·ba /ˈrəmbə; ˈroom-; ˈroom-/ (also **rhum·ba**) ▸*n.* a rhythmic dance with Spanish and African elements, originating in Cuba. ■ a piece of music for this dance or in a similar style. ■ a ballroom dance imitative of this dance.
▸*v.* (**-bas, -baed** /-bəd/, **-ba·ing**) [*intr.*] dance the rumba.

rum·ble /ˈrəmbəl/ ▸*v.* **1** [*intr.*] make a continuous deep, resonant sound: *thunder rumbled, lightning flickered.* ■ [*tr.*] utter in a deep, resonant voice: *the man's low voice rumbled an instruction.* ■ (of a person's stomach) make a deep, resonant sound due to hunger. **2** [*intr.*] *inf.* take part in a street fight between gangs or large groups: *the five of them rumbled with the men in the other car.*
▸*n.* **1** a continuous deep, resonant sound like distant thunder: *the steady rumble of traffic | fig. rumbles of discontent.* **2** *inf.* a street fight between gangs or large groups.

ru·men /'rōōmən/ ▶ n. (pl. **-mens** or **-mi·na** /-mənə/) Zool. the first stomach of a ruminant.

ru·mi·nant /'rōōmənənt/ ▶ n. an artiodactyl that chews the cud regurgitated from its rumen. The ruminants comprise the cattle, sheep, antelopes, deer, giraffes, and their relatives.

ru·mi·nate /'rōōmə,nāt/ ▶ v. [intr.] **1** think deeply about something: we sat ruminating on the nature of existence. **2** (of a ruminant) chew the cud. —**ru·mi·na·tion** /,rōōmə'nāsHən/ n. —**ru·mi·na·tive** /-,nātiv/ adj. —**ru·mi·na·tive·ly** /-,nātivlē/ adv. —**ru·mi·na·tor** /-,nātər/ n.

rum·mage /'rəmij/ ▶ v. [intr.] search unsystematically and untidily through a mass or receptacle: he rummaged in his pocket for a handkerchief | [tr.] he rummaged the drawer for his false teeth. ■ [tr.] find (something) by searching in this way: Mick rummaged up his skateboard. ■ [tr.] (of a customs officer) make a thorough search of (a vessel): our brief was to rummage as many of the vessels as possible.
▶ n. an unsystematic and untidy search through a mass or receptacle.
▷ late 15th cent.: from Old French arrumage, from arrumer 'stow (in a hold),' from Middle Dutch ruim 'room.' In early use the word referred to the arranging of items such as casks in the hold of a ship, giving rise (early 17th cent.) to the verb sense 'make a search of (a vessel).' —**rum·mag·er** n.

rum·mage sale ▶ n. a sale of miscellaneous secondhand articles, typically held in order to raise money for a charity or a special event.

rum·my /'rəmē/ ▶ n. a card game, sometimes played with two decks, in which the players try to form sets and sequences of cards.

ru·mor /'rōōmər/ (Brit. **ru·mour**) ▶ n. a currently circulating story or report of uncertain or doubtful truth: they were investigating rumors of a massacre.
▶ v. (**be rumored**) be circulated as an unverified account: it's rumored that he lives on a houseboat.

rump /rəmp/ ▶ n. the hind part of the body of a mammal or the lower back of a bird. ■ chiefly humorous a person's buttocks. **2** a small or unimportant remnant of something originally larger: once the profitable enterprises have been sold the unprofitable rump will be left. —**rump·less** adj.

rum·ple /'rəmpəl/ ▶ v. [tr.] [usu. as adj.] (**rumpled**) give a creased, ruffled, or disheveled appearance to: a rumpled bed.
▶ n. an untidy state. —**rum·ply** /'rəmp(ə)lē/ adj.

rum·pus /'rəmpəs/ ▶ n. (pl. **-pus·es**) inf. a noisy disturbance; a commotion: he caused a rumpus with his flair for troublemaking.

rum·pus room ▶ n. a room, typically in the basement of a house, used for games and recreation.

run /rən/ ▶ v. (**run·ning**; past **ran** /ran/; past part. **run**) **1** move at a speed faster than a walk, never having both or all the feet on the ground at the same time: the dog ran across the road. ■ enter (a racehorse) for a race. ■ (of hounds) chase or hunt their quarry. ■ (of a boat) sail directly before the wind, esp. in bad weather. ■ (of a migratory fish) go upriver from the sea, or onto a beach, in order to spawn. **2** move about in a hurried and hectic way: I've spent the whole day running around after the kids. ■ (**run to**) have rapid recourse to (someone) for support or help: don't come running to me for a handout. **3** pass or cause to pass quickly or smoothly in a particular direction: the rumor ran through the pack of photographers. ■ move or cause to move somewhere forcefully or with a particular result: the tanker ran aground off the Aleutian Islands | a woman ran a stroller into the back of my legs. ■ inf. fail to stop at (a red traffic light). ■ navigate (rapids or a waterfall) in a boat. ■ extend or cause to extend in a particular direction: cobbled streets run down to a tiny harbor | he ran a wire under the carpet. ■ (**run in**) (of a quality or trait) be common or inherent in members of (a particular family), esp. over several generations: weight problems run in my family. ■ pass into or reach a specified state or level: inflation is running at 11 percent | the decision ran counter to previous government commitments. **4** (of a liquid) flow in a specified direction: tears were running down her face. ■ cause (a liquid) to flow: she ran cold water into the sink. ■ cause water to flow over (something): I ran my hands under the faucet. ■ fill (a bath) with water: I'll run you a nice hot bath. ■ (**run with**) be covered or streaming with (a particular liquid): his face was running with sweat. ■ emit or exude a liquid: she was weeping loudly, and her nose was running. ■ (of a solid substance) melt and become fluid: it was so hot that the butter ran. ■ (of the sea, the tide, or a river) rise higher or flow more quickly: there was still a heavy sea running. ■ (of dye or color in fabric or paper) dissolve and spread when the fabric or paper becomes wet: the red dye ran when the socks were washed. ■ (of a stocking or pair of tights) develop a ravel. **5** (of a bus, train, ferry, or other form of transportation) make a regular journey on a particular route: buses run into town every half hour. ■ put (a particular form of public transportation) in service: the group is drawing up plans to run trains on key routes. ■ take (someone) somewhere in a car: I'll

run you home. **6** be in charge of; manage: Andrea runs her own catering business | (**-run**) an attractive family-run hotel. ■ (of a system, organization, or plan) operate or proceed in a particular way: everything's running according to plan. ■ organize and make available for other people: we decided to run a series of seminars. ■ carry out (a test or procedure): he asked the army to run tests on the anti nerve-gas pills. ■ own, maintain, and use (a vehicle). ■ be in or cause to be in operation; function or cause to function: the car runs on unleaded fuel | a number of peripherals can be run off one SCSI port. **7** continue or be valid or operative for a particular period of time: the course ran for two days. ■ happen or arrive at the specified time: the program was running fifteen minutes late. ■ (of a play or exhibition) be staged or presented: the play ran on Broadway last year. **9** be a candidate in a political election: he announced that he intended to run for President. ■ (esp. of a political party) sponsor (a candidate) in an election: they ran their first candidate for the school board. **10** publish or be published in a newspaper or magazine: the tabloids ran the story | when the story ran, there was a big to-do. ■ (of a story, argument, or piece of writing) have a specified wording or contents: "Tapestries slashed!" ran the dramatic headline. **11** bring (goods) into a country illegally and secretly; smuggle: they run drugs for the cocaine cartels. **12** (of an object or act) cost (someone) (a specified amount): a new photocopier will run us about $1,300.

▶ phrasal v. □ **run across** meet or find by chance: I just thought you might have run across him before. □ **run along** [in imper.] inf. go away (used typically to address a child): run along now, there's a good girl. □ **run away with 1** (of one's imagination or emotions) work wildly, so as to overwhelm (one): Susan's imagination was running away with her. **2** excel in or win (a competition) easily: the Yankees ran away with the series. □ **run something by** (or **past**) tell (someone) about something, esp. in order to ascertain their opinion or reaction. □ **run someone/something down 1** (of a vehicle or its driver) hit a person or animal and knock them to the ground. ■ (of a boat) collide with another vessel. **2** find someone or something after a search: she finally ran the professor down. **3** Baseball (of two or more fielders) try to tag out a base runner who is trapped between two bases, in the process throwing the ball back and forth. □ **run something down** (or **run down**) reduce (or become reduced) in size, numbers, or resources: hardwood stocks in some countries are rapidly running down. ■ lose (or cause to lose) power; stop (or cause to stop) functioning: the battery has run down. ■ gradually deteriorate (or cause to deteriorate) in quality or condition: the property had been allowed to run down. □ **run into 1** collide with: he ran into a lamp post. ■ meet by chance: I ran into Stasia and Katie on the way home. ■ experience (a problem or difficult situation): the bank ran into financial difficulties. **2** reach (a level or amount): debts running into millions of dollars. **3** blend into or appear to coalesce with: her words ran into each other. □ **run something off** reproduce copies of a piece of writing on a machine. □ **run on 1** continue without stopping; go on longer than is expected: the story ran on for months. ■ talk incessantly. **2** Printing continue on the same line as the preceding matter. □ **run out 1** (of a supply of something) be used up: our food is about to run out. ■ use up one's supply of something: we've run out of gasoline. ■ become no longer valid: her contract runs out at the end of the year. □ **run someone/something over** (of a vehicle or its driver) knock a person or animal down and pass over their body: I almost ran over that raccoon. □ **run through** use or spend recklessly or rapidly: her husband had long since run through her money. □ **run something up** allow a debt or bill to accumulate quickly: he ran up debts of $153,000. ■ achieve a particular score in a game or match: North Carolina ran up a 62–44 lead. □ **run up against** experience or meet (a difficulty or problem): the proposal has been dropped because it could run up against Federal regulations.

▶ n. **1** an act or spell of running: I usually go for a run in the morning | a cross-country run. ■ a running pace: Bobby set off at a run. ■ an opportunity or attempt to achieve something: their absence means the Russians will have a clear run at the title. ■ a preliminary test of the efficiency of a procedure or system: if you are styling your hair yourself, have a practice run. ■ an attempt to secure election to political office: his run for the Republican nomination. ■ an annual mass migration of fish up a river or onto a beach to spawn, or their return migration afterward: the annual salmon runs. **2** a journey accomplished or route taken by a vehicle, aircraft, or boat, esp. on a regular basis: the New York-Washington run. **3** Baseball a point scored when a base runner reaches home plate after touching the other bases. **4** a continuous spell of a particular situation or condition: he's had a run of bad luck. ■ a continuous series of performances: *the play had a long run on Broadway.* ■ a quantity or amount of something produced at one time: *a production run of only 150 cars.* ■ a continuous stretch or length of something: *long runs of copper piping.* ■ a rapid series of musical notes forming a scale. ■ a sequence of cards of the same suit. **5** (**a run on**) a widespread and sudden or continuous demand for (a particular currency or commodity): *there's been a big run on nostalgia toys this year.* ■ a sudden demand for repayment from a bank made by a large number of lenders: *growing nervousness among investors led to a run on some banks.* **6** (**the run of**) free and unrestricted use of or access to: *her cats were given the run of the house.* **7** (**the run**) the average or usual type of person or thing: *she stood out from the general run of varsity cheerleaders.* **8** an enclosed area in which domestic animals or birds can run freely in the open: *a chicken run.* ■ a track made or regularly used by a particular animal: *a badger run.* ■ a sloping snow-covered course or track used for skiing, bobsledding, or tobogganing: *a ski run.* **9** a line of unraveled stitches in stockings or tights. **10** (**the runs**) *inf.* diarrhea. ▷Old English *rinnan, irnan* (verb), of Germanic origin, probably reinforced in Middle English by Old Norse *rinna, renna.* The current form with -u- in the present tense is first recorded in the 16th cent. —**run·na·ble** *adj.*

▶ □ **give someone/something a** (**good**) **run for their money** provide someone or something with challenging competition or opposition. □ **on the run** trying to avoid being captured: *a kidnapper on the run from the FBI.* □ **run afoul** (or **foul**) **of 1** *Naut.* collide or become entangled with (an obstacle or another vessel): *another ship ran afoul of us.* **2** come into conflict with; go against: *the act may run afoul of consumer protection legislation.* □ **run low** (or **short**) become depleted: *supplies had run short.* ■ have too little of something: *we're **running short** of time.* □ **run off at the mouth** *inf.* talk excessively or indiscreetly. □ **run the show** *inf.* dominate or be in charge of a project, undertaking, or domain.

run·a·bout /ˈrənəˌbout/ ▶ *n.* a small motorboat, esp. one used for short trips.

run·a·round /ˈrənəˌround/ *inf.* ▶ *n.* difficult or awkward treatment, esp. in which someone is evasive or avoids a question: *the times he got the **runaround** looking for work.*

run·a·way /ˈrənəˌwā/ ▶ *n.* a person who has run away, esp. from their family or an institution. ■ [often as *adj.*] an animal or vehicle that is running out of control: *a runaway train.* ■ [as *adj.*] denoting something happening or done quickly, easily, or uncontrollably: *the runaway success of the book.*

run·down ▶ *n.* /ˈrənˌdoun/ **1** an analysis or summary of something by a knowledgeable person: *he gave his teammates **a rundown** on the opposition.* **2** a reduction in the productivity or activities of a company or institution: *a rundown in the business would be a devastating blow to the local economy.*

▶ *adj.* /ˈrənˈdoun/ (usu. **run-down**) **1** (esp. of a building or area) in a poor or neglected state after having been prosperous: *a run-down, vandalized inner-city area.* ■ (of a company or industry) in a poor economic state. **2** tired and somewhat unwell, esp. through overwork: *feeling tired and generally run-down.*

rune /rōōn/ ▶ *n.* a letter of an ancient Germanic alphabet, related to the Roman alphabet. ■ a similar mark of mysterious or magic significance. ■ (**runes**) small stones, pieces of bone, etc., bearing such marks, and used as divinatory symbols: *the casting of the runes.* ■ a spell or incantation. —**ru·nic** /ˈrōōnik/ *adj.*

rung[1] /rəNG/ ▶ *n.* **1** a horizontal support on a ladder for a person's foot. ■ *fig.* a level in a hierarchical structure, esp. a class or career structure: *we must ensure that the unskilled do not get trapped on the bottom rung.* **2** a strengthening crosspiece in the structure of a chair. —**runged** *adj.* —**rung·less** *adj.*

rung[2] ▶ past participle of RING[2].

run-in ▶ *n. inf.* a disagreement or fight, esp. with someone in an official position: *a run-in with armed police in Rio | humorous a run-in with a parking meter.*

run·nel /ˈrənl/ ▶ *n.* a narrow channel in the ground for liquid to flow through. ■ a small stream of a particular liquid: *a runnel of sweat.*

run·ner /ˈrənər/ ▶ *n.* **1** a person who runs, esp. in a specified way: *a fast runner.* ■ a horse that runs in a particular race: *there were only four runners.* ■ a messenger, collector, or agent for a bank, bookmaker, or other organization. ■ *Baseball* a base runner. ■ a messenger in the army. **2** [in *comb.*] a person who smuggles specified goods into or out of a country or area: *a drug-runner.* **3** a rod, groove, or blade on which something slides. ■ each of the long pieces on the underside of a sled that forms the contact in sliding. ■ (often **runners**) a roller for moving a heavy article. ■ a ring capable of slipping or sliding along a strap or rod or through which something may be passed or drawn. ■ *Naut.* a

rope run through a block. **4** a shoot, typically leafless, that grows from the base of a plant along the surface of the ground and can take root at points along its length. ■ a plant that spreads by means of such shoots. ■ a twining plant. **5** a long, narrow rug or strip of carpet, esp. for a hall or stairway.

run·ner-up ▶ *n.* (*pl.* **run·ners-up**) a competitor or team taking second place in a contest: *he was runner-up in the 200 m individual medley.* ■ a competitor finishing behind the winner in the specified position: *third runner-up in last year's election.*

run·ning /ˈrəniNG/ ▶ *n.* **1** the action or movement of a runner: *he accounted for 31 touchdowns with his running and passing.* ■ the sport of racing on foot: *marathon running.* ■ an act of running a race: *the 122nd running of the Derby.* **2** the action of managing or operating something: *the day-to-day running of the office.*

▶ *adj.* **1** denoting something that runs, in particular: ■ (of water) flowing naturally or supplied to a building through pipes and taps: *hot and cold running water.* ■ (of a sore or a part of the body) exuding liquid or pus: *a running sore.* ■ continuous or recurring over a long period: *a running joke.* ■ done while running: *a running jump.* ■ (of a measurement) in a straight line: *today, those same lots are worth $6,000 a running foot.* **2** consecutive; in succession: *he failed to produce an essay for the third week running.*

▶ □ **in** (or **out of**) **the running** in (or no longer in) contention for an award, victory, or a place on a team: *he is in the running for an Oscar.*

run·ning board ▶ *n.* a footboard extending along the side of a vehicle, typically found on trucks, SUVs, and some early models of automobiles.

run·ning com·men·ta·ry ▶ *n.* a verbal description of events, given as they occur.

run·ning lights ▶ *pl. n.* small lights on a motor vehicle that remain illuminated while the vehicle is running.

run·ning mate ▶ *n.* **1** an election candidate for the lesser of two closely associated political offices: *a rationale offered by a presidential candidate for choosing his vice presidential running mate.* **2** a horse entered in a race in order to set the pace for another horse from the same stable, which is intended to win.

run·ning stitch ▶ *n.* a simple needlework stitch consisting of a line of small even stitches that run in and out through the cloth without overlapping.

run·ny /ˈrənē/ ▶ *adj.* (**-ni·er, -ni·est**) **1** somewhat liquid; not firm: *the soufflé was hard on top and quite runny underneath.* **2** (of a person's nose) producing or discharging mucus; running. ■ dripping: *a runny spout.*

run·off /ˈrənˌôf/ (also **run-off**) ▶ *n.* **1** a further competition, election, race, etc., after a tie or inconclusive result. **2** the draining away of water (or substances carried in it) from the surface of an area of land, a building or structure, etc. ■ the water or other material that drains freely off the surface of something.

run-of-the-mill ▶ *adj.* lacking unusual or special aspects; ordinary: *a run-of-the-mill job.*

runt /rənt/ ▶ *n.* an animal that is smaller than average, esp. the smallest in a litter. ■ *fig., derog.* an undersized or weak person. —**runt·y** *adj.*

run-through ▶ *n.* **1** a rehearsal: *a run-through of the whole show.* **2** a brief outline or summary: *the textbooks provide a run-through of research findings.*

run-time li·cense ▶ *n.* a relatively broad software license enabling the holder to operate software on a network and in some cases to distribute it with other products.

run·way /ˈrənˌwā/ ▶ *n.* **1** a leveled strip of smooth ground along which aircraft take off and land. **2** a raised aisle extending into the audience from a stage, esp. as used for fashion shows. **3** an animal run, esp. one made by small mammals in grass, under snow, etc. **4** an incline or chute down which something slides or runs.

ru·pee /rōōˈpē, ˈrōō,pē/ ▶ *n.* the basic monetary unit of India, Pakistan, Sri Lanka, Nepal, Mauritius, and the Seychelles, equal to 100 paisa in India, Pakistan, and Nepal, and 100 cents in Sri Lanka, Mauritius, and the Seychelles.

rup·ture /ˈrəpCHər/ ▶ *v.* [*intr.*] (esp. of a pipe, a vessel, or a bodily part such as an organ or membrane) break or burst suddenly: *if the main artery ruptures he could die.* ■ [*tr.*] cause to break or burst suddenly and completely: *the impact ruptured both fuel tanks.* ■ [*tr.*] suffer such a bursting of (a bodily part): *it was her first match since rupturing an Achilles tendon.* ■ (**be ruptured** or **rupture oneself**) suffer an abdominal hernia: *one of the boys was ruptured and needed to be fitted with a truss.* ■ [*tr.*] *fig.* breach or disturb (a harmonious feeling or situation): *once trust has been ruptured it can be difficult to regain.*

▶ *n.* an instance of breaking or bursting suddenly and completely: *a small hairline crack could develop into a rupture.* ■ *fig.* a breach of a harmonious relationship: *the rupture with his father would never be healed.* ■ an abdominal hernia.

ru·ral /ˈro͝orəl/ ▶ *adj.* in, relating to, or characteristic of the countryside rather than the town: *remote rural areas.* —**ru·ral·ism** *n.* —**ru·ral·ist** *n.* —**ru·ral·i·ty** /ro͝oˈralitē/ *n.* —**ru·ral·i·za·tion** /ˌro͝orələˈzāSHən/ *n.* —**ru·ral·ize** *v.* —**ru·ral·ly** *adv.*

ruse /ro͞oz; ro͞os/ ▶ *n.* an action intended to deceive someone; a trick: *Eleanor tried to think of a ruse to get Paul out of the house.*

rush[1] /rəSH/ ▶ *v.* **1** move with urgent haste: *Jason rushed after her* | *I rushed outside and hailed a taxi.* ■ (of air or a liquid) flow strongly: *the water rushed in through the great oaken gates.* ■ force (someone) to act hastily: *I don't want to rush you into something.* ■ take (someone) somewhere with great haste: *an ambulance was waiting to rush him to the hospital.* ■ deliver (something) quickly to (someone): *we'll rush you a copy at once.* ■ dash toward (someone or something) in an attempt to attack or capture them or it: *he rushed the stronghold.* **2** [*tr.*] *Football* advance rapidly toward (an offensive player, esp. the quarterback). ■ [*intr.*] gain a specified amount of yardage or score a touchdown or conversion by running from scrimmage with the ball: *he rushed for 100 yards on 22 carries.* **3** [*tr.*] entertain (a new student) in order to assess their suitability for membership in a college fraternity or sorority. ■ (of a student) visit (a college fraternity or sorority) with a view toward joining it: *he rushed three fraternities.*
▶ *n.* **1** a sudden quick movement toward something, typically by a number of people: *there was a **rush** for the door.* ■ a flurry of hasty activity: *the pre-Christmas rush* | [as *adj.*] *a rush job.* ■ a sudden strong demand for a commodity: *there's been a **rush** on the Tribune because of the murder.* ■ a sudden flow or flood: *she felt a rush of cold air.* ■ a sudden intense feeling: *Mark felt a rush of anger.* ■ a sudden thrill or feeling of euphoria such as experienced after taking certain drugs: *users experience a rush.* **2** *Football* a rapid advance by a defensive player or players, esp. toward the quarterback. ■ an act of running from scrimmage with the ball to gain yardage. **3** the process whereby college fraternities or sororities entertain new students in order to assess suitability for membership: *ranking pledges during rush* | [as *adj.*] *rush week.* **4** (**rushes**) the first prints made of a movie after a period of shooting. —**rush·er** *n.* —**rush·ing·ly** *adv.*

rush[2] ▶ *n.* **1** a marsh or waterside plant (genus *Juncus*, family Juncaceae) with slender stemlike pith-filled leaves. ■ used in names of similar plants of wet habitats, e.g., **flowering rush.** ■ a stem of such a plant. ■ such plants used as a material. **2** *archaic* a thing of no value (used for emphasis): *not one of them is worth a rush.* —**rush·like** /-ˌlīk/ *adj.*

rush hour ▶ *n.* a time during each day when traffic is at its heaviest.

rusk /rəsk/ ▶ *n.* a light, dry biscuit or piece of rebaked bread, esp. one prepared for use as baby food. ■ rebaked bread used as extra filling, for sausages and, formerly as rations at sea.

rus·set /ˈrəsət/ ▶ *adj.* **1** reddish brown in color: *gardens of russet and gold chrysanthemums.* **2** *archaic* rustic; homely.
▶ *n.* **1** a reddish-brown color: *the woods in autumn are a riot of russet and gold.* **2** an apple of a variety with a slightly rough greenish-brown skin.
▶ *v.* (**-set·ed, -set·ing**) make or become russet in color. ■ (of smooth-skinned fruit) develop a rough reddish-brown or yellowish-brown skin, or patches of such: [*tr.*] *a week of humid weather has russeted the pears* | [*intr.*] *this variety of apple tends not to russet.* —**rus·set·y** *adj.*

Rus·sian /ˈrəSHən/ ▶ *adj.* of or relating to Russia, its people, or their language.
▶ *n.* **1** a native or national of Russia. ■ a person of Russian descent. ■ *hist.* (in general use) a national of the former Soviet Union. **2** the East Slavic language of Russia. —**Rus·sian·i·za·tion** /ˌrəSHənəˈzāSHən/ *n.* —**Rus·sian·ize** /-ˌnīz/ *v.* —**Rus·sian·ness** *n.*

Rus·sian rou·lette ▶ *n.* the practice of loading a bullet into one chamber of a revolver, spinning the cylinder, and then pulling the trigger while pointing the gun at one's own head. ■ *fig.* an activity that is potentially very dangerous.

rust /rəst/ ▶ *n.* **1** a reddish- or yellowish-brown flaky coating of iron oxide that is formed on iron or steel by oxidation, esp. in the presence of moisture. ■ *fig.* a state of deterioration or disrepair resulting from neglect or lack of use: *they are here to scrape the rust off the derelict machinery of government.* **2** a disease of plants that results in reddish or brownish patches, caused by a fungus (*Puccinia* and other genera,

order Uredinales, class Teliomycetes). **3** a reddish-brown color: [in comb.] *his rust-colored hair.*
▶ *v.* [*intr.*] be affected with rust: *the blades had **rusted** away* | [as *adj.*] (**rusting**) *rusting machinery.* ■ *fig.* deteriorate through neglect or lack of use. —**rust·less** *adj.*

rus·tic /ˈrəstik/ ▶ *adj.* **1** having a simplicity and charm that is considered typical of the countryside: *bare plaster walls and a terra-cotta floor give a rustic feel.* ■ *often derog.* lacking the sophistication of the city; backward and provincial: *you are a rustic halfwit.* **2** constructed or made in a plain and simple fashion, in particular: ■ made of untrimmed branches or rough timber: *a rustic oak bench.* ■ *Archit.* with rough-hewn or roughened surface or with deeply sunk joints: *a rustic bridge.*
▶ *n. often derog.* an unsophisticated country person. —**rus·ti·cal·ly** /-ik(ə)lē/ *adv.* —**rus·tic·i·ty** /rəˈstisətē/ *n.*

rus·ti·cate /ˈrəstiˌkāt/ ▶ *v.* **1** [*intr.*] go to, live in, or spend time in the country. **2** [*tr.*] fashion (masonry) in large blocks with sunk joints and a roughened surface: [as *adj.*] (**rusticated**) *the stable block was built of rusticated stone.* —**rus·ti·ca·tion** /ˌrəstiˈkāSHən/ *n.*

rus·tle /ˈrəsəl/ ▶ *v.* **1** [*intr.*] make a soft, muffled crackling sound like that caused by the movement of dry leaves or paper: *she came closer, her skirt swaying and rustling.* ■ move with such sound: *a nurse rustled in with a syringe.* ■ [*tr.*] move (something), causing it to make such a sound: *Dolly rustled the paper.* **2** [*tr.*] round up and steal (cattle, horses, or sheep). **3** [*intr.*] *inf.* move or act quickly or energetically; hustle: *rustle around the kitchen, see what there is.*
▶ *phrasal v.* □ **rustle something up** *inf.* produce something quickly when it is needed: *see if you can rustle up a cup of coffee for Paula and me, please.*
▶ *n.* a soft, muffled crackling sound like that made by the movement of dry leaves or paper: *there was a rustle in the undergrowth behind her.* —**rus·tler** /ˈrəs(ə)lər/ *n.*

rust·proof /ˈrəstˌpro͞of/ ▶ *adj.* (of metal or a metal object) not susceptible to corrosion by rust.
▶ *v.* [*tr.*] make resistant to corrosion by rust.

rust·y /ˈrəstē/ ▶ *adj.* (**rust·i·er, rust·i·est**) **1** (of a metal object) affected by rust: *a rusty hinge.* ■ rust-colored: *green grass turning a rusty brown.* **2** (of knowledge or a skill) impaired by lack of recent practice: *my typing is a little rusty.* ■ stiff with age or disuse: *it was my first race for three months and I felt a bit rusty.* **3** (of a voice) croaking: *her voice sounded rusty.* —**rust·i·ly** /ˈrəstəlē/ *adv.* —**rust·i·ness** *n.*

rut[1] /rət/ ▶ *n.* a long deep track made by the repeated passage of the wheels of vehicles. ■ *fig.* a habit or pattern of behavior that has become dull and unproductive but is hard to change: *the administration was stuck in a rut and was losing its direction.* —**rut·ted** *adj.* —**rut·ty** *adj.*

rut[2] ▶ *n.* (**the rut**) an annual period of sexual activity in deer and some other mammals, during which the males fight each other for access to the females.
▶ *v.* (**rut·ted, rut·ting**) [*intr.*] [often as *adj.*] (**rutting**) engage in such activity: *a rutting stag.* —**rut·tish** *adj.*

ru·ta·ba·ga /ˈro͞otəˌbāgə; ˈro͞ot-/ ▶ *n.* **1** a large, round, yellow-fleshed root that is eaten as a vegetable. **2** the European plant (*Brassica napus*) of the cabbage family that produces this root.

ru·the·ni·um /ro͞oˈTHēnēəm/ ▶ *n.* the chemical element of atomic number 44, a hard silvery-white metal of the transition series. (Symbol: **Ru**)

ruth·er·for·di·um /ˌrəTHərˈfôrdēəm/ ▶ *n.* the chemical element of atomic number 104, a very unstable element made by high-energy atomic collisions. (Symbol: **Rf**)

ruth·less /ˈro͞oTHləs/ ▶ *adj.* having or showing no pity or compassion for others: *a ruthless manipulator.* —**ruth·less·ly** *adv.* —**ruth·less·ness** *n.*

RV ▶ *abbr.* ■ recreational vehicle. ■ a rendezvous point. ■ Revised Version (of the Bible).

RVer /ˈärˈvēər/ ▶ *n.* a user of a recreational vehicle.

rye /rī/ ▶ *n.* **1** a wheatlike cereal plant (*Secale cereale*) that tolerates poor soils and low temperatures. ■ grains of this, used mainly for making bread or whiskey and for fodder. **2** (also **rye whiskey**) whiskey in which a significant amount of the grain used in distillation is fermented rye. **3** (also **rye bread**) bread made with all or part rye flour, typically with caraway seeds added: *pastrami on rye.* ▷Old English *ryge*, of Germanic origin; related to Dutch *rogge* and German *Roggen*.

rye·grass /ˈrīˌgras/ ▶ *n.* a Eurasian grass (genus *Lolium*) that is widely grown as forage.

Ss

S[1] /es/ (also **s**) ▶*n.* (*pl.* **Ss** or **S's** /esiz/) **1** the nineteenth letter of the alphabet. ■ denoting the next after R in a set of items, categories, etc. **2** a shape like that of a capital S: [in *comb.*] *an S-bend.*

S[2] ▶*abbr.* ■ (chiefly in Catholic use) Saint: *S Ignatius Loyola.* ■ small (as a clothes size). ■ South or Southern: *65° S.*
▶*symb.* ■ the chemical element sulfur. ■ *Chem.* entropy.

s ▶*abbr.* ■ second(s). ■ *Law* section (of an act). ■ shilling(s). ■ *Gram.* singular. ■ *Chem.* solid. ■ (in genealogies) son(s). ■ succeeded. ■ *Chem.* denoting electrons and orbitals possessing zero angular momentum and total symmetry: *s-electrons.*
▶*symb.* (in mathematical formulae) distance.

's *inf.* ▶*contr. of* ■ is: *it's raining.* ■ has: *she's gone.* ■ us: *let's go.* ■ does: *what's he do?*

's- ▶*prefix archaic* (used chiefly in oaths) God's: *'sblood.*

SA ▶*abbr.* ■ Salvation Army.

sab·bath /'sabəTH/ ▶*n.* **1** (often **the Sabbath**) a day of religious observance and abstinence from work, kept by Jews from Friday evening to Saturday evening, and by most Christians on Sunday. **2** (also **witch·es' sab·bath**) a supposed annual midnight meeting of witches with the Devil.

sab·bat·i·cal /sə'batikəl/ ▶*n.* a period of paid leave granted to a college teacher for study or travel, traditionally every seventh year: *she's away on sabbatical.*

sa·ber /'sābər/ (*Brit.* **sa·bre**) ▶*n.* a heavy cavalry sword with a curved blade and a single cutting edge. ■ a light fencing sword with a tapering blade. ▷late 17th cent.: from French, alteration of obsolete *sable*, from German *Sabel* (local variant of *Säbel*), from Hungarian *szablya.*

sa·ber-rat·tling ▶*n.* the display or threat of military force.

sa·ber·tooth /'sābər,tōōTH/ ▶*n.* **1** (also **sa·ber-toothed cat** or **sa·ber-toothed tiger**) a large extinct carnivorous mammal (genus *Smilodon* of the American Pleistocene and genus *Machairodus* of the Old World Pliocene) of the cat family, with massive, curved upper canine teeth. **2** a large extinct marsupial mammal (genus *Thylacosmilus*, family Borhyaenidae) with similar teeth, of the South American Pliocene.

cavalry saber

Sa·bi·an /'sābēən/ ▶*adj.* of or relating to a non-Muslim sect classed in the Koran with Jews, Christians, and Zoroastrians as having a faith revealed by the true God. It is not known who the original Sabians were, but the name was adopted by some groups in order to escape religious persecution by Muslims.
▶*n.* a member of this sect.

Sa·bine /'sā,bīn; -,bin/ ▶*adj.* of, relating to, or denoting an ancient Oscan-speaking people of the central Apennines in Italy, northeast of Rome, who feature in early Roman legends and were incorporated into the Roman state in 290 BC.
▶*n.* a member of this people.

sa·ble[1] /'sābəl/ ▶*n.* a marten (*Martes zibellina*) with a short tail and dark brown fur, native to Japan and Siberia and valued for its fur. ■ the fur of the sable.

sa·ble[2] ▶*adj. poetic/lit.* black.
▶*n.* **1** *poetic/lit.* black. **2** (also **sable antelope**) a large African antelope (*Hippotragus niger*) with long curved horns, the male of which has a black coat and the female a russet coat, both having a white belly.

sab·ot /sa'bō/ ▶*n.* a kind of simple shoe, shaped and hollowed out from a single block of wood, traditionally worn by French and Breton peasants. —**sa·boted** /sa'bōd/ *adj.*

sab·o·tage /'sabə,täzH/ ▶*v.* [*tr.*] deliberately destroy, damage, or obstruct (something), esp. for political or military advantage.
▶*n.* the action of sabotaging something.

sabot

sab·o·teur /,sabə'tər/ ▶*n.* a person who engages in sabotage.

sa·bra /'säbrə/ ▶*n.* a Jew born in Israel (or before 1948 in Palestine).

SAC /sak/ ▶*abbr.* Strategic Air Command.

Sac ▶*n.* variant spelling of **SAUK**.

sac /sak/ ▶*n.* a hollow, flexible structure resembling a bag or pouch: *a fountain pen with an ink sac.* ■ a cavity enclosed by a membrane within a living organism, containing air, liquid, or solid structures. —**sac·like** *adj.*

sac·cha·rin /'sak(ə)rən/ ▶*n.* a sweet-tasting synthetic compound used in food and drink as a substitute for sugar.

sac·cha·rine /'sak(ə)rin; -,rēn; -,rīn/ ▶*adj.* excessively sweet or sentimental.
▶*n.* another term for **SACCHARIN**.

sac·er·do·tal /,sasər'dōtl; ,sakər-/ ▶*adj.* relating to priests or the priesthood; priestly.

sa·chem /'sāCHəm/ ▶*n.* (among some American Indian peoples) a chief or leader. ■ *inf.* a boss or leader.

sa·chet /sa'SHā/ ▶*n.* a small perfumed bag used to scent clothes. ▷mid 19th cent.: from French, 'little bag,' diminutive of *sac*, from Latin *saccus* 'sack, bag.'

sack[1] /sak/ ▶*n.* **1** a large bag made of a strong material such as burlap, thick paper, or plastic, used for storing and carrying goods. ■ the contents of such a bag or the amount it can contain: *a sack of flour.* **2** a loose, unfitted, or shapeless garment, in particular: **3** (**the sack**) *inf.* bed, esp. as regarded as a place for sex. **4** (**the sack**) *inf.* dismissal from employment: *he got the sack for swearing.* **5** *inf. Baseball* a base. **6** *Football* an act of tackling a quarterback behind the line of scrimmage before he can throw a pass.
▶*v.* [*tr.*] **1** *inf.* dismiss from employment: *any official found to be involved would be sacked on the spot.* **2** (**sack out**) *inf.* go to sleep or bed. **3** *Football* tackle (a quarterback) behind the line of scrimmage before he can throw a pass. —**sack·a·ble** *adj.* —**sack·ful** *adj.* —**sack·like** /-,līk/ *adj.*
▶ □ **hit the sack** *inf.* go to bed. □ **a sack of potatoes** *inf.* used in similes to refer to clumsiness, inertness, or unceremonious treatment of the person or thing in question: *he drags me in like a sack of potatoes.*

sack[2] ▶*v.* [*tr.*] *chiefly hist.* plunder and destroy (a captured town, building, or other place).
▶*n.* the pillaging of a town or city.

sack·cloth /'sak,klôTH; -,klä TH/ ▶*n.* a very coarse, rough fabric woven from flax or hemp.

sack·ing /'sakiNG/ ▶*n.* **1** an act of sacking someone or something. **2** coarse material for making sacks; sackcloth.

sack race ▶*n.* a race in which competitors, typically children, stand in sacks up to the waist or neck and jump forward.

sa·cra /'sakrə; 'sā-/ ▶ plural form of **SACRUM**.

sa·cral /'sakrəl; 'sā-/ ▶*adj.* **1** *Anat.* of or relating to the sacrum.

2 *Anthropol. & Religion* of, for, or relating to sacred rites or symbols: *sacral horns of a Minoan type.* —**sa·cral·i·ty** /sā'kralētē; sə-/ *n.*

sac·ra·ment /'sakrəmənt/ ▶*n.* a religious ceremony or act of the Christian Church that is regarded as an outward and visible sign of inward and spiritual divine grace, in particular: ■ (in the Roman Catholic and many Orthodox Churches) the rites of baptism, confirmation, the Eucharist, penance, anointing of the sick, ordination, and matrimony. ■ (among Protestants) baptism and the Eucharist. ■ (in Roman Catholic use) the consecrated elements of the Eucharist, esp. the Host: *he heard Mass and received the sacrament.* ■ a thing of mysterious and sacred significance; a religious symbol. ▷Middle English: from Old French *sacrement*, from Latin *sacramentum* 'solemn oath' (from *sacrare* 'to hallow,' from *sacer* 'sacred'), used in Christian Latin as a translation of Greek *mustērion* 'mystery.' —**sac·ra·men·tal** /sakrə'mentl/ *adj.*

sac·ra·ment of rec·on·cil·i·a·tion (also **sacrament of penance**) ▶*n.* (chiefly in the Roman Catholic Church) the practice of private confession of sins to a priest and the receiving of absolution.

sa·cred /'sākrid/ ▶*adj.* connected with God (or the gods) or dedicated to a religious purpose and so deserving veneration: *sacred rites.* ■ religious rather than secular: *sacred music.* ■ (of writing or text) embodying the laws or doctrines of a religion: *a sacred Hindu text.* ■ regarded with great respect and reverence by a particular religion, group, or individual: *an animal sacred to Mexican culture.* ■ sacrosanct: *to a police officer nothing is sacred.* —**sa·cred·ly** *adv.* —**sa·cred·ness** *n.*

sa·cred cow ▶*n.* an idea, custom, or institution held, esp. unreasonably, to be above criticism (with reference to the Hindus' respect for the cow as a holy animal).

sa·cred lo·tus ▶*n.* see LOTUS (sense 1).

sac·ri·fice /'sakrə,fīs/ ▶*n.* an act of slaughtering an animal or person or surrendering a possession as an offering to God or to a divine or supernatural figure: *they offer sacrifices to the spirits.* ■ an animal, person, or object offered in this way. ■ an act of giving up something valued for the sake of something else regarded as more important or worthy: *we must all be prepared to make sacrifices.* ■ *Christian Church* the Eucharist regarded either (in Catholic terms) as a propitiatory offering of the body and blood of Christ or (in Protestant terms) as an act of thanksgiving. ■ *Chess* a move intended to allow the opponent to win a pawn or piece, for strategic or tactical reasons. ■ (also **sacrifice bunt** or **sacrifice hit**) *Baseball* a bunted ball that puts the batter out but allows a base runner or runners to advance. ■ (also **sacrifice bid**) *Bridge* a bid made in the belief that it will be less costly to be defeated in the contract than to allow the opponents to make a contract.
▶*v.* [*tr.*] offer or kill as a religious sacrifice: *the goat was sacrificed at the shrine.* ■ give up (something important or valued) for the sake of other considerations: *working hard doesn't mean sacrificing your social life.* ■ *Chess* deliberately allow one's opponent to win (a pawn or piece). ■ *Baseball* advance (a base runner) by a sacrifice. ■ [*intr.*] *Bridge* make a sacrifice bid. —**sac·ri·fi·cial** /,sakrə'fiSHəl/ *adj.*

sac·ri·lege /'sakrəlij/ ▶*n.* violation or misuse of what is regarded as sacred: *putting ecclesiastical vestments to secular use was considered sacrilege.* —**sac·ri·le·gious** /,sakrə'lijəs/ *adj.* —**sac·ri·le·gious·ly** /,sakrə'lijəslē/ *adv.*

sac·ris·ty /'sakristē/ ▶*n.* (pl. **-ties**) a room in a church where a priest prepares for a service, and where vestments and other things used in worship are kept.

sac·ro·il·i·ac /,sakrō'ilē,ak/ ▶*adj.* *Anat.* relating to the sacrum and the ilium. ■ denoting the rigid joint at the back of the pelvis between the sacrum and the ilium.

sac·ro·sanct /'sakrō,saNG(k)t/ ▶*adj.* (esp. of a principle, place, or routine) regarded as too important or valuable to be interfered with: *the individual's right to work has been upheld as sacrosanct.* —**sac·ro·sanc·ti·ty** /,sakrō'saNG(k)titē/ *n.*

sac·rum /'sakrəm; 'sā-/ ▶*n.* (pl. **sac·ra** /'sakrə; 'sā-/ or **sac·rums**) *Anat.* a triangular bone in the lower back formed from fused vertebrae and situated between the two hipbones of the pelvis.

SAD ▶*abbr.* seasonal affective disorder.

sad /sad/ ▶*adj.* (**sad·der, sad·dest**) **1** feeling or showing sorrow; unhappy: *I was sad and subdued.* ■ causing or characterized by sorrow or regret; unfortunate and regrettable: *he told her the sad story of his life.* **2** *inf.* pathetically inadequate or unfashionable: *somebody's priorities are pretty sad.* —**sad·dish** *adj.* —**sad·ly** *adv.* —**sad·ness** *n.*

sad·den /'sadn/ ▶*v.* [*tr.*] (often **be saddened**) cause to feel sorrow; make unhappy: *he was greatly saddened by the death of his only son.*

sad·dle /'sadl/ ▶*n.* **1** a seat fastened on the back of a horse or other animal for riding, typically made of leather and raised at the front and rear. ■ a seat on a bicycle or motorcycle. **2** something resembling a saddle in appearance, function, or position, in particular: ■ a low part

of a ridge between two higher points or peaks. ■ *Math.* a low region of a curve between two high points, esp. (in three dimensions) one representing the highest point of a curve in one direction and the lowest point in another direction. ■ a shaped support on which a cable, wire, or pipe rests. **3** a large cut of meat consisting of the two loins.
▶*v.* [*tr.*] put a saddle on (a horse): *he was in the stable saddling up his horse.* ■ (usu. **be saddled with**) burden (someone) with an onerous responsibility or task: *he's saddled with debts of $12 million.*

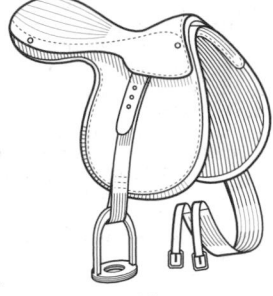
saddle

▶ □ **in the saddle** in a position of control or responsibility.

sad·dle·back /'sadl,bak/ ▶*n.* **1** *Archit.* a tower roof that has two gables connected by a pitched section. **2** a hill with a concave ridge along the top. —**sad·dle·backed** *adj.*

sad·dle·bag /'sadl,bag/ ▶*n.* each of a pair of bags attached behind the saddle on a horse, bicycle, or motorcycle. ■ (**saddlebags**) excess fat around the hips and thighs.

sad·dle·blan·ket /'sadl,blaNGkit/ ▶*n.* a cloth laid on a horse's back under the saddle.

sad·dler /'sadlər/ ▶*n.* someone who makes, repairs, or deals in saddles, bridles, and other equipment for horses.

sad·dle shoe ▶*n.* a white oxford shoe with a piece of leather in a contrasting color (typically black or brown) stitched across the instep.

sad·dle·sore /'sadl,sôr/ ▶*n.* a bruise or sore on a horse's back, caused by pressure or chafing of an ill-fitting saddle.
▶*adj.* (of a person) chafed from riding on a saddle.

Sad·du·cee /'saje,sē; 'sadyə-/ ▶*n.* a member of a Jewish sect or party of the time of Jesus Christ that denied the resurrection of the dead, the existence of spirits, and the obligation of oral tradition, emphasizing acceptance of the written Law alone. Compare with PHARISEE. —**Sad·du·ce·an** /,saje'sēən; ,sadyə-/ *adj.*

sa·dism /'sā,dizəm/ ▶*n.* the tendency to derive pleasure, esp. sexual gratification, from inflicting pain, suffering, or humiliation on others. ■ (in general use) deliberate cruelty. —**sa·dist** *n.* —**sa·dis·tic** /sə'distik/ *adj.* —**sa·dis·ti·cal·ly** /sə'distik(ə)lē/ *adv.*

sa·do·mas·o·chism /,sādō'masə,kizəm; ,sadō-/ ▶*n.* psychological tendency or sexual practice characterized by both sadism and masochism. —**sa·do·mas·o·chist** *n.* —**sa·do·mas·o·chis·tic** /',sādō-,masə'kistik; ,sadō-/ *adj.*

sad sack ▶*n. inf.* an inept, blundering person.

sa·fa·ri /sə'färē/ ▶*n.* (pl. **-ris**) an expedition to observe or hunt animals in their natural habitat, esp. in East Africa: *one week on safari.* ▷late 19th cent.: from Kiswahili, from Arabic *safara* 'to travel.'

safe /sāf/ ▶*adj.* **1** protected from or not exposed to danger or risk; not likely to be harmed or lost: *she felt safer with them than alone.* ■ *Baseball* having reached a base without being put out: *Davis was safe when the right fielder dropped a fly ball.* ■ not likely to cause or lead to harm or injury; not involving danger or risk: *we have to cross the river where it's safe for us to do so.* ■ (of a place) affording security or protection: *put it in a safe place.* **2** uninjured; with no harm done: *they had returned safe and sound.*
▶*n.* **1** a strong fireproof cabinet with a complex lock, used for the storage of valuables. **2** a condom. —**safe·ly** *adv.* —**safe·ness** *n.*

safe con·duct ▶*n.* immunity from arrest or harm when passing through an area. ■ a document securing such a privilege.

safe·guard /'sāf,gärd/ ▶*n.* a measure, such as a law or procedure, designed to prevent something undesirable: *there were multiple safeguards to prevent the accidental release of a virus.*
▶*v.* [*tr.*] protect against something undesirable in this way: *low interest rates are offering the opportunity to safeguard their financial futures.*

safe ha·ven ▶*n.* **1** a place of refuge or security. **2** *Law* temporary refuge given to asylum seekers. ■ a country or area within a country where this is provided.

safe house ▶*n.* a house in a secret location, used by spies or criminals in hiding.

safe·keep·ing /'sāf'kēpiNG/ ▶*n.* preservation in a safe place: *she'd put her wedding ring in her purse for safekeeping.*

Pronunciation Key ə *ago,* up; ər *over, fur;* a *hat;* ā *ate;* ä *car;* CH *chin;* e *let;* ē *see;* e(ə)r *air,* i *fit;* ī *by;* i(ə)r *ear;* NG *sing;* ō *go;* ô *law, for;* oi *toy;* oo *good;* oo *goo;* ou *out;* SH *she;* TH *thin;* TH *then;* (h)w *why;* ZH *vision*

S

safe room ▶ *n.* a room in a house or other building that is invulnerable to attack or intrusion, and from which security operations can be directed. Also called PANIC ROOM.

safe sex ▶ *n.* sexual activity in which people take precautions to protect themselves against sexually transmitted diseases such as AIDS.

safe·ty /ˈsāftē/ ▶ *n.* (*pl.* **-ties**) **1** the condition of being protected from or unlikely to cause danger, risk, or injury: *they should leave for their own safety.* ■ *inf.* a condom. **2** *Football* a defensive back who normally is positioned well behind the line of scrimmage. ■ a play in which the offense downs the ball (by action of the defense, or intentionally) in their own end zone, scoring two points for the defense.

safe·ty belt ▶ *n.* another term for SEAT BELT.

safe·ty glass ▶ *n.* **1** glass that has been toughened or laminated so that it is less likely to splinter when broken. **2** (**safety glasses**) toughened glasses or goggles for protecting the eyes when using power tools or industrial or laboratory equipment.

safe·ty har·ness ▶ *n.* a system of belts or restraints to hold a person to prevent falling or injury.

safe·ty match ▶ *n.* a match igniting only when struck on a specially prepared surface, esp. the side of a matchbook or matchbox.

safe·ty net ▶ *n.* a net placed to catch an acrobat or similar performer in case of a fall. ■ *fig.* a safeguard against possible hardship or adversity: *a safety net for workers who lose their jobs.*

safe·ty pin ▶ *n.* a pin with a point that is bent back to the head and is held in a guard when closed.

safe·ty ra·zor ▶ *n.* a razor with a guard to reduce the risk of cutting the skin.

safe·ty valve ▶ *n.* a valve opening automatically to relieve excessive pressure, esp. in a boiler. ■ *fig.* a means of giving harmless vent to feelings of tension or stress.

saf·flow·er /ˈsafˌlou(-ə)r/ ▶ *n.* an orange-flowered, thistlelike Eurasian plant (*Carthamus tinctorius*) of the daisy family, with seeds that yield an edible oil and petals that were formerly used to produce a red or yellow dye. ■ (**saf·flow·er oil**) the edible oil obtained from the seeds of this plant.

saf·fron /ˈsafrən/ ▶ *n.* **1** an orange-yellow flavoring, food coloring, and dye made from the dried stigmas of a crocus: [as *adj.*] *saffron buns.* ■ the orange-yellow color of this. **2** (also **saffron crocus**) an autumn-flowering crocus (*Crocus sativus*) with reddish-purple flowers, native to warmer regions of Eurasia. Enormous numbers of flowers are required to produce a small quantity of the large red stigmas used for the spice. —**saf·fron·y** *adj.*

sag /sag/ ▶ *v.* (**sagged**, **sag·ging**) [*intr.*] sink or subside gradually under weight or pressure or through lack of strength: *he closed his eyes and sagged against the wall.* ■ hang down loosely or unevenly: *stockings that sagged at the knees.* ■ have a downward bulge or curve: *the bed sagged in the middle.* ■ *fig.* decline to a lower level, usually temporarily: *exports are forging ahead while home sales sag.*
▶ *n.* a downward curve or bulge in a structure caused by weakness or excessive weight or pressure: *a sag in the middle necessitated a third set of wheels.* ■ *Geom.* the amount of this, measured as the perpendicular distance from the middle of the curve to the straight line between the two supporting points. ■ *fig.* a decline, esp. a temporary one. —**sag·gy** *adj.*

sa·ga /ˈsägə/ ▶ *n.* a long story of heroic achievement, esp. a medieval prose narrative in Old Norse or Old Icelandic. ■ a long, involved story, account, or series of incidents: *the saga of her engagement.*

sa·ga·cious /səˈgāsʜəs/ ▶ *adj.* having or showing keen mental discernment and good judgment; shrewd: *they were sagacious enough to avoid any outright confrontation.* —**sa·ga·cious·ly** *adv.* —**sa·gac·i·ty** /-ˈgasitē/ *n.*

sage[1] /sāj/ ▶ *n.* **1** an aromatic plant (*Salvia officinalis*) of the mint family, with grayish-green leaves that are used as a culinary herb, native to southern Europe and the Mediterranean. **2** (also **white sage**) a bushy North American plants with silvery-gray leaves, esp. an aromatic plant (*Artemisia ludoviciana*) of the daisy family.

sage[2] ▶ *n.* a profoundly wise man, esp. one who features in ancient history or legend.
▶ *adj.* having, showing, or indicating profound wisdom: *they nodded in agreement with these sage remarks.* —**sage·ly** *adv.* —**sage·ness** *n.*

sage·brush /ˈsājˌbrəsʜ/ ▶ *n.* a shrubby aromatic North American plant (genus *Artemisia*) of the daisy family. ■ scrub dominated by such shrubs, occurring chiefly in semiarid regions of western North America.

Sag·it·tar·i·us /ˌsajiˈte(ə)rēəs/ ▶ **1** *Astron.* a large constellation (the Archer), said to represent a centaur carrying a bow and arrow. The

center of the Galaxy is situated within it. **2** *Astrol.* the ninth sign of the zodiac, which the sun enters about November 22. ■ (**a Sagittarius**) (*pl.* same) a person born when the sun is in this sign.

sa·go /ˈsāgō/ ▶ *n.* (*pl.* **-os**) **1** edible starch that is obtained from a palm and is a staple food in parts of the tropics. ■ (also **sago pudding**) a sweet dish made from sago and milk. **2** (**sago palm**) the palm (*Metroxylon sagu*) from which most sago is obtained, growing in freshwater swamps in Southeast Asia. ■ any of a number of other palms or cycads that yield a similar starch.

sa·gua·ro /səˈ(g)wärō/ (also **saguaro cactus**) ▶ *n.* (*pl.* **-os**) a giant cactus (*Carnegiea gigantea*) that can grow to 66 feet (20 m) in height and whose branches are shaped like candelabra, native to Mexico and the southwestern U.S. Its reddish-purple fruit is consumable as food and drink.

Sa·hap·ti·an /säˈhaptēən/ ▶ *adj.* denoting, belonging to, or relating to a family of North American Indian languages, including Nez Percé and Sahaptin, spoken in southern Washington, northern Oregon, and central Idaho.
▶ *n.* this family of languages.

Sa·hap·tin /säˈhaptin/ ▶ *n.* **1** any of several native American peoples of southern Washington and northern Oregon. **2** the Sahaptian language spoken by these peoples.

sa·hib /ˈsä(h)ib/ ▶ *n. Indian* a polite title or form of address for a man: *the Doctor Sahib.*

said /sed/ ▶ past and past participle of SAY.
▶ *adj.* used in legal language or humorously to refer to someone or something already mentioned or named: *acting in pursuance of the said agreement.*

sail /sāl/ ▶ *n.* **1** a piece of material extended on a mast to catch the wind and propel a boat, ship, or other vessel: *all the sails were unfurled.* ■ the use of sailing ships as a means of transport: *this led to bigger ships as steam replaced sail.* ■ a voyage or excursion in a ship, esp. a sailing ship or boat: *they went for a sail.* ■ something resembling a sail in shape or function, in particular: ■ a wind-catching apparatus, typically one consisting of canvas or a set of boards, attached to the arm of a windmill. ■ the conning tower of a submarine.
▶ *v.* [*intr.*] **1** travel in a boat with sails, esp. as a sport or recreation: *Ian took us out sailing on the lake.* ■ travel in a ship or boat using sails or engine power: *the ferry caught fire sailing between Caen and Portsmouth.* ■ begin a voyage; leave a harbor: *the catamaran sails at 3:30.* ■ [*tr.*] travel by ship on or across (a sea) or on (a route): *plastic ships could be sailing the oceans soon.* ■ [*tr.*] navigate or control (a boat or ship): *I stole a small fishing boat and sailed it to the Delta.* **2** move smoothly and rapidly or in a stately or confident manner: *she sailed into the conference room at 2:30 sharp.* —**sail·a·ble** *adj.* —**sailed** *adj.* [in *comb.*] *a black-sailed ship.*

sail·board /ˈsālˌbôrd/ ▶ *n.* a board with a mast attached to it by a swivel joint, and a sail, used in windsurfing. —**sail·board·er** *n.* —**sail·board·ing** *n.*

sail·boat /ˈsālˌbōt/ ▶ *n.* a boat propelled by sails.

sail·cloth /ˈsālˌklôтʜ; -ˌkläтʜ/ ▶ *n.* canvas or other material used for making sails. ■ a canvaslike fabric used for making durable weatherproof clothes.

sail·fish /ˈsālˌfisʜ/ ▶ *n.* (*pl.* same or **-fishes**) a fish with a high, sail-like dorsal fin, in particular: ■ an edible migratory billfish that is a prized game fish (genus *Istiophorus*, esp. *I. platypterus*). ■ a small tropical freshwater fish of Sulawesi, popular in aquariums (*Telmatherina ladigesi*, family Atherinidae).

sail·or /ˈsālər/ ▶ *n.* a person whose job it is to work as a member of the crew of a commercial or naval ship or boat, esp. one who is below the rank of officer. ■ a person who goes sailing as a sport or recreation. —**sail·or·ly** *adj.*

saint /sānt/ ▶ *n.* **1** a person acknowledged as holy or virtuous and typically regarded as being in heaven after death. ■ (in the Catholic and Orthodox Churches) a person formally recognized or canonized by the Church after death, who may be the object of veneration and prayers for intercession. ■ a person who is admired or venerated because of their virtue: *he was considered a living saint by recipients of his generosity.* ■ (in or alluding to biblical use) a Christian believer. ■ (**Saint**) a member of the Church of Jesus Christ of Latter-Day Saints; a Mormon. **2** (**Saint**) (abbr.: **St.** or **S.**) used in titles of religious saints: *the epistles of Saint Paul.* ■ used in place names or other dedications: *St. Louis.*
▶ *v.* [*tr.*] [as *adj.*] (**sainted**) worthy of being a saint; very virtuous: *the story of his sainted sister Eileen.* ▷ Middle English, from Old French *seint*, from Latin *sanctus* 'holy,' past participle of *sancire* 'consecrate.' —**saint·hood** *n.* —**saint·like** *adj.*

saint·ly /ˈsāntlē/ ▶ *adj.* (**-li·er**, **-li·est**) very holy or virtuous: *a truly saintly woman.* —**saint·li·ness** *n.*

saith /seTH; 'sāiTH/ ▶ archaic third person singular present of SAY.

sake[1] /sāk/ ▶n. **1** (**for the sake of something** or **for something's sake**) for the purpose of; in the interest of; in order to achieve or preserve: *the couple moved to the coast for the sake of her health.* ■ used in phrases to comment on the speaker's purpose in choosing a particular way of wording a text or presenting an argument: *let us say, for the sake of argument, that the plotter and the assassin are one and the same person.* ■ (**for its own sake** or **something for something's sake** or **for the sake of it**) used to indicate something that is done as an end in itself rather than to achieve some other purpose: *new ideas amount to change for change's sake.* **2** (**for the sake of someone** or **for someone's sake**) out of consideration for or in order to help someone: *I felt I couldn't give up, for my own sake or the baby's.* ■ in order to please: *he'd even kill a man for my sake.* **3** (**for God's** or **goodness**, etc., **sake**) used to express impatience, annoyance, urgency, or desperation: *"Oh, for God's sake!" snarled Dyson.*

sa·ke[2] /'säkē; -kä/ (also **saki**) ▶n. a Japanese alcoholic drink made from fermented rice, traditionally drunk warm in small porcelain cups.

sa·laam /sə'läm/ ▶interj. a common greeting in many Arabic-speaking and Muslim countries.
▶n. a gesture of greeting or respect, with or without a spoken salutation, typically consisting of a low bow of the head and body with the hand or fingers touching the forehead. ■ (**salaams**) respectful compliments.

sal·a·ble /'sāləbəl/ (also **sale·a·ble**) ▶adj. fit or able to be sold. —**sal·a·bil·i·ty** /,sālə'bilitē/ n.

sa·la·cious /sə'lāsHəs/ ▶adj. (of writing, pictures, or talk) treating sexual matters in an indecent way and typically conveying undue interest in or enjoyment of the subject: *salacious stories.* ■ lustful; lecherous: *his salacious grin faltered.* —**sa·la·cious·ly** adv. —**sa·la·cious·ness** n. —**sa·lac·i·ty** /-'lasitē/ n. (*dated*).

sal·ad /'saləd/ ▶n. a cold dish of various mixtures of raw or cooked vegetables, usually seasoned with oil, vinegar, or other dressing and sometimes accompanied by meat, fish, or other ingredients. ■ a mixture containing a specified ingredient served with a dressing: *a red pepper filled with tuna salad.* ▷late Middle English: from Old French *salade*, from Provençal *salada*, based on Latin *sal* 'salt.'

sal·ad days ▶pl. n. (**one's salad days**) the period when one is young and inexperienced. ■ the peak or heyday of something.

sal·ad dress·ing ▶n. see DRESSING (sense 1).

sal·a·man·der /'salə,mandər/ ▶n. **1** a newtlike amphibian (Salamandridae and other families, order Urodela) that typically has bright markings, and that once was thought to be able to endure fire. **2** a mythical lizardlike creature able to withstand fire. —**sal·a·man·drine** /,salə'mandrin/ adj.

sa·la·mi /sə'lämē/ ▶n. (*pl.* same or **-mis**) a type of highly seasoned sausage, originally from Italy, usually eaten cold in slices. ■ *inf. Baseball* a grand slam home run.

sal·a·ry /'salərē/ ▶n. (*pl.* **-ries**) a fixed regular payment, typically paid on a monthly or biweekly basis but often expressed as an annual sum, made by an employer to an employee, esp. a professional or white-collar worker: [as adj.] *a 15 percent salary increase.*

sale /sāl/ ▶n. **1** the exchange of a commodity for money; the action of selling something: *we withdrew it from sale.* ■ (**sales**) a quantity or amount sold: *price cuts failed to boost sales.* ■ (**sales**) the activity or business of selling products: *director of sales and marketing.* **2** an event for the rapid disposal of goods at reduced prices for a period, esp. at the end of a season: *a clearance sale.* ■ a public or charitable event at which goods are sold. ■ a public auction.
▶ □ (**up**) **for sale** offered for purchase; to be bought: *cars for sale at reasonable prices.* □ **on sale** offered for purchase: *the November issue is on sale now.* ■ offered for purchase at a reduced price.

sale·a·ble ▶adj. variant spelling of SALABLE.

sales·clerk /'sālz,klərk/ (also **sales clerk**) ▶n. an assistant who sells goods in a retail store.

sales·girl /'sālz,gərl/ ▶n. a female salesclerk.

sales·la·dy /'sālz,lādē/ ▶n. (*pl.* **-dies**) a saleswoman, esp. one working as a salesclerk.

sales·man /'sālzmən/ ▶n. (*pl.* **-men**) a man whose job involves selling or promoting commercial products, either in a store or visiting locations to get orders: *an insurance salesman.* —**sales·man·ship** /-,SHip/ n.

sales·per·son /'sālz,pərsən/ ▶n. (*pl.* **-per·sons** or **-peo·ple**) a salesman or saleswoman (used as a neutral alternative).

sales·room /'sālz,rōōm; -,rŏŏm/ ▶n. a room in which items are sold at auction. ■ a showroom displaying goods offered for sale.

sales tax ▶n. a tax on sales or on the receipts from sales.

sales·wom·an /'sālz,wŏŏmən/ ▶n. (*pl.* **-wom·en**) a woman whose job involves selling or promoting commercial products.

sal·i·cyl·ic ac·id /,salə'silik/ ▶n. *Chem.* a bitter compound, $C_6H_4(OH)(COOH)$, present in certain plants. It is used as a fungicide and in the manufacture of aspirin and dyestuffs. —**sa·lic·y·late** /sə'lisə,lāt; -lit/ n.

sa·li·ent /'sālyənt; -lēənt/ ▶adj. most noticeable or important: *it succinctly covered all the salient points of the case.* ■ prominent; conspicuous: *it was always the salient object in my view.* ■ (of an angle) pointing outward.
▶n. a piece of land or section of fortification that juts out to form an angle. ■ an outward bulge in a line of military attack or defense. —**sa·li·ence** n. —**sa·li·en·cy** n. —**sa·li·ent·ly** adv.

sa·line /'sā,lēn; -,līn/ ▶adj. containing or impregnated with salt: *saline alluvial soils.* ■ *chiefly Med.* (of a solution) containing sodium chloride and/or a salt or salts of magnesium or another alkali metal.
▶n. a saline solution used in medicine. —**sa·lin·i·ty** /sə'linitē/ n. —**sal·i·ni·za·tion** /,salənə'zāsHən/ n. —**sal·i·nize** /'salə,nīz/ v.

sa·li·va /sə'līvə/ ▶n. watery liquid secreted into the mouth by glands, providing lubrication for chewing and swallowing, and aiding digestion. —**sal·i·var·y** /'salə,verē/ adj.

sal·i·vate /'salə,vāt/ ▶v. [intr.] secrete saliva, esp. in anticipation of food. ■ *fig.* display great relish at the sight or prospect of something: *I was fairly salivating at the prospect of a $10 million loan.* —**sal·i·va·tion** /,salə'vāsHən/ n.

Salk vac·cine /sô(l)k/ ▶n. the first vaccine developed against polio, made from viruses of the three immunological types inactivated with formalin. ▷1950s: Named after Jonas Edward *Salk* (1914–95), U.S. microbiologist, who developed the vaccine in 1954.

sal·low[1] /'salō/ ▶adj. (**-low·er**, **-low·est**) (of a person's face or complexion) of an unhealthy yellow or pale brown color.
▶v. [tr.] *rare* make sallow. —**sal·low·ish** adj. —**sal·low·ness** n.

sal·ly /'salē/ ▶n. (*pl.* **-lies**) a sudden charge out of a besieged place against the enemy; a sortie. ■ a brief journey or sudden start into activity. ■ a witty or lively remark, esp. one made as an attack or as a diversion in an argument; a retort.
▶v. (**-lies**, **-lied**) [intr.] make a military sortie: *they sallied out to harass the enemy.* ■ *formal* or *humorous* set out from a place to do something: *I made myself presentable and sallied forth.*

sal·ma·gun·di /,salmə'gəndē/ ▶n. (*pl.* **-dis**) a dish of chopped meat, anchovies, eggs, onions, and seasoning. ■ a general mixture; a miscellaneous collection.

salm·on /'samən/ ▶n. (*pl.* same or (esp. of types) **salmons**) **1** a large edible game fish, much prized for its pink flesh. Salmon mature in the sea but migrate to freshwater streams to spawn. The **Atlantic salmon** (*Salmo salar*) may return to spawn two or three times, but the five species of Pacific salmon (genus *Oncorhynchus*) always die after spawning. The **salmon family** (Salmonidae) also includes trout, char, whitefish, and their relatives. ■ the flesh of this fish as food. **2** any of a number of fishes that resemble the true salmons. **3** a pale pinkish orange color. —**salm·on·y** adj.

sal·mo·nel·la /,salmə'nelə/ ▶n. (*pl.* **salmonellae** /-'nelē/) a bacterium that occurs mainly in the intestine, esp. a type causing food poisoning. ■ food poisoning caused by infection with a such a bacterium: *an outbreak of salmonella.* —**sal·mo·nel·lo·sis** /-,ne'lōsis/ n.

sa·lon /sə'län; sa'lôn/ ▶n. **1** an establishment where a hairdresser, beautician, or couturier conducts business. **2** a reception room in a large house. ■ *hist.* a social gathering of eminent people (esp. writers and artists). at the house of a woman prominent in high society.

sa·loon /sə'lōōn/ ▶n. a public room or building used for a specified purpose: *a billiard saloon.* ■ *hist.* or *humorous* a place where alcoholic drinks may be bought and drunk. ■ a large public room for use as a lounge on a ship.

salp /salp/ ▶n. a free-swimming marine invertebrate related to the sea squirts with a transparent, barrel-shaped body.

sal·sa /'sälsə/ ▶n. **1** a type of Latin American dance music incorporating elements of jazz and rock. ■ a dance performed to this music. **2** (esp. in Latin American cooking) a spicy tomato sauce.

SALT /sôlt/ ▶abbr. Strategic Arms Limitation Talks.

salt /sôlt/ ▶n. **1** (also **common salt**) sodium chloride (NaCl), a white crystalline substance that gives seawater its characteristic taste and is used for seasoning or preserving food. ■ *poetic/lit.* something that adds freshness or piquancy. **2** *Chem.* any chemical compound formed from

---

Pronunciation Key ə *ago*, *up*; ər *over*, *fur*; a *hat*; ā *ate*; ä *car*; CH *chin*; e *let*; ē *see*; e(ə)r *air*; i *fit*; ī *by*; i(ə)r *ear*; NG *sing*; ō *go*; ô *law*, *for*; oi *toy*; ŏŏ *good*; ōō *goo*; ou *out*; SH *she*; TH *thin*; TH *then*; (h)w *why*; ZH *vision*

the reaction of an acid with a base, with all or part of the hydrogen of the acid replaced by a metal or other cation. **3** (usu. **old salt**) *inf.* an experienced sailor.

▶*adj.* **1** impregnated with, treated with, or tasting of salt: *salt water* | *salt beef.* **2** (of a plant) growing on the coast or in salt marshes.

▶*v.* [*tr.*] **1** [usu. as *adj.*] (**salted**) season or preserve with salt: *cook the carrots in boiling salted water.* ■ *fig.* make (something) piquant or more interesting. **2** *inf.* fraudulently make (a mine) appear to be a paying one by placing rich ore into it.

▶*phrasal v.* ☐ **salt something away** *inf.* secretly store or put by something, esp. money.

▶ ☐ **the salt of the earth** a person or group of people of great kindness, reliability, or honesty. ☐ **take something with a grain** (or **pinch**) **of salt** regard something as exaggerated; believe only part of something. ☐ **worth one's salt** good or competent at the job or profession specified.

salt-and-pep·per ▶*adj.* flecked or speckled with intermingled dark and light shades: *his salt-and-pepper hair.*

sal·ta·rel·lo /ˌsältəˈrelō; ˌsôl-/ ▶*n.* (*pl.* **-rel·los** or **-rel·li** /-ˈrelē/) an energetic Italian or Spanish dance for one couple, characterized by leaps and skips.

salt·cel·lar /ˈsôltˌselər/ ▶*n.* a dish or container for storing salt, now typically a closed container with perforations in the lid for sprinkling.

sal·tine /ˌsôlˈtēn/ ▶*n.* a thin, crisp, savory cracker sprinkled with salt.

salt lake ▶*n.* a lake of salt water.

salt lick ▶*n.* a place where animals go to lick salt from the ground. ■ a block of salt provided for animals to lick.

salt marsh ▶*n.* an area of coastal grassland that is regularly flooded by seawater.

salt pan ▶*n.* a shallow container or depression in the ground in which salt water evaporates to leave a deposit of salt.

salt·pe·ter /ˈsôltˌpētər/ (*Brit.* **salt·pe·tre**) ▶*n.* another term for POTASSIUM NITRATE.

salt shak·er ▶*n.* a perforated container for sprinkling salt.

salt·wa·ter /ˈsôltˌwôtər; -ˌwätər/ ▶*adj.* of or found in salt water; living in the sea: *saltwater fish.*

salt·wort /ˈsôltwərt; -ˈwôrt/ ▶*n.* a plant (genus *Salsola*) of the goosefoot family that typically grows in salt marshes. It is rich in alkali, and its ashes were formerly used in soap-making.

salt·y /ˈsôltē/ ▶*adj.* (**salt·i·er**, **salt·i·est**) tasting of, containing, or preserved with salt. ■ (of language or humor) down-to-earth; coarse. —**salt·i·ness** *n.*

sa·lu·bri·ous /səˈlōōbrēəs/ ▶*adj.* health-giving; healthy: *salubrious weather.* ■ (of a place) pleasant; not run-down. —**sa·lu·bri·ous·ly** *adv.* —**sa·lu·bri·ous·ness** *n.*

Sa·lu·ki /səˈlōōkē/ (also **sa·lu·ki**) ▶*n.* (*pl.* **-kis**) a tall, swift, slender dog of a silky-coated breed with large drooping ears and fringed feet.

sal·u·tar·y /ˈsalyəˌterē/ ▶*adj.* (esp. with reference to something unwelcome or unpleasant) producing good effects; beneficial: *a salutary reminder of where we came from.*

sal·u·ta·tion /ˌsalyəˈtāSHən/ ▶*n.* a gesture or utterance made as a greeting or acknowledgment of another's arrival or departure: *we greeted them but no one returned our salutations.* ■ a standard formula of words used in a letter to address the person being written to. —**sal·u·ta·tion·al** /-SHənl/ *adj.*

sa·lu·ta·to·ri·an /səˌlōōtəˈtôrēən/ ▶*n.* the student who ranks second highest in a graduating class and delivers the salutatory. Compare with VALEDICTORIAN.

sa·lu·ta·to·ry /səˈlōōtəˌtôrē/ ▶*n.* (*pl.* **-ries**) an address of welcome, esp. one given as an oration by the student ranking second highest in a graduating class at a high school or college.

sa·lute /səˈlōōt/ ▶*n.* a gesture of respect, homage, or polite recognition or acknowledgment, esp. one made to or by a person when arriving or departing: *he raises his arms in a triumphant salute.* ■ a prescribed or specified movement, typically a raising of a hand to the head, made by a member of a military or similar force as a formal sign of respect or recognition. ■ the discharge of a gun or guns as a formal or ceremonial sign of respect or celebration: *a twenty-one-gun salute.* ■ *Fencing* the formal performance of certain guards or other movements by fencers before engaging.

▶*v.* [*tr.*] make a formal salute to: *don't you usually salute a superior officer?* ■ greet: *he saluted her with a smile.* ■ show or express admiration and respect for: *we salute a truly great photographer.*

sal·vage /ˈsalvij/ ▶*v.* [*tr.*] rescue (a wrecked or disabled ship or its cargo) from loss at sea: *an emerald and gold cross was salvaged from the wreck.*

■ retrieve or preserve (something) from potential loss or adverse circumstances: *it was the only crumb of comfort he could salvage from the ordeal.*

▶*n.* the rescue of a wrecked or disabled ship or its cargo from loss at sea: [as *adj.*] *a salvage operation was under way.* ■ the cargo saved from a wrecked or sunken ship: *salvage taken from a ship that had sunk in the river.* ■ the rescue of property or material from potential loss or destruction. ■ *Law* payment made or due to a person who has saved a ship or its cargo. —**sal·vage·a·ble** *adj.* —**sal·vag·er** *n.*

sal·va·tion /salˈvāSHən/ ▶*n. Theol.* deliverance from sin and its consequences, believed by Christians to be brought about by faith in Christ. ■ preservation or deliverance from harm, ruin, or loss: *they try to sell it to us as economic salvation.* ■ (**one's salvation**) a source or means of being saved in this way: *his only salvation was to outpace the enemy.*

salve /sav; säv/ ▶*n.* an ointment used to promote healing of the skin or as protection. ■ *fig.* something that is soothing or consoling for wounded feelings or an uneasy conscience: *the idea provided him with a salve for his guilt.*

▶*v.* soothe (wounded pride or one's conscience): *charity salves our conscience.*

sal·ver /ˈsalvər/ ▶*n.* a tray, typically one made of silver and used in formal circumstances.

sal·vo /ˈsalˌvō/ ▶*n.* (*pl.* **-vos** or **-voes**) a simultaneous discharge of artillery or other guns in a battle. ■ a number of weapons released from one or more aircraft in quick succession. ■ *fig.* a sudden, vigorous, or aggressive act or series of acts: *the pardons provoked a salvo of accusations.*

sal vo·la·ti·le /ˌsal vəˈlatl-ē/ ▶*n.* a scented solution of ammonium carbonate in alcohol, used as smelling salts.

SAM /sam/ ▶*abbr.* surface-to-air missile.

sa·ma·dhi /səˈmädē/ ▶*n.* (*pl.* **-dhis**) *Hinduism & Buddhism* a state of intense concentration achieved through meditation. In Hindu yoga this is regarded as the final stage, at which union with the divine is reached.

sam·a·ra /ˈsamərə; səˈme(ə)rə/ ▶*n. Bot.* a winged nut or achene containing one seed, as in ash and maple.

Sa·mar·i·tan /səˈmaritn; -ˈme(ə)r-/ ▶*n.* **1** (usu. **good Samaritan**) a charitable or helpful person. **2** a member of a people inhabiting Samaria in biblical times, or of the modern community in the region of Nablus claiming descent from them, adhering to a form of Judaism accepting only its own ancient version of the Pentateuch as Scripture. **3** the dialect of Aramaic formerly spoken in Samaria.

▶*adj.* of or relating to Samaria or the Samaritans. —**Sa·mar·i·tan·ism** /-ˌizəm/ *n.*

sa·mar·i·um /səˈme(ə)rēəm/ ▶*n.* the chemical element of atomic number 62, a hard, silvery-white metal of the lanthanide series. (Symbol: **Sm**)

sam·ba /ˈsambə; ˈsäm-/ ▶*n.* a Brazilian dance of African origin. ■ a piece of music for this dance. ■ a lively modern ballroom dance imitating this dance.

▶*v.* (**-bas**, **-baed** /-bəd/ or **-ba'd**, **-ba·ing** /-bə,iNG/) [*intr.*] dance the samba.

Sam Browne belt /sam ˈbroun/ ▶*n.* a leather belt with a supporting strap that passes over the right shoulder, worn by army and police officers.

same /sām/ ▶*adj.* (**the same**) **1** identical; not different; unchanged: *he's worked at the same place for quite a few years.* ■ (**this/that same**) referring to a person or thing just mentioned: *that same year I went to Boston.* **2** of an identical type: *they all wore the same clothes.*

▶*pron.* **1** (**the same**) the same thing as something previously mentioned: *I'll resign and encourage everyone else to do the same.* ■ people or things that are identical or share the same characteristics: *there are several brands and they're not all the same.* **2** (chiefly in formal or legal use) the person or thing just mentioned: *sighted sub, sank same.*

▶*adv.* similarly; in the same way: *treating women the same as men.* —**same·ness** *n.*

▶ ☐ **all** (or **just**) **the same** in spite of this; nevertheless: *she knew they had meant it kindly, but it had hurt all the same.* ■ in any case; anyway: *I can manage alone, thanks all the same.* ☐ **at the same time 1** simultaneously. **2** on the other hand; nevertheless: *it's a very creative place, but at the same time it's very relaxing.* ■ **be all the same to** be unimportant to (someone) what happens: *it was all the same to me where it was being sold.* ☐ **one and the same** the same person or thing (used for emphasis): *the guy in the glasses and Superman were one and the same.* ☐ **same difference** *inf.* used to express the speaker's belief that two or more things are essentially the same, in spite of apparent differences. ☐ **same here** *inf.* the same applies to me. ☐ (**the**) **same to you!** may you do or have the same thing (a response to a greeting or insult).

same-sex ▶*adj.* relating to or involving people of the same sex: *same-sex friendships* ■ relating to or denoting a sexual relationship in which both partners are of the same sex: *same-sex marriage.*

same-store sales /'sām ,stôr ,sālz/ ▶*n. Finance* a figure used to determine what amount of sales growth is attributable to new store openings, based on sales made by stores that have been open more than one year.

Sa·mo·an /sə'mōən/ ▶*adj.* of or relating to Samoa, its people, or their language.
▶*n.* **1** a native or inhabitant of Samoa. **2** the Polynesian language of Samoa, spoken in Samoa, New Zealand, the U.S., and elsewhere.

sam·o·var /'samə,vär/ ▶*n.* a highly decorated tea urn used in Russia.

Sam·o·yed /'samə,yed; sə'moiyid/ ▶*n.* **1** a member of a group of mainly nomadic peoples of northern Siberia, who traditionally live as reindeer herders. **2** any of several Samoyedic languages of these peoples. **3** a dog of a white Arctic breed.

sam·pan /'sam,pan/ ▶*n.* a small boat of a kind used in the Far East, typically with an oar or oars at the stern. ▷early 17th cent.: from Chinese *san-ban*, from *san* 'three' + *ban* 'board.'

sampan

sam·phire /'sam,fīr/ ▶*n.* **1** an aromatic, fleshy-leafed European plant (*Crithmum maritimum*) of the parsley family that grows on rocks and cliffs by the sea. **2** another term for GLASSWORT.

sam·ple /'sampəl/ ▶*n.* a small part or quantity intended to show what the whole is like: *investigations involved analyzing samples of handwriting.* ■ a specimen taken for scientific testing or analysis: *a urine sample.* ■ *Statistics* a portion drawn from a population, the study of which is intended to lead to statistical estimates of the attributes of the whole population. ■ a small amount of a food or other commodity, esp. one given to a prospective customer. ■ a sound created by sampling.
▶*v.* [*tr.*] take a sample or samples of (something) for analysis: *bone marrow cells were sampled.* ■ try the qualities of (food or drink) by tasting it. ■ get a representative experience of: *sample the pleasures of Saint Maarten.* ■ *Electr.* ascertain the momentary value of (an analog signal) many times a second so as to convert the signal to digital form. ■ record or extract a small piece of music or sound digitally for reuse as part of a composition or song.

sam·pler /'samplər/ ▶*n.* **1** a piece of embroidery worked in various stitches as a specimen of skill, typically containing the alphabet and some mottoes. **2** a representative collection or example of something: *a few superb samplers of West Indian dishes.* **3** a person or device that takes and analyzes samples. ■ an electronic device for sampling music and sound.

sam·pling /'sampliNG/ ▶*n.* **1** the taking of a sample or samples. **2** the technique of digitally encoding music or sound and reusing it as part of a composition or recording.

sam·sa·ra /səm'särə/ ▶*n. Hinduism & Buddhism* the cycle of death and rebirth to which life in the material world is bound. —**sam·sa·ric** /-'särik/ *adj.*

sam·u·rai /'samə,rī/ ▶*n.* (*pl.* same) *hist.* a member of a powerful military caste in feudal Japan, esp. a member of the class of military retainers.

San /sän/ ▶*n.* **1** a member of the aboriginal peoples of southern Africa commonly called Bushmen. See BUSHMAN. **2** any of the Khoisan languages spoken by these peoples.
▶*adj.* of or relating to the San or their languages.

san·a·to·ri·um /,sanə'tôrēəm/ ▶*n.* (*pl.* **-ri·ums** or **-ri·a** /-rēə/) another term for SANITARIUM.

sanc·ti·fy /'saNG(k)tə,fī/ ▶*v.* (**-fies, -fied**) [*tr.*] set apart as or declare holy; consecrate: *a small Christian shrine was built to sanctify the site.* ■ (often **be sanctified**) make legitimate or binding by religious sanction: *they see their love sanctified by the sacrament of marriage.* ■ free from sin; purify. ■ (often **be sanctified**) *fig.* give the appearance of being right or good;

legitimize: *they looked to royalty to sanctify their cause.* —**sanc·ti·fi·ca·tion** /-fi'kāSHən/ *n.* —**sanc·ti·fi·er** *n.*

sanc·ti·mo·ni·ous /,saNG(k)tə'mōnēəs/ ▶*adj. derog.* making a show of being morally superior to other people: *what happened to all the sanctimonious talk about putting his family first?* —**sanc·ti·mo·ni·ous·ly** *adv.* —**sanc·ti·mo·ni·ous·ness** *n.* —**sanc·ti·mo·ny** /-nē/ *n.*

sanc·tion /'saNG(k)SHən/ ▶*n.* **1** a threatened penalty for disobeying a law or rule: *a range of sanctions aimed at deterring insider abuse.* ■ (**sanctions**) measures taken by a nation to coerce another to conform to an international agreement or norms of conduct, typically in the form of restrictions on trade or on participation in official sporting events. ■ *Ethics* a consideration operating to enforce obedience to any rule of conduct. **2** official permission or approval for an action: *he appealed to the bishop for his sanction.* ■ official confirmation or ratification of a law.
▶*v.* [*tr.*] **1** (often **be sanctioned**) give official permission or approval for (an action): *only two treatments have been sanctioned by the Food and Drug Administration.* **2** impose a sanction or penalty on.

sanc·ti·ty /'saNG(k)titē/ ▶*n.* (*pl.* **-ties**) the state or quality of being holy, sacred, or saintly: *the tomb was a place of sanctity for the ancient Egyptians.* ■ ultimate importance and inviolability: *the sanctity of human life.*

sanc·tu·ar·y /'saNG(k)CHŌō,erē/ ▶*n.* (*pl.* **-ar·ies**) **1** a place of refuge or safety: *people automatically sought a sanctuary in time of trouble.* ■ immunity from arrest: *he has been **given sanctuary** in the U.S. Embassy in Beijing.* **2** a nature reserve: *a bird sanctuary.* **3** a holy place; a temple or church. ■ the inmost recess or holiest part of a temple or church. ■ the part of the chancel of a church containing the high altar. ▷Middle English: from Old French *sanctuaire*, from Latin *sanctuarium*, from *sanctus* 'holy.' The early sense 'a church or other sacred place where a fugitive was immune from arrest' gave rise to senses 1 and 2.

sanc·tum /'saNG(k)təm/ ▶*n.* (*pl.* **-tums**) a sacred place, esp. a shrine within a temple or church. ■ *fig.* a private place from which most people are excluded.

Sanc·tus /'saNG(k)təs/ ▶*n. Christian Church* a hymn beginning *Sanctus, sanctus, sanctus* (Holy, holy, holy) forming a set part of the Mass.

sand /sand/ ▶*n.* a loose granular substance, typically pale yellowish brown, resulting from the erosion of siliceous and other rocks and forming a major constituent of beaches, riverbeds, the seabed, and deserts. ■ (**sands**) an expanse of sand, typically along a shore. ■ a light yellow-brown color like that of sand.
▶*v.* [*tr.*] **1** smooth or polish with sandpaper or a mechanical sander: *sand the rusty areas until you expose bare metal.* **2** sprinkle or overlay with sand, to give better purchase on a surface. —**sand·er** *n.* —**sand·like** /-,līk/ *adj.*

san·dal /'sandl/ ▶*n.* a light shoe with either an openwork upper or straps attaching the sole to the foot. —**san·daled** /'sandld/ *adj.*

san·dal·wood /'sandl,wŏod/ ▶*n.* a widely cultivated Indian tree (*Santalum album*) that yields fragrant timber and oil. ■ a perfume or incense derived from this timber.

sand·bag /'san(d),bag/ ▶*n.* a bag filled with sand, typically used for defensive purposes or for protection from flooding.
▶*v.* (**-bagged, -bag·ging**) [*tr.*] **1** [usu. as *adj.*] (**sandbagged**) barricade using sandbags. **2** hit or fell with or as if with a blow from a sandbag. **3** [*intr.*] deliberately underperform in a race or competition to gain an unfair advantage. —**sand·bag·ger** *n.*

sand·bank /'san(d),baNGk/ ▶*n.* a deposit of sand forming a shallow area in the sea or a river.

sand·bar /'san(d),bär/ ▶*n.* a long, narrow sandbank, esp. at the mouth of a river.

sand·blast /'san(d),blast/ ▶*v.* [*tr.*] roughen or clean (a surface) with a jet of sand driven by compressed air or steam. —**sand·blast·er** *n.*

sand·box /'san(d),bäks/ ▶*n.* **1** a shallow box or hollow in the ground partly filled with sand for children to play in. ■ *Comput.* a virtual space in which software or Web sites can be tested, evaluated, or developed before being made generally available. **2** (also **sandbox tree**) a tropical American tree (*Hura crepitans*) of the spurge family whose seed cases were formerly used to hold sand for blotting ink.

sand cas·tle (also **sand·cas·tle**) ▶*n.* a model of a castle built out of sand, typically by children.

sand dol·lar ▶*n.* a flattened sea urchin (order Clypeasteroida) that lives partly buried in sand, feeding on detritus. Several genera and species include the **common sand dollar** (*Echinarachnius parma*) found mostly along the coasts of North America and Japan.

Pronunciation Key ə *ago, up;* ər *over, fur;* a *hat;* ā *ate;* ä *car;* CH *chin;* e *let;* ē *see;* e(ə)r *air;* i *fit;* ī *by;* i(ə)r *ear;* NG *sing;* ō *go;* ô *law, for;* oi *toy;* ŏŏ *good;* ōō *goo;* ou *out;* SH *she;* TH *thin;* TH *then;* (h)w *why;* ZH *vision*

sand·er /'sandər/ ▸n. a power tool used for smoothing a surface with sandpaper or other abrasive material.

sand·fly /'san,flī/ ▸n. (pl. **-flies**) a small, hairy, biting fly of tropical and subtropical regions that transmits a number of diseases, including leishmaniasis.

sand·hog /'san(d),hôg; -,häg/ ▸n. a person who does construction work underground or under water, such as laying foundations or building a tunnel.

sand·lot /'san(d),lät/ ▸n. a piece of unoccupied land used by children for games.

sand·man /'san(d),man/ ▸n. (**the sandman**) a fictional man supposed to make children sleep by sprinkling sand in their eyes.

sand·pa·per /'san(d),pāpər/ ▸n. paper with sand or another abrasive stuck to it, used for smoothing or polishing woodwork or other surfaces. ▪ used to refer to something that feels rough or has a very rough surface.
▸v. [tr.] smooth with sandpaper. —**sand·pa·per·y** adj.

sand·pi·per /'san(d),pīpər/ ▸n. a wading bird (Calidris, Tringa, and Actitis, and other genera) with a long bill and typically long legs, nesting on the ground near water. The **sandpiper family** (Scolopacidae) also includes the godwits, curlews, turnstones, woodcock, and snipe.

sand·pit /'san(d),pit/ ▸n. a quarry from which sand is excavated.

sand·stone /'san(d),stōn/ ▸n. sedimentary rock consisting of sand or quartz grains cemented together, typically red, yellow, or brown in color.

sand·storm /'san(d),stôrm/ ▸n. a strong wind carrying clouds of sand with it, esp. in a desert.

sand·wich /'san,(d)wiCH/ ▸n. an item of food consisting of two pieces of bread with meat, cheese, or other filling between them, eaten as a light meal: a ham sandwich. ▪ something that is constructed like or has the form of a sandwich.
▸v. [tr.] (usu. **be sandwiched between**) insert or squeeze (someone or something) between two other people or things, typically in a restricted space or so as to be uncomfortable: the girl was sandwiched between two burly men in the back of the car.

sand·wich board ▸n. a pair of advertisement boards connected by straps by which they are hung over a person's shoulders.

sand·y /'sandē/ ▸adj. (**sand·i·er, sand·i·est**) **1** covered in or consisting mostly of sand: pine woods and a fine sandy beach. **2** (esp. of hair) light yellowish brown. —**sand·i·ness** n. —**sand·y·ish** adj.

sane /sān/ ▸adj. (of a person) of sound mind; not mad or mentally ill: hard work kept me sane. ▪ (of an undertaking or manner) reasonable; sensible. ▷early 17th cent.: from Latin sanus 'healthy.' —**sane·ly** adv. —**sane·ness** n.

sang /saNG/ ▸ past of SING.

sang·froid /säNG'frwä/ (also **sang-froid**) ▸n. composure or coolness, sometimes excessive, as shown in danger or under trying circumstances.

san·gri·a /saNG'grēə/ ▸n. a Spanish drink of red wine mixed with lemonade, fruit, and spices.

san·guine /'saNGgwin/ ▸adj. cheerfully optimistic: they are not sanguine about the prospect.
▸n. a blood-red color. ▪ a deep red-brown crayon or pencil containing iron oxide. —**san·guine·ly** adv. —**san·guine·ness** n.

San·hed·rin /san'hedrən; -'hēdrən; sän-/ ▸the highest court of justice and the supreme council in ancient Jerusalem.

san·i·tar·i·um /,sani'te(ə)rēəm/ ▸n. (pl. **-tar·i·ums** or **-tar·i·a** /-'te(ə)rēə/) an establishment for the medical treatment of people who are convalescing or have a chronic illness.

san·i·tar·y /'sani,terē/ ▸adj. of or relating to the conditions that affect hygiene and health, esp. the supply of sewage facilities and clean drinking water: a sanitary engineer. ▪ hygienic and clean: the most convenient and sanitary way to get rid of food waste from your kitchen. —**san·i·tar·i·ly** /-,terəlē/ adv. —**san·i·tar·i·ness** n.

san·i·tar·y nap·kin ▸n. an absorbent pad worn by women to absorb menstrual blood.

san·i·ta·tion /,sani'tāSHən/ ▸n. conditions relating to public health, esp. the provision of clean drinking water and adequate sewage disposal.

san·i·tize /'sani,tīz/ ▸v. [tr.] make clean and hygienic: new chemicals for sanitizing a pool. ▪ (usu. **be sanitized**) derog. alter (something regarded as less acceptable) so as to make it more palatable: lawyers sanitized documents that could have exposed the company to lawsuits. —**san·i·ti·za·tion** /,sanətə'zāSHən/ n. —**san·i·tiz·er** n.

san·i·ty /'sanitē/ ▸n. the ability to think and behave in a normal and rational manner; sound mental health: I began to doubt my own sanity. ▪ reasonable and rational behavior.

sans /sanz/ ▸prep. poetic/lit., humorous without: flavorful vegetarian dishes sans meat, eggs, or milk.

San·skrit /'sanskrit/ ▸n. an ancient Indic language of India, in which the Hindu scriptures and classical Indian epic poems are written and from which many northern Indian languages are derived.
▸adj. of or relating to this language. —**San·skrit·ic** /san'skritik/ adj. —**San·skrit·ist** /'san,skritist/ n.

sans ser·if /,san(z) 'serəf/ Printing ▸n. a style of type without serifs.
▸adj. without serifs.

San·ta Claus /'santə ,klôz/ (also **San·ta**) ▸an imaginary figure said to bring presents for children on Christmas. He is conventionally pictured as a jolly old man from the far north, with a long white beard and red garments trimmed with white fur.

sap[1] /sap/ ▸n. the fluid, chiefly water with dissolved sugars and mineral salts, that circulates in the vascular system of a plant. ▪ fig. vigor or energy, esp. sexual vitality: the hot, heady days of youth when the sap was rising.
▸v. (**sapped, sap·ping**) [tr.] gradually weaken or destroy (a person's strength or power): our energy is being sapped by bureaucrats and politicians. ▪ (**sap someone of**) drain someone of (strength or power): her illness had sapped her of energy and life. —**sap·less** adj.

sap[2] ▸n. inf. a foolish and gullible person: He fell for it! What a sap!

sap[3] inf. ▸n. a bludgeon or club.
▸v. (**sapped, sap·ping**) [tr.] hit with a bludgeon or club.

sap·id /'sapid/ ▸adj. having a strong, pleasant taste. ▪ (of talk or writing) pleasant or interesting. —**sa·pid·i·ty** /sə'piditē/ n.

sa·pi·ent /'sāpēənt/ ▸adj. **1** formal wise, or attempting to appear wise. ▪ (chiefly in science fiction) intelligent: sapient life forms. **2** of or relating to the human species (Homo sapiens): our sapient ancestors of 40,000 years ago.
▸n. a human of the species Homo sapiens. —**sa·pi·ence** n. —**sa·pi·ent·ly** adv.

sap·ling /'sapliNG/ ▸n. a young tree, esp. one with a slender trunk.

sap·o·dil·la /,sapə'dilə/ ▸n. a large, evergreen, tropical American tree (Manilkara zapota, family Sapotaceae) that yields chicle and has edible fruit and hard, durable wood. ▪ (also **sapodilla plum**) the sweet, brownish, bristly fruit of this tree.

sap·o·nin /'sapənən/ ▸n. Chem. a toxic compound that is present in soapwort and makes foam when shaken with water. ▪ any of the class of steroid and terpenoid glycosides typified by this, examples of which are used in detergents and foam fire extinguishers.

sap·per /'sapər/ ▸n. a military engineer who lays or detects and disarms mines.

sap·phic /'safik/ ▸adj. **1** formal or humorous of or relating to lesbians or lesbianism: sapphic lovers. **2** (**Sapphic**) of or relating to Sappho or her poetry.

sap·phire /'sa,fīr/ ▸n. a transparent precious stone, typically blue, which is a variety of corundum. ▪ a bright blue color. ▷Middle English: from Old French safir, via Latin from Greek sappheiros, probably denoting lapis lazuli. —**sap·phir·ine** /'safərin; -,rēn; -,rīn/ adj.

sap·py /'sapē/ ▸adj. (**-pi·er, -pi·est**) inf. oversentimental; mawkish. —**sap·pi·ly** /-əlē/ adv. —**sap·pi·ness** n.

sap·ro·gen·ic /,saprō'jenik/ ▸adj. Biol. causing or produced by putrefaction or decay.

sap·ro·phyte /'saprə,fīt/ ▸n. Biol. a plant, fungus, or microorganism that lives on dead or decaying organic matter. —**sap·ro·phyt·ic** /,saprə'fitik/ adj. —**sap·ro·phyt·i·cal·ly** /-ik(ə)lē/ adv.

sap·suck·er /'sap,səkər/ ▸n. an American woodpecker (genus Sphyrapicus varius) that pecks rows of small holes in trees and visits them for sap and insects.

sap·wood /'sap,wŏod/ ▸n. the soft outer layers of recently formed wood between the heartwood and the bark, containing the functioning vascular tissue.

sar·a·band /'sarə,band/ (also **sar·a·bande**) ▸n. a slow, stately Spanish dance in triple time. ▪ a piece of music written for such a dance.

Sar·a·cen /'sarəsən/ ▸n. an Arab or Muslim, esp. at the time of the Crusades. ▪ a nomad of the Syrian and Arabian desert at the time of the Roman Empire. —**Sar·a·cen·ic** /,serə'senik/ adj.

sa·ra·pe ▸n. variant spelling of SERAPE.

sar·casm /'sär,kazəm/ ▸n. the use of irony to mock or convey contempt: his voice, hardened by sarcasm, could not hide his resentment.

sar·cas·tic /sär'kastik/ ▸adj. marked by or given to using irony in order to mock or convey contempt: *sarcastic comments on their failures* | *she's witty and sarcastic.* —**sar·cas·ti·cal·ly** /-ik(ə)lē/ *adv.*

sar·co·ma /särˈkōmə/ ▶*n.* (*pl.* **-mas** or **-ma·ta** /-mətə/) *Med.* a malignant tumor of connective or other nonepithelial tissue. —**sar·co·ma·to·sis** /ˌsärˌkōmə'tōsis/ *n.* —**sar·co·ma·tous** /-mətəs/ *adj.*

sar·coph·a·gus /särˈkäfəgəs/ ▶*n.* (*pl.* **-gi** /-ˌjī/) a stone coffin, typically adorned with a sculpture or inscription and associated with the ancient civilizations of Egypt, Rome, and Greece.

sar·dine /särˈdēn/ ▶*n.* a young pilchard or other young or small herringlike fish.

sar·don·ic /särˈdänik/ ▶*adj.* grimly mocking or cynical: *Starkey attempted a sardonic smile.* —**sar·don·i·cal·ly** /-ik(ə)lē/ *adv.* —**sar·don·i·cism** /-ˈdänəˌsizəm/ *n.*

sarge /särj/ ▶*n. inf.* sergeant.

sa·ri /ˈsärē/ (also **sa·ree**) ▶*n.* (*pl.* **-ris** or **-rees**) a garment consisting of a length of cotton or silk elaborately draped around the body, traditionally worn by women from the Indian subcontinent.

sa·rong /səˈrông; -ˈräng/ ▶*n.* a garment consisting of a long piece of cloth worn wrapped around the body and tucked in at the waist or under the armpits, traditionally worn in Southeast Asia and now also by women in the West.

sar·sa·pa·ril·la /ˌsärs(ə)pəˈrilə; ˌsaspə-/ ▶*n.* **1** a preparation of the dried rhizomes of various plants, esp. smilax, used to flavor some drinks and medicines and formerly as a tonic. ■ a sweet drink flavored with this. **2** the tropical American climbing plant (genus *Smilax*) of the lily family from which these rhizomes are generally obtained, esp. *S. regelii*, which is the chief source of commercial sarsaparilla.

sar·sen /ˈsärsən/ (also **sarsen stone**) ▶*n. Geol.* a silicified sandstone boulder of a kind that occurs on the chalk downs of southern England. Such stones were used in constructing Stonehenge and other prehistoric monuments.

sar·to·ri·al /särˈtôrēəl/ ▶*adj.* of or relating to tailoring, clothes, or style of dress: *sartorial elegance.* —**sar·to·ri·al·ly** *adv.*

sar·to·ri·us /särˈtôrēəs/ (also **sartorius muscle**) ▶*n. Anat.* a long, narrow muscle running obliquely across the front of each thigh from the hipbone to the inside of the leg below the knee.

SASE ▶*abbr.* self-addressed stamped envelope.

sash[1] /sash/ ▶*n.* a long strip or loop of cloth worn over one shoulder or around the waist, esp. as part of a uniform or official dress. —**sashed** /sasht/ *adj.* —**sash·less** *adj.*

sash[2] ▶*n.* a frame holding the glass in a window, typically one of two sliding frames. —**sashed** *adj.*

sa·shay /saˈSHā/ ▶*v.* [*intr.*] *inf.* walk in an ostentatious yet casual manner, typically with exaggerated movements of the hips and shoulders: *Louise was sashaying along in a red satin dress.*
▶*n.* a square dancing figure in which partners circle each other by taking sideways steps.

sa·shi·mi /säˈSHēmē/ ▶*n.* a Japanese dish of bite-sized pieces of raw fish eaten with soy sauce and horseradish paste: *tuna sashimi.*

Sas·quatch /ˈsaskwäch; -kwäch/ ▶*n.* another term for **Bigfoot**.

sass /sas/ *inf.* ▶*n.* impudence; cheek: *a boy who wouldn't give you any sass.*
▶*v.* [*tr.*] be cheeky or rude to (someone): *we wouldn't have dreamed of sassing our parents.* ▷mid 19th cent.: variant of *sauce*.

sas·sa·fras /ˈsasəˌfras/ ▶*n.* a deciduous North American tree (*Sassafras albidum*) of the laurel family, with aromatic leaves and bark. The leaves are infused to make tea or ground into filé. ■ an extract of the leaves or bark of this tree, used medicinally or in perfumery.

sas·sy /ˈsasē/ ▶*adj.* (**-si·er**, **-si·est**) *inf.* lively, bold, and full of spirit; cheeky. —**sas·si·ly** /-əlē/ *adv.* —**sas·si·ness** *n.*

sas·tru·gi /səˈstrōōgē; sa'-; ˈsastrə-/ ▶*pl. n.* parallel wavelike ridges caused by winds on the surface of hard snow, esp. in polar regions.

SAT /ˈes ˌā ˈtē/ ▶*n.* trademark a test of a student's academic skills, used for admission to U.S. colleges.

sat /sat/ ▶ past and past participle of **sit**.

Sat. ▶*abbr.* Saturday.

Sa·tan /ˈsātn/ ▶the Devil; Lucifer.

sa·tan·ic /səˈtanik; sā'-/ ▶*adj.* of or characteristic of Satan. ■ connected with satanism: *a satanic cult.* ■ extremely evil or wicked. —**sa·tan·i·cal·ly** /-ik(ə)lē/ *adv.*

sa·tan·ism /ˈsātnˌizəm/ (also **Sa·tan·ism**) ▶*n.* the worship of Satan,

typically involving a travesty of Christian symbols and practices, such as placing a cross upside down. —**sa·tan·ist** *n. & adj.* —**sa·tan·ize** *v.*

sa·tay /ˈsä,tā/ (also **sa·té**) ▶*n.* an Southeast Asian dish of small pieces of skewered meat grilled and usually served with a spiced sauce.

satch·el /ˈsaCHəl/ ▶*n.* a bag carried on the shoulder by a long strap and typically closed by a flap.

sate /sāt/ ▶*v.* [*tr.*] satisfy (a desire or an appetite) to the full: *sate your appetite at the resort's restaurant.* ■ supply (someone) with as much as or more of something than is desired or can be managed.
▶*adj.* satisfied completely; fulfilled: *afterward, sated and happy, they both slept.* —**sate·less** *adj.* (*poetic/lit.*).

sa·teen /saˈtēn/ ▶*n.* a cotton fabric woven like satin with a glossy surface.

sat·el·lite /ˈsatlˌīt/ ▶*n.* **1** an artificial body placed in orbit around the earth or moon or another planet in order to collect information or for communication. ■ [as *adj.*] transmitted by satellite; using or relating to satellite technology: *satellite broadcasting.* ■ satellite television: *a news service on satellite.* **2** *Astron.* a celestial body orbiting the earth or another planet. **3** [usu. as *adj.*] something that is separated from or on the periphery of something else but is nevertheless dependent on or controlled by it: *satellite offices in London and New York.* ■ a small country or state politically or economically dependent on another.

sat·el·lite dish ▶*n.* a bowl-shaped antenna with which signals are transmitted to or received from a communications satellite.

Sa·ti /ˌsəˈtē; ˈsə,tē/ *Hinduism* ▶the wife of Shiva, reborn as Parvati. According to some accounts, she died by throwing herself into the sacred fire.

sa·ti ▶*n.* variant spelling of **suttee**.

sa·ti·ate /ˈsāsHē,āt/ ▶*v.* another term for **sate**[1] : *he folded up his newspaper, his curiosity satiated.* —**sa·tia·ble** /-SHəbəl/ *adj.* (*archaic*) —**sa·ti·a·tion** /ˌsāsHē'āsHən/ *n.*

sat·in /ˈsatn/ ▶*n.* a smooth, glossy fabric, typically of silk, produced by a weave in which the threads of the warp are caught and looped by the weft only at certain intervals. ■ [as *adj.*] denoting or having a surface or finish resembling this fabric, produced on metal or other material: *an aluminum alloy with a black satin finish.* —**sat·in·y** *adj.*

sat·in·wood /ˈsatn,wŏod/ ▶*n.* **1** glossy yellowish timber from a tropical tree, valued for cabinetwork. **2** either of two species (*Chloroxylon swietenia* and *Zanthoxylum flava*) of tropical hardwood trees of the rue family that produces this timber.

sat·ire /ˈsa,tīr/ ▶*n.* the use of humor, irony, exaggeration, or ridicule to expose and criticize people's stupidity or vices, particularly in the context of contemporary politics and other topical issues. ■ a play, novel, film, or other work that uses satire: *a stinging satire on American politics.* ■ a genre of literature characterized by the use of satire. —**sat·i·rist** /ˈsatərist/ *n.*

sa·tir·i·cal /səˈti(ə)rikəl/ (also **sa·tir·ic** /-ˈti(ə)rik/) ▶*adj.* containing or using satire: *a New York-based satirical magazine.* —**sa·tir·i·cal·ly** *adv.*

sat·i·rize /ˈsatə,rīz/ ▶*v.* [*tr.*] deride and criticize by means of satire: *Aristophanes satirized the lack of respect for the laws.* —**sat·i·ri·za·tion** *n.*

sat·is·fac·tion /ˌsatis'fakSHən/ ▶*n.* fulfillment of one's wishes, expectations, or needs, or the pleasure derived from this: *he smiled with satisfaction.* ■ *Law* the payment of a debt or fulfillment of an obligation or claim: *in full and final satisfaction of the claim.* ■ what is felt to be owed or due to one, esp. in reparation of an injustice or wrong: *the work will come to a halt if the electricity and telephone people don't get satisfaction.* ■ *hist.* the opportunity to defend one's honor in a duel: *I demand the satisfaction of a gentleman.*
▶ □ **to one's satisfaction** so that one is satisfied: *some amendments were made, not entirely to his satisfaction.*

sat·is·fac·to·ry /ˌsatis'fakt(ə)rē/ ▶*adj.* fulfilling expectations or needs; acceptable, though not outstanding or perfect: *the brakes are satisfactory if not particularly powerful.* ■ (of a patient in a hospital) not deteriorating or likely to die. —**sat·is·fac·to·ri·ly** /-t(ə)rəlē/ *adv.* —**sat·is·fac·to·ri·ness** *n.*

sat·is·fice /ˈsatis,fīs/ ▶*v.* accept an available option as satisfactory: *it talks about telling you not to just satisfice but to always look for the best.*

sat·is·fy /ˈsatis,fī/ ▶*v.* (**-fies**, **-fied**) [*tr.*] meet the expectations, needs, or desires of (someone): *I have never been satisfied with my job.* ■ fulfill (a desire or need): *social services is trying to satisfy the needs of so many different groups.* ■ provide (someone) with adequate information or proof so that they are convinced about something: [*tr.*] *people need to be satisfied that the environmental assessments are accurate.* ■ adequately meet or comply with (a condition, obligation, or demand): *the whole team is working to satisfy demand.* ■ *Math.* (of a quantity) make (an equation) true. ■ pay off (a debt or creditor): *there was insufficient collateral to satisfy the loan.* —**sat·is·fi·a·bil·i·ty** /ˌsatis,fīəˈbilitē/ *n.* —**sat·is·fi·a·ble** *adj.* —**sat·is·fy·ing** *adj.*

sa·to·ri /səˈtôrē/ ▶*n. Buddhism* sudden enlightenment: *the road that leads to satori.*

sa·trap /ˈsā,trap; ˈsa-/ ▶*n.* a provincial governor in the ancient Persian empire. ■ any subordinate or local ruler.

sat·u·rate ▶*v.* /ˈsaCHə,rāt/ [*tr.*] (usu. **be saturated**) cause (something) to become thoroughly soaked with liquid so that no more can be absorbed: *the soil is saturated.* ■ cause (a substance) to combine with, dissolve, or hold the greatest possible quantity of another substance: *the groundwater is **saturated** with calcium hydroxide.* ■ (usu. **be saturated with**) *fig.* fill (something or someone) with something until no more can be held or absorbed: *they've become thoroughly saturated with powerful and seductive messages from the media.* ■ supply (a market) beyond the point at which the demand for a product is satisfied: *Japan's electronics industry began to saturate the world markets.*

▶*n.* /-rət/ (usu. **saturates**) a saturated fat. —**sat·u·ra·ble** /-əbəl/ *adj.* (technical).

sat·u·ra·tion /ˌsaCHəˈrāSHən/ ▶*n.* the state or process that occurs when no more of something can be absorbed, combined with, or added. ■ *Chem.* the degree or extent to which something is dissolved or absorbed compared with the maximum possible, usually expressed as a percentage. ■ [as *adj.*] to a very full extent, esp. beyond the point regarded as necessary or desirable: *saturation bombing.* ■ (also **color saturation**) (esp. in photography) the intensity of a color, expressed as the degree to which it differs from white.

sat·u·ra·tion point ▶*n. Chem.* the stage at which no more of a substance can be absorbed into a vapor or dissolved into a solution. ■ *fig.* the stage beyond which no more of something can be absorbed or accepted.

Sat·ur·day /ˈsatər,dā; -dē/ ▶*n.* the day of the week before Sunday and following Friday, and (with Sunday) forming part of the weekend.

Sat·ur·day night spe·cial ▶*n. inf.* a cheap, low-caliber pistol or revolver, easily obtained and concealed.

Sat·urn /ˈsatərn/ ▶ **1** *Roman Mythol.* an ancient god, regarded as a god of agriculture. **2** *Astron.* the sixth planet from the sun in the solar system, circled by a system of broad, flat rings. **3** a series of American space rockets, of which the very large *Saturn V* was used as the launch vehicle for the Apollo missions of 1969–72.

Sat·ur·na·li·a /ˌsatərˈnālēə; -ˈnālyə/ ▶*n.* [treated as *sing.* or *pl.*] the ancient Roman festival of Saturn in December, which was a period of general merrymaking and was the predecessor of Christmas. ■ (**saturnalia**) an occasion of wild revelry. —**sat·ur·na·li·an** *adj.*

sat·ur·nine /ˈsatər,nīn/ ▶*adj.* (of a person or their manner) slow and gloomy: *a saturnine temperament.* ■ (of a person or their features) dark in coloring and moody or mysterious: *his saturnine face and dark, watchful eyes.* —**sat·ur·nine·ly** *adv.*

sat·ya·gra·ha /səˈtyägrəhə; ˈsətyə,grəhə/ ▶*n.* a policy of passive political resistance, esp. that advocated by Mahatma Gandhi against British rule in India.

sa·tyr /ˈsatər; ˈsātər/ ▶*n.* **1** *Greek Mythol.* one of a class of lustful, drunken woodland gods represented as a man with a horse's or goat's ears and tail. ■ a man who has strong sexual desires. **2** a butterfly with chiefly dark brown wings. —**sa·tyr·ic** /səˈtirik/ *adj.*

sauce /sôs/ ▶*n.* **1** thick liquid served with food, usually savory dishes, to add moistness and flavor: *tomato sauce.* ■ stewed fruit, esp. apples, eaten as dessert or used as a garnish. **2** (**the sauce**) *inf.* alcoholic drink: *she's been **on the sauce** for years.*

▶*v.* [*tr.*] **1** (usu. **be sauced**) provide a sauce for (something); season with a sauce. ■ *fig.* make more interesting and exciting. **2** *inf.* be rude or impudent to (someone). ▷Middle English: from Old French, based on Latin *salsus* 'salted,' past participle of *salere* 'to salt,' from *sal* 'salt.'

sauce·pan /ˈsôs,pan/ ▶*n.* a deep cooking pan, typically round, made of metal, and with one long handle and a lid. —**sauce·pan·ful** /-,f>ool/ *n.* (*pl.* **-fuls**).

sau·cer /ˈsôsər/ ▶*n.* a shallow dish, typically having a circular indentation in the center, on which a cup is placed. —**sau·cer·ful** /-,fool/ *n.* (*pl.* **-fuls**). —**sau·cer·less** *adj.*

▶ □ **have eyes like saucers** have one's eyes opened wide in amazement.

sau·cy /ˈsôsē/ ▶*adj.* (**-ci·er**, **-ci·est**) *inf.* **1** impudent; flippant: *a saucy*

remark. **2** bold and lively; smart-looking: *a hat with a saucy brim.* —**sau·ci·ly** /-səlē/ *adv.* —**sau·ci·ness** *n.*

Sau·di /ˈsoudē; ˈsô-/ ▶*adj.* of or relating to Saudi Arabia or its ruling dynasty.

▶*n.* (*pl.* **-dis**) a citizen of Saudi Arabia, or a member of its ruling dynasty.

sau·er·kraut /ˈsou(ə)r,krout/ ▶*n.* chopped cabbage that has been pickled in brine.

Sauk /sôk/ (also **Sac**) ▶*n.* (*pl.* same or **Sauks**) **1** a member of an American Indian people inhabiting parts of the central U.S. **2** the Algonquian language of this people.

▶*adj.* of or relating to this people or their language.

sau·na /ˈsônə; ˈsou-/ ▶*n.* a small room used as a hot-air or steam bath for cleaning and refreshing the body. ■ a session in such a room.

saun·ter /ˈsôntər/ ▶*v.* [*intr.*] walk in a slow, relaxed manner, without hurry or effort: *Adam sauntered into the room.*

▶*n.* a leisurely stroll: *a quiet saunter down the road.* —**saun·ter·er** *n.*

sau·ri·an /ˈsôrēən/ ▶*adj.* of or like a lizard.

▶*n.* any large reptile, esp. a dinosaur or other extinct form.

sau·ro·pod /ˈsôrə,päd/ ▶*n.* a very large quadrupedal herbivorous dinosaur (infraorder Sauropoda, suborder Sauropodomorpha, order Saurischia) with a long neck and tail, small head, and massive limbs.

sau·sage /ˈsôsij/ ▶*n.* a short cylindrical tube of minced pork, beef, or other meat encased in a skin, typically sold raw to be grilled, boiled, or fried before eating. ■ a cylindrical tube of minced pork, beef, or other meat seasoned and cooked or preserved, sold mainly to be eaten cold in slices: *smoked sausage.* ■ [usu. as *adj.*] used in references to the characteristic cylindrical shape of sausages: *mold into a sausage shape.*

sau·té /sôˈtā; sō-/ ▶*adj.* **1** fried quickly in a little hot fat: *sauté potatoes.* **2** *Ballet* (of a step) performed while jumping.

▶*n.* a dish cooked in such a way.

▶*v.* (**-tés**, **-téed** /-ˈtād/ or **-téd**, **-téing** /-ˈtāiNG/) [*tr.*] cook in such a way: *sauté the onions in the olive oil.*

sav·age /ˈsavij/ ▶*adj.* (of an animal or force of nature) fierce, violent, and uncontrolled: *tales of a savage beast.* ■ cruel and vicious; aggressively hostile: *they launched a savage attack on the budget.* ■ primitive; uncivilized. ■ (of something bad or negative) very great; severe: *this would deal a savage blow to the government's fight.*

▶*n. chiefly hist.* or *poetic/lit.* a member of a people regarded as primitive and uncivilized. ■ a brutal or vicious person.

▶*v.* [*tr.*] (esp. of a dog or wild animal) attack ferociously and maul: *ewes savaged by marauding dogs.* ■ subject to a vicious verbal attack; criticize brutally: *Fowler savaged her in his last review.* —**sav·age·ly** *adv.* —**sav·age·ness** *n.* —**sav·age·ry** /-rē/ *n.*

sa·van·na /səˈvanə/ (also **sa·van·nah**) ▶*n.* a grassy plain in tropical and subtropical regions, with few trees.

sa·vant /saˈvänt; sə-/ ▶*n.* a learned person, esp. a distinguished scientist. See also **IDIOT SAVANT**.

save[1] /sāv/ ▶*v.* [*tr.*] **1** keep safe or rescue (someone or something) from harm or danger: *she **saved** a boy **from** drowning.* ■ prevent (someone) from dying: *the doctors did everything they could to save him.* ■ (in Christian use) preserve (a person's soul) from damnation. **2** keep and store up (something, esp. money) for future use: *she had never been able to save much from her salary.* ■ *Comput.* keep (data) by moving a copy to a storage location, esp. from memory: *save it to a new file.* ■ preserve (something) by not expending or using it: *save your strength till later.* ■ [in *imper.*] (**save it**) *inf.* used to tell someone to stop talking: *save it, Joey—I'm in big trouble now.* **3** avoid the need to use up or spend (money, time, or other resources): *save $20 on a new camcorder.* ■ avoid, lessen, or guard against: *this approach saves wear and tear on the books.* **4** prevent an opponent from scoring (a goal or point) in a game or from winning (the game): *the powerful German saved three match points.* ■ *Baseball* (of a relief pitcher in certain game situations) finish (a game) while preserving a winning position gained by another pitcher. ■ *Soccer & Hockey* (of a goalkeeper) stop (a shot) from entering the goal.

▶*n. Baseball* an instance of a relief pitcher saving a game. ■ *chiefly Soccer & Hockey* an act of preventing an opponent's scoring: *the keeper made a great save.*

save[2] ▶*prep. & conj. formal* or *poetic/lit.* except; other than: *no one needed to know save herself.*

sav·er /ˈsāvər/ ▶*n.* **1** a person who regularly saves money through a bank or recognized scheme. **2** [in *comb.*] an object, action, or process that prevents a particular kind of resource from being used up or expended: *a great space-saver.*

sav·in /'savin/ ▶ n. a bushy Eurasian juniper (*Juniperus sabina*) that typically has horizontally spreading branches.

sav·ing /'sāviNG/ ▶ n. **1** an economy of or reduction in money, time, or another resource: *this resulted in a considerable* **saving in** *development costs.* **2** (usu. **one's savings**) the money one has saved, esp. through a bank or official scheme: *the agents were cheating them out of their* **life savings**. ▶ adj. [in *comb.*] preventing waste of a particular resource: *an energy-saving light bulb.* ▶ prep. with the exception of; except.

sav·ing grace ▶ n. [*mass noun*] the redeeming grace of God. ■ a redeeming quality or characteristic.

sav·ings ac·count ▶ n. a bank account that earns interest.

sav·ings and loan (also **savings and loan association**) ▶ n. an institution that accepts savings at interest and lends money to savers chiefly for home mortgage loans and may offer checking accounts and other services.

sav·ings bank ▶ n. a financial institution that receives savings accounts and pays interest to depositors.

sav·ior /'sāvyər/ (*Brit.* **sav·iour**) ▶ n. a person who saves someone or something (esp. a country or cause) from danger, and who is regarded with the veneration of a religious figure. ■ (**the/our Savior**) (in Christianity) God or Jesus Christ as the redeemer of sin and saver of souls.

sav·oir faire /ˌsavwär 'fe(ə)r/ (also **sav·oir-faire**) ▶ n. the ability to act or speak appropriately in social situations.

sa·vor /'sāvər/ (*Brit.* **sa·vour**) ▶ v. **1** [*tr.*] taste (good food or drink) and enjoy it completely: *gourmets will want to savor our game specialties.* ■ *fig.* enjoy or appreciate (something pleasant) completely, esp. by dwelling on it: *I wanted to savor every moment.* **2** [*intr.*] (**savor of**) have a suggestion or trace of (something, esp. something bad): *glad to escape anything that savored of work.* ▶ n. a characteristic taste, flavor, or smell, esp. a pleasant one: *the subtle savor of wood smoke.* ■ a suggestion or trace, esp. of something bad. —**sa·vor·less** *adj.*

sa·vor·y[1] /'sāv(ə)rē/ ▶ n. an aromatic plant (genus *Satureja*) of the mint family, used as a culinary herb, esp. the annual **summer savory** (*S. hortensis*).

sa·vor·y[2] (*Brit.* **sa·vour·y**) ▶ adj. **1** (of food) belonging to the category that is salty or spicy rather than sweet. **2** morally wholesome or acceptable: *a front for less savory operations.* —**sa·vor·i·ly** /-rəlē/ *adv.* —**sa·vor·i·ness** *n.*

sa·voy /sə'voi/ (also **savoy cabbage**) ▶ n. a cabbage of a hardy variety with densely wrinkled leaves.

sav·vy /'savē/ (also **sav·vi·ness**) *inf.* ▶ n. shrewdness and practical knowledge, esp. in politics or business: *the financiers lacked the necessary political savvy.* ▶ v. (**-vies, -vied**) know or understand: *I want to make sure. Savvy?* ▶ adj. (**-vi·er, -vi·est**) shrewd and knowledgeable in the realities of life.

saw[1] /sô/ ▶ n. a hand tool for cutting wood or other materials, typically with a long, thin serrated steel blade and operated using a backward and forward movement. ■ a mechanical power-driven tool for cutting, typically with a toothed rotating disk or moving band. ▶ v. (*past part.* **sawed** or **sawn** /sôn/) [*tr.*] cut (something, esp. wood or a tree) using a saw: *the top of each post is* **sawed off** *at railing height.* ■ make or form (something) using a saw: *the seats are sawed from well-seasoned oak planks.* ■ cut (something) as if with a saw, esp. roughly or so as to leave rough or unfinished edges: *the woman who* **sawed off** *all my lovely hair.* —**saw·like** /-ˌlīk/ *adj.*

saw[2] ▶ past of SEE[1].

saw[3] ▶ n. a proverb or maxim.

saw·buck /'sô,bək/ ▶ n. **1** a sawhorse. **2** *inf.* a $10 bill.

saw·dust /'sô,dəst/ ▶ n. powdery particles of wood produced by sawing.

sawed-off /'sôd 'ôf/ (also *chiefly Brit.* **sawn-off**) ▶ adj. (of a gun) having a specially shortened barrel to make handling easier and to give a wider field of fire.

saw·fish /'sô,fiSH/ ▶ n. (*pl.* same or **-fishes**) a large tropical mainly marine fish (family Pristidae) related to the rays, with an elongated flattened snout that bears large blunt teeth along each side.

saw·fly /'sô,flī/ ▶ n. (*pl.* **-flies**) an insect related to the wasps, with a sawlike egg-laying tube used to cut into plant tissue before depositing the eggs. The larvae resemble caterpillars and can be serious pests of crops and foliage.

saw·horse /'sô,hôrs/ ▶ n. a frame or trestle that supports wood for sawing.

saw·mill /'sô,mil/ ▶ n. a factory in which logs are sawed into lumber by machine.

sawn /sôn/ ▶ past participle of SAW[1].

saw·tooth /'sô,tōōTH/ (also **saw·toothed** or **saw-tooth** or **saw-toothed** /-ˌtōōTHt/) ▶ adj. shaped like the teeth of a saw with alternate steep and gentle slopes.

saw-whet owl ▶ n. a small North and Central American owl (genus *Aegolius*, family Strigidae) with a call that resembles the sound of a saw blade being sharpened.

saw·yer /'sôyər/ ▶ n. **1** a person who saws timber for a living. **2** an uprooted tree floating in a river but held fast at one end. **3** a large longhorn beetle (genus *Monochamus*, family Cerambycidae) whose larvae bore tunnels in the wood of injured or recently felled trees, producing an audible chewing sound.

sax /saks/ ▶ n. *inf.* a saxophone. —**sax·ist** *n.*

sax·horn /'saks,hôrn/ ▶ n. a member of a family of brass instruments with valves and a funnel-shaped mouthpiece, used mainly in military and brass bands.

Sax·on /'saksən/ ▶ n. **1** a member of a Germanic people that inhabited parts of central and northern Germany from Roman times, many of whom conquered and settled in southern England in the 5th–6th centuries. ■ a native of modern Saxony in Germany. **2** the language of the Saxons, in particular: ■ (**Old Saxon**) the West Germanic language of the ancient Saxons. ■ the Low German dialect of modern Saxony. ▶ adj. **1** of or relating to the Anglo-Saxons, their language (Old English), or their period of dominance in England (5th–11th centuries). **2** of or relating to Saxony or the continental Saxons or their language. —**Sax·on·ize** /-ˌnīz/ *v.*

sax·o·phone /'saksə,fōn/ ▶ n. a member of a family of metal wind instruments with a single-reed mouthpiece, used esp. in jazz and dance music. —**sax·o·phon·ic** /ˌsaksə'fänik/ *adj.* —**sax·o·phon·ist** *n.*

saxophone

say /sā/ ▶ v. (**says** /sez/; *past* and *past part.* **said** /sed/) **1** utter words so as to convey information, an opinion, a feeling or intention, or an instruction: [with *direct speech*] *"Thank you," he said.* ■ (of a text or a symbolic representation) convey specified information or instructions: *the law says such behavior is an offense.* ■ [*tr.*] enable a listener or reader to learn or understand something by conveying or revealing (information or ideas): *I don't want to say too much.* ■ [*tr.*] (of a clock or watch) indicate (a specified time): *the clock says ten past two.* ■ (**be said**) be asserted or reported (often used to avoid committing the speaker or writer to the truth of the assertion): *they were said to be training freedom fighters.* ■ [*tr.*] (**say something for**) present a consideration in favor of or excusing (someone or something): *all I can say for him is that he's a better writer than some.* ■ [*tr.*] utter the whole of (a speech or other set of words, typically one learned in advance): *we say the Pledge of Allegiance each morning.* **2** assume something in order to work out what its consequences would be; make a hypothesis: *let's say we pay five thousand dollars in the first year.* ■ used parenthetically to indicate that something is being suggested as possible or likely but not certain: *the form might include, say, a dozen questions.* ▶ n. an opportunity for stating one's opinion or feelings: *the voters are entitled to* **have their say** *on the treaty.* ■ an opportunity to influence developments and policy: *the assessor will* **have a say** *in how the money is spent.* ▷Old English *secgan*, of Germanic origin; related to Dutch *zeggen* and German *sagen*. —**say·a·ble** *adj.* —**say·er** *n.* [usu. in *comb.*] *naysayers.* ▶ □ **go without saying** be obvious: *it goes without saying that teachers must be selected with care.* □ **not to say** used to introduce a stronger alternative or addition to something already said: *it is easy to become sensitive, not to say paranoid.* □ **say the word** give permission or instructions to do something. □ **when all is said and done** when everything is taken into account (used to indicate that one is making a generalized judgment about a situation). □ **you don't say!** *inf.* used to express amazement or disbelief.

say·ing /'sāiNG/ ▶ n. a short, pithy expression that generally contains

---

Pronunciation Key ə *ago,* up; ər *over, fur;* a *hat;* ā *ate;* ä *car;* CH *chin;* e *let;* ē *see;* e(ə)r *air;* i *fit;* ī *by;* i(ə)r *ear;* NG *sing;* ō *go;* ô *law, for;* oi *toy;* ōō *good;* ōō *goo;* ou *out;* SH *she;* TH *thin;* TH *then;* (h)w *why;* ZH *vision*

advice or wisdom. ■ (**sayings**) a collection of such expressions identified with a particular person, esp. a political or religious leader.

▶ □ **as** (or **so**) **the saying goes** used to introduce or append an expression, drawing attention to its status as a saying or as not part of one's normal language: *I am, as the saying goes, burned out.*

say-so ▶ *n. inf.* the power or act of deciding or allowing something: *no new employees come into the organization without his say-so.* ■ (usu. **on someone's say-so**) a person's arbitrary or unauthorized assertion or instruction: *I don't stop on the say-so of anybody's assistant.*

SB ▶ *abbr.* ■ Bachelor of Science. ■ simultaneous broadcast. ■ South Britain (England and Wales).

Sb ▶ *symb.* the chemical element antimony.

SBA ▶ *abbr.* Small Business Administration.

Sc ▶ *symb.* the chemical element scandium.

sc. ▶ *abbr.* that is to say (used to introduce a word to be supplied or an explanation of an ambiguity).

scab /skab/ ▶ *n.* **1** a dry, rough protective crust that forms over a cut or wound during healing. ■ mange or a similar skin disease in animals. ■ any of a number of fungal diseases of plants in which rough patches develop, esp. on apples and potatoes. **2** *fig.* or *inf.* a person or thing regarded with dislike and disgust. ■ *derog.* a person who refuses to strike or to join a labor union or who takes over the job responsibilities of a striking worker.

▶ *v.* (**scabbed, scab·bing**) [*intr.*] **1** [usu. as *adj.*] (**scabbed**) become encrusted or covered with a scab or scabs: *she rested her scabbed fingers on his arm.* **2** act or work as a scab. —**scab·by** *adj.* —**scab·like** /-,līk/ *adj.*

scab·bard /'skabərd/ ▶ *n.* a sheath for the blade of a sword or dagger, typically made of leather or metal. ■ a sheath for a gun or other weapon or tool.

sca·bies /'skābēz/ ▶ *n.* a contagious skin disease marked by itching and small raised red spots, caused by the itch mite.

scab·rous /'skabrəs/ ▶ *adj.* **1** rough and covered with, or as if with, scabs. **2** indecent; salacious: *scabrous publications.* —**scab·rous·ly** *adv.* —**scab·rous·ness** *n.*

scads /skadz/ ▶ *pl. n. inf.* a large number or quantity: *they raised scads of children.*

scaf·fold /'skafəld; -,fōld/ ▶ *n.* **1** a raised wooden platform used formerly for the public execution of criminals. **2** a structure made of scaffolding. —**scaf·fold·er** *n.*

scaf·fold·ing /'skafəldiNG; -,fōl-/ ▶ *n.* a temporary structure on the outside of a building, made usually of wooden planks and metal poles, used by workers while building, repairing, or cleaning the building. ■ the materials used in such a structure.

scag /skag/ ▶ *n. inf.* **1** an unkempt or despicable person; sleazeball. **2** variant spelling of SKAG.

scal·a·ble /'skāləbəl/ ▶ *adj.* **1** able to be scaled or climbed. **2** able to be changed in size or scale: *scalable fonts.* ■ (of a computing process) able to be used or produced in a range of capabilities: *it is scalable across a range of systems.* **3** *technical* able to be measured or graded according to a scale. —**scal·a·bil·i·ty** /,skālə'bilitē/ *n.*

sca·lar /'skālər/ *Math. Physics* ▶ *adj. Math. & Physics* (of a quantity) having only magnitude, not direction.

▶ *n. Math. & Physics* a scalar quantity.

scal·a·wag /'skalə,wag/ (also **scal·ly·wag** /'skalē-/) ▶ *n. inf.* a person who behaves badly but in an amusingly mischievous rather than harmful way; a rascal. ■ *hist.* a white Southerner who collaborated with northern Republicans during Reconstruction, often for personal profit.

scald /skôld/ ▶ *v.* [*tr.*] injure with very hot liquid or steam: *the tea scalded his tongue.* ■ heat (milk or other liquid) to near boiling point. ■ immerse (something) briefly in boiling water for various purposes, such as to facilitate the removal of skin from fruit or to preserve meat. ■ cause to feel a searing sensation like that of boiling water on skin: *hot tears scalding her eyes.*

▶ *n.* a burn or other injury caused by hot liquid or steam. ■ any of a number of plant diseases that produce a similar effect to that of scalding, esp. a disease of fruit marked by browning and caused by excessive sunlight, bad storage conditions, or atmospheric pollution.

scale¹ /skāl/ ▶ *n.* **1** each of the small, thin horny or bony plates protecting the skin of fish and reptiles, typically overlapping one another. **2** something resembling a fish scale in appearance or function, in particular: ■ a thick dry flake of skin. ■ a rudimentary leaf, feather, or bract. ■ each of numerous microscopic tilelike structures covering the wings of butterflies and moths. **3** a flaky deposit, in particular: ■ a white deposit formed in a kettle, boiler, etc., by the evaporation of

water containing lime. ■ tartar formed on teeth. ■ a coating of oxide formed on heated metal.

▶ *v.* **1** [*tr.*] remove scale or scales from: *he scales the fish and removes the innards.* ■ remove tartar from (teeth) by scraping them. **2** [*intr.*] (often as *n.*] (**scaling**) (esp. of the skin) form scales: *moisturizers can ease off drying and scaling.* ■ come off in scales or thin pieces; flake off: *the paint was scaling from the brick walls.* —**scaled** /skāld/ *adj.* [often in *comb.*] *a rough-scaled fish.* —**scale·less** /'skāl(l)is/ *adj.* —**scal·er** *n.*

scale² ▶ *n.* (usu. **scales**) an instrument for weighing. Scales were originally simple balances (**pairs of scales**) but are now usually devices with an internal weighing mechanism housed under a platform on which the thing to be weighed is placed, with a gauge or electronic display showing the weight.

scale³ ▶ *n.* **1** a graduated range of values forming a standard system for measuring or grading something: *company employees have hit the top of their pay scales.* ■ a series of marks at regular intervals in a line used in measuring something: *the mean delivery time is plotted against a scale on the right.* ■ a device having such a series of marks: *she read the exact distance off a scale.* ■ a rule determining the distances between such marks: *the vertical axis is given on a logarithmic scale.* **2** the relative size or extent of something: *no one foresaw the scale of the disaster.* ■ [often as *adj.*] a ratio of size in a map, model, drawing, or plan: *a one-fifth scale model of a seven-story building.* ■ (in full **scale of notation**) *Math.* a system of numerical notation in which the value of a digit depends upon its position in the number, successive positions representing successive powers of a fixed base: *the conversion of the number to the binary scale.* ■ *Photog.* the range of exposures over which a photographic material will give an acceptable variation in density. **3** *Mus.* an arrangement of the notes in any system of music in ascending or descending order of pitch: *the scale of C major.*

▶ *v.* [*tr.*] **1** climb up or over (something high and steep): *thieves scaled an 8-foot fence.* **2** represent in proportional dimensions; reduce or increase in size according to a common scale: [as *adj.*] (**scaled**) *scaled plans of the house.* ■ [*intr.*] (of a quantity or property) be variable according to a particular scale. **3** estimate the amount of timber that will be produced from (a log or uncut tree).

▶ *phrasal v.* □ **scale something back** reduce something in size, number, or extent, esp. by a constant proportion across the board: *in the short term, even scaling back defense costs money.* □ **scale something down** (or **scale down**) reduce something (or be reduced) in size, number or extent, esp. by a constant proportion across the board: *manufacturing capacity has been scaled down | his whole income scaled down by 20 percent.* □ **scale something up** (or **scale up**) increase something (or be increased) in size or number: *one cannot suddenly scale up a laboratory procedure by a thousandfold.* ▷late Middle English: from Latin *scala* 'ladder' (the verb via Old French *escaler* or medieval Latin *scalare* 'climb'), from the base of Latin *scandere* 'to climb.' —**scal·er** *n.*

▶ □ **play** (or **sing** or **practice**) **scales** *Mus.* perform the notes of a scale as an exercise for the fingers or voice. □ **to scale** with a uniform reduction or enlargement: *it is hard to build models to scale from a drawing.*

scale in·sect ▶ *n.* a small insect with a protective shieldlike scale. It spends most of its life attached by its mouth to a single plant, sometimes occurring in such large numbers that it becomes a serious pest.

sca·lene /skā'lēn/ ▶ *adj.* (of a triangle) having sides unequal in length.

▶ *n.* (also **scalene muscle**) *Anat.* another term for SCALENUS.

sca·le·nus /skā'lēnəs/ ▶ *n.* (pl. **-ni** /-'lēnī/) any of several muscles extending from the neck to the first and second ribs.

scal·lion /'skalyən/ ▶ *n.* a long-necked onion with a small bulb, in particular a shallot or green onion.

scal·lop /'skäləp; 'skal-/ ▶ *n.* **1** an edible bivalve mollusk (family Pectinidae) with a ribbed fan-shaped shell. Scallops swim by rapidly opening and closing the shell valves. ■ a small pan or dish shaped like a scallop shell and used for baking or serving food. **2** (usu. **scallops**) each of a series of convex rounded projections forming an ornamental edging cut in material or worked in lace or knitting.

▶ *v.* (**-loped, -lop·ing**) **1** [*tr.*] [usu. as *adj.*] (**scalloped**) ornament (an edge or material) with scallops: *a scalloped neckline.* **2** [*intr.*] [usu. as *n.*] (**scalloping**) gather or dredge for scallops. **3** [*tr.*] bake with milk or a sauce: [as *adj.*] (**scalloped**) *scalloped potatoes.* —**scal·lop·er** *n.*

scal·ly·wag /'skalē,wag/ ▶ *n.* variant spelling of SCALAWAG.

scalp /skalp/ ▶ *n.* the skin covering the head, excluding the face. ■ *hist.* the scalp with the hair belonging to it cut or torn away from an enemy's head as a battle trophy, esp. by an American Indian.

▶ *v.* [*tr.*] *hist.* take the scalp of (an enemy). ■ *inf.* sell (a ticket) for a popular event at a price higher than the official one: *tickets were scalped for forty times their face value.* ▷Middle English (denoting the skull or cranium): probably of Scandinavian origin. —**scalp·er** *n.*

scal·pel /ˈskalpəl/ ▸*n.* a knife with a small, sharp, sometimes detachable blade, as used by a surgeon.

scal·y /ˈskālē/ ▸*adj.* (**scal·i·er**, **scal·i·est**) covered in scales. ■ (of skin) dry and flaking. —**scal·i·ness** *n.*

scam /skam/ ▸*n. inf.* a dishonest scheme; a fraud: *an insurance scam.*
▸*v.* (**scammed**, **scam·ming**) [*tr.*] swindle. —**scam·mer** *n.*

scamp /skamp/ ▸*n. inf.* a person, esp. a child, who is mischievous in a likable or amusing way. ■ a wicked or worthless person; a rogue. —**scamp·ish** *adj.*

scamp·er /ˈskampər/ ▸*v.* [*intr.*] (esp. of a small animal or child) run with quick light steps, esp. through fear or excitement: *he scampered in like an overgrown puppy.*

scam·pi /ˈskampē/ ▸*pl. n.* large shrimp or prawns, esp. when prepared or cooked. ■ a dish of shrimp or prawns, typically sautéed in garlic and butter and often topped with bread crumbs.

scan /skan/ ▸*v.* (**scanned**, **scan·ning**) [*tr.*] **1** look at all parts of (something) carefully in order to detect some feature: *he raised his binoculars to scan the coast.* ■ look quickly but not very thoroughly through (a document or other text) in order to identify relevant information: *we scan the papers for news from the trouble spots.* ■ cause (a surface, object, or part of the body) to be traversed by a detector or an electromagnetic beam: *their brains are scanned so that researchers can monitor the progress of the disease.* ■ resolve (a picture) into its elements of light and shade in a prearranged pattern for the purposes of television transmission. ■ convert (a document or picture) into digital form for storage or processing on a computer: *text and pictures can be scanned into the computer.* **2** analyze the meter of (a line of verse) by reading with the emphasis on its rhythm or by examining the pattern of feet or syllables. ■ [*intr.*] (of verse) conform to metrical principles.
▸*n.* an act of scanning someone or something: *a quick scan of the sports page.* ■ a medical examination using a scanner: *a brain scan.* ■ an image obtained by scanning or with a scanner. —**scan·na·ble** *adj.*

scan·dal /ˈskandl/ ▸*n.* an action or event regarded as morally or legally wrong and causing general public outrage: *a bribery scandal involving one of his key supporters.* ■ the outrage or anger caused by such an action or event: *divorce was cause for scandal on the island.* ■ rumor or malicious gossip about such events or actions: *I know that you would want no scandal attached to her name.* ■ a state of affairs regarded as wrong or reprehensible and causing general public outrage or anger: *it's a scandal that many older patients are dismissed as untreatable.* ▷Middle English: from Old French *scandale*, from ecclesiastical Latin *scandalum* 'cause of offense,' from Greek *skandalon* 'snare, stumbling block.' —**scan·dal·ous** *adj.* —**scan·dal·ous·ly** *adv.*

scan·dal·ize /ˈskandl,īz/ ▸*v.* [*tr.*] shock or horrify (someone) by a real or imagined violation of propriety or morality: *their lack of manners scandalized their hosts.* —**scan·dal·i·za·tion** /ˌskandl-əˈzāSHən/ *n.* —**scan·dal·iz·er** *n.*

scan·dal sheet ▸*n. derog.* a newspaper or magazine giving prominence to scandalous stories or gossip.

Scan·di·na·vi·an /ˌskandəˈnāvēən/ ▸*adj.* of or relating to Scandinavia, its people, or their languages.
▸*n.* **1** a native or inhabitant of Scandinavia, or a person of Scandinavian descent. **2** the North Germanic languages (Danish, Norwegian, Swedish, Icelandic, Faeroese) descended from Old Norse.

scan·di·um /ˈskandēəm/ ▸*n.* the chemical element of atomic number 21, a soft silvery-white metal resembling the rare earth elements. (Symbol: **Sc**)

scan·ner /ˈskanər/ ▸*n.* a device for examining, reading, or monitoring something, in particular: ■ *Med.* a machine that examines the body through the use of radiation, ultrasound, or magnetic resonance imaging, as a diagnostic aid. ■ *Electr.* a device that scans documents or images and converts them into digital data.

scan·sion /ˈskanSHən/ ▸*n.* the action of scanning a line of verse to determine its rhythm. ■ the rhythm of a line of verse.

scant /skant/ ▸*adj.* barely sufficient or adequate: *companies with scant regard for the safety of future generations.* ■ barely amounting to a specified number or quantity: *she weighed a scant two pounds.*
▸*v.* [*tr.*] provide grudgingly or in insufficient amounts: *he does not scant his attention to the later writings.* ■ deal with inadequately; neglect: *the press regularly scants a host of issues relating to safety and health.* —**scant·ly** *adv.* —**scant·ness** *n.*

scant·y /ˈskantē/ ▸*adj.* (**scant·i·er**, **scant·i·est**) small or insufficient in

quantity or amount: *scanty wages.* ■ (of clothing) revealing; skimpy. —**scant·i·ly** /ˈskantəlē; ˈskantl-ē/ *adv.* —**scant·i·ness** *n.*

scape /skāp/ ▸*n. Bot.* a long, leafless flower stalk coming directly from a root.

scape·goat /ˈskāp,gōt/ ▸*n.* a person who is blamed for the wrongdoings, mistakes, or faults of others, esp. for reasons of expediency. —**scape·goat·er** *n.* —**scape·goat·ing** *n.* —**scape·goat·ism** /-,izəm/ *n.*

scap·u·la /ˈskapyələ/ ▸*n.* (*pl.* **-lae** /-,lē/ or **-las**) *Anat.* technical term for **SHOULDER BLADE**.

scap·u·lar /ˈskapyələr/ ▸*adj. Anat. & Zool.* of or relating to the shoulder or shoulder blade.
▸*n.* a short monastic cloak covering the shoulders. ■ a symbol of affiliation to an ecclesiastical order, consisting of two strips of cloth hanging down the breast and back and joined across the shoulders.

scar /skär/ ▸*n.* a mark left on the skin or within body tissue where a wound, burn, or sore has not healed quite completely and fibrous connective tissue has developed: *a faint scar ran the length of his left cheek.* ■ *fig.* a lasting effect of grief, fear, or other emotion left on a person's character by a traumatic experience: *the attack has left mental scars on Terry and his family.* ■ a mark left on something following damage of some kind: *Max could see scars of the blast.* ■ a mark left at the point of separation of a leaf, frond, or other part from a plant.
▸*v.* (**scarred**, **scar·ring**) [*tr.*] (often **be scarred**) mark with a scar or scars: *he is likely to be **scarred for life** after injuries to his face, arms, and legs* | [as *adj.*, in *comb.*] *battle-scarred troops.* ▷late Middle English: from Old French *escharre*, via late Latin from Greek *eskhara* 'scab.'

scar·ab /ˈskarəb; ˈsker-/ ▸*n.* (also **scarab beetle**) a large dung beetle (*Scarabaeus sacer*) of the eastern Mediterranean area, regarded as sacred in ancient Egypt. The **scarab family** (Scarabaeidae) also includes the smaller dung beetles and chafers, together with some very large tropical species. ■ an ancient Egyptian gem cut in the form of this beetle, sometimes depicted with the wings spread, and engraved with hieroglyphs on the flat underside.

scarce /ske(ə)rs/ ▸*adj.* (esp. of food, money, or some other resource) insufficient for the demand: *as raw materials became scarce, synthetics were developed.* ■ occurring in small numbers or quantities; rare: *the freshwater shrimp becomes scarce in soft water.* —**scarce·ness** *n.* —**scar·ci·ty** /ˈskersitē/ *n.*
▸ □ **make oneself scarce** *inf.* leave a place, esp. so as to avoid a difficult situation.

scarce·ly /ˈske(ə)rslē/ ▸*adv.* only just; almost not: *her voice is so low I can scarcely hear what she is saying.* ■ only a very short time before: *she had scarcely dismounted before the door swung open.* ■ used to suggest that something is unlikely to be or certainly not the case: *they could scarcely all be wrong.*

scare /ske(ə)r/ ▸*v.* [*tr.*] cause great fear or nervousness in; frighten: *the rapid questions were designed to **scare** her **into** blurting out the truth.* ■ [*tr.*] drive or keep (someone) away by frightening them: *the threat of bad weather scared away the crowds.* ■ [*intr.*] become scared: *I don't scare easily.*
▸*phrasal v.* □ **scare something up** *inf.* manage to find or obtain something: *for a price, the box office can usually scare up a pair of tickets.*
▸*n.* a sudden attack of fright: *gosh, that gave me a scare!* ■ a general feeling of anxiety or alarm about something: *they were forced to leave the building because of a bomb scare.* —**scar·er** *n.*

scare·crow /ˈske(ə)r,krō/ ▸*n.* an object, usually made to resemble a human figure, set up to scare birds away from a field where crops are growing. ■ *inf.* a person who is very badly dressed, odd-looking, or thin.

scared·y-cat /ˈske(ə)rdē ,kat/ ▸*n. inf.* a timid person.

scare·mon·ger /ˈske(ə)r,məNGgər; -,mäNGgər/ ▸*n.* a person who spreads frightening or ominous reports or rumors. —**scare·mon·ger·ing** *n. & adj.*

scare quotes ▸*plural n.* quotation marks used around a word or phrase when they are not required, thereby eliciting attention or doubts: *putting the term "global warming" in scare quotes serves to subtly cast doubt on the reality of such a phenomenon.*

scarf[1] /skärf/ ▸*n.* (*pl.* **scarves** /skärvz/ or **scarfs** /skärfs/) a length or square of fabric worn around the neck or head. —**scarfed** /skärft/ (also **scarved**) *adj.*

scarf[2] ▸*v.* [*tr.*] join the ends of (two pieces of timber or metal) by beveling or notching them so that they fit over or into each other.
▸*n.* (also **scarf joint**) a joint connecting two pieces of timber or metal in

which the ends are beveled or notched so that they fit over or into each other.

scarf³ ▶ *v.* [*tr.*] *inf.* eat or drink (something) hungrily or enthusiastically: *he scarfed down the waffles.*

scar·i·fy¹ /'skarə,fī/ ▶ *v.* (**-fies, -fied**) [*tr.*] make cuts or scratches in (the surface of something), in particular: ■ break up the surface of (soil or pavement). ■ make shallow incisions in (the skin), esp. as a medical procedure or traditional cosmetic practice: *she scarified the bite with a paring knife.* ■ *fig.* criticize severely and hurtfully. —**scar·i·fi·ca·tion** /-fi-'kāSHən/ *n.*

scar·i·fy² /'ske(ə)rə,fī/ ▶ *v.* (**-fies, -fied**) [*tr.*] [usu. as *adj.*] (**scarifying**) *inf.* frighten: *a scarifying mix of extreme violence and absurdist humor.*

scar·la·ti·na /,skärlə'tēnə/ ▶ *n.* another term for **SCARLET FEVER.**

scar·let /'skärlit/ ▶ *adj.* **1** of a brilliant red color: *a mass of scarlet berries.* **2** *chiefly dated* (of an offense or sin) wicked; heinous. ■ immoral, esp. promiscuous or unchaste.
▶ *n.* a brilliant red color: *papers lettered* **in scarlet** *and black.* ■ clothes or material of this color.

scar·let fe·ver ▶ *n.* an infectious bacterial disease affecting esp. children, and causing fever and a scarlet rash.

scar·let pim·per·nel ▶ *n.* a small plant (*Anagallis arvensis arvensis*) of the primrose family, with scarlet flowers that close in rainy or cloudy weather.

scarp /skärp/ ▶ *n.* a very steep bank or slope; an escarpment.

scarves /skärvz/ ▶ plural form of **SCARF**¹.

scar·y /'ske(ə)rē/ ▶ *adj.* (**scar·i·er, scar·i·est**) *inf.* frightening; causing fear: *a scary movie.* ■ uncannily striking or surprising: *it was scary the way they bonded with each other.* —**scar·i·ly** /-əlē/ *adv.* —**scar·i·ness** *n.*

scat¹ /skat/ ▶ *v.* (**scat·ted, scat·ting**) [*intr.*] *inf.* go away; leave: *Scat! Leave me alone.*

scat² (also **scat sing·ing**) ▶ *n.* improvised jazz singing in which the voice is used in imitation of an instrument.
▶ *v.* (**scat·ted, scat·ting**) [*intr.*] sing in such a way.

scat³ ▶ *n.* droppings, esp. those of carnivorous mammals.

scathe /skāTH/ *archaic* ▶ *v.* [*tr.*] (usu. **be scathed**) harm; injure: *he was barely scathed.*
▶ *n.* harm; injury.

sca·tol·o·gy /skə'täləjē/ ▶ *n.* an interest in or preoccupation with excrement and excretion. ■ obscene literature that is concerned with excrement and excretion. —**scat·o·log·i·cal** /'skatl'äjikəl/ *adj.*

scat·ter /'skatər/ ▶ *v.* [*tr.*] throw in various directions: *scatter the coconut over the icing.* ■ (**be scattered**) [usu.] occur or be found at intervals rather than all together: *there are many mills scattered throughout the marshlands.* ■ (of a group of people or animals) separate and move off quickly in different directions: *the roar made the dogs scatter.* ■ [*tr.*] cause (a group or people or animals) to act in such a way: *he charged across the foyer, scattering people.* ■ (usu. **be scattered with**) cover (a surface) with objects thrown or spread randomly over it: *sandy beaches scattered with driftwood.* ■ *Physics* deflect or diffuse (electromagnetic radiation or particles).
▶ *n.* a small, dispersed amount of something: *a scatter of houses on the north shore.* ■ *Statistics* the degree to which repeated measurements or observations of a quantity differ. —**scat·ter·a·ble** *adj.* —**scat·ter·a·tion** /,skatə'rāSHən/ *n.* —**scat·ter·er** *n.*

scat·ter·brain /'skatər,brān/ ▶ *n.* a person who tends to be disorganized and lacking in concentration. —**scat·ter·brained** *adj.*

scat·ter·shot /'skatər,SHät/ ▶ *adj.* denoting something that is broad but random and haphazard in its range: *a scattershot collection of stories.*

scav·enge /'skavənj/ ▶ *v.* [*tr.*] search for and collect (anything usable) from discarded waste: *people sell junk* **scavenged** *from the garbage* | [*intr.*] *the city dump where the squatters scavenge to survive.* ■ (of an animal) search for (carrion) as food. ■ search for discarded items or food in (a place): *the mink is still commonly seen scavenging the beaches of California.* ■ remove (combustion products) from the cylinder of an internal combustion engine on the return stroke of the piston.

scav·en·ger /'skavənjər/ ▶ *n.* an animal that feeds on carrion, dead plant material, or refuse. ■ a person who searches for and collects discarded items. ■ *Chem.* a substance that reacts with and removes particular molecules, radicals, etc.

sce·nar·i·o /sə'ne(ə)rē,ō; -'när-/ ▶ *n.* (*pl.* **-os**) a written outline of a movie, novel, or stage work giving details of the plot and individual scenes: *imagine the scenarios for four short stories.* ■ a postulated sequence or development of events: *a possible scenario is that he was attacked after opening the front door.* ■ a setting, in particular for a work of art or literature: *the scenario is World War II.*

scene /sēn/ ▶ *n.* **1** the place where an incident in real life or fiction occurs or occurred: *the emergency team were among the first* **on the scene.** ■ a place, with the people, objects, and events in it, regarded as having a particular character or making a particular impression: *a scene of carnage.* ■ a landscape: *thick snow had turned the scene outside into a picture postcard.* ■ an incident of a specified nature: *there had already been some scenes of violence.* ■ a place or representation of an incident: *scenes of 1930s America.* ■ a specified area of activity or interest: *the country music scene.* ■ a public display of emotion or anger: *she was loath to* **make a scene** *in the office.* **2** a sequence of continuous action in a play, movie, opera, or book: *a scene from Brando's first film.* ■ a subdivision of an act of a play in which the time is continuous and the setting fixed and which does not usually involve a change of characters: *beginning at Act One, Scene One.* ■ [usu. as *adj.*] the pieces of scenery used in a play or opera: *scene changes.*
▶ □ **behind the scenes** out of sight of the public at a theater or organization. ■ *fig.* secretly: *diplomatic maneuvers going on behind the scenes.* □ **come** (or **appear** or **arrive**) **on the scene** arrive; appear. □ **not one's scene** *inf.* not something one enjoys or is interested in: *sorry, that witchcraft stuff is not my scene.* □ **set the scene** describe a place or situation in which something is about to happen. ■ create the conditions for a future event: *the congressman's speech* **set the scene** *for a bitter debate.*

scen·er·y /'sēn(ə)rē/ ▶ *n.* the natural features of a landscape considered in terms of their appearance, esp. when picturesque: *spectacular views of mountain scenery.* ■ the painted background used to represent natural features or other surroundings on a theater stage or movie set.
▶ *phrasal v.* □ **chew** (**up**) **the scenery** (of an actor) overact: *he chews up the courtroom scenery as the unscrupulous attorney.*
▶ □ **change of scenery** a move to different surroundings: *we spent the weekend in Seattle just for a change of scenery.*

sce·nic /'sēnik/ ▶ *adj.* providing or relating to views of impressive or beautiful natural scenery: *the scenic route to Brussels.* ■ of or relating to theatrical scenery: *a scenic artist from the Metropolitan Opera House.* ■ (of a picture) representing an incident: *the trend to scenic figural work.* —**sce·ni·cal·ly** /-ik(ə)lē/ *adv.*

scent /sent/ ▶ *n.* a distinctive smell, esp. one that is pleasant: *the scent of freshly cut hay.* ■ pleasant-smelling liquid worn on the skin; perfume: *she sprayed scent over her body.* ■ a trail indicated by the characteristic smell of an animal, perceptible to hounds or other animals: *the hound followed the scent.* ■ *fig.* a trail of evidence or other signs assisting someone in a search or investigation: *once their interest is aroused, they follow the scent with sleuthlike pertinacity.*
▶ *v.* [*tr.*] **1** (usu. **be scented with**) impart a pleasant scent to: *a glass of tea scented with lemon balm* | [as *adj.*] (**scented**) *scented soap.* **2** discern by the sense of smell: *a shark can scent blood from well over half a mile away.* ■ *fig.* sense the presence, existence, or imminence of: *a commander who scented victory.* ■ sniff (the air) for a scent: *the bull advanced, scenting the breeze at every step.* —**scent·less** *adj.*
▶ □ **put** (or **throw**) **someone off the scent** mislead someone in the course of a search or investigation.

scent gland ▶ *n.* an animal gland that secretes an odorous pheromone or defensive substance, esp. one under the tail of a carnivorous mammal such as a civet or skunk.

scep·ter /'septər/ (*Brit.* **scep·tre**) ▶ *n.* an ornamented staff carried by rulers on ceremonial occasions as a symbol of sovereignty. —**scep·tered** *adj.*

scha·den·freu·de /'SHädən,froidə/ (also **Scha·den·freu·de**) ▶ *n.* pleasure derived by someone from another person's misfortune.

sched·ule /'skejool; -jəl/ ▶ *n.* **1** a plan for carrying out a process or procedure, giving lists of intended events and times: *we have drawn up an engineering schedule.* ■ (usu. **one's schedule**) one's day-to-day plans or timetable: *take a moment out of your busy schedule.* ■ a timetable: *information on airline schedules.* **2** *chiefly Law* an appendix to a formal document or statute, esp. as a list, table, or inventory.
▶ *v.* [*tr.*] (often **be scheduled**) arrange or plan (an event) to take place at a particular time: *the release of the single is* **scheduled** *for April.* ■ make arrangements for (someone or something) to do something: [*tr.*] *he is scheduled to be released from prison this spring.* ▶*late Middle English* (in the sense 'scroll, explanatory note, appendix'): from Old French *cedule*, from late Latin *schedula* 'slip of paper,' diminutive of *scheda*, from Greek *skhedē* 'papyrus leaf.' The verb dates from the mid 19th cent. —**sched·ul·er** *n.*

sche·ma /'skēmə/ ▶ *n.* (*pl.* **-ma·ta** /-mətə/ or **-mas**) a representation of a

scepter

plan or theory in the form of an outline or model: *a schema of scientific reasoning.*

sche·mat·ic /skə'matik; skē-/ ▸*adj.* (of a diagram or other representation) symbolic and simplified. ■ (of thought, ideas, etc.) simplistic or formulaic in character, usually to an extent inappropriate to the complexities of the subject matter: *a highly schematic reading of the play.*
▸*n.* (in technical contexts) a schematic diagram, in particular of an electric or electronic circuit. —**sche·mat·i·cal·ly** /-ik(ə)lē/ *adv.*

scheme /skēm/ ▸*n.* a large-scale systematic plan or arrangement for attaining some particular object or putting a particular idea into effect: *a clever marketing scheme.* ■ a secret or underhanded plan; a plot: *police uncovered a scheme to steal paintings worth more than $250,000.* ■ a particular ordered system or arrangement: *a classical rhyme scheme.*
▸*v.* [*intr.*] make plans, in a devious way or with intent to do something illegal or wrong: *he schemed to bring about the collapse of the government.* ▷mid 16th cent. (denoting a figure of speech): from Latin *schema,* from Greek. An early sense was 'diagram of the position of celestial objects,' giving rise to 'diagram, outline.' —**schem·er** *n.*
▸ □ **the scheme of things** a supposed or apparent overall system, within which everything has a place and in relation to which individual details are ultimately to be assessed: *in the overall scheme of things, we didn't do badly.*

schem·ing /'skēmiNG/ ▸*adj.* given to or involved in making secret and underhanded plans: *they had mean, scheming little minds.*
▸*n.* the activity or practice of making such plans. —**schem·ing·ly** *adv.*

scher·zan·do /skərt'sändō/ *Mus.* ▸*adv. & adj.* (esp. as a direction) in a playful manner.

scher·zo /'skertsō/ ▸*n.* (*pl.* **-zos** or **-zi** /-tsē/) *Mus.* a vigorous, light, or playful composition, typically comprising a movement in a symphony or sonata.

schil·ling /'sHiliNG/ ▸*n.* the basic monetary unit of Austria (until replaced by the euro), equal to 100 groschen.

schism /'s(k)izəm/ ▸*n.* a split or division between strongly opposed sections or parties, caused by differences in opinion or belief. ■ the formal separation of a church into two churches or the secession of a group owing to doctrinal and other differences. ▷late Middle English: from Old French *scisme,* via ecclesiastical Latin from Greek *skhisma* 'cleft,' from *skhizein* 'to split.'

schis·mat·ic /s(k)iz'matik/ ▸*adj.* of, characterized by, or favoring schism. —**schis·mat·i·cal·ly** /-ik(ə)lē/ *adv.*

schist /sHist/ ▸*n. Geol.* a coarse-grained metamorphic rock that consists of layers of different minerals and can be split into thin irregular plates. —**schis·tose** /-,tōs/ *adj.* —**schis·tous** /-təs/ *adj.*

schis·to·some /'sHistə,sōm/ ▸*n. Zool. Med.* a parasitic flatworm that needs two hosts to complete its life cycle. The immature form infests freshwater snails, and the adult lives in the blood vessels of birds and mammals, causing bilharzia in humans.

schi·zan·thus /ski'zanTHəs/ ▸*n.* a South American plant (genus *Schizanthus*) of the nightshade family, with irregularly lobed showy flowers marked with one or more contrasting colors.

schiz·o /'skitsō/ *inf., offens.* ▸*adj.* (of a person or their behavior) schizophrenic.
▸*n.* (*pl.* **-os**) a schizophrenic.

schiz·oid /'skit,soid/ ▸*adj. Psychiatry* denoting or having a personality type characterized by emotional aloofness and solitary habits. ■ *inf.* (in general use) resembling schizophrenia in having inconsistent or contradictory elements; mad or crazy: *it's a frenzied, schizoid place.*
▸*n.* a schizoid person.

schiz·o·phre·ni·a /,skitsə'frēnēə; -'frenēə/ ▸*n.* a long-term mental disorder of a type involving a breakdown in the relation between thought, emotion, and behavior, leading to faulty perception, inappropriate actions and feelings, withdrawal from reality and personal relationships into fantasy and delusion, and a sense of mental fragmentation. ■ (in general use) a mentality or approach characterized by inconsistent or contradictory elements. —**schiz·o·phren·ic** /-'frenik/ *adj. & n.*

schle·miel /sHlə'mēl/ (also **shle·miel**) ▸*n. inf.* a stupid, awkward, or unlucky person.

schlep /sHlep/ (also **schlepp** or **shlep**) *inf.* ▸*v.* (**schlepped**, **schlep·ping**) [*tr.*] haul or carry (something heavy or awkward): *she schlepped her groceries home.* ■ [*intr.*] (of a person) go or move reluctantly or with effort: *I would have preferred not to schlep all the way over there to run an errand.*
▸*n.* a tedious or difficult journey.

schlock /sHläk/ (also **shlock**) ▸*n. inf.* cheap or inferior goods or material; trash: *they peddle their schlock to willing tourists.* —**schlock·y** *adj.*

schmaltz /sHmälts; sHmôlts/ (also **schmalz**) ▸*n. inf.* excessive sentimentality, esp. in music or movies. —**schmaltz·y** *adj.*

schmuck /sHmək/ (also **shmuck**) ▸*n. inf.* a foolish or contemptible person.

schnapps /sHnäps; sHnaps/ ▸*n.* a strong alcoholic drink resembling gin and often flavored with fruit: *peach schnapps.*

schnau·zer /'sHnouzər/ ▸*n.* a medium- or small-sized dog of a German breed with a close wiry coat and heavy whiskers around the muzzle.

schnit·zel /'sHnitsəl/ ▸*n.* a thin slice of veal or other light meat, coated in breadcrumbs and fried.

schol·ar /'skälər/ ▸*n.* a specialist in a particular branch of study, esp. the humanities; a distinguished academic: *a Hebrew scholar.* —**schol·ar·ly** *adj.*

schol·ar·ship /'skälər,sHip/ ▸*n.* **1** academic study or achievement; learning of a high level. **2** a grant or payment made to support a student's education, awarded on the basis of academic or other achievement.

scho·las·tic /skə'lastik/ ▸*adj.* of or concerning schools and education: *scholastic achievement.* ■ of or relating to secondary schools. —**scho·las·ti·cal·ly** /-ik(ə)lē/ *adv.* —**scho·las·ti·cism** *n.*

school [1] /skool/ ▸*n.* **1** an institution for educating children. ■ the buildings used by such an institution: *the cost of building a new school.* ■ [treated as *pl.*] the students and staff of a school: *the principal was addressing the whole school.* ■ a day's work at school; lessons: *school started at 7 a.m.* ■ *fig.* used to describe the type of circumstances in which someone was brought up: *I was brought up in a hard school and I don't forget it.* **2** any institution at which instruction is given in a particular discipline: *a dancing school.* ■ *inf.* another term for **UNIVERSITY**. ■ a department or faculty of a college concerned with a particular subject of study: *the School of Dental Medicine.* **3** a group of people, particularly writers, artists, or philosophers, sharing the same or similar ideas, methods, or style: *the Frankfurt school of critical theory.* ■ a style, approach, or method of a specified character: *filmmakers are tired of the skin-deep school of cinema.* —**school·work** *n.*
▸*v.* [*tr.*] *chiefly formal* send to school; educate: *a scientist born in Taiwan and schooled in California.* ■ train or discipline (someone) in a particular skill or activity: *he schooled her in horsemanship.*
▸ □ **leave school** discontinue one's education: *he left school at 16.* □ **school of thought** a particular way of thinking, typically one disputed by the speaker: *a school of thought that calls into question the constitutional foundations of this country.*

school [2] ▸*n.* a large group of fish or sea mammals.
▸*v.* [*intr.*] (of fish or sea mammals) form a large group.

school age ▸*n.* the age range of children normally attending school. —**school-age** or **school-aged** *adj.*

school board ▸*n.* a local board or authority responsible for the provision and maintenance of schools.

school·boy /'skool,boi/ ▸*n.* a boy attending school. ■ [as *adj.*] characteristic of or associated with schoolboys, esp. in being immature: *schoolboy humor.*

school·child /'skool,cHīld/ ▸*n.* (*pl.* **-child·ren**) a child attending school.

school·days /'skool,dāz/ ▸*pl. n.* the period in someone's life when they attended school: *a close friend from their schooldays.*

school·girl /'skool,gərl/ ▸*n.* a girl attending school. ■ [as *adj.*] characteristic of or associated with schoolgirls, esp. in being elementary or immature: *schoolgirl French.*

school·house /'skool,hous/ ▸*n.* a building used as a school, esp. in a small community or village.

school·ing /'skooliNG/ ▸*n.* education or training received, esp. at school: *his parents paid for his schooling.*

school·marm /'skool,mä(r)m/ ▸*n.* a female schoolteacher (typically used with reference to a woman regarded as prim, strict, and brisk in manner). —**school·marm·ish** *adj.*

school·mate /'skool,māt/ ▸*n. inf.* a person who attends or attended the same school as oneself.

school·room /'skool,room; -,room/ ▸*n.* a room in which a class of students is taught. ■ (**the schoolroom**) used to refer to school as an institution: *I got most of my education outside of the schoolroom.*

school·teach·er /'skool,tēcHər/ ▸*n.* a person who teaches in a school. —**school·teach·ing** /-,tēcHiNG/ *n.*

Pronunciation Key ə *ago,* up; ər *over,* fur; a *hat;* ā *ate;* ä *car;* cH *chin;* e *let;* ē *see;* e(ə)r *air;* i *fit;* ī *by;* i(ə)r *ear;* NG *sing;* ō *go;* ô *law, for;* oi *toy;* oo *good;* oo *goo;* ou *out;* sH *she;* TH *thin;* TH *then;* (h)w *why;* zH *vision*

school vouch·er ▸*n.* a government-funded voucher redeemable for tuition fees at a school other than the public school that a student could attend free.

schoon·er /'sko͞onər/ ▸*n.* **1** a sailing ship with two or more masts, typically with the foremast smaller than the mainmast, and having gaff-rigged lower masts. **2** a tall beer glass.

schooner

schot·tische /'SHätiSH/ ▸*n.* a slow polka.

schuss /SHo͞os; SHo͝os/ ▸*v.* [*intr.*] make a straight downhill run on skis.

schwa /SHwä/ ▸*n.* *Phonet.* the unstressed central vowel (as in *a* moment *a*go), represented by the symbol (ə) in the International Phonetic Alphabet.

sci·at·ic /sī'atik/ ▸*adj.* of or relating to the hip. ■ of or affecting the sciatic nerve. ■ suffering from or liable to sciatica. —**sci·at·i·cal·ly** /-ik(ə)lē/ *adv.*

sci·at·i·ca /sī'atikə/ ▸*n.* pain affecting the back, hip, and outer side of the leg, caused by compression of a spinal nerve root in the lower back, often owing to degeneration of an intervertebral disk.

sci·at·ic nerve ▸*n. Anat.* a major nerve extending from the lower end of the spinal cord down the back of the thigh, and dividing above the knee joint. It is the nerve with the largest diameter in the human body.

sci·ence /'sīəns/ ▸*n.* the intellectual and practical activity encompassing the systematic study of the structure and behavior of the physical and natural world through observation and experiment: *the world of science and technology.* ■ a particular area of this: *veterinary science.* ■ a systematically organized body of knowledge on a particular subject: *the science of criminology.* ▷Middle English (denoting knowledge): from Old French, from Latin *scientia*, from *scire* 'know.'

sci·ence fic·tion (abbr.: **SF** or **sci-fi**) ▸*n.* fiction based on imagined future scientific or technological advances and major social or environmental changes, frequently portraying space or time travel and life on other planets.

sci·ence park ▸*n.* an area devoted to scientific research or the development of science-based or technological industries.

sci·en·tif·ic /ˌsīən'tifik/ ▸*adj.* based on or characterized by the methods and principles of science: *the scientific study of earthquakes.* ■ relating to or used in science: *scientific instruments.* ■ *inf.* systematic; methodical: *how many people buy food in an organized, scientific way?* —**sci·en·tif·i·cal·ly** /-ik(ə)lē/ *adv.*

sci·en·tist /'sīəntist/ ▸*n.* a person who is studying or has expert knowledge of one or more of the natural or physical sciences.

Sci·en·tol·o·gy /ˌsīən'täləjē/ ▸*n.* *trademark* a religious system based on the seeking of self-knowledge and spiritual fulfillment through graded courses of study and training. It was founded by science-fiction writer L. Ron Hubbard (1911–86) in 1955. —**Sci·en·tol·o·gist** /-jist/ *n.*

sci-fi /'sī 'fī/ ▸*n. inf.* short for SCIENCE FICTION.

scil·i·cet /'silə,set/ ▸*adv.* that is to say; namely (introducing a word to be supplied or an explanation of an ambiguity).

scil·la /'silə/ ▸*n.* a plant (genus *Scilla*) of the lily family that typically bears small blue star- or bell-shaped flowers and glossy straplike leaves, native to Eurasia and temperate Africa.

scim·i·tar /'simətər; -ˌtär/ ▸*n.* a short sword with a curved blade that broadens toward the point, used originally in Eastern countries.

scin·tig·ra·phy /sin'tigrəfē/ ▸*n. Med.* a technique in which a scintillation counter or similar

detector is used with a radioactive tracer to obtain an image of a bodily organ or a record of its functioning. —**scin·ti·graph·ic** /ˌsinti'grafik/ *adj.*

scin·til·la /sin'tilə/ ▸*n.* a tiny trace or spark of a specified quality or feeling: *a scintilla of doubt.*

scin·til·late /'sin(t)l,āt/ ▸*v.* [*intr.*] emit flashes of light; sparkle. —**scin·til·lant** /-ənt/ *adj.* & *n.*

scin·til·la·tion /ˌsin(t)l'āSHən/ ▸*n.* a flash or sparkle of light. ■ the process or state of emitting flashes of light.

sci·on /'sīən/ ▸*n.* **1** a young shoot or twig of a plant, esp. one cut for grafting or rooting. **2** a descendant of a notable family or one with a long lineage: *he was the scion of a wealthy family.*

si·roc·co /SHə'räkō; sə-/ ▸*n.* variant spelling of SIROCCO.

scis·sion /'siZHən; 'siSH-/ ▸*n. technical* the action or state of cutting or being cut, in particular: ■ *chiefly Biochem.* breakage of a chemical bond, esp. one in a long chain molecule so that two smaller chains result. ■ a division or split between people or parties; a schism. —**scis·sile** /'sisəl; -īl/ *adj.*

scis·sor /'sizər/ ▸*v.* [*tr.*] move (one's legs) move back and forth in a way resembling the action of scissors: *he was still hanging on, scissoring his legs uselessly.*

▸*n.* see SCISSORS.

scis·sors /'sizərz/ ▸*pl. n.* an instrument used for cutting cloth, paper, and other thin material, consisting of two blades laid one on top of the other and fastened in the middle so as to allow them to be opened and closed by a thumb and finger inserted through rings on the end of their handles. ■ (also **scis·sor**) [often as *adj.*] an action in which two things cross each other or open and close like the blades of a pair of scissors: *as the fish swims, the tail lobes open and close in a slight scissor action.*

scle·ra /'skli(ə)rə/ ▸*n. Anat.* the white outer layer of the eyeball. At the front of the eye it is continuous with the cornea. —**scle·ral** *adj.*

scle·ro·sis /sklə'rōsis/ ▸*n. Med.* abnormal hardening of body tissue. ■ see MULTIPLE SCLEROSIS. ■ *fig.* excessive resistance to change: *the challenge was to avoid institutional sclerosis.*

scle·rot·ic /sklə'rätik/ ▸*adj.* **1** *Med.* of or having sclerosis. ■ *fig.* becoming rigid and unresponsive; losing the ability to adapt: *sclerotic management.* **2** *Anat.* of or relating to the sclera.

scoff[1] /skôf; skäf/ ▸*v.* [*intr.*] speak to someone or about something in a scornfully derisive or mocking way: *department officials scoffed at the allegations* | [with *direct speech*] *"You, a scientist?" he scoffed.* —**scoff·er** *n.* —**scoff·ing·ly** *adv.*

scoff[2] ▸*inf.* ▸*v.* [*tr.*] eat (something) quickly and greedily: *she scoffed down several chops* | *a lizard scoffing up insects.*

scold /skōld/ ▸*v.* [*tr.*] remonstrate with or rebuke (someone) angrily: *Mom took Anna away, scolding her for her bad behavior.*

▸*n. archaic* a woman who nags or grumbles constantly. —**scold·er** *n.* —**scold·ing** *n.* & *adj.*

sco·li·o·sis /ˌskōlē'ōsis/ ▸*n. Med.* abnormal lateral curvature of the spine. —**sco·li·ot·ic** /-'ätik/ *adj.*

scol·lop /'skäləp; 'skal-/ ▸*n.* & *v.* archaic spelling of SCALLOP.

sconce /skäns/ ▸*n.* **1** a candle holder, or a holder of another light source, that is attached to a wall with an ornamental bracket. **2** a flaming torch or candle secured in such a holder. ▷late Middle English (originally denoting a portable lantern with a screen to protect the flame): shortening of Old French *esconse* 'lantern,' or from medieval Latin *sconsa*, from Latin *absconsa (laterna)* 'dark (lantern),' literally 'hidden (lantern)' (i.e., a lantern with a device for concealing the light), from *abscondere* 'to hide.'

scone /skōn; skän/ ▸*n.* a small unsweetened or lightly sweetened biscuitlike cake made from flour, fat, milk, and sometimes fruit.

scoop /sko͞op/ ▸*n.* **1** a utensil resembling a spoon, with a long handle and a deep bowl, used for removing powdered, granulated, or semi-solid substances (such as ice cream) from a container. ■ a short-handled deep shovel used for moving grain, coal, etc. ■ a moving bowl-shaped part of a digging machine, dredger, or other mechanism into which material is gathered. ■ a quantity taken up by a scoop: *an apple pie with scoops of ice cream on top.* **2** *inf.* a piece of news published by a newspaper or broadcast by a television or radio station in advance of its rivals. ■ (**the scoop**) the latest information about something.

▸*v.* [*tr.*] **1** pick up and move (something) with a scoop: *Philip began to scoop grain into his bag.* ■ create (a hollow or hole) with or as if with a scoop: *a hole was scooped out in the floor of the hut.* ■ pick up (someone or something) in a swift, fluid movement: *he scooped her up in his arms.* **2** *inf.* publish a news story before (a rival reporter, newspaper, or radio or television station). —**scoop·er** *n.* —**scoop·ful** *n.*

scimitar

scoot /skoōt/ ▶v. [intr.] inf. go or leave somewhere quickly: *I'd better scoot | they scooted off on their bikes.*

scoot·er /'skoōtər/ ▶n. **1** (also **motor scooter**) a light two-wheeled open motor vehicle on which the driver sits over an enclosed engine with legs together and feet resting on a floorboard. ■ any small, light, vehicle able to travel quickly across water, ice, or snow. **2** a recreational vehicle consisting of a footboard mounted on two wheels and a long steering handle, propelled by resting one foot on the footboard and pushing the other against the ground.
▶v. [intr.] travel or ride on a scooter. **—scoot·er·ist** /-ist/ n.

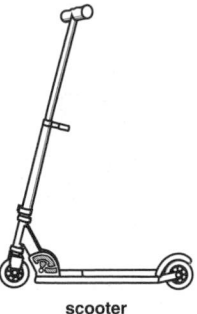

scooter

scope¹ /skōp/ ▶n. the extent of the area or subject matter that something deals with or to which it is relevant: *we widened the scope of our investigation.* ■ the opportunity or possibility to do or deal with something: *the scope for major change is always limited by political realities.*

scope² inf. ▶n. a telescope, microscope, or other device having a name ending in -scope.
▶v. [tr.] inf. look at carefully; scan: *they watched him scoping the room, looking for Michael.* ■ assess; weigh up: *they'd scoped out their market.*

sco·pol·a·mine /skə'pälə,mēn/ ▶n. Chem. a poisonous plant alkaloid used for motion sickness and as a preoperative medication for examination of the eye.

scor·bu·tic /skôr'byoōtik/ ▶adj. relating to or affected with scurvy.

scorch /skôrCH/ ▶v. **1** [tr.] burn the surface of (something) with flame or heat: *surrounding houses were scorched by heat from the blast.* ■ [intr.] become burned when exposed to heat or a flame: *the meat had scorched.* ■ [often as adj.] (**scorched**) (of the heat of the sun) cause (vegetation or a place) to become dried out and lifeless: *a desolate, scorched landscape.* **2** [intr.] inf. (of a person or vehicle) move very fast: *a sports car scorching along the expressway.*
▶n. the burning or charring of the surface of something: [as adj.] *a scorch mark.*

scorched earth pol·i·cy ▶n. a military strategy of burning or destroying buildings, crops, or other resources that might be of use to an invading enemy force. ■ fig. a strategy that involves taking extreme action: *a lawyer renowned for his scorched earth policy in divorce cases.*

scorch·er /'skôrCHər/ ▶n. inf. **1** a day or period of very hot weather: *next week could be a real scorcher.* **2** a remarkable or extreme example of something, in particular: ■ a very powerfully struck ball: *Winfield hit a scorcher over the left field fence.* ■ sensational book or film. ■ a heated or violent argument.

score /skôr/ ▶n. **1** the number of points, goals, runs, etc., achieved in a game: *the final score was 25–16 in favor of Washington.* ■ the number of points, goals, runs, etc., achieved by an individual player or a team in a game: *his highest score of the season.* ■ inf. an act of gaining a point, goal, or run in a game. ■ a rating or grade, such as a mark achieved in a test: *an IQ score of 161.* ■ (**the score**) inf. the state of affairs; the real facts about the present situation: *"Hey, what's the score here, what's goin' on?"* ■ inf. an act of buying illegal drugs. **2** (pl. same) a group or set of twenty or about twenty: *a score of men lost their lives in the battle.* ■ (**scores of**) a large amount or number of something: *he sent scores of enthusiastic letters to friends.* **3** a written representation of a musical composition showing all the vocal and instrumental parts arranged one below the other. ■ the music composed for a movie or play. **4** a notch or line cut or scratched into a surface.
▶v. [tr.] **1** gain (a point, goal, run, etc.) in a competitive game: *Penn State scored two touchdowns in the fourth quarter.* ■ decide on the score to be awarded to (a competitor): *the judge must score each dog against this standard.* ■ gain (a number of points) for a competitor; be worth: *each correct answer scores ten points.* ■ decide on the scores to be awarded in (a game or competition). ■ [intr.] record the score during a game; act as scorer. ■ Baseball cause (a teammate) to score: *McNab singled, scoring Reynolds and Diaz.* ■ inf. secure (a success or an advantage): *the band scored a hit single.* ■ [intr.] inf. be successful: *his new movie scored big.* ■ inf. buy or acquire (something, typically illegal drugs): *Sally had scored some acid.* ■ [intr.] inf. succeed in attracting a sexual partner, typically for a casual encounter. **2** orchestrate or arrange (a piece of music), typically for a specified instrument or instruments: *it was scored for clarinet, saxophone, trumpet, trombone, and percussion.* ■ compose the music for (a movie or play). **3** cut or scratch a notch or line on (a surface): *score the card until you cut through.* **—score·less** adj. **—scor·er** n.

▶ □ **know the score** inf. be aware of the essential facts about a situation. □ **on that** (or **this**) **score** so far as that (or this) is concerned: *my priority was to blend new faces into the team, and we have succeeded on that score.* □ **score points** outdo another person, esp. in an argument. □ **settle a** (or **the**) **score** take revenge on someone for a past act.

score·board /'skôr,bôrd/ ▶n. a large board on which the score in a game or match is displayed.

score·card /'skôr,kärd/ (also **score·sheet** or **score·book**) ▶n. (in sports) a card, sheet, or book in which scores are entered.

scorn /skôrn/ ▶n. the feeling or belief that someone or something is worthless or despicable; contempt: *I do not wish to become the object of scorn.*
▶v. [tr.] feel or express contempt or derision for: *he accused America of scorning the Arab nation.* ■ reject (something) in a contemptuous way: *opponents scorned Noriega's offer to negotiate.* ■ [intr.] refuse to do something because one is too proud: *at her lowest ebb, she would have scorned to stoop to such tactics.* ▷Middle English: shortening of Old French *escarn* (noun), *escharnir* (verb), of Germanic origin. **—scorn·er** n. (rare).
▶ □ **pour** (or **heap**) **scorn on** speak with contempt or mockery of.

scorn·ful /'skôrnfəl/ ▶adj. feeling or expressing contempt or derision: *the justices have been scornful of the government's conduct.* **—scorn·ful·ly** adv. **—scorn·ful·ness** n.

Scor·pi·o /'skôrpē,ō/ Astrol. ▶the eighth sign of the zodiac (the Scorpion), which the sun enters about October 23. ■ (**a Scorpio**) (pl. **-os**) a person born when the sun is in this sign.

scor·pi·on /'skôrpēən/ ▶n. a terrestrial arachnid (order Scorpiones) with lobsterlike pincers and a poisonous sting at the end of its jointed tail, which it can hold curved over the back. Most kinds live in tropical and subtropical areas. ■ used in names of other arachnids and insects resembling a scorpion, e.g., **false scorpion**, **water scorpion**.

Scot /skät/ ▶n. a native of Scotland or a person of Scottish descent. ■ a member of a Gaelic people that migrated from Ireland to Scotland around the late 5th century.

Scotch /skäCH/ ▶adj. old-fashioned term for **Scottish**.
▶n. **1** short for **Scotch whisky**. **2** [as pl. n.] (**the Scotch**) dated the people of Scotland. **3** dated the form of English spoken in Scotland.

scotch /skäCH/ ▶v. [tr.] decisively put an end to: *a spokesman has scotched the rumors.*

Scotch broth ▶n. a traditional Scottish soup made from beef or mutton stock with pearl barley and vegetables.

Scotch pine ▶n. a long-lived, medium-sized Eurasian pine tree (*Pinus sylvestris*) extensively planted for its timber and other products. It is well established in the northeastern U.S.

Scotch whis·ky (also **Scotch whis·key**) ▶n. whisky distilled in Scotland, esp. from malted barley.

scot-free ▶adv. without suffering any punishment or injury: *the people who kidnapped you will get off scot-free.*

Scot·land Yard ▶the headquarters of the London Metropolitan Police, situated from 1829 to 1890 in Great Scotland Yard off Whitehall, from 1890 until 1967 in New Scotland Yard on the Thames Embankment, and from 1967 in New Scotland Yard, Westminster. ■ used to allude to the Criminal Investigation Department of the London Metropolitan Police force.

sco·to·ma /skə'tōmə/ ▶n. (pl. **-mas** or **-ma·ta** /-mətə/) Med. a partial loss of vision or a blind spot in an otherwise normal visual field. **—sco·tom·a·tous** /-mətəs/ adj.

Scots /skäts/ ▶adj. another term for **Scottish**: *a Scots accent.*
▶n. the form of English used in Scotland.

Scots·man /'skätsmən/ (also fem. **Scots·wom·an**) ▶n. (pl. **-men**) a male native or national of Scotland or a man of Scottish descent.

Scot·tie /'skätē/ ▶n. inf. (also **Scottie dog**) a Scottish terrier.

Scot·tish /'skätish/ ▶adj. of or relating to Scotland or its people: *the Scottish Highlands | Scottish dancing.*
▶n. [as pl. n.] (**the Scottish**) the people of Scotland. See also **Scots**. **—Scot·tish·ness** n.

Scot·tish ter·ri·er ▶n. a small terrier of a rough-haired short-legged breed.

scoun·drel /'skoundrəl/ ▶n. a dishonest or unscrupulous person; a rogue. **—scoun·drel·ism** /-,lizəm/ n. **—scoun·drel·ly** adj.

scour¹ /skou(ə)r/ ▶v. [tr.] clean or brighten the surface of (something) by rubbing it hard, typically with an abrasive or detergent: *he scoured the* *bathtub.* ■ remove (dirt or unwanted matter) by rubbing in such a way: *use an electric toothbrush to scour off plaque.* ■ (of water or a watercourse) make (a channel or pool) by flowing forcefully over something and removing soil or rock: *a stream came crashing through a narrow cavern to scour out a round pool below.*

▶*n.* **1** the action of scouring or the state of being scoured, esp. by swift-flowing water. ■ an act of rubbing something hard to clean or brighten it: *give the floor a good scour.* **2** (also **scours**) diarrhea in livestock, esp. cattle and pigs. —**scour·er** *n.*

scour² ▶*v.* [*tr.*] subject (a place, text, etc.) to a thorough search in order to locate something: *David scoured each newspaper for an article on the murder.*

scourge /skərj/ ▶*n.* **1** *hist.* a whip used as an instrument of punishment. **2** a person or thing that causes great trouble or suffering: *the scourge of mass unemployment.*

▶*v.* [*tr.*] **1** *hist.* whip (someone) as a punishment. **2** cause great suffering to: *political methods used to scourge and oppress workers.* —**scourg·er** *n.* (*hist.*).

scout /skout/ ▶*n.* **1** a soldier or other person sent out ahead of a main force so as to gather information about the enemy's position, strength, or movements. ■ a ship or aircraft employed for reconnaissance, esp. a small fast aircraft. ■ short for **TALENT SCOUT**. ■ an instance of gathering information, esp. by reconnoitering an area: *a lengthy scout around the area.* **2** (also **Scout**) a Boy Scout or Girl Scout. **3** *inf., dated* a man or boy: *I've got nothing against Harrison—he's a good scout.*

▶*v.* [*intr.*] make a search for someone or something in various places: *I was sent to scout around for a place to park the camper | we scouted for clues.* ■ (esp. of a soldier) go ahead of a main force so as to gather information about an enemy's position, strength, or movements. ■ [*tr.*] explore or examine (a place or area of business) so as to gather information about it: *American companies are keen to scout out business opportunities.* ■ look for suitably talented people for recruitment to one's own organization or sports team: *Johnson has been scouting for the Pirates.* —**scout·er** *n.*

scout·mas·ter /'skout,mastər/ ▶*n.* the adult in charge of a group of Boy Scouts.

scow /skou/ ▶*n.* a wide-beamed sailing dinghy. ■ a flat-bottomed boat with sloping ends used as a lighter and in dredging and other harbor services.

scowl /skoul/ ▶*n.* an angry or bad-tempered expression.

▶*v.* [*intr.*] frown in an angry or bad-tempered way: *she scowled at him defiantly.* —**scowl·er** *n.*

scrab·ble /'skrabəl/ ▶*v.* [*intr.*] scratch or grope around with one's fingers to find, collect, or hold on to something: *she scrabbled at the grassy slope, desperate for a firm grip.* ■ (of an animal) scratch at something with its claws: *a dog was scrabbling at the door.* ■ make great efforts to get somewhere or achieve something: *I had to scrabble around to find this apartment.*

▶*n.* **1** an act of scratching or scrambling for something: *he heard the scrabble of claws behind him.* ■ a struggle to get somewhere or achieve something: *a scrabble among the salesmen to avoid going to the bottom of the heap.* **2** (**Scrabble**) *trademark* a board game in which players use lettered tiles to create words in a crossword fashion. —**scrab·bler** *n.*

scrag·gly /'skrag(ə)lē/ (also **scrag·gy** /'skragē/) ▶*adj.* (**-gli·er, -gli·est**) (of a person or animal) thin and bony. ■ ragged, thin, or untidy in form or appearance: *a man with a scraggly beard.* ■ (of a plant, tree, or shrubbery) sparsely foliated or having thin, uneven growth: *it was the scraggliest Christmas tree I had ever seen.* —**scrag·gi·ly** /-əlē/ *adv.* —**scrag·gli·ness** or **scrag·gi·ness** *n.*

scram /skram/ ▶*v.* (**scrammed, scram·ming**) **1** [*intr.*, usu. in *imper.*] *inf.* go away or get out of somewhere quickly: *get out of here, you miserable wretches—scram!* **2** [*tr.*] *inf.* shut down (a nuclear reactor) in an emergency.

▶*n.* *inf.* the emergency shutdown of a nuclear reactor: *the power plant was cited for its high rate of scrams over the past year.*

scram·ble /'skrambəl/ ▶*v.* **1** [*intr.*] make one's way quickly or awkwardly up a steep slope or over rough ground by using one's hands as well as one's feet: *we scrambled over the wet boulders.* ■ move hurriedly or clumsily from or into a particular place or position: *she scrambled out of the car.* ■ (**scramble into**) put (clothes) on hurriedly: *Robbie scrambled into jeans and a T-shirt.* ■ [*tr.*] *inf.* perform (an action) or achieve (a result) hurriedly, clumsily, or with difficulty. ■ struggle or compete with others for something in an eager or uncontrolled and undignified way: *firms scrambled to win public-sector contracts.* ■ [*tr.*] (often **be scrambled**) order (a fighter aircraft or its pilot) to take off immediately in an

emergency or for action. ■ [*intr.*] (of a fighter aircraft or its pilot) take off in such a way. ■ [*intr.*] *Football* (of a quarterback) run around with the ball behind the line of scrimmage while looking for an open receiver. ■ [*intr.*] *Football* run forward with the ball when unable to pass to an open receiver. **2** [*tr.*] make (something) jumbled or muddled: *maybe the alcohol has scrambled his brains.* ■ prepare (eggs) by beating them with a little liquid and then cooking and stirring them gently. ■ make (a broadcast transmission, a telephone message, or electronic data) unintelligible unless received by an appropriate decoding device: [as *adj.*] (**scrambled**) *scrambled television signals.*

▶*n.* **1** a difficult or hurried clamber up or over something: *an undignified scramble over the wall.* ■ a walk up steep terrain involving the use of one's hands. ■ an eager or uncontrolled and undignified struggle with others to obtain or achieve something: *a scramble for high-priced concert seats.* **2** a disordered mixture of things: *the encryptor produced a scramble of the letters of the alphabet.* ▷late 16th cent.: imitative; compare with the dialect words *scamble* 'stumble' and *cramble* 'crawl.' —**scram·bling** /-b(ə)liNG/ *n.*

scram·bler /'skramb(ə)lər/ ▶*n.* a person or thing that scrambles, esp. a device for scrambling a broadcast transmission, a telephone message, or electronic data.

scrap¹ /skrap/ ▶*n.* **1** a small piece or amount of something, esp. one that is left over after the greater part has been used: *I scribbled her address on a scrap of paper.* ■ (**scraps**) bits of uneaten food left after a meal, esp. when fed to animals: *he filled Sammy's bowls with fresh water and scraps.* ■ used to emphasize the lack or smallness of something: *there was not a scrap of aggression in him.* ■ *inf.* a small person or animal, esp. one regarded with affection or sympathy: *poor little scrap, she's too hot in that coat.* ■ a particularly small thing of its kind: *she was wearing a short black skirt and a tiny scrap of a top.* **2** (also **scrap metal**) discarded metal for reprocessing: *the steamer was eventually sold for scrap.* ■ [often as *adj.*] any waste articles or discarded material, esp. that which can be put to another purpose: *we're burning scrap lumber.*

▶*v.* (**scrapped, scrap·ping**) [*tr.*] (often **be scrapped**) discard or remove from service (a retired, old, or inoperative vehicle, vessel, or machine), esp. so as to convert it to scrap metal: *the decision was made to scrap the entire fleet.* ■ abolish or cancel (something, esp. a plan, policy, or law) that is now regarded as unnecessary, unwanted, or unsuitable: *the station scrapped plans to televise the contest live.*

scrap² *inf.* ▶*n.* a fight or quarrel, esp. a minor or spontaneous one.

▶*v.* (**scrapped, scrap·ping**) [*intr.*] engage in such a fight or quarrel. ■ compete fiercely: *the talk-show producers are scrapping for similar audiences.* —**scrap·per** *n.*

scrap·book /'skrap,bŏŏk/ ▶*n.* a book of blank pages for sticking clippings, drawings, or pictures in.

▶*v.* [*intr.*] [usually as *n.*] (**scrapbooking**) create scrapbooks as a hobby: *I scrapbook with the kids nearly every weekend.*

scrape /skrāp/ ▶*v.* **1** [*tr.*] push or pull a hard or sharp implement across (a surface or object) so as to remove dirt or other matter: *rinse off the carrots and scrape them.* ■ use a sharp or hard implement to remove (dirt or unwanted matter) from something: *she scraped the mud off her shoes.* ■ make (a hollow) by scraping away soil or rock: *he found a ditch, scraped a hole, and put the bag in it.* **2** rub or cause to rub by accident against a rough or hard surface, causing damage or injury: [*intr.*] *he smashed into the wall and felt his knee scrape against the plaster | [tr.] she reversed in a reckless sweep, scraping the left front fender.* ■ [*tr.*] draw or move (something) along or over something else, making a harsh noise: *she scraped back her chair and stood up.* ■ [*intr.*] move with or make such a sound: *she lifted the gate to prevent its scraping along the ground.* ■ [*intr.*] *humorous* play a violin or similar stringed instrument tunelessly. **3** [*tr.*] just manage to achieve; accomplish with great effort or difficulty. ■ (**scrape something together/up**) collect or accumulate something with difficulty: *they could hardly scrape up enough money for one ticket, let alone two.* ■ [*intr.*] try to save as much money as possible; economize. ■ [*intr.*] (**scrape by/along**) manage to live with difficulty: *she has to scrape by on Social Security.* ■ [*intr.*] barely manage to succeed in a particular undertaking: *Clinton scraped into office in 1992.*

▶*n.* **1** an act or sound of scraping: *he heard the scrape of his mother's key in the lock.* ■ an injury or mark caused by scraping: *there was a long, shallow scrape on his shin.* ■ *Med.* a procedure of dilatation of the cervix and curettage of the uterus, or the result of this. **2** *inf.* an embarrassing or difficult predicament caused by one's own unwise behavior: *he'd been in worse scrapes than this before now.*

▶ □ **scrape the bottom of the barrel** *inf.* be reduced to using things or people of the poorest quality because there is nothing else available.

scrap·er /'skrāpər/ ▶n. a tool or device used for scraping, esp. for removing dirt, paint, ice, or other unwanted matter from a surface.

scrap heap ▶n. a pile of discarded materials or articles: *cars on a scrap heap.*

scrap·py /'skrapē/ ▶adj. (**-pi·er, -pi·est**) **1** consisting of disorganized, untidy, or incomplete parts: *scrappy lecture notes piled up unread.* **2** inf. determined, argumentative, or pugnacious: *he played the part of a scrappy detective.* —**scrap·pi·ly** /-əlē/ adv. —**scrap·pi·ness** n.

scrap·yard /'skrap,yärd/ ▶n. a place where scrap metal is collected and processed.

scratch /skraCH/ ▶v. **1** [tr.] score or mark the surface of (something) with a sharp or pointed object: *the car's paintwork was battered and scratched.* ■ make a long, narrow superficial wound in the skin of: *her arms were scratched by the thorns.* ■ rub (a part of one's body) with one's fingernails to relieve itching: *Jessica lifted her sunglasses and scratched her nose.* ■ make (a mark or hole) by scoring a surface with a sharp or pointed object: *I found two names scratched on one of the windowpanes.* ■ write (something) hurriedly or awkwardly: *pass me my writing things—I'll scratch a few letters before I get up.* ■ [intr.] make a rasping or grating noise by scraping something over a hard surface: *the dog scratched to be let in.* ■ [intr.] [often as n.] (**scratching**) play a record using the scratch technique (see sense 1 of the n. below). ■ [intr.] (of a bird or mammal, esp. a chicken) rake the ground with the beak or claws in search of food. ■ accomplish (something) with great effort or difficulty: *he scratches out a living growing strawberries.* **2** [tr.] cancel or strike out (writing) with a pen or pencil: *the name of Dr. McNab was scratched out and that of Dr. Daniels substituted.* ■ withdraw (a competitor) from a competition: *Oswald's Zephyr was the second horse to be scratched from a race today.* ■ cancel or abandon (an undertaking or project): *the original filming schedule has been scratched.*
▶n. **1** a mark or wound made by scratching: *the scratches on her arm were throbbing.* ■ inf. a slight or insignificant wound or injury: *it's nothing—just a scratch.* ■ an act or spell of scratching oneself to relieve itching: *he gave his scalp a good scratch.* ■ a rasping or grating noise produced by something rubbing against a hard surface: *the scratch of a match lighting a cigarette.* ■ a rough hiss, caused by the friction of the stylus in the groove, heard when a record is played. ■ a technique, used esp. in rap music, of stopping a record by hand and moving it back and forth to give a rhythmic scratching effect. **2** the starting point in a handicap for a competitor receiving no odds. ■ *Golf* a handicap of zero, indicating that a player is good enough to achieve par on a course. **3** inf. money: *he was working to get some scratch together.*
▶adj. **1** assembled or made from whatever is available, and so unlikely to be of the highest quality: *at least two vessels set sail with scratch crews.* **2** (of a sports competitor or event) with no handicap given. —**scratch·er** n.
▶ ■ **from scratch** from the very beginning, esp. without utilizing or relying on any previous work for assistance: *he built his own computer company from scratch.* □ **scratch one's head** inf. think hard in order to find a solution to something. ■ feel or express bewilderment. □ **scratch the surface 1** deal with a matter only in the most superficial way: *research has only scratched the surface of the paranormal.* **2** initiate the briefest investigation to discover something concealed: *they have a boring image, but scratch the surface and it's fascinating.* □ **up to scratch** up to the required standard; satisfactory: *her German was not up to scratch.*

scratch·pad /'skraCH,pad/ (also **scratch pad**) ▶n. a notepad. ■ *Comput.* a small, fast memory for the temporary storage of data.

scratch·y /'skraCHē/ ▶adj. (**scratch·i·er, scratch·i·est**) (esp. of a fabric or garment) having a rough, uncomfortable texture and tending to cause itching or discomfort. ■ (of a voice or sound) rough; grating: *she dropped her voice to a scratchy whisper.* ■ (of a record) making a crackling or rough sound because of scratches on the surface. ■ (of writing or a drawing) done with quick and jagged strokes: *a scratchy ink sketch of a man on horseback.* —**scratch·i·ly** /-əlē/ adv. —**scratch·i·ness** n.

scrawl /skrôl/ ▶v. [tr.] write (something) in a hurried, careless way: *Charlie scrawled his signature.*
▶n. an example of hurried, careless writing: *reams of handwritten scrawl.* —**scrawl·er** n. —**scrawl·y** adj.

scrawn·y /'skrônē/ ▶adj. (**scrawn·i·er, scrawn·i·est**) (of a person or animal) unattractively thin and bony. ■ (of vegetation) meager or stunted. —**scrawn·i·ness** n.

scream /skrēm/ ▶v. [intr.] give a long, loud, piercing cry or cries expressing excitement, great emotion, or pain: *they could hear him screaming in pain.* ■ cry something in a high-pitched, frenzied way: [intr.] *I ran to the house screaming for help.* ■ urgently and vociferously call attention to one's views or feelings, esp. ones of anger or distress: *his supporters*

scream that he is being done an injustice. ■ make a loud, high-pitched sound: *sirens were screaming from all over the city.* ■ move very rapidly with or as if with such a sound: *a shell screamed overhead.*
▶n. a long, loud, piercing cry expressing extreme emotion or pain: *they were awakened by screams for help.* ■ a high-pitched cry made by an animal: *the screams of the seagulls.* ■ a loud, piercing sound: *the scream of a falling bomb.* ■ inf. an irresistibly funny person, thing, or situation: *the movie's a scream.*

scree /skrē/ ▶n. a mass of small loose stones that form or cover a slope on a mountain. ■ a slope covered with such stones.

screech /skrēCH/ ▶v. [intr.] (of a person or animal) give a loud, harsh, piercing cry: *she hit her brother, causing him to screech with pain.* ■ make a loud, harsh, squealing sound: [as adj.] (**screeching**) *she brought the car to a screeching halt.* ■ [intr.] move rapidly with such a sound: *the van screeched around the corner at top speed.*
▶n. a loud, harsh, piercing cry. ■ a loud, harsh, squealing sound: *a screech of brakes.* —**screech·er** n. —**screech·y** adj. (**screech·i·er, screech·i·est**).

screech owl ▶n. a small American owl (*Otus asio*, family Strigidae) with a screeching call and distinctive ear tufts.

screed /skrēd/ ▶n. **1** a long speech or piece of writing, typically one regarded as tedious. **2** a leveled layer of material (e.g., cement) applied to a floor or other surface. ■ a strip of plaster or other material placed on a surface as a guide to thickness.
▶v. [trans.] level (wet concrete, e.g.) with a straight edge using a back and forth motion while moving across the surface.

screen /skrēn/ ▶n. **1** a fixed or movable upright partition used to divide a room, to give shelter from drafts, heat, or light, or to provide concealment or privacy. ■ a thing providing concealment or protection: *his jeep was discreetly parked behind a screen of trees.* ■ *Mil.* a detachment of troops or ships detailed to cover the movements of the main body. ■ *Archit.* a partition of carved wood or stone separating the nave of a church from the chancel, choir, or sanctuary. See also ROOD SCREEN. ■ a frame with fine wire netting used in a window or doorway to keep out insects: [as adj.] *screen door.* **2** the surface of a cathode-ray tube or similar electronic device, esp. that of a television, VDT, or monitor, on which images and data are displayed. ■ a blank, typically white or silver surface on which a photographic image is projected: *the world's largest movie screen.* ■ (**the screen**) movies or television; the motion-picture industry: *she's a star of the stage as well as the screen.* ■ the data or images displayed on a computer screen: *pressing the F1 key at any time will display a help screen.* ■ *Photog.* a flat piece of ground glass on which the image formed by a camera lens is focused. **3** *Printing* a transparent, finely ruled plate or film used in halftone reproduction. **4** a large sieve or riddle, esp. one for sorting substances such as grain or coal into different sizes.
▶v. [tr.] **1** conceal, protect, or shelter (someone or something) with a screen or something forming a screen: *her hair swung across to screen her face.* ■ (**screen something off**) separate something from something else with or as if with a screen: *an area had been screened off as a waiting room.* ■ protect (someone) from something dangerous or unpleasant: *in my country, a man of my rank would be screened completely from any risk of attack.* ■ prevent from causing or protect from electromagnetic interference: *ensure that your microphone leads are properly screened from hum pickup.* **2** show (a movie or video) or broadcast (a television program): *the show is to be screened by HBO later this year.* **3** test (a person or substance) for the presence of a disease or contaminant: *outpatients were screened for cervical cancer.* ■ check on or investigate (someone), typically to ascertain whether they are suitable for or can be trusted in a particular situation or job. ■ evaluate or analyze (something) for its suitability for a particular purpose or application. ■ (**screen someone/something out**) exclude someone or something after such evaluation or investigation. **4** pass (a substance such as grain or coal) through a large sieve or screen, esp. so as to sort it into different sizes. **5** *Printing* project (a photograph or other image) through a transparent ruled plate so as to be able to reproduce it as a halftone. ▷Middle English: shortening of Old Northern French *escren*, of Germanic origin. —**screen·a·ble** adj. —**screen·er** n. —**screen·ful** /-,fool/ n.

screen·ing /'skrēniNG/ ▶n. **1** a showing of a movie, video, or television program. **2** the evaluation or investigation of something as part of a methodical survey, to assess suitability for a particular role or purpose. ■ the testing of a person or group of people for the presence of

---

Pronunciation Key ə *ago,* up; ər *over, fur;* a *hat;* ā *ate;* ä *car;* CH *chin;* e *let;* ē *see;* e(ə)r *air;* i *fit;* ī *by;* i(ə)r *ear;* NG *sing;* ō *go;* ô *law, for;* oi *toy;* ŏŏ *good;* ōō *goo;* ou *out;* SH *she;* TH *thin;* <u>TH</u> *then;* (h)w *why;* ZH *vision*

a disease or other condition: *prenatal screening for Down syndrome.* **3** (**screenings**) refuse separated by sieving grain.

screen·play /ˈskrēnˌplā/ ▶*n.* the script of a movie, including acting instructions and scene directions.

screen-print ▶*v.* [*tr.*] [often as *adj.*] (**screen-printed**) force ink or metal onto (a surface) through a prepared screen of fine material so as to create a picture or pattern.
▶*n.* (**screen print**) a picture or design produced by screen-printing.

screen test ▶*n.* a filmed test to ascertain whether an actor is suitable for a movie role.
▶*v.* (**screen-test**) [*tr.*] give such a test to (an actor).

screen·writ·er /ˈskrēnˌrītər/ ▶*n.* a person who writes a screenplay. —**screen·writ·ing** /-ˌrītiNG/ *n.*

screw /skroō/ ▶*n.* **1** a short, slender, sharp-pointed metal pin with a raised helical thread running around it and a slotted head, used to join things together by being rotated so that it pierces wood or other material and is held tightly in place. ■ a cylinder with a helical ridge or thread running around the outside (a **male screw**) that can be turned to seal an opening, apply pressure, adjust position, etc., esp. one fitting into a corresponding internally grooved or threaded piece (a **female screw**). ■ (also **screw propeller**) a ship's or aircraft's propeller (considered as acting like a screw in moving through water or air). **2** an act of turning a screw or other object having a thread. **3** *inf.* a prisoner's derogatory term for a prison guard or warden. **4** *vulgar slang* an act of sexual intercourse. ■ a sexual partner of a specified ability.
▶*v.* **1** [*tr.*] fasten or tighten with a screw or screws: *screw the hinge to your new door.* ■ rotate (something) so as to fit it into or on to a surface or object by means of a spiral thread: *Philip screwed the top on the flask.* ■ [*intr.*] (of an object) be attached or removed by being rotated in this way: *a connector that screws on to the gas cylinder.* **2** [*tr.*] (usu. **be screwed**) *inf.* cheat or swindle (someone), esp. by charging them too much for something: *if you do what they tell you, you're screwed.* ■ (**screw something out of**) extort or force something, esp. money, from (someone) by putting them under strong pressure: *your grandmother screwed cash out of him for ten years.* **3** [*tr.*] *vulgar slang* have sexual intercourse with. ■ [*intr.*] (of a couple) have sexual intercourse. ■ [in *imper.*] *inf.* used to express anger or contempt: *Screw him!*
▶*phrasal v.* □ **screw around 1** *vulgar slang* have many different sexual partners. **2** *inf.* fool around. □ **screw someone over** *inf.* treat someone unfairly; cheat or swindle someone. □ **screw up** *inf.* completely mismanage or mishandle a situation: *I'm sorry, Susan, I screwed up.* □ **screw someone up** *inf.* cause someone to be emotionally or mentally disturbed: *this job can really screw you up.* □ **screw something up 1** tense the muscles of one's face or around one's eyes, typically so as to register an emotion or because of bright light. **2** *inf.* cause something to fail or go wrong: *why are you trying to screw up your life?* **3** summon up one's courage: *now Stephen had to screw up his courage and confess.* —**screw·a·ble** *adj.* —**screw·er** *n.*
▶ □ **have a screw loose** *inf.* be slightly eccentric or mentally disturbed. □ **turn** (or **tighten**) **the screw** (or **screws**) *inf.* exert strong pressure on someone.

screw·ball /ˈskroōˌbôl/ ▶*n.* **1** *Baseball* a pitched ball that moves in a direction opposite to that of a curveball. **2** *inf.* a crazy or eccentric person.
▶*adj. inf.* crazy; absurd. ■ relating to or denoting a style of fast-moving comedy film involving eccentric characters or ridiculous situations. —**screw·ball·er** *n.*

screw·driv·er /ˈskroōˌdrīvər/ ▶*n.* **1** a tool with a flattened, cross-shaped, or star-shaped tip that fits into the head of a screw to turn it. **2** a cocktail made from vodka and orange juice.

screwed /skroōd/ ▶*adj. inf.* cheated or swindled. ■ ruined; rendered ineffective.

screw thread ▶*n.* see THREAD (sense 4).

screw·y /ˈskroōē/ ▶*adj.* (**screw·i·er, screw·i·est**) *inf.* rather odd or eccentric. —**screw·i·ness** *n.*

scrib·ble /ˈskribəl/ ▶*v.* [*tr.*] write or draw (something) carelessly or hurriedly: *he took the clipboard and scribbled something illegible.* ■ [*intr.*] *inf.* write for a living or as a hobby: *she spent her last years scribbling and painting.*
▶*n.* a piece of writing or a picture produced in this way: *illegible scribbles.* —**scrib·bler** *n.* —**scrib·bly** /ˈskrib(ə)lē/ *adj.*

scribe /skrīb/ ▶*n.* **1** *hist.* a person who copies out documents, esp. one employed to do this before printing was invented. ■ *inf., often humorous* a writer, esp. a journalist. **2** (also **Scribe**) *Judaism* an ancient Jewish record-keeper or, later, a professional theologian and jurist.

scrim /skrim/ ▶*n.* strong, coarse fabric, chiefly used for heavy-duty lining or upholstery, or for diffusing light.

scrim·mage /ˈskrimij/ ▶*n.* **1** a confused struggle or fight. **2** *Football* the beginning of each down of play, with the ball placed on the ground between the offensive and defensive lines with its longest axis at right angles to the goal line. ■ offensive plays begun in this way. ■ *chiefly Football* a session in which teams practice by playing a simulated game.
▶*v.* [*intr.*] *chiefly Football* engage in a simulated game. —**scrim·mag·er** *n.*

scrimp /skrimp/ ▶*v.* [*intr.*] be thrifty or parsimonious; economize: *I have scrimped and saved to give you a good education.*

scrim·shaw /ˈskrimˌSHô/ ▶*n.* whalebone, ivory, shells, or other materials with carved or colored designs.

scrip¹ /skrip/ ▶*n.* **1** a provisional certificate of money subscribed to a bank or company, entitling the holder to a formal certificate and dividends. ■ such certificates collectively. ■ (also **scrip issue** or **dividend**) *Finance* an issue of additional shares to shareholders in proportion to the shares already held. **2** a certificate entitling the holder to acquire possession of certain portions of public land.

scrip² ▶*n.* another term for SCRIPT².

script¹ /skript/ ▶*n.* **1** handwriting as distinct from print; written characters: *her neat, tidy script.* ■ printed type imitating handwriting. ■ writing using a particular alphabet: *Russian script.* **2** the written text of a play, movie, or broadcast. ■ *Comput.* an automated series of instructions carried out in a specific order. ■ *Psychol.* the social role or behavior appropriate to particular situations that an individual absorbs through cultural influences and association with others.
▶*v.* [*tr.*] write a script for (a play, movie, or broadcast).

script² ▶*n. inf.* a doctor's prescription.

scrip·tur·al /ˈskripcHərəl/ ▶*adj.* of, from, or relating to the Bible: *scriptural quotations from Genesis.* —**scrip·tur·al·ly** *adv.*

scrip·ture /ˈskripcHər/ ▶*n.* (often **Scripture** or **Scriptures**) the sacred writings of Christianity contained in the Bible: *passages of scripture* | *the fundamental teachings of the Scriptures.* ■ the sacred writings of another religion.

script·writ·er /ˈskriptˌrītər/ ▶*n.* a person who writes a script for a play, movie, or broadcast. —**script·writ·ing** /-ˌrītiNG/ *n.*

scrod /skräd/ ▶*n.* a young cod, haddock, or similar fish, esp. one prepared for cooking.

scrof·u·la /ˈskrôfyələ/ ▶*n. chiefly hist.* a disease with glandular swellings, probably a form of tuberculosis. —**scrof·u·lous** /-ləs/ *adj.*

scroll /skrōl/ ▶*n.* **1** a roll of parchment or paper for writing or painting on. ■ an ancient book or document on such a roll. ■ an ornamental design or carving resembling a partly unrolled scroll of parchment, e.g., on the capital of a column, or at the end of a stringed instrument. ■ *Art* a depiction of a narrow ribbon bearing a motto or inscription. **2** [usu. as *adj.*] the facility that moves a display on a VDT screen in order to view new material.
▶*v.* **1** [*intr.*] move displayed text or graphics in a particular direction on a computer screen in order to view different parts of them: *she scrolled through her file.* ■ (of displayed text or graphics) move up, down, or across a computer screen. **2** [*tr.*] cause to move like paper rolling or unrolling: *the wind scrolled back the uppermost layer of loose dust.* —**scroll·a·ble** *adj.*

scroll·work /ˈskrōlˌwərk/ ▶*n.* decoration consisting of spiral lines or patterns, esp. as cut by a scroll saw.

Scrooge /skroōj/ Ebenezer, a miserly curmudgeon in Charles Dickens's novel *A Christmas Carol* (1843). ■ [as *n.*] (**a Scrooge**) a person who is miserly.

scro·tum /ˈskrōtəm/ ▶*n.* (*pl.* **scro·ta** or **scro·tums**) a pouch of skin containing the testicles. —**scro·tal** /ˈskrōtl/ *adj.*

scrounge /skrounj/ *inf.* ▶*v.* [*tr.*] seek to obtain (something, typically food or money) at the expense or through the generosity of others or by stealth: *he had managed to scrounge a free meal.*
▶*n.* an act of seeking to obtain something in such a way. —**scroung·er** *n.*

scrub¹ /skrəb/ ▶*v.* (**scrubbed, scrub·bing**) [*tr.*] rub (someone or something) hard so as to clean them, typically with a brush and water: *he had to scrub the floor.* ■ (**scrub something away/off**) remove dirt by rubbing hard: *it took ages to scrub off the muck.* ■ [*intr.*] (**scrub up**) thoroughly clean one's hands and arms, esp. before performing surgery: *the doctor scrubbed up and put on a protective gown.* ■ *inf.* cancel or abandon (something): *opposition leaders suggested she should scrub the trip to China.* ■ remove impurities from (gas or vapor).
▶*n.* **1** an act of scrubbing something or someone: *give the floor a good scrub.* **2** a semiabrasive cosmetic lotion applied to the face or body in order to cleanse the skin. **3** (**scrubs**) informal term for SCRUB SUIT. —**scrub·ba·ble** *adj.*

scrub[2] ▶*n.* **1** vegetation consisting mainly of brushwood or stunted forest growth. ■ land covered with such vegetation. **2** [as *adj.*] denoting a shrubby or small form of a plant: *scrub apple trees.* ■ denoting an animal of inferior breed or physique: *a scrub bull.* —**scrub·by** *adj.*

scrub suit ▶*n.* a hygienic outfit worn by surgeons and other surgical staff while performing or assisting at an operation.

scruff /skrəf/ ▶*n.* the back of a person's or animal's neck: *he grabbed him by the scruff of his neck.*

scruff·y /'skrəfē/ ▶*adj.* (**scruff·i·er**, **scruff·i·est**) shabby and untidy or dirty: *dressed in scruffy jeans and a baggy T-shirt.* —**scruff·i·ly** /-əlē/ *adv.* —**scruff·i·ness** *n.*

scrum /skrəm/ ▶*n.* *Rugby* an ordered formation of players, used to restart play, in which the forwards of a team form up with arms interlocked and heads down, and push forward against a similar group from the opposing side. The ball is thrown into the scrum and the players try to gain possession of it by kicking it backward toward their own side.

▶*v.* (**scrummed**, **scrum·ming**) [*intr.*] *Rugby* form or take part in a scrum.

scrump·tious /'skrəm(p)SHəs/ ▶*adj. inf.* (of food) extremely appetizing or delicious. ■ (of a person) very attractive. —**scrump·tious·ly** *adv.* —**scrump·tious·ness** *n.*

scrunch /skrənCH/ ▶*v.* [*intr.*] make a loud crunching noise: *crisp yellow leaves scrunched underfoot.* ■ [*tr.*] crush or squeeze (something) into a compact mass: *Gloria scrunched the handkerchief into a ball.* ■ [*intr.*] become crushed or squeezed in such a way: *their faces* **scrunch up** *with concentration.*

scrunch·ie /'skrənCHē/ ▶*n.* a circular band of fabric-covered elastic used for fastening the hair.

scru·ple /'skroopəl/ ▶*n.* (usu. **scruples**) a feeling of doubt or hesitation with regard to the morality or propriety of a course of action: *I had no scruples about eavesdropping.*

▶*v.* [*intr.*] hesitate or be reluctant to do something that one thinks may be wrong: *she doesn't scruple to ask her parents for money.*

scru·pu·lous /'skroopyələs/ ▶*adj.* (of a person or process) diligent, thorough, and extremely attentive to details: *the research has been carried out with scrupulous attention to detail.* ■ very concerned to avoid doing wrong: *she's too scrupulous to have an affair with a married man.* —**scru·pu·los·i·ty** /,skroopyə'läsitē/ *n.* —**scru·pu·lous·ly** *adv.* *she was scrupulously polite.* —**scru·pu·lous·ness** *n.*

scru·ti·nize /'skrootn,īz/ ▶*v.* [*tr.*] examine or inspect closely and thoroughly: *customers were warned to scrutinize the small print.* —**scru·ti·ni·za·tion** /,skrootn-i'zāsHən/ *n.* —**scru·ti·niz·er** *n.*

scru·ti·ny /'skrootn-ē/ ▶*n.* (*pl.* **-nies**) critical observation or examination: *every aspect of local government was placed* **under scrutiny.**

scry /skrī/ ▶*v.* (**scries**, **scried**) [*intr.*] foretell the future using a crystal ball or other reflective object or surface. —**scry·er** *n.*

SCSI /'skəzē/ *Computing* ▶*abbr.* small computer system interface, a bus standard for connecting computers and their peripherals.

scu·ba /'skoobə/ ▶*n.* an aqualung. ■ scuba diving.

scu·ba div·ing ▶*n.* the sport or pastime of swimming underwater using scuba gear. —**scu·ba dive** (also **scu·ba-dive**) *v.* —**scu·ba div·er** *n.*

scud /skəd/ ▶*v.* (**scud·ded**, **scud·ding**) [*intr.*] move fast in a straight line because of or as if driven by the wind: *we lie watching the clouds* **scudding** *across the sky.*

▶*n.* (**Scud**) (also **Scud missile**) a type of long-range surface-to-surface guided missile able to be fired from a mobile launcher.

scuff /skəf/ ▶*v.* [*tr.*] scrape or brush the surface of (a shoe or other object) against something: *I scuffed the heel of my shoe on a stone.* ■ mark (a surface) by scraping or brushing it, esp. with one's shoes: *the linoleum on the floor was scuffed.* ■ [*intr.*] (of an object or surface) become marked by scraping or brushing: *these shoes won't scuff.* ■ drag (one's feet or heels) when walking: *he scuffed his feet boyishly.* ■ [*intr.*] walk in such a way: *she scuffed along in her slippers.*

▶*n.* a mark made by scraping or grazing a surface or object: *dark colors don't show scuffs.*

scuf·fle /'skəfəl/ ▶*n.* **1** a short, confused fight or struggle at close quarters: *there were minor* **scuffles with** *police.* **2** an act or sound of moving in a hurried, confused, or shuffling manner: *he heard the scuffle of feet.*

▶*v.* [*intr.*] **1** engage in a short, confused fight or struggle at close quarters: *the teacher noticed two students scuffling in the corridor.* **2** move in a hurried, confused, or awkward way, making a rustling or shuffling sound: *a drenched woman scuffled through the doorway.*

scull /skəl/ ▶*n.* each of a pair of small oars used by a single rower. ■ an oar placed over the stern of a boat to propel it by a side-to-side motion,

reversing the blade at each turn. ■ a light, narrow boat propelled with a scull or a pair of sculls.

▶*v.* [*intr.*] [*intr.*] (of an aquatic animal) propel itself with fins or flippers.

scul·ler·y /'skəl(ə)rē/ ▶*n.* (*pl.* **-ler·ies**) a small kitchen or room at the back of a house used for washing dishes and other dirty household work.

scul·pin /'skəlpən/ ▶*n.* a chiefly marine fish (Cottidae and related families) of the northern hemisphere, with a broad flattened head and spiny scales and fins. Many genera and numerous species include the bullheads.

sculpt /skəlpt/ (also **sculp** /skəlp/) ▶*v.* [*tr.*] create or represent (something) by carving, casting, or other shaping techniques: *sculpting human figures from ivory* | [*intr.*] *she was teaching him how to sculpt.*

sculp·tor /'skəlptər/ ▶*n.* an artist who makes sculptures.

sculp·ture /'skəlpCHər/ ▶*n.* the art of making two- or three-dimensional representative or abstract forms, esp. by carving stone or wood or by casting metal or plaster. ■ a work of such a kind: *a bronze sculpture.* ■ *Zool. & Bot.* raised or sunken patterns or texture on the surface of a shell, pollen grain, cuticle, or other biological structure.

▶*v.* [*tr.*] make or represent (a form) by carving, casting, or other shaping techniques: *the choir stalls were each carefully sculptured.* ■ form, shape, or mark as if by sculpture, esp. with strong, smooth curves. ▷late Middle English: from Latin *sculptura*, from *sculpere* 'carve.' —**sculp·tur·al** /-CHərəl/ *adj.*

scum /skəm/ ▶*n.* a layer of dirt or froth on the surface of a liquid: *green scum found on stagnant pools.* ■ *inf.* a worthless or contemptible person or group of people: *you drug dealers are the scum of the earth.*

▶*v.* (**scummed**, **scum·ming**) [*intr.*] (of a liquid) become covered with a layer of dirt or froth: *the lagoon scummed over.* ■ [*tr.*] form a layer of dirt or froth on (a liquid): *litter scummed the surface of the harbor.* —**scum·my** *adj.* (**-mi·er**, **-mi·est**) .

scum·bag /'skəm,bag/ ▶*n. inf.* a contemptible or objectionable person.

scum·ble /'skəmbəl/ *Art* ▶*v.* [*tr.*] modify (a painting or color) by applying a very thin coat of opaque paint to give a softer or duller effect. ■ modify (a drawing) in a similar way with light shading in pencil or charcoal.

▶*n.* a thin, opaque coat of paint or layer of shading applied to give a softer or duller effect. ■ the effect produced by adding such a coat or layer.

scup /skəp/ ▶*n.* (*pl.* same) a common porgy (*Stenotomus chrysops*) with faint dark vertical bars, occurring off the coasts of the northwestern Atlantic.

scup·per[1] /'skəpər/ ▶*n.* (usu. **scuppers**) a hole in a ship's side to carry water overboard from the deck. ■ an outlet in the side of a building for draining water.

scup·per[2] ▶*v.* [*tr.*] chiefly *Brit.* sink (a ship or its crew) deliberately. ■ *inf.* prevent from working or succeeding; thwart: *plans for a casino were scuppered by a public inquiry.*

scurf /skərf/ ▶*n.* flakes on the surface of the skin that form as fresh skin develops below, occurring esp. as dandruff. ■ a similar flaky deposit on any surface, esp. one on a plant resulting from a fungal infection. —**scurf·y** *adj.*

scur·ril·ous /'skərələs/ ▶*adj.* making or spreading scandalous claims about someone with the intention of damaging their reputation: *a scurrilous attack on his integrity.* —**scur·ril·i·ty** /skə'rilitē/ *n.* (*pl.* **-ties**) —**scur·ril·ous·ly** *adv.* —**scur·ril·ous·ness** *n.*

scur·ry /'skərē/ ▶*v.* (**-ries**, **-ried**) [*intr.*] (of a person or small animal) move hurriedly with short quick steps: *pedestrians scurried for cover.*

scur·vy /'skərvē/ ▶*n.* a disease caused by a deficiency of vitamin C, characterized by swollen bleeding gums and the opening of previously healed wounds, which particularly affected poorly nourished sailors until the end of the 18th century.

▶*adj.* (**-vi·er**, **-vi·est**) *archaic* worthless or contemptible: *that was a scurvy trick.* —**scur·vi·ly** /-vəlē/ *adv.*

scutch·eon /'skəCHən/ ▶*n.* archaic spelling of ESCUTCHEON.

scu·tel·lum /sk(y)oo'teləm/ ▶*n.* (*pl.* **-tel·la** /-'telə/) *Bot. & Zool.* a small shieldlike structure, in particular: ■ a modified cotyledon in the embryo of a grass seed. —**scu·tel·lar** /-'telər/ *adj.*

scut·tle[1] /'skətl/ ▶*n.* (in full **coal scut·tle**) a metal container with a sloping hinged lid and a handle, used to fetch and store coal for a domestic fire. ■ the amount of coal held in such a container: *carrying endless scuttles of coal up from the cellar.*

---

scut·tle[2] ▶ v. [intr.] run hurriedly or furtively with short quick steps: *a mouse scuttled across the floor.*

scut·tle[3] ▶ v. [tr.] sink (a ship) deliberately by holing it or opening its sea-cocks to let water in. ■ deliberately cause (a scheme) to fail: *some of the stockholders are threatening to scuttle the deal.*
▶ n. an opening with a lid in a ship's deck or side.

scut·tle·butt /ˈskətlˌbət/ ▶ n. inf. rumor; gossip: *the scuttlebutt has it that he was a spy.*

scuzz /skəz/ ▶ n. inf. something regarded as disgusting, sordid, or disreputable. ■ a disreputable or unpleasant person. —**scuzz·y** adj.

scythe /sīTH/ ▶ n. a tool used for cutting crops such as grass or wheat, with a long curved blade at the end of a long pole attached to which are one or two short handles.
▶ v. [tr.] cut with a scythe. ■ [intr.] move through or penetrate something rapidly and forcefully: *attacking players can scythe through defenses.*

SDI ▶ abbr. Strategic Defense Initiative.

SE ▶ abbr. southeast or southeastern.

Se ▶ symb. the chemical element selenium.

sea /sē/ ▶ n. (often **the sea**) the expanse of salt water that covers most of the earth's surface and surrounds its landmasses: *a ban on dumping radioactive wastes in the sea.* ■ [often in *place names*] a roughly definable area of this: *the Black Sea.* ■ [in *place names*] a large lake: *the Sea of Galilee.* ■ used to refer to waves as opposed to calm sea: *there was still some sea running.* ■ (**seas**) large waves: *the lifeboat met seas of thirty-five feet head-on.* ■ fig. a vast expanse or quantity of something: *she scanned the sea of faces for Stephen.* ▷Old English *sǣ*, of Germanic origin; related to Dutch *zee* and German *See*.
▶ □ **at sea** (also **all at sea**) confused or unable to decide what to do: *he feels at sea with economics.*

sea a·nem·o·ne ▶ n. a sedentary marine coelenterate (order Actiniaria, class Anthozoa) with a columnar body that bears a ring of stinging tentacles around the mouth.

sea bass /bas/ ▶ n. any of a number of marine fishes that are related to or resemble the common perch, in particular: ■ a mainly tropical fish of a large family (Serranidae), the **sea bass family**), esp. one of the genus *Centropristis*, including the **giant sea bass** (*C. stiata*). The sea bass family also includes the groupers. ■ (**white sea bass**) a large game fish (*Cynoscion nobilis*) of the drum family, found along the Pacific coast of North America.

sea·bed /ˈsēˌbed/ ▶ n. the ground under the sea; the ocean floor.

sea·bird /ˈsēˌbərd/ ▶ n. a bird that frequents the sea or coast.

sea·board /ˈsēˌbôrd/ ▶ n. a region bordering the sea; the coastline.

sea·bor·gi·um /sēˈbôrgēəm/ ▶ n. the chemical element of atomic number 106, a very unstable element made by high-energy atomic collisions. (Symbol: **Sg**)

sea·borne /ˈsēˌbôrn/ ▶ adj. transported or traveling by sea: *seaborne trade.*

sea bream ▶ n. a deep-bodied marine fish that resembles the freshwater bream, in particular: ■ several genera and species in the family Sparidae (the **sea bream family**), which also includes the porgies. ■ a fish (*Seriolella brama*, family Centrolophidae) of Australasian coastal waters, with a purple back and silver underside.

sea change ▶ n. a profound or notable transformation.

sea·coast /ˈsēˌkōst/ ▶ n. the land adjacent to the sea.

sea·cock /ˈsēˌkäk/ ▶ n. a valve in an opening through a ship's hull below or near the waterline (esp. one connecting a ship's engine-cooling system to the sea).

sea cow ▶ n. a sirenian, esp. a manatee.

sea cu·cum·ber ▶ n. an echinoderm (class Holothuroidea) that has a thick, wormlike body with tentacles around the mouth. They typically have rows of tube feet along the body.

sea dog ▶ n. inf. an old or experienced sailor.

sea·far·ing /ˈsēˌfe(ə)riNG/ ▶ adj. (of a person) traveling by sea, esp. regularly. —**sea·far·er** /-ˌfe(ə)rər/ n.

sea·food /ˈsēˌfo͞od/ ▶ n. shellfish and sea fish, served as food.

sea·go·ing /ˈsēˌgōiNG/ ▶ adj. (of a ship) suitable or designed for voyages

on the sea. ■ characterized by or relating to traveling by sea, esp. habitually: *a seagoing life.*

sea-green ▶ adj. of a pale bluish green color.

sea·gull /ˈsēˌgəl/ ▶ n. a popular name for a gull.

sea hare ▶ n. a large sea slug (*Aplysia* and other genera, class Gastropoda) that has a minute internal shell and lateral extensions to the foot. Most species can swim, and many secrete distasteful chemicals to deter predators.

sea hol·ly ▶ n. a spiny-leaved plant (*Eryngium maritimum*) of the parsley family, with metallic blue teasel-like flowers, growing in sandy places by the sea and native to Europe.

sea·horse /ˈsēˌhôrs/ (also **sea horse**) ▶ n. **1** a small marine fish (genus *Hippocampus*, family Syngnathidae) with segmented bony armor, an upright posture, and a head and neck suggestive of a horse. Many species include the American *H. hudsonius.* **2** a mythical creature with a horse's head and fish's tail.

SEAL /sēl/ ▶ n. a member of an elite force within the U.S. Navy specializing in guerrilla warfare and counterinsurgency.

seal[1] /sēl/ ▶ n. **1** a device or substance that is used to join two things together so as to prevent them from coming apart or to prevent anything from passing between them: *blue smoke from the exhaust suggests worn valve seals.* ■ the state or fact of being joined or rendered impervious by such a substance or device: *many fittings have tapered threads for a better seal.* **2** a piece of wax, lead, or other material with an individual design stamped into it, attached to a document to show that it has come from the person who claims to have issued it. ■ a design embossed in paper for this purpose. ■ an engraved device used for stamping a design that authenticates a document. ■ a thing regarded as a confirmation or guarantee of something: *the International Monetary Fund is likely to give a seal of approval to the Mexican plan.*
▶ v. [tr.] fasten or close securely: *he folded it, sealed the envelope, and walked to the mailbox.* ■ (**seal something off**) isolate an area by preventing or monitoring entrance to and exit from it: *anti-terrorist squad officers sealed off the area to search for possible bombs.* ■ apply a nonporous coating to (a surface) to make it impervious: *seal the finish with a satin varnish.* ■ fix a piece of wax or lead stamped with a design to (a document) to authenticate it. ■ conclude, establish, or secure (something) definitively, excluding the possibility of reversal or loss: *to seal the deal he offered Thornton a place on the board of the nascent company.* —**seal·a·ble** adj. —**seal·er** n.
▶ □ **my** (or **his**, etc.) **lips are sealed** used to convey that one will not discuss or reveal something. □ **set** (or **put**) **one's seal on** mark with one's distinctive character: *it was the Stewart dynasty which most markedly set its seal on the place.*

seal[2] ▶ n. a fish-eating aquatic mammal with a streamlined body and feet developed as flippers, returning to land to breed or rest. Two families: Phocidae (the **true seals**) and Otariidae (the **eared seals**, including the fur seals and sea lions). ■ another term for **SEALSKIN**.
▶ v. [intr.] [usu. as n.] (**sealing**) hunt for seals.

seal·ant /ˈsēlənt/ ▶ n. material used for sealing something so as to make it airtight or watertight.

sea lav·en·der ▶ n. a chiefly maritime plant (genus *Limonium*, family Plumbaginaceae) with small pink or lilac funnel-shaped flowers. Several kinds are cultivated and some are used as everlasting flowers.

sea legs ▶ pl. n. (**one's sea legs**) a person's ability to keep their balance and not feel seasick when on board a moving ship.

sea lev·el ▶ n. the level of the sea's surface, used in reckoning the height of geographical features such as hills and as a barometric standard: *it is only 500 feet above sea level.*

sea lil·y ▶ n. a sedentary marine echinoderm (class Crinoidea) that has a small body on a long jointed stalk, with featherlike arms to trap food.

seal·ing wax ▶ n. a mixture of shellac and rosin with turpentine and pigment, softened by heating and used to make seals.

sea li·on ▶ n. an eared seal occurring mainly on Pacific coasts, the large male of which has a mane on the neck and shoulders.

seal·skin /ˈsēlˌskin/ ▶ n. [often as adj.] the skin or prepared fur of a seal, esp. when made into a garment.

seam /sēm/ ▶ n. **1** a line along which two pieces of fabric are sewn together in a garment or other article. ■ a line where the edges of two pieces of wood, wallpaper, or another material touch each other. ■ a long thin indentation or scar: *a sun-scorched face fissured with delicate seams.* **2** an underground layer, as of coal.
▶ v. [tr.] **1** join with a seam. **2** [usu. as adj.] (**seamed**) make a long narrow indentation in: *men in middle age have seamed faces.* —**seam·er** n. —**seam·less** adj.

▶ □ **bursting** (or **bulging**) **at the seams** *inf.* (of a place or building) full to overflowing. □ **come** (or **fall**) **apart at the seams** *inf.* (of a person or system) be in a very poor condition and near to collapse: *the attitude of the airport guard was symptomatic of a system falling apart at the seams.*

sea·man /'sēmən/ ▶*n.* (*pl.* **-men**) a person who works as a sailor, esp. one below the rank of officer. ■ a sailor of the lowest rank in the U.S. Navy or Coast Guard, ranking below petty officer. ■ a person regarded in terms of their ability to captain or crew a boat or ship: *he's the best seaman on the coast.* —**sea·man·like** /-,līk/ *adj.* —**sea·man·ly** *adj.*

sea·man·ship /'sēmən,SHip/ ▶*n.* the skill, techniques, or practice of handling a ship or boat at sea.

sea mile ▶*n.* a unit of distance equal to a minute of arc of a great circle and varying (because the earth is not a perfect sphere) between approx. 2,014 yards (1,842 meters) at the equator and 2,035 yards (1,861 meters) at the pole.

seam·stress /'sēmstris/ ▶*n.* a woman who sews, esp. one who earns her living by sewing.

seam·y /'sēmē/ ▶*adj.* (**seam·i·er, seam·i·est**) sordid and disreputable: *a seamy sex scandal.* —**seam·i·ness** *n.*

se·ance /'sā,äns/ ▶*n.* a meeting at which people attempt to make contact with the dead, esp. through the agency of a medium.

sea ot·ter ▶*n.* an entirely aquatic marine otter (*Enhydra lutris*) of North Pacific coasts, formerly hunted for its dense fur.

sea·plane /'sē,plān/ ▶*n.* an aircraft with floats, designed to land on and take off from water.

sea·port /'sē,pôrt/ ▶*n.* a town or city with a harbor for seagoing ships.

sear /si(ə)r/ ▶*v.* [*tr.*] burn or scorch the surface of (something) with a sudden, intense heat: *the water got so hot that it seared our lips.* ■ [*intr.*] (of pain) be experienced as a sudden, burning sensation: *a crushing pain seared through his chest.* ■ brown (food) quickly at a high temperature so that it will retain its juices in subsequent cooking: [as *adj.*] (**seared**) *seared chicken livers.*

▶*adj. poetic/lit.* variant spelling of SERE.

search /sərCH/ ▶*v.* [*intr.*] try to find something by looking or otherwise seeking carefully and thoroughly: *I searched among the rocks, but there was nothing.* ■ [*tr.*] examine (a place, vehicle, or person) thoroughly in order to find something or someone: *she searched the house from top to bottom.* ■ [as *adj.*] (**searching**) scrutinizing thoroughly, esp. in a disconcerting way: *you have to ask yourselves some searching questions.*

▶*n.* an act of searching for someone or something: *the police carried out a thorough search of the premises.* ▷Middle English: from Old French *cerchier* (verb), from late Latin *circare* 'go around,' from Latin *circus* 'circle.' —**search·a·ble** *adj.* —**search·er** *n.* —**search·ing·ly** *adv.*

search en·gine ▶*n. Comput.* a program for the retrieval of data from a database or network, esp. the Internet.

search·light /'sərCH,līt/ ▶*n.* a powerful outdoor electric light with a concentrated beam that can be turned in the required direction.

search par·ty ▶*n.* a group of people organized to look for someone or something that is lost.

search war·rant ▶*n.* a legal document authorizing a police officer or other official to enter and search premises.

sea salt ▶*n.* salt produced by the evaporation of seawater.

sea·scape /'sē,skāp/ ▶*n.* a view of an expanse of sea. ■ a picture of such a view.

sea ser·pent ▶*n.* a legendary serpentlike sea monster.

sea·shell /'sē,SHel/ ▶*n.* the shell of a marine mollusk.

sea·shore /'sē,SHôr/ ▶*n.* (usu. **the seashore**) an area of sandy, stony, or rocky land bordering and level with the sea. ■ the land between high- and low-water marks.

sea·sick /'sē,sik/ ▶*adj.* suffering from sickness or nausea caused by the motion of a ship at sea. —**sea·sick·ness** *n.*

sea·side /'sē,sīd/ ▶*n.* (usu. **the seaside**) a place by the sea, esp. a beach area or vacation resort.

sea·son /'sēzən/ ▶*n.* each of the four divisions of the year (spring, summer, autumn, and winter) marked by particular weather patterns and daylight hours, resulting from the earth's changing position with regard to the sun. ■ a period of the year characterized by a particular climatic feature or marked by a particular activity, event, or festivity: *the rainy season* | *the season for gathering pine needles.* ■ a fixed time in the year when a particular sport is played: *basketball season is over.* ■ the time of year when a particular fruit, vegetable, or other food is plentiful and in good condition: *the pies are made with fruit that is in season.* ■ an indefinite or unspecified period of time; a while: *this most beautiful soul, who walked with me for a season in this world.*

▶*v.* [*tr.*] **1** add salt, herbs, pepper, or other spices to (food): *season the soup* to taste with salt and pepper. ■ add a quality or feature to (something), esp. so as to make it more lively or exciting: *his conversation is seasoned liberally with exclamation points and punch lines.* **2** make (wood) suitable for use as timber by adjusting its moisture content to that of the environment in which it will be used: [as *adj.*] (**seasoned**) *it was made from seasoned, untreated oak.* ■ [as *adj.*] (**seasoned**) accustomed to particular conditions; experienced: *she is a seasoned traveler.*

sea·son·a·ble /'sēzənəbəl/ ▶*adj.* usual for or appropriate to a particular season of the year: *seasonable temperatures.* —**sea·son·a·bil·i·ty** /,sēzənə-'bilitē/ *n.* —**sea·son·a·ble·ness** *n.* —**sea·son·a·bly** /-blē/ *adv.*

sea·son·al /'sēzənəl/ ▶*adj.* of, relating to, or characteristic of a particular season of the year: *a selection of seasonal fresh fruit.* ■ fluctuating or restricted according to the season or time of year: *seasonal rainfall.* —**sea·son·al·i·ty** /,sēzə'nalitē/ *n.* —**sea·son·al·ly** *adv.*

sea·son·al af·fec·tive dis·or·der ▶*n.* depression associated with late autumn and winter and thought to be caused by a lack of light.

sea·son·ing /'sēzəniNG/ ▶*n.* **1** salt, herbs, or spices added to food to enhance the flavor. **2** the process of adjusting the moisture content of wood to make it more suitable for use as lumber.

sea squirt ▶*n.* a marine invertebrate that has a baglike body with orifices through which water flows into and out of a central pharynx.

seat /sēt/ ▶*n.* **1** a thing made or used for sitting on, such as a chair or stool. ■ the roughly horizontal part of a chair, on which one's weight rests directly. ■ a sitting place for a passenger in a vehicle or for a member of an audience: *we have a fairly small theater with about 1,300 seats.* ■ a place in an elected legislative or other body: *he lost his seat in the 1998 election.* ■ a site or location of something specified: *Washington, the seat of the federal government.* ■ short for COUNTY SEAT. ■ a part of a machine that supports or guides another part. ■ the stationary interior part of a valve against which the moving part is tightened in order to stop the flow of fluid. **2** a person's buttocks. ■ the part of a garment that covers the buttocks. ■ a manner of sitting on a horse: *he's got the worst seat on a horse of anyone I've ever seen.*

▶*v.* [*tr.*] arrange for (someone) to sit somewhere: *he seated her next to her husband.* ■ (**seat oneself** or **be seated**) sit down: *she invited them to be seated.* ■ (of a place such as a theater or restaurant) have seats for (a specified number of people): *a large tent that seats 100 to 150 people.* ■ [*tr.*] fit in position: *upper boulders were simply seated in the interstices below.* —**seat·less** *adj.*

▶ □ **by the seat of one's pants** *inf.* by instinct rather than logic or knowledge. □ **take one's seat** sit down, typically in a seat assigned to one.

seat belt (also **seat·belt**) ▶*n.* a belt or strap securing a person to prevent injury, esp. in a vehicle or aircraft.

seat·ing /'sētiNG/ ▶*n.* **1** the seats with which a building or room is provided: *the restaurant has seating for 80.* **2** the act of directing people to seats: *reservations are only taken for large parties at early seatings.*

SEATO /'sētō/ ▶*abbr.* Southeast Asia Treaty Organization.

sea tur·tle ▶*n.* see TURTLE (sense 2).

sea ur·chin ▶*n.* a marine echinoderm that has a spherical or flattened shell covered in mobile spines, with a mouth on the underside and calcareous jaws. Several families and genera and numerous species include the **Atlantic purple sea urchin** (*Arbacia punctulata*, family Arbaciidae).

sea wall ▶*n.* a wall or embankment erected to prevent the sea from encroaching on or eroding an area of land.

sea·ward /'sēwərd/ ▶*adv.* toward the sea: *after about a mile they turned seaward.*

▶*adj.* going or pointing toward the sea: *there was a seaward movement of water on the bottom.* ■ nearer or nearest to the sea: *the seaward end of the village.*

sea·wa·ter /'sē,wôtər; -,wätər/ ▶*n.* water in or taken from the sea.

sea·way /'sē,wā/ ▶*n.* **1** an inland waterway capable of accommodating seagoing ships. ■ a natural channel connecting two areas of sea. ■ a route across the sea used by ships. **2** a stretch of water in which a sea is running: *with the engine mounted amidship, the boat pitches less in a seaway.*

sea·weed /'sē,wēd/ ▶*n.* large algae growing in the sea or on rocks below the high-water mark.

sea·wor·thy /'sē,wərTHē/ ▶*adj.* (of a vessel) in a good enough condition to sail on the sea. —**sea·wor·thi·ness** *n.*

Pronunciation Key ə *ago,* up; ər *over,* fur; a *hat;* ā *ate;* ä *car;* CH *chin;* e *let;* ē *see;* e(ə)r *air;* i *fit;* ī *by;* i(ə)r *ear;* NG *sing;* ō *go;* ô *law, for;* oi *toy;* o͞o *good;* o͞o *goo;* ou *out;* SH *she;* TH *thin;* TH *then;* (h)w *why;* ZH *vision*

se·ba·ceous /səˈbāsHəs/ ▶ *adj.* technical of or relating to oil or fat. ■ of or relating to a sebaceous gland or its secretion.

seb·or·rhe·a /ˌsebəˈrēə/ (*Brit.* **seb·or·rhoe·a**) ▶ *n. Med.* excessive discharge of sebum from the sebaceous glands. **—seb·or·rhe·ic** /-ˈrē-ik/ *adj.*

se·bum /ˈsēbəm/ ▶ *n.* an oily secretion of the sebaceous glands.

SEC ▶ *abbr.* Securities and Exchange Commission, a U.S. governmental agency that monitors trading in securities and company takeovers.

sec¹ /sek/ ▶ *abbr.* secant.

sec² ▶ *n.* (**a sec**) *inf.* a second; a very short space of time: *stay put, I'll be back in a sec.*

sec³ ▶ *adj.* (of wine) dry.

Sec. ▶ *abbr.* secretary.

sec. ▶ *abbr.* second(s).

se·cant /ˈsēˌkant; -kənt/ ▶ *n.* **1** (abbr.: **sec**) *Math.* the ratio of the hypotenuse to the shorter side adjacent to an acute angle (in a right-angled triangle); the reciprocal of a cosine. **2** *Geom.* a straight line that cuts a curve in two or more parts.

se·cede /siˈsēd/ ▶ *v.* [*intr.*] withdraw formally from membership in a federal union, an alliance, or a political or religious organization: *the kingdom of Belgium seceded from the Netherlands in 1830.* **—se·ced·er** *n.*

se·ces·sion /səˈseSHən/ ▶ *n.* the action of withdrawing formally from membership of a federation or body, esp. a political state: *the republics want secession from the union.* ■ (**the Secession**) *hist.* the withdrawal of eleven Southern states from the Union in 1860, leading to the Civil War. **—se·ces·sion·al** /-SHənl/ *adj.* **—se·ces·sion·ism** /-ˌnizəm/ *n.* **—se·ces·sion·ist** /-ist/ *adj.*

se·clude /siˈklo͞od/ ▶ *v.* [*tr.*] keep (someone) away from other people: *I secluded myself up here for a life of study and meditation.*

se·clu·sion /siˈklo͞oZHən/ ▶ *n.* the state of being private and away from other people: *they enjoyed ten days of peace and seclusion.* **—se·clu·sive** /-siv/ *adj.*

sec·ond¹ /ˈsekənd/ ▶ *ordinal number* **1** constituting number two in a sequence; coming after the first in time or order; 2nd: *he married for a second time.* ■ secondly (used to introduce a second point or reason): *second, they are lightly regulated; and third, they do business with nonresident clients.* ■ alternating; other: *auctions are held every second week.* ■ *Mus.* an interval spanning two consecutive notes in a diatonic scale. ■ the note that is higher by this interval than the tonic of a diatonic scale or root of a chord. ■ the second in a sequence of a vehicle's gears: *he took the corner in second.* ■ *Baseball* second base. ■ (**seconds**) *inf.* a second course or second helping of food at a meal. ■ denoting someone or something regarded as comparable to or reminiscent of a better-known predecessor: *a fear that the conflict would turn into a second Vietnam.* ■ an act or instance of seconding. **2** subordinate or inferior in position, rank, or importance: *it was second only to Copenhagen among Baltic ports.* ■ additional to that already existing, used, or possessed: *a second home.* ■ the second finisher or position in a race or competition: *he finished second.* ■ *Brit.* a place in the second-highest grade in an examination, esp. for a degree: *she got a first in moral sciences and a second in history.* ■ *Mus.* performing a lower or subordinate of two or more parts for the same instrument or voice: *the second violins.* ■ (**seconds**) goods of an inferior quality. **3** an assistant, in particular: ■ an attendant assisting a combatant in a duel or boxing match.

▶ *v.* [*tr.*] formally support or endorse (a nomination or resolution or its proposer) as a necessary preliminary to adoption or further discussion: *Bertonazzi seconded Birmingham's nomination.* ■ express agreement with: *her view is seconded by most Indian leaders today.* **—sec·ond·er** *n.*

▶ □ **in the second place** as a second consideration or point. □ **second to none** the best, worst, fastest, etc.

sec·ond² ▶ *n.* **1** (abbr.: **s**) a sixtieth of a minute of time, which as the SI unit of time is defined in terms of the natural periodicity of the radiation of a cesium-133 atom. (Symbol: ″) ■ *inf.* a very short time: *his eyes met Charlotte's for a second.* **2** (also **arc second** or **second of arc**) a sixtieth of a minute of angular distance. (Symbol: ″)

sec·ond·ar·y /ˈsekənˌderē/ ▶ *adj.* coming after, less important than, or resulting from someone or something else that is primary: *luck plays a role, but it's ultimately secondary to local knowledge.* ■ of or relating to education for children from the age of eleven to sixteen or eighteen: *a secondary school.* ■ relating to or denoting the output side of a device using electromagnetic induction, esp. in a transformer.

▶ *n.* (*pl.* **-ar·ies**) **1** short for: ■ a secondary color. ■ *Ornithol.* a secondary feather. ■ a secondary coil or winding in an electrical transformer. **2** *Football* the players in the defensive backfield; the area these players cover. **—sec·ond·ar·i·ly** /-ˌderəlē/ *adv.* **—sec·ond·ar·i·ness** *n.*

sec·ond·ar·y col·or ▶ *n.* a color resulting from the mixing of two primary colors.

sec·ond class ▶ *n.* a set of people or things grouped together as the second best. ■ the second-best accommodations in an aircraft, train, or ship.

▶ *adj. & adv.* of the second-best quality or in the second division: [as *adj.*] *until 1914 women were thought of as second-class citizens.* ■ of or relating to the second-best accommodations in an aircraft, train, or ship: [as *adj.*] *I want second-class tickets* | [as *adv.*] *they don't fly second-class.* ■ of or relating to a class of mail having lower priority than first-class mail: [as *adj.*] *second-class postage stamps.* ■ (in North America) denoting a class of mail that includes newspapers and periodicals.

sec·ond cous·in ▶ *n.* see COUSIN.

sec·ond-de·gree ▶ *adj.* **1** *Med.* denoting burns that cause blistering but not permanent scars. **2** *Law* denoting a category of a crime, esp. murder, that is less serious than a first-degree crime.

sec·ond-gen·er·a·tion ▶ *adj.* **1** denoting the offspring of parents who have immigrated to a particular country: *she was a second-generation American.* **2** of a more advanced stage of technology than previous models or systems.

sec·ond-guess ▶ *v.* [*tr.*] **1** anticipate or predict (someone's actions or thoughts) by guesswork: *he had to second-guess what the environmental regulations would be in five years' time.* **2** judge or criticize (someone) with hindsight: *the prime minister was willing to second-guess senior ministers in public.* **—sec·ond-guess·er** *n.*

sec·ond·hand /ˈsekən(d)ˈhand/ (also **sec·ond·hand**) ▶ *adj.* **1** (of goods) having had a previous owner; not new: *a secondhand car.* ■ denoting a store or shop where such goods can be bought: *a secondhand bookstore.* **2** (of information or experience) accepted on another's authority and not from original investigation: *secondhand knowledge of her country.*

▶ *adv.* **1** on the basis that something has had a previous owner: *tips on the pitfalls to avoid when buying secondhand.* **2** on the basis of what others have said; indirectly: *I was discounting anything I heard secondhand.*

sec·ond hand ▶ *n.* an extra hand in some watches and clocks that moves around to indicate the seconds.

sec·ond lieu·ten·ant ▶ *n.* a commissioned officer of the lowest rank in the U.S. Army, Air Force, and Marine Corps ranking above chief warrant officer and below first lieutenant.

sec·ond·ly /ˈsekən(d)lē/ ▶ *adv.* in the second place (used to introduce a second point or reason).

sec·ond na·ture ▶ *n.* a characteristic or habit in someone that appears to be instinctive because that person has behaved in a particular way so often: *deceit was becoming second nature to her.*

sec·ond-rate ▶ *adj.* of mediocre or inferior quality: *a second-rate theater.* **—sec·ond-rat·ed·ness** *n.* **—sec·ond-rat·er** *n.*

sec·ond sight ▶ *n.* the supposed ability to perceive future or distant events; clairvoyance. **—sec·ond-sight·ed** *adj.*

sec·ond string ▶ *n.* **1** (in sports) the players who are available to replace or relieve those who start a game: [as *adj.*] *the second-string quarterback.* **2** an alternative resource or course of action in case another one fails. **—sec·ond-string·er** *n.*

sec·ond thoughts (also **sec·ond thought**) ▶ *pl. n.* a change of opinion or resolve reached after considering something again: *on second thought, perhaps he was right.*

sec·ond wind /wind/ ▶ *n.* a person's ability to breathe freely during exercise, after having been out of breath. ■ a new strength or energy to continue something that is an effort: *she gained a second wind during the campaign and turned the opinion polls around.*

se·cre·cy /ˈsēkrəsē/ ▶ *n.* the action of keeping something secret or the state of being kept secret: *the bidding is conducted in secrecy.*

se·cret /ˈsēkrit/ ▶ *adj.* not known or seen or not meant to be known or seen by others: *how did you guess I had a secret plan?* ■ not meant to be known as such by others: *a secret drinker.* ■ (of information or documents) given the security classification above confidential and below top secret.

▶ *n.* something that is kept or meant to be kept unknown or unseen by others: *a state secret.* ■ something that is not properly understood; a mystery: *I'm not trying to explain the secrets of the universe in this book.* ■ a valid but not commonly known or recognized method of achieving or maintaining something: *the secret of a happy marriage is compromise.* ▷ late Middle English: from Old French, from Latin *secretus* (adjective) 'separate, set apart,' from the verb *secernere*, from *se-* 'apart' + *cernere* 'sift.' **—se·cret·ly** *adv.*

▶ □ **be in on the secret** be among the few who know something. □ **in secret** without others knowing. □ **make no secret of something** make something perfectly clear.

se·cret a·gent ▶ *n.* a spy acting for a country.

sec·re·taire /ˌsekriˈte(ə)r/ ▸n. a small writing desk; an escritoire.

sec·re·tar·i·at /ˌsekriˈte(ə)rēət/ ▸n. a permanent administrative office or department, esp. a governmental one. ■ [treated as *sing.* or *pl.*] the staff working in such an office.

sec·re·tar·y /ˈsekriˌterē/ ▸n. (*pl.* **-tar·ies**) a person employed by an individual or in an office to assist with correspondence, keep records, make appointments, and carry out similar tasks. ■ an official of a society or other organization who conducts its correspondence and keeps its records. ■ an official in charge of a government department: [as *title*] *Secretary of the Treasury.* ■ a writing desk with shelves on top of it. —**sec·re·tar·i·al** /-ˈte(ə)rēəl/ *adj.* —**sec·re·tar·y·ship** /-ˌ SHip/ *n.*

sec·re·tar·y bird ▸n. a slender, long-legged African bird of prey (*Sagittarius serpentarius*) that feeds on snakes, having a crest likened to a quill pen stuck behind the ear.

sec·re·tar·y-gen·er·al ▸n. (*pl.* **sec·re·tar·ies-gen·er·al**) a title given to the principal administrator of some organizations, most notably the United Nations.

sec·re·tar·y of state ▸n. **1** (in the U.S.) the head of the State Department, responsible for foreign affairs. **2** (in the UK) the head of a major government department. **3** (in Canada) a government minister responsible for a specific area within a department.

se·cret bal·lot ▸n. a ballot in which votes are cast in secret.

se·crete[1] /siˈkrēt/ ▸v. [*tr.*] (of a cell, gland, or organ) produce and discharge (a substance): *insulin is secreted in response to rising levels of glucose in the blood.* —**se·cre·tor** /-tər/ *n.* —**se·cre·to·ry** /-tərē/ *adj.*

se·crete[2] ▸v. [*tr.*] conceal; hide: *the assets had been secreted in Swiss bank accounts.*

se·cre·tion /siˈkrēSHən/ ▸n. a process by which substances are produced and discharged from a cell, gland, or organ for a particular function in the organism or for excretion. ■ a substance discharged in such a way.

se·cre·tive /ˈsēkritiv/ ▸adj. (of a person or an organization) inclined to conceal feelings and intentions or not to disclose information: *she was very secretive about her past.* ■ (of a person's expression or manner) having an enigmatic or conspiratorial quality: *a secretive smile.* —**se·cre·tive·ly** *adv.* —**se·cre·tive·ness** *n.*

se·cret po·lice ▸n. [treated as *pl.*] a police force working in secret against a government's political opponents.

se·cret serv·ice ▸n. **1** a government department concerned with espionage. **2** (**Secret Service**) (in the U.S.) a branch of the Treasury Department dealing with counterfeiting and providing protection for the president.

se·cret shop·per ▸n. a person employed by a manufacturer or retailer to pose as a shopper in order to evaluate the quality of customer service. Also called MYSTERY SHOPPER.

sect /sekt/ ▸n. a group of people with somewhat different religious beliefs (typically regarded as heretical) from those of a larger group to which they belong. ■ often derog. a group that has separated from an established church; a nonconformist church. ■ a philosophical or political group, esp. one regarded as extreme or dangerous.

sec·tar·i·an /sekˈte(ə)rēən/ ▸adj. denoting or concerning a sect or sects: *among the sectarian offshoots of Ismailism were the Druze of Lebanon.* ■ (of an action) carried out on the grounds of membership of a sect, denomination, or other group. ■ rigidly following the doctrines of a sect or other group: *the sectarian Bolshevism advocated by Moscow.* ▸n. a member of a sect. ■ a person who rigidly follows the doctrines of a sect or other group. —**sec·tar·i·an·ism** /-ˌnizəm/ *n.* —**sec·tar·i·an·ize** /-ˌnīz/ *v.*

sec·tion /ˈsekSHən/ ▸n. **1** any of the more or less distinct parts into which something is or may be divided or from which it is made up: *arrange orange sections on a platter.* ■ a relatively distinct part of a book, newspaper, statute, or other document. ■ a measure of land, equal to one square mile. **2** a distinct group within a larger body of people or things: *the children's section of the library.* ■ a group of players of a family of instruments within an orchestra: *the brass section.* ■ a small class of students who are part of a larger course but are taught separately: *graduate students lead discussion sections for professors' lecture courses.* **3** the shape resulting from cutting a solid along a plane. ■ a representation of the internal structure of something as if it has been cut through vertically or horizontally. ■ *Biol.* a thin slice of plant or animal tissue prepared for microscopic examination. ▸v. [*tr.*] divide into sections: *she began to section the grapefruit.* ■ *Biol.* cut (animal or plant tissue) into thin slices for microscopic examination.

sec·tion·al /ˈsekSHənl/ ▸adj. of or relating to a section or subdivision of a larger whole: *a sectional championship.* ■ of or relating to a section or group within a community: *the chairman of the commission looked on*

sectional interests as a danger to the common good. ■ of or relating to a view of the structure of an object in section: *sectional drawings.* ▸n. a sofa made in sections that can be used separately as chairs. —**sec·tion·al·ism** /-ˌīz/ *v.* —**sec·tion·al·ly** *adv.*

sec·tor /ˈsektər/ ▸n. **1** an area or portion that is distinct from others. ■ a distinct part or branch of a nation's economy or society or of a sphere of activity such as education: *the industrial and commercial sector.* ■ *Mil.* a subdivision of an area for military operations. ■ *Comput.* a subdivision of a track on a magnetic disk. **2** the plane figure enclosed by two radii of a circle or ellipse and the arc between them. —**sec·tor·al** /-rəl/ *adj.*

sec·u·lar /ˈsekyələr/ ▸adj. **1** denoting attitudes, activities, or other things that have no religious or spiritual basis: *secular buildings.* Contrasted with SACRED. **2** *Astron.* of or denoting slow changes in the motion of the sun or planets. **3** *Econ.* (of a fluctuation or trend) occurring or persisting over an indefinitely long period: *there is evidence that the slump is not cyclical but secular.* **4** occurring once every century or similarly long period (used esp. in reference to celebratory games in ancient Rome). —**sec·u·lar·ism** /-ˌrizəm/ *n.* —**sec·u·lar·ist** /-rist/ *n.* —**sec·u·lar·i·ty** /ˌsekyəˈlaritē/ *n.* —**sec·u·lar·i·za·tion** /ˌsekyələrəˈzāSHən/ *n.* —**sec·u·lar·ize** /-ˌrīz/ *v.* —**sec·u·lar·ly** *adv.*

se·cure /siˈkyo͝or/ ▸adj. fixed or fastened so as not to give way, become loose, or be lost: *check to ensure that all nuts and bolts are secure.* ■ not subject to threat; certain to remain or continue safe and unharmed: *they are working to ensure that their market share remains secure against competition.* ■ protected against attack or other criminal activity. ■ (of a place of detention) having provisions against the escape of inmates: *a secure unit for youthful offenders.* ■ feeling safe, stable, and free from fear or anxiety: *everyone needs to have a home and to feel secure and wanted.* ▸v. [*tr.*] fix or attach (something) firmly so that it cannot be moved or lost: *pins secure the handle to the main body.* ■ make (a door or container) hard to open; fasten or lock: *doors are likely to be well secured at night.* ■ protect against threats; make safe. ■ capture (a person or animal): *the suspect is secured and in the back of a patrol car.* ■ succeed in obtaining (something), esp. with difficulty: *the division secured a major contract.* ■ seek to guarantee repayment of (a loan) by having a right to take possession of an asset in the event of nonpayment: *a loan secured on your home.* —**se·cur·a·ble** *adj.* —**se·cure·ly** *adv.* —**se·cure·ment** *n.*

se·cu·ri·ty /siˈkyo͝oritē/ ▸n. (*pl.* **-ties**) **1** the state of being free from danger or threat: *the system is designed to provide maximum security against toxic spills.* ■ the safety of a state or organization against criminal activity such as terrorism, theft, or espionage: *a matter of national security.* ■ procedures followed or measures taken to ensure such safety. ■ the state of feeling safe, stable, and free from fear or anxiety: *this man could give the emotional security she needed.* **2** a private police force that guards a building, campus, park, etc. **3** a thing deposited or pledged as a guarantee of the fulfillment of an undertaking or the repayment of a loan, to be forfeited in case of default. **4** (often **securities**) a certificate attesting credit, the ownership of stocks or bonds, or the right to ownership connected with tradable derivatives.
▸ □ **on security of something** using something as a guarantee.

se·cu·ri·ty blan·ket ▸n. a blanket or other familiar object that is a comfort to someone, typically a child.

Se·cu·ri·ty Coun·cil ▸a permanent body of the United Nations seeking to maintain peace and security. It consists of fifteen members, of which five (China, France, Russia, the UK, and the U.S.) are permanent and have the power of veto. The other members are elected for two-year terms.

se·cu·ri·ty guard ▸n. a person employed to protect something, esp. a building, against intruders or damage.

se·cu·ri·ty patch ▸n. a software or operating-system patch that is intended to correct a vulnerability to hacking or viral infection.

se·dan /siˈdan/ ▸n. **1** an enclosed automobile for four or more people, having two or four doors. **2** (also **sedan chair**) *chiefly hist.* an enclosed chair for conveying one person, carried between horizontal poles by two or more porters.

se·date[1] /siˈdāt/ ▸adj. calm, dignified, and unhurried: *in the old days, business was carried on at a rather more sedate pace.* ■ quiet and rather dull: *sedate suburban domesticity.* —**se·date·ly** *adv.* —**se·date·ness** *n.*

se·date[2] ▸v. [*tr.*] calm (someone) or make them sleep by administering a sedative drug: *she was heavily sedated.*

se·da·tion /siˈdāSHən/ ▸n. the administering of a sedative drug to produce a state of calm or sleep: *he was distraught with grief and under sedation.*

sed·a·tive /'sedətiv/ ▶*adj.* promoting calm or inducing sleep: *the seeds have a sedative effect.*

▶*n.* a drug taken for its calming or sleep-inducing effect.

sed·en·tar·y /'sedn,terē/ ▶*adj.* (of a person) tending to spend much time seated; somewhat inactive. ■ (of work or a way of life) characterized by little physical exercise. ■ (of a position) sitting; seated. ■ *Zool. & Anthropol.* inhabiting the same locality throughout life; not migratory or nomadic. —**sed·en·tar·i·ly** /-,te(ə)rəlē/ *adv.* —**sed·en·tar·i·ness** *n.*

sedge /sej/ ▶*n.* a grasslike plant (*Carex* and other genera, family Cyperaceae) with triangular stems and inconspicuous flowers, widely distributed throughout temperate and cold regions, growing typically in wet ground. ▷Old English *secg*, of Germanic origin, from an Indo-European root shared by Latin *secare* 'to cut.' —**sedg·y** /'sejē/ *adj.*

sed·i·ment /'sedəmənt/ ▶*n.* matter that settles to the bottom of a liquid; dregs. ■ *Geol.* particulate matter that is carried by water or wind and deposited on the surface of the land or the bottom of a body of water, and may in time become consolidated into rock. —**sed·i·men·ta·ry** /,sedə'ment(ə)rē/ *adj.* —**sed·i·men·ta·tion** /,sedəmen'tāsHən/ *n.*

se·di·tion /si'disHən/ ▶*n.* conduct or speech inciting people to rebel against the authority of a state or monarch. —**se·di·tious** *adj.*

se·duce /si'd(y)ōōs/ ▶*v.* [*tr.*] attract (someone) to a belief or into a course of action that is inadvisable or foolhardy: *they should not be seduced into thinking that their success ruled out the possibility of a relapse.* ■ entice into sexual activity. ■ attract powerfully: *the melody seduces the ear with warm string tones.* —**se·duc·er** *n.* —**se·duc·i·ble** *adj.*

se·duc·tion /si'dəksHən/ ▶*n.* the action of seducing someone: *if seduction doesn't work, she can play on his sympathy.* ■ (often **seductions**) a tempting or attractive thing: *the seductions of the mainland.*

se·duc·tive /si'dəktiv/ ▶*adj.* tempting and attractive; enticing: *a seductive voice.* —**se·duc·tive·ly** *adv.* —**se·duc·tive·ness** *n.*

se·duc·tress /si'dəktris/ ▶*n.* a woman who seduces someone, esp. one who entices a man into sexual activity.

sed·u·lous /'sejələs/ ▶*adj.* (of a person or action) showing dedication and diligence: *he watched himself with the most sedulous care.* —**se·du·li·ty** /sə'jōōlitē/ *n.* —**sed·u·lous·ly** *adv.* —**sed·u·lous·ness** *n.*

se·dum /'sēdəm/ ▶*n.* a widely distributed fleshy-leaved plant (genus *Sedum*) of the stonecrop family, with small star-shaped yellow, pink, or white flowers, grown as an ornamental.

see[1] /sē/ ▶*v.* (**sees** /sēz/; **see·ing** /'sē-iNG/; past **saw** /sô/; past part. **seen** /sēn/) [*tr.*] **1** perceive with the eyes; discern visually: *in the distance she could see the blue sea.* ■ be or become aware of something from observation or from a written or other visual source: *I see from your appraisal report that you have asked for training.* ■ be a spectator of (a film, game, or other entertainment); watch: *I went to see King Lear at the Old Vic.* ■ visit (a place) for the first time: *see Alaska in style.* ■ experience or witness (an event or situation): *I shall not live to see it* | [*tr.*] *I can't bear to see you so unhappy.* ■ be the time or setting of (something): *the 1970s saw the beginning of a technological revolution.* ■ observe without being able to affect: *they see their rights being taken away.* ■ (**see something in**) find good or attractive qualities in (someone): *I don't know what I see in you.* **2** discern or deduce mentally after reflection or from information; understand: *I can't see any other way to treat it.* ■ ascertain after inquiring, considering, or discovering an outcome: *I'll go along to the club and see if I can get a game.* ■ [*tr.*] regard in a specified way: *he saw himself as a good teacher.* ■ foresee; view or predict as a possibility: *I can't see him earning any more anywhere else.* ■ used to ascertain or express comprehension, agreement, or continued attention, or to emphasize that an earlier prediction was correct: *it has to be the answer, don't you see?* **3** meet (someone one knows) socially or by chance: *I went to see Caroline.* ■ meet regularly as a boyfriend or girlfriend: *some guy she was seeing was messing her around.* ■ consult (a specialist or professional): *you may need to see a lawyer.* ■ give an interview or consultation to (someone): *the doctor will see you now.* **4** [*tr.*] escort or conduct (someone) to a specified place: *don't bother seeing me out.* ■ [*intr.*] attend to; provide for the wants of: *I'll see to Dad's tea.* ■ [*intr.*] ensure: *Lucy saw to it that everyone got enough to eat and drink* | *see that no harm comes to him.* **5** (in poker) equal the bet of (an opponent).

▶*phrasal v.* □ **see about** attend to; deal with: *he had gone to see about a job he had heard of.* □ **see something of** spend a specified amount of time with (someone) socially: *we saw a lot of the Bakers.* ■ spend some time in (a place): *I want to see something of those countries.* □ **see through** not be deceived by; detect the true nature of: *he can see through her lies and deceptions.*

▶ □ **as far as I can see** to the best of my understanding or belief. □ **as**

I see it in my opinion. □ **have seen better days** have declined from former prosperity or good condition: *this part of South London has seen better days.* □ **see something coming** foresee or be prepared for an event, typically an unpleasant one.

see[2] ▶*n.* the place in which a cathedral church stands, identified as the seat of authority of a bishop or archbishop.

seed /sēd/ ▶*n.* **1** a flowering plant's unit of reproduction, capable of developing into another such plant. ■ a quantity of these: *grass seed* | *you can grow artichokes from seed.* ■ *fig.* the cause or latent beginning of a feeling, process, or condition: *the conversation sowed a tiny seed of doubt in his mind.* ■ *archaic* (chiefly in biblical use) a person's offspring or descendants. ■ a man's semen. ■ (also **seed crystal**) a small crystal introduced into a liquid to act as a nucleus for crystallization. ■ a small container for radioactive material placed in body tissue during radiotherapy. **2** any of a number of stronger competitors in a sports tournament who have been assigned a specified position in an ordered list with the aim of ensuring that they do not play each other in the early rounds: *he knocked the top seed out of the championships.*

▶*v.* **1** [*tr.*] sow (land) with seeds: *the shoreline is seeded with a special grass.* ■ sow (a particular kind of seed) on or in the ground. ■ *fig.* cause (something) to begin to develop or grow: *his severance pay helped seed their new business.* ■ place a crystal or crystalline substance in (something) in order to cause crystallization or condensation (esp. in a cloud to produce rain). **2** [*intr.*] (of a plant) produce or drop seeds: *mulches encourage many plants to seed freely.* ■ (**seed itself**) (of a plant) reproduce itself by means of its own seeds: *feverfew will seed itself readily.* **3** [*tr.*] remove the seeds from (vegetables or fruit): *stem and seed the chilies.* **4** [*tr.*] give (a competitor) the status of seed in a tournament: *Jeff Tarango, seeded five, was defeated by fellow American Todd Witsken.* —**seed·less** *adj.*

▶ □ **go** (or **run**) **to seed** (of a plant) cease flowering as the seeds develop. ■ deteriorate in condition, strength, or efficiency: *Mark knows he has allowed himself to go to seed.*

seed·bed /'sēd,bed/ ▶*n.* a bed of fine soil in which seedlings are germinated.

seed·er /'sēdər/ ▶*n.* **1** a machine for sowing seed mechanically. **2** a plant that produces seeds in a particular way or under particular conditions: [in *comb.*] *a beautiful, hardy annual self-seeder.*

seed·ling /'sēdliNG/ ▶*n.* a young plant, esp. one raised from seed and not from a cutting.

seed mon·ey ▶*n.* money allocated to initiate a project.

seed pearl ▶*n.* a very small pearl.

seed·pod /'sēd,päd/ ▶*n.* see POD[1] (sense 1).

seed·y /'sēdē/ ▶*adj.* (**seed·i·er**, **seed·i·est**) **1** sordid and disreputable: *his seedy affair with a soft-porn starlet.* ■ shabby and squalid: *an increasingly seedy and dilapidated property.* **2** *dated* unwell: *she felt weak and seedy.* —**seed·i·ly** /'sēdl-ē/ *adv.* —**seed·i·ness** *n.*

see·ing /'sē-iNG/ ▶*conj.* because; since: *seeing as Stuart's an old friend, I thought I might help him out.*

▶*n.* the action of seeing someone or something. ■ *Astron.* the quality of observed images as determined by atmospheric conditions.

seek /sēk/ ▶*v.* (past **sought** /sôt/) [*tr.*] attempt to find (something): *they came here to seek shelter from biting winter winds.* ■ attempt or desire to obtain or achieve (something): *the new regime sought his extradition.* ■ ask for (something) from someone. ■ (**seek someone/something out**) search for and find someone or something: *it's his job to seek out new customers.* —**seek·er** *n.* [often in *comb.*] *a pleasure-seeker.*

seem /sēm/ ▶*v.* [*intr.*] give the impression or sensation of being something or having a particular quality: *Dawn seemed annoyed.* ■ used to make a statement or description of one's thoughts, feelings, or actions less assertive or forceful: *I seem to remember giving you very precise instructions.* ■ (**cannot seem to do something**) be unable to do something, despite having tried: *he couldn't seem to remember his lines.* ■ (**it seems** or **it would seem**) used to suggest in a cautious, guarded, or polite way that something is true or a fact: *it would seem that he has been fooling us all.*

seem·ing /'sēmiNG/ ▶*adj.* appearing to be real or true, but not necessarily being so; apparent: *Ellen's seeming indifference to the woman's fate.* ■ [in *comb.*] giving the impression of having a specified quality: *an angry-seeming man.* —**seem·ing·ly** *adv.*

seem·ly /'sēmlē/ ▶*adj.* conforming to accepted notions of propriety or good taste; decorous: *I felt it was not seemly to observe too closely.* —**seem·li·ness** *n.*

seen /sēn/ ▶ past participle of SEE[1].

seep /sēp/ ▶*v.* [*intr.*] (of a liquid) flow or leak slowly through porous material or small holes: *water began to seep through the soles of his boots.*

▶*n.* a place where petroleum or water oozes slowly out of the ground.

seep·age /ˈsēpij/ ▸*n.* the slow escape of a liquid or gas through porous material or small holes. ■ the quantity of liquid or gas that seeps out.

seer /ˈsēər; siˈ(ə)r/ ▸*n.* a person who is supposed to be able, through supernatural insight, to see what the future holds. ■ an expert who provides forecasts of the economic or political future: *our seers have grown gloomier about prospects for growth.*

seer·suck·er /ˈsi(ə)rˌsəkər/ ▸*n.* a printed cotton or synthetic fabric that has a surface consisting of puckered and flat sections, typically in a striped pattern.

see·saw /ˈsēˌsô/ (also **see-saw**) ▸*n.* a long plank balanced in the middle on a fixed support, on each end of which children sit and swing up and down by pushing the ground alternately with their feet. ■ *fig.* a situation characterized by rapid, repeated changes from one state or condition to another: *the emotional seesaw of a first love affair.*
▸*v.* [*intr.*] change rapidly and repeatedly from one position, situation, or condition to another and back again: *the market seesawed as rumors spread of an imminent cabinet reshuffle.* ■ [*tr.*] cause (something) to move back and forth or up and down rapidly and repeatedly.

seethe /sēTH/ ▸*v.* [*intr.*] (of a liquid) bubble up as a result of being boiled: *the brew foamed and seethed.* ■ (of a river or the sea) foam as if it were boiling; be turbulent: *the gray ocean seethed.* ■ [*intr.*] (of a person) be filled with intense but unexpressed anger: *inwardly he was seething at the slight to his authority.* ■ (of a place) be crowded with people or things moving about in a rapid or hectic way: *the entire cellar was **seething with** spiders.*

see-through ▸*adj.* (esp. of clothing) translucent: *this shirt's a bit see-through when it's wet.*

seg·ment ▸*n.* /ˈsegmənt/ **1** each of the parts into which something is or may be divided. ■ a portion of time allocated to a particular broadcast item on radio or television. ■ a separate broadcast item, typically one of a number that make up a particular program. ■ *Phonet.* the smallest distinct part of a spoken utterance, in particular the vowels and consonants as opposed to stress and intonation. ■ *Zool.* each of the series of similar anatomical units of which the body and appendages of some animals are composed, such as the visible rings of an earthworm's body. **2** *Geom.* a part of a figure cut off by a line or plane intersecting it, in particular: ■ the part of a circle enclosed between an arc and a chord. ■ the part of a line included between two points.
▸*v.* /ˈsegˌment; segˈment/ [*tr.*] divide (something) into parts or sections: *the unemployed are segmented into two groups.* ■ [*intr.*] divide into separate parts or sections: *the market is beginning to segment into a number of well-defined categories.* ▷late 16th cent. (as a term in geometry): from Latin *segmentum*, from *secare* 'to cut.' The verb dates from the mid 19th cent. —**seg·men·tal** /segˈmentl/ *adj.* —**seg·men·tar·y** /-ˌterē/ *adj.* —**seg·men·ta·tion** /ˌsegmənˈtāSHən/ *n.*

se·go /ˈsēgō/ (in full **sego lily**) ▸*n.* (*pl.* **-os**) a plant (*Calochortus nuttalli*) of the lily family, with green and white bell-shaped flowers, native to the western U.S.

seg·re·gate /ˈsegriˌgāt/ ▸*v.* [*tr.*] (usu. **be segregated**) set apart from the rest or from each other; isolate or divide: *handicapped people should not be segregated from the rest of society.* ■ separate or divide (people, activities, or institutions) along racial, sexual, or religious lines: *blacks were segregated in churches, schools, and colleges* | [as *adj.*] (**segregated**) *segregated education systems.* ■ [*intr.*] *Genetics* (of pairs of alleles) be separated at meiosis and transmitted independently via separate gametes. —**seg·re·ga·ble** /-gəbəl/ *adj.* —**seg·re·ga·tive** /-ˌgātiv/ *adj.*

seg·re·ga·tion /ˌsegriˈgāSHən/ ▸*n.* the action or state of setting someone or something apart from other people or things or being set apart: *the segregation of pupils with learning difficulties.* ■ the enforced separation of different racial groups in a country, community, or establishment: *an official policy of racial segregation.* ■ *Genetics* the separation of pairs of alleles at meiosis and their independent transmission via separate gametes. —**seg·re·ga·tion·al** /-SHənl/ *adj.* —**seg·re·ga·tion·ist** /-ist/ *adj. & n.*

se·gue /ˈsegwā; ˈsā-/ ▸*v.* (**se·gues, se·gued** /ˈsegwād; ˈsā-/, **se·gue·ing** /ˈsegwā-iNG; ˈsā-/) [*intr.*] (in music and film) move without interruption from one song, melody, or scene to another: *allowing one song to segue into the next.*

sei·cen·to /sāˈCHenˌtō/ ▸*n.* [often as *adj.*] the style of Italian art and literature of the 17th century: *Florentine seicento painting.* —**sei·cen·tist** /-tist/ *n.*

seiche /sāSH/ ▸*n.* a temporary disturbance or oscillation in the water level of a lake or partially enclosed body of water, esp. one caused by changes in atmospheric pressure.

sei·gneur /sānˈyər/ ▸*n.* chiefly *hist.* a feudal lord; the lord of a manor. —**sei·gneu·ri·al** /-ˈyŏŏrēəl/ *adj.*

seine /sān/ ▸*n.* (also **seine net**) a fishing net that hangs vertically in the water with floats at the top and weights at the bottom edge, the ends being drawn together to encircle the fish.
▸*v.* [*tr.*] catch (fish) with a seine: *they seine whitefish and salmon.* —**sein·er** *n.*

seis·mic /ˈsīzmik/ ▸*adj.* of or relating to earthquakes or other vibrations of the earth and its crust. ■ relating to or denoting geological surveying methods involving vibrations produced artificially by explosions. ■ *fig.* of enormous proportions or effect: *there are seismic pressures threatening American society.* —**seis·mi·cal** *adj.* —**seis·mi·cal·ly** /-ik(ə)lē/ *adv.*

seis·mo·graph /ˈsīzməˌgraf/ ▸*n.* an instrument that measures and records details of earthquakes, such as force and duration. —**seis·mo·graph·ic** /ˌsīzməˈgrafik/ *adj.* —**seis·mo·graph·i·cal** /ˌsīzməˈgrafikəl/ *adj.*

seis·mol·o·gy /sīzˈmäləjē/ ▸*n.* the branch of science concerned with earthquakes and related phenomena. —**seis·mo·log·i·cal** /ˌsīzmə-ˈläjikəl/ *adj.* —**seis·mo·log·i·cal·ly** /ˌsīzməˈläjik(ə)lē/ *adv.* —**seis·mol·o·gist** /-jist/ *n.*

seize /sēz/ ▸*v.* **1** [*tr.*] take hold of suddenly and forcibly: *she jumped up and seized his arm* | *she **seized hold of** the door handle.* ■ capture (a place) using force: *army rebels seized an air force base.* ■ assume (power or control) by force: *the current president seized power in a coup.* ■ (of the police or another authority) take possession of (something) by warrant or legal right; confiscate; impound: *police have seized 726 lb of cocaine.* ■ take (an opportunity or initiative) eagerly and decisively: *he seized his chance to attack as Delaney hesitated.* ■ (of a feeling or pain) affect (someone) suddenly or acutely: *he was seized by the most dreadful fear.* ■ strongly appeal to or attract (the imagination or attention): *the story of the king's escape seized the public imagination.* **2** [*intr.*] (of a machine with moving parts or a moving part in a machine) become stuck or jammed: *the engine **seized up** after only three weeks.*
▸*phrasal v.* □ **seize on/upon** take eager advantage of (something); exploit for one's own purposes: *the government has eagerly seized on the evidence to deny any link between deprivation and crime.* —**seiz·a·ble** *adj.* —**seiz·er** *n.*

sei·zure /ˈsēZHər/ ▸*n.* **1** the action of capturing someone or something using force: *the seizure of the embassy.* ■ the action of confiscating or impounding property by warrant of legal right. **2** a sudden attack of illness, esp. a stroke or an epileptic fit: *the patient **had a seizure**.*

sel·dom /ˈseldəm/ ▸*adv.* not often; rarely: *Islay is seldom visited by tourists* | [in comb.] *an old seldom-used church.*

se·lect /səˈlekt/ ▸*v.* [*tr.*] carefully choose as being the best or most suitable: *students must select their own program* | [*intr.*] *you can **select from** a range of quality products.* ■ [*intr.*] (**select for/against**) *Biol.* (in terms of evolution) determine whether (a characteristic or organism) will survive: *a phenotype can be selected against.* ■ use a mouse or keystrokes to mark (something) on a computer screen for a particular operation.
▸*adj.* (of a group of people or things) carefully chosen from a larger number as being the best or most valuable: *he joined his select team of young Intelligence operatives.* ■ (of a place or group of people) only used by or consisting of a wealthy or sophisticated elite; exclusive: *the opera was seen by a small and highly select audience.* ▷mid 16th cent.: from Latin *select-* 'chosen,' from the verb *seligere*, from *se-* 'apart' + *legere* 'choose.' —**se·lect·a·ble** *adj.* —**se·lect·ness** *n.*

se·lec·tion /səˈlekSHən/ ▸*n.* **1** the action or fact of carefully choosing someone or something as being the best or most suitable: *such men decided the selection of candidates.* ■ a number of carefully chosen things. ■ a range of things from which a choice may be made: *the restaurant offers a wide selection of hot and cold dishes.* **2** *Comput.* data highlighted on a computer screen that is a target for various manipulations: *your selection may not contain two different data types.* **3** *Biol.* a process in which environmental or genetic influences determine which types of organism thrive better than others, regarded as a factor in evolution. See also NATURAL SELECTION.

se·lec·tive /səˈlektiv/ ▸*adj.* relating to or involving the selection of the most suitable or best qualified: *the mini-cow is the result of generations of selective breeding.* ■ (of a person) tending to choose carefully: *he is very **selective in** his reading.* ■ (of a process or agent) affecting some things and not others: *modern pesticides are more selective in effect.* —**se·lec·tive·ly** *adv.* —**se·lec·tive·ness** *adj.* —**se·lec·tiv·i·ty** /səlekˈtivitē/ *n.*

se·lec·tive serv·ice ▸*n.* service in the armed forces under conscription.

se·lec·tor /səˈlektər/ ▸*n.* a person or thing that selects something, in particular: ■ a device for selecting a particular gear or other setting of a machine or device.

---

se·le·ni·um /səˈlēnēəm/ ▶*n.* the chemical element of atomic number 34, a gray crystalline nonmetal with semiconducting properties. (Symbol: **Se**) —**sel·e·nide** /ˈseləˌnīd; -nid/ *n.*

self /self/ ▶*n.* (*pl.* **selves** /selvz/) a person's essential being that distinguishes them from others, esp. considered as the object of introspection or reflexive action: *our alienation from our true selves.* ■ a person's particular nature or personality; the qualities that make a person individual or unique: *by the end of the round he was back to his old self.* ■ one's own interests or pleasure: *to love in an unpossessive way implies the total surrender of self.*
▶*pron.* (*pl.* **selves**) oneself, in particular: ■ (**one's self**) used ironically to refer in specified glowing terms to oneself or someone else: *the only side worth supporting is your own sweet self.*
▶*v.* [*tr.*] chiefly *Bot.* self-pollinate; self-fertilize. ■ [usu. as *adj.*] (**selfed**) *Genetics* cause (an animal or plant) to breed with or fertilize one of the same hybrid origin or strain: *progeny were derived from selfed crosses.*

self-a·buse /əˈbyoōs/ ▶*n.* behavior that causes damage or harm to oneself. ■ used euphemistically to refer to masturbation.

self-ad·dressed ▶*adj.* (esp. of an envelope) bearing one's own address: *enclose a self-addressed stamped envelope.*

self-ad·he·sive ▶*adj.* coated with a sticky substance; adhering without requiring moistening.

self-ad·just·ing ▶*adj.* (chiefly of machinery) adjusting itself to meet varying requirements. —**self-ad·just·ment** *n.*

self-ag·gran·dize·ment ▶*n.* the action or process of promoting oneself as being powerful or important. —**self-ag·gran·diz·ing** *adj.*

self-a·nal·y·sis ▶*n.* the analysis of oneself, in particular one's motives and character. —**self-an·a·lyz·ing** *adj.*

self-ap·point·ed ▶*adj.* having assumed a position or role without the endorsement of others: *self-appointed experts.*

self-as·sem·bly ▶*n.* *Biol.* the spontaneous formation of a ribosome, virus, or other body in a medium containing the appropriate components. ■ a manufacturing process in which atoms, molecules, and components arrange themselves into ordered, functioning entities with no active human involvement —**self-as·sem·ble** *v.*

self-as·ser·tion ▶*n.* the confident and forceful expression or promotion of oneself, one's views, or one's desires. —**self-as·sert·ing** *adj.* —**self-as·ser·tive** *adj.* —**self-as·ser·tive·ness** *n.*

self-as·sur·ance ▶*n.* confidence in one's own abilities or character. —**self-as·sured** *adj.* —**self-as·sur·ed·ly** *adv.*

self-a·ware·ness ▶*n.* conscious knowledge of one's own character, feelings, motives, and desires: *the process can be painful but it leads to greater self-awareness.* —**self-a·ware** *adj.*

self-be·tray·al ▶*n.* the intentional or inadvertent revelation of the truth about one's actions or thoughts.

self-cen·tered ▶*adj.* preoccupied with oneself and one's affairs: *he's far too self-centered to care what you do.* —**self-cen·tered·ly** *adv.* —**self-cen·tered·ness** *n.*

self-clean·ing ▶*adj.* (of an object or apparatus) able to clean itself: *a self-cleaning oven.*

self-con·dem·na·tion ▶*n.* the blaming of oneself: *guilt and self-condemnation were riding her hard.* ■ the inadvertent revelation of one's wrongdoing. —**self-con·demned** *adj.* —**self-con·demn·ing** *adj.*

self-con·fessed ▶*adj.* having openly admitted to being a person with certain characteristics: *a self-confessed control freak.* —**self-con·fess·ed·ly** /-ˈfesidlē/ *adv.* —**self-con·fes·sion** *n.* —**self-con·fes·sion·al** *adj.*

self-con·fi·dence ▶*n.* a feeling of trust in one's abilities, qualities, and judgment. —**self-con·fi·dent** *adj.* —**self-con·fi·dent·ly** *adv.*

self-con·scious ▶*adj.* feeling undue awareness of oneself, one's appearance, or one's actions: *I feel a bit self-conscious parking my scruffy old car* | *a self-conscious laugh.* ■ *Philos. & Psychol.* having knowledge of one's own existence, esp. the knowledge of oneself as a conscious being. ■ (esp. of an action or intention) deliberate and with full awareness, esp. affectedly so: *her self-conscious identification with the upper classes.* —**self-con·scious·ly** *adv.* —**self-con·scious·ness** *n.*

self-con·tained ▶*adj.* **1** (of a thing) complete, or having all that is needed, in itself. **2** (of a person) quiet and independent; not depending on or influenced by others. —**self-con·tain·ment** *n.*

self-con·tra·dic·tion ▶*n.* inconsistency between aspects or parts of a whole: *deconstruction is interested in revealing self-contradiction and instability.* —**self-con·tra·dict·ing** *adj.* —**self-con·tra·dic·to·ry** *adj.*

self-con·trol ▶*n.* the ability to control oneself, in particular one's emotions and desires or the expression of them in one's behavior, esp. in difficult situations: *Lucy silently struggled for self-control.* —**self-con·trolled** *adj.*

self-cor·rect·ing ▶*adj.* correcting oneself or itself without external help: *the process is self-correcting.* —**self-cor·rect** *v.* —**self-cor·rec·tion** *n.*

self-de·cep·tion ▶*n.* the action or practice of allowing oneself to believe that a false or unvalidated feeling, idea, or situation is true: *Jane remarked on men's capacity for self-deception.* —**self-de·ceit** *n.* —**self-de·ceiv·ing** *adj.* —**self-de·cep·tive** *adj.*

self-de·feat·ing ▶*adj.* (of an action or policy) unable, because of its inherent qualities, to achieve the end it is designed to bring about.

self-de·fense ▶*n.* the defense of one's person or interests, esp. through the use of physical force, which is permitted in certain cases as an answer to a charge of violent crime: *he claimed self-defense in the attempted murder charge* | [as *adj.*] *self-defense classes.* —**self-de·fen·sive** *adj.*

self-de·ni·al ▶*n.* the denial of one's own interests and needs; self-sacrifice. —**self-de·ny·ing** *adj.*

self-dep·re·cat·ing ▶*adj.* modest about or critical of oneself, esp. humorously so: *self-deprecating jokes.* —**self-dep·re·cat·ing·ly** *adv.* —**self-dep·re·ca·tion** *n.* —**self-dep·re·ca·to·ry** *adj.*

self-de·struct ▶*v.* [*intr.*] (of a thing) destroy itself by exploding or disintegrating automatically, having been preset to do so: *the tape would automatically self-destruct after twenty minutes.* —**self-de·struc·tion** *n.* —**self-de·struc·tive** *adj.* —**self-de·struc·tive·ly** *adv.*

self-de·ter·mi·na·tion ▶*n.* the process by which a country determines its own statehood and forms its own allegiances and government: *the changes cannot be made until the country's right to self-determination is recognized.* ■ the process by which a person controls their own life.

self-dis·ci·pline ▶*n.* the ability to control one's feelings and overcome one's weaknesses; the ability to pursue what one thinks is right despite temptations to abandon it. —**self-dis·ci·plined** *adj.*

self-doubt ▶*n.* lack of confidence in oneself and one's abilities: *his later years were plagued by self-doubt.*

self-ed·u·cat·ed ▶*adj.* educated largely through one's own efforts, rather than by formal instruction: *he was a self-made and almost self-educated businessman.* —**self-ed·u·ca·tion** *n.*

self-ef·fac·ing ▶*adj.* not claiming attention for oneself; retiring and modest: *his demeanor was self-effacing, gracious, and polite.* —**self-ef·face·ment** *n.* —**self-ef·fac·ing·ly** *adv.*

self-em·ployed ▶*adj.* working for oneself as a freelancer or the owner of a business rather than for an employer: *a self-employed builder.* —**self-em·ploy·ment** *n.*

self-es·teem ▶*n.* confidence in one's own worth or abilities; self-respect: *assertiveness training for those with low self-esteem.*

self-ev·i·dent ▶*adj.* not needing to be demonstrated or explained; obvious: *self-evident truths.* —**self-ev·i·dence** *n.* —**self-ev·i·dent·ly** *adv.*

self-ex·am·i·na·tion ▶*n.* the study of one's own behavior and motivations: *a period of considerable self-doubt and self-examination.* ■ the action of examining one's own body for signs of illness.

self-ex·plan·a·to·ry ▶*adj.* easily understood; not needing explanation: *the film's title is fairly self-explanatory.*

self-ex·pres·sion ▶*n.* the expression of one's feelings, thoughts, or ideas, esp. in writing, art, music, or dance. —**self-ex·pres·sive** *adj.*

self-fer·ti·li·za·tion ▶*n.* *Biol.* the fertilization of plants and some invertebrate animals by their own pollen or sperm rather than that of another individual. —**self-fer·ti·lized** *adj.* —**self-fer·ti·liz·ing** *adj.*

self-ful·fill·ing ▶*adj.* (of an opinion or prediction) bound to be proved correct or to come true as a result of behavior caused by its being expressed: *expecting something to be bad can turn out to be a self-fulfilling prophecy.*

self-ful·fill·ment (*Brit.* **self-ful·fil·ment**) ▶*n.* the fulfillment of one's hopes and ambitions: *it is the striving for self-fulfillment which guides our lives.*

self-gen·er·at·ing ▶*adj.* generated by itself, rather than by some external force: *the strident activity of the industrial scene seems to be self-generating.*

self-gov·ern·ment ▶*n.* **1** government of a country by its own people, esp. after having been a colony. **2** another term for SELF-CONTROL. —**self-gov·erned** *adj.* —**self-gov·ern·ing** *adj.*

self-heal (also **self-heal**) ▶*n.* a purple-flowered plant (*Prunella vulgaris*) of the mint family that was formerly widely used for healing wounds.

self-help ▶*n.* the use of one's own efforts and resources to achieve things without relying on others: *what government does is not a substitute for what people can do with encouragement and self-help.* ■ [as *adj.*] designed to assist people in achieving things for themselves: *a self-help group for drug abusers.*

self-im·age ▶*n.* the idea one has of one's abilities, appearance, and personality: *sickness is an affront to one's self-image and dignity.*

self-im·por·tance ▶*n.* an exaggerated sense of one's own value or importance: *he was a big, blustering, opinionated cop, full of self-importance.* —**self-im·por·tant** *adj.* —**self-im·por·tant·ly** *adv.*

self-im·posed ▶*adj.* (of a task or circumstance) imposed on oneself, not by an external force: *he went into self-imposed exile.*

self-im·prove·ment ▶*n.* the improvement of one's knowledge, status, or character by one's own efforts.

self-in·duced ▶*adj.* brought about by oneself: *self-induced vomiting.*

self-in·dul·gent ▶*adj.* characterized by doing or tending to do exactly what one wants, esp. when this involves pleasure or idleness: *a self-indulgent extra hour of sleep.* ■ (of a creative work) lacking economy and control. —**self-in·dul·gence** *n.* —**self-in·dul·gent·ly** *adv.*

self-in·flict·ed ▶*adj.* (of a wound or other harm) inflicted on oneself.

self-in·ter·est ▶*n.* one's personal interest or advantage, esp. when pursued without regard for others. —**self-in·ter·est·ed** *adj.*

self·ish /'selfiSH/ ▶*adj.* (of a person, action, or motive) lacking consideration for others; concerned chiefly with one's own personal profit or pleasure: *I joined them for selfish reasons.* —**self·ish·ly** *adv.* —**self·ish·ness** *n.*

self-jus·ti·fi·ca·tion ▶*n.* the justification or excusing of oneself or one's actions. —**self-jus·tif·i·ca·to·ry** *adj.* —**self-jus·ti·fy·ing** *adj.*

self-knowl·edge ▶*n.* understanding of oneself or one's own motives or character.

self·less /'selfləs/ ▶*adj.* concerned more with the needs and wishes of others than with one's own; unselfish: *an act of selfless devotion.* —**self·less·ly** *adv.* —**self·less·ness** *n.*

self-love ▶*n.* regard for one's own well-being and happiness (chiefly considered as a desirable rather than narcissistic characteristic). —**self-lov·ing** *adj.*

self-made ▶*adj.* having become successful or rich by one's own efforts: *a self-made millionaire.* ■ made by oneself: *his self-made fortune.*

self-med·i·cate ▶*v.* [*intr.*] choose and take medicines oneself, rather than by prescription or on expert advice. ■ take addictive or habituating drugs to relieve stress or other conditions. —**self-med·i·ca·tion** *n.*

self-mo·ti·vat·ed ▶*adj.* motivated to do or achieve something because of one's own enthusiasm or interest, without needing pressure from others: *she's a very independent, self-motivated individual.* —**self-mo·ti·vat·ing** *adj.* —**self-mo·ti·va·tion** *n.*

self-o·pin·ion·at·ed ▶*adj.* having an arrogantly high regard for oneself or one's own opinions: *a pompous, self-opinionated bully.* —**self-o·pin·ion** *n.*

self-per·pet·u·at·ing ▶*adj.* perpetuating itself or oneself without external agency or intervention: *the self-perpetuating power of the bureaucracy.* —**self-per·pet·u·a·tion** *n.*

self-pit·y ▶*n.* excessive, self-absorbed unhappiness over one's own troubles. —**self-pit·y·ing** *adj.*

self-pol·li·na·tion ▶*n.* *Bot.* the pollination of a flower by pollen from the same flower or from another flower on the same plant. —**self-pol·li·nat·ed** *adj.* —**self-pol·li·nat·ing** *adj.* —**self-pol·li·na·tor** *n.*

self-por·trait ▶*n.* a portrait of an artist produced or created by that artist. —**self-por·trai·ture** *n.*

self-pos·sessed ▶*adj.* calm, confident, and in control of one's feelings; composed. —**self-pos·ses·sion** *n.*

self-pres·er·va·tion ▶*n.* the protection of oneself from harm or death, esp. regarded as a basic instinct in human beings and animals.

self-pro·claimed ▶*adj.* described as or proclaimed to be such by oneself, without endorsement by others: *exercise books written by self-proclaimed experts.*

self-pro·pelled ▶*adj.* moving or able to move without external propulsion or agency: *a self-propelled weapon.* —**self-pro·pel·ling** *adj.*

self-re·al·i·za·tion ▶*n.* fulfillment of one's own potential.

self-re·gard ▶*n.* regard or consideration for oneself; self-respect. ■ conceit; vanity. —**self-re·gard·ing** *adj.*

self-reg·u·lat·ing ▶*adj.* regulating itself without intervention from external bodies: *advertising is governed by a self-regulating system.* —**self-reg·u·la·tion** *n.* —**self-reg·u·la·to·ry** *adj.*

self-re·li·ance ▶*n.* reliance on one's own powers and resources rather than those of others. —**self-re·li·ant** *adj.* —**self-re·li·ant·ly** *adv.*

self-re·spect ▶*n.* pride and confidence in oneself; a feeling that one is behaving with honor and dignity. —**self-re·spect·ing** *n.*

self-re·straint ▶*n.* restraint imposed by oneself on one's own actions; self-control. —**self-re·strained** *adj.*

self-right·eous ▶*adj.* having or characterized by a certainty, esp. an unfounded one, that one is totally correct or morally superior: *self-righteous indignation and complacency.* —**self-right·eous·ly** *adv.* —**self-right·eous·ness** *n.*

self-right·ing ▶*adj.* (of a boat) designed to right itself when capsized.

self-ris·ing flour ▶*n.* flour that has a leavening agent already added.

self-rule ▶*n.* another term for SELF-GOVERNMENT (sense 1).

self-sac·ri·fice ▶*n.* the giving up of one's own interests or wishes in order to help others or to advance a cause. —**self-sac·ri·fi·cial** *adj.* —**self-sac·ri·fic·ing** *adj.*

self·same /'self,sām/ ▶*adj.* (usu. **the selfsame**) exactly the same: *he was standing in the selfsame spot you're filling now.*

self-sat·is·fied ▶*adj.* excessively and unwarrantedly satisfied with oneself or one's achievements; smugly complacent. —**self-sat·is·fac·tion** *n.*

self-seal·ing ▶*adj.* sealing itself without the usual process or procedure, in particular: ■ (of a tire, fuel tank, etc.) able to seal small punctures automatically. ■ (of an envelope) self-adhesive.

self-se·lect ▶*v.* **1** choose for oneself: [*tr.*] *participants were asked to self-select their titles, which were divided into executive and non-executive.* **2** [*intr.*] determine one's own status with regard to membership in a group: *the crowd self-selects because this isn't a club for the passing trade.*

self-se·lec·tion ▶*n.* the action of putting oneself forward for something. —**self-se·lect·ing** *adj.*

self-serv·ice ▶*adj.* denoting a store, restaurant, or service station where customers select goods for themselves or service their car for themselves and pay a cashier: *a self-service cafeteria.*
▶*n.* the system whereby customers select goods for themselves or service their car for themselves and pay a cashier: *providing quick self-service.*

self-serv·ing ▶*adj.* having concern for one's own welfare and interests before those of others: *public accountability is replaced by self-serving propaganda.*

self-start·er ▶*n.* a person who is sufficiently motivated or ambitious to start a new career or business or to pursue further education without the help of others: *he was the self-starter who worked his way up from messenger boy to account executive.* —**self-start·ing** *adj.*

self-styled ▶*adj.* using a description or title that one has given oneself: *self-styled experts* | *the self-styled president of Bougainville.*

self-suf·fi·cient ▶*adj.* needing no outside help in satisfying one's basic needs, esp. with regard to the production of food: *I don't think Botswana, due to the climate, could ever be self-sufficient in food.* ■ emotionally and intellectually independent: *their son was a little bit of a loner and very self-sufficient.* —**self-suf·fi·cien·cy** *n.* —**self-suf·fi·cient·ly** *adv.*

self-sup·port·ing ▶*adj.* **1** having the resources to be able to survive without outside assistance. **2** staying up or upright without being supported by something else: *arches were originally self-supporting structures.* —**self-sup·port** *n.*

self-sus·tain·ing ▶*adj.* able to continue in a healthy state without outside assistance: *his puny farms were years from being self-sustaining.* —**self-sus·tained** *adj.*

self-taught ▶*adj.* having acquired knowledge or skill on one's own initiative rather than through formal instruction or training: *a self-taught graphic artist.*

self-willed ▶*adj.* obstinately doing what one wants in spite of the wishes or orders of others: *the child may be very obstinate and self-willed.* —**self-will** *n.*

self-wind·ing /'wīndiNG/ ▶*adj.* (chiefly of a watch) wound by some automatic means, such as an electric motor or the movement of the wearer, rather than by hand.

sell /sel/ ▶*v.* (*past* and *past part.* **sold** /sōld/) [*tr.*] **1** give or hand over (something) in exchange for money: *they had sold the car.* ■ have a stock of (something) available for sale: *the store sells hi-fis, TVs, videos, and other electrical goods.* ■ [*intr.*] (of a thing) be purchased: *this magazine of yours won't sell.* ■ (of a publication or recording) attain sales of (a specified number of copies): *the album sold 6 million copies in the U.S.* ■ [*intr.*] (**sell for/at**) be available for sale at (a specified price): *these antiques sell for about $375.* ■ [*intr.*] (**sell out**) sell all of one's stock of something: *they had nearly sold out of the initial run of 75,000 copies.* ■ [*intr.*] (**sell out**) be all sold: *it was clear that the performances would not sell out.* ■ (**sell oneself**) have sex in exchange for money: *if she was going to sell herself then it would be as well not to come too cheap.* ■ (**sell someone out**) betray someone for one's own financial or material benefit: *But if they're not careful, these "friends" will sell them out instead.* ■ [*intr.*] (**sell out**) abandon one's principles for reasons of expedience: *the prime minister has come under fire for selling out*

---

to the U.S. **2** persuade someone of the merits of: *he sold the idea of making a film about Tchaikovsky.* ■ be the reason for (something) being bought: *what sells CDs to most people is convenience.* ■ cause (someone) to become enthusiastic about: [as *adj.*] (**sold**) *I'm just not **sold** on the idea.*
▸ *n. inf.* **1** an act of selling or attempting to sell something: *the excitement of scientific achievement is too subtle a sell to stir the public.* **2** a disappointment, typically one arising from being deceived as to the merits of something: *actually, Hawaii's a bit of a sell.* —**sell·a·ble** *adj.* —**sell·er** *n.*
▸ □ **sell someone/something short** fail to recognize or state the true value of: *don't sell yourself short—you've got what it takes.* □ **sell one's soul (to the devil)** do or be willing to do anything, no matter how wrong it is, in order to achieve one's objective: *universities are selling their souls for commercial success.*

sell-by date ▸ *n.* a date marked on a perishable product indicating the recommended time by which it should be sold: *milk past its sell-by date.*

sell·ing point ▸ *n.* a feature of a product for sale that makes it attractive to customers.

sell·out /ˈselˌout/ ▸ *n.* **1** the selling of an entire stock of something, esp. tickets for an entertainment or sports event. ■ an event for which all tickets are sold: *the game is sure to be a sellout.* **2** a sale of a business or company. ■ a betrayal of one's principles for reasons of expedience: *the sellout of socialist economic policy.*

selt·zer /ˈseltsər/ (also **seltzer water**) ▸ *n.* soda water.

sel·vage /ˈselvij/ ▸ *n.* an edge produced on woven fabric during manufacture that prevents it from unraveling.

selves /selvz/ ▸ plural form of SELF.

sem·a·code /ˈseməˌkōd/ ▸ *n.* an optical pattern that encodes a URL for recognition by cellular-phone cameras, enabling the user to access a Web page by scanning the code with the telephone.

se·man·tic /səˈmantik/ ▸ *adj.* relating to meaning in language or logic. —**se·man·ti·cal·ly** /-ik(ə)lē/ *adv.*

se·man·tics /səˈmantiks/ ▸ *pl. n.* [usu. treated as *sing.*] the branch of linguistics and logic concerned with meaning. **Formal semantics** studies the logical aspects of meaning, such as sense, reference, implication, and logical form; **lexical semantics** studies word meanings and word relations; and **conceptual semantics** studies the cognitive structure of meaning. ■ the meaning of a word, phrase, sentence, or text: *such quibbling over semantics may seem petty stuff.* —**se·man·ti·cian** /ˌsemanˈtishən/ *n.* —**se·man·ti·cist** *n.*

sem·a·phore /ˈseməˌfôr/ ▸ *n.* **1** a system of sending messages by holding the arms or two flags or poles in certain positions according to an alphabetic code. ■ a signal sent by semaphore. **2** an apparatus for signaling in this way, consisting of an upright with movable parts. —**sem·a·phor·ic** /ˌseməˈfôrik/ *adj.* —**sem·a·phor·i·cal·ly** /ˌseməˈfôrik(ə)lē/ *adv.*

sem·blance /ˈsembləns/ ▸ *n.* the outward appearance or apparent form of something, esp. when the reality is different: *she tried to force her thoughts back into some semblance of order.*

se·men /ˈsēmən/ ▸ *n.* the male reproductive fluid, containing spermatozoa in suspension.

se·mes·ter /səˈmestər/ ▸ *n.* a half-year term in a school or college, typically lasting fifteen to eighteen weeks. ▷early 19th cent.: from German *Semester*, from Latin *semestris* 'six-monthly,' from *sex* 'six' + *mensis* 'month.'

sem·i /ˈsemī/ ▸ *n.* (*pl.* **sem·is**) *inf.* **1** a tractor-trailer: *she pulled into the path of a semi.* **2** a semifinal: *they defeated them in the semi.*

semi- ▸ *prefix* **1** half: *semicircular.* ■ occurring or appearing twice in a specified period: *semiannual.* **2** partly; in some degree or particular: *semiconscious.* ■ almost: *semidarkness.*

sem·i·an·nu·al /ˌsemēˈanyooəl; ˌsemˌī-/ ▸ *adj.* occurring twice a year; half-yearly: *their semiannual meetings.* ■ (of a plant) living for half a year only. —**sem·i·an·nu·al·ly** *adv.*

sem·i·au·to·mat·ic /ˌsemēˌôtəˈmatik; ˌsemˌī-/ ▸ *adj.* partially automatic: *a semiautomatic climate-control system.* ■ (of a firearm) having a mechanism for self-loading but not for continuous firing: *semiautomatic rifles.*
▸ *n.* a semiautomatic firearm.

sem·i·cir·cle /ˈsemēˌsərkəl; ˈsemˌī-/ ▸ *n.* a half of a circle or of its circumference. ■ a set of objects arranged in a semicircle: *chairs were in a semicircle around the hearth.* —**sem·i·cir·cu·lar** *adj.*

sem·i·co·lon /ˈsemiˌkōlən; ˈsemˌī-/ ▸ *n.* a punctuation mark (;) indicating a pause, typically between two main clauses, that is more pronounced than that indicated by a comma.

sem·i·con·duct·ing /ˈsemēkənˌdəktiNG; ˌsemˌī-/ ▸ *adj.* (of a material or device) having the properties of a semiconductor.

sem·i·con·duc·tor /ˈseměkənˌdəktər; ˌsemˌī-/ ▸ *n.* a solid substance that

has a conductivity between that of an insulator and that of most metals, either due to the addition of an impurity or because of temperature effects. Devices made of semiconductors, notably silicon, are essential components of most electronic circuits.

sem·i·con·scious /ˌseměˈkänsHəs; ˌsemˌī-/ ▸ *adj.* (of a person) only partially conscious: *he dragged out the semiconscious pilot.*

sem·i·de·tached /ˌsemědiˈtacHt; ˌsemˌī-/ ▸ *adj.* (of a house) joined to another house on one side only by a common wall.

sem·i·di·am·e·ter /ˌsemědīˈamitər; ˌsemˌī-/ ▸ *n. Astron.* & *Geom.* half of a diameter; radius.

sem·i·fi·nal /ˌseměˈfīnl; ˌsemˌī-/ ▸ *n.* a game or round immediately preceding the final, the winner of which goes on to the final. —**sem·i·fi·nal·ist** *n.*

sem·i·for·mal /ˌseměˈfôrməl; ˌsemˌī-/ ▸ *adj.* combining formal and informal elements: *in the semiformal atmosphere irritations can be aired.* ■ used to describe clothing that is neither formal nor casual and that is typically worn for a dance, wedding, or other event: *the casino has a semiformal dress code (men must wear a tie and jacket).*
▸ *n.* an event at which semiformal attire is expected: *it had organized its own spring semiformal at a nearby hotel.*

sem·i·lu·nar /ˌseměˈloonər; ˌsemˌī-/ ▸ *adj. chiefly Anat.* shaped like a half-moon or crescent.

sem·i·nal /ˈsemənl/ ▸ *adj.* **1** (of a work, event, moment, or figure) strongly influencing later developments: *his seminal work on chaos theory.* **2** of, relating to, or denoting semen. —**sem·i·nal·ly** *adv.*

sem·i·nar /ˈseməˌnär/ ▸ *n.* a conference or other meeting for discussion or training. ■ a class at a college or university in which a topic is discussed by a teacher and a small group of students.

sem·i·nar·y /ˈseməˌnerē/ ▸ *n.* (*pl.* **-nar·ies**) a college that prepares students to be priests, ministers, or rabbis. ■ *archaic* a private school or college, esp. one for young women. —**sem·i·nar·i·an** /ˌsemə'ne(ə)rēən/ *n.* —**sem·i·na·rist** /-nərist/ *n.*

Sem·i·nole /ˈseməˌnōl/ ▸ *n.* (*pl.* same or **-noles**) **1** a member of an American Indian people of the Creek confederacy and their descendants, noted for resistance in the 19th century to encroachment on their land in Georgia and Florida. Many were resettled in Oklahoma. **2** either of the Muskogean languages, usually Creek, spoken by the Seminole.
▸ *adj.* of or relating to the Seminole or their language.

sem·i·of·fi·cial /ˌseměəˈfisHəl; ˌsemˌī-/ ▸ *adj.* having some, but not full, official authority or recognition: *a semiofficial visit.* —**sem·i·of·fi·cial·ly** *adv.*

se·mi·ot·ics /ˌsēmēˈätiks; ˌsēmē-; ˌsemˌī-/ ▸ *pl. n.* [treated as *sing.*] the study of signs and symbols and their use or interpretation. —**se·mi·ot·ic** *adj.* —**se·mi·ot·i·cal·ly** /-ik(ə)lē/ *adv.* —**se·mi·o·ti·cian** /ˌsemēəˈtisHən; ˌsēmēə-/ *n.*

sem·i·per·me·a·ble /ˌseměˈpərmēəbəl; ˌsemˌī-/ ▸ *adj.* (of a material or membrane) allowing certain substances to pass through it but not others, esp. allowing the passage of a solvent but not of certain solutes.

sem·i·pre·cious /ˌseměˈpresHəs; ˌsemˌī-/ ▸ *adj.* denoting minerals that can be used as gems but are considered to be less valuable than precious stones.

sem·i·pro /ˌseměˈprō; ˌsemī-/ & *adj.* /ˈsemēˌprō; ˈsemī-/ (*pl.* **-pros**) *inf.* short for SEMIPROFESSIONAL.

sem·i·pro·fes·sion·al /ˌseměprəˈfesHənl; ˌsemˌī-/ ▸ *adj.* receiving payment for an activity but not relying entirely on it for a living: *a semiprofessional musician.* ■ involving or suitable for people engaged in an activity on such a basis: *training at the semiprofessional level.*
▸ *n.* a person who is engaged in an activity on such a basis.

sem·i·skilled /ˌseměˈskild; ˌsemˌī-/ ▸ *adj.* (of work or a worker) having or needing some, but not extensive, training: *assembly lines of semiskilled workers.*

sem·i·sol·id /ˌseměˈsälid; ˌsemˌī-/ ▸ *adj.* highly viscous; slightly thicker than semifluid.

sem·i·sweet /ˌseměˈswēt; ˌsemˌī-/ ▸ *adj.* (of food) slightly sweetened, but less so than normal: *semisweet chocolates.* ■ (of wine) neither dry nor sweet; slightly sweeter than medium dry.

Sem·ite /ˈsemīt/ ▸ *n.* a member of any of the peoples who speak or spoke a Semitic language, including in particular the Jews and Arabs.

Se·mit·ic /səˈmitik/ ▸ *adj.* **1** relating to or denoting a family of languages that includes Hebrew, Arabic, and Aramaic and certain ancient languages such as Phoenician and Akkadian, constituting the main subgroup of the Afro-Asiatic family. **2** of or relating to the peoples who speak these languages, esp. Hebrew and Arabic.

sem·i·tone /ˈseměˌtōn; ˈsemˌī-/ ▸ *n. Mus.* the smallest interval used in classical Western music, equal to a twelfth of an octave or half a tone; a half step.

sem·i·trail·er /'semē,trālər; 'sem,ī-/ ▶ *n.* a trailer having wheels at the back but supported at the front by a towing vehicle.

sem·i·vow·el /'semē,vouəl; 'sem,ī-/ ▶ *n.* a speech sound intermediate between a vowel and a consonant, e.g., *w* or *y*.

sem·i·week·ly /,semē'wēklē; ,sem,ī-/ ▶ *adj.* occurring twice a week.

sem·o·li·na /,semə'lēnə/ ▶ *n.* the hard grains left after the milling of flour, used in puddings and in pasta.

sem·pi·ter·nal /,sempə'tərnl/ ▶ *adj.* eternal and unchanging; everlasting: *his writings have the sempiternal youth of poetry.* —**sem·pi·ter·nal·ly** *adv.* —**sem·pi·ter·ni·ty** /-'tərnitē/ *n.*

sem·pli·ce /'sempli,CHā/ ▶ *adv. Mus.* (as a direction) in a simple style of performance.

sem·pre /'sem,prā/ ▶ *adv. Mus.* (in directions) throughout; always: *sempre forte.*

Sen. ▶ *abbr.* ■ Senate. ■ Senator. ■ Senior.

sen·ate /'senit/ ▶ *n.* any of various legislative or governing bodies, in particular: ■ the smaller upper assembly in the U.S. Congress, most U.S. states, France, and other countries. ■ the state council of the ancient Roman republic and empire, which shared legislative power with the popular assemblies, administration with the magistrates, and judicial power with the knights. ▷Middle English: from Old French *senat,* from Latin *senatus,* from *senex* 'old man.'

sen·a·tor /'senitər/ ▶ *n.* a member of a senate. —**sen·a·to·ri·al** /,senə'tôrēəl/ *adj.* —**sen·a·tor·ship** /-,SHip/ *n.*

send /send/ ▶ *v.* (past **sent** /sent/) **1** [*tr.*] cause to go or be taken to a particular destination; arrange for the delivery of, esp. by mail: *we sent a reminder letter but received no reply.* ■ order or instruct to go to a particular destination or in a particular direction: *Clemons sent me to Bangkok for R&R.* ■ [*intr.*] send a message or letter: *he sent to invite her to supper.* ■ [*tr.*] cause to move sharply or quickly; propel: *the volcano sent clouds of ash up four miles into the air.* **2** [*tr.*] *inf.* affect with powerful emotion; put into ecstasy: *it's the spectacle and music that send us, not the words.*
▶ *phrasal v.* □ **send for** order or instruct (someone) to come to one; summon: *if you don't go I shall send for the police.* ■ order by mail: *send for our mail order catalog.* □ **send something in** submit material to be considered for a competition or possible publication: *don't forget to send in your entries for our summer competition.* □ **send someone off** instruct someone to go; arrange for someone's departure: *she sent him off to a lecturing engagement.* □ **send something off** dispatch something by mail: *please take a moment or two to send off a check to a good cause.* □ **send out for something** order delivery of something: *we sent out for pizza.* □ **send something out 1** produce or give out something; emit something: *radar signals were sent out in powerful pulses.* **2** dispatch items to a number of people; distribute something widely: *the company sent out written information about the stock.* □ **send someone up** sentence someone to imprisonment: *he was sent up for arson.* □ **send someone/something up** *inf.* give an exaggerated imitation of someone or something in order to ridicule them: *the humorist who sent up sacred cows like school spirit.* —**send·a·ble** *adj.* —**send·er** *n.*

send-off ▶ *n.* a celebratory demonstration of goodwill at a person's departure: *I got an affectionate send-off from my colleagues.*

send-up /'send,əp/ ▶ *n. inf.* an act of imitating someone or something in order to ridicule them; a parody: *a delicious sendup of a speech given by a trendy academic.*

Sen·e·ca /'senəkə/ ▶ *n.* (*pl.* same or **-cas**) **1** a member of an American Indian people that was one of the Five Nations. **2** the Iroquoian language of this people.
▶ *adj.* of or relating to this people or their language.

se·nesce /sə'nes/ ▶ *v.* [*intr.*] *Biol.* (of a living organism) deteriorate with age. —**se·nes·cence** /-'nesəns/ *n.*

se·nile /'sē,nīl; 'sen-/ ▶ *adj.* (of a person) having or showing the weaknesses or diseases of old age, esp. a loss of mental faculties: *she couldn't cope with her senile husband.* ■ (of a condition) characteristic of or caused by old age: *senile decay.* —**se·nil·i·ty** /si'nilitē/ *n.*

se·nile de·men·tia ▶ *n.* severe mental deterioration in old age, characterized by loss of memory and control of bodily functions.

sen·ior /'sēnyər/ ▶ *adj.* **1** of a more advanced age: *he is 20 years senior to Leonard.* ■ of or for students in the final year of college or high school. ■ relating to or denoting competitors of above a certain age or of the highest status in a particular sport. ■ (often **Senior**) (in names) denoting the elder of two who have the same name in a family, esp. a father as distinct from his son: *Henry James senior.* **2** holding a high and authoritative position: *he is a senior Finance Ministry official.*

▶ *n.* a person who is a specified number of years older than someone else: *she was only two years his senior.* ■ an elderly person, esp. one who is retired and living on a pension. ■ a student in the final year of college or high school. ■ a competitor of above a certain age or of the highest status in a particular sport: *at fourteen you move up to the seniors.* —**sen·ior·i·ty** /sēn'yôritē; -'yär-/ *n.*

sen·ior cit·i·zen ▶ *n.* an elderly person, esp. one who is retired and living on a pension.

sen·ior mo·ment ▶ *n. inf.* a temporary mental lapse (humorously attributed to the gradual loss of one's mental faculties as one grows older).

sen·na /'senə/ ▶ *n.* the cassia tree. ■ a laxative prepared from the dried pods of this tree.

se·ñor /sān'yôr; sen-/ ▶ *n.* (*pl.* **se·ñores** /sān'yôrāz; sen'yôres/ or **se·ñors**) a title or form of address used of or to a Spanish-speaking man, corresponding to *Mr.* or *sir*: *he is certain his information is correct, señor.*

se·ño·ra /sān'yôrə; sen-/ ▶ *n.* a title or form of address used of or to a Spanish-speaking woman, corresponding to *Mrs.* or *madam*: *Señora Dolores.*

se·ño·ri·ta /,sānyə'rētə; ,sen-/ ▶ *n.* a title or form of address used of or to a Spanish-speaking unmarried woman, corresponding to *Miss*: *a beautiful señorita.*

sen·sate /'sen,sāt/ ▶ *adj. poetic/lit.* able to perceive with the senses; sensing: *the infant stretches, sensate, wakening.* ■ perceived by the senses: *you are immersed in an illusory, yet sensate, world.*

sen·sa·tion /sen'sāSHən/ ▶ *n.* **1** a physical feeling or perception resulting from something that happens to or comes into contact with the body: *a burning sensation in the middle of the chest.* ■ the capacity to have such feelings or perceptions: *they had lost sensation in one or both forearms.* ■ an inexplicable awareness or impression: *she had the eerie sensation that she was being watched.* **2** a widespread reaction of interest and excitement: *his arrest for poisoning caused a sensation.* ■ a person, object, or event that arouses such interest and excitement: *Catherine's line of bookmarks is the latest sensation among local readers.*

sen·sa·tion·al /sen'sāSHənl/ ▶ *adj.* (of an event, a person, or a piece of information) causing great public interest and excitement: *a sensational trial.* ■ (of an account or a publication) presenting information in a way that is intended to provoke public interest and excitement, at the expense of accuracy: *sensational reports.* ■ *inf.* very good indeed; very impressive or attractive: *you look sensational.* —**sen·sa·tion·al·ly** *adv.*

sen·sa·tion·al·ism /sen'sāSHənl,izəm/ ▶ *n.* (esp. in journalism) the use of exciting or shocking stories or language at the expense of accuracy, in order to provoke public interest or excitement: *media sensationalism.* —**sen·sa·tion·al·ist** *n.* & *adj.* —**sen·sa·tion·al·is·tic** /sen,sāSHənl'istik/ *adj.* —**sen·sa·tion·al·ize** *v.*

sense /sens/ ▶ *n.* **1** a faculty by which the body perceives an external stimulus; one of the faculties of sight, smell, hearing, taste, and touch: *the bear has a keen sense of smell that enables it to hunt at dusk.* **2** a feeling that something is the case: *she had the sense of being a political outsider.* ■ an awareness or feeling that one is in a specified state: *you can improve your general health and sense of well-being.* ■ (**sense of**) a keen intuitive awareness of or sensitivity to the presence or importance of something: *she had a fine sense of comic timing.* **3** a sane and realistic attitude to situations and problems: *he earned respect by the good sense he showed at meetings.* ■ a reasonable or comprehensible rationale: *I can't see the sense in leaving all the work to you.* **4** a way in which an expression or a situation can be interpreted; a meaning: *it is not clear which sense of the word "characters" is intended in this passage.* **5** chiefly *Math. Physics* a property, e.g., direction of motion, distinguishing a pair of objects, quantities, effects, etc., that differ only in that each is the reverse of the other. ■ [as *adj.*] *Genetics* relating to or denoting a coding sequence of nucleotides, complementary to an antisense sequence.
▶ *v.* [*tr.*] perceive by a sense or senses: *with the first frost, they could sense a change in the days.* ■ be aware of: *she could sense her father's anger rising.* ■ be aware that something is the case without being able to define exactly how one knows: *he could sense that he wasn't liked.* ■ (of a machine or similar device) detect: *an optical fiber senses a current flowing in a conductor.*
▶ □ **bring someone to their** (or **come to one's**) **senses** restore someone to (or regain) consciousness. ■ cause someone to (or start to) think and behave reasonably after a period of folly or irrationality. □ **in a** (or **one**) **sense** used to indicate a particular interpretation of a statement

---

Pronunciation Key ə *ago,* up; ər *over, fur;* a *hat;* ā *ate;* ä *car;* CH *chin;* e *let;* ē *see;* e(ə)r *air;* i *fit;* ī *by;* i(ə)r *ear;* NG *sing;* ō *go;* ô *law, for;* oi *toy;* o͝o *good;* o͞o *goo;* ou *out;* SH *she;* TH *thin;* <u>TH</u> *then;* (h)w *why;* ZH *vision*

or situation: *in a sense, behavior cannot develop independently of the environment.* □ **in one's senses** fully aware and in control of one's thoughts and words: *would any man in his senses invent so absurd a story?* □ **make sense** be intelligible, justifiable, or practicable. □ **make sense of** find meaning or coherence in: *she must try to make sense of what was going on.* □ **out of one's senses** in or into a state of insanity. □ **take leave of one's senses** (in hyperbolic use) go insane.

sense·less /ˈsensləs/ ▸*adj.* **1** (of a person) unconscious: *the attack left a policeman beaten senseless.* ▪ incapable of sensation: *she knocked the glass from the girl's senseless fingers.* **2** (esp. of violent or wasteful action) without discernible meaning or purpose: *in Vietnam, I saw the senseless waste of human beings.* ▪ lacking common sense; wildly foolish: *it was as senseless as crossing Death Valley on foot.* —**sense·less·ly** *adv.* —**sense·less·ness** *n.*

sen·si·bil·i·ty /ˌsensəˈbilitē/ ▸*n.* (*pl.* -**ties**) the ability to appreciate and respond to complex emotional or aesthetic influences; sensitivity: *the study of literature leads to a growth of intelligence and sensibility.* ▪ (**sensibilities**) a person's delicate sensitivity that makes them readily offended or shocked: *the photos shocked people's sensibilities.*

sen·si·ble /ˈsensəbəl/ ▸*adj.* (of a statement or course of action) chosen in accordance with wisdom or prudence; likely to be of benefit: *I cannot believe that it is sensible to spend so much | a sensible diet.* ▪ (of a person) possessing or displaying prudence: *he was a sensible and capable boy.* ▪ (of an object) practical and functional rather than decorative: *Mom always made me have sensible shoes.* —**sen·si·ble·ness** *n.* —**sen·si·bly** /-blē/ *adv.*

sen·si·tive /ˈsensitiv/ ▸*adj.* **1** quick to detect or respond to slight changes, signals, or influences: *the new method of protein detection was more sensitive than earlier ones.* ▪ easily damaged, injured, or distressed by slight changes: *the committee called for improved protection of wildlife in environmentally sensitive areas.* ▪ (of photographic materials) prepared so as to respond rapidly to the action of light. ▪ (of a market) unstable and liable to quick changes of price because of outside influences. **2** (of a person or a person's behavior) having or displaying a quick and delicate appreciation of others' feelings: *I pay tribute to the Minister for his sensitive handling of the bill.* ▪ easily offended or upset: *I suppose I shouldn't be so sensitive.* **3** kept secret or with restrictions on disclosure to avoid endangering security: *he was suspected of passing sensitive information to other countries.*

▸*n.* a person who is believed to respond to occult influences. —**sen·si·tive·ly** *adv.* —**sen·si·tive·ness** *n.*

sen·si·tive plant ▸*n.* a tropical American plant (*Mimosa pudica*) of the pea family, whose leaflets fold together and leaves bend down when touched.

sen·si·tiv·i·ty /ˌsensiˈtivitē/ ▸*n.* (*pl.* -**ties**) the quality or condition of being sensitive: *a total lack of common decency and sensitivity | he has a sensitivity to cow's milk.* ▪ (**sensitivities**) a person's feelings which might be easily offended or hurt; sensibilities: *the only rules that matter are practical ones that respect local sensitivities.*

sen·si·tize /ˈsensiˌtīz/ ▸*v.* [*tr.*] cause (someone or something) to respond to certain stimuli; make sensitive: *the introductory section aims to sensitize students to the methodology of the course.* ▪ make (photographic film) sensitive to light: *the kit sensitizes any 35 mm film in hours.* ▪ (often **be sensitized to**) make (an organism) abnormally sensitive to a foreign substance: *the workers must then be immunologically sensitized to the enzyme.* —**sen·si·ti·za·tion** /ˌsensitiˈzāSHən/ *n.* —**sen·si·tiz·er** *n.*

sen·sor /ˈsensər/ ▸*n.* a device that detects or measures a physical property and records, indicates, or otherwise responds to it.

sen·so·ry /ˈsensərē/ ▸*adj.* of or relating to sensation or the physical senses; transmitted or perceived by the senses: *sensory input.* —**sen·so·ri·ly** /-rəlē/ *adv.*

sen·su·al /ˈsensHo͞oəl/ ▸*adj.* of or arousing gratification of the senses and physical, esp. sexual, pleasure: *the production of the ballet is sensual and passionate.* —**sen·su·al·ism** /-ˌlizəm/ *n.* —**sen·su·al·ist** /-ist/ *n.* —**sen·su·al·ize** /-ˌlīz/ *v.* —**sen·su·al·ly** *adv.*

sen·su·al·i·ty /ˌsensHo͞oˈalitē/ ▸*n.* the enjoyment, expression, or pursuit of physical, esp. sexual, pleasure: *he ate the grapes with surprising sensuality.* ▪ the condition of being pleasing or fulfilling to the senses: *life can dazzle with its sensuality, its color.*

sen·su·ous /ˈsensHo͞oəs/ ▸*adj.* **1** relating to or affecting the senses rather than the intellect: *the work showed a deliberate disregard of the more sensuous and immediately appealing aspects of painting.* **2** attractive or gratifying physically, esp. sexually: *her voice was rather deep but very sensuous.* —**sen·su·ous·ly** *adv.* —**sen·su·ous·ness** *n.*

sent /sent/ ▸ past and past participle of SEND[1].

sen·tence /ˈsentns/ ▸*n.* **1** a set of words that is complete in itself,

typically containing a subject and predicate, conveying a statement, question, exclamation, or command, and consisting of a main clause and sometimes one or more subordinate clauses. **2** the punishment assigned to a defendant found guilty by a court: *her husband is serving a three-year sentence for fraud.*

▸*v.* [*tr.*] declare the punishment decided for (an offender): *ten army officers were sentenced to death.* ▷Middle English (in the senses 'way of thinking, opinion,' 'court's declaration of punishment,' and 'gist (of a piece of writing)'): via Old French from Latin *sententia* 'opinion,' from *sentire* 'feel, be of the opinion.'

▸ □ **under sentence of** having been condemned to: *he was under sentence of death.*

sen·ten·tious /senˈtenCHəs/ ▸*adj.* given to moralizing in a pompous or affected manner: *he tried to encourage his men with sententious rhetoric.* —**sen·ten·tious·ly** *adv.* —**sen·ten·tious·ness** *n.*

sen·tient /ˈsenCH(ē)ənt/ ▸*adj.* able to perceive or feel things: *she had been instructed from birth in the equality of all sentient life forms.* —**sen·tience** *n.* —**sen·tient·ly** *adv.*

sen·ti·ment /ˈsen(t)əmənt/ ▸*n.* **1** a view of or attitude toward a situation or event; an opinion: *I agree with your sentiments regarding the road bridge.* ▪ general feeling or opinion: *the council sought steps to control the rise of racist sentiment.* **2** a feeling or emotion: *an intense sentiment of horror.* ▪ exaggerated and self-indulgent feelings of tenderness, sadness, or nostalgia: *many of the appeals rely on treacly sentiment.*

sen·ti·men·tal /ˌsen(tə)ˈmen(t)l/ ▸*adj.* of or prompted by feelings of tenderness, sadness, or nostalgia: *she felt a sentimental attachment to the place creep over her.* ▪ (of a work of literature, music, or art) dealing with feelings of tenderness, sadness, or nostalgia in an exaggerated and self-indulgent way: *a sentimental ballad.* ▪ (of a person) excessively prone to feelings of tenderness, sadness, or nostalgia: *I'm a sentimental old fool.* —**sen·ti·men·tal·ism** *n.* —**sen·ti·men·tal·i·ty** /ˌsentəmenˈtalitē/ *n.* —**sen·ti·men·tal·ize** *v.* —**sen·ti·men·tal·ly** *adv.*

▸ □ **sentimental value** the value of something to someone because of personal or emotional associations rather than material worth.

sen·ti·nel /ˈsentn-əl/ ▸*n.* a soldier or guard whose job is to stand and keep watch. ▪ *fig.* something that appears to be standing guard or keeping watch. ▪ *Med.* a thing that acts as an indicator of the presence of disease.

▸*v.* (**-neled, -nel·ing**; *chiefly Brit.* **-nelled, -nel·ling**) [*tr.*] station a soldier or guard by (a place) to keep watch: *an area sentineled with police.*

sen·try /ˈsentrē/ ▸*n.* (*pl.* -**tries**) a soldier stationed to keep guard or to control access to a place.

sen·try box ▸*n.* a structure providing shelter for a standing sentry.

se·pal /ˈsēpəl/ ▸*n.* *Bot.* each of the parts of the calyx of a flower, enclosing the petals and typically green and leaflike.

sep·a·ra·ble /ˈsep(ə)rəbəl/ ▸*adj.* able to be separated or treated separately: *body and soul are not separable.* ▪ *Gram.* (of a German prefix) separated from the base verb when inflected. ▪ *Gram.* (of a German verb) consisting of a prefix and a base verb that are separated when inflected, e.g., *einführen.* ▪ *Gram.* (of an English phrasal verb) allowing the insertion of the direct object between the base verb and the particle, e.g., *look it over* as opposed to *go over it.* —**sep·a·ra·bil·i·ty** /ˌsep(ə)rəˈbilitē/ *n.* —**sep·a·ra·ble·ness** *n.* —**sep·a·ra·bly** /-blē/ *adv.*

sep·a·rate ▸*adj.* /ˈsep(ə)rit/ forming or viewed as a unit apart or by itself: *this raises two separate issues.* ▪ not joined or touching physically: *hostels with separate quarters for men and women.* ▪ different; distinct: *melt the white and dark chocolate in separate bowls.*

▸*v.* /ˈsepəˌrāt/ **1** [*tr.*] cause to move or be apart: *police were trying to separate two rioting mobs.* ▪ form a distinction or boundary between (people, places, or things): *only a footpath separated their garden from the shore.* ▪ [*intr.*] become detached or disconnected: *the second stage of the rocket failed to separate.* ▪ [*intr.*] leave another person's company: *they separated at the corner, agreeing to meet within two hours.* ▪ [*intr.*] stop living together as a couple: *after her parents separated, she was brought up by her mother* | [as *adj.*] (**separated**) *her parents are separated.* ▪ (often **be separated**) discharge or dismiss (someone) from service or employment: *this year one million veterans will be separated from the service.* **2** divide or cause to divide into constituent or distinct elements: [*intr.*] *the milk had separated into curds and whey* | [*tr.*] *separate the eggs and beat the yolks.* ▪ [*tr.*] extract or remove for use or rejection: *the skins are separated from the juice before fermentation.* ▪ [*tr.*] distinguish between; consider individually: *we cannot separate his thinking from his activity.* ▪ (of a factor or quality) distinguish (someone or something) from others: *his position separates him from those who might share his interests.*

▸*n.* (**separates**) things forming units by themselves, in particular: ▪ individual items of clothing, such as skirts, jackets, or pants, suitable for wearing in different combinations. ■ the self-contained, freestanding components of a sound-reproduction system. **—sep·a·rate·ly** adv. **—sep·a·rate·ness** n.

▸ □ **separate but equal** hist. racially segregated but ostensibly ensuring equal opportunities to all races.

sep·a·ra·tion /ˌsepəˈrāsʜən/ ▸n. **1** the action or state of moving or being moved apart: *the damage that might arise from the separation of parents and children.* ■ the state in which a husband and wife remain married but live apart: *legal grounds for divorce or separation.* **2** the division of something into constituent or distinct elements: *prose structured into short sentences with meaningful separation into paragraphs.* ■ the process of distinguishing between two or more things: *religion involved the separation of the sacred and the profane* | *the constitution imposed a clear separation between church and state.* ■ the process of sorting and then extracting or removing a specified substance for use or rejection.

▸ □ **separation of powers** an act of vesting the legislative, executive, and judicial powers of government in separate bodies.

sep·a·ra·tist /ˈsep(ə)rətist/ ▸n. a person who supports the separation of a particular group of people from a larger body on the basis of ethnicity, religion, or gender: *religious separatists.*

▸adj. of or relating to such separation or those supporting it: *a separatist rebellion.* **—sep·a·rat·ism** n.

sep·a·ra·tor /ˈsepəˌrātər/ ▸n. a machine or device that separates something into its constituent or distinct elements: *a magnetic separator.* ■ something that keeps two or more things apart: *use commas as separators between addresses.*

Se·phar·di /səˈfärdē/ ▸n. (pl. **-phar·dim** /-ˈfärdim; -ˌfärˈdēm/) a Jew of Spanish or Portuguese descent. They retain their own distinctive customs and rituals, preserving Babylonian Jewish traditions rather than the Palestinian ones of the Ashkenazim. Compare with Ashkenazi. ■ any Jew of the Middle East or North Africa. **—Se·phar·dic** /-dik/ adj.

se·pi·a /ˈsēpēə/ ▸n. a reddish-brown color associated particularly with monochrome photographs of the 19th and early 20th centuries. ■ a brown pigment prepared from a black fluid secreted by cuttlefish, used in monochrome drawing and in watercolors. ■ a drawing done with this pigment. ■ a blackish fluid secreted by a cuttlefish as a defensive screen.

▸adj. of a reddish-brown color: *old sepia photographs.*

sep·sis /ˈsepsis/ ▸n. Med. the presence in tissues of harmful bacteria and their toxins, typically through infection of a wound. ▷late 19th cent.: modern Latin, from Greek *sēpsis*, from *sēpein* 'make rotten.'

Sept. ▸abbr. ■ September. ■ Septuagint.

sep·ta /ˈseptə/ ▸ plural form of SEPTUM.

sept·cen·ten·ary /ˌsep(t)senˈtenərē; -ˈsentnˌerē/ ▸n. (pl. **-ar·ies**) the seven-hundredth anniversary of a significant event.

▸adj. of or relating to a seven-hundredth anniversary.

Sep·tem·ber /sepˈtembər/ ▸n. the ninth month of the year, in the northern hemisphere usually considered the first month of autumn. | [as adj.] *a warm September evening.*

sep·ten·ni·al /sepˈtenēəl/ ▸adj. recurring every seven years. ■ lasting for or relating to a period of seven years.

sep·tet /sepˈtet/ (also **sep·tette**) ▸n. a group of seven people playing music or singing together. ■ a composition for such a group.

sep·tic /ˈseptik/ ▸adj. **1** (chiefly of a wound or a part of the body) infected with bacteria. **2** denoting a drainage system incorporating a septic tank.

▸n. a drainage system incorporating a septic tank. **—sep·ti·cal·ly** /-ik(ə)lē/ adv. **—sep·tic·i·ty** /sepˈtisitē/ n.

sep·ti·ce·mi·a /ˌseptiˈsēmēə/ (Brit. **sep·ti·cae·mi·a**) ▸n. blood poisoning, esp. that caused by bacteria or their toxins. **—sep·ti·ce·mic** /-mik/ adj.

sep·tic tank ▸n. a tank, typically underground, in which sewage is collected and allowed to decompose through bacterial activity before draining by means of a leaching field.

sep·tu·a·ge·nar·i·an /ˌsepcʜōōəjəˈne(ə)rēən/ ▸n. a person who is from 70 to 79 years old.

Sep·tu·a·gint /ˈsepcʜōōəˌjint/ ▸n. a Greek version of the Hebrew Bible (or Old Testament), including the Apocrypha, made for Greek-speaking Jews in Egypt in the 3rd and 2nd centuries BC and adopted by the early Christian Churches.

sep·tum /ˈseptəm/ ▸n. (pl. **-ta** /-tə/) chiefly Anat. Biol. a partition separating two chambers, such as that between the nostrils or the chambers of the heart.

sep·tup·let /sepˈtəplit; sepˈt(y)ōō-/ ▸n. **1** (usu. **septuplets**) each of seven children born at one birth. **2** Mus. a group of seven notes to be performed in the time of four or six.

sep·ul·cher /ˈsepəlkər/ (Brit. **sep·ul·chre**) ▸n. a small room or monument, cut in rock or built of stone, in which a dead person is laid or buried.

se·pul·chral /səˈpəlkrəl/ ▸adj. of or relating to a tomb or interment: *sepulchral monuments.* ■ gloomy; dismal: *a speech delivered in sepulchral tones.* **—se·pul·chral·ly** adv.

se·quel /ˈsēkwəl/ ▸n. a published, broadcast, or recorded work that continues the story or develops the theme of an earlier one. ■ something that takes place after or as a result of an earlier event: *this encouragement to grow potatoes had a disastrous sequel some fifty years later.*

se·que·la /siˈkwelə/ ▸n. (pl. **-que·lae** /-ˈkwelē; -ˈkwelī/) (usu. **sequelae**) Med. a condition that is the consequence of a previous disease or injury: *the long-term sequelae of infection.*

se·quence /ˈsēkwəns/ ▸n. **1** a particular order in which related events, movements, or things follow each other: *the content of the program should follow a logical sequence.* ■ Mus. a repetition of a phrase or melody at a higher or lower pitch. ■ Biochem. the order in which amino acid or nucleotide residues are arranged in a protein, DNA, etc. **2** a set of related events, movements, or things that follow each other in a particular order: *a grueling sequence of exercises* | *a sonnet sequence.* ■ a set of three or more playing cards of the same suit next to each other in value, for example 10, 9, 8. ■ Math. an infinite ordered series of numerical quantities. **3** a part of a film dealing with one particular event or topic: *the famous underwater sequence.*

▸v. [tr.] **1** arrange in a particular order: *trainee librarians decide how a set of misfiled cards could be sequenced.* ■ Biochem. ascertain the sequence of amino acid or nucleotide residues in (a protein, DNA, etc.). **2** play or record (music) with a sequencer.

▸ □ **in sequence** in a given order.

se·quenc·er /ˈsēkwənsər/ ▸n. a programmable electronic device for storing sequences of musical notes, chords, or rhythms and transmitting them when required to an electronic musical instrument.

se·quen·tial /siˈkwencʜəl/ ▸adj. forming or following in a logical order or sequence: *a series of sequential steps.* ■ chiefly Comput. performed or used in sequence: *sequential processing of data files.* **—se·quen·ti·al·i·ty** /siˌkwencʜēˈalitē/ n. **—se·quen·tial·ly** adv.

se·ques·ter /səˈkwestər/ ▸v. [tr.] **1** isolate or hide away (someone or something): *Tiberius was sequestered on an island.* ■ isolate (a jury) from outside influences during a trial: *the jurors had been sequestered since Monday.* ■ Chem. [intr.] form a chelate or other stable compound with (an ion, atom, or molecule) so that it is no longer available for reactions. **2** take legal possession of (assets) until a debt has been paid or other claims have been met: *the power of courts to sequester the assets of unions.* ■ take forcible possession of (something); confiscate: *compensation for Jewish property sequestered by the Libyan regime.* ■ legally place (the property of a bankrupt) in the hands of a trustee for division among the creditors: [as adj.] (**sequestered**) *a trustee in a sequestered estate.* **—se·ques·tra·ble** /siˈkwestrəbəl/ adj. **—se·ques·tra·tor** /ˈsēkwiˌstrātər; ˈsek-; siˈkwesˌtrātər/ n.

se·ques·trate /ˈsēkwiˌstrāt; ˈsek-; səˈkwesˌtrāt/ ▸v. another term for SEQUESTER. **—se·ques·tra·tion** n.

se·quin /ˈsēkwin/ ▸n. **1** a small, shiny disk sewn as one of many onto clothing for decoration. **2** hist. a Venetian gold coin. **—se·quined** (also **se·quinned**) adj.

se·quoi·a /səˈk(w)oi-ə/ ▸n. a redwood tree, esp. the California redwood.

se·ra /ˈsi(ə)rə/ ▸ plural form of SERUM.

se·ragl·io /səˈrälyō/ ▸n. (pl. **-ios**) **1** the women's apartments (harem) in a Muslim palace. ■ another term for HAREM (sense 2). **2** (**the Seraglio**) hist. a Turkish palace, esp. the Sultan's court and government offices at Constantinople.

se·ra·pe /səˈräpē/ (also **sa·ra·pe**) ▸n. a shawl or blanket worn as a cloak in Latin America.

ser·aph /ˈserəf/ ▸n. (pl. **ser·a·phim** /ˈserəˌfim/ or **ser·aphs**) an angelic being, regarded in traditional Christian theology as belonging to the highest order of the ninefold celestial hierarchy, associated with light, ardor, and purity.

se·raph·ic /səˈrafik/ ▸adj. characteristic of or resembling a seraph or seraphim: *a seraphic smile.* **—se·raph·i·cal·ly** /-ik(ə)lē/ adv.

Serb /sərb/ ▸n. a native or national of Serbia. ■ a person of Serbian descent.

▸adj. of or relating to Serbia, the Serbs, or their language.

Pronunciation Key ə *ago,* up; ər *over,* fur; a *hat*; ā *ate*; ä *car*; cʜ *chin*; e *let*; ē *see*; e(ə) *air*; i *fit*; ī *by*; i(ə)r *ear*; NG *sing*; ō *go*; ô *law, for*; oi *toy*; ōō *good*; o͞o *goo*; ou *out*; sʜ *she*; тн *thin*; ᴛ͟ʜ *then*; (h)w *why*; zʜ *vision*

Ser·bi·an /ˈsərbēən/ ▶n. **1** the dialect of Serbo-Croat used by the Serbs. See **Serbo-Croat**. **2** another term for **Serb**.
▶adj. of or relating to Serbia, the Serbs, or their language.

Ser·bo-Cro·at /ˈsərbō ˈkrōˌat; ˈkrōt/ (also **Ser·bo-Cro·a·tian** /krōˈāshən/)
▶n. the South Slavic language spoken in Serbia, Croatia, and elsewhere in the former Yugoslavia. Serbo-Croat is generally classed as one language, but comprises two closely similar forms: Serbian, written in the Cyrillic alphabet, and Croat, written in the Roman alphabet.
▶adj. of or relating to this language.

sere¹ /si(ə)r/ (also **sear**) ▶adj. dry; arid: *a harsh life on the sere granite ledges of those remote offshore islands*. ▪ (esp. of plants) withered.

sere² ▶n. Ecol. a natural succession of plant (or animal) communities, esp. a full series from uncolonized habitat to the appropriate climax vegetation.

ser·e·nade /ˌserəˈnād/ ▶n. a piece of music sung or played in the open air, typically by a man at night under the window of his lover.
▶v. [tr.] entertain (someone) with a serenade: *a strolling guitarist serenades the diners*. —**ser·e·nad·er** n.

ser·en·dip·i·ty /ˌserənˈdipitē/ ▶n. the occurrence and development of events by chance in a happy or beneficial way: *a fortunate stroke of serendipity*. —**ser·en·dip·i·tous** /-ˈdipitəs/ adj. —**ser·en·dip·i·tous·ly** adv.

se·rene /səˈrēn/ ▶adj. **1** calm, peaceful, and untroubled; tranquil: *their serene faces*. **2** (**Serene**) (in a title) used as a term of respect for members of some European royal families: *His Serene Highness*.
▶n. (usu. **the serene**) archaic an expanse of clear sky or calm sea: *not a cloud obscured the deep serene*. —**se·rene·ly** adv.

se·ren·i·ty /səˈrenitē/ ▶n. (pl. **-ties**) the state of being calm, peaceful, and untroubled: *an oasis of serenity in the bustling city*.

serf /sərf/ ▶n. an agricultural laborer bound under the feudal system to work on his lord's estate. —**serf·age** /-fij/ n. —**serf·dom** /-dəm/ n.

serge /sərj/ ▶n. a durable twilled woolen or worsted fabric.
▶v. [tr.] overcast (the edge of a piece of material) to prevent fraying.

ser·geant /ˈsärjənt/ ▶n. a noncommissioned officer in the armed forces, in particular (in the U.S. Army or Marine Corps) an NCO ranking above corporal and below staff sergeant, or (in the U.S. Air Force) an NCO ranking above airman and below staff sergeant. ▪ a police officer ranking below a lieutenant. —**ser·gean·cy** /-jənsē/ n. (pl. **-cies**)

ser·geant ma·jor ▶n. **1** a noncommissioned officer in the US Army or Marine Corps of the highest rank, above master sergeant and below warrant officer. **2** a boldly striped fish (*Abudefduf saxatilis*, family Pomacentridae) that lives in warm seas, esp. on coral reefs.

se·ri·al /ˈsi(ə)rēəl/ ▶adj. **1** consisting of, forming part of, or taking place in a series: *a serial publication*. ▪ Mus. using transformations of a fixed series of notes. ▪ Comput. (of a device) involving the transfer of data as a single sequence of bits. ▪ Comput. (of a processor) running only a single task, as opposed to multitasking. ▪ Linguistics (of verbs) used in sequence to form a construction, as in *they wanted, needed, longed for peace*. **2** (of a criminal) repeatedly committing the same offense and typically following a characteristic, predictable behavior pattern: *a suspected serial rapist*. ▪ denoting an action or behavior pattern that is committed or followed repeatedly: *serial killings*.
▶n. a story or play appearing in regular installments on television or radio or in a magazine or newspaper: *a new three-part drama serial*. ▪ (usu. **serials**) (in a library) a periodical. —**se·ri·al·i·ty** /ˌsi(ə)rēˈalitē/ n. —**se·ri·al·ly** adv.

se·ri·al·ism /ˈsi(ə)rēəˌlizəm/ ▶n. Mus. a compositional technique in which a fixed series of notes, esp. the twelve notes of the chromatic scale, are used to generate the harmonic and melodic basis of a piece and are subject to change only in specific ways. —**se·ri·al·ist** adj. & n.

se·ri·al·ize /ˈsi(ə)rēəˌlīz/ ▶v. [tr.] **1** publish or broadcast (a story or play) in regular installments: *sections of the book were serialized in the New Yorker*. **2** arrange (something) in a series. —**se·ri·al·i·za·tion** /ˌsi(ə)rēələˈzāshən/ n.

se·ri·al num·ber ▶n. a number showing the position of an item in a series, esp. one printed on paper currency or on a manufactured article for the purposes of identification.

ser·i·cul·ture /ˈseriˌkəlchər/ ▶n. the production of silk and the rearing of silkworms for this purpose. —**ser·i·cul·tur·al** /ˌseriˈkəlchərəl/ adj. —**ser·i·cul·tur·ist** /ˌseriˈkəlchərist/ n.

se·ries /ˈsi(ə)rēz/ ▶n. (pl. **same**) a number of things, events, or people of a similar kind or related nature coming one after another: *the explosion was the latest in a series of accidents*. ▪ a set of related television or radio programs, esp. of a specified kind: *a new drama series*. ▪ a set of books, maps, periodicals, or other documents published in a common format or under a common title. ▪ a set of games played between two teams: *a playoff series against Portland*. See also **World Series**. ▪ a line of

products, esp. vehicles or machines, sharing features of design or assembly and marketed with a separate number from other lines: [as adj.] *a series III SWB Land Rover*. ▪ a set of stamps, banknotes, or coins issued at a particular time or having a common design or theme. ▪ [as adj.] denoting electrical circuits or components arranged so that the current passes through each successively. The opposite of **parallel**. ▪ Geol. a range of strata corresponding to an epoch in time, being a subdivision of a system and itself subdivided into stages: *the Pliocene series*. ▪ Chem. a set of elements with common properties or of compounds related in composition or structure: *the metals of the lanthanide series*. ▪ Math. a set of quantities constituting a progression or having the several values determined by a common relation. ▪ Mus. another term for **tone row**. ▷early 17th cent.: from Latin, literally 'row, chain,' from *serere* 'join, connect.'
▶ □ **in series** (of a set of batteries or electrical components) arranged so that the current passes through each successively.

ser·if /ˈserəf/ ▶n. a slight projection finishing off a stroke of a letter, as in T contrasted with T. —**ser·iffed** adj.

ser·i·graph /ˈseriˌgraf/ ▶n. a printed design produced by means of a silkscreen.

se·ri·o·com·ic /ˌsi(ə)rēōˈkämik/ ▶adj. combining the serious and the comic; serious in intention but jocular in manner or vice versa: *a telling seriocomic critique*. —**se·ri·o·com·i·cal·ly** adv.

se·ri·ous /ˈsi(ə)rēəs/ ▶adj. **1** (of a person) solemn or thoughtful in character or manner: *her face grew serious*. ▪ (of a subject, state, or activity) demanding careful consideration or application: *marriage is a serious matter*. ▪ (of thought or discussion) careful or profound: *we give serious consideration to safety recommendations*. ▪ (of music, literature, or other art forms) requiring deep reflection and inviting a considered response: *he bridges the gap between serious and popular music*. **2** acting or speaking sincerely and in earnest, rather than in a joking or half-hearted manner: *suddenly he wasn't teasing any more—he was deadly serious*. **3** significant or worrying because of possible danger or risk; not slight or negligible: *she escaped serious injury* | *Haydn was Mozart's only serious rival*. **4** inf. substantial in terms of size, number, or quality: *he suddenly had serious money to spend*. —**se·ri·ous·ness** n.

se·ri·ous·ly /ˈsi(ə)rēəslē/ ▶adv. **1** in a solemn or considered manner: *the doctor looked seriously at him*. **2** with earnest intent; not lightly or superficially: *I seriously considered canceling my subscription*. ▪ really or sincerely (used esp. to indicate a response of surprise or shock): *do you seriously believe that I would jeopardize my career by such acts?* ▪ used to add sincerity to a statement that is to follow, esp. after a facetious exchange of remarks: *seriously though, shortcuts rarely work*. ▪ inf. used to indicate surprise at what someone has said and to check whether they really meant it: *"I'm dying to know." "Seriously?" "Of course."* **3** to a degree that is significant or worrying because of possible danger or risk: *the amount of fat you eat can seriously affect your health*. **4** inf. very: *he was seriously rich*.
▶ □ **take someone/something seriously** regard someone or something as important and worthy of attention.

ser·mon /ˈsərmən/ ▶n. a talk on a religious or moral subject, esp. one given during a church service and based on a passage from the Bible. ▪ a printed transcript of such a talk: *a volume of sermons*. ▪ inf. a long or tedious piece of admonition or reproof; a lecture. —**ser·mon·ic** /sərˈmänik/ adj.

ser·mon·ette /ˌsərməˈnet/ ▶n. a short sermon.

ser·mon·ize /ˈsərməˌnīz/ ▶v. [intr.] compose or deliver a sermon. ▪ deliver an opinionated and dogmatic talk to someone: *they confidently sermonize on the fixed nature of identity* | [tr.] *I just don't like being sermonized*. —**ser·mon·iz·er** n.

se·rol·o·gy /siˈräləjē/ ▶n. the scientific study or diagnostic examination of blood serum, esp. with regard to the response of the immune system to pathogens or introduced substances. —**se·ro·log·ic** /ˌsi(ə)rəˈläjik/ adj. —**se·ro·log·i·cal** adj. —**se·ro·log·i·cal·ly** adv. —**se·rol·o·gist** /-jist/ n.

ser·o·tine /ˈserətin; -ˌtīn/ ▶n. a medium-sized insectivorous bat (family Vespertilionidae), esp. a chiefly Eurasian bat (genus *Eptesicus*) and an African bat (genus *Pipistrellus*).

se·ro·to·nin /ˌserəˈtōnən; ˌsir-/ ▶n. Biochem. a compound present in blood platelets and serum that constricts the blood vessels and acts as a neurotransmitter.

se·rous /ˈsi(ə)rəs/ ▶adj. Physiol. of, resembling, or producing serum. —**se·ros·i·ty** /siˈräsitē/ n.

ser·pent /ˈsərpənt/ ▶n. chiefly poetic/lit. a large snake. ▪ (**the Serpent**) a biblical name for Satan (see Gen. 3, Rev. 20). ▪ a dragon or other mythical snakelike reptile. ▪ fig. a sly or treacherous person, esp. one who exploits a position of trust in order to betray it.

ser·pen·tine /'sərpən,tēn; -,tīn/ ▶ *adj.* of or like a serpent or snake: *serpentine coils.* ■ winding and twisting like a snake: *serpentine country lanes.* ■ complex, cunning, or treacherous: *his charm was too subtle and serpentine for me.*
▶ *n.* **1** a dark green mineral consisting of hydrated magnesium silicate, sometimes mottled or spotted like a snake's skin. **2** a thing in the shape of a winding curve or line.

ser·ra·no /sə'ränō/ ▶ *n.* a small, very hot chili that is used fresh or dried in Mexican cooking.

ser·rat·ed /'ser,ātid; sə'rātid/ ▶ *adj.* having or denoting a jagged edge; sawlike: *a knife with a serrated edge.* —**ser·ra·tion** *n.*

ser·ried /'serēd/ ▶ *adj.* (of rows of people or things) standing close together: *serried ranks of soldiers | the serried rows of vines.*

se·rum /'si(ə)rəm/ ▶ *n.* (*pl.* **se·ra** /'si(ə)rə/ or **se·rums**) an amber-colored, protein-rich liquid that separates out when blood coagulates.

ser·val /'sərvəl; sər'val/ ▶ *n.* a slender African wildcat (*Felis serval*) with long legs, large ears, and a black-spotted orange-brown coat.

serv·ant /'sərvənt/ ▶ *n.* a person who performs duties for others, esp. a person employed in a house on domestic duties or as a personal attendant. ■ a person employed in the service of a government. See also CIVIL SERVANT, PUBLIC SERVANT. ■ a devoted and helpful follower or supporter: *a tireless servant of God.* —**serv·ant·hood** /-,hŏŏd/ *n.*

serve /sərv/ ▶ *v.* [*tr.*] **1** perform duties or services for (another person or an organization): *Malcolm has served the church very faithfully.* ■ provide (an area or group of people) with a product or service: *a telecommunications company that serves southern New England.* ■ [*intr.*] be employed as a member of the armed forces: *a military engineer who served with the army.* ■ spend (a period) in office, in an apprenticeship, or in prison: *he is serving a ten-year jail sentence.* **2** present (food or drink) to someone: *they serve wine instead of beer.* ■ present (someone) with food or drink: *I'll serve you with coffee and cake.* ■ (of food or drink) be enough for: *the recipe serves four people.* ■ attend to (a customer in a store): *she turned to serve the impatient customer.* ■ supply (goods) to a customer. **3** *Law* deliver (a document such as a summons or writ) in a formal manner to the person to whom it is addressed: *a warrant was served on Jack Sherman.* ■ deliver a document to (someone) in such a way: *they were just about to serve him with a writ.* **4** be of use in achieving or satisfying: *this book will serve a useful purpose.* ■ [*intr.*] be of some specified use: *the island's one pub serves as a café by day.* ■ [*tr.*] function for or treat (someone) in a specified way: *the strategy served him well.* ■ (of a male breeding-animal) copulate with (a female). **5** [*intr.*] (in tennis and other racket sports) hit the ball or shuttlecock to begin play: *he tossed the ball up to serve* | [*tr.*] *serve the ball onto the front wall.* ■ [*tr.*] (in tennis and other racket sports) begin play for each point in (a game).
▶ *n.* (in tennis and other racket sports) an act or turn of hitting the ball or shuttlecock to start play: *he was let down by an erratic serve.*
▶ □ **serve someone right** a person's deserved punishment or misfortune: *it would serve you right if Jeff walked out on you.* □ **serve one's time** (also **serve time**) spend time in office, in an apprenticeship, or in prison.

serv·er /'sərvər/ ▶ *n.* a person or thing that provides a service or commodity, in particular: ■ a computer or computer program that manages access to a centralized resource or service in a network. ■ (in tennis and other racket sports) the player who serves. ■ a waiter or waitress. ■ *Christian Church* a person assisting the celebrant at the celebration of the Eucharist. ■ a large utensil for serving food. ■ a sideboard or similar piece of furniture, on which food to be served is placed.

serv·ice /'sərvis/ ▶ *n.* **1** the action of helping or doing work for someone: *millions are involved in voluntary service.* ■ an act of assistance: *he has done us a great service.* ■ assistance or advice given to customers during and after the sale of goods: *they aim to provide better quality of service.* ■ work done for a customer other than manufacturing: *scheduled commercial airline service.* ■ the action or process of serving food and drinks to customers: *they complained of poor bar service.* ■ short for SERVICE CHARGE: *service is included in the final bill.* **2** a period of employment with a company or organization: *he retired after 40 years' service.* ■ employment as a servant: *the pitifully low wages gained from domestic service.* ■ the use that can be made of a machine: *the computer should provide good service for years.* ■ the provision of the necessary maintenance work for a machine: *they phoned for service on their air conditioning.* ■ a periodic routine inspection and maintenance of a vehicle or other machine: *he took his car in for service.* ■ (**the services**) the armed forces: *troops from all branches of the services.* **2** a system supplying a public need such as transport, communications, or utilities such as electricity and water: *a regular bus service.* ■ a public department or organization run by the

government: *the U.S. Fish and Wildlife Service.* **3** a ceremony of religious worship according to a prescribed form; the prescribed form for such a ceremony: *a funeral service.* **4** a set of matching dishes and utensils used for serving a particular meal: *a dinner service.* **5** (in tennis and other racket sports) the action or right of serving to begin play. ■ a serve. **6** *Law* the formal delivery of a document such as a writ or summons.
▶ *v.* [*tr.*] **1** (usu. **be serviced**) perform routine maintenance or repair work on (a vehicle or machine): *have your car serviced regularly.* ■ supply and maintain systems for public utilities and transportation and communications in (an area): *the town is small but well serviced.* ■ perform a service or services for (someone): *the state's biggest health maintenance organization servicing the poor.* ■ pay interest on (a debt): *taxpayers are paying $250 million just to service that debt.* **2** (of a male animal) mate with (a female animal). ■ *vulgar slang* (of a man) have sexual intercourse with (a woman).
▶ □ **in service** in or available for use. □ **out of service** not available for use.

serv·ice·a·ble /'sərvəsəbəl/ ▶ *adj.* fulfilling its function adequately; usable: *an aging but still serviceable water supply system.* ■ functional and durable rather than attractive: *only twelve aircraft were fully serviceable this morning.* ■ in working order: —**serv·ice·a·bil·i·ty** /,sərvəsə'bilitē/ *n.* —**serv·ice·a·bly** /-blē/ *adv.*

serv·ice ar·e·a ▶ *n.* **1** a roadside area where services are available to motorists. **2** the area covered by the signal of a broadcasting station.

serv·ice charge (also **service fee**) ▶ *n.* an extra charge assessed for a service.

serv·ice in·dus·try ▶ *n.* a business that does work for a customer, and occasionally provides goods, but is not involved in manufacturing.

serv·ice·man /'sərvəs,mən; -,man/ ▶ *n.* (*pl.* **-men**) **1** a man serving in the armed forces. **2** a person providing maintenance on machinery, esp. domestic appliances.

serv·ice pack ▶ *n.* (abbr. **SP**) a periodically released update to software from a manufacturer, consisting of enhancements to the program and fixes for known bugs.

serv·ice pro·vid·er ▶ *n.* *Comput.* a company that provides its subscribers access to the Internet.

serv·ice road ▶ *n.* another term for FRONTAGE ROAD.

serv·ice sta·tion ▶ *n.* an establishment selling gasoline and oil and typically having the facilities to provide automotive repairs and maintenance.

serv·ice·wom·an /'sərvəs,wŏŏmən/ ▶ *n.* (*pl.* **-wom·en**) a woman serving in the armed forces.

ser·vi·ette /,sərvē'et/ ▶ *n.* *Brit. & Can.* a table napkin.

ser·vile /'sərvəl; -,vīl/ ▶ *adj.* **1** having or showing an excessive willingness to serve or please others: *bowing his head in a servile manner.* **2** of or characteristic of a slave or slaves. —**ser·vile·ly** *adv.* —**ser·vil·i·ty** /sər'vilitē/ *n.*

serv·ing /'sərviNG/ ▶ *n.* a quantity of food suitable for or served to one person: *a large serving of spaghetti.*

ser·vi·tude /'sərvi,t(y)ŏŏd/ ▶ *n.* the state of being a slave or completely subject to someone more powerful.

serv·let /'sərvlit/ ▶ *n.* *Comput.* a small, server-resident program that typically runs automatically in response to user input: *students will build servlets that generate Web pages and communicate with other Java servers.*

ser·vo·mech·an·ism /'sərvō,mekə,nizəm/ ▶ *n.* a powered mechanism producing motion or forces at a higher level of energy than the input level, e.g., in the brakes and steering of large motor vehicles, esp. where feedback is employed to make the control automatic.

ses·a·me /'sesəmē/ ▶ *n.* a tall annual herbaceous plant (*Sesamum indicum*, family Pedaliaceae) of tropical and subtropical areas of the Old World, cultivated for its oil-rich seeds. ■ (**ses·a·me seed**) the edible seeds of this plant, which are used whole or have the oil extracted. ▷ late Middle English: via Latin from Greek *sēsamon, sēsamē*; compare with Arabic *simsim.*

ses·qui·cen·ten·ni·al /,seskwisen'tenēəl/ ▶ *adj.* of or relating to the one-hundred-and-fiftieth anniversary of a significant event.
▶ *n.* a one-hundred-and-fiftieth anniversary.

ses·sile /'sesəl; -īl/ ▶ *adj.* *Biol.* (of an organism, e.g., a barnacle) fixed in one place; immobile. ■ (of a plant or animal structure) attached directly by its base without a stalk or peduncle.

ses·sion /'seSHən/ ▶ *n.* **1** a meeting of a deliberative or judicial body to conduct its business. ■ a period during which such meetings are regularly held: *legislation to curb wildcat strikes will be introduced during the coming parliamentary session.* **2** a period devoted to a particular activity: *gym is followed by a training session.* ■ *inf.* a period of heavy or sustained drinking. ■ a period of recording music in a studio, esp. by a session musician: *he did the sessions for a Great Country Hits album.* ■ an academic year. ■ the period during which a school has classes. —**ses·sion·al** /-sHənl/ *adj.*

▶ □ **in session** assembled for or proceeding with business.

ses·tet /ses'tet/ ▶ *n.* Prosody the last six lines of a sonnet.

ses·ti·na /se'stēnə/ ▶ *n.* Prosody a poem with six stanzas of six lines and a final triplet, all stanzas having the same six words at the line-ends in six different sequences that follow a fixed pattern, and with all six words appearing in the closing three-line envoi.

set[1] /set/ ▶ *v.* (**set·ting**; *past* **set**) **1** [*tr.*] put, lay, or stand (something) in a specified place or position: *Dana set the mug of tea down.* ■ (**be set**) be situated or fixed in a specified place or position: *the village was set among olive groves on a hill.* ■ represent (a story, play, movie, or scene) as happening at a specified time or in a specified place: *a spy novel set in Berlin.* ■ mount a precious stone in (something, typically a piece of jewelry): *a bracelet set with emeralds.* ■ mount (a precious stone) in something. ■ *Printing* arrange (type) as required. ■ prepare (a table) for a meal by placing cutlery, dishes, etc., on it in their proper places. ■ (**set something to**) provide (music) so that a written work can be produced in a musical form: *she set his poem to music.* ■ give the teeth of (a saw) alternating outward inclinations. ■ *Sailing* put (a sail) up in position to catch the wind: *a safe distance from shore all sails were set.* **2** [*tr.*] put or bring into a specified state: *plunging oil prices set in motion an economic collapse in Houston.* ■ [*tr.*] cause (someone or something) to start doing something: *the incident set me thinking.* ■ [*tr.*] instruct (someone) to do something: *he'll set a man to watch you.* ■ give someone (a task): *the problem we have been set.* ■ devise (a test) and give it to someone to do. ■ establish as (an example) for others to follow, copy, or try to achieve: *the scheme sets a precedent for other companies.* ■ establish (a record): *his time in the 25-meter freestyle set a national record.* ■ decide on: *they set a date for a full hearing at the end of February.* ■ fix (a price, value, or limit) on something: *the unions had set a limit on the size of the temporary workforce.* **3** [*tr.*] adjust the hands of (a clock or watch), typically to show the right time. ■ adjust (an alarm clock) to sound at the required time. ■ adjust (a device or its controls) so that it performs a particular operation: *you have to be careful not to set the volume too high.* **4** [*intr.*] harden into a solid or semisolid state: *cook for a further thirty-five minutes until the filling has set.* ■ [*tr.*] arrange (the hair) while damp so that it dries in the required style: *she had set her hair on small rollers.* ■ [*tr.*] put parts of (a broken or dislocated bone or limb) into the correct position for healing. ■ (of a bone) be restored to its normal condition by knitting together again after being broken: *dogs' bones soon set.* ■ (with reference to a person's face) assume or cause to assume a fixed or rigid expression: [*intr.*] *her features never set into a civil parade of attention* | [*tr.*] *Travis's face was set as he looked up.* ■ (of the eyes) become fixed in position or in the feeling they are expressing: *his bright eyes set in an expression of mocking amusement.* ■ (of a hunting dog) adopt a rigid attitude indicating the presence of game. **5** [*intr.*] (of the sun, moon, or another celestial body) appear to move toward and below the earth's horizon as the earth rotates: *the sun was setting and a warm, red glow filled the sky.* **6** [*intr.*] (of a tide or current) take or have a specified direction or course: *a fair tide can be carried well past Lands End before the stream sets to the north.* **7** [*tr.*] start (a fire). **8** [*intr.*] (of blossom or a tree) develop into or produce (fruit). ■ (of a plant) produce (seed): *the herb has flowered and started to set seed.*

▶ *phrasal v.* □ **set about** start doing something with vigor or determination: *it would be far better to admit the problem openly and set about tackling it.* □ **set someone apart** give someone an air of unusual superiority: *his blunt views set him apart.* □ **set something apart** separate something and keep it for a special purpose: *there were books and rooms set apart as libraries.* □ **set something aside 1** save or keep something, typically money or time, for a particular purpose: *the bank expected to set aside about $700 million for restructuring.* ■ remove land from agricultural production. **2** annul a legal decision or process. □ **set someone/something back 1** delay or impede the progress of someone or something: *this incident undoubtedly set back research.* **2** *inf.* (of a purchase) cost someone a particular amount of money: *that must have set you back a bit.* □ **set something down** record something in writing. ■ establish something authoritatively as a rule or principle to be followed: *the Association set down codes of practice for all members to comply with.* □ **set forth** begin a journey or trip. □ **set something forth** state or describe something in writing or speech: *the principles and aims set forth in the Charter.* □ **set in**

(of something unpleasant or unwelcome) begin and seem likely to continue: *less hardy plants should be brought inside before cold weather sets in.* □ **set off** begin a journey. □ **set someone off** cause someone to start doing something, esp. laughing or talking: *anything will set him off laughing.* □ **set something off 1** detonate a bomb. ■ cause an alarm to go off. ■ cause a series of things to occur: *the fear is that this could set off a chain reaction in other financial markets.* **2** serve as decorative embellishment to: *a pink carnation set off nicely by a red bow tie and cream shirt.* □ **set on** (or **upon**) attack (someone) violently. □ **set someone/something on** (or **upon**) cause or urge a person or animal to attack: *I was asked to leave and threatened with having dogs set upon me.* □ **set out** begin a journey. ■ aim or intend to do something: *she drew up a plan of what her organization should set out to achieve.* □ **set something out** arrange or display something in a particular order or position. ■ present information or ideas in a well-ordered way in writing or speech: *this chapter sets out the debate surrounding pluralism.* □ **set someone up 1** establish someone in a particular capacity or role: *his father set him up in business.* **2** restore or enhance the health of someone: *after my operation, the doctor recommended a cruise to set me up again.* **3** *inf.* make an innocent person appear guilty of something: *suppose Zielinski had set him up for Ingram's murder?* □ **set something up 1** place or erect something in position: *police set up a roadblock on Tenth Street.* **2** establish a business, institution, or other organization. ■ make the arrangements necessary for something: *he asked if I would like him to set up a meeting with the president.* **3** begin making a loud sound. □ **set oneself up as** establish oneself in (a particular occupation): *he set himself up as an attorney in St. Louis.* ■ claim to be or act like a specified kind of person (used to indicate skepticism as to someone's right or ability to do so): *he set himself up as a crusader for higher press and broadcasting standards.*

▶ □ **set one's heart** (or **hopes**) **on** have a strong desire for or to do: *she had her heart set on going to college.* □ **set sail** hoist the sails of a vessel. ■ begin a voyage: *tomorrow we set sail for France.* □ **set one's teeth** clench one's teeth together. ■ become resolute: *they have set their teeth against a change which would undermine their prospects of forming a government.* □ **set someone straight** inform someone of the truth of a situation. □ **set the wheels in motion** do something to begin a process or put a plan into action.

set[2] ▶ *n.* **1** a group or collection of things that belong together, resemble one another, or are usually found together: *a set of false teeth.* ■ a collection of implements, containers, or other objects customarily used together for a specific purpose: *an electric fondue set.* ■ a group of people with common interests or occupations or of similar social status: *it was a fashionable haunt of the literary set.* ■ (in tennis, darts, and other games) a group of games counting as a unit toward a match, only the player or side that wins a defined number or proportion of the games being awarded a point toward the final score: *he took the first set 6-3.* ■ (in jazz or popular music) a sequence of songs or pieces performed together: *a four-song set.* ■ a group of people making up the required number for a square dance or similar country dance. ■ a fixed number of repetitions of a particular bodybuilding exercise; compare with **REP**[4]. ■ *Math. & Logic* a collection of distinct entities regarded as a unit, being either individually specified or (more usually) satisfying specified conditions: *the set of all positive integers.* **2** the way in which something is set, disposed, or positioned: *the shape and set of the eyes.* ■ the posture or attitude of a part of the body, typically in relation to the impression this gives of a person's feelings or intentions: *the determined set of her upper torso.* ■ the flow of a current or tide in a particular direction: *the rudder kept the dinghy straight against the set of the tide.* ■ an arrangement of the hair when damp so that it dries in the required style: *a shampoo and set.* ■ the alternating outward inclinations of the teeth of a saw, or the amount of this. ■ a warp or bend in wood, metal, or another material caused by continued strain or pressure. **3** a radio or television receiver: *a TV set.* **4** a collection of scenery, stage furniture, and other articles used for a particular scene in a play or film. ■ the place or area in which filming is taking place or a play is performed: *the magazine has interviews on set with top directors.* **5** a cutting, young plant, or bulb used in the propagation of new plants. ■ a young fruit that has just formed.

set[3] ▶ *adj.* **1** fixed or arranged in advance: *there is no set procedure.* ■ (of a view or habit) unlikely to change: *I've been on my own a long time and I'm rather set in my ways.* ■ (of a person's expression) held for an unnaturally long time without changing, typically as a reflection of determination. ■ (of a meal or menu in a restaurant) offered at a fixed price with a limited choice of dishes. ■ having a conventional or predetermined wording; formulaic: *witnesses often delivered their testimony according to a set speech.* **2** ready, prepared, or likely to do something: *"All set for tonight?" he asked.* ■ (**set against**) firmly opposed to: *an approach* set against tradition and authority. ■ (**set on**) determined to do (something): *he's set on marrying that girl.*

se·ta /'sētə/ ▸*n.* (*pl.* **-tae** /-tē/) *chiefly Zool.* a stiff hairlike or bristlelike structure, esp. in an invertebrate. —**se·ta·ceous** /si'tāsHəs/ *adj.* —**se·tal** *adj.*

set·back /'set,bak/ ▸*n.* **1** a reversal or check in progress: *a serious setback for the peace process.* **2** *Archit.* a plain, flat offset in a wall. **3** the distance by which a building or part of a building is set back from the property line.

set point ▸*n.* (in tennis and other sports) a point that, if won by a contestant, will also win the set.

set screw ▸*n.* a screw for adjusting or clamping parts of a machine.

set square ▸*n.* a right-angled triangular plate for drawing lines, esp. at 90°, 45°, 60°, or 30°. ■ a form of T-square with an additional arm turning on a pivot for drawing lines at fixed angles to the head.

set·tee /se'tē/ ▸*n.* a long upholstered seat for more than one person, typically with a back and arms.

set·ter /'setər/ ▸*n.* **1** a dog of a large, long-haired breed trained to stand rigid when scenting game. **2** [usu. in *comb.*] a person or thing that sets something: *trend-setters in Hollywood.*

set the·o·ry ▸*n.* the branch of mathematics that deals with the formal properties of sets as units (without regard to the nature of their individual constituents) and the expression of other branches of mathematics in terms of sets. —**set-the·o·ret·ic** *adj.* —**set-the·o·ret·i·cal** *adj.*

set·ting /'setiNG/ ▸*n.* **1** the place or type of surroundings where something is positioned or where an event takes place: *cozy waterfront cottage in a peaceful country setting.* ■ the place and time at which a play, novel, or film is represented as happening: *short stories with a contemporary setting.* ■ a piece of metal in which a precious stone or gem is fixed to form a piece of jewelry. ■ a piece of vocal or choral music composed for particular words: *a setting of Yevtushenko's bleak poem.* ■ short for PLACE SETTING. **2** a speed, height, or temperature at which a machine or device can be adjusted to operate: *if you find the room getting too hot, check the thermostat setting.*

set·tle /'setl/ ▸*v.* **1** [*tr.*] resolve or reach an agreement about (an argument or problem): *every effort was made to settle the dispute.* ■ end (a legal dispute) by mutual agreement: *the matter was settled out of court* | [*intr.*] *he sued for libel and then settled out of court.* ■ determine; decide on: *exactly what goes into the legislation has not been settled.* ■ pay (a debt or account): *his bill was settled by charge card.* ■ complete the administration and distribution of a decedent's estate. ■ [*intr.*] (**settle for**) accept or agree to (something that one considers to be less than satisfactory): *it was too cold for champagne so they settled for a cup of tea.* **2** [*intr.*] adopt a more steady or secure style of life, esp. in a permanent job and home: *one day I will **settle down** and raise a family.* ■ make one's permanent home somewhere: *in 1863 the family settled in London.* ■ begin to feel comfortable or established in a new home, situation, or job: *she settled in happily with a foster family.* ■ [*tr.*] establish a colony in: *European immigrants settled much of Australia.* ■ (**settle down to**) turn one's attention to; apply oneself to: *Catherine settled down to her studies.* ■ become or make calmer or quieter: [*intr.*] *after a few months the controversy settled down* | [*tr.*] *try to settle your puppy down before going to bed.* **3** [*intr.*] sit or come to rest in a comfortable position: *he settled into an armchair.* ■ [*tr.*] move or adjust (something) so that it rests securely: *she settled her bag on her shoulder.* ■ fall or come down on to a surface: *dust from the mill had settled on the roof.* ■ [*intr.*] (of suspended particles) sink slowly in a liquid to form sediment; (of a liquid) become clear or still through this process: *sediment settles near the bottom of the tank* | *he pours a glass and leaves it on the bar to settle.* ■ [*intr.*] (of an object or objects) gradually sink down under its or their own weight: *they listened to the soft ticking and creaking as the house settled.* ■ [*intr.*] (of a ship or boat) sink gradually. —**set·tle·a·ble** *adj.* —**set·tled·ness** *n.*

▸ □ **settle one's affairs** make any necessary arrangements, such as writing a will, before one's death.

set·tle·ment /'setlmənt/ ▸*n.* **1** an official agreement intended to resolve a dispute or conflict: *unions succeeded in reaching a pay settlement.* ■ a formal arrangement made between the parties to a lawsuit in order to resolve it, esp. out of court: *the owner reached an out-of-court settlement with the plaintiffs.* **2** a place, typically one that has hitherto been uninhabited, where people establish a community: *the little settlement of Buttermere.* ■ the process of settling in such a place: *the early settlement of Queensland.* ■ the action of allowing or helping people to do this: *Israel's settlement of immigrants in the occupied territories.* **3** *Law* an arrangement whereby property passes to a succession of people as dictated by the settlor. ■ the amount or property given. **4** the action or process of settling an account.

set·tler /'setl-ər; 'setlər/ ▸*n.* a person who settles in an area, typically one with no or few previous inhabitants.

set·tlor /'setl-ər; 'setlər/ ▸*n.* *Law* a person who makes a settlement, esp. of a property.

set-to ▸*n.* (*pl.* **-tos**) *inf.* a fight or argument: *we had a little set-to about her piano practicing.*

set·up /'set,əp/ ▸*n.* *inf.* **1** the way in which something, esp. an organization or equipment, is organized, planned, or arranged: *would you feel comfortable in a smaller setup?* ■ an organization or arrangement: *Moses and Jesus came from strange family setups.* ■ a set of equipment needed for a particular activity or purpose: *I have a recording setup in my house.* ■ (in a ball game) a pass or play intended to provide an opportunity for another player to score. **2** a scheme or trick intended to incriminate or deceive someone: *"Listen. He didn't die. It was a setup."* ■ a contest with a prearranged outcome.

sev·en /'sevən/ ▸*cardinal number* equivalent to the sum of three and four; one more than six, or three less than ten; 7: *two sevens are fourteen.* (Roman numeral: **vii, VII**.) ■ a group or unit of seven people or things: *animals were offered for sacrifice in sevens.* ■ seven years old: *my mother died when I was seven.* ■ seven o'clock: *the meeting doesn't finish until seven.* ■ a size of garment or other merchandise denoted by seven. ■ a playing card with seven pips. ▷Old English *seofon,* of Germanic origin; related to Dutch *zeven* and German *sieben,* from an Indo-European root shared by Latin *septem* and Greek *hepta.*

sev·en dead·ly sins ▸*pl. n.* (**the seven deadly sins**) (in Christian tradition) the sins of pride, covetousness, lust, anger, gluttony, envy, and sloth.

sev·en·fold /'sevən,fōld/ ▸*adj.* seven times as great or as numerous: *stock fund sales were up sevenfold from December.* ■ having seven parts or elements: *the sevenfold purpose of religious education.*

▸*adv.* by seven times; to seven times the number or amount: *his rent had gone up sevenfold.*

Sev·en Sis·ters (**the Seven Sisters**) ▸ **1** *Astronomy* the star cluster of the Pleiades. **2** a group of women's (or formerly women's) colleges in the eastern U.S. having high academic and social prestige. It includes Barnard, Bryn Mawr, Mount Holyoke, Radcliffe, Smith, Vassar, and Wellesley.

sev·en·teen /,sevən'tēn; 'sevən,tēn/ ▸*cardinal number* one more than sixteen, or seven more than ten; 17: *seventeen years later.* (Roman numeral: **xvii, XVII**) ■ seventeen years old: *he joined the Marines at seventeen.* ■ a set or team of seventeen individuals. —**sev·en·teenth** /,sevən-'tēnTH; 'sevən,tēnTH/ *adj. & n.*

sev·en·teen-year lo·cust ▸*n.* the nymph of the northern species of the periodical cicada. See PERIODICAL CICADA.

sev·enth /'sevənTH/ ▸*ordinal number* constituting number seven in a sequence; 7th: *his seventh goal of the season.* ■ (**a seventh/one seventh**) each of seven equal parts into which something is or may be divided. ■ the seventh finisher or position in a race or competition: *he finished seventh in the tournament.* ■ seventhly (used to introduce a seventh point or reason). ■ the seventh grade of a school. ■ *Mus.* an interval spanning seven consecutive notes in a diatonic scale. ■ *Mus.* the note that is higher by this interval than the tonic of a diatonic scale or root of a chord. ■ *Mus.* a chord in which the seventh note of the scale forms an important component. —**sev·enth·ly** *adv.*

Sev·enth-Day Ad·vent·ist ▸*n.* a member of a Protestant sect that preaches the imminent return of Christ to Earth (originally expecting the Second Coming in 1844) and observes Saturday as the sabbath. See also ADVENTIST.

sev·en·ty /'sevəntē/ ▸*cardinal number* (*pl.* **-ties**) the number equivalent to the product of seven and ten; ten less than eighty; 70: *about seventy people attended.* (Roman numeral: **lxx, LXX**) ■ (**seventies**) the numbers from seventy to seventy-nine, esp. the years of a century or of a person's life: *Dad was now in his seventies.* ■ seventy years old: *she was nearly seventy.* ■ seventy miles an hour: *doing about seventy.* —**sev·en·ti·eth** /-tēəTH/ *ordinal number* —**sev·en·ty·fold** /-,fōld/ *adj. & adv.*

sev·en-year itch ▸*n.* a supposed tendency to infidelity after seven years of marriage.

sev·er /'sevər/ ▸*v.* [*tr.*] divide by cutting or slicing, esp. suddenly and forcibly: *the head was **severed** from the body.* ■ put an end to (a connection or relationship); break off: *he severed his relations with Lawrence.* —**sev·er·a·ble** *adj.*

sev·er·al /'sev(ə)rəl/ ▸*adj. & pron.* more than two but not many: [as *adj.*]

the author of several books | [as *pron.*] *Van Gogh was just one of several artists who gathered at Auvers.*

▶*adj.* separate or respective: *the two levels of government sort out their several responsibilities.* ■ *Law* applied or regarded separately. —**sev·er·al·ly** *adv.*

sev·er·ance /ˈsev(ə)rəns/ ▶*n.* the action of ending a connection or relationship: *the severance and disestablishment of the Irish Church | a complete severance of links with the Republic.* ■ dismissal or discharge from employment: [as *adj.*] *employees were offered severance terms.* ■ short for SEVERANCE PAY.

sev·er·ance pay ▶*n.* an amount paid to an employee upon dismissal or discharge from employment.

se·vere /səˈvi(ə)r/ ▶*adj.* **1** (of something bad or undesirable) very great; intense: *a severe shortage of technicians.* ■ demanding great ability, skill, or resilience: *a severe test of stamina.* **2** strict or harsh: *the charges would have warranted a severe sentence.* **3** very plain in style or appearance: *she wore another severe suit, gray this time.* —**se·vere·ly** *adv.* —**se·ver·i·ty** /-ˈveritē/ *n.*

sew /sō/ ▶*v.* (*past part.* **sewn** /sōn/ or **sewed** /sōd/) [*tr.*] join, fasten, or repair (something) by making stitches with a needle and thread or a sewing machine: *she sewed the seams and hemmed the border* | [*intr.*] *I don't even sew very well.* ■ [*tr.*] attach (something) to something else by sewing: *she could sew the veil on properly in the morning.* ■ make (a garment) by sewing.

▶*phrasal v.* □ **sew something up** *inf.* bring something to a favorable conclusion: *he sank a 3-pointer to sew up a 120-118 victory.* ■ achieve exclusive control over something: *the U.S. courier market has been more or less sewn up by two companies.*

sew·age /ˈsōij/ ▶*n.* waste water and excrement conveyed in sewers.

sew·er[1] /ˈsōər/ ▶*n.* an underground conduit for carrying off drainage water and waste matter.

sew·er[2] /ˈsōər/ ▶*n.* a person who sews.

sew·er·age /ˈsōərij/ ▶*n.* the provision of drainage by sewers. ■ another term for SEWAGE.

sew·ing /ˈsō-iNG/ ▶*n.* the action or activity of sewing. ■ work that is to be or is being sewn: *she put down her sewing.*

sew·ing ma·chine ▶*n.* a machine with a mechanically driven needle for sewing or stitching cloth.

sewn /sōn/ ▶ past participle of SEW.

sex /seks/ ▶*n.* **1** (chiefly with reference to people) sexual activity, including specifically sexual intercourse: *he enjoyed talking about sex.* **2** either of the two main categories (male and female) into which humans and many other living things are divided on the basis of their reproductive functions: *adults of both sexes.* ■ the fact of belonging to one of these categories: *direct discrimination involves treating someone less favorably on the grounds of their sex.* ■ the group of all members of either of these categories: *she was well known for her efforts to improve the social condition of her sex.*

▶*v.* [*tr.*] **1** determine the sex of: *sexing chickens.* **2** (**sex someone up**) *inf.* arouse or attempt to arouse someone sexually. —**sex·er** *n.*

sex·a·ge·nar·i·an /ˌseksəjəˈne(ə)rēən/ ▶*n.* a person who is from 60 to 69 years old.

sex·a·ges·i·mal /ˌseksəˈjesəməl/ ▶*adj.* **1** of, relating to, or reckoning by sixtieths. **2** of or relating to the number sixty.

▶*n.* (also **sexagesimal fraction**) a fraction based on sixtieths (i.e., with a denominator equal to a power of sixty), as in the divisions of the degree and hour. —**sex·a·ges·i·mal·ly** *adv.*

sex ap·peal ▶*n.* the quality of being attractive in a sexual way: *she just oozes sex appeal.*

sex·cen·ten·ar·y /ˌseksenˈtenərē/ ▶*n.* (*pl.* **-ar·ies**) the six-hundredth anniversary of a significant event.

▶*adj.* of or relating to a six-hundredth anniversary.

sex chro·mo·some ▶*n.* a chromosome involved with determining the sex of an organism, typically one of two kinds.

sex hor·mone ▶*n.* a hormone, such as estrogen or testosterone, affecting sexual development or reproduction.

sex·ism /ˈsekˌsizəm/ ▶*n.* prejudice, stereotyping, or discrimination, typically against women, on the basis of sex. —**sex·ist** *adj.* & *n.*

sex·less /ˈseksləs/ ▶*adj.* **1** lacking in sexual desire, interest, activity, or attractiveness: *I've no patience with pious, sexless females.* **2** neither male nor female: *the stylized and sexless falsetto.* —**sex·less·ly** *adv.* —**sex·less·ness** *n.*

sex ob·ject ▶*n.* a person regarded by another only in terms of their sexual attractiveness or availability: *we're now in a period when it is permissible for women to make men into sex objects.*

sex·ol·o·gy /sekˈsäləjē/ ▶*n.* the study of human sexual life or relationships. —**sex·o·log·i·cal** /ˌseksəˈläjikəl/ *adj.* —**sex·ol·o·gist** /-jist/ *n.*

sex·ploi·ta·tion /ˌseksploiˈtāsHən/ ▶*n. inf.* the commercial exploitation of sex, sexual attractiveness, or sexually explicit material.

sex·pot /ˈseksˌpät/ ▶*n. inf.* a sexy person.

sex sym·bol ▶*n.* a person widely noted for their sexual attractiveness.

sext /sekst/ ▶*n.* a service forming part of the Divine Office of the Western Christian Church, traditionally said (or chanted) at the sixth hour of the day (i.e., noon).

sex·tant /ˈsekstənt/ ▶*n.* an instrument with a graduated arc of 60° and a sighting mechanism, used for measuring the angular distances between objects and esp. for taking altitudes in navigation. ▷late 16th cent. (denoting the sixth part of a circle): from Latin *sextans, sextant-* 'sixth part,' from *sextus* 'sixth.'

sex·tet /sekˈstet/ (also **sex·tette**) ▶*n.* a group of six people playing music or singing together. ■ a composition for such a group. ■ a set of six people or things: *a sextet of new releases.*

sex·ton /ˈsekstən/ ▶*n.* a person who looks after a church and churchyard, sometimes acting as bell-ringer and formerly as a gravedigger.

sex·tu·ple /sekˈst(y)o͞opəl; -ˈtəpəl/ ▶*adj.* consisting of six parts or things. ■ six times as much or as many.

▶*n.* a sixfold number or amount.

▶*v.* [*tr.*] multiply by six; increase sixfold. —**sex·tu·ply** /-plē/ *adv.*

sex·tu·plet /sekˈstəplit; -ˈst(y)o͞oplət/ ▶*n.* **1** each of six children born at one birth. **2** *Mus.* a group of six notes to be performed in the time of four.

sex·u·al /ˈseksHo͞oəl/ ▶*adj.* **1** relating to the instincts, physiological processes, and activities connected with physical attraction or intimate physical contact between individuals: *she had felt the thrill of a sexual attraction.* **2** of or relating to the two sexes or to gender: *sensitivity about sexual stereotypes.* ■ of or characteristic of one sex or the other: *the hormones which control the secondary sexual characteristics.* ■ *Biol.* being of one sex or the other; capable of sexual reproduction. —**sex·u·al·i·ty** /ˌseksHo͞oˈalitē/ *n.* —**sex·u·al·ly** *adv.*

sex·u·al in·ter·course ▶*n.* sexual contact between individuals involving penetration, esp. the insertion of a man's erect penis into a woman's vagina, typically culminating in orgasm and the ejaculation of semen.

sex·u·al o·ri·en·ta·tion ▶*n.* a person's sexual attraction toward members of the same, opposite, or both genders: *a draft ordinance that would prohibit discrimination on the basis of sexual orientation.*

sex·y /ˈseksē/ ▶*adj.* (**sex·i·er**, **sex·i·est**) sexually attractive or exciting: *sexy French underwear.* ■ sexually aroused: *neither of them was feeling sexy.* ■ *inf.* exciting; appealing: *I've climbed most of the really sexy west coast mountains.* —**sex·i·ly** /-səlē/ *adv.* —**sex·i·ness** *n.*

sfor·zan·do /sfôrtˈsändō/ (also **sfor·za·to** /sfôrtˈsätō/) *Mus.* ▶*adv.* & *adj.* (esp. as a direction) with sudden emphasis.

▶*n.* (*pl.* **-dos** or **-di** /-dē/) a sudden or marked emphasis.

sfu·ma·to /sfo͞oˈmätō/ ▶*n. Art* the technique of allowing tones and colors to shade gradually into one another, producing softened outlines or hazy forms.

sfz *Mus.* ▶*abbr.* sforzando.

SG ▶*abbr.* ■ *Physics* specific gravity.

Sg ▶*symb.* the chemical element seaborgium.

Sgt (also **SGT**) ▶*abbr.* sergeant.

shab·by /ˈsHabē/ ▶*adj.* (**-bi·er**, **-bi·est**) in poor condition through long or hard use or lack of care: *a conscript in a shabby uniform saluted the car.* ■ dressed in old or worn clothes. ■ (of behavior) mean and shameful: *shabby, disrespectful treatment.* ■ inferior in performance or quality: *The gain jumps to 67 percent. Not too shabby.* —**shab·bi·ly** /-əlē/ *adv.* —**shab·bi·ness** *n.*

shack /sHak/ ▶*n.* a roughly built hut or cabin.

▶*v.* [*intr.*] (**shack up**) *inf.* move in or live with someone as a lover.

shack·le /ˈsHakəl/ ▶*n.* **1** (**shackles**) a pair of fetters connected together by a chain, used to fasten a prisoner's wrists or ankles together. ■ *fig.* used in reference to something that restrains or impedes: *society is going to throw off* **the shackles of** *racism and colonialism.* **2** a metal link, typically U-shaped and closed by a bolt, used to secure a chain or rope to something. ■ a pivoted link connecting a spring in a vehicle's suspension to the body of the vehicle.

▶*v.* [*tr.*] chain with shackles. ■ *fig.* restrain; limit: *they seek to shackle the oil and gas companies by imposing new controls.*

shad /sHad/ ▶*n.* (*pl.* same or **shads**) a fish (genera *Alosa* and *Caspialosa*) of the herring family that spends much of its life in the sea, typically entering rivers to spawn. It is an important food fish in many regions.

shade /SHād/ ▶ *n.* **1** comparative darkness and coolness caused by shelter from direct sunlight: *sitting in the shade.* ■ the darker part of a picture. ■ *fig.* a position of relative inferiority or obscurity: *her elegant pink and black ensemble would put most outfits in the shade.* **2** a color, esp. with regard to how light or dark it is or as distinguished from one nearly like it: *various shades of blue.* ■ *Art* a slight degree of difference between colors. ■ a slightly differing variety of something: *politicians of all shades of opinion.* ■ a slight amount of something: *there is a shade of wistfulness in his rejection.* **3** a lampshade. ■ (often **shades**) a screen or blind on a window. ■ an eyeshade. ■ (**shades**) *inf.* sunglasses.

▶ *v.* **1** screen from direct light: *she shaded her eyes against the sun.* ■ cover, moderate, or exclude the light of: *he shaded the flashlight with his hand.* **2** darken or color (an illustration or diagram) with parallel pencil lines or a block of color: *she shaded in the outline of a chimney.* ■ [*intr.*] (of a color or something colored) gradually change into another color: *the sky shaded from turquoise to night blue.* **3** make a slight reduction in the amount, rate, or price of: *banks may shade the margin over base rate they charge customers.* —**shade·less** *adj.* —**shad·er** *n.*

▶ □ **a shade —** a little —: *he was a shade hung over.* □ **shades of —** used to suggest reminiscence of or comparison with someone or something specified: *colleges were conducting campaigns to ban Jewish societies—shades of Nazi Germany.*

shad·ing /ˈSHādiNG/ ▶ *n.* the darkening or coloring of an illustration or diagram with parallel lines or a block of color. ■ a very slight variation, typically in color or meaning: *the shadings of opinion even among those who are in broad agreement.*

shad·ow /ˈSHadō/ ▶ *n.* **1** a dark area or shape produced by a body coming between rays of light and a surface: *trees cast long shadows.* ■ partial or complete darkness, esp. as produced in this way: *the north side of the cathedral was deep in shadow.* ■ the shaded part of a picture. ■ a dark patch or area on a surface: *there are dark shadows beneath your eyes.* ■ a region of opacity on a radiograph: *shadows on his lungs.* ■ short for EYESHADOW. **2** *fig.* used in reference to proximity, ominous oppressiveness, or sadness and gloom: *the shadow of war fell across Europe.* ■ used in reference to something insubstantial or fleeting: *a freedom that was more shadow than substance.* ■ used in reference to a position of relative inferiority or obscurity: *he lived in the shadow of his father.* ■ the slightest trace of something: *she knew without a shadow of a doubt that he was lying.* ■ a weak or inferior remnant or version of something: *this fine-looking, commanding man had become a shadow of his former self.* ■ an expression of perplexity or sadness: *a shadow crossed Maria's face.* **3** an inseparable attendant or companion: *her faithful shadow, a Yorkshire terrier called Heathcliffe.* ■ a person secretly following and observing another. ■ a person who accompanies someone in their daily activities at work in order to gain experience at or insight into a job. ■ [as *adj.*] unofficial or alternative: *the Committee of Twenty-Five, a shadow government of unelected businessmen.*

▶ *v.* [*tr.*] **1** (often **be shadowed**) envelop in shadow; cast a shadow over: *the market is shadowed by St. Margaret's church.* **2** follow and observe (someone) closely and typically secretly: *he had been up all night shadowing a team of poachers.* ■ accompany (someone) in their daily activities at work in order to gain experience at or insight into a job. —**shad·ow·er** *n.* —**shad·ow·less** *adj.*

shad·ow·box /ˈSHadō,bäks/ ▶ *v.* [*intr.*] spar with an imaginary opponent as a form of training.

shad·ow·y /ˈSHadōē/ ▶ *adj.* (**-ow·i·er, -ow·i·est**) full of shadows: *the shadowy back streets of Stringtown.* ■ of uncertain identity or nature: *a shadowy figure appeared through the mist.* ■ insubstantial; unreal: *they were attacked by a swarm of shadowy, ethereal forms.* —**shad·ow·i·ness** *n.*

shad·y /ˈSHādē/ ▶ *adj.* (**shad·i·er, shad·i·est**) situated in or full of shade: *shady woods.* ■ giving shade from sunlight: *they sprawled under a shady carob tree.* ■ *inf.* of doubtful honesty or legality: *he was involved in his grandmother's shady deals.* —**shad·i·ly** *adv.* —**shad·i·ness** *n.*

shaft /SHaft/ ▶ *n.* **1** a long, narrow part or section forming the handle of a tool or club, the body of a spear or arrow, or a similar implement: *the shaft of a golf club.* ■ an arrow or spear. ■ a column, esp. the main part between the base and capital. ■ a long cylindrical rotating rod for the transmission of motive power in a machine. ■ each of the pair of poles between which a horse is harnessed to a vehicle. ■ a ray of light or bolt of lightning: *a shaft of sunlight.* ■ *vulgar slang* a penis. ■ (**the shaft**) *inf.* harsh or unfair treatment: *the executives continue to raise their pay while the workers get the shaft.* **2** a long, narrow, typically vertical hole that gives access to a mine, accommodates an elevator in a building, or provides ventilation.

▶ *v.* **1** [*intr.*] (of light) shine in beams: *brilliant sunshine shafted through the skylight.* **2** [*tr.*] *vulgar slang* (of a man) have sexual intercourse with (a

woman). ■ *inf.* treat (someone) harshly or unfairly: *I suppose she'll get a lawyer and I'll be shafted.* ▷Old English *scæft, sceaft* 'handle, pole,' of Germanic origin; related to Dutch *schaft,* German *Schaft,* and perhaps also to *scepter.* Early senses of the verb (late Middle English) were 'fit with a handle' and 'send out shafts of light.' —**shaft·ed** *adj.* [in *comb.*] *a long-shafted harpoon.*

shag¹ /SHag/ ▶ *n.* **1** [usu. as *adj.*] a carpet or rug with a long, rough pile: *wall-to-wall shag carpet.* ■ cloth with a velvet nap on one side. **2** a thick, tangled hairstyle or mass of hair: *her hair was cut short in a boyish shag.* **3** (also **shag tobacco**) a coarse kind of cut tobacco.

shag² ▶ *n.* a western European and Mediterranean cormorant (*Phalacrocorax aristotelis*) with greenish-black plumage and a long curly crest in the breeding season.

shag³ ▶ *v.* [*tr.*] *Baseball* chase or catch (fly balls) for practice.

shag⁴ *Brit., vulgar slang* ▶ *v.* (**shagged, shag·ging**) [*tr.*] have sexual intercourse with (someone). —**shag·ger** *n.*

shag·gy /ˈSHagē/ ▶ *adj.* (**-gi·er, -gi·est**) (of hair or fur) long, thick, and unkempt: *the mountain goat has a long, shaggy coat.* ■ having long, thick, unkempt hair or fur: *a huge shaggy English sheepdog.* ■ of or having a covering resembling rough, thick hair. —**shag·gi·ly** /-əlē/ *adv.* —**shag·gi·ness** *n.*

▶ □ **shaggy-dog story** a long, rambling story or joke, typically one that is amusing only because it is absurdly inconsequential or pointless.

sha·green /SHəˈgrēn/ ▶ *n.* **1** sharkskin used as a decorative material or, for its natural rough surface of pointed scales, as an abrasive. **2** a kind of untanned leather with a rough granulated surface. ▷late 17th cent.: variant of *chagrin* from French, literally 'rough skin.'

shah /SHä/ ▶ *n. hist.* a title of the former monarch of Iran. —**shah·dom** /-dəm/ *n.*

shake /SHāk/ ▶ *v.* (past **shook** /SHo͝ok/; past part. **shak·en** /ˈSHākən/) **1** [*intr.*] (of a structure or area of land) tremble or vibrate: *buildings shook in Sacramento and tremors were felt in Reno.* ■ cause to tremble or vibrate: *a severe earthquake shook the area.* ■ (of a person, a part of the body, or the voice) tremble uncontrollably from a strong emotion such as fear or anger: *Luke was shaking with rage | her voice shook with passion.* **2** [*tr.*] move (an object) up and down or from side to side with rapid, forceful, jerky movements: *she stood in the hall and shook her umbrella.* ■ [*tr.*] remove (an object or substance) from something by movements of this kind: *they shook the sand out of their shoes.* ■ *inf.* get rid of or put an end to (something unwanted): *he was unable to shake off the memories of the trenches.* ■ grasp (someone) and move them roughly to and fro, either in anger or to rouse them from sleep: [*tr.*] *he gently shook the driver awake and they set off.* ■ brandish in anger or as a warning; make a threatening gesture with: *men shook their fists and shouted.* **3** [*tr.*] upset the composure of; shock or astonish: *rumors of a further loss shook the market.* ■ [*tr.*] cause a change of mood or attitude by shocking or disturbing (someone): *he had to shake himself out of his lethargy.* ■ weaken or impair (confidence, a belief, etc.), esp. by shocking or disturbing: *the escalation in costs is certain to shake the confidence of private investors.*

▶*phrasal v.* □ **shake someone down** *inf.* extort money from someone. □ **shake something down** cause something to fall or settle by shaking. □ **shake someone off** get away from someone by shaking their grip loose. ■ manage to evade or outmaneuver someone who is following or pestering one: *he thought he had shaken off his pursuer.* ■ (in sports, esp. a race) outdistance another competitor: *in the final lap she looked as though she had shaken off the Dutch girl.* □ **shake something off** successfully deal with or recover from an illness or injury: *she has shaken off a virus.* □ **shake on it** confirm (an agreement) by shaking hands: *they shook on the deal.* □ **shake someone up** rouse someone from lethargy, apathy, or complacency: *he had to do something to shake the team up—we lacked spark.* □ **shake something up 1** mix ingredients by shaking: *use soap flakes shaken up in the water to make bubbles.* **2** make radical changes to the organization or structure of an institution or system: *he presented plans to shake up the legal profession.*

▶*n.* **1** an act of shaking: *with a shake of its magnificent antlers the stag charged down the slope.* ■ an earth tremor. ■ an amount of something that is sprinkled by shaking a container: *add a few shakes of sea salt and black pepper.* ■ short for MILK SHAKE. ■ (**the shakes**) *inf.* a fit of trembling or shivering: *I wouldn't go in there, it gives me the shakes.* **2** *Mus.* a trill.

▶ □ **get** (or **give someone**) **a fair shake** *inf.* get (or give someone) just treatment or a fair chance: *I do not believe he gave the industry a fair shake.* □ **in two shakes** (**of a lamb's tail**) *inf.* very quickly: *I'll be back to you in*

---

two shakes. □ **more —— than one can shake a stick at** inf. used to emphasize the largeness of an amount: *a team with more experience than you can shake a stick at.* □ **no great shakes** inf. not very good or significant: *it is no great shakes as a piece of cinema.* □ **shake the dust off one's feet** leave indignantly or disdainfully. □ **shake hands (with someone)** (or **shake someone by the hand** or **shake someone's hand**) clasp someone's right hand in one's own at meeting or parting, in reconciliation or congratulation, or as a sign of agreement. □ **shake one's head** turn one's head from side to side in order to indicate refusal, denial, disapproval, or incredulity: *she shook her head in disbelief.* □ **shake a leg** inf. make a start; rouse oneself: *come on, shake a leg.*

shake·down /ˈSHākˌdoun/ ▶n. inf. **1** a radical change or restructuring, particularly in a hierarchical organization or group: *after the collapse of the Soviet Union, a shakedown of the Russian press was inevitable.* ■ a thorough search of a person or place: *harassment and shakedowns by persons in police uniforms.* ■ a swindle; a piece of extortion: *he wants to eliminate bribery, shakedowns, and bid-rigging in New York City's construction industry.* ■ a test of a new product or model, esp. a vehicle or ship: *the high-orbit shakedown of the lunar module had its merits.* **2** a makeshift bed.

shake·out /ˈSHākˌout/ ▶n. inf. an upheaval or reorganization of a business, market, or organization due to competition and typically involving streamlining and layoffs.

shak·er /ˈSHākər/ ▶n. **1** a container used for mixing ingredients by shaking: *a cocktail shaker.* ■ a container with a pierced top from which a powdered substance such as flour or salt is poured by shaking. **2** (**Shaker**) a member of an American religious sect, the United Society of Believers in Christ's Second Coming, established in England *c.*1750 and living simply in celibate mixed communities. ■ [as adj.] denoting a style of elegantly functional furniture traditionally produced by Shaker communities. —**Shak·er·ism** /-ˌrizəm/ n.

shake-up (also **shake·up**) ▶n. inf. a radical reorganization.

shak·o /ˈSHakō; ˈSHā-/ ▶n. (pl. **-os**) a cylindrical or conical military hat with a brim and a plume or pom-pom.

shak·y /ˈSHākē/ ▶adj. (**shak·i·er, shak·i·est**) shaking or trembling: *she managed a shaky laugh.* ■ unstable because of poor construction or heavy use: *a cracked, dangerously shaky table.* ■ not safe or reliable; liable to fail or falter: *thoroughly shaky evidence.* —**shak·i·ly** /-kilē/ adv. —**shak·i·ness** n.

shale /SHāl/ ▶n. soft, fine-grained sedimentary rock that formed from consolidated mud or clay and can be split easily into fragile slabs. —**shal·y** (also **shal·ey**) adj.

shale oil ▶n. oil obtained from bituminous shale.

shall /SHal/ ▶modal verb (3rd sing. present **shall**) **1** (in the first person) expressing the future tense: *this time next week I shall be in Scotland.* **2** expressing a strong assertion or intention: *they shall succeed.* **3** expressing an instruction or command: *you shall not steal.* **4** used in questions indicating offers or suggestions: *shall I send you the book?*

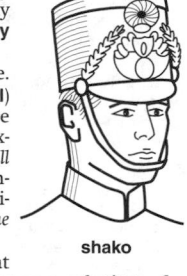

shako

shal·lot /SHəˈlät; ˈSHalət/ ▶n. **1** a small bulb that resembles an onion and is used for pickling or as a substitute for onion. **2** the plant (*Allium ascalonicum*) of the lily family that produces these bulbs, each mature bulb producing a cluster of smaller bulbs.

shal·low /ˈSHalō/ ▶adj. of little depth: *serve the noodles in a shallow bowl* | *being fairly shallow, the water was warm.* ■ situated at no great depth: *the shallow bed of the North Sea.* ■ varying only slightly from a specified or understood line or direction, esp. the horizontal: *a shallow roof.* ■ not exhibiting, requiring, or capable of serious thought: *a shallow analysis of contemporary society.* ■ (of breathing) taking in little air.
▶n. (**shallows**) an area of the sea, a lake, or a river where the water is not very deep.
▶v. [intr.] (of the sea, a lake, or a river) become less deep over time or in a particular place: *the boat ground to a halt where the water shallowed.* —**shal·low·ly** adv. —**shal·low·ness** n.

sha·lom /SHäˈlōm; SHə-/ ▶interj. used as salutation by Jews at meeting or parting, meaning "peace."

shalt /SHalt/ ▶ archaic second person singular of **SHALL**.

sham /SHam/ ▶n. **1** a thing that is not what it is purported to be: *the proposed legislation is a farce and a sham.* ■ pretense: *it all turned out to be sham and hypocrisy.* ■ a person who pretends to be someone or something they are not: *he was a sham, totally unqualified for his job as a senior doctor.* **2** short for **PILLOW SHAM**.
▶adj. bogus; false: *a clergyman who arranged a sham marriage.*

▶v. (**shammed, sham·ming**) [intr.] falsely present something as the truth: *was he ill or was he shamming?* ■ [tr.] pretend to be or to be experiencing: *she shams indifference.* —**sham·mer** n.

sha·man /ˈSHämən; ˈSHā-/ ▶n. (pl. **-mans**) a person regarded as having access to, and influence in, the world of good and evil spirits, esp. among some peoples of northern Asia and North America. —**sha·man·ic** /SHəˈmanik/ adj. —**sha·man·ism** /-ˌnizəm/ n. —**sha·man·ist** /-nist/ n. & adj. —**sha·man·is·tic** /ˌSHämənˈistik; ˌSHā-/ adj.

sham·ble /ˈSHambəl/ ▶v. [intr.] (of a person) move with a slow, shuffling, awkward gait: *he shambled off down the corridor* | [as adj.] (**shambling**) *a big, shambling, shy man.*
▶n. a slow, shuffling, awkward gait.

sham·bles /ˈSHambəlz/ ▶pl. n. [treated as sing.] **1** inf. a state of total disorder: *my career was in a shambles.* **2** a butcher's slaughterhouse (archaic except in place names). ■ a scene of carnage: *the room was a shambles—their throats had been cut and they lay in a waste of blood.*

shame /SHām/ ▶n. a painful feeling of humiliation or distress caused by the consciousness of wrong or foolish behavior: *she was hot with shame.* ■ a loss of respect or esteem; dishonor: *the incident had brought shame on his family.* ■ used to reprove someone for something of which they should be ashamed: *shame on you for hitting a woman.* ■ a regrettable or unfortunate situation or action: *it is a shame that they are not better known.* ■ a person, action, or situation that brings a loss of respect or honor: *ignorance of Latin would be a disgrace and a shame to any public man.*
▶v. [tr.] (of a person, action, or situation) make (someone) feel ashamed: *I tried to shame him into giving some away.* ■ cause (someone) to feel ashamed or inadequate by outdoing or surpassing them: *she shames me with her eighty-year-old energy.*

shame·faced /ˈSHāmˌfāst/ ▶adj. feeling or expressing shame or embarrassment: *all the boys looked shamefaced.* —**shame·fac·ed·ly** /-ˌfāsidlē/ -ˌfāstlē/ adv. —**shame·fac·ed·ness** /-ˌfāsidnis/ n.

shame·ful /ˈSHāmfəl/ ▶adj. worthy of or causing shame or disgrace: *a shameful accusation.* —**shame·ful·ly** adv. *record companies are shamefully slow in fulfilling orders.* —**shame·ful·ness** n.

shame·less /ˈSHāmlis/ ▶adj. (of a person or their conduct) characterized by or showing a lack of shame: *his shameless hypocrisy.* —**shame·less·ly** adv. —**shame·less·ness** n.

sham·my /ˈSHamē/ (also **shammy leather**) ▶n. (pl. **-mies**) informal term for **CHAMOIS** (sense 2).

sham·poo /SHamˈpōō/ ▶n. a liquid preparation containing detergent or soap for washing the hair: *he smelt clean, of soap and shampoo* | *an anti-dandruff shampoo.* ■ a similar substance for cleaning a carpet, soft furnishings, or a car. ■ an act of washing or cleaning something, esp. the hair, with shampoo: *a shampoo and set.*
▶v. (**-poos, -pooed** /-ˈpōōd/) [tr.] wash or clean (something, esp. the hair) with shampoo: *Dolly was sitting in the bath shampooing her hair.*

sham·rock /ˈSHamˌräk/ ▶n. a low-growing, cloverlike plant (esp. *Trifolium minus*) of the pea family, with three-lobed leaves, used as the national emblem of Ireland. ■ a spray or leaf of this plant. ▷late 16th cent.: from Irish *seamróg* 'trefoil' (diminutive of *seamar* 'clover').

shang·hai /ˈSHaNGˌhī/ ▶v. (**-hais, -haied** /-ˌhīd/, **-hai·ing** /-ˌhī-iNG/) [tr.] hist. force (someone) to join a ship lacking a full crew by drugging them or using other underhanded means. ■ inf. coerce or trick (someone) into a place or position or into doing something: *Brady shanghaied her into his Jaguar and roared off.*

Shan·gri-La /ˈSHaNGgri ˈlä/ ▶a Tibetan utopia in James Hilton's novel *Lost Horizon* (1933). ■ [as n.] (**a Shangri-La**) a place regarded as an earthly paradise, esp. when involving a retreat from the pressures of modern civilization.

shank /SHaNGk/ ▶n. **1** (often **shanks**) a person's leg, esp. the part from the knee to the ankle: *the old man's thin, bony shanks showed through his trousers.* ■ the lower part of an animal's foreleg. ■ this part of an animal's leg as a cut of meat. **2** the shaft or stem of a tool or implement, in particular: ■ a long narrow part of a tool connecting the handle to the operational end. ■ the cylindrical part of a bit by which it is held in a drill. ■ the long stem of a key, spoon, anchor, etc. ■ the straight part of a nail or fishhook. **3** a part or appendage by which something is attached to something else, esp. a wire loop attached to the back of a button. ■ the band of a ring rather than the setting or gemstone. **4** the narrow middle of the sole of a shoe. **5** inf. a dagger made by a prison inmate from available materials.
▶v. [tr.] Golf strike (the ball) with the heel of the club: *even a pro can shank a drive now and then.* —**shanked** adj. [usu. in comb.] *a long-shanked hook.*

shan't /SHant/ ▶contr. of shall not.

shan·ty[1] /ˈSHantē/ ▶n. (pl. **-ties**) a small, crudely built shack.

shan·ty[2] ▶n. (pl. **-ties**) variant spelling of **CHANTEY**.

shan·ty·town /ˈsHantē,toun/ ▶ *n.* a deprived area on the outskirts of a town consisting of large numbers of crude dwellings.

SHAPE /sHāp/ ▶ *abbr.* Supreme Headquarters Allied Powers Europe, one of NATO's two main military commands.

shape /sHāp/ ▶ *n.* **1** the external form or appearance characteristic of someone or something; the outline of an area or figure: *she liked the shape of his nose.* ■ a person or thing that is difficult to see and identify clearly: *he saw a shape through the mist.* ■ a specific form or guise assumed by someone or something: *a fiend in human shape.* ■ a piece of material, paper, etc., made or cut in a particular form: *stick paper shapes on for the puppet's eyes and nose.* **2** the particular condition or state of someone or something: *he was in no shape to drive.* ■ the distinctive nature or qualities of something: *the future shape and direction of the country.* ■ definite or orderly arrangement: *check that your structure will* **give shape** *to your essay.*

▶ *v.* [*tr.*] (often **be shaped**) give a particular shape or form to: *most caves are shaped by the flow of water through limestone.* ■ make (something) fit the form of something else: [*tr.*] *suits have been shaped to fit so snugly that no curve is undefined.* ■ determine the nature of; have a great influence on: *his childhood was shaped by a loving relationship with his elder brother.* ■ [*intr.*] develop in a particular way; progress: *the yacht was shaping well in trials.* ■ form or produce (a sound or words).

▶ *phrasal v.* □ **shape up** develop or happen in a particular way: *it was shaping up to be another bleak year.* ■ *inf.* improve performance or behavior: *we have never been afraid to tell our children to shape up* ■ become physically fit: *I need to shape up.* —**shap·a·ble** (also **shape·a·ble**) *adj.* —**shaped** *adj.* [usu. in comb.] *egg-shaped | X-shaped.* —**shap·er** *n.*

▶ □ **get into shape** (or **get someone into shape**) become (or make someone) physically fitter by exercise: *if you're thinking of getting into shape, take it easy and build up slowly.* □ **in** (**good**) **shape** in good physical condition. □ **in the shape of** represented or embodied by: *retribution arrived in the shape of my irate father.* □ **out of shape 1** (of an object) not having its usual or original shape, esp. after being bent or knocked: *check that the pipe end and compression nut are not bent out of shape.* **2** (of a person) in poor physical condition; unfit. □ **take shape** assume a distinct form; develop into something definite or tangible: *the past few months have seen the state's health insurance legislation begin to take shape.*

shape·less /ˈsHāplis/ ▶ *adj.* (esp. of a garment) lacking a distinctive or attractive shape: *women in shapeless cotton dresses.* —**shape·less·ly** *adv.* —**shape·less·ness** *n.*

shape·ly /ˈsHāplē/ ▶ *adj.* (**-li·er, -li·est**) (esp. of a woman or part of her body) having an attractive or well-proportioned shape: *however much she ate made no difference to her shapely figure.* —**shape·li·ness** *n.*

shard /sHärd/ ▶ *n.* a piece of broken ceramic, metal, glass, or rock, typically having sharp edges: *shards of glass flew in all directions.*

share /sHe(ə)r/ ▶ *n.* a part or portion of a larger amount that is divided among a number of people, or to which a number of people contribute: *under the proposals, investors would pay a greater share of the annual fees required.* ■ one of the equal parts into which a company's capital is divided, entitling the holder to a proportion of the profits: *bought 33 shares of American Standard.* ■ part proprietorship of property held by joint owners: *Jake had a share in a large seagoing vessel.* ■ the allotted or due amount of something that a person expects to have or to do, or that is expected to be accepted or done by them: *she's done more than her fair share of globe-trotting.*

▶ *v.* [*tr.*] have a portion of (something) with another or others: *he* **shared** *the pie* **with** *her.* ■ [*tr.*] give a portion of (something) to another or others: *money raised will be shared between the two charities.* ■ use, occupy, or enjoy (something) jointly with another or others: *they once shared a house in the Hamptons.* ■ possess (a view or quality) in common with others: *other countries don't share our reluctance to eat goat meat.* ■ [*intr.*] (**share in**) (of a number of people or organizations) have a part in (something, esp. an activity): *the companies would share in the development of three oil platforms.* ■ tell someone about (something), esp. something personal: *she had never* **shared** *the secret* **with** *anyone before.* —**share·a·ble** (also **shar·a·ble**) *adj.* —**shar·er** *n.*

share·crop·per /ˈsHe(ə)r,kräpər/ ▶ *n.* a tenant farmer who gives a part of each crop as rent. —**share·crop** *v.* (**-cropped, -crop·ping**).

share·hold·er /ˈsHe(ə)r,hōldər/ ▶ *n.* an owner of shares in a company. —**share·hold·ing** /-,hōldiNG/ *n.*

share·ware /ˈsHe(ə)r,we(ə)r/ ▶ *n. Comput.* software that is available free of charge and often distributed informally for evaluation, after which a fee may be requested for continued use.

sha·ri·a /sHäˈrēə/ (also **sha·ri·ah**) ▶ *n.* Islamic canonical law based on the teachings of the Koran and the traditions of the Prophet (Hadith and Sunna), prescribing both religious and secular duties and sometimes retributive penalties for lawbreaking. It has generally been supplemented by legislation adapted to the conditions of the day, though the manner in which it should be applied in modern states is a subject of dispute between Islamic fundamentalists and modernists.

sha·rif /sHəˈrēf/ (also **she·reef** or **she·rif**) ▶ *n.* **1** a descendant of Muhammad through his daughter Fatima, entitled to wear a green turban or veil. **2** a Muslim ruler, magistrate, or religious leader. —**sha·rif·i·an** *adj.*

shark[1] /sHärk/ ▶ *n.* **1** a long-bodied chiefly marine fish with a cartilaginous skeleton, a prominent dorsal fin, and toothlike scales. Most sharks are predatory, although the largest kinds feed on plankton. **2** a small Southeast Asian freshwater fish of the minnow family with a sharklike tail, popular in aquariums.

shark[2] ▶ *n. inf.* **1** a person who unscrupulously exploits or swindles others: *Coleby was a shark, not the sort of man to pay more when he could pay less.* See also **LOAN SHARK. 2** an expert in a specified field: *a pool shark.*

shark·skin /ˈsHärk,skin/ ▶ *n.* the rough scaly skin of a shark, sometimes used as shagreen. ■ a stiff, slightly lustrous synthetic fabric.

sharp /sHärp/ ▶ *adj.* **1** (of an object) having an edge or point that is able to cut or pierce something: *cut the cake with a very sharp knife | keep tools sharp.* ■ producing a sudden, piercing physical sensation or effect: *I suddenly felt a sharp pain in my back.* ■ (of a food, taste, or smell) acidic and intense: *sharp goats' milk cheese.* ■ (of a sound) sudden and penetrating: *there was a sharp crack of thunder.* ■ (of words or a speaker) intended or intending to criticize or hurt: *she feared his sharp tongue.* ■ (of an emotion or experience) felt acutely or intensely; painful: *her sharp disappointment was tinged with embarrassment.* **2** tapering to a point or edge: *a sharp pencil.* ■ distinct in outline or detail; clearly defined: *the job was a sharp contrast from her past life.* ■ *inf.* (of clothes or their wearer) neat and stylish: *they were greeted by a young man in a sharp suit.* **3** (of an action or change) sudden and marked: *there was a sharp increase in interest rates.* ■ (of a bend, angle, or turn) making a sudden change of direction: *a sharp turn in the river.* ■ having or showing speed of perception, comprehension, or response: *her sharp eyes missed nothing.* ■ quick to take advantage, esp. in an unscrupulous or dishonest way: *Paul's a sharp operator.* **4** (of musical sound) above true or normal pitch. ■ [in comb.] (of a note) a semitone higher than a specified note: *the quartet in C-sharp minor.* ■ (of a key) having a sharp or sharps in the key signature: *recorder players are most comfortable in sharp keys.*

▶ *adv.* **1** precisely (used after an expression of time): *the meeting starts at 7:30 sharp.* **2** in a sudden or abrupt way: *the creek bent sharp left.* **3** above the true or normal pitch of musical sound: *he heard him playing a little sharp on the high notes.*

▶ *n.* **1** a musical note raised a semitone above natural pitch. ■ the sign (♯) indicating this. **2** a long, sharply pointed sewing needle. ■ (usu. **sharps**) a thing with a sharp edge or point, such as a hypodermic needle, a blade, or a fragment of glass: *the safe disposal of sharps and clinical waste.* **3** *inf.* a swindler or cheat. See also **CARD SHARP.**

▶ *v.* [*tr.*] (usu. as *adj.*) (**sharped**) *Mus.* raise the pitch of (a note). —**sharp·ly** *adv.* —**sharp·ness** *n.*

sharp·en /ˈsHärpən/ ▶ *v.* make or become sharp: [*tr.*] *she sharpened her pencil* | [*intr.*] *her tone sharpened to exasperation.* ■ improve or cause to improve: [*intr.*] *they must* **sharpen up** *or risk losing half their business* | [*tr.*] *students will* **sharpen up** *their reading skills.* —**sharp·en·er** *n.*

sharp·er /ˈsHärpər/ ▶ *n. inf.* a swindler, esp. at cards.

sharp·shoot·er /ˈsHärp,sHo͞otər/ ▶ *n.* a person who is very skilled in shooting. —**sharp·shoot·ing** /-,sHo͞otiNG/ *n. & adj.*

sharp·wit·ted ▶ *adj.* (of a person) quick to notice and understand things. —**sharp·wit·ted·ly** *adv.* —**sharp·wit·ted·ness** *n.*

shat·ter /ˈsHatər/ ▶ *v.* break or cause to break suddenly and violently into pieces: [*intr.*] *bullets riddled the bar top, glasses shattered, bottles exploded* | [*tr.*] *the window was shattered by a stone.* ■ [*tr.*] damage or destroy (something abstract): *the crisis will shatter their confidence.* ■ [*tr.*] upset (someone) greatly: *everyone was shattered by the news* | [as *adj.*] (**shattering**) *he found it a shattering experience.* —**shat·ter·er** *n.* —**shat·ter·ing·ly** *adv.* —**shat·ter·proof** /-,pro͞of/ *adj.*

shave /sHāv/ ▶ *v.* **1** [*intr.*] cut the hair off one's face with a razor: *he washed, shaved, and had breakfast.* ■ [*tr.*] cut the hair off (a part of the body) with a razor: *she shaved her legs.* ■ [*tr.*] cut the hair off the face or another part of the body of (someone) with a razor: *his wife washed and shaved him.* ■ cut (hair) off with a razor: *professional male swimmers* **shave** *off their body hair.* **2** [*tr.*] cut (a thin slice or slices) from the surface of

---

Pronunciation Key ə *ago,* up; ər *over, fur;* a *hat;* ā *ate;* ä *car;* cH *chin;* e *let;* ē *see;* e(ə)r *air;* i *fit;* ī *by;* i(ə)r *ear;* NG *sing;* ō *go;* ô *law, for;* oi *toy;* o͞o *good;* o͞o *goo;* ou *out;* sH *she;* tH *thin;* tH *then;* (h)w *why;* zH *vision*

something: *scrape a large, sharp knife across the surface*, **shaving off** *rolls of very fine chocolate*. ■ reduce by a small amount: *they shaved profit margins*. ■ remove (a small amount) from something: *she shaved 0.5 seconds off the record*. **3** [*tr.*] pass or send something close to (something else), missing it narrowly: *Scott shaved the post in the 29th minute*.

▸*n.* **1** an act of shaving hair from the face or a part of the body: *he always needed a shave*. **2** a tool used for shaving very thin slices or layers from wood or other material.

shav·er /ˈSHāvər/ ▸*n.* **1** an electric razor. **2** *inf.* a young lad: *little shavers and their older brothers*.

shav·ing /ˈSHāviNG/ ▸*n.* **1** a thin strip cut off a surface: *she brushed wood shavings from her knees*. **2** the action of shaving.

sha·war·ma /SHəˈwärmə/ ▸*n.* roasted meat, especially when cooked on a revolving spit and shaved for serving in sandwiches.

shawl /SHôl/ ▸*n.* a piece of fabric worn by women over the shoulders or head or wrapped around a baby. ▷from Urdu and Persian *SHāl*, probably from *SHāliāt*, the name of a town in India. —**shawled** *adj.*

Shaw·nee /SHôˈnē/ ▸*n.* (*pl.* same or **-nees**) **1** a member of an American Indian people living formerly in the eastern U.S. and now chiefly in Oklahoma. **2** the Algonquian language of this people.

▸*adj.* of or relating to the Shawnee or their language.

she /SHē/ ▸*pron.* [*third person sing.*] used to refer to a woman, girl, or female animal previously mentioned or easily identified: *my sister told me that she was not happy*. ■ used to refer to a ship, vehicle, country, or other inanimate thing regarded as female: *I was aboard the St. Roch shortly before she sailed for the Northwest Passage*. ■ used to refer to a person or animal of unspecified sex: *only include your child if you know she won't distract you*. ■ any female person: *she who rocks the cradle rules the world*.

▸*n.* a female; a woman: *society would label him a slut if he were a she*. ■ [in *comb.*] female: *a she-bear* | *a she-wolf*.

s/he /SHē ər ˈhē; ˈSHē ˈhē/ ▸*pron.* a written representation of "he or she" used as a neutral alternative to indicate someone of either sex.

sheaf /SHēf/ ▸*n.* (*pl.* **sheaves** /SHēvz/) a bundle of grain stalks laid lengthwise and tied together after reaping. ■ a bundle of objects of one kind, esp. papers: *he waved a sheaf of papers in the air*.

shear /SHi(ə)r/ ▸*v.* (*past part.* **shorn** /SHôrn/ or **sheared**) **1** [*tr.*] cut the wool off (a sheep or other animal). ■ cut off (something such as hair, wool, or grass), with scissors or shears: *I'll shear off all that fleece*. ■ (**be shorn of**) have something cut off: *they were shorn of their hair*. **2** break off or cause to break off, owing to a structural strain: [*intr.*] *the derailleur sheared and jammed in the rear wheel* | [*tr.*] *the left wing had been almost completely sheared off*.

▸*n.* a strain in the structure of a substance produced by pressure, when its layers are laterally shifted in relation to each other. —**shear·er** *n.*

shear·wa·ter /ˈSHir,wôtər; -,wätər/ ▸*n.* **1** a long-winged seabird (*Puffinus* and other genera, family Procellariidae) related to the petrels, often flying low over the surface of the water far from land. **2** North American term for SKIMMER (sense 2).

sheath /SHēTH/ ▸*n.* (*pl.* **sheaths** /SHēT͟Hz; SHēTHS/) a close-fitting cover for something, esp. something that is elongated in shape, in particular: ■ a cover for the blade of a knife or sword. ■ a structure in living tissue that closely envelops another: *the fatty sheath around nerve fibers*. ■ a woman's close-fitting dress: *a tight sheath of black and gold lurex*. ■ a protective covering around an electric cable. ■ a condom. —**sheath·less** *adj.*

sheathe /SHēT͟H/ ▸*v.* [*tr.*] put (a weapon such as a knife or sword) into a sheath. ■ (often **be sheathed in**) encase (something) in a close-fitting or protective covering: *her legs were sheathed in black stockings*.

sheath·ing /ˈSHēT͟HiNG/ ▸*n.* protective casing or covering. ■ sheets of rigid material (often plywood) attached to the framework of a building to strengthen it and to underlie siding or roofing.

sheaves /SHēvz/ ▸ plural form of SHEAF.

she·bang /SHəˈbaNG/ ▸*n. inf.* a matter, operation, or set of circumstances: *the Mafia boss who's running the whole shebang*.

shed¹ /SHed/ ▸*n.* a simple roofed structure, typically made of wood or metal, used as a storage space, a shelter for animals, or a workshop. ■ a larger structure, typically with one or more sides open, for storing or maintaining vehicles or other machinery: *a shed is required for the three shunt engines*.

▸*v.* (**shed·ded, shed·ding**) [*tr.*] (usu. **be shedded**) park (a vehicle) in a depot.

shed² ▸*v.* (**shed·ding**; *past* and *past part.* **shed**) [*tr.*] (of a tree or other plant) allow (leaves or fruit) to fall to the ground: *both varieties shed leaves in winter*. ■ (of a reptile, insect, etc.) allow (its skin or shell) to come off, to be replaced by another one that has grown underneath. ■

■ (of a mammal) lose (hair) as a result of molting, disease, or age. ■ take off (clothes). ■ discard (something undesirable, superfluous, or outdated): *what they lacked was a willingness to shed the arrogance of the past*. ■ have the property of preventing (something) from being absorbed: *this leather has a superior ability to shed water, sweat, and salt*. ■ eliminate part of (an electrical power load) by disconnecting circuits.

she'd /SHed/ ▸ *contr.* of she had; she would.

she-dev·il ▸*n.* a malicious or spiteful woman.

sheen /SHēn/ ▸*n.* a soft luster on a surface: *black crushed velvet with a slight sheen*.

▸*v. poetic/lit.* shine or cause to shine softly: [*tr.*] *men entered with rain sheening their steel helms* | [*intr.*] *her black hair sheened in the sun*. —**sheen·y** *adj.*

sheep /SHēp/ ▸*n.* (*pl.* same) **1** a domesticated ruminant (*Ovis aries*) of the cattle family with a thick woolly coat and (typically only in the male) curving horns. ■ a wild mammal related to this, such as the bighorn. **2** a person too easily influenced or led.

sheep·dog /ˈSHēp,dôg; -,däg/ ▸*n.* a dog trained to guard and herd sheep. ■ a dog of a breed suitable for this.

sheep·fold /ˈSHēp,fōld/ ▸*n.* a sheep pen.

sheep·ish /ˈSHēpiSH/ ▸*adj.* (of a person or expression) showing embarrassment from shame or a lack of self-confidence: *a sheepish grin*. —**sheep·ish·ly** *adv.* —**sheep·ish·ness** *n.*

sheep·skin /ˈSHēp,skin/ ▸*n.* a sheep's skin with the wool on, esp. when made into a garment or rug: [as *adj.*] *a sheepskin coat*. ■ leather from a sheep's skin used in bookbinding. ■ *inf.* a diploma.

sheer¹ /SHi(ə)r/ ▸*adj.* **1** nothing other than; unmitigated (used for emphasis): *she giggled with sheer delight*. **2** (esp. of a cliff or wall) perpendicular or nearly so: *the sheer ice walls*. **3** (of a fabric) very thin; diaphanous: *sheer white silk chiffon*.

▸*adv.* perpendicularly: *the ridge fell sheer, in steep crags*.

▸*n.* a very fine or diaphanous fabric or article. —**sheer·ly** *adv.* —**sheer·ness** *n.*

sheer² ▸*v.* [*intr.*] (typically of a boat or ship) swerve or change course quickly: *the boat sheered off to beach further up the coast*. ■ *fig.* avoid or move away from an unpleasant topic: *her mind sheered away from images she didn't want to dwell on*.

sheer³ ▸*n.* the upward slope of a ship's lines toward the bow and stern.

sheer·legs /ˈSHi(ə)r,legz/ ▸*pl. n.* [treated as *sing.*] a hoisting apparatus made from poles joined at or near the top and separated at the bottom, used for masting ships, installing engines, and lifting other heavy objects.

sheet¹ /SHēt/ ▸*n.* **1** a large rectangular piece of cotton or other fabric, used on a bed to cover the mattress and as a layer beneath blankets when these are used. ■ used in comparisons to describe the pallor of a person who is ill or has had a shock: *Are you OK? You're as white as a sheet*. ■ a broad flat piece of material such as metal or glass: *the small pipe has been formed from a flat sheet of bronze*. **2** a rectangular piece of paper, esp. one of a standard size produced commercially and used for writing and printing on: *a sheet of unmarked paper*. ■ a quantity of text or other information contained on such a piece of paper: *he produced yet another sheet of figures*. ■ a flat piece of paper as opposed to a reel of continuous paper, the bound pages of a book, or a folded map. ■ all the postage stamps printed on one piece of paper: *a sheet of stamps*. ■ a map, esp. one part of a series covering a larger area. **3** an extensive unbroken surface area of something: *a sheet of ice*. ■ a broad moving mass of flames or water: *the rain was still falling in sheets*.

sheet² *Naut.* ▸*n.* **1** a rope attached to the lower corner of a sail for securing or extending the sail or for altering its direction. **2** (**sheets**) the space at the bow or stern of an open boat.

▸ □ **two** (or **three**) **sheets to the wind** *inf.* drunk.

sheet·ing /ˈSHētiNG/ ▸*n.* material formed into a sheet: *a window covered with plastic sheeting*.

sheet light·ning ▸*n.* lightning with its brightness diffused by reflection within clouds.

sheet met·al ▸*n.* metal formed into thin sheets, typically by rolling or hammering.

sheet mu·sic ▸*n.* printed music, as opposed to performed or recorded music. ■ music published in single or interleaved sheets, not bound.

sheikh /SHēk; SHāk/ (also **sheik**) ▸*n.* **1** an Arab leader, in particular the chief or head of an Arab tribe, family, or village. **2** a leader in a Muslim community or organization. —**sheikh·dom** /-dəm/ *n.*

shei·la /ˈSHēlə/ ▸*n. Austral./NZ informal* a girl or young woman.

shek·el /ˈSHekəl/ ▸*n.* the basic monetary unit of modern Israel, equal to 100 agora. ■ (**shekels**) *inf.* money; wealth.

shel·drake /ˈSHelˌdrāk/ ▶n. another name for SHELDUCK (specifically a male).

shel·duck /ˈSHelˌdək/ ▶n. (pl. same or **shelducks**) a large gooselike Old World duck (genus *Tadorna*) with brightly colored plumage, typically showing black and white wings in flight.

shelf /SHelf/ ▶n. (pl. **shelves** /SHelvz/) a flat length of wood or rigid material, attached to a wall or forming part of a piece of furniture, that provides a surface for the storage or display of objects. ■ a ledge of rock or protruding strip of land. ■ a submarine bank, or a part of the continental shelf. ▷Middle English: from Middle Low German *schelf*; related to Old English *scylfe* 'partition,' *scylf* 'crag.' —**shelf·ful** /-ˌfool/ n. (pl. **-fuls**) —**shelf·like** /-ˌlīk/ adj.
▶ □ **off the shelf** not designed or made to order but taken from existing stock or supplies: *off-the-shelf software packages.*

shelf life ▶n. the length of time for which an item remains usable, fit for consumption, or saleable.

shell /SHel/ ▶n. **1** the hard protective outer case of a mollusk or crustacean: *cowrie shells.* ■ the thin outer covering of an animal's egg, which is hard and fragile in that of a bird but leathery in that of a reptile. ■ the outer case of a nut kernel or seed. ■ the carapace of a tortoise, turtle, or terrapin. ■ (**one's shell**) *fig.* used with reference to a state of shyness or introversion: *she'll soon come out of her shell with the right encouragement.* **2** something resembling or likened to a shell because of its shape or its function as an outer case: *pasta shells.* ■ the walls of an unfinished or gutted building or other structure: *the hotel was a shell, the roof having collapsed completely.* ■ *fig.* an outer form without substance: *he was a shell of the man he had been previously.* ■ a light racing boat used in the sport of crew. ■ a woman's sleeveless sweater or blouse. ■ the metal framework of a vehicle body. ■ *Physics* each of a set of orbitals around the nucleus of an atom, occupied or able to be occupied by electrons of similar energies. **3** an explosive artillery projectile or bomb: *the sound of the shell passing over, followed by the explosion.* ■ a hollow metal or paper case used as a container for fireworks, explosives, or cartridges. ■ a cartridge.
▶v. **1** [tr.] bombard with shells: *the guns started shelling their positions.* **2** [tr.] remove the shell or pod from (a nut or seed): *they were shelling peas.*
▶*phrasal v.* □ **shell something out** (or **shell out**) *inf.* pay a specified amount of money, esp. an amount that is resented as being excessive: *it doesn't make sense to shell out $8.50 for an elevator ride.* —**shelled** adj. [in comb.]: *a soft-shelled clam.* —**shell·less** adj. —**shell·like** /-ˌlīk/ adj. —**shell·y** /ˈSHelē/ adj.

she'll /SHēl/ ▶contr. of she shall; she will.

shel·lac /SHəˈlak/ ▶n. lac resin melted into thin flakes, used for making varnish. ■ a thin varnish containing this resin.
▶v. (**-lacked** /-ˈlakt/, **-lack·ing** /-ˈlakiNG/) [tr.] **1** [often as adj.] (**shellacked**) varnish (something) with shellac. **2** (usu. **be shellacked**) *inf.* defeat or beat (someone) decisively: *they were shellacked in the 1982 election.*

shell·fish /ˈSHelˌfiSH/ ▶n. (pl. same) an aquatic shelled mollusk (e.g., an oyster or cockle) or a crustacean (e.g., a crab or shrimp), esp. one that is edible. ■ such mollusks or crustaceans as food.

shell pro·gram ▶n. *Comput.* a program that provides an interface between the user and the operating system.

shell shock ▶n. see COMBAT FATIGUE (sense 1). —**shell-shocked** adj.

shel·ter /ˈSHeltər/ ▶n. a place giving temporary protection from bad weather or danger. ■ a place providing food and accommodations for the homeless. ■ an animal sanctuary. ■ a shielded or safe condition; protection: *he hung back in the shelter of a rock.*
▶v. [tr.] protect or shield from something harmful, esp. bad weather: *the hut sheltered him from the cold wind.* ■ [intr.] find refuge or take cover from bad weather or danger: *people were sheltering under store canopies and trees.* ■ prevent (someone) from having to do or face something difficult or unpleasant: [as adj.] (**sheltered**) *she led a sheltered life until her mother and father went through a bitter divorce.* ■ protect (income) from taxation. —**shel·ter·er** n. —**shel·ter·less** adj.

shelve[1] /SHelv/ ▶v. [tr.] place or arrange (items, esp. books) on a shelf. ■ *fig.* decide not to proceed with (a project or plan), either temporarily or permanently: *plans to reopen the school have been shelved.*

shelve[2] ▶v. [intr.] (of ground) slope downward in a specified manner or direction: *the ground shelved gently down to the water.*

shelves /SHelvz/ ▶ plural form of SHELF.

she·nan·i·gans /SHəˈnanəgənz/ ▶pl. n. *inf.* secret or dishonest activity or maneuvering: *widespread financial shenanigans had ruined the fortunes of many.* ■ silly or high-spirited behavior; mischief.

shep·herd /ˈSHepərd/ ▶n. a person who tends and rears sheep. ■ *fig.* a member of the clergy who provides spiritual care and guidance for a congregation. ■ short for GERMAN SHEPHERD.
▶v. [tr.] [usu. as n.] (**shepherding**) tend (sheep) as a shepherd. ■ [tr.] guide or direct in a particular direction: *we were shepherded around with great ceremony.* ■ give guidance to (someone), esp. on spiritual matters: *she had to submit the control of her career and money to a group who shepherded her.*

sher·bet /ˈSHərbit/ ▶n. a frozen dessert made with fruit juice added to milk or cream, egg white, or gelatin. ■ a frozen fruit juice and sugar mixture served as a dessert or between courses of a meal to cleanse the palate.

sherd /SHərd/ ▶n. another term for POTSHERD.

she·reef /SHəˈrēf/ (also **she·rif**) ▶n. variant spelling of SHARIF.

sher·iff /ˈSHerif/ ▶n. an elected officer in a county who is responsible for keeping the peace.

Sher·pa /ˈSHərpə/ ▶n. (pl. same or **-pas**) a member of a Himalayan people living on the borders of Nepal and Tibet, renowned for their skill in mountaineering. ■ a civil servant or diplomat who undertakes preparatory political work prior to a summit conference.

sher·ry /ˈSHerē/ ▶n. (pl. **-ries**) a fortified wine originally and mainly from southern Spain, often drunk as an aperitif.

she's /SHēz/ ▶contr. of she is; she has.

Shet·land po·ny ▶n. a pony of a small, hardy, rough-coated breed.

Shet·land sheep·dog ▶n. a small dog of a collielike breed.

Shet·land wool ▶n. a type of fine loosely twisted wool from Shetland sheep.

shew /SHō/ ▶v. old-fashioned variant spelling of SHOW.

Shi·a /ˈSHēˌä/ (also **Shi'a**) ▶n. (pl. same or **Shi·as**) one of the two main branches of Islam, followed esp. in Iran, that rejects the first three Sunni caliphs and regards Ali, the fourth caliph, as Muhammad's first true successor. Compare with SUNNI. ■ a Muslim who adheres to this branch of Islam.

shi·at·su /SHēˈätsoō/ ▶n. a form of therapy of Japanese origin based on the same principles as acupuncture, in which pressure is applied to certain points on the body using the hands.

shib·bo·leth /ˈSHibəliTH; -ˌleTH/ ▶n. a custom, principle, or belief distinguishing a particular class or group of people, esp. a long-standing one regarded as outmoded or no longer important: *the party began to break with the shibboleths of the left.*

shield /SHēld/ ▶n. **1** a broad piece of metal or another suitable material, held by straps or a handle attached on one side, used as a protection against blows or missiles. **2** something shaped like a shield, in particular: ■ a police officer's badge. ■ *Heraldry* a stylized representation of a shield used for displaying a coat of arms. ■ *Geol.* a large rigid area of the earth's crust, typically of Precambrian rock, that has been unaffected by later orogenic episodes, e.g., the Canadian Shield. **3** a person or thing providing protection: *a protective coating of grease provides a shield against abrasive dirt.* ■ a protective plate or screen on machinery or equipment. ■ a device or material that prevents or reduces the emission of light or other radiation.
▶v. [tr.] protect (someone or something) from a danger, risk, or unpleasant experience: *he pulled the cap lower to shield his eyes from the glare.* ■ prevent from being seen: *the rocks she sat behind shielded her from the lodge.* ■ enclose or screen (a piece of machinery) to protect the user. ■ prevent or reduce the escape of sound, light, or other radiation from (something). ▷Old English *scild* (noun), *scildan* (verb), of Germanic origin; related to Dutch *schild* and German *Schild*, from a base meaning 'divide, separate.' —**shield·less** adj.

shi·er /ˈSHīər/ ▶ a comparative of SHY[1].

shi·est /ˈSHīəst/ ▶ a superlative of SHY[1].

shift /SHift/ ▶v. move or cause to move from one place to another, esp. over a small distance: [tr.] *I shift the weight back to the other leg* | [intr.] *the roof cracked and shifted.* ■ [intr.] change the position of one's body, esp. because one is nervous or uncomfortable: *he shifted a little in his chair.* ■ [tr.] change the emphasis, direction, or focus of: *she's shifting the blame onto me.* ■ [intr.] change in emphasis, direction, or focus: *the wind had shifted to the east.* ■ *Comput.* move (data) one or more places to the right or left in a register: *the partial remainder is shifted left.* ■ [intr.] press the shift key on a typewriter or computer keyboard. ■ [intr.] change gear in a vehicle: *she shifted down to fourth.*
▶n. **1** a slight change in position, direction, or tendency: *a shift of wind took us by surprise.* ■ (also **shift key**) a key on a typewriter or computer keyboard used to switch between two sets of characters or functions,

principally between lowercase and uppercase letters. ■ the gearshift or gear-changing mechanism in a motor vehicle. ■ *Building* the positioning of successive rows of bricks so that their ends do not coincide. ■ *Comput.* a movement of the digits of a word in a register one or more places to left or right, equivalent to multiplying or dividing the corresponding number by a power of whatever number is the base. ■ *Football* a change of position by two or more players before the ball is put into play. **2** one of two or more recurring periods in which different groups of workers do the same jobs in relay: *the night shift.* ■ a group of workers who work in this way. **3** a woman's straight, unwaisted dress. —**shift·a·ble** /ˈSHiftəbəl/ *adj.*

▶ □ **shift for oneself** manage as best one can without help.

shift·less /ˈSHiftlis/ ▶*adj.* (of a person or action) characterized by laziness, indolence, and a lack of ambition: *a shiftless lot of good-for-nothings.* —**shift·less·ly** *adv.* —**shift·less·ness** *n.*

shift·y /ˈSHiftē/ ▶*adj.* (**shift·i·er, shift·i·est**) *inf.* (of a person or their manner) appearing deceitful or evasive: *a shifty, fast-talking lawyer.* —**shift·i·ly** /-əlē/ *adv.* —**shift·i·ness** *n.*

Shi·ite /ˈSHēˌīt/ (also **Shi'ite**) ▶*n.* an adherent of the Shia branch of Islam.

▶*adj.* of or relating to Shia. —**Shi·ism** /ˈSHēˌizəm/ (also **Shi'ism**) *n.*

shill /SHil/ *inf.* ▶*n.* an accomplice of a hawker, gambler, or swindler who acts as an enthusiastic customer to entice or encourage others.

▶*v.* [*intr.*] act or work as such a person.

shil·le·lagh /SHəˈlālē/ ▶*n.* a thick stick of blackthorn or oak used in Ireland, typically as a weapon.

shil·ling /ˈSHiliNG/ ▶*n.* **1** a former British coin and monetary unit equal to one twentieth of a pound or twelve pence. **2** the basic monetary unit in Kenya, Tanzania, and Uganda, equal to 100 cents.

shil·ly-shal·ly /ˈSHilē ˌSHalē/ ▶*v.* (**-lies, -lied**) [*intr.*] fail to act resolutely or decisively: *the government shilly-shallied about the matter.*

▶*n.* indecisive behavior. —**shil·ly-shal·ly·er** /-ˌSHalēər/ (also **shil·ly-shal·li·er**) *n.*

shim /SHim/ ▶*n.* a washer or thin strip of material used to align parts, make them fit, or reduce wear.

▶*v.* (**shimmed, shim·ming**) [*tr.*] wedge (something) or fill up (a space) with a shim.

shim·mer /ˈSHimər/ ▶*v.* [*intr.*] shine with a soft tremulous light: *the sea shimmered in the sunlight.*

▶*n.* a light with such qualities: *a pale shimmer of moonlight.* —**shim·mer·ing·ly** *adv.* —**shim·mer·y** *adj.*

shim·my /ˈSHimē/ ▶*n.* (pl. **-mies**) a kind of ragtime dance in which the whole body shakes or sways. ■ shaking, esp. abnormal vibration of the wheels of a motor vehicle: *a shimmy caused by oversized tires.*

▶*v.* (**-mies, -mied**) [*intr.*] dance the shimmy. ■ shake or vibrate abnormally: *he braked hard and felt the car shimmy.* ■ move with a graceful swaying motion: *her hair swung as she shimmied down the catwalk.*

shin /SHin/ ▶*n.* the front of the leg below the knee.

▶*v.* (**shinned, shin·ning**) [*intr.*] (**shin up/down**) climb quickly up or down by gripping with one's arms and legs: *he shinned up a tree.*

shin·bone /ˈSHinˌbōn/ ▶*n.* the tibia.

shin·dig /ˈSHinˌdig/ ▶*n. inf.* a large, lively party, esp. one celebrating something.

shine /SHīn/ ▶*v.* (*past* **shone** /SHōn/ or **shined**) **1** [*intr.*] (of the sun or another source of light) give out a bright light: *the sun shone through the window.* ■ glow or be bright with reflected light: *I could see his eyes shining in the light of the fire.* ■ [*tr.*] direct (a flashlight or other light) somewhere in order to see something in the dark: *an usher shines his flashlight into the boys' faces.* ■ (of something with a smooth surface) reflect light because clean or polished: *my shoes were polished until they shone like glass.* ■ (of a person's eyes) be bright with the expression of a particular emotion: *his eyes shone with excitement.* ■ [often as *adj.*] (**shining**) *fig.* be brilliant or excellent at something: *he has set a shining example with his model behavior* | *she shines at comedy.* ■ (**shine through**) *fig.* (of a quality or skill) be clearly evident: *at Regis his talent shone through.* **2** (*past* **shined**) [*tr.*] make (an object made of leather, metal, or wood) bright by rubbing it; polish: *his shoes were shined to perfection.*

▶*n.* a quality of brightness, esp. through reflecting light: *a shine of saliva on his chin.* ■ a high polish or sheen; a luster: *use shoe polish to get a shine.* ■ an act of rubbing something to give it a shiny surface. —**shin·ing·ly** /-niNGlē/ *adv.*

▶ □ **take the shine off** spoil the brilliance or excitement of: *the absence of new jobs has taken some of the shine off his stellar popularity ratings.* □ **take a shine to** *inf.* develop a liking for.

shin·er /ˈSHīnər/ ▶*n.* **1** [in *comb.*] a person or thing that polishes something: *shoeshiners.* **2** *inf.* a black eye. **3** a small silvery North American

freshwater fish (*Notropis* and other genera) of the minnow family that typically has colorful markings.

shin·gle[1] /ˈSHiNGgəl/ ▶*n.* a mass of small rounded pebbles, esp. on a seashore. —**shin·gly** /-g(ə)lē/ *adj.*

shin·gle[2] ▶*n.* **1** a rectangular tile of asphalt composite, wood, metal, or slate used on walls or roofs. **2** a small signboard, esp. one found outside a doctor's or lawyer's office.

▶*v.* [*tr.*] roof or clad with shingles.

▶ □ **hang out one's shingle** begin to practice a profession.

shin·gles /ˈSHiNGgəlz/ ▶*pl. n.* [treated as *sing.*] *Med.* an acute, painful inflammation of the nerve ganglia, with skin eruptions. It is caused by the same virus as chicken pox. Also called **HERPES ZOSTER**.

shin·ny[1] /ˈSHinē/ ▶*v.* (**-nies, -nied**) another term for **SHIN**: *he loved to shinny up that tree.*

shin·ny[2] (also **shinny hockey**) ▶*n.* an informal form of ice hockey played esp. by children, on the street or on ice, often with a ball or other object in place of a puck: *we used to play shinny on the canal with tin cans.*

Shin·to /ˈSHinˌtō/ ▶*n.* a Japanese religion dating from the early 8th century and incorporating the worship of ancestors and nature spirits and a belief in sacred power in both animate and inanimate things. It was the state religion of Japan until 1945. —**Shin·to·ism** /-izəm/ *n.* —**Shin·to·ist** /-ist/ *n.*

shin·y /ˈSHinē/ ▶*adj.* (**shin·i·er, shin·i·est**) (of a smooth surface) reflecting light, typically because very clean or polished: *shiny hair* | *shiny black shoes.* —**shin·i·ly** /-əlē/ *adv.* —**shin·i·ness** *n.*

ship /SHip/ ▶*n.* a vessel larger than a boat for transporting people or goods by sea. ■ a sailing vessel with a bowsprit and three or more square-rigged masts. ■ a spaceship. ■ an aircraft.

▶*v.* (**shipped, ship·ping**) **1** [*tr.*] (often **be shipped**) transport (goods or people) on a ship: *the wounded soldiers were shipped home.* ■ transport by some other means: *the freight would be shipped by rail.* ■ [*tr.*] send (a package) somewhere via the mail service or a private company. ■ [*tr.*] *Electr.* make (a product) available for purchase. **2** [*tr.*] (of a boat) take in (water) over the side. **3** [*tr.*] take (oars) from the oarlocks and lay them inside a boat. ■ fix (something such as a rudder or mast) in its place on a ship. —**ship·less** *adj.* —**ship·pa·ble** *adj.*

▶ □ **ship out** (of a naval force or one of its members) go to sea from a home port: *Bob got sick a week before we shipped out.*

ship·board /ˈSHipˌbôrd/ ▶*n.* [as *adj.*] used or occurring on board a ship: *playing in a shipboard jazz orchestra.*

ship·build·er /ˈSHipˌbildər/ ▶*n.* a person or company whose job or business is the design and construction of ships. —**ship·build·ing** /-ˌbildiNG/ *n.*

ship·load /ˈSHipˌlōd/ ▶*n.* as much cargo or as many people as a ship can carry.

ship·mate /ˈSHipˌmāt/ ▶*n.* a fellow member of a ship's crew.

ship·ment /ˈSHipmənt/ ▶*n.* the action of shipping goods: *logs waiting for shipment* | *shipments begin this month.* ■ a quantity of goods shipped; a consignment: *coal and oil shipments.*

ship·per /ˈSHipər/ ▶*n.* a person or company that sends or transports goods by sea, land, or air.

ship·ping /ˈSHipiNG/ ▶*n.* ships considered collectively, esp. those in a particular area or belonging to a particular country: *the volume of shipping using these ports.* ■ the transport of goods by sea or some other means. ■ a charge imposed by a retail company to send merchandise to a customer: *statues were available at $20 plus $4 for shipping and handling.*

ship·shape /ˈSHipˌSHāp/ ▶*adj.* in good order; trim and neat: *he checked that everything was shipshape.*

ship·wreck /ˈSHipˌrek/ ▶*n.* the destruction of a ship at sea by sinking or breaking up, e.g., in a storm or after running aground. ■ a ship so destroyed: *the detritus of a forgotten shipwreck in an Arctic sea.*

▶*v.* (**be shipwrecked**) (of a person or ship) suffer a shipwreck: *he was shipwrecked off the coast of Sardinia and nearly drowned.*

ship·wright /ˈSHipˌrīt/ ▶*n.* a shipbuilder.

ship·yard /ˈSHipˌyärd/ ▶*n.* a place where ships are built and repaired.

shire /SHī(ə)r/ ▶*n. Brit.* a county, esp. in England. ▷Old English *scīr* 'care, official charge, county,' of Germanic origin.

shirk /SHərk/ ▶*v.* [*tr.*] avoid or neglect (a duty or responsibility): *their sole motive is to shirk responsibility and rip off the company.* —**shirk·er** *n.*

shirr /SHər/ ▶*v.* [*tr.*] **1** gather (an area of fabric or part of a garment) by means of drawn or elasticated threads in parallel rows: [as *adj.*] (**shirred**) *a swimsuit with a shirred front.* **2** bake (an egg without its shell).

shirt /SHərt/ ▶*n.* a garment for the upper body made of cotton or a similar fabric, with a collar, sleeves, and buttons down the front. ■ a similar garment of stretchable material with few or no buttons, typically worn as casual wear or for sports. ▷Old English *scyrte*, of Germanic origin; related to Old Norse *skyrta*, Dutch *schort*, German *Schürze* 'apron,' also to *short*; probably from a base meaning 'short garment.' **—shirt·ed** adj. **—shirt·less** adj.

▶ □ **keep your shirt on** *inf.* don't lose your temper; stay calm. □ **lose one's shirt** *inf.* lose all one's possessions. □ **the shirt off one's back** *inf.* one's last remaining possessions: *we share things—we'd give our shirt off our back to another.*

shirt·dress /ˈSHərt,dres/ ▶n. a dress with a collar and buttons in the style of a shirt, typically cut without a seam at the waist.

shirt·front /ˈSHərt,frənt/ ▶n. the breast of a shirt, in particular the part that shows when a suit is worn.

shirt·sleeve /ˈSHərt,slēv/ ▶n. (usu. **shirtsleeves**) the sleeve of a shirt: *he rolled up his shirtsleeves.* ▶adj. **1** (of weather) warm enough to wear a shirt with no jacket: *the shirtsleeve November days before the hard cold set in.* **2** (of work or an atmosphere) straightforward and unpretentious, with hard work being done: *thousands have used this shirtsleeve workshop to improve their company profits.* **—shirt·sleeved** adj.

▶ □ **in (one's) shirtsleeves** wearing a shirt with nothing over it.

shirt·tail /ˈSHər,tāl/ ▶n. (also **shirt·tails**) the lower, typically curved, part of a shirt that comes below the waist. ▶adj. (of relatives) distantly related: *if you checked back far enough, they were shirttail cousins of Curly's parents.*

shirt·waist /ˈSHərt,wāst/ ▶n. a woman's blouse that resembles a shirt. ■ (also **shirtwaist dress**) a woman's dress with a seam at the waist, its bodice incorporating a collar and buttons in the style of a shirt.

shish ke·bab /ˈSHiSH kə,bäb/ ▶n. a dish of pieces of marinated meat and vegetables cooked and served on skewers.

shit /SHit/ *vulgar slang* ▶v. (**shit·ting**; *past* and *past part.* **shit·ted** or **shit** or **shat** /SHat/) [intr.] expel feces from the body. ■ (**shit oneself**) soil one's clothes as a result of expelling feces accidentally. ■ (**shit oneself**) *fig.* be very frightened. ▶n. feces. ■ an act of defecating. ■ a contemptible or worthless person. ■ something worthless; garbage; nonsense. ■ unpleasant experiences or treatment. ■ personal belongings; stuff. ■ any psychoactive drug, e.g., marijuana. ▶interj. an exclamation of disgust, anger, or annoyance.

▶ □ **be shitting bricks** be extremely nervous or frightened. □ **get one's shit together** organize oneself so as to be able to deal with or achieve something. □ **in deep shit** (or **in the shit**) in trouble; in a difficult situation. □ **no shit** used to seek confirmation of the truth of a statement or to confirm the truth of a statement. □ **not know shit** not know anything. □ **shit on someone** show contempt or disregard for someone. □ **be up shit creek** (**without a paddle**) be in an awkward predicament. □ **the shit hits the fan** the disastrous consequences of something become public.

shit·ty /ˈSHitē/ ▶adj. (**-ti·er, -ti·est**) *vulgar slang* **1** (of a person or action) contemptible; worthless. **2** (of an experience or situation) unpleasant; awful. **2** covered with excrement.

Shi·va /ˈSHēvə/ (also **Si·va**) ▶(in Indian religion) a god associated with the powers of reproduction and dissolution.

shiv·er /ˈSHivər/ ▶v. [intr.] (of a person or animal) shake slightly and uncontrollably as a result of being cold, frightened, or excited: *they shivered in the damp foggy cold.* ▶n. a momentary trembling movement: *she gave a little shiver as the wind flicked at her bare arms.* ■ (**the shivers**) a spell or an attack of trembling, typically as a result of fear or horror: *a look that gave him the shivers.* **—shiv·er·er** n. **—shiv·er·ing·ly** adv. **—shiv·er·y** /ˈSHiv(ə)rē/ adj.

shiv·er² ▶n. (usu. **shivers**) each of the small fragments into which something such as glass is shattered when broken; a splinter.

shie·miel /ˈSHlə'məl/ ▶n. variant spelling of SCHLEMIEL.

shlep ▶v. & n. variant spelling of SCHLEP.

shlock ▶n. variant spelling of SCHLOCK.

shmuck ▶n. variant spelling of SCHMUCK.

shoal¹ /SHōl/ ▶n. a large number of fish swimming together: *a shoal of bream.* Compare with SCHOOL². ■ *inf.* a large number of people. ▶v. [intr.] (of fish) form shoals.

shoal² ▶n. an area of shallow water, esp. as a navigational hazard. ■ a submerged sandbank visible at low water. ■ (usu. **shoals**) *fig.* a hidden danger or difficulty: *he alone could safely guide them through Hollywood's treacherous shoals.* ▶v. [intr.] (of water) become shallower. ▶adj. (of water) shallow. **—shoal·y** adj.

shoat /SHōt/ ▶n. a young pig, esp. one that is newly weaned.

shock¹ /SHäk/ ▶n. **1** a sudden upsetting or surprising event or experience: *it was a shock to face such hostile attitudes when I arrived.* ■ a feeling of disturbed surprise resulting from such an event: *her death gave us all a terrible shock.* ■ an acute medical condition associated with a fall in blood pressure, caused by such events as loss of blood, severe burns, bacterial infection, allergic reaction, or sudden emotional stress, and marked by cold, pallid skin, irregular breathing, rapid pulse, and dilated pupils: *he died of shock due to massive abdominal hemorrhage.* ■ a disturbance causing instability in an economy: *trading imbalances caused by the two oil shocks.* ■ short for ELECTRIC SHOCK. **2** a violent shaking movement caused by an impact, explosion, or tremor: *earthquake shocks.* ■ short for SHOCK ABSORBER.

▶v. [tr.] (often **be shocked**) cause (someone) to feel surprised and upset: *she was shocked at the state of his injuries.* ■ offend the moral feelings of; outrage: *the revelations shocked the nation.* ■ [intr.] experience such feelings: *he shocked so easily.* ■ (usu. **be shocked**) affect with physiological shock, or with an electric shock. **—shock·a·bil·i·ty** /-ə'bilitē/ n. **—shock·a·ble** adj.

shock² ▶n. a group of sheaves of grain stacked upright and supporting each other to allow the grain to dry and ripen.

shock³ ▶n. an unkempt or thick mass of hair: *a slender man with an untamable shock of black hair.*

shock ab·sorb·er ▶n. a device for absorbing jolts and vibrations, esp. on a motor vehicle.

shock·er /ˈSHäkər/ ▶n. *inf.* something that shocks, esp. through being unacceptable or sensational: *the play's penultimate sequence is a shocker.*

shock·ing /ˈSHäkiNG/ ▶adj. causing indignation or disgust; offensive: *shocking behavior.* ■ causing a feeling of surprise and dismay: *she brought shocking news.* **—shock·ing·ly** adv. **—shock·ing·ness** n.

shock·proof /ˈSHäk,proōf/ ▶adj. **1** designed to resist damage when dropped or knocked: *a shockproof watch.* **2** not easily shocked: *the teacher puts them at ease by her shockproof attitude toward ignorance.*

shock ther·a·py (also **shock treatment**) ▶n. treatment of chronic mental conditions by electroconvulsive therapy or by inducing physiological shock. ■ *fig.* sudden and drastic measures taken to solve an intractable problem.

shock troops ▶pl. n. a group of soldiers trained specially for carrying out a sudden assault. ■ a group of people likened to such soldiers: *the volunteers became the shock troops in his upset victory over Oregon's senator.*

shock wave ▶n. a sharp change of pressure in a narrow region traveling through a medium, esp. air, caused by explosion or by a body moving faster than sound: *charting the shock waves of the explosion.*

shod /SHäd/ ▶ past and past participle of SHOE.

shod·dy /ˈSHädē/ ▶adj. (**-di·er, -di·est**) badly made or done: *we're not paying good money for shoddy goods.* ■ *fig.* lacking moral principle; sordid: *a shoddy misuse of the honor system.* **—shod·di·ly** /-əlē/ adv. **—shod·di·ness** n.

shoe /SHoō/ ▶n. **1** a covering for the foot, typically made of leather, with a sturdy sole and not reaching above the ankle. ■ a horseshoe. **2** something resembling a shoe in shape or use, in particular: ■ a drag for a wheel. ■ short for BRAKE SHOE. ■ a socket, esp. on a camera, for fitting a flash unit or other accessory.

▶v. (**shoes, shoe·ing** /ˈSHoōiNG/; *past* and *past part.* **shod** /SHäd/) [tr.] (often **be shod**) fit (a horse) with a shoe or shoes. ■ (**be shod**) (of a person) be wearing shoes of a specified kind: *his large feet were shod in sneakers.* ■ protect (the end of an object such as a pole) with a metal shoe: *the four wooden beams were each shod with heavy iron heads.* **—shoe·less** adj.

▶ □ **be** (or **put oneself**) **in another person's shoes** be (or put oneself) in another person's situation or predicament: *if I'd been in your shoes I'd have walked out on him.* □ **if the shoe fits, wear it** used as a way of suggesting that someone should accept a generalized remark or criticism as applying to themselves. □ **the shoe is on the other foot** the situation, in particular the holding of advantage, has reversed. □ **shoe leather** *inf.* used in reference to the wear on shoes through walking: *you can save on shoe leather by giving us your instructions over the telephone.* □ **wait for the other shoe to drop** *inf.* be prepared for a further or consequential event or complication to occur.

shoe·box /ˈSHoō,bäks/ ▶n. a box in which a pair of shoes is delivered or sold. ■ used in references to small or uniform rooms or spaces: *a shoebox of a room.*

S

Pronunciation Key ə *ago*, *up*; ər *over*, *fur*; a *hat*; ā *ate*; ä *car*; CH *chin*; e *let*; ē *see*; e(ə)r *air*; i *fit*; ī *by*; i(ə)r *ear*; NG *sing*; ō *go*; ô *law, for*; oi *toy*; ŏŏ *good*; ōō *goo*; ou *out*; SH *she*; TH *thin*; TH *then*; (h)w *why*; ZH *vision*

shoe·horn /'sнōō,hôrn/ ▶n. a curved instrument used to ease one's heel into a shoe.
▶v. [tr.] force into an inadequate space: *people were shoehorned into cramped corners.*

shoe·lace /'sнōō,lās/ ▶n. a cord or leather strip passed through eyelets or hooks on opposite sides of a shoe and pulled tight and fastened.

shoe·mak·er /'sнōō,mākər/ ▶n. a person who makes shoes and other footwear as a profession. —**shoe·mak·ing** /-,mākiNG/ n.

shoe·shine /'sнōō,sнīn/ ▶n. an act of polishing someone's shoes, esp. for payment: [as adj.] *a shoeshine boy.* —**shoe·shin·er** n.

shoe·string /'sнōō,striNG/ ▶n. **1** inf. a small or inadequate budget: *they proved capable of producing high-quality material on a shoestring.* **2** a shoelace.
▶adj. (of a save, tackle, or catch in sports) near or around the ankles or feet, or just above the ground.

shoe tree ▶n. a shaped block inserted into a shoe when it is not being worn, to keep the shoe in shape.

sho·far /'sнōfər; sнō'fär/ ▶n. (pl. **sho·fars** or **sho·froth** /sнō'frōt; -'frōs/) a ram's-horn trumpet used by ancient Jews in religious ceremonies and as a battle signal, now sounded at Rosh Hashanah and Yom Kippur.

sho·gun /'sнōgən/ ▶n. a hereditary commander-in-chief in feudal Japan.

shone /sнōn/ ▶ past and past participle of SHINE.

shoo /sнōō/ ▶interj. a word said to frighten or drive away a person or animal.
▶v. (**shoos, shooed** /sнōōd/) [tr.] make (a person or animal) go away by waving one's arms at them, saying "shoo," or otherwise acting in a discouraging manner: *I went to comfort her but she shooed me away.*

shoo-in ▶n. a person or thing that is certain to succeed, esp. someone who is certain to win a competition: *he was a shoo-in for reelection.*

shook /sнōōk/ past of SHAKE. ▶adj. (**shook up**) inf. emotionally or physically disturbed; upset: *she looks pretty shook up from the letter.*

shoot /sнōōt/ ▶v. (past **shot** /sнät/) **1** [tr.] kill or wound (a person or animal) with a bullet or arrow: *he was shot in the leg during an armed robbery.* ■ [intr.] fire a bullet from a gun or discharge an arrow from a bow: *he shot at me twice* | [tr.] *they shot a volley of arrows into the village.* ■ cause (a gun) to fire. ■ [tr.] damage or remove (something) with a bullet or missile: *Guy, shoot their hats off.* ■ [intr.] hunt game with a gun: *we go to Scotland to shoot every autumn.* **2** [intr.] move suddenly and rapidly in a particular direction: *the car shot forward.* ■ [tr.] cause to move suddenly and rapidly in a particular direction: *he would have fallen if Marc hadn't shot out a hand to stop him.* ■ [tr.] direct (a glance, question, or remark) at someone: *Luke shot her a quick glance.* ■ [intr.] used to invite a comment or question: *"May I just ask you one more question?" "Shoot."* ■ (of a pain) move with a sharp stabbing sensation: *Claudia felt a shaft of pain shoot through her chest.* ■ [tr.] (of a boat) sweep swiftly down or under (rapids, a waterfall, or a bridge). ■ [tr.] (of a motor vehicle) pass (a traffic light at red). ■ extend sharply in a particular direction: *a road that seemed to just shoot upward at a terrifying angle.* ■ [tr.] move (a door bolt) to fasten or unfasten a door. **3** [intr.] (in soccer, hockey, basketball, etc.) kick, hit, or throw the ball or puck in an attempt to score a goal: *Williams twice shot wide.* ■ [tr.] inf. make (a specified score) for a round of golf: *in the second round he shot a 65.* ■ [tr.] inf. play a game of (pool or dice). **4** [tr.] film or photograph (a scene, film, etc.): *she has just been commissioned to shoot a video* | [intr.] *point the camera and just shoot.* **5** [tr.] inf. inject oneself or another person with (a narcotic drug): *he shot dope into his arm.*
▶phrasal v. □ **shoot someone/something down** kill or wound someone by shooting them, esp. in a ruthless way: *troops shot down 28 demonstrators.* ■ bring down an aircraft, missile, or pilot by shooting at it. ■ fig. crush someone or their opinions by forceful criticism or argument: *she tried to argue and got shot down in flames for her trouble.* □ **shoot up** (esp. of a child) grow taller rapidly: *when she hit thirteen she shot up to a startling 5 foot 9.* ■ (of a price or amount) rise suddenly. □ **shoot someone/something up 1** cause great damage to something by shooting; kill or wound someone by shooting: *the police shot up our building.* **2** (also **shoot up**) inf. inject someone with a narcotic drug: *she went home and shot up alone in her room.*
▶n. **1** a young branch or sucker springing from the main stock of a tree or other plant: *he nipped off the new shoots that grew where the leaves joined the stems.* **2** an occasion when a group of people hunt and shoot game for sport: *a grouse shoot.* ■ a shooting match or contest: *activities include a weekly rifle shoot.* **3** an occasion when a professional photographer takes photographs or when a film or movie is being made: *a photo shoot.* **4** variant spelling of CHUTE[1]. **5** a rapid in a stream: *follow the portages that skirt all nine shoots of whitewater.*
▶interj. inf. used as a euphemism for 'shit': *shoot, it was a great day to be

alive.* ▷Old English *scēotan*, of Germanic origin; related to Dutch *schieten* and German *schiessen*. —**shoot·a·ble** adj.
▶ □ **shoot the breeze** inf. have a casual conversation. □ **shoot from the hip** inf. react suddenly or without careful consideration of one's words or actions. □ **shoot oneself in the foot** inf. inadvertently make a situation worse for oneself. □ **shoot one's mouth off** inf. talk boastfully or indiscreetly.

shoot·er /'sнōōtər/ ▶n. **1** a person who uses a gun either regularly or on a particular occasion. ■ inf. a gun. **2** a member of a team in games such as basketball whose role is to attempt to score goals. ■ a person who throws a die or dice. **3** a marble used to shoot at other marbles.

shoot·ing /'sнōōtiNG/ ▶n. the action or practice of shooting: *the unprovoked shooting of civilians by soldiers.* ■ the sport or pastime of shooting with a gun. ■ the right of shooting game over an area of land. ■ an estate or other area rented to shoot over.
▶adj. moving or growing quickly: *shooting beams of light played over the sea.* ■ (of a pain) sudden and piercing.

shoot·ing gal·ler·y ▶n. a room or fairground booth used for recreational shooting at targets with guns or air guns. ■ inf. a place used for taking drugs, esp. injecting heroin.

shoot·ing range ▶n. an area provided with targets for the controlled practice of shooting.

shoot·ing star[1] ▶n. a small, rapidly moving meteor burning up on entering the earth's atmosphere.

shoot·ing star[2] ▶n. a North American plant (genus *Dodecatheon*) of the primrose family, with white, pink, or purple hanging flowers with backward curving petals.

shoot-out ▶n. inf. a decisive gun battle. ■ (also **penalty shoot-out**) Soccer a tiebreaker decided by each side taking a specified number of penalty kicks.

shop /sнäp/ ▶n. **1** a building or part of a building where goods or services are sold; a store: *a card shop* | *a barber shop.* ■ inf. an act of going shopping: *she slogged her way around the supermarket doing the weekly shop.* **2** a place where things are manufactured or repaired; a workshop: *an auto repair shop.* ■ a room or department in a factory where a particular stage of production is carried out: *the machine shop.* ■ short for SHOP CLASS: *I got an A in shop last year.* ■ a profession, trade, business, etc., esp. as a subject of conversation: *when mathematicians talk shop, they do it at the blackboard.*
▶v. (**shopped, shop·ping**) [intr.] go to a store or stores to buy goods: *she shopped for groceries twice a week.* ■ (**shop around**) look for the best available price or rate for something: *shopping around for cheaper food.*

shop class ▶n. a class in which practical skills such as woodworking are taught.

shop·keep·er /'sнäp,kēpər/ ▶n. the owner and manager of a shop. —**shop·keep·ing** /-,kēpiNG/ n.

shop·lift·ing /'sнäp,liftiNG/ ▶n. the criminal action of stealing goods from a shop while pretending to be a customer. —**shop·lift** v. —**shop·lift·er** /-,liftər/ n.

shop·per /'sнäpər/ ▶n. a person who is shopping.

shop·ping /'sнäpiNG/ ▶n. [often as adj.] the purchasing of goods from stores: *a busy shopping area.* ■ goods bought from stores, esp. food and household goods: *I unloaded all the shopping.*

shop·ping cen·ter ▶n. an area or complex of stores with adjacent parking.

shop·ping mall ▶n. see MALL (sense 1).

shop stew·ard ▶n. a person elected by workers, for example in a factory, to represent them in dealings with management.

shop·worn /'sнäp,wôrn/ ▶adj. (of an article) made dirty or imperfect by being displayed or handled in a store: *he brought out some shopworn lettuce.*

shore[1] /sнôr/ ▶n. the land along the edge of a sea, lake, or other large body of water: *I took the tiller and made for the shore.* ■ Law the land between ordinary high- and low-water marks. —**shore·less** adj. —**shore·ward** /-wərd/ adj. & adv. —**shore·wards** /-wərdz/ adv.

shore[2] ▶n. a prop or beam set obliquely against something weak or unstable as a support.
▶v. [tr.] support or hold up (something) with such props or beams: *rescue workers had to shore up the building, which was in danger of collapse.*

shore leave ▶n. leisure time spent ashore by a sailor: *the hall was full of sailors on shore leave.*

shore·line /'sнôr,līn/ ▶n. the line along which a large body of water meets the land: *he walked along the shoreline.*

shorn /sнôrn/ ▶ past participle of SHEAR.

short /sнôrt/ ▶adj. **1** measuring a small distance from end to end: *short,*

dark hair. ■ (of a journey) covering a small distance: *the hotel is a short walk from the sea.* ■ (of a garment or sleeves on a garment) only covering the top part of a person's arms or legs: *a short skirt.* ■ (of a person) small in height: *he is short and tubby.* ■ short for **SHORTSTOP. 2** lasting or taking a small amount of time: *visiting London for a short break.* ■ seeming to last less time than is the case; passing quickly: *in 10 short years all this changed.* ■ (of a person's memory) retaining things for only a small amount of time: *he has a short memory for past misdeeds.* ■ *Stock Market* (of stocks or other securities or commodities) sold in advance of being acquired, with reliance on the price falling so that a profit can be made. ■ *Stock Market* (of a broker, position in the market, etc.) buying or based on such stocks or other securities or commodities. ■ denoting or having a relatively early date for the maturing of a bill of exchange. **3** relatively small in extent: *a short speech.* ■ (**short of/on**) not having enough of (something); lacking or deficient in: *they were short of provisions.* ■ in insufficient supply: *food is short.* ■ (of a person) terse; uncivil: *he was often sharp and rather short with her.* **4** *Phonet.* (of a vowel) categorized as short with regard to quality and length (e.g., in standard English the vowel in *good* is short as distinct from the long vowel in *food*). ■ *Prosody* (of a vowel or syllable) having the lesser of two recognized durations. **5** (of odds or a chance) reflecting or representing a high level of probability: *they have been backed at short odds to win thousands.* **6** (of pastry) containing a high proportion of fat to flour and therefore crumbly.
▶*adv.* (chiefly in sports) at, to, or over a relatively small distance: *you go deep and you go short.* ■ not as far as the point aimed at; not far enough: *all too often you pitch the ball short.*
▶*n.* **1** a short film as opposed to a feature film. ■ a short sound such as a short signal in Morse code or a short vowel or syllable: *her call was two longs and a short.* ■ a short circuit. **2** *Stock Market* (**shorts**) stocks due for early payment or redemption.
▶*v.* short-circuit or cause to short-circuit: [*intr.*] *the electrical circuit had shorted out* | [*tr.*] *if the contact terminals are shorted, the battery quickly overheats.* **—short·ish** *adj.* **—short·ness** *n.*
▶ ■ **be caught short** be put at a disadvantage: *the troubled company has been caught short by price competition in a recession-stricken market.* □ **come (up) short** fail to reach a goal or standard: *we're so close to getting the job done, but we keep coming up short.* □ **for short** as an abbreviation or nickname: *the File Transfer Protocol, or ftp for short.* □ **go short** not have enough of something, esp. food: *you won't go short when I die.* □ **in short** to sum up; briefly: *he was a faithful, orthodox party member; a Stalinist in short.* □ **in short order** immediately; rapidly: *after the killing the camp had been shut down in short order.* □ **in the short run** in the near future. □ **the short term** in the near future. □ **make short work of** accomplish, consume, or destroy quickly: *we made short work of our huge portions.* □ **the short end of the stick** an outcome in which one has less advantage than others. □ **short for** an abbreviation or nickname for: *I'm Robbie—short for Roberta.* □ **short of** less than: *he died at sixty-one, four years short of his pensionable age.* ■ not reaching as far as: *a rocket failure left a satellite tumbling in an orbit far short of its proper position.* ■ without going so far as (some extreme action): *short of putting out an all-persons alert, there's little else we can do.* □ **stop short** stop suddenly or abruptly. □ **stop short of** not go as far as (some extreme action): *the measures stopped short of establishing direct trade links.*

short·age /'SHôrtij/ ▶*n.* a state or situation in which something needed cannot be obtained in sufficient amounts: *a shortage of hard cash.*

short·bread /'SHôrt,bred/ ▶*n.* a crisp, rich, crumbly type of cookie made with butter, flour, and sugar.

short·cake /'SHôrt,kāk/ ▶*n.* **1** a small cake made of biscuit dough and typically served with fruit and whipped cream as a dessert. ■ a small circular sponge cake used in the same way. **2** a dessert made from shortcake topped with fruit, typically strawberries, and whipped cream.

short·change /'SHôrt'CHānj/ (also **short-change**) ▶*v.* [*tr.*] cheat by giving insufficient money as change: *I'm sure I was shortchanged at the bar.* ■ treat unfairly by withholding something of value: *residents perennially complain about their own children's needs being shortchanged.*

short cir·cuit ▶*n.* in a device, an electrical circuit of lower resistance than that of a normal circuit, typically resulting from the unintended contact of components and consequent accidental diversion of the current.
▶*v.* (**short-cir·cuit**) (with reference to an electrical device) malfunction or fail, or cause to do this, as a result of a short circuit across it: [*intr.*] *the birds caused the electricity supply to short-circuit* | [*tr.*] *water had leaked into the washing machine's motor, short-circuiting it.* ■ [*tr.*] *fig.* shorten (a process or activity) by using a more direct (but often improper) method: *the normal processes of a democracy should not be short-circuited.*

short·com·ing /'SHôrt,kəmiNG/ ▶*n.* (usu. **shortcomings**) a fault or failure to meet a certain standard, typically in a person's character, a plan, or a system: *he is forthright about his shortcomings.*

short·cut /'SHôrt,kət/ ▶*n.* an shorter alternative route. ■ *fig.* an accelerated way of doing or achieving something: *the promise of a shortcut to optimum health and fitness is a tantalizing one.*

short·en /'SHôrtn/ ▶*v.* make or become shorter: [*tr.*] *he shortened his stride* | [*intr.*] *around mid-September, days shorten and temperatures dip.* ■ [*tr.*] *Sailing* reduce the amount of (sail) exposed to the wind. ■ (with reference to gambling odds) make or become shorter; decrease: [*intr.*] *the odds had shortened to 14-1.* ■ [*tr.*] *Prosody & Phonet.* make (a vowel or syllable) short.

short·en·ing /'SHôrtlē; 'SHôrtn-iNG/ ▶*n.* butter or other fat used for making pastry or bread.

short·fall /'SHôrt,fôl/ ▶*n.* a deficit of something required or expected: *they are facing an expected $10 billion shortfall in revenue.*

short·hand /'SHôrt,hand/ ▶*n.* a method of rapid writing by means of abbreviations and symbols, used esp. for taking dictation. The major systems of shorthand are those devised in 1837 by Sir Isaac Pitman and in 1888 by John R. Gregg (1867–1948). ■ a short and simple way of expressing or referring to something: *poetry for him is simply a shorthand for literature that has aesthetic value.*

short-hand·ed ▶*adj.* **1** not having enough or the usual number of staff or crew: *the kitchen was a bit short-handed.* **2** *Ice Hockey* (of a goal) scored by a team playing with fewer players on the ice than their opponent.
▶*adv.*

short haul ▶*n.* a relatively short distance in terms of travel or the transport of goods: *it is only a short haul over the mountains to Los Angeles.*

short·horn /'SHôrt,hôrn/ ▶*n.* an animal of a breed of cattle with short horns.

short list (also **short·list**) ▶*n.* a list of selected candidates from which a final choice is made: *a short list of four companies.*
▶*v.* [*tr.*] (**short-list**) put (someone or something) on a short list: *the novel was short-listed for the Booker Prize.*

short-lived /'livd; 'līvd/ ▶*adj.* lasting only a short time: *a short-lived romance* | *these benefits are likely to be short-lived.*

short·ly /'SHôrtlē/ ▶*adv.* **1** in a short time; soon: *the new database will shortly be available for consultation.* **2** abruptly, sharply, or curtly: *"Do you like football?" "I do not," she said shortly.*

short or·der ▶*n.* an order or dish of food that can be quickly prepared and served: *a short order of fries* | [as *adj.*] *I'm a short-order cook.*

short-range ▶*adj.* **1** (esp. of a vehicle or missile) only able to be used or be effective over short distances: *short-range nuclear weapons.* **2** of or over a short period of future time: *short-range forecasting.*

shorts /SHôrts/ ▶*pl. n.* short pants that reach only to the thighs or knees: *cycling shorts.* ■ men's underpants.

short shrift ▶*n.* rapid and unsympathetic dismissal; curt treatment: *the judge gave short shrift to an argument based on the right to free speech.*

short-sight·ed /'SHôrt'sītid/ (also **short-sight·ed**) ▶*adj.* lacking imagination or foresight: *expedient, shortsighted solutions to problems.* **—short-sight·ed·ly** *adv.* **—short-sight·ed·ness** *n.*

short-sleeved ▶*adj.* having sleeves that do not reach below the elbow: *a short-sleeved silk top.*

short·stop /'SHôrt,stäp/ ▶*n.* *Baseball* a fielder positioned in the infield between second and third base, or the position itself.

short sto·ry ▶*n.* a story with a fully developed theme but significantly shorter and less elaborate than a novel.

short tem·per ▶*n.* a tendency to lose one's temper quickly. **—short-tem·pered** *adj.*

short-term ▶*adj.* occurring in or relating to a relatively short period of time: *it might be a wise short-term investment.*

short ton ▶*n.* see TON¹.

short·wave /'SHôrt'wāv/ ▶*n.* a radio wave of a wavelength between about 10 and 100 m (and a frequency of about 3 to 30 MHz): [as *adj.*] *a shortwave transmitter.* ■ broadcasting using radio waves of this wavelength: [as *adj.*] *shortwave radio.*

short-wind·ed /'windid/ ▶*adj.* (of a person) out of breath or quickly becoming so.

short·y /'SHôrtē/ (also **short·ie**) ▶*n.* (*pl.* **short·ies**) *inf.* a person who is shorter than average (often used as a nickname).

Sho·sho·ne /shōˈshōnē/ ▶ n. (pl. same or **-nes**) **1** a member of an American Indian people living chiefly in Wyoming, Idaho, and Nevada. **2** the Uto-Aztecan language of this people.
▶ adj. of or relating to the Shoshone or their language.

shot¹ /shät/ ▶ n. **1** the firing of a gun or cannon: *he brought down a caribou with a single shot to the neck.* ■ an attempt to hit a target by shooting: *he asked me if I would like to have a shot at a pheasant.* ■ the range of a gun or cannon: *six more desperadoes came galloping up and halted just out of rifle shot.* ■ *fig.* a critical or aggressive remark: *Paul tried one last shot—"You realize what you want will cost more money?"* ■ a person with a specified level of ability in shooting: *he was an excellent shot at short and long distances.* **2** a hit, stroke, or kick of the ball in sports such as basketball, tennis, or golf: *his partner pulled off a winning backhand shot.* ■ an attempt to drive a ball into a goal; an attempt to score: *he took a shot that the goalie stopped.* ■ *inf.* an attempt to do something: *several of the competitors will have a shot at the title.* **3** (pl. same.) a ball of stone or metal used as a missile fired from a large gun or cannon. ■ tiny lead pellets used in quantity in a single charge or cartridge in a shotgun. ■ a heavy ball thrown by a shot-putter. **4** a photograph: *she took a shot of me holding a lamp near my face.* ■ a film sequence photographed continuously by one camera: *the movie's opening shot is of a character walking across a featureless landscape.* ■ the range of a camera's view: *a prop man was standing just out of shot.* **5** *inf.* a small drink, esp. of distilled liquor: *he took a shot of whiskey.* ■ an injection of a drug or vaccine: *Jerry gave the monkey a shot of a sedative.* **6** the launch of a space rocket: *a moon shot.*
▶ □ **give it one's best shot** *inf.* do the best that one can. □ **a shot in the arm** *inf.* an encouraging stimulus: *the movie was a real shot in the arm for our crew.*

shot² past and past participle of **SHOOT.** ▶ adj. **1** (of colored cloth) woven with a warp and weft of different colors, giving a contrasting iridescent effect when looked at from different angles: *a dress of shot silk.* ■ interspersed with a different color: *dark hair shot with silver.* **2** *inf.* ruined or worn out: *a completely shot engine will put you out of the race.* ■ drunk.

shot·gun /ˈshät,gən/ ▶ n. **1** a smoothbore gun for firing small shot at short range. **2** (also **shotgun formation**) *Football* an offensive formation in which the quarterback receives the snap while standing several yards behind the line of scrimmage.
▶ adj. **1** aimed at a wide range of things; with no specific target: *many companies use the shotgun approach, aiming advertising at the widest possible audience.* **2** (of a house or other structure) with the rooms lined up one behind another, forming a long narrow whole: *his family lived in a shotgun shack in South Memphis.*

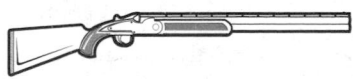

shotgun

shot put ▶ n. an athletic contest in which a very heavy round ball is thrown (that is, pushed from the shoulder) as far as possible. —**shot-put·ter** n. —**shot-put·ting** n.

should /shŏŏd/ ▶ modal verb (3rd sing. **should**) **1** used to indicate obligation, duty, or correctness, typically when criticizing someone's actions: *he should have been careful.* ■ indicating a desirable or expected state: *by now students should be able to read with a large degree of independence.* ■ used to give or ask advice or suggestions: *you should go back to bed | what should I wear?* ■ (**I should**) used to give advice: *I should hold out if I were you.* **2** used to indicate what is probable: *$348 million should be enough to buy him out.* **3** *formal* expressing the conditional mood: ■ (in the first person) indicating the consequence of an imagined event: *if I were to obey my first impulse, I should spend my days writing letters.* ■ referring to a possible event or situation: *if you should change your mind, I'll be at the hotel.* **4** used in a clause with "that" after a main clause describing feelings: *it is astonishing that we should find violence here.* **5** used in a clause with "that" expressing purpose: *in order that training should be effective it must be planned systematically.* **6** (in the first person) expressing a polite request or acceptance: *we should be grateful for your advice.* **7** (in the first person) expressing a conjecture or hope: *he'll have a sore head, I should imagine.* **8** used to emphasize to a listener how striking an event is or was: *you should have seen Marge's face.*

shoul·der /ˈshōldər/ ▶ n. **1** the upper joint of the human arm and the part of the body between this and the neck. ■ (in quadrupeds) the joint of the upper forelimb and the adjacent part of the back. ■ the part of a bird or insect at which the wing is attached. ■ a large cut of meat from the upper foreleg and shoulder blade of an animal: *a shoulder of lamb.* ■ a part of a garment covering the shoulder: *a jacket with padded shoulders.* ■ (**shoulders**) the upper part of the back and arms: *a tall youth with broad shoulders.* ■ (**shoulders**) *fig.* this part of the body regarded as bearing responsibility or hardship or providing strength: *all accounts place the blame squarely on his shoulders.* **2** a part of something resembling a shoulder in shape, position, or function: *the shoulder of a pulley.* **3** a paved strip alongside a road for stopping on in an emergency.
▶ v. **1** [tr.] put (something heavy) over one's shoulder or shoulders to carry: *we shouldered our crippling backpacks and set off slowly up the hill.* ■ *fig.* take on (a burden or responsibility): *she shouldered the blame for the incident.* **2** [tr.] push (someone or something) out of one's way with one's shoulder: *she shouldered him brusquely aside.* ■ [intr.] move in this way: *he shouldered past a woman with a baby.* ▷Old English *sculdor*; related to Dutch *schouder* and German *Schulter.* —**shoul·dered** /ˈshōldərd/ adj. [in comb.] *broad-shouldered.*
▶ □ **be looking over one's shoulder** be anxious or insecure about a possible danger: *takeovers are the thing that keeps suppliers looking over their shoulders.* □ **shoulder arms** hold a rifle against the side of the body, barrel upward. □ **shoulder to shoulder** side by side: *everyone is bunched together shoulder to shoulder.* ■ acting together toward a common aim; with united effort: *we fought shoulder to shoulder with the rest of the country.*

shoul·der blade ▶ n. either of the large, flat, triangular bones that lie against the ribs in the upper back and provide attachments for the bone and muscles of the upper arm. Also called **SCAPULA.**

should·n't /ˈshŏŏdnt/ ▶ contr. of should not.

shout /shout/ ▶ v. [intr.] (of a person) utter a loud call or cry, typically as an expression of a strong emotion: *she shouted for joy.* ■ say something very loudly; call out: [tr.] *he leaned out of his window and shouted abuse at them.* ■ [tr.] (**shout someone down**) prevent someone from speaking or being heard by shouting: *he was shouted down as he tried to explain the decision.*
▶ n. a loud cry expressing a strong emotion or calling attention: *his words were interrupted by warning shouts.* —**shout·er** n.

shout-out ▶ n. *inf.* a message of congratulation, support, or appreciation: *a special shout-out to Marlon Brando, Al Pacino, James Gandolfini, and Robert De Niro for being such kick-ass cinematic mobsters.*

shove /shəv/ ▶ v. [tr.] push (someone or something) roughly: *police started pushing and shoving people down the street* | [intr.] *kids pushed, kicked, and shoved.* ■ [intr.] make one's way by pushing someone or something: *Woody shoved past him.* ■ [tr.] put (something) somewhere carelessly or roughly: *she shoved the books into her briefcase.* ■ (**shove it**) *inf.* used to express angry dismissal of something: *I should have told the boss to shove it.*
▶ phrasal v. □ **shove off 1** (usu. in imper.) *inf.* go away: *shove off—you're bothering the customers.* **2** push away from the shore or another vessel in a boat.
▶ n. a strong push: *she gave him a hefty shove and he nearly fell.*

shov·el /ˈshəvəl/ ▶ n. a tool with a broad flat blade and typically upturned sides, used for moving coal, earth, snow or other material. ■ a machine or part of a machine having a similar shape or function. ■ an amount of something carried or moved with shovel: *a few shovels of earth.*
▶ v. (**-eled, -el·ing**; Brit. **-elled, -el·ling**) [tr.] move (coal, earth, snow, or similar material) with a shovel: *she shoveled coal on the fire.* ■ [tr.] remove snow from (an area) with a shovel: *shovel the walk.* ■ *inf.* put or push (something, typically food) somewhere quickly and in large quantities: *Dave was shoveling pasta into his mouth.* —**shov·el·ful** /-,fŏŏl/ n. (pl. **-fuls**).

show /shō/ ▶ v. (past part. **shown** /shōn/ or **showed**) **1** be or allow or cause to be visible: [intr.] *wrinkles were starting to show on her face* | [tr.] *a white blouse will show the blood.* ■ [tr.] offer, exhibit, or produce (something) for scrutiny or inspection: *an alarm salesperson should show an ID card.* ■ [tr.] put on display in an exhibition or competition: *he ceased early in his career to show his work* | [intr.] *other artists who showed there included Robert Motherwell.* ■ [tr.] present (a movie or television program) on a screen for public viewing: [intr.] (of a movie) be presented in this way: *a movie showing at the Venice Film Festival.* ■ [tr.] indicate (a particular time, measurement, etc.): *a travel clock showing the time in different cities.* ■ [tr.] represent or depict in art: *a postcard showing the Wicklow Mountains.* ■ [intr.] *inf.* arrive or turn up for an appointment or at a gathering: *her date failed to show.* ■ [intr.] finish third or in the first three in a race. ■ [intr.] *inf.* (of a woman) be visibly pregnant: *Shirley was four months pregnant and just starting to show.* **2** [tr.] display or allow to be perceived (a quality, emotion, or characteristic): *it was Frank's turn to show his frustration.* ■ accord or treat someone with (a specified quality): *he urged his soldiers to fight them and show no mercy.* ■ [intr.] (of an emotion) be noticeable: *he tried not to let his relief show*. **3** [*tr.*] demonstrate or prove: *experts say this shows the benefit of regular inspections*. ▪ (**show oneself**) prove or demonstrate oneself to be: *she showed herself to be a harsh critic*. ▪ cause to understand or be capable of doing something by explanation or demonstration: *he showed the boy how to operate the machine*. ▪ [*tr.*] conduct or lead: *show them in, please*.

▸*phrasal v.* □ **show off** *inf.* make a deliberate or pretentious display of one's abilities or accomplishments. □ **show someone/something off** display or cause others to take notice of someone or something that is a source of pride: *his jeans were tight-fitting, showing off his compact figure*. □ **show through** (of one's real feelings) be revealed inadvertently. □ **show up 1** be conspicuous or clearly visible. **2** *inf.* arrive or turn up for an appointment or gathering. □ **show someone up** *inf.* embarrass or humiliate someone: *she says I showed her up in front of her friends.*

▸*n.* **1** a spectacle or display of something, typically an impressive one: *spectacular shows of bluebells*. **2** a public entertainment, in particular: ▪ a play or other stage performance, esp. a musical. ▪ a program on television or radio. ▪ an event or competition involving the public display or exhibition of animals, plants, or products: *the annual agricultural show*. ▪ *inf.* an undertaking, project, or organization: *I man a desk in a little office. I don't run the show.* ▪ *inf.* an opportunity for doing something; a chance: *I didn't have a show*. **3** an outward appearance or display of a quality or feeling: *Joanie was frightened of any show of affection*. ▪ an outward display intended to give a particular, false impression: *Drew made a show of looking around for firewood*. **4** *Med.* a discharge of blood and mucus from the vagina at the onset of labor or menstruation.

▸ □ **for show** for the sake of appearance rather than for use. □ **get** (or **keep**) **the show on the road** *inf.* begin (or succeed in continuing with) an undertaking or enterprise: *"Let's get this show on the road—we're late already."* □ **have something** (or **nothing**) **to show for** have a (or no) visible result of (one's work or experience): *a year later, he had nothing to show for his efforts.* □ **show cause** *Law* produce satisfactory grounds for application of (or exemption from) a procedure or penalty. □ **show one's face** appear in public: *she had been up in court and was so ashamed she could hardly show her face*. □ **show one's hand** (in a card game) reveal one's cards. ▪ *fig.* disclose one's plans: *he needed hard evidence, and to get it he would have to show his hand*. □ **show of force** a demonstration of the forces at one's command and of one's readiness to use them. □ **show of hands** the raising of hands among a group of people to indicate a vote for or against something, with numbers typically being estimated rather than counted.

show biz ▸*n.* informal term for **show business**. —**show·biz·zy** /ˈSHō-ˌbizē/ *adj.*

show·boat /ˈSHō,bōt/ ▸*n.* a river steamboat on which theatrical performances are given. ▪ *inf.* a show-off; an exhibitionist.

▸*v.* [*intr.*] *inf.* show off: [as *adj.*] (**showboating**) *a lot of showboating politicians.* —**show·boat·er** *n.*

show busi·ness ▸*n.* the theater, movies, television, and pop music as a profession or industry.

show·case /ˈSHō,kās/ ▸*n.* a glass case used for displaying articles in a store or museum. ▪ a place or occasion for presenting something favorably to general attention: *the gallery will provide a showcase for Atlanta's young photographers.*

▸*v.* [*tr.*] exhibit; display: *the albums showcase his production skills.*

show·down /ˈSHō,doun/ ▸*n.* a final test or confrontation intended to settle a dispute. ▪ (in poker) the requirement at the end of a round that the players who remain in must show their cards to determine which is the strongest hand.

show·er /ˈSHou(-ə)r/ ▸*n.* **1** a brief and usually light fall of rain, hail, sleet, or snow. ▪ a mass of small things falling or moving at the same time: *a shower of dust sprinkled his face*. ▪ *fig.* a large number of things happening or given to someone at the same time: *he was pleased by the shower of awards*. **2** an enclosure in which a person stands under a spray of water to wash. ▪ the apparatus that produces such a spray of water. ▪ (also **shower bath**) an act of washing oneself in a shower. **3** a party at which presents are given to someone, typically a woman who is about to get married or have a baby: *she loved going to baby showers.*

▸*v.* **1** [*intr.*] (of a mass of small things) fall or be thrown in a shower: *bits of broken glass showered over me*. ▪ [*tr.*] cause (a mass of small things) to fall in a shower: *his hooves showered sparks across the concrete floor*. ▪ [*tr.*] (**shower someone with**) give someone a great number of (things): *he showered her with kisses*. ▪ [*tr.*] (**shower something on/upon**) give a great number of (things) to (someone): *senior officers showered praise on their young cadet.* **2** [*intr.*] wash oneself in a shower. —**show·er·y** *adj.*

▸ □ **send someone to the showers** *inf.* cause someone to fail early on in a race or contest.

show·er·proof /ˈSHou(-ə)r,proŏf/ ▸*adj.* (of a garment) resistant to light rain.

show·girl /ˈSHō,gərl/ ▸*n.* an actress who sings and dances in musicals, variety acts, and similar shows.

show jump·ing ▸*n.* the competitive sport of riding horses over a course of fences and other obstacles in an arena, with penalty points for errors. —**show jump** *n.* —**show jumper** *n.*

show·man /ˈSHōmən/ ▸*n.* (*pl.* **-men**) a person who produces or presents shows as a profession, esp. the proprietor, manager, or MC of a circus, fair, or other variety show. ▪ a person skilled in dramatic or entertaining presentation, performance, or publicity. —**show·man·ship** /-,SHip/ *n.*

shown /SHōn/ ▸ past participle of **show**.

show-off ▸*n. inf.* a person who acts pretentiously or who publicly parades themselves, their possessions, or their accomplishments.

show·piece /ˈSHō,pēs/ ▸*n.* something that attracts attention or admiration as an outstanding example of its type: *the factory has expanded and become a showpiece of American industry*. ▪ something that offers a particular opportunity for a display of skill: *the serenade was a showpiece for the wind section*. ▪ an item of work presented for exhibition or display.

show·place /ˈSHō,plās/ ▸*n.* a place of beauty or interest attracting many visitors.

show·room /ˈSHō,roŏm; -,roŏm/ ▸*n.* a room used to display goods for sale, such as appliances, cars, or furniture.

show·stop·per ▸*n. inf.* a performance or item receiving prolonged applause. ▪ something that is striking or has great popular appeal: *a show-stopper of a smile*. —**show·stop·ping** *adj.*

show·y /ˈSHō-ē/ ▸*adj.* (**show·i·er**, **show·i·est**) having a striking appearance or style, typically by being excessively bright, colorful, or ostentatious: *showy flowers*. —**show·i·ly** /-əlē/ *adv.* —**show·i·ness** *n.*

shrank /SHraNGk/ ▸ past of **shrink**.

shrap·nel /ˈSHrapnəl/ ▸*n.* fragments of a bomb, shell, or other object thrown out by an explosion.

shred /SHred/ ▸*n.* (usu. **shreds**) a strip of some material, such as paper, cloth, or food, that has been torn, cut, or scraped from something larger: *her beautiful dress was torn to shreds* *fig.* *my reputation will be in shreds*. ▪ a very small amount: *there was not a shred of evidence that linked him to the fire.*

▸*v.* (**shredded**, **shredding**) [*tr.*] tear or cut into shreds.

shred·der /ˈSHredər/ ▸*n.* **1** a machine or other device for shredding something, esp. documents. **2** *inf.* a snowboarder.

shrew /SHroŏ/ ▸*n.* a small mouselike insectivorous mammal (*Sorex, Crocidura*, and other genera, family Soricidae) with a long pointed snout and tiny eyes. ▪ a bad-tempered or aggressively assertive woman. —**shrew·ish** *adj.* —**shrew·ish·ly** *adv.* —**shrew·ish·ness** *n.*

shrewd /SHroŏd/ ▸*adj.* having or showing sharp powers of judgment; astute: *she was shrewd enough to guess the motive behind his gesture*. ▷Middle English (in the sense 'evil in nature or character'): from *shrew* (Old English *scrēawa, scrǣwa*, of Germanic origin) in the sense 'evil person or thing,' or as the past participle of obsolete *shrew* 'to curse.' The word developed the sense 'cunning,' and gradually gained a favorable connotation during the 17th cent. —**shrewd·ly** *adv.* —**shrewd·ness** *n.*

shriek /SHrēk/ ▸*v.* [*intr.*] utter a high-pitched piercing sound or words, esp. as an expression of terror, pain, or excitement: *the audience shrieked with laughter* | [*tr.*] *she was shrieking abuse at a taxi driver*. ▪ (of something inanimate) make a high-pitched screeching sound: *the wheels shrieked as the car sped away*. ▪ *fig.* be very obvious or strikingly discordant: *the patterned carpets shrieked at Betsy from the shabby store.*

▸*n.* a high-pitched piercing cry or sound; a scream: *shrieks of laughter*. —**shriek·er** *n.*

shrike /SHrīk/ ▸*n.* a songbird (family Laniidae) with a strong sharply hooked bill, often impaling its prey of small birds, lizards, and insects on thorns.

shrill /SHril/ ▸*adj.* (of a voice or sound) high-pitched and piercing: *a shrill laugh*. ▪ *derog.* (esp. of a complaint or demand) loud and forceful: *a concession to their shrill demands.*

▸*v.* [*intr.*] make a shrill noise.

▸*n.* a shrill sound or cry: *the rising shrill of women's voices*. ▷late Middle English: of Germanic origin; related to Low German *schrell* 'sharp in tone or taste.' —**shrill·ness** *n.* —**shril·ly** /ˈSHri(l)lē/ *adv.*

shrimp /SHrimp/ ▶*n.* (*pl.* same or **shrimps**) a small free-swimming crustacean (*Pandalus, Penaeus, Crangon,* and other genera, order Decapoda) with an elongated body, typically marine and frequently harvested for food. Its numerous species include the commercially important **pink shrimp** (*Penaeus duorarum*). ■ *inf., derog.* a small, physically weak person.
▶*v.* [*intr.*] fish for shrimp: [as *adj.*] (**shrimping**) *a shrimping net.* —**shrimp·er** *n.* —**shrimp·y** *adj.*

shrine /SHrīn/ ▶*n.* a place regarded as holy because of its associations with a divinity or a sacred person or relic, typically marked by a building or other construction. ■ a place associated with or containing memorabilia of a particular revered person or thing: *her grave has become a shrine for fans from all over the world.* ■ a casket containing sacred relics; a reliquary. ■ a niche or enclosure containing a religious statue or other object.

shrink /SHriNGk/ ▶*v.* (*past* **shrank** /SHraNGk/; *past part.* **shrunk** /SHrəNGk/ or (esp. as *adj.*) **shrunk·en** /ˈSHrəNGkən/) **1** become or make smaller in size or amount; contract or cause to contract: [*intr.*] *the workforce has shrunk to less than a thousand* | [*tr.*] *the summer sun had shrunk and dried the wood.* ■ [as *adj.*] (**shrunken**) (esp. of a person's face or other part of the body) withered, wrinkled, or shriveled through old age or illness: *a tiny shrunken face and enormous eyes.* **2** [*intr.*] move back or away, esp. because of fear or disgust: *she shrank away from him, covering her face.* ■ (**shrink from**) be averse to or unwilling to do (something difficult or unappealing): *I don't shrink from my responsibilities.*
▶*n. inf.* a clinical psychologist, psychiatrist, or psychotherapist: *you should see a shrink.* —**shrink·a·ble** *adj.* —**shrink·er** *n.* —**shrink·ing·ly** *adv.*

shrink·age /ˈSHriNGkij/ ▶*n.* the process, fact, or amount of shrinking: *give long curtains good hems to allow for shrinkage.* ■ an allowance made for reduction in the earnings of a business due to wastage or theft.

shrink-fit ▶*adj.* designed to fit perfectly after anticipated shrinkage: *a shrink-fit chuck.*
▶*n.* a system that uses shrink-fit parts or fittings.

shrink·ing vi·o·let ▶*n. inf.* an exaggeratedly shy person: *Dorothy is no shrinking violet when it comes to expressing her views.*

shrink-wrap ▶*v.* [*tr.*] package (an article) by enclosing it in clinging transparent plastic film that shrinks tightly onto it: [as *adj.*] (**shrink-wrapped**) *shrink-wrapped blocks of cheese.* ■ [as *adj.*] (**shrink-wrapped**) *Comput.* (of a product) sold commercially as a ready-made software package.
▶*n.* clinging transparent plastic film used to enclose an article as packaging.

shriv·el /ˈSHrivəl/ ▶*v.* (**-eled, -el·ing;** *Brit.* **-elled, -el·ling**) wrinkle and contract or cause to wrinkle and contract, esp. due to loss of moisture: [*intr.*] *the flowers simply shriveled up* | [*tr.*] *a heat wave so intense that it shriveled the grapes in every vineyard.* ■ [*intr.*] *fig.* lose momentum, will, or desire; become insignificant or ineffectual: *under the reign of the Nazis, German universities shriveled as centers of learning.* ■ [*tr.*] *fig.* cause to feel worthless or insignificant: *she shriveled him with one glance.*

shroud /SHroud/ ▶*n.* **1** a length of cloth or an enveloping garment in which a dead person is wrapped for burial: *he was buried in a linen shroud.* ■ *fig.* a thing that envelops or obscures something: *a shroud of mist* | *they operate behind a shroud of secrecy.* ■ *technical* a protective casing or cover. **2** one of a set of ropes supporting the mast of a sailing vessel from the sides. ■ (also **shroud line**) each of the lines joining the canopy of a parachute to the harness.
▶*v.* [*tr.*] wrap or dress (a body) in a shroud for burial. ■ *fig.* cover or envelop so as to conceal from view: *mountains shrouded by cloud.*

Shrove Tues·day /SHrōv/ ▶*n.* the day before Ash Wednesday. Though named for its former religious significance, it is chiefly marked by feasting and celebration, which traditionally preceded the observance of the Lenten fast.

shrub[1] /SHrəb/ ▶*n.* a woody plant that is smaller than a tree and has several main stems arising at or near the ground. —**shrub·by** *adj.*

shrub[2] ▶*n.* **1** a drink made of sweetened fruit juice and liquor, typically rum or brandy. **2** a slightly acid cordial made from fruit juice and water.

shrub·ber·y /ˈSHrəb(ə)rē/ ▶*n.* shrubs collectively. ■ (*pl.* **-ber·ies**) an area planted with shrubs.

shrug /SHrəg/ ▶*v.* (**shrugged, shrug·ging**) [*tr.*] raise (one's shoulders) slightly and momentarily to express doubt, ignorance, or indifference: *Jimmy looked inquiringly at Pete, who shrugged his shoulders* | [*intr.*] *he just shrugged and didn't look interested.* ■ (**shrug something off**) dismiss something as unimportant: *the managing director shrugged off the criticism.*
▶*n.* **1** an act or instance of shrugging one's shoulders: *she gave him a*

dismissive shrug. **2** a woman's close-fitting cardigan or jacket, cut short at the front and back so that only the arms and shoulders are covered.

shrunk /SHrəNGk/ (also **shrunk·en**) ▶ past participle of **SHRINK**.

shtick /SHtik/ ▶*n. inf.* an attention-getting or theatrical routine, gimmick, or talent.

shuck /SHək/ ▶*n.* **1** an outer covering such as a husk or pod, esp. the husk of an ear of corn. ■ the shell of an oyster or clam. **2** *inf.* a person or thing regarded as worthless or contemptible: *William didn't dig the idea at all and said it was a shuck.*
▶*interj.* (**shucks**) *inf.* used to express surprise, regret, irritation, or, in response to praise, self-deprecation: *"Thank you for getting it." "Oh, shucks, it was nothing."*
▶*v.* [*tr.*] remove the shucks from corn or shellfish: *shuck and drain the oysters.* —**shuck·er** *n.*

shud·der /ˈSHədər/ ▶*v.* [*intr.*] (of a person) tremble convulsively, typically as a result of fear or repugnance: *he shuddered with revulsion.* ■ (esp. of a vehicle, machine, or building) shake or vibrate deeply: *the train shuddered and edged forward.* ■ [usu. as *adj.*] (**shuddering**) (of a person's breathing) be unsteady, esp. as a result of emotional disturbance: *he drew a deep, shuddering breath.*
▶*n.* an act of shuddering: *the elevator rose with a shudder.* —**shud·der·ing·ly** *adv.* —**shud·der·y** *adj.*
▶ □ **give someone the shudders** *inf.* cause someone to feel repugnance or fear: *it gives me the shudders to hear you use words like that.*

shuf·fle /ˈSHəfəl/ ▶*v.* **1** [*intr.*] walk by dragging one's feet along or without lifting them fully from the ground: *I stepped into my skis and shuffled to the edge of the steep slope.* ■ shift one's position while sitting or move one's feet while standing, typically because of boredom, nervousness, or embarrassment: *Christine shuffled uneasily in her chair.* **2** [*tr.*] rearrange (a deck of cards) by sliding the cards over each other quickly. ■ move (people or things) around so as to occupy different positions or to be in a different order: *she shuffled her papers into a neat pile.* ■ [*intr.*] (**shuffle through**) sort or look through (a number of things) hurriedly: *he shuffled through the papers on his desk.* **3** [*tr.*] (**shuffle something off**) get out of or avoid a responsibility or obligation: *some hospitals can shuffle off their responsibilities by claiming to have no suitable facilities.*
▶*n.* **1** a shuffling movement, walk, or sound: *there was a shuffle of approaching feet.* ■ a quick dragging or scraping movement of the feet in dancing. ■ a dance performed with such steps. ■ a piece of music for or in the style of such a dance. ■ a rhythmic motif based on such a dance step and typical of early jazz, consisting of alternating quarter notes and eighth notes in a triplet pattern. **2** an act of shuffling a deck of cards. ■ a change of order or relative positions; a reshuffle: *the president will deliver a speech short on economic details Cabinet shuffles but long on fight.* ■ a facility on a CD player for playing tracks in an arbitrary order: [as *adj.*] *a fully programmable CD changer with shuffle play.* —**shuf·fler** /ˈSHəf(ə)lər/ *n.*
▶ □ **be** (or **get**) **lost in the shuffle** *inf.* be overlooked or missed in a confused or crowded situation.

shuf·fle·board /ˈSHəfəlˌbôrd/ ▶*n.* a game played by pushing disks with a long-handled cue over a marked surface.

shun /SHən/ ▶*v.* (**shunned, shun·ning**) [*tr.*] persistently avoid, ignore, or reject (someone or something) through antipathy or caution: *he shunned fashionable society.*

shunt /SHənt/ ▶*v.* **1** [*tr.*] push or pull (a train or part of a train) from the main line to a siding or from one track to another: *their train had been shunted into a siding.* ■ (usu. **be shunted**) push or shove (someone or something): *chairs were being shunted back and forth.* ■ direct or divert (someone or something) to a less important place or position: *amateurs were gradually being shunted to filing jobs.* **2** [*tr.*] provide (an electrical current) with a conductor joining two points of a circuit, through which more or less of the current may be diverted.
▶*n.* **1** an act of pushing or shoving something. **2** an electrical conductor joining two points of a circuit, through which more or less of a current may be diverted. ■ *Surgery* an alternative path for the passage of the blood or other body fluid: [as *adj.*] *shunt surgery.* —**shunt·er** *n.*

shush /SHŏŏSH; SHəSH/ ▶*interj.* be quiet: *"Shush! Do you want to wake everyone?"*
▶*n.* an utterance of "shush": *the thumps were followed by shushes from the aunts.*
▶*v.* [*tr.*] tell or signal (someone) to be silent: *she shushed him with a wave.* ■ [*intr.*] become or remain silent: *Beth told her to shush.*

shut /SHət/ ▶*v.* (**shut·ting;** *past* **shut**) [*tr.*] move (something) into position so that it blocks an opening: *shut the window, please.* ■ [*intr.*] (of something that can block an opening) move or be moved into position: *the* *door shut behind him.* ■ block an opening into (something) by moving something into position: *he shut the box and locked it.* ■ keep (someone or something) in a place by closing something such as a door: *it was his own dog that he had accidentally shut outside.* ■ fold or bring together the sides of (something) so as to close it: *he shut his book.* ■ prevent access to or along: *they ought to shut the path up to that terrible cliff.* ■ make or become unavailable for business or service, either permanently or until due to be open again; close: *we shut the shop for lunch.*

▸*phrasal v.* □ **shut down** (or **shut something down**) cease (or cause something to cease) business or operation: *the plant's operators decided to shut down the reactor.* □ **shut someone/something in** keep someone or something inside a place by closing something such as a door: *her parents shut her in an upstairs room.* ■ enclose or surround a place: *the village is shut in by the mountains on either side.* ■ trap something by shutting a door or drawer on it: *you shut your finger in the door.* □ **shut off** (or **shut something off**) (used esp. in relation to water, electricity, or gas) stop (or cause something to stop) flowing: *he was about to shut off the power.* ■ stop (or cause something to stop) working: *the engines shut off automatically.* ■ **shut something off**) block the entrances and exits of something: *the six compartments were being shut off from each other.* □ **shut oneself off** isolate oneself from other people. □ **shut someone/something out** keep someone or something out of a place or situation: *the door swung closed behind them, shutting out some of the noise.* ■ prevent an opponent from scoring in a game. ■ screen someone or something from view: *clouds shut out the stars.* ■ prevent something from occurring: *there was a high-mindedness that shut out any consideration of alternatives.* ■ block something such as a painful memory from the mind: *anything he didn't like he shut out.* □ **shut up** (or **shut someone up**) [often in *imper.*] *inf.* stop (or cause someone to stop) talking: *just shut up and listen.* ▷Old English *scyttan* 'put (a bolt) in position to hold fast'; related to Dutch *schutten* 'shut up, obstruct,' also to *shoot.*
▸ □ **shut your face** (or **mouth** or **trap**)! *inf.* used as a rude or angry way of telling someone to be quiet.

shut·down /ˈSHət,doun/ ▸*n.* a closure of a factory or system, typically a temporary closure due to a malfunction or for maintenance. ■ a turning off of a computer or computer system.

shut-eye ▸*n. inf.* sleep: *we'd better get some shut-eye.*

shut-in ▸*n.* **1** a person confined indoors, esp. as a result of physical or mental disability. **2** a state or period in which an oil or gas well has available but unused capacity.

shut·out /ˈSHət,out/ ▸*n.* a competition or game in which the losing side fails to score.

shut·ter /ˈSHətər/ ▸*n.* **1** each of a pair of hinged panels, often louvered, fixed inside or outside a window that can be closed for security or privacy or to keep out light. **2** *Photog.* a device that opens and closes to expose the film in a camera. **3** *Mus.* the blind enclosing the swell box in an organ, used for controlling the volume of sound.
▸*v.* [*tr.*] close the shutters of (a window or building): *the windows were shuttered against the afternoon heat.* ■ close (a business): *the city was gripped by economic forces that were squeezing its tax base and shuttering its factories.* —**shut·ter·less** *adj.*

shut·ter·bug /ˈSHətər,bəg/ ▸*n. inf.* an enthusiastic amateur photographer.

shut·tle /ˈSHətl/ ▸*n.* **1** a form of transportation that travels regularly between two places: *the nine o'clock shuttle from Boston* | [as *adj.*] *a shuttle bus service from the city center.* ■ short for **SPACE SHUTTLE**. **2** a wooden device with two pointed ends holding a bobbin, used for carrying the weft thread between the warp threads in weaving. ■ a bobbin carrying the lower thread in a sewing machine. **3** short for **SHUTTLECOCK**.
▸*v.* [*intr.*] travel regularly between two or more places: *a container ship that shuttled between Rotterdam and the Persian Gulf.* ■ [*tr.*] transport in a shuttle.

shut·tle·cock /ˈSHətl,käk/ ▸*n.* a cork to which feathers are attached to form a cone shape, or a similar object of plastic, struck with rackets in the games of badminton and battledore.

shut·tle di·plo·ma·cy ▸*n.* negotiations conducted by a mediator who travels between two or more parties that are reluctant to hold direct discussions.

shy¹ /SHī/ ▸*adj.* (**shy·er**, **shy·est**) **1** being reserved or having or showing nervousness or timidity in the company of other people: *I was pretty shy at school.* ■ (**shy about**) slow or reluctant to do (something): *she has never been shy about discussing her efforts to raise aesthetic standards.* ■ [in *comb.*] having a dislike of or aversion to a

shuttlecock

specified thing: *they were a little camera-shy.* ■ (of a wild mammal or bird) reluctant to remain in sight of humans. **2** (**shy of**) *inf.* less than; short of: *he won the championship with a score three points shy of a world record.* ■ before: *he left school just shy of his fourteenth birthday.*
▸*v.* (**shies**, **shied**) [*intr.*] (esp. of a horse) start suddenly aside in fright at an object, noise, or movement. ■ (**shy from**) avoid doing or becoming involved in (something) due to nervousness or a lack of confidence: *don't shy away from saying what you think.*
▸*n.* a sudden startled movement, esp. of a frightened horse. —**shy·er** /ˈSHī(ə)r/ *n.* —**shy·ly** *adv.* —**shy·ness** *n.*

shy² *dated* ▸*v.* (**shies**, **shied**) [*tr.*] fling or throw (something) at a target: *he tore the glasses off and shied them at her.*
▸*n.* (*pl.* **shies**) an act of flinging or throwing something at a target.

shy·ster /ˈSHīstər/ ▸*n. inf.* a person, esp. a lawyer, who uses unscrupulous, fraudulent, or deceptive methods in business.

SI ▸*abbr.* ■ the international system of units of measurement.

Si ▸*symb.* the chemical element silicon.

si /sē/ ▸*n. Mus.* another term for **TI**.

si·a·mang /ˈsēə,mäNG/ ▸*n.* a large black gibbon (*Hylobates syndactylus*) native to Sumatra and the Malay peninsula.

Si·a·mese /ˌsīəˈmēz/ ▸*n.* (*pl.* same) **1** *dated* a native of Siam (now Thailand). **2** old-fashioned term for **THAI** (the language). **3** (also **Siamese cat**) a cat of a lightly built short-haired breed characterized by slanting blue eyes and typically pale fur with darker points.

Si·a·mese twin ▸*n.* dated term for **CONJOINED TWIN**.

sib /sib/ ▸*n.* **1** *chiefly Zool.* a brother or sister; a sibling. **2** *Anthropol.* a group of people recognized by an individual as his or her kindred.

sib·i·lant /ˈsibələnt/ ▸*adj. Phonet.* (of a speech sound) sounded with a hissing effect, for example *s*, *sh*. ■ making or characterized by a hissing sound: *his sibilant whisper.*
▸*n. Phonet.* a sibilant speech sound. —**sib·i·lance** *n.*

sib·ling /ˈsibliNG/ ▸*n.* each of two or more children or offspring having one or both parents in common; a brother or sister.

sib·yl /ˈsibəl/ ▸*n.* a woman in ancient times supposed to utter the oracles and prophecies of a god. ■ *poetic/lit.* a woman able to foretell the future.

sic¹ /sik/ ▸*adv.* used in brackets after a copied or quoted word that appears odd or erroneous to show that the word is quoted exactly as it stands in the original, as in *a story must hold a child's interest and "enrich his [sic] life."*

sic² (also **sick**) ▸*v.* (**sicced**, **sic·cing** or **sicked**, **sick·ing**) [*tr.*] (**sic something on**) set a dog or other animal on (someone or something): *the plan was to surprise the heck out of the grizzly by sicking the dog on him.* ■ (**sic someone on**) *inf.* set someone to pursue, keep watch on, or accompany (another).

sick¹ /sik/ ▸*adj.* **1** affected by physical or mental illness: *nursing very sick children* | [as *pl. n.*] (**the sick**) *visiting the sick and the elderly.* ■ of or relating to those who are ill: *the company organized a sick fund for its workers.* ■ *fig.* (of an organization, system, or society) suffering from serious problems, esp. of a financial nature: *their economy remains sick.* **2** feeling nauseous and wanting to vomit: *he was starting to feel sick.* ■ (of an emotion) so intense as to cause one to feel unwell or nauseous: *he had a sick fear of returning.* ■ *inf.* disappointed, mortified, or miserable: *he looked pretty sick at that, but he eventually agreed.* **3** (**sick of**) intensely annoyed with or bored by (someone or something) as a result of having had too much of them: *I'm absolutely sick of your moods.* **4** *inf.* (esp. of humor) having something unpleasant such as death, illness, or misfortune as its subject and dealing with it in an offensive way: *this was someone's idea of a sick joke.* ■ (of a person) having abnormal or unnatural tendencies; perverted: *he is a deeply sick man from whom society needs to be protected.* —**sick·ish** *adj.*
▸ □ **be sick 1** be ill. **2** vomit. □ **make someone sick** cause someone to vomit or feel nauseous or unwell: *sherry makes me sick and so do cigars.* ■ cause someone to feel intense annoyance or disgust: *you're so damned self-righteous you make me sick!* □ —— **oneself sick** do something to such an extent that one feels nauseous or unwell (often used for emphasis): *she was worrying herself sick about Mike.* □ **sick and tired of** *inf.* annoyed about or bored with (something) and unwilling to put up with it any longer: *I am sick and tired of all the criticism.* □ (**as**) **sick as a dog** *inf.* extremely ill. □ **sick to death of** *inf.* another way of saying **SICK AND TIRED OF** above.

sick² ▸*v.* variant of **SIC²**.

sick·bay /ˈsikˌbā/ (also **sick bay**) ▶*n.* a room or building set aside for the treatment or accommodation of the sick, esp. within a military base or on board a ship.

sick·bed /ˈsikˌbed/ ▶*n.* an invalid's bed (often used to refer to the state or condition of being an invalid): *he had climbed from his sickbed to help the club.*

sick·en /ˈsikən/ ▶*v.* **1** [*tr.*] (often **be sickened**) make (someone) feel disgusted or appalled: *she was sickened by the bomb attack.* **2** [*intr.*] become ill: *Dawson sickened unexpectedly and died in 1916.*

sick·le /ˈsikəl/ ▶*n.* a short-handled farming tool with a semicircular blade, used for reaping, lopping, or trimming. ▷Old English *sicol, sicel,* of Germanic origin; related to Dutch *sikkel* and German *Sichel,* based on Latin *secula,* from *secare* 'to cut.'

sick leave ▶*n.* leave of absence granted because of illness.

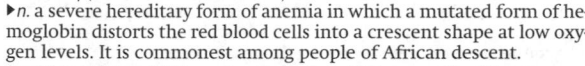

sickle

sick·le cell a·ne·mi·a /ˈsikəl sel əˈnēmēə/ (also **sickle cell disease**) ▶*n.* a severe hereditary form of anemia in which a mutated form of hemoglobin distorts the red blood cells into a crescent shape at low oxygen levels. It is commonest among people of African descent.

sick·ly /ˈsiklē/ ▶*adj.* (**-li·er, -li·est**) **1** often ill; in poor health: *she was a thin, sickly child.* ■ (of a person's complexion or expression) indicative of poor health: *his usual sickly pallor.* ■ (of a place, climate, or time) causing or characterized by unhealthiness: *a deep sickly vaporous swamp.* **2** (of a flavor, smell, color, or light) so unpleasant as to induce discomfort or nausea: *the walls were painted a sickly green.* ■ excessively sentimental or mawkish: *a sickly fable of delicate young lovers.* —**sick·li·ness** *n.*

sick·ness /ˈsiknis/ ▶*n.* **1** the state of being ill: *she was absent through sickness.* ■ a particular type of illness or disease: *botulism causes fodder sickness of horses.* **2** the feeling or fact of being affected with nausea or vomiting: *she felt a wave of sickness wash over her.*

sick·o /ˈsikō/ ▶*n.* (*pl.* **-os**) *inf.* a mentally ill or perverted person, esp. one who is sadistic.

sick·room /ˈsikˌrōōm/ ▶*n.* a room occupied by an ill person.

side /sīd/ ▶*n.* **1** a position to the left or right of an object, place, or central point: *a town on the other side of the river.* ■ either of the two halves of an object, surface, or place regarded as divided by an imaginary central line: *she lay on her side of the bed.* ■ the right or the left part of a person's or animal's body, esp. of the human torso: *he has been paralyzed on his right side since birth.* ■ a place or position closely adjacent to someone: *his wife stood at his side.* ■ either of the lateral halves of the body of a butchered animal, or an animal or fish prepared for eating: *a side of beef.* **2** an upright or sloping surface of a structure or object that is not the top or bottom and generally not the front or back: *a car crashed into the side of the house.* ■ each of the flat surfaces of a solid object. ■ either of the two surfaces of something flat and thin, such as paper or cloth. ■ either of the two faces of a record or of the two separate tracks on a length of recording tape. **3** a part or region near the edge and away from the middle of something: *a minivan was parked at the side of the road.* ■ [as *adj.*] subsidiary to or less important than something: *a side dish of fresh vegetables.* ■ a dish served as subsidiary to the main one: *a side of German potato salad.* ■ each of the lines forming the boundary of a plane rectilinear figure: *the farm buildings formed three sides of a square.* **4** a person or group opposing another or others in a dispute, contest, or debate: *the two sides agreed to resume border trade.* ■ *chiefly Brit.* a sports team. ■ the position, interests, or attitude of one person or group, esp. when regarded as being in opposition to another or others: *Mrs. Burt hasn't kept her side of the bargain.* ■ a particular aspect of something, esp. a situation or a person's character: *her ability to put up with his disagreeable side.* ■ a person's kinship or line of descent as traced through either their father or mother: *Richard was of French descent on his mother's side.*

▶*v.* [*intr.*] (**side with/against**) support or oppose in a conflict, dispute, or debate: *he felt that Max had betrayed him by siding with Beatrice.* —**side·less** *adj.*

▶ □ **by the side of** close to: *a house by the side of the road.* □ **from side to side 1** alternately left and right from a central point: *I shook my head frantically from side to side.* **2** across the entire width; right across: *the fleet stretched four miles from side to side.* □ **have something on one's side** (or **something is on one's side**) something is operating to one's

advantage: *now that he had time on his side, Tom relaxed a little.* □ **on the —— side** tending toward being ——; rather —— (used to qualify an adjective): *these shoes are a bit on the tight side.* □ **on the side 1** in addition to one's regular job or as a subsidiary source of income: *no one lived in the property, but the caretaker made a little on the side by renting rooms out.* **2** secretly, esp. with regard to a relationship in addition to one's legal or regular partner: *Brian had a mistress on the side.* **3** served separately from the main dish: *a club sandwich with french fries on the side.* □ **side by side** (of two or more people or things) close together and facing the same way: *on we jogged, side by side, for a mile.* ■ together: *we have been using both systems, side by side, for two years.* ■ (of people or groups) supporting each other; in cooperation: *the two institutions worked side by side in complete harmony.* □ **take sides** support one person or cause against another or others in a dispute, conflict, or contest: *I do not want to take sides in this matter.* □ **this side of 1** before (a particular time, date, or event): *this side of midnight.* ■ yet to reach (a particular age): *I'm this side of forty-five.* **2** *inf.* used in superlative expressions to denote that something is comparable with a paragon or model of its kind: *the finest coffee this side of Brazil.* □ **to one side** out of one's way; aside. ■ to be dealt with or considered later, esp. because tending to distract one from something more important: *before the kickoff a player has to set his disappointments and frustrations to one side.*

side·arm (also **side arm**) ▶*n.* a weapon worn at a person's side, such as a pistol or other small firearm (or, formerly, a sword or bayonet).

side·band /ˈsīdˌband/ ▶*n.* Telecomm. one of two frequency bands on either side of the carrier wave, containing the modulated signal.

side·bar /ˈsīdˌbär/ ▶*n.* a short article in a newspaper or magazine, typically boxed, placed alongside a main article, and containing additional or explanatory material. ■ a secondary, additional, or incidental thing; a side issue. ■ (also **sidebar conference**) (in a court of law) a discussion between the lawyers and the judge held out of earshot of the jury.

side·board /ˈsīdˌbôrd/ ▶*n.* **1** a flat-topped piece of furniture with cupboards and drawers, placed along a wall and used for storing dishes, glasses, and table linen. **2** a board forming the side, or a part of the side, of a structure, esp. a removable board at the side of a truck or trailer.

side·burn /ˈsīdˌbərn/ ▶*n.* (usu. **sideburns**) a strip of hair grown by a man down each side of the face in front of his ears.

side·car /ˈsīdˌkär/ ▶*n.* **1** a small, low vehicle attached to the side of a motorcycle for carrying passengers. **2** a cocktail of brandy and lemon juice with orange liqueur.

sid·ed /ˈsīdid/ ▶*adj.* [in *comb.*] having sides of a specified number or type: *narrow, steep-sided canyons.* —**sid·ed·ly** *adv.* [in *comb.*] . —**sid·ed·ness** *n.*

side dish ▶*n.* a dish served as subsidiary to the main one: *both were served with an excellent side dish of fresh vegetables.*

side ef·fect ▶*n.* a secondary, typically undesirable effect of a drug or medical treatment: *many anticancer drugs now in use have toxic side effects.*

side·grade /ˈsīd ˌgrād/ ▶*n.* a marketing incentive aimed at persuading a consumer to switch to a competitor's product: *a competitive sidegrade to Canvas or CorelDraw.*

▶*v.* switch to a competitive product: *I'd prefer to sidegrade to Windows Media Player 10 at some point.*

side·kick /ˈsīdˌkik/ ▶*n.* *inf.* a person's assistant or close associate, esp. one who has less authority than that person.

side·light /ˈsīdˌlīt/ ▶*n.* a light placed at the side of something. ■ (**sidelights**) a ship's port (red) and starboard (green) navigation lights. ■ *fig.* a piece of incidental information that helps to clarify or enliven a subject. ■ natural light coming from the side.

side·line /ˈsīdˌlīn/ ▶*n.* **1** an activity done in addition to one's main job, esp. to earn extra income: [as *adj.*] *a sideline career as a stand-up comic.* ■ an auxiliary line of goods or business: *electronic handbooks are a lucrative sideline for the firm.* **2** (usu. **sidelines**) either of the two lines bounding the longer sides of a football field, basketball court, tennis court, or similar playing area. ■ the area immediately outside such lines as a place for nonplayers, substitutes, or spectators: *his son watched from the sidelines.*

▶*v.* [*tr.*] (often **be sidelined**) cause (a player) to be unable to play on a team or in a game: *he has been sidelined for the last six weeks with a fractured wrist.* ■ *fig.* remove from the center of activity or attention; place in a less influential position: *a respected lawyer will be sidelined by alcohol abuse.*

▶ □ **on** (or **from**) **the sidelines** in (or from) a position where one is observing a situation but is unable or unwilling to be directly involved in it.

side·long /ˈsīdˌlôNG/ ▶adj. & adv. directed to or from one side; sideways: [as adj.] *Steve gave her a sidelong glance* | [as adv.] *he looked sidelong at her.*

si·de·re·al /sīˈdi(ə)rēəl/ ▶adj. of or with respect to the distant stars (i.e., the constellations or fixed stars, not the sun or planets).

si·de·re·al day ▶n. Astron. the time between two consecutive transits of the First Point of Aries. It represents the time taken by the earth to rotate on its axis relative to the stars, and is almost four minutes shorter than the solar day because of the earth's orbital motion.

sid·er·ite /ˈsīdəˌrīt/ ▶n. a brown mineral consisting of ferrous carbonate, occurring as the main component of some kinds of iron ore or as rhombohedral crystals in mineral veins. —**sid·er·it·ic** /ˌsīdəˈritik/ adj.

side·sad·dle /ˈsīdˌsadl/ (also **side-sad·dle**) ▶n. a saddle in which the rider has both feet on the same side of the horse. It is typically used by a woman rider wearing a skirt.
▶adv. sitting in this position on a horse.

side·show /ˈsīdˌSHō/ ▶n. a small show or stall at an exhibition, fair, or circus. ■ fig. a minor or diverting incident or issue, esp. one that distracts attention from something more important.

side·slip /ˈsīdˌslip/ (also **side-slip**) ▶n. a sideways skid or slip. ■ Aeron. a sideways movement of an aircraft, esp. downward toward the inside of a turn.

side·split·ting /ˈsīdˌsplitiNG/ ▶adj. inf. extremely amusing; causing violent laughter: *sidesplitting anecdotes.*

side·step /ˈsīdˌstep/ ▶v. (-**stepped**, -**step·ping**) [tr.] avoid (someone or something) by stepping sideways: *she sidestepped the cracks in the pavement.* ■ fig. avoid dealing with or discussing (something problematic or disagreeable): *he neatly sidestepped the questions about riots.* —**side·step·per** n.

side·stroke /ˈsīdˌstrōk/ ▶n. a swimming stroke similar to the breaststroke in which the swimmer lies on their side.

side·swipe /ˈsīdˌswīp/ ▶v. [tr.] strike (someone or something) with or as if with a glancing blow: *Curtis jerked the wheel hard over and sideswiped the other car.*

side·track /ˈsīdˌtrak/ ▶v. [tr.] (usu. **be/get sidetracked**) **1** cause (someone) to be distracted from an immediate or important issue: *he does not let himself get sidetracked by fads and trends.* ■ divert (a project or debate) away from a central issue or previously determined plan: *the effort at reform has been sidetracked for years.* **2** direct (a train) onto a branch line or siding. ■ divert (a well or borehole) to reach a productive deposit or to avoid an obstruction.
▶n. a railroad branch line or siding.

side·walk /ˈsīdˌwôk/ ▶n. a paved path for pedestrians at the side of a road.

side·wall /ˈsīdˌwôl/ ▶n. **1** (often **side wall**) a wall forming the side of a structure or room. **2** the side of a tire, typically untreaded and sometimes marked or colored distinctively.

side·ward /ˈsīdwərd/ ▶adj. another term for SIDEWAYS.
▶adv. (also **side·wards** /-wərdz/) another term for SIDEWAYS.

side·ways /ˈsīdˌwāz/ (also **side·wise**) ▶adv. & adj. to, toward, or from the side: [as adv.] *she tilted her body sideways* | [as adj.] *he hurried toward his office without a sideways glance.* ■ [as adv.] with one side facing forward: *the truck slid sideways across the road.* ■ so as to occupy a job or position at the same level as one previously held rather than be promoted or demoted: [as adj.] *after the reshuffle there were sideways moves for managers.* ■ by an unexpected way: [as adv.] *he came into politics sideways, as campaign manager for the president.* ■ [as adj.] from an unconventional or unorthodox viewpoint: *take a sideways look at daily life.*

side·wind·er¹ /ˈsīdˌwīndər/ ▶n. a pale-colored, nocturnal, burrowing rattlesnake (*Crotalus cerastes*) of North American deserts. It moves sideways by throwing its body into S-shaped curves.

side·wind·er² ▶n. a heavy blow with the fist delivered from or on the side.

sid·ing /ˈsīdiNG/ ▶n. **1** a short track at the side of and opening onto a railroad line. **2** cladding material for the outside of a building.

si·dle /ˈsīdl/ ▶v. [intr.] walk in a furtive, unobtrusive, or timid manner, esp. sideways or obliquely: *I sidled up to her.*

SIDS /sidz/ ▶abbr. sudden infant death syndrome.

siege /sēj/ ▶n. a military operation in which enemy forces surround a town or building, cutting off essential supplies, with the aim of compelling the surrender of those inside: *Verdun had withstood a siege of ten weeks.* ■ a similar operation by a police or other force to compel the surrender of an armed person. ■ a prolonged period of misfortune: *I've been having a siege of headaches.*
▶ □ **lay siege to** conduct a siege of (a place): *government forces laid siege to*

the building. fig. *the press laid siege to her apartment.* □ **under siege** (of a place) undergoing a siege.

sie·mens /ˈsēmənz/ (abbr.: **S**) ▶n. Physics the SI unit of conductance, equal to one reciprocal ohm.

si·er·ra /sēˈerə/ ▶n. **1** a long jagged mountain chain. **2** a code word representing the letter S, used in radio communication.

si·es·ta /sēˈestə/ ▶n. an afternoon rest or nap, esp. one taken during the hottest hours of the day in a hot climate.

sieve /siv/ ▶n. a utensil consisting of a wire or plastic mesh held in a frame, used for straining solids from liquids, for separating coarser from finer particles, or for reducing soft solids to a pulp. ■ used figuratively with reference to the fact that a sieve does not hold all its contents: *she's forgotten all the details already—she's got a mind like a sieve.*
▶v. [tr.] put (a food substance or other material) through a sieve. ■ [intr.] (**sieve through**) fig. examine in detail: *lawyers had sieved through her contract.* —**sieve·like** /-ˌlīk/ adj.

sift /sift/ ▶v. [tr.] put (a fine, loose, or powdery substance) through a sieve so as to remove lumps or large particles: *sift the flour into a large bowl.* ■ fig. examine (something) thoroughly so as to isolate that which is most important or useful: *until we sift the evidence ourselves, we can't comment objectively.* ■ cause to pass as through a sieve: *Melanie sifted the warm sand through her fingers.* ■ [intr.] (of snow, ash, light, or something similar) descend or float down lightly or sparsely as if sprinkled from a sieve. —**sift·er** n.

sigh /sī/ ▶v. [intr.] emit a long, deep, audible breath expressing sadness, relief, tiredness, or a similar feeling: *Harry sank into a chair and sighed with relief.* ■ fig. (of the wind or something through which the wind blows) make a sound resembling this: *a breeze made the treetops sigh.*
▶n. a long, deep, audible exhalation expressing sadness, relief, tiredness, or a similar feeling: *she let out a long sigh of despair.* ■ fig. a gentle sound resembling this, esp. one made by the wind.

sight /sīt/ ▶n. **1** the faculty or power of seeing: *Joseph lost his sight as a baby.* ■ the action or fact of seeing someone or something: *I've always been scared of the sight of blood.* ■ the area or distance within which someone can see or something can be seen: *he now refused to let Rose out of his sight.* **2** a thing that one sees or that can be seen: *John was a familiar sight in the bar for many years.* ■ (**sights**) places of interest to tourists and visitors in a city, town, or other place: *she offered to show me the sights.* ■ (**a sight**) inf. a person or thing having a ridiculous, repulsive, or disheveled appearance: "*I must look a frightful sight,*" *she said.* **3** (usu. **sights**) a device on a gun or optical instrument used for assisting a person's precise aim or observation.
▶v. **1** [tr.] manage to see or observe (someone or something); catch an initial glimpse of: *tell me when you sight London Bridge* | [as n.] (**sighting**) *the unseasonal sighting of a cuckoo.* **2** [intr.] take aim by looking through the sights of a gun: *she sighted down the barrel.* ■ take a detailed visual measurement of something with or as with a sight. ■ [tr.] adjust the sight of (a firearm or optical instrument). —**sight·er** n.
▶ □ **at first sight** on first seeing or meeting someone: *it was love at first sight.* ■ after an initial impression (which is then found to be different from what is experienced): *the debate is more complex than it seems at first sight.* □ **in sight** visible: *no other vehicle was in sight.* ■ near at hand; close to being achieved or realized: *the minister insisted that agreement was in sight.* □ **in** (or **within**) **sight of** so as to see or be seen from: *I climbed the hill and came in sight of the house.* ■ within reach of; close to attaining: *he was safe for the moment and in sight of victory.* □ **in** (or **within**) **one's sights** visible, esp. through the sights of one's gun. ■ within the scope of one's ambitions or expectations: *he had the prize firmly in his sights.* □ **lose sight of** be no longer able to see. ■ fail to consider, be aware of, or remember: *we should not lose sight of the fact that the issues involved are moral ones.* □ **on** (or **at**) **sight** as soon as someone or something has been seen: *in Africa, paramilitary game wardens shoot poachers on sight.* □ **out of sight 1** not visible: *she saw them off, waving until the car was out of sight.* **2** [often as interj.] inf. extremely good; excellent: [as adj.] *these headphones are an out-of-sight choice.* □ **a sight** —— inf. or dial. used to indicate that something is so described to a considerable extent: *the old lady is a sight cleverer than Sarah.* □ **a sight for sore eyes** inf. a person or thing that one is extremely pleased or relieved to see.

sight de·pos·it ▶n. Finance a bank deposit that can be withdrawn immediately without notice or penalty.

sight·ed /ˈsītid/ ▶adj. (of a person) having the ability to see; not blind: *a*

---

sighted guide is needed | [as *pl. n.*] (**the sighted**) *the blind leading the sighted, I thought.* ■ [in *comb.*] having a specified kind of sight: *the keen-sighted watcher may catch a glimpse.*

sight-less /ˈsītlis/ ▶ *adj.* unable to see; blind: *blank, sightless eyes.* ■ *poetic/lit.* invisible. —**sight-less-ly** *adv.* —**sight-less-ness** *n.*

sight-ly /ˈsītlē/ ▶ *adj.* pleasing to the eye: *metal guards can also be used but are less sightly.* —**sight-li-ness** *n.*

sight-see-ing /ˈsītˌsēiNG/ ▶ *n.* the activity of visiting places of interest in a particular location: *our two-week trip combines spectacular sightseeing and superb hospitality.* —**sight-see** *v.* —**sight-se-er** /ˈsītˌsēər/ *n.*

sig-ma /ˈsigmə/ ▶ *n.* the eighteenth letter of the Greek alphabet (Σ, σ), transliterated as 's.'
▶ *symb.* ■ (Σ) mathematical sum. ■ (σ) standard deviation.

sign /sīn/ ▶ *n.* **1** an object, quality, or event whose presence or occurrence indicates the probable presence or occurrence of something else: *flowers are often given as a sign of affection.* ■ something regarded as an indication or evidence of what is happening or going to happen: *the signs are that counterfeiting is growing at an alarming rate.* ■ used to indicate that someone or something is not present where they should be or are expected to be: *there was still no sign of her.* ■ *Med.* an indication of a disease detectable by a medical practitioner even if not apparent to the patient. ■ a miracle regarded as evidence of supernatural power (chiefly in biblical and literary use). ■ any trace of a wild animal, esp. its tracks or droppings: *wolverine sign.* **2** a gesture or action used to convey information or instructions: *she gave him the thumbs-up sign.* ■ a notice that is publicly displayed giving information or instructions in a written or symbolic form: *I didn't see the stop sign.* ■ an action or reaction that conveys something about someone's state or experiences: *she gave no sign of having seen him.* ■ a gesture used in a system of sign language.
■ short for SIGN LANGUAGE. ■ a symbol or word used to represent an operation, instruction, concept, or object in algebra, music, or other subjects. ■ a word or gesture given according to prior arrangement as a means of identification; a password. **3** (also **zodiacal sign**) *Astrol.* each of the twelve equal sections into which the zodiac is divided, named from the constellations formerly situated in each, and associated with successive periods of the year according to the position of the sun on the ecliptic: *a person born under the sign of Virgo.* **4** *Math.* the positiveness or negativeness of a quantity.
▶ *v.* **1** [*tr.*] write one's name on (a letter, card, or similar item) to identify oneself as the writer or sender: *the card was signed by the whole class.* ■ indicate agreement with or authorization of the contents of (a document or other written or printed material) by attaching a signature: *the two countries signed a nonaggression treaty.* ■ write (one's name) for purposes of identification or authorization: *she signed her name in the book* | [*tr.*] *she signed herself Ingrid* | [*intr.*] *he signed on the dotted line.* ■ engage (someone, typically a sports player or a musician) to work for one by signing a contract with them: *the company signed 30 bands.* ■ [*intr.*] sign a contract committing oneself to work for a particular person or organization: *Sherman has signed for another two seasons.* **2** [*intr.*] use gestures to convey information or instructions: *she signed to her husband to leave the room.* ■ communicate in sign language: *she was learning to sign.* ■ [*tr.*] express or perform (something) in sign language: [as *adj.*] (**signed**) *the theater routinely puts on signed performances.*
▶ *phrasal v.* □ **sign something away/over** officially relinquish rights or property by signing a deed: *I have no intention of signing away my inheritance.* □ **sign for** sign a receipt to confirm that one has received (something delivered or handed over). □ **sign in** sign a register on arrival, typically in a hotel. □ **sign off** conclude a letter, broadcast, or other message: *he signed off with a few words of advice.* ■ sign to record that one is leaving work for the day. ■ *Bridge* indicate by a conventional bid that one is seeking to end the bidding. □ **sign off on** *inf.* assent or give one's approval to: *it was hard to get celebrities to sign off on these issues.* □ **sign on** *chiefly Brit.* commit oneself to employment, membership in a society, or some other undertaking: *I'll sign on with an advertising agency.* □ **sign someone on** take someone into one's employment. □ **sign out** sign a register to record one's departure, typically from a hotel. □ **sign something out** sign to indicate that one has borrowed or hired something: *I signed out the keys.* □ **sign up** commit oneself to a period of employment or education or to some other undertaking: *he signed up for a ten-week course.* ■ enlist in the armed forces. □ **sign someone up** formally engage someone in employment. ▷Middle English: from Old French *signe* (noun), *signer* (verb), from Latin *signum* 'mark, token.' —**sign-er** *n.*
▶ □ **sign of the cross** a Christian sign made in blessing or prayer by tracing a cross from the forehead to the chest and to each shoulder, or in the air. □ **sign of the times** something judged to exemplify or

indicate the nature or quality of a particular period, typically something unwelcome or unpleasant: *the theft was a sign of the times.*

sig-nal¹ /ˈsignəl/ ▶ *n.* **1** a gesture, action, or sound that is used to convey information or instructions, typically by prearrangement between the parties concerned: *the firing of the gun was the signal for a chain of beacons to be lit* | *the policeman raised his hand as a signal to stop.* ■ an indication of a state of affairs: *the markets are waiting for a clear signal about the direction of policy.* ■ an event or statement that provides the impulse or occasion for something specified to happen: *the champion's announcement that he was retiring was the signal for scores of journalists to gather at his last match.* ■ an apparatus on a railroad, typically a colored light or a semaphore, informing the train crew whether or not the line is clear. ■ *Bridge* a prearranged convention of bidding or play intended to convey information to one's partner. **2** an electrical impulse or radio wave transmitted or received: *equipment for receiving TV signals.*
▶ *v.* (**-naled, -nal-ing;** *chiefly Brit.* **-nalled, -nal-ling**) [*intr.*] transmit information or instructions by means of a gesture, action, or sound: *hold your fire until I signal.* ■ [*tr.*] instruct (someone) to do something by means of gestures or signs rather than explicit orders: *she signaled Charlotte to be silent.* ■ (of a cyclist, motorist, or vehicle) indicate an intention to turn in a specified direction using an extended arm or flashing indicator: *Stone signaled right* | *the truck signaled to turn left.* ■ [*tr.*] indicate the existence or occurrence of (something) by actions or sounds: *they could signal displeasure by refusing to cooperate.* ■ give an indication of a state of affairs: *she gave a glance that signaled that her father was being secretive.* —**sig-nal-er** *n.*

sig-nal² ▶ *adj.* striking in extent, seriousness, or importance; outstanding: *he attacked the administration for its signal failure of leadership.* —**sig-nal-ly** *adv.*

sig-nal-ize /ˈsignəˌlīz/ ▶ *v.* [*tr.*] mark or indicate (something), esp. in a striking or conspicuous manner: *people seek to change their name to signalize a change in status that has taken place.*

sig-na-to-ry /ˈsignəˌtôrē/ ▶ *n.* (pl. **-ries**) a party that has signed an agreement, esp. a country that has signed a treaty: *Bulgaria is a signatory to a variety of international human rights conventions.*

sig-na-ture /ˈsignəCHər; -ˌCHo͝or/ ▶ *n.* **1** a person's name written in a distinctive way as a form of identification in authorizing a check or document or concluding a letter. ■ the action of signing a document: *the license was sent to the customer for signature.* ■ a distinctive pattern, product, or characteristic by which someone or something can be identified: *the chef produced the pâté that was his signature* | [as *adj.*] *his signature dish.* **2** *Mus.* short for KEY SIGNATURE or TIME SIGNATURE. **3** *Printing* a letter or figure printed at the foot of one or more pages of each sheet of a book as a guide in binding. ■ a printed sheet after being folded to form a group of pages. **4** the part of a medical prescription that gives instructions about the use of the medicine or drug prescribed.

sign-board /ˈsīnˌbôrd/ ▶ *n.* a board displaying the name or logo of a business or product. ■ a board displaying a sign to direct traffic or travelers.

sig-net /ˈsignit/ ▶ *n.* *hist.* a small seal, esp. one set in a ring, used instead of or with a signature to give authentication to an official document.

sig-nif-i-cance /sigˈnifikəns/ ▶ *n.* **1** the quality of being worthy of attention; importance: *adolescent education was felt to be a social issue of some significance.* **2** the meaning to be found in words or events. **3** (also **statistical significance**) the extent to which a result deviates from that expected to arise simply from random variation or errors in sampling.

sig-nif-i-cant /sigˈnifikənt/ ▶ *adj.* **1** sufficiently great or important to be worthy of attention; noteworthy: *a significant increase in sales.* **2** having a particular meaning; indicative of something: *in times of stress her dreams seemed to her especially significant.* ■ suggesting a meaning or message that is not explicitly stated: *she gave him a significant look.* **3** *Statistics* of, relating to, or having significance. —**sig-nif-i-cant-ly** *adv.*

sig-nif-i-cant oth-er ▶ *n.* a person with whom someone has an established romantic or sexual relationship.

sig-ni-fy /ˈsignəˌfī/ ▶ *v.* (**-fies, -fied**) **1** [*tr.*] be an indication of: *this decision signified a fundamental change in their priorities.* ■ be a symbol of; have as meaning: *the church used this image to signify the Holy Trinity.* ■ (of a person) indicate or declare (a feeling or intention): *signify your agreement by signing the letter below.* ■ [*intr.*] be of importance: *the locked door doesn't necessarily signify.* **2** [*intr.*] *inf.* (among black Americans) exchange boasts or insults as a game or ritual. —**sig-ni-fi-ca-tion** /ˌsignəfiˈkāSHən/ *n.* —**sig-ni-fi-er** *n.*

sign lan-guage ▶ *n.* a system of communication using visual gestures and signs, as used by deaf people.

si·gnor /sēn'yôr/ ▶ n. (pl. **si·gno·ri** /sēn'yôrē/) a title or form of address used of or to an Italian-speaking man, corresponding to *Mr.* or *sir.*

si·gno·ra /sēn'yôrə/ ▶ n. a title or form of address used of or to an Italian-speaking married woman, corresponding to *Mrs.* or *madam.*

si·gno·ri·na /ˌsēnyə'rēnə/ ▶ n. a title or form of address used of or to an Italian-speaking unmarried woman, corresponding to *Miss.*

sign·post /'sīn,pōst/ ▶ n. a sign giving information such as the direction and distance to a nearby town, typically found at a crossroads. ■ *fig.* something that acts as guidance or a clue to an unclear or complicated issue: *there are few unambiguous signposts for doctors facing ethical issues.*

si·ka /'sēkə/ (also **si·ka deer**) ▶ n. a forest-dwelling deer (*Cervus nippon*) with a grayish winter coat that turns yellowish-brown with white spots in summer. It is native to Japan and Southeast Asia and naturalized elsewhere.

Sikh /sēk/ ▶ n. an adherent of Sikhism.
▶ adj. of or relating to Sikhs or Sikhism.

Sikh·ism /'sēkizəm/ ▶ n. a monotheistic religion founded in Punjab in the 15th century by Guru Nanak.

si·lage /'sīlij/ ▶ n. grass or other green fodder compacted and stored in airtight conditions, typically in a silo, without first being dried, and used as animal feed in the winter.

sil·den·a·fil cit·rate /sil'denə,fil/ ▶ n. an off-white crystalline compound that works by inhibiting the breakdown of enzymes that leads to loss of erection. Also called **VIAGRA** (*trademark*).

si·lence /'sīləns/ ▶ n. complete absence of sound: *sirens pierce the silence of the night.* ■ the fact or state of abstaining from speech: *Karen had withdrawn into sullen silence.* ■ the avoidance of mentioning or discussing something: *politicians keep their silence on the big questions.* ■ the state of standing still and not speaking as a sign of respect for someone deceased or in an opportunity for prayer: *a moment of silence presided over by a local minister.*
▶ v. [tr.] (often **be silenced**) cause to become silent; prohibit or prevent from speaking: *the team's performance silenced their critics.*

si·lenc·er /'sīlənsər/ ▶ n. a device for reducing the noise emitted by a gun or other loud mechanism.

si·lent /'sīlənt/ ▶ adj. not <u>making or</u> accompanied by any sound: *the woods were still and silent.* ■ (of a person) not speaking: *she fell silent for a moment.* ■ not expressed aloud: *a silent prayer.* ■ (of a letter) written but not pronounced, e.g., *b* in *doubt.* ■ (of a movie) without an accompanying soundtrack. ■ saying or recording nothing on a particular subject: *the poems are silent on the question of marriage.* ■ (of a person) not prone to speak much; taciturn: *I'm the strong, silent type.* —**si·lent·ly** adv.
▶ □ **the silent majority** the majority of people, regarded as holding moderate opinions but rarely expressing them. □ **the silent treatment** a stubborn refusal to talk to someone, esp. after a recent argument or disagreement.

si·lent com·merce ▶ n. a group of technologies based on wireless communications and sensing devices that permit various business and marketing activities to proceed without direct human intervention, on the basis of communications between tagged products and controlling software.

si·lent part·ner ▶ n. a partner not sharing in the actual work of a firm.

sil·hou·ette /ˌsiloo'et/ ▶ n. the dark shape and outline of someone or something visible against a lighter background, esp. in dim light. ■ a representation of someone or something showing the shape and outline only, typically colored in solid black.
▶ v. [tr.] (usu. **be silhouetted**) cast or show (someone or something) as a dark shape and outline against a lighter background: *the castle was silhouetted against the sky.*

sil·i·ca /'silikə/ ▶ n. a hard, unreactive, colorless compound, SiO_2, that occurs as the mineral quartz and as a principal constituent of sandstone, granite, and other rocks. —**si·li·ceous** /sə'lishəs/ (also **si·li·cious**) adj.

sil·i·ca gel ▶ n. hydrated silica in a hard granular hygroscopic form used as a desiccant.

sil·i·cate /'silə,kāt; -kit/ ▶ n. *Chem.* any of the many minerals consisting primarily of $SiO_4{}^{2-}$ combined with metal ions, forming a major component of the rocks of the earth's crust.

sil·i·con /'silə,kän; -kən/ ▶ n. the chemical element of atomic number 14, a nonmetal with semiconducting properties, used in making electronic circuits. (Symbol: **Si**)

sil·i·con chip ▶ n. a microchip.

sil·i·cone /'silə,kōn/ ▶ n. any of a class of synthetic materials that are polymers with a chemical structure based on chains of alternate silicon and oxygen atoms, with organic groups attached to the silicon atoms. Such compounds are typically resistant to chemical attack and insensitive to temperature changes and are used to make rubber, plastics, polishes, and lubricants.

sil·i·co·sis /ˌsilə'kōsis/ ▶ n. *Med.* lung fibrosis caused by the inhalation of dust containing silica. —**sil·i·cot·ic** /ˌsilə'kätik/ adj.

silk /silk/ ▶ n. a fine, strong, soft, lustrous fiber produced by silkworms in making cocoons and collected to make thread and fabric. ■ a similar fiber spun by some other insect larvae and by most spiders. ■ [often as adj.] thread or fabric made from the fiber produced by the silkworm: *a silk shirt.* ■ (**silks**) garments made from such fabric, esp. as worn by a jockey in the colors of a particular horse owner. ■ any silklike threads that grow in plants, such as at the end of an ear of corn or in a milkweed pod. —**silk·like** /'silk,līk/ adj.

silk·en /'silkən/ ▶ adj. made of silk: *a silken ribbon.* ■ soft or lustrous like silk: *silken hair.*

silk·screen /'silk,skrēn/ (also **silk screen**) ▶ n. a screen of fine mesh used in screen-printing. ■ a print made by screen-printing.
▶ v. [tr.] print, decorate, or reproduce using a silkscreen.

silk·worm /'silk,wərm/ ▶ n. the commercially bred caterpillar of the domesticated Asian silkworm moth (*Bombyx mori*, family Bombycidae), which spins a silk cocoon that is processed to yield silk fiber. ■ a commercial silk-yielding caterpillar of certain large moths of a different family (Saturniidae).

silk·y /'silkē/ ▶ adj. (**silk·i·er**, **silk·i·est**) of or resembling silk, esp. in being soft, fine, and lustrous: *the fur felt silky and soft.* ■ (of a person or their speech or manner) suave and smooth, esp. in a way intended to be persuasive: *a silky, seductive voice.* —**silk·i·ly** /'silkəlē/ adv. —**silk·i·ness** n.

sill /sil/ ▶ n. a shelf or slab of stone, wood, or metal at the foot of a window or doorway. ■ a strong horizontal member at the base of any structure, e.g., in the frame of a motor or rail vehicle. ■ *Geol.* a tabular sheet of igneous rock intruded between and parallel with the existing strata. ▷Old English *syll*, *sylle* 'horizontal beam forming a foundation,' of Germanic origin; related to German *Schwelle* 'threshold.'

sil·ly /'silē/ ▶ adj. (**-li·er**, **-li·est**) having or showing a lack of common sense or judgment; absurd and foolish: *another of his silly jokes.* ■ ridiculously trivial or frivolous: *he would brood about silly things.* ■ used to convey that an activity or process has been engaged in to such a degree that someone is no longer capable of thinking or acting sensibly: *he often drank himself silly.*
▶ n. (pl. **-lies**) *inf.* a foolish person (often used as a form of address): *Come on, silly.* —**sil·li·ly** /'siləlē/ adv. —**sil·li·ness** n.

si·lo /'sīlō/ ▶ n. (pl. **-los**) **1** a tower or pit on a farm used to store grain. ■ a pit or other airtight structure in which green crops are compressed and stored as silage. **2** an underground chamber in which a guided missile is kept ready for firing.

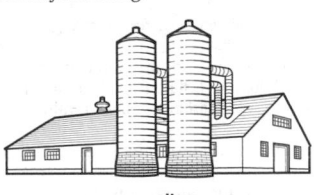

silos

silt /silt/ ▶ n. fine sand, clay, or other material carried by running water and deposited as a sediment, esp. in a channel or harbor.
▶ v. [intr.] become filled or blocked with silt: *the river's mouth had silted up.* ■ [tr.] fill or block with silt. —**sil·ta·tion** /sil'tāshən/ n. —**silt·y** adj.

sil·va /'silvə/ (also **syl·va**) ▶ n. the trees of a region, epoch, or environment.

sil·ver /'silvər/ ▶ n. **1** a precious shiny grayish-white metal, the chemical element of atomic number 47. (Symbol: **Ag**) **2** a shiny gray-white color or appearance like that of silver: *the dark hair was now highlighted with silver.* **3** silver dishes, containers, or cutlery: *thieves stole $5,000 worth of silver* | *the family silver.* ■ household cutlery of any material: *it is important to wash table silver in hot soapy water immediately after each meal.* **4** coins made from silver or from a metal that resembles silver.

▶*adj.* made wholly or chiefly of silver: *silver jewelry.* ■ colored like silver: *a silver Mercedes.* ■ denoting a twenty-fifth anniversary.

▶*v.* [tr.] [often as *adj.*] (**silvered**) coat or plate with silver: *large silvered candlesticks.* ■ provide (mirror glass) with a backing of a silver-colored material in order to make it reflective. ■ turn (a person's hair) gray or white. ■ [intr.] (of a person's hair) turn gray or white.

▶ □ **the silver screen** the movie industry; movies collectively: *stars of the silver screen.*

sil·ver birch ▶*n.* a European birch (*Betula pendula*) with silver-gray bark, common on poorer soils to the northern limit of tree growth.

sil·ver·fish /ˈsilvərˌfiSH/ ▶*n.* (*pl.* same or **-fishes**) **1** a chiefly nocturnal silvery bristletail (*Lepisma saccharina*, family Lepismatidae) that frequents houses and other buildings, feeding on starchy materials. **2** a silver-colored fish, esp. a goldfish of an unpigmented variety.

sil·ver med·al ▶*n.* a medal made of or colored silver, awarded for second place in a race or competition.

sil·ver plate ▶*n.* a thin layer of silver electroplated or otherwise applied as a coating to another metal. ■ plates, dishes, etc., made of silver.

sil·ver·smith /ˈsilvərˌsmiTH/ ▶*n.* a person who makes silver articles. —**sil·ver·smith·ing** *n.*

Sil·ver Star ▶*n.* a decoration bestowed by the U.S. Army upon a soldier for gallantry in action.

sil·ver tongue ▶*n.* a tendency to be eloquent and persuasive in speaking. —**sil·ver-tongued** *adj.*

sil·ver·ware /ˈsilvərˌwer/ ▶*n.* dishes, containers, or cutlery made of or coated with silver. ■ eating and serving utensils made of any material.

sil·ver·y /ˈsilvərē/ ▶*adj.* like silver in color or appearance; shiny and gray-white: *shoals of silvery fish.* ■ (of a person's hair) gray-white and lustrous. ■ (of a sound) gentle, clear, and melodious: *a little silvery laugh.* —**sil·ver·i·ness** *n.*

sil·vi·cul·ture /ˈsilviˌkəlCHər/ ▶*n.* the cultivation of trees. —**sil·vi·cul·tur·al** /ˌsilviˈkəlCHərəl/ *adj.* —**sil·vi·cul·tur·ist** /ˌsilviˈkəlCHərist/ *n.*

sim·i·an /ˈsimēən/ ▶*adj.* relating to, resembling, or affecting apes or monkeys: *simian immunodeficiency virus.*

▶*n.* an ape or monkey. ▷early 17th cent.: from Latin *simia* 'ape,' perhaps via Latin from Greek *simos* 'flat-nosed.'

sim·i·lar /ˈsimələr/ ▶*adj.* resembling without being identical: *a soft cheese similar to Brie | northern India and similar areas.* ■ *Geom.* (of geometric figures) having the same shape, with the same angles and proportions, though not necessarily of the same size. —**sim·i·lar·i·ty** /ˌsiməˈlaritē/ *n.* —**sim·i·lar·ly** *adv.*

sim·i·le /ˈsiməlē/ ▶*n.* a figure of speech involving the comparison of one thing with another thing of a different kind, used to make a description more emphatic or vivid (e.g., *as brave as a lion, crazy like a fox*). ■ the use of such a method of comparison.

si·mil·i·tude /siˈmiləˌt(y) o͞od/ ▶*n.* the quality or state of being similar to something.

sim·mer /ˈsimər/ ▶*v.* [intr.] (of water or food) stay just below the boiling point while being heated: *the goulash was simmering slowly in the oven.* ■ [tr.] keep (something) at such a point when cooking or heating it: *simmer the sauce gently until thickened.* ■ be in a state of suppressed anger or excitement: *she was simmering with resentment.* ■ (**simmer down**) become calmer and quieter.

▶*n.* a state or temperature just below the boiling point: *bring the water to a simmer.*

simp /simp/ ▶*n. inf.* a silly or foolish person.

sim·pa·ti·co /simˈpatiˌkō/ ▶*adj.* (of a person) likable and easy to get along with. ■ having or characterized by shared attributes or interests; compatible: *a simpatico relationship.*

sim·per /ˈsimpər/ ▶*v.* [intr.] smile or gesture in an affectedly coquettish, coy, or ingratiating manner: *she simpered, looking pleased with herself.*

▶*n.* an affectedly coquettish, coy, or ingratiating smile or gesture: *an exaggerated simper.* —**sim·per·ing·ly** *adv.*

sim·ple /ˈsimpəl/ ▶*adj.* (**-pler, -plest**) **1** easily understood or done; presenting no difficulty: *a simple solution.* ■ plain, basic, or uncomplicated in form, nature, or design; without much decoration or ornamentation: *a simple white blouse.* ■ used to emphasize the fundamental and straightforward nature of something: *the simple truth.* **2** composed of a single element; not compound. ■ *Math.* denoting a group that has no proper normal subgroup. ■ *Bot.* (of a leaf or stem) not divided or branched. ■ (of a lens, microscope, etc.) consisting of a single lens or component. ■ (in English grammar) denoting a tense formed without an auxiliary, e.g., *sang* as opposed to *was singing.* ■ (of interest) payable on the sum loaned only. **3** of or characteristic of low rank or status;

humble and unpretentious: *a simple Buddhist monk.* **4** of low or abnormally low intelligence. —**sim·ple·ness** *n.*

sim·ple eye ▶*n.* a small eye of an insect or other arthropod that has only one lens, typically present in one or more pairs.

sim·ple frac·ture ▶*n.* a fracture of the bone only, without damage to the surrounding tissues or breaking of the skin. Compare with COMPOUND FRACTURE.

sim·ple-mind·ed /ˈsimpəlˈmīndid/ ▶*adj.* having or showing very little intelligence or judgment. —**sim·ple-mind·ed·ly** *adv.* —**sim·ple-mind·ed·ness** *n.*

sim·ple·ton /ˈsimpəltən/ ▶*n.* a foolish or gullible person.

sim·plex /ˈsimpleks/ ▶*adj. technical* composed of or characterized by a single part or structure. ■ (of a communications system, computer circuit, etc.) only allowing transmission of signals in one direction at a time.

▶*n.* a simple or uncompounded word.

sim·plic·i·ty /simˈplisitē/ ▶*n.* the quality or condition of being easy to understand or do: *for the sake of simplicity, this chapter will concentrate on one theory.* ■ the quality or condition of being plain or natural: *the grandeur and simplicity of Roman architecture.* ■ a thing that is plain, natural, or easy to understand: *the simplicities of pastoral living.*

sim·pli·fy /ˈsimpləˌfī/ ▶*v.* (**-fies, -fied**) [tr.] make (something) simpler or easier to do or understand: *an overhaul of court procedure to simplify litigation.* —**sim·pli·fi·ca·tion** /ˌsimpləfiˈkāSHən/ *n.*

sim·plism /ˈsimplizəm/ ▶*n. rare* the oversimplification of an issue.

sim·plis·tic /simˈplistik/ ▶*adj.* treating complex issues and problems as if they were much simpler than they really are: *simplistic solutions.* —**sim·plis·ti·cal·ly** *adv.*

sim·ply /ˈsimplē/ ▶*adv.* **1** in a straightforward or plain manner: *speaking simply and from the heart.* **2** merely; just: *simply complete the application form.* ■ absolutely; completely (used for emphasis): *it makes Terry simply furious.* ■ used to introduce a short summary of a situation: *quite simply, some things have to be taught.*

sim·u·late /ˈsimyəˌlāt/ ▶*v.* [tr.] imitate the appearance or character of: *red ocher intended to simulate blood.* ■ pretend to have or feel (an emotion): *it was impossible to force a smile, to simulate pleasure.* ■ produce a computer model of: *future population changes were simulated by computer.* —**sim·u·la·tion** /ˌsimyəˈlāSHən/ *n.* —**sim·u·la·tive** /-ˌlātiv/ *adj.*

sim·u·la·tor /ˈsimyəˌlātər/ ▶*n.* a machine with a similar set of controls designed to provide a realistic imitation of the operation of a vehicle, aircraft, or other complex system, used for training purposes. ■ (also **simulator program**) a program enabling a computer to execute programs written for a different computer.

si·mul·cast /ˈsīməlˌkast/ ▶*n.* a simultaneous transmission of the same program on radio and television, or on two or more channels. ■ a live transmission of a public celebration or sports event: *simulcasts of live races.*

▶*v.* [tr.] broadcast (a program) in such a way: *it will be simulcast live to 201 countries.*

si·mul·ta·ne·ous /ˌsīməlˈtānēəs/ ▶*adj.* occurring, operating, or done at the same time: *a simultaneous withdrawal of all troops.* —**si·mul·ta·ne·i·ty** /ˌsīməltəˈnēitē/ *n.* —**si·mul·ta·ne·ous·ly** *adv.* —**si·mul·ta·ne·ous·ness** *n.*

sin¹ /sin/ ▶*n.* an immoral act considered to be a transgression against divine law: *a sin in the eyes of God.* ■ an act regarded as a serious or regrettable fault, offense, or omission: *he committed the unforgivable sin of refusing to give interviews | humorous it's a sin to stay inside.*

▶*v.* (**sinned, sin·ning**) [intr.] commit a sin: *I sinned and brought shame down on us.* ■ (**sin against**) offend against (God, a person, or a principle): *I had sinned against my master.* —**sin·less** *adj.* —**sin·less·ly** *adv.* —**sin·less·ness** *n.*

▶ □ **live in sin** *inf., dated* live together as though married. □ **sin of commission** a sinful action. □ **sin of omission** a sinful failure to perform an action.

sin² /sin/ ▶*abbr.* sine.

since /sins/ ▶*prep., conj., & adv.* **1** in the intervening period between (the time mentioned) and the time under consideration, typically the present: [as *prep.*] *she has suffered from cystic fibrosis since 1984* | [as *conj.*] *I've felt better since I've been here* | [as *adv.*] *she ran away on Friday and we haven't seen her since.* **2** [*conj.*] for the reason that: because: *delegates were delighted, since better protection of rhino reserves will help protect other rare species.* **3** [*adv.*] ago: *the settlement had vanished long since.*

sin·cere /sinˈsi(ə)r/ ▶*adj.* (**-cer·er, -cer·est**) free from pretense or deceit; proceeding from genuine feelings: *they offer their sincere thanks to Paul.* ■ (of a person) saying what they genuinely feel or believe; not dishonest or hypocritical. —**sin·cere·ness** *n.* —**sin·cer·i·ty** /sinˈseritē/ *n.*

sin·cere·ly /sin'si(ə)rlē/ ▶adv. in a sincere or genuine way: *I sincerely hope that we shall have a change of government* | *sincerely held differences of belief.* ■ (also **sincerely yours**) a formula used to end a letter, typically a formal one in which the recipient is addressed by name.

sin·ci·put /'sinsəpət/ ▶n. Anat. the front of the skull from the forehead to the crown. —**sin·cip·i·tal** /sin'sipitl/ adj.

sine /sīn/ ▶n. Math. the trigonometric function that is equal to the ratio of the side opposite a given angle (in a right triangle) to the hypotenuse.

si·ne·cure /'sīnə,kyŏŏr; 'si-/ ▶n. a position requiring little or no work but giving the holder status or financial benefit. ▷mid 17th cent.: from Latin *sine cura* 'without care.' —**si·ne·cur·ism** /'sīnəkyŏŏrizəm; si-/ n. —**si·ne·cur·ist** /'sīnə,kyŏŏrist; si-/ n.

si·ne qua non /,sini ,kwä 'nōn; ,sini ,kwä 'nän/ ▶n. an essential condition; a thing that is absolutely necessary: *grammar and usage are the sine qua non of language teaching and learning.*

sin·ew /'sinyōō/ ▶n. a piece of tough fibrous tissue uniting muscle to bone or bone to bone; a tendon or ligament. ■ (usu. **sinews**) fig. the parts of a structure, system, or thing that give it strength or bind it together: *the sinews of government.* —**sin·ew·less** adj. —**sin·ew·y** /-wē/ adj.

sin·fo·ni·a /,sinfə'nēə/ ▶n. Mus. a symphony. ■ (in the 17th and 18th centuries) an orchestral piece used as an introduction, interlude, or postlude to an opera, oratorio, cantata, or suite.

sin·fo·niet·ta /,sinfən'yetə/ ▶n. Mus. a short or simple symphony. ■ a small symphony orchestra.

sin·ful /'sinfəl/ ▶adj. wicked and immoral; committing or characterized by the committing of sins: *sinful men* | *a sinful way of life.* ■ highly reprehensible: *a sinful waste.* —**sin·ful·ly** adv. —**sin·ful·ness** n.

sing /sing/ ▶v. (past **sang** /sang/; past part. **sung** /səng/) [intr.] make musical sounds with the voice, esp. words with a set tune: *Bella sang to the baby.* ■ [tr.] perform (a song, words, or tune) in this way: *someone started singing "God Bless America"* | [as n.] (**singing**) *the singing of hymns in Latin.* ■ (**sing along**) sing in accompaniment to a song or piece of music. ■ (**sing something out**) call something out loudly; shout: *he sang out a greeting.* ■ (of a bird) make characteristic melodious whistling and twittering sounds: *the birds were singing in the chestnut trees.* ■ make a high-pitched whistling or buzzing sound: *the kettle was beginning to sing.* ■ inf. act as an informer to the police: *a leading terrorist was **singing like a canary.*** ■ [tr.] recount or celebrate in a work of literature, esp. poetry: *poetry should sing the strangeness and variety of the human race* | [intr.] *these poets sing of the North American experience.* ▶n. inf. an act or spell of singing. ■ a meeting for amateur singing. —**sing·a·ble** adj. —**sing·er** n. —**sing·ing·ly** adv.

sing. ▶abbr. singular.

singe /sinj/ ▶v. (**singe·ing**) [tr.] burn (something) superficially or lightly: *fire singed his eyebrows.* ■ [intr.] be burned in this way: *I could feel the hairs on my hands singe.* ■ burn the bristles or down off (the carcass of a pig or fowl) to prepare it for cooking. ▶n. a superficial burn.

Singh /sing/ ▶n. a title or surname adopted by certain warrior castes of northern India.

Sin·gha·lese /,singgə'lēz; -'lēs/ ▶n. & adj. variant spelling of **Sinhalese**.

sin·gle /'singgəl/ ▶adj. **1** only one; not one of several: *a single red rose.* ■ regarded separately or as distinct from each other or others in a group: *she wrote down every single word.* ■ even one (used for emphasis): *they didn't receive a single reply.* ■ designed or suitable for one person: *a single bed.* **2** unmarried or not involved in a stable sexual relationship: *a single mother.* **3** consisting of one part: *the studio was a single large room.* ■ (of a flower) having only one whorl of petals. ■ denoting an alcoholic drink that consists of one measure of liquor: *a single whiskey.* ▶n. **1** an individual person or thing rather than part of a pair or a group. ■ a short record with one song on each side. ■ (**singles**) people who are unmarried or not involved in a stable sexual relationship: [as adj.] *a singles bar.* ■ a bedroom, esp. in a hotel, that is suitable for one person. ■ a single measure of liquor. ■ inf. a one-dollar bill. **2** Baseball a hit that allows the batter to reach first base safely. **3** (**singles**) (esp. in tennis and badminton) a game or competition for individual players, not pairs or teams. ▶v. [tr.] **1** (**single someone/something out**) choose someone or something from a group for special treatment: *one newspaper was **singled out for criticism.*** **2** [intr.] Baseball hit a single: *Aaron singled to center.* ■ (**single in**) [tr.] cause (a run) to be scored by hitting a single: *they each singled in a run.* ■ [tr.] advance (a runner) by hitting a single. —**sin·gle·ness** n. —**sin·gly** /-glē/ adv.

sin·gle-breast·ed ▶adj. (of a jacket or coat) showing only one row of buttons at the front when fastened.

sin·gle file ▶n. a line of people or things arranged one behind another: *we trooped along in single file* | [as adj.] *a single-file column.* ▶adv. one behind another: *we walked single file.*

sin·gle-hand·ed (also **sin·gle-hand·ed** /'singgəl'handid/) ▶adv. & adj. **1** done without help from anyone else. **2** done or designed to be used with one hand. —**sin·gle-hand·ed·ly** (or **sin·gle·hand·ed·ly**) adv. —**sin·gle-hand·ed·ness** (or **sin·gle·hand·ed·ness**) n.

sin·gle-lens re·flex ▶adj. denoting a reflex camera in which the lens that forms the image on the film also provides the image in the viewfinder.

sin·gle-mind·ed (also **sin·gle-mind·ed** /'singgəl'mīndid/) ▶adj. having or concentrating on only one aim or purpose: *the single-minded pursuit of profit.* —**sin·gle-mind·ed·ly** (or **sin·gle·mind·ed·ly**) adv. —**sin·gle-mind·ed·ness** (or **sin·gle·mind·ed·ness**) n.

sin·gle par·ent ▶n. a person bringing up a child or children without a partner.

sin·gle·ton /'singgəltən/ ▶n. a single person or thing of the kind under consideration: *splitting the clumps of plants into singletons.* ■ [often as adj.] a child or animal born singly, rather than one of a multiple birth: *singleton boys.* ■ (in card games, esp. bridge) a card that is the only one of its suit in a hand. ■ Math. & Logic a set that contains exactly one element.

sin·gle·tree /'singgəl,trē/ ▶n. a crossbar pivoted in the middle, to which the traces are attached in a horse-drawn wagon or plow.

sing·song /'sing,sông/ (also **sing-song**) ▶adj. (of a person's voice) having a repeated rising and falling rhythm: *the singsong voices of children reciting tables.*

sin·gu·lar /'singgyələr/ ▶adj. **1** exceptionally good or great; remarkable: *the singular beauty of the desert.* ■ strange or eccentric in some respect: *no explanation accompanied this rather singular statement.* ■ Math. possessing unique properties. ■ Math. (of a square matrix) having a zero determinant. ■ Math. denoting a point that is a singularity. **2** Gram. (of a word or form) denoting or referring to just one person or thing. **3** single; unique: *she always thought of herself as singular, as his only daughter.* ▶n. (usu. **the singular**) Gram. the singular form of a word: *the first person singular.* —**sin·gu·lar·ly** adv.

sin·gu·lar·i·ty /,singgyə'laritē/ ▶n. (pl. **-ties**) **1** the state, fact, quality, or condition of being singular: *he believed in the singularity of all cultures.* ■ a peculiarity or odd trait. **2** Physics & Math. a point at which a function takes an infinite value, esp. in space-time when matter is infinitely dense, as at the center of a black hole.

Sin·ha·lese /,sinhə'lēz; -'lēs/ (also **Sin·gha·lese** /,singə-/, **Sin·ha·la** /sin'hälə/) ▶n. (pl. same) **1** a member of a people originally from northern India, now forming the majority of the population of Sri Lanka. **2** the Indic language of this people. ▶adj. of or relating to this people or language.

sin·is·ter /'sinistər/ ▶adj. **1** giving the impression that something harmful or evil is happening or will happen: *there was something sinister about that murmuring voice.* ■ wicked or criminal. **2** archaic of, on, or toward the left-hand side. The opposite of **dexter**[1]. —**sin·is·ter·ly** adv. —**sin·is·ter·ness** n.

sink[1] /singk/ ▶v. (past **sank** /sangk/ or **sunk** /səngk/; past part. **sunk** /səngk/) **1** [intr.] go down below the surface of something, esp. of a liquid; become submerged: *he saw the coffin sink below the surface of the waves.* ■ (of a ship) go to the bottom of the sea or some other body of water because of damage or a collision. ■ [tr.] cause (a ship) to go to the bottom of the sea or other body of water: *a freak wave sank their boat near the shore.* ■ [tr.] fig. cause to fail: *she apparently wishes to sink the company.* ■ [tr.] fig. conceal, keep in the background, or ignore: *they agreed to sink their differences.* **2** [intr.] descend; drop: *Sam felt the ground sinking beneath his feet.* ■ (of a person) lower oneself or drop gently: *she sank back onto her pillow.* ■ gradually penetrate the surface of something: *her feet sank into the thick pile of the carpet.* ■ (**sink in**) fig. (of words or facts) be fully understood or realized: *Peter read the letter twice before its meaning sank in.* ■ [tr.] (**sink something into**) cause something sharp to penetrate (a surface): *the dog sank its teeth into her arm.* **3** [intr.] gradually decrease or decline in value, amount, quality, or intensity: *their output sank to a third of the prewar figure* | *the reputation of the mayor sank to a very low level.* ■ lapse or fall into a particular state or condition, typically one that is unwelcome or unpleasant: *he sank into a coma after suffering a brain hemorrhage.* ■ be overwhelmed by a darker mood; become depressed: *her heart sank as she thought of Craig.* ■ approach death: *the doctor concluded*

S

that Sanders was sinking fast. **4** [*tr.*] insert beneath a surface by digging or hollowing out: *rails attached with screws sunk below the surface of the wood.* ■ excavate (a well) or bore (a shaft) more or less vertically downward. ■ pocket (a ball) in billiards. ■ *Golf* hit the ball into the hole with (a putt or other shot). ■ [*tr.*] insert into something: *Kelly stood watching, her hands sunk deep into her pockets.* ■ [*intr.*] (of eyes) appear unusually deep or receded: *her eyes had sunk deep into their sockets.* **5** [*tr.*] (**sink something into**) put money or energy into (something); invest something in: *many investors sank their life savings into the company.* —**sink·a·ble** *adj.* —**sink·age** /ˈsiNGkij/ *n.*

sink² ▶ *n.* a fixed basin with a water supply and a drain. ■ short for SINK-HOLE. ■ a pool or marsh in which a river's water disappears by evaporation or percolation. ■ *technical* a body or process that acts to absorb or remove energy or a particular component from a system. The opposite of SOURCE. ■ *fig.* a place of vice or corruption: *a sink of unnatural vice, pride, and luxury.*

sink·er /ˈsiNGkər/ ▶ *n.* **1** a weight used to sink a fishing line or sounding line. **2** (also **sinker ball**) *Baseball* a pitch that drops markedly as it nears home plate. **3** a doughnut.

sink·hole /ˈsiNGk,hōl/ ▶ *n.* a cavity in the ground, esp. in limestone bedrock, caused by water erosion and providing a route for surface water to disappear underground.

sink·ing fund ▶ *n.* a fund formed by periodically setting aside money for the gradual repayment of a debt or replacement of a wasting asset.

sin·ner /ˈsinər/ ▶ *n.* a person who transgresses against divine law by committing an immoral act or acts.

Sinn Fein /ˈsHin ˈfān/ ▶ a political movement and party seeking a united republican Ireland. —**Sinn Fein·er** *n.*

si·no·a·tri·al node /ˌsīnōˈātrēəl/ ▶ *n. Anat.* a small body of specialized muscle tissue in the wall of the right atrium of the heart that acts as a pacemaker by producing a contractile signal at regular intervals.

Si·nol·o·gy /sīˈnäləjē/ ▶ *n.* the study of Chinese language, history, customs, and politics. —**Si·no·log·i·cal** /ˌsīnlˈäjikəl; ˌsin-/ *adj.* —**Si·nol·o·gist** /-jist/ *n.*

sin·u·ate /ˈsinyoˌāt, -it/ ▶ *adj. Bot.* & *Zool.* having a wavy or sinuous margin; with alternate rounded notches and lobes.

sin·u·os·i·ty /ˌsinyooˈäsitē/ ▶ *n.* (*pl.* **-ties**) the ability to curve or bend easily and flexibly. ■ a bend, esp. in a stream or road.

sin·u·ous /ˈsinyooəs/ ▶ *adj.* having many curves and turns: *the river follows a sinuous trail through the forest.* ■ lithe and supple: *the sinuous grace of a cat.* —**sin·u·ous·ly** *adv.* —**sin·u·ous·ness** *n.*

si·nus /ˈsīnəs/ ▶ *n.* **1** (often **sinuses**) *Anat.* & *Zool.* a cavity within a bone or other tissue, esp. one in the bones of the face or skull connecting with the nasal cavities. ■ an irregular venous or lymphatic cavity, reservoir, or dilated vessel. **2** [as *adj.*] *Physiol.* relating to or denoting the sinoatrial node of the heart or its function as a pacemaker: *sinus rhythm.*

si·nus·i·tis /ˌsīnəˈsītis/ ▶ *n. Med.* inflammation of a nasal sinus.

si·nus·oid /ˈsīnəˌsoid/ ▶ *n.* a curve having the form of a sine wave. —**si·nus·oi·dal** /ˌsīnəˈsoidl/ *adj.* —**si·nus·oi·dal·ly** /ˌsīnəˈsoidəlē/ *adv.*

Sion /ˈsīən/ ▶ *n.* variant spelling of ZION.

-sion ▶ *suffix* forming nouns such as *mansion, persuasion.*

Sioux /soo/ ▶ *n.* (*pl.* same) another term for the Dakota people or their language. See DAKOTA.

▶ *adj.* of or relating to this people or their language.

sip /sip/ ▶ *v.* (**sipped, sip·ping**) [*tr.*] drink (something) by taking small mouthfuls: *I sat sipping coffee* | [*intr.*] *she sipped at her tea.*

▶ *n.* a small mouthful of liquid: *she took a sip of the red wine.* —**sip·per** *n.*

si·phon /ˈsīfən/ (also **sy·phon**) ▶ *n.* a pipe or tube used to convey liquid upward from a container and then down to a lower level by gravity, the liquid being made to enter the pipe by atmospheric pressure. ■ *Zool.* a tubular organ in an aquatic animal, esp. a mollusk, through which water is drawn in or expelled.

▶ *v.* [*tr.*] draw off or convey (liquid) by means of a siphon. ■ *fig.* draw off or transfer over a period of time, esp. illegally or unfairly: *he's been siphoning money off the firm.* ▷late Middle English: from French, or via Latin from Greek *siphōn* 'pipe.' The verb dates from the mid 19th cent. —**si·phon·age** /-nij/ *n.* —**si·phon·al** /-nəl/ *adj.* (*Zool.*) —**si·phon·ic** /sīˈfänik/ *adj.*

Sir. ▶ *abbr.* (in biblical references) Sirach (Apocrypha).

sir /sər/ (also **Sir**) ▶ *n.* used as a polite or respectful way of addressing a man, esp. one in a position of authority: *excuse me, sir.* ■ used to address a man at the beginning of a formal or business letter: *Dear Sir.* ■ (in Britain) used as a title before the given name of a knight or baronet. ■ another expression for SIREE.

sire /sīr/ ▶ *n.* **1** the male parent of an animal, esp. a stallion or bull kept for breeding. **2** *archaic* a respectful form of address for someone of high social status, esp. a king. ■ a father or other male forebear.

▶ *v.* [*tr.*] be the male parent of (an animal).

sir·ee /səˈrē/ (also **sir·ree**) ▶ *interj. inf.* used for emphasis, esp. after *yes* and *no*: *he's not the type to treat young employees like mud, no siree.*

si·ren /ˈsīrən/ ▶ *n.* **1** a device that makes a loud prolonged signal or warning sound. **2** *Greek Mythol.* each of a number of women or winged creatures whose singing lured unwary sailors onto rocks. ■ a woman considered to be alluring or fascinating but also dangerous in some way. **3** an eellike American amphibian (genera *Siren* and *Pseudobranchus*, family Sirenidae) with tiny forelimbs, no hind limbs, small eyes, and external gills, typically living in muddy pools.

sir·loin /ˈsərloin/ ▶ *n.* the choicer part of a loin of beef: [as *adj.*] *fresh sirloin steaks.*

si·roc·co /səˈräkō/ (also **sci·roc·co** /sHəˈräkō; sə-/) ▶ *n.* (*pl.* **-cos**) a hot wind blowing from North Africa across the Mediterranean to southern Europe.

sir·up ▶ *n.* variant spelling of SYRUP.

sis /sis/ ▶ *n. inf.* a person's sister (often used as a form of address): *where are you going, sis?*

si·sal /ˈsisəl; ˈsī-/ ▶ *n.* a Mexican agave (*Agave sisalana*) with large fleshy leaves, cultivated for fiber production. ■ the fiber made from this plant, used esp. for ropes or matting.

sis·sy /ˈsisē/ *inf.* ▶ *n.* (*pl.* **-sies**) a person regarded as effeminate or cowardly. ■ *chiefly offens.* an effeminate homosexual.

▶ *adj.* (**-si·er, -si·est**) feeble and cowardly. —**sis·si·fied** /ˈsisə,fīd/ *adj.* —**sis·si·ness** *n.* —**sis·sy·ish** *adj.*

sis·ter /ˈsistər/ ▶ *n.* a woman or girl in relation to other daughters and sons of her parents. ■ a half-sister, stepsister, or foster sister. ■ a sister-in-law. ■ a close female friend or associate, esp. a female fellow member of a labor union or other organization. ■ (often **Sister**) a member of a religious order or congregation of women. ■ a fellow woman seen in relation to feminist issues. ■ *inf.* a black woman (chiefly used as a term of address by other black people). ■ [usu. as *adj.*] a thing, esp. an organization, that bears a relationship to another of common origin or allegiance or mutual association: *Eastern's sister airline, Continental* | *a sister ship.* ▷Old English, of Germanic origin; related to Dutch *zuster* and German *Schwester*, from an Indo-European root shared by Latin *soror.* —**sis·ter·li·ness** *n.* —**sis·ter·ly** *adj.*

sis·ter·hood /ˈsistər,hŏŏd/ ▶ *n.* **1** the relationship between sisters. ■ the feeling of kinship with and closeness to a group of women or all women. **2** (often **Sisterhood**) an association, society, or community of women linked by a common interest, religion, or trade.

sis·ter-in-law ▶ *n.* (*pl.* **sis·ters-in-law**) the sister of one's wife or husband. ■ the wife of one's brother or brother-in-law.

Sis·tine /ˈsistēn/ ▶ *adj.* of or relating to any of the popes called Sixtus, esp. Sixtus IV: *the Sistine Chapel.*

Sis·y·phe·an /ˌsisəˈfēən/ ▶ *adj.* (of a task) such that it can never be completed.

sit /sit/ ▶ *v.* (**sit·ting**; *past* **sat** /sat/) **1** [*intr.*] adopt or be in a position in which one's weight is supported by one's buttocks rather than one's feet and one's back is upright: *you'd better sit down.* ■ [*tr.*] cause to adopt or be in such a position. ■ (of an animal) rest with the hind legs bent and the body close to the ground: *it is important for a dog to sit when instructed.* ■ (of a bird) rest on a branch; perch. ■ (of a bird) remain on its nest to incubate its egg: [as *adj.*] (**sitting**) *a sitting hen.* ■ [*tr.*] ride or keep one's seat on (a horse). ■ [*tr.*] not use (a player) in a game: *the manager must decide who to sit in the World Series.* ■ [*tr.*] (of a table, room, or building) be large enough for (a specified number of seated people): *the cathedral sat about 3,000 people.* ■ (**sit for**) pose, typically in a seated position, for (an artist or photographer): *Walter Deverell asked her to sit for him.* ■ [*intr.*] be or remain in a particular position or state: *the fridge was sitting in a pool of water.* ■ (of an item of clothing) fit a person well or badly as specified: *the blue uniform sat well on his big frame.* ■ (**sit with**) be harmonious with: *his shyness doesn't sit easily with Hollywood tradition.* **2** [*intr.*] (of a legislature, committee, court of law, etc.) be engaged in its business: *Congress continued sitting until March 16.* ■ serve as a member of a council, jury, or other official body: *they were determined that women jurists should sit on the tribunal.* **3** [*intr.*] [usu. in *comb.*] stay in someone's house while they are away and look after their house or pet: *Kelly had been cat-sitting for me.* ■ babysit.

▶ *phrasal v.* □ **sit back** relax: *sit back and enjoy the music.* ■ take no action; choose not to become involved: *I can't just sit back and let Betsy do all the work.* □ **sit by** take no action in order to prevent something undesirable from occurring: *I'm not going to sit by and let an innocent man go to*

jail. □ **sit in 1** (of a group of people) occupy a place as a form of protest. **2** attend a meeting or discussion without taking an active part in it: *I sat in on a training session for therapists.* □ **sit in for** temporarily carry out the duties of (another person). □ **sit on** *inf.* **1** fail to deal with: *she sat on the article until a deadline galvanized her into putting words to paper.* **2** subdue (someone), typically by saying something intended to discomfit or embarrass them. ■ suppress (something): *tell them to sit on this story until we hear from Quinlan.* □ **sit something out** not take part in a particular event or activity: *he had to sit out the first playoff game.* ■ wait without moving or taking action until a particular unwelcome situation or process is over: *most of the workers seem to be sitting the crisis out, waiting to see what will happen.* □ **sit up 1** move from a lying or slouching to a sitting position: *Amy sat up and rubbed her eyes.* **2** refrain from going to bed until a later time than usual: *we sat up late to watch a horror film.*
▸ *n.* a period of sitting: *a sit in the shade.*
▸ □ **sit on one's hands** take no action. □ **sit tight** *inf.* remain firmly in one's place. ■ refrain from taking action or changing one's mind: *we're advising our clients to sit tight and neither to buy nor to sell.*

si·tar /sɪˈtär/ ▸ *n.* a large, long-necked Indian lute with movable frets, played with a wire pick. —**si·tar·ist** /-ist/ *n.*

sit·com /ˈsɪtˌkäm/ ▸ *n. inf.* a situation comedy.

sit-down ▸ *adj.* (of a meal) eaten sitting at a table. ■ (of a protest) in which demonstrators occupy their workplace or sit down on the ground in a public place, refusing to leave until their demands are met.
▸ *n.* a period of sitting down; a short rest. ■ a sit-down protest.

site /sɪt/ ▸ *n.* an area of ground on which a town, building, or monument is constructed: *the proposed site of a hydroelectric dam.* ■ a place where a particular event or activity is occurring or has occurred: *the site of the Battle of Antietam.* ■ short for **WEB SITE**.
▸ *v.* [*tr.*] (usu. **be sited**) fix or build (something) in a particular place: *the rectory is sited behind the church.*

sit-in ▸ *n.* a form of protest in which demonstrators occupy a place, refusing to leave until their demands are met.

sit·ter /ˈsɪtər/ ▸ *n.* [usu. in comb.] a person who looks after children, pets, or a house while the parents or owners are away: *a house-sitter.* ■ a person who provides care and companionship for people who are ill.

sit·ting /ˈsɪtɪNG/ ▸ *n.* a continuous period of being seated, esp. when engaged in a particular activity: *the whole roast was eaten at one sitting.* ■ a period of time spent as a model for an artist or photographer. ■ a scheduled period of time when a group of people are served a meal, esp. in a restaurant: *there will be two sittings for Christmas lunch.* ■ a period of time during which a committee or legislature is engaged in its normal business.
▸ *adj.* **1** denoting a person who has sat down or the position of such a person: *a sitting position.* ■ (of an animal or bird) not running or flying. **2** (of an elected representative) current; present: *the resignation of the sitting congressman.*

sit·ting duck (also **sitting target**) ▸ *n. inf.* a person or thing with no protection against an attack or other source of danger.

sit·ting room ▸ *n.* a room in a house or hotel in which people can sit down and relax.

sit·u·ate ▸ *v.* /ˈsɪCHŌ̅ōˌāt/ [*tr.*] (usu. **be situated**) fix or build (something) in a certain place or position: *the pilot light is usually situated at the front of the boiler.* ■ put in context; describe the circumstances surrounding (something): *it is necessary to situate these ideas in the wider context of the economy.* ■ (**be situated**) be in a specified financial or marital position: *Amy is now comfortably situated.*

sit·u·a·tion /ˌsɪCHŌ̅ōˈāSHən/ ▸ *n.* **1** a set of circumstances in which one finds oneself; a state of affairs: *the situation between her and Jake had come to a head | the political situation in Russia.* **2** the location and surroundings of a place: *the situation of the town is pleasant.* **3** *formal* a position of employment; a job. —**sit·u·a·tion·al** /-SHənl/ *adj.* —**sit·u·a·tion·al·ly** *adv.*

sit·u·a·tion com·e·dy ▸ *n.* a television or radio series in which the same set of characters are involved in various amusing situations.

sit-up ▸ *n.* a physical exercise designed to strengthen the abdominal muscles, in which a person sits up from a supine position without using the arms for leverage.

sitar

Si·va /ˈSHēvə; ˈsē-/ ▸variant spelling of **SHIVA**.

six /sɪks/ ▸ *cardinal number* equivalent to the product of two and three; one more than five, or four less than ten; 6: *she's lived here six months | six of the people arrested have been charged | a six-week tour.* (Roman numeral: **vi**, **VI**.) ■ a group or unit of six people or things. ■ six years old: *a child of six.* ■ six o'clock: *it's half past six.* ■ a size of garment or other merchandise denoted by six. ■ a playing card or domino with six pips. —**six·fold** *adj.*

six-gun ▸ *n.* another term for **SIX-SHOOTER**.

Six Na·tions ▸ *pl. n.* (**the Six Nations**) the Five Nations of the original Iroquois confederacy after the Tuscarora joined them in 1722.

six-pack ▸ *n.* **1** a pack of six cans of beer or soft drinks typically held together with a plastic fastener. **2** *inf.* a set of well-developed abdominal muscles: [as adj.] *six-pack abs.*

six-shoot·er ▸ *n.* a revolver with six chambers.

six·teen /sɪkˈstēn; ˈsɪkˌstēn/ ▸ *cardinal number* equivalent to the product of four and four; one more than fifteen, or six more than ten; 16: *sixteen miles east of Detroit.* (Roman numeral: **xvi**, **XVI**.) ■ a size of garment or other merchandise denoted by sixteen. ■ sixteen years old: *I'm sixteen.* —**six·teenth** /sɪkˈstēnTH; ˈsɪkˌstēnTH/ *ordinal number* .

six·teenth note /ˌsɪksˈtēnTH/ ▸ *n. Mus.* a note having the time value of a sixteenth of a whole note or half an eighth note, represented by a large dot with a two-hooked stem.

sixth /sɪksTH/ ▸ *ordinal number* constituting number six in a sequence; 6th: *her sixth novel | the sixth of the month.* ■ (**a sixth/one sixth**) each of six equal parts into which something is or may be divided: *a sixth of the total population.* ■ the sixth finisher or position in a race or other competition: *he could only finish sixth.* ■ the sixth grade of a school. ■ sixthly (used to introduce a sixth point or reason): *sixth, given all the facts there is no logical reason why we can't make a decision.* ■ *Mus.* an interval spanning six consecutive notes in a diatonic major or minor scale, e.g., C to A (**major sixth**) or A to F (**minor sixth**). ■ *Mus.* the note that is higher by this interval than the tonic of a scale or root of a chord. —**sixth·ly** *adv.*

sixth sense ▸ *n.* a supposed intuitive faculty giving awareness not explicable in terms of normal perception: *some sixth sense told him he was not alone.*

six·ty /ˈsɪkstē/ ▸ *cardinal number* (pl. **-ties**) the number equivalent to the product of six and ten; ten more than fifty; 60: *a crew of sixty | sixty bedrooms.* (Roman numeral: **lx**, **LX**.) ■ (**sixties**) the numbers from sixty to sixty-nine, esp. the years of a century or of a person's life: *Morris was in his early sixties | the flower children of the sixties.* ■ sixty miles an hour: *they were doing sixty.* ■ sixty years old: *he retired at sixty.* —**six·ti·eth** /-iTH/ *ordinal number* —**six·ty·fold** /-ˈfōld/ *adj. & adv.*

six·ty-nine ▸ *n. inf.* sexual activity between two people involving mutual oral stimulation of their genitals.

siz·a·ble /ˈsīzəbəl/ (also **size·a·ble**) ▸ *adj.* fairly large: *a sizable proportion of the population | a sizable apartment.* —**siz·a·bly** /-blē/ *adv.*

size[1] /sīz/ ▸ *n.* **1** the relative extent of something; a thing's overall dimensions or magnitude; how big something is: *the schools varied in size.* ■ extensive dimensions or magnitude: *she seemed slightly awed by the size of the building.* **2** each of the classes, typically numbered, into which garments or other articles are divided according to how large they are: *I can never find anything in my size.* ■ a person or garment corresponding to such a numbered class: *she's a size 10.*
▸ *v.* [*tr.*] alter or sort in terms of size or according to size: *some drills are sized in millimeters.* ■ (**size someone/something up**) *inf.* form an estimate or rough judgment of someone or something: *the two men sized each other up.*
▸ *adj.* [in comb.] having a specified size; sized: *marble-size chunks of hail.* —**siz·er** *n.*

size[2] ▸ *n.* a gelatinous solution used in gilding paper, stiffening textiles, and preparing plastered walls for decoration.
▸ *v.* [*tr.*] treat with size to glaze or stiffen.

size·a·ble ▸ *adj.* variant spelling of **SIZABLE**.

siz·zle /ˈsɪzəl/ ▸ *v.* [*intr.*] (of food) make a hissing sound when frying or cooking: *the bacon began to sizzle in the pan.* ■ [often as adj.] (**sizzling**) *inf.* be very hot: *the sizzling summer temperatures.* ■ [often as adj.] (**sizzling**) *inf.* be very exciting or passionate, esp. sexually: *that was the start of a sizzling affair.*
▸ *n.* a hissing sound, as of food frying or cooking: *the sizzle of hot dogs.* ■ *inf.* a state or quality of great excitement or passion: *a dance routine with lots of sizzle.* —**siz·zler** /ˈsɪz(ə)lər/ *n.*

Pronunciation Key ə *ago,* up; ər *over,* fur; a *hat;* ā *ate;* ä *car;* CH *chin;* e *let;* ē *see;* e(ə)r *air;* i *fit;* ī *by;* i(ə)r *ear;* NG *sing;* ō *go;* ô *law, for;* oi *toy;* ŏŏ *good;* ōō *goo;* ou *out;* SH *she;* TH *thin;* ̲TH *then;* (h)w *why;* ZH *vision*

ska /skä/ ▸ *n.* a style of fast popular music having a strong offbeat and originating in Jamaica in the 1960s, a forerunner of reggae.

skald /skôld; skäld/ ▸ *n. hist.* (in ancient Scandinavia) a composer and reciter of poems honoring heroes and their deeds. —**skald·ic** /-ik/ *adj.*

skate¹ /skāt/ ▸ *n.* an ice skate or roller skate. ■ a device, typically with wheels on the underside, used to move a heavy or unwieldy object. ▸ *v.* [*intr.*] move on ice skates or roller skates in a gliding fashion: *the boys were skating on the ice.* ■ ride on a skateboard. ■ (**skate through**) *fig.* make quick and easy progress through: *he admits he had expected to skate through the system.* —**skat·er** *n.*

skate² ▸ *n.* (*pl.* same or **skates**) a typically large marine fish of the ray family (Rajidae) with a cartilaginous skeleton and a flattened diamond-shaped body, in particular the commercially valuable *Raja batis.* ■ the flesh of a skate used as food.

skate·board /ˈskāt,bôrd/ ▸ *n.* a short narrow board with two small wheels fixed to the bottom of either end, on which (as a recreation or sport) a person can ride in a standing or crouching position, propelling themselves by occasionally pushing one foot against the ground. ▸ *v.* [*intr.*] [often as *n.*] (**skateboarding**) ride on a skateboard. —**skate·board·er** *n.*

skat·ing rink ▸ *n.* an expanse of ice artificially made for skating, or a floor used for roller skating.

ske·dad·dle /skiˈdadl/ ▸ *v.* [*intr.*] *inf.* depart quickly or hurriedly; run away: *when he saw us, he skedaddled.*

skeet /skēt/ (also **skeet shooting**) ▸ *n.* a shooting sport in which a clay target is thrown from a trap to simulate the flight of a bird. —**skeet shoot·er** *n.*

skee·ter /ˈskētər/ ▸ *n. inf.* a mosquito.

skeg /skeg/ (also **skag** skag) ▸ *n.* a tapering or projecting stern section of a vessel's keel, which protects the propeller and supports the rudder.

skein /skān/ ▸ *n.* a length of thread or yarn, loosely coiled and knotted. ■ a tangled or complicated arrangement, state, or situation: *the skeins of her long hair* | *fig.* *a skein of lies.* ■ a flock of wild geese or swans in flight, typically in a V-shaped formation.

skel·e·ton /ˈskelitn/ ▸ *n.* an internal or external framework of bone, cartilage, or other rigid material supporting or containing the body of an animal or plant. ■ used in exaggerated reference to a very thin or emaciated person or animal: *she was no more than a skeleton at the end.* ■ the remaining part of something after its life or usefulness is gone: *the chapel was stripped to a skeleton of its former self.* ■ the supporting framework, basic structure, or essential part of something: *the concrete skeleton of an unfinished building.* ■ [as *adj.*] denoting the essential or minimum number of people, things, or parts necessary for something: *there was only a skeleton staff on duty.* —**skel·e·tal** /-itl/ *adj.* —**skel·e·ton·ize** /-,īz/ *v.*

▸ □ **skeleton in the closet** a discreditable or embarrassing fact that someone wishes to keep secret.

skel·e·ton key ▸ *n.* a key designed to fit many locks by having the interior of the bit hollowed.

skep·tic /ˈskeptik/ (*Brit.* **scep·tic**) ▸ *n.* **1** a person inclined to question or doubt all accepted opinions. ■ a person who doubts the truth of Christianity and other religions; an atheist or agnostic. **2** *Philos.* an ancient or modern philosopher who denies the possibility of knowledge, or even rational belief, in some sphere. ▸ *adj.* another term for SKEPTICAL. —**skep·ti·cism** /ˈskeptə,sizəm/ (*Brit.* **scep·ti·cism**) *n.*

skep·ti·cal /ˈskeptikəl/ (*Brit.* **scep·ti·cal**) ▸ *adj.* **1** not easily convinced; having doubts or reservations: *the public were deeply skeptical about some of the proposals.* **2** *Philos.* relating to the theory that certain knowledge is impossible. —**skep·ti·cal·ly** /-ik(ə)lē/ (*Brit.* **scep·ti·cal·ly**) *adv.*

sketch /skeCH/ ▸ *n.* **1** a rough or unfinished drawing or painting, often made to assist in making a more finished picture: *a charcoal sketch.* ■ a brief written or spoken account or description of someone or something, giving only basic details: *a biographical sketch of Ernest Hemingway.* ■ a rough or unfinished version of any creative work. **2** a short humorous play or performance, consisting typically of one scene in a comedy program. **3** *inf.* a comical or amusing person or thing. ▸ *v.* [*tr.*] make a rough drawing of: *Modigliani began to sketch her* | [*intr.*] *Jean sketched whenever she had the time.* ■ give a brief account or general outline of: *they sketched out the prosecution case.* —**sketch·er** *n.*

sketch·book /ˈskeCH,bʊk/ ▸ *n.* (also **sketch·pad** /-,pad/) a pad or book of drawing paper for sketching on. ■ a book of drawings or literary sketches.

sketch·y /ˈskeCHē/ ▸ *adj.* (**sketch·i·er**, **sketch·i·est**) not thorough or

detailed: *the information they had was sketchy.* —**sketch·i·ly** /ˈskeCHəlē/ *adv.* —**sketch·i·ness** *n.*

skew /skyoo/ ▸ *adj.* **1** neither parallel nor at right angles to a specified or implied line; askew; crooked: *his hat was slightly skew.* ■ *Statistics* (of a statistical distribution) not symmetrical. **2** *Math.* (of a pair of lines) neither parallel nor intersecting. ■ (of a curve) not lying in a plane. ▸ *n.* an oblique angle; a slant. ■ a bias toward one particular group or subject: *the paper had a working-class skew.* ■ *Statistics* the state of not being symmetrical. ▸ *v.* [*intr.*] suddenly change direction or position: *the car had skewed across the track.* ■ twist or turn or cause to do this: *he skewed around in his saddle* | [*tr.*] *his leg was skewed in and pushed against the other one.* ■ [*tr.*] make biased or distorted in a way that is regarded as inaccurate, unfair, or misleading: *the curriculum is skewed toward the practical subjects.* ■ [*tr.*] *Statistics* cause (a distribution) to be asymmetrical. —**skew·ness** *n.*

skew·er /ˈskyooər/ ▸ *n.* a long piece of wood or metal used for holding pieces of food, typically meat, together during cooking. ▸ *v.* [*tr.*] fasten together or pierce with a pin or skewer: [as *adj.*] (**skewered**) *skewered meat and fish.* ■ *inf.* criticize (someone) sharply.

ski /skē/ ▸ *n.* (*pl.* **skis**) each of a pair of long narrow pieces of hard flexible material, typically pointed and turned up at the front, fastened under the feet for gliding over snow. ■ a similar device attached beneath a vehicle or aircraft. ■ [as *adj.*] of, relating to, or used for skiing: *a ski instructor* | *ski boots.* ■ another term for WATERSKI. ▸ *v.* (**skis**, **skied** /skēd/, **ski·ing** /ˈskē-iNG/) [*intr.*] travel over snow on skis; take part in the sport or recreation of skiing: *they skied down the mountain.* ■ [*tr.*] ski on (a particular ski run or type of snow): *spring snow is not always easy to ski.* ▷mid 18th cent.: from Norwegian, from Old Norse *skíth* 'stick of wood, snowshoe.' —**ski·a·ble** *adj.*

skid /skid/ ▸ *v.* (**skid·ded**, **skid·ding**) [*intr.*] (of a vehicle) slide, typically sideways or obliquely, on slippery ground or as a result of stopping or turning too quickly: *the taxicab skidded to a halt.* ■ slip; slide: *Barbara's foot skidded, and she fell to the floor.* ■ [*tr.*] move a heavy object on skids: *they skidded the logs down the hill to the waterfront.* ■ *fig.* decline; deteriorate: *its shares have skidded 29% since March.* ▸ *n.* **1** an act of skidding or sliding: *the Volvo went into a skid.* **2** a runner attached to the underside of an aircraft for use when landing on snow or grass.

skid row /rō/ ▸ *n. inf.* a run-down part of a town frequented by vagrants, alcoholics, and drug addicts. ■ *fig.* a desperately unfortunate or difficult situation: *I don't want to end up on skid row.*

ski·er /ˈskēər/ ▸ *n.* a person who skis.

skiff /skif/ ▸ *n.* a shallow, flat-bottomed open boat with sharp bow and square stern.

ski lift ▸ *n.* a system used to transport skiers up a slope to the top of a run, typically consisting of moving seats attached to an overhead cable.

skill /skil/ ▸ *n.* the ability to do something well; expertise: *difficult work, taking great skill.* ■ a particular ability: *the basic skills of cooking.*

skilled /skild/ ▸ *adj.* having or showing the knowledge, ability, or training to perform a certain activity or task well: *a lab technician skilled in electronics* | *skilled draftsmen.* ■ based on such training or experience; showing expertise: *skilled legal advice.* ■ (of work) requiring special abilities or training: *a highly skilled job.*

skil·let /ˈskilit/ ▸ *n.* a frying pan.

skill·ful /ˈskilfəl/ ▸ *adj.* having or showing skill: *a skillful infielder* | *his skillful use of propaganda.* —**skill·ful·ly** *adv.* —**skill·ful·ness** *n.*

skim /skim/ ▸ *v.* (**skimmed**, **skim·ming**) **1** [*tr.*] remove (a substance) from the surface of a liquid: *as the scum rises, skim it off.* ■ remove a substance from the surface of (a liquid): *bring to the boil, then skim it to remove any foam.* ■ *inf.* steal or embezzle (money), esp. in small amounts over a period of time: *she was skimming money from the household kitty.* ■ [often as *n.*] (**skimming**) fraudulently copy (credit or debit card details) with a card swipe or other device. **2** go or move quickly and lightly over or on a surface or through the air: *he let his fingers skim across her shoulders.* ■ [*tr.*] read (something) quickly or cursorily so as to note only the important points: *he sat down and skimmed the report* | [*intr.*] *she skimmed through the newspaper.* ■ (**skim over**) deal with or treat (a subject) briefly or superficially. ▸ *n.* **1** a thin layer of a substance on the surface of a liquid: *a skim of ice.* **2** an act of reading something quickly or superficially: *a quick skim through the pamphlet.*

skim·mer /ˈskimər/ ▸ *n.* **1** a person or thing that skims, in particular: ■ a utensil or device for removing a substance from the surface of a liquid. ■ a device or craft designed to collect oil spilled on water. ■ a hydroplane, hydrofoil, hovercraft, or other vessel that has little or no displacement when traveling. **2** a long-winged seabird (genus *Rynchops*) related to the terns, feeding by flying low over the water surface with its knifelike extended lower mandible immersed. **3** a flat, broad-brimmed straw hat. **4** a broad-bodied dragonfly (Libellulidae and related families) commonly found at ponds and swamps.

skim milk (also **skimmed milk**) ▶ *n.* milk from which the cream has been removed.

skimp /skimp/ ▶ *v.* [*intr.*] expend or use less time, money, or material on something than is necessary in an attempt to economize: *don't skimp on insurance when you travel overseas.*

skimp·y /'skimpē/ ▶ *adj.* (**skimp·i·er**, **skimp·i·est**) (of clothes) short and revealing: *a skimpy dress.* ■ providing or consisting of less than is needed; meager: *my knowledge of music is extremely skimpy.* —**skimp·i·ly** /'skimpəlē/ *adv.* —**skimp·i·ness** *n.*

skin /skin/ ▶ *n.* **1** the thin layer of tissue forming the natural outer covering of the body of a person or animal: *I use lotion to keep my skin soft.* ■ the skin of a dead animal with or without the fur, used as material for clothing or other items: *is this real crocodile skin?* ■ a container made from the skin of an animal such as a goat, used for holding liquids. **2** an outer layer or covering, in particular: ■ the peel or outer layer of certain fruits or vegetables. ■ the thin outer covering of a sausage. ■ a thin layer forming on the surface of certain hot liquids, such as milk, as they cool. ■ the outermost layer of a structure such as a building or aircraft. ■ *Comput.* a customized graphic user interface for an application or operating system. **3** (usu. **skins**) *inf.* (esp. in jazz) a drum or drum head. **4** [as *adj.*] *inf.* relating to or denoting pornographic literature or films: *the skin trade.*
▶ *v.* (**skinned**, **skin·ning**) [*tr.*] remove the skin from (an animal or a fruit or vegetable). ■ (in hyperbolic use) punish severely: *Dad would skin me alive if I forgot it.* ■ scratch or scrape the skin off (a part of one's body): *he scrambled down from the tree with such haste that he skinned his knees.* ■ *inf.* take money from or swindle (someone). —**skin·less** *adj.*
▶ □ **by the skin of one's teeth** by a very narrow margin; barely: *I only got away by the skin of my teeth.* □ **get under someone's skin** *inf.* **1** annoy or irritate someone intensely: *it was the sheer effrontery of them that got under my skin.* **2** fill someone's mind in a compelling and persistent way. **3** reach or display a deep understanding of someone: *movies that get under the skin of our national character.* □ **give someone** (**some**) **skin** *inf.* shake or slap hands together as a gesture or friendship or solidarity. □ **it's no skin off my nose** (or **off my back**) *inf.* (usually spoken with emphasis on "my") used to indicate that one is not offended or adversely affected by something: *it's no skin off my nose if you don't want dessert.* □ **make someone's skin** (or **flesh**) **crawl** (or **creep**) cause someone to feel fear, horror, or disgust: *a person dying in a fire—doesn't it make your skin crawl?*

skin-deep ▶ *adj.* not deep or lasting; superficial: *their left-wing attitudes were only skin-deep.*

skin div·ing ▶ *n.* the action or sport of swimming under water without a diving suit, typically in deep water using an aqualung and flippers. —**skin-dive** *v.* —**skin div·er** *n.*

skin flick (also **skin-flick**) ▶ *n. inf.* a pornographic film.

skin·flint /'skin,flint/ ▶ *n. inf.* a person who spends as little money as possible; a miser.

skin graft ▶ *n.* a surgical operation in which a piece of healthy skin is transplanted to a new site on the body. ■ a piece of skin transferred in this way.

skin·head /'skin,hed/ ▶ *n.* a young person with close-cropped hair, often perceived as aggressive, violent, and racist, and having neo-Nazi tendencies.

skin·ny /'skinē/ ▶ *adj.* (**-ni·er**, **-ni·est**) *inf.* (of a person or part of their body) very thin: *his skinny arms.* ■ (of an article of clothing) tight-fitting: *a skinny black dress.*
▶ *n.* (**the skinny**) confidential information on a particular person or topic: *the inside skinny is that he didn't know the deal was in the works.* —**skin·ni·ness** *n.*

skin·ny-dip ▶ *v.* [*intr.*] *inf.* swim naked.
▶ *n.* a naked swim.

skin·tight /'skin'tīt/ (also **skin-tight**) ▶ *adj.* (of a garment) very close-fitting.

skip /skip/ ▶ *v.* (**skipped**, **skip·ping**) [*intr.*] move along lightly, stepping from one foot to the other with a hop or bounce: *she began to skip down the path.* ■ [*intr.*] jump over a rope that is held at both ends by oneself or two other people and turned repeatedly over the head and under the feet, as a game or for exercise. ■ [*tr.*] omit (part of a book that one is reading, or a stage in a sequence that one is following): *the video manual allows the viewer to skip sections he's not interested in.* ■ [*tr.*] fail to attend

or deal with as appropriate; miss: *I wanted to skip my English lesson.* ■ [*intr.*] move quickly and in an unmethodical way from one point or subject to another: *Marian skipped halfheartedly through the book.* ■ [*tr.*] *inf.* depart quickly and secretly from: *she skipped her home amid rumors of a romance.* ■ [*intr.*] run away; disappear: *I'm not giving them a chance to skip off again.* ■ (**skip it**) *inf.* abandon an undertaking, conversation, or activity: *after several wrong turns in our journey, we almost decided to skip it.* ■ [*tr.*] throw (a stone) so that it ricochets off the surface of water.
▶ *n.* a light, bouncing step; a skipping movement: *he moved with a strange, dancing skip.* ■ *Comput.* an act of passing over part of a sequence of data or instructions. ■ *inf.* a person who defaults or absconds.

ski pole ▶ *n.* either of two lightweight poles held by a skier to assist in balance or propulsion.

skip·per[1] /'skipər/ *inf.* ▶ *n.* the captain of a ship or boat. ■ the captain of an aircraft.
▶ *v.* [*tr.*] act as captain of.

skip·per[2] ▶ *n.* **1** a person or thing that skips. ■ used in names of small insects and crustaceans that skip or hop. **2** a small brownish moth-like butterfly (family Hesperiidae) with rapid darting flight.

skirl /skərl/ ▶ *n.* a shrill sound, esp. that of bagpipes.

skir·mish /'skərmiSH/ ▶ *n.* an episode of irregular or unpremeditated fighting, esp. between small or outlying parts of armies or fleets. ■ a short argument: *there was a skirmish over the budget.*
▶ *v.* [*intr.*] (often as *n.*) (**skirmishing**) engage in a skirmish: *reports of skirmishing along the border.* —**skir·mish·er** *n.*

skirt /skərt/ ▶ *n.* a woman's outer garment fastened around the waist and hanging down around the legs. ■ the part of a coat or dress that hangs below the waist. ■ *inf., chiefly offens.* a woman or women regarded as objects of sexual desire: *so, Al, off to chase some skirt?* ■ the curtain that hangs around the base of a hovercraft to contain the air cushion. ■ a surface that conceals or protects the wheels or underside of a vehicle or aircraft.
▶ *v.* [*tr.*] go around or past the edge of: *he did not go through the city but skirted it.* ■ be situated along or around the edge of: *the fields that skirted the highway were full of cattle.* ■ [*intr.*] (**skirt along/around**) go along or around (something) rather than directly through or across it: *the valley skirts along the northern slopes.* ■ attempt to ignore; avoid dealing with: *there was a subject she was always skirting.* —**skirt·ed** *adj.* [in *comb.*] *a full-skirted dress.*

ski run ▶ *n.* a track on a slope for skiing.

skit /skit/ ▶ *n.* a short comedy sketch or piece of humorous writing, esp. a parody: *a skit on daytime magazine programs.*

skit·ter /'skitər/ ▶ *v.* [*intr.*] **1** [*intr.*] move lightly and quickly or hurriedly: *the girls skittered up the stairs.* **2** [*tr.*] draw (bait) jerkily across the surface of the water as a technique in fishing.

skit·ter·y /'skitərē/ ▶ *adj.* restless; skittish: *a skittery horse.*

skit·tish /'skitiSH/ ▶ *adj.* lively and unpredictable; playful: *my skittish and immature mother.* ■ (esp. of a horse) nervous; inclined to shy. —**skit·tish·ly** *adv.* —**skit·tish·ness** *n.*

skit·tle /'skitl/ ▶ *n.* **1** (**skittles**) [treated as *sing.*] a game played with wooden pins, typically nine, set up at the end of an alley to be bowled down with a wooden ball or disk. **2** a pin used in the game of skittles.

skiv·vy /'skivē/ ▶ *n.* (*pl.* **-vies**) **1** (**skivvies**) *trademark* underwear, esp. a set consisting of undershirt and underpants, or just the underpants. **2** a lightweight high-necked, long-sleeved garment. ■ an undershirt or T-shirt.

skoal /skōl/ ▶ *interj.* used to express friendly feelings toward one's companions before drinking.

skul·dug·ger·y /skəl'dəgərē/ (also **skull·dug·ger·y**) ▶ *n.* underhanded or unscrupulous behavior; trickery: *a firm that investigates commercial skulduggery.*

skulk /skəlk/ ▶ *v.* [*intr.*] keep out of sight, typically with a sinister or cowardly motive: *don't skulk outside the door like a spy!* ■ shirk duty.
▶ *n.* a group of foxes. —**skulk·er** *n.*

skull /skəl/ ▶ *n.* a framework of bone or cartilage enclosing the brain of a vertebrate; the skeleton of a person's or animal's head. ■ *inf.* a person's head or brain: *a skull crammed with too many thoughts.* —**skulled** *adj.* [in *comb.*] *long-skulled.*
▶ □ **out of one's skull** *inf.* **1** out of one's mind; crazy. **2** very drunk. □ **skull and crossbones** a representation of a skull with two thigh bones crossed below it as an emblem of piracy or death.

skull·cap /'skəl,kap/ ▶ *n.* **1** a small close-fitting cap without a bill. **2** a widely distributed plant (genus *Scutellaria*) of the mint family, whose tubular flowers have a helmet-shaped cup at the base.

skunk /skəNGk/ ▶ *n.* a cat-sized American mammal (*Mephitis* and other genera) of the weasel family, with distinctive black-and-white-striped fur. When threatened, it squirts a fine spray of foul-smelling irritant liquid from its anal glands toward its attacker. ■ the fur of the skunk. ■ *inf.* a contemptible person.
▶ *v.* [*tr.*] *inf.* (often **be skunked**) defeat (someone) overwhelmingly in a game or contest, esp. by preventing them from scoring at all. ▷mid 17th cent.: from Massachusett *squunck*.

skunk cab·bage ▶ *n.* a North American plant (genera *Lysichitum* and *Symplocarpus*) of the arum family, the flower of which has a distinctive smell.

sky /skī/ ▶ *n.* (*pl.* **skies**) (often **the sky**) the region of the atmosphere and outer space seen from the earth: *hundreds of stars shining in the sky.*
▶ *v.* (**skies**, **skied**) [*tr.*] *inf.* hit (a ball) high into the air: *he skied his tee shot.* ■ hang (a picture) very high on a wall, esp. in an exhibition. —**sky·less** *adj.*

sky·box /'skī,bäks/ ▶ *n.* a luxurious enclosed seating area located high in a sports arena.

sky·cap /'skī,kap/ ▶ *n.* a porter at an airport.

sky·div·ing /'skī,dīviNG/ ▶ *n.* the sport of jumping from an aircraft and performing acrobatic maneuvers in the air during free fall before landing by parachute. —**sky·dive** *v.* —**sky·div·er** *n.*

Skye ter·ri·er ▶ *n.* a small long-haired terrier of a slate-colored or beige-colored Scottish breed.

sky-high ▶ *adv. & adj.* as if reaching the sky; very high: [as *adv.*] *they saved a president from being blown sky-high.* ■ at or to a very high level; very great: [as *adj.*] *sky-high premiums.*

sky·jack /'skī,jak/ ▶ *v.* [*tr.*] hijack (an aircraft).
▶ *n.* an act of skyjacking. —**sky·jack·er** *n.*

sky·lark /'skī,lärk/ ▶ *n.* a common Eurasian and North African lark (genus *Alauda*, family Alaudidae) of farmland and open country, noted for its prolonged song given in hovering flight.
▶ *v.* [*intr.*] pass time by playing tricks or practical jokes; indulge in horseplay: *he was skylarking with a friend when he fell into a pile of boxes.*

sky·light /'skī,līt/ ▶ *n.* a window installed in a roof or ceiling.

sky·line /'skī,līn/ ▶ *n.* an outline of land and buildings defined against the sky: *the skyline of the city.* ■ the line along which the horizon is visible.

sky·rock·et /'skī,räkit/ ▶ *n.* a rocket designed to explode high in the air as a signal or firework.
▶ *v.* (**-rock·et·ed**, **-rock·et·ing**) [*intr.*] *inf.* (of a price, rate, or amount) increase very steeply or rapidly: *the cost of housing has skyrocketed.*

sky·scrap·er /'skī,skrāpər/ ▶ *n.* a very tall building of many stories.

sky·walk /'skī,wôk/ ▶ *n.* an enclosed overhead walkway between buildings.

sky·ward /'skīwərd/ ▶ *adv.* (also **sky·wards**) toward the sky: *flames were now shooting skyward.*

sky·way /'skī,wā/ ▶ *n.* **1** another term for SKYWALK. **2** an elevated highway.

sky·writ·ing /'skī,rītiNG/ ▶ *n.* words in the form of smoke trails made by an airplane, esp. for advertising. —**sky·writ·er** /-tər/ *n.*

slab /slab/ ▶ *n.* a large, thick, flat piece of stone, concrete, or wood, typically rectangular: *paving slabs* | *she settled on a slab of rock.* ■ a large, thick slice or piece of cake, bread, chocolate, etc.: *a slab of bread and cheese.* ■ an outer piece of timber sawn from a log. ■ a table used for laying a body on in a morgue. —**slab·by** *adj.*

slack /slak/ ▶ *adj.* **1** not taut or held tightly in position; loose: *a slack rope.* **2** (of business) characterized by a lack of work or activity; quiet: *business was rather slack.* ■ having or showing laziness or negligence: *slack accounting procedures.* **3** (of a tide) neither ebbing nor flowing.
▶ *n.* **1** the part of a rope or line that is not held taut; the loose or unused part: *I picked up the rod and wound in the slack.* **2** (**slacks**) casual trousers. **3** *inf.* a spell of inactivity or laziness: *he slept deeply, refreshed by a little slack in the daily routine.*
▶ *v.* [*tr.*] loosen (something, esp. a rope). ■ reduce the intensity or speed of (something); slacken: *the horse slacked his pace.* ■ [*intr.*] (**slack off**) decrease in quantity or intensity: *the flow of blood slacked off.* ■ [*intr.*] (**slack up**) slow down: *the animal doesn't slack up until he reaches the trees.*
▶ *adv.* loosely: *their heads were hanging slack in attitudes of despair.* —**slack·ly** *adv.* —**slack·ness** *n.*
▶ □ **cut someone some slack** *inf.* allow someone some leeway in their conduct. □ **take** (or **pick**) **up the slack** **1** use up a surplus or improve the use of resources to avoid an undesirable lull in business: *as domestic demand starts to flag, foreign demand will help pick up the slack.* **2** pull on the loose end or part of a rope in order to make it taut.

slack·en /'slakən/ ▶ *v.* make or become slack: [*tr.*] *he slackened his grip* | [*intr.*] *the pace never slackens.*

slack·er /'slakər/ ▶ *n. inf.* a person who avoids work or effort. ■ a person who evades military service. ■ a young person (esp. in the 1990s) of a subculture characterized by apathy and aimlessness.

slag /slag/ ▶ *n.* stony waste matter separated from metals during the smelting or refining of ore. —**slag·gy** *adj.* (**-gi·er**, **-gi·est**).

slain /slān/ ▶ past participle of SLAY.

slake /slāk/ ▶ *v.* [*tr.*] **1** quench or satisfy (one's thirst): *slake your thirst with some lemonade.* ■ *fig.* satisfy (desires): *restaurants worked to slake the Italian obsession with food.* **2** combine (quicklime) with water to produce calcium hydroxide.

slaked lime ▶ *n.* see LIME[1].

sla·lom /'släləm/ ▶ *n.* a ski race down a winding course marked by flags or poles. ■ a sporting event on water with a winding course marked by obstacles, typically a canoe or sailing race.
▶ *v.* [*intr.*] move or race in a winding path, avoiding obstacles: *she drove with reckless speed, slaloming in and out of the stalled cars.* ▷1920s: from Norwegian *slalåm*, literally 'sloping track.' —**sla·lom·er** *n.*

slam[1] /slam/ ▶ *v.* (**slammed**, **slam·ming**) [*tr.*] shut (a door, window, or lid) forcefully and loudly: *he slams the door behind him as he leaves.* ■ [*intr.*] be closed forcefully and loudly: *she heard a car door slam.* ■ [*tr.*] push or put somewhere with great force: *Charlie slammed down the phone.* ■ [*intr.*] (**slam into**) crash into; collide heavily with: *the car mounted the sidewalk, slamming into a lamppost.* ■ [*tr.*] *inf.* hit (something) with great force in a particular direction: *he slammed a shot into the net.* ■ put (something) into action suddenly or forcefully: *I slammed on the brakes.* ■ [*tr.*] (usu. **be slammed**) *inf.* criticize severely: *his efforts to slam the president destroyed his own campaign.* ■ [*tr.*] *inf.* score points against or gain a victory over (someone) easily: *the Blue Devils slammed Kansas to win the title.* ■ [*tr.*] [often as *n.*] (**slamming**) (of a telephone company) take over the account of (a telephone customer) without their permission.
▶ *n.* **1** a loud bang caused by the forceful shutting of something such as a door: *the back door closed with a slam.* **2** (usu. **the slam**) *inf.* prison. **3** a poetry contest in which competitors recite their entries and are judged by members of the audience, the winner being elected after several elimination rounds.

slam[2] ▶ *n.* Bridge a grand slam (all thirteen tricks) or small slam (twelve tricks), for which bonus points are scored if bid and made.

slam-danc·ing ▶ *n.* a form of dancing to rock music in which the dancers deliberately collide with one another. —**slam dance** *v.* —**slam danc·er** *n.*

slam dunk ▶ *n. Basketball* a shot in which a player thrusts the ball forcefully down through the basket. ■ [usu. as *adj.*] *inf.* something reliable or unfailing; a foregone conclusion or certainty: *a movie predicted to be the season's one slam-dunk hit.*
▶ *v.* (**slam-dunk**) [*tr.*] thrust (the ball) forcefully down through the basket. ■ *inf.* defeat or dismiss decisively: *they continue to slam-dunk every proposal we make.*

slam·mer /'slamər/ ▶ *n.* **1** (usu. **the slammer**) *inf.* prison. **2** a person who deliberately collides with others when slam-dancing.

slan·der /'slandər/ ▶ *n. Law* the action or crime of making a false spoken statement damaging to a person's reputation: *he is suing the TV network for slander.* Compare with LIBEL. ■ a false and malicious spoken statement: *I've had just about all I can stomach of your slanders.*
▶ *v.* [*tr.*] make false and damaging statements about (someone): *they were accused of slandering the head of state.* —**slan·der·er** *n.* —**slan·der·ous** /-rəs/ *adj.* —**slan·der·ous·ly** /-rəslē/ *adv.*

slang /slaNG/ ▶ *n.* a type of language that consists of words and phrases that are regarded as very informal, are more common in speech than writing, and are typically restricted to a particular context or group of people: *grass is slang for marijuana* | *army slang.*
▶ *v.* [*tr.*] *inf.* attack (someone) using abusive language: *he watched ideological groups slanging one another.*

slant /slant/ ▶ *v.* [*intr.*] slope or lean in a particular direction; diverge from the vertical or horizontal: *a plowed field slanted up to the skyline.* ■ (esp. of light or shadow) fall in an oblique direction: *the early sun slanted across the mountains.* ■ [*tr.*] cause (something) to lean or slope in such a way: *slant your skis as you turn to send up a curtain of water.* ■ [*tr.*] [often as *adj.*] (**slanted**) present or view (information) from a particular angle, esp. in a biased or unfair way: *slanted news coverage.*
▶ *n.* **1** a sloping position: *the hedge grew at a slant.* **2** a particular point of view from which something is seen or presented: *a new slant on*

science. **3** *inf., offens.* a contemptuous term for an East Asian or Southeast Asian person.
▶ *adj.* sloping: *slant pockets.*

slap /slap/ ▶ *v.* (**slapped, slap·ping**) [*tr.*] hit (someone or something) with the palm of one's hand or a flat object: *my sister slapped my face.* ■ [*intr.*] hit against or into something with the sound of such an action: *water slapped against the boat.* ■ (**slap someone down**) *inf.* reprimand someone forcefully. ■ [*tr.*] put or apply (something) somewhere quickly, carelessly, or forcefully: *slap on a bit of makeup.* ■ (**slap something on**) *inf.* impose a fine or other penalty on: *the government had slapped an embargo on imports.*
▶ *n.* a blow with the palm of the hand or a flat object: *he gave her a slap across her cheek.* ■ a sound made or as if made by such an action: *she heard the slap of water against the harbor wall.*
▶ *adv. inf.* suddenly and directly: *she ran slap into Luke.*
▶ □ **slap in the face** an unexpected rejection or affront. □ **slap on the back** congratulations or commendations: *they deserve a hearty slap on the back for their efforts.* □ **slap on the wrist** a mild reprimand or punishment.

slap-dash /ˈslapˌdaSH/ ▶ *adj.* done too hurriedly and carelessly: *he gave a slapdash performance.*

slap-hap·py /ˈslapˌhapē/ (also **slap-hap·py**) ▶ *adj. inf.* **1** casual or flippant in a cheerful and often irresponsible way: *he possessed slaphappy courage.* ■ (of an action or operation) unmethodical; poorly thought out: *slaphappy surveying methods.* **2** dazed or stupefied from happiness or relief: *she's a bit slaphappy after such a narrow escape.*

slap-jack /ˈslapˌjak/ ▶ *n.* a pancake.

slap shot ▶ *n. Ice Hockey* a hard shot made by raising the stick about waist-high before striking the puck with a sharp slapping motion.

slap-stick /ˈslapˌstik/ ▶ *n.* comedy based on deliberately clumsy actions and humorously embarrassing events: [as *adj.*] *slapstick humor.*

slash[1] /slaSH/ ▶ *v.* [*tr.*] cut (something) with a violent sweeping movement, typically using a knife or sword: *a tire was slashed on my car* | [*intr.*] *the man slashed at him with a sword.* ■ *inf.* reduce (a price, quantity, etc.) greatly: *the workforce has been slashed by 2,000.*
▶ *n.* **1** a cut made with a wide, sweeping stroke: *the man took a mighty slash at his head with a large sword.* ■ a wound or gash made by such an action: *he staggered over with a crimson slash across his temple.* ■ *fig.* a bright patch or flash of color or light: *yellow and gold foliage, with the odd slash of red.* **2** an oblique stroke (/) in print or writing, used between alternatives (e.g., *and/or*), in fractions (e.g., 3/4), in ratios (e.g., *miles/day*), or between separate elements of a text. ■ [as *adj.*] denoting or belonging to a genre of fiction, chiefly published in fanzines, in which any of various male pairings from the popular media is portrayed as having a homosexual relationship. **3** debris resulting from the felling or destruction of trees. —**slash·er** *n.*

slash[2] ▶ *n.* a tract of swampy ground, esp. in a coastal region.

slat /slat/ ▶ *n.* a thin, narrow piece of wood, plastic, or metal, esp. one of a series that overlap or fit into each other, as in a fence or a Venetian blind. —**slat·ted** *adj.*

slate /slāt/ ▶ *n.* **1** a fine-grained gray, green, or bluish metamorphic rock easily split into smooth, flat pieces. ■ a flat piece of such rock used as roofing material. **2** a flat piece of slate used for writing on, typically framed in wood, formerly used in schools. ■ a list of candidates for election to a post or office, typically a group sharing a set of political views: *another slate of candidates will be picked for the state convention.* ■ a range of something offered: *the company has revealed details of a $60 million slate of film productions.* ■ a board showing the identifying details of a take of a motion picture, which is held in front of the camera at its beginning and end. **3** [usu. as *adj.*] a bluish-gray color: *suits of slate gray.*
▶ *v.* [*tr.*] **1** cover (something, esp. a roof) with slates. **2** (usu. **be slated**) schedule; plan: *renovations are slated for late June.* ■ (usu. **be slated**) nominate (someone) as a candidate for an office or post: *I understand that I am being slated for promotion.* **3** identify (a movie take) using a slate. —**slat·y** *adj.*

slath·er /ˈslaT͟Hər/ ▶ *n.* (often **slathers**) *inf.* a large amount.
▶ *v.* [*tr.*] *inf.* spread or smear (a substance) thickly or liberally: *slather on some tanning lotion.* | *biscuits slathered with butter.*

slat·tern /ˈslatərn/ ▶ *n. dated* a dirty, untidy woman. —**slat·tern·li·ness** *n.* —**slat·tern·ly** *adj.*

slaugh·ter /ˈslôtər/ ▶ *n.* the killing of animals for food. ■ the killing of a large number of people or animals in a cruel or violent way; massacre: *the slaughter of 20 peaceful demonstrators.* ■ *inf.* a thorough defeat: *an absolute slaughter by the Red Sox.*
▶ *v.* [*tr.*] (usu. **be slaughtered**) kill (animals) for food. ■ kill (people or

animals) in a cruel or violent way, typically in large numbers: *innocent civilians are being slaughtered.* ■ *inf.* defeat (an opponent) thoroughly: *our team was slaughtered in the finals.* —**slaugh·ter·er** *n.* —**slaugh·ter·ous** /-rəs/ *adj.*

slaugh·ter·house /ˈslôtərˌhous/ ▶ *n.* a place where animals are slaughtered for food.

Slav /släv/ ▶ *n.* a member of a group of peoples in central and eastern Europe speaking Slavic languages.
▶ *adj.* another term for SLAVIC.

slave /slāv/ ▶ *n. chiefly hist.* a person who is the legal property of another and is forced to obey them. ■ a person who works very hard without proper remuneration or appreciation: *by the time I was ten, I had become her slave, doing all the housework.* ■ a person who is excessively dependent upon or controlled by something: *the poorest people of the world are slaves to the banks* | *she was no slave to fashion.* ■ a device, or part of one, directly controlled by another: [as *adj.*] *a slave cassette deck.* ■ an ant captured in its pupal state by an ant of another species, for which it becomes a worker.
▶ *v.* [*intr.*] work excessively hard: *after slaving away for fourteen years, all he gets is two thousand.* ■ [*tr.*] subject (a device) to control by another: *should the need arise, the two channels can be slaved together.*

slave driv·er ▶ *n.* a person who oversees and urges on slaves at work. ■ a person who works others very hard. —**slave-drive** *v.*

slav·er[1] /ˈslāvər/ ▶ *n. chiefly hist.* a person dealing in or owning slaves. ■ a ship used for transporting slaves.

slav·er[2] /ˈslavər/ ▶ *n.* saliva running from the mouth.
▶ *v.* [*intr.*] let saliva run from the mouth: *the Labrador was slavering at the mouth.* ■ show excessive desire: *suburbanites slavering over drop-dead models.*

slav·er·y /ˈslāvərē/ ▶ *n.* the state of being a slave: *thousands had been sold into slavery.* ■ the practice or system of owning slaves. ■ a condition compared to that of a slave in respect of exhausting labor or restricted freedom: *female domestic slavery.* ■ excessive dependence on or devotion to something: *slavery to tradition.*

slave ship ▶ *n. hist.* a ship transporting slaves, esp. one carrying slaves from Africa.

slave trade ▶ *n. chiefly hist.* the procuring, transporting, and selling of human beings as slaves, in particular the former trade in African blacks as slaves by European countries and North America. —**slave trad·er** *n.*

Slav·ic /ˈslävik/ ▶ *adj.* of, relating to, or denoting the branch of the Indo-European language family that includes Russian, Ukrainian, and Belorussian (**East Slavic**), Polish, Czech, Slovak, and Sorbian (**West Slavic**), and Bulgarian, Serbo-Croat, Macedonian, and Slovene (**South Slavic**). ■ of, relating to, or denoting the peoples of central and eastern Europe who speak any of these languages.
▶ *n.* the Slavic languages collectively. See also SLAVONIC.

slav·ish /ˈslāviSH/ ▶ *adj.* relating to or characteristic of a slave, typically by behaving in a servile or submissive way: *he noted the slavish, feudal respect they had for her.* ■ showing no attempt at originality, constructive interpretation, or development: *a slavish adherence to protocol.* —**slav·ish·ly** *adv.* —**slav·ish·ness** *n.*

Sla·von·ic /sləˈvänik/ ▶ *adj. & n.* another term for SLAVIC.

slay /slā/ ▶ *v.* (*past* **slew** /slo͞o/; *past part.* **slain** /slān/) [*tr.*] *archaic, poetic/lit.* kill (a person or animal) in a violent way: *St. George slew the dragon.* ■ (usu. **be slain**) murder (someone) (used chiefly in journalism): *a man was slain with a shotgun* | [as *n.*] (**slaying**) *a gangland slaying.* ■ *inf.* greatly impress or amuse (someone): *you slay me, you really do.* —**slay·er** *n.*

sleaze /slēz/ ▶ *n.* immoral, sordid, and corrupt behavior or material, esp. in business or politics: *political campaigns that are long on sleaze and short on substance.* ■ *inf.* a sordid, corrupt, or immoral person.
▶ *v.* [*intr.*] *inf.* behave in a sordid way: *sleazing around bars.*

slea·zy /ˈslēzē/ ▶ *adj.* (**-zi·er, -zi·est**) (of a person or situation) sordid, corrupt, or immoral. ■ (of a place) squalid and seedy: *a sleazy all-night café.* —**slea·zi·ly** /ˈslēzəlē/ *adv.* —**slea·zi·ness** *n.*

sled /sled/ ▶ *n.* a vehicle on runners for traveling over snow or ice, either pushed or pulled, drawn by horses, dogs, or a motor vehicle, or allowed to slide downhill. ■ another term for SLEDGE[1]. ■ another term for SNOWMOBILE.
▶ *v.* (**sled·ded, sled·ding**) [*intr.*] ride on a sled: *they sledded down the slopes in the frozen snow* | [as *n.*] (**sledding**) *the sledding has been excellent this year.*

sledge[1] /slej/ ▶ *n.* a vehicle on runners for conveying loads or passengers esp. over snow or ice, often pulled by draft animals. ■ British term for SLED.

▶ *v.* [*tr.*] carry (a load or passengers) on a sledge: *the task of sledging lifeboats across tundra.*

sledge[2] ▶ *n.* a sledgehammer.

sledge·ham·mer /'slej,hamər/ ▶ *n.* a large, heavy hammer used for such jobs as breaking rocks and driving in fence posts. ■ [as *adj.*] powerful; forceful: *sledgehammer blows.* ■ [as *adj.*] *fig.* ruthless, insensitive, or using unnecessary force: *under his sledgehammer direction, anything of subtlety is swamped.*

▶ *v.* [*tr.*] hit with a sledgehammer.

sleek /slēk/ ▶ *adj.* (of hair, fur, or skin) smooth and glossy: *he was tall, with sleek, dark hair.* ■ (of a person or animal) having smooth, glossy skin, hair, or fur, often taken as a sign of physical fitness: *a sleek black cat.* ■ (of a person) having a wealthy and well-groomed appearance: *his sleek and elegant sisters.* ■ (of an object) having an elegant, streamlined shape or design: *his sleek black car slid through the traffic.* ■ ingratiating; unctuous: *she gave Guy a sleek smile to underline her words.*

▶ *v.* [*tr.*] make (the hair) smooth and glossy, typically by applying pressure or moisture to it: *her black hair was sleeked down.* —**sleek·ly** *adv.* —**sleek·ness** *n.* —**sleek·y** *adj.*

sleep /slēp/ ▶ *n.* a condition of body and mind such as that which typically recurs for several hours every night, in which the nervous system is relatively inactive, the eyes closed, the postural muscles relaxed, and consciousness practically suspended: *I was on the verge of sleep.* ■ *chiefly poetic/lit.* a state compared to or resembling this, such as death or complete silence or stillness: *a photograph of the poet in his last sleep.* ■ a gummy or gritty secretion found in the corners of the eyes after sleep: *she sat up, rubbing the sleep from her eyes.*

▶ *v.* (*past* and *past part.* **slept** /slept/) [*intr.*] rest in such a condition; be asleep: *she slept for half an hour* | [as *adj.*] (**sleeping**) *he looked at the sleeping child.* ■ (**sleep through**) fail to be woken by: *he was so tired he slept through the alarm.* ■ have sexual intercourse or be involved in a sexual relationship: *I won't sleep with a man who doesn't respect me.* ■ [*tr.*] (**sleep something off/away**) dispel the effects of or recover from something by going to sleep: *she thought it wise to let him sleep off his hangover.* ■ [*tr.*] provide (a specified number of people) with beds, rooms, or places to stay the night: *studios sleeping two people cost $70 a night.* ■ *fig.* be inactive or dormant: *Copenhagen likes to be known as the city that never sleeps.* ■ *poetic/lit.* be at peace in death; lie buried: *he sleeps beneath the silver birches.*

▶ *phrasal v.* □ **sleep around** *inf.* have many casual sexual partners. □ **sleep in** remain asleep or in bed later than usual in the morning. ■ sleep by night at one's place of work. □ **sleep over** spend the night at a place other than one's own home: *Katie was asked to sleep over with Jenny.* ▷Old English *slēp, slæp* (noun), *slēpan, slæpan* (verb), of Germanic origin; related to Dutch *slapen* and German *schlafen.*

▶ □ **put someone to sleep** make someone unconscious by the use of drugs, alcohol, or an anesthetic. ■ (also **send someone to sleep**) bore someone greatly. □ **put something to sleep** kill an animal, esp. an old, sick, or badly injured one, painlessly (used euphemistically). ■ *Comput.* put a computer on standby while it is not being used, esp. in order to reduce power consumption. □ **sleep like a log** (or **top**) sleep very soundly. □ **sleep on it** *inf.* delay making a decision on something until the following day so as to have more time to consider it. □ **the sleep of the just** deep, untroubled sleep. □ **sleep tight** [usu. in *imper.*] sleep well (said to someone when parting from them at night).

sleep·er /'slēpər/ ▶ *n.* **1** a person or animal who is asleep. ■ a person with a specified sleep pattern: *a light sleeper.* **2** a thing used for or connected with sleeping, in particular: ■ a train carrying sleeping cars. ■ a sleeping car. ■ a berth in a sleeping car. ■ (often **sleepers**) one-piece coverall pajamas for a baby or small child. ■ a sofa or chair that converts into a bed. **3** a movie, book, play, etc., that achieves sudden unexpected success. **4** a stocky fish (*Dormitator* and other genera, family Gobiidae, or Eleotridae) with mottled coloration that occurs widely in warm seas and fresh water.

sleep·er cell ▶ *n.* a secretive group with suspected links to a terrorist organization that is planning or believed capable of carrying out an attack.

sleep·ing bag ▶ *n.* a warm lined padded bag to sleep in, esp. when camping.

sleep·ing car ▶ *n.* a railroad car provided with beds or berths.

sleep·ing pill ▶ *n.* a tablet of a drug that helps to induce sleep.

sleep·ing sick·ness ▶ *n.* a tropical disease caused by a parasitic protozoan that is transmitted by the bite of the tsetse fly. It causes fever,

chills, pain in the limbs, and anemia, and eventually affects the nervous system causing extreme lethargy and death.

sleep·less /'slēplis/ ▶ *adj.* characterized by or experiencing lack of sleep: *another sleepless night* | *Lisa lay sleepless.* —**sleep·less·ly** *adv.* —**sleep·less·ness** *n.*

sleep·walk /'slēp,wôk/ ▶ *v.* [*intr.*] walk around and sometimes perform other actions while asleep.

▶ *n.* an instance of such activity. —**sleep·walk·er** *n.* —**sleep·walk·ing** *n.*

sleep·y /'slēpē/ ▶ *adj.* (**sleep·i·er, sleep·i·est**) needing or ready for sleep: *the wine had made her sleepy.* ■ showing the effects of sleep: *she rubbed her sleepy eyes.* ■ inducing sleep; soporific: *the sleepy heat of the afternoon.* ■ (of a place) without much activity: *he turned off the road into a sleepy little town.* ■ (of a business, organization, or industry) lacking the ability or will to respond to change; not dynamic: *it was once a sleepy subsidiary of Foster & Sykes.* —**sleep·i·ly** /'slēpəlē/ *adv.* —**sleep·i·ness** *n.*

sleet /slēt/ ▶ *n.* a form of precipitation consisting of ice pellets, often mixed with rain or snow. ■ a thin coating of ice formed by rain freezing on contact with a cold surface.

▶ *v.* [*intr.*] (**it sleets, it is sleeting,** etc.) sleet falls: *it was sleeting so hard we could barely see.* —**sleet·y** *adj.*

sleeve /slēv/ ▶ *n.* the part of a garment that wholly or partly covers a person's arm: *a shirt with the sleeves rolled up.* ■ a protective paper or cardboard cover for a record or album. ■ a protective or connecting tube fitting over or enclosing a rod, spindle, or smaller tube. —**sleeved** *adj.* [often in *comb.*] *a cap-sleeved shirt.* —**sleeve·less** *adj.*

▶ □ **up one's sleeve** (of a strategy, idea, or resource) kept secret and in reserve for use when needed: *I wonder what's up his sleeve.*

sleigh /slā/ ▶ *n.* a sled drawn by horses or reindeer, esp. one used for passengers.

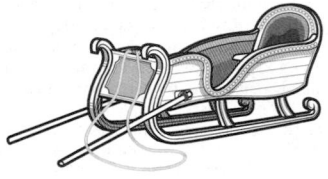

sleigh

sleigh bell ▶ *n.* a tinkling bell attached to the harness of a sleigh horse.

sleight of hand /slīt/ ▶ *n.* manual dexterity, typically in performing tricks: *a nifty bit of sleight of hand got the ashtray into the correct position.* ■ skillful deception: *this is financial sleight of hand of the worst sort.*

slen·der /'slendər/ ▶ *adj.* (**-der·er, -der·est**) **1** (of a person or part of the body) gracefully thin: *her slender neck.* ■ (esp. of a rod or stem) of small girth or breadth: *slender iron railings.* **2** (of something abstract) barely sufficient in amount or basis: *a slender majority of four.* —**slen·der·ly** *adv.* —**slen·der·ness** *n.*

slen·der·ize /'slendə,rīz/ ▶ *v.* [*tr.*] [usu. as *adj.*] (**slenderizing**) make (a person or a part of their body) appear more slender: *my mother has always held that dark colors are slenderizing.* ■ [*intr.*] (of a person) lose weight; become slim.

slept /slept/ ▶ past and past participle of SLEEP.

sleuth /slōōTH/ *inf.* ▶ *n.* a detective.

▶ *v.* [*intr.*] [often as *n.*] (**sleuthing**) carry out a search or investigation in the manner of a detective: *scientists began their genetic sleuthing for honey mushrooms four years ago.*

slew[1] /slōō/ (also **slue**) ▶ *v.* [*intr.*] (of a vehicle or person) turn or slide violently or uncontrollably in a particular direction: *the Chevy slewed from side to side in the snow.* ■ [*tr.*] turn or slide (something, esp. a vehicle) in such a way: *he managed to slew the aircraft around before it settled on the runway.*

slew[2] ▶ past of SLAY.

slew[3] ▶ *n.* *inf.* a large number or quantity of something: *he asked me a slew of questions.*

slice /slīs/ ▶ *n.* **1** a thin, broad piece of food, such as bread, meat, or cake, cut from a larger portion: *four slices of bread.* ■ a portion or share of something: *a huge slice of public spending.* **2** *Golf* a stroke that makes the ball curve away to the right (for a left-handed player, the left), typically inadvertently. Compare with HOOK. ■ (in other sports) a shot or stroke made with glancing contact to impart spin. **3** a utensil with a broad, flat blade for lifting foods such as cake and fish.

▶ *v.* [*tr.*] **1** cut (something, esp. food) into slices: *slice the onion into rings.* ■ (**slice something off/from**) cut something or a piece of something off or from (something larger), typically with one clean cut: *he sliced a* *corner from a fried egg.* ■ cut with or as if with a sharp implement: *the bomber's wings were slicing the air with some efficiency.* ■ [*intr.*] move easily and quickly: *Senna then sliced past Berger to take third place.* **2** *Golf* strike (the ball) or play (a stroke) so that the ball curves away to the right (for a left-handed player, the left), typically inadvertently. ■ (in other sports) propel (the ball) with a glancing contact to impart spin: *Evans went and sliced a corner into his own net.* —**slice·a·ble** *adj.* —**slic·er** *n.* [often in *comb.*] *a cheese-slicer.*

slice and dice ▶*v.* rearrange or analyze in a number of different ways, often arbitrarily: [trans.] *each network has analysis teams that slice and dice the exit poll information to find a conclusion.*

slick /slik/ ▶*adj.* **1** (of an action or thing) done or operating in an impressively smooth, efficient, and apparently effortless way: *a slick piece of software.* ■ (of a thing) superficially impressive or efficient in presentation: *the brands are backed by slick advertising.* ■ (of a person or their behavior) adroit or clever; glibly assured: *he's a slick con man.* **2** (of skin or hair) smooth and glossy: *a dandy-looking dude with a slick black ponytail.* ■ (of a surface) smooth, wet, and slippery: *she tumbled back against the slick, damp wall.*

▶*n.* **1** an oil slick. ■ a small smear or patch of a glossy or wet substance, esp. a cosmetic: *a slick of lip balm.* **2** (usu. **slicks**) a race car or bicycle tire without a tread, for use in dry weather conditions. **3** *inf.* a glossy magazine.

▶*v.* **1** [*tr.*] make (one's hair) flat, smooth, and glossy by applying water, oil, or cream to it: *his damp hair was slicked back* | [as *adj.* in *comb.*] (**slicked**) *his slicked-down hair.* ■ cover with a film of liquid; make wet or slippery: *she woke to find her body slicked with sweat* | [as *adj.* in *comb.*] (**-slicked**) *a rain-slicked road.* **2** (**slick someone/something up**) make someone or something smart, tidy, or stylish. —**slick·ly** *adv.* —**slick·ness** *n.*

slick·er /ˈslikər/ ▶*n.* **1** *inf.* a crook or swindler. ■ short for CITY SLICKER. **2** a raincoat made of smooth material.

slide /slīd/ ▶*v.* (past **slid** /slid/) [*intr.*] move along a smooth surface while maintaining continuous contact with it: *she slid down the bank into the water* | [as *adj.*] (**sliding**) *the tank should have a sliding glass cover.* ■ [*tr.*] move (something) along a surface in such a way: *she slid the keys over the table.* ■ move smoothly, quickly, or unobtrusively: *I quickly slid into a seat at the back of the hall.* ■ [*tr.*] move (something) in such a way: *she slid the bottle into her pocket.* ■ change gradually to a worse condition or lower level: *the country faces the prospect of sliding from recession into slump.*

▶*n.* **1** a structure with a smooth sloping surface for children to slide down. ■ a smooth stretch or slope of ice or packed snow for sledding on. ■ an act of moving along a smooth surface while maintaining continuous contact with it: *use an ice ax to halt a slide on ice and snow.* ■ *Baseball* a sliding approach to a base along the ground. ■ a decline in value or quality: *the current slide in house prices.* **2** a part of a machine or musical instrument that slides. ■ the place on a machine or instrument where a sliding part operates. ■ slide guitar: *I'd been playing slide for years.* **3** a rectangular piece of glass on which an object is mounted or placed for examination under a microscope. ■ a mounted transparency, typically one placed in a projector for viewing on a screen: [as *adj.*] *a slide show.* —**slid·a·ble** *adj.* —**slid·er** *n.*

▶ □ **let something slide** negligently allow something to deteriorate: *Papa had let the business slide after Mama's death.*

slide rule ▶*n.* a ruler with a sliding central strip, marked with logarithmic scales and used for making rapid calculations, esp. multiplication and division.

slid·ing door ▶*n.* a door drawn across an aperture on a groove or suspended from a track, rather than turning on hinges.

slid·ing scale ▶*n.* a scale of fees, taxes, wages, etc., that varies in accordance with variation of some standard.

slight /slīt/ ▶*adj.* **1** small in degree; inconsiderable: *a slight increase.* ■ (esp. of a creative work) not profound or substantial; somewhat trivial or superficial: *a slight plot.* **2** (of a person or their build) not sturdy and strongly built: *she was slight and delicate-looking.*

▶*v.* [*tr.*] insult (someone) by treating or speaking of them without proper respect or attention: *he was careful not to slight a guest.*

▶*n.* an insult caused by a failure to show someone proper respect or attention: *an unintended slight can create grudges.* —**slight·ing·ly** *adv.* —**slight·ish** *adj.* —**slight·ly** *adv.* —**slight·ness** *n.*

sli·ly ▶*adv.* variant spelling of SLYLY (see SLY).

slim /slim/ ▶*adj.* (**slim·mer**, **slim·mest**) **1** (of a person or their build) gracefully thin; slenderly built (used approvingly): *her slim figure.* ■ (of a thing) small in width and typically long and narrow in shape: *a slim gold band encircled her wrist.* ■ (of a garment) cut with slender lines; designed to make the wearer appear slim: *a pair of slim, immaculately cut*

slacks. ■ (of a business or other organization) reduced to a smaller size in the hope that it will become more efficient. **2** (of something abstract, esp. a chance or margin) very small: *there was just a slim chance of success.*

▶*v.* (**slimmed**, **slim·ming**) [*intr.*] make oneself thinner by dieting and sometimes exercising: *I need to slim down a bit* | [as *n.*] (**slimming**) *an aid to slimming.* ■ [*tr.*] make (a person or a bodily part) thinner in such a way: *how can I slim down my hips?* ■ [*tr.*] reduce (a business or other organization) to a smaller size in the hope of making it more efficient: *restructuring and slimming down the organization.* —**slim·ly** *adv.* —**slim·ness** *n.*

slime /slīm/ ▶*n.* a moist, soft, and slippery substance, typically regarded as repulsive: *the cold stone was wet with slime.*

slim·y /ˈslīmē/ ▶*adj.* (**slim·i·er**, **slim·i·est**) covered by or having the feel or consistency of slime: *the thick, slimy mud* | *the walls were slimy with lichens.* ■ *inf.* disgustingly immoral, dishonest, or obsequious: *he was a slimy people-pleaser.* —**slim·i·ly** /-məlē/ *adv.* —**slim·i·ness** *n.*

sling¹ /sliNG/ ▶*n.* **1** a flexible strap or belt used in the form of a loop to support or raise a weight: *the horse had to be supported by a sling fixed to the roof.* ■ a bandage or soft strap looped around the neck to support an injured arm: *she had her arm in a sling.* ■ a pouch or frame for carrying a baby, supported by a strap around the neck or shoulders. **2** a simple weapon in the form of a strap or loop, used to hurl stones or other small missiles.

▶*v.* (past **slung** /sləNG/) **1** [*tr.*] suspend or arrange (something), esp. with a strap or straps, so that it hangs loosely in a particular position: *a hammock was slung between two trees.* ■ carry (something, esp. a garment) loosely and casually: *he had his jacket slung over one shoulder.* **2** [*tr.*] *inf.* throw; fling (often used to express the speaker's casual attitude): *sling a few things into your knapsack.* ■ hurl (a stone or other missile) from a sling or similar weapon. ■ hoist or transfer (something) with a sling: *horse after horse was slung up from the barges.* —**sling·er** *n.*

▶ □ **slings and arrows** used with reference to adverse factors or circumstances: *the slings and arrows of outrageous critics.*

sling² ▶*n.* a sweetened drink of liquor, esp. gin, and water.

sling·shot /ˈsliNG,SHät/ ▶*n.* a forked stick, to which an elastic strap (or a pair of elastic bands connected by a small sling) is fastened to the two prongs, typically used for shooting small stones. ■ [often as *adj.*] the effect of the gravitational pull of a celestial body in accelerating and changing the course of another body or a spacecraft.

▶*v.* (**-shot·ting**; past and past part. **-shot** or **-shot·ted**) forcefully accelerate or cause to accelerate through use of gravity.

slink /sliNGk/ ▶*v.* (past **slunk** /sləNGk/) [*intr.*] move smoothly and quietly with gliding steps, in a stealthy or sensuous manner: *the fox came slinking through the woods.* ■ come or go unobtrusively or furtively.

slinkshot

slink·y /ˈsliNGkē/ ▶*adj.* (**slink·i·er**, **slink·i·est**) *inf.* graceful and sinuous in movement, line, or figure: *a slinky black evening dress.*

▶*n.* (**Slinky**) *trademark* a toy consisting of a flexible helical spring that can be made to somersault down steps. —**slink·i·ly** /ˈsliNGkəlē/ *adv.* —**slink·i·ness** *n.*

slip¹ /slip/ ▶*v.* (**slipped**, **slip·ping**) **1** [*intr.*] (of a person or animal) slide unintentionally for a short distance, typically losing one's balance or footing: *I slipped on the ice.* ■ (of a thing) accidentally slide or move out of position or from someone's grasp: *the envelope slipped through Luke's fingers.* ■ fail to grip or make proper contact with a surface: *the front wheels began to slip* | [as *adj.*] (**slipping**) *a badly slipping clutch.* ■ go or move quietly or quickly, without attracting notice: *we slipped out by a back door.* ■ pass or change to a lower, worse, or different condition, typically in a gradual or imperceptible way: *many people feel standards have slipped.* ■ (**be slipping**) *inf.* be behaving in a way that is not up to one's usual level of performance: *you're slipping, Joe—you need a vacation.* ■ (**slip away/by**) (of time) elapse: *the night was slipping away.* ■ [*tr.*] put (something) in a particular place or position quietly, quickly, or stealthily: *she slipped the map into her pocket.* ■ (**slip into/out of**) put on or take off (a garment) quickly and easily. ■ (**slip something in**) insert a remark smoothly or adroitly into a conversation. **2** [*tr.*] escape or get loose from (a means of restraint): *the giant balloon slipped its moorings.*

Pronunciation Key ə *ago*, *up*; ər *over*, *fur*; a *hat*; ā *ate*; ä *car*; CH *chin*; e *let*; ē *see*; e(ə)r *air*; i *fit*; ī *by*; i(ə)r *ear*; NG *sing*; ō *go*; ô *law*, *for*; oi *toy*; o͝o *good*; o͞o *goo*; ou *out*; SH *she*; TH *thin*; <u>TH</u> *then*; (h)w *why*; ZH *vision*

■ [*intr.*] (**slip out**) (of a remark) be uttered inadvertently. ■ (of a thought or fact) fail to be remembered by (one's mind or memory); elude (one's notice): *a beautiful woman's address was never likely to slip his mind.* ■ *Knitting* move (a stitch) to the other needle without knitting it. ■ release (the clutch of a motor vehicle) slightly or briefly.

▶*phrasal v.* □ **slip away** depart without saying goodbye; leave quietly or surreptitiously. ■ slowly disappear; recede or dwindle: *his ability to concentrate is slipping away.* ■ die peacefully (used euphemistically): *he lay there and quietly slipped away.* □ **slip something over on** *inf.* take advantage of (someone) by trickery. □ **slip up** *inf.* make a careless error: *they often slipped up when it came to spelling.*

▶*n.* **1** an act of sliding unintentionally for a short distance: *a single slip could send them plummeting down the mountainside.* ■ a fall to a lower level or standard: *a continued slip in house prices.* ■ relative movement of an object or surface and a solid surface in contact with it. ■ a reduction in the movement of a pulley or other mechanism due to slipping of the belt, rope, etc. ■ a sideways movement of an aircraft in flight, typically downward toward the center of curvature of a turn. ■ *Geol.* the extent of relative horizontal displacement on either side of a fault plane. **2** a minor or careless mistake: *the judge made a slip in his summing up.* **3** a woman's loose-fitting, dress- or skirt-length undergarment, suspended by shoulder straps (**full slip**) or by an elasticized waistband (**half slip**): *a silk slip.* **4** a space in which to dock a boat or ship, esp. between two wharves or piers. **5** (also **slip leash**) a leash that enables a dog to be released quickly.

▶ □ **give someone the slip** *inf.* evade or escape from someone. □ **let something slip** reveal something inadvertently in the course of a conversation: *Alex had let slip he was married.* □ **slip of the pen** (or **the tongue**) a minor mistake in writing (or speech).

slip² ▶*n.* **1** a small piece of paper, typically a form for writing on or one giving printed information: *his monthly salary slip.* ■ a long, narrow strip of a thin material such as wood. **2** a cutting taken from a plant for grafting or planting; a scion.

slip³ ▶*n.* a creamy mixture of clay, water, and typically a pigment, used esp. for decorating earthenware.

slip-case /ˈslipˌkās/ ▶*n.* a close-fitting case open at one side or end for an object such as a book.

slip-cov-er /ˈslipˌkəvər/ ▶*n.* a removable fitted cloth cover for a chair or sofa. ■ a jacket or slipcase for a book.

slip knot ▶*n.* **1** a knot that can be undone by a pull. **2** a running knot.

slip-on ▶*adj.* (esp. of shoes or clothes) having no (or few) fasteners and therefore able to be put on and taken off quickly.
▶*n.* a shoe or garment that can be easily slipped on and off.

slip-page /ˈslipij/ ▶*n.* the action or process of something slipping or subsiding; the amount or extent of this. ■ failure to meet a standard or deadline; the extent of this: *slippage on any job will entail slippage on the overall project.*

slipped disc (also **slipped disk**) ▶*n.* a vertebral disc that is displaced or partly protruding, pressing on nearby nerves and causing back pain or sciatica. See **DISK** *noun* sense 3.

slip-per /ˈslipər/ ▶*n.* a comfortable slip-on shoe that is worn indoors. ■ a light slip-on shoe, esp. one used for dancing. —**slip-pered** *adj.*

slip-per-y /ˈslipərē/ ▶*adj.* (of a surface or object) difficult to hold firmly or stand on because it is smooth, wet, or slimy: *slippery ice.* ■ (of a person) evasive and unpredictable; not to be relied on: *Martin's a slippery customer.* ■ (of a word or concept) elusive in meaning because changing according to one's point of view: *the word "intended" is a decidedly slippery one.* —**slip-per-i-ly** /ˈslipərəlē/ *adv.* —**slip-per-i-ness** *n.*

▶ □ **slippery slope** an idea or course of action that will lead to something unacceptable, wrong, or disastrous.

slip-shod /ˈslipˌSHäd/ ▶*adj.* (typically of a person or method of work) characterized by a lack of care, thought, or organization: *he'd caused many problems with his slipshod management.*

slip stitch ▶*n.* **1** (in sewing) a loose stitch joining layers of fabric and not visible externally. **2** [often as *adj.*] *Knitting* a type of stitch in which the stitches are moved from one needle to the other without being knitted.
▶*v.* (**slip-stitch**) [*tr.*] sew or knit with such stitches.

slip-stream /ˈslipˌstrēm/ ▶*n.* a current of air or water driven back by a revolving propeller or jet engine. ■ the partial vacuum created in the wake of a moving vehicle, often used by other vehicles in a race to assist in passing. ■ *figurative* an assisting force regarded as drawing something along behind something else: *when the U.S. economy booms, the rest of the world is pulled along in the slipstream.*
▶*v.* [*intrans.*] (esp. in auto racing) another term for **DRAFT** (sense 4).

■ [*trans.*] travel in the slipstream of (someone), esp. in order to overtake them.

slip-up ▶*n. inf.* a mistake or blunder.

slip-way /ˈslipˌwā/ ▶*n.* another term for **SLIP¹** (sense 4).

slit /slit/ ▶*n.* a long, narrow cut or opening.
▶*v.* (**slit-ting**; *past* **slit**) [*tr.*] make a long, narrow cut in (something): *give me the truth or I will slit your throat.* ■ cut (something) into strips. ■ (*past* **slit-ted**) form (one's eyes) into slits; squint. —**slit-ter** *n.*

slith-er /ˈsliT͟Hər/ ▶*v.* [*intr.*] move smoothly over a surface with a twisting or oscillating motion: *I spied a baby adder slithering away.*
▶*n.* a movement in such a manner: *a snakelike slither across the grass.* —**slith-er-y** *adj.*

sliv-er /ˈslivər/ ▶*n.* a small, thin, narrow piece of something cut or split off a larger piece: *a sliver of cheese.* ■ a strip of loose untwisted textile fibers produced by carding.
▶*v.* [*tr.*] [usu. as *adj.*] (**slivered**) cut or break (something) into small, thin, narrow pieces: *slivered almonds.*

slob /släb/ ▶*n. inf.* a lazy and slovenly person. ▷late 18th cent.: from Irish *slab* 'mud,' from Anglo-Irish *slab* 'ooze, sludge,' probably of Scandinavian origin. —**slob-bish** *adj.* —**slob-by** *adj.*

slob-ber /ˈsläbər/ ▶*v.* [*intr.*] have saliva dripping copiously from the mouth: *Fido tended to slobber* | [as *adj.*] (**slobbering**) *big slobbering kisses.* ■ (**slobber over**) *fig.* be excessively sentimental; show excessive enthusiasm for: *news executives slobbered over him for autographs.*
▶*n.* saliva dripping copiously from the mouth. —**slob-ber-y** *adj.*

sloe /slō/ ▶*n.* another term for **BLACKTHORN**. ■ the small bluish-black fruit of the blackthorn, with a sharp sour taste.

sloe-eyed ▶*adj.* having attractive dark, typically almond-shaped eyes.

sloe gin ▶*n.* a liqueur made by steeping sloes in gin.

slog /släg/ ▶*v.* (**slogged, slog-ging**) **1** [*intr.*] work hard over a period of time: *they were slogging away to meet a deadline.* ■ walk or move with difficulty or effort: *he slogged home through the gray slush.* **2** [*intr.*] hit forcefully and typically wildly, esp. in boxing: *the fighters were slogging away.* ■ (**slog it out**) fight or compete at length or fiercely.
▶*n.* a spell of difficult, tiring work or traveling: *it would be a hard slog back to the camp.* —**slog-ger** *n.*

slo-gan /ˈslōgən/ ▶*n.* a short and striking or memorable phrase used in advertising. ■ a motto associated with a political party or movement or other group.

sloop /slo͞op/ ▶*n.* a one-masted sailboat with a fore-and-aft mainsail and a jib.

slop /släp/ ▶*v.* (**slopped, slop-ping**) **1** [*intr.*] (of a liquid) spill or flow over the edge of a container, typically as a result of careless handling: *water slopped over the edge of the sink.* ■ [*tr.*] cause (a liquid) to spill or overflow in such a way: *in spite of his care he slopped some water.* ■ [*tr.*] apply or put (something) somewhere in a casual or careless manner: *they spent their weekend slopping on paint.* **2** [*tr.*] feed slops to (an animal, esp. a pig).
▶*n.* **1** (usu. **slops**) waste water from a kitchen, bathroom, or chamber pot that has to be emptied by hand: *sink slops.* ■ (usu. **slops**) semiliquid kitchen refuse, often used as animal food. ■ unappetizing weak, semiliquid food: *they fed us some slop in a bowl.* **2** sentimental language or material: *country music is not all commercial slop.*

slope /slōp/ ▶*n.* **1** a surface of which one end or side is at a higher level than another; a rising or falling surface: *he slithered helplessly down the slope.* ■ a difference in level or sideways position between the two ends or sides of a thing: *the roof should have a slope sufficient for proper drainage.* ■ (often **slopes**) a part of the side of a hill or mountain, esp. as a place for skiing: *a ten-minute cable-car ride delivers you to the slopes.* ■ the gradient of a graph at any point. **2** *inf., offens.* an Asian person, esp. a Vietnamese or other Southeast Asian.
▶*v.* [*intr.*] (of a surface or line) be inclined from a horizontal or vertical line; slant up or down: *the garden sloped down to a stream* | *the ceiling sloped.* ■ [*tr.*] place or arrange in such a position or inclination: *Poole sloped his shoulders.* | [as *adj.*] (**sloped**) *a sloped leather writing surface.*

slop-py /ˈsläpē/ ▶*adj.* (**slop-pi-er, slop-pi-est**) **1** (of semifluid matter) containing too much liquid; watery and disagreeable or unsatisfactory: *do not make the concrete too sloppy.* **2** careless and unsystematic; excessively casual: *your speech has always been sloppy.* ■ (of a garment) casual and loose-fitting: *wearing a sloppy sweater and jeans.* **3** (of literature or behavior) weakly or foolishly sentimental: *lovers of sloppy romance.* —**slop-pi-ly** /ˈsläpəlē/ *adv.* —**slop-pi-ness** *n.*

slosh /släSH/ ▶*v.* [*intr.*] (of liquid in a container) move irregularly with a splashing sound: *water in the boat sloshed around under our feet.* ■ (of a person) move through liquid with a splashing sound: *they sloshed up the tracks in the dank woods.* ■ [*tr.*] pour (liquid) clumsily: *she sloshed coffee into a cracked cup.*

▶ *n.* an act or sound of splashing: *the distant slosh of the washing machine in the basement.*

sloshed /släsht/ ▶ *adj. inf.* drunk: *I drank a lot of wine and got sloshed.*

Slot /slät/ ▶(**the Slot**) name given in World War II by U.S. forces to New Georgia Sound, in the central Solomon Islands. Japanese forces trying to defend Guadalcanal were seen as coming consistently down this passage from the northwest.

slot /slät/ ▶ *n.* **1** a long, narrow aperture or slit in a machine for something to be inserted: *he slid a coin into the slot of the jukebox.* ■ a groove or channel into which something fits or in which something works, such as one in the head of a screw. **2** an allotted place in an arrangement or plan such as a broadcasting schedule: *a late-night television slot.*
▶ *v.* (**slot·ted, slot·ting**) [*tr.*] place (something) into a long, narrow aperture: *the plates come in sections that can be slotted together.* ■ [*intr.*] be placed or able to be placed into such an aperture: *the processors will slot into a personal computer.* —**slot·ted** *adj.*

sloth /slôth; släth; slōth/ ▶ *n.* **1** reluctance to work or make an effort; laziness. **2** a slow-moving tropical American mammal that hangs upside down from the branches of trees using its long limbs and hooked claws. Two families: Bradypodidae (three species of **three-toed sloth**, genus *Bradypus*) and Megalonychidae (two species of **two-toed sloth**, genus *Choloepus*).

slot ma·chine ▶ *n.* a machine worked by the insertion of a coin, in particular: ■ a game machine that generates random combinations of symbols on a dial, certain combinations winning varying amounts of money for the player.

slouch /slouch/ ▶ *v.* [*intr.*] stand, move, or sit in a lazy, drooping way: *he slouched against the wall* | (**be slouched**) *he was slouched in his chair.*
▶ *n.* **1** a lazy, drooping posture or movement: *his stance was a round-shouldered slouch.* **2** *inf.* an incompetent person: *my brother was no slouch at making a buck.* **3** a downward bend of a hat brim. —**slouch·y** *adj.*

slough[1] /slou; slō/ ▶ *n.* a swamp. ■ *fig.* a situation characterized by lack of progress or activity: *the economic slough of the interwar years.* ■ a muddy side channel or inlet. —**slough·y** *adj.*

slough[2] /sləf/ ▶ *v.* [*tr.*] (of an animal, esp. a snake, or a person) cast off or shed (an old skin or dead skin): *a snake sloughs off its old skin.* ■ [*intr.*] (**slough off**) (of dead skin) drop off; be shed. —**slough·y** *adj.*

Slo·vak /'slōväk; -vak/ ▶ *n.* **1** a native or national of Slovakia, or a person of Slovak descent. **2** the West Slavic language of Slovakia, closely related to Czech.
▶ *adj.* of or relating to this people or their language.

Slo·vene /'slōvēn/ ▶ *n.* **1** a native or national of Slovenia, or a person of Slovene descent. **2** the South Slavic language of this people.
▶ *adj.* of or relating to Slovenia, its people, or their language.

slov·en·ly /'sləvənlē; 'slä-/ ▶ *adj.* (esp. of a person or their appearance) messy and dirty: *he was upbraided for his slovenly appearance.* ■ (esp. of a person or action) careless; excessively casual: *slovenly speech.* —**slov·en·li·ness** *n.*

slow /slō/ ▶ *adj.* **1** moving or operating, or designed to do so, only at a low speed; not quick or fast: *a time when diesel cars were slow and noisy.* ■ taking a long time to perform a specified action: *she was a slow reader.* ■ lasting or taking a long time: *a slow process.* ■ not allowing or intended for fast travel: *the slow lane.* ■ (of a playing field) likely to make the ball bounce or run slowly or to prevent competitors from traveling fast. **2** (of a clock or watch) showing a time earlier than the correct time: *the clock was five minutes slow.* **3** not prompt to understand, think, or learn: *he's so slow, so unimaginative.* **4** uneventful and rather dull: *a slow and mostly aimless narrative.* ■ (of business) with little activity; slack: *sales were slow.* **5** *Photog.* (of a film) needing long exposure. ■ (of a lens) having a small aperture. **6** (of a fire or oven) burning or giving off heat gently: *bake the dish in a preheated slow oven.*
▶ *adv.* at a slow pace; slowly: *the train went slower and slower* | [in *comb.*] *a slow-moving river.*
▶ *v.* [*intr.*] reduce one's speed or the speed of a vehicle or process: *the train slowed to a halt* | [*tr.*] *he slowed the car.* —**slow·ish** *adj.* —**slow·ly** *adv.* —**slow·ness** *n.*

slow·down /'slō,doun/ ▶ *n.* an act of slowing down: *a traffic slowdown in the passing lane.* ■ a decline in economic activity.

slow mo·tion ▶ *n.* the action of showing film or playing back video more slowly than it was made or recorded, so that the action appears slower than in real life: *the scene was shown in slow motion.*

slow-worm ▶ *n.* a small snakelike Eurasian legless lizard (*Anguis fragilis*, family Anguidae) that is typically brownish or copper-colored and that gives birth to live young.

SLR ▶ *abbr.* ■ self-loading rifle. ■ single-lens reflex.

sludge /sləj/ ▶ *n.* thick, soft, soft mud or a similar viscous mixture of liquid and solid components, esp. the product of an industrial or refining process. ■ dirty oil, esp. in the sump of an internal combustion engine. —**sludg·y** *adj.*

slue ▶ *v.* & *n.* variant spelling of **SLEW**[1].

slug[1] /sləg/ ▶ *n.* **1** a tough-skinned terrestrial mollusk (order Stylommatophora, class Gastropoda) that typically lacks a shell and secretes a film of mucus for protection. It can be a serious plant pest. **2** a slow, lazy person; a sluggard. **3** an amount of an alcoholic drink, typically liquor, that is gulped or poured: *he took a slug of whiskey.* **4** an elongated, typically rounded piece of metal. ■ a counterfeit coin; a token. ■ a bullet, esp. one of lead. ■ a missile for an air gun. ■ a line of type in Linotype printing. ■ *Printing* a metal bar used in spacing.
▶ *v.* (**slugged, slugging**) [*tr.*] drink (something, typically alcohol) in a large draft; swig.

slug[2] *inf.* ▶ *v.* (**slugged, slug·ging**) [*tr.*] strike (someone) with a hard blow: *he was the one who'd get slugged.* ■ (**slug it out**) settle a dispute or contest by fighting or competing fiercely: *they went outside to slug it out.*
▶ *n.* a hard blow. —**slug·ger** *n.*

slug·gard /'sləgərd/ ▶ *n.* a lazy, sluggish person. —**slug·gard·li·ness** *n.* —**slug·gard·ly** *adj.*

slug·gish /'sləgish/ ▶ *adj.* slow-moving or inactive: *a sluggish stream.* ■ lacking energy or alertness: *Alex woke late feeling tired and sluggish.* ■ slow to respond or make progress: *the car had been sluggish all morning.* —**slug·gish·ly** *adv.* —**slug·gish·ness** *n.*

sluice /slōōs/ ▶ *n.* **1** (also **sluice gate**) a sliding gate or other device for controlling the flow of water, esp. one in a lock gate. ■ (also **sluice·way** /-,wā/) an artificial water channel for carrying off overflow or surplus water. ■ (in gold mining) a channel or trough constructed with grooves into which a current of water is directed in order to separate gold from the sand or gravel containing it. **2** an act of rinsing or showering with water: *a sluice with cold water.*
▶ *v.* [*tr.*] wash or rinse freely with a stream or shower of water: *crews sluiced down the decks of their ship.* ■ [*intr.*] (of water) pour, flow, or shower freely: *the waves sluiced over them.*

slum /sləm/ ▶ *n.* a squalid and overcrowded urban street or district inhabited by very poor people. ■ a house or building unfit for human habitation.
▶ *v.* (**slummed, slum·ming**) [*intr.*] *inf.* spend time at a lower social level than one's own through curiosity or for charitable purposes: *rich tourists slumming among the quaintly dangerous natives.* ■ (**slum it**) put up with conditions that are less comfortable or of a lower quality than one is used to. —**slum·mer** *n.* —**slum·mi·ness** *n.* —**slum·my** *adj.*

slum·ber /'sləmbər/ *poetic/lit.* ▶ *v.* [*intr.*] sleep: *Sleeping Beauty slumbered.*
▶ *n.* (often **slumbers**) a sleep: *scaring folk from their slumbers.* —**slum·ber·er** *n.* —**slum·brous** /-brəs/ (also **slum·ber·ous** /-bərəs/) *adj.*

slump /sləmp/ ▶ *v.* [*intr.*] **1** sit, lean, or fall heavily and limply, esp. with a bent back: *she slumped against the cushions* | (**be slumped**) *Denis was slumped in his seat.* **2** undergo a sudden severe or prolonged fall in price, value, or amount: *land prices slumped.* ■ fail or decline substantially: *the Giants slumped to an 8–8 record.*
▶ *n.* a sudden severe or prolonged fall in the price, value, or amount of something: *a slump in annual profits.* ■ a prolonged period of abnormally low economic activity, typically bringing widespread unemployment. ■ a period of substantial failure or decline: *the organization's recent slump.* ▷late 17th cent. (in the sense 'fall into a bog'): probably imitative and related to Norwegian *slumpe* 'to fall.' —**slump·y** *adj.*

slung /sləNG/ ▶ past and past participle of **SLING**[1].

slunk /sləNGk/ ▶ past and past participle of **SLINK**.

slur /slər/ ▶ *v.* (**slurred, slur·ring**) [*tr.*] **1** speak (words or speech) indistinctly so that the sounds run into one another: *he was slurring his words like a drunk.* ■ [*intr.*] (of words or speech) be spoken in this way: *his speech was beginning to slur.* ■ pass over (a fact or aspect) so as to conceal or minimize it: *essential attributes are being slurred over or ignored.* **2** *Mus.* perform (a group of two or more notes) legato: [as *adj.*] (**slurred**) *a group of slurred notes.* ■ mark (notes) with a slur. **3** make damaging or insulting insinuations or allegations about: *try and slur the integrity of the police to secure an acquittal.*
▶ *n.* **1** an insinuation or allegation about someone that is likely to insult them or damage their reputation: *the comments were a slur on the staff* | *a racial slur.* **2** an act of speaking indistinctly so that sounds or words run into one another or a tendency to speak in such a way: *there was a mean slur in his voice.* **3** *Mus.* a curved line used to show that a

---

group of two or more notes is to be sung to one syllable or played or sung legato.

slurp /slərp/ ▶ *v.* [*tr.*] eat or drink (something) with a loud sloppy sucking noise: *she slurped her coffee* | [*intr.*] *he slurped noisily from a wine cup.*
▶ *n.* a loud sucking sound made while eating or drinking: *she drank it down with a loud slurp.* —**slurp·y** *adj.*

slur·ry /'slərē/ ▶ *n.* (*pl.* **-ries**) a semiliquid mixture, typically of fine particles of manure, cement, or coal suspended in water.

slush /sləsh/ ▶ *n.* **1** partially melted snow or ice: *the snow was turning into brown slush in the gutters.* ■ watery mud. **2** *inf.* excessive sentiment: *the slush of Hollywood's romantic fifties films.*

slush·y /'sləshē/ ▶ *adj.* (**slush·i·er**, **slush·i·est**) **1** resembling, consisting of, or covered with slush: *slushy snow.* **2** *inf.* excessively sentimental: *slushy novels.* —**slush·i·ness** *n.*

slut /slət/ ▶ *n.* a slovenly or promiscuous woman. —**slut·tish** *adj.* —**slut·tish·ness** *n.*

sly /slī/ ▶ *adj.* (**sly·er**, **sly·est**) having or showing a cunning and deceitful nature: *her sly personality.* ■ (of a remark, glance, or facial expression) showing in an insinuating way that one has some secret knowledge that may be harmful or embarrassing: *his sly grin.* ■ (of an action) surreptitious: *a sly sip of water.* —**sly·ly** (also **sli·ly**) *adv.* —**sly·ness** *n.*
▶ □ **on the sly** in a secretive fashion: *she was drinking on the sly.*

SM ▶ *abbr.* ■ service mark. ■ sadomasochism. ■ sergeant major.

Sm ▶ *symb.* the chemical element samarium.

S-M (also **s-m**, **S/M**, **s/m**) ▶ *abbr.* ■ (also **S&M**) sadomasochism. ■ sadomasochistic.

smack¹ /smak/ ▶ *n.* a sharp slap or blow, typically one given with the palm of the hand: *she gave Mark a smack across the face.* ■ a loud, sharp sound made by such a blow or a similar action: *she closed the ledger with a smack.* ■ a loud kiss: *I was saluted with two hearty smacks on my cheeks.*
▶ *v.* [*tr.*] strike (someone or something), typically with the palm of the hand and as a punishment: *Jessica smacked his face quite hard.* ■ [*tr.*] smash, drive, or put forcefully into or onto something: *he smacked a fist into the palm of a black-gloved hand.* ■ part (one's lips) noisily in eager anticipation or enjoyment of food, drink, or other pleasures.
▶ *adv. inf.* **1** in a sudden and violent way: *I ran smack into the back of a parked truck.* **2** exactly; precisely: *our mother's house was smack in the middle of the city.*

smack² ▶ *v.* [*intr.*] (**smack of**) have a flavor of; taste of: *the tea smacked of peppermint.* ■ suggest the presence or effects of (something wrong or unpleasant): *the whole thing smacks of a cover-up.*
▶ *n.* (**a smack of**) a flavor or taste of: *anything with even a modest smack of hops dries the palate.* ■ a trace or suggestion of: *I hear the smack of collusion between them.*

smack³ ▶ *n. inf.* heroin.

smack·er /'smakər/ (also **smack·er·oo** /ˌsmakə'rōō/) ▶ *n. inf.* **1** a dollar: *it set me back fifteen smackers.* **2** a loud kiss.

small /smôl/ ▶ *adj.* of a size that is less than normal or usual: *the room was small and quiet.* ■ not great in amount, number, strength, or power: *a small amount of money.* ■ not fully grown or developed; young: *as a small boy, he spent his days either reading or watching TV.* ■ used as the first letter of a word that has both a general and a specific use to show that in this case the general use is intended: *I meant "catholic" with a small c.* ■ insignificant; unimportant: *these are small points.* ■ (of a voice) lacking strength and confidence: *"I'm scared," she said in a small voice.* ■ little; hardly any: *the captain had been paying small attention.* ■ (of a business or its owner) operating on a modest scale: *a small farmer.*
▶ *adv.* into small pieces: *the okra cut up small.* ■ in a small size: *you shouldn't write so small.* —**small·ish** *adj.* —**small·ness** *n.*
▶ □ **the small of the back** the part of a person's back where the spine curves toward the front at the level of the waist. □ **small wonder** not very surprising: *it's small wonder that her emotions had seesawed.*

small arms ▶ *pl. n.* portable firearms, esp. rifles, pistols, and light machine guns.

small-claims court ▶ *n.* a local court in which claims for small sums of money can be heard and decided quickly and cheaply, without legal representation.

small fry ▶ *pl. n.* young fish, animals, or children. ■ insignificant people or things: *high officials walked, but the small fry got busted.*

small in·tes·tine ▶ *n.* the part of the intestine that runs between the stomach and the large intestine; the duodenum, jejunum, and ileum collectively.

small-mind·ed ▶ *adj.* having or showing rigid opinions or a narrow outlook; petty. —**small-mind·ed·ly** *adv.* —**small-mind·ed·ness** *n.*

small·pox /'smôlˌpäks/ ▶ *n.* an acute contagious viral disease, with fever

and pustules usually leaving permanent scars. It was effectively eradicated through vaccination by 1979. Also called VARIOLA.

small print ▶ *n.* another term for FINE PRINT.

small-scale ▶ *adj.* of limited size or extent: *a small-scale research project.*

small talk ▶ *n.* polite conversation about unimportant or uncontroversial matters, esp. as engaged in on social occasions: *propriety required that he face these people and make small talk.*

small-time ▶ *adj. inf.* unimportant; minor: *a small-time gangster.* —**small-tim·er** *n.*

smart /smärt/ ▶ *adj.* **1** *inf.* having or showing a quick-witted intelligence: *if he was that smart he would never have been tricked.* ■ (of a device) capable of independent and seemingly intelligent action: *hi-tech smart weapons.* ■ showing impertinence by making clever or sarcastic remarks: *don't get smart or I'll whack you one.* **2** (of a person) clean, neat, and well-dressed: *you look very smart.* ■ (of clothes) attractively neat and stylish: *a smart blue skirt.* ■ (of a thing) bright and fresh in appearance: *a smart green van.* ■ (of a person or place) fashionable and upscale: *a smart restaurant.* **3** quick; brisk: *I gave him a smart salute.* ■ painfully severe: *a dog that snaps is given a smart blow.*
▶ *v.* [*intr.*] (of a wound or part of the body) cause a sharp, stinging pain: *the wound was smarting* | [as *adj.*] (**smarting**) *Susan rubbed her smarting eyes.* ■ (of a person) feel upset and annoyed: *chiefs of staff are still smarting from the government's cuts.*
▶ *n.* **1** (**smarts**) *inf.* intelligence; acumen: *I don't think I have the smarts for it.* **2** sharp stinging pain: *the smart of the recent blood-raw cuts.* ■ *archaic* mental pain or suffering: *sorrow is the effect of smart, and smart the effect of faith.*
▶ *adv. archaic* in a quick or brisk manner: *it is better for tenants to be compelled to pay up smart.* —**smart·ing·ly** *adv.* —**smart·ly** *adv.* —**smart·ness** *n.*

smart al·eck (also **smart al·ec**) *inf.* ▶ *n.* a person considered irritating because they know a great deal or always have a clever answer to a question.
▶ *adj.* having or showing an irritating, know-it-all attitude: *a smart-aleck answer.* —**smart-al·eck·y** *adj.*

smart-ass ▶ *n. inf.* another term for SMART ALECK.

smart bomb ▶ *n.* a radio-controlled or laser-guided bomb, often with a built-in computer.

smart·en /'smärtn/ ▶ *v.* [*tr.*] make (something) smarter in appearance: *he spent part of the proceeds on smartening up his office.* ■ [*intr.*] (**smarten up**) acquire more common sense; behave more wisely: *if you don't smarten up soon, you'll find yourself out on the street.* ■ [*intr.*] (**smarten up**) make one's appearance smarter: *I'd like to smarten up and shave.*

smart growth ▶ *n.* planned economic and community development that attempts to curb urban sprawl and worsening environmental conditions.

smart·y /'smärtē/ ▶ *n.* (*pl.* **smart·ies**) *inf.* **1** a know-it-all or a smart aleck. **2** *dated* a smartly dressed person; a member of the smart set.

smart·y-pants ▶ *n.* another term for SMARTY (sense 1).

smash /smash/ ▶ *v.* **1** [*tr.*] violently break (something) into pieces: *the thief smashed a window to get into the car* | *gone are the days when he smashed up hotels.* ■ [*intr.*] be violently broken into pieces; shatter: *the glass ball smashed instantly on the pavement.* ■ violently knock down or crush inward: *soldiers smashed down doors.* ■ crash and severely damage (a vehicle): *my Volvo's been smashed up.* ■ hit or attack (someone) very violently: *Donald smashed him over the head.* ■ easily or comprehensively beat (a record): *he smashed the course record.* ■ completely defeat, destroy, or foil (something regarded as hostile or dangerous): *a deliberate attempt to smash the union movement.* **2** [*intr.*] move so as to hit or collide with something with great force and impact: *their plane smashed into a mountainside.* ■ [*tr.*] (in sports) strike (the ball) or score (a goal, run, etc.) with great force: *he smashed that one into the bleachers for another two-run homer.* ■ [*tr.*] (in tennis, badminton, and similar sports) strike (the ball or shuttlecock) downward with a hard overhand stroke.
▶ *n.* **1** an act or sound of something smashing: *he heard the smash of glass.* ■ a violent collision or impact between vehicles: *a car smash.* ■ a violent blow: *a forearm smash.* ■ a stroke in tennis, badminton, and similar sports in which the ball is hit downward with a hard overhand volley. ■ *inf., dated* a bankruptcy or financial failure. **2** (also **smash hit**) *inf.* a very successful song, film, show, or performer: *a box-office smash.*
▷ early 18th cent. (as a noun): probably imitative, representing a blend of words such as *smack*, *smite* with *bash*, *mash*, etc.

smash·ing /'smashing/ ▶ *adj. inf., chiefly Brit.* excellent; wonderful: *you look smashing!* —**smash·ing·ly** *adv.*

smash-up ▶ *n. inf.* a violent collision, esp. of cars.

smat·ter·ing /'smatəring/ (also **smat·ter**) ▶ *n.* a slight superficial knowledge of a language or subject: *Edward had only a smattering of Spanish.* ■ a small amount of something: *a smattering of* snow.

smear /smi(ə)r/ ▶*v.* [*tr.*] coat or mark (something) messily or carelessly with a greasy or sticky substance: *his face was smeared with dirt.* ■ [*tr.*] spread (a greasy, oily, or sticky substance) over something: *Barbara smeared peanut butter on a slice of bread.* ■ *fig.* damage the reputation of (someone) by false accusations; slander: *someone was trying to smear her by faking letters.* ■ messily blur the outline of (something such as writing or paint); smudge: *her lipstick was smeared.*
▶*n.* a mark or streak of a greasy or sticky substance: *there was an oil smear on his jacket.* ■ *fig.* a false accusation intended to damage someone's reputation: *the media were indulging in unwarranted smears.* ■ a sample of material spread thinly on a microscope slide for examination, typically for medical diagnosis: *most of the smears were positive.* —**smear·y** *adj.* —**smear·er** *n.*

smeg·ma /'smegmə/ ▶*n.* a sebaceous secretion in the folds of the skin, esp. under a man's foreskin.

smell /smel/ ▶*n.* the faculty or power of perceiving odors or scents by means of the organs in the nose: *a highly developed sense of smell | dogs locate the bait by smell.* ■ a quality in something that is perceived by this faculty; an odor or scent: *lingering kitchen smells | a smell of coffee.* ■ an unpleasant odor: *twenty-seven cats lived there—you can imagine the smell!* ■ an act of inhaling in order to ascertain an odor or scent: *have a smell of this.*
▶*v.* (*past* and *past part.* **smelled** or **smelt** /smelt/) **1** [*tr.*] perceive or detect the odor or scent of (something): *I think I can smell something burning.* ■ sniff at (something) in order to perceive or detect its odor or scent: *the dogs smell each other.* ■ [*intr.*] have or use a sense of smell: *becoming deaf or blind or unable to smell.* ■ (**smell something out**) detect or discover something by the faculty of smell: *his nose can smell out an animal from ten miles away.* ■ detect or suspect (something) by means of instinct or intuition: *he can smell trouble long before it gets serious | he can smell out weakness in others.* **2** [*intr.*] emit an odor or scent of a specified kind: *it smelled like cough medicine | the food smelled and tasted good | [as adj., in comb.] (-smelling) pungent-smelling food.* ■ have a strong or unpleasant odor: *if I don't get a bath soon I'll start to smell | it smells in here.* ■ appear in a certain way; be suggestive of something: *it smells like a hoax to me.* —**smell·a·ble** *adj.* —**smell·er** *n.*
▶ □ **smell blood** discern weakness or vulnerability in an opponent. □ **smell a rat** *inf.* suspect trickery or deception. □ **smell the roses** *inf.* enjoy or appreciate what is often ignored. □ **smell something up** permeate an area with a bad smell: *he smelled up the whole house.*

smell·ing salts ▶*pl. n. chiefly hist.* a pungent substance sniffed as a restorative in cases of faintness or headache, typically consisting of ammonium carbonate mixed with perfume.

smell·y /'smelē/ ▶*adj.* (**smell·i·er**, **smell·i·est**) having a strong or unpleasant smell: *smelly feet.* —**smell·i·ness** *n.*

smelt[1] /smelt/ ▶*v.* [*tr.*] [often as *n.*] (**smelting**) extract (metal) from its ore by a process involving heating and melting: *tin smelting.* ■ extract a metal from (ore) in this way. —**smelt·er** *n.*

smelt[2] ▶ past and past participle of SMELL.

smelt[3] ▶*n.* (*pl.* same or **smelts** /smelts/) a small silvery food fish (*Osmerus* and other genera, family Osmeridae) that lives in both marine and fresh water and is sometimes fished commercially.

smid·gen /'smijin/ (also **smid·geon** or **smid·gin**) ▶*n. inf.* a small amount of something: *add a smidgen of cayenne.*

smi·lax /'smīlaks/ ▶*n.* **1** a widely distributed climbing shrub (genus *Smilax*) of the lily family, with hooks and tendrils. Several South American species yield sarsaparilla from their roots, and some are cultivated as ornamentals. **2** a climbing asparagus (*Asparagus* (or **Myrsiphyllum**) *asparagoides*), the decorative foliage of which is used by florists.

smile /smīl/ ▶*v.* [*intr.*] form one's features into a pleased, kind, or amused expression, typically with the corners of the mouth turned up and the front teeth exposed: *she was smiling | he smiled at Shelley | [as adj.] (smiling) smiling faces.* ■ [*tr.*] express (a feeling) with such an expression: *he smiled his admiration of the great stone circle.* ■ [*tr.*] give (a smile) of a specified kind: *Guy smiled a grim smile.* ■ (**smile at/on/upon**) regard favorably or indulgently: *at first fortune smiled on him.* ■ [often as *adj.*] (**smiling**) *poetic/lit.* (esp. of a landscape) have a bright or pleasing aspect: *smiling groves and terraces.*
▶*n.* a pleased, kind, or amused facial expression, typically with the corners of the mouth turned up and the front teeth exposed: *he flashed his most winning smile | she greeted us all with a smile.* —**smil·er** *n.* —**smil·ing·ly** *adv.*
▶ □ **be all smiles** *inf.* (of a person) look very cheerful and pleased, esp. in contrast to a previous mood. □ **come up smiling** *inf.* recover from adversity and cheerfully face what is to come.

smirch /smərCH/ ▶*v.* [*tr.*] make (something) dirty; soil: *the window was smirched by heat and smoke.* ■ *fig.* discredit (a person or their reputation); taint: *I am not accustomed to having my honor smirched.*
▶*n.* a dirty mark or stain. ■ *fig.* a blot on someone's character; a flaw.

smirk /smərk/ ▶*v.* [*intr.*] smile in an irritatingly smug, conceited, or silly way: *Dr. Ali smirked in triumph.*
▶*n.* a smug, conceited, or silly smile: *Gloria pursed her mouth in a self-satisfied smirk.* —**smirk·er** *n.* —**smirk·i·ly** /-kəlē/ *adv.* —**smirk·ing·ly** *adv.* —**smirk·y** *adj.*

smit /smit/ *archaic* ▶ past participle of SMITE.

smite /smīt/ ▶*v.* (*past* **smote** /smōt/; *past part.* **smit·ten** /'smitn/) [*tr.*] *poetic/lit.* strike with a firm blow: *he smites the water with his sword.* ■ *archaic* defeat or conquer (a people or land): *he may smite our enemies.* ■ (usu. **be smitten**) *fig.* (esp. of disease) attack or affect severely: *various people had been smitten with untimely summer flu.* ■ (**be smitten**) be strongly attracted to someone or something: *she was so smitten with the boy.*
▶*n. archaic* a heavy blow or stroke with a weapon or the hand. —**smit·er** *n.*

smith /smiTH/ ▶*n.* a worker in metal. ■ short for BLACKSMITH.
▶*v.* [*tr.*] treat (metal) by heating, hammering, and forging it: *tin-bronze was cast into ingots before being smithed into bracelets.*

smith·er·eens /ˌsmiTHə'rēnz/ ▶*pl. n. inf.* small pieces: *a grenade blew him to smithereens.*

smith·y /'smiTHē/ ▶*n.* (*pl.* **smith·ies**) a blacksmith's workshop; a forge. ■ a blacksmith.

smit·ten /'smitn/ ▶ past participle of SMITE.

smock /smäk/ ▶*n.* a loose dress or blouse, with the upper part closely gathered in smocking. ■ a loose garment worn over one's clothes to protect them: *an artist's smock.* ■ (also **smock-frock**) *hist.* a smocked linen overgarment worn by an agricultural worker.
▶*v.* [*tr.*] [usu. as *adj.*] (**smocked**) decorate (something) with smocking: *smocked dresses.*

smock·ing /'smäkiNG/ ▶*n.* decoration on a garment created by gathering a section of the material into tight pleats and holding them together with parallel stitches in an ornamental pattern.

smog /smäg/ ▶*n.* fog or haze combined with smoke and other atmospheric pollutants. —**smog·gy** *adj.*

smoke /smōk/ ▶*n.* a visible suspension of carbon or other particles in air, typically one emitted from a burning substance: *bonfire smoke.* ■ an act of smoking tobacco: *I'm dying for a smoke.* ■ *inf.* a cigarette or cigar.
▶*v.* **1** [*intr.*] emit smoke or visible vapor: *heat the oil until it just smokes | [as adj.] (smoking) they huddled around his smoking fire in the winter damp.* ■ inhale and exhale the smoke of tobacco or a drug: *Janine was sitting at the kitchen table smoking | [as n.] (smoking) the effect of smoking on health | [tr.] he smoked forty cigarettes a day.* **2** [*tr.*] [often as *adj.*] (**smoked**) cure or preserve (meat or fish) by exposure to smoke: *smoked salmon.* ■ treat (glass) so as to darken it: *the smoked glass of his lenses.* ■ fumigate, cleanse, or purify by exposure to smoke. ■ subdue (insects, esp. bees) by exposing them to smoke. ■ (**smoke someone/something out**) drive someone or something out of a place by using smoke: *we will fire the roof and smoke him out.* ■ (**smoke someone out**) *fig.* force someone to make something known: *as the press smokes him out on other human rights issues, he will be revealed as a social conservative.* **3** [*intr.*] be aggressive or energetic: [as *adj.*] (**smoking**) *the band responds with a smoking first set.* ■ [*tr.*] kill (someone) by shooting. ■ defeat overwhelmingly in a fight or contest. **4** [*tr.*] *archaic* make fun of (someone): *we baited her and smoked her.* —**smok·a·ble** (also **smoke·a·ble**) *adj.*
▶ □ **blow smoke** try to mislead or threaten someone by giving false or exaggerated information: *the coach has been blowing smoke for the past three years about our program.* □ **go up in smoke** *inf.* be destroyed by fire. ■ *fig.* (of a plan) come to nothing: *more than one dream is about to go up in smoke.* □ **smoke and mirrors** the obscuring or embellishing the truth of a situation with misleading or irrelevant information: *the budget process is an exercise in smoke and mirrors.* □ **smoke like a chimney** smoke tobacco incessantly.

smoke·less /'smōkləs/ ▶*adj.* producing or emitting little or no smoke: *smokeless fuel.*

smoke screen (also **smoke·screen**) ▶*n.* a cloud of smoke created to conceal military operations. ■ *fig.* a ruse designed to disguise someone's real intentions or activities: *he tried to create a smokescreen by quibbling about the statistics.*

Pronunciation Key ə *ago,* up; ər *over,* fur; a *hat;* ā *ate;* ä *car;* CH *chin;* e *let;* ē *see;* e(ə)r *air;* i *fit;* ī *by;* i(ə)r *ear;* NG *sing;* ō *go;* ô *law, for;* oi *toy;* o͞o *good;* o͞o *goo;* ou *out;* SH *she;* TH *thin;* TH *then;* (h)w *why;* ZH *vision*

smoke·stack /'smōk,stak/ ▸*n.* a chimney or funnel for discharging smoke from a locomotive, ship, factory, etc. and helping to induce a draft. ▪ [as *adj.*] pertaining to heavy industry: *America's smokestack cities and blue-collar suburbs.*

smok·y /'smōkē/ ▸*adj.* (**smok·i·er, smok·i·est**) filled with or smelling of smoke: *a smoky office.* ▪ producing or obscured by a great deal of smoke: *smoky factory chimneys.* ▪ having the taste or aroma of smoked food: *smoky bacon.* ▪ like smoke in color or appearance: *smoky eyes.* —**smok·i·ly** /-kəlē/ *adv.* —**smok·i·ness** *n.*

smol·der /'smōldər/ ▸*v.* [*intr.*] burn slowly with smoke but no flame: *the bonfire still smoldered, the smoke drifting over the paddock.* ▪ show or feel barely suppressed anger, hatred, or another powerful emotion: *Anna smoldered with indignation* | [as *adj.*] (**smoldering**) *he met her smoldering eyes.* ▪ exist in a suppressed or concealed state: *the controversy smoldered on for several years* | [as *adj.*] (**smoldering**) *smoldering rage.*
▸*n.* smoke coming from a fire that is burning slowly without a flame: *the last acrid smolder of his cigarette.* —**smol·der·ing·ly** *adv.*

smolt /smōlt/ ▸*n.* a young salmon (or trout) after the parr stage, when it becomes silvery and migrates to the sea for the first time.

smooch /smōōCH/ *inf.* ▸*v.* [*intr.*] kiss and cuddle amorously: *the young lovers smooched in their car.*
▸*n.* a kiss or a spell of amorous kissing and cuddling: *a slurpy smooch on the ear.* —**smooch·er** *n.* —**smooch·y** *adj.* (**smooch·i·er, smooch·i·est**).

smooth /smōōTH/ ▸*adj.* **1** having an even and regular surface or consistency; free from perceptible projections, lumps, or indentations: *smooth flat rocks.* ▪ (of a person's face or skin) not wrinkled, pitted, or hairy: *a smooth skin tans more easily.* ▪ (of a liquid) with an even consistency; without lumps: *cook gently until the sauce is smooth.* ▪ (of the sea or another body of water) without heavy waves; calm: *the smooth summer sea.* ▪ (of movement) without jerks: *the trucks gave a smooth ride* | *graphics are excellent, with fast, smooth scrolling.* ▪ (of an action, event, or process) without problems or difficulties: *the group's expansion into the U.S. market was not quite so smooth.* **2** (of food or drink) without harshness or bitterness: *a lovely, smooth, very fruity wine.* ▪ (of a person or their manner, actions, or words) suavely charming in a way considered to be unctuous: *his voice was infuriatingly smooth.*
▸*v.* [*tr.*] give (something) a flat, regular surface or appearance by running one's hand over it: *she smoothed out the newspaper.* ▪ rub off the rough edges of (something): *you can use sandpaper to smooth the joint.* ▪ deal successfully with (a problem, difficulty, or perceived fault): *these doctrinal disputes were smoothed over.* ▪ free (a course of action) from difficulties or problems: *a conference would be held to smooth the way for the establishment of the provisional government.* ▪ modify (a graph, curve, etc.) so as to lessen irregularities: *values are collected over a long period of time so that fluctuations are smoothed out.*
▸*adv. archaic* in a way that is without difficulties: *the course of true love never did run smooth.* —**smooth·a·ble** *adj.* —**smooth·er** *n.* —**smooth·ish** *adj.* —**smooth·ly** *adv.* —**smooth·ness** *n.*

smooth·bore /'smōōTH,bôr/ ▸*n.* [often as *adj.*] a gun with an unrifled barrel: *smoothbore muskets.*

smooth·ie /'smōōTHē/ ▸*n.* **1** *inf.* a man with a smooth, suave manner: *a smoothie with an eye for a pretty girl.* **2** a thick, smooth drink of fresh fruit puréed with milk, yogurt, or ice cream.

smooth talk ▸*n.* charming or flattering language, esp. when used to persuade someone to do something.
▸*v.* (**smooth-talk**) [*tr.*] use such language to (someone), esp. to persuade them to do something: *don't try to smooth-talk me* | [as *adj.*] (**smooth-talking**) *a smooth-talking salesman.* —**smooth talk·er** *n.*

smooth tongue ▸*n.* the ability or tendency to use insincere flattery or persuasion: *your smooth tongue could even turn your mistakes to your advantage.* —**smooth-tongued** *adj.*

smor·gas·bord /'smôrgəs,bôrd/ ▸*n.* a buffet offering a variety of hot and cold meats, salads, hors d'oeuvres, etc. ▪ *fig.* a wide range of something; a variety: *the album is a smorgasbord of different musical styles.*

smor·zan·do /smôrt'sändō/ *Mus.* ▸*adv. & adj.* (esp. as a direction) dying away.

smote /smōt/ ▸ past of **SMITE**.

smoth·er /'sməTHər/ ▸*v.* [*tr.*] kill (someone) by covering their nose and mouth so that they suffocate. ▪ extinguish (a fire) by covering it. ▪ (**smother someone/something in/with**) cover someone or something entirely with: *rich orange sorbets smothered in fluffy whipped cream* | *fig. he smothered her with kisses.* ▪ make (someone) feel trapped and oppressed by acting in an overly protective manner toward them: *it's time for you to leave the house—she'll smother you if you remain.* ▪ suppress (a feeling or an action): *she smothered a sigh.* ▪ (in sports) stop the motion of (the ball or a shot) by falling on it and covering it: *the goalkeeper was able to smother the ball.* ▪ cook in a covered container, typically with a sauce and vegetables on top: [as *adj.*] (**smothered**) *smothered fried chicken.*
▸*n.* a mass of something that stifles or obscures: *all this vanished in a smother of foam.* —**smoth·er·y** *adj.*

SMTP ▸*abbr. Comput.* simple mail transfer protocol, a data transmission format used to send and receive e-mail.

smudge[1] /sməj/ ▸*n.* a blurred or smeared mark on the surface of something: *a smudge of blood on the floor.* ▪ an indistinct or blurred view or image: *the low smudge of hills on the horizon.*
▸*v.* [*tr.*] cause (something) to become messily smeared by rubbing it: *she dabbed her eyes, careful not to smudge her makeup.* ▪ [*intr.*] become smeared when rubbed: *mascaras that smudge or flake around the eyes.* ▪ make blurred or indistinct: *the photograph had been smudged by the photocopier and was by no means as clear as the original.* —**smudge·less** *adj.*

smudge[2] ▸*n.* a smoky outdoor fire that is lit to keep off insects or protect plants against frost.

smudg·y /'sməjē/ ▸*adj.* (**smudg·i·er, smudg·i·est**) smeared or blurred from being smudged: *a smudgy photograph.* —**smudg·i·ly** /-jəlē/ *adv.* —**smudg·i·ness** *n.*

smug /sməg/ ▸*adj.* (**smug·ger, smug·gest**) having or showing an excessive pride in oneself or one's achievements: *he was feeling smug after his win.* ▷mid 16th cent. (originally in the sense 'neat, spruce'): from Low German *smuk* 'pretty.' —**smug·ly** *adv.* —**smug·ness** *n.*

smug·gle /'sməgəl/ ▸*v.* [*tr.*] move (goods) illegally into or out of a country: *he's been smuggling cigarettes from Gibraltar into Spain* | [as *n.*] (**smuggling**) *cocaine smuggling has increased alarmingly.* ▪ [*tr.*] convey (someone or something) somewhere secretly and illicitly: *he smuggled out a message.* —**smug·gler** /'sməg(ə)lər/ *n.*

smut /smət/ ▸*n.* **1** a small flake of soot or other dirt. ▪ a mark or smudge made by such a flake. **2** a disease of grains in which parts of the ear change to black powder, caused by a fungus of the order Ustilaginales. **3** obscene or lascivious talk, writing, or pictures. —**smut·ti·ly** /-təlē/ *adv.* —**smut·ti·ness** *n.* —**smut·ty** *adj.*

Sn ▸*symb.* the chemical element tin.

snack /snak/ ▸*n.* a small amount of food eaten between meals. ▪ a light meal that is eaten in a hurry or in a casual manner.
▸*v.* [*intr.*] eat a snack: *she likes to snack on yogurt.*

snack bar ▸*n.* a place where snacks are sold.

snaf·fle /'snafəl/ ▸*n.* (also **snaffle bit**) (on a bridle) a simple bit, typically a jointed one, used with a single set of reins. ▪ (also **snaffle bridle**) a bridle with such a bit.

sna·fu /sna'fōō/ *inf.* ▸*n.* a confused or chaotic state; a mess: *an enormous amount of my time was devoted to untangling snafus.*
▸*adj.* in utter confusion or chaos: *our refrigeration plant is snafu.*
▸*v.* [*tr.*] throw (a situation) into chaos: *you ignored his orders and snafued everything.*

snag /snag/ ▸*n.* **1** an unexpected or hidden obstacle or drawback: *the picture's U.S. release hit a snag.* **2** a sharp, angular, or jagged projection: *keep an emery board handy in case of nail snags.* ▪ a rent or tear in fabric caused by such a projection. **3** a dead tree.
▸*v.* (**snagged, snag·ging**) [*tr.*] catch or tear (something) on a projection: *thorns snagged his sweater.* ▪ [*intr.*] become caught on a projection: *radio aerials snagged on bushes and branches.* ▪ *inf.* catch or obtain (someone or something): *it's the first time they've snagged the star for a photo.* —**snag·gy** *adj.*

snail /snāl/ ▸*n.* a mollusk (class Gastropoda) with a single spiral shell into which the whole body can be withdrawn. ▪ (in metaphorical use) any person or thing that moves exceedingly slowly. —**snail·like** /-,līk/ *adj.*

snake /snāk/ ▸*n.* **1** a long limbless reptile (suborder Ophidia or Serpentes) that has no eyelids, and jaws that are capable of considerable extension. Some snakes have a venomous bite. ▪ (in general use) a limbless lizard or amphibian. **2** (also **snake in the grass**) a treacherous or deceitful person. **3** (in full **plumber's snake**) a long flexible wire for clearing obstacles in pipes.
▸*v.* [*intr.*] move or extend with the twisting motion of a snake: *a rope snaked down.* —**snake·like** /-,līk/ *adj.*

snake charm·er ▸*n.* an entertainer who appears to make snakes move by playing music.

snake oil ▸*n. inf.* a substance with no real medicinal value sold as a remedy for all diseases: *some kelp products are snake oil, but the good ones promote plant growth* | *fig. the president's foreign policy is snake oil.*

snake pit ▸*n.* a pit containing poisonous snakes. ▪ *fig.* a scene of vicious behavior or ruthless competition: *the literary snake pits of New York.* ▪ *fig.* a place of overcrowded squalor, esp. a poorly run mental hospital: *the* *clinic opened in 1949, when most drug and alcohol sanitariums were still snake pits.*

snak·y /'snākē/ ▶*adj.* (**snak·i·er, snak·i·est**) like a snake in appearance; long and sinuous: *a long snaky whip.* ■ of the supposed nature of a snake in showing coldness, venom, or cunning: *a snaky friend.* ■ infested with snakes. —**snak·i·ly** /-kəlē/ *adv.* —**snak·i·ness** *n.*

snap /snap/ ▶*v.* (**snapped, snap·ping**) **1** break or cause to break suddenly and completely, typically with a sharp cracking sound: [*intr.*] *guitar strings kept snapping* | [*tr.*] *dead twigs can be* **snapped off.** | [*intr.*] emit a sudden, sharp cracking sound: *banners snapping in the breeze.* ■ [*intr.*] (of an animal) make a sudden audible bite: *a dog was* **snapping** *at his heels.* ■ cause to move or alter in a specified way with a brisk movement and typically a sharp sound: *Rosa snapped her bag shut.* ■ [*intr.*] move or alter in this way: *his mouth snapped into a tight, straight line.* ■ [*intr.*] *fig.* suddenly lose one's self-control: *she claims she snapped after years of violence.* ■ say something quickly and irritably to someone: [*intr.*] *McIlvanney* **snapped at** *her* | [with *direct speech*] *"I really don't much care," she snapped.* **2** [*tr.*] take a snapshot of: *he planned to spend the time snapping rare wildlife* | [*intr.*] *photographers were* **snapping away** *at her.* **3** [*tr.*] *Football* put (the ball) into play by a quick backward movement from the ground. **4** [*tr.*] fasten with snaps: *he pulled a white rubber swim hat over his head and snapped it under his chin.*

▶*phrasal v.* □ **snap back** recover quickly and easily from an illness or period of difficulty: *our bodies can snap back pretty well from short-term bouts of stress.* □ **snap out of** [often in *imper.*] *inf.* get out of (a bad or unhappy mood) by a sudden effort: *come on, Fran—snap out of it!* □ **snap something up** quickly and eagerly buy or secure something that is in short supply or being sold cheaply: *all the tickets have been snapped up.*

▶*n.* **1** a sudden, sharp cracking sound or movement: *she closed her purse with a snap.* ■ a hurried, irritable tone or manner: *"I'm still waiting," he said with a snap.* ■ vigor or liveliness of style or action; zest: *the snap of the dialogue.* **2** (usu. **snaps**) a small fastener on clothing, engaged by pressing its two halves together. **3** *inf.* an easy task: *a control panel that makes operation a snap.* **4** *Football* a quick backward movement of the ball from the ground that begins a play. **5** a snapshot.

▶*adj.* done or taken on the spur of the moment, unexpectedly, or without notice: *a snap judgment* | *he could call a snap election.* —**snap·ping·ly** *adv.*

▶ □ **in a snap** *inf.* in a moment; almost immediately: *gourmet-quality meals are ready in a snap.* □ **snap one's fingers** make a sharp clicking sound by bending the last joint of the middle finger against the thumb and suddenly releasing it, typically in order to attract attention in a peremptory way or to accompany the beat of music.

snap·drag·on /'snap,dragən/ ▶*n.* a plant (genus *Antirrhinum*) of the figwort family, bearing spikes of brightly colored two-lobed flowers that gape like a mouth when a bee lands on the curved lip.

snap·per /'snapər/ ▶*n.* **1** a marine fish of a widespread tropical family (Lutjanidae, the **snapper family**) that snaps its toothed jaws. **2** another term for SNAPPING TURTLE.

snap·ping tur·tle ▶*n.* a large American freshwater turtle (family Chelydridae) with a long neck and strong hooked jaws. Two North American species include the **common snapping turtle** (*Chelydra serpentina*) and the larger **alligator snapping turtle** (*Macroclemys temminckii*).

snap·pish /'snapish/ ▶*adj.* (of a dog) irritable and inclined to bite. ■ irritable and curt: *she was often snappish with the children.* —**snap·pish·ly** *adv.* —**snap·pish·ness** *n.*

snap·py /'snapē/ ▶*adj.* (**snap·pi·er, snap·pi·est**) *inf.* **1** irritable and inclined to speak sharply; snappish: *anything unusual made her snappy and nervous.* **2** cleverly concise; neat: *snappy catchphrases.* ■ neat and elegant: *a snappy dresser.* —**snap·pi·ly** /-pəlē/ *adv.* —**snap·pi·ness** *n.*

▶ □ **make it snappy** be quick about it: *into bed and make it snappy!*

snap·shot /'snap,SHät/ ▶*n.* **1** an informal photograph taken quickly, typically with a small hand-held camera. ■ a brief look or summary: *this excellent book can only be a snapshot of a complex industry.* ■ *Comput.* a record of the contents of a storage location or data file at a given time. **2** (**snap shot**) a shot taken quickly by a hunter.

snare /sne(ə)r/ ▶*n.* **1** a trap for catching birds or animals, typically one having a noose of wire or cord. ■ *fig.* a thing likely to lure or tempt someone into harm or error: *the wickedness and snares of the Devil.* ■ *Surgery* a wire loop for severing polyps or other growths. **2** a length of wire, gut, or hide stretched across a drumhead to produce a rattling sound. ■ short for SNARE DRUM.

▶*v.* [*tr.*] catch (a bird or mammal) in a snare. ■ *fig.* catch or trap (someone): *I snared a passing waiter.* —**snar·er** *n.*

snare drum ▶*n.* a short cylindrical drum with a membrane at each end, the upper one being struck with hard sticks and the lower one fitted with snares.

snarl¹ /snärl/ ▶*v.* [*intr.*] (of an animal such as a dog) make an aggressive growl with bared teeth: [as *adj.*] (**snarling**) *snarling Dobermans.* ■ (of a person) say something in an angry, bad-tempered voice: *I used to snarl at anyone I disliked* | [with *direct speech*] *"Shut your mouth!" he snarled* | [*tr.*] *he snarled a few choice remarks at them.*

▶*n.* an act or sound of snarling: *the cat drew its mouth back in a snarl.* —**snarl·er** *n.* —**snarl·ing·ly** *adv.* —**snarl·y** *adj.*

snarl² ▶*v.* [*tr.*] **1** entangle or impede (something): *the bus got snarled up in the downtown traffic.* ■ [*intr.*] become entangled or impeded: *the promising opening soon snarls up in a mess of motives.* **2** decorate (metalwork) with raised shapes by hammering the underside.

▶*n.* a knot or tangle: *snarls of wild raspberry plants* | *our hair hung in damp snarls.*

snatch /snaCH/ ▶*v.* [*tr.*] quickly seize (something) in a rude or eager way: *she snatched a cookie from the plate* | *fig. a victory snatched from the jaws of defeat.* ■ *inf.* steal (something) or kidnap (someone), typically by seizing or grabbing suddenly: *a mission to snatch Winston Churchill.* ■ [*intr.*] (**snatch at**) hastily or ineffectually attempt to seize (something): *she snatched at the handle.* ■ quickly secure or obtain (something) when a chance presents itself: *snatching a few hours' sleep.* ■ [*intr.*] (**snatch at**) eagerly take or accept (an offer or opportunity): *I snatched at the chance.*

▶*n.* **1** an act of snatching or quickly seizing something: *a quick snatch of breath.* ■ a short spell of doing something: *brief snatches of sleep.* ■ a fragment of song or talk: *picking up snatches of conversation.* ■ *inf.* a kidnapping or theft. **2** *Weightlifting* the rapid raising of a weight from the floor to above the head in one movement. **3** *vulgar slang* a woman's genitals. —**snatch·er** *n.* —**snatch·y** *adj.*

snaz·zy /'snazē/ ▶*adj.* (**snaz·zi·er, snaz·zi·est**) *inf.* stylish and attractive: *snazzy little silk dresses.* —**snaz·zi·ly** /-zəlē/ *adv.* —**snaz·zi·ness** *n.*

sneak /snēk/ ▶*v.* (past **sneaked** or *inf.* **snuck** /'snək/) [*intr.*] move or go in a furtive or stealthy manner: *I sneaked out by the back exit.* ■ [*tr.*] convey (someone or something) in such a way: *someone sneaked a camera inside.* ■ [*tr.*] do or obtain (something) in a stealthy or furtive way: *she sneaked a glance at her watch.* ■ (**sneak up on**) creep up on (someone) without being detected: *he sneaks up on us slyly.*

▶*n. inf.* **1** a furtive and contemptible person: *he was branded a prying sneak for eavesdropping on intimate conversation.* **2** (usu. **sneaks**) short for SNEAKER.

▶*adj.* acting or done surreptitiously, unofficially, or without warning: *a sneak thief* | *a sneak preview.* ▷late 16th cent.: probably dialect; perhaps related to obsolete *snike* 'to creep.'

sneak·er /'snēkər/ ▶*n.* a soft shoe with a rubber sole worn for sports or casual occasions.

sneak·y /'snēkē/ ▶*adj.* (**sneak·i·er, sneak·i·est**) furtive; sly: *sneaky, underhanded tactics.* ■ (of a feeling) secret; reluctant: *I developed a sneaky fondness for the old lady.* —**sneak·i·ly** /-kəlē/ *adv.* —**sneak·i·ness** *n.*

sneer /sni(ə)r/ ▶*n.* a contemptuous or mocking smile, remark, or tone: *he acknowledged their presence with a condescending sneer.*

▶*v.* [*intr.*] smile or speak in a contemptuous or mocking manner: *she had sneered at their bad taste* | [with *direct speech*] *"I see you're conservative in your ways," David sneered.* —**sneer·er** *n.* —**sneer·ing·ly** *adv.*

sneeze /snēz/ ▶*v.* [*intr.*] make a sudden involuntary expulsion of air from the nose and mouth due to irritation of one's nostrils: *the smoke made her sneeze.*

▶*n.* an act or the sound of expelling air from the nose in such a way: *he stopped a sudden sneeze.* —**sneez·er** *n.* —**sneez·y** *adj.*

▶ □ **not to be sneezed at** *inf.* not to be rejected without careful consideration; worth having or taking into account: *a saving of $550 was not to be sneezed at.*

snick·er /'snikər/ ▶*v.* [*intr.*] give a smothered or half-suppressed laugh; snigger. ■ (of a horse) whinny.

▶*n.* a smothered laugh; a snigger. ■ a whinny. —**snick·er·ing·ly** *adv.*

snide /snīd/ ▶*adj.* derogatory or mocking in an indirect way: *snide remarks about my mother.* ■ (of a person) devious and underhanded: *a snide divorce lawyer.* —**snide·ly** *adv.* —**snide·ness** *n.* —**snide·y** *adj.*

sniff /snif/ ▶*v.* [*intr.*] draw in air audibly through the nose to detect a smell, to stop it from running, or to express contempt: *his dog sniffed at my trousers* | [with *direct speech*] *"You're behaving in an unladylike fashion," sniffed Mother.* ■ [*tr.*] draw in (a scent, substance, or air) through the nose. ■ (**sniff at**) show contempt or dislike for: *the price is not to be sniffed* *at.* ■ (**sniff around**) *inf.* investigate covertly, esp. to find out confidential or incriminating information about someone. ■ [*tr.*] (**sniff something out**) *inf.* discover something by investigation: *he made millions upon millions sniffing out tax loopholes for companies.*

▶*n.* an act or sound of drawing air through the nose: *he gave a sniff of disapproval.* ■ an amount of air or other substance taken up in such a way: *his drug use was confined to a sniff of amyl nitrite.* ■ *inf.* a trace, hint, or small amount: *they're off at the first sniff of trouble.*

sniff·er /ˈsnifər/ ▶*n.* **1** a person who sniffs, esp. one who sniffs a drug or toxic substance: *a glue sniffer.* ■ *inf.* a device for detecting an invisible and dangerous substance, such as gas or radiation: *electronic sniffers are used to detect the presence of a nuclear mass.* **2** *inf.* a person's nose. **3** (also **sniffer program**) a computer program that detects and records a variety of restricted information, esp. the secret passwords needed to gain access to files or networks.

snif·fle /ˈsnifəl/ ▶*v.* [*intr.*] sniff slightly or repeatedly, typically because of a cold or fit of crying.

▶*n.* an act of sniffing in such a way: *he was restraining his sniffles rather well.* ■ a head cold causing a running nose and sniffing: *she had a slight cough and a sniffle* | *they may get damp and catch the sniffles.* —**snif·fler** /ˈsnif(ə)lər/ *n.* —**snif·fly** /ˈsnif(ə)lē/ *adj.*

snif·fy /ˈsnifē/ ▶*adj.* (**snif·fi·er, snif·fi·est**) *inf.* scornful; contemptuous: *some people are sniffy about tea bags.* —**sniff·i·ly** /-fəlē/ *adv.* —**sniff·i·ness** *n.*

snif·ter /ˈsniftər/ ▶*n.* a footed glass that is wide at the bottom and tapers to the top, used for brandy and other drinks. ■ *inf.* a small quantity of an alcoholic drink: *care to join me for a snifter?*

snig·ger /ˈsnigər/ ▶*n.* a smothered or half-suppressed laugh.

▶*v.* [*intr.*] give such a laugh: *the boys at school were sure to snigger at him behind his back* | [with *direct speech*] *"Doesn't he look like a fool?" they sniggered.* —**snig·ger·er** *n.* —**snig·ger·ing·ly** *adv.*

snip /snip/ ▶*v.* (**snipped, snip·ping**) [*tr.*] cut (something) with scissors or shears, typically with small quick strokes: *she snipped layers into the hair around her face* | [*intr.*] *she inspected the embroidery, snipping at loose threads.*

▶*n.* **1** an act of cutting something in such a way: *he took a snip at a dandelion on the grass.* ■ a small piece of something that has been cut off: *the collage consists of snips of wallpaper.* **2** *inf.* a small or insignificant person: *imagine that little snip telling me I was wrong!* **3** (**snips**) hand shears, esp. for cutting metal: *use tin snips.*

snipe /snīp/ ▶*n.* (*pl.* same or **snipes**) a wading bird (*Gallinago* and other genera) of the sandpiper family, living in marshes and wet meadows, with brown camouflaged plumage and a long straight bill.

▶*v.* [*intr.*] shoot at someone from a hiding place, esp. at long range. ■ make a sly or petty verbal attack: *the brothers sniped at each other.* —**snip·er** *n.*

snip·pet /ˈsnipit/ ▶*n.* a small piece or brief extract: *snippets of information about the war.* —**snip·pet·y** *adj.*

snip·py /ˈsnipē/ ▶*adj.* (**snip·pi·er, snip·pi·est**) *inf.* curt or sharp, esp. in a condescending way: *a snippy note from our landlord.* —**snip·pi·ly** /-pəlē/ *adv.* —**snip·pi·ness** *n.*

snit /snit/ ▶*n.* *inf.* a fit of irritation; a sulk: *the ambassador and delegation had withdrawn in a snit.*

snitch /snicH/ *inf.* ▶*v.* **1** [*tr.*] steal. **2** [*intr.*] inform on someone: *she wouldn't tell who snitched on me.*

▶*n.* an informer.

sniv·el /ˈsnivəl/ ▶*v.* (**sniv·eled, sniv·el·ing**; *Brit.* **sniv·elled, sniv·el·ling**) [*intr.*] cry and sniffle: *Kate started to snivel, looking sad and stunned.* ■ complain in a whining or tearful way: *he shouldn't snivel about his punishment* | [as *adj.*] (**sniveling**) *you sniveling little brat!*

▶*n.* a slight sniff indicating suppressed emotion or crying: *Lucy's torrent of howls weakened to a snivel.* —**sniv·el·er** *n.* —**sniv·el·ing·ly** *adv.*

snob /snäb/ ▶*n.* a person with an exaggerated respect for high social position or wealth who seeks to associate with social superiors and dislikes people or activities regarded as lower-class. ■ a person who believes that their tastes in a particular area are superior to those of other people: *a musical snob.* —**snob·ber·y** /-bərē/ *n.* (*pl.* **-ber·ies**) —**snob·bish** *adj.* —**snob·bism** /-ˌbizəm/ *n.* —**snob·by** *adj.* (**-bi·er, -bi·est**).

snood /sno͞od/ ▶*n.* **1** an ornamental hairnet or fabric bag worn over the hair at the back of a woman's head. ■ *hist.* a ribbon or band worn by unmarried women in Scotland to confine their hair. **2** a wide ring of knitted material worn as a hood or scarf. **3** a short line attaching a hook to a main line in sea fishing.

snook[1] /sno͞ok/ ▶*n.* a large edible game fish (*Centropomus undecimalis*, family Centropomidae) of the Caribbean that is sometimes found in brackish water.

snook[2] ▶*n.* (in phrase **cock a snook**) *inf., chiefly Brit.* place one's hand so that the thumb touches one's nose and the fingers are spread out, in order to express contempt: *you wouldn't be so quick to cock a snook if she were actually looking at you.* ■ *fig.* openly show contempt or a lack of respect for someone or something; thumb one's nose: *he spent a lifetime cocking a snook at the art world.*

snook·er /ˈsno͞okər/ ▶*n.* a game played with cues on a billiard table in which the players use a cue ball (white) to pocket the other balls (fifteen red and six colored) in a set order. ■ a position in a game of snooker or pool in which a player cannot make a direct shot at any permitted ball; a shot placing an opponent in such a position: *he needed a snooker to have a chance of winning the frame.*

▶*v.* [*tr.*] subject (oneself or one's opponent) to a snooker. ■ *fig.* leave (someone) in a difficult position; thwart. ■ *fig.* trick, entice, or trap: *they were snookered into buying books at prices that were too high.*

snoop /sno͞op/ *inf.* ▶*v.* [*intr.*] investigate or look around furtively in an attempt to find out something, esp. about someone's private affairs: *your sister might find the ring if she goes snooping around* | [as *adj.*] (**snooping**) *snooping neighbors.*

▶*n.* an act of looking around in such a way: *I could go back to her cottage and have another snoop.* ■ a person who investigates in such a way; a detective. —**snoop·er** *n.* —**snoop·y** *adj.*

snoot /sno͞ot/ ▶*n.* **1** *inf.* a person's nose. **2** *inf.* a person who shows contempt for those considered to be of a lower social class: *the snoots complain that the paper has lowered its standards.* **3** a tubular or conical attachment used to produce a narrow beam from a spotlight.

snoot·y /ˈsno͞otē/ ▶*adj.* (**snoot·i·er, snoot·i·est**) *inf.* showing disapproval or contempt toward others, esp. those considered to belong to a lower social class: *snooty neighbors.* —**snoot·i·ly** /-təlē/ *adv.* —**snoot·i·ness** *n.*

snooze /sno͞oz/ *inf.* ▶*n.* a short, light sleep, esp. during the day: *he settled in the grass for a snooze.* ■ a boring event or person: *months go by and the job's a snooze.*

▶*v.* [*intr.*] have a short, light sleep: *the children play beach games while the adults snooze in the sun.* —**snooz·er** /ˈsno͞ozər/ *n.* —**snooz·y** /ˈsno͞ozē/ *adj.*

snore /snôr/ ▶*n.* a snorting or grunting sound in a person's breathing while asleep: *she lay on the mattress listening to Sally's snores.* ■ *inf.* a thing that is extremely boring: *she sings a version of "Passionate Kisses" that's a certified snore.*

▶*v.* [*intr.*] breathe with a snorting or grunting sound while asleep: *he was snoring loudly* | [as *n.*] (**snoring**) *you keep me awake all night with your snoring.* —**snor·er** *n.*

snor·kel /ˈsnôrkəl/ ▶*n.* **1** a short curved tube for a swimmer to breathe through while keeping the face under water. ■ a tube used by a submarine just below the surface as a fresh-air intake. **2** (**Snorkel**) *trademark* a type of hydraulically elevated platform for firefighting.

▶*v.* (**-keled, -kel·ing**; *Brit.* **-kel·led, -kel·ling**) [*intr.*] [often as *n.*] (**snorkeling**) swim using a snorkel: *the sea is incredibly clear, which is ideal for snorkeling* | *snorkel around the unspoiled coral reefs.* —**snor·kel·er** *n.*

snort /snôrt/ ▶*n.* an explosive sound made by the sudden forcing of breath through a person's nose, used to express indignation, derision, or incredulity: *he gave a snort of disgust.* ■ a similar sound made by an animal, typically when excited or frightened. ■ *inf.* an inhaled dose of an illegal powdered drug, esp. cocaine: *they were high on a few snorts.* ■ *inf.* a measure of an alcoholic drink: *a bottle of rum was opened and they took a good long snort.*

▶*v.* [*intr.*] make a sudden sound through one's nose, esp. to express indignation or derision: *she snorted with laughter* | [with *direct speech*] *"How perfectly ridiculous!" he snorted.* ■ (of an animal) make such a sound, esp. when excited or frightened. ■ [*tr.*] *inf.* inhale (an illegal drug).

snot /snät/ ▶*n.* *inf.* nasal mucus. ■ an arrogant or conceited person. ■ a contemptible or worthless person.

snot·ty /ˈsnätē/ ▶*adj.* (**-ti·er, -ti·est**) *inf.* **1** full of or covered with nasal mucus: *a snotty nose.* **2** having or showing a superior or conceited attitude: *a snotty letter.* —**snot·ti·ly** /-təlē/ *adv.* —**snot·ti·ness** *n.*

snout /snout/ ▶*n.* the projecting nose and mouth of an animal, esp. a mammal. ■ *derog.* a person's nose. ■ the projecting front or end of something such as a pistol. —**snout·ed** *adj.* [often in *comb.*] *long-snouted baboons.* —**snout·y** *adj.*

snow /snō/ ▶*n.* **1** atmospheric water vapor frozen into ice crystals and falling in light white flakes or lying on the ground as a white layer: *we were trudging through deep snow* | *the first snow of the season.* **2** something that resembles snow in color or texture, in particular: ■ a mass of flickering white spots on a television or radar screen, caused by

snifter

interference or a poor signal. ■ *inf.* cocaine. ■ a dessert or other dish resembling snow: *vanilla snow*. ■ a frozen gas resembling snow: *carbon dioxide snow*.

▶*v.* **1** [*intr.*] (**it snows**, **it is snowing**, etc.) snow falls: *it's not snowing so heavily now*. ■ (**be snowed in**) be confined or blocked by a large quantity of snow: *I was snowed in for a week*. ■ [*tr.*] *fig.* used to describe the arrival of an overwhelming quantity of something: *in the last week it had snowed letters and business*. ■ [*tr.*] sprinkle or scatter (something), causing it to fall like snow: *the ceiling is snowing green flakes of paint onto the seats*. **2** [*tr.*] *inf.* mislead or charm (someone) with elaborate and insincere words: *they would snow the public into believing that all was well*.

▶**phrasal v.** □ **snow someone under** (usu. **be snowed under**) overwhelm someone with a large quantity of something, esp. work: *he's been snowed under with urgent cases*. —**snow·less** *adj.* —**snow·like** /-ˌlīk/ *adj.*

snow·ball /ˈsnōˌbôl/ ▶*n.* a ball of packed snow, esp. one made for throwing at other people for fun. ■ *fig.* a thing that grows rapidly in intensity or importance: *the small speculator jumps in for a quick profit, adding his weight to the snowball, and the price goes up*.

▶*v.* **1** [*tr.*] throw snowballs at: *I made sure the other kids stopped snowballing Celia*. **2** [*intr.*] increase rapidly in size, intensity, or importance: *the campaign was snowballing*.

▶ □ **a snowball's chance** (**in hell**) *inf.* no chance at all: *the plan has a snowball's chance in hell of being accepted*.

snow·ber·ry /ˈsnōˌberē/ ▶*n.* a North American shrub (*Symphoricarpos albus*) of the honeysuckle family, bearing white berries and often cultivated as an ornamental or for hedging.

snow·bird /ˈsnōˌbərd/ ▶*n.* **1** *inf.* a northerner who moves to a warmer southern state in the winter. **2** a widespread and variable junco (*Junco hyemalis*) with gray or brown upper parts and a white belly.

snow·blink /ˈsnōˌbliNGk/ ▶*n.* a white reflection in the sky of snow or ice on the ground.

snow·board /ˈsnōˌbôrd/ ▶*n.* a board resembling a short, broad ski, used for sliding downhill on snow.

▶*v.* [*intr.*] slide downhill on such a board: [as *n.*] (**snowboarding**) *the thrills of snowboarding*. —**snow·board·er** *n.*

snow·bound /ˈsnōˌbound/ ▶*adj.* prevented from traveling or going out by snow or snowy weather: *he was snowbound in the nearby mountains*. ■ covered in snow or inaccessible because of it: *a snowbound Alpine village*.

snow·cap /ˈsnōˌkap/ ▶*n.* a covering of snow on the top of a mountain. —**snow·capped** *adj.*

snow·drift /ˈsnōˌdrift/ ▶*n.* a bank of deep snow heaped up by the wind.

snow·drop /ˈsnōˌdräp/ ▶*n.* a widely cultivated bulbous European plant (*Galanthus nivalis*) of the lily family that bears drooping white flowers during the late winter.

snow·fall /ˈsnōˌfôl/ ▶*n.* a fall of snow: *heavy snowfalls made travel absolutely impossible*. ■ the quantity of snow falling within a given area in a given time: *winters with above-average snowfall*.

snow·field /ˈsnōˌfēld/ ▶*n.* a permanent wide expanse of snow in mountainous or polar regions.

snow·flake /ˈsnōˌflāk/ ▶*n.* **1** a flake of snow, esp. a feathery ice crystal, typically displaying delicate sixfold symmetry. **2** a white-flowered Eurasian plant (Genus *Leucojum*) related to and resembling the snowdrop, typically blooming in the summer or autumn.

snow job ▶*n. inf.* a deception or concealment of one's real motive in an attempt to flatter or persuade: *we need to do a snow job on him*.

snow leop·ard ▶*n.* a rare large Asian cat (*Panthera uncia*) that has pale gray fur patterned with dark blotches and rings. Also called OUNCE.

snow·man /ˈsnōˌman/ ▶*n.* (*pl.* **-men**) a representation of a human figure created with compressed snow.

snow·mo·bile /ˈsnōmōˌbēl/ ▶*n.* a motor vehicle, esp. one with runners in the front and caterpillar tracks in the rear, for traveling over snow.

▶*v.* [*intr.*] travel by snowmobile: [as *n.*] (**snowmobiling**) *the county offers snowmobiling, ice fishing, kayaking, and rafting*. —**snow·mo·bil·er** *n.*

snowmobile

snow·plow /ˈsnōˌplou/ ▶*n.* **1** an implement or vehicle for clearing roads of snow by pushing it aside. **2** *Skiing* an act of turning the points of one's skis inward in order to slow down or turn.

▶*v.* [*intr.*] ski with the tips of one's skis pointing inward in order to slow down or turn.

snow·shoe /ˈsnōˌSHoo/ ▶*n.* a flat device resembling a racket that is attached to the sole of a boot and used for walking on snow.

▶*v.* [*intr.*] travel wearing snowshoes: *we snowshoed down into the next valley*. —**snow·sho·er** /-ər/ *n.* —**snow·shoe·ing** /-iNG/ *n.*

snow·storm /ˈsnōˌstôrm/ ▶*n.* a heavy fall of snow, esp. with a high wind. ■ *fig.* a shower or large quantity of something: *it swam away in a flurry of wings and flippers, raising a snowstorm of foam*.

snow-white ▶*adj.* of a pure white color: *perfect spotless utensils on a snow-white tablecloth*.

snow·y /ˈsnōē/ ▶*adj.* (**snow·i·er**, **snow·i·est**) covered with snow: *snowy mountains*. ■ (of weather or a period of time) characterized by snowfall: *a snowy January day*. ■ of or like snow, esp. in being pure white: *snowy hair*. —**snow·i·ly** /ˈsnōəlē/ *adv.* —**snow·i·ness** *n.*

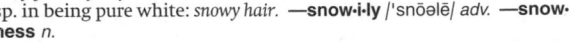

snowshoes

snow·y owl ▶*n.* a large northern owl (*Nyctea scandiaca*) that breeds mainly in the Arctic tundra, the male being entirely white and the female having darker markings.

snub /snəb/ ▶*v.* (**snubbed**, **snub·bing**) [*tr.*] **1** rebuff, ignore, or spurn disdainfully: *he snubbed faculty members and students alike | he snubbed her request to wind up the debate*. **2** check the movement of (a horse or boat), esp. by a rope wound around a post: *a horse snubbed to a tree*.

▶*n.* an act of showing disdain or a lack of cordiality by rebuffing or ignoring someone or something: *he couldn't help thinking that the whole thing was meant to be taken as a snub*.

▶*adj.* (of a person's or animal's nose) short and turned up at the end: [in *comb.*] snub-nosed.

snuff[1] /snəf/ ▶*v.* [*tr.*] extinguish (a candle): *a breeze snuffed out the candle*. ■ put an end to (something) in a brutal manner: *his life was snuffed out by a sniper's bullet*. ■ *inf.* kill: *I lost track of the number of people he snuffed who were wearing bulletproof fabric*. ■ (**snuff it**) *Brit., inf.* die. ■ *dated* trim the charred wick from (a candle).

▶*n.* the charred part of a candle wick.

snuff[2] ▶*n.* powdered tobacco that is sniffed up the nostril rather than smoked: *a pinch of snuff*.

▶*v.* [*tr.*] inhale or sniff at (something): *they stood snuffing up the keen cold air*. ■ [*intr.*] *archaic* sniff up powdered tobacco.

▶ □ **up to snuff** *inf.* **1** meeting the required standard: *they need a million dollars to get their facilities up to snuff*. ■ in good health: *he hadn't felt up to snuff all summer*. **2** *Brit., archaic* not easily deceived; knowing: *an up-to-snuff old vagabond*.

snuff·box /ˈsnəfˌbäks/ ▶*n.* a small ornamental box for holding snuff.

snuff·er /ˈsnəfər/ (also **can·dle·snuff·er**) ▶*n.* a small hollow metal cone on the end of a handle, used to extinguish a candle by smothering the flame. ■ (usu. **snuffers** or **candlesnuffers**) an implement resembling scissors with an inverted metal cup attached to one blade, used to extinguish a candle or trim its wick.

snuff·y[1] /ˈsnəfē/ ▶*adj.* (**snuff·i·er**, **snuff·i·est**) *archaic* supercilious or contemptuous: *some snuffy old stockbroker*. ■ easily offended; annoyed.

snuff·y[2] ▶*adj. archaic* resembling powdered tobacco in color or substance.

snug /snəg/ ▶*adj.* (**snug·ger**, **snug·gest**) **1** comfortable, warm, and cozy; well protected from the weather or cold: *she was safe and snug in Ruth's arms | a snug cottage*. ■ *archaic* (of an income or employment) allowing one to live in comfort and comparative ease. **2** (esp. of clothing) very tight or close-fitting: *a well-shaped hood for a snug fit*.

▶*v.* [*tr.*] place (something) safely or cozily: *she tucks him in, snugging the blanket up to his chin*. ■ [*intr.*] settle comfortably and cozily: *the passengers snugged down among the cargo*. —**snug·ly** *adv.* —**snug·ness** *n.*

▶ □ **snug as a bug (in a rug)** *humorous* in an extremely comfortable position or situation.

snug·gle /ˈsnəgəl/ ▶ *v.* settle or move into a warm, comfortable position: [*intr.*] **I snuggled down** in my sleeping bag | [*tr.*] she snuggled her head into his shoulder.

so[1] /sō/ ▶ *adv.* **1** to such a great extent: *the words tumbled out so fast that I could barely hear them* | *don't look so worried* | *I'm not so foolish* **as to** *say that.* ■ extremely; very much (used for emphasis): *she looked so pretty* | *I do love it so.* ■ *inf.* used to emphasize a clause or negative statement: *that's so not fair* | *you are so going to regret this.* ■ *inf.* used with a gesture to indicate size: *the bird was about so long.* **2** to the same extent (used in comparisons): *he isn't so bad as you'd think* | *without his parents' support, he would not have done so well.* **3** referring back to something previously mentioned: ■ *that is the case: "Is it going to rain?" "I think so."* | *if she notices, she never says so.* ■ the truth: *I hear that you're a writer—is that so?* ■ similarly; and also: *times have changed and so have I.* ■ expressing agreement: *"It's cold in here." "So it is."* ■ *inf.* used to emphatically contradict a negative statement: *it is so!* **4** in the way described or demonstrated; thus: *hold your arms so* | *so it was that he was still a bachelor.*

▶ *conj.* **1** and for this reason; therefore: *it was still painful, so I went to see a specialist* | *you know I'm telling the truth, so don't interrupt.* ■ (**so that**) with the result that: *it was overgrown with brambles, so that I had difficulty making any progress.* **2** (**so that**) with the aim that; in order that: *they whisper to each other so that no one else can hear.* **3** and then; as the next step: *and so to the finals.* **4** introducing a question: *so, what did you do today?* ■ introducing a question following on from what was said previously: *so what did he do about it?* ■ (also **so what?**) *inf.* why should that be considered significant?: *"Marv is wearing a suit." "So?"* | *so what if he failed?* **5** introducing a statement that is followed by a defensive comment: *so I like anchovies—what's wrong with that?* **6** introducing a concluding statement: *so that's that.* **7** in the same way; correspondingly: *just as bad money drives out good, so does bad art drive out the good.*

▶ □ **and so on** (or **forth**) and similar things; et cetera: *these snacks include cheeses, cold meats, and so on.* □ **just so much** *chiefly derog.* emphasizing a large amount of something: *it's just so much ideological cant.* □ **not so much —— as ——** but rather ——: *the novel was not so much unfinished as unfinishable.* □ **only so much** a limited amount: *there is only so much you can do to protect yourself.* □ **so be it** an expression of acceptance or resignation. □ **so long!** *inf.* goodbye until we meet again. □ **so many** (or **much**) indicating a particular but unspecified quantity: *so many hours at such-and-such a speed.* □ **so much as** even: *he sat down without so much as a word to anyone.* □ **so much for 1** indicating that one has finished talking about something: *So much for the melodic line. We now turn our attention to the accompaniment.* **2** suggesting that something has not been successful or useful: *so much for that idea!* □ **so much so that** to such an extent that: *I was fascinated by the company, so much so that I wrote a book about it.* □ **so to speak** (or **say**) used to highlight the fact that one is describing something in an unusual or metaphorical way: *delving into the body's secrets, I looked death in the face, so to speak.*

so[2] ▶ *n.* alternate spelling of **SOL**[1].

So. ▶ *abbr.* South.

soak /sōk/ ▶ *v.* [*tr.*] **1** make or allow (something) to become thoroughly wet by immersing it in liquid: *soak the beans overnight in water.* ■ [*intr.*] be immersed in water or another liquid: *she spent some time soaking in a hot bath.* ■ (of a liquid) cause (something or someone) to become extremely wet: *the rain poured down, soaking their hair.* ■ [*intr.*] (of a liquid) penetrate or permeate completely: *cold water was soaking into my shoes.* ■ (**soak something off/out**) remove something by immersing it in water for a period of time: *don't disturb the wound—soak the dressing off if necessary.* ■ (**soak oneself in**) immerse oneself in (a particular experience, activity, or interest): *he soaked himself in the music of Mozart.* **2** *inf.* impose heavy charges or taxation on: *few of us common people care how much tax Congress soaks on racing motorboats.* **3** [*intr.*] *archaic, inf.* drink heavily: *you keep soaking in taverns.*

▶ *phrasal v.* ■ **soak something up** absorb a liquid: *use clean tissues to soak up any droplets of water.* ■ *fig.* expose oneself to or experience (something beneficial or enjoyable): *lie back and soak up the Mediterranean sun* | *he spends his time painting and soaking up the culture.* ■ *inf.* cost or use up money: *the project had soaked up over $1 billion.*

▶ *n.* **1** an act of immersing someone or something in liquid for a period of time: *I'm looking forward to a long soak in the tub.* **2** *inf.* a heavy drinker: *his daughter stayed up to put the old soak to bed.* —**soak·age** /ˈsōkij/ *n.* —**soak·er** *n.* —**soak·ing** *adj.*

so-and-so ▶ *n.* (pl. **-sos**) a person or thing whose name the speaker does not need to specify or does not know or remember. ■ *inf.* a person who is disliked or is considered to have a particular characteristic, typically an unfavorable one: *nosy old so-and-so!*

soap /sōp/ ▶ *n.* **1** a substance used with water for washing and cleaning, made of a compound of natural oils or fats with sodium hydroxide or another strong alkali, and typically having perfume and coloring added: *a bar of soap.* **2** *inf.* a soap opera: *the soaps are at the top of the ratings.*

▶ *v.* [*tr.*] wash with soap: *she soaped her face.* —**soap·less** *adj.*

▶ □ **no soap** *inf.* used to convey that there is no chance of something happening or occurring: *They needed a writer with some enthusiasm. No soap.*

soap·ber·ry /ˈsōpˌberē/ ▶ *n.* any of several trees or shrubs with berries that produce a soapy froth when crushed, in particular a plant (genus *Sapindus*, family Sapindaceae) with saponin-rich berries that are used as a soap substitute. ■ the berry of any of these plants.

soap·box /ˈsōpˌbäks/ ▶ *n.* a box or crate used as a makeshift stand by a public speaker: [as *adj.*] *a soapbox orator.* ■ *fig.* a thing that provides an opportunity for someone to air their views publicly: *fanzines are soapboxes for critical sports fans.* ■ *chiefly hist.* a box or crate in which soap is packed and transported.

soap op·er·a ▶ *n.* a television or radio drama series dealing typically with daily events in the lives of the same group of characters.

soap·stone /ˈsōpˌstōn/ ▶ *n.* a soft rock consisting largely of talc.

soap·suds /ˈsōpˌsədz/ ▶ *plural n.* froth made from soap and water.

soap·wort /ˈsōpwərt; -ˌwôrt/ ▶ *n.* a plant (*Saponaria officinalis*) of the pink family, with fragrant pink or white flowers and leaves that were formerly used to make soap.

soap·y /ˈsōpē/ ▶ *adj.* (**soap·i·er**, **soap·i·est**) **1** containing or covered with soap: *hot soapy water.* ■ of or like soap: *his hands smelled soapy.* ■ (of a person or behavior) unpleasantly flattering and ingratiating: *a soapy, fawning look.* **2** *inf.* characteristic of a soap opera: *soapy little turns of plot.* —**soap·i·ly** /-pəlē/ *adv.* —**soap·i·ness** *n.*

soar /sôr/ ▶ *v.* [*intr.*] fly or rise high in the air: *the bird spread its wings and soared into the air* | *fig. when she heard his voice, her spirits soared.* ■ maintain height in the air without flapping wings or using engine power: *the gulls soared on the summery winds.* ■ increase rapidly above the usual level: *the cost of living continued to soar* | [as *adj.*] (**soaring**) *the soaring crime rate.* ▷ late Middle English: shortening of Old French *essorer*, based on Latin *ex-* 'out of' + *aura* 'breeze.' —**soar·er** *n.* —**soar·ing·ly** *adv.*

SOB ▶ *abbr.* son of a bitch.

sob /säb/ ▶ *v.* (**sobbed**, **sob·bing**) [*intr.*] cry noisily, making loud, convulsive gasps: *he broke down and sobbed like a child* | [*tr.*] *he sobbed himself to sleep.* ■ [*tr.*] say while crying noisily: [with *direct speech*] *"I thought they'd killed you," he sobbed weakly.*

▶ *n.* an act or sound of sobbing: *with a sob of despair she threw herself onto the bed.* —**sob·bing·ly** *adv.*

so·ber /ˈsōbər/ ▶ *adj.* (**-ber·er**, **-ber·est**) not affected by alcohol; not drunk. ■ serious, sensible, and solemn: *a sober view of life* | *his expression became sober.* ■ free from alcoholism; not habitually drinking alcohol: *I've been clean and sober for five years.* ■ muted in color: *a sober gray suit.*

▶ *v.* make or become sober after drinking alcohol: [*tr.*] *that coffee sobered him up* | [*intr.*] *I ought to sober up a bit.* ■ make or become more serious, sensible, and solemn: [*intr.*] *his expression sobered her* | [as *adj.*] (**sobering**) *a sobering thought.* —**so·ber·ing·ly** *adv.* —**so·ber·ly** *adv.*

so·bri·e·ty /səˈbrīətē; sō-/ ▶ *n.* the state of being sober: *the price of beer compelled me to maintain a certain level of sobriety.* ■ the quality of being staid or solemn.

so·bri·quet /ˈsōbriˌkā; -ˌket/ (also **sou·bri·quet** /ˈsoōbri-/) ▶ *n.* a person's nickname.

sob sto·ry ▶ *n.* *inf.* a story or explanation intended to make someone feel sympathy for the person relating it.

Soc. ▶ *abbr.* ■ Socialist. ■ Society.

so-called ▶ *adj.* used to show that something or someone is commonly designated by the name or term specified: *the worst oils are the so-called "tropical" oils like coconut and palm oil.* ■ used to express one's view that such a name or term is inappropriate: *she could trust him more than any of her so-called friends.*

soc·cer /ˈsäkər/ ▶ *n.* a game played by two teams of eleven players with a round ball that may not be touched with the hands or arms during play except by the goalkeepers. The object of the game is to score goals by kicking or heading the ball into the opponents' goal.

so·cia·ble /ˈsōsHəbəl/ ▶ *adj.* willing to talk and engage in activities with other people; friendly: *being a sociable person, Eva loved entertaining.* ■ (of a place, occasion, or activity) marked by friendliness: *a very sociable little* *village.* —**so·cia·bil·i·ty** /ˌsōSHəˈbilitē/ *n.* —**so·cia·ble·ness** *n.* —**so·cia·bly** /-blē/ *adv.*

so·cial /ˈsōSHəl/ ▶*adj.* **1** of or relating to society or its organization: *alcoholism is recognized as a major social problem* | *a traditional Japanese social structure.* ▪ of or relating to rank and status in society: *a recent analysis of social class in Britain* | *her mother is a lady of the highest social standing.* ▪ needing companionship and therefore best suited to living in communities: *we are social beings as well as individuals.* ▪ relating to or designed for activities in which people meet each other for pleasure: *Guy led a full social life.* **2** *Zool.* (of a bird) gregarious; breeding or nesting in colonies. ▪ (of an insect) living together in organized communities, typically with different castes, as ants, bees, wasps, and termites do. ▪ (of a mammal) living together in groups, typically in a hierarchical system with complex communication.
▶*n.* an informal social gathering, esp. one organized by the members of a particular club or group: *a church social.* —**so·cial·i·ty** /ˌsōSHēˈalədē/ *n.* —**so·cial·ly** /ˈsōSHəlē/ *adv. families who are socially disadvantaged.*

so·cial climb·er ▶*n. derog.* a person who is eager to gain a higher social status. —**so·cial climb·ing** *n.*

so·cial con·tract ▶*n.* an implicit agreement among the members of a society to cooperate for social benefits, for example by sacrificing some individual freedom for state protection. Theories of a social contract became popular in the 16th, 17th, and 18th centuries among theorists such as Thomas Hobbes, John Locke, and Jean-Jacques Rousseau, as a means of explaining the origin of government and the obligations of subjects.

so·cial dis·ease ▶*n. inf.* a venereal disease.

so·cial·ism /ˈsōSHəˌlizəm/ ▶*n.* a political and economic theory of social organization that advocates that the means of production, distribution, and exchange should be owned or regulated by the community as a whole. ▪ policy or practice based on this theory. ▪ (in Marxist theory) a transitional social state between the overthrow of capitalism and the realization of communism. —**so·cial·ist** *n. & adj.* —**so·cial·is·tic** /ˌsōSHəˈlistik/ *adj.* —**so·cial·is·ti·cal·ly** /ˌsōSHəˈlistik(ə)lē/ *adv.*

so·cial·ite /ˈsōSHəˌlīt/ ▶*n.* a person who is well known in fashionable society and is fond of social activities and entertainment.

so·cial·ize /ˈsōSHəˌlīz/ ▶*v.* **1** [*intr.*] mix socially with others: *he didn't mind socializing with his staff.* **2** [*tr.*] make (someone) behave in a way that is acceptable to their society: *newcomers are socialized into orthodox ways* | [as *adj.*] (**socializing**) *a socializing effect.* **3** [*tr.*] organize according to the principles of socialism: [as *adj.*] (**socialized**) *socialized economies.* —**so·cial·i·za·tion** /ˌsōSHəli'zāSHən/ *n.*

so·cial sci·ence ▶*n.* the scientific study of human society and social relationships. ▪ a subject within this field, such as economics or politics. —**so·cial sci·en·tist** *n.*

so·cial se·cu·ri·ty ▶*n.* any government system that provides monetary assistance to people with an inadequate or no income. ▪ (**Social Security**) (in the U.S.) a federal insurance program that provides benefits to retired persons, the unemployed, and the disabled.

so·cial serv·ice ▶*n.* (**social services**) government services provided for the benefit of the community, such as education, medical care, and housing. ▪ activity aiming to promote the welfare of others.

so·cial work ▶*n.* work carried out by trained personnel with the aim of alleviating the conditions of those in need of help or welfare. —**so·cial work·er** *n.*

so·ci·e·ty /səˈsīətē/ ▶*n.* (*pl.* **-ties**) **1** the aggregate of people living together in a more or less ordered community: *drugs, crime, and other dangers to society.* ▪ the community of people living in a particular country or region and having shared customs, laws, and organizations: *the high incidence of violence in American society* | *modern industrial societies.* ▪ a specified section or subset of a community: *no one in polite society uttered the word.* ▪ (also **high society**) the aggregate of people who are fashionable, wealthy, and influential, regarded as forming a distinct group in a community: [as *adj.*] *a society wedding.* ▪ a plant or animal community. **2** an organization or club formed for a particular purpose or activity: [in *names*] *the American Society for the Prevention of Cruelty to Animals.* **3** the situation of being in the company of other people: *she shunned the society of others.* —**so·ci·e·tal** *adj.*

So·ci·e·ty of Je·sus ▶*official name of the* Jesuits (see **JESUIT**).

so·ci·o·cul·tur·al /ˌsōsēōˈkəlCHərəl/ ▶*adj.* combining social and cultural factors. —**so·ci·o·cul·tur·al·ly** *adv.*

so·ci·o·ec·o·nom·ic /ˌsōsēōˌēkəˈnämik; -ekə-/ ▶*adj.* relating to or concerned with the interaction of social and economic factors. —**so·ci·o·ec·o·nom·i·cal·ly** *adv.*

so·ci·o·lin·guis·tics /ˌsōsēōˌliNGˈgwistiks/ ▶*pl. n.* [treated as *sing.*] the study of language in relation to social factors, including differences of

regional, class, and occupational dialect, gender differences, and bilingualism. —**so·ci·o·lin·guist** /-ˈliNGgwist/ *n.* —**so·ci·o·lin·guis·tic** *adj.* —**so·ci·o·lin·guis·ti·cal·ly** /-ik(ə)lē/ *adv.*

so·ci·ol·o·gy /ˌsōsēˈäləjē/ ▶*n.* the study of the development, structure, and functioning of human society. ▪ the study of social problems. —**so·ci·o·log·i·cal** /ˌsōsēōˈläjikəl/ *adj.* —**so·ci·o·log·i·cal·ly** /ˌsōsēō-ˈläjik(ə)lē/ *adv.* —**so·ci·ol·o·gist** /-jist/ *n.*

so·ci·o·path /ˈsōsēōˌpaTH/ ▶*n.* a person with a personality disorder manifesting itself in extreme antisocial attitudes and behavior and a lack of conscience. —**so·ci·o·path·ic** /ˌsōsēōˈpaTHik/ *adj.* —**so·ci·op·a·thy** /ˌsōsēˈäpəTHē/ *n.*

sock /säk/ ▶*n.* **1** a garment for the foot and lower part of the leg, typically knitted from wool, cotton, or nylon. ▪ a removable inner sole placed inside a shoe or boot for added warmth or to improve the fit. ▪ a white marking on the lower part of a horse's leg, not extending as far as the knee or hock. **2** *inf.* a hard blow: *a sock on the jaw.* ▪ force or emphasis: *we have enough speed and sock in our lineup to score runs.*
▶*v. inf.* [*tr.*] hit forcefully: *Jess socked his father across the face.* ▪ (often **be socked with**) affect disadvantageously: *consumers have been socked with huge price increases.*
▶*phrasal v.* ▫ **sock something away** put money aside as savings: *you'll need to sock away about $900 a month.* ▫ **sock something in** (or **sock in**) (of weather) envelop: *the beach was socked in with fog.*
▶ ▫ **knock** (or **blow**) **someone's socks off** *inf.* amaze or impress someone. ▫ **knock the socks off** *inf.* surpass or beat: *it will knock the socks off the opposition.* ▫ ——— **one's socks off** *inf.* do something with great energy and enthusiasm: *she acted her socks off.* ▫ **put a sock in it** [usu. in *imper.*] *inf.* stop talking. ▫ **sock it to someone** *inf.* attack or make a forceful impression on someone.

sock·et /ˈsäkit/ ▶*n.* **1** a natural or artificial hollow into which something fits or in which something revolves: *the eye socket.* **2** an electrical device receiving a plug or light bulb to make a connection.
▶*v.* (**-et·ed**, **-et·ing**) [*tr.*] place in or fit with a socket.

So·crat·ic /səˈkratik/ ▶*adj.* of or relating to Socrates or his philosophy.
▶*n.* a follower of Socrates. —**So·crat·i·cal·ly** /-ik(ə)lē/ *adv.*

sod[1] /säd/ ▶*n.* (**the sod**) the surface of the ground, with the grass growing on it. ▪ a piece of this, usually sold in rolls and used to start a new lawn, athletic field, etc.
▶*v.* (**sod·ded**, **sod·ding**) [*tr.*] cover with sod or pieces of turf: *the stadium has been sodded.*

sod[2] *chiefly Brit., vulgar slang* ▶*n.* an unpleasant or obnoxious person. ▪ a person of a specified kind. ▪ something that is difficult or causes problems.
▶*v.* (**sod·ded**, **sod·ding**) [*tr.*] used to express one's anger or annoyance at someone or something. ▪ [*intr.*] (**sod off**) [in *imper.*] go away. ▪ [as *adj.*] (**sodding**) used as a general term of contempt.
▶ ▫ **sod all** absolutely nothing.

so·da /ˈsōdə/ ▶*n.* **1** (also **soda water** or **club soda**) carbonated water (originally made with sodium bicarbonate) drunk alone or with liquor or wine: *a whiskey and soda.* ▪ (also **soda pop**) a carbonated soft drink: *a can of soda.* **2** sodium carbonate, esp. as a natural mineral or as an industrial chemical. ▪ sodium in chemical combination: *nitrate of soda.*

so·da foun·tain ▶*n.* a device that dispenses soda water or soft drinks. ▪ a shop or counter selling drinks from such a device.

sod·den /ˈsädn/ ▶*adj.* saturated with liquid, esp. water; soaked through: *his clothes were sodden.* ▪ [in *comb.*] having drunk an excessive amount of a particular alcoholic drink: *a whiskey-sodden criminal.*
▶*v.* [*tr.*] *archaic* saturate (something) with water. —**sod·den·ly** *adv.* —**sod·den·ness** *n.*

so·di·um /ˈsōdēəm/ ▶*n.* the chemical element of atomic number 11, a soft silver-white reactive metal of the alkali metal group. (Symbol: **Na**)

so·di·um bi·car·bon·ate ▶*n.* a soluble white powder, $NaHCO_3$, used in fire extinguishers and effervescent drinks and as a leavening agent in baking. Also called **BAKING SODA.**

so·di·um chlo·ride ▶*n.* a colorless crystalline compound, $NaCl$, occurring naturally in seawater and halite; common salt.

so·di·um hy·drox·ide ▶*n.* a strongly alkaline white deliquescent compound, $NaOH$, used in many industrial processes, e.g., the manufacture of soap and paper.

Sod·om /ˈsädəm/ ▶*a town in ancient Palestine, probably south of the Dead Sea. According to Genesis it was destroyed by fire from heaven,

---

Pronunciation Key ə *ago, up;* ər *over, fur;* a *hat;* ā *ate;* ä *car;* CH *chin;* e *let;* ē *see;* e(ə)r *air;* i *fit;* ī *by;* i(ə)r *ear;* NG *sing;* ō *go;* ô *law, for;* oi *toy;* o͝o *good;* o͞o *goo;* ou *out;* SH *she;* TH *thin;* T̷H *then;* (h)w *why;* ZH *vision*

together with Gomorrah, for the wickedness of its inhabitants. ■ [as *n.*] (**a Sodom**) a wicked or depraved place.

sod·om·ite /'sädə,mīt/ ▶*n.* a person who engages in sodomy. —**sod·o·mit·ic** /,sädə'mitik/, /,sädə'mitikəl/ *adj.*

sod·om·y /'sädəmē/ ▶*n.* sexual intercourse involving anal or oral copulation. —**sod·om·ize** /'sädə,mīz/ *v.*

so·ev·er /sō'evər/ ▶*adv.* archaic or poetic/lit. of any kind; to any extent: *how great soever the assurance is.*

so·fa /'sōfə/ ▶*n.* a long upholstered seat with a back and arms, for two or more people.

so·fa bed ▶*n.* a sofa that can be converted into a bed, typically for occasional use.

sof·fit /'säfit/ ▶*n.* the underside of an architectural structure, such as an arch, a balcony, or overhanging eaves.

soft /sôft/ ▶*adj.* **1** easy to mold, cut, compress, or fold; not hard or firm to the touch: *soft margarine | the ground was soft beneath their feet.* ■ having a smooth surface or texture that is pleasant to touch; not rough or coarse: *soft crushed velvet | her hair felt very soft.* ■ rounded; not angular: *the soft edges of their adobe home.* **2** having a pleasing quality involving a subtle effect or contrast rather than sharp definition: *the soft glow of the lamps | the moon's pale light cast soft shadows.* ■ (of a voice or sound) quiet and gentle: *they spoke in soft whispers.* ■ (of rain, wind, or other natural force) not strong or violent: *a soft breeze rustled the trees.* ■ (of a consonant) pronounced as a fricative (as *c* in *ice*). ■ (of a market, currency, or commodity) falling or likely to fall in value. **3** sympathetic, lenient, or compassionate, esp. to a degree perceived as excessive; not strict or sufficiently strict: *the administration is not becoming soft on crime | Julia's soft heart was touched by his grief.* ■ (of words or language) not harsh or angry; conciliatory; soothing: *he was no good with soft words, gentle phrases.* ■ not strong or robust: *soft, out-of-shape executives in a computer company.* ■ inf. (of a job or way of life) requiring little effort. ■ (of news or other journalism) regarded more as entertainment than as basic news: *fashion is regarded as soft news.* ■ willing to compromise in political matters; moderate: *candidates ranging from far right to soft left.* ■ inf. foolish; silly: *he must be going soft in the head.* ■ (**soft on**) inf. infatuated with: *was Brendan soft on her?* **4** (of a drink) not alcoholic: *all they had was ginger ale and a few other soft drinks.* ■ (of a drug) not likely to cause addiction. ■ (of water) free from mineral salts that inhibit lathering. ■ (of radiation) having little penetrating power. ■ (of a detergent) biodegradable. ■ (also **soft-core**) (of pornography) suggestive or erotic but not explicit.
▶*adv.* softly: *I can just speak soft and she'll hear me.* ■ in a weak or foolish way: *don't talk soft.* ▷Old English *sōfte* 'agreeable, calm, gentle'; related to Dutch *zacht* and German *sanft.* —**soft·ish** *adj.* —**soft·ness** *n.*
▶ □ **have a soft spot for** be fond of or affectionate toward. □ **soft option** an easier alternative: *probation should in no sense be seen as a soft option by the judiciary.* □ **soft touch** (also **easy touch**) inf. a person who readily gives or does something if asked.

soft·ball /'sôf(t),bôl/ ▶*n.* a modified form of baseball played on a smaller field with a larger ball, seven rather than nine innings, and underarm pitching. The game evolved in the U.S. during the late 19th century from a form of indoor baseball. ■ the ball used in this game.

soft-boiled ▶*adj.* (of an egg) boiled for a short time, leaving the yolk soft or liquid. ■ fig. gentle or sentimental: *she's perfected the soft-boiled New York type she's played in most of her movies.*

soft·cov·er /'sôf(t),kəvər/ ▶*adj.* & *n.* another term for PAPERBACK.

soft drink ▶*n.* a nonalcoholic drink, esp. one that is carbonated.

soft·en /'sôfən/ ▶*v.* make or become less hard: [*tr.*] *plant extracts to soften and moisturize the skin* | [*intr.*] *let the vegetables soften over a low heat.* ■ make or become less severe: [*intr.*] *her expression softened at the sight of Diane's white face.* ■ [*tr.*] undermine the resistance of (someone): *the blockade appears a better weapon with which to soften them up for eventual surrender.* ■ [*tr.*] remove mineral salts from (water). —**soft·en·er** *n.*

soft fo·cus ▶*n.* deliberate slight blurring or lack of definition in a photograph or movie.
▶*adj.* (**soft-focus**) characterized by or producing such a lack of definition. ■ denoting a point of view or style of presentation that obscures or avoids sharp definition in order to be more widely acceptable: *soft-focus, nonpolitical essays about American life.*

soft-head·ed (also **soft-head·ed**) ▶*adj.* lacking wisdom or intelligence. —**soft-head·ed·ness** *n.*

soft-heart·ed /'sôft'härtid/ ▶*adj.* kind and compassionate. —**soft-heart·ed·ness** *n.*

soft·ie /'sôftē/ (also **soft·y**) ▶*n.* (*pl.* **soft·ies**) inf. a softhearted, weak, or sentimental person.

soft·ly /'sôf(t)lē/ ▶*adv.* in a quiet voice or manner: *"Can't you sleep?" she*

asked softly | *the door opened softly.* ■ with a gentle or slow movement: *he touched her cheek softly.* ■ in a pleasantly subdued manner: *the room was softly lit by a lamp.*

soft pal·ate /'palit/ ▶*n.* the fleshy, flexible part toward the back of the roof of the mouth.

soft ped·al ▶*n.* a pedal on a piano that can be pressed to make the tone softer.
▶*v.* (**soft-ped·al**) [*tr.*] *Mus.* play with the soft pedal down. ■ refrain from emphasizing the more unpleasant aspects of; play down: *the administration's decision to soft-pedal the missile program.*

soft sell ▶*n.* subtly persuasive selling.
▶*v.* (**soft-sell**) [*tr.*] sell (something) by using such a method.

soft-shell clam (also **soft·shell clam**) ▶*n.* a marine bivalve mollusk (genus *Mya*, family Myidae, esp. *M. arenaria*) with a thin shell and a long siphon, valued as food on the east coast of North America. Also called **soft clam**, **steam·er**.

soft soap ▶*n.* **1** a semifluid soap, esp. one made with potassium rather than sodium salts. **2** inf. persuasive flattery.
▶*v.* (**soft-soap**) [*tr.*] inf. use flattery in order to persuade or cajole (someone) to do something.

soft-spo·ken ▶*adj.* speaking or said with a gentle, quiet voice.

soft·ware /'sôft,we(ə)r/ ▶*n.* the programs and other operating information used by a computer. Compare with HARDWARE.

soft·ware li·brar·y ▶*n.* see LIBRARY.

soft·y ▶*n.* variant spelling of SOFTIE.

sog·gy /'sägē/ ▶*adj.* (**-gi·er**, **-gi·est**) wet and soft: *the sandbags were soggy and split open* | fig. *the chorus sings powerfully but the interpretation is ultimately soggy.* —**sog·gi·ly** /'sägəlē/ *adv.* —**sog·gi·ness** *n.*

soil[1] /soil/ ▶*n.* the upper layer of earth in which plants grow, a black or dark brown material typically consisting of a mixture of organic remains, clay, and rock particles: *blueberries need very acid soil* | fig. *the Garden State has provided fertile soil for the specialty beer market.* ■ the territory of a particular nation: *the stationing of U.S. troops on Japanese soil.* —**soil·less** *adj.*

soil[2] ▶*v.* [*tr.*] make dirty: *he might soil his expensive suit* | [as *adj.*] (**soiled**) *a soiled T-shirt.* ■ (esp. of a child, patient, or pet) make (something) dirty by defecating in or on it. ■ fig. bring discredit to; tarnish: *what good is there in soiling your daughter's reputation?*
▶*n.* waste matter, esp. sewage containing excrement. ■ archaic a stain or discoloring mark.

soil[3] ▶*v.* [*tr.*] rare feed (cattle) on fresh-cut green fodder (originally for the purpose of purging them).

soi·rée /swä'rā/ ▶*n.* an evening party or gathering, typically in a private house, for conversation or music.

so·journ /'sōjərn/ formal ▶*n.* a temporary stay: *her sojourn in Rome.*
▶*v.* [*intr.*] stay somewhere temporarily: *she had sojourned once in Egypt.* —**so·journ·er** *n.*

SOL ▶*abbr.* vulgar slang shit out of luck.

Sol /säl; sōl/ *Roman Mythol.* ▶the sun, esp. when personified as a god.

sol[1] /sōl/ (also **so**) ▶*n.* *Mus.* (in solmization) the fifth note of a major scale. ■ the note G in the fixed-do system.

sol[2] /säl; sōl/ ▶*n. Chem.* a fluid suspension of a colloidal solid in a liquid.

sol[3] /sōl; sôl/ ▶*n.* (*pl.* **so·les** /'sōlāz; 'sôles/) the basic monetary unit of Peru, equal to 100 centavos. It replaced the inti in 1991.

sol·ace /'sälis/ ▶*n.* comfort or consolation in a time of distress or sadness: *she sought solace in her religion.*
▶*v.* [*tr.*] give solace to.

so·lar[1] /'sōlər/ ▶*adj.* of, relating to, or determined by the sun or its radiant energy: *solar heating.*

so·lar[2] ▶*n. Brit.* an upper chamber in a medieval house.

so·lar bat·ter·y (also **solar cell**) ▶*n.* a device converting solar radiation into electricity.

so·lar·i·um /sə'le(ə)rēəm; sō-/ ▶*n.* (*pl.* **-lar·i·ums** or **-lar·i·a** /-'le(ə)rēə/) a room fitted with extensive areas of glass to admit sunlight. ■ a room equipped with sunlamps or tanning beds that can be used to acquire an artificial suntan.

so·lar·ize /'sōlə,rīz/ ▶*v.* [*tr.*] *Photog.* change the relative darkness of (a part of an image) by overexposure to light. —**so·lar·i·za·tion** /,sōləri'zāsHən/ *n.*

so·lar pan·el ▶*n.* a panel designed to absorb the sun's rays as a source of energy for generating electricity or heating.

so·lar plex·us /'pleksəs/ ▶*n.* a complex of ganglia and radiating nerves of the sympathetic system at the pit of the stomach. ■ the area of the body near the base of the sternum: *she felt as if someone had punched her in the solar plexus.*

so·lar sys·tem ▸*n.* *Astron.* the collection of nine planets and their moons in orbit around the sun, together with smaller bodies in the form of asteroids, meteoroids, and comets.

sold /sōld/ ▸ past and past participle of SELL.

sol·der /ˈsädər/ ▸*n.* a low-melting alloy, esp. one based on lead and tin or (for higher temperatures) on brass or silver, used for joining less fusible metals.
▸*v.* [*tr.*] join with solder. —**sol·der·a·ble** *adj.* —**sol·der·er** *n.*

sol·dier /ˈsōljər/ ▸*n.* **1** a person who serves in an army. ■ a private in an army. **2** *Entomol.* a wingless caste of ant or termite with a large specially modified head and jaws, involved chiefly in defense.
▸*v.* [*intr.*] serve as a soldier: [as *n.*] (**soldiering**) *soldiering was what the colonel understood.* ■ (**soldier on**) *inf.* carry on doggedly; persevere: *Gary wasn't enjoying this, but he soldiered on.* ■ *inf.* work more slowly than one's capacity; loaf or malinger: *is it the reason you've been soldiering on the job?* —**sol·dier·ly** *adj.* —**sol·dier·ship** /-ˌSHip/ *n.* (*archaic*).

sol·dier of for·tune ▸*n.* a person who works as a soldier for any country or group that will pay them; a mercenary.

sole[1] /sōl/ ▸*n.* the undersurface of a person's foot: *the soles of their feet were nearly black with dirt.* ■ the section forming the underside of a piece of footwear (typically excluding the heel when this forms a distinct part). ■ the undersurface of a tool or implement such as a plane or the head of a golf club. ■ the floor of a ship's cabin or cockpit.
▸*v.* [*tr.*] (usu. **be soled**) put a new sole onto (a shoe). —**soled** *adj.* [in comb.] *rubber-soled shoes.*

sole[2] ▸*n.* a marine flatfish of almost worldwide distribution, important as a food fish. Several species are in the families Soleidae, Pleuronectidae, and Bothidae.

sole[3] ▸*adj.* one and only: *my sole aim was to contribute to the national team.* ■ belonging or restricted to one person or group of people: *loans can be in sole or joint names* | *the health club is for the sole use of our guests.* ■ *archaic* (esp. of a woman) unmarried. ■ *archaic* alone; unaccompanied. —**sole·ly** *adv.*

sol·e·cism /ˈsäləˌsizəm; ˈsō-/ ▸*n.* a grammatical mistake in speech or writing. ■ a breach of good manners; a piece of incorrect behavior. —**sol·e·cis·tic** /ˌsäləˈsistik; ˌsō-/ *adj.*

sol·emn /ˈsäləm/ ▸*adj.* formal and dignified: *a solemn procession.* ■ not cheerful or smiling; serious: *Tim looked very solemn.* ■ characterized by deep sincerity: *he swore a solemn oath to keep faith.* —**sol·emn·ly** *adv.* —**sol·emn·ness** *n.*

so·lem·ni·ty /səˈlemnitē/ ▸*n.* (*pl.* **-ties**) the state or quality of being serious and dignified: *his ashes were laid to rest with great solemnity.* ■ (usu. **solemnities**) a formal, dignified rite or ceremony: *the ritual of the church was observed in all its solemnities.*

sol·em·nize /ˈsäləmˌnīz/ ▸*v.* [*tr.*] duly perform (a ceremony, esp. that of marriage). ■ mark with a formal ceremony. —**sol·em·ni·za·tion** /ˌsäləmniˈzāSHən/ *n.*

so·le·noid /ˈsōləˌnoid/ ▸*n.* a cylindrical coil of wire acting as a magnet when carrying electric current. ▷early 19th cent.: from French *solénoïde,* from Greek *sōlēn* 'channel, pipe.' —**so·le·noi·dal** /ˌsōləˈnoidl/ *adj.*

sol-fa /ˌsōl ˈfä/ ▸*n.* short for TONIC SOL-FA.
▸*v.* (**-fas, -faed** /-ˈfäd/, **-fa·ing**) [*tr.*] sing using the sol-fa syllables.

sol·fège /sälˈfeZH/ ▸*n.* *Music* **1** solmization. ■ an exercise in singing using solmization syllables. **2** the study of singing and musicianship using solmization syllables.

sol·feg·gio /sälˈfejē,ō/ ▸*n.* (*pl.* **-gi** /-jē/) another term for SOLFÈGE, esp. sense 1.

so·li /ˈsōlē/ ▸ plural form of SOLO.

so·lic·it /səˈlisit/ ▸*v.* (**-it·ed, -it·ing**) [*tr.*] ask for or try to obtain (something) from someone: *he called a meeting to solicit their views.* ■ ask (someone) for something: *historians and critics are solicited for opinions by the auction houses.* ■ [*intr.*] accost someone and offer one's or someone else's services as a prostitute: [as *n.*] (**soliciting**) *although prostitution was not itself an offense, soliciting was.* —**so·lic·i·ta·tion** /sə,lisəˈtāSHən/ *n.*

so·lic·i·tor /səˈlisitər/ ▸*n.* **1** a person who tries to obtain business orders, advertising, etc.; a canvasser. **2** the chief law officer of a city, town, or government department. ■ *Brit.* a member of the legal profession qualified to deal with conveyancing, the drawing up of wills, and other legal matters. Compare with BARRISTER.

so·lic·i·tor gen·er·al ▸*n.* (*pl.* **so·lic·i·tors gen·er·al**) the law officer directly below the attorney general in the Department of Justice, responsible for arguing cases before the Supreme Court. ■ a similar position in some states.

so·lic·i·tous /səˈlisitəs/ ▸*adj.* characterized by or showing interest or

concern: *she was always solicitous about the welfare of her students* | *a solicitous inquiry.* ■ *archaic* eager or anxious to do something: *he was solicitous to cultivate her mamma's good opinion.* —**so·lic·i·tous·ly** *adv.* —**so·lic·i·tous·ness** *n.*

so·lic·i·tude /səˈlisiˌt(y)ōōd/ ▸*n.* care or concern for someone or something: *I was touched by his solicitude.*

sol·id /ˈsälid/ ▸*adj.* (**-id·er, -id·est**) **1** firm and stable in shape; not liquid or fluid: *the stream was frozen solid* | *solid fuels.* ■ strongly built or made of strong materials; not flimsy or slender: *a solid door with good, secure locks.* ■ having three dimensions: *a solid figure with six plane faces.* ■ concerned with objects having three dimensions: *solid geometry.* **2** not hollow or containing spaces or gaps: *a sculpture made out of solid rock* | *a solid mass of flowers* | *the stores were packed solid.* ■ consisting of the same substance throughout: *solid silver cutlery.* ■ (of typesetting) without extra space between the lines of characters. ■ (of a line or surface) without spaces; unbroken: *the solid outline encloses the area within which we measured.* ■ (of time) uninterrupted; continuous: *a solid day of meetings* | *it poured for two hours solid.* **3** dependable; reliable: *the defense is solid* | *there is solid evidence of lower inflation.* ■ sound but without any special qualities or flair: *the rest of the acting is solid.* ■ unanimous or undivided: *they received solid support from their teammates.* ■ financially sound: *the company is very solid and will come through the current recession.* ■ (**solid with**) *inf.* on good terms with: *he thought he could put himself in solid with you by criticizing her.*
▸*n.* a substance or object that is solid rather than liquid or fluid. ■ (**solids**) food that is not liquid: *she drinks only milk and rarely eats solids.* ■ *Geom.* a body or geometric figure having three dimensions. —**sol·id·ly** *adv.* —**sol·id·ness** *n.*

sol·i·dar·i·ty /ˌsäləˈde(ə)ritē/ ▸*n.* **1** unity or agreement of feeling or action, esp. among individuals with a common interest; mutual support within a group: *factory workers voiced solidarity with the striking students.* **2** (**Solidarity**) an independent trade union movement in Poland that developed into a mass campaign for political change and inspired popular opposition to communist regimes across eastern Europe during the 1980s.

sol·i·di /ˈsäliˌdī/ ▸ plural form of SOLIDUS.

so·lid·i·fy /səˈlidəˌfī/ ▸*v.* (**-fies, -fied**) make or become hard or solid: [*intr.*] *the magma slowly solidifies and forms crystals.* ■ [*tr.*] *fig.* make stronger; reinforce: *social and political pressures helped to solidify national identities.* —**so·lid·i·fi·ca·tion** /sə,lidəfiˈkāSHən/ *n.* —**so·lid·i·fi·er** /-ər/ *n.*

so·lid·i·ty /səˈliditē/ ▸*n.* the quality or state of being firm or strong in structure: *the sheer strength and solidity of Romanesque architecture.* ■ the quality of being substantial or reliable in character: *he exuded an aura of reassuring solidity.*

sol·id state ▸*n.* the state of matter in which materials are not fluid but retain their boundaries without support, the atoms or molecules occupying fixed positions with respect to one another and unable to move freely.
▸*adj.* (**sol·id-state**) (of a device) making use of the electronic properties of solid semiconductors (as opposed to electron tubes).

sol·i·dus /ˈsälidəs/ ▸*n.* (*pl.* **-di** /-ˌdī/) **1** another term for SLASH[1] (sense 2). **2** (also **solidus curve**) *Chem.* a curve in a graph of the temperature and composition of a mixture, below which the substance is entirely solid. **3** *hist.* a gold coin of the later Roman Empire.

so·lil·o·quy /səˈliləkwē/ ▸*n.* (*pl.* **-quies**) an act of speaking one's thoughts aloud when by oneself or regardless of any hearers, esp. by a character in a play. ■ a part of a play involving such an act. —**so·lil·o·quist** /-kwist/ *n.* —**so·lil·o·quize** /-ˌkwīz/ *v.*

sol·ip·sism /ˈsälipˌsizəm/ ▸*n.* the view or theory that the self is all that can be known to exist. —**sol·ip·sist** *n.* —**sol·ip·sis·tic** /ˌsälipˈsistik/ *adj.* —**sol·ip·sis·ti·cal·ly** /ˌsälipˈsistik(ə)lē/ *adv.*

sol·i·taire /ˈsäləˌter/ ▸*n.* **1** any of various card games played by one person, the object of which is to use up all one's cards by forming particular arrangements and sequences. **2** a diamond or other gem set in a piece of jewelry by itself. ■ a ring set with such a gem. **3** a large American thrush (genus *Myadestes*) with mainly gray plumage and a short bill.

sol·i·tar·y /ˈsäləˌterē/ ▸*adj.* done or existing alone: *I live a pretty solitary life* | *tigers are essentially solitary.* ■ (of a place) secluded or isolated: *solitary farmsteads.* ■ single; only: *we have not a solitary shred of evidence to go on.* ■ (of a bird, mammal, or insect) living alone or in pairs, esp. in contrast to related social forms: *a solitary wasp.* ■ (of a flower or other part) borne singly.

Pronunciation Key ə *ago, up;* ər *over, fur;* a *hat;* ā *ate;* ä *car;* CH *chin;* e *let;* ē *see;* e(ə)r *air;* i *fit;* ī *by;* i(ə)r *ear;* NG *sing;* ō *go;* ô *law, for;* oi *toy;* ōō *good;* ōō *goo;* ou *out;* SH *she;* TH *thin;* TH *then;* (h)w *why;* ZH *vision*

▶ *n.* (*pl.* **-tar·ies**) **1** a recluse or hermit. **2** *inf.* short for **SOLITARY CONFINEMENT.** —**sol·i·tar·i·ly** /-rəlē/ *adv.* —**sol·i·tar·i·ness** *n.*

sol·i·tar·y con·fine·ment ▶ *n.* the isolation of a prisoner in a separate cell as a punishment.

sol·i·tude /'sälə,t(y)ōōd/ ▶ *n.* the state or situation of being alone: *she savored her few hours of freedom and solitude.* ▪ a lonely or uninhabited place.

sol·mi·za·tion /,sälmi'zāshən; sōl-/ ▶ *n. Mus.* a system of associating each note of a scale with a particular syllable, esp. to teach singing.

so·lo /'sōlō/ ▶ *n.* (*pl.* **-los**) a thing done by one person unaccompanied, in particular: ▪ (*pl.* **so·los** or **so·li** /'sōlē/) a piece of vocal or instrumental music or a dance, or a part or passage in one, for one performer. ▪ an unaccompanied flight by a pilot in an aircraft.
▶ *adj. & adv.* for or done by one person alone; unaccompanied: [as *adj.*] *a solo album* | [as *adv.*] *she'd spent most of her life flying solo.*
▶ *v.* (**so·loes**, **so·loed**) [*intr.*] perform something unaccompanied, in particular: ▪ perform an unaccompanied piece of music or a part or passage in one. ▪ fly an aircraft unaccompanied. ▪ undertake solo climbing.

so·lo·ist /'sōlōist/ ▶ *n.* a singer or other musician who performs a solo.

sol·stice /'sōlstis/ ▶ *n.* either of the two times in the year, the **summer solstice** and the **winter solstice**, when the sun reaches its highest or lowest point in the sky at noon, marked by the longest and shortest days. —**sol·sti·tial** /sōl'stishəl/ *adj.*

sol·u·ble /'sälyəbəl/ ▶ *adj.* **1** (of a substance) able to be dissolved, esp. in water: *the poison is soluble in alcohol.* **2** (of a problem) able to be solved. —**sol·u·bil·i·ty** /,sälyə'bilitē/ *n.*

sol·ute /'säl,yōōt/ ▶ *n.* the minor component in a solution, dissolved in the solvent.

so·lu·tion /sə'lōōshən/ ▶ *n.* **1** a means of solving a problem or dealing with a difficult situation: *there are no easy solutions to financial and marital problems.* ▪ the correct answer to a puzzle: *the solution to this month's crossword.* **2** a liquid mixture in which the minor component (the solute) is uniformly distributed within the major component (the solvent). ▪ the process or state of being dissolved in a solvent. **3** *archaic* the action of separating or breaking down; dissolution: *the solution of British supremacy in South Africa.*

solv·ate /'sälvāt/ ▶ *n. Chem.* a more or less loosely bonded complex formed between a solvent and a dissolved species. —**solv·a·tion** /säl'vāshən/ *n.*

solve /sälv; sôlv/ ▶ *v.* [*tr.*] find an answer to, explanation for, or means of effectively dealing with (a problem or mystery): *the policy could solve the town's housing crisis* | *a murder investigation that has never been solved.* —**solv·a·ble** *adj.* —**solv·er** *n.*

sol·vent /'sälvənt/ ▶ *adj.* **1** having assets in excess of liabilities; able to pay one's debts: *interest rate rises have very severe effects on normally solvent companies.* **2** able to dissolve other substances: *osmotic, chemical, or solvent action.*
▶ *n.* the liquid in which a solute is dissolved to form a solution. ▪ a liquid, typically one other than water, used for dissolving other substances. ▪ *fig.* something that acts to weaken or dispel a particular attitude or situation: *an unrivaled solvent of social prejudices.* —**sol·ven·cy** *n.*

so·ma /'sōmə/ ▶ *n.* [usu. in *sing.*] *Biology* the parts of an organism other than the reproductive cells. ▪ the body as distinct from the soul, mind, or psyche. ▷late 19th cent.: from Greek *sōma* 'body.'

So·ma·li /sə'mälē/ ▶ *n.* (*pl.* same or **-lis**) a member of a mainly Muslim people of Somalia. ▪ the Cushitic language that is the official language of Somalia, also spoken in Djibouti and parts of Kenya and Ethiopia. ▪ a native or national of Somalia.
▶ *adj.* of or relating to Somalia, the Somalis, or their language. —**So·ma·li·an** /-lēən/ *adj. & n.*

so·mat·ic /sə'matik; sō-/ ▶ *adj.* of or relating to the body, esp. as distinct from the mind. ▪ *Biol.* of or relating to the soma. ▪ *Anat.* of or relating to the outer wall of the body, as opposed to the viscera. —**so·mat·i·cal·ly** *adv.*

so·mat·i·za·tion /sə,matə'zāshən; 'sōmə-/ ▶ *n. Psychiatry* the production of recurrent and multiple medical symptoms with no discernible organic cause.

so·mat·o·tro·pin /sə,matə'trōpən/ (also **so·mat·o·tro·phin** /-fin/) ▶ *n. Biochem.* a growth hormone secreted by the anterior pituitary gland.

som·ber /'sämbər/ (*Brit.* also **som·bre**) ▶ *adj.* dark or dull in color or tone; gloomy: *the night skies were somber and starless.* ▪ oppressively solemn or sober in mood; grave: *he looked at her with a somber expression.* ▷mid 18th cent.: from French, based on Latin *sub* 'under' + *umbra* 'shade.' —**som·ber·ly** *adv.* —**som·ber·ness** *n.*

som·bre·ro /säm'bre(ə)rō/ ▶ *n.* (*pl.* **-ros**) a broad-brimmed felt or straw hat, typically worn in Mexico and the southwestern U.S.

some /səm/ ▶ *adj.* **1** an unspecified amount or number of: *I made some money running errands* | *he played some records for me.* **2** used to refer to someone or something that is unknown or unspecified: *she married some newspaper magnate twice her age* | *there must be some mistake* | *he's in some kind of trouble.* **3** (used with a number) approximately: *some thirty different languages are spoken.* **4** a considerable amount or number of: *he went to some trouble* | *I've known you for some years now.* **5** at least a small amount or number of: *he liked some music but generally wasn't musical.* **6** expressing admiration of something notable: *that was some goal.* ▪ used ironically to express disapproval or disbelief: *Mr. Power gave his stock reply. Some help.*
▶ *pron.* **1** an unspecified number or amount of people or things: *here are some of our suggestions* | *if you want whiskey I'll give you some.* **2** at least a small amount or number of people or things: *surely some have noticed.*
▶ *adv. inf.* to some extent; somewhat: *when you get to the majors, the rules change some.*
▶ □ **and then some** *inf.* and plenty more than that: *we got our money's worth and then some.* □ **some little** a considerable amount of: *we are going to be working together for some little time yet.*

-some[1] ▶ *suffix* forming adjectives meaning: **1** productive of: *loathsome.* **2** characterized by being: *wholesome.* ▪ apt to: *tiresome.*

-some[2] ▶ *suffix* (forming nouns) denoting a group of a specified number: *foursome.*

some·bod·y /'səm,bädē/ ▶ *pron.* **1** some person; someone. **2** a person of importance or authority: *I'd like to be somebody* | [as *n.*] *nobodies who want to become somebodies.*

some·day /'səm,dā/ ▶ *adv.* at some time in the future: *I know someday my whole family will be together and happy.*

some·how /'səm,hou/ ▶ *adv.* in some way; by some means: *somehow I managed to get the job done.* ▪ for a reason that is not known or specified: *he looked different somehow.*

some·one /'səm,wən/ ▶ *pron.* **1** an unknown or unspecified person; some person: *there's someone at the door.* **2** a person of importance or authority: *a small-time lawyer keen to be someone.*

some·place /'səm,plās/ ▶ *adv. & pron. inf.* another term for **SOMEWHERE.**

som·er·sault /'səmər,sôlt/ ▶ *n.* an acrobatic movement in which a person turns head over heels in the air or on the ground and lands or finishes on their feet: *a backward somersault.* ▪ *fig.* a dramatic upset or reversal of policy or opinion: *those who perform doctrinal somersaults almost overnight.*
▶ *v.* [*intr.*] perform such an acrobatic feat, or make a similar movement accidentally: *his car somersaulted into a ditch.*

some·thing /'səm,THiNG/ ▶ *pron.* **1** a thing that is unspecified or unknown: *we stopped for something to eat.* **2** used in various expressions indicating that a description or amount being stated is not exact: *a wry look, something between amusement and regret.*
▶ *adv.* **1** *inf.* used for emphasis with a following adjective functioning as an adverb: *my back hurts something terrible.* **2** *archaic* or *dial.* to some extent; somewhat: *the people were something scared.*
▶ □ **thirty-something (forty-something,** etc.) *inf.* an unspecified age between thirty and forty (forty and fifty, etc.): *I'm guessing she's forty-something.* ▪ of or relating to a person between thirty and forty (forty and fifty, etc.): *this music appeals more to your thirty-something crowd.*

some·time /'səm,tīm/ ▶ *adv.* at some unspecified or unknown time: *you must come and have supper sometime.*
▶ *adj.* **1** former: *the sometime editor of the paper.* **2** occasional: *a sometime contributor.*

some·times /'səm,tīmz/ ▶ *adv.* occasionally, rather than all of the time: *sometimes I want to do things on my own.*

some·what /'səm,(h)wät/ ▶ *adv.* to a moderate extent or by a moderate amount: *matters have improved somewhat since then.*
▶ □ **somewhat of** something of: *it was somewhat of a disappointment.*

some·when /'səm,(h)wen/ ▶ *adv. inf.* at some time: *somewhen between 1918 and 1930.*

some·where /'səm,(h)we(ə)r/ ▶ *adv.* in or to some place: *I've seen you somewhere before* | *can we go somewhere warm?* ▪ used to indicate an approximate amount: *it cost somewhere around two thousand dollars.*
▶ *pron.* some unspecified place: *in search of somewhere to live.*
▶ □ **get somewhere** *inf.* make progress; achieve success.

som·nam·bu·lism /säm'nambyə,lizəm/ ▶ *n.* sleepwalking. —**som·nam·bu·lant** /-lənt/ *adj.* —**som·nam·bu·lant·ly** /-ləntlē/ *adv.* —**som·nam·bu·list** *n.* —**som·nam·bu·lis·tic** /-,nambyə'listik/ *adj.* —**som·nam·bu·lis·ti·cal·ly** /-,nambyə'listik(ə)lē/ *adv.*

som·no·lent /ˈsämnələnt/ ▸ *adj.* sleepy; drowsy. ■ causing or suggestive of drowsiness: *a somnolent summer day.* —**som·no·lence** *n.* —**som·no·len·cy** *n.* —**som·no·lent·ly** *adv.*

son /sən/ ▸ *n.* a boy or man in relation to either or both of his parents. ■ a male offspring of an animal. ■ a male descendant: *the sons of Adam.* ■ (**the Son**) (in Christian belief) the second person of the Trinity; Christ. ■ a man considered in relation to his native country or area: *one of Nevada's most famous sons.* ■ a man regarded as the product of a particular person, influence, or environment: *sons of the French Revolution.* ■ used by an elder person as a form of address for a boy or young man: *"You're on private land, son."*
▸ □ **son of a bitch** used as a general term of contempt or abuse. □ **son of a gun** *inf.* a jocular or affectionate way of addressing or referring to someone: *he's a pretentious son of a gun, but he's got a heart of gold.*

so·nar /ˈsōˌnär/ ▸ *n.* a system for the detection of objects under water and for measuring the water's depth by emitting sound pulses and detecting or measuring their return after being reflected. ■ an apparatus used in this system. ■ the method of echolocation used in air or water by animals such as whales and bats.

so·na·ta /səˈnätə/ ▸ *n.* a classical composition for an instrumental soloist, often with a piano accompaniment. It is typically in several movements.

son·a·ti·na /ˌsänəˈtēnə/ ▸ *n.* a simple or short sonata.

Song ▸ variant spelling of **Sung**.

song /sôNG/ ▸ *n.* a short poem or other set of words set to music or meant to be sung. ■ singing or vocal music: *the young airmen broke into song.* ■ a musical composition suggestive of a song. ■ the musical phrases uttered by some birds, whales, and insects, typically forming a recognizable and repeated sequence and used chiefly for territorial defense or for attracting mates. ■ a poem, esp. one in rhymed stanzas: *The Song of Hiawatha.* ■ *archaic* poetry.
▸ □ **a song and dance** *inf.* a long explanation that is pointless or deliberately evasive. ■ *chiefly Brit.* a fuss or commotion: *she would be sure to make a song and dance about her aching feet.*

song·bird /ˈsôNGˌbərd/ ▸ *n.* **1** a bird with a musical song. **2** *Ornithol.* a perching bird of a group distinguished by having a vocal organ that is capable of producing a variety of notes.

song·smith /ˈsôNGˌsmiTH/ ▸ *n.* *inf.* a person who writes popular songs.

song·ster /ˈsôNGstər/ ▸ *n.* a person who sings, esp. fluently and skillfully. ■ a person who writes songs or verse. ■ a songbird.

song·writ·er /ˈsôNGˌrītər/ ▸ *n.* a person who writes popular songs or the music for them. —**song·writ·ing** *n.*

son·ic /ˈsänik/ ▸ *adj.* relating to or using sound waves. ■ denoting or having a speed equal to that of sound. —**son·i·cal·ly** /-ik(ə)lē/ *adv.*

son·ic bar·ri·er ▸ *n.* another term for **SOUND BARRIER**.

son·ic boom ▸ *n.* a loud explosive noise caused by the shock wave from an aircraft traveling faster than the speed of sound.

son-in-law ▸ *n.* (*pl.* **sons-in-law**) the husband of one's daughter.

son·net /ˈsänit/ ▸ *n.* a poem of fourteen lines using any of a number of formal rhyme schemes, in English typically having ten syllables per line.
▸ *v.* (**-net·ed**, **-net·ing**) [*intr.*] *archaic* compose sonnets. ■ [*tr.*] celebrate in a sonnet.

son·ny /ˈsənē/ ▸ *n.* *inf.* used by an older person as a familiar form of address to a young boy. ■ used as a humorous or patronizing way of addressing a man: *look, sonny, that's all I can tell you.*

so·no·rous /ˈsänərəs/ ▸ *adj.* (of a person's voice or other sound) imposingly deep and full. ■ capable of producing a deep or ringing sound: *the alloy is sonorous and useful in making bells.* ■ (of a speech or style) using imposing language: *they had expected the lawyers to deliver sonorous lamentations.* ■ having a pleasing sound: *she used the misleadingly sonorous name "melanoma" to describe it.* —**so·nor·i·ty** /səˈnôritē/ *n.* —**so·no·rous·ly** *adv.* —**so·no·rous·ness** *n.*

sook /sŏŏk; sək/ ▸ *n.* a female crab.

soon /sŏŏn/ ▸ *adv.* **1** in or after a short time: *everyone will soon know the truth.* ■ early: *it's a pity you have to leave so soon | I wish you'd told me sooner.* **2** used to indicate one's preference in a particular matter: *I'd just as soon Tim did it | I would sooner resign than transfer to Toronto.* —**soon·ish** *adv.*

soot /sŏŏt/ ▸ *n.* a black powdery or flaky substance consisting largely of amorphous carbon, produced by the incomplete burning of organic matter.
▸ *v.* [*tr.*] cover or clog (something) with soot.

sooth /sŏŏTH/ ▸ *n.* *archaic* truth.
▸ □ **in sooth** in truth; really.

soothe /sŏŏTH/ ▸ *v.* [*tr.*] gently calm (a person or their feelings): *a shot of brandy might soothe his nerves | [as *adj.*] (**soothing**) *she put on some soothing music.* ■ reduce pain or discomfort in (a part of the body): *to soothe the skin try chamomile or thyme.* ■ relieve or ease (pain): *it contains a mild anesthetic to soothe the pain.* —**sooth·er** *n.* —**sooth·ing·ly** *adv.*

sooth·say·er /ˈsŏŏTHˌsāər/ ▸ *n.* a person supposed to be able to foresee the future. —**sooth·say·ing** *n.*

soot·y /ˈsŏŏtē/ ▸ *adj.* (**soot·i·er**, **soot·i·est**) covered with or colored like soot: *the front of the fireplace was blackened and sooty | his olive skin and sooty eyes.* ■ used in names of birds and other animals that are mainly blackish or brownish black, e.g., **sooty tern.** —**soot·i·ly** /ˈsŏŏtəlē/ *adv.* —**soot·i·ness** *n.*

SOP ▸ *abbr.* ■ Standard Operating Procedure.

sop /säp/ ▸ *n.* **1** a thing given or done as a concession of no great value to appease someone whose main concerns or demands are not being met: *my agent telephones as a sop but never finds me work.* **2** a piece of bread dipped in gravy, soup, or sauce.
▸ *v.* (**sopped**, **sop·ping**) [*tr.*] (**sop something up**) soak up liquid using an absorbent substance: *he used some bread to sop up the sauce.* ■ wet thoroughly; soak.

soph. ▸ *abbr.* sophomore.

soph·ism /ˈsäfizəm/ ▸ *n.* a fallacious argument, esp. one used deliberately to deceive.

soph·ist /ˈsäfist/ ▸ *n.* a paid teacher of philosophy and rhetoric in ancient Greece, associated in popular thought with moral skepticism and specious reasoning. ■ a person who reasons with clever but fallacious arguments. ▷mid 16th cent.: via Latin from Greek *sophistēs*, from *sophizesthai* 'devise, become wise,' from *sophos* 'wise.' —**so·phis·tic** /səˈfistik/ *adj.* —**so·phis·ti·cal** /səˈfistikəl/ *adj.* —**so·phis·ti·cal·ly** /səˈfistik(ə)lē/ *adv.*

so·phis·ti·cate ▸ *v.* /səˈfistəˌkāt/ [*tr.*] cause (a person or their thoughts, attitudes, and expectations) to become less simple or straightforward through education or experience: *readers who have been sophisticated by modern literary practice.* ■ develop (something such as a piece of equipment or a technique) into a more complex form: *functions that other software applications have sophisticated.*
▸ *n.* /səˈfistəˌkāt; -kit/ a person with much worldly experience and knowledge of fashion and culture: *he is still the butt of jokes made by New York sophisticates.* —**so·phis·ti·ca·tion** /səˌfistiˈkāSHən/ *n.*

so·phis·ti·cat·ed /səˈfistiˌkātid/ ▸ *adj.* (of a machine, system, or technique) developed to a high degree of complexity: *highly sophisticated computer systems.* ■ (of a person or their thoughts, reactions, and understanding) aware of and able to interpret complex issues; subtle: *discussion and reflection are necessary for a sophisticated response to a text.* ■ having, revealing, or proceeding from a great deal of worldly experience and knowledge of fashion and culture: *a chic, sophisticated woman | a young man with sophisticated tastes.* ■ appealing to people with such knowledge of experience: *a sophisticated restaurant.* —**so·phis·ti·cat·ed·ly** *adv.*

soph·ist·ry /ˈsäfəstrē/ ▸ *n.* (*pl.* **-ries**) the use of fallacious arguments, esp. with the intention of deceiving. ■ a fallacious argument.

soph·o·more /ˈsäf(ə)ˌmôr/ ▸ *n.* a second-year college or high school student.

soph·o·mor·ic /ˌsäf(ə)ˈmôrik/ ▸ *adj.* of, relating to, or characteristic of a sophomore: *my sophomoric years.* ■ pretentious or juvenile: *sophomoric double entendres.*

sop·o·rif·ic /ˌsäpəˈrifik/ ▸ *adj.* tending to induce drowsiness or sleep: *the motion of the train had a somewhat soporific effect.* ■ sleepy or drowsy: *some medicine made her soporific.* ■ tediously boring or monotonous: *a libel trial is in large parts intensely soporific.*
▸ *n.* a drug or other agent of this kind. —**sop·o·rif·i·cal·ly** /-ik(ə)lē/ *adv.*

sop·ping /ˈsäpiNG/ ▸ *adj.* saturated with liquid; wet through: *get those sopping clothes off.*

sop·py /ˈsäpē/ ▸ *adj.* (**-pi·er**, **-pi·est**) *inf.* self-indulgently sentimental: *I look at babies with a soppy smile on my face.* —**sop·pi·ly** /ˈsäpəlē/ *adv.* —**sop·pi·ness** *n.*

so·pran·o /səˈpranō/ ▸ *n.* (*pl.* **-pran·os**) the highest of the four standard singing voices: *a piece composed for soprano, flute, and continuo.* ■ a female or boy singer with such a voice. ■ a part written for such a voice. ■ [usu. as *adj.*] an instrument of a high or the highest pitch in its family: *a soprano saxophone.*

Pronunciation Key ə *ago*, *up*; ər *over*, *fur*; a *hat*; ā *ate*; ä *car*; CH *chin*; e *let*; ē *see*; e(ə)r *air*; i *fit*; ī *by*; i(ə)r *ear*; NG *sing*; ō *go*; ô *law*, *for*; oi *toy*; ŏŏ *good*; ŏŏ *goo*; ou *out*; SH *she*; TH *thin*; <u>TH</u> *then*; (h)w *why*; ZH *vision*

sor·bet /sôr'bā; 'sôrbit/ ▶n. a dessert consisting of frozen fruit juice or flavored water and sugar.

sor·cer·er /'sôrsərər/ ▶n. a person who claims or is believed to have magic powers; a wizard.

sor·cer·y /'sôrsərē/ ▶n. the use of magic, esp. black magic. —**sor·cer·ous** /-rəs/ adj.

sor·did /'sôrdid/ ▶adj. involving ignoble actions and motives; arousing moral distaste and contempt: *the story paints a sordid picture of bribes and scams.* ■ dirty or squalid: *the overcrowded housing conditions were sordid and degrading.* —**sor·did·ly** adv. —**sor·did·ness** n.

sor·di·no /sôr'dēnō/ ▶n. (pl. **-ni** /-nē/) Mus. a mute. ■ (**sordini**) (on a piano) the dampers.

sore /sôr/ ▶adj. (of a part of one's body) painful or aching: *my feet were sore and my head ached.* ■ suffering pain from a part of one's body: *he was sore from the long ride.* ■ inf. upset and angry: *I didn't even know they were sore at us.* ■ severe; urgent: *we're in sore need of him.*
▶n. a raw or painful place on the body: *we had sores on our hands.* ■ a cause or source of distress or annoyance: *there's no point raking over the past and opening old sores.*
▶adv. archaic extremely; severely: *they were sore afraid.* —**sore·ness** n.
▶ □ **sore point** a subject or issue about which someone feels distressed or annoyed: *the glamorous image of their paramilitary rivals was always a sore point with the police.* □ **stand** (or **stick**) **out like a sore thumb** be obviously different from the surrounding people or things.

sore·head /'sôr,hed/ ▶n. inf. a person who is in a bad temper or easily irritated.

sore·ly /'sôrlē/ ▶adv. to a very high degree or level of intensity (esp. of an unwelcome or unpleasant state or emotion): *she would sorely miss his company.*

sor·ghum /'sôrgəm/ ▶n. a widely cultivated cereal (genus *Sorghum*) native to warm regions of the Old World. ■ a syrupy sweetener made from a type of this cereal.

so·ror·i·ty /sə'rôritē, -'rä-/ ▶n. (pl. **-ties**) a society for female students in a university or college, typically for social purposes.

sor·rel[1] /'sôrəl/ ▶n. a European plant (genus *Rumex*) of the dock family, with arrow-shaped leaves that are used in salads and cooking for their acidic flavor.

sor·rel[2] ▶n. a horse with a light reddish-brown coat. ■ [usu. as adj.] a light reddish-brown color: *a sorrel mare with four white socks.*

sor·row /'särō/ ▶n. a feeling of deep distress caused by loss, disappointment, or other misfortune suffered by oneself or others: *he understood the sorrow and discontent underlying his brother's sigh.* ■ an event or circumstance that causes such a feeling: *it was a great sorrow to her when they separated.* ■ the outward expression of grief; lamentation.
▶v. [intr.] feel or display deep distress: [as adj.] (**sorrowing**) *the sorrowing widower found it hard to relate to his sons.*

sor·row·ful /'särəfəl/ ▶adj. feeling or showing grief: *she looked at him with sorrowful eyes.* ■ causing grief: *the sorrowful news of his father's death.* —**sor·row·ful·ly** adv. —**sor·row·ful·ness** n.

sor·ry /'särē; 'sô-/ ▶adj. (**-ri·er, -ri·est**) **1** feeling distress, esp. through sympathy with someone else's misfortune: *I was sorry to hear about what happened to your family.* ■ (**sorry for**) filled with compassion for: *he couldn't help feeling sorry for her.* ■ feeling regret or penitence: *he said he was sorry he had upset me.* ■ used as an expression of apology: *sorry—I was trying not to make a noise.* ■ used as a polite request that someone should repeat something that one has failed to hear or understand: *Sorry? In case I what?* **2** in a poor or pitiful state or condition: *he looks a sorry sight with his broken jaw.* ■ unpleasant and regrettable, esp. on account of incompetence or misbehavior: *we feel so ashamed that we keep quiet about the whole sorry business.* —**sor·ri·ly** /'särəlē; sô-/ adv. —**sor·ri·ness** n.
▶ □ **sorry for oneself** sad and self-pitying.

sort /sôrt/ ▶n. **1** a category of things or people having some common feature; a type: *if only we knew the sort of people she was mixing with.* ■ inf. a person of a specified character or nature: *Frank was a genuinely friendly sort.* **2** Comput. the arrangement of data in a prescribed sequence.
▶v. [tr.] **1** arrange systematically in groups; separate according to type, class, etc.: *she sorted out the clothes, some to be kept, some to be thrown away.* ■ (**sort through**) look at (a group of things) one after another in order to classify them or make a selection: *she sat down and sorted through her mail.* **2** resolve (a problem or difficulty): *the teacher helps the children to sort out their problems.* ■ resolve the problems or difficulties of (oneself): *I need time to sort myself out.*
▶phrasal v. □ **sort something out 1** separate something from a mixed group: *she started sorting out the lettuce from the spinach.* **2** arrange;

prepare: *they are anxious to sort out traveling arrangements.* —**sort·a·ble** adj. —**sort·er** n.
▶ □ **nothing of the sort** used as an emphatic way of denying permission or refuting an earlier statement or assumption: *"I'll pay." "You'll do nothing of the sort."* □ **of a sort** (or **of sorts**) inf. of an atypical and typically inferior type: *the training camp actually became a tourist attraction of sorts.* □ **out of sorts** slightly unwell: *feeling nauseous and generally out of sorts.* ■ in low spirits; irritable: *the trying events of the day had put him out of sorts.* □ **sort of** inf. to some extent; in some way or other (used to convey inexactness or vagueness): *"Do you see what I mean?" "Sort of," answered Jean cautiously.*

sor·ta·tion /sôr'tāsHən/ ▶n. (especially in data processing) the process of sorting or its result.

sort·ie /'sôrtē; 'sôrtē/ ▶n. an attack made by troops coming out from a position of defense. ■ an operational flight by a single military aircraft. ■ a short trip or journey: *I went on a shopping sortie.*
▶v. (**-ies, -ied, -ie·ing**) [intr.] come out from a defensive position to make an attack.

SOS ▶n. (pl. **SOSs**) an international code signal of extreme distress, used esp. by ships at sea. ■ an urgent appeal for help.

so-so ▶adj. neither very good nor very bad: *a happy ending to a so-so season.*

sos·te·nu·to /,sästə'nōōtō/ Mus. ▶adj. (of a passage of music) to be played in a sustained or prolonged manner.
▶n. (pl. **-tos**) performance in this manner.

sot /sät/ ▶n. a habitual drunkard. —**sot·tish** adj.

sot·to vo·ce /'sätō 'vōchē/ ▶adv. & adj. (of singing or a spoken remark) in a quiet voice, if not to be overheard: [as adv.] *"It won't be cheap," he added sotto voce* | [as adj.] *a sotto voce remark.*

sou /sōō/ ▶n. hist. a former French coin of low value. ■ inf. a very small amount of money: *he didn't have a sou.*

sou·bri·quet ▶n. variant spelling of SOBRIQUET.

souf·flé /sōō'flā/ ▶n. a light, spongy baked dish made typically by adding flavored egg yolks to stiffly beaten egg whites. ■ any of various light dishes made with beaten egg whites.

sought /sôt/ ▶ past and past participle of SEEK.

sought af·ter ▶adj. in demand; generally desired: *this print will be much sought after by collectors.*

soul /sōl/ ▶n. **1** the spiritual or immaterial part of a human being or animal, regarded as immortal. ■ a person's moral or emotional nature or sense of identity: *in the depths of her soul, she knew he would betray her.* ■ the essence of something: *integrity is the soul of intellectual life.* ■ emotional or intellectual energy or intensity, esp. as revealed in a work of art or an artistic performance: *their interpretation lacked soul.* **2** a person regarded as the embodiment of a specified quality: *he was the soul of discretion.* ■ an individual person: *I'll never tell a soul.* ■ a person regarded with affection or pity: *she's a nice old soul.* **3** African-American culture or ethnic pride. ■ short for SOUL MUSIC. ▷Old English *sāwol, sāw(e)l,* of Germanic origin; related to Dutch *ziel* and German *Seele.* —**souled** adj. [in comb.] *she was a great-souled character.*

soul food ▶n. traditional southern African-American food.

soul·ful /'sōlfəl/ ▶adj. expressing or appearing to express deep and often sorrowful feeling: *she gave him a soulful glance.* —**soul·ful·ly** adv. —**soul·ful·ness** n.

soul·less /'sōl,lis/ ▶adj. (of a building, room, or other place) lacking character and individuality: *she found the apartment beautiful but soulless.* ■ (of an activity) tedious and uninspiring: *soulless, nonproductive work.* ■ lacking or suggesting the lack of human feelings and qualities: *two soulless black eyes were watching her.* —**soul·less·ly** adv. —**soul·less·ness** n.

soul mate (also **soul·mate**) ▶n. a person ideally suited to another as a close friend or romantic partner.

soul mu·sic ▶n. a kind of music incorporating elements of rhythm and blues and gospel music, popularized by African-Americans. Characterized by an emphasis on vocals and an impassioned improvisatory delivery, it is associated with performers such as Marvin Gaye, Aretha Franklin, James Brown, and Otis Redding.

sound[1] /sound/ ▶n. vibrations that travel through the air or another medium and can be heard when they reach a person's or animal's ear: *light travels faster than sound.* ■ a group of vibrations of this kind; a thing that can be heard: *she heard the sound of voices in the hall.* ■ the area or distance within which something can be heard:. ■ the ideas or impressions conveyed by words: *you've had a hard day, by the sound of it.* ■ sound produced by continuous and regular vibrations, as opposed to noise. ■ music, speech, and sound effects when recorded, used to

accompany a film or video production, or broadcast: [as *adj.*] *a sound studio.* ■ broadcasting by radio as distinct from television. ■ the distinctive quality of the music of a particular composer or performer or of the sound produced by a particular musical instrument: *the sound of the Beatles.* ■ (**sounds**) *inf.* music, esp. popular music: *sounds of the sixties.*
▶*v.* [*intr.*] emit sound: *a loud buzzer sounded.* ■ [*tr.*] cause (something) to emit sound: *she sounded the horn.* ■ [*tr.*] say (something); utter: *he sounded a warning that a coup was imminent.* ■ [*tr.*] convey a specified impression when heard: *he sounded worried.* ■ (of something or someone that has been described to one) convey a specified impression: *it sounds as though you really do believe that.* ■ [*tr.*] test (the lungs or another body cavity) by noting the sound they produce: *the doctor sounded her chest.*
▶*phrasal v.* □ **sound off** express one's opinions in a loud or forceful manner. —**sound·less** *adj.* —**sound·less·ly** *adv.* —**sound·less·ness** *n.*
sound² ▶*adj.* **1** in good condition; not damaged, injured, or diseased: *they returned safe and sound* | *he was of sound mind.* ■ based on reason, sense, or judgment: *sound advice for healthy living.* ■ competent, reliable, or holding acceptable views: *he's a bit stuffy, but he's very sound on his law.* ■ financially secure: *she could get her business on a sound footing for the first time.* **2** (of sleep) deep and undisturbed. ■ (of a person) tending to sleep deeply: *I am a sound sleeper.* **3** severe: *such people should be given a sound thrashing.*
▶*adv.* soundly: *he was sound asleep.* —**sound·ly** *adv.* —**sound·ness** *n.*
sound³ ▶*v.* **1** [*tr.*] ascertain (the depth of water), typically by means of a weighted line or pole or using sound echoes. **2** [*tr.*] question (someone), typically in a cautious or discreet way, as to their opinions or feelings on a subject: *we'll sound out our representatives first.* ■ inquire into (someone's opinions of feelings) in this way: *officials arrived to sound out public opinion at meetings in factories.* **3** [*intr.*] (esp. of a whale) dive down steeply to a great depth.
▶*n.* a long surgical probe, typically with a curved, blunt end. —**sound·er** *n.*
sound⁴ ▶*n.* a narrow stretch of water forming an inlet or connecting two wider areas of water such as two seas or a sea and a lake.
sound bar·ri·er ▶*n.* (**the sound barrier**) the increased drag, reduced controllability, and other effects that occur when an aircraft approaches the speed of sound, formerly regarded as an obstacle to supersonic flight.
sound bite ▶*n.* a short extract from a recorded interview, chosen for its pungency or appropriateness.
sound·board /'soun(d),bôrd/ (also **sounding board**) ▶*n.* a thin sheet of wood over which the strings of a piano or similar instrument are positioned to increase the sound produced.
sound ef·fect ▶*n.* a sound other than speech or music made artificially for use in a play, movie, or other broadcast production: *the play used sound effects of galley oars and blood-curdling yells.*
sound·ing /'soundiNG/ ▶*n.* the action or process of measuring the depth of the sea or other body of water. ■ a measurement taken by sounding. ■ the determination of any physical property at a depth in the sea or at a height in the atmosphere. ■ (**soundings**) *fig.* information or evidence ascertained as a preliminary step before deciding on a course of action: *he's been **taking soundings** about the possibility of moving his offices.*
sound·ing board ▶*n.* **1** a board or screen placed over or behind a pulpit or stage to reflect a speaker's voice forward. ■ another term for SOUNDBOARD. **2** a person or group whose reactions to suggested ideas are used as a test of their validity or likely success before they are made public: *I considered him mainly as a sounding board for my impressions.* ■ a channel through which ideas are disseminated.
sound·proof /'soun(d),proof/ ▶*adj.* preventing, or constructed of material that prevents, the passage of sound: *there was a soundproof, state-of-the-art recording studio.*
▶*v.* [*tr.*] make (a room or building) resistant to the passage of sound. —**sound·proof·ing** *n.*
sound·track /'soun(d),trak/ ▶*n.* a recording of the musical accompaniment to a movie: *she has requested a collaboration for the soundtrack to her forthcoming movie.*
sound wave ▶*n.* Physics a wave of compression and rarefaction, by which sound is propagated in an elastic medium such as air.
soup /soop/ ▶*n.* **1** a liquid dish, typically made by boiling meat, fish, or vegetables, etc., in stock or water: *a bowl of tomato soup.* ■ *fig.* a substance or mixture perceived to resemble soup in appearance or consistency: *the waves and the water beyond have become a thick brown soup.* **2** *inf.* the chemicals in which film is developed. —**soup·like** *adj.*
▶*phrasal v.* □ **soup something up** *inf.* increase the power and efficiency

of an engine or other machine. ■ make something more elaborate or impressive: *we had to soup up the show for the new venue.*
soup·çon /soop'sôN/ ▶*n.* a very small quantity of something: *a soupçon of mustard.*
soup kitch·en ▶*n.* a place where free food is served to those who are homeless or destitute.
soup·spoon /'soop,spoon/ (also **soup spoon**) ▶*n.* a large spoon with a round bowl, used for eating soup.
soup·y /'soopē/ ▶*adj.* (**soup·i·er**, **soup·i·est**) having the appearance or consistency of soup: *a soupy stew.* ■ (of the air or climate) humid. ■ *inf.* mawkishly sentimental: *soupy nostalgia.* —**soup·i·ly** /'soopəlē/ *adv.* —**soup·i·ness** *n.*
sour /'sou(ə)r/ ▶*adj.* having an acid taste like lemon or vinegar: *she sampled the wine and found it was sour.* ■ (of food, esp. milk) spoiled because of fermentation. ■ having a rancid smell: *her breath was always sour.* ■ *fig.* feeling or expressing resentment, disappointment, or anger: *she was quite a different woman from the sour, bored creature I had known.* ■ (of petroleum or natural gas) having a relatively high sulfur content.
▶*n.* a drink made by mixing an alcoholic beverage with lemon juice or lime juice: *a rum sour.*
▶*v.* make or become sour: [*tr.*] *water soured with tamarind* | [as *adj.*] (**soured**) *soured cream* | [*intr.*] *a bowl of milk was souring in the sun.* ■ make or become unpleasant, acrimonious, or difficult: [*tr.*] *a dispute soured relations between the two countries for over a year* | [*intr.*] *many friendships have soured over borrowed money.* —**sour·ish** *adj.* —**sour·ly** *adv.* —**sour·ness** *n.*
▶ □ **sour grapes** an attitude in which someone disparages or affects to despise something because they cannot have it themselves: *government officials dismissed many of the complaints as sour grapes.*
source /sôrs/ ▶*n.* a place, person, or thing from which something comes or can be obtained: *mackerel is a good source of fish oil.* ■ a spring or fountainhead from which a river or stream issues: *the source of the Nile.* ■ a person who provides information: *military sources announced a reduction in strategic nuclear weapons.* ■ a book or document used to provide evidence in research. ■ *technical* a body or process by which energy or a particular component enters a system. The opposite of SINK².
▶*v.* [*tr.*] (often **be sourced**) obtain from a particular source: *each type of coffee is sourced from one country.* ■ find out where (something) can be obtained: *she was called upon to source a supply of carpet.* —**source·less** *adj.*
source·book /'sôrs,book/ ▶*n.* a collection of writings and articles on a particular subject, esp. one used as a basic introduction to that subject.
sour cream ▶*n.* cream that has been deliberately fermented by the addition of certain bacteria.
sour·dough /'sou(ə)r,dō/ ▶*n.* **1** leaven for making bread, consisting of fermenting dough, typically that left over from a previous batch. ■ bread made using such leaven. **2** an experienced prospector in the western U.S. or Canada; an old-timer.
sour·puss /'sou(ə)r,poos/ ▶*n.* *inf.* a bad-tempered or habitually sullen person.
souse /sous/ ▶*v.* [*tr.*] soak in or drench with liquid. ■ [often as *adj.*] (**soused**) put (gherkins, fish, etc.) in a pickling solution or a marinade: *soused herring.* ■ [as *adj.*] (**soused**) *inf.* drunk: *I was soused to the eyeballs.*
south /souTH/ ▶*n.* (usu. **the south**) **1** the direction toward the point of the horizon 90° clockwise from east, or the point on the horizon itself: *the breeze came from the south.* ■ the compass point corresponding to this. **2** the southern part of the world or of a specified country, region, or town: *he was staying in the south of France.* **3** (**South**) Bridge the player sitting opposite and partnering North.
▶*adj.* **1** lying toward, near, or facing the south: *the south coast.* ■ (of a wind) blowing from the south. **2** of or denoting the southern part of a specified area, city, or country or its inhabitants: *Telegraph Hill in South Boston.*
▶*adv.* to or toward the south: *they journeyed south along the valley.*
south·bound /'souTH,bound/ ▶*adj.* traveling or leading toward the south: *southbound traffic.*
south·east /,souTH'ēst/ ▶*n.* **1** (usu. **the southeast**) the direction toward the point of the horizon midway between south and east, or the point on the horizon itself: *a ship was coming in from the southeast.* ■ the compass point corresponding to this. **2** (also **the Southeast**) the southeastern part of a country, region, or town: *most "Mexican" foods in the southeast are actually Texan.*

▸*adj.* **1** lying toward, near, or facing the southeast: *a table stood in the southeast corner.* ■ (of a wind) blowing from the southeast. **2** of or denoting the southeastern part of a specified country, region, or town or its inhabitants: *Southeast Asia.*
▸*adv.* to or toward the southeast: —**south·east·er·ly** *adv.* —**south·east·ern** /-ərn/ *adj.*

south·east·er /ˌsoutʰˈēstər/ ▸*n.* a wind blowing from the southeast.

south·er·ly /ˈsəтнərlē/ ▸*adj. & adv.* in a southward position or direction: [as *adj.*] *the most southerly of the Greek islands.* ■ (of a wind) blowing from the south: [as *adj.*] *a southerly gale* | [as *adv.*] *the wind had backed southerly.*
▸*n.* (often **southerlies**) a wind blowing from the south.

south·ern /ˈsəтнərn/ ▸*adj.* **1** situated in the south or directed toward or facing the south: *the southern hemisphere.* **2** living in or originating from the south: *the southern rural poor.* ■ of, relating to, or characteristic of the south or its inhabitants: *a faintly southern accent.* —**south·ern·most** /-ˌmōst/ *adj.*

South·ern Cross *Astron.* ▸the smallest constellation but the most familiar one to observers in the southern hemisphere.

South·ern·er (also **south·ern·er**) /ˈsəтнərnər/ ▸*n.* a native or inhabitant of the south, esp. of the southern U.S.

south·ern lights ▸another name for the aurora australis. See **AURORA**.

south·ing /ˈsouтнiNG/ ▸*n.* distance traveled or measured southward, esp. at sea.

south·paw /ˈsouтн,pô/ ▸*n.* a left-handed person, esp. a boxer who leads with the right hand or a baseball pitcher .

South Pole ▸*n.* see **POLE**[2].

south·ward /ˈsouтнwərd/ *Naut.* ▸*adj.* in a southerly direction: *employment and people began a southward drift.*
▸*adv.* (also **south·wards**) toward the south.
▸*n.* (**the southward**) the direction or region to the south: *cool air from the ocean to the southward.* —**south·ward·ly** *adv.*

south·west /ˌsouтнˈwest/ ▸*n.* **1** (usu. **the southwest**) the direction toward the point of the horizon midway between south and west, or the point of the horizon itself: *clouds uncoiled from the southwest.* ■ the compass point corresponding to this. **2** the southwestern part of a country, region, or town: *the beach is in the southwest of the island.* ■ (usu. **the Southwest**) the southwestern part of the U.S.: *the desert turtle population in the Southwest.*
▸*adj.* **1** lying toward, near, or facing the southwest: *the southwest tower collapsed in a storm.* ■ (of a wind) blowing from the southwest. **2** of or denoting the southwestern part of a specified country, region, or town or its inhabitants: *fishing in southwest Alaska's Bristol Bay area.*
▸*adv.* to or toward the southwest: *they drove directly southwest.* —**south·west·er·ly** *adv.* —**south·west·ern** /-ərn/ *adj.*

south·west·er /ˌsouтнˈwestər/ ▸*n.* a wind blowing from the southwest.

sou·ve·nir /ˌso͞ovəˈnir/ ▸*n.* a thing that is kept as a reminder of a person, place, or event.
▸*v.* [*tr.*] *inf.* take as a memento: *many parts of the aircraft have been souvenired.*

sou'·west·er /ˌsou'westər/ ▸*n.* a waterproof hat with a broad flap covering the neck.

sou'wester

sov·er·eign /ˈsäv(ə)rən/ ▸*n.* a supreme ruler, esp. a monarch.
▸*adj.* possessing supreme or ultimate power: *in modern democracies the people's will is in theory sovereign.* ■ (of a nation or state) fully independent and determining its own affairs: *a sovereign, democratic republic.* ■ (of affairs) subject to a specified state's control without outside interference: *criticism was seen as interference in China's sovereign affairs.* —**sov·er·eign·ly** *adv.*

sov·er·eign·ty /ˈsäv(ə)rəntē/ ▸*n.* (*pl.* **-ties**) supreme power or authority: *how can we hope to wrest sovereignty away from the oligarchy and back to the people?* ■ the authority of a state to govern itself or another state: *national sovereignty.* ■ a self-governing state. ▷late Middle English: from Old French *sovereinete*, from *soverain.*

so·vi·et /ˈsōvēit; -,et/ ▸*n.* **1** an elected local, district, or national council in the former USSR. ■ a revolutionary council of workers or peasants in Russia before 1917. **2** (**Soviet**) a citizen of the former USSR.
▸*adj.* (**So·vi·et**) of or concerning the former Soviet Union: *the Soviet leader.* ▷early 20th cent.: from Russian *sovet* 'council.' —**So·vi·et·i·za·tion** /ˌsōvēiti'zāSHən/ *n.* —**So·vi·et·ize** /-ˌtīz/ *v.*

So·vi·et·ol·o·gist /ˌsōvēi'täləjist/ ▸*n.* a person who studies the former Soviet Union. —**So·vi·et·o·log·i·cal** /-tə'läjikəl/ *adj.* —**So·vi·et·o·log·y** /-jē/ *n.*

sow[1] /sō/ ▸*v.* (*past* **sowed**; *past part.* **sown** /sōn/ or **sowed**) [*tr.*] plant (seed) by scattering it on or in the earth: *fill a pot with compost and sow a* thin layer of seeds on top. ■ plant the seeds of (a plant or crop): *the corn had just been sown.* ■ plant (a piece of land) with seed: *the field used to be sown with oats.* ■ cause to appear or spread: *the new policy has sown confusion and doubt.* —**sow·er** *n.*
▸ □ **sow the seeds** (or **seed**) **of** do something that will eventually bring about (a particular result, esp. a disastrous one): *the seeds of dissension had been sown.*

sow[2] /sou/ ▸*n.* an adult female pig, esp. one that has farrowed. ■ the female of certain other mammals, e.g., the guinea pig.

sown /sōn/ ▸ past participle of **SOW**[1].

sox /säks/ ▸*n.* nonstandard plural spelling of **SOCK** (sense 1).

soy /soi/ ▸*n.* another term for **SOYBEAN**.

soy·bean /ˈsoi,bēn/ ▸*n.* a leguminous plant, *Glycine max*, native to Asia and widely cultivated for its edible seeds. ■ the fruit of this plant, used in a variety of foods and fodder, esp. as a replacement for animal protein.

soy·meal /ˈsoi,mēl/ ▸*n.* a high-protein foodstuff made by cracking, heating, flaking, cooking, and grinding soybeans. Also called **soybean meal**.

SP ▸*abbr.* ■ starting price. ■ service pack (usually followed by a number): *Windows 2000 SP3 and SP4.*

spa /spä/ ▸*n.* a mineral spring considered to have health-giving properties. ■ a place or resort with such a spring. ■ a commercial establishment offering health and beauty treatment through such means as steam baths, exercise equipment, and massage. ■ a bath or small pool containing hot aerated water.

space /spās/ ▸*n.* **1** a continuous area or expanse that is free, available, or unoccupied: *a table took up much of the space.* ■ an area of land that is not occupied by buildings: *she had a love of open spaces.* ■ an empty area left between one-, two-, or three-dimensional points or objects: *the space between a wall and a utility pipe.* ■ a blank between printed, typed, or written words, characters, numbers, etc. ■ *Mus.* each of the four gaps between the five lines of a staff. ■ an interval of time (often used to suggest that the time is short, considering what has happened or been achieved in it): *both their cars were stolen in the space of three days.* ■ pages in a newspaper, or time between television or radio programs, available for advertising. ■ (also **commercial space**) an area rented or sold as business premises. ■ the amount of paper used or needed to write about a subject: *there is no space to give further details.* ■ the freedom and scope to live, think, and develop in a way that suits one: *a teenager needing her own space.* **2** the dimensions of height, depth, and width within which all things exist and move: *the work gives the sense of a journey in space and time.* ■ (also **outer space**) the physical universe beyond the earth's atmosphere. ■ the near vacuum extending between the planets and stars, containing small amounts of gas and dust. ■ *Math.* a mathematical concept generally regarded as a set of points having some specified structure.
▸*v.* **1** [*tr.*] (usu. **be spaced**) position (two or more items) at a distance from one another: *the houses are spaced out.* ■ (in printing or writing) put blanks between (words, letters, or lines): [as *n.*] (**spacing**) *the default setting is single line spacing.* **2** (usu. **be spaced out** or **space out**) *inf.* be or become distracted, euphoric, or disoriented, esp. from taking drugs; cease to be aware of one's surroundings: *I was so tired that I began to feel totally spaced out.* —**spac·er** *n.*

space age ▸*n.* (**the space age** or **the Space Age**) the era starting when the exploration of space became possible: *as the Space Age evolved, massive amounts of data gushed in.*
▸*adj.* (**space-age**) very modern; technologically advanced: *a space-age control room.*

space ca·det ▸*n.* *inf.* a person perceived as out of touch with reality, as though high on drugs.

space cap·sule ▸*n.* a small spacecraft or the part of a larger one that contains the instruments or crew.

space·craft /ˈspās,kraft/ ▸*n.* (*pl.* same or **-crafts**) a vehicle used for traveling in space.

space heat·er ▸*n.* a self-contained appliance, usually electric, for heating an enclosed room. —**space-heat·ed** *adj.* —**space heat·ing** *n.*

space·man /ˈspās,man; -mən/ ▸*n.* (*pl.* **-men**) a male astronaut.

space·ship /ˈspā(s),SHip/ ▸*n.* a spacecraft, esp. one controlled by a crew.

space shut·tle ▸*n.* a rocket-launched spacecraft, able to land like an unpowered aircraft, used to make repeated journeys between the earth and earth orbit.

space sta·tion ▸*n.* a large artificial satellite used as a long-term base for manned operations in space.

space·suit /ˈspāsˌso͞ot/ ▸ n. a garment designed to allow an astronaut to survive in space.

spac·ey /ˈspāsē/ (also **spac·y**) ▸ adj. (**spac·i·er, spac·i·est**) inf. out of touch with reality, as though high on drugs: *I remember babbling, high and spacey.* ■ (of popular, esp. electronic music) drifting and ethereal.

spa·cial ▸ adj. variant spelling of SPATIAL.

spa·cious /ˈspāSHəs/ ▸ adj. (esp. of a room or building) having ample space. —**spa·cious·ly** adv. —**spa·cious·ness** n.

spade[1] /spād/ ▸ n. a tool with a sharp-edged, typically rectangular, metal blade and a long handle, used for digging or cutting earth, sand, turf, etc.
▸ v. [tr.] dig in (ground) with a spade: *while spading the soil, I think of the flowers.* ■ [tr.] move (soil) with a spade: *earth is spaded into the grave.* —**spade·ful** /-ˌfo͝ol/ n. (pl. -**fuls**).
▸ □ **call a spade a spade** speak plainly without avoiding unpleasant or embarrassing issues.

spade[2] ▸ n. 1 (**spades**) one of the four suits in a conventional deck of playing cards, denoted by a black inverted heart-shaped figure with a small stalk. ■ (**a spade**) a card of this suit. 2 inf., offens. a black person.
▸ □ **in spades** inf. to a very high degree: *he got his revenge now in spades.*

spa·dix /ˈspādiks/ ▸ n. (pl. **spa·di·ces** /-dəsēz/) Bot. a spike of minute flowers closely arranged around a fleshy axis and typically enclosed in a spathe, characteristic of the arums.

spae /spā/ ▸ v. [trans.] (**spaes, spaed, spae·ing**) chiefly Scottish foretell; prophesy: *she did spae that Nora would marry well* | [intrans.] *I wish that he would spae no more.*

spa·ghet·ti /spəˈɡetē/ ▸ n. pasta made in long, slender, solid strings. ■ an Italian dish consisting largely of this, typically with a sauce. ■ fig. a tangle of stringlike objects, resembling a plate of cooked spaghetti: *a clumsy spaghetti of coils and wires.* ■ Electr. a type of narrow tubing that encases and insulates wire. ▷Italian, plural of the diminutive of *spago* 'string.'

spa·ghet·ti west·ern ▸ n. inf. a western movie made cheaply in Europe by an Italian director.

spake /spāk/ archaic poetic/lit. ▸ past of SPEAK.

spall /spôl/ ▸ v. [tr.] [intr.] (of ore, rock, or stone) break off in fragments: *cracks below the surface cause slabs of material to **spall off**.*

spam /spam/ ▸ n. 1 (**Spam**) trademark a canned meat product made mainly from ham. 2 irrelevant or inappropriate messages sent on the Internet to a large number of recipients.
▸ v. [tr.] send the same message indiscriminately to (large numbers of recipients) on the Internet. —**spam·mer** n.

span /span/ ▸ n. the full extent of something from end to end; the amount of space that something covers: *a warehouse with a span of 28 feet.* ■ the length of time for which something lasts: *a short concentration span.* ■ the wingspan of an aircraft or a bird. ■ an arch or part of a bridge between piers or supports. ■ the maximum distance between the tips of the thumb and little finger, taken as the basis of a measurement equal to 9 inches.
▸ v. (**spanned, span·ning**) [tr.] (of a bridge, arch, etc.) extend from side to side of: *the stream was spanned by a narrow bridge.* ■ extend across (a period of time or a range of subjects): *their interests span almost all the conventional disciplines.* ■ cover or enclose with the length of one's hand: *her waist was slender enough for him to span with his hands.*

span·drel /ˈspandrəl/ ▸ n. Archit. the almost triangular space between one side of the outer curve of an arch, a wall, and the ceiling or framework. ■ the space between the shoulders of adjoining arches and the ceiling or molding above.

spang /spaNG/ ▸ adv. inf. directly; completely: *looking the general right spang in the eye.*

span·gle /ˈspaNGgəl/ ▸ n. a small thin piece of glittering material, typically used in quantity to ornament a dress; a sequin. ■ a small sparkling object; a spot of bright color or light.
▸ v. [tr.] [usu. as adj.] (**spangled**) cover with spangles or other small sparkling objects: *a spangled Christmas doll.* —**span·gly** adj.

span·iel /ˈspanyəl/ ▸ n. a dog of a breed with a long silky coat and drooping ears. ■ used in similes and metaphors as a symbol of devotion or obsequiousness: *I followed my uncles around as faithfully as any spaniel.*

Span·ish /ˈspaniSH/ ▸ adj. of or relating to Spain, its people, or its language.
▸ n. 1 [as pl. n.] (**the Spanish**) the people of Spain. 2 the Romance language of most of Spain and of much of Central and South America and several other countries. —**Span·ish·ness** n.

Span·ish fly ▸ n. a bright green European blister beetle (*Lytta vesicatoria*) with a mousy smell. ■ a toxic preparation of the dried bodies of these beetles, formerly used in medicine as a counterirritant and sometimes taken as an aphrodisiac. Also called CANTHARIDES.

Span·ish In·qui·si·tion /ˌiNGkwiˈziSHən/ ▸ an ecclesiastical court established in Roman Catholic Spain in 1478 and directed originally against converts from Judaism and Islam but later also against Protestants. It operated with great severity until suppressed in the early 19th century.

spank /spaNGk/ ▸ v. [tr.] slap with one's open hand or a flat object, esp. on the buttocks as a punishment: *she was spanked for spilling ink on the carpet.*
▸ n. a slap of this type.

spank·er /ˈspaNGkər/ ▸ n. a fore-and-aft sail set on the after side of a ship's mast, esp. the mizzenmast.

spank·ing /ˈspaNGkiNG/ ▸ adj. 1 (esp. of a horse or its gait) lively; brisk: *a spanking trot.* 2 inf. very good: *we had a spanking time.* ■ fine and impressive: *a spanking white Rolls Royce.*
▸ n. an act of slapping, esp. on the buttocks as a punishment for children: *you deserve a good spanking.*

spar[1] /spär/ ▸ n. a thick, strong pole such as is used for a mast or yard on a ship. ■ the main longitudinal beam of an airplane wing.

spar[2] ▸ v. (**sparred, spar·ring**) [intr.] make the motions of boxing without landing heavy blows, as a form of training: *one contestant broke his nose while sparring.* ■ engage in argument, typically of a kind that is prolonged or repeated but not violent: *mother and daughter spar regularly over drink, drugs, and career.* ■ (of a gamecock) fight with the feet or spurs.

spar[3] ▸ n. [usu. in comb.] a crystalline, easily cleavable, light-colored mineral. —**spar·ry** adj.

spare /spe(ə)r/ ▸ adj. 1 additional to what is required for ordinary use: *few people had spare cash for inessentials.* ■ not currently in use or occupied: *the spare bedroom.* 2 with no excess fat; thin: *a spare, bearded figure.* ■ elegantly simple: *her clothes are smart and spare in style.* ■ meager; nearly inadequate: *the furnishings were spare and unadorned.*
▸ n. 1 an item kept in case another item of the same type is lost, broken, or worn out. ■ a spare tire: *make sure there are no problems with any of the tires, including the spare.* 2 (in tenpin bowling) an act of knocking down all the pins with two consecutive rolls of the ball.
▸ v. 1 give (something of which one has enough) to (someone); afford to give to: *she asked if I could spare her a dollar or two.* ■ make free or available: *I'm sure you can spare me a moment.* 2 [tr.] refrain from killing, injuring, or distressing: *there was no way the men would spare her.* ■ refrain from inflicting (something) on (someone): *the country had until now been spared the violence occurring elsewhere.* ■ (**spare oneself**) try to ensure or satisfy one's own comfort or needs: *in her concern to help others, she has never spared herself.* —**spare·ly** adv. —**spare·ness** n. —**spar·er** n. (rare).

spare·ribs /ˈspe(ə)rˌribz/ (also **spare ribs**) ▸ pl. n. closely trimmed ribs of pork or sometimes beef.

spare tire ▸ n. an extra tire carried in a motor vehicle for emergencies. ■ inf. a roll of fat around a person's waist.

spar·ing /ˈspe(ə)riNG/ ▸ adj. moderate; economical: *physicians advised sparing use of the ointment.* —**spar·ing·ly** adv. —**spar·ing·ness** n.

spark /spärk/ ▸ n. a small fiery particle thrown off from a fire, alight in ashes, or produced by striking together two hard surfaces such as stone or metal. ■ a light produced by a sudden disruptive electrical discharge through the air. ■ a discharge such as this serving to ignite the explosive mixture in an internal combustion engine. ■ a small bright object or point: *there was a spark of light.* ■ a trace of a specified quality or intense feeling: *a tiny spark of anger flared within her.* ■ a sense of liveliness and excitement: *there was a spark between them at their first meeting.*
▸ v. 1 [intr.] emit sparks of fire or electricity: *the ignition sparks as soon as the gas is turned on.* 2 [tr.] ignite: *the explosion sparked a fire.* ■ fig. provide the stimulus for (a dramatic event or process): *the severity of the plan sparked off street protests.* —**spark·er** n. —**spark·less** adj. —**spark·y** adj.

spar·kle /ˈspärkəl/ ▸ v. [intr.] shine brightly with flashes of light: *her earrings sparkled as she turned her head* | [as adj.] (**sparkling**) *her sparkling blue eyes.* ■ be vivacious and witty: *after a glass of wine, she began to sparkle.* ■ [as adj.] (**sparkling**) (of wine and similar drinks) effervescent;
▸ n. a glittering flash of light: *there was a sparkle in his eyes.* ■ vivacity and wit: *she's got a kind of sparkle.* —**spar·kling·ly** adv. —**spar·kly** adj.

spar·kler /ˈspärk(ə)lər/ ▸ n. 1 a thing that sparkles, in particular: ■ a hand-held firework that emits sparks. ■ inf. a gemstone, esp. a diamond. **2** a nozzle attached to the spout on a beer pump to give the beer a frothy head.

spark plug ▶*n.* a device for firing the explosive mixture in an internal combustion engine.

spar·ring part·ner ▶*n.* a boxer employed to engage in sparring with another as training. ■ a person with whom one continually argues or contends.

spar·row /ˈsparō/ ▶*n.* **1** a small finchlike Old World bird (*Passer* and other genera, family Passeridae or Ploceidae) related to the weavers, typically with brown and gray plumage. **2** any of a number of birds that resemble true sparrows in size or color, including an American bunting.

spar·row hawk ▶*n.* a small Old World woodland hawk (genus *Accipiter*) that preys on small birds. ■ the American kestrel (see KESTREL).

sparse /spärs/ ▶*adj.* thinly dispersed or scattered: *areas of sparse population.* ■ austere; meager: *an elegantly sparse chamber.* ▷early 18th cent. (used to describe writing in the sense 'widely spaced'): from Latin *sparsus,* past participle of *spargere* 'scatter.' —**sparse·ly** *adv.* —**sparse·ness** *n.* —**spar·si·ty** /ˈspärsitē/ *n.*

Spar·tan /ˈspärtn/ ▶*adj.* of or relating to Sparta in ancient Greece. ■ (usu. **spartan**) showing the indifference to comfort or luxury traditionally associated with ancient Sparta: *spartan but adequate rooms.* ▶*n.* a citizen of Sparta.

spasm /ˈspazəm/ ▶*n.* a sudden involuntary muscular contraction or convulsive movement. ■ a sudden and brief spell of an activity or sensation: *a spasm of coughing woke him.* ■ prolonged involuntary muscle contraction: *the airways in the lungs go into spasm.*

spas·mod·ic /spazˈmädik/ ▶*adj.* occurring or done in brief, irregular bursts: *spasmodic fighting continued.* ■ caused by, subject to, or in the nature of a spasm or spasms: *a spasmodic cough.* —**spas·mod·i·cal·ly** /-ik(ə)lē/ *adv.*

spas·tic /ˈspastik/ ▶*adj.* relating to or affected by muscle spasm. ■ relating to or denoting a form of muscular weakness (**spastic paralysis**) typical of cerebral palsy, caused by damage to the brain or spinal cord. ■ (of a person) affected with cerebral palsy. ■ *inf., offens.* incompetent or uncoordinated. ▶*n.* a person with cerebral palsy. ■ *inf., offens.* an incompetent or uncoordinated person. —**spas·ti·cal·ly** *adv.* —**spas·tic·i·ty** /spaˈstisitē/ *n.*

spat[1] /spat/ ▶ past and past participle of SPIT[1].

spat[2] ▶*n.* (usu. **spats**) *hist.* a short cloth gaiter covering the instep and ankle.

spat[3] *inf.* ▶*n.* a petty quarrel.

spat[4] ▶*n.* the spawn or larvae of shellfish, esp. oysters.

spate /spāt/ ▶*n.* a large number of similar things or events appearing or occurring in quick succession: *a spate of attacks on travelers.* ▶ □ **in (full) spate** (of a river) overflowing due to a sudden flood. ■ *fig.* (of a person or action) at the height of activity: *work was in full spate.*

spat

spathe /spāTH/ ▶*n.* *Bot.* a large sheathing bract enclosing the flower cluster of certain plants, esp. the spadix of arums and palms.

spa·tial /ˈspāSHəl/ (also **spa·cial**) ▶*adj.* of or relating to space: *the spatial distribution of population.* —**spa·ti·al·i·ty** /ˌspāSHēˈalitē/ *n.* —**spa·tial·i·za·tion** /ˌspāSHələˈzāSHən/ *n.* —**spa·tial·ize** /ˈspāSHəˌlīz/ *v.* —**spa·tial·ly** *adv.*

spat·ter /ˈspatər/ ▶*v.* [*tr.*] cover with drops or spots of something: *passing vehicles spattered his shoes and pants with mud.* ■ scatter or splash (liquid, mud, etc.) over a surface: *he spatters grease all over the stove.* ■ [*intr.*] fall so as to be scattered over an area: *she watched the raindrops spatter down.* ▶*n.* a spray or splash of something. ■ a sprinkling: *there was a spatter of freckles over her nose.* ■ a short outburst of sound: *the sharp spatter of shots.*

spat·u·la /ˈspaCHələ/ ▶*n.* an implement with a broad, flat, blunt blade, used for mixing and spreading things, esp. in cooking and painting.

spat·u·late /ˈspaCHələt/ ▶*adj.* having a broad, rounded end: *his thick, spatulate fingers.* ■ (also **spath·u·late** /ˈspaTHyələt/) *Bot. & Zool.* broad at the apex and tapered to the base: *large spatulate leaves.*

spawn /spôn/ ▶*v.* [*intr.*] (of a fish, frog, mollusk, crustacean, etc.) release or deposit eggs: *the fish spawn among fine-leaved plants.* ■ [*tr.*] *a large brood is spawned.* ■ (**be spawned**) (of a fish, frog, etc.) be laid as eggs. ■ [*tr.*] (of a person) produce (offspring, typically offspring regarded as undesirable): *why had she married a man who could spawn a boy like that?* ■ [*tr.*] produce or generate, esp. in large numbers: *the decade spawned a bewildering variety of books on the forces.* ■ *Comput.* [*tr.*] generate (a dependent or subordinate computer process): *from time to time it spawns two copies of the ip-up program, other times only one.* ▶*n.* the eggs of fish, frogs, etc.: *the fish covers its spawn with gravel.* ■ the process of producing such eggs. ■ the product or offspring of a person or place (used to express distaste or disgust): *the spawn of chaos: demons and sorcerers.* ■ the mycelium of a fungus, esp. a cultivated mushroom. —**spawn·er** *n.*

spay /spā/ ▶*v.* [*tr.*] (usu. **be spayed**) sterilize (a female animal) by removing the ovaries:.

SPCA ▶*abbr.* Society for the Prevention of Cruelty to Animals.

speak /spēk/ ▶*v.* (past **spoke** /spōk/; past part. **spo·ken** /ˈspōkən/) [*intr.*] **1** say something in order to convey information, an opinion, or a feeling: *in his agitation he was unable to speak.* ■ have a conversation: *I wish to speak privately with you.* ■ [*tr.*] utter (a word, message, speech, etc.): *patients copy words spoken by the therapist.* ■ [*tr.*] communicate in or be able to communicate in (a specified language): *my mother spoke Russian.* ■ make a speech before an audience, or make a contribution to a debate: *twenty thousand people attended to hear him speak.* ■ (**speak for**) express the views or position of (another person or group): *he claimed to speak for the majority of local people.* ■ convey one's views or position indirectly: *speaking through his attorney, he refused to join the debate.* ■ (of behavior, a quality, an event, etc.) serve as evidence for something: *her harping on him spoke strongly of a crush.* ■ (of an object that typically makes a sound when it functions) make a characteristic sound: *the gun spoke again.* ■ (of an organ pipe or other musical instrument) make a sound: *insufficient air circulates for the pipes to speak.* **2** (**speak to**) talk to in order to reprove or advise: *she tried to speak to Seth about his drinking.* ■ talk to in order to give or extract information: *he had spoken to the police.* ■ discuss or comment on formally: *the Church wants to speak to real issues.* ■ appeal or relate to: *the story spoke to him directly.*
▶*phrasal v.* □ **speak out** (or **up**) express one's feelings or opinions frankly and publicly: *the administration will be forthright in speaking out against human rights abuses.* —**speak·a·ble** *adj.*
▶ □ **speak one's mind** express one's feelings or opinions frankly.

speak·eas·y /ˈspēkˌēzē/ ▶*n.* (pl. **-eas·ies**) *inf.* (during Prohibition) an illicit liquor store or nightclub.

speak·er /ˈspēkər/ ▶*n.* **1** a person who speaks. ■ a person who delivers a speech or lecture. ■ a person who speaks a specified language: *he is a fluent English and French speaker.* **2** (**Speaker**) the presiding officer in a legislative assembly, esp. the House of Representatives. **3** short for LOUDSPEAKER: *a cassette player with two speakers.*

speak·er·phone /ˈspēkərˌfōn/ ▶*n.* a telephone with a loudspeaker and microphone, allowing it to be used without picking up the handset.

speak·ing /ˈspēkiNG/ ▶*n.* the action of conveying information or expressing one's thoughts and feelings in spoken language. ■ the activity of delivering speeches or lectures: *public speaking.* ▶*adj.* used for or engaged in speech: *you have a clear speaking voice.* ■ able to communicate in a specified language: *an English-speaking guide.*
▶ □ **on speaking terms 1** slightly acquainted. **2** sufficiently friendly to talk to each other: *she parted from her mother barely on speaking terms.*

spear /spi(ə)r/ ▶*n.* a weapon with a long shaft and a pointed tip, typically of metal, used for thrusting or throwing. ■ a similar barbed instrument used for catching fish. ■ a plant shoot, esp. a pointed stem of asparagus or broccoli. ▶*v.* [*tr.*] pierce or strike with a spear or other pointed object: *she speared her last French fry with her fork.* ■ quickly extend the arm to catch (a fast-moving ball or other object): *he hit a line drive that Bogar speared back-handed.*

spear·head /ˈspi(ə)rˌhed/ ▶*n.* the point of a spear. ■ an individual or group chosen to lead an attack or movement: *she became the spearhead of a health education program.* ▶*v.* [*tr.*] lead (an attack or movement): *Alex is spearheading a campaign to clean up the Hattie Pynn Clubhouse.*

spear·mint /ˈspirˌmint/ ▶*n.* the common garden mint (*Mentha spicata*), used as a culinary herb and to flavor candy, chewing gum, etc.

spec[1] /spek/ ▶*n.* (in phrase **on spec**) *inf.* in the hope of success but without any specific commission or instructions: *he built the factory on spec and hoped someone would buy it.*

spec[2] ▶*n.* *inf.* a detailed working description: *I'll have to look at the specs on the equipment.*

spe·cial /ˈspeSHəl/ ▶*adj.* better, greater, or otherwise different from what is usual: *they always made a special effort at Christmas.* ■ exceptionally good or precious: *she's a very special person.* ■ belonging specifically to a particular person or place: *we want to preserve our town's special character.* ■ designed or organized for a particular person, purpose, or occasion: *we will return by special coaches.* ■ (of a subject) studied in particular depth. ■ used to denote education for children with particular needs, esp. those with learning difficulties.

▸*n.* a thing, such as an event, product, or broadcast, that is designed or organized for a particular occasion or purpose: *television's election night specials.* ■ a dish not on the regular menu at a restaurant but served on a particular day. ■ *inf.* a product or service offered at a temporarily reduced price. —**spe·cial·ly** *adv.* —**spe·cial·ness** *n.*

spe·cial de·liv·er·y ▸*n.* a former express mail service of the U.S. Postal Service that involved expedited delivery of mail, often by special courier. ■ any mail service that involves special handling or expedited delivery. ■ a letter or parcel sent by a special-delivery service.

spe·cial ef·fects ▸*pl. n.* illusions created for movies and television by props, camerawork, computer graphics, etc.

Spe·cial For·ces ▸*n.* an elite force within the U.S. Army specializing in guerrilla warfare and counterinsurgency.

spe·cial in·ter·est (also **special interest group**) ▸*n.* a group of people or an organization seeking or receiving special advantages, typically through political lobbying.

spe·cial·ist /'speSHəlist/ ▸*n.* a person who concentrates primarily on a particular subject or activity; a person highly skilled in a specific and restricted field. ■ a physician highly trained in a particular branch of medicine. ■ (in the U.S. Army) an enlisted person who has technical or administrative duties but does not exercise command.
▸*adj.* possessing or involving detailed knowledge or study of a restricted topic: *the project may involve people with specialist knowledge.* —**spe·cial·ism** /-,lizəm/ *n.*

spe·cial·ize /'speSHə,līz/ ▸*v.* [*intr.*] concentrate on and become expert in a particular subject or skill: *he could specialize in tropical medicine.* ■ confine oneself to providing a particular product or service: *the company specialized in commercial brochures.* ■ make a habit of engaging in a particular activity: *a group of writers has specialized in attacking the society they live in.* ■ [*tr.*] (often **be specialized**) *Biol.* adapt or set apart (an organ or part) to serve a special function or to suit a particular way of life: *zooids specialized for different functions.* —**spe·cial·i·za·tion** /,speSHəli'zāSHən/ *n.*

spe·cial·ty /'speSHəltē/ ▸*n.* (*pl.* **-ties**) a pursuit, area of study, or skill to which someone has devoted much time and effort and in which they are expert: *his specialty was watercolors.* ■ a particular branch of medicine or surgery. ■ a product, esp. a type of food, that a person or region is famous for making well: *the local specialties are all seafood.* ■ [as *adj.*] meeting particular tastes or needs: *specialty potatoes for salads.*

spe·ci·a·tion /,speSHē'āSHən; ,spēsē-/ ▸*n. Biol.* the formation of new and distinct species in the course of evolution. —**spe·ci·ate** /'spēSHē-,āt; spēsē-/ *v.*

spe·cie /'spēSHē; -sē/ ▸*n.* money in the form of coins rather than notes.
▸ □ **in specie 1** in coin. **2** *Law* in the real, precise, or actual form specified: *the plaintiff could not be sure of recovering his goods in specie.*

spe·cies /'spēsēz; -sHēz/ ▸*n.* (*pl.* same) (abbr.: **sp.**, **spp.**) *Biol.* a group of living organisms consisting of similar individuals capable of exchanging genes or interbreeding. The species is the principal natural taxonomic unit, ranking below a genus and denoted by a Latin binomial, e.g., *Homo sapiens.* ■ a kind or sort: *a species of invective at once tough and suave.* ■ used humorously to refer to people who share a characteristic or occupation: *a political species that is becoming more common, the environmental statesman.* ■ *Chem. & Physics* a particular kind of atom, molecule, ion, or particle: *a new molecular species.* ▷late Middle English: from Latin, literally 'appearance, form, beauty,' from *specere* 'to look.'

spe·cif·ic /spə'sifik/ ▸*adj.* **1** clearly defined or identified: *increasing the electricity supply only until it met specific development needs.* ■ precise and clear in making statements or issuing instructions: *when ordering goods be specific.* ■ belonging or relating uniquely to a particular subject: *information needs are often very specific to companies and individuals.* **2** *Biol.* of, relating to, or connected with species or a species. **3** (of a duty or a tax) levied at a fixed rate per physical unit of the thing taxed, regardless of its price. **4** *Physics* of or denoting a number equal to the ratio of the value of some property of a given substance to the value of the same property of some other substance used as a reference, such as water, or of a vacuum, under equivalent conditions. ■ of or denoting a physical quantity expressed in terms of a unit mass, volume, or other measure, in order to give a value independent of the properties or scale of the particular system studied.
▸*n.* (usu. **specifics**) a precise detail: *he worked through the specifics of the contract.* —**spe·cif·i·cal·ly** *adv.* —**spec·i·fic·i·ty** /,spesə'fisitē/ *n.*

spec·i·fi·ca·tion /,spesəfi'kāSHən/ ▸*n.* an act of describing or identifying something precisely or of stating a precise requirement: *give a full specification of the job advertised.* ■ (usu. **specifications**) a detailed description of the design and materials used to make something. ■ a

standard of workmanship, materials, etc., required to be met in a piece of work: *everything was built to a higher specification.*

spec·i·fy /'spesə,fī/ ▸*v.* (**-fies**, **-fied**) [*tr.*] identify clearly and definitely: *the coup leader promised an election but did not specify a date.* ■ state a fact or requirement clearly and precisely: *the agency failed to specify that the workers were not their employees.* ■ include in an architect's or engineer's specifications: *naval architects specified circular portholes.* —**spec·i·fi·a·ble** /,spesə'fīəbəl/ *adj.*

spec·i·men /'spesəmən/ ▸*n.* an individual animal, plant, piece of a mineral, etc., used as an example of its species or type for scientific study or display. ■ an example of something such as a product or piece of work, regarded as typical of its class or group. ■ a sample for medical testing, esp. of urine. ■ *inf.* used to refer humorously to a person or animal: *in her he found himself confronted by a sorrier specimen than himself.*

spe·cious /'spēSHəs/ ▸*adj.* superficially plausible, but actually wrong: *a specious argument.* ■ misleading in appearance, esp. misleadingly attractive: *the music trade gives Golden Oldies a specious appearance of novelty.* —**spe·cious·ly** *adv.* —**spe·cious·ness** *n.*

speck /spek/ ▸*n.* a tiny spot: *the figure in the distance had become a mere speck.* ■ a small particle of a substance: *specks of dust.*
▸*v.* [*tr.*] (usu. **be specked**) mark with small spots: *their skin was specked with goose pimples.* —**speck·less** *adj.*

speck·le /'spekəl/ ▸*n.* (usu. **speckles**) a small spot or patch of color.
▸*v.* [*tr.*] (often as *adj.*] (**speckled**) mark with a large number of small spots or patches of color: *a large speckled brown egg.*

specs /'speks/ ▸*pl. n. inf.* **1** a pair of spectacles. **2** plural form of SPEC[2].

spec·ta·cle /'spektəkəl/ ▸*n.* a visually striking performance or display: *the acrobatic feats make a good spectacle.* ■ an event or scene regarded in terms of its visual impact.

spec·ta·cles /'spektəkəlz/ ▸*pl. n.* another term for GLASSES.

spec·tac·u·lar /spek'takyələr/ ▸*adj.* beautiful in a dramatic and eye-catching way: *spectacular mountain scenery.* ■ strikingly large or obvious: *the party suffered a spectacular loss in the election.*
▸*n.* an event such as a pageant or musical, produced on a large scale and with striking effects. —**spec·tac·u·lar·ly** *adv.*

spec·ta·tor /'spek,tātər/ ▸*n.* a person who watches at a show, game, or other event.

spec·ta·tor sport ▸*n.* a sport that many people find entertaining to watch.

spec·ter /'spektər/ (*Brit.* **spec·tre**) ▸*n.* a ghost. ■ something widely feared as a possible unpleasant or dangerous occurrence: *the specter of nuclear holocaust.*

spec·tra /'spektrə/ ▸ plural form of SPECTRUM.

spec·tral /'spektrəl/ ▸*adj.* **1** of or like a ghost. **2** of or concerning spectra or the spectrum. —**spec·tral·ly** *adv.*

spec·trom·e·ter /spek'trämitər/ ▸*n.* an apparatus used for recording and measuring spectra, esp. as a method of analysis. —**spec·tro·met·ric** /,spektrə'metrik/ *adj.* —**spec·trom·e·try** /spek'trämətrē/ *n.*

spec·trum /'spektrəm/ ▸*n.* (*pl.* **-tra** /-trə/) **1** a band of colors, as seen in a rainbow, produced by separation of the components of light by their different degrees of refraction according to wavelength. ■ (**the spectrum**) the entire range of wavelengths of electromagnetic radiation. ■ an image or distribution of components of any electromagnetic radiation arranged in a progressive series according to wavelength. ■ a similar image or distribution of components of sound, particles, etc., arranged according to such characteristics as frequency, charge, and energy. **2** used to classify something, or suggest that it can be classified, in terms of its position on a scale between two extreme or opposite points: *the left or the right of the political spectrum.* ■ a wide range.

spec·u·la /'spekyələ/ ▸ plural form of SPECULUM.

spec·u·late /'spekyə,lāt/ ▸*v.* [*intr.*] **1** form a theory or conjecture about a subject without firm evidence: *my colleagues speculate about my private life.* **2** invest in stocks, property, or other ventures in the hope of gain but with the risk of loss. —**spec·u·la·tion** /,spekyə'lāSHən/ *n.* —**spec·u·la·tor** /-,lātər/ *n.*

spec·u·la·tive /'spekyə,lātiv; -lətiv/ ▸*adj.* **1** engaged in, expressing, or based on conjecture rather than knowledge: *discussion of the question is largely speculative.* **2** (of an investment) involving a high risk of loss. ■ (of a business venture) undertaken on the chance of success, without a preexisting contract. —**spec·u·la·tive·ly** *adv.* —**spec·u·la·tive·ness** *n.*

spec·u·lum /'spekyələm/ ▶ *n.* (*pl.* **-la** /-lə/) **1** *Med.* a metal or plastic instrument that is used to dilate an orifice or canal in the body to allow inspection. **2** *Ornithol.* a bright patch of plumage on the wings of certain birds, esp. a strip of metallic sheen on the secondary flight feathers of many ducks.

sped /sped/ ▶ past and past participle of SPEED.

speech /spēCH/ ▶ *n.* **1** the expression of or the ability to express thoughts and feelings by articulate sounds: *he was born deaf and without the power of speech.* ■ a person's style of speaking: *she wouldn't accept his correction of her speech.* ■ the language of a nation, region, or group: *the distinctive rhythms of their speech.* **2** a formal address or discourse delivered to an audience: *the headmistress made a speech about how much they would miss her.* ■ a sequence of lines written for one character in a play.

speech·i·fy /'spēcHə,fī/ ▶ *v.* (**-fies, -fied**) [*intr.*] deliver a speech, esp. in a tedious or pompous way: *writers should write, not speechify.* —**speech·i·fi·ca·tion** /,spēcHəfi'kāSHən/ *n.* —**speech·i·fi·er** *n.*

speech·less /'spēcHlis/ ▶ *adj.* unable to speak, esp. as the temporary result of shock or some strong emotion: *he was speechless with rage.* ■ unable to be expressed in words: *surges of speechless passion.* —**speech·less·ly** *adv.* —**speech·less·ness** *n.*

speech sound ▶ *n.* a phonetically distinct unit of speech.

speed /spēd/ ▶ *n.* **1** rapidity of movement or action: *the accident was due to excessive speed.* ■ the rate at which someone or something is able to move or operate: *the car has a top speed of 147 mph.* ■ each of the possible gear ratios of a bicycle or motor vehicle. ■ the sensitivity of photographic film to light. ■ the light-gathering power or f-number of a camera lens. ■ the duration of a photographic exposure. **2** *inf.* an amphetamine drug, esp. methamphetamine. **3** *inf.* something that matches one's tastes or inclinations: *oak tables and chairs are more his speed.*
▶ *v.* (*past* **sped** /sped/ or **speed·ed**) [*intr.*] move quickly: *I got into the car and home we sped.* ■ [*intr.*] (of a motorist) travel at a speed that is greater than the legal limit: *the car that crashed was speeding.* ■ (**speed up**) move or work more quickly: *you force yourself to speed up because you don't want to keep others waiting.* ■ [*tr.*] cause to move, act, or happen more quickly: *recent initiatives have sought to speed up decision-making.* —**speed·er** *n.*

speed·ball /'spēd,bôl/ ▶ *n. inf.* a mixture of cocaine and heroin.

speed·boat /'spēd,bōt/ ▶ *n.* a motorboat designed for high speed. —**speed·boat·ing** *n.*

speed bump (*chiefly Brit.* also **speed hump**) ▶ *n.* a ridge set in a road surface, typically at intervals, to control the speed of vehicles.

speed·om·e·ter /spē'dämitər/ ▶ *n.* an instrument on a vehicle's dashboard indicating its speed.

speed·way /'spēd,wā/ ▶ *n.* a stadium or track used for automobile or motorcycle racing. ■ a highway for fast motor traffic.

speed·y /'spēdē/ ▶ *adj.* (**speed·i·er, speed·i·est**) **1** done or occurring quickly: *a speedy recovery.* **2** moving quickly: *a speedy center fielder.* —**speed·i·ly** /'spēdəlē/ *adv.* —**speed·i·ness** *n.*

spe·le·ol·o·gy /,spēlē'äləjē/ ▶ *n.* the study or exploration of caves. —**spe·le·o·log·i·cal** /,spēlēə'läjikəl/ *adj.* —**spe·le·ol·o·gist** /-jist/ *n.*

spell¹ /spel/ ▶ *v.* (*past* and *past part.* **spelled** /speld/ or *chiefly Brit.* **spelt** /spelt/) write or name the letters that form (a word) in correct sequence: *Dolly spelled her name* ■ (of letters) make up or form (a word): *the letters spell the word "how."* ■ be recognizable as a sign or characteristic of: *she had the chic, efficient look that spells Milan.* ■ lead to: *the plans would spell disaster for the economy.*

spell² ▶ *n.* a form of words used as a magical charm or incantation. ■ a state of enchantment caused by such a form of words: *the magician may cast a spell on himself.* ■ an ability to control or influence people as though one had magical power over them: *she is afraid that you are waking from her spell.*

spell³ ▶ *n.* a short period: *I want to get away from racing for a spell.* ■ a period spent in an activity: *a spell of greenhouse work.* ■ a period of a specified kind of weather: *an early cold spell in autumn.* ■ a period of suffering from a specified kind of illness: *she plunges off a yacht and suffers a spell of amnesia.*
▶ *v.* [*tr.*] allow (someone) to rest briefly by taking their place in some activity: *I got sleepy and needed her to spell me for a while at the wheel.*

spell·bind /'spel,bīnd/ ▶ *v.* (*past* and *past part.* **-bound**) [*tr.*] hold the complete attention of (someone) as though by magic; fascinate: [as *adj.*] (**spellbinding**) *she told the spellbinding story of her life* | [as *adj.*] (**spellbound**) *the killer whale gave the spellbound audience a good soaking.* —**spell·bind·er** *n.* —**spell·bind·ing·ly** *adv.*

spell·er /'spelər/ ▶ *n.* a person who spells with a specified ability: *a very weak speller.* ■ a book for teaching spelling.

spell·ing /'speliNG/ ▶ *n.* the process or activity of writing or naming the letters of a word. ■ the way a word is spelled: *the spelling of his name was influenced by French.* ■ a person's ability to spell words: *her spelling was deplorable.* ■ a school subject.

spell·ing bee ▶ *n.* a spelling competition.

spe·lunk·ing /spi'ləNGkiNG/ ▶ *n.* the exploration of caves, esp. as a hobby. —**spe·lunk·er** /-kər/ *n.*

spend /spend/ ▶ *v.* (*past* and *past part.* **spent** /spent/) [*tr.*] pay out (money) in buying or hiring goods or services: *the firm has spent $100,000 on hardware and software.* ■ pay out (money) for a particular person's benefit or for the improvement of something: *the college spent $140 on each of its students.* ■ used to show the activity in which someone is engaged or the place where they are living over a period of time: *she spent a lot of time traveling.* ■ use or give out the whole of; exhaust: *she couldn't buy any more because she had already spent her money.* —**spend·a·ble** *adj.* —**spend·er** *n.*

spend·thrift /'spen(d),THrift/ ▶ *n.* a person who spends money in an extravagant, irresponsible way.

sperm /spərm/ ▶ *n.* (*pl.* same or **sperms**) short for SPERMATOZOON. ■ *inf.* semen.

sper·ma·cet·i /,spərmə'setē/ ▶ *n.* a white waxy substance produced by the sperm whale, formerly used in candles and ointments. It is present in a rounded organ in the head, where it focuses acoustic signals and aids in the control of buoyancy. ▷late 15th cent.: from medieval Latin, from late Latin *sperma* 'sperm' + *ceti* 'of a whale' (genitive of *cetus*, from Greek *kētos* 'whale'), from the belief that it was whale spawn.

sper·mat·ic cord ▶ *n.* a bundle of nerves, ducts, and blood vessels connecting the testicles to the abdominal cavity.

sper·mat·o·cyte /spər'matə,sīt/ ▶ *n. Biol.* a cell produced at the second stage in the formation of spermatozoa, formed from a spermatogonium and dividing by meiosis into spermatids.

sper·mat·o·gen·e·sis /,spərmətə'jenəsis; spər,ma-/ ▶ *n. Biol.* the production or development of mature spermatozoa.

sper·mat·o·phyte /'spər'matə,fīt/ ▶ *n. Bot.* a plant of a large division (Spermatophyta) that comprises those that bear seeds, including the gymnosperms and angiosperms.

sper·ma·to·zo·on /,spərmətə'zōən; spər,ma-/ ▶ *n.* (*pl.* **-zo·a** /-'zōə/) *Biol.* the mature motile male sex cell of an animal, by which the ovum is fertilized, typically having a compact head and one or more long flagella for swimming. —**sper·ma·to·zo·al** /-zōəl/ *adj.* —**sper·ma·to·zo·an** /-'zōən/ *adj.*

sper·mi·cide /'spərmə,sīd/ ▶ *n.* a substance that kills spermatozoa, used as a contraceptive. —**sper·mi·cid·al** /,spərmə'sīdl/ *adj.*

sperm whale ▶ *n.* a toothed whale of the family Physeteridae (esp. the very large *Physeter macrocephalus*), with a massive head, typically feeding at great depths on squid, formerly valued for the spermaceti and sperm oil in its head and the ambergris in its intestines.

spew /spyōō/ ▶ *v.* [*tr.*] expel large quantities of (something) rapidly and forcibly: *buses were spewing out black clouds of exhaust.* ■ [*intr.*] be poured or forced out in large quantities: *oil spewed out of the damaged tanker.* ■ [*intr.*] *inf.* vomit. —**spew·er** *n.*

SPF ▶ *abbr.* sun protection factor (indicating the effectiveness of protective skin preparations).

sphere /sfi(ə)r/ ▶ *n.* **1** a round solid figure, or its surface, with every point on its surface equidistant from its center. ■ an object having this shape; a ball or globe. ■ a globe representing the earth. ■ *chiefly poetic/lit.* a celestial body. ■ *poetic/lit.* the sky perceived as a vault upon or in which celestial bodies are represented as lying. ■ each of a series of revolving concentrically arranged spherical shells in which celestial bodies were formerly thought to be set in a fixed relationship. **2** an area of activity, interest, or expertise: *his new wife's skill in the domestic sphere.* ■ a section of society or an aspect of life distinguished and unified by a particular characteristic: *political reforms to match those in the economic sphere.* —**spher·al** /-əl/ *adj.* (*archaic*).
▶ □ **music** (or **harmony**) **of the spheres** the natural harmonic tones supposedly produced by the movement of the celestial spheres or the bodies fixed in them.

spher·ic /'sfi(ə)rik; 'sfer-/ ▶ *adj.* spherical. —**sphe·ric·i·ty** /sfi'risitē/ *n.*

spher·i·cal /'sfi(ə)rikəl; 'sfer-/ ▶ *adj.* shaped like a sphere. ■ of or relating to the properties of spheres. ■ formed inside or on the surface of a sphere. —**spher·i·cal·ly** *adv.*

sphe·roid /'sfi(ə)r,oid/ ▶ *n.* a spherelike but not perfectly spherical body. ■ a solid generated by a half-revolution of an ellipse about its major axis (**prolate spheroid**) or minor axis (**oblate spheroid**). —**sphe·roi·dal** /sfi'roidl/ adj. —**sphe·roi·dic·i·ty** /,sfi(ə)roi'disitē/ n.

spher·ule /'sfi(ə)r(y)o͞ol; 'sfer-/ ▶n. a small sphere. —**spher·u·lar** /-yo͞olər/ adj.

spher·u·lite /'sfi(ə)r(y)ə,līt; 'sfer-/ ▶n. chiefly Geol. a small spheroidal mass of crystals (esp. of a mineral) grouped radially around a point. —**spher·u·lit·ic** /,sfi(ə)r(y)ə'litik; ,sfer-/ adj.

sphinc·ter /'sfiNGktər/ ▶n. Anat. a ring of muscle surrounding and serving to guard or close an opening or tube, such as the anus or the openings of the stomach. ▷late 16th cent.: via Latin from Greek *sphinktēr*, from *sphingein* 'bind tight.' —**sphinc·ter·al** /-əl/ adj. —**sphinc·ter·ic** /,sfiNGk'terik/ adj.

sphinx /sfiNGks/ ▶n. **1** (**Sphinx**) *Greek Mythol.* a winged monster of Thebes, having a woman's head and a lion's body. ▪ (**the Sphinx**) an ancient Egyptian stone figure having a lion's body and a human or animal head, esp. the huge statue near the Pyramids at Giza. ▪ (usu. **sphinx**) an enigmatic or inscrutable person. **2** (also **sphinx moth**) another term for HAWK MOTH.

sphyg·mo·ma·nom·e·ter /,sfigmōmə'nämitər/ ▶n. an instrument for measuring blood pressure, typically consisting of an inflatable rubber cuff that is applied to the arm. —**sphyg·mo·ma·nom·e·try** /-mətrē/ n.

spice /spīs/ ▶n. **1** an aromatic or pungent vegetable substance used to flavor food, e.g., cloves, pepper, or mace: *enjoy the taste and aroma of freshly ground spices.* ▪ an element providing interest and excitement: *healthy rivalry adds spice to the game.* **2** a russet color.
▶v. [tr.] [often as adj.] (**spiced**) flavor with spice: *turbot with a spiced sauce.* ▪ add an interesting or piquant quality to; make more exciting: *she was probably adding details to spice up the story.*

spick-and-span /'spik ən 'span/ (also **spic-and-span**) ▶adj. spotlessly clean and well looked after: *spick-and-span shining bathrooms.*

spic·ule /'spikyo͞ol/ ▶n. **1** technical a minute sharp-pointed object or structure that is typically present in large numbers, such as a fine particle of ice. ▪ Zool. each of the small needlelike or sharp-pointed structures of calcite or silica that make up the skeleton of a sponge. **2** Astron. a short-lived, relatively small radial jet of gas in the chromosphere or lower corona of the sun. —**spic·u·lar** /-yələr/ adj. —**spic·u·late** /-yəlit; -yə,lāt/ adj. —**spic·u·la·tion** n.

spic·y /'spīsē/ ▶adj. (**spic·i·er, spic·i·est**) flavored with or fragrant with spice: *pasta in a spicy tomato sauce.* —**spic·i·ly** adv.

spi·der /'spīdər/ ▶n. an eight-legged predatory arachnid with an unsegmented body consisting of a fused head and thorax and a rounded abdomen. Spiders have fangs that inject poison into their prey, and most kinds spin webs in which to capture insects. ▪ used in names of similar or related arachnids, e.g., **sea spider**. ▪ any object resembling a spider, esp. one having numerous or prominent legs or radiating spokes. —**spi·der·ish** adj.

spi·der crab ▶n. a crab (*Macropodia* and other genera) with long thin legs and a compact pear-shaped body, which is camouflaged in some kinds by attached sponges and seaweed.

spi·der mon·key ▶n. a South American monkey (genus *Brachyteles*, family Cebidae) with very long limbs and a long prehensile tail.

spi·der·y /'spīdərē/ ▶adj. resembling a spider, esp. having long, thin, angular lines like a spider's legs: *the letters were written in a spidery hand.*

spiel /spēl; SHpēl/ inf. ▶n. a long or fast speech or story, typically one intended as a means of persuasion or as an excuse but regarded with skepticism or contempt by those who hear it: *he delivers a breathless and effortless spiel in promotion of his new novel.*
▶v. [tr.] reel off; recite: *he solemnly spieled all he knew.* ▪ [intr.] speak glibly or at length.

spiff·y /'spifē/ ▶adj. (**spiff·i·er, spiff·i·est**) inf. smart in appearance: *a spiffy new outfit.* —**spif·fi·ly** /'spifəlē/ adv.

spig·ot /'spigət/ ▶n. **1** a small peg or plug, esp. for insertion into the vent of a cask. **2** a faucet.

spike¹ /spīk/ ▶n. **1** a thin, pointed piece of metal, wood, or another rigid material. ▪ a large stout nail, esp. one used to fasten a rail to a railroad tie. ▪ each of several metal points set into the sole of an athletic shoe to prevent slipping. ▪ (**spikes**) a pair of athletic shoes with such metal points. ▪ short for SPIKE HEEL. ▪ inf. a hypodermic needle. **2** a sharp increase in the magnitude or concentration of something: *the oil price spike.* ▪ Electr. a pulse of very short duration in which a rapid increase in voltage is followed by a rapid decrease.
▶v. [tr.] **1** impale on or pierce with a sharp point: *she spiked another oyster.* ▪ Baseball injure (a player) with the spikes on one's shoes. ▪ (of a newspaper editor) reject (a story) by or as if by filing it on a spike: *the editors deemed the article in bad taste and spiked it.* ▪ stop the progress of (a plan or undertaking); put an end to: *he doubted they would spike the*

entire effort over this one negotiation. **2** form into or cover with sharp points: *his hair was matted and spiked with blood.* ▪ [intr.] take on a sharp, pointed shape: *lightning spiked across the sky.* ▪ [intr.] increase and then decrease sharply; reach a peak: *oil prices would spike and fall again.* **3** inf. add alcohol or a drug to contaminate (drink or food) surreptitiously: *she bought me an orange juice and spiked it with vodka.* ▪ add sharp or pungent flavoring to (food or drink): *spike the liquid with lime or lemon juice.* ▪ enrich (a nuclear reactor or its fuel) with a particular isotope. **4** (in volleyball) hit (the ball) forcefully from a position near the net so that it moves downward into the opposite court.

spike² ▶n. Bot. a flower cluster formed of many flowerheads attached directly to a long stem. —**spike·let** n.

spike heel ▶n. a high tapering heel on a woman's shoe.

spik·y /'spīkē/ ▶adj. (**spik·i·er, spik·i·est**) like a spike or spikes or having many spikes: *he has short spiky hair.* ▪ inf. easily offended or annoyed. —**spik·i·ly** /-kəlē/ adv. —**spik·i·ness** n.

spill /spil/ ▶v. (past **spilled** or **spilt** /spilt/) [tr.] cause or allow (liquid) to flow over the edge of its container, esp. unintentionally: *you'll spill that coffee if you're not careful.* ▪ [intr.] (of liquid) flow over the edge of its container: *some of the wine spilled onto the floor.* ▪ [intr.] (of the contents of something) be emptied out onto a surface: *passengers' baggage had spilled out of the hold.* ▪ cause or allow (the contents of something) to be emptied out: *injured cells tend to swell up and burst, spilling their contents.* ▪ [intr.] (of a number of people) move out of somewhere quickly: *students began to spill out of the building.* ▪ inf. reveal (confidential information) to someone: *he was reluctant to spill her address.* ▪ cause (someone) to fall off a horse or bicycle: *the horse was wrenched off course, spilling his rider.*
▶n. **1** a quantity of liquid that has spilled or been spilled: *a 25-ton oil spill.* ▪ an instance of a liquid spilling or being spilled. **2** a fall from a horse or bicycle: *Granddad took a spill while riding the bay mare.* —**spill·age** /'spilij/ n. —**spill·er** n.
▶ □ **spill the beans** inf. reveal secret information unintentionally or indiscreetly.

spill·o·ver /'spil,ōvər/ ▶n. an instance of overflowing or spreading into another area: *there has been a spillover into public schools of the ethos of private schools.* ▪ a thing that spreads or has spread into another area: *the village was a spillover from a neighboring, larger village.* ▪ [usu. as adj.] an unexpected consequence, repercussion, or byproduct: *the spillover effect of the quarrel.*

spill·way /'spil,wā/ ▶n. a passage for surplus water from a dam. ▪ a natural drainage channel cut by water from melting glaciers or ice fields.

spin /spin/ ▶v. (**spin·ning**; past and past part. **spun** /spən/) **1** turn or cause to turn or whirl around quickly: [intr.] *the girl spun around in alarm* | [tr.] *he fiddled with the radio, spinning the dial.* ▪ [intr.] (of a person's head) give a sensation of dizziness: *the figures were enough to make her head spin.* ▪ [intr.] travel or move through the air with such a revolving motion. ▪ [tr.] give (a news story or other information) a particular interpretation, esp. a favorable one. ▪ [tr.] shape (sheet metal) by pressure applied during rotation on a lathe: [as adj.] (**spun**) *spun metal components.* **2** draw out (wool, cotton, or other material) and convert it into threads, either by hand or with machinery: *they spin wool into the yarn for weaving* | [as adj.] (**spun**) *spun glass.* ▪ make (threads) in this way: *this method is used to spin filaments from syrups.* ▪ (of a spider or a silkworm or other insect) produce (gossamer or silk) or construct (a web or cocoon) by extruding a fine viscous thread from a special gland.
▶phrasal v. □ **spin something off** (of a parent company) turn a subsidiary into a new and separate company. □ **spin out** (of a driver or car) lose control, esp. in a skid.
▶n. **1** a rapid turning or whirling motion: *he concluded the dance with a double spin.* ▪ revolving motion imparted to a ball in a game such as baseball, cricket, tennis, or billiards: *this racket enables the player to impart more spin to the ball.* ▪ a particular bias, interpretation, or point of view, intended to create a favorable (or sometimes, unfavorable) impression when presented to the public: *he tried to put a positive spin on the president's campaign.* ▪ a fast revolving motion of an aircraft as it descends rapidly: *he tried to stop the plane from going into a spin.* ▪ Physics the intrinsic angular momentum of a subatomic particle. **2** inf. a brief trip in a vehicle for pleasure: *a spin around town.* ▷Old English *spinnan* 'draw out and twist (fiber)'; related to German *spinnen.* The noun dates from the mid 19th cent.
▶ □ **spin one's wheels** inf. waste one's time or efforts.

spi·na bif·i·da /ˈspīnə ˈbifidə/ ▶ n. a congenital defect of the spine in which part of the spinal cord and its meninges are exposed through a gap in the backbone. It often causes paralysis of the lower limbs, and sometimes mental handicap.

spin·ach /ˈspinicH/ ▶ n. a widely cultivated edible Asian plant (*Spinacia oleracea*) of the goosefoot family, with large, dark green leaves that are eaten raw or cooked as a vegetable.

spi·nal /ˈspīnl/ ▶ adj. of or relating to the spine: *spinal injuries*. —**spi·nal·ly** adv.

spi·nal col·umn ▶ n. the spine; the backbone.

spi·nal cord ▶ n. the cylindrical bundle of nerve fibers and associated tissue that is enclosed in the spine and connects nearly all parts of the body to the brain, with which it forms the central nervous system.

spin·dle /ˈspindl/ ▶ n. **1** a slender rounded rod with tapered ends used in hand spinning to twist and wind thread from a mass of wool or flax held on a distaff. ■ a pin or rod used on a spinning wheel to twist and wind the thread. ■ a pin bearing the bobbin of a spinning machine. ■ a pointed metal rod on a base, used to impale paper items for temporary filing. ■ a turned piece of wood used as a banister or chair leg. **2** a rod or pin serving as an axis that revolves or on which something revolves.

spin·dly /ˈspin(d)lē/ ▶ adj. (of a person or limb) long or tall and thin: *spindly arms and legs*. ■ (of a thing) thin and weak or insubstantial in construction: *spindly chairs*.

spin doc·tor ▶ n. inf. a spokesperson employed to give a favorable interpretation of events to the media, esp. on behalf of a political party.

spin·drift /ˈspinˌdrift/ ▶ n. spray blown from the crests of waves by the wind.

spine /spīn/ ▶ n. **1** a series of vertebrae extending from the skull to the small of the back, enclosing the spinal cord and providing support for the thorax and abdomen; the backbone. ■ fig. a thing's central feature or main source of strength: *players who will form the spine of our team*. ■ fig. resolution or strength of character. ■ the part of a book's jacket or cover that encloses the inner edges of the pages, facing outward when the book is on a shelf and typically bearing the title and the author's name. **2** *Zool. & Bot.* any hard pointed defensive projection or structure, such as a prickle of a hedgehog, a spikelike projection on a sea urchin, a sharp ray in a fish's fin, or a spike on the stem of a plant. —**spined** adj. [in comb.] *broken-spined paperbacks*.

spine-chill·er ▶ n. a story or movie that inspires terror and excitement. —**spine-chill·ing** adj.

spine·less /ˈspīnlis/ ▶ adj. **1** having no spine or backbone; invertebrate. ■ fig. (of a person) lacking resolution; weak and purposeless: *a spineless coward*. **2** (of an animal or plant) lacking spines: *spineless forms of prickly pear have been selected*. —**spine·less·ly** adv. —**spine·less·ness** n.

spin·et /ˈspinit/ ▶ n. a type of small upright piano.

spine-tin·gling ▶ adj. inf. thrilling or pleasurably frightening: *a spine-tingling adventure*.

spin·na·ker /ˈspinəkər/ ▶ n. a large three-cornered sail, typically bulging when full, set forward of the mainsail of a yacht when running before the wind.

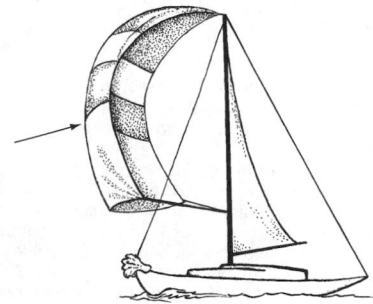

spinnaker

spin·ner /ˈspinər/ ▶ n. **1** a person occupied in making thread by spinning. **2** a person or thing that spins. **3** (also **spin·ner·bait** /-ˌbāt/) *Fishing* a lure designed to revolve when pulled through the water.

spin·ner·et /ˌspinəˈret/ ▶ n. *Zool.* any of a number of different organs through which the silk, gossamer, or thread of spiders, silkworms, and certain other insects is produced. ■ (in the production of manmade fibers) a cap or plate with a number of small holes through which a fiber-forming solution is forced.

spin·ning /ˈspiniNG/ ▶ n. the action or process of converting fibers into thread or yarn.

spin·ning jen·ny ▶ n. hist. a machine for spinning with more than one spindle at a time, patented by James Hargreaves in 1770.

spin·ning mule ▶ n. see MULE[1] (sense 3).

spin·ning wheel ▶ n. an apparatus for spinning yarn or thread, with a spindle driven by a wheel attached to a crank or treadle.

spin-off (also **spin·off**) ▶ n. a byproduct or incidental result of a larger project: *the commercial spin-off from defense research*. ■ a product marketed by its association with a popular television program, movie, personality, etc.: [as adj.] *spin-off merchandising*. ■ a business or organization developed out of or by members of another organization, in particular a subsidiary of a parent company that has been sold off, creating a new company.

spin·ster /ˈspinstər/ ▶ n. derog. an unmarried woman, typically an older woman beyond the usual age for marriage. —**spin·ster·hood** /-ˌho͝od/ n. —**spin·ster·ish** adj.

spin·y /ˈspinē/ ▶ adj. (**spin·i·er**, **spin·i·est**) full of or covered with prickles: *a spiny cactus*. ■ inf. difficult to understand or handle: *a spiny problem*. —**spin·i·ness** n.

spin·y lob·ster ▶ n. a large edible crustacean (*Palinuris* and other genera, family Palinuridae) with a spiny shell and long heavy antennae, but lacking the large claws of true lobsters.

spi·ral /ˈspīrəl/ ▶ adj. winding in a continuous and gradually widening (or tightening) curve, either around a central point on a flat plane or about an axis so as to form a cone: *a spiral pattern*. ■ winding in a continuous curve of constant diameter about a central axis, as though along a cylinder; helical. ■ (of a staircase) constantly turning in one direction as it rises, around a solid or open center.
▶ n. **1** a spiral curve, shape, or pattern: *he spotted a spiral of smoke*. **2** a progressive rise or fall of prices, wages, etc., each responding to an upward or downward stimulus provided by a previous one: *an inflationary spiral*. ■ a process of deterioration through the continuous increase or decrease of a specified feature: *a downward spiral of sex and drink*. **3** *Football* a pass or kick that moves smoothly through the air while spinning on its long axis.
▶ v. (**-raled, -ral·ing**; *Brit.* **-ralled, -ral·ling**) **1** [intr.] move in a spiral course: *a wisp of smoke spiraled up from the trees*. ■ [tr.] cause to have a spiral shape or follow a spiral course: *spiral the bandage around the injured limb*. **2** [intr.] show a continuous and dramatic increase: *inflation continued to spiral* | [as adj.] (**spiraling**) *he needed to relax after the spiraling tensions of the day*. ■ (**spiral down/downward**) decrease or deteriorate continuously: *he expects the figures to spiral down further*. —**spi·ral·ly** adv.

spi·ral-bound ▶ adj. (of a book or notepad) bound with a wire or plastic spiral threaded through a row of holes along one edge.

spi·ral gal·ax·y ▶ n. a galaxy in which the stars and gas clouds are concentrated mainly in one or more spiral arms.

spire[1] /spī(ə)r/ ▶ n. a tapering conical or pyramidal structure on the top of a building, typically a church tower. ■ a long tapering object: *spires of delphiniums*. —**spired** adj. —**spir·y** adj.

spire[2] ▶ n. *Zool.* the upper tapering part of the spiral shell of a gastropod mollusk, comprising all but the whorl containing the body.

spi·ril·lum /spīˈriləm/ ▶ n. (pl. **spirilla** /-lə/) a bacterium with a rigid spiral structure, found in stagnant water and sometimes causing disease.

spir·it /ˈspirit/ ▶ n. **1** the nonphysical part of a person that is the seat of emotions and character; the soul: *we seek a harmony between body and spirit*. ■ such a part regarded as a person's true self and as capable of surviving physical death or separation: *a year after he left, his spirit is still present*. ■ such a part manifested as an apparition after their death; a ghost. ■ a supernatural being: *shrines to nature spirits*. ■ (**the Spirit**) short for HOLY SPIRIT. **2** those qualities regarded as forming the definitive or typical elements in the character of a person, nation, or group or in the thought and attitudes of a particular period: *the university is a symbol of the nation's egalitarian spirit*. ■ a person identified with their most prominent mental or moral characteristics or with their role in a group or movement: *he was a leading spirit in the conference*. ■ a specified emotion or mood, esp. one prevailing at a particular time: *I hope the team will build on this spirit of confidence*. ■ (**spirits**) a person's mood: *the warm weather lifted everyone's spirits after the winter*. ■ the quality of courage, energy, and determination or assertiveness: *his visitors admired his spirit and good temper*. ■ the attitude or intentions with which someone undertakes or regards something: *he confessed in a spirit of self-respect, not defiance*. ■ the real meaning or the intention behind something as opposed to its strict verbal interpretation: *the rule had been broken in spirit if not in letter*. **3** (usu. **spirits**) strong distilled liquor such as brandy, whiskey, gin, or rum. ■ a volatile liquid, esp. a fuel, prepared by distillation: *spirits of turpentine.* | *aviation spirit.*

▸ *v.* (**-it·ed, -it·ing**) [*tr.*] convey rapidly and secretly: *stolen cows were spirited away some distance to prevent detection.* ▷Middle English: from Anglo-Norman French, from Latin *spiritus* 'breath, spirit,' from *spirare* 'breathe.' —**spir·it·ous** *adj.*

spir·it·ed /ˈspiritid/ ▸ *adj.* **1** full of energy, enthusiasm, and determination: *a spirited campaigner for women's rights.* **2** [in *comb.*] having a specified character, outlook on life, or mood: *he was a warmhearted, generous-spirited man.* —**spir·it·ed·ly** *adv.* —**spir·it·ed·ness** *n.*

spir·it·less /ˈspiritlis/ ▸ *adj.* lacking courage, vigor, or vivacity: *Ruth and I played a spiritless game of Scrabble.* —**spir·it·less·ly** *adv.* —**spir·it·less·ness** *n.*

spir·it·u·al /ˈspiriCHOŌəl/ ▸ *adj.* **1** of, relating to, or affecting the human spirit or soul as opposed to material or physical things: *I'm responsible for his spiritual welfare* | *the spiritual values of life.* ■ (of a person) not concerned with material values or pursuits. **2** of or relating to religion or religious belief: *Iran's spiritual leader.*

▸ *n.* (also **Negro spiritual**) a religious song of a kind associated with black Christians of the southern U.S. —**spir·it·u·al·i·ty** /ˌspiriCHOŌˈalitē/ *n.* —**spir·it·u·al·ly** *adv.*

▸ □ **one's spiritual home** a place in which one feels a profound sense of belonging: *I had always thought of Italy as my spiritual home.*

spir·it·u·al·ism /ˈspiriCHOŌəˌlizəm/ ▸ *n.* a system of belief or religious practice based on supposed communication with the spirits of the dead, esp. through mediums. —**spir·it·u·al·ist** *n.* —**spir·it·u·al·is·tic** /ˌspiriCHOŌəˈlistik/ *adj.*

spi·ro·chete /ˈspīrəˌkēt/ ▸ *n.* a flexible spirally twisted bacterium, esp. one that causes syphilis.

spi·ro·gy·ra /ˌspīrəˈjīrə/ ▸ *n. Bot.* a filamentous freshwater green alga (genus *Spirogyra*, division Chlorophyta) containing spiral bands of chloroplasts.

spit[1] /spit/ ▸ *v.* (**spit·ting**; *past* and *past part.* **spit** or **spat** /spat/) [*intr.*] eject saliva forcibly from one's mouth, sometimes as a gesture of contempt or anger: *Todd spit in Hugh's face.* ■ [*tr.*] forcibly eject (food or liquid) from one's mouth: *he spits out his piece of coconut.* ■ (**spit up**) (esp. of a baby) vomit or regurgitate food. ■ [*tr.*] utter in a hostile or aggressive way: *she spat abuse at the jury.* ■ be extremely angry or frustrated: *he was spitting with sudden fury.* ■ (of a fire or something being cooked) emit small bursts of sparks or hot fat with a series of short, explosive noises. ■ (of a cat) make a hissing noise as a sign of anger or hostility.

▸ *n.* **1** saliva, typically that which has been ejected from a person's mouth. **2** an act of spitting. —**spit·ter** *n.*

spit[2] ▸ *n.* **1** a long, thin metal rod pushed through meat in order to hold and turn it while it is roasted over an open fire: *chicken cooked on a spit.* **2** a narrow point of land projecting into the sea: *a narrow spit of land shelters the bay.*

▸ *v.* (**spit·ted, spit·ting**) [*tr.*] put a spit through (meat) in order to roast it over an open fire: *I spitted the squirrel meat and turned it over the flames.*

spit and pol·ish ▸ *n.* thorough or exaggerated cleaning and polishing, esp. by a soldier: *they gave the dining room some extra spit and polish.*

spit·ball /ˈspitˌbôl/ ▸ *n.* **1** a piece of paper that has been chewed and shaped into a ball for use as a missile. **2** *Baseball* an illegal pitch made with a ball moistened with saliva or another substance to make it move erratically.

▸ *v.* [*tr.*] *inf.* throw out (a suggestion) for discussion: *I'm just spitballing a few ideas.* —**spit·ball·er** *n.*

spite /spīt/ ▸ *n.* a desire to hurt, annoy, or offend someone: *he'd think I was saying it out of spite.* ■ *archaic* an instance of such a desire; a grudge: *it seemed as if the wind had a spite at her.*

▸ *v.* [*tr.*] deliberately hurt, annoy, or offend (someone): *he put the house up for sale to spite his family.*

▸ □ **in spite of** without being affected by the particular factor mentioned: *he was suddenly cold in spite of the sun.*

spite·ful /ˈspītfəl/ ▸ *adj.* showing or caused by malice: *the teachers made spiteful little jokes about me.* —**spite·ful·ly** *adv.* —**spite·ful·ness** *n.*

spit·fire /ˈspitˌfīr/ ▸ *n.* a person with a fierce temper.

spit·ting im·age ▸ *n.* (**the spitting image of**) *inf.* the exact double of (another person or thing): *she's the spitting image of her mom.*

spit·tle /ˈspitl/ ▸ *n.* saliva, esp. as ejected from the mouth. —**spit·tly** *adj.*

spit·toon /spiˈtoōn/ ▸ *n.* a metal or earthenware pot typically having a funnel-shaped top, used for spitting into.

splash /splaSH/ ▸ *n.* a sound made by something striking or falling into liquid: *we hit the water with a mighty splash.* ■ a spell of moving about in water energetically: *the girls joined them for a final splash in the pool.* ■ a small quantity of liquid that has fallen or been dashed against a

surface: *a splash of gravy.* ■ a small quantity of liquid added to a drink: *a splash of lemonade.* ■ a bright patch of color: *add a red scarf to give a splash of color.* ■ *inf.* a prominent or sensational news feature or story: *a front-page splash.* ■ a striking, ostentatious, or exciting effect or event: *there's going to be a big splash when Mike returns to the ring.*

▸ *v.* [*tr.*] cause (liquid) to strike or fall on something in irregular drops: *she splashed cold water onto her face.* ■ [*tr.*] make wet by doing this: *they splashed each other with water.* ■ [*intr.*] (of a liquid) fall or be scattered in irregular drops: *a tear fell and splashed onto the pillow.* ■ [*intr.*] strike or move around in a body of water, causing it to fly about noisily. ■ (**be splashed with**) be decorated with scattered patches of: *a field splashed with purple clover.* ■ [*tr.*] print (a story or photograph, esp. a sensational one) in a prominent place in a newspaper or magazine: *the story was splashed across the front pages.*

▸ *phrasal v.* □ **splash down** (of a spacecraft) land on water. —**splash·y** *adj.*

▸ □ **make a splash** *inf.* attract a great deal of attention.

splash·down /ˈsplaSHˌdoun/ ▸ *n.* the alighting of a returning spacecraft on the sea, with the assistance of parachutes.

splat /splat/ ▸ *inf.* ▸ *n.* a sound of something soft and wet or heavy striking a surface: *the goblin makes a huge splat as he hits the ground.*

▸ *adv.* with a sound of this type: *he lands splat on his right elbow.*

▸ *v.* (**splat·ted, splat·ting**) [*tr.*] crush or squash (something) with a sound of this type: *he was splatting a bug.* ■ [*intr.*] land or be squashed with a sound of this type.

splat·ter /ˈsplatər/ ▸ *v.* [*tr.*] splash with a sticky or viscous liquid: *a passing cart rolled by, splattering him with mud.* ■ splash (such a liquid) over a surface or object. ■ [*intr.*] (of such a liquid) splash: *heavy droplets of rain splatter onto the windshield.* ■ *inf.* prominently or sensationally publish (a story) in a newspaper: *the story is splattered over pages two and three.*

▸ *n.* **1** a spot or trail of a sticky or viscous liquid splashed over a surface or object: *each puddle we crossed threw a splatter of mud on the windshield.* **2** [as *adj.*] *inf.* denoting or referring to films featuring many violent and gruesome deaths: *a splatter movie.*

splay /splā/ ▸ *v.* [*tr.*] thrust or spread (things, esp. limbs or fingers) out and apart: *her hands were splayed across his broad shoulders.* ■ [*intr.*] (esp. of limbs or fingers) be thrust or spread out and apart: *his legs splayed out in front of him.* ■ [*tr.*] (of a thing) diverge in shape or position; become wider or more separated. ■ [usu. as *adj.*] (**splayed**) construct (a window, doorway, or aperture) so that it diverges or is wider at one side of the wall than the other: *the walls are pierced by splayed window openings.*

▸ *n.* **1** a widening or outward tapering of something, in particular: ■ a tapered widening of a road at an intersection to increase visibility. **2** a surface making an oblique angle with another, such as the splayed side of a window or embrasure. ■ the degree of bevel or slant of a surface.

▸ *adj.* [usu. in *comb.*] turned outward or widened: *the girls were sitting splay-legged.*

spleen /splēn/ ▸ *n.* **1** *Anat.* an abdominal organ involved in the production and removal of blood cells in most vertebrates and forming part of the immune system. **2** bad temper; spite: *he could **vent his spleen** on the institutions that had duped him.* ▷Middle English: shortening of Old French *esplen,* via Latin from Greek *splēn.*

splen·did /ˈsplendid/ ▸ *adj.* magnificent; very impressive: *a splendid view of Windsor Castle.* ■ *inf.* excellent; very good: *a splendid fellow.* —**splen·did·ly** *adv.* *a splendidly ornate style.* —**splen·did·ness** *n.*

splen·dif·er·ous /splenˈdifərəs/ ▸ *adj. inf., humorous* splendid: *a splendiferous Sunday dinner.* —**splen·dif·er·ous·ly** *adv.* —**splen·dif·er·ous·ness** *n.*

splen·dor /ˈsplendər/ (*Brit.* **splen·dour**) ▸ *n.* magnificent and splendid appearance; grandeur: *the splendor of the Florida Keys.* ■ (**splendors**) magnificent features or qualities: *the splendors of the imperial court.*

splen·ec·to·my /spləˈnektəmē/ ▸ *n.* (*pl.* **-mies**) a surgical operation involving removal of the spleen.

sple·net·ic /spləˈnetik/ ▸ *adj.* bad-tempered; spiteful: *a splenetic outburst.* —**sple·net·i·cal·ly** *adv.*

splen·ic /ˈsplēnik/ ; 'sple-/ ▸ *adj.* of or relating to the spleen: *the splenic artery.*

sple·ni·tis /spləˈnītis/ ; sple-/ ▸ *n. Med.* inflammation of the spleen.

splice /splīs/ ▸ *v.* [*tr.*] join or connect (a rope or ropes) by interweaving the strands: *we learned how to weave and splice ropes* | *a cord was spliced on.* ■ join (pieces of timber, film, or tape) at the ends: *commercials can be spliced in later.* ■ *Genetics* join or insert (a gene or gene fragment).

▶*n.* a union of two ropes, pieces of timber, or similar materials spliced together at the ends. —**splic·er** *n.*

spline /splīn/ ▶*n.* **1** a rectangular key fitting into grooves in the hub and shaft of a wheel, esp. one formed integrally with the shaft that allows movement of the wheel on the shaft. ■ a corresponding groove in a hub along which the key may slide. **2** a slat. ■ a flexible wood or rubber strip used esp. in drawing large curves.

splint /splint/ ▶*n.* **1** a strip of rigid material used for supporting and immobilizing a broken bone when it has been set: *she had to wear splints on her legs.* **2** a long, thin strip of wood used to light a fire. ■ a rigid or flexible strip, esp. of wood, used in basketwork.
▶*v.* [*tr.*] secure (a broken limb) with a splint or splints: *his leg was splinted.*

splin·ter /'splin(t)ər/ ▶*n.* a small, thin, sharp piece of wood, glass, or similar material broken off from a larger piece: *a splinter of ice.*
▶*v.* break or cause to break into small sharp fragments: [*intr.*] *the soap box splintered.* | [*tr.*] *he crashed into a fence, splintering the wooden barricade.* —**splin·ter·y** *adj.*

splin·ter group (also **splinter party**) ▶*n.* a small organization, typically a political party, that has broken away from a larger one.

split /split/ ▶*v.* (**split·ting**; *past* and *past part.* **split**) **1** break or cause to break forcibly into parts, esp. into halves or along the grain: [*intr.*] *the ice cracked and heaved and split* | [*tr.*] *split and toast the muffins.* ■ remove or be removed by breaking, separating, or dividing: [*tr.*] *the point was pressed against the edge of the flint to split off flakes.* ■ divide or cause to divide into parts or elements: [*tr.*] *splitting water into oxygen and hydrogen.* ■ [*tr.*] divide and share (something, esp. resources or responsibilities): *they met up and split the booty.* ■ [*tr.*] cause the fission of (an atom). ■ [*tr.*] issue new shares of (stock) to existing stockholders in proportion to their current holdings. **2** (with reference to a group of people) divide into two or more groups: [*intr.*] *let's split up and find the other two* | [*tr.*] *once again the family was split up.* ■ [*intr.*] end a marriage or an emotional or working relationship: *I split with my boyfriend a year ago.* ■ [*tr.*] (often **be split**) (of an issue) cause (a group) to be divided because of opposing views: *the party was deeply split over its future direction.* **3** [*intr.*] *inf.* (of one's head) suffer great pain from a headache: *my head is splitting* | [as *adj.*] (**splitting**) *a splitting headache.* **4** [*intr.*] *inf.* leave a place, esp. suddenly: *"Let's split," Harvey said.*
▶*n.* **1** a tear, crack, or fissure in something, esp. down the middle or along the grain: *light squeezed through a small split in the curtain.* ■ an instance or act of splitting or being split; a division: *the split between the rich and the poor.* ■ a separation into parties or within a party; a schism: *the accusations caused a split in the party.* ■ an ending of a marriage or an emotional or working relationship: *a much-publicized split with his wife.* ■ short for STOCK SPLIT. **2** (**a split** or **the splits**) (in gymnastics and dance) an act of leaping in the air or sitting down with the legs straight and at right angles to the upright body, one in front and the other behind, or one at each side: *I could never do a split before.* **3** a thing that is divided or split, in particular: ■ half a bottle or glass of champagne or other liquor. ■ (in bowling) a formation of standing pins after the first ball in which there is a gap between two pins or groups of pins, making a spare unlikely. ■ a drawn game or series. ■ a split-level house. **4** the time taken to complete a recognized part of a race, or the point in the race where such a time is measured. —**split·ter** *n.*
▶ □ **split the difference** take the average of two proposed amounts.

split in·fin·i·tive ▶*n.* a construction consisting of an infinitive with an adverb or other word inserted between *to* and the verb, e.g., *she seems to really like it.*

split-lev·el ▶*adj.* (of a building) having a room or rooms higher than others by less than a whole story: *a large split-level house.* ■ (of a room) having its floor on two levels.
▶*n.* a split-level building.

split pea ▶*n.* a pea dried and split in half for cooking.

split per·son·al·i·ty ▶*n.* less common term for MULTIPLE PERSONALITY.

split screen ▶*n.* a movie, television, or computer screen on which two or more separate images are displayed.

split sec·ond ▶*n.* a very brief moment of time: *for a split second, I hesitated.*
▶*adj.* very rapid or accurate: *split-second timing is crucial.*

splotch /spläCH/ *inf.* ▶*n.* a daub, blot, or smear of something, typically a liquid: *a splotch of red in a larger area of yellow.*
▶*v.* [*tr.*] (usu. **be splotched**) make such a daub, blot, or smear on: *a rag splotched with grease.* —**splotch·y** *adj.*

splurge /splərj/ *inf.* ▶*n.* an act of spending money freely or extravagantly: *the annual pre-Christmas splurge.* ■ a large or excessive amount of something: *there has recently been a splurge of teach-yourself books.*

▶*v.* [*tr.*] spend (money) freely or extravagantly: *I'd splurged about $2,500 on clothes* | [*intr.*] *we splurged on T-bone steaks.*

splut·ter /'splətər/ ▶*v.* [*intr.*] make a series of short explosive spitting or choking sounds: *she coughed and spluttered, tears coursing down her face.* ■ say something rapidly, indistinctly, and with a spitting sound, as a result of anger, embarrassment, or another strong emotion: [*tr.*] *he began to splutter excuses.* ■ [*tr.*] spit (something) out from one's mouth noisily and in small splashes: *spluttering brackish water, he struggled to regain his feet.*
▶*n.* a short explosive spitting or choking noise. —**splut·ter·er** *n.* —**splut·ter·ing·ly** *adv.*

spoil /spoil/ ▶*v.* (*past* and *past part.* **spoiled** or *chiefly Brit.* **spoilt** /spoilt/) [*tr.*] **1** diminish or destroy the value or quality of: *I wouldn't want to spoil your fun.* ■ prevent someone from enjoying (an occasion or event): *she was afraid of spoiling Christmas for the rest of the family.* ■ [*intr.*] (of food) become unfit for eating: *I've got some ham that'll spoil if we don't eat it tonight.* **2** harm the character of (a child) by being too lenient or indulgent: *the last thing I want to do is spoil Thomas* | [as *adj.*] (**spoiled**) *a spoiled child.* ■ treat with great or excessive kindness, consideration, or generosity: *Susanna would go to the North Street house whenever she needed to be spoiled.* **3** [*intr.*] (**be spoiling for**) be extremely or aggressively eager for: *Cooper was spoiling for a fight.*
▶*n.* **1** (usu. **spoils**) goods stolen or taken forcibly from a person or place: *the looters carried their spoils away.* **2** waste material generated during an excavation or a dredging or mining operation.

spoil·age /'spoilij/ ▶*n.* the action of spoiling, esp. the deterioration of food and perishable goods.

spoil·er /'spoilər/ ▶*n.* **1** a person or thing that spoils. ■ (esp. in a political context) a person who obstructs or prevents an opponent's success while having no chance of winning a contest themselves. ■ an electronic device for preventing unauthorized copying of sound recordings by means of a disruptive signal inaudible on the original. **2** a flap on an aircraft or glider that can be projected from the surface of a wing in order to create drag and so reduce speed. ■ a similar device on a motor vehicle intended to prevent it from being lifted off the road when traveling at very high speeds.

spoil·sport /'spoil,spôrt/ ▶*n.* a person who behaves in a way that spoils others' pleasure, esp. by not joining in an activity.

spoils sys·tem ▶*n.* the practice of a successful political party giving public office to its supporters.

spoke[1] /spōk/ ▶*n.* each of the bars or wire rods connecting the center of a wheel to its outer edge. ■ each of a set of radial handles projecting from a ship's wheel. ■ each of the metal rods in an umbrella to which the material is attached. —**spoked** *adj.* [in *comb.*] *a wire-spoked wheel.*

spoke[2] ▶ *past* of SPEAK.

spo·ken /'spōkən/ ▶ *past participle* of SPEAK.
▶*adj.* [in *comb.*] speaking in a specified way: *a blunt-spoken man.*
▶ □ **be spoken for** be already claimed, owned, or reserved. ■ (of a person) already have a romantic commitment: *he knows Claudine is spoken for.*

spoke·shave /'spōk,SHāv/ ▶*n.* a small plane with a handle on each side of its blade, used for shaping curved surfaces (originally wheel spokes).
▶*v.* [*tr.*] shape with a plane of this type.

spokes·man /'spōksmən/ ▶*n.* (*pl.* **-men**) a person, esp. a man, who makes statements on behalf of another individual or a group: *a spokesman for Greenpeace.*

spokes·per·son /'spōks,pərsən/ ▶*n.* (*pl.* **-per·sons** or **-peo·ple** /-,pēpəl/) a spokesman or spokeswoman (used as a neutral alternative).

spo·li·a·tion /,spōlē'āSHən/ ▶*n.* **1** the action of ruining or destroying something: *the spoliation of the countryside.* **2** the action of taking goods or property from somewhere by illegal or unethical means: *the spoliation of the Church.* —**spo·li·a·tor** /'spōlē,ātər/ *n.*

spon·dee /'spändē/ ▶*n.* Prosody a foot consisting of two long (or stressed) syllables.

sponge /spənj/ ▶*n.* **1** a primitive sedentary aquatic invertebrate with a soft porous body that is typically supported by a framework of fibers or calcareous or glassy spicules. **2** a piece of a soft, light, porous substance originally consisting of the fibrous skeleton of such an invertebrate but now usually made of synthetic material. Sponges absorb liquid and are used for washing and cleaning. ■ an act of wiping or cleaning with a sponge: *they gave him a quick sponge down.* ■ a piece of such a substance impregnated with spermicide and inserted into a woman's vagina as a form of barrier contraceptive. ■ *inf.* a heavy drinker. ■ metal in a porous form, typically prepared by reduction without fusion or by electrolysis: *platinum sponge.* **3** (also **sponge pudding**) a steamed or baked pudding of fat, flour, and eggs. **4** *inf.* a person who lives at someone else's expense.

▶*v.* (**sponging** or **spongeing**) **1** [*tr.*] wipe, rub, or clean with a wet sponge or cloth: *she sponged him down in an attempt to cool his fever.* ■ remove or wipe away (liquid or a mark) in such a way: *I'll go and sponge this orange juice off my dress.* ■ give a decorative mottled or textured effect to (a painted wall or surface) by applying a different shade of paint with a sponge. **2** [*intr.*] *inf.* obtain or accept money or food from other people without doing or intending to do anything in return: *they found they could earn a perfectly good living by sponging off others.* ■ [*tr.*] obtain (something) in such a way: *he edged closer, clearly intending to sponge money from her.* —**sponge·a·ble** *adj.* —**sponge·like** /ˈspənjˌlīk/ *adj.*

sponge cake /ˈspənj ˌkāk/ ▶*n.* a very light sweet cake of spongelike consistency, made with eggs and with little or no fat.

spong·er /ˈspənjər/ ▶*n.* **1** *inf.* a person who lives at others' expense. **2** a person who applies paint to pottery using a sponge.

spon·gy /ˈspənjē/ ▶*adj.* (**-gi·er, -gi·est**) like a sponge, esp. in being porous, compressible, elastic, or absorbent: *a soft, spongy blanket of moss.* ■ (of metal) having an open, porous structure: *spongy platinum.* ■ (chiefly of a motor vehicle's braking system) lacking firmness. —**spon·gi·ly** /ˈspənjəlē/ *adv.* —**spon·gi·ness** *n.*

spon·sor /ˈspänsər/ ▶*n.* a person or organization that provides funds for a project or activity carried out by another, in particular: ■ an individual or organization that pays some or all of the costs involved in staging a sporting or artistic event in return for advertising. ■ a person who pledges to donate a certain amount of money to another person after they have participated in a fund-raising event organized on behalf of a charity. ■ a business or organization that pays for or contributes to the costs of a radio or television program in return for advertising. **2** a person who introduces and supports a proposal for legislation: *a leading sponsor of the bill.* ■ a person taking official responsibility for the actions of another: *they act as informants, sponsors, and contacts for new immigrants.* ■ a godparent at a child's baptism. ■ (esp. in the Roman Catholic Church) a person presenting a candidate for confirmation.

▶*v.* [*tr.*] **1** provide funds for (a project or activity or the person carrying it out): *Joe is being sponsored by his church.* ■ pay some or all of the costs involved in staging a (sporting or artistic event) in return for advertising. ■ pledge to donate a certain sum of money to (someone) after they have participated in a fund-raising event organized on behalf of a charity. **2** introduce and support (a proposal) in a legislative assembly: *Senator Hardin sponsored the bill.* ■ propose and organize (negotiations or talks) between other people or groups: *the U.S. sponsored negotiations between the two sides.* ▷mid 17th cent. (as a noun): from Latin, from *spondere* 'promise solemnly'. The verb dates from the late 19th cent. —**spon·sor·ship** /-ˌSHip/ *n.*

spon·ta·ne·ous /spänˈtānēəs/ ▶*adj.* performed or occurring as a result of a sudden inner impulse or inclination and without premeditation or external stimulus: *the audience broke into spontaneous applause.* ■ (of a person) having an open, natural, and uninhibited manner. ■ (of a process or event) occurring without apparent external cause: *spontaneous miscarriages.* ■ *Biol.* (of movement or activity in an organism) instinctive or involuntary: *the spontaneous mechanical activity of circular smooth muscle.* —**spon·ta·ne·i·ty** /ˌspäntəˈnēitē; -ˈnā-/ *n.* —**spon·ta·ne·ous·ly** *adv.*

spon·ta·ne·ous com·bus·tion ▶*n.* the ignition of organic matter (e.g., hay or coal) without apparent cause, typically through heat generated internally by rapid oxidation.

spon·ta·ne·ous gen·er·a·tion ▶*n.* *hist.* the supposed production of living organisms from nonliving matter, as inferred from the apparent appearance of life in some infusions.

spoof /spo͞of/ *inf.* ▶*n.* **1** a humorous imitation of something, typically a film or a particular genre of film, in which its characteristic features are exaggerated for comic effect: *a Robin Hood spoof.* **2** a trick played on someone as a joke.

▶*v.* [*tr.*] **1** imitate (something) while exaggerating its characteristic features for comic effect: *it is a movie that spoofs other movies.* **2** hoax or trick (someone): *they proceeded to spoof Western intelligence with false information.* ■ interfere with (radio or radar signals) so as to make them useless. —**spoof·er** *n.* —**spoof·er·y** /ˈspo͞ofərē/ *n.*

spook /spo͞ok/ *inf.* ▶*n.* **1** a ghost. **2** a spy: *a CIA spook.*

▶*v.* [*tr.*] frighten; unnerve: *they spooked a couple of grizzly bears.* ■ [*intr.*] (esp. of an animal) take fright suddenly: *he'll spook if we make any noise.*

spook·y /ˈspo͞okē/ ▶*adj.* (**spook·i·er, spook·i·est**) *inf.* **1** sinister or ghostly in a way that causes fear and unease: *I bet this place is really spooky late*

at night. **2** (of a person or animal) easily frightened; nervous. —**spook·i·ly** /ˈspo͞okəlē/ *adv.* —**spook·i·ness** *n.*

spool[1] /spo͞ol/ ▶*n.* a cylindrical device on which film, magnetic tape, thread, or other flexible materials can be wound; a reel: *spools of electrical cable.* ■ a cylindrical device attached to a fishing rod and used for winding and unwinding the line as required. ■ [as *adj.*] denoting furniture of a style popular in England in the 17th century and North America in the 19th century, typically ornamented with a series of small knobs resembling spools: *a narrow spool bed.*

▶*v.* **1** [*tr.*] wind (magnetic tape or thread) on to a spool: *he was trying to spool his tapes back into the cassettes with a pencil eraser.* ■ [*intr.*] be wound on or off a spool: *the plastic reel allows the line to run free as it spools out.* **2** [*intr.*] (of an engine) increase its speed of rotation, typically to that required for operation: *a jet engine can take up to six seconds to spool up.*

spool[2] ▶*v.* [*tr.*] *Comput.* send (data that is intended for printing or processing on a peripheral device) to an intermediate store: *users can set which folder they wish to spool files to.*

spoon /spo͞on/ ▶*n.* **1** an implement consisting of a small, shallow oval or round bowl on a long handle, used for eating, stirring, and serving food. ■ the contents of such an implement: *three spoons of sugar.* ■ (**spoons**) a pair of spoons held in the hand and beaten together rhythmically as a percussion instrument. **2** a thing resembling a spoon in shape, in particular: ■ (also **spoon bait**) a fishing lure designed to wobble when pulled through the water.

▶*v.* **1** [*tr.*] convey (food) somewhere by using a spoon: *Rosie spooned sugar into her mug.* ■ hit (a ball) up into the air with a soft or weak stroke: *he spooned his shot high over the bar.* **2** [*intr.*] *inf., dated* (of two people) behave in an amorous way; kiss and cuddle: *I saw them spooning on the beach.* ■ (of two people) lie close together sideways and front to back with bent knees, so as to fit together like spoons. —**spoon·er** *n.* —**spoon·ful** /-ˌfo͞ol/ *n.* (*pl.* **-fuls** /-ˌfo͞olz/).

spoon·bill /ˈspo͞onˌbil/ ▶*n.* a tall mainly white or pinkish wading bird (genera *Platalea* and *Ajaia*) of the ibis family, having a long bill with a very broad flat tip.

spoon·er·ism /ˈspo͞onəˌrizəm/ ▶*n.* a verbal error in which a speaker accidentally transposes the initial sounds or letters of two or more words, often to humorous effect, as in the sentence *you have hissed the mystery lectures,* accidentally spoken instead of the intended sentence *you have missed the history lectures.*

spoon-feed ▶*v.* [*tr.*] feed (someone) by using a spoon. ■ *fig.* provide (someone) with so much help or information that they do not need to think for themselves.

spo·rad·ic /spəˈradik/ ▶*adj.* occurring at irregular intervals or only in a few places; scattered or isolated: *sporadic fighting broke out.* —**spo·rad·i·cal·ly** /-ik(ə)lē/ *adv.*

spo·ran·gi·um /spəˈranjēəm/ ▶*n.* (*pl.* **-gi·a** /-jēə/) *Bot.* (in ferns and lower plants) a receptacle in which asexual spores are formed. —**spo·ran·gi·al** /-jēəl/ *adj.*

spore /spôr/ ▶*n.* *Biol.* a minute, typically one-celled, reproductive unit capable of giving rise to a new individual without sexual fusion, characteristic of lower plants, fungi, and protozoans. ■ *Bot.* (in a plant exhibiting alternation of generations) a haploid reproductive cell that gives rise to a gametophyte. ■ *Microbiology* (in bacteria) a rounded resistant form adopted by a bacterial cell in adverse conditions.

spo·ro·phyte /ˈspôrəˌfīt/ ▶*n.* *Bot.* (in the life cycle of plants with alternating generations) the asexual and usually diploid phase, producing spores from which the gametophyte arises. It is the dominant form in vascular plants, e.g., the frond of a fern. —**spo·ro·phyt·ic** /ˌspôrəˈfitik/ *adj.*

sport /spôrt/ ▶*n.* **1** an activity involving physical exertion and skill in which an individual or team competes against another or others for entertainment: *team sports such as baseball and soccer.* **2** *inf.* a person who behaves in a good or specified way in response to teasing, defeat, or a similarly trying situation: *go on, be a sport!* **3** *Biol.* an animal or plant showing abnormal or striking variation from the parent type, esp. in form or color, as a result of spontaneous mutation.

▶*v.* **1** [*tr.*] wear or display (a distinctive or noticeable item): *he was sporting a huge handlebar mustache.* **2** [*intr.*] amuse oneself or play in a lively, energetic way: *the children sported in the water.* —**sport·er** *n.*

sport coat (also **sports coat** or **sport jacket** or **sports jacket**) ▶*n.* a man's jacket resembling a suit jacket, for informal wear.

sport·ing /ˈspôrtiNG/ ▶*adj.* **1** connected with or interested in sports: *a*

---

major sporting event. **2** fair and generous in one's behavior or treatment of others, esp. in a game or contest: *it was not very sporting of Smith to hit Gonzales with that pitch.* —**sport·ing·ly** *adv.*

spor·tive /'spôrtiv/ ▸*adj.* playful; lighthearted. —**spor·tive·ly** *adv.* —**spor·tive·ness** *n.*

sports car ▸*n.* a low-built car designed for performance at high speeds.

sports·cast /'spôrts,kast/ ▸*n.* a broadcast of sports news or a sports event. —**sports·cast·er** *n.* —**sports·cast·ing** *n.*

sports·man /'spôrtsmən/ ▸*n.* (*pl.* -**men**) a man who takes part in a sport, esp. as a professional. ■ a person who behaves sportingly. ■ *dated* a man who hunts or shoots wild animals as a pastime. —**sports·man·like** /-,līk/ *adj.* —**sports·man·ship** /-,SHip/ *n.*

sports·wear /'spôrts,we(ə)r/ ▸*n.* clothes worn for casual outdoor use or for such sports activities as jogging, cycling, tennis, sailing, etc.

sport·y /'spôrtē/ ▸*adj.* (**sport·i·er, sport·i·est**) *inf.* flashy or showy in dress or behavior. ■ (of clothing) casual yet attractively stylish: *a sporty outfit.* ■ (of a car) compact and with fast acceleration: *a sporty red coupe.* ■ fond of or good at sports. —**sport·i·ly** /'spôrtəlē/ *adv.* —**sport·i·ness** *n.*

spot /spät/ ▸*n.* **1** a small round or roundish mark, differing in color or texture from the surface around it: *ladybugs have black spots on their red wing covers.* ■ a small mark or stain: *a spot of mildew on the wall.* ■ a pimple. ■ a pip on a domino, playing card, or die. ■ [in *comb.*] *inf.* a banknote of a specified value: *a ten-spot.* **2** a particular place or point: *a nice secluded spot.* ■ a small feature or part of something with a particular quality: *his bald spot.* ■ a position within a listing; a ranking: *the runner-up spot.* ■ *Sports* an advantage allowed to a player as a handicap. ■ a place for an individual item within a show: *she couldn't do her usual singing spot in the club.* **3** *inf., chiefly Brit.* a small amount of something: *a spot of rain.* **4** [as *adj.*] denoting a system of trading in which commodities or currencies are delivered and paid for immediately after a sale: *trading in the spot markets.* **5** short for SPOTLIGHT.
▸*v.* (**spot·ted, spot·ting**) **1** [*tr.*] see, notice, or recognize (someone or something) that is difficult to detect or that one is searching for: *Andrew spotted the ad in the paper.* ■ (usu. **be spotted**) recognize that (someone) has a particular talent, esp. for sports or show business: *we were spotted by a talent scout.* **2** [*tr.*] (usu. **be spotted**) mark with spots: *the velvet was spotted with stains.* ■ [*intr.*] become marked with spots: *a damp atmosphere causes the flowers to spot.* ■ cover (a surface or area) thinly: *thorn trees spotted the land.* **3** [*tr.*] place (a billiard ball or football) on its designated starting point. **4** *inf.* give or lend (money) to (someone): *I'll spot you $300.* ■ allow (an advantage) to (someone) in a game or sport: *the higher-rated team spots the lower-rated team the difference in their handicaps.* **5** [*tr.*] observe or assist (a gymnast) during a performance in order to minimize the chance of injury to the gymnast.
▸ □ **on the spot 1** without any delay; immediately: *he offered me the job on the spot.* **2** at the scene of an action or event: *journalists on the spot reported no progress.*

spot·less /'spätlis/ ▸*adj.* absolutely clean or pure; immaculate: *a spotless white apron.* —**spot·less·ly** *adv.* —**spot·less·ness** *n.*

spot·light /'spät,līt/ ▸*n.* a lamp projecting a narrow, intense beam of light directly onto a place or person, esp. a performer on stage. ■ a beam of light from a lamp of this kind: *the knife flashed in the spotlight.* ■ (**the spotlight**) *fig.* intense scrutiny or public attention: *she was constantly in the media spotlight.*
▸*v.* (*past* and *past part.* -**light·ed** or -**lit** /-lit/) [*tr.*] illuminate with a spotlight: *the dancers are spotlighted from time to time throughout the evening.* ■ *fig.* direct attention to (a particular problem or situation): *the protest spotlighted the overcrowding in federal prisons.*

spot·ted /'spätid/ ▸*adj.* marked or decorated with spots. —**spot·ted·ness** *n.*

spot·ter /'spätər/ ▸*n. inf.* a person employed by a company or business to keep watch on employees or customers. ■ an aviator or aircraft employed in locating or observing enemy positions: [as *adj.*] *spotter planes.* ■ a person who observes or assists a gymnast or weightlifter during a performance or practice in order to minimize the chance of injury to the gymnast or weightlifter.

spot·ty /'spätē/ ▸*adj.* (-**ti·er, -ti·est**) marked with spots: *a spotty purple flower.* ■ of uneven quality; patchy: *his spotty record on the environment.* —**spot·ti·ly** /'spätəlē/ *adv.* —**spot·ti·ness** *n.*

spouse /spous/ ▸*n.* a husband or wife, considered in relation to their partner.

spout /spout/ ▸*n.* **1** a tube or lip projecting from a container, through which liquid can be poured: *a teapot with a chipped spout.* ■ a pipe or trough through which water may be carried away or from which it can flow out. ■ a sloping trough for conveying something to a lower

level; a chute. **2** a stream of liquid issuing from somewhere with great force: *the tall spouts of geysers.* ■ the plume of water vapor ejected from the blowhole of a whale: *the spout of an occasional whale.*
▸*v.* [*tr.*] **1** send out (liquid) forcibly in a stream: *volcanoes spouted ash and lava.* ■ [*intr.*] (of a liquid) flow out of somewhere in such a way: *blood was spouting from the cuts on my hand.* ■ (of a whale or dolphin) eject (water vapor and air) through its blowhole. **2** express (one's views or ideas) in a lengthy, declamatory, and unreflecting way: *he was spouting platitudes about animal rights* | [*intr.*] *they like to spout off at each other.* ▷Middle English (as a verb): from Middle Dutch *spouten,* from an imitative base shared by Old Norse *spýta* 'to spit.' —**spout·ed** *adj.* —**spout·er** *n.* —**spout·less** *adj.*

sprain /sprān/ ▸*v.* [*tr.*] wrench or twist the ligaments of (an ankle, wrist, or other joint) violently so as to cause pain and swelling but not dislocation: *he left in a wheelchair after spraining an ankle.*
▸*n.* the result of such a wrench or twist of a joint.

sprang /spraNG/ ▸ past of SPRING.

sprat /sprat/ ▸*n.* a small marine fish (*Sprattus* and other genera) of the herring family, widely caught for food and fish products.

sprawl /sprôl/ ▸*v.* [*intr.*] sit, lie, or fall with one's arms and legs spread out in an ungainly or awkward way: *the door shot open, sending him sprawling across the pavement.* ■ spread out over a large area in an untidy or irregular way: *the town sprawled along several miles of cliff top.* | [as *adj.*] (**sprawling**) *the sprawling suburbs.*
▸*n.* an ungainly or carelessly relaxed position in which one's arms and legs are spread out: *she fell into a sort of luxurious sprawl.* ■ a group or mass of something that has spread out in an untidy or irregular way: *a sprawl of buildings.* ■ the expansion of an urban or industrial area into the adjoining countryside in a way perceived to be disorganized and unattractive: *the growth of urban sprawl.* ■ such an area: *Washington's suburban sprawl.* —**sprawl·ing·ly** *adv.*

spray¹ /sprā/ ▸*n.* liquid that is blown or driven through the air in the form of tiny drops: *a torrent of white foam and spray.* ■ a liquid preparation that can be forced out of a can or other container in such a form: *a can of insect spray.* ■ a can or container holding such a preparation. ■ an act of applying such a preparation: *refresh your flowers with a quick spray.*
▸*v.* [*tr.*] apply (liquid) to someone or something in the form of a shower of tiny drops: *the product can be sprayed on to wet or dry hair.* ■ [*tr.*] sprinkle or cover (someone or something) with a shower of tiny drops of liquid: *she sprayed herself with perfume.* ■ [*intr.*] (of liquid) be driven through the air or forced out of something in such a form: *water sprayed into the air.* ■ [*tr.*] treat (a plant) with insecticide or herbicide in such a way: *avoid spraying your plants with pesticides.* ■ scatter (something) somewhere with great force: *the truck shuddered to a halt, spraying gravel from under its wheels.* ■ [*tr.*] fire a rapid succession of bullets at: *enemy gunners sprayed the decks of the warships.* ■ [*tr.*] (of a male cat) direct a stream of urine over (an object or area) to mark a territory. ■ [*tr.*] (in a sporting context) kick, hit, or throw (the ball) in an unpredictable or inaccurate direction: *he began his round by spraying his fairway shots.* —**spray·a·ble** *adj.* —**spray·er** *n.*

spray² ▸*n.* a stem or small branch of a tree or plant, bearing flowers and foliage: *a spray of honeysuckle.* ■ a bunch of cut flowers arranged in an attractive way.

spray gun ▸*n.* a device resembling a gun that is used to spray a liquid such as paint or pesticide under pressure.

spray-paint ▸*v.* [*tr.*] (often **be spray-painted**) paint (an image or message) onto a surface with a spray. ■ paint (a surface) with a spray: *they were spray-painting the chairs.*
▸*n.* (**spray paint**) paint that is contained in an aerosol can for the purpose of spraying onto a surface.

spread /spred/ ▸*v.* (*past* and *past part.* **spread**) **1** [*tr.*] open out (something) so as to extend its surface area, width, or length: *I spread a towel on the sand and sat down.* ■ stretch out (arms, legs, hands, fingers, or wings) so that they are far apart: *the swan spread its wings.* **2** [no *obj.*] extend over a large or increasing area: *she stood at the window looking at the town spread out below.* ■ (**spread out**) (of a group of people) move apart so as to cover a wider area: *the Marines spread out across the docks.* ■ distribute or disperse (something) over a certain area: *volcanic eruptions spread dust high into the stratosphere.* ■ gradually reach or cause to reach a larger and larger area or more and more people: [*intr.*] *the violence spread from the city to the suburbs* | [*tr.*] *she's always spreading rumors about other people.* ■ (of people, animals, or plants) become distributed over a large or larger area: *the owls have spread as far north as Yellowknife.* ■ distribute (something) in a specified way: *you can spread the payments over as long a period as you like.* **3** apply (a substance) to an object or

surface in an even layer: *he sighed, spreading jam on a croissant.* ■ cover (a surface) with a substance in such a way: *spread each slice thinly with mayonnaise.* ■ [no *obj.*] be able to be applied in such a way: *the whipped butter spreads easily.*
▶*n.* **1** the fact or process of spreading over an area: *the spread of AIDS | the spread of the urban population into rural areas.* **2** the extent, width, or area covered by something: *the male's antlers can attain a spread of six feet.* ■ the wingspan of a bird. ■ an expanse or amount of something: *the green spread of the park.* ■ a large farm or ranch. **3** the range or variety of something: *a wide spread of ages.* ■ the difference between two rates or prices: *the very narrow spread between borrowing and deposit rates.* ■ short for **POINT SPREAD.** **4** a soft paste that can be applied in a layer to bread or other food. **5** an article or advertisement covering several columns or pages of a newspaper or magazine, esp. one on two facing pages: *a double-page spread.* ■ a bedspread. **6** *inf.* a large and impressively elaborate meal. **—spread·a·ble** *adj.* **—spread·er** *n.*

spread-ea·gle ▶*v.* [*tr.*] (usu. **be spread-eagled**) stretch (someone) out with their arms and legs extended: *he lay spread-eagled in the road.* ■ [*intr.*] *Skating* perform a spread eagle.
▶*n.* (**spread ea·gle**) *Figure Skating* a straight glide made with the feet in a line, with the heels touching, and the arms stretched out to either side.
▶*adj.* **1** stretched out with one's arms and legs extended: *prisoners are chained to their beds, spread-eagle.* **2** loudly or aggressively patriotic about the U.S.: *spread-eagle oratory.*

spread·sheet /'spred,SHēt/ ▶*n.* a computer program used chiefly for accounting, in which figures arranged in the rows and columns of a grid can be manipulated and used in calculations.

spree /sprē/ ▶*n.* a spell or sustained period of unrestrained activity of a particular kind: *he went on a six-month crime spree | a shopping spree.* ■ a spell of unrestrained drinking.

sprig /sprig/ ▶*n.* a small stem bearing leaves or flowers, taken from a bush or plant: *a sprig of holly.* ■ a descendant or younger member of a family or social class: *a sprig of the French nobility.* **—sprig·gy** *adj.*

spright·ly /'sprītlē/ ▶*adj.* (**-li·er, -li·est**) (esp. of an old person) lively; full of energy: *she was quite sprightly for her age.* **—spright·li·ness** *n.*

spring /spriNG/ ▶*v.* (*past* **sprang** /spraNG/ or **sprung** /sprəNG/; *past part.* **sprung**) **1** [*intr.*] move or jump suddenly or rapidly upward or forward: *I sprang out of bed.* ■ [*intr.*] move rapidly or suddenly from a constrained position by or as if by the action of a spring: *the drawer sprang open.* ■ operate or cause to operate by means of a mechanism: [*tr.*] *he prepared to spring his trap* | [*intr.*] *the engine sprang into life.* ■ [*tr.*] cause (a game bird) to rise from cover. ■ [*tr.*] *inf.* bring about the escape or release of (a prisoner): *the president sought to spring the hostages.* **2** [*intr.*] (**spring from**) originate or arise from: *madness and creativity could spring from the same source.* ■ appear suddenly or unexpectedly from: *tears sprang from his eyes.* ■ (**spring up**) suddenly develop or appear: *a terrible storm sprang up.* ■ [*tr.*] (**spring something on**) present or propose something suddenly or unexpectedly to (someone): *we decided to spring a surprise on them.* **3** [*tr.*] (usu. as *adj.*) (**sprung**) cushion or fit (a vehicle or item of furniture) with springs: *a fully sprung mattress.* **4** [*intr.*] (esp. of wood) become warped or split. **5** [*intr.*] (**spring for**) *inf.* pay for, esp. as a treat for someone else: *he's never offered to spring for dinner.*
▶*n.* **1** the season after winter and before summer, in which vegetation begins to appear, in the northern hemisphere from March to May and in the southern hemisphere from September to November. ■ *Astron.* the period from the vernal equinox to the summer solstice. **2** a resilient device, typically a helical metal coil, that can be pressed or pulled but returns to its former shape when released, used chiefly to exert constant tension or absorb movement. ■ the ability to spring back strongly; elasticity: *the mattress has lost its spring.* **3** a sudden jump upward or forward: *with a sudden spring, he leapt onto the table.* **4** a place where water or oil wells up from an underground source, or the basin or flow formed in such a way: [as *adj.*] *spring water.* ■ *fig.* the origin or a source of something: *the place was a spring of musical talent.* **—spring·less** *adj.* **—spring·like** /-,līk/ *adj.*
▶ □ **spring a leak** (of a boat or container) develop a leak.

spring·board /'spriNG,bôrd/ ▶*n.* a strong, flexible board from which someone can jump in order to gain added impetus when performing a dive or a gymnastic movement. ■ *fig.* a thing that lends impetus or assistance to a particular action, enterprise, or development: *an economic plan that may be the springboard for recovery.*

spring chick·en ▶*n.* *inf.* a young person: *you're no spring chicken yourself anymore.*

spring·er /'spriNGər/ ▶*n.* **1** (usu. **spring·er span·iel**) a small spaniel of a breed originally used to spring game. There are two main breeds, the

English **springer spaniel**, typically black and white or brown and white, and the less common red and white **Welsh springer spaniel**. **2** *Archit.* the lowest stone in an arch, where the curve begins.

spring fe·ver ▶*n.* a feeling of restlessness and excitement felt at the beginning of spring.

spring-load·ed ▶*adj.* containing a compressed or stretched spring pressing one part against another: *a spring-loaded clothespin.*

spring peep·er ▶*n.* see PEEPER².

spring roll ▶*n.* an Asian snack consisting of rice paper filled with minced vegetables and usually meat, rolled into a cylinder and fried.

spring·tail /'spriNG,tāl/ ▶*n.* a minute primitive wingless insect that has a springlike organ under the abdomen that enables it to leap when disturbed. Springtails are abundant in the soil and leaf litter.

spring tide /'spriNG ,tīd/ ▶*n.* a tide just after a new or full moon, when there is the greatest difference between high and low water. Compare with NEAP.

spring·time /'spriNG,tīm/ ▶*n.* the season of spring. ■ *fig.* or *poetic/lit.* the early part or first stage of something: *the springtime of their marriage.*

spring·y /'spriNGē/ ▶*adj.* (**spring·i·er, spring·i·est**) springing back quickly when squeezed or stretched; elastic: *the springy turf.* ■ (of movements) light and confident: *he left the room with a springy step.* **—spring·i·ly** /'spriNGəlē/ *adv.* **—spring·i·ness** *n.*

sprin·kle /'spriNGkəl/ ▶*v.* **1** [*tr.*] scatter or pour small drops or particles of a substance over (an object or surface): *I sprinkled the floor with water.* ■ scatter or pour (small drops or particles of a substance) over an object or surface: *sprinkle sesame seeds over the top.* ■ *fig.* distribute or disperse something randomly or irregularly throughout (something): *he sprinkled his conversation with quotations.* ■ *fig.* place or attach (a number of things) at irregularly spaced intervals: *a dress with little daisies sprinkled all over it.* **2** [*intr.*] (**it sprinkles, it is sprinkling,** etc.) rain very lightly: *it began to sprinkle.*
▶*n.* **1** a small quantity or amount of something scattered over an object or surface: *a generous sprinkle of pepper.* **2** a light rain. **3** (**sprinkles**) tiny sugar shapes, typically strands and balls, used for decorating cakes and desserts.

sprin·kler /'spriNGk(ə)lər/ ▶*n.* a device that sprays water. ■ a device used for watering lawns. ■ an automatic fire extinguisher installed in the ceilings of a building.

sprin·kling /'spriNGk(ə)liNG/ ▶*n.* a small thinly distributed amount of something: *a sprinkling of gray in his hair.*

sprint /sprint/ ▶*v.* [*intr.*] run at full speed over a short distance: *I saw Charlie sprinting through the traffic toward me.*
▶*n.* an act or short spell of running at full speed. ■ a short, fast race in which the competitors run a distance of 400 meters or less: *the 100 meters sprint.* ■ a short, fast race or exercise in cycling, swimming, horse racing, etc. **—sprint·er** *n.*

sprit /sprit/ ▶*n.* *Sailing* a small spar reaching diagonally from low on a mast to the upper outer corner of a quadrangular fore-and-aft sail.

sprite /sprīt/ ▶*n.* **1** an elf or fairy. **2** a computer graphic that may be moved on-screen and otherwise manipulated as a single entity.

sprit·sail /'sprit,sāl; -səl/ ▶*n.* a sail set from by a sprit.

spritz /sprits/ ▶*v.* [*tr.*] squirt or spray something at or onto (something) in quick short bursts: *she spritzed her neck with cologne.*
▶*n.* an act or an instance of squirting or spraying in quick short bursts.

spritz·er /'spritsər/ ▶*n.* a mixture of wine and soda water.

sprock·et /'spräkit/ ▶*n.* each of several projections on the rim of a wheel that engage with the links of a chain or with holes in film, tape, or paper. ■ (also **sprocket wheel**) a wheel with teeth of this kind.

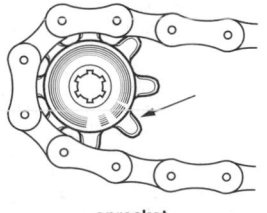

sprocket

sprout /sprout/ ▶*v.* [*intr.*] (of a plant) put forth shoots: *the weeds begin to sprout.* ■ [*tr.*] grow (plant shoots or hair): *many black cats sprout a few white hairs.* ■ [*intr.*] (of a plant, flower, or hair) start to grow; spring up: *crocuses sprouted up from the grass.*
▶*n.* **1** a shoot of a plant. ■ (**sprouts**) young shoots eaten as a vegetable, esp. the shoots of alfalfa, mung beans, or soybeans. **2** short for BRUSSELS SPROUT.

spruce[1] /spro�͞os/ ▸*n.* a widespread coniferous tree (genus *Picea*) of the pine family that has a distinctive conical shape and hanging cones, widely grown for timber, pulp, and Christmas trees.

spruce[2] ▸*adj.* neat in dress and appearance: *he looked as spruce as if he were getting married.*

▸*v.* [*tr.*] (**spruce someone/something up**) make a person or place smarter or tidier: *the fund will be used to spruce up historic buildings.* —**spruce·ly** *adv.* —**spruce·ness** *n.*

sprung /sprəŋ/ ▸ past and past participle of SPRING.

spry /sprī/ ▸*adj.* (**spry·er, spry·est** or **spri·er, spri·est**) (esp. of an old person) active; lively: *he continued to look spry and active well into his eighties.* —**spry·ly** *adv.* —**spry·ness** *n.*

spud /spəd/ ▸*n.* **1** *inf.* a potato. **2** a small, narrow spade for cutting the roots of plants, esp. weeds.

▸*v.* (**spud·ded, spud·ding**) [*tr.*] **1** dig up or cut (plants, esp. weeds) with a spud. **2** make the initial drilling for (an oil well).

spu·man·te /spə'mäntē; spyə-/ ▸*n.* an Italian sparkling white wine.

spun /spən/ ▸ past and past participle of SPIN.

spunk /spəŋk/ ▸*n.* **1** *inf.* courage and determination. **2** tinder.

spunk·y /'spəŋkē/ ▸*adj.* (**spunk·i·er, spunk·i·est**) *inf.* courageous and determined: *a spunky performance.* —**spunk·i·ly** /'spəŋkəlē/ *adv.* —**spunk·i·ness** *n.*

spur /spər/ ▸*n.* **1** a device with a small spike or a spiked wheel that is worn on a rider's heel and used for urging a horse forward. ■ *fig.* a thing that prompts or encourages someone; an incentive: *profit was both the spur and the reward of enterprise.* ■ a hard spike on the back of the leg of a cock or male game bird, used in fighting. ■ a steel point fastened to the leg of a gamecock. ■ a climbing iron. **2** a thing that projects or branches off from a main body, in particular: ■ a projection from a mountain or mountain range. ■ a short branch road or rail line. ■ *Bot.* a slender tubular projection from the base of a flower, e.g., a honeysuckle or orchid, typically containing nectar. ■ a short fruit-bearing side shoot.

spur

▸*v.* (**spurred, spur·ring**) [*tr.*] urge (a horse) forward by digging one's spurs into its sides: *she spurred her horse toward the hedge.* ■ give an incentive or encouragement to (someone): *her sons' passion for computer games spurred her on to set up a software store.* ■ cause or promote the development of; stimulate: *governments cut interest rates to spur demand.* —**spur·less** *adj.* —**spurred** *adj.*

▸ □ **on the spur of the moment** on a momentary impulse; without premeditation.

spurge /spərj/ ▸*n.* a herbaceous plant or shrub (genus *Euphorbia*, family Euphorbiaceae) with milky latex and very small typically greenish flowers.

spu·ri·ous /'spyoͅoͅorēəs/ ▸*adj.* not being what it purports to be; false or fake: *separating authentic and spurious claims.* ■ (of a line of reasoning) apparently but not actually valid: *this spurious reasoning results in nonsense.* —**spu·ri·ous·ly** *adv.* —**spu·ri·ous·ness** *n.*

spurn /spərn/ ▸*v.* [*tr.*] reject with disdain or contempt: *he spoke gruffly, as if afraid that his invitation would be spurned.* ▷Old English *spurnan, spornan*; related to Latin *spernere* 'to scorn,' also to *spur.* —**spurn·er** *n.*

spurt /spərt/ ▸*v.* [*intr.*] gush out in a sudden and forceful stream: *he cut his finger, and blood spurted over the sliced potatoes.* ■ [*tr.*] cause to gush out suddenly: *the kettle boiled and spurted scalding water everywhere.* ■ move with a sudden burst of speed: *the other car had spurted to the top of the ramp.*

▸*n.* a sudden gushing stream: *a sudden spurt of blood gushed into her eyes.* ■ a sudden marked burst or increase of activity or speed: *late in the race he put on a spurt and reached second place.*

Sput·nik /'spətnik; 'spoͅoͅot-/ ▸*n.* each of a series of Soviet artificial satellites, the first of which (launched on October 4, 1957) was the first satellite to be placed in orbit.

sput·ter /'spətər/ ▸*v.* **1** [*intr.*] make a series of soft explosive sounds, typically when being heated or as a symptom of a fault: *the engine sputtered and stopped.* ■ speak in a series of incoherent bursts as a result of indignation or some other strong emotion: [with *direct speech*] *"But . . . but . . ." she sputtered.* ■ [*tr.*] emit with a spitting sound: *the goose is in the oven, sputtering fat.* ■ *fig.* proceed or develop in a spasmodic and feeble way: *strikes in the public services sputtered on.* **2** [*tr.*] *Physics* deposit (metal) on a surface by using fast ions to eject particles of it from a target.

▸*n.* a series of soft explosive sounds, typically produced by an engine or

by something heating or burning: *the sputter of the motor died away.* —**sput·ter·er** *n.*

spu·tum /'spyoͅoͅotəm/ ▸*n.* a mixture of saliva and mucus coughed up from the respiratory tract, typically as a result of infection or other disease and often examined microscopically to aid medical diagnosis.

spy /spī/ ▸*n.* (*pl.* **spies**) a person who secretly collects and reports information on the activities, movements, and plans of an enemy or competitor. ■ a person who keeps watch on others secretly: [as *adj.*] *a spy camera.*

▸*v.* (**spies, spied, spy·ing**) [*intr.*] work for a government or other organization by secretly collecting information about enemies or competitors: *he agreed to spy for the West.* ■ (**spy on**) observe (someone) furtively: *the couple were spied on by reporters.* ■ [*tr.*] discern or make out, esp. by careful observation: *he could spy a figure in the distance.* ■ [*tr.*] (**spy something out**) collect information about something to use in deciding how to act: *he would go and spy out the land.*

spy·glass /'spī,glas/ ▸*n.* a small hand-held telescope.

sq ▸*abbr.* square: *51,100 sq km.*

squab /skwäb/ ▸*n.* a young unfledged pigeon. ■ the flesh of such a bird as food: *roast squab.*

squab·ble /'skwäbəl/ ▸*n.* a noisy quarrel about something petty or trivial: *family squabbles.*

▸*v.* [*intr.*] quarrel noisily over a trivial matter: *the boys were squabbling over a ball.* —**squab·bler** /'skwäb(ə)lər/ *n.*

squad /skwäd/ ▸*n.* [treated as *sing.* or *pl.*] a small group of people having a particular task: *an assassination squad.* ■ a small number of soldiers assembled for drill or assigned to some special task, esp. an infantry unit forming part of a platoon. ■ a group of sports players or competitors from which a team is chosen: *eleven first-string players on the Nebraska squad.* ■ a division of a police force dealing with a particular crime or type of crime: *the narcotics crime squad.*

squad car ▸*n.* a police patrol car.

squad·ron /'skwädrən/ ▸*n.* an operational unit in an air force consisting of two or more flights of aircraft and the personnel required to fly them. ■ a principal division of an armored or cavalry regiment, consisting of two or more troops. ■ a group of warships detached on a particular duty or under the command of a flag officer. ■ *inf.* a large group of people or things: *he immediately commissioned a squadron of architects.*

squal·id /'skwälid/ ▸*adj.* (of a place) extremely dirty and unpleasant, esp. as a result of poverty or neglect: *the squalid, overcrowded prison.* ■ showing or involving a contemptible lack of moral standards: *a squalid attempt to save themselves from electoral embarrassment.* —**squal·id·ly** *adv.* —**squal·id·ness** *n.*

squall /skwôl/ ▸*n.* a sudden violent gust of wind or a localized storm, esp. one bringing rain, snow, or sleet: *low clouds and squalls of driving rain.* ■ a loud cry: *he emitted a short mournful squall.*

▸*v.* [*intr.*] (of a baby or small child) cry noisily and continuously: *Sarah was squalling in her crib.* —**squall·y** *adj.*

squal·or /'skwälər/ ▸*n.* a state of being extremely dirty and unpleasant, esp. as a result of poverty or neglect: *they lived in squalor and disease.*

squan·der /'skwändər/ ▸*v.* [*tr.*] waste (something, esp. money or time) in a reckless and foolish manner: *entrepreneurs squander their profits on expensive cars.* ■ allow (an opportunity) to pass or be lost: *the team squandered several good scoring chances.* —**squand·er·er** *n.*

square /skwe(ə)r/ ▸*n.* **1** a plane figure with four equal straight sides and four right angles. ■ a thing having such a shape or approximately such a shape: *she tore a bit of cloth into a four-inch square.* ■ a thing having the shape or approximate shape of a cube: *a small square of chocolate.* ■ an open (typically four-sided) area surrounded by buildings in a town, village, or city: *a market square.* ■ an open area at the meeting of streets. ■ a small square area on the board used in a game. ■ a block of buildings bounded by four streets. ■ a unit of 100 square ft. used as a measure of flooring, roofing, etc. **2** the product of a number multiplied by itself: *a circle's area is proportional to the square of its radius.* **3** an L-shaped or T-shaped instrument used for obtaining or testing right angles: *a carpenter's square.* **4** *inf.* a person considered to be old-fashioned or boringly conventional in attitude or behavior. **5** *inf.* a square meal: *three squares a day.*

▸*adj.* **1** having the shape or approximate shape of a square: *a square table.* ■ having the shape or approximate shape of a cube: *a square box.* ■ having or in the form of two right angles: *a suitable length of wood with square ends.* ■ having an outline resembling two corners of a square: *his square jaw.* ■ broad and solid in shape: *he was short and square.* **2** denoting a unit of measurement equal to the area of a square whose side is of the unit specified: *30,000 square feet of new gallery space.* ■ denoting the length of each side of a square shape or object: *the office was fifteen* *feet square.* **3** at right angles; perpendicular: *these lines must be square to the top and bottom marked edges.* **4** level or parallel: *place one piece of wood on top of the other, ensuring that they are exactly square.* ■ properly arranged; in good order: *we should get everything square before we leave.* ■ compatible or in agreement: *he wanted to make sure we were square with the court's decision and not subject to a lawsuit.* ■ fair and honest: *she'd been as square with him as anybody could be.* ■ (of two people) owing nothing to each other: *an acknowledgment that we are square.* ■ with both players or sides having equal scores in a game: *the goal brought the match all square once again.* **6** *inf.* old-fashioned or boringly conventional: *Elvis was anything but square.* **7** (of rhythm) simple and straightforward.

▸ *adv.* directly; straight: *it hit me square in the forehead* ■ *inf.* fairly; honestly: *I'd acted square and on the level with him.*

▸ *v.* [*tr.*] **1** make square or rectangular; give a square or rectangular cross section to: *you can square off the other edge.* ■ [usu. as *adj.*] (**squared**) mark out in squares. **2** multiply (a number) by itself: *5 squared equals 25.* ■ [usu. as *adj.*] (**squared**) convert (a linear unit of measurement) to a unit of area equal to a square whose side is of the unit specified: *there were only three square per kilometer squared.* **3** make compatible; reconcile: *I'm able to square my profession with my religious beliefs.* ■ [*intr.*] be compatible: *do those announcements really square with the facts?* **4** balance (an account): *they're anxious to square their books before the audit.* ■ make the score of (a match or game) even: *his goal squared the match 1-1.* ■ *inf.* secure the help, acquiescence, or silence of (someone), esp. by offering an inducement: *trying to square the press.* **5** bring (one's shoulders) into a position in which they appear square and broad, typically to prepare oneself for a difficult task or event: *chin up, shoulders squared, she stepped into the room.* ■ (**square oneself**) adopt a posture of defense. —**square·ly** *adv.* —**square·ness** *n.* —**squar·er** *n.* —**squar·ish** *adj.*

▸ □ **back to** (or **at**) **square one** *inf.* back to where one started, with no progress having been made.

square dance ▸ *n.* a country dance that starts with four couples facing one another in a square, with the steps and movements shouted out by a caller.

▸ *v.* (**square dance**) [*intr.*] [often as *n.*] (**square dancing**) participate in a square dance. —**square danc·er** *n.*

square deal ▸ *n.* a fair bargain or treatment: *the workers feel they are not getting a square deal.*

square knot ▸ *n.* a type of double knot that is made symmetrically to hold securely and to be easy to untie.

square meal ▸ *n.* a substantial, satisfying, and balanced meal: *three square meals a day.*

square meas·ure ▸ *n.* a unit of measurement relating to area.

square root ▸ *n.* a number that produces a specified quantity when multiplied by itself: *7 is a square root of 49.*

square sail ▸ *n.* a four-cornered sail supported by a yard attached to a mast.

square shoot·er ▸ *n.* a person who is honest, fair, and straightforward.

square-should·ered ▸ *adj.* (of a person) having broad shoulders that do not slope.

squash¹ /skwäsh; skwôsh/ ▸ *v.* [*tr.*] crush or squeeze (something) with force so that it becomes flat, soft, or out of shape: *wash and squash the cans for the recycling bin.* ■ [*tr.*] squeeze or force (someone or something) into a small or restricted space: *she squashed some of her clothes inside the bag.* ■ [*intr.*] make one's way into a small or restricted space: *I squashed into the middle of the crowd.* ■ suppress, stifle, or subdue (a feeling, conjecture, or action): *the mournful sound did nothing to squash her high spirits.* ■ firmly reject (an idea or suggestion).

▸ *n.* **1** a state of being squeezed or forced into a small or restricted space: *it was a tight squash but he didn't seem to mind.* **2** a game in which two players use rackets to hit a small, soft rubber ball against the walls of a closed court. **3** *Biol.* a preparation of softened tissue that has been made thin for microscopic examination by gently compressing or tapping it. —**squash·y** *adj.*

squash² ▸ *n.* (*pl.* same or **squashes**) **1** an edible gourd, the flesh of which may be cooked and eaten as a vegetable. **2** the trailing plant (genus *Cucurbita*) of the gourd family that produces this fruit.

squat /skwät/ ▸ *v.* (**squat·ted**, **squat·ting**) **1** [*intr.*] crouch or sit with one's knees bent and one's heels close to or touching one's buttocks or the back of one's thighs: *I squatted down in front of him.* ■ [*tr.*] *Weightlifting* crouch down in such a way and rise again while holding (a specified weight) at one's shoulders: *he can squat 850 pounds.* **2** [*intr.*] unlawfully occupy an uninhabited building or settle on a piece of land: *eight families are squatting in the house.* ■ [*tr.*] occupy (an uninhabited building) in such a way.

▸ *adj.* (**squat·ter**, **squat·test**) short and thickset; disproportionately broad or wide: *he was muscular and squat.*

▸ *n.* **1** a position in which one's knees are bent and one's heels are close to or touching one's buttocks or the back of one's thighs. ■ *Weightlifting* an exercise in which a person squats down and rises again while holding a barbell at shoulder level. ■ (in gymnastics) an exercise involving a squatting movement or action. **2** *inf.* short for DIDDLY-SQUAT: *I didn't know squat about writing plays.* —**squat·ly** *adv.* —**squat·ness** *n.*

squat·ter /'skwätər/ ▸ *n.* a person who unlawfully occupies an uninhabited building or unused land. ■ *hist.* a settler with no legal title to the land occupied, typically one on land not yet allocated by a government.

squaw /skwô/ ▸ *n. offens.* an American Indian woman or wife. ■ a woman or wife.

squawk /skwôk/ ▸ *v.* [*intr.*] (of a bird) make a loud, harsh noise: *the geese flew upriver, squawking.* ■ complain or protest about something.

▸ *n.* a loud, harsh or discordant noise made by a bird or a person. ■ a complaint or protest: *her plan provoked a loud squawk from her friends.* —**squawk·er** *n.*

squeak /skwēk/ ▸ *n.* a short, high-pitched sound or cry: *the door opened with a slight squeak.* ■ a single remark, statement, or communication: *I didn't hear a squeak from him for months.*

▸ *v.* [*intr.*] **1** make a high-pitched sound or cry: *he oiled the hinges to stop them from squeaking.* **2** *inf.* succeed in achieving something by a very narrow margin: *the bill squeaked through with just six votes to spare.* ■ (**squeak by**) make or have just enough money for basic necessities: *she was squeaking by on her minimum-wage job.*

squeak·er /'skwēkər/ ▸ *n.* a person or thing that squeaks. ■ *inf.* a competition or election won or likely to be won by a narrow margin.

squeak·y /'skwēkē/ ▸ *adj.* (**squeak·i·er**, **squeak·i·est**) having or making a high-pitched sound or cry: *a high, squeaky voice.* —**squeak·i·ly** /-kəlē/ *adv.* —**squeak·i·ness** *n.*

squeal /skwēl/ ▸ *n.* a long, high-pitched cry or noise: *we heard a splash and a squeal.*

▸ *v.* [*intr.*] **1** make such a cry or noise: *the girls squealed with delight.* ■ complain or protest about something: *the bookies only squealed because we beat them.* **2** *inf.* inform on someone to the police or a person in authority: *she feared they would victimize her for squealing on their pals.* —**squeal·er** *n.*

squeam·ish /'skwēmish/ ▸ *adj.* (of a person) easily made to feel sick, faint, or disgusted, esp. by unpleasant images, such as the sight of blood: *he was a bit squeamish at the sight of the giant needles.* ■ (of a person) having strong moral views; scrupulous: *she was not squeamish about using her social influence in support of her son.* —**squeam·ish·ly** *adv.* —**squeam·ish·ness** *n.*

squee·gee /'skwē,jē/ ▸ *n.* a scraping implement with a rubber-edged blade set on a handle, typically used for cleaning windows. ■ a similar small instrument or roller used esp. in photography for squeezing water out of prints. ■ [usu. as *adj.*] *inf.* a person who cleans the windshield of a car stopped in traffic and then demands payment from the driver: *squeegee guys at every corner.*

▸ *v.* (**-gees**, **-geed**, **-gee·ing**) [*tr.*] clean or scrape (something) with a squeegee: *squeegee the shower doors while the surfaces are still wet.*

squeeze /skwēz/ ▸ *v.* **1** [*tr.*] firmly press (something soft or yielding), typically with one's fingers: *Kate squeezed his hand affectionately* | [*intr.*] *he squeezed with all his strength.* ■ [*tr.*] extract (liquid or a soft substance) from something by compressing or twisting it firmly: *squeeze out as much juice as you can.* ■ [*tr.*] obtain (something) from someone with difficulty: *a governor who wants to squeeze as much money out of taxpayers as he can.* ■ *inf.* pressure (someone) in order to obtain something from them: *she used the opportunity to squeeze him for information.* ■ (esp. in a financial or commercial context) have a damaging or restricting effect on: *the economy is being squeezed by foreign debt repayments.* ■ (**squeeze off**) *inf.* shoot a round or shot from a gun: *squeeze off a few well-aimed shots.* ■ (**squeeze off**) *inf.* take a photograph: *he squeezed off a half-dozen Polaroids.* **2** [*intr.*] manage to get into or through a narrow or restricted space: *Sarah squeezed in beside her.* ■ [*tr.*] manage to force into or through such a space: *she squeezed herself into her tightest pair of jeans.* ■ [*intr.*] (**squeeze up**) move closer to someone or something so that one is pressed tightly against them or it: *he guided her toward a seat, motioning for everyone to squeeze up and make room.* ■ [*tr.*] (**squeeze someone/something in**) manage to find time for someone or something: *the* *doctor can squeeze you in at noon.* ■ [*tr.*] (**squeeze someone/something out**) force someone or something out of a domain or activity: *workers have been squeezed out of their jobs.*

▶*n.* **1** an act of pressing something with one's fingers: *a gentle squeeze of the trigger.* ■ a hug. ■ a state of forcing oneself or being forced into a small or restricted space: *it was a tight squeeze in the tiny hall.* ■ a strong financial demand or pressure, typically a restriction on borrowing, spending, or investment in a financial crisis: *industry faced higher costs and a squeeze on profits.* ■ a molding or cast of an object, or an impression or copy of a design, obtained by pressing a pliable substance around or over it. ■ *inf.* money illegally extorted or exacted from someone: *he was out to extract some squeeze from her.* ■ *Bridge* a tactic that forces an opponent to discard an important card. ■ (also **squeeze play**) *Baseball* an act of bunting a ball in order to enable a runner on third base to start for home as soon as the ball is pitched. **2** *inf.* a person's girlfriend or boyfriend: *the poor guy just lost his main squeeze.* —**squeez·a·ble** *adj.* —**squeez·er** *n.*

squelch /skwelCH/ ▶*v.* [*intr.*] make a soft sucking sound such as that made by walking heavily through mud: *bedraggled guests squelched across the lawn to seek shelter.* ■ [*tr.*] *inf.* forcefully silence or suppress: *property developers tried to squelch public protest.*

▶*n.* **1** a soft sucking sound made when pressure is applied to liquid or mud: *the squelch of their feet.* **2** (also **squelch circuit**) *Electr.* a circuit that suppresses the output of a radio receiver if the signal strength falls below a certain level. —**squelch·er** *n.* —**squelch·y** *adj.*

squib /skwib/ ▶*n.* **1** a small firework that burns with a hissing sound before exploding. ■ a short piece of satirical writing. ■ a short news item or filler in a newspaper. **2** a small, slight, or weak person, esp. a child. **3** *Football* a short kick on a kickoff. ■ *Baseball* (also **squib·ber**) a blooper or infield grounder that becomes a base hit.

▶*v.* (**squibbed, squib·bing**) [*tr.*] *Football* kick (the ball) a comparatively short distance on a kickoff; execute (a kick) in this way.

squick /skwik/ ▶*v.* [*trans.*] *inf.* cause immediate and thorough revulsion: *was anyone else squicked by the potential adoptive parents?*

▶*n.* a person or thing that causes immediate and thorough revulsion.

squid /skwid/ ▶*n.* (*pl.* same or **squids**) an elongated, fast-swimming cephalopod mollusk with ten arms (technically, eight arms and two long tentacles), typically able to change color. ■ this mollusk used as food. ■ *inf.* a sailor.

squig·gle /ˈskwigəl/ ▶*n.* a short line that curls and loops in an irregular way: *some prescriptions are a series of meaningless squiggles.*

▶*v.* [*intr.*] wriggle; squirm: *a worm that squiggled in his palm.* ■ [*tr.*] squeeze (something) from a tube so as to make irregular, curly lines on a surface. —**squig·gly** /ˈskwig(ə)lē/ *adj.*

squinch /skwinCH/ ▶*v.* [*tr.*] tense up the muscles of (one's eyes or face): *Gina squinched her face up.* ■ [*intr.*] (of a person's eyes) narrow so as to be almost closed, typically in reaction to strong light: *he flicked on the light, which made my eyes squinch up.* ■ [*intr.*] crouch down in order to make oneself seem smaller or to occupy less space: *I squinched down under the sheet.*

squint /skwint/ ▶*v.* **1** [*intr.*] look at someone or something with one or both eyes partly closed in an attempt to see more clearly or as a reaction to strong light: *the bright sun made them squint.* ■ [*tr.*] partly close (one's eyes) for such reasons. **2** [*intr.*] have eyes that look in different directions: *Melanie did not squint.*

▶*n.* **1** a permanent deviation in the direction of the gaze of one eye: *I had a bad squint.* **2** *inf.* a quick or casual look: *let me have a squint.* —**squint·er** *n.* —**squint·y** *adj.* [often in *comb.*] *squinty-eyed.*

squire /ˈskwīr/ ▶*n.* **1** a man of high social standing who owns and lives on an estate in a rural area, esp. the chief landowner in such an area: *the squire of Radbourne Hall.* **2** *hist.* a young nobleman acting as an attendant to a knight before becoming a knight himself.

▶*v.* [*tr.*] (of a man) accompany or escort (a woman): *she was squired around Rome by a reporter.* —**squire·dom** /-dəm/ *n.* —**squire·ship** /-ˌSHip/ *n.*

squirm /skwərm/ ▶*v.* [*intr.*] wriggle or twist the body from side to side, esp. as a result of nervousness or discomfort: *all my efforts to squirm out of his grasp were useless.* ■ show or feel embarrassment or shame.

▶*n.* a wriggling movement. —**squirm·er** *n.* —**squirm·y** *adj.*

squir·rel /ˈskwərl/ ▶*n.* an agile tree-dwelling rodent (*Sciurus* and other genera, family Sciuridae) with a bushy tail, typically feeding on nuts and seeds. ■ a related rodent of this family (see GROUND SQUIRREL, FLYING SQUIRREL). ■ the fur of the squirrel.

▶*v.* (**squirreled, squirreling**) [*tr.*] (**squirrel something away**) hide money or something of value in a safe place: *the money was squirreled away in foreign bank accounts.* ▷Middle English: shortening of Old French *esquireul,* from a diminutive of Latin *sciurus,* from Greek *skiouros,* from

skia 'shade' + *oura* 'tail.' Current verb senses date from the early 20th cent.

squir·rel·ly /ˈskwər(ə)lē/ ▶*adj.* **1** relating to or resembling a squirrel: *the chipmunks were little squirrelly things.* **2** *inf.* restless, nervous, or unpredictable. ■ eccentric or insane.

squir·rel mon·key ▶*n.* a small South American monkey (genus *Saimiri,* family Cebidae) with a nonprehensile tail, typically moving through trees by leaping.

squirt /skwərt/ ▶*v.* [*tr.*] cause (a liquid) to be ejected from a small opening in something in a thin, fast stream or jet: *she squirted soda into a glass.* ■ cause (a container of liquid) to eject its contents in this way: *some youngsters squirted a water pistol in her face.* ■ [*tr.*] wet (someone or something) with a jet or stream of liquid in this way: *she squirted me with the juice from her lemon wedge.* ■ [*intr.*] (of a liquid) be ejected from something in this way. ■ [*intr.*] (of an object) move suddenly and unpredictably: *he got his glove on the ball but it squirted away.*

▶*n.* **1** a thin stream or small quantity of liquid ejected from something: *a quick squirt of perfume.* **2** *inf.* a person perceived to be insignificant, impudent, or presumptuous: *what did he see in this patronizing little squirt?* —**squirt·er** *n.*

squish /skwiSH/ ▶*v.* [*intr.*] make a soft squelching sound when walked on or in: *the mud squished under my shoes.* ■ yield easily to pressure when squeezed or squashed. ■ [*tr.*] *inf.* squash (something): *Naomi was furiously squishing her ice cream in her bowl.*

▶*n.* a soft squelching sound. —**squish·y** *adj.* (**squish·i·er, squish·i·est**)

Sr ▶*symb.* the chemical element strontium.

Sr. ▶*abbr.* ■ senior (in names): *E. T. Krebs, Sr.* ■ Señor. ■ Signor. ■ Sister (in a religious order).

SRO ▶*abbr.* ■ (in the UK) self-regulatory organization, a body that regulates the activities of investment businesses. ■ single room occupancy. ■ standing room only.

SS[1] ▶*abbr.* ■ Saints: *the Church of SS Peter and Paul.* ■ *Baseball* shortstop. ■ social security. ■ (in prescriptions) in the strict sense. ■ steamship: *the SS Canberra.*

SS[2] ▶the Nazi special police force. Founded in 1925 by Hitler as a personal bodyguard, the SS provided security forces (including the Gestapo) and administered the concentration camps.

SSA ▶*abbr.* ■ Social Security Act. ■ Social Security Administration.

SSE ▶*abbr.* south-south-east.

SST ▶*abbr.* supersonic transport.

SSW ▶*abbr.* south-southwest.

ST ▶*abbr.* stokes.

St. ▶*abbr.* ■ Saint: *St. George.*

Sta. ▶*abbr.* station (in particular, a railroad station).

stab /stab/ ▶*v.* (**stabbed, stab·bing**) [*tr.*] (of a person) thrust a knife or other pointed weapon into (someone) so as to wound or kill: *he stabbed him in the stomach* | [as *n.*] (**stabbing**) *the fatal stabbings of four rival gang members.* ■ [*intr.*] make a thrusting gesture or movement at something with a pointed object: *she stabbed at the earth with the fork* | [*tr.*] *she stabbed the air with her forefinger* ■ [*intr.*] (**stab into/through**) (of a sharp or pointed object) violently pierce: *a sharp end of wicker stabbed into his sole.* ■ [*intr.*] (**stab at**) (of a pain or painful thing) cause a sudden sharp sensation: [as *adj.*] (**stabbing**) *I felt a stabbing pain in my chest.*

▶*n.* **1** a thrust with a knife or other pointed weapon: [as *adj.*] *multiple stab wounds.* ■ a wound made in such a way: *she had a deep stab in the back.* ■ a thrusting movement with a finger or other pointed object: *impatient stabs of his finger.* ■ a sudden sharp feeling or pain: *she felt a stab of jealousy.* **2** (**stab at**) *inf.* an attempt to do (something): *Meredith made a feeble stab at joining in.* —**stab·ber** *n.*

▶ ◻ **a stab in the back** a treacherous act or statement.

sta·bil·i·ty /stəˈbilitē/ ▶*n.* the state of being stable: *there are fears for the political stability of the area.*

sta·bil·i·ty ball ▶*n.* another term for EXERCISE BALL.

sta·bi·lize /ˈstābəˌlīz/ ▶*v.* make or become stable: [*intr.*] *his condition appears to have stabilized* | [*tr.*] *an emergency program designed to stabilize the economy.* ■ [*tr.*] cause (an object or structure) to be unlikely to overturn: *the craft was stabilized by throwing out the remaining ballast.* —**sta·bi·li·za·tion** /ˌstābəliˈzāSHən/ *n.*

sta·bi·liz·er /ˈstābəˌlīzər/ ▶*n.* a thing used to keep something steady or stable, in particular: ■ another term for HORIZONTAL STABILIZER. ■ a gyroscopically controlled system used to reduce the rolling of a ship. ■ a substance that prevents the breakdown of emulsions, esp. in foods and paints.

sta·ble[1] /ˈstābəl/ ▶*adj.* (**-bler, -blest**) not likely to change or fail; firmly established: *a stable relationship.* ■ (of a patient or a medical condition) not deteriorating in health after an injury or operation: *he is now in a stable condition in the hospital.* ■ (of a person) sane and sensible; not easily upset or disturbed: *the officer concerned is mentally and emotionally stable.* ■ (of an object or structure) not likely to give way or overturn; firmly fixed: *specially designed dinghies that are very stable.* ■ not liable to undergo chemical decomposition, radioactive decay, or other physical change. —**sta·bly** /-b(ə)lē/ *adv.*

sta·ble² ▶*n.* a building set apart and adapted for keeping horses. ■ an establishment where racehorses are kept and trained. ■ the racehorses of a particular training establishment. ■ an organization or establishment providing the same background or training for its members: *the player comes from the same stable as Agassi.* ■ a group of people trained by the same person or under one management: *the agent looked after a big stable of European golfers.*

▶*v.* [*tr.*] put or keep (a horse) in a specially adapted building. ■ put or base (a train) in a depot. —**sta·ble·ful** /'stābəl,fŏŏl/ *n.* (*pl.* **-fuls**).

sta·bling /'stāb(ə)liNG/ ▶*n.* accommodations for horses.

stac·ca·to /stə'kätō/ *chiefly Mus.* ▶*adv.* & *adj.* with each sound or note sharply detached or separated from the others: [as *adj.*] *a staccato rhythm.* Compare with LEGATO.

▶*n.* (*pl.* **-tos**) performance in this manner. ■ a noise or speech resembling a series of short, detached musical notes: *her heels made a rapid staccato on the polished boards.*

stack /stak/ ▶*n.* **1** a pile of objects, typically one that is neatly arranged: *a stack of boxes.* ■ (**a stack of/stacks of**) *inf.* a large quantity of something: *there's stacks of work for me now.* ■ a rectangular or cylindrical pile of hay or straw or of grain in sheaf. ■ a vertical arrangement of stereo or guitar amplification equipment. ■ a number of aircraft flying in circles at different altitudes around the same point while waiting for permission to land at an airport. ■ (**the stacks**) the part of a library in which books are stored on shelves. ■ *Comput.* a set of storage locations that store data in such a way that the most recently stored item is the first to be retrieved. **2** a chimney, esp. one on a factory, or a vertical exhaust pipe on a vehicle. ■ a column of rock standing in the sea, remaining after erosion of cliffs.

▶*v.* [*tr.*] **1** arrange (a number of things) in a pile, typically a neat one: *the books had been **stacked up** in three piles.* ■ fill or cover (a place or surface) with piles of things, typically neat ones: *he spent most of the time stacking shelves.* ■ cause (an aircraft) to fly in circles while waiting for permission to land at an airport: *I hope we aren't stacked for hours over Kennedy.* **2** shuffle or arrange (a deck of cards) dishonestly so as to gain an unfair advantage. ■ (**be stacked against/in favor of**) used to refer to a situation that is such that an unfavorable or a favorable outcome is overwhelmingly likely: *the odds were stacked against Fiji in the World Cup.* **3** [*intr.*] (in snowboarding) fall over.

▶*phrasal v.* □ **stack up** *inf.* measure up; compare: *our rural schools stack up well against their urban counterparts.* ■ make sense; correspond to reality: *to blame the debacle on the antics of a rogue trader is not credible—it doesn't stack up.* —**stack·a·ble** *adj.* —**stack·er** *n.*

sta·di·um /'stādēəm/ ▶*n.* (*pl.* **-di·ums** or **-di·a** /-dēə/) a sports arena with tiers of seats for spectators. ■ (in ancient Rome or Greece) a track for a foot race or chariot race.

staff /staf/ ▶*n.* **1** [treated as *sing.* or *pl.*] all the people employed by a particular organization: *a staff of 600.* ■ the teachers in a school or college: [as *adj.*] *a staff meeting.* **2** [treated as *sing.* or *pl.*] a group of officers assisting an officer in command of an army formation or administration headquarters. **3** a long stick used as a support when walking or climbing or as a weapon. ■ a rod or scepter held as a sign of office or authority. ■ short for FLAGSTAFF. **4** (*pl.* **staves** /stāvz/) (also *Brit.* **stave**) *Mus.* a set of five parallel lines and the spaces between them, on which notes are written to indicate their pitch.

▶*v.* [*tr.*] (usu. **be staffed**) provide (an organization, business, etc.) with staff: *legal advice centers are staffed by volunteer lawyers.*

▶ □ **the staff of life** a staple food, esp. bread.

staff·er /'stafər/ ▶*n.* a member of the staff of an organization, esp. of a newspaper.

staff ser·geant ▶*n.* a noncommissioned officer in the armed forces.

stag /stag/ ▶*n.* a male deer. ■ [usu. as *adj.*] a social gathering attended by men only: *a stag event.* ■ a person who attends a social gathering unaccompanied by a partner.

▶*adv.* without a partner at a social gathering: *a lot of boys went stag.* ▷Middle English (as a noun): related to Old Norse *steggr* 'male bird,' Icelandic *steggi* 'tomcat.'

stage /stāj/ ▶*n.* **1** a point, period, or step in a process or development: *there is no need at this stage to give explicit details.* ■ a section of a journey or race. ■ each of two or more sections of a rocket or spacecraft that

have their own engines and are jettisoned in turn when their propellant is exhausted. ■ *Electr.* a specified part of a circuit, typically one consisting of a single amplifying transistor or electron tube with the associated equipment. **2** a raised floor or platform, typically in a theater, on which actors, entertainers, or speakers perform: *there are only two characters on stage.* ■ (**the stage**) the acting or theatrical profession: *I've always wanted to go on the stage.* ■ a scene of action or forum of debate, esp. in a particular political context: *Argentina is playing a leading role on the international stage.* **3** a floor or level of a building or structure: *the upper stage was added in the 17th century.* ■ (on a microscope) a raised and usually movable plate on which a slide or object is placed for examination. **4** *Geol.* a range of strata corresponding to an age in time, forming a subdivision of a series.

▶*v.* [*tr.*] present a performance of (a play or other show): *the show is being staged at the Goodspeed Opera House.* ■ (of a person or group) organize and participate in (a public event): *UDF supporters staged a demonstration in Sofia.* ■ cause (something dramatic or unexpected) to happen: *the president's attempt to stage a comeback.* —**stage·a·bil·i·ty** /,stājə'bilitē/ *n.* —**stage·a·ble** *adj.* —**stage·er** *n.*

▶ □ **set the stage for** prepare the conditions for (the occurrence or beginning of something): *these churchmen helped to set the stage for popular reform.*

stage·coach /'stāj,kōCH/ ▶*n.* a large, closed horse-drawn vehicle formerly used to carry passengers and often mail along a regular route between two places.

stagecoach

stage·craft /'stāj,kraft/ ▶*n.* skill or experience in writing or staging plays.

stage door ▶*n.* an actors' and workers' entrance from the street to the area of a theater behind the stage.

stage fright ▶*n.* nervousness before or during an appearance before an audience.

stage·hand /'stāj,hand/ ▶*n.* a person who moves scenery or props before or during the performance of a play.

stage name ▶*n.* a name assumed for professional purposes by an actor or other performer.

stage-struck ▶*adj.* having a passionate desire to become an actor.

stage·y ▶*adj.* variant spelling of STAGY.

stag·fla·tion /,stag'flāSHən/ ▶*n.* *Econ.* persistent high inflation combined with high unemployment and stagnant demand in a country's economy.

stag·ger /'stagər/ ▶*v.* **1** [*intr.*] walk or move unsteadily, as if about to fall: *he staggered to his feet, swaying a little.* ■ *fig.* continue in existence or operation uncertainly or precariously: *the council staggered from one crisis to the next.* **2** [*tr.*] astonish or deeply shock: *I was staggered to find it was six o'clock.* **3** [*tr.*] arrange (events, payments, hours, etc.) so that they do not occur at the same time; spread over a period of time: *meetings are staggered throughout the day.* ■ arrange (objects or parts of an object) in a zigzag order or so that they are not in line: *stagger the screws at each joint.*

▶*n.* **1** an unsteady walk or movement: *she walked with a stagger.* **2** an arrangement of things in a zigzag order or so that they are not in line. —**stag·ger·er** *n.* —**stag·ger·ing·ly** *adv. a staggeringly unjust society.*

stag·ing /'stājiNG/ ▶*n.* **1** an instance or method of presenting a play or other dramatic performance: *one of the better stagings of this classic.* ■ an instance of organizing a public event or protest: *the fourteenth staging of the championships.* **2** a stage or set of stages or temporary platforms arranged as a support for performers or between different levels of scaffolding.

stag·ing ar·e·a ▶*n.* a stopping place or assembly point en route to a destination: *a vast staging area for guerrilla attacks* | *the geese's major staging area on the St. Lawrence River.*

S

stag·nant /'stagnənt/ ▶*adj.* (of a body of water or the atmosphere of a confined space) having no current or flow and often having an unpleasant smell as a consequence: *a stagnant ditch.* ■ *fig.* showing no activity; dull and sluggish: *a stagnant economy.* —**stag·nan·cy** /-nənsē/ *n.* —**stag·nant·ly** *adv.*

stag·nate /'stag,nāt/ ▶*v.* [*intr.*] (of water or air) cease to flow or move; become stagnant. ■ *fig.* cease developing; become inactive or dull: *teaching can easily stagnate into a set of routines.* —**stag·na·tion** /stag'nāSHən/ *n.*

stag·y /'stājē/ (also **stag·ey**) ▶*adj.* (**stag·i·er**, **stag·i·est**) excessively theatrical; exaggerated: *a stagy melodramatic voice.* —**stag·i·ly** /-jilē/ *adv.* —**stag·i·ness** *n.*

staid /stād/ ▶*adj.* sedate, respectable, and unadventurous: *staid law firms.* —**staid·ly** *adv.* —**staid·ness** *n.*

stain /stān/ ▶*v.* [*tr.*] **1** mark (something) with colored patches or dirty marks that are not easily removed: *her clothing was stained with blood.* ■ [*intr.*] be marked or be liable to be marked with such patches. ■ *fig.* damage or bring disgrace to (the reputation or image of someone or something): *the awful events would unfairly stain the city's reputation.* **2** color (a material or object) by applying a penetrative dye or chemical: *wood can always be stained to a darker shade.*
▶*n.* **1** a colored patch or dirty mark that is difficult to remove: *there were mud stains on my shoes.* ■ a thing that damages or brings disgrace to someone or something's reputation: *he regarded his time in jail as a stain on his character.* ■ a patch of brighter or deeper color that suffuses something: *the sun left a red stain behind as it retreated.* **2** a penetrative dye or chemical used in coloring a material or object. ■ *Biol.* a special dye used to color organic tissue so as to make the structure visible for microscopic examination. ▷late Middle English (as a verb): shortening of archaic *distain*, from Old French *desteindre* 'tinge with a color different from the natural one.' The noun was first recorded (mid 16th cent.) in the sense 'defilement, disgrace.' —**stain·a·ble** *adj.* —**stain·er** *n.*

stained glass ▶*n.* colored glass used to form decorative or pictorial designs, notably for church windows, both by painting and esp. by setting contrasting pieces in a lead framework like a mosaic.

stain·less /'stānlis/ ▶*adj.* unmarked by or resistant to stains or discoloration.

stain·less steel ▶*n.* a form of steel containing chromium, resistant to corrosion.

stair /ste(ə)r/ ▶*n.* (usu. **stairs**) a set of steps leading from one floor of a building to another, typically inside the building: *he came up the stairs.* ■ single step in such a set: *the bottom stair.*

stair·case /'ste(ə)r,kās/ ▶*n.* a set of stairs and its surrounding walls or structure.

stair·way /'ste(ə)r,wā/ ▶*n.* a set of steps or stairs and its surrounding walls or structure.

stair·well /'ste(ə)r,wel/ ▶*n.* a shaft in a building in which a staircase is built.

stake¹ /stāk/ ▶*n.* **1** a strong wooden or metal post with a point at one end, driven into the ground to support a tree, form part of a fence, act as a boundary mark, etc. **2** (**the stake**) *hist.* a wooden post to which a person was tied before being burned alive as a punishment.
▶*v.* [*tr.*] **1** support (a tree or plant) with a stake or stakes. **2** (**stake something out**) mark an area with stakes so as to claim ownership of it: *the boundary between the two ranches was properly staked out.* ■ be assertive in defining and defending a position or policy: *Elena was staking out a role for herself.*
▶*phrasal v.* □ **stake someone/something out** *inf.* continuously watch a place or person in secret: *they'd staked out Culley's house for half a day.*
▶ □ **stake a claim** assert one's right to something.

stake² ▶*n.* (usu. **stakes**) a sum of money or something else of value gambled on the outcome of a risky game or venture: *playing dice for high stakes.* ■ a share or interest in a business, situation, or system: *GM acquired a 50 percent stake in Saab.* ■ (**stakes**) prize money, esp. in horse racing. ■ [*in names*] (**stakes**) a horse race in which all the owners of the racehorses running contribute to the prize money: *the horse is to run in the Lexington Stakes.*
▶*v.* [*tr.*] **1** gamble (money or something else of value) on the outcome of a game or race: *one gambler staked everything he'd got and lost.* **2** *inf.* give financial or other support to: *he staked him to an education at the École des Beaux-Arts.*
▶ □ **at stake 1** to be won or lost; at risk: *people's lives could be at stake.* **2** at issue or in question: *the logical response is to give up, but there's more at stake than logic.*

stake·out /'stāk,out/ ▶*n.* *inf.* a period of secret surveillance of a building or an area by police in order to observe someone's activities.

sta·lac·tite /stə'lak,tīt/ ▶*n.* a tapering structure hanging like an icicle from the roof of a cave, formed of calcium salts deposited by dripping water. Compare with STALAGMITE. —**sta·lac·tit·ic** /,stalək'titik/ *adj.*

sta·lag·mite /stə'lag,mīt/ ▶*n.* a mound or tapering column rising from the floor of a cave, formed of calcium salts deposited by dripping water and often uniting with a stalactite. —**stal·ag·mit·ic** /,staləg'mitik/ *adj.*

stale /stāl/ ▶*adj.* (**stal·er**, **stal·est**) (of food) no longer fresh and pleasant to eat; hard, musty, or dry: *stale bread.* ■ no longer new and interesting or exciting: *their marriage had gone stale.* ■ (of a person) no longer able to perform well or creatively because of having done something for too long: *a top executive tends to get stale.*
▶*v.* make or become stale. —**stale·ly** /'stā(l)lē/ *adv.* —**stale·ness** *n.*

stale·mate /'stāl,māt/ ▶*n.* *Chess* a position counting as a draw, in which a player is not in check but cannot move except into check. ■ a situation in which further action or progress by opposing or competing parties seems impossible: *the war had again reached stalemate.*
▶*v.* [*tr.*] bring to or cause to reach stalemate.

Sta·lin·ism /'stālə,nizəm/ ▶*n.* the ideology and policies adopted by Joseph Stalin, based on centralization, totalitarianism, and the pursuit of communism. ■ any rigid centralized authoritarian form of communism. —**Sta·lin·ist** *n. & adj.*

stalk¹ /stôk/ ▶*n.* the main stem of a herbaceous plant: *he chewed a stalk of grass.* ■ the slender attachment or support of a leaf, flower, or fruit: *the acorns grow on stalks.* ■ a similar support for a sessile animal, or for an organ in an animal. ■ a slender support or stem of something: *drinking glasses with long stalks.* —**stalked** *adj.* [in *comb.*] *rough-stalked meadow grass.* —**stalk·less** *adj.* —**stalk·like** /-,līk/ *adj.* —**stalk·y** *adj.*

stalk² ▶*v.* **1** [*tr.*] pursue or approach stealthily: *a cat stalking a bird.* ■ harass or persecute (someone) with unwanted and obsessive attention: *for five years she was stalked by a man who would taunt and threaten her.* ■ *chiefly poetic/lit.* move silently or threateningly through (a place): *the tiger stalks the jungle | fig. fear stalked the camp.* **2** [*intr.*] stride somewhere in a proud, stiff, or angry manner: *without another word she turned and stalked out.*
▶*n.* **1** a stealthy pursuit of someone or something. **2** a stiff, striding gait. —**stalk·er** *n.*

stall /stôl/ ▶*n.* **1** a stand, booth, or compartment for the sale of goods in a market or large covered area: *fruit and vegetable stalls.* **2** an individual compartment for an animal in a stable or barn, enclosed on three sides. ■ a stable. ■ a marked-out parking space for a vehicle. ■ a compartment for one person in a shower room, toilet, or similar facility. **3** a fixed seat in the choir or chancel of a church, more or less enclosed at the back and sides and often canopied, typically reserved for a particular member of the clergy. **4** an instance of an engine, vehicle, aircraft, or boat stalling: *speed must be maintained to avoid a stall and loss of control.*
▶*v.* **1** [*intr.*] (of a motor vehicle or its engine) stop running, typically because of an overload on the engine: *her car stalled at the crossroads.* ■ (of an aircraft or its pilot) reach a condition in which the speed is too low to allow effective operation of the controls. ■ [*tr.*] cause (an engine, vehicle, aircraft, or boat) to stall. **2** [*intr.*] (of a situation or process) stop making progress: *his career had stalled, hers taken off.* ■ [*tr.*] delay, obstruct, or block the progress of (something): *the government has stalled the much-needed project.* ■ speak or act in a deliberately vague way in order to gain more time to deal with a question or issue; prevaricate: *she was stalling for time.* ■ [*tr.*] delay or divert (someone) by acting in such a way: *stall him until I've had time to take a look.* **3** [*tr.*] put or keep (an animal) in a stall, esp. in order to fatten it.

stal·lion /'stalyən/ ▶*n.* an uncastrated adult male horse.

stal·wart /'stôlwərt/ ▶*adj.* loyal, reliable, and hardworking: *he remained a stalwart supporter of the cause.*
▶*n.* a loyal, reliable, and hardworking supporter or participant in an organization or team: *the stalwarts of the Ladies' Auxiliary.* —**stal·wart·ly** *adv.* —**stal·wart·ness** *n.*

sta·men /'stāmin/ ▶*n.* *Bot.* the male fertilizing organ of a flower, typically consisting of a pollen-containing anther and a filament.

stam·i·na /'stamənə/ ▶*n.* the ability to sustain prolonged physical or mental effort: *their secret is stamina rather than speed.*

stam·i·nate /'stamə,nāt/ ▶*adj.* *Bot.* (of a plant or flower) having stamens but no pistils.

stam·mer /'stamər/ ▶*v.* [*intr.*] speak with sudden involuntary pauses and a tendency to repeat the initial letters of words. ■ [*tr.*] utter (words) in such a way: *I stammered out my history.*
▶*n.* a tendency to stammer: *as a young man, he had a dreadful stammer.* —**stam·mer·er** *n.* —**stam·mer·ing·ly** *adv.*

stamp /stamp/ ▶*v.* [*tr.*] **1** bring down (one's foot) heavily on the ground or on something on the ground: *he stamped his foot in frustration* | [*intr.*] *he threw his cigarette down and stamped on it.* ■ [*tr.*] crush, flatten, or remove with a heavy blow from one's feet: *he stamped out the flames before they could grow.* ■ **(stamp something out)** suppress or put an end to something by taking decisive action: *urgent action is required to stamp out corruption.* ■ [*intr.*] walk with heavy, forceful steps: *John stamped off, muttering.* **2** impress a pattern or mark, esp. an official one, on (a surface, object, or document) using an engraved or inked block or die or other instrument: *the woman stamped my passport.* ■ impress (a pattern or mark) on something in such a way: *a key with a number stamped on the shaft.* ■ make (something) by cutting it out with a die or mold: *the knives are stamped out from a flat strip of steel.* ■ *fig.* reveal or mark out as having a particular character, quality, or ability: *his style stamps him as a player to watch.* **3** affix a postage stamp or stamps onto (a letter or package): *Annie stamped the envelope for her.*

▶*n.* **1** an instrument for stamping a pattern or mark, in particular an engraved or inked block or die. ■ a mark or pattern made by such an instrument, esp. one indicating official validation or certification: *passports with visa stamps.* ■ *fig.* a characteristic or distinctive impression or quality: *the whole project has the stamp of authority.* ■ a particular class or type or person or thing: *empiricism of this stamp has been esp. influential in British philosophy.* **2** a small adhesive piece of paper stuck to something to show that an amount of money has been paid, in particular a postage stamp: *a first-class stamp.* **3** an act or sound of stamping with the foot: *the stamp of boots on the bare floor.* —**stamp·er** *n.*

stam·pede /stam'pēd/ ▶*n.* a sudden panicked rush of a number of horses, cattle, or other animals. ■ a sudden rapid movement or reaction of a mass of people in response to a particular circumstance or stimulus: *a stampede of bargain hunters.* ■ a rodeo: *the Calgary Stampede.*

▶*v.* [*intr.*] (of horses, cattle, or other animals) rush wildly in a sudden mass panic: *the nearby sheep stampeded as if they sensed impending danger.* ■ [*intr.*] (of people) move rapidly in a mass: *the children stampeded through the kitchen, playing tag or hide-and-seek.* ■ [*tr.*] cause (people or animals) to move in such a way: *the raiders stampeded 200 mules* | *fig. don't let them stampede us into anything.* —**stam·ped·er** *n.*

stance /stans/ ▶*n.* the way in which someone stands, esp. when deliberately adopted (as in baseball, golf, and other sports); a person's posture: *she altered her stance, resting all her weight on one leg.* ■ the attitude of a person or organization toward something; a standpoint: *the party is changing its stance on the draft.*

stanch[1] /stônCH; stänCH/ (also **staunch**) ▶*v.* [*tr.*] stop or restrict (a flow of blood) from a wound: *colleagues may have saved her life by stanching the flow.*

stanch[2] ▶*adj.* variant spelling of **STAUNCH**[1] (sense 2).

stan·chion /'stanCHən/ ▶*n.* an upright bar, post, or frame forming a support or barrier. —**stan·chioned** *adj.*

stand /stand/ ▶*v.* (*past* **stood** /stŏŏd/) **1** [*intr.*] have or maintain an upright position, supported by one's feet: *Lionel stood in the doorway.* ■ rise to one's feet: *the two men stood up and shook hands.* ■ [*intr.*] move to and remain in a specified position: *she stood aside to let them enter.* ■ [*tr.*] place or set in an upright or specified position: *don't stand the plant in direct sunlight.* **2** [*intr.*] (of an object, building, or settlement) be situated in a particular place or position: *the town stood on a hill.* ■ (of a building or other vertical structure) remain upright and entire rather than fall into ruin or be destroyed: *after the heavy storms, only one house was left standing.* ■ remain valid or unaltered: *my decision stands* | *his strikeout record stood for 38 years.* ■ (esp. of a vehicle) remain stationary: *the train now standing on track 3.* ■ (of a liquid) collect and remain motionless: *avoid planting in soil where water stands in winter.* ■ (of food, a mixture, or liquid) rest without disturbance, typically so as to infuse or marinate: *pour boiling water over the fruit and leave it to stand for 5 minutes.* **3** [*intr.*] be in a specified state or condition: *since mother's death, the house had stood empty* | *sorry, darling—I stand corrected.* ■ adopt a particular attitude toward a matter or issue: *students should consider where they stand on this issue.* ■ be of a specified height: *Sampson was a small man, standing 5 ft. 4 in. tall.* ■ **(stand at)** be at (a particular level or value): *the budget stood at $14 million per annum.* ■ [*intr.*] be in a situation where one is likely to do something: *investors stood to lose heavily.* ■ act in a specified capacity: *he stood watch all night.* **4** [*tr.*] withstand (an experience or test) without being damaged: *small boats that could stand the punishment of heavy seas.* ■ *inf.* be able to endure or tolerate: *I can't stand the way Mom talks to him.* ■ *inf.* strongly dislike: *I can't stand brandy.* **5** [*intr.*] *Brit.* be a candidate in an election: *he stood for Parliament in 1968.* **6** provide (food or drink) for someone at one's own expense: *somebody in the bar would stand him a beer.*

▶*phrasal v.* □ **stand aside** take no action to prevent, or not involve

oneself in, something that is happening: *the army had stood aside as the monarchy fell.* □ **stand by 1** be present while something bad is happening but fail to take any action to stop it: *he was beaten to the ground as onlookers stood by.* **2** support or remain loyal to (someone), typically in a time of need: *she had stood by him during his years in prison.* ■ adhere to or abide by (something promised, stated, or decided): *the government must stand by its pledges.* **3** be ready to deal or assist with something: *two battalions were on their way, and a third was standing by.* □ **stand for 1** be an abbreviation of or symbol for: *NASA stands for National Aeronautics and Space Administration.* **2** *inf.* refuse to endure or tolerate: *I won't stand for any nonsense.* **3** support (a cause or principle): *we stand for animal welfare.* □ **stand out** project from a surface: *the veins in his neck stood out.* ■ be easily noticeable: *he was one of those men who stood out in a crowd.* ■ be clearly better or more significant than someone or something: *four issues stand out as being of crucial importance.* □ **stand up** (of an argument, claim, evidence, etc.) remain valid after close scrutiny or analysis: *but will your story stand up in court?*

▶*n.* **1** an attitude toward a particular issue; a position taken in an argument: *the party's tough stand on welfare* | *his traditionalist stand.* ■ a determined effort to resist or fight for something: *this was not the moment to make a stand for independence.* ■ an act of holding one's ground against or halting to resist an opposing force: *Custer's legendary last stand.* **2** a place where, or an object on which, someone or something stands, sits, or rests, in particular: ■ a large raised tiered structure for spectators, typically at a sports arena: *her parents watched from the stands.* ■ a rack, base, or piece of furniture for holding, supporting, or displaying something: *a microphone stand.* ■ a small stall or booth in a street, market, or public building from which goods are sold: *a hot-dog stand.* ■ a raised platform for a band, orchestra, or speaker. ■ **(the stand)** (also **witness stand**) a witness box: *Sergeant Harris took the stand.* ■ a place where vehicles, typically taxicabs, wait for passengers. **3** each halt made on a touring theatrical production to give one or more performances. **4** a group of growing plants of a specified kind, esp. trees: *a stand of poplars.* ▷Old English *standan* (verb), *stand* (noun), of Germanic origin, from an Indo-European root shared by Latin *stare* and Greek *histanai*, also by the noun *stead.* —**stand·er** *n.*

stand·ard /'standərd/ ▶*n.* **1** a level of quality or attainment: *their restaurant offers a high standard of service.* ■ a required or agreed level of quality or attainment: *half of the beaches fail to comply with EPA standards.* **2** an idea or thing used as a measure, norm, or model in comparative evaluations: *the wages are low by today's standards.* ■ **(standards)** principles of conduct informed by notions of honor and decency: *a decline in moral standards.* ■ a form of language that is widely accepted as the correct form. ■ the prescribed weight of fine metal in gold or silver coins: *the sterling standard for silver.* ■ a system by which the value of a currency is defined in terms of gold or silver or both. **3** an object that is supported in an upright position, in particular: ■ a military or ceremonial flag carried on a pole or hoisted on a rope. ■ an upright water or gas pipe. **4** a tune or song of established popularity.

▶*adj.* used or accepted as normal or average: *the standard rate of income tax.* ■ (of a size, measure, design, etc.) such as is regularly used or produced; not special or exceptional: *all these doors come in a range of standard sizes.* ■ (of a work, repertoire, or writer) viewed as authoritative or of permanent value and so widely read or performed: *his essays on the interpretation of reality became a standard text.* ■ denoting or relating to the spoken or written form of a language widely accepted as usual and correct: *speakers of standard English.* —**stand·ard·ly** *adv.*

stand·ard-bear·er ▶*n.* a leading figure in a cause or movement: *the announcement made her a standard-bearer for gay rights.*

stand·ard·ize /'standər,dīz/ ▶*v.* [*tr.*] cause (something) to conform to a standard: *Jones's effort to standardize oriental spelling.* —**stand·ard·iz·a·ble** *adj.* —**stand·ard·i·za·tion** /,standərdi'zāSHən/ *n.* —**stand·ard·iz·er** *n.*

stand·ard of liv·ing ▶*n.* the degree of wealth and material comfort available to a person or community.

stand·ard time ▶*n.* a uniform time for places in approximately the same longitude, established in a country or region by law or custom.

stand·by /'stan(d),bī/ ▶*n.* (*pl.* **-bys**) readiness for duty or immediate deployment: *buses were placed on standby for the trip to Washington.* ■ the state of waiting to secure an unreserved place for a journey or performance, allocated on the basis of earliest availability: *passengers were obliged to go on standby.* ■ a person waiting to secure such a place. ■ a person or thing ready to be deployed immediately, esp. if needed as backup in an emergency: *a generator was kept as a standby in case of power failure.* ▪ an operational mode of an electrical appliance in which the power is switched on but the appliance is not actually functioning.

stand·ee /stan'dē/ ▸ *n.* a person who stands, esp. in a passenger vehicle when all the seats are occupied or at a performance or sporting event.

stand-in ▸ *n.* a person who stands in for another, esp. in a performance; a substitute: *his stand-in does all the dancing sequences.*

stand·ing /'standiNG/ ▸ *n.* **1** position, status, or reputation: *their standing in the community.* ▪ (**standings**) the table of scores indicating the relative positions of competitors in a sports contest: *she heads the world championship standings.* **2** used to specify the length of time that something has lasted or that someone has fulfilled a particular role: *an interdepartmental squabble of long standing.*
▸ *adj.* **1** (of a jump or a start in a running race) performed from rest or an upright position, without a run-up or the use of starting blocks. **2** remaining in force or use; permanent: *a standing army.* **3** (of water) stagnant or still. **4** (of grain) not yet reaped and so still erect.

stand·off·ish /,stand'ôfiSH; -'äfiSH/ ▸ *adj. inf.* distant and cold in manner; unfriendly. —**stand·off·ish·ly** *adv.* —**stand·off·ish·ness** *n.*

stand·out /'stand,out/ *inf.* ▸ *n.* a person or thing of exceptional ability or high quality: *standouts include the homemade ravioli and the pizzas.*
▸ *adj.* exceptionally good: *he became a standout quarterback in the NFL.*

stand·pipe /'stan(d),pīp/ ▸ *n.* a vertical pipe extending from a water supply, esp. for use in fighting fires.

stand·point /'stan(d),point/ ▸ *n.* an attitude to or outlook on issues, typically arising from one's circumstances or beliefs: *she writes on religion from the standpoint of a believer.* ▪ the position from which someone is able to view a scene or an object.

stand·still /'stan(d),stil/ ▸ *n.* a situation or condition in which there is no movement or activity at all: *the traffic came to a standstill.*

stand-up (also **stand·up** /'stand,əp/) ▸ *adj.* **1** involving, done by, or engaged in by people standing up: *a stand-up party.* ▪ such that people have to stand rather than sit: *a stand-up bar.* ▪ (of a comedian) performing by standing in front of an audience and telling jokes. ▪ (of comedy) performed in such a way: *his stand-up routine depends on improvised observations.* **2** *inf.* courageous and loyal in a combative way: *he was a stand-up kind of guy* **3** designed to stay upright or erect.
▸ *n.* a comedian who performs by standing in front of an audience and telling jokes. ▪ comedy performed in such a way: *he began doing stand-up when he was fifteen.*

stank /staNGk/ ▸ past of STINK.

stan·za /'stanzə/ ▸ *n.* a group of lines forming the basic recurring metrical unit in a poem; a verse. ▪ a group of four lines in some Greek and Latin meters. —**stan·zaed** *adj.* —**stan·za·ic** /stan'zā-ik/ *adj.*

sta·pes /'stāpēz/ ▸ *n.* (*pl.* same) *Anat.* a small stirrup-shaped bone in the middle ear, transmitting vibrations from the incus to the inner ear. Also called STIRRUP.

staph·y·lo·coc·cus /,staf(ə)lō'käkəs/ ▸ *n.* (*pl.* **staphylococci** /-'käk,sī; -,sē/) a bacterium of a genus that includes many pathogenic kinds that cause pus formation, esp. in the skin and mucous membranes. —**staph·y·lo·coc·cal** /-'käkəl/ *adj.*

sta·ple[1] /'stāpəl/ ▸ *n.* a piece of bent metal or wire pushed through something or clipped over it as a fastening, in particular: ▪ a piece of thin wire with a long center portion and two short end pieces that are driven by a stapler through sheets of paper to fasten them together. ▪ a small U-shaped metal bar with pointed ends for driving into wood to hold attachments such as fencing or electric wires of cloth in place.
▸ *v.* [*tr.*] attach or secure with a staple or staples: *Mark stapled a batch of papers together.* —**sta·pler** *n.*

sta·ple[2] ▸ *n.* **1** a main or important element of something, esp. of a diet: *bread, milk, and other staples.* ▪ a main item of trade or production: *rubber became the staple of the Malayan economy.* **2** the fiber of cotton or wool considered with regard to its length and degree of fineness: [in *comb.*] *long-staple Egyptian cotton.*
▸ *adj.* main or important, esp. in terms of consumption: *the staple foods of the poor.* ▪ most important in terms of trade or production: *rice was the staple crop grown in most villages.*

sta·ple gun ▸ *n.* a hand-held mechanical tool for driving staples.

star /stär/ ▸ *n.* **1** a fixed luminous point in the night sky that is a large, remote incandescent body like the sun. **2** a conventional or stylized representation of a star, typically one having five or more points: *the walls were painted with silver moons and stars.* ▪ a symbol of this shape used to indicate a category of excellence: *the hotel has three stars.* ▪ an asterisk. ▪ a white patch on the forehead of a horse or other animal.

▪ (also **star network**) [usu. as *adj.*] a data or communication network in which all nodes are independently connected to one central unit: *computers in a star layout.* **3** a famous or exceptionally talented performer in the world of entertainment or sports: *a pop star.* ▪ an outstandingly good or successful person or thing in a group: *a rising star in the party.* **4** *Astrol.* a planet, constellation, or configuration regarded as influencing someone's fortunes or personality: *his golf destiny was written in the stars.*
▸ *v.* (**starred**, **star·ring**) [*tr.*] **1** (of a movie, play, or other show) have (someone) as a principal performer: *a film starring Liza Minnelli.* ▪ [*intr.*] (of a performer) have a principal role in a movie, play, or other show: *McQueen had starred in such epics as* The Magnificent Seven. ▪ [*intr.*] (of a person) perform brilliantly or prominently in a particular endeavor or event: *Vitt starred at third base for the Detroit Tigers.* **2** decorate or cover with star-shaped marks or objects: *thick grass starred with flowers.* ▪ mark (something) for special notice or recommendation with an asterisk or other star-shaped symbol: *the activities listed below are starred according to their fitness ratings* | [as *adj.*, in *comb.*] (**-starred**) *Michelin-starred restaurants.* ▷Old English *steorra*, of Germanic origin; related to Dutch *ster*, German *Stern*, from an Indo-European root shared by Latin *stella* and Greek *astēr.* —**star·dom** *n.* —**star·less** *adj.* —**star·like** /-,līk/ *adj.*

star·board /'stär,bôrd/ ▸ *n.* the side of a ship or aircraft that is on the right when one is facing forward. The opposite of PORT[3].
▸ *v.* [*tr.*] turn (a ship or its helm) to starboard.

star·burst /'stär,bərst/ ▸ *n.* a pattern of lines or rays radiating from a central object or source of light: [as *adj.*] *a starburst pattern.* ▪ an explosion producing such an effect. ▪ a camera lens attachment that produces a pattern of rays around the image of a source of light. ▪ a period of intense activity in a galaxy involving the formation of stars.

starch /stärCH/ ▸ *n.* an odorless tasteless white substance occurring widely in plant tissue and obtained chiefly from cereals and potatoes. It is a polysaccharide that functions as a carbohydrate reserve and is an important constituent of the human diet. ▪ food containing this substance. ▪ powder or spray made from this substance and used before ironing to stiffen fabric or clothing. ▪ *fig.* stiffness of manner or character: *the starch in her voice.*
▸ *v.* [*tr.*] stiffen (fabric or clothing) with starch: [as *adj.*] (**starched**) *his immaculately starched shirt.* —**starch·er** *n.*

starch·y /'stärCHē/ ▸ *adj.* (**starch·i·er**, **starch·i·est**) **1** (of food or diet) containing a relatively high amount of starch. **2** (of clothing) stiff with starch. ▪ *inf.* very stiff, formal, or prim in manner or character: *the manager is usually a bit starchy.* —**starch·i·ly** /-CHəlē/ *adv.* —**starch·i·ness** *n.*

star-crossed ▸ *adj. poetic/lit.* (of a person or a plan) thwarted by bad luck.

star·dust /'stär,dəst/ ▸ *n.* (esp. in the context of success in the world of entertainment or sports) a magical or charismatic quality or feeling: *a gang of Hollywood stars anointing us with sparkling stardust.*

stare /ste(ə)r/ ▸ *v.* [*intr.*] look fixedly or vacantly at someone or something with one's eyes wide open: *he stared at her in amazement.* ▪ (of a person's eyes) be wide open, with a fixed or vacant expression: *her gray eyes stared back at him.* ▪ [*intr.*] (of a thing) be unpleasantly prominent or striking: *the obituaries stared out at us.*
▸ *phrasal v.* □ **stare someone down** look fixedly at someone until they feel forced to lower their eyes or turn away.
▸ *n.* a long fixed or vacant look: *she gave him a cold stare.* —**star·er** *n.*

star·fish /'stär,fiSH/ ▸ *n.* (*pl.* same or **-fishes**) a marine echinoderm with five or more radiating arms.

star·gaz·er /'stär,gāzər/ ▸ *n.* **1** *inf.* an astronomer or astrologer. ▪ a daydreamer. **2** a fish (families Uranoscopidae and Dactyloscopidae) of warm seas that normally lies buried in the sand with only its eyes, which are on top of the head, protruding. —**star·gaze** *v.*

stark /stärk/ ▸ *adj.* **1** severe or bare in appearance or outline: *the ridge formed a stark silhouette against the sky.* ▪ unpleasantly or sharply clear; impossible to avoid: *his position on civil rights is in stark contrast to that of his liberal opponent.* **2** complete; sheer: *he came running back in stark terror.* ▪ *rare* completely naked. —**stark·ly** *adv. the reality is starkly different.* —**stark·ness** *n.*

star·let /'stärlit/ ▸ *n. inf.* a young actress with aspirations to become a star: *a Hollywood starlet.*

star·light /'stär,līt/ ▸ *n.* the light that comes from the stars.

star·ling /'stärliNG/ ▸ *n.* a gregarious Old World songbird (*Sturnus* and other genera) with a straight bill, typically with dark lustrous or iridescent plumage but sometimes brightly colored. The **starling family** (Sturnidae) also includes the mynahs and grackles.

star·lit /'stär,lit/ ▸ *adj.* lit or made brighter by stars: *a clear starlit night.*

Star of Beth·le·hem ▸*n.* a resplendent star that is said to have guided the Magi to the birthplace of the infant Jesus.

Star of Da·vid ▸*n.* a six-pointed figure consisting of two interlaced equilateral triangles, used as a Jewish and Israeli symbol.

star route ▸*n.* a postal delivery route served by a private contractor.

star·ry /'stärē/ ▸*adj.* (**-ri·er, -ri·est**) full of or lit by stars: *a starry sky.* ■ resembling a star in brightness or shape: *tiny white starry flowers.* —**star·ri·ness** *n.*

star·ry-eyed ▸*adj.* naively enthusiastic or idealistic; failing to recognize the practical realities of a situation.

Star of David

Stars and Bars ▸*pl. n.* [treated as *sing.*] *hist.* the flag of the Confederate States of America. It had a horizontal white stripe between two red stripes, and in the upper left corner was a blue field with a circle of seven white stars, one for each of the original seven seceded states.

Stars and Stripes ▸*pl. n.* [treated as *sing.*] the national flag of the U.S. It has 13 horizontal stripes, alternating red and white, which represent the original Thirteen Colonies. In the upper left corner is a field of blue with 50 white stars, which represent the 50 states.

star shell ▸*n.* an explosive projectile designed to burst in the air and light up an enemy's position.

star-span·gled ▸*adj. poetic/lit. fig.* glitteringly successful: *a star-spangled career.*

star-stud·ded ▸*adj.* **1** (of the night sky) filled with stars. **2** *inf.* featuring a number of famous people, esp. actors or sports players: *a star-studded cast.*

START /stärt/ ▸*abbr.* Strategic Arms Reduction Talks.

start /stärt/ ▸*v.* **1** [*intr.*] come into being; begin or be reckoned from a particular point in time or space: *the season starts in September.* ■ embark on a continuing action or a new venture: *I started to chat to him.* ■ use a particular point, action, or circumstance as an opening for a course of action: *the teacher can start by capitalizing on children's curiosity.* ■ [*intr.*] begin to move or travel: *we started out into the snow.* ■ [*tr.*] begin to attend (an educational establishment) or engage in (an occupation, esp. a profession): *she will start school today.* ■ begin one's working life: *she started off as a general practitioner.* ■ [*tr.*] begin to live through (a period distinguished by a specified characteristic): *they started their married life.* ■ cost at least a specified amount: *fees start at around $300.* **2** [*tr.*] cause (an event or process) to happen: *two men started the blaze that caused the explosion.* ■ bring (a project or an institution) into being; cause to take effect or begin to work or operate: *I'm starting a campaign to get the law changed.* ■ cause (a machine) to begin to work: *we had trouble starting the car.* ■ [*intr.*] (of a machine or device) begin operating or being used: *the noise of a tractor starting up.* ■ cause or enable (someone or something) to begin doing or pursuing something: *his father started him off in business.* ■ give a signal to (competitors) to start in a race. **3** [*intr.*] give a small jump or make a sudden jerking movement from surprise or alarm: *"Oh my!" she said, starting.* ■ (of eyes) bulge so as to appear to burst out of their sockets: *his eyes started out of his head like a hare's.*

▸*phrasal v.* □ **start on** begin to work on or deal with: *I'm starting on a new book.* □ **start out** (or **up**) embark on a venture or undertaking, esp. a commercial one. □ **start over** make a new beginning: *could you face going back to school and starting over?*

▸*n.* **1** the point in time or space at which something has its origin; the beginning of something: *he takes over as chief executive at the start of next year* | *his bicycle was found close to the start of a forest trail.* ■ the point or moment at which a race begins. ■ an act of beginning to do or deal with something: *I can make a start on cleaning up.* ■ used to indicate that a useful initial contribution has been made but that more remains to be done: *if he would tell her who had put him up to it, it would be a start.* ■ a person's position or circumstances at the beginning of their life, esp. a position of advantage: *she's anxious to give her baby the best start in life.* ■ an advantage consisting in having set out in a race or on journey earlier than one's rivals or opponents: *he would have a ninety-minute start on them.* **2** a sudden movement of surprise or alarm: *she awoke with a start* | *the woman gave a nervous start.*

start·er /'stärtər/ ▸*n.* a person or thing that starts an event, activity, or process, in particular: ■ an automatic device for starting a machine, esp. the engine of a vehicle. ■ a person who gives the signal for the start of a race. ■ a horse, competitor, or player taking part in a race or game at the start: *the trainer has confirmed Cool Ground as a definite starter.* ■ *Baseball* the pitcher who starts the game. ■ *Baseball* a pitcher who

normally starts games, and seldom is used as a relief pitcher. ■ a person or thing that starts in a specified way, esp. with reference to time or speed: *he was a late starter in photography.* ■ a topic, question, or other item with which to start a group discussion or course of study: *material to act as a starter for discussion.* ■ (also **starter culture**) a bacterial culture used to initiate souring in making yogurt, cheese, or butter.

start·ing block ▸*n.* (usu. **starting blocks**) a shaped rigid block for bracing the feet of a runner at the start of a race.

start·ing gate ▸*n.* (usu. **the starting gate**) a restraining structure incorporating a barrier that is raised at the start of a race, typically in horse racing and skiing, to ensure a simultaneous start.

star·tle /'stärtl/ ▸*v.* [*tr.*] cause (a person or animal) to feel sudden shock or alarm: *a sudden sound in the doorway startled her.* —**star·tler** *n.*

star·tling /'stärtl-iNG/ ▸*adj.* very surprising, astonishing, or remarkable: *he bore a startling likeness to their father.* —**star·tling·ly** *adv. a startlingly good memory.*

starve /stärv/ ▸*v.* [*intr.*] (of a person or animal) suffer severely or die from hunger: *she left her animals to starve.* ■ [*tr.*] cause (a person or animal) to suffer severely or die from hunger: *for a while she had considered starving herself.* ■ (**be starving** or **starved**) *inf.* feel very hungry: *I don't know about you, but I'm starving.* ■ (**starve someone out** or **into**) force someone out of a place or into a specified state by stopping supplies of food: *the Royalists were starved out after eleven days.* ■ [*tr.*] (usu. **be starved of** or **for**) deprive of something necessary: *the arts are being starved of funds.* —**star·va·tion** /-'vāSHən/ *n.*

Star Wars ▸ an informal name for the Strategic Defense Initiative.

stash¹ /staSH/ *inf.* ▸*v.* [*tr.*] store (something) safely and secretly in a specified place: *their wealth had been stashed away in Swiss banks.*

▸*n.* a secret store of something: *the man grudgingly handed over a stash of notes.* ■ a quantity of an illegal drug, esp. one kept for personal use: *one prisoner tried to swallow his stash.*

stash² ▸*n. inf.* a mustache.

sta·sis /'stāsis/ ▸*n. formal* or *technical* a period or state of inactivity or equilibrium. ■ *Med.* a stoppage of flow of a body fluid.

stat¹ /stat/ *inf.* ▸*abbr.* ■ photostat. ■ statistic. ■ statistics: [as *adj.*] *a stat sheet.* ■ thermostat.

stat² ▸*adv.* (in a medical direction or prescription) immediately.

state /stāt/ ▸*n.* **1** the particular condition that someone or something is in at a specific time: *the state of the company's finances.* ■ a physical condition as regards internal or molecular form or structure: *water in a liquid state.* ■ (**a state**) *inf.* an agitated or anxious condition: *don't get into a state.* ■ *inf.* a dirty or untidy condition: *look at the state of you—what a mess!* **2** a nation or territory considered as an organized political community under one government: *the state of Israel.* ■ an organized political community or area forming part of a federal republic: *the German state of Bavaria.* **3** the civil government of a country: *services provided by the state* | *state-owned companies.* **4** pomp and ceremony associated with monarchy or high levels of government: *he was buried in state.* **5** an impression taken from an etched or engraved plate at a particular stage. ■ a particular printed version of the first edition of a book, distinguished from others by prepublication changes.

▸*adj.* **1** of, provided by, or concerned with the civil government of a country: *a state secret.* **2** used or done on ceremonial occasions; involving the ceremony associated with a head of state: *a state visit to Hungary by Queen Elizabeth.*

▸*v.* express something definitely or clearly in speech or writing: *the report stated that more than 51 percent of voters failed to participate.* ■ [*tr.*] *chiefly Law* specify the facts of (a case) for consideration: *judges must give both sides an equal opportunity to state their case.* —**stat·a·ble** *adj.*

▸ □ **state of affairs** (or **things**) a situation or set of circumstances: *the survey revealed a sorry state of affairs in schools.* ■ **state of the art** the most recent stage in the development of a product, incorporating the newest ideas and the most up-to-date features. ■ [as *adj.*] incorporating the newest ideas and the most up-to-date features: *a new state-of-the-art hospital.* □ **state of emergency** a situation of national danger or disaster in which a government suspends normal constitutional procedures in order to regain control: *the government has declared a state of emergency.* □ **state of grace** a condition of being free from sin. □ **state of war** a situation when war has been declared or is in progress.

state·craft /'stāt,kraft/ ▸*n.* the skillful management of state affairs; statesmanship: *issues of statecraft require great deliberation.*

State De·part·ment ▶the department in the U.S. government dealing with foreign affairs.

state·hood /ˈstātˌho͝od/ ▶n. the status of being a recognized independent nation: *the Jewish struggle for statehood.* ■ the status of being a state of the U.S.: *a proposed referendum on statehood for Puerto Rico.*

state house (also **state·house**) ▶n. the building where a state legislature meets.

state·less /ˈstātlis/ ▶adj. (of a person) not recognized as a citizen of any country. —**state·less·ness** /ˈstātləsnəs/ n.

state·ly /ˈstātlē/ ▶adj. (**-li·er**, **-li·est**) having a dignified, unhurried, and grand manner; majestic in manner and appearance: *a stately procession.* —**state·li·ness** n.

state·ment /ˈstātmənt/ ▶n. a definite or clear expression of something in speech or writing: *do you agree with this statement?* ■ an official account of facts, views, or plans, esp. one for release to the media: *the officials issued a joint statement calling for negotiations.* ■ a formal account of events given by a witness, defendant, or other party to the police or in a court of law: *she made a statement to the police.* ■ a document setting out items of debit and credit between a bank or other organization and a customer. ■ the expression of an idea or opinion through something other than words: *their humorous kitschiness makes a statement of serious wealth.* ■ Mus. the occurrence of a musical idea or motive within a composition.

state·room /ˈstātˌro͞om; -ˌro͝om/ ▶n. a private compartment on a ship. ■ a captain's or superior officer's room on a ship. ■ a private compartment on a train.

state's ev·i·dence ▶n. Law evidence for the prosecution given by a participant in or accomplice to the crime being tried.
▶ □ **turn state's evidence** give such evidence: *persuading one-time gang members to turn state's evidence.*

state·side /ˈstātˌsīd/ ▶adj. & adv. inf. of, in, or toward the U.S. (used in reference to the U.S. from elsewhere or from the geographically separate states of Alaska and Hawaii): [as adj.] *stateside police departments* | [as adv.] *they were headed stateside.*

states·man /ˈstātsmən/ ▶n. (pl. **-men**) a skilled, experienced, and respected political leader or figure. —**states·man·like** /-ˌlīk/ adj. —**states·man·ship** /-ˌSHip/ n.

state so·cial·ism ▶n. a political system in which the state has control of industries and services.

states' rights ▶pl. n. the rights and powers held by individual U.S. states rather than by the federal government.

state u·ni·ver·si·ty ▶n. a university managed by the public authorities of a particular U.S. state.

stat·ic /ˈstatik/ ▶adj. **1** lacking in movement, action, or change, esp. in a way viewed as undesirable or uninteresting: *demand has grown in what was a fairly static market.* ■ Comput. (of a process or variable) not able to be changed during a set period, for example, while a program is running. **2** Physics concerned with bodies at rest or forces in equilibrium. ■ (of an electric charge) having gathered on or in an object that cannot conduct a current. ■ acting as weight but not moving. **3** Comput. (of a memory or store) not needing to be periodically refreshed by an applied voltage.
▶n. crackling or hissing noises on a telephone, radio, or other telecommunications system. ■ short for STATIC ELECTRICITY. ■ inf. angry or critical talk or behavior: *the reception was going sour, breaking up into static.* —**stat·i·cal·ly** /-ik(ə)lē/ adv. —**stat·ick·y** /-ikē/ adj.

stat·ice /ˈstatisē; ˈstatis/ ▶n. another term for SEA LAVENDER, esp. when cultivated as a garden plant.

stat·ic e·lec·tric·i·ty ▶n. a stationary electric charge, typically produced by friction, that causes sparks or crackling or the attraction of dust or hair.

stat·ics /ˈstatiks/ ▶pl. n. [usu. treated as sing.] the branch of mechanics concerned with bodies at rest and forces in equilibrium.

sta·tion /ˈstāSHən/ ▶n. **1** a regular stopping place on a public transportation route, esp. one on a railroad line with a platform and often one or more buildings. **2** a place or building where a specified activity or service is based: *coastal radar stations.* ■ a small military base, esp. of a specified kind: *a naval station.* ■ a police station. ■ a subsidiary post office. ■ Austral./NZ a large sheep or cattle farm. **3** a company involved in broadcasting of a specified kind: *a radio station.* **4** the place where someone or something stands or is placed on military or other duty: *the lookout resumed his station in the bow.* ■ dated one's social rank or position: *Karen was getting ideas above her station.*
▶v. [tr.] put in or assign to a specified place for a particular purpose, esp. a military one: *troops were stationed in the town.*

sta·tion·ar·y /ˈstāSHəˌnerē/ ▶adj. not moving or not intended to be moved: *a car collided with a stationary vehicle.* ■ not changing in quantity or condition: *a stationary population.*

sta·tion break ▶n. a pause between broadcast programs for an announcement of the identity of the station transmitting them, typically also containing commercials.

sta·tion·er /ˈstāSH(ə)nər/ ▶n. a person or store selling paper, pens, and other writing and office materials.

sta·tion·er·y /ˈstāSHəˌnerē/ ▶n. writing paper, esp. with matching envelopes. ■ writing and other office materials.

Sta·tion of the Cross ▶n. (usu. **Stations of the Cross**) one of a series of images representing Jesus' progress from Pilate's house to his crucifixion at Calvary, before which devotions are performed in some churches.

sta·tion wag·on ▶n. a car with a longer body than usual, incorporating a large carrying area behind the seats and having an extra door at the rear for easy loading.

stat·ism /ˈstātˌizəm/ ▶n. a political system in which the state has substantial centralized control over social and economic affairs: *the rise of authoritarian statism.* —**stat·ist** n. & adj.

sta·tis·tic /stəˈtistik/ ▶n. a fact or piece of data from a study of a large quantity of numerical data: *the statistics show that the crime rate has increased.* ■ an event or person regarded as no more than such a piece of data (used to suggest an inappropriately impersonal approach): *he was just another statistic.*
▶adj. another term for STATISTICAL. —**stat·is·ti·cian** /ˌstatisˈtiSHən/ n.

sta·tis·ti·cal /stəˈtistikəl/ ▶adj. of or relating to the use of statistics: *a statistical comparison.* —**sta·tis·ti·cal·ly** /-ik(ə)lē/ adv. *these differences were not statistically significant.*

sta·tis·ti·cal sig·nif·i·cance ▶n. see SIGNIFICANCE.

sta·tis·tics /stəˈtistiks/ ▶pl. n. [treated as sing.] the practice or science of collecting and analyzing numerical data in large quantities, esp. for the purpose of inferring proportions in a whole from those in a representative sample.

stat·u·ar·y /ˈstaCHo͞oˌerē/ ▶n. sculpture consisting of statues; statues regarded collectively: *fragments of broken statuary.* ■ archaic the art or practice of making statues.

stat·ue /ˈstaCHo͞o/ ▶n. a carved or cast figure of a person or animal, esp. one that is life-size or larger. —**stat·ued** adj.

stat·u·esque /ˌstaCHo͞oˈesk/ ▶adj. (esp. of a woman) attractively tall and dignified: *her statuesque beauty.* —**stat·u·esque·ly** adv. —**stat·u·esque·ness** n.

stat·u·ette /ˌstaCHo͞oˈet/ ▶n. a small statue or figurine, esp. one that is smaller than life-size.

stat·ure /ˈstaCHər/ ▶n. a person's natural height: *a man of short stature.* ■ importance or reputation gained by ability or achievement: *an architect of international stature.* —**stat·ured** adj. [in comb.] *a short-statured fourteen-year-old.*

sta·tus /ˈstātəs; ˈstatəs/ ▶n. **1** the relative social, professional, or other standing of someone or something: *an improvement in the status of women.* ■ high rank or social standing: *those who enjoy wealth and status.* ■ the official classification given to a person, country, or organization, determining their rights or responsibilities: *the duchy had been elevated to the status of a principality.* **2** the position of affairs at a particular time, esp. in political or commercial contexts: *an update on the status of the bill.*

sta·tus quo /ˈstātəs ˈkwō; ˈstatəs/ ▶n. (usu. **the status quo**) the existing state of affairs, esp. regarding social or political issues: *they have a vested interest in maintaining the status quo.*

stat·ute /ˈstaCHo͞ot/ ▶n. a written law passed by a legislative body: *violation of the hate crimes statute.* ■ a rule of an organization or institution: *the appointment will be subject to the statutes of the university.*

stat·ute mile ▶n. see MILE.

stat·ute of lim·i·ta·tions ▶n. Law a statute prescribing a period of limitation for the bringing of certain kinds of legal action.

stat·u·to·ry /ˈstaCHəˌtôrē/ ▶adj. required, permitted, or enacted by statute: *the courts did award statutory damages to each of the plaintiffs.* ■ of or relating to statutes: *constitutional and statutory interpretation.* —**stat·u·to·ri·ly** /-ˌtôrəlē/ adv.

stat·u·to·ry rape ▶n. Law sexual intercourse with a minor.

staunch[1] /stônCH; stänCH/ ▶adj. **1** loyal and committed in attitude: *a staunch supporter of the antinuclear lobby.* **2** (of a wall) of strong or firm construction. —**staunch·ly** adv. —**staunch·ness** n.

staunch[2] ▶v. variant spelling of STANCH[1].

stave /stāv/ ▶n. **1** any of the lengths of wood attached side by side to

make a barrel, bucket, or other container. **2** *Mus.* another term for STAFF[1] (sense 4). **3** a verse or stanza of a poem.
▶*v.* [*tr.*] **1** (*past* and *past part.* **staved** or **stove** /stōv/) (**stave something in**) break something by forcing it inward or piercing it roughly: *the door was staved in.* **2** (*past* and *past part.* **staved**) (**stave something off**) avert or delay something bad or dangerous: *a reassuring presence can stave off a panic attack.*

staves /stāvz/ ▶ plural of STAFF *n.* sense 4.

stay[1] /stā/ ▶*v.* **1** [*intr.*] remain in the same place: *he stayed with the firm as a consultant.* ▪ (**stay down**) (of food) remain in the stomach, rather than be thrown up as vomit. ▪ (**stay with**) remain in the mind or memory of (someone): *Gary's words stayed with her all evening.* **2** [*intr.*] remain in a specified state or position: *her ability to stay calm.* ▪ (**stay with**) continue or persevere with (an activity or task): *the incentive needed to stay with a healthy diet.* ▪ (**stay with**) (of a competitor or player) keep up with (another) during a race or match. **3** [*intr.*] (of a person) live somewhere temporarily as a visitor or guest: *the girls had gone to stay with friends.* **4** [*tr.*] stop, delay, or prevent (something), in particular suspend or postpone (judicial proceedings) or refrain from pressing (charges). ▪ assuage (hunger) for a short time: *I grabbed something to stay the pangs of hunger.* ▪ *poetic/lit.* curb; check: *he tries to stay the destructive course of barbarism.*
▶*phrasal v.* □ **stay over** (of a guest or visitor) sleep somewhere, esp. at someone's home, for the night. □ **stay up** not go to bed: *they stayed up all night.*
▶*n.* **1** a period of staying somewhere, in particular of living somewhere temporarily as a visitor or guest: *an overnight stay at a luxury hotel.* **2** *poetic/lit.* a curb or check: *there is likely to be a good public library as a stay against boredom.* ▪ *Law* a suspension or postponement of judicial proceedings: *a stay of prosecution.* **3** a device used as a brace or support.
—**stay·er** *n.*
▶ □ **stay the course** (or **distance**) keep going strongly to the end of a race or contest. ▪ pursue a difficult task or activity to the end. □ **stay put** (of a person or object) remain somewhere without moving or being moved.

stay[2] ▶*n.* a rope, wire, or rod used to support a ship's mast, leading from the masthead to another mast or spar or down to the deck.

St. Ber·nard /bər'närd/ (also **St. Bernard dog**) ▶*n.* a large dog of a breed originally kept to rescue travelers by the monks of the Hospice on the Great St. Bernard Pass in the Swiss Alps.

STD ▶*abbr.* ▪ Doctor of Sacred Theology. ▪ sexually transmitted disease.

std. ▶*abbr.* standard.

stead /sted/ ▶*n.* the place or role that someone or something should have or fill (used in referring to a substitute): *you wish to have him superseded and to be appointed in his stead.*
▶ □ **stand someone in good stead** be advantageous or useful to someone over time or in the future: *his early training stood him in good stead.*

stead·fast /'sted,fast/ ▶*adj.* resolutely or dutifully firm and unwavering: *steadfast loyalty.* —**stead·fast·ly** *adv.* —**stead·fast·ness** *n.*

stead·y /'stedē/ ▶*adj.* (**stead·i·er, stead·i·est**) **1** firmly fixed, supported, or balanced; not shaking or moving: *the lighter the camera, the harder it is to hold steady.* ▪ not faltering or wavering; controlled: *a steady gaze.* ▪ (of a person) sensible, reliable, and self-restrained: *a solid, steady young man.* ▪ (of a ship) following a straight course: *steady as she goes.* **2** regular, even, and continuous in development, frequency, or intensity: *a steady decline in the national birth rate.* ▪ not changing; regular and established: *I thought I'd better get a steady job.*
▶*v.* (**stead·ies, stead·ied**) make or become steady: [*tr.*] *I took a deep breath to steady my nerves* [as *adj.*] (**steadying**) *she's the one steadying influence in his life* | [*intr.*] *by the beginning of May prices had steadied.*
▶*n.* (*pl.* **stead·ies**) a person's regular boyfriend or girlfriend: *his steady chucked him two weeks ago.* —**stead·i·er** *n.* —**stead·i·ly** /'stedəlē/ *adv.* —**stead·i·ness** *n.*
▶ □ **go steady** *inf.* have a regular romantic or sexual relationship with a particular person.

steak /stāk/ ▶*n.* high-quality beef taken from the hindquarters of the animal, typically cut into thick slices that are cooked by broiling or frying: *he liked his steak rare.* ▪ a thick slice of such beef or other high-quality meat or fish: *a salmon steak.* ▪ poorer-quality beef that is cubed or ground and cooked more slowly by braising or stewing. ▷Middle English: from Old Norse *steik*; related to *steikja* 'roast on a spit' and *stikna* 'be roasted.'

steak·house /'stāk,hous/ ▶*n.* a restaurant that specializes in serving steaks.

steal /stēl/ ▶*v.* (*past* **stole** /stōl/; *past part.* **sto·len** /'stōlən/) **1** [*tr.*] take (another person's property) without permission or legal right and without intending to return it: *thieves stole her bicycle* | [*intr.*] *she was found guilty of stealing from her employers.* ▪ dishonestly pass off (another person's ideas) as one's own: *accusations that one group had stolen ideas from the other were soon flying.* ▪ take the opportunity to give or share (a kiss) when it is not expected or when people are not watching: *he was allowed to steal a kiss in the darkness.* ▪ (in various sports) gain (an advantage, a run, or possession of the ball) unexpectedly or by exploiting the temporary distraction of an opponent. ▪ *Baseball* (of a base runner) advance safely to (the next base) by running to it as the pitcher begins the delivery: *Rickey stole third base.* ▪ attract the most notice in (a scene or a theatrical production) while not being the featured performer: *why not be a big ham, and steal as many scenes as possible.* **2** [*intr.*] move somewhere quietly or surreptitiously: *he stole down to the kitchen.* ▪ [*tr.*] direct (a look) quickly and unobtrusively: *he stole a furtive glance at her.*
▶*n.* **1** *inf.* a bargain: *for $5 it was a steal.* **2** an act of stealing something: *New York's biggest art steal.* ▪ an idea taken from another work. ▪ *Baseball* an act of stealing a base. —**steal·er** *n.* [in *comb.*] *a sheep-stealer.*

stealth /stelTH/ ▶*n.* cautious and surreptitious action or movement: *the silence and stealth of a hungry cat.*
▶*adj.* (chiefly of aircraft) designed in accordance with technology that makes detection by radar or sonar difficult: *a stealth bomber.* ▪ secretive; trying to avoid notice: *she has been ducking the press as befits a stealth candidate.*

stealth·y /'stelTHē/ ▶*adj.* (**stealth·i·er, stealth·i·est**) behaving, done, or made in a cautious and surreptitious manner, so as not to be seen or heard: *stealthy footsteps.* —**stealth·i·ly** /-THəlē/ *adv.* —**stealth·i·ness** *n.*

steam /stēm/ ▶*n.* the vapor into which water is converted when heated, forming a white mist of minute water droplets in the air. ▪ the invisible gaseous form of water, formed by boiling, from which this vapor condenses. ▪ the expansive force of this vapor used as a source of power for machines: *the equipment was originally powered by steam.* ▪ locomotives and railroad systems powered in this way: *the last years of steam.* ▪ *fig.* energy and momentum or impetus: *the anticorruption drive gathered steam.*
▶*v.* **1** [*intr.*] give off or produce steam: *a mug of coffee was steaming at her elbow.* ▪ (**steam up** or **steam something up**) become or cause to become covered or misted over with steam: [*intr.*] *the glass keeps steaming up* | [*tr.*] *the warm air had begun to steam up the windows.* ▪ (often **be/get steamed up**) *inf.* be or become extremely agitated or angry: *you got all steamed up over nothing!* **2** [*tr.*] cook (food) by heating it in steam from boiling water: *steam the vegetables until just tender.* ▪ [*intr.*] (of food) cook in this way: *add the mussels and leave them to steam.* ▪ clean or otherwise treat with steam: *he steamed his shirts in the bathroom to remove the wrinkles.* ▪ apply steam to (something fixed with adhesive) so as to open or loosen it: *he'd steamed the letter open and then resealed it.* ▪ operate (a steam locomotive). **3** [*intr.*] (of a ship or train) travel somewhere under steam power: *the 11:54 steamed into the station.* ▪ *inf.* come, go, or move somewhere rapidly or in a forceful way: *Jerry steamed in ten minutes late.*
▶ □ **pick up** (or **get up**) **steam** (of a project in its early stages) gradually gain more impetus and driving force: *his campaign steadily picked up steam.* □ **let** (or **blow**) **off steam** *inf.* (of a person) get rid of pent-up energy or strong emotion. □ **run out of** (or **lose**) **steam** *inf.* lose impetus or enthusiasm: *a rebellion that had run out of steam.*

steam age ▶*n.* the time when trains were drawn by steam locomotives.

steam·boat /'stēm,bōt/ ▶*n.* a boat that is propelled by a steam engine, esp. a paddle-wheel craft of a type used widely on rivers in the 19th century.

steam en·gine ▶*n.* an engine that uses the expansion or rapid condensation of steam to generate power. ▪ a steam locomotive.

steam·er /'stēmər/ ▶*n.* **1** a ship or boat powered by steam. ▪ *inf.* a steam locomotive. **2** a type of saucepan in which food can be steamed. ▪ a device used to direct a jet of hot steam onto a garment in order to remove creases. **3** (in full **steam·er clam**) another term for SOFT-SHELL CLAM.

steam·roll·er /'stēm,rōlər/ ▶*n.* a heavy, slow-moving vehicle with a roller, formerly powered by steam, used to flatten the surfaces of roads during construction. ▪ *fig.* an oppressive and relentless power or force: *victims of an ideological steamroller.*
▶*v.* (also **steam·roll**) [*tr.*] (of a government or other authority) forcibly pass (a measure) by restricting debate or otherwise overriding opposition: *they would have to work together to steamroller the necessary bills past the smaller parties.* ▪ force (someone) into doing or accepting something: *an*

attempt to **steamroller** *the country* **into** *political reforms.* ■ [*intr.*] proceed forcefully and seemingly invincibly: *they steamrolled through the playoffs undefeated.*

steam·ship /'stēm,SHip/ ▶ *n.* a ship that is propelled by a steam engine.

steam·y /'stēmē/ ▶ *adj.* (**steam·i·er**, **steam·i·est**) producing, filled with, or clouded with steam: *a small steamy kitchen.* ■ (of a place or its atmosphere) hot and humid: *the hot, steamy jungle.* ■ *inf.* depicting or involving erotic sexual activity: *steamy sex scenes* | *a steamy affair.* —**steam·i·ly** /-məlē/ *adv.* —**steam·i·ness** /-ēnis/ *n.*

ste·ar·ic ac·id /stē'ärik; 'stir-/ ▶ *n. Chem.* a solid saturated fatty acid obtained from animal or vegetable fats. —**ste·a·rate** /'stē(ə),rāt/ *n.*

ste·a·rin /'stēərin; 'stī(ə)rin/ ▶ *n.* a white crystalline substance that is the main constituent of tallow and suet.

ste·a·tite /'stēə,tīt/ ▶ *n.* the mineral talc occurring in consolidated form, esp. as soapstone. —**ste·a·tit·ic** /,stēə'titik/ *adj.*

steed /stēd/ ▶ *n. archaic* or *poetic/lit.* a horse being ridden or available for riding.

steel /stēl/ ▶ *n.* a hard, strong, gray or bluish-gray alloy of iron with carbon and usually other elements, used extensively as a structural and fabricating material. ■ used as a symbol or embodiment of strength and firmness: *nerves of steel.* ■ a rod of roughened steel on which knives are sharpened.
▶ *v.* [*tr.*] mentally prepare (oneself) to do or face something difficult: *I speak quickly,* **steeling myself for** *a mean reply.*

steel band ▶ *n.* a band that plays music on steel drums.

steel drum ▶ *n.* a percussion instrument originating in Trinidad, made out of an oil drum with one end beaten down and divided by grooves into sections to give different notes. Also called **PAN**[1] (esp. by players).

steel·head /'stēl,hed/ (also **steelhead trout**) ▶ *n.* a rainbow trout of a large migratory variety.

steel wool ▶ *n.* fine strands of steel matted together into a mass, used as an abrasive.

steel·works /'stēl,wərks/ ▶ *pl. n.* [usu. treated as *sing.*] an industrial plant where steel is manufactured. —**steel·work·er** /-,wərkər/ *n.*

steel·y /'stēlē/ ▶ *adj.* (**steel·i·er**, **steel·i·est**) resembling steel in color, brightness, or strength: *a steely blue.* ■ *fig.* coldly determined; hard: *there was a steely edge to his questions.* —**steel·i·ness** *n.*

steel·yard /'stēl,yärd/ ▶ *n.* an apparatus for weighing that has a short arm taking the item to be weighed and a long graduated arm along which a weight is moved until it balances.

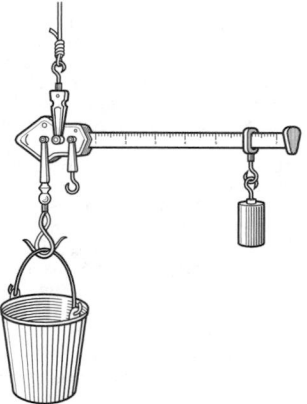

steep[1] /stēp/ ▶ *adj.* **1** (of a slope, flight of stairs, angle, ascent, etc.) rising or falling sharply; nearly perpendicular: *she pushed the bike up the steep hill.* ■ (of a rise or fall in an amount) large or rapid: *the steep rise in unemployment.* **2** *inf.* (of a price or demand) not reasonable; excessive: *a steep membership fee.* —**steep·en** *v.* —**steep·ish** *adj.* —**steep·ly** *adv.* —**steep·ness** *n.*

steep[2] ▶ *v.* [*tr.*] soak (food or tea) in water or other liquid so as to extract its flavor or to soften it: *the chilies are steeped in olive oil* | [*intr.*]

steelyard

the noodles should be left to steep for 3–4 minutes. ■ soak or saturate (cloth) in water or other liquid. ■ (usu. **be steeped in**) *fig.* surround or fill with a quality or influence: *a city steeped in history.*

stee·ple /'stēpəl/ ▶ *n.* a church tower and spire. ■ a spire on the top of a church tower or roof. —**stee·pled** *adj.*

stee·ple·chase /'stēpəl,CHās/ ▶ *n.* a horse race run on a racecourse having ditches and hedges as jumps. ■ a running race in which runners must clear hurdles and water jumps. —**stee·ple·chas·er** *n.* —**stee·ple·chas·ing** *n.*

stee·ple·jack /'stēpəl,jak/ ▶ *n.* a person who climbs tall structures such as chimneys and steeples in order to carry out repairs.

steer[1] /sti(ə)r/ ▶ *v.* [*tr.*] (of a person) guide or control the movement of (a vehicle, vessel, or aircraft), for example by turning a wheel or operating a rudder: *he steered the boat slowly toward the busy quay* | [*intr.*] *he let Lily steer.* ■ [*intr.*] (of a vehicle, vessel, or aircraft) be guided in a specified direction in such a way: *the ship* **steered into** *port.* ■ [*tr.*] follow (a course) in

a specified direction: *the fishermen were steering a direct course for Kodiak.* ■ [*tr.*] guide the movement or course of (someone or something): *he had steered her to a chair.*
▶ *n. inf.* a piece of advice or information concerning the development of a situation: *the need for the school to be given a clear steer as to its future direction.* —**steer·a·ble** /'sti(ə)rəbəl/ *adj.* —**steer·er** *n.* —**steer·ing** *adj.*

steer[2] ▶ *n.* a male domestic bovine animal that has been castrated and is raised for beef.

steer·age /'sti(ə)rij/ ▶ *n. hist.* the part of a ship providing accommodations for passengers with the cheapest tickets: *poor emigrants in steerage.*

steer·ing com·mit·tee ▶ *n.* a committee that decides on the priorities or order of business of an organization and manages the general course of its operations.

steer·ing wheel ▶ *n.* a wheel that a driver rotates in order to steer a vehicle.

steers·man /'sti(ə)rzmən/ ▶ *n.* (*pl.* **-men**) a person who is steering a boat or ship.

steg·o·saur /'stegə,sôr/ (also **steg·o·sau·rus** /,stegə'sôrəs/) ▶ *n.* a small-headed quadrupedal herbivorous dinosaur (*Stegosaurus* and other genera) of the Jurassic and early Cretaceous periods, with a double row of large bony plates or spines along the back. ▷modern Latin, from Greek *stegē* 'covering' + *sauros* 'lizard.'

stein /stīn/ ▶ *n.* a large earthenware beer mug.

ste·la /'stēlə/ ▶ *n.* (*pl.* **-lae** /-,lē/) *Archaeol.* an upright stone slab or column typically bearing a commemorative inscription or relief design, often serving as a gravestone.

stel·lar /'stelər/ ▶ *adj.* of or relating to a star or stars: *stellar structure and evolution.* ■ *inf.* featuring or having the quality of a star performer or performers: *a stellar cast had been assembled* | *Susanna gave another stellar performance between the goalposts.* ■ *inf.* exceptionally good; outstanding: *his restaurant has received stellar ratings in the guides.* —**stel·li·form** /'stelə,fôrm/ *adj.*

stel·late /'stelit; -,āt/ ▶ *adj. technical* arranged in a radiating pattern like that of a star. —**stel·lat·ed** *adj.*

St. El·mo's fire /'elmōz/ ▶ *n.* a phenomenon in which a luminous electrical discharge appears on a ship or aircraft during a storm.

stem[1] /stem/ ▶ *n.* **1** the main body or stalk of a plant or shrub, typically rising above ground but occasionally subterranean. ■ the stalk supporting a fruit, flower, or leaf, and attaching it to a larger branch, twig, or stalk. **2** a long and thin supportive or main section of something: *the main stem of the wing feathers.* ■ the slender part of a wineglass between the base and the bowl. ■ the tube of a tobacco pipe. ■ a rod or cylinder in a mechanism, e.g., the winding pin of a watch. ■ a vertical stroke in a letter or musical note. **3** *Gram.* the root or main part of a noun, adjective, or other word, to which inflections or formative elements are added. **4** the main upright structural piece at the bow of a ship, to which the ship's sides are joined. **5** *inf.* a pipe used for smoking crack or opium.
▶ *v.* (**stemmed**, **stem·ming**) **1** [*intr.*] (**stem from**) originate in or be caused by: *many of the universities' problems stem from rapid expansion.* **2** [*tr.*] remove the stems from (fruit or tobacco leaves). **3** [*tr.*] (of a boat) make headway against (the tide or current). —**stemmed** *adj.* —**stem·less** *adj.* —**stem·like** /-,līk/ *adj.*
▶ □ **from stem to stern** ■ along the entire length of something; throughout: *the album is a joy from stem to stern.*

stem[2] ▶ *v.* (**stemmed**, **stem·ming**) **1** [*tr.*] stop or restrict (the flow of something): *a nurse did her best to stem the bleeding.* **2** [*intr.*] *Skiing* slide the tail of one ski or both skis outward in order to turn or slow down.

stem cell ▶ *n. Biol.* an undifferentiated cell of a multicellular organism that is capable of giving rise to indefinitely more cells of the same type, and from which certain other kinds of cell arise by differentiation.

stem·ware /'stem,we(ə)r/ ▶ *n.* goblets and stemmed glasses regarded collectively.

stench /stenCH/ ▶ *n.* a strong and very unpleasant smell: *the stench of rotting fish.*

sten·cil /'stensəl/ ▶ *n.* a thin sheet of cardboard, plastic, or metal with a pattern or letters cut out of it, used to produce the cut design on the surface below by the application of ink or paint through the holes. ■ a design produced by such a sheet: *a floral stencil around the top of the room.*
▶ *v.* (**-ciled**, **-cil·ing**; *Brit.* **-cilled**, **-cil·ling**) [*tr.*] decorate (a surface) with such a design: *the walls had been* **stenciled with** *designs* | [as *n.*] (**stenciling**) *the art of stenciling.* ■ produce (a design) with a stencil: *stencil a border around the door* | [as *adj.*] (**stenciled**) *the stenciled letters.*

sten·o /'stenō/ ▸ *n.* (*pl.* **-os**) *inf.* a stenographer: *it was written by the steno herself.*

ste·nog·ra·phy /stə'nägrəfē/ ▸ *n.* the action or process of writing in shorthand or taking dictation. —**ste·nog·ra·pher** /-fər/ *n.* —**sten·o·graph·ic** /ˌstenə'grafik/ *adj.*

ste·no·sis /stə'nōsis/ ▸ *n.* (*pl.* **-ses** /-ˌsēz/) *Med.* the abnormal narrowing of a passage in the body. —**ste·nosed** /stə'nōst; -'nōzd/ *adj.* —**ste·nos·ing** /-'nōsiNG; -'nōz-/ *adj.* —**ste·not·ic** /stə'nätik/ *adj.*

sten·o·type /'stenəˌtīp/ ▸ *n.* a machine resembling a typewriter that is used for recording speech in syllables or phonemes. —**sten·o·typ·ist** /-ˌtīpist/ *n.* —**sten·o·typ·y** /-ˌtīpē/ *n.*

step /step/ ▸ *n.* **1** an act or movement of putting one leg in front of the other in walking or running: *Ron took a step back.* ■ the distance covered by such a movement: *Richard came a couple of steps nearer.* ■ a person's particular way of walking: *she left the room with a springy step.* ■ one of the sequences of movement of the feet that make up a dance. ■ a short or easily walked distance: *the market is only a short step from the end of the lake.* **2** a flat surface, esp. one in a series, on which to place one's foot when moving from one level to another: *the bottom step of the staircase.* ■ a doorstep: *there was a pint of milk on the step.* ■ a rung of a ladder. ■ *Climbing* a foothold cut in a slope of ice. ■ a block, typically fixed to the vessel's keel, on which the base of a mast is seated. ■ *Physics* an abrupt change in the value of a quantity, esp. voltage. **3** a measure or action, esp. one of a series taken in order to deal with or achieve a particular thing: *the government must take steps to discourage age discrimination.* ■ a stage in a gradual process: *sales are up, which is a step in the right direction.* ■ a particular position or grade on an ascending or hierarchical scale: *the first step on the managerial ladder.* **4** *Mus.* an interval in a scale; a tone (whole step) or semitone (half step). **5** step aerobics: [as *adj.*] *a step class.*

▸ *v.* (**stepped, step·ping**) [*intr.*] lift and set down one's foot or one foot after the other in order to walk somewhere or move to a new position: *I accidentally stepped on his foot.* ■ [as *imper.*] used as a polite or deferential way of asking someone to walk a short distance for a particular purpose: *please step this way.*

▸ *phrasal v.* □ **step back** mentally withdraw from a situation in order to consider it objectively. □ **step down** withdraw or resign from an important position or office: *Mr. Krenz stepped down as party leader a week ago.* □ **step in** become involved in a difficult or problematic situation, esp. in order to help or prevent something from happening. ■ act as a substitute for someone: *Lucy stepped in at very short notice to take Joan's place.* □ **step something up** increase the amount, speed, or intensity of something: *police decided to step up security plans for the game.* —**step·like** /-ˌlīk/ *adj.* —**stepped** *adj.*

▸ □ **in** (or **out of**) **step** conforming (or not conforming) to what others are doing or thinking: *the party is clearly out of step with voters.* ■ *Physics* (of two or more oscillations or other cyclic phenomena) having (or not having) the same frequency and always in the same phase. □ **step** (or **tread**) **on someone's toes** offend someone by encroaching on their area of responsibility.

step aer·o·bics ▸ *pl. n.* [often treated as *sing.*] a type of aerobics that involves stepping up onto and down from a portable block.

step·broth·er /'stepˌbrəT͟Hər/ ▸ *n.* a son of one's stepparent, by a marriage other than that with one's own father or mother.

step·child /'stepˌCHīld/ ▸ *n.* (*pl.* **-chil·dren**) a child of one's husband or wife by a previous marriage.

step·daugh·ter /'stepˌdôtər/ ▸ *n.* a daughter of one's husband or wife by a previous marriage.

step·fa·ther /'stepˌfäT͟Hər/ ▸ *n.* a man who is married to one's mother after the divorce of one's parents or the death of one's father.

step·lad·der /'stepˌladər/ ▸ *n.* a short folding ladder with flat steps and a small platform.

step·moth·er /'stepˌməT͟Hər/ ▸ *n.* a woman who is married to one's father after the divorce of one's parents or the death of one's mother.

step·par·ent /'ste(p)ˌparənt; -ˌpe(ə)r-/ ▸ *n.* a stepfather or stepmother.

steppe /step/ ▸ *n.* (often **steppes**) a large area of flat unforested grassland in southeastern Europe or Siberia.

step·ping·stone /'stepiNGˌstōn/ ▸ *n.* a raised stone used singly or in a series as a place on which to step when crossing a stream or muddy area. ■ *fig.* an undertaking or event that helps one to make progress toward a specified goal: *the school championships are a steppingstone to international competition.*

step·sis·ter /'stepˌsistər/ ▸ *n.* a daughter of one's stepparent by a marriage other than one with one's own father or mother.

step·son /'stepˌsən/ ▸ *n.* a son of one's husband or wife by a previous marriage.

step stool (also **step·stool**) ▸ *n.* a stool with usu. folding steps used to reach high shelves, etc.

step·well /'stepˌwel/ ▸ *n.* the stairwell of a bus.

ste·ra·di·an /stə'rādēən/ (abbr.: **sr**) ▸ *n.* the SI unit of solid angle, equal to the angle at the center of a sphere subtended by a part of the surface equal in area to the square of the radius. ▷late 19th cent.: from Greek *stereos* 'solid' + *radian* (from the Latin *radius*, literally 'spoke, ray.'

stere /sti(ə)r/ ▸ *n.* a unit of volume equal to one cubic meter.

ster·e·o /'sterē-ō; 'sti(ə)r-/ ▸ *n.* (*pl.* **-os**) sound that is directed through two or more speakers so that it seems to surround the listener and to come from more than one source; stereophonic sound. ■ a sound system, typically including a CD, tape, or record player, that has two or more speakers and produces stereo sound.

▸ *adj.* short for STEREOPHONIC: *stereo equipment* | *stereo sound.*

ster·e·o·chem·is·try /ˌsterē-ō'keməstrē; ˌsti(ə)r-/ ▸ *n.* the branch of chemistry concerned with the three-dimensional arrangement of atoms and molecules and the effect of this on chemical reactions. —**ster·e·o·chem·i·cal** /-'kemikəl/ *adj.* —**ster·e·o·chem·i·cal·ly** *adv.*

ster·e·og·ra·phy /ˌsterē'ägrəfē; ˌsti(ə)r-/ ▸ *n.* the depiction or representation of three-dimensional things by projection onto a two-dimensional surface, e.g., in cartography. —**ster·e·o·graph** /'sterēəˌgraf; 'sti(ə)r-/ *n.* —**ster·e·o·graph·ic** /ˌsterēə'grafik; ˌsti(ə)r-/ *adj.*

ster·e·o·i·so·mer /ˌsterē-ō'īsəmər; ˌsti(ə)r-/ ▸ *n. Chem.* each of two or more compounds differing only in the spatial arrangement of their atoms. —**ster·e·o·i·so·mer·ic** /-ˌīsə'merik/ *adj.* —**ster·e·o·i·som·er·ism** /-ī'säməˌrizəm/ *n.*

ster·e·o·phon·ic /ˌsterē-ə'fänik; ˌsti(ə)r-/ ▸ *adj.* (of sound recording and reproduction) using two or more channels of transmission and reproduction so that the reproduced sound seems to surround the listener and to come from more than one source. —**ster·e·o·phon·i·cal·ly** *adv.* —**ster·e·oph·o·ny** /-'äfənē/ *n.*

ster·e·o·scope /'sterēəˌskōp; 'sti(ə)r-/ ▸ *n.* a device by which two photographs of the same object taken at slightly different angles are viewed together, creating an impression of depth and solidity. —**ster·e·o·scop·ic** /ˌsterēə'skäpik; ˌsti(ə)r-/ *adj.* —**ster·e·o·scop·i·cal·ly** *adv.* —**ster·e·os·co·py** /ˌsterē'äskəpē; ˌsti(ə)r-/ *n.*

ster·e·o·type /'sterēəˌtīp; 'sti(ə)r-/ ▸ *n.* **1** a widely held but fixed and oversimplified image or idea of a particular type of person or thing: *the stereotype of the woman as the carer* | *sexual and racial stereotypes.* ■ a person or thing that conforms to such an image: *don't treat anyone as a stereotype.* **2** a relief printing plate cast in a mold made from composed type or an original plate.

▸ *v.* [*tr.*] view or represent as a stereotype: *the city is too easily stereotyped as an industrial wasteland.* —**ster·e·o·typ·ic** /ˌsterēə'tipik/ *adj.* —**ster·e·o·typ·i·cal** *adj.* —**ster·e·o·typ·i·cal·ly** *adv.*

ster·ile /'sterəl/ ▸ *adj.* **1** not able to produce children or young: *the disease had made him sterile.* ■ (of a plant) not able to produce fruit or seeds. ■ (of land or soil) too poor in quality to produce crops. ■ lacking in imagination, creativity, or excitement; uninspiring or unproductive: *he found the fraternity's teachings sterile.* **2** free from bacteria or other living microorganisms; totally clean: *a sterile needle and syringes.* ▷late Middle English: from Old French, or from Latin *sterilis*; related to Greek *steira* 'barren cow.' Sense 2 dates from the late 19th cent. —**ster·ile·ly** /'sterə(l)lē/ *adv.* —**ste·ril·i·ty** /stə'rilitē/ *n.*

ster·i·lize /'sterəˌlīz/ ▸ *v.* [*tr.*] **1** make (something) free from bacteria or other living microorganisms: *babies' feeding equipment can be cleaned and sterilized.* **2** (usu. **be sterilized**) deprive (a person or animal) of the ability to produce offspring, typically by removing or blocking the sex organs. ■ make (land or water) unable to produce crops or support life. —**ster·i·liz·a·ble** *adj.* —**ster·i·li·za·tion** /ˌsterələ'zāSHən/ *n.* —**ster·i·liz·er** *n.*

ster·ling /'stərliNG/ ▸ *n.* British money: *prices are shown in sterling.* ■ short for STERLING SILVER: [as *adj.*] *a sterling spoon.*

▸ *adj.* (of a person or their work, efforts, or qualities) excellent or valuable: *this organization does sterling work for youngsters.*

ster·ling sil·ver ▸ *n.* silver of 92¹/₄ percent purity.

stern[1] /stərn/ ▸ *adj.* (of a person or their manner) serious and unrelenting, esp. in the assertion of authority and exercise of discipline: *Mama looked stern.* ■ (of an act or statement) strict and severe; using extreme measures or terms: *stern measures to restrict growth of traffic.* ■ (of competition or opposition) putting someone or something under extreme pressure: *the past year has been a stern test of the ability of local industry.* —**stern·ly** *adv.* —**stern·ness** *n.*

stern² ▶*n.* the rearmost part of a ship or boat: *he stood at the stern of the yacht.* ■ *humorous* a person's bottom: *my stern can't take too much sun.* —**sterned** /stərnd/ *adj.* [in comb.] *a square-sterned vessel.* —**stern·most** /-ˌmōst/ *adj.* —**stern·ward** /-wərd/ *adv.*

ster·num /ˈstərnəm/ ▶*n.* (*pl.* **-nums** or **-na** /-nə/) the breastbone.

ste·roid /ˈsterˌoid/ ˈsti(ə)r-/ ▶*n. Biochem.* any of a large class of organic compounds with a characteristic molecular structure containing four rings of carbon atoms (three six-membered and one five). They include many hormones, alkaloids, and vitamins. ■ short for ANABOLIC STEROID. —**ste·roi·dal** /steˈroidl/ sti-/ *adj.*

ster·ol /ˈsterôl, -äl/ ˈsti(ə)r-/ ▶*n. Biochem.* any of a group of naturally occurring unsaturated steroid alcohols, typically waxy solids.

ster·to·rous /ˈstərtərəs/ ▶*adj.* (of breathing) noisy and labored. —**ster·to·rous·ly** *adv.*

stet /stet/ ▶*v.* (**stet·ted, stet·ting**) [*intr.*] let it stand (used as an instruction on a printed proof to indicate that a correction or alteration should be ignored). ■ [*tr.*] write such an instruction against (something corrected or deleted).
▶*n.* such an instruction made on a printed proof.

steth·o·scope /ˈstethəˌskōp/ ▶*n.* a medical instrument for listening to the action of someone's heart or breathing, typically having a small disk-shaped resonator that is placed against the chest, and two tubes connected to earpieces. —**steth·o·scop·ic** /ˌstethəˈskäpik/ *adj.*

Stet·son /ˈstetsən/ ▶*n. trademark* a hat with a high crown and a wide brim, traditionally worn by cowboys and ranchers in the U.S.

ste·ve·dore /ˈstēvəˌdôr/ ▶*n.* a person employed, or a contractor engaged, at a dock to load and unload cargo from ships.

ste·vi·a /ˈstēvēə/ ˈstev-/ ▶*n.* a composite herb native to South America (Genus *Stevia*, especially *S. rebaudiana*, native to Paraguay) whose leaves are the source of a noncaloric sweetener. ■ a food supplement prepared from this, used as a sweetener.

stethoscope

stew¹ /st(y)o͞o/ ▶*n.* **1** a dish of meat and vegetables cooked slowly in liquid in a closed dish or pan: *lamb stew.* **2** *inf.* a state of great anxiety or agitation: *I suppose he's all in a stew.*
▶*v.* cook (meat, fruit, or other food) slowly in liquid in a closed dish or pan: *a new way to stew rhubarb.* ■ [*intr.*] (of meat, fruit, or other food) be cooked in such a way. ■ [*intr.*] *inf.* remain in a heated or stifling atmosphere: *sweaty clothes left to stew in a plastic bag.* ■ [*intr.*] *inf.* worry about something, esp. on one's own: *James will be expecting us, so we will let him stew a bit.*

stew² ▶*n. Brit.* a pond or large tank for keeping fish for eating. ■ an artificial oyster bed.

stew³ ▶*n. inf.* an air steward or stewardess.

stew·ard /ˈst(y)o͞oərd/ ▶*n.* **1** a person who looks after the passengers on a ship, aircraft, or train and brings them meals. ■ a person responsible for supplies of food to a college, club, or other institution. **2** an official appointed to supervise arrangements or keep order at a large public event, for example a sporting event. ■ short for SHOP STEWARD. **3** a person employed to manage another's property, esp. a large house or estate. ■ a person whose responsibility it is to take care of something: *farmers pride themselves on being stewards of the countryside.*
▶*v.* [*tr.*] **1** (of an official) supervise arrangements or keep order at (a large public event): *the event was organized and stewarded properly.* **2** manage or look after (another's property). —**stew·ard·ship** *n.*

stew·ard·ess /ˈst(y)o͞oərdis/ ▶*n.* a woman who is employed to provide meals for and otherwise look after the passengers on a ship or aircraft.

stick¹ /stik/ ▶*n.* **1** a thin piece of wood that has fallen or been cut from a tree. **2** a thin piece of wood that has been trimmed for a particular purpose, in particular: ■ a long piece of wood used for support in walking or as a weapon with which to hit someone or something. ■ (in hockey, polo, and other games) a long implement, typically made of wood, with a head or blade of varying form that is used to hit or direct the ball or puck. ■ a short piece of wood used to impale food: *Popsicle sticks.* ■ *fig.* a piece of basic furniture: *every **stick of furniture** just vanished.* ■ (**sticks**) (in field hockey) the foul play of raising the stick above the shoulder. **3** something resembling or likened to a stick, in particular: ■ a long, thin piece of something: *cinnamon sticks.* ■ a quarter-pound

rectangular block of butter or margarine. ■ a conductor's baton. ■ a gear or control lever. ■ (in extended and metaphorical use) a very thin person or limb: *the girl was a stick.* ■ a number of bombs or paratroopers dropped rapidly from an aircraft. ■ *inf.* a marijuana cigarette. **4** a threat of punishment or unwelcome measures (often contrasted with the offer of reward as a means of persuasion): *training that relies more on the carrot than on the stick.* **5** (**the sticks**) *inf., derog.* rural areas far from cities: *a small, dusty town out in the sticks.* —**stick·like** /-ˌlīk/ *adj.*

stick² ▶*v.* (*past* **stuck** /stək/) **1** [*tr.*] (**stick something in/into/through**) push a sharp or pointed object into or through (something): *he stuck his fork into the sausage.* ■ (**stick something on**) fix something on (a point or pointed object): *stick the balls of wool on knitting needles.* ■ [*intr.*] (**stick in/into/through**) (of a pointed object) be or remain fixed with its point embedded in (something): *there was a slim rod sticking into the ground beside me.* ■ [*tr.*] insert, thrust, or push: *a youth with a cigarette stuck behind one ear.* ■ [*intr.*] protrude or extend in a certain direction: *his front teeth stick out.* ■ [*tr.*] put somewhere, typically in a quick or careless way: *just stick that sandwich on my desk.* ■ *inf.* used to express angry dismissal of a particular thing: *he told them they could stick the job—he didn't want it anyway.* ■ *inf.* cause to incur an expense or loss: *she stuck me for all of last month's rent.* ■ stab or pierce with a sharp object: [as *adj.*] (**stuck**) *he screamed like a stuck pig.* **2** [*intr.*] adhere or cling to a substance or surface: *the plastic seats stuck to my skin.* ■ [*tr.*] fasten or cause to adhere to an object or surface: *she stuck the stamp on the envelope.* ■ be or become fixed or jammed in one place as a result of an obstruction: *he drove into a bog, where his wheels stuck fast.* ■ remain in a static condition; fail to progress. ■ (of a feeling or thought) remain persistently in one's mind: *one particular incident sticks in my mind.* ■ *inf.* be or become convincing, established, or regarded as valid: *the authorities couldn't make the charges stick.* ■ (in blackjack and similar card games) decline to add to one's hand. **3** (**be stuck**) be fixed in a particular position or unable to move or be moved: *Sara tried to open the window but it was stuck | we got stuck in a traffic jam.* ■ be unable to progress with a task or find the answer or solution to something: *I'm doing the crossword and I'm stuck.* ■ *inf.* be or remain in a specified place or situation, typically one perceived as tedious or unpleasant: *I don't want to be stuck in an office all my life.* ■ (**be stuck for**) be at a loss for or in need of: *I'm not usually stuck for words.* ■ (**be stuck with**) *inf.* be unable to get rid of or escape from: *like it or not, she and Grant were stuck with each other.* **4** (**stick it out**) *inf.* put up with or persevere with something difficult or disagreeable.
▶*phrasal v.* □ **stick around** *inf.* remain in or near a place: *I'd like to stick around and watch the game.* □ **stick by 1** continue to support or be loyal to (someone), typically during difficult times: *I love him and whatever happens, I'll stick by him.* **2** another way of saying STICK TO in sense 2 below. □ **stick out** be extremely noticeable: *many important things had happened to him, but one stuck out.* □ **stick to 1** continue or confine oneself to doing or using (a particular thing): *I'll stick to bitter lemon, thanks.* ■ not move or digress from (a path or a subject). **2** adhere to (a commitment, belief, or rule): *the government stuck to its election pledges.* □ **stick up for** support or defend (a person or cause). □ **stick with** *inf.* **1** persevere or continue with: *I'm happy to stick with the present team.* **2** another way of saying STICK BY above.
▶ □ **stick in one's throat** (or **craw**) be difficult or impossible to accept; be a source of continuing annoyance. ■ (of words) be difficult or impossible to say: *she couldn't say "Thank you"—the words stuck in her throat.*

stick·ball /ˈstikˌbôl/ ▶*n.* an informal game resembling baseball, played with a stick and a (usually rubber) ball.

stick-built /ˈstikˌbilt/ (also **stick-built**) ▶*adj.* (of houses or other buildings) built piece-by-piece on the premises, rather than constructed from prefabricated units.

stick·er /ˈstikər/ ▶*n.* an adhesive label or notice, generally printed or illustrated. ■ short for STICKER PRICE.

stick·er price ▶*n.* the advertised retail price of an item, esp. the price listed on a sticker attached to the window of a new automobile.

stick·er shock ▶*n. inf.* shock or dismay experienced by the potential buyers of a particular product on discovering its high or increased price: *drugstore consumers are feeling the pain of sticker shock as never before.*

stick·ing point ▶*n.* a point at which an obstacle arises in progress toward an agreement or goal: *Jerusalem emerged as a key sticking point in Israeli–Palestinian negotiations.*

stick-in-the-mud ▶*n. inf.* a person who is dull and unadventurous and who resists change.

stick·le·back /ˈstikəlˌbak/ ▶*n.* a small fish (family Gasterosteidae) with sharp spines along its back, able to live in both salt and fresh water and found in both Eurasia and North America.

stick·ler /ˈstik(ə)lər/ ▶*n.* **1** a person who insists on a certain quality or type of behavior: *a stickler for accuracy* | *a stickler when it comes to time-keeping.* **2** a difficult problem; a conundrum.

stick·pin /'stik,pin/ ▶ *n.* a straight pin with an ornamental head, worn to keep a tie in place or as a brooch.

stick shift ▶ *n.* a manual transmission.

stick·up /'stik,əp/ ▶ *n. inf.* an armed robbery in which a gun is used to threaten people.

stick·y /'stikē/ ▶ *adj.* (**stick·i·er, stick·i·est**) **1** tending or designed to stick to things on contact or covered with something that sticks. ■ (of a substance) glutinous; viscous: *the dough should be moist but not sticky.* ■ (of prices, interest rates, or wages) slow to change or react to change. **2** (of the weather) hot and damp; muggy: *it was an unusually hot and sticky summer.* ■ damp with sweat: *she felt hot and sticky and changed her clothes.* **3** *inf.* involving problems; difficult or awkward: *the relationship is going through a sticky patch.* —**stick·i·ly** /'stikəlē/ *adv.* —**stick·i·ness** *n.*

stiff /stif/ ▶ *adj.* **1** not easily bent or changed in shape; rigid: *a stiff black collar.* ■ not moving as freely as is usual or desirable; difficult to turn or operate: *the faucet in the shower is a little stiff.* ■ (of a person or part of the body) unable to move easily and without pain: *he was stiff from sitting on the desk.* ■ (of a person or their manner) not relaxed or friendly; constrained: *she greeted him with stiff politeness.* ■ viscous; thick: *add wheat until the mixture is quite stiff.* **2** severe or strong: *a stiff increase in taxes.* ■ (of a wind) blowing strongly: *a stiff breeze stirring the lake.* ■ requiring strength or effort; difficult: *a long stiff climb up the bare hillside.* ■ (of an alcoholic drink) strong: *a stiff measure of brandy.* **3** (—— **stiff**) *inf.* having a specified unpleasant feeling to an extreme extent: *she was scared stiff.*
▶ *n. inf.* **1** a dead body. **2** a boring, conventional person: *ordinary working stiffs in respectable offices.* ■ *inf.* a fellow: *the lucky stiff!*
▶ *v.* [*tr.*] *inf.* **1** (often **be stiffed**) cheat (someone) out of something, esp. money: *several workers were stiffed out of their pay.* ■ fail to leave (someone) a tip. **2** ignore deliberately; snub. ■ fail to appear for a promised engagement or appointment: *he stiffed us and didn't show up.* **3** kill: *I want to get those pigs who stiffed your doctor.* ■ [*intr.*] be unsuccessful: *as soon as he began singing about the wife and kids, his albums stiffed.* —**stiff·ish** *adj.* —**stiff·ly** *adv.* —**stiff·ness** *n.*
▶ □ **a stiff upper lip** a quality of uncomplaining stoicism: *senior managers had to keep a stiff upper lip and remain optimistic.*

stiff·en /'stifən/ ▶ *v.* make or become stiff or rigid: [*tr.*] *he stiffened his knees in an effort to prevent them from trembling* | [*intr.*] *my back stiffens up and I can't bend.* ■ [*tr.*] support or strengthen (a garment or fabric), typically by adding tape or an adhesive layer. ■ *fig.* make or become stronger or more steadfast: [*tr.*] *outrage over the murders stiffened the government's resolve to confront the Mafia* | [*intr.*] *the regime's resistance stiffened.* —**stiff·en·er** /'stif(ə)nər/ *n.* —**stiff·en·ing** *n.*

stiff-necked ▶ *adj.* (of a person or their behavior) haughty and stubborn.

sti·fle /'stīfəl/ ▶ *v.* [*tr.*] **1** make (someone) unable to breathe properly; suffocate: *those in the streets were stifled by the fumes.* **2** restrain (a reaction) or stop oneself acting on (an emotion): *she stifled a giggle* | *she stifled a desire to turn and flee.* ■ prevent or constrain (an activity or idea): *high taxes were stifling private enterprise.* —**sti·fler** /-f(ə)lər/ *n.* —**sti·fling·ly** /-f(ə)liNGlē/ *adv.* *a stiflingly hot day.*

stig·ma /'stigmə/ ▶ *n.* (*pl.* **stig·mas** or esp. in sense 2 **stig·ma·ta** /stig'mätə; 'stigmətə/) **1** a mark of disgrace associated with a particular circumstance, quality, or person: *the stigma of mental disorder* | *to be a nonreader carries a social stigma.* **2** (**stigmata**) (in Christian tradition) marks corresponding to those left on Jesus' body by the Crucifixion, said to have been impressed by divine favor on the bodies of St. Francis of Assisi and others. **3** *Bot.* (in a flower) the part of a pistil that receives the pollen during pollination. ▷late 16th cent. (denoting a mark made by pricking or branding): via Latin from Greek *stigma* 'a mark made by a pointed instrument, a dot.'

stig·ma·tize /'stigmə,tīz/ ▶ *v.* [*tr.*] (usu. **be stigmatized**) describe or regard as worthy of disgrace or great disapproval: *the institution was stigmatized as a last resort for the destitute.* —**stig·ma·ti·za·tion** /,stigməti'zāSHən/ *n.*

stile[1] /stīl/ ▶ *n.* an arrangement of steps that allows people but not animals to climb over a fence or wall.

stile[2] ▶ *n.* a vertical piece in the frame of a paneled door or sash window.

sti·let·to /stə'letō/ ▶ *n.* (*pl.* **-tos**) **1** a short dagger with a tapering blade. ■ a sharp-pointed tool for making eyelet holes. **2** (also **stiletto heel**) a thin, high, tapering heel on a woman's shoe: [as *adj.*] *the rapid click of stiletto heels on pavement.* ■ a shoe with such a heel.

still[1] /stil/ ▶ *adj.* not moving or making a sound: *the still body of the young*

man. ■ (of air or water) undisturbed by wind, sound, or current; calm and tranquil: *her voice carried on the still air.* ■ (of a drink such as wine) not effervescent;
▶ *n.* **1** deep silence and calm; stillness: *the still of the night.* **2** an ordinary static photograph as opposed to a motion picture, esp. a single shot from a movie.
▶ *adv.* **1** without moving: *the sheriff commanded him to stand still and drop the gun.* **2** up to and including the present or the time mentioned; even now (or then) as formerly: *it was still raining.* ■ referring to something that will or may happen in the future: *we could still win.* **3** nevertheless; all the same: *I'm afraid he's crazy. Still, he's harmless.* **4** even (used with comparatives for emphasis): *write, or better still, type, captions for the pictures.*
▶ *v.* make or become still; quiet: [*tr.*] *she raised her hand, stilling Erica's protests* | [*intr.*] *the din in the hall stilled.* —**still·ness** *n.*

still[2] ▶ *n.* an apparatus for distilling alcoholic drinks such as whiskey.

still·birth /'stil,bərTH/ ▶ *n.* the birth of an infant that has died in the womb (strictly, after having survived through at least the first 28 weeks of pregnancy, earlier instances being regarded as abortion or miscarriage).

still·born /'stil,bôrn/ ▶ *adj.* (an infant) born dead. ■ *fig.* (of a proposal or plan) having failed to develop or succeed; unrealized: *the proposed wealth tax was stillborn.*

still life ▶ *n.* (*pl.* **still lifes** /,līfs/) a painting or drawing of an arrangement of objects, typically including fruit and flowers and objects contrasting with these in texture, such as bowls and glassware. ■ this type or genre of painting or drawing.

stilt /stilt/ ▶ *n.* **1** either of a pair of upright poles with supports for the feet enabling the user to walk at a distance above the ground. ■ each of a set of posts or piles supporting a building above the ground. ■ a small, flat, three-pointed support for ceramic ware in a kiln. **2** a long-billed wading bird (*Himantopus* and other genera) with predominantly black and white plumage and long slender reddish legs.

stilt·ed /'stiltid/ ▶ *adj.* (of a manner of talking or writing) stiff and self-conscious or unnatural: *we made stilted conversation.* —**stilt·ed·ly** *adv.* —**stilt·ed·ness** *n.*

Stil·ton /'stiltn/ ▶ *n. trademark* a kind of strong rich cheese, often with blue veins, originally made in Leicestershire, England.

stim·u·lant /'stimyələnt/ ▶ *n.* a substance that raises levels of physiological or nervous activity in the body. ■ something that increases activity, interest, or enthusiasm in a specified field: *population growth is a major stimulant to industrial development.*
▶ *adj.* raising levels of physiological or nervous activity in the body: *caffeine has stimulant effects on the heart.*

stim·u·late /'stimyə,lāt/ ▶ *v.* [*tr.*] raise levels of physiological or nervous activity in (the body or any biological system): *the women are given fertility drugs to stimulate their ovaries.* ■ encourage interest or activity in (a person or animal): *the reader could not fail to be stimulated by the ideas presented.* ■ encourage development of or increased activity in (a state or process): *the courses stimulate a passion for learning.* —**stim·u·la·ble** /-ləbəl/ *adj.* —**stim·u·lat·ing·ly** *adv.* —**stim·u·la·tion** /,stimyə'lāSHən/ *n.* —**stim·u·la·tive** /-,lātiv; -lətiv/ *adj.* —**stim·u·la·tor** /-,lātər/ *n.* —**stim·u·la·to·ry** /-lə,tôrē/ *adj.*

stim·u·lus /'stimyələs/ ▶ *n.* (*pl.* **-li** /-,lī/) a thing or event that evokes a specific functional reaction in an organ or tissue: *areas of the brain which respond to auditory stimuli.* ■ a thing that rouses activity or energy in someone or something; a spur or incentive: *if the tax were abolished, it would act as a stimulus to exports.* ■ an interesting and exciting quality: *she loved the stimulus of the job.* ▷late 17th cent.: from Latin, 'goad, spur, incentive.'

sting /stiNG/ ▶ *n.* **1** a small sharp-pointed organ at the end of the abdomen of bees, wasps, ants, and scorpions, capable of inflicting a painful or dangerous wound by injecting poison. ■ any of a number of minute hairs or other organs of plants, jellyfishes, etc., that inject a poisonous or irritating fluid when touched. ■ a wound from such an animal or plant organ: *a wasp or bee sting.* ■ a sharp tingling or burning pain or sensation: *I felt the sting of the cold, bitter air.* ■ *fig.* a hurtful quality or effect: *she smiled to take the sting out of her words.* **2** *inf.* a carefully planned operation, typically one involving deception: *five blackmailers were snared in a police sting.*
▶ *v.* (*past* and *past part.* **stung** /stəNG/) **1** [*tr.*] wound or pierce with a sting: *he was stung by a jellyfish* | [*intr.*] *a nettle stings if you brush it lightly.* **2** feel or

cause to feel a sharp tingling or burning pain or sensation: [*intr.*] *her eyes stung* | [*tr.*] *the brandy stung his throat* | [as *adj.*] (**stinging**) *a stinging pain.* ■ [*tr.*] *fig.* (typically of something said) hurt or upset (someone): *stung by her mockery, Frank hung his head.* ■ (**sting someone into**) provoke someone to do (something) by causing annoyance or offense: *he was stung into action by an article in the paper.* **3** [*tr.*] *inf.* swindle or exorbitantly overcharge (someone): *an elaborate fraud that stung a bank for thousands.* —**sting·ing·ly** *adv.* —**sting·less** *adj.*

sting·er /ˈstiNGər/ ▶*n.* **1** an insect or animal that stings, such as a bee or jellyfish. ■ the part of an insect or animal that holds a sting. ■ *inf.* a painful blow: *he suffered a stinger on his right shoulder.* **2** a cocktail including crème de menthe and brandy. **3** (**Stinger**) a heat-seeking ground-to-air missile that is launched from the shoulder.

sting·ray /ˈstiNGˌrā/ ▶*n.* a bottom-dwelling marine ray with a flattened diamond-shaped body and a long poisonous serrated spine at the base of the tail. Two families: Dasyatidae (the **long-tailed stingrays**) and Urolophidae (the **short-tailed stingrays**).

stin·gy /ˈstinjē/ ▶*adj.* (**-gi·er**, **-gi·est**) unwilling to give or spend; ungenerous: *his employer is stingy and idle.* —**stin·gi·ly** /-lē/ *adv.* —**stin·gi·ness** *n.*

stink /stiNGk/ ▶*v.* (*past* **stank** /staNGk/ *or* **stunk** /stəNGk/; *past part.* **stunk**) [*intr.*] **1** have a strong unpleasant smell: *the place stank like a sewer* | *his breath stank of drink.* **2** *inf.* be very unpleasant, contemptible, or scandalous: *the industry's reputation stinks.* ■ (**stink of**) be highly suggestive of (something regarded with disapproval): *the whole affair stinks of a setup.* ■ (**stink of**) have or appear to have a scandalously large amount of (something, esp. money): *the whole place was luxurious and stank of money.* ▶*n.* **1** a strong unpleasant smell; a stench: *the stink of the place hit me as I went in.* **2** *inf.* a commotion or fuss: *we go to the Four Seasons where Brad makes a big stink about getting a prime table.*

stink·er /ˈstiNGkər/ ▶*n.* *inf.* a person or thing that smells very bad. ■ a very bad or unpleasant person or thing: *have those little stinkers been bullying you?* ■ a difficult task: *Tackled the crossword yet? It's a stinker.*

stink·ing /ˈstiNGkiNG/ ▶*adj.* foul-smelling: *he was locked in a stinking cell.* ■ *inf.* very bad or unpleasant: *a stinking cold.* ▶*adv.* *inf.* extremely: *she is obviously stinking rich* | *I want to get stinking drunk and forget.* —**stink·ing·ly** *adv.*

stink·o /ˈstiNGkō/ ▶*adj.* *inf.* **1** extremely drunk: *they took three-hour lunches and came back stinko.* **2** worthless or contemptible: *the plot and cast of characters are just plain stinko.*

stink·pot /ˈstiNGkˌpät/ ▶*n.* *inf.* an unpleasant person (used as a term of abuse). ■ a vehicle that emits foul-smelling exhaust fumes, esp. a motorboat as opposed to a sailboat.

stink·weed /ˈstiNGkˌwēd/ ▶*n.* any of a number of plants with a strong or fetid smell, e.g., jimson weed.

stint¹ /stint/ ▶*v.* [*tr.*] supply an ungenerous or inadequate amount of (something): *stowage room hasn't been stinted.* ■ [*intr.*] be economical or frugal about spending or providing something: *he doesn't stint on wining and dining.* ■ restrict (someone) in the amount of something (esp. money) given or permitted: *to avoid having to stint yourself, budget in advance.* ▶*n.* **1** a person's fixed or allotted period of work: *his varied career included a stint as a magician.* **2** limitation of supply or effort: *a collector with an eye for quality and the means to indulge it without stint.*

stint² ▶*n.* a small short-legged sandpiper (genus *Calidris*) of northern Eurasia and Alaska, with a brownish back and white underparts.

sti·pend /ˈstīˌpend; -pənd/ ▶*n.* a fixed regular sum paid as a salary or allowance.

sti·pen·di·ar·y /stīˈpendē,erē/ ▶*adj.* receiving a stipend; working for payment rather than on a voluntary, unpaid basis: *stipendiary clergy.* ■ of, relating to, or of the nature of a stipend: *stipendiary obligations.*

stip·ple /ˈstipəl/ ▶*v.* [*tr.*] (in drawing, painting, and engraving) mark (a surface) with numerous small dots or specks: [as *n.*] (**stippling**) *the artist's use of stippling.* ■ produce a decorative effect on (paint or other material) by roughening its surface when it is wet. ▶*n.* the process or technique of stippling a surface, or the effect so created. —**stip·pler** /ˈstip(ə)lər/ *n.*

stip·u·late /ˈstipyəˌlāt/ ▶*v.* [*tr.*] demand or specify (a requirement), typically as part of a bargain or agreement: *he stipulated certain conditions before their marriage* | [as *adj.*] (**stipulated**) *the stipulated time has elapsed.* —**stip·u·la·tion** /ˌstipyəˈlāsнən/ *n.* —**stip·u·la·tor** /-ˌlātər/ *n.*

stir¹ /stər/ ▶*v.* (**stirred**, **stir·ring**) **1** [*tr.*] move a spoon or other implement around in (a liquid or other substance) in order to mix it thoroughly: *stir the batter until it is just combined.* ■ (**stir something in/into**) add an ingredient to (a liquid or other substance) in such a way: *stir in the flour and cook gently for two minutes.* **2** [*intr.*] move or begin to move slightly: *nothing stirred except the wind.* ■ [*tr.*] cause to move or be disturbed

slightly: *a gentle breeze stirred the leaves.* ■ (of a person or animal) rise or wake from sleep: *no one else had stirred yet.* ■ (**stir from**) (of a person) leave or go out of (a place): *as he grew older, he seldom stirred from his apartment.* ■ begin or cause to begin to be active or to develop: [*intr.*] *the 1960s, when the civil rights movement stirred.* **3** [*tr.*] arouse strong feelings in (someone); move or excite: *they will be stirred to action by what is written* | *he stirred up the sweating crowd.* ■ arouse or prompt (a feeling or memory) or inspire (the imagination): *the story stirred many memories of my childhood* | *the rumors had stirred up his anger.* ▶*n.* **1** a slight physical movement: *I stood, straining eyes and ears for the faintest stir.* ■ a commotion: *the event caused quite a stir.* ■ an initial sign of a specified feeling: *Caroline felt a stir of anger deep within her breast.* **2** an act of mixing food or drink with a spoon or other implement: *he gives his chocolate milk a stir.* —**stir·rer** *n.*

stir² ▶*n.* *inf.* prison: *I've spent twenty-eight years in stir.*

stir-cra·zy ▶*adj.* *inf.* psychologically disturbed, esp. as a result of being confined or imprisoned.

stir-fry ▶*v.* [*tr.*] fry (meat, fish, or vegetables) rapidly over a high heat while stirring briskly: [as *adj.*] (**stir-fried**) *stir-fried beef.* ▶*n.* a dish cooked by such a method.

stir·ring /ˈstəriNG/ ▶*adj.* causing great excitement or strong emotion; rousing: *stirring songs.* ▶*n.* an initial sign of activity, movement, or emotion: *the first stirrings of anger.* —**stir·ring·ly** *adv.*

stir·rup /ˈstərəp; ˈstəˌrəp; ˈstir-/ ▶*n.* **1** each of a pair of devices attached to each side of a horse's saddle, in the form of a loop with a flat base to support the rider's foot. **2** (**stir·rups**) a pair of metal supports in which a woman's heels may be placed during gynecological examinations and childbirth, to hold her legs in a position that will facilitate medical examination or intervention. **3** (also **stirrup bone**) another term for STAPES.

stirrup

stitch /stiCH/ ▶*n.* **1** a loop of thread or yarn resulting from a single pass or movement of the needle in sewing, knitting, or crocheting. ■ a loop of thread used to join the edges of a wound or surgical incision: *a neck wound requiring forty stitches.* ■ a method of sewing, knitting, or crocheting producing a particular pattern or design: *basic embroidery stitches.* ■ *inf.* the smallest item of clothing: *a man answered the door without a stitch on.* **2** a sudden sharp pain in the side of the body, caused by strenuous exercise: *she ran with a stitch in her side.* ▶*v.* [*tr.*] make, mend, or join (something) with stitches: *stitch a plain seam with right sides together.* | [as *adj.*], [in *comb.*] (**stitched**) *hand-stitched English dresses.* —**stitch·er** *n.* —**stitch·er·y** *n.* ▶ □ **in stitches** *inf.* laughing uncontrollably: *he had his audiences in stitches.*

stitch·wort /ˈstiCHwərt; -ˌwôrt/ ▶*n.* a straggling plant (genus *Stellaria*) of the pink family with a slender stem and white starry flowers. It was formerly thought to cure a stitch in the side.

St. John's wort (also **St. Johns wort**) ▶*n.* a herbaceous plant or shrub (*Hypericum*, family Guttiferae) with distinctive yellow five-petaled flowers and paired oval leaves, used to treat various disorders, including depression.

sto·a /ˈstōə/ ▶*n.* a classical portico or roofed colonnade.

stoat /stōt/ ▶*n.* a small carnivorous mammal (*Mustela erminea*) of the weasel family that has chestnut fur with white underparts and a black-tipped tail. It is native to both Eurasia and North America, and in northern areas the coat turns white in winter. Compare with ERMINE.

sto·chas·tic /stəˈkastik/ ▶*adj.* randomly determined; having a random probability distribution or pattern that may be analyzed statistically but may not be predicted precisely. —**sto·chas·ti·cal·ly** /-ik(ə)lē/ *adv.*

stock /stäk/ ▶*n.* **1** the goods or merchandise kept on the premises of a business or warehouse and available for sale or distribution. ■ a supply or quantity of something accumulated or available for future use: *my stock of wine.* ■ farm animals such as cattle, pigs, and sheep, bred and kept for their meat or milk; livestock. ■ (also **film stock**) photographic film that has not been exposed or processed. ■ the undealt cards of the deck, left on the table to be drawn from in some card games. **2** the capital raised by a business or corporation through the issue and subscription of shares: *the company's stock rose by 86%.* ■ (also **stocks**) a portion of this as held by an individual or group as an investment. ■ (also **stocks**) the shares of a particular company, type of

company, or industry: *blue-chip stocks.* ■ securities issued by the government in fixed units with a fixed rate of interest. ■ *fig.* a person's reputation or popularity. **3** liquid made by cooking bones, meat, fish, or vegetables slowly in water, used as a basis for the preparation of soup, gravy, or sauces. ■ the raw material from which a specified commodity can be manufactured. **4** a person's ancestry or line of descent: *her mother was of French stock.* **5** a herbaceous European plant (genus *Matthiola*) of the cabbage family, widely cultivated for its fragrant flowers, which are typically lilac, pink, or white. **6** (**the stocks**) [treated as *sing.* or *pl.*] *hist.* an instrument of punishment consisting of an adjustable wooden structure with holes for securing a person's feet and hands, in which criminals were locked and exposed to public ridicule or assault. **7** the part of a rifle or other firearm to which the barrel and firing mechanism are attached, held against one's shoulder when firing the gun. ■ the crosspiece of an anchor. ■ the handle of something such as a whip or fishing rod. **8** (**stocks**) a frame used to support a ship or boat out of water, esp. when under construction.
▶*adj.* **1** (of a product or type of product) usually kept in stock and thus regularly available for sale: *25 percent off stock items.* **2** (of a phrase or expression) so regularly used as to be automatic or hackneyed: *their stock response was "We can't take everyone."* ■ denoting a conventional character type or situation that recurs in a particular genre of literature, theater, or film.
▶*v.* [*tr.*] **1** have or keep a supply of (a particular product or type or product) available for sale. ■ provide or fill with goods, items, or a supply of something. ■ [*intr.*] (**stock up**) amass supplies of something, typically for a particular occasion or purpose. **2** fit (a rifle or other firearm) with a stock.
▶ □ **in** (or **out of**) **stock** (of goods) available (or unavailable) for immediate sale in a store. □ **take stock** review or make an overall assessment of a particular situation, typically as a prelude to making a decision: *he needed to **take stock** of his life.*
stock·ade /stäˈkād/ ▶*n.* a barrier formed from upright wooden posts or stakes, esp. as a defense against attack or as a means of confining animals. ■ an enclosure bound by such a barrier: *we got ashore and into the stockade.* ■ a military prison.
▶*v.* [*tr.*] [usu. as *adj.*] (**stockaded**) enclose (an area) by erecting such a barrier.
stock·breed·er /ˈstäkˌbrēdər/ ▶*n.* a farmer who breeds livestock. —**stock·breed·ing** /-ˌbrēdiNG/ *n.*
stock·bro·ker /ˈstäkˌbrōkər/ ▶*n.* a broker who buys and sells securities on a stock exchange on behalf of clients. —**stock·bro·ker·age** /-ˌbrōk(ə)rij/ *n.* —**stock·brok·ing** /-ˌbrōkiNG/ *n.*
stock car ▶*n.* **1** an ordinary car that has been modified for racing. **2** a railroad car for transporting livestock.
stock com·pa·ny ▶*n.* a repertory company that is largely based in one theater.
stock ex·change ▶*n.* a market in which securities are bought and sold: *the company was floated **on the Stock Exchange**.* ■ (**the Stock Exchange**) the level of prices in such a market: *a plunge in the Stock Exchange during the election campaign.*
stock·feed /ˈstäkˌfēd/ ▶*n.* food for livestock: *meat and bonemeal stockfeed has been banned for all livestock.*
stock·hold·er /ˈstäkˌhōldər/ ▶*n.* a shareholder. —**stock·hold·ing** /-ˌhōldiNG/ *n.*
stock·i·nette /ˌstäkəˈnet/ (also **stock·i·net**) ▶*n.* a soft, loosely knitted stretch fabric, formerly used for making underwear and now used for cleaning, wrapping, or bandaging.
stock·ing /ˈstäkiNG/ ▶*n.* a women's garment, typically made of translucent nylon or silk, that fits closely over the foot and is held up by garters or an elasticized strip at the upper thigh. ■ a cylindrical bandage or other medical covering for the leg resembling a stocking, esp. an elasticized support used in the treatment of disorders of the veins. ■ a white marking of the lower part of a horse's leg, extending as far as, or just beyond, the knee or hock. —**stock·inged** /ˈstäkiNGd/ *adj.* [in *comb.*] *her black-stockinged legs.* —**stock·ing·less** *adj.*
stock·ing cap ▶*n.* a knitted conical hat with a long tapered end, often bearing a tassel, that hangs down.
stock·ing stuff·er ▶*n.* a small present suitable for putting in a Christmas stocking.
stock-in-trade ▶*n.* the typical subject or commodity a person, company, or profession uses or deals in: *information is our stock-in-trade.* ■ qualities, ideas, or behavior characteristic of a person or their work: *flippancy is his stock-in-trade.*
stock·man /ˈstäkmən; -ˌman/ ▶*n.* (*pl.* **-men**) **1** a person who looks after livestock. **2** a person who looks after a stockroom or warehouse.

stock mar·ket ▶*n.* (usu. **the stock market**) a stock exchange.
stock·pile /ˈstäkˌpīl/ ▶*n.* a large accumulated stock of goods or materials, esp. one held in reserve for use at a time of shortage or other emergency.
▶*v.* [*tr.*] accumulate a large stock of (goods or materials): *he claimed that the weapons were being stockpiled.* —**stock·pil·er** *n.*
stock·pot /ˈstäkˌpät/ ▶*n.* a pot in which stock for soup is prepared by long, slow cooking.
stock·room /ˈstäkˌro͞om; -ˌro͝om/ ▶*n.* a room in which quantities of goods are stored.
stock split ▶*n.* an issue of new shares in a company to existing shareholders in proportion to their current holdings.
stock-still ▶*adv.* without any movement; completely still: *he stood stock-still.*
stock swap ▶*n.* **1** acquisition of a company in which payment consists of stock in the buying company. **2** a means of exercising stock options in which shares already owned are traded for a greater number of shares at the exercise price.
stock·tak·ing /ˈstäkˌtākiNG/ ▶*n.* the action or process of recording the amount of stock held by a business: *the store is closed for stocktaking.* ■ the action of reviewing and assessing one's situation and options: *she had some mental stocktaking to do.* —**stock·take** *n.* —**stock·tak·er** /-ˌtākər/ *n.*
stock·y /ˈstäkē/ ▶*adj.* (**stock·i·er**, **stock·i·est**) (of a person) broad and sturdily built. —**stock·i·ly** /ˈstäkəlē/ *adv.* —**stock·i·ness** *n.*
stock·yard /ˈstäkˌyärd/ ▶*n.* a large yard containing pens and sheds, typically adjacent to a slaughterhouse, in which livestock is kept and sorted.
stodg·y /ˈstäjē/ ▶*adj.* (**stodg·i·er**, **stodg·i·est**) dull and uninspired: *some of the material is rather stodgy and top-heavy with facts.* —**stodg·i·ly** /ˈstäjəlē/ *adv.* —**stodg·i·ness** *n.*
sto·gie /ˈstōgē/ (also **sto·gy**) ▶*n.* (*pl.* **-gies**) a long, thin, inexpensive cigar.
sto·ic /ˈstō-ik/ ▶*n.* **1** a person who can endure pain or hardship without showing their feelings or complaining. **2** (**Stoic**) a member of the ancient philosophical school of Stoicism.
▶*adj.* **1** another term for STOICAL. **2** (**Stoic**) of or belonging to the Stoics or their school of philosophy.
sto·i·cal /ˈstō-ikəl/ ▶*adj.* enduring pain and hardship without showing one's feelings or complaining: *he taught a stoical acceptance of suffering.* —**sto·i·cal·ly** /-ik(ə)lē/ *adv.*
sto·i·cism /ˈstō-iˌsizəm/ ▶*n.* **1** the endurance of pain or hardship without a display of feelings and without complaint. **2** (**Stoicism**) an ancient Greek school of philosophy founded at Athens by Zeno of Citium. The school taught that virtue, the highest good, is based on knowledge, and that the wise live in harmony with the divine Reason (also identified with Fate and Providence) that governs nature, and are indifferent to the vicissitudes of fortune and to pleasure and pain.
stoke /stōk/ ▶*v.* [*tr.*] add coal or other solid fuel to (a fire, furnace, or boiler). ■ encourage or incite (a strong emotion or tendency): *his composure had the effect of stoking her anger.* ■ [often as *adj.*] (**stoked**) *inf.* excite or thrill: *when they told me I was on the team, I was stoked.* ■ [*intr.*] *inf.* consume a large quantity of food or drink to give one energy.
stoke·hole /ˈstōkˌhōl/ ▶*n.* a space in front of a furnace in which a stoker works.
stok·er /ˈstōkər/ ▶*n.* a person who tends the furnace on a steamship or steam locomotive. ■ a mechanical device for supplying fuel to a firebox or furnace, esp. on a steam locomotive.
STOL /ˈestôl; stôl/ ▶*abbr.* *Aeron.* short takeoff and landing.
stole[1] /stōl/ ▶*n.* a woman's long scarf or shawl, esp. fur or similar material, worn loosely over the shoulders. ■ of a strip of fabric used as an ecclesiastical vestment, worn over the shoulders and hanging down to the knee or below.
stole[2] ▶ past of STEAL.
sto·len /ˈstōlən/ ▶ past participle of STEAL.
stol·id /ˈstälid/ ▶*adj.* (of a person) calm, dependable, and showing little emotion or animation. —**sto·lid·i·ty** /stəˈliditē/ *n.* —**stol·id·ly** *adv.* —**stol·id·ness** *n.*
sto·ma /ˈstōmə/ ▶*n.* (*pl.* **sto·mas** or **sto·ma·ta** /-mətə; ˌstōˈmätə/) *Bot.* any of the minute pores in the epidermis of the leaf or stem of a plant, forming a slit of variable width that allows movement of gases in and

---

Pronunciation Key ə *ago,* up; ər *over,* fur; a *hat;* ā *ate;* ä *car;* CH *chin;* e *let;* ē *see;* e(ə)r *air;* i *fit;* ī *by;* i(ə)r *ear;* NG *sing;* ō *go;* ô *law, for;* oi *toy;* o͞o *good;* o͞o *goo;* ou *out;* SH *she;* TH *thin;* ͟TH *then;* (h)w *why;* ZH *vision*

out of the intercellular spaces. ■ *Med.* an artificial opening made into a hollow organ, esp. one on the surface of the body leading to the gut or trachea. —**sto·mal** *adj. (Med.).*

stom·ach /ˈstəmək/ ▸*n.* **1** the internal organ in which the first part of digestion occurs, being (in humans and many mammals) a pear-shaped enlargement of the alimentary canal linking the esophagus to the small intestine. ■ each of four such organs in a ruminant. ■ any of a number of analogous organs in lower animals. ■ the front part of the body between the chest and thighs; the belly: *Blake hit him in the stomach.* ■ the stomach viewed as the seat of hunger, nausea, anxiety, or other unsettling feelings: *Virginia had a sick feeling in her stomach.* **2** an appetite for food or drink: *she doesn't have the stomach to eat anything.* ■ a desire or inclination for something involving conflict, difficulty, or unpleasantness: *the teams proved to have no stomach for a fight.*
▸*v.* [*tr.*] (usu. **cannot stomach**) consume (food or drink) without feeling or being sick: *if you cannot stomach orange juice, try apple juice.* ■ endure or accept (an obnoxious thing or person): *I can't stomach the self-righteous attitude of some managers.* ▷Middle English: from Old French *estomac, stomaque,* via Latin from Greek *stomakhos* 'gullet,' from *stoma* 'mouth.' The early sense of the verb was 'be offended at, resent' (early 16th cent.). —**stom·ach·ful** /-ˌfŏŏl/ *n.* (*pl.* **-fuls**).

stom·ach·ache /ˈstəmək͵āk/ ▸*n.* a pain in a person's belly: *most childhood stomachaches aren't serious.*

sto·ma·ta /ˈstōmətə; stōˈmätə/ ▸ plural form of STOMA.

stomp /stämp; stômp/ ▸*v.* [*intr.*] tread heavily and noisily, typically in order to show anger: *Martin stomped off to the spare room.* ■ [*intr.*] (**stomp on**) tread heavily or stamp on: *I stomped on the accelerator.* ■ [*tr.*] deliberately trample or tread heavily on: *Cobb proceeded to kick and stomp him viciously.* ■ [*tr.*] stamp (one's feet). ■ [*intr.*] dance with heavy stamping steps.
▸*n. inf.* (in jazz or popular music) a tune or song with a fast tempo and a heavy beat. ■ a lively dance performed to such music, involving heavy stamping. —**stomp·er** *n.* —**stomp·y** *adj.*

stone /stōn/ ▸*n.* **1** the hard, solid, nonmetallic mineral matter of which rock is made, esp. as a building material: *the houses are built of stone.* ■ a small piece of rock found on the ground. ■ (in metaphorical use) weight or lack of feeling, expression, or movement: *Isabel stood as if turned to stone.* ■ *Astron.* a meteorite made of rock, as opposed to metal. ■ *Med.* a calculus; a gallstone or kidney stone. **2** a piece of stone shaped for a purpose, esp. one of commemoration, ceremony, or demarcation: *a memorial stone.* ■ a gem or jewel. ■ a round piece or counter, originally made of stone, used in various board games such as backgammon. **3** a hard seed in a cherry, plum, peach, and some other fruits. **4** (*pl.* same) *Brit.* a unit of weight equal to 14 pounds (6.35 kg): *I weighed 10 stone.* **5** a natural shade of whitish-gray or brownish-gray: [as *adj.*] *stone stretch trousers.*
▸*v.* [*tr.*] throw stones at: *policemen were stoned by the crowd.* ■ *chiefly hist.* execute (someone) by throwing stones at them: *Stephen was stoned to death in Jerusalem.* —**stone·less** *adj.*
▸ □ **be written** (or **engraved** or **set**) **in stone** used to emphasize that something is fixed and unchangeable: *anything can change—nothing is written in stone.* □ **leave no stone unturned** try every possible course of action in order to achieve something. □ **a stone's throw** a short distance: *wild whales blowing a stone's throw from the boat.*

Stone Age ▸ a prehistoric period when weapons and tools were made of stone or of organic materials such as bone, wood, or horn.

stone·crop /ˈstōn͵kräp/ ▸*n.* a small fleshy-leaved plant (genus *Sedum,* family Crassulaceae) that typically has star-shaped yellow or white flowers and grows among rocks or on walls.

stone·cut·ter /ˈstōn͵kətər/ ▸*n.* a person who cuts stone from a quarry or who shapes and carves it for use.

stoned /stōnd/ ▸*adj. inf.* under the influence of drugs, esp. marijuana: *he was up in the deck chair getting stoned.* ■ very drunk.

stone deaf ▸*adj.* completely deaf: *the stone-deaf person relies entirely on sight.*

stone·fish /ˈstōn͵fiSH/ ▸*n.* (*pl.* same or **-fishes**) a chiefly marine fish (*Synanceia* and other genera, family Synanceiidae) of bizarre appearance that lives in the tropical Indo-Pacific. It rests motionless in the sand with its venomous dorsal spines projecting.

stone fruit ▸*n.* a fruit with flesh or pulp enclosing a stone, such as a peach, plum, or cherry.

stone·ground /ˈstōn͵ground/ ▸*adj.* (of flour) ground with millstones.

stone·ma·son /ˈstōn͵māsən/ ▸*n.* a person who cuts, prepares, and builds with stone. —**stone·ma·son·ry** /-͵māsənrē/ *n.*

stone·wall /ˈstōn͵wôl/ ▸*v.* [*tr.*] delay or block (a request, process, or

person) by refusing to answer questions or by giving evasive replies, esp. in politics: *the highest level of bureaucracy stonewalled us.* —**stone·wall·er** *n.*

stoneware /ˈstōn͵we(ə)r/ ▸*n.* a type of pottery that is impermeable and partly vitrified but opaque.

stone·washed /ˈstōn͵wôSHt; -͵wäSHt/ (also **stone-wash**) ▸*adj.* (of a garment or fabric, esp. denim) washed with abrasives to produce a worn or faded appearance.

stone·work /ˈstōn͵wərk/ ▸*n.* the parts of a building that are made of stone. ■ the work of a mason: *a masterpiece of clever stonework.* —**stone·work·er** *n.*

stone·wort /ˈstōnwərt; -͵wôrt/ ▸*n.* a freshwater plant (*Chara* and other genera, class Charophyceae) with whorls of slender leaves, related to green algae. Many kinds become encrusted with chalky deposits, giving them a stony feel.

ston·y /ˈstōnē/ ▸*adj.* (**ston·i·er, ston·i·est**) covered with or full of small pieces of rock: *rough stony paths.* ■ made of or resembling stone: *stony steps.* ■ not having or showing feeling or sympathy: *Lorenzo's hard, stony eyes* | [in *comb.*] *he walked away, stony-faced.* ■ *Astron.* (of a meteorite) consisting mostly of rock, as opposed to metal. —**ston·i·ly** /-nəlē/ *adv.* —**ston·i·ness** *n.*

stood /stŏŏd/ ▸ past and past participle of STAND.

stooge /stōōj/ ▸*n. derog.* a person who serves merely to support or assist others, particularly in doing unpleasant work: *you fell for that helpless-female act and let her make you a stooge.* ■ a person who is employed to assume a particular role while keeping their true identity hidden: *a police stooge.*

stool /stōōl/ ▸*n.* **1** a seat without a back or arms, typically resting on three or four legs or on a single pedestal. ■ a support on which to stand in order to reach high objects. ■ short for FOOTSTOOL. **2** a piece of feces.
▸*v.* [*intr.*] (of a plant) throw up shoots from the root. ■ [*tr.*] cut back (a plant) to or near ground level in order to induce new growth.

stool·ie /ˈstōōlē/ ▸*n. inf.* short for STOOL PIGEON.

stool pi·geon ▸*n.* a police informer. ■ a person acting as a decoy.

stoop¹ /stōōp/ ▸*v.* [*intr.*] **1** bend one's head or body forward and downward: *he stooped down and reached toward the coin.* | [*tr.*] *the man stoops his head.* ■ have the head and shoulders habitually bent forward: *he tends to stoop when he walks.* **2** lower one's moral standards so far as to do something reprehensible: *Craig wouldn't stoop to thieving.* ■ condescend to do something.
▸*n.* **1** a posture in which the head and shoulders are habitually bent forward: *a tall, thin man with a stoop.* **2** the downward swoop of a bird of prey.

stoop² ▸*n.* a porch with steps in front of a house or other building.

stop /stäp/ ▸*v.* (**stopped, stop·ping**) **1** [*intr.*] (of an event, action, or process) come to an end; cease to happen: *his laughter stopped as quickly as it had begun.* ■ cease to perform a specified action or have a specified experience: *she stopped giggling.* ■ abandon a specified practice or habit: *I've stopped eating meat.* ■ stop moving or operating: *he stopped to look at the view.* ■ (of a bus or train) call at a designated place to pick up or let off passengers: *main-line trains stop at platform 7.* **2** [*tr.*] cause (an action, process, or event) to come to an end: *this harassment has got to be stopped.* ■ prevent (an action or event) from happening: *a security guard was killed trying to stop a raid.* ■ prevent or dissuade (someone) from continuing in an activity or achieving an aim: *a campaign is under way to stop the bombers.* ■ [*tr.*] prevent (someone or something) from performing a specified action or undergoing a specified experience: *you can't stop me from getting what I want.* ■ cause or order to cease moving or operating: *he stopped his car by the house.* ■ *inf.* be hit by (a bullet). ■ instruct a bank to withhold payment on (a check). ■ refuse to supply as usual; withhold or deduct: *the union has threatened to stop the supply of minerals.* **3** [*tr.*] block or close up (a hole or leak): *the drain has been stopped up.* ■ plug the upper end of (an organ pipe), giving a note an octave lower. ■ obtain the required pitch from (the string of a violin or similar instrument) by pressing at the appropriate point with the finger.
▸*n.* **1** a cessation of movement or operation: *all business came to a stop.* ■ a break or halt during a journey: *allow an hour or so for driving and as long as you like for stops.* ■ a place designated for a bus or train to pick up or drop off passengers: *the bus was pulling up at her stop.* ■ an object or part of a mechanism that is used to prevent something from moving: *the shelves have special stops to prevent them from being pulled out too far.* ■ used in telegrams to indicate a period: *MEET YOU AT THE AIRPORT STOP.* ■ *Phonet.* a consonant produced with complete closure of the vocal tract. **2** a set of organ pipes of a particular tone and range of pitch. ■ (also **stop knob**) a knob, lever, or similar device in an organ or

harpsichord that brings into play a set of pipes or strings of a particular tone and range of pitch. **3** *Photog.* the effective diameter of a lens. ■ a device for reducing this. ■ a unit of change of relative aperture or exposure (with a reduction of one stop equivalent to halving it). —**stop·pa·ble** *adj.*

▶ □ **pull out all the stops** make a very great effort to achieve something: *the director pulled out all the stops to meet the impossible deadline.* ■ do something very elaborately or on a grand scale: *they gave a Christmas party and pulled out all the stops.*

stop-and-go ▶*n.* [usu. as *adj.*] alternate stopping and restarting of progress: *stop-and-go driving.*

stop·cock /'stäp,käk/ ▶*n.* an externally operated valve regulating the flow of a liquid or gas through a pipe.

stop·gap /'stäp,gap/ ▶*n.* a temporary way of dealing with a problem or satisfying a need: *transplants are only a stopgap until more sophisticated alternatives can work.*

stop·light /'stäp,līt/ ▶*n.* another term for TRAFFIC LIGHT. ■ a red traffic light.

stop-off ▶*n.* another term for STOPOVER.

stop·o·ver /'stäp,ōvər/ ▶*n.* a break in a journey: *the one-day stopover in Honolulu.* ■ a place where a journey is broken.

stop·page /'stäpij/ ▶*n.* an instance of movement, activity, or supply stopping or being stopped: *the result of the air raid was complete stoppage of production.* ■ a blockage in a narrow passage, such as the barrel of a gun. ■ a cessation of work by employees protesting the terms set by their employers.

stop·per /'stäpər/ ▶*n.* **1** a plug for sealing a hole, esp. in the neck of a bottle or other container. **2** a person or thing that halts or obstructs a specified thing: [in *comb.*] *a crime-stopper.* ■ (in soccer and other sports) a player whose function is to block attacks on goal from the middle of the field. ■ *Baseball* a starting pitcher depended on to win a game or stop a losing streak, or a relief pitcher used to prevent the opposing team from scoring. ■ (in sailing or climbing) a rope or clamp for preventing a rope or cable from running out.
▶*v.* [usu. as *adj.*] (**stoppered**) use a stopper to seal (a bottle or other container): *a small stoppered jar.*

stop·watch /'stäp,wäcH/ ▶*n.* a special watch with buttons that start, stop, and then zero the hands, used to time races.

stor·age /'stôrij/ ▶*n.* the action or method of storing something for future use: *the chair can be folded flat for easy storage.* ■ the retention of retrievable data on a computer or other electronic system; memory. ■ space available for storing something, esp. allocated space in a warehouse: *Cooper had put much of the furniture into storage.* ■ the cost of storing something in a warehouse.

stor·age bat·ter·y (also **storage cell**) ▶*n.* a battery (or cell) used for storing electrical energy.

store /stôr/ ▶*n.* **1** a retail establishment selling items to the public: *a health-food store.* ■ [as *adj.*] store-bought: *there's a loaf of store bread.* **2** a quantity or supply of something kept for use as needed: *the squirrel has a store of food.* ■ a place where things are kept for future use or sale: *a grain store.* ■ (**stores**) supplies of equipment and food kept for use by members of an army, navy, or other institution, or the place where they are kept.
▶*v.* [*tr.*] keep or accumulate (something) for future use: *a small room used for storing furniture.* ■ retain or enter (information) for future electronic retrieval: *the data is stored on disk.* ■ (**be stored with**) have a supply of (something useful): *a mind well stored with esoteric knowledge.* ■ [*intr.*] remain fresh while being stored: *they do not ship or store well.* —**stor·a·ble** *adj.* —**stor·er** *n.*

▶ □ **in store 1** in a safe place while not being used or displayed: *items held in store.* **2** coming in the future; about to happen: *he did not yet know what lay in store for him.*

store·front /'stôr,frənt/ ▶*n.* **1** the facade of a store. **2** a room or set of rooms facing the street on the ground floor of a commercial building, typically used as a store: [as *adj.*] *a bright storefront eatery.*

store·house /'stôr,hous/ ▶*n.* a building used for storing goods. ■ a large supply of something: *an enormous storehouse of facts.*

store·keep·er /'stôr,kēpər/ ▶*n.* **1** a person who owns or runs a store. **2** a person responsible for stored goods.

store·room /'stôr,rōōm; -,rŏŏm/ ▶*n.* a room in which items are stored.

sto·ried /'stôrēd/ ▶*adj. poetic/lit.* celebrated in or associated with stories or legends: *the island's storied past.*

stork /stôrk/ ▶*n.* a tall long-legged wading bird (family Ciconiidae) with a long heavy bill and typically with white and black plumage, esp. the

European **white stork** (*Ciconia ciconia*), which often nests on tall buildings. ■ the white stork as the pretended bringer of babies.

storm /stôrm/ ▶*n.* **1** a violent disturbance of the atmosphere with strong winds and usually rain, thunder, lightning, or snow. ■ (also **storm system**) an intense low-pressure weather system; a cyclone. ■ a wind of force 10 on the Beaufort scale (48–55 knots or 55-63 mph). ■ a heavy discharge of missiles or blows: *two men were taken by a storm of bullets.* **2** a tumultuous reaction; an uproar or controversy: *the book caused a storm in South America.* ■ a violent or noisy outburst of a specified feeling or reaction: *the disclosure raised a storm of protest.* **3** (**storms**) storm windows.
▶*v.* **1** [*intr.*] move angrily or forcefully in a specified direction: *she burst into tears and stormed off.* ■ [with *direct speech*] shout (something) angrily; rage: "*Don't patronize me!*" *she stormed.* ■ move forcefully and decisively to a specified position in a game or contest: *he barged past and stormed to the checkered flag.* **2** [*tr.*] (of troops) suddenly attack and capture (a building or other place) by means of force: *Indian commandos stormed a hijacked plane early today.* **3** [*intr.*] (of the weather) be violent, with strong winds and usually rain, thunder, lightning, or snow: *when it stormed in the day, I shoveled the drive before Harry came home.* —**storm·proof** /-,prōōf/ *adj.*

▶ □ **take something by storm** (of troops) capture a place by a sudden and violent attack. ■ have great and rapid success in a particular place or with a particular group of people: *his first collection took the fashion world by storm.*

storm door ▶*n.* an additional outer door for protection in bad weather or winter.

storm pet·rel ▶*n.* a small seabird (*Hydrobates* and other genera, family Hydrobatidae) of the open ocean, typically having blackish plumage and a white rump, and formerly believed to be a harbinger of bad weather.

storm sail ▶*n.* a sail used in stormy weather, of smaller size and stronger material than the corresponding one used in ordinary weather.

storm sig·nal ▶*n.* a lamp, flag, or other device used to give a visible warning of an approaching storm.

storm troops ▶*pl. n.* another term for SHOCK TROOPS. ■ (**Storm Troops**) *hist.* the Nazi political militia. —**storm troop·er** *n.*

storm win·dow ▶*n.* a window installed outside a normal window for protection and insulation in bad weather or winter.

storm·y /'stôrmē/ ▶*adj.* (**storm·i·er, storm·i·est**) (of weather) characterized by strong winds and usually rain, thunder, lightning, or snow: *a dark and stormy night.* ■ (of the sea or sky) having large waves or dark clouds because of windy or rainy conditions: *gray and stormy skies.* ■ full of angry or violent outbursts of feeling: *a long and stormy debate.* —**storm·i·ly** /-məlē/ *adv.* —**storm·i·ness** *n.*

sto·ry[1] /'stôrē/ ▶*n.* (pl. **-ries**) **1** an account of imaginary or real people and events told for entertainment: *an adventure story.* ■ a plot or story line: *the novel has a good story.* ■ a report of an item of news in a newspaper, magazine, or news broadcast: *stories in the local papers.* ■ a piece of gossip; a rumor: *there have been lots of stories going around, as you can imagine.* ■ *inf.* a false statement or explanation; a lie: *Ellie never told stories—she had always believed in the truth.* **2** an account of past events in someone's life or in the evolution of something: *the story of modern farming.* ■ a particular person's representation of the facts of a matter, esp. as given in self-defense: *during police interviews, Harper changed his story.* ■ a situation viewed in terms of the information known about it or its similarity to another: *having such information is useful, but it is not the whole story.*

sto·ry[2] (*Brit.* also **sto·rey**) ▶*n.* a part of a building comprising all the rooms that are on the same level: [in *comb.*] *a three-story building.* —**sto·ried** (*Brit.* also **sto·reyed**) *adj.* [in *comb.*] *four-storied houses.*

sto·ry·board /'stôrē,bôrd/ ▶*n.* a sequence of drawings, typically with some directions and dialogue, representing the shots planned for a movie or television production.

sto·ry·book /'stôrē,bŏŏk/ ▶*n.* a book containing a story or collection of stories intended for children. ■ [as *adj.*] denoting something that is as idyllically perfect as things typically are in storybooks: *it was a storybook finish to an illustrious career.*

sto·ry·tell·er /'stôrē,telər/ ▶*n.* a person who tells stories. —**sto·ry·tell·ing** /-,teliNG/ *n.* & *adj.*

stout /stout/ ▶*adj.* **1** (of a person) somewhat fat or of heavy build: *stout* *middle-aged men.* ■ (of an object) strong and thick: *stout walking boots.* **2** (of an act, quality, or person) brave and determined: *he put up a stout defense in court.*

▶*n.* a kind of strong, dark beer brewed with roasted malt or barley. —**stout·ish** *adj.* (in sense 1). —**stout·ly** *adv.* —**stout·ness** *n.*

stout·heart·ed /'stout'härtid/ ▶*adj.* courageous or determined. —**stout·heart·ed·ly** *adv.* —**stout·heart·ed·ness** *n.*

stove¹ /stōv/ ▶*n.* an apparatus for cooking or heating that operates by burning fuel or using electricity.

stove² ▶ past and past participle of **STAVE**.

stove·pipe /'stōv,pīp/ ▶*n.* **1** the pipe taking the smoke and gases from a stove up through a roof or to a chimney. **2** an information conduit that traverses vertical levels efficiently but does not disperse widely: [as *adj.*] *a computer system that was expected to integrate 40 different stovepipe entities that previously were unable to communicate with one another.*

▶*v.* [*tr.*] transmit (information) directly through levels of a hierarchy: *neocons who stovepiped lies straight up to the White House.*

stove·pipe hat ▶*n.* a silk hat resembling a top hat but much taller.

stow /stō/ ▶*v.* [*tr.*] pack or store (an object) carefully and neatly in a particular place: *the bathhouse offers baskets in which to stow your clothes.*

▶*phrasal v.* □ **stow away** conceal oneself on a ship, aircraft, or other passenger vehicle in order to travel secretly or without paying the fare.

stow·age /'stōij/ ▶*n.* the action or manner of stowing something. ■ space for stowing something in: *there is plenty of stowage beneath the berth.*

stow·a·way /'stōə,wā/ ▶*n.* a person who stows away.

STP ▶*abbr.* ■ *Chem.* standard temperature and pressure.

stra·bis·mus /strə'bizməs/ ▶*n.* abnormal alignment of the eyes; the condition of having a squint. —**stra·bis·mic** /-mik/ *adj.*

strad·dle /'stradl/ ▶*v.* [*tr.*] sit or stand with one leg on either side of: *he turned the chair around and straddled it.* ■ place (one's legs) wide apart: *he shifted his legs, straddling them to keep his balance.* ■ extend across or be situated on both sides of: *a mountain range straddling the Franco-Swiss border.* ■ take up or maintain an equivocal position with regard to (a political issue): *a man who had straddled the issue of taxes.*

▶*n.* **1** an act of sitting or standing with one's legs wide apart. **2** *Stock Market* a simultaneous purchase of options to buy and to sell a security or commodity at a fixed price, allowing the purchaser to make a profit whether the price of the security or commodity goes up or down. —**strad·dler** *n.*

Strad·i·var·i·us /,stradə've(ə)rēəs/ ▶*n.* a violin or other stringed instrument made by Antonio Stradivari or his followers.

strafe /strāf/ ▶*v.* [*tr.*] attack repeatedly with bombs or machine-gun fire from low-flying aircraft: *military aircraft strafed the village.*

▶*n.* an attack from low-flying aircraft. ▷ early 20th cent.: humorous adaptation of the German World War I catchphrase *Gott strafe England* 'may God punish England.'

strag·gle /'stragəl/ ▶*v.* [*intr.*] move along slowly, typically in a small irregular group, so as to remain some distance behind the person or people in front: *half the men were already straggling back into the building.* ■ grow, spread, or be laid out in an irregular, untidy way: *her hair was straggling over her eyes.*

▶*n.* an untidy or irregularly arranged mass or group of something: *a straggle of cottages.* —**strag·gler** /'strag(ə)lər/ *n.* —**strag·gly** /'strag(ə)lē/ *adj.*

straight /strāt/ ▶*adj.* **1** extending or moving uniformly in one direction only; without a curve or bend: *a long, straight road.* ■ *Geom.* (of a line) lying on the shortest path between any two of its points. ■ (of an aim, blow, or course) going direct to the intended target: *a straight punch to the face.* ■ (of hair) not curly or wavy. ■ (of a garment) not flared or fitted closely to the body: *a straight skirt.* ■ (of an arch) flat-topped. **2** properly positioned so as to be level, upright, or symmetrical: *he made sure his tie was straight.* ■ in proper order or condition: *it'll take a long time to get the place straight.* **3** not evasive; honest: *a straight answer.* ■ simple; straightforward: *a straight choice between nuclear power and penury.* ■ (of a look) bold and steady: *he gave her a straight, no-nonsense look.* ■ (of thinking) clear, logical, and unemotional. ■ not addicted to drugs. **4** in continuous succession: *he scored his fourth straight win.* ■ supporting all the principles and candidates of one political party: *he generally voted a straight ticket.* **5** (of an alcoholic drink) undiluted; neat: *straight brandy.* **6** (esp. of drama) serious as opposed to comic or musical; employing the conventional techniques of its art form: *a straight play.* ■ *inf.* (of a person) conventional or respectable: *she looked pretty straight in her school clothes.* ■ *inf.* heterosexual.

▶*adv.* **1** in a straight line; directly: *he was gazing straight at her.* ■ with no

delay or diversion; directly or immediately: *after dinner we went straight back to our hotel.* **2** in or into a level, even, or upright position: *he pulled his clothes straight.* **3** correctly; clearly: *I'm so tired I can hardly think straight.* ■ honestly and directly; in a straightforward manner: *I told her straight—the kid's right.* **4** without a break; continuously: *he remembered working sixteen hours straight.*

▶*n.* **1** a part of something that is not curved or bent, esp. the concluding stretch of a racetrack: *he pulled away in the straight to win by half a second.* **2** *Poker* a continuous sequence of five cards. **3** *inf.* a conventional person. ■ a heterosexual. —**straight·ish** *adj.* —**straight·ly** *adv.* —**straight·ness** *n.*

▶ □ **a straight face** a blank or serious facial expression, esp. when trying not to laugh: *my father kept a straight face when he joked.*

straight·a·way /'strātə,wā/ ▶*adv.* immediately.

▶*adj.* extending or moving in a straight line.

▶*n.* a straight section of a road or racetrack.

straight·edge /'strāt,ej/ ▶*n.* a bar with one accurately straight edge, used for testing whether something else is straight, or for drawing a straight line.

straight·en /'strātn/ ▶*v.* make or become straight: [*tr.*] *she helped him straighten his tie* | [*intr.*] *where the river straightened he took his chance to check the barometer.* ■ [*tr.*] make tidy or put in order again: *he sat down at his desk, straightening his things that Lee had moved.* ■ [*intr.*] stand or sit erect after bending: *he straightened up, using the bedside table for support.* ■ [*intr.*] (**straighten up**) (of a vehicle, ship, or aircraft) stop turning and move in a straight line. —**straight·en·er** *n.*

straight·for·ward /,strāt'fôrwərd/ ▶*adj.* uncomplicated and easy to do or understand: *in a straightforward case no fees will be charged.* ■ (of a person) honest and frank: *a straightforward young man.* —**straight·for·ward·ly** *adv.* —**straight·for·ward·ness** *n.*

straight·jack·et ▶*n. & v.* variant spelling of **STRAITJACKET**.

straight-laced ▶*adj.* variant spelling of **STRAIT-LACED**.

straight man ▶*n.* the person in a comedy duo who speaks lines that give a comedian the opportunity to make jokes.

straight ra·zor ▶*n.* a razor having a long blade set in a handle, usually folding like a penknife.

strain¹ /strān/ ▶*v.* **1** [*tr.*] force (a part of one's body or oneself) to make a strenuous or unusually great effort: *I stopped and listened, straining my ears for any sound.* ■ injure (a limb, muscle, or organ) by overexerting it or twisting it awkwardly: *on cold days you are more likely to strain a muscle.* ■ [*intr.*] make a strenuous and continuous effort: *his voice was so quiet that I had to strain to hear it.* ■ make severe or excessive demands on: *he strained her tolerance to the limit.* ■ [*intr.*] pull or push forcibly at something: *the bear strained at the chain around its neck.* ■ stretch (something) tightly: *the barbed wire fence was strained to posts six feet high.* **2** [*tr.*] pour (a mainly liquid substance) through a porous or perforated device or material in order to separate out any solid matter: *strain the custard into a bowl.* ■ cause liquid to drain off (food that has been boiled, soaked, or canned) by using such a device. ■ drain off (liquid) in this way: *strain off the surplus fat.*

▶*n.* **1** a force tending to pull or stretch something to an extreme or damaging degree: *the usual type of chair puts an enormous strain on the spine* | *aluminum may bend under strain.* ■ *Physics* the magnitude of a deformation, equal to the change in the dimension of a deformed object divided by its original dimension. ■ an injury to a part of the body caused by overexertion or twisting a muscle awkwardly: *he has a slight groin strain.* **2** a severe or excessive demand on the strength, resources, or abilities of someone or something: *the accusations put a strain on relations between the two countries.* ■ a state of tension or exhaustion resulting from this: *the telltale signs of nervous strain.* **3** (usu. **strains**) the sound of a piece of music as it is played or performed: *through the open windows came the strains of a hurdy-gurdy playing in the street.* —**strain·a·ble** *adj.*

strain² ▶*n.* **1** a breed, stock, or variety of an animal or plant developed by breeding. ■ a natural or cultured variety of a microorganism with a distinct form, biochemistry, or virulence. **2** a particular tendency as part of a person's character: *there was a powerful strain of insanity on her mother's side of the family.* ■ a variety of a particular abstract thing: *a strain of feminist thought.*

strained /strānd/ ▶*adj.* **1** (of an atmosphere, situation, or relationship) not relaxed or comfortable; tense or uneasy: *there was a strained silence.* ■ (of a person) showing signs of tiredness or nervous tension: *Jean's pale, strained face.* ■ (of an appearance or performance) produced by deliberate effort rather than natural impulse; artificial or forced: *I put on my strained smile for the next customer.* ■ (of a statement or representation) labored or far-fetched: *my example may seem a little strained and artificial.* **2** (of a limb or muscle) injured by overexertion or twisting.

3 (of a mainly liquid substance) having been strained to separate out any solid matter.

strain·er /ˈstrānər/ ▶ *n.* a device having holes punched in it or made of crossed wires for separating solid matter from a liquid: *a tea strainer.*

strait /strāt/ ▶ *n.* **1** (also **straits**) a narrow passage of water connecting two seas or other large bodies of water: [in *place names*] *the Strait of Gibraltar.* **2** (**straits**) used in reference to a situation characterized by a specified degree of trouble or difficulty: *the economy is in dire straits.* ▷Middle English: shortening of Old French *estreit* 'tight, narrow,' from Latin *strictus* 'drawn tight,' from the verb *stringere.* —**strait·ly** *adv.* —**strait·ness** *n.*

strait·jack·et /ˈstrāt.jakət/ (also **straight·jack·et**) ▶ *n.* a strong garment with long sleeves that can be tied together to confine the arms of a violent prisoner or mental patient. ■ used in reference to something that restricts freedom of action, development, or expression: *the government is operating in an economic straitjacket.*
▶ *v.* (**-jack·et·ed, -jack·et·ing**) [*tr.*] restrain with a straitjacket. ■ impose severely restrictive measures on (a person or activity): *the treaty should not be used as a tool to straitjacket international trade.*

strait-laced (also **straight-laced**) ▶ *adj.* having or showing very strict moral attitudes.

strand[1] /strand/ ▶ *v.* [*tr.*] drive or leave (a boat, sailor, or sea creature) aground on a shore: *the ships were stranded in shallow water.* ■ leave (someone) without the means to move from somewhere: *they were stranded in St. Louis by the blizzard.*
▶ *n. poetic/lit.* the shore of a sea, lake, or large river: *a heron glided to rest on a pebbly strand.*

strand[2] ▶ *n.* a single thin length of something such as thread, fiber, or wire, esp. as twisted together with others: *a strand of cotton.* ■ a string of beads or pearls. ■ an element that forms part of a complex whole: *Marxist theories evolved from different strands of social analysis.*

strange /strānj/ ▶ *adj.* **1** unusual or surprising in a way that is unsettling or hard to understand: *children have some strange ideas.* **2** not previously visited, seen, or encountered; unfamiliar or alien: *she found herself in bed in a strange place.* **3** *Physics* having a nonzero value for strangeness. —**strange·ly** *adv. the house was strangely quiet* | *strangely enough, people were able to perform this task without difficulty.* —**strange·ness** *n.*

stran·ger /ˈstrānjər/ ▶ *n.* a person whom one does not know or with whom one is not familiar: *don't talk to strangers* | *she remained a stranger to him.* ■ a person who does not know, or is not known in, a particular place or community: *I'm a stranger in these parts* | *he must have been a stranger to the village.* ■ (**stranger to**) a person entirely unaccustomed to (a feeling, experience, or situation): *he is no stranger to controversy.*

stran·gle /ˈstranGgəl/ ▶ *v.* [*tr.*] squeeze or constrict the neck of (a person or animal), esp. so as to cause death: *the victim was strangled with a scarf.* ■ [as *adj.*] (**strangled**) sounding as though the speaker's throat is constricted: *a series of strangled gasps.* ■ suppress (an impulse, action, or sound): *she strangled a sob.* ■ hamper or hinder the development or activity of: *overrestrictive policies that strangle growth.* —**stran·gler** /ˈstranGg(ə)lər/ *n.*

stran·gle·hold /ˈstranGgəl.hōld/ ▶ *n.* a grip around the neck of another person that can kill by asphyxiation if held for long enough. ■ complete or overwhelming control: *he broke the union that held a stranglehold on bus service.*

stran·gu·late /ˈstranGgyə.lāt/ ▶ *v.* [*tr.*] [often as *adj.*] (**strangulated**) *Med.* prevent circulation of the blood supply through (a part of the body, esp. a hernia) by constriction: *a strangulated hernia.*

stran·gu·la·tion /ˌstranGgyəˈlāSHən/ ▶ *n.* **1** the action or state of strangling or being strangled: *death due to strangulation.* ■ the process or state of severely restricting the activities or supplies of an area or community or of undergoing such restrictions: *economic strangulation.* **2** *Med.* the condition in which circulation of blood to a part of the body (esp. a hernia) is cut off by constriction.

strap /strap/ ▶ *n.* a strip of leather, cloth, or other flexible material, often with a buckle, used to fasten, secure, or carry something or to hold on to something: *her bra strap.* ■ a strip of metal, often hinged, used to fasten or secure something. ■ (**the strap**) punishment by beating with a strip of leather. ■ variant form of **STROP**.
▶ *v.* (**strapped, strap·ping**) **1** [*tr.*] fasten or secure in a specified place or position with a strap or seat belt: *I had to strap the bag to my bicycle.* **2** [*tr.*] beat (someone) with a strip of leather: *I expected when my dad walked in that he'd strap him.* —**strap·py** *adj.*

strap·hang·er /ˈstrap.haNGər/ ▶ *n. inf.* a standing passenger in a bus or train. ■ a person who commutes to work by public transportation. —**strap·hang** *v.*

strap·less /ˈstrapləs/ ▶ *adj.* (esp. of a dress or bra) without shoulder straps.

strap·ping[1] /ˈstrapiNG/ ▶ *adj.* (esp. of a young person) big and strong: *they had three strapping sons.*

strap·ping[2] ▶ *n.* strips of leather or pliable metal used to hold, strengthen, or fasten something.

stra·ta /ˈstrātə; ˈstratə/ ▶ plural form of **STRATUM**.

strat·a·gem /ˈstratəjəm/ ▶ *n.* a plan or scheme, esp. one used to outwit an opponent or achieve an end: *a series of devious stratagems.*

stra·te·gic /strəˈtējik/ ▶ *adj.* relating to the identification of long-term or overall aims and interests and the means of achieving them: *the company should take strategic actions to cope with fundamental changes in the environment.* ■ carefully designed or planned to serve a particular purpose or advantage: *alarms are positioned at strategic points around the prison.* ■ relating to the gaining of overall or long-term military advantage: *New Orleans was of strategic importance.* ■ (of human or material resources) essential in fighting a war: *the strategic forces on Russian territory.* ■ (of bombing or weapons) done or for use against industrial areas and communication centers of enemy territory as a long-term military objective: *strategic nuclear missiles.* —**stra·te·gi·cal** *adj.* —**stra·te·gi·cal·ly** /-ik(ə)lē/ *adv. a strategically placed mirror.*

Strategic Defense Initiative (abbr.: **SDI**) ▶ a military defense strategy proposed by President Ronald Reagan in 1983, in which enemy weapons would be destroyed in space by lasers, antiballistic missiles, etc., launched or directed from orbiting military satellites.

strat·e·gy /ˈstratəjē/ ▶ *n.* (*pl.* **-gies**) a plan of action or policy designed to achieve a major or overall aim: *time to develop a coherent economic strategy.* ■ the art of planning and directing overall military operations and movements in a war or battle. ■ a plan for such military operations and movements: *nonprovocative defense strategies.* —**strat·e·gist** *n.*

strat·i·fy /ˈstratə.fī/ ▶ *v.* (**-fies, -fied**) [*tr.*] [usu. as *adj.*] (**stratified**) form or arrange into strata: *socially stratified cities* | [*intr.*] *the residues have begun to stratify.* ■ arrange or classify: *stratifying patients into well-defined risk groups.* —**strat·i·fi·ca·tion** /ˌstratəfiˈkāSHən/ *n.*

stra·tig·ra·phy /strəˈtigrəfē/ ▶ *n.* the branch of geology concerned with the order and relative position of strata and their relationship to the geological time scale. ■ the analysis of the order and position of layers of archaeological remains. ■ the structure of a particular set of strata. —**stra·tig·ra·pher** /-fər/ *n.* —**strat·i·graph·ic** /ˌstratəˈgrafik/ *adj.* —**strat·i·graph·i·cal** /ˌstratəˈgrafikəl/ *adj.*

stra·to·cu·mu·lus /ˌstratōˈkyo͞omyələs; ˌstrā-/ ▶ *n.* cloud forming a low layer of clumped or broken gray masses.

strat·o·sphere /ˈstratə.sfi(ə)r/ ▶ *n.* the layer of the earth's atmosphere above the troposphere, extending to about 50 km above the earth's surface (the lower boundary of the mesosphere). ■ *fig.* the very highest levels of a profession or other sphere, or of prices or other quantities: *her next big campaign launched her into the fashion stratosphere.* —**strat·o·spher·ic** /ˌstratəˈsfi(ə)rik; -ˈsferik/ *adj.*

stra·tum /ˈstrātəm; ˈstra-/ ▶ *n.* (*pl.* **stra·ta** /ˈstrātə; ˈstra-/) **1** a layer or a series of layers of rock or unconsolidated material in the ground: *a stratum of sandstone.* ■ a thin layer within any structure: *thin strata of air.* **2** a level or class to which people are assigned according to their social status, education, or income: *members of other social strata.* ■ *Statistics* a group into which members of a population are divided in stratified sampling.

stra·tus /ˈstrātəs; ˈstra-/ ▶ *n.* cloud forming a continuous horizontal gray sheet, often with rain or snow.

straw /strô/ ▶ *n.* **1** dried stalks of grain, used esp. as fodder or as material for thatching, packing, or weaving: [as *adj.*] *a straw hat.* ■ a pale yellow color like that of straw: [as *adj.*] *a dull straw color.* ■ used in reference to something insubstantial or worthless: *it seemed as if the words were merely straw.* ■ anything or at all (used to emphasize how little something is valued): *if he finds you here, my life won't be worth a straw.* **2** a single dried stalk of grain: *the tramp sat chewing a straw.* ■ a stalk of grain or something similar used in drawing lots: *we had to draw straws for the food we had.* **3** a thin hollow tube of paper or plastic for sucking drink from a glass or bottle.
▶ □ **grasp** (or **clutch** or **catch**) **at straws** (or **a straw**) be in such a desperate situation as to resort to even the most unlikely means of salvation. □ **draw the short straw** be the unluckiest of a group of people, esp. in being chosen to perform an unpleasant task. □ **the last** (or **final**) **straw** a further difficulty or annoyance, typically minor in itself

but coming on top of a whole series of difficulties, that makes a situation unbearable: *his affair was the last straw.*

straw·ber·ry /ˈstrôˌberē; -bərē/ ▶*n.* **1** a sweet soft red fruit with a seed-studded surface. **2** the low-growing plant (genus *Fragaria*) of the rose family that produces this fruit, having white flowers, lobed leaves, and runners, and found throughout north temperate regions. **3** a deep pinkish-red color.

straw·ber·ry blond (also **strawberry blonde**) ▶*adj.* (of hair) of a light reddish-blond color. ■ (of a person) having hair of such a color.
▶*n.* a light reddish-blond hair color. ■ a person who has hair of such a color.

straw·ber·ry mark ▶*n.* a soft red birthmark.

straw poll (also **straw vote**) ▶*n.* an unofficial ballot conducted as a test of opinion: *I took a straw poll among my immediate colleagues.*

stray /strā/ ▶*v.* [*intr.*] move without a specific purpose or by mistake, esp. so as to get lost or arrive somewhere where one should not be: *I strayed a few blocks in the wrong direction.* ■ move so as to escape from control or leave the place where one belongs: *dog owners are urged not to allow their dogs to stray.* ■ [*intr.*] (of the eyes or a hand) move idly or casually in a specified direction: *her eyes strayed to the telephone.* ■ (of a person who is married or in a long-term relationship) be unfaithful: *men who stray are seen as more exciting and desirable.*
▶*adj.* **1** not in the right place; not where it should be or where other items of the same kind are: *he pushed a few stray hairs from her face.* ■ appearing somewhere by chance or accident; not part of a general pattern or plan: *she was killed by a stray bullet.* ■ (of a domestic animal) having no home or having wandered away from home: *stray dogs.* **2** *Physics* (of a physical quantity) arising as a consequence of the laws of physics, not by deliberate design, and usually having a detrimental effect on the operation or efficiency of equipment: *stray capacitance.*
▶*n.* **1** a stray person or thing, esp. a domestic animal. **2** (**strays**) electrical phenomena interfering with radio reception. —**stray·er** *n.*

streak /strēk/ ▶*n.* **1** a long, thin line or mark of a different substance or color from its surroundings: *a streak of oil.* **2** an element of a specified kind in someone's character: *there's a streak of insanity in the family.* ■ a continuous period of specified success or luck: *the theater is on a winning streak.*
▶*v.* **1** [*tr.*] cover (a surface) with streaks: *his beard was streaked with gray.* ■ dye (hair) with long, thin lines of a different, typically lighter color than one's natural hair color: [*tr.*] *hair that was streaked blond.* ■ *Microbiology* smear (a needle, swab, etc.) over the surface of a solid culture medium to initiate a culture. **2** [*intr.*] move very fast in a specified direction: *the cat leaped free and streaked across the street.* **3** [*intr.*] *inf.* run naked in a public place so as to shock or amuse others. —**streak·er** *n.*
▶ □ **like a streak** *inf.* very fast: *he is off like a streak.* □ **streak of lightning** a flash of lightning.

streak·y /ˈstrēkē/ ▶*adj.* (**streak·i·er, streak·i·est**) having streaks of different colors or textures: *streaky blond hair.* ■ *inf.* variable in quality; not predictable or reliable: *King has always been a famously streaky hitter.* —**streak·i·ly** /-lē/ *adv.* —**streak·i·ness** *n.*

stream /strēm/ ▶*n.* **1** a small, narrow river. **2** a continuous flow of liquid, air, or gas: *Frank blew out a stream of smoke.* ■ a current within a larger body of water or in the ocean. ■ (**a stream/streams of**) a mass of people or things moving continuously in the same direction: *there is a steady stream of visitors.* ■ (**a stream/streams of**) a large number of things that happen or come one after the other: *a woman shouted a stream of abuse.* ■ *Comput.* a continuous flow of data or instructions, typically one having a constant or predictable rate.
▶*v.* **1** [*intr.*] (of liquid) run or flow in a continuous current in a specified direction: *she sat with tears streaming down her face.* ■ (of a mass of people or things) move in a continuous flow in a specified direction: *he was watching the taxis streaming past.* **2** [*intr.*] (usu. **be streaming**) (of a person or part of the body) produce a continuous flow of liquid; run with liquid: *my eyes were streaming.* **3** [*intr.*] (of hair, clothing, etc.) float or wave at full extent in the wind: *her black cloak streamed behind her.* **4** *Comput.* [*tr.*] transmit (audio or video data) continuously, so that the parts arriving first can be viewed or listened to while the remainder is downloading. **5** British term for **TRACK** *verb* sense 4. ▷Old English *strēam* (noun), of Germanic origin; related to Dutch *stroom*, German *Strom*, from an Indo-European root shared by Greek *rhein* 'to flow.'
▶ □ **on stream** in or into operation or existence; available: *more jobs are coming on stream.*

stream·er /ˈstrēmər/ ▶*n.* a long, narrow strip of material used as a decoration or symbol: *plastic party streamers.* ■ [usu. as *adj.*] a banner headline in a newspaper: *his appearance was announced with a streamer headline.* ■ [usu. as *adj.*] *Fishing* a fly with feathers attached: *a streamer fly.*

stream·ing /ˈstrēmiNG/ ▶*n.* a method of relaying data (especially video and audio material) over a computer network as a steady continuous stream, allowing playback to proceed while subsequent data is being received.
▶*adj. Comput.* (of data) transmitted in a continuous stream while earlier parts are being used.

stream·line /ˈstrēmˌlīn/ ▶*v.* [*tr.*] [usu. as *adj.*] (**streamlined**) design or provide with a form that presents very little resistance to a flow of air or water, increasing speed and ease of movement: *streamlined passenger trains.* ■ *fig.* make (an organization or system) more efficient and effective by employing faster or simpler working methods: *the company streamlined its operations by removing whole layers of management.*
▶*n.* a line along which the flow of a moving fluid is least turbulent.

stream of con·scious·ness ▶*n. Psychol.* a person's thoughts and conscious reactions to events, perceived as a continuous flow. The term was introduced by William James in his *Principles of Psychology* (1890). ■ a literary style in which a character's thoughts, feelings, and reactions are depicted in a continuous flow uninterrupted by objective description or conventional dialogue. James Joyce, Virginia Woolf, and Marcel Proust are among its notable early exponents.

street /strēt/ ▶*n.* a public road in a city or town, typically with houses and buildings on one or both sides: *the narrow, winding streets of Greenwich Village.* ■ (**the street**) used to refer to the financial markets and activities on Wall Street. ■ (**the street/streets**) the roads or public areas of a city or town: *every week, fans stop me in the street.* ■ [as *adj.*] of or relating to the outlook, values, or lifestyle of those young people who are perceived as composing a fashionable urban subculture: *New York City street culture.* ■ [as *adj.*] denoting someone who is homeless: *he ministered to street people in storefront missions.* ■ [as *adj.*] performing or being performed on the street: *street theater.* —**street·ed** *adj.* [in *comb.*] *a many-streeted tangle of low, brick buildings.* —**street·ward** /-wərd/ *adj. & adv.*
▶ □ **on the streets 1** homeless. **2** working as a prostitute.

street·car /ˈstrētˌkär/ ▶*n.* another term for **TROLLEY CAR.**

street·light /ˈstrētˌlīt/ (also **street·lamp**) ▶*n.* a light illuminating a road, typically mounted on a tall pole.

street-smart ▶*adj. inf.* having the skills and knowledge necessary for dealing with modern urban life, esp. the difficult or criminal aspects of it: *a street-smart hustler on a motorcycle.*
▶*n.* (**street smarts**) these skills and knowledge: *take the advice of somebody who's got a little more street smarts than you.*

street val·ue ▶*n.* the price a commodity, esp. an amount of drugs, would fetch if sold illicitly: *detectives seized drugs with a street value of $300,000.*

street·walk·er /ˈstrētˌwôkər/ ▶*n.* a prostitute who seeks customers in the street. —**street·walk·ing** /-ˌwôkiNG/ *n. & adj.*

street·wise /ˈstrētˌwīz/ ▶*adj.* another term for **STREET SMART.** ■ reflective of modern urban life, esp. that of urban youth: *streetwise fashion.*

strength /streNG(k)TH; strenTH/ ▶*n.* **1** the quality or state of being strong, in particular: ■ physical power and energy: *cycling can help you build up your strength.* ■ the emotional or mental qualities necessary in dealing with situations or events that are distressing or difficult: *many people find strength in religion.* ■ the capacity of an object or substance to withstand great force or pressure: *they were taking no chances with the strength of the retaining wall.* ■ the influence or power possessed by a person, organization, or country: *the political and military strength of European governments.* ■ the degree of intensity of a feeling or belief: *street protests demonstrated the strength of feeling against the president.* ■ the cogency of an argument or case: *the strength of the argument for property taxation.* ■ the potency, intensity, or speed of a force or natural agency: *the wind had markedly increased in strength.* ■ the potency or degree of concentration of a drug, chemical, or drink: *it's double the strength of your average beer.* **2** a good or beneficial quality or attribute of a person or thing: *his strength was his obsessive single-mindedness.* ■ *poetic/lit.* a person or thing perceived as a source of mental or emotional support: *he was my closest friend, my strength and shield.* **3** the number of people comprising a group, typically a team or army: *the peacetime strength of the army was 415,000.* ■ a number of people required to make such a group complete: *we are now more than 100 officers below strength.* —**strength·less** *adj.*
▶ □ **in strength** in large numbers: *security forces were out in strength.* □ **on the strength of** on the basis or with the justification of: *she got into Princeton on the strength of her essays.*

strength·en /ˈstreNG(k)THən; ˈstren-/ ▶*v.* make or become stronger: [*tr.*] *he advises an application of fluoride to strengthen the teeth* | [*intr.*] *the wind won't strengthen until after dark.* —**strength·en·er** *n.*

stren·u·ous /ˈstrenyōōəs/ ▶*adj.* requiring or using great exertion: *Beijing's strenuous efforts to join the World Trade Organization.* —**stren·u·ous·ly** *adv.* —**stren·u·ous·ness** *n.*

strep /strep/ ▶*n. inf. Med.* short for STREPTOCOCCUS.

strep throat ▶*n.* an acute sore throat caused by hemolytic streptococci and characterized by fever and inflammation.

strep·to·coc·cus /ˌstreptəˈkäkəs/ ▶*n.* (*pl.* **streptococci** /-ˈkäksī; -sē/) a bacterium of a genus that includes the agents of souring of milk and dental decay, and hemolytic pathogens causing various infections such as scarlet fever and pneumonia. —**strep·to·coc·cal** /-ˈkäkəl/ *adj.*

strep·to·my·cin /ˌstreptəˈmīsin/ ▶*n. Med.* an antibiotic produced by the bacterium *Streptomyces griseus.*

STRESS /stres/ ▶*n. Comput.* a language designed for use in solving civil engineering structural analysis problems.

stress /stres/ ▶*n.* **1** pressure or tension exerted on a material object: *the distribution of stress is uniform across the bar.* ■ the degree of this measured in units of force per unit area. **2** a state of mental or emotional strain or tension resulting from adverse or very demanding circumstances: *he's obviously **under** a lot of **stress** | [in comb.] stress-related illnesses.* ■ something that causes such a state: *the stresses and strains of public life.* **3** particular emphasis or importance: *he has started to **lay** greater **stress** on the government's role in industry.* ■ emphasis given to a particular syllable or word in speech, typically through a combination of relatively greater loudness, higher pitch, and longer duration: *normally, the stress falls on the first syllable.*
▶*v.* **1** give particular emphasis or importance to (a point, statement, or idea) made in speech or writing: [tr.] *they stressed the need for reform.* ■ [tr.] give emphasis to (a syllable or word) when pronouncing it. **2** [tr.] subject to pressure or tension: *this type of workout does stress the shoulder and knee joints.* **3** [tr.] cause mental or emotional strain or tension in: *I avoid many of the things that used to stress me before* | [as adj.] (**stressed**) *she should see a doctor if she is feeling particularly **stressed out**.* ■ [intr.] *inf.* become tense or anxious; worry: *don't stress—there's plenty of time to get a grip on the situation.* —**stress·less** *adj.*

stress·ful /ˈstresfəl/ ▶*adj.* causing mental or emotional stress: *corporate finance work can be stressful.* —**stress·ful·ly** *adv.* —**stress·ful·ness** *n.*

stretch /strecH/ ▶*v.* [intr.] **1** (of something soft or elastic) be made or be capable of being made longer or wider without tearing or breaking: *my sweater stretched in the wash.* ■ [tr.] cause to do this: *stretch the elastic.* ■ [tr.] pull (something) tightly from one point to another or across a space: *small squares of canvas were stretched over the bamboo frame.* ■ last or cause to last longer than expected: *her nap had stretched to two hours* | [tr.] *stretch your weekend into a mini summer vacation.* ■ [tr.] make great demands on the capacity or resources of: *the cost of the court case has **stretched** their finances **to the limit**.* ■ [tr.] adapt or extend the scope of (something) in a way that exceeds a reasonable or acceptable limit: *to describe her as sweet would be stretching it a bit.* **2** straighten or extend one's body or a part of one's body to its full length, typically so as to tighten one's muscles or in order to reach something: *the cat yawned and stretched.* **3** [intr.] extend or spread over an area or period of time: *the beach stretches for over four miles.*
▶*n.* **1** an act of stretching one's limbs or body: *I got up and had a stretch.* ■ the fact or condition of a muscle being stretched: *she could feel the stretch and pull of the muscles in her legs.* ■ *Baseball* a phase of a pitcher's delivery, during which the arms are raised above and behind the head. ■ *Baseball* a shortened form of a pitcher's windup, typically used to prevent base runners from stealing or gaining a long lead. ■ [usu. as adj.] the capacity of a material or garment to stretch or be stretched; elasticity: *stretch jeans.* ■ a difficult or demanding task: *it was a stretch for me sometimes to come up with the rent.* **2** a continuous area or expanse of land or water: *a treacherous stretch of road.* ■ a continuous period of time: *long stretches of time.* ■ *inf.* a period of time spent in prison: *a four-year stretch for tax fraud.* ■ a straight part of a racetrack, typically the homestretch: *he made a promising start, but faded down the stretch.* **3** [usu. as adj.] *inf.* a motor vehicle or aircraft modified so as to have extended seating or storage capacity: *a black stretch limo.* —**stretch·a·bil·i·ty** /-ə-ˈbilitē/ *n.* —**stretch·a·ble** *adj.* —**stretch·y** *adj.*
▶ □ **at a stretch** in one continuous period: *I often had to work for over twenty hours at a stretch.*

stretch·er /ˈstrecHər/ ▶*n.* **1** a framework of two poles with a long piece of canvas slung between them, used for carrying sick, injured, or dead people. ■ a gurney. **2** a thing that stretches something, in particular: ■ a wooden frame over which a canvas is spread and tautened ready for painting. **3** a rod or bar joining and supporting chair legs. ■ a crosspiece in the bottom of a boat on which a rower's feet

are braced. **4** a brick or stone laid with its long side along the face of a wall.

stretch marks ▶*pl. n.* streaks or stripes on the skin, esp. on the abdomen, caused by distension of the skin from obesity or during pregnancy.

strew /strōō/ ▶*v.* (*past part.* **strewn** /strōōn/ or **strewed**) [tr.] (usu. **be strewn**) scatter or spread (things) untidily over a surface or area: *a small room with newspapers strewn all over the floor.* ■ (usu. **be strewn with**) cover (a surface or area) with untidily scattered things: *the table was strewn with books and papers* | [as adj., in comb.] (**strewn**) *boulder-strewn slopes.* ■ be scattered or spread untidily over (a surface or area): *leaves strewed the path.* —**strew·er** *n.*

stri·a /ˈstrīə/ ▶*n.* (*pl.* **stri·ae** /ˈstrī-ē/) *technical* a linear mark, slight ridge, or groove on a surface, often one of a number of similar parallel features. ■ *Anat.* any of a number of longitudinal collections of nerve fibers in the brain.

stri·ate /ˈstrī-āt/ *technical* ▶*adj.* marked with striae: *the striate cortex.*
▶*v.* [tr.] [usu. as adj.] (**striated**) mark with striae: *striated bark.* —**stri·a·tion** /strīˈāsHən/ *n.*

strick·en /ˈstrikən/ ▶ past participle of STRIKE.
▶*adj.* seriously affected by an undesirable condition or unpleasant feeling: *the pilot landed the stricken aircraft* | *Raymond was stricken with grief* | [in comb.] *the farms were drought-stricken.* ■ (of a face or look) showing great distress: *she looked at Anne's stricken face, contorted with worry.*

strict /strikt/ ▶*adj.* demanding that rules concerning behavior are obeyed and observed: *a strict upbringing.* ■ (of a rule or discipline) demanding total obedience or observance; rigidly enforced: *civil servants are bound by strict rules on secrecy.* ■ (of a person) following rules or beliefs exactly: *a strict vegetarian.* ■ exact in correspondence or adherence to something; not allowing or admitting deviation or relaxation: *a strict interpretation of the law.* —**strict·ness** *n.*

strict·ly /ˈstrik(t)lē/ ▶*adv.* **1** in a way that involves rigid enforcement or that demands obedience: *he's been brought up strictly.* **2** used to indicate that one is applying words or rules exactly or rigidly: ***strictly speaking,** ham is a cured, cooked leg of pork.* ■ with no exceptions; completely or absolutely: *these foods are strictly forbidden.* ■ no more than; purely: *that visit was strictly business.*

stric·ture /ˈstrikcHər/ ▶*n.* **1** a restriction on a person or activity: *religious strictures on everyday life.* **2** a sternly critical or censorious remark or instruction: *his strictures on their lack of civic virtue.* **3** *Med.* abnormal narrowing of a canal or duct in the body: *a colonic stricture.* —**stric·tured** *adj.*

stride /strīd/ ▶*v.* (*past* **strode** /strōd/; *past part.* **strid·den** /ˈstridn/) [intr.] walk with long, decisive steps in a specified direction: *he strode across the road* | *fig. striding confidently toward the future.* ■ [tr.] walk about or along (a street or other place) in this way: *a woman striding the cobbled streets.*
▶*n.* **1** a long, decisive step: *he crossed the room in a couple of strides.* ■ the length of a step or manner of taking steps in walking or running: *the horse shortened its stride.* **2** (usu. **strides**) a step or stage in progress toward an aim: *great strides have been made toward equality.* ■ (**one's stride**) a good or regular rate of progress, esp. after a slow or hesitant start: *after months of ineffective campaigning, he seems to have **hit his stride**.* **3** [as adj.] denoting or relating to a rhythmic style of jazz piano playing in which the left hand alternately plays single bass notes on the downbeat and chords an octave higher on the upbeat: *a stride pianist.* —**strid·er** *n.*
▶ □ **take something in (one's) stride** deal with something difficult or unpleasant in a calm and accepting way: *we took each new disease in stride.*

stri·dent /ˈstrīdnt/ ▶*adj.* loud and harsh; grating: *his voice had become increasingly sharp, almost strident.* ■ presenting a point of view, esp. a controversial one, in an excessively and unpleasantly forceful way: *public pronouncements on the crisis became less strident.* ▷mid 17th cent.: from Latin *strident-* 'creaking,' from the verb *stridere.* —**stri·den·cy** *n.* —**stri·dent·ly** *adv.*

strife /strīf/ ▶*n.* angry or bitter disagreement over fundamental issues; conflict: *strife within the community.*

strike /strīk/ ▶*v.* (*past* **struck** /strək/) **1** [tr.] hit forcibly and deliberately with one's hand or a weapon or other implement: *he raised his hand, as if to strike me* | [intr.] *Edgar struck out at her.* ■ inflict (a blow): *he struck her two blows on the leg.* ■ accidentally hit (a part of one's body) against

something: *she fell, striking her head against the side of the boat.* ■ come into forcible contact or collision with: *he was struck by a car on Whitepark Road.* ■ (of a beam or ray of light or heat) fall on (an object or surface): *the light struck her ring, reflecting off the diamond.* ■ [*intr.*] (of a clock) indicate the time by sounding a chime or stroke: *the church clock struck twelve.* ■ ignite (a match) by rubbing it briskly against an abrasive surface. ■ produce (fire or a spark) as a result of friction: *his iron stick struck sparks from the pavement.* ■ bring (an electric arc) into being. **2** [*tr.*] (of a disaster, disease, or other unwelcome phenomenon) occur suddenly and have harmful or damaging effects on: *an earthquake struck the island* | [*intr.*] *tragedy struck when he was killed in a car crash* | [as *adj.* in *comb.*] (**struck**) *storm-struck areas.* ■ [*intr.*] carry out an aggressive or violent action, typically without warning: *it was eight months before the murderer struck again.* ■ (usu. **be struck down**) kill or seriously incapacitate (someone): *he was struck down by a mystery virus.* ■ (**strike something into**) cause or create a particular strong emotion in (someone): *drugs—a subject guaranteed to strike fear into parents' hearts.* ■ [*tr.*] cause (someone) to be in a specified state: *he was struck dumb.* **3** [*tr.*] (of a thought or idea) come into the mind of (someone) suddenly or unexpectedly: *a disturbing thought struck Melissa.* ■ cause (someone) to have a particular impression: *it struck him that Marjorie was unusually silent* | *the idea struck her as odd.* ■ (**be struck by/with**) find particularly interesting, noticeable, or impressive: *Lucy was struck by the ethereal beauty of the scene.* **4** [*intr.*] (of employees) refuse to work as a form of organized protest, typically in an attempt to obtain a particular concession or concessions from their employer: *workers may strike over threatened job losses.* ■ [*tr.*] undertake such action against (an employer). **5** [*tr.*] cancel, remove, or cross out with or as if with a pen: *strike his name from the list.* ■ (**strike someone off**) officially remove someone from membership of a professional group: *he had been struck off as a disgrace to the profession.* ■ (**strike something down**) abolish a law or regulation: *the law was struck down by the Supreme Court.* **6** [*tr.*] make (a coin or medal) by stamping metal. ■ (in cinematography) make (another print) of a film. ■ reach, achieve, or agree to (something involving agreement, balance, or compromise): *the team has struck a deal with a sports marketing agency.* ■ (in financial contexts) reach (a figure) by balancing an account: *last year's loss was struck after allowing for depreciation of 67 million dollars.* **7** [*tr.*] discover (gold, minerals, or oil) by drilling or mining. ■ [*intr.*] (**strike on/upon**) discover or think of, esp. unexpectedly or by chance: *pondering, she struck upon a brilliant idea.* ■ come to or reach: *several days out of the village, we struck the Gilgit Road.* **8** [*intr.*] move or proceed vigorously or purposefully: *she struck out into the lake with a practiced crawl.* ■ (**strike out**) start out on a new or independent course or endeavor: *after two years he was able to strike out on his own.* **9** [*tr.*] take down (a tent or the tents of an encampment): *it took ages to strike camp.* ■ dismantle (theatrical scenery): *the minute we finish this evening, they'll start striking the set.* ■ lower or take down (a flag or sail), esp. as a salute or to signify surrender: *the ship struck her German colors.* **10** [*intr.*] *Fishing* secure a hook in the mouth of a fish by jerking or tightening the line after it has taken the bait or fly.
▸*phrasal v.* □ **strike back** retaliate: *he struck back at critics who claim he is too negative.* □ **strike someone out** (or **strike out**) *Baseball* put a batter out (or be put out) from play as a batter by means of three strikes. ■ (**strike out**) *inf.* fail or be unsuccessful: *the company struck out the first time it tried to manufacture personal computers.* □ **strike up** (or **strike something up**) (of a band or orchestra) begin to play a piece of music: *they struck up the "Star-Spangled Banner"* ■ (**strike something up**) begin a friendship or conversation with someone, typically in a casual way.
▸*n.* **1** a refusal to work organized by a body of employees as a form of protest, typically in an attempt to gain a concession or concessions from their employer: *miners voted for an all-out strike.* ■ a refusal to do something expected or required, typically by a body of people, with a similar aim: *a rent strike.* **2** a sudden attack, typically a military one: *the threat of nuclear strikes.* ■ (in bowling) an act of knocking down all the pins with one's first ball. ■ *Fishing* an act or instance of jerking or tightening the line to secure a fish that has already taken the bait or fly. **3** a discovery of gold, minerals, or oil by drilling or mining: *the Lena goldfields strike of 1912.* **4** *Baseball* a pitch that is counted against the batter, in particular one that the batter swings at and misses, or that passes through the strike zone without the batter swinging, or that the batter hits foul (unless two strikes have already been called). A batter accumulating three strikes is out. ■ a pitch that passes through the strike zone and is not hit. ■ something to one's discredit: *when they returned from Vietnam they had two strikes against them.* **5** the horizontal or compass direction of a stratum, fault, or other geological feature.

▸ □ **strike a blow for** (or **at/against**) do something to help (or hinder) a cause, belief, or principle: *just by finishing the race, she hopes to strike a blow for womankind.* □ **strike a pose** (or **attitude**) hold one's body in a particular position to create an impression: *striking a dramatic pose, Antonia announced that she was leaving.* □ **strike while the iron is hot** make use of an opportunity immediately.
strike-bound /ˈstrīkˌbound/ ▸*adj.* immobilized or closed by a strike.
strike-break-er /ˈstrīkˌbrākər/ ▸*n.* a person who works or is employed in place of others who are on strike, thereby making the strike ineffectual. —**strike-break** v. —**strike-break-ing** /-ˌbrākiNG/ *n.*
strike-out /ˈstrīkˌout/ ▸*n. Baseball* an out called when a batter accumulates three strikes.
▸*adj. Comput.* (of text) having a horizontal line through the middle; crossed out.
strik-er /ˈstrīkər/ ▸*n.* **1** an employee on strike. **2** (chiefly in soccer) a forward or attacker: *a gifted striker of the ball.*
strike zone ▸*n. Baseball* an area over home plate extending approximately from the armpits to the knees of a batter when in the batting position. The ball must be pitched through this area in order for a strike to be called.
strik-ing /ˈstrīkiNG/ ▸*adj.* **1** attracting attention by reason of being unusual, extreme, or prominent: *the murder bore a striking similarity to an earlier shooting.* ■ dramatically good-looking or beautiful: *she is naturally striking.* **2** (of an employee) on strike: *striking mine workers.*
▸*n.* the action of striking: *substantial damage was caused by the striking of a submerged object.* —**strik-ing-ly** *adv. a strikingly beautiful girl.*
string /striNG/ ▸*n.* **1** material consisting of threads of cotton, hemp, or other material twisted together to form a thin length. ■ a piece of such material used to tie around or attach to something. ■ a piece of catgut or similar material interwoven with others to form the head of a sports racket. ■ a length of catgut or wire on a musical instrument, producing a note by vibration. ■ (**strings**) the stringed instruments in an orchestra. ■ [as *adj.*] of, relating to, or consisting of stringed instruments: *a string quartet.* **2** a set of things tied or threaded together on a thin cord: *she wore a string of agates around her throat.* ■ a sequence of similar items or events: *a string of burglaries.* ■ *Comput.* a linear sequence of characters, words, or other data. ■ a group of racehorses trained at one stable. ■ a team or player holding a specified position in an order of preference: *Gary was first string on the varsity football team.* **3** a tough piece of fiber in vegetables, meat, or other food, such as a tough elongated piece connecting the two halves of a bean pod. **4** a hypothetical one-dimensional subatomic particle having the dynamical properties of a flexible loop. ■ (also **cosmic string**) (in cosmology) a hypothetical threadlike concentration of energy within the structure of space-time.
▸*v.* (*past* **strung** /strəNG/) **1** [*tr.*] hang (something) so that it stretches in a long line: *lights were strung across the promenade.* ■ thread (a series of small objects) on a string: *he collected stones with holes in them and strung them on a strong cord.* ■ (**be strung**) be arranged in a long line: *the houses were strung along the road.* ■ (**string something together**) add items to one another to form a series or coherent whole: *he can't string two sentences together.* **2** [*tr.*] fit a string or strings to (a musical instrument, a racket, or a bow): *the harp had been newly strung.* **3** [*tr.*] remove the strings from (a bean).
▸*phrasal v.* □ **string someone along** *inf.* mislead someone deliberately over a length of time, esp. about one's intentions: *she had no plans to marry him—she was just stringing him along.* □ **string something out** cause something to stretch out; prolong something. ■ (**be strung out**) be nervous or tense: *I often felt strung out by daily stresses.* ■ (**be strung out**) be under the influence of alcohol or drugs: *he died, strung out on booze and cocaine.* □ **string someone/something up** kill someone by hanging. —**string-less** *adj.* —**string-like** /-ˌlīk/ *adj.*
▸ □ **no strings attached** *inf.* used to show that an offer or opportunity carries no special conditions or restrictions. □ **on a string** under one's control or influence: *I've got the world on a string.*
string bass /bās/ ▸*n.* (esp. among jazz musicians) a double bass.
string bean ▸*n.* **1** any of various beans eaten in their fibrous pods, such as scarlet runners. **2** *inf.* a tall thin person.
stringed /striNGd/ ▸*adj.* (of a musical instrument) having strings: [in *comb.*] *a three-stringed fiddle.*
strin-gent /ˈstrinjənt/ ▸*adj.* (of regulations, requirements, or conditions) strict, precise, and exacting: *California's air pollution guidelines are stringent.* —**strin-gen-cy** *n.* —**strin-gent-ly** *adv.*
string-er /ˈstriNGər/ ▸*n.* **1** a longitudinal structural piece in a framework, esp. that of a ship or aircraft. **2** *inf.* a newspaper correspondent not on the regular staff of a newspaper, esp. one retained on

a part-time basis to report on events in a particular place. **3** a side of a staircase, which supports the treads and risers. **4** [in *comb.*] a sports player holding a specified position in an order of preference: *a third-stringer on the football team.*

string·y /ˈstriNGē/ ▶ *adj.* (**string·i·er, string·i·est**) (esp. of hair) resembling string; long, thin, and lusterless. ■ (of a person) tall, wiry, and thin. ■ (of food) containing tough fibers and so hard to eat. ■ (of a liquid) viscous; forming strings. —**string·i·ly** /-lē/ *adv.* —**string·i·ness** *n.*

strip¹ /strip/ ▶ *v.* (**stripped, strip·ping**) [*tr.*] **1** remove all coverings from: *they stripped the bed.* ■ remove the clothes from (someone): [*tr.*] *the man had been stripped naked.* ■ [*intr.*] take off one's clothes: *they stripped and showered.* ■ pull or tear off (a garment or covering): *she stripped off her shirt.* ■ remove bark and branches from (a tree). ■ remove paint from (a surface) with solvent. ■ remove (paint) in this way: *strip off the existing paint.* ■ remove the stems from (tobacco). ■ milk (a cow) dry. **2** leave bare of accessories or fittings: *thieves stripped the room of luggage.* ■ remove the accessory fittings of or take apart (a machine, motor vehicle, etc.) to inspect or adjust it: *the tank was stripped down piece by piece.* **3** (**strip someone of**) deprive someone of (rank, power, or property): *the lieutenant was stripped of his rank.* **4** sell off (the assets of a company) for profit. ■ *Finance* divest (a bond) of its interest coupons so that it and they may be sold separately. **5** tear the thread or teeth from (a screw, gear, etc.). ■ [*intr.*] (of a screw, gear, etc.) lose its thread or teeth.
▶ *n.* an act of undressing, esp. in a striptease: *she got drunk and did a strip on top of the piano.* ■ [as *adj.*] used for or involving the performance of stripteases: *a campaigner against strip joints.*

strip² ▶ *n.* **1** a long, narrow piece of cloth, paper, plastic, or some other material: *a strip of linen.* ■ a long, narrow area of land. ■ a main road in or leading out of a town, lined with shops, restaurants, and other facilities. ■ steel or other metal in the form of narrow flat bars. **2** a comic strip.

stripe /strīp/ ▶ *n.* **1** a long narrow band or strip, typically of the same width throughout its length, differing in color or texture from the surface on either side of it: *a pair of blue shorts with pink stripes.* **2** a chevron sewn onto a uniform to denote military rank. ■ a type or category: *entrepreneurs of all stripes are joining in the offensive.*
▶ *v.* [*tr.*] (usu. **be striped**) mark with stripes: *her body was striped with bands of sunlight.*

striped /strīpt/ ▶ *adj.* marked with or having stripes: [in *comb.*] *a green-striped coat.*

striped bass /bas/ ▶ *n.* (also **strip·er** /ˈstrīpər/) a large bass (*Morone saxatilis*, family Perchicthyidae) of North American coastal waters, with dark horizontal stripes along the upper sides.

strip·ling /ˈstripliNG/ ▶ *n. humorous* a young man.

strip-mine ▶ *v.* [*tr.*] obtain (ore or coal) by open-pit mining: *lignite coal is strip-mined at depths of 45 to 100 feet* | [as *n.*] (**strip-mining**) *protected lands opened up to strip-mining for coal.*
▶ *n.* (**strip mine**) a mine worked by this method.

strip·per /ˈstripər/ ▶ *n.* **1** a device used for stripping something: *plier-style wire strippers.* ■ solvent for removing paint. **2** a striptease performer.

strip-search ▶ *v.* [*tr.*] search (someone) for concealed items, typically drugs or weapons, in a way that involves the removal of all their clothes.
▶ *n.* (**strip search**) an act of searching someone in such a way.

strip·tease /ˈstripˌtēz/ ▶ *n.* a form of entertainment in which a performer gradually undresses to music in a way intended to be sexually exciting. —**strip·teas·er** *n.*

strip·y /ˈstrīpē/ (also **strip·ey**) ▶ *adj.* striped: *a stripy T-shirt.*

strive /strīv/ ▶ *v.* (*past* **strove** /strōv/ or **strived**; *past part.* **striv·en** /ˈstrivən/ or **strived**) [*intr.*] make great efforts to achieve or obtain something: *national movements were striving for independence.* ■ struggle or fight vigorously: *scholars must strive against bias.* —**striv·er** *n.*

strobe /strōb/ *inf.* ▶ *n.* **1** a stroboscope. ■ a stroboscopic lamp: [as *adj.*] *strobe lights dazzled her.* **2** an electronic flash for a camera.
▶ *v.* [*intr.*] **1** flash intermittently: *the light of the fireworks strobed around the room.* ■ [*tr.*] light as if with a stroboscope: *a neon sign strobed the room.* **2** exhibit or give rise to strobing: *he explained that the stripes I was wearing would strobe.*

stro·bo·scope /ˈstrōbəˌskōp/ ▶ *n. Physics* an instrument for studying periodic motion or determining speeds of rotation by shining a momentary bright light at intervals so that a moving object appears stationary. ■ a lamp made to flash intermittently, esp. for this purpose. —**stro·bo·scop·ic** /ˌstrōbəˈskäpik/ *adj.* —**stro·bo·scop·i·cal·ly** /ˌstrōbə-ˈskäpik(ə)lē/ *adv.*

strode /strōd/ ▶ past of **STRIDE**.

stro·ga·noff /ˈstrôgəˌnôf; ˈstrō-/ ▶ *n.* a dish in which the central ingredient, typically strips of beef, is cooked in a sauce containing sour cream.

stroke /strōk/ ▶ *n.* **1** an act of hitting or striking someone or something; a blow: *he received three strokes of the cane.* ■ a method of striking the ball in sports or games. ■ *Golf* an act of hitting the ball with a club, as a unit of scoring: *won by two strokes.* ■ the sound made by a striking clock: *the stroke of midnight.* **2** an act of moving one's hand or an object across a surface, applying gentle pressure: *massage the cream into your skin using light upward strokes.* ■ a mark made by drawing a pen, pencil, or paintbrush in one direction across paper or canvas: *the paint had been applied in careful, regular strokes.* ■ a line forming part of a written or printed character. ■ a short printed or written diagonal line typically separating characters or figures. **3** a movement, esp. one of a series, in which something moves out of its position and back into it; a beat: *the ray swam with effortless strokes of its huge wings.* ■ the whole motion of a piston in either direction. ■ the rhythm to which a series of repeated movements is performed: *the rowers sing to keep their stroke.* ■ a movement of the arms and legs forming one of a series in swimming. ■ style of moving the arms and legs in swimming: *front crawl is a popular stroke.* ■ (in rowing) the mode or action of moving the oar. ■ (also **stroke oar**) the oar or oarsman nearest the stern of a boat, setting the timing for the other rowers. **4** a sudden disabling attack or loss of consciousness caused by an interruption in the flow of blood to the brain, esp. through thrombosis.
▶ *v.* [*tr.*] **1** move one's hand with gentle pressure over (a surface, esp. hair, fur, or skin), typically repeatedly; caress: *he put his hand on her hair and stroked it.* ■ [*tr.*] apply (something) to a surface using a gentle movement: *she strokes blue eyeshadow on her eyelids.* ■ *inf.* reassure or flatter (someone), esp. in order to gain their cooperation: *production executives were expert at stroking stars and brokering talent.* **2** act as the stroke of (a boat or crew). **3** hit or kick (a ball) smoothly and deliberately: *Miller calmly stroked three-pointers throughout the tournament.*
▶ □ **at a** (or **one**) **stroke** by a single action having immediate effect: *attitudes cannot be changed at one stroke.* □ **on the stroke of** — precisely at the specified time: *he arrived on the stroke of two.* □ **stroke of genius** an outstandingly brilliant and original idea. □ **stroke of luck** (or **good luck**) a fortunate occurrence that could not have been predicted or expected.

stroll /strōl/ ▶ *v.* [*intr.*] walk in a leisurely way: *I strolled around the city.*
▶ *n.* a short leisurely walk. ■ *fig.* a victory or objective that is easily achieved.

stroll·er /ˈstrōlər/ ▶ *n.* **1** a chair on wheels, typically folding, in which a baby or young child can be pushed along. **2** a person taking a leisurely walk: *shady gardens where strollers could relax.*

stro·ma /ˈstrōmə/ ▶ *n.* (*pl.* **-ma·ta** /-mətə/) *Anat. & Biol.* the supportive tissue of an epithelial organ, tumor, gonad, etc., consisting of connective tissues and blood vessels. ■ the spongy framework of protein fibers in a red blood cell or platelet. —**stro·mal** *adj.* (*chiefly Anat.*) —**stro·mat·ic** /strōˈmatik/ *adj.* (*chiefly Bot.*).

strong /strôNG/ ▶ *adj.* (**strong·er** /ˈstrôNGgər/, **strong·est** /ˈstrôNGgist/) **1** having the power to move heavy weights or perform other physically demanding tasks: *she cut through the water with her strong arms.* ■ able to perform a specified action well and powerfully: *he was not a strong swimmer.* ■ exerting great force: *a strong current.* ■ (of an argument or case) likely to succeed because of sound reasoning or convincing evidence: *there is a strong argument for decentralization.* ■ possessing skills and qualities that create a likelihood of success: *the competition was too strong.* ■ powerfully affecting the mind, senses, or emotions: *his imagery made a strong impression on the critics.* ■ used after a number to indicate the size of a group: *a hostile crowd several thousand strong.* **2** able to withstand great force or pressure: *cotton is strong, hard-wearing, and easy to handle.* ■ (of a person's constitution) not easily affected by disease or hardship. ■ (of a person's nervous or emotional state) not easily disturbed or upset: *driving on these highways requires strong nerves.* ■ (of a person's character) showing determination, self-control, and good judgment: *only a strong will enabled him to survive.* ■ in a secure financial position: *the company's chip business remains strong.* ■ (of a market) having steadily high or rising prices. ■ offering security and advantage: *the company was in a strong position to negotiate a deal.* ■ (of a belief or feeling) intense and firmly held. ■ (of a relationship) lasting and remaining warm despite difficulties. **3** (of light) very intense. ■ (of something seen or heard) not soft or muted; clear or prominent: *she should wear strong colors.* ■ (of food or its flavor) distinctive and pungent: *strong cheese.* ■ (of a solution or drink) containing a large proportion of a particular substance; concentrated: *a cup of strong coffee.* ■ (of an acid) highly ionized. ■ *Chem.* (of an acid or base) fully ionized into cations and anions in solution; having (respectively) a very low or a very high pH. ■ (of language or actions) forceful and extreme, esp. excessively or unacceptably so: *the government was urged to take strong measures against the perpetrators of violence.* **4** *Gram.* denoting a class of verbs in Germanic languages that form the past tense and past participle by a change of vowel within the stem rather than by addition of a suffix (e.g., swim, swam, swum); **5** *Physics* of, relating to, or denoting the strongest of the known kinds of force between particles, which acts between nucleons and other hadrons when closer than about 10^{-13} cm. —**strong·ish** *adj.* —**strong·ly** *adv.*

▶ □ **come on strong** *inf.* **1** behave aggressively or assertively, esp. in making sexual advances to someone. **2** improve one's position considerably: *he came on strong toward the end of the round.* □ **going strong** *inf.* continuing to be healthy, vigorous, or successful: *the program is still going strong after twelve episodes.*

strong-arm ▶ *adj.* using or characterized by force or violence: *they were furious at what they said were government strong-arm tactics.*
▶ *v.* [*tr.*] use force or violence against: *the culprit shouted before being strong-armed out of the door.*

strong·box /'strôNG,bäks/ ▶ *n.* a small lockable box, typically made of metal, in which valuables may be kept.

strong·hold /'strôNG,hōld/ ▶ *n.* a place that has been fortified so as to protect it against attack. ■ a place where a particular cause or belief is strongly defended or upheld: *a Republican stronghold.*

strong·room /'strôNG,rōōm; -,rŏŏm/ ▶ *n.* a room, typically one in a bank, designed to protect valuable items against fire and theft.

strong suit ▶ *n.* (in bridge) a holding of a number of high cards of one suit in a hand. ■ a desirable quality that is particularly prominent in someone's character or an activity at which they excel: *compassion is not Jack's strong suit.*

stron·ti·um /'stränCHēəm; -tēəm/ ▶ *n.* the chemical element of atomic number 38, a soft, silver-white metal of the alkaline earth series. (Symbol: **Sr**)

stron·ti·um 90 ▶ *n.* a radioactive isotope of strontium, used in radiotherapy. It is one of the chief products of the fission of uranium 235 and can pass from fallout into plants and animals and hence into human tissue, where it is concentrated in bones and teeth.

strop /sträp/ ▶ *n.* a device, typically a strip of leather, for sharpening straight razors. ■ (also **strap**) *Naut.* a rope sling for handling cargo.
▶ *v.* (**stropped, strop·ping**) [*tr.*] sharpen on or with a strop: *he stropped a knife razor-sharp on his belt.*

stro·phe /'strōfē/ ▶ *n.* the first section of an ancient Greek choral ode or of one division of it. ■ a structural division of a poem containing stanzas of varying line-length, especially an ode or free verse poem. —**stroph·ic** /-fik; 'strä-/ *adj.*

strove /strōv/ ▶ past of STRIVE.

struck /strək/ ▶ past and past participle of STRIKE.

struc·tur·al /'strəkCHərəl/ ▶ *adj.* of, relating to, or forming part of the structure of an object or other item: *the blast left ten buildings with major structural damage.* ■ of or relating to the arrangement of and relations between the parts or elements of a complex whole: *there have been structural changes in the industry.* —**struc·tur·al·ly** *adv.*

struc·tur·al·ism /'strəkCHərə,lizəm/ ▶ *n.* the doctrine that structure is more important than function. —**struc·tur·al·ist** *n. & adj.*

struc·ture /'strəkCHər/ ▶ *n.* the arrangement of and relations between the parts or elements of something complex. ■ the organization of a society or other group and the relations between its members, determining its working. ■ a building or other object constructed from several parts. ■ the quality of being organized: *we shall use three headings to give some structure to the discussion.*
▶ *v.* [*tr.*] (often **be structured**) construct or arrange according to a plan; give a pattern or organization to: *the game is structured so that there are five ways to win.* —**struc·ture·less** *adj.*

stru·del /'strōōdl/ ▶ *n.* a confection of thin pastry rolled up around a fruit filling and baked.

strug·gle /'strəgəl/ ▶ *v.* [*intr.*] make forceful or violent efforts to get free of restraint or constriction: *before she could struggle, he lifted her up.* ■ strive to achieve or attain something in the face of difficulty or resistance: *many families struggle to make ends meet.* ■ (**struggle with**) have difficulty handling or coping with: *passengers struggle with bags and*

briefcases. ■ engage in conflict: *politicians continued to struggle over familiar issues.* ■ [*intr.*] make one's way with difficulty: *he struggled to the summit of the world's highest mountain.* ■ have difficulty in gaining recognition or a living: *new authors are struggling in the present climate.*
▶ *n.* a forceful or violent effort to get free of restraint or resist attack. ■ a conflict or contest: *a power struggle for the leadership.* ■ a great physical effort: *with a struggle, she pulled the stroller up the slope.* ■ a determined effort under difficulties: *the center is the result of the scientists' struggle to realize their dream.* ■ a very difficult task: *it was a struggle to make herself understood.* —**strug·gler** /'strəg(ə)lər/ *n.*

strum /strəm/ ▶ *v.* (**strummed, strum·ming**) [*tr.*] play (a guitar or similar instrument) by sweeping the thumb or a plectrum up or down the strings. ■ play (a tune) in such a way: *he strummed a few chords.* ■ [*intr.*] play casually or unskillfully on a stringed or keyboard instrument.
▶ *n.* the sound made by strumming: *the brittle strum of acoustic guitars.* ■ an instance or spell of strumming. —**strum·mer** *n.*

strung /strəNG/ ▶ past and past participle of STRING.

strut /strət/ ▶ *n.* **1** a rod or bar forming part of a framework and designed to resist compression. **2** a stiff, erect, and apparently arrogant or conceited gait: *that old confident strut and swagger has returned.*
▶ *v.* (**strut·ted, strut·ting**) **1** [*intr.*] walk with a stiff, erect, and apparently arrogant or conceited gait: *peacocks strut through the grounds.* **2** [*tr.*] brace (something) with a strut or struts: *the holes were close-boarded and strutted.* ▷Old English *strūtian* 'protrude stiffly,' of Germanic origin. Current senses date from the late 16th cent. —**strut·ter** *n.* —**strut·ting·ly** *adv.*

strych·nine /'strik,nīn; -,nēn/ ▶ *n.* a bitter and highly poisonous compound alkaloid compound.

Sts. ▶ *abbr.* Saints.

Stu·art /'stōōərt/ (also **Stew·art**) ▶ *adj.* of or relating to the royal family ruling Scotland 1371–1714 and Britain 1603–49 and 1660–1714.
▶ *n.* a member of this family.

stub /stəb/ ▶ *n.* **1** the truncated remnant of a pencil, cigarette, or similar-shaped object after use. ■ a truncated or unusually short thing: *he wagged his little stub of tail.* ■ [as *adj.*] denoting a projection or hole that goes only part of the way through a surface: *a stub tenon.* **2** the part of a check, receipt, ticket, or other document torn off and kept as a record.
▶ *v.* (**stubbed, stub·bing**) [*tr.*] **1** accidentally strike (one's toe) against something: *I stubbed my toe, swore, and tripped.* **2** extinguish (a lighted cigarette) by pressing the lighted end against something: *she stubbed out her cigarette in the overflowing ashtray.*

stub·ble /'stəbəl/ ▶ *n.* the cut stalks of grain plants left sticking out of the ground after the grain is harvested. ■ short, stiff hairs growing on a man's face when he has not shaved for a while. —**stub·bled** *adj.* —**stub·bly** /'stəb(ə)lē/ *adj.*

stub·born /'stəbərn/ ▶ *adj.* having or showing dogged determination not to change one's attitude or position on something, esp. in spite of good arguments or reasons to do so: *he accused her of being a silly, stubborn old woman.* ■ difficult to move, remove, or cure: *the removal of stubborn screws.* —**stub·born·ly** *adv.* —**stub·born·ness** *n.*

stub·by /'stəbē/ ▶ *adj.* (**-bi·er, -bi·est**) short and thick: *Bloom pointed with a stubby finger.* —**stub·bi·ly** /-əlē/ *adv.* —**stub·bi·ness** *n.*

stuc·co /'stəkō/ ▶ *n.* fine plaster used for coating wall surfaces or molding into architectural decorations.
▶ *v.* (**-coes, -coed**) [*tr.*] [usu. as *adj.*] (**stuccoed**) coat or decorate with such plaster: *a stuccoed house.*

stuck /stək/ ▶ past and past participle of STICK[2].

stuck-up ▶ *adj. inf.* staying aloof from others because one thinks one is superior.

stud[1] /stəd/ ▶ *n.* **1** a large-headed piece of metal that pierces and projects from a surface, esp. for decoration. ■ a small, simple piece of jewelry for wearing in pierced ears or nostrils. ■ a fastener consisting of two buttons joined with a bar, used in formal wear to fasten a shirtfront or to fasten a collar to a shirt. ■ (usu. **studs**) a small projection fixed to the base of footwear, esp. athletic shoes, to allow the wearer to grip the ground. ■ (usu. **studs**) a small metal piece set into the tire of a motor vehicle to improve traction in slippery conditions. **2** an upright support in the wall of a building to which sheathing, drywall, etc., are attached.
▶ *v.* (**stud·ded, stud·ding**) [*tr.*] [usu. **be studded**] decorate or augment (something) with many studs or similar small objects: *a dagger studded with precious diamonds.* ■ strew or cover (something) with a scattering of small objects or features: *the sky was clear and studded with stars.*

stud[2] ▶ *n.* **1** an establishment where horses or other domesticated animals are kept for breeding: [as *adj.*] *a stud farm* | *the horse was retired to* *stud.* ■ a collection of horses or other domesticated animals belonging to one person. ■ (also **stud horse**) a stallion. ■ *inf.* a young man thought to be very active sexually or regarded as a good sexual partner. **2** (also **stud poker**) a form of poker in which the first card of a player's hand is dealt face down and the others face up, with betting after each round of the deal.

stu·dent /'st(y)ōōdnt/ ▸*n.* a person who is studying at a school or college. ■ [as *adj.*] denoting someone who is studying in order to enter a particular profession: *a group of student nurses.* ■ a person who takes an interest in a particular subject: *a student of the free market.*

stu·dio /'st(y)ōōdē,ō/ ▸*n.* (*pl.* **-os**) **1** a room where an artist, photographer, sculptor, etc., works. ■ a place where performers, esp. dancers, practice and exercise. ■ a room where musical or sound recordings can be made. ■ a room from which television or radio programs are broadcast, or in which they are recorded. ■ a place where movies are made or produced. **2** a film or television production company. **3** a studio apartment.

stu·dio a·part·ment ▸*n.* an apartment containing one main room.

stu·dio couch ▸*n.* a sofa bed.

stu·di·ous /'st(y)ōōdēəs/ ▸*adj.* spending a lot of time studying or reading: *he was quiet and studious.* ■ done deliberately or with a purpose in mind: *his studious absence from public view.* ■ showing great care or attention: *a studious inspection.* —**stu·di·ous·ly** *adv.* —**stu·di·ous·ness** *n.*

stud·y /'stədē/ ▸*n.* (*pl.* **stud·ies**) **1** the devotion of time and attention to acquiring knowledge on an academic subject, esp. by means of books. ■ (**studies**) activity of this type as pursued by one person: *some students may not be able to resume their studies.* ■ an academic book or article on a particular topic: *a study of Jane Austen's novels.* ■ (**studies**) used in the title of an academic subject: *a major in East Asian studies.* **2** a detailed investigation and analysis of a subject or situation: *a study of a sample of 5,000 children.* ■ a portrayal in literature or another art form of an aspect of behavior or character: *a study of a man devoured by awareness of his own mediocrity.* ■ a person who learns a skill or acquires knowledge at a specified speed: *I'm a quick study.* **3** a room used or designed for reading, writing, or academic work. **4** a piece of work, esp. a drawing, done for practice or as an experiment. ■ a musical composition designed to develop a player's technical skill. **5** (**a study in**) a thing or person that is an embodiment or good example of something: *he perched on the edge of the bed, a study in confusion and misery.* ■ *inf.* an amusing or remarkable thing or person: *Ira's face was a study as he approached the car.*
▸*v.* (**stud·ies, stud·ied**) [*tr.*] **1** devote time and attention to acquiring knowledge on (an academic subject), esp. by means of books: *she studied biology and botany.* ■ investigate and analyze (a subject or situation) in detail: *he has been studying mink for many years.* ■ [*intr.*] apply oneself to study: *he spent his time listening to the radio rather than studying.* ■ [*intr.*] acquire academic knowledge at an educational establishment: *he studied at the Kensington School of Art.* ■ [*intr.*] (**study up**) learn intensively about something, esp. in preparation for a test of knowledge: *a graduate student studies up for her doctoral exams.* ■ (of an actor) try to learn (the words of one's role). **2** look at closely in order to observe or read: *she bent her head to study the plans.*

stuff /stəf/ ▸*n.* **1** matter, material, articles, or activities of a specified or indeterminate kind that are being referred to, indicated, or implied: *a pickup truck picked the stuff up.* ■ a person's belongings, equipment, or baggage: *he took his stuff and went.* ■ *Brit., inf., dated* worthless or foolish ideas, speech, or writing: rubbish: [as *interj.*] *stuff and nonsense!* ■ *inf.* drink or drugs. ■ (**one's stuff**) things in which one is knowledgeable and experienced; one's area of expertise: *he knows his stuff and can really write.* **2** the basic constituents or characteristics of something or someone: *Healey was made of sterner stuff.* **3** (in sports) spin given to a ball to make it vary its course. ■ *Baseball* a pitcher's ability to produce such spin or control the speed of delivery of a pitch.
▸*v.* [*tr.*] fill (a receptacle or space) tightly with something: *an old teapot stuffed full of cash.* ■ *inf.* force or cram (something) tightly into a receptacle or space: *he stuffed a thick wad of cash into his jacket pocket.* ■ *inf.* hastily or clumsily push (something) into a space: *Sadie took the coin and stuffed it in her coat pocket.* ■ fill (the cavity of an item of food) with a savory or sweet mixture, esp. before cooking: *chicken stuffed with mushrooms and breadcrumbs.* ■ (**be stuffed up**) (of a person) have one's nose blocked up with mucus as a result of a cold. ■ *inf.* fill (oneself) with large amounts of food: *he stuffed himself with potato chips.* ■ fill out the skin of (a dead animal or bird) with material to restore the original shape and appearance: *he took the bird to a taxidermist to be stuffed.* ■ *inf.* fill (envelopes) with identical copies of printed matter: *they spent the*

whole time in a back room stuffing envelopes. ■ place bogus votes in (a ballot box). —**stuff·er** *n.* [in *comb.*] *a sausage-stuffer.*
▸ □ **stuff it** *inf.* said to express indifference, resignation, or rejection: *Stuff it, I'm 61, what do I care?* □ **that's the stuff** *inf.* said in approval of what has just been done or said.

stuffed shirt ▸*n. inf.* a conservative, pompous person.

stuff·ing /'stəfiNG/ ▸*n.* **1** a mixture used to stuff poultry or meat before cooking. **2** padding used to stuff cushions, furniture, or soft toys.
▸ □ **knock** (or **take**) **the stuffing out of** *inf.* severely impair the confidence or strength of (someone).

stuff·y /'stəfē/ ▸*adj.* (**stuff·i·er, stuff·i·est**) (of a place) lacking fresh air or ventilation: *a stuffy, overcrowded office.* ■ (of a person's nose) blocked up and making breathing difficult, typically as a result of illness. ■ (of a person) not receptive to new or unusual ideas and behavior; conventional and narrow-minded: *he was steady and rather stuffy.* —**stuff·i·ly** /'stəfəlē/ *adv.* —**stuff·i·ness** *n.*

stul·ti·fy /'stəltə,fī/ ▸*v.* (**-fies, -fied**) [*tr.*] **1** [usu. as *adj.*] (**stultifying**) cause to lose enthusiasm and initiative, esp. as a result of a tedious or restrictive routine: *the mentally stultifying effects of a disadvantaged home.* **2** cause (someone) to appear foolish or absurd: *Counsel is not expected to stultify himself in an attempt to advance his client's interests.* —**stul·ti·fi·ca·tion** /,stəltəfi'kāSHən/ *n.* —**stul·ti·fi·er** *n.*

stum·ble /'stəmbəl/ ▸*v.* [*intr.*] trip or momentarily lose one's balance; almost fall: *her foot caught a shoe and she stumbled.* ■ trip repeatedly as one walks: *his legs still weak, he stumbled after them.* ■ make a mistake or repeated mistakes in speaking: *she stumbled over the words.* ■ (**stumble across/on/upon**) find or encounter by chance: *they stumbled across a farmer selling 25 acres.*
▸*n.* an act of stumbling. ■ a stumbling walk: *he parodied my groping stumble across the stage.* —**stum·bler** /-b(ə)lər/ *n.* —**stum·bling·ly** /-b(ə)liNGlē/ *adv.*

stum·ble·bum /'stəmbəl,bəm/ ▸*n. inf.* a clumsy or inept person.

stum·bling block ▸*n.* a circumstance that causes difficulty or hesitation: *bashfulness is a great stumbling block to some men.*

stump /stəmp/ ▸*n.* **1** the bottom part of a tree left projecting from the ground after most of the trunk has fallen or been cut down. ■ the small projecting remnant of something that has been cut or broken off or worn away: *the stump of an amputated arm.* **2** [as *adj.*] engaged in or involving political campaigning: *he is an inspiring stump speaker.*
▸*v.* [*tr.*] **1** (usu. **be stumped**) (of a question or problem) be too hard for; baffle: *education chiefs were stumped by some of the exam questions.* ■ (**be stumped**) be at a loss; be unable to work out what to do or say: *detectives are stumped for a reason for the attack.* **2** [*intr.*] walk stiffly and noisily: *he stumped away on short thick legs.* **3** travel around (a district) making political speeches: *there is no chance that he will be well enough to stump the country* | [*intr.*] *the two men had come to the city to stump for the presidential candidate.*

stump·age /'stəmpij/ ▸*n.* a price on standing timber and the right to harvest it, reckoned as a unit value per stump. ■ such a price calculated in board feet, cubic meters, or some other measure.

stump·er /'stəmpər/ ▸*n. inf.* a puzzling question.

stump·y /'stəmpē/ ▸*adj.* (**stump·i·er, stump·i·est**) short and thick; squat: *weak stumpy legs.* —**stump·i·ly** /-pəlē/ *adv.* —**stump·i·ness** *n.*

stun /stən/ ▸*v.* (**stunned, stun·ning**) [*tr.*] knock unconscious or into a dazed or semiconscious state: *the man was strangled after being stunned by a blow to the head.* ■ (usu. **be stunned**) astonish or shock (someone) so that they are temporarily unable to react: *the community was stunned by the tragedy.* ■ (of a sound) deafen temporarily: *a blast like that could stun anybody.* ■ Middle English: shortening of Old French *estoner* 'astonish.'

stung /stəNG/ ▸ past and past participle of STING.

stunk /stəNGk/ ▸ past and past participle of STINK.

stun·ner /'stənər/ ▸*n. inf.* a strikingly beautiful or impressive person or thing: *the girl was a stunner.* ■ an amazing turn of events.

stun·ning /'stəniNG/ ▸*adj.* extremely impressive or attractive: *she looked stunning.* —**stun·ning·ly** *adv.*

stunt¹ /stənt/ ▸*v.* [*tr.*] [often as *adj.*] (**stunted**) retard the growth or development of: *trees damaged by acid rain had stunted branches.* ■ frustrate and spoil: *she was concerned at the stunted lives of those around her.* —**stunt·ed·ness** *n.*

stunt² ▸*n.* an action or performance displaying spectacular skill and daring. ■ something unusual done to attract attention: *the story was spread as a publicity stunt to help sell books.*

stunt·man /ˈstəntˌman/ ▶*n.* (*pl.* **-men**) a man employed to take an actor's place in performing dangerous stunts.

stu·pa /ˈstoōpə/ ▶*n.* a dome-shaped structure erected as a Buddhist shrine.

stu·pe·fy /ˈst(y)oōpəˌfī/ ▶*v.* (**-fies**, **-fied**) [*tr.*] make (someone) unable to think or feel properly: *the offense of administering drugs to a woman with intent to stupefy her.* ■ astonish and shock: *the amount they spend on clothes would appall their parents and stupefy their grandparents.* —**stu·pe·fac·tion** /ˌst(y)oōpəˈfakSHən/ *n.* —**stu·pe·fi·er** *n.* —**stu·pe·fy·ing·ly** *adv.* *a stupefyingly tedious task.*

stu·pen·dous /st(y)oōˈpendəs/ ▶*adj. inf.* extremely impressive: *a stupendous display of technique.* —**stu·pen·dous·ly** *adv.* —**stu·pen·dous·ness** *n.*

stu·pid /ˈst(y)oōpid/ ▶*adj.* (**-pid·er**, **-pid·est**) lacking intelligence or common sense: *I was stupid enough to think she was perfect.* ■ dazed and unable to think clearly: *apprehension was numbing her brain and making her stupid.* ■ *inf.* used to express exasperation or boredom: *she told him to stop messing with his stupid painting.*
▶*n. inf.* a stupid person (often used as a term of address): *you're not a coward, stupid!* —**stu·pid·i·ty** /st(y)oōˈpiditē/ *n.* —**stu·pid·ly** *adv.*

stu·por /ˈst(y)oōpər/ ▶*n.* a state of near-unconsciousness or insensibility: *a drunken stupor.* —**stu·por·ous** /-rəs/ *adj.*

stur·dy /ˈstərdē/ ▶*adj.* (**-di·er**, **-di·est**) (of a person or their body) strongly and solidly built: *he had a sturdy, muscular physique.* ■ strong enough to withstand rough work or treatment: *the bike is sturdy enough to cope with bumpy tracks.* ■ showing confidence and determination: *the townspeople have a sturdy independence.* —**stur·died** *adj.* (from the *noun*) —**stur·di·ly** /-dl-ē/ *adv.* —**stur·di·ness** *n.*

stur·geon /ˈstərjən/ ▶*n.* a very large primitive fish (family Acipenseridae) with bony plates on the body. It occurs in temperate seas and rivers of the northern hemisphere, esp. central Eurasia, and is of commercial importance for its caviar and flesh.

Sturm und Drang /ˈSHtoŏrm ŏŏn(d) ˈdräNG/ ▶*n.* a literary and artistic movement in Germany in the late 18th century, influenced by Jean-Jacques Rousseau and characterized by the expression of emotional unrest and a rejection of neoclassical literary norms.

stut·ter /ˈstətər/ ▶*v.* [*intr.*] talk with continued involuntary repetition of sounds, esp. initial consonants: *the child was stuttering in fright.* ■ [*tr.*] utter in such a way: *he shyly **stuttered out** an invitation to the movies.* ■ (of a machine or gun) produce a series of short, sharp sounds: *she flinched as a machine gun stuttered nearby.*
▶*n.* a tendency to stutter while speaking. ■ a series of short, sharp sounds produced by a machine or gun. —**stut·ter·er** *n.* —**stut·ter·ing·ly** *adv.*

stut·ter tone ▶*n.* a dial tone interrupted by several short gaps, indicating the arrival of new voicemail messages to the user.

St. Vi·tus's dance ▶*n.* old-fashioned term for SYDENHAM'S CHOREA.

sty¹ /stī/ ▶*n.* a pigpen.

sty² (also **stye**) ▶*n.* (*pl.* **sties** or **styes**) an inflamed swelling on the edge of an eyelid, caused by bacterial infection of the gland at the base of an eyelash.

style /stīl/ ▶*n.* **1** a manner of doing something: *different styles of management.* ■ a way of painting, writing, composing, building, etc., characteristic of a particular period, place, person, or movement. ■ a way of using language: *he never wrote in a journalistic style.* ■ a way of behaving or approaching a situation that is characteristic of or favored by a particular person: *backing out isn't my style.* ■ an official or legal title: *the partnership traded **under the style of** Storr and Mortimer.* **2** a distinctive appearance, typically determined by the principles according to which something is designed: *the pillars are no exception to the general style.* ■ a particular design of clothing. ■ a way of arranging the hair. **3** elegance and sophistication: *a sophisticated nightspot with style and taste.* **4** a rodlike object or part, in particular: ■ *Bot.* (in a flower) a narrow, typically elongated extension of the ovary, bearing the stigma.
▶*v.* [*tr.*] **1** design or make in a particular form: *the yacht is well proportioned and conservatively styled.* ■ arrange (hair) in a particular way: *he styled her hair by twisting it up to give it body.* **2** [*tr.*] designate with a particular name, description, or title: *the official is styled principal and vice chancellor of the university.* —**style·less** /ˈstīl(l)is/ *adj.* —**style·less·ness** /ˈstīl(l)isnis/ *n.* —**styl·er** *n.*

sty·li /ˈstīlī/ ▶ plural form of STYLUS.

styl·ish /ˈstīliSH/ ▶*adj.* having or displaying a good sense of style: *these are elegant and stylish performances.* ■ fashionably elegant: *a stylish and innovative range of jewelry.* —**styl·ish·ly** *adv.* —**styl·ish·ness** *n.*

styl·ist /ˈstīlist/ ▶*n.* **1** a person who works creatively in the fashion and beauty industry, in particular: ■ a designer of fashionable styles of clothing. ■ a hairdresser. **2** a person noted for elegant work or performance, in particular: ■ a writer noted for taking great pains over the style in which he or she writes. ■ (in sports or music) a person who performs with style.

sty·lis·tic /stīˈlistik/ ▶*adj.* of or concerning style, esp. literary style: *the stylistic conventions of magazine stories.* —**styl·is·ti·cal·ly** /-ik(ə)lē/ *adv.*

sty·lis·tics /stīˈlistiks/ ▶*pl. n.* [treated as *sing.*] the study of the distinctive styles found in particular literary genres and in the works of individual writers.

styl·ize /ˈstīˌlīz/ ▶*v.* [*tr.*] [usu. as *adj.*] (**stylized**) depict or treat in a mannered and nonrealistic style: *gracefully shaped vases decorated with stylized but recognizable white lilies.* —**styl·i·za·tion** /ˌstīliˈzāSHən/ *n.*

sty·loid proc·ess ▶*n. Anat.* a slender projection of bone, such as that from the lower surface of the temporal bone of the skull, or those at the lower ends of the ulna and radius.

sty·lus /ˈstīləs/ ▶*n.* (*pl.* **-li** /-ˌlī/, or **-lus·es**) **1** a hard point, typically of diamond or sapphire, following a groove in a phonograph record and transmitting the recorded sound for reproduction. ■ a similar point producing such a groove when recording sound. **2** an ancient writing implement, consisting of a small rod with a pointed end for scratching letters on wax-covered tablets. ■ an implement of similar shape used esp. for engraving and tracing. ■ *Comput.* a penlike device used to input handwritten text or drawings directly into a computer or for input on a touch-sensitive monitor.

sty·mie /ˈstīmē/ ▶*v.* (**-mies**, **-mied**, **-my·ing** or **-mie·ing**) [*tr.*] *inf.* prevent or hinder the progress of: *the changes must not be allowed to stymie new medical treatments.*

styp·tic /ˈstiptik/ *Med.* ▶*adj.* (of a substance) capable of causing bleeding to stop when it is applied to a wound.
▶*n.* a substance of this kind.

styp·tic pen·cil ▶*n.* a stick of a styptic substance, used to treat small cuts.

sty·rene /ˈstīrēn/ ▶*n. Chem.* an unsaturated liquid hydrocarbon obtained as a petroleum byproduct. It is easily polymerized and is used to make plastics and resins.

sty·ro·foam /ˈstīrəˌfōm/ ▶*n. trademark* a kind of expanded polystyrene.

Styx /stiks/ *Greek Mythology* ▶ one of the rivers in the underworld, over which Charon ferried the souls of the dead. ▷from Greek *Stux*, from *stugnos* 'hateful, gloomy.'

suave /swäv/ ▶*adj.* (**suav·er**, **suav·est**) (esp. of a man) charming, confident, and elegant: *all the waiters were suave and deferential.* —**suave·ly** *adv.* —**suave·ness** *n.* —**suav·i·ty** /-itē/ *n.* (*pl.* **-ties**)

sub /səb/ *inf.* ▶*n.* **1** a submarine. ■ short for SUBMARINE SANDWICH. **2** a subscription. **3** a substitute.
▶*v.* (**subbed**, **sub·bing**) [*intr.*] act as a substitute for someone: *he subbed for Scott as weatherman.*

sub. ▶*abbr.* ■ subordinated. ■ subscription. ■ substitute. ■ suburb. ■ suburban. ■ subway.

sub·a·cute /ˌsəbəˈkyoōt/ ▶*adj. Med.* (of a condition) between acute and chronic.

sub·al·pine /ˌsəbˈalpīn/ ▶*adj.* of or situated on the higher slopes of mountains just below the timberline.

sub·al·tern ▶*n.* /səbˈôltərn/ an officer in the British army below the rank of captain, esp. a second lieutenant.

sub·a·quat·ic /ˌsəbəˈkwätik, -ˈkwa-/ ▶*adj.* underwater: *a narrow, subaquatic microclimate.*

sub·a·que·ous /səbˈākwēəs, -ˈak-/ ▶*adj.* existing, formed, or taking place underwater. ■ *fig.* lacking in substance or strength: *the light that filtered through the leaves was pale, subaqueous.*

sub·arc·tic /ˌsəbˈärktik, -ˈärtik/ ▶*adj.* of or relating to the region immediately south of the Arctic Circle.

sub·a·tom·ic /ˌsəbəˈtämik/ ▶*adj.* smaller than or occurring within an atom.

sub·a·tom·ic par·ti·cle ▶*n.* a particle smaller than an atom (e.g., a neutron) or a cluster of such particles (e.g., an alpha particle). Compare with ELEMENTARY PARTICLE.

sub·cat·e·go·ry /ˈsəbˌkatəˌgôrē/ ▶*n.* (*pl.* **-ries**) a secondary or subordinate category. —**sub·cat·e·go·ri·za·tion** /ˌsəbˌkatəgəriˈzāSHən/ *n.* —**sub·cat·e·go·rize** /ˌsəbˈkatəgəˌrīz/ *v.*

sub·cla·vi·an /səbˈklāvēən/ ▶*adj. Anat.* relating to or denoting an artery or vein that serves the neck and arm on the left or right side of the body.

sub·clin·i·cal /ˌsəbˈklinikəl/ ▶*adj. Med.* relating to or denoting a disease that is not severe enough to present definite or readily observable symptoms.

sub·com·mit·tee /ˈsəbkəˌmitē/ ▶n. a committee composed of some members of a larger committee, board, or other body and reporting to it.

sub·com·pact /səbˈkämpakt/ ▶n. a motor vehicle that is smaller than a compact.

sub·con·scious /səbˈkänsHəs/ ▶adj. of or concerning the part of the mind of which one is not fully aware but which influences one's actions and feelings: *my subconscious fear.*
▶n. (**one's/the subconscious**) this part of the mind (not in technical use in psychoanalysis, where *unconscious* is preferred). —**sub·con·scious·ly** adv. —**sub·con·scious·ness** n.

sub·con·ti·nent /ˌsəbˈkäntə)nənt/ ▶n. a large, distinguishable part of a continent, such as North America or southern Africa. —**sub·con·ti·nen·tal** /-ˌkäntəˈnen(t)l/ adj.

sub·con·tract ▶v. /ˌsəbkənˈtrakt/ [tr.] employ a business or person outside one's company to do (work) as part of a larger project: *we would subcontract the translation work out.* ■ [intr.] (of a business or person) carry out work for a company as part of a larger project.
▶n. /səbˈkäntrakt/ a contract for a company or person to do work for another company as part of a larger project. —**sub·con·trac·tor** /-ˈtraktər/ n.

sub·cul·ture /ˈsəbˌkəlCHər/ ▶n. a cultural group within a larger culture, often having beliefs or interests at variance with those of the larger culture. —**sub·cul·tur·al** /ˌsəbˈkəlCHərəl/ adj.

sub·cu·ta·ne·ous /ˌsəbkyo͞oˈtānēəs/ ▶adj. Anat. & Med. situated or applied under the skin: *subcutaneous fat.* —**sub·cu·ta·ne·ous·ly** adv.

sub·di·vide /ˈsəbdəˌvīd/ ▶v. [tr.] divide (something that has already been divided or that is a separate unit): *the heading was subdivided into eight separate sections.*

sub·di·vi·sion /ˈsəbdəˌviZHən/ ▶n. the action of subdividing or being subdivided. ■ a secondary or subordinate division. ■ an area of land divided into plots for sale; an area of housing. ■ Biol. any taxonomic subcategory, esp. (in botany) one that ranks below division and above class.

sub·dom·i·nant /səbˈdämənənt/ ▶n. Mus. the fourth note of the diatonic scale of any key.

sub·duc·tion /səbˈdəkSHən/ ▶n. Geol. the sideways and downward movement of the edge of a plate of the earth's crust into the mantle beneath another plate. ▷1970s: via French from Latin *subductio(n-)*, from *subduct-* 'drawn from below,' from the verb *subducere.* —**sub·duct** /-ˈdəkt/ v.

sub·due /səbˈd(y)o͞o/ ▶v. (**-dues, -dued, -du·ing**) [tr.] overcome, quiet, or bring under control (a feeling or person): *she managed to subdue an instinct to applaud.* ■ bring (a country or people) under control by force: *Charles went on a campaign to subdue the Saxons.* —**sub·du·a·ble** adj.

sub·fam·i·ly /ˈsəbˌfam(ə)lē/ ▶n. (pl. **-lies**) a subdivision of a group. ■ Biol. a taxonomic category that ranks below family and above tribe or genus, usually ending in *-inae* (in zoology) or *-oideae* (in botany).

sub·floor /ˈsəbˌflôr/ ▶n. the foundation for a floor in a building.

sub·gla·cial /ˌsəbˈglāSHəl/ ▶adj. Geol. situated or occurring underneath a glacier or ice sheet.

sub·group /ˈsəbˌgro͞op/ ▶n. a subdivision of a group. ■ Math. a group whose members are all members of another group, both being subject to the same operations.

sub·head·ing /ˈsəbˌhediNG/ (also **sub·head**) ▶n. a heading given to a subsection of a piece of writing.

sub·hu·man /səbˈ(h)yo͞omən/ ▶adj. of a lower order of being than the human. ■ Zool. (of a primate) closely related to humans. ■ derog. (of people or their behavior) not worthy of a human being; debased or depraved: *he regards all PR people as subhuman.*
▶n. a subhuman creature or person.

subj. ▶abbr. ■ subject. ■ subjective. ■ subjectively. ■ subjunctive.

sub·ject ▶n. /ˈsəbjekt/ **1** a person or thing that is being discussed, described, or dealt with: *I've said all there is to be said on the subject.* ■ a person or circumstance giving rise to a specified feeling, response, or action: *the incident was the subject of international condemnation.* ■ Gram. a noun phrase functioning as one of the main components of a clause, being the element about which the rest of the clause is predicated. ■ Logic the part of a proposition about which a statement is made. ■ Mus. a theme of a fugue or of a piece in sonata form; a leading phrase or motif. ■ a person who is the focus of scientific or medical attention or experiment. **2** a branch of knowledge studied or taught in a school,

college, or university. **3** a citizen or member of a state other than its supreme ruler.
▶adj. /ˈsəbjekt/ (**subject to**) **1** likely or prone to be affected by (a particular condition or occurrence, typically an unwelcome or unpleasant one): *he was subject to bouts of manic depression.* **2** dependent or conditional upon: *the proposed merger is subject to the approval of the shareholders.* **3** under the authority of: *legislation making Congress subject to the laws it passes.* ■ under the control or domination of (another ruler, country, or government): *the Greeks were the first subject people to break free from Ottoman rule.*
▶adv. /ˈsəbjekt/ (**subject to**) conditionally upon: *subject to bankruptcy court approval, the company expects to begin liquidation of its inventory.*
▶v. /səbˈjekt/ [tr.] **1** (**subject someone/something to**) cause or force to undergo (a particular experience of form of treatment): *he'd subjected her to a terrifying ordeal.* **2** bring (a person or country) under one's control or jurisdiction, typically by using force. —**sub·jec·tion** /səbˈjekSHən/ n. —**sub·ject·less** /ˈsəbjək(t)ləs/ adj.

sub·jec·tive /səbˈjektiv/ ▶adj. **1** based on or influenced by personal feelings, tastes, or opinions: *his views are highly subjective.* Contrasted with OBJECTIVE. ■ dependent on the mind or on an individual's perception for its existence. **2** Gram. of, relating to, or denoting a case of nouns and pronouns used for the subject of a sentence. —**sub·jec·tive·ly** adv. —**sub·jec·tive·ness** n. —**sub·jec·tiv·i·ty** /ˌsəbjekˈtivitē/ n.

sub·ject mat·ter ▶n. the topic dealt with or the subject represented in a debate, exposition, or work of art.

sub·join /səbˈjoin/ ▶v. [tr.] formal add (comments or supplementary information) at the end of a speech or text.

sub·ju·gate /ˈsəbjəˌgāt/ ▶v. [tr.] bring under domination or control, esp. by conquest: *the invaders had soon subjugated most of the native population.* ■ (**subjugate someone/something to**) make someone or something subordinate to: *the new ruler firmly subjugated the Church to the state.* —**sub·ju·ga·tion** /ˌsəbjəˈgāSHən/ n. —**sub·ju·ga·tor** /-ˌgātər/ n.

sub·junc·tive /səbˈjəNG(k)tiv/ Gram. ▶adj. relating to or denoting a mood of verbs expressing what is imagined or wished or possible. Compare with INDICATIVE.
▶n. a verb in the subjunctive mood. ■ (**the subjunctive**) the subjunctive mood. —**sub·junc·tive·ly** adv.

sub·lease ▶n. /ˈsəbˌlēs/ a lease of a property by a tenant to a subtenant.
▶v. /səbˈlēs/ another term for SUBLET.

sub·let ▶v. /səbˈlet/ (**-let·ting**; past and past part. **-let**) [tr.] lease (a property) to a subtenant: *I quit my job and sublet my apartment.*

sub·li·mate ▶v. /ˈsəbləˌmāt/ **1** [tr.] (esp. in psychoanalytic theory) divert or modify (an instinctual impulse) into a culturally higher or socially more acceptable activity: *people who will sublimate sexuality into activities which help to build up and preserve civilization.* **2** Chem. [intr.] another term for SUBLIME.
▶n. /-ˌmit; -ˌmāt/ Chem. a solid deposit of a substance that has sublimed. —**sub·li·ma·tion** /ˌsəbləˈmāSHən/ n.

sub·lime /səˈblīm/ ▶adj. (**-lim·er, -lim·est**) of such excellence, grandeur, or beauty as to inspire great admiration or awe: *Mozart's sublime piano concertos* | [as n.] (**the sublime**) *experiences that ranged from the sublime to the ridiculous.* ■ used to denote the extreme or unparalleled nature of a person's attitude or behavior: *he had the sublime confidence of youth.*
▶v. [intr.] Chem. (of a solid substance) change directly into vapor when heated, typically forming a solid deposit again on cooling. ■ [tr.] cause (a substance) to do this: *the crystals could be sublimed under a vacuum.* —**sub·lime·ly** adv. —**sub·lim·i·ty** /-ˈblimitē/ n.

sub·lim·i·nal /səˈblimənl/ ▶adj. Psychol. (of a stimulus or mental process) below the threshold of sensation or consciousness; perceived by or affecting someone's mind without their being aware of it. —**sub·lim·i·nal·ly** adv.

sub·lim·i·nal ad·ver·tis·ing ▶n. the use by advertisers of images and sounds to influence consumers' responses without their being conscious of it.

sub·ma·chine gun /ˌsəbməˈSHēn/ ▶n. a hand-held, lightweight machine gun.

sub·ma·rine /ˌsəbməˈrēn; ˈsəbməˌrēn/ ▶n. a warship with a streamlined hull designed to operate completely submerged in the sea for long periods, equipped with an internal store of air and a periscope and typically armed with torpedoes and/or missiles. ■ a submersible craft of any kind. ■ a submarine sandwich.

Pronunciation Key ə *ago,* up; ər *over, fur;* a *hat;* ā *ate;* ä *car;* CH *chin;* e *let;* ē *see;* e(ə)r *air;* i *fit;* ī *by;* i(ə)r *ear;* NG *sing;* ō *go;* ô *law, for;* oi *toy;* o͞o *good;* o͞o *goo;* ou *out;* SH *she;* TH *thin;* TH *then;* (h)w *why;* ZH *vision*

▸*adj.* existing, occurring, done, or used under the surface of the sea: *submarine volcanic activity.* —**sub·ma·rin·er** /səb'marənər; -mə'rēnər/ *n.*

sub·ma·rine sand·wich ▸*n.* a sandwich made of a long roll typically filled with meat, cheese, and vegetables such as lettuce, tomato, and onions.

sub·merge /səb'mərj/ ▸*v.* [*tr.*] (usu. **be submerged**) cause to be under water: *houses had been flooded and cars submerged.* ■ [*intr.*] descend below the surface of an area of water: *the U-boat had had time to submerge.* ■ completely cover or obscure: *the tensions submerged earlier in the campaign now came to the fore.* —**sub·mer·gence** /-jəns/ *n.* —**sub·mer·gi·ble** /-jəbəl/ *adj.*

sub·merse /səb'mərs/ ▸*v.* [*tr.*] submerge: *pellets were then submersed in agar.*

▸*adj.* (**submersed**) *Bot.* denoting or characteristic of a plant growing entirely underwater. Contrasted with **EMERSED**. —**sub·mer·sion** /-'mərzHən; -sHən/ *n.*

sub·mers·i·ble /səb'mərsəbəl/ ▸*adj.* designed to be completely submerged or to operate while submerged.

▸*n.* a small boat or other craft of this kind, esp. one designed for research and exploration.

sub·mi·cro·scop·ic /,səbmīkrə'skäpik/ ▸*adj.* too small to be seen by an ordinary light microscope.

sub·mis·sion /səb'misHən/ ▸*n.* **1** the action or fact of accepting or yielding to a superior force or to the will or authority of another person: *they were forced into submission.* **2** the action of presenting a proposal, application, or other document for consideration or judgment: *reports should be prepared for submission at partners' meetings.* ■ a proposal, application, or other document presented in this way.

sub·mis·sive /səb'misiv/ ▸*adj.* ready to conform to the authority or will of others; meekly obedient or passive. —**sub·mis·sive·ly** *adv.* —**sub·mis·sive·ness** *n.*

sub·mit /səb'mit/ ▸*v.* (**-mit·ted, -mit·ting**) **1** [*intr.*] accept or yield to a superior force or to the authority or will of another person: *the original settlers were forced to submit to Bulgarian rule.* ■ (**submit oneself**) consent to undergo a certain treatment: *he submitted himself to a body search.* ■ [*tr.*] subject to a particular process, treatment, or condition: *samples submitted to low pressure.* ■ agree to refer a matter to a third party for decision or adjudication: *the U.S. refused to submit to arbitration.* **2** [*tr.*] present (a proposal, application, or other document) to a person or body for consideration or judgment: *the panel's report was submitted to a parliamentary committee.* ■ (esp. in judicial contexts) suggest; argue: *he submitted that such measures were justified.* —**sub·mit·ter** *n.*

sub·nor·mal /səb'nôrməl/ ▸*adj.* not meeting standards or reaching a level regarded as usual, esp. with respect to intelligence or development. —**sub·nor·mal·i·ty** /,səbnôr'malitē/ *n.*

sub·or·der /'səb,ôrdər/ ▸*n. Biol.* a taxonomic category that ranks below order and above family.

sub·or·di·nate ▸*adj.* /sə'bôrdnit/ lower in rank or position: *his subordinate officers.* ■ of less or secondary importance: *in adventure stories, character must be subordinate to action.*

▸*n.* /sə'bôrdnit/ a person under the authority or control of another within an organization.

▸*v.* /-,āt/ [*tr.*] treat or regard as of lesser importance than something else: *practical considerations were subordinated to political expediency.* ■ make subservient to or dependent on something else. —**sub·or·di·nate·ly** *adv.* —**sub·or·di·na·tion** /-,bôrdn'āsHən/ *n.* —**sub·or·di·na·tive** /-ətiv/ *adj.*

sub·or·di·nate clause ▸*n.* a clause, typically introduced by a conjunction, that forms part of and is dependent on a main clause (e.g., "when it rang" in "she answered the phone when it rang").

sub·orn /sə'bôrn/ ▸*v.* [*tr.*] bribe or otherwise induce (someone) to commit an unlawful act such as perjury: *he was accused of conspiring to suborn witnesses.* —**sub·or·na·tion** /,səbôr'nāsHən/ *n.* —**sub·orn·er** *n.*

sub·plot /'səb,plät/ ▸*n.* a subordinate plot in a play, novel, or similar work.

sub·poe·na /sə'pēnə/ *Law* ▸*n.* a writ ordering a person to attend a court: *a subpoena may be issued to compel their attendance | they were all under subpoena to appear.*

▸*v.* (**-nas, -naed** /-nəd/, **-na·ing**) [*tr.*] summon (someone) with a subpoena: *the Queen is above the law and cannot be subpoenaed.* ■ require (a document or other evidence) to be submitted to a court of law: *the decision to subpoena government records.* ▷late Middle English (as a noun): from Latin *sub poena* 'under penalty' (the first words of the writ). Use as a verb dates from the mid 17th cent.

sub·ro·ga·tion /,səbrə'gāsHən/ ▸*n. Law* the substitution of one person or group by another in respect of a debt or insurance claim, accompanied by the transfer of any associated rights and duties. —**sub·ro·gate** /'səbrə,gāt/ *v.*

sub ro·sa /,səb 'rōzə/ ▸*adj.* & *adv. formal* happening or done in secret: [as *adv.*] *the committee operates sub rosa* | [as *adj.*] *sub rosa inspections.*

sub·rou·tine /'səbrōō,tēn/ ▸*n. Comput.* a set of instructions designed to perform a frequently used operation within a program.

sub·scribe /səb'skrīb/ ▸*v.* **1** [*intr.*] arrange to receive something regularly, typically a publication, by paying in advance: *subscribe to the magazine for twelve months and receive a free T-shirt.* ■ arrange for access to an online service: *I subscribe to an Internet newsgroup.* ■ (**subscribe to**) *fig.* express or feel agreement with (an idea or proposal): *we prefer to subscribe to an alternative explanation.* ■ [*intr.*] apply to participate in: *the course has been fully subscribed.* ■ apply for or undertake to pay for an offering of shares of stock: *investors would subscribe electronically to the initial stock offerings* | [*tr.*] *yesterday's offering was fully subscribed.* ■ [*tr.*] (of a bookseller) agree before publication to take (a certain number of copies of a book): *most of the first print run of 15,000 copies has been subscribed.* **2** [*tr.*] *formal* sign (a will, contract, or other document): *he subscribed the will as a witness.* ▷late Middle English (in the sense 'sign at the bottom of a document'): from Latin *subscribere,* from *sub-* 'under' + *scribere* 'write.' —**sub·scrib·er** *n.*

sub·script /'səb,skript/ ▸*adj.* (of a letter, figure, or symbol) written or printed below the line.

▸*n.* a subscript letter, figure, or symbol. ■ *Comput.* a symbol (notionally written as a subscript but in practice usually not) used in a program, alone or with others, to specify one of the elements of an array.

sub·scrip·tion /səb'skripsHən/ ▸*n.* the action of making or agreeing to make an advance payment in order to receive or participate in something: *the newsletter is available only on subscription.* ■ an arrangement by which access is granted to an online service. ■ a system in which the production of a book is wholly or partly financed by advance orders.

sub·sec·tion /'səb,seksHən/ ▸*n.* a division of a section.

sub·se·quent /'səbsəkwənt/ ▸*adj.* coming after something in time; following: *the theory was developed subsequent to the earthquake of 1906.* —**sub·se·quent·ly** *adv.*

sub·serve /səb'sərv/ ▸*v.* [*tr.*] help to further or promote: *officers are appointed to subserve their own profit and convenience.*

sub·ser·vi·ent /səb'sərvēənt/ ▸*adj.* prepared to obey others unquestioningly: *she was subservient to her parents.* ■ less important; subordinate: *Marxism makes freedom subservient to control.* ■ serving as a means to an end: *the whole narration is subservient to the moral plan of exemplifying twelve virtues in twelve knights.* —**sub·ser·vi·ence** *n.* —**sub·ser·vi·en·cy** *n.* —**sub·ser·vi·ent·ly** *adv.*

sub·set /'səb,set/ ▸*n.* a part of a larger group of related things. ■ *Math.* a set of which all the elements are contained in another set.

sub·side /səb'sīd/ ▸*v.* **1** become less intense, violent, or severe: *I'll wait a few minutes until the storm subsides.* ■ lapse into silence or inactivity: *Fred opened his mouth to protest again, then subsided.* **2** (of water) go down to a lower or the normal level: *the floods subside almost as quickly as they arise.* ■ (of the ground) cave in; sink: *the island is subsiding.* ■ (of a swelling) reduce until gone: *it took seven days for the swelling to subside completely.*

sub·sid·i·ar·y /səb'sidē,erē/ ▸*adj.* less important than but related or supplementary to: *the cause of animal rights is subsidiary to that of protecting the environment.* ■ (of a company) controlled by a holding or parent company.

▸*n.* (*pl.* **-ar·ies**) a company controlled by a holding company. —**sub·sid·i·ar·i·ly** /-,sidē'e(ə)rəlē/ *adv.* (*rare*).

sub·si·dize /'səbsə,dīz/ ▸*v.* [*tr.*] support (an organization or activity) financially: *it was beyond the power of a state to subsidize a business.* ■ pay part of the cost of producing (something) to reduce prices for the buyer: *the government subsidizes basic goods including sugar, petroleum, and wheat.* —**sub·si·di·za·tion** /,səbsədi'zāsHən/ *n.* —**sub·si·diz·er** *n.*

sub·si·dy /'səbsidē/ ▸*n.* (*pl.* **-dies**) a sum of money granted by the government or a public body to assist an industry or business so that the price of a commodity or service may remain low or competitive: *a farm subsidy.* ■ a sum of money granted to support an arts organization or other undertaking held to be in the public interest. ■ a sum of money paid by one government to another for the preservation of neutrality, the promotion of war, or to repay military aid. ■ a grant or contribution of money.

sub·sist /səb'sist/ ▸*v.* [*intr.*] **1** maintain or support oneself, esp. at a minimal level: *thousands of refugees subsist on international handouts.* **2** *chiefly Law* remain in being, force, or effect. —**sub·sist·ent** /-ənt/ *adj.*

sub·sist·ence /səb'sistəns/ ▸*n.* **1** the action or fact of maintaining or supporting oneself at a minimum level: *the minimum income needed for* subsistence. ■ the means of doing this: *the garden provided not only subsistence but a little cash crop.* ■ [as adj.] denoting or relating to production at a level sufficient only for one's own use or consumption, without any surplus for trade: *subsistence agriculture.* **2** *chiefly Law* the state of remaining in force or effect: *rights of occupation normally only continue during the subsistence of the marriage.*

sub·soil /'səb,soil/ ▶*n.* the soil lying immediately under the surface soil.

sub·son·ic /,səb'sänik/ ▶*adj.* relating to or flying at a speed or speeds less than that of sound. —**sub·son·i·cal·ly** /-ik(ə)lē/ *adv.*

sub·spe·cies /'səb,spēsēz; -sēz/ (abbr.: **subsp.** or **ssp.**) ▶*n.* (*pl.* same) *Biology* a taxonomic category that ranks below species, usually a fairly permanent geographically isolated race. Compare with FORM and VARIETY.

subst. ▶*abbr.* ■ substantive. ■ substantively. ■ substitute.

sub·stance /'səbstəns/ ▶*n.* **1** a particular kind of matter with uniform properties: *a steel tube coated with a waxy substance.* ■ an intoxicating, stimulating, or narcotic chemical or drug, esp. an illegal one. **2** the real physical matter of which a person or thing consists and which has a tangible, solid presence: *proteins compose much of the actual substance of the body.* ■ the quality of having a solid basis in reality or fact: *the claim has no substance.* ■ the quality of being dependable or stable: *some were inclined to knock her for her lack of substance.* **3** the quality of being important, valid, or significant: *he had yet to accomplish anything of substance.* ■ the most important or essential part of something; the real or essential meaning: *the substance of the treaty.* ■ the subject matter of a text, speech, or work of art, esp. as contrasted with the form or style in which it is presented: *a woman of substance.* ■ wealth and possessions: *a woman of substance.*

sub·stand·ard /səb'standərd/ ▶*adj.* **1** below the usual or required standard: *substandard housing.* **2** another term for NONSTANDARD.

sub·stan·tial /səb'stanCHəl/ ▶*adj.* **1** of considerable importance, size, or worth: *a substantial amount of cash.* ■ strongly built or made: *a row of substantial Victorian villas.* ■ (of a meal) large and filling. ■ important in material or social terms; wealthy: *a substantial Devon family.* **2** concerning the essentials of something: *there was substantial agreement on changing policies.* **3** real and tangible rather than imaginary: *spirits are shadowy, human beings substantial.* —**sub·stan·tial·ly** *adv.* —**sub·stan·ti·al·i·ty** /-,stanCHē'alitē/ *n.*

sub·stan·ti·ate /səb'stanCHē,āt/ ▶*v.* [*tr.*] provide evidence to support or prove the truth of: *they had found nothing to substantiate the allegations.* —**sub·stan·ti·a·tion** /-,stanCHē'āSHən/ *n.*

sub·stan·tive /'səbstəntiv/ ▶*adj.* **1** having a firm basis in reality and therefore important, meaningful, or considerable: *there is no substantive evidence for the efficacy of these drugs.* **2** (of law) defining rights and duties as opposed to giving the rules by which such things are established. ▶*n. Gram.* a noun. —**sub·stan·ti·val** /,səbstən'tīvəl/ *adj.* —**sub·stan·tive·ly** *adv.*

sub·sta·tion /'səb,stāSHən/ ▶*n.* **1** a set of equipment reducing the high voltage of electrical power transmission to that suitable for supply to consumers. **2** a subordinate station for the police or fire department. ■ a small post office, for example one situated within a larger store.

sub·stit·u·ent /səb'stiCHŌŌənt/ ▶*n. Chem.* an atom or group of atoms taking the place of another atom or group or occupying a specified position in a molecule.

sub·sti·tute /'səbsti,t(y)ōōt/ ▶*n.* a person or thing acting or serving in place of another: *soy milk is used as a **substitute for** dairy milk.* ■ a sports player nominated as eligible to replace another after a game has begun. ■ *Psychol.* a person or thing that becomes the object of love or other emotion deprived of its natural outlet: *a father substitute.*
▶*v.* [*tr.*] use or add in place of: *dried rosemary can be **substituted for** the fresh herb.* ■ [*intr.*] act or serve as a substitute: *I found someone to **substitute for** me.* ■ replace (someone or something) with another: *customs officers **substituted** the drugs **with** another substance.* ■ replace (a sports player) with a substitute during a contest: *he was substituted for Nichols in the fifth inning.* ■ *Chem.* replace (an atom or group in a molecule, esp. a hydrogen atom) with another. ▷late Middle English (denoting a deputy or delegate): from Latin *substitutus* 'put in place of,' past participle of *substituere,* based on *statuere* 'set up.' —**sub·sti·tut·a·bil·i·ty** /,səbstə,t(y)ōōtə'bilitē/ *n.* —**sub·sti·tut·a·ble** *adj.* —**sub·sti·tu·tion** /,səbsti't(y)ōōSHən/ *n.* —**sub·sti·tu·tive** /-,t(y)ōōtiv/ *adj.*

sub·strate /'səb,strāt/ ▶*n.* a substance or layer that underlies something, or on which some process occurs, in particular: ■ the surface or material on or from which an organism lives, grows, or obtains its nourishment. ■ the substance on which an enzyme acts. ■ a material that provides the surface on which something is deposited or inscribed, for example the silicon wafer used to manufacture integrated circuits.

sub·stra·tum /'səb,strātəm; -,stra-/ ▶*n.* (*pl.* **-ta** /-tə/) an underlying layer or substance, in particular, a layer of rock or soil beneath the surface of the ground. ■ a foundation or basis of something: *there is a broad **substratum** of truth in it.*

sub·struc·ture /'səb,strəkCHər/ ▶*n.* an underlying or supporting structure. —**sub·struc·tur·al** /,səb'strəkCHərəl/ *adj.*

sub·sume /səb'sōōm/ ▶*v.* [*tr.*] (often **be subsumed**) include or absorb (something) in something else: *most of these phenomena can be **subsumed** **under** two broad categories.* —**sub·sum·a·ble** *adj.* —**sub·sump·tion** /-'səm(p)SHən/ *n.*

sub·ten·ant /səb'tenənt/ ▶*n.* a person who leases property from a tenant. —**sub·ten·an·cy** /'tenənsē/ *n.*

sub·ter·fuge /'səbtər,fyōōj/ ▶*n.* deceit used in order to achieve one's goal. ■ a statement or action resorted to in order to deceive.

sub·ter·ra·ne·an /,səbtə'rānēən/ ▶*adj.* existing, occurring, or done under the earth's surface. ■ secret; concealed: *the subterranean world of Islam's radical fringe.* —**sub·ter·ra·ne·ous·ly** /-'rānēəslē/ *adv.*

sub·text /'səb,tekst/ ▶*n.* an underlying and often distinct theme in a piece of writing or conversation.

sub·ti·tle /'səb,tītl/ ▶*n.* **1** (**subtitles**) captions displayed at the bottom of a movie or television screen that translate or transcribe the dialogue or narrative. **2** a subordinate title of a published work or article giving additional information about its content.
▶*v.* [*tr.*] (usu. **be subtitled**) **1** provide (a movie or program) with subtitles: *much of the film is subtitled.* **2** provide (a published work or article) with a subtitle: *the novel was aptly subtitled.*

sub·tle /'sətl/ ▶*adj.* (**-tler, -tlest**) (esp. of a change or distinction) so delicate or precise as to be difficult to analyze or describe: *his language expresses rich and subtle meanings.* ■ (of a mixture or effect) delicately complex and understated: *subtle lighting.* ■ making use of clever and indirect methods to achieve something: *he tried a more subtle approach.* ■ capable of making fine distinctions: *a subtle mind.* ■ arranged in an ingenious and elaborate way. —**sub·tle·ness** *n.* —**sub·tly** *adv.*

sub·tle·ty /'sətltē/ ▶*n.* (*pl.* **-ties**) the quality or state of being subtle: *the textural subtlety of Degas.* ■ a subtle distinction, feature, or argument: *the subtleties of English grammar.*

sub·ton·ic /səb'tänik/ ▶*n. Mus.* the note below the tonic, the seventh note of the diatonic scale of any key.

sub·to·tal /'səb,tōtl/ ▶*n.* the total of one set of a larger group of figures to be added.
▶*v.* (**-taled, -tal·ing;** *Brit.* **-talled, -tal·ling**) [*tr.*] add (numbers) so as to obtain a subtotal.

sub·tract /səb'trakt/ ▶*v.* [*tr.*] take away (a number or amount) from another to calculate the difference: *subtract 43 from 60.* ■ take away (something) from something else so as to decrease the size, number, or amount: *programs were added and subtracted as called for.* —**sub·tract·er** *n.* —**sub·trac·tion** *n.* —**sub·trac·tive** /-tiv/ *adj.*

sub·trop·ics /səb'träpiks/ ▶*pl. n.* (**the subtropics**) the regions adjacent to or bordering on the tropics. —**sub·trop·i·cal** /-'träpikəl/ *adj.*

sub·urb /'səbərb/ ▶*n.* an outlying district of a city, esp. a residential one.

sub·ur·ban /sə'bərbən/ ▶*adj.* of or characteristic of a suburb: *suburban life.* ■ contemptibly dull and ordinary: *Elizabeth despised Ann's house-proudness as deeply suburban.* —**sub·ur·ban·ite** *n.* —**sub·ur·ban·i·za·tion** /sə,bərbənə'zāSHən/ *n.* —**sub·ur·ban·ize** *v.*

sub·ur·bi·a /sə'bərbēə/ ▶*n.* the suburbs or their inhabitants viewed collectively.

sub·ven·tion /səb'venCHən/ ▶*n.* a grant of money, esp. from a government.

sub·ver·sive /səb'vərsiv/ ▶*adj.* seeking or intended to subvert an established system or institution: *subversive literature.*
▶*n.* a person with such aims. —**sub·ver·sive·ly** *adv.* —**sub·ver·sive·ness** *n.*

sub·vert /səb'vərt/ ▶*v.* [*tr.*] undermine the power and authority of (an established system or institution): *an attempt to subvert our democratic government.* —**sub·ver·sion** /-'vərzHən; -SHən/ *n.* —**sub·vert·er** *n.*

sub·way /'səb,wā/ ▶*n.* an underground electric railroad.

sub·ze·ro /,səb'zi(ə)rō/ ▶*adj.* below zero on the Fahrenheit scale (–18 Celsius); very cold. ■ below zero on the Celsius scale; below freezing.

suc·ceed /sək'sēd/ ▶*v.* **1** [*intr.*] achieve what one aims or wants to: *he succeeded in winning a pardon.* ■ (of a plan, request, or undertaking) lead to the desired result: *a mission which could not possibly succeed.* **2** [*tr.*] take

---

Pronunciation Key ə *ago,* up; ər *over, fur;* a *hat;* ā *ate;* ä *car;* CH *chin;* e *let;* ē *see;* e(ə)r *air;* i *fit;* ī *by;* i(ə)r *ear;* NG *sing;* ō *go;* ô *law, for;* oi *toy;* ōō *good;* ōō *goo;* ou *out;* SH *she;* TH *thin;* TH *then;* (h)w *why;* ZH *vision*

over a throne, inheritance, office, or other position from: *he would succeed Hawke as prime minister.* ■ [*intr.*] become the new rightful holder of an inheritance, office, title, or property: *he succeeded to his father's kingdom.* ■ come after and take the place of: *her embarrassment was succeeded by fear.* —**suc·ceed·er** *n.* (*archaic*).

suc·cess /sək'ses/ ▶*n.* the accomplishment of an aim or purpose: *the president had some success in restoring confidence.* ■ the attainment of popularity or profit: *the success of his play.* ■ a person or thing that achieves desired aims or attains prosperity: *I must make a success of my business.*

suc·cess·ful /sək'sesfəl/ ▶*adj.* accomplishing an aim or purpose: *a successful attack on the town.* ■ having achieved popularity, profit, or distinction: *a successful actor.* —**suc·cess·ful·ly** *adv.* —**suc·cess·ful·ness** *n.*

suc·ces·sion /sək'seshən/ ▶*n.* **1** a number of people or things sharing a specified characteristic and following one after the other: *she had been secretary to a succession of board directors.* **2** the action or process of inheriting a title, office, property, etc.: *the new king was already elderly at the time of his succession.* ■ the right or sequence of inheriting a position, title, etc.: *the succession to the Crown was disputed.* ■ *Ecol.* the process by which a plant or animal community successively gives way to another until a stable climax is reached. —**suc·ces·sion·al** /-shənl/ *adj.*

▶ □ **in succession** following one after the other without interruption: *she won the race for the second year in succession.*

suc·ces·sive /sək'sesiv/ ▶*adj.* following one another or following others: *they were looking for their fifth successive win.* —**suc·ces·sive·ly** *adv.* —**suc·ces·sive·ness** *n.*

suc·ces·sor /sək'sesər/ ▶*n.* a person or thing that succeeds another: *Schoenberg saw himself as a natural successor to the German romantic school.*

suc·cinct /sə(k)'siNG(k)t/ ▶*adj.* (esp. of something written or spoken) briefly and clearly expressed: *use short, succinct sentences.* —**suc·cinct·ly** *adv.* —**suc·cinct·ness** *n.*

suc·cor /'səkər/ (*Brit.* **suc·cour**) ▶*n.* assistance and support in times of hardship and distress. —**suc·cor·less** *adj.*

suc·co·tash /'səkə,tash/ ▶*n.* a dish of corn and lima beans cooked together.

Suc·coth /soō'kôt; 'soōkəs/ (also **Suk·koth**) ▶*n.* a major Jewish festival held in the autumn (beginning on the 15th day of Tishri) to commemorate the sheltering of the Israelites in the wilderness.

suc·cu·bus /'səkyəbəs/ ▶*n.* (*pl.* **-bi** /-,bī/) a female demon believed to have sexual intercourse with sleeping men.

suc·cu·lent /'səkyələnt/ ▶*adj.* (of food) tender, juicy, and tasty. ▶*n. Bot.* a plant having thick fleshy leaves or stems adapted to storing water. —**suc·cu·lence** *n.* —**suc·cu·lent·ly** *adv.*

suc·cumb /sə'kəm/ ▶*v.* [*intr.*] fail to resist (pressure, temptation, or some other negative force): *he has become the latest to succumb to the strain.* ■ die from the effect of a disease or injury.

such /səCH/ ▶*adj. & pron.* **1** of the type previously mentioned: [as *adj.*] *I have been involved in many such courses* | [as *pron.*] *we were second-class citizens and they treated us as such.* **2** (**such —— as/that**) of the type about to be mentioned: [as *adj.*] *there is no such thing as a free lunch* | [as *pron.*] *the wound was such that I had to have stitches.* **3** to so high a degree; so great (often used to emphasize a quality): [as *adj.*] *this material is of such importance that it has a powerful bearing on the case* | [as *pron.*] *such is the elegance of his typeface that it is still a favorite of designers.*

such·like /'səCH,līk/ ▶*pron.* things of the type mentioned: *carpets, old chairs, tables, and suchlike.* ▶*adj.* of the type mentioned: *food, drink, clothing, and suchlike provisions.*

suck /sək/ ▶*v.* **1** [*tr.*] draw into the mouth by contracting the muscles of the lip and mouth to make a partial vacuum: *they suck mint juleps through straws.* ■ hold (something) in the mouth and draw at it by contracting the lip and cheek muscles: *she sucked a mint* | [*intr.*] *the child sucked on her thumb.* ■ draw milk, juice, or other fluid from (something) into the mouth or by suction: *she sucked each segment of the orange carefully.* ■ [*tr.*] draw in a specified direction by creating a vacuum: *he was sucked under the surface of the river.* ■ *fig.* involve (someone) in something without their choosing: *I didn't want to be sucked into the role of dutiful daughter.* ■ [*intr.*] (of a pump) make a gurgling sound as a result of drawing air. **2** [*intr.*] *inf.* be very bad, disagreeable, or disgusting: *I love your country, but the weather sucks.*

▶*phrasal v.* □ **suck up** *inf.* behave obsequiously, esp. for one's own advantage: *he has risen to where he is mainly by sucking up to the president.*

▶*n.* an act of sucking something. ■ the sound made by water retreating and drawing at something: *the soft suck of the sea against the sand.*

▶ □ **suck someone in** cheat or deceive someone: *we were sucked in by his charm and good looks.*

suck·er /'səkər/ ▶*n.* **1** a person or thing that sucks, in particular: ■ a flat or concave organ enabling an animal to cling to a surface by suction. ■

the piston of a suction pump. ■ a pipe through which liquid is drawn by suction. **2** *inf.* a gullible or easily deceived person. ■ (**a sucker for**) a person especially susceptible to or fond of a specified thing: *I always was a sucker for a good fairy tale.* **3** *inf.* a thing or person not specified by name: *he's one strong sucker.* **4** *Bot.* a shoot springing from the base of a tree or other plant, esp. one arising from the root below ground level at some distance from the main stem or trunk. ■ a side shoot from an axillary bud, as in tomato plants. **5** a freshwater fish (family Catostomidae) with thick lips that are used to suck up food from the bottom, native to North America and Asia. **6** *inf.* a lollipop.

▶*v.* **1** [*intr.*] *Bot.* (of a plant) produce suckers: *it spread rapidly after being left undisturbed to sucker.* **2** [*tr.*] *inf.* fool or trick (someone): *they got suckered into accepting responsibility.*

suck·le /'səkəl/ ▶*v.* [*tr.*] feed (a baby or young animal) from the breast or teat: *a mother pig suckling a huge litter.* ■ [*intr.*] (of a baby or young animal) feed by sucking the breast or teat: *the infant's biological need to suckle.*

suck·ling /'səkliNG/ ▶*n.* an unweaned child or animal: [as *adj.*] *roast suckling pig.*

su·crose /'soō,krōs/ ▶*n. Chem.* the sugar that is the chief component of cane and beet sugar.

suc·tion /'səkshən/ ▶*n.* the production of a partial vacuum by the removal of air in order to force fluid into a vacant space or procure adhesion.

▶*v.* [*tr.*] remove (something) using suction: *physicians used a tube to suction out the gallstones.*

sud·den /'sədn/ ▶*adj.* occurring or done quickly and unexpectedly or without warning: *a sudden bright flash.* —**sud·den·ly** *adv.* —**sud·den·ness** *n.*

sud·den death ▶*n. inf.* a means of deciding the winner in a tied contest, in which play continues and the winner is the first side or player to score: [as *adj.*] *a sudden-death playoff.*

sud·den in·fant death syn·drome (abbr. **SIDS**) ▶*n.* the death of a seemingly healthy baby in its sleep, due to an apparent spontaneous cessation of breathing.

su·do·ku /soō'dōkoō/ ▶*n.* a logic-based puzzle consisting of squares that form grids within a grid. Into each smaller grid, the numerals 1 through 9 are entered but not repeated, and they may not be repeated in any row or column of the larger grid.

suds /sədz/ ▶*pl. n.* short for SOAPSUDS. ■ *inf.* beer.

▶*v.* [*tr.*] lather, cover, or wash in soapy water: *Martha sudsed my back.* —**suds·y** *adj.*

sue /soō/ ▶*v.* (**sues**, **sued**, **su·ing**) **1** [*tr.*] institute legal proceedings against (a person or institution), typically for redress: *she is to sue the baby's father* | [*intr.*] *I sued for breach of contract.* **2** [*intr.*] *formal* appeal formally to a person for something: *the rebels were forced to sue for peace.* ▷Middle English: from Anglo-Norman French *suer*, based on Latin *sequi* 'follow.' Early senses were very similar to those of the verb *follow*. —**su·er** /'soōər/ *n.*

suede /swād/ ▶*n.* leather, esp. kid, with the flesh side rubbed to make a velvety nap.

su·et /'soōit/ ▶*n.* the hard white fat on the kidneys and loins of cattle, sheep, and other animals, used in cooking. —**su·et·y** *adj.*

suf. ▶*abbr.* suffix.

suf·fer /'səfər/ ▶*v.* [*tr.*] **1** experience or be subjected to (something bad or unpleasant): *he'd suffered intense pain* | [*intr.*] *he'd suffered a great deal since his arrest* | [as *n.*] (**suffering**) *weapons that cause unnecessary suffering.* ■ [*intr.*] (**suffer from**) be affected by or subject to (an illness or ailment): *his daughter suffered from agoraphobia.* ■ [*intr.*] become or appear worse in quality: *his relationship with Anne did suffer.* **2** *dated* tolerate: *France will no longer suffer the existing government.* ■ allow (someone) to do something: *my conscience would not suffer me to accept any more.* —**suf·fer·a·ble** /'səf(ə)rəbəl/ *adj.* —**suf·fer·er** /'səf(ə)rər/ *n.*

suf·fer·ance /'səf(ə)rəns/ ▶*n.* absence of objection rather than genuine approval; toleration: *Charles was only here on sufferance.*

suf·fice /sə'fīs/ ▶*v.* [*intr.*] be enough or adequate: *a quick look should suffice.* ■ [*tr.*] meet the needs of: *simple mediocrity cannot suffice them.*

suf·fi·cien·cy /sə'fishənsē/ ▶*n.* (*pl.* **-cies**) the condition or quality of being adequate or sufficient. ■ an adequate amount of something, esp. of something essential: *a sufficiency of good food.*

suf·fi·cient /sə'fishənt/ ▶*adj.* enough; adequate: *a small income that was sufficient for her needs.* —**suf·fi·cient·ly** *adv.*

suf·fix ▶*n.* /'səfiks/ a morpheme added at the end of a word to form a derivative, e.g., *-ation*, *-fy*, *-ing*, *-itis*.

▶*v.* /'səfiks; sə'fiks/ [*tr.*] append, esp. as a suffix. —**suf·fix·a·tion** /,səfik·'sāshən/ *n.*

suf·fo·cate /'səfəˌkāt/ ▶ v. die or cause to die from lack of air or inability to breathe: [intr.] *ten detainees suffocated in an airless police cell.* | [tr.] *she was suffocated by the fumes.* ■ have or cause to have difficulty in breathing: [intr.] *he was suffocating, his head jammed up against the back of the sofa* | [tr.] *you're suffocating me—I can scarcely breathe* | [as adj.] (**suffocating**) *the suffocating heat.* ■ fig. feel or cause to feel trapped and oppressed: [as adj.] (**suffocated**) *I felt suffocated by my marriage.* —**suf·fo·cat·ing·ly** adv. —**suf·fo·ca·tion** /ˌsəfəˈkāsHən/ n.

suf·frage /'səfrij/ ▶ n. the right to vote in political elections.

suf·fra·gette /ˌsəfrəˈjet/ ▶ n. hist. a woman seeking the right to vote through organized protest.

suf·fra·gist /'səfrəjist/ ▶ n. chiefly hist. a person advocating the extension of suffrage, esp. to women. —**suf·fra·gism** /-ˌjizəm/ n.

suf·fuse /səˈfyōōz/ ▶ v. [tr.] gradually spread through or over: *her cheeks were suffused with color.* —**suf·fu·sion** /-ˈfyōōzHən/ n. —**suf·fu·sive** /-ˈfyōōsiv/ adj.

Su·fi /'sōōfē/ ▶ n. (pl. -fis) a Muslim ascetic and mystic. —**Su·fic** /-fik/ adj.

sug·ar /'sHŏŏgər/ ▶ n. **1** a sweet crystalline substance obtained from various plants, esp. sugar cane and sugar beet, consisting essentially of sucrose, and used as a sweetener in food and drink. ■ a lump or teaspoonful of this, used to sweeten tea or coffee: *I'll have mine black with two sugars.* ■ inf. used as a term of endearment or an affectionate form of address: *what's wrong, sugar?* ■ [as interj.] inf. used as a euphemism for "shit." ■ inf. a psychoactive drug in the form of white powder, esp. heroin or cocaine. **2** Biochem. any of the class of soluble, crystalline, typically sweet-tasting carbohydrates found in living tissues and exemplified by glucose and sucrose.
▶ v. [tr.] sweeten, sprinkle, or coat with sugar: *she absentmindedly sugared her tea.* ■ fig. make more agreeable or palatable: *the novel was preachy but sugared heavily with jokes.* ▷Middle English: from Old French *sukere*, from Italian *zucchero*, probably via medieval Latin from Arabic *sukkar.* —**sug·ar·less** adj.

sug·ar beet ▶ n. beet of a variety from which sugar is extracted.

sug·ar cane (also **sug·ar-cane** /'sHŏŏgərˌkān/) ▶ n. a perennial tropical grass (genus *Saccharum*) with tall stout jointed stems from which sugar is extracted.

sug·ar·coat /'sHŏŏgərˌkōt/ ▶ v. [tr.] coat (an item of food) with sugar: [as adj.] (**sugarcoated**) *sugarcoated almonds.* ■ make superficially attractive or acceptable: *you won't see him sugarcoat the truth.* ■ make excessively sentimental: *the filmmakers' proficiency is overpowered by their tendency to sugarcoat the material.*

sug·ar dad·dy ▶ n. inf. a rich older man who lavishes gifts on a young woman in return for her company or sexual favors.

sug·ar ma·ple ▶ n. see MAPLE.

sug·ar·plum /'sHŏŏgərˌpləm/ ▶ n. a small round candy.

sug·ar·y /'sHŏŏgərē/ ▶ adj. containing much sugar: *energy-restoring, sugary drinks.* ■ resembling or coated in sugar: *a sugary texture.* ■ excessively sentimental: *sugary romance.* —**sug·ar·i·ness** n.

sug·gest /sə(g)ˈjest/ ▶ v. put forward for consideration: *I suggest that we wait a day or two* | [tr.] *Ruth suggested a vacation.* ■ [tr.] cause one to think that (something) exists or is the case: *finds of lead coffins suggested a cemetery north of the river.* ■ state or express indirectly: *are you suggesting that I should ignore her?* | [tr.] *the seduction scenes suggest his guilt and her loneliness.* ■ [tr.] evoke: *the theatrical interpretation of weather and water almost suggests El Greco.* —**sug·gest·er** n.

sug·gest·i·ble /sə(g)ˈjestəbəl/ ▶ adj. open to suggestion; easily swayed: *a suggestible client would comply.* —**sug·gest·i·bil·i·ty** /-ˌjestəˈbilitē/ n.

sug·ges·tion /sə(g)ˈjescHən/ ▶ n. an idea or plan put forward for consideration. ■ the action of doing this: *at my suggestion, the museum held an exhibition of his work.* ■ something that implies or indicates a certain fact or situation: *there is no suggestion that he was involved in any wrongdoing.* ■ a slight trace or indication of something: *there was a suggestion of a smile on his lips.* ■ the action or process of calling up an idea or thought in someone's mind by associating it with other things: *the power of suggestion.* ■ Psychol. the influencing of a person to accept an idea, belief, or impulse uncritically, esp. as a technique in hypnosis or other therapies. ■ Psychol. a belief or impulse of this type.

sug·ges·tive /sə(g)ˈjestiv/ ▶ adj. tending to suggest an idea: *there were various suggestive pieces of evidence.* ■ indicative or evocative: *flavors suggestive of coffee and blackberry.* ■ making someone think of sex and sexual relationships: *a suggestive remark.* —**sug·ges·tive·ly** adv. —**sug·ges·tive·ness** n.

su·i·cid·al /ˌsōōiˈsīdl/ ▶ adj. deeply unhappy or depressed and likely to commit suicide: *far from being suicidal, he was clearly enjoying life.* ■ relating to or likely to lead to suicide: *I began to take her suicidal tendencies*

seriously. ■ likely to have a disastrously damaging effect on oneself or one's interests: *a suicidal career move.* —**su·i·cid·al·ly** adv.

su·i·cide /'sōōiˌsīd/ ▶ n. the action of killing oneself intentionally: *he committed suicide at the age of forty.* ■ a person who does this. ■ a course of action that is disastrously damaging to oneself or one's own interests: *it would be political suicide to restrict criteria for unemployment benefits.* ■ [as adj.] relating to or denoting a violent act or attack carried out by a person who does not expect to survive it: *a suicide bombing.*

su·i ge·ne·ris /ˌsōō.ī ˈjenərəs; ˌsōōē/ ▶ adj. unique: *the sui generis nature of animals.*

suit /sōōt/ ▶ n. **1** a set of outer clothes made of the same fabric and designed to be worn together, typically consisting of a jacket and trousers or a jacket and skirt. ■ a set of clothes to be worn on a particular occasion or for a particular activity: *a jogging suit.* ■ a complete set of pieces of armor for covering the whole body. ■ (usu. **suits**) inf. an executive in a business or organization, typically one regarded as exercising influence in an impersonal way: *maybe now the suits in Washington will listen.* **2** any of the sets distinguished by their pictorial symbols into which a deck of playing cards is divided, in conventional decks comprising spades, hearts, diamonds, and clubs. **3** short for LAWSUIT. ■ the process of trying to win a woman's affection, typically with a view to marriage: *he could not compete with John's charms in Marian's eyes and his suit came to nothing.*
▶ v. **1** [tr.] be convenient for or acceptable to: *he lied whenever it suited him* | [intr.] *the apartment has two bedrooms—if it suits, you can have one of them.* ■ go well with or enhance the features, figure, or character of (someone): *the dress didn't suit her.* **2** [intr.] put on clothes, typically for a particular activity: *I suited up and entered the water.* ▷Middle English: from Anglo-Norman French *siwte*, from a feminine past participle of a Romance verb based on Latin *sequi* 'follow.' Early senses included 'attendance at a court' and 'legal process'; senses 1 and 2 derive from an earlier meaning 'set of things to be used together.' The verb sense 'make appropriate' dates from the late 16th cent.

suit·a·ble /'sōōtəbəl/ ▶ adj. right or appropriate for a particular person, purpose, or situation: *these toys are not suitable for children under five.* —**suit·a·bil·i·ty** /ˌsōōtəˈbilitē/ n. —**suit·a·ble·ness** n. —**suit·a·bly** /-blē/ adv.

suit·case /'sōōtˌkās/ ▶ n. a case with a handle and a hinged lid, used for carrying clothes and other personal possessions. —**suit·case·ful** /-ˌfŏŏl/ n. (pl. -fuls).

suite /swēt/ ▶ n. **1** a set of things belonging together, in particular: ■ a set of rooms designated for one person's or family's use or for a particular purpose. ■ a set of furniture of the same design. ■ Mus. a set of instrumental compositions, originally in dance style, to be played in succession. ■ Mus. a set of selected pieces from an opera or musical, arranged to be played as one instrumental work. ■ Comput. a set of programs with a uniform design and the ability to share data. ■ Geol. a group of minerals, rocks, or fossils occurring together and characteristic of a location or period. **2** a group of people in attendance on a monarch or other person of high rank.

suit·or /'sōōtər/ ▶ n. a man who pursues a relationship with a particular woman, with a view to marriage. ■ a prospective buyer of a business or corporation.

su·ki·ya·ki /ˌsōŏkēˈyäkē/ ▶ n. a Japanese dish of sliced meat, esp. beef, cooked rapidly with vegetables and sauce.

Suk·koth ▶ variant spelling of SUCCOTH.

sul·fa /'səlfə/ (chiefly Brit. also **sul·pha**) ▶ n. [usu. as adj.] the sulfonamide family of drugs: *a succession of life-saving sulfa drugs.*

sul·fate /'səlˌfāt/ (chiefly Brit. also **sul·phate**) ▶ n. Chem. a salt or ester of sulfuric acid, containing the anion $SO_4{}^{2-}$ or the divalent group $-OSO_2O-$.

sul·fide /'səlˌfīd/ (chiefly Brit. also **sul·phide**) ▶ n. Chem. a binary compound of sulfur with another element or group.

sul·fite /'səlˌfīt/ (chiefly Brit. also **sul·phite**) ▶ n. Chem. a salt of sulfurous acid, containing the anion $SO_3{}^{2-}$.

sul·fon·a·mide /səlˈfänəˌmīd/ (chiefly Brit. also **sul·phon·a·mide**) ▶ n. Med. any of a class of synthetic drugs that are able to prevent the multiplication of some pathogenic bacteria.

sul·fur /'səlfər/ (also chiefly Brit. **sul·phur**) ▶ n. **1** the chemical element of atomic number 16, a yellow combustible nonmetal. (Symbol: **S**) ■ the material of which hellfire and lightning were believed to consist. ■ a pale greenish-yellow color: [as adj.] *the bird's sulfur-yellow throat.* **2** an

American butterfly (*Colias, Phoebis,* and other genera, family Pieridae) with predominantly yellow wings that may bear darker patches. —**sul·fur·y** *adj.*

sul·fur di·ox·ide ▶*n. Chem.* a colorless pungent toxic gas, SO_2.

sul·fu·re·ous /səlˈfyŏŏrēəs/ (*chiefly Brit.* also **sul·phu·re·ous**) ▶*adj.* of, like, or containing sulfur.

sul·fu·ric /səlˈfyŏŏrik/ (*chiefly Brit.* also **sul·phu·ric**) ▶*adj.* containing sulfur or sulfuric acid: *the sulfuric byproducts of wood fires.*

sul·fu·ric ac·id ▶*n.* a strong acid made by oxidizing solutions of sulfur dioxide, H_2SO_4, and used as an industrial and laboratory reagent. The concentrated form is an oily, dense, corrosive liquid.

sul·fur·ous /ˈsəlfərəs/ (*chiefly Brit.* also **sul·phur·ous**) ▶*adj.* (chiefly of vapor or smoke) containing or derived from sulfur: *wafts of sulfurous fumes.* ■ sulfureous. ■ like sulfur in color; pale yellow. ■ marked by bad temper, anger, or profanity: *a sulfurous glance.*

sulk /səlk/ ▶*v.* [*intr.*] be silent, morose, and bad-tempered out of annoyance or disappointment: *he was sulking over the breakup of his band.*
▶*n.* a period of gloomy and bad-tempered silence stemming from annoyance and resentment: *she was in a fit of the sulks.* —**sulk·er** *n.*

sulk·y /ˈsəlkē/ ▶*adj.* (**sulk·i·er, sulk·i·est**) morose, bad-tempered, and resentful; refusing to be cooperative or cheerful: *disappointment was making her sulky.* ■ expressing or suggesting gloom and bad temper: *she had a sultry, sulky mouth.* ■ *fig.* not quick to work or respond: *a sulky fire.*
▶*n.* (*pl.* **sulk·ies**) a light two-wheeled horse-drawn vehicle for one person, used chiefly in harness racing. —**sulk·i·ly** /-kəlē/ *adv.* —**sulk·i·ness** *n.*

sul·len /ˈsələn/ ▶*adj.* bad-tempered and sulky; gloomy: *a sullen pout.* —**sul·len·ly** *adv.* —**sul·len·ness** *n.*

sul·ly /ˈsəlē/ ▶*v.* (**-lies, -lied**) [*tr.*] *poetic/lit.* or *ironic* damage the purity or integrity of; defile: *they were outraged that anyone should sully their good name.*

sul·tan /ˈsəltn/ ▶*n.* a Muslim sovereign. ■ (**the Sultan**) *hist.* the sultan of Turkey. —**sul·tan·ate** /-ˌāt/ *n.*

sul·tan·a /səlˈtanə/ ▶*n.* **1** a small, light brown, seedless raisin used in foods such as puddings and cakes. **2** a wife or concubine of a sultan. ■ any other woman in a sultan's family.

sul·try /ˈsəltrē/ ▶*adj.* (**-tri·er, -tri·est**) **1** (of the air or weather) hot and humid. **2** (of a person, esp. a woman) attractive in a way that suggests a passionate nature. —**sul·tri·ly** /-trəlē/ *adv.* —**sul·tri·ness** *n.*

sum /səm/ ▶*n.* **1** a particular amount of money: *they could not afford such a sum.* **2** (**the sum of**) the total amount resulting from the addition of two or more numbers, amounts, or items: *the sum of two prime numbers.* ■ the total amount of something that exists: *the sum of his own knowledge.*
▶*v.* (**summed, sum·ming**) [*tr.*] *technical* find the sum of (two or more amounts): *if we sum these equations we obtain x.* ■ [*intr.*] (**sum to**) (of two or more amounts) add up to a specified total: *these additional probabilities must sum to 1.*
▶*phrasal v.* □ **sum up** give a brief summary of something: *Gerard will open the debate and I will sum up.* ■ *Law* (of a judge) review the evidence at the end of a case, and direct the jury regarding points of law.
▶ □ **in sum** to sum up; in summary: *this interpretation does little, in sum, to add to our understanding.*

su·mac /ˈsŏŏmak; ˈshŏŏ-/ (also **su·mach**) ▶*n.* a shrub or small tree (genera *Rhus* and *Cotinus*) of the cashew family, with compound leaves, fruits in conical clusters, and bright autumn colors. Its several species include **staghorn sumac** (*R. typhina*), with densely clustered reddish hairy fruits, and **poison sumac** (*R. vernix*), with loosely clustered greenish-white fruits. Touching any part of the poison sumac can cause severe dermatitis.

su·ma·trip·tan /ˌsŏŏməˈtripˌtan; -tən/ ▶*n.* a drug used for the acute treatment of migraines.

Su·me·ri·an /səˈmerēən; -ˈmiər-/ ▶*adj.* of or relating to the ancient Mesopotamian state of Sumer, its ancient language, or the early, non-Semitic element it contributed to Babylonian civilization.
▶*n.* **1** a member of the indigenous non-Semitic people of ancient Babylonia. **2** the Sumerian language.

sum·ma cum lau·de /ˈsŏŏmə ˌkŏŏm ˈloudē; ˈloudē/ ▶*adv.* & *adj.* with the highest distinction: [as *adv.*] *he graduated summa cum laude.*

sum·ma·rize /ˈsəməˌrīz/ ▶*v.* [*tr.*] give a brief statement of the main points of (something): *these results can be summarized in the following table.* —**sum·ma·ri·za·tion** /ˌsəməriˈzāSHən/ *n.* —**sum·ma·riz·er** *n.*

sum·ma·ry /ˈsəmərē/ ▶*n.* (*pl.* **-ries**) a brief statement or account of the main points of something: *a summary of Chapter Three.*
▶*adj.* **1** dispensing with needless details or formalities; brief: *summary financial statements.* **2** *Law* (of a judicial process) conducted without the customary legal formalities: *summary arrest.* ■ (of a conviction) made

by a judge or magistrate without a jury. —**sum·mar·i·ly** /səˈme(ə)rəlē; ˈsəmərəlē/ *adv.* —**sum·mar·i·ness** /səˈmerēnis/ *n.*

sum·ma·tion /səˈmāSHən/ ▶*n.* **1** the process of adding things together: *the summation of numbers of small pieces of evidence.* ■ a sum total of things added together. **2** the process of summing something up: *these will need summation in a single document.* ■ a summary. ■ *Law* an attorney's closing speech at the conclusion of the giving of evidence. —**sum·ma·tion·al** /-SHənl/ *adj.* —**sum·ma·tive** /ˈsəmətiv/ *adj.*

sum·mer /ˈsəmər/ ▶*n.* the warmest season of the year, in the northern hemisphere from June to August and in the southern hemisphere from December to February. ■ *Astron.* the period from the summer solstice to the autumnal equinox. ■ (**summers**) *poetic/lit.* years, esp. of a person's age: *a girl of sixteen or seventeen summers.*
▶*v.* [*intr.*] spend the summer in a particular place: *well over 100 birds summered there in 1976.* —**sum·mer·y** *adj.*

sum·mer·house /ˈsəmərˌhous/ (also **sum·mer house**) ▶*n.* a small, typically rustic building in a garden or park, used for sitting in during the summer months. ■ (usu. **summer house**) a cottage or house use as a second residence, esp. during the summer.

sum·mer·sault ▶*n.* & *v.* archaic spelling of **SOMERSAULT**.

sum·mer sol·stice ▶*n.* the solstice that marks the onset of summer, at the time of the longest day, about June 21 in the northern hemisphere and December 22 in the southern hemisphere. ■ *Astron.* the solstice in June.

sum·mer squash ▶*n.* a squash (*Cucurbita pepo melopepo*) that is eaten before the seeds and rind have hardened.

sum·mer·time /ˈsəmərˌtīm/ ▶*n.* the season or period of summer: *in summertime trains run every ten minutes.*

sum·ming-up ▶*n.* a restatement of the main points of an argument, case, etc.

sum·mit /ˈsəmit/ ▶*n.* **1** the highest point of a hill or mountain. ■ *fig.* the highest attainable level of achievement: *the dramas are considered to form one of the summits of world literature.* **2** a meeting between heads of government: [as *adj.*] *a summit conference.*

sum·mon /ˈsəmən/ ▶*v.* [*tr.*] authoritatively or urgently call on (someone) to be present, esp. as a defendant or witness in a law court: *the pope summoned Anselm to Rome.* ■ urgently demand (help): *she summoned medical assistance.* ■ call people to attend (a meeting): *he summoned a meeting of head delegates.* ■ bring to the surface (a particular quality or reaction) from within oneself: *she managed to summon up a smile.* ■ (**summon something up**) call an image to mind: *names that summon up images of far-off places.* —**sum·mon·a·ble** *adj.* —**sum·mon·er** *n.*

sum·mons /ˈsəmənz/ ▶*n.* (*pl.* **-mons·es**) an order to appear before a judge or magistrate, or the writ containing it: *a summons for nonpayment of a parking ticket.* ■ an authoritative or urgent call to someone to be present or to do something: *they might receive a summons to fly to France next day.*
▶*v.* [*tr.*] *chiefly Law* serve (someone) with a summons: [*tr.*] *he has been summonsed to appear in court next month.*

su·mo /ˈsŏŏmō/ ▶*n.* (*pl.* **-mos**) a Japanese form of heavyweight wrestling, in which a wrestler wins a bout by forcing his opponent outside a marked circle or by making him touch the ground with any part of his body except the soles of his feet. ■ a sumo wrestler.

sump /səmp/ ▶*n.* a pit or hollow in which liquid collects, in particular: ■ the base of an internal combustion engine, which serves as a reservoir of oil for the lubrication system. ■ a depression in the floor of a mine or basement in which water collects. ■ a cesspool.

sump·tu·ous /ˈsəm(p)CHŏŏs/ ▶*adj.* splendid and expensive-looking: *the banquet was a sumptuous, luxurious meal.* —**sump·tu·os·i·ty** /ˌsəm(p)CHŏŏˈäsitē/ *n.* —**sump·tu·ous·ly** *adv.* —**sump·tu·ous·ness** *n.*

sum to·tal ▶*n.* another term for **SUM** (sense 2).

sun /sən/ ▶*n.* **1** (also **Sun**) the star around which the earth orbits. ■ any similar star in the universe, with or without planets. **2** (usu. **the sun**) the light or warmth received from the earth's sun: *we sat outside in the sun.* ■ *poetic/lit.* a person or thing regarded as a source of glory or inspiration or understanding: *the rhetoric faded before the sun of reality.*
▶*v.* (**sunned, sun·ning**) (**sun oneself**) sit or lie in the sun: *Buzz could see Clare sunning herself on the terrace below.* ■ [*tr.*] expose (something) to the sun, esp. to warm or dry it: *the birds are sunning their wings.* —**sun·less** *adj.* —**sun·less·ness** *n.* —**sun·like** /-ˌlīk/ *adj.* —**sun·ward** /-wərd/ *adj.* & *adv.* —**sun·wards** /-wərdz/ *adv.*
▶ □ **under the sun** on earth; in existence (used in expressions emphasizing the large number of something): *they exchanged views on every subject under the sun.*

Sun. ▶*abbr.* Sunday.

sun·bathe /'sən,bāтн/ ▶v. [intr.] sit or lie in the sun, esp. to tan the skin: [as n.] (**sunbathing**) *it was too hot for sunbathing.* —**sun·bath·er** n.

sun·beam /'sən,bēm/ ▶n. a ray of sunlight.

sun·belt /'sən,belt/ (also **sun belt**) ▶n. a strip of territory receiving a high amount of sunshine.

sun·block /'sən,bläk/ ▶n. a cream or lotion for protecting the skin from the sun and preventing sunburn.

sun·burn /'sən,bərn/ ▶n. reddening, inflammation, and, in severe cases, blistering and peeling of the skin caused by overexposure to the ultraviolet rays of the sun.
▶v. (past and past part. **-burned** or **-burnt**) (**be sunburned**) (of a person or bodily part) suffer from sunburn: *most of us managed to get sunburnt.* ■ [usu. as adj.] (**sunburned** or **sunburnt**) ruddy from exposure to the sun: *a handsome sunburned face.* ■ [intr.] suffer from sunburn: *a complexion that sunburned easily.*

sun·burst /'sən,bərst/ ▶n. a sudden brief appearance of the full sun from behind clouds. ■ a decoration or ornament resembling the sun and its rays: [as adj.] *a pair of sunburst diamond earrings.* ■ a pattern of irregular concentric bands of color with the brightest at the center.

sun·dae /'sən,dā/ ▶n. a dish of ice cream with added ingredients such as fruit, nuts, syrup, and whipped cream.

Sun·day /'sən,dā; -dē/ ▶n. the day of the week before Monday and following Saturday, observed by Christians as a day of rest and religious worship and (together with Saturday) forming part of the weekend.
▶adv. on Sunday: *the concert will be held Sunday.* ■ (**Sundays**) on Sundays; each Sunday: *the program is repeated Sundays at 9 p.m.*

Sun·day best ▶n. (**one's Sunday best**) a person's best clothes, worn to church or on special occasions.

Sun·day school ▶n. a class held on Sundays to teach children about their religion.

sun·der /'səndər/ ▶v. [tr.] poetic/lit. split apart: *the crunch of bone when it is sundered.*

sun·di·al /'sən,dīl/ ▶n. **1** an instrument showing the time by the shadow of a pointer cast by the sun onto a plate marked with the hours of the day. **2** (also **sundial shell**) a mollusk (family Architectonicidae) with a flattened spiral shell that is typically patterned in shades of brown, living in tropical and subtropical seas.

sun·down /'sən,doun/ ▶n. the time in the evening when the sun disappears or daylight fades.

sun·dress /'sən,dres/ ▶n. a light, loose, sleeveless dress, typically having a wide neckline and thin shoulder straps.

sun·dry /'səndrē/ ▶adj. of various kinds; several: *lemon rind and sundry herbs.*
▶as pl. n. (**sundries**) various items not important enough to be mentioned individually: *a drugstore selling magazines, newspapers, and sundries.*

sun·fish /'sən,fiSH/ ▶n. (pl. same or **-fishes**) **1** a large deep-bodied marine fish (family Molidae) of warm seas, with tall dorsal and anal fins near the rear of the body and a very short tail. Its several species include the very large **ocean sunfish** (*Mola mola*), also known as **mola mola**. **2** a nest-building freshwater fish native to North America and popular in aquariums. The **freshwater sunfish family** (Centrarchidae) also includes sport fish such as various basses.

sun·flow·er /'sən,flou(-ə)r/ ▶n. a tall North American plant (*Helianthus annuus*) of the daisy family, with very large golden-rayed flowers. Sunflowers are cultivated for their edible seeds, which are an important source of oil for cooking and margarine.

Sung /sŏŏNG/ (also **Song**) ▶a dynasty that ruled in China AD 960–1279.

sung /səNG/ ▶ past participle of SING.

sun·glass·es /'sən,glasiz/ ▶pl. n. glasses tinted to protect the eyes from sunlight or glare.

sunk /səNGk/ ▶ past and past participle of SINK¹.

sunk·en /'səNGkən/ ▶adj. **1** having sunk or been submerged in water: *the wreck of a sunken ship.* ■ having sunk below the usual or expected level: *the inspector looked at his sunken head with compassion.* ■ at a lower level than the surrounding area: *a sunken garden.* ■ (of a person's eyes or cheeks) deeply recessed, esp. as a result of illness, hunger, or stress: *her face was white, with sunken cheeks.*

sun·lamp /'sən,lamp/ ▶n. a lamp emitting ultraviolet rays used as a substitute for sunlight, typically to produce an artificial suntan or in therapy.

sun·light /'sən,līt/ ▶n. light from the sun: *a shaft of sunlight.*

sun·lit /'sən,lit/ ▶adj. illuminated by direct light from the sun: *clear sunlit waters.*

Sun·ni /'sŏŏnē/ ▶n. (pl. same or **-nis**) one of the two main branches of

Islam, commonly described as orthodox, and differing from Shia in its understanding of the Sunna, the traditional portion of Muslim law based on Muhammad's words or acts, and in its acceptance of the first three caliphs. Compare with SHIA. ■ a Muslim who adheres to this branch of Islam. —**Sun·nite** /sŏŏnīt/ adj. & n.

sun·ny /'sənē/ ▶adj. (**-ni·er**, **-ni·est**) bright with sunlight: *a sunny day.* ■ (of a place) receiving much sunlight: *find a sunny patch for the dahlia tubers.* ■ (of a person or their temperament) cheery and bright: *he had a sunny disposition.* ■ suggestive of the warmth or brightness of the sun: *the room was done up in nice sunny colors.* —**sun·ni·ly** /'sənəlē/ adv. —**sun·ni·ness** n.

sun·ny side ▶n. the side of something that receives the sun for longest: *a well-known hotel on the sunny side of the island.* ■ the more cheerful or pleasant aspect of a state of affairs: *he was fond of the sunny side of life.*
▶ □ **sunny side up** (of an egg) fried on one side only.

sun·rise /'sən,rīz/ ▶n. the time in the morning when the sun appears or full daylight arrives: *an hour before sunrise.* ■ the colors and light visible in the sky on an occasion of the sun's first appearance in the morning, considered as a view or spectacle: *a spectacular sunrise over the summit of the mountain.*

sun·rise in·dus·try ▶n. a new and growing industry, esp. in electronics or telecommunications.

sun·roof /'sən,rŏŏf/ -,rŏŏf/ ▶n. a panel in the roof of a car that can be opened for extra ventilation.

sun·screen /'sən,skrēn/ ▶n. a cream or lotion rubbed onto the skin to protect it from the sun. ■ an active ingredient of creams and lotions of this kind and other preparations for the skin.

sun·set /'sən,set/ ▶n. the time in the evening when the sun disappears or daylight fades: *sunset was still a couple of hours away.* ■ the colors and light visible in the sky on an occasion of the sun's disappearance in the evening, considered as a view or spectacle: *a blue and gold sunset.* ■ fig. a period of decline, esp. the last years of a person's life: *the sunset of his life.*

sun·set law ▶n. Law a law that automatically terminates a regulatory agency, board, or function of government on a certain date, unless renewed.

sun·shade /'sən,SHād/ ▶n. a parasol, awning, or other device giving protection from the sun.

sun·shine /'sən,SHīn/ ▶n. direct sunlight unbroken by cloud, esp. over a comparatively large area: *we walked in the warm sunshine.* ■ fig. cheerfulness; happiness: *their colorful music can bring a ray of sunshine.* —**sun·shin·y** adj.

sun·spot /'sən,spät/ ▶n. Astron. a spot or patch appearing from time to time on the sun's surface.

sun·stroke /'sən,strōk/ ▶n. heatstroke brought about by excessive exposure to the sun.

sun·tan /'sən,tan/ ▶n. a browning of skin caused by exposure to the sun: *he had acquired quite a suntan.* ■ a light or medium brownish color.
▶v. [tr.] [usu. as adj.] (**suntanned**) expose to the sun in order to achieve such a brown color: *a suntanned face.*

sun·up /'sən,əp/ ▶n. the time in the morning when the sun appears or full daylight arrives: *they worked from sunup to sundown.*

su·per /'sŏŏpər/ ▶adj. **1** inf. very good or pleasant; excellent: *Julie was a super girl* | [as interj.] *You're both coming in? Super!* **2** (of a manufactured product) superfine: *a super quality binder.*
▶adv. inf. especially; particularly: *he's been super understanding.*
▶n. inf. a superintendent.

super. ▶abbr. ■ superintendent. ■ superior.

su·per·a·ble /'sŏŏpərəbəl/ ▶adj. able to be overcome.

su·per·a·bun·dant /,sŏŏpərə'bəndənt/ ▶adj. excessive in quantity; more than sufficient; overabundant. —**su·per·a·bun·dance** n. —**su·per·a·bun·dant·ly** adv.

su·per·an·nu·ate /,sŏŏpər'anyŏŏ,āt/ ▶v. [tr.] (usu. **be superannuated**) retire (someone) with a pension: *his pilot's license was withdrawn and he was superannuated.* ■ [as adj.] (**superannuated**) (of a position or employee) belonging to a superannuation plan: *she is not superannuated and has no paid vacation.* ■ [usu. as adj.] (**superannuated**) cause to become obsolete through age or new technological or intellectual developments: *superannuated computing equipment.* —**su·per·an·nu·a·ble** /-'anyŏŏəbəl/ adj.

su·per·an·nu·a·tion /,sŏŏpər,anyŏŏ'āSHən/ ▶n. [usu. as adj.] regular payment made into a fund by an employee toward a future pension: *a superannuation fund.*

su·perb /soo'pərb; sə-/ ▶*adj.* **1** excellent: *a superb performance.* **2** impressively splendid: *a superb Egyptian statue of Osiris.* ▷mid 16th cent. (sense 2): from Latin *superbus* 'proud, magnificent.' —**su·perb·ly** *adv.* —**su·perb·ness** *n.*

su·per·cal·en·der /'soopər,kaləndər/ ▶*v.* [*tr.*] give a highly glazed finish to (paper) by calendering it more than normally calendered paper: [as *adj.*] (**supercalendered**) *a supercalendered art paper.*

su·per·car·go /'soopər,kärgō/ ▶*n.* (*pl.* **-goes** or **-gos**) an agent on board a merchant ship, responsible for overseeing the cargo and its sale.

su·per·charge /'soopər,cHärj/ ▶*v.* [*tr.*] fit or design (an internal combustion engine) with a supercharger: [as *adj.*] (**supercharged**) *a supercharged 3.8-liter V6.* ■ [usu. as *adj.*] (**supercharged**) supply with extra energy or power: *a supercharged computer.* ■ [as *adj.*] (**supercharged**) having powerful emotional overtones or associations: *appeasement is one of those supercharged words, like terrorism and fascism.*

su·per·charg·er /'soopər,cHärjər/ ▶*n.* a device that increases the pressure of the fuel-air mixture in an internal combustion engine, used in order to achieve greater efficiency.

su·per·cil·i·ous /,soopər'silēəs/ ▶*adj.* behaving or looking as though one thinks one is superior to others: *a supercilious lady's maid.* —**su·per·cil·i·ous·ly** *adv.* —**su·per·cil·i·ous·ness** *n.*

su·per·com·put·er /'soopərkəm,pyootər/ ▶*n.* a particularly powerful mainframe computer. —**su·per·com·put·ing** /-,pyootiNG/ *n.*

su·per·con·duc·tiv·i·ty /,soopər,kän,dək'tivitē/ ▶*n.* Physics the property of zero electrical resistance in some substances at very low absolute temperatures. —**su·per·con·duct** /-kən'dəkt/ *v.* —**su·per·con·duct·ing** /-kən'dəktiNG/ *adj.* —**su·per·con·duc·tive** /-kən'dəktiv/ *adj.*

su·per·con·duc·tor /'soopərkən,dəktər/ ▶*n.* Physics a substance capable of becoming superconducting at sufficiently low temperatures. ■ a substance in the superconducting state.

su·per·cool /,soopər'kool/ ▶*v.* [*tr.*] Chem. cool (a liquid) below its freezing point without solidification or crystallization. ■ [*intr.*] Biol. (of a living organism) survive body temperatures below the freezing point of water.

▶*adj. inf.* extremely attractive, impressive, or calm: *the supercool tracks in this collection.*

su·per·crit·i·cal /,soopər'kritikəl/ ▶*adj.* Physics above a critical threshold, in particular: ■ (in nuclear physics) containing or involving more than the critical mass. ■ (of a flow of fluid) faster than the speed at which waves travel in the fluid. ■ of, relating to, or denoting a fluid at a temperature and pressure greater than its critical temperature and pressure.

su·per·du·per /'soopər 'doopər/ ▶*adj. humorous* very good; marvelous: *this new line of toys is super-duper.* ■ tremendous or colossal in size or degree: *a super-duper ice sculpture.*

su·per·e·go /,soopər'ēgō/ ▶*n.* (*pl.* **-gos**) Psychoanal. the part of a person's mind that acts as a self-critical conscience, reflecting social standards learned from parents and teachers. Compare with EGO and ID.

su·per·fam·i·ly /'soopər,fam(ə)lē/ ▶*n.* (*pl.* **-lies**) Biol. a taxonomic category that ranks above family and below order.

su·per·fi·cial /,soopər'fishəl/ ▶*adj.* existing or occurring at or on the surface: *the building suffered only superficial damage.* ■ situated or occurring on the skin or immediately beneath it: *the superficial muscle groups.* ■ appearing to be true or real only until examined more closely: *the resemblance between the breeds is superficial.* ■ not thorough, deep, or complete; cursory: *he had only the most superficial knowledge of foreign countries.* ■ not having or showing any depth of character or understanding: *perhaps I was a superficial person.* —**su·per·fi·ci·al·i·ty** /-,fishē'alitē/ *n.* (*pl.* **-ties**) —**su·per·fi·cial·ly** *adv.* —**su·per·fi·cial·ness** *n.*

su·per·fine /,soopər'fīn/ ▶*adj.* **1** of especially high quality: *superfine upholstery.* **2** consisting of especially small particles: *superfine sugar.*

su·per·fine sug·ar ▶*n.* finely granulated white sugar that dissolves quickly and is used in cold drinks and baking.

su·per·flu·i·ty /,soopər'flooitē/ ▶*n.* (*pl.* **-ties**) an unnecessarily or excessively large amount or number of something: *a superfluity of unoccupied time.* ■ an unnecessary thing: *they thought the garrison a superfluity.* ■ the state of being superfluous: *servants who had nothing to do but to display their own superfluity.*

su·per·flu·ous /soo'pərflooəs/ ▶*adj.* unnecessary, esp. through being more than enough: *the purchaser should avoid asking for superfluous information.* —**su·per·flu·ous·ly** *adv.* —**su·per·flu·ous·ness** *n.*

su·per·food /'soopər,food/ ▶*n.* (not in technical use) a natural food regarded as especially beneficial because of its nutrient profile or its

health-protecting qualities: *he touts broccoli sprouts and salmon as two of the most perfect superfoods.*

su·per·heat /,soopər'hēt/ Physics ▶*v.* [*tr.*] heat (a liquid) under pressure above its boiling point without vaporization. ■ heat (a vapor) above its temperature of saturation. ■ heat to a very high temperature. —**su·per·heat·er** *n.*

su·per·high·way /'soopər,hīwā; ,soopər'hī,wā/ ▶*n.* an expressway.

su·per·hu·man /,soopər'(h)yoomən/ ▶*adj.* having or showing exceptional ability or powers: *the pilot made one last superhuman effort not to come down right on our heads.* —**su·per·hu·man·ly** *adv.*

su·per·im·pose /,soopərim'pōz/ ▶*v.* [*tr.*] place or lay (one thing) over another, typically so that both are still evident: *the number will appear on the screen, superimposed on a flashing button.* —**su·per·im·pos·a·ble** *adj.* —**su·per·im·po·si·tion** /-,impə'zisHən/ *n.*

su·per·in·tend /,soopərin'tend/ ▶*v.* [*tr.*] be responsible for the management or arrangement of (an activity or organization); oversee: *he superintended a land reclamation program.* —**su·per·in·tend·ence** /-dəns/ *n.* —**su·per·in·tend·en·cy** /-dənsē/ *n.*

su·per·in·tend·ent /,soopərin'tendənt/ ▶*n.* a person who manages or superintends an organization or activity: *the construction superintendent.* ■ a high-ranking official, esp. the head of a large urban police department. ■ the caretaker of a building.

su·pe·ri·or /sə'pi(ə)rēər/ ▶*adj.* **1** higher in rank, status, or quality: *a superior officer.* ■ of high standard or quality: *superior malt whiskeys.* ■ greater in size or power: *deploying superior force.* ■ (**superior to**) above yielding to or being influenced by: *I felt superior to any accusation of anti-Semitism.* ■ having or showing an overly high opinion of oneself; supercilious: *that girl was frightfully superior.* **2** chiefly Anat. further above or out; higher in position. ■ Astron. (of a planet) having an orbit further from the sun than the earth's.

▶*n.* a person or thing superior to another in rank, status, or quality, esp. a colleague in a higher position: *obeying their superiors' orders.* ■ the head of a monastery or other religious institution. —**su·pe·ri·or·ly** *adv.*

su·pe·ri·or·i·ty /sə,pi(ə)rē'ôritē; -'äritē/ ▶*n.* the state of being superior: *an attempt to establish superiority over others.* ■ a supercilious manner or attitude: *he attacked the media's smug superiority.*

su·pe·ri·or·i·ty com·plex ▶*n.* an attitude of superiority that conceals actual feelings of inferiority and failure.

su·per·la·tive /sə'pərlətiv/ ▶*adj.* **1** of the highest quality or degree: *a superlative piece of skill.* **2** Gram. (of an adjective or adverb) expressing the highest or a very high degree of a quality (e.g., *bravest, most fiercely*). Contrasted with and COMPARATIVE.

▶*n.* **1** Gram. a superlative adjective or adverb. ■ (**the superlative**) the highest degree of comparison. **2** (usu. **superlatives**) an exaggerated or hyperbolical expression of praise: *the critics ran out of superlatives to describe him.* **3** something or someone embodying excellence. —**su·per·la·tive·ly** *adv. he was superlatively fit.* —**su·per·la·tive·ness** *n.*

su·per·lu·na·ry /,soopər'loonərē/ ▶*adj.* belonging to a higher world; celestial.

su·per·man /'soopə,man/ ▶*n.* (*pl.* **-men**) (**a superman**) *inf.* a man with exceptional physical or mental ability. ▷early 20th cent.: from *super-* 'exceptional' + *man*, coined by G. B. Shaw in imitation of German *Übermensch* (used by Nietzsche).

su·per·mar·ket /'soopər,märkit/ ▶*n.* a large self-service store selling foods and household goods.

su·per·nat·u·ral /,soopər'nacH(ə)rəl/ ▶*adj.* (of a manifestation or event) attributed to some force beyond scientific understanding or the laws of nature: *a supernatural being.* ■ unnaturally or extraordinarily great: *a woman of supernatural beauty.*

▶*n.* (**the supernatural**) manifestations or events considered to be of supernatural origin, such as ghosts. —**su·per·nat·u·ral·ism** *n.* —**su·per·nat·u·ral·ist** *n.* —**su·per·nat·u·ral·ly** *adv. the monster was supernaturally strong.*

su·per·no·va /'soopər,nōvə/ ▶*n.* (*pl.* **-no·vae** /-,nōvē/ or **-no·vas**) Astron. a star that suddenly increases greatly in brightness because of a catastrophic explosion that ejects most of its mass.

su·per·nu·mer·a·ry /,soopər'n(y)oomə,rerē/ ▶*adj.* present in excess of the normal or requisite number, in particular: ■ (of a person) not belonging to a regular staff but engaged for extra work. ■ not wanted or needed; redundant. ■ (of an actor) appearing on stage but not speaking.

▶*n.* (*pl.* **-ar·ies**) a supernumerary person or thing.

su·per·pose /,soopər'pōz/ ▶*v.* [*tr.*] place (something) on or above something else, esp. so that they coincide: [as *adj.*] (**superposed**) *a border of superposed triangles.* —**su·per·pos·a·ble** *adj.* —**su·per·po·si·tion** /-pə'zisHən/ *n.*

su·per·pow·er /ˈsoopər,pouər/ ▶n. a very powerful and influential nation (used esp. with reference to the U.S. and the former USSR when these were perceived as the two most powerful nations in the world). ■ a dominant or preeminent individual or organization, esp. in a particular field.

su·per·sat·u·rate /ˌsoopər'sacHə,rāt/ ▶v. [tr.] Chem. increase the concentration of (a solution) beyond saturation point. —**su·per·sat·u·ra·tion** /-,sacHə'rāsHən/ n.

su·per·scribe /ˌsoopər'skrīb/ ▶v. [tr.] write or print (an inscription) at the top of or on the outside of a document: they had superscribed "Top Secret" across the cover page. ■ write or print an inscription at the top of or on the outside of a document): he invariably will want to superscribe the memo with one of his banal mottoes. ■ write or print (a letter, word, symbol, or line of writing or printing) above an existing letter, word, or line. —**su·per·scrip·tion** /-ˈskripsHən/ n.

su·per·script /ˈsoopər,skript/ ▶adj. (of a letter, figure, or symbol) written or printed above the line.
▶n. a superscript letter, figure, or symbol.

su·per·sede /ˌsoopər'sēd/ ▶v. [tr.] take the place of (a person or thing previously in authority or use); supplant: the older models have now been superseded. —**su·per·ses·sion** /-ˈsesHən/ n.

su·per·size /ˈsoopər,sīz/ ▶v. [tr.] produce or serve something in a larger size: click here to supersize the picture.
▶adj. larger than normal: this supersize clock has black 2-inch numbers on white face in a simple lightweight black frame.

su·per·son·ic /ˌsoopər'sänik/ ▶adj. involving or denoting a speed greater than that of sound. —**su·per·son·i·cal·ly** /-ik(ə)lē/ adv.

su·per·star /ˈsoopər,stär/ ▶n. a high-profile and extremely successful performer or athlete. —**su·per·star·dom** /-dəm/ n.

su·per·sti·tion /ˌsoopər'stisHən/ ▶n. excessively credulous belief in and reverence for supernatural beings: he dismissed the ghost stories as mere superstition. ■ a widely held but unjustified belief in supernatural causation leading to certain consequences of an action or event, or a practice based on such a belief: she touched her locket for luck, a superstition she had had since childhood. —**su·per·sti·tious** /-ˈstisHəs/ adj. —**su·per·sti·tious·ly** /-ˈstisHəslē/ adv. —**su·per·sti·tious·ness** /-ˈstisHəsnəs/ n.

su·per·store /ˈsoopər,stôr/ ▶n. a retail store, as a grocery store or bookstore, with more than the average amount of space and variety of stock.

su·per·struc·ture /ˈsoopər,strəkcHər/ ▶n. a structure built on top of something else. ■ the parts of a ship, other than masts and rigging, built above its hull and main deck. ■ the part of a building above its foundations. ■ a concept or idea based on others. —**su·per·struc·tur·al** /ˌsoopər'strəkcHərəl/ adj.

su·per·tank·er /ˈsoopər,taNGkər/ ▶n. a very large oil tanker, specifically one whose dead-weight capacity exceeds 75,000 tons.

su·per·ton·ic /ˈsoopər,tänik/ ▶n. Mus. the second note of the diatonic scale of any key; the note above the tonic.

su·per·vene /ˌsoopər'vēn/ ▶v. [intr.] occur later than a specified or implied event or action, typically in such a way as to change the situation: [as adj.] (supervening) any plan that is made is liable to be disrupted by supervening events. —**su·per·ven·ient** /-ˈvēnyənt/ adj. —**su·per·ven·tion** /-ˈvencHən/ n.

su·per·vise /ˈsoopər,vīz/ ▶v. [tr.] observe and direct the execution of (a task, project, or activity): the sergeant left to supervise the loading of the trucks. ■ observe and direct the work of (someone): nurses were supervised by a consulting psychiatrist. ■ keep watch over (someone) in the interest of their or others' security: prisoners were supervised by two officers. —**su·per·vi·sion** /ˌsoopər'vizHən/ n. —**su·per·vi·sor** /-,vīzər/ n. —**su·per·vi·so·ry** /ˌsoopər'vīzərē/ adj.

su·per·wom·an /ˈsoopər,woomən/ ▶n. (pl. -wom·en) inf. a woman with exceptional strength or ability, esp. one who successfully manages a home, brings up children, and has a full-time job.

su·pi·nate /ˈsoopə,nāt/ ▶v. [tr.] technical 1 put or hold (a hand, foot, or limb) with the palm or sole turned upward: [as adj.] (supinated) a supinated foot. Compare with PRONATE. 2 walk or run with most of the weight on the inside of the feet. —**su·pi·na·tion** /ˌsoopə'nāsHən/ n.

su·pi·na·tor /ˈsoopə,nātər/ ▶n. Anat. 1 a muscle whose contraction produces or assists in the supination of a limb or part of a limb. ■ any of several muscles in the forearm. 2 one who supinates when walking or running.

su·pine /ˈsoo,pīn/ ▶adj. 1 (of a person) lying face upward. ■ technical having the front or ventral part upward. ■ (of the hand) with the palm upward. 2 failing to act or protest as a result of moral weakness or

indolence: supine in the face of racial injustice. —**su·pine·ly** adv. —**su·pine·ness** n.

sup·per /ˈsəpər/ ▶n. an evening meal, typically a light or informal one: we had a delicious cold supper. ■ a late-night dinner. ■ an evening social event at which food is served. —**sup·per·less** adj.

sup·plant /sə'plant/ ▶v. [tr.] supersede and replace: the socialist society that Marx believed would eventually supplant capitalism. —**sup·plant·er** n.

sup·ple /ˈsəpəl/ ▶adj. (-pler, -plest) bending and moving easily and gracefully; flexible: her supple fingers. ■ not stiff or hard; easily manipulated: this body oil leaves your skin feeling deliciously supple.
▶v. [tr.] make more flexible. —**sup·ple·ly** /ˈsəp(ə)lē/ (also **sup·ply**) adv. —**sup·ple·ness** n.

sup·ple·ment ▶n. /ˈsəpləmənt/ 1 something that completes or enhances something else when added to it: the handout is a **supplement** to the official manual. ■ a substance taken to remedy the deficiencies in a person's diet: vitamin supplements. ■ a part added to a book to provide further or corrected information but separate from the main body of the text. ■ a separate section, esp. a color magazine, added to a newspaper or periodical. 2 Geom. the amount by which an angle is less than 180°.
▶v. /ˈsəplə,ment; -mənt/ [tr.] add an extra element or amount to: she took the job to supplement her husband's income. —**sup·ple·men·tal** /ˌsəplə'mentl/ adj. —**sup·ple·men·tal·ly** /ˌsəplə'mentl-ē/ adv. —**sup·ple·men·ta·tion** /ˌsəplə,men'tāsHən/ n.

sup·ple·men·ta·ry /ˌsəplə'mentərē/ ▶adj. completing or enhancing something: the center's work was to be seen as **supplementary to** orthodox treatment and not a substitute for it. —**sup·ple·men·tar·i·ly** /-,men'te(ə)rəlē/ adv.

sup·pli·ant /ˈsəplēənt/ ▶n. a person making a humble plea to someone in power or authority.
▶adj. making or expressing a plea, esp. to someone in power or authority: their faces were suppliant. —**sup·pli·ant·ly** adv.

sup·pli·cate /ˈsəpli,kāt/ ▶v. [intr.] ask or beg for something earnestly or humbly: the plutocracy supplicated to be made peers. —**sup·pli·cant** /-kənt/ adj. & n. —**sup·pli·ca·tion** /ˌsəpli'kāsHən/ n. —**sup·pli·ca·to·ry** /-kə,tôrē/ adj.

sup·ply[1] /sə'plī/ ▶v. (-plies, -plied) [tr.] make (something needed or wanted) available to someone; provide: the farm supplies apples to cider makers. ■ provide (someone) with something needed or wanted: they struggled to **supply** the besieged island **with** aircraft. ■ be a source of (something needed): eat foods that supply a significant amount of dietary fiber. ■ be adequate to satisfy (a requirement or demand): the two reservoirs supply about 1% of the city's needs.
▶n. (pl. -plies) a stock of a resource from which a person or place can be provided with the necessary amount of that resource: there were fears that the drought would limit the exhibition's water supply. ■ the action of providing what is needed or wanted: the deal involved the supply of forty fighter aircraft. ■ Econ. the amount of a good or service offered for sale. ■ (supplies) the provisions and equipment necessary for an army or for people engaged in a particular project or expedition. ■ [as adj.] providing necessary goods and equipment: a supply ship. —**sup·pli·er** n.
▶ □ **supply and demand** the amount of a good or service available and the desire of buyers for it, considered as factors regulating its price: by the law of supply and demand the cost of health care will plummet.

sup·ply[2] /ˈsəp(ə)lē/ ▶adv. variant spelling of SUPPLELY (see SUPPLE).

sup·ply-side ▶adj. Econ. denoting or relating to a policy designed to increase output and employment by changing the conditions under which goods and services are supplied, esp. by measures that reduce government involvement in the economy and allow the free market to operate. —**sup·ply-sid·er** n.

sup·port /sə'pôrt/ ▶v. [tr.] 1 bear all or part of the weight of; hold up: the dome was supported by a hundred white columns. ■ produce enough food and water for; be capable of sustaining: the land had lost its capacity to support life. ■ be capable of fulfilling (a role) adequately: tutors gain practical experience that helps them support their tutoring role. ■ endure; tolerate. 2 give assistance to, esp. financially; enable to function or act: the government gives $2.5 billion a year to support the activities of the voluntary sector. ■ provide with a home and the necessities of life. ■ give comfort and emotional help to: I like to visit her to support her. ■ approve of and encourage: the proposal was supported by many delegates. ■ suggest the truth of; corroborate: the studies support our findings. ■ be actively interested in and concerned for the success of (a particular sports team).

Pronunciation Key ə *ago,* up; ər *over,* fur; a *hat;* ā *ate;* ä *car;* CH *chin;* e *let;* ē *see;* e(ə)r *air;* i *fit;* ī *by;* i(ə)r *ear;* NG *sing;* ō *go;* ô *law, for;* oi *toy;* oo *good;* oo *goo;* ou *out;* SH *she;* TH *thin;* TH *then;* (h)w *why;* ZH *vision*

■ [as *adj.*] (**supporting**) (of an actor or a role) important in a play or film but subordinate to the leading parts. ■ (of a pop or rock group or performer) function as a secondary act to (another) at a concert. **3** *Comput.* (of a computer or operating system) allow the use or operation of (a program, language, or device): *the new versions do not support the graphical user interface standard.*

▶*n.* **1** a thing that bears the weight of something or keeps it upright: *the best support for a camera is a tripod.* ■ the action or state of bearing the weight of something or someone or of being so supported: *she clutched the sideboard for support.* **2** material assistance: *he urged that military support be sent to protect humanitarian convoys.* ■ comfort and emotional help offered to someone in distress: *she's been through a bad time and needs our support.* ■ approval and encouragement. ■ a secondary act at a pop or rock concert. ■ technical help given to the user of a computer or other product. —**sup·port·a·bil·i·ty** /səˌpôrtəˈbilitē/ *n.* —**sup·port·a·ble** *adj.*

sup·port·er /səˈpôrtər/ ▶*n.* **1** a person who approves of and encourages someone or something (typically a public figure, a movement or party, or a policy): *Reagan supporters.* ■ a person who is actively interested in and wishes success for a particular sports team. **2** (in full **athletic supporter**) another term for JOCKSTRAP.

sup·port·ive /səˈpôrtiv/ ▶*adj.* providing encouragement or emotional help: *the staff are extremely supportive of each other.* —**sup·port·ive·ly** *adv.* —**sup·port·ive·ness** *n.*

sup·pose /səˈpōz/ ▶*v.* **1** assume that something is the case on the basis of evidence or probability but without proof or certain knowledge: *I suppose I got there about half past eleven.* ■ used to make a reluctant or hesitant admission: *I'm quite a good actress, I suppose.* ■ used to introduce a hypothesis and trace or ask about what follows from it: *suppose he had been murdered—what then?* ■ [in *imper.*] used to introduce a suggestion: *suppose we leave this to the police.* ■ (of a theory or argument) assume or require that something is the case as a precondition: *the procedure supposes that a will has already been proved* | [*tr.*] *the theory supposes a predisposition to interpret utterances.* ■ [*tr.*] believe to exist or to possess a specified characteristic: *he **supposed** the girl **to be** about twelve* [as *adj.*] (**supposed**) often /səˈpōzid/ *people admire their supposed industriousness.* **2** (**be supposed to do something**) be required to do something because of the position one is in or an agreement one has made: *I'm supposed to be meeting someone at the airport.* ■ be forbidden to do something: *I shouldn't have been in the kitchen—I'm not supposed to go in there.* —**sup·pos·a·ble** *adj.*

sup·pos·ed·ly /səˈpōzidlē/ ▶*adv.* according to what is generally assumed or believed (often used to indicate that the speaker doubts the truth of the statement): *the ads are aimed at women, supposedly because they do the shopping.*

sup·po·si·tion /ˌsəpəˈziSHən/ ▶*n.* an uncertain belief: *they were working on the supposition that his death was murder.* —**sup·po·si·tion·al** /-SHənl/ *adj.*

sup·pos·i·to·ry /səˈpäzəˌtôrē/ ▶*n.* (*pl.* **-ries**) a solid medical preparation in a roughly conical or cylindrical shape, designed to be inserted into the rectum or vagina to dissolve and be absorbed.

sup·press /səˈpres/ ▶*v.* [*tr.*] forcibly put an end to: *the uprising was savagely suppressed.* ■ prevent the development, action, or expression of (a feeling, impulse, idea, etc.); restrain: *she could not suppress a rising panic.* ■ prevent the dissemination of (information): *the report had been suppressed.* ■ prevent or inhibit (a process or reaction): *use of the drug suppressed the immune response.* ■ *Psychoanalysis* consciously inhibit (an unpleasant idea or memory) to avoid considering it. —**sup·press·i·ble** *adj.* —**sup·pres·sion** *n.* —**sup·pres·sive** /-siv/ *adj.* —**sup·pres·sor** /-sər/ *n.*

sup·pres·sant /səˈpresənt/ ▶*n.* a drug or other substance that acts to suppress or restrain something: *an appetite suppressant.*

sup·pu·rate /ˈsəpyəˌrāt/ ▶*v.* [*intr.*] undergo the formation of pus; fester. —**sup·pu·ra·tion** /ˌsəpyəˈrāSHən/ *n.* —**sup·pu·ra·tive** /-ˌrātiv/ *adj.*

su·pra /ˈso͞oprə/ ▶*adv.* *formal* used in academic or legal texts to refer to someone or something mentioned above or earlier: *the recent work by McAuslan and others (supra).*

su·pra·na·tion·al /ˌso͞oprəˈnaSHənl/ ▶*adj.* having power or influence that transcends national boundaries or governments: *supranational law.* —**su·pra·na·tion·al·ism** /-ˌizəm/ *n.* —**su·pra·na·tion·al·i·ty** /-ˌnaSHəˈnalitē/ *n.*

su·prem·a·cist /səˈpreməsist; so͞o-/ ▶*n.* an advocate of the supremacy of a particular group, esp. one determined by race or sex: *a white supremacist.*

▶*adj.* relating to or advocating such supremacy. —**su·prem·a·cism** /-ˌsizəm/ *n.*

su·prem·a·cy /səˈpreməsē; so͞o-/ ▶*n.* the state or condition of being superior to all others in authority, power, or status: *the supremacy of the king.*

su·preme /səˈprēm; so͞o-/ ▶*adj.* (of authority or an office, or someone holding it) superior to all others: *a unified force with a supreme commander.* ■ strongest, most important, or most powerful: *on the racetrack he reigned supreme.* ■ very great or intense; extreme: *he was nerving himself for a supreme effort.* ■ (of a penalty or sacrifice) involving death: *our comrades who made the supreme sacrifice.* ■ used to indicate that someone or something is very good at or well known for a specified activity: *here was the gift supreme.* —**su·preme·ly** *adv.*

▶ □ **the Supreme Being** a name for God.

Su·preme Court ▶*n.* the highest judicial court in most U.S. states. ■ (in full **U.S. Supreme Court**) the highest federal court in the U.S.

su·pre·mo /so͞oˈprēmō/ ▶*n.* (*pl.* **-mos**) *chiefly Brit. informal* a person in charge. ■ a person having supreme power or authority.

Supt. ▶*abbr.* Superintendent.

su·ra /ˈso͞orə/ (also **su·rah**) ▶*n.* a chapter or section of the Koran. ▷from Arabic *sūra.*

sur·cease /sərˈsēs/ ▶*n.* cessation: *he teased us without surcease.* ■ relief or consolation: *drugs are taken to provide surcease from intolerable psychic pain.* ▶*v.* [*intr.*] *archaic* cease.

sur·charge /ˈsərˌCHärj/ ▶*n.* an additional charge or payment: *we guarantee that no surcharges will be added to the cost of your trip.* ■ a charge made by assessors as a penalty for false returns of taxable property. ■ the showing of an omission in an account for which credit should have been given.

▶*v.* [*tr.*] exact an additional charge or payment from: *retailers will be able to surcharge credit-card users.*

sur·cin·gle /ˈsərˌsiNGgəl/ ▶*n.* a wide strap that runs over the back and under the belly of a horse, used to keep a blanket or other equipment in place.

surd /sərd/ ▶*adj.* **1** *Math.* (of a number) irrational. **2** *Phonet.* (of a speech sound) uttered with the breath and not the voice (e.g., *f, k, p, s, t*).

▶*n.* **1** *Math.* a surd number, esp. the irrational root of an integer. **2** *Phonet.* a surd consonant.

sure /SHo͝or/ ▶*adj.* confident in what one thinks or knows; having no doubt that one is right: *I'm sure I've seen that dress before.* ■ (**sure of**) having a certain prospect or confident anticipation of: *Ripken can be sure of a place in the Hall of Fame.* ■ certain to do something: *it's sure to rain before morning.* ■ true beyond any doubt: *what is sure is that learning is a complex business.* ■ able to be relied on or trusted: *her neck was red—a sure sign of agitation.* ■ confident; assured: *the drawings impress by their sure sense of rhythm.*

▶*adv. inf.* certainly (used for emphasis): *Texas sure was a great place to grow up.* ■ [as *interj.*] used to show assent: *"Are you serious?" "Sure."* ▷Middle English: from Old French *sur*, from Latin *securus* 'free from care.' —**sure·ness** *n.*

▶ □ **to be sure** used to concede the truth of something that conflicts with another point that one wishes to make: *the ski runs are very limited, to be sure, but excellent for beginners.* ■ used for emphasis: *what an extraordinary woman she was, to be sure.*

sure-fire ▶*adj. inf.* certain to succeed: *bad behavior is a sure-fire way of getting attention.*

sure-foot·ed (also **sure-foot·ed**) ▶*adj.* unlikely to stumble or slip: *tough, sure-footed ponies.* ■ confident and competent: *the challenges of the 1990s demand a responsible and sure-footed government.* —**sure-foot·ed·ly** *adv.* —**sure-foot·ed·ness** *n.*

sure·ly /ˈSHo͝orlē/ ▶*adv.* **1** used to emphasize the speaker's firm belief that what they are saying is true and often their surprise that there is any doubt of this: *if there is no will, then surely the house goes automatically to you.* ■ without doubt; certainly: *if he did not heed the warning, he would surely die.* ■ [as *interj.*] *inf.* of course; yes: *"You'll wait for me?" "Surely."* **2** with assurance or confidence: *no one knows how to move the economy quickly and surely in that direction.*

sure·ty /ˈSHo͝oritē/ ▶*n.* (*pl.* **-ties**) a person who takes responsibility for another's performance of an undertaking, for example their appearing in court or the payment of a debt. ■ money given to support an undertaking that someone will perform a duty, pay their debts, etc.; a guarantee: *the judge granted bail with a surety of $500.* ■ the state of being sure or certain of something: *I was enmeshed in the surety of my impending fatherhood.* —**sur·e·ty·ship** /-ˌSHip/ *n.*

surf /sərf/ ▶*n.* the mass or line of foam formed by waves breaking on a seashore or reef: *the roar of the surf.* ■ a spell of surfing: *he went for an early surf.*

▶*v.* [*intr.*] ride on the crest of a wave, typically toward the shore while riding on a surfboard: *learning to surf.* ▪ [*tr.*] ride (a wave) toward the shore in such a way: *he has built a career out of surfing big waves.* ▪ short for **CHANNEL-SURF.** ▪ [*tr.*] move from site to site on (the Internet). —**surf·er** *n.* —**surf·y** *adj.*

sur·face /'sərfis/ ▸*n.* **1** the outside part or uppermost layer of something (often used when describing its texture, form, or extent): *the earth's surface | poor road surfaces.* ▪ the level top of something: *roll out the dough on a floured surface.* ▪ (also **surface area**) the area of such an outer part or uppermost layer: *the surface area of a cube.* ▪ the upper limit of a body of liquid: *fish floating on the surface of the water.* ▪ what is apparent on a casual view or consideration of someone or something, esp. as distinct from feelings or qualities that are not immediately obvious: *Tom was a womanizer, but on the surface he remained respectable.* **2** *Geom.* a set of points that has length and breadth but no thickness.
▸*adj.* of, relating to, or occurring on the upper or outer part of something: *surface workers at the copper mines.* ▪ denoting ships that travel on the surface of the water as distinct from submarines: *the surface fleet.* ▪ carried by or denoting transportation by sea or overland as contrasted with by air: *surface mail.*
▸*v.* **1** [*intr.*] rise or come up to the surface of the water or the ground: *he surfaced from his dive.* ▪ come to people's attention; become apparent: *the quarrel first surfaced two years ago.* ▪ *inf.* (of a person) appear after having been asleep: *it was almost noon before Anthony surfaced.* **2** [*tr.*] (usu. **be surfaced**) provide (something, esp. a road) with a particular upper or outer layer: *a small path surfaced with terra-cotta tiles.* —**sur·faced** *adj.* [often in comb.] *a smooth-surfaced cylinder.* —**sur·fac·er** *n.*

sur·face ten·sion ▸*n.* the tension of the surface film of a liquid caused by the attraction of the particles in the surface layer by the bulk of the liquid, which tends to minimize surface area.

sur·fac·tant /sər'faktənt/ ▸*n.* a substance that tends to reduce the surface tension of a liquid in which it is dissolved.

surf·board /'sərf,bôrd/ ▸*n.* a long, narrow streamlined board used in surfing.

surf·cast·ing /'sərf,kastiNG/ (also **surf cast·ing** or **surf-cast·ing**) ▸*n.* fishing by casting a line into the sea from the shore or near the shore. —**surf·cast·er** /-,kastər/ *n.*

sur·feit /'sərfit/ ▸*n.* an excessive amount of something: *a surfeit of food and drink.*
▸*v.* (**-feit·ed, -feit·ing**) [*tr.*] (usu. **be surfeited with**) cause (someone) to desire no more of something as a result of having consumed or done it to excess: *I am surfeited with shopping.*

surg. ▸*abbr.* ▪ surgeon. ▪ surgery. ▪ surgical.

surge /sərj/ ▸*n.* a sudden powerful forward or upward movement, esp. by a crowd or by a natural force such as the waves or tide: *flooding caused by tidal surges.* ▪ a sudden large increase, typically a brief one that happens during an otherwise stable or quiescent period: *the firm predicted a 20% surge in sales.* ▪ a powerful rush of an emotion or feeling: *Sophie felt a surge of anger.* ▪ a sudden marked increase in voltage or current in an electric circuit.
▸*v.* [*intr.*] (of a crowd or a natural force) move suddenly and powerfully forward or upward: *the journalists surged forward.* ▪ increase suddenly and powerfully, typically during an otherwise stable or quiescent period: *shares surged to a record high.* ▪ (of an emotion or feeling) affect someone powerfully and suddenly: *indignation surged up within her.* ▪ (of an electric voltage or current) increase suddenly.

sur·geon /'sərjən/ ▸*n.* a medical practitioner qualified to practice surgery.

sur·geon gen·er·al ▸*n.* (*pl.* **sur·geons gen·er·al**) the head of a public health service or of an armed forces medical service.

sur·ger·y /'sərjərē/ ▸*n.* (*pl.* **-ger·ies**) the branch of medicine concerned with treatment of injuries or disorders of the body by incision or manipulation, esp. with instruments: *cardiac surgery.* ▪ such treatment, as performed by a surgeon: *he had surgery on his ankle.*

sur·gi·cal /'sərjikəl/ ▸*adj.* of, relating to, or used in surgery: *a surgical dressing.* ▪ (of a special garment or appliance) worn to correct or relieve an injury, illness, or deformity: *surgical stockings.* ▪ *fig.* denoting something done with great precision, esp. a swift and highly accurate military attack from the air: *surgical bombing.* —**sur·gi·cal·ly** /-ik(ə)lē/ *adv.*

sur·ly /'sərlē/ ▸*adj.* (**-li·er, -li·est**) bad-tempered and unfriendly: *he left with a surly expression.* —**sur·li·ly** /-ləlē/ *adv.* —**sur·li·ness** *n.*

sur·mise ▸*v.* /sər'mīz/ [*intr.*] suppose that something is true without having evidence to confirm it: *he surmised that something must be wrong.*
▸*n.* /sər'mīz; 'sər,mīz/ a supposition that something may be true, even though there is no evidence to confirm it: *Charles was glad to have his surmise confirmed.* ▷late Middle English (in the senses 'formal allegation' and 'allege formally'): from Anglo-Norman French and Old

French *surmise,* feminine past participle of *surmettre* 'accuse,' from late Latin *supermittere* 'put in afterward,' from *super-* 'over' + *mittere* 'send.'

sur·mount /sər'mount/ ▸*v.* [*tr.*] **1** overcome (a difficulty or obstacle): *all manner of cultural differences were surmounted.* **2** (usu. **be surmounted**) stand or be placed on top of: *the tomb was surmounted by a sculptured angel.* —**sur·mount·a·ble** *adj.*

sur·name /'sər,nām/ ▸*n.* a hereditary name common to all members of a family, as distinct from a given name.

sur·pass /sər'pas/ ▸*v.* [*tr.*] exceed; be greater than: *prewar levels of production were surpassed in 1929.* ▪ be better than: *he continued to surpass me at all games.* ▪ (**surpass oneself**) do or be better than ever before: *the organist was surpassing himself.* —**sur·pass·a·ble** *adj.* —**sur·pass·ing·ly** *adv.*

sur·plice /'sərplis/ ▸*n.* a loose white linen vestment varying from hip-length to calf-length, worn over a cassock by clergy, acolytes, and choristers at Christian church services. —**sur·pliced** *adj.*

sur·plus /'sərpləs/ ▸*n.* an amount of something left over when requirements have been met; an excess of production or supply over demand: *exports of food surpluses.* ▪ an excess of income or assets over expenditure or liabilities in a given period, typically a fiscal year: *a trade surplus of $1.4 billion.* ▪ the excess value of a company's assets over the face value of its stock.
▸*adj.* more than what is needed or used; excess: *make the most of your surplus cash.* ▪ denoting a store selling excess or out-of-date military equipment or clothing: *she had picked up her boots in an army surplus store.*

sur·prise /sə(r)'prīz/ ▸*n.* an unexpected or astonishing event, fact, or thing: *the announcement was a complete surprise.* ▪ a feeling of mild astonishment or shock caused by something unexpected: *much to her surprise, she'd missed him.* ▪ [as *adj.*] denoting something made, done, or happening unexpectedly: *a surprise attack.*
▸*v.* [*tr.*] (often **be surprised**) (of something unexpected) cause (someone) to feel mild astonishment or shock: *I was surprised at his statement.* | [as *adj.*] *Joe was surprised that he enjoyed the journey* | [as *adj.*] (**surprising**) *a surprising sequence of events.* ▪ capture, attack, or discover suddenly and unexpectedly; catch unawares: *he surprised a gang stealing scrap metal.* ▷late Middle English (in the sense 'unexpected seizure of a place, or attack on troops'): from Old French, feminine past participle of *surprendre,* from medieval Latin *superprehendere* 'seize.' —**sur·pris·ed·ly** /-z(i)dlē/ *adv.* —**sur·pris·ing·ly** *adv.* *the profit margin in advertising is surprisingly low* | *not surprisingly, his enthusiasm knew no bounds.* —**sur·pris·ing·ness** *n.*

sur·re·al /sə'rēəl/ ▸*adj.* having the qualities of surrealism; bizarre: *a surreal mix of fact and fantasy.* —**sur·re·al·i·ty** /,sərē'alitē/ *n.* —**sur·re·al·ly** *adv.*

sur·re·al·ism /sə'rēə,lizəm/ ▸*n.* a 20th-century avant-garde movement in art and literature that sought to release the creative potential of the unconscious mind, for example by the irrational juxtaposition of images. —**sur·re·al·ist** *n.* & *adj.* —**sur·re·al·is·tic** /sə,rēə'listik/ *adj.* —**sur·re·al·is·ti·cal·ly** /sə,rēə'listik(ə)lē/ *adv.*

sur·ren·der /sə'rendər/ ▸*v.* [*intr.*] cease resistance to an enemy or opponent and submit to their authority: *over 140 rebels surrendered to the authorities.* ▪ [*tr.*] give up or hand over (a person, right, or possession), typically on compulsion or demand: *in 1815 Denmark surrendered Norway to Sweden.* ▪ [*tr.*] (in a sports contest) lose (a point, game, or advantage): *she surrendered only twenty games in her five qualifying matches.* ▪ (**surrender to**) abandon oneself entirely to (a powerful emotion or influence); give in to: *he was surprised that Miriam should surrender to this sort of jealousy.* ▪ [*tr.*] (of an insured person) cancel (a life insurance policy) and receive back a proportion of the premiums paid.
▸*n.* the action of surrendering. ▪ the action of surrendering a life insurance policy.

sur·rep·ti·tious /,sərəp'tiSHəs/ ▸*adj.* kept secret, esp. because it would not be approved of: *they carried on a surreptitious affair.* —**sur·rep·ti·tious·ly** *adv.* —**sur·rep·ti·tious·ness** *n.*

sur·rey /'sərē/ ▸*n.* (*pl.* **-reys**) *hist.* a light four-wheeled carriage with two seats facing forward.

sur·ro·gate /'sərəgit; -,gāt/ ▸*n.* a substitute, esp. a person deputizing for another in a specific role or office: *she was regarded as the surrogate for the governor during his final illness.* ▪ a judge in charge of probate, inheritance, and guardianship. —**sur·ro·ga·cy** /-gəsē/ *n.*

sur·ro·gate moth·er ▸*n.* a woman who bears a child on behalf of another woman, either from her own egg fertilized by the other woman's partner, or from the implantation in her uterus of a fertilized egg from the other woman.

Pronunciation Key ə *ago,* up; ər *over,* fur; a *hat;* ā *ate;* ä *car;* CH *chin;* e *let;* ē *see;* e(ə)r *air;* i *fit;* ī *by;* i(ə)r *ear;* NG *sing;* ō *go;* ô *law, for;* oi *toy;* o͞o *good;* o͞o *goo;* ou *out;* SH *she;* TH *thin;* T͟H *then;* (h)w *why;* ZH *vision*

sur·round /sə'round/ ▸*v.* [*tr.*] (usu. **be surrounded**) be all around (someone or something): *the hotel is surrounded by its own gardens.* ■ (of troops, police, etc.) encircle (someone or something) so as to cut off communication or escape: *troops surrounded the parliament building.* ■ be associated with: *the killings were surrounded by controversy.*
▸*n.* a thing that forms a border or edging around an object: *an oak fireplace surround.* ■ (usu. **surrounds**) the area encircling something; surroundings: *the beautiful surrounds of Moosehead Lake.*

sur·round·ings /sə'roundiNGz/ ▸*pl. n.* the things and conditions around a person or thing: *I took up the time admiring my surroundings.*

sur·tax /'sər,taks/ ▸*n.* an additional tax on something already taxed, such as a higher rate of tax on incomes above a certain level.

sur·veil·lance /sər'vāləns/ ▸*n.* close observation, esp. of a suspected spy or criminal: *he found himself put **under surveillance** by military intelligence.*

sur·vey ▸*v.* /sər'vā/ [*tr.*] **1** (of a person or their eyes) look carefully and thoroughly at (someone or something), esp. so as to appraise them: *I surveyed the options.* ■ investigate the opinions or experience of (a group of people) by asking them questions: *95% of patients surveyed were satisfied with the health service.* ■ investigate (behavior or opinions) by questioning a group of people: *the investigator surveyed the attitudes and beliefs held by residents.* **2** examine and record the area and features of (an area of land) so as to construct a map, plan, or description: *he surveyed the coasts of New Zealand.*
▸*n.* /'sər,vā/ **1** a general view, examination, or description of someone or something: *the author provides a survey of the relevant literature.* ■ an investigation of the opinions or experience of a group of people, based on a series of questions. **2** an act of surveying an area of land: *the flight involved a detailed aerial survey of military bases.* ■ a map, plan, or detailed description obtained in such a way. ■ a department carrying out the surveying of land: *the U.S. Geological Survey.*

sur·vey·or /sər'vāər/ ▸*n.* a person who surveys, esp. one whose profession is the surveying of land. ■ a person who investigates or examines something, esp. boats for seaworthiness or cargo for damage: *a marine surveyor.* —**sur·vey·or·ship** /-,SHip/ *n.*

sur·viv·al /sər'vīvəl/ ▸*n.* the state or fact of continuing to live or exist, typically in spite of an accident, ordeal, or difficult circumstances: *the animal's chances of survival were pretty low.* ■ an object or practice that has continued to exist from an earlier time: *his shorts were a survival from his army days.*
▸ □ **survival of the fittest** *Biol.* the continued existence of organisms that are best adapted to their environment, with the extinction of others, as a concept in the Darwinian theory of evolution. Compare with NATURAL SELECTION.

sur·viv·al·ism /sər'vīvə,lizəm/ ▸*n.* **1** the policy of trying to ensure one's own survival or that of one's social or national group. **2** the practicing of outdoor survival skills as a sport or hobby. —**sur·viv·al·ist** *n. & adj.*

sur·viv·al kit ▸*n.* a pack of emergency equipment, including food, medical supplies, and tools, esp. as carried by members of the armed forces. ■ a collection of items to help someone in a particular situation: *a substitute teacher survival kit.*

sur·vive /sər'vīv/ ▸*v.* [*intr.*] continue to live or exist, esp. in spite of danger or hardship: *against all odds the child survived.* ■ [*tr.*] continue to live or exist in spite of (an accident or ordeal): *he has survived several assassination attempts.* ■ [*tr.*] remain alive after the death of (a particular person): *he was survived by his wife and six children.* ■ [*intr.*] manage to keep going in difficult circumstances: *she had to work day and night and survive on two hours sleep.*

sur·vi·vor /sər'vīvər/ ▸*n.* a person who survives, esp. a person remaining alive after an event in which others have died: *the sole survivor of the massacre.* ■ the remainder of a group of people or things: *a survivor from last year's team.* ■ a person who copes well with difficulties in their life: *she is a born survivor.* ■ *Law* a joint tenant who has the right to the whole estate on the other's death.

sus·cep·ti·bil·i·ty /sə,septə'bilitē/ ▸*n.* (*pl.* **-ties**) **1** the state or fact of being likely or liable to be influenced or harmed by a particular thing: *lack of exercise increases susceptibility to disease.* ■ (**susceptibilities**) a person's feelings, typically considered as being easily hurt: *I was so careful not to offend their susceptibilities.* **2** *Physics* the ratio of magnetization to a magnetizing force.

sus·cep·ti·ble /sə'septəbəl/ ▸*adj.* **1** likely or liable to be influenced or harmed by a particular thing: *patients with liver disease may be **susceptible** to infection.* ■ (of a person) easily influenced by feelings or emotions; sensitive: *they only do it to tease him—he's too susceptible.* **2** (**susceptible of**) capable of or admitting of: *the problem is not susceptible of a simple solution.* —**sus·cep·ti·bly** /-blē/ *adv.*

su·shi /'sooshē/ ▸*n.* a Japanese dish consisting of small balls or rolls of vinegar-flavored cold cooked rice served with a garnish of raw fish, vegetables, or egg.

sus·pect ▸*v.* /sə'spekt/ [*tr.*] **1** have an idea or impression of the existence, presence, or truth of (something) without certain proof: *if you suspect a gas leak, do not turn on an electric light* | [as *adj.*] (**suspected**) *a suspected heart condition.* ■ believe or feel that (someone) is guilty of an illegal, dishonest, or unpleasant act, without certain proof: *parents **suspected** of child abuse.* **2** doubt the genuineness or truth of: *a broker whose honesty he had no reason to suspect.*
▸*n.* /'səs,pekt/ a person thought to be guilty of a crime or offense: *the police have arrested a suspect.*
▸*adj.* /'səs,pekt/ not to be relied on or trusted; possibly dangerous or false: *a suspect package was found on the platform.*

sus·pend /sə'spend/ ▸*v.* [*tr.*] (usu. **be suspended**) **1** temporarily prevent from continuing or being in force or effect: *work on the dam was suspended.* ■ officially prohibit (someone) from holding their usual post or carrying out their usual role for a particular length of time: *two officers were **suspended from** duty pending the outcome of the investigation.* ■ defer or delay (an action, event, or judgment): *the judge suspended judgment until January 15.* ■ *Law* (of a judge or court) cause (an imposed sentence) to be unenforced as long as no further offense is committed within a specified period: *the sentence was suspended for six months.* **2** hang (something) from somewhere: *the light was **suspended from** the ceiling.* **3** (**be suspended**) (of solid particles) be dispersed throughout the bulk of a fluid: *the paste contains collagen suspended in a salt solution.*

sus·pend·ed an·i·ma·tion ▸*n.* the temporary cessation of most vital functions without death, as in a dormant seed or a hibernating animal.

sus·pend·ers /sə'spendərz/ ▸*pl. n.* a pair of straps that pass over the shoulders and fasten to the waistband of a pair of trousers or a skirt at the front and back to hold it up.

sus·pense /sə'spens/ ▸*n.* a state or feeling of excited or anxious uncertainty about what may happen: *come on, Fran, don't keep us **in suspense**!* ■ a quality in a work of fiction that arouses excited expectation or uncertainty about what may happen: *a tale of mystery and suspense.* —**sus·pense·ful** /-fəl/ *adj.*

sus·pen·sion /sə'spenSHən/ ▸*n.* **1** the action of suspending someone or something or the condition of being suspended, in particular: ■ the temporary prevention of something from continuing or being in force or effect: *the suspension of military action.* ■ the official prohibition of someone from holding their usual post or carrying out their usual role for a particular length of time: *the investigation led to the suspension of several officers* | *a four-game suspension.* ■ *Mus.* a discord made by prolonging a note of a chord into the following chord. **2** the system of springs and shock absorbers by which a vehicle is cushioned from road conditions: *the car's rear suspension.* **3** a mixture in which particles are dispersed throughout a fluid: *a suspension of corn starch in peanut oil.* ■ the state of being dispersed in such a way: *the agitator in the vat keeps the slurry in suspension.*

sus·pen·sion bridge ▸*n.* a bridge in which the weight of the deck is supported by vertical cables suspended from larger cables that run between towers and are anchored in abutments at each end.

sus·pi·cion /sə'spiSHən/ ▸*n.* **1** a feeling or thought that something is possible, likely, or true: *she had a sneaking **suspicion that** he was laughing at her.* ■ a feeling or belief that someone is guilty of an illegal, dishonest, or unpleasant action: *police would not say what aroused their suspicions.* ■ cautious distrust: *her activities were regarded with suspicion by the headmistress.* **2** a very slight trace of something: *a suspicion of a smile.*

sus·pi·cious /sə'spiSHəs/ ▸*adj.* having or showing a cautious distrust of someone or something: *he was **suspicious of** her motives.* ■ causing one to have the idea or impression that something or someone is of questionable, dishonest, or dangerous character or condition: *they are not treating the fire as suspicious.* ■ having the belief or impression that someone is involved in an illegal or dishonest activity: *police were called when staff became suspicious.* —**sus·pi·cious·ly** *adv. it's suspiciously cheap* —**sus·pi·cious·ness** *n.*

sus·tain /sə'stān/ ▸*v.* [*tr.*] **1** strengthen or support physically or mentally: *this thought had sustained him throughout the years.* ■ cause to continue or be prolonged for an extended period or without interruption: *he cannot sustain a normal conversation.* ■ (of a performer) represent (a part or character) convincingly: *he sustained the role with burly resilience.* ■ bear (the weight of an object) without breaking or falling: *he sagged against her so that she could barely sustain his weight.* **2** undergo or suffer (something unpleasant, esp. an injury): *he died after sustaining severe* *head injuries.* **3** uphold, affirm, or confirm the justice or validity of: *the allegations of discrimination were sustained.*

▶*n. Mus.* an effect or facility on a keyboard or electronic instrument whereby a note can be sustained after the key is released. ▷Middle English: from Old French *soustenir,* from Latin *sustinere,* from *sub-* 'from below' + *tenere* 'hold.' —**sus·tain·a·ble** *adj.* —**sus·tain·ed·ly** /-nidlē/ *adv.* —**sus·tain·er** *n.* —**sus·tain·ment** *n.*

sus·te·nance /ˈsəstənəns/ ▶*n.* food and drink regarded as a source of strength; nourishment: *poor rural economies turned to potatoes for sustenance.* ■ the maintaining of someone or something in life or existence: *he kept two or three cows for the sustenance of his family | the sustenance of democracy.*

su·tra /ˈso͞otrə/ ▶*n.* a rule or aphorism in Sanskrit literature, or a set of these on a technical subject. See also **KAMA SUTRA.** ■ a Buddhist or Jain scripture.

sut·tee /səˈtē; ˈsə·ˌtē/ (also **sa·ti** *pronunc.* same) ▶*n.* (*pl.* **sut·tees;** also **sa·tis** /səˈtēz; ˈsə·ˌtēz/) the former Hindu practice of a widow immolating herself on her husband's funeral pyre.

su·ture /ˈso͞oCHər/ ▶*n.* **1** a stitch or row of stitches holding together the edges of a wound or surgical incision. ■ a thread or wire used for this. ■ the action of stitching together the edges of a wound or incision. **2** a seamlike immovable junction between two bones, such as those of the skull. ■ *Zool.* a similar junction, such as between the parts of the exoskeleton of an insect's body.

▶*v.* [*tr.*] stitch up (a wound or incision) with a suture: *the small incision was sutured.* —**su·tur·al** /-CHərəl/ *adj.*

SUV ▶*abbr.* sport utility vehicle.

su·ze·rain /ˈso͞ozərən; -ˌrān/ ▶*n.* a sovereign or state having some control over another state that is internally autonomous. —**su·ze·rain·ty** /-rəntē; -ˌrāntē/ *n.*

svelte /svelt; sfelt/ ▶*adj.* (of a person) slender and elegant.

SW ▶*abbr.* ■ southwest. ■ southwestern.

swab /swäb/ ▶*n.* **1** an absorbent pad or piece of material used in surgery and medicine for cleaning wounds, applying medication, or taking specimens. ■ a specimen of a secretion taken with a swab for examination: *he had taken throat swabs.* ■ a piece of absorbent material used for cleaning the bore of a firearm, a woodwind instrument, etc. **2** a mop or other absorbent device for cleaning or mopping up a floor or other surface.

▶*v.* (**swabbed, swab·bing**) [*tr.*] clean (a wound or surface) with a swab: *swabbing down the decks | swab a patch of skin with alcohol.* ■ absorb or clear (moisture) with a swab: *the blood was swabbed away.*

swad·dle /ˈswädl/ ▶*v.* [*tr.*] wrap (someone, esp. a baby) in garments or cloth: *she swaddled the baby tightly.*

swag /swag/ ▶*n.* **1** an ornamental festoon of flowers, fruit, and greenery: *ribbon-tied swags of flowers.* ■ a carved or painted representation of such a festoon: *fine plaster swags.* ■ a curtain or piece of fabric fastened so as to hang in a drooping curve. **2** *Austral./NZ* a traveler's or miner's bundle of personal belongings.

▶*v.* (**swagged, swag·ging**) [*tr.*] arrange in or decorate with a swag or swags of fabric: *swag the fabric gracefully over the curtain tie-backs.*

swag·ger /ˈswagər/ ▶*v.* [*intr.*] walk or behave in a very confident and typically arrogant or aggressive way: *he swaggered along the corridor.*

▶*n.* a very confident and typically arrogant or aggressive gait or manner: *they strolled around the camp with an exaggerated swagger.* —**swag·ger·er** /ˈswag(ə)rər/ *n.* —**swag·ger·ing·ly** /ˈswag(ə)riNGlē/ *adv.*

swag·ger stick ▶*n.* a short cane carried by a military officer.

Swa·hi·li /swäˈhēlē/ ▶*n.* **1** a Bantu language widely used as a lingua franca in East Africa and having official status in several countries. Also called **KISWAHILI.** **2** a member of a people of Zanzibar and nearby coastal regions, descendants of the original speakers of Swahili.

swain /swān/ ▶*n. archaic* a country youth. ■ *poetic/lit.* a young lover or suitor.

swal·low[1] /ˈswälō/ ▶*v.* [*tr.*] cause or allow (something, esp. food or drink) to pass down the throat: *she swallowed a mouthful slowly.* ■ [*intr.*] perform the muscular movement of the esophagus required to do this, esp. through fear or nervousness: *she swallowed hard, sniffing back her tears.* ■ put up with or meekly accept (something insulting or unwelcome): *he seemed ready to swallow any insult.* ■ believe unquestioningly (a lie or unlikely assertion): *she had swallowed his story hook, line, and sinker.* ■ resist expressing (a feeling) or uttering (words): *he swallowed his pride.* ■ take in and cause to disappear; engulf: *the dark mist swallowed him up.* ■ completely use up (money or resources): *debts swallowed up most of the money he had gotten for the house.*

▶*n.* an act of swallowing something, esp. food or drink: *he downed his*

drink in one swallow. ■ an amount of something swallowed in one action: *he said he'd like just a swallow of pie.* —**swal·low·a·ble** *adj.* —**swal·low·er** *n.*

swal·low[2] ▶*n.* a migratory swift-flying songbird (*Hirundo* and other genera, family Hirundinidae) with a forked tail and long pointed wings, feeding on insects in flight. Its numerous species include the widespread **barn swallow** (*H. rustica*).

swal·low·tail /ˈswälō·ˌtāl/ ▶*n.* (also **swallowtail butterfly**) a large brightly colored butterfly (family Papilionidae) with tail-like projections (suggestive of a swallow's tail) on the hind wings.

swam /swam/ ▶ past of **SWIM.**

swa·mi /ˈswämē/ ▶*n.* (*pl.* **-mis**) a Hindu male religious teacher.

swamp /swämp/ ▶*n.* an area of low-lying, uncultivated ground where water collects; a bog or marsh. ■ used to emphasize the degree to which a piece of ground is waterlogged: *the ceaseless deluge had turned the lawn into a swamp.*

▶*v.* [*tr.*] overwhelm or flood with water: *a huge wave swamped the canoes.* ■ *fig.* overwhelm with an excessive amount of something; inundate: *feelings of guilt suddenly swamped her.* —**swamp·y** *adj.*

swan /swän/ ▶*n.* a large waterbird (genus *Cygnus,* family Anatidae) with a long flexible neck, short legs, webbed feet, a broad bill, and typically all-white plumage. —**swan·like** /-ˌlīk/ *adj.*

swan dive ▶*n.* a dive performed with one's arms outspread until close to the water.

swank /swaNGk/ *inf.* ▶*v.* [*intr.*] display one's wealth, knowledge, or achievements in a way that is intended to impress others: *swanking about, playing the dashing young master spy.*

▶*n.* behavior, talk, or display intended to impress others: *a little money will buy you a good deal of swank.*

▶*adj.* another term for **SWANKY:** *coming out of some swank nightclub.*

swank·y /ˈswaNGkē/ ▶*adj.* (**swank·i·er, swank·i·est**) *inf.* stylishly luxurious and expensive: *directors with swanky company cars.* ■ using one's wealth, knowledge, or achievements to try to impress others. —**swank·i·ly** /-kəlē/ *adv.* —**swank·i·ness** *n.*

swans·down /ˈswänz·ˌdoun/ (also **swan's down**) ▶*n.* **1** the fine down of a swan, used for trimmings and powder puffs. **2** a thick cotton fabric with a soft nap on one side, used esp. for baby clothes.

swan song ▶*n.* a person's final public performance or professional activity before retirement: *he has decided to make this tour his swan song.*

swap /swäp/ (also **swop**) ▶*v.* (**swapped, swap·ping**) [*tr.*] take part in an exchange of: *we swapped phone numbers | I was wondering if you'd like to swap with me.* ■ give (one thing) and receive something else in exchange: *swap one of your sandwiches for a cheese and pickle?* ■ substitute (one thing) for another: *I swapped my busy life on Wall Street for a peaceful mountain retreat.*

▶*n.* an act of exchanging one thing for another: *let's do a swap.* ■ a thing that has been or may be given in exchange for something else: *I've got one already, but I'll keep this as a swap.* ■ *Finance* an exchange of liabilities between two borrowers, either so that each acquires access to funds in a currency they need or so that a fixed interest rate is exchanged for a floating rate. —**swap·pa·ble** *adj.* —**swap·per** *n.*

swap meet ▶*n.* a gathering at which enthusiasts or collectors trade or exchange items of common interest: *a computer swap meet.* ■ a flea market.

sward /swôrd/ ▶*n.* an expanse of short grass.

swarm[1] /swôrm/ ▶*n.* a large or dense group of insects, esp. flying ones. ■ a large number of honeybees that leave a hive en masse with a newly fertilized queen in order to establish a new colony. ■ (a **swarm/swarms of**) a large number of people or things: *a swarm of journalists.* ■ a series of similar-sized earthquakes occurring together, typically near a volcano. ■ *Astron.* a large number of minor celestial objects occurring together in space, esp. a dense shower of meteors.

▶*v.* **1** [*intr.*] (of insects) move in or form a swarm: [as *adj.*] (**swarming**) *swarming locusts.* ■ (of honeybees, ants, or termites) issue from the nest in large numbers with a newly fertilized queen in order to found new colonies: *the bees had swarmed and left the hive.* **2** [*intr.*] move somewhere in large numbers: *protesters were swarming into the building.* ■ (**swarm with**) (of a place) be crowded or overrun with (moving people or things): *the place was swarming with police.*

swarm[2] ▶*v.* [*intrans.*] climb up or upon a pole, tree, or the like, by clasping it with the arms and legs alternately: *pursued by a dog, a raccoon will* swarm like lightning | the object is to **swarm up** the flagpole in less than a minute | [trans.] he swarmed the mast.

swarth·y /ˈswôrᴛʜē/ ▶adj. (**swarth·i·er**, **swarth·i·est**) dark-skinned: she looked frail standing next to her strong and swarthy brother. —**swarth·i·ly** /-ᴛʜəlē/ adv. —**swarth·i·ness** n.

swash·buck·le /ˈswôsʜˌbəkəl; ˈswāsʜ-/ ▶v. [intrans.] [usu. as adj.] (**swash-buckling**) engage in daring and romantic adventures with ostentatious bravado or flamboyance: a crew of swashbuckling buccaneers.

swash·buck·ler /ˈswôsʜˌbəklər; ˈswāsʜ-/ ▶n. a swashbuckling person.

swas·ti·ka /ˈswästikə/ ▶n. an ancient symbol in the form of an equal-armed cross with each arm continued at a right angle, used (in clockwise form) as the emblem of the German Nazi Party.

swastika

swat /swät/ ▶v. (**swat·ted**, **swat·ting**) [tr.] hit or crush (something, esp. an insect) with a sharp blow from a flat object: I swatted a mosquito that had landed on my wrist | [intr.] swatting at a fly. ■ hit (someone) with a sharp blow: she swatted him over the head with a rolled-up magazine.
▶n. such a sharp blow: the dog gave the hedgehog a sideways swat.

swatch /swäcʜ/ ▶n. a sample, esp. of fabric. ■ a patch or area of a material or surface: the sunset had filled the sky with swatches of deep orange.

swath /swäᴛʜ; swôᴛʜ/ (also **swathe** /swāᴛʜ; swôᴛʜ; swäᴛʜ/) ▶n. (pl. **swaths** /swäᴛʜs; swôᴛʜs/ or **swathes** /swäᴛʜz/) **1** a strip left clear by the passage of a mowing machine or scythe: the combine had cut a deep swath around the border of the fields. **2** a broad strip or area of something: vast swaths of countryside.

swathe /swāᴛʜ; swôᴛʜ/ ▶v. [tr.] (usu. **be swathed in**) wrap in several layers of fabric: his hands were swathed in bandages.
▶n. a piece or strip of material in which something is wrapped.

sway /swā/ ▶v. move or cause to move slowly or rhythmically backward and forward or from side to side: [intr.] he swayed slightly on his feet wind rattled and swayed the trees. ■ [tr.] control or influence (a person or course of action): he's easily swayed by other people.
▶n. **1** a rhythmical movement from side to side: the easy sway of her hips. **2** rule; control: the part of the continent under Russia's sway.
▶ □ **hold sway** have great power or influence over a particular person, place, or domain.

swear /swe(ə)r/ ▶v. (past **swore** /swôr/; past part. **sworn** /swôrn/) **1** make a solemn statement or promise undertaking to do something or affirming that something is the case: [tr.] they were reluctant to swear allegiance. ■ take (an oath): he forced them to swear an oath of loyalty to him. ■ [tr.] take a solemn oath as to the truth of (a statement): I asked him if he would swear a statement to this effect. ■ [tr.] (**swear someone in**) admit someone to a particular office or position by directing them to take a formal oath: he was sworn in as president on July 10. ■ [tr.] make (someone) promise to observe a certain course of action: I've been sworn to secrecy. ■ [intr.] (**swear to**) express one's assurance that something is the case: I couldn't swear to it, but I'm pretty sure it's his writing. ■ [intr.] (**swear off**) inf. promise to abstain from: I'd sworn off alcohol. ■ [intr.] (**swear by**) inf. have or express great confidence in the use, value, or effectiveness of: Iris swears by her yoga. **2** [intr.] use offensive language, esp. as an expression of anger: Peter swore under his breath.
▶phrasal v. □ **swear something out** Law obtain the issue of (a warrant for arrest) by making a charge on oath. —**swear·er** n.

sweat /swet/ ▶n. **1** moisture exuded through the pores of the skin, typically in profuse quantities as a reaction to heat, physical exertion, fever, or fear. ■ an instance of exuding moisture in this way over a period of time: even thinking about him made me **break out in a sweat**. ■ inf. a state of flustered anxiety or distress: I don't believe he'd **get into such a sweat** about a girl. ■ inf. hard work; effort: computer graphics take a lot of the sweat out of animation. **2** (**sweats**) informal term for ꜱᴡᴇᴀᴛꜱᴜɪᴛ or ꜱᴡᴇᴀᴛᴘᴀɴᴛꜱ. ■ [as adj.] denoting loose casual garments made of thick, fleecy cotton: sweat tops and bottoms.
▶v. (past **sweat·ed** or **sweat**) [intr.] exude sweat: he was sweating profusely. ■ [tr.] (**sweat something out/off**) get rid of (something) from the body by exuding sweat: a well-hydrated body sweats out waste products more efficiently. ■ [tr.] cause (a person or animal) to exude sweat by exercise or exertion: cold as it was, the climb had sweated him. ■ (of food or an object) ooze or exude beads of moisture onto its surface: cheese stored at room temperature will quickly sweat. ■ (of a person) exert a great deal of strenuous effort: I've **sweated over** this for six months. ■ (of a person) be or remain in a state of extreme anxiety, typically for a prolonged period: I let her sweat for a while, then I asked her out again. ■ [tr.] inf. worry about (something): he's not going to have a lot of time to sweat the details.

▷Old English swāt (noun), swǣtan (verb), of Germanic origin; related to Dutch zweet and German Schweiss, from an Indo-European root shared by Latin sudor.

▶ □ **no sweat** inf. used to convey that one perceives no difficulty or problem with something: "We haven't any decaf, I'm afraid." "No sweat." □ **sweat blood** inf. make an extraordinarily strenuous effort to do something: she's sweated blood to support her family. ■ be extremely anxious: we've been sweating blood over the question of what is right. □ **sweat bullets** inf. be extremely anxious or nervous. □ **sweat it out** inf. wait in a state of extreme anxiety for something to happen or be resolved: he sweated it out until the lab report was back.

sweat·band /ˈswetˌband/ ▶n. a band of absorbent material worn around the head or wrist to soak up sweat, esp. by participants in sports. ■ a band of absorbent material lining a hat.

sweat·er /ˈswetər/ ▶n. a knitted garment typically with long sleeves, worn over the upper body.

sweat gland ▶n. a small gland that secretes sweat, situated in the dermis of the skin. Such glands are found over most of the body, and have a simple coiled tubular structure.

sweat·pants /ˈswetˌpants/ ▶pl. n. loose, warm trousers with an elasticized or drawstring waist, worn when exercising or as leisurewear.

sweat·shirt /ˈswetˌsʜərt/ ▶n. a loose, heavy shirt, typically made of cotton, worn when exercising or as leisurewear.

sweat·shop /ˈswetˌsʜäp/ ▶n. a factory or workshop, esp. in the clothing industry, where manual workers are employed at very low wages for long hours and under poor conditions.

sweat·suit /ˈswetˌsᴏᴏt/ ▶n. a suit consisting of a sweatshirt and sweatpants, worn when exercising or as leisurewear.

sweat·y /ˈswetē/ ▶adj. (**sweat·i·er**, **sweat·i·est**) exuding, soaked in, or inducing sweat: my feet got so hot and sweaty. —**sweat·i·ly** /ˈswetəlē/ adv. —**sweat·i·ness** n.

Swede /swēd/ ▶n. a native or national of Sweden, or a person of Swedish descent.

Swed·ish /ˈswēdisʜ/ ▶adj. of or relating to Sweden, its people, or their language.
▶n. the North Germanic language of Sweden, also spoken in parts of Finland.

sweep /swēp/ ▶v. (past **swept** /swept/) **1** [tr.] clean (an area) by brushing away dirt or litter: I've swept the floor. ■ [tr.] move or remove (dirt or litter) in such a way: she swept the tea leaves into a dustpan. ■ [tr.] move or push (someone or something) with great force: I was swept along by the crowd. ■ [tr.] brush (hair) back from one's face or upward: long hair swept up into a high chignon. ■ search (an area) for something: the detective swept the room for hair and fingerprints. ■ examine (a place or thing) for electronic listening devices: the line is swept every fifteen minutes. ■ cover (an entire area) with a gun: they were trying to get the Lewis gun up behind some trees from where they would sweep the trench. **2** [intr.] move swiftly and smoothly: a large black car swept past the open windows. ■ [tr.] cause to move swiftly and smoothly: he swept his hand around the room. ■ (of a person) move in a confident and stately manner: she swept magnificently from the hall. ■ (of a geographical or natural feature) extend continuously in a particular direction, esp. in a curve: green forests swept down the hillsides. ■ [tr.] look swiftly over: her eyes swept the room. ■ affect (an area or place) swiftly and widely: violence swept the country | [intr.] the rebellion had swept through all four of the country's provinces. ■ [tr.] win all the games in (a series); take each of the winning or main places in (a contest or event): we knew we had to sweep these three home games.
▶n. **1** an act of sweeping something with a brush: I was giving the floor a quick sweep. **2** a long, swift, curving movement: a grandiose sweep of his hand. ■ a comprehensive search or survey of a place or area: the police finished their sweep through the woods. ■ (often **sweeps**) a survey of the ratings of broadcast stations, carried out at regular intervals to determine advertising rates. **3** a long, typically curved stretch of road, river, country, etc.: we could see a wide sweep of country perhaps a hundred miles across. ■ fig. the range or scope of something: the whole sweep of the history of the USSR. **4** inf. a sweepstake. **5** an instance of winning every event, award, or place in a contest: a World Series sweep. **6** a long heavy oar used to row a barge or other vessel. **7** a long pole mounted as a lever for raising buckets from a well.

sweep·er /ˈswēpər/ ▶n. a person or device that cleans a floor or road by sweeping.

sweep·ing /ˈswēpiNG/ ▶adj. wide in range or effect: we cannot recommend any sweeping alterations. ■ extending or performed in a long, continuous curve: sweeping, desolate moorlands. ■ (of a statement) taking no account of particular cases or exceptions; too general: a sweeping assertion.

▶ *n.* (**sweepings**) dirt or refuse collected by sweeping: *the sweepings from the house.* —**sweep·ing·ly** *adv.* —**sweep·ing·ness** *n.*

sweep·stakes /ˈswēpˌstāks/ ▶ *n.* (also **sweep·stake**) a form of gambling, esp. on horse races, in which all the stakes are divided among the winners. ■ a race on which money is bet in this way. ■ a prize or prizes won in a sweepstakes.

sweet /swēt/ ▶ *adj.* **1** having the pleasant taste characteristic of sugar or honey; not salty, sour, or bitter: *a cup of hot sweet tea.* ■ (of air, water, or food) fresh, pure, and untainted: *lungfuls of the clean, sweet air.* ■ [often in *comb.*] smelling pleasant like flowers or perfume; fragrant: *sweet-smelling flowers.* **2** pleasing in general; delightful: *it was the sweet life he had always craved.* ■ highly satisfying or gratifying: *some sweet, short-lived revenge.* ■ working, moving, or done smoothly or easily: *the sweet handling of this motorcycle.* ■ (of sound) melodious or harmonious: *the sweet notes of the flute.* ■ denoting music, esp. jazz, played at a steady tempo without improvisation. **3** (of a person or action) pleasant and kind or thoughtful: *a very sweet nurse came along.* ■ (esp. of a person or animal) charming and endearing: *a sweet little cat.* ■ dear; beloved: *my sweet love.* **4** used for emphasis in various phrases and exclamations: *What had happened? Sweet nothing.*

▶ *n.* **1** (**sweets**) sweet foods, collectively: *Americans eat too many sweets.* **2** used as an affectionate form of address to a person one is very fond of: *hello, my sweet.* —**sweet·ish** *adj.* —**sweet·ly** *adv.*

sweet·bread /ˈswētˌbred/ ▶ *n.* the thymus gland (or, rarely, the pancreas) of an animal, esp. as used for food.

sweet·bri·er /ˈswētˌbrīər/ (also **sweet·bri·ar**) ▶ *n.* a Eurasian wild rose (*Rosa eglanteria*) with fragrant leaves and flowers.

sweet clov·er /swēt ˈklōvər/ ▶ *n.* another term for MELILOT.

sweet corn ▶ *n.* corn of a variety with kernels that have a high sugar content. It is grown for human consumption and is harvested while slightly immature. ■ the kernels of this plant eaten as a vegetable.

sweet·en /ˈswētn/ ▶ *v.* make or become sweet or sweeter, esp. in taste: [*tr.*] *a cup of coffee sweetened with saccharin* | [*intr.*] *her smile sweetened.* ■ [*tr.*] make more agreeable or acceptable: *there is no way to sweeten the statement.* ■ [*tr.*] *inf.* induce (someone) to be well disposed or helpful to oneself: *I am in the process of sweetening him up.*

▶ □ **sweeten the pot** add to the total sum of bets made in poker. ■ add an inducement, typically in the form of money or a concession: *he is trying to sweeten the pot, offering workers a 50-cent raise.*

sweet·en·er /ˈswētn-ər; ˈswētnər/ ▶ *n.* a substance used to sweeten food or drink, esp. one other than sugar. ■ *inf.* an inducement, typically in the form of money or a concession: *these sweeteners made rental cars a bargain.*

sweet·heart /ˈswētˌhärt/ ▶ *n.* used as a term of endearment or affectionate form of address: *don't worry, sweetheart, I've got it all worked out.* ■ a person that one is in love with: *the pair were childhood sweethearts.* ■ a particularly lovable or pleasing person or thing: *he is an absolute sweetheart.* ■ [as *adj.*] *inf.* denoting an arrangement reached privately by two sides, esp. an employer and a labor union, in their own interests: *a sweetheart agreement.*

sweet·ie /ˈswētē/ *inf.* ▶ *n.* (also **sweetie pie**) used as a term of endearment (esp. as a form of address).

sweet mar·jo·ram ▶ *n.* see MARJORAM.

sweet·ness /ˈswētnis/ ▶ *n.* the quality of being sweet. ■ used as an affectionate form of address, though often ironically: *I've just got to go, sweetness.*

sweet pea ▶ *n.* a climbing plant (genus *Lathyrus*) of the pea family, widely cultivated for its colorful fragrant flowers.

sweet pep·per ▶ *n.* a large green, yellow, orange, or red variety of capsicum (*Capsicum annuum annuum*) that has a mild or sweet flavor and is often eaten raw.

sweet po·ta·to ▶ *n.* **1** an edible tropical tuber with pinkish orange, slightly sweet flesh. **2** the widely cultivated Central American climbing plant (*Ipomoea batatas*) of the morning glory family that yields this tuber. **3** *inf.* another term for OCARINA.

sweet talk *inf.* ▶ *v.* (**sweet-talk**) [*tr.*] insincerely praise (someone) in order to persuade them to do something: *detectives sweet-talked them into confessing.*

▶ *n.* insincere praise used to persuade someone to do something.

sweet tooth ▶ *n.* (*pl.* **sweet tooths**) a great liking for sweet-tasting foods. —**sweet-toothed** *adj.*

sweet wil·liam (also **sweet Wil·liam**) ▶ *n.* a fragrant garden plant (*Dianthus barbatus*) of the pink family, with flattened clusters of vivid red, pink, or white flowers.

swell /swel/ ▶ *v.* (*past part.* **swol·len** /ˈswōlən/ or **swelled**) [*intr.*] (esp. of a part of the body) become larger or rounder in size, typically as a result of an accumulation of fluid: *her bruised knee was already swelling up.* ■ become or make greater in intensity, number, amount, or volume: [*intr.*] *the murmur swelled to a roar* | [as *adj.*] (**swelling**) *the swelling ranks of Irish singer-songwriters* | [*tr.*] *the population was swollen by refugees.* ■ be intensely affected or filled with a particular emotion: *she felt herself swell with pride.*

▶ *n.* **1** a full or gently rounded shape or form: *the soft swell of her breast.* ■ a gradual increase in sound, amount, or intensity: *there was a swell of support in favor of him.* ■ a welling up of a feeling: *a swell of pride swept over George.* **2** a slow, regular movement of the sea in rolling waves that do not break: *there was a heavy swell.* **3** a mechanism for producing a crescendo or diminuendo in an organ or harmonium.

▶ *adj. inf., dated* excellent; very good: *you're looking swell.*

▶ *adv. inf., dated* excellently; very well: *everything was just going swell.*

swell·ing /ˈsweling/ ▶ *n.* an abnormal enlargement of a part of the body, typically as a result of an accumulation of fluid. ■ a natural rounded protuberance: *the lobes are prominent swellings on the base of the brain.*

swel·ter /ˈsweltər/ ▶ *v.* [*intr.*] (of a person or the atmosphere at a particular time or place) be uncomfortably hot: *Barney sweltered in his doorman's uniform* | [as *adj.*] (**sweltering**) *the sweltering afternoon heat.*

▶ *n.* an uncomfortably hot atmosphere: *the swelter of an August day.* —**swel·ter·ing·ly** *adv.*

swept /swept/ ▶ past and past participle of SWEEP.

swerve /swərv/ ▶ *v.* change or cause to change direction abruptly: [*intr.*] *a car swerved around a corner* | [*tr.*] *he swerved the truck, narrowly missing a teenager on a skateboard.*

▶ *n.* an abrupt change of direction: *do not make sudden swerves, particularly around parked vehicles.* —**swerv·er** *n.*

swift /swift/ ▶ *adj.* happening quickly or promptly: *a remarkably swift recovery.* ■ moving or capable of moving at high speed: *the water was very swift.*

▶ *adv. poetic/lit.* [except in *comb.*] swiftly: *streams that ran swift and clear* | *a swift-acting poison.*

▶ *n.* **1** a swift-flying insectivorous bird (family Apodidae) with long slender wings and a superficial resemblance to a swallow, spending most of its life on the wing. **2** (also **swift moth**) a moth (*Hepialus* and other genera, family Hepialidae), typically yellow-brown in color, with fast darting flight. —**swift·ly** *adv.* —**swift·ness** *n.*

swig /swig/ *inf.* ▶ *v.* (**swigged** /swigd/, **swig·ging**) [*tr.*] drink in large gulps: *Dave swigged the wine in five gulps* | [*intr.*] *old men swigged from bottles of plum brandy.*

▶ *n.* a large draft of drink: *he took a swig of tea.* —**swig·ger** *n.*

swill /swil/ ▶ *v.* [*tr.*] drink (something) greedily or in large quantities: *they whiled away their evening swilling pints of beer.* ■ accompany (food) with large quantities of drink: *a feast swilled down with pints of cider.*

▶ *n.* **1** kitchen refuse and scraps of waste food mixed with water for feeding to pigs. ■ alcohol of inferior quality: *the beer was just warm swill.* **2** a large mouthful of a drink: *a swill of ale.* —**swill·er** *n.* [usu. in *comb.*] *beer-swillers.*

swim /swim/ ▶ *v.* (**swim·ming**; *past* **swam** /swam/; *past part.* **swum** /swəm/) **1** [*intr.*] propel the body through water by using the limbs, or, (in the case of a fish or other aquatic animal) by using fins, tail, or other bodily movement: *they swam ashore.* ■ [*tr.*] cross (a particular stretch of water) in this way: *she swam the Channel.* ■ float on or at the surface of a liquid: *bubbles swam on the surface.* ■ [*tr.*] cause to float or move across water: *the Russians were able to swim their infantry carriers across.* **2** [*intr.*] be immersed in or covered with liquid: *mashed potatoes swimming in gravy.* **3** [*intr.*] appear to reel or whirl before one's eyes: *Emily rubbed her eyes as the figures swam before her eyes.* ■ experience a dizzily confusing sensation in one's head: *the drink made his head swim.*

▶ *n.* **1** an act or period of swimming: *we went for a swim in the river.* **2** a pool in a river that is a particularly good spot for fishing: *he landed two 5 lb chub from the same swim.* —**swim·ma·ble** *adj.* —**swim·mer** *n.*

swim blad·der ▶ *n. Zool.* a gas-filled sac present in the body of many bony fishes, used to maintain and control buoyancy.

swim·ming·ly /ˈswimingglē/ ▶ *adv.* smoothly and satisfactorily: *things are going swimmingly.*

swim·ming pool ▶ *n.* an artificial pool for swimming in.

swim·suit /ˈswimˌso͞ot/ (also **swim·ming suit**) ▶ *n.* a garment worn for swimming. —**swim·suit·ed** *adj.*

swim·wear /'swim,we(ə)r/ ▶ n. clothing worn for swimming.

swin·dle /'swindl/ ▶ v. [tr.] use deception to deprive (someone) of money or possessions: *a businessman swindled investors out of millions of dollars.* ■ obtain (money) fraudulently: *he was said to have swindled $62.5 million from the pension fund.*
▶ n. a fraudulent scheme or action: *he is mixed up in a $10 million insurance swindle.* —**swin·dler** n.

swine /swīn/ ▶ n. (pl. same) **1** a pig. **2** (pl. same or **swines**) inf. a person regarded by the speaker with contempt and disgust: *what an arrogant, unfeeling swine!* —**swin·ish** adj. —**swin·ish·ly** adv. —**swin·ish·ness** n.

swing /swiNG/ ▶ v. (past **swung** /swəNG/) **1** move or cause to move back and forth or from side to side while or as if suspended: [intr.] *her long black skirt swung about her legs* | [tr.] *a priest began swinging a censer* | [as adj.] (**swinging**) *local girls with their castanets and their swinging hips.* ■ move or cause to move in alternate directions or in either direction on an axis: [intr.] *a wooden gate swinging crazily on its hinges* | [tr.] *he swung the heavy iron door shut.* ■ [intr.] inf. be executed by hanging: *now he was going to swing for it.* **2** [intr.] move by grasping a support from below and leaping: *we swung across like two trapeze artists* | (**swing oneself**) *the Irishman swung himself into the saddle.* ■ move quickly around to the opposite direction: *Ronni had swung around to face him.* **3** move or cause to move in a smooth, curving line: [tr.] *he swung her bag up onto the rack* | [intr.] *the cab swung into the parking lot.* ■ [tr.] bring down (something held) with a curving movement, typically in order to hit an object: *I swung the club and missed the ball.* ■ [intr.] (**swing at**) attempt to hit or punch, typically with a wide curving movement of the arm: *he swung at me with the tire iron.* ■ [tr.] throw (a punch) with such a movement: *she swung a punch at him.* **4** shift or cause to shift from one opinion, mood, or state of affairs to another: [intr.] *opinion swung in the chancellor's favor* | [tr.] *the failure to seek a peace could swing sentiment the other way.* ■ [tr.] have a decisive influence on (something, esp. a vote or election): *an attempt to swing the vote in their favor.* ■ [tr.] inf. succeed in bringing about: *with us backing you we might be able to swing something.* **5** [intr.] play music with an easy flowing but vigorous rhythm: *the band swung on.* ■ (of music) be played with such a rhythm. **6** [intr.] inf. (of an event, place, or way of life) be lively, exciting, or fashionable. **7** [intr.] inf. be promiscuous, typically by engaging in group sex or swapping sexual partners.
▶ n. **1** a seat suspended by ropes or chains, on which someone may sit and swing back and forth. ■ a spell of swinging on such an apparatus. **2** an act of swinging: *with the swing of her arm, the knife flashed through the air.* ■ the manner in which a golf club or a bat is swung: *improve your golf swing.* ■ the motion of swinging: *this short cut gave her hair new movement and swing.* ■ a smooth flowing rhythm or action: *they came with a steady swing up the last reach.* **3** a discernible change in opinion: *the South's swing to the right.* **4** a style of jazz or dance music with an easy flowing but vigorous rhythm. ■ the rhythmic feeling or drive of such music. **5** a swift tour involving a number of stops, esp. one undertaken as part of a political campaign. —**swing·er** n.

swing bridge ▶ n. a bridge over water that can be rotated horizontally to allow ships through.

swing·ing /'swiNGiNG/ ▶ adj. inf. (of a person, place, or way of life) lively, exciting, and fashionable: *a swinging resort.* ■ sexually liberated or promiscuous. —**swing·ing·ly** adv.

swing shift ▶ n. a work shift from mid-afternoon to around midnight.

swing-wing ▶ n. [usu. as adj.] an aircraft wing that can move from a right-angled to a swept-back position: *swing-wing fighter bombers.* ■ an aircraft with wings of this design.

swing·y /'swiNGē/ ▶ adj. (**swing·i·er**, **swing·i·est**) **1** (of music) characterized by swing (see **SWING** (sense 4 of the noun)). **2** (of a skirt, coat, or other garment) cut so as to swing as the wearer moves.

swipe /swīp/ inf. ▶ v. [tr.] **1** hit or try to hit with a swinging blow: *she swiped me right across the nose* | [intr.] *she lifted her hand to swipe at a cat.* **2** steal: *someone swiped one of his sausages.* **3** pass (a card with a magnetic strip) through an electronic device that reads it.
▶ n. a sweeping blow: *he missed the ball with his first swipe.* ■ an attack or criticism: *he took a swipe at his critics.* —**swip·er** n.

swirl /swərl/ ▶ v. [intr.] move in a twisting or spiraling pattern: *the smoke was swirling around him.* ■ [tr.] cause to move in such a pattern: *swirl a little cream into the soup.*
▶ n. a quantity of something moving in such a pattern: *swirls of dust swept across the floor.* ■ a twisting or spiraling movement or pattern: *she emerged with a swirl of skirts* | *swirls of color.* —**swirl·y** adj.

swish /swiSH/ ▶ v. [intr.] move with a hissing or rushing sound: *a car swished by.* ■ [tr.] cause to move with such a sound: *a girl came in, swishing her long skirts.* ■ aim a swinging blow at something: *he swished at a*

bramble with a piece of stick. ■ [tr.] *Basketball* sink (a shot) without the ball touching the backboard or rim.
▶ n. **1** a hissing or rustling sound: *he could hear the swish of a distant car.* ■ a rapid swinging movement: *the cow gave a swish of its tail.* ■ *Basketball, inf.* a shot that goes through the basket without touching the backboard or rim. **2** inf., offens. an effeminate male homosexual.
▶ adj. inf., offens. effeminate. —**swish·y** adj.

Swiss /swis/ ▶ adj. of or relating to Switzerland or its people. ■ [as pl. n.] (**the Swiss**) the people of Switzerland.
▶ n. (pl. same) a native or national of Switzerland, or a person of Swiss descent. ▷early 16th cent.: from French *Suisse*, from Middle High German *Swīz* 'Switzerland.'

Swiss chard ▶ n. see **CHARD**.

Swiss cheese ▶ n. cheese of a style originating in Switzerland, typically containing large holes. ■ used figuratively to refer to something that is full of holes, gaps, or defects: *the team has Swiss cheese for a defense.*

switch /swiCH/ ▶ n. **1** a device for making and breaking the connection in an electric circuit: *the guard hit a switch and the gate swung open.* ■ *Comput.* a program variable that activates or deactivates a certain function of a program. **2** an act of adopting one policy or way of life, or choosing one type of item, in place of another; a change, esp. a radical one: *his friends were surprised at his switch from newspaper owner to farmer.* **3** a slender flexible shoot cut from a tree. **4** a junction of two railroad tracks, with a pair of linked tapering rails that can be moved laterally to allow a train to pass from one line to the other.
▶ v. [tr.] change the position, direction, or focus of: *the company switched the boats to other routes.* ■ adopt (something different) in place of something else; change: *she's managed to switch careers.* ■ [intr.] adopt a new policy, position, way of life, etc.: *she worked as a librarian and then switched to journalism.* ■ substitute (two items) for each other; exchange: *after ten minutes, listener and speaker switch roles.* —**switch·a·ble** adj. —**switch·er** n.

switch·back /'swiCH,bak/ ▶ n. a 180° bend in a road or path, esp. one leading up the side of a mountain.
▶ v. [intr.] (of a road or vehicle) make a series of switchback turns: *a road that switchbacked up blue and distant hills.*

switch·blade /'swiCH,blād/ ▶ n. a knife with a blade that springs out from the handle when a button is pressed.

switch·board /'swiCH,bôrd/ ▶ n. an installation for the manual control of telephone connections in an office, hotel, or other large building. ■ another term for **HELPLINE**. ■ an apparatus for varying connections between electric circuits in other applications.

switch-hit·ter ▶ n. *Baseball* a batter who can hit from either side of home plate. ■ inf. a bisexual. —**switch-hit** v. —**switch-hit·ting** adj.

swiv·el /'swivəl/ ▶ n. a coupling between two parts enabling one to revolve without turning the other.
▶ v. (**-eled**, **-el·ing**; *Brit.* **-elled**, **-el·ling**) turn around a point or axis or on a swivel: [intr.] *he swiveled in the chair* | [tr.] *she swiveled her eyes around.*

swiz·zle stick ▶ n. a stick used for stirring still drinks or taking the fizz out of sparkling ones.

swol·len /'swōlən/ ▶ past participle of **SWELL**.

swoon /swoon/ ▶ v. [intr.] faint from extreme emotion: *I don't want a nurse who swoons at the sight of blood.* ■ be emotionally affected by someone or something that one admires; become ecstatic: *teenagers swoon over Japanese pop singers.*
▶ n. an occurrence of fainting: *her strength ebbed away and she fell into a swoon.*

swoop /swoop/ ▶ v. **1** [intr.] (esp. of a bird) move rapidly downward through the air: *the barn owl can swoop down on a mouse in total darkness.* ■ carry out a sudden attack, esp. in order to make a capture or arrest: *investigators swooped on the Graf family home.* **2** [tr.] inf. seize with a sweeping motion: *she swooped up the hen in her arms.*
▶ n. a swooping or snatching movement or action: *four members were arrested following a swoop by detectives on their homes.*

swoosh /swooSH; swooSH/ ▶ n. the sound produced by a sudden rush of air or liquid: *the swoosh of surf.*
▶ v. [intr.] move with such a sound: *swooshing down beautiful ski slopes.*

swop /swäp/ ▶ v. & n. chiefly *Brit.* variant spelling of **SWAP**.

sword /sôrd/ ▶ n. a weapon with a long metal blade and a hilt with a hand guard, used for thrusting or striking and now typically worn as part of ceremonial dress. ■ (**the sword**) poetic/lit. military power, violence, or destruction: *not many perished by the sword.* —**sword-like** /-,līk/ adj.

sword·fish /'sôrd,fiSH/ ▶ n. (pl. same or **-fishes**) a large edible marine fish (*Xiphias gladius*, family Xiphiidae) with a streamlined body and a long flattened swordlike snout.

sword·play /'sôrd,plā/ ▶*n.* the activity or skill of fencing with swords or foils. ■ *fig.* repartee; skillful debate: *this intellectual swordplay went on for several minutes.*

swords·man /'sôrdzmən/ ▶*n.* (*pl.* **-men**) a man who fights with a sword (typically with his level of skill specified): *an expert swordsman.* —**swords·man·ship** /-,SHip/ *n.*

sword·tail /'sôrd,tāl/ ▶*n.* a livebearing freshwater fish (*Xiphophorus helleri*, family Poeciliidae) of Central America, popular in aquariums.

swore /swôr/ ▶ past of SWEAR.

sworn /swôrn/ ▶ past participle of SWEAR.
▶*adj.* **1** (of testimony or evidence) given under oath: *he made a sworn statement.* **2** determined to remain in the role or condition specified: *they were sworn enemies.*

swum /swəm/ ▶ past participle of SWIM.

swung /swəNG/ ▶ past and past participle of SWING.

syb·a·rite /'sibə,rīt/ ▶*n.* a person who is self-indulgent in their fondness for sensuous luxury. —**syb·a·rit·ic** /,sibə'ritik/ *adj.* —**syb·a·rit·ism** /-rīt,izəm/ *n.*

syc·a·more /'sikə,môr/ ▶*n.* an American plane tree, esp. *P. occidentalis*, the largest deciduous tree in the U.S.

syc·o·phant /'sikəfənt/ -,fant/ ▶*n.* a person who acts obsequiously toward someone in order to gain advantage; a servile flatterer. —**syc·o·phan·cy** /-fənsē/ -,fansē/ *n.* —**syc·o·phan·tic** /,sikə'fantik/ *adj.* —**syc·o·phan·ti·cal·ly** /,sikə'fantik(ə)lē/ *adv.*

Sy·den·ham's cho·rea /'sidn-əmz kô'rēə/ ▶*n.* a form of chorea chiefly affecting children, associated with rheumatic fever. Formerly called ST. VITUS'S DANCE.

syl. ▶*abbr.* syllable.

syl·la·bar·y /'silə,berē/ ▶*n.* (*pl.* **-bar·ies**) a set of written characters representing syllables and (in some languages or stages of writing) serving the purpose of an alphabet.

syl·la·bi /'silə,bī/ ▶ plural form of SYLLABUS.

syl·lab·ic /sə'labik/ ▶*adj.* of, relating to, or based on syllables: *a system of syllabic symbols.* ■ *Prosody* based on the number of syllables in a line: *the recreation of classical syllabic meters.* ■ (of a consonant) constituting a whole syllable, such as the *m* in *Mbabane* or the *l* in *bottle.* ■ articulated in syllables: *syllabic singing.*
▶*n.* a written character that represents a syllable: *Inuit syllabics.* —**syl·lab·i·cal·ly** /-ik(ə)lē/ *adv.* —**syl·la·bic·i·ty** /,silə'bisitē/ *n.*

syl·la·bize /'silə,bīz/ ▶*v.* [*tr.*] divide into or articulate by syllables.

syl·la·ble /'siləbəl/ ▶*n.* a unit of pronunciation having one vowel sound, with or without surrounding consonants, forming the whole or a part of a word; e.g., there are two syllables in *water* and three in *inferno.* ■ a character or characters representing a syllable: *syl·la·bled adj.* [usu. in *comb.*] *poems of few-syllabled lines.*

syl·la·bub /'silə,bəb/ ▶*n.* a whipped cream dessert, typically flavored with white wine or sherry.

syl·la·bus /'siləbəs/ ▶*n.* (*pl.* **-bus·es** or **-bi** /-,bī/) an outline of the subjects in a course of study or teaching: *there isn't time to cover the syllabus.*

syl·lep·sis /sə'lepsis/ ▶*n.* (*pl.* **-ses** /-sēz/) a figure of speech in which a word is applied to two others in different senses (e.g., *caught the train and a bad cold*) or to two others of which it grammatically suits only one (e.g., *neither they nor it is working*). —**syl·lep·tic** /-tik/ *adj.*

syl·lo·gism /'silə,jizəm/ ▶*n.* an instance of a form of reasoning in which a conclusion is drawn (whether validly or not) from two given or assumed propositions (premises), each of which shares a term with the conclusion, and shares a common or middle term not present in the conclusion (e.g., *all dogs are animals; all animals have four legs; therefore all dogs have four legs*). —**syl·lo·gis·tic** /,silə'jistik/ *adj.* —**syl·lo·gis·ti·cal·ly** /,silə'jistik(ə)lē/ *adv.*

sylph /silf/ ▶*n.* an imaginary spirit of the air. ■ a slender woman or girl. —**sylph·like** *adj.*

syl·va /'silvə/ ▶ variant spelling of SILVA.

syl·van /'silvən/ (also **sil·van**) ▶*adj. chiefly poetic/lit.* consisting of or associated with woods; wooded: *trees and contours all add to a sylvan setting.* ■ pleasantly rural or pastoral: *vistas of sylvan charm.*

sym. ▶*abbr.* ■ symbol. ■ *Chem.* symmetrical. ■ symphony. ■ symptom.

sym·bi·ont /'simbē,änt; -bī-/ ▶*n. Biol.* either of two organisms that live in symbiosis with one another.

sym·bi·o·sis /,simbē'ōsis; -bī-/ ▶*n.* (*pl.* **-ses** /-,sēz/) *Biol.* interaction between two different organisms living in close physical association, typically to the advantage of both. ■ a mutually beneficial relationship between different people or groups: *a perfect mother and daughter symbiosis.* —**sym·bi·ot·ic** /-'ätik/ *adj.* —**sym·bi·ot·i·cal·ly** /-'ätik(ə)lē/ *adv.*

sym·bol /'simbəl/ ▶*n.* a thing that represents or stands for something else, esp. a material object representing something abstract: *the limousine was another symbol of his wealth and authority.* ■ a mark or character used as a conventional representation of an object, function, or process, e.g., the letter or letters standing for a chemical element or a character in musical notation. ■ a shape or sign used to represent something such as an organization, e.g., a red cross or a Star of David.

sym·bol·ic /sim'bälik/ ▶*adj.* **1** serving as a symbol: *a repeating design symbolic of eternity.* ■ significant purely in terms of what is being represented or implied: *the release of the dissident was an important symbolic gesture.* **2** involving the use of symbols or symbolism: *the symbolic meaning of motifs and designs.* —**sym·bol·i·cal** *adj.* —**sym·bol·i·cal·ly** /-ik(ə)lē/ *adv.*

sym·bol·ism /'simbə,lizəm/ ▶*n.* the use of symbols to represent ideas or qualities: *in China, symbolism in gardens achieved great subtlety.* ■ symbolic meaning attributed to natural objects or facts: *the old-fashioned symbolism of flowers.* ■ (also **Sym·bol·ism**) an artistic and poetic movement or style using symbolic images and indirect suggestion to express mystical ideas, emotions, and states of mind. —**sym·bol·ist** *n.* & *adj.*

sym·bol·ize /'simbə,līz/ ▶*v.* [*tr.*] be a symbol of: *the ceremonial dagger symbolizes justice.* ■ represent by means of symbols: *a tendency to symbolize the father as the sun.* —**sym·bol·i·za·tion** /,simbəli'zāsHən/ *n.*

sym·bol·o·gy /sim'bäləjē/ ▶*n.* the study or use of symbols. ■ symbols collectively: *the use of religious symbology.*

sym·met·ri·cal /sə'metrikəl/ ▶*adj.* made up of exactly similar parts facing each other or around an axis; showing symmetry. —**sym·met·ric** *adj.* —**sym·met·ri·cal·ly** /-ik(ə)lē/ *adv.*

sym·me·try /'simitrē/ ▶*n.* (*pl.* **-tries**) the quality of being made up of exactly similar parts facing each other or around an axis: *this series has a line of symmetry through its center.* ■ correct or pleasing proportion of the parts of a thing: *an overall symmetry making the poem pleasant to the ear.* ■ similarity or exact correspondence between different things: *a lack of symmetry between men and women.* ■ *Physics* & *Math.* a law or operation in which a physical property or process has an equivalence in two or more directions. —**sym·me·trize** /-,trīz/ *v.*

sym·pa·thet·ic /,simpə'THetik/ ▶*adj.* **1** feeling, showing, or expressing sympathy: *he was sympathetic toward staff with family problems.* ■ showing approval of or favor toward an idea or action: *he was sympathetic to evolutionary ideas.* **2** pleasant or agreeable, in particular: ■ (of a person) attracting the liking of others: *Audrey develops as a sympathetic character.* ■ (of a structure) designed in a sensitive or fitting way: *buildings that were sympathetic to their surroundings.* **3** relating to or denoting the part of the autonomic nervous system consisting of nerves arising from ganglia near the middle part of the spinal cord, supplying the internal organs, blood vessels, and glands. **4** relating to, producing, or denoting an effect that arises in response to a similar action elsewhere. —**sym·pa·thet·i·cal·ly** /-ik(ə)lē/ *adv.*

sym·pa·thize /'simpə,THīz/ ▶*v.* [*intr.*] **1** feel or express sympathy: *it is easy to understand and sympathize with his predicament.* **2** agree with a sentiment or opinion: *they sympathize with critiques of traditional theory.* —**sym·pa·thiz·er** *n.*

sym·pa·thy /'simpəTHē/ ▶*n.* (*pl.* **-thies**) **1** feelings of pity and sorrow for someone else's misfortune: *they had great sympathy for the flood victims.* ■ (**one's sympathies**) formal expression of such feelings; condolences: *all Tony's friends joined in sending their sympathies to his widow Jean.* **2** understanding between people; common feeling: *the special sympathy between the two boys was obvious to all.* ■ (**sympathies**) support in the form of shared feelings or opinions: *his sympathies lay with his constituents.* ■ agreement with or approval of an opinion or aim; a favorable attitude: *I have some sympathy for this view.* ■ (**in sympathy**) relating harmoniously to something else; in keeping: *repairs had to be in sympathy with the original structure.* ▷late 16th cent. (sense 2): via Latin from Greek *sumpatheia,* from *sumpathēs,* from *sun-* 'with' + *pathos* 'feeling.'

sym·phon·ic /sim'fänik/ ▶*adj.* (of music) relating to or having the form or character of a symphony: *Franck's Symphonic Variations.* ■ relating to or written for a symphony orchestra: *symphonic and chamber music.* —**sym·phon·i·cal·ly** /-ik(ə)lē/ *adv.*

sym·phon·ic po·em ▶*n.* another term for TONE POEM.

sym·pho·ny /'simfənē/ ▶*n.* (*pl.* **-nies**) an elaborate musical composition for full orchestra, typically in four movements, at least one of which is traditionally in sonata form. ■ something regarded, typically favorably, as a composition of different elements: *autumn is a symphony of texture and pattern.* ■ (esp. in names of orchestras) short for SYMPHONY ORCHESTRA: *the Boston Symphony.*

Pronunciation Key ə *ago, up*; ər *over, fur*; a *hat*; ā *ate*; ä *car*; CH *chin*; e *let*; ē *see*; e(ə)r *air*; i *fit*; ī *by*; i(ə)r *ear*; NG *sing*; ō *go*; ô *law, for*; oi *toy*; o͝o *good*; o͞o *goo*; ou *out*; SH *she*; TH *thin*; T͟H *then*; (h)w *why*; ZH *vision*

sym·pho·ny or·ches·tra ▶*n.* a large classical orchestra, including string, wind, brass, and percussion instruments.

sym·po·si·um /sim'pōzēəm/ ▶*n.* (*pl.* **-si·a** /-zēə/ or **-si·ums**) a conference or meeting to discuss a particular subject. ■ a collection of essays or papers on a particular subject by a number of contributors.

symp·tom /'sim(p)təm/ ▶*n. Med.* a physical or mental feature that is regarded as indicating a condition of disease, particularly such a feature that is apparent to the patient: *dental problems may be a symptom of other illness.* ■ a sign of the existence of something, esp. of an undesirable situation: *the government was plagued by leaks—a symptom of divisions and poor morale.* —**symp·tom·less** *adj.*

symp·to·mat·ic /,sim(p)tə'matik/ ▶*adj.* serving as a symptom or sign, esp. of something undesirable: *the closings are symptomatic of a decaying city.* ■ exhibiting or involving symptoms: *patients with symptomatic celiac disease.* —**symp·to·mat·i·cal·ly** /-ik(ə)lē/ *adv.*

syn. ▶*abbr.* ■ synonym. ■ synonymous. ■ synonymy.

syn·a·gogue /'sinə,gäg/ ▶*n.* the building where a Jewish assembly or congregation meets for religious worship and instruction. ■ such a Jewish assembly or congregation. —**syn·a·gog·al** /,sinə'gägəl; -'gôgəl/ *adj.* —**syn·a·gog·i·cal** /,sinə'gäjikəl/ *adj.*

syn·apse /'sin,aps/ ▶*n.* a junction between two nerve cells, consisting of a minute gap across which impulses pass by diffusion of a neurotransmitter.

syn·ap·sis /sə'napsis/ ▶*n. Biol.* the fusion of chromosome pairs at the start of meiosis.

syn·ap·tic /sə'naptik/ ▶*adj. Anat.* of or relating to a synapse or synapses between nerve cells: *the synaptic membrane.* —**syn·ap·ti·cal·ly** /-ik(ə)lē/ *adv.*

sync /singk/ (also **synch**) *inf.* ▶*n.* synchronization: *images flash onto your screen in sync with the music.*
▶*v.* [*tr.*] synchronize: *the flash needs to be synced to your camera.*
▶ □ **in** (or **out of**) **sync** working well (or badly) together; in (or out of) agreement: *her eyes and her brain seemed to be seriously out of sync.*

syn·chro /'singkrō/ ▶*n.* **1** synchronized or synchronization: *tape editing with synchro start.* **2** short for SYNCHRONIZED SWIMMING. **3** short for SYNCHROMESH.

syn·chro·mesh /'singkrō,mesh/ ▶*n.* a system of gear changing, esp. in motor vehicles, in which the driving and driven gearwheels are made to revolve at the same speed during engagement by means of a set of friction clutches, thereby easing the change.

syn·chron·ic /sing'kränik/ ▶*adj.* concerned with something, esp. a language, as it exists at one point in time: *synchronic linguistics.* —**syn·chron·i·cal·ly** /-ik(ə)lē/ *adv.*

syn·chro·nize /'singkrə,nīz/ ▶*v.* [*tr.*] cause to occur or operate at the same time or rate: *soldiers used watches to synchronize movements.* ■ [*intr.*] occur at the same time or rate: *sometimes converging swells will synchronize to produce a peak.* ■ adjust (a clock or watch) to show the same time as another: *It is now 5:48. Synchronize watches.* ■ [*intr.*] tally; agree: *their version failed to synchronize with the police view.* ■ coordinate; combine: *both media synchronize national interests with multinational scope.* —**syn·chro·ni·za·tion** /,singkrənə'zāshən/ *n.* —**syn·chro·niz·er** *n.*

syn·chro·nized swim·ming ▶*n.* a sport in which members of a team of swimmers perform coordinated or identical movements in time to music. —**syn·chro·nized swim·mer** *n.*

syn·chro·nous /'singkrənəs/ ▶*adj.* **1** existing or occurring at the same time: *major changes in the relative position of land and sea must have been approximately synchronous globally.* **2** (of a satellite or its orbit) making or denoting an orbit around the earth or another celestial body in which one revolution is completed in the period taken for the body to rotate about its axis. —**syn·chro·nous·ly** *adv.*

syn·chro·ny /'singkrənē/ ▶*n.* simultaneous action, development, or occurrence. ■ the state of operating or developing according to the same time scale as something else: *some individuals do not remain in synchrony with the twenty-four-hour day.*

syn·cline /'sin,klīn/ ▶*n. Geol.* a trough or fold of stratified rock in which the strata slope upward from the axis. —**syn·cli·nal** /sin'klīnl/ *adj.*

syn·co·pate /'singkə,pāt/ ▶*v.* [*tr.*] **1** [usu. as *adj.*] (**syncopated**) displace the beats or accents in (music or a rhythm) so that strong beats become weak and vice versa: *syncopated dance music.* **2** shorten (a word) by dropping sounds or letters in the middle, as in *symbology* for *symbolology*, or *Gloster* for *Gloucester*. —**syn·co·pa·tion** /,singkə'pāshən/ *n.* —**syn·co·pa·tor** /-,pātər/ *n.*

syn·co·pe /'singkəpē/ ▶*n.* **1** *Med.* temporary loss of consciousness caused by a fall in blood pressure. **2** *Gram.* the omission of sounds or letters from within a word, e.g., when *probably* is pronounced /'präblē/. —**syn·co·pal** /-pəl/ *adj.*

syn·cy·tium /sin'sishəm/ ▶*n.* (*pl.* **-cy·tia** /-'sishə/) *Biol.* a single cell or cytoplasmic mass containing several nuclei, formed by fusion of cells or by division of nuclei. ■ *Embryology* material of this kind forming the outermost layer of the trophoblast. ▷late 19th cent.: from *syn-* 'together' + *-cyte* 'cell' + *-ium* (noun suffix denoting a biological structure). —**syn·cy·tial** /-shəl/ *adj.*

syn·di·cal·ism /'sindəkə,lizəm/ ▶*n. hist.* a movement for transferring the ownership and control of the means of production and distribution to workers' unions. Syndicalism developed in French labor unions during the late 19th century. —**syn·di·cal·ist** *n.* & *adj.*

syn·di·cate ▶*n.* /'sindikit/ a group of individuals or organizations combined to promote some common interest: *large-scale buyouts involving a syndicate of financial institutions.* ■ an association or agency supplying material simultaneously to a number of newspapers or periodicals.
▶*v.* /'sindi,kāt/ [*tr.*] (usu. **be syndicated**) control or manage by a syndicate: *the loans are syndicated to a group of banks.* ■ publish or broadcast (material) simultaneously in a number of newspapers, television stations, etc.: *his reports were syndicated to 200 other papers.* —**syn·di·ca·tion** /,sindi'kāshən/ *n.* —**syn·di·ca·tor** /-,kātər/ *n.*

syn·drome /'sin,drōm/ ▶*n.* a group of symptoms that consistently occur together or a condition characterized by a set of associated symptoms: *a rare syndrome in which the production of white blood cells is damaged.* ■ a characteristic combination of opinions, emotions, or behavior: *the "Not In My Backyard" syndrome.* ▷mid 16th cent.: modern Latin, from Greek *sundromē*, from *sun-* 'together' + *dramein* 'to run.' —**syn·drom·ic** /sin'drämik/ *adj.*

syndrome X ▶*n.* a group of risk factors (including glucose intolerance, high triglycerides, obesity, and hypertension) that indicate predisposition to diabetes.

syn·ec·do·che /si'nekdəkē/ ▶*n.* a figure of speech in which a part is made to represent the whole or vice versa, as in *Cleveland won by six runs* (meaning "Cleveland's baseball team"). —**syn·ec·doch·ic** /,sinek'däkik/ *adj.* —**syn·ec·doch·i·cal** /,sinek'däkikəl/ *adj.* —**syn·ec·doch·i·cal·ly** /-'däkik(ə)lē/ *adv.*

syn·e·col·o·gy /,sini'käləjē/ ▶*n.* the ecological study of whole plant or animal communities. —**syn·e·co·log·i·cal** /sin,ekə'läjikəl; -,ēkə-/ *adj.* —**syn·e·col·o·gist** /-jist/ *n.*

syn·er·gist /'sinərjist/ ▶*n.* a substance, organ, or other agent that participates in an effect of synergy. —**syn·er·gis·tic** /,sinər'jistik/ *adj.* —**syn·er·gis·ti·cal·ly** /',sinər'jistik(ə)lē/ *adv.*

syn·er·gy /'sinərjē/ (also **syn·er·gism** /-,jizəm/) ▶*n.* the interaction or cooperation of two or more organizations, substances, or other agents to produce a combined effect greater than the sum of their separate effects: *the synergy between artist and record company.* —**syn·er·get·ic** /,sinər'jetik/ *adj.* —**syn·er·gic** /sə'nərjik/ *adj.*

syn·od /'sinəd/ ▶*n.* an assembly of the clergy and sometimes also the laity in a diocese or other division of a particular church.

syn·o·nym /'sinə,nim/ ▶*n.* a word or phrase that means exactly or nearly the same as another word or phrase in the same language, for example *shut* is a synonym of *close*. ■ a person or thing so closely associated with a particular quality or idea that the mention of their name calls it to mind: *the Victorian age is a synonym for sexual puritanism.* ■ *Biol.* a taxonomic name that has the same application as another, esp. one that has been superseded and is no longer valid. —**syn·o·nym·ic** /,sinə'nimik/ *adj.* —**syn·o·nym·i·ty** /,sinə'nimitē/ *n.*

syn·on·y·mous /sə'nänəməs/ ▶*adj.* (of a word or phrase) having the same or nearly the same meaning as another word or phrase in the same language: *aggression is often taken as synonymous with violence.* ■ closely associated with or suggestive of something: *his deeds had made his name synonymous with victory.* —**syn·on·y·mous·ly** *adv.* —**syn·on·y·mous·ness** *n.*

syn·on·y·my /sə'nänəmē/ ▶*n.* the state of being synonymous.

syn·op·sis /sə'näpsis/ ▶*n.* (*pl.* **-ses** /-,sēz/) a brief summary or general survey of something: *a synopsis of the accident.* ■ an outline of the plot of a book, play, movie, or episode of a television show. —**syn·op·size** /-,sīz/ *v.*

syn·op·tic /sə'näptik/ ▶*adj.* of or forming a general summary or synopsis: *a synoptic outline of the contents.* ■ taking or involving a comprehensive mental view: *a synoptic model of higher education.* —**syn·op·ti·cal** *adj.* —**syn·op·ti·cal·ly** /-ik(ə)lē/ *adv.*

syn·o·vi·al /sə'nōvēəl/ ▶*adj.* relating to or denoting a type of joint that is surrounded by a thick flexible membrane forming a sac into which is secreted a viscous fluid that lubricates the joint.

syn·tac·tic /sin'taktik/ ▸adj. of or according to syntax: *syntactic analysis.* —**syn·tac·ti·cal** *adj.* —**syn·tac·ti·cal·ly** /-ik(ə)lē/ *adv.*

syn·tax /'sin,taks/ ▸n. the arrangement of words and phrases to create well-formed sentences in a language: *the syntax of English.* ▪ a set of rules for or an analysis of this: *generative syntax.* ▪ the branch of linguistics that deals with this.

syn·the·sis /'sinTHəsis/ ▸n. (*pl.* -**ses** /-,sēz/) combination or composition, in particular: ▪ the combination of ideas to form a theory or system: *the synthesis of intellect and emotion in his work.* Often contrasted with ANALYSIS. ▪ the production of chemical compounds by reaction from simpler materials: *the synthesis of methanol from carbon monoxide and hydrogen.* ▪ *Linguistics* the use of inflected forms rather than word order to express grammatical structure. —**syn·the·sist** *n.*

syn·the·size /'sinTHi,sīz/ ▸v. [*tr.*] make (something) by synthesis, esp. chemically: *man synthesizes new chemical poisons and sprays the countryside wholesale.* ▪ combine (a number of things) into a coherent whole: *pupils should synthesize the data they have gathered.* ▪ produce (sound) electronically: *trigger chips that synthesize speech.*

syn·the·siz·er /'sinTHə,sīzər/ ▸n. an electronic musical instrument, typically operated by a keyboard, producing a wide variety of sounds by generating and combining signals of different frequencies.

syn·thet·ic /sin'THetik/ ▸adj. relating to or using synthesis. ▪ (of a substance) made by chemical synthesis, esp. to imitate a natural product: *synthetic rubber.* ▪ (of an emotion or action) not genuine; insincere: *their tears are a bit synthetic.* ▪ *Linguistics* (of a language) characterized by the use of inflections rather than word order to express grammatical structure.
▸n. (often **synthetics**) a synthetic material or chemical, esp. a textile fiber. —**syn·thet·i·cal** *adj.* —**syn·thet·i·cal·ly** /-ik(ə)lē/ *adv.*

syn·thet·ic res·in ▸n. see RESIN.

syph·i·lis /'sifəlis/ ▸n. a chronic bacterial disease caused by the spirochete *Treponema pallidum.* It is contracted chiefly by infection during sexual intercourse. —**syph·i·lit·ic** /,sifə-'litik/ *adj.* & *n.*

sy·phon ▸n. & v. variant spelling of SIPHON.

sy·rin·ga /sə'riNGgə/ ▸n. **1** a plant of the genus *Syringa* in the olive family, esp. (in gardening) the lilac. **2** *inf.* another term for MOCK ORANGE.

sy·ringe /sə'rinj; 'sirinj/ ▸n. *Med.* a tube with a nozzle and piston or bulb for sucking in and ejecting liquid in a thin stream, used for cleaning wounds or body cavities, or fitted with a hollow needle for injecting or withdrawing fluids. ▪ any similar device used in gardening or cooking.

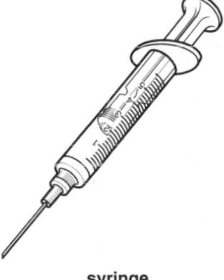

syringe

syr·up /'sirəp; 'sər-/ (also **sir·up**) ▸n. a thick sweet liquid made by dissolving sugar in boiling water, often used for preserving fruit. ▪ a thick sweet liquid containing medicine or used as a drink: *cough syrup.* ▪ a thick sticky liquid derived from a sugar-rich plant, esp. sugar cane, corn, and maple. ▪ *fig.* excessive sweetness or sentimentality of style or manner: *Mr. Gurney's poems are almost all of them syrup.* —**syr·up·y** *adj.*

sys·tem /'sistəm/ ▸n. **1** a set of connected things or parts forming a complex whole, in particular: ▪ a set of things working together as parts of a mechanism or an interconnecting network: *the state railroad system.* ▪ *Physiol.* a set of organs in the body with a common structure or function: *the digestive system.* ▪ the human or animal body as a whole: *you need to get the cholesterol out of your system.* ▪ *Comput.* a group of related hardware units or programs or both, esp. when dedicated to a single application. **2** a set of principles or procedures according to which something is done; an organized scheme or method: *the public school system.* ▪ orderliness; method: *there was no system at all in the company.* ▪ a method of choosing one's procedure in gambling. ▪ a set of rules used in measurement or classification: *the metric system.* ▪ (**the system**) the prevailing political or social order, esp. when regarded as oppressive and intransigent: *don't try bucking the system.* ▷early 17th cent.: from French *système* or late Latin *systema,* from Greek *sustēma,* from *sun-* 'with' + *histanai* 'set up.' —**sys·tem·less** *adj.*

sys·tem·at·ic /,sistə'matik/ ▸adj. done or acting according to a fixed plan or system; methodical: *a systematic search of the whole city.* —**sys·tem·at·i·cal·ly** /-ik(ə)lē/ *adv.* —**sys·tem·a·tist** /'sistəmə,tist/ *n.*

sys·tem·at·ics /,sistə'matiks/ ▸*pl. n.* [treated as *sing.*] the branch of biology that deals with classification and nomenclature; taxonomy.

sys·tem·a·tize /'sistəmə,tīz/ ▸v. [*tr.*] arrange according to an organized system; make systematic: *Galen set about systematizing medical thought.* —**sys·tem·a·ti·za·tion** /,sistəməti'zāsHən/ *n.* —**sys·tem·a·tiz·er** *n.*

sys·tem·ic /sə'stemik/ ▸adj. **1** of or relating to a system, esp. as opposed to a particular part: *the disease is localized rather than systemic.* ▪ (of an insecticide, fungicide, or similar substance) entering the plant via the roots or shoots and passing through the tissues. **2** *Physiol.* denoting the part of the circulatory system concerned with the transportation of oxygen to and carbon dioxide from the body in general, esp. as distinct from the pulmonary part concerned with the transportation of oxygen from and carbon dioxide to the lungs. —**sys·tem·i·cal·ly** /-ik(ə)lē/ *adv.*

sys·tems an·a·lyst ▸n. a person who analyzes a complex process or operation in order to improve its efficiency, esp. by applying a computer system. —**sys·tems a·nal·y·sis** *n.*

sys·to·le /'sistəlē/ ▸n. *Physiol.* the phase of the heartbeat when the heart muscle contracts and pumps blood from the chambers into the arteries. Often contrasted with DIASTOLE. —**sys·tol·ic** /si'stälik/ *adj.*

S

Tt

T¹ /tē/ (also **t**) ▶ *n.* (*pl.* **Ts** or **T's**) **1** the twentieth letter of the alphabet. ■ denoting the next after S in a set of items, categories, etc. **2** (**T**) (also **tee**) a shape like that of a capital T: [in *comb.*] make a *T-shaped* wound in the rootstock and insert the cut bud.

▶ □ **to a T** *inf.* exactly; to perfection: *I baked it to a T, and of course it was delicious.*

T² ▶ *abbr.* ■ [in *comb.*] (in units of measurement) tera- (10¹²): *12 Tbytes of data storage.* ■ tesla.

▶ *symb.* ■ temperature. ■ *Chem.* the hydrogen isotope tritium.

t ▶ *abbr.* long, short or metric ton(s).

▶ *symb.* (*t*) *Statistics* a number characterizing the distribution of a sample taken from a population with a normal distribution.

't ▶ *contr. of* the word "it," attached to the end of a verb, esp. in the transcription of regional spoken use: *I'll never do 't again.*

Ta ▶ *symb.* the chemical element tantalum.

ta /tä/ ▶ *interj.* Brit. *inf.* thank you.

tab¹ /tab/ ▶ *n.* **1** a small flap or strip of material attached to or projecting from something, used to hold or manipulate it, or for identification and information. ■ a similar piece of material forming part of a garment. ■ a strip or ring of metal attached to the top of a canned drink and pulled to open the can. **2** *inf.* a restaurant or bar bill. **3** *Aeron.* a part of a control surface, typically hinged, that modifies the action or response of the surface.

▶ *v.* (**tabbed**, **tab·bing**) [*tr.*] mark or identify with a projecting piece of material: *a page tabbed by a cloth bookmark.* ■ *fig.* identify as being of a specified type or suitable for a specified position: *he was tabbed by the president as the next Republican National Committee chairman.* —**tabbed** *adj.*

▶ □ **keep tabs** (or **a tab**) **on** *inf.* monitor the activities or development of; keep under observation. □ **pick up the tab** *inf.* pay for something.

tab² ▶ *n.* a facility in a word-processing program, or a device on a typewriter, used for advancing to a sequence of set positions in tabular work: *set tabs at 1.4 inches and 3.4 inches.*

▶ *v.* (**tabbed**, **tab·bing**) **1** short for TABULATE. **2** [*intr.*] activate the tab feature on a word processor or typewriter: *the user can tab to the phrase and press Enter.*

tab³ ▶ *n. inf.* a tablet containing a dose of a drug.

tab⁴ ▶ *n. inf.* a tabloid newspaper.

Ta·bas·co /təˈbaskō/ (also **Tabasco sauce**) ▶ *n. trademark* a pungent sauce made from the fruit of a capsicum pepper (*Capsicum frutescens*).

tab·bou·leh /təˈbo͞olē/ (also **ta·bou·li**) ▶ *n.* an Arab salad of cracked wheat mixed with finely chopped tomatoes, onions, and parsley.

tab·by /ˈtabē/ ▶ *n.* (*pl.* **-bies**) **1** (also **tabby cat**) a cat whose fur is mottled or streaked with dark stripes. ■ *inf.* any domestic cat. **2** a fabric with a watered pattern, typically silk. **3** a plain weave. **4** a type of concrete made of lime, shells, gravel, and stones that dries very hard.

▶ *adj.* (of a cat) gray or brownish in color and streaked with dark stripes.

tab·er·na·cle /ˈtabərˌnakəl/ ▶ *n.* **1** (in biblical use) a fixed or movable habitation, typically of light construction. ■ a tent used as a sanctuary for the Ark of the Covenant by the Israelites during the Exodus and until the building of the Temple. **2** a meeting place for worship used by some Protestants or Mormons. **3** an ornamented receptacle or cabinet in which a pyx or ciborium containing the reserved sacrament may be placed in Catholic churches, usually on or above an altar. ▷Middle English: via French from Latin *tabernaculum* 'tent,' diminutive of *taberna* 'hut, tavern.' —**tab·er·na·cled** *adj.*

ta·bla /ˈtäblə/ ▶ *n.* a pair of small hand drums attached together, used in

Indian music; one is slightly larger than the other and is played using pressure from the heel of the hand to vary the pitch.

ta·ble /ˈtābəl/ ▶ *n.* **1** a piece of furniture with a flat top and one or more legs, providing a level surface on which objects may be placed, and that can be used for such purposes as eating, writing, working, or playing games. ■ food provided in a restaurant or household: *he was reputed to have the finest French table of the time.* ■ a group seated at a table for a meal: *the whole table was in gales of laughter.* ■ (**the table**) a meeting place for formal discussions held to settle an issue or dispute: *the negotiating table.* ■ *Bridge* the dummy hand (which is exposed on the table): *they made the hand easily with the aid of a club ruff on the table.* **2** a set of facts or figures systematically displayed, esp. in columns: *the population has grown, as shown in table 1 | a table of contents.* ■ *Comput.* a collection of data stored in memory as a series of records, each defined by a unique key stored with it. **3** a flat surface, in particular: ■ *Archit.* a flat, typically rectangular, vertical surface. ■ a horizontal molding, esp. a cornice. ■ a slab of wood or stone bearing an inscription. ■ a flat surface of a gem. ■ a cut gem with two flat faces. ■ each half or quarter of a folding board for backgammon.

▶ *v.* [*tr.*] **1** postpone consideration of: *I'd like the issue to be tabled for the next few months.* **2** *Brit.* present formally for discussion or consideration at a meeting: *an MP tabled an amendment to the bill.* —**ta·ble·ful** /-ˌfo͝ol/ *n.* (*pl.* **-fuls**).

▶ □ **at table** seated at a table eating a meal. □ **lay something on the table 1** make something known so that it can be freely and sensibly discussed. **2** postpone something indefinitely. □ **on the table** offered for discussion: *our offer remains on the table.* □ **turn the tables** reverse one's position relative to someone else, esp. by turning a position of disadvantage into one of advantage: *police invited householders to a seminar on how to turn the tables on burglars.* □ **under the table 1** *inf.* very drunk: *by 3:30 everybody was under the table.* **2** (esp. of making a payment) secretly or covertly: *he accepted a slew of payoffs under the table.* ■ another term for UNDER THE COUNTER (see COUNTER¹).

ta·bleau /ˈtablō/ ▶ *n.* (*pl.* **tab·leaux** /ˌtaˈblōz/) a group of models or motionless figures representing a scene from a story or from history.

ta·ble·cloth /ˈtābəlˌklôTH; -ˌkläTH/ ▶ *n.* a cloth spread over a table, esp. during meals.

ta·ble·land /ˈtābəlˌ(l)and/ ▶ *n.* a broad, high, level region; a plateau.

ta·ble man·ners ▶ *pl. n.* a pattern of behavior that is conventionally required of someone while eating.

ta·ble nap·kin ▶ *n.* see NAPKIN (sense 1).

ta·ble·spoon /ˈtābəlˌspo͞on/ ▶ *n.* a large spoon for serving food. ■ (abbr.: **tbsp.** or **tbs.** or **T.**) a measurement in cooking, equivalent to 1/2 fluid ounce, three teaspoons, or 15 ml. —**ta·ble·spoon·ful** /-ˌfo͝ol/ *n.* (*pl.* **-fuls**).

tab·let /ˈtablit/ ▶ *n.* a flat slab of stone, clay, or wood, used esp. for an inscription. ■ a small disk or cylinder of a compressed solid substance, typically a measured amount of a medicine or drug; a pill. ■ a writing pad. ■ *Archit.* another term for TABLE (sense 3).

ta·ble ten·nis ▶ *n.* an indoor game based on tennis, played with small paddles and a ball bounced on a table divided by a net.

ta·ble·top /ˈtābəlˌtäp/ ▶ *n.* the horizontal top part of a table. ■ [as *adj.*] small or portable enough to be placed or used on a table: *a tabletop hockey game.*

ta·ble·ware /ˈtābəlˌwer/ ▶ *n.* dishes, utensils, and glassware used for serving and eating meals at a table.

tab·loid /ˈtabˌloid/ ▶ *n.* a newspaper having pages half the size of those of a standard newspaper, typically popular in style and dominated by headlines, photographs, and sensational stories. ■ [as *adj.*] sensational in a lurid or vulgar way.

ta·boo /tə'bōō; ta-/ (also **ta·bu**) ▸*n.* (*pl.* **-boos** also **-bus** /tə'bōōz/) a social or religious custom prohibiting or restricting a particular practice or forbidding association with a particular person, place, or thing.
▸*adj.* prohibited or restricted by social custom: *sex was a taboo subject.* ■ designated as sacred and prohibited.

ta·bor /'tābər/ ▸*n. hist.* a small drum, esp. one used simultaneously by the player of a simple pipe.

tab·u·lar /'tabyələr/ ▸*adj.* **1** (of data) consisting of or presented in columns or tables: *a tabular presentation of running costs.* **2** broad and flat like the top of a table: *a huge tabular iceberg.* ■ (of a crystal) relatively broad and thin, with two well-developed parallel faces. —**tab·u·lar·ly** *adv.*

tab·u·late /'tabyə,lāt/ ▸*v.* [*tr.*] arrange (data) in tabular form: [as *adj.*] (**tabulated**) *tabulated results.* —**tab·u·la·tion** /,tabyə'lāSHən/ *n.*

tab·u·la·tor /'tabyəlātər/ ▸*n.* **1** a person or thing that arranges data in tabular form. **2** another term for TAB[2].

tach /tak/ ▸*n. inf.* short for TACHOMETER.

tach·ism /'ta,SHizəm/ ▸*n.* a style of painting adopted by some French artists from the 1940s, involving the use of dabs or splotches of color, similar in aims to abstract expressionism.

ta·chom·e·ter /ta'kämitər; tə-/ ▸*n.* an instrument that measures the working speed of an engine (esp. in a road vehicle), typically in revolutions per minute.

tach·y·car·di·a /,taki'kärdēə/ ▸*n.* an abnormally rapid heart rate.

tac·it /'tasit/ ▸*adj.* understood or implied without being stated: *your silence may be taken to mean tacit agreement.* ▷early 17th cent. (in the sense 'wordless, noiseless'): from Latin *tacitus,* past participle of *tacere* 'be silent.' —**tac·it·ly** *adv.*

tac·i·turn /'tasi,tərn/ ▸*adj.* (of a person) reserved or uncommunicative in speech; saying little. —**tac·i·tur·ni·ty** /,tasi'tərnitē/ *n.* —**tac·i·turn·ly** *adv.*

tack[1] /tak/ ▸*n.* **1** a small, sharp, broad-headed nail. ■ a thumbtack. **2** a long stitch used to fasten fabrics together temporarily, prior to permanent sewing. **3** *Sailing* an act of changing course by turning a vessel's head into and through the wind, so as to bring the wind on the opposite side. ■ a boat's course relative to the direction of the wind. ■ *fig.* a method of dealing with a situation or problem; a course of action or policy: *as she could not stop him from going she tried another tack.* **4** *Sailing* a rope for securing the weather clew of a course. ■ the weather clew of a course, or the lower forward corner of a fore-and-aft sail. **5** the quality of being sticky: *cooking the sugar to caramel gives tack to the texture.*
▸*v.* **1** [*tr.*] fasten or fix in place with tacks. ■ fasten (pieces of cloth) together temporarily with long stitches. ■ (**tack something on**) add or append something to something already existing: *long-term savings plans with some life insurance tacked on.* **2** [*intr.*] *Sailing* change course by turning a boat's head into and through the wind. ■ *fig.* make a change in one's conduct, policy, or direction of attention. —**tack·er** *n.*

tack[2] ▸*n.* equipment used in horseback riding, including the saddle and bridle.
▸*v.* [*tr.*] (usu. **tack up**) put tack on (a horse).

tack·le /'takəl/ ▸*n.* **1** the equipment required for a task or sport: *fishing tackle.* **2** a mechanism consisting of ropes, pulley blocks, hooks, or other things for lifting heavy objects. ■ the running rigging and gear used to work a boat's sails. **3** *Football & Rugby* an act of seizing and stopping a player in possession of the ball by knocking them to the ground. ■ (in soccer and other games) an act of taking the ball, or attempting to take the ball, from an opponent. **4** *Football* a player who lines up inside the end along the line of scrimmage.
▸*v.* [*tr.*] make determined efforts to deal with (a problem or difficult task). ■ *Football & Rugby* stop the forward progress of (the ball carrier) by seizing them and knocking them to the ground. ■ *chiefly Soccer* try to take the ball from (an opponent). —**tack·ler** /'tak(ə)lər/ *n.*

tack·le block ▸*n.* a pulley over which a rope runs.

tack·y[1] /'takē/ ▸*adj.* (**tack·i·er, tack·i·est**) (of glue, paint, or other substances) retaining a slightly sticky feel; not fully dry. —**tack·i·ness** *n.*

tack·y[2] ▸*adj.* (**tack·i·er, tack·i·est**) *inf.* showing poor taste and quality: *her tacky costumes.* —**tack·i·ly** /'takəlē/ *adv.* —**tack·i·ness** *n.*

ta·co /'täkō/ ▸*n.* (*pl.* **-cos**) a Mexican dish consisting of a fried tortilla, typically folded, filled with various mixtures, such as seasoned meat, beans, lettuce, and tomatoes.

tact /takt/ ▸*n.* adroitness and sensitivity in dealing with others or with difficult issues: *the inspector broke the news to me with tact.*

tact·ful /'tak(t)fəl/ ▸*adj.* having or showing tact: *they need a tactful word of advice.* —**tact·ful·ly** *adv.* —**tact·ful·ness** *n.*

tac·tic /'taktik/ ▸*n.* an action or strategy carefully planned to achieve a specific end. ■ (**tactics**) [also treated as *sing.*] the art of disposing armed forces in order of battle and of organizing operations, esp. during contact with an enemy. —**tac·ti·cian** /tak'tiSHən/ *n.*

tac·ti·cal /'taktikəl/ ▸*adj.* of, relating to, or constituting actions carefully planned to gain a specific military end: *as a tactical officer in the field he had no equal.* ■ (of bombing or weapons) done or for use in immediate support of military or naval operations. ■ (of a person or their actions) showing adroit planning; aiming at an end beyond the immediate action. —**tac·ti·cal·ly** /-ik(ə)lē/ *adv.*

tac·tile /'taktl; 'tak,tīl/ ▸*adj.* of or connected with the sense of touch: *vocal and visual signals become less important as tactile signals intensify.* ■ perceptible by touch or apparently so; tangible: *an almost tactile memory.* ■ designed to be perceived by touch: *tactile exhibitions help blind people enjoy sculpture.* ■ (of a person) given to touching others, esp. as an unselfconscious expression of sympathy or affection. —**tac·til·i·ty** /tak'tilitē/ *n.*

tact·less /'taktləs/ ▸*adj.* having or showing a lack of adroitness and sensitivity in dealing with others or with difficult issues: *a tactless remark.* —**tact·less·ly** *adv.* —**tact·less·ness** *n.*

tad /tad/ *inf.* ▸*adv.* (**a tad**) to a small extent; somewhat: *Mark looked a tad embarrassed.*
▸*n.* a small amount of something: *sweetened with a tad of honey.*

tad·pole /'tad,pōl/ ▸*n.* the tailed aquatic larva of an amphibian (frog, toad, newt, or salamander), breathing through gills and lacking legs until its later stages of development.

tae kwon do /'tī 'kwän 'dō/ ▸*n.* a modern Korean martial art similar to karate.

taf·fe·ta /'tafitə/ ▸*n.* a fine lustrous silk or similar synthetic fabric with a crisp texture.

taf·fy /'tafē/ ▸*n.* (*pl.* **-fies**) **1** a candy made from sugar or molasses, boiled with butter and pulled until glossy. **2** *inf.* insincere flattery.

tag[1] /tag/ ▸*n.* **1** a label attached to someone or something for the purpose of identification or to give other information. ■ an electronic device that can be attached to someone or something for monitoring purposes, e.g., to deter shoplifters. ■ a nickname or description popularly given to someone or something. ■ a license plate of a motor vehicle. ■ *Comput.* a character or set of characters appended to or enclosing an item of data in order to identify it. **2** a small piece or part that is attached to a main body. ■ a ragged lock of wool on a sheep. ■ the tip of an animal's tail when it is distinctively colored. ■ a loose or spare end of something; a leftover. ■ a metal or plastic point at the end of a shoelace that stiffens it, making it easier to insert through an eyelet. **3** a frequently repeated quotation or stock phrase. ■ *Theater* a closing speech addressed to the audience. ■ the refrain of a song. ■ a musical phrase added to the end of a piece. ■ *Gram.* a short phrase or clause added to an already complete sentence, as in *I like it, I do.*
▸*v.* (**tagged, tag·ging**) [*tr.*] **1** attach a label to: *the bears were tagged and released.* ■ [*tr.*] give a specified name or description to: *he left because he didn't want to be tagged as a soap star.* ■ attach an electronic tag to. ■ *Comput.* add a character or set of characters to (an item of data) in order to identify it for later retrieval. ■ *Biol. & Chem.* label (something) with a radioactive isotope, fluorescent dye, or other marker: *pieces of DNA tagged with radioactive particles.* **2** [*tr.*] add to something, esp. as an afterthought or with no real connection: *she meant to tag her question on at the end of her remarks.* ■ [*intr.*] follow or accompany someone, esp. without invitation: *that'll teach you not to tag along where you're not wanted.* **3** shear away ragged locks of wool from (sheep).

tag[2] ▸*n.* a children's game in which one chases the rest, and anyone who is touched then becomes the pursuer. ■ *Baseball* the action of tagging out a runner or tagging a base.
▸*v.* (**tagged, tag·ging**) [*tr.*] touch (someone being chased) in a game of tag. ■ (**tag out**) *Baseball* put out (a runner) by touching them with the ball or with the glove holding the ball: *catching their fastest runner in a rundown and tagging him out.* ■ [*intr.*] (usu. **tag up**) *Baseball* (of a base runner) touch the base one has occupied after a fly ball is caught, before running to the next base: *when the ball was hit, he went back to the bag to tag up.*

Ta·ga·log /tə'gäləg; -lôg/ ▸*n.* **1** a member of a people originally of central Luzon in the Philippine Islands. **2** the Austronesian language of this people.

▶*adj.* of or relating to this people or their language.

Ta·hi·tian /təˈhēsHən/ ▶*n.* **1** a native or national of Tahiti, or a person of Tahitian descent. **2** the Polynesian language of Tahiti.

▶*adj.* of or relating to Tahiti, its people, or their language.

t'ai chi ch'uan /ˈtī ˌCHē ˈCHwän; ˌjē/ (also **t'ai chi** /ˈtī ˈCHē/) ▶*n.* **1** a Chinese martial art and system of calisthenics, consisting of sequences of very slow controlled movements. **2** (in Chinese philosophy) the ultimate source and limit of reality, from which spring yin and yang and all of creation.

tai·ga /ˈtīgə/ ▶*n.* (often **the taiga**) the sometimes swampy coniferous forest of high northern latitudes, esp. that between the tundra and steppes of Siberia and North America.

tail /tāl/ ▶*n.* **1** the hindmost part of an animal, esp. when prolonged beyond the rest of the body, such as the flexible extension of the backbone in a vertebrate, the feathers at the hind end of a bird, or a terminal appendage in an insect. ■ a thing resembling an animal's tail in its shape or position, typically something extending downward or outward at the end of something: *the trailed tail of a capital Q.* ■ the rear part of an airplane, with the horizontal stabilizer and rudder. ■ the lower or hanging part of a garment, esp. the back of a shirt or coat. ■ (**tails**) *inf.* a tailcoat; a man's formal evening suit with such a coat. ■ the luminous stream of particles ejected from a comet when it is near the sun; it extends away from the sun. **2** the end of a long train or line of people or vehicles: *an armored truck at the tail of the convoy.* ■ the final, more distant, or weaker part of something: *the forecast says we're in for the tail of a hurricane.* ■ *inf.* a person secretly following another to observe their movements. **3** *inf.* a person's buttocks. ■ *vulgar slang* a woman's genitals. ■ *inf., chiefly offens.* women collectively regarded as a means of sexual gratification: *chasing tail.* **4** (**tails**) the reverse side of a coin (used when tossing a coin).

▶*v.* [*tr.*] **1** *inf.* follow and observe (someone) closely, esp. in secret: *a flock of paparazzi had tailed them all over Paris.* ■ [*intr.*] follow: *they went to their favorite café—Bill and Sally tailed along.* **2** [*intr.*] (of an object in flight) drift or curve in a particular direction: *the next pitch tailed in on me at the last second.* **3** *rare* provide with a tail. **4** *archaic* join (one thing) to another: *each new row of houses tailed on its drains to those of its neighbors.*

▶*phrasal v.* ■ **tail off** (or **away**) gradually diminish in amount, strength, or intensity. ■ **tailed** *adj.* [in *comb.*] *a white-tailed deer.* ■ **tail·less** *adj.* ■ **tail·less·ness** *n.*

▶ □ **chase one's** (**own**) **tail** *inf.* rush around ineffectually. □ **on someone's tail** following someone closely: *a police car stayed on his tail for half a mile.* □ **with one's tail between one's legs** *inf.* in a state of dejection or humiliation.

tail·back /ˈtālˌbak/ ▶*n. Football* (in some offensive formations) the back who is positioned farthest from the line of scrimmage.

tail·coat /ˈtālˌkōt/ ▶*n.* a man's formal morning or evening coat, with a long skirt divided at the back into tails and cut away in front.

tail·gate /ˈtālˌgāt/ ▶*n.* a hinged flap at the back of a truck that can be lowered or removed when loading or unloading the vehicle. ■ the door at the back of a station wagon. ■ [as *adj.*] relating to or denoting an informal meal served from the back of a parked vehicle, typically in the parking lot of a sports stadium: *a huge tailgate party.* ■ [as *adj.*] denoting a style of jazz trombone playing characterized by improvisation in the manner of the early New Orleans musicians.

▶*v. inf.* **1** [*tr.*] drive too closely behind another vehicle: *he started tailgating the car in front* | [*intr.*] *drivers who will tailgate at 90 mph.* ■ (of a person or vehicle) gain unauthorized entry to a secured area by closely following someone with authority to enter: *a Toyota pickup that tailgated the delivery vehicle into the prison.* **2** [*intr.*] eat a meal from the back of a parked vehicle. ■ **tail·gat·er** *n.*

tail·light /ˈtālˌ(l)īt/ (also **tail·lamp**) ▶*n.* a red light at the rear of a motor vehicle, train, or bicycle.

tai·lor /ˈtālər/ ▶*n.* **1** a person whose occupation is making fitted clothes such as suits, pants, and jackets to fit individual customers. **2** (also **tai·lor·fish**) another term for BLUEFISH.

▶*v.* [*tr.*] (usu. **be tailored**) make (clothes) to fit individual customers: *a sports coat that had been tailored in New York.* ■ make or adapt for a particular purpose or person: *arrangements can be tailored to meet individual requirements.* ▷Middle English: from Anglo-Norman French *taillour*, literally 'cutter,' based on late Latin *taliare* 'to cut.' The verb dates from the mid 17th cent. ■ **tail·or·ing** *n.*

tai·lored /ˈtālərd/ ▶*adj.* **1** (of clothes) smart, fitted, and well cut: *a tailored charcoal-gray suit.* ■ (of clothes) cut in a particular way: *her clothes*

were well tailored and expensive. **2** made or adapted for a particular purpose or person: *specially tailored courses can be run on request.*

tai·lor-made ▶*adj.* (of clothes) made by a tailor for a particular customer: *tailor-made suits.* ■ made, adapted, or suited for a particular purpose or person: *he was tailor-made for the job.*

tail·piece /ˈtālˌpēs/ ▶*n.* a final or end part of something, in particular: ■ a part added to the end of a story or piece of writing. ■ a small decorative design at the foot of a page or the end of a chapter or book. ■ the piece at the base of a violin or other stringed instrument to which the strings are attached.

tail·pipe /ˈtālˌpīp/ ▶*n.* the rear section of the exhaust system of a motor vehicle.

tail·spin /ˈtālˌspin/ ▶*n.* an aircraft's diving descent combined with rotation. ■ a state or situation characterized by chaos, panic, or loss of control: *the rise in interest rates sent the stock market into a tailspin.*

▶*v.* (**-spin·ning**; *past* and *past part.* **-spun**) [*intr.*] become out of control.

tail·wheel /ˈtālˌ(h)wēl/ ▶*n.* a wheel supporting the tail of an aircraft, designed to ease handling while on the ground.

tail·wind /ˈtālˌwind/ ▶*n.* a wind blowing in the direction of travel of a vehicle or aircraft; a wind blowing from behind.

taint /tānt/ ▶*n.* a trace of a bad or undesirable quality or substance: *the taint of corruption that adhered to the regime.* ■ a thing whose influence or effect is perceived as contaminating or undesirable. ■ an unpleasant smell.

▶*v.* [*tr.*] (often **be tainted**) contaminate or pollute (something): *the air was tainted by fumes from the cars.* ■ affect with a bad or undesirable quality: *his administration was tainted by scandal.* ■ [*intr.*] *archaic* (of food or water) become contaminated or polluted. —**taint·less** *adj.* (*poetic/lit.*).

tai·pan /ˈtīˌpan/ ▶*n.* a foreigner who is head of a business in China or Hong Kong.

take /tāk/ ▶*v.* (*past* **took** /to͝ok/; *past part.* **tak·en** /ˈtākən/) [*tr.*] **1** lay hold of (something) with one's hands; reach for and hold: *he leaned forward to take her hand.* ■ [*tr.*] remove (someone or something) from a particular place: *he took an envelope from his inside pocket.* ■ consume as food, drink, medicine, or drugs: *take an aspirin and lie down.* ■ capture or gain possession of by force or military means: *the French took Ghent.* ■ (in bridge, hearts, and similar card games) win (a trick). ■ *Chess* capture (an opposing piece or pawn). ■ dispossess someone of (something); steal or illicitly remove: *someone must have sneaked in and taken it.* ■ cheat (someone) of something: *can I get taken by buying mutual funds?* ■ subtract: *take two from ten.* ■ occupy (a place or position): *we found that all the seats were taken.* ■ buy or rent (a house). ■ agree to buy (an item): *I'll take the one on the end.* ■ gain or acquire (possession or ownership of something). ■ (**be taken**) *humorous* (of a person) already be married or in an emotional relationship. ■ [in *imper.*] use or have ready to use: *take half the marzipan and roll out.* ■ [usu. in *imper.*] use as an instance or example in support of an argument: *let's take Napoleon, for instance.* ■ regularly buy or subscribe to (a particular newspaper or periodical). ■ ascertain by measurement or observation: *the nurse takes my blood pressure.* ■ write down: *he was taking notes.* ■ make (a photograph) with a camera. ■ (usu. **be taken**) (esp. of illness) suddenly strike or afflict (someone): *he was taken with a seizure of some kind.* ■ have sexual intercourse with. **2** [*tr.*] carry or bring with one; convey: *he took along a portfolio of his drawings* | *I took him a letter.* ■ accompany or guide (someone) to a specified place: *I'll take you to your room.* ■ bring into a specified state: *the invasion took Europe to the brink of war.* ■ use as a route or a means of transportation: *take 95 north to Baltimore.* **3** accept or receive (someone or something): *she was advised to take any job offered.* ■ understand or accept as valid: *I take your point.* ■ acquire or assume (a position, state, or form): *he took office in September.* ■ achieve or attain (a victory or result): *John Martin took the men's title.* ■ act on (an opportunity): *he took his chance to get out while the house was quiet.* ■ experience or be affected by: *the lad took a savage beating.* ■ tolerate, stand: *I can't take the humidity.* ■ [*tr.*] react to or regard (news or an event) in a specified way: *she took the news well* | *everything you say, he takes it the wrong way.* ■ [*tr.*] deal with (a physical obstacle or course) in a specified way: *he takes the corners with no concern for his own safety.* ■ *Baseball* (of a batter) allow (a pitch) to go by without attempting to hit the ball. ■ regard or view in a specified way: *he somehow took it as a personal insult.* ■ (**be taken by/with**) be attracted or charmed by: *Billie was very taken with him.* ■ submit to, tolerate, or endure: *they refused to take it any more.* ■ (**take it**) assume: *I take it that someone is coming to meet you.* **4** make, undertake, or perform (an action or task): *Lucy took a deep breath.* ■ be taught or be examined in (a subject): *some degrees require a student to take a secondary subject.* ■ *Brit.* obtain (an academic degree) after fulfilling the required conditions: *she took a degree in English.* **5** require or use up (a specified amount of time): *the jury took an hour to find McPherson guilty | it takes me a quarter of an hour to walk to work.* ■ (of a task or situation) need or call for (a particular person or thing): *it will take an electronics expert to dismantle it.* ■ hold; accommodate: *an exclusive island hideaway that takes just twenty guests.* ■ wear or require (a particular size of garment or type of complementary article): *he takes size 5 boots.* **6** [*intr.*] (of a plant or seed) take root or begin to grow; germinate. ■ (of an added substance) become successfully established. **7** *Gram.* have or require as part of the appropriate construction: *verbs that take both the infinitive and the finite clause as their object.*

▶*phrasal v.* □ **take after** resemble (a parent or ancestor): *the rest of us take after our mother.* □ **take something apart** dismantle something. ■ (**take someone/something apart**) *inf.* attack, criticize, or defeat someone or something in a vigorous or forceful way. □ **take away from** detract from. □ **take someone back** strongly remind someone of a past time: *if "Disco Inferno" doesn't take you back, the bell-bottom pants will.* □ **take something back 1** retract a statement. **2** return unsatisfactory goods to a store. ■ (of a store) accept such goods. □ **take something down 1** write down spoken words. **2** dismantle and remove a structure. □ **take from** another way of saying TAKE AWAY FROM. □ **take someone in 1** accommodate someone as a lodger or because they are homeless or in difficulties. **2** cheat, fool, or deceive someone: *she tried to pass this off as an amusing story, but nobody was taken in.* □ **take something in 1** undertake work at home: *she took in laundry on weekends.* **2** make a garment tighter by altering its seams. ■ *Sailing* furl a sail. **3** receive a specified amount of money as payment or earnings: *our club took in $800,000 in its first year.* **4** include or encompass something: *the sweep of his arm took in most of Main Street.* ■ fully understand or absorb something heard or seen: *she took in the scene at a glance.* **5** visit or attend a place or event in a casual way or on the way to another: *he'd maybe take in a movie.* □ **take off 1** (of an aircraft or bird) become airborne. ■ (of an enterprise) become successful or popular: *the newly launched electronic newspaper has really taken off.* **2** depart hastily. □ **take something off 1** remove clothing from one's or another's body. **2** deduct part of an amount. **3** choose to have a period away from work: *I took the next day off.* □ **take someone on 1** hire an employee. **2** be willing or ready to meet an adversary or opponent, esp. a stronger one: *a group of villagers has taken on the planners.* □ **take something on 1** undertake a task or responsibility, esp. a difficult one. **2** acquire a particular meaning or quality: *the subject has taken on a new significance in the past year.* □ **take someone out** to escort, as on a date. □ **take someone/something out** *inf.* kill, destroy, or disable someone or something. □ **take something out 1** obtain an official document or service: *you can take out a loan for a specific purchase.* ■ get a license or summons issued. **2** buy food at a café or restaurant for eating elsewhere: *he ordered a lamb madras to take out.* □ **take something out on** relieve frustration or anger by attacking or mistreating (a person or thing not responsible for such feelings). □ **take something over** (also **take over**) assume control of something. ■ (of a company) buy out another. ■ become responsible for a task in succession to another: *he will take over as chief executive in April.* □ **take to 1** begin or fall into the habit of: *he took to hiding some secret supplies in his desk.* **2** form a liking for: *Mrs. Brady never took to Moran.* ■ develop an ability for (something), esp. quickly or easily. **3** go to (a place) to escape danger or an enemy: *they took to the hills.* □ **take something up 1** become interested or engaged in a pursuit: *she took up tennis at the age of 11.* ■ begin to hold or fulfill a position or post: *an appointment as a missionary.* ■ accept an offer or challenge. **2** occupy time, space, or attention: *I don't want to take up any more of your time.* **3** pursue a matter later or further: *he'll have to take it up with the bishop.* ■ (also **take up**) resume speaking after an interruption: *I took up where I had left off.* **4** shorten a garment by turning up the hem. □ **take someone up on 1** accept (an offer or challenge) from someone. **2** challenge or question a speaker on (a particular point). □ **take up with** begin to associate with (someone), esp. in a way disapproved of by the speaker: *he's taken up with a divorced woman, I understand.*

▶*n.* **1** a scene or sequence of sound or vision photographed or recorded continuously at one time. ■ a particular version of or approach to something: *his own whimsical take on life.* **2** an amount of something gained or acquired from one source or in one session: *the take from commodity taxation.* ■ the money received at a theater, arena, etc., for seats. —**tak·a·ble** /ˈtākəbəl/ (also **take·a·ble**) *adj.*

▶ □ **be on the take** *inf.* take bribes. □ **have what it takes** *inf.* have the necessary qualities for success. □ **take the cake** *inf.* (of a person or incident) be the most remarkable or foolish of their kind. □ **take five** (or **ten**) take a five (or ten) minute break before resuming work or another activity. □ **take a lot of** (or **some**) —— be difficult to do or effect in the specified way: *he might take some convincing.* □ **take someone in**

hand undertake to control or reform someone. □ **take something in hand** start doing or dealing with a task. □ **take the heat** *inf.* accept blame or withstand disapproval. □ **take it from me** I can assure you: *take it from me, kid—I've been there.* □ **take it on one** (or **oneself**) **to do something** decide to do something without asking for permission or advice. □ **take it or leave it** [usu. in *imper.*] said to express that the offer one has made is not negotiable and that one is indifferent to another's reaction to it: *that's the deal—take it or leave it.* □ **take it out of** exhaust the strength of (someone): *parties can take it out of you, especially if you are over 65.* □ **take sick** (or **ill**) *inf.* become ill, esp. suddenly. □ **take the stand** testify at a trial. □ **take that!** exclaimed when hitting someone or taking decisive action against them. □ **take one's time** not hurry.

take-home pay ▶*n.* the pay received by an employee after the deduction of taxes and other obligations.

take·off /ˈtākˌôf; -ˌäf/ (also **take-off**) ▶*n.* **1** the action of becoming airborne: *the plane accelerated down the runway for takeoff.* **2** an act of mimicking someone or something.

take·out /ˈtākˌout/ (also **take-out**) ▶*n.* **1** food that is cooked and sold by a restaurant or store to be eaten elsewhere: *cartons of Chinese takeout for late-night dinners* | [as *adj.*] *takeout pizza.* **2** *Bridge* a bid in a different suit made in response to a bid or double by one's partner.

take·o·ver /ˈtākˌōvər/ ▶*n.* an act of assuming control of something, esp. the buying out of one company by another.

tak·er /ˈtākər/ ▶*n.* **1** [in *comb.*] a person who takes a specified thing: *a risk-taker.* **2** a person who takes a bet or accepts an offer or challenge: *there were plenty of takers when I offered a small wager.*

tak·ing /ˈtākiNG/ ▶*n.* **1** the action or process of taking something: *the taking of life.* **2** (**takings**) the amount of money earned by a business from the sale of goods or services: *box-office takings were scant.*

▶*adj.* *dated* (of a person) captivating in manner; charming: *he was not a very taking person, she felt.* —**tak·ing·ly** *adv.*

▶ □ **for the taking** ready or available for someone to take advantage of: *the big money is out there for the taking.*

talc /talk/ ▶*n.* talcum powder. ■ a white, gray, or pale green soft magnesium-silicate mineral with a greasy feel, occurring as translucent masses or laminae.

▶*v.* (**talced, talc·ing**) [*tr.*] powder or treat (something) with talc. —**talc·ose** /ˈtalkōs/ *adj.* (*Geol.*). —**talc·y** /ˈtalkē/ *adj.*

tal·cum /ˈtalkəm/ (also **talcum powder**) ▶*n.* a cosmetic or toilet preparation consisting of the mineral talc in powdered form, typically perfumed.

▶*v.* (**-cumed, -cum·ing**) [*tr.*] powder (something) with this substance.

tale /tāl/ ▶*n.* a fictitious or true narrative or story, esp. one that is imaginatively recounted. ■ a lie.

tal·ent /ˈtalənt/ ▶*n.* **1** natural aptitude or skill: *he possesses more talent than any other player* | *she displayed a talent for garden design.* ■ people possessing such aptitude or skill: *I signed all the talent in Rome.* ■ *inf.* people regarded as sexually attractive or as prospective sexual partners:. **2** a former weight and unit of currency, used esp. by the ancient Romans and Greeks. —**tal·ent·less** *adj.*

tal·ent·ed /ˈtaləntid/ ▶*adj.* having a natural aptitude or skill for something: *a talented young musician.*

tal·ent scout ▶*n.* a person whose job is to search for talented performers who can be employed or promoted, esp. in sports and entertainment.

ta·li /ˈtā,lī/ ▶ plural form of TALUS[1].

tal·is·man /ˈtalismən; -iz-/ ▶*n.* (*pl.* **-mans**) an object, typically an inscribed ring or stone, that is thought to have magic powers and to bring good luck. —**tal·is·man·ic** /ˌtaliz'manik/ *adj.*

talk /tôk/ ▶*v.* [*intr.*] speak in order to give information or express ideas or feelings; converse or communicate by spoken words: *the two men talked* | *we'd sit and talk about jazz* | [*tr.*] *you're talking rubbish.* ■ have the power of speech: *he can talk as well as you or I can.* ■ discuss personal or intimate feelings: *we need to talk, Maggie.* ■ have formal dealings or discussions; negotiate: *they won't talk to the regime that killed their families.* ■ (**talk something over/through**) discuss something thoroughly. ■ (**talk at**) address (someone) in a hectoring or self-important way without listening to their replies. ■ (**talk to**) reprimand or scold (someone). ■ [*tr.*] (**be talking**) *inf.* used to emphasize the seriousness, importance, or extent of the thing one is mentioning or in the process of discussing: *we're talking big money.* ■ [*tr.*] use (a particular language) in speech: *we were* *talking German.* ■ [*tr.*] persuade or cause (someone) to do something by talking: *don't try to talk me into acting as a go-between.* ■ reveal secret or confidential information; betray secrets. ■ gossip.

▸**phrasal v.** □ **talk back** reply defiantly or insolently. □ **talk down to** speak patronizingly or condescendingly to. □ **talk someone through** enable someone to perform (a task) by giving them continuous instruction. □ **talk someone/something up** (or **down**) discuss someone or something in a way that makes them seem more (or less) interesting or attractive.

▸*n.* conversation; discussion: *there was a slight but noticeable lull in the talk.* ■ a period of conversation or discussion, esp. a relatively serious one: *my mother had a talk with Louis.* ■ an informal address or lecture. ■ rumor, gossip, or speculation: *there is talk of an armistice.* ■ empty promises or boasting: *he's all talk.* ■ (**the talk of**) a current subject of widespread gossip or speculation in (a particular place): *within days I was the talk of the town.* ■ (**talks**) formal discussions or negotiations over a period: *peace talks.* —**talk·er** *n.*

▸ □ **don't talk to me about** —— *inf.* said in protest when someone introduces a subject of which the speaker has had bitter personal experience. □ **know what one is talking about** be expert or authoritative on a specified subject. □ **look who's talking** another way of saying YOU SHOULDN'T TALK. □ **you shouldn't** (or **should**) **talk** *inf.* used to convey that a criticism made applies equally well to the person who has made it: *"He'd chase anything in a skirt!" "You shouldn't talk!"* □ **talk about** ——! *inf.* used to emphasize that something is an extreme or striking example of a particular situation, state, or experience: *Talk about hangovers! But aching head or not we were getting ready.* □ **talk sense into** persuade (someone) to behave more sensibly. □ **talk through one's hat** *inf.* talk foolishly, wildly, or ignorantly.

talk·a·tive /'tôkətiv/ ▸*adj.* fond of or given to talking: *the talkative driver hadn't stopped chatting.* —**talk·a·tive·ly** *adv.* —**talk·a·tive·ness** *n.*

talk·ie /'tôkē/ ▸*n. inf.* a movie with a soundtrack, as distinct from a silent film.

talk·ing /'tôkiNG/ ▸*adj.* engaging in speech. ■ (of an animal or object) able to make sounds similar to those of speech: *the world's greatest talking bird.* ■ silently expressive: *he did have talking eyes.*

▸*n.* the action of talking; speech or discussion: *I'll do the talking—you just back me up.*

▸ □ **talking of** —— while we are on the subject of —— (said when one is reminded of something by the present topic of conversation): *talking of cards, you'd better take a couple of my business cards.*

talk·ing book ▸*n.* a recorded reading of a book, originally designed for use by the blind.

talk·ing head ▸*n. inf.* a commentator or reporter on television who addresses the camera and is viewed in close-up.

talk·ing-to ▸*n. inf.* a sharp reprimand in which someone is told that they have done wrong.

talk show ▸*n.* a television or radio show in which various topics are discussed informally and listeners, viewers, or the studio audience are invited to participate in the discussion.

tall /tôl/ ▸*adj.* **1** of great or more than average height, esp. (with reference to an object) relative to width: *a tall, broad-shouldered man.* ■ (after a measurement and in questions) measuring a specified distance from top to bottom: *he was over six feet tall | how tall are you?* ■ [as *adv.*] used in reference to proud and confident movement or behavior: *stop wishing that you were somehow different—start to walk tall!* **2** *inf.* (of an account) fanciful and difficult to believe; unlikely: *sometimes it's hard to tell a legend from a tall tale.* —**tall·ish** *adj.* —**tall·ness** *n.*

▸ □ **a tall order** an unreasonable or difficult demand.

tall·boy /'tôl,boi/ ▸*n. chiefly Brit.* a tall chest of drawers, typically one mounted on legs and in two sections, one standing on the other. Compare with HIGHBOY.

tal·lith /'tälis; tä'lēt/ (also **tal·lis**) ▸*n.* a fringed shawl traditionally worn by Jewish men at prayer.

tal·low /'talō/ ▸*n.* a hard fatty substance made from rendered animal fat, used in making candles and soap.

▸*v.* [*tr.*] *archaic* smear (something, esp. the bottom of a boat) with such a substance. —**tal·low·y** *adj.*

tall ship ▸*n.* a sailing ship with high masts.

tal·ly /'talē/ ▸*n.* (*pl.* -lies) **1** a current score or amount: *that takes his tally to 10 goals in 10 games.* ■ a record of a score or amount: *I kept a running tally of David's debt.* ■ a particular number taken as a group or unit to facilitate counting. ■ a mark registering such a number. ■ (also **tally stick**) *hist.* a piece of wood scored across with notches for the items of an account and then split into halves, each party keeping one. ■ an account kept in such a way. ■ *archaic* a counterpart or duplicate of

something. **2** a label attached to a plant or tree, or stuck in the ground beside it, that gives information about it, such as its name and class.

▸*v.* (-lies, -lied) **1** [*intr.*] agree or correspond: *their signatures should tally with their names on the register.* **2** [*tr.*] calculate the total number of: *the votes were being tallied with abacuses.* —**tal·li·er** *n.*

tal·ly·ho /'talē'hō/ (also **tal·ly-ho**) ▸*interj.* a huntsman's cry to the hounds on sighting a fox.

▸*n.* (*pl.* -hos) **1** an utterance of this. **2** *hist.* a fast horse-drawn coach.

▸*v.* (-hoes, -hoed) [*intr.*] utter a cry of "tallyho."

Tal·mud /'täl,mŏŏd; 'talməd/ ▸*n.* (**the Talmud**) the body of Jewish civil and ceremonial law and legend comprising the Mishnah and the Gemara. —**Tal·mud·ic** /tal'm(y)ŏŏdik; -'mŏŏdik/ *adj.* —**Tal·mud·i·cal** /tal-'m(y)ŏŏdikəl; -'mŏŏd-/ *adj.* —**Tal·mud·ist** /'talmŏŏdist; 'talməd-/ *n.*

tal·on /'talən/ ▸*n.* **1** a claw, esp. one belonging to a bird of prey. **2** (in various card games) the cards remaining undealt. —**tal·oned** *adj.*

ta·lus¹ /'tāləs/ ▸*n.* (*pl.* **ta·li** /'tālī/) *Anat.* the large bone in the ankle that articulates with the tibia of the leg and the calcaneum and navicular bone of the foot.

ta·lus² ▸*n.* (*pl.* **ta·lus·es**) a sloping mass of rock fragments at the foot of a cliff. ■ the sloping side of an earthwork, or of a wall that tapers to the top.

ta·ma·le /tə'mälē/ ▸*n.* a Mexican dish of seasoned meat wrapped in cornmeal dough and steamed or baked in corn husks. ▷from Mexican Spanish *tamal*, plural *tamales*, from Nahuatl *tamalli.*

tam·a·rack /'tamə,rak/ ▸*n.* a slender North American larch (*Larix laricina*).

tam·a·rind /'tamə,rind/ ▸*n.* **1** sticky brown acidic pulp from the pod of a tree of the pea family, widely used as a flavoring in Asian cooking. ■ the pod from which this pulp is extracted. **2** the tropical African tree (*Tamarindus indica*) that yields these pods, cultivated throughout the tropics and also grown as an ornamental and shade tree.

tam·a·risk /'tamə,risk/ ▸*n.* an Old World shrub or small tree (genus *Tamarix*, family Tamaricaceae) with tiny scalelike leaves borne on slender branches, giving it a feathery appearance.

tam·bour /'tam,bŏŏr/ ▸*n.* **1** *hist.* a small drum. **2** something resembling a drum in shape or construction, in particular: ■ a circular frame for holding fabric taut while it is being embroidered. ■ *Archit.* a wall of circular plan, such as one supporting a dome or surrounded by a colonnade. ■ *Archit.* each of a sequence of cylindrical stones forming the shaft of a column. ■ [usu. as *adj.*] a sliding flexible shutter or door on a piece of furniture, made of strips of wood attached to a backing of canvas.

tam·bou·ra /tam'bŏŏrə/ (also **tam·bu·ra**) ▸*n.* **1** a large four-stringed lute used in Indian music as a drone accompaniment. **2** a long-necked lute or mandolin of Balkan countries.

tam·bou·rine /,tambə'rēn/ ▸*n.* a percussion instrument resembling a shallow drum with small metal disks in slots around the edge, played by being shaken or hit with the hand. —**tam·bou·rin·ist** *n.*

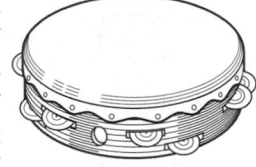
tambourine

tame /tām/ ▸*adj.* **1** (of an animal) not dangerous or frightened of people; domesticated: *the fish are so tame you have to push them away from your face mask.* ■ not exciting, adventurous, or controversial: *network TV on Saturday night is a pretty tame affair.* ■ *inf.* (of a person) willing to cooperate. **2** (of a plant) produced by cultivation.

▸*v.* [*tr.*] domesticate (an animal). ■ make less powerful and easier to control: *the battle to tame inflation.* ■ cultivate (land or wilderness). —**tam·a·ble** (also **tame·a·ble**) *adj.* —**tame·ly** *adv.* —**tame·ness** *n.* —**tam·er** *n.*

Tam·il /'taməl/ ▸*n.* **1** a member of a people inhabiting parts of southern India and Sri Lanka. **2** the Dravidian language of the Tamils.

▸*adj.* of or relating to this people or their language. —**Tam·il·i·an** /tə-'milēən/ *adj. & n.*

tam-o'-shan·ter /'tam ə ,sHantər/ ▸*n.* a round woolen or cloth cap of Scottish origin, with a pom-pom in the center.

tamp /tamp/ ▸*v.* [*tr.*] pack (a blast hole) full of clay or sand to concentrate the force of the explosion: *when the hole was tamped to the top, gunpowder was inserted.* ■ [*tr.*] ram or pack (a substance) down or into something firmly: *he tamped down the tobacco with his thumb.*

tam·per /'tampər/ ▸*v.* **1** [*intr.*] (**tamper with**) interfere with (something) in order to cause damage or make unauthorized alterations: *someone tampered with the brakes on my car.* **2** [*intr.*] (**tamper with**) exert a secret or corrupt influence upon (someone).

▶*n.* a person or thing that tamps something down, esp. a machine or tool for tamping down earth or ballast. —**tam·per·er** *n.* —**tam·per·proof** *adj.*

tam·pon /'tam,pän/ ▶*n.* a plug of soft material inserted into the vagina to absorb menstrual blood. ■ *Med.* a plug of material used to stop a wound or block an opening in the body and absorb blood or secretions. ▶*v.* (**-poned, -pon·ing**) [*tr.*] plug with a tampon.

tam·tam /'təm ,təm; 'tam ,tam/ ▶*n.* a large metal gong with indefinite pitch.

tan[1] /tan/ ▶*n.* **1** a yellowish-brown color: *the overall color scheme of tan and cream.* ■ a golden-brown shade of skin developed by pale-skinned people after exposure to the sun. **2** (also **tan·bark** /'tan,bärk/) bark of oak or other trees, bruised and used as a source of tannin for converting hides into leather. ■ such bark from which the tannin has been extracted, used for covering the ground for walking, riding, children's play, etc., and in gardening. ▶*v.* (**tanned, tan·ning**) **1** [*intr.*] (of a pale-skinned person or their skin) become brown or browner after exposure to the sun: *you'll tan very quickly in the pure air.* ■ [*tr.*] [usu. as *adj.*] (of the sun) cause (a pale-skinned person or their skin) to become brown or browner. **2** [*tr.*] convert (animal skin) into leather by soaking in a liquid containing tannic acid, or by the use of other chemicals. **3** [*tr.*] *inf., dated* beat (someone) repeatedly, esp. as a punishment: *"If Mickey touches a fishing net, I'll tan his hide!"* ▶*adj.* of a yellowish-brown color: *a tan baseball cap with orange piping.* ■ (of a pale-skinned person) having golden-brown skin after exposure to the sun: *she looks tall, tan, and healthy.* —**tan·na·ble** *adj.* —**tan·nish** *adj.*

tan[2] ▶*abbr.* tangent.

tan·a·ger /'tanəjər/ ▶*n.* a small American songbird (*Tangara* and other genera) of the bunting family, the male of which typically has brightly colored plumage.

tan·bark /'tan,bärk/ ▶*n.* see **TAN**[1] (sense 2).

tan·dem /'tandəm/ ▶*n.* (also **tandem bicycle**) a bicycle with seats and pedals for two riders, one behind the other. ■ a carriage driven by two animals harnessed one in front of the other. ■ a group of two people or machines working together. ■ a truck with two rear drive axles. ▶*adv.* with two or more horses harnessed one behind another: *I rode tandem to Paris.* ■ alongside each other; together. ▶*adj.* having two things arranged one in front of the other: *satisfactory steering angles can be maintained with tandem trailers.* ▶ □ **in tandem** alongside each other; together. ■ one behind another.

tan·door /tan'dŏŏr; tän-/ ▶*n.* a clay oven of a type used originally in northern India and Pakistan.

tan·door·i /tan'dŏŏrē; tän-/ ▶*adj.* denoting or relating to a style of Indian cooking based on the use of a tandoor: *tandoori chicken.* ▶*n.* food or cooking of this type. ■ a restaurant serving such food.

Tang /tang/ ▶a dynasty ruling China 618–c.906, a period noted for territorial conquest and great wealth and regarded as the golden age of Chinese poetry and art.

tang[1] /tang/ ▶*n.* **1** a strong taste, flavor, or smell: *the clean salty tang of the sea.* ■ a characteristic quality: *the tang of finality hovers throughout Tolstoy's story.* **2** the projection on the blade of a tool such as a knife, by which the blade is held firmly in the handle.

tang[2] ▶*v.* [*intr.*] make a loud ringing or clanging sound. ▶*n.* a tanging sound.

tang[3] ▶*n.* a deep-bodied and brightly colored tropical marine fish (genus *Acanthurus*, family Acanthuridae) with a scalpel-like spine on each side of the tail. It occurs around reefs and rocky areas, where it browses on algae.

tan·ge·lo /'tanjə,lō/ ▶*n.* (*pl.* **-los**) a hybrid of the tangerine and grapefruit.

tan·gent /'tanjənt/ ▶*n.* **1** a straight line or plane that touches a curve or curved surface at a point, but if extended does not cross it at that point. ■ *fig.* a completely different line of thought or action: *she went off on a tangent about how she and her husband had driven past a department store window.* **2** *Math.* the trigonometric function that is equal to the ratio of the sides (other than the hypotenuse) opposite and adjacent to an angle in a right triangle. ▶*adj.* (of a line or plane) touching, but not intersecting, a curve or curved surface. —**tan·gen·cy** /-jənsē/ *n.*

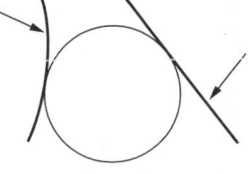

tangent

tan·gen·tial /tan'jenCHəl/ ▶*adj.* of, relating to, or along a tangent: *a tangential line.* ■ diverging from a previous course or line; erratic: *tangential*

thoughts. ■ hardly touching a matter; peripheral: *the reforms were tangential to efforts to maintain a basic standard of life.* —**tan·gen·tial·ly** *adv.*

tan·ge·rine /,tanjə'rēn/ ▶*n.* **1** a small citrus fruit with a loose skin, esp. one of a variety with deep orange-red skin. ■ a deep orange-red color. **2** the tree (*Citrus reticulata*) that bears this fruit.

tan·gi·ble /'tanjəbəl/ ▶*adj.* perceptible by touch: *the atmosphere of neglect and abandonment was almost tangible.* ■ clear and definite; real: *the emphasis is now on tangible results.* ▶*n.* (usu. **tangibles**) a thing that is perceptible by touch. —**tan·gi·bil·i·ty** /,tanjə'bilitē/ *n.* —**tan·gi·ble·ness** *n.* —**tan·gi·bly** /-blē/ *adv.*

tan·gle /'tanggəl/ ▶*v.* [*tr.*] twist together into a confused mass: *the broom got tangled up in my long skirt.* ■ [*intr.*] (**tangle with**) *inf.* become involved in a conflict or fight with: *there'll be trouble if I try to tangle with him.* ▶*n.* a confused mass of something twisted together: *a tangle of golden hair.* ■ a confused or complicated state; a muddle. ■ *inf.* a fight, argument, or disagreement. —**tan·gly** /-g(ə)lē/ *adj.* ▶ □ **a tangled web** a complex, difficult, and confusing situation or thing.

tan·go /'tanggō/ ▶*n.* (*pl.* **-gos**) **1** a ballroom dance originating in Buenos Aires, characterized by marked rhythms and postures and abrupt pauses. ■ a piece of music written for or in the style of this dance, typically in a slow dotted duple rhythm. **2** a code word representing the letter T, used in voice communication by radio. ▶*v.* (**-goes, -goed**) [*intr.*] dance the tango.

tan·gram /'tan,gram/ ▶*n.* a Chinese geometric puzzle consisting of a square cut into seven pieces that can be arranged to make various other shapes.

tang·y /'tangē/ ▶*adj.* (**tang·i·er, tang·i·est**) having a strong, piquant flavor or smell: *a tangy salad.* —**tang·i·ness** *n.*

tank /tangk/ ▶*n.* **1** a large receptacle or storage chamber, esp. for liquid or gas. ■ the container holding the fuel supply in a motor vehicle. ■ a receptacle with transparent sides in which to keep fish; an aquarium. **2** a heavy armored fighting vehicle carrying guns and moving on a continuous articulated metal track. **3** *inf.* a cell in a police station or jail. ▶*v.* **1** [*intr.*] fill the tank of a vehicle with fuel: *the cars stopped to tank up.* ■ (**be/get tanked up**) *inf.* drink heavily; become drunk: *they get tanked up before the game.* **2** [*intr.*] *inf.* fail completely, esp. at great financial cost. ■ [*tr.*] *inf.* (in sports) deliberately lose or fail to finish (a game): *the lackluster performance prompted speculation that he tanked the second set.* —**tank·ful** /-,fŏŏl/ *n.* (*pl.* **-fuls**). —**tank·less** *adj.*

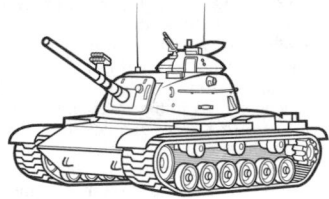

tank

tan·kard /'tangkərd/ ▶*n.* a tall beer mug, typically made of silver or pewter, with a handle and sometimes a hinged lid. ■ the contents of or an amount held by such a mug: *I've downed a tankard of ale.*

tank·er /'tangkər/ ▶*n.* **1** a ship, road vehicle, or aircraft for carrying liquids, esp. petroleum, in bulk. **2** *Mil.* member of a tank crew.

tank top ▶*n.* a close-fitting sleeveless top.

tan·ner /'tanər/ ▶*n.* **1** a person who tans animal hides, esp. to earn a living. **2** a lotion or cream designed to promote the development of a suntan or produce a similar skin color artificially.

tan·ner·y /'tanərē/ ▶*n.* (*pl.* **-ner·ies**) a place where animal hides are tanned; the workshop of a tanner.

tan·nic /'tanik/ ▶*adj.* of or related to tannin.

tan·nic ac·id ▶*n.* another term for TANNIN. —**tan·nate** /'tanāt/ *n.*

tan·nin /'tanin/ ▶*n.* a yellowish or brownish bitter-tasting organic substance present in some galls, barks, and other plant tissues, consisting of derivatives of gallic acid, used in leather production and ink manufacture.

tan·sy /'tanzē/ ▶*n.* a plant (genus *Tanacetum*) of the daisy family, with yellow flat-topped buttonlike flowerheads and aromatic leaves.

Pronunciation Key ə *ago,* up; ər *over,* fur; a *hat;* ā *ate;* ä *car;* CH *chin;* e *let;* ē *see;* e(ə)r *air;* i *fit;* ī *by;* i(ə)r *ear;* NG *sing;* ō *go;* ô *law, for;* oi *toy;* ŏŏ *good;* ōō *goo;* ou *out;* SH *she;* TH *thin;* <u>TH</u> *then;* (h)w *why;* ZH *vision*

tan·ta·lize /ˈtantlˌīz/ ▸v. [tr.] torment or tease (someone) with the sight or promise of something that is unobtainable: *such ambitious questions have long tantalized the world's best thinkers.* ■ excite the senses or desires of (someone): *she still tantalized him* | [as *adj.*] (**tantalizing**) *the tantalizing fragrance of fried bacon.* —**tan·ta·li·za·tion** /ˌtantliˈzāsʜən/ *n.* —**tan·ta·liz·er** *n.* —**tan·ta·liz·ing·ly** *adv.*

tan·ta·lum /ˈtantl-əm/ ▸n. the chemical element of atomic number 73, a hard silver-gray metal of the transition series. (Symbol: **Ta**) —**tan·tal·ic** /tanˈtalik/ *adj.*

tan·ta·mount /ˈtantəˌmount/ ▸adj. (**tantamount to**) equivalent in seriousness to; virtually the same as: *the resignations were tantamount to an admission of guilt.*

Tan·tra /ˈtəntrə; ˈtan-/ ▸n. a Hindu or Buddhist mystical or ritual text, dating from the 6th to the 13th centuries. ■ adherence to the doctrines or principles of the tantras, involving mantras, meditation, yoga, and ritual. —**tan·tric** /-trik/ *adj.* —**tan·trism** /-ˌtrizəm/ *n.* —**tan·trist** /-trist/ *n.*

tan·trum /ˈtantrəm/ ▸n. an uncontrolled outburst of anger and frustration, typically in a young child: *he has **temper tantrums** if he can't get his own way.*

Tao·ism /ˈdouˌizəm; ˈtou-/ ▸n. a Chinese philosophy based on the writings of Lao-tzu (*fl.* 6th century BC), advocating humility and religious piety. —**Tao·ist** *n.* & *adj.* —**Tao·is·tic** /touˈistik/ *adj.*

tap[1] /tap/ ▸n. **1** a device by which a flow of liquid or gas from a pipe or container can be controlled. ■ a device connected to a telephone used for listening secretly to someone's conversations. ■ an act of listening secretly to someone's telephone conversation. ■ (also **tap·ping**) an electrical connection made to some point between the end terminals of a transformer coil or other component. **2** an instrument for cutting a threaded hole, esp. in metal.
▸v. (**tapped**, **tap·ping**) [tr.] **1** draw liquid through the tap or spout of (a cask, barrel, or other container). ■ draw (liquid) from a cask, barrel, or other container: *the butlers were tapping new and old ale.* ■ connect a device to (a telephone) so that conversation can be listened to secretly: *the telephones were tapped by the state security police.* ■ *inf.* obtain money or information from (someone): *he considered whom he could tap for information.* ■ exploit or draw a supply from (a resource): *clients from industry seeking to tap Philadelphia's resources of expertise* | [intr.] *these magazines have **tapped into** a target market of consumers.* ■ draw sap from (a tree) by cutting into it. **2** cut a thread in (something) to accept a screw. —**tap·pa·ble** *adj.*
▸ □ **on tap** ready to be poured from a tap. ■ *inf.* freely available whenever needed. ■ *inf.* on schedule to occur.

tap[2] ▸v. (**tapped**, **tap·ping**) [tr.] **1** strike (someone or something) with a quick light blow or blows: *one of my staff tapped me on the shoulder.* ■ strike (something) against something else with a quick light blow or blows: *Gloria was tapping her feet in time to the music.* ■ (**tap something out**) produce (a rhythm) with a series of quick light blows on a surface: *drums tapped out a rumba beat.* ■ write or enter (something) using a keyboard or keypad: *he **tapped out** a few words on the keyboard.* **2** *inf.* designate or select (someone) for a task or honor, esp. membership in an organization or committee: *he had been tapped to serve in Costa Rica.*
▸n. **1** a quick light blow or the sound of such a blow. **2** tap dancing. ■ a piece of metal attached to the toe and heel of a tap dancer's shoe to make a tapping sound. **3** (**taps**) [treated as *sing.* or *pl.*] a bugle call for lights to be put out in army quarters. ■ a similar call sounded at a military funeral. —**tap·per** *n.*

tap dance ▸n. a dance performed wearing shoes fitted with metal taps, characterized by rhythmical tapping of the toes and heels.
▸v. [intr.] (**tap-dance**) perform such a dance. —**tap danc·er** *n.* —**tap danc·ing** *n.*

tape /tāp/ ▸n. a narrow strip of material, typically used to hold or fasten something: *a roll of tape.* ■ long narrow flexible material with magnetic properties, used for recording sound, pictures, or computer data. ■ a cassette or reel containing such material. ■ a recording on such a cassette or reel. ■ a strip of paper or plastic coated with adhesive, used to stick things together. ■ a strip of material stretched across the finish line of a race, to be broken by the winner. ■ a strip of white material at the top of a tennis net. ■ a strip of material used to mark off an area. ■ a tape measure.
▸v. [tr.] **1** record (sound or pictures) on audio or videotape. **2** fasten or attach (something) with adhesive tape. **3** (**tape something off**) seal or mark off an area or thing with tape.
▸ □ **on tape** recorded on magnetic tape.

tape deck ▸n. a piece of equipment for playing audiotapes, esp. as part of a stereo system.

tape meas·ure ▸n. a length of tape or thin flexible metal, marked at intervals for measuring.

ta·per /ˈtāpər/ ▸n. a slender candle. ■ a wick coated with wax, used for conveying a flame. ■ a gradual narrowing: *the current industry standard taper of 5 degrees.*
▸v. diminish or reduce or cause to diminish or reduce in thickness toward one end: [intr.] *the tail tapers to a rounded tip* | [tr.] *David asked my dressmaker to taper his trousers.* ■ [intr.] gradually lessen: *the impact of the dollar's depreciation started to **taper off**.*

tape re·cord·er ▸n. an apparatus for recording sounds on magnetic tape and later reproducing them. —**tape-record** *v.* —**tape re·cord·ing** *n.*

tap·es·try /ˈtapistrē/ ▸n. (*pl.* **-tries**) a piece of thick textile fabric with pictures or designs formed by weaving colored weft threads or by embroidering on canvas, used as a wall hanging or furniture covering. ■ *fig.* used in reference to an intricate or complex combination of things or sequence of events: *a tapestry of cultures, races, and customs.* —**tap·es·tried** *adj.*

tape·worm /ˈtāpˌwərm/ ▸n. a parasitic flatworm (class Cestoda), the adult of which lives in the intestine of humans and other vertebrates. It has a long ribbonlike body with many segments that can become independent, and a small head bearing hooks and suckers.

tap·i·o·ca /ˌtapēˈōkə/ ▸n. a starchy substance in the form of hard white grains, obtained from cassava and used in cooking puddings and other dishes.

ta·pir /ˈtāpər/ ▸n. a nocturnal hoofed mammal (genus *Tapirus*, family Tapiridaae) with a stout body, sturdy limbs, and a short flexible proboscis, native to the forests of tropical America and Malaysia.

tap·pet /ˈtapit/ ▸n. a lever or projecting part on a machine that intermittently makes contact with a cam or other part so as to give or receive motion.

tap·room /ˈtapˌrōōm; -ˌrōōm/ ▸n. a room in which alcoholic drinks, esp. beer, are available on tap; a bar in a hotel or inn.

tap·root /ˈtapˌrōōt; -ˌrōōt/ ▸n. a straight tapering root growing vertically downward and forming the center from which subsidiary rootlets spring.

tap wa·ter ▸n. water from a piped supply.

tar[1] /tär/ ▸n. another term for ASPHALT. ■ a dark, thick, flammable liquid distilled from wood or coal, consisting of a mixture of hydrocarbons, resins, alcohols, and other compounds. ■ a similar substance formed by burning tobacco or other material: [in *comb.*] *low-tar cigarettes.*
▸v. (**tarred**, **tar·ring**) [tr.] cover (something) with tar.

tar[2] ▸n. *inf., dated* a sailor.

tar·an·tel·la /ˌtarənˈtelə/ (also **tar·an·telle** /-ˈtel/) ▸n. a rapid whirling dance originating in southern Italy. ■ a piece of music written in fast 6/8 time in the style of this dance.

ta·ran·tu·la /təˈranCHələ/ ▸n. **1** a large hairy spider found chiefly in tropical and subtropical America. **2** a large black wolf spider (*Lycosa tarentula*) of southern Europe.

tar·dy /ˈtärdē/ ▸adj. (**-di·er, -di·est**) delaying or delayed beyond the right or expected time; late: *please forgive this tardy reply.* ■ slow in action or response; sluggish. ▷mid 16th cent.: from French *tardif, -ive*, from Latin *tardus* 'slow.' —**tar·di·ly** /ˈtärdl-ē/ *adv.* —**tar·di·ness** *n.*

tare[1] /te(ə)r/ ▸n. a vetch, esp. the common vetch.

tare[2] ▸n. an allowance made for the weight of the packaging in order to determine the net weight of goods. ■ the weight of a motor vehicle, railroad car, or aircraft without its fuel or load.

tar·get /ˈtärgit/ ▸n. a person, object, or place selected as the aim of an attack. ■ a mark or point at which someone fires or aims, esp. a round or rectangular board marked with concentric circles used in archery or shooting. ■ an objective or result toward which efforts are directed: *the car met its sales target in record time.* ■ *Phonet.* an idealization of the articulation of a speech sound, with reference to which actual utterances can be described. ■ a person or thing against whom criticism or abuse is or may be directed.
▸v. (**-get·ed, -get·ing**) [tr.] select as an object of attention or attack: *two men were targeted by the attackers.* ■ aim or direct (something): *a significant nuclear capability targeted on the U.S.* —**tar·get·a·ble** *adj.*
▸ □ **on target** accurately hitting the thing aimed at. ■ proceeding or improving at a good enough rate to achieve an objective.

tar·iff /ˈtarif/ ▸n. a tax or duty to be paid on a particular class of imports or exports. ■ a list of these taxes. ■ a table of the fixed charges made by a business, esp. in a hotel or restaurant.

T

▶ *v.* [*tr.*] fix the price of (something) according to a tariff: *these services are tariffed by volume.*

Tar·mac /ˈtärˌmak/ ▶ *n.* (usu. **tarmac**) *trademark* material used for surfacing roads or other outdoor areas, consisting of crushed rock mixed with tar. ■ (**the tarmac**) a runway or other area surfaced with such material.

tarn /tärn/ ▶ *n.* a small mountain lake.

tar·na·tion /tärˈnāsHən/ ▶ *n. & interj.* used as a euphemism for "damnation."

tar·nish /ˈtärnisH/ ▶ *v.* lose or cause to lose luster, esp. as a result of exposure to air or moisture: [*intr.*] *silver tarnishes too easily* | [*tr.*] *lemon juice would tarnish the gilded metal.* ■ *fig.* make or become less valuable or respected: [*tr.*] *his regime had not been tarnished by human rights abuses.*
▶ *n.* dullness of color; loss of brightness. ■ a film or stain formed on an exposed surface of a mineral or metal. ■ *fig.* damage or harm done to something. —**tar·nish·a·ble** *adj.*

ta·ro /ˈtärō; ˈterō/ ▶ *n.* a tropical Asian plant (*Colocasia esculenta esculenta*) of the arum family that has edible starchy corms and edible fleshy leaves, esp. a variety with a large central corm grown as a staple in the Pacific. ■ the corm of this plant.

ta·rot /ˈtarō; ˈte(ə)rō; təˈrō/ ▶ *n.* (**the Tarot**) playing cards, traditionally a pack of 78 with five suits, used for fortune-telling and (esp. in Europe) in certain games.

tarp /tärp/ ▶ *n. inf.* a tarpaulin sheet or cover.

tar·pau·lin /tärˈpôlən; ˈtärpə-/ ▶ *n.* heavy-duty waterproof cloth, originally of tarred canvas. ■ a sheet or covering of this.

tar·pon /ˈtärpən/ ▶ *n.* a large tropical marine fish (family Megalopidae) of herringlike appearance. Two species: *Tarpon atlanticus*, a prized Atlantic game fish, and *Megalops cyprinoides* of the Indo-Pacific.

tar·ra·gon /ˈtarəˌgän; -gən; ˈtər-/ ▶ *n.* a perennial plant (*Artemisia dracunculus*) of the daisy family, with narrow aromatic leaves that are used as a culinary herb.

tar·ry[1] /ˈtärē/ ▶ *adj.* (**-ri·er, -ri·est**) of, like, or covered with tar: *a length of tarry rope.* —**tar·ri·ness** *n.*

tar·ry[2] /ˈtarē/ ▶ *v.* (**-ries, -ried**) [*intr.*] *dated* stay longer than intended; delay leaving a place: *she could tarry a bit and not get home until four.* —**tar·ri·er** *n.* (*rare*).

tar·sal /ˈtärsəl/ ▶ *adj. Anat. & Zool.* of or relating to the tarsus: *the tarsal claws of beetles.*
▶ *n.* a bone of the tarsus.

tar·si·er /ˈtärsēər/ ▶ *n.* a small insectivorous, tree-dwelling, nocturnal primate (genus *Tarsius*, family Tarsiidae) with large eyes, a long tufted tail, and long hind limbs, native to the islands of Southeast Asia.

tar·sus /ˈtärsəs/ ▶ *n.* (pl. **tar·si** /ˈtärsī; -sē/) **1** *Anat.* a group of small bones between the main part of the hind limb and the metatarsus in terrestrial vertebrates. The seven bones of the human tarsus form the ankle and upper part of the foot. ■ *Zool.* the shank of the leg of a bird or reptile. **2** *Anat.* a thin sheet of fibrous connective tissue which supports the edge of each eyelid.

tart[1] /tärt/ ▶ *n.* an open pastry case containing a filling. —**tart·let** /-lit/ *n.*

tart[2] ▶ *n. inf., derog.* a prostitute or a promiscuous woman.
▶ *v.* [*tr.*] (**tart oneself up**) *inf., chiefly Brit.* dress or make oneself up in order to look attractive or eye-catching. ■ (**tart something up**) decorate or improve the appearance of something.

tart[3] ▶ *adj.* sharp or acid in taste: *a tart apple.* ■ (of a remark or tone of voice) cutting, bitter, or sarcastic: *I bit back a tart reply.* —**tart·ly** *adv.* —**tart·ness** *n.*

tar·tan[1] /ˈtärtn/ ▶ *n.* a woolen cloth woven in one of several patterns of plaid, esp. of a design associated with a particular Scottish clan.
▶ *adj.* used allusively in reference to Scotland or the Scots.

tar·tan[2] ▶ *n. hist.* a lateen-rigged, single-masted ship used in the Mediterranean.

Tar·tar /ˈtärtər/ ▶ *n. hist.* a member of the combined forces of central Asian peoples, including Mongols and Turks, who under Genghis Khan conquered much of Asia and eastern Europe in the early 13th century, and under Tamerlane (14th century) established an empire. See also TATAR. ■ (**tartar**) a harsh, fierce, or intractable person. —**Tar·tar·i·an** /tärˈte(ə)rēən/ *adj.*

tar·tar /ˈtärtər/ ▶ *n.* a hard calcified deposit that forms on the teeth and contributes to their decay. ■ a deposit of impure potassium hydrogen tartrate formed during the fermentation of wine. See also CREAM OF TARTAR.

tar·tar·ic ac·id ▶ *n. Chem.* a crystalline acid, COOH(CHOH)$_2$COOH, that is used in baking powders and as a food additive.

tar·tar sauce (also **tar·tare sauce**) ▶ *n.* a cold sauce, typically eaten with

fish, consisting of mayonnaise mixed with chopped pickles, capers, etc.

task /task/ ▶ *n.* a piece of work to be done or undertaken.
▶ *v.* [*tr.*] assign such a piece of work to: *NATO troops are tasked with separating the warring parties.* ■ make great demands on (someone's resources or abilities): *it tasked his diplomatic skill to effect his departure.*
▶ □ **take someone to task** reprimand or criticize someone severely for a fault or mistake.

task force ▶ *n.* an armed force organized for a special operation. ■ a unit specially organized for a task: *aides say his plans include a task force on hate crimes.*

task·mas·ter /ˈtaskˌmastər/ ▶ *n.* a person who imposes a harsh or onerous workload on someone.

Tas·ma·ni·an dev·il /tazˈmānēən; -ˈmānyən/ ▶ *n.* a heavily built marsupial (*Sarcophilus harrisii*, family Dasyuridae) with a large head, powerful jaws, and mainly black fur, found only in Tasmania.

tas·sel /ˈtasəl/ ▶ *n.* a tuft of loosely hanging threads, cords, or other material knotted at one end and attached for decoration to home furnishings, clothing, or other items. ■ the tufted head of some plants, esp. a flowerhead with prominent stamens at the top of a cornstalk.
▶ *v.* (**-seled, -sel·ing**; *Brit.* **-selled, -sel·ling**) [*intr.*] (of corn or other plants) form tassels.

taste /tāst/ ▶ *n.* **1** the sensation of flavor perceived in the mouth and throat on contact with a substance: *the wine had a fruity taste.* ■ the faculty of perceiving this quality: *a highly developed sense of taste.* ■ a small portion of food or drink taken as a sample: *try a taste of Gorgonzola.* ■ a brief experience of something, conveying its basic character: *his first taste of serious action.* **2** a person's liking for particular flavors: *this pudding is too sweet for my taste.* ■ a person's tendency to like and dislike certain things: *he found the competitiveness of the profession was not to his taste.* ■ (**taste for**) a liking for or interest in (something): *have you lost your taste for fancy restaurants?* ■ the ability to discern what is of good quality or of a high aesthetic standard: *she has awful taste in literature.* ■ conformity or failure to conform with generally held views concerning what is offensive or acceptable: *that's a joke in bad taste.*
▶ *v.* [*tr.*] perceive or experience the flavor of: *she had never tasted ice cream before.* ■ [*intr.*] have a specified flavor: *the spinach tastes delicious.* ■ sample or test the flavor of (food or drink) by taking it into the mouth: *the waiter poured some wine for him to taste.* ■ eat or drink a small portion of. ■ have experience of: *the team has not yet tasted victory at home.*
▶ □ **a bad** (or **bitter**) **taste in someone's mouth** *inf.* a feeling of distress or disgust following an experience: *this incident has left a bad taste in all our mouths.* □ **to taste** in the amount needed to give a flavor pleasing to someone eating a dish: *add salt and pepper to taste.*

taste bud ▶ *n.* (usu. **taste buds**) any of the clusters of bulbous nerve endings on the tongue and in the lining of the mouth that provide the sense of taste.

taste·ful /ˈtāstfəl/ ▶ *adj.* showing good aesthetic judgment or appropriate behavior. —**taste·ful·ly** *adv.* —**taste·ful·ness** *n.*

taste·less /ˈtāstlis/ ▶ *adj.* **1** lacking flavor. **2** considered to be lacking in aesthetic judgment or to offend against what is regarded as appropriate behavior: *a tasteless joke.* —**taste·less·ly** *adv.* —**taste·less·ness** *n.*

tast·er /ˈtāstər/ ▶ *n.* a person employed to test food or drink for quality by tasting it. ■ a small cup used by a person tasting wine in such a way. ■ an instrument for extracting a small sample from within a cheese.

tast·ing /ˈtāstiNG/ ▶ *n.* a gathering at which people sample, compare, and evaluate different wines, or other drinks or food: *we did a tasting of over forty of the cheaper champagnes.* See also WINE TASTING.

tast·y /ˈtāstē/ ▶ *adj.* (**tast·i·er, tast·i·est**) (of food) having a pleasant, distinct flavor: *a tasty snack.* —**tast·i·ly** /-stilē/ *adv.* —**tast·i·ness** *n.*

tat[1] /tat/ ▶ *v.* (**tat·ted, tat·ting**) make tatting.

tat[2] ▶ *n.* (in phrase **tit for tat**) see TIT[3].

ta·ta /tä ˈtä/ ▶ *interj. inf., chiefly Brit.* goodbye.

Ta·tar /ˈtätər/ ▶ *n.* **1** a member of a Turkic people living in Tatarstan and various other parts of Russia and Ukraine. They are the descendants of the Tartars who ruled central Asia in the 14th century. **2** the Turkic language of this people.
▶ *adj.* of or relating to this people or their language.

ta·ter /ˈtātər/ ▶ *n. inf.* a potato.

---

tat·tered /ˈtatərd/ ▸adj. torn, old, and in generally poor condition; in tatters: *an old woman in tattered clothes.* ■ *fig.* virtually destroyed; ruined.

tat·ters /ˈtatərz/ ▸pl. n. irregularly torn pieces of cloth, paper, or other material.

▸ □ **in tatters** *inf.* torn in many places; in shreds: *wallpaper hung in tatters.* ■ *fig.* destroyed; ruined: *the cease-fire was in tatters within hours.*

tat·ting /ˈtatiNG/ ▸n. a kind of knotted lace made by hand with a small shuttle, used chiefly for trimming. ■ the process of making such lace.

tat·tle /ˈtatl/ ▸v. [intr.] report another's wrongdoing: *he never tattled or told tales | I would tattle on her whenever I had hard evidence.* ■ gossip idly.
▸n. gossip; idle talk. —**tat·tler** n.

tat·tle·tale /ˈtatlˌtāl/ ▸n. a person, esp. a child, who reveals secrets or informs on others; a telltale.

tat·too[1] /taˈto͞o/ ▸n. (pl. **-toos**) an evening drum or bugle signal recalling soldiers to their quarters. ■ a rhythmic tapping or drumming.

tat·too[2] ▸v. (**-toos, -tooed** /-ˈto͞od/) [tr.] mark (a person or a part of the body) with an indelible design by inserting pigment into punctures in the skin: *his cheek was tattooed with a winged fist.* ■ make (a design) in such a way: *he has a heart tattooed on his left hand.*
▸n. (pl. **-toos**) a design made in such a way. —**tat·too·er** n. —**tat·too·ist** /taˈto͞oist/ n.

tau /tou; tô/ ▸n. the nineteenth letter of the Greek alphabet (T, τ), transliterated as 't.' ■ (in full **tau particle** or **tau lepton**) *Physics* an unstable subatomic particle of the lepton class, with a charge of −1 and a mass roughly 3,500 times that of the electron.

taught /tôt/ ▸ past and past participle of TEACH.

taunt /tônt/ ▸n. a remark made in order to anger, wound, or provoke someone.
▸v. [tr.] provoke or challenge (someone) with insulting remarks: *students began taunting her about her weight.* ■ reproach (someone) with something in a contemptuous way. —**taunt·er** n. —**taunt·ing·ly** adv.

taupe /tōp/ ▸n. gray with a tinge of brown: [as adj.] *a taupe overcoat.* ▷early 20th cent.: from French, literally 'mole, moleskin,' from Latin *talpa.*

Tau·rus /ˈtôrəs/ ▸ **1** *Astron.* a constellation (the Bull), having many bright stars including Aldebaran, as well as the Crab Nebula and the star clusters of the Hyades and the Pleiades. **2** *Astrol.* the second sign of the zodiac, which the sun enters on about April 21. ■ (**a Taurus**) (pl. same) a person born when the sun is in this sign.

taut /tôt/ ▸adj. stretched or pulled tight; not slack: *the fabric stays taut without adhesive.* ■ (esp. of muscles or nerves) tense; not relaxed. ■ *fig.* (of writing, music, etc.) concise and controlled. —**taut·en** /ˈtôtn/ v. —**taut·ly** adv. —**taut·ness** n.

tau·tog /tôˈtäg; tôˈtôg/ ▸n. a grayish-olive edible wrasse (*Tautoga onitis*) that occurs off the Atlantic coast of North America.

tau·tol·o·gy /tôˈtäləjē/ ▸n. (pl. **-gies**) the saying of the same thing twice in different words, generally considered to be a fault of style (e.g., *they arrived one after the other in succession*). ■ a phrase or expression in which the same thing is said twice in different words. —**tau·to·log·i·cal** /ˌtôtl-ˈäjikəl/ adj. —**tau·to·log·i·cal·ly** /ˌtôtlˈäjik(ə)lē/ adv. —**tau·tol·o·gist** /-jist/ n. —**tau·tol·o·gize** /-ˌjīz/ v. —**tau·tol·o·gous** /-gəs/ adj.

tav·ern /ˈtavərn/ ▸n. an establishment for the sale of beer and other drinks to be consumed on the premises, sometimes also serving food.

taw·dry /ˈtôdrē/ ▸adj. (**-dri·er, -dri·est**) showy but cheap and of poor quality: *tawdry jewelry.* ■ sordid or unpleasant: *the tawdry business of politics.*
▸n. archaic cheap and gaudy finery. ▷early 17th cent.: short for *tawdry lace*, a fine silk lace or ribbon worn as a necklace in the 16th–17th centuries, contraction of *St. Audrey's lace*: *Audrey* was a later form of *Etheldrida* (died 679), patron saint of Ely, England, where tawdry laces, along with cheap imitations and other cheap finery, were traditionally sold at a fair. —**taw·dri·ly** /-drəlē/ adv. —**taw·dri·ness** n.

taw·ny /ˈtônē/ ▸adj. (**-ni·er, -ni·est**) of an orange-brown or yellowish-brown color: *tawny eyes.*
▸n. an orange-brown or yellowish-brown color. —**taw·ni·ness** n.

tax /taks/ ▸n. a compulsory contribution to state revenue, levied by the government on workers' income and business profits or added to the cost of some goods, services, and transactions. ■ *fig.* a strain or heavy demand: *a heavy tax on the reader's attention.*
▸v. [tr.] **1** impose a tax on (someone or something): *hardware and software is taxed at 7.5 percent.* ■ *fig.* make heavy demands on (someone's powers or resources). **2** confront (someone) with a fault or wrongdoing. —**tax·a·ble** adj. —**tax·er** n.

tax·a·tion /takˈsāsHən/ ▸n. the levying of tax. ■ money paid as tax.

tax-de·duct·i·ble ▸adj. able to be deducted from taxable income when calculating income tax due.

tax e·va·sion ▸n. the illegal nonpayment or underpayment of tax.

tax-ex·empt ▸adj. not liable or obligated to pay taxes: *the foundation has applied for tax-exempt status.* ■ bearing interest on which no taxes are imposed: *ask about our tax-exempt savings plans.*

tax ex·emp·tion ▸the process of exempting a person or organization from paying taxes, usu. on a specified amount of income. ■ a taxpayer's dependent exempted in this way.

tax ha·ven ▸n. a country or independent area where taxes are levied at a low rate.

tax·i /ˈtaksē/ ▸n. (pl. **tax·is**) short for TAXICAB. ■ a boat or other means of transportation used to convey passengers in return for payment of a fare.
▸v. (**tax·is, tax·ied, tax·i·ing** or **tax·y·ing**) [intr.] **1** (of an aircraft) move slowly along the ground before takeoff or after landing: *the plane taxis up to a waiting limousine.* ■ [tr.] (of a pilot) cause (an aircraft) to move in such a way. **2** take a taxi as a means of transport.

tax·i·cab /ˈtaksēˌkab/ ▸n. a car licensed to transport passengers in return for payment of a fare, usually fitted with a taximeter.

tax·i·der·my /ˈtaksəˌdərmē/ ▸n. the art of preparing, stuffing, and mounting the skins of animals with lifelike effect. —**tax·i·der·mal** /ˌtaksəˈdərməl/ adj. —**tax·i·der·mic** /ˌtaksəˈdərmik/ adj. —**tax·i·der·mi·cal·ly** /ˌtaksəˈdərmik(ə)lē/ adv. —**tax·i·der·mist** n.

tax·i·me·ter /ˈtaksēˌmētər/ ▸n. a device used in taxicabs that automatically records the distance traveled and the fare payable.

tax·i stand ▸n. a place where taxicabs park while waiting to be engaged.

tax·man /ˈtaksˌman/ ▸n. (pl. **-men**) *inf.*, chiefly Brit. a collector of taxes. ■ (**the taxman**) the government department that collects tax.

tax·on /ˈtaksän/ ▸n. (pl. **tax·a** /ˈtaksə/) *Biol.* a taxonomic group of any rank, such as a species, family, or class.

tax·on·o·my /takˈsänəmē/ ▸n. chiefly Biol. the branch of science concerned with classification, esp. of organisms; systematics. ■ the classification of something, esp. organisms. ■ a scheme of classification. —**tax·o·nom·ic** /ˌtaksəˈnämik/ adj. —**tax·o·nom·i·cal** /ˌtaksəˈnämikəl/ adj. —**tax·o·nom·i·cal·ly** /ˌtaksəˈnämik(ə)lē/ adv. —**tax·on·o·mist** /-mist/ n.

tax·pay·er /ˈtaksˌpāər/ ▸n. a person who pays taxes.

tax re·turn ▸n. a form on which a taxpayer makes an annual statement of income and personal circumstances, used by the tax authorities to assess liability for tax.

tax shel·ter ▸n. a financial arrangement made to avoid or minimize taxes.

TB ▸abbr. ■ terabyte(s). ■ (also **t.b.**) tubercle bacillus. ■ (also **t.b.**) tuberculosis.

Tb ▸abbr. ■ terabyte(s). ■ Bible Tobit.
▸symb. the chemical element terbium.

T-bar ▸n. **1** a beam or bar shaped like the letter T. ■ (also **T-bar lift**) a type of ski lift in the form of a series of inverted T-shaped bars for towing two skiers at a time uphill. **2** the horizontal line of the letter T.

T-bone ▸n. (also **T-bone steak**) a large choice piece of loin steak containing a T-shaped bone.
▸v. [tr.] crash head-on into the side of (another vehicle): *his car rolled over and was T-boned by an oncoming vehicle.*

tbsp. (also **tbs.**) (pl. same or **tbsps.**) ▸abbr. tablespoon; tablespoonful.

Tc ▸symb. the chemical element technetium.

T cell (also **T-cell**) ▸n. *Physiol.* a lymphocyte of a type produced or processed by the thymus gland and actively participating in the immune response.

TCP/IP trademark, Comput. ▸abbr. transmission control protocol/Internet protocol, used to govern the connection of computer systems to the Internet.

TD ▸abbr. ■ Football touchdown. ■ Treasury Department.

Te ▸symb. the chemical element tellurium.

tea /tē/ ▸n. **1** a hot drink made by infusing the dried, crushed leaves of the tea plant in boiling water. ■ the dried leaves used to make such a drink. ■ (also **iced tea**) such a drink served cold with ice cubes. ■ a hot drink made from the infused leaves, fruits, or flowers of other plants: *herbal tea.* **2** (also **tea plant**) the evergreen shrub or small tree (*Camellia sinensis*, family Theaceae) that produces these leaves, native to South and eastern Asia and grown as a major cash crop. **3** chiefly Brit. a light afternoon meal consisting typically of tea to drink, sandwiches, and cakes. ■ Brit. a cooked evening meal. See also HIGH TEA. **4** *inf.* another term for MARIJUANA. ▷mid 17th cent.: probably via Malay from Chinese (Min dialect) *te.*

tea bag ▸n. a small porous bag containing tea leaves or powdered tea, onto which boiling water is poured in order to make a drink of tea.

tea ball ▸*n.* a hollow ball of perforated metal to hold tea leaves, over which boiling water is poured in order to make a drink of tea.

tea cad·dy ▸*n.* a small container in which tea is kept for daily use.

tea cer·e·mo·ny ▸*n.* an elaborate Japanese ritual of serving and drinking tea, as an expression of Zen Buddhist philosophy.

teach /tēCH/ ▸*v.* (*past* **taught** /tôt/) [*tr.*] show or explain to (someone) how to do something: *she taught him to read.* ■ [*tr.*] give information about or instruction in (a subject or skill): *he came to teach painting* | *she teaches me French.* ■ [*intr.*] give such instruction professionally: *she teaches at the local high school.* ■ [*tr.*] encourage someone to accept (something) as a fact or principle: *the philosophy teaches self-control.* ■ cause (someone) to learn or understand something: *she'd been taught that it paid to be passive.* ■ induce (someone) by example or punishment to do or not to do something: *my upbringing taught me never to be disrespectful to elders.* ■ *inf.* make (someone) less inclined to do something: *"I'll teach you to mess with girls!"* ▸*n. inf.* a teacher.

teach·a·ble /ˈtēCHəbəl/ ▸*adj.* **1** (of a person) able to learn by being taught. **2** (of a subject) able to be taught. **—teach·a·bil·i·ty** /ˌtēCHə-ˈbilitē/ *n.* **—teach·a·ble·ness** *n.*

teach·er /ˈtēCHər/ ▸*n.* a person who teaches, esp. in a school. **—teach·er·ly** *adj.*

teach·ing /ˈtēCHiNG/ ▸*n.* **1** the occupation, profession, or work of a teacher. **2** (**teachings**) ideas or principles taught by an authority.

tea co·zy ▸*n.* a thick or padded cover placed over a teapot to keep the tea hot.

tea·cup /ˈtē,kəp/ ▸*n.* a cup from which tea is drunk. ■ an amount held by this, about 150 ml. **—tea·cup·ful** /-ˌfŏŏl/ *n.* (*pl.* **-fuls**).

teak /tēk/ ▸*n.* **1** hard durable timber used in shipbuilding and for making furniture. **2** the large deciduous tree (*Tectona grandis*, family Verbenaceae) native to India and Southeast Asia that yields this timber.

tea·ket·tle /ˈtē,ketl/ ▸*n.* a typically metal container with a lid, spout, and handle, used for boiling water.

teal /tēl/ ▸*n.* (*pl.* same or **teals**) a small freshwater duck (genus *Anas*), typically with a greenish band on the wing that is most prominent in flight. ■ (also **teal blue**) a dark greenish-blue color.

team /tēm/ ▸*n.* [treated as *sing.* or *pl.*] a group of players forming one side in a competitive game or sport. ■ two or more people working together: *a team of researchers* | [as *adj.*] *a team effort.* ■ two or more animals, esp. horses, harnessed together to pull a vehicle. ▸*v.* **1** [*intr.*] (**team up**) come together as a team to achieve a common goal: *he teamed up with the band to produce the album.* **2** [*tr.*] (usu. **team something with**) match or coordinate a garment with (another). **3** [*tr.*] harness (animals, esp. horses) together to pull a vehicle.

team·mate /ˈtē(m),māt/ ▸*n.* a fellow member of a team.

team·ster /ˈtēmstər/ ▸*n.* **1** a truck driver. ■ a member of the Teamsters Union, including truck drivers, chauffeurs, and warehouse workers. **2** a driver of a team of animals.

team·work /ˈtēm,wərk/ ▸*n.* the combined action of a group of people, esp. when effective and efficient.

tea·pot /ˈtē,pät/ ▸*n.* a pot with a handle, spout, and lid, in which tea is brewed and from which it is poured. ■ a teakettle.

tear[1] /te(ə)r/ ▸*v.* (*past* **tore** /tôr/; *past part.* **torn** /tôrn/) **1** [*tr.*] pull or rip (something) apart or to pieces with force: *I tore up the letter.* ■ remove by pulling or ripping forcefully: *Sanna couldn't wait to tear up the pink carpeting* | *he tore off his belt.* ■ (**be torn between**) *fig.* have great difficulty in choosing between: *he was torn between his duty and his better instincts.* ■ [*tr.*] make a hole or split in (something) by ripping or pulling at it: *she was always tearing her clothes.* ■ make (a hole or split) in something by force: *the blast tore a hole in the wall.* ■ [*intr.*] come apart; rip. ■ [*tr.*] damage (a muscle or ligament) by overstretching it. **2** [*intr.*] *inf.* move very quickly, typically in a reckless or excited manner: *she tore along the footpath on her bike.*

▸*phrasal v.* □ **tear someone/something apart 1** destroy something, esp. good relations between people: *a bloody civil war had torn the country apart.* **2** upset someone greatly. **3** search a place thoroughly. **4** criticize someone or something harshly. □ **tear oneself away** leave despite a strong desire to stay: *she couldn't tear herself away from the view.* □ **tear something down** demolish something, esp. a building. □ **tear someone down** *inf.* criticize or punish someone severely. □ **tear into 1** attack verbally. **2** make an energetic or enthusiastic start on: *a jazz trio is tearing into the tune with gusto.*

▸*n.* **1** a hole or split in something caused by it having been pulled apart forcefully. **2** *inf.* a spell of great success or excellence in performance: *he went on a tear, winning three out of every four hands.* ■ a brief spell of erratic behavior; a binge or spree. **—tear·a·ble** *adj.* **—tear·er** *n.*

▸ □ **tear one's hair out** *inf.* act with or show extreme desperation. □ **tear**

someone/something **to shreds** (or **pieces**) *inf.* criticize someone or something forcefully or aggressively.

tear[2] /ti(ə)r/ ▸*n.* a drop of clear salty liquid secreted from glands in a person's eye when they cry or when the eye is irritated. ■ a drop of such liquid secreted continuously to lubricate the surface of the eyeball under the eyelid. ■ (**tears**) the state or action of crying: *he was so hurt by her attitude he was nearly in tears* | *sock puppets that moved Jack to tears.* ▸*v.* [*intr.*] (of the eye) produce tears. **—tear·like** /-,līk/ *adj.*

tear·drop /ˈti(ə)r,dräp/ ▸*n.* a single tear. ■ [as *adj.*] shaped like a single tear: *a wardrobe with brass teardrop handles.*

tear duct /ti(ə)r/ ▸*n.* a passage through which tears pass from the lachrymal glands to the eye or from the eye to the nose.

tear·ful /ˈti(ə)rfəl/ ▸*adj.* crying or inclined to cry. ■ causing tears; sad or emotional: *a tearful farewell.* **—tear·ful·ly** *adv.* **—tear·ful·ness** *n.*

tear gas /ti(ə)r/ ▸*n.* gas that causes severe irritation to the eyes, chiefly used in riot control to force crowds to disperse. ▸*v.* (**tear-gas**) [*tr.*] attack with tear gas.

tear·jerk·er /ˈti(ə)r,jərkər/ ▸*n. inf.* a sentimental story, movie, or song, calculated to evoke sadness or sympathy. **—tear·jerk·ing** /-,jərkiNG/ *n.* & *adj.*

tea·room /ˈtē,rŏŏm; -,rŏŏm/ (also **tea room**) ▸*n.* a small restaurant or café where tea and other light refreshments are served.

tease /tēz/ ▸*v.* [*tr.*] **1** make fun of or attempt to provoke (a person or animal) in a playful way: *Brenda teased her father about the powerboat that he bought but seldom used* | [*intr.*] *she was just teasing.* ■ tempt (someone) sexually with no intention of satisfying the desire aroused. **2** [*tr.*] gently pull or comb (something tangled, esp. wool or hair) into separate strands: *she was teasing out the curls into her usual hairstyle.* ■ (**tease something out**) *fig.* find something out from a mass of irrelevant information: *a historian who tries to tease out the truth.* ■ comb (hair) in the reverse direction of its natural growth in order to make it appear fuller. ■ *archaic* comb (the surface of woven cloth) to raise a nap.

▸*n.* *inf.* a person who makes fun of someone playfully or unkindly. ■ a person who tempts someone sexually with no intention of satisfying the desire aroused. ■ an act of making fun of or tempting someone: *she couldn't resist a gentle tease.* **—teas·ing·ly** *adv.*

tea·sel /ˈtēzəl/ ▸*n.* a tall prickly Eurasian plant (genus *Dipsacus*) with spiny purple flowerheads. Its several species include **fuller's teasel.** ■ a large, dried, spiny head from such a plant, or a device serving as a substitute for one of these, used in the textile industry to raise a nap on woven cloth.

teas·er /ˈtēzər/ ▸*n.* **1** *inf.* a difficult or tricky question or task. **2** a person who makes fun of or provokes others in a playful or unkind way. ■ a person who tempts someone sexually with no intention of satisfying the desire aroused. ■ a short introductory advertisement for a product, esp. one that does not mention the name of the thing being advertised. ■ *Fishing* a lure or bait trailed behind a boat to attract fish.

tea set (also **tea service**) ▸*n.* a set of dishes, typically of china or silver, used for serving tea.

tea·spoon /ˈtē,spŏŏn/ ▸*n.* a small spoon used typically for adding sugar to and stirring hot drinks or for eating some soft foods. ■ (abbr.: **tsp.** or **t.**) a measurement used in cooking, equivalent to 1/6 fluid ounce, 1/3 tablespoon, or 4.9 ml. **—tea·spoon·ful** /-,fŏŏl/ *n.* (*pl.* **-fuls**).

teat /tēt/ ▸*n.* a nipple of the mammary gland of a female mammal, from which the milk is sucked by the young. ■ *Brit.* a thing resembling this, esp. a perforated plastic bulb by which an infant or young animal can suck milk from a bottle.

tech /tek/ (*Brit.* also **tec**) ▸*n. inf.* technology. See also HIGH-TECH. ■ a technician. ■ *Basketball* a technical. ▸*adj.* technical: *I was in tech school then.*

tech·ne·ti·um /tekˈnēsH(ē)əm/ ▸*n.* the chemical element of atomic number 43, a radioactive metal. (Symbol: **Tc**)

tech·ni·cal /ˈteknikəl/ ▸*adj.* **1** of or relating to a particular subject, art, or craft, or its techniques: *technical terms.* ■ (esp. of a book or article) requiring special knowledge to be understood: *a technical report.* **2** of, involving, or concerned with applied and industrial sciences: *an important technical achievement.* **3** resulting from mechanical failure: *a technical fault.* **4** according to a strict application or interpretation of the law or rules: *the arrest was a technical violation of the treaty.* **—tech·ni·cal·ly** *adv.*

tech·ni·cal foul ▸*n. Basketball* a violation of certain rules of the game, not usually involving physical contact, but often involving unsportsmanlike actions.

tech·ni·cal·i·ty /ˌtekniˈkalitē/ ▸ *n.* (*pl.* **-ties**) a point of law or a small detail of a set of rules: *their convictions were overturned on a technicality.* ■ (**technicalities**) the specific details or terms belonging to a particular field: *he has great expertise in the technicalities of the game.* ■ the state of being technical; the use of technical terms or methods: *the extreme technicality of the proposed constitution.*

tech·ni·cal knock·out (abbr.: **TKO**) ▸ *n. Boxing* the ending of a fight by the referee on the grounds of one contestant's inability to continue, the opponent being declared the winner.

tech·ni·cian /tekˈnishən/ ▸ *n.* a person employed to look after technical equipment or do practical work in a laboratory. ■ an expert in the practical application of a science. ■ a person skilled in the technique of an art or craft.

Tech·ni·col·or /ˈtekniˌkələr/ ▸ *n. trademark* a process of color cinematography using synchronized monochrome films, each of a different color, to produce a movie in color. ■ (**technicolor**) *inf.* vivid color: [as *adj.*] *a technicolor bruise.* —**tech·ni·col·ored** *adj.*

tech·nique /tekˈnēk/ ▸ *n.* a way of carrying out a particular task, esp. the execution or performance of an artistic work or a scientific procedure. ■ skill or ability in a particular field: *he has excellent technique | an established athlete with a very good technique.* ■ a skillful or efficient way of doing or achieving something: *tape recording is a good technique for evaluating our own communications.*

tech·no /ˈteknō/ ▸ *n.* a style of fast, heavy electronic dance music, typically with few or no vocals. ▷1980s: abbreviation of *technological.*

tech·no·bab·ble /ˈteknōˌbabəl/ ▸ *n. inf.* incomprehensible technical jargon.

tech·noc·ra·cy /tekˈnäkrəsē/ ▸ *n.* (*pl.* **-cies**) the government or control of society or industry by an elite of technical experts. ■ an instance or application of this. ■ an elite of technical experts.

tech·no·crat /ˈteknəˌkrat/ ▸ *n.* an exponent or advocate of technocracy. ■ a member of a technically skilled elite. —**tech·no·crat·ic** /ˌteknəˈkratik/ *adj.* —**tech·no·crat·i·cal·ly** /ˌteknəˈkratik(ə)lē/ *adv.*

tech·no·log·i·cal /ˌteknəˈläjikəl/ ▸ *adj.* of, relating to, or using technology. —**tech·no·log·i·cal·ly** /-ik(ə)lē/ *adv.*

tech·nol·o·gy /tekˈnäləjē/ ▸ *n.* (*pl.* **-gies**) the application of scientific knowledge for practical purposes, esp. in industry: *advances in computer technology | recycling technologies.* ■ machinery and equipment developed from such scientific knowledge. ■ the branch of knowledge dealing with engineering or applied sciences. —**tech·nol·o·gist** /-jist/ *n.* —**tech·nol·o·gize** /-ˌjīz/ *v.*

tec·ton·ic /tekˈtänik/ ▸ *adj.* **1** *Geol.* of or relating to the structure of the earth's crust and the large-scale processes that take place within it. **2** of or relating to building or construction. —**tec·ton·i·cal·ly** /-ik(ə)lē/ *adv.*

tec·ton·ics /tekˈtäniks/ ▸ *pl. n.* [treated as *sing.* or *pl.*] *Geol.* large-scale processes affecting the structure of the earth's crust.

ted·dy /ˈtedē/ ▸ *n.* (*pl.* **-dies**) **1** (also **teddy bear**) a soft toy bear. **2** a woman's all-in-one undergarment.

te·di·ous /ˈtēdēəs/ ▸ *adj.* too long, slow, or dull: tiresome or monotonous: *a tedious journey.* —**te·di·ous·ly** *adv.* —**te·di·ous·ness** *n.*

te·di·um /ˈtēdēəm/ ▸ *n.* the state of being tedious. ▷mid 17th cent.: from Latin *taedium*, from *taedere* 'be weary of.'

tee[1] /tē/ ▸ *n.* see **T**[1] (sense 2).

tee[2] ▸ *n.* **1** a cleared space on a golf course, from which the ball is struck at the beginning of play for each hole. ■ a small peg with a concave head that can be placed in the ground to support a golf ball before it is struck from such an area. ■ *Football* a small stand on which the ball is placed for a placekick. **2** a mark aimed at in lawn bowling, quoits, curling, and other similar games.

▸ *v.* (**tees, teed, tee·ing**) [*intr.*] (usu. **tee up**) *Golf* place the ball on a tee ready to make the first stroke of the round or hole: *he had not missed a par as he teed up for the last hole* | [*tr.*] *she fished in her pocket for a ball and teed it.* ■ [*tr.*] place (something) in position, esp. to be struck: *a shining white radar dome was teed up on top of the mountain.*

▸ *phrasal v.* □ **tee off** *Golf* play the ball from a tee; begin a round or hole of golf: *we spend ten minutes practicing putting before we tee off.* ■ *inf.* make a start on something. □ **tee someone off** *inf.* make someone angry or annoyed: *Tommy was really teed off at Ernie.*

tee[3] ▸ *n. inf.* a T-shirt.

tee-hee /tē ˈhē/ ▸ *n.* a giggle or titter.

▸ *v.* (**-hees, -heed, -hee·ing**) [*intr.*] titter or giggle in such a way.

teem[1] /tēm/ ▸ *v.* [*intr.*] (**teem with**) be full of or swarming with: *every garden is teeming with wildlife.*

teem[2] ▸ *v.* [*intr.*] (of water, esp. rain) pour down; fall heavily: *with the rain teeming down at the manor, Italy seemed a long way off.*

teen /tēn/ *inf.* ▸ *adj.* of or relating to teenagers: *a teen idol.* ▸ *n.* a teenager.

teen·age /ˈtēnˌāj/ ▸ *adj.* denoting a person between 13 and 19 years old: *a teenage girl.* ■ relating to or characteristic of people of this age: *teenage magazines.* —**teen·aged** *adj.*

teen·ag·er /ˈtēnˌājər/ ▸ *n.* a person aged from 13 to 19 years.

teens /tēnz/ ▸ *pl. n.* the years of a person's age from 13 to 19: *they were both in their late teens.*

teen·sy /ˈtēnsē/ ▸ *adj.* (**-si·er, -si·est**) *inf.* tiny.

tee·ny /ˈtēnē/ ▸ *adj.* (**-ni·er, -ni·est**) *inf.* tiny: *a teeny bit of criticism.*

tee·ny·bop·per /ˈtēnēˌbäpər/ ▸ *n. inf.* a young teenager, esp. a girl, who keenly follows the latest fashions in clothes and pop music. —**tee·ny·bop** *adj.*

tee·pee ▸ *n.* variant spelling of **TEPEE**.

tee shirt ▸ *n.* variant spelling of **T-SHIRT**.

tee·ter /ˈtētər/ ▸ *v.* [*intr.*] move or balance unsteadily; sway back and forth. ■ (often **teeter between**) *fig.* be unable to decide between different courses; waver: *she teetered between tears and anger.*

teeth /tēth/ ▸ plural form of **TOOTH**.

teethe /tēTH/ ▸ *v.* [*intr.*] grow or cut teeth, esp. milk teeth. —**teeth·ing** *adj.*

tee·to·tal /ˈtēˌtōtl/ ▸ *adj.* choosing or characterized by abstinence from alcohol: *a teetotal lifestyle.* —**tee·to·tal·ism** /-ˌizəm/ *n.*

tee·to·tal·er /ˈtēˌtōtl-ər/ (*Brit.* **tee·to·tal·ler**) ▸ *n.* a person who never drinks alcohol.

Tef·lon /ˈtefˌlän/ ▸ *n.* trademark for **POLYTETRAFLUOROETHYLENE**.

▸ *adj.* able to withstand criticism or attack with no apparent effect: *the head of the crime family is known as the Teflon Don because of his acquittals in three previous trials.*

tel·e·cast /ˈteləˌkast/ ▸ *n.* a television broadcast.

▸ *v.* [*tr.*] transmit by television: *the program will be telecast simultaneously to nearly 150 cities.* —**tel·e·cast·er** *n.*

tel·e·com·mu·ni·ca·tion /ˌteləkəˌmyo͞oniˈkāshən/ ▸ *n.* communication over a distance by cable, telegraph, telephone, or broadcasting. ■ (**telecommunications**) [treated as *sing.*] the branch of technology concerned with such communication. ■ *formal* a message sent by such means.

tel·e·com·mute /ˌteləkəˈmyo͞ot/ ▸ *v.* [*intr.*] work from home, communicating with the workplace using equipment such as telephones, fax machines, and modems. —**tel·e·com·mut·er** *n.*

tel·e·con·fer·ence /ˈteləˌkänf(ə)rəns/ ▸ *n.* a conference with participants in different locations linked by telecommunications devices.

▸ *v.* [*intr.*] participate in a teleconference: *he teleconferenced with everyone who had been in attendance.* —**tel·e·con·fer·enc·ing** /ˌteləˈkänf(ə)rənsiNG/ *n.*

tel·e·gen·ic /ˌteləˈjenik/ ▸ *adj.* having an appearance or manner that is appealing on television: *his telegenic charm appears to be his major asset.* —**tel·e·gen·i·cal·ly** /-ik(ə)lē/ *adv.*

tel·e·gram /ˈteləˌgram/ ▸ *n.* a message sent by telegraph and then delivered in written or printed form.

tel·e·graph /ˈteləˌgraf/ ▸ *n.* a system for transmitting messages from a distance along a wire, esp. one creating signals by making and breaking an electrical connection: *news came from the outside world by telegraph.* ■ a device for transmitting messages in such a way.

▸ *v.* [*tr.*] send (someone) a message by telegraph. ■ send (a message) by telegraph. ■ convey (an intentional or unconscious message), esp. with facial expression or body language: *a tiny movement of her arm telegraphed her intention to strike.* —**te·leg·ra·pher** /təˈlegrəfər/ *n.*

tel·e·graph·ic /ˌteləˈgrafik/ ▸ *adj.* **1** of or by telegraphs or telegrams: *the telegraphic transfer of the funds.* **2** (esp. of speech) omitting inessential words; concise. —**tel·e·graph·i·cal·ly** /-ik(ə)lē/ *adv.*

te·leg·ra·phy /təˈlegrəfē/ ▸ *n.* the science or practice of using or constructing communications systems for the transmission or reproduction of information.

tel·e·im·mer·sion /ˌtelə iˈmərzhən; -shən/ ▸ *n.* two-way remote communication in which each party gets an audio and three-dimensional visual representation of the other, via high-speed data exchange: *teleimmersion allows users to climb into a computer screen.*

tel·e·ki·ne·sis /ˌteləkiˈnēsis/ ▸ *n.* the supposed ability to move objects at a distance by mental power or other nonphysical means. —**tel·e·ki·net·ic** /-ˈnetik/ *adj.*

tel·e·mark /ˈtelə₁märk/ *Skiing* ▸*n.* a turn in downhill skiing or a landing style in ski jumping with one ski advanced and the knees bent.
▸*v.* [*intr.*] perform such a turn while skiing.

tel·e·mar·ket·ing /ˈtelə₁märkidiNG/ ▸*n.* the marketing of goods or services by means of telephone calls, typically unsolicited, to potential customers. **—tel·e·mar·ket·er** /-₁märkidər/ *n.*

te·lem·e·ter ▸*n.* /təˈlemitər; ˈtelə₁mētər/ an apparatus for recording the readings of an instrument and transmitting them by radio.
▸*v.* /ˈtelə₁mētər/ [*tr.*] transmit (readings) to a distant receiving set or station. **—tel·e·met·ric** /ˌteləˈmetrik/ *adj.* **—te·lem·e·try** /təˈlemitrē/ *n.*

tel·e·ol·o·gy /ˌtelēˈäləjē; ˌtēlē-/ ▸*n.* (*pl.* **-gies**) *Philos.* the explanation of phenomena by the purpose they serve rather than by postulated causes. **—tel·e·o·log·ic** /-əˈläjik/ *adj.* **—tel·e·o·log·i·cal** /-əˈläjikəl/ *adj.* **—tel·e·o·log·i·cal·ly** /-əˈläjik(ə)lē/ *adv.* **—tel·e·ol·o·gism** /-₁jizəm/ *n.* **—tel·e·ol·o·gist** /-jist/ *n.*

tel·e·path /ˈteləˌpaTH/ ▸*n.* a person with the ability to communicate using telepathy.

te·lep·a·thy /təˈlepəTHē/ ▸*n.* the supposed communication of thoughts or ideas by means other than the known senses. **—tel·e·path·ic** /ˌteləˈpaTHik/ *adj.* **—tel·e·path·i·cal·ly** /ˌteləˈpaTHik(ə)lē/ *adv.* **—te·lep·a·thist** /-THist/ *n.*

tel·e·phone /ˈteləˌfōn/ ▸*n.* **1** a system that converts acoustic vibrations to electrical signals in order to transmit sound, typically voices, over a distance using wire or radio. ▪ an instrument used as part of such a system, typically a single unit including a handset with a transmitting microphone and a set of numbered buttons by which a connection can be made to another such instrument. **2** a game in which a message is distorted by being passed around in a whisper.
▸*v.* [*tr.*] call or speak to (someone) using the telephone: *he had just finished telephoning his wife.* ▪ [*intr.*] make a telephone call: *she telephoned for help.* ▪ send (a message) by telephone. **—tel·e·phon·er** *n.* **—tel·e·phon·ic** /ˌteləˈfänik/ *adj.* **—tel·e·phon·i·cal·ly** /ˌteləˈfänik(ə)lē/ *adv.*

tel·e·phone booth ▸*n.* a public booth or enclosure housing a pay phone.

te·leph·o·ny /təˈlefənē; ˈteləˌfōnē/ ▸*n.* the working or use of telephones.

tel·e·pho·to lens /ˈteləˌfōtō/ ▸*n.* a lens with a longer focal length than standard, giving a narrow field of view and a magnified image.

tel·e·pho·tog·ra·phy /ˌteləfəˈtägrəfē/ ▸*n.* the photographing of distant objects with a telephoto lens.

tel·e·port /ˈteləˌpôrt/ ▸*v.* (esp. in science fiction) transport or be transported across space and distance instantly.
▸*n.* **1** a center providing interconnections between different forms of telecommunications, esp. one that links satellites to ground-based communications. **2** an act of teleporting. **—tel·e·por·ta·tion** /ˌteləˌpôrˈtāSHən/ *n.*

tel·e·print·er /ˈteləˌprin(t)ər/ ▸*n.* a device for transmitting telegraph messages as they are keyed, and for printing messages received.

Tel·e·Promp·Ter /ˈteləˌpräm(p)tər/ ▸*n. trademark* a device used in television and moviemaking to project a speaker's script out of sight of the audience.

tel·e·scope /ˈteləˌskōp/ ▸*n.* an optical instrument designed to make distant objects appear nearer, containing an arrangement of lenses, or of curved mirrors and lenses, by which rays of light are collected and focused and the resulting image magnified. ▪ short for **RADIO TELESCOPE**.
▸*v.* [*tr.*] cause (an object made of concentric tubular parts) to slide into itself, so that it becomes smaller. ▪ [*intr.*] be capable of sliding together in this way: *five steel sections that telescope into one another.* ▪ crush (a vehicle) by the force of an impact. ▪ *fig.* condense or conflate so as to occupy less space or time: *a way of telescoping many events into a relatively brief period.*

tel·e·scop·ic /ˌteləˈskäpik/ ▸*adj.* **1** of, relating to, or made with a telescope. ▪ capable of viewing and magnifying distant objects. ▪ visible only through a telescope. **2** having or consisting of concentric tubular sections designed to slide into one another. **—tel·e·scop·i·cal·ly** /-ik(ə)lē/ *adv.*

tel·e·scop·ic sight ▸*n.* a small telescope used for sighting, typically mounted on a rifle.

tel·e·sur·ger·y /ˈteləˌsərjərē/ ▸*n.* surgery performed by a doctor considerably distant from the patient, using medical robotics and multimedia image communication. **—tel·e·sur·geon** /ˈteləˌsərjən/ *n.*

tel·e·text /ˈteləˌtekst/ ▸*n.* a news and information service in the form of text and graphics, transmitted using the spare capacity of existing television channels to televisions with appropriate receivers.

tel·e·thon /ˈteləˌTHän/ ▸*n.* a very long television program, typically one broadcast to raise money for a charity.

Tel·e·type /ˈteləˌtīp/ (often **tele·type**) ▸*n. trademark* a kind of teleprinter. ▪ a message received and printed by a teleprinter.
▸*v.* [*tr.*] send (a message) by means of a teleprinter.

tel·e·type·writ·er /ˌteləˈtīp₁rītər/ ▸*n.* a teleprinter.

tel·e·van·ge·list /ˌteləˈvanjəlist/ ▸*n.* an evangelical preacher who appears regularly on television to preach and appeal for funds. **—tel·e·van·gel·i·cal** /ˌteləˌvanˈjelikəl/ *adj.* **—tel·e·van·ge·lism** /-₁lizəm/ *n.*

tel·e·vise /ˈteləˌvīz/ ▸*v.* [*tr.*] transmit by television: *a live televised debate between the party leaders.* **—tel·e·vis·a·ble** *adj.*

tel·e·vi·sion /ˈteləˌviZHən/ ▸*n.* **1** a system for transmitting visual images and sound that are reproduced on screens, chiefly used to broadcast programs for entertainment, information, and education. ▪ the activity, profession, or medium of broadcasting on television: *neither of my children showed an inclination to follow me into television* | [as *adj.*] *television news.* ▪ television programs. **2** (also **television set**) a box-shaped device that receives television signals and reproduces them on a screen.
▸ □ **on (the) television** being broadcast by television; appearing in a television program: *Norman was on television yesterday.*

tel·ex /ˈteleks/ ▸*n.* an international system of telegraphy of printed messages using the public telecommunications network. ▪ a device used for this. ▪ a message sent by this system.
▸*v.* [*tr.*] communicate with (someone) by telex. ▪ send (a message) by telex.

tell[1] /tel/ ▸*v.* (*past* **told** /tōld/) **1** [*tr.*] communicate information, facts, or news to someone in spoken or written words: *I told her you were coming* | *"We have nothing in common," she told him* | *he's telling the truth* | *we must be told the facts.* ▪ order, instruct, or advise (someone) to do something: *tell him to go away.* ▪ [*tr.*] narrate or relate (a tale or story). ▪ reveal (information) to someone in a nonverbal way: *the figures tell a different story* | *the smile on her face told him everything.* ▪ [*intr.*] divulge confidential or private information: *promise you won't tell.* ▪ [*intr.*] (**tell on**) *inf.* inform someone of the misdemeanors of: *friends don't tell on each other.* **2** [*tr.*] decide or determine correctly or with certainty: *you can tell they're in love.* ▪ distinguish (one person or thing) from another; perceive (the difference) between one person or thing and another: *I can't tell the difference between margarine and butter.* **3** [*intr.*] (of an experience or period of time) have a noticeable, typically harmful, effect on someone: *the strain of supporting the family was beginning to tell on him.* ▪ (of a particular factor) play a part in the success or otherwise of someone or something: *lack of fitness told against him on his first run of the season.* **4** [*tr.*] *archaic* count (the members of a series or group): *the shepherd had told all his sheep.*
▸*phrasal v.* □ **tell someone off** *inf.* reprimand or scold someone.
▸*n.* (esp. in poker) an unconscious behavior that is thought to betray an attempted deception. **—tell·a·ble** *adj.*
▸ □ **as far as one can tell** judging from the available information. □ **I (or I'll) tell you what** used to introduce a suggestion: *I tell you what, why don't we meet for lunch tomorrow?* □ **I told you (so)** used as a way of pointing out that one's warnings, although ignored, have been proved to be well founded. □ **tell it like it is** *inf.* describe the facts of a situation no matter how unpleasant they may be. □ **tell tales** make known or gossip about another person's secrets, wrongdoings, or faults. □ **tell time** be able to ascertain the time from reading the face of a clock or watch. □ **tell someone where to get off** (or **where they get off**) *inf.* angrily dismiss or rebuke someone. □ **tell someone where to put** (or **what to do with**) **something** *inf.* angrily or emphatically reject something: *I told him what he could do with his diamond.* □ **there is no telling** used to convey the impossibility of knowing what has happened or will happen: *there's no telling how she will react.* □ **to tell (you) the truth** used as a preface to a confession or admission of something. □ **you're telling me!** *inf.* used to emphasize that one is already well aware of something or in complete agreement with a statement.

tell[2] ▸*n. Archaeol.* (in the Middle East) an artificial mound formed by the accumulated remains of ancient settlements.

tell·er /ˈtelər/ ▸*n.* **1** a person employed to deal with customers' transactions in a bank. ▪ an automated teller machine. **2** a person who tells something: *a foul-mouthed teller of lies.* **3** a person appointed to count votes, esp. in a legislature.

tell·ing /ˈteliNG/ ▸*adj.* having a striking or revealing effect; significant: *a telling argument against this theory.* **—tell·ing·ly** *adv.*

---

tell·tale /'tel,tāl/ ▶*adj.* revealing, indicating, or betraying something: *the telltale bulge of a concealed weapon.*
▶*n.* **1** a person, esp. a child, who reports others' wrongdoings or reveals their secrets. **2** a device or object that automatically gives a visual indication of the state or presence of something.

tel·lu·ri·an /tə'loŏrēən/ ▶*adj. formal* or *poetic/lit.* of or inhabiting the earth.
▶*n. formal* or *poetic/lit.* an inhabitant of the earth.

tel·lu·ri·um /tə'loŏrēəm/ ▶*n.* the chemical element of atomic number 52, a brittle, shiny, silvery-white semiconducting semimetal resembling selenium and occurring mainly in small amounts in metallic sulfide ores. (Symbol: **Te**) —**tel·lu·ride** /'telyə,rīd/ *n.*

te·mer·i·ty /tə'meritē/ ▶*n.* excessive confidence or boldness; audacity. ▷late Middle English: from Latin *temeritas*, from *temere* 'rashly.'

temp[1] /temp/ *inf.* ▶*n.* a temporary employee, typically an office worker who finds employment through an agency.
▶*v.* [*intr.*] work as a temporary employee.

temp[2] ▶*abbr.* temperature.

tem·per /'tempər/ ▶*n.* **1** a person's state of mind seen in terms of their being angry or calm: *he rushed out in a very bad temper.* ■ a tendency to become angry easily: *I know my temper gets the better of me at times.* ■ an angry state of mind: *Drew had walked out* **in a temper** | *I only said it in* **a fit of temper.** ■ a character or mode of thought: *the temper of the late sixties.* **2** the degree of hardness and elasticity in steel or other metal: *the blade rapidly heats up and the metal loses its temper.*
▶*v.* [*tr.*] **1** improve the hardness and elasticity of (steel or other metal) by reheating and then cooling it. ■ improve the consistency or resiliency of (a substance) by heating it or adding particular substances to it. **2** serve as a neutralizing or counterbalancing force to (something): *their idealism is tempered with realism.* **3** tune (a piano or other instrument) so as to adjust the note intervals correctly. ▷Old English *temprian* 'bring something into the required condition by mixing it with something else,' from Latin *temperare* 'mingle, restrain oneself.' Sense development was probably influenced by Old French *temprer* 'to temper, moderate.' The noun originally denoted a proportionate mixture of elements or qualities, also the combination of the four bodily humors, believed in medieval times to be the basis of temperament, hence sense 1 (late Middle English).
▶ □ **keep** (or **lose**) **one's temper** refrain (or fail to refrain) from becoming angry. □ **out of temper** in an irritable mood.

tem·per·a /'tempərə/ ▶*n.* a method of painting with pigments dispersed in an emulsion miscible with water, typically egg yolk. The method was used in Europe for fine painting, mainly on wood panels, from the 12th or early 13th century until the 15th, when it began to give way to oils. ■ emulsion used in this method of painting.

tem·per·a·ment /'temp(ə)rəmənt/ ▶*n.* **1** a person's or animal's nature, esp. as it permanently affects their behavior: *she had an artistic temperament.* ■ the tendency to behave angrily or emotionally. **2** the adjustment of intervals in tuning a piano or other musical instrument so as to fit the scale for use in different keys; in **equal temperament**, the octave consists of twelve equal semitones.

tem·per·a·men·tal /,temp(ə)rə'mentl/ ▶*adj.* **1** (of a person) liable to unreasonable changes of mood. **2** of or relating to a person's temperament. —**tem·per·a·men·tal·ly** *adv.*

tem·per·ance /'temp(ə)rəns/ ▶*n.* abstinence from alcoholic drink: [as *adj.*] *the temperance movement.* ■ moderation or self-restraint, esp. in eating and drinking.

tem·per·ate /'temp(ə)rət/ ▶*adj.* **1** of, relating to, or denoting a region or climate characterized by mild temperatures. **2** showing moderation or self-restraint: *Charles was temperate in his consumption of both food and drink.* —**tem·per·ate·ly** *adv.* —**tem·per·ate·ness** *n.*

tem·per·a·ture /'temp(ə)rəCHər/ -,CHoŏr/ ▶*n.* the degree or intensity of heat present in a substance or object, esp. as expressed according to a comparative scale and shown by a thermometer or perceived by touch. ■ *Med.* the degree of internal heat of a person's body: *I'll* **take her temperature.** ■ *inf.* a body temperature above the normal; fever: *he was* **running a temperature.** ■ the degree of excitement or tension in a discussion or confrontation.

tem·pest /'tempist/ ▶*n.* a violent windy storm.
▶ □ **a tempest in a teapot** great commotion about a trivial matter.

tem·pes·tu·ous /tem'pesCHoŏəs/ ▶*adj.* **1** characterized by strong and turbulent or conflicting emotion: *he had a reckless and tempestuous streak.* **2** very stormy: *a tempestuous wind.* —**tem·pes·tu·ous·ly** *adv.* —**tem·pes·tu·ous·ness** *n.*

tem·plate /'templət/ ▶*n.* a shaped piece of metal, wood, card, plastic, or other material used as a pattern for processes such as painting, cutting out, shaping, or drilling. ■ *fig.* something that serves as a model for others to copy: *the plant was to serve as the template for change throughout the company.* ■ *Comput.* a preset format for a document or file, used so that the format does not have to be recreated each time it is used: *a memo template.* ■ *Comput.* a guide that fits over all or part of a computer keyboard to describe the functions of each key for a particular software application. ■ *Biochem.* a nucleic acid molecule that acts as a pattern for the sequence of assembly of a protein, nucleic acid, or other large molecule.

tem·ple[1] /'tempəl/ ▶*n.* a building devoted to the worship, or regarded as the dwelling place, of a god or gods or other objects of religious reverence. ■ (**the Temple**) either of two successive religious buildings of the Jews in Jerusalem. The first (957–586 BC) was built by Solomon. The second (515 BC–AD 70) was destroyed by the Romans during a Jewish revolt. ■ a synagogue. ■ a place of Christian public worship, esp. a Protestant church in France.

tem·ple[2] ▶*n.* the flat part of either side of the head between the forehead and the ear.

tem·po /'tempō/ ▶*n.* (*pl.* **-pos** or **-pi** /-pē/) **1** *Mus.* the speed at which a passage of music is or should be played. **2** the rate or speed of motion or activity; pace: *the tempo of life dictated by a heavy workload.*

tem·po·ral[1] /'temp(ə)rəl/ ▶*adj.* **1** relating to worldly as opposed to spiritual affairs; secular. **2** of or relating to time. ■ *Gram.* relating to or denoting time or tense. —**tem·po·ral·ly** *adv.*

tem·po·ral[2] ▶*adj. Anat.* of or situated in the temples of the head.

tem·po·ral lobe ▶*n.* each of the paired lobes of the brain lying beneath the temples, including areas concerned with the understanding of speech.

tem·po·rar·y /'tempə,rerē/ ▶*adj.* lasting for only a limited period of time; not permanent: *a temporary job.*
▶*n.* (*pl.* **-rar·ies**) a person employed on a temporary basis, typically an office worker who finds employment through an agency. See also TEMP[1]. —**tem·po·rar·i·ly** /,tempə're(ə)rəlē; 'tempə,rer-/ *adv.* —**tem·po·rar·i·ness** *n.*

tem·po·rize /'tempə,rīz/ ▶*v.* **1** [*intr.*] avoid making a decision or committing oneself in order to gain time. **2** temporarily adopt a particular course in order to conform to the circumstances: *their unwillingness to temporize had driven their country straight into conflict with France.* —**tem·po·ri·za·tion** /,tempəri'zāsHən/ *n.* —**tem·po·riz·er** *n.*

tempt /tem(p)t/ ▶*v.* [*tr.*] entice or attempt to entice (someone) to do or acquire something that they find attractive but know to be wrong or not beneficial: *jobs that involve entertaining may tempt you to drink more than you intend.* ■ (**be tempted to do something**) have an urge or inclination to do something: *I was tempted to look at my watch, but didn't dare.* ■ attract; allure: *he was tempted out of retirement to save the team.* ■ *archaic* risk provoking (a deity or abstract force), usually with undesirable consequences.
▶ □ **tempt fate** (or **providence**) do something that one knows to be risky or dangerous.

temp·ta·tion /tem(p)'tāsHən/ ▶*n.* a desire to do something, esp. something wrong or unwise: *he resisted the temptation to call Celia at the office* | *we almost gave in to temptation.* ■ a thing or course of action that attracts or tempts someone: *the temptations of life in New York.*

tempt·er /'tem(p)tər/ ▶*n.* a person or thing that tempts. ■ (**the Tempter**) the Devil.

tempt·ing /'tem(p)tiNG/ ▶*adj.* appealing to or attracting someone, even if wrong or inadvisable: *a tempting financial offer.* —**tempt·ing·ly** *adv.*

tempt·ress /'tem(p)tris/ ▶*n.* a woman who tempts someone to do something, typically a sexually attractive woman who sets out to allure or seduce someone.

tem·pu·ra /tem'poŏrə/ ▶*n.* a Japanese dish of fish, shellfish, or vegetables, fried in batter.

ten /ten/ ▶*cardinal number* equivalent to the product of five and two; one more than nine; 10. (Roman numeral: **x**, **X**) ■ a group or unit of ten people or things: *count in tens.* ■ ten years old. ■ ten o'clock. ■ a size of garment or other merchandise denoted by ten. ■ a ten-dollar bill: *he took the money in tens.* ■ a playing card with ten pips. ■ (**a ten**) used to indicate that someone has done something well; the highest mark on a scale of one to ten: *I would have to give them a ten for all the work they did.* ▷Old English *tēn*, *tien*, of Germanic origin; related to Dutch *tien* and German *zehn*, from an Indo-European root shared by Sanskrit *daśa*, Greek *deka*, and Latin *decem.*

ten·a·ble /'tenəbəl/ ▶*adj.* **1** able to be maintained or defended against attack or objection: *such a simplistic approach is no longer tenable.* **2** (of an office, position, scholarship, etc.) able to be held or used. —**ten·a·bil·i·ty** /,tenə'bilitē/ *n.*

te·na·cious /təˈnāSHəs/ ▸*adj.* not readily letting go of, giving up, or separated from an object that one holds, a position, or a principle: *a tenacious grip.* ■ not easily dispelled or discouraged; persisting in existence or in a course of action: *you're tenacious and you get at the truth.* —**te·na·cious·ly** *adv.* —**te·na·cious·ness** *n.* —**te·nac·i·ty** /-ˈnasitē/ *n.*

ten·an·cy /ˈtenənsē/ ▸*n.* (*pl.* **-cies**) possession of land or property as a tenant: *Holding took over the tenancy of the farm.*

ten·ant /ˈtenənt/ ▸*n.* a person who occupies land or property rented from a landlord. ■ *Law* a person holding real property by private ownership.
▸*v.* [*tr.*] (usu. **be tenanted**) occupy (property) as a tenant. —**ten·ant·a·ble** *adj.* (*formal*) —**ten·ant·less** *adj.*

tend[1] /tend/ ▸*v.* [*intr.*] regularly or frequently behave in a particular way or have a certain characteristic: *written language tends to be formal.* ■ [*intr.*] (**tend to/toward**) be liable to possess or display (a particular characteristic): *Walter tended toward corpulence.* ■ [*intr.*] go or move in a particular direction: *the road tends west around small mountains.* ■ [*intr.*] (**tend to**) *Math.* approach (a quantity or limit): *the Fourier coefficients tend to zero.*

tend[2] ▸*v.* [*tr.*] care for or look after; give one's attention to: *Viola tended plants on the roof* | [*intr.*] *he tended to business.* ■ direct or manage; work in: *I've been tending bar at the airport lounge.* ■ *archaic* wait on as an attendant or servant. —**tend·ance** /ˈtendəns/ *n.* (*archaic*).

ten·den·cy /ˈtendənsē/ ▸*n.* (*pl.* **-cies**) an inclination toward a particular characteristic or type of behavior: *for students, there is a tendency to socialize in the evenings* | *criminal tendencies.* ■ a group within a larger political party or movement: *the dominant tendency in the party.*

ten·den·tious /tenˈdenSHəs/ ▸*adj.* expressing or intending to promote a particular cause or point of view, esp. a controversial one: *a tendentious reading of history.* —**ten·den·tious·ly** *adv.* —**ten·den·tious·ness** *n.*

ten·der[1] /ˈtendər/ ▸*adj.* (**-der·er, -der·est**) **1** showing gentleness and concern or sympathy: *he was being so kind and tender.* ■ (**tender of**) *archaic* solicitous of; concerned for: *be tender of a lady's reputation.* **2** (of food) easy to cut or chew; not tough: *tender green beans.* ■ (of a plant) easily injured by severe weather and therefore needing protection. ■ (of a part of the body) sensitive to pain: *the pale, tender skin of her forearm.* ■ young, immature, and vulnerable: *at the tender age of five.* ■ requiring tact or careful handling: *the issue of conscription was a particularly tender one.* ■ *Naut.* (of a ship) leaning or readily inclined to roll in response to the wind. —**ten·der·ly** *adv.* —**ten·der·ness** *n.*

ten·der[2] ▸*v.* [*tr.*] offer or present (something) formally: *he tendered his resignation as leader.* ■ offer (money) as payment: *she tendered her fare.* ■ [*intr.*] make a formal written offer to carry out work, supply goods, or buy land, shares, or another asset for a stated fixed price: *firms of interior decorators have been tendering for the work.* ■ [*tr.*] make such an offer giving (a stated fixed price): *what price should we tender for a contract?*
▸*n.* an offer to carry out work, supply goods, or buy land, shares, or another asset at a stated fixed price. —**ten·der·er** *n.*

ten·der[3] ▸*n.* **1** [usu. in *comb.*] a person who looks after someone else or a machine or place. **2** a boat used to ferry people and supplies to and from a ship. **3** a rail car coupled to a steam locomotive to carry fuel and water.

ten·der·foot /ˈtendərˌfo͝ot/ ▸*n.* (*pl.* **-foots** or **-feet**) **1** a newcomer or novice, esp. a person unaccustomed to the hardships of pioneer life. **2** a Boy Scout of the lowest rank.

ten·der·ize /ˈtendəˌrīz/ ▸*v.* make (meat) more tender by beating or slow cooking. —**ten·der·iz·er** *n.*

ten·der·loin /ˈtendərˌloin/ ▸*n.* **1** the tenderest part of a loin of beef, pork, etc., taken from under the short ribs in the hindquarters. ■ the undercut of a sirloin. **2** *inf.* a district of a city where vice and corruption are prominent.

ten·don /ˈtendən/ ▸*n.* a flexible but inelastic cord of strong fibrous collagen tissue attaching a muscle to a bone. ■ the hamstring of a quadruped. —**ten·di·ni·tis** /ˌtendəˈnītis/ *n.* —**ten·di·nous** /-dənəs/ *adj.*

ten·dril /ˈtendrəl/ ▸*n.* a slender threadlike appendage of a climbing plant, often growing in a spiral form, that stretches out and twines around any suitable support. ■ something resembling a plant tendril, esp. a slender curl or ringlet of hair.

ten·e·ment /ˈtenəmənt/ ▸*n.* **1** a room or a set of rooms forming a separate residence within a house or block of apartments. ■ (also **tenement house**) a house divided into and rented in such separate residences, esp. one that is run-down and overcrowded. **2** a piece of land held by an owner. ■ *Law* any kind of permanent property, e.g., lands or rents, held from a superior.

ten·et /ˈtenit/ ▸*n.* a principle or belief, esp. one of the main principles of a religion or philosophy: *the tenets of classical liberalism.*

ten·fold /ˈtenˌfōld/ ▸*adj.* ten times as great or as numerous: *a tenfold increase in the use of insecticides.* ■ having ten parts or elements.
▸*adv.* by ten times; to ten times the number or amount.

ten·nis /ˈtenis/ ▸*n.* a game in which two or four players strike a ball with rackets over a net stretched across a court. The usual form (originally called **lawn tennis**) is played with a felt-covered hollow rubber ball on a grass, clay, or artificial surface.

ten·nis el·bow ▸*n.* inflammation of the tendons of the elbow caused by overuse of the muscles of the forearm.

ten·nis shoe ▸*n.* a light canvas or leather soft-soled shoe suitable for tennis or casual wear.

ten·on /ˈtenən/ ▸*n.* a projecting piece of wood made for insertion into a mortise in another piece. —**ten·on·er** *n.*

ten·or[1] /ˈtenər/ ▸*n.* a singing voice between baritone and alto or countertenor, the highest of the ordinary adult male range. ■ a singer with such a voice. ■ a part written for such a voice. ■ [usu. as *adj.*] an instrument, esp. a saxophone, trombone, tuba, or viol, of the lowest pitch but one in its family: *a tenor sax.* ■ (in full **tenor bell**) the largest and deepest bell of a ring or set.

ten·or[2] ▸*n.* **1** (usu. **the tenor of**) the general meaning, sense, or content of something: *the general tenor of the debate.* ■ the subject to which a metaphor refers, e.g., "a large, difficult challenge" conveyed by *bear* in *this one is going to be a bear.* **2** (usu. **the tenor of**) a settled or prevailing character or direction, esp. the course of a person's life or habits: *the even tenor of life in the kitchen was disrupted the following day.* **3** *Finance* the time that must elapse before a bill of exchange or promissory note becomes due for payment.

ten·pin bowl·ing ▸*n.* a game in which ten wooden pins are set up at the end of a lane (typically one of several in a large, automated alley) and bowled down with hard rubber or plastic balls.

tense[1] /tens/ ▸*adj.* (esp. of a muscle or someone's body) stretched tight or rigid. ■ (of a person) unable to relax because of nervousness, anxiety, or stimulation. ■ (of a situation, event, etc.) causing or showing anxiety and nervousness: *relations between the two neighboring states had been tense.* ■ *Phonet.* (of a speech sound, esp. a vowel) pronounced with the vocal muscles stretched tight. The opposite of **LAX**.
▸*v.* [*intr.*] become tense, typically through anxiety or nervousness: *her body tensed up.* ■ [*tr.*] make (a muscle or one's body) tight or rigid: *carefully stretch and then tense your muscles.* —**tense·ly** *adv.* —**tense·ness** *n.* —**ten·si·ty** /ˈtensitē/ *n.* (*dated*).

tense[2] ▸*n. Gram.* a set of forms taken by a verb to indicate the time (and sometimes also the continuance or completeness) of the action in relation to the time of the utterance: *the past tense.* —**tense·less** *adj.*

ten·sile /ˈtensəl; -ˌsīl/ ▸*adj.* **1** of or relating to tension. **2** capable of being drawn out or stretched. —**ten·sil·i·ty** /tenˈsilitē/ *n.*

ten·sile strength ▸*n.* the resistance of a material to breaking under tension.

ten·sion /ˈtenSHən/ ▸*n.* **1** the state of being stretched tight: *the parachute keeps the cable under tension as it drops.* ■ the state of having the muscles stretched tight, esp. as causing strain or discomfort: *the elimination of neck tension can relieve headaches.* ■ a strained state or condition resulting from forces acting in opposition to each other. ■ the degree of tightness of stitches in knitting and machine sewing. **2** mental or emotional strain. ■ a strained political or social state or relationship. | *racial tensions.* ■ a relationship between ideas or qualities with conflicting demands or implications: *the basic tension between freedom and control.* —**ten·sion·al** /-SHənl/ *adj.* —**ten·sion·al·ly** /-SHənl-ē/ *adv.* —**ten·sion·er** *n.* —**ten·sion·less** *adj.*

tent /tent/ ▸*n.* a portable shelter made of cloth, supported by one or more poles and stretched tight by cords or loops attached to pegs driven into the ground.
▸*v.* **1** [*tr.*] cover with or as if with a tent: *the garden had been completely tented over for supper.* ■ arrange in a shape that looks like a tent: *Tim tented his fingers.* ■ [as *adj.*] (**tented**) composed of or provided with tents: *they were living in large tented camps.* **2** [*intr.*] (esp. of traveling circus people) live in a tent.

ten·ta·cle /ˈten(t)əkəl/ ▸*n.* a slender flexible limb or appendage in an animal, esp. around the mouth of an invertebrate, used for grasping, moving about, or bearing sense organs. ■ something resembling a tentacle in shape or flexibility: *trailing tentacles of vapor.* ■ (usu. **tentacles**)

Pronunciation Key ə *ago,* up; ər *over,* fur; a *hat;* ā *ate;* ä *car;* CH *chin;* e *let;* ē *see;* e(ə)r *air;* i *fit;* ī *by;* i(ə)r *ear;* NG *sing;* ō *go;* ô *law, for;* oi *toy;* o͝o *good;* o͞o *goo;* ou *out;* SH *she;* TH *thin;* T͟H *then;* (h)w *why;* ZH *vision*

fig. an insidious spread of influence and control. **—ten·ta·cled** *adj.* [also in *comb.*] **—ten·tac·u·lar** /ten'takyələr/ *adj.* **—ten·tac·u·late** /ten-'takyələt/ *adj.*

ten·ta·tive /'tentətiv/ ▶*adj.* not certain or fixed; provisional: *a tentative conclusion.* ■ done without confidence; hesitant. **—ten·ta·tive·ly** *adv.* **—ten·ta·tive·ness** *n.*

tent cat·er·pil·lar ▶*n.* a chiefly American moth caterpillar (family Lasiocampidae) that lives in groups inside communal silken webs in a tree, which it often defoliates.

ten·ter·hook /'ten(t)ər,ho͝ok/ ▶*n.* (in the phrase **on tenterhooks**) in a state of suspense or agitation because of uncertainty about a future event.

tenth /tenTH/ ▶*n.* constituting number ten in a sequence; 10th: *the tenth century | the tenth of September | the tenth-floor locker room.* ■ (**a tenth/one tenth**) each of ten equal parts into which something is or may be divided. ■ the tenth grade of a school. ■ *Mus.* an interval or chord spanning an octave and a third in the diatonic scale, or a note separated from another by this interval. **—tenth·ly** *adv.*

tent peg ▶*n.* see PEG (sense 1).

ten·u·ous /'tenyo͞oəs/ ▶*adj.* very weak or slight: *the tenuous link between interest rates and investment.* ■ very slender or fine; insubstantial: *a tenuous cloud.* **—ten·u·ous·ly** *adv.* **—ten·u·ous·ness** *n.*

ten·ure /'tenyər; -,yo͝or/ ▶*n.* **1** the conditions under which land or buildings are held or occupied. **2** the holding of an office: *his tenure of the premiership would be threatened.* ■ a period for which an office is held. **3** guaranteed permanent employment, esp. as a teacher or professor, after a probationary period. ▶*v.* [tr.] give (someone) a permanent post, esp. as a teacher or professor: *I had recently been tenured and then promoted to full professor.* ■ [as *adj.*] (**tenured**) having or denoting such a post: *a tenured faculty member.* ▷late Middle English: from Old French, from *tenir* 'to hold,' from Latin *tenere*.

te·pee /'tē,pē/ (also **tee·pee**) ▶*n.* a portable conical tent made of skins, cloth, or canvas on a frame of poles, used by American Indians of the Plains and Great Lakes regions.

tep·id /'tepid/ ▶*adj.* (esp. of a liquid) only slightly warm; lukewarm. ■ *fig.* showing little enthusiasm: *the applause was tepid.* **—te·pid·i·ty** /tə-'piditē/ *n.* **—tep·id·ly** *adv.* **—tep·id·ness** *n.*

tepee

te·qui·la /tə'kēlə/ ▶*n.* a Mexican liquor made from an agave.

ter·a·byte /'terə,bīt/ (abbr.: **Tb** or **TB**) ▶*n. Comput.* a unit of information equal to one million million (10^{12}) or strictly, 2^{40} bytes.

ter·bi·um /'tərbēəm/ ▶*n.* the chemical element of atomic number 65, a silvery-white metal of the lanthanide series. (Symbol **Tb**)

terce /tərs/ ▶*n.* a service forming part of the Divine Office of the Western Christian Church, traditionally said (or chanted) at the third hour of the day (i.e., 9 a.m.).

ter·cen·ten·ni·al /,tərsen'tenēəl/ ▶*adj.* & *n.* another term for TRICENTENNIAL.

ter·e·binth /'terə,binTH/ ▶*n.* a small southern European tree (*Pistacia terebinthus*) of the cashew family that was formerly a source of turpentine.

ter·gi·ver·sate /'tərˈjivər,sāt; 'tərjivər-/ ▶*v.* [intr.] **1** make conflicting or evasive statements; equivocate. **2** change one's loyalties; be apostate. **—ter·gi·ver·sa·tion** /,tərjivər'sāsHən/ *n.* **—ter·gi·ver·sa·tor** /-,sātər/ *n.*

ter·i·ya·ki /,terē'yäkē/ ▶*n.* a Japanese dish consisting of fish or meat marinated in soy sauce and grilled. ■ (also **teriyaki sauce**) a mixture of soy sauce, sake, ginger, and other flavorings, used in Japanese cooking as a marinade or glaze for such dishes.

term /tərm/ ▶*n.* **1** a word or phrase used to describe a thing or to express a concept, esp. in a particular kind of language or branch of study: *the musical term "leitmotiv".* ■ (**terms**) language used on a particular occasion; a way of expressing oneself: *a protest in the strongest possible terms.* ■ *Logic* a word or words that may be the subject or predicate of a proposition. **2** a fixed or limited period for which something, e.g., office, imprisonment, or investment, lasts or is intended to last: *elected for a single four-year term.* ■ *archaic* the duration of a person's life. ■ the completion of a normal length of pregnancy: *there can be as much as a 15% error in the estimated weight at term.* ■ *Law* a tenancy of a fixed

period. ■ *archaic* a boundary or limit, esp. of time. **3** each of the periods in the year, alternating with holidays or vacations, during which instruction is given in a school, college, or university, or during which a court holds sessions: *the summer term.* **4** (**terms**) conditions under which an action may be undertaken or agreement reached; stipulated or agreed-upon requirements: *the contract's terms.* ■ conditions with regard to payment for something; stated charges: *loans on favorable terms.* ■ agreed conditions under which a war or other dispute is brought to an end: *a deal in Bosnia that could force the Serbs to come to terms.* **5** *Math.* each of the quantities in a ratio, series, or mathematical expression. **6** *Archit.* another term for TERMINUS.
▶*v.* [tr.] give a descriptive name to; call by a specified name.
▶ □ **come to terms with** come to accept (a new and painful or difficult event or situation); reconcile oneself to. □ **in terms of** (or **in —— terms**) with regard to the particular aspect or subject specified: *replacing the printers is difficult to justify in terms of cost.* □ **on —— terms** in a specified relation or on a specified footing: *we are all on friendly terms.*

ter·ma·gant /'tərməgənt/ ▶*n.* a harsh-tempered or overbearing woman.

ter·mi·na·ble /'tərmənəbəl/ ▶*adj.* **1** able to be terminated. **2** coming to an end after a certain time.

ter·mi·nal /'tərmənl/ ▶*adj.* **1** of, forming, or situated at the end or extremity of something: *the terminal tip of the probe.* ■ of or forming a transportation terminal. ■ *Zool.* situated at, forming, or denoting the end of a part or series of parts furthest from the center of the body. ■ *Bot.* (of a flower, inflorescence, etc.) borne at the end of a stem or branch. **2** (of a disease) predicted to lead to death, esp. slowly; incurable. ■ suffering from or relating to such a disease: *a hospice for terminal cases.* ■ (of a condition) forming the last stage of such a disease. ■ *inf.* extreme and usually beyond cure or alteration (used to emphasize the extent of something regarded as bad or unfortunate): *you're making a terminal ass of yourself.*
▶*n.* **1** an end or extremity of something, in particular: ■ the end of a railroad or other transport route, or a station at such a point. ■ a departure and arrival building for air passengers at an airport. ■ an installation where oil or gas is stored at the end of a pipeline or at a port. **2** a point of connection for closing an electric circuit. **3** a device at which a user enters data or commands for a computer system and that displays the received output. **4** (also **terminal figure**) another term for TERMINUS (sense 3). **—ter·mi·nal·ly** *adv.*

ter·mi·nal ve·loc·i·ty ▶*n. Physics* the constant speed that a freely falling object eventually reaches when the resistance of the medium through which it is falling prevents further acceleration.

ter·mi·nate /'tərmə,nāt/ ▶*v.* [tr.] bring to an end. ■ [intr.] (**terminate in**) (of a thing) have its end at (a specified place) or of (a specified form): *the chain terminated in an iron ball covered with spikes.* ■ [intr.] (of a train, bus, or boat service) end its journey: *the train will terminate at Stratford.* ■ end (a pregnancy) before term by artificial means. ■ end the employment of (someone); dismiss. ■ assassinate (someone, esp. an intelligence agent). **—ter·mi·na·tion** /,tərmə'nāsHən/ *n.* **—ter·mi·na·tor** /,nātər/ *n.*

ter·mi·nol·o·gy /,tərmə'näləjē/ ▶*n.* (pl. **-gies**) the body of terms used with a particular technical application in a subject of study, theory, profession, etc. **—ter·mi·no·log·i·cal** /-nə'läjikəl/ *adj.* **—ter·mi·no·log·i·cal·ly** /-nə'läjik(ə)lē/ *adv.* **—ter·mi·nol·o·gist** /-jist/ *n.*

ter·mi·nus /'tərmənəs/ ▶*n.* (pl. **-ni** /-nī/ or **-nus·es**) **1** a final point in space or time; an end or extremity: *the exhibition's terminus is 1962.* **2** chiefly *Brit.* the end of a railroad or other transportation route, or a station at such a point; a terminal. ■ an oil or gas terminal. **3** *Archit.* a figure of a human bust or an animal ending in a square pillar from which it appears to spring, originally used as a boundary marker in ancient Rome.

ter·mite /'tər,mīt/ ▶*n.* a small, pale soft-bodied insect that lives in large colonies with several different castes, typically within a mound of cemented earth. Many kinds feed on wood and can be highly destructive to trees and timber. Also called WHITE ANT.

term life in·sur·ance ▶*n.* life insurance that pays a benefit in the event of the death of the insured during a specified term. Compare with WHOLE LIFE INSURANCE.

term pa·per ▶*n.* a student's lengthy essay on a subject drawn from the work done during a school or college term.

tern[1] /tərn/ ▶*n.* a seabird (*Sterna* and other genera, family Sternidae, or Laridae) related to the gulls, typically smaller and more slender, with long pointed wings and a forked tail.

tern[2] ▶*n. rare* a set of three, esp. three lottery numbers that when drawn together win a large prize.

ter·na·ry /'tərnərē/ ▶*adj.* composed of three parts. ■ *Math.* using three as a base.

terp·si·cho·re·an /ˌtərpsikəˈrēən; -ˈkôrēən/ ▶*adj.* formal or humorous of or relating to dancing.
▶*n.* formal or humorous a dancer.

terr. ▶*abbr.* ■ terrace. ■ territorial. ■ territory.

ter·race /ˈteris/ ▶*n.* **1** a level paved area or platform next to a building; a patio or veranda. ■ each of a series of flat areas made on a slope, used for cultivation. ■ *Geol.* a natural horizontal shelflike formation, such as a raised beach. **2** chiefly Brit. a block of row houses. ■ a row house.
▶*v.* [*tr.*] make or form (sloping land) into a number of level flat areas resembling a series of steps.

ter·ra cot·ta /ˈterə ˈkätə/ (also **ter·ra-cot·ta**) ▶*n.* unglazed, typically brownish-red earthenware, used chiefly as an ornamental building material and in modeling. ■ a statuette or other object made of such earthenware. ■ a strong brownish-red or brownish-orange color.

ter·ra fir·ma /ˈterə ˈfərmə/ ▶*n.* dry land; the ground as distinct from the sea or air.

ter·rain /təˈrān/ ▶*n.* **1** a stretch of land, esp. with regard to its physical features: *rough terrain.* **2** *Geol.* variant form of TERRANE.

ter·rane /təˈrān; ˈterˌān/ (also **ter·rain**) ▶*n.* *Geol.* a fault-bounded area or region with a distinctive stratigraphy, structure, and geological history.

ter·ra·pin /ˈterəˌpin/ ▶*n.* **1** a small turtle (*Malaclemys terrapin*) with lozenge-shaped markings on its shell, found in coastal marshes of the eastern US. **2** a freshwater turtle, esp. one of the smaller kinds of the Old World.

ter·rar·i·um /təˈre(ə)rēəm/ ▶*n.* (*pl.* **-rar·i·ums** or **-rar·i·a** /-ˈre(ə)rēə/) an enclosure, container, or structure for smaller land animals, esp. reptiles, amphibians, or terrestrial invertebrates, typically in the form of a glass-fronted case. ■ a sealed transparent globe or similar container in which plants are grown.

ter·res·tri·al /təˈrestrēəl; -ˈreschəl/ ▶*adj.* of, on, or relating to the earth: *increased ultraviolet radiation may disrupt terrestrial ecosystems.* ■ denoting television broadcast using equipment situated on the ground rather than by satellite: *terrestrial and cable technology.* ■ of or on dry land. ■ (of an animal) living on or in the ground; not aquatic, arboreal, or aerial. ■ (of a plant) growing on land or in the soil; not aquatic or epiphytic. ■ *Astron.* (of a planet) similar in size or composition to the earth, esp. being one of the four inner planets of our solar system. ■ *archaic* of or relating to the earth as opposed to heaven.
▶*n.* an inhabitant of the earth. —**ter·res·tri·al·ly** *adv.*

ter·ri·ble /ˈterəbəl/ ▶*adj.* extremely and shockingly or distressingly bad or serious: *terrible pain.* ■ causing or likely to cause terror; sinister: *the stranger gave a terrible smile.* ■ of extremely poor quality: *the terrible conditions in which the people lived.* ■ *inf.* used to emphasize the extent of something unpleasant or bad: *what a terrible mess.* ■ extremely incompetent or unskillful: *she is terrible at managing her money.* ■ feeling or looking extremely unwell: *I was sick all night and felt terrible for two solid days.* ■ (of a person or their feelings) troubled or guilty: *Maria felt terrible because she had forgotten the woman's name.* —**ter·ri·ble·ness** *n.*

ter·ri·bly /ˈterəblē/ ▶*adv.* **1** very; extremely: *I'm terribly sorry.* **2** very badly or unpleasantly: *they beat me terribly.* ■ very greatly (used to emphasize something bad, distressing, or unpleasant): *your father misses you terribly.*

ter·ri·er /ˈterēər/ ▶*n.* a small dog of a breed originally used for turning out foxes and other burrowing animals from their lairs. ▷late Middle English: from Old French (*chien*) *terrier* 'earth (dog),' from medieval Latin *terrarius*, from Latin *terra* 'earth.'

ter·rif·ic /təˈrifik/ ▶*adj.* **1** of great size, amount, or intensity: *there was a terrific bang.* ■ *inf.* extremely good; excellent: *it's been such a terrific day | you look terrific.* **2** *archaic* causing terror. —**ter·rif·i·cal·ly** /-ik(ə)lē/ *adv.*

ter·ri·fy /ˈterəˌfī/ ▶*v.* (**-fies, -fied**) [*tr.*] cause to feel extreme fear: *the thought terrifies me | he is terrified of spiders | [as adj.] (terrifying) the terrifying events of the past few weeks.* —**ter·ri·fi·er** *n.* —**ter·ri·fy·ing·ly** /ˈterəˌfī-iNGlē/ *adv.* *the bombs are terrifyingly accurate.*

ter·ri·to·ri·al /ˌteriˈtôrēəl/ ▶*adj.* **1** of or relating to the ownership of an area of land or sea: *territorial disputes.* ■ *Zool.* (of an animal or species) defending a territory: *these sharks are aggressively territorial.* ■ of or relating to an animal's territory or its defense. **2** of or relating to a particular territory, district, or locality: *a bizarre territorial rite.* ■ (usu. **Territorial**) of or relating to a Territory, in the U.S. or Canada. —**ter·ri·to·ri·al·i·ty** /-ˌtôrēˈalitē/ *n.* —**ter·ri·to·ri·al·ly** *adv.*

ter·ri·to·ri·al wa·ters ▶*pl. n.* the waters under the jurisdiction of a state, esp. the part of the sea within a stated distance of the shore (traditionally three miles from low-water mark).

ter·ri·to·ry /ˈterəˌtôrē/ ▶*n.* (*pl.* **-ries**) **1** an area of land under the jurisdiction of a ruler or state: *sorties into enemy territory.* ■ *Zool.* an area

defended by an animal or group of animals against others of the same sex or species. ■ an area defended by a team or player in a game or sport. ■ an area in which one has certain rights or for which one has responsibility with regard to a particular type of activity: *a sales rep for a large territory.* ■ *fig.* an area of knowledge, activity, or experience: *the way she felt now—she was in unknown territory.* ■ land with a specified characteristic: *woodland territory.* **2** (**Territory**) (esp. in the U.S., Canada, or Australia) an organized division of a country that is not yet admitted to the full rights of a state.
▶ □ **go** (or **come**) **with the territory** be an unavoidable result of a particular situation.

ter·ror /ˈterər/ ▶*n.* **1** extreme fear: *people fled in terror | a terror of darkness.* ■ the use of such fear to intimidate people, esp. for political reasons: *weapons of terror.* ■ a person or thing that causes extreme fear: *his unyielding scowl became **the terror** of the Chicago mob.* ■ *inf.* a person whose excellence in a particular field or endeavor intimidates others engaged in the same activity: *Stone is the terror of Halo video games.* ■ (**the Terror**) the period of the French Revolution between mid 1793 and July 1794 when the ruling Jacobins executed anyone considered a threat to their regime. Also called REIGN OF TERROR. **2** *inf.* a person, esp. a child, who causes trouble or annoyance.

ter·ror·ism /ˈterəˌrizəm/ ▶*n.* the use of violence and intimidation in the pursuit of political aims.

ter·ror·ist /ˈterərist/ ▶*n.* a person who uses terrorism in the pursuit of political aims. ▷late 18th cent.: from French *terroriste*, from Latin *terror* 'terror,' from *terrere* 'frighten.' The word was originally applied to supporters of the Jacobins in the French Revolution, who advocated repression and violence in pursuit of the principles of democracy and equality. —**ter·ror·is·tic** /ˌterəˈristik/ *adj.* —**ter·ror·is·ti·cal·ly** *adv.*

ter·ror·ize /ˈterəˌrīz/ ▶*v.* [*tr.*] create and maintain a state of extreme fear and distress in (someone); fill with terror: *he used his private army to terrorize the population.* —**ter·ror·i·za·tion** /ˌterərəˈzāSHən/ *n.* —**ter·ror·iz·er** *n.*

ter·ror-strick·en (also **ter·ror-struck** /-ˌstrək/) ▶*adj.* feeling or expressing extreme fear.

ter·ry /ˈterē/ (also **terry cloth**) ▶*n.* (*pl.* **-ries**) a fabric with raised uncut loops of thread covering both surfaces, used esp. for towels.

terse /tərs/ ▶*adj.* (**ters·er, ters·est**) sparing in the use of words; abrupt: *a terse statement.* —**terse·ly** *adv.* —**terse·ness** *n.*

ter·ti·ar·y /ˈtərSHē,erē; -SHərē/ ▶*adj.* **1** third in order or level: *most of the enterprises were of tertiary importance.* **2** (**Tertiary**) *Geol.* of, relating to, or denoting the first period of the Cenozoic era, between the Cretaceous and Quaternary periods, and comprising the Paleogene and Neogene subperiods.

tes·sel·late /ˈtesəˌlāt/ (also **tes·se·late**) ▶*v.* [*tr.*] cover (a plane surface) by repeated use of a single shape, without gaps or overlapping. —**tes·sel·la·tion** /ˌtesəˈlāSHən/ (also **tes·se·la·tion**) *n.*

tes·si·tu·ra /ˌtesiˈto͝orə/ ▶*n.* *Mus.* the range within which most notes of a vocal part fall.

test¹ /test/ ▶*n.* a procedure intended to establish the quality, performance, or reliability of something, esp. before it is taken into widespread use. ■ a short written or spoken examination of a person's proficiency or knowledge: *a spelling test.* ■ an event or situation that reveals the strength or quality of someone or something by putting them under strain: *the first test of the peace agreement.* ■ an examination of part of the body or a body fluid for medical purposes, esp. by means of a chemical or mechanical procedure rather than simple inspection: *a test for HIV.* ■ the result of a medical examination or analytical procedure: *a positive test for protein.* ■ a means of establishing whether an action, item, or situation is an instance of a specified quality, esp. one held to be undesirable: *a statutory test of obscenity.*
▶*v.* [*tr.*] take measures to check the quality, performance, or reliability of (something), esp. before putting it into widespread use or practice: *this product has not been tested on animals.* ■ reveal the strengths or capabilities of (someone or something) by putting them under strain: *such behavior would severely test any marriage.* ■ give (someone) a short written or oral examination of their proficiency or knowledge. ■ judge or measure (someone's proficiency or knowledge) by means of such an examination. ■ carry out a medical test on (a person, a part of the body, or a body fluid). ■ [*intr.*] produce a specified result in a medical test, esp. a drug test or AIDS test: *he tested positive for steroids.* ■ *Chem.* examine (a substance) by means of a reagent. ■ touch or taste

(something) to check that it is acceptable before proceeding further: *she tested the water with the tip of her elbow.* —**test·a·bil·i·ty** /ˌtestəˈbilitē/ *n.* —**test·a·ble** *adj.* —**test·ee** /-ˈtē/ *n.*

▶ □ **put someone/something to the test** find out how useful, strong, or effective someone or something is. □ **stand the test of time** last or remain popular for a long time.

test² ▶*n. Zool.* the shell or integument of some invertebrates and protozoans, such as the tough outer layer of a tunicate.

Test. ▶*abbr.* Testament.

test. ▶*abbr.* ■ testator. ■ testimony.

tes·ta /ˈtestə/ ▶*n. (pl.* **-tae** /-tē/) *Bot.* the protective outer covering of a seed; the seed coat.

tes·ta·ment /ˈtestəmənt/ ▶*n.* **1** a person's will, esp. the part relating to personal property. **2** something that serves as a sign or evidence of a specified fact, event, or quality: *growing attendance figures are a testament to the event's popularity.* **3** (in biblical use) a covenant or dispensation. ■ (**Testament**) a division of the Bible. See also **OLD TESTAMENT, NEW TESTAMENT.** ■ (**Testament**) a copy of the New Testament.

tes·ta·men·ta·ry /ˌtestəˈmen(t)ərē/ ▶*adj.* of, relating to, or bequeathed or appointed through a will.

tes·tate /ˈtesˌtāt/ ▶*adj.* having made a valid will before one dies.
▶*n.* a person who has died leaving such a will.

tes·ta·tor /ˈtestātər/ ▶*n. Law* a person who has made a will.

test case ▶*n. Law* a case that sets a precedent for other cases involving the same question of law.

test drive ▶*n.* an act of driving a motor vehicle that one is considering buying in order to determine its quality. ■ *fig.* a test of a product before purchase or release.
▶*v.* (**test-drive**) [*tr.*] drive (a vehicle) to determine its qualities with a view to buying it. ■ *fig.* test (a product) before purchase or release.

test·er¹ /ˈtestər/ ▶*n.* a person who tests something, esp. a new product. ■ a person who tests another's proficiency. ■ a device that tests the functioning of something: *a cake tester.* ■ a sample of a product provided so that customers can try it before buying it.

test·er² ▶*n.* a canopy over a four-poster bed.

tes·tes /ˈtestēz/ ▶ plural form of **TESTIS.**

test flight ▶*n.* a flight during which the performance of an aircraft or its equipment is tested. —**test-fly** *v.*

tes·ti·cle /ˈtestikəl/ ▶*n.* either of the two oval organs that produce sperm in men and other male mammals, enclosed in the scrotum behind the penis. Also called **TESTIS.** —**tes·tic·u·lar** /teˈstikyələr/ *adj.*

tes·ti·fy /ˈtestəˌfī/ ▶*v.* (**-fies, -fied**) [*intr.*] give evidence as a witness in a law court: *he testified against his own commander* | [*tr.*] *he testified that he had supplied Barry with crack.* ■ serve as evidence or proof of something's existing or being the case: *the bleak lines **testify** to inner torment.* —**tes·ti·fi·er** *n.*

tes·ti·mo·ni·al /ˌtestəˈmōnēəl/ ▶*n.* a formal statement testifying to someone's character and qualifications. ■ a public tribute to someone and to their achievements.

tes·ti·mo·ny /ˈtestəˌmōnē/ ▶*n. (pl.* **-nies**) a formal written or spoken statement, esp. one given in a court of law. ■ evidence or proof provided by the existence or appearance of something. ■ a public recounting of a religious conversion or experience.

tes·tis /ˈtestis/ ▶*n. (pl.* **-tes** /-ˌtēz/) *Anat. & Zool.* an organ that produces spermatozoa.

tes·tos·ter·one /teˈstästəˌrōn/ ▶*n.* a steroid hormone that stimulates development of male secondary sexual characteristics, produced mainly in the testes, but also in the ovaries and adrenal cortex.

test pat·tern ▶*n.* a geometric design broadcast by a television station so that viewers can adjust the quality of their reception.

test pi·lot ▶*n.* a pilot who flies an aircraft to test its performance.

test tube ▶*n.* a thin glass tube closed at one end, used to hold small amounts of material for laboratory testing or experiments. ■ [as *adj.*] denoting things produced or processes performed in a laboratory: *new forms of test-tube life.*

tes·ty /ˈtestē/ ▶*adj.* easily irritated; impatient and somewhat bad-tempered. —**tes·ti·ly** /ˈtestəlē/ *adv.* —**tes·ti·ness** *n.*

tet·a·nus /ˈtetn-əs/ ▶*n.* **1** a bacterial disease marked by rigidity and spasms of the voluntary muscles. See also **TRISMUS. 2** *Physiol.* the prolonged contraction of a muscle caused by rapidly repeated stimuli. —**tet·a·nize** /-ˌīz/ *v.* —**tet·a·noid** /-ˌoid/ *adj.*

tetch·y /ˈtecHē/ ▶*adj.* bad-tempered and irritable. —**tetch·i·ly** /ˈtecHəlē/ *adv.* —**tetch·i·ness** *n.*

tête-à-tête /ˈtāt ə ˈtāt; ˈtet ə ˈtet/ ▶*n.* **1** a private conversation between

two people. **2** an S-shaped sofa on which two people can sit face to face.
▶*adj. & adv.* involving or happening between two people in private: [as *adj.*] *a tête-à-tête meal* | [as *adv.*] *his business was conducted tête-à-tête.*

teth·er /ˈteTHər/ ▶*n.* a rope or chain with which an animal is tied to restrict its movement.
▶*v.* [*tr.*] tie (an animal) with a rope or chain so as to restrict its movement.

tet·ra /ˈtetrə/ ▶*n.* a small tropical freshwater fish (family Characidae) that is typically brightly colored. Native to Africa and America, many tetras are popular in aquariums.

tet·ra·chord /ˈtetrəˌkôrd/ ▶*n. Mus.* a scale of four notes, the interval between the first and last being a perfect fourth.

tet·ra·cy·cline /ˌtetrəˈsī,klēn; -klin/ ▶*n. Med.* any of a large group of antibiotics with a molecular structure containing four rings.

tet·rad /ˈte,trad/ ▶*n. technical* a group or set of four.

tet·ra·gon /ˈtetrəˌgän/ ▶*n.* a plane figure with four angles and four sides.

te·trag·o·nal /teˈtragənl/ ▶*adj.* of or denoting a crystal system or three-dimensional geometric arrangement having three axes at right angles, two of them equal. —**te·trag·o·nal·ly** *adv.*

tet·ra·gram /ˈtetrəˌgram/ ▶*n.* a word consisting of four letters or characters.

tet·ra·he·dron /ˌtetrəˈhēdrən/ ▶*n. (pl.* **-dra** /-drə/ or **-drons**) a solid having four plane triangular faces; a triangular pyramid. —**tet·ra·he·dral** /-drəl/ *adj.*

te·tral·o·gy /teˈträləjē/ ▶*n. (pl.* **-gies**) a group of four related literary or operatic works. ■ a series of four ancient Greek dramas, three tragedies and one satyr play, originally presented together.

te·tram·e·ter /teˈtramitər/ ▶*n. Prosody* a verse of four measures.

tet·ra·ple·gi·a /ˌtetrəˈplēj(ē)ə/ ▶*n.* another term for **QUADRIPLEGIA.** —**tet·ra·ple·gic** /-ˈplējik/ *adj. & n.*

tetrahedron

tet·ra·ploid /ˈtetrəˌploid/ *Biol.* ▶*adj.* (of a cell or nucleus) containing four homologous sets of chromosomes. ■ (of an organism or species) composed of such cells.
▶*n.* an organism, variety, or species of this type. —**tet·ra·ploi·dy** *n.*

tet·ra·pod /ˈtetrəˌpäd/ ▶*n. Zool.* a four-footed animal, esp. a member of a group that includes all vertebrates higher than fishes. ■ an object or structure with four feet, legs, or supports.

te·trarch /ˈteˌträrk/ ▶*n.* (in the Roman Empire) the governor of one of four divisions of a country or province. ■ one of four joint rulers. ■ *archaic* a subordinate ruler. —**te·trar·chy** *n. (pl.* **-chies**)

tet·ra·va·lent /ˌtetrəˈvālənt/ ▶*adj. Chem.* having a valence of four.

Teu·ton /ˈt(y)ōōtn/ ▶*n.* a member of a people who lived in Jutland in the 4th century BC and fought the Romans in France in the 2nd century BC. ■ *often derog.* a German.

Teu·ton·ic /t(y)ōōˈtänik/ ▶*adj.* **1** of or relating to the Teutons. ■ *inf., often derog.* displaying the characteristics popularly attributed to Germans. **2** *archaic* denoting the Germanic branch of the Indo-European language family.
▶*n. archaic* the language of the Teutons. —**Teu·ton·i·cism** /-ˈtänəˌsizəm/ *n.*

Tex-Mex /ˈteks ˈmeks/ ▶*adj.* (esp. of cooking and music) having a blend of Mexican and southern American features originally characteristic of the border regions of Texas and Mexico.
▶*n.* **1** music or cooking of such a type. **2** a variety of Mexican Spanish spoken in Texas.

text /tekst/ ▶*n.* **1** a book or other written or printed work, regarded in terms of its content rather than its physical form: *a text which explores pain and grief.* ■ a piece of written or printed material regarded as conveying the authentic or primary form of a particular work: *the text of the lecture was available to guests.* ■ written or printed words, typically forming a connected piece of work: *stylistic features of journalistic text.* ■ *Comput.* data in written form, esp. when stored, processed, or displayed in a word processor. ■ a text message. ■ the main body of a book or other piece of writing, as distinct from other material such as notes, appendices, and illustrations: *the pictures relate well to the text.* ■ a script or libretto. ■ a written work chosen or assigned as a subject of study: *the book is intended as a secondary text for religion courses.* ■ a textbook. ■ a passage from the Bible or other religious work, esp. when used as the subject of a sermon. ■ a subject or theme for a discussion or exposition: *he took as his text the fact that Australia is paradise.* **2** (also **text-hand**) fine, large handwriting, used esp. for manuscripts.

▶*v.* to send a text message: *I thought it was fantastic that he took the trouble to text me.* —**text·less** *adj.*

text·book /'teks(t),bŏŏk/ ▶*n.* a book used as a standard work for the study of a particular subject.

▶*adj.* conforming to or corresponding to a standard or type that is prescribed or widely held by theorists: *he had the presence of mind to carry out a textbook emergency descent.* —**text·book·ish** *adj.*

text ed·i·tor ▶*n.* Comput. a system or program that allows a user to edit text.

tex·tile /'tek,stīl/ ▶*n.* (usu. **textiles**) cloth or woven fabric: *a fascinating range of pottery, jewelry, and textiles.* ■ (**textiles**) the branch of industry involved in the manufacture of cloth.

▶*adj.* of or relating to fabric or weaving: *the textile industry.* ▷early 17th cent.: from Latin *textilis*, from *text-* 'woven,' from the verb *texere*.

text mes·sage ▶*n.* an electronic communication sent and received by cellular phone. —**text mes·sag·ing** *n.*

tex·tu·al /'tekschŏŏəl/ ▶*adj.* of or relating to a text or texts: *textual analysis.* —**tex·tu·al·ly** *adv.*

tex·tu·al·ist /'tekschŏŏəlist/ ▶*n.* a person who adheres strictly to a text, esp. that of the scriptures. —**tex·tu·al·ism** /-,lizəm/ *n.*

tex·ture /'tekschər/ ▶*n.* the feel, appearance, or consistency of a surface or a substance: *the cheese is firm in texture* | *the different colors and textures of bark.* ■ the character or appearance of a textile fabric as determined by the arrangement and thickness of its threads: *a dark shirt of rough texture.* ■ *Art* the tactile quality of the surface of a work of art. ■ the quality created by the combination of the different elements in a work of music or literature: *a closely knit symphonic texture.*

▶*v.* [*tr.*] give (a surface, esp. of a fabric or wall covering) a rough or raised texture. —**tex·tur·al** /-rəl/ *adj.* —**tex·tur·al·ly** /-rəlē/ *adv.* —**tex·ture·less** *adj.*

tex·tur·ize /'tekschə,rīz/ ▶*v.* [*tr.*] impart a particular texture to (a product, esp. a fabric or foodstuff) in order to make it more attractive. ■ cut (hair) in such a way as to remove its weight and create extra fullness.

Th ▶*symb.* the chemical element thorium.

Th. ▶*abbr.* Thursday.

Thai /tī/ ▶*adj.* of or relating to Thailand, its people, or their language.

▶*n.* (*pl.* same or **Thais**) **1** a native or national of Thailand. ■ a member of the largest ethnic group in Thailand. ■ a person of Thai descent. **2** the Tai language that is the official language of Thailand.

thal·a·mus /'THaləməs/ ▶*n.* (*pl.* **-mi** /-,mī/) *Anat.* either of two masses of gray matter lying between the cerebral hemispheres on either side of the third ventricle, relaying sensory information and acting as a center for pain perception. —**tha·lam·ic** /THə'lamik/ *adj.*

tha·lid·o·mide /THə'lidə,mīd/ ▶*n.* a drug formerly used as a sedative, but withdrawn in the early 1960s after it was found to cause congenital malformation or absence of limbs in children whose mothers took the drug during early pregnancy.

thal·li·um /'THalēəm/ ▶*n.* the chemical element of atomic number 81, a soft silvery-white metal that occurs naturally in small amounts in pyrite and other ores. (Symbol: **Tl**)

thal·lus /'THaləs/ ▶*n.* (*pl.* **thal·li** /'THalī/) *Bot.* a plant body that is not differentiated into stem and leaves and lacks true roots and a vascular system. Thalli are typical of algae, fungi, lichens, and some liverworts. —**thal·loid** /'THaloid/ *adj.*

than /THan; THən/ ▶*conj. & prep.* **1** introducing the second element in a comparison: [as *prep.*] *he was much smaller than his son* | [as *conj.*] *Jack doesn't know any more than I do.* **2** used in expressions introducing an exception or contrast: [as *prep.*] *he claims not to own anything other than his home* | [as *conj.*] *they observe rather than act.* **3** [*conj.*] used in expressions indicating one thing happening immediately after another: *scarcely was the work completed than it was abandoned.*

thank /THangk/ ▶*v.* [*tr.*] express gratitude to (someone), esp. by saying "Thank you": *Mac thanked her for the meal and left.* ■ used ironically to assign blame or responsibility for something: *you have only yourself to thank for the plight you are in.*

▶ □ **thank goodness** (or **God** or **heavens**) an expression of relief: *thank goodness no one was badly injured.*

thank·ful /'THangkfəl/ ▶*adj.* pleased and relieved: *they were thankful that the war was over* | *I was very thankful to be alive.* ■ expressing gratitude and relief: *an earnest and thankful prayer.* —**thank·ful·ness** *n.*

thank·ful·ly /'THangkfəlē/ ▶*adv.* in a thankful manner: *she thankfully accepted the armchair she was offered.* ■ used to express pleasure or relief at

the situation or outcome that one is reporting; fortunately: *thankfully, everything went smoothly.*

thank·less /'THangklis/ ▶*adj.* (of a job or task) difficult or unpleasant and not likely to bring one pleasure or the appreciation of others. ■ (of a person) not expressing or feeling gratitude. —**thank·less·ly** *adv.* —**thank·less·ness** *n.*

thanks·giv·ing /,THangks'giving/ ▶*n.* **1** the expression of gratitude, esp. to God. **2** (**Thanksgiving** or **Thanksgiving Day**) (in North America) an annual national holiday held in the U.S. on the fourth Thursday in November and marked by religious observances and a traditional meal including turkey. A similar holiday is held in Canada, usually on the second Monday in October.

thank you ▶*interj.* a polite expression used when acknowledging a gift, service, or compliment, or accepting or refusing an offer: *thank you for your letter* | *no thank you, I don't believe I will.*

▶*n.* an instance or means of expressing thanks: *Lucy planned a party as a thank you to the nurses* | [as *adj.*] *thank-you letters.*

that /THat; THət/ ▶*pron.* (*pl.* **those** /THōz/) **1** used to identify a specific person or thing observed by the speaker: *that's his wife over there.* ■ referring to the more distant of two things near to the speaker (the other, if specified, being identified by "this"): *this is stronger than that.* **2** referring to a specific thing previously mentioned, known, or understood: *that's a good idea.* **3** used in singling out someone or something and ascribing a distinctive feature to them: *it is part of human nature to be attracted to that which is aesthetically pleasing* | *they care about the rights of those less privileged than themselves.* **4** (*pl.* **that**) [*relative pron.*] used to introduce a defining or restrictive clause, esp. one essential to identification: ■ instead of "which," "who," or "whom": *the book that I've just written.* ■ instead of "when" after an expression of time: *the year that Anna was born.*

▶*adj.* (*pl.* **those**) **1** used to identify a specific person or thing observed or heard by the speaker: *look at that man there.* ■ referring to the more distant of two things near to the speaker (the other, if specified, being identified by "this"). **2** referring to a specific thing previously mentioned, known, or understood: *he lived in Mysore at that time.* **3** used in singling out someone or something and ascribing a distinctive feature to them: *I have always envied those people who make their own bread.* **4** referring to a specific person or thing assumed as understood or familiar to the person being addressed: *where is that son of yours?*

▶*adv.* to such a degree; so: *I would not go that far.* ■ used with a gesture to indicate size: *it was that big, perhaps even bigger.* ■ *inf.* very: *he wasn't that far away.*

▶*conj.* **1** introducing a subordinate clause expressing a statement or hypothesis: *she said that she was satisfied.* ■ expressing a reason or cause: *he seemed pleased that I wanted to continue.* ■ expressing a result: *she was so tired that she couldn't think.* ■ expressing a purpose, hope, or intention: *I eat that I may live.* **2** *poetic/lit.* expressing a wish or regret: *oh that he could be restored to health.*

▶ □ **and all that** *inf.* and that sort of thing; and so on: *other people depend on them for food and clothing and all that.* □ **like that 1** of that nature or in that manner: *don't talk like that.* **2** *inf.* with no preparation or introduction; instantly or effortlessly: *he can't just leave like that.* □ **not all that** — not very — : *it was not all that long ago.* □ **that is** (or **that is to say**) a formula introducing or following an explanation or further clarification of a preceding word or words: *let us be Christians—that is to say, let us love our brothers.* □ **that said** even so (introducing a concessive statement): *It's just a gimmick. That said, I'd love to do it.* □ **that's that** there is nothing more to do or say about the matter.

thatch /THACH/ ▶*n.* a roof covering of straw, reeds, palm leaves, or a similar material. ■ straw or a similar material used for such a covering. ■ *inf.* the hair on a person's head, esp. if thick or unruly. ■ a matted layer of dead stalks, moss, and other material in a lawn.

▶*v.* [*tr.*] cover (a roof or a building) with straw or a similar material. —**thatch·er** *n.*

thaw /THô/ ▶*v.* [*intr.*] (of ice, snow, or another frozen substance, such as food) become liquid or soft as a result of warming. ■ (**it thaws, it is thawing,** etc.) the weather becomes warmer and melts snow and ice. ■ [*tr.*] make (something) warm enough to become liquid or soft: *European exporters simply thawed their beef before unloading.* ■ (of a part of the body) become warm enough to stop feeling numb: *Ryan began to feel his ears and toes thaw out.* ■ become friendlier or more cordial: *she thawed*

---

out sufficiently to allow a smile to appear. ▪ [*tr.*] make friendlier or more cordial.
▶*n.* a period of warmer weather that thaws ice and snow: *the thaw came yesterday afternoon.* ▪ an increase in friendliness or cordiality.

the /T͟Hē; T͟Hə/ [called the *definite article*] ▶*adj.* **1** denoting one or more people or things already mentioned or assumed to be common knowledge: *what's the matter?* | *call the doctor.* Compare with **A**. ▪ used to refer to a person, place, or thing that is unique: *the Queen* | *the Mona Lisa.* ▪ *inf.* denoting a disease or affliction: *I've got the flu.* ▪ (with a unit of time) the present; the current: *dish of the day.* ▪ *inf.* used instead of a possessive to refer to someone with whom the speaker or person addressed is associated: *how's the family?* ▪ used with a surname to refer to a family or married couple: *the Johnsons were wealthy.* ▪ used before the surname of the chief of a Scottish or Irish clan: *the O'Donoghue.* **2** used to point forward to a following qualifying or defining clause or phrase: *the top of a bus.* ▪ (chiefly with rulers and family members with the same name) used after a name to qualify it: *George the Sixth.* **3** used to make a generalized reference to something rather than identifying a particular instance: *worry about the future.* ▪ used with a singular noun to indicate that it represents a whole species or class: *they placed the African elephant on their endangered list.* ▪ used with an adjective to refer to those people who are of the type described: *the unemployed.* ▪ used with an adjective to refer to something of the class or quality described: *accomplish the impossible.* ▪ used with the name of a unit to state a rate: *they can do 120 miles **to the** gallon.* **4** enough of (a particular thing): *he hoped to publish monthly, if only he could find the money.* **5** (pronounced stressing "the") used to indicate that someone or something is the best known or most important of that name or type: *he was **the** hot young piano prospect in jazz.* **6** used adverbially with comparatives to indicate how one amount or degree of something varies in relation to another: ***the** more she thought about it, **the** more devastating it became.* ▪ (usu. **all the ——**) used to emphasize the amount or degree to which something is affected: *coins made all the more desirable by their rarity.*

the·a·ter /ˈT͟Hēətər/ (also **the·a·tre**) ▶*n.* a building or outdoor area in which plays and other dramatic performances are given. ▪ (often **the theater**) the activity or profession of acting in, producing, directing, or writing plays. ▪ a play or other activity or presentation considered in terms of its dramatic quality: *this is intense, moving, and inspiring theater.* ▪ a movie theater. ▪ a room or hall for lectures, etc., with seats in tiers. ▪ the area in which something happens: *a new **theater of war** has been opened up.* ▪ [as *adj.*] denoting weapons for use in a particular region between tactical and strategic: *he was working on theater defense missiles.*
▷late Middle English (originally as 'theatre'), from Old French, or from Latin *theatrum,* from Greek *theatron,* from *theasthai* 'behold.'

the·a·ter-in-the-round ▶*n.* a form of theatrical presentation in which the audience is seated in a circle around the stage or on at least three of its sides.

the·at·ric /T͟Hēˈatrik/ ▶*adj.* another term for **THEATRICAL**.

the·at·ri·cal /T͟Hēˈatrikəl/ ▶*adj.* of, for, or relating to acting, actors, or the theater: *theatrical productions.* ▪ exaggerated and excessively dramatic: *Henry looked over his shoulder with theatrical caution.* —**the·at·ri·cal·ism** /-ˌlizəm/ *n.* —**the·at·ri·cal·i·ty** /-ˌatriˈkalitē/ *n.* —**the·at·ri·cal·i·za·tion** /-ˌatrikəliˈzāSHən/ *n.* —**the·at·ri·cal·ize** /-ˌīz/ *v.* —**the·at·ri·cal·ly** /-ik(ə)lē/ *adv.*

thee /T͟Hē/ ▶*pron.* [*second person sing.*] archaic or dialect form of **YOU**, as the singular object of a verb or preposition: *we beseech thee O lord.* Compare with **THOU**[1].

theft /T͟Heft/ ▶*n.* the action or crime of stealing: *he was convicted of theft* | *the latest theft happened at a garage.*

their /T͟Hə(ə)r/ ▶*possessive adj.* **1** belonging to or associated with the people or things mentioned or easily identified: *her taunts had lost their power to touch him.* ▪ belonging to or associated with a person of unspecified sex: *she heard someone blow their nose loudly.* **2** (**Their**) used in titles: *a double portrait of Their Majesties.*

theirs /T͟Hə(ə)rz/ ▶*possessive pron.* used to refer to a thing or things belonging to or associated with two or more people or things previously mentioned: *they think everything is theirs* | *a favorite game **of theirs**.*

the·ism /ˈT͟Hēˌizəm/ ▶*n.* belief in the existence of a god or gods, esp. belief in one god as creator of the universe, intervening in it and sustaining a personal relation to his creatures. Compare with **DEISM**. —**the·ist** *n.* —**the·is·tic** /T͟Hēˈistik/ *adj.*

them /T͟Hem; T͟Həm/ ▶*pron.* [*third person pl.*] used as the object of a verb or preposition to refer to two or more people or things previously mentioned or easily identified: *I bathed the kids and read them stories.* Compare with **THEY**. ▪ used after the verb "to be" and after "than" or "as":

we're better than them. ▪ referring to a person of unspecified sex: *how well do you have to know someone before you call them a friend?*
▶*adj. inf.* or *dial.* those: *look at them eyes.*

the·mat·ic /T͟Hiˈmatik/ ▶*adj.* **1** having or relating to subjects or a particular subject. ▪ *Linguistics* belonging to, relating to, or denoting the theme of a sentence. ▪ *Mus.* of, relating to, or containing melodic subjects. **2** *Linguistics* of or relating to the theme of an inflected word. ▪ (of a vowel) connecting the theme of a word to its inflections. ▪ (of a word) having a vowel connecting its theme to its inflections.
▶*n.* **1** (**thematics**) [treated as *sing.* or *pl.*] a body of topics for study or discussion. **2** *Philately* British term for **TOPICAL**. —**the·mat·i·cal·ly** /-ik(ə)lē/ *adv.*

theme /T͟Hēm/ ▶*n.* **1** the subject of a talk, a piece of writing, a person's thoughts, or an exhibition; a topic: *the theme of the sermon was reverence.* ▪ *Linguistics* the first major constituent of a clause, indicating the subject matter, typically being the subject but optionally other constituents, as in "*poor* he is not." ▪ an idea that recurs in or pervades a work of art or literature. ▪ *Mus.* a prominent or frequently recurring melody or group of notes in a composition. ▪ [as *adj.*] (of music) frequently recurring in or accompanying the beginning and end of a film, play, or musical: *a theme song.* ▪ a setting or ambience given to a leisure venue or activity: *a family fun park with a western theme.* ▪ [as *adj.*] denoting a restaurant or bar in which the decor and the food and drink served are intended to suggest a particular foreign country, historical period, or other ambience: *a New Deal theme restaurant.* ▪ [in *comb.*] (**-themed**) (mainly in journalism) characterized by a theme or pervasive influence: *a golf-themed business park.* ▪ an essay written by a student on an assigned subject. **2** *Linguistics* the stem of a noun or verb; the part to which inflections are added, esp. one composed of the root and an added vowel. **3** *hist.* any of the twenty-nine provinces in the Byzantine empire.
▶*v.* [*tr.*] give a particular setting or ambience to (a venue or activity).
▷Middle English: via Old French from Latin *thema,* from Greek, literally 'proposition'; related to *tithenai* 'to set or place.'

theme park ▶*n.* an amusement park with a unifying setting or idea.

them·selves /T͟Həmˈselvz; T͟Hem-/ ▶*pron.* [*third person pl.*] **1** [*reflexive*] used as the object of a verb or preposition to refer to a group of people or things previously mentioned as the subject of the clause: *countries unable to look after themselves.* **2** used to emphasize a particular group of people or things mentioned: *excellent at organizing others, they may well be disorganized themselves.* **3** used instead of "himself" or "herself" to refer to a person of unspecified sex: *anyone who fancies themselves as a racing driver.*

then /T͟Hen/ ▶*adv.* **1** at that time; at the time in question: *I was living in Cairo then* | [as *adj.*] *a hotel where the then prime minister, Margaret Thatcher, was staying.* **2** after that; next; afterward: *she won the first and then the second game.* ▪ also; in addition: *I'm paid a generous salary, and then there's the money I've made at the races.* **3** in that case; therefore: *well, that's okay then.* ▪ used at the end of a sentence to emphasize an inference being drawn: *so you're still here, then.* ▪ used to finish off a conversation: *see you in an hour, then.*
▶ □ **but then** (**again**) after all; on the other hand (introducing a contrasting comment). □ **then and there** immediately.

thence /T͟Hens/ (also **from thence**) ▶*adv. formal* from a place or source previously mentioned: *they intended to cycle on into France and thence home via Belgium.* ▪ as a consequence: *studying maps to assess past latitudes and thence an indication of climate.* ▪ from that time: *four months thence I stood once again in the dooryard.*

thence·forth /T͟HensˈfôrT͟H/ (also **from thence·forth**) ▶*adv.* archaic or *poetic/lit.* from that time, place, or point onward.

thence·for·ward /T͟Hensˈfôrwərd/ ▶*adv.* another term for **THENCEFORTH**.

the·o·cen·tric /ˌT͟Hēōˈsentrik/ ▶*adj.* having God as a central focus.

the·oc·ra·cy /T͟Hēˈäkrəsē/ ▶*n.* (pl. **-cies**) a system of government in which priests rule in the name of God or a god. —**the·o·crat** /ˈT͟Hēəˌkrat/ *n.* —**the·o·crat·ic** /T͟Hēəˈkratik/ *adj.* —**the·o·crat·i·cal·ly** /T͟Hēəˈkratik(ə)lē/ *adv.*

the·od·o·lite /T͟Hēˈädəˌlīt/ ▶*n.* a surveying instrument with a rotating telescope for measuring horizontal and vertical angles. —**the·od·o·lit·ic** /-ˌädəˈlitik/ *adj.*

theol. ▶*abbr.* ▪ theologian. ▪ theological. ▪ theology.

the·o·lo·gian /T͟Hēəˈlōjən/ ▶*n.* a person who engages or is an expert in theology.

the·o·log·i·cal /T͟Hēəˈläjikəl/ ▶*adj.* of or relating to the study of theology. —**the·o·log·i·cal·ly** /-ik(ə)lē/ *adv.*

the·ol·o·gy /T͟Hēˈäləjē/ ▶*n.* (pl. **-gies**) the study of the nature of God and religious belief. ■ religious beliefs and theory when systematically developed: *Christian theology.* —**the·ol·o·gist** /-jist/ *n.*

the·o·rem /ˈᴛʜēərəm; ˈᴛʜi(ə)r-/ ▸*n. Physics & Math.* a general proposition not self-evident but proved by a chain of reasoning; a truth established by means of accepted truths. ■ a rule in algebra or other branches of mathematics expressed by symbols or formulae. —**the·o·re·mat·ic** /ˌᴛʜēərəˈmatik; ˌᴛʜi(ə)rə-/ *adj.*

the·o·ret·i·cal /ᴛʜēəˈretikəl/ ▸*adj.* concerned with or involving the theory of a subject or area of study rather than its practical application: *a theoretical physicist.* ■ based on or calculated through theory rather than experience or practice: *the theoretical value of their work.* —**the·o·ret·i·cal·ly** /-ik(ə)lē/ *adv.*

the·o·re·ti·cian /ˌᴛʜēərəˈtiSHən; ˌᴛʜi(ə)rə-/ ▸*n.* a person who forms, develops, or studies the theoretical framework of a subject.

the·o·rist /ˈᴛʜēərist; ˈᴛʜi(ə)r-/ ▸*n.* a person concerned with the theoretical aspects of a subject; a theoretician.

the·o·rize /ˈᴛʜēəˌrīz; ˈᴛʜi(ə)r,īz/ ▸*v.* [*intr.*] form a theory or set of theories about something. ■ [*tr.*] create a theoretical premise or framework for (something): *women should be doing feminism rather than theorizing it.* —**the·o·ri·za·tion** /ˌᴛʜēərəˈzāSHən; ˌᴛʜi(ə)r-/ *n.* —**the·o·riz·er** *n.*

the·o·ry /ˈᴛʜēərē; ˈᴛʜi(ə)rē/ ▸*n.* (*pl.* **-ries**) a supposition or a system of ideas intended to explain something, esp. one based on general principles independent of the thing to be explained: *Darwin's theory of evolution.* ■ a set of principles on which the practice of an activity is based: *music theory.* ■ an idea used to account for a situation or justify a course of action: *my theory is that the place has been seriously mismanaged.* ■ *Math.* a collection of propositions to illustrate the principles of a subject.
▸ □ **in theory** used in describing what is supposed to happen or be possible, usually with the implication that it does not in fact happen.

the·os·o·phy /ᴛʜēˈäsəfē/ ▸*n.* any of a number of philosophies maintaining that a knowledge of God may be achieved through spiritual ecstasy, direct intuition, or special individual relations. —**the·os·o·pher** /-fər/ *n.* —**the·o·soph·ic** /ˌᴛʜēəˈsäfik/ *adj.* —**the·o·soph·i·cal** /ˌᴛʜēəˈsäfikəl/ *adj.* —**the·o·soph·i·cal·ly** /ˌᴛʜēəˈsäfik(ə)lē/ *adv.* —**the·os·o·phist** /-fist/ *n.*

ther·a·peu·tic /ˌᴛʜerəˈpyo͞otik/ ▸*adj.* of or relating to the healing of disease: *therapeutic facilities.* ■ administered or applied for reasons of health: *a therapeutic shampoo.* ■ having a good effect on the body or mind; contributing to a sense of well-being. —**ther·a·peu·ti·cal** *adj.* —**ther·a·peu·ti·cal·ly** /-ik(ə)lē/ *adv.* —**ther·a·peu·tist** /-tist/ *n.* (*archaic*)

ther·a·peu·tics /ˌᴛʜerəˈpyo͞otiks/ ▸*pl. n.* [treated as *sing.*] the branch of medicine concerned with the treatment of disease and the action of remedial agents.

ther·a·py /ˈᴛʜerəpē/ ▸*n.* (*pl.* **-pies**) treatment intended to relieve or heal a disorder: *a course of antibiotic therapy | cancer therapies.* ■ the treatment of mental or psychological disorders by psychological means: *he is currently in therapy* | [as *adj.*] *therapy sessions.* —**ther·a·pist** /-pist/ *n.*

there /ᴛʜe(ə)r/ ▸*adv.* **1** in, at, or to that place or position: *we went on to Paris and stayed there eleven days | I'm not going in there—it's freezing.* ■ used when pointing or gesturing to indicate the place in mind: *my house is there on the right.* ■ at that point (in speech, performance, writing, etc.): *"I'm quite—" There she stopped.* ■ in that respect; on that issue: *I don't agree with you there.* ■ used to indicate one's role in a particular situation: *at the end of the day, we are there to make money.* **2** used in attracting someone's attention or calling attention to someone or something: *hello there!* **3** used to indicate the fact or existence of something: *there's a restaurant around the corner | there comes a point where you give up.*
▸*interj.* **1** used to focus attention on something and express satisfaction or annoyance at it: *there, I told you she wouldn't mind!* **2** used to comfort someone: *there, there, you must take all of this philosophically.*
▸ □ **be there for someone** be available to provide support or comfort for someone, esp. at a time of adversity. □ **not all there** (of a person) not fully alert and functioning. □ **so there** *inf.* used to express one's defiance or awareness that someone will not like what one has decided or is saying: *you can't, so there!* □ **there goes —— ** used to express the destruction or failure of something: *there goes my career.* □ **there you are** (or **go**) *inf.* **1** this is what you wanted: *there you are—that'll be $3.80 please.* **2** expressing confirmation, triumph, or resignation: *sometimes it is embarrassing, but there you go.*

there·a·bouts /ˈᴛʜe(ə)rəˌbouts/ (also **there·a·bout**) ▸*adv.* near that place: *the land is dry in places thereabouts.* ■ used to indicate that a date or figure is approximate: *the notes were written in 1860 or thereabouts.*

there·af·ter /ᴛʜe(ə)rˈaftər/ ▸*adv. formal* after that time: *thereafter their fortunes suffered a steep decline.*

there·by /ᴛʜe(ə)rˈbī/ ▸*adv.* by means; as a result of that: *students*

perform in hospitals, thereby gaining a deeper awareness of the therapeutic power of music.

there·fore /ˈᴛʜe(ə)r,fôr/ ▸*adv.* for that reason; consequently: *he was injured and therefore unable to play.*

there·up·on /ˈᴛʜe(ə)rə,pän/ ▸*adv. formal* immediately or shortly after that: *he thereupon returned to Moscow.*

therm /ᴛʜərm/ ▸*n.* a unit of heat equivalent to 100,000 Btu or 1.055×10^8 joules.

ther·mal /ˈᴛʜərməl/ ▸*adj.* of or relating to heat. ■ another term for GEO-THERMAL. ■ (of a garment) made of a fabric that provides exceptional insulation to keep the body warm: *thermal underwear.*
▸*n.* an upward current of warm air, used by gliders, balloons, and birds to gain height. —**ther·mal·ly** *adv.*

ther·mal print·er ▸*n.* a printer in which small heated pins form characters on heat-sensitive paper.

ther·mo·cou·ple /ˈᴛʜərmō,kəpəl/ ▸*n.* a thermoelectric device for measuring temperature, consisting of two wires of different metals connected at two points, a voltage being developed between the two junctions in proportion to the temperature difference.

ther·mo·dy·nam·ics /ˌᴛʜərmōdīˈnamiks/ ▸*pl. n.* [treated as *sing.*] the branch of physical science that deals with the relations between heat and other forms of energy (such as mechanical, electrical, or chemical energy), and, by extension, the relationships and interconvertibility of all forms of energy. —**ther·mo·dy·nam·ic** *adj.* —**ther·mo·dy·nam·i·cal** /-ikəl/ *adj.* —**ther·mo·dy·nam·i·cal·ly** /-ik(ə)lē/ *adv.* —**ther·mo·dy·nam·i·cist** /-,dīˈnamisist/ *n.*

ther·mo·graph /ˈᴛʜərmə,graf/ ▸*n.* an instrument that produces a trace or image representing a record of the varying temperature or infrared radiation over an area or during a period of time.

ther·mog·ra·phy /ᴛʜərˈmägrəfē/ ▸*n.* **1** the use of thermograms to study heat distribution in structures or regions, for example in detecting tumors. **2** a printing technique in which a wet ink image is fused by heat or infrared radiation with a resinous powder to produce a raised impression. —**ther·mo·graph·ic** /ˌᴛʜərməˈgrafik/ *adj.*

ther·mo·la·bile /ˌᴛʜərmōˈlā,bīl; -bəl/ ▸*adj. chiefly Biochem.* (of a substance) readily destroyed or deactivated by heat.

ther·mo·lu·mi·nes·cence /ˌᴛʜərmō,lo͞oməˈnesəns/ ▸*n.* the property of some materials that have accumulated energy over a long period of becoming luminescent when pretreated and subjected to high temperatures, used as a means of dating ancient ceramics and other artifacts. —**ther·mo·lu·mi·nes·cent** *adj.*

ther·mom·e·ter /ᴛʜərˈmämitər/ ▸*n.* an instrument for measuring and indicating temperature, typically one consisting of a narrow, hermetically sealed glass tube marked with graduations and having at one end a bulb containing mercury or alcohol that expands and contracts in the tube with heating and cooling. ▷mid 17th cent.: from French *thermomètre* or modern Latin *thermometrum,* from *thermo-* 'of heat' + *-metrum* 'measure.' —**ther·mo·met·ric** /ˌᴛʜərməˈmetrik/ *adj.* —**ther·mo·met·ri·cal** /ˌᴛʜərməˈmetrikəl/ *adj.* —**ther·mom·e·try** /-trē/ *n.*

ther·mo·nu·cle·ar /ˌᴛʜərmōˈn(y)o͞oklēər; -kli(ə)r/ ▸*adj.* relating to or using nuclear reactions that occur only at very high temperatures. ■ of, relating to, or involving weapons in which explosive force is produced by thermonuclear reactions.

ther·mo·phile /ˈᴛʜərmə,fīl/ ▸*n. Microbiol.* a bacterium or other microorganism that grows best at higher than normal temperatures. —**ther·mo·phil·ic** /ˌᴛʜərməˈfilik/ *adj.*

ther·mo·plas·tic /ˌᴛʜərməˈplastik/ *Chem.* ▸*adj.* denoting substances (esp. synthetic resins) that become plastic on heating and harden on cooling and are able to repeat these processes.

ther·mos /ˈᴛʜərməs/ (also **thermos bot·tle**) ▸*n.* a container that keeps a drink or other fluid hot or cold by means of a double wall enclosing a vacuum.

ther·mo·sphere /ˈᴛʜərmō,sfir/ ▸*n.* the region of the atmosphere above the mesosphere and below the height at which the atmosphere ceases to have the properties of a continuous medium.

ther·mo·stat /ˈᴛʜərmə,stat/ ▸*n.* a device that automatically regulates temperature, or that activates a device when the temperature reaches a certain point. —**ther·mo·stat·ic** /ˌᴛʜərməˈstatik/ *adj.* —**ther·mo·stat·i·cal·ly** /ˌᴛʜərməˈstatik(ə)lē/ *adv.*

the·sau·rus /ᴛʜəˈsôrəs/ ▸*n.* (*pl.* **-sau·ri** /-ˈsôrī/ or **-sau·rus·es**) a book that

---

lists words in groups of synonyms and related concepts. ■ *archaic* a dictionary or encyclopedia.

these /T͟Hēz/ ▶ plural form of THIS.

the·sis /ˈT͟Hēsis/ ▶*n.* (*pl.* **-ses** /-sēz/) **1** a statement or theory that is put forward as a premise to be maintained or proved: *his central thesis is that psychological life is not part of the material world.* **2** a long essay or dissertation involving personal research, written by a candidate for a college degree: *a doctoral thesis.* **3** *Prosody* an unstressed syllable or part of a metrical foot in Greek or Latin verse.

thes·pi·an /ˈT͟Hespēən/ *formal humorous* ▶*adj.* of or relating to drama and the theater: *thespian talents.*
▶*n.* an actor or actress.

the·ta /ˈT͟Hātə; ˈT͟Hē-/ ▶*n.* the eighth letter of the Greek alphabet (Θ, ϑ), transliterated as 'th.' ■ [as *adj.*] denoting electrical activity observed in the brain under certain conditions, consisting of oscillations having a frequency of 4 to 7 hertz: *theta rhythm.*
▶*symb.* ■ (θ) a plane angle. ■ (ϑ) a polar coordinate.

they /T͟Hā/ ▶*pron.* [third person *pl.*] **1** used to refer to two or more people or things previously mentioned or easily identified: *the two men could get life sentences if they are convicted.* ■ people in general: *the rest, as they say, is history.* ■ *inf.* a group of people in authority regarded collectively: *they cut my water off.* **2** used to refer to a person of unspecified sex: *ask someone if they could help.*

they'd /T͟Hād/ ▶*contr. of* they had. ■ they would.

they'll /T͟Hāl/ ▶*contr. of* they shall; they will.

they're /T͟He(ə)r/ ▶*contr. of* they are.

they've /T͟Hāv/ ▶*contr. of* they have.

thi·a·mine /ˈT͟Hīəmin; -mēn/ (also **thi·a·min** /-min/) ▶*n. Biochem.* a vitamin of the B complex, found in unrefined grains, beans, and liver, a deficiency of which causes beriberi. Also called VITAMIN B₁ (see VITAMIN B).

thick /T͟Hik/ ▶*adj.* **1** with opposite sides or surfaces that are a great or relatively great distance apart: *thick slices of bread.* ■ (of a garment or other knitted or woven item) made of heavy material for warmth or comfort: *a thick sweater.* ■ of large diameter: *thick metal cables.* ■ (of script or type) consisting of broad lines. ■ made up of a large number of things or people close together: *his hair was long and thick.* ■ (**thick with**) densely filled or covered with: *the room was thick with smoke.* ■ (of air, the atmosphere, or an odor carried by them) heavy or dense. ■ (of darkness or a substance in the air) so black or dense as to be impossible or difficult to see through: *thick fog.* **3** (of a liquid or a semiliquid substance) relatively firm in consistency; not flowing freely: *thick mud.* **4** *inf.* of low intelligence; stupid. **5** (of a voice) not clear or distinct; hoarse or husky. ■ (of an accent) very marked and difficult to understand. **6** *inf.* having a very close, friendly relationship: *he's very thick with the new boss.*
▶*n.* (**the thick**) *rare* the busiest or most crowded part of something; the middle of something: *the thick of battle.*
▶*adv.* in or with deep, dense, or heavy mass: *bread spread thick with butter.* —**thick·ish** *adj.* —**thick·ly** *adv.* *thickly carpeted corridors.*
▶ □ **thick and fast** rapidly and in great numbers. □ **through thick and thin** under all circumstances, no matter how difficult: *they stuck together through thick and thin.*

thick·en /ˈT͟Hikən/ ▶*v.* make or become thick or thicker: [*tr.*] *thicken the sauce with flour* | [*intr.*] *the fog had thickened.* —**thick·en·er** *n.*
▶ □ **the plot thickens** used when a situation is becoming more and more complicated and puzzling.

thick·et /ˈT͟Hikit/ ▶*n.* a dense group of bushes or trees.

thick·head /ˈT͟Hik,hed/ ▶*n. inf.* a stupid person. —**thick·head·ed** *adj.* —**thick·head·ed·ness** *n.*

thick·ness /ˈT͟Hiknis/ ▶*n.* **1** the distance between opposite sides of something: *the gateway is several feet in thickness.* ■ the quality of being broad or deep: *the immense thickness of the walls.* ■ a layer of a specified material: *two thicknesses of plasterboard.* ■ a broad or deep part of a specified thing: *the beams were set into the thickness of the wall.* **2** the quality of being dense. ■ the state or quality of being made up of many closely packed parts: *the thickness of his hair.*

thick·set /ˈT͟Hik,set/ ▶*adj.* (of a person or animal) heavily or solidly built; stocky.

thief /T͟Hēf/ ▶*n.* (*pl.* **thieves** /T͟Hēvz/) a person who steals another person's property, esp. by stealth and without using force or violence.

thieve /T͟Hēv/ ▶*v.* [*intr.*] be a thief; steal something: *they began thieving.*

thiev·er·y /ˈT͟Hēv(ə)rē/ ▶*n.* the action of stealing another person's property.

thieves /T͟Hēvz/ ▶ plural form of THIEF.

thigh /T͟Hī/ ▶*n.* the part of the human leg between the hip and the knee. ■ the corresponding part in other animals. —**thighed** *adj.* [in *comb.*].

thim·ble /ˈT͟Himbəl/ ▶*n.* a metal or plastic cap with a closed end, worn to protect the finger and push the needle in sewing. ■ a short metal tube or ferrule. ■ *Naut.* a metal ring, concave on the outside, around which a loop of rope is spliced.

thim·ble·ful /ˈT͟Himbəl,fõõl/ ▶*n.* (*pl.* **-fuls**) a small quantity of liquid, esp. alcohol: *a thimbleful of brandy.*

thin /T͟Hin/ ▶*adj.* (**thin·ner**, **thin·nest**) **1** having opposite surfaces or sides close together; of little thickness or depth: *thin slices of bread.* ■ (of a person) having little, or too little, flesh or fat on their body. ■ (of a garment or other knitted or woven item) made of light material for coolness or elegance. ■ (of a garment) having had a considerable amount of fabric worn away. ■ (of script or type) consisting of narrow lines. **2** having few parts or members relative to the area covered or filled; sparse: *a depressingly thin crowd.* ■ not dense: *the thin cold air of the mountains.* ■ containing much liquid and not much solid substance: *thin soup.* ■ *Climbing* denoting a route on which the holds are small or scarce. **3** (of a sound) faint and high-pitched: *a thin voice.* ■ (of a smile) weak and forced. ■ too weak to justify a result or effect; inadequate: *the evidence is rather thin.*
▶*adv.* [often in *comb.*] with little thickness or depth: *cut the meat as thin as possible.*
▶*v.* (**thinned**, **thin·ning**) **1** make or become less dense, crowded, or numerous: [*tr.*] *the remorseless fire of archers thinned their ranks* | [*intr.*] *the trees began to thin out.* ■ [*tr.*] remove some plants from (a row or area) to allow the others more room to grow: *thin out overwintered rows of peas.* ■ make or become weaker or more watery: [*tr.*] *if the soup is too thick, add a little water to thin it down* | [*intr.*] *the blood thins.* **2** make or become smaller in width or thickness: [*tr.*] *their effect in thinning the ozone layer is probably slowing the global warming trend* | [*intr.*] *the trees have thinned and diminished in size.* ▷Old English *thynne,* of Germanic origin; related to Dutch *dun* and German *dünn,* from an Indo-European root shared by Latin *tenuis.* —**thin·ly** *adv.* —**thin·ness** *n.* —**thin·nish** *adj.*
▶ □ **thin air** used to refer to the state of being invisible or nonexistent: *she just vanished into thin air.*

thine /T͟Hīn/ ▶*possessive pron.* archaic form of YOURS; the thing or things belonging to or associated with thee: *his spirit will take courage from thine.*
▶*possessive adj.* form of THY used before a vowel: *inquire into thine own heart.*

thing /T͟HiNG/ ▶*n.* **1** an object that one need not, cannot, or does not wish to give a specific name to: *there are lots of things I'd like to buy.* ■ (**things**) personal belongings or clothing. ■ (**things**) objects, equipment, or utensils used for a particular purpose: *they cleared away the last few lunch things.* ■ (**a thing**) anything (used for emphasis): *she couldn't find a thing to wear.* ■ used to express one's disapproval or contempt for something: *you won't find me smoking those filthy things.* ■ (**things**) all that can be described in the specified way: *his love for all things Italian.* **2** an inanimate material object as distinct from a living sentient being: *I'm not a thing, not a work of art to be cherished.* ■ a living creature or plant: *all living things.* ■ used to express and give a reason for one's pity, affection, approval, or contempt for a person or animal: *the lamb was a puny little thing.* **3** an action, activity, event, thought, or utterance: *the only thing I could do well was cook.* ■ (**things**) circumstances, conditions, or matters that are unspecified: *how are things with you?* ■ an abstract entity or concept: *mourning and depression are not the same thing.* ■ a quality or attribute: *they had one thing in common—they were men of action.* ■ a specimen or type of something: *the game is the latest thing in family fun.* ■ (**one's thing**) *inf.* one's special interest or concern: *reading isn't my thing.* ■ (**a thing**) *inf.* a situation or activity of a specified type or quality: *your being here is just a friendship thing, OK?* **4** (**the thing**) *inf.* what is needed or required: *you need a tonic—and here's just the thing.* ■ what is socially acceptable or fashionable: *it wouldn't be the thing to go to a royal garden party in boots.* ■ used to introduce or draw attention to an important fact or consideration: *the thing is, I am going to sell this house.*
▶ □ **be on to a good thing** *inf.* have found a job, situation, or lifestyle that is pleasant, profitable, or easy. □ **be hearing** (or **seeing**) **things** imagine that one can hear (or see) something that is not in fact there. □ **do one's own thing** *inf.* follow one's own interests or inclinations regardless of others. □ **do things to** *inf.* have a powerful emotional effect on: *it just does things to me when we kiss.* □ **for one thing** used to introduce one of two or more possible reasons for something, the remainder of which may or may not be stated: *Why hadn't he arranged to see her at the house? For one thing, it would have been warmer.* □ **have a thing about** *inf.* have an obsessive interest in or dislike of: *she had a thing about men who*

wore glasses. □ **make a (big) thing of** (or **about**) *inf.* make (something) seem more important than it actually is. □ **of all things** out of all conceivable possibilities (used to express surprise): *What had he been thinking about? A kitten, of all things.* □ **a thing of the past** a thing that no longer happens or exists. □ **a thing or two** *inf.* used to refer to useful information that can be imparted or learned: *Teddy taught me a thing or two about wine.*

thing·a·ma·jig /ˈTHiNGəməˌjig/ (also **thing·u·ma·jig**; **thing·a·ma·bob** or **thing·um·a·bob** /-ˌbäb/) ▶ *n. inf.* used to refer to or address a person or thing whose name one has forgotten, does not know, or does not wish to mention.

thing·y /ˈTHiNGē/ ▶ *n.* (*pl.* **thing·ies**) another term for **THINGAMAJIG**.

think /THiNGk/ ▶ *v.* (*past* and *past part.* **thought** /THôt/) **1** [*tr.*] have a particular opinion, belief, or idea about someone or something: *she thought that nothing would be the same again* | [*intr.*] *what would John think of her?* | (**be thought**) *it's thought he may have collapsed from shock.* ■ used in questions to express anger or surprise: *What do you think you're doing?* ■ (**I think**) used in speech to reduce the force of a statement or opinion, or to politely suggest or refuse something: *I thought we could go out for a meal.* **2** [*intr.*] direct one's mind toward someone or something; use one's mind actively to form connected ideas: *he was thinking about Colin* | [*tr.*] *any writer who so rarely produces a book is not thinking deep thoughts.* ■ (**think of/about**) take into account or consideration when deciding on a course of action: *you can live how you like, but there's the children to think about.* ■ (**think of/about**) consider the possibility or advantages of (a course of action): *he was thinking of becoming a zoologist.* ■ have a particular mental attitude or approach: *he thought like a general.* ■ (**think of**) have a particular opinion of: *I think of him as a friend.* ■ call something to mind; remember: *lemon thyme is a natural pair with any chicken dish you can think of.* ■ imagine (an actual or possible situation): *think of being paid a salary to hunt big game!* | [*tr.*] expect: *I never thought we'd raise so much money.*
▶ *phrasal v.* □ **think back** recall a past event or time: *I keep thinking back to school.* □ **think on** think of or about. □ **think something out** consider something in all its aspects before taking action. □ **think something over** consider something carefully. □ **think something through** consider all the possible effects or implications of something. □ **think something up** *inf.* use one's ingenuity to invent or devise something.
▶ *n. inf.* an act of thinking: *I went for a walk to have a think.* —**think·a·ble** *adj.*
▶ □ **think again** reconsider something, typically so as to alter one's intentions or ideas. □ **think out loud** express one's thoughts as soon as they occur. □ **think better of** decide not to do (something) after reconsideration. □ **think for oneself** have an independent mind or attitude. □ **think nothing** (or **little**) **of** consider (an activity others regard as odd, wrong, or difficult) as straightforward or normal. □ **think twice** consider a course of action carefully before embarking on it.

think·er /ˈTHiNGkər/ ▶ *n.* a person who thinks deeply and seriously. ■ a person with highly developed intellectual powers, esp. one whose profession involves intellectual activity: *a leading scientific thinker.*

think·ing /ˈTHiNGkiNG/ ▶ *adj.* using thought or rational judgment; intelligent: *he seemed to be a thinking man.*
▶ *n.* the process of using one's mind to consider or reason about something: *they have done some thinking about welfare reform.* ■ a person's ideas or opinions: *his thinking is reflected in his later autobiography.* ■ (**thinkings**) *archaic* thoughts; meditations.

think tank ▶ *n.* a body of experts providing advice and ideas on specific political or economic problems. —**think tank·er** *n.*

thin·ner /ˈTHinər/ ▶ *n.* a volatile solvent used to make paint or other mixtures less viscous.

Thin·su·late /ˈTHinsəlit/ ▶ *n. trademark* a thin, highly insulating fabric made from polypropylene fibers, used to make outdoor clothing and sleeping bags.

thi·o·pen·tal /ˌTHĪ-ōˈpentəl; -tôl/ ▶ *n. Med.* a sulfur-containing barbiturate drug used as a general anesthetic and hypnotic, and (reputedly) as a truth serum.

third /THərd/ ▶ *ordinal number* constituting number three in a sequence; 3rd: *the third century* | *the third of October* | *Edward the Third.* ■ (**a third/one third**) each of three equal parts into which something is or may be divided: *a third of a mile.* ■ the third finisher or position in a race or competition: *Hill finished third.* ■ the third in a sequence of a vehicle's gears. ■ *Baseball* third base. ■ the third grade of a school. ■ thirdly (used to introduce a third point or reason): *second, they are lightly regulated; and third, they do business with nonresident clients.* ■ *Mus.* an interval spanning three consecutive notes in a diatonic scale, e.g., C to E (**major third**, equal to two tones) or A to C (**minor third**, equal to a tone and a semitone). ■ *Mus.* the note that is higher by this interval than the tonic of

a diatonic scale or root of a chord. ■ *Brit.* a place in the third-highest grade in an examination, esp. that for a degree. —**third·ly** *adv.*

third class ▶ *n.* a group of people or things considered together as third best. ■ *Brit.* a university degree or examination result in the third-highest classification. ■ a cheap class of mail for advertising and other printed material that weighs less than 16 ounces and is unsealed. ■ *chiefly hist.* the cheapest and least comfortable accommodations in a train or ship.
▶ *adj. & adv.* of the third-best quality or of lower status: [as *adj.*] *many indigenous groups are still viewed as third-class citizens.* ■ of or relating to a cheap class of mail including advertising and other printed material weighing less than 16 ounces: [as *adj.*] *third-class mail.* ■ *chiefly hist.* of or relating to the cheapest and least comfortable accommodations in a train or ship: [as *adj.*] *a third-class compartment* [as *adv.*] *I traveled third class.*

third-de·gree ▶ *adj.* **1** denoting burns of the most severe kind, affecting tissue below the skin. **2** *Law* denoting the least serious category of a crime, esp. murder.
▶ *n.* (**the third degree**) long and harsh questioning, esp. by police, to obtain information or a confession.

third par·ty ▶ *n.* a person or group besides the two primarily involved in a situation, esp. a dispute. ■ a political party organized as an alternative to the major parties in a two-party system.
▶ *adj.* of or relating to a person or group besides the two primarily involved in a situation: *third-party suppliers.*

third-rate ▶ *adj.* of inferior or very poor quality. —**third-rat·er** *n.*

Third Reich ▶ the Nazi regime, 1933–45.

Third World ▶ *n.* (usu. **the Third World**) the developing countries of Asia, Africa, and Latin America.

thirst /THərst/ ▶ *n.* a feeling of needing or wanting to drink something: *they quenched their thirst with spring water.* ■ lack of the liquid needed to sustain life: *tens of thousands died of thirst and starvation.* ■ (usu. **thirst for**) *poetic/lit.* a strong desire for something.
▶ *v.* [*intr.*] *archaic* (of a person or animal) feel a need to drink something. ■ (usu. **thirst for/after**) *poetic/lit.* have a strong desire for something: *an opponent thirsting for revenge.*

thirst·y /ˈTHərstē/ ▶ *adj.* (**thirst·i·er**, **thirst·i·est**) feeling a need to drink something. ■ (of land, plants, or skin) in need of water: dry or parched. ■ (of an engine, plant, or crop) consuming a lot of fuel or water. ■ having or showing a strong desire for causing the feeling: *thirsty for scandal.* ■ *inf.* (of activity, weather, or a time) causing the feeling of a need to drink something. —**thirst·i·ly** /-stəlē/ *adv.* —**thirst·i·ness** *n.*

thir·teen /ˌTHərˈtēn; ˈTHərˌtēn/ ▶ *cardinal number* equivalent to the sum of six and seven; one more than twelve, or seven less than twenty; 13: *thirteen miles away.* | *thirteen of the bishops voted against the motion.* (Roman numeral: **xiii, XIII**.) ■ a size of garment or other merchandise denoted by thirteen. ■ thirteen years old. —**thir·teenth** /ˌTHərˈtēnTH; ˈTHərˌtēnTH/ *ordinal number.*

Thir·teen Col·o·nies ▶ the British colonies that ratified the Declaration of Independence in 1776 and thereby became founding states of the U.S. The colonies were Virginia, Massachusetts, Maryland, Connecticut, Rhode Island, North Carolina, South Carolina, New York, New Jersey, Delaware, New Hampshire, Pennsylvania, and Georgia.

thir·ty /ˈTHərtē/ ▶ *cardinal number* (*pl.* **-ties**) the number equivalent to the product of three and ten; ten less than forty; 30: *thirty years ago* | *thirty were hurt* | *thirty of her school friends.* (Roman numeral: **xxx, XXX**.) ■ (**thirties**) the numbers from thirty to thirty-nine, esp. the years of a century or of a person's life: *a woman in her thirties.* ■ thirty years old. ■ thirty miles an hour: *doing about thirty.* —**thir·ti·eth** /-iTH/ *ordinal number* —**thir·ty-fold** /-ˌfōld/ *adj. & adv.*

this /THis/ ▶ *pron.* (*pl.* **these** /THēz/) **1** used to identify a specific person or thing close at hand or being indicated or experienced: *is this your bag?* ■ used to introduce someone or something: *listen to this.* ■ referring to the nearer of two things close to the speaker (the other, if specified, being identified by "that"): *this is different from that.* **2** referring to a specific thing or situation just mentioned: *the company was transformed, and Ward had played a vital role in bringing this about.*
▶ *adj.* (*pl.* **these**) **1** used to identify a specific person or thing close at hand or being indicated or experienced: *don't listen to this guy.* ■ referring to the nearer of two things close to the speaker (the other, if specified, being identified by "that"): *this one or that one?* **2** referring to a specific thing or situation just mentioned: *there was a court case resulting*

from this incident. **3** used with periods of time related to the present: *busy all this week.* ▪ referring to a period of time that has just passed: *I haven't left my bed these three days.* **4** *inf.* used (chiefly in narrative) to refer to a person or thing previously unspecified: *I've got this problem and I need help.*
▸*adv.* to the degree or extent indicated: *they can't handle a job this big.*

this·tle /ˈTHisəl/ ▸*n.* **1** a widely distributed herbaceous plant (*Carlina, Cirsium, Carduus,* and other genera) of the daisy family, which typically has a prickly stem and leaves and rounded heads of purple flowers. Its numerous species include the **bull thistle** (*Cirsium vulgare*). **2** a plant of this type as the Scottish national emblem, esp. the **Scotch thistle** (*Onopordum acanthium*). —**this·tly** /ˈTHis(ə)lē/ *adj.*

this·tle·down /ˈTHisəlˌdoun/ ▸*n.* light fluffy down that is attached to thistle seeds, enabling them to be blown about in the wind.

thith·er /ˈTHiTHər/ ▸*adv. archaic* or *poetic/lit.* to or toward that place: *no trickery had been necessary to attract him thither.*

thix·ot·ro·py /THikˈsätrəpē/ ▸*n. Chem.* the property of becoming less viscous when subjected to an applied stress, shown for example by some gels that become temporarily fluid when shaken or stirred. —**thix·o·trop·ic** /ˌTHiksəˈträpik; -ˈtrōpik/ *adj.*

tho /THō/ (also **tho'**) ▸*conj. & adv.* informal spelling of THOUGH.

thong /THôNG; THäNG/ ▸*n.* **1** a narrow strip of leather or other material, used esp. as a fastening or as the lash of a whip. **2** an item of clothing fastened by or including such a narrow strip, in particular: ▪ a skimpy bathing suit or pair of underpants like a G-string. ▪ another term for FLIP-FLOP (sense 1).
▸*v.* [*tr.*] *archaic* flog or lash (someone) with a whip. —**thonged** *adj.* —**thong·y** *adj.*

tho·rac·ic /THəˈrasik/ ▸*adj. Anat. & Zool.* of or relating to the thorax.

tho·rax /ˈTHôrˌaks/ ▸*n.* (pl. **tho·rax·es** or **tho·ra·ces** /ˈTHôrəˌsēz/) *Anat. & Zool.* the part of the body of a mammal between the neck and the abdomen containing the chief organs of circulation and respiration; the chest. ▪ *Zool.* the corresponding part of a bird, reptile, amphibian, or fish. ▪ *Entomol.* the middle section of the body of an insect, between the head and the abdomen, bearing the legs and wings.

tho·ri·um /ˈTHôrēəm/ ▸*n.* the chemical element of atomic number 90, a white radioactive metal of the actinide series. (Symbol: **Th**)

thorn /THôrn/ ▸*n.* **1** a stiff, sharp-pointed, straight or curved woody projection on the stem or other part of a plant. ▪ *fig.* a source of discomfort, annoyance, or difficulty; an irritation or an obstacle: *the issue has become a thorn in renewing the peace talks.* **2** (also **thorn bush** or **thorn tree**) a thorny bush, shrub, or tree, esp. a hawthorn. **3** an Old English and Icelandic runic letter, Þ or þ, representing the dental fricatives /TH/ and /ᴛʜ/. In English it was eventually superseded by the digraph *th.* Compare with ETH.
▸ □ **a thorn in someone's side** (or **flesh**) a source of continual annoyance or trouble: *the pastor has long been a thorn in the side of the regime.*

thorn·y /ˈTHôrnē/ ▸*adj.* (**thorn·i·er, thorn·i·est**) having many thorns or thorn bushes. ▪ *fig.* causing distress, difficulty, or trouble: *a thorny problem for our team to solve.* —**thorn·i·ly** /-nəlē/ *adv.* —**thorn·i·ness** *n.*

thor·ough /ˈTHərō/ ▸*adj.* complete with regard to every detail; not superficial or partial: *a thorough understanding of the subject.* ▪ performed or written with great care and completeness: *a thorough examination of the wreckage.* ▪ taking pains to do something carefully and completely: *the authorities are very thorough.* ▪ absolute (used to emphasize the degree of something, typically something unwelcome or unpleasant): *a thorough nuisance.* —**thor·ough·ly** *adv.* —**thor·ough·ness** *n.*

thor·ough bass /bäs/ ▸*n. Mus.* basso continuo (see CONTINUO).

thor·ough·bred /ˈTHərəˌbred/ ▸*adj.* (of a horse) of pure breed, esp. a breed originating from English mares and Arab stallions and widely used as racehorses. ▪ *inf.* of outstanding quality.
▸*n.* a horse of a thoroughbred breed. ▪ *inf.* an outstanding or first-class person or thing: *this is a real thoroughbred of a record.*

thor·ough·fare /ˈTHərəˌfer/ ▸*n.* a road or path forming a route between two places. ▪ a main road in a town.

thor·ough·go·ing /ˈTHərəˌgōiNG/ ▸*adj.* involving or attending to every detail or aspect of something: *a thoroughgoing reform of the whole economy.* ▪ exemplifying a specified characteristic fully; absolute: *a thoroughgoing appraisal.*

those /THōz/ ▸ plural form of THAT.

thou[1] /THou/ ▸*pron.* [*second person sing.*] *archaic* or *dialect* form of YOU, as the singular subject of a verb: *thou art fair, o my beloved.* Compare with THEE.

thou[2] /THou/ ▸*n.* (pl. same or **thous**) *inf.* a thousand. ▪ one thousandth of an inch.

though /THō/ ▸*conj.* despite the fact that; although: *though they were speaking in undertones, Philip could hear them.* ▪ even if (introducing a possibility): *you will be informed of its progress, slow though that may be.* ▪ however; but (introducing something opposed to or qualifying what has just been said): *her name was Rose, though no one called her that.*
▸*adv.* however (indicating that a factor qualifies or imposes restrictions on what was said previously): *I was hunting for work. Jobs were scarce though.*

thought[1] /THôt/ ▸*n.* **1** an idea or opinion produced by thinking or occurring suddenly in the mind: *Maggie had a sudden thought.* ▪ an idea or mental picture, imagined and contemplated: *the mere thought of Peter with Nicole made her see red.* ▪ (**one's thoughts**) one's mind or attention: *he's very much in our thoughts and prayers.* ▪ an act of considering or remembering someone or something: *she hadn't given a thought to Max.* ▪ (usu. **thought of**) an intention, hope, or idea of doing or receiving something: *he had given up all thoughts of making Manhattan his home.* **2** the action or process of thinking: *Sophie sat deep in thought.* ▪ the formation of opinions, esp. as a philosophy or system of ideas, or the opinions so formed: *the freedom of thought and action.* ▪ careful consideration or attention: *I haven't given it much thought.* ▪ concern for another's well-being or convenience: *he is carrying on the life of a single man, with no thought for me.*

thought[2] ▸ past and past participle of THINK.

thought·ful /ˈTHôtfəl/ ▸*adj.* absorbed in or involving thought: *brows drawn together in thoughtful consideration.* ▪ showing consideration for the needs of other people. ▪ showing careful consideration or attention: *her work is thoughtful and provocative.* —**thought·ful·ly** *adv.* —**thought·ful·ness** *n.*

thought·less /ˈTHôtləs/ ▸*adj.* (of a person or their behavior) not showing consideration for the needs of other people. ▪ without consideration of the possible consequences: *to think a few minutes of thoughtless pleasure could end in this.* —**thought·less·ly** *adv.* —**thought·less·ness** *n.*

thought-pro·vok·ing ▸*adj.* stimulating careful consideration or attention: *thought-provoking questions.*

thou·sand /ˈTHouzənd/ ▸*cardinal number* (pl. **-sands** /ˈTHouzndz/ or (with numeral or quantifying word) same) (**a/one thousand**) the number equivalent to the product of a hundred and ten; 1,000: *a thousand meters | thousands have been killed.* (Roman numeral: **m, M**) ▪ (**thousands**) the numbers from one thousand to 9,999: *the cost of repairs could be in the thousands.* ▪ (usu. **thousands**) *inf.* an unspecified large number: *I have imagined it a thousand times.* —**thou·sand·fold** /-ˌfōld/ *adj. & adv.* —**thou·sandth** /-zən(t)TH/ *ordinal number.*

thrall /THrôl/ ▸*n. poetic/lit.* the state of being in someone's power or having great power over someone: *she was in thrall to her abusive husband.* ▪ *hist.* a slave, servant, or captive. ▷Old English *thræl* 'slave,' from Old Norse *thræll.* —**thrall·dom** /-dəm/ (also **thral·dom**) *n.*

thrash /THrasH/ ▸*v.* [*tr.*] beat (a person or animal) repeatedly and violently with a stick or whip. ▪ hit (something) hard and repeatedly: *the wind screeched and the mast thrashed the deck.* ▪ [*intr.*] make a repeated crashing by or as if by hitting something: *the surf thrashed and thundered.* ▪ [*intr.*] move in a violent and convulsive way: *he lay on the ground thrashing around in pain* | [*tr.*] *she thrashed her arms, attempting to swim.* ▪ [*intr.*] (**thrash around**) struggle in a wild or desperate way to do something: *two months of thrashing around on my own.* ▪ *inf.* defeat (someone) heavily in a contest or match. ▪ [*intr.*] move with brute determination or violent movements: *I wrench the steering wheel back and thrash on up the hill.* ▪ rare term for THRESH (sense 1).
▸*phrasal v.* □ **thrash something out** discuss something thoroughly and honestly. ▪ produce a conclusion by such discussion.
▸*n.* **1** a violent or noisy movement, typically involving hitting something repeatedly: *the thrash of the waves.* **2** (also **thrash metal**) a style of fast, loud, harsh-sounding rock music, combining elements of punk and heavy metal. ▪ a short, fast, loud piece or passage of rock music.

thrash·er[1] /ˈTHrasHər/ ▸*n.* a person or thing that thrashes.

thrash·er[2] ▸*n.* a thrushlike American songbird (*Toxostoma* and other genera) of the mockingbird family, with mainly brown or gray plumage, a long tail, and a down-curved bill.

thread /THred/ ▸*n.* **1** a long, thin strand of cotton, nylon, or other fibers used in sewing or weaving. ▪ (**threads**) *inf.* clothes. **2** a thing resembling a thread in length or thinness, in particular: ▪ *chiefly poetic/lit.* a long, thin line or piece of something: *the river was a thread of silver below them.* ▪ something abstract or intangible, regarded as weak or fragile: *the tenuous thread of life.* ▪ a theme or characteristic, typically forming one of several, running throughout a situation or piece of writing: *a common thread running through the scandals was the failure to conduct audits.* **3** *Comput.* a group of linked messages posted on the Internet that

share a common subject or theme. ■ a programming structure or process formed by linking a number of separate elements or subroutines, esp. each of the tasks executed concurrently in multithreading. **4** (also **screw thread**) a helical ridge on the outside of a screw, bolt, etc., or on the inside of a cylindrical hole, to allow two parts to be screwed together.
▸ v. [tr.] **1** pass a thread through the eye of (a needle) or through the needle and guides of (a sewing machine). ■ [tr.] pass (a long, thin object or piece of material) through something and into the required position for use: *he threaded the rope through a pulley.* ■ [intr.] move carefully or skillfully in and out of obstacles: *she **threaded her way** through the tables.* ■ interweave or intersperse as if with threads: *his hair had become **threaded with gray.*** ■ put (beads, chunks of food, or other small objects) together or singly on a thread, chain, or skewer that runs through the center of each one. **2** cut a screw thread in or on (a hole, screw, or other object). —**thread·er** n. —**thread·like** /-ˌlīk/ adj.
▸ □ **hang by a thread** be in a highly precarious state. □ **lose the** (or **one's**) **thread** be unable to follow what someone is saying or remember what one is going to say next.

thread·bare /ˈTHredˌber/ ▸ adj. (of cloth, clothing, or soft furnishings) becoming thin and tattered with age: ■ (of a person, building, or room) poor or shabby in appearance.

thread·worm /ˈTHredˌwərm/ ▸ n. a very slender parasitic nematode worm, esp. a pinworm.

threat /THret/ ▸ n. **1** a statement of an intention to inflict pain, injury, damage, or other hostile action on someone in retribution for something done or not done: *members of her family have received **death threats.*** ■ *Law* a menace of bodily harm, such as may restrain a person's freedom of action. **2** a person or thing likely to cause damage or danger: *hurricane damage poses a major threat.* ■ the possibility of trouble, danger, or ruin: *the company faces the threat of bankruptcy.*

threat·en /ˈTHretn/ ▸ v. [tr.] state one's intention to take hostile action against someone in retribution for something done or not done: *the unions threatened a general strike.* ■ [tr.] express one's intention to harm or kill (someone): *the men **threatened** the customers **with** a handgun.* ■ cause (someone or something) to be vulnerable or at risk; endanger: *a broken finger threatened his career.* ■ (of a situation or weather conditions) seem likely to produce an unpleasant or unwelcome result. | [tr.] *the air was raw and threatened rain.* ■ [intr.] (of something undesirable) seem likely to occur: *unless war threatened, national politics remained the focus of attention.* —**threat·en·er** /ˈTHretn-ər/ n. —**threat·en·ing** adj. —**threat·en·ing·ly** adv.

three /THrē/ ▸ cardinal number equivalent to the sum of one and two; one more than two; 3: *her three children | a crew of three | a three-bedroom house.* (Roman numeral: **iii, III**) ■ a group or unit of three people or things: *students clustered in twos or threes.* ■ three years old:. ■ three o'clock. ■ a size of garment or other merchandise denoted by three. ■ a playing card or domino with three pips.

three-di·men·sion·al ▸ adj. having or appearing to have length, breadth, and depth: *a three-dimensional object.* ■ *fig.* (of a literary or dramatic work) sufficiently full in characterization and representation of events to be believable. —**three-di·men·sion·al·i·ty** /ˌdīˌmensHəˈnalətē/ n. —**three-di·men·sion·al·ly** adv.

three·fold /ˈTHrēˌfōld/ ▸ adj. three times as great or as numerous: *a threefold increase in the number of stolen cars.* ■ having three parts or elements. ▸ adv. by three times; to three times the number or amount.

three-leg·ged race /ˈlegəd/ ▸ n. a race run by pairs of people, one member of each pair having their left leg tied to the right leg of the other.

three-par·ent ▸ adj. **1** *Genetics* containing a chromosomal complement from a mother and father and the mitochondrial DNA from the egg of a donor: *three-parent embryos.* **2** having or regarding three different adults in a parental role: *kids in three-parent homes.*

three-piece ▸ adj. consisting of three separate and complementary items, in particular: ■ (of a set of furniture) consisting of a sofa and two armchairs. ■ (of a set of clothes) consisting of slacks or a skirt with a vest and jacket.
▸ n. a set of three separate and complementary items. ■ a group consisting of three musicians.

three-point land·ing ▸ n. a landing of an aircraft on the two main wheels and the tailwheel or skid simultaneously.

three-ring cir·cus ▸ n. a circus with three rings for simultaneous performances. ■ a public spectacle, esp. one with little substance.

three·score /ˈTHrēˈskôr/ ▸ cardinal number *poetic/lit.* sixty.

three·some /ˈTHrēsəm/ ▸ n. a group of three people engaged in the same activity. ■ a game or activity for three people.

three-wheel·er ▸ n. a vehicle with three wheels, esp. a child's tricycle.

thren·o·dy /ˈTHrenədē/ ▸ n. (pl. **-dies**) a lament. ▷mid 17th cent.: from Greek *thrēnōidia*, from *thrēnos* 'wailing' + *ōidē* 'song.' —**thre·no·di·al** /THrəˈnōdēəl/ adj. —**thre·nod·ic** /THrəˈnädik/ adj. —**thren·o·dist** /-dist/ n.

thresh /THresH/ ▸ v. [tr.] **1** separate grain from (a plant), typically with a flail or by the action of a revolving mechanism: *machinery that can reap and thresh corn in the same process* [as n.] (**threshing**) *farm workers started the afternoon's threshing.* **2** variant spelling of THRASH (in the sense of violent movement).

thresh·er /ˈTHresHər/ ▸ n. **1** a person or machine that separates grain from the plants by beating. **2** (also **thresher shark**) a surface-living shark (*Alopias vulpinus,* family Alopidae) with a long upper lobe to the tail. Threshers often hunt in pairs, lashing the water with their tails to herd fish into a tightly packed shoal.

thresh·old /ˈTHresH,(h)ōld/ ▸ n. **1** a strip of wood, metal, or stone forming the bottom of a doorway and crossed in entering a house or room. ■ a point of entry or beginning: *she was **on the threshold** of a dazzling career.* ■ the beginning of an airport runway on which an aircraft is attempting to land. **2** the magnitude or intensity that must be exceeded for a certain reaction, phenomenon, result, or condition to occur or be manifested: *nothing happens until the signal passes the threshold.* ■ the maximum level of radiation or a concentration of a substance considered to be acceptable or safe: *their water would meet the safety threshold of 50 milligrams of nitrates per liter.* ■ *Physiol. & Psychol.* a limit below which a stimulus causes no reaction: *his low pain threshold.*

threw /THrōō/ ▸ past of THROW.

thrice /THrīs/ ▸ adv. *chiefly formal poetic/lit.* three times: *a dose of 25 mg thrice daily.* ■ extremely; very: *I was thrice blessed.*

thrift /THrift/ ▸ n. the quality of using money and other resources carefully and not wastefully: *the values of thrift and self-reliance.* ■ another term for SAVINGS AND LOAN.

thrift shop (also **thrift store**) ▸ n. a store selling secondhand clothes and other household goods, typically to raise funds for a charitable institution.

thrift·y /ˈTHriftē/ ▸ adj. (**thrift·i·er, thrift·i·est**) (of a person or their behavior) using money and other resources carefully and not wastefully. —**thrift·i·ly** /-lē/ adv. —**thrift·i·ness** n.

thrill /THril/ ▸ n. a sudden feeling of excitement and pleasure: *the thrill of jumping out of an airplane.* ■ an experience that produces such a feeling. ■ a wave or nervous tremor of emotion or sensation: *a thrill of excitement ran through her.* ■ *archaic* a throb or pulsation.
▸ v. **1** [tr.] cause (someone) to have a sudden feeling of excitement and pleasure: *his kiss thrilled and excited her.* ■ [intr.] experience such feeling: *thrill to the magic of the world 's greatest guitarist.* **2** [intr.] (of an emotion or sensation) pass with a nervous tremor: *the shock of alarm thrilled through her.* ■ [intr.] *poetic/lit.* quiver or throb. —**thrill·ing·ly** adv.

thrill·er /ˈTHrilər/ ▸ n. a novel, play, or movie with an exciting plot, typically involving crime or espionage. ■ a person, thing, or experience that thrills: *the Rockies could make Game 4 another thriller.*

thrips /THrips/ (also **thrip**) ▸ n. (pl. same) a minute black winged insect that sucks plant sap and can be a serious pest of ornamental and food plants when present in large numbers.

thrive /THrīv/ ▸ v. (past **throve** /THrōv/ or **thrived;** past part. **thriv·en** /ˈTHrivən/ or **thrived**) [intr.] (of a child, animal, or plant) grow or develop well or vigorously. ■ prosper; flourish: *education groups **thrive on** organization.*

throat /THrōt/ ▸ n. the passage that leads from the back of the mouth of a person or animal. ■ the front part of a person's or animal's neck, behind which the esophagus, trachea, and blood vessels serving the head are situated. ■ *poetic/lit.* a voice of a person or a songbird. ■ a thing compared to a throat, esp. a narrow passage, entrance, or exit. —**throat·ed** adj. [in comb.] *a full-throated baritone | a ruby-throated hummingbird.*
▸ □ **be at each other's throats** (of people or organizations) quarrel or fight persistently. □ **cut one's own throat** bring about one's own downfall by one's actions. □ **force** (or **shove** or **ram**) **something down someone's throat** force ideas or material on a person's attention by repeatedly putting them forward.

throat·y /ˈTHrōtē/ ▸ adj. (**throat·i·er, throat·i·est**) (of a sound such as a person's voice or the noise of an engine) deep and rasping: *rich, throaty laughter.* —**throat·i·ly** /-təlē/ adv. —**throat·i·ness** n.

throb /THräb/ ▸ v. (**throbbed, throb·bing**) [intr.] beat or sound with a

strong, regular rhythm; pulsate steadily: *the war drums throbbed.* ■ feel pain in a series of regular beats: *her foot throbbed with pain.*
▸ *n.* a strong, regular beat or sound; a steady pulsation: *the throb of the ship's engines.* ■ a feeling of pain in a series of regular beats.

throes /THrōz/ ▸ *pl. n.* intense or violent pain and struggle, esp. accompanying birth, death, or great change: *in his death throes.*
▸ □ **in the throes of** in the middle of doing or dealing with something very difficult or painful: *a friend was in the throes of a divorce.*

throm·bo·cyte /'THrämbə,sīt/ ▸ *n.* another term for **PLATELET**.

throm·bo·sis /THräm'bōsis/ ▸ *n.* (*pl.* **-ses** /-,sēz/) local coagulation or clotting of the blood in a part of the circulatory system: *he died of a coronary thrombosis.* —**throm·bot·ic** /-'bätik/ *adj.*

throm·bus /'THrämbəs/ ▸ *n.* (*pl.* **-bi** /-,bī/) a blood clot formed in situ within the vascular system of the body and impeding blood flow.

throne /THrōn/ ▸ *n.* a ceremonial chair for a sovereign, bishop, or similar figure. ■ (**the throne**) used to signify sovereign power: *the heir to the throne.* ■ *humorous* a toilet.

throng /THrông; THräNG/ ▸ *n.* a large, densely packed crowd of people or animals: *he pushed his way through the throng* | *a throng of birds.*
▸ *v.* [*tr.*] (of a crowd) fill or be present in (a place or area): *a crowd thronged the station* | *the streets were thronged with people.* ■ [*intr.*] flock or be present in great numbers: *tourists thronged to the picturesque village.*

throt·tle /'THrätl/ ▸ *n.* **1** a device controlling the flow of fuel or power to an engine: *the engines were at full throttle.* **2** *archaic* a throat, gullet, or windpipe.
▸ *v.* [*tr.*] **1** attack or kill (someone) by choking or strangling them. **2** control (an engine or vehicle) with a throttle. ■ [*intr.*] (**throttle back** or **down**) reduce the power of an engine or vehicle by use of the throttle. —**throt·tler** /'THrätl-ər; 'THrätlər/ *n.*

through /THrōō/ ▸ *prep. & adv.* **1** moving in one side and out of the other side of (an opening, channel, or location): [as *prep.*] *stepping boldly through the doorway* | [as *adv.*] *as soon as we opened the gate, they came streaming through.* ■ so as to make a hole or opening in (a physical object): [as *prep.*] *the truck smashed through a brick wall* | [as *adv.*] *a cucumber, slit, but not all the way through.* ■ moving around or from one side to the other within (a crowd or group): [as *prep.*] *making my way through the guests.* ■ so as to be perceived from the other side of (an intervening obstacle): [as *prep.*] *the sun was streaming in through the window* | [as *adv.*] *the glass in the front door where the moonlight streamed through.* ■ [*prep.*] expressing the position or location of something beyond or at the far end of (an opening or an obstacle): *the approach to the church is through a gate.* ■ expressing the extent of turning from one orientation to another: [as *prep.*] *each joint can move through an angle within fixed limits.* **2** continuing in time toward completion of (a process or period): [as *adv.*] *to struggle through until payday.* ■ so as to complete (a particular stage or trial) successfully: [as *prep.*] *she had come through her sternest test* | [as *adv.*] *I will struggle through alone.* ■ from beginning to end of (an experience or activity, typically a tedious or stressful one): [as *prep.*] *we sat through some boring speeches* | [as *adv.*] *Karl will see you through, Ingrid.* **3** so as to inspect all or part of (a collection, inventory, or publication): [as *prep.*] *flipping through the pages* | [as *adv.*] *she read the letter through carefully.* **4** [*prep.*] up to and including (a particular point in an ordered sequence): *they will be in town from March 24 through May 7.* **5** [*prep.*] by means of (a process or intermediate stage): *dioxins get into mothers' milk through contaminated food.* ■ by means of (an intermediary or agent): *seeking justice through the proper channels.* **6** [*adv.*] so as to be connected by telephone: *he put a call through to the senator.*
▸ *adj.* **1** (of a means of public transportation or a ticket) continuing or valid to the final destination: *a through train from Boston.* **2** denoting traffic that passes from one side of a place to another in the course of a longer journey: *neighborhoods from which through traffic would be excluded.* ■ denoting a road that is open at both ends, allowing traffic free passage from one end to the other: *the shopping center is on a busy through road.* **3** (of a room) running the whole length of a building. **4** *inf.* having no prospect of any future relationship, dealings, or success: *she told him she was through with him.*
▸ □ **through and through** in every aspect; thoroughly or completely.

through·out /THrōō'out/ ▸ *prep. & adv.* all the way through, in particular: ■ in every part of (a place or object): [as *prep.*] *it had repercussions throughout Europe* | [as *adv.*] *the house is in good order throughout.* ■ from beginning to end of (an event or period of time): [as *prep.*] *throughout her life* | [as *adv.*] *both sets of parents retained a smiling dignity throughout.*

through·put /'THrōō,pŏŏt/ ▸ *n.* the amount of material or items passing through a system or process.

through·way ▸ *n.* another spelling of **THRUWAY**.

throve /THrōv/ ▸ past of **THRIVE**.

throw /THrō/ ▸ *v.* (*past* **threw** /THrōō/; *past part.* **thrown** /THrōn/) **1** [*tr.*] propel (something) with force through the air by a movement of the arm and hand: *I threw a brick through the window.* ■ [*tr.*] push or force (someone or something) violently and suddenly into a particular physical position or state: *the pilot and one passenger were thrown clear and survived.* ■ put in place or erect quickly: *the stewards had thrown a cordon across the fairway.* ■ move (a part of the body) quickly or suddenly in a particular direction: *she threw her head back and laughed.* ■ project or cast (light or shadow) in a particular direction: *a chandelier threw its bright light over the walls.* ■ deliver (a punch). ■ direct (a particular kind of look or facial expression): *she threw a withering glance at him.* ■ project (one's voice) so that it appears to come from someone or something else, as in ventriloquism. ■ (**throw something off/on**) put on or take off a garment hastily: *I threw on my housecoat and went to the door.* ■ move (a switch or lever) so as to operate a device. ■ roll (dice). ■ obtain (a specified number) by rolling dice. ■ *inf.* lose (a race or contest) intentionally, esp. in return for a bribe. **2** [*tr.*] cause to enter suddenly a particular state or condition: *he threw all her emotions into turmoil.* ■ put (someone) in a particular place or state, esp. in a rough, abrupt, or summary fashion: *these guys should be thrown in jail.* ■ [*tr.*] disconcert; confuse: *she frowned, thrown by this apparent change of tack.* **3** [*tr.*] send (one's opponent) to the ground in wrestling, judo, or similar activity. ■ (of a horse) unseat (its rider). ■ (of a horse) lose (a shoe). **4** [*tr.*] form (ceramic ware) on a potter's wheel: *further on, a potter was throwing pots.* ■ turn (wood or other material) on a lathe. **5** [*tr.*] have (a fit or tantrum). **6** [*tr.*] give or hold (a party).
▸ *phrasal v.* □ **throw oneself at** appear too eager to become the sexual partner of. □ **throw something away 1** discard something as useless or unwanted. ■ waste or fail to make use of an opportunity or advantage. ■ discard a playing card in a game. **2** (of an actor) deliver a line with deliberate underemphasis for increased dramatic effect. □ **throw something in 1** include something, typically at no extra cost, with something that is being sold or offered: *they cut the price by $100 and threw in an AC adaptor.* **2** make a remark casually as an interjection in a conversation. □ **throw oneself into** start to do (something) with enthusiasm and vigor: *Eve threw herself into her work.* □ **throw something off 1** rid oneself of something: *give roses a boost that may help them throw off a pest on their own.* **2** write or utter in an offhand manner: *Thomas threw off the question lightly.* □ **throw oneself on** (or **upon**) attack (someone) vigorously: *they threw themselves on the enemy.* □ **throw someone out 1** expel someone unceremoniously from a place, organization, or activity. **2** *Baseball* put out a runner by a throw to the base being approached, followed by a tag. □ **throw something out 1** discard something as unwanted. **2** (of a court, legislature, or other body) dismiss or reject something brought before it: *the charges were thrown out by the judge.* **3** put forward a suggestion tentatively: *a suggestion that Dunne threw out caught many a reader's fancy.* **4** emit or radiate something: *a big range fire that threw out heat like a furnace.* **5** (of a plant) rapidly develop a side shoot, bud, etc. □ **throw people together** bring people into contact, esp. by chance. □ **throw something together** make or produce something hastily, without careful planning or arrangement. □ **throw up** vomit. □ **throw something up 1** abandon or give up something, esp. one's job. **2** *inf.* vomit something one has eaten or drunk. **3** produce something and bring it to notice: *he saw the prayers of the Church as a living and fruitful tradition that threw up new ideas.* **4** erect a building or structure hastily.
▸ *n.* **1** an act of throwing something. ■ an act of throwing one's opponent in wrestling, judo, or similar sport: *a shoulder throw.* **2** a light cover for furniture. **3** short for **THROW OF THE DICE** (see **DICE**). **4** *Geol.* the extent of vertical displacement between the two sides of a fault. **5** the action or motion of a slide valve or of a crank, eccentric wheel, or cam. ■ the extent of such motion. ■ the distance moved by the pointer of an instrument. **6** (**a throw**) *inf.* used to indicate how much a single item, turn, or attempt costs: *he was offering to draw portraits at $25 a throw.* —**throw·a·ble** *adj.* —**throw·er** *n.*
▸ □ **throw one's hand in** withdraw from a card game, poker, because one has a poor hand. ■ withdraw from a contest or activity; give up. □ **throw in the towel** (of boxers or their seconds) throw a towel into the ring as a token of defeat. ■ abandon a struggle; admit defeat. □ **throw up one's hands** raise both hands in the air as an indication of one's exasperation.

throw·a·way /'THrōə,wā/ ▸ *adj.* **1** denoting or relating to products that are intended to be discarded after being used once or a few times: *a throwaway camera.* **2** (of a remark) expressed in a casual or understated way: *some people overreacted to a few throwaway lines.*
▸ *n.* a thing intended or destined to be discarded after brief use or appeal. ■ a casual or understated remark or idea.

throw·back /'THrō,bak/ ▶ n. a reversion to an earlier ancestral characteristic. ■ a person or thing having the characteristics of a former time: *a lot of his work is a throwback to the fifties.*

throw rug ▶ n. a small decorative rug designed to be placed with a casual effect and moved as required.

thru /THrōō/ ▶ prep., adv., & adj. informal spelling of **THROUGH**.

thrum¹ /THrəm/ ▶ v. (**thrummed, thrum·ming**) [*intr.*] make a continuous rhythmic humming sound: *the boat's huge engines thrummed in his ears.* ■ [*tr.*] strum (the strings of a musical instrument) in a rhythmic way. ▶ n. a continuous rhythmic humming sound.

thrum² ▶ n. (in weaving) an unwoven end of a warp thread, or a fringe of such ends, left in the loom when the finished cloth is cut away. ■ any short loose thread.
▶ v. (**thrummed, thrum·ming**) [*tr.*] cover or adorn (cloth or clothing) with ends of thread. —**thrum·mer** n. —**thrum·my** adj.

thrush¹ /THrəSH/ ▶ n. a small or medium-sized songbird (*Turdus* and other genera), typically having a brown back, spotted breast, and loud song. The **thrush family** (Muscicapidae) includes the robins, bluebirds, and blackbirds.

thrush² ▶ n. **1** infection of the mouth and throat, producing whitish patches, caused by a yeastlike fungus. Also called **CANDIDIASIS**. ■ infection of the female genitals with the same fungus. **2** a chronic condition affecting the frog of a horse's foot, causing the accumulation of a dark, foul-smelling substance.

thrust /THrəst/ ▶ v. (*past* **thrust**) [*tr.*] push (something or someone) suddenly or violently in the specified direction: *she thrust her hands into her pockets* | *fig. Howard was thrust into the limelight* | [*intr.*] *he thrust at his opponent with his sword.* ■ [*tr.*] (of a person) move or advance forcibly: *she thrust through the bramble canes.* ■ [*intr.*] (of a thing) extend so as to project conspicuously: *a jetty thrust out into the water.* ■ (**thrust something on/upon**) force (someone) to accept or deal with something: *he felt that fame had been thrust upon him.* ■ [*tr.*] (of a man) penetrate the vagina or anus of a sexual partner with forceful movements of the penis.
▶ n. **1** a sudden or violent lunge with a pointed weapon or a bodily part. ■ a forceful attack or effort: *executives led a new thrust in business development.* ■ the principal purpose or theme of a course of action or line of reasoning: *anti-Americanism became the main thrust of their policy.* **2** the propulsive force of a jet or rocket engine. ■ the lateral pressure exerted by an arch or other support in a building. **3** (also **thrust fault**) *Geol.* a reverse fault of low angle, with older strata displaced horizontally over younger.

thru·way /'THrōō,wā/ (also **through·way**) ▶ n. a major road or highway.

thud /THəd/ ▶ n. a dull, heavy sound, such as that made by an object falling to the ground: *Jean heard the thud of the closing door.*
▶ v. (**thud·ded, thud·ding**) [*intr.*] move, fall, or strike something with a dull, heavy sound: *the bullets thudded into the dusty ground.* ▷late Middle English (originally Scots): probably from Old English *thyddan* 'to thrust, push'; related to *thoden* 'violent wind.' The noun is recorded first denoting a sudden blast or gust of wind, later the sound of a thunderclap, whence a dull, heavy sound. The verb dates from the early 16th cent.

thug /THəg/ ▶ n. a violent person, esp. a criminal. —**thug·ger·y** /-gərē/ n. —**thug·gish** adj. —**thug·gish·ly** adv. —**thug·gish·ness** n.

thu·li·um /'TH(y)ōōlēəm/ ▶ n. the chemical element of atomic number 69, a soft silvery-white metal of the lanthanide series. (Symbol: **Tm**)

thumb /THəm/ ▶ n. the short, thick first digit of the human hand, set lower and apart from the other four and opposable to them. ■ the corresponding digit of primates or other mammals. ■ the part of a glove intended to cover the thumb.
▶ v. [*tr.*] press, move, or touch (something) with one's thumb. ■ turn over (pages) with or as if with one's thumb: *I've thumbed my address book and found a range of smaller hotels* | [*intr.*] *he was **thumbing through** that magazine.* ■ wear or soil (a book's pages) by repeated handling: *his dictionaries were thumbed and ink-stained.* ■ request or obtain (a free ride in a passing vehicle) by signaling with one's thumb: *three cars passed me and I tried to **thumb a ride*** | [*intr.*] *he was **thumbing his way** across France.* —**thumbed** adj. —**thumb·less** adj.
▶ □ **be all thumbs** *inf.* be clumsy or awkward in one's actions. □ **thumb one's nose at** *inf.* show disdain or contempt for. □ **thumbs up** (or **down**) *inf.* an indication of satisfaction or approval (or of rejection or failure). □ **under someone's thumb** completely under someone's influence or control.

thumb drive ▶ n. *Comput.* another term for **USB FLASH DRIVE**.

thumb·nail /'THəm,nāl/ ▶ n. **1** the nail of the thumb. **2** [usu. as adj.] a very small or concise description, representation, or summary: *a thumbnail sketch.* ■ *Comput.* a small picture of an image or page layout.

thumb·print /'THəm,print/ ▶ n. an impression or mark made on a surface by the inner part of the top joint of the thumb, esp. as used for identifying individuals from the unique pattern of whorls and lines. ■ *fig.* a distinctive identifying characteristic.

thumb·screw /'THəm,skrōō/ ▶ n. **1** a screw with a protruding winged or flattened head for turning with the thumb and forefinger. **2** (usu. **thumbscrews**) an instrument of torture for crushing the thumbs.

thumb·tack /'THəm,tak/ ▶ n. a short flat-headed pin, used for fastening paper to a wall or other surface.

thump /THəmp/ ▶ v. [*tr.*] hit (someone or something) heavily, esp. with the fist or a blunt implement: *Holman thumped the desk with his hand* | [*intr.*] *she thumped on the door.* ■ [*tr.*] move (something) forcefully, noisily, or decisively: *she picked up the kettle then thumped it down again.* ■ [*intr.*] move or do something with a heavy deadened sound: *Philip thumped down on the sofa.* ■ [*intr.*] (of a person's heart or pulse) beat or pulsate strongly, typically because of fear or excitement. ■ *inf.* defeat heavily.
▶ n. a heavy dull blow with a person's fist or a blunt implement: *I felt a thump on my back.* ■ a loud deadened sound. ■ a strong heartbeat, esp. one caused by fear or excitement. —**thump·er** n.

thun·der /'THəndər/ ▶ n. a loud rumbling or crashing noise heard after a lightning flash due to the expansion of rapidly heated air. ■ a resounding loud deep noise.
▶ v. [*intr.*] (**it thunders, it is thundering**, etc.) thunder sounds: *it began to thunder.* ■ make a loud, deep resounding noise: *the train thundered through the night.* ■ [*tr.*] strike powerfully: *McGwire thundered that one out of the stadium.* ■ speak loudly and forcefully or angrily, esp. to denounce or criticize: *he **thundered against** the evils of the age* | *"Sit down!" thundered Morse with immense authority.* —**thun·der·er** n. —**thun·der·y** /-d(ə)rē/ adj.

thun·der·bolt /'THəndər,bōlt/ ▶ n. *poetic/lit.* a flash of lightning with a simultaneous crash of thunder. ■ a supposed bolt or shaft believed to be the destructive agent in a lightning flash, esp. as an attribute of a god. ■ used in similes and comparisons to refer to a very sudden or unexpected event or item of news, esp. of an unpleasant nature: *the full force of what she had been told hit her like a thunderbolt.* ■ *inf.* a very fast and powerful shot, throw, or stroke.

thun·der·clap /'THəndər,klap/ ▶ n. a crash of thunder: *the door opened like a thunderclap.* ■ *fig.* something startling or unexpected.

thun·der·cloud /'THəndər,kloud/ ▶ n. a cumulus cloud with a towering or spreading top, charged with electricity and producing thunder and lightning. ■ *fig.* something ominous.

thun·der·head /'THəndər,hed/ ▶ n. a rounded, projecting head of a cumulus cloud, which portends a thunderstorm.

thun·der·ous /'THənd(ə)rəs/ ▶ adj. of, relating to, or giving warning of thunder: *a thunderous gray cloud.* ■ very loud: *thunderous applause.* ■ very powerful or intense. —**thun·der·ous·ly** adv. —**thun·der·ous·ness** n.

thun·der·show·er /'THəndər,SHou(ə)r/ ▶ n. a brief rain shower accompanied by thunder and lightning.

thun·der·storm /'THəndər,stôrm/ ▶ n. a storm with thunder and lightning and typically also heavy rain or hail.

thun·der·struck /'THəndər,strək/ ▶ adj. extremely surprised or shocked.

Thur. ▶ abbr. Thursday.

Thurs. ▶ abbr. Thursday.

Thurs·day /'THərz,dā; -dē/ ▶ n. the day of the week before Friday and following Wednesday.
▶ adv. on Thursday: *he called her up Thursday.* ■ (**Thursdays**) on Thursdays; each Thursday: *the column is published Thursdays.*

thus /THəs/ ▶ adv. *poetic/lit.* or *formal* **1** as a result or consequence of this; therefore: *Burke knocked out Byrne, thus becoming champion.* **2** in the manner now being indicated or exemplified; in this way: *she phoned Susan, and while she was thus engaged, Charles summoned the doctor.* **3** to this point; so: *the Web site has been hacked three times thus far.*

thwart /THwôrt/ ▶ v. [*tr.*] prevent (someone) from accomplishing something: *he was thwarted in his desire to punish Uncle Fred.* ■ oppose (a plan, attempt, or ambition) successfully: *the government had been able to thwart all attempts by opposition leaders to form new parties.*
▶ n. a structural crosspiece sometimes forming a seat for a rower in a boat.
▶ prep. & adv. *archaic* or *poetic/lit.* from one side to another side of; across: [as prep.] *a pink-tinged cloud spread thwart the shore.*

Pronunciation Key ə *ago, up*; ər *over, fur*; a *hat*; ā *ate*; ä *car*; CH *chin*; e *let*; ē *see*; e(ə)r *air*; i *fit*; ī *by*; i(ə)r *ear*; NG *sing*; ō *go*; ô *law, for*; oi *toy*; ōō *good*; ōō *goo*; ou *out*; SH *she*; TH *thin*; <u>TH</u> *then*; (h)w *why*; ZH *vision*

thy /T͟Hī/ (also **thine** before a vowel) ▶*possessive adj.* archaic or dialect form of **YOUR:** *honor thy father and thy mother.*

thyme /tīm/ ▶*n.* a low-growing aromatic plant (genus *Thymus*) of the mint family, with small leaves used as a culinary herb. ▷Middle English: from Old French *thym,* via Latin from Greek *thumon,* from *thuein* 'burn, sacrifice.' —**thym·y** /ˈtīmē/ *adj.*

thy·mine /ˈTHīˌmēn; -min/ ▶*n.* Biochem. a pyrimidine derivative that is one of the four constituent bases of nucleic acids. It is paired with adenine in double-stranded DNA.

thy·mus /ˈTHīməs/ (also **thymus gland**) ▶*n.* (*pl.* **-mus·es** or **-mi** /-mī/) a lymphoid organ situated in the neck of vertebrates that produces T cells for the immune system.

thy·roid /ˈTHīˌroid/ ▶*n.* **1** (also **thyroid gland**) a large ductless gland in the neck that secretes hormones regulating growth and development through the rate of metabolism. ■ an extract prepared from the thyroid gland of animals and used in treating deficiency of thyroid hormones. **2** (also **thyroid cartilage**) a large cartilage of the larynx, a projection of which forms the Adam's apple in humans.

thy·rox·ine /THīˈräksēn; -sin/ (also **thy·rox·in** /-ˌräksin/) ▶*n.* Biochem. the main hormone, $C_{15}H_{11}NO_4I_4$, produced by the thyroid gland, acting to increase metabolic rate and so regulating growth and development.

thy·self /THīˈself/ ▶*pron.* [second person sing.] archaic or dialect form of **YOURSELF**, corresponding to the subject **THOU**[1] : *thou shalt love thy neighbor as thyself.*

Ti ▶*symb.* the chemical element titanium.

ti /tē/ ▶*n.* (in solmization) the seventh note of a major scale. ■ the note B in the fixed-do system.

ti·ar·a /tēˈärə; -ˈarə; -ˈe(ə)rə/ ▶*n.* a jeweled ornamental band worn on the head.

Ti·bet·an /təˈbetn/ ▶*n.* **1** a native of Tibet or a person of Tibetan descent. **2** the Tibeto-Burman language of Tibet, also spoken in neighboring areas of China, India, and Nepal.
▶*adj.* of or relating to Tibet, its people, or its language.

tib·i·a /ˈtibēə/ ▶*n.* (*pl.* **tib·i·ae** /ˈtibēˌē/ or **tib·i·as**) Anat. the inner and typically larger of the two bones between the knee and the ankle (or the equivalent joints in other terrestrial vertebrates), parallel with the fibula. —**tib·i·al** *adj.*

tic /tik/ ▶*n.* a habitual spasmodic contraction of the muscles, most often in the face. ■ a characteristic or recurrent behavioral trait; idiosyncrasy.

tick[1] /tik/ ▶*n.* **1** a regular short, sharp sound, esp. that made every second by a clock or watch. ■ *Brit. inf.* a moment: *I'll be with you in a tick.* **2** *chiefly Brit.* a check mark. **3** *Stock Market* the smallest recognized amount by which a price of a security or future may fluctuate.
▶*v.* **1** [intr.] (of a clock or other mechanical device) make regular short sharp sounds, typically for every second of time passing. ■ (**tick away/by/past**) (of time) pass (used esp. when someone is pressed for time or keenly awaiting an event): *the minutes were ticking away till the actor's appearance.* ■ [tr.] (**tick something away**) (of a clock or watch) mark the passing of time with regular short sharp sounds: *the little clock ticked the precious minutes away.* ■ proceed or progress: *her book was ticking along nicely.* **2** *chiefly Brit.* [tr.] mark (an item) with a check mark, typically to show that it has been chosen, checked, or approved: *just tick the appropriate box below.* ■ (**tick something off**) list items one by one in one's mind or during a speech: *he ticked the points off on his fingers.*
▶ □ **what makes someone tick** *inf.* what motivates someone.

tick[2] ▶*n.* a parasitic arachnid that attaches itself to the skin of a terrestrial vertebrate from which it sucks blood, leaving the host when sated. Some species transmit diseases, including Lyme disease. ■ *inf.* a parasitic louse fly.

tick[3] ▶*n.* a fabric case stuffed with feathers or other material to form a mattress or pillow. ■ short for **TICKING**.

tick·er /ˈtikər/ ▶*n.* **1** *inf.* a watch. ■ a person's heart. **2** a telegraphic or electronic machine that prints out data on a strip of paper, esp. stock market information or news reports.

tick·er tape ▶*n.* a paper strip on which messages are recorded in a telegraphic tape machine. ■ [as *adj.*] denoting a parade or other event in which this or similar material is thrown from windows.

tick·et /ˈtikit/ ▶*n.* **1** a piece of paper or small card that gives the holder a certain right, esp. to enter a place, travel by public transport, or participate in an event. ■ (**ticket to/out of**) a method of getting into or out of (a specified state or situation): *drugs are seen as the only ticket out of poverty.* **2** a certificate or warrant, in particular: ■ an official notice of a traffic offense. ■ a certificate of qualification as a ship's master, pilot, or other crew member. **3** a label attached to a retail product,

giving its price, size, and other details. **4** a list of candidates put forward by a party in an election: *the Republican ticket.* ■ a set of principles or policies supported by a party in an election. **5** (**the ticket**) *inf.,* dated the desirable or correct thing: *a wet spring would be just the ticket for the garden.*
▶*v.* (**-et·ed, -et·ing**) [tr.] **1** issue (someone) with an official notice of a traffic or other offense. **2** (**be ticketed**) (of a passenger) be issued with a travel ticket: *passengers can now get electronically ticketed.* ■ be destined or heading for a specified state or position: *they were sure that Downing was ticketed for greatness.* **3** (**be ticketed**) (of a retail product) be marked with a label giving its price, size, and other details.

tick·et·less /ˈtikitlis/ ▶*adj.* & *adv.* **1** not requiring a paper ticket: [as *adj.*] *all seats are assigned, all travel is ticketless.* **2** not in possession of a valid ticket: [as *adv.*] *activists on Monday traveled ticketless in suburban trains to protest the hike in fares.*

tick·ing /ˈtikiNG/ ▶*n.* a strong, durable material, typically striped, used to cover mattresses and pillows.

tick·le /ˈtikəl/ ▶*v.* [tr.] **1** lightly touch or prod (a person or a part of the body) in a way that causes itching and often laughter: *she tickled me under the chin.* ■ [intr.] (of a part of the body) give a sensation of mild discomfort similar to that caused by being touched in this way: *his throat had stopped tickling.* ■ touch with light finger movements: *tickling the safe open took nearly ninety minutes.* **2** appeal to (someone's taste, sense of humor, curiosity, etc.): *here are a couple of anecdotes that might tickle your fancy.* ■ cause (someone) amusement or pleasure: *he is tickled by the idea.*
▶*n.* an act of tickling someone. ■ a sensation like that of being lightly touched or prodded. —**tick·ler** *n.* —**tick·ly** *adj.*
▶ □ **be tickled pink** (or **to death**) *inf.* be extremely amused or pleased. □ **tickle the ivories** *inf.* play the piano.

tick·lish /ˈtik(ə)liSH/ ▶*adj.* **1** sensitive to being tickled. ■ (of a cough) characterized by persistent irritation in the throat. **2** (of a situation or problem) difficult to deal with; requiring careful handling. ■ (of a person) easily upset. —**tick·lish·ly** *adv.* —**tick·lish·ness** *n.*

tick·tack·toe ▶*n.* variant spelling of **TIC-TAC-TOE**.

tick·y-tack·y /ˈtikē ˌtakē/ *inf.* ▶*n.* inferior or cheap material, esp. as used in suburban building.
▶*adj.* (esp. of a building or housing development) made of inferior material; cheap or in poor taste: *ticky-tacky little houses.*

tic-tac-toe /ˈtik ˌtak ˈtō/ (also **tick-tack-toe**) ▶*n.* a game in which two players seek in alternate turns to complete a row, a column, or a diagonal with either three O's or three X's drawn in the spaces of a grid of nine squares.

tid·al /ˈtīdl/ ▶*adj.* of, relating to, or affected by tides. —**tid·al·ly** *adv.*

tid·al bore ▶*n.* a large wave caused by the funneling of a flood tide as it enters a long, narrow, shallow inlet.

tid·al wave ▶*n.* an exceptionally large ocean wave, esp. one caused by an underwater earthquake or volcanic eruption (used as a nontechnical term for **TSUNAMI**). ■ *fig.* a widespread or overwhelming manifestation of an emotion or phenomenon: *a tidal wave of crime.*

tid·bit /ˈtidˌbit/ ▶*n.* a small piece of tasty food. ■ a small and particularly interesting item of gossip or information.

tid·dly·wink /ˈtidlēˌwiNGk/ (also **tid·dle·dy·wink** /ˈtidl-dē-/) ▶*n.* **1** (**tiddlywinks**) a game in which small plastic counters are flicked into a central receptacle by being pressed on the edge with a larger counter. **2** a counter used in such a game.

tide /tīd/ ▶*n.* the alternate rising and falling of the sea, usually twice in each lunar day at a particular place, due to the attraction of the moon and sun. ■ the water as affected by this: *the rising tide covered the wharf.* ■ *fig.* a powerful surge of feeling or trend of events: *we must reverse the growing tide of racism.* —**tide·less** *adj.*
▶*phrasal v.* □ **tide someone over** help someone through a difficult period, esp. with financial assistance.
▶ □ **turn the tide** reverse the trend of events.

tide·land /ˈtīdˌland/ ▶*n.* (also **tidelands**) land that is submerged at high tide.

tide·wa·ter ▶*n.* water brought or affected by tides. ■ an area that is affected by tides: [as *adj.*] *tidewater country.*

ti·dings /ˈtīdiNGz/ ▶*pl. n. poetic/lit.* news; information: *glad tidings.*

ti·dy /ˈtīdē/ ▶*adj.* (**-di·er, -di·est**) **1** arranged neatly and in order: *his tidy apartment* | *fig. the lives they lead don't fit into tidy patterns.* ■ (of a person) inclined to keep things or one's appearance neat and in order. ■ not messy; neat and controlled: *he wrote down her replies in a small, tidy hand.* **2** *inf.* (of an amount, esp. of money) considerable: *the book will bring in a tidy sum.*
▶*v.* (**-dies, -died**) [tr.] (often **tidy someone/something up**) bring order to;

arrange neatly: *I'd better try to tidy my desk up a bit* | [*intr.*] *I'll just go and tidy up.* —**ti·di·ly** /-dilē/ *adv.* —**ti·di·ness** *n.*

tie /tī/ ▶*v.* (**ty·ing** /'tī-ɪNG/) **1** [*tr.*] attach or fasten (someone or something) with string or similar cord: *they tied Max to a chair.* ■ fasten (something) to or around someone or something by means of its strings or by forming the ends into a knot or bow: *Lewis tied on his apron.* ■ form (a string, ribbon, or lace) into a knot or bow. ■ form (a knot or bow) in this way. ■ [*intr.*] be fastened with a knot or bow: *a sarong that ties at the waist.* ■ restrict or limit (someone) to a particular situation, occupation, or place: *she didn't want to be like her mother, tied to a feckless man.* **2** [*tr.*] connect; link: *self-respect is closely tied up with the esteem in which one is held by one's peers.* ■ hold together by a crosspiece or tie. ■ *Mus.* unite (written notes) by a tie. ■ *Mus.* perform (two notes) as one unbroken note. **3** [*intr.*] achieve the same score or ranking as another competitor or team: *he tied for second in the league* | [*tr.*] *Toronto tied the score in the fourth inning.*

▶*phrasal v.* □ **tie someone down** restrict someone to a particular situation or place. □ **tie something in** (or **tie in**) cause something to fit or harmonize with something else (or fit or harmonize with something): *she may have developed ideas that don't necessarily tie in with mine.* □ **tie into** *inf.* attack or get to work on vigorously. □ **tie someone up** bind someone's legs and arms together or bind someone to something so that they cannot move or escape. ■ *inf.* occupy someone to the exclusion of any other activity: *she would be tied up at the meeting all day.* □ **tie something up 1** bind or fasten something securely with rope, cord, or string. ■ moor a vessel. ■ invest or reserve capital so that it is not immediately available for use. **2** bring something to a satisfactory conclusion; settle.

▶*n.* (*pl.* **ties**) **1** a piece of string, cord, or the like used for fastening or tying something. ■ (usu. **ties**) *fig.* a thing that unites or links people: *family ties.* ■ (usu. **ties**) *fig.* a thing that restricts someone's freedom of action: *some cities and merchants were freed from feudal ties.* ■ a rod or beam holding parts of a structure together. ■ a wooden or concrete beam laid transversely under a railroad track to support it. ■ *Mus.* a curved line above or below two notes of the same pitch indicating that they are to be played for the combined duration of their time values. **2** a strip of material worn around the collar and tied in a knot at the front with the ends hanging down, typically forming part of a man's business or formal outfit. **3** a result in a game or other competitive situation in which two or more competitors or teams have the same score or ranking; a draw. —**tie·less** *adj.*

▶ □ **tie one on** *inf.* get drunk.

tie-back (also **tie·back**) ▶*n.* a decorative strip of fabric or cord, typically used for holding an open curtain off to the side of the window.

tie-break·er /'tī,brākər/ ▶*n.* a means of deciding a winner from competitors who have tied, in particular (in tennis) a special game to decide the winner of a set when the score is six games all.

tie-dye ▶*n.* [often as *adj.*] a method of producing textile patterns by tying parts of the fabric to shield it from the dye: *tie-dye T-shirts.*

▶*v.* [*tr.*] dye (a garment or piece of cloth) by such a process. —**tie-dye·ing** *n.*

tie-in ▶*n.* a connection or association: *there's a tie-in to another case I'm working on.* ■ a book, movie, or other product produced to take advantage of a related work in another medium. ■ [as *adj.*] denoting sales made conditional on the purchase of an additional item or items from the same supplier.

tie-pin /'tī,pin/ ▶*n.* an ornamental pin for holding a tie in place.

tier /tir/ ▶*n.* a row or level of a structure, typically one of a series of rows placed one above the other and successively receding or diminishing in size: *a tier of seats* | [in *comb.*] *the room was full of three-tier metal bunks.* ■ one of a number of successively overlapping ruffles or flounces on a garment. ■ a level or grade within the hierarchy of an organization or system: *companies have taken out a tier of management to save money.* —**tiered** /ti(ə)rd/ *adj.*

TIFF /tif/ ▶*Comput. abbr.* tagged image file format, widely used in desktop publishing.

tiff /tif/ ▶*n. inf.* a petty quarrel, esp. one between friends or lovers.

ti·ger /'tīgər/ ▶*n.* a very large solitary cat (*Panthera tigris*) with a yellow-brown coat striped with black, native to the forests of Asia. ■ used to refer to someone fierce, determined, or ambitious: *despite his wound, he still fought like a tiger* | *one of the sport's young tigers.* ■ (also **tiger economy**) a dynamic economy of one of the smaller eastern Asian countries, esp. that of Singapore, Taiwan, or South Korea. ▷Middle English: from Old French *tigre*, from Latin *tigris*, from Greek. —**ti·ger·ish** *adj.*

ti·ger cat ▶*n.* a small forest cat (*Felis tigrina*) that has a light brown coat with dark stripes and blotches, native to Central and South America.

■ any moderate-sized striped cat, such as the ocelot, serval, or margay. ■ a domestic cat with markings like a tiger's.

ti·ger lil·y ▶*n.* a tall lily (*Lilium lancifolium* , or *L. tigrinum*) that has orange flowers spotted with black or purple.

ti·ger's eye (also **ti·ger eye**) ▶*n.* a yellowish-brown semiprecious variety of quartz with a silky luster. This gem is typically cut en cabochon, which reveals a band of bright reflected light in the stone.

tight /tīt/ ▶*adj.* **1** fixed, fastened, or closed firmly; hard to move, undo, or open: *a tight knot.* ■ (of clothes or shoes) close-fitting, esp. uncomfortably so. ■ (of a grip) very firm so as not to let go: *she released her tight hold on the dog.* ■ (of a ship, building, or object) well sealed against something such as water or air: [in *comb.*] *a light-tight container.* ■ (of a formation or a group of people or things) closely or densely packed together. ■ (of a community or other group of people) having close relations; secretive: *the tenants were far too tight to let anyone know.* **2** (of a rope, fabric, or surface) stretched so as to leave no slack; not loose: *the belt pulls tight.* ■ (of a part of the body or a bodily sensation) feeling painful and constricted, as a result of anxiety or illness. ■ (of appearance or manner) tense, irritated, or angry: *she gave him a tight smile.* ■ (of a rule, policy, or form of control) strictly imposed: *security was tight at yesterday's ceremony.* ■ (of a game or contest) with evenly matched competitors; very close: *he won in a tight finish.* ■ (of a written work or form) concise, condensed, or well structured: *a tight argument.* ■ (of an organization or group of people) disciplined or professional; well coordinated. **3** (of an area or space) having or allowing little room for maneuver. ■ (of a bend, turn, or angle) changing direction sharply; having a short radius. ■ (of money or time) limited or restricted: *an ability to work to tight deadlines.* ■ *inf.* (of a person) not willing to spend or give much money; stingy. **4** *inf.* drunk: *later, at the club, he got tight on brandy.*

▶*adv.* very firmly, closely, or tensely: *he went downstairs, holding tight to the banisters.* —**tight·ly** *adv.* —**tight·ness** *n.*

▶ □ **run a tight ship** be very strict in managing an organization or operation. □ **a tight corner** (or **spot** or **place**) a difficult situation.

tight·en /'tītn/ ▶*v.* make or become tight or tighter: [*tr.*] *tighten the bolts* | [*intr.*] *the revenue laws were tightening up.*

tight-fist·ed /'tīt'fistid/ (also **tight-fist·ed**) ▶*adj. inf.* not willing to spend or give much money; miserly.

tight-fit·ting ▶*adj.* (of a garment) fitting close to and showing the contours of the body. ■ (of a lid or cover) forming a tight seal when placed on a container.

tight-lipped ▶*adj.* with the lips firmly closed, esp. as a sign of suppressed emotion or determined reticence.

tight·rope /'tīt,rōp/ ▶*n.* a rope or wire stretched tightly high above the ground, on which acrobats perform feats of balancing.

▶*v.* [*intr.*] walk or perform on such a rope.

tights /tīts/ ▶*pl. n.* a woman's thin, close-fitting garment, typically made of nylon, cotton, or wool, covering the lower half of the body. ■ a similar garment worn by a dancer or acrobat.

tight·wad /'tīt,wäd/ ▶*n. inf.* a mean or miserly person.

ti·gress /'tīgris/ ▶*n.* a female tiger. ■ *fig.* a fierce or passionate woman.

tike ▶*n.* variant spelling of TYKE.

ti·la·pi·a /təˈläpēə/ ▶*n.* an African freshwater cichlid (*Tilapia* and related genera) that has been widely introduced to many areas for food.

til·de /'tildə/ ▶*n.* an accent (˜) placed over Spanish *n* when pronounced *ny* (as in *señor*) or Portuguese *a* or *o* when nasalized (as in *São Paulo*), or over a vowel in phonetic transcription, indicating nasalization. ■ the same symbol as a part of a URL. ■ a similar symbol used in mathematics to indicate similarity, and in logic to indicate negation.

tile /tīl/ ▶*n.* a thin rectangular slab of baked clay, concrete, or other material, used in overlapping rows for covering roofs. ■ a thin square slab of ceramic, cork, linoleum, or other material for covering floors, walls, or other surfaces. ■ a thin, flat piece used in Scrabble, mahjongg, and other games. ■ *Math.* a plane shape used in tiling.

▶*v.* [*tr.*] cover (something) with tiles: *the lobby was tiled in blue.* ■ *Comput.* arrange (two or more windows) on a computer screen so that they do not overlap.

til·ing /'tīlɪNG/ ▶*n.* the action of laying tiles. ■ a surface covered by tiles: *an area of plain tiling.* ■ tiles collectively, when used to cover a roof, floor, etc. ■ a technique for displaying several nonoverlapping windows on a computer screen. ■ *Math.* a way of arranging identical polygons so that they completely cover an area without overlapping.

---

till¹ /til/ ▶*prep.* & *conj.* less formal way of saying **UNTIL**.

till² ▶*n.* a cash register or drawer for money in a store, bank, or restaurant.

till³ ▶*v.* [*tr.*] prepare and cultivate (land) for crops. —**till·a·ble** *adj.*

till⁴ ▶*n. Geol.* an unstratified sediment consisting of particles of various sizes and deposited by melting glaciers or ice sheets.

till·age /'tilij/ ▶*n.* the preparation of land for growing crops. ■ land under cultivation: *forty acres of tillage.*

till·er¹ /'tilər/ ▶*n.* a horizontal bar fitted to the head of a boat's rudder post and used as a lever for steering.

till·er² ▶*n.* an implement or machine for breaking up soil; a plow or cultivator.

till·er³ ▶*n.* a lateral shoot from the base of the stem, esp. in a grass or cereal.
▶*v.* [*intr.*] [usu. as *n.*] (**tillering**) develop tillers.

tilt /tilt/ ▶*v.* **1** move or cause to move into a sloping position: [*intr.*] *the floor tilted slightly* fig. *the balance of industrial power tilted toward the workers* | [*tr.*] *he tilted his head to one side.* ■ *fig.* incline or cause to incline toward a particular opinion: [*intr.*] *he is tilting toward a new economic course.* ■ [*tr.*] move (a camera) in a vertical plane. **2** [*intr.*] (**tilt at**) *hist.* (in jousting) thrust at with a lance or other weapon. ■ (**tilt with**) *archaic* engage in a contest with.
▶*n.* **1** a sloping position or movement: *the tilt of her head.* ■ an upward or downward pivoting movement of a camera. ■ an inclination or bias: *the paper's tilt toward the Republicans.* **2** *hist.* a combat for exercise or sport between two men on horseback with lances; a joust. ■ (**tilt at**) an attempt at winning (something) or defeating (someone), esp. in sports: *a tilt at the championship.* —**tilt·er** *n.*
▶ □ (**at**) **full tilt** with maximum energy or force; at top speed. □ **tilt at windmills** attack imaginary enemies or evils.

tim·bale /'timbəl; tim'bäl/ ▶*n.* **1** a dish of finely minced meat or fish cooked with other ingredients in a pastry shell or in a mold. **2** (**timbales**) paired cylindrical drums played with sticks in Latin American dance music.

tim·ber /'timbər/ ▶*n.* wood prepared for use in building and carpentry: [as *adj.*] *a small timber building.* ■ trees grown for such wood. ■ (usu. **timbers**) a wooden beam or board used in building a house, ship, or other structure. ■ [as *interj.*] used to warn that a tree is about to fall after being cut: *we cried "Timber!" as our tree fell.* ■ personal qualities or character, esp. as seen as suitable for a particular role: *she is frequently hailed as presidential timber.* ▷Old English in the sense 'a building,' also 'building material,' of Germanic origin; related to German *Zimmer* 'room,' from an Indo-European root meaning 'build.'

tim·bered /'timbərd/ ▶*adj.* **1** (of a building) made wholly or partly of timber. ■ (of the walls or other surface of a room) covered with wooden panels. **2** having many trees; wooded.

tim·ber·land /'timbər,land/ ▶*n.* (also **timberlands**) land covered with forest suitable or managed for timber.

tim·ber·line /'timbər,līn/ ▶*n.* (on a mountain) the line or altitude above which no trees grow. ■ (in high northern (or southern) latitudes) the line north (or south) of which no trees grow.

tim·ber wolf ▶*n.* a wolf of a large variety found mainly in northern North America, with gray brindled fur.

tim·bre /'tambər; 'tăNbrə/ ▶*n.* the character or quality of a musical sound or voice as distinct from its pitch and intensity.

time /tīm/ ▶*n.* **1** the indefinite continued progress of existence and events in the past, present, and future regarded as a whole: *travel through space and time* | *one of the greatest wits of all time.* ■ the progress of this as affecting people and things: *things were getting better as time passed.* ■ time or an amount of time as reckoned by a conventional standard: *it's eight o'clock Eastern Standard Time.* ■ (**Time** or **Father Time**) the personification of time, typically as an old man with a scythe and hourglass. **2** a point of time as measured in hours and minutes past midnight or noon: *the time is 9:30.* ■ a moment or definite portion of time allotted, used, or suitable for a purpose: *the scheduled departure time* | *should we set a time for the meeting?* ■ (often **time for/to do something**) the favorable or appropriate time to do something; the right moment: *it was time to go* | *it's time for bed.* ■ (**a time**) an indefinite period: *traveling always distorts one's feelings for a time.* ■ (also **times**) a more or less definite portion of time in history or characterized by particular events or circumstances: *Victorian times* | *at the time of Galileo* | *the park is beautiful at this time of year.* ■ (also **times**) the conditions of life during a particular period: *times have changed.* ■ (**the Times**) used in names of newspapers: *The New York Times.* ■ (**one's time**) one's lifetime: *I've known a lot of women in my time.* ■ (**one's time**) the successful, fortunate, or influential part of a person's life or career: *in my time that was unheard of.*

■ (**one's time**) the appropriate or expected time for something, in particular childbirth or death: *he seemed old before his time.* ■ an apprenticeship: *all of our foremen served their time on the loading dock.* ■ dated a period of menstruation or pregnancy. ■ the normal rate of pay for time spent working: *if called out on weekends, they are paid time and a half.* ■ the length of time taken to run a race or complete an event or journey: *his time for the mile was 3:49.31.* ■ (in sports) a moment at which play is stopped temporarily within a game, or the act of calling for this: *the umpire called time.* ■ *Soccer* the end of the game: *he scored five minutes from time.* **3** time as allotted, available, or used: *we need more time* | *it would be a waste of time.* ■ *inf.* a prison sentence: *he was doing time for fraud.* **4** an instance of something happening or being done; an occasion: *this is the first time I have gotten into debt* | *the nurse came in four times a day.* ■ an event, occasion, or period experienced in a particular way: *we had a good time* | *she was having a rough time of it.* **5** (**times**) (following a number) expressing multiplication: *five goes into fifteen three times* | *it burns calories four times faster than walking.* **6** the rhythmic pattern of a piece of music, as expressed by a time signature: *tunes in waltz time.* ■ the tempo at which a piece of music is played or marked to be played.
▶*v.* **1** [*tr.*] plan, schedule, or arrange when (something) should happen or be done: *the first track race is timed for 11:15* | *the bomb had been timed to go off an hour later.* ■ perform (an action) at a particular moment: *Williams timed his pass perfectly from about thirty yards.* **2** [*tr.*] measure the time taken by (a process or activity, or a person doing it): *we were timed and given certificates according to our speed* | *I timed how long it took to empty that tanker.* **3** [*tr.*] (**time something out**) *Comput.* (of a computer or a program) cancel an operation automatically because a predefined interval of time has passed without a certain event happening.
▶ □ **about time** used to convey that something now happening or about to happen should have happened earlier: *it's about time I came clean and admitted it.* □ **against time** with utmost speed, so as to finish by a specified time: *he was working against time.* □ **ahead of time** earlier than expected or required. □ **ahead of one's time** having ideas too enlightened or advanced to be accepted by one's contemporaries. □ **all the time** at all times. ■ very frequently or regularly: *we were in and out of each other's houses all the time.* □ **at one time** in or during a known but unspecified past period: *she was a nurse at one time.* □ **at the same time 1** simultaneously; at once. **2** nevertheless (used to introduce a fact that should be taken into account): *I can't really explain it, but at the same time I'm not convinced.* □ **at a time** separately in the specified groups or numbers: *he took the stairs two at a time.* □ **at times** sometimes; on occasions. □ **before time** before the due or expected time. □ **behind time** late. □ **behind the times** not aware of or using the latest ideas or techniques; out of date. □ **for the time being** for the present; until some other arrangement is made. □ **give someone the time of day** be pleasantly polite or friendly to someone: *I wouldn't give him the time of day if I could help it.* □ **half the time** as often as not. □ **have no time for** be unable or unwilling to spend time on: *he had no time for anything except essays and projects.* ■ dislike or disapprove of: *he's got no time for airheads.* □ **have the time 1** be able to spend the time needed to do something: *she didn't have the time to look very closely.* **2** know from having a watch what time it is. □ **in** (**less than**) **no time** very quickly or very soon: *the video has sold 30,000 copies in no time.* □ **in one's own time** (also **in one's own good time**) at a time and a rate decided by oneself. □ **in time 1** not late; punctual: *I came back in time for Molly's party.* **2** eventually: *there is the danger that he might, in time, not be able to withstand temptation.* **3** in accordance with the appropriate musical rhythm or tempo. □ **keep good** (or **bad**) **time 1** (of a clock or watch) record time accurately (or inaccurately). **2** (of a person) be habitually punctual (or not punctual). □ **keep time** play or rhythmically accompany music in time. □ **lose no time** do a specified thing immediately or as soon as possible: *the administration lost no time in trying to regain the initiative.* □ **no time** a very short interval or period: *the renovations were done in no time.* □ **on one's own time** outside working hours; without being paid. □ **on time** punctual; punctually: *the train was on time* | *we paid our bills on time.* □ **out of time 1** at the wrong time or period: *I felt that I was born out of time.* ■ not following or maintaining the correct rhythm (of music): *every time we get to this part in the song, you are out of time.* **2** with no time remaining to continue or complete something, esp. a task for which a specific amount of time had been allowed: *I knew the answers to all the essay questions, but I ran out of time.* □ **pass the time of day** exchange greetings or casual remarks. □ **time after time** (also **time and again** or **time and time again**) on very many occasions; repeatedly. □ **time immemorial** used to refer to a point of time in the past that was so long ago that people have no knowledge or memory of it: *markets had been held there from time immemorial.* □ **the time of one's life** a

period or occasion of exceptional enjoyment. □ **time out of mind** another way of saying TIME IMMEMORIAL. □ **time was** there was a time when: *time was, each street had its own specialized trade.* □ **(only) time will tell** the truth or correctness of something will (only) be established at some time in the future.

time bomb ▸*n.* a bomb designed to explode at a preset time. ■ *fig.* a process or procedure causing a problem that will eventually become dangerous if not addressed: *an environmental time bomb.*

time cap·sule ▸*n.* a container storing a selection of objects chosen as being typical of the present time, buried for discovery in the future.

time·card /'tīm,kärd/ ▸*n.* a card used to record an employee's starting and quitting times, usually stamped by a time clock.

time clock ▸*n.* a clock with a device for recording employees' times of arrival and departure.

time ex·po·sure ▸*n.* the exposure of photographic film for longer than the maximum normal shutter setting.

time frame ▸*n.* a period of time, esp. a specified period in which something occurs or is planned to take place.

time-hon·ored ▸*adj.* (of a custom or tradition) respected or valued because it has existed for a long time.

time·keep·er /'tīm,kēpər/ ▸*n.* **1** a person who measures or records the amount of time taken, esp. in a sports competition. **2** a person regarded as being punctual or not punctual: *we were good timekeepers.* ■ a watch or clock regarded as recording time accurately or inaccurately. —**time·keep·ing** /-,kēpiNG/ *n.*

time lag ▸*n.* see LAG¹ (n. sense 1).

time-lapse ▸*adj.* denoting the photographic technique of taking a sequence of frames at set intervals to record changes that take place slowly over time. When the frames are shown at normal speed, or in quick succession, the action seems much faster.

time·less /'tīmlis/ ▸*adj.* not affected by the passage of time or changes in fashion. —**time·less·ly** *adv.* —**time·less·ness** *n.*

time·ly /'tīmlē/ ▸*adj.* done or occurring at a favorable or useful time; opportune: *a timely warning.* —**time·li·ness** *n.*

time off ▸*n.* time for rest or recreation away from one's usual work or studies: *we're too busy to take time off.*

time out ▸*n.* **1** time for rest or recreation away from one's usual work or studies: *she is taking time out from her hectic tour.* ■ (usu. **timeout** or **time-out**) a brief break in play in a game or sport: *he inadvertently called for a timeout with two seconds remaining.* ■ (also **timeout** or **time-out**) an imposed temporary suspension of activities, esp. the separation of a misbehaving child from one or more playmates as a disciplinary measure: *it's the third time this week he's been in time-out.* **2** (usu. **timeout**) *Comput.* a cancellation or cessation that automatically occurs when a predefined interval of time has passed without a certain event occurring.

time·piece /'tīm,pēs/ ▸*n.* an instrument, such as a clock or watch, for measuring time.

tim·er /'tīmər/ ▸*n.* **1** an automatic mechanism for activating a device at a preset time: *a video timer.* ■ a person or device that measures or records the amount of time taken by a process or activity. **2** [in *comb.*] used to indicate how many times someone has done something: *for most first-timers the success rate is 45 percent.*

time·scale /'tīm,skāl/ ▸*n.* the time allowed for or taken by a process or sequence of events: *climatic changes on a timescale of thousands of years.*

time·share /'tīm,SHe(ə)r/ ▸*n.* the arrangement whereby several joint owners have the right to use a property as a vacation home under a time-sharing scheme. ■ a property owned in such a way.

time-shar·ing ▸*n.* **1** the operation of a computer system by several users for different operations at the same time. **2** the use of a property as a vacation home at specified times by several joint owners.

time sheet (also **time·sheet** /'tīm,SHēt/) ▸*n.* a piece of paper for recording the number of hours worked.

time sig·na·ture ▸*n. Mus.* an indication of rhythm following a clef, generally expressed as a fraction with the denominator defining the beat as a division of a whole note and the numerator giving the number of beats in each bar.

time·ta·ble /'tīm,tābəl/ ▸*n.* a chart showing the departure and arrival times of trains, buses, or planes. ■ a plan of times at which events are scheduled to take place, esp. toward a particular end. ▸*v.* [*tr.*] schedule (something) to take place at a particular time.

time warp ▸*n.* (esp. in science fiction) an imaginary distortion of space in relation to time whereby people or objects of one period can be moved to another.

time·worn /'tīm,wôrn/ (also **time-worn**) ▸*adj.* damaged or impaired, or made less striking or attractive, as a result of age or much use.

time zone ▸*n.* see ZONE (sense 1).

tim·id /'timid/ ▸*adj.* (**-id·er, -id·est**) showing a lack of courage or confidence; easily frightened: *I was too timid to ask for what I wanted.* —**ti·mid·i·ty** /tə'miditē/ *n.* —**tim·id·ly** *adv.* —**tim·id·ness** *n.*

tim·ing /'tīmiNG/ ▸*n.* the choice, judgment, or control of when something should be done. ■ a particular point or period of time when something happens. ■ (in an internal combustion engine) the times when the valves open and close, and the time of the ignition spark, in relation to the movement of the piston in the cylinder.

tim·or·ous /'timərəs/ ▸*adj.* showing or suffering from nervousness, fear, or a lack of confidence. —**tim·or·ous·ly** *adv.* —**tim·or·ous·ness** *n.*

tim·pa·ni /'timpənē/ (also **tym·pa·ni**) ▸*pl. n.* kettledrums, esp. when played in an orchestra. —**tim·pa·nist** /-nist/ *n.*

tin /tin/ ▸*n.* **1** a silvery-white metal, the chemical element of atomic number 50. (Symbol: **Sn**) ■ short for TINPLATE. **2** a metal container, in particular: ■ *chiefly Brit.* another term for TIN CAN. ■ a lidded airtight container made of tinplate or aluminum: *Albert got out the cookie tin.* ▸*v.* (**tinned** /tind/, **tin·ning**) [*tr.*] cover with a thin layer of tin. ▸ □ **have a tin ear** be tone-deaf.

tin can ▸*n.* a container made of plated steel or aluminum and used for for preserving food, esp. an empty one.

tinc·ture /'tiNGkCHər/ ▸*n.* **1** a medicine made by dissolving a drug in alcohol: *a bottle containing tincture of iodine.* **2** a slight trace of something: *she could not keep a tincture of bitterness out of her voice.* ▸*v.* (**be tinctured**) be tinged, flavored, or imbued with a slight amount of: *Arthur's affability was tinctured with faint sarcasm.*

tin·der /'tindər/ ▸*n.* dry, flammable material, such as wood or paper, used for lighting a fire. —**tin·der·y** *adj.*

tin·der·box /'tindər,bäks/ ▸*n. hist.* a box containing tinder, flint, a steel, and other items for kindling fires. ■ *fig.* a thing that is readily ignited: *dry winds and no rain have turned parts of the state into a tinderbox.* ■ *fig.* a volatile situation, or a person who is readily aroused, esp. to anger.

tine /'tīn/ ▸*n.* a prong or sharp point, such as that on a fork or antler. —**tined** *adj.* [in *comb.*] *a three-tined fork.*

ting /tiNG/ ▸*n.* a sharp, clear ringing sound, such as when a glass is struck by a metal object. ▸*v.* [*intr.*] emit such a sound.

tinge /tinj/ ▸*v.* (**ting·ing** or **tinge·ing**) [*tr.*] color slightly: *a mass of white blossom tinged with pink.* ■ *fig.* have a slight influence on: *this visit will be tinged with sadness.* ▸*n.* a tendency toward or trace of some color: *there was a pink tinge to the sky.* ■ *fig.* a slight trace of a feeling or quality. ▷late 15th cent.: from Latin *tingere* 'to dip or color.' The noun dates from the mid 18th cent.

tin·gle /'tiNGgəl/ ▸*v.* [*intr.*] (of a person or a part of their body) experience a slight prickling or stinging sensation: *she was tingling with excitement.* ■ [*tr.*] cause to experience such a sensation: *a standing ovation that tingled your spine.* ■ [*intr.*] (of such a sensation) be experienced in a part of one's body: *shivers tingled down the length of her spine.* ▸*n.* a slight prickling or stinging sensation.

tin·gly /'tiNGg(ə)lē/ ▸*adj.* (**-gli·er, -gli·est**) causing or experiencing a slight prickling or stinging sensation: *a tingly sense of excitement.*

tin·horn /'tin,hôrn/ ▸*n. inf.* a contemptible person, esp. one pretending to have money, influence, or ability: [as *adj.*] *tinhorn politicians.*

tin·ker /'tiNGkər/ ▸*n.* **1** (esp. in former times) a person who travels from place to place mending metal utensils as a way of making a living. ■ a person who makes minor mechanical repairs, esp. on a variety of appliances and apparatuses, usually for a living. ■ *Brit., chiefly derog.* a gypsy or other person living in an itinerant community. **2** an act of attempting to repair something. ▸*v.* [*intr.*] attempt to repair or improve something in a casual or desultory way, often to no useful effect: *he spent hours tinkering with the car.* —**tin·ker·er** *n.* ▸ □ **not give a tinker's damn** *inf.* not care at all.

tin·kle /'tiNGkəl/ ▸*v.* **1** make or cause to make a light, clear ringing sound: [*intr.*] *cool water tinkled in the stone fountains* | [*tr.*] *the maid tinkled a bell.* **2** [*intr.*] *inf.* urinate. ▸*n.* **1** a light, clear ringing sound. **2** *inf.* an act of urinating. —**tin·kly** /-k(ə)lē/ *adj.*

tin·ni·tus /'tinitəs; ti'nī-/ ▸*n. Med.* ringing or buzzing in the ears.

Pronunciation Key ə *ago,* up; ər *over, fur;* a *hat;* ā *ate;* ä *car;* CH *chin;* e *let;* ē *see;* e(ə)r *air;* i *fit;* ī *by;* i(ə)r *ear;* NG *sing;* ō *go;* ô *law, for;* oi *toy;* o͝o *good;* o͞o *goo;* ou *out;* SH *she;* TH *thin;* TH *then;* (h)w *why;* ZH *vision*

tin·ny /'tinē/ ▶*adj.* (**-ni·er**, **-ni·est**) having a displeasingly thin, metallic sound. ■ (of an object) made of thin or poor-quality metal: *a tinny little car.* ■ having an unpleasantly metallic taste: *canned artichokes taste somewhat tinny.* —**tin·ni·ly** /'tinilē/ *adv.* —**tin·ni·ness** *n.*

Tin Pan Al·ley ▶the name given to a district in New York City (not associated with any particular street, but with the area around 28th Street, between 5th Avenue and Broadway) where many songwriters, arrangers, and music publishers were formerly based. ■ [as *n.*] [usu. as *adj.*] the world of composers and publishers of popular music.

tin·pot /'tin,pät/ (also **tin-pot**) ▶*adj. inf.* (esp. of a country or its leader) having or showing poor leadership or organization: *a tinpot dictator.*

tin·sel /'tinsəl/ ▶*n.* a form of decoration consisting of thin strips of shiny metal foil. ■ showy or superficial attractiveness or glamour: *his taste for the tinsel of the art world.* —**tin·seled** *adj.* —**tin·sel·ly** *adj.*

tint /tint/ ▶*n.* **1** a shade or variety of color: *the sky was taking on an apricot tint.* ■ a trace of something: *a tint of glamour.* **2** an artificial dye for coloring the hair. ■ an application of such a substance.
▶*v.* [*tr.*] color (something) slightly; tinge: *her skin was tinted with delicate color.* ■ dye (someone's hair) with a tint. —**tint·er** *n.*

tin·tin·nab·u·la·tion /,tintə,nabyə'lāsHən/ ▶*n.* a ringing or tinkling sound.

ti·ny /'tīnē/ ▶*adj.* (**-ni·er**, **-ni·est**) very small: *a tiny hummingbird.* —**ti·ni·ly** /-nəlē/ *adv.* —**ti·ni·ness** *n.*

tip[1] /tip/ ▶*n.* the pointed or rounded end or extremity of something slender or tapering: *the northern tip of Maine.* ■ a small piece or part fitted to the end of an object: *the rubber tip of the walking stick.*
▶*v.* (**tipped**, **tip·ping**) [*tr.*] **1** attach to or cover the end or extremity of: *mountains tipped with snow* | [in comb.] *steel-tipped spears.* ■ color (something) at its end or edge: *red petals tipped with white.* **2** (**tip a page in**) (in bookbinding) paste a single page, typically an illustration, to the neighboring page of a book by a thin line of paste down its inner margin.
▶ □ **on the tip of one's tongue** used to indicate that someone is almost but not quite able to bring a particular word or name to mind. ■ used to indicate that someone is about to utter a comment or question but thinks better of it.

tip[2] ▶*v.* (**tipped**, **tip·ping**) **1** overbalance or cause to overbalance so as to fall or turn over: [*intr.*] *the hay caught fire when the candle **tipped over*** | [*tr.*] *a youth sprinted past, **tipping over** her glass.* ■ be or cause to be in a sloping position with one end or side higher than the other: [*tr.*] *I tipped my seat back* | [*intr.*] *the car tipped to one side.* **2** [*tr.*] strike or touch lightly. ■ [*tr.*] cause (an object) to move somewhere by striking or touching it in this way: *the ball was tipped over the rim by Erving.* **3** [*intr.*] (**tip off**) *Basketball* put the ball in play by throwing it up between two opponents.
▶*n. Baseball* a pitched ball that is slightly deflected by the bat. —**tip·py** *adj.*
▶ □ **tip one's hand** *inf.* reveal one's intentions inadvertently. □ **tip one's hat** (or **cap**) raise or touch one's hat or cap as a way of greeting or acknowledging someone. □ **tip the scales** (or **balance**) (of a circumstance or event) be the deciding factor; make the critical difference: *her proven current form **tips the scales in her favor.*** □ **tip the scales at** have a weight of (a specified amount): *this phone tips the scales at only 5 ounces.*

tip[3] ▶*n.* **1** a sum of money given to someone as a reward for their services. **2** a small but useful piece of practical advice. ■ a prediction or piece of expert information about the likely winner of a race or contest: *Barry had a **hot tip**.*
▶*v.* (**tipped**, **tip·ping**) [*tr.*] give (someone) a sum of money as a way of rewarding them for their services: *I tipped her five dollars* | [*intr.*] *that sort of person never tips.* —**tip·per** *n.*
▶ □ **tip someone off** *inf.* give someone information about something, typically in a discreet or confidential way.

tip-off (also **tip·off**) ▶*n.* **1** *inf.* a piece of information, typically one given in a discreet or confidential way. **2** (usu. **tipoff**) a jump ball that begins each period in a basketball game (used esp. in reference to the first tipoff of the game).

tip·ple[1] /'tipəl/ ▶*v.* [*intr.*] drink alcohol, esp. habitually.
▶*n. inf.* an alcoholic drink. —**tip·pler** *n.*

tip·ple[2] ▶*n.* a revolving frame or cage in which a truck or freight car is inverted to discharge its load. ■ a place where such loads, esp. from a coal mine, are dumped.

tip·sy /'tipsē/ ▶*adj.* (**-si·er**, **-si·est**) slightly drunk. —**tip·si·ly** /-səlē/ *adv.* —**tip·si·ness** *n.*

tip·toe /'tip,tō/ ▶*v.* (**-toes**, **-toed**, **-toe·ing**) [*intr.*] walk quietly and carefully with one's heels raised and one's weight on the balls of the feet.

tip-top (also **tip·top**) ▶*adj.* of the very best class or quality; excellent.

▶*n.* **1** the highest part or point of excellence. **2** a line guide on a fishing rod.

ti·rade /'tī,rād; ,tī'rād/ ▶*n.* a long, angry speech of criticism or accusation: *a tirade of abuse.*

tire[1] /tīr/ ▶*v.* [*intr.*] become in need of rest or sleep; grow weary: *soon the ascent grew steeper and he began to tire.* ■ [*tr.*] cause to feel in need of rest or sleep; weary: *the journey had tired her* | *the training **tired us out**.* ■ (**tire of**) lose interest in; become bored with: *she will stay with him until he tires of her.* ■ [*tr.*] exhaust the patience or interest of; bore.

tire[2] (*Brit.* **tyre**) ▶*n.* a rubber covering, typically inflated or surrounding an inflated inner tube, placed around a wheel to form a flexible contact with the road. ■ a strengthening band of metal fitted around the rim of a wooden wheel.

tired /tīrd/ ▶*adj.* in need of sleep or rest; weary: *Fisher rubbed his tired eyes* | *she was **tired out** now that the strain was over.* ■ (**tired of**) bored with. ■ (of a thing) no longer fresh or in good condition: *tired vegetables.* ■ (esp. of a statement or idea) boring or uninteresting because overfamiliar: *tired clichés.* —**tired·ly** *adv.* —**tired·ness** *n.*

tire·less /'tīrlis/ ▶*adj.* having or showing great effort or energy: *a tireless campaigner.* —**tire·less·ly** *adv.* —**tire·less·ness** *n.*

tire·some /'tīrsəm/ ▶*adj.* causing one to feel bored or annoyed. —**tire·some·ly** *adv.* —**tire·some·ness** *n.*

ti·ro ▶*n.* cheifly British spelling of TYRO.

'tis /tiz/ *chiefly poetic/lit.* ▶*contr.* of it is.

tis·sue /'tisHoō/ ▶*n.* **1** any of the distinct types of material of which animals or plants are made, consisting of specialized cells and their products: *inflammation is a reaction of living tissue to infection or injury* (**tissues**) *the organs and tissues of the body.* **2** tissue paper. ■ a disposable piece of absorbent paper, used esp. as a handkerchief or for cleaning the skin. ■ rich or fine material of a delicate or gauzy texture: [as *adj.*] *the blue and silver tissue sari.* **3** an intricate structure or network made from a number of connected items: *such scandalous stories are **a tissue of lies**.* —**tis·su·ey** *adj.*

tis·sue pa·per ▶*n.* thin, soft paper, typically used for wrapping or protecting fragile or delicate articles.

tit[1] /tit/ ▶*n.* a titmouse. ■ used in names of similar or related birds, e.g., **New Zealand tit**.

tit[2] ▶*n. vulgar slang chiefly N. Amer.* a woman's breast or nipple.

tit[3] ▶*n.* (in phrase **tit for tat**) the infliction of an injury or insult in return for one that one has suffered.

Ti·tan /'tītn/ ▶ **1** *Greek Mythol.* any of the older gods who preceded the Olympians and were the children of Uranus (Heaven) and Gaia (Earth). ■ [as *n.*] (usu. **a titan**) a person or thing of very great strength, intellect, or importance: *a titan of American industry.* **2** *Astron.* the largest satellite of Saturn.

ti·tan·ic /tī'tanik/ ▶*adj.* of exceptional strength, size, or power: *a series of titanic explosions.* —**ti·tan·i·cal·ly** /-ik(ə)lē/ *adv.*

ti·ta·ni·um /tī'tānēəm/ ▶*n.* the chemical element of atomic number 22, a hard silver-gray metal of the transition series, used in strong, light, corrosion-resistant alloys. (Symbol: **Ti**)

tithe /tīTH/ ▶*n.* one tenth of annual produce or earnings, formerly taken as a tax for the support of the church and clergy. ■ (in certain religious denominations) a tenth of an individual's income pledged to the church.
▶*v.* [*tr.*] pay or give as a tithe: *he tithes 10 percent of his income to the church.* ▷Old English *tēotha* (adjective in the ordinal sense 'tenth,' used in a specialized sense as a noun), *tēothian* (verb).

tit·il·late /'titl,āt/ ▶*v.* [*tr.*] stimulate or excite (someone), esp. in a sexual way: *these journalists are paid to titillate the public.* ■ *archaic* lightly touch; tickle. —**tit·il·lat·ing·ly** *adv.* —**tit·il·la·tion** /,titl'āsHən/ *n.*

ti·tle /'tītl/ ▶*n.* **1** the name of a book, composition, or other artistic work. ■ (usu. as **titles**) a caption or credit in a movie or broadcast. ■ a book, magazine, or newspaper considered as a publication. **2** a name that describes someone's position or job: *Leese assumed the title of director general.* ■ a word that is used before someone's name, or a form that is used instead of someone's name, to indicate high social or official rank: *the title of the Duke of Marlborough.* ■ a word such as *Mrs.* or *Dr.* that is used before someone's name to indicate their profession or marital status. ■ a descriptive or distinctive name that is earned or chosen: *Nata's deserved the title of Best Restaurant of the Year.* **3** the position of being the champion of a major sports competition: *Davis won the world title.* **4** *Law* a right or claim to the ownership of property or to a rank or throne: *a local family had **title to** the property.*
▶*v.* [*tr.*] give a name to (a book, composition, or other work).

ti·tled /'tītld/ ▸*adj.* (of a person) having a title indicating high social or official rank.

ti·tle role ▸*n.* the part in a play, movie, television show, etc., from which the work's title is taken.

tit·mouse /'tit,mous/ ▸*n.* (*pl.* **titmice** /-,mīs/) a small songbird (*Parus* and other genera, family Paridae) that searches acrobatically for insects among foliage and branches. Its numerous species include the chickadees and the **tufted titmouse** (*P. bicolor*).

ti·trate /'tī,trāt/ ▸*v.* [*tr.*] *Chem.* ascertain the amount of a constituent in (a solution) by measuring the volume of a known concentration of reagent required to complete a reaction with it, typically using an indicator. ■ *Med.* continuously measure and adjust the balance of (a physiological function or drug dosage). —**ti·tra·ta·ble** *adj.* —**ti·tra·tion** /,tī'trāsHən/ *n.*

tit·ter /'titər/ ▸*v.* [*intr.*] give a short, half-suppressed laugh; giggle. ▸*n.* a short, half-suppressed laugh. —**tit·ter·er** *n.* —**tit·ter·ing·ly** *adv.*

tit·tle /'titl/ ▸*n.* a tiny amount or part of something: *the rules have **not** been altered **one jot or tittle** since.* ■ *archaic* a small written or printed stroke or dot, indicating omitted letters in a word.

tit·tle-tat·tle ▸*n.* idle talk; gossip. ▸*v.* [*intr.*] engage in such talk.

tit·u·lar /'tiCHələr/ ▸*adj.* **1** holding or constituting a purely formal position or title without any real authority: *the queen is titular head of the Church of England.* **2** denoting a person or thing from whom or which the name of an artistic work or similar is taken: *the work's titular song.* —**tit·u·lar·ly** *adv.*

tiz·zy /'tizē/ ▸*n.* (*pl.* **-zies**) *inf.* a state of nervous excitement or agitation: *he got **into a tizzy** and was talking absolute nonsense.*

TKO *Boxing* ▸*abbr.* technical knockout.

Tl ▸*symb.* the chemical element thallium.

TLC *inf.* ▸*abbr.* tender loving care.

Tlin·git /'tliNG(g)it/ ▸*n.* (*pl.* same or **-gits**) **1** a member of an American Indian people of the coasts and islands of southeastern Alaska and adjacent British Columbia. **2** the Na-Dene language of this people. ▸*adj.* of or relating to this people or their language.

TM *trademark* ▸*abbr.* Transcendental Meditation.

Tm ▸*symb.* the chemical element thulium.

tn ▸*abbr.* ■ ton(s). ■ town. ■ train.

TNT ▸*n.* a high explosive, $C_7H_5(NO_2)_3$.

to /tōō/ ▸*prep.* **1** expressing motion in the direction of (a particular location): *my first visit to Africa.* ■ expressing location, typically in relation to a specified point of reference: *forty miles to the south of the site.* ■ expressing a point reached at the end of a range or after a period of time: *from 1938 to 1945.* ■ (in telling the time) before (the hour specified): *it's five to ten.* ■ approaching or reaching (a particular condition): *she was close to tears.* ■ expressing the result of a process or action: *smashed to smithereens.* **2** identifying the person or thing affected: *you were terribly unkind to her.* ■ identifying the recipient or intended recipient of something: *he wrote a letter to the parents.* **3** identifying a particular relationship between one person and another: *he is married to Jan's cousin.* ■ in various phrases indicating how something is related to something else (often followed by a noun without a determiner): *a prelude to disaster.* ■ indicating a rate of return on something, e.g., the distance traveled in exchange for fuel used, or an exchange rate that can be obtained in one currency for another: *it only does ten miles to the gallon.* ■ (**to the**) *Math.* indicating the power (exponent) to which a number is raised: *ten to the minus thirty-three.* **4** indicating that two things are attached: *he had left his bike chained to a fence.* **5** concerning or likely to concern (something, esp. something abstract): *a threat to world peace.* **6** governing a phrase expressing someone's reaction to something: *to her astonishment, he smiled.* **7** used to introduce the second element in a comparison: *it's nothing to what it once was.*
▸*infinitive marker* **1** used with the base form of a verb to indicate that the verb is in the infinitive, in particular: ■ expressing purpose or intention: *we tried to help.* ■ expressing an outcome, result, or consequence: *he was left to die.* ■ expressing a cause: *I'm sorry to hear that.* ■ indicating a desired or advisable action: *I'd love to go to France this summer.* ■ indicating a proposition that is known, believed, or reported about a specified person or thing: *a house that people believed to be haunted.* ■ (**about to**) forming a future tense with reference to the immediate future: *he was about to sing.* ■ after a noun, indicating its function or purpose: *something to eat.* ■ after a phrase containing an ordinal number: *the first person to arrive.* **2** used without a verb following when the missing verb is clearly understood: *he asked her to come but she said she didn't want to.*
▸*adv.* so as to be closed or nearly closed: *he pulled the door to behind him.*

toad /tōd/ ▸*n.* **1** a tailless amphibian with a short stout body and short legs, typically having dry warty skin that can exude poison. **2** a contemptible or detestable person (used as a general term of abuse). —**toad·ish** *adj.*

toad·flax /'tōd,flaks/ ▸*n.* a Eurasian plant (*Linaria* and related genera) of the figwort family, typically having yellow or purplish snapdragonlike flowers and slender leaves.

toad·stool /'tōd,stōōl/ ▸*n.* the spore-bearing fruiting body of a fungus, typically in the form of a rounded cap on a stalk, esp. one that is believed to be inedible or poisonous. See also MUSHROOM.

toad·y /'tōdē/ ▸*n.* (*pl.* **toad·ies**) a person who behaves obsequiously to someone important. ▸*v.* (**toad·ies**, **toad·ied**) [*intr.*] act in an obsequious way: *she imagined him toadying to his rich clients.* —**toad·y·ish** *adj.* —**toad·y·ism** /-,izəm/ *n.*

to and fro (also **to-and-fro**) ▸*adv.* in a constant movement backward and forward or from side to side.

toast¹ /tōst/ ▸*n.* **1** sliced bread browned on both sides by exposure to radiant heat. **2** a call to a gathering of people to raise their glasses and drink together in honor of a person or thing, or an instance of drinking in this way: *he raised his glass in a toast to his son.* ■ a person or thing that is very popular or held in high regard by a particular group of people: *he found himself **the toast of** the baseball world.* ▸*v.* [*tr.*] **1** cook or brown (food, esp. bread or cheese) by exposure to a grill, fire, or other source of radiant heat: [as *adj.*] *toasted marshmallows.* ■ [*intr.*] (of food) cook or become brown in this way: *broil until the nuts have toasted.* ■ warm (oneself or part of one's body) in front of a fire or other source or heat. **2** drink to the health or in honor of (someone or something) by raising one's glass together with others: *happy families toasting each other's health.* ▸ □ **be toast** *inf.* be or be likely to become finished, defunct, or dead: *one mistake and you're toast.*

toast² ▸*v.* [*intr.*] [usu. as *n.*] (**toasting**) (of a DJ) accompany a reggae backing track or music with improvised rhythmic speech. —**toast·er** *n.*

toast·er /'tōstər/ ▸*n.* an electrical device for making toast.

toast·mas·ter /'tōs(t),mastər/ ▸*n.* an official responsible for proposing toasts, introducing speakers, and making other formal announcements at a large social event.

toast·y /'tōstē/ ▸*adj.* of or resembling toast. ■ comfortably warm.

to·bac·co /tə'bakō/ ▸*n.* (*pl.* **-os**) **1** a preparation of the nicotine-rich leaves of an American plant, which are cured by a process of drying and fermentation for smoking or chewing. **2** (also **tobacco plant**) the plant (*Nicotiana tabacum*) of the nightshade family that yields these leaves, native to tropical America.

to·bac·co·nist /tə'bakənist/ ▸*n.* a dealer in cigarettes, tobacco, cigars, and other items used by smokers.

to·bog·gan /tə'bägən/ ▸*n.* a long narrow sled used for the sport of coasting downhill over snow or ice. It typically is made of a lightweight board that is curved upward and backward at the front. ▸*v.* [*intr.*] ride on a toboggan. —**to·bog·gan·er** *n.* —**to·bog·gan·ist** /-nist/ *n.*

toboggan

toc·ca·ta /tə'kätə/ ▸*n.* a musical composition for a keyboard instrument designed to exhibit the performer's touch and technique.

to·coph·er·ol /tə'käfə,rôl; -,räl/ ▸*n.* *Biochem.* any of several closely related compounds, found in wheat germ oil, egg yolk, and leafy vegetables, that collectively constitute vitamin E.

to·day /tə'dā/ ▸*adv.* on or in the course of this present day: *she's thirty today* | *he will appear in court today.* ■ at the present period of time; nowadays: *millions of people today cannot afford adequate housing.* ▸*n.* this present day: *today is a day of rest* | *today's game against the Blue Jays.* ■ the present period of time: *the powerful computers of today.*

tod·dle /'tädl/ ▸*v.* [*intr.*] (of a young child) move with short unsteady steps while learning to walk. ■ *inf.* walk or go somewhere in a casual or leisurely way: *they would go for a drink and then toddle off home.* ▸*n.* a young child's unsteady walk.

tod·dler /'tädlər/ ▸*n.* a young child who is just beginning to walk. —**tod·dler·hood** /-,hōōd/ *n.*

tod·dy /'tädē/ ▶n. (pl. **-dies**) **1** a drink made of alcoholic liquor with hot water, sugar, and sometimes spices. **2** the sap of some kinds of palm, fermented to produce arrack.

to-do /tə 'dōō/ ▶n. inf. a commotion or fuss.

toe /tō/ ▶n. **1** any of the five digits at the end of the human foot. ■ any of the digits of the foot of a quadruped or bird. ■ the part of an item of footwear that covers a person's toes. **2** the lower end, tip, or point of something, in particular: ■ the foot or base of a cliff, slope, or embankment. ■ a flattish portion at the foot of an otherwise steep curve on a graph. ■ a section of a rhizome or similar fleshy root from which a new plant may be propagated.
▶v. (**toes, toed, toe·ing**) **1** [tr.] push, touch, or kick (something) with one's toe: *he toed off his shoes and flexed his feet.* **2** [intr.] (**toe in/out**) walk with the toes pointed in (or out): *he toes out when he walks.* ■ (of a pair of wheels) converge (**toe in**) or diverge (**toe out**) slightly at the front: *on a turn, the inner wheel toes out more.* —**toed** adj. [in comb.] *three-toed feet.* —**toe·less** adj.
▶ □ **on one's toes** ready for any eventuality; alert. □ **toe the line** accept the authority, principles, or policies of a particular group, esp. under pressure.

toe cap (also **toe-cap**) ▶n. a piece of steel or leather constituting or fitted over the front part of a boot or shoe as protection or reinforcement.

toe clip ▶n. a clip on a bicycle pedal to prevent the foot from slipping.

toe·nail /'tō,nāl/ ▶n. **1** the nail at the tip of each toe. **2** a nail driven obliquely through a piece of wood to secure it.
▶v. [tr.] fasten (a piece of wood) in this way.

tof·fee /'tôfē; 'täfē/ ▶n. (pl. **-fees**) a kind of firm or hard candy that softens when sucked or chewed, made by boiling together sugar and butter, often with other ingredients or flavorings added. ■ a small shaped piece of such candy.

to·fu /'tōfōō/ ▶n. curd made from mashed soybeans, used chiefly in Asian and vegetarian cooking.

tog /täg/ inf. ▶n. (**togs**) clothes: *running togs.*
▶v. (**togged, tog·ging**) (**be/get togged up/out**) be or get dressed for a particular occasion or activity: *we got togged up in our glad rags.*

to·ga /'tōgə/ ▶n. a loose flowing outer garment worn by the citizens of ancient Rome, made of a single piece of cloth and covering the whole body apart from the right arm. ■ a robe of office; a mantle of responsibility, etc. ▷Latin; related to *tegere* 'to cover.'

to·geth·er /tə'geTHər/ ▶adv. **1** with or in proximity to another person or people: *they stood together in the kitchen.* ■ so as to touch or combine: *pieces of wood nailed together.* ■ in combination; collectively: *taken together, these measures would improve people's chances of surviving a tornado.* ■ into companionship or close association: *the experience has brought us together.* ■ (of two people) married or in a sexual relationship with each other: *they split up after ten years together.* ■ so as to be united or in agreement: *he won the confidence of the government and the rebels, but could not bring the two sides together.* **2** at the same time: *they both spoke together.* **3** without interruption; continuously: *she sits for hours together in the lotus position.*
▶adj. inf. self-confident, level-headed, or well organized.
▶ □ **together with** as well as; along with.

to·geth·er·ness /tə'geTHərnəs/ ▶n. the state of being close to another person or other people: *the sense of family togetherness.*

tog·gle /'tägəl/ ▶n. **1** a short rod of wood or plastic sewn to one side of a coat or other garment, pushed through a hole or loop on the other side and twisted so as to act as a fastener. ■ a pin or other crosspiece put through the eye of a rope or a link of a chain to keep it in place. ■ (also **toggle bolt**) a kind of wall fastener for use on hollow walls, having a part that springs open or turns through 90° after it is inserted so as to prevent withdrawal. **2** (also **toggle switch** or **toggle key**) Comput. a key or command that is operated the same way but with opposite effect on successive occasions.
▶v. **1** [intr.] Comput. switch from one effect, feature, or state to another by using a toggle. **2** [tr.] provide or fasten with a toggle or toggles.

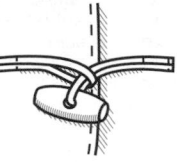

toggle

tog·gle switch ▶n. **1** an electric switch operated by means of a projecting lever that is moved up and down. **2** Comput. another term for TOGGLE.

toil /toil/ ▶v. [intr.] work extremely hard or incessantly: *we toiled away.* ■ move slowly and with difficulty: *she began to toil up the cliff path.*
▶n. exhausting physical labor: *a life of toil.* ▷Middle English (in the senses 'contend verbally' and 'strife'): from Anglo-Norman French *toiler* 'strive, dispute,' *toil* 'confusion,' from Latin *tudiculare* 'stir around,' from *tudicula* 'machine for crushing olives,' related to *tundere* 'crush.' —**toil·er** n.

toile /twäl/ ▶n. **1** an early version of a garment made in cheap material so that the design can be tested and perfected. **2** a translucent linen or cotton fabric, used for making clothes.

toi·let /'toilit/ ▶n. **1** a large bowl for urinating or defecating into, typically plumbed into a sewage system and with a flushing mechanism. ■ a room, building, or cubicle containing one or more of these. **2** the process of washing oneself, dressing, and attending to one's appearance: *her toilet completed, she finally went back downstairs.* ■ [as adj.] denoting articles used in this process: *a bathroom cabinet stocked with toilet articles.* ■ the cleansing of part of a person's body as a medical procedure.
▶v. (**-let·ed, -let·ing**) [tr.] assist or supervise (someone, esp. an infant or invalid) in using a toilet. ▷mid 16th cent.: from French *toilette* 'cloth, wrapper,' diminutive of *toile* 'cloth, web,' from Latin *tela* 'web.' The word originally denoted a cloth used as a wrapper for clothes; then (in the 17th cent.) a cloth cover for a dressing table, the articles used in dressing, and the process of dressing, later also of washing oneself (sense 2). In the 19th cent. the word came to denote a dressing room, and, in the U.S., one with washing facilities; hence, a lavatory (early 20th cent.).

toi·let pa·per ▶n. paper in sheets or on a roll for wiping oneself clean after urination or defecation.

toi·let·ries /'toilitrēz/ ▶pl. n. articles used in washing and taking care of one's body, such as soap, shampoo, and toothpaste.

toi·lette /twä'let/ ▶n. dated the process of washing oneself, dressing, and attending to one's appearance: *Emily got up to begin her morning toilette.*

toi·let wa·ter ▶n. a dilute form of perfume. Also called EAU DE TOILETTE.

toil·some /'toilsəm/ ▶adj. archaic or poetic/lit. involving hard or tedious work. —**toil·some·ly** adv. —**toil·some·ness** n.

to·ken /'tōkən/ ▶n. **1** a thing serving as a visible or tangible representation of something abstract: *mistletoe was cut from an oak tree as a token of good fortune.* ■ a thing given to or done for someone as an expression of one's feelings: *I wanted to offer you a small token of my appreciation.* ■ archaic a characteristic or distinctive sign or mark, esp. a badge or favor worn to indicate allegiance to a particular person or party. ■ archaic a word or object conferring authority on or serving to authenticate the speaker or holder. ■ Comput. a sequence of bits used in a certain network architecture in which the ability to transmit information is conferred on a particular node by the arrival there of this sequence, which is passed continuously between nodes in a fixed order. ■ a person chosen by way of tokenism as a nominal representative of a minority or underrepresented group. **2** a voucher that can be exchanged for goods or services, typically one given as a gift or offered as part of a promotional offer. ■ a metal or plastic disk used to operate a machine or in exchange for particular goods or services. **3** an individual occurrence of a symbol or string, in particular: ■ Linguistics an individual occurrence of a linguistic unit in speech or writing, as contrasted with the type or class of linguistic unit of which it is an instance. ■ Comput. the smallest meaningful unit of information in a sequence of data for a compiler.
▶adj. done for the sake of appearances or as a symbolic gesture: *cases like these often bring just token fines from the courts.* ■ (of a person) chosen by way of tokenism as a representative of a particular minority or underrepresented group: *the token woman on the force.*
▶ □ **by the same token** in the same way or for the same reason. □ **in token of** as a sign or symbol of.

to·ken·ism /'tōkə,nizəm/ ▶n. the practice of making only a perfunctory or symbolic effort to do a particular thing, esp. by recruiting a small number of people from underrepresented groups in order to give the appearance of sexual or racial equality within a workforce. —**to·ken·is·tic** /,tōkə'nistik/ adj.

told /tōld/ ▶ past and past participle of TELL[1].

tol·er·a·ble /'tälərəbəl/ ▶adj. able to be endured: *a stimulant to make life more tolerable.* ■ fairly good; mediocre: *he was fond of music and had a tolerable voice.* —**tol·er·a·bil·i·ty** /,täl(ə)rə'bilitē/ n. —**tol·er·a·bly** /-blē/ adv.

tol·er·ance /'täl(ə)rəns/ ▶n. **1** the ability or willingness to tolerate something, in particular the existence of opinions or behavior that one does not necessarily agree with: *an advocate of religious tolerance.* ■ the capacity to endure continued subjection to something, esp. a drug, transplant, antigen, or environmental conditions, without adverse reaction: *the desert camel shows the greatest tolerance to dehydration.* ■ diminution in the body's response to a drug after continued use. **2** an allowable amount of variation of a specified quantity, esp. in the dimensions of a machine or part.

tol·er·ant /'tälərənt/ ▸*adj.* **1** showing willingness to allow the existence of opinions or behavior that one does not necessarily agree with: *we must be **tolerant of** others.* **2** (of a plant, animal, or machine) able to endure (specified conditions or treatment): *rye is reasonably **tolerant of** drought.* —**tol·er·ant·ly** *adv.*

tol·er·ate /'tälə,rāt/ ▸*v.* [*tr.*] allow the existence, occurrence, or practice of (something that one does not necessarily like or agree with) without interference. ■ accept or endure (someone or something unpleasant or disliked) with forbearance: *how was it that she could tolerate such noise?* ■ be capable of continued subjection to (a drug, toxin, or environmental condition) without adverse reaction: *lichens grow in conditions that no other plants tolerate.* —**tol·er·a·tor** /-,rātər/ *n.*

tol·er·a·tion /,tälə'rāSHən/ ▸*n.* the practice of tolerating something, in particular differences of opinion or behavior.

toll¹ /tōl/ ▸*n.* **1** a charge payable for permission to use a particular bridge or road: *turnpike tolls* | [as *adj.*] *a toll bridge.* ■ a charge for a long-distance telephone call. **2** the number of deaths, casualties, or injuries arising from particular circumstances, such as a natural disaster, conflict, or accident. ■ the cost or damage resulting from something: *the environmental toll of the policy has been high.*
▸*v.* [*tr.*] [usu. as *n.*] (**tolling**) charge a toll for the use of (a bridge or road): *the report advocates expressway tolling.*
▸ □ **take its toll** (or **take a heavy toll**) have an adverse effect, esp. so as to cause damage, suffering, or death.

toll² ▸*v.* [*intr.*] (of a bell) sound with a slow, uniform succession of strokes, as a signal or announcement. ■ [*tr.*] cause (a bell) to make such a sound. ■ (of a bell) announce or mark (the time, a service, or a person's death): *the bell of St. Mary's began to toll the curfew.*
▸*n.* a single ring of a bell.

toll·booth /'tōl,bōōTH/ ▸*n.* a booth where drivers must pay to use a bridge or road.

toll·gate /'tōl,gāt/ ▸*n.* a barrier across a road where drivers or pedestrians must pay to go further.

toll·house /'tōl,hous/ ▸*n.* a small house by a tollgate or toll bridge where money is collected from road users.

Tol·tec /'tōl,tek; 'täl-/ ▸*n.* **1** a member of an American Indian people that flourished in Mexico before the Aztecs. **2** the language of this people.
▸*adj.* of or relating to this people. —**Tol·tec·an** /tōl'tekən; täl-/ *adj.*

tol·u·ene /'tälyōō,ēn/ ▸*n.* *Chem.* a colorless liquid hydrocarbon present in coal tar and petroleum and used as a solvent and in organic synthesis. Also called METHYLBENZENE.

tom /täm/ ▸*n.* **1** the male of various animals, esp. a turkey or domestic cat. **2** (**Tom**) *inf.* short for UNCLE TOM.
▸*v.* (**Tom**) (**Tommed**, **Tom·ming**) [*intr.*] *inf.*, *derog.* (of a black person) behave in an excessively obedient or servile way.

tom·a·hawk /'tämə,hôk/ ▸*n.* *hist.* a light ax used as a tool or weapon originally by American Indians.
▸*v.* [*tr.*] strike or cut with or as if with a tomahawk. ▷early 17th cent.: from a Virginia Algonquian language.

to·ma·to /tə'mātō; -'mätō/ ▸*n.* (*pl.* **-oes**) **1** a glossy red, or occasionally yellow, pulpy edible fruit that is typically eaten as a vegetable or in salad. ■ the bright red color of a ripe tomato. **2** the widely cultivated South American plant (*Lycopersicon esculentum*) of the nightshade family that produces this fruit. —**to·ma·to·ey** /-'mätō-ē; -'mätō-ē/ *adj.*

tomb /tōōm/ ▸*n.* a large vault, typically an underground one, for burying the dead. ■ an enclosure for a corpse cut in the earth or in rock. ■ a monument to the memory of a dead person, erected over their burial place. ■ used in similes and metaphors to refer to a place or situation that is extremely cold, quiet, or dark, or that forms a confining enclosure: *as quiet as a tomb.* ■ (**the tomb**) *poetic/lit.* death.

tom·boy /'täm,boi/ ▸*n.* a girl who enjoys rough, noisy activities traditionally associated with boys. —**tom·boy·ish** *adj.* —**tom·boy·ish·ness** *n.*

tomb·stone /'tōōm,stōn/ ▸*n.* **1** a large, flat inscribed stone standing or laid over a grave. **2** (also **tombstone advertisement** or **tombstone ad**) an advertisement listing the underwriters or firms associated with a new issue of securities.

tom·cat /'täm,kat/ ▸*n.* a male domestic cat. ■ *inf.* a sexually aggressive man; a womanizer.
▸*v.* (**-cat·ted**, **-cat·ting**) [*intrans.*] *informal* pursue women promiscuously for sexual gratification: *tomcatting all night and sleeping until noon.*

tome /tōm/ ▸*n.* chiefly humorous a book, esp. a large, heavy, scholarly one: *a weighty tome.*

tom·fool /'täm'fōōl/ ▸*n.* dated a foolish person: [as *adj.*] *she was destined to take part in some tomfool caper.*

tom·fool·er·y /täm'fōōl(ə)rē/ ▸*n.* foolish or silly behavior.

tom·my gun /'tämē/ ▸*n.* *inf.* a type of submachine gun.

to·mog·ra·phy /tə'mägrəfē/ ▸*n.* a technique for displaying a representation of a cross section through a human body or other solid object using X-rays or ultrasound. —**to·mo·graph·ic** /,tōmə'grafik/ *adj.*

to·mor·row /tə'môrō; -'märō/ ▸*adv.* on the day after today: *the show opens tomorrow.* ■ in the future, esp. the near future: *East Germany will not disappear tomorrow.*
▸*n.* the day after today: *tomorrow is going to be a special day.* ■ the future, esp. the near future: *today's engineers are tomorrow's buyers.*

tom·tit /täm'tit/ ▸*n.* a popular name for any of a number of small active songbirds, esp. a tit or a chickadee.

tom-tom ▸*n.* a medium-sized cylindrical drum beaten with the hands and used in jazz bands, etc. ■ an early drum, of Native American or Asian origin, typically played with the hands.

ton¹ /tən/ (abbr.: **t** also **tn**) ▸*n.* **1** (also **short ton**) a unit of weight equal to 2,000 pounds avoirdupois (907.19 kg). ■ (also **long ton**) a unit of weight equal to 2,240 pounds avoirdupois (1016.05 kg). ■ short for METRIC TON. ■ a unit of measurement of a ship's weight representing the weight of water it displaces. **2** (usu. **a ton of/tons of**) *inf.* a large number or amount: *I had tons of friends.*

ton² /tôn/ ▸*n.* fashionable style or distinction. ■ (**the ton**) [treated as *sing.* or *pl.*] fashionable society.

ton·al /'tōnl/ ▸*adj.* of or relating to the tone of music, color, or writing: *his ear for tonal color* | *the poem's tonal lapses.* ■ of or relating to music written using conventional keys and harmony. ■ *Phonet.* (of a language) expressing semantic differences by varying the intonation given to words or syllables of a similar sound. —**ton·al·ly** *adv.*

to·nal·i·ty /tō'nalitē/ ▸*n.* (*pl.* **-ties**) **1** the character of a piece of music as determined by the key in which it is played or the relations between the notes of a scale or key. ■ the harmonic effect of being in a particular key: *the first bar would seem set to create a tonality of C major.* ■ the use of conventional keys and harmony as the basis of musical composition. **2** the color scheme or range of tones used in a picture.

tone /tōn/ ▸*n.* **1** the overall quality of a musical or vocal sound: *the piano tone appears lacking in warmth.* ■ a modulation of the voice expressing a particular feeling or mood: *a firm tone of voice.* ■ a manner of expression in writing: *a general tone of ill-concealed glee in the reporting.* **2** the general character of a group of people or a place or event: *a bell would lower the tone of the place.* ■ *inf.* an atmosphere of respectability or class. **3** a musical sound, esp. one of a definite pitch and character. ■ a musical note, warble, or other sound used as a particular signal on a telephone or answering machine. ■ *Phonet.* (in some languages, such as Chinese) a particular pitch pattern on a syllable used to make semantic distinctions. ■ *Phonet.* (in some languages, such as English) intonation on a word or phrase used to add functional meaning: *tone of voice.* **4** (also **whole tone**) a basic interval in classical Western music, equal to two semitones; a major second or whole step. **5** the particular quality of brightness, deepness, or hue of a tint or shade of a color: *stained glass in vivid tones of red and blue.* ■ the general effect of color or of light and shade in a picture. ■ a slight degree of difference in the intensity of a color. **6** (also **muscle tone**) the normal level of firmness or slight contraction in a resting muscle.
▸*v.* [*tr.*] **1** give greater strength or firmness to (the body or a part of it): *exercise **tones up** the muscles.* ■ [*intr.*] (**tone up**) (of a muscle or bodily part) became stronger or firmer. **2** [*intr.*] (**tone with**) harmonize with (something) in terms of color. **3** *Photog.* give a (monochrome picture) an altered color in finishing by means of a chemical solution.
▸*phrasal v.* □ **tone something down** make something less harsh in sound or color. ■ make something less extreme or intense. —**toned** *adj.* [in *comb.*] *the fresh-toned singing.* —**tone·less** *adj.* —**tone·less·ly** *adv.*

tone-deaf ▸*adj.* (of a person) unable to perceive differences of musical pitch accurately. —**tone-deaf·ness** *n.*

tone po·em ▸*n.* a piece of orchestral music, typically in one movement, on a descriptive or rhapsodic theme.

ton·er /'tōnər/ ▸*n.* **1** an astringent liquid applied to the skin to reduce oiliness and improve its condition. ■ [with *adj.*] a device or exercise for making a specified part of the body firmer and stronger: *a tummy toner.* **2** a black and colored powder used making photocopies. ■ [usu. with *adj.*] a chemical bath for changing the color or shade of a photographic print, esp. as specified: *sepia or blue toners.*

---

tone row ▸*n.* a particular sequence of the twelve notes of the chromatic scale used as a basis for twelve-tone (serial) music.

tongs /tôngz; tăngz/ ▸*pl. n.* an instrument with two movable arms that are joined at one end, used for picking up and holding things: *ice tongs.*

tongue /təng/ ▸*n.* **1** the fleshy muscular organ in the mouth of a mammal, used for tasting, licking, swallowing, and (in humans) articulating speech. ■ the equivalent organ in other vertebrates, sometimes used (in snakes) as a scent organ or (in chameleons) for catching food. ■ an analogous organ in insects, formed from some of the mouthparts and used in feeding. ■ the tongue of a hoofed mammal, in particular an ox or lamb, as food. ■ used in reference to a person's style or manner of speaking: *a debater with a caustic tongue.* ■ a particular language: *the prioress chatted to the peddler in a strange tongue.* **2** a thing resembling or likened to a tongue, in particular: ■ a long, low promontory of land. ■ a strip of leather or fabric under the laces in a shoe, attached only at the front end. ■ the pin of a buckle. ■ a projecting strip on a wooden board fitting into a groove on another. ■ the vibrating reed of a musical instrument or organ pipe. ■ a jet of flame.
▸*v.* (**tongues, ton·gued, ton·guing** /'təNGGiNG/) [*tr.*] **1** *Mus.* sound (a note) distinctly on a wind instrument by interrupting the air flow with the tongue. **2** lick or caress with the tongue. ▷Old English *tunge,* of Germanic origin; related to Dutch *tong,* German *Zunge* and Latin *lingua.* —**tongued** *adj.*
▸ □ **speak in tongues** speak in an unknown language during religious worship. □ (**with**) **tongue in cheek** without really meaning what one is saying or writing.

tongue and groove ▸*n.* wooden planking in which adjacent boards are joined by means of interlocking ridges and grooves down their sides. —**tongued-and-grooved** *adj.*

tongue de·pres·sor ▸*n.* an instrument, typically a small flat piece of wood, used to press down the tongue in order to examine the mouth or throat.

tongue-in-cheek ▸*adj. & adv.* with ironic or flippant intent: [as *adj.*] *her delightful tongue-in-cheek humor* | [as *adv.*] *"I swear there's a female conspiracy against men!" he complained, tongue-in-cheek.*

tongue-lash·ing ▸*n.* a loud or severe scolding: *the incensed boss gave him a tongue-lashing.* —**tongue-lash** *v.*

tongue-tied ▸*adj.* **1** too shy or embarrassed to speak. **2** having a malformation restricting the movement of the tongue.

tongue-twist·er ▸*n.* a sequence of words or sounds, typically of an alliterative kind, that are difficult to pronounce quickly and correctly, as, for example, *tie twine to three tree twigs.* —**tongue-twist·ing** *adj.*

ton·ic /'tänik/ ▸*n.* **1** a medicinal substance taken to give a feeling of vigor or well-being. ■ something with an invigorating effect: *being needed is a tonic for someone at my age.* **2** short for TONIC WATER. **3** *Mus.* the first note in a scale that, in conventional harmony, provides the keynote of a piece of music.
▸*adj.* **1** giving a feeling of vigor or well-being; invigorating. **2** *Mus.* relating to or denoting the first degree of a scale. **3** *Phonet.* denoting or relating to the syllable within a tone group that has greatest prominence, because it carries the main change of pitch. **4** relating to or restoring normal tone to muscles or other organs. ■ *Physiol.* relating to, denoting, or producing continuous muscular contraction. —**ton·i·cal·ly** /-ik(ə)lē/ *adv.*

ton·ic sol-fa /ˌsōl 'fä/ ▸*n.* a system of naming the notes of the scale (usually **do, re, mi, fa, sol, la, ti**) developed in England and used esp. to teach singing, with do as the keynote of all major keys and la as the keynote of all minor keys. See SOLMIZATION.

ton·ic wa·ter ▸*n.* a bitter carbonated soft drink made with quinine, used esp. as a mixer with gin or other liquors.

to·night /tə'nīt/ ▸*adv.* on the present or approaching evening or night: *are you doing anything tonight?*
▸*n.* the evening or night of the present day: *tonight is a night to remember.*

ton·nage /'tənij/ ▸*n.* weight in tons, esp. of cargo or freight: *road convoys carry more tonnage.* ■ the size or carrying capacity of a ship measured in tons. ■ shipping considered in terms of total carrying capacity.

tonne /tən/ ▸*n.* another term for METRIC TON.

ton·sil /'tänsəl/ ▸*n.* either of two small masses of lymphoid tissue in the throat, one on each side of the root of the tongue. —**ton·sil·lar** /-sələr/ *adj.*

ton·sil·lec·to·my /ˌtänsə'lektəmē/ ▸*n.* (*pl.* **-mies**) a surgical operation to remove the tonsils.

ton·sil·li·tis /ˌtänsə'lītis/ ▸*n.* inflammation of the tonsils.

ton·so·ri·al /tän'sôrēəl/ ▸*adj. formal* or *humorous* of or relating to hairdressing.

ton·sure /'tänsHər/ ▸*n.* a part of a monk's or priest's head left bare on top by shaving off the hair. ■ an act of shaving the top of a monk's or priest's head as a preparation for entering a religious order.
▸*v.* [*tr.*] shave the hair on the crown of.

To·ny /'tōnē/ ▸*n.* (*pl.* **To·nys**) any of a number of awards given annually in the U.S. for outstanding achievement in the theater in various categories.

ton·y /'tōnē/ ▸*adj.* (**ton·i·er, ton·i·est**) *inf.* fashionable among wealthy or stylish people: *a tony restaurant.*

too /tōō/ ▸*adv.* **1** to a higher degree than is desirable, permissible, or possible; excessively: *he was driving too fast.* ■ *inf.* very: *you're too kind.* **2** in addition; also: *is he coming too?* ■ moreover (used when adding a further point): *she is a grown woman, and a strong one too.*
▸ □ **all too** —— used to emphasize that something is the case to an extreme or unwelcome extent: *failures are all too common.* □ **none too** —— far from; not very: *her sight's none too good.*

took /tŏŏk/ ▸ past of TAKE.

tool /tōōl/ ▸*n.* **1** a device or implement, esp. one held in the hand, used to carry out a particular function: *gardening tools.* ■ a thing used in an occupation or pursuit: *computers are an essential tool.* ■ a person used or exploited by another. ■ *Comput.* a piece of software that carries out a particular function, typically creating or modifying another program. **2** a distinct design in the tooling of a book. ■ a small stamp or roller used to make such a design. **3** *vulgar slang* a man's penis. ■ *inf.* a dull, slow-witted, or socially inept person.
▸*v.* **1** [*tr.*] impress a design on (leather, esp. a leather book cover): *volumes bound in green leather and tooled in gold.* ■ dress (stone) with a chisel. **2** equip or be equipped with tools for industrial production: [*tr.*] *the factory must be tooled to produce the models* | [*intr.*] *they were tooling up for production.* **3** [*intr.*] *inf.* drive or ride in a casual or leisurely manner: *tooling around town in a pink convertible.* —**tool·er** *n.*

tool·bar /'tōōlˌbär/ ▸*n. Comput.* (in a program with a graphical user interface) a strip of icons used to perform certain functions.

tool·mak·er /'tōōlˌmākər/ ▸*n.* a maker of tools, esp. a person who makes and maintains tools for use in a manufacturing process. —**tool·mak·ing** /-ˌmākiNG/ *n.*

toot /tōōt/ ▸*n.* **1** a short, sharp sound made by a horn, trumpet, or similar instrument. **2** *inf.* a snort of a drug, esp. cocaine. ■ cocaine. **3** *inf.* a spell of drinking and lively enjoyment; a spree: *a sales manager on a toot.*
▸*v.* [*tr.*] **1** sound (a horn or similar instrument) with a short, sharp sound: *behind us an impatient driver tooted a horn.* ■ [*intr.*] make such a sound: *a car tooted at us.* **2** *inf.* snort (cocaine). —**toot·er** *n.*

tooth /tōōTH/ ▸*n.* (*pl.* **teeth** /tēTH/) **1** each of a set of hard, bony enamel-coated structures in the jaws of most vertebrates, used for biting and chewing. ■ a similar hard, pointed structure in invertebrate animals, typically functioning in the mechanical breakdown of food. ■ an appetite or liking for a particular thing. ■ roughness given to a surface to allow color or glue to adhere. ■ (**teeth**) *fig.* genuine force or effectiveness of a body or in a law or agreement. **2** a projecting part on a tool or other instrument, esp. one of a series that function or engage together, such as a cog on a gearwheel or a point on a saw or comb. ■ a projecting part on an animal or plant, esp. one of a jagged or dentate row on the margin of a leaf or shell. —**toothed** *adj.* —**tooth·less** *adj.* —**tooth·like** /-ˌlīk/ *adj.*
▸ □ **armed to the teeth** formidably armed. □ **fight tooth and nail** fight fiercely. □ **get** (or **sink**) **one's teeth into** work energetically and productively on (a task).

tooth·ache /'tōōTHˌāk/ ▸*n.* a pain in a tooth or teeth: *he has a toothache.*

tooth·brush /'tōōTHˌbrəsH/ ▸*n.* a small brush with a long handle, used for cleaning the teeth.

tooth·paste /'tōōTHˌpāst/ ▸*n.* a paste used on a toothbrush for cleaning the teeth.

tooth·pick /'tōōTHˌpik/ ▸*n.* a short pointed piece of wood or plastic used for removing bits of food lodged between the teeth.

tooth·some /'tōōTHsəm/ ▸*adj.* (of food) temptingly tasty: *a toothsome morsel.* ■ *inf.* (of a person) good-looking; attractive. —**tooth·some·ly** *adv.* —**tooth·some·ness** *n.*

tooth·y /'tōōTHē/ ▸*adj.* (**tooth·i·er, tooth·i·est**) having or showing large, numerous, or prominent teeth: *a toothy smile.* —**tooth·i·ly** /-THəlē/ *adv.*

too·tle /'tōōtl/ ▸*v.* **1** [*intr.*] casually make a series of sounds on a horn, trumpet, or similar instrument: *he tootled on the horn.* ■ [*tr.*] play (an instrument) or make (a sound or tune) in such a way: *the video games tootled their tunes.* **2** [*intr.*] *inf.* go or travel in a leisurely way: *they were tootling along the coast.*

▸*n.* **1** an act or sound of casual playing on an instrument such as a horn or trumpet. **2** *inf.* a leisurely journey.

top[1] /täp/ ▸*n.* **1** the highest or uppermost point, part, or surface of something: *Eileen stood at the top of the stair.* ■ (usu. **tops**) the leaves, stems, and shoots of a plant, esp. those of a vegetable grown for its root. ■ *chiefly Brit.* the end of something that is furthest from the speaker or a point of reference: *at the top of the road.* **2** a thing or part placed on, fitted to, or covering the upper part of something, in particular: ■ a garment covering the upper part of the body and worn with a skirt, pants, or shorts. ■ a lid, cover, or cap for something. ■ a platform at the head of a ship's mast, esp. (in a sailing ship) a platform around the head of each of the lower masts, serving to extend the topmast shrouds. **3** (**the top**) the highest or most important rank, level, or position: *her talent will take her right to the top.* ■ a person or thing occupying such a position: *North Korea was top of the agenda.* ■ (**tops**) *inf.* a person or thing regarded as particularly good or pleasant: *Davison is tops in its market.* ■ the utmost degree or the highest level: *she shouted at the top of her voice.* ■ the high-frequency component of reproduced sound. **4** *Baseball* the first half of an inning: *the top of the eighth.* **5** *Physics* one of six flavors of quark. **6** *inf.* a male who takes the active role in homosexual intercourse, esp. anal intercourse.

▸*adj.* highest in position, rank, or degree: *a top executive.*

▸*v.* (**topped, top·ping**) [*tr.*] **1** exceed (an amount, level, or number); be more than: *losses are expected to top $100 million this year.* ■ be at the highest place or rank in (a list, poll, chart, or league). ■ be taller than. ■ surpass (a person or previous achievement or action); outdo: *he was baffled as to how he could top his past work.* ■ appear as the chief performer or attraction at: *Hopper topped a great night of boxing.* ■ reach the top of (a hill or other stretch of rising ground). **2** provide with a top or topping: *baked potatoes topped with melted cheese.* ■ complete (an outfit) with an upper garment, hat, or item of jewelry: *a white dress topped by a dark cardigan.* ■ remove the top of (a vegetable or fruit) in preparation for cooking. **3** *Golf* mishit (the ball or a stroke) by hitting above the center of the ball.

▸*phrasal v.* □ **top something off 1** finish something in a memorable or notable way: *the festivities were topped off with the awarding of prizes.* **2** *inf.* fill up a nearly full tank with fuel. □ **top out** reach an upper limit. □ **top something out** put the highest structural feature on a building, typically as a ceremony to mark the building's completion. □ **top something up** *chiefly Brit.* add to a number or amount to bring it up to a certain level: *a 0.5 percent bonus is offered to top up savings rates.* ■ fill up a glass or other partly full container.

▸*adv.* (**tops**) *inf.* at the most: *he makes $28,000 a year, tops.* —**top·most** /-ˌmōst/ *adj.* —**topped** *adj.* [in *comb.*] *a glass-topped table.*

▸ □ **at the top of one's lungs** as loudly as possible. □ **from top to bottom** completely; thoroughly. □ **from top to toe** completely; all over. □ **from the top** *inf.* from the beginning: *they rehearsed Act One from the top.* □ **on top 1** on the highest point or uppermost surface. ■ on the upper part of the head. **2** in a leading or the dominant position: *his party came out on top in last month's elections.* □ **on top of 1** on the highest point or uppermost surface of: *a town perched on top of a hill.* ■ so as to cover; over: *trays stacked one on top of another.* ■ in close proximity to: *we all lived on top of each other.* **2** in command or control of: *he couldn't get on top of his work.* **3** in addition to: *on top of everything else, he's a brilliant linguist.* □ **on top of the world** *inf.* happy and elated. □ **over the top** /ˌōvər T͟Hə 'tap/ *inf.* to an excessive or exaggerated degree, in particular so as to go beyond reasonable or acceptable limits: *his reactions had been a bit over the top.* **2** *chiefly hist.* over the parapet of a trench and into battle. □ **top dollar** *inf.* a very high price. □ **to top it all** as a culminating, typically unpleasant, event or action in a series.

top[2] ▸*n.* a conical, spherical, or pear-shaped toy that with a quick or vigorous twist may be set to spin.

to·paz /'tōpaz/ ▸*n.* **1** a precious stone, typically colorless, yellow, or pale blue, consisting of a fluorine-containing aluminum silicate. ■ a dark yellow color. **2** a large tropical American hummingbird (genus *Topaza*) with a yellowish throat and a long tail.

top brass ▸*n.* see BRASS.

top·coat /'täpˌkōt/ ▸*n.* **1** an overcoat. **2** an outer coat of paint.

top dog ▸*n.* *inf.* a person who is successful or dominant in their field.

top draw·er ▸*n.* the uppermost drawer in a chest or desk. ■ (**the top drawer**) *inf.* high social position or class.

▸*adj.* (**top-draw·er**) *inf.* of the highest quality or social class.

tope[1] /tōp/ ▸*v.* [*intr.*] *archaic* or *poetic/lit.* drink alcohol to excess, esp. on a regular basis. —**top·er** *n.*

tope[2] ▸*n.* a small grayish slender-bodied shark (genus *Galeorhinus*, family Carcharhinidae), occurring chiefly in inshore waters.

top hat ▸*n.* a man's formal hat with a high cylindrical crown.

top-heav·y ▸*adj.* disproportionately heavy at the top so as to be in danger of toppling. ■ (of an organization) having a disproportionately large number of people in senior administrative positions. ■ *inf.* (of a woman) having a disproportionately large bust. —**top-heav·i·ly** *adv.* —**top-heav·i·ness** *n.*

top hat

to·pi·ar·y /'tōpēˌerē/ ▸*n.* (pl. **-ar·ies**) the art or practice of clipping shrubs or trees into ornamental shapes. ■ shrubs or trees clipped into ornamental shapes in such a way: *a cottage surrounded by topiary and flowers.* —**to·pi·ar·i·an** /ˌtōpē'e(ə)rēən/ *adj.* —**to·pi·a·rist** /-ərist/ *n.*

top·ic /'täpik/ ▸*n.* a matter dealt with in a text, discourse, or conversation; a subject: *her favorite topic of conversation is her partner.* ■ *Linguistics* that part of a sentence about which something is said, typically the first major constituent.

top·i·cal /'täpikəl/ ▸*adj.* **1** (of a subject) of immediate relevance, interest, or importance owing to its relation to current events. ■ relating to a particular subject; classified according to subject: *annotated links to resources in eleven topical categories.* **2** *chiefly Med.* relating or applied directly to a part of the body.

▸*n.* *Philately* a postage stamp forming part of a set or collection with designs connected with the same subject. —**top·i·cal·i·ty** /ˌtäpə'kalitē/ *n.* —**top·i·cal·ly** /-ik(ə)lē/ *adv.*

top·knot /'täpˌnät/ ▸*n.* a knot of hair arranged on the top of the head. ■ a decorative knot or bow of ribbon worn on the top of the head, popular in the 18th century. ■ (in an animal or bird) a tuft or crest of hair or feathers.

top·less /'täpləs/ ▸*adj.* (of a woman or a woman's item of clothing) having or leaving the breasts uncovered: *a topless dancer.* ■ (of a place such as a bar or beach) where there are women wearing such clothes. —**top·less·ness** *n.*

top-lev·el ▸*adj.* of the highest level of importance or prestige.

top·mast /'täpˌmast; -məst/ ▸*n.* the second section of a square-rigged sailing ship's mast, immediately above the lower mast.

top-notch ▸*adj.* *inf.* of the highest quality; excellent: *a top-notch hotel.* —**top-notch·er** *n.*

to·pog·ra·phy /tə'pägrəfē/ ▸*n.* the arrangement of the natural and artificial physical features of an area: *the topography of the island.* ■ a detailed description or representation on a map of such features. —**to·pog·ra·pher** /-fər/ *n.* —**top·o·graph·ic** /ˌtäpə'grafik/ *adj.* —**top·o·graph·i·cal** *adj.*

to·poi /'tōpoi/ ▸ plural form of TOPOS.

to·pol·o·gy /tə'päləjē/ ▸*n.* **1** *Math.* the study of geometric properties and spatial relations unaffected by the continuous change of shape or size of figures. ■ a family of open subsets of an abstract space such that the union and the intersection of any two of them are members of the family, and that includes the space itself and the empty set. **2** the way in which constituent parts are interrelated or arranged: *the topology of a computer network.* —**top·o·log·i·cal** /ˌtäpə'läjikəl/ *adj.* —**top·o·log·i·cal·ly** /ˌtäpə'läjik(ə)lē/ *adv.* —**to·pol·o·gist** /-jist/ *n.*

top·o·nym /'täpəˌnim/ ▸*n.* a place name, esp. one derived from a topographical feature. —

to·pon·y·my /tə'pänəmē/ ▸*n.* the study of place names. —**top·o·nym·ic** /ˌtäpə'nimik/ *adj.*

to·pos /'täpōs/ ▸*n.* (pl. **-poi** /-poi/) a traditional theme or formula in literature.

top·ping /'täpiNG/ ▸*n.* a layer of food poured or spread over a base of a different type of food to add flavor: *a cake with a marzipan topping.*

▸*adj.* *Brit., inf., dated* excellent: *that really is a topping dress.*

top·ple /'täpəl/ ▸*v.* [*intr.*] overbalance or become unsteady and fall slowly: *she toppled over when I touched her.* ■ [*tr.*] cause to fall in such a way: *the push almost toppled him to the ground* | *fig. disagreement had threatened to topple the government.*

top·sail /'täpsəl; -ˌsāl/ ▸*n.* a sail set on a ship's topmast.

top se·cret ▸*adj.* of the highest secrecy; highly confidential. ■ (of information or documents) given the highest security classification, above secret.

top·side /'täpˌsīd/ ▸*n.* (often **topsides**) the upper part of a ship's side, above the waterline.

top·soil /ˈtäpˌsoil/ ▸ n. the top layer of soil.

top·spin /ˈtäpˌspin/ ▸ n. a fast forward spinning motion imparted to a ball when throwing or hitting it, often resulting in a curved path or a strong forward motion on rebounding. —**top·spin·ner** n.

top·sy-tur·vy /ˈtäpsē ˈtərvē/ ▸ adj. upside down: *the fairground ride turned riders topsy-turvy.* ■ in a state of confusion.
▸ n. a state of utter confusion. —**top·sy-tur·vi·ly** /ˈtərvəlē/ adv. —**top·sy-tur·vi·ness** n.

toque /tōk/ ▸ n. a woman's small hat, typically having a narrow, closely turned-up brim. ■ hist. a small cap or bonnet of such a type worn by a man or woman. ■ a tall white hat with a full pouched crown, worn by chefs.

tor /tôr/ ▸ n. a hill or rocky peak.

To·rah /ˈtôrə; -ˈtô-; tôˈrä/ ▸ n. (usu. **the Torah**) (in Judaism) the law of God as revealed to Moses and recorded in the first five books of the Hebrew scriptures (the Pentateuch). ■ a scroll containing this. ▷from Hebrew *tōrāh* 'instruction, doctrine, law,' from *yārāh* 'show, direct, instruct.'

torch /tôrCH/ ▸ n. chiefly hist. a portable means of illumination such as a piece of wood or cloth soaked in tallow or an oil lamp on a pole, sometimes carried ceremonially. ■ (usu. **the torch**) fig. used to refer to a valuable quality, principle, or cause that needs to be protected and maintained: *mountain warlords carried the torch of Greek independence.* ■ a blowtorch. ■ inf. an arsonist. ■ British term for FLASHLIGHT.
▸ v. [tr.] inf. set fire to: *the shops had been looted and torched.*
▸ □ **carry a torch for** suffer from unrequited love for.

torch·light /ˈtôrCHˌlīt/ ▸ n. the light of a torch or torches. —**torch·lit** /-lit/ adj.

torch song ▸ n. a sad or sentimental song of unrequited love. —**torch sing·er** n.

tore[1] /tôr/ ▸ past of TEAR[1].

tor·e·a·dor /ˈtôrēəˌdôr/ ▸ n. a bullfighter.

tor·e·a·dor pants ▸ pl. n. women's tight-fitting calf-length trousers.

to·ri /ˈtôrī/ ▸ plural form of TORUS.

tor·ment ▸ n. /ˈtôrment/ severe physical or mental suffering. ■ a cause of such suffering.
▸ v. /tôrˈment/ [tr.] cause to experience severe mental or physical suffering. ■ annoy or provoke in a deliberately unkind way. —**tor·ment·ed·ly** /tôrˈmentədlē/ adv. —**tor·ment·ing·ly** /tôrˈmentiNGlē/ adv. —**tor·men·tor** /tôrˈmentər/ n.

torn /tôrn/ ▸ past participle of TEAR[1].

tor·na·do /tôrˈnādō/ ▸ n. (pl. -**does** or -**dos**) a mobile, destructive vortex of violently rotating winds having the appearance of a funnel-shaped cloud and advancing beneath a large storm system. ■ fig. a person or thing characterized by violent or devastating action or emotion: *a tornado of sexual confusion.* —**tor·nad·ic** /-ˈnädik; -ˈnadik/ adj.

to·ro /ˈtôrō/ ▸ n. a pale, fatty cut of tuna used for sushi and sashimi.

to·roi·dal /tôˈroidl/ ▸ adj. Geom. of or resembling a torus. —**to·roi·dal·ly** adv.

tor·pe·do /tôrˈpēdō/ ▸ n. (pl. -**does**) **1** a cigar-shaped self-propelled underwater missile designed to be fired from a ship or submarine or dropped into the water from an aircraft and to explode on reaching a target. ■ a signal placed on a railroad track, exploding as the train passes over it. ■ a firework exploding on impact with a hard surface. ■ inf. a submarine sandwich. ■ inf. a gangster hired to commit a murder or other violent act. ■ an explosive device lowered into oil wells to clear obstructions. ■ (also **torpedo ray**) an electric ray.
▸ v. (-**does**, -**doed**) [tr.] attack or sink (a ship) with a torpedo or torpedoes. ■ fig. destroy or ruin (a plan or project). —**tor·pe·do·like** /-ˌlīk/ adj.

tor·pid /ˈtôrpid/ ▸ adj. mentally or physically inactive; lethargic: *we sat around in a torpid state.* ■ (of an animal) dormant, esp. during hibernation. —**tor·pid·i·ty** /tôrˈpiditē/ n. —**tor·pid·ly** adv.

tor·por /ˈtôrpər/ ▸ n. a state of physical or mental inactivity; lethargy.

torque /tôrk/ ▸ n. Mechanics a twisting force that tends to cause rotation.
▸ v. [tr.] apply torque or a twisting force to (an object). —**tor·quey** adj.

torque con·vert·er ▸ n. a device that transmits or multiplies torque generated by an engine.

tor·rent /ˈtôrənt; ˈtär-/ ▸ n. a strong and fast-moving stream of water or other liquid. ■ (**a torrent of** or **torrents of**) a sudden, violent, and copious outpouring of (something, typically words or feelings): *she was subjected to a torrent of abuse* | *banks plowed torrents of money into the booming stock and property markets.*

tor·ren·tial /tôˈrenCHəl; tə-/ ▸ adj. (of rain) falling rapidly and in copious quantities: *a torrential downpour.* ■ (of water) flowing rapidly and with force. —**tor·ren·tial·ly** adv.

tor·rid /ˈtôrəd; ˈtär-/ ▸ adj. very hot and dry. ■ full of passionate or highly charged emotions arising from sexual love. ■ full of difficulty or tribulation: *Wall Street is in for a torrid time in the next few weeks.* —**tor·rid·i·ty** /təˈriditē/ n. —**tor·rid·ly** adv.

tor·rid zone (also **Tor·rid Zone**) ▸ n. the hot central belt of the earth bounded by the tropics of Cancer and Capricorn.

tor·sion /ˈtôrSHən/ ▸ n. the action of twisting or the state of being twisted, esp. of one end of an object relative to the other. —**tor·sion·al** /-SHənl/ adj. —**tor·sion·al·ly** /-SHənl-ē/ adv. —**tor·sion·less** adj.

tor·sion bar ▸ n. a bar forming part of a vehicle suspension, twisting in response to the motion of the wheels and absorbing their vertical movement.

tor·so /ˈtôrsō/ ▸ n. (pl. -**sos** or -**si** /-sē/) the trunk of the human body. ■ the trunk of a statue without, or considered independently of, the head and limbs. ■ fig. an unfinished or mutilated thing, esp. a work of art or literature: *the Requiem mass was preceded by the cantata.*

tort /tôrt/ ▸ n. Law a wrongful act or an infringement of a right (other than under contract) leading to legal liability.

torte /tôrt; ˈtôrtə/ ▸ n. (pl. **tortes** or German **tor·ten** /ˈtôrtn/) a sweet cake or tart. ▷from German *Torte*, via Italian from late Latin *torta* 'round loaf, cake.'

tor·til·la /tôrˈtē(y)ə/ ▸ n. (in Mexican cooking) a thin, flat pancake of cornmeal or flour, eaten hot or cold, typically with a savory filling. ■ (in Spanish cooking) a thick omelet containing potato and other vegetables, typically served cut into wedges.

tor·toise /ˈtôrtəs/ ▸ n. a turtle, typically a herbivorous one that lives on land. ■ inf. anything exceptionally slow-moving. —**tor·toise·like** /-ˌlīk/ adj. & adv.

tor·toise·shell /ˈtôrtə(s)ˌSHel/ ▸ n. **1** the semitransparent mottled yellow and brown shell of certain turtles, typically used to make jewelry or ornaments. ■ a synthetic substance made in imitation of this. **2** short for TORTOISESHELL BUTTERFLY.

tor·toise·shell but·ter·fly ▸ n. a butterfly (genera *Aglais* and *Nymphalis*, family Nymphalidae) with mottled orange, yellow, and black markings, and wavy wing margins.

tor·toise·shell cat ▸ n. a domestic cat with markings resembling tortoiseshell.

tor·to·ni /tôrˈtōnē/ ▸ n. an Italian ice cream made with eggs and cream, typically served in a small cup and topped with chopped almonds or crumbled macaroons.

tor·tu·ous /ˈtôrCHo͞oəs/ ▸ adj. full of twists and turns. ■ excessively lengthy and complex: *a tortuous argument.* —**tor·tu·os·i·ty** /ˌtôrCHo͞oˈäsitē/ n. (pl. -**ties**) —**tor·tu·ous·ly** adv. —**tor·tu·ous·ness** n.

tor·ture /ˈtôrCHər/ ▸ n. the action or practice of inflicting severe pain on someone as a punishment or to force them to do or say something, or for the pleasure of the person inflicting the pain. ■ great physical or mental suffering or anxiety: *the torture I've gone through because of loving you so.* ■ a cause of such suffering or anxiety.
▸ v. [tr.] inflict severe pain on. ■ cause great mental suffering or anxiety to: *he was tortured by grief.* —**tor·tur·er** n. —**tor·tur·ous** adj.

to·rus /ˈtôrəs/ ▸ n. (pl. **to·ri** /ˈtôrī/ or **to·rus·es**) Geom. a surface or solid formed by rotating a closed curve, esp. a circle, around a line that lies in the same plane but does not intersect it (e.g., like a ring-shaped doughnut).

To·ry /ˈtôrē/ ▸ n. (pl. -**ries**) **1** an American colonist who supported the British side during the American Revolution. **2** (in the UK) a member or supporter of the Conservative Party. ■ a member of the English political party opposing the exclusion of James II from the succession. It remained the name for members of the English, later British, parliamentary party supporting the established religious and political order until the emergence of the Conservative Party in the 1830s. Compare with WHIG (sense 1).
▸ adj. of or relating to the British Conservative Party or its supporters: *Tory voters.* —**To·ry·ism** /-ˌizəm/ n.

toss /tôs; täs/ ▸ v. **1** [tr.] throw (something) somewhere lightly, easily, or casually: *Suzy tossed her bag onto the sofa* | *she tossed me a box of matches.* ■ [tr.] (of a horse) throw (a rider) off its back. ■ [tr.] throw (a coin) into the air in order to make a decision between two alternatives, based on which side of the coin faces up when it lands. ■ [tr.] settle a matter with (someone) by doing this. ■ move or cause to move from side to side or back and forth: [intr.] *the tops of the olive trees swayed and tossed* | [tr.] *the yachts were tossed around in the harbor like toys* [as adj. in comb.] (-**tossed**) *a storm-tossed sea.* ■ [tr.] jerk (one's head or hair) sharply backward. ■ [tr.] shake or turn (food) in a liquid, so as to coat it lightly. **2** [tr.] inf. search (a place).
▸ phrasal v. □ **toss something off 1** drink something rapidly or all at once. **2** produce something rapidly or without thought or effort.

▶*n.* an action or instance of tossing something. ■ **(the toss)** the action of tossing a coin as a method of deciding which team has the right to make a particular decision at the beginning of a game. —**toss·er** *n.*
▶ □ **toss one's cookies** *inf.* vomit.

toss-up ▶*n. inf.* the tossing of a coin to make a decision between two alternatives. ■ a situation in which all outcomes or options are equally possible or equally attractive.

tos·ta·da /tōˈstädə/ (also **tos·ta·do** /-dō/) ▶*n.* (*pl.* **-das** also **-dos**) a Mexican deep-fried tortilla topped with a seasoned mixture of beans, ground meat, and vegetables.

tot[1] /tät/ ▶*n.* **1** a very young child. **2** *chiefly Brit.* a small amount of a strong alcoholic drink such as whiskey or brandy: *a tot of brandy.*

tot[2] ▶*v.* (**tot·ted, tot·ting**) [*tr.*] *chiefly Brit.* (**tot something up**) add up numbers or amounts. ■ accumulate something over a period of time: *he has already totted up 89 victories.*

to·tal /ˈtōtl/ ▶*adj.* **1** comprising the whole number or amount: *a total cost of $4,000.* **2** complete; absolute: *a total stranger.*
▶*n.* the whole number or amount of something: *he scored a total of thirty-three points* | *in total, 200 people were interviewed.*
▶*v.* (**-taled, -tal·ing**; *Brit.* **-talled, -tal·ling**) [*tr.*] amount in number to: *they were left with debts totaling $6,260.* ■ add up the full number or amount of: *the scores were totaled.* **2** [*tr.*] *inf.* damage (something, typically a vehicle) beyond repair; wreck.

to·tal e·clipse ▶*n.* an eclipse in which the whole of the disk of the sun or moon is obscured.

to·tal·i·tar·i·an /tōˌtaliˈte(ə)rēən/ ▶*adj.* of or relating to a system of government that is centralized and dictatorial and requires complete subservience to the state: *a totalitarian regime.*
▶*n.* a person advocating such a system of government. —**to·tal·i·tar·i·an·ism** /-ˌnizəm/ *n.*

to·tal·i·ty /tōˈtalitē/ ▶*n.* the whole of something: *the totality of their current policies.* ■ *Astron.* the moment or duration of total obscuration of the sun or moon during an eclipse.
▶ □ **in its totality** as a whole: *a deeper exploration of life in its totality.*

to·tal·ly /ˈtōtl-ē/ ▶*adv.* completely; absolutely: *the building was totally destroyed by the fire* | *they came from totally different backgrounds.*

to·tal re·call ▶*n.* the ability to remember with clarity every detail of the events of one's life or of a particular event, object, or experience.

to·tal war ▶*n.* a war that is unrestricted in terms of the weapons used, the territory or combatants involved, or the objectives pursued, esp. one in which the laws of war are disregarded.

tote[1] /tōt/ ▶*v.* [*tr.*] *inf.* carry, wield, or convey (something heavy or substantial): *here are books well worth toting home* | [as *adj.*, in *comb.*] (**-toting**) *a gun-toting loner.*
▶*n.* short for TOTE BAG. —**tot·er** *n.* [in *comb.*] *a gun-toter.*

tote[2] ▶*n.* (**the tote**) *inf.* a system of betting in which dividends are calculated according to the amount staked rather than odds offered.

tote bag ▶*n.* a large bag used for carrying a number of items.

to·tem /ˈtōtəm/ ▶*n.* a natural object or animal believed by a particular society to have spiritual significance and adopted by it as an emblem. —**to·tem·ic** /tōˈtemik/ *adj.* —**to·tem·ism** /-ˌmizəm/ *n.* —**to·tem·ist** /-mist/ *n.* —**to·tem·is·tic** /ˌtōdəˈmistik/ *adj.*

to·tem pole ▶*n.* a pole on which totems are hung or on which the images of totems are carved. ■ *fig.* a hierarchy: *the social totem pole.*

tot·ter /ˈtätər/ ▶*v.* [*intr.*] move in a feeble or unsteady way: *a hunched figure tottering down the path.* ■ [usu. as *adj.*] (**tottering**) (of a building) shake or rock as if about to collapse. ■ *fig.* be insecure or about to collapse: *the pharmaceutical industry has tottered from crisis to crisis.*
▶*n.* a feeble or unsteady gait. —**tot·ter·er** *n.* —**tot·ter·y** *adj.*

tou·can /ˈtoōˌkan; -ˌkän/ ▶*n.* a tropical American fruit-eating bird (genera *Ramphastos* and *Andigena*, family Ramphastidae) with a massive bill and typically brightly colored plumage.

touch /təCH/ ▶*v.* [*tr.*] **1** come so close to (an object) as to be or come into contact with it: *the dog had one paw outstretched, not quite touching the ground.* ■ bring one's hand or another part of one's body into contact with something: *he touched a strand of her hair.* ■ (**touch something to**) move a part of one's

totem pole

body to bring it into contact with: *he gently touched his lips to her cheek.* ■ lightly press or strike (a button or key on a device or instrument) to operate or play it. ■ [*intr.*] (of two people or two or more things, typically ones of the same kind) come into contact with each other: *for a moment their fingers touched.* ■ cause (two or more things, typically ones of the same kind) to come into contact: *we touched wheels and nearly came off the road.* ■ *Geom.* be tangent to (a curve or surface) at a certain point. ■ *inf.* reach (a specified level or amount). ■ *inf.* be comparable to in quality or excellence: *there's no one who can touch him at lightweight judo.* **2** handle in order to manipulate, alter, or otherwise affect, esp. in an adverse way: *I didn't touch any of her stuff.* ■ cause harm to (someone): *I've got friends who'll pull strings—nobody will dare touch me.* ■ take some of (a store, esp. of money) for use: *in three years I haven't touched a cent of the money.* ■ consume a small amount of (food or drink): *the beer by his right hand was hardly touched.* ■ used to indicate that something is avoided or rejected: *he was good only for the jobs that nobody else would touch.* ■ (**touch someone for**) *inf.* ask someone for (money or some other commodity) as a loan or gift. **3** have an effect on; make a difference to. ■ be relevant to. ■ (of a quality or feature) be visible or apparent in the appearance or character of (something): *the trees were beginning to be touched by the colors of autumn.* ■ reach and affect the appearance of: *a wry smile touched his lips.* ■ (**touch something in**) *chiefly Art* lightly mark in features or other details with a brush or pencil. ■ produce feelings of affection, gratitude, or sympathy in: *she was touched by her friend's loyalty.* ■ [as *adj.*] (**touched**) *inf.* slightly insane.
▶*phrasal v.* □ **touch at** (of a ship or someone in it) call briefly at (a port). □ **touch down** (of an aircraft or spacecraft) make contact with the ground in landing. □ **touch something off** cause something to ignite or explode by touching it with a match. ■ cause something to happen, esp. suddenly. □ **touch on** (or **upon**) **1** deal briefly with (a subject) in written or spoken discussion. **2** come near to being. □ **touch something up** make small improvements to something.
▶*n.* **1** an act of bringing a part of one's body, typically one's hand, into contact with someone or something: *her touch on his shoulder.* ■ an act of lightly pressing or striking something in order to move or operate it: *you can manipulate images on the screen at the touch of a key.* ■ the faculty of perception through physical contact, esp. with the fingers: *reading by touch.* ■ a musician's manner of playing keys or strings. ■ the manner in which a musical instrument's keys or strings respond to being played: *Viennese instruments with their too delicate touch.* ■ a light stroke with a pen, pencil, etc. ■ *inf., dated* an act of asking for and getting money or some other commodity from someone as a loan or gift: *he was good for a touch now and then.* ■ *archaic* a thing or an action that tries out the worth or character of something; a test: *you must put your fate to the touch.* **2** a small amount; a trace. ■ a detail or feature, typically one that gives something a distinctive character. ■ a distinctive manner or method of dealing with something. ■ an ability to deal with something successfully: *getting caught looks so incompetent, as though we're losing our touch.* **3** *Bell-ringing* a series of changes shorter than a peal. —**touch·a·ble** *adj.* —**touch·er** *n.*
▶ □ **in touch** **1** in or into communication: *we need to keep in touch with the latest developments.* **2** possessing up-to-date knowledge: *we need to keep in touch with the latest developments.* ■ having an intuitive or empathetic awareness: *you need to be in touch with your feelings.* □ **lose touch** **1** cease to correspond or be in communication. **2** cease to be aware or informed: *we cannot lose touch with political reality.* □ **out of touch** lacking knowledge or information concerning current events and developments. ■ lacking in awareness or sympathy: *we have been betrayed by a government out of touch with our values.* □ **to the touch** used to describe the qualities of something perceived by touching it or the sensations felt by someone who is touched: *the silk was slightly rough to the touch.* □ **touch bottom** reach the bottom of a body of water with one's feet or a pole. ■ be at the lowest or worst point. □ **would not touch something with a ten-foot pole** *inf.* used to express a refusal to have anything to do with someone or something.

touch and go ▶*adj.* (of an outcome, esp. one that is desired) possible but very uncertain: *it was touch and go there for a while whether they would make it.*
▶*n.* (**touch-and-go**) (*pl.* **touch-and-goes**) a maneuver in which an aircraft touches the ground as in landing, and immediately takes off again.

touch·back /ˈtəCHˌbak/ ▶*n.* *Football* a ball one downs deliberately behind one's own goal line or that is kicked through one's end zone. It is taken to the 20-yard line to resume play.

---

touch·down /'təcʜ,doun/ ▸n. **1** the moment at which an aircraft's wheels or part of a spacecraft make contact with the ground during landing. **2** Football a six-point score made by carrying or passing the ball into the end zone of the opposing side, or by recovering it there following a fumble or blocked kick. ■ Rugby an act of touching the ground with the ball behind the opponents' goal line, scoring a try.

tou·ché /tōō'sʜā/ ▸interj. (in fencing) used as an acknowledgment of a hit by one's opponent. ■ used as an acknowledgment during a discussion of a good or clever point made at one's expense by another person.

touch foot·ball ▸n. a form of football in which a ball carrier is downed by touching instead of tackling.

touch·ing /'təcʜɪɴɢ/ ▸adj. arousing strong feelings of sympathy, appreciation, or gratitude.
▸prep. concerning; about: evidence touching the facts of Roger's case. —**touch·ing·ly** adv. —**touch·ing·ness** n.

touch-me-not ▸n. a plant (genus Impatiens) of the balsam family whose ripe seed capsules burst when touched, scattering seeds over some distance.

touch·point /'təcʜ,point/ ▸n. **1** Commerce any point of contact between a buyer and a seller. **2** Comput. on some laptop computers, a device like a miniature joystick with a rubber tip, manipulated with a finger to move the screen pointer. ■ a time, condition, or circumstance that is vulnerable or unstable enough to precipitate a highly unfavorable, possibly devastating outcome: so much remains to be done to take the fleeting opportunities there may be still in the Middle East to make it a safer and less terrible touchpoint for world conflagration. ■ Psychol. the time in a child's development that precedes an appreciable leap in physical, emotional, or cognitive growth. This phase is often associated with outbursts of uncharacteristic behavior.

touch screen (also **touch·screen**) ▸n. a display device that allows a user to interact with a computer by touching areas on the screen.

touch·stone /'təcʜ,stōn/ ▸n. a piece of fine-grained dark rock formerly used for testing alloys of gold by observing the color of the mark that they made on it. ■ a standard or criterion by which something is judged or recognized.

touch-tone (also **Touch-Tone**) ▸adj. (of a telephone) having push buttons and generating tones to dial rather than pulses. ■ (of a service) accessed or controlled by the tones generated by these telephones.
▸n. trademark a telephone of this type. ■ one of the set of tones generated by these telephones.

touch-type ▸v. [intr.] (often as n.] (touch-typing) type using all one's fingers and without looking at the keys. —**touch-typ·ist** n.

touch·y /'təcʜē/ ▸adj. (touch·i·er, touch·i·est) (of a person) oversensitive and irritable. ■ (of an issue or situation) requiring careful handling; delicate. —**touch·i·ly** /'təcʜəlē/ adv. —**touch·i·ness** n.

tough /təf/ ▸adj. **1** (of a substance or object) strong enough to withstand adverse conditions or rough or careless handling. ■ (of a person or animal) able to endure hardship or pain; physically robust. ■ able to protect one's own interests or maintain one's own opinions without being intimidated by opposition; confident and determined: she's both sensitive and tough. ■ demonstrating a strict and uncompromising attitude or approach. ■ (of a person) strong and prone to violence. ■ (of an area) notorious for violence and crime. ■ (of food, esp. meat) difficult to cut or chew. **2** involving considerable difficulty or hardship; requiring great determination or effort: he had a tough time getting into a good college. ■ used to express sympathy with someone in an unpleasant or difficult situation: Poor kid. It's tough on her. ■ [often as interj.] used to express a lack of sympathy with someone: I feel the way I feel, and if you don't like it, tough.
▸n. a tough person, esp. a gangster or criminal. —**tough·ish** adj. —**tough·ly** adv. —**tough·ness** n.
▸ □ **tough it out** inf. endure a period of hardship or difficulty.

tough·en /'təfən/ ▸v. make or become tougher: [tr.] he tried to toughen his son up by sending him to public school | [intr.] if removed from the oven too soon meringues shrink and toughen. ■ [tr.] make (rules or a policy) stricter and more harsh: new congressional efforts to toughen the laws. —**tough·en·er** n.

tou·pee /tōō'pā/ ▸n. a small wig or artificial hairpiece worn to cover a bald spot.

tour /tōōr/ ▸n. **1** a journey for pleasure in which several different places are visited: an airline tour of Alaska. ■ a short trip to or through a place in order to view or inspect something: a tour of the White House. **2** a journey made by performers or an athletic team, in which they perform or play in several different places: she joined the Royal Shakespeare Company on tour. ■ (the tour) (in golf, tennis, and other sports) the annual round of events in which top professionals compete. **3** (also **tour of duty**) a period of duty on military or diplomatic service.
▸v. [tr.] make a tour of (an area): he decided to tour France | [intr.] they had toured in a little minivan. ■ take (a performer, production, etc.) on tour. ▷Middle English (sense 3; also denoting a circular movement): from Old French, 'turn,' via Latin from Greek tornos 'lathe.' Sense 1 dates from the mid 17th cent.

tour de force /,tōōr də 'fôrs/ ▸n. (pl. **tours de force** pronunc. same or /'tōōrz/) an impressive performance or achievement that has been accomplished or managed with great skill: his novel is a tour de force.

tour·ism /'tōōr,izəm/ ▸n. the commercial organization and operation of vacations and visits to places of interest.

tour·ist /'tōōrist/ ▸n. a person who is traveling or visiting a place for pleasure.
▸v. [intr.] rare travel as a tourist: American families touristing abroad. —**tour·is·tic** /tōō'ristik/ adj. —**tour·is·ti·cal·ly** /tōō'ristik(ə)lē/ adv.

tour·ist class ▸n. the cheapest accommodations or seating for passengers in a ship, aircraft, or hotel.
▸adj. & adv. of, relating to, or by such accommodations or seating: [as adj.] a tourist-class hotel

tour·ma·line /'tōōrmələn; -,lēn/ ▸n. a brittle typically black or blackish opaque aluminosilicate mineral that has pyroelectric and polarizing properties, and is used in electrical and optical instruments. Its colorful transparent varieties are used as gemstones.

tour·na·ment /'tərnəmənt; 'tōōr-/ ▸n. **1** (in a sport or game) a series of contests between a number of competitors, who compete for an overall prize. **2** (in the Middle Ages) a sporting event in which two knights (or two groups of knights) jousted on horseback with blunted weapons, each trying to knock the other off.

tour·ne·dos /'tōōrnə,dō/ ▸n. (pl. same) a small round thick cut from a fillet of beef.

tour·ney /'tərnē; 'tōōr-/ ▸n. (pl. **-neys**) a tournament.
▸v. (**-neys, -neyed**) [intr.] take part in a tournament.

tour·ni·quet /'tərnikit; 'tōōr-/ ▸n. a device for stopping the flow of blood through an artery, typically by compressing a limb with a cord or tight bandage.

tou·sle /'touzəl/ ▸v. [tr.] make (something, esp. a person's hair) untidy.
▸n. an act of tousling something, esp. hair. ■ a tousled mass, esp. of hair: he'd gently brush back my tousle.

tout[1] /tout/ ▸v. **1** [tr.] attempt to sell (something), typically by pestering people in an aggressive or bold manner. ■ (often **be touted**) attempt to persuade people of the merits of (someone or something): the facility was touted as the best. **2** [intr.] offer racing tips for a share of any resulting winnings. ■ [tr.] chiefly Brit. spy out the movements and condition of (a racehorse in training) in order to gain information to be used when betting.
▸n. **1** a person soliciting custom or business, typically in an aggressive or bold manner. **2** a person who offers racing tips for a share of any resulting winnings. —**tout·er** n.

tout[2] /tōō/ ▸adj. (often **le tout**) used before the name of a city to refer to its high society or people of importance: le tout Washington adored him.

tow[1] /tō/ ▸v. [tr.] (of a motor vehicle or boat) pull (another vehicle or boat) along with a rope, chain, or tow bar. ■ (of a person) pull (someone or something) along behind one.
▸n. an act of towing a vehicle or boat. ■ a rope or line used to tow a vehicle or boat. —**tow·a·ble** adj.
▸ □ **in tow 1** being towed by another vehicle or boat. **2** accompanying or following someone: trying to shop with three children in tow.

tow[2] ▸n. the coarse and broken part of flax or hemp prepared for spinning. ■ a bundle of untwisted natural or man-made fibers. —**tow·y** adj.

to·ward /tôrd; t(ə)'wôrd/ ▸prep. (also **to·wards**) **1** in the direction of: I walked toward the door. ■ getting closer to achieving (a goal): a move toward freedom. ■ close or closer to (a particular time): toward the end of April. **2** as regards; in relation to: our attitude toward death. ■ paying homage to, esp. in a superficial or insincere way: he gave a nod toward the good work done by the fund. **3** contributing to the cost of (something): the council provided a grant toward the cost of new buses.

tow·el /'toul/ ▸n. a piece of thick absorbent cloth or paper used for drying oneself or wiping things dry.
▸v. (**-eled, -el·ing**; Brit. **-elled, -el·ling**) [tr.] wipe or dry (a person or thing) with a towel: [tr.] she toweled her hair dry | [intr.] quickly we'd towel off and dress for dinner.

tow·er /'tou(-ə)r/ ▸n. **1** a tall narrow building, either freestanding or forming part of a building such as a church or castle. ■ a tall structure that houses machinery, operators, etc. ■ a tall structure used as a receptacle or for storage: *a CD tower.* ■ a tall pile or mass of something. **2** a place of defense; a protection.

▶*v.* [*intr.*] **1** rise to or reach a great height: *he seemed to **tower over** everyone else.* **2** (of a bird) soar to a great height, esp. (of a falcon) so as to be able to swoop down on the quarry. **—tow·ered** *adj.* (*chiefly poetic/lit.*).

tow·head /'tō,hed/ ▶*n.* a head of tow-colored or very blond hair. ■ a person with such hair. **—tow·head·ed** *adj.*

town /toun/ ▶*n.* an urban area that has a name, defined boundaries, and local government, and that is larger than a village and generally smaller than a city. ■ the particular town under consideration, esp. one's own town: *Carson was **in town**.* ■ the central part of a neighborhood, with its business or shopping area: *Rachel left to drive back **into town**.* ■ a densely populated area, esp. as contrasted with the country or suburbs. ■ a town's community: *the whole town is talking about it.* ■ the permanent residents of a college town as distinct from the members of the college. ■ another term for TOWNSHIP (sense 3). ▷Old English *tūn* 'enclosed piece of land, homestead, village,' of Germanic origin; related to Dutch *tuin* 'garden' and German *Zaun* 'fence.'

▶ □ **go to town** *inf.* do something thoroughly, enthusiastically, or extravagantly. □ **on the town** *inf.* enjoying the entertainments, esp. the nightlife, of a city or town: *a lot of guys out for **a night on the town**.*

town clerk ▶*n.* a public official in charge of the records of a town.

town cri·er ▶*n. hist.* a person employed to make public announcements in the streets or marketplace of a town.

town hall ▶*n.* a building used for the administration of local government.

town·ie /'tounē/ ▶*n.* a person who lives in a town (used esp. with reference to their supposed lack of familiarity with rural affairs). ■ a resident in a college town, rather than a student.

town·scape /'toun,skāp/ ▶*n.* the visual appearance of a town or urban area; an urban landscape. ■ a picture of a town.

town·ship /'toun,SHip/ ▶*n.* **1** a division of a county with some corporate powers. ■ a district six miles square. **2** (in South Africa) a suburb or city of predominantly black occupation, formerly officially designated for black occupation by apartheid legislation.

towns·peo·ple /'tounz,pēpəl/ (also **towns·folk** /-,fōk/) ▶*pl. n.* the people living in a particular town or city.

tox·e·mi·a /täk'sēmēə/ ▶*n.* blood poisoning by toxins from a local bacterial infection. ■ (also **toxemia of pregnancy**) another term for PREECLAMPSIA. **—tox·e·mic** /-'sēmik/ *adj.*

tox·ic /'täksik/ ▶*adj.* poisonous: *the dumping of toxic waste.* ■ of or relating to poison: *toxic hazards.* ■ caused by poison: *toxic liver injury.*

▶*n.* (**toxics**) poisonous substances. **—tox·i·cal·ly** /-sik(ə)lē/ *adv.* **—tox·ic·i·ty** /täk'sisitē/ *n.*

tox·i·col·o·gy /,täksi'käləjē/ ▶*n.* the branch of science concerned with the nature, effects, and detection of poisons. **—tox·i·co·log·ic** /-kə'läjik/ *adj.* **—tox·i·co·log·i·cal** /-kə'läjikəl/ *adj.* **—tox·i·co·log·i·cal·ly** *adv.* **—tox·i·col·o·gist** /-'kälejist/ *n.*

tox·in /'täksin/ ▶*n.* an antigenic poison or venom of plant or animal origin, esp. one produced by or derived from microorganisms and causing disease when present at low concentration in the body.

toy /toi/ ▶*n.* **1** an object for a child to play with, typically a model or miniature replica of something: [as *adj.*] *a toy car.* ■ an object, esp. a gadget or machine, regarded as providing amusement for an adult: *in 1914 the car was still a rich man's toy.* ■ a person treated by another as a source of pleasure or amusement rather than with due seriousness: *a man needed a friend, an ally, not an idol or a toy.* **2** [as *adj.*] denoting a diminutive breed or variety of dog: *a toy poodle.* **—toy·like** /-,līk/ *adj.*

▶*phrasal v.* □ **toy with** **1** consider (an idea, movement, or proposal) casually or indecisively. ■ treat (someone) without due seriousness, esp. in a superficially amorous way. **2** move or handle (an object) absentmindedly or nervously. ■ eat or drink in an unenthusiastic or restrained way.

toy·book /'toi,bŏŏk/ ▶*n.* a children's book with features that enable it to be played with as well as read.

tp. ▶*abbr.* ■ township. ■ troop.

trace¹ /trās/ ▶*v.* [*tr.*] **1** find or discover by investigation: *police are trying to trace a white van seen in the area.* ■ find or describe the origin or development of: *Bob's book traces his flying career with the Marines.* ■ follow or mark the course or position of (something) with one's eye, mind, or finger: *through the binoculars, I traced the path I had taken the night before.* ■ take (a particular path or route): *a tear traced a lonely path down her cheek.* **2** copy (a drawing, map, or design) by drawing over its lines on a superimposed piece of transparent paper. ■ draw (a pattern or line), esp. with one's finger or toe. ■ give an outline of: *the article **traces out** some of the connections between education, qualifications, and the labor market.*

▶*n.* **1** a mark, object, or other indication of the existence or passing of something: *remove all traces of the old adhesive* | *the aircraft disappeared without trace.* ■ a beaten path or small road; a track. ■ a physical change in the brain presumed to be caused by a process of learning and memory. ■ a procedure to investigate the source of something, such as the place from which a telephone call was made, or the origin of an error in a computer program. **2** a very small quantity, esp. one too small to be accurately measured: *his body contained traces of amphetamines* [as *adj.*] *trace quantities of PCBs.* ■ a slight indication or barely discernible hint of something: *just a trace of a smile.* **3** a line or pattern displayed by an instrument using a moving pen or a luminous spot on a screen to show the existence or nature of something that is being investigated. ■ a line that represents the projection of a curve or surface on a plane or the intersection of a curve or surface with a plane. **4** *Math.* the sum of the elements in the principle diagonal of a square matrix. **—trace·a·bil·i·ty** /,trāsə'bilitē/ *n.* **—trace·a·ble** *adj.* **—trace·less** *adj.*

trace² ▶*n.* each of the two side straps, chains, or ropes by which a horse is attached to a vehicle that it is pulling.

trace el·e·ment ▶*n.* a chemical element present only in minute amounts in a particular sample or environment. ■ a chemical element required only in minute amounts by living organisms for normal growth.

trace min·er·al ▶*n.* a trace element required for nutrition.

trac·er /'trāsər/ ▶*n.* a person or thing that traces something or by which something may be traced, in particular: ■ a projectile whose course is made visible in flight by a trail of flames or smoke, used to assist in aiming. ■ a substance introduced into a biological organism or other system so that its subsequent distribution can be readily followed from its color, fluorescence, radioactivity, or other distinctive property. ■ a device that transmits a signal and so can be located when attached to a moving vehicle or other object.

trac·er·y /'trāsərē/ ▶*n.* (pl. **-er·ies**) *Archit.* ornamental stone openwork, typically in the upper part of a Gothic window. ■ a delicate branching pattern: *a tracery of red veins.* **—trac·er·ied** *adj.*

tra·che·a /'trākēə/ ▶*n.* (pl. **-che·ae** /-kē,ē/ or **-che·as**) *Anat.* a large membranous tube reinforced by rings of cartilage, extending from the larynx to the bronchial tubes and conveying air to and from the lungs; the windpipe. ■ *Entomol.* each of a number of fine chitinous tubes in the body of an insect, conveying air directly to the tissues. **—tra·che·al** *adj.* **—tra·che·ate** /-it, -,āt/ *adj.*

tra·che·id /'trākēid/ ▶*n. Bot.* a type of water-conducting cell in the xylem that lacks perforations in the cell wall.

tra·che·ot·o·my /,trākē'ätəmē/ (also **tra·che·os·to·my** /-'ästəmē/) ▶*n.* (pl. **-mies**) *Med.* an incision in the windpipe made to relieve an obstruction to breathing.

tra·cho·ma /trə'kōmə/ ▶*n.* a contagious bacterial infection of the eye in which there is inflamed granulation on the inner surface of the lids. ▷late 17th cent.: from Greek *trakhōma* 'roughness,' from *trakhus* 'rough.' **—tra·chom·a·tous** /-mətəs/ *adj.*

trac·ing /'trāsiNG/ ▶*n.* a copy of a drawing, map, or design made by tracing it. ■ a faint or delicate mark or pattern: *tracings of apple blossoms against the deep greens of pines.* ■ *Figure Skating* the marking out of a figure on the ice when skating.

track /trak/ ▶*n.* **1** a rough path or minor road, typically one beaten by use rather than constructed: *follow the track to the farm.* ■ a prepared course or circuit for athletes, horses, motor vehicles, bicycles, or dogs to race on. ■ the sport of running on such a track. ■ (usu. **tracks**) a mark or line of marks left by a person, animal, or vehicle in passing. ■ the course or route followed by someone or something (used esp. in talking about their pursuit by others): *I didn't want the Russians **on my track**.* ■ *fig.* a course of action; a way of proceeding. **2** a continuous line of rails on a railroad. ■ a metal or plastic strip or rail from which a curtain or spotlight may be hung or fitted. ■ a continuous articulated band of metal plates around the wheels of a heavy vehicle such as a tank or bulldozer, intended to facilitate movement over rough or soft ground. **3** a section of a record, compact disc, or cassette tape containing one song or piece of music. ■ a lengthwise strip of magnetic tape containing one sequence of signals. ■ the soundtrack of a film or video. **4** the transverse distance between a vehicle's wheels. **5** a group in which schoolchildren of the same age and ability are taught.

▶*v.* [*tr.*] **1** follow the course or trail of (someone or something), typically in order to find them or note their location at various points: *he*

---

tracked Anna to her room. ■ *fig.* follow and note the course or progress of: *they are tracking the girth and evolution of stars.* ■ [*intr.*] follow a particular course: *the storm was tracking across the ground at 30 mph.* ■ [*intr.*] (of a film or television camera) move in relation to the subject being filmed. ■ (**track something up**) leave a trail of dirty footprints on a surface. ■ (**track something in**) leave a trail of dirt, debris, or snow from one's feet. **2** [*intr.*] (of wheels) run so that the back ones are exactly in the track of the front ones. **3** assign (a student) to a course of study according to ability.
▸*phrasal v.* ▢ **track someone/something down** find someone or something after a thorough or difficult search.
▸ ▢ **in one's tracks** *inf.* where one or something is at that moment; suddenly: *Turner immediately stopped dead in his tracks.* ▢ **keep** (or **lose**) **track of** keep (or fail to keep) fully aware of or informed about. ▢ **make tracks (for)** *inf.* leave hurriedly (for a place). ▢ **off the track** departing from the right course of thinking or behavior. ▢ **on the right** (or **wrong**) **track** acting or thinking in a way that is likely to result in success (or failure). ▢ **on track** acting or thinking in a way that is likely to achieve what is required: *formulas for keeping the economy on track.* ▢ **the wrong** (or **right**) **side of the tracks** *inf.* a poor, less prestigious (or wealthy, prestigious) part of town.

track and field ▸*n.* athletic events that take place on a running track and a nearby field; track events and field events.

track·ing /ˈtrakiNG/ ▸*n.* **1** the action of tracking someone or something. ■ *Electr.* the maintenance of a constant difference in frequency between two or more connected circuits or components. ■ the alignment of the wheels of a vehicle. ■ a control in a videocassette recorder that electronically adjusts the manner in which the head receives signals from the videotape, providing a clearer playback. **2** the practice of putting schoolchildren in groups of the same age and ability to be taught together.

track·ing sta·tion ▸*n.* a place from which the movements of missiles, aircraft, or satellites are tracked by radar or radio.

track·less /ˈtrakləs/ ▸*adj.* **1** (of land) having no paths or tracks on it: *leading travelers into trackless wastelands.* ■ *poetic/lit.* not leaving a track or trace. **2** (of a vehicle or component) not running on a track or tracks.

track rec·ord ▸*n.* the best recorded performance in a particular track-and-field event at a particular track. ■ the past achievements or performance of a person, organization, or product.

track shoe ▸*n.* a running shoe.

tract[1] /trakt/ ▸*n.* **1** an area of indefinite extent, typically a large one: *large tracts of natural forest.* ■ *poetic/lit.* an indefinitely large extent of something: *vast tracts of time.* **2** a major passage in the body, large bundle of nerve fibers, or other continuous elongated anatomical structure or region: *the digestive tract.*

tract[2] ▸*n.* a short treatise in pamphlet form, typically on a religious subject.

trac·ta·ble /ˈtraktəbəl/ ▸*adj.* (of a person or animal) easy to control or influence. ■ (of a situation or problem) easy to deal with. —**trac·ta·bil·i·ty** /ˌtraktəˈbilitē/ *n.* —**trac·ta·bly** /-blē/ *adv.*

trac·tion /ˈtraksHən/ ▸*n.* **1** the action of drawing or pulling a thing over a surface, esp. a road or track: *a primitive vehicle used in animal traction.* ■ motive power provided for such movement, esp. on a railroad: *the changeover to diesel and electric traction.* ■ locomotives collectively. **2** *Med.* the application of a sustained pull on a limb or muscle, esp. in order to maintain the position of a fractured bone or to correct a deformity: *his leg is in traction.* **3** the grip of a tire on a road or a wheel on a rail: *his car hit a patch of ice and lost traction.*

trac·tor /ˈtraktər/ ▸*n.* a powerful motor vehicle with large rear wheels, used chiefly on farms for hauling equipment and trailers. ■ a short truck consisting of the driver's cab, designed to pull a large trailer.

trac·tor-trail·er ▸*n.* a transport vehicle consisting of a semi-tractor and attached trailer.

trade /trād/ ▸*n.* **1** the action of buying and selling goods and services: *a significant increase in foreign trade.* ■ *dated, chiefly derog.* the practice of making one's living in business, as opposed to in a profession or from unearned income: *the aristocratic classes were contemptuous of those in trade.* ■ (in sports) a transfer; an exchange. **2** a skilled job, typically one requiring manual skills and special training: *the fundamentals of the construction trade.* ■ (**the trade**) [treated as *sing.* or *pl.*] the people engaged in a particular area of business: *in the trade this sort of computer is called "a client-based system."* ■ *inf.* a person in gay male sexual encounters who is not penetrated sexually and usually considers himself to be heterosexual. **3** (usu. **trades**) a trade wind.
▸*v.* [*intr.*] buy and sell goods and services: *middlemen trading in luxury goods.* ■ [*tr.*] buy or sell (a particular item or product): *she has traded*

millions of dollars' worth of metals. ■ (esp. of shares or currency) be bought and sold at a specified price: *the dollar was trading where it was in January.* ■ [*tr.*] exchange (something) for something else, typically as a commercial transaction: *they trade shark livers for fish oil* | *the hostages were traded for arms.* ■ [*tr.*] *fig.* give and receive (typically insults or blows). ■ [*tr.*] transfer (a player) to another club or team.
▸*phrasal v.* ▢ **trade down** (or **up**) sell something in order to buy something similar but less (or more) expensive. ▢ **trade something in** exchange a used article in part payment for another. ▢ **trade something off** exchange something of value, esp. as part of a compromise: *the government traded off economic advantages for political gains.* ▢ **trade on** take advantage of (something), esp. in an unfair way: *the government is trading on fears of inflation.* —**trad·a·ble** (or **trade·a·ble**) *adj.*

trade def·i·cit ▸*n.* the amount by which the cost of a country's imports exceeds the value of its exports.

trad·ed op·tion ▸*n. Finance* an option on a stock exchange or futures exchange which can itself be bought and sold.

trade-in ▸*n.* [usu. as *adj.*] a used article accepted by a retailer in partial payment for another: *the trade-in value of the old car.*

trade jour·nal (also **trade magazine**) ▸*n.* a periodical containing news and items of interest concerning a particular trade.

trade·mark /ˈtrādˌmärk/ ▸*n.* a symbol, word, or words legally registered or established by use as representing a company or product. ■ *fig.* a distinctive characteristic or object: *it had all the trademarks of a Mafia hit.*
▸*v.* [*tr.*] [usu. as *adj.*] (**trademarked**) provide with a trademark. ■ *fig.* identify (a habit, quality, or way of life) as typical of someone.

trade name ▸*n.* **1** a name that has the status of a trademark. **2** a name by which something is known in a particular trade or profession.

trade-off ▸*n.* a balance achieved between two desirable but incompatible features; a compromise: *a trade-off between objectivity and relevance.*

trad·er /ˈtrādər/ ▸*n.* a person who buys and sells goods, currency, or stocks. ■ a merchant ship.

trade se·cret ▸*n.* a secret device or technique used by a company in manufacturing its products.

trades·man /ˈtrādzmən/ ▸*n.* (*pl.* **-men**) a person engaged in trading or a trade, typically on a relatively small scale.

trade un·ion ▸*n.* an organized association of workers in a trade, group of trades, or profession, formed to protect and further their rights and interests.

trade wind /wind/ ▸*n.* a wind blowing steadily toward the equator from the northeast in the northern hemisphere or the southeast in the southern hemisphere, esp. at sea.

trad·ing /ˈtrādiNG/ ▸*n.* the action of engaging in trade.

trad·ing post ▸*n.* a store or small settlement established for trading, typically in a remote place.

trad·ing stamp ▸*n.* a stamp given by some stores to a customer according to the amount spent, and exchangeable in the appropriate number for various articles.

tra·di·tion /trəˈdisHən/ ▸*n.* **1** the transmission of customs or beliefs from generation to generation, or the fact of being passed on in this way: *every shade of color is fixed by tradition and governed by religious laws.* ■ a long-established custom or belief that has been passed on in this way: *Japan's unique cultural traditions.* ■ an artistic or literary method or style established by an artist, writer, or movement, and subsequently followed by others: *visionary works in the tradition of William Blake.* **2** *Theol.* a doctrine believed to have divine authority though not in the scriptures, in particular: ■ (in Christianity) doctrine not explicit in the Bible but held to derive from the oral teaching of Jesus and the Apostles. ■ (in Judaism) an ordinance of the oral law not in the Torah but held to have been given by God to Moses. ■ (in Islam) a saying or act ascribed to the Prophet but not recorded in the Koran. See **Hadith**.
▷late Middle English: from Old French *tradicion*, or from Latin *traditio(n-)*, from *tradere* 'deliver, betray,' from *trans-* 'across' + *dare* 'give.' —**tra·di·tion·ist** /-nist/ *n.*

tra·di·tion·al /trəˈdisHənl/ ▸*adj.* existing in or as part of a tradition; long-established: *the traditional festivities of the church year.* ■ produced, done, or used in accordance with tradition: *a traditional fish soup.* ■ habitually done, used, or found: *the traditional drinks in the clubhouse.* ■ (of a person or group) adhering to tradition, or to a particular tradition. ■ (of jazz) in the style of the early 20th century. —**tra·di·tion·al·ly** *adv.*

tra·di·tion·al·ism /trəˈdisHənlˌizəm/ ▸*n.* the upholding or maintenance of tradition, esp. so as to resist change. ■ *chiefly hist.* the theory that all moral and religious truth comes from divine revelation passed on by tradition, human reason being incapable of attaining it. —**tra·di·tion·al·ist** *n.* & *adj.* —**tra·di·tion·al·is·tic** /trəˌdisHənlˈistik/ *adj.*

T

tra·duce /trəˈd(y) o͞os/ ▶ v. [tr.] speak badly of or tell lies about (someone) so as to damage their reputation. —**tra·duce·ment** n. —**tra·duc·er** n.

traf·fic /ˈtrafik/ ▶ n. **1** vehicles moving on a road or public highway: *a stream of heavy traffic.* ■ a large number of such vehicles. ■ the movement of other forms of transportation or of pedestrians: *managing the air traffic.* ■ the transportation of goods or passengers. ■ the messages or signals transmitted through a communications system: *data traffic between remote workstations.* **2** the action of dealing or trading in something illegal: *the traffic in stolen cattle.* **3** archaic dealings or communication between people.
▶ v. (**-ficked, -fick·ing**) [intr.] deal or trade in something illegal: *the government will vigorously pursue individuals who traffic in drugs.* —**traf·fic·er** n. —**traf·fic·less** adj.

traf·fic cir·cle ▶ n. a road junction at which traffic moves in one direction around a central island.

traf·fic jam ▶ n. road traffic at or near a standstill because of road construction, an accident, or heavy congestion.

traf·fic light (also **traffic signal**) ▶ n. a set of automatically operated colored lights, typically red, amber, and green, for controlling traffic at road junctions and crosswalks.

tra·ge·di·an /trəˈjēdēən/ ▶ n. an actor who specializes in tragic roles. ■ a writer of tragedies.

tra·ge·di·enne /trə͟ˌjēdēˈen/ ▶ n. an actress who specializes in tragic roles.

trag·e·dy /ˈtrajidē/ ▶ n. (pl. **-dies**) **1** an event causing great suffering, destruction, and distress, such as a serious accident, crime, or natural catastrophe: **2** a play dealing with tragic events and having an unhappy ending, esp. one concerning the downfall of the main character. ■ the dramatic genre represented by such plays: *Greek tragedy.* Compare with COMEDY.

trag·ic /ˈtrajik/ ▶ adj. causing or characterized by extreme distress or sorrow: *the shooting was a tragic accident.* ■ suffering extreme distress or sorrow: *the tragic parents reached the end of their tether.* ■ of or relating to tragedy in a literary work. —**trag·i·cal** adj. —**trag·i·cal·ly** /-ik(ə)lē/ adv.
trag·ic i·ro·ny ▶ n. see IRONY[1].

trag·i·com·e·dy /ˌtrajəˈkämidē/ ▶ n. (pl. **-dies**) a play or novel containing elements of both comedy and tragedy. ■ such works as a genre. —**trag·i·com·ic** /-ˈkämik/ adj. —**trag·i·com·i·cal·ly** /-ˈkämik(ə)lē/ adv.

trail /trāl/ ▶ n. **1** a mark or a series of signs or objects left behind by the passage of someone or something: *a trail of blood.* ■ a track or scent used in following someone or hunting an animal: *police followed his trail to Atlantic City.* ■ a part, typically long and thin, stretching behind or hanging down from someone or something: *trails of ivy.* ■ a line of people or things following behind each other: *a trail of ants.* **2** a beaten path through rough country such as a forest or moor. ■ a route planned or followed for a particular purpose: *a Democratic candidate on the campaign trail.* ■ a downhill ski run or cross-country ski route.
▶ v. **1** draw or be drawn along the ground or other surface behind someone or something: [tr.] *Alex trailed a hand through the clear water* | [intr.] *her robe trailed along the ground.* ■ [intr.] (typically of a plant) grow or hang over the edge of something or along the ground. ■ [tr.] follow (a person or animal), typically by using marks, signs, or scent left behind. ■ [intr.] be losing to an opponent in a game or contest. **2** [intr.] walk or move slowly or wearily: *she trailed behind, whimpering at intervals.* ■ (of the voice or a speaker) fade gradually before stopping: *her voice trailed away.*

trail·blaz·er /ˈtrālˌblāzər/ ▶ n. a person who makes a new track through wild country. ■ a pioneer; an innovator: *he was a trailblazer for many ideas that are now standard fare.* —**trail·blaz·ing** /-ˌblāziNG/ n. & adj.

trail·er /ˈtrālər/ ▶ n. **1** an unpowered vehicle towed by another, in particular: ■ the rear section of a tractor-trailer. ■ an open cart. ■ a platform for transporting a boat. ■ an unpowered vehicle equipped for living in, typically used during vacations. **2** an excerpt or series of excerpts from a movie or program used to advertise it, esp. in advance. **3** a thing that trails, esp. a trailing plant.
▶ v. [tr.] transport (something) by trailer.

trail·er park (also **trailer court**) ▶ n. an area with special amenities where trailers are parked and used for recreation or as permanent homes.

train /trān/ ▶ v. **1** [tr.] teach (a person or animal) a particular skill or type of behavior through practice and instruction over a period of time. ■ [intr.] be taught in such a way: *he trained as a flight engineer.* ■ cause (a mental or physical faculty) to be sharp, discerning, or developed as a result of instruction or practice. ■ cause (a plant) to grow in a particular direction or into a required shape. ■ [intr.] undertake a course of exercise and diet in order to maintain or reach a high level of physical fitness, typically in preparation for participating in a specific sport or event: *she trains three times a week.* ■ cause to undertake such a course of exercise: *the horse was trained in Paris.* **2** [tr.] (**train something on**) point or aim something, typically a gun or camera, at. **3** [intr.] dated go by train. **4** [tr.] archaic entice (someone) by offering pleasure or a reward.
▶ n. **1** a series of railroad cars moved as a unit by a locomotive or by integral motors. **2** a succession of vehicles or pack animals traveling in the same direction: *a camel train.* ■ a retinue of attendants accompanying an important person. ■ a series of connected events: *you may be setting in motion a train of events that will cause harm.* ■ a series of gears or other connected parts in machinery. **3** a long piece of material attached to the back of a formal dress or robe that trails along the ground. **4** a trail of gunpowder for firing an explosive charge. —**train·a·bil·i·ty** /ˌtrānəˈbilitē/ n. —**train·a·ble** adj.
▶ □ **in someone/something's train** (or **in the train of**) following behind someone or something. ■ fig. as a sequel or consequence: *unemployment brings great difficulties in its train.* □ **train of thought** the way in which someone reaches a conclusion; a line of reasoning.

train·ee /trāˈnē/ ▶ n. a person undergoing training for a particular job or profession. —**train·ee·ship** /-ˌSHip/ n.

train·er /ˈtrānər/ ▶ n. **1** a person who trains people or animals. ■ inf. an aircraft or simulator used to train pilots. **2** a person whose job is to provide medical assistance to athletes. **3** Brit. a soft shoe, suitable for sports or casual wear.

train·ing /ˈtrāniNG/ ▶ n. the action of teaching a person or animal a particular skill or type of behavior. ■ the action of undertaking a course of exercise and diet in preparation for a sporting event.
▶ □ **in** (or **out of**) **training** undergoing (or no longer undergoing) physical training for a sporting event. ■ physically fit (or unfit) as a result of the amount of training one has undertaken.

train·man /ˈtrānmən; -ˌman/ ▶ n. (pl. **-men**) a railroad employee who works on trains.

traipse /trāps/ ▶ v. [intr.] walk or move wearily or reluctantly: *students had to traipse all over Washington to attend lectures.* ■ walk about casually or needlessly: *there's people traipsing in and out all the time.*
▶ n. **1** a tedious or tiring journey on foot. **2** archaic a slovenly woman.

trait /trāt/ ▶ n. a distinguishing quality or characteristic, typically one belonging to a person. ■ a genetically determined characteristic. ▷mid 16th cent.: from French, from Latin *tractus* 'drawing, pulling,' from *trahere* 'draw, pull.' An early sense was 'stroke of the pen or pencil in a picture,' giving rise to the sense 'a particular feature of mind or character' (mid 18th cent.).

trai·tor /ˈtrātər/ ▶ n. a person who betrays a friend, country, principle, etc. —**trai·tor·ous** /-tərəs/ adj. —**trai·tor·ous·ly** adv.
▶ □ **turn traitor** betray a group or person.

tra·jec·to·ry /trəˈjektərē/ ▶ n. (pl. **-ries**) **1** the path described by a projectile flying or an object moving under the action of given forces. **2** Geom. a curve or surface cutting a family of curves or surfaces at a constant angle.

tram /tram/ (also **tram·car** /-ˌkär/) ▶ n. **1** Brit. a trolley car. **2** a cable car.

tram·mel /ˈtraməl/ ▶ n. **1** (usu. **trammels**) poetic/lit. a restriction or impediment to someone's freedom of action. **2** (also **trammel net**) a fishing net consisting of three layers of netting, designed so that a fish entering through one of the large-meshed outer sections will push part of the finer-meshed central section through the large meshes on the further side, forming a pocket in which the fish is trapped.
▶ v. (**-meled, -mel·ing**; Brit. **-melled, -mel·ling**) [tr.] deprive of freedom of action: *those less trammeled by convention than himself.*

tramp /tramp/ ▶ v. [intr.] walk heavily or noisily: *he tramped around the room.* ■ walk through or over a place wearily or reluctantly and for long distances: *we have tramped miles over mountain and moorland.* ■ [tr.] tread or stamp on: *one of the few wines still tramped by foot.*
▶ n. **1** a person who travels from place to place on foot in search of work or as a vagrant or beggar. **2** the sound of heavy steps, typically of several people. **3** a long walk, typically a tiring one. **4** [usu. as adj.] a cargo vessel that carries goods among many different ports rather than sailing a fixed route: *a tramp steamer.* **5** inf. a promiscuous woman. **6** a metal plate protecting the sole of a boot. ■ the top of the blade of a spade. —**tramp·er** n. —**tramp·ish** adj.

tram·ple /ˈtrampəl/ ▶ v. [tr.] tread on and crush: *the fence had been trampled*

Pronunciation Key ə *ago,* up; ər *over, fur;* a *hat;* ā *ate;* ä *car;* CH *chin;* e *let;* ē *see;* e(ə)r *air;* i *fit;* ī *by;* i(ə)r *ear;* NG *sing;* ō *go;* ô *law, for;* oi *toy;* o͞o *good;* o͞o *goo;* ou *out;* SH *she;* TH *thin;* TH *then;* (h)w *why;* ZH *vision*

down | [*intr.*] *her dog* trampled on *his tulips.* ■ [*intr.*] (**trample on/over**) *fig.* treat with contempt.
▶*n. poetic/lit.* an act or sound of trampling. —**tram·pler** /-p(ə)lər/ *n.*

tram·po·line /'trampə,lēn/ ▶*n.* a strong fabric sheet connected by springs to a frame, used as a springboard and landing area in doing acrobatic or gymnastic exercises.
▶*v.* [*intr.*] do acrobatic or gymnastic exercises on a trampoline as a recreation or sport. ■ [*intr.*] leap or rebound from something with a springy base. ▷late 18th cent.: from Italian *trampolino,* from *trampoli* 'stilts.' —**tram·po·lin·er** *n.* —**tram·po·lin·ist** /-nist/ *n.*

trance /trans/ ▶*n.* a half-conscious state characterized by an absence of response to external stimuli, typically as induced by hypnosis or entered by a medium: *she put him into a light trance.* ■ a state of abstraction: *the kind of trance he went into whenever illness was discussed.* ■ (also **trance music**) a type of electronic dance music characterized by hypnotic rhythms and sounds.
▶*v.* [*tr.*] *poetic/lit.* put into a trance: *she's been tranced and may need waking.* —**tranced·ly** /'transtlē; 'transid-/ *adv.* —**trance·like** /-,līk/ *adj.*

tran·quil /'traNGkwəl/ ▶*adj.* free from disturbance; calm: *her tranquil gaze.* —**tran·quil·i·ty** /,traNG'kwilitē/ (also **tran·quil·li·ty**) *n.* —**tran·quil·ly** *adv.*

tran·quil·ize /'traNGkwə,līz/ (*Brit.* **tran·quil·lize**) ▶*v.* [*tr.*] (of a drug) have a calming or sedative effect on. ■ administer such a drug to (a person or animal): *the stray elk was tranquilized and relocated.* ■ *poetic/lit.* make tranquil: *joys that tranquilize the mind.*

tran·quil·iz·er /'traNGkwə,līzər/ (*Brit.* **tran·quil·liz·er**) ▶*n.* a medicinal drug taken to reduce tension or anxiety.

trans /tranz; trans/ ▶*adj. Chem.* denoting or relating to a molecular structure in which two particular atoms or groups lie on opposite sides of a given plane in the molecule.

trans. ▶*abbr.* ■ transaction; transactions. ■ transfer. ■ transferred. ■ transformer. ■ transit. ■ transitive. ■ translated. ■ translation. ■ translator. ■ transparent. ■ transportation. ■ transverse.

trans·act /tran'sakt; -'zakt/ ▶*v.* [*tr.*] conduct or carry out (business). —**trans·ac·tor** /-tər/ *n.*

trans·ac·tion /tran'saksHən; -'zak-/ ▶*n.* an instance of buying or selling something; a business deal: *in an ordinary commercial transaction a delivery date is essential.* ■ the action of conducting business. ■ an exchange or interaction between people: *intellectual transactions in the classroom.* ■ (**transactions**) published reports of proceedings at the meetings of a learned society. ■ an input message to a computer system that must be dealt with as a single unit of work. —**trans·ac·tion·al** /-sHənl/ *adj.* —**trans·ac·tion·al·ly** /-sHənl-ē/ *adv.*

trans·al·pine /trans'alpīn; tranz-/ ▶*adj.* of, related to, or situated in the area beyond the Alps, in particular as viewed from Italy. ■ crossing the Alps: *transalpine road freight.*

trans·at·lan·tic /,transət'lantik; ,tranz-/ ▶*adj.* crossing the Atlantic: *a transatlantic flight.* ■ concerning countries on both sides of the Atlantic: *the transatlantic relationship.* ■ of, relating to, or situated on the other side of the Atlantic; British or European (from an American point of view). —**trans·at·lan·ti·cal·ly** /-ik(ə)lē/ *adv.*

trans·ax·le /trans'aksəl; tranz-/ ▶*n.* an integral driving axle and differential gear in a motor vehicle.

tran·scend /tran'send/ ▶*v.* [*tr.*] be or go beyond the range or limits of (something abstract, typically a conceptual field or division): *an issue transcending party politics.* ■ surpass (a person or an achievement).

tran·scen·dent /tran'sendənt/ ▶*adj.* beyond or above the range of normal or merely physical human experience. ■ surpassing the ordinary; exceptional: *the conductor was described as a "transcendent genius."* ■ (of God) existing apart from and not subject to the limitations of the material universe. Often contrasted with IMMANENT. —**tran·scend·ence** *n.* —**tran·scend·en·cy** *n.* —**tran·scend·ent·ly** *adv.*

tran·scen·den·tal /,transen'dentl/ ▶*adj.* **1** of or relating to a spiritual or nonphysical realm. ■ relating to or denoting Transcendentalism. **2** *Math.* (of a number, e.g., *e* or π) real but not a root of an algebraic equation with rational roots. ■ (of a function) not capable of being produced by the algebraical operations of addition, multiplication, and involution, or the inverse operations. —**tran·scen·den·tal·ize** /-,īz/ *v.* —**tran·scen·den·tal·ly** *adv.*

tran·scen·den·tal·ism /,tran,sen'dentl,izəm/ ▶*n.* (**Transcendentalism**) an idealistic philosophical and social movement that developed in New England around 1836. It taught that divinity pervades all nature and humanity, and its members held progressive views. Ralph Waldo Emerson and Henry David Thoreau were central figures. —**tran·scen·den·tal·ist** (also **Tran·scen·den·tal·ist**) *n. & adj.*

Tran·scen·den·tal Med·i·ta·tion (abbr.: **TM**) ▶*n.* trademark a technique for detaching oneself from anxiety and promoting harmony and self-

realization by meditation, repetition of a mantra, and other yogic practices.

trans·con·ti·nen·tal /,transkäntə'nentl; ,tranz-/ ▶*adj.* (esp. of a railroad line) crossing a continent. ■ extending across or relating to two or more continents: *a transcontinental radio audience.*
▶*n.* a transcontinental railroad or train. —**trans·con·ti·nen·tal·ly** *adv.*

tran·scribe /tran'skrīb/ ▶*v.* [*tr.*] put (thoughts, speech, or data) into written or printed form. ■ transliterate (foreign characters) or write or type out (shorthand, notes, or other abbreviated forms) into ordinary characters or full sentences. ■ arrange (a piece of music) for a different instrument, voice, or group of these: *his largest early work was transcribed for organ.* ■ *Biochem.* synthesize (a nucleic acid, typically RNA) using an existing nucleic acid, typically DNA, as a template, thus copying the genetic information in the latter. —**tran·scrib·er** *n.*

tran·script /'tran,skript/ ▶*n.* a written or printed version of material originally presented in another medium. ■ an official record of a student's work, showing courses taken and grades achieved. —**tran·scrip·tive** /,tran'skriptiv/ *adj.*

tran·scrip·tion /tran'skripsHən/ ▶*n.* a written or printed representation of something. ■ the action or process of transcribing something: *the funding covers transcription of nearly illegible photocopies.* ■ an arrangement of a piece of music for a different instrument, voice, or number of these: *a transcription for voice and lute.* ■ a form in which a speech sound or a foreign character is represented. ■ *Biochemistry* the process by which genetic information represented by a sequence of DNA nucleotides is copied into newly synthesized molecules of RNA, with the DNA serving as a template. ▷late 16th cent.: from French, or from Latin *transcriptio(n-),* from the verb *transcribere* 'transcribe,' from *trans-* 'across' + *scribere* 'write.' —**tran·scrip·tion·al** /-sHənl/ *adj.* —**tran·scrip·tion·al·ly** /-sHənl-ē/ *adv.* —**tran·scrip·tion·ist** /-nist/ *n.*

trans·duc·er /trans'd(y)ōōsər; tranz-/ ▶*n.* a device that converts variations in a physical quantity, such as pressure or brightness, into an electrical signal, or vice versa. —**trans·duce** *v.* —**trans·duc·tion** /-'dəksHən/ *n.*

tran·sect /tran'sekt/ *technical* ▶*v.* [*tr.*] cut across or make a transverse section in.
▶*n.* a straight line or narrow section through an object or natural feature or across the earth's surface, along which observations are made or measurements taken. —**tran·sec·tion** /-'seksHən/ *n.*

tran·sept /'tran,sept/ ▶*n.* (in a cross-shaped church) either of the two parts forming the arms of the cross shape, projecting at right angles from the nave: *the north transept.* —**tran·sep·tal** /tran'septl/ *adj.*

trans·fer ▶*v.* /trans'fər; 'transfər/ (**-ferred, -fer·ring**) [*tr.*] move (someone or something) from one place to another: *he would have to transfer money to his own account.* ■ move or cause to move to another group, occupation, or service: [*intr.*] *she transferred to the Physics Department* | [*tr.*] *employees have been transferred to the installation team.* ■ [*intr.*] enroll in a different school or college. ■ (in professional sports) move or cause to move to another team: [*intr.*] *he transferred to the Dodgers* | [*tr.*] *when a player is transferred to the minors by a major league club.* ■ [*intr.*] change to another place, route, or means of transportation during a journey: *transfer from Rome airport to the railroad station.* ■ make over the possession of (property, a right, or a responsibility) to someone else. ■ convey (a drawing or design) from one surface to another. ■ change (the sense of a word or phrase) by extension or metaphor. ■ redirect (a telephone call) to another line or extension.
▶*n.* /'transfər/ an act of moving something or someone to another place. ■ a change of employment, typically within an organization or field: *she was going to ask her boss for a transfer to the city.* ■ *Brit.* an act of selling or moving an athlete to another team. ■ a student who has enrolled in a different school or college: [as *adj.*] *the impact of transfer students on enrollment figures.* ■ a conveyance of property, esp. stocks, from one person to another. ■ a small colored picture or design on paper that can be transferred to another surface by being pressed or heated: *T-shirts with iron-on transfers.* ■ a ticket allowing a passenger to change from one public transportation vehicle to another as part of a single journey. —**trans·fer·ee** /,transfə'rē/ *n.* —**trans·fer·or** /trans'fərər; 'transfərər/ *n.* (*chiefly Law*) —**trans·fer·rer** *n.*

trans·fer·a·ble /trans'fərəbəl; 'transfərə-/ ▶*adj.* (typically of financial assets, liabilities, or legal rights) able to be transferred or made over to the possession of another person. —**trans·fer·a·bil·i·ty** /,transfərə-'bilitē/ *n.*

trans·fer·ence /trans'fərəns; 'transfərəns/ ▶*n.* the action of transferring something or the process of being transferred. ■ *Psychoanalysis* the redirection to a substitute, usually a therapist, of emotions that were

T

originally felt in childhood (in a phase of analysis called **transference neurosis**).

trans·fer RNA ▸*n. Biochem.* RNA consisting of folded molecules that transport amino acids from the cytoplasm of a cell to a ribosome.

trans·fig·u·ra·tion /ˌtransˌfigyəˈrāSHən/ ▸*n.* a complete change of form or appearance into a more beautiful or spiritual state. ■ (**the Transfiguration**) Christ's appearance in radiant glory to three of his disciples. ■ the church festival commemorating this, held on August 6.

trans·fig·ure /transˈfigyər/ ▸*v.* [*tr.*] transform into something more beautiful or elevated: *the world is made luminous and is transfigured.*

trans·fix /transˈfiks/ ▸*v.* [*tr.*] **1** cause (someone) to become motionless with horror, wonder, or astonishment: *he was transfixed by the pain in her face.* **2** pierce with a sharp implement or weapon. —**trans·fix·ion** /-ˈfiksHən/ *n.*

trans·form /transˈfôrm/ ▸*v.* [*tr.*] make a thorough or dramatic change in the form, appearance, or character of: *lasers have transformed cardiac surgery.* ■ [*intr.*] undergo such a change: *an automobile that transformed into a boat.* ■ change the voltage of (an electric current). ■ *Math.* change (a mathematical entity) by transformation.
▸*n.* /ˈtransfôrm/ *Math. & Linguistics* the product of a transformation. ■ a rule for making a transformation. —**trans·form·a·ble** *adj.* —**trans·form·a·tive** /-mətiv/ *adj.*

trans·for·ma·tion /ˌtransfərˈmāSHən/ ▸*n.* a thorough or dramatic change in form or appearance. ■ a metamorphosis during the life cycle of an animal. ■ *Linguistics* a process by which an element in the underlying deep structure of a sentence is converted to an element in the surface structure. ■ *Biol.* the genetic alteration of a cell by introduction of extraneous DNA, esp. by a plasmid. ■ *Biol.* the heritable modification of a cell from its normal state to a malignant state. —**trans·for·ma·tion·al** *adj.*

trans·form·er /transˈfôrmər/ ▸*n.* **1** an apparatus for reducing or increasing the voltage of an alternating current. **2** a person or thing that transforms something.

trans·fuse /transˈfyōōz/ ▸*v.* [*tr.*] **1** *Med.* transfer (blood or its components) from one person or animal to another. ■ inject (liquid) into a blood vessel to replace lost fluid. **2** cause (something or someone) to be permeated or infused by something. —**trans·fu·sion** *n.*

trans·gen·der /tranzˈjendər; trans-/ (also **trans·gen·dered**) ▸*adj.* identified with a gender other than the biological one: *a transgender activist and author.*

trans·gress /transˈgres; tranz-/ ▸*v.* [*tr.*] infringe or go beyond the bounds of (a moral principle or other established standard of behavior): *she had transgressed an unwritten social law* | [*intr.*] *they must control the impulses that lead them to transgress.* ■ *Geol.* (of the sea) spread over (an area of land). —**trans·gres·sion** /-ˈgreSHən/ *n.* —**trans·gres·sive** *adj.* —**trans·gres·sor** /-ˈgresər/ *n.*

tran·sient /ˈtransHənt; -zHənt; -zēənt/ ▸*adj.* lasting only for a short time; impermanent. ■ staying or working in a place for only a short time.
▸*n.* **1** a person who is staying or working in a place for only a short time. **2** a momentary variation in current, voltage, or frequency. ▷late 16th cent.: from Latin *transient-* 'going across,' from the verb *transire*, from *trans-* 'across' + *ire* 'go.' —**tran·sience** *n.* —**tran·sien·cy** *n.* —**tran·sient·ly** *adv.*

tran·sis·tor /tranˈzistər/ ▸*n.* a semiconductor device with three connections, capable of amplification in addition to rectification. ■ (also **transistor radio**) a portable radio using circuits containing transistors rather than vacuum tubes.

tran·sit /ˈtranzit/ ▸*n.* **1** the carrying of people or goods from one place to another: *a painting was damaged in transit.* ■ an act of passing through or across a place: *the transit of the Northwest Passage.* ■ the conveyance of passengers on public transportation. ■ *Astron.* the passage of an inferior planet across the face of the sun, or of a moon or its shadow across the face of a planet. ■ *Astron.* the apparent passage of a celestial body across the meridian of a place. ■ *Astrol.* the passage of a celestial body through a specified sign, house, or area of a chart. **2** (in full **transit theodolite**) a tool used by surveyors to measure horizontal angles.
▸*v.* (**-sit·ed, -sit·ing**) [*tr.*] pass across or through (an area). ■ *Astron.* (of a planet or other celestial body) pass across (a meridian or the face of another body). ■ *Astrol.* (of a celestial body) pass across (a specified sign, house, or area of a chart).

tran·si·tion /tranˈziSHən; -ˈsiSHən/ ▸*n.* the process or a period of changing from one state or condition to another: *a transition to democracy.* ■ a passage in a piece of writing that smoothly connects two topics or sections to each other. ■ *Mus.* a momentary modulation from one key to another. ■ *Physics* a change of an atom, nucleus, electron, etc., from

one quantum state to another, with emission or absorption of radiation.
▸*v.* undergo or cause to undergo a process or period of transition: [*tr.*] *to be built by the government and transitioned into private industry* | [*intr.*] *we have transitioned from a combat operation to a support role in the community.* —**tran·si·tion·al** /-sHənl/ *adj.* —**tran·si·tion·a·ry** /-ˌnerē/ *adj.*

tran·si·tive /ˈtransitiv; ˈtranz-/ ▸*adj. Gram.* (of a verb or a sense or use of a verb) able to take a direct object (expressed or implied), e.g., *saw* in *he saw the donkey.* The opposite of INTRANSITIVE.
▸*n.* a transitive verb. —**tran·si·tive·ly** *adv.* —**tran·si·tive·ness** *n.* —**tran·si·tiv·i·ty** /ˌtransəˈtivitē; -zə-/ *n.*

tran·si·to·ry /ˈtransiˌtôrē; ˈtranzi-/ ▸*adj.* not permanent. —**tran·si·to·ri·ly** /-rəlē/ *adv.* —**tran·si·to·ri·ness** *n.*

tran·sit vi·sa ▸*n.* a visa allowing its holder to pass through a country but not to stay there.

trans·late /transˈlāt; tranz-/ ▸*v.* [*tr.*] **1** express the sense of (words or text) in another language. ■ [*intr.*] be expressed or be capable of being expressed in another language: *shiatsu literally translates as "finger pressure."* ■ (**translate something into/translate into**) convert or be converted into (another form or medium): [*tr.*] *few of Shakespeare's other works have been translated into ballets.* **2** move from one place or condition to another: *to be translated from familiar surroundings to a foreign court.* ■ *Biol.* convert (a sequence of nucleotides in messenger RNA) to an amino-acid sequence in a protein or polypeptide during synthesis. **3** *Physics* cause (a body) to move so that all its parts travel in the same direction, without rotation or change of shape. ■ *Math.* transform (a geometric figure) in an analogous way. —**trans·lat·a·bil·i·ty** /ˌtransˌlātə-ˈbilətē; ˌtranz-/ *n.* —**trans·lat·a·ble** *adj.*

trans·la·tion /transˈlāSHən; tranz-/ ▸*n.* **1** the process of translating words or text from one language into another. ■ a written or spoken rendering of the meaning of a word, speech, book, or other text, in another language. ■ the conversion of something from one form or medium into another: *the translation of research findings into clinical practice.* ■ *Biol.* the process by which a sequence of nucleotide triplets in a messenger RNA molecule gives rise to a specific sequence of amino acids during synthesis of a polypeptide or protein. **2** *formal* or *technical* the process of moving something from one place to another: *the translation of the relics of St. Thomas of Canterbury.* ■ *Math.* movement of a body from one point of space to another such that every point of the body moves in the same direction and over the same distance, without any rotation, reflection, or change in size. —**trans·la·tion·al** /-sHənl/ *adj.* —**trans·la·tion·al·ly** /-sHənl-ē/ *adv.*

trans·la·tor /ˈtransˌlātər; ˈtranz-/ ▸*n.* a person who translates from one language into another, esp. as a profession. ■ a program that translates from one programming language into another.

trans·lit·er·ate /transˈlitəˌrāt; tranz-/ ▸*v.* [*tr.*] write or print (a letter or word) using the closest corresponding letters of a different alphabet or language. —**trans·lit·er·a·tion** /transˌlitəˈrāSHən; tranz-/ *n.* —**trans·lit·er·a·tor** /-ˌrātər/ *n.*

trans·lu·cent /transˈlōōsnt; tranz-/ ▸*adj.* (of a substance) allowing light, but not detailed images, to pass through; semitransparent. —**trans·lu·cence** *n.* —**trans·lu·cen·cy** *n.* —**trans·lu·cent·ly** *adv.*

trans·mi·grate /transˈmīˌgrāt; tranz-/ ▸*v.* [*intr.*] (of the soul) pass into a different body after death. —**trans·mi·gra·tion** /ˌtransˌmīˈgrāSHən; ˌtranz-/ *n.* —**trans·mi·gra·tor** /-ˌgrātər/ *n.* —**trans·mi·gra·to·ry** /-grəˌtôrē/ *adj.*

trans·mis·sion /transˈmiSHən; tranz-/ ▸*n.* **1** the action or process of transmitting something or the state of being transmitted. ■ a program or signal that is broadcast or sent out. **2** the mechanism by which power is transmitted from an engine to the wheels of a motor vehicle.

trans·mit /tranzˈmit; trans-/ ▸*v.* (**-mit·ted, -mit·ting**) [*tr.*] cause (something) to pass on from one place or person to another. ■ broadcast or send out (an electrical signal or a radio or television program). ■ pass on (a disease or trait) to another: *sexually transmitted diseases.* ■ allow (heat, light, sound, electricity, or other energy) to pass through a medium: *the three bones transmit sound waves to the inner ear.* ■ communicate or be a medium for (an idea or emotion). —**trans·mis·si·bil·i·ty** /-ˌmisəˈbilitē/ *n.* (*chiefly Med.*). —**trans·mis·si·ble** /-ˈmisəbəl/ *adj.* (*chiefly Med.*). —**trans·mis·sive** /-ˈmisiv/ *adj.* —**trans·mit·ta·ble** *adj.* —**trans·mit·tal** /-ˈmitl/ *n.*

trans·mit·ter /transˈmitər; tranz-/ ▸*n.* a set of equipment used to generate and transmit electromagnetic waves carrying messages or signals, esp. those of radio or television. ■ a person or thing that transmits something. ■ short for NEUROTRANSMITTER.

trans·mog·ri·fy /transˈmägrə,fī; tranz-/ ▶v. (-fies, -fied) [tr.] (often be **transmogrified**) *chiefly humorous* transform, esp. in a surprising or magical manner. —**trans·mog·ri·fi·ca·tion** /-,mägrəfiˈkāSHən/ n.

trans·mute /transˈmyo͞ot; tranz-/ ▶v. change in form, nature, or substance: [tr.] *the raw material of his experience was* transmuted *into stories* | [intr.] *the discovery that elements can transmute by radioactivity.* ■ [tr.] subject (base metals) to alchemical conversion: *the quest to* transmute *lead into gold.* —**trans·mut·a·bil·i·ty** /-,myo͞otəˈbilitē/ n. —**trans·mut·a·ble** adj. —**trans·mu·ta·tion** /,transmyo͞oˈtāSHən; ,tranz-/ n. —**trans·mu·ta·tive** /-ˈmyo͞otətiv/ adj. —**trans·mut·er** n.

trans·na·tion·al /transˈnaSHənl; tranz-/ ▶adj. extending or operating across national boundaries: *transnational advertising agencies.*
▶n. a large company operating internationally; a multinational. —**trans·na·tion·al·ism** /-,izəm/ n. —**trans·na·tion·al·ly** adv.

trans·o·ce·an·ic /,transōSHēˈanik; ,tranz-/ ▶adj. crossing an ocean: *the transoceanic cable system.* ■ coming from or situated beyond an ocean.

tran·som /ˈtransəm/ ▶n. the flat surface forming the stern of a vessel. ■ a horizontal beam reinforcing the stern of a vessel. ■ a strengthening crossbar, in particular one set above a window or door. Compare with MULLION. ■ short for TRANSOM WINDOW. —**tran·somed** adj.
▶ □ **over the transom** *inf.* offered or sent without prior agreement; unsolicited: *the editors receive about ten manuscripts a week over the transom.*

tran·som win·dow ▶n. a window set above the transom of a door or larger window; a fanlight.

trans·par·en·cy /tranˈsparənsē/ ▶n. (pl. -cies) **1** the condition of being transparent: *the transparency of ice.* **2** an image, text, or positive transparent photograph printed on transparent plastic or glass, able to be viewed using a projector.

trans·par·ent /tranˈspe(ə)rənt; -ˈspar-/ ▶adj. (of a material or article) allowing light to pass through so that objects behind can be distinctly seen: *transparent blue water.* ■ easy to perceive or detect: *the residents will see through any* transparent *attempt to buy their votes* | *the meaning of the poem is not* transparent. ■ having thoughts, feelings, or motives that are easily perceived: *you'd be no good at poker—you're too* transparent. ■ (of an organization or its activities) open to public scrutiny: *if you had transparent government procurement, corruption would go away.* ■ *Comput.* (of a process or interface) functioning without the user being aware of its presence. —**trans·par·ent·ly** adv. *a transparently feeble argument.*

tran·spire /tranˈspī(ə)r/ ▶v. [intr.] **1** occur; happen. ■ prove to be the case: *as it transpired, he was right.* ■ (of a secret or something unknown) come to be known; be revealed: *Yaddo, it transpired, had been under FBI surveillance for some time.* **2** *Bot.* (of a plant or leaf) give off water vapor through the stomata. —**tran·spi·ra·tion** /-spəˈrāSHən/ n.

trans·plant ▶v. /transˈplant/ [tr.] move or transfer (something) to another place or situation, typically with some effort or upheaval. ■ replant (a plant) in another place. ■ remove (living tissue or an organ) and implant it in another part of the body or in another body.
▶n. /ˈtrans,plant/ an operation in which an organ or tissue is transplanted: *a heart transplant.* ■ an organ or tissue that is transplanted. ■ a plant that has been or is to be transplanted. ■ a person or thing that has been moved to a new place or situation. —**trans·plant·a·ble** /transˈplantəbəl/ adj. —**trans·plan·ta·tion** /-,planˈtāSHən/ n. —**trans·plant·er** n.

tran·spon·der /tranˈspändər/ ▶n. a device for receiving a radio signal and automatically transmitting a different signal.

trans·port ▶v. /transˈpôrt/ [tr.] take or carry (people or goods) from one place to another by means of a vehicle, aircraft, or ship. ■ *fig.* cause (someone) to feel that they are in another place or time: *for a moment she was transported to a warm summer garden on the night of a ball.* ■ overwhelm (someone) with a strong emotion, esp. joy: *she was* transported *with pleasure.* ■ *hist.* send (a convict) to a penal colony.
▶n. /ˈtrans,pôrt/ **1** a system or means of conveying people or goods from place to place by means of a vehicle, aircraft, or ship: *air transport.* ■ the action of transporting something or the state of being transported. ■ a large vehicle, ship, or aircraft used to carry troops or stores. **2** (usu. **transports**) an overwhelmingly strong emotion: *art can send people into* transports *of delight.* —**trans·port·a·ble** adj.

trans·por·ta·tion /,transpərˈtāSHən/ ▶n. **1** the action of transporting someone or something or the process of being transported. ■ a system or means of transporting people or goods. **2** *hist.* the action or practice of transporting convicts to a penal colony.

trans·port·er /transˈpôrtər/ ▶n. a person or thing that transports something, in particular: ■ a large vehicle used to carry heavy objects, e.g.,

cars. ■ (in science fiction) a device that conveys people or things instantaneously from one place to another.

trans·pose /transˈpōz/ ▶v. [tr.] **1** cause (two or more things) to change places with each other. **2** transfer to a different place or context: *the problems of civilization are* transposed *into a rustic setting.* ■ write or play (music) in a different key from the original: *the basses are* transposed *down an octave.* ■ *Math.* transfer (a term), with its sign changed, to the other side of an equation. ■ change into a new form: *he* transposed *a gaffe by the mayor into a public-relations advantage.* —**trans·pos·a·ble** adj. —**trans·pos·al** /-ˈspōzəl/ n. —**trans·pos·er** n.

trans·po·si·tion /,transpəˈziSHən/ ▶n. the action of transposing something. ■ a thing that has been produced by transposing something. —**trans·po·si·tion·al** /-SHənl/ adj.

trans·sex·u·al /tran(s)ˈsekSHo͞oəl/ ▶n. a person born with the physical characteristics of one sex who emotionally and psychologically feels that they belong to the opposite sex. ■ a person who has undergone surgery and hormone treatment in order to acquire the physical characteristics of the opposite sex.
▶adj. of or relating to such a person. —**trans·sex·u·al·ism** /-,lizəm/ n. —**trans·sex·u·al·i·ty** /-,sekSHo͞oˈalitē/ n.

trans·ship /tran(s)ˈSHip/ (also **tran·ship**) ▶v. (-shipped, -ship·ping) [tr.] transfer (cargo) from one ship or other form of transport to another. —**trans·ship·ment** n.

tran·sub·stan·ti·a·tion /,transəb,stanCHēˈāSHən/ ▶n. *Christian Theol.* (esp. in the Roman Catholic Church) the conversion of the substance of the Eucharistic elements into the body and blood of Christ at consecration, only the appearances of bread and wine still remaining. ■ *formal* a change in the form or substance of something.

trans·verse /transˈvərs; tranz-/ ▶adj. situated or extending across something: *a transverse beam supports the dashboard.* —**trans·verse·ly** adv.

trans·ves·tite /transˈves,tīt; tranz-/ ▶n. a person, typically a man, who derives pleasure from dressing in clothes appropriate to the opposite sex. —**trans·ves·tism** /-,tizəm/ n. —**trans·ves·tist** /-tist/ n. (dated). —**trans·ves·ti·tism** /-ti,tizəm/ n.

trap[1] /trap/ ▶n. **1** a device or enclosure designed to catch and retain animals, typically by allowing entry but not exit or by catching hold of a part of the body. ■ a curve in the waste pipe from a bathtub, sink, or toilet that is always full of liquid and prevents gases from coming up the pipe into the building. ■ a container or device used to collect a specified thing. ■ a bunker or other hollow on a golf course. ■ the compartment from which a greyhound is released at the start of a race. ■ *fig.* a trick by which someone is misled into giving themselves away or otherwise acting contrary to their interests or intentions. ■ *fig.* an unpleasant situation from which it is hard to escape: *they fell into the* trap *of relying too little on equity financing.*

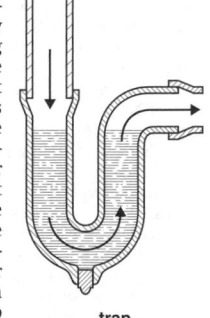

trap

2 a device for hurling an object such as a clay pigeon into the air to be shot at. **3** *chiefly hist.* a light, two-wheeled carriage pulled by a horse or pony. **4** *inf.* a person's mouth (used in expressions to do with speaking). **5** (usu. **traps**) *inf.* percussion instruments, typically in a jazz band. **6** *Baseball & Football* an act of trapping the ball.
▶v. (**trapped, trap·ping**) [tr.] catch (an animal) in a trap. ■ prevent (someone) from escaping from a place. ■ have (something, typically a part of the body) held tightly by something so that it cannot move or be freed. ■ induce (someone), by means of trickery or deception, to do something they would not otherwise want to do. ■ *Baseball & Football* catch (the ball) after it has briefly touched the ground. ■ *Soccer* bring (the ball) under control with the feet or other part of the body on receiving it. —**trap·like** /-,līk/ adj.

trap[2] ▶v. (**trapped, trap·ping**) [tr.] *archaic* put trappings on (a horse, etc.)

trap[3] (also **trap·rock**) ▶n. basalt or a similar dark, fine-grained igneous rock.

trap·door /ˈtrap,dôr/ (also **trap door**) ▶n. a hinged or removable panel in a floor, ceiling, or roof. ■ a feature or defect of a computer system that allows surreptitious unauthorized access to data belonging to other users.

tra·peze /trəˈpēz; tra-/ ▶n. **1** a horizontal bar hanging by two ropes (usually high in the air) and free to swing, used by acrobats in a circus. **2** *Sailing* a harness attached by a cable to a sailboat's mast, enabling one to balance the boat by leaning backward out over the windward side.

tra·pe·zi·um /trəˈpēzēəm/ ▶ n. (pl. **-zi·a** /-zēə/ or **-zi·ums**) **1** *Geom.* a quadrilateral with no sides parallel. **2** *Anat.* a bone in the wrist below the base of the thumb.

trap·e·zoid /ˈtrapiˌzoid/ ▶ n. **1** *Geom.* a quadrilateral with only one pair of parallel sides. **2** (also **trapezoid bone**) *Anat.* a small carpal bone in the base of the hand, articulating with the metacarpal of the index finger. **—trap·e·zoi·dal** /ˌtrapiˈzoidl/ *adj.*

trapezium

trapezoid

trap·per /ˈtrapər/ ▶ n. a person who traps wild animals, esp. for their fur.

trap·pings /ˈtrapiNGZ/ ▶ pl. n. the outward signs, features, or objects associated with a particular situation, role, or thing: *I had the trappings of success.* ■ a horse's ornamental harness.

Trap·pist /ˈtrapist/ ▶ adj. of, relating to, or denoting a branch of the Cistercian order of monks founded in 1664 and noted for an austere rule including a vow of silence.
▶ n. a member of this order. ▷early 19th cent.: from French *trappiste*, from *La Trappe* in Normandy.

trash /trasH/ ▶ n. discarded matter; refuse. ■ writing, art, or other cultural items of poor quality: *if they read at all, they read trash.* ■ a person or people regarded as being of very low social standing: *she would have been considered trash.* ■ nonsense.
▶ v. [tr.] **1** *inf.* damage or wreck: *my apartment's been totally trashed.* ■ discard: *they trashed the tapes and sent her back into the studio.* ■ *Comput.* kill (a file or process) or wipe (a disk): *she almost trashed the e-mail window.* ■ criticize severely: *trade associations trashed the legislation as deficient.* ■ [as adj.] (**trashed**) intoxicated with alcohol or drugs: *there was pot, there was booze, but nobody really got trashed.* **2** strip (sugar cane) of its outer leaves to ripen it faster.

trash·y /ˈtrasHē/ ▶ adj. (**trash·i·er**, **trash·i·est**) (esp. of items of popular culture) of poor quality: *trashy novels and formulaic movies.* **—trash·i·ly** /ˈtrasHəlē/ *adv.* **—trash·i·ness** *n.*

trat·to·ri·a /ˌträtəˈrēə/ ▶ n. an Italian restaurant serving simple food.

trau·ma /ˈtroumə; ˈtrô-/ ▶ n. (pl. **-mas** or **-ma·ta** /-mətə/) a deeply distressing or disturbing experience. ■ emotional shock following a stressful event or a physical injury, which may be associated with physical shock and sometimes leads to long-term neurosis. ■ *Med.* physical injury. ▷late 17th cent.: from Greek, literally 'wound.' **—trau·ma·tize** *v.*

trau·mat·ic /trəˈmatik; trou-; trô-/ ▶ adj. emotionally disturbing or distressing. ■ relating to or causing psychological trauma. ■ *Med.* relating to or denoting physical injury. **—trau·mat·i·cal·ly** /-ik(ə)lē/ *adv.*

tra·vail /trəˈvāl; ˈtrav,āl/ *poetic/lit.* ▶ n. (also **travails**) painful or laborious effort.
▶ v. [intr.] engage in painful or laborious effort. ■ (of a woman) be in labor.

trav·el /ˈtravəl/ ▶ v. (**-eled**, **-el·ing**; also *chiefly Brit.* **-elled**, **-el·ling**) **1** [intr.] make a journey, typically of some length or abroad. ■ [tr.] journey along (a road) or through (a region): *he traveled the world with the army.* ■ go or be moved from place to place: *a traveling exhibition.* ■ *inf.* resist motion sickness, damage, or some other impairment on a journey: *he usually travels well.* ■ be enjoyed or successful away from the place of origin: *accordion music travels well.* ■ *dated* go from place to place as a sales representative. ■ (of an object or radiation) move, typically in a constant or predictable way: *light travels faster than sound.* ■ *inf.* (esp. of a vehicle) move quickly. **2** [intr.] *Basketball* take more than the allowed number of steps (typically two) while holding the ball without dribbling it.
▶ n. the action of traveling, typically abroad. ■ (**travels**) journeys, esp. long or exotic ones. ■ [as adj.] (of a device) designed so as to be sufficiently compact for use on a journey: *a travel iron.* ■ the range, rate, or mode of motion of a part of a machine.

trav·el a·gen·cy ▶ n. an agency that makes the necessary arrangements for travelers, esp. the booking of airline tickets and hotel rooms. **—trav·el a·gent** *n.*

trav·eled /ˈtravəld/ ▶ adj. [often in comb.] **1** having traveled to many places: *he was widely traveled.* **2** used by people traveling: *a lightly traveled route.*

trav·el·er /ˈtrav(ə)lər/ (*Brit.* **trav·el·ler**) ▶ n. a person who is traveling or who often travels.

trav·el·er's check ▶ n. a check for a fixed amount that can be cashed or used in payment after endorsement with the holder's signature.

trav·el·ing sales·man ▶ n. a representative of a company who visits stores and other businesses to show samples and gain orders.

trav·e·logue /ˈtravəˌlôg; -ˌläg/ ▶ n. a movie, book, or illustrated lecture about the places visited and experiences encountered by a traveler.

trav·erse /trəˈvərs/ ▶ v. [tr.] **1** travel across or through. ■ extend across or through: *a moving catwalk that traversed a vast cavernous space.* ■ [intr.] cross a hill or mountain by means of a series of sideways movements: *I often use this route, eventually traversing around the cliff.* ■ ski diagonally across (a slope), with only a slight descent. ■ *fig.* consider or discuss the whole extent of (a subject). **2** [tr.] move (something) back and forth or sideways. ■ turn (a large gun or other device on a pivot) to face a different direction. **3** *Law* deny (an allegation) in pleading.
▶ n. **1** an act of traversing something, or a sideways movement, or a series of such movements, across a rock face from one line of ascent or descent to another. ■ a place where a movement of this type is necessary. ■ a movement following a diagonal course made by a skier descending a slope. ■ a zigzag course followed by a ship because winds or currents prevent it from sailing directly toward its destination. **2** a part of a structure that extends or is fixed across something. ■ a gallery extending from side to side of a church or other building. **3** a mechanism enabling a large gun to be turned to face a different direction. ■ the sideways movement of a part in a machine. **4** a single line of survey, usually plotted from compass bearings and chained or paced distances between angular points. ■ a tract surveyed in this way.
▶ adj. (of a curtain rod) allowing the curtain to be opened and closed by sliding it along the rod. **—tra·vers·a·ble** *adj.* **—tra·vers·al** /-səl/ *n.* **—tra·vers·er** *n.*

trav·es·ty /ˈtravistē/ ▶ n. (pl. **-ties**) a false, absurd, or distorted representation of something: *the absurdly lenient sentence is a travesty of justice.*

tra·vois /trəˈvoi; ˈtrav,oi/ ▶ n. (pl. same) a type of sled formerly used by North American Indians to carry goods, consisting of two joined poles dragged by a horse or dog.

trawl /trôl/ ▶ v. [intr.] fish with a trawl net or seine: *the boats trawled for flounder.* ■ sift through as part of a search: *they trawled through confidential files* | [tr.] *he trawled his memory.* ■ [tr.] drag or trail (something) through water or other liquid.
▶ n. **1** an act of sifting through something as part of a search: *a constant trawl for information.* **2** (also **trawl net**) a large wide-mouthed fishing net dragged by a vessel along the bottom or in the midwater of the sea or a lake.

trawl·er /ˈtrôlər/ ▶ n. a fishing boat used for trawling.

tray /trā/ ▶ n. a flat, shallow container with a raised rim, typically used for carrying food and drink, or for holding small items. **—tray·ful** /-ˌfool/ *n.* (pl. **-fuls**).

trayf /trāf/ (also **treyf**) ▶ adj. (of food) not satisfying the requirements of Jewish law: *I asked her if she ever ate food that was trayf.*

treach·er·ous /ˈtrecHərəs/ ▶ adj. guilty of or involving betrayal or deception. ■ (of ground, water, conditions, etc.) hazardous because of presenting hidden or unpredictable dangers. **—treach·er·ous·ly** *adv.* **—treach·er·ous·ness** *n.*

treach·er·y /ˈtrecHərē/ ▶ n. (pl. **-er·ies**) betrayal of trust; deceptive action or nature: *his resignation was perceived as an act of treachery.*

trea·cle /ˈtrēkəl/ ▶ n. British term for MOLASSES. ■ *fig.* cloying sentimentality or flattery. **—trea·cly** /ˈtrēk(ə)lē/ *adj.*

tread /tred/ ▶ v. (past **trod** /träd/ /träd/; past part. **trod·den** /ˈträdn/ or **trod**) [intr.] walk in a specified way: *he trod lightly* | *fig. the administration had to tread carefully so as not to offend the judiciary.* ■ (**tread on**) set one's foot down on top of. ■ [tr.] walk on or along. ■ [tr.] press down into the ground or another surface with the feet: *food and cigarette butts had been trodden into the carpet.* ■ [tr.] crush or flatten something with the feet: *the snow had been trodden down by the horses.*
▶ n. **1** a manner or the sound of someone walking: *I heard the heavy tread of Dad's boots.* **2** the top surface of a step or stair. **3** the thick molded part of a vehicle tire that grips the road. **—tread·er** *n.*
▶ □ **tread water** (past **tread·ed**) maintain an upright position in deep water by moving the feet with a walking movement and the hands with a downward circular motion. ■ *fig.* fail to advance or make progress: *men who are treading water in their careers.*

trea·dle /ˈtredl/ ▶ n. a lever worked by the foot that imparts motion to a machine. ■ any of a row of metal spikes set on an angle on a spring within a plate laid across the entrance or exit of a parking facility, used to prevent drivers from using the facility without paying.
▶ v. [tr.] operate (a machine) using a treadle.

tread·mill /'trɛd,mil/ ▶*n. hist.* a device used for driving machinery, consisting of a large wheel with steps fitted into its inner surface. It was turned by the weight of people or animals treading the steps. ■ an exercise machine, typically with a continuous belt, that allows one to walk or run in place. ■ *fig.* a job or situation that is tiring, boring, or unpleasant and from which it is hard to escape.

trea·son /'trēzən/ ▶*n.* (also **high treason**) the crime of betraying one's country, esp. by attempting to kill the sovereign or overthrow the government. ■ the action of betraying someone or something. ▷Middle English: from Anglo-Norman French *treisoun*, from Latin *traditio(n-)* 'handing over,' from the verb *tradere*. —**trea·son·a·ble** *adj.* —**trea·son·ous** /'trēzənəs/ *adj.*

treas·ure /'trɛzʜər/ ▶*n.* a quantity of precious metals, gems, or other valuable objects. ■ a very valuable object. ■ *inf.* a person whom the speaker loves or who is valued for the assistance they can give.
▶*v.* [*tr.*] keep carefully (a valuable or valued item). ■ value highly.

treas·ure hunt ▶*n.* a search for treasure. ■ a game in which players search for hidden objects by following a trail of clues.

treas·ur·er /'trɛzʜərər/ ▶*n.* a person appointed to administer or manage the financial assets and liabilities of a society, company, local authority, or other body. —**treas·ur·er·ship** /-,ʃHip/ *n.*

treas·ure trove ▶*n.* valuables of unknown ownership that are found hidden, in some cases declared the property of the finder. ■ a hidden store of valuable or delightful things.

treas·ur·y /'trɛzʜərē/ ▶*n.* (*pl.* **-ur·ies**) **1** the funds or revenue of a government, corporation, or institution. ■ (**Treasury**) (in some countries) the government department responsible for budgeting for and controlling public expenditure, management of the national debt, and the overall management of the economy. **2** a place or building where treasure is stored. ■ a store or collection of valuable or delightful things: *the old town is a treasury of ancient monuments.*

Treas·ur·y bill ▶*n.* a short-dated government security, yielding no interest but issued at a discount on its redemption price.

treat /trēt/ ▶*v.* [*tr.*] **1** behave toward or deal with in a certain way: *she had been brutally treated.* ■ (**treat something as**) regard something as being of a specified nature with implications for one's actions concerning it: *the names are being treated as classified information.* ■ give medical care or attention to; try to heal or cure. ■ apply a process or a substance to (something) to protect or preserve it or to give it particular properties: *linen creases badly unless it is treated with the appropriate finish.* ■ present or discuss (a subject). **2** (**treat someone to**) provide someone with (food, drink, or entertainment) at one's own expense. ■ give someone (something) as a favor: *he treated her to one of his smiles.* ■ (**treat oneself**) do or have something that gives one great pleasure. **3** [*intr.*] negotiate terms with someone, esp. an opponent: *he was treating with the enemy.*
▶*n.* an event or item that is out of the ordinary and gives great pleasure. ■ used with a possessive adjective to indicate that the person specified is paying for food, entertainment, etc., for someone else: *"My treat," he insisted, reaching for the bill.* —**treat·a·ble** *adj.* —**treat·er** *n.*

trea·tise /'trētis/ ▶*n.* a written work dealing formally and systematically with a subject: *a comprehensive treatise on electricity and magnetism.*

treat·ment /'trētmənt/ ▶*n.* the manner in which someone behaves toward or deals with someone or something: *equal treatment for men and women.* ■ medical care given to a patient for an illness or injury. ■ a session of medical care or the administration of a dose of medicine. ■ the use of a chemical, physical, or biological agent to preserve or give particular properties to something: *the treatment of hazardous waste.* ■ the presentation or discussion of a subject: *analysis of the treatment of women in her painting.* ■ (**the full treatment**) *inf.* used to indicate that something is done enthusiastically, vigorously, or to an extreme degree: *I gave them the full treatment, and they were just falling over themselves.*

trea·ty /'trētē/ ▶*n.* (*pl.* **-ties**) a formally concluded and ratified agreement between countries.

tre·ble¹ /'trɛbəl/ ▶*adj.* consisting of three parts; threefold: *the fish were caught with large treble hooks dragged through the water.* ■ multiplied or occurring three times: *she turned back to make a double and treble check.*
▶three times as much or as many: *the tip was at least treble what she would normally have given.*
▶*n.* a threefold quantity or thing, in particular: ■ a drink of liquor of three times the standard measure.
▶*pron.* a number or amount that is three times as large as a contrasting or usual number or amount: *by virtue of having paid treble, he had a double room to himself.*
▶*v.* make or become three times as large or numerous: [*tr.*] *rents were doubled and probably trebled* | [*intr.*] *his salary has trebled in a couple of years.*

tre·ble² ▶*n.* a high-pitched voice, esp. a boy's singing voice. ■ a boy or girl with such a singing voice. ■ a part written for a high voice or an instrument of a high pitch. ■ [as *adj.*] denoting a relatively high-pitched member of a family of similar instruments: *a treble viol.* ■ (also **treble bell**) the smallest and highest-pitched bell of a set. ■ the high-frequency output of an audio system or radio, corresponding to the treble in music.

tre·ble clef ▶*n.* a clef placing G above middle C on the second-lowest line of the staff.

tre·cen·to /trā'CHentō/ ▶*n.* (**the trecento**) the 14th century as a period of Italian art, architecture, or literature.

tree /trē/ ▶*n.* **1** a woody perennial plant, typically having a single stem or trunk growing to a considerable height and bearing lateral branches at some distance from the ground. ■ (in general use) any bush, shrub, or herbaceous plant with a tall erect stem, e.g., a banana plant. **2** a wooden structure or part of a structure. ■ *archaic* or *poetic/lit.* the cross on which Jesus Christ was crucified. ■ *archaic* a gallows or gibbet. **3** a thing that has a branching structure resembling that of a tree. ■ (also **tree diagram**) a diagram with a structure of branching connecting lines, representing different processes and relationships.
▶*v.* (**trees, treed, tree·ing**) [*tr.*] force (a hunted animal) to take refuge in a tree. ■ *inf.* force (someone) into a difficult situation. —**tree·less** *adj.* —**tree·less·ness** *n.* —**tree·like** /-,līk/ *adj.*
▶ □ **out of one's tree** *inf.* completely stupid; insane. □ **up a tree** *inf.* in a difficult situation without escape; cornered.

tree·creep·er /'trē,krēpər/ ▶*n.* a small songbird with drab plumage and a down-curved bill that creeps around on the trunks of trees to search for insects. Two families: Certhiidae of Eurasia and North America, and Climacteridae of Australia.

tree frog ▶*n.* an arboreal frog that has long toes with adhesive disks and is typically small and brightly colored.

tree house (also **tree·house**) ▶*n.* a structure built in the branches of a tree for children to play in.

tree ring ▶*n.* each of a number of concentric rings in the cross section of a tree trunk, representing a single year's growth.

tree sur·geon ▶*n.* a person who prunes and treats old or damaged trees in order to preserve them. —**tree sur·ger·y** *n.*

tree toad ▶*n.* another term for TREE FROG.

tree·top /'trē,täp/ ▶*n.* (usu. **treetops**) the uppermost part of a tree.

tre·foil /'trē,foil; 'tref,oil/ ▶*n.* a small plant (genera *Trifolium* and *Lotus*) of the pea family with yellow flowers and three-lobed cloverlike leaves. ■ a similar or related plant with three-lobed leaves. ■ an ornamental design of three rounded lobes like a clover leaf, used typically in architectural tracery. ■ a thing having three parts; a set of three. ■ [as *adj.*] denoting something shaped in the form of a trefoil leaf. —**tre·foiled** *adj.*

trek /trɛk/ ▶*n.* a long arduous journey, esp. one made on foot: *a trek to the South Pole.* ■ a tourist hike.
▶*v.* (**trekked, trek·king**) [*intr.*] go on a long arduous journey, typically on foot. ■ *chiefly S. Afr., hist.* migrate or journey with one's belongings by ox-wagon. ■ [*intr.*] *S. Afr.* (of an ox) draw a vehicle or pull a load. ■ *S. Afr.* travel constantly from place to place; lead a nomadic life. ▷mid 19th cent.: from South African Dutch *trek* (noun), *trekken* (verb) 'pull, travel.' —**trek·ker** *n.*

trel·lis /'trɛlis/ ▶*n.* a framework of light wooden or metal bars, chiefly used as a support for fruit trees or climbing plants.
▶*v.* (**-lised, -lis·ing**) [*tr.*] provide with or enclose in a trellis: *a trellised archway.* ■ support (a climbing plant) with a trellis.

trem·ble /'trɛmbəl/ ▶*v.* [*intr.*] shake involuntarily, typically as a result of anxiety, excitement, or frailty: *Isobel was trembling with excitement.* ■ be in a state of extreme apprehension: *I tremble to think that we could ever return to conditions like these.* ■ (of a person's voice) sound unsteady or hesitant. ■ shake or quiver slightly: *the earth trembled beneath their feet.*
▶*n.* **1** a trembling feeling, movement, or sound. **2** (**the trembles**) *inf.* a physical or emotional condition marked by trembling. —**trem·bling·ly** /-b(ə)liNGlē/ *adv.*

tre·men·dous /trə'mendəs/ ▶*adj.* very great in amount, scale, or intensity: *a tremendous explosion.* ■ *inf.* extremely good or impressive; excellent: *a tremendous job.* —**tre·men·dous·ly** *adv.* —**tre·men·dous·ness** *n.*

trem·o·lo /'trɛmə,lō/ ▶*n.* (*pl.* **-los**) *Mus.* a wavering effect in a musical tone, typically produced by rapid reiteration of a note, or sometimes by rapid repeated variation in the pitch of a note or by sounding two notes of slightly different pitches to produce prominent overtones. Compare with VIBRATO. ■ a mechanism in an organ producing such an effect. ■ (also **tremolo arm**) a lever on an electric guitar, used to produce such an effect.

trem·or /'trɛmər/ ▶*n.* an involuntary quivering movement: *a disorder that* causes *tremors and muscle rigidity.* ■ a slight earthquake. ■ a sudden feeling of fear or excitement: *a tremor of unease.* ■ a tremble or quaver in a person's voice.

trem·u·lous /ˈtremyələs/ ▶*adj.* shaking or quivering slightly. ■ timid; nervous. —**trem·u·lous·ly** *adv.* —**trem·u·lous·ness** *n.*

trench /trenCH/ ▶*n.* a long, narrow ditch. ■ such a ditch dug by troops to provide a place of shelter from enemy fire. ■ (**trenches**) a connected system of such ditches forming an army's line. ■ (**the trenches**) the battlefields of northern France and Belgium in World War I: *the slaughter in the trenches created a new cynicism* | *fig. entry-level teachers are taught the latest classroom techniques by colleagues with experience in the trenches.* ■ a long, narrow, deep depression in the ocean floor, typically one running parallel to a plate boundary and marking a subduction zone.
▶*v.* [*tr.*] dig a trench or trenches in (the ground): *she trenched the terrace to a depth of 6 feet.* ■ turn over the earth of (a field or garden) by digging a succession of adjoining ditches.

trench·ant /ˈtrenCHənt/ ▶*adj.* **1** vigorous or incisive in expression or style. **2** *archaic* or *poetic/lit.* (of a weapon or tool) having a sharp edge: *a trenchant blade.* —**trench·an·cy** /-CHənsē/ *n.* —**trench·ant·ly** *adv.*

trench coat ▶*n.* a loose, belted, double-breasted raincoat in a military style. ■ a lined or padded waterproof coat worn by soldiers.

trench·er[1] /ˈtrenCHər/ ▶*n.* **1** *hist.* a wooden plate or platter for food. ■ a thick slice of bread used as a plate or platter. **2** old-fashioned term for MORTARBOARD (sense 1).

trench·er[2] ▶*n.* a machine or attachment used in digging trenches.

trench·er·man /ˈtrenCHərmən/ ▶*n.* (*pl.* **-men**) *humorous* a person who eats in a specified manner, typically heartily: *he is a hearty trencherman.*

trench war·fare ▶*n.* a type of combat in which opposing troops fight from trenches facing each other.

trend /trend/ ▶*n.* a general direction in which something is developing or changing: *an upward trend in sales and profit margins.* ■ a fashion.
▶*v.* [*intr.*] (esp. of geographical features) bend or turn away in a specified direction: *the Richelieu River trending southward.* ■ change or develop in a general direction: *unemployment has been trending upward.*

trend·set·ter /ˈtren(d)ˌsetər/ ▶*n.* a person who leads the way in fashion or ideas. —**trend·set·ting** /-ˌsetiNG/ *adj.*

trend·y /ˈtrendē/ *inf.* ▶*adj.* (**trend·i·er, trend·i·est**) very fashionable or up to date in style or influence.
▶*n.* (*pl.* **trend·ies**) a person who is very fashionable or up to date. —**trend·i·ly** /-dəlē/ *adv.* —**trend·i·ness** *n.*

trep·i·da·tion /ˌtrepiˈdāSHən/ ▶*n.* a feeling of fear or agitation about something that may happen: *the men set off in fear and trepidation.* —**trep·i·da·tious** /-SHəs/ *adj.*

tres·pass /ˈtrespəs; -ˌpas/ ▶*v.* [*intr.*] **1** enter the owner's land or property without permission: *there is no excuse for trespassing on railroad property.* ■ (**trespass on**) make unfair claims on or take advantage of (something): *she really must not trespass on his hospitality.* **2** (**trespass against**) *archaic* or *poetic/lit.* commit an offense against (a person or a set of rules): *a man who had trespassed against Judaic law.*
▶*n.* **1** *Law* entry to a person's land or property without their permission. **2** *archaic* or *poetic/lit.* a sin; an offense: *the worst trespass against the goddess Venus is to see her naked and asleep.* —**tres·pass·er** *n.*

tress /tres/ ▶*n.* (usu. **tresses**) a long lock of a woman's hair.
▶*v.* [*tr.*] *archaic* arrange (a person's hair) into long locks. —**tressed** *adj.* [often in *comb.*] *a blonde-tressed sex symbol.* —**tress·y** *adj.*

tres·tle /ˈtresəl/ ▶*n.* a framework consisting of a horizontal beam supported by two pairs of sloping legs, used in pairs to support a flat surface such as a tabletop. ■ (also **tres·tle·work** /-ˌwərk/) an open crossbraced framework used to support an elevated structure such as a bridge.

treyf /trāf/ ▶*adj.* variant spelling of TRAYF.

tri·ad /ˈtrīˌad/ ▶*n.* **1** a group or set of three connected people or things. ■ a chord of three musical notes, consisting of a given note with the third and fifth above it. ■ a Welsh form of literary composition with an arrangement of subjects or statements in groups of three. **2** (also **Tri·ad**) a secret society originating in China, typically involved in organized crime. ■ a member of such a society. —**tri·ad·ic** /trīˈadik/ *adj.*

tri·age /trēˈäZH; ˈtrēˌäZH/ ▶*n.* **1** the action of sorting according to quality. **2** (in medical use) the assignment of degrees of urgency to wounds or illnesses to decide the order of treatment of a large number of patients. ▷*early 18th cent.:* from French, from *trier* 'separate out.' The medical sense dates from the 1930s, from the military system of assessing the wounded on the battlefield.

tri·al /ˈtrī(ə)l/ ▶*n.* **1** a formal examination of evidence by a judge, typically before a jury, in order to decide guilt in a case of criminal or civil proceedings. **2** a test of the performance, qualities, or suitability of someone or something: *clinical trials must establish whether the new hip replacements are working.* ■ an athletic contest to test the ability of players eligible for selection to a team. ■ (**trials**) an event in which horses, dogs, or other animals compete or perform: *horse trials.* **3** a person, thing, or situation that tests a person's endurance or forbearance: *the trials and tribulations of married life.*
▶ □ **on trial** being tried in a court of law. □ **trial and error** the process of experimenting with various methods of doing something until one finds the most successful.

tri·al run ▶*n.* a test of the operation of a new system or product.

tri·an·gle /ˈtrīˌaNGgəl/ ▶*n.* a plane figure with three straight sides and three angles: *an equilateral triangle.*

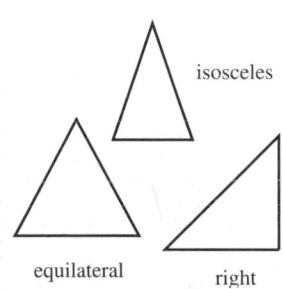

isosceles

equilateral   right

triangles

■ a thing shaped like such a figure: *a small triangle of grass.* ■ a situation involving three people or things, esp. an emotional relationship involving a couple and a third person with whom one of them is involved. ■ a musical instrument consisting of a steel rod bent into a triangle and sounded by being struck with a small steel rod. ■ a frame used to position the balls in pool and snooker. ■ a drawing instrument in the form of a right triangle.

tri·an·gu·lar /trīˈaNGgyələr/ ▶*adj.* shaped like a triangle; having three sides and three corners. ■ involving three people or parties. ■ (of a pyramid) having a three-sided base. —**tri·an·gu·lar·i·ty** /trīˌaNGgyə-ˈlaritē/ *n.* —**tri·an·gu·lar·ly** *adv.*

tri·an·gu·late /trīˈaNGgyəˌlāt/ ▶*v.* **1** [*tr.*] divide (an area) into triangles for surveying purposes. ■ measure and map (an area) by the use of triangles with a known base length and base angles. ■ determine (a height, distance, or location) in this way. **2** [*tr.*] form into a triangle or triangles: *the brackets triangulate the frame.* —**tri·an·gu·la·tion** /trīˌaNGgyə-ˈlāSHən/ *n.*

Tri·as·sic /trīˈasik/ ▶*adj.* *Geol.* of, relating to, or denoting the earliest period of the Mesozoic era, between the Permian and Jurassic periods. ■ [as *n.*] (**the Triassic** or **the Trias**) the Triassic period or the system of rocks deposited during it.

tri·ath·lon /trīˈaTHlən; -ˌlän/ ▶*n.* an athletic contest consisting of three different events, typically swimming, cycling, and long-distance running. —**tri·ath·lete** /-ˌlēt/ *n.*

tri·a·tom·ic /ˌtrīəˈtämik/ ▶*adj.* *Chem.* consisting of three atoms.

tri·ax·i·al /trīˈaksēəl/ ▶*adj.* having or relating to three axes, esp. in mechanical or astronomical contexts.

trib. ▶*abbr.* tributary.

trib·al /ˈtrībəl/ ▶*adj.* of or characteristic of a tribe or tribes: *tribal people in Malaysia.* ■ *chiefly derog.* characterized by a tendency to form groups or by strong group loyalty.
▶*n.* (**tribals**) members of tribal communities, esp. in the Indian subcontinent. —**trib·al·ly** *adv.*

trib·al·ism /ˈtrībəˌlizəm/ ▶*n.* the state or fact of being organized in a tribe or tribes. ■ *chiefly derog.* the behavior and attitudes that stem from strong loyalty to one's own tribe or social group: *an ethnic group demanding the paraphernalia of campus tribalism.* —**trib·al·ist** *n.*

tribe /trīb/ ▶*n.* **1** a social division in a traditional society consisting of families or communities linked by social, economic, religious, or blood ties, with a common culture and dialect, typically having a recognized leader: *indigenous Indian tribes.* ■ (in ancient Rome) each of several political divisions, originally three, later thirty, ultimately thirty-five. ■ *inf.* family: *the entire tribe is coming for Thanksgiving.* ■ *derog.* a distinctive close-knit social or political group: *the social codes of her English middle-class tribe.* ■ *derog.* a group or class of people or things: *an outburst against the whole tribe of theoreticians.* ■ (often **tribes**) *inf.* large numbers of people or animals: *tribes of children.* **2** *Biol.* a taxonomic category that ranks above genus and below family or subfamily, usually ending in *-ini* (in zoology) or *-eae* (in botany).

tribes·man /ˈtrībzmən/ ▶*n.* (*pl.* **-men**) a man belonging to a tribe in a traditional society or group.

trib·u·la·tion /ˌtrībyəˈlāSHən/ ▶*n.* (usu. **tribulations**) a cause of great trouble or suffering. ■ a state of great trouble or suffering. ■ **(the tribu-lation** or **the Great Tribulation)** *Christian Theol.* a period of great suffering expected during the end times.

tri·bu·nal /trī'byōōnl; trə-/ ▶ *n.* a court of justice: *an international war crimes tribunal.* ■ a seat or bench for a judge or judges.

trib·une /'tribyōōn; tri'byōōn/ ▶ *n.* an official in ancient Rome chosen by the plebeians to protect their interests. ■ a Roman legionary officer. ■ *fig.* a popular leader; a champion of the people. ■ used in names of newspapers: *the Chicago Tribune.* —**trib·u·nate** /'tribyənit; trī'byōōnit; -,nāt/ *n.* —**trib·une·ship** /-,SHip/ *n.*

trib·u·tar·y /'tribyə,terē/ ▶ *n.* (*pl.* **-tar·ies**) **1** a river or stream flowing into a larger river or lake. **2** *hist.* a person or state that pays tribute to another state or ruler.

trib·ute /'tribyōōt/ ▶ *n.* **1** an act, statement, or gift that is intended to show gratitude, respect, or admiration: *the video is a tribute to the musicals of the '40s.* ■ something resulting from something else and indicating its worth: *his victory in the championship was **a tribute to** his persistence.* **2** *hist.* payment made periodically by one state or ruler to another, esp. as a sign of dependence.

trice /trīs/ ▶ *n.* (in phrase **in a trice**) in a moment; very quickly.

tri·cen·ten·ni·al /,trīsen'tenēəl/ ▶ *n.* the three-hundredth anniversary of a significant event.
▶ *adj.* of or relating to a three-hundredth anniversary: *the tricentennial year.*

tri·ceps /'trī,seps/ ▶ *n.* (*pl.* same) *Anat.* any of several muscles having three points of attachment at one end, particularly the large muscle at the back of the upper arm.

tri·cer·a·tops /trī'serə,täps/ ▶ *n.* a large quadrupedal herbivorous dinosaur (genus *Triceratops*) living at the end of the Cretaceous period.

tri·chi·na /tri'kīnə/ ▶ *n.* (*pl.* **trichinae** /-nē/) a parasitic nematode (genus *Trichinella*, class Aphasmida) of humans and other mammals, the adults of which live in the small intestine. The larvae form hard cysts in the muscles.

trich·i·no·sis /,trikə'nōsis/ ▶ *n.* a disease caused by certain nematodes, typically from infected meat, esp. pork, characterized by digestive disturbance, fever, and muscular rigidity.

tri·chot·o·my /trī'kätəmē/ ▶ *n.* (*pl.* **-mies**) a division into three categories: *the pragmatics–semantics–syntax trichotomy.* ■ the division of the human person into body, soul, and spirit.

trick /trik/ ▶ *n.* **1** a cunning or skillful act or scheme intended to deceive or outwit someone. ■ a mischievous practical joke: *she thought Elaine was **playing** some **trick** on her.* ■ a skillful act performed for entertainment or amusement: *he did conjuring tricks for his daughters.* ■ an illusion: *I thought I saw a flicker of emotion, but it was probably **a trick of the light.*** ■ a clever or particular way of doing something: *the trick is to put one ski forward and kneel.* **2** a peculiar or characteristic habit or mannerism. **3** (in bridge, whist, and similar card games) a sequence of cards forming a single round of play. One card is laid down by each player, the highest card being the winner. **4** *inf.* a prostitute's client. **5** a sailor's turn at the helm, usually lasting for two or four hours.
▶ *v.* [*tr.*] deceive or outwit (someone) by being cunning or skillful: *buyers can be tricked by savvy sellers.* ■ **(trick someone into)** use deception to make someone do (something). ■ **(trick someone out of)** use deception to deprive someone of (something).
▶ *phrasal v.* □ **trick someone/something out** (or **up**) dress or decorate someone or something in an elaborate or showy way.
▶ *adj.* **1** intended or used to deceive or mystify, or to create an illusion: *a trick question.* **2** liable to fail; defective: *a trick knee.* —**trick·er** *n.*
▶ □ **do the trick** *inf.* achieve the required result. □ **every trick in the book** *inf.* every available method of achieving what one wants. □ **the oldest trick in the book** a ruse so hackneyed that it should no longer deceive anyone. □ **trick or treat** a children's custom of calling at houses at Halloween with the threat of pranks if they are not given a small gift (often used as a greeting by children doing this). □ **tricks of the trade** special ingenious techniques used in a profession or craft, esp. those that are little known by outsiders. □ **turn a trick** *inf.* (of a prostitute) have a session with a client. □ **up to one's (old) tricks** *inf.* misbehaving in a characteristic way.

trick·er·y /'trikərē/ ▶ *n.* (*pl.* **-er·ies**) the practice of deception.

trick·le /'trikəl/ ▶ *v.* [*intr.*] (of a liquid) flow in a small stream: *a solitary tear trickled down her cheek.* ■ [*tr.*] cause (a liquid) to flow in a small stream. ■ come or go slowly or gradually: *the details began to trickle out.*
▶ *phrasal v.* □ **trickle down** (of wealth) gradually benefit the poorest as a result of the increasing wealth of the richest.
▶ *n.* a small flow of liquid: *a trickle of blood.* ■ a small group or number of people or things moving slowly: *the traffic had dwindled to a trickle.*

trick·ster /'trikstər/ ▶ *n.* a person who cheats or deceives people.

trick·y /'trikē/ ▶ *adj.* (**trick·i·er, trick·i·est**) (of a task, problem, or situation) requiring care and skill because difficult or awkward: *applying eyeliner can be a tricky business.* ■ (of a person or act) deceitful, crafty, or skillful. —**trick·i·ly** /'trikəlē/ *adv.* —**trick·i·ness** *n.*

tri·clin·ic /trī'klinik/ ▶ *adj.* of or denoting a crystal system or three-dimensional geometric arrangement having three unequal oblique axes.

tri·col·or /'trī,kələr/ (*Brit.* **tri·col·our**) ▶ *n.* a flag with three bands or blocks of different colors, esp. the French national flag with equal upright bands of blue, white, and red.
▶ *adj.* (also **tri·col·ored**) having three colors.

tri·corne /'trī,kôrn/ (also **tri·corn**) ▶ *adj.* (of a hat) having a brim turned up on three sides.
▶ *n.* a hat of this kind.

tri·cot /'trēkō/ ▶ *n.* a fine knitted fabric made of a natural or man-made fiber.

tri·cy·cle /'trīsikəl; -,sikəl/ ▶ *n.* a vehicle similar to a bicycle, but having three wheels, two at the back and one at the front.
▶ *v.* [*intr.*] ride on a tricycle. —**tri·cy·clist** /-ist/ *n.*

tri·dent /'trīdnt/ ▶ *n.* a three-pronged spear, esp. as an attribute of Poseidon (Neptune) or Britannia. ■ **(Trident)** a U.S. design of submarine-launched long-range ballistic missile.

tried /trīd/ ▶ past and past participle of TRY.
▶ *adj.* used in various phrases to describe something that has proved effective or reliable before: *novel applications of **tried-and-tested** methods.*
▶ □ **the tried and true** something that has proved effective or reliable before: *supermarkets generally stick to the tried and true.*

tri·en·ni·al /trī'enēəl/ ▶ *adj.* recurring every three years: *the triennial meeting of the Association.* ■ lasting for or relating to a period of three years. —**tri·en·ni·al·ly** *adv.*

tri·fid /'trīfid/ ▶ *adj.* *chiefly Biol.* partly or wholly split into three divisions or lobes.

tri·fle /'trīfəl/ ▶ *n.* **1** a thing of little value or importance. ■ a small amount of something: *the thousand yen he'd paid seemed the merest trifle.* **2** *chiefly Brit.* a cold dessert of sponge cake and fruit covered with layers of custard, jelly, and cream.
▶ *v.* [*intr.*] **(trifle with)** treat (someone or something) without seriousness or respect: *men who trifle with women's affections.* —**tri·fler** /-f(ə)lər/ *n.*
▶ □ **a trifle** a little; somewhat: *his methods are a trifle eccentric.*

tri·fling /'trīf(ə)liNG/ ▶ *adj.* unimportant or trivial. —**tri·fling·ly** *adv.*

tri·fo·cal /'trī,fōkəl/ ▶ *adj.* (of a pair of glasses) having lenses with three parts with different focal lengths.
▶ *n.* **(trifocals)** a pair of glasses with such lenses.

tri·fo·li·ate /trī'fōlē-it; -,āt/ ▶ *adj.* (of a compound leaf) having three leaflets: *dark green trifoliate leaves.*

trig¹ /trig/ ▶ *n.* *inf.* trigonometry.

trig² ▶ *adj.* neat and smart in appearance.
▶ *v.* (**trigged, trig·ging**) [*tr.*] make neat and smart in appearance.

trig·ger /'trigər/ ▶ *n.* a small device that releases a spring or catch and so sets off a mechanism, esp. in order to fire a gun. ■ an event or thing that causes something to happen: *the trigger for the strike was the closure of a mine.*
▶ *v.* [*tr.*] cause (an event or situation) to happen or exist: *an allergy triggered by stress.* ■ cause (a device) to function. ▷early 17th cent.: from dialect *tricker,* from Dutch *trekker,* from *trekken* 'to pull.' —**trig·gered** *adj.*
▶ □ **quick on the trigger** quick to respond.

trig·ger·fish /'trigər,fiSH/ ▶ *n.* (*pl.* same or **-fishes**) a marine fish (family Balistidae) occurring chiefly in tropical inshore waters. It has a large, stout dorsal spine that can be erected and locked into place, allowing the fish to wedge itself into crevices.

trig·ger-hap·py ▶ *adj.* ready to react violently, esp. by shooting, on the slightest provocation: *territory controlled by trigger-happy bandits.*

trig·o·nom·e·try /,trigə'nämitrē/ ▶ *n.* the branch of mathematics dealing with the relations of the sides and angles of triangles and with the relevant functions of any angles. —**trig·o·no·met·ric** /-nə'metrik/ *adj.* —**trig·o·no·met·ri·cal** /-nə'metrikəl/ *adj.*

tri·gram /'trī,gram/ ▶ *n.* **1** another term for TRIGRAPH. **2** each of the

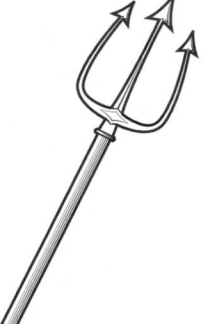
trident

eight figures formed of three parallel lines, each either whole or broken, combined to form the sixty-four hexagrams of the *I Ching*.

tri·graph /ˈtrīˌgraf/ ▶ *n.* a group of three letters representing one sound, for example German *sch-*.

tri·he·dron /trīˈhēdrən/ ▶ *n.* (*pl.* **-drons** or **-dra** /-drə/) a solid figure having three sides or faces (in addition to the base or ends).

trike /trīk/ *inf.* ▶ *n.* a tricycle.

tri·lat·er·al /trīˈlat(ə)rəl/ ▶ *adj.* shared by or involving three parties: *trilateral negotiations.* ■ *Geom.* of, on, or with three sides.
▶ *n.* a triangle.

tril·by /ˈtrilbē/ ▶ *n.* (*pl.* **-bies**) chiefly *Brit.* a soft felt hat with a narrow brim and indented crown.

tri·lin·gual /trīˈliNGgwəl/ ▶ *adj.* (of a person) speaking three languages fluently. ■ (of a text or an activity) written or conducted in three languages. **—tri·lin·gual·ism** /-ˌlizəm/ *n.*

trill /tril/ ▶ *n.* a quavering or vibratory sound, esp. a rapid alternation of sung or played notes: *the caged bird launched into a piercing trill.* ■ the pronunciation of a consonant, esp. *r*, with rapid vibration of the tongue against the hard or soft palate or the uvula.
▶ *v.* [*intr.*] produce a quavering or warbling sound: *a skylark was trilling overhead.* ■ [*tr.*] sing (a note or song) with a warbling or quavering sound. ■ [*tr.*] pronounce (a consonant) by rapid vibration of the tongue against the hard or soft palate or the uvula.

tril·lion /ˈtrilyən/ ▶ *cardinal number* (*pl.* **-lions** or (with numeral) same) a million million (1,000,000,000,000, or 10¹²). ■ (**trillions**) *inf.* a very large number or amount. **—tril·lionth** /-yənTH/ *ordinal number.*

tri·lo·bite /ˈtrīləˌbīt/ ▶ *n.* an extinct marine arthropod abundant during the Paleozoic era, with a carapace over the forepart, and a segmented hindpart divided longitudinally into three lobes.

tril·o·gy /ˈtriləjē/ ▶ *n.* (*pl.* **-gies**) a group of three related novels, plays, films, operas, or albums. ■ (in ancient Greece) a series of three tragedies performed one after the other. ■ *fig.* a group or series of three related things: *a trilogy of cases reflected this development.*

trim /trim/ ▶ *v.* (**trimmed**, **trim·ming**) [*tr.*] **1** make (something) neat or of the required size or form by cutting away irregular or unwanted parts: *trim the grass using a sharp mower.* ■ [*tr.*] cut off (irregular or unwanted parts): *he was trimming the fat off some pork chops.* ■ *fig.* reduce the size, amount, or number of (something, typically expenditure or costs). ■ [*intr.*] (**trim down**) (of a person) lose weight; become slimmer. ■ firm up or lose weight from (a part of one's body). **2** decorate (something), typically with contrasting items or pieces of material: *a pair of black leather gloves trimmed with fake fur.* **3** adjust (sails) to take best advantage of the wind. ■ adjust the forward and after drafts of (a vessel) by changing the distribution of weight on board, esp. cargo and ballast. ■ stow (a bulk cargo) properly in a ship's hold by use of manual labor or machinery. ■ keep or adjust the degree to which (an aircraft) can be maintained at a constant altitude without any control forces being present. **4** *inf.*, *dated* get the better of (someone), typically by cheating them out of money. **5** *inf.*, *dated* rebuke (someone) angrily.
▶ *n.* **1** additional decoration, typically along the edges of something and in contrasting color or material. ■ decorative additions to a vehicle, typically the upholstery or interior lining of a car. **2** an act of cutting off part of something in order to neaten it: *his hair needs a trim.* ■ a short piece of film cut out during the final editing stage. **3** the state of being in good order or condition: *no one had been there for months— everything was out of trim.* **4** the degree to which an aircraft can be maintained at a constant altitude without any control forces being present. **5** the difference between a vessel's forward and after drafts, esp. as it affects its navigability.
▶ *adj.* (**trim·mer**, **trim·mest**) neat and smart in appearance; in good order: *a trim little villa.* ■ (of a person or their body) slim and fit. **—trim·ly** *adv.* **—trim·ness** *n.*
▶ □ **in trim** slim and fit. ■ *Naut.* in good order. □ **trim one's sails (to the wind)** make changes to suit one's new circumstances.

tri·ma·ran /ˈtrīməˌran/ ▶ *n.* a yacht with three hulls in parallel.

tri·mes·ter /trīˈmestər; ˈtrīˌmes-/ ▶ *n.* a period of three months, esp. as a division of the duration of pregnancy. ■ each of the three terms in an academic year. **—tri·mes·tral** /trīˈmestrəl/ *adj.* **—tri·mes·tri·al** /trīˈmestrēəl/ *adj.*

trim·e·ter /ˈtrimitər/ ▶ *n. Prosody* a line of verse consisting of three metrical feet. **—tri·met·ric** /trīˈmetrik/ *adj.* **—tri·met·ri·cal** /trīˈmetrikəl/ *adj.*

trim·ming /ˈtrimiNG/ ▶ *n.* **1** the action of cutting off the unwanted or untidy parts of something: *he keeps his hair short by continual trimming.* ■ (**trimmings**) small pieces cut off in such a way: *hedge trimmings.* **2** decoration, esp. for clothing: *a party dress with lace trimming.* ■ (**the**

trimmings) *inf.* the traditional accompaniments to something, esp. a meal or special occasion: *roast turkey with all the trimmings.*

tri·ni·tro·tol·u·ene /trīˌnītrōˈtälyəˌwēn/ ▶ *n.* see **TNT**.

trin·i·ty /ˈtrinitē/ ▶ *n.* (*pl.* **-ties**) (also **the Trin·i·ty** or **the Holy Trinity**) the Christian Godhead as one God in three persons: Father, Son, and Holy Spirit. ■ a group of three people or things. ■ the state of being three.

trin·ket /ˈtriNGkit/ ▶ *n.* a small ornament or item of jewelry that is of little value. **—trin·ket·ry** /-trē/ *n.*

tri·no·mi·al /trīˈnōmēəl/ ▶ *adj.* **1** (of an algebraic expression) consisting of three terms. **2** *Biol.* (of a systematic name for a taxon) consisting of three terms of which the first is the name of the genus, the second that of the species, and the third that of the subspecies or variety.

tri·o /ˈtrē-ō/ ▶ *n.* (*pl.* **-os**) a set or group of three people or things: *a trio of brothers.* ■ a group of three musicians: *a jazz trio.* ■ a composition written for three musicians: *Chopin's G minor Trio.* ■ the central, typically contrasting, section of a minuet, scherzo, or march. ■ (in piquet) a set of three aces, kings, queens, jacks, or tens held in one hand.

trip /trip/ ▶ *v.* (**tripped**, **trip·ping**) **1** [*intr.*] catch one's foot on something and stumble or fall: *he tripped over his cat.* ■ [*tr.*] cause (someone) to do this. ■ (**trip up**) make a mistake: *taxpayers often trip up by not declaring taxable income.* ■ [*tr.*] (**trip someone up**) detect or expose someone in an error, blunder, or inconsistency: *the man was determined to trip him up on his economics.* **2** [*intr.*] walk, run, or dance with quick light steps: *they tripped up the terrace steps.* ■ (of words) flow lightly and easily: *a name that trips off the tongue.* **3** [*tr.*] activate (a mechanism), esp. by contact with a switch, catch, or other electrical device: *an intruder trips the alarm.* ■ [*intr.*] (of part of an electric circuit) disconnect automatically as a safety measure: *the plugs will trip as soon as any change in current is detected.* **4** [*intr.*] *inf.* experience hallucinations induced by taking a psychedelic drug, esp. LSD: *they prance around tripping out on their hallucinogens.* **5** [*intr.*] go on a short journey: *when tripping through the Yukon, take some time to explore our museums.*
▶ *n.* **1** a journey or excursion, esp. for pleasure. ■ an act of going to a place and returning. **2** a stumble or fall due to catching one's foot on something. ■ *archaic* a mistake. **3** *inf.* a hallucinatory experience caused by taking a psychedelic drug, esp. LSD. ■ an exciting or stimulating experience: *it was a trip seeing him again.* ■ a self-indulgent attitude or activity: *politics was a sixties trip.* **4** a device that activates or disconnects a mechanism, circuit, etc. ■ an instance of a device deactivating or the power supply disconnecting as a safety measure. ▷Middle English: from Old French *triper*, from Middle Dutch *trippen* 'to skip, hop.'

tri·par·tite /trīˈpärˌtīt/ ▶ *adj.* consisting of three parts: *a tripartite classification.* ■ shared by or involving three parties: *a tripartite coalition government.* **—tri·par·tite·ly** *adv.* **—tri·par·ti·tion** /ˌtrīpärˈtiSHən/ *n.*

tripe /trīp/ ▶ *n.* **1** the first or second stomach of a cow or other ruminant used as food. **2** *inf.* nonsense; rubbish: *you do talk tripe sometimes.*

tri·plane /ˈtrīˌplān/ ▶ *n.* an early type of airplane with three pairs of wings, one above the other.

tri·ple /ˈtripəl/ ▶ *adj.* consisting of or involving three parts, things, or people: *a triple murder.* ■ having three times the usual size, quality, or strength: *a triple dark rum.* ■ (of a person or animal) having done or won something three times: *a triple champion.*
▶ *n.* **1** a set of three things or parts. ■ an amount that is three times as large as another: *the triples of numbers.* **2** (**Triples**) *Bell-ringing* a system of change ringing using seven bells, with three pairs changing places each time. **3** *Baseball* a hit that enables the batter to reach third base.
▶ *v.* [*intr.*] **1** become three times as much or as many: *grain prices were expected to triple.* ■ [*tr.*] multiply (something) by three. **2** *Baseball* hit a triple. **—trip·ly** /ˈtriplē/ *adv.*

tri·ple crown ▶ *n.* (**Triple Crown**) an award or honor for winning a group of three important events in a sport, in particular victory by one horse in the Kentucky Derby, the Preakness, and the Belmont Stakes.

tri·ple jump ▶ *n.* **1** (**the triple jump**) a track-and-field event in which competitors attempt to jump as far as possible by performing a hop, a step, and a jump from a running start. **2** *Skating* a jump in which the skater makes three full turns while in the air.
▶ *v.* (**tri·ple-jump**) [*intr.*] (of an athlete) perform a triple jump. **—tri·ple jump·er** *n.*

tri·ple play ▶ *n. Baseball* a defensive play in which three runners are put out.

Pronunciation Key ə *ago*, *up*; ər *over*, *fur*; a *hat*; ā *ate*; ä *car*; CH *chin*; e *let*; ē *see*; e(ə)r *air*; i *fit*; ī *by*; i(ə)r *ear*; NG *sing*; ō *go*; ô *law*, *for*; oi *toy*; o͝o *good*; o͞o *goo*; ou *out*; SH *she*; TH *thin*; T͟H *then*; (h)w *why*; ZH *vision*

tri·plet /ˈtriplit/ ▶n. **1** (usu. **triplets**) one of three children or animals born at the same birth. **2** a set or succession of three similar things. ■ *Mus.* a group of three equal notes to be performed in the time of two or four. ■ a set of three rhyming lines of verse.

tri·plet code ▶n. *Biol.* the standard version of the genetic code, in which a sequence of three nucleotides in a DNA or RNA molecule codes for a specific amino acid in protein synthesis.

trip·li·cate ▶adj. /ˈtriplikit/ existing in three copies or examples.
▶n. /ˈtriplikit/ *archaic* a thing that is part of a set of three copies or corresponding parts: *the triplicate of a letter to the Governor.*
▶v. /-ˌkāt/ [tr.] make three copies of (something); multiply by three. —**trip·li·ca·tion** /ˌtripləˈkāSHən/ n.
▶ □ **in triplicate** three times in exactly the same way: *the procedure was repeated in triplicate.* ■ existing as a set of three exact copies.

trip·loid /ˈtriploid/ *Genetics* ▶adj. (of a cell or nucleus) containing three homologous sets of chromosomes. ■ (of an organism or species) composed of triploid cells.
▶n. a triploid organism, variety, or species. —**trip·loi·dy** /ˈtriˌploidē/ n.

trip·me·ter /ˈtripˌmētər/ ▶n. a vehicle instrument that can be set to record the distance of individual journeys.

tri·pod /ˈtrīpäd/ ▶n. **1** a three-legged stand for supporting a camera or other apparatus. **2** *archaic* a stool, table, or cauldron resting on three legs. ■ *hist.* the bronze altar at Delphi on which a priestess sat to utter oracles. —**trip·o·dal** /ˈtrīˌpōdl/ adj.

trip·tych /ˈtriptik/ ▶n. a picture or relief carving on three panels, typically hinged together side by side and used as an altarpiece. ■ a set of three associated artistic, literary, or musical works intended to be appreciated together.

trip·wire /ˈtripˌwīr/ ▶n. a wire stretched close to the ground, working a trap, explosion, or alarm when disturbed and serving to detect or prevent people or animals entering an area. ■ a comparatively weak military force employed as a first line of defense, engagement with which will trigger the intervention of strong forces.

tri·reme /ˈtrīˌrēm/ ▶n. an ancient Greek or Roman war galley with rowers three to a bench on each side.

tri·sac·cha·ride /trīˈsakəˌrīd/ ▶n. *Chem.* any of the class of sugars whose molecules contain three monosaccharide molecules.

tri·sect /trīˈsekt/ ▶v. [tr.] divide (something) into three parts, typically three equal parts. —**tri·sec·tion** /-ˈsekSHən/ n. —**tri·sec·tor** /-tər/ n.

tris·mus /ˈtrizməs/ ▶n. *Med.* spasm of the jaw muscles, causing the mouth to remain tightly closed, typically as a symptom of tetanus. Also called LOCKJAW.

trite /trīt/ ▶adj. (of a remark, opinion, or idea) overused and consequently of little import; lacking originality or freshness. ▷mid 16th cent.: from Latin *tritus,* past participle of *terere* 'to rub.' —**trite·ly** adv. —**trite·ness** n.

trit·i·um /ˈtritēəm/ 'triSH-/ ▶n. *Chem.* a radioactive isotope of hydrogen with a mass approximately three times that of the common protium isotope. (Symbol: **T**)

trit·u·rate /ˈtriCHəˌrāt/ ▶v. [tr.] *technical* grind to a fine powder. ■ chew or grind (food) thoroughly. —**trit·u·ra·tion** /ˌtriCHəˈrāSHən/ n. —**trit·u·ra·tor** /-ˌrātər/ n.

tri·umph /ˈtrīəmf/ ▶n. **1** a great victory or achievement: *Napoleon's many triumphs.* ■ the state of being triumphant or successful: *the king returned home in triumph.* ■ joy or satisfaction resulting from a success or victory: *"Here it is!" Helen's voice rose in triumph.* ■ a highly successful example of something: *the marriage had been a triumph of togetherness.* **2** the processional entry of a victorious general into ancient Rome.
▶v. [intr.] achieve a victory; be successful: *capitalism triumphed over socialism.* ■ rejoice or exult at a victory or success: *"There!" triumphed Alima.*

tri·um·phal /trīˈəmfəl/ ▶adj. made, carried out, or used in celebration of a great victory or achievement: *a vast triumphal arch.*

tri·um·phant /trīˈəmfənt/ ▶adj. having won a battle or contest; victorious. ■ feeling or expressing jubilation after having won a victory or mastered a difficulty: *a triumphant smile.* —**tri·um·phant·ly** adv.

tri·um·vir /trīˈəmvər/ ▶n. (pl. **-virs** or **-vi·ri** /-vəˌrī/) (in ancient Rome) each of three public officers jointly responsible for overseeing any of the administrative departments. —**tri·um·vi·ral** /-rəl/ adj.

tri·um·vi·rate /trīˈəmvərit; -ˌrāt/ ▶n. **1** (in ancient Rome) a group of three men holding power. ■ a group of three powerful or notable people or things existing in relation to each other. **2** the office of triumvir in ancient Rome.

tri·va·lent /trīˈvālənt/ ▶adj. *Chem.* having a valence of three.

triv·et /ˈtrivit/ ▶n. an iron tripod placed over a fire for a cooking pot or

kettle to stand on. ■ an iron bracket designed to hook onto bars of a grate for a similar purpose. ■ a small plate placed under a hot serving dish to protect a table.

triv·i·a /ˈtrivēə/ ▶pl. n. details, considerations, or pieces of information of little importance or value: *we fill our days with meaningless trivia.*

triv·i·al /ˈtrivēəl/ ▶adj. of little value or importance: *huge fines were imposed for trivial offenses | trivial details.* ■ (of a person) concerned only with trifling or unimportant things. ■ *Math.* denoting a subgroup that either contains only the identity element or is identical with the given group. —**triv·i·al·i·ty** /ˌtrivēˈalitē/ n. (pl. **-ties**) —**triv·i·al·ly** adv.

triv·i·al·ize /ˈtrivēəˌlīz/ ▶v. [tr.] make (something) seem less important, significant, or complex than it really is: *the problem was either trivialized or ignored by teachers.* —**triv·i·al·i·za·tion** /ˌtrivēəliˈzāSHən/ n.

tro·chee /ˈtrōkē/ ▶n. *Prosody* a foot consisting of one long or stressed syllable followed by one short or unstressed syllable.

troch·le·a /ˈträklēə/ ▶n. (pl. **-le·ae** /-lē,ē/) *Anat.* a structure resembling or acting like a pulley, such as the groove at the lower end of the humerus forming part of the elbow joint.

tro·choid /ˈtrōˌkoid/ ▶adj. **1** *Anat.* denoting a joint in which one element rotates on its own axis. **2** *Geom.* denoting a curve traced by a point on a radius of a circle rotating along a straight line or another circle. —**tro·choi·dal** /trōˈkoidl/ adj.

trod /träd/ ▶ past and past participle of TREAD.

trod·den /ˈträdn/ ▶ past participle of TREAD.

trog·lo·dyte /ˈträgləˌdīt/ ▶n. (esp. in prehistoric times) a person who lived in a cave. ■ a hermit. ■ a person who is regarded as being deliberately ignorant or old-fashioned. —**trog·lo·dyt·ic** /ˌträgləˈditik/ adj. —**trog·lo·dyt·ism** /-dī,tizəm/ n.

troi·ka /ˈtroikə/ ▶n. **1** a Russian vehicle pulled by a team of three horses abreast. ■ a team of three horses for such a vehicle. **2** a group of three people working together, esp. in an administrative or managerial capacity.

troil·ism /ˈtroi,lizəm/ ▶n. sexual activity involving three participants.

Tro·jan /ˈtrōjən/ ▶adj. of or relating to ancient Troy in Asia Minor.
▶n. a native or inhabitant of ancient Troy.

Tro·jan Horse ▶n. *Greek Mythol.* a hollow wooden statue of a horse in which the Greeks concealed themselves in order to enter Troy. ■ (also **Trojan horse**) *fig.* a person or thing intended secretly to undermine or bring about the downfall of an enemy or opponent: *the rebels may use this peace accord as a Trojan horse to try and take over.* ■ (also **Trojan horse**) *Comput.* a program designed to breach the security of a computer system while ostensibly performing some innocuous function.

troll[1] /trōl/ ▶n. a mythical, cave-dwelling being depicted in folklore as either a giant or a dwarf, typically having a very ugly appearance.

troll[2] ▶v. [intr.] **1** fish by trailing a baited line along behind a boat: *we trolled for mackerel.* ■ search for something: *a group of companies trolling for partnership opportunities.* **2** [tr.] sing (something) in a happy and carefree way: *troll the ancient Yuletide carol.* **3** [tr.] *inf. Comput.* send (an e-mail message or posting on the Internet) intended to provoke a response from the reader by containing errors. **4** *chiefly Brit.* walk; stroll: *we all trolled into town.*
▶n. **1** the action of trolling for fish. ■ a line or bait used in such fishing. **2** *inf. Comput.* an e-mail message or posting on the Internet intended to provoke an indignant response in the reader. —**troll·er** n.

trol·ley /ˈträlē/ ▶n. (pl. **-leys**) **1** short for TROLLEY CAR. **2** (also **trolley wheel**) a wheel attached to a pole, used for collecting current from an overhead electric wire to drive a streetcar or trolley bus. **3** a large metal basket or frame on wheels, resembling a shopping cart and used for transporting luggage at an airport or railroad station.
▶ □ **off one's trolley** *inf.* mad; insane.

trol·ley car ▶n. a passenger vehicle powered by electricity obtained from an overhead cable by means of a trolley wheel. Also called STREETCAR.

trol·lop /ˈträləp/ ▶n. *dated* or *humorous* a woman perceived as sexually disreputable or promiscuous.

trom·bone /trämˈbōn; trəm-/ ▶n. a large brass wind instrument with straight tubing in three sections, ending in a bell over the player's left shoulder, different fundamental notes being made using a forward-pointing extendable slide. —**trom·bon·ist** n.

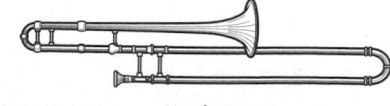

trombone

trompe l'oeil /ˌtrômp ˈloi/ ▸n. (pl. **trompe l'oeils** pronunc. same) visual illusion in art, esp. as used to trick the eye into perceiving a painted detail as a three-dimensional object. ■ a painting or design intended to create such an illusion.

troop /tro͞op/ ▸n. **1** a group of soldiers, esp. a cavalry unit commanded by a captain, or an airborne unit. ■ (**troops**) soldiers or armed forces. ■ a unit of 18 to 24 Girl Scouts or Boy Scouts organized under a troop leader. **2** a group of people or animals of a particular kind: *a troop of musicians.*
▸v. [intr.] (of a group of people) come or go together or in large numbers: *the girls trooped in for dinner.* ■ (of a lone person) walk at a slow or steady pace: *Caroline trooped wearily home from work.*

troop·er /ˈtro͞opər/ ▸n. **1** a state police officer. ■ a mounted police officer. **2** a private soldier in a cavalry, armored, or airborne unit. ■ a cavalry horse.

tro·phy /ˈtrōfē/ ▸n. (pl. **-phies**) **1** a cup or other decorative object awarded as a prize for a victory or success. ■ a souvenir of an achievement, esp. a part of an animal taken when hunting. **2** (in ancient Greece or Rome) the weapons and other spoils of a defeated army set up as a memorial of victory. ■ a representation of such a memorial; an ornamental group of symbolic objects arranged for display.

tro·phy wife ▸n. inf., derog. a young, attractive wife regarded as a status symbol for an older man.

trop·ic[1] /ˈträpik/ ▸n. the parallel of latitude 23°26′ north (**tropic of Cancer**) or south (**tropic of Capricorn**) of the equator. ■ Astron. each of two corresponding circles on the celestial sphere where the sun appears to turn after reaching its greatest declination, marking the northern and southern limits of the ecliptic. ■ (**the tropics**) the region between the tropics of Cancer and Capricorn.
▸adj. another term for TROPICAL (sense 1).

trop·ic[2] ▸adj. Biol. relating to, consisting of, or exhibiting tropism.

trop·i·cal /ˈträpəkəl/ ▸adj. of, typical of, or peculiar to the tropics: *a tropical rain forest.* ■ resembling the tropics, esp. in being very hot and humid. —**trop·i·cal·ly** /-ik(ə)lē/ adv.

trop·i·cal storm ▸n. a localized, very intense low-pressure wind system, forming over tropical oceans and with winds of hurricane force.

tro·pism /ˈtrō,pizəm/ ▸n. Biol. the turning of all or part of an organism in a particular direction in response to an external stimulus.

trop·o·sphere /ˈträpə,sfi(ə)r; ˈtrō-/ ▸n. the lowest region of the atmosphere, extending from the earth's surface to a height of about 6–10 km (the lower boundary of the stratosphere). —**trop·o·spher·ic** /ˌträpə-ˈsfi(ə)rik; -ˈsferik; ˌtrō-/ adj.

trot /trät/ ▸v. (**trot·ted**, **trot·ting**) (of a horse or other quadruped) proceed at a pace faster than a walk, lifting each diagonal pair of legs alternately. ■ [tr.] cause (a horse) to move at such a pace. ■ [intr.] (of a person) run at a moderate pace. ■ [intr.] inf. go or walk briskly: *he trotted over to the bonfire.*
▸phrasal v. □ **trot something out 1** inf. produce the same information, story, or explanation that has been produced many times before. **2** cause a horse to trot to show its paces.
▸n. **1** a trotting pace: *our horses slowed to a trot.* **2** (**the trots**) inf. diarrhea: *a bad case of the trots.* **3** inf. a literal translation of a foreign language text for use by students, esp. in a surreptitious way.

troth /trôTH; trōTH/ ▸n. **1** archaic or formal faith or loyalty when pledged in a solemn agreement or undertaking: *a token of troth.* **2** archaic truth.
▸ □ **pledge** (or **plight**) **one's troth** make a solemn pledge of commitment or loyalty, esp. in marriage.

trou·ba·dour /ˈtro͞obə,dôr; -,do͝or/ ▸n. a French medieval lyric poet composing and singing in Provençal in the 11th to 13th centuries, esp. on the theme of courtly love. ■ a poet who writes verse to music.

trou·ble /ˈtrəbəl/ ▸n. **1** difficulty or problems: *I had trouble finding somewhere to park.* ■ the malfunction of something such as a machine or a part of the body: *their helicopter developed engine trouble.* ■ effort or exertion made to do something, esp. when inconvenient: *I wouldn't want to put you to any trouble.* ■ a cause of worry or inconvenience: *the kid had been no trouble.* ■ a particular aspect or quality of something regarded as unsatisfactory or as a source of difficulty: *that's **the trouble with** capitalism.* ■ a situation in which one is liable to incur punishment or blame: *he's been **in trouble with** the police.* ■ inf., dated used to refer to the condition of a pregnant unmarried woman: *she's not the first girl who's got herself **into trouble.*** **2** public unrest or disorder: *the cops are preparing for trouble.*
▸v. [tr.] **1** (often **be troubled**) cause distress or anxiety to: *he was not troubled by doubts.* ■ [intr.] (**trouble about/over/with**) be distressed or anxious about: *there is nothing you need trouble about.* ■ cause (someone) pain. ■ cause (someone) inconvenience (typically used as a polite way of

asking someone to do or provide something): *sorry to trouble you.* ■ [intr.] make the effort required to do something: *oh, don't trouble to answer.* **2** disturb or agitate (the surface in a pool or other body of water): *the waters were troubled.* —**trou·bler** /-b(ə)lər/ n.
▸ □ **ask for trouble** inf. act in a way that is likely to incur problems or difficulties. □ **look for trouble** inf. behave in a way that is likely to provoke an argument or fight.

trou·bled /ˈtrəbəld/ ▸adj. beset by problems or conflict: *his troubled private life.* ■ showing distress or anxiety: *his troubled face.*
▸ □ **troubled waters** a difficult situation or time.

trou·ble·mak·er /ˈtrəbəl,mākər/ ▸n. a person who habitually causes difficulty or problems, esp. by inciting others to defy those in authority. —**trou·ble·mak·ing** /-,mākiNG/ n. & adj.

trou·ble·shoot /ˈtrəbəl,SHo͞ot/ ▸v. [intr.] solve serious problems for a company or other organization. ■ trace and correct faults in a mechanical or electronic system. —**trou·ble·shoot·er** n.

trou·ble·some /ˈtrəbəlsəm/ ▸adj. causing difficulty or annoyance: *a troublesome injury.* —**trou·ble·some·ly** adv. —**trou·ble·some·ness** n.

trou·ble spot ▸n. a place where difficulties regularly occur, esp. a country or area where there is a continuous cycle of violence.

trough /trôf/ ▸n. a long, narrow open container for animals to eat or drink out of: *a water trough.* ■ a container of a similar shape used for a purpose such as growing plants or mixing chemicals. ■ a channel used to convey a liquid. ■ a long hollow in the earth's surface: *a vast glacial trough.* ■ an elongated region of low atmospheric pressure. ■ a hollow between two wave crests in the sea. ■ a low level of economic activity. ■ Math. a region around the minimum on a curve of variation of a quantity. ■ a point of low achievement or satisfaction.

trounce /trouns/ ▸v. [tr.] defeat heavily in a contest: *the Knicks trounced the Rockets on Sunday.* ■ rebuke or punish severely. —**trounc·er** n.

troupe /tro͞op/ ▸n. a group of dancers, actors, or other entertainers who tour to different venues.

troup·er /ˈtro͞opər/ ▸n. an actor or other entertainer, typically one with long experience. ■ a reliable and uncomplaining person: *a **real trouper**, Ma concealed her troubles.*

trou·ser /ˈtrouzər/ ▸n. [as adj.] relating to trousers: *his trouser pocket.* ■ a trouser leg: *his trouser was torn.*

trou·sers /ˈtrouzərz/ ▸pl. n. an outer garment covering the body from the waist to the ankles, with a separate part for each leg. —**trou·sered** /-zərd/ adj.

trous·seau /ˈtro͞o,sō; ˌtro͞oˈsō/ ▸n. (pl. **-seaux** pronunc. same, or **-seaus**) the clothes, household linen, and other belongings collected by a bride for her marriage.

trout /trout/ ▸n. (pl. same or **trouts**) a chiefly freshwater fish (genera *Salmo* and *Salvelinus*) of the salmon family, found in Eurasia and North America and highly valued as food and game. ▷late Old English *truht*, from late Latin *tructa*, based on Greek *trōgein* 'gnaw.'

trove /trōv/ ▸n. a store of valuable or delightful things.

trow·el /ˈtrouəl/ ▸n. **1** a small hand-held tool with a flat, pointed blade, used to apply and spread mortar or plaster. **2** a small hand-held tool with a curved scoop for lifting plants or earth.
▸v. (**-eled, -el·ing**; Brit. **-elled, -el·ling**) [tr.] apply or spread with or as if with a trowel.

troy /troi/ (in full **troy weight**) ▸n. a system of weights used mainly for precious metals and gems, with a pound of 12 ounces or 5,760 grains. Compare with AVOIRDUPOIS.

tru·ant /ˈtro͞oənt/ ▸n. a student who stays away from school without leave or explanation.
▸adj. (of a student) being a truant. ■ wandering; straying.
▸v. [intr.] another way of saying PLAY TRUANT below. —**tru·an·cy** /-ənsē/ n.
▸ □ **play truant** stay away from school or work without permission or explanation; play hooky.

truce /tro͞os/ ▸n. an agreement between enemies or opponents to stop fighting or arguing for a certain time.

truck[1] /trək/ ▸n. **1** a wheeled vehicle, in particular: ■ a large, heavy motor vehicle, used for transporting goods, materials, or troops. ■ a low flat-topped cart used for moving heavy items. **2** an undercarriage with four to six wheels pivoted beneath the end of a railroad car. ■ each of two axle units on a skateboard, to which the wheels are attached.
▸v. [tr.] convey by truck. ■ [intr.] drive a truck. ■ [intr.] inf. go or proceed,

---

Pronunciation Key ə *ago*, *up*; ər *over*, *fur*; a *hat*; ā *ate*; ä *car*; CH *chin*; e *let*; ē *see*; e(ə) *air*; i *fit*; ī *by*; i(ə) *ear*; NG *sing*; ō *go*; ô *law*, *for*; oi *toy*; o͞o *good*; o͞o *goo*; ou *out*; SH *she*; TH *thin*; TH *then*; (h)w *why*; ZH *vision*

esp. in a casual or leisurely way: *he walked confidently behind them and trucked on through!* —**truck·age** /-kij/ *n.*

truck² ▶*n.* **1** *archaic* barter. ■ *chiefly hist.* the payment of workers in kind or with vouchers rather than money. **2** *chiefly archaic* small wares. ■ *inf.* odds and ends. **3** market-garden produce, esp. vegetables: [as *adj.*] *a truck garden.*
▶*v.* [*tr.*] *archaic* barter or exchange.
▶ □ **have** (or **want**) **no truck with** avoid or wish to avoid dealings or being associated with: *we have no truck with that style of gutter journalism.*

truck·er /'trəkər/ ▶*n.* a long-distance truck driver.

truck·le ▶*v.* [*intr.*] submit or behave obsequiously: *she despised her husband, who truckled to her.* —**truck·ler** /'trək(ə)lər/ *n.*

truck stop ▶*n.* a large roadside service station and restaurant for truck drivers on interstate highways.

truc·u·lent /'trəkyələnt/ ▶*adj.* eager or quick to argue or fight; aggressively defiant. —**truc·u·lence** *n.* —**truc·u·lent·ly** *adv.*

trudge /trəj/ ▶*v.* [*intr.*] walk slowly and with heavy steps, typically because of exhaustion or harsh conditions: *I trudged up the stairs.*
▶*n.* a difficult or laborious walk: *the long trudge back.* —**trudg·er** *n.*

true /trōō/ ▶*adj.* (**tru·er, tru·est**) **1** in accordance with fact or reality: *a true story.* ■ rightly or strictly so called; genuine: *we believe in true love.* ■ real or actual: *he has guessed my true intentions.* ■ said when conceding a point in argument or discussion: *true, it faced north, but you got used to that.* **2** accurate or exact: *a true depiction.* ■ (of a note) exactly in tune. ■ (of a compass bearing) measured relative to true north: *steer 085 degrees true.* ■ correctly positioned, balanced, or aligned; upright or level. **3** loyal or faithful: *he was a true friend.* ■ (**true to**) accurately conforming to (a standard or expectation); faithful to: *this entirely new production remains true to the essence of Lorca's play.* **4** *chiefly archaic* honest: *we appeal to all good men and true to rally to us.*
▶*adv.* **1** *chiefly poetic/lit.* truly: *Hobson spoke truer than he knew.* **2** accurately or without variation.
▶*v.* (**trues, trued, tru·ing** or **true·ing**) [*tr.*] bring (an object, wheel, or other construction) into the exact shape, alignment, or position required. —**true·ness** *n.*
▶ □ **come true** actually happen or become the case: *dreams can come true.* □ **out of true** not in the correct or exact shape or alignment. □ **true to form** (or **type**) being or behaving as expected. □ **true to life** accurately representing real events or objects.

true-blue ▶*adj.* extremely loyal or orthodox.

true north ▶*n.* north according to the earth's axis, not magnetic north.

truf·fle /'trəfəl/ ▶*n.* **1** a strong-smelling underground fungus (*Tuber* and other genera) that resembles an irregular, rough-skinned potato. It is considered a culinary delicacy. **2** a soft candy made of a chocolate mixture, typically flavored with rum and covered with cocoa.

tru·ism /'trōō,izəm/ ▶*n.* a statement that is obviously true and says nothing new or interesting. —**tru·is·tic** /trōō'istik/ *adj.*

tru·ly /'trōōlē/ ▶*adv.* **1** in a truthful way: *he speaks truly.* ■ used to emphasize emotional sincerity or seriousness: *what we truly want | it is truly a privilege to be here | I'm truly sorry | truly, I don't understand you.* **2** to the fullest degree; genuinely or properly: *management does not truly care about the residents.* ■ absolutely or completely (used to emphasize a description): *a truly dreadful song.* **3** in fact or without doubt; really: *this is truly a miracle.*
▶ □ **yours truly** used as a formula for ending a letter. ■ *humorous* used to refer to oneself: *the demos will be organized by yours truly.*

trump¹ /trəmp/ ▶*n.* (in bridge, whist, and similar card games) a playing card of the suit chosen to rank above the others, which can win a trick where a card of a different suit has been led. ■ (**trumps**) the suit having this rank in a particular game: *the ace of trumps.* ■ (also **trump card**) *fig.* a valuable resource that may be used, esp. as a surprise, in order to gain an advantage. ■ *inf., dated* a helpful or admirable person.
▶*v.* [*tr.*] (in bridge, whist, and similar card games) play a trump on (a card of another suit), having no cards of the suit led. ■ *fig.* beat (someone or something) by saying or doing something better.
▶*phrasal v.* □ **trump something up** invent a false accusation or excuse.

trump² ▶*n.* *archaic* a trumpet or a trumpet blast.

trump·er·y /'trəmpərē/ ▶*n.* (pl. **-er·ies**) *archaic* attractive articles of little value or use. ■ practices or beliefs that are superficially or visually appealing but have little real value or worth.

trum·pet /'trəmpit/ ▶*n.* **1** a brass musical instrument with a flared bell and a bright, penetrating tone. The modern instrument has the tubing looped to form a straight-sided coil, with three valves. ■ something shaped like a trumpet, esp. the tubular corona of a daffodil flower. ■ a sound resembling that of a trumpet, esp. the loud cry of an

elephant. **2** (**trumpets**) a North American pitcher plant (genus *Sarracenia*).
▶*v.* (**trum·pet·ed, trum·pet·ing**) **1** [*intr.*] play a trumpet. ■ make a loud, penetrating sound resembling that of a trumpet: *wild elephants trumpeting in the bush.* **2** [*tr.*] proclaim widely or loudly.

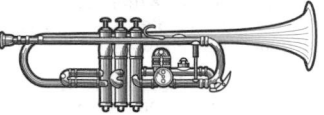

trumpet

trum·pet·er /'trəmpitər/ ▶*n.* **1** a person who plays a trumpet. **2** a large gregarious ground-dwelling bird (genus *Psophia*) of tropical South American forests, with mainly black plumage and loud trumpeting calls. **3** a pigeon of a domestic breed that makes a trumpetlike sound.

trum·pet·er swan ▶*n.* a large migratory swan (*Cygnus buccinator*) with a black and yellow bill and a honking call, breeding in northern North America.

trun·cate /'trəNG,kāt/ ▶*v.* [*tr.*] shorten (something) by cutting off the top or the end: *discussion was truncated by the arrival of tea.* ■ *Crystallog.* replace (an edge or an angle) by a plane, typically so as to make equal angles with the adjacent faces.
▶*adj. Bot. & Zool.* (of a leaf, feather, or other part) ending abruptly as if cut off across the base or tip. —**trun·ca·tion** /,trəNG'kāSHən/ *n.*

trun·cheon /'trənCHən/ ▶*n.* *chiefly Brit.* a short, thick stick carried as a weapon by a police officer. ■ a staff or baton acting as a symbol of authority.

trun·dle /'trəndl/ ▶*v.* [*intr.*] (of a wheeled vehicle or its occupants) move slowly and heavily, typically in a noisy or uneven way. ■ (of a person) move in a similar way. ■ [*tr.*] cause (something, typically a wheeled vehicle) to roll or move in such a way.
▶*n.* an act of moving in such a way.

trun·dle bed ▶*n.* a low bed on wheels that can be stored under a larger bed.

trunk /trəNGk/ ▶*n.* **1** the main woody stem of a tree as distinct from its branches and roots. ■ the main part of an artery, nerve, or other anatomical structure from which smaller branches arise. ■ an enclosed shaft or conduit for cables or ventilation. **2** a person's or animal's body apart from the limbs and head. **3** the elongated, prehensile nose of an elephant. **4** a large box with a hinged lid for storing or transporting clothes and other articles. ■ the space at the back of a car for carrying luggage and other goods. —**trunk·ful** /-,fŏŏl/ *n.* (pl. **-fuls**) —**trunk·less** *adj.*

trunk line ▶*n.* a main line of a railroad, telephone system, or other network.

truss /trəs/ ▶*n.* **1** a framework, typically consisting of rafters, posts, and struts, supporting a roof, bridge, or other structure: *roof trusses.* ■ a surgical appliance worn to support a hernia, typically a padded belt. ■ a large projection of stone or timber, typically one supporting a cornice. **2** a compact cluster of flowers or fruit growing on one stalk.
▶*v.* [*tr.*] **1** tie up the wings and legs of (a chicken or other bird) before cooking. ■ tie up (someone) with their arms at their sides. **2** support (a roof, bridge, or other structure) with a truss or trusses. —**truss·er** *n.*

trust /trəst/ ▶*n.* **1** firm belief in the reliability, truth, ability, or strength of someone or something: *relations have to be built on trust.* ■ acceptance of the truth of a statement without evidence or investigation: *I used only primary sources, taking nothing on trust.* ■ the state of being responsible for someone or something: *a man in a position of trust.* ■ *poetic/lit.* a person or duty for which one has responsibility: *rulership is a trust from God.* ■ *poetic/lit.* a hope or expectation: *all the great trusts of womanhood.* **2** *Law* confidence placed in a person by making that person the nominal owner of property to be held or used for the benefit of one or more others. ■ an arrangement whereby property is held in such a way: *property held in trust for his son.* **3** a body of trustees. ■ an organization or company managed by trustees: *a charitable trust.* ■ *dated* a large company that has or attempts to gain monopolistic control of a market.
▶*v.* [*tr.*] **1** believe in the reliability, truth, ability, or strength of. ■ (**trust someone with**) allow someone to have, use, or look after (someone or something of importance or value) with confidence. ■ (**trust some-one/something to**) commit (someone or something) to the safekeeping of: *they don't like to **trust** their money **to** anyone outside the family.* ■ have confidence; hope (used as a polite formula in conversation): *I trust that you have enjoyed this book.* ■ [*intr.*] have faith or confidence: *she*

trusted in the powers of justice. ■ [*intr.*] (**trust to**) place reliance on (luck, fate, or something else over which one has little control): *trusting to the cover of night, I ventured out.* **2** *chiefly archaic* allow credit to (a customer). ▷Middle English: from Old Norse *traust*, from *traustr* 'strong'; the verb from Old Norse *treysta*, assimilated to the noun. —**trust·a·ble** *adj.* —**trust·er** *n.*

▶ □ **trust someone to** —— it is characteristic or predictable for someone to act in the specified way: *trust Sam to have all the inside information.*

trust·ee /trəˈstē/ ▶*n. Law* an individual person or member of a board given control or powers of administration of property in trust with a legal obligation to administer it solely for the purposes specified. —**trust·ee·ship** /-ˌSHip/ *n.*

trust·ful /ˈtrəs(t)fəl/ ▶*adj.* having or marked by a total belief in the reliability, truth, ability, or strength of someone. —**trust·ful·ly** *adv.* —**trust·ful·ness** *n.*

trust fund ▶*n.* a fund consisting of assets belonging to a trust, held by the trustees for the beneficiaries.

trust·ing /ˈtrəstiNG/ ▶*adj.* showing or tending to have a belief in a person's honesty or sincerity; not suspicious. —**trust·ing·ly** *adv.* —**trust·ing·ness** *n.*

trust·wor·thy /ˈtrəstˌwərᴛʜē/ ▶*adj.* able to be relied on as honest or truthful. —**trust·wor·thi·ly** /-ᴛʜəlē/ *adv.* —**trust·wor·thi·ness** *n.*

trust·y /ˈtrəstē/ ▶*adj.* (**trust·i·er, trust·i·est**) *archaic* or *humorous* having served for a long time and regarded as reliable or faithful. ▶*n.* (*pl.* **trust·ies**) a prisoner who is given special privileges or responsibilities in return for good behavior. —**trust·i·ly** /-təlē/ *adv.* —**trust·i·ness** *n.*

truth /trooᴛʜ/ ▶*n.* (*pl.* **truths** /trooᴛʜz; trooᴛʜs/) the quality or state of being true: *to accept the truth of her accusation.* ■ (also **the truth**) that which is true or in accordance with fact or reality: *tell me the truth.* ■ a fact or belief that is accepted as true: *scientific truths.*

▶ □ **in truth** really; in fact: *in truth, she was more than a little unhappy.* □ **to tell the truth** (or **truth to tell** or **if truth be told**) to be frank (used esp. when making an admission or when expressing an unwelcome or controversial opinion): *I think, if truth be told, we were all a little afraid of him.*

truth·ful /ˈtrooᴛʜfəl/ ▶*adj.* (of a person or statement) telling or expressing the truth; honest. ■ (of artistic or literary representation) characterized by accuracy or realism. —**truth·ful·ly** *adv.* —**truth·ful·ness** *n.*

try /trī/ ▶*v.* (**tries, tried**) **1** [*intr.*] make an attempt or effort to do something: *none of them tried very hard* | [*tr.*] *three times he tried the maneuver and three times he failed.* ■ (**try for**) attempt to achieve or attain: *they decided to try for another baby.* ■ [*tr.*] use, test, or do (something new or different) in order to see if it is suitable, effective, or pleasant: *everyone wanted to know if I'd tried jellied eel.* ■ (**try out for**) compete or audition in order to join (a team) or be given (a position). ■ [*tr.*] go to (a place) or attempt to contact (someone), typically in order to obtain something: *I've tried the apartment, but the number is busy.* ■ [*tr.*] push or pull (a door or window) to determine whether it is locked. ■ [*tr.*] make severe demands on (a person or a quality, typically patience). **2** [*tr.*] (usu. **be tried**) subject (someone) to trial: *he was tried for the murder.* ■ investigate and decide (a case or issue) in a formal trial: *the most serious criminal cases must be tried by a jury.* **3** [*tr.*] extract (oil or fat) by heating: *some of the fat may be tried out and used.*

▶*phrasal v.* ■ **try something on** put on an item of clothing to see if it fits or suits one. □ **try someone/something out** test someone or something new or different to assess their suitability or effectiveness.

▶*n.* (*pl.* **tries**) **1** an effort to accomplish something; an attempt. ■ an act of doing, using, or testing something new or different to see if it is suitable, effective, or pleasant: *give the idea a try.* **2** *Rugby* an act of touching the ball down behind the opposing goal line, scoring points and entitling the scoring side to a goal kick.

▶ □ **try something on for size** assess whether something is suitable. □ **try one's hand at** attempt to do (something) for the first time, typically in order to find out if one is good at it. □ **try me** used to suggest that one may be willing to do something unexpected or unlikely: *"You won't use a gun up here." "Try me."*

try·ing /ˈtrī-iNG/ ▶*adj.* difficult or annoying; hard to endure: *it had been a very trying day.* —**try·ing·ly** *adv.*

tryp·to·phan /ˈtriptəˌfan/ ▶*n. Biochem.* an amino acid that is a constituent of most proteins. It is an essential nutrient in the diet of vertebrates.

tryst /trist/ *poetic/lit.* ▶*n.* a private, romantic rendezvous between lovers: *a moonlight tryst.*

▶*v.* [*intr.*] keep a rendezvous of this kind: [as *n.*] (**trysting**) *a trysting place.* —**trys·ter** *n.*

tsar /zär/ (also **czar** or **tzar**) ▶*n.* an emperor of Russia before 1917: *Tsar*

Nicholas II. ■ a South Slav ruler in former times, esp. one reigning over Serbia in the 14th century. ■ —**tsar·dom** /-dəm/ *n.* —**tsar·ism** /-ˌizəm/ *n.* —**tsar·ist** /-ist/ *n. & adj.*

tsa·ri·na /zäˈrēnə/ (*t*)sä-/ (also **cza·ri·na** or **tza·ri·na**) ▶*n. hist.* an empress of Russia before 1917.

tset·se /ˈ(t)setsē; ˈ(t)set-/ (also **tsetse fly**) ▶*n.* an African bloodsucking fly (genus *Glossina*, family Tabanidae) that bites humans and other mammals, transmitting sleeping sickness and other diseases.

T-shirt (also **tee shirt**) ▶*n.* a short-sleeved casual top, generally made of cotton, having the shape of a T when spread out flat.

tsp. ▶*abbr.* (*pl.* same or **tsps.**) teaspoon; teaspoonful.

T-square (also **T square**) ▶*n.* a T-shaped instrument for drawing or testing right angles.

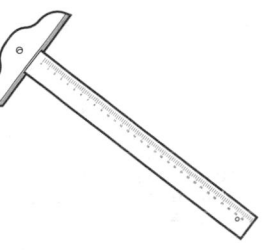
T-square

tsu·na·mi /(t)sooˈnämē/ ▶*n.* (*pl.* same or **-mis**) a long high sea wave caused by an earthquake, submarine landslide, or other disturbance. ▷late 19th cent.: from Japanese, from *tsu* 'harbor' + *nami* 'wave.'

tub /təb/ ▶*n.* **1** a wide, open, deep, typically round container with a flat bottom used for holding liquids, growing plants, etc.. ■ a similar small plastic or cardboard container in which food is bought or stored: *a margarine tub.* ■ the contents of such a container or the amount it can contain. ■ a washtub. ■ *inf.* a bathtub. **2** *inf.* an old, awkward, or run-down vessel. —**tub·ful** /-ˌfool/ *n.* (*pl.* **-fuls**).

tu·ba /ˈt(y)oobə/ ▶*n.* a large brass wind instrument of bass pitch, with three to six valves and a broad bell typically facing upward.

tub·al /ˈt(y)oobəl/ ▶*adj.* of, relating to, or occurring in a tube, esp. the fallopian tubes.

tub·by /ˈtəbē/ ▶*adj.* (**-bi·er, -bi·est**) **1** *inf.* (of a person) short and rather fat. **2** (of a sound) lacking resonance; dull. —**tub·bi·ness** *n.*

tube /t(y)oob/ ▶*n.* **1** a long, hollow cylinder of metal, plastic, glass, etc., for holding or transporting something, chiefly liquids or gases. ■ the inner tube of a bicycle tire. ■ material in such a cylindrical form; tubing: *the firm manufactures steel tube.* **2** a thing in the form of or resembling such a cylinder, in

tuba

particular: ■ a flexible metal or plastic container sealed at one end and having a screw cap at the other, for holding a semiliquid substance ready for use: *a tube of toothpaste.* ■ a rigid cylindrical container: *a tube of lipstick.* ■ *Anat., Zool.,, & Bot.* a hollow cylindrical organ or structure in an animal body or in a plant (e.g., a Eustachian tube). ■ (**tubes**) *inf.* a woman's fallopian tubes. ■ a woman's close-fitting garment, typically without darts or other tailoring and made from a single piece of knitted or elasticized fabric: [as *adj.*] *stretchy tube skirts.* ■ (in surfing) the hollow curve under the crest of a breaking wave. **3** (**the tube**) *Brit., inf.* the subway system in London. ■ a train running on this system. **4** a sealed container, typically of glass and either evacuated or filled with gas, containing two electrodes between which an electric current can be made to flow. ■ a cathode-ray tube, esp. in a television set. ■ (**the tube**) *inf.* television. ■ a vacuum tube. —**tube·less** *adj.* —**tube·like** /-ˌlīk/ *adj.*

▶ □ **go down the tubes** (or **tube**) *inf.* be completely lost or wasted; fail utterly.

tu·ber /ˈt(y)oobər/ ▶*n.* a much thickened underground part of a stem or rhizome, e.g., in the potato, serving as a food reserve and bearing buds from which new plants arise. ■ a tuberous root, e.g., of the dahlia.

tu·ber·cle /ˈt(y)oobərkəl/ ▶*n.* **1** *Anat., Zool., & Bot.* a small rounded projection or protuberance, esp. on a bone or on the surface of an animal or plant. **2** *Med.* a small nodular lesion in the lungs or other tissues, characteristic of tuberculosis. —**tu·ber·cu·late** /t(y)ooˈbərkyəˌlāt; -lit/ *adj.*

tu·ber·cu·lar /təˈbərkyələr/ ▶*adj. Med.* of, relating to, or affected with tuberculosis. ■ *Biol. & Med.* having or covered with tubercles. ▶*n.* a person with tuberculosis.

tu·ber·cu·lin /t(y)ōˈbərkyəlin/ ▶n. a sterile protein extract from cultures of tubercle bacillus, used in a test by hypodermic injection for infection with or immunity to tuberculosis.

tu·ber·cu·lo·sis /tə,bərkyəˈlōsis; t(y)ōō-/ (abbr.: **TB**) ▶n. an infectious disease characterized by the growth of nodules (tubercles) in the tissues, esp. the lungs.—**tu·ber·cu·lous** /-ˈbərkyələs/ adj.

tu·ber·ose /ˈt(y)ōōbə,rōs; -,rōz/ ▶n. **1** a Mexican plant (*Polianthes tuberosa*) of the agave family, with scented white waxy flowers and a bulblike base. It was formerly cultivated as a flavoring for chocolate, and the flower oil is used in perfumery. **2** variant spelling of TUBEROUS.

tu·ber·ous /ˈt(y)ōōbərəs/ (also **tu·ber·ose** /-bə,rōs/) ▶adj. **1** Bot. of the nature of a tuber. ■ (of a plant) having tubers or a tuberous root. **2** Med. characterized by or affected by rounded swellings: *tuberous sclerosis.* —**tu·ber·os·i·ty** /,t(y)ōōbəˈräsitē/ n.

tub·ing /ˈt(y)ōōbiNG/ ▶n. **1** a length or lengths of metal, plastic, glass, etc., in tubular form. **2** the leisure activity of riding on water or snow on a large inflated inner tube.

tu·bu·lar /ˈt(y)ōōbyələr/ ▶adj. long, round, and hollow like a tube. ■ made from a tube or tubes. ■ Surfing (of a wave) hollow and well curved. ■ inf., dated excellent: *U2's brand of really tubular new-wave sounds.*

tu·bu·lar bells ▶pl. n. an orchestral instrument consisting of a row of vertically suspended metal tubes struck with a mallet.

tu·bule /ˈt(y)ōō,byōōl/ ▶n. a minute tube, esp. as an anatomical structure: *kidney tubules.*

tuck /tək/ ▶v. **1** [tr.] push, fold, or turn (the edges or ends of something, esp. a garment or bedclothes) so as to hide them or hold them in place. ■ (**tuck someone in**) make someone, esp. a child, comfortable in bed by pulling the edges of the bedclothes firmly under the mattress. ■ draw (something, esp. part of one's body) together into a small space: *she tucked her legs under her.* ■ put (something) away in a specified place or way so as to be hidden, safe, comfortable, or tidy. **2** [tr.] make a flattened, stitched fold in (a garment or material), typically so as to shorten or tighten it, or for decoration.

▶phrasal v. □ **tuck something away 1** store something in a secure place: *employees can tuck away a percentage of their pretax salary.* ■ put or keep someone or something in an inconspicuous or concealed place: *the police station was tucked away in a square behind the main street.* **2** inf. eat a lot of food. □ **tuck in** (or **into**) inf. eat heartily.

▶n. **1** a flattened, stitched fold in a garment or material, typically one of several parallel folds put in a garment for shortening, tightening, or decoration. ■ inf. a surgical operation to reduce surplus flesh or fat: *a tummy tuck.* **2** (also **tuck position**) (in diving, gymnastics, downhill skiing, etc.) a position with the knees bent and held close to the chest, often with the hands clasped around the shins.

tuck·er /ˈtəkər/ ▶n. hist. a piece of lace or linen worn in or around the top of a bodice or as an insert at the front of a low-cut dress.

▶v. [tr.] (usu. **be tuckered out**) inf. exhaust; wear out.

Tu·dor /ˈt(y)ōōdər/ ▶adj. of or relating to the English royal dynasty that held the throne from the accession of Henry VII in 1485 until the death of Elizabeth I in 1603. ■ of, denoting, or relating to the prevalent architectural style of the Tudor period.

▶n. a member of this dynasty.

Tues. (also **Tue.**) ▶abbr. Tuesday.

Tues·day /ˈt(y)ōōz,dā; -dē/ ▶n. the day of the week before Wednesday and following Monday: *come to dinner on Tuesday* | *the following Tuesday* | [as adj.] *Tuesday afternoons.*

▶adv. on Tuesday: *they're all leaving Tuesday.* ■ (**Tuesdays**) on Tuesdays; each Tuesday: *she works late Tuesdays.*

tu·fa /ˈt(y)ōōfə/ ▶n. a porous rock composed of calcium carbonate and formed by precipitation from water, e.g., around mineral springs. ■ another term for TUFF. —**tu·fa·ceous** /t(y)ōōˈfāSHəs/ adj.

tuff /təf/ ▶n. a light, porous rock formed by consolidation of volcanic ash. —**tuff·a·ceous** /təˈfāSHəs/ adj.

tuft /təft/ ▶n. a bunch or collection of something, typically threads, grass, or hair, held or growing together at the base.

▶v. [tr.] **1** provide (something) with a tuft or tufts. **2** make depressions at regular intervals in (a mattress or cushion) by passing a thread through it. —**tuft·y** adj.

tuft·ed /ˈtəftid/ ▶adj. having or growing in a tuft or tufts: *tufted grass.*

tug /təg/ ▶v. (**tugged, tug·ging**) [tr.] pull (something) hard or suddenly: *she tugged off her boots* | [intr.] *he tugged at Tom's coat sleeve.*

▶n. **1** a hard or sudden pull: *another tug and it came loose* | fig. *a tug of attraction.* **2** short for TUGBOAT. —**tug·ger** n.

tug·boat ▶n. a powerful, stoutly built boat used for towing larger vessels, esp. in harbor.

tugboat

tug of war ▶n. a contest in which two teams pull at opposite ends of a rope until one drags the other over a central line. ■ fig. a situation in which two evenly matched people or factions are striving to keep or obtain the same thing: *a tug of war between builders and environmentalists.*

tu·i·tion /t(y)ōōˈiSHən/ ▶n. a sum of money charged for teaching or instruction by a school, college, or university. ■ teaching or instruction, esp. of individual pupils or small groups. —**tu·i·tion·al** /-SHənl/ adj.

tu·la·re·mi·a /,t(y)ōōləˈrēmēə/ (Brit. **tu·la·rae·mi·a**) ▶n. a severe infectious bacterial disease of animals transmissible to humans, characterized by ulcers at the site of infection, fever, and loss of weight. Compare with RABBIT FEVER. ▷1920s: modern Latin, from *Tulare*, the county in California where it was first observed. —**tu·la·re·mic** /ˈrēmik/ adj.

tu·lip /ˈt(y)ōōlip/ ▶n. a bulbous spring-flowering plant (genus *Tulipa*) of the lily family, with boldly colored cup-shaped flowers. ▷late 16th cent.: from French *tulipe*, via Turkish from Persian *dulband* 'turban.'

tu·lip tree ▶n. a deciduous North American tree (*Liriodendron tulipifera*) of the magnolia family, with large distinctively lobed leaves and insignificant tuliplike flowers. Also called YELLOW POPLAR (see POPLAR).

tulle /tōōl/ ▶n. a soft, fine silk, cotton, or nylon material like net, used for making veils and dresses.

tum·ble /ˈtəmbəl/ ▶v. **1** [intr.] (typically of a person) fall suddenly, clumsily, or headlong: *she pitched forward, tumbling down the stairs.* ■ move or rush in a headlong or uncontrolled way: *police tumbled from the vehicle.* ■ (of something abstract) fall rapidly in amount or value: *property prices tumbled.* ■ [tr.] rumple; disarrange. ■ [tr.] inf. have sexual intercourse with (someone). **2** [intr.] perform acrobatic or gymnastic exercises, typically handsprings and somersaults in the air. **3** [tr.] clean (castings, gemstones, etc.) in a tumbling barrel.

▶n. **1** a sudden or headlong fall: *I took a tumble in the nettles.* ■ a rapid fall in amount or value. ■ an untidy or confused arrangement or state: *her hair was a tumble of curls.* ■ inf. an act of sexual intercourse. ■ a handspring, somersault in the air, or other acrobatic feat. **2** inf. a friendly sign of recognition, acknowledgment, or interest: *not a soul gave him a tumble.* ▷Middle English (as a verb, also in the sense 'dance with contortions'): from Middle Low German *tummelen*; compare with Old English *tumbian* 'to dance.' The sense was probably influenced by Old French *tomber* 'to fall.' The noun, first in the sense 'tangled mass,' dates from the mid 17th cent.

tum·ble·down /ˈtəmbəl,doun/ ▶adj. (of a building or structure) falling or fallen into ruin; dilapidated.

tum·ble dry ▶v. (**dries, dried**) dry washed clothes by spinning them in hot air inside a dryer.

tum·bler /ˈtəmblər/ ▶n. **1** a drinking glass with straight sides and no handle or stem. **2** an acrobat or gymnast, esp. one who performs somersaults. **3** a pivoted piece in a lock that holds the bolt until lifted by a key. ■ a notched pivoted plate in a gunlock. **4** a revolving drum containing an abrasive substance, in which castings, gemstones, or other hard objects can be cleaned and polished by friction. —**tum·bler·ful** /-,fŏŏl/ n. (pl. **-fuls**).

tum·ble·weed /ˈtəmbəl,wēd/ ▶n. a plant of arid regions that breaks off near the ground in late summer, forming light globular masses that are tumbled about by the wind. Its two genera are *Salsola* of the goosefoot family and *Amaranthus* of the amaranth family.

tum·bril /ˈtəmbrəl/ (also **tum·brel**) ▶n. hist. a cart that tilted backward to empty out its load, in particular one used to convey condemned prisoners to the guillotine during the French Revolution.

tu·mes·cent /t(y)ōōˈmesənt/ ▶adj. swollen or becoming swollen, esp. as a response to sexual arousal. ■ fig. (esp. of language or literary style) pompous or pretentious. —**tu·mes·cence** n. —**tu·mes·cent·ly** adv.

tum·my /ˈtəmē/ ▶n. (pl. **-mies**) inf. a person's stomach or abdomen.

tu·mor /ˈt(y)ōōmər/ (Brit. **tu·mour**) ▶n. a swelling of a part of the body, generally without inflammation, caused by an abnormal growth of tissue, whether benign or malignant. —**tu·mor·ous** /-mərəs/ adj.

tu·mult /ˈt(y)ōō,məlt/ ▶n. a loud, confused noise, esp. one caused by a large mass of people. ■ confusion or disorder: *the neighborhood was in a state of tumult* | fig. *his personal tumult ended when he began writing.*

tu·mul·tu·ous /t(y)ōō'melcHōōes; tə-/ ▶*adj.* making a loud, confused noise; uproarious: *tumultuous applause.* ■ excited, confused, or disorderly: *a tumultuous crowd | fig. a tumultuous personal life.* —**tu·mul·tu·ous·ly** *adv.* —**tu·mul·tu·ous·ness** *n.*

tun /tən/ ▶*n.* **1** a large beer or wine cask. ■ a brewer's fermenting vat. **2** (also **tun shell**) a large marine mollusk that has a rounded barrel-like shell with broad spirals.
▶*v.* (**tunned, tunning**) [*tr.*] *archaic* store (wine or other alcoholic drinks) in a tun.

tu·na[1] /'t(y)ōōnə/ ▶*n.* (*pl.* same or **tunas**) a large and active predatory schooling fish (*Thunnus* and other genera) of the mackerel family. Found in warm seas, it is extensively fished commercially and is popular as a game fish. ■ (also **tuna fish**) the flesh of this fish as food, usually canned.

tu·na[2] ▶*n.* **1** the edible fruit of a prickly pear cactus. **2** a cactus that produces such fruit, in particular *Opuntia tuna* of Central America and the Caribbean.

tun·dra /'təndrə/ ▶*n.* a vast, flat, treeless Arctic region of Europe, Asia, and North America in which the subsoil is permanently frozen.

tune /t(y)ōōn/ ▶*n.* a melody, esp. one that characterizes a certain piece of music: *she left the theater humming a cheerful tune.*
▶*v.* [*tr.*] adjust (a musical instrument) to the correct or uniform pitch. ■ adjust (a receiver circuit such as a radio or television) to the frequency of the required signal: *the radio was tuned to the CBC* | [*intr.*] *they tuned in to watch the game.* ■ (often **tune up**) adjust (an engine) or balance (mechanical parts) so that a vehicle or other machine runs smoothly and efficiently: *the suspension was tuned for a softer ride* | *fig. officials tuning up an emergency plan.* ■ *fig.* adjust or adapt (something) to a particular purpose or situation: *the animals are finely tuned to life in the desert.* ■ [*intr.*] (**tune into**) *fig.* become sensitive to.
▶*phrasal v.* □ **tune out** *inf.* stop listening or paying attention. □ **tune someone out** not listen or pay attention to someone. □ **tune up** (of a musician) adjust one's instrument to the correct or uniform pitch. —**tun·a·ble** (also **tune·a·ble**) *adj.* —**tun·ing** *n.*
▶ □ **be tuned in** *inf.* be aware of, sensitive to, or able to understand something. □ **in** (or **out of**) **tune** with correct (or incorrect) pitch or intonation. ■ (of an engine or other machine) properly (or poorly) adjusted. ■ *fig.* in (or not in) agreement or harmony: *he was out of tune with conventional belief.* □ **to the tune of** *inf.* amounting to or involving (a specified considerable sum): *he was in debt to the tune of forty thousand pounds.*

tune·ful /'t(y)ōōnfəl/ ▶*adj.* having a pleasing tune; melodious. —**tune·ful·ly** *adv.* —**tune·ful·ness** *n.*

tune·less /'t(y)ōōnləs/ ▶*adj.* not pleasing to listen to; unmelodious. —**tune·less·ly** *adv.* —**tune·less·ness** *n.*

tun·er /'t(y)ōōnər/ ▶*n.* a person who tunes musical instruments, esp. pianos. ■ an electronic device for tuning a guitar or other instrument. ■ an electronic device for varying the frequency to which a radio or television is tuned. ■ a separate unit for detecting and preamplifying a program signal and supplying it to an audio amplifier.

tung·sten /'təNGstən/ ▶*n.* the chemical element of atomic number 74, a hard steel-gray metal of the transition series. It has a very high melting point (3410°C) and is used to make electric light filaments. (Symbol: **W**)

tung·sten car·bide ▶*n.* a very hard gray compound, WC (or W$_2$C), used in making cutting and drilling tools, etc.

tu·nic /'t(y)ōōnik/ ▶*n.* **1** a loose garment, typically sleeveless and reaching to the wearer's knees, as worn in ancient Greece and Rome. ■ a loose, thigh-length garment, worn typically by women over a skirt or trousers. **2** a close-fitting short coat as part of a uniform, esp. a police or military uniform. **3** *Biol. & Anat.* an integument or membrane enclosing or lining an organ or part.

tu·ni·cate /'t(y)ōōni,kāt/ ▶*n.* *Zool.* a marine invertebrate of a group that includes the sea squirts and salps. They have a rubbery or hard outer coat and two siphons to draw water into and out of the body.

tun·ing fork ▶*n.* a two-pronged steel device used by musicians, which vibrates when struck to give a note of specific pitch.

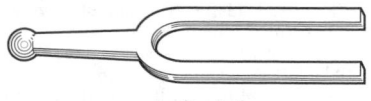

tuning fork

tun·nel /'tənl/ ▶*n.* an artificial underground passage, esp. one built through a hill or under a building, road, or river. ■ an underground passage dug by a burrowing animal.

▶*v.* (**-neled, -nel·ing**; *Brit.* **-nelled, -nel·ling**) **1** [*intr.*] dig or force a passage underground or through something: *he tunneled under the fence* | (**tunnel one's way**) *the insect tunnels its way out of the plant.* **2** [*intr.*] *Physics* (of a particle) pass through a potential barrier. —**tun·nel·er** *n.*

tun·nel vi·sion ▶*n.* defective sight in which objects cannot be properly seen if not close to the center of the field of view. ■ *inf.* the tendency to focus exclusively on a single or limited goal or point of view.

tu·pe·lo /'t(y)ōōpə,lō/ ▶*n.* (*pl.* **-los**) a North American or Asian tree (genus *Nyssa*) of moist habitats.

Tu·pi /'tōōpē; tōō'pē/ ▶*n.* (*pl.* same or **-pis**) **1** a member of a group of American Indian peoples living in scattered areas throughout the Amazon basin. **2** any of the languages of these peoples, a branch of the Tupi-Guarani language family.
▶*adj.* of or relating to these peoples or their languages. —**Tu·pi·an** /-pēən/ *adj.*

tup·pence ▶*n. Brit.* variant spelling of TWOPENCE.

tup·pen·ny /'təp(ə)nē/ ▶*adj. Brit.* variant spelling of TWOPENNY.

tuque /t(y)ōōk/ ▶*n. Can.* a close-fitting knitted stocking cap.

tur·ban /'tərbən/ ▶*n.* a man's headdress, consisting of a long length of cotton or silk wound around a cap or the head, worn esp. by Muslims and Sikhs. ▷mid 16th cent.: via French from Turkish *tülbent*, from Persian *dulband*. —**tur·baned** *adj.*

tur·bid /'tərbid/ ▶*adj.* (of a liquid) cloudy, opaque, or thick with suspended matter: *the turbid estuary* | *fig. a turbid piece of cinéma vérité.* —**tur·bid·i·ty** /tər'biditē/ *n.* —**tur·bid·ly** *adv.* —**tur·bid·ness** *n.*

tur·bine /'tər,bīn; -bin/ ▶*n.* a machine for producing continuous power in which a wheel or rotor, typically fitted with vanes, is made to revolve by a fast-moving flow of water, steam, gas, air, or other fluid.

tur·bo /'tərbō/ ▶*n.* (*pl.* **-bos**) short for TURBOCHARGER. ■ a motor vehicle equipped with a turbocharger. ■ a computer program, machine, or other object equipped to operate at high speed.

tur·bo·charg·er /'tərbō,cHärjər/ ▶*n.* a supercharger driven by a turbine powered by the engine's exhaust gases.

tur·bo·fan /'tərbō,fan/ ▶*n.* a jet engine in which a turbine-driven fan provides additional thrust. ■ an aircraft powered by such an engine.

tur·bo·jet /'tərbō,jet/ ▶*n.* a jet engine in which the jet gases also operate a turbine-driven compressor for compressing the air drawn into the engine. ■ an aircraft powered by such an engine.

tur·bo·prop /'tərbō,präp/ ▶*n.* a jet engine in which a turbine is used to drive a propeller. ■ an aircraft powered by such an engine.

tur·bot /'tərbət/ ▶*n.* (*pl.* same or **turbots**) a European flatfish (*Scophthalmus maximus*, family Scophthalmidae) of inshore waters that has large bony tubercles on the body and is prized as food. ■ used in names of similar flatfishes.

tur·bu·lence /'tərbyələns/ ▶*n.* violent or unsteady movement of air or water, or of some other fluid. ■ *fig.* conflict; confusion.

tur·bu·lent /'tərbyələnt/ ▶*adj.* characterized by conflict, disorder, or confusion; not controlled or calm. ■ (of air or water) moving unsteadily or violently: *the turbulent sea.* ■ *technical* of, relating to, or denoting flow of a fluid in which the velocity at any point fluctuates irregularly and there is continual mixing rather than a steady or constant flow pattern. —**tur·bu·lent·ly** *adv.*

turd /tərd/ ▶*n.* *vulgar slang* a lump of excrement. ■ a person regarded as obnoxious or contemptible.

tu·reen /t(y)ōō'rēn/ ▶*n.* a deep covered dish from which soup is served.

turf /tərf/ ▶*n.* (*pl.* **turfs** or **turves** /tərvz/) **1** grass and the surface layer of earth held together by its roots. ■ *Brit.* a piece of such grass and earth cut from the ground. ■ peat used for fuel. **2** (**the turf**) horse racing or racecourses generally. **3** *inf.* an area regarded as someone's personal territory; one's home ground: *the team will play Canada on their home turf.* ■ a person's sphere of influence or activity.
▶*v.* [*tr.*] cover (a patch of ground) with turf: *a turfed lawn.*

tur·gid /'tərjid/ ▶*adj.* swollen and distended or congested: *a turgid and fast-moving river.* ■ (of language or style) tediously pompous. —**tur·gid·i·ty** /tər'jiditē/ *n.* —**tur·gid·ly** *adv.*

Turk /tərk/ ▶*n.* **1** a native or national of Turkey, or a person of Turkish descent. **2** *hist.* a member of any of the ancient central Asian peoples who spoke Turkic languages. **3** *archaic* a member of the ruling Muslim population of the Ottoman Empire.

tur·key /'tərkē/ ▶*n.* (*pl.* **-keys**) **1** a large mainly domesticated game bird (*Meleagris gallopavo*, family Meleagridae or Phasianidae) native to North

Pronunciation Key ə *ago, up;* ər *over, fur;* a *hat;* ā *ate;* ä *car;* cH *chin;* e *let;* ē *see;* e(ə)r *air;* i *fit;* ī *by;* i(ə)r *ear;* NG *sing;* ō *go;* ô *law, for;* oi *toy;* ōō *good;* ōō *goo;* ou *out;* sH *she;* TH *thin;* ᴛʜ *then;* (h)w *why;* zH *vision*

America, having a bald head and (in the male) red wattles. It is prized as food, esp. on festive occasions such as Thanksgiving and Christmas. ■ the flesh of the turkey as food. **2** *inf.* something that is extremely or completely unsuccessful, esp. a play or movie. ■ a stupid or inept person.

▶ □ **talk turkey** *inf.* discuss something frankly and straightforwardly.

tur·key vul·ture ▶*n.* a common American vulture (*Cathartes aura*) with black plumage and a bare red head.

Turk·ish /'tərkiSH/ ▶*adj.* of or relating to Turkey or to the Turks or their language. ■ *hist.* relating to or associated with the Ottoman Empire. ▶*n.* the Turkic language that is the official language of Turkey.

Turk·ish bath ▶*n.* a cleansing or relaxing treatment that involves a period of time spent sitting in a room filled with very hot air or steam, generally followed by washing and massage. ■ a building or room where such a treatment is available.

Turk·ish tow·el ▶*n.* a towel made of cotton terry toweling.

tur·mer·ic /'tərmərik/ ▶*n.* **1** a bright yellow aromatic powder obtained from the rhizome of a plant of the ginger family, used for flavoring and coloring in Asian cooking and formerly as a fabric dye. **2** the Asian plant (*Curcuma longa*) from which this rhizome is obtained.

tur·moil /'tər,moil/ ▶*n.* a state of great disturbance, confusion, or uncertainty: *the country was in turmoil | he endured years of inner turmoil.*

turn /tərn/ ▶*v.* **1** move or cause to move in a circular direction wholly or partly around an axis or point: [*intr.*] *the big wheel was turning* | [*tr.*] *I turned the key in the door and crept in.* ■ [*tr.*] move (something) so that it is in a different position in relation to its surroundings or its previous position: *we waited in suspense for him to turn the cards over.* ■ [*tr.*] move (a page) over so that it is flat against the previous or next page: *she turned a page noisily* | [*intr.*] *turn to page five.* ■ change or cause to change direction: [*intr.*] *we turned around and headed back to the house.* ■ [*tr.*] aim, point, or direct (something): *she turned her head toward me.* ■ [*intr.*] change the position of one's body so that one is facing in a different direction. ■ [*intr.*] (of the tide) change from flood to ebb or vice versa. ■ [*tr.*] perform (a somersault or cartwheel). ■ [*tr.*] twist or sprain (an ankle). ■ [*tr.*] fold or unfold (fabric or a piece of a garment) in the specified way: *he turned up the collar of his coat.* ■ [*tr.*] remake (a garment or a sheet), putting the worn outer side on the inside. ■ [*tr.*] *archaic* bend back (the edge of a blade) so as to make it blunt. **2** [*intr.*] change in nature, state, form, or color; become: *Emmeline turned pale.* ■ cause to change in such a way; cause to become: *potatoes are covered with sacking to keep the light from turning them green.* ■ [*intr.*] (of leaves) change color in the autumn. ■ [*tr.*] pass the age or time of: *I've just turned forty.* ■ (with reference to milk) make or become sour: [*tr.*] *the thunder had turned the milk.* ■ (with reference to the stomach) make or become nauseated: [*tr.*] *the smell was bad enough to turn the strongest stomach.* ■ send or put into a specified place or condition: *the dogs were turned loose on the crowd.* **3** [*intr.*] (**turn to**) start doing or becoming involved with. ■ go on to consider next: *we can now turn to another aspect of the problem.* ■ go to for help, advice, or information: *who can she turn to?* ■ have recourse to (something, esp. something dangerous or unhealthy). **4** [*tr.*] shape (something) on a lathe. ■ give a graceful or elegant form to: [as *adj.*] (**turned**) *a production full of so many finely turned words.* ■ make (a profit).

▶*phrasal v.* □ **turn against** (or **turn someone against**) become (or cause someone to become) hostile toward. □ **turn around** move so as to face in the opposite direction. □ **turn something around 1** prepare a ship or aircraft for its return journey. **2** reverse the previously poor performance of something, esp. a company. □ **turn someone away** refuse to allow someone to enter or pass through a place. □ **turn back** (or **turn someone/something back**) go (or cause to go) back in the direction in which one has come. □ **turn someone down** reject an offer or application made by someone. □ **turn something down 1** reject something offered or proposed. **2** adjust a control on a device to reduce the volume, heat, etc. □ **turn in** *inf.* go to bed in the evening. □ **turn someone in** hand someone over to the authorities. □ **turn something in** give something to someone in authority: *I've turned in my resignation.* ■ produce or achieve a particular score or a performance of a specified quality. □ **turn off** leave one road in order to join another. □ **turn someone off** *inf.* induce a feeling of boredom or disgust in someone. □ **turn something off** stop the operation or flow of something by means of a valve, switch, or button. ■ operate a valve or switch in order to do this. □ **turn on 1** suddenly attack (someone) physically or verbally. **2** have as the main topic or point of interest: *the central questions will turn on taxation.* □ **turn someone on** *inf.* excite or stimulate the interest of someone, esp. sexually. □ **turn something on** start the flow or operation of something by means of a valve, switch, or button. ■ operate a valve or switch in order to do this. □ **turn someone on to** *inf.*

cause someone to become interested or involved in (something, esp. drugs). □ **turn out 1** prove to be the case. **2** go somewhere in order to do something, esp. to attend a meeting, to play a game, or to vote. □ **turn someone out 1** eject or expel someone from a place. **2** *Mil.* call a guard from the guardroom. **3** (**be turned out**) be dressed in the manner specified: *she was smartly turned out.* □ **turn something out 1** extinguish a light. **2** produce something. **3** empty something, esp. one's pockets. **4** tip prepared food from a mold or other container. □ **turn over** (of an engine) start or continue to run properly. □ **turn someone over to** deliver someone to the care or custody of (another person or body, esp. one in authority). □ **turn something over 1** cause an engine to run. **2** transfer control or management of something to someone else. **3** change the function or use of something: *the works was turned over to the production of aircraft parts.* **4** (of a business) have a turnover of a specified amount. □ **turn up 1** be found, esp. by chance, after being lost. **2** put in an appearance; arrive. □ **turn something up 1** increase the volume or strength of sound, heat, etc., by turning a knob or switch on a device. **2** reveal or discover something. **3** shorten a garment by raising the hem.

▶*n.* **1** an act of moving something in a circular direction around an axis or point. ■ a change of direction when moving: *they made a left turn.* ■ a development or change in circumstances or a course of events: *life has taken a turn for the better.* ■ a time when one specified period of time ends and another begins: *the turn of the century.* ■ a bend or curve in a road, path, river, etc.: *the twists and turns in the passageways.* ■ a place where a road meets or branches off another. ■ (**the turn**) the beginning of the second nine holes of a round of golf. ■ a change of the tide from ebb to flow or vice versa. ■ one round in a coil of rope or other material. **2** an opportunity or obligation to do something that comes successively to each of a number of people: *his turn to speak.* ■ a short performance, esp. one of a number given by different performers in succession: *a comic turn.* ■ a performer giving such a performance. **3** a short walk or ride: *why don't you take a turn around the garden?* **4** *inf.* a shock: *you gave us quite a turn!* ■ a brief feeling or experience of illness. **5** the difference between the buying and selling price of stocks or other financial products. ■ a profit made from such a difference. **6** *Mus.* a melodic ornament consisting of the principal note with those above and below it.

▶ □ **at every turn** on every occasion; continually. □ **by turns** one after the other; alternately. □ **do someone a good** (or **bad**) **turn** do something that is helpful (or unhelpful) for someone. □ **in turn** in succession; one after the other. □ **not know which way** (or **where**) **to turn** not know what to do; be completely at a loss. □ **out of turn** at a time when it is not one's turn. □ **speak** (or **talk**) **out of turn** speak in a tactless or foolish way. □ **take turns** (of two or more people) do something alternately or in succession. □ **to a turn** to exactly the right degree (used esp. in relation to cooking): *hamburgers done to a turn.* □ **turn the corner** pass the critical point and start to improve. □ **turn over a new leaf** start to act or behave in a better or more responsible way. □ **turn something over in one's mind** think about or consider something thoroughly. □ **turn tail** *inf.* turn around and run away.

turn·a·bout /'tərnə,bout/ ▶*n.* a sudden and complete change or reversal of policy, opinion, or of a situation.

turn·a·round /'tərnə,round/ ▶*n.* **1** an abrupt or unexpected change, esp. one that results in a more favorable situation. **2** the process of completing or the time needed to complete a task, esp. one involving receiving something, processing it, and sending it out again: *a seven-day turnaround.* ■ the process of or time taken for unloading and reloading a ship, aircraft, or vehicle. **3** a space for vehicles to turn around in, esp. one at the end of a driveway or dead end street.

turn·coat /'tərn,kōt/ ▶*n.* a person who deserts one party or cause in order to join an opposing one.

turn·down /'tərn,doun/ ▶*n.* **1** a rejection or refusal. **2** a decline in something; a downturn. ▶*adj.* **1** (of a collar) turned down. **2** denoting a hotel service in which the sheets are turned back in preparation for sleeping.

turn·ing /'tərniNG/ ▶*n.* **1** a place where a road branches off another. **2** the action or skill of using a lathe. ■ (**turnings**) shavings of wood or metal resulting from turning something on a lathe.

turn·ing point ▶*n.* a time at which a decisive change in a situation occurs, esp. one with beneficial results.

tur·nip /'tərnəp/ ▶*n.* **1** a round root with white or cream flesh that is eaten as a vegetable and also has edible leaves. ■ a similar or related root, esp. a rutabaga. **2** the European plant (*Brassica rapa*) of the cabbage family that produces this root.

turn·key /'tərn,kē/ ▶*n.* (*pl.* **-keys**) *archaic* a jailer.

▶*adj.* of or involving the provision of a complete product or service that is ready for immediate use: *turnkey systems for telecommunications customers.*

turn·off /ˈtərnˌôf/ (also **turn-off**) ▶*n.* **1** a junction at which a road branches off from a main road. **2** *inf.* a person or thing that causes someone to feel bored, disgusted, or sexually repelled. **3** an instance of turning or switching something off.

turn·on ▶*n.* **1** *inf.* a person or thing that causes someone to feel excited or sexually aroused: *tight jeans are a real turn-on.* **2** an instance of turning or switching something on.

turn·out /ˈtərnˌout/ ▶*n.* **1** the number of people attending or taking part in an event, esp. the number of people voting in an election. **2** a turn in a road. ■ a point at which a railroad track diverges. ■ a widened place in a road for cars to pass each other or park temporarily. **3** the way in which a person or thing is equipped or dressed.

turn·o·ver /ˈtərnˌōvər/ ▶*n.* **1** the amount of money taken by a business in a particular period. ■ *Stock Market* the volume of shares traded during a particular period, as a percentage of total shares listed. **2** the rate at which employees leave a workforce and are replaced. ■ the rate at which goods are sold and replaced in a store. **3** a small pie made by folding a piece of pastry over on itself to enclose a filling. **4** (in a game) a loss of possession of the ball to the opposing team.

turn·pike /ˈtərnˌpīk/ ▶*n.* an expressway, esp. one on which a toll is charged. ■ *hist.* a toll gate. ■ (also **turnpike road**) *hist.* a road on which a toll was collected at such a gate.

turn sig·nal ▶*n.* a flashing light on a vehicle to show that it is about to change lanes or turn.

turn·stile /ˈtərnˌstīl/ ▶*n.* a mechanical gate consisting of revolving horizontal arms fixed to a vertical post, allowing only one person at a time to pass through.

turn·stone /ˈtərnˌstōn/ ▶*n.* a small, short-billed wading bird (genus *Arenaria*) of the sandpiper family that turns over stones to feed on small animals beneath them.

turn·ta·ble /ˈtərnˌtābəl/ ▶*n.* a circular revolving plate supporting a phonograph record as it is played. ■ a circular revolving platform for turning a railroad locomotive or rail car.

tur·pen·tine /ˈtərpənˌtīn/ ▶*n.* **1** a volatile pungent oil distilled from gum turpentine or pine wood, used in mixing paints and varnishes and in liniment. ■ an oleoresin secreted by certain trees, esp. pines, and distilled to make rosin and oil of turpentine. **2** (also **turpentine tree**) any of a number of trees that yield turpentine or a similar resin, in particular the terebinth, or a coniferous tree (*Larix*, *Pinus*, and other genera) of the pine family.

tur·pi·tude /ˈtərpiˌt(y)ōōd/ ▶*n.* depravity; wickedness: *moral turpitude.*

turps /tərps/ ▶*n. inf.* turpentine.

tur·quoise /ˈtərˌk(w)oiz/ ▶*n.* **1** a semiprecious stone, typically opaque and of a greenish-blue or sky-blue color, consisting of a hydrated phosphate of copper and aluminum. **2** a greenish-blue color like that of this stone: [as *adj.*] *the turquoise waters of the bay.*

tur·ret /ˈtərit/ ▶*n.* **1** a small tower on top of a larger tower or at the corner of a building or wall, typically of a castle. ■ a low, flat armored tower, typically one that revolves, for a gun and gunners in a ship, aircraft, fort, or tank. ■ a rotating holder for tools, esp. on a lathe. **2** (also **turret shell**) a mollusk (*Turritella* and other genera) with a long, slender, pointed spiral shell, typically brightly colored and living in tropical seas. ▷Middle English: from Old French *tourete*, diminutive of *tour* 'tower.' —**tur·ret·ed** *adj.*

turret

tur·tle /ˈtərtl/ ▶*n.* **1** a slow-moving reptile (family Testudinidae) of warm climates, enclosed in a scaly or leathery domed shell into which it can retract its head and thick legs. **2** (also **sea turtle**) a large marine reptile (families Cheloniidae and Dermochelyidae) with a bony or leathery shell and flippers, coming ashore annually on sandy beaches to lay eggs. ■ the flesh of a sea turtle, esp. the green turtle, used chiefly for soup. **3** a freshwater reptile (Emydidae and other families) related to the turtles, typically having a flattened shell. Called TERRAPIN in South Africa and India and TORTOISE in Australia. ■ any reptile of this order, including the terrapins and tortoises. **4** *Comput.* a directional cursor in a computer graphics system that can be instructed to move around a screen. **5** short for TURTLENECK.

▶ □ **turn turtle** (chiefly of a boat) capsize.

tur·tle·dove /ˈtərtlˌdəv/ ▶*n.* a small Old World dove (genus *Streptopelia*) with a soft purring call, noted for the apparent affection shown for its mate.

tur·tle·neck /ˈtərtlˌnek/ ▶*n.* a high, close-fitting, turned-over collar on a garment, typically a shirt or sweater: [as *adj.*] *a turtleneck sweater.* ■ a shirt or sweater with a neck of this type.

Tus·can /ˈtəskən/ ▶*adj.* **1** of or relating to Tuscany, its inhabitants, or the form of Italian spoken there, which is the standard variety taught to foreign learners. **2** relating to or denoting a classical order of architecture resembling the Doric but lacking all ornamentation.

▶*n.* **1** a native or inhabitant of Tuscany. **2** the form of Italian spoken in Tuscany. **3** the Tuscan order of architecture.

Tus·ca·ro·ra /ˌtəskəˈrôrə/ ▶*n.* (*pl.* same or **-ras**) **1** an American Indian people forming part of the Six Nations, originally inhabiting the Carolinas and later New York. **2** the Iroquoian language of this people.

▶*adj.* of or relating to the Tuscarora or their language.

tush /təsh/ ▶*interj. archaic* or *humorous* expressing disapproval, impatience, or dismissal: *tush, these are trifles and mere old wives' tales.*

tush[2] /tōōsh/ ▶*n. inf.* a person's buttocks.

tusk /təsk/ ▶*n.* a long, pointed tooth, esp. one specially developed so as to protrude from the closed mouth, as in the elephant, walrus, or wild boar. —**tusked** *adj.* —**tusk·y** *adj.* (*poetic/lit.*).

tus·sle /ˈtəsəl/ ▶*n.* a vigorous struggle or scuffle, typically in order to obtain or achieve something: *there was a tussle for the ball.*

▶*v.* [*intr.*] engage in such a struggle or scuffle.

tus·sock /ˈtəsək/ ▶*n.* **1** a small area of grass that is thicker or longer than the grass growing around it. **2** (also **tussock moth**) a woodland moth (family Lymantriidae) whose adults and brightly colored caterpillars both bear tufts of irritant hairs. The caterpillars can be a pest of trees, damaging fruit and stripping leaves. —**tus·sock·y** *adj.*

tu·te·lage /ˈt(y)ōōtl-ij/ ▶*n.* protection of or authority over someone or something; guardianship. ■ instruction; tuition: *he felt privileged to be under the tutelage of an experienced actor.*

tu·te·lar·y /ˈt(y)ōōtlˌerē/ (also **tu·te·lar** /-tl-ər/) ▶*adj.* serving as a protector, guardian, or patron: *the tutelary spirits of these regions.* ■ of or relating to protection or a guardian.

tu·tor /ˈt(y)ōōtər/ ▶*n.* a private teacher, typically one who teaches a single student or a small group. ■ *chiefly Brit.* a university or college teacher responsible for the teaching and supervision of assigned students. ■ an assistant lecturer in a college or university.

▶*v.* [*tr.*] act as a tutor to (a single student or a small group). ▷late Middle English: from Old French *tutour* or Latin *tutor*, from *tueri* 'to watch, guard.' —**tu·tor·age** /-rij/ *n.* —**tu·tor·ship** /-ˌship/ *n.*

tu·to·ri·al /t(y)ōōˈtôrēəl/ ▶*adj.* of or relating to a tutor or a tutor's instruction: *tutorial sessions.*

▶*n.* a period of instruction given by a university or college tutor to an individual or very small group. ■ an account or explanation of a subject, printed or on a computer screen, intended for private study.

tut·ti /ˈtōōtē/ *Mus.* ▶*adv.* & *adj.* (esp. as a direction after a solo section) with all voices or instruments together.

tut·ti-frut·ti /ˈtōōtē ˈfrōōtē/ ▶*n.* (*pl.* **-frut·tis**) a type of ice cream containing or flavored with mixed fruits and sometimes nuts.

tu·tu /ˈtōōˌtōō/ ▶*n.* a female ballet dancer's costume consisting of a bodice and an attached skirt incorporating numerous layers of fabric.

tux /təks/ ▶*n. inf.* a tuxedo.

tux·e·do /təkˈsēdō/ ▶*n.* (*pl.* **-dos** or **-does**) a man's dinner jacket. ■ a suit of formal evening clothes including such a jacket. —**tux·e·doed** *adj.*

TV ▶*abbr.* ■ television (the system or a set). ■ transvestite.

TVA ▶*abbr.* Tennessee Valley Authority.

twad·dle /ˈtwädl/ *inf.* ▶*n.* trivial or foolish speech or writing; nonsense.

▶ *v.* [*intr.*] *archaic* talk or write in a trivial or foolish way: *what is that old fellow twaddling about?* —**twad·dler** /'twädlər; 'wädl-ər/ *n.*

twain /twān/ ▶*cardinal number archaic* term for **two**: *he split it in twain.*

twang /twaNG/ ▶*n.* a strong ringing sound such as that made by the plucked string of a musical instrument or a released bowstring. ■ a nasal or other distinctive manner of pronunciation or intonation characteristic of the speech of an individual, area, or country.
▶*v.* make or cause to make such a sound: [*intr.*] *a spring twanged beneath him.* ■ [*tr.*] utter (something) with a nasal twang. —**twang·y** *adj.*

'twas /twəz/ ▶*archaic* or *poetic/lit. contr. of* it was.

tweak /twēk/ ▶*v.* [*tr.*] **1** twist or pull (something) sharply: *he tweaked the boy's ear.* **2** *inf.* improve (a mechanism or system) by making fine adjustments to it: *engineers tweak the car's operating systems during the race.*
▶*n.* **1** a sharp twist or pull. **2** *inf.* a fine adjustment to a mechanism or system.

tweed /twēd/ ▶*n.* a rough-surfaced woolen cloth, typically of mixed flecked colors, originally produced in Scotland: [as *adj.*] *a tweed sports jacket.* ■ (**tweeds**) clothes made of this material.

tweed·y /'twēdē/ ▶*adj.* (**tweed·i·er, tweed·i·est**) (of a garment) made of tweed cloth. ■ *inf.* (of a person) habitually wearing tweed clothes. ■ of a refined, traditional, upscale character. —**tweed·i·ly** /-dilē/ *adv.* —**tweed·i·ness** *n.*

'tween /twēn/ ▶*archaic* or *poetic/lit. contr. of* between.

tweet /twēt/ (also **tweet tweet**) ▶*n.* the chirp of a small or young bird.
▶*v.* [*intr.*] make a chirping noise: *the birds were tweeting in the branches.*

tweet·er /'twētər/ ▶*n.* a loudspeaker designed to reproduce high frequencies.

tweeze /twēz/ ▶*v.* [*tr.*] pluck, grasp, or pull with or as if with tweezers.

'tweez·ers /'twēzərz/ ▶*pl. n.* a small instrument like a pair of pincers for plucking out hairs and picking up small objects.

twelfth /twelftH/ ▶*ordinal number* constituting number twelve in a sequence; 12th: *the twelfth of November* | *his twelfth birthday.* ■ (**a twelfth/one twelfth**) each of twelve equal parts into which something is or may be divided. ■ the twelfth grade of a school. ■ *Mus.* an interval or chord spanning an octave and a fifth in the diatonic scale, or a note separated from another by this interval. —**twelfth·ly** *adv.* —**twelve-fold** /'twel(v),fōld/ *adj. & adv.*

twelve /twelv/ ▶*cardinal number* equivalent to the product of three and four; two more than ten; 12. (Roman numeral: **xii, XII.**) ■ a group or unit of twelve people or things. ■ twelve years old. ■ twelve o'clock. ■ a size of garment or other merchandise denoted by twelve. ■ (**the Twelve**) the twelve Apostles.

twen·ty /'twentē/ ▶*cardinal number* (*pl.* **-ties**) the number equivalent to the product of two and ten; ten less than thirty; 20. (Roman numeral: **xx, XX.**) ■ (**twenties**) the numbers from twenty to twenty-nine, esp. the years of a century or of a person's life. ■ twenty years old. ■ twenty miles an hour. ■ a size of garment or other merchandise denoted by twenty. ■ a twenty-dollar bill. —**twen·ti·eth** /-tēitH/ *ordinal number* —**twen·ty·fold** /-,fōld/ *adj. & adv.*

twen·ty-one ▶*n.* the card game blackjack.

twen·ty-twen·ty (also **20/20**) ▶*adj.* denoting vision of normal acuity.

'twere /twər/ *archaic poetic/lit. contr. of* it were.

twerp /twərp/ (also **twirp**) ▶*n. inf.* a silly or annoying person.

twice /twīs/ ▶*adv.* two times; on two occasions: *she had been married twice.* ■ double in degree or quantity: *I'm twice your age.*

twid·dle /'twidl/ ▶*v.* [*tr.*] twist, move, or fiddle with (something), typically in a purposeless or nervous way: *she twiddled the dials* | [*intr.*] *he began twiddling with the cord.*
▶*n.* an act of twisting or fiddling with something: *one twiddle of a button.* —**twid·dler** /'twidlr; 'twidl-ər/ *n.* —**twid·dly** /'twidlē; 'twidl-ē/ *adj.*
▶ □ **twiddle one's thumbs** rotate one's thumbs around each other with the fingers linked together. ■ be bored or idle.

twig¹ /twig/ ▶*n.* a slender woody shoot growing from a branch or stem of a tree or shrub. —**twigged** *adj.* —**twig·gy** *adj.*

twi·light /'twī,līt/ ▶*n.* the soft glowing light from the sky when the sun is below the horizon, caused by the refraction and scattering of the sun's rays from the atmosphere. ■ the period of the evening during which this takes place, between daylight and darkness: *a pleasant walk in the woods at twilight.* ■ *fig.* a period or state of obscurity, ambiguity, or gradual decline: *he was in the twilight of his career.*

twi·light zone ▶*n.* **1** a conceptual area that is undefined or intermediate: *the twilight zone between the middle and working classes.* ■ a sphere of experience that appears sinister or dangerous because of its uncertainty, unpredictability, or ambiguity. **2** the lowest level of the ocean to which light can penetrate.

twi·lit /'twī,lit/ ▶*adj.* dimly illuminated by or as if by twilight: *the deserted twilit street.* ■ relating to or denoting the period of twilight: *twilit hours.*

twill /twil/ ▶*n.* a fabric so woven as to have a surface of diagonal parallel ridges.
▶*v.* [*tr.*] weave (fabric) in this way: *twilled cotton.*

'twill /twil/ *archaic poetic/lit.* ▶*contr. of* it will.

twin /twin/ ▶*n.* **1** one of two children or animals born at the same birth. ■ a person or thing that is exactly like another. ■ (**the Twins**) the zodiacal sign or constellation Gemini. **2** something containing or consisting of two matching or similar parts, in particular: ■ a twin-bedded room. ■ a twin-engined aircraft.
▶*adj.* forming, or being one of, a pair born at one birth: *her twin sister.* ■ forming a matching, complementary, or closely connected pair. ■ *Bot.* growing in pairs: *twin seed leaves.* ■ (of a bedroom) containing two single beds.
▶*v.* (**twinned, twin·ning**) [*tr.*] link; combine.

twin bed ▶*n.* a bed designed or suitable for one person; a single bed, esp. one of a pair of matching single beds. —**twin-bed·ded** *adj.*

twine /twīn/ ▶*n.* strong thread or string consisting of two or more strands of hemp, cotton, or nylon twisted together.
▶*v.* [*tr.*] cause to wind or spiral round something: *she twined her arms around his neck.* ■ [*intr.*] (of a plant) grow so as to spiral around a support. ■ interlace. ▷Old English *twīn* 'thread, linen,' from the Germanic base of *twi-* 'two'; related to Dutch *twijn*. —**twin·er** *n.*

twinge /twinj/ ▶*n.* a sudden, sharp localized pain. ■ a brief experience of an emotion, typically an unpleasant one: *Kate felt a twinge of guilt.*
▶*v.* (**twinge·ing** or **twing·ing** /-jiNG/) [*intr.*] (of a part of the body) suffer a sudden, sharp localized pain: *the ankle still twinged, but the pain was slight.*

twin·kle /'twiNGkəl/ ▶*v.* [*intr.*] (of a star or light, or a shiny object) shine with a gleam that varies repeatedly between bright and faint. ■ (of a person's eyes) sparkle, esp. with amusement. ■ smile so that one's eyes sparkle. ■ [*intr.*] (of a person's feet) move lightly and rapidly.
▶*n.* a sparkle or gleam in a person's eyes. ■ a light that appears continually to grow brighter and fainter: *the distant twinkle of the lights.* —**twin·kler** /-k(ə)lər/ *n.* —**twin·kly** /-k(ə)lē/ *adj.*
▶ □ **in a twinkling** (or **the twinkling of an eye**) in an instant.

twirl /twərl/ ▶*v.* [*intr.*] spin quickly and lightly around, esp. repeatedly: *she twirled in delight to show off her new dress.* ■ [*tr.*] cause to rotate: *she twirled her fork in the pasta.* ■ [*tr.*] *Baseball* pitch (the ball).
▶*n.* an act of spinning. ■ a spiraling or swirling shape, esp. a flourish made with a pen. —**twirl·er** *n.* —**twirl·y** *adj.*

twist /twist/ ▶*v.* [*tr.*] **1** form into a bent, curling, or distorted shape: *a strip of metal is twisted to form a hollow tube.* ■ [*tr.*] form (something) into a particular shape by taking hold of one or both ends and turning them: *she twisted her handkerchief into a knot.* ■ [*tr.*] turn or bend into a specified position or in a specified direction: *he grabbed the man and twisted his arm behind his back.* ■ (**twist something off**) remove something by pulling and rotating it. ■ [*intr.*] move one's body so that the shoulders and hips are facing in different directions: *she twisted in her seat to look at the buildings.* ■ [*intr.*] move in a wriggling or writhing fashion: *he twisted himself free.* ■ injure (a joint) by wrenching it. ■ distort or misrepresent the meaning of (words). ■ [as *adj.*] (**twisted**) (of a personality or a way of thinking) unpleasantly or unhealthily abnormal: *a man with a twisted mind.* **2** cause to rotate around something that remains stationary; turn: *she twisted her ring around and around on her finger.* ■ [*tr.*] wind around or through something: *she twisted a lock of hair around her finger.* ■ move or cause to move around each other; interlace: [*tr.*] *she twisted her hands together nervously.* ■ make (something) by interlacing or winding strands together. ■ [*intr.*] take or have a winding course: *the road twisted through a dozen villages.* **3** [*intr.*] dance the twist.
▶*n.* **1** an act of turning something so that it moves in relation to something that remains stationary. ■ an act of turning one's body or part of one's body. ■ (**the twist**) a dance with a twisting movement of the body, popular in the 1960s. ■ the extent of twisting of a rod or other object. ■ force producing twisting; torque. ■ the rifling in the bore of a gun: *barrels with a 1:24 inch twist.* **2** a thing with a spiral shape: *a licorice twist.* ■ a curled piece of lemon peel used to flavor a drink. **3** a distorted shape: *he had a cruel twist to his mouth.* ■ an unusual feature of a person's personality, typically an unhealthy one. **4** a point at which something turns or bends: *the twists and turns of the mountain road.* ■ an unexpected development of events: *it was soon time for the next twist of fate in his career.* ■ a new treatment or outlook; a variation: *she takes conventional subjects and gives them a twist.* **5** a strong thread consisting of twisted strands of cotton or silk. **6** *Brit.* a drink consisting of two ingredients mixed together. —**twist·y** *adj.*

▶ □ **twist someone's arm** *inf.* persuade someone to do something that they are or might be reluctant to do. □ **twist in the wind** be left in a state of suspense or uncertainty.

twist·er /'twistər/ ▶*n.* a tornado.

twit¹ /twit/ ▶*n. inf.* a silly or foolish person. —**twit·tish** *adj.*

twit² ▶*v.* (**twit·ted, twit·ting**) [*tr.*] *dated* tease or taunt (someone), esp. in a good-humored way.

▶*n.* a state of nervous excitement: *we're in a twit about your visit.*

twitch /twicH/ ▶*v.* **1** give or cause to give a short, sudden jerking or convulsive movement: [*intr.*] *he saw her lips twitch and her eyelids flutter* | [*tr.*] *the dog twitched his ears.* ■ [*tr.*] cause to move in a specified direction by giving a sharp pull. **2** [*tr.*] apply a sudden pull or jerk to (a horse).

▶*n.* **1** a short, sudden jerking or convulsive movement. ■ a sudden pull or jerk. ■ a sudden sharp sensation; a pang: *he felt a twitch of annoyance.* **2** a stick with a small noose attached to one end. The noose may be twisted around the upper lip or the ear of a horse to subdue it. —**twitch·y** *adj.*

twit·ter /'twitər/ ▶*v.* [*intr.*] (of a bird) give a call consisting of repeated light tremulous sounds. ■ talk in a light, high-pitched voice. ■ talk rapidly and at length in an idle or trivial way.

▶*n.* a series of short, high-pitched calls or sounds: *his words were cut off by a faint electronic twitter.* ■ idle or ignorant talk: *drawing-room twitter.* —**twit·ter·er** *n.* —**twit·ter·y** *adj.*

▶ ■ **in** (or of) **a twitter** *inf.* in a state of agitation or excitement.

'twixt /twikst/ ▶*contr. of* betwixt.

two /tōō/ ▶*cardinal number* equivalent to the sum of one and one; one less than three; 2. (Roman numeral: **ii, II.**) ■ a group or unit of two people or things: *they would straggle home in ones and twos.* ■ two years old. ■ two o'clock: *the bar closed at two.* ■ a size of garment or other merchandise denoted by two. ■ a playing card or domino with two pips.

▶ ■ □ **a —— or two** (or **two or three ——**) used to denote a small but unspecified number: *a minute or two had passed* | *I called him two or three times.* □ **in two** in or into two halves or pieces: *he tore the piece of paper in two.* □ **put two and two together** draw an obvious conclusion from what is known or evident. □ **two by two** side by side in pairs.

two-bit ▶*adj. inf.* insignificant, cheap, or worthless: *some two-bit town.*

two-by-four ▶*n.* a piece of lumber with a rectangular cross section nominally two inches by four inches. ■ [usu. as *adj.*] a small or insignificant thing, typically a building: *they lived in a two-by-four shack.*

two-di·men·sion·al ▶*adj.* having or appearing to have length and breadth but no depth. ■ lacking depth or substance; superficial. —**two-di·men·sion·al·i·ty** *n.* —**two-di·men·sion·al·ly** *adv.*

two-faced ▶*adj.* insincere and deceitful.

two·fold /'tōō,fōld/ ▶*adj.* twice as great or as numerous: *a twofold increase in the risk.* ■ having two parts or elements.

▶*adv.* so as to double; to twice the number or amount.

two-hand·ed ▶*adj.* & *adv.* having, using, or requiring the use of two hands. —**two-hand·ed·ly** *adv.*

two·pence /'təpəns/ ▶*n. Brit.* the sum of two pence, esp. before decimalization (1971). ■ *inf.* a trivial sum; anything at all: *he didn't care twopence for her.*

two-ply ▶*adj.* (of a material or yarn) consisting of two layers or strands.

two·some /'tōōsəm/ ▶*n.* a pair of people considered together. ■ a game or dance for or involving two people.

two-step ▶*n.* a round dance with a sliding step in march or polka time.

two-stroke ▶*adj.* denoting an internal combustion engine whose power cycle is completed in one up-and-down movement of the piston. ■ denoting a vehicle having such an engine.

▶*n.* a two-stroke engine or vehicle.

two-time ▶*v.* [*tr.*] *inf.* deceive or be unfaithful to (a lover or spouse).

▶*adj.* denoting someone who has done or experienced something twice: *a two-time winner of the award.* —**two-tim·er** *n.*

two-tone (also **two-toned**) ▶*adj.* having two different shades or colors: *a two-tone jacket.* ■ emitting or consisting of two different sounds, typically alternating and at intervals: *a two-tone pulse signal.*

'twould /twōōd/ ▶*archaic* ▶*contr. of* it would.

two-way ▶*adj.* allowing or involving movement or communication in opposite directions: *a two-way radio.* ■ involving two participants. ■ (of a switch) permitting a current to be switched on or off from either of two points.

▶ □ **two-way street** a situation or relationship involving mutual or reciprocal action or obligation: *trust is a two-way street.*

two-way mir·ror ▶*n.* a panel of glass that can be seen through from one side but is a mirror on the other.

ty·coon /tī'kōōn/ ▶*n.* **1** a wealthy, powerful person in business or industry: *a newspaper tycoon.* **2** a title applied by foreigners to the shogun of Japan in power between 1857 and 1868.

ty·ing /'tī-iNG/ ▶ present participle of TIE.

tyke /tīk/ (also **tike**) ▶*n.* **1** *inf.* a small child: *is the little tyke up to his tricks again?* ■ [usu. as *adj.*] *Can.* an initiation level of sports competition for young children: *tyke hockey.* **2** a dog, esp. a mongrel.

ty·lo·sin /'tīlə,sin/ ▶*n.* an antibiotic that is routinely fed to livestock as a growth promoter and that may contribute to antibiotic resistance in humans.

tym·pa·na /'timpənə/ ▶ plural form of TYMPANUM.

tym·pa·ni ▶*pl. n.* variant spelling of TIMPANI.

tym·pan·ic /tim'panik/ ▶*adj.* **1** *Anat.* of, relating to, or having a tympanum. **2** resembling or acting like a drumhead.

tym·pan·ic mem·brane ▶*n.* a membrane forming part of the organ of hearing, which vibrates in response to sound waves. In humans and other higher vertebrates it forms the eardrum.

tym·pa·num /'timpənəm/ ▶*n.* (*pl.* -**nums** or -**na** /-nə/) **1** *Anat.* & *Zool.* the tympanic membrane or eardrum. ■ *Entomol.* a membrane covering the hearing organ on the leg or body of some insects, sometimes adapted for producing sound. **2** *Archit.* a vertical recessed triangular space forming the center of a pediment, typically decorated. ■ a similar space over a door between the lintel and the arch.

type /tīp/ ▶*n.* **1** a category of people or things having common characteristics. ■ a person, thing, or event considered as a representative of such a category: *it's not the type of car I'd want my daughter to drive.* ■ *inf.* a person of a specified character or nature: *professor types in tweed.* ■ (**one's type**) *inf.* the sort of person one likes or finds attractive: *she's not my type.* ■ *Linguistics* an abstract category or class of linguistic item or unit, as distinct from actual occurrences in speech or writing. **2** a person or thing symbolizing or exemplifying the ideal or defining characteristics of something: *she characterized his witty sayings as the type of modern wisdom.* ■ an object, conception, or work of art serving as a model for subsequent artists. ■ *Bot.* & *Zool.* an organism or taxon chosen as having the essential characteristics of its group. **3** printed characters or letters: *bold or italic type.* ■ pieces of metal with raised letters or characters on their upper surfaces, for use in letterpress printing. **4** a design on either side of a medal or coin.

▶*v.* [*tr.*] **1** write (something) on a typewriter or computer by pressing the keys: *he typed out the second draft* | [*intr.*] *I am learning how to type.* **2** *Med.* determine the type to which (a person or their blood or tissue) belongs. **3** short for TYPECAST.

type·cast /'tīp,kast/ ▶*v.* (*past* and *past part.* -**cast**) [*tr.*] (usu. **be typecast**) assign (an actor or actress) repeatedly to the same type of role, as a result of the appropriateness of their appearance or previous success in such roles. ■ represent or regard (a person or their role) as a stereotype: *people are not as likely to be typecast by their accents as they once were.*

type·face /'tīp,fās/ ▶*n.* *Printing* a particular design of type.

type·script /'tīp,skript/ ▶*n.* a typed copy of a text.

type·set /'tīp,set/ ▶*v.* (-**set·ting**; *past* and *past part.* -**set**) [*tr.*] arrange or generate the type for (a piece of text to be printed). —**type·set·ting** *n.*

type·set·ter /'tīp,setər/ ▶*n.* *Printing* a person who typesets text. ■ a typesetting machine.

type·writ·er /'tīp,rītər/ ▶*n.* an electric, electronic, or manual machine with keys for producing printlike characters one at a time on paper inserted around a roller. —**type·writ·ing** /-,rītiNG/ *n.* —**type·writ·ten** /-,ritn/ *adj.*

ty·phoid /'tī,foid/ (also **typhoid fever**) ▶*n.* an infectious bacterial fever with an eruption of red spots on the chest and abdomen and severe intestinal irritation. —**ty·phoi·dal** /tī'foidl/ *adj.*

ty·phoon /tī'fōōn/ ▶*n.* a tropical storm in the region of the Indian or western Pacific oceans. —**ty·phon·ic** /-'fänik/ *adj.*

ty·phus /'tīfəs/ ▶*n.* an infectious disease caused by rickettsiae, characterized by a purple rash, headaches, fever, and usually delirium. There are several forms, transmitted by vectors such as lice, ticks, mites, and rat fleas. —**ty·phous** /-fəs/ *adj.*

typ·i·cal /'tipikəl/ ▶*adj.* having the distinctive qualities of a particular type of person or thing: *a typical day.* ■ characteristic of a particular person or thing: *he brushed the incident aside with typical good humor.* ■ *inf.*

showing the characteristics expected of or popularly associated with a particular person, situation, or thing: *"Typical woman!"* John said disapprovingly. ■ representative as a symbol; symbolic: *the pit is typical of hell.* —**typ·i·cal·i·ty** /ˌtipiˈkalitē/ *n.* —**typ·i·cal·ly** /-ik(ə)lē/ *adv.*

typ·i·fy /ˈtipəˌfī/ ▶*v.* (**-fies, -fied**) [*tr.*] be characteristic or a representative example of. ■ represent; symbolize: *the sun typified the Greeks, and the moon the Persians.* —**typ·i·fi·ca·tion** /ˌtipəfiˈkāsʜən/ *n.* —**typ·i·fi·er** *n.*

typ·ist /ˈtīpist/ ▶*n.* a person who is skilled in using a typewriter or computer keyboard, esp. one who is employed for this purpose.

ty·po /ˈtīpō/ ▶*n.* (*pl.* **-pos**) *inf.* a typographical error.

ty·pog·ra·phy /tīˈpägrəfē/ ▶*n.* the art or process of setting and arranging types and printing from them. ■ the style and appearance of printed matter. —**ty·pog·ra·pher** /-fər/ *n.* —**ty·po·graph·ic** /ˌtīpəˈgrafik/ *adj.* —**ty·po·graph·i·cal** /ˌtīpəˈgrafikəl/ *adj.* —**ty·po·graph·i·cal·ly** /ˌtīpəˈgrafik(ə)lē/ *adv.*

ty·ran·ni·cal /təˈranikəl/ ▶*adj.* exercising power in a cruel or arbitrary way. ■ characteristic of tyranny; oppressive and controlling: *a momentary quieting of her tyrannical appetite.* —**ty·ran·ni·cal·ly** /-ik(ə)lē/ *adv.*

tyr·an·nize /ˈtirəˌnīz/ ▶*v.* [*tr.*] rule or treat (someone) despotically or cruelly: *she tyrannized her family* | [*intr.*] *he* **tyrannizes over** *the servants.*

ty·ran·no·saur /təˈranəˌsôr/ (also **ty·ran·no·sau·rus** /təˌranəˈsôrəs/) ▶*n.* a very large bipedal carnivorous dinosaur (family Tyrannosauridae, infraorder Carnosauria, suborder Theopoda) of the late Cretaceous period, with powerful jaws and small clawlike front legs.

tyr·an·ny /ˈtirənē/ ▶*n.* (*pl.* **-nies**) cruel and oppressive government or rule. ■ a nation under such cruel and oppressive government. ■ cruel, unreasonable, or arbitrary use of power or control. ■ (esp. in ancient Greece) rule by one who has absolute power without legal right. —**tyr·an·nous** /-nəs/ *adj.* —**tyr·an·nous·ly** /-nəslē/ *adv.*

ty·rant /ˈtīrənt/ ▶*n.* a cruel and oppressive ruler: *the tyrant was deposed by popular demonstrations.* ■ a person exercising power or control in a cruel, unreasonable, or arbitrary way. ■ (esp. in ancient Greece) a ruler who seized power without legal right.

ty·rant fly·catch·er ▶*n.* see FLYCATCHER.

ty·ro /ˈtīrō/ (also *chiefly Brit.* **ti·ro**) ▶*n.* (*pl.* **-ros**) a beginner or novice. ▷late Middle English: from Latin *tiro*, medieval Latin *tyro* 'recruit.'

T

Uu

U¹ /yōō/ (also **u**) ▶*n.* (*pl.* **Us** or **U's**) **1** the twenty-first letter of the alphabet. ■ denoting the next after T in a set of items, categories, etc. **2** (**U**) a shape like that of a capital U, esp. a cross section: [in *comb.*] *U-shaped glaciated valleys.*

U² ▶*symb.* the chemical element uranium.

u·biq·ui·tous /yōō'bikwətəs/ ▶*adj.* present, appearing, or found everywhere: *his ubiquitous influence was felt by all the family | cowboy hats are ubiquitous among the male singers.* —**u·biq·ui·tous·ly** *adv.* —**u·biq·ui·tous·ness** *n.* —**u·biq·ui·ty** /-wətē/ *n.*

U-boat ▶*n.* a German submarine used in World War I or World War II.

ud·der /'ədər/ ▶*n.* the mammary gland of female cattle, sheep, goats, horses, and related ungulates, a baglike organ with two or more teats hanging near the hind legs. —**ud·dered** *adj.* [in *comb.*] .

UFO ▶*n.* (*pl.* **UFOs**) a mysterious object seen in the sky for which, it is claimed, no orthodox scientific explanation can be found.

u·fol·o·gy /yōō'fäləjē/ ▶*n.* the study of UFOs. —**u·fo·log·i·cal** /ˌyōōfə-'läjikəl/ *adj.* —**u·fol·o·gist** /-jist/ *n.*

ugh /əg; əкн; ōōкн/ ▶*interj. inf.* used to express disgust or horror.

Ug·li fruit /'əglē/ ▶*n.* (*pl.* same) *trademark* a mottled green and yellow citrus fruit that is a hybrid of grapefruit and tangerine, obtained from the tree *Citrus × tangelo.*

ug·ly /'əglē/ ▶*adj.* (**-li·er, -li·est**) unpleasant or repulsive, esp. in appearance: *an ugly wart.* | [as *n.*] (**the ugly**) *he instinctively shrinks from the ugly.* ■ (of a situation or mood) involving or likely to involve violence or other unpleasantness. ■ unpleasantly suggestive; causing disquiet. ■ morally repugnant. ▷Middle English: from Old Norse *uggligr* 'to be dreaded,' from *ugga* 'to dread.' —**ug·li·fi·ca·tion** /ˌəgləfi'kāsHən/ *n.* —**ug·li·fy** /'əglə,fī/ *v.* —**ug·li·ly** /-lēlē/ *adv.* —**ug·li·ness** *n.*

ug·ly duck·ling ▶*n.* a person, esp. a child, who turns out to be beautiful or talented against all expectations.

UHF ▶*abbr.* ultrahigh frequency.

uh-huh /ə 'hə; əн 'həн/ ▶*interj.* used to express assent or as a noncommittal response to a question or remark.

u·kase /yōō'kās; -'kāz/ ▶*n.* an edict of the Russian government. ■ an arbitrary command: *defying the publisher in the very building from which he had issued his ukase.*

U·krain·i·an /yōō'krānēən/ ▶*n.* **1** a native or national of Ukraine, or a person of Ukrainian descent. **2** the East Slavic language of Ukraine. ▶*adj.* of or relating to Ukraine, its people, or their language.

u·ku·le·le /ˌyōōkə'lālē/ ▶*n.* a small four-stringed guitar of Hawaiian origin.

ul·cer /'əlsər/ ▶*n.* an open sore on an external or internal surface of the body, caused by a break in the skin or mucous membrane that fails to heal. ■ *fig.* a moral blemish or corrupting influence. —**ul·cered** *adj.* —**ul·cer·ous** /'əls(ə)rəs/ *adj.*

ul·cer·ate /'əlsə,rāt/ ▶*v.* [*intr.*] develop into or become affected by an ulcer. —**ul·cer·a·tion** /ˌəlsə'rāsHən/ *n.* —**ul·cer·a·tive** /-rətiv; -,rātiv/ *adj.*

ul·na /'əlnə/ ▶*n.* (*pl.* **-nae** /-,nē; -,nī/ or **-nas**) the thinner and longer of the two bones in the human forearm, on the side opposite to the thumb. Compare with **RADIUS** (sense 2). ■ the corresponding bone in a quadruped's foreleg or a bird's wing. —**ul·nar** *adj.*

ul·ster /'əlstər/ ▶*n.* a man's long, loose overcoat of rough cloth, typically with a belt at the back.

ult. ▶*abbr.* ▪ ultimate. ▪ ultimo.

ul·te·ri·or /əl'ti(ə)rēər/ ▶*adj.* existing beyond what is obvious or admitted; intentionally hidden: *could there be an ulterior motive behind his request?* ■ beyond what is immediate or present; coming in the future.

ul·ti·ma·ta /ˌəltə'mätə; -'mätə/ ▶ plural form of **ULTIMATUM**.

ul·ti·mate /'əltəmit/ ▶*adj.* being or happening at the end of a process; final: *their ultimate aim was to force his resignation.* ■ being the best or most extreme example of its kind: *the ultimate accolade.* ■ basic or fundamental: *the ultimate constituents of anything that exists are atoms.* ▶*n.* **1** (**the ultimate**) the best achievable or imaginable of its kind: *the ultimate in decorative luxury.* **2** a final or fundamental fact or principle. —**ul·ti·ma·cy** /-məsē/ *n.* (*pl.* **-cies**) —**ul·ti·mate·ly** *adv.*

ul·ti·ma·tum /ˌəltə'mātəm; -'mät-/ ▶*n.* (*pl.* **-ma·tums** or **-ma·ta** /-'mātə; -'mätə/) a final demand or statement of terms, the rejection of which will result in retaliation or a breakdown in relations.

ul·tra /'əltrə/ *inf.* ▶*adv.* very; extremely: *the play was not just boring, it was ultra boring.*

ultra- ▶*prefix* **1** beyond; on the other side of: *ultramontane.* **2** extreme; to an extreme degree: *ultramicroscopic | ultraradical.*

ul·tra·high fre·quen·cy /'əltrə,hī; ˌəltrə'hī/ (abbr.: **UHF**) ▶*n.* a radio frequency in the range 300 to 3,000 MHz.

ul·tra·ism /'əltrə,izəm/ ▶*n.* the holding of extreme opinions: *there is ultraism on both sides of the issue.* —**ul·tra·ist** *n.*

ul·tra·light ▶*adj.* /ˌəltrə'līt; 'əltrə,līt/ extremely lightweight. ▶*n.* /'əltrə,līt/ a small, light, single-seater aircraft.

ul·tra·ma·rine /ˌəltrəmə'rēn/ ▶*n.* a brilliant deep blue pigment originally obtained from lapis lazuli. ■ an imitation of such a pigment, made from powdered fired clay, sodium carbonate, sulfur, and resin. ■ a brilliant deep blue color.

ul·tra·son·ic /ˌəltrə'sänik/ ▶*adj.* of or involving sound waves with a frequency above the upper limit of human hearing. —**ul·tra·son·i·cal·ly** /-ik(ə)lē/ *adv.*

ul·tra·son·ics /ˌəltrə'säniks/ ▶*pl. n.* [treated as *sing.*] the science and application of ultrasonic waves. ■ [treated as *sing.* or *pl.*] ultrasonic waves; ultrasound.

ul·tra·sound /'əltrə,sound/ ▶*n.* sound or other vibrations having an ultrasonic frequency, particularly as used in medical imaging. ■ an ultrasound scan, esp. one of a pregnant woman to examine the fetus.

ul·tra·struc·ture /'əltrə,strəkcHər/ ▶*n. Biol.* a fine structure, esp. within a cell, that can be seen only with the high magnification obtainable with an electron microscope. —**ul·tra·struc·tur·al** /-cHərəl/ *adj.*

ul·tra·vi·o·let /ˌəltrə'vī(ə)lət/ *Physics* ▶*adj.* (of electromagnetic radiation) having a wavelength shorter than that of the violet end of the visible spectrum but longer than that of X-rays. ■ (of equipment or techniques) using or concerned with this radiation: *an ultraviolet telescope.* ▶*n.* the ultraviolet part of the spectrum; ultraviolet radiation.

ul·u·late /'əlyə,lāt; 'yōōl-/ ▶*v.* [*intr.*] howl or wail as an expression of strong emotion, typically grief: *women were ululating as the body was laid out.* —**ul·u·lant** /-lənt/ *adj.* —**ul·u·la·tion** /ˌəlyə'lāsHən; ˌyōōl-/ *n.*

um /(ə)m/ ▶*interj.* expressing hesitation or a pause in speech.

um·bel /'əmbəl/ ▶*n. Bot.* a flower cluster in which stalks of nearly equal length spring from a common center and form a flat or curved surface, characteristic of the parsley family. —**um·bel·late** /'əmbəlit; -,lāt; ,əm'belit/ *adj.*

um·ber /'əmbər/ ▶*n.* a natural pigment resembling but darker than ocher, normally dark yellowish-brown in color (**raw umber**) or dark brown when roasted (**burnt umber**). ■ the color of this pigment.

um·bil·i·cal /ˌəm'bilikəl/ ▶*adj.* relating to or affecting the navel or umbilical cord: *the umbilical artery.* ■ *fig.* extremely close; inseparable: *their*

umbilical attachment to the state. ■ (of a pipe, cable, etc.) connecting someone or something to a source of essential supplies.
▶*n.* short for UMBILICAL CORD. **—um·bil·i·cal·ly** /-ik(ə)lē/ *adv.*

um·bil·i·cal cord ▶*n.* a flexible cordlike structure containing blood vessels and attaching a human or other mammalian fetus to the placenta during gestation. ■ a flexible cable, pipe, or other line carrying essential services or supplies.

um·bil·i·cus /ˌəmˈbilikəs/ ▶*n.* (*pl.* **-ci** /-ˌkī/ -ˌsī; -ˌkē/ or **-cus·es**) *Anat.* the navel. ▷late 17th cent.: from Latin: related to Greek *omphalos,* also to *navel.*

um·bra /ˈəmbrə/ ▶*n.* (*pl.* **-bras** or **-brae** /-ˌbrē; -ˌbrī/) the fully shaded inner region of a shadow cast by an opaque object, esp. the area on the earth or moon experiencing the total phase of an eclipse. Compare with PENUMBRA. **—um·bral** *adj.*

um·brage /ˈəmbrij/ ▶*n.* offense or annoyance: *she took umbrage at his remarks.* **—um·bra·geous** /ˌəmˈbrājəs/ *adj.*

um·brel·la /ˌəmˈbrelə/ ▶*n.* **1** a device consisting of a circular canopy of cloth on a folding metal frame supported by a central rod, used as protection against rain or sometimes sun. ■ *fig.* a protecting force or influence: *the American nuclear umbrella over the west.* ■ a screen of fighter aircraft or antiaircraft artillery. ■ [usu. as *adj.*] a thing that includes or contains many different elements or parts. **2** *Zool.* the gelatinous disk of a jellyfish, which it contracts and expands to move through the water. **—um·brel·laed** *adj.* **—um·brel·la·like** /-ˌlīk/ *adj.*

u·mi·ak /ˈo͞omēˌak/ ▶*n.* an Eskimo open boat made with skin stretched over a wooden frame.

um·laut /ˈo͞omˌlout/ *Linguistics* ▶*n.* a mark (|die|) used over a vowel, as in German or Hungarian, to indicate a different vowel quality, usually fronting or rounding.

ump /əmp/ ▶*n.* & *v. inf.* short for UMPIRE.

um·pire /ˈəmˌpī(ə)r/ ▶*n.* (in some sports) an official who watches a game or match closely to enforce the rules and arbitrate on matters arising from the play. ■ a person chosen to arbitrate between contending parties.
▶*v.* [*intr.*] act as an umpire. ■ [*tr.*] act as umpire in (a game or match). **—um·pir·age** /-ˌpīrij/ *n.* **—um·pire·ship** /-ˌSHip/ *n.*

ump·teen /ˈəm(p)ˌtēn/ *inf.* ▶*cardinal number* indefinitely many; a lot of. **—ump·teenth** /-ˌtēnTH/ *ordinal number* .

UN (also **U.N.**) ▶*abbr.* United Nations.

un-[1] ▶*prefix* **1** (added to adjectives, participles, and their derivatives) denoting the absence of a quality or state; not: *unabashed | unacademic | unrepeatable.* ■ the reverse of (usually with an implication of approval or disapproval, or with another special connotation): *unselfish | unprepossessing | unworldly.* **2** (added to nouns) a lack of: *unrest | untruth.*

un-[2] ▶*prefix* added to verbs: **1** denoting the reversal or cancellation of an action or state: *untie.* **2** denoting deprivation, separation, or reduction to a lesser state: *unmask.* ■ denoting release: *unhand.*

un·a·bat·ed /ˌənəˈbātid/ ▶*adj.* without any reduction in intensity or strength: *the storm was raging unabated.* **—un·a·bat·ed·ly** *adv.*

---

un·ab·sorbed *adj.*
un·ac·cent·ed *adj.*
un·ac·com·mo·dat·ing *adj.*
un·ac·knowl·edged *adj.*
un·ac·quaint·ed *adj.*
un·a·dapt·a·ble *adj.*
un·a·dapt·ed *adj.*
un·ad·ja·cent *adj.*
un·ad·ven·tur·ous *adj.*
un·af·fec·tion·ate *adj.*
un·af·fil·i·at·ed *adj.*
un·a·fraid *adj.*
un·ag·gres·sive *adj.*
un·a·ligned *adj.*
un·a·like *adj. & adv.*
un·al·lied *adj.*
un·al·low·a·ble *adj.*
un·am·bi·tious *adj.*
un·am·bi·tious·ly *adv.*
un·am·biv·a·lent *adj.*
un·am·pli·fied *adj.*
un·an·chored *adj.*
un·ap·peal·ing *adj.*
un·ap·peal·ing·ly *adv.*
un·ap·peased *adj.*
un·ap·plied *adj.*
un·ap·pre·hend·ed *adj.*
un·apt *adj.*
un·ar·rest·ing *adj.*
un·ar·tis·tic *adj.*
un·as·cer·tained *adj.*
un·as·ser·tive *adj.*
un·as·ser·tive·ly *adv.*
un·as·signed *adj.*
un·as·so·ci·at·ed *adj.*
un·at·trac·tive *adj.*
un·at·trac·tive·ness *n.*
un·au·dit·ed *adj.*
un·au·then·ti·cat·ed *adj.*
un·au·thor·ized *adj.*
un·a·vail·a·bil·i·ty *n.*
un·a·vail·a·ble *adj.*
un·a·vowed *adj.*
un·awed *adj.*
un·be·fit·ting *adj.*
un·be·fit·ting·ly *adv.*
un·bid·da·ble *adj.*
un·bleached *adj.*
un·blend·ed *adj.*
un·brand·ed *adj.*

un·breach·a·ble *adj.*
un·break·a·ble *adj.*
un·bridge·a·ble *adj.*
un·bruised *adj.*
un·bur·ied *adj.*
un·burned *adj.*
un·burnt *adj.*
un·busi·ness·like *adj.*
un·caged *adj.*
un·ca·non·i·cal *adj.*
un·car·pet·ed *adj.*
un·cashed *adj.*
un·caught *adj.*
un·cen·sored *adj.*
un·change·a·ble *adj. & n.*
un·changed *adj.*
un·chang·ing *adj.*
un·chap·er·oned *adj.*
un·char·ac·ter·is·tic *adj.*
un·char·ac·ter·is·ti·cal·ly *adv.*
un·char·tered *adj.*
un·chiv·al·rous *adj.*
un·cho·sen *adj.*
un·clas·si·fi·a·ble *adj.*
un·clut·tered *adj.*
un·coat·ed *adj.*
un·combed *adj.*
un·com·pan·ion·a·ble *adj.*
un·com·plet·ed *adj.*
un·con·clud·ed *adj.*
un·con·fi·dent *adj.*
un·con·gen·ial *adj.*
un·con·jec·tur·a·ble *adj.*
un·con·quered *adj.*
un·con·se·crat·ed *adj.*
un·con·sent·ing *adj.*
un·con·strained *adj.*
un·con·strict·ed *adj.*
un·con·tam·i·nat·ed *adj.*
un·con·ten·tious *adj.*
un·con·tra·dict·ed *adj.*
un·con·trived *adj.*
un·con·trol·la·ble *adj. & n.*
un·con·trol·la·bly *adv.*
un·con·tro·ver·sial *adj.*
un·cooked *adj.*
un·cor·rect·ed *adj.*
un·cor·rob·o·rat·ed *adj.*
un·cor·rupt·ed *adj.*
un·cropped *adj.*

un·crowd·ed *adj.*
un·crushed *adj.*
un·cul·tured *adj.*
un·curbed *adj.*
un·cured *adj.*
un·cur·tained *adj.*
un·dam·aged *adj.*
un·dec·o·rat·ed *adj.*
un·de·feat·ed *adj.*
un·de·fend·ed *adj.*
un·de·liv·ered *adj.*
un·de·mand·ing *adj.*
un·dem·o·crat·ic *adj.*
un·de·nied *adj.*
un·de·nom·i·na·tion·al *adj.*
un·de·pend·a·ble *adj.*
un·de·sir·ous *adj.*
un·de·tect·a·ble *adj.*
un·de·tect·ed *adj.*
un·de·terred *adj.*
un·de·vi·at·ing *adj.*
un·di·ag·nosed *adj.*
un·di·gest·ed *adj.*
un·dig·ni·fied *adj.*
un·di·lut·ed *adj.*
un·di·min·ished *adj.*
un·dis·cern·ing *adj.*
un·dis·charged *adj.*
un·dis·ci·plined *adj.*
un·dis·closed *adj.*
un·dis·cov·ered *adj.*
un·dis·crim·i·nat·ing *adj.*
un·dis·solved *adj.*
un·dis·trib·ut·ed *adj.*
un·dis·turbed *adj.*
un·do·mes·ti·cat·ed *adj.*
un·drink·a·ble *adj.*
un·dyed *adj.*
un·eat·a·ble *adj.*
un·eat·en *adj.*
un·ed·it·ed *adj.*
un·em·bel·lished *adj.*
un·em·phat·ic *adj.*
un·en·closed *adj.*
un·en·cum·bered *adj.*
un·en·dowed *adj.*
un·en·force·a·ble *adj.*
un·en·gaged *adj.*
un·en·joy·a·ble *adj.*
un·en·light·ened *adj.*

un·en·ter·pris·ing *adj.*
un·en·thu·si·as·tic *adj.*
un·en·thu·si·as·ti·cal·ly *adv.*
un·en·vied *adj.*
un·e·quipped *adj.*
un·es·tab·lished *adj.*
un·e·vent·ful *adj.*
un·ex·am·ined *adj.*
un·ex·cit·ing *adj.*
un·ex·e·cut·ed *adj.*
un·ex·er·cised *adj.*
un·ex·plod·ed *adj.*
un·fad·ing *adj.*
un·fal·ter·ing *adj.*
un·fash·ion·a·ble *adj.*
un·fash·ion·a·bly *adv.*
un·fa·ther·ly *adj.*
un·fath·om·a·ble *adj.*
un·fath·omed *adj.*
un·fazed *adj.*
un·fea·si·ble *adj.*
un·fea·si·bly *adv.*
un·fed *adj.*
un·fem·i·nine *adj.*
un·fenced *adj.*
un·fer·ment·ed *adj.*
un·fer·tile *adj.*
un·fer·ti·lized *adj.*
un·filled *adj.*
un·flat·ter·ing *adj.*
un·fore·see·a·ble *adj.*
un·fore·seen *adj.*
un·for·giv·en *adj.*
un·for·got·ten *adj.*
un·for·mu·lat·ed *adj.*
un·for·ti·fied *adj.*
un·framed *adj.*
un·fund·ed *adj.*
un·gal·lant *adj.*
un·gal·lant·ly *adv.*
un·gen·er·ous *adj.*
un·gen·er·ous·ly *adv.*
un·gen·tle *adj.*
un·gen·tle·man·ly *adj.*
un·gent·ly *adv.*
un·glam·or·ous *adj.*
un·grace·ful *adj.*
un·grace·ful·ly *adv.*
un·grace·ful·ness *n.*
un·grudg·ing *adj.*

un·a·bridged /ˌənəˈbrijd/ ▸*adj.* (of a text) not cut or shortened; complete: *an unabridged edition.*

un·ac·com·pa·nied /ˌənəˈkəmp(ə)nēd/ ▸*adj.* having no companion or escort: *no unaccompanied children allowed.* ■ (of a piece of music) sung or played without instrumental accompaniment: *an unaccompanied violin elegy.* ■ (of a state, condition, or event) taking place without something specified taking place at the same time.

un·ac·com·plished /ˌənəˈkämplishT/ ▸*adj.* **1** showing little skill. **2** not carried out.

un·ac·count·a·ble /ˌənəˈkountəbəl/ ▸*adj.* **1** unable to be explained. ■ (of a person or their behavior) unpredictable and strange. **2** (of a person, organization, or institution) not required or expected to justify actions or decisions; not responsible for results or consequences. —**un·ac·count·a·bil·i·ty** /-ˌkountəˈbilətē/ *n.* —**un·ac·count·a·bly** /-blē/ *adv.*

un·ac·count·ed /ˌənəˈkountid/ ▸*adj.* (**unaccounted for**) not included in (an account or calculation) through being lost or disregarded.

un·ac·cus·tomed /ˌənəˈkəstəmd/ ▸*adj.* not familiar or usual; out of the ordinary. ■ (**unaccustomed to**) not familiar with or used to. —**un·ac·cus·tomed·ly** *adv.*

un·a·dul·ter·at·ed /ˌənəˈdəltəˌrātid/ ▸*adj.* not mixed or diluted with any different or extra elements; complete and absolute: *pure, unadulterated jealousy.* ■ (of food or drink) having no inferior added substances; pure.

un·ad·vis·ed·ly /ˌənədˈvīzidlē/ ▸*adv.* in an unwise or rash manner.

un·af·fect·ed /ˌənəˈfektid/ ▸*adj.* **1** feeling or showing no effects or

changes. **2** (of a person) without artificiality or insincerity. —**un·af·fect·ed·ly** *adv.* —**un·af·fect·ed·ness** *n.*

un·al·ien·a·ble /ˌənˈālyənəbəl; -ˈālēə-/ ▸*adj.* another term for INALIENABLE.

un·A·mer·i·can /ˌənəˈmerikən/ ▸*adj.* not in accordance with American characteristics: *such un-American concepts as subsidized medicine.* ■ *chiefly hist.* contrary to the interests of the U.S. and therefore treasonable. —**un·A·mer·i·can·ism** /-ˌnizəm/ *n.*

u·nan·i·mous /yo͞oˈnanəməs/ ▸*adj.* (of two or more people) fully in agreement. ■ (of an opinion, decision, or vote) held or carried by everyone involved. —**u·na·nim·i·ty** /ˌyo͞onəˈnimətē/ *n.* —**u·nan·i·mous·ly** *adv.*

un·an·swer·a·ble /ˌənˈans(ə)rəbəl/ ▸*adj.* unable to be answered: *unanswerable questions concerning our own mortality.* ■ unable to be disclaimed or proved wrong. —**un·an·swer·a·bly** /-blē/ *adv.*

un·ap·proach·a·ble /ˌənəˈprōCHəbəl/ ▸*adj.* (of a person or institution) not welcoming or friendly. —**un·ap·proach·a·bil·i·ty** /-ˌprōCHəˈbilətē/ *n.* —**un·ap·proach·a·bly** /-blē/ *adv.*

un·ar·gu·a·ble /ˌənˈärgyəwəbəl/ ▸*adj.* not open to disagreement; indisputable. ■ not able to be discussed or asserted. —**un·ar·gu·a·bly** /-blē/ *adv.*

un·armed /ˌənˈärmd/ ▸*adj.* not equipped with or carrying weapons.

un·a·shamed /ˌənəˈsHāmd/ ▸*adj.* expressed or acting openly and without guilt or embarrassment: *an unashamed emotionalism.* —**un·a·sham·ed·ly** /-ˈsHāmidlē/ *adv.* —**un·a·sham·ed·ness** /-ˈsHām(i)dnis/ *n.*

---

un·grudg·ing·ly *adv.*	**un·la·bored** *adj.*	**un·proud** *adj.*	**un·safe** *adj.*
un·ham·pered *adj.*	**un·lib·er·at·ed** *adj.*	**un·pub·li·cized** *adj.*	**un·salt·ed** *adj.*
un·har·mo·ni·ous *adj.*	**un·locked** *adj.*	**un·pun·ish·a·ble** *adj.*	**un·sanc·ti·fied** *adj.*
un·hatched *adj.*	**un·loved** *adj.*	**un·pu·ri·fied** *adj.*	**un·sanc·tioned** *adj.*
un·healed *adj.*	**un·lov·ing** *adj.*	**un·quench·a·ble** *adj.*	**un·san·i·tar·y** *adj.*
un·heat·ed *adj.*	**un·mar·ket·a·ble** *adj.*	**un·quenched** *adj.*	**un·sat·is·fied** *adj.*
un·heed·ed *adj.*	**un·mar·ried** *adj. & n.*	**un·quot·a·ble** *adj.*	**un·sat·is·fy·ing** *adj.*
un·heed·ing *adj.*	**un·ma·tured** *adj.*	**un·reach·a·ble** *adj.*	**un·scent·ed** *adj.*
un·help·ful *adj.*	**un·meant** *adj.*	**un·reached** *adj.*	**un·sched·uled** *adj.*
un·help·ful·ly *adv.*	**un·me·lo·di·ous** *adj.*	**un·re·al·is·tic** *adj.*	**un·searched** *adj.*
un·he·ro·ic *adj.*	**un·mem·o·ra·ble** *adj.*	**un·re·al·is·ti·cal·ly** *adv.*	**un·seg·re·gat·ed** *adj.*
un·hes·i·tat·ing *adj.*	**un·me·thod·i·cal** *adj.*	**un·rec·og·niz·a·ble** *adj.*	**un·se·lect** *adj.*
un·hin·dered *adj.*	**un·mod·ern·ized** *adj.*	**un·rec·om·pensed** *adj.*	**un·se·lec·tive** *adj.*
un·hon·ored *adj.*	**un·mod·i·fied** *adj.*	**un·rec·on·ciled** *adj.*	**un·sep·a·rat·ed** *adj.*
un·hurt *adj.*	**un·mount·ed** *adj.*	**un·re·cord·ed** *adj.*	**un·sewn** *v.*
un·hy·gi·en·ic *adj.*	**un·mown** *adj.*	**un·rec·ti·fied** *adj.*	**un·shape·ly** *adj.*
un·hy·phen·at·ed *adj.*	**un·neigh·bor·ly** *adj.*	**un·re·deem·a·ble** *adj.*	**un·shel·tered** *adj.*
un·i·de·al *adj.*	**un·ob·scured** *adj.*	**un·re·deemed** *adj.*	**un·shield·ed** *adj.*
un·i·den·ti·fied *adj.*	**un·ob·serv·ant** *adj.*	**un·re·formed** *adj.*	**un·shock·a·ble** *adj.*
un·il·lu·mi·nat·ed *adj.*	**un·ob·struct·ed** *adj.*	**un·re·lat·ed** *adj.*	**un·solv·a·ble** *adj.*
un·il·lus·trat·ed *adj.*	**un·ob·served** *adj.*	**un·re·laxed** *adj.*	**un·solved** *adj.*
un·im·ag·i·na·tive *adj.*	**un·ob·tain·a·ble** *adj.*	**un·re·li·a·ble** *adj.*	**un·sort·ed** *adj.*
un·im·ped·ed *adj.*	**un·of·fend·ing** *adj.*	**un·re·li·a·bly** *adv.*	**un·soured** *adj.*
un·im·por·tant *adj.*	**un·of·fi·cial** *adj.*	**un·re·mem·bered** *adj.*	**un·spe·cial·ized** *adj.*
un·im·pos·ing *adj.*	**un·oiled** *adj.*	**un·re·morse·ful** *adj.*	**un·spot·ted** *adj.*
un·im·pres·sion·a·ble *adj.*	**un·o·pened** *adj.*	**un·re·mov·a·ble** *adj.*	**un·stained** *adj.*
un·im·pres·sive *adj.*	**un·op·posed** *adj.*	**un·re·newed** *adj.*	**un·sub·dued** *adj.*
un·in·fect·ed *adj.*	**un·or·di·nar·y** *adj.*	**un·re·pealed** *adj.*	**un·sub·ju·gat·ed** *adj.*
un·in·flamed *adj.*	**un·or·na·ment·ed** *adj.*	**un·rep·re·sent·ed** *adj.*	**un·suc·cess** *n.*
un·in·flu·enced *adj.*	**un·os·ten·ta·tious** *adj.*	**un·re·proved** *adj.*	**un·suc·cess·ful** *adj.*
un·in·flu·en·tial *adj.*	**un·paint·ed** *adj.*	**un·re·quest·ed** *adj.*	**un·suc·cess·ful·ly** *adv.*
un·in·form·a·tive *adj.*	**un·pas·teur·ized** *adj.*	**un·re·sist·ed** *adj.*	**un·sul·lied** *adj.*
un·in·formed *adj.*	**un·pat·ent·ed** *adj.*	**un·re·sist·ing** *adj.*	**un·sum·moned** *adj.*
un·in·hab·it·ed *adj.*	**un·pa·tri·ot·ic** *adj.*	**un·re·solv·a·ble** *adj.*	**un·tal·ent·ed** *adj.*
un·in·jured *adj.*	**un·pa·tron·iz·ing** *adj.*	**un·re·spon·sive** *adj.*	**un·trimmed** *adj.*
un·in·spir·ing *adj.*	**un·paved** *adj.*	**un·rest·ful** *adj.*	**un·twist·ed** *adj.*
un·in·su·lat·ed *adj.*	**un·peeled** *adj.*	**un·re·vealed** *adj.*	**un·var·y·ing** *adj.*
un·in·sured *adj.*	**un·pen·i·tent** *adj.*	**un·re·veal·ing** *adj.*	**un·ver·i·fi·a·ble** *adj.*
un·in·tend·ed *adj.*	**un·per·cep·tive** *adj.*	**un·re·voked** *adj.*	**un·ver·i·fied** *adj.*
un·in·ten·tion·al	**un·per·fect·ed** *adj.*	**un·re·ward·ing** *adj.*	**un·war·like** *adj.*
un·in·ter·est·ing *adj.*	**un·per·fo·rat·ed** *adj.*	**un·rhymed** *adj.*	**un·warmed** *adj.*
un·in·ven·tive *adj.*	**un·per·formed** *adj.*	**un·rhyth·mic** *adj.*	**un·watched** *adj.*
un·in·ves·ti·gat·ed *adj.*	**un·per·sua·sive** *adj.*	**un·rhyth·mi·cal** *adj.*	**un·watch·ful** *adj.*
un·in·vit·ing *adj.*	**un·pit·ied** *adj.*	**un·ripe** *adj.*	**un·wea·ry** *adj.*
un·in·volved *adj.*	**un·plucked** *adj.*	**un·ris·en** *adj.*	**un·wet·ted** *adj.*
un·joined *adj.*	**un·pol·lut·ed** *adj.*	**un·ro·man·tic** *adj.*	**un·wound·ed** *adj.*
un·joint·ed *adj.*	**un·pre·scribed** *adj.*		
un·jus·ti·fied *adj.*	**un·priced** *adj.*		
un·la·beled *adj.*	**un·pro·claimed** *adj.*		
	un·pro·cur·a·ble *adj.*		

Pronunciation Key ə *ago,* up; ər *over, fur;* a *hat;* ā *ate;* ä *car;* CH *chin;* e *let;* ē *see;* eər *air;* i *fit;* ī *by;* i(ə)r *ear;* NG *sing;* ō *go;* ô *law, for;* oi *toy;* o͝o *good;* o͞o *goo;* ou *out;* sH *she;* TH *thin;* TH *then;* (h)w *why;* ZH *vision*

un·as·sail·a·ble /ˌənəˈsāləbəl/ ▶*adj.* unable to be attacked, questioned, or defeated: *an unassailable lead.* —**un·as·sail·a·bil·i·ty** /-ˌsāləˈbilətē/ *n.* —**un·as·sail·a·bly** /-blē/ *adv.*

un·as·sum·ing /ˌənəˈsōōmiNG/ ▶*adj.* not pretentious or arrogant; modest. —**un·as·sum·ing·ly** *adv.* —**un·as·sum·ing·ness** *n.*

un·at·tached /ˌənəˈtacHt/ ▶*adj.* not working for or belonging to a particular body or organization. ■ not fastened to anything; loose. ■ not married or having an established partner; single.

un·at·tend·ed /ˌənəˈtendid/ ▶*adj.* not noticed or dealt with: *her behavior went unnoticed and **unattended to**.* ■ not supervised or looked after.

un·at·trib·ut·ed /ˌənəˈtribyətid/ ▶*adj.* (of a quotation, story, or work of art) not ascribed to any source; of unknown provenance. —**un·at·trib·ut·a·ble** /-ˈtribyətəbəl/ —**un·at·trib·ut·a·bly** /-yətəblē/ *adv.*

un·a·void·a·ble /ˌənəˈvoidəbəl/ ▶*adj.* not able to be avoided, prevented, or ignored; inevitable: *the natural and unavoidable consequences of growing old.* —**un·a·void·a·bil·i·ty** /-ˌvoidəˈbilətē/ *n.* —**un·a·void·a·bly** /-blē/ *adv.*

un·a·ware /ˌənəˈwe(ə)r/ ▶*adj.* having no knowledge of a situation or fact: *they were **unaware of** his absence.*
▶*adv.* variant of UNAWARES. —**un·a·ware·ness** *n.*

un·a·wares /ˌənəˈwe(ə)rz/ (also **un·a·ware**) ▶*adv.* without being aware of a situation: *it will be flagged so that people don't stumble on it unawares.*

un·bal·ance /ˌənˈbaləns/ ▶*v.* [*tr.*] make (someone or something) unsteady so that they tip or fall. ■ upset or disturb the equilibrium of (a state of affairs or someone's state of mind).
▶*n.* a lack of symmetry, balance, or stability.

un·bear·a·ble /ˌənˈbe(ə)rəbəl/ ▶*adj.* not able to be endured or tolerated: *the heat was getting unbearable.* —**un·bear·a·ble·ness** *n.* —**un·bear·a·bly** /-blē/ *adv.* *it was unbearably hot.*

un·beat·a·ble /ˌənˈbētəbəl/ ▶*adj.* not able to be defeated or exceeded in a contest or commercial market: *the shop sells bikes at unbeatable prices.* ■ extremely good; outstanding. —**un·beat·a·bly** /-blē/ *adv.*

un·beat·en /ˌənˈbētn/ ▶*adj.* not defeated or surpassed: *they were the only team to remain unbeaten.* ■ not stirred or whipped.

un·be·com·ing /ˌənbiˈkəmiNG/ ▶*adj.* (esp. of clothing or a color) not flattering: *a stout lady in an unbecoming striped sundress.* ■ (of a person's attitude or behavior) not fitting or appropriate; unseemly. —**un·be·com·ing·ly** *adv.* —**un·be·com·ing·ness** *n.*

un·be·known /ˌənbiˈnōn/ (also **un·be·knownst** /-ˈnōnst/) ▶*adj.* (**unbeknown to**) without the knowledge of (someone).

un·be·lief /ˌənbəˈlēf/ ▶*n.* lack of religious belief; an absence of faith. ■ another term for DISBELIEF. —**un·be·liev·er** /-ˈlēvər/ *n.* —**un·be·liev·ing** /-ˈlēviNG/ *adj.* —**un·be·liev·ing·ly** /-ˈlēviNGlē/ *adv.*

un·be·liev·a·ble /ˌənbəˈlēvəbəl/ ▶*adj.* not able to be believed; unlikely to be true. ■ so great or extreme as to be difficult to believe; extraordinary. —**un·be·liev·a·bil·i·ty** /-ˌlēvəˈbilətē/ *n.* —**un·be·liev·a·bly** /-ˈlēvəblē/ *adv.* *he worked unbelievably long hours.*

un·bend /ˌənˈbend/ ▶*v.* (*past* and *past part.* **-bent**) make or become straight from a bent or twisted form or position: [*intr.*] *he unbent from the cockpit as she passed.* ■ [*intr.*] become less reserved, formal, or strict.

un·bend·ing /ˌənˈbendiNG/ ▶*adj.* stiff; inflexible. ■ strict and austere in one's behavior or attitudes: *they were unbending in their demands | his unbending iron will.* —**un·bend·ing·ly** *adv.* —**un·bend·ing·ness** *n.*

un·bi·ased /ˌənˈbīəst/ (also *chiefly Brit.* **un·bi·assed**) ▶*adj.* showing no prejudice for or against something; impartial.

un·bind /ˌənˈbīnd/ ▶*v.* (*past* and *past part.* **-bound**) [*tr.*] release from bonds or restraints.

un·blink·ing /ˌənˈbliNGkiNG/ ▶*adj.* (of a person or their gaze or eyes) not blinking. ■ (of a portrayal or scrutiny) direct, thorough, and honest. —**un·blink·ing·ly** *adv.*

un·block /ˌənˈbläk/ ▶*v.* [*tr.*] remove an obstruction from: *balloon catheters are used to unblock occluded arteries.*

un·bolt /ˌənˈbōlt/ ▶*v.* [*tr.*] open by drawing back a bolt.

un·born /ˌənˈbôrn/ ▶*adj.* (of a baby) not yet born: *the sound of an unborn baby's heartbeat | fig. without training, your full talent remains unborn | [as pl. n.] the side with the most power will determine how America treats its unborn.*

un·bound /ˌənˈbound/ ▶ past and past participle of UNBIND.
▶*adj.* not bound or tied up: *her hair was unbound | fig. they were unbound by convention.* ■ (of printed sheets) not bound together. ■ (of a book) not provided with a proper or permanent cover.

un·bound·ed /ˌənˈboundid/ ▶*adj.* having or appearing to have no limits. —**un·bound·ed·ly** *adv.* —**un·bound·ed·ness** *n.*

un·bri·dle /ˌənˈbrīdl/ ▶*v.* [*tr.*] remove the bridle from (a horse or mule). ■ release from restraint: [as *adj.*] *the forces of the world capitalist market were unbridled and spread quickly.*

un·bro·ken /ˌənˈbrōkən/ ▶*adj.* not broken, fractured, or damaged: *an unbroken glass.* ■ not interrupted or disturbed; continuous: *a night of sleep unbroken by nightmares.* ■ (of a record) not surpassed: *a 13-year unbroken record of increasing profits.* ■ (of a horse) not tamed or accustomed to being ridden. —**un·bro·ken·ly** *adv.* —**un·bro·ken·ness** *n.*

un·buck·le /ˌənˈbəkəl/ ▶*v.* [*tr.*] unfasten the buckle of.

un·bur·den /ˌənˈbərdn/ ▶*v.* [*tr.*] relieve (someone) of something that is causing anxiety or distress: *the need to **unburden yourself to** someone who will listen.* ■ (usu. **be unburdened**) not cause (someone) hardship or distress: *they are unburdened by expectations of success.*

un·but·ton /ˌənˈbətn/ ▶*v.* [*tr.*] unfasten the buttons of (a garment). ■ [*intr.*] *inf.* relax and become less inhibited: *unbutton a little, Molly.*

un·called /ˌənˈkôld/ ▶*adj.* not summoned or invited. ■ (**uncalled for**) (esp. of a person's behavior) undesirable and unnecessary.

un·can·ny /ˌənˈkanē/ ▶*adj.* (**-ni·er, -ni·est**) strange or mysterious, esp. in an unsettling way: *Bonnet Boy bears an uncanny resemblance to Boy George.* —**un·can·ni·ly** /-ˈkanəl-ē/ *adv.* —**un·can·ni·ness** *n.*

un·cap /ˌənˈkap/ ▶*v.* (**-capped, -cap·ping**) [*tr.*] remove the lid or cover from. ■ remove a limit or restriction on (a price, rate, or amount).

un·cared /ˌənˈke(ə)rd/ ▶*adj.* (**uncared for**) not looked after properly: *it was sad to see the old place uncared for and neglected.*

un·car·ing /ˌənˈke(ə)riNG/ ▶*adj.* not displaying sympathy or concern for others. ■ not feeling interest in or attaching importance to something: *she fled out the door, **uncaring of** the rain.* —**un·car·ing·ly** *adv.*

un·ceas·ing /ˌənˈsēsiNG/ ▶*adj.* not coming to an end; continuous: *the unceasing efforts of the staff.* —**un·ceas·ing·ly** *adv.*

un·cer·e·mo·ni·ous /ˌənserəˈmōnēəs/ ▶*adj.* having or showing a lack of formality: *her entertaining was gracious but unceremonious.* ■ abrupt or discourteous: *they make their unceremonious exit from the window.* —**un·cer·e·mo·ni·ous·ly** *adv.* —**un·cer·e·mo·ni·ous·ness** *n.*

un·cer·tain /ˌənˈsərtn/ ▶*adj.* not able to be relied on; not known or definite: *an uncertain future.* ■ (of a person) not completely confident or sure of something: *I was uncertain how to proceed.* —**un·cer·tain·ly** *adv.*

un·cer·tain·ty /ˌənˈsərtntē/ ▶*n.* (pl. **-ties**) the state of being uncertain: *times of uncertainty and danger.* ■ (usu. **uncertainties**) something that is uncertain or that causes one to feel uncertain: *financial uncertainties.*

un·chain /ˌənˈcHān/ ▶*v.* [*tr.*] remove the chains fastening or securing (someone or something).

un·char·i·ta·ble /ˌənˈcHaritəbəl/ ▶*adj.* (of a person's behavior or attitude toward others) unkind; unsympathetic: *an uncharitable remark.* —**un·char·i·ta·ble·ness** *n.* —**un·char·i·ta·bly** /-blē/ *adv.*

un·chart·ed /ˌənˈcHärtid/ ▶*adj.* (of an area of land or sea) not mapped or surveyed.

un·checked /ˌənˈcHekt/ ▶*adj.* (esp. of something undesirable) not controlled or restrained. ■ not examined, esp. in order to determine the accuracy, quality, or condition of something.

un·chris·tian /ˌənˈkriscHən/ ▶*adj.* not professing Christianity or its teachings. ■ (of a person or their behavior) unkind, unfair, or morally wrong. —**un·chris·tian·ly** *adv.*

un·ci·al /ˈənsHəl; -sēəl/ ▶*adj.* of or written in a majuscule script with rounded unjoined letters that is found in European manuscripts of the 4th–8th centuries and from which modern capital letters are derived.
▶*n.* an uncial letter or script.

un·cir·cum·cised /ˌənˈsərkəmˌsīzd/ ▶*adj.* (of a boy or man) not circumcised. —**un·cir·cum·ci·sion** /-ˌsərkəmˈsizHən/ *n.*

un·civ·il /ˌənˈsivəl/ ▶*adj.* discourteous; impolite. —**un·civ·il·ly** *adv.*

un·civ·i·lized /ˌənˈsivəˌlīzd/ ▶*adj.* considered not to be socially, culturally, or morally advanced. ■ impolite; bad-mannered.

un·clasp /ˌənˈklasp/ ▶*v.* [*tr.*] unfasten (a clasp or similar device): *they unclasped their seat belts.* ■ release the grip of.

un·clas·si·fied /ˌənˈklasəˌfīd/ ▶*adj.* not arranged in or assigned to classes or categories. ■ (of information or documents) not designated as officially secret.

un·cle /ˈəNGkəl/ ▶*n.* the brother of one's father or mother or the husband of one's aunt. ■ *inf.* an unrelated older male friend, esp. of a child. ▷Middle English: from Old French *oncle*, from late Latin *auunculus*, alteration of Latin *avunculus* 'maternal uncle,' diminutive of *avus* 'grandfather.'
▶ □ **cry** (or **say**) **uncle** *inf.* surrender or admit defeat.

un·clean /ˌənˈklēn/ ▶*adj.* dirty. ■ morally wrong: *unclean thoughts.* ■ (of food) regarded in a particular religion as impure and unfit to be eaten. ■ (in biblical use) ritually impure; (of a spirit) evil. —**un·clean·li·ness** /ˌənˈklenlēnis/ *n.* —**un·clean·ness** *n.*

un·clear /ˌənˈkli(ə)r/ ▶*adj.* not easy to see, hear, or understand: *the motive for this killing is unclear.* ■ not obvious or definite; ambiguous. ■ having or feeling doubt or confusion. —**un·clear·ly** *adv.* —**un·clear·ness** *n.*

Un·cle Sam /sam/ ▶a personification of the federal government or citizens of the U.S., typically portrayed as a tall, thin, bearded man wearing a suit of red, white, and blue.

Un·cle Tom /tăm/ ▶n. derog. a black man considered to be excessively obedient or servile. —**Un·cle Tom·ism** /'tăm,izəm/ n.

un·clog /,ən'klôg; -'kläg/ ▶v. (-clogged, -clog·ging) [tr.] remove accumulated matter from: exfoliation unclogs pores and prevents blackheads.

un·clothe /,ən'klōTH/ ▶v. [tr.] remove the clothes from.

un·cloud·ed /,ən'kloudid/ ▶adj. (of the sky) not dark or overcast. ■ not troubled or spoiled by anything: six months of unclouded happiness.

un·col·ored /,ən'kələrd/ (Brit. **un·col·oured**) ▶adj. having no color; neutral in color. ■ not influenced, esp. in a negative way.

un·com·fort·a·ble /,ən'kəmfərtəbəl; -'kəmftərbəl/ ▶adj. causing or feeling slight pain or physical discomfort: athlete's foot is a painful and uncomfortable condition. ■ causing or feeling unease or awkwardness: an uncomfortable silence. —**un·com·fort·a·ble·ness** n. —**un·com·fort·a·bly** /-blē/ adv. the house was dark and uncomfortably cold.

un·com·mit·ted /,ənkə'mitid/ ▶adj. not committed to a particular course or policy: uncommitted voters. ■ (of resources) not pledged or set aside for future use: there is very little uncommitted money to fund new policies. ■ (of a person) not pledged to remain in a long-term emotional relationship with someone.

un·com·mon /,ən'kämən/ ▶adj. out of the ordinary; unusual: an uncommon name. ■ remarkably great (used for emphasis): an uncommon amount of noise. —**un·com·mon·ly** adv. an uncommonly large crowd. —**un·com·mon·ness** n.

un·com·mu·ni·ca·tive /,ənkə'myōōnəkətiv; -,kātiv/ ▶adj. (of a person) unwilling to talk or impart information. ■ (of something such as writing or art) not conveying much or any meaning or sense. —**un·com·mu·ni·ca·tive·ly** adv. —**un·com·mu·ni·ca·tive·ness** n.

un·com·pro·mis·ing /,ən'kämprə,mīziNG/ ▶adj. showing an unwillingness to make concessions to others, esp. by changing one's ways or opinions. ■ harsh or relentless: the uncompromising ugliness of her home. —**un·com·pro·mis·ing·ly** adv. —**un·com·pro·mis·ing·ness** n.

un·con·cern /,ən'kənsərn/ ▶n. a lack of worry or interest, esp. when surprising or callous. —**un·con·cerned** adj.

un·con·di·tion·al /,ənkən'disHənl; -'disHnəl/ ▶adj. not subject to any conditions: unconditional surrender. —**un·con·di·tion·al·i·ty** /-,disHə'nalətē/ n. —**un·con·di·tion·al·ly** adv.

un·con·di·tioned /,ənkən'disHənd/ ▶adj. **1** not subject to conditions or to an antecedent condition; unconditional: pure and unconditioned love. **2** relating to or denoting instinctive reflexes or other behavior not formed or influenced by conditioning or learning: an unconditioned response. **3** not subjected to a conditioning process.

un·con·nect·ed /,ənkə'nektid/ ▶adj. not joined together or to something else. ■ not associated or linked in a sequence. ■ not having relatives in important or influential positions. —**un·con·nect·ed·ly** adv. —**un·con·nect·ed·ness** n.

un·con·scion·a·ble /,ən'känsH(ə)nəbəl/ ▶adj. not right or reasonable: the unconscionable conduct of his son. ■ unreasonably excessive. —**un·con·scion·a·bly** /-blē/ adv.

un·con·scious /,ən'känsHəs/ ▶adj. not conscious: the boy was beaten unconscious. ■ done or existing without one realizing. ■ (**unconscious of**) unaware of: "What is it?" he said again, unconscious of the repetition.
▶n. (**the unconscious**) the part of the mind that is inaccessible to the conscious mind but that affects behavior and emotions. —**un·con·scious·ly** adv. —**un·con·scious·ness** n.

un·con·sti·tu·tion·al /,ən,känstə't(y)ōōsHənl/ ▶adj. not in accordance with a political constitution, esp. the U.S. Constitution, or with procedural rules. —**un·con·sti·tu·tion·al·i·ty** /-,t(y)ōōsHə'nalətē/ n. —**un·con·sti·tu·tion·al·ly** adv.

un·con·ven·tion·al /,ənkən'vensHənl/ ▶adj. not based on or conforming to what is generally done or believed. —**un·con·ven·tion·al·i·ty** /-,vensHə'nalətē/ n. —**un·con·ven·tion·al·ly** adv.

un·cool /,ən'kōōl/ ▶adj. inf. not fashionable or impressive.

un·co·or·di·nat·ed /,ənkō'ôrdn,ātid/ ▶adj. **1** badly organized. **2** (of a person or their movements) clumsy.

un·cork /,ən'kôrk/ ▶v. [tr.] pull the cork out of (a bottle or other container). ■ fig. allow (feelings) to be vented: there are those who have tried to uncork some of the mounting frustrations and pressures of the job by turning to the bottle. ■ inf. (in a game or sport) deliver (a kick, throw, or punch).

un·count·ed /,ən'kountid/ ▶adj. not counted. ■ very numerous.

un·couth /,ən'kōōTH/ ▶adj. (of a person or their appearance or behavior) lacking good manners, refinement, or grace. ■ (esp. of art or language)

lacking sophistication or delicacy: uncouth sketches of peasants. —**un·couth·ly** adv. —**un·couth·ness** n.

un·cov·er /,ən'kəvər/ ▶v. [tr.] remove a cover or covering from. ■ discover (something previously secret or unknown).

un·cross /,ən'krôs; -'kräs/ ▶v. [tr.] move (something) back from a crossed position: the reporter uncrossed his legs.

un·crown /,ən'kroun/ ▶v. [tr.] deprive of a ruling position.

unc·tion /'əNG(k)sHən/ ▶n. **1** formal the action of anointing someone with oil or ointment as a religious rite or as a symbol of investiture as a monarch. ■ the oil or ointment so used. ■ short for EXTREME UNCTION. **2** a manner of expression arising or apparently arising from deep emotion, esp. as intended to flatter.

unc·tu·ous /'əNG(k)CHōōəs/ ▶adj. (of a person) excessively or ingratiatingly flattering; oily. —**unc·tu·ous·ly** adv. —**unc·tu·ous·ness** n.

un·cut /,ən'kət/ ▶adj. not cut. ■ (of a text, movie, or performance) complete; unabridged. ■ (of a stone, esp. a diamond) not shaped by cutting. ■ (of alcohol or a drug) not diluted or adulterated: large amounts of uncut heroin.

un·de·cid·ed /,əndi'sīdid/ ▶adj. (of a person) not having made a decision: the jury remained undecided. ■ not settled or resolved.
▶n. a person who has not decided how they are going to vote in an election. —**un·de·cid·ed·ly** adv.

un·de·mon·stra·tive /,əndi'mänstrətiv/ ▶adj. (of a person) not tending to express feelings, esp. of affection, openly. —**un·de·mon·stra·tive·ly** adv. —**un·de·mon·stra·tive·ness** n.

un·de·ni·a·ble /,əndi'nīəbəl/ ▶adj. unable to be denied or disputed: ornate fireplaces give the place undeniable class. —**un·de·ni·a·bly** /-blē/ adv. the topic is undeniably an important one.

un·der /'əndər/ ▶prep. **1** extending or directly below: vast stores of oil under Alaska. ■ below (something covering or protecting): under several feet of water. **2** at a lower level or layer than: the room under his study. ■ behind (a physical surface). ■ behind or hidden behind (an appearance or disguise). ■ lower in grade or rank than: under him in the hierarchy. **3** used to express dominance or control: I was under his spell. ■ during (a specified time period, reign, or administration). ■ as a reaction to or undergoing the pressure of (something): the sofa creaked under his weight. ■ as provided for by the rules of; in accordance with: flowers supplied under contract by a local florist. ■ used to express grouping or classification: published under his own name. ■ Comput. within the environment of (a particular operating system): the program runs under DOS. **4** lower than (a specified amount, rate, or norm): they averaged just under 2.8 percent. **5** undergoing (a process): under construction. ■ in an existent state of. ■ planted with: fields under wheat.
▶adv. **1** extending or directly below something. **2** under water.
▶adj. **1** denoting the lowest part or surface of something; on the underside: the under part of the shell is concave. **2** unconscious, typically as a result of general anesthesia: she was only under for 15 minutes. ▷Old English, of Germanic origin; related to Dutch onder and German unter. —**un·der·most** /-,mōst/ adj.
▶ □ **under way** having started and making progress.

under- ▶prefix **1** below; beneath: underclothes | undercover. ■ lower in status; subordinate: undersecretary. **2** insufficiently; incompletely.

un·der·a·chieve /,əndərə'CHēv/ ▶v. [intr.] do less well than is expected, esp. in schoolwork. —**un·der·a·chieve·ment** n. —**un·der·a·chiev·er** n.

un·der·age /,əndər'āj/ ▶adj. (of a person) too young to engage legally in a particular activity, esp. drinking alcohol or having sex. ■ (of an activity) engaged in by people who are underage: underage drinking.

un·der·arm /'əndər,ärm/ ▶adj. & adv. another term for UNDERHAND (sense 2).
▶n. a person's armpit: [as adj.] use an underarm deodorant.

un·der·bel·ly /'əndər,belē/ ▶n. (pl. **-lies**) the soft underside or abdomen of an animal. ■ fig. an area vulnerable to attack. ■ fig. a hidden unpleasant or criminal part of society.

un·der·bid ▶v. /,əndər'bid/ (-bid·ding; past and past part. -bid) [tr.] (in an auction or when seeking a contract) make a lower bid than (someone). ■ Bridge make a lower bid on (one's hand) than its strength warrants.
▶n. /'əndər,bid/ a bid that is lower than another or than is justified. —**un·der·bid·der** /,əndər'bidər/ n.

un·der·brush /'əndər,brəsH/ ▶n. shrubs and small trees forming the undergrowth in a forest.

un·der·car·riage /'əndər,karij/ ▶n. a wheeled structure beneath an aircraft, typically retracted when not in use, that receives the impact on landing and supports the aircraft on the ground. ■ the supporting frame under the body of a vehicle.

un·der·charge ▶v. /ˌəndərˈCHärj/ [tr.] charge (someone) a price or amount that is too low.
▶n. /ˈəndərˌCHärj/ a charge that is insufficient.

un·der·class /ˈəndərˌklas/ ▶n. the lowest social stratum in a country or community, consisting of the poor and unemployed.

un·der·clothes /ˈəndərˌklō(TH)z/ ▶pl. n. clothes worn under others, typically next to the skin.

un·der·cloth·ing /ˈəndərˌklōTHiNG/ ▶n. underclothes.

un·der·coat /ˈəndərˌkōt/ ▶n. 1 a layer of paint applied after the primer and before the topcoat. 2 an animal's underfur or down.
▶v. [tr.] apply a coat of undercoat to (something).

un·der·cov·er /ˌəndərˈkəvər/ ▶adj. (of a person or their activities) involved in or involving secret work within a community or organization, esp. for the purposes of police investigation or espionage.
▶adv. as an undercover agent.

un·der·cur·rent /ˈəndərˌkərənt/ ▶n. a current of water below the surface, moving in a different direction from any surface current. ■ fig. an underlying feeling or influence, esp. one that is contrary to the prevailing atmosphere and is not expressed openly.

un·der·cut ▶v. /ˌəndərˈkət/ (-cut·ting; past and past part. -cut) [tr.] 1 offer goods or services at a lower price than (a competitor). 2 cut or wear away the part below or under (something, esp. a cliff). ■ fig. weaken; undermine. ■ cut away material to leave (a carved design) in relief. 3 (in sports such as tennis or golf) strike (a ball) with a chopping motion so as to give it backspin.
▶n. /ˈəndərˌkət/ a space formed by the removal or absence of material from the lower part of something, such as a cliff, a coal seam, or part of a carving in relief.

un·der·de·vel·oped /ˌəndərdiˈveləpt/ ▶adj. not fully developed: underdeveloped kidneys. ■ (of a country or region) not advanced economically. ■ (of photographic film) not developed sufficiently to give a normal image. —un·der·de·vel·op·ment /-əpmənt/ n.

un·der·dog /ˈəndərˌdôg; -ˌdäg/ ▶n. a competitor thought to have little chance of winning a fight or contest. ■ a person who has little status in society.

un·der·done /ˌəndərˈdən/ ▶adj. (of food) insufficiently cooked.

un·der·dress /ˌəndərˈdres/ ▶v. [intr.] (also be underdressed) dress too plainly or too informally: without a pinstripe you'd be underdressed.

un·der·em·ployed /ˌəndərimˈploid/ ▶adj. (of a person) not doing work that makes full use of their skills and abilities. ■ (of a person) not having enough paid work. —un·der·em·ploy·ment /-ˈploimənt/ n.

un·der·es·ti·mate ▶v. /ˌəndərˈestəˌmāt/ [tr.] estimate (something) to be smaller or less important than it actually is. ■ regard (someone) as less capable than they really are.
▶n. /-mit/ an estimate that is too low. —un·der·es·ti·ma·tion /-ˌestə-ˈmāSHən/ n.

un·der·ex·pose /ˌəndərikˈspōz/ ▶v. [tr.] Photog. expose (film or an image) for too short a time. —un·der·ex·po·sure /-ˈspōZHər/ n.

un·der·foot /ˌəndərˈfo͝ot/ ▶adv. under one's feet; on the ground: fig. genuine rights were being trodden underfoot. ■ constantly present and in one's way.

un·der·gar·ment /ˈəndərˌgärmənt/ ▶n. an article of underclothing.

un·der·glaze /ˈəndərˌglāz/ ▶adj. (of decoration on pottery) done before the glaze is applied. ■ (of colors) used in such decoration.
▶n. a color or design applied in this way.

un·der·go /ˌəndərˈgō/ ▶v. (-goes; past -went; past part. -gone) [tr.] experience or be subjected to (something, typically something unpleasant, painful, or arduous): the baby underwent a life-saving brain operation.

un·der·grad·u·ate /ˌəndərˈgrajəwit/ ▶n. a student at a college or university who has not yet earned a bachelor's or equivalent degree.

un·der·ground ▶adv. /ˌəndərˈground/ beneath the surface of the ground: miners working underground. ■ in or into secrecy or hiding, esp. as a result of carrying out subversive political activities.
▶adj. /ˈəndərˌground/ situated beneath the surface of the ground: underground parking garages. ■ of or relating to the secret activities of people working to subvert an established order: Czech underground literature. ■ of or denoting a group or movement seeking to explore alternative forms of lifestyle or artistic expression; radical and experimental.
▶n. /ˈəndərˌground/ 1 a group or movement organized secretly to work against an existing regime: I got involved with the French underground. ■ a group or movement seeking to explore alternative forms of lifestyle

or artistic expression: the late sixties underground. 2 (the Underground) Brit. a subway, esp. the one in London: travel chaos on the Underground.

Un·der·ground Rail·road ▶a secret network for helping slaves escape from the South to the North and to Canada in the years before the Civil War.

un·der·growth /ˈəndərˌgrōTH/ ▶n. a dense growth of shrubs and other plants, esp. under trees in woodland.

un·der·hand /ˈəndərˌhand/ ▶adj. 1 (of a throw or stroke in sports) made with the arm or hand below shoulder level: [as adv.] I served underhand. ■ with the palm of the hand upward or outward: an underhand grip. 2 another term for UNDERHANDED.

un·der·hand·ed /ˌəndərˈhandəd/ ▶adj. acting or done in a secret or dishonest way. —un·der·hand·ed·ly adv.

un·der·lay¹ ▶v. /ˌəndərˈlā/ (past and past part. -laid) [tr.] (usu. be underlaid) place something under (something else), esp. to support or raise it: fig. a whine underlaid by an occasional choking sob.
▶n. /ˈəndərˌlā/ something placed under or behind something else, esp. material laid under a carpet for protection or support.

un·der·lay² ▶ past tense of UNDERLIE.

un·der·lie /ˌəndərˈlī/ ▶v. (-ly·ing; past -lay; past part. -lain) [tr.] (esp. of a layer of rock or soil) lie or be situated under (something). ■ be the cause or basis of (something): the fundamental issue that underlies the conflict | [as adj.] (underlying) the underlying causes of poverty.

un·der·line /ˈəndərˌlīn/ ▶v. [tr.] draw a line under (a word or phrase) to give emphasis or indicate special type. ■ emphasize (something).
▶n. a line drawn under a word or phrase, esp. for emphasis.

un·der·ling /ˈəndərliNG/ ▶n. (usu. underlings) chiefly derog. a person lower in status or rank.

un·der·ly·ing /ˌəndərˈlī-iNG/ ▶ present participle of UNDERLIE.

un·der·man /ˌəndərˈman/ ▶v. (-manned, -man·ning) [tr.] (usu. be undermanned) fail to provide with enough workers or crew.

un·der·mine /ˌəndərˈmīn; ˈəndərˌmīn/ ▶v. [tr.] erode the base or foundation of (a rock formation). ■ dig or excavate beneath (a building or fortification) so as to make it collapse. ■ fig. damage or weaken (someone or something), esp. gradually or insidiously. —un·der·min·er n.

un·der·neath /ˌəndərˈnēTH/ ▶prep. & adv. 1 situated directly below (something else): [as prep.] our bedroom is right underneath theirs | [as adv.] his eyes were red-rimmed with black bags underneath | [as adj.] on longer hair, the underneath layers can be permed to give extra body. ■ situated on a page directly below (a picture or another piece of writing): [as prep.] four names written neatly underneath one another | [as adv.] there was writing underneath. 2 so as to be concealed by (something else): [as prep.] money changed hands underneath the table | fig. underneath his aloof air, Nicky was a warm and open young man | [as adv.] paint peeling off in flakes to reveal grayish plaster underneath. ■ partly or wholly concealed by (a garment): [as prep.] she could easily see the broadness of his shoulders underneath a tailored white shirt | [as adv.] I wear button-downs, and my T-shirts show underneath.
▶n. the part or side of something facing toward the ground; the underside.

un·der·nour·ished /ˌəndərˈnəriSHt; -ˈnə-risht/ ▶adj. having insufficient food or other substances for good health and condition: undernourished children. —un·der·nour·ish·ment n.

un·der·paid /ˌəndərˈpād/ ▶ past and past participle of UNDERPAY.

un·der·pants /ˈəndərˌpan(t)s/ ▶pl. n. an undergarment covering the lower part of the torso and having two holes for the legs.

un·der·part /ˈəndərˌpärt/ ▶n. a lower part or portion of something. ■ (underparts) the underside of an animal's body.

un·der·pass /ˈəndərˌpas/ ▶n. a road or pedestrian tunnel passing under another road or a railroad.

un·der·pay /ˌəndərˈpā/ ▶v. (past and past part. -paid) [tr.] pay too little to (someone). ■ pay less than is due for (something): [as adj.] (underpaid) late or underpaid tax. —un·der·pay·ment /ˌəndərˈpāmənt; ˈəndərˌpā-/ n.

un·der·pin·ning /ˈəndərˌpiniNG/ ▶n. a solid foundation laid below ground level to support or strengthen a building. ■ a set of ideas, motives, or devices that justify or form the basis for something.

un·der·play /ˌəndərˈplā; ˈəndərˌplā/ ▶v. [tr.] perform (something) in a restrained way: the violins underplayed the romantic element in the music. ■ represent (something) as being less important than it actually is.

un·der·priv·i·leged /ˌəndərˈpriv(ə)lijd/ ▶adj. (of a person) not enjoying the same standard of living or rights as the majority of people in a society.

un·der·rate /ˌəndə(r)ˈrāt/ ▶v. [tr.] [often as adj.] (underrated) underestimate the extent, value, or importance of (someone or something).

un·der·score ▶v. /ˌəndərˈskôr; ˈəndərˌskôr/ another term for UNDERLINE.
▶n. /ˈəndərˌskôr/ another term for UNDERLINE (sense 1).

un·der·sea /ˌəndərˈsē/ ▶adj. below the sea or the surface of the sea.

un·der·sec·re·tar·y /ˌəndərˈsekriˌterē/ ▶n. (pl. **-tar·ies**) a subordinate official, in particular the principal assistant to a member of the cabinet.

un·der·sell /ˌəndərˈsel/ ▶v. (past and past part. **-sold**) [tr.] sell something at a lower price than (a competitor): *we can equal or undersell mail order.* ■ promote or rate (something) insufficiently; undervalue.

un·der·sexed /ˌəndərˈsekst/ ▶adj. having weak sexual desires.

un·der·shirt /ˈəndərˌSHərt/ ▶n. an undergarment worn under a shirt.

un·der·shoot ▶v. /ˌəndərˈSHo͞ot/ (past and past part. **-shot**) [tr.] fall short of (a point or target). ■ (of an aircraft) land short of (the runway).
▶n. /ˈəndərSHo͞ot/ an act of undershooting.

un·der·shorts /ˈəndərˌSHôrts/ ▶pl. n. underpants, esp. those worn by men or boys.

un·der·side /ˈəndərˌsīd/ ▶n. the bottom or lower side or surface of something. ■ fig. the less favorable aspect of something: *the sordid underside of the glamorous 1980s.*

un·der·signed /ˈəndərˌsīnd/ ▶adj. [usu. as pl. n.] (**the undersigned**) formal whose signature is appended.

un·der·sized /ˌəndərˈsīzd/ (also **un·der·size**) ▶adj. of less than the usual size.

un·der·skirt /ˈəndərˌskərt/ ▶n. a skirt worn under another; a petticoat.

un·der·staff /ˌəndərˈstaf/ ▶v. [tr.] provide (an organization) with too few staff members to operate effectively: [as adj.] (**understaffed**) *the department is understaffed and overworked.* —**un·der·staff·ing** n.

un·der·stand /ˌəndərˈstand/ ▶v. (past and past part. **-stood**) **1** [tr.] perceive the intended meaning of (words, a language, or speaker): *he could usually **make himself understood** | she understood what he was saying.* ■ perceive the significance, explanation, or cause of (something): *he couldn't understand why we burst out laughing.* ■ be sympathetically or knowledgeably aware of the character or nature of: *Picasso understood color | I understand how you feel.* ■ interpret or view (something) in a particular way: *as the term is usually understood, legislation refers to regulations and directives.* **2** infer something from information received (often used as a polite formula in conversation): *I understand you're at art school.* ■ [tr.] (often **be understood**) regard (a missing word, phrase, or idea) as present; supply mentally: *"present company excepted" is always understood when sweeping generalizations are being made.* ■ [tr.] (often **be understood**) assume to be the case; take for granted. —**un·der·stand·able** adj. —**un·der·stand·er** n.

un·der·stand·ing /ˌəndərˈstandiNG/ ▶n. the ability to understand something; comprehension: *foreign visitors with little understanding of English.* ■ the power of abstract thought; intellect. ■ an individual's perception or judgment of a situation: *my understanding was that he would try to find a new supplier.* ■ sympathetic awareness or tolerance. ■ an informal or unspoken agreement or arrangement: *he and I have an understanding.*
▶adj. sympathetically aware of other people's feelings; tolerant and forgiving. —**un·der·stand·ing·ly** adv.

un·der·state /ˌəndərˈstāt/ ▶v. [tr.] describe or represent (something) as being smaller, worse, or less important than it actually is: *the press has understated the extent of the problem.* —**un·der·state·ment** n. —**un·der·stat·er** /ˈəndərˌstātər/ n.

un·der·stood /ˌəndərˈsto͝od/ ▶ past and past participle of UNDERSTAND.

un·der·stud·y /ˈəndərˌstədē/ ▶n. (pl. **-stud·ies**) (in the theater) a person who learns another's role in order to be able to act as a replacement at short notice.
▶v. (**-stud·ies**, **-stud·ied**) [tr.] learn (a role) or the role played by (an actor).

un·der·take /ˌəndərˈtāk/ ▶v. (past **-took**; past part. **-tak·en**) [tr.] commit oneself to and begin (an enterprise or responsibility); take on: *a firm of builders undertook the construction work.* ■ promise to do a particular thing: *the firm undertook to keep price increases to a minimum.* ■ guarantee or affirm something; give as a formal pledge.

un·der·tak·er /ˈəndərˌtākər/ ▶n. a person whose business is preparing dead bodies for burial or cremation and making arrangements for funerals.

un·der·tak·ing /ˈəndərˌtākiNG, ˌəndərˈtā-/ ▶n. **1** a formal pledge or promise to do something: *I give **an undertaking that** we shall proceed with the legislation.* ■ a task that is taken on; an enterprise. ■ the action of undertaking to do something. **2** /ˈəndərˌtākiNG/ the management of funerals as a profession.

un·der·things /ˈəndərˌTHiNGZ/ ▶pl. n. underclothes, esp. those worn by a woman or girl.

un·der·tone /ˈəndərˌtōn/ ▶n. a subdued or muted tone of sound or color: *they were talking in undertone.* ■ an underlying quality or feeling.

un·der·took /ˌəndərˈto͝ok/ ▶ past participle of UNDERTAKE.

un·der·tow /ˈəndərˌtō/ ▶n. another term for RIP CURRENT, used in the incorrect belief that rip currents drag swimmers below the surface: *I was*

swept away by the undertow. ■ fig. an implicit quality, emotion, or influence underlying the superficial aspects of something and leaving a particular impression.

un·der·use ▶v. /ˌəndərˈyo͞oz/ [tr.] [usu. as adj.] (**underused**) use (something) below the optimum level: *the owner noted a lot of underused space in that garage.*
▶n. /ˌəndərˈyo͞os/ insufficient use: *underuse of existing services.*

un·der·val·ue /ˌəndərˈvalyo͞o/ ▶v. (**-val·ues**, **-val·ued**, **-val·u·ing**) [tr.] [often as adj.] (**undervalued**) rate (something) insufficiently highly; fail to appreciate: *the skills of the housewife remain undervalued in society.* ■ underestimate the financial value of (something): *the company's assets were undervalued in its balance sheet.* —**un·der·val·u·a·tion** /-ˌvalyo͞oˈāSHən/ n.

un·der·wa·ter /ˌəndərˈwôtər, -ˈwätər/ ▶adj. & adv. situated, occurring, or done beneath the surface of the water: [as adj.] *there are underwater volcanoes in the region* | [as adv.] *they learn to navigate underwater at night.*

un·der·way /ˌəndərˈwā/ ▶adv. (of a vessel) having begun to move through the water: *the ship was so huge and silent, I hadn't realized we had gotten underway.* ■ (of a process, project, activity, etc.) having begun, in progress; being done or carried out: *the remodeling should be underway by July* | *is the party already underway?*

un·der·wear /ˈəndərˌwer/ ▶n. clothing worn under other clothes, typically next to the skin.

un·der·weight /ˈəndərˌwāt, ˌəndərˈwāt/ ▶adj. below a weight considered normal or desirable: *he was thirty pounds underweight.* ■ Finance (also **un·der·weight·ed**) having less investment in a particular area than is considered desirable or appropriate: *underweighted in technology.*
▶v. [tr.] apply too little weight to (something): *fig. clinicians tend to overweight parent and underweight child information when deriving diagnoses.*
▶n. insufficient weight.

un·der·went /ˌəndərˈwent/ ▶ past of UNDERGO.

un·der·whelm /ˌəndərˈ(h)welm/ ▶v. [tr.] (usu. **be underwhelmed**) humorous fail to impress or make a positive impact on; disappoint.

un·der·wire /ˈəndərˌwīr/ ▶n. a semicircular wire support stitched under each cup of a bra. —**un·der·wired** adj.

un·der·work /ˌəndərˈwərk/ ▶v. [tr.] (usu. **be underworked**) impose too little work on (someone).

un·der·world /ˈəndərˌwərld/ ▶n. **1** the world of criminals or of organized crime. **2** the mythical abode of the dead, imagined as being under the earth.

un·der·write /ˈəndə(r)ˌrīt, ˌəndə(r)ˈrīt/ ▶v. (past **-wrote**; past part. **-writ·ten**) [tr.] **1** sign and accept liability under (an insurance policy), thus guaranteeing payment in case loss or damage occurs. ■ accept (a liability or risk) in this way. **2** (of a bank or other financial institution) engage to buy all the unsold shares in (an issue of new securities). ■ undertake to finance or otherwise support or guarantee (something). —**un·der·writ·er** /ˈəndə(r)ˌrītər/ n.

un·de·sir·a·ble /ˌəndiˈzīrəbəl/ ▶adj. not wanted or desirable because harmful, objectionable, or unpleasant: *the drug's undesirable side effects.*
▶n. a person considered to be objectionable in some way. —**un·de·sir·a·bil·i·ty** n. —**un·de·sir·a·ble·ness** n. —**un·de·sir·a·bly** /-blē/ adv.

un·de·ter·mined /ˌəndiˈtərmənd/ ▶adj. not authoritatively decided or settled. ■ not known.

un·did /ˌənˈdid/ ▶ past of UNDO.

un·dies /ˈəndēz/ ▶pl. n. inf. articles of underwear, esp. those of a woman or girl.

un·dis·put·ed /ˌəndiˈspyo͞otid/ ▶adj. not disputed or called into question; accepted.

un·di·vid·ed /ˌəndiˈvīdid/ ▶adj. not divided, separated, or broken into parts. ■ concentrated on or devoted completely to one object.

un·do /ˌənˈdo͞o/ ▶v. (**-does** /-ˈdəz/; past **-did**; past part. **-done**) [tr.] **1** unfasten, untie, or loosen (something). **2** cancel or reverse the effects or results of (a previous action or measure). ■ cancel (the last one or more commands executed by a computer). **3** formal cause the downfall or ruin of: *Iago's hatred of women undoes him.*
▶n. Comput. a feature of a computer program that allows a user to cancel or reverse the last one or more commands executed.

un·do·cu·ment·ed /ˌənˈdäkyəˌmentid/ ▶adj. **1** not recorded in or proved by documents. **2** not having the appropriate legal document or license: *undocumented immigrants.*

un·do·ing /ˌənˈdo͞oiNG/ ▶n. a person's ruin or downfall: *he knew of his ex-partner's role in his undoing.* ■ the cause of such ruin or downfall.

Pronunciation Key ə *ago, up;* ər *over, fur;* a *hat;* ā *ate;* ä *car;* CH *chin;* e *let;* ē *see;* e(ə)r *air;* i *fit;* ī *by;* i(ə)r *ear;* NG *sing;* ō *go;* ô *law, for;* oi *toy;* o͝o *good;* o͞o *goo;* ou *out;* SH *she;* TH *thin;* T͟H *then;* (h)w *why;* ZH *vision*

un·done /ˌənˈdən/ ▸ past participle of UNDO.
▸*adj.* **1** not tied or fastened. **2** not done or finished: *he had left his homework undone.* **3** *formal* or *humorous* (of a person) ruined by a disastrous or devastating setback or reverse: *I am undone!*

un·doubt·ed /ˌənˈdoutid/ ▸*adj.* not questioned or doubted by anyone: *her undoubted ability.* —**un·doubt·ed·ly** *adv.*

un·dreamed /ˌənˈdrēmd/ (*Brit.* also **un·dreamt** /-ˈdremt/) ▸*adj.* (**undreamed of**) not thought to be possible (used to express pleasant surprise at the amount, extent, or level of something): *she is now enjoying undreamed-of success.*

un·dress /ˌənˈdres/ ▸*v.* [*intr.*] take off one's clothes: *I went into the bathroom to get undressed.* ■ [*tr.*] take the clothes off (someone else).
▸*n.* **1** the state of being naked or only partially clothed: *women in various states of undress.* **2** *Mil.* ordinary clothing or uniform, as opposed to that worn on ceremonial occasions.

un·dressed /ˌənˈdrest/ ▸*adj.* **1** wearing no clothes. **2** not treated, processed, or prepared for use: *undressed skins of elk.* **3** (of food) not having a dressing.

un·due /ˌənˈd(y)o͞o/ ▸*adj.* unwarranted or inappropriate because excessive or disproportionate. —**un·du·ly** /-ˈd(y)o͞olē/ *adv.*

un·du·lant /ˈənjələnt; ˈəndyə-/ ▸*adj.* having a rising and falling motion or appearance like that of waves; undulating. —**un·du·lance** *n.*

un·du·late /ˈənjəˌlāt; ˈəndyə-/ ▸*v.* [*intr.*] move with a smooth wavelike motion. ■ [usu. *adj.*] (**undulating**) have a wavy form or outline: *delightful views over undulating countryside.* ▷mid 17th cent.: from late Latin *undulatus*, from Latin *unda* 'a wave.' —**un·du·late·ly** /-litlē/ *adv.* —**un·du·la·tion** /ˌənjəˈlāSHən; ˌəndyə-/ *n.* —**un·du·la·to·ry** /ˈənjələˌtôrē; ˈəndyə-/ *adj.*

un·dy·ing /ˌənˈdī-iNG/ ▸*adj.* (esp. of an emotion) lasting forever: *promises of undying love.* —**un·dy·ing·ly** *adv.*

un·earned in·come ▸*n.* income from investments rather than from work.

un·earth /ˌənˈərTH/ ▸*v.* [*tr.*] find (something) in the ground by digging. ■ discover (something hidden, lost, or kept secret) by investigation or searching: *they have done all they can to unearth the truth.*

un·earth·ly /ˌənˈərTHlē/ ▸*adj.* **1** unnatural or mysterious, esp. in a disturbing way: *unearthly quiet.* **2** *inf.* unreasonably early or inconvenient: *a job that involves getting up at an unearthly hour.* —**un·earth·li·ness** *n.*

un·ease /ˌənˈēz/ ▸*n.* anxiety or discontent.

un·eas·y /ˌənˈēzē/ ▸*adj.* (**-eas·i·er, -eas·i·est**) causing or feeling anxiety; troubled or uncomfortable: *an uneasy silence.* —**un·eas·i·ly** /-zəlē/ *adv.* —**un·eas·i·ness** *n.*

un·ec·o·nom·i·cal /ˌənˌekəˈnämikəl; -ˌēkə-/ ▸*adj.* wasteful of money or other resources; not economical. —**un·ec·o·nom·i·cal·ly** /-ik(ə)lē/ *adv.*

un·em·ployed /ˌənimˈploid/ ▸*adj.* (of a person) without a paid job but available to work: [as *pl. n.*] (**the unemployed**) *a training program for the long-term unemployed.* ■ (of a thing) not in use.

un·em·ploy·ment /ˌənimˈploimənt/ ▸*n.* the state of being unemployed. ■ the number or proportion of unemployed people: *a time of high unemployment.* ■ (also **unemployment benefit**) a payment made by a government or a labor union to an unemployed person. ■ (also **unemployment compensation**) money that substitutes for wages or salary, paid to recently unemployed workers under a government- or union-run program.

un·e·qual /ˌənˈēkwəl/ ▸*adj.* **1** not equal in quantity, size, or value: *two rooms of unequal size* | *unequal odds.* ■ not fair, evenly balanced, or having equal advantage. **2** not having the ability or resources to meet a challenge: *she felt unequal to the task before her.*
▸*n.* a person or thing considered to be different from another in status or level. —**un·e·qual·ly** *adv.*

un·e·qualed /ˌənˈēkwəld/ ▸*adj.* superior to all others in performance or extent: *trout of unequaled quality.*

un·e·quiv·o·cal /ˌənəˈkwivəkəl/ ▸*adj.* leaving no doubt; unambiguous. —**un·e·quiv·o·cal·ly** /-ik(ə)lē/ *adv.* —**un·e·quiv·o·cal·ness** *n.*

un·err·ing /ˌənˈəriNG; -ˈer-/ ▸*adj.* always right or accurate: *an unerring sense of direction.* —**un·err·ing·ly** *adv.* —**un·err·ing·ness** *n.*

UNESCO /yo͞oˈneskō/ (also **Unesco**) ▸an agency of the United Nations established in 1945 to promote the exchange of information, ideas, and culture. In 1984 the U.S. withdrew from the organization.

un·eth·i·cal /ˌənˈeTHikəl/ ▸*adj.* not morally correct: *it is unethical to torment any creature for entertainment.* —**un·eth·i·cal·ly** /-ik(ə)lē/ *adv.*

un·e·ven /ˌənˈēvən/ ▸*adj.* not level or smooth. ■ not regular, consistent, or equal: *the uneven distribution of resources.* ■ (of a contest) not equally balanced. —**un·e·ven·ly** *adv.* —**un·e·ven·ness** *n.*

un·ex·am·pled /ˌənigˈzampəld/ ▸*adj.* *formal* having no precedent or parallel: *a regime that brought such unexampled disaster on its people.*

un·ex·cep·tion·a·ble /ˌənikˈsepSH(ə)nəbəl/ ▸*adj.* not open to objection. —**un·ex·cep·tion·a·ble·ness** *n.* —**un·ex·cep·tion·a·bly** /-blē/ *adv.*

un·ex·cep·tion·al /ˌənikˈsepSHənl/ ▸*adj.* not out of the ordinary; usual: *an unexceptional movie.* —**un·ex·cep·tion·al·ly** *adv.*

un·ex·pect·ed /ˌənikˈspektid/ ▸*adj.* not expected or regarded as likely to happen: *his death was totally unexpected* | [as *n.*] (**the unexpected**) *he seemed to have a knack for saying the unexpected.* —**un·ex·pect·ed·ly** *adv. an unexpectedly high price* —**un·ex·pect·ed·ness** *n.*

un·fail·ing /ˌənˈfāliNG/ ▸*adj.* without error or fault: *his unfailing memory for names.* ■ reliable or constant. —**un·fail·ing·ly** *adv.* —**un·fail·ing·ness** *n.*

un·fair /ˌənˈfe(ə)r/ ▸*adj.* not based on or behaving according to the principles of equality and justice. ■ unkind, inconsiderate, or unreasonable. ■ not following the rules of a game or sport. —**un·fair·ly** *adv.* —**un·fair·ness** *n.*

un·faith·ful /ˌənˈfāTHfəl/ ▸*adj.* not faithful, in particular: ■ engaging in sexual relations with a person other than one's regular partner in contravention of a previous promise or understanding: *you haven't been unfaithful to him, have you?* | *her unfaithful husband.* ■ disloyal, treacherous, or insincere. —**un·faith·ful·ly** *adv.* —**un·faith·ful·ness** *n.*

un·fas·ten /ˌənˈfasən/ ▸*v.* [*tr.*] open the fastening of; undo (something): [as *adj.*] (**unfastened**) *he had left the door unfastened.* ■ [*intr.*] become loose or undone.

un·fa·vor·a·ble /ˌənˈfāv(ə)rəbəl/ ▸*adj.* **1** expressing or showing a lack of approval or support. **2** adverse; inauspicious. —**un·fa·vor·a·ble·ness** *n.* —**un·fa·vor·a·bly** /-blē/ *adv.*

un·feel·ing /ˌənˈfēliNG/ ▸*adj.* unsympathetic, harsh, or callous. ■ lacking physical sensation or sensitivity. —**un·feel·ing·ly** *adv.* —**un·feel·ing·ness** *n.*

un·feigned /ˌənˈfānd/ ▸*adj.* genuine; sincere: *their unfeigned gratitude.* —**un·feign·ed·ly** /-ˈfānidlē/ *adv.*

un·fet·ter /ˌənˈfetər/ ▸*v.* [*tr.*] [usu. as *adj.*] (**unfettered**) release from restraint or inhibition: *his imagination is unfettered by the laws of logic.*

un·fit /ˌənˈfit/ ▸*adj.* **1** (of a thing) not of the necessary quality or standard to meet a particular purpose: *the land is unfit for food crops.* ■ (of a person) not having the requisite qualities or skills to undertake something competently: *she is unfit to have care and control of her children.* ■ *Biol.* (of a species) not able to produce viable offspring or survive in a particular environment. **2** (of a person) not in good physical condition, typically as a result of failure to exercise regularly. —**un·fit·ly** *adv.* —**un·fit·ness** *n.*

un·fit·ting /ˌənˈfitiNG/ ▸*adj.* not fitting or suitable; unbecoming. —**un·fit·ting·ly** *adv.*

un·flag·ging /ˌənˈflagiNG/ ▸*adj.* tireless; persistent: *his unflagging enthusiasm.* —**un·flag·ging·ly** *adv.*

un·flap·pa·ble /ˌənˈflapəbəl/ ▸*adj.* *inf.* having or showing calmness in a crisis. —**un·flap·pa·bil·i·ty** /-ˌflapəˈbilətē/ *n.* —**un·flap·pa·bly** /-blē/ *adv.*

un·fold /ˌənˈfōld/ ▸*v.* open or spread out from a folded position: [*intr.*] *a Chinese paper flower that unfolds in water.* ■ [*tr.*] reveal or disclose (thoughts or information): *Miss Eva unfolded her secret exploits to Mattie.* ■ [*intr.*] (of information or a sequence of events) be revealed or disclosed: *there was a fascinating scene unfolding before me.* —**un·fold·ment** *n.*

un·forced /ˌənˈfôrst/ ▸*adj.* not produced by effort; natural: *an unforced cheerfulness.* ■ not compelled or constrained: *her unforced departure.* —**un·forc·ed·ly** /-ˈfôrsədlē/ *adv.*

un·for·get·ta·ble /ˌənfərˈgetəbəl/ ▸*adj.* impossible to forget; very memorable: *that unforgettable first kiss.* —**un·for·get·ta·bly** /-blē/ *adv.*

un·for·tu·nate /ˌənˈfôrCHənət/ ▸*adj.* having or marked by bad fortune; unlucky: *the unfortunate Cunningham was fired.* ■ (of a circumstance) unfavorable or inauspicious: *the delay at the airport was an unfortunate start to our vacation.* ■ regrettable or inappropriate.
▸*n.* (often **unfortunates**) a person who suffers bad fortune.

un·for·tu·nate·ly /ˌənˈfôrCHənətlē/ ▸*adv.* it is unfortunate that: *unfortunately, we do not have the time to interview every applicant.*

un·found·ed /ˌənˈfoundid/ ▸*adj.* having no foundation or basis in fact. —**un·found·ed·ly** *adv.* —**un·found·ed·ness** *n.*

un·friend·ly /ˌənˈfren(d)lē/ ▸*adj.* (**-li·er, -li·est**) not friendly: *she shot him an unfriendly glance* | *environmentally unfriendly activities.* —**un·friend·li·ness** *n.*

un·fruit·ful /ˌənˈfro͞otfəl/ ▸*adj.* **1** not producing good or helpful results; unproductive: *the meeting was unfruitful.* **2** not producing fruit or crops; unfertile. —**un·fruit·ful·ly** *adv.* —**un·fruit·ful·ness** *n.*

un·fun·ny /ˌənˈfənē/ ▸*adj.* (**-ni·er, -ni·est**) (typically of something intended to be funny) not amusing: *a hideously unfunny spoof film.* —**un·fun·ni·ly** /-ˈfənəlē/ *adv.* —**un·fun·ni·ness** *n.*

un·furl /ən'fərl/ ▶v. make or become spread out from a rolled or folded state, esp. in order to be open to the wind: [intr.] *the flags unfurl.*

un·gain·ly /ən'gānlē/ ▶adj. (of a person or movement) awkward; clumsy: *an ungainly walk.* —**un·gain·li·ness** *n.*

un·god·ly /ən'gädlē/ ▶adj. irreligious or immoral: *ungodly lives of self-obsession, lust, and pleasure.* ■ *inf.* unreasonably early or inconvenient: *I've been troubled by telephone calls at ungodly hours.* —**un·god·li·ness** *n.*

un·gov·ern·a·ble /ən'gəvərnəbəl/ ▶adj. impossible to control or govern. —**un·gov·ern·a·bil·i·ty** /-,gəvərnə'bilətē/ *n.* —**un·gov·ern·a·bly** /-blē/ *adv.*

un·gra·cious /ən'grāSHəs/ ▶adj. **1** not polite or friendly. **2** not graceful or elegant. —**un·gra·cious·ly** *adv.* —**un·gra·cious·ness** *n.*

un·gram·mat·i·cal /,əngrə'matikəl/ ▶adj. not conforming to grammatical rules; not well formed: *ungrammatical sentences.* —**un·gram·mat·i·cal·i·ty** /-,mati'kalətē/ *n.* (*pl.* **-ties**) . —**un·gram·mat·i·cal·ly** /-ik(ə)lē/ *adv.* —**un·gram·mat·i·cal·ness** *n.*

un·guard·ed /ən'gärdid/ ▶adj. without protection or a guard: *the museum was unguarded at night.* ■ not well considered; careless: *an unguarded remark.* —**un·guard·ed·ly** *adv.* —**un·guard·ed·ness** *n.*

un·guent /'əNGgwənt/ ▶n. a soft greasy or viscous substance used as an ointment or for lubrication.

un·guid·ed /ən'gīdid/ ▶adj. not guided in a particular path or direction; left to take its own course.

un·gu·late /'əNGgyələt/ ▶n. *Zool.* a hoofed mammal of the former order Ungulata, now divided into two unrelated orders: the **artiodactyl** (even-toed ungulate) and the **perissodactyl** (odd-toed ungulate) groups.

un·hand /ən'hand/ ▶v. [tr.] [usu. in *imper.*] *archaic* or *humorous* release (someone) from one's grasp: *"Unhand me, sir!" she cried.*

un·hand·y /ən'handē/ ▶adj. **1** not easy to handle or manage; awkward. **2** not skillful in using the hands. —**un·hand·i·ly** /-dəlē/ *adv.* —**un·hand·i·ness** *n.*

un·hap·py /ən'hapē/ ▶adj. (**-pi·er**, **-pi·est**) not happy. ■ (**unhappy at/about/with**) not satisfied or pleased with (a situation). ■ unfortunate: *an unhappy coincidence.* —**un·hap·pi·ly** *adv.* —**un·hap·pi·ness** *n.*

un·health·y /ən'helTHē/ ▶adj. (**-health·i·er**, **-health·i·est**) harmful to health. ■ not having or showing good health. ■ (of a person's attitude or behavior) not sensible or well balanced; abnormal and harmful. —**un·health·i·ly** /-THəlē/ *adv.* —**un·health·i·ness** *n.*

un·heard /ən'hərd/ ▶adj. not heard or listened to. ■ (**unheard of**) not previously known of or done: *wines from unheard-of villages.*

un·hinge /ən'hinj/ ▶v. [tr.] **1** [usu. as *adj.*] (**unhinged**) make (someone) mentally unbalanced: *I thought she must be unhinged by grief.* ■ deprive of stability or fixity; throw into disorder. **2** take (a door) off its hinges.

un·ho·ly /ən'hōlē/ ▶adj. (**-li·er**, **-li·est**) sinful; wicked. ■ not holy; unconsecrated: *an unholy marriage.* ■ denoting an alliance with potentially harmful implications between two or more parties that are not natural allies. ■ *inf.* awful; dreadful (used for emphasis): *she was making an unholy racket.* —**un·ho·li·ness** *n.*

un·hook /ən'hŏŏk/ ▶v. [tr.] unfasten or detach (something that is held or caught by a hook).

un·horse /ən'hôrs/ ▶v. [tr.] cause to fall from a horse: *fig. her mission is to unhorse fashionable literary theories.*

un·hu·man /ən'(h)yōōmən/ ▶adj. not resembling or having the qualities of a human being.

u·ni·cam·er·al /,yōōnə'kam(ə)rəl/ ▶adj. (of a legislative body) having a single legislative chamber.

u·ni·cast /'yōōni,kast/ ▶n. transmission of a data package or an audiovisual signal to a single recipient.

UNICEF /'yōōnə,sef/ ▶an agency of the United Nations established in 1946 to help governments (esp. in developing countries) improve the health and education of children and their mothers.

u·ni·cel·lu·lar /,yōōnə'selyələr/ ▶adj. *Biol.* (of protozoans, certain algae and spores, etc.) consisting of a single cell.

u·ni·corn /'yōōnə,kôrn/ ▶n. a mythical animal typically represented as a horse with a single straight horn projecting from its forehead. ▷Middle English: via Old French from Latin *unicornis*, from *uni-* 'single' + *cornu* 'horn,' translating Greek *monokerōs*.

u·ni·cy·cle /'yōōnə,sīkəl/ ▶n. a cycle with a single wheel, typically used by acrobats. —**u·ni·cy·clist** /-,sīklist/ *n.*

u·ni·fi·ca·tion /,yōōnəfi'kāSHən/ ▶n. the process of being united or made into a whole. —**u·ni·fi·ca·to·ry** /-'kātərē/ *adj.*

u·ni·form /'yōōnə,fôrm/ ▶adj. **1** not changing in form or character; remaining the same in all cases and at all times: *blocks of stone of uniform size.* ■ of a similar form or character to another or others: *a uniform*

package of amenities at a choice of hotels. **2** denoting a garment forming part of a person's uniform: *black uniform jackets.*
▶n. **1** the distinctive clothing worn by members of the same organization or body or by children attending certain schools. | *an officer in uniform.* ■ *inf.* a police officer wearing a uniform. **2** a code word representing the letter U, used in radio communication.
▶v. [tr.] **1** make uniform. **2** provide or dress (someone) in a uniform. —**u·ni·form·ly** /'yōōnə,fôrmlē; ,yōōnə'fôrm-/ *adv.*

u·ni·form·i·ty /,yōōnə'fôrmətē/ ▶n. (*pl.* **-ties**) the quality or state of being uniform: *an attempt to impose administrative and cultural uniformity.*

u·ni·fy /'yōōnə,fī/ ▶v. (**-fies**, **-fied**) make or become united, uniform, or whole: [tr.] *the government hoped to centralize and unify the nation* | [as *adj.*] (**unified**) *a unified system of national education.* —**u·ni·fi·er** *n.*

u·ni·lat·er·al /,yōōnə'latərəl; -'latrəl/ ▶adj. (of an action or decision) performed by or affecting only one person, group, or country involved in a particular situation, without the agreement of another or the others. —**u·ni·lat·er·al·ly** *adv.*

u·ni·lat·er·al·ism /,yōōnə'latərə,lizəm; -'latrə-/ ▶n. the process of acting, reaching a decision, or espousing a principle unilaterally. —**u·ni·lat·er·al·ist** *n.* & *adj.*

u·ni·lin·gual /,yōōnə'liNGg(yə)wəl/ ▶adj. conducted in, concerned with, or speaking only one language. —**u·ni·lin·gual·ly** *adv.*

un·im·peach·a·ble /,ənim'pēCHəbəl/ ▶adj. not able to be doubted, questioned, or criticized; entirely trustworthy: *an unimpeachable witness.* —**un·im·peach·a·bly** /-blē/ *adv.*

un·im·proved /,ənim'prōōvd/ ▶adj. not made better. ■ (of land) not cleared or cultivated.

un·in·cor·po·rat·ed /,ənin'kôrpə,rātid; ,əniNG-/ ▶adj. **1** (of a company or other organization) not formed into a legal corporation: *an unincorporated business.* **2** not included as part of a whole. ■ (of territory) not designated as belonging to a particular country, town, or area.

un·in·i·ti·at·ed /,ənə'niSHē,ātid/ ▶adj. without special knowledge or experience: *a bachelor neither prudish nor uninitiated* | [as *pl. n.*] (**the uninitiated**) *the discussion wasn't easy to follow for the uninitiated.*

un·in·ter·est·ed /ən'intristid; -'intə,restid/ ▶adj. not interested in or concerned about something or someone: *I was totally uninterested in boys* | *an uninterested voice.* —**un·in·ter·est·ed·ly** *adv.* —**un·in·ter·est·ed·ness** *n.*

un·ion /'yōōnyən/ ▶n. **1** the action or fact of joining or being joined, esp. in a political context: *he was opposed to closer political or economic union with Europe* | *a currency union between the two countries.* ■ a state of harmony or agreement: *they live in perfect union.* ■ a marriage: *their union had not been blessed with children.* **2** an organized association of workers formed to protect and further their rights and interests; a labor union: *the National Farmers' Union.* ■ a club, society, or association formed by people with a common interest or purpose: *members of the Students' Union.* **3** (also **Un·ion**) a political unit consisting of a number of states or provinces with the same central government, in particular: ■ the U.S., esp. from its founding by the original thirteen states in 1787–90 to the secession of the Confederate states in 1860–61. ■ (also **the Federal Union**) the northern states of the U.S. that opposed the seceding Confederate states in the Civil War. **4** a building at a college or university used by students for recreation and other nonacademic activities. **5** *Math.* the set that comprises all the elements (and no others) contained in any of two or more given sets. ■ the operation of forming such a set. **6** a pipe coupling.

un·ion·ist /'yōōnyənist/ ▶n. **1** a member of a labor union. ■ an advocate or supporter of labor unions. **2** (**Un·ion·ist**) a person who opposed secession during the Civil War. —**un·ion·ism** /-,nizəm/ *n.* —**un·ion·is·tic** /,yōōnyə'nistik/ *adj.*

un·ion·ize /'yōōnyə,nīz/ ▶v. become or cause to become members of a labor union. —**un·ion·i·za·tion** /,yōōnyəni'zāSHən; -,nī'zā-/ *n.*

Un·ion Jack ▶n. the national flag of the United Kingdom, consisting of red and white crosses on a blue background.

un·ion shop ▶n. a place of work where employers may hire nonunion workers who must join a labor union within an agreed time.

un·ion suit ▶n. *dated* a single undergarment combining shirt and pants.

u·ni·po·lar /,yōōnə'pōlər/ ▶adj. having or relating to a single pole or kind of polarity: *a unipolar magnetic charge.* ■ (of psychiatric illness) characterized by either depressive or (more rarely) manic episodes but not both. Compare with **BIPOLAR DISORDER**. ■ (of a nerve cell) having only one axon or process. —**u·ni·po·lar·i·ty** *n.*

Pronunciation Key ə *ago*, *up*; ər *over*, *fur*; a *hat*; ā *ate*; ä *car*; CH *chin*; e *let*; ē *see*; e(ə)r *air*; i *fit*; ī *by*; i(ə)r *ear*; NG *sing*; ō *go*; ô *law*, *for*; oi *toy*; ŏŏ *good*; ōō *goo*; ou *out*; SH *she*; TH *thin*; <u>TH</u> *then*; (h)w *why*; ZH *vision*

u·nique /yŏŏ'nēk/ ▶*adj.* being the only one of its kind; unlike anything else. ■ particularly remarkable, special, or unusual: *a unique opportunity to see the spectacular Bolshoi Ballet.* ■ (**unique to**) belonging or connected to (one particular person, group, or place): *a style of architecture that is unique to Portugal.* —**u·nique·ly** *adv.* —**u·nique·ness** *n.*

u·ni·sex /'yŏŏnə‚seks/ ▶*adj.* (esp. of clothing or hairstyles) designed to be suitable for both sexes.
▶*n.* a style in which men and women look and dress in a similar way.

u·ni·sex·u·al /‚yŏŏnə'seksHŏŏəl/ ▶*adj.* (of an organism) either male or female; not hermaphrodite. —**u·ni·sex·u·al·i·ty** /-‚seksHŏŏ'alitē/ *n.* —**u·ni·sex·u·al·ly** *adv.*

u·ni·son /'yŏŏnəsən; -zən/ ▶*n.* **1** simultaneous performance of action or utterance of speech: *"Yes, sir," said the girls in unison.* **2** *Mus.* coincidence in pitch of sounds or notes. ■ a combination of notes, voices, or instruments at the same pitch or (esp. when singing) in octaves: *good unisons are formed by flutes, oboes, and clarinets.*
▶*adj.* performed in unison. —**u·nis·o·nous** /yŏŏ'nisənəs/ *adj.*

u·nit /'yŏŏnit/ ▶*n.* **1** an individual thing or person regarded as single and complete, esp. for purposes of calculation: *the family unit.* ■ each of the individuals or smaller groups into which a complex whole may be divided: *the sentence as a unit of grammar.* ■ a device that has a specified function, esp. one forming part of a complex mechanism: *the gearbox and transmission unit.* ■ a piece of furniture or equipment for fitting with others like it or made of complementary parts: *a sink unit.* ■ a self-contained section of accommodations in a larger building or group of buildings: *one- and two-bedroom units.* ■ a part of an institution such as a hospital having a special function: *the intensive care unit.* ■ a subdivision of a larger military grouping: *he returned to Germany with his unit.* ■ an amount of educational instruction, typically determined by the number of hours spent in class. ■ an item manufactured: [as *adj.*] *unit cost.* ■ a police car. **2** a quantity chosen as a standard in terms of which other quantities may be expressed: *a unit of measurement.* **3** the number one. ■ (**units**) the digit before the decimal point in decimal notation, representing an integer less than ten.

u·ni·tard /'yŏŏnə‚tärd/ ▶*n.* a tight-fitting one-piece garment of stretchable fabric that covers the body from the neck to the knees or feet.

U·ni·tar·i·an /‚yŏŏni'te(ə)rēən/ ▶*n.* *Theol.* a person, esp. a Christian, who asserts the unity of God and rejects the doctrine of the Trinity. ■ a member of a church or religious body maintaining this belief and typically rejecting formal dogma in favor of a rationalist and inclusivist approach to belief.
▶*adj.* of or relating to the Unitarians. —**U·ni·tar·i·an·ism** /-‚nizəm/ *n.*

u·ni·tar·y /'yŏŏni‚terē/ ▶*adj.* **1** single; uniform: *a sort of unitary wholeness.* ■ of or relating to a system of government or organization in which the powers of the separate constituent parts are vested in a central body: *a unitary rather than a federal state.* **2** unified; whole. —**u·ni·tar·i·ly** /'yŏŏnə‚terəlē; ‚yŏŏnə'te(ə)r-/ *adv.* —**u·ni·tar·i·ty** /‚yŏŏnə'te(ə)ritē/ *n.*

u·nite /yŏŏ'nīt/ ▶*v.* come or bring together for a common purpose or action: [*intr.*] *he called on the party to unite* | [*tr.*] *they are united by their love of cars.* ■ come or bring together to form a unit or whole, esp. in a political context: [*intr.*] *the two Germanys officially united* | [*tr.*] *he aimed to unite Italy and Sicily under his imperial crown* | *his work unites theory and practice.* —**u·ni·tive** /'yŏŏnətiv; yŏŏ'nī-/ *adj.*

u·nit·ed /yŏŏ'nītid/ ▶*adj.* joined together politically, for a common purpose, or by common feelings. —**u·nit·ed·ly** *adv.*

U·nit·ed Na·tions (abbr.: **UN**) ▶ an international organization of countries set up in 1945, in succession to the League of Nations, to promote international peace, security, and cooperation.

unit pric·ing ▶*n.* identification of and labeling of items for sale with the retail price per unit, permitting easier price comparisons among similar products in different sized containers.

u·ni·ty /'yŏŏnətē/ ▶*n.* (pl. **-ties**) the state of being united or joined as a whole, esp. in a political context: *European unity* | *economic unity.* ■ harmony or agreement between people or groups: *their leaders called for unity between opposing factions.* ■ the state of forming a complete and pleasing whole, esp. in an artistic context: *the repeated phrase gives the piece unity and cohesion.* ■ a thing forming a complex whole: *they speak of the three parts as a unity.*

Univ. ▶*abbr.* University.

univ. ▶*abbr.* ■ universal.

u·ni·va·lent /*adj.* /‚yŏŏnə'vālənt; yŏŏ'nivələnt/ *Biol.* (of a chromosome) remaining unpaired during meiosis.

u·ni·valve /'yŏŏnə‚valv/ *Zool.* ▶*adj.* having one valve or shell.
▶*n.* another term for GASTROPOD.

u·ni·ver·sal /‚yŏŏnə'vərsəl/ ▶*adj.* of, affecting, or done by all people or things in the world or in a particular group; applicable to all cases: *the incidents caused universal concern.* ■ (of a tool or machine) adjustable to or appropriate for all requirements; not restricted to a single purpose or position.
▶*n.* a person or thing having universal effect, currency, or application, in particular: —**u·ni·ver·sal·i·ty** /-vər'salətē/ *n.*

u·ni·ver·sal·ist /‚yŏŏnə'vərsəlist/ ▶*n.* **1** *Christian Theol.* a person who believes that all humankind will eventually be saved. ■ (usu. **Universalist**) a member of an organized body of Christians who hold such beliefs. **2** a person advocating loyalty to and concern for others without regard to national or other allegiances.
▶*adj.* **1** *Christian Theol.* of or relating to universalists. **2** universal in scope or character. —**u·ni·ver·sal·ism** /-‚lizəm/ *n.* —**u·ni·ver·sal·is·tic** /-‚vərsə'listik/ *adj.*

u·ni·ver·sal joint (also **universal coupling**) ▶*n.* a coupling or joint that can transmit rotary power by a shaft through a range of angles.

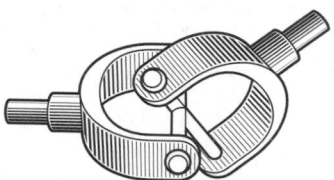

universal joint

u·ni·ver·sal·ly /‚yŏŏnə'vərsəlē/ ▶*adv.* by everyone; in every case: *progress is not always universally welcomed.*

U·ni·ver·sal Prod·uct Code ▶*n.* more formal term for BAR CODE.

U·ni·ver·sal Time ▶see GREENWICH MEAN TIME.

u·ni·verse /'yŏŏnə‚vərs/ ▶*n.* (**the universe**) all existing matter and space considered as a whole; the cosmos. ■ a particular sphere of activity, interest, or experience: *the front parlor was the hub of her universe.* ▷late Middle English: from Old French *univers* or Latin *universum*, neuter of *universus* 'combined into one, whole,' from *uni-* 'one' + *versus* 'turned' (past participle of *vertere*).

u·ni·ver·si·ty /‚yŏŏnə'vərsətē/ ▶*n.* (pl. **-ties**) an educational institution designed for instruction, examination, or both, of students in many branches of advanced learning, conferring degrees in various faculties, and often embodying colleges and similar institutions: *the university buildings* | *a university professor.* ■ the members of this collectively. ■ the grounds and buildings of such an institution.

u·niv·o·cal /‚yŏŏnə'vōkəl; yŏŏ'nivə-/ ▶*adj.* *Philos.* & *Linguistics* (of a word or term) having only one possible meaning; unambiguous: *a univocal set of instructions.* —**u·niv·o·cal·i·ty** /‚yŏŏnə‚vō'kalətē/ *n.* —**u·niv·o·cal·ly** *adv.*

U·nix /'yŏŏniks/ (also **UNIX**) ▶*n.* *trademark, Comput.* a widely used multiuser operating system.

un·just /‚ən'jəst/ ▶*adj.* not based on or behaving according to what is morally right and fair: *resistance to unjust laws.* —**un·just·ly** *adv.* —**un·just·ness** *n.*

un·kempt /‚ən'kem(p)t/ ▶*adj.* (esp. of a person) having an untidy or disheveled appearance. —**un·kempt·ly** *adv.* —**un·kempt·ness** *n.*

un·kept /‚ən'kept/ ▶*adj.* **1** (of a commitment or undertaking) not honored or fulfilled. **2** not tidy or cared for.

un·kind /‚ən'kīnd/ ▶*adj.* inconsiderate and harsh to others: *you were terribly unkind to her.* —**un·kind·ly** *adv.* —**un·kind·ness** *n.*

un·know·a·ble /‚ən'nōəbəl/ ▶*adj.* not able to be known: *the total cost is unknowable.* —**un·know·a·bil·i·ty** /-‚nōə'bilətē/ *n.*

un·know·ing /‚ən'nō-iNG/ ▶*adj.* not knowing or aware.
▶*n.* lack of awareness or knowledge. —**un·know·ing·ly** *adv.* —**un·know·ing·ness** *n.*

un·known /‚ən'nōn/ ▶*adj.* not known or familiar. ■ (of a performer or artist) not well known or famous.
▶*n.* an unknown person or thing: *she is a relative unknown.* ■ *Math.* an unknown quantity or variable: *find the unknown in the following equations.* ■ (**the unknown**) that which is unknown: *our fear of the unknown.* —**un·known·ness** *n.*

Un·known Sol·dier ▶*n.* an unidentified representative member of a country's armed forces killed in war, given burial with special honors in a national memorial.

un·lace /‚ən'lās/ ▶*v.* [*tr.*] undo the laces of (a shoe or garment).

un·law·ful /‚ən'lôfəl/ ▶*adj.* not conforming to, permitted by, or recognized by law or rules. —**un·law·ful·ly** /-f(ə)lē/ *adv.* —**un·law·ful·ness** *n.*

un·lead·ed /,ən'ledid/ ▶*adj.* (esp. of gasoline) without added tetraethyl lead. ■ *humorous* (of coffee) decaffeinated.
▶*n.* gasoline without added lead.

un·learn /,ən'lərn/ ▶*v.* [tr.] discard (something learned, esp. a bad habit or false or outdated information) from one's memory.

un·learn·ed[1] /,ən'lərnid/ ▶*adj.* (of a person) not well educated. —**un·learn·ed·ly** *adv.*

un·learned[2] /,ən'lərnd/ ▶*adj.* not having been learned: *she found herself on the stage, lines unlearned.* ■ not needing to be learned because innate.

un·leash /,ən'lēSH/ ▶*v.* [tr.] release from a leash or restraint: *fig. the failure of the talks could unleash more fighting.*

un·leav·ened /,ən'levənd/ ▶*adj.* (of bread) made without yeast or other leavening agent.

un·less /ən'les; ,ən-/ ▶*conj.* except if (used to introduce a case in which a statement being made is not true or valid): *unless you have a photographic memory, repetition is vital.*

un·let·tered /,ən'letərd/ ▶*adj.* (of a person) poorly educated or illiterate.

un·like /,ən'līk/ ▶*prep.* different from; not similar to: *a large house not unlike Mr. Shaw's.* ■ in contrast to; differently from. ■ uncharacteristic of (someone): *he sounded irritable, which was unlike him.*
▶*adj.* dissimilar or different from each other. —**un·like·ness** *n.*

un·like·ly /,ən'līklē/ ▶*adj.* (**-li·er, -li·est**) not likely to happen, be done, or be true; improbable: *it is unlikely that they will ever be used.* —**un·like·li·hood** /-,hŏŏd/ *n.* —**un·like·li·ness** *n.*

un·lim·it·ed /,ən'limitid/ ▶*adj.* not limited or restricted in terms of number, quantity, or extent. —**un·lim·it·ed·ly** *adv.* —**un·lim·it·ed·ness** *n.*

un·lined[1] /,ən'līnd/ ▶*adj.* not marked or covered with lines: *unlined paper.*

un·lined[2] ▶*adj.* (of a container or garment) without a lining: *unlined curtains.*

un·link /,ən'liNGk/ ▶*v.* [tr.] make no longer connected. ■ [as *adj.*] (**unlinked**) unconnected: *three previously unlinked murders.*

un·list·ed /,ən'listid/ ▶*adj.* not included on a list. ■ (of a person or telephone number) not listed in a telephone directory or available through directory assistance, at the wish of the subscriber. ■ denoting or relating to a company whose shares are not listed on a stock exchange.

un·lived-in /,ən'liv ,din/ ▶*adj.* not appearing to be used or inhabited; not homey or comfortable.

un·load /,ən'lōd/ ▶*v.* [tr.] **1** remove goods from (a vehicle, ship, container, etc.). ■ remove (goods) from a vehicle, ship, container, etc. ■ [intr.] (of a vehicle, ship, container, etc.) have goods removed: *the street was jammed with trucks unloading.* ■ *inf.* get rid of (something unwanted): *he had unloaded his depreciating stock on his unsuspecting wife.* ■ *inf.* give expression to (oppressive thoughts or feelings): *it was a chance for her to unload some of her feelings about her son.* **2** remove (ammunition) from a gun or (film) from a camera. —**un·load·er** *n.*

un·lock /,ən'läk/ ▶*v.* [tr.] undo the lock of (something) by using a key. ■ make (something previously inaccessible or unexploited) available for use.

un·looked-for /,ən'lŏŏkt ,fôr/ ▶*adj.* unexpected; unforeseen.

un·loose /,ən'lōōs/ (also **un·loos·en**) ▶*v.* [tr.] undo; let free: *his first action was to unloose that knotted necktie* | *fig. she unloosed a salvo of condescension.*

un·luck·y /,ən'ləkē/ ▶*adj.* (**-luck·i·er, -luck·i·est**) having, bringing, or resulting from bad luck: *the visitors were unlucky to have a goal disallowed.* —**un·luck·i·ly** /-'ləkəlē/ *adv.* —**un·luck·i·ness** *n.*

un·made /,ən'mād/ ▶*adj.* (of a bed) not having the bedclothes neatly arranged for sleeping in.

un·make /,ən'māk/ ▶*v.* (*past* and *past part.* **-made**) [tr.] reverse or undo the making of; annul: *Watergate made the independent prosecutor law necessary; Whitewater may unmake it.* ■ ruin; destroy: *human beings make cities and unmake them.*

un·man·age·a·ble /,ən'manijəbəl/ ▶*adj.* difficult or impossible to manage, manipulate, or control: *his behavior was becoming unmanageable at home.* —**un·man·age·a·ble·ness** *n.* —**un·man·age·a·bly** /-blē/ *adv.*

un·manned /,ən'mand/ ▶*adj.* not having or needing a crew or staff: *an unmanned space flight.*

un·man·ner·ly /,ən'manərlē/ ▶*adj.* not having or showing good manners: *uncouth, unmannerly fellows.* —**un·man·ner·li·ness** *n.*

un·marked /,ən'märkt/ ▶*adj.* not marked: *an unmarked police car.*

un·mask /,ən'mask/ ▶*v.* [tr.] expose the true character of or hidden truth about: *the trial unmasked him as a complete charlatan.* ■ [often as *adj.*] (**unmasked**) remove the mask from: *an unmasked gunman.* —**un·mask·er** *n.*

un·matched /,ən'macHt/ ▶*adj.* not matched or equaled.

un·men·tion·a·ble /,ən'menCHənəbəl/ ▶*adj.* too embarrassing, offensive, or shocking to be spoken about.
▶*n.* (usu. **unmentionables**) *chiefly humorous* a person or thing that is too shocking or embarrassing to be mentioned by name: *wearing nothing but fig leaves over their unmentionables.* ■ (**unmentionables**) underwear. —**un·men·tion·a·bil·i·ty** /-,menCHənə'bilətē/ *n.* —**un·men·tion·a·ble·ness** *n.* —**un·men·tion·a·bly** /-blē/ *adv.*

un·mer·ci·ful /,ən'mərsəfəl/ ▶*adj.* cruel or harsh; showing no mercy. —**un·mer·ci·ful·ly** /-f(ə)lē/ *adv.* —**un·mer·ci·ful·ness** *n.*

un·met /,ən'met/ ▶*adj.* (of a requirement) not achieved or fulfilled.

un·mis·tak·a·ble /,ənmə'stākəbəl/ (also **un·mis·take·a·ble**) ▶*adj.* not able to be mistaken for anything else; very distinctive. —**un·mis·tak·a·bil·i·ty** /-,stākə'bilətē/ *n.* —**un·mis·tak·a·bly** /-blē/ *adv.*

un·mit·i·gat·ed /,ən'mitə,gātid/ ▶*adj.* absolute; unqualified: *an unmitigated disaster.* —**un·mit·i·gat·ed·ly** *adv.*

un·mor·al /,ən'môrəl; -'mär-/ ▶*adj.* not influenced by or concerned with morality. Compare with **IMMORAL**. —**un·mo·ral·i·ty** /-mə'ralətē; -mô-/ *n.* —**un·mor·al·ly** *adv.*

un·moved /,ən'mōōvd/ ▶*adj.* not affected by emotion or excitement: *he was unmoved by her outburst.* ■ not changed in one's purpose or intention: *her opponents were unmoved and plan to return to court.* ■ not changed in position. —**un·mov·a·ble** /-vəbəl/ (also **un·move·a·ble**) *adj.*

un·mu·si·cal /,ən'myōōzikəl/ ▶*adj.* not pleasing to the ear. ■ unskilled in or indifferent to music. —**un·mu·si·cal·i·ty** /-,myōōzi'kalətē/ *n.* —**un·mu·si·cal·ly** /-zik(ə)lē/ *adv.* —**un·mu·si·cal·ness** *n.*

un·named /,ən'nāmd/ ▶*adj.* not having a name: *a new but yet unnamed African violet.* ■ not identified by name: *an old couple in an unnamed American city.*

un·nat·u·ral /,ən'nacH(ə)rəl/ ▶*adj.* contrary to the ordinary course of nature; abnormal: *death by unnatural causes.* ■ not existing in nature; artificial. ■ affected or stilted. ■ lacking feelings of kindness and sympathy that are considered to be natural: *they condemned her as an unnatural woman.* —**un·nat·u·ral·ly** *adv.* —**un·nat·u·ral·ness** *n.*

un·nec·es·sar·y /,ən'nesə,serē/ ▶*adj.* not needed. ■ more than is needed; excessive: *the police used unnecessary force.* ■ (of a remark) not appropriate and likely to be offensive or impertinent.
▶*pl. n.* (**unnecessaries**) unnecessary things. —**un·nec·es·sar·i·ly** /-,nesə-'se(ə)rəlē/ *adv.* —**un·nec·es·sar·i·ness** *n.*

un·nerve /,ən'nərv/ ▶*v.* [tr.] make (someone) lose courage or confidence: [as *adj.*] (**unnerving**) *an unnerving experience.* —**un·nerv·ing·ly** *adv.*

un·num·bered /,ən'nəmbərd/ ▶*adj.* **1** not marked with or assigned a number. **2** not counted, typically because very great.

un·ob·jec·tion·a·ble /,ənəb'jeksHənəbəl/ ▶*adj.* not objectionable; acceptable.

un·ob·tru·sive /,ənəb'trōōsiv/ ▶*adj.* not conspicuous or attracting attention. —**un·ob·tru·sive·ly** *adv.* —**un·ob·tru·sive·ness** *n.*

un·or·gan·ized /,ən'ôrgə,nīzd/ ▶*adj.* not organized. ■ not represented by or formed into a trade union: *unorganized white-collar workers.*

un·pack /,ən'pak/ ▶*v.* [tr.] open and remove the contents of (a suitcase, bag, or package): *she unpacked her suitcase* | [intr.] *he unpacked and put everything away.* ■ remove (something) from a suitcase, bag, or package: *we unpacked the sandwiches.* ■ *fig.* analyze (something) into its component elements: *let us unpack this question.* —**un·pack·er** *n.*

un·paired /,ən'pe(ə)rd/ ▶*adj.* **1** not arranged in pairs. **2** not forming one of a pair.

un·pal·at·a·ble /,ən'palətəbəl/ ▶*adj.* not pleasant to taste. ■ difficult to tolerate or accept. —**un·pal·at·a·bil·i·ty** /-,palətə'bilitē/ *n.* —**un·pal·at·a·bly** /-blē/ *adv.*

un·par·al·leled /,ən'parə,leld/ ▶*adj.* having no parallel or equal; exceptional: *the sudden rise in unemployment is unparalleled in the postwar period.*

un·peo·ple /,ən'pēpəl/ ▶*v.* [usu. as *adj.*] (**unpeopled**) empty of people; depopulate.

un·per·son /'ən'pərsən; -,pər-/ ▶*n.* (*pl.* **-per·sons**) a person whose name or existence is denied or ignored, esp. because of a political misdemeanor.

un·pin /,ən'pin/ ▶*v.* (**-pinned, -pin·ning**) [tr.] unfasten or detach by removing a pin or pins.

un·placed /,ən'plāst/ ▶*adj.* not having or assigned to a specific place.

un·plug /,ən'pləg/ ▶*v.* (**-plugged, -plug·ging**) [tr.] **1** disconnect (an electrical device) by removing its plug from a socket. ■ sever the connection between a peripheral device and a computer. **2** remove an obstacle or blockage from: *a procedure to unplug blocked arteries.*

3 [intrans.] *inf.* relax by disengaging from normal activities: *they've gone up to the cabin to unplug.*

un·pol·ished /ˌənˈpälisHt/ ▶*adj.* unrefined in style or behavior: *his work is unpolished and sometimes incoherent.*

un·pop·u·lar /ˌənˈpäpyələr/ ▶*adj.* not liked or popular: *Luke was unpopular with most of the teachers.* —**un·pop·u·lar·i·ty** /-ˌpäpyəˈlaritē/ *n.*

un·prac·ticed /ˌənˈpraktist/ ▶*adj.* (of a person or faculty) not trained or experienced: *to the unpracticed eye, the result might appear.* ■ (of an action or performance) not often done before.

un·prec·e·dent·ed /ˌənˈpresəˌdentid/ ▶*adj.* never done or known before. —**un·prec·e·dent·ed·ly** *adv.*

un·pre·ten·tious /ˌənpriˈtenCHəs/ ▶*adj.* not attempting to impress others with an appearance of greater importance, talent, or culture than is actually possessed. ■ (of a place) pleasantly simple and functional; modest. —**un·pre·ten·tious·ly** *adv.* —**un·pre·ten·tious·ness** *n.*

un·prin·ci·pled /ˌənˈprinsəpəld/ ▶*adj.* (of a person or their behavior) not acting in accordance with moral principles.

un·print·a·ble /ˌənˈprintəbəl/ ▶*adj.* (of words, comments, or thoughts) too offensive or shocking to be published. —**un·print·a·bly** /-blē/ *adv.*

un·pro·fes·sion·al /ˌənprəˈfeSHənl/ ▶*adj.* below or contrary to the standards expected in a particular profession: *a report on unprofessional conduct.* —**un·pro·fes·sion·al·ism** /-ˌizəm/ *n.* —**un·pro·fes·sion·al·ly** *adv.*

un·prom·is·ing /ˌənˈpräməsiNG/ ▶*adj.* not giving hope of future success or good results. —**un·prom·is·ing·ly** *adv.*

un·prompt·ed /ˌənˈpräm(p)tid/ ▶*adv.* without being encouraged or assisted to say or do something: *those are the notions they volunteered unprompted.*
▶*adj.* said, done, or acting without being encouraged or assisted: *unprompted remarks.*

un·prov·en /ˌənˈproōvən/ (also **un·proved** /-ˈproōvd/) ▶*adj.* not demonstrated by evidence or argument as true or existing. ■ (of a new or alternative product, system, or treatment) not tried and tested.

un·pro·vid·ed /ˌənprəˈvīdid/ ▶*adj.* not provided. ■ (**unprovided with**) not equipped with (something useful or necessary). ■ (**unprovided for**) (of a dependent) not supplied with sufficient money to cover the cost of living: *he left a widow and children totally unprovided for.*

un·pro·voked /ˌənprəˈvōkt/ ▶*adj.* (of an attack, or a display of aggression or emotion) not caused by anything done or said: *acts of unprovoked aggression.* ■ (of a person) not provoked to do something.

un·qual·i·fied /ˌənˈkwäləˌfīd/ ▶*adj.* **1** (of a person) not officially recognized as a practitioner of a particular profession or activity through having satisfied the relevant conditions or requirements. ■ not competent or sufficiently knowledgeable to do something. **2** without reservation or limitation; total: *the experiment was not an unqualified success.* —**un·qual·i·fied·ly** /-ˌfī(i)dlē/ *adv.*

un·ques·tion·a·ble /ˌənˈkwesCHənəbəl/ ▶*adj.* not able to be disputed or doubted: *his musicianship is unquestionable.* —**un·ques·tion·a·bil·i·ty** /-ˈkwesCHənəˈbilətē/ *n.* —**un·ques·tion·a·bly** /-blē; -ˈkwesH-/ *adv. unquestionably,* the loss of his father was a grievous blow.

un·ques·tioned /ˌənˈkwesCHənd/ ▶*adj.* not disputed or doubted; certain: *his loyalty to John is unquestioned.* ■ not examined or inquired into: *an unquestioned assumption.*

un·ques·tion·ing /ˌənˈkwesCHəniNG/ ▶*adj.* accepting something without dissent or doubt: *an unquestioning acceptance of the traditional curriculum.* —**un·ques·tion·ing·ly** *adv.*

un·qui·et /ˌənˈkwīət/ ▶*adj.* not inclined to be quiet or inactive; restless: *she prowled at night like an unquiet spirit.* ■ uneasy; anxious: *her unquiet desperation.* —**un·qui·et·ly** *adv.* —**un·qui·et·ness** *n.*

un·quote /ˌənˈkwōt; ˈənˌkwōt/ ▶*v.* see QUOTE —— UNQUOTE at QUOTE.

un·rav·el /ˌənˈravəl/ ▶*v.* (**-rav·eled, -rav·el·ing**) [*tr.*] **1** undo (twisted, knitted, or woven threads). ■ [*intr.*] (of twisted, knitted, or woven threads) become undone. ■ unwind (something wrapped around another object): *he unraveled the cellophane from a small cigar.* **2** investigate and solve or explain (something complicated or puzzling): *they were attempting to unravel the cause of death.* ■ [*intr.*] begin to fail or collapse.

un·read /ˌənˈred/ ▶*adj.* (of a book or document) not read.

un·read·a·ble /ˌənˈrēdəbəl/ ▶*adj.* not clear enough to read; illegible. ■ too dull or difficult to be worth reading: *a heavy, unreadable novel.* ■ (of a facial expression) unable to be interpreted: *an unreadable expression in his eyes.* —**un·read·a·bil·i·ty** /-ˌrēdəˈbilətē/ *n.* —**un·read·a·bly** /-blē/ *adv.*

un·re·al /ˌənˈrē(ə)l/ ▶*adj.* so strange as to appear imaginary; not seeming real: *in the half-light the tiny cottages seemed unreal.* ■ unrealistic. ■ *inf.* incredible; amazing. —**un·re·al·i·ty** /-rēˈalətē/ *n.* —**un·re·al·ly** *adv.*

un·rea·son /ˌənˈrēzən/ ▶*n.* inability to act or think reasonably.

un·rea·son·a·ble /ˌənˈrēz(ə)nəbəl/ ▶*adj.* not guided by or based on good sense: *your attitude is completely unreasonable.* ■ beyond the limits of acceptability or fairness: *an unreasonable request.* —**un·rea·son·a·ble·ness** *n.* —**un·rea·son·a·bly** /-blē/ *adv.*

un·re·lent·ing /ˌənriˈlentiNG/ ▶*adj.* not yielding in strength, severity, or determination: *the heat was unrelenting.* ■ (of a person or their behavior) not giving way to kindness or compassion: *unrelenting opponents.* —**un·re·lent·ing·ly** *adv.* —**un·re·lent·ing·ness** *n.*

un·re·mark·a·ble /ˌənriˈmärkəbəl/ ▶*adj.* not particularly interesting or surprising: *an unremarkable house.* —**un·re·mark·a·bly** /-blē/ *adv.*

un·re·mit·ting /ˌənriˈmitiNG/ ▶*adj.* never relaxing or slackening; incessant. —**un·re·mit·ting·ly** *adv.* —**un·re·mit·ting·ness** *n.*

un·re·peat·a·ble /ˌənriˈpētəbəl/ ▶*adj.* not able to be done or made again. ■ too offensive or shocking to be said again.

un·re·quit·ed /ˌənriˈkwītid/ ▶*adj.* (of a feeling, esp. love) not returned or rewarded. —**un·re·quit·ed·ly** *adv.* —**un·re·quit·ed·ness** *n.*

un·re·served /ˌənriˈzərvd/ ▶*adj.* **1** without reservations; complete: *he has had their unreserved support.* ■ frank and open: *a tall, unreserved young man.* **2** not set apart for a particular purpose or booked in advance. —**un·re·serv·ed·ly** /-ˈzərvidlē/ *adv.* —**un·re·serv·ed·ness** /-ˈzərvədnəs/ *n.*

un·re·solved /ˌənriˈzälvd; -ˈzôlvd/ ▶*adj.* (of a problem, question, or dispute) not resolved: *a number of issues remain unresolved.* —**un·re·solv·ed·ly** /-ˈzälvidlē; -ˈzôl-/ *adv.* —**un·re·solv·ed·ness** /-ˈzälvidnəs; -ˈzôl-/ *n.*

un·right·eous /ˌənˈrīCHəs/ ▶*adj. formal* not righteous; wicked. —**un·right·eous·ly** *adv.* —**un·right·eous·ness** *n.*

un·ri·valed /ˌənˈrīvəld/ ▶*adj.* better than everyone or everything of the same type: *the paper's coverage of foreign news is unrivaled.*

un·roll /ˌənˈrōl/ ▶*v.* open or cause to open out from a rolled-up state.

un·ruf·fled /ˌənˈrəfəld/ ▶*adj.* not disordered or disarranged: *the unruffled waters of the lake.* ■ (of a person) not agitated or disturbed; calm.

un·ru·ly /ˌənˈroōlē/ ▶*adj.* (**-li·er, -li·est**) disorderly and disruptive and not amenable to discipline or control: *complaints about unruly behavior.* ■ (of hair) difficult to keep neat and tidy. —**un·ru·li·ness** *n.*

un·said /ˌənˈsed/ ▶*adj.* not said or uttered: *the rest of the remark he left unsaid.*

un·sat·is·fac·to·ry /ˌənˌsatəsˈfakt(ə)rē/ ▶*adj.* unacceptable because poor or not good enough: *an unsatisfactory situation.* —**un·sat·is·fac·to·ri·ly** /-ˈfakt(ə)rəlē/ *adv.* —**un·sat·is·fac·to·ri·ness** *n.*

un·sat·u·rat·ed /ˌənˈsaCHəˌrātid/ ▶*adj. Chem.* (of organic molecules) having carbon–carbon double or triple bonds and therefore not containing the greatest possible number of hydrogen atoms for the number of carbons. —**un·sat·u·ra·tion** /-ˌsaCHəˈrāSHən/ *n.*

un·sa·vor·y /ˌənˈsāv(ə)rē/ (*Brit.* **un·sa·vour·y**) ▶*adj.* disagreeable and unpleasant because morally disreputable: *an unsavory reputation.* —**un·sa·vor·i·ly** /-rəlē/ *adv.* —**un·sa·vor·i·ness** *n.*

un·scathed /ˌənˈskāTHd/ ▶*adj.* without suffering any injury, damage, or harm: *I came through all those perils unscathed.*

un·schooled /ˌənˈskoōld/ ▶*adj.* not educated at or made to attend school: *unschooled children.* ■ lacking knowledge or training in a particular field: *she was unschooled in the niceties of royal behavior.* ■ not affected or artificial; natural and spontaneous.

un·sci·en·tif·ic /ˌənˌsīənˈtifik/ ▶*adj.* **1** not in accordance with scientific principles or methodology. **2** lacking knowledge of or interest in science. —**un·sci·en·tif·i·cal·ly** /-ik(ə)lē/ *adv.*

un·scram·ble /ˌənˈskrambəl/ ▶*v.* [*tr.*] restore (something that has been scrambled) to an intelligible, readable, or viewable state. —**un·scram·bler** /-b(ə)lər/ *n.*

un·screw /ˌənˈskroō/ ▶*v.* (with reference to a lid or other object held in place by a spiral thread) unfasten or be unfastened by twisting. ■ [*tr.*] detach, open, or slacken (something) by removing or loosening the screws holding it in place.

un·script·ed /ˌənˈskriptid/ ▶*adj.* said or delivered without a prepared script; impromptu.

un·scru·pu·lous /ˌənˈskroōpyələs/ ▶*adj.* having or showing no moral principles; not honest or fair. —**un·scru·pu·lous·ly** *adv.* —**un·scru·pu·lous·ness** *n.*

un·seal /ˌənˈsēl/ ▶*v.* [*tr.*] remove or break the seal of.

un·sea·son·a·ble /ˌənˈsēzənəbəl/ ▶*adj.* (of weather) unusual for the time of year. ■ untimely; inopportune: *we visited the place at an unseasonable time.* —**un·sea·son·a·ble·ness** *n.* —**un·sea·son·a·bly** /-blē/ *adv.*

un·sea·soned /ˌənˈsēzənd/ ▶*adj.* **1** (of food) not flavored with salt, pepper, or other spices or seasonings. **2** (of timber) not treated or matured. ■ (of a person) inexperienced.

un·seat /ˌənˈsēt/ ▶*v.* [*tr.*] cause (someone) to fall from a horse or bicycle. ■ remove from a position of power or authority.

un·see·ing /ˌənˈsēiNG/ ▶adj. with one's eyes open but without noticing or seeing anything. —**un·see·ing·ly** adv.

un·seem·ly /ˌənˈsēmlē/ ▶adj. (of behavior or actions) not proper or appropriate: an unseemly squabble. —**un·seem·li·ness** n.

un·self·ish /ˌənˈselfiSH/ ▶adj. willing to put the needs or wishes of others before one's own: unselfish devotion. —**un·self·ish·ly** adv. —**un·self·ish·ness** n.

un·set·tle /ˌənˈsetl/ ▶v. [tr.] cause to feel anxious or uneasy; disturb: the crisis has unsettled financial markets | [as adj.] (**unsettling**) an unsettling conversation. —**un·set·tle·ment** n. | —**un·set·tling·ly** adv.

un·set·tled /ˌənˈsetld/ ▶adj. **1** lacking stability: an unsettled childhood. ■ worried and uneasy: she felt edgy and unsettled. ■ liable to change; unpredictable: a spell of unsettled weather. ■ not yet resolved. ■ (of a bill) not yet paid. **2** (of an area) having no settlers or inhabitants. —**un·set·tled·ness** n.

un·shack·le /ˌənˈSHakəl/ ▶v. [tr.] (usu. **be unshackled**) release from shackles, chains, or other physical restraints. ■ fig. liberate; set free.

un·shak·a·ble /ˌənˈSHākəbəl/ (also **un·shake·a·ble**) ▶adj. (of a belief, feeling, or opinion) strongly felt and unable to be changed: an unshakable faith in God. ■ unable to be disputed or questioned: an unshakable alibi. —**un·shak·a·bil·i·ty** /-ˌSHākəˈbilətē/ n. —**un·shak·a·bly** /-blē/ adv.

un·sheathe /ˌənˈSHēTH/ ▶v. [tr.] draw or pull out (a knife, sword, or similar weapon) from its sheath or covering.

un·shrink·ing /ˌənˈSHriNGkiNG/ ▶adj. unhesitating; fearless. —**un·shrink·ing·ly** adv.

un·sight·ly /ˌənˈsītlē/ ▶adj. unpleasant to look at; ugly: unsightly warts. —**un·sight·li·ness** n.

un·skilled /ˌənˈskild/ ▶adj. not having or requiring special skill or training: unskilled manual workers.

un·so·cia·ble /ˌənˈsōSHəbəl/ ▶adj. not enjoying or making an effort to behave sociably in the company of others. ■ not conducive to friendly social relations: watching TV is a fairly unsociable activity. —**un·so·cia·bil·i·ty** /-ˌsōSHəˈbilətē/ n. —**un·so·cia·ble·ness** n. —**un·so·cia·bly** /-blē/ adv.

un·so·lic·it·ed /ˌənsəˈlisitid/ ▶adj. not asked for; given or done voluntarily: unsolicited junk mail. —**un·so·lic·it·ed·ly** adv.

un·so·phis·ti·cat·ed /ˌənsəˈfistəˌkātid/ ▶adj. lacking refined worldly knowledge or tastes. ■ not complicated or highly developed; basic: unsophisticated computer software. ■ not artificial. —**un·so·phis·ti·cat·ed·ly** adv. —**un·so·phis·ti·cat·ed·ness** n. —**un·so·phis·ti·ca·tion** /-ˌfisti-ˈkāSHən/ n.

un·sound /ˌənˈsound/ ▶adj. not safe or robust; in poor condition: the tower is structurally unsound. ■ not based on sound evidence or reasoning and therefore unreliable or unacceptable. ■ (of a person) not competent, reliable, or holding acceptable views. ■ injured, ill, or diseased, esp. (of a horse) lame. —**un·sound·ly** adv. —**un·sound·ness** n.

un·spar·ing /ˌənˈspe(ə)riNG/ ▶adj. **1** merciless; severe: he is unsparing in his criticism of the arms trade. **2** given freely and generously. —**un·spar·ing·ly** adv. —**un·spar·ing·ness** n.

un·speak·a·ble /ˌənˈspēkəbəl/ ▶adj. not able to be expressed in words: I felt an unspeakable tenderness toward her. ■ too bad or horrific to express in words. —**un·speak·a·ble·ness** n. —**un·speak·a·bly** /-blē/ adv.

un·spoiled /ˌənˈspoild/ ▶adj. not spoiled, in particular (of a place) not marred by development: unspoiled countryside.

un·sports·man·like /ˌənˈspôrtsmənˌlīk/ ▶adj. not fair, generous, or sportsmanlike: a penalty against us for unsportsmanlike conduct.

un·sta·ble /ˌənˈstābəl/ ▶adj. (**-bler**, **-blest**) prone to change, fail, or give way; not stable: the unstable cliff tops | an unstable government. ■ prone to psychiatric problems or sudden changes of mood: he was mentally unstable. —**un·sta·ble·ness** n. —**un·sta·bly** /-blē/ adv.

un·stead·y /ˌənˈstedē/ ▶adj. (**-stead·i·er**, **-stead·i·est**) **1** liable to fall or shake; not firm: he was very unsteady on his feet. **2** not uniform or regular. —**un·stead·i·ly** /-ˈstedl-ē/ adv. —**un·stead·i·ness** n.

un·stick /ˌənˈstik/ ▶v. (past and past part. **-stuck**) [tr.] cause to become no longer stuck together.
▶ □ **come** (or **get**) **unstuck** become separated or unfastened.

un·stint·ing /ˌənˈstintiNG/ ▶adj. given or giving without restraint; unsparing: he was unstinting in his praise. —**un·stint·ing·ly** adv.

un·stop·pa·ble /ˌənˈstäpəbəl/ ▶adj. impossible to stop or prevent. —**un·stop·pa·bil·i·ty** /-ˌstäpəˈbilətē/ n. —**un·stop·pa·bly** /-blē/ adv.

un·strap /ˌənˈstrap/ ▶v. (**-strapped**, **-strap·ping**) [tr.] undo the strap or straps of. ■ release (someone or something) by undoing straps.

un·stressed /ˌənˈstrest/ ▶adj. **1** Phonet. (of a syllable) not pronounced with stress: an unstressed syllable. **2** not subjected to stress.

un·struc·tured /ˌənˈstrəkCHərd/ ▶adj. without formal organization or structure: an unstructured interview.

un·stuck /ˌənˈstək/ ▶ past and past participle of **UNSTICK**.

un·stud·ied /ˌənˈstədēd/ ▶adj. not labored or artificial; natural: she had an unstudied grace in every step. —**un·stud·ied·ly** adv.

un·sub·scribe /ˌənsəbˈskrīb/ ▶v. [intr.] cancel a subscription, esp. to an Internet newsletter, newsgroup, or electronic mailing list.

un·sub·stan·tial /ˌənsəbˈstanCHəl/ ▶adj. having little or no solidity, reality, or factual basis. —**un·sub·stan·ti·al·i·ty** /-ˌstanCHēˈalitē/ n. —**un·sub·stan·tial·ly** adv.

un·sung /ˌənˈsəNG/ ▶adj. not celebrated or praised.

un·sure /ˌənˈSHoŏr/ ▶adj. not feeling, showing, or done with confidence and certainty: she was feeling nervous, unsure of herself. ■ (of a fact) not fixed or certain: the date is unsure. —**un·sure·ly** adv. —**un·sure·ness** n.

un·swerv·ing /ˌənˈswərviNG/ ▶adj. not changing or becoming weaker; steady or constant: unswerving loyalty. —**un·swerv·ing·ly** adv.

un·tan·gle /ˌənˈtaNGgəl/ ▶v. [tr.] free from a tangled or twisted state: fishermen untangle their nets. ■ make (something complicated or confusing) easier to understand or deal with.

un·tapped /ˌənˈtapt/ ▶adj. **1** (of a resource) not yet exploited or used. **2** (of a telephone, etc.) free from listening devices.

un·taught /ˌənˈtôt/ ▶adj. (of a person) not trained by teaching: she is totally untaught and will not listen. ■ not acquired by teaching; natural or spontaneous: by untaught instinct they know that scent means food.

un·teach /ˌənˈtēCH/ ▶v. (past and past part. **-taught**) **1** cause (someone) to forget or discard previous knowledge. **2** remove from the mind (something known or taught) by different teaching.

un·ten·a·ble /ˌənˈtenəbəl/ ▶adj. (esp. of a position or view) not able to be maintained or defended against attack or objection. —**un·ten·a·bil·i·ty** /-ˌtenəˈbilitē/ n. —**un·ten·a·bly** /-blē/ adv.

un·think·a·ble /ˌənˈTHiNGkəbəl/ ▶adj. (of a situation or event) too unlikely or undesirable to be considered a possibility: it was unthinkable that John could be dead | [as n.] (**the unthinkable**) the unthinkable happened—I spoke up. —**un·think·a·bil·i·ty** /-ˌTHiNGkəˈbilitē/ n. —**un·think·a·bly** /-blē/ adv. a land of unthinkably vast spaces.

un·think·ing /ˌənˈTHiNGkiNG/ ▶adj. expressed, done, or acting without proper consideration of the consequences: she was at pains to correct unthinking prejudices. —**un·think·ing·ly** adv. —**un·think·ing·ness** n.

un·tie /ˌənˈtī/ ▶v. (**-tied**, **-ty·ing**) [tr.] undo or unfasten (a cord or knot): she knelt to untie her laces. ■ undo a cord or similar fastening that binds (someone or something): Morton untied the parcel.

un·tied /ˌənˈtīd/ ▶adj. not fastened or knotted.

un·til /ˌənˈtil; ən-/ ▶prep. & conj. up to (the point in time or the event mentioned): [as conj.] you don't know what you can achieve until you try.

un·time·ly /ˌənˈtīmlē/ ▶adj. (of an event or act) happening or done at an unsuitable time: Dave's untimely return. ■ (of a death or end) happening too soon or sooner than normal. —**un·time·li·ness** n.

un·tir·ing /ˌənˈtīriNG/ ▶adj. (of a person or their actions) continuing at the same rate without loss of vigor; indefatigable. —**un·tir·ing·ly** adv.

un·ti·tled /ˌənˈtītld/ ▶adj. **1** (of a book, composition, or other artistic work) having no name. **2** (of a person) not having a title indicating high social or official rank: lesser untitled officials.

un·told /ˌənˈtōld/ ▶adj. **1** too much or too many to be counted or measured: thieves caused untold damage. **2** (of a story or event) not narrated or recounted: no event, however boring, is left untold.

un·touch·a·ble /ˌənˈtəCHəbəl/ ▶adj. **1** not able or allowing to be touched or affected. ■ unable to be matched or rivaled: we took the silver medal behind the untouchable U.S. team. **2** of or belonging to the lowest-caste Hindu group or the people outside the caste system.
▶n. a member of the lowest-caste Hindu group or a person outside the caste system. Contact with untouchables is traditionally held to defile members of higher castes. —**un·touch·a·bil·i·ty** /-ˌtəCHəˈbilitē/ n.

un·touched /ˌənˈtəCHt/ ▶adj. **1** not handled, used, or tasted. ■ (of a subject) not treated in writing or speech; not discussed: no detail is left untouched. **2** not affected, changed, or damaged in any way: Prague was relatively untouched by the war.

un·to·ward /ˌənˈtôrd; -t(ə)ˈwôrd/ ▶adj. unexpected and inappropriate or inconvenient: both tried to behave as if nothing untoward had happened. —**un·to·ward·ly** adv. —**un·to·ward·ness** n.

un·treat·a·ble /ˌənˈtrētəbəl/ ▶adj. (of a patient, a disease or other condition) for whom or which no medical care is available or possible.

un·tried /ˌənˈtrīd/ ▶adj. **1** not tested to discover quality or reliability;

inexperienced: *he chose two untried actors for leading roles.* **2** *Law* (of an accused person) not yet subjected to a trial in court.

un·trou·bled /ˌənˈtrəbəld/ ▶ *adj.* not feeling, showing, or affected by anxiety or problems: *a man untroubled by a guilty conscience.*

un·true /ˌənˈtroō/ ▶ *adj.* **1** not in accordance with fact or reality; false or incorrect. **2** not faithful or loyal. —**un·tru·ly** /-ˈtroōlē/ *adv.*

un·truth /ˌənˈtroōTH/ ▶ *n.* (*pl.* -**truths** /-ˈtroōTHz; -ˈtroōTHs/) a lie or false statement (often used euphemistically). ▪ the quality of being false. —**un·truth·ful** *adj.*

un·ty·ing /ˌənˈtī-iNG/ ▶ present participle of UNTIE.

un·used /ˌənˈyoōzd;/ ▶ *adj.* **1** not being, or never having been, used: *an unused bedpan.* **2** /-ˈyoōst/ (**unused to**) not familiar with or accustomed to something: *unused to spicy food, she took a long mouthful of water.*

un·u·su·al /ˌənˈyoōzHoōəl/ ▶ *adj.* not habitually or commonly occurring or done. ▪ remarkable or interesting because different from or better than others: *a man of unusual talent.* —**un·u·su·al·ly** *adv. he made an unusually large number of mistakes.* —**un·u·su·al·ness** *n.*

un·ut·ter·a·ble /ˌənˈətərəbəl/ ▶ *adj.* too great, intense, or awful to describe: *those private moments of unutterable grief.* —**un·ut·ter·a·bly** /-blē/ *adv. Juliet climbed the stairs, feeling unutterably weary.*

un·val·ued /ˌənˈvalyoōd/ ▶ *adj.* not considered to be important or beneficial: *he felt unvalued.*

un·var·nished /ˌənˈvärnisHt/ ▶ *adj.* not covered with varnish. ▪ (of a statement or manner) plain and straightforward.

un·veil /ˌənˈvāl/ ▶ *v.* [*tr.*] remove a veil or covering from, esp. uncover (a new monument or work of art) as part of a public ceremony: *the mayor unveiled a plaque* | [as *n.*] (**unveiling**) *the unveiling of the memorial.* ▪ show or announce publicly for the first time.

un·war·rant·ed /ˌənˈwôrəntid; -ˈwär-/ ▶ *adj.* not justified or authorized.

un·war·y /ˌənˈwe(ə)rē/ ▶ *adj.* not cautious; not aware of possible dangers or problems: (**the unwary**) *hidden traps for the unwary.* —**un·war·i·ly** /-ˈwe(ə)rəlē/ *adv.* —**un·war·i·ness** *n.*

un·washed /ˌənˈwôsHt; -ˈwäsHt/ ▶ *adj.* not having been washed.
▶ □ **the** (**great**) **unwashed** *derog.* the mass or multitude of ordinary people; the working class.

un·wea·ried /ˌənˈwi(ə)rēd/ ▶ *adj.* not tired or becoming tired. —**un·wea·ried·ly** *adv.*

un·wed /ˌənˈwed/ (also **un·wed·ded**) ▶ *adj.* not married: *an unwed teenage mother.* —**un·wed·ded·ness** *n.*

un·wel·come /ˌənˈwelkəm/ ▶ *adj.* (of a guest or new arrival) not gladly received. ▪ not much needed or desired: *unwelcome attentions from men.* —**un·wel·come·ly** *adv.* —**un·wel·come·ness** *n.*

un·well /ˌənˈwel/ ▶ *adj.* sick: *consult a doctor if you feel unwell.*

un·whole·some /ˌənˈhōlsəm/ ▶ *adj.* not characterized by or conducive to health or moral well-being. —**un·whole·some·ly** *adv.* —**un·whole·some·ness** *n.*

un·wield·y /ˌənˈwēldē/ ▶ *adj.* (-**wield·i·er**, -**wield·i·est**) difficult to carry or move because of its size, shape, or weight. ▪ (of a system or bureaucracy) too big or badly organized to function efficiently. —**un·wield·i·ly** *adv.* —**un·wield·i·ness** *n.*

un·will·ing /ˌənˈwiliNG/ ▶ *adj.* not ready, eager, or prepared to do something. —**un·will·ing·ly** *adv.* —**un·will·ing·ness** *n.*

un·wind /ˌənˈwīnd/ ▶ *v.* (*past* and *past part.* -**wound** /-ˈwound/) undo or be undone after winding or being wound. ▪ [*intr.*] relax after a period of work or tension: *the Grand Hotel is a superb place to unwind.*

un·wise /ˌənˈwīz/ ▶ *adj.* (of a person or action) not wise or sensible; foolish: *unwise policy decisions.* —**un·wise·ly** *adv. unwisely, she repeated the remark to her mother.*

un·wit·ting /ˌənˈwitiNG/ ▶ *adj.* (of a person) not aware of the full facts: *an unwitting accomplice.* ▪ not done on purpose; unintentional. —**un·wit·ting·ly** *adv. quite unwittingly, you played right into my hands that night.* —**un·wit·ting·ness** *n.*

un·wont·ed /ˌənˈwôntid/ ▶ *adj.* unaccustomed or unusual: *there was an unwonted gaiety in her manner.* —**un·wont·ed·ly** *adv. she was unwontedly shy and subdued.* —**un·wont·ed·ness** *n.*

un·world·ly /ˌənˈwərldlē/ ▶ *adj.* (of a person) not having much awareness of the realities of life, in particular, not motivated by material or practical considerations: *she was so shrewd in some ways, but hopelessly unworldly in others.* ▪ not seeming to belong to this planet; strange: *the unworldly monolith loomed four stories high.* —**un·world·li·ness** *n.*

un·worn /ˌənˈwôrn/ ▶ *adj.* not damaged or shabby-looking as a result of much use. ▪ (of a garment) never worn.

un·wor·thy /ˌənˈwərTHē/ ▶ *adj.* (-**thi·er**, -**thi·est**) not deserving effort, attention, or respect: *he was **unworthy of trust** and unfit to hold office.* ▪ (of a person's action or behavior) not acceptable, esp. from someone with

a good reputation or social position. ▪ having little value or merit: *many pieces are unworthy and ungrammatical.* —**un·wor·thi·ly** /-THəlē/ *adv.* —**un·wor·thi·ness** *n.*

un·wrap /ˌənˈrap/ ▶ *v.* (-**wrapped**, -**wrap·ping**) [*tr.*] remove the wrapping from a package.

un·writ·ten /ˌənˈritn/ ▶ *adj.* not recorded in writing. ▪ (esp. of a law) resting originally on custom or judicial decision rather than on statute. ▪ (of a convention) understood and accepted by everyone, although not formally established: *the unwritten rules of social life.*

un·yield·ing /ˌənˈyēldiNG/ ▶ *adj.* (of a mass or structure) not giving way to pressure; hard or solid: *the Atlantic hurled its waves at the unyielding rocks.* ▪ (of a person or their behavior) unlikely to be swayed; resolute: *his unyielding faith.* —**un·yield·ing·ly** *adv.* —**un·yield·ing·ness** *n.*

un·zip /ˌənˈzip/ ▶ *v.* (-**zipped**, -**zip·ping**) [*tr.*] unfasten the zipper of (an item of clothing): *he unzipped his black jacket.* ▪ *Comput.* decompress (a file) that has previously been compressed.

up /əp/ ▶ *adv.* **1** toward the sky or a higher position: *he jumped up* | *two of the men hoisted her up* | *the curtain went up.* ▪ upstairs: *she made her way up to bed.* ▪ out of bed: *Miranda hardly ever got up for breakfast* | *he had been up for hours.* ▪ (of the sun) visible in the sky after daybreak: *the sun was already up when they set off.* ▪ expressing movement toward or position in the north: *I drove up to Detroit.* ▪ to or at a place perceived as higher: *going for a walk up to the stores.* ▪ (of food that has been eaten) regurgitated from the stomach: *I was sick and vomited up everything.* ▪ [as *interj.*] used as a command to a soldier or an animal to stand up and be ready to move or attack: *up, boys, and at 'em.* **2** to the place where someone is: *Dot didn't hear Mrs. Parvis come creeping up behind her.* **3** at or to a higher level of intensity, volume, or activity: *she turned the volume up* | *liven up the graphics* | *U.S. environmental groups had been stepping up their attack on GATT.* ▪ at or to a higher price, value, or rank: *sales are up 22.8 percent at $50.2 million* | *unemployment is up and rising.* ▪ winning or at an advantage by a specified margin: *there they were in the fourth quarter, up by 11 points* | *we came away 300 bucks up on the evening.* **4** into the desired or a proper condition: *the mayor agreed to set up a committee.* ▪ so as to be finished or closed: *I've got a bit of paperwork to finish up* | *I zipped up my sweater.* **5** into a happy mood: *I don't think anything's going to cheer me up.* **6** displayed on a bulletin board or other publicly visible site: *he put up posters around the city.* **7** *Baseball* at bat: *every time up, he had a different stance.*
▶ *prep.* from a lower to a higher point on (something); upward along: *she climbed up a flight of steps.* ▪ from one end to another of (a street or other area), not necessarily on an upward slope: *bicycling up Pleasant Avenue toward Maywood Avenue* | *walking up the street.* ▪ to a higher part of (a river or stream), away from the sea: *a cruise up the Rhine.*
▶ *adj.* **1** directed or moving toward a higher place or position: *the up escalator.* **2** in a cheerful mood; ebullient: *the mood here is resolutely up.* **3** (of a computer system or industrial process) functioning properly: *the system is now up.* **4** at an end: *his contract was up in three weeks.*
▶ *v.* (**upped**, **up·ping**) **1** [*intr.*] (**up and do something**) *inf.* do something abruptly or boldly: *she upped and left him.* **2** [*tr.*] cause (a level or amount) to be increased. **3** [*tr.*] lift (something) up: *everybody was cheering and upping their glasses.* ▷Old English *up(p)*, *uppe*, of Germanic origin; related to Dutch *op* and German *auf*.
▶ □ **get it up** *vulgar slang* have a penile erection. □ **on the up and up** *inf.* honest or sincere. □ **something is up** *inf.* something unusual or undesirable is happening or afoot. □ **up against** close to or in contact with. ▪ *inf.* confronted with or opposed by: *I began to think of what teachers are up against today.* □ **up and about** no longer in bed (after sleep or an illness). □ **up and down 1** moving upward and downward: *bouncing up and down.* **2** to and fro. ▪ [as *prep.*] to and fro along: *strolling up and down the corridor.* **3** in various places throughout: *in clubs up and down the country.* **4** *inf.* in varying states or moods; changeable: *my relationship with her was up and down.* □ **up and running** (esp. of a computer system) in operation; functioning: *the new computer is up and running.* □ **up the ante** see ANTE. □ **up before** appearing for a hearing in the presence of: *we'll have to come up before a magistrate.* □ **up for 1** available for sale: *the house next door is up for sale.* **2** being considered for: *he had been up for promotion.* **3** due for: *his contract was up for renewal in June.* □ **up for it** *inf.* ready to take part in a particular activity: *Nick wasn't really up for it.* □ **up on** well informed about: *he was up on the latest methods.* □ **up to 1** as far as: *I could reach just up to his waist.* ▪ (also **up until**) until: *up to now I hadn't had a relationship.* **2** indicating a maximum amount: *the process is expected to take up to two years.* **3** as good as; good enough for: *I was not up to her standards.* ▪ capable of or fit for: *he is simply not up to the job.* **4** the duty, responsibility, or choice of (someone): *it was up to them to gauge*

the problem. **5** *inf.* occupied or busy with: *what's he been up to?* □ **what's up?** *inf.* **1** what's going on? **2** what's the matter?: *what's up with you?*

up·and·com·ing ▶*adj.* (of a person beginning a particular activity or occupation) making good progress and likely to become successful: *up-and-coming young players.* —**up-and-com·er** *n.*

up·beat /ˈəpˌbēt/ ▶*n.* (in music) an unaccented beat preceding an accented beat.
▶*adj. inf.* cheerful; optimistic.

up·braid /ˌəpˈbrād/ ▶*v.* [*tr.*] find fault with (someone); scold: *he was upbraided for his slovenly appearance.*

up·bring·ing /ˈəpˌbriNGiNG/ ▶*n.* the treatment and instruction received by a child from its parents throughout its childhood.

UPC ▶*abbr.* ■ Universal Product Code.

up·chuck /ˈəpˌCHək/ *inf.* ▶*v.* vomit: [*intr.*] *don't let her upchuck on him.*
▶*n.* matter vomited from the stomach.

up·com·ing /ˈəpˌkəmiNG/ ▶*adj.* forthcoming; about to happen.

up·coun·try /ˌəpˈkəntrē; ˈəpˌkəntrē/ ▶*adv. & adj.* in or toward the interior of a country; inland: *a little upcountry town.*

up·date ▶*v.* /ˌəpˈdāt; ˈəpˌdāt/ [*tr.*] make (something) more modern or up to date: [as *adj.*] (**updated**) *an updated list of subscribers.* ■ give (someone) the latest information about something: *the reporter promised to keep the viewers updated.*
▶*n.* /ˈəpˌdāt/ an act of bringing something or someone up to date, or an updated version of something. —**up·dat·a·ble** *adj.* (*Comput.*).

up·draft /ˈəpˌdraft/ ▶*n.* an upward current or draft of air.

up·end /ˌəpˈend/ ▶*v.* [*tr.*] set or turn (something) on its end or upside down: [as *adj.*] (**upended**) *an upended box.* ■ [*intr.*] (of a swimming duck or other waterbird) submerge the head and foreparts in order to feed, so that the tail is raised in the air.

up·front /ˌəpˈfrənt/ *inf.* ▶*adv.* (usu. **up front**) **1** at the front; in front. **2** (of a payment) in advance: *the salesmen are paid commission up front.*
▶*adj.* **1** bold, honest, and frank: *he'd been upfront about his intentions.* **2** (of a payment) made in advance. **3** at the front or the most prominent position.

up·grade ▶*v.* /ˈəpˌgrād; ˌəpˈgrād/ [*tr.*] raise (something) to a higher standard, in particular improve (equipment or machinery) by adding or replacing components: [as *adj.*] (**upgraded**) *upgraded computers.* ■ raise (an employee) to a higher grade or rank.
▶*n.* /ˈəpˌgrād/ an act of upgrading something. ■ an improved or more modern version of something, esp. a piece of computing equipment. —**up·grad·a·bil·i·ty** /ˌəpˌgrādəˈbilitē/ (also **up·grade·a·bil·i·ty**) *n.* —**up·grad·a·ble** /ˈəpˌgrādəbəl/ (also **up·grade·a·ble**) *adj.*

up·heav·al /ˌəpˈhēvəl/ ▶*n.* a violent or sudden change or disruption to something. ■ an upward displacement of part of the earth's crust.

up·hill ▶*adv.* /ˌəpˈhil/ in an ascending direction up a hill or slope.
▶*adj.* /ˈəpˌhil/ sloping upward; ascending: *the journey is slightly uphill.* ■ *fig.* requiring great effort; difficult: *an uphill struggle to gain worldwide recognition.*
▶*n.* /ˈəpˌhil/ an upward slope.

up·hold /ˌəpˈhōld/ ▶*v.* (*past* and *past part.* **-held**) [*tr.*] confirm or support (something that has been questioned): *the court upheld his claim for damages.* ■ maintain (a custom or practice). —**up·hold·er** *n.*

up·hol·ster /əpˈhōlstər; əˈpōl-/ ▶*v.* [*tr.*] provide (furniture) with a soft, padded covering: *the chairs were upholstered in red velvet.* ■ cover the walls or furniture in (a room) with textiles. —**up·hol·ster·er** *n.*

up·hol·ster·y /əpˈhōlst(ə)rē; əˈpōl-/ ▶*n.* soft, padded textile covering that is fixed to furniture such as armchairs and sofas.

up·keep /ˈəpˌkēp/ ▶*n.* the process of keeping something in good condition. ■ financial or material support of a person or animal: *payments for the children's upkeep.*

up·land /ˈəplənd; -ˌland/ ▶*n.* (also **uplands**) an area of high or hilly land.

up·lift ▶*v.* /ˌəpˈlift/ [*tr.*] **1** [usu. as *adj.*] (**uplifted**) lift (something) up; raise: *her uplifted face.* ■ (**be uplifted**) (of an island, mountain, etc.) be created by an upward movement of the earth's surface. **2** elevate or stimulate (someone) morally or spiritually: [as *adj.*] (**uplifting**) *an uplifting tune.*
▶*n.* /ˈəpˌlift/ **1** an act of raising something. **2** a morally or spiritually elevating influence. —**up·lift·er** /ˌəpˈliftər/ *n.*

up·load /ˈəpˌlōd/ *Comput.* ▶*v.* [*tr.*] transfer (data) to another computer system; transmit (data). Compare with **DOWNLOAD.**
▶*n.* the action or process of transferring data in such a way.

up·mar·ket /ˌəpˈmärkit; ˈəpˌmär-/ (also **up·mar·ket**) ▶*adj.* upscale.

up·most /ˈəpˌmōst/ ▶*adj.* another term for **UPPERMOST.**

up·on /əˈpän; əˈpôn/ ▶*prep.* more formal term for **ON,** esp. in abstract senses: *it was based upon two principles.*

up·per[1] /ˈəpər/ ▶*adj.* **1** situated above another part. ■ higher in position or status: *the upper end of the social scale.* **2** situated on higher ground. ■ situated to the north: [in place names] *Upper California.*
▶*n.* **1** the part of a boot or shoe above the sole. **2** (**uppers**) upper dentures or teeth.
▶ □ **have** (or **gain**) **the upper hand** have or gain advantage or control over someone or something.

up·per[2] ▶*n.* (usu. **uppers**) *inf.* a stimulating drug, esp. amphetamine.

up·per·case /ˈəpərˈkās/ (also **up·per case**) ▶*n.* capital letters as opposed to small letters (lowercase): *uppercase letters.*

up·per class ▶*n.* [treated as *sing.* or *pl.*] the social group that has the highest status in society, esp. the aristocracy.
▶*adj.* of, relating to, or characteristic of such a group: *upper-class accents.*

up·per crust ▶*n.* (**the upper crust**) *inf.* the upper classes.

up·per·cut /ˈəpərˌkət/ ▶*n.* a punch delivered with an upward motion and the arm bent.
▶*v.* [*tr.*] hit with an uppercut.

up·per house ▶*n.* the smaller house in a bicameral legislature or parliament. ■ (**the Upper House**) (in the UK) the House of Lords.

up·per·most /ˈəpərˌmōst/ ▶*adj.* (also **up·most**) highest in place, rank, or importance: *the uppermost windows | her father was uppermost in her mind.*
▶*adv.* at or to the highest or most important position.

up·pi·ty /ˈəpətē/ ▶*adj. inf.* self-important; arrogant: *an uppity sister-in-law.*

up·right /ˈəpˌrīt/ ▶*adj.* **1** vertical; erect. ■ (of a piano) having vertical strings. ■ greater in height than breadth: *an upright freezer.* ■ denoting a device designed to be used in a vertical position: *an upright vacuum cleaner.* **2** (of a person or their behavior) strictly honorable or honest: *an upright member of the community.*
▶*adv.* in or into a vertical position: *she was sitting upright in bed.*
▶*n.* a post or rod fixed vertically, esp. as a structural support: *the stone uprights of the parapet.* ■ (**uprights**) *Football* the vertical posts extending up from the goal post, between which a field goal must pass to score. —**up·right·ly** *adv.* —**up·right·ness** *n.*

up·ris·ing /ˈəpˌrīziNG/ ▶*n.* an act of resistance or rebellion; a revolt.

up·riv·er /ˈəpˈrivər/ ▶*adv. & adj.* toward or situated at a point nearer the source of a river.

up·roar /ˈəpˌrôr/ ▶*n.* a loud and impassioned noise or disturbance: *the assembly dissolved in uproar.* ■ a public expression of protest or outrage.

up·roar·i·ous /ˌəpˈrôrēəs/ ▶*adj.* characterized by or provoking loud noise or uproar: *an uproarious party.* ■ provoking loud laughter; very funny. —**up·roar·i·ous·ly** *adv.* —**up·roar·i·ous·ness** *n.*

up·root /ˌəpˈrōōt; -ˈrŏŏt/ ▶*v.* [*tr.*] pull (something, esp. a tree or plant) out of the ground: *the elephant's trunk is powerful enough to uproot trees.* ■ move (someone) from their home or a familiar location. ■ *fig.* eradicate; destroy: *a revolution to uproot the social order.* —**up·root·er** *n.*

ups and downs ▶*pl. n.* a succession of both good and bad experiences: *I have my ups and downs.* ■ rises and falls, esp. in the value or success of something: *the ups and downs of the market.*

up·scale /ˌəpˈskāl; ˈəpˌskāl/ ▶*adj. & adv.* toward or relating to the more expensive or affluent sector of the market: [as *adv.*] *once known as the low-cost cousin of beef, fish has moved upscale.*

up·set /ˌəpˈset/ ▶*v.* (**-set·ting**; *past* and *past part.* **-set**) [*tr.*] **1** make (someone) unhappy, disappointed, or worried: [as *adj.*] (**upsetting**) *a painful and upsetting divorce.* **2** knock (something) over: *he upset a tureen of soup.* ■ cause disorder in (something); disrupt: *the dam will upset the ecological balance.* ■ disturb the digestion of (a person's stomach); cause (someone) to feel nauseous or unwell.
▶*n.* /ˈəpˌset/ **1** a state of being unhappy, disappointed, or worried: *domestic upsets.* **2** an unexpected result or situation, esp. in a sports competition: *they caused one of last season's league upsets by winning 27–15.* **3** a disturbance of a person's digestive system: *a stomach upset.*
▶*adj.* /ˌəpˈset/ **1** unhappy, disappointed, or worried. **2** (of a person's stomach) having disturbed digestion, esp. because of something eaten. —**up·set·ter** /ˌəpˈsetər/ *n.* —**up·set·ting·ly** *adv.*

up·shot /ˈəpˌSHät/ ▶*n.* the final or eventual outcome or conclusion of a discussion, action, or series of events.

up·side down ▶*adv. & adj.* with the upper part where the lower part should be; in an inverted position. ■ in or into total disorder or confusion: [as *adv.*] *burglars have **turned** our house **upside down**.*

up·side-down cake ▶*n.* a cake that is baked over a layer of fruit in syrup and inverted for serving.

up·si·lon /ˈəpsəˌlän; ˈ(y)o͞op-/ ▶*n.* the twentieth letter of the Greek alphabet (Υ, υ), transliterated in the traditional Latin style as 'y' (as in *cycle*) or in the modern style as 'u.'

up·stage /ˌəpˈstāj/ ▶*adv. & adj.* at or toward the back of a theater stage: [as *adv.*] *Hamlet turns to face upstage* | [as *adj.*] *an upstage exit.*
▶*v.* [*tr.*] divert attention from (someone) toward oneself; outshine: *they were totally upstaged by their costar in the film.* ■ (of an actor) move toward the back of a stage to make (another actor) face away from the audience.

up·stairs ▶*adv.* /ˌəpˈste(ə)rz/ on or to an upper floor of a building. ■ used to refer to someone's mental health: *is he all right upstairs?*
▶*adj.* /ˈəpˈsterz/ situated on an upper floor: *an upstairs bedroom.*
▶*n.* /ˌəpˈsterz; ˈəpˌsterz/ an upper floor: *she was cleaning the upstairs.*

up·stand·ing /ˌəpˈstandiNG; ˈəpˌstan-/ ▶*adj.* **1** honest; respectable: *an upstanding member of the community.* **2** standing up; erect.

up·start /ˈəpˌstärt/ ▶*n. derog.* a person who has risen suddenly to wealth or high position, esp. one who behaves arrogantly: *the upstarts who dare to challenge the legitimacy of his rule* | [as *adj.*] *an upstart leader.*

up·state /ˈəpˈstāt/ ▶*adj. & adv.* of, in, or to a part of a state remote from its large cities, esp. the northern part.
▶*n.* such an area: *visiting farmers from upstate.* ■ (also **Upstate**) in New York, parts of the state north of New York City, thought of as distinct culturally and politically: *the small community college in upstate New York.* **—up·stat·er** *n.*

up·stream /ˌəpˈstrēm/ ▶*adv. & adj.* moving or situated in the opposite direction from that in which a stream or river flows; nearer to the source: [as *adv.*] *a salmon swimming upstream* | [as *adj.*] *the upstream stretch of the Platte.* ■ at a stage in the process of gas or oil extraction and production before the raw material is ready for refining.

up·surge /ˈəpˌsərj/ ▶*n.* an upward surge in the strength or quantity of something; an increase: *an upsurge in separatist activity.*

up·swept /ˈəpˌswept/ ▶*adj.* curved, sloping, or directed upward: *an upswept mustache.* ■ (of the hair) brushed or held upward and off the face.

up·swing /ˈəpˌswiNG/ ▶*n.* an increase in strength or quantity; an upward trend: *cigar smoking has been **on the upswing**.*

up·take /ˈəpˌtāk/ ▶*n.* the action of taking up or making use of something that is available: *a recent uptake in cigar smoking.* ■ the taking in or absorption of a substance by a living organism or bodily organ: *the uptake of glucose into the muscles.*
▶ □ **be quick** (or **slow**) **on the uptake** *inf.* be quick (or slow) to understand something.

up·tight /ˌəpˈtīt/ ▶*adj. inf.* anxious or angry in a tense and overly controlled way: *don't get so uptight about everything.*

up to date ▶*adj.* incorporating the latest developments and trends: *a modern, up-to-date hospital.* ■ incorporating or aware of the latest information: *the book will keep you up to date.*

up-to-the-min·ute ▶*adj.* incorporating the very latest information or developments: *an up-to-the-minute news broadcast.*

up·town ▶*adj.* /ˌəpˈtoun/ of, in, or characteristic of the residential area of a city or town. ■ of or characteristic of an affluent area or people: *I don't pay uptown prices.*
▶*adv.* /ˌəpˈtoun/ in or into such an area.
▶*n.* /ˈəpˌtoun/ a residential area in a town or city. **—up·town·er** /ˌəpˈtounər/ *n.*

up·turn ▶*n.* /ˈəpˌtərn/ an improvement or upward trend, esp. in economic conditions or someone's fortunes: *an upturn in the economy.*
▶*v.* /ˈəpˌtərn; ˌəpˈtərn/ [*tr.*] [usu. as *adj.*] (**upturned**) turn (something) upward or upside down: *a sea of upturned faces.*

up·ward /ˈəpwərd/ ▶*adv.* (also **up·wards**) toward a higher place, point, or level: *she peered upward at the sky.*
▶*adj.* moving, pointing, or leading to a higher place, point, or level: *an upward trend in sales.* **—up·ward·ly** *adv.*
▶ □ **upwards** (or **upward**) **of** more than: *upwards of 3,500 copies* | *Gooden can throw the ball at upward of 95 miles per hour.*

up·ward·ly mo·bile /ˈəpwərdlē/ ▶*adj.* moving to a higher social class; acquiring wealth and status. **—up·ward mo·bil·i·ty** *n.*

up·weight /ˈəpˌwāt/ ▶*v.* [*tr.*] **1** give increased importance, rank or weighting to: *some advertisers upweighted TV, while others upweighted press.* **2** *Finance* increase the proportion of (an asset or asset class) in a portfolio or fund: *an opportunity to upweight equities where feasible within your risk profile.*

up·wind /ˌəpˈwind/ ▶*adv. & adj.* against the direction of the wind: [as *adv.*] *you learn how to sail upwind* | [as *adj.*] *the upwind wing tip.*

u·ra·ni·um /yo͞oˈrānēəm/ ▶*n.* the chemical element of atomic number 92, a gray, dense radioactive metal used as a fuel in nuclear reactors. (Symbol: **U**)

U·ra·nus /ˈyo͝orənəs; yo͝oˈrā-/ ▶ **1** *Greek Mythol.* a personification of heaven or the sky, the most ancient of the Greek gods and first ruler of the universe. He was overthrown and castrated by his son Cronus. **2** *Astron.* a distant planet of the solar system, seventh in order from the sun, discovered by William Herschel in 1781.

ur·ban /ˈərbən/ ▶*adj.* in, relating to, or characteristic of a city or town: *the urban population.*

ur·bane /ərˈbān/ ▶*adj.* (of a person, esp. a man) suave, courteous, and refined in manner. **—ur·bane·ly** *adv.*

ur·ban·ite /ˈərbəˌnīt/ ▶*n. inf.* a person who lives in a city or town.

ur·ban·i·ty /ˌərˈbanitē/ ▶*n.* **1** suavity, courteousness, and refinement of manner. **2** urban life.

ur·ban·ize /ˈərbəˌnīz/ ▶*v.* make or become urban in character: [*tr.*] *once an agrarian society, the island has recently been urbanized* | [as *adj.*] (**urbanized**) *urbanized areas.* **—ur·ban·i·za·tion** /ˌərbənəˈzāSHən/ *n.*

ur·ban re·new·al ▶*n.* the redevelopment of areas within a large city, typically involving the clearance of slums.

ur·ban sprawl ▶*n.* the uncontrolled expansion of urban areas.

ur·chin /ˈərCHin/ ▶*n.* **1** a mischievous young child, esp. one who is poorly or raggedly dressed. ■ *archaic* a goblin. **2** short for **SEA URCHIN**. ▷Middle English *hirchon, urchon* 'hedgehog,' from Old Northern French *herichon*, based on Latin *hericius* 'hedgehog.'

Ur·du /ˈo͝ordo͞o; ˈər-/ ▶*n.* a form of Hindustani written in Persian script, with many loanwords from Persian and Arabic. It is an official language of Pakistan and is widely used in India and elsewhere.

u·re·a /yo͝oˈrēə/ ▶*n. Biochem.* a colorless crystalline compound that is the main nitrogenous breakdown product of protein metabolism in mammals and is excreted in urine.

u·re·mi·a /yo͝oˈrēmēə/ (*Brit.* **u·rae·mi·a**) ▶*n. Med.* a raised level in the blood of urea and other nitrogenous waste compounds that are normally eliminated by the kidneys. **—u·re·mic** /yo͝oˈrēmik/ *adj.*

u·re·ter /ˈyo͝oritər; yo͝oˈrētər/ ▶*n. Anat. & Zool.* the duct by which urine passes from the kidney to the bladder or cloaca. **—u·re·ter·al** /yo͝oˈrētərəl/ *adj.* **—u·re·ter·ic** /ˌyo͝oriˈterik/ *adj.*

u·re·thane /ˈyo͝orəˌTHān/ ▶*n. Chem.* a synthetic crystalline compound used in making pesticides and fungicides. ■ short for **POLYURETHANE**.

u·re·thra /yo͝oˈrēTHrə/ ▶*n. Anat. & Zool.* the duct by which urine is conveyed out of the body from the bladder, and which in male vertebrates also conveys semen. **—u·re·thral** *adj.*

u·re·thri·tis /ˌyo͝orəˈTHrītis/ ▶*n. Med.* inflammation of the urethra.

urge /ərj/ ▶*v.* [*tr.*] try earnestly or persistently to persuade (someone) to do something: *"Try to relax," she urged.* ■ recommend or advocate (something) strongly: *I urge caution in interpreting these results.* ■ [*tr.*] encourage (a person or animal) to move more quickly or in a particular direction: *drawing up outside the house, he urged her inside.* ■ (**urge someone on**) encourage someone to continue or succeed in something: *he could hear her voice urging him on.*
▶*n.* a strong desire or impulse: *the urge for revenge.*

ur·gent /ˈərjənt/ ▶*adj.* (of a state or situation) requiring immediate action or attention. ■ (of action or an event) done or arranged in response to such a situation: *she needs urgent treatment.* ■ (of a person or their manner) earnest and persistent in response to such a situation: *an urgent whisper.* **—ur·gen·cy** *n.* **—ur·gent·ly** *adv.*

u·ric ac·id /ˈyo͝orik/ ▶*n. Biochem.* an almost insoluble compound which is a breakdown product of nitrogenous metabolism. **—u·rate** /ˈyo͝orˌāt/ *n.*

u·ri·nal /ˈyo͝orənl/ ▶*n.* a bowl or other receptacle, typically attached to a wall in a public toilet, into which men may urinate.

u·ri·nar·y /ˈyo͝orəˌnerē/ ▶*adj.* of or relating to urine. ■ of, relating to, or denoting the system of organs, structures, and ducts by which urine is produced and discharged, in mammals comprising the kidneys, ureters, bladder, and urethra.

u·ri·nate /ˈyo͝orəˌnāt/ ▶*v.* [*intr.*] discharge urine; pass water. **—u·ri·na·tion** /ˌyo͝orəˈnāSHən/ *n.*

u·rine /ˈyo͝orən/ ▶*n.* a watery, typically yellowish fluid stored in the bladder and discharged through the urethra.

URL ▶*abbr. Comput.* uniform (or universal) resource locator, the address of a World Wide Web page.

urn /ərn/ ▶*n.* **1** a tall, rounded vase with a base, and often a stem, esp. one used for storing the ashes of a cremated person. **2** a large metal container with a tap, in which tea or coffee is made and kept hot, or water for making such drinks is boiled: *a tea urn.*

u·ro·gen·i·tal /ˌyo͞orō'jenətl; ˌyoͦōrə-/ ▶*adj.* of, relating to, or denoting both the urinary and genital organs.

u·rol·o·gy /yoͦō'räləjē/ ▶*n.* the branch of medicine and physiology concerned with the function and disorders of the urinary system. —**u·ro·log·ic** /ˌyoͦōrə'läjik/ *adj.* —**u·ro·log·i·cal** *adj.* —**u·rol·o·gist** /-jist/ *n.*

Ur·sa Ma·jor /'ərsə 'mäjər/ *Astron.* ▶one of the largest and most prominent northern constellations (the Great Bear). The seven brightest stars are known by various names (esp. the Big Dipper and the Plow) and include the Pointers.

Ur·sa Mi·nor /'ərsə 'mīnər/ *Astron.* ▶a northern constellation (the Little Bear) that contains the north celestial pole and the polar star Polaris. The brightest stars form what is also known as the Little Dipper.

ur·sine /'ər,sīn; -,sēn/ ▶*adj.* of, relating to, or resembling bears. ▷mid 16th cent.: from Latin *ursinus,* from *ursus* 'bear.'

ur·ti·car·i·a /ˌərti'ke(ə)rēə/ ▶*n. Med.* a rash of round, red welts on the skin that itch intensely, sometimes with dangerous swelling, caused by an allergic reaction, typically to specific foods. Also called HIVES.

us /əs/ ▶*pron.* [first person pl.] **1** used by a speaker to refer to himself or herself and one or more other people as the object of a verb or preposition: *let us know* | *both of us.* Compare with WE. ■ used after the verb "to be" and after "than" or "as": *it's us or them.* ■ *inf.* to or for ourselves: *we got us some good hunting.* **2** *inf.* me: *give us a kiss.*

us·a·ble /'yoͦōzəbəl/ (also **use·a·ble**) ▶*adj.* able or fit to be used: *usable information.* —**us·a·bil·i·ty** /ˌyoͦōzə'bilətē/ *n.*

U.S.A.F. (also **USAF**) ▶*abbr.* United States Air Force.

us·age /'yoͦōsij; -zij/ ▶*n.* the action of using something or the fact of being used: *a survey of water usage* | *the usage of equipment.* ■ the way in which a word or phrase is normally and correctly used. ■ habitual or customary practice, esp. as creating a right, obligation, or standard.

USB ▶*abbr. Comput.* universal serial bus, a connection technology for attaching peripheral devices to a computer, providing fast data exchange.

USB flash drive ▶*n. Comput.* an external flash drive, small enough to carry on a key ring, that can be used with any computer with a USB port.

U.S.C.G. (also **USCG**) ▶*abbr.* United States Coast Guard.

use ▶*v.* **1** /yoͦōz/ [tr.] take, hold, or deploy (something) as a means of accomplishing a purpose or achieving a result; employ: *she used her key to open the front door* | *the poem uses simple language.* ■ take or consume (an amount) from a limited supply of something: *we have used all the available funds.* ■ exploit (a person or situation) for one's own advantage: *I couldn't help feeling that she was using me.* ■ [tr.] treat (someone) in a particular way: *use your troops well and they will not let you down.* ■ apply (a name or title) to oneself: *she still used her maiden name professionally.* ■ **(one could use)** *inf.* one would like or benefit from: *I could use another cup of coffee.* ■ *inf.* take (an illegal drug): *they were using heroin daily* | [intr.] *had she been using again?* **2** /yoͦōst/ [in past] **(used to)** describing an action or state of affairs that was done repeatedly or existed for a period in the past: *this road used to be a dirt track* | *I used to give him lifts home.* **3** /yoͦōst/ **(be/get used to)** be or become familiar with someone or something through experience: *she was used to getting what she wanted* | *he's weird, but you just have to get used to him.*

▶*n.* /yoͦōs/ the action of using something or the state of being used for some purpose: *a member of staff is present when the pool is in use* | *theater owners were charging too much for the use of their venues.* ■ the ability or power to exercise or manipulate something, esp. one's mind or body: *the horse lost the use of his hind legs.* ■ a purpose for or way in which something can be used: *the herb has various culinary uses.* ■ the value or advantage of something: *it was no use trying to persuade her* | *what's the use of crying?* ■ the action of taking or habitual consumption of a drug.

use·ful /'yoͦōsfəl/ ▶*adj.* able to be used for a practical purpose or in several ways. —**use·ful·ly** *adv.* —**use·ful·ness** *n.*

use·less /'yoͦōsləs/ ▶*adj.* not fulfilling or not expected to achieve the intended purpose or desired outcome: *a piece of useless knowledge* | *we tried to pacify him, but it was useless.* ■ *inf.* having no ability or skill in a specified activity or area. —**use·less·ly** *adv.* —**use·less·ness** *n.*

us·er /'yoͦōzər/ ▶*n.* a person who uses or operates something, esp. a computer or other machine. ■ a person who takes illegal drugs; a drug user: *the drug causes long-term brain damage in users* | *a heroin user.* ■ a person who manipulates others for their own gain: *he was a gifted user of other people.*

us·er-friend·ly ▶*adj.* (of a machine or system) easy to use or understand: *the search software is user-friendly.* —**us·er-friend·li·ness** *n.*

ush·er /'əsHər/ ▶*n.* a person who shows people to their seats, esp. in a theater or at a wedding. ■ an official in a court whose duties include swearing in jurors and witnesses and keeping order.

▶*v.* [tr.] show or guide (someone) somewhere. ■ *fig.* cause or mark the start of (something new): *the railroads ushered in an era of cheap mass travel.*

U.S.M.C. (also **USMC**) ▶*abbr.* ■ United States Marine Corps.

U.S.N. (also **USN**) ▶*abbr.* United States Navy.

USO ▶*abbr.* ■ United Service Organizations.

USPS (also **U.S.P.S.**) ▶*abbr.* ■ United States Postal Service.

U.S.S. (also **USS**) ▶*abbr.* United States Ship, used in the names of ships in the U.S. Navy: *the U.S.S. Maine was launched in 1895.*

usu. ▶*abbr.* ■ usual; usually.

u·su·al /'yoͦōZHoͦoəl/ ▶*adj.* habitually or typically occurring or done; customary: *their room was a shambles as usual.*

▶*n.* **(the/one's usual)** *inf.* the drink someone habitually orders or prefers. ■ the thing that is typically done or present: *it's a nice change from the usual.* —**u·su·al·ly** *adv.* —**u·su·al·ness** *n.*

u·surp /yoͦō'sərp/ ▶*v.* [tr.] take (a position of power or importance) illegally or by force: *Richard usurped the throne.* ■ take the place of (someone in a position of power) illegally: supplant: *the Hanovers had usurped the Stuarts.* —**u·sur·pa·tion** /ˌyoͦōsər'pāsHən/ *n.* —**u·surp·er** *n.*

u·su·ry /'yoͦōZH(ə)rē/ ▶*n.* the illegal action or practice of lending money at unreasonably high rates of interest. ■ *archaic* interest at such rates. —**un·su·rer** *n.*

UT ▶*abbr.* Universal Time.

u·tah·rap·tor /'yoͦō,tô,raptər; -,tä-/ ▶*n.* a large carnivorous bipedal dinosaur (genus *Utahraptor,* family Dromaeosauridae), the remains of which were discovered in Utah in 1992.

Ute /yoͦōt/ ▶*n.* (pl. same or **Utes**) **1** a member of an American Indian people living chiefly in Colorado and Utah. **2** the Uto-Aztecan language of this people.

u·ten·sil /yoͦō'tensəl/ ▶*n.* an implement, container, or other article, esp. for household use.

u·ter·ine /'yoͦōtərin; -,rīn/ ▶*adj.* of or relating to the uterus or womb: *uterine contractions.* ■ born of the same mother but not having the same father: *a uterine sister.*

u·ter·us /'yoͦōtərəs/ ▶*n.* (pl. **u·ter·i** /'yoͦōtə,rī; -,rē/) the organ in the lower body of a woman or female mammal where offspring are conceived and in which they gestate before birth; the womb.

u·til·i·tar·i·an /yoͦō,tili'te(ə)rēən/ ▶*adj.* designed to be useful or practical rather than attractive.

u·til·i·tar·i·an·ism /yoͦō,tilə'te(ə)rēə,nizəm/ ▶*n.* the doctrine that actions are right if they are useful or for the benefit of a majority. ■ the doctrine that an action is right insofar as it promotes happiness, and that the greatest happiness of the greatest number should be the guiding principle of conduct.

u·til·i·ty /yoͦō'tilətē/ ▶*n.* (pl. **-ties**) **1** the state of being useful, profitable, or beneficial: *he had a poor opinion of the utility of book learning.* ■ (in game theory or economics) a measure of that which is sought to be maximized in any situation involving a choice. **2** a public utility. ■ stocks and bonds in public utilities. **3** *Comput.* a utility program.

▶*adj.* **1** useful, esp. through being able to perform several functions: *a utility truck.* **2** functional rather than attractive: *utility clothing.* **3** of or relating to the lowest U.S. government grade of beef.

u·ti·lize /'yoͦōtl,īz/ ▶*v.* [tr.] make practical and effective use of: *vitamin C helps your body utilize the iron present in your diet.* —**u·ti·liz·a·ble** /ˌyoͦōtl-'īzəbəl; 'yoͦōtl,ī-/ *adj.* —**u·ti·li·za·tion** /ˌyoͦōtl-ə'zāsHən/ *n.* —**u·ti·liz·er** *n.*

ut·most /'ət,mōst/ ▶*adj.* most extreme; greatest: *a matter of the utmost importance.*

▶*n.* **(the utmost)** the greatest or most extreme extent or amount: *a plot that stretches credulity to the utmost.*

U·to·pi·a /yoͦō'tōpēə/ (also **u·to·pi·a**) ▶*n.* an imagined place or state of things in which everything is perfect. ▷based on Greek *ou* 'not' + *topos* 'place.'

U·to·pi·an /yoͦō'tōpēən/ (also **u·to·pi·an**) ▶*adj.* modeled on or aiming for a state in which everything is perfect; idealistic.

▶*n.* an idealistic reformer. —**U·to·pi·an·ism** /-,nizəm/ *n.*

ut·ter¹ /'ətər/ ▶*adj.* complete; absolute: *Charles stared at her in utter amazement.* —**ut·ter·ly** *adv.* *he looked utterly ridiculous.* .

ut·ter² ▶*v.* [tr.] make (a sound) with one's voice: *he uttered an exasperated* *snort.* ■ say (something) aloud: *they are busily scribbling down every word she utters.* —**ut·ter·a·ble** *adj.* —**ut·ter·er** *n.*

ut·ter·ance /'ətərəns/ ▶ *n.* a spoken word, statement, or vocal sound. ■ the action of saying or expressing something aloud: *the simple utterance of a few platitudes.* ■ *Linguistics* an uninterrupted chain of spoken or written language.

ut·ter·most /'ətər,mōst/ ▶ *adj.* & *n.* another term for UTMOST.

U-turn ▶ *n.* the turning of a vehicle in a U-shaped course so as to face in the opposite direction. ■ *fig.* a change of plan, esp. a reversal of political policy: *another U-turn by the government.*

UV ▶ *abbr.* ultraviolet.

u·ve·a /'yōōvēə/ ▶ *n.* the pigmented layer of the eye, lying beneath the sclera and cornea, and comprising the iris, choroid, and ciliary body. —**u·ve·al** *adj.*

u·vu·la /'yōōvyələ/ ▶ *n.* (*pl.* **-lae** /-,lē; -,līi/) *Anat.* a fleshy extension at the back of the soft palate that hangs above the throat. ■ a similar fleshy hanging structure in any organ of the body, particularly one at the opening of the bladder.

u·vu·lar /'yōōvyələr/ ▶ *adj.* **1** *Phonet.* (of a sound) articulated with the back of the tongue and the uvula, as *r* in French and *q* in Arabic. **2** *Anat.* of or relating to the uvula.

ux·o·ri·al /,ək'sôrēəl; əg'zôr-/ ▶ *adj.* of or relating to a wife.

ux·o·ri·ous /,ək'sôrēəs; ,əg'zôr-/ ▶ *adj.* having or showing an excessive or submissive fondness for one's wife. —**ux·o·ri·ous·ly** *adv.* —**ux·o·ri·ous·ness** *n.*

Vv

V¹ /vē/ (also **v**) ▸*n.* (*pl.* **Vs** or **V's**) **1** the twenty-second letter of the alphabet. ■ denoting the next after U in a set of items, categories, etc. **2** (also **vee**) a shape like that of a letter V: [in *comb.*] *deep, V-shaped valleys.* ■ [as *adj.*] denoting an internal combustion engine with a number of cylinders arranged in two rows at an angle to each other in a V-shape: *a V-engine.* **3** the Roman numeral for five.

V² ▸*abbr.* ■ volt(s).
▸*symb.* ■ the chemical element vanadium. ■ voltage or potential difference: $V = IR$. ■ (in mathematical formulae) volume: $pV = nRT$.

v. ▸*abbr.* ■ *Gram.* verb. ■ (in textual references) verse. ■ verso. ■ versus. ■ very. ■ (in textual references) vide.
▸*symb.* velocity.

VA ▸*abbr.* Veterans Affairs (formerly Veterans Administration).

va·can·cy /'vākənsē/ ▸*n.* (*pl.* **-cies**) **1** an unoccupied position or job: *a vacancy for a shorthand typist.* ■ an available room in a hotel or other establishment providing accommodations. **2** empty space: *Cathy stared into vacancy, seeing nothing.* ■ emptiness of mind; lack of intelligence or understanding: *vacancy, vanity, and inane deception.*

va·cant /'vākənt/ ▸*adj.* (of premises) having no fixtures, furniture, or inhabitants; empty. ■ (of a position or office) not filled: *the post was left vacant.* ■ (of a person or their expression) having or showing no intelligence or interest: *a vacant stare.* —**va·cant·ly** *adv.*

va·cate /'vā,kāt/ ▸*v.* [*tr.*] **1** leave (a place that one previously occupied): *rooms must be vacated by noon.* ■ give up (a position or office): *he will vacate a job in government sales.* **2** *Law* cancel or annul (a judgment, contract, or charge).

va·ca·tion /vā'kāSHən; və-/ ▸*n.* **1** an extended period of recreation, esp. one spent away from home or in traveling: *people come here on vacation* ■ a fixed holiday period between terms in schools and law courts. **2** the action of leaving something one previously occupied: *his marriage was the reason for the vacation of his fellowship.*
▸*v.* [*intr.*] take a vacation: *vacationing in Europe.* —**va·ca·tion·er** *n.*

vac·ci·nate /'vaksə,nāt/ ▸*v.* [*tr.*] treat with a vaccine to produce immunity against a disease; inoculate: *all the children were **vaccinated against** diphtheria.* —**vac·ci·na·tion** /,vaksə'nāSHən/ *n.* —**vac·ci·na·tor** *n.*

vac·cine /vak'sēn/ ▸*n.* *Med.* a substance used to stimulate the production of antibodies and provide immunity against one or several diseases. ■ *Comput.* a program designed to detect computer viruses, and inactivate them. ▷late 18th cent.: from Latin *vaccinus,* from *vacca* 'cow' (because of the early use of the cowpox virus against smallpox).

vac·il·late /'vasə,lāt/ ▸*v.* [*intr.*] alternate or waver between different opinions or actions; be indecisive: *vacillated between teaching and journalism.* —**vac·il·la·tion** /,vasə'lāSHən/ *n.* —**vac·il·la·tor** *n.*

vac·u·a /'vakyəwə/ ▸ plural form of VACUUM.

vac·u·ole /'vakyŌ͞o,ōl/ ▸*n.* *Biol.* a space or vesicle within the cytoplasm of a cell, enclosed by a membrane and typically containing fluid. —**vac·u·o·lar** /,vakyŌ͞o'ōlər; 'vakyŌ͞oōələr/ *adj.* —**vac·u·o·la·tion** /,vakyŌ͞oə'lāSHən/ *n.*

vac·u·ous /'vakyəwəs/ ▸*adj.* having or showing a lack of thought or intelligence; mindless: *a vacuous smile* | *vacuous slogans.* ■ *archaic* empty. —**va·cu·i·ty** /va'kyŌ͞oətē; və-/ *n.* —**vac·u·ous·ly** *adv.* —**vac·u·ous·ness** *n.*

vac·u·um /'vak,yŌ͞o(ə)m; -yəm/ ▸*n.* (*pl.* **-u·ums** or **-u·a** /-yŌ͞oə/) **1** a space entirely devoid of matter. ■ a space or container from which the air has been completely or partly removed. ■ a gap left by the loss, death, or departure of someone or something formerly playing a significant part in a situation or activity: *the political vacuum left by the death of the Emperor.* **2** (*pl.* **-u·ums**) a vacuum cleaner.
▸*v.* [*tr.*] clean with a vacuum cleaner: *the room needs to be vacuumed.*
▸ □ **in a vacuum** (of an activity or a problem to be considered) isolated from the context normal to it and in which it can best be understood or assessed.

vac·u·um clean·er ▸*n.* an electrical apparatus that by means of suction collects dust and small particles from floors and other surfaces.

vac·u·um-pack ▸*v.* [*tr.*] seal (a product) in packaging after any air has been removed so that the packaging is tight and firm: *it is quickly vacuum-packed in foil pouches to ensure freshness.*

vac·u·um tube ▸*n.* an electron tube containing a near-vacuum that allows the free passage of electric current.

vag·a·bond /'vagə,bänd/ ▸*n.* a person who wanders from place to place without a home or job. ■ *inf., dated* a rascal; a rogue.
▸*adj.* having no settled home. —**vag·a·bond·age** /-dij/ *n.*

va·gar·y /'vāgərē/ ▸*n.* (*pl.* **-gar·ies**) (usu. **vagaries**) an unexpected and inexplicable change in a situation or in someone's behavior.

va·gi·na /və'jīnə/ ▸*n.* (*pl.* **-nas** or **-nae** /-nē; -nī/) the muscular tube leading from the external genitals to the cervix of the uterus in women and most other female mammals. —**vag·i·nal** /'vajənl/ *adj.*

vag·i·ni·tis /,vajə'nītis/ *n.* inflammation of the vagina.

va·grant /'vāgrənt/ ▸*n.* a person without a settled home or regular work who wanders from place to place and lives by begging. ■ *archaic* a wanderer. ■ *Ornithol.* a bird that has strayed or been blown from its usual range or migratory route. Also called ACCIDENTAL.
▸*adj.* characteristic of, relating to, or living the life of a vagrant: *vagrant beggars.* ■ moving from place to place; wandering: *vagrant whales.* ■ *poetic/lit.* moving or occurring unpredictably; inconstant: *the vagrant heart of my mother.* —**va·gran·cy** /-grənsē/ *n.* —**va·grant·ly** *adv.*

vague /vāg/ ▸*adj.* of uncertain, indefinite, or unclear character or meaning: *many patients suffer vague symptoms.* ■ thinking or communicating in an unfocused or imprecise way: *he had been very vague about his activities.* —**vague·ly** *adv.* —**vague·ness** *n.* —**vagu·ish** *adj.*

vain /vān/ ▸*adj.* **1** having or showing an excessively high opinion of one's appearance, abilities, or worth: *their flattery made him vain.* **2** producing no result; useless: *a vain attempt to tidy up the room.* ■ having no meaning or likelihood of fulfillment: *a vain boast.* ▷Middle English (in the sense 'devoid of real worth'): via Old French from Latin *vanus* 'empty, without substance.' —**vain·ly** *adv.*
▸ □ **in vain** without success or a result: *they waited in vain for a response.* □ **take someone's name in vain** use someone's name in a way that shows a lack of respect.

vain·glo·ry /'vān,glôrē; ,vān'glôrē/ ▸*n.* *poetic/lit.* inordinate pride in oneself or one's achievements; excessive vanity. —**vain·glo·ri·ous** /,vān'glôrēəs/ *adj.* —**vain·glo·ri·ous·ly** *adv.* —**vain·glo·ri·ous·ness** *n.*

val·ance /'valəns/ ▸*n.* a length of decorative drapery attached to the canopy or frame of a bed in order to screen the structure or the space beneath it. ■ a length of decorative drapery hung above a window to screen the curtain fittings. ■ a lighting fixture extending along the top of an interior wall and providing indirect light. —**val·anced** *adj.*

vale /vāl/ ▸*n.* a valley (used in place names or as a poetic term).

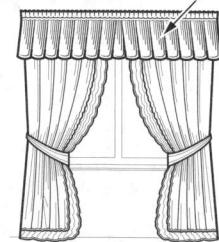

valance

▶ □ **vale of tears** *poetic/lit.* the world regarded as a scene of trouble or sorrow.

val·e·dic·tion /ˌvaləˈdiksHən/ ▶n. the action of saying farewell: *he spread his palm in valediction.* ■ a statement or address made at or as a farewell.

val·e·dic·to·ri·an /ˌvaləˌdikˈtôrēən/ ▶n. a student, typically having the highest academic achievements of the class, who delivers the valedictory at a graduation ceremony. Compare with **SALUTATORIAN**.

val·e·dic·to·ry /ˌvaləˈdikt(ə)rē/ ▶adj. serving as a farewell: *a valedictory wave.*
▶n. (pl. **-ries**) a farewell address.

va·lence /ˈvāləns/ ▶n. *Chem.* the combining power of an element, esp. as measured by the number of hydrogen atoms it can displace or combine with: *carbon always has a valence of 4.* ■ [as adj.] relating to or denoting electrons involved in or available for chemical bond formation: *molecules with unpaired valence electrons.*

val·en·tine /ˈvalənˌtīn/ ▶n. a card sent on St. Valentine's Day (February 14) to a person one loves or is attracted to. ■ a person to whom one sends such a card or whom one asks to be one's sweetheart.

va·le·ri·an /vəˈli(ə)rēən/ ▶n. a plant (family Valerianaceae) that typically bears clusters of small pink or white flowers. Native to Eurasia, several species have been introduced to North America. Its several species include the **common valerian** (*Valeriana officinalis*), a valued medicinal herb. ■ a drug obtained from the root of common valerian, used as a sedative and antispasmodic.

val·et /vaˈlā; ˈvalā; ˈvalit/ ▶n. **1** a man's personal male attendant, responsible for his clothes and appearance. ■ a hotel employee performing such duties for guests. ■ a rack or stand on which to hang clothing. **2** a person employed to park cars.
▶v. (**-eted, -et·ing**) [tr.] act as a valet to (a particular man). ■ [intr.] work as a valet.

Val·hal·la /valˈhalə; välˈhälə/ *Scandinavian Mythol.* ▶a hall in which heroes killed in battle were believed to feast with Odin for eternity.

val·iant /ˈvalyənt/ ▶adj. possessing or showing courage or determination: *she made a valiant effort to hold her anger in check.* —**val·iant·ly** adv.

val·id /ˈvalid/ ▶adj. actually supporting the intended point or claim; acceptable as cogent: *a valid criticism.* ■ legally binding due to having been executed in compliance with the law: *a valid contract.* ■ legally acceptable: *the visas are valid for thirty days.* —**va·lid·i·ty** /vəˈlidətē/ n. —**val·id·ly** adv.

val·i·date /ˈvaləˌdāt/ ▶v. [tr.] check or prove the validity or accuracy of (something): *these estimates have been validated by periodic surveys.* ■ demonstrate or support the truth or value of: *in a healthy family a child's feelings are validated.* ■ make or declare legally valid. —**val·i·da·tion** /ˌvaləˈdāsHən/ n.

va·lise /vəˈlēs/ ▶n. a small traveling bag or suitcase.

Val·i·um /ˈvalēəm/ ▶n. trademark for **DIAZEPAM**.

Val·kyr·ie /valˈki(ə)rē; ˈvalkərē/ ▶n. *Scandinavian Mythol.* each of Odin's twelve handmaidens who conducted the slain warriors of their choice from the battlefield to Valhalla.

val·ley /ˈvalē/ ▶n. (pl. **-leys**) **1** a low area of land between hills or mountains, typically with a river or stream flowing through it. **2** *Archit.* an internal angle formed by the intersecting planes of a roof, or by the slope of a roof and a wall.

val·or /ˈvalər/ (*Brit.* **val·our**) ▶n. great courage in the face of danger, esp. in battle: *the medals are awarded for acts of valor.* —**val·or·ous** /-ərəs/ adj.

val·u·a·ble /ˈvaly(oō)əbəl/ ▶adj. worth a great deal of money: *a valuable antique.* ■ extremely useful or important: *my time is valuable.*
▶n. (usu. **valuables**) a thing that is of great worth, esp. a small item of personal property: *put all your valuables in the hotel safe.* —**val·u·a·bly** /-blē/ adv.

val·u·a·tion /ˌvalyoōˈāsHən/ ▶n. an estimation of something's worth, esp. one carried out by a professional appraiser: *it is wise to obtain an independent valuation.* ■ the monetary worth of something, esp. as estimated by an appraiser. —**val·u·ate** /ˈvalyoōˌāt/ v. —**val·u·a·tor** n.

val·ue /ˈvalyoō/ ▶n. **1** the regard that something is held to deserve; the importance or preciousness of something: *your support is of great value.* ■ the material or monetary worth of something: *prints seldom rise in value.* ■ the worth of something compared to the price paid or asked for it: *the book is a good value.* ■ the usefulness of something considered in respect of a particular purpose: *some new drugs are of great value in treating cancer.* ■ the relative rank, importance, or power of a playing card, chess piece, etc., according to the rules of the game. **2** (**values**) a person's principles or standards of behavior; one's judgment of what is important in life: *they internalize their parents' rules and values.* **3** the numerical amount denoted by an algebraic term; a magnitude,

quantity, or number: *an accurate value for the mass of Venus.* **4** *Mus.* the relative duration of the sound signified by a note. **5** *Linguistics* the quality or tone of a spoken sound; the sound represented by a letter. **6** *Art* the relative degree of lightness or darkness of a particular color.
▶v. (**-ues, -ued, -u·ing**) [tr.] **1** (often **be valued**) estimate the monetary worth of (something): *his estate was valued at $45,000.* **2** consider (someone or something) to be important or beneficial; have a high opinion of: [as adj.] (**valued**) *a valued friend.*

val·ue-add·ed tax (abbr.: **VAT**) ▶n. a tax on the amount by which the value of an article has been increased at each stage of its production or distribution.

val·ue judg·ment /ˈvalyoō ˌjəjmənt/ ▶n. an assessment of something as good or bad in terms of one's standards or priorities.

va·lu·ta /vəˈloōtə/ ▶n. the value of one currency with respect to its exchange rate with another. ■ foreign currency: *these internal flights supply valuta to the cash-starved confederation.*

valve /valv/ ▶n. a device for controlling the passage of fluid through a pipe or duct. ■ an automatic device allowing flow in one direction only. ■ *Mus.* a cylindrical mechanism in a brass instrument that, when depressed or turned, admits air into different sections of tubing and so extends the range of available notes.

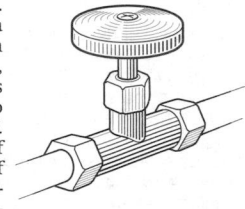
valve

■ *Anat. & Zool.* a membranous fold in a hollow organ or tubular structure, such as a blood vessel or the digestive tract, that maintains the flow of the contents in one direction by closing in response to any pressure from reverse flow. ■ *Zool.* each of the halves of the hinged shell of a bivalve mollusk or brachiopod, or of the parts of the compound shell of a barnacle. —**valved** adj. [in comb.] *a two-valved outer covering* —**valve·less** adj.

val·vu·lar /ˈvalvyələr/ ▶adj. relating to, having, or acting as a valve or valves: *valvular heart disease.*

va·moose /vaˈmoōs; və-/ ▶v. [intr.] *inf.* depart hurriedly: *we'd better vamoose before we're caught.*

vamp¹ /vamp/ ▶n. **1** the upper front part of a boot or shoe. **2** (in jazz and popular music) a short, simple introductory passage, usually repeated until otherwise instructed.
▶v. **1** [tr.] attach a new upper to (a boot or shoe). ■ (**vamp something up**) *inf.* repair or improve something: *the production values have been vamped up.* **2** [intr.] repeat a short, simple passage of music.

vamp² ▶n. a woman who uses sexual attraction to exploit men.
▶v. [tr.] **1** blatantly set out to attract: *she had not vamped him like some wicked Jezebel.* **2** (in fiction) turn (someone) into a vampire. —**vamp·ish** adj. —**vamp·ish·ly** adv. —**vamp·y** adj.

vam·pire /ˈvamˌpī(ə)r/ ▶n. **1** a corpse supposed, in European folklore, to leave its grave at night to drink the blood of the living by biting their necks with long pointed canine teeth. ■ *fig.* a person who preys ruthlessly on others. **2** (also **vampire bat**) a small bat (family Desmodontidae) that feeds on the blood of mammals or birds using its two sharp incisor teeth and anticoagulant saliva, found mainly in tropical America. —**vam·pir·ic** /vamˈpirik/ adj. —**vam·pir·ism** n.

van¹ /van/ ▶n. a covered boxlike motor vehicle, typically having a rear door and sliding doors on the side panels, used for transporting goods or people. ■ a covered truck used for moving goods, esp. furniture.

van² ▶n. (**the van**) the foremost part of a company of people moving or preparing to move forward, esp. the foremost division of an advancing military force: *in the van were the foremost chiefs and some of the warriors astride horses.* ■ *fig.* the forefront: *he was in the van of the movement.*

va·na·di·um /vəˈnādēəm/ ▶n. the chemical element of atomic number 23, a hard gray metal of the transition series, used to make alloy steels. (Symbol: **V**)

Van Al·len belt ▶n. each of two regions of intense radiation partly surrounding the earth at heights of several thousand kilometers.

van·dal /ˈvandl/ ▶n. **1** a person who deliberately destroys or damages public or private property: *the rear window was smashed by vandals.* **2** (**Vandal**) a member of a Germanic people that ravaged Gaul, Spain, and North Africa in the 4th–5th centuries and sacked Rome in AD 455.

van·dal·ism /ˈvandlˌizəm/ ▶n. action involving deliberate destruction of or damage to public or private property. —**van·dal·is·tic** /ˌvandlˈistik/ adj. —**van·dal·is·ti·cal·ly** /ˌvandlˈistik(ə)lē/ adv.

van·dal·ize /ˈvandlˌīz/ ▶v. [tr.] deliberately destroy or damage (public or private property).

Van·dyke (also **van·dyke**) ▶n. **1** a broad lace or linen collar with an edge deeply cut into large points, fashionable in the 18th century. **2** (also **Vandyke beard**) a neat, pointed beard.

vane /vān/ ▸*n.* a broad blade attached to a rotating axis or wheel that pushes or is pushed by wind or water and forms part of a machine or device such as a windmill, propeller, or turbine. ■ a broad, flat projecting surface designed to guide the motion of a projectile, such as a feather on an arrow or a fin on a torpedo. ▷late Middle English: dialect variant of obsolete *fane* 'banner,' of Germanic origin. —**vaned** *adj.* [usu. in *comb.*] *a three-vaned windmill.*

van·guard /'van,gärd/ ▸*n.* a group of people leading the way in new developments or ideas: *the modernist vanguard.* ■ a position at the forefront of new developments or ideas: *the prototype was in the vanguard of technical development.* ■ the foremost part of an advancing army or naval force. —**van·guard·ism** *n.* —**van·guard·ist** *n.*

va·nil·la /və'nilə/ ▸*n.* **1** a substance obtained from vanilla beans or produced artificially and used to flavor sweet foods or to impart a fragrant scent to cosmetic preparations: [as *adj.*] *vanilla ice cream.* ■ ice cream flavored with vanilla: *a scoop of vanilla.* **2** a tropical climbing orchid (genus *Vanilla*) that has fragrant flowers and long podlike fruit. Its many species include *V. planifolia,* the chief commercial source of vanilla beans. ■ (also **vanilla bean** or **vanilla pod**) the fruit of this plant, which is cured and then either used in cooking or processed to extract an essence that is used for flavor and fragrance.
▸*adj.* having no special or extra features; ordinary: *vanilla sex.*

va·nil·lin /və'nilin; 'vanl-/ ▸*n. Chem.* a fragrant aldehyde that is the essential constituent of vanilla.

van·ish /'vanisH/ ▸*v.* [*intr.*] **1** disappear suddenly and completely: *Mary vanished without a trace.* ■ gradually cease to exist: *the days of the extended family are vanishing.* **2** *Math.* become zero.

van·ish·ing point ▸*n.* **1** the point at which receding parallel lines viewed in perspective appear to converge. **2** the point at which something that has been growing smaller or increasingly faint disappears altogether: *custody fees have dropped close to the vanishing point.*

van·i·ty /'vanətē/ ▸*n.* (*pl.* **-ties**) **1** excessive pride in or admiration of one's own appearance or achievements: *it flattered his vanity to think I was in love with him.* ■ [as *adj.*] denoting a person or company that publishes works at the author's expense: *a vanity press.* **2** the quality of being worthless or futile: *the vanity of human wishes.* **3** a dressing table. ■ a bathroom unit consisting of a washbasin typically set into a counter with a cabinet beneath.

van·quish /'vaNGkwish/ ▸*v.* [*tr.*] defeat thoroughly: *Mexican forces vanquished the French army in a battle in Puebla.* —**van·quish·er** *n.*

van·tage /'vantij/ ▸*n.* (usu. **vantage point**) ▸*n.* a place or position affording a good view of something: *from my vantage point I could see into the front garden* | *fig. from the vantage point of the present.*

vap·id /'vapid/ ▸*adj.* offering nothing that is stimulating or challenging: *tuneful but vapid musical comedies.* —**va·pid·i·ty** /va'pidətē/ *n.* —**vap·id·ly** *adv.*

va·por /'vāpər/ (*Brit.* **va·pour**) ▸*n.* a substance diffused or suspended in the air, esp. one normally liquid or solid: *dense clouds of smoke and toxic vapor.* ■ *Physics* a gaseous substance that is below its critical temperature, and can therefore be liquefied by pressure alone.
▸*v.* [*intr.*] talk in a vacuous, boasting, or pompous way: *he was vaporing on about the days of his youth.* —**va·por·ous** /'vāpərəs/ *adj.* —**va·por·ous·ness** *n.* —**va·por·y** *adj.*

va·por·ize /'vāpə,rīz/ ▸*v.* convert or be converted into vapor: [*intr.*] *cold gasoline does not vaporize readily.* —**va·por·iz·a·ble** *adj.* —**va·por·i·za·tion** /,vāpərə'zāshən; -,rī'zā-/ *n.*

va·por·iz·er /'vāpə,rīzər/ ▸*n.* a device that emits a particular substance in the form of vapor, esp. for medicinal inhalation.

vapor trail ▸*n.* another term for CONTRAIL.

VAR ▸*abbr.* ■ value-added reseller, a company that adds extra features to products it has bought before selling them. ■ value at risk, a method of quantifying the risk of holding a financial asset.

var·i·a·ble /'ve(ə)rēəbəl/ ▸*adj.* **1** not consistent or having a fixed pattern; liable to change: *the quality of hospital food is highly variable.* ■ (of a wind) tending to change direction. ■ *Math.* (of a quantity) able to assume different numerical values. ■ *Bot. & Zool.* (of a species) liable to deviate from the typical color or form, or to occur in different colors or forms. **2** able to be changed or adapted: *the drill has variable speed.* ■ (of a gear) designed to give varying ratios or speeds.
▸*n.* an element, feature, or factor that is liable to vary or change: *there are too many variables involved to make any meaningful predictions.* ■ *Math.* a quantity that during a calculation is assumed to vary or be capable of varying in value. ■ *Comput.* a data item that may take on more than one value within or between programs. ■ *Astron.* short for VARIABLE

STAR. ■ (**variables**) the region of light, variable winds to the north of the northeast trade winds or (in the southern hemisphere) between the southeast trade winds and the westerlies. —**var·i·a·bil·i·ty** /,ve(ə)rēə'bilitē/ *n.* —**var·i·a·ble·ness** *n.* —**var·i·a·bly** /-blē/ *adv.*

var·i·a·ble-rate mort·gage ▸*n.* another term for ADJUSTABLE RATE MORTGAGE.

var·i·a·ble star ▸*n.* *Astron.* a star whose brightness changes, either irregularly or regularly.

var·i·ance /'ve(ə)rēəns/ ▸*n.* the fact or quality of being different, divergent, or inconsistent: *her light tone was at variance with her sudden trembling.* ■ the state or fact of disagreeing or quarreling: *they were at variance with all their previous allies.* ■ *chiefly Law* a discrepancy between two statements or documents. ■ *Law* an official dispensation from a rule or regulation, typically a building regulation. ■ *Statistics* a quantity equal to the square of the standard deviation. ■ (in accounting) the difference between expected and actual costs, profits, output, etc., in a statistical analysis.

var·i·ant /'ve(ə)rēənt/ ▸*n.* a form or version of something that differs in some respect from other forms of the same thing or from a standard: *clinically distinct variants of malaria* | [as *adj.*] *a variant spelling.*

var·i·a·tion /,ve(ə)rē'āshən/ ▸*n.* **1** a change or difference in condition, amount, or level, typically with certain limits: *regional variations in house prices.* ■ *Math.* a change in the value of a function due to small changes in the values of its argument or arguments. ■ the angular difference between true north and magnetic north at a particular place. ■ *Biol.* the occurrence of an organism in more than one distinct color or form. **2** a different or distinct form or version of something: *hurling is an Irish variation of field hockey.* ■ *Mus.* a version of a theme, modified in melody, rhythm, harmony, or ornamentation, so as to present it in a new but still recognizable form: *there is an eleven-bar theme followed by seven variations and a coda.* —**var·i·a·tion·al** /-sHənl/ *adj.*

var·i·cel·la /,ve(ə)rə'selə/ ▸*n. Med.* technical term for CHICKEN POX. ■ (also **var·i·cel·la-zos·ter** /'zästər/) a herpes virus that causes chicken pox and shingles; herpes zoster.

var·i·col·ored /'ve(ə)ri,kələrd/ (*Brit.* **var·i·col·oured**) ▸*adj.* consisting of several different colors.

var·i·cose /'varə,kōs/ ▸*adj.* affected by a condition causing the swelling and tortuous lengthening of veins, most often in the legs: *varicose veins.* —**var·i·cosed** *adj.* —**var·i·cos·i·ty** /,vari'käsitē/ *n.*

var·ied /'ve(ə)rēd/ ▸*adj.* incorporating a number of different types or elements; showing variation or variety: *a long and varied career.* —**var·ied·ly** *adv.*

var·i·e·gat·ed /'ver(ē)ə,gātid/ ▸*adj.* exhibiting different colors, esp. as irregular patches or streaks: *variegated yellow bricks.* ■ *Bot.* (of a plant or foliage) having or consisting of leaves that are edged or patterned in a second color. ■ marked by variety: *his variegated and amusing observations.* —**var·i·e·gate** *v.* —**var·i·e·ga·tion** *n.*

var·i·e·tal /və'rīətl/ ▸*adj.* (of a wine or grape) made from or belonging to a single specified variety of grape.
▸*n.* a varietal wine. —**va·ri·e·tal·ly** *adv.*

va·ri·e·ty /və'rīətē/ ▸*n.* (*pl.* **-ties**) **1** the quality or state of being different or diverse; the absence of uniformity, sameness, or monotony: *it's the variety that makes my job so enjoyable.* ■ (**a variety of**) a number or range of things of the same general class that are different or distinct in character or quality: *a variety of leisure activities.* ■ a thing that differs in some way from others of the same general class or sort; a type: *fifty varieties of fresh and frozen pasta.* ■ a form of television or theater entertainment consisting of a series of different types of acts, such as singing, dancing, and comedy: [as *adj.*] *a variety show.* **2** *Biol.* a taxonomic category that ranks below subspecies (where present) or species, its members differing from others of the same subspecies or species in minor but permanent or heritable characteristics. Compare with FORM and SUBSPECIES. ■ a cultivated form of a plant. See CULTIVAR. ■ a plant or animal that varies in some trivial respect from its immediate parent or type.

va·ri·o·la /və'rīələ; ,ve(ə)rē'ōlə/ ▸*n. Med.* technical term for SMALLPOX. —**va·ri·o·lar** /-lər/ *adj.* —**va·ri·o·lous** /-ləs/ *adj.* (*archaic*)

var·i·o·rum /,ve(ə)rē'ôrəm/ ▸*adj.* (of an edition of an author's works) having notes by various editors or commentators.
▸*n.* a variorum edition.

var·i·ous /'ve(ə)rēəs/ ▸*adj.* different from one another; of different

kinds or sorts: *dresses of various colors.* ■ having or showing different properties or qualities: *their environments are locally various.*
▶*adj. & pron.* more than one; individual and separate: [as *adj.*] *various people arrived* | [as *pron.*] *various of her friends had called.* —**var·i·ous·ly** *adv.* —**var·i·ous·ness** *n.*

var·let /ˈvärlət/ ▶*n. hist. archaic* an unprincipled rogue or rascal.

var·mint /ˈvärmənt/ ▶*n. dial., inf.* a troublesome wild animal, esp. a fox. ■ a troublesome and mischievous person, esp. a child.

var·nish /ˈvärnisʜ/ ▶*n.* resin dissolved in a liquid for applying on wood, metal, or other materials to form a hard, clear, shiny surface when dry.
▶*v.* [*tr.*] apply varnish to: *we stripped the floor and varnished it.* ■ disguise or gloss over (a fact): *the White House is varnishing over the defeat of the president's proposal.* —**var·nish·er** *n.*

var·si·ty /ˈvärsətē/ ▶*n.* (*pl.* **-ties**) a sports team representing a school or college: [as *adj.*] *girls' varsity basketball.*

var·y /ˈve(ə)rē/ ▶*v.* (**var·ies, var·ied**) [*intr.*] differ in size, amount, degree, or nature from something else of the same general class: *the properties vary in price* | [as *adj.*] (**varying**) *varying degrees of success.* ■ change from one condition, form, or state to another: *your skin's moisture content varies according to climatic conditions.* ■ [*tr.*] introduce modifications or changes into (something) so as to make it different or less uniform: *he tried to vary his diet.* —**var·y·ing·ly** *adv.*

vas /vas/ ▶*n.* (*pl.* **va·sa** /ˈvāsə; -zə/) *Anat.* a vessel or duct. ▷late 16th cent.: from Latin, literally 'vessel.'

vas·cu·lar /ˈvaskyələr/ ▶*adj. Anat., Zool., & Med.* of, relating to, affecting, or consisting of a vessel or vessels, esp. those that carry blood: *vascular disease.* ■ *Bot.* relating to or denoting the plant tissues (xylem and phloem) that conduct water, sap, and nutrients in flowering plants, ferns, and their relatives. —**vas·cu·lar·i·ty** /ˌvaskyəˈlaritē/ *n.*

vas def·er·ens /ˌvas ˈdefərenz; -ˌrenz/ ▶*n.* (*pl.* **va·sa def·er·en·ti·a** /ˌvāsə ˌdefəˈrensʜ(ē)ə; ˌvāzə/) *Anat.* the duct that conveys sperm from the testicle to the urethra.

vase /vās; vāz; väz/ ▶*n.* a decorative container, typically made of glass or china and used as an ornament or for displaying cut flowers. —**vase·ful** /-ˌfo͝ol/ *n.* (*pl.* **-fuls**) .

vas·ec·to·my /vəˈsektəmē; va-/ ▶*n.* (*pl.* **-mies**) the surgical cutting and sealing of part of each vas deferens, typically as a means of sterilization. —**va·sec·to·mize** /-ˌmīz/ *v.*

Vas·e·line /ˌvasəˈlēn; ˈvasəˌlēn/ ▶*n. trademark* a type of petroleum jelly used as an ointment and lubricant.
▶*v.* [*tr.*] cover or smear with this.

vas·o·ac·tive /ˌvāzōˈaktiv; ˌvasō-/ ▶*adj. Physiol.* affecting the diameter of blood vessels (and hence blood pressure).

vas·o·con·stric·tion /ˌvāzōkənˈstriksʜən; ˌvasō-/ ▶*n.* the constriction of blood vessels, which increases blood pressure. —**vas·o·con·stric·tive** /-ˈstriktiv/ *adj.* —**vas·o·con·stric·tor** /-ˈstriktər/ *n.*

vas·o·di·la·tion /ˌvāzōdīˈlāsʜən; ˌvasō-/ (also **vas·o·di·la·ta·tion** /-ˌdīlə-ˈtāsʜən/) ▶*n.* the dilatation of blood vessels, which decreases blood pressure. —**vas·o·di·la·tor** /-ˈdīˌlātər/ *n.* —**vas·o·dil·a·to·ry** /-ˈdīləˌtôrē/ *adj.*

vas·o·mo·tor /ˌvāzōˈmōtər; ˌvaso-/ ▶*adj.* causing or relating to the constriction or dilatation of blood vessels. ■ denoting a region in the medulla of the brain (the **vasomotor center**) that regulates blood pressure by controlling reflex alterations in the heart rate and the diameter of the blood vessels.`

vas·o·pres·sin /ˌvāzōˈpresən; ˌvasō-/ ▶*n. Biochem.* a pituitary hormone that acts to promote the retention of water by the kidneys and increase blood pressure.

vas·sal /ˈvasəl/ ▶*n. hist.* a holder of land by feudal tenure on conditions of homage and allegiance. ■ a person or country in a subordinate position to another: [as *adj.*] *a vassal state of the Chinese empire.* —**vas·sal·age** /-əlij/ *n.*

vast /vast/ ▶*adj.* of very great extent or quantity; immense: *a vast plain of buffalo grass.* —**vast·ly** *adv.* —**vast·ness** *n.* —**vast·y** *adj.*

VAT /vat/ ▶*abbr.* value added tax.

vat /vat/ ▶*n.* **1** a large tank or tub used to hold liquid, esp. in industry: *a vat of hot tar.* **2** (also **vat dye**) a water-insoluble dye, such as indigo, that is applied to a fabric in a soluble form, the color being obtained on subsequent oxidation in the fabric fibers.
▶*v.* (**vat·ted, vat·ting**) [*tr.*] (often **be vatted**) place or treat in a vat.

Vat·i·can /ˈvatikən/ ▶*n.* (usu. **the Vatican**) the palace and official residence of the pope in Rome. ■ the administrative center of the Roman Catholic Church.

vaude·ville /ˈvôd(ə)ˌvil; -vəl/ ▶*n.* a type of entertainment popular in the early 20th century, featuring a mixture of specialty acts such as

burlesque comedy and song and dance. —**vaude·vil·lian** /ˌvôd(ə)ˈvilyən; -ˈvilēən/ *adj. & n.*

vault¹ /vôlt/ ▶*n.* **1** a roof in the form of an arch or a series of arches, typical of churches and other large, formal buildings. ■ *poetic/lit.* a thing resembling an arched roof, esp. the sky: *the vault of heaven.* ■ *Anat.* the arched roof of a cavity, esp. that of the skull: *the cranial vault.* **2** a large room or chamber used for storage, esp. an underground one. ■ a secure room in a bank in which valuables are stored. ■ a chamber beneath a church or in a graveyard used for burials.
▶*v.* [*tr.*] [usu. as *adj.*] (**vaulted**) provide (a building or room) with an arched roof or roofs: *a vaulted arcade.*

vault² ▶*v.* [*intr.*] leap or spring while supporting or propelling oneself with one or both hands or with the help of a pole: *he vaulted over the gate.* ■ [*tr.*] jump over (an obstacle) in such a way.
▶*n.* an act of vaulting. —**vault·er** *n.*

vault·ing /ˈvôltiNG/ ▶*n.* **1** ornamental work in a vaulted roof or ceiling. **2** the action of vaulting as a gymnastic or athletic exercise.

vault·ing horse ▶*n.* a padded wooden block used for vaulting over by gymnasts and athletes.

vaunt /vônt; vänt/ ▶*v.* [*tr.*] [usu. as *adj.*] (**vaunted**) boast about or praise (something), esp. excessively: *the much vaunted information superhighway.* —**vaunt·er** *n.* —**vaunt·ing·ly** *adv.*

VC ▶*abbr.* ■ Vice-Chairman. ■ Vice-Chancellor. ■ Vice-Consul. ■ Vietcong.

V-chip ▶*n.* a computer chip installed in a television receiver that can be programmed by the user to block or scramble material containing a special code in its signal indicating that it is deemed violent or sexually explicit.

VCR ▶*abbr.* videocassette recorder.

VD ▶*abbr.* venereal disease.

VDT ▶*abbr.* video display terminal.

've *inf.* ▶*abbr.* have (usually after the pronouns *I, you, we,* and *they*): *we've tried our best.*

veal /vēl/ ▶*n.* the flesh of a calf, used as food.

vec·tor /ˈvektər/ ▶*n.* **1** *Math. & Physics* a quantity having direction as well as magnitude, esp. as determining the position of one point in space relative to another. ■ *Math.* a matrix with one row or one column. ■ a course to be taken by an aircraft. ■ [as *adj.*] *Comput.* denoting a type of graphical representation using straight lines to construct the outlines of objects. **2** an organism, typically a biting insect or tick, that transmits a disease or parasite from one animal or plant to another. ■ *Genetics* a bacteriophage or plasmid that transfers genetic material into a cell, or from one bacterium to another. ▷mid 19th cent.: from Latin, literally 'carrier,' from *vehere* 'convey.' —**vec·tor·i·za·tion** /ˌvektərəˈzāsʜən/ *n.* —**vec·tor·ize** /-ˌrīz/ *v.*

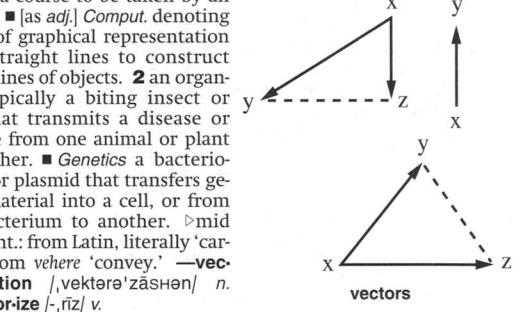

vectors

Ve·da /ˈvādə; ˈvēdə/ ▶*n.* [treated as *sing.* or *pl.*] the most ancient Hindu scriptures, written in early Sanskrit and containing hymns, philosophy, and guidance on ritual for the priests of Vedic religion.

Ve·dan·ta /vāˈdäntə; və-/ ▶*n.* a Hindu philosophy based on the doctrine of the Upanishads. —**Ve·dan·tic** /-tik/ *adj.* —**Ve·dan·tist** /-tist/ *n.*

V-E Day ▶*n.* the day (May 8) marking the Allied victory in Europe in 1945.

Ve·dic /ˈvādik; ˈvēdik/ ▶*adj.* of or relating to the Veda or Vedas.
▶*n.* the language of the Vedas, an early form of Sanskrit.

vee /vē/ ▶*n.* the letter V. ■ a thing shaped like a V: *a broken vee of birds.*

vee·jay /ˈvēˌjā/ ▶*n. inf.* a person who introduces and plays popular music videos.

veer /vi(ə)r/ ▶*v.* [*intr.*] change direction suddenly: *an oil tanker that had veered off course.* ■ *fig.* suddenly change an opinion, subject, type of behavior, etc.: *the conversation eventually veered away from theatrical things.* ■ (of the wind) change direction clockwise around the points of the compass: *the wind veered southwest.*
▶*n.* a sudden change of direction.

veg·an /ˈvēgən; ˈvejən/ ▶*n.* a person who does not eat or use animal products: *I'm a strict vegan* | [as *adj.*] *a vegan diet.*

veg·e·ta·ble /ˈvejtəbəl; ˈvejətə-/ ▶*n.* **1** a plant or part of a plant used as food, typically as accompaniment to meat or fish, such as a cabbage,

potato, carrot, or bean. **2** *inf., offens.* a person who is incapable of normal mental or physical activity, esp. through brain damage. ■ *inf.* a person with a dull or inactive life.
▶ *adj.* of or relating to vegetables as food: *a vegetable garden | vegetable soup.* ■ of or relating to plants or plant life, esp. as distinct from animal life or mineral substances: *vegetable matter.*

veg·e·ta·ble mar·row ▶ *n.* see MARROW (sense 2).

veg·e·tal /'vejətl/ ▶ *adj.* **1** *formal* of or relating to plants: *a vegetal aroma.* **2** *Embryology* of or relating to that pole of the ovum or embryo that contains the less active cytoplasm, and frequently most of the yolk, in the early stages of development: *vegetal cells | the vegetal region.*

veg·e·tar·i·an /ˌveji'te(ə)rēən/ ▶ *n.* a person who does not eat meat, and sometimes other animal products, esp. for moral, religious, or health reasons.
▶ *adj.* of or relating to the exclusion of meat or other animal products from the diet: *a vegetarian restaurant.* —**veg·e·tar·i·an·ism** /-ˌnizəm/ *n.*

veg·e·tate /'vejəˌtāt/ ▶ *v.* [*intr.*] live or spend a period of time in a dull, inactive, unchallenging way: *if she left him there alone, he'd sit in front of the television set and vegetate.*

veg·e·ta·tion /ˌvejə'tāSHən/ ▶ *n.* **1** plants considered collectively, esp. those found in a particular area or habitat: *the chalk cliffs are mainly sheer with little vegetation.* **2** the action or process of vegetating. **3** *Med.* an abnormal growth on or in the body. —**veg·e·ta·tion·al** /-SHənl/ *adj.*

veg·e·ta·tive /'vejəˌtātiv/ ▶ *adj.* **1** *Biol.* of, relating to, or denoting reproduction or propagation achieved by asexual means, either naturally (budding, rhizomes, runners, bulbs, etc.) or artificially (grafting, layering, or taking cuttings): *vegetative spores.* ■ of, relating to, or concerned with growth rather than sexual reproduction: *environmental factors trigger the switch from vegetative to floral development.* **2** of or relating to vegetation or plant life: *diverse vegetative types.* **3** *Med.* (of a person) alive but comatose and without apparent brain activity or responsiveness. See PERSISTENT VEGETATIVE STATE. —**veg·e·ta·tive·ly** *adv.* —**veg·e·ta·tive·ness** *n.*

veg·gie /'vejē/ (also **veg·ie**) ▶ *n. & adj. inf.* **1** another term for VEGETABLE. **2** another term for VEGETARIAN.

ve·he·ment /'vēəmənt/ ▶ *adj.* showing strong feeling; forceful, passionate, or intense. —**ve·he·mence** *n.* —**ve·he·ment·ly** *adv.*

ve·hi·cle /'vēəkəl; 'vē,hikəl/ ▶ *n.* **1** a thing used for transporting people or goods, esp. on land, such as a car, truck, or cart. **2** a thing used to express, embody, or fulfill something: *I use paint as a* **vehicle for** *my ideas.* ■ a substance that facilitates the use of a drug, pigment, or other material mixed with it. ■ a film, television program, song, etc., that is intended to display the leading performer to the best advantage. —**ve·hic·u·lar** /vē'hikyələr/ *adj.* .

veil /vāl/ ▶ *n.* a piece of fine material worn by women to protect or conceal the face: *a white bridal veil.* ■ a piece of linen or other fabric forming part of a nun's headdress, resting on the head and shoulders. ■ a thing that conceals, disguises, or obscures something: *shrouded in an eerie veil of mist.*
▶ *v.* [*tr.*] cover with or as though with a veil: *she veiled her face.* ■ [usu. as *adj.*] (**veiled**) partially conceal, disguise, or obscure: *a thinly veiled threat.*

vein /vān/ ▶ *n.* **1** any of the tubes forming part of the blood circulation system of the body, carrying in most cases oxygen-depleted blood toward the heart. Compare with ARTERY. ■ (in general and figurative use) a blood vessel: *he felt the adrenaline course through his veins.* ■ (in plants) a slender rib running through a leaf or bract, typically dividing or branching, and containing a vascular bundle. ■ (in insects) a hardened branching rib that forms part of the supporting framework of a wing. ■ a streak or stripe of a different color in wood, marble, cheese, etc. ■ a fracture in rock containing a deposit of minerals or ore and typically having an extensive course underground. ■ subsurface water, esp. as considered a source or potential source of water for a well or wells and thought of as flowing in a channel. ■ *fig.* a source of a specified quality or other abstract resource: *he managed to tap into the thick vein of discontent with his own advantage.* **2** a distinctive quality, style, or tendency: *he closes his article in a somewhat humorous vein.* —**vein·less** *adj.* —**vein·let** /-lit/ *n.* —**vein·y** *adj.* (**vein·i·er, vein·i·est**) .

ve·la /'vēlə/ ▶ plural form of VELUM.

ve·lar /'vēlər/ ▶ *adj.* **1** of or relating to a veil or velum. **2** *Phonet.* (of a speech sound) pronounced with the back of the tongue near the soft palate, as in *k* and *g* in English.

Vel·cro /'velkrō/ ▶ *n. trademark* a fastener for clothes or other items, consisting of two strips of thin plastic sheet, one covered with tiny loops and the other with tiny flexible hooks, which adhere when pressed together and can be separated when pulled apart deliberately.
▶ *v.* [*tr.*] fasten, join, or fix with such a fastener.

veld /velt/ (also **veldt**) ▶ *n.* open, uncultivated country or grassland in southern Africa.

vel·lum /'veləm/ ▶ *n.* **1** fine parchment made originally from the skin of a calf. **2** smooth writing paper imitating vellum.

ve·loc·i·pede /və'läsəˌpēd/ ▶ *n. hist.* an early form of bicycle propelled by working pedals on cranks fitted to the front axle. ■ a child's tricycle.

ve·loc·i·rap·tor /və'läsəˌraptər/ ▶ *n.* a small dinosaur (genus *Velociraptor*) of the late Cretaceous period.

ve·loc·i·ty /və'läsətē/ ▶ *n.* (pl. **-ties**) the speed of something in a given direction: *the velocities of the emitted particles.* ■ (in general use) speed. ■ (also **velocity of circulation**) *Econ.* the rate at which money changes hands within an economy.

ve·lo·drome /'velə,drōm; 'vēlə-/ ▶ *n.* a cycle-racing track, typically with steeply banked curves. ■ a stadium containing such a track.

ve·lour /və'lŏŏr/ (also **ve·lours**) ▶ *n.* a plush woven fabric resembling velvet, chiefly used for soft furnishings, clothing, and hats.

ve·lum /'vēləm/ ▶ *n.* (pl. **ve·la** /-lə/) a membrane or membranous structure, typically covering another structure or partly obscuring an opening, in particular: ■ *Anat.* the soft palate. ■ *Zool.* a membrane, typically bordering a cavity, esp. in certain mollusks, medusae, and other invertebrates.

vel·vet /'velvət/ ▶ *n.* a closely woven fabric of silk, cotton, or nylon, that has a thick short pile on one side. ■ soft downy skin that covers a deer's antler while it is growing. —**vel·vet·ed** *adj.* —**vel·vet·y** *adj.*

vel·vet·een /'velvə,tēn; ,velvə'tēn/ ▶ *n.* a cotton fabric with a pile resembling velvet.

ve·na ca·va /,vēnə 'kāvə; 'kāvə/ ▶ *n.* (pl. **ve·nae ca·vae** /'vēnē 'kāvē; 'kāvē; 'vēnī 'kāvī; 'kāvī/) a large vein carrying deoxygenated blood into the heart. There are two in humans, the **inferior vena cava** (carrying blood from the lower body) and the **superior vena cava** (carrying blood from the upper body).

ve·nal /'vēnl/ ▶ *adj.* showing or motivated by susceptibility to bribery: *their generosity had been at least partly venal.* —**ve·nal·i·ty** /vē'nalətē; və-/ *n.* —**ve·nal·ly** *adv.*

vend /vend/ ▶ *v.* [*tr.*] offer (small items, esp. food) for sale, esp. either from a stall or from a slot machine: *a man vending sticky cakes and ices.* ■ *Law* or *formal* sell (something). —**vend·i·ble** (also **vend·a·ble**) *adj.*

ven·det·ta /ven'detə/ ▶ *n.* a blood feud in which the family of a murdered person seeks vengeance on the murderer or the murderer's family. ■ a prolonged bitter quarrel with or campaign against someone: *he has accused the British media of pursuing a vendetta against him.*

vend·ing ma·chine ▶ *n.* a machine that dispenses small articles such as food, drinks, or cigarettes when a coin, bill, or token is inserted.

ven·dor /'vendər; -,dôr/ (also **vend·er**) ▶ *n.* a person or company offering something for sale, esp. a trader in the street: *an Italian ice cream vendor.* ■ a person or company whose principal product lines are office supplies and equipment. ■ *Law* the seller, esp. of property.

ve·neer /və'ni(ə)r/ ▶ *n.* a thin decorative covering of fine wood applied to a less expensive wood or other material. ■ a layer of wood used to make plywood. ■ an attractive appearance that covers or disguises someone or something's true nature or feelings: *her veneer of composure cracked a little.*
▶ *v.* [*tr.*] [usu. as *adj.*] (**veneered**) cover (something) with a decorative layer of fine wood. ■ cover or disguise (someone or something's true nature) with an attractive appearance.

ven·er·a·ble /'ven(ə)rəbəl/ ▶ *adj.* accorded a great deal of respect, esp. because of age, wisdom, or character: *a venerable statesman.* —**ven·er·a·bil·i·ty** /,venərə'bilətē/ *n.* —**ven·er·a·bly** /-blē/ *adv.*

ven·er·ate /'venə,rāt/ ▶ *v.* [*tr.*] (often **be venerated**) regard with great respect; revere: *Mother Teresa is venerated as a saint.* —**ven·er·a·tion** /,venə-'rāSHən/ *n.* —**ven·er·a·tor** /-,rātər/ *n.*

ve·ne·re·al /və'ni(ə)rēəl/ ▶ *adj.* of or relating to sexual desire or sexual intercourse. ■ of or relating to venereal disease. —**ve·ne·re·al·ly** *adv.*

ve·ne·re·al dis·ease ▶ *n.* a disease typically contracted by sexual contact with a person already infected; a sexually transmitted disease.

Ve·ne·tian /və'nēSHən/ ▶ *adj.* of or relating to Venice or its people.
▶ *n.* a native or citizen of Venice. ■ the dialect of Italian spoken in Venice.

ve·ne·tian blind ▶ *n.* a window blind consisting of horizontal slats that can be pivoted to control the amount of light that passes through it.

Pronunciation Key ə *ago*, *up*; ər *over*, *fur*; a *hat*; ā *ate*; ä *car*; CH *chin*; e *let*; ē *see*; e(ə)r *air*; i *fit*; ī *by*; i(ə)r *ear*; NG *sing*; ō *go*; ô *law*, *for*; oi *toy*; ŏŏ *good*; ōō *goo*; ou *out*; SH *she*; TH *thin*; TH̲ *then*; (h)w *why*; ZH *vision*

venge·ance /ˈvenjəns/ ▶ n. punishment inflicted or retribution exacted for an injury or wrong.

▶ □ **with a vengeance** with intensity: *her headache was back with a vengeance.*

venge·ful /ˈvenjfəl/ ▶ adj. seeking to harm someone in return for a perceived injury: *a vengeful ex-con.* —**venge·ful·ly** adv. —**venge·ful·ness** n.

ve·ni·al /ˈvēnēəl; ˈvēnyəl/ ▶ adj. *Christian Theol.* denoting a sin that is not regarded as depriving the soul of divine grace. Often contrasted with MORTAL. ■ (of a fault or offense) slight and pardonable. —**ve·ni·al·i·ty** /ˌvēnēˈalətē/ n. —**ve·ni·al·ly** adv.

ven·i·son /ˈvenəsən; -zən/ ▶ n. meat from a deer.

Venn di·a·gram /ven/ ▶ n. a diagram representing mathematical or logical sets pictorially as circles or closed curves within an enclosing rectangle (the universal set), common elements of the sets being represented by the areas of overlap among the circles.

ven·om /ˈvenəm/ ▶ n. poisonous fluid secreted by animals such as snakes and scorpions and typically injected into prey or aggressors by biting or stinging. ■ *fig.* extreme malice and bitterness shown in someone's attitudes, speech, or actions: *his voice was full of venom.* ▷Middle English: from Old French *venim*, variant of *venin*, from an alteration of Latin *venenum* 'poison.'

ven·om·ous /ˈvenəməs/ ▶ adj. (of animals, esp. snakes, or their parts) secreting venom; capable of injecting venom by means of a bite or sting. ■ *fig.* (of a person or their behavior) full of malice or spite: *she replied with a venomous glance.* —**ven·om·ous·ly** adv. —**ven·om·ous·ness** n.

ve·nous /ˈvēnəs/ ▶ adj. of or relating to a vein or the veins. ■ of or relating to the dark red, oxygen-poor blood in the veins and pulmonary artery. —**ve·nos·i·ty** /viˈnäsətē/ n. —**ve·nous·ly** adv.

vent[1] /vent/ ▶ n. an opening that allows air, gas, or liquid to pass out of or into a confined space. ■ *fig.* release or expression of a strong emotion, energy, etc.: *children give vent to their anger in various ways.* ■ the opening of a volcano, through which lava and other materials are emitted. ■ the anus, esp. one in a lower animal such as a fish that serves for both excretion and reproduction.

▶ v. **1** give free expression to (a strong emotion): *he had come to vent his rage and despair.* **2** provide with an outlet for air, gas, or liquid: *clothes dryers must be vented to the outside.* ■ discharge or expel (air, gas, or liquid) through an outlet. ■ permit air to enter (a beer cask).

vent[2] ▶ n. a slit in a garment, esp. in the lower edge of the back of a coat through the seam.

ven·ti·late /ˈventəˌlāt/ ▶ v. [*tr.*] **1** cause air to enter and circulate freely in (a room, building, etc.). [as *adj.,* in *comb.*] (**-ventilated**) *well-ventilated rooms.* ■ *Med.* subject to artificial respiration. **2** discuss or examine (an opinion, issue, complaint, etc.) in public: *to ventilate an ongoing complaint.*

ven·ti·la·tion /ˌventəˈlāSHən/ ▶ n. **1** the provision of fresh air to a room, building, etc. ■ *Med.* the supply of air to the lungs, esp. by artificial means. **2** public discussion or examination of an opinion, issue, complaint, etc. ▷late Middle English (in the sense 'current of air'): from Old French, or from Latin *ventilatio(n-)*, from *ventilare* 'to blow, winnow,' from *ventus* 'wind.'

ven·ti·la·tor /ˈventəˌlātər/ ▶ n. **1** an appliance or aperture for ventilating a room or other space. **2** *Med.* an appliance for artificial respiration; a respirator.

ven·tral /ˈventrəl/ ▶ adj. *Anat., Zool., & Bot.* of, on, or relating to the underside of an animal or plant; abdominal: *a ventral nerve cord | the ventral part of the head.* Compare with DORSAL. —**ven·tral·ly** adv.

ven·tri·cle /ˈventrikəl/ ▶ n. *Anat.* a hollow part or cavity in an organ, in particular: ■ each of the two main chambers of the heart, left and right. ■ each of the four connected fluid-filled cavities in the center of the brain. —**ven·tric·u·lar** /venˈtrikyələr/ adj.

ven·tril·o·quist /venˈtriləkwist/ ▶ n. a person who can speak or utter sounds so that they seem to come from somewhere else, esp. an entertainer who makes their voice appear to come from a dummy. —**ven·tril·o·qui·al** /ˌventrəˈlōkwēəl/ adj. —**ven·tril·o·quism** /-ˌkwizəm/ n. —**ven·tril·o·quize** /-ˌkwīz/ v. —**ven·tril·o·quy** /-kwē/ n.

ven·ture /ˈvenCHər/ ▶ n. a risky or daring journey or undertaking. ■ a business enterprise involving considerable risk.

▶ v. [*intr.*] dare to do something or go somewhere that may be dangerous or unpleasant: *she ventured out into the blizzard.* ■ dare to do or say something that may be considered audacious (often used as a polite expression of hesitation or apology): *may I venture to add a few comments?* | [*tr.*] *he ventured the opinion that Putt was now dangerously insane.* ■ [*tr.*] expose (something) to the risk of loss: *his fortune was ventured in an expedition over which he has no control.*

ven·ture cap·i·tal ▶ n. capital invested in a project in which there is a

substantial element of risk, typically a new or expanding business. —**ven·ture cap·i·tal·ist** n.

ven·ture·some /ˈvenCHərsəm/ ▶ adj. willing to take risks or embark on difficult or unusual courses of action. —**ven·ture·some·ly** adv. —**ven·ture·some·ness** n.

ven·ue /ˈvenˌyoo/ ▶ n. the place where something happens, esp. an organized event such as a concert, conference, or sports event: *the river could soon be the venue for a powerboat world championship event.* ■ *Law* the county or district within which a criminal or civil case must be heard.

ven·ule /ˈvenˌyool/ ▶ n. *Anat.* a very small vein, esp. one collecting blood from the capillaries.

Ve·nus /ˈvēnəs/ ▶ **1** *Roman Mythol.* a goddess, worshiped as the goddess of love in classical Rome. ■ [as *n.*] (**a Venus**) *chiefly poetic/lit.* a beautiful woman. **2** *Astron.* the second planet from the sun in the solar system, the brightest celestial object after the sun and moon and frequently appearing in the twilight sky as the evening or morning star. **3** (also **venus**) a burrowing marine bivalve mollusk (*Venus, Venerupis,* and other genera, family Veneridae) with clearly defined growth lines on the shell. —**Ve·nu·si·an** /vəˈn(y)ooSH(ē)ən; -ZHən; -sēən/ adj. & n.

Ve·nus fly·trap (also **Venus's flytrap**) ▶ n. a small carnivorous bog plant (*Dionaea muscipula,* family Droseraceae) with hinged leaves that spring shut on and digest insects that land on them.

ve·ra·cious /vəˈrāSHəs/ ▶ adj. *formal* speaking or representing the truth. —**ve·ra·cious·ly** adv. —**ve·ra·cious·ness** n.

ve·rac·i·ty /vəˈrasətē/ ▶ n. conformity to facts; accuracy: *officials expressed doubts concerning the veracity of the story.* ■ habitual truthfulness.

ve·ran·da /vəˈrandə/ (also **ve·ran·dah**) ▶ n. a roofed platform along the outside of a house, level with the ground floor. —**ve·ran·daed** adj.

verb /vərb/ ▶ n. *Gram.* a word used to describe an action, state, or occurrence, and forming the main part of the predicate of a sentence, such as *hear, become, happen.* —**verb·less** adj.

ver·bal /ˈvərbəl/ ▶ adj. **1** relating to or in the form of words: *the root of the problem is visual rather than verbal | verbal abuse.* ■ spoken rather than written; oral: *a verbal agreement.* ■ tending to talk a lot: *he's very verbal.* **2** *Gram.* of, relating to, or derived from a verb: *a verbal adjective.*

▶ n. *Gram.* a word or words functioning as a verb. ■ a verbal noun. —**ver·bal·ly** adv.

ver·bal·ism /ˈvərbəˌlizəm/ ▶ n. concentration on forms of expression rather than content. ■ a verbal expression. ■ excessive or empty use of language. —**ver·bal·ist** n. —**ver·bal·is·tic** /ˌvərbəˈlistik/ adj.

ver·bal·ize /ˈvərbəˌlīz/ ▶ v. **1** [*tr.*] express (ideas or feelings) in words, esp. by speaking out loud: *they are unable to verbalize their real feelings.* **2** [*intr.*] speak, esp. at excessive length and with little real content: *the dangers of verbalizing about art.* **3** [*tr.*] make (a word, esp. a noun) into a verb. —**ver·bal·iz·a·ble** adj. —**ver·bal·i·za·tion** /ˌvərbələˈzāSHən; -ˌlīˈzā-/ n.

ver·bal noun ▶ n. *Gram.* a noun formed by inflection of a verb and partly sharing its constructions, such as *smoking* in *smoking is forbidden.*

ver·ba·tim /vərˈbātəm/ ▶ adv. & adj. in exactly the same words as were used originally: [as *adv.*] *subjects were instructed to recall the passage verbatim* | [as *adj.*] *your quotations must be verbatim.*

ver·be·na /vərˈbēnə/ ▶ n. a chiefly American herbaceous plant (genus *Verbena,* family Verbenaceae) that bears heads of bright showy flowers, widely cultivated as a garden ornamental.

ver·bi·age /ˈvərbē-ij/ ▶ n. speech or writing that uses too many words or excessively technical expressions.

ver·bose /vərˈbōs/ ▶ adj. using or expressed in more words than are needed: *much academic language is obscure and verbose.* —**ver·bose·ly** adv. —**ver·bos·i·ty** /-ˈbäsətē/ n.

ver·bo·ten /fərˈbōtn; vər-/ ▶ adj. forbidden, esp. by an authority.

ver·dant /ˈvərdnt/ ▶ adj. (of countryside) green with grass or other rich vegetation. ■ of the bright green color of lush grass: *a deep, verdant green.* —**ver·dan·cy** /ˈvərdn-sē/ n. —**ver·dant·ly** adv.

ver·dict /ˈvərdikt/ ▶ n. a decision on a disputed issue in a civil or criminal case or an inquest: *the jury returned a verdict of 'not guilty.'* ■ an opinion or judgment: *I'm anxious to know your verdict on me.* ▷Middle English: from Anglo-Norman French *verdit,* from Old French *veir* 'true' (from Latin *verus*) + *dit* (from Latin *dictum* 'saying').

ver·di·gris /ˈvərdəˌgrēs; -ˌgris; -ˌgrē/ ▶ n. a bright bluish-green encrustation or patina formed on copper or brass by atmospheric oxidation, consisting of basic copper carbonate.

ver·dure /ˈvərjər/ ▶ n. lush green vegetation. ■ the fresh green color of such vegetation. —**ver·dured** adj. —**ver·dur·ous** /-jərəs/ adj.

verge[1] /vərj/ ▶ n. an edge or border: *the verge of the lake.* ■ an extreme limit beyond which something specified will happen: *I was on the verge of tears.*

▶ *v.* [*intr.*] (**verge on**) approach (something) closely; be close or similar to (something): *despair verging on the suicidal.*

verge² ▶ *v.* [*intr.*] incline in a certain direction or toward a particular state: *his style verged into the art nouveau school.*

ver·i·fi·ca·tion /ˌverəfiˈkāSHən/ ▶ *n.* the process of establishing the truth, accuracy, or validity of something: *the verification of official documents.* ■ the process of ensuring that procedures laid down in weapons limitation agreements are followed.

ver·i·fy /ˈverəˌfī/ ▶ *v.* (**-fies, -fied**) [*tr.*] (often **be verified**) make sure or demonstrate that (something) is true, accurate, or justified: *his conclusions have been verified by later experiments.* ■ *Law* swear to or support (a statement) by affidavit. —**ver·i·fi·a·ble** /ˈverəˌfīəbəl; ˌverəˈfī-/ *adj.* —**ver·i·fi·a·bly** /-blē/ *adv.* —**ver·i·fi·er** *n.*

ver·i·ly /ˈverəlē/ ▶ *adv.* archaic truly; certainly: *I verily believed myself to be a free woman.*

ver·i·si·mil·i·tude /ˌverəsəˈmiliˌt(y) o͞od/ ▶ *n.* the appearance of being true or real: *the detail gives the novel some verisimilitude.* —**ver·i·sim·i·lar** /-ˈsimələr/ *adj.*

ve·ris·mo /vəˈrizmō; ve-/ ▶ *n.* realism in the arts, esp. late 19th-century Italian opera. ■ this genre of opera, as composed principally by Puccini, Mascagni, and Leoncavallo.

ver·i·ta·ble /ˈverətəbəl/ ▶ *adj.* used as an intensifier, often to qualify a metaphor: *the early 1970s witnessed a veritable price explosion.* —**ver·i·ta·bly** /-blē/ *adv.*

ver·i·ty /ˈverətē/ ▶ *n.* (*pl.* **-ties**) a true principle or belief, esp. one of fundamental importance: *the eternal verities.* ■ truth: *irrefutable, objective verity.*

ver·meil /ˈvərməl; -ˌmāl; vərˈmā(l)/ ▶ *n.* [often as *adj.*] **1** gilded silver or bronze. **2** *poetic/lit.* vermilion.

ver·mi·cel·li /ˌvərməˈCHelē; -ˈselē/ ▶ *n.* pasta made in long slender threads.

ver·mi·cide /ˈvərməˌsīd/ ▶ *n.* a substance that is poisonous to worms.

ver·mic·u·lar /vərˈmikyələr/ ▶ *adj.* **1** like a worm in form or movement; vermiform. **2** marked with close wavy lines.

ver·mic·u·lite /vərˈmikyəˌlīt/ ▶ *n.* a yellow or brown mineral used for insulation or as a moisture-retentive medium for growing plants.

ver·mi·form /ˈvərməˌfôrm/ ▶ *adj.* chiefly *Zool.* or *Anat.* resembling or having the form of a worm.

ver·mi·form ap·pen·dix ▶ *n.* technical term for APPENDIX (sense 1).

ver·mil·ion /vərˈmilyən/ (also **ver·mil·lion**) ▶ *n.* a brilliant red pigment made from cinnabar. ■ a brilliant red color: [as *adj.*] *vermilion streaks of sunset.*

ver·min /ˈvərmən/ ▶ *n.* [treated as *pl.*] wild mammals and birds that are believed to be harmful to crops, farm animals, or game, or that carry disease, e.g., foxes, rodents, and insect pests. ■ parasitic worms or insects. ■ *fig.* people perceived as despicable and as causing problems for the rest of society: *the vermin who ransacked her house.* —**ver·min·ous** /-mənəs/ *adj.*

ver·mouth /vərˈmo͞oTH/ ▶ *n.* a red or white wine flavored with aromatic herbs, made chiefly in France and Italy and used in cocktails.

ver·nac·u·lar /vərˈnakyələr/ ▶ *n.* **1** (usu. **the vernacular**) the language or dialect spoken by the ordinary people in a particular country or region: *he wrote in the vernacular to reach a larger audience.* ■ the terminology used by people belonging to a specified group or engaging in a specialized activity: *gardening vernacular.* **2** architecture concerned with domestic and functional rather than monumental buildings.
▶ *adj.* **1** (of language) spoken as one's mother tongue; not learned or imposed as a second language. ■ (of speech or written works) using such a language: *vernacular literature.* **2** (of architecture) concerned with domestic and functional rather than monumental buildings. —**ver·nac·u·lar·ism** /-ˌrizəm/ *n.* —**ver·nac·u·lar·ize** /-ˌrīz/ *v.* —**ver·nac·u·lar·ly** *adv.*

ver·nal /ˈvərnl/ ▶ *adj.* of, in, or appropriate to spring: *the vernal freshness of the land.* —**ver·nal·ly** *adv.*

ver·nal e·qui·nox ▶ *n.* the equinox in spring, on about March 20 in the northern hemisphere and September 22 in the southern hemisphere.■ *Astron.* the equinox in March. ■ *Astron.* the point on the celestial sphere where the path of the sun crosses the celestial equator from south to north in March, marking the zero point of right ascension. Owing to precession of the equinoxes, it has moved from Aries into Pisces, and is now approaching Aquarius.

ver·nier /ˈvərnēər/ ▶ *n.* a small movable graduated scale for obtaining fractional parts of subdivisions on a fixed main scale of a measuring instrument.

ve·ro·nal /ˈverəˌnôl; -ənl/ ▶ *n.* trademark another term for BARBITAL.

ve·ron·i·ca /vəˈränəkə/ ▶ *n.* a herbaceous plant (genus *Veronica*) of the figwort family, typically with upright stems bearing narrow pointed leaves and spikes of blue or purple flowers, found in north temperate regions.

ver·sa·tile /ˈvərsətl/ ▶ *adj.* able to adapt or be adapted to many different functions or activities: *he was versatile enough to play either position.* —**ver·sa·tile·ly** *adv.* —**ver·sa·til·i·ty** /ˌvərsəˈtilətē/ *n.*

verse /vərs/ ▶ *n.* writing arranged with a metrical rhythm, typically having a rhyme: *a lament in verse.* ■ a group of lines that form a unit in a poem or song; a stanza: *the second verse.* ■ each of the short numbered divisions of a chapter in the Bible or other scripture. ■ a versicle.

versed /vərst/ ▶ *adj.* (**versed in**) experienced or skilled in; knowledgeable about: *a native Icelander well versed in her country's medieval literature.*

ver·si·cle /ˈvərsikəl/ ▶ *n.* (usu. **versicles**) a short sentence said or sung by the minister in a church service, to which the congregation responds.

ver·si·fy /ˈvərsəˌfī/ ▶ *v.* (**-fies, -fied**) [*tr.*] turn into or express in verse: *he versifies others' ideas.* —**ver·si·fi·ca·tion** /ˌvərsəfiˈkāSHən/ *n.* —**ver·si·fi·er** *n.*

ver·sion /ˈvərzHən/ ▶ *n.* a particular form of something differing in certain respects from an earlier form or other forms of the same type of thing: *a revised version of the paper was produced for a later meeting.* ■ a particular edition or translation of a book or other work: *the English version will be published next year.* ■ an adaptation of a novel, piece of music, etc., into another medium or style: *a film version of a wonderfully funny cult novel.* ■ a particular updated edition of a piece of computer software. ■ an account of a matter from a particular person's point of view: *he told her his version of events.* ▷late Middle English (in the sense 'translation'): from French, or from medieval Latin *versio(n-)*, from Latin *vertere* 'to turn.' —**ver·sion·al** /-zHənl/ *adj.*

vers li·bre /ˌver ˈlēbrə/ ▶ *n.* another term for FREE VERSE.

ver·so /ˈvərsō/ ▶ *n.* (*pl.* **-sos**) **1** a left-hand page of an open book, or the back of a loose document. Contrasted with RECTO. **2** the reverse of something such as a coin or painting.

ver·sus /ˈvərsəs; -səz/ (abbr. **v.** or **vs.**) ▶ *prep.* against (esp. in sports and legal use): *Penn versus Princeton.* ■ as opposed to; in contrast to: *weighing the pros and cons of organic versus inorganic produce.*

ver·te·bra /ˈvərtəbrə/ ▶ *n.* (*pl.* **-brae** /-ˌbrē; -ˌbrā/) each of the series of small bones forming the backbone, having several projections for articulation and muscle attachment, and a hole through which the spinal cord passes. —**ver·te·bral** /-brəl; vərˈtē-/ *adj.*

ver·te·brate /ˈvərtəbrət; -ˌbrāt/ ▶ *n.* an animal of a large group distinguished by the possession of a backbone or spinal column, including mammals, birds, reptiles, amphibians, and fishes. Compare with IN-VERTEBRATE.
▶ *adj.* of or relating to the vertebrates.

ver·tex /ˈvərˌteks/ ▶ *n.* (*pl.* **-ti·ces** /-təˌsēz/ or **-tex·es**) **1** the highest point; the top or apex. **2** *Geom.* each angular point of a polygon, polyhedron, or other figure. ■ a meeting point of two lines that form an angle. ■ the point at which an axis meets a curve or surface.

ver·ti·cal /ˈvərtikəl/ ▶ *adj.* involving different levels of a hierarchy or progression, in particular: ■ involving all the stages from the production to the sale of a class of goods. ■ (esp. of the transmission of disease or genetic traits) passed from one generation to the next.
▶ *n.* **1** (usu. **the vertical**) a vertical line or plane: *the columns incline several degrees away from the vertical.* **2** an upright structure: *we remodeled the opening with a simple lintel and unadorned verticals.* **3** the distance between the highest and lowest points of a ski area: *the resort claims a vertical of 2100 meters.* —**ver·ti·cal·i·ty** /ˌvərtiˈkalətē/ *n.* —**ver·ti·cal·ize** /-ˌlīz/ *v.* —**ver·ti·cal·ly** /-ik(ə)lē/ *adv.*

ver·ti·go /ˈvərtəˌgō/ ▶ *n.* a sensation of whirling and loss of balance, associated particularly with looking down from a great height, or caused by disease affecting the inner ear or the vestibular nerve.

verve /vərv/ ▶ *n.* vigor and spirit or enthusiasm: *sings with verve.*

ver·y /ˈverē/ ▶ *adv.* used for emphasis: ■ in a high degree: *very large* | *very quickly.* ■ used to emphasize that the following description applies without qualification: *the very best quality.*
▶ *adj.* actual; precise (used to emphasize the exact identity of a particular person or thing): *those were his very words.* ■ emphasizing an extreme point in time or space: *from the very beginning of the book.* ■ with no addition of or contribution from anything else; mere: *the very thought of drink made him feel sick.* ■ archaic real; genuine: *the very God of Heaven.*
▶ □ **not very 1** in a low degree: *"Bad news?" "Not very."* **2** far from being: *I'm not very impressed.* □ **very good** (or **well**) an expression of consent.

ve·ry high fre·quen·cy ▶*n.* (abbr.: **VHF**) the band of frequencies between 30 and 300 megahertz, typically used for broadcasting television signals.

ve·si·cal /'vesəkəl/ ▶*adj. Anat. & Med.* of, relating to, or affecting the urinary bladder: *the vesical artery.*

ve·si·cle /'vesikəl/ ▶*n.* a fluid- or air-filled cavity or sac, in particular: ■ *Anat. & Zool.* a small fluid-filled bladder, sac, cyst, or vacuole within the body. ■ *Bot.* an air-filled swelling in a plant, esp. a seaweed. ■ *Geol.* a small cavity in volcanic rock, produced by gas bubbles in the molten lava. ■ *Med.* a small blister full of clear fluid. —**ve·sic·u·lar** /və'sikyələr/ *adj.* —**ve·sic·u·lat·ed** /və'sikyə,lātid/ *adj.* —**ve·sic·u·la·tion** /və,sikyə-'lāsHən/ *n.*

ves·per /'vespər/ ▶*n.* evening prayer: [as *adj.*] *vesper service.* See also **VES·PERS.**

ves·pers /'vespərz/ ▶*n.* a service of evening prayer in the Divine Office of the Western Christian Church (sometimes said earlier in the day). ■ a service of evening prayer in other churches.

ves·sel /'vesəl/ ▶*n.* **1** a ship or large boat. **2** a hollow container, esp. one used to hold liquid, such as a bowl or cask. **3** *Anat. & Zool.* a duct or canal holding or conveying blood or other fluid. See also **BLOOD VES·SEL.** ■ *Bot.* any of the tubular structures in the vascular system of a plant, serving to conduct water and mineral nutrients from the root.

vest /vest/ ▶*n.* a close-fitting waist-length garment, typically having no sleeves or collar and buttoning down the front. ■ a similar garment worn on the upper part of the body for a particular purpose or activity: *a bulletproof vest.* ■ *Brit.* an undershirt.
▶*v.* **1** [*tr.*] (usu. **be vested in**) confer or bestow (power, authority, property, etc.) on someone: *executive power is vested in the president.* ■ (usu. **be vested with**) give (someone) the legal right to power, property, etc.: *vested with the power of legislation.* ■ [*intr.*] (**vest in**) (of power, property, etc.) come into the possession of: *the bankrupt's property vests in his trustee.* **2** [*intr.*] put on vestments.

ves·tal /'vestl/ ▶*adj.* chaste; pure.

vest·ed in·ter·est ▶*n.* a personal stake or involvement in an undertaking or state of affairs, esp. one with an expectation of financial gain: *banks have **a vested interest in** the growth of their customers.* ■ a person or group having such a personal stake or involvement. ■ *Law* an interest (usually in land and money held in trust) recognized as belonging to a particular person.

ves·tib·u·lar /ve'stibyələr; və-/ ▶*adj. chiefly Anat.* of or relating to a vestibule, particularly that of the inner ear, or more generally to the sense of balance.

ves·ti·bule /'vestə,byōōl/ ▶*n.* **1** an antechamber, hall, or lobby next to the outer door of a building. ■ an enclosed entrance compartment in a railroad car. **2** *Anat.* a chamber or channel communicating with or opening into another, in particular: ■ the central cavity of the labyrinth of the inner ear. ■ the part of the mouth outside the teeth. ■ the space in the vulva into which both the urethra and vagina open. —**ves·tib·u·lar** /ves'tibyələr/ *adj.* —**ves·ti·buled** *adj.*

ves·tige /'vestij/ ▶*n.* a trace of something that is disappearing or no longer exists: *the last vestiges of colonialism.* ■ the smallest amount (used to emphasize the absence of something): *he waited patiently, but without a vestige of sympathy.* ■ *Biol.* a part or organ of an organism that has become reduced or functionless in the course of evolution.

ves·tig·i·al /ve'stij(ē)əl/ ▶*adj.* forming a very small remnant of something that was once much larger or more noticeable: *he felt a vestigial flicker of anger from last night.* ■ *Biol.* (of an organ or part of the body) degenerate, rudimentary, or atrophied, having become functionless in the course of evolution. —**ves·tig·i·al·ly** *adv.*

vest·ment /'ves(t)mənt/ ▶*n.* (usu. **vestments**) a chasuble or other robe worn by the clergy or choristers during services.

ves·try /'vestrē/ ▶*n.* (*pl.* **-tries**) a room or building attached to a church, used as an office and for changing into vestments. ■ a meeting of parishioners, originally in a vestry, for the conduct of parochial business. ■ a body of parishioners meeting in such a way.

vet[1] /vet/ ▶*n. inf.* a veterinary surgeon.
▶*v.* (**vet·ted, vet·ting**) [*tr.*] make a careful and critical examination of (something): *proposals for vetting large takeover bids.* ■ (often **be vetted**) investigate (someone) thoroughly, esp. in order to ensure that they are suitable for a job requiring secrecy, loyalty, or trustworthiness: *each applicant will be vetted by police.*

vet[2] ▶*n. inf.* a veteran.

vetch /vecH/ ▶*n.* a widely distributed herbaceous plant (genus *Vicia*) of the pea family that is cultivated as a silage or fodder crop.

vet·er·an /'vet(ə)rən/ ▶*n.* a person who has had long experience in a particular field. ■ a person who has served in the military.

Vet·er·ans Day ▶*n.* a public holiday held on the anniversary of the end of World War I (November 11) to honor U.S. veterans and victims of all wars. It replaced Armistice Day in 1954.

vet·er·i·nar·i·an /,vet(ə)rə'ne(ə)rēən/ ▶*n.* a person qualified to treat diseased or injured animals.

vet·er·i·nar·y /'vet(ə)rə,nerē/ ▶*adj.* of or relating to the diseases, injuries, and treatment of animals: *veterinary medicine* | *a veterinary nurse.*

ve·to /'vētō/ ▶*n.* (*pl.* **-toes**) a constitutional right to reject a decision or proposal made by a law-making body: *the legislature would have a veto over appointments to key posts.* ■ such a rejection. ■ a prohibition.
▶*v.* (**-toes, -toed**) [*tr.*] exercise a veto against (a decision or proposal made by a law-making body): *the president vetoed the bill.* ■ refuse to accept or allow: *the film star often has a right to veto publicity pictures.* ▷early 17th cent.: from Latin, literally 'I forbid,' used by Roman tribunes of the people when opposing measures of the Senate.

vex /veks/ ▶*v.* [*tr.*] make (someone) feel annoyed, frustrated, or worried, esp. with trivial matters: *the memory of the conversation still vexed him* | [as *adj.*] (**vexing**) *vexing questions.* —**vex·er** *n.* —**vex·ing·ly** *adv.*

vex·a·tion /vek'sāsHən/ ▶*n.* the state of being annoyed, frustrated, or worried: *Jenny bit her lip in vexation.* ■ something that causes annoyance, frustration, or worry: *the cares and vexations of life.*

vex·a·tious /vek'sāsHəs/ ▶*adj.* causing or tending to cause annoyance, frustration, or worry: *the vexatious questions posed by software copyrights.* ■ *Law* denoting an action or the bringer of an action that is brought without sufficient grounds for winning, purely to cause annoyance to the defendant. —**vex·a·tious·ly** *adv.* —**vex·a·tious·ness** *n.*

vexed /vekst/ ▶*adj.* **1** (of a problem or issue) difficult and much debated; problematic: *the vexed question of exactly how much money the government is going to spend.* **2** annoyed, frustrated, or worried: *I'm very vexed with you!* —**vex·ed·ly** /'veksədlē/ *adv.*

VHF ▶*abbr.* very high frequency, denoting radio waves of a frequency of about 30–300 MHz (and a wavelength of about 1–10 meters).

vi·a /'vīə; 'vēə/ ▶*prep.* traveling through (a place) en route to a destination: *they came to Europe via Turkey.* ■ by way of; through: *they can see the artists' works via a camera hookup.* ■ by means of: *a file sent via e-mail.*

vi·a·ble /'vīəbəl/ ▶*adj.* capable of working successfully; feasible: *the proposed investment was economically viable.* ■ *Bot.* (of a seed or spore) able to germinate. ■ *Biol.* (of a plant, animal, or cell) capable of surviving or living successfully, esp. under particular environmental conditions. ■ *Med.* (of a fetus or unborn child) able to live after birth. —**vi·a·bil·i·ty** /,vīə'bilətē/ *n.* —**vi·a·bly** /-blē/ *adv.*

vi·a·duct /'vīə,dəkt/ ▶*n.* a long bridgelike structure, typically a series of arches, carrying a road or railroad across a valley or other low ground.

Vi·ag·ra /vī'agrə/ ▶*n.* trademark for **SILDENAFIL CITRATE.**

vi·al /'vī(ə)l/ ▶*n.* a small container, typically cylindrical and made of glass, used esp. for holding liquid medicines.

vi·and /'vīənd/ ▶*n.* (usu. **viands**) *poetic/lit.* an item of food: *an unlimited assortment of viands.*

vibe /vīb/ ▶*n. inf.* **1** (usu. **vibes**) a person's emotional state or the atmosphere of a place as communicated to and felt by others: *moody people giving off **bad vibes**.* **2** (**vibes**) another term for **VIBRAPHONE.**

vi·brant /'vībrənt/ ▶*adj.* full of energy and enthusiasm: *a vibrant cosmopolitan city.* ■ quivering; pulsating: *Rose was vibrant with anger.* ■ (of color) bright and striking. ■ (of sound) strong or resonating: *a vibrant male voice.* —**vi·bran·cy** /-brənsē/ *n.* —**vi·brant·ly** *adv.*

vi·bra·phone /'vībrə,fōn/ ▶*n.* a musical percussion instrument with a double row of tuned metal bars, each above a tubular resonator containing a motor-driven rotating vane, giving a vibrato effect. —**vi·bra·phon·ist** *n.*

vibraphone

vi·brate /'vī,brāt/ ▶ *v.* move or cause to move continuously and rapidly to and fro: [*intr.*] *the cabin started to vibrate* | [*tr.*] *the bumblebee vibrated its wings for a few seconds.* ■ [*intr.*] (**vibrate with**) quiver with (a quality or emotion): *his voice vibrated with terror.* ■ [*intr.*] (of a sound) resonate; continue to be heard: *a low rumbling sound that began to vibrate through the car.* ■ [*intr.*] (of a pendulum) swing to and fro.

vi·bra·tion /vī'brāSHən/ ▶ *n.* an instance of vibrating: *powerful vibrations from an earthquake.* ■ *Physics* an oscillation of the parts of a fluid or an elastic solid whose equilibrium has been disturbed, or of an electromagnetic wave. ■ (**vibrations**) *inf.* a person's emotional state, the atmosphere of a place, or the associations of an object, as communicated to and felt by others. —**vi·bra·tion·al** /-SHənl/ *adj.*

vi·bra·to /və'brätō; vī-/ ▶ *n. Mus.* a rapid, slight variation in pitch in singing or playing some musical instruments, producing a stronger or richer tone. Compare with TREMOLO.

vi·bra·tor /'vī,brātər/ ▶ *n.* a device that vibrates or causes vibration, in particular: ■ a device used for massage or sexual stimulation. ■ *Mus.* a reed in a reed organ.

vi·bra·to·ry /'vībrə,tôrē/ ▶ *adj.* of, relating to, or causing vibration.

vi·bur·num /vī'bərnəm/ ▶ *n.* a shrub or small tree (genus *Viburnum*) of the honeysuckle family, typically bearing flat or rounded clusters of small white flowers. Its many species and ornamental hybrids include the guelder rose and wayfaring tree.

vic·ar /'vikər/ ▶ *n.* (in the Roman Catholic Church) a representative or deputy of a bishop. ■ (in the Episcopal Church) a member of the clergy in charge of a chapel. ■ (in the Church of England) an incumbent of a parish where tithes formerly passed to a chapter or religious house or layman. ■ (in other Anglican Churches) a member of the clergy deputizing for another. —**vic·ar·ship** /-,SHip/ *n.*

vic·ar·age /'vikərij/ ▶ *n.* the residence of a vicar.

vi·car·i·ous /vī'ke(ə)rēəs; vi-/ ▶ *adj.* experienced in the imagination through the feelings or actions of another person: *I could glean vicarious pleasure from the struggles of my imaginary film friends.* ■ acting or done for another: *a vicarious atonement.* ■ *Physiol.* of or pertaining to the performance by one organ of the functions normally discharged by another. —**vi·car·i·ous·ly** *adv.* —**vi·car·i·ous·ness** *n.*

vice[1] /vīs/ ▶ *n.* immoral or wicked behavior. ■ criminal activities involving prostitution, pornography, or drugs. ■ an immoral or wicked personal characteristic. ■ a weakness of character or behavior; a bad habit: *cigars happen to be my father's vice.* —**vice·less** *adj.*

vice[2] ▶ *n.* British spelling of VISE.

vice[3] /vīs; 'vīsē; 'vīsə/ ▶ *prep.* as a substitute for: *the letter was drafted by David Hunt, vice the chairman who was ill.*

vice ad·mi·ral /vīs/ ▶ *n.* a naval officer of very high rank, in particular an officer in the U.S. Navy or Coast Guard ranking above rear admiral and below admiral.

vice chan·cel·lor /vīs/ ▶ *n.* a deputy chancellor, esp. one of a British university.

vice pres·i·dent /vīs/ ▶ *n.* an official or executive ranking below and deputizing for a president. —**vice pres·i·den·cy** *n.* (*pl.* **-cies**) —**vice pres·i·den·tial** *adj.*

vice·re·gal /,vīs'rēgəl/ ▶ *adj.* of or relating to a viceroy.

vice·roy /'vīs,roi/ ▶ *n.* **1** a ruler exercising authority in a colony on behalf of a sovereign. **2** a migratory orange and black butterfly (*Limenitis archippus*) that closely resembles the monarch but is typically somewhat smaller. —**vice·roy·al** /,vīs'roi-əl/ *adj.* —**vice·roy·al·ty** *n.*

vice squad /vīs/ ▶ *n.* a department or division of a police force that enforces laws against prostitution, drug abuse, illegal gambling, etc.

vice ver·sa /'vīs 'vərsə; 'vīsə/ ▶ *adv.* with the main items in the preceding statement the other way around: *science must be at the service of man, and not vice versa.*

vi·chys·soise /,vēSHē'swäz; ,viSHē-; 'vēSHē,swäz; 'viSHē-/ ▶ *n.* a soup made with potatoes, leeks, and cream and typically served chilled.

Vi·chy wa·ter /'viSHē/ ▶ *n.* an effervescent mineral water from springs in Vichy, France, or an imitation of this.

vi·cin·i·ty /və'sinətē/ ▶ *n.* (*pl.* **-ties**) the area near or surrounding a particular place: *the number of people living in the immediate vicinity was small.*

vi·cious /'viSHəs/ ▶ *adj.* deliberately cruel or violent: *a vicious assault.* ■ (of an animal) wild and dangerous to people. ■ *fig.* serious or dangerous: *a vicious flu bug.* —**vi·cious·ly** *adv.* —**vi·cious·ness** *n.*

vi·cis·si·tude /və'sisə,t(y)ōōd/ ▶ *n.* (usu. **vicissitudes**) a change of circumstances or fortune, typically one that is unwelcome or unpleasant: *her husband's sharp vicissitudes of fortune.* —**vi·cis·si·tu·di·nous** /-,sisə't(y)ōōdn-əs; -'t(y)ōōdnəs/ *adj.*

vic·tim /'viktəm/ ▶ *n.* a person harmed, injured, or killed as a result of a crime, accident, or other event or action. ■ a person who is tricked or duped: *the victim of a hoax.* ■ a living creature killed as a religious sacrifice.

▶ □ **fall victim to** be hurt, killed, damaged, or destroyed by: *many streams have fallen victim to the recent drought.*

vic·tim·ize /'viktə,mīz/ ▶ *v.* [*tr.*] single (someone) out for cruel or unjust treatment: *scam artists who victimize senior citizens.* —**vic·tim·i·za·tion** /,viktəmə'zāSHən/ *n.* —**vic·tim·iz·er** *n.*

vic·tor /'viktər/ ▶ *n.* **1** a person who defeats an enemy or opponent in a battle, game, or other competition. **2** a code word representing the letter V, used in radio communication.

Vic·to·ri·an /vik'tôrēən/ ▶ *adj.* of or relating to the reign of Queen Victoria: *a Victorian house.* ■ of or relating to the attitudes and values of this period, regarded as characterized esp. by a stifling and prudish moral earnestness.

▶ *n.* a person who lived during the Victorian period. —**Vic·to·ri·an·ism** /-,nizəm/ *n.*

Vic·to·ri·an·a /vik,tôrē'anə; -'änə/ ▶ *pl. n.* articles, esp. collectors' items, from the Victorian period. ■ matters or attitudes relating to or characteristic of this period.

vic·to·ri·ous /vik'tôrēəs/ ▶ *adj.* having won a victory; triumphant: *a victorious army.* ■ of or characterized by victory: *the victorious campaigns of the Franco-Prussian War.* —**vic·to·ri·ous·ly** *adv.* —**vic·to·ri·ous·ness** *n.*

vic·to·ry /'vikt(ə)rē/ ▶ *n.* (*pl.* **-ries**) an act of defeating an enemy or opponent in a battle, game, or other competition: *an election victory.*

vict·ual /'vitl/ *dated* ▶ *n.* (**victuals**) food or provisions, typically as prepared for consumption.

▶ *v.* (**-ualed**, **-ual·ing**; *Brit.* **-ualled**, **-ual·ling**) [*tr.*] provide with food or other stores: *the ship wasn't even properly victualed.*

vi·cu·ña /vī'k(y)ōōnə və-; 'kōōnyə/ ▶ *n.* a mammal (*Vicugna vicugna*) of the camel family, a wild relative of the llama, inhabiting mountainous regions of South America and valued for its fine silky wool. ■ cloth made from this wool, or an imitation of it.

vi·de /'vēdē; 'vē,dā; 'vīdē/ ▶ *v.* [*tr.*] see; consult (used as an instruction in a text to refer the reader to a specified passage, book, author, etc., for fuller or further information): *vide the comments cited in Schlosser.*

vi·de·li·cet /və'delə,set; -set; -'dälə,ket/ ▶ *adv.* more formal term for VIZ.

vid·e·o /'vidē,ō/ ▶ *n.* (*pl.* **-os**) the system of recording, reproducing, or broadcasting moving visual images on or from videotape. ■ a movie or other piece of material recorded on videotape. ■ a videocassette: *the film will soon be released on video.* ■ a short movie made by a pop or rock group to accompany a song when broadcast on television.

vid·e·o ar·cade ▶ *n.* an indoor area containing coin-operated video games.

vid·e·o cam·er·a ▶ *n.* a camera for recording images on videotape or for transmitting them to a monitor screen.

vid·e·o·cas·sette /,vidēōkə'set/ ▶ *n.* a cassette of videotape.

vid·e·o·cas·sette re·cord·er (abbr.: **VCR**) ▶ *n.* a device used for recording on videotapes and playing them on a TV.

vid·e·o·disc /'vidēō,disk/ (also **vid·e·o·disk**) ▶ *n.* a CD-ROM or other disk used to store visual images and sound.

vid·e·o dis·play ter·min·al (abbr.: **VDT**) ▶ *n. Comput.* a device for displaying input signals as characters on a screen, typically a monitor.

vid·e·o game ▶ *n.* a game played by electronically manipulating images produced by a computer program on a television screen or other display screen.

vid·e·o jock·ey ▶ *n.* a person who introduces and plays music videos for a broadcast, party, or other entertainment.

vid·e·o·phone /'vidēō,fōn/ ▶ *n.* a telephone device transmitting and receiving a visual image as well as sound.

vid·e·o·tape /'vidēō,tāp/ ▶ *n.* magnetic tape for recording and reproducing visual images and sound. ■ a videocassette. ■ a film or other piece of material recorded on videotape.

▶ *v.* [*tr.*] make a video recording of (an event or broadcast): *his arrest was videotaped.*

vie /vī/ ▶ *v.* (**vy·ing**) [*intr.*] compete eagerly with someone in order to do or achieve something: *rival mobs vying for control of the liquor business.*

Vi·et·nam·ese /vē,etnə'mēz; ,vyet-; ,vēət-; -'mēs/ ▶ *adj.* of or relating to Vietnam, its people, or their language.

▶ *n.* (*pl.* same) **1** a native or national of Vietnam, or a person of Vietnamese descent. **2** the language of Vietnam.

Pronunciation Key ə *ago*, *up*; ər *over*, *fur*; a *hat*; ā *ate*; ä *car*; CH *chin*; e *let*; ē *see*; e(ə)r *air*; i *fit*; ī *by*; i(ə)r *ear*; NG *sing*; ō *go*; ô *law*, *for*; oi *toy*; ōō *good*; ōō *goo*; ou *out*; SH *she*; TH *thin*; TH *then*; (h)w *why*; ZH *vision*

view /vyo͞o/ ▸*n.* **1** the ability to see something or to be seen from a particular place: *the end of the tunnel came into view.* ■ a sight or prospect, typically of attractive natural scenery, that can be taken in by the eye from a particular place: *a fine view of the castle.* ■ a work of art depicting such a sight. ■ the visual appearance or an image of something when looked at in a particular way: *an aerial view of the military earthworks.* ■ an inspection of things for sale by prospective purchasers, esp. of works of art at an exhibition. **2** a particular way of considering or regarding something; an attitude or opinion: *strong political views.*
▸*v.* **1** [*tr.*] look at or inspect (something): *the public can view the famous hall with its unique staircase.* **2** [*tr.*] regard in a particular light or with a particular attitude: *farmers are viewing the rise in rabbit numbers with concern.* ▷Middle English: from Anglo-Norman French *vieue*, feminine past participle of *veoir* 'see,' from Latin *videre*. The verb dates from the early 16th cent. —**view·a·ble** *adj.*
▸ ◻ **in view** visible to someone: *the youth was keeping him in view.* ■ as one's aim or objective: *his arrest is the principal object I* **have in view.** ◻ **in view of** because or as a result of. ◻ **with a view to** with the hope, aim, or intention of.

view·er /ˈvyo͞oər/ ▸*n.* **1** a person who looks at or inspects something. ■ a person watching television or a movie. **2** a device for looking at slides or similar photographic images.

view·find·er /ˈvyo͞oˌfīndər/ ▸*n.* a device on a camera showing the field of view of the lens, used in framing and focusing the picture.

view·ing /ˈvyo͞oiNG/ ▸*n.* the action of inspecting or looking at something: *viewing by appointment.* ■ the action of watching something on television: *unsuitable for family viewing.* ■ an opportunity to see something, esp. a work of art.

view·point /ˈvyo͞oˌpoint/ ▸*n.* another term for POINT OF VIEW.

vig·il /ˈvijəl/ ▸*n.* **1** a period of keeping awake during the time usually spent asleep, esp. to keep watch or pray: *as he lay in a coma the family kept vigil.* ■ a stationary, peaceful demonstration in support of a particular cause, typically without speeches. **2** (in the Christian Church) the eve of a festival or holy day as an occasion of religious observance. ■ (**vigils**) nocturnal devotions.

vig·i·lance /ˈvijələns/ ▸*n.* the action or state of keeping careful watch for possible danger or difficulties.

vig·i·lant /ˈvijələnt/ ▸*adj.* keeping careful watch for possible danger or difficulties: *a burglar spotted by vigilant neighbors.* —**vig·i·lant·ly** *adv.*

vig·i·lan·te /ˌvijəˈlantē/ ▸*n.* a member of a self-appointed group of citizens who undertake law enforcement in their community without legal authority. —**vig·i·lan·tism** /-ˌtizəm/ *n.*

vi·gnette /vinˈyet/ ▸*n.* **1** a brief evocative description, account, or episode. **2** a small illustration or portrait photograph that fades into its background without a definite border. ■ a small ornamental design filling a space in a book or carving, typically based on foliage. —**vi·gnet·tist** /-ˈyetist/ *n.*

vig·or /ˈvigər/ (*Brit.* **vig·our**) ▸*n.* physical strength and good health. ■ effort, energy, and enthusiasm: *they set about the new task with vigor.* ■ strong, healthy growth of a plant. —**vig·or·less** /ˈvigərləs/ *adj.*

vig·or·ous /ˈvig(ə)rəs/ ▸*adj.* (of a person) strong, healthy, and full of energy. ■ characterized by or involving physical strength, effort, or energy: *vigorous exercise.* ■ (of language) forceful: *a vigorous denial.* ■ (of a plant) growing strongly. —**vig·or·ous·ly** *adv.* —**vig·or·ous·ness** *n.*

Vi·king /ˈvīkiNG/ ▸*n.* any of the Scandinavian seafaring pirates and traders who raided and settled in many parts of northwestern Europe in the 8th–11th centuries.
▸*adj.* of or relating to the Vikings or the period in which they lived.

vile /vīl/ ▸*adj.* extremely unpleasant: *he has a vile temper.* ■ morally bad; wicked: *as vile a rogue as ever lived.* —**vile·ly** *adv.* —**vile·ness** *n.*

vil·i·fy /ˈviləˌfī/ ▸*v.* (**-fies, -fied**) [*tr.*] speak or write about in an abusively disparaging manner: *he has been vilified in the press.* —**vil·i·fi·ca·tion** /ˌviləfiˈkāSHən/ *n.* —**vil·i·fi·er** *n.*

vil·la /ˈvilə/ ▸*n.* (esp. in continental Europe) a large and luxurious country residence. ■ a large country house of Roman times, having an estate and consisting of farm and residential buildings arranged around a courtyard.

vil·lage /ˈvilij/ ▸*n.* a group of houses and associated buildings, larger than a hamlet and smaller than a town, situated in a rural area. ■ a self-contained district or community within a town or city, regarded as having features characteristic of village life: *the Olympic village.* ■ a small municipality with limited corporate powers. —**vil·lag·er** *n.*

vil·lain /ˈvilən/ ▸*n.* a person guilty or capable of a crime or wickedness. ■ the person or thing responsible for specified trouble, harm, or damage: *the industrialized nations are the real environmental villains.* ■ (in a play

or novel) a character whose evil actions or motives are important to the plot. —**vil·lain·ess** /ˈvilənəs/ *n.*

vil·lain·ous /ˈvilənəs/ ▸*adj.* relating to, constituting, or guilty of wicked or criminal behavior: *the villainous crimes.* ■ *inf.* extremely bad or unpleasant: *a villainous smell.* —**vil·lain·ous·ly** *adv.* —**vil·lain·ous·ness** *n.*

vil·lain·y /ˈvilənē/ ▸*n.* (*pl.* **-lain·ies**) wicked or criminal behavior: *the villainy of professional racketeers* | *minor villainies.*

vil·lein /ˈvilən; -ˌān/ ▸*n. hist.* (in medieval England) a feudal tenant entirely subject to a lord or manor to whom he paid dues and services in return for land.

vil·lus /ˈviləs/ (*pl.* **vil·li** /ˈvilī; ˈvilē/) ▸*n. Anat.* any of numerous minute elongated projections set closely together on a surface, typically increasing its surface area for the absorption of substances, in particular: ■ a fingerlike projection of the lining of the small intestine.

vim /vim/ ▸*n. inf.* energy; enthusiasm: *full of vim and vigor.*

VIN /vin/ ▸*abbr.* vehicle identification number.

vin /van; van/ ▸*n.* French wine: *vin blanc.*

vin·ai·grette /ˌvinəˈgret/ ▸*n.* (also **vinaigrette dressing**) salad dressing of oil, wine vinegar, and seasoning.

vin·di·cate /ˈvindəˌkāt/ ▸*v.* [*tr.*] clear (someone) of blame or suspicion: *hospital staff were vindicated by the inquest verdict.* ■ show or prove to be right, reasonable, or justified: *more sober views were vindicated by events.* —**vin·di·ca·tion** /ˌvindəˈkāSHən/ *n.* —**vin·di·ca·tor** /-ˌkātər/ *n.* —**vin·di·ca·to·ry** /-kəˌtôrē/ *adj.*

vin·dic·tive /vinˈdiktiv/ ▸*adj.* having or showing a strong or unreasoning desire for revenge: *the criticism was both vindictive and personalized.* —**vin·dic·tive·ly** *adv.* —**vin·dic·tive·ness** *n.*

vine /vīn/ ▸*n.* a climbing or trailing woody-stemmed plant (*Vitis* and other genera) of the grape family. ■ used in names of climbing or trailing plants of other families, e.g., **potato vine**. ■ the slender stem of a trailing or climbing plant. —**vin·y** *adj.*

vin·e·gar /ˈvinəgər/ ▸*n.* a sour-tasting liquid containing acetic acid, obtained by fermenting dilute alcoholic liquids, typically wine, cider, or beer, and used as a condiment or for pickling. ■ *fig.* sourness or peevishness of behavior, character, or speech: *her aggrieved tone held a touch of vinegar.* —**vin·e·gar·ish** *adj.* —**vin·e·gar·y** *adj.*

vine·yard /ˈvinyərd/ ▸*n.* a plantation of grapevines, typically producing grapes used in winemaking. ■ *fig.* a sphere of action or labor: *women professors laboring in feminist vineyards.*

vin·i·cul·ture /ˈvinəˌkəlCHər/ ▸*n.* the cultivation of grapevines for winemaking. —**vin·i·cul·tur·al** /ˌvinəˈkəlCHərəl/ *adj.* —**vin·i·cul·tur·ist** *n.*

vi·no /ˈvēnō/ ▸*n.* (*pl.* **-nos**) Spanish or Italian wine.

vin·tage /ˈvintij/ ▸*n.* the year or place in which wine, esp. wine of high quality, was produced. ■ a wine of high quality made from the crop of a single identified district in a good year. ■ *poetic/lit.* wine. ■ the harvesting of grapes for winemaking. ■ the grapes or wine produced in a particular season. ■ the time that something of quality was produced: *rifles of various sizes and vintages.*
▸*adj.* of, relating to, or denoting wine of high quality: *vintage claret.* ■ denoting something of high quality, esp. something from the past or characteristic of the best period of a person's work: *a vintage Sherlock Holmes adventure.*

vint·ner /ˈvintnər/ ▸*n.* **1** a wine merchant. **2** a wine maker.

vi·nyl /ˈvīnl/ ▸*n.* **1** synthetic resin or plastic consisting of polyvinyl chloride or a related polymer, used esp. for wallpapers and other covering materials and for phonograph records: *light-reflecting vinyls can be hung in the usual way.* ■ vinyl used as the standard material for phonograph records: *fans had to wait almost a year before the song eventually appeared on vinyl.* **2** [as *adj.*] *Chem.* of or denoting the unsaturated hydrocarbon radical −CH=CH₂: *a vinyl group.*

vi·ol /ˈvīəl/ ▸*n.* a musical instrument of the Renaissance and baroque periods, typically six-stringed, held vertically and played with a bow.

vi·o·la¹ /vīˈōlə; vē-; ˈvīələ/ ▸*n.* an instrument of the violin family, larger than the violin and tuned a fifth lower.

vi·o·la² /vēˈōlə/ ▸*n.* a plant of a genus (*Viola*) that includes the pansies and violets.

vi·o·late /ˈvīəˌlāt/ ▸*v.* [*tr.*] break or fail to comply with (a rule or formal agreement): *they violated the terms of a cease-fire.* ■ fail to respect (someone's peace, privacy, or rights): *they denied that human rights were being violated.* ■ treat (something sacred) with irreverence or disrespect: *he was accused of violating a tomb.* ■ rape or sexually assault (someone). —**vi·o·la·tor** /-ˌlātər/ *n.* —**vi·o·la·ble** /-ləbəl/ *adj.* (*rare*). —**vi·o·la·tive** *adj.* —**vi·o·la·tion** *n.*

vi·o·lence /ˈvī(ə)ləns/ ▸*n.* behavior involving physical force intended to hurt, damage, or kill someone or something. ■ strength of emotion or an unpleasant or destructive natural force: *the violence of her own feelings*. ■ *Law* the unlawful exercise of physical force or intimidation by the exhibition of such force.

vi·o·lent /'vī(ə)lənt/ ▸*adj.* using or involving physical force intended to hurt, damage, or kill someone or something: *a violent confrontation with riot police.* ■ (esp. of an emotion or unpleasant or destructive natural force) very strong or powerful: *violent dislike.* ■ (of a color) vivid. ■ *Law* involving an unlawful exercise or exhibition of force. —**vi·o·lent·ly** *adv.*

vi·o·let /'vī(ə)lət/ ▸*n.* **1** a herbaceous plant (genus *Viola*, family Violaceae) of temperate regions, typically having purple, blue, or white five-petaled flowers. ■ used in names of similar-flowered plants of other families, e.g., **African violet. 2** a bluish-purple color seen at the end of the spectrum opposite red.
▸*adj.* of a purplish-blue color.

vi·o·lin /ˌvīə'lin/ ▸*n.* a stringed musical instrument of treble pitch, played with a horsehair bow. The classical European violin was developed in the 16th century. It has four strings and a body of characteristic rounded shape, narrowed at the middle and with two f-shaped sound holes. —**vi·o·lin·ist** *n.*

vi·o·list ▸*n.* **1** /vē'ōlist/ a viola player. **2** /'vīəlist/ a viol player.

vi·o·lon·cel·lo /ˌvīələn'CHelō; ˌvē-/ ▸*n.* formal term for **CELLO**. —**vi·o·lon·cel·list** /-'CHelist/ *n.*

VIP ▸*abbr.* very important person.

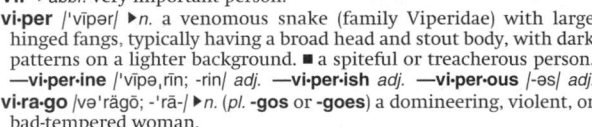
violin

vi·per /'vīpər/ ▸*n.* a venomous snake (family Viperidae) with large hinged fangs, typically having a broad head and stout body, with dark patterns on a lighter background. ■ a spiteful or treacherous person. —**vi·per·ine** /'vīpə,rīn; -rin/ *adj.* —**vi·per·ish** *adj.* —**vi·per·ous** /-əs/ *adj.*

vi·ra·go /və'rägō; -'rä-/ ▸*n.* (*pl.* **-gos** or **-goes**) a domineering, violent, or bad-tempered woman.

vi·ral /'vīrəl/ ▸*adj.* of the nature of, caused by, or relating to a virus or viruses. —**vi·ral·ly** *adv.*

vi·ral load ▸*n.* a measurement of the amount of a virus in an organism, typically in the bloodstream.

vir·e·o /'virē,ō/ ▸*n.* (*pl.* **-os**) a small American songbird (genus *Vireo*, family Vireonidae), typically having a green or gray back and yellow or white underparts.

vir·gin /'vərjən/ ▸*n.* a person, typically a woman, who has never had sexual intercourse. ■ a naive, innocent, or inexperienced person, esp. in a particular context: *a political virgin.* ■ (**the Virgin**) the mother of Jesus; the Virgin Mary. ■ a woman who has taken a vow to remain a virgin. ■ (**the Virgin**) the zodiacal sign or constellation Virgo.
▸*adj.* **1** being, relating to, or appropriate for a virgin: *his virgin bride.* **2** not yet touched, used, or exploited: *acres of virgin forests.* ■ (of clay) not yet fired. ■ (of wool) not yet, or only once, spun or woven. ■ (of olive oil) obtained from the first pressing of olives.

vir·gin·al /'vərjənl/ ▸*adj.* being, relating to, or appropriate for a virgin: *virginal shyness.*
▸*n.* (usu. **virginals**) an early spinet with the strings parallel to the keyboard, typically rectangular. —**vir·gin·al·ly** *adv.*

Vir·gin·ia creep·er ▸*n.* a North American vine (genus *Parthenocissus*) of the grape family, chiefly cultivated for its red autumn foliage.

Vir·gin·ia reel ▸*n.* a lively American country dance performed by a number of couples facing each other in parallel lines.

vir·gin·i·ty /vər'jinətē/ ▸*n.* the state of never having had sexual intercourse: *he lost his virginity in college.* ■ the state of being naive, innocent, or inexperienced in a particular context: *his political virginity.*

Vir·go /'vərgō/ ▸ **1** *Astron.* a large constellation (the Virgin), said to represent a maiden or goddess associated with the harvest. It contains several bright stars, the brightest of which is Spica. **2** *Astrol.* the sixth sign of the zodiac, which the sun enters about August 23. ■ (**a Virgo**) (*pl.* **-gos**) a person born when the sun is in this sign.

vir·gule /'vər,gyool/ ▸*n.* another term for **SLASH**[1] (sense 2). ▷mid 19th cent.: from French, literally 'comma,' from Latin *virgula*, diminutive of *virga* 'rod.'

vi·rid·i·an /və'ridēən/ ▸*n.* a bluish-green pigment consisting of hydrated chromium hydroxide. ■ the bluish-green color of this.

vir·ile /'virəl/ ▸*adj.* (of a man) having strength, energy, and a strong sex drive. ■ having or characterized by strength and energy: *a strong, virile performance.* —**vi·ril·i·ty** /və'rilitē/ *n.*

vi·rol·o·gy /vī'räləjē/ ▸*n.* the branch of science that deals with the study of viruses. —**vi·ro·log·i·cal** /ˌvīrə'läjikəl/ *adj.* —**vi·ro·log·i·cal·ly** *adv.* —**vi·rol·o·gist** /-jist/ *n.*

vir·tu·al /'vərCHooəl/ ▸*adj.* almost or nearly as described, but not completely or according to strict definition: *the virtual absence of border controls.* ■ *Comput.* not physically existing as such but made by software to appear to do so: *a virtual computer.* See also **VIRTUAL REALITY.** ■ *Optics* relating to the points at which rays would meet if produced backward. ■ *Physics* denoting particles or interactions with extremely short lifetimes and indefinitely great energies, postulated as intermediates in some processes. —**vir·tu·al·i·ty** /ˌvərCHoo'alitē/ *n.*

vir·tu·al·ly /'vərCHooəlē/ ▸*adv.* nearly; almost: *virtually all those arrested were accused | the college became virtually bankrupt.* ■ *Comput.* by means of virtual reality techniques.

vir·tu·al re·al·i·ty ▸*n. Comput.* the computer-generated simulation of a three-dimensional image or environment that can be interacted with in a seemingly real or physical way by a person using special electronic equipment, such as a helmet with a screen inside or gloves fitted with sensors.

vir·tue /'vərCHoo/ ▸*n.* behavior showing high moral standards: *paragons of virtue.* ■ a quality considered morally good or desirable in a person: *patience is a virtue.* ■ a good or useful quality of a thing: *Mike was extolling the virtues of the car.*
▸ □ **by** (or **in**) **virtue of** because or as a result of.

vir·tu·o·so /ˌvərCHoo'ōsō/ ▸*n.* (*pl.* **-si** /-sē/ or **-sos**) a person highly skilled in music or another artistic pursuit: *a celebrated clarinet virtuoso |* [as *adj.*] *virtuoso guitar playing.* ■ a person with a special knowledge of or interest in works of art or curios. —**vir·tu·os·ic** /-'äsik; -'ōsik/ *adj.* —**vir·tu·os·i·ty** /-'äsitē/ *n.*

vir·tu·ous /'vərCHəwəs/ ▸*adj.* having or showing high moral standards: *she considered herself very virtuous because she neither drank nor smoked.* ■ *archaic* (esp. of a woman) chaste. —**vir·tu·ous·ly** *adv.* —**vir·tu·ous·ness** *n.*

vir·u·lent /'vir(y)ələnt/ ▸*adj.* **1** (of a disease or poison) extremely severe or harmful in its effects. ■ (of a pathogen, esp. a virus) highly infective. **2** bitterly hostile: *a virulent attack on liberalism.* —**vir·u·lence** *n.* —**vir·u·lent·ly** *adv.*

vi·rus /'vīrəs/ ▸*n.* an infective agent that typically consists of a nucleic acid molecule in a protein coat, is too small to be seen by light microscopy, and is able to multiply only within the living cells of a host: [as *adj.*] *a virus infection.* ■ *inf.* an infection or disease caused by such an agent. ■ *fig.* a harmful or corrupting influence: *the virus of cruelty that is latent in all human beings.* ■ (also **computer virus**) a piece of code that is capable of copying itself and typically has a detrimental effect, such as corrupting the system or destroying data.

vi·sa /'vēzə/ ▸*n.* an endorsement on a passport indicating that the holder is allowed to enter, leave, or stay for a specified period of time in a country.

vis·age /'vizij/ ▸*n. poetic/lit.* a person's face, with reference to the form or proportions of the features: *an elegant, angular visage.* ■ a person's facial expression: *his visage of cheerfulness.* ■ *fig.* the surface of an object presented to view: *the moonlit visage of the port's whitewashed buildings.* —**vis·aged** *adj.* [in *comb.*] *a stern-visaged old man.*

vis-à-vis /'vēz ə 'vē/ ▸*prep.* in relation to; with regard to: *many agencies now have a unit to deal with women's needs vis-à-vis employment.* ■ as compared with; as opposed to: *the advantage for U.S. exports is the value of the dollar vis-à-vis other currencies.*
▸*n.* (*pl.* same) a face-to-face meeting: *the dreaded vis-à-vis with his boss.*

vis·cer·a /'visərə/ ▸*pl. n.* the internal organs in the main cavities of the body, esp. those in the abdomen, e.g., the intestines.

vis·cer·al /'vis(ə)rəl/ ▸*adj.* of or relating to the viscera: *the visceral nervous system.* ■ relating to deep inward feelings rather than to the intellect: *the voters' visceral fear of change.* —**vis·cer·al·ly** *adv.*

vis·cid /'visid/ ▸*adj.* glutinous; sticky: *the viscid mucus lining of the intestine.* —**vis·cid·i·ty** /və'sidətē/ *n.*

vis·cose /'vis,kōs; -,kōz/ ▸*n.* a viscous orange-brown solution made from cellulose used to make rayon fiber and transparent cellulose film. ■ rayon fabric or fiber made from this.

vis·cos·i·ty /ˌvi'skäsitē/ ▸*n.* (*pl.* **-ties**) the state of being thick, sticky, and semifluid in consistency, due to internal friction. ■ a quantity expressing the magnitude of such friction, as measured by the force per unit area resisting a flow in which parallel layers unit distance apart have unit speed relative to one another.

V

vis·count /ˈvīˌkount/ ▸ n. a British nobleman ranking above a baron and below an earl. —**vis·count·cy** /-ˌkountsē/ n.

vis·count·ess /ˈvīˌkountəs/ ▸ n. the wife or widow of a viscount. ■ a woman holding the rank of viscount in her own right.

vis·cous /ˈviskəs/ ▸ adj. having a thick, sticky consistency between solid and liquid; having a high viscosity: *viscous lava.* —**vis·cous·ly** adv. —**vis·cous·ness** n.

vise /vīs/ (*Brit.* **vice**) ▸ n. a metal tool with movable jaws that are used to hold an object firmly in place while work is done on it, typically attached to a workbench. —**vise·like** adj.

Vish·nu /ˈvishˌnoō/ *Hinduism* ▸ a god, originally a minor Vedic god, now regarded by his worshipers as the supreme deity and savior, by others as the preserver of the cosmos in a triad with Brahma and Shiva. Vishnu is considered by Hindus to have had nine earthly incarnations or avatars, including Rama, Krishna, and the historical Buddha; the tenth avatar will herald the end of the world. —**Vish·nu·ism** /-ˌizəm/ n. —**Vish·nu·ite** /-ˌīt/ n. & adj.

vis·i·bil·i·ty /ˌvizəˈbilitē/ ▸ n. the state of being able to see or be seen: *a reduction in police presence and visibility on the streets.* ■ the distance one can see as determined by light and weather conditions: *visibility was down to 15 yards.* ■ the degree to which something has attracted general attention; prominence: *the issue began to lose its visibility.*

vis·i·ble /ˈvizəbəl/ ▸ adj. **1** able to be seen: *the church spire is visible from miles away.* ■ *Physics* (of light) within the range of wavelengths to which the eye is sensitive. ■ able to be perceived or noticed easily: *a visible improvement.* ■ in a position of public prominence: *a highly visible member of the royal entourage.* **2** of or relating to imports or exports of tangible commodities: *the visible trade gap.* —**vis·i·ble·ness** n. —**vis·i·bly** /-blē/ adv. *he was visibly uncomfortable.*

Vis·i·goth /ˈvizəˌgäth/ ▸ n. a member of the branch of the Goths who invaded the Roman Empire between the 3rd and 5th centuries AD and ruled much of Spain until overthrown by the Moors in 711. —**Vis·i·goth·ic** /ˌvizəˈgäthik/ adj.

vi·sion /ˈvizHən/ ▸ n. **1** the faculty or state of being able to see: *she had defective vision.* ■ the ability to think about or plan the future with imagination or wisdom: *the organization had lost its vision and direction.* ■ a mental image of what the future will or could be like: *a socialist vision of society.* **2** an experience of seeing someone or something in a dream or trance, or as a supernatural apparition: *the idea came to him in a vision.* ■ (often **visions**) a vivid mental image, esp. a fanciful one of the future: *he **had visions of** becoming the Elton John of his time.* ■ a person or sight of unusual beauty.
▸ v. [tr.] *rare* imagine. —**vi·sion·al** /-zHənl/ adj. —**vi·sion·less** adj.

vi·sion·ar·y /ˈvizHəˌnerē/ ▸ adj. **1** (esp. of a person) thinking about or planning the future with imagination or wisdom: *a visionary leader.* **2** of, relating to, or able to see visions in a dream or trance, or as a supernatural apparition: *a visionary experience.*
▸ n. (pl. **-ar·ies**) a person with original ideas about what the future will or could be like. —**vi·sion·ar·i·ness** n.

vis·it /ˈvizit/ ▸ v. (**-it·ed**, **-it·ing**) [tr.] **1** go to see and spend time with (someone) socially: *I came to visit my grandmother.* ■ go to see and spend time in (a place) as a tourist. ■ stay temporarily with (someone) or at (a place) as a guest: *we hope you enjoy your stay and will visit us again* | [intr.] *I don't live here—I'm only visiting.* ■ go to see (someone or something) for a specific purpose, such as to make an inspection or to receive or give professional advice or help: *inspectors visit all the hotels.* ■ [intr.] (**visit with**) go to see (someone) socially: *he went out to visit with his pals.* ■ [intr.] *inf. chat: there was nothing to do but visit with one another.* ■ go to (a Web site or Web page): *visit us at www.flycreekcidermill.com.* ■ (chiefly in biblical use) (of God) come to (a person or place) in order to bring comfort or salvation. **2** (often **be visited**) inflict (something harmful or unpleasant) on someone: *the mockery visited upon him by his schoolmates.* ■ (of something harmful or unpleasant) afflict (someone): *they were visited with epidemics of a strange disease.*
▸ n. an act of going or coming to see a person or place socially, as a tourist, or for some other purpose: *a visit to the doctor.* ■ a temporary stay with a person or at a place. ■ an informal conversation. ▷Middle English: from Old French *visiter* or Latin *visitare* 'go to see,' frequentative of *visare* 'to view,' from *videre* 'to see.'

vis·it·a·tion /ˌvizəˈtāsHən/ ▸ n. **1** an official or formal visit, in particular: ■ (in church use) an official visit of inspection, esp. one by a bishop to a church in the bishop's diocese. ■ the appearance of a divine or supernatural being. ■ a gathering with the family of a deceased person before the funeral. ■ *Law* a divorced person's right to spend time with their children in the custody of a former spouse. **2** a disaster or difficulty regarded as a divine punishment: *a visitation of the plague.*

vis·it·ing /ˈviziting/ ▸ adj. (of a person) on a visit to a person or place: *a visiting speaker.* ■ (of an academic) working for a fixed period of time at another institution: *a visiting professor.*

vis·it·ing nurse ▸ n. a nurse who visits and treats patients in their homes, operating as part of a social service agency.

vis·i·tor /ˈvizitər/ ▸ n. a person visiting a person or place, esp. socially or as a tourist. ■ (usu. **visitors**) a member of a sports team on tour or playing away from home. ■ *Ornithol.* a migratory bird present in a locality for only part of the year. ▷late Middle English: from Anglo-Norman French *visitour,* from Old French *visiter* 'go to see,' from Latin *visitare,* frequentative of *visare* 'to view,' from *videre* 'to see.'

vi·sor /ˈvīzər/ ▸ n. a stiff brim at the front of a cap. ■ a movable part of a helmet that can be pulled down to cover the face. ■ a screen for protecting the eyes from unwanted light, esp. one at the top of a vehicle windshield. —**vi·sored** adj.

VISTA /ˈvistə/ ▸ abbr. Volunteers in Service to America.

vis·ta /ˈvistə/ ▸ n. a pleasing view, esp. one seen through a long, narrow opening: *a vista of church spires.* ■ a mental view of a succession of remembered or anticipated events: *vistas of freedom seemed to open.*

vis·u·al /ˈvizHoōəl/ ▸ adj. of or relating to seeing or sight: *visual perception.*
▸ n. (usu. **visuals**) a picture, piece of film, or display used to illustrate or accompany something. —**vis·u·al·i·ty** /ˌvizHoōˈalitē/ n. —**vis·u·al·ly** adv.

vis·u·al aid ▸ n. (usu. **visual aids**) an item of illustrative matter, such as a film, slide, or model, designed to supplement written or spoken information so that it can be understood more easily.

vis·u·al·ize /ˈvizHoōəˌlīz/ ▸ v. [tr.] **1** form a mental image of; imagine: *it is not easy to visualize the future.* **2** make (something) visible to the eye: *the cells were better visualized by staining.* —**vis·u·al·iz·a·ble** adj. —**vis·u·al·i·za·tion** /ˌvizHoōələˈzāsHən/ n.

vi·tal /ˈvītl/ ▸ adj. **1** absolutely necessary or important; essential: *secrecy is of vital importance.* ■ indispensable to the continuance of life: *the vital organs.* **2** full of energy; lively: *a beautiful, vital girl.*
▸ n. (**vitals**) the body's important internal organs, esp. the gut or the genitalia. ■ short for VITAL SIGNS. —**vi·tal·ly** adv.

vi·tal·ism /ˈvītlˌizəm/ ▸ n. the theory that the origin and phenomena of life are dependent on a force or principle distinct from purely chemical or physical forces. —**vi·tal·ist** n. & adj. —**vi·tal·is·tic** /ˌvītlˈistik/ adj.

vi·tal·i·ty /vīˈtalitē/ ▸ n. the state of being strong and active; energy: *changes that will give renewed vitality to our democracy.* ■ the power giving continuance of life, present in all living things: *the vitality of seeds.*

vi·tal·ize /ˈvītlˌīz/ ▸ v. [tr.] give strength and energy to: *yoga calms and vitalizes body and mind.* —**vi·tal·i·za·tion** /ˌvītl-əˈzāsHən/ n.

vi·tal signs /ˈvīdl sīnz/ ▸ pl. n. clinical measurements, specifically pulse rate, temperature, respiration rate, blood pressure, and blood oxygen saturation, that indicate the state of a patient's essential body functions.

vi·tal sta·tis·tics /ˈvīdl stəˈtistiks/ ▸ pl. n. **1** quantitative data concerning a population, such as the number of births, marriages, and deaths. **2** *inf.* the measurements of a woman's bust, waist, and hips.

vi·ta·min /ˈvītəmən/ ▸ n. any of a group of organic compounds that are essential for normal growth and nutrition and are required in small quantities in the diet because they cannot be synthesized by the body.

vi·ta·min A ▸ n. another term for RETINOL.

vi·ta·min B ▸ n. any of a group of substances (the **vitamin B complex**) that are essential for the working of certain enzymes in the body and are generally found together in the same foods. They include thiamine (**vitamin B₁**), riboflavin (**vitamin B₂**), pyridoxine (**vitamin B₆**), and cyanocobalamin (**vitamin B₁₂**).

vi·ta·min C ▸ n. another term for ASCORBIC ACID.

vi·ta·min D ▸ n. any of a group of vitamins found in liver and fish oils, essential for the absorption of calcium and the prevention of rickets in children and softening of the bones in adults. They include calciferol (**vitamin D₂**) and cholecalciferol (**vitamin D₃**).

vi·ta·min E ▸ n. another term for TOCOPHEROL.

vi·ta·min K ▸ n. any of a group of vitamins found mainly in green leaves and essential for the blood-clotting process. They include phylloquinone (**vitamin K₁**) and menaquinone (**vitamin K₂**).

vi·ti·ate /ˈvishēˌāt/ ▸ v. [tr.] *formal* spoil or impair the quality or efficiency of: *development programs have been vitiated by the rise in population.* ■ destroy or impair the legal validity of. —**vi·ti·a·tion** /ˌvishēˈāsHən/ n. —**vi·ti·a·tor** /-ˌātər/ n.

vit·i·cul·ture /ˈvitiˌkəlcHər/ ▸ n. the cultivation of grapevines. ■ the study of grape cultivation. —**vit·i·cul·tur·al** /ˌvitiˈkəlcHərəl/ adj. —**vit·i·cul·tur·ist** /-rist/ n.

vit·re·ous /ˈvitrēəs/ ▸ adj. like glass in appearance or physical properties.

■ (of a substance) derived from or containing glass: *the toilet and bidet are made of vitreous china.* —**vit·re·ous·ness** *n.*

vit·re·ous hu·mor ▶*n.* the transparent jellylike tissue filling the eyeball behind the lens. Compare with AQUEOUS HUMOR.

vit·ri·form /'vitrə,fôrm/ ▶*adj.* having the form or appearance of glass.

vit·ri·fy /'vitrə,fī/ ▶*v.* (**-fies, -fied**) [*tr.*] (often **be vitrified**) convert (something) into glass or a glasslike substance, typically by exposure to heat. —**vit·ri·fac·tion** /,vitrə'fakSHən/ *n.* —**vit·ri·fi·a·ble** /'vitrə,fīəbəl; ,vitrə'fī-/ *adj.* —**vit·ri·fi·ca·tion** /,vitrəfi'kāSHən/ *n.*

vit·ri·ol /'vitrēəl; -,ôl/ ▶*n. archaic* or *poetic/lit.* sulfuric acid. ■ *fig.* cruel and bitter criticism: *her mother's sudden gush of fury and vitriol.* —**vit·ri·ol·ic** /,vitrē'älik/ *adj.*

vi·tu·per·a·tion /və,t(y)o͞opə'rāSHən, vī-/ ▶*n.* bitter and abusive language: *no one else attracted such vituperation from him.*

vi·tu·per·a·tive /və't(y)o͞opə,rātiv, vī-; -p(ə)rətiv/ ▶*adj.* bitter and abusive: *the criticism soon turned into a vituperative attack.*

vi·va /'vēvə/ ▶*interj.* long live! (used to express acclaim or support for a specified person or thing): *"Viva Mexico!"*
▶*n.* a cry of this as a salute or cheer.

vi·va·ce /vē'vä,CHā; -CHē/ *Mus.* ▶*adv. & adj.* (esp. as a direction) in a lively and brisk manner.

vi·va·cious /və'vāSHəs; vī-/ ▶*adj.* (esp. of a woman) attractively lively and animated. —**vi·va·cious·ly** *adv.* —**vi·va·cious·ness** *n.* —**vi·vac·i·ty** /və'vasitē; vī-/ *n.*

vi·va vo·ce /,vēvə 'vōCHā; ,vīvə 'vōsē/ ▶*adj.* (esp. of an examination) oral rather than written.
▶*adv.* orally rather than in writing.

viv·id /'vivid/ ▶*adj.* producing powerful feelings or strong, clear images in the mind: *memories of that evening were still vivid.* ■ (of a color) intensely deep or bright. —**viv·id·ly** *adv.* —**viv·id·ness** *n.*

vi·vip·a·rous /vī'vip(ə)rəs; vi-/ ▶*adj. Zool.* (of an animal) bringing forth live young that have developed inside the body of the parent. ■ *Bot.* (of a plant) reproducing from buds that form plantlets while still attached to the parent plant, or from seeds that germinate within the fruit. —**vi·vi·par·i·ty** /,vivə'paritē; ,vīvə-/ *n.* —**vi·vip·a·rous·ly** *adv.*

viv·i·sec·tion /,vivə'sekSHən/ ▶*n.* the practice of performing operations on live animals for the purpose of experimentation or scientific research (used only by people who are opposed to such work). ■ *fig.* ruthlessly sharp and detailed criticism or analysis: *the vivisection of America's seamy underbelly.* —**viv·i·sec·tion·ist** /-ist/ *n. & adj.*

vix·en /'viksən/ ▶*n.* a female fox. ■ a spiteful or quarrelsome woman. —**vix·en·ish** *adj.*

viz. /viz/ or said as /'nāmlē/ ▶*adv.* namely; in other words (used esp. to introduce a gloss or explanation): *the first music reproducing media, viz., the music box and the player piano.*

vi·zier /və'zi(ə)r/ ▶*n. hist.* a high official in some Muslim countries, esp. in Turkey under Ottoman rule.

VJ ▶*abbr.* video jockey.

V-neck ▶*n.* a neckline of a garment, having straight sides meeting at a point. ■ a garment with a neckline of this type. —**V-necked** *adj.*

vocab. ▶*abbr.* ■ vocabulary.

vo·cab·u·lar·y /vō'kabyə,lerē; vi-/ ▶*n.* (*pl.* **-lar·ies**) the body of words used in a particular language. ■ a part of such a body of words used on a particular occasion or in a particular sphere: *the vocabulary of law.* ■ the body of words known to an individual person: *he had a wide vocabulary.* ■ a list of difficult or unfamiliar words with an explanation of their meanings, accompanying a piece of specialist or foreign-language text. ■ a range of artistic or stylistic forms, techniques, or movements: *dance companies have their own vocabularies of movement.*

vo·cal /'vōkəl/ ▶*adj.* **1** of or relating to the human voice: *nonlinguistic vocal effects like laughs and sobs.* ■ *Anat.* used in the production of speech sounds: *the vocal apparatus.* ■ *Phonet.* (of a sound in speech) made with the voice rather than the breath alone; voiced. **2** expressing opinions or feelings freely or loudly: *he was vocal in condemning the action.* **3** (of music) consisting of or incorporating singing.
▶*n.* (often **vocals**) a part of a piece of music that is sung. ■ a musical performance involving singing. —**vo·cal·i·ty** /vō'kalətē/ *n.* —**vo·cal·ly** *adv.*

vo·cal cords (also **vocal folds**) ▶*pl. n.* folds of membranous tissue that project inward from the sides of the larynx to form a slit across the glottis in the throat, and whose edges vibrate in the airstream to produce the voice.

vo·cal·ism /'vōkə,lizəm/ ▶*n.* the use of the voice or vocal organs in speech. ■ the skill or art of exercising the voice in singing.

vo·cal·ist /'vōkəlist/ ▶*n.* a singer, typically one who regularly performs with a jazz or pop group.

vo·cal·ize /'vōkə,līz/ ▶*v.* [*tr.*] utter (a sound or word): *the child vocalizes a number of distinct sounds* | [*intr.*] *a warbler vocalized from a reed bed.* ■ express (something) with words: *Gillie could scarcely vocalize her responses.* —**vo·cal·i·za·tion** /,vōkələ'zāSHən/ *n.* —**vo·cal·iz·er** *n.*

vo·ca·tion /vō'kāSHən/ ▶*n.* a strong feeling of suitability for a particular career or occupation. ■ a person's employment or main occupation, esp. regarded as particularly worthy and requiring great dedication: *her vocation as a poet.* ■ a trade or profession.

vo·ca·tion·al /vō'kāSHənl/ ▶*adj.* of or relating to an occupation or employment: *they supervised prisoners in vocational activities.* ■ (of education or training) directed at a particular occupation and its skills: *vocational school* | *specialized vocational courses.* —**vo·ca·tion·al·ism** /-,izəm/ *n.* —**vo·ca·tion·al·ize** /-,īz/ *v.* —**vo·ca·tion·al·ly** *adv.*

voc·a·tive /'väkətiv/ *Gram.* ▶*adj.* relating to or denoting a case of nouns, pronouns, and adjectives in Latin and other languages, used in addressing or invoking a person or thing.
▶*n.* a word in the vocative case. ■ (**the vocative**) the vocative case.

vo·cif·er·ate /və'sifə,rāt; vō-/ ▶*v.* [*intr.*] shout, complain, or argue loudly or vehemently: *he then began to vociferate pretty loudly* | [*tr.*] *he entered, vociferating curses.* —**vo·cif·er·ant** /-rənt/ *adj.* —**vo·cif·er·a·tion** /-,sifə-'rāSHən/ *n.*

vo·cif·er·ous /və'sifərəs; vō-/ ▶*adj.* (esp. of a person or speech) vehement or clamorous: *he was a vociferous opponent of the takeover.* —**vo·cif·er·ous·ly** *adv.* —**vo·cif·er·ous·ness** *n.*

vod·ka /'vädkə/ ▶*n.* an alcoholic spirit of Russian origin made by distilling rye, wheat, or potatoes.

vogue /vōg/ ▶*n.* the prevailing fashion or style at a particular time: *the vogue is to make realistic films.* ■ general acceptance or favor; popularity: *the 1920s and 30s, when art deco was much in vogue.*
▶*adj.* popular; fashionable: *the government's new vogue word.*
▶*v.* (**vogued, vogueing** or **vogu·ing**) [*intr.*] dance to music in such a way as to imitate the characteristic poses struck by a model on a catwalk. —**vogu·ish** *adj.*

voice /vois/ ▶*n.* **1** the sound produced in a person's larynx and uttered through the mouth, as speech or song: *Meg raised her voice.* ■ an agency by which a particular point of view is expressed or represented: *the proud voice of middle-class conservatism.* ■ the means of expressing an opinion: *the new electoral system gives minority parties a voice.* ■ a particular opinion or attitude expressed: *a dissenting voice.* ■ the ability to speak or sing: *she'd lost her voice.* ■ (usu. **voices**) the supposed utterance of a guiding spirit, typically giving instructions or advice. ■ the distinctive tone or style of a literary work or author: *she had strained and falsified her literary voice.* **2** *Mus.* the range of pitch or type of tone with which a person sings, such as soprano or tenor. ■ a vocal part in a composition. ■ each of the notes or sounds able to be produced simultaneously by a musical instrument (esp. an electronic one) or a computer. **3** *Gram.* a form or set of forms of a verb showing the relation of the subject to the action: *the passive voice.*
▶*v.* [*tr.*] **1** express (something) in words: *get teachers to voice their opinions on important subjects.* **2** [usu. as *adj.*] (**voiced**) *Phonet.* utter (a speech sound) with resonance of the vocal cords (e.g., *b, d, g, v, z*). **3** *Mus.* regulate the tone quality of (organ pipes). ▷Middle English: from Old French *vois*, from Latin *vox, voc-.* —**voiced** *adj.* [in *comb.*] *deep-voiced.*
▶ □ **give voice to** allow (a particular emotion, opinion, or point of view) to be expressed. ■ allow (a person or group) to express their emotions, opinion, or point of view. □ **with one voice** in complete agreement; unanimously.

voice box ▶*n.* the larynx.

voice·less /'voislis/ ▶*adj.* mute; speechless: *how could he have remained voiceless in the face of her cruelty?* ■ not expressed: *the air was charged with voiceless currents of thought.* ■ (of a person or group) lacking the power or right to express an opinion or exert control over affairs. ■ *Phonet.* (of a speech sound) uttered without resonance of the vocal cords, e.g., *f* as opposed to *v*, *p* as opposed to *b*, and *s* as opposed to *z*. —**voice·less·ly** *adv.* —**voice·less·ness** *n.*

voice mail (also **voice-mail**) ▶*n.* a centralized electronic system that can store messages from telephone callers.

voice-o·ver ▶*n.* a piece of narration in a movie or broadcast, not accompanied by an image of the speaker.

void /void/ ▶*adj.* **1** not valid or legally binding: *the contract was void.* ■ (of speech or action) ineffectual; useless: *all the stratagems you've worked out are rendered void.* **2** completely empty: *void spaces surround the tanks.*

■ (**void of**) free from; lacking: *what were once the masterpieces of literature are now void of meaning.* ■ *formal* (of an office or position) vacant.
▶*n.* a completely empty space: *the nothingness of the black void.* ■ an emptiness caused by the loss of something: *the void left by the collapse of communism.* ■ an unfilled space in a wall, building, or structure.
▶*v.* [*tr.*] **1** declare that (something) is not valid or legally binding: *the Supreme Court voided the statute.* **2** discharge or drain away (water, gases, etc.). ■ *chiefly Med.* excrete (waste matter). ■ [usu. as *adj.*] (**voided**) empty or evacuate (a container or space).

void·ance /'voidns/ ▶*n. chiefly Law* an annulment of a contract.

voile /voil/ ▶*n.* a thin, plain-weave, semitransparent fabric of cotton, wool, or silk.

vol. ▶*abbr.* volume.

vo·lant /'vōlənt/ ▶*adj. Zool.* (of an animal) able to fly or glide: *newly volant young.* ■ of, relating to, or characterized by flight: *volant ways of life.*

vol·a·tile /'välətl/ ▶*adj.* **1** (of a substance) easily evaporated at normal temperatures. **2** liable to change rapidly and unpredictably, esp. for the worse: *the political situation was becoming more volatile.* ■ (of a person) liable to display rapid changes of emotion. ■ (of a computer's memory) retaining data only as long as there is a power supply connected.
▶*n.* (usu. **volatiles**) a volatile substance. —**vol·a·til·i·ty** /,välə'tilitē/ *n.*

vol·a·til·ize /'välətl,īz/ ▶*v.* [*tr.*] cause (a substance) to evaporate or disperse in vapor. ■ [*intr.*] become volatile; evaporate. —**vol·a·til·iz·a·ble** *adj.* —**vol·a·til·i·za·tion** /,välətl-ə'zāSHən/ *n.*

vol·can·ic /väl'kanik; vôl-/ ▶*adj.* of, relating to, or produced by a volcano or volcanoes. ■ *fig.* (esp. of a feeling or emotion) bursting out or liable to burst out violently: *the kind of volcanic passion she'd felt last night.* —**vol·can·i·cal·ly** /-ik(ə)lē/ *adv.*

vol·ca·no /väl'kānō; vôl-/ ▶*n.* (*pl.* **-noes** or **-nos**) a mountain or hill, typically conical, having a crater or vent through which lava, rock fragments, hot vapor, and gas are or have been erupted from the earth's crust. ■ *fig.* an intense suppressed emotion or situation liable to burst out suddenly: *a volcano of emotion boiling inside that youngster.*

vol·can·ol·o·gy /,välkə'näləjē; ,vôl-/ (also **vul·can·ol·o·gy**) ▶*n.* the scientific study of volcanoes. —**vol·can·o·log·i·cal** /,välkənl'äjikəl; ,vôl-/ *adj.* —**vol·can·ol·o·gist** *n.*

vole /vōl/ ▶*n.* a small, typically burrowing, mouselike rodent (*Microtus* and other genera, subfamily Microtinae) with a rounded muzzle, found in both Eurasia and North America.

vo·li·tion /və'liSHən; vō-/ ▶*n.* the faculty or power of using one's will: *without conscious volition she backed into her office.* —**vo·li·tion·al** /-SHənl/ *adj.* —**vo·li·tion·al·ly** /-SHənl-ē/ *adv.*

vol·ley /'välē/ ▶*n.* (*pl.* **-leys**) **1** a number of bullets, arrows, or other projectiles discharged at one time: *the infantry let off a couple of volleys.* ■ a series of utterances directed at someone in quick succession: *he unleashed a volley of angry questions.* ■ *Tennis* an exchange of shots. **2** (in sports, esp. tennis or soccer) a strike or kick of the ball made before it touches the ground.
▶*v.* (**-leys**, **-leyed**) [*tr.*] (in sports, esp. tennis or soccer) strike or kick (the ball) before it touches the ground: *he volleyed home the ball.* ■ score (a goal) with such a shot. ■ [*intr.*] (in tennis and similar games) play a pregame point, sometimes in order to determine who will serve first. —**vol·ley·er** *n.*

vol·ley·ball /'välē,bôl/ ▶*n.* a game for two teams, usually of six players, in which a large ball is hit by hand over a high net, the aim being to score points by making the ball reach the ground on the opponent's side of the court. ■ the inflated ball used in this game.

volt /vōlt/ (abbr.: **V**) ▶*n.* the SI unit of electromotive force, the difference of potential that would drive one ampere of current against one ohm resistance.

volt·age /'vōltij/ ▶*n. Physics* an electromotive force or potential difference expressed in volts.

volt·me·ter /'vōlt,mētər/ ▶*n.* an instrument for measuring electric potential in volts.

vol·u·ble /'välyəbəl/ ▶*adj.* speaking or spoken incessantly and fluently: *she was as voluble as her husband was silent.* —**vol·u·bil·i·ty** /,välyə'bilətē/ *n.* —**vol·u·ble·ness** *n.* —**vol·u·bly** /-blē/ *adv.*

vol·ume /'välyəm; -,yōōm/ ▶*n.* **1** a book forming part of a work or series. ■ a single book or a bound collection of printed sheets. ■ a consecutive sequence of issues of a periodical. **2** the amount of space that a substance or object occupies, or that is enclosed within a container, esp. when great: *the sewer could not cope with the volume of rainwater.* ■ the amount or quantity of something, esp. when great: *changes in the volume of consumer spending.* ■ (**a volume of/volumes of**) a certain, typically large amount of something: *the volumes of data handled are vast.*

■ fullness or expansive thickness of something, esp. of a person's hair. **3** quantity or power of sound; degree of loudness: *he turned the volume up on the radio.*

vo·lu·mi·nous /və'lōōmənəs/ ▶*adj.* occupying or containing much space; large in volume, in particular: ■ (of clothing or drapery) loose and ample. ■ (of writing) very lengthy and full. ■ (of a writer) producing many books. —**vo·lu·mi·nous·ly** *adv.* —**vo·lu·mi·nous·ness** *n.*

vol·un·ta·rism /'väləntə,rizəm/ ▶*n.* the principle of relying on voluntary action (used esp. with reference to the involvement of voluntary organizations in social welfare). —**vol·un·ta·rist** *n.* & *adj.* —**vol·un·ta·ris·tic** /,väləntə'ristik/ *adj.*

vol·un·tar·y /'välən,terē/ ▶*adj.* done, given, or acting of one's own free will: *we are funded by voluntary contributions.* ■ working, done, or maintained without payment: *a voluntary helper.* ■ supported by contributions rather than taxes or dues: *voluntary hospitals.* ■ *Physiol.* under the conscious control of the brain. ■ *Law* (of a conveyance or disposition) made without return in money or other consideration.
▶*n.* (*pl.* **-tar·ies**) an organ solo played before, during, or after a church service. —**vol·un·tar·i·ly** /,välən'te(ə)rəlē; 'välən,ter-/ *adv.* —**vol·un·tar·i·ness** *n.*

vol·un·teer /,välən'tir/ ▶*n.* a person who freely offers to take part in an enterprise or undertake a task. ■ a person who works for an organization without being paid. ■ a person who freely enrolls for military service rather than being conscripted, esp. a member of a force formed by voluntary enrollment and distinct from the regular army. ■ a plant that has not been deliberately planted.
▶*v.* [*intr.*] freely offer to do something: *he volunteered for the job* | *I rashly volunteered to be a contestant.* ■ [*tr.*] offer (help) in such a way: *he volunteered his services as a driver for the convoy.* ■ say or suggest something without being asked: [*tr.*] *it never paid to volunteer information.* ■ work for an organization without being paid. ■ [*tr.*] commit (someone) to a particular undertaking, typically without consulting them: *he was volunteered for parachute training by friends.*

vo·lup·tu·ar·y /və'ləpcHŌŌ,erē/ ▶*n.* (*pl.* **-ar·ies**) a person devoted to luxury and sensual pleasure.
▶*adj.* concerned with luxury and sensual pleasure: *a voluptuary decade when high living was in style.*

vo·lup·tu·ous /və'ləpcHwəs/ ▶*adj.* of, relating to, or characterized by luxury or sensual pleasure: *long curtains in voluptuous crimson velvet.* ■ (of a woman) curvaceous and sexually attractive. ▷late Middle English: from Old French *voluptueux* or Latin *voluptuosus*, from *voluptas* 'pleasure.' —**vo·lup·tu·ous·ly** *adv.* —**vo·lup·tu·ous·ness** *n.*

vo·lute /və'lōōt/ ▶*n.* **1** *Archit.* a spiral scroll characteristic of Ionic capitals and also used in Corinthian and composite capitals. **2** a deep-water marine mollusk (*Voluta* and other genera, family Volutidae) with a thick spiral shell that is colorful and prized by collectors. —**vo·lut·ed** *adj.*

volute

vom·it /'vämət/ ▶*v.* (**-it·ed**, **-it·ing**) [*intr.*] eject matter from the stomach through the mouth: *the sickly stench made him want to vomit* | [*tr.*] *she used to vomit up her food.* ■ [*tr.*] emit (something) in an uncontrolled stream or flow: *the machine vomited fold after fold of paper.*
▶*n.* matter vomited from the stomach. —**vom·it·er** *n.*

voo·doo /'vōō,dōō/ ▶*n.* a black religious cult practiced in the Caribbean and the southern U.S., combining elements of Roman Catholic ritual with traditional African magical and religious rites, and characterized by sorcery and spirit possession. ■ a person skilled in such practice. —**voo·doo·ism** /-,izəm/ *n.* —**voo·doo·ist** /-ist/ *n.*

vo·ra·cious /və'rāSHəs/ ▶*adj.* wanting or devouring great quantities of food: *he had a voracious appetite.* ■ having a very eager approach to an activity: *his voracious reading of literature.* —**vo·ra·cious·ly** *adv.* —**vo·ra·cious·ness** *n.* —**vo·rac·i·ty** /-'rasitē/ *n.*

vor·tex /'vôr,teks/ ▶*n.* (*pl.* **-tex·es** or **-ti·ces** /-tə,sēz/) a mass of whirling fluid or air, esp. a whirlpool or whirlwind. ■ *fig.* something regarded as a whirling mass: *the vortex of existence.* —**vor·ti·cal** /'vôrtikəl/ *adj.* —**vor·ti·cal·ly** /'vôrtik(ə)lē/ *adv.* —**vor·tic·i·ty** /vôr'tisitē/ *n.*

vor·ti·cel·la /,vôrtə'selə/ ▶*n. Zool.* a sedentary, single-celled aquatic animal (genus *Vorticella*, phylum Ciliophora) with a bell-shaped body bearing a ring of cilia.

vo·ta·ry /'vōtərē/ ▶*n.* (*pl.* **-ries**) a person, such as a monk or nun, who has made vows of dedication to religious service. ■ a devoted follower, adherent, or advocate of someone or something: *he was a votary of John Keats.* —**vo·ta·rist** /-rist/ *n.*

vote /vōt/ ▶*n.* a formal indication of a choice between two or more candidates or courses of action, expressed typically through a ballot or a show of hands or by voice. ■ an act of expressing such an indication of choice: *they are ready to **put it to a vote**.* ■ **(the vote)** the choice expressed collectively by a body of electors or by a specified group: *the Republican vote in Florida.* ■ **(the vote)** the right to indicate a choice in an election.
▶*v.* [*intr.*] give or register a vote: *they voted against the resolution.* ■ [*tr.*] cause (someone) to gain or lose a particular post or honor by means of a vote: *incompetent judges are voted out of office.* ■ *inf.* used to express a wish to follow a particular course of action: *I vote we have one more game.* ■ [*tr.*] (of a legislature) grant or confer by vote. ■ [*tr.*] (**vote something down**) reject (something) by means of a vote. —**vote·less** *adj.*
▶ □ **vote of confidence** a vote showing that a majority continues to support the policy of a leader or governing body. □ **vote of no confidence** (or **vote of censure**) a vote showing that a majority does not support the policy of a leader or governing body.

vot·er /'vōtər/ ▶*n.* a person who votes or has the right to vote at an election.

vo·tive /'vōtiv/ ▶*adj.* offered or consecrated in fulfillment of a vow: *votive offerings.*
▶*n.* an object offered in this way, such as a candle used as a vigil light.

vouch /vou̇CH/ ▶*v.* [*intr.*] (**vouch for**) assert or confirm as a result of one's own experience that something is true or accurately so described: *they say New York is the city that never sleeps, and I can certainly **vouch for** that.* ■ confirm that someone is who they say they are or that they are of good character: *he was refused entrance until someone could vouch for him.*

vouch·er /'vou̇CHər/ ▶*n.* a small printed piece of paper that entitles the holder to a discount or that may be exchanged for goods or services. ■ a receipt.

vouch·safe /vou̇CH'sāf; 'vou̇CH,sāf/ ▶*v.* (often **be vouchsafed**) give or grant (something) to (someone) in a gracious or condescending manner: *it is a blessing vouchsafed him by heaven.* ■ [*tr.*] reveal or disclose (information): *you'd never vouchsafed that interesting tidbit before.*

vow /vou̇/ ▶*n.* a solemn promise. ■ (**vows**) a set of such promises committing one to a prescribed role, calling, or course of action, typically to marriage or a monastic career.
▶*v.* solemnly promise to do a specified thing: *he vowed that his government would not tolerate a repeat of the disorder.*

vow·el /'vou̇əl/ ▶*n.* a speech sound that is produced in a comparatively open vocal tract, with vibration of the vocal cords but without audible friction and is a unit of the sound system of a language that forms the nucleus of a syllable. Contrasted with CONSONANT. ■ a letter representing such a vowel, such as *a, e, i, o, u.*

vox po·pu·li /'väks 'päpyə,lī; -,lē/ ▶*n.* the opinions or beliefs of the majority.

voy·age /'voi-ij/ ▶*n.* a long journey involving travel by sea or in space: *a six-year voyage to Jupiter* | *fig. writing a biography is a **voyage of discovery**.*
▶*v.* [*intr.*] go on a long journey, typically by sea or in space: *he has voyaged through places like Venezuela and Peru.* —**voy·age·a·ble** *adj.* (*archaic*) —**voy·ag·er** *n.*

vo·yeur /voi'yər; vwä-/ ▶*n.* a person who gains sexual pleasure from watching others when they are naked or engaged in sexual activity. ■ a person who enjoys seeing the pain or distress of others. —**vo·yeur·ism** *n.* —**voy·eur·is·tic** *adj.* —**voy·eur·is·ti·cal·ly** *adv.*

VP ▶*abbr.* Vice President.

V-sign ▶*n.* a sign resembling the letter V made with the palm of the hand facing outward, used as a symbol or gesture of victory.

VTOL /'vē,täl; -,tôl/ ▶*abbr.* vertical takeoff and landing.

vul·can·ize /'vəlkə,nīz/ ▶*v.* [*tr.*] harden (rubber or rubberlike material) by treating it with sulfur at a high temperature. —**vul·can·iz·a·ble** *adj.* —**vul·can·i·za·tion** /,vəlkənə'zāSHən/ *n.* —**vul·can·iz·er** *n.*

vul·can·ol·o·gy /,vəlkə'näləjē/ ▶*n.* variant spelling of VOLCANOLOGY.

vul·gar /'vəlgər/ ▶*adj.* lacking sophistication or good taste; unrefined: *the vulgar trappings of wealth.* ■ making explicit and offensive reference to sex or bodily functions; coarse and rude: *a vulgar joke.* ■ *dated* characteristic of or belonging to the masses. —**vul·gar·i·ty** /,vəl'garitē/ *n.* (*pl.* **-ties**) —**vul·gar·ly** *adv.*

vul·gar·i·an /,vəl'ge(ə)rēən/ ▶*n.* an unrefined person, esp. one with newly acquired power or wealth.

vul·gar·ism /'vəlgə,rizəm/ ▶*n.* a word or expression that is considered inelegant, esp. one that makes explicit and offensive reference to sex or bodily functions.

vul·gar·ize /'vəlgə,rīz/ ▶*v.* [*tr.*] make less refined: *her voice, vulgarized by its accent, was full of caressing tones.* ■ make commonplace or less subtle or complex: [as *adj.*] (**vulgarized**) *a vulgarized version of the argument.* —**vul·gar·i·za·tion** /,vəlgərə'zāSHən/ *n.*

Vul·gate /'vəl,gāt; -gət/ ▶*n.* **1** the principal Latin version of the Bible, prepared mainly by St. Jerome in the late 4th century, and (as revised in 1592) adopted as the official text for the Roman Catholic Church. **2** (**vul·gate**) *formal* common or colloquial speech.

vul·ner·a·ble /'vəln(ə)rəbəl/ ▶*adj.* susceptible to physical or emotional attack or harm: *we were in a vulnerable position.* ■ *Bridge* (of a partnership) liable to higher penalties, either by convention or through having won one game toward a rubber. ▷early 17th cent.: from late Latin *vulnerabilis,* from Latin *vulnerare* 'to wound,' from *vulnus* 'wound.' —**vul·ner·a·bil·i·ty** /,vəln(ə)rə'bilitē/ *n.* (*pl.* **-ties**) —**vul·ner·a·ble·ness** *n.* —**vul·ner·a·bly** /-blē/ *adv.*

vul·pine /'vəl,pīn/ ▶*adj.* of or relating to a fox or foxes. ■ crafty; cunning: *Karl gave a vulpine smile.*

vul·ture /'vəlCHər/ ▶*n.* **1** a large bird of prey with the head and neck more or less bare of feathers, feeding chiefly on carrion. They are classified as **Old World vultures** (family Accipitridae) and **New World vultures** (family Cathartidae). **2** a contemptible person who preys on or exploits others. —**vul·tur·ine** /-,rīn/ *adj.* —**vul·tur·ish** *adj.* —**vul·tur·ous** /-CH(ə)rəs/ *adj.*

vul·va /'vəlvə/ ▶*n.* *Anat.* the female external genitals. ■ *Zool.* the external opening of the vagina or reproductive tract in a female mammal or nematode. —**vul·val** *adj.* —**vul·var** *adj.*

vv. ▶*abbr.* ■ verses. ■ volumes.

vy·ing /'vī-iNG/ ▶ present participle of VIE.

Ww

W¹ /'dəbəl,yōō/ (also **w**) ▶*n.* (*pl.* **Ws** or **W's**) **1** the twenty-third letter of the alphabet. ■ denoting the next after V in a set of items, categories, etc. **2** a shape like that of a letter W: [in *comb.*] *the W-shaped northern constellation of Cassiopeia.*

W² ▶*abbr.* ■ Wales. ■ *Baseball* WALK (sense 3 of the *noun*). ■ warden. ■ (in tables of sports results) games won. ■ watt(s). ■ Wednesday. ■ week. ■ (w) weight. ■ Welsh. ■ West or Western: *104° W | W Europe.* ■ (in personal ads) White. ■ width: *23 in. H x 20.5 in. W x 16 in. D.* ■ (in personal ads) widowed. ■ (in genealogies) wife. ■ women's (clothes size). ■ *Physics* work.
▶*symb.* ■ the chemical element tungsten.

Wa /wä/ ▶*n.* (*pl.* same or **Was**) **1** a member of a hill people living on the border between China and Myanmar (Burma). **2** the Mon-Khmer language of this people.
▶*adj.* of, relating to, or denoting this people or their language.

WAC /wak/ ▶*abbr.* Women's Army Corps. ■ (also **Wac**) a member of the Women's Army Corps.

wack·o /'wakō/ (also **whack·o**) *inf.* ▶*adj.* mad; insane: *wacko ideas.*
▶*n.* (*pl.* **-os**) a crazy person.

wack·y /'wakē/ (also **whack·y**) ▶*adj.* (**wack·i·er, wack·i·est**) *inf.* funny or amusing in a slightly odd or peculiar way: *a wacky chase movie.* —**wack·i·ly** /'wakəlē/ *adv.* —**wack·i·ness** *n.*

wad /wäd/ ▶*n.* **1** a lump or bundle of a soft material, used for padding, stuffing, or wiping: *a wad of cotton.* ■ *chiefly hist.* a disk, usu. of felt, used to keep powder or shot in place in a gun barrel. ■ a portion of chewing gum, or of tobacco or another narcotic when used for chewing. **2** a bundle of paper, banknotes, or documents: *a thick wad of index cards.* ■ *inf.* a large amount of something, esp. money: *wads of money.*
▶*v.* (**wad·ded, wad·ding**) [*tr.*] [usu. as *adj.*] (**wadded**) **1** compress (a soft material) into a lump or bundle: *a wadded handkerchief.* **2** stop up (an aperture or a gun barrel) with a bundle or lump of soft material. ■ line or stuff (a garment or piece of furniture) with wadding.

wad·ding /'wädiNG/ ▶*n.* soft, thick material used to line garments or pack fragile items, esp. absorbent cotton. ■ a material from which wads for guns are made.

wad·dle /'wädl/ ▶*v.* [*intr.*] walk with short steps and a clumsy swaying motion: *three geese waddled across the road.*
▶*n.* a waddling gait: *I walk with a waddle.* —**wad·dler** *n.*

wade /wād/ ▶*v.* [*intr.*] walk through water or another liquid or soft substance: *we waded ashore.* ■ [*tr.*] walk through (something filled with water): *firefighters waded the waist-deep flood water.* ■ (**wade through**) read laboriously through (a long piece of writing). ■ (**wade into**) *inf.* get involved in (something) vigorously or forcefully: *he waded into the yelling, fighting crowd.*
▶*n.* an act of wading. —**wad·a·ble** (also **wade·a·ble**) *adj.*

wad·er /'wādər/ ▶*n.* **1** a person or animal, esp. a bird, that wades, in particular: ■ a wading bird of the group that comprises the herons, storks, and ibises. **2** (**waders**) high waterproof boots used esp. by anglers when fishing.

wa·di /'wädē/ ▶*n.* (*pl.* **-dis** or **-dies**) (in certain Arabic-speaking countries) a valley, ravine, or channel that is dry except in the rainy season.

wa·fer /'wāfər/ ▶*n.* a very thin, light, crisp, sweet cookie or cracker, esp. one of a kind eaten with ice cream. ■ a thin disk of unleavened bread used in the Eucharist. ■ *Electr.* a very thin slice of a semiconductor crystal used as the substrate for solid-state circuitry. ■ a round, thin piece of something: *a wafer of ice.* —**wa·fer·y** *adj.*

wa·fer-thin ▶*adj.* & *adv.* very thin or thinly: [as *adj.*] *plates of wafer-thin metal* | [as *adv.*] *slicing meats wafer-thin.*

waf·fle¹ /'wäfəl; 'wô-/ *inf.* ▶*v.* [*intr.*] fail to make up one's mind: *Joseph had been waffling over where to go.*
▶*n.* a failure to make up one's mind: *his waffle on abortion.* —**waf·fler** /'wäf(ə)lər; 'wô-/ *n.* —**waf·fly** /'wäf(ə)lē; 'wô-/ *adj.*

waf·fle² ▶*n.* a small crisp batter cake, baked in a waffle iron and eaten hot with butter or syrup.
▶*adj.* denoting a style of fine honeycomb weaving.

waf·fle i·ron ▶*n.* a utensil, typically consisting of two shallow metal pans hinged together, used for baking waffles.

waft /wäft; waft/ ▶*v.* pass or cause to pass easily or gently through or as if through the air: [*intr.*] *the smell of stale fat wafted out from the café* | [*tr.*] *each breeze would waft pollen around the house.*
▶*n.* a gentle movement of air. ■ a scent or odor carried on such a movement of air.

wag¹ /wag/ ▶*v.* (**wagged, wag·ging**) (with reference to an animal's tail) move or cause to move rapidly to and fro: [*intr.*] *his tail began to wag* | [*tr.*] *the dog went out, wagging its tail.* ■ [*tr.*] move (an upward-pointing finger) from side to side to signify a warning or reprimand: *she wagged a finger at Elinor.* ■ [*intr.*] (used of a tongue, jaw, or chin, as representing a person) talk, esp. in order to gossip or spread rumors: *this is a small island, and tongues are beginning to wag.*
▶*n.* a single rapid movement from side to side: *a chirpy wag of the head.*

wag² ▶*n.* *dated* a person who makes facetious jokes.

wage /wāj/ ▶*n.* (usu. **wages**) a fixed regular payment, typically paid on a daily or weekly basis, made by an employer to an employee, esp. to a manual or unskilled worker: *we were struggling to get better wages.* ■ (**wages**) *Econ.* the part of total production that is the return to labor as earned income as distinct from the remuneration received by capital as unearned income. ■ *fig.* the result or effect of doing something considered wrong or unwise: *the wages of sin is death.*
▶*v.* [*tr.*] carry on (a war or campaign): *it is necessary to destroy their capacity to wage war.*

wa·ger /'wājər/ ▶*n.* & *v.* more formal term for BET.

wag·gish /'wagiSH/ ▶*adj.* *dated* humorous in a playful, mischievous, or facetious manner: *a waggish riposte.* —**wag·gish·ly** *adv.* —**wag·gish·ness** *n.*

wag·gle /'wagəl/ ▶*v.* *inf.* move or cause to move with short quick movements from side to side or up and down: [*intr.*] *his arm waggled* | [*tr.*] *Mary waggled a glass at them.* ■ [*tr.*] swing (a golf club) loosely to and fro over the ball before playing a shot.
▶*n.* an act of waggling.

wag·gly /'wag(ə)lē/ ▶*adj.* moving with quick short movements from side to side or up and down: *a waggly tail.*

wag·on /'wagən/ (*Brit.* also **wag·gon**) ▶*n.* a vehicle used for transporting goods or another specified purpose: *a coal wagon.* ■ a four-wheeled trailer for agricultural use, or a small version of this for use as a child's toy. ■ a horse-drawn vehicle, esp. a covered wagon used by early settlers in North America and elsewhere. ■ a wheeled cart or hut used as a food stall. ■ a small cart or wheeled table used for serving drinks or food. ■ a vehicle like a camper used by gypsies or circus performers. ■ *inf.* short for STATION WAGON.
▶ □ **off the wagon** (of an alcoholic) drinking after a period of abstinence: *she fell off the wagon two days after making a resolution to quit.* □ **on the wagon** *inf.* (of an alcoholic) abstaining from drinking.

wag·tail /'wag,tāl/ ▶*n.* a slender Eurasian and African songbird (genera

Motacilla and *Dendronanthus*, family Motacillidae) with a long tail that is frequently wagged up and down, typically living by water.

wa·hoo ▶*a* large predatory tropical marine fish (*Acanthocybium solanderi*) of the mackerel family, prized as a game fish.

waif /wāf/ ▶*n.* a homeless and helpless person, esp. a neglected or abandoned child: *she is foster-mother to various **waifs and strays**.* ■ an abandoned pet animal. **—waif·ish** *adj.*

wail /wāl/ ▶*n.* a prolonged high-pitched cry of pain, grief, or anger. ■ a sound resembling this: *the wail of an air-raid siren.*
▶*v.* [*intr.*] give such a cry of pain, grief, or anger: *Tina ran off wailing.* ■ make a sound resembling such a cry: *the wind wailed and buffeted the timber structure.* ʻ**—wail·er** *n.* **—wail·ing·ly** *adv.*

wain·scot /ˈwān,skōt; -skət; -,skät/ ▶*n.* an area of wooden paneling on the lower part of the walls of a room.
▶*v.* (**-scot·ed**, **-scot·ing** or **-scot·ted**, **-scot·ting**) [*tr.*] line (a room or wall) with wooden paneling.

wain·scot·ing /ˈwān,skōtiNG; -,skä-/ (also **wain·scot·ting**) ▶*n.* wooden paneling that lines the lower part of the walls of a room. ■ material for such paneling.

waist /wāst/ ▶*n.* the part of the human body below the ribs and above the hips. ■ the circumference of this: *her waist is 28 inches.* ■ a narrowing of the trunk of the body at this point: *the last time you had a waist was around 1978.* ■ the part of a garment encircling or covering the waist. ■ the point at which a garment is shaped so as to narrow between the rib cage and the hips: *a jacket with a high waist.* ■ a blouse or bodice. ■ a narrow part in the middle of anything, such as a violin, an hourglass, the body of wasp, etc. ■ the middle part of a ship, between the forecastle and the quarterdeck. **—waist·ed** *adj.* [in *comb.*] high-waisted. **—waist·less** *adj.*

waist·band /ˈwās(t),band/ ▶*n.* a strip of cloth forming the waist of a garment such as a skirt or a pair of trousers.

waist·coat /ˈwās(t),kōt; ˈweskət/ ▶*n.* Brit. a vest, esp. one worn by men over a shirt and under a jacket.

waist·line /ˈwās(t),līn/ ▶*n.* an imaginary line around a person's body at the waist, esp. with respect to its size: *eliminating inches from the waistline.* ■ the shaping and position of the waist of a garment.

wait /wāt/ ▶*v.* [*intr.*] **1** stay where one is or delay action until a particular time or until something else happens: *he did not **wait for** a reply* | [*tr.*] *I had to wait my turn to play.* ■ remain in readiness for some purpose: *he found the car waiting on the platform.* ■ be left until a later time before being dealt with: *we shall need a statement later, but that will have to wait.* ■ [*tr.*] *inf.* defer (a meal) until a person's arrival: *he will wait supper for me.* **2** (**cannot wait**) used to indicate that one is eagerly impatient to do something or for something to happen: *I can't wait for tomorrow.* **3** act as a waiter or waitress, serving food and drink: *a local man was employed to **wait on** them at table* | [*tr.*] *we had to wait tables in the mess hall.*
▶*phrasal v.* □ **wait on** (or **upon**) act as an attendant to (someone): *a maid was appointed to wait on her.* ■ serve (a customer) in a store. ■ *archaic* pay a respectful visit to. □ **wait up 1** not go to bed until someone arrives or something happens. **2** go more slowly or stop until someone catches up.
▶*n.* a period of waiting: *we had a long wait.*

wait·er /ˈwātər/ ▶*n.* **1** a man whose job is to serve customers at their tables in a restaurant. **2** a person who waits for a time, event, or opportunity. **3** a small tray; a salver.

wait·ing /ˈwātiNG/ ▶*n.* **1** the action of staying where one is or delaying action until a particular time or until something else happens. **2** Brit. official attendance at court. See also LADY-IN-WAITING.

wait·ing game ▶*n.* a tactic in which one refrains from action for a time in order to act more effectively at a later date or stage.

wait·per·son /ˈwāt,pərsən/ ▶*n.* a waiter or waitress (used as a neutral alternative).

wait·ress /ˈwātris/ ▶*n.* a woman whose job is to serve customers at their tables in a restaurant.

waive /wāv/ ▶*v.* [*tr.*] refrain from insisting on or using (a right or claim): *he will waive all rights to the money.* ■ refrain from applying or enforcing (a rule, restriction, or fee): *her tuition fees would be waived.*

waiv·er /ˈwāvər/ ▶*n.* an act or instance of waiving a right or claim. ■ a document recording such waiving of a right or claim.

wake¹ /wāk/ ▶*v.* (*past* **woke** /wōk/ or **waked**; *past part.* **wok·en** /ˈwōkən/ or **waked**) **1** emerge or cause to emerge from a state of sleep; stop sleeping: [*intr.*] *she woke up feeling better* | [*tr.*] *I wake him gently.* ■ [*intr.*] (**wake up to**) become alert to or aware of: *he needs to wake up to reality.* ■ [*tr.*] *fig.*

cause (something) to stir or come to life: *it wakes desire in others.* **2** [*tr.*] *dial.* hold a vigil beside (someone who has died): *we waked Jim last night.*
▶*n.* a watch or vigil held beside the body of someone who has died, sometimes accompanied by ritual observances including eating and drinking.

wake² ▶*n.* a trail of disturbed water or air left by the passage of a ship or aircraft. ■ *fig.* used to refer to the aftermath or consequences of something: *the committee was set up **in the wake of** the inquiry.*

wake·ful /ˈwākfəl/ ▶*adj.* (of a person) unable or not needing to sleep: *he had been wakeful all night.* ■ alert and vigilant. ■ (of a period of time) passed with little or no sleep: *wakeful nights.* **—wake·ful·ly** *adv.* **—wake·ful·ness** *n.*

wak·en /ˈwākən/ ▶*v.* poetic/literary term for WAKE¹ (sense 1).

wal·do /ˈwôldō/ ▶*n.* (*pl.* **-dos**) a remote manipulator, as for puppets, operated either mechanically or electronically.

wale /wāl/ ▶*n.* **1** a ridge on a textured woven fabric such as corduroy. **2** a horizontal band around a woven basket. ▷late Old English *walu* 'stripe, weal.'

walk /wôk/ ▶*v.* **1** [*intr.*] move at a regular and fairly slow pace by lifting and setting down each foot in turn, never having both feet off the ground at once: *I walked across the lawn.* ■ use similar movements but of a different part of one's body or a support: *he could walk on his hands, carrying a plate on one foot.* ■ go on foot for recreation and exercise: *you can walk in 21,000 acres of mountain and moorland.* ■ [*tr.*] travel along or over (a route or area) on foot: *the police department has encouraged officers to walk the beat.* ■ (of a quadruped) proceed with the slowest gait, always having at least two feet on the ground at once. ■ [*tr.*] ride (a horse) at this pace: *he walked his horse toward her.* ■ *inf.* abandon or suddenly withdraw from a job, commitment, or situation: *they can **walk away** from the deal* | *we were expecting the merger with Bell to go through—we didn't expect Bell to **walk on** the deal.* ■ *inf.* be released from suspicion or from a charge: *had any of the others come clean during the trial, he might have walked.* ■ used to suggest that someone has achieved a state or position easily or undeservedly: *no one has the right to **walk** straight **into** a well-paid job for life.* ■ (of a ghost) be present and visible: *the ghosts of Bannockburn walked abroad.* ■ *Baseball* be awarded first base after not swinging at four balls pitched outside the strike zone. ■ [*tr.*] *Baseball* allow or enable (a batter) to do this. ■ *Baseball* (of a pitcher) give a walk with the bases loaded so as to force in (a run). ■ *Basketball* another term for TRAVEL (sense 2). **2** [*tr.*] cause or enable (someone or something) to walk or move as though walking: *she walked her fingers over the dresses.* ■ guide, accompany, or escort (someone) on foot: *he walked her home to her door.* ■ [*tr.*] take (a domestic animal, typically a dog) out for exercise: *a man walking his retriever.* ■ push (a bicycle or motorcycle) while walking alongside it.
▶*phrasal v.* □ **walk away** easily, casually, or irresponsibly abandon a situation in which one is involved or for which one is responsible. □ **walk off with** *inf.* **1** steal. **2** win: *the team walked off with a silver medal.* □ **walk out** depart suddenly or angrily. ■ leave one's job suddenly. ■ go on strike. ■ abandon someone or something toward which one has responsibilities: *he walked out on his wife.* □ **walk through** rehearse (a play or other piece), reading the lines aloud from a script and performing the actions of the characters. ■ act or perform in a perfunctory or lackluster manner.
▶*n.* **1** an act of traveling or an excursion on foot: *he was too restless to sleep, so he went out for a walk.* ■ used to indicate the time that it will take someone to reach a place on foot or the distance that they must travel: *the library is within five minutes' walk.* ■ a route recommended or marked out for recreational walking. ■ a sidewalk or path. **2** an unhurried rate of movement on foot: *they crossed the field at a leisurely walk.* ■ the slowest gait of an animal. ■ a person's manner of walking: *the spring was back in his walk.* **3** *Baseball* an instance of being awarded (or allowing a batter to reach) first base after not swinging at four balls pitched outside the strike zone. **—walk·a·ble** /ˈwôkəbəl/ *adj.*
▶ □ **walk all over** *inf.* treat in a thoughtless, disrespectful, and exploitative manner: *they thought they could come in and walk all over us.* ■ defeat easily. □ **walk on eggshells** be extremely cautious about one's words or actions.

walk·a·thon /ˈwôkə,THän/ ▶*n. inf.* a long-distance walk organized as a fund-raising event.

walk·er /ˈwôkər/ ▶*n.* a person who walks, esp. for exercise or enjoyment. ■ a device for helping a baby learn to walk, consisting of a harness set into a frame on wheels. ■ a frame used by disabled or infirm people for support while walking, typically made of metal tubing with small wheels or rubber-tipped feet.

walk·ie-talk·ie /ˈwôkē ˈtôkē/ ▶ n. a portable two-way radio.

walk·ing pa·pers ▶ pl. n. inf. notice of dismissal from a job: *the reporter has been given his walking papers.*

walk·ing wound·ed /ˈwoʊndid/ ▶ pl. n. (usu. **the walking wounded**) people who have been injured in a battle or major accident but who are still able to walk. ■ people who have suffered emotional wounds.

Walk·man /ˈwôkmən; -ˌman/ ▶ n. (pl. **-mans** or **-men**) trademark a type of personal stereo.

walk-on ▶ adj. denoting a small nonspeaking part in a play or film.
▶ n. a person who plays such a part, or the part itself. ■ a sports player with no regular status in a team.

walk·out /ˈwôkˌout/ ▶ n. a sudden angry departure, esp. as a protest or strike.

walk·o·ver /ˈwôkˌōvər/ ▶ n. an easy victory: *they won in a 12–2 walkover.* ■ a win by forfeit.

walk-up ▶ adj. (of a building) allowing access to the upper floors by stairs only; having no elevator: *a walk-up hotel.* ■ (of a room or apartment) accessed in this way. ■ (of a building or service) easily accessible to pedestrians: *a walk-up food stand.* ■ (of a travel fare) at the price charged for immediate use rather than at the lower level for and advance reservation: *the one-way walk-up fare from Baltimore to San Francisco.*
▶ n. a building allowing access to the upper floors by stairs only.

walk·way /ˈwôkˌwā/ ▶ n. a passage or path for walking along, esp. a raised passageway connecting different sections of a building or a wide path in a park or garden.

wall /wôl/ ▶ n. a continuous vertical brick or stone structure that encloses or divides an area of land: *a garden wall.* ■ a side of a building or room, typically forming part of the building's structure. ■ any high vertical surface or facade, esp. one that is imposing in scale: *the eastern wall of the valley.* ■ a thing perceived as a protective or restrictive barrier: *a wall of silence.* ■ Soccer a line of defenders forming a barrier against a free kick taken near the penalty area. ■ Anat. & Zool. the membranous outer layer or lining of an organ or cavity: *the wall of the stomach.*
▶ v. [tr.] enclose (an area) within walls, esp. to protect it or lend it some privacy: *housing areas that are walled off from the indigenous population.*
▷Old English, from Latin *vallum* 'rampart,' from *vallus* 'stake.'
▶ □ **drive someone up the wall** inf. make someone very irritated or angry. □ **go to the wall** inf. **1** (of a business) fail; go out of business. **2** support someone or something, no matter what the cost to oneself: *the tendency for poets to go to the wall for their beliefs.* □ **hit the wall** (of an athlete) experience a sudden loss of energy in a long race. □ **off the wall** inf. **1** eccentric or unconventional. **2** (of a person) angry: *the president was off the wall about the article.* **3** (of an accusation) without basis or foundation. □ **wall-to-wall** (of a carpet or other floor covering) fitted to cover an entire floor. ■ inf. denoting great extent or number: *wall-to-wall customers.*

wal·la·by /ˈwäləbē/ ▶ n. (pl. **-ies**) an Australasian marsupial (family Macropodidae) that is similar to, but smaller than, a kangaroo.

wall·board /ˈwôlˌbôrd/ ▶ n. a type of board made from wood pulp, plaster, or other material, used for covering walls and ceilings. ■ a piece of such board.

wal·let /ˈwälit; ˈwô-/ ▶ n. a pocket-sized, flat, folding holder for money and plastic cards.

wall·eye /ˈwôlˌī/ ▶ n. **1** an eye with a streaked or opaque white iris. ■ an eye squinting outward. **2** a North American pikeperch (*Stizostedion vitreum*) with large, opaque silvery eyes. It is a commercially valuable food fish and a popular sporting fish. —**wall-eyed** adj.

wall·flow·er /ˈwôlˌflou(-ə)r/ ▶ n. **1** a southern European plant (*Cheiranthus cheiri*) of the cabbage family, with fragrant yellow, orange-red, dark red, or brown flowers, cultivated for its early spring blooming. **2** inf. a person who has no one to dance with or who feels shy, awkward, or excluded at a party.

Wal·loon /wäˈloʊn/ ▶ n. **1** a member of a people who speak a French dialect and live in southern and eastern Belgium and neighboring parts of France. Compare with FLEMING. **2** the French dialect spoken by this people.
▶ adj. of or concerning the Walloons or their language.

wal·lop /ˈwäləp/ inf. ▶ v. (**-loped**, **-lop·ing**) [tr.] strike or hit (someone or something) very hard: *they walloped the back of his head with a stick.* ■ heavily defeat (an opponent).

▶ n. a heavy blow or punch. ■ fig. a potent effect: *the script packs a wallop.* —**wal·lop·er** n. —**wal·lop·ing** adj.

wal·low /ˈwälō/ ▶ v. [intr.] **1** (chiefly of large mammals) roll about or lie relaxed in mud or water, esp. to keep cool, avoid biting insects, or spread scent: *watering places where buffalo liked to wallow.* ■ (of a boat or aircraft) roll from side to side: *the small jet wallowed in the sky.* **2** (**wallow in**) (of a person) indulge in an unrestrained way in (something that creates a pleasurable sensation): *he had been wallowing in self-pity.*
▶ n. **1** an act of wallowing: *a wallow in nostalgia.* **2** an area of mud or shallow water where mammals go to wallow, typically developing into a depression in the ground over long use. —**wal·low·er** n.

wall·pa·per /ˈwôlˌpāpər/ ▶ n. paper that is pasted in vertical strips over the walls of a room to provide a decorative or textured surface. ■ Comput. an optional background pattern or picture on a computer screen.
▶ v. [tr.] apply wallpaper to (a wall or room).

wal·nut /ˈwôlˌnət/ ▶ n. **1** the large wrinkled edible seed of a deciduous tree, consisting of two halves contained within a hard shell that is enclosed in a green fruit. **2** (also **walnut tree**) the tall tree (genus *Juglans*, family Juglandaceae) that produces this nut, with compound leaves and valuable ornamental timber.

wal·rus /ˈwôlrəs; ˈwä-/ ▶ n. a large gregarious marine mammal (*Odobenus rosmarus*) related to the eared seals, having two large downward-pointing tusks and found in the Arctic Ocean.

waltz /wôlts/ ▶ n. a dance in triple time performed by a couple who as a pair turn rhythmically around and around as they progress around the dance floor. ■ a piece of music written for or in the style of this dance.
▶ v. [intr.] dance a waltz: *I waltzed across the floor with the lieutenant.* ■ [tr.] guide (someone) in or as if in a waltz: *he waltzed her around the table.* ■ [intr.] move or act lightly, casually, or inconsiderately: *you can't just waltz in and expect to make a mark.* —late 18th cent.: from German *Walzer*, from *walzen* 'revolve.' —**waltz·er** n.

wam·pum /ˈwämpəm/ ▶ n. hist. a quantity of small cylindrical beads made by North American Indians from seashells, strung together and worn as a decorative belt or other decoration or used as money.

WAN /wan/ ▶ abbr. ■ Comput. wide area network.

wan /wän/ ▶ adj. (of a person's complexion or appearance) pale and giving the impression of illness or exhaustion: *she was looking wan and bleary-eyed.* ■ (of light) pale; weak: *the wan dawn light.* ■ (of a smile) weak; strained. —**wan·ly** adv. —**wan·ness** n.

wand /wänd/ ▶ n. a long, thin stick or rod, in particular: ■ a stick or rod thought to have magic properties, held by a magician, fairy, or conjuror and used in casting spells or performing tricks: *the fairy godmother waves her magic wand and grants the heroine's wishes.* ■ a staff or rod held as a symbol of office. ■ inf. a conductor's baton. ■ a hand-held electronic device that can be passed over a bar code to read the encoded data. ■ a hand-held metal detector, used as a security device. ■ a device emitting a laser beam, used esp. to create a pointer on a projected image or text. ■ a small stick with a brush at one end used for the application of mascara.

wan·der /ˈwändər/ ▶ v. [intr.] walk or move in a leisurely, casual, or aimless way. ■ move slowly away from a fixed point or place: *please don't wander off again* | *fig. his attention had wandered.* ■ (of a road or river) wind with gentle twists and turns in a particular direction; meander. ■ [tr.] move or travel slowly through or over (a place or area): *he found her wandering the streets.*
▶ n. an act or instance of wandering. —**wan·der·er** n.

wan·der·lust /ˈwändərˌləst/ ▶ n. a strong desire to travel: *a man consumed by wanderlust.*

wane /wān/ ▶ v. [intr.] (of the moon) have a progressively smaller part of its visible surface illuminated, so that it appears to decrease in size. ■ (esp. of a condition or feeling) decrease in vigor, power, or extent; become weaker: *confidence in the dollar waned.*

wan·gle /ˈwaNGgəl/ inf. ▶ v. [tr.] obtain (something that is desired) by persuading others to comply or by manipulating events: *I wangled an invitation to her party.* —**wan·gler** /ˈwaNG(ə)lər/ n.

wan·na·be /ˈwänəbē; ˈwô-/ ▶ n. inf., derog. a person who tries to be like someone else or to fit in with a particular group of people: *a star-struck wannabe.*

want /wänt; wônt/ ▶ v. **1** [tr.] have a desire to possess or do (something); wish for: *I want an apple* | [tr.] *she wanted me to go to her room* | [intr.] *I'll give you a lift into town if you want.* ■ wish to consult or speak to (someone): *Tony wants me in the studio.* ■ (usu. **be wanted**) (of the police) desire to question or apprehend (a suspected criminal): *he is wanted by the police in connection with an arms theft.* ■ desire (someone) sexually: *I've wanted you since the first moment I saw you.* ■ inf., chiefly Brit. (of a thing) require to be attended to in a specified way: *the wheel wants greasing.* ■ *inf.* ought, should, or need to do something: *you don't want to believe everything you hear.* ■ [*intr.*] (**want in/into/out/away**) *inf.* desire to be in or out of a particular place or situation: *if anyone wants out, there's the door.* **2** [*intr.*] chiefly archaic lack or be short of something desirable or essential: *you shall **want for nothing** while you are with me.*

▶ *n.* **1** a lack or deficiency of something: *Victorian houses which are in want of repair.* ■ the state of being poor and in need of essentials; poverty: *freedom from want.* **2** a desire for something: *the expression of our wants and desires.* ▷Middle English: the noun from Old Norse *vant*, neuter of *vanr* 'lacking'; the verb from Old Norse *vanta* 'be lacking.' The original notion of "lack" was early extended to "need," and from this developed the sense 'desire.'

want ad ▶ *n. inf.* a classified advertisement in a newspaper or magazine; a small ad.

want·ing /'wäntiNG, wônt-/ ▶ *adj.* lacking in a certain required or necessary quality: *they weren't **wanting in** confidence.*

wan·ton /'wäntn/ ▶ *adj.* **1** (of a cruel or violent action) deliberate and unprovoked: *sheer wanton vandalism.* **2** (esp. of a woman) sexually immodest or promiscuous. —**wan·ton·ly** *adv.* —**wan·ton·ness** *n.*

wap·i·ti /'wäpitē/ ▶ *n.* (*pl.* **-tis**) another term for ELK.

war /wôr/ ▶ *n.* a state of armed conflict between different nations or states or different groups within a nation or state: *Japan **declared war** on Germany.* ■ a particular armed conflict: *after the war, they emigrated to America.* ■ a state of competition, conflict, or hostility between different people or groups: *she was **at war with** her parents.* ■ a sustained effort to deal with or end a particular unpleasant or undesirable situation or condition: *the authorities are **waging war against** all forms of smuggling* | *a **war on** drugs.*

▶ *v.* (**warred**, **war·ring**) [*intr.*] engage in a war: *small states warred against each another.* ▷late Old English *werre*, from an Anglo-Norman French variant of Old French *guerre*, from a Germanic base.

war·ble¹ /'wôrbəl/ ▶ *v.* [*intr.*] (of a bird) sing softly and with a succession of constantly changing notes: *larks were warbling in the trees.* ■ (of a person) sing in a trilling or quavering voice.

▶ *n.* a warbling sound or utterance.

war·ble² ▶ *n.* a swelling or abscess beneath the skin on the back of cattle, horses, and other mammals, caused by the presence of the larva of a warble fly.

war·ble fly ▶ *n.* a large fly (genus *Hypoderma*, family Oestridae) that lays its eggs on the legs of mammals such as cattle and horses. The larvae migrate internally to the host's back, where they form a small lump with a breathing hole, dropping to the ground later when fully grown.

war·bler /'wôrb(ə)lər/ ▶ *n.* **1** any of a number of small insectivorous songbirds that typically have a warbling song, in particular: ■ a New World bird (subfamily Parulinae) of the bunting family. **2** *inf.* a person who sings in a trilling or quavering voice.

war cry ▶ *n.* a call made to rally soldiers for battle or to gather participants in a campaign.

ward /wôrd/ ▶ *n.* **1** a separate room in a hospital, typically one allocated to a particular type of patient: *a children's ward.* ■ one of the divisions of a prison. **2** an administrative division of a city or borough that typically elects and is represented by a councilor or councilors. **3** a person, usually a minor, under the care and control of a guardian appointed by their parents or a court. **4** (usu. **wards**) any of the internal ridges or bars in a lock that prevent the turning of any key that does not have grooves of corresponding form or size. ■ the corresponding grooves in the bit of a key.

▶ *phrasal v.* □ **ward someone/something off** prevent from harming or affecting one: *she put up a hand as if to ward him off.*

war·den /'wôrdn/ ▶ *n.* a person responsible for the supervision of a particular place or thing or for ensuring that regulations associated with it are obeyed: *the warden of a local nature reserve.* ■ the head official in charge of a prison. —**war·den·ship** /-,SHip/ *n.*

ward heel·er ▶ *n. inf.*, chiefly derog. a person who assists in a political campaign by canvassing votes for a party and performing menial tasks for its leaders.

ward·robe /'wôr,drōb/ ▶ *n.* a large, tall cabinet in which clothes may be hung or stored. ■ a person's entire collection of clothes: *her wardrobe is extensive.* ■ the costume department or costumes of a theater or movie company: [as *adj.*] *a wardrobe assistant.* ■ a department of a royal or noble household in charge of clothing.

ward·room /'wôrd,rōōm, -,rŏŏm/ ▶ *n.* a commissioned officers' mess on board a warship.

ware /we(ə)r/ ▶ *n.* pottery, typically of a specified type: *blue-and-white majolica ware.* ■ manufactured articles of a specified type: *crystal ware.*

■ (**wares**) articles offered for sale: *traders in the street markets displayed their wares.*

ware·house ▶ *n.* /'we(ə)r,hous/ a large building where raw materials or manufactured goods may be stored before their export or distribution for sale. ■ a large wholesale or retail store: *a discount warehouse.*

▶ *v.* /-,hous; -,houz/ [*tr.*] store (goods) in a warehouse. ■ place (imported goods) in a bonded warehouse pending the payment of import duty. ■ *inf.* place (someone, typically a prisoner or a psychiatric patient) in a large, impersonal institution in which their problems are not satisfactorily addressed.

war·fare /'wôr,fe(ə)r/ ▶ *n.* engagement in or the activities involved in war or conflict: *guerrilla warfare.*

war game ▶ *n.* a military exercise carried out to test or improve tactical expertise. ■ a simulated military conflict carried out as a game, leisure activity, or exercise in personal development.

▶ *v.* [*tr.*] (**war-game**) engage in (a campaign or course of action) using the strategies of such a military exercise: *there seemed to be no point war-gaming an election 15 months away.* —**war-gam·er** *n.*

war·head /'wôr,hed/ ▶ *n.* the explosive head of a missile, torpedo, or similar weapon.

war·horse /'wôr,hôrs/ ▶ *n.* (in historical contexts) a large, powerful horse ridden in battle. ■ *inf.* an elderly person such as a soldier, politician, or sports player who has fought many campaigns or contests. ■ a musical, theatrical, or literary work that has been heard or performed repeatedly: *that old warhorse Liszt's "Hungarian Rhapsody No. 2."*

war·like /'wôr,līk/ ▶ *adj.* disposed toward or threatening war; hostile: *a warlike clan.* ■ (of plans, preparations, or munitions) directed toward or prepared for war.

war·lock /'wôr,läk/ ▶ *n.* a man who practices witchcraft; a sorcerer.

war·lord /'wôr,lôrd/ ▶ *n.* a military commander, esp. an aggressive regional commander with individual autonomy.

warm /wôrm/ ▶ *adj.* **1** of or at a fairly or comfortably high temperature: *a warm September evening.* ■ (of clothes or coverings) made of a material that helps the body to retain heat; suitable for cold weather: *a warm winter coat.* ■ (of a color) containing red, yellow, or orange tones: *her fair coloring suited soft, warm shades.* **2** having, showing, or expressive of enthusiasm, affection, or kindness: *they exchanged warm, friendly smiles.* **3** *inf.* (esp. in children's games) close to discovering something or guessing the correct answer: *you're getting warmer.*

▶ *v.* make or become warm: [*tr.*] *I stamped my feet to **warm** them **up*** | [*intr.*] *it's a bit chilly in here, but it'll soon **warm up**.*

▶ *phrasal v.* □ **warm up** prepare for physical exertion or a performance by exercising or practicing gently beforehand: *the band was warming up.* ■ (of an engine or electrical appliance) reach a temperature high enough to allow it to operate efficiently. ■ become livelier or more animated: *after several more rounds, things began to warm up in the bar.* ▷Old English *wearm* (adjective), *werman*, *wearmian* (verb), of Germanic origin; related to Dutch *warm* and German *warm*, from an Indo-European root shared by Latin *formus* 'warm' and Greek *thermos* 'hot.' —**warm·er** *n.* [usu. in *comb.*] *a towel-warmer.* —**warm·ly** *adv.* —**warm·ness** *n.*

warm-blood·ed ▶ *adj.* **1** relating to or denoting animals (chiefly mammals and birds) that maintain a constant body temperature, typically above that of the surroundings, by metabolic means. **2** ardent; passionate. —**warm-blood·ed·ness** *n.*

warmed-o·ver ▶ *adj.* **1** (also **warmed-up**) (of food or drink) reheated: *warmed-over chicken and pasta.* **2** (of an idea or product) secondhand; stale: *warmed-over communism.*

warm-heart·ed /'wôrm 'härtəd/ ▶ *adj.* (of a person or their actions) sympathetic and kind. —**warm-heart·ed·ly** *adv.* —**warm-heart·ed·ness** *n.*

war·mon·ger /'wôr,məNGgər; -,mäNG-/ ▶ *n.* a sovereign or political leader or activist who promotes aggression or warfare toward other nations or groups. —**war·mon·ger·ing** *n. & adj.*

warmth /wôrmTH/ ▶ *n.* the quality, state, or sensation of being warm; moderate and comfortable heat: *the warmth of the sun on her skin.* ■ enthusiasm, affection, or kindness: *she smiled with real warmth.* ■ vehemence or intensity of emotion: *"Of course not," he snapped, with a warmth that he regretted.*

warm-up (also **warm-up**) ▶ *n.* a period or act of preparation for a game, performance, or exercise session, involving gentle exercise or practice. ■ (**warm-ups**) a garment worn during light exercise or training; a sweatsuit. ■ a period before a stage performance in which the audience is amused or entertained in order to make it more receptive to the main act.

warn /wôrn/ ▶v. inform someone in advance of an impending or possible danger, problem, or other unpleasant situation: [tr.] *his father had warned him of what might happen.* ■ give someone forceful or cautionary advice about their actions or conduct: [tr.] *friends warned her against the marriage* | [intr.] *they warned against false optimism.* —**warn·er** *n.*

warn·ing /ˈwôrniNG/ ▶n. a statement or event that indicates a possible or impending danger, problem, or other unpleasant situation: *a warning about heavy thunderstorms.* ■ cautionary advice: *a word of warning—don't park illegally.* ■ advance notice of something: *she had only had four days' warning before leaving Berlin.* ■ an experience or sight that serves as a cautionary example to others: *his death should be a warning to everyone.* —**warn·ing·ly** *adv.*

warn·ing track ▶n. *Baseball* a grassless strip around the outside of the outfield grass that warns fielders that they are approaching the outfield wall.

warp /wôrp/ ▶v. become or cause to become bent or twisted out of shape, typically as a result of the effects of heat or dampness: [intr.] *wood has a tendency to warp* | [tr.] *moisture had warped the box.* ■ [tr.] cause to become abnormal or strange; have a distorting effect on: *your judgment has been warped by your obvious dislike of him.*
▶n. **1** a twist or distortion in the shape or form of something: *the head of the racket had a curious warp.* ■ *fig.* an abnormality or perversion in a person's character. ■ [as adj.] relating to or denoting (fictional or hypothetical) space travel by means of distorting space-time: *the craft possessed warp drive.* **2** (in weaving) the threads on a loom over and under which other threads (the weft) are passed to make cloth: *fig. rugby is woven into the warp and weft of South African society.* —**warp·age** /ˈwôrpij/ *n.* .

war·path /ˈwôrˌpaTH/ ▶n. (in phrase **on the warpath**) in an angry and aggressive state about a conflict of dispute: *he intends to go on the warpath with a national campaign to reverse the decision.*

war·rant /ˈwôrənt; ˈwä-/ ▶n. **1** a document issued by a legal or government official authorizing the police or some other body to make an arrest, search premises, or carry out some other action relating to the administration of justice: *magistrates issued a warrant for his arres.* ■ a document that entitles the holder to receive goods, money, or services: *we'll issue you with a travel warrant.* ■ *Finance* a negotiable security allowing the holder to buy shares at a specified price at or before some future date. ■ justification or authority for an action, belief, or feeling: *there is no warrant for this assumption.* **2** an official certificate of appointment issued to an officer of lower rank than a commissioned officer.
▶v. [tr.] justify or necessitate (a certain course of action): *that offense is serious enough to warrant a court marshal.* ■ officially affirm or guarantee: *the vendor warrants the accuracy of the report.* —**war·rant·a·ble** *adj.* —**war·rant·er** *n.* —**war·ran·tor** /-ˌentər/ *n.*

war·ran·ty /ˈwôrəntē; ˈwä-/ ▶n. (pl. **-ties**) a written guarantee, issued to the purchaser of an article by its manufacturer, promising to repair or replace it if necessary within a specified period of time: *the car comes with a three-year warranty.* ■ (in contract law) a promise that something in furtherance of the contract is guaranteed by one of the contractors, esp. the seller's promise that the thing being sold is as promised or represented. ■ (in an insurance contract) an engagement by the insured party that certain statements are true or that certain conditions shall be fulfilled, the breach of it invalidating the policy. ■ (in property law) a covenant by which the seller binds themselves and their heirs to secure to the buyer the estate conveyed in the deed. ■ (in contract law) a term or promise in a contract, breach of which entitles the innocent party to damages but not to treat the contract as discharged by breach.

war·ran·ty deed ▶n. *Law* a deed that guarantees a clear title to the buyer of real property.

war·ren /ˈwôrən; ˈwä-/ ▶n. (also **rabbit warren**) a network of interconnecting rabbit burrows. ■ a densely populated or labyrinthine building or district: *a warren of narrow gas-lit streets.*

war·ri·or /ˈwôrēər/ ▶n. (esp. in former times) a brave or experienced soldier or fighter.

war·ship /ˈwôrˌSHip/ ▶n. a ship equipped with weapons and designed to take part in warfare at sea.

wart /wôrt/ ▶n. a small, hard, benign growth on the skin, caused by a virus. ■ any rounded excrescence on the skin of an animal or the surface of a plant. ■ *inf.* an obnoxious or objectionable person. ■ an undesirable or disfiguring feature: *few products are without their warts.* —**wart·y** /ˈwôrtē/ *adj.*

wart·hog /ˈwôrtˌhäg/ ▶n. an African wild pig (*Phacochoerus aethiopicus*) with bristly gray skin, a large head, warty lumps on the face, and curved tusks.

war·time /ˈwôrˌtīm/ ▶n. a period during which a war is taking place.

war·y /ˈwe(ə)rē/ ▶adj. (**war·i·er**, **war·i·est**) feeling or showing caution about possible dangers or problems: *dogs that have been mistreated often remain very wary of strangers* | *a wary look.* —**war·i·ly** /-rəlē/ *adv.* —**war·i·ness** *n.*

was /wəz/ ▶ first and third person singular past of BE.

wash /wäSH; wôSH/ ▶v. **1** [tr.] clean with water and, typically, soap or detergent: *I stripped and washed myself all over.* ■ [intr.] clean oneself, esp. one's hands and face with soap and water. ■ (of an animal) clean (itself or another) by licking. ■ [tr.] remove (a stain or dirt) from something by cleaning with water and detergent: *they have to keep washing the mold off the walls.* ■ [intr.] (of dirt or a stain) be removed in such a way: *the dirt on his clothes would easily wash out.* ■ [intr.] (of fabric, a garment, or dye) withstand cleaning to a specified degree without shrinking or fading: *a linen-mix yarn that washes well.* **2** [tr.] (of flowing water) carry (someone or something) in a particular direction: *floods washed away the bridges.* ■ [intr.] be carried by flowing water: *an oil slick washed up on the beaches.* ■ [intr.] (esp. of waves) sweep, move, or splash in a particular direction: *the sea began to wash along the decks.* ■ [tr.] (usu. **be washed**) (of a river, sea, or lake) flow through or lap against (a country, coast, etc.): *offshore islands washed by warm blue seas.* ■ [intr.] (**wash over**) (of a feeling) affect (someone) suddenly: *a deep feeling of sadness washed over her.* ■ [intr.] (**wash over**) occur all around without greatly affecting (someone): *she allowed the babble of conversation to wash over her.* **3** [tr.] (usu. **be washed**) brush with a thin coat of diluted paint or ink: *the walls were washed with shades of umber.* ■ (**wash something with**) coat inferior metal with (a film of gold or silver from a solution). **4** [intr.] *inf.* seem convincing or genuine: *charm won't wash with this crew.*
▶*phrasal v.* □ **wash something out 1** (usu. **be washed out**) cause an event to be postponed or canceled because of rain: *the game was washed out.* **2** (of a flood or downpour) make a breach in a road.
▶n. **1** an act of washing something or an instance of being washed. ■ a quantity of clothes needing to be or just having been washed: *she hung out her Tuesday wash.* ■ a medicinal or cleansing solution: *mouth wash.* **2** the disturbed water or air behind a moving boat or aircraft or the sound made by this: *the wash of a motorboat.* ■ the surging of water or breaking of waves or the sound made by this: *the wash of waves on the pebbled beach.* **3** a layer of paint or metal spread thinly on a surface: *the walls were covered with a pale lemon wash.* **4** silt or gravel carried by a stream or river and deposited as sediment. ■ a sandbank exposed only at low tide. **5** *inf.* a situation or result that is of no benefit to either of two opposing sides: *the plan's impact on jobs would be a wash, creating as many as it costs.*
▶ □ **come out in the wash** *inf.* be resolved eventually with no lasting harm: *he's not happy, but he assures me it'll all come out in the wash.* □ **wash one's hands of** disclaim responsibility for: *the social services washed their hands of his daughter.*

wash·a·ble /ˈwäSHəbəl; ˈwôSH-/ ▶adj. (esp. of fabric or clothes) able to be washed without shrinkage or other damage: *washable curtains* | [as n.] *fine washables.* —**wash·a·bil·i·ty** /ˌwäSHəˈbilitē; ˌwôSH-/ *n.*

wash·ba·sin /ˈwäSHˌbāsən; ˈwôSH-/ ▶n. a basin, typically fixed to a wall or on a pedestal, used for washing one's hands and face.

wash·board /ˈwäSHˌbôrd; ˈwôSH-/ ▶n. a board made of ridged wood or a sheet of corrugated zinc, used when washing clothes as a surface against which to scrub them. ■ a similar board played as a percussion instrument by scraping. ■ the surface of a worn, uneven road. ■ [as adj.] denoting a man's stomach that is lean and has well-defined muscles.
▶v. [tr.] [usu. as adj.] (**washboarded**) cause ridges to develop in (a road or road surface): *a road left washboarded by winter frost.*

wash·cloth /ˈwäSHˌklôTH; ˈwôSH-/ ▶n. a cloth for washing one's face and body, typically made of terry or other absorbent material.

washed-out ▶adj. faded by or as if by sunlight or repeated washing: *washed-out jeans.* ■ (of a person) pale and tired.

washed-up ▶adj. deposited by the tide on a shore: *washed-up jellyfish.* ■ *inf.* no longer effective or successful: *a washed-up actress.*

wash·er /ˈwäSHər; ˈwôSH-/ ▶n. **1** a person or device that washes something: *a glass washer.* ■ a washing machine. **2** a small flat ring made of metal, rubber, or plastic fixed under a nut or the head of a bolt to spread the pressure when tightened or between two joining surfaces as a spacer or seal.

wash·er·wom·an /ˈwäSHərˌwoŏmən; ˈwôSH-/ ▶n. (pl. **-wom·en**) a woman whose occupation is washing clothes.

wash·ing /ˈwäSHiNG; ˈwôSH-/ ▶n. the action of washing oneself or laundering clothes, bed linen, etc. ■ a quantity of clothes, bed linen, etc., that is to be washed or has just been washed.

wash·ing ma·chine ▸*n.* a machine for washing clothes, bed linens, etc.

wash·out /'wäSH,out; 'wôSH-/ ▸*n.* **1** *inf.* an event that is spoiled by constant or heavy rain. ■ a disappointing failure: *the film was a washout.* **2** a breach in a road or railroad track caused by flooding.

wash·room /'wäSH,rōōm; 'wôSH-; -,rŏŏm/ ▸*n.* a room with washing and toilet facilities.

wash·stand /'wäSH,stand; 'wôSH-/ ▸*n.* chiefly *hist.* a piece of furniture designed to hold a jug, bowl, or basin for the purpose of washing one's hands and face.

wash·tub /'wäSH,təb; 'wôSH-/ ▸*n.* a large metal tub used for washing clothes and linen.

wash·y /'wäSHē; 'wôSHē/ ▸*adj.* (**wash·i·er, wash·i·est**) **1** lacking in strength or vigor; insipid: *a weak and washy production.* **2** (of a color) having a faded look. —**wash·i·ness** *n.*

was·n't /'wəzənt/ ▸*contr. of* was not.

Wasp /wäsp/ (also **WASP**) ▸*n.* an upper- or middle-class American white Protestant, considered to be a member of the most powerful group in society. ▷*1950s: acronym from* white Anglo-Saxon Protestant. —**Wasp·ish** *adj.* —**Wasp·y** *adj.*

wasp /wäsp/ ▸*n.* **1** a social winged insect (*Vespula, Polistes,* and other genera, family Vespidae) that has a narrow waist and a sting. It constructs a paper nest from wood pulp and raises the larvae on a diet of insects. **2** a solitary winged insect (several superfamilies) with a narrow waist, mostly distantly related to the social wasps and including many parasitic kinds.

wasp·ish /'wäspiSH/ ▸*adj.* readily expressing anger or irritation: *he had a waspish tongue.* —**wasp·ish·ly** *adv.* —**wasp·ish·ness** *n.*

was·sail /'wäsəl; -,sāl/ *archaic* ▸*n.* spiced ale or mulled wine drunk during celebrations for Twelfth Night and Christmas Eve. ■ lively and noisy festivities involving the drinking of plentiful amounts of alcohol; revelry.
▸*v.* **1** [*intr.*] drink plentiful amounts of alcohol and enjoy oneself with others in a noisy, lively way. **2** go from house to house at Christmas singing carols: *here we go a-wassailing.* ▷*Middle English* wæs hæil 'be in (good) health!': *from Old Norse* ves heill. The drinking formula *wassail* (and the reply *drinkhail* 'drink good health') were probably introduced by Danish-speaking inhabitants of England, and then spread, so that by the 12th cent. the usage was considered by the Normans to be characteristic of Englishmen. —**was·sail·er** *n.*

wast·age /'wāstij/ ▸*n.* **1** the action or process of losing or destroying something by using it carelessly or extravagantly: *the wastage of natural resources.* ■ the amount of something lost or destroyed in such a way: *wastage was cut by 50 percent.* **2** the weakening or deterioration of a part of the body, typically as a result of illness or lack of use: *the wastage of muscle tissue.*

waste /wāst/ ▸*v.* **1** [*tr.*] use or expend carelessly, extravagantly, or to no purpose: *we can't afford to waste electricity.* ■ (usu. **be wasted on**) bestow or expend on an unappreciative recipient: *her small talk was wasted on this guest.* ■ (usu. **be wasted**) fail to make full or good use of: *we're wasted in this job.* **2** [*intr.*] (of a person or a part of the body) become progressively weaker and more emaciated: *she was dying of AIDS, visibly wasting away.* **3** *inf.* kill or severely injure (someone): *I saw them waste the guy I worked for.*
▸*adj.* **1** (of a material, substance, or byproduct) eliminated or discarded as no longer useful or required after the completion of a process: *ensure that waste materials are disposed of responsibly* | *plants produce oxygen as a waste product.* **2** (of an area of land, typically in a city or town) not used, cultivated, or built on: *a patch of waste ground.*
▸*n.* **1** an act or instance of using or expending something carelessly, extravagantly, or to no purpose: *it's always a waste of time trying to argue with him.* **2** material that is not wanted; the unusable remains or byproducts of something: *bodily waste* | (**wastes**) *hazardous industrial wastes.* **3** (usu. **wastes**) a large area of barren, typically uninhabited land: *the icy wastes of the Antarctic.* **4** *Law* damage to an estate caused by an act or by neglect, esp. by a life-tenant.

waste·bas·ket /'wāst,baskit/ (also **wastepaper basket**) ▸*n.* a receptacle for small quantities of rubbish.

waste·ful /'wāstfəl/ ▸*adj.* (of a person or action) using or expending something of value carelessly, extravagantly, or to no purpose: *wasteful energy consumption.* —**waste·ful·ly** *adv.* —**waste·ful·ness** *n.*

waste·land /'wāst,land/ ▸*n.* an unused area of land that has become barren or overgrown. ■ a bleak, unattractive, and unused or neglected urban or industrial area: *the restoration of industrial wasteland* | *fig. the mid 70s are now seen as something of a cultural wasteland.*

waste·pa·per /'wāst,pāpər/ ▸*n.* discarded paper.

wast·er /'wāstər/ ▸*n.* a wasteful person or thing: *you are a great waster of time.* ■ *inf.* a person who does little or nothing of value.

was·trel /'wāstrəl/ ▸*n. poetic/lit.* a wasteful or good-for-nothing person.

watch /wäCH/ ▸*v.* [*tr.*] look at or observe attentively, typically over a period of time: *Lucy watched him go* | [*intr.*] *as she watched, two women came into the garden.* ■ keep under careful or protective observation: *a large set of steel doors, watched over by a single guard.* ■ secretly follow or spy on: *he told me my telephones were tapped and I was being watched.* ■ follow closely or maintain an interest in: *the girls watched the development of this relationship with incredulity.* ■ exercise care, caution, or restraint about: *most women watch their diet during pregnancy.* ■ [*intr.*] (**watch for**) look out or be on the alert for: *in spring and summer, watch for kingfishers* ■ [*intr.*] [usu. in *imper.*] (**watch out**) be careful: *credit-card fraud is on the increase, so watch out.* ■ (**watch it/yourself**) [usu. in *imper.*] *inf.* be careful (used as a warning or threat): *if anyone finds out, you're dead meat; so watch it.*
▸*n.* **1** a small timepiece worn typically on a strap on one's wrist. **2** an act or instance of carefully observing someone or something over a period of time: *the security forces have been **keeping a close watch on** our activities.* ■ a period of vigil during which a person is stationed to look out for danger or trouble, typically during the night: *Murray took the last watch before dawn.* ■ a fixed period of duty on a ship, usually lasting four hours. ■ the officers and crew on duty during one such period. ■ *fig.* the period someone spends in a particular role or job. ■ (usu. **the watch**) *hist.* a watchman or group of watchmen who patrolled and guarded the streets of a town before the introduction of the police force. —**watch·a·ble** *adj.* —**watch·er** *n.* [often in *comb.*] *a bird-watcher.*

watch chain ▸*n.* a metal chain securing a pocket watch.

watch·dog /'wäCH,dôg/ ▸*n.* a dog kept to guard private property. ■ a person or group whose function is to monitor the practices of companies providing a particular service or utility: *a watchdog for the global banking industry.*
▸*v.* (**-dogged, -dog·ging**) [*tr.*] maintain surveillance over (a person, activity, or situation): *how can we watchdog our investments?*

watch·ful /'wäCHfəl/ ▸*adj.* watching or observing someone or something closely; alert and vigilant: *they attended dances under the watchful eye of their father.* —**watch·ful·ly** *adv.* —**watch·ful·ness** *n.*

watch·man /'wäCHmən/ ▸*n.* (*pl.* **-men**) a man employed to look after an empty building, esp. at night. ■ *hist.* a member of a body of people employed to keep watch in a town at night.

watch·tow·er /'wäCH,tou(-ə)r/ ▸*n.* a tower built to create an elevated observation point.

watch·word /'wäCH,wərd/ ▸*n.* a word or phrase expressing a person's or group's core aim or belief: *the watchword is be prepared for anything.*

wa·ter /'wôtər; 'wä-/ ▸*n.* **1** a colorless, transparent, odorless, tasteless liquid that forms the seas, lakes, rivers, and rain and is the basis of the fluids of living organisms. Water is a compound of oxygen and hydrogen, H_2O, with highly distinctive physical and chemical properties: it is able to dissolve many other substances; its solid form (ice) is less dense than the liquid form; its boiling point, viscosity, and surface tension are unusually high for its molecular weight, and it is partially dissociated into hydrogen and hydroxyl ions. ■ this as supplied to houses or commercial establishments through pipes and taps: *each bedroom has a washbasin with hot and cold water* | [as *adj.*] *water pipes.* ■ one of the four elements in ancient and medieval philosophy and in astrology: [as *adj.*] *a water sign.* ■ (usu. **the waters**) the water of a mineral spring, typically as used medicinally for bathing in or drinking: *resorts where invalids came to take the waters.* ■ a solution of a specified substance in water: *ammonia water.* ■ *urine: drinking alcohol will make you need to pass water more often.* ■ (**waters**) the amniotic fluid surrounding a fetus in the womb, esp. as discharged in a flow shortly before birth: *I think my waters have broken.* **2** (**the water**) a stretch or area of water, such as a river, sea, or lake: *the lawns ran down to the water's edge.* ■ the surface of such an area of water: *she ducked under the water.* ■ [as *adj.*] found in, on, or near such areas of water: *a water plant.* ■ (**waters**) the water of a particular sea, river, or lake: *the waters of Hudson Bay* | *fig. the government is taking us into unknown waters with this legislation.* ■ (**waters**) an area of sea regarded as under the jurisdiction of a particular country: *Japanese coastal waters.* **3** *Finance* capital stock that represents a book value greater than the true assets of a company.
▸*v.* **1** [*tr.*] pour or sprinkle water over (a plant or an area of ground), typically in order to encourage plant growth: *I went out to water the*

geraniums. ■ give a drink of water to (an animal): *they stopped to water the horses.* ■ [*intr.*] (of an animal) drink water. ■ (usu. **be watered**) (of a river) flow through (an area of land): *the valley is watered by the Pines River.* ■ take a fresh supply of water on board (a ship or steam train). ■ *Finance* increase (a company's debt, or nominal capital) by the issue of new shares without a corresponding addition to assets. **2** [*intr.*] (of the eyes) become full of moisture or tears: *Rory blinked, his eyes watering.* ■ (of the mouth) produce saliva, typically in response to the sight or smell of appetizing food: *the smell of frying bacon made Hilary's mouth water.* **3** [*tr.*] dilute or adulterate (a drink, typically an alcoholic one) with water: *staff at the club had been watering down the drinks.* ■ (**water something down**) make a statement or proposal less forceful or controversial by changing or leaving out certain details: *the army's report of its investigation was considerably watered down.* ▷Old English *wæter* (noun), *wæterian* (verb), of Germanic origin; related to Dutch *water*, German *Wasser*, from an Indo-European root shared by Russian *voda* 'water,' also by Latin *unda* 'wave' and Greek *hudōr* 'water.' —**wa·ter·er** *n.* —**wa·ter·less** *adj.*

wa·ter·bed /ˈwôtərˌbed; ˈwä-/ ▶*n.* a bed with a water-filled rubber or plastic mattress.

wa·ter·bird /ˈwôtərˌbərd; ˈwä-/ ▶*n.* a bird that frequents water, esp. one that habitually wades or swims in fresh water.

wa·ter buf·fa·lo ▶*n.* a large black domesticated buffalo (*Bubalus bubalis*) with heavy swept-back horns, used as a beast of burden throughout the tropics.

wa·ter chest·nut ▶*n.* **1** the tuber of a tropical sedge that is widely used in Asian cooking, its white flesh remaining crisp after cooking. **2** the sedge (*Eleocharis tuberosa*) that yields this tuber, which is cultivated in flooded fields in Southeast Asia. **3** (also **water caltrop**) an aquatic plant (*Trapa natans*, family Trapaceae) with small white flowers, producing an edible rounded seed with two large projecting horns.

wa·ter·col·or /ˈwôtərˌkələr; ˈwä-/ ▶*n.* (also **watercolors**) artists' paint made with a water-soluble binder such as gum arabic, and thinned with water rather than oil, giving a transparent color. ■ a picture painted with watercolors. ■ the art of painting with watercolors, esp. using a technique of producing paler colors by diluting rather than by adding white. —**wa·ter·col·or·ist** *n.*

wa·ter cool·er ▶*n.* a dispenser of cooled drinking water, typically used in office workplaces. ■ [*as adj.*] *inf.* denoting the type of informal conversation or socializing among office workers that takes place in the communal area in which such a dispenser is located: *a water-cooler chat about the president.*

wa·ter·course /ˈwôtərˌkôrs; ˈwä-/ ▶*n.* a brook, stream, or artificially constructed water channel. ■ the bed along which this flows.

wa·ter·cress /ˈwôtərˌkres; ˈwä-/ ▶*n.* a cress (*Nasturtium officinale*) that grows in running water and whose pungent leaves are used in salad.

wa·ter·fall /ˈwôtərˌfôl; ˈwä-/ ▶*n.* a cascade of water falling from a height, formed when a river or stream flows over a precipice or steep incline.

wa·ter flea ▶*n.* another term for DAPHNIA.

wa·ter·fowl /ˈwôtərˌfoul; ˈwä-/ ▶*pl. n.* ducks, geese, or other large aquatic birds, esp. when regarded as game.

wa·ter·front /ˈwôtərˌfrənt; ˈwä-/ ▶*n.* a part of a town that borders a body of water.

wa·ter·hole /ˈwôtərˌhōl; ˈwä-/ ▶*n.* a depression in which water collects, esp. one from which animals regularly drink.

wa·ter·ing hole ▶*n.* a waterhole from which animals regularly drink. ■ *inf.* a tavern or bar.

wa·ter lil·y ▶*n.* an aquatic plant (family Nymphaeaceae) with large round floating leaves and large, typically cup-shaped, floating flowers. Several genera and many species include the white-flowered **fragrant water lily** (*Nymphaea odorata*) of eastern North America. ■ a closely related aquatic plant (family Nelumbonaceae) that includes the lotuses.

wa·ter·line /ˈwôtərˌlīn; ˈwä-/ ▶*n.* the line to which a vessel's hull is immersed when loaded in a specified way. ■ the level reached by the sea or a river visible as a line on a rock face, beach, or riverbank.

wa·ter·logged /ˈwôtərˌlôgd; ˈwä-/ ▶*adj.* saturated with or full of water: *the race was called off after parts of the course were found to be waterlogged.*

wa·ter main ▶*n.* a main line in a water supply system.

wa·ter·man /ˈwôtərmən; ˈwä-/ ▶*n.* (*pl.* -men) a boatman. ■ an oarsman who has attained a particular level of knowledge or skill.

wa·ter·mark /ˈwôtərˌmärk; ˈwä-/ ▶*n.* a faint design made in some paper during manufacture, that is visible when held against the light and typically identifies the maker.
▶*v.* [*tr.*] mark with such a design.

wa·ter·mel·on /ˈwôtərˌmelən; ˈwä-/ ▶*n.* **1** the large melonlike fruit of a

plant of the gourd family, with smooth green skin, red pulp, and watery juice. **2** the widely cultivated African plant (*Citrullus lanatus*) that yields this fruit.

wa·ter pipe ▶*n.* **1** a pipe for conveying water. **2** a pipe for smoking tobacco, cannabis, etc., that draws the smoke through water to cool it.

wa·ter pis·tol ▶*n.* a toy pistol that shoots a jet of water.

wa·ter plan·tain ▶*n.* an aquatic or marshland plant (genus *Alisma*, family Alismataceae) of north temperate regions, with leaves that resemble those of plantains and a tall stem bearing numerous white or pink flowers.

wa·ter po·lo ▶*n.* a seven-a-side game played by swimmers in a pool, with a ball like a volleyball that is thrown into the opponent's net.

wa·ter·proof /ˈwôtərˌpro͞of; ˈwä-/ ▶*adj.* impervious to water: *a waterproof hat.* ■ not liable to be washed away by water: *waterproof ink.*
▶*v.* [*tr.*] make impervious to water. —**wa·ter·proof·er** *n.*

wa·ter·re·pel·lent ▶*adj.* not easily penetrated by water, esp. as a result of being treated for such a purpose with a surface coating.

wa·ter·shed /ˈwôtərˌshed; ˈwä-/ ▶*n.* an area or ridge of land that separates waters flowing to different rivers, basins, or seas. ■ an area or region drained by a river, river system, or other body of water. ■ an event or period marking a turning point in a course of action or state of affairs: *these works mark a watershed in the history of music.*

wa·ter·ski /ˈwôtərˌskē; ˈwä-/ ▶*n.* (*pl.* -skis) each of a pair of skis enabling the wearer to skim the surface of the water when towed by a motorboat.
▶*v.* [*intr.*] skim the surface of water on waterskis. —**wa·ter·ski·er** *n.*

wa·ter·spout /ˈwôtərˌspout; ˈwä-/ ▶*n.* a rotating column of water and spray formed by a whirlwind occurring over the sea or other body of water.

wa·ter ta·ble ▶*n.* the level below which the ground is saturated with water.

wa·ter·tight /ˈwôtərˌtīt; ˈwä-/ ▶*adj.* closely sealed, fastened, or fitted so that no water enters or passes through: *a watertight seal.* ■ (of an argument or account) unable to be disputed or questioned: *their alibis are watertight.*

wa·ter·way /ˈwôtərˌwā; ˈwä-/ ▶*n.* a river, canal, or other route for travel by water.

wa·ter·wheel /ˈwôtərˌ(h)wēl; ˈwä-/ ▶*n.* a large wheel driven by flowing water, used to work machinery or to raise water to a higher level.

waterwheel

wa·ter wings ▶*pl. n.* inflated floats that may be fixed to the arms of someone learning to swim to give increased buoyancy.

wa·ter·works /ˈwôtərˌwərks; ˈwä-/ ▶*pl. n.* **1** [treated as *sing.*] an establishment for managing a water supply. **2** *inf.* the shedding of tears: *"Don't turn on the waterworks,"* he advised.

wa·ter·y /ˈwôtərē; ˈwä-/ ▶*adj.* consisting of, containing, or resembling water: *a watery fluid.* ■ thin or tasteless as a result of containing too much water: *watery coffee.* ■ weak; pale: *watery sunshine.* ■ (of a person's eyes) full of or running with tears. —**wa·ter·i·ness** *n.*

watt /wät/ (abbr.: **W**) ▶*n.* the SI unit of power, equivalent to one joule per second, corresponding to the power in an electric circuit in which the potential difference is one volt and the current one ampere.

watt·age /ˈwätij/ ▶*n.* a measure of electrical power expressed in watts. ■ the operating power of a lamp or other electrical appliance expressed in watts.

watt-hour ▶*n.* a measure of electrical energy equivalent to a power consumption of one watt for one hour.

wat·tle[1] /'wätl/ ▸*n.* a material for making fences, walls, etc., consisting of rods or stakes interlaced with twigs or branches.
▸*v.* [*tr.*] make, enclose, or fill up with wattle.

wat·tle[2] ▸*n.* a colored fleshy lobe hanging from the head or neck of domestic chickens, turkeys, and some other birds. —**wat·tled** *adj.*

wave /wāv/ ▸*v.* **1** [*intr.*] move one's hand to and fro in greeting or as a signal: *he waved to me from the train.* ■ [*tr.*] move (one's hand or arm, or something held in one's hand) to and fro: *he waved a sheaf of papers in the air.* ■ move to and fro with a swaying or undulating motion while remaining fixed to one point: *the flag waved in the wind.* ■ [*tr.*] convey (a greeting or other message) by moving one's hand or something held in it to and fro: *we waved our farewells.* ■ [*tr.*] instruct (someone) to move in a particular direction by moving one's hand: *he waved her back.* **2** [*tr.*] style (hair) so that it curls slightly: *her hair had been carefully waved for the evening.* ■ [*intr.*] (of hair) grow with a slight curl: [as *adj.*] (**waving**) *thick, waving gray hair sprouted back from his forehead.*
▸*n.* **1** a long body of water curling into an arched form and breaking on the shore. ■ a ridge of water between two depressions in open water: *gulls and cormorants bobbed on the waves.* ■ a shape seen as comparable to a breaking wave: *a wave of treetops stretched to the horizon.* ■ (usu. **the wave**) an effect resembling a moving wave produced by successive sections of the crowd in a stadium standing up, raising their arms, lowering them, and sitting down again. ■ (**the waves**) *poetic/lit.* the sea. ■ an intense burst of a particular feeling or emotion: *horror came over me in waves.* ■ a sudden occurrence of or increase in a specified phenomenon: *a wave of strikes had effectively paralyzed the government.* **2** a gesture or signal made by moving one's hand to and fro: *he gave a little wave and walked off.* **3** a slightly curling lock of hair: *his hair was drying in unruly waves.* ■ a tendency to curl in a person's hair: *her hair has a slight natural wave.* **4** *Physics* a periodic disturbance of the particles of a substance that may be propagated without net movement of the particles, such as in the passage of undulating motion, heat, or sound. ■ a single curve in the course of this motion. ■ a similar variation of an electromagnetic field in the propagation of light or other radiation through a medium or vacuum. —**wave·less** *adj.* —**wave·like** *adj.* & *adv.*
▸ □ **make waves** *inf.* create a significant impression: *made waves as a sculptor.* ■ cause trouble: *I don't want to risk her welfare by making waves.*

wave·band /'wāv,band/ ▸*n.* a range of wavelengths falling between two given limits, used in radio transmission.

wave·length /'wāv,leNGTH/ ▸*n. Physics* the distance between successive crests of a wave, esp. points in a sound wave or electromagnetic wave. (Symbol: λ) ■ this distance as a distinctive feature of radio waves from a transmitter. ■ *fig.* a person's ideas and way of thinking, esp. as it affects their ability to communicate with others: *when we met we hit it off immediately—we're* **on the same wavelength.**

wave·let /'wāvlit/ ▸*n.* a small wave of water; a ripple.

wa·ver /'wāvər/ ▸*v.* [*intr.*] shake with a quivering motion: *the flame wavered in the draft.* ■ become unsteady or unreliable: *his love for her had never wavered.* ■ be undecided between two opinions or courses of action; be irresolute: *she never wavered from her intention.* —**wa·ver·er** *n.* —**wa·ver·ing·ly** *adv.* —**wa·ver·y** *adj.*

wav file /wāv/ (also **wave file**) ▸*n. Comput.* a format for storing audio files that produces CD-quality audio.

wav·y /'wāvē/ ▸*adj.* (**wav·i·er, wav·i·est**) (of a line or surface) having or consisting of a series of undulating and wavelike curves: *she had long, wavy hair.* —**wav·i·ly** /'wāvəlē/ *adv.* —**wav·i·ness** *n.*

wax[1] /waks/ ▸*n.* a sticky yellowish moldable substance secreted by honeybees as the material of honeycomb; beeswax. ■ a white translucent material obtained by bleaching and purifying this substance and used for such purposes as making candles, modeling, and as a basis of polishes. ■ a similar viscous substance, typically a lipid or hydrocarbon. ■ earwax. ■ *inf.* used in reference to phonograph records: *he didn't get* **on wax** *until 1959.*
▸*v.* [*tr.*] **1** cover or treat (something) with wax or a similar substance, typically to polish or protect it: *I washed and waxed the floor.* ■ remove unwanted hair from (a part of the body) by applying wax and then peeling off the wax and hairs together. **2** *inf.* make a recording of: *he waxed a series of tracks that emphasized his lead guitar work.* —**wax·er** *n.*

wax[2] ▸*v.* [*intr.*] **1** (of the moon between new and full) have a progressively larger part of its visible surface illuminated, increasing its apparent size. ■ *poetic/lit.* become larger or stronger: *his anger waxed.* ■ begin to speak or write about something in the specified manner: *they* **waxed** *lyrical about the old days.*
▸ □ **wax and wane** undergo alternate increases and decreases: *companies whose fortunes wax and wane with the economic cycle.*

waxed pa·per (also **wax paper**) ▸*n.* paper that has been impregnated with wax to make it waterproof or greaseproof, used esp. in cooking and the wrapping of foodstuffs.

wax·en /'waksən/ ▸*adj.* having a smooth, pale, translucent surface or appearance like that of wax: *a canopy of waxen, creamy blooms.*

wax·work /'waks,wərk/ ▸*n.* (**waxworks**) [treated as *sing.*] an exhibition of wax dummies.

wax·y /'waksē/ ▸*adj.* (**wax·i·er, wax·i·est**) resembling wax in consistency or appearance: *waxy potatoes.* —**wax·i·ly** /'waksəlē/ *adv.* —**wax·i·ness** *n.*

way /wā/ ▸*n.* **1** a method, style, or manner of doing something: *worry was their way of showing how much they care.* ■ a person's characteristic or habitual manner of behavior or expression: *it was not his way to wait passively for things to happen.* ■ (**ways**) the customary modes of behavior or practices of a group: *foreigners who adopt French ways.* ■ the typical manner in which something happens or in which someone or something behaves: *he was showing off, as is the way with adolescent boys.* **2** a road, track, path, or street for traveling along: [in *place names*] *No. 3, Church Way.* ■ a course of travel or route taken in order to reach a place: *can you tell me the way to Duffy Square?* ■ a means of entry or exit from somewhere, such as a door or gate: *we're going in the back way.* ■ (also *inf.* **ways**) a distance traveled or to be traveled; the distance from one place to another: *they still had a long way ahead of them.* ■ a period between one point in time and another: *September was a long way off.* ■ travel or motion along a particular route; the route along which someone or something would travel if unobstructed: *Christine tried to follow but Martin blocked her way.* ■ a specified direction: *we just missed another car coming the other way.* ■ (often **ways**) parts into which something divides or is divided: *the national vote split three ways* | [in *comb.*] *a five-way bidding war.* ■ (**one's way**) used with a verb and adverbial phrase to intensify the force of an action or to denote movement or progress: *I shouldered my way to the bar.* ■ forward or backward motion of a ship or boat through water: *the dinghy lost way and drifted toward the shore.* **3** *inf.* a particular area or locality: *I've got a sick cousin over Fayetteville way.* **4** a particular aspect of something; a respect: *I have changed in every way.* **5** a specified condition or state: *the family was in a poor way.* **6** (**ways**) a sloping structure down which a new ship is launched.
▸*adv. inf.* at or to a considerable distance or extent; far (used before an adverb or preposition for emphasis): *his understanding of what constitutes good writing is way off target* ■ much: *I was cycling way too fast.* ■ extremely; really (used for emphasis): *the guys behind the bar were way cool.* ▷Old English *weg*, of Germanic origin; related to Dutch *weg* and German *Weg*, from a base meaning 'move, carry.'
▸ □ **by the way 1** incidentally (used to introduce a minor topic not connected with what was being spoken about previously): *by the way, pay in advance if you can.* **2** during the course of a journey: *you will have a fine view of Moray Firth by the way.* □ **by way of 1** so as to pass through or across; via: *we approached the Berlin Wall by way of Checkpoint Charlie.* **2** constituting; as a form of: *"I can't help it," shouted Tom by way of apology.* **3** by means of: *noncompliance with the regulations is punishable by way of a fine.* □ **give way 1** yield to someone or something: *he was not a man to give way to this kind of pressure.* ■ (of a support or structure) be unable to carry a load or withstand a force; collapse or break. ■ (**give way to**) allow oneself to be overcome by or to succumb to (an emotion or impulse): *she gave way to a burst of weeping.* **2** allow someone or something to be or go first: *give way to traffic coming from the right.* ■ (**give way to**) be replaced or superseded by: *Alan's discomfort gave way to anger.* □ **go all the** (or **go the whole**) **way** continue a course of action to its conclusion. ■ *inf.* have sexual intercourse with someone. □ **go out of one's way** make a special effort to do something: *Mrs. Mott went out of her way to be courteous to Sara.* □ **have a way with** have a particular talent for dealing with or ability in: *she's got a way with animals.* □ **know one's way around** be familiar with (an area, procedure, or subject). □ **look the other way** deliberately avoid seeing or noticing someone or something. □ **way of life** the typical pattern of behavior of a person or group: *the rural way of life.* □ **ways and means** the methods and resources at someone's disposal for achieving something: *the company is seeking ways and means of safeguarding jobs.*

way·far·er /'wā,fe(ə)rər/ ▸*n. poetic/lit.* a person who travels on foot. —**way·far·ing** *n.*

way·lay /'wā,lā/ ▸*v.* (*past* and *past part.* **-laid**) [*tr.*] stop or interrupt (someone) and detain them in conversation or trouble them in some other way: *he waylaid me on the stairs.* —**way·lay·er** *n.*

way·side /ˈwāˌsīd/ ▶*n.* the edge of a road.
▷ □ **fall by the wayside** fail to persist in an endeavor or undertaking: *many readers will fall by the wayside as the terminology becomes more complicated.*

way·ward /ˈwāwərd/ ▶*adj.* difficult to control or predict because of unusual or perverse behavior: *her wayward, difficult sister* | *fig. his wayward emotions.* —**way·ward·ly** *adv.* —**way·ward·ness** *n.*

we /wē/ ▶*pron.* [first person pl.] **1** used by a speaker to refer to himself or herself and one or more other people considered together: *shall we have a drink?* ■ used to refer to the speaker together with other people regarded in the same category: *nobody knows kids better than we teachers do.* ■ people in general: *we should eat as varied and well-balanced a diet as possible.* **2** used in formal contexts for or by a royal person, or by a writer or editor, to refer to himself or herself: *in this section we discuss the reasons.* **3** used condescendingly to refer to the person being addressed: *how are we today?*

weak /wēk/ ▶*adj.* **1** lacking the power to perform physically demanding tasks; lacking physical strength and energy: *she was recovering from the flu and was very weak.* ■ lacking political or social power or influence: *the central government had grown too weak to impose order* | [as pl. n.] (**the weak**) *the new king used his powers to protect the weak.* ■ (of a crew, team, or army) containing too few members or members of insufficient quality. ■ (of a faculty or part of the body) not able to fulfill its functions properly: *he had a weak stomach.* ■ of a low standard; performing or performed badly: *the choruses on this recording are weak.* ■ not convincing or logically forceful: *the argument is an extremely weak one.* ■ exerting only a small force: *a weak magnetic field.* **2** liable to break or give way under pressure; easily damaged: *the salamander's tail may be broken off at a weak spot near the base.* ■ lacking the force of character to hold to one's own decisions, beliefs, or principles; irresolute. ■ (of a belief, emotion, or attitude) not held or felt with such conviction or intensity as to prevent its being abandoned or dispelled: *their commitment to the project is weak.* ■ not in a secure financial position: *people have no faith in weak banks.* ■ (of prices or a market) having a downward tendency. **3** lacking intensity or brightness: *a weak light from a single street lamp.* ■ (of a liquid or solution) lacking flavor or effectiveness because of being heavily diluted: *a cup of weak coffee.* ■ (of an acid) only slightly ionized. ■ displaying or characterized by a lack of enthusiasm or energy: *she managed a weak, nervous smile.* ■ (of features) not striking or strongly marked: *his beard covered a weak chin.* ■ (of a syllable) unstressed. **4** *Gram.* denoting a class of verbs in Germanic languages that form the past tense and past participle by addition of a suffix (in English, typically -*ed*); **5** *Physics* of, relating to, or denoting the weakest of the known kinds of force between particles, which acts only at distances less than about 10^{-15} cm and is very much weaker than the electromagnetic and the strong interactions. ▷Old English *wāc* 'pliant,' 'of little worth,' 'not steadfast,' reinforced in Middle English by Old Norse *veikr*, from a Germanic base meaning 'yield, give way.' —**weak·ish** *adj.*

weak·en /ˈwēkən/ ▶*v.* make or become weaker in power, resolve, or physical strength: [tr.] *fault lines had weakened and shattered the rocks* | [intr.] *his resistance had weakened.* —**weak·en·er** *n.*

weak-kneed ▶*adj.* weak and shaky as a result of fear or excitement. ■ lacking in resolve or courage; cowardly.

weak·ling /ˈwēkliNG/ ▶*n.* a person or animal that is physically weak and frail. ■ an ineffectual or cowardly person.

weak·ly /ˈwēklē/ ▶*adv.* in a way that lacks strength or force: *she leaned weakly against the wall.*
▶*adj.* (-li·er, -li·est) sickly; not robust. —**weak·li·ness** *n.*

weak-mind·ed ▶*adj.* lacking determination, emotional strength, or intellectual capacity. —**weak-mind·ed·ness** *n.*

weak·ness /ˈwēknis/ ▶*n.* the state or condition of lacking strength: *the country's weakness in international dealings.* ■ a quality or feature regarded as a disadvantage or fault: *you must recognize your product's strengths and weaknesses.* ■ a person or thing that one is unable to resist or likes excessively: *you're his one weakness—he should never have met you.* ■ (**weakness for**) a self-indulgent liking for: *he had a great weakness for Scotch whisky.*

weal[1] /wēl/ (also *chiefly Med.* **wheal**) ▶*n.* a red, swollen mark left on flesh by a blow or pressure. ■ *Med.* an area of the skin that is temporarily raised, typically reddened, and usually accompanied by itching.

weal[2] ▶*n. formal* that which is best for someone or something: *I am holding this trial behind closed doors in the public weal.*

wealth /welTH/ ▶*n.* an abundance of valuable possessions or money: *he used his wealth to bribe officials.* ■ the state of being rich; material prosperity: *some people buy boats and cars to display their wealth.* ■ plentiful supplies of a particular resource: *the country's mineral wealth.* ■ a plentiful supply of a particular desirable thing: *the tables and maps contain a wealth of information.* ■ *archaic* well-being; prosperity.

wealth·y /ˈwelTHē/ ▶*adj.* (**wealth·i·er, wealth·i·est**) having a great deal of money, resources, or assets; rich: *the wealthy nations of the world* | [as pl. n.] (**the wealthy**) *the burden of taxation on the wealthy.* —**wealth·i·ly** /-THəlē/ *adv.*

wean /wēn/ ▶*v.* [tr.] accustom (an infant or other young mammal) to food other than its mother's milk. ■ accustom (someone) to managing without something on which they have become dependent or of which they have become excessively fond: *the doctor tried to wean her off the sleeping pills.* ■ (**be weaned on**) be strongly influenced by (something), esp. from an early age: *I was weaned on a regular diet of Hollywood fantasy.*

weap·on /ˈwepən/ ▶*n.* a thing designed or used for inflicting bodily harm or physical damage: *nuclear weapons.* ■ *fig.* a means of gaining an advantage or defending oneself in a conflict or contest: *resignation threats had long been a weapon in his armory.* —**weap·oned** *adj.* —**weap·on·less** *adj.*

weap·on·ize ▶*v.* [tr.] **1** convert to use as a weapon: *a list of pathogens that terrorists might weaponize.* **2** supply or equip with weapons: *a plan to weaponize space.* —**weap·on·i·za·tion** *n.*

weap·on·ry /ˈwepənrē/ ▶*n.* [treated as *sing.* or *pl.*] weapons regarded collectively.

wear /we(ə)r/ ▶*v.* (*past* **wore** /wôr/; *past part.* **worn** /wôrn/) **1** [tr.] have on one's body or a part of one's body as clothing, decoration, protection, or for some other purpose: *he was wearing a dark suit.* ■ habitually have on one's body or be dressed in: *although she was a widow, she didn't wear black.* ■ exhibit or present (a particular facial expression or appearance): *they wear a frozen smile on their faces.* ■ have (one's hair or beard) at a specified length or arranged in a specified style: *the students wore their hair long.* **2** [tr.] damage, erode, or destroy by friction or use: *the track has been worn down in part to bare rock.* ■ [intr.] undergo such damage, erosion, or destruction: *mountains are wearing down with each passing second.* ■ [tr.] form (a hole, path, etc.) by constant friction or use: *the water was forced up through holes it had worn.* ■ [intr.] (**wear on**) cause weariness or fatigue to: *some losses can wear on you.* **3** [intr.] withstand continued use or life in a specified way: *a carpet-type finish seems to wear well.* **4** [intr.] (**wear on**) (of a period of time) pass, esp. slowly or tediously: *as the afternoon wore on, he began to look unhappy.*
▷*phrasal v.* □ **wear someone/something down** overcome or exhaust someone or something by persistence. □ **wear off** lose effectiveness or intensity. □ **wear something out** (or **wear out**) **1** use or be used until no longer in good condition or working order: *wearing out the stair carpet.* **2** (**wear someone/something out**) exhaust or tire someone or something: *an hour of this wandering wore out Lampard's patience.*
▶*n.* **1** the wearing of something or the state of being worn as clothing: *some new tops for wear in the evening.* **2** clothing suitable for a particular purpose or of a particular type: *evening wear.* **3** damage or deterioration sustained from continuous use: *you need to make a deduction for wear and tear on all your belongings.* ■ the capacity for withstanding continuous use without such damage: *old things were relegated to the bedrooms because there was plenty of wear left in them.* —**wear·a·ble** *adj.* —**wear·a·bil·i·ty** *n.* —**wear·er** *n.*
▷ □ **wear thin** be gradually used up or become less convincing or acceptable: *his patience was wearing thin* | *the joke had started to wear thin.*

wear·i·some /ˈwi(ə)rēsəm/ ▶*adj.* causing one to feel tired or bored. —**wea·ri·some·ly** *adv.* —**wea·ri·some·ness** *n.*

wear·y /ˈwi(ə)rē/ ▶*adj.* (**wear·i·er, wear·i·est**) feeling or showing tiredness, esp. as a result of excessive exertion or lack of sleep: *he gave a long, weary sigh.* ■ reluctant to see or experience any more of (something); tired of: *she was weary of their constant arguments* | [in *comb.*] *war-weary Americans.* ■ calling for a great amount of energy or endurance; tiring and tedious: *the weary journey began again.*
▶*v.* (**wear·ies, wear·ied**) [tr.] cause to become tired: *she was wearied by her persistent cough.* ■ [intr.] (**weary of**) grow tired of or bored with: *she wearied of the sameness of her life.* —**wea·ri·ly** /ˈwirəlē/ *adv.* —**wea·ri·ness** *n.* —**wea·ry·ing·ly** *adv.*

wea·sel /ˈwēzəl/ ▶*n.* a small, slender, carnivorous mammal (genus *Mustela*), esp. *M. nivalis* of northern Eurasia and northern North America, related to, but generally smaller than, the stoat. The **weasel family** (Mustelidae) also includes the polecats, minks, martens, skunks, otters, and badgers. ■ *fig., inf.* a deceitful or treacherous person.
▶*v.* (-seled, -sel·ing; *Brit.* -selled, -sel·ling) [intr.] achieve something by

use of cunning or deceit: *she suspects me of trying to* **weasel** *my way into his affections.* ■ behave or talk evasively. —**wea·sel·ly** *adj.*

weath·er /ˈweT͟Hər/ ▶*n.* the state of the atmosphere at a place and time as regards heat, cloudiness, dryness, sunshine, wind, rain, etc.: *if the weather's good, we can go for a walk.* ■ a report on such conditions as broadcast on radio or television. ■ cold, wet, and unpleasant or unpredictable atmospheric conditions; the elements: *stone walls provide shelter from wind and weather.* ■ [as *adj.*] denoting the side from which the wind is blowing, esp. on board a ship; windward.
▶*v.* [*tr.*] **1** wear away or change the appearance or texture of (something) by long exposure to the atmosphere: [*tr.*] *his skin was weathered almost black by his long outdoor life* | [as *adj.*] (**weathered**) *chemically weathered rock.* ■ [*intr.*] (of rock or other material) be worn away or altered by such processes: *the ice sheet preserves specimens that would* **weather away** *more quickly in other regions.* **2** come safely through (a storm). ■ withstand (a difficulty or danger): *this year has tested our ability to weather recession.* ■ *Sailing* (of a ship) get to the windward of (a cape or other obstacle).

weath·er·cock /ˈweT͟Hərˌkäk/ ▶*n.* a weathervane in the form of a rooster.

weath·er·man /ˈweT͟Hərˌman/ ▶*n.* (*pl.* **-men**) a man who broadcasts a description and forecast of weather conditions.

weath·er·proof /ˈweT͟Hərˌpro͞of/ ▶*adj.* resistant to the effects of bad weather, esp. rain: *the building is structurally sound and weatherproof.*
▶*v.* [*tr.*] make (something) resistant to the effects of bad weather, esp. rain.

weath·er·strip /ˈweT͟Hərˌstrip/ ▶*n.* a strip of rubber, metal, or other material used to seal the edges of a door or window against rain and wind.
▶*v.* (**-stripped**, **-strip·ping**) [*tr.*] apply such a strip to (a door or window). —**weath·er·strip·ping** *n.*

weath·er·vane /ˈweT͟Hərˌvān/ ▶*n.* a revolving pointer to show the direction of the wind, typically mounted on top of a building.

weathervane

weave[1] /wēv/ ▶*v.* (*past* **wove**; *past part.* **woven** or **wove**) [*tr.*] form (fabric or a fabric item) by interlacing long threads passing in one direction with others at a right angle to them. ■ form (thread) into fabric in this way: *thick mohair can be difficult to weave.* ■ [*intr.*] [usu. as *n.*] (**weaving**) make fabric in this way typically by working at a loom: *cotton spinning and weaving was done in mills.* ■ (**weave something into**) include something as an integral part or element of (a woven fabric): *a gold pattern was woven into the material.* ■ make (basketwork or a wreath) by interlacing rods or flowers. ■ make (a complex story or pattern) from a number of interconnected elements: *he weaves colorful, cinematic plots.* ■ (**weave something into**) include an element in (such a story or pattern): *interpretative comments are woven into the narrative.*
▶*n.* a particular style or manner in which something is woven: *scarlet cloth of a very fine weave.*

weave[2] ▶*v.* [*intr.*] twist and turn from side to side while moving somewhere in order to avoid obstructions: *he had to* **weave his way** *through the crowds.* ■ take evasive action in an aircraft, typically by moving it from side to side.

weav·er /ˈwēvər/ ▶*n.* **1** a person who weaves fabric. **2** (also **weav·er·bird**) a finchlike songbird (*Ploceus* and other genera, family Ploceidae) of tropical Africa and Asia. They build elaborately woven nests.

web /web/ ▶*n.* **1** a network of fine threads constructed by a spider from fluid secreted by its spinnerets, used to catch its prey. ■ a similar filmy network spun by some insect larvae, esp. communal caterpillars. ■ *fig.* a complex system of interconnected elements, esp. one perceived as a trap or danger: *he found himself caught up in* **a web of** *bureaucracy.* ■ (**the Web**) short for WORLD WIDE WEB. **2** a membrane between the toes of a swimming bird or other aquatic animal. ■ a thin flat part connecting thicker or more solid parts in machinery. **3** a roll of paper used in a continuous printing process. **4** a piece of woven fabric.
▶*v.* (**webbed**, **web·bing**) [*intr.*] move or hang so as to form a weblike shape: *an intricate transportation network webs from coast to coast.* ■ [*tr.*] (usu. **be webbed**) cover with or as though with a web: *she noticed his tanned skin, webbed with fine creases.* —**web·like** /-ˌlīk/ *adj.*

web·bing /ˈwebiNG/ ▶*n.* **1** strong, closely woven fabric used for making items such as straps and belts, and for supporting the seats of

upholstered chairs. **2** the part of a baseball glove between the thumb and forefinger.

web-foot·ed ▶*adj.* (of a swimming bird or other aquatic animal) having webbed feet.

Web host·ing ▶*n.* Comput. the activity or business of providing storage space and access for Web sites.

web·log /ˈwebˌlôg; -ˌläg/ ▶*n.* another term for BLOG. ▷1990s: from *web* in the sense 'World Wide Web' and *log* in the sense 'regular record of incidents.' —**web·log·ger** *n.*

Web·mail /ˈwebˌmāl/ (also **web-mail**) ▶*n.* e-mail available for use online and stored in the Internet server mailbox, and that is not downloaded to an e-mail program or used offline.

Web site (also **web site** or **web·site**) ▶*n.* Comput. a location connected to the Internet that maintains one or more pages on the World Wide Web.

web·zine /ˈwebˌzēn/ ▶*n.* a magazine published on the Internet.

wed /wed/ ▶*v.* **wed·ding**; *past* and *past part.* **wed·ded** or **wed**) [*tr.*] *chiefly formal* or *archaic* get married to: *he was to wed the king's daughter.* ■ [*intr.*] get married: *they wed a week after meeting* | (**be wed**) *after a three-month engagement, they were wed in London.* ■ give or join in marriage: *will you wed your daughter to him?* ■ [as *adj.*] (**wedded**) of or concerning marriage: *a celebration of 25 years'* **wedded bliss.** ■ combine (two factors or qualities, esp. desirable ones): *in this recording he weds an excellent program with a distinctive vocal style.* ■ (**be wedded to**) be obstinately attached or devoted to (an activity, belief, or system): *foreign policy has remained wedded to outdated assumptions.*

we'd /wēd/ ▶*contr. of* we had: *we'd already been on board.* ■ we should or we would: *we'd like to make you an offer.*

Wed. ▶*abbr.* Wednesday.

wed·ding /ˈwediNG/ ▶*n.* a marriage ceremony, esp. considered as including the associated celebrations.

wedding march ▶*n.* a piece of march music played at the entrance of the bride or the exit of the couple at a wedding.

wedge /wej/ ▶*n.* a piece of wood, metal, or some other material having one thick end and tapering to a thin edge, that is driven between two objects or parts of an object to secure or separate them. ■ an object or piece of something having such a shape: *a wedge of cheese.* ■ a formation of people or animals with such a shape. ■ a golf club with a low, angled face for maximum loft. ■ a shoe, typically having a fairly high heel, of which the heel and sole form a solid block, with no gap under the instep. ■ a heel of this kind.
▶*v.* **1** [*tr.*] fix in position using a wedge: [*tr.*] *the door was wedged open.* **2** [*tr.*] force into a narrow space: *I wedged the bags into the back seat.*
▶ □ **drive a wedge between** separate: *the general aimed to drive a wedge between the city and its northern defenses.* ■ cause disagreement or hostility between: *I'm not trying to drive a wedge between you and your father.*

wedg·ie /ˈwejē/ ▶*n. inf.* **1** a shoe with a wedged heel. **2** an uncomfortable tightening of the underpants between the buttocks, typically produced when someone pulls the underpants up from the back as a practical joke.

wed·lock /ˈwedˌläk/ ▶*n.* the state of being married.

Wednes·day /ˈwenzˌdā; -ˌdē/ ▶*n.* the day of the week before Thursday and following Tuesday.
▶*adv.* on Wednesday: *see you Wednesday.* ■ (**Wednesdays**) on Wednesdays; each Wednesday: *Wednesdays, the jazz DJ hosts a jam session.*

wee /wē/ ▶*adj.* (**we·er**, **we·est**) *chiefly Scot.* little: *just a wee drop.*
▶ □ **the wee hours** the early hours of the morning after midnight: *nights of dining and dancing until the wee hours.*

weed /wēd/ ▶*n.* a wild plant growing where it is not wanted and in competition with cultivated plants. ■ any wild plant growing in salt or fresh water. ■ *inf.* marijuana. ■ (**the weed**) *inf.* tobacco.
▶*v.* [*tr.*] remove unwanted plants from (an area of ground or the plants cultivated in it): *I was weeding a flower bed.* ■ (**weed something out**) remove something, esp. inferior or unwanted items or members from a group or collection: *we must raise the level of research and weed out the poorest work.* —**weed·er** *n.* —**weed·less** *adj.*

weed·y /ˈwēdē/ ▶*adj.* (**weed·i·er**, **weed·i·est**) **1** containing or covered with many weeds: *a weedy path led to the gate.* ■ of the nature of or resembling a weed: *a weedy species of plant.* **2** *inf.* (of a person) thin and physically weak in appearance. —**weed·i·ness** *n.*

week /wēk/ ▶*n.* a period of seven days. ■ the period of seven days generally reckoned from and to midnight on Saturday night: *she has an art class twice a week.* ■ workdays as opposed to the weekend; the five days from Monday to Friday: *I work during the week, so I can only get to this shop on Saturdays.* ■ the time spent working in this period of five to seven days: *she works a 48-hour week.* ■ a period of five or seven days devoted to a specified purpose or beginning on a specified day: *Super Bowl week | the week of June 23.* ■ *inf., chiefly Brit.* used after the name of a day to indicate that something will happen seven days after that day: *the program will be broadcast on Sunday week.*

week·day /ˈwēkˌdā/ ▶*n.* a day of the week other than Saturday or Sunday.

week·end /ˈwēkˌend/ ▶*n.* the period from Friday evening through Sunday evening, esp. regarded as a time for leisure: *she spent the weekend camping* | [as *adj.*] *a weekend break.* ■ (also **long weekend**) this period plus one or two days immediately before or after: *the long holiday weekend.*

▶*v.* [*intr.*] *inf.* spend a weekend somewhere: *weekending in the country.*

week-long (also **week·long**) ▶*adj.* lasting for a week: *a week-long visit to New Zealand.*

week·ly /ˈwēklē/ ▶*adj.* done, produced, or occurring once a week: *there was a weekly dance on Wednesdays.* ■ relating to or calculated in terms of a week: *the difference in weekly income is $290.*

▶*adv.* once a week: *interviews were given weekly.*

▶*n.* (pl. **-lies**) a newspaper or periodical issued every week.

wee·nie /ˈwēnē/ ▶*n.* **1** another term for WIENER). **2** *vulgar slang* a man's penis. ■ *informal* a weak, socially inept, or boringly studious person: *newer programming languages are a favorite of the tech weenies.*

weep /wēp/ ▶*v.* (past and past part. **wept** /wept/) [*intr.*] **1** shed tears: *a grieving mother wept over the body of her daughter* | [*tr.*] *he wept bitter tears at her cruelty.* ■ utter or express with tears: [with *direct speech*] *"No!" she wept.* **2** exude liquid: *she rubbed one of the sores, making it weep.*

▶*n.* a fit or spell of shedding tears. —**weep·er** *n.*

weep·y /ˈwēpē/ ▶*adj.* (**weep·i·er**, **weep·i·est**) *inf.* tearful; inclined to weep: *a weepy clingy child.* ■ sentimental: *a weepy made-for-TV movie.* —**weep·i·ly** /-əlē/ *adv.* —**weep·i·ness** *n.*

wee·vil /ˈwēvəl/ ▶*n.* a small beetle (Curculionidae and other families) with an elongated snout, the larvae of which typically develop inside seeds, stems, or other plant parts. Many are pests of crops or stored foodstuffs. ■ *inf.* any small insect that damages stored grain. —**wee·vil·y** *adj.*

wee-wee *inf.* ▶*n.* a child's word for urine.

▶*v.* [*intr.*] urinate.

weft /weft/ ▶*n.* (in weaving) the crosswise threads on a loom over and under which other threads (the warp) are passed to make cloth.

weigh /wā/ ▶*v.* **1** [*tr.*] find out how heavy (someone or something) is, typically using scales: *weigh yourself on the day you begin the diet.* ■ have a specified weight: *when the twins were born, they weighed ten pounds.* ■ balance in the hands to guess or as if to guess the weight of: *she picked up the brick and weighed it in her right hand.* ■ (**weigh something out**) measure and take from a larger quantity of a substance a portion of a particular weight: *she weighed out two ounces of loose tobacco.* ■ [*intr.*] (**weigh on**) be depressing or burdensome to: *his unhappiness would weigh on my mind so much.* **2** assess the nature or importance of, esp. with a view to a decision or action: *the consequences of the move would need to be very carefully weighed.* ■ (**weigh something against**) compare the importance of one factor with that of (another): *they need to weigh benefit against risk.* ■ [*intr.*] influence a decision or action; be considered important: *the evidence weighed heavily against him.*

▶*phrasal v.* □ **weigh someone down** be heavy and cumbersome to someone: *my waders and fishing gear weighed me down.* ■ be oppressive or burdensome to someone: *she was weighed down by family responsibilities.* ▷Old English *wegan*, of Germanic origin; related to *wagon* and *wain*, and to Dutch *wegen* 'weigh,' German *bewegen* 'move,' from an Indo-European root shared by Latin *vehere* 'convey.' Early senses included 'transport from one place to another' and 'raise up.'

▶ □ **weigh one's words** carefully choose the way one expresses something.

weight /wāt/ ▶*n.* **1** a body's relative mass or the quantity of matter contained by it, giving rise to a downward force; the heaviness of a person or thing: *he was at least 175 pounds in weight.* ■ *Physics* the force exerted on the mass of a body by a gravitational field. Compare with MASS. ■ the quality of being heavy: *as he came upstairs the boards creaked under his weight.* ■ a unit or system of units used for expressing how much an object or quantity of matter weighs. ■ a piece of metal known to weigh a definite amount and used on scales to determine how heavy an object or quantity of a substance is. ■ any of several

divisions based on relative lightness and heaviness into which boxers and wrestlers are classified for competition. ■ the surface density of cloth, used as a measure of its quality. ■ *Printing* the degree of blackness of a type font. **2** a heavy object, esp. one being lifted or carried. ■ a heavy object used to give an impulse or act as a counterweight in a mechanism. ■ (**weights**) blocks or discs of metal or other heavy material used in weightlifting or weight training. ■ a burden or responsibility. ■ the ability of someone or something to influence decisions or actions: *a recommendation by the committee will carry great weight.* ■ the importance attached to something: *individuals differ in the weight they attach to various aspects of a job.* ■ *Statistics* a factor associated with one of a set of numerical quantities, used to represent its importance relative to the other members of the set.

▶*v.* [*tr.*] **1** hold (something) down by placing a heavy object on top of it: *a mug half filled with coffee weighted down a stack of papers.* ■ make (something) heavier by attaching a heavy object to it, esp. so as to make it stay in place: *the jugs were covered with muslin veils weighted with colored beads.* **2** attach importance or value to: *speaking, reading, and writing should be weighted equally in the assessment.* ■ (**be weighted**) be planned or arranged so as to put a specified person, group, or factor in a position of advantage or disadvantage: *the balance of power is weighted in favor of the government.* ■ *Statistics* multiply the components of (an average) by factors to take account of their importance.

▶ □ **throw one's weight around** *inf.* be unpleasantly self-assertive.
□ **throw one's weight behind** *inf.* use one's influence to help support.

weight·less /ˈwātlis/ ▶*adj.* (of a body, esp. in an orbiting spacecraft) not apparently acted on by gravity. —**weight·less·ly** *adv.* —**weight·less·ness** *n.*

weight·lift·ing /ˈwātˌliftiNG/ ▶*n.* the sport or activity of lifting barbells or other heavy weights. —**weight·lift·er** *n.*

weight·y /ˈwātē/ ▶*adj.* (**weight·i·er**, **weight·i·est**) weighing a great deal; heavy: *a weighty vase.* ■ of great seriousness and importance: *he threw off all weighty considerations of state.* ■ having a great deal of influence on events or decisions. —**weight·i·ly** /-təlē/ *adv.* —**weight·i·ness** *n.*

weir /wi(ə)r/ ▶*n.* a low dam built across a stream to raise the level of water upstream or regulate its flow. ■ an enclosure of stakes set in a stream as a trap for fish.

weird /wi(ə)rd/ ▶*adj.* suggesting something supernatural; uncanny: *the weird crying of a seal.* ■ *inf.* very strange; bizarre: *a weird coincidence.*

▶*v.* [*tr.*] (**weird someone out**) *inf.* induce a sense of disbelief or alienation in someone. —**weird·ly** *adv.* —**weird·ness** *n.*

weird·o /ˈwi(ə)rdō/ ▶*n.* (pl. **-dos**) *inf.* a person whose dress or behavior seems strange or eccentric.

welch /welCH/ ▶*v.* variant spelling of WELSH.

wel·come /ˈwelkəm/ ▶*n.* an instance or manner of greeting someone: *you will receive a warm welcome.*

▶*interj.* used to greet someone in a glad or friendly way: *welcome to the Wildlife Park.*

▶*v.* [*tr.*] greet (someone arriving) in a glad, polite, or friendly way: *hotels should welcome guests in their own language* | [as *adj.*] (**welcoming**) *a welcoming smile.* ■ be glad to entertain (someone) or receive (something): *we welcome any comments.* ■ react with pleasure or approval to (an event or development): *the bank's decision to cut its rates was widely welcomed.*

▶*adj.* (of a guest or new arrival) gladly received: *visitors with disabilities are always welcome.* ■ very pleasing because much needed or desired: *after your walk, the café serves a welcome pot of coffee.* ■ allowed or invited to do a specified thing: *anyone is welcome to join them at their midday meal.* ■ (**welcome to**) used to indicate that one is relieved to be relinquishing the control or possession of something to another: *the job is all yours and you're welcome to it!* —**wel·come·ly** *adv.* —**wel·come·ness** *n.* —**wel·com·er** *n.* —**wel·com·ing·ly** *adv.*

▶ □ **you're welcome** used as a polite response to thanks.

weld /weld/ ▶*v.* [*tr.*] join together (metal pieces or parts) by heating the surfaces to the point of melting with a blowpipe, electric arc, or other means, and uniting them by pressing, hammering, etc.: *the truck had spikes welded to the back.* ■ forge (an article) by such means. ■ unite (pieces of plastic or other material) by melting or softening of surfaces in contact. ■ *fig.* cause to combine and form a harmonious or effective whole: *his efforts to weld together the religious parties ran into trouble.*

▶*n.* a welded joint. —**weld·a·bil·i·ty** /ˌweldəˈbilitē/ *n.* —**weld·a·ble** *adj.* —**weld·er** *n.*

wel·fare /ˈwelˌfe(ə)r/ ▶*n.* the health, happiness, and fortunes of a person or group: *they don't give a damn about the welfare of their families.* ■ statutory procedure or social effort designed to promote the basic physical

and material well-being of people in need: *the protection of rights to education, housing, and welfare.* ■ financial support given for this purpose.
▶ □ **on welfare** receiving government financial assistance for basic material needs.
wel·far·ism /'welfə(ə),rizəm/ ▶ *n.* the principles or policies associated with a welfare state. **—wel·far·ist** *n.* & *adj.*
well¹ /wel/ ▶ *adv.* (**bet·ter, best**) **1** in a good or satisfactory way: *the whole team played well.* ■ in a way that is appropriate to the facts or circumstances: *you did well to come and tell me* | [in comb.] *a well-timed exit.* ■ so as to have a fortunate outcome: *his campaign did not go well.* ■ in a kind way: *the animals will remain loyal to humans if treated well.* ■ with praise or approval: *people spoke well of him.* ■ with equanimity: *she took it very well, all things considered.* ■ profitably; advantageously: *she would marry well or not at all.* ■ in a condition of prosperity or comfort: *they lived well and were generous with their money.* **2** in a thorough manner: *add the mustard and lemon juice and mix well.* ■ to a great extent or degree (often used for emphasis): *the visit had been planned well in advance* | [in comb.] *a well-loved mother.* ■ intimately; closely: *he knew my father very well.* **3** very probably; in all likelihood: *being short of breath may well be the first sign of asthma.* ■ without difficulty: *she could well afford to pay for the reception herself.* ■ with good reason: *"What are we doing here?" "You may well ask."*
▶ *adj.* (**bet·ter, best**) **1** in good health; free or recovered from illness: *I don't feel very well.* ■ in a satisfactory state or position: *all is not well in post-Soviet Russia.* **2** sensible; advisable: *it would be well to know just what this suggestion entails.*
▶ *interj.* used to express a range of emotions including surprise, anger, resignation, or relief: *Well, really! The manners of some people!* ■ used when pausing to consider one's next words: *well, I suppose I could fit you in at 3:45.* ■ used to express agreement or acceptance, often in a qualified or slightly reluctant way: *well, all right, but be quick.* ■ used to introduce the resumption of a narrative or a change of subject. ■ used to mark the end of a conversation or activity: *well, cheers, Tom—I must run.* ■ used to indicate that one is waiting for an answer or explanation from someone: *Well? You promised to tell me all about it.* ▷Old English *wel(l)*, of Germanic origin; related to Dutch *wel* and German *wohl.* **—well·ness** *n.*
▶ □ **as well 1** in addition; too: *the museum provides hours of fun and a few surprises as well.* **2** (**as well** or **just as well**) with equal reason or an equally good result: *I may as well have a look.* ■ sensible, appropriate, or desirable: *it would be as well to let him go.* □ **leave** (or **let**) **well enough alone** refrain from interfering with or trying to improve something that is satisfactory or adequate as it is. □ **very well** used to express agreement or understanding, sometimes grudging: *oh very well then, come in.*
well² ▶ *n.* **1** a shaft sunk into the ground to obtain water, oil, or gas. ■ a plentiful source or supply: *she could feel a deep well of sympathy and compassion.* ■ a depression made to hold liquid: *put the flour on a flat surface and make a well to hold the eggs.* **2** an enclosed space in the middle of a building, giving room for stairs or an elevator, or to allow light or ventilation. **3** *Physics* a region of minimum potential: *a gravity well.*
▶ *v.* [*intr.*] (of a liquid) rise to the surface and spill or be about to spill: *tears were beginning to well in her eyes.* ■ (of an emotion) arise and become more intense: *all the old bitterness began to well up inside her again.*
we'll /wēl/ ▶ *contr.* of we shall; we will.
well-ad·vised ▶ *adj.* sensible; wise: *you would be well advised to obtain legal advice.*
well-ap·point·ed ▶ *adj.* (of a building or room) having a high standard of equipment or furnishing.
well-bal·anced ▶ *adj.* **1** sensible; sane. ■ (of a meal or a diet) nutritionally sound; providing an appropriate selection of nutrients: *a hotdog with cheese fries is hardly a well-balanced dinner.* **2** having a symmetrical or orderly arrangement of parts.
well-be·ing ▶ *n.* the state of being comfortable, healthy, or happy: *an improvement in the patient's well-being.*
well-born ▶ *adj.* from a noble or wealthy family.
well-dis·posed ▶ *adj.* having a positive, sympathetic, or friendly attitude toward someone or something: *the company is well-disposed to the idea of partnership.*
well-done ▶ *adj.* **1** (of a task or undertaking) carried out successfully or satisfactorily: *the decoration is very well done.* **2** (of meat) thoroughly cooked: *well-done roast beef.*
▶ *interj.* used to express congratulation or approval: *Well done—you've worked very hard!*

well-found·ed ▶ *adj.* (esp. of a suspicion or belief) based on good evidence or reasons: *their apprehensions were well founded.*
well-groomed ▶ *adj.* (esp. of a person) clean, tidy, and well dressed.
well-ground·ed ▶ *adj.* based on good evidence or reasons. ■ having a good training in or knowledge of a subject: *boys who are well grounded in traditional academic subjects.*
well-head /'wel,hed/ ▶ *n.* **1** the place where a spring comes out of the ground. **2** the structure over a well, typically an oil or gas well.
well-in·formed ▶ *adj.* having or showing much knowledge about a wide range of subjects, or about one particular subject.
well-in·ten·tioned ▶ *adj.* having or showing good intentions despite a lack of success or fortunate results: *well-intentioned advice.*
well-known ▶ *adj.* known widely or thoroughly: *a well-known television personality.*
well-mean·ing ▶ *adj.* well intentioned: *well-meaning friends.*
well-off ▶ *adj.* wealthy: *her family is quite well off.* ■ in a favorable situation or circumstances: *they were well off without her.*
well-oiled ▶ *adj.* **1** *inf.* drunk. **2** (esp. of an organization) operating smoothly: *the ruling party's well-oiled political machine.*
well-pre·served ▶ *adj.* (of something old) having remained in good condition. ■ (of an old person) showing little sign of aging.
well-read /red/ ▶ *adj.* knowledgeable through much reading.
well-round·ed ▶ *adj.* having a smooth, curved shape: *well-rounded quartz pebbles.* ■ (of a person) plump. ■ pleasingly varied or balanced: *a dry, robust, well-rounded wine.* ■ (of a person) having a personality that is fully developed in all aspects. ■ (of a phrase or sentence) carefully composed and balanced. ■ (of an education) covering well the necessary areas of instruction.
well-spo·ken ▶ *adj.* (of a person) speaking in an educated and refined manner.
well-thought-of ▶ *adj.* having a good reputation; esteemed; respected.
well-to-do ▶ *adj.* wealthy; prosperous: *a well-to-do family.*
well-worn ▶ *adj.* showing the signs of extensive use or wear: *a well-worn leather armchair.* ■ (of a phrase, idea, or joke) used or repeated so often that it no longer has interest or significance.
Welsh /welsh/ ▶ *adj.* of or relating to Wales, its people, or their Celtic language.
▶ *n.* **1** the Celtic language of Wales, spoken by about 500,000 people (mainly bilingual in English). Descended from the Brythonic language spoken in most of Roman Britain, it has been strongly revived after a long decline. **2** [as *pl. n.*] (**the Welsh**) the people of Wales collectively. **—Welsh·ness** *n.*
welsh /welsh/ (also **welch**) ▶ *v.* [*intr.*] (**welsh on**) fail to honor (a debt or obligation incurred through a promise or agreement): *the banks began welshing on their agreement not to convert dollar reserves into gold.* **—welsh·er** *n.*
Welsh cor·gi ▶ *n.* (pl. **Welsh cor·gis**) a dog of a short-legged breed with a foxlike head. ▷1920s: from Welsh, from *cor* 'dwarf' + *ci* 'dog.'
Welsh·man /'welshmən/ ▶ *n.* (pl. **-men**) a male native or national of Wales, or a man of Welsh descent.
Welsh rare·bit (also **Welsh rabbit**) ▶ *n.* another term for RAREBIT.
Welsh·wom·an /'welsh,woŏmən/ ▶ *n.* (pl. **-wom·en**) a female native or national of Wales, or a woman of Welsh descent.
welt /welt/ ▶ *n.* **1** a leather rim sewn around the edge of a shoe upper to which the sole is attached. ■ a ribbed, reinforced, or decorative border of a garment or pocket. **2** a red, swollen mark left on flesh by a blow or pressure. ■ a heavy blow.
▶ *v.* [*tr.*] **1** provide with a welt. **2** strike (someone or something) hard and heavily: *I could have welted her.* ■ [*intr.*] develop a raised scar: *his lip was beginning to thicken and welt from the blow.*
wel·ter /'weltər/ ▶ *n.* a large number of items in no order; a confused mass: *there's such a welter of conflicting rules.* ■ a state of general disorder: *the attack petered out in a welter of bloody, confused fighting.*
wel·ter·weight /'weltər,wāt/ ▶ *n.* a weight in boxing and other sports intermediate between lightweight and middleweight. In the amateur boxing scale it ranges from 140 to 147 pounds (63.5–67 kg). ■ a boxer or other competitor of this weight.
wen¹ /wen/ ▶ *n.* a boil or other swelling or growth on the skin, esp. a sebaceous cyst.
wen² (also **wyn** /win/) ▶ *n.* a runic letter, used in Old and Middle English, later replaced by *w.*

---

wench /wench/ ▶ *n. archaic* or *humorous* a girl or young woman. —**wench·er** *n.*

wend /wend/ ▶ *v.* [*intr.*] (**wend one's way**) go in a specified direction, typically slowly or by an indirect route: *they wended their way across the city.*

went /went/ ▶ past of GO[1].

wept /wept/ ▶ past and past participle of WEEP.

were /wər/ ▶ second person singular past, plural past, and past subjunctive of BE.

we're /wi(ə)r/ ▶ *contr. of* we are.

weren't /wər(ə)nt/ ▶ *contr. of* were not.

were·wolf /'we(ə)r,wŏŏlf/ ▶ *n.* (*pl.* **-wolves**) (in myth or fiction) a person who changes for periods of time into a wolf, typically when there is a full moon.

west /west/ ▶ *n.* (usu. **the west**) **1** the direction toward the point of the horizon where the sun sets at the equinoxes, on the left-hand side of a person facing north, or the part of the horizon lying in this direction: *the evening sun glowed from the west.* ■ the compass point corresponding to this. **2** the western part of the world or of a specified country, region, or town: *it will become windy in the west.* ■ (usu. **the West**) Europe and its culture seen in contrast to other civilizations. ■ (usu. **the West**) *hist.* the noncommunist states of Europe and North America, contrasted with the former communist states of eastern Europe. **3** (**West**) *Bridge* the player sitting to the right of North and partnering East.
▶ *adj.* **1** lying toward, near, or facing the west: *the west coast.* ■ (of a wind) blowing from the west. **2** of or denoting the western part of a specified area, city, or country or its inhabitants: *West Africa.*
▶ *adv.* to or toward the west: *he faced west and watched the sunset* | *the accident happened a mile west of Bowes.*

west·er·ly /'westərlē/ ▶ *adj. & adv.* in a westward position or direction: [as *adj.*] *the westerly end of Sunset Boulevard* | [as *adv.*] *our plan was to keep westerly.* ■ (of a wind) blowing from the west: [as *adj.*] *a stiff westerly breeze.*
▶ *n.* (often **westerlies**) a wind blowing from the west. ■ (**westerlies**) the belt of prevailing westerly winds in the mid-latitudes of the northern and southern hemispheres.

west·ern /'western/ ▶ *adj.* **1** situated in the west, or directed toward or facing the west: *there will be showers in some western areas.* **2** (usu. **Western**) living in or originating from the west, in particular Europe or the U.S.: *Western society.* ■ of, relating to, or characteristic of the west or its inhabitants: *the history of western art.* ■ *hist.* of or originating from the noncommunist states of Europe and North America in contrast to the Eastern bloc.
▶ *n.* (also **West·ern**) a film, television drama, or novel about cowboys in western North America, esp. in the late 19th and early 20th centuries. —**West·ern·er** *n.* —**west·ern·most** /-,mōst/ *adj.*

west·ern·ize /'westər,nīz/ ▶ *v.* [*tr.*] (usu. **be westernized**) cause (a country, person, or system) to adopt or be influenced by the cultural, economic, or political systems of Europe and North America: *the agreement provided for the legal system to be westernized.* ■ [*intr.*] be in the process of adopting or being influenced by the systems of the West: [as *adj.*] (**westernizing**) *a westernizing tribe.* —**west·ern·i·za·tion** /,westərni-'zāshən/ *n.* —**west·ern·iz·er** *n.*

West Nile vi·rus ▶ *n.* a flavivirus of African origin that can be spread to humans and other mammals via mosquitoes, causing encephalitis and flulike symptoms, with some fatalities.

west-north·west ▶ *n.* the direction or compass point midway between west and northwest.

west-south·west ▶ *n.* the direction or compass point midway between west and southwest.

west·ward /'westwərd/ ▶ *adj.* toward the west: *the journey covers eight time zones in a westward direction.*
▶ *adv.* (also **west·wards**) in a westerly direction: *the vast prairie lands extending from northern Ohio westward.*
▶ *n.* (**the westward**) a direction or region toward the west: *he sees a light to the westward.* —**west·ward·ly** *adv.*

wet /wet/ ▶ *adj.* (**wet·ter**, **wet·test**) **1** covered or saturated with water or another liquid: *she followed, slipping on the wet rock.* ■ (of the weather) rainy: *a wet, windy evening.* ■ (of paint, ink, plaster, or a similar substance) not yet having dried or hardened. ■ (of a baby or young child) having urinated in its diaper or underwear. ■ involving the use of water or liquid: *wet methods of photography.* **2** *inf.* (of a country or region or of its legislation) allowing the sale of alcoholic beverages. ■ (of a person) addicted to alcohol.
▶ *v.* (**wet·ting**; past and past part. **wet** or **wet·ted**) [*tr.*] cover or touch with liquid; moisten: *he wet a finger and flicked through the pages* | [as *n.*]

(**wetting**) *the wetting caused an aggravation of his gout.* ■ (esp. of a baby or young child) urinate in or on: *the child wet the bed.* ■ (**wet oneself**) urinate involuntarily.
▶ *n.* liquid that makes something damp: *I could feel the wet of his tears.* ■ (**the wet**) rainy weather: *the race was held in the wet.* ■ a person opposed to the prohibition of alcoholic beverages. —**wet·ly** *adv.* —**wet·ness** *n.* —**wet·ta·ble** *adj.*
▶ □ **all wet** completely wrong. □ **wet behind the ears** *inf.* lacking experience; immature.

wet·back /'wet,bak/ ▶ *n. inf., derog.* a Mexican living in the U.S., esp. one who is an illegal immigrant.

wet cell ▶ *n.* a primary electric cell in which the electrolyte is a liquid. Compare with DRY CELL.

wet dream ▶ *n.* an erotic dream associated with involuntary ejaculation of semen.

wet·land /'wet,land; -lənd/ ▶ *n.* (also **wetlands**) land consisting of marshes or swamps; saturated land.

wet nurse ▶ *n. chiefly hist.* a woman employed to suckle another woman's child.

wet·suit /'wet,sŏŏt/ ▶ *n.* a close-fitting garment of neoprene or similar material typically covering most of the body but not designed to exclude water, worn for warmth in water sports or diving.

we've /wēv/ ▶ *contr. of* we have.

whack /(h)wak/ *inf.* ▶ *v.* [*tr.*] strike forcefully with a sharp blow: *his attacker whacked him on the head* | [*intr.*] *she found a stick to whack at the branches.* ■ murder: *he was whacked while sitting in his car.*
▶ *n.* **1** a sharp or resounding blow. **2** a try or attempt: *we decided to take a whack at spotting the decade's trends.* —**whack·er** *n.* —**whack·ing** *adj.*
▶ □ **out of whack** out of order; not working: *all their calculations were out of whack.*

whack·o ▶ *adj. & n.* (*pl.* **-os**) variant spelling of WACKO.

whack·y ▶ *adj.* variant spelling of WACKY.

whale[1] /(h)wāl/ ▶ *n.* (*pl.* same or **whales**) a very large cetacean with a streamlined hairless body, a horizontal tail fin, and a blowhole on top of the head for breathing. See BALEEN WHALE.

whale[2] ▶ *v.* [*tr.*] *inf.* beat; hit: *Dad came upstairs and whaled me* | [*intr.*] *they whaled at the water with their paddles.*

whale·bone /'(h)wāl,bōn/ ▶ *n.* an elastic horny substance that grows in a series of thin parallel plates in the upper jaw of some whales and is used by them to strain plankton from the seawater. Also called BALEEN. ■ strips of this substance, much used formerly as stays in corsets and dresses: [as *adj.*] *a whalebone bodice.* ■ bone or ivory from a whale or walrus.

whal·er /'(h)wālər/ ▶ *n.* a whaling ship. ■ a seaman engaged in whaling.

whal·ing /'(h)wāliNG/ ▶ *n.* the practice or industry of hunting and killing whales for their oil, meat, or whalebone.

wham /(h)wam/ *inf.* ▶ *interj.* used to express the sound of a forcible impact: *the bombs landed—wham!—right on target.* ■ used to express the idea of a sudden, dramatic, and decisive occurrence: *he asked me out for a drink, and—wham!—that was it.*
▶ *v.* (**whammed**, **wham·ming**) [*intr.*] strike something forcefully: *trucks whammed into each other.* ■ make a loud sound as of a forceful impact: *my heart was whamming away like a drum.*

wham·my /'(h)wamē/ ▶ *n.* (*pl.* **-mies**) *inf.* an event with a powerful and unpleasant effect; a blow: *the third whammy was the degradation of the financial system.* ■ an evil or unlucky influence: *I've threatened to put the whammy on them.*

wharf /(h)wôrf/ ▶ *n.* (*pl.* **wharves** /(h)wôrvz/ or **wharfs**) a level dockside area to which a ship may be moored to load and unload.

wharves /(h)wôrvz/ ▶ plural form of WHARF.

what /(h)wət; (h)wät/ ▶ *pron.* **1** [*interrog. pron.*] asking for information specifying something: *what is your name?* | *I'm not sure what you mean.* ■ asking for repetition of something not heard or confirmation of something not understood: *what? I can't hear you.* **2** [*relative pron.*] the thing or things that (used in specifying something): *what we need is a commitment.* ■ (referring to the whole of an amount) whatever: *what I want to do what I can to make a difference.* ■ *dial.* who or that: *the one what got to my house.* **3** (in exclamations) emphasizing something surprising or remarkable: *what some people do for attention!*
▶ *adj.* **1** asking for information specifying something: *what time is it?* **2** (referring to the whole of an amount) whatever: *he had been robbed of what little money he had.* **3** (in exclamations) how great or remarkable: [as *adj.*] *what luck!*
▶ *adv.* **1** to what extent?: *what does it matter?* **2** used to indicate an estimate or approximation: *see you, what, about four?* ▷Old English *hwæt,* of

Germanic origin; related to Dutch *wat* and German *was*, from an Indo-European root shared by Latin *quod*.

▸ □ **and** (or **or**) **what have you** *inf.* and/or anything else similar: *for a binder try soup, gravy, cream, or what have you.* □ **and what not** *inf.* and other similar things. □ **what about ——?** **1** used when asking for information or an opinion on something: *what about the practical angle?* **2** used to make a suggestion: *what about a walk?* □ **what if ——?** **1** what would result if ——?: *what if nobody shows up?* **2** what does it matter if ——?: *what if our house is a mess? I'm clean.* □ **what's what** *inf.* what is useful or important: *I'll teach her what's what.* □ **what with** because of (used usually to introduce several causes of something): *what with the drought and the neglect, the garden is in a sad condition.*

what·ev·er /'(h)wət'evər; ˌ(h)wät-/ ▸*relative pron. & adj.* used to emphasize a lack of restriction in referring to any thing or amount, no matter what: [as *pron.*] *do whatever you like* | [as *adj.*] *take whatever action is needed.* ■ regardless of what: [as *pron.*] *you have our support, whatever you decide* | [as *adj.*] *whatever decision he made I would support it.*
▸*interrog. pron.* used for emphasis instead of "what" in questions, typically expressing surprise or confusion: *whatever is the matter?*
▸*adv.* **1** at all; of any kind (used for emphasis): *they received no help whatever.* **2** *inf.* no matter what happens: *we told him we'd back him whatever.*
▸*interj.* used to express skepticism or exasperation: *Joseph's commentary amounted to "Yeah, well. Whatever."*

what·not /'(h)wät,nät; '(h)wät-/ ▸*n.* **1** *inf.* used to refer to an item or items that are not identified but are felt to have something in common with items already named: *little flashing digital displays, electric zooms and whatnots.* **2** a stand with shelves for small objects.

what·so·ev·er /ˌ(h)wətsō'evər; ˌ(h)wät-/ ▸*adv.* at all (used for emphasis): *I have no doubt whatsoever.*

wheal /(h)wēl/ ▸*n.* see WEAL¹.

wheat /(h)wēt/ ▸*n.* a cereal plant (genus *Triticum*) that is the most important kind grown in temperate countries, the grain of which is ground to make flour for bread, pasta, pastry, etc. ■ the grain of this plant.

wheat·en /'(h)wētn/ ▸*adj.* (esp. of bread) made of wheat. ■ of a color resembling that of wheat; a pale yellow-beige.

wheat germ ▸*n.* a nutritious foodstuff of a dry floury consistency consisting of the extracted embryos of grains of wheat.

whee /(h)wē/ ▸*interj.* used to express delight, excitement, or exhilaration: *as the car began to bump down the track he felt a lightening of his spirits—whee!*

whee·dle /'(h)wēdl/ ▸*v.* [*intr.*] employ endearments or flattery to persuade someone to do something or give one something: *you can contrive to **wheedle your way** onto a court.* ■ [*tr.*] (**wheedle someone into doing something**) coax or persuade someone to do something. ■ [*tr.*] (**wheedle something out of**) coax or persuade (someone) to say or give something. —**whee·dler** *n.* —**whee·dling·ly** *adv.*

wheel /(h)wēl/ ▸*n.* **1** a circular object that revolves on an axle and is fixed below a vehicle or other object to enable it to move easily over the ground. ■ a circular object that revolves on an axle and forms part of a machine. ■ (**the wheel**) used in reference to the cycle of a specified condition or set of events: *the final release from the wheel of life.* **2** a machine or structure having a wheel as its essential part. ■ (**the wheel**) a steering wheel (used in reference to driving or steering a vehicle or vessel): *his crew knows when he wants to **take the wheel**.* ■ a vessel's propeller or paddle wheel. ■ a device with a revolving disk or drum used in various games of chance. ■ a system, or a part of a system, regarded as a relentlessly moving machine: *the wheels of justice.* **3** (**wheels**) *inf.* a car: *she's got wheels now.* ■ a bicycle. **4** a thing resembling a wheel in form or function, in particular a cheese made in the form of a disk. **5** an instance of wheeling; a turn or rotation.
▸*v.* **1** [*tr.*] push or pull (a vehicle with wheels): *the sea sled was **wheeled** out to the flight deck.* ■ [*tr.*] carry (someone or something) in or on a vehicle with wheels: *a young woman is wheeled into the operating room.* ■ (**wheel something in/on/out**) *inf.* produce something that is unimpressive because it has been frequently seen or heard before: *the old journalistic arguments have to be wheeled out.* **2** [*intr.*] (of a bird or aircraft) fly in a wide circle or curve: *the birds wheeled and dived.* ■ turn around quickly so as to face another way: *Robert **wheeled around** to see the face of Mr. Mafouz.* ■ turn or seem to turn on an axis or pivot: *the stars wheeled through the sky.* ▷Old English *hwēol* (noun), of Germanic origin, from an Indo-European root shared by Sanskrit *cakra* 'wheel, circle' and Greek *kuklos* 'circle.' —**wheeled** *adj.* [in comb.] *a four-wheeled cart.*
▸ □ **wheel and deal** engage in commercial or political scheming, esp. unscrupulously: [as *n.*] (**wheeling and dealing**) *the wheeling and dealing of the Wall Street boom years.*

wheel·bar·row /'(h)wēl,barō/ ▸*n.* a small cart with a single wheel at the front and two supporting legs and two handles at the rear, used typically for carrying loads in building-work or gardening.
▸*v.* [*tr.*] carry (a load) in a wheelbarrow.

wheel·base /'(h)wēl,bās/ ▸*n.* the distance between the front and rear axles of a vehicle: *a short-wheelbase model.*

wheel·chair /'(h)wēl,CHe(ə)r/ ▸*n.* a chair built on wheels for an invalid or disabled person, pushed by another person or propelled by the occupant, or motorized.

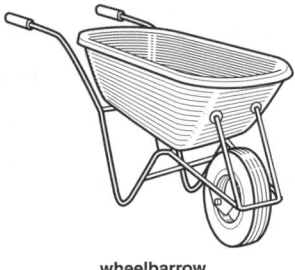
wheelbarrow

wheel·er-deal·er (also **wheel·er and deal·er**) ▸*n.* a person who engages in commercial or political scheming. —**wheel·er-deal·ing** *n.*

wheel·house /'(h)wēl,hous/ ▸*n.* a part of a boat or ship serving as a shelter for the person at the wheel.

wheel·ie /'(h)wēlē/ ▸*n.* *inf.* a trick or maneuver whereby a bicycle or motorcycle is ridden for a short distance with the front wheel raised off the ground.

wheeze /(h)wēz/ ▸*v.* [*intr.*] (of a person) breathe with a whistling or rattling sound in the chest, as a result of obstruction in the air passages: *the illness often leaves her wheezing.* ■ [*tr.*] utter with such a sound: *he could barely wheeze out his pleas for a handout.* ■ [*intr.*] walk or move slowly with such a sound: *she wheezed up the hill toward them.* ■ (of a device) make an irregular rattling or spluttering sound: *the engine coughed, wheezed, and shrieked into life.*
▸*n.* a sound of or as of a person wheezing: *I talk with a wheeze.* —**wheez·er** *n.* —**wheez·ing·ly** *adv.* —**wheez·y** *adj.*

whelk /(h)welk/ ▸*n.* a predatory marine mollusk (family Buccinidae) with a heavy, pointed spiral shell, some kinds of which are edible.

whelp /(h)welp/ ▸*n.* a puppy. ■ a cub. ■ a boy or young man (often as a disparaging form of address).
▸*v.* [*tr.*] (of a female dog) give birth to (a puppy): *Copper whelped seven puppies* | [*intr.*] *a bitch due to whelp.*

when /(h)wen/ ▸*interrog. adv.* at what time: *when did you last see him?* | *since when have you been interested?* ■ how soon: *when can I see you?* ■ in what circumstances: *when would such a rule be justifiable?*
▸*relative adv.* at or on which (referring to a time or circumstance): *Saturday is the day when I get my hair done.*
▸*conj.* **1** at or during the time that: *I loved math when I was in school.* ■ after: *call me when you're finished.* ■ at any time that; whenever: *can you spare five minutes when it's convenient?* **2** after which; and just then (implying suddenness): *he had just drifted off to sleep when the phone rang.* **3** in view of the fact that; considering that: *why bother to paint it when you can photograph it with the same effect?* **4** although; whereas: *I'm saying it now when I should have told you long ago.*

whence /(h)wens/ (also **from whence**) ▸*interrog. adv. formal* or *archaic* from what place or source: *whence does Congress derive this power?*
▸*relative adv. formal* or *archaic* from which; from where: *the Ural mountains, whence the ore is procured.* ■ to the place from which: *he will be sent back whence he came.* ■ as a consequence of which: *whence it followed that the strategies were obsolete.*

when·ev·er /(h)wen'evər/ ▸*conj.* at whatever time; on whatever occasion (emphasizing a lack of restriction): *you can ask for help whenever you need it.* ■ every time that: *the springs in the armchair creak whenever I change position.*
▸*interrog. adv.* used for emphasis instead of "when" in questions, typically expressing surprise or confusion: *whenever shall we get there?*

where /(h)we(ə)r/ ▸*interrog. adv.* in or to what place or position: *where do you live?* ■ in what direction or respect: *where does the argument lead?* ■ in or from what source: *where did you read that?* ■ in or to what situation or condition: *where is all this leading us?*
▸*relative adv.* **1** at, in, or to which (used after reference to a place or situation): *I first saw him in Paris, where I lived in the early sixties.* **2** the place or situation in which: *this is where I live.* ■ in or to a place or situation in which: *sit where I can see you.* ■ in or to any place in which; wherever: *he was free to go where he liked.*

Pronunciation Key ə *ago, up;* ər *over, fur;* a *hat;* ā *ate;* ä *car;* CH *chin;* e *let;* ē *see;* e(ə)r *air;* i *fit;* ī *by;* i(ə)r *ear;* NG *sing;* ō *go;* ô *law, for;* oi *toy;* oȯ *good;* oō *goo;* ou *out;* SH *she;* TH *thin;* T͟H *then;* (h)w *why;* ZH *vision*

▶*conj. inf.* **1** that: *I see where the hotel has changed hands again.* **2** whereas: *where some caregivers burn out, others become too involved.*

▶*n.* [(prec. by the)] the place; the scene of something (see **when** *n.*).

where·a·bouts /'(h)we(ə)rə,bouts/ ▶*interrog. adv.* where or approximately where: *whereabouts do you come from?*

▶*n.* [treated as *sing.* or *pl.*] the place where someone or something is: *his whereabouts remain secret.*

where·as /(h)we(ə)r'az/ ▶*conj.* in contrast or comparison with the fact that: *you treat the matter lightly, whereas I myself was never more serious.* ■ (esp. in legal preambles) taking into consideration the fact that.

where·by /(h)we(ə)r'bī/ ▶*relative adv.* by which: *a system whereby people could vote by telephone.*

where·fore /'(h)we(ə)r,fôr/ *archaic* ▶*interrog. adv.* for what reason: *she took an ill turn, but wherefore I cannot say.*

▶*relative adv. & conj.* as a result of which: [as *conj.*] *truly he cared for me, wherefore I title him with all respect.*

where·in /(h)we(ə)r'in/ *formal* ▶*adv.* **1** [*relative adv.*] in which: *the situation wherein the information will eventually be used.* **2** [*interrog. adv.*] in what place or respect?: *so wherein lies the difference?*

where·of /(h)we'räv; -'əv/ ▶*relative adv. formal* of what or which: *I know whereof I speak.*

where·up·on /,(h)we(ə)rə'pän/ ▶*conj.* immediately after which: *he qualified in February, whereupon he was promoted to sergeant.*

wher·ev·er /(h)we(ə)r'evər/ ▶*relative adv.* in or to whatever place (emphasizing a lack of restriction): *meet me wherever you like.* ■ in all places; regardless of where: *it should be available wherever you go to shop.*

▶*interrog. adv.* used for emphasis instead of "where" in questions, typically expressing surprise or confusion: *wherever can he have gone to?*

▶*conj.* in every case when: *use whole grain cereals wherever possible.*

where·with·al /'(h)we(ə)rwiтн,ôl; -wiтн-/ ▶*n.* (**the wherewithal**) the resources needed for a particular purpose: *they lacked the wherewithal to pay.*

whet /(h)wet/ ▶*v.* (**whet·ted, whet·ting**) [*tr.*] sharpen the blade of (a tool or weapon): *her husband is whetting his knife.* ■ excite or stimulate (someone's desire, interest, or appetite): *here's an extract to whet your appetite.*

wheth·er /'(h)weтнər/ ▶*conj.* expressing a doubt or choice between alternatives: *he seemed undecided **whether** to go **or** stay.* ■ expressing an inquiry or investigation (often used in indirect questions): *I'll see whether she's at home.* ■ indicating that a statement applies whichever of the alternatives mentioned is the case: *I'm going **whether** you like it **or not.***

whet·stone /'(h)wet,stōn/ ▶*n.* a fine-grained stone used for sharpening cutting tools.

whew /hyoo͞; hwyoo͞/ ▶*interj.* used to express surprise, relief, or a feeling of being very hot or tired: *Whew—and I thought it was serious!*

whey /(h)wā/ ▶*n.* the watery part of milk that remains after the formation of curds.

which /(h)wiCH/ ▶*interrog. pron. & adj.* asking for information specifying one or more people or things from a definite set: [as *pron.*] *which are the best grapes for long keeping?* | [as *adj.*] *which way is the wind blowing?*

▶*relative pron. & adj.* used referring to something previously mentioned when introducing a clause giving further information: [as *pron.*] *a conference in Vienna, which ended on Friday* | [after *prep.*] *it was a crisis for which he was totally unprepared.*

which·ev·er /,(h)wiCH'evər/ ▶*relative adj. & pron.* used to emphasize a lack of restriction in selecting one of a definite set of alternatives: [as *adj.*] *choose whichever brand you prefer* | [as *pron.*] *their pension should be increased annually in line with earnings or prices, whichever is the higher.* ■ regardless of which: [as *adj.*] *they were in a position to intercept him whichever way he ran* | [as *pron.*] *whichever they choose, we must accept it.*

whiff /(h)wif/ ▶*n.* **1** a smell that is only smelled briefly or faintly: *I caught a **whiff** of peachy perfume.* ■ an act of sniffing or inhaling, typically so as to determine or savor a scent: *one whiff of clothing and Fido was off.* ■ a trace or hint of something bad, menacing, or exciting: *here was a man with a whiff of danger about him.* **2** a puff or breath of air or smoke. **3** *inf.* (chiefly in baseball or golf) an unsuccessful attempt to hit the ball.

▶*v.* **1** [*tr.*] get a brief or faint smell of: *he screwed up his nose as if he'd whiffed Limburger.* **2** [*intr.*] *inf.* (chiefly in baseball or golf) try unsuccessfully to hit the ball.

Whig /(h)wig/ *hist.* ▶*n.* **1** a member of the British reforming and constitutional party that sought the supremacy of Parliament and was eventually succeeded in the 19th century by the Liberal Party. **2** an American colonist who supported the American Revolution. ■ a member of

an American political party in the 19th century, succeeded by the Republicans.

while /(h)wīl/ ▶*n.* **1** a period of time: *she retired a little while ago.* ■ (**a while**) for some time: *can I keep it a while?* **2** (**the while**) at the same time; meanwhile: *he starts to draw, talking the while.*

▶*conj.* **1** during the time that; at the same time as: *nothing much changed while he was away.* **2** whereas (indicating a contrast): *one person wants out, while the other wants the relationship to continue.* ■ in spite of the fact that; although: *while I wouldn't recommend a night-time visit, by day the area is full of interest.*

▶*relative adv.* during which: *the period while the animal remains alive.*

▶*v.* [*tr.*] (often **while away the time**) pass time in a leisurely manner: *a diversion to while away the long afternoons.*

▶ □ **worth one's while** worth the time or effort spent.

whim /(h)wim/ ▶*n.* a sudden desire or change of mind, esp. one that is unusual or unexplained: *she bought it **on a whim.***

whim·per /'(h)wimpər/ ▶*v.* [*intr.*] (of a person or animal) make a series of low, feeble sounds expressive of fear, pain, or discontent: *a child in a bed nearby began to whimper.* ■ [with *direct speech*] say something in a low, feeble voice expressive of such emotions: *"He's not dead, is he?" she whimpered.*

▶*n.* a low, feeble sound expressive of such emotions: *she gave a little whimper of protest.* ■ (**a whimper**) a feeble or anticlimactic tone or ending: *their first appearance in the top flight ended with a whimper rather than a bang.* —**whim·per·er** *n.* —**whim·per·ing·ly** *adv.*

whim·si·cal /'(h)wimzikəl/ ▶*adj.* **1** playfully quaint or fanciful, esp. in an appealing and amusing way: *a whimsical sense of humor.* **2** acting or behaving in a capricious manner: *the whimsical arbitrariness of autocracy.* —**whim·si·cal·i·ty** /,(h)wimzi'kalitē/ *n.* —**whim·si·cal·ly** /-ik(ə)lē/ *adv.*

whim·sy /'(h)wimzē/ (also **whim·sey**) ▶*n.* (*pl.* **-sies** or **-seys**) playfully quaint or fanciful behavior or humor: *the film is an awkward blend of whimsy and moralizing.* ■ a whim. ■ a thing that is fanciful or odd: *the stone carvings and whimsies.*

whine /(h)wīn/ ▶*n.* a long, high-pitched complaining cry: *the dog gave a small whine.* ■ a long, high-pitched unpleasant sound: *the whine of the engine.* ■ a complaining tone of voice. ■ a feeble or petulant complaint: *a constant whine about the quality of public services.*

▶*v.* [*intr.*] give or make a long, high-pitched complaining cry or sound: *the dog whined and scratched at the back door.* ■ complain in a feeble or petulant way: [*intr.*] *the waitress whined about the increased work.* —**whin·er** *n.* —**whin·ing·ly** *adv.* —**whin·y** *adj.*

whin·ny /'(h)winē/ ▶*n.* (*pl.* **-nies**) a gentle, high-pitched neigh.

▶*v.* (**-nies, -nied**) [*intr.*] (of a horse) make such a sound: *the pony whinnied and tossed his head happily.*

whip /(h)wip/ ▶*n.* **1** a strip of leather or length of cord fastened to a handle, used for flogging or beating a person or for urging on an animal. ■ *fig.* a thing causing mental or physical pain or acting as a stimulus to action: *councils are attempting to find new sites **under the whip** of a powerful agency.* **2** a thing or person resembling a whip in form or function: *a licorice whip.* ■ a utensil such as a whisk or an eggbeater for beating cream, eggs, or other food. ■ a slender, unbranched shoot or plant. **3** an official of a political party appointed to maintain discipline among its members in Congress or Parliament, esp. so as to ensure attendance and voting in debates. **4** a dessert consisting of cream or eggs beaten into a light fluffy mass with fruit, chocolate, or other ingredients. **5** a violent striking or beating movement. ■ in metaphorical use referring to something that acts as a stimulus to work or action: *the governor **cracked the whip** in the city.*

▶*v.* (**whipped, whip·ping**) [*tr.*] **1** beat (a person or animal) with a whip or similar instrument, esp. as a punishment or to urge them on. ■ (of a flexible object or rain or wind) strike or beat violently: *the wind whipped their faces* | [*intr.*] *ferns and brambles whipped at him.* ■ beat (cream, eggs, or other food) into a froth. ■ (**whip someone into**) urge or rouse someone into (a specified state or position): *the radio host whipped his listeners into a frenzy.* ■ *inf.* (of a player or team) defeat (a person or team) heavily in a sporting contest. **2** [*intr.*] move fast or suddenly in a specified direction: *I whipped around the corner.* ■ [*tr.*] take out or move (something) fast or suddenly: *he whipped out his revolver and shot him.* **3** bind (something) with spirally wound twine. ■ sew or gather (something) with overcast stitches.

▶*phrasal v.* □ **whip something out** (or **off**) write something hurriedly: *you'll find the software ideal for whipping out memos and proposals.* □ **whip something up** **1** cause water, sand, etc., to rise up and be flung up in a violent manner: *the sea was whipped up by a force-nine gale.* ■ stimulate a particular feeling in someone: *we tried hard to whip up interest in*

the products. **2** make or prepare something, typically something to eat, very quickly. —**whip·like** /-,līk/ *adj.* —**whip·per** *n.*

whip·lash /'(h)wip,lasH/ ▶*n.* **1** the lashing action of a whip: *fig. he cringed before the icy whiplash of Curtis's tongue.* ■ the flexible part of a whip or something resembling it. **2** injury caused by a severe jerk to the head, typically in a motor-vehicle accident.
▶*v.* [*tr.*] jerk or jolt (someone or something) suddenly, typically so as to cause injury: *the force of impact had whiplashed the man's head.* ■ [*intr.*] move suddenly and forcefully, like a whip being cracked: *he rammed the yacht, sending its necklace of lights whiplashing from the bridge.*

whip·per·snap·per /'(h)wipər,snapər/ ▶*n. inf.* a young and inexperienced person considered to be presumptuous or overconfident.

whip·pet /'(h)wipit/ ▶*n.* a dog of a small slender breed originally produced as a cross between the greyhound and the terrier or spaniel, bred for racing. ▷early 17th cent.: partly from obsolete *whippet* 'move briskly.'

whip·ping /'(h)wipiNG/ ▶*n.* **1** a thrashing or beating with a whip or similar implement: *she saw scars on his back from the whippings.* **2** cord or twine used to bind or cover a rope.

whip·ping boy ▶*n.* a person who is blamed or punished for the faults or incompetence of others.

whip·poor·will /'(h)wipər,wil/ (also **whip-poor-will**) ▶*n.* a North and Central American nightjar (*Caprimulgus vociferus*) with a distinctive call.

whir /(h)wər/ (also **whirr**) ▶*v.* (**whirred, whir·ring**) [*intr.*] (esp. of a machine or a bird's wings) make a low, continuous, regular sound: *the ceiling fans whirred in the smoky air.*
▶*n.* a sound of such a type: *the whir of the projector.*

whirl /(h)wərl/ ▶*v.* move or cause to move rapidly around and around: [*intr.*] *leaves whirled in eddies of wind* | [*tr.*] *I whirled her around the dance floor.* ■ move or cause to move rapidly: [*intr.*] *Sybil stood waving as they whirled past* | [*tr.*] *he was whirled into the bushes.* ■ [*intr.*] (of the head, mind, or senses) seem to spin around: *Kate made her way back to the office, her mind whirling.* ■ [*intr.*] (of thoughts or mental images) follow each other in bewildering succession: *a kaleidoscope of images whirled through her brain.*
▶*n.* a rapid movement around and around. ■ frantic activity of a specified kind: *the event was all part of the mad social whirl.* ■ a specified kind of candy or cookie with a spiral shape: *a hazelnut whirl.* —**whirl·er** *n.* —**whirl·ing·ly** *adv.*
▶ □ **give something a whirl** *inf.* give something a try. □ **in a whirl** in a state of confusion.

whirl·i·gig /'(h)wərli,gig/ ▶*n.* **1** a toy that spins around, for example a top or windmill. ■ another term for MERRY-GO-ROUND. **2** a thing regarded as hectic or constantly changing: *the whirligig of time.* **3** (also **whirligig beetle**) a small black predatory beetle (*Gyrinus* and other genera, family Gyrinidae) that swims rapidly in circles on the surface of still or slow-moving water and dives when alarmed.

whirl·ing der·vish ▶*n.* see DERVISH.

whirl·pool /'(h)wərl,pōōl/ ▶*n.* a rapidly rotating mass of water in a river or sea into which objects may be drawn, typically caused by the meeting of conflicting currents. ■ *fig.* a turbulent situation from which it is hard to escape: *he was drawing her down into an emotional whirlpool.* ■ (also **whirlpool bath**) a heated pool in which hot, typically aerated water is continuously circulated.

whirl·wind /'(h)wərl,wind/ ▶*n.* a column of air moving rapidly around and around in a cylindrical or funnel shape. ■ used in similes and metaphors to describe a very energetic or tumultuous person or process: *a whirlwind of activity* [as *adj.*] *a whirlwind romance.*

whirr ▶*n.* & *v.* variant spelling of WHIR.

whisk /(h)wisk/ ▶*v.* **1** [*tr.*] take or move (someone or something) in a particular direction suddenly and quickly: *his jacket was whisked away for dry cleaning.* ■ move (something) through the air with a light, sweeping movement: *hippopotamuses spread their scents by whisking their tails.* **2** [*tr.*] beat or stir (a substance, esp. cream or eggs) with a light, rapid movement. **3** brush with a whisk broom.
▶*n.* **1** a utensil for whipping eggs or cream. **2** a bunch of grass, twigs, or bristles for removing dust or flies.

whisk broom ▶*n.* a small, stiff, short-handled broom used esp. to brush clothing.

whisk·er /'(h)wiskər/ ▶*n.* **1** a long projecting hair or bristle growing from the face or snout of many mammals. ■ (**whiskers**) the hair growing on a man's face, esp. on his cheeks. ■ a single crystal of a material in the form of a filament with no dislocations. **2** (a **whisker**) *inf.* a very small amount: *they won the election by a whisker.* —**whiskered** *adj.* —**whiskery** *adj.*

whis·key /'(h)wiskē/ ▶*n.* (*pl.* **-keys**) **1** (also **whis·ky** (*pl.* **-kies**)) a spirit

distilled from malted grain, esp. barley or rye. **2** a code word representing the letter W, used in radio communication.

whis·per /'(h)wispər/ ▶*v.* [*intr.*] speak very softly using one's breath without one's vocal cords, esp. for the sake of privacy: *Alison was whispering in his ear* | [*tr.*] *he managed to whisper a faint goodbye.* ■ *poetic/lit.* (of leaves, wind, or water) rustle or murmur softly. ■ (**be whispered**) be rumored: *it was whispered that he would soon die.*
▶*n.* a soft or confidential tone of voice; a whispered word or phrase: *she spoke in a whisper.* ■ *poetic/lit.* a soft rustling or murmuring sound: *the thunder of the surf became a muted whisper.* ■ a rumor or piece of gossip: *whispers of a blossoming romance.* ■ a slight trace; a hint: *he didn't show even a whisper of interest.* —**whis·per·er** *n.* —**whis·per·y** *adj.*

whist /(h)wist/ ▶*n.* a card game, usually for two pairs of players, in which points are scored according to the number of tricks won.

whis·tle /'(h)wisəl/ ▶*n.* a clear, high-pitched sound made by forcing breath through a small hole between partly closed lips, or between one's teeth. ■ a similar sound, esp. one made by a bird, machine, or the wind. ■ an instrument used to produce such a sound.
▶*v.* [*intr.*] emit a clear, high-pitched sound by forcing breath through a small hole between one's lips or teeth: *the audience cheered and whistled* | [as *adj.*] (**whistling**) *a whistling noise.* ■ express surprise, admiration, or derision by making such a sound: *Bob whistled. "You look beautiful!" he said.* ■ [*tr.*] produce (a tune) in such a way. ■ (esp. of a bird or machine) produce a similar sound: *the kettle began to whistle.* ■ [*intr.*] produce such a sound by moving rapidly through the air or a narrow opening: *the wind was whistling down the chimney.* ■ blow an instrument that makes such a sound, esp. as a signal: *the referee did not whistle for a foul.*
▶ □ **blow the whistle on** *inf.* bring an illicit activity to an end by informing on the person responsible. □ (**as**) **clean as a whistle** extremely clean or clear. ■ *inf.* free of incriminating evidence: *the cops raided the warehouse but the place was clean as a whistle.*

whis·tle-blow·er (also **whis·tle·blow·er**) ▶*n.* a person who informs on someone engaged in an illicit activity. —**whis·tle-blow·ing** *n.*

whit /(h)wit/ ▶*n.* a very small part or amount: *the last whit of warmth was drawn off by the setting sun.*

white /(h)wīt/ ▶*adj.* **1** of the color of milk or fresh snow, due to the reflection of most wavelengths of visible light; the opposite of black: *a sheet of white paper.* ■ approaching such a color; very pale: *her face was white with fear.* ■ *fig.* morally or spiritually pure; innocent and untainted: *he is as pure and white as the driven snow.* ■ (of a plant) having white flowers or pale-colored fruit. ■ (of a tree) having light-colored bark. ■ (of wine) made from white grapes, or dark grapes with the skins removed, and having a yellowish color. ■ (of glass) transparent; colorless. ■ (of bread) made from a light-colored, sifted, or bleached flour. **2** (also **White**) belonging to or denoting a human group having light-colored skin (chiefly used of peoples of European extraction): *a white farming community.* ■ of or relating to such people: *white Australian culture.* **3** *hist.* counter-revolutionary or reactionary.
▶*n.* **1** white color or pigment: *garnet-red flowers flecked with white* | *the woodwork was an immaculate white.* ■ white clothes or material: *he was dressed from head to foot in white.* ■ (**whites**) white clothes, esp. as worn for playing tennis, or as naval uniform, or in the context of washing:

whisks

wash whites separately. ■ **white wine.** ■ (**White**) the player of the white pieces in chess or checkers. ■ the white pieces in chess. ■ a white thing, in particular the white ball (the cue ball) in billiards. ■ the outer part (white when cooked) that surrounds the yolk of an egg; the albumen. ■ white bread: *tuna on white.* **2** the visible pale part of the eyeball around the iris. **3** (also White) a member of a light-skinned people, esp. one of European extraction. **4** a white or cream butterfly (family Pieridae) that has dark veins or spots on the wings. It can be a serious crop pest. —**white·ly** *adv.* —**white·ness** *n.* —**whit·ish** *adj.*

white ant ▸*n.* another term for TERMITE.

white·cap /'(h)wīt,kap/ ▸*n.* a small wave with a foamy crest.

white cell ▸*n.* less technical term for LEUKOCYTE.

white choc·o·late ▸*n.* a white candy in which cocoa butter supplies most or all of the fat.

white-col·lar ▸*adj.* of or relating to the work done or those who work in an office or other professional environment. ■ denoting nonviolent crime committed by white-collar workers, esp. fraud.

white el·e·phant ▸*n.* a possession that is useless or troublesome, esp. one that is expensive to maintain or difficult to dispose of.

white·fish /'(h)wīt,fiSH/ ▸*n.* (*pl.* same or **-fishes**) a mainly freshwater fish (*Coregonus* and other genera) of the salmon family, widely used as food.

white flag ▸*n.* a white flag or cloth used as a symbol of surrender, truce, or a desire to parley.

white·fly /'(h)wīt,flī/ ▸*n.* (*pl.* same or **-flies**) a minute winged bug (family Aleyrodidae) covered with powdery white wax, damaging plants by feeding on the sap and coating them with honeydew.

white goods ▸*pl. n.* large electrical goods used domestically such as refrigerators and washing machines, typically white in color.

white·head /'(h)wīt,hed/ ▸*n. inf.* a pale or white-topped pustule on the skin.

white heat ▸*n.* the temperature or state of something that is so hot that it emits white light. ■ *fig.* a state of intense passion or activity.

white-hot ▸*adj.* at white heat: *a shower of white-hot embers.*

White House ▸ **1** the official residence of the U.S. president in Washington, D.C. ■ the U.S. president, presidency, or government: *the White House denounced the charge.* **2** the Russian parliament building.

white lie ▸*n.* a harmless or trivial lie, esp. one told to avoid hurting someone's feelings.

white light ▸*n.* apparently colorless light, for example ordinary daylight. It contains all the wavelengths of the visible spectrum at equal intensity.

white meat ▸*n.* pale meat such as poultry, veal, and rabbit.

whit·en /'(h)wītn/ ▸*v.* make or become white. —**whit·en·er** *n.*

white noise ▸*n. Physics* noise containing many frequencies with equal intensities.

white·out /'(h)wīt,out/ ▸*n.* **1** a blizzard, esp. in polar regions, that reduces visibilities to near zero. ■ a weather condition in which the features and horizon of snow-covered country are indistinguishable due to uniform light diffusion. **2** white correction fluid for covering typing or writing mistakes. **3** a loss of color vision due to rapid acceleration, often before a loss of consciousness.

white sage ▸*n.* see SAGE[1] (sense 2).

white sale ▸*n.* a store's sale of household linens.

white sauce ▸*n.* a sauce of flour, melted butter, and milk or cream.

white slave ▸*n.* a woman tricked or forced into prostitution, typically one taken to a foreign country for this purpose. —**white slav·er** *n.* —**white slav·er·y** *n.*

white tie ▸*n.* a white bow tie worn by men as part of full evening dress. ■ full evening dress with a white bow tie: *white tie and tails.*

▸*adj.* (of an event) requiring full evening dress to be worn, including a white bow tie.

white·wall /'(h)wīt,wôl/ ▸*n.* **1** (also **whitewall tire**) a tire with a white stripe around the outside, or a white sidewall. **2** [as *adj.*] denoting a haircut in which the sides of the head are shaved and the top and back are left longer.

white·wash /'(h)wīt,wäSH; -,wôSH/ ▸*n.* **1** a solution of lime and water or of whiting, size, and water, used for painting walls white. ■ (also **white·wash·ing**) a deliberate concealment of someone's mistakes or faults in order to clear their name. **2** a victory in a game in which the loser scores no points.

▸*v.* [*tr.*] **1** [usu. as *adj.*] (**whitewashed**) paint (a wall, building, or room) with whitewash. ■ try to clear (someone or their name) by deliberately concealing their mistakes or faults: *his wife must have wanted to whitewash his reputation.* ■ deliberately conceal (someone's mistakes or

faults): *meant to whitewash the political practice of the government.* **2** defeat (an opponent), keeping them from scoring. —**white·wash·er** *n.*

white-wa·ter /'(h)wīt'wôtər; 'wä-/ (also **white wa·ter**) ▸*n.* [often as *adj.*] (also **white·wa·ter**) fast shallow stretches of water in a river: *whitewater rafting.*

whit·ey /'(h)wītē/ ▸*n.* (*pl.* **-eys**) *inf., offens.* a contemptuous term used by black people to refer to a white person. ■ white people collectively: *her ambitions in publishing have been thwarted by whitey.*

whith·er /'(h)wiTHər/ ▸*interrog. adv.* archaic or poetic/lit. to what place or state: *whither are we bound?* ■ what is the likely future of: *whither modern architecture?*

▸*relative adv.* archaic or poetic/lit. to which (with reference to a place): *the barbecue had been set up by the lake, whither Matthew and Sara were conducted.* ■ to whatever place; wherever: *we could drive whither we pleased.*

whit·ing[1] /'(h)wītiNG/ ▸*n.* (*pl.* same) **1** a slender-bodied marine fish (*Merlangius merlangus*) of the cod family. It lives in shallow European waters and is a commercially important food fish. **2** any of a number of similar marine fishes, in particular the northern kingfish of eastern North America.

whit·ing[2] ▸*n.* ground chalk used for purposes such as whitewashing and cleaning metal plate.

Whit·sun·day /'(h)wit'sən,dā/ ▸*n.* another term for PENTECOST (sense 1).

whit·tle /'(h)witl/ ▸*v.* [*tr.*] carve (wood) into an object by repeatedly cutting small slices from it. ■ carve (an object) from wood in this way. ■ (**whittle something away/down**) reduce something in size, amount, or extent by a gradual series of steps: *the short list of fifteen was whittled down to five* | [*intr.*] *the censors had whittled away at the racy dialogue.* —**whit·tler** *n.*

whiz /(h)wiz/ (also **whizz**) ▸*v.* (**whizzed**, **whiz·zing**) **1** [*intr.*] move quickly through the air with a whistling or whooshing sound: *fig. the weeks whizzed by.* ■ (**whiz through**) do or deal with quickly: *Audrey would whiz through a few chores in the shop.* **2** [*intr.*] *inf.* urinate.

▸*n.* **1** a whistling or whooshing sound made by something moving fast through the air. **2** (also **wiz**) *inf.* a person who is extremely clever at something: *a computer whiz.* **3** *inf.* an act of urinating.

whiz kid ▸*n. inf.* a young person who is outstandingly skillful or successful at something: *a computer whiz kid.*

WHO ▸*abbr.* World Health Organization.

who /hoō/ ▸*pron.* **1** [*interrog. pron.*] what or which person or people: *who is that woman?* **2** [*relative pron.*] used to introduce a clause giving further information about a person or people previously mentioned: *Joan Fontaine plays the mouse who married the playboy.*

whoa /wō/ ▸*interj.* used as a command to a horse to make it stop or slow down. ■ *inf.* used as a greeting, to express surprise or interest, or to command attention: *whoa, that's huge!*

who'd /hoōd/ ▸*contr. of* ■ who had: *some Americans who'd arrived after lunch.* ■ who would: *he knew many of the people who'd be there.*

who-dun·it /hoō'dənit/ (*Brit.* **who-dun·nit**) ▸*n. inf.* a story or play about a murder in which the identity of the murderer is not revealed until the end.

who-ev·er /hoō'evər/ ▸*relative pron.* the person or people who; any person who: *whoever did it hated him.* ■ regardless of who: *come out, whoever you are.*

▸*interrog. pron.* used for emphasis instead of "who" in questions, typically expressing surprise or confusion: *whoever would want to make up something like that?*

whole /hōl/ ▸*adj.* **1** all of; entire: *he spent the whole day walking* | *she wasn't telling the whole truth.* ■ used to emphasize a large extent or number: *whole shelves in libraries are devoted to the subject.* **2** in an unbroken or undamaged state; in one piece: *owls usually swallow their prey whole.* ■ (of milk, blood, or other substances) with no part removed. ■ healthy: *all people should be whole in body, mind, and spirit.*

▸*n.* **1** a thing that is complete in itself: *the subjects of the curriculum form a coherent whole.* **2** (**the whole**) all of something: *the effects will last for the whole of his life.*

▸*adv. inf.* used to emphasize the novelty or distinctness of something: *the man who's given a whole new meaning to the term "cowboy."* —**whole·ness** *n.*

▸ □ **as a whole** as a single unit and not as separate parts; in general: *a healthy economy is in the best interests of society as a whole.* □ **on the whole** taking everything into account; in general.

whole bod·y scan ▸*n.* a CT scan of the torso, especially one obtained for health screening purposes. —**whole bod·y scan·ning** *n.*

whole·heart·ed /'hōl'härtid/ ▸*adj.* showing or characterized by complete sincerity and commitment: *you have my wholehearted support.* —**whole·heart·ed·ly** adv. —**whole·heart·ed·ness** n.

whole-life ▸adj. relating to or denoting a life insurance policy that pays a specified amount only on the death of the person insured.

whole life in·sur·ance ▸n. life insurance that pays a benefit on the death of the insured and also accumulates a cash value. Compare with TERM LIFE INSURANCE.

whole note ▸n. *Mus.* a note having the time value of two half notes or four quarter notes, represented by a ring with no stem. It is the longest note now in common use.

whole num·ber ▸n. a number without fractions; an integer.

whole·sale /'hōl,sāl/ ▸n. the selling of goods in large quantities to be retailed by others.
▸adv. being sold in such a way: *bottles from this region sell wholesale at about $72 a case.* ■ on a large scale: *the safety clauses seem to have been taken wholesale from union documents.*
▸adj. done on a large scale; extensive: *the wholesale destruction of Iraqi communications.*
▸v. [tr.] sell (goods) in large quantities at low prices to be retailed by others. —**whole·sal·er** n.

whole·some /'hōlsəm/ ▸adj. conducive to or suggestive of good health and physical well-being: *the food is plentiful and very wholesome.* ■ conducive to or promoting moral well-being: *good wholesome fun.* —**whole·some·ly** adv. —**whole·some·ness** n.

whole step ▸n. *Mus.* an interval of a (whole) tone.

whole tone ▸n. see TONE (sense 4).

whole-tone scale ▸n. *Mus.* a scale consisting entirely of intervals of a tone, with no semitones.

whole-wheat ▸adj. denoting flour or bread made from whole grains of wheat, including the husk or outer layer.
▸n. whole-wheat bread or flour.

who·lism /'hōlizəm/ ▸n. variant spelling of HOLISM. —**who·lis·tic** adj. —**who·lis·ti·cal·ly** adv.

whol·ly /'hōl(l)ē/ ▸adv. entirely; fully: *she found herself given over wholly to sensation* | *the distinction is not wholly clear.*

whom /hōōm/ ▸pron. used instead of "who" as the object of a verb or preposition: [interrog. pron.] *whom did he marry?* | [relative pron.] *her mother, in whom she confided, said it wasn't easy for her.*

whom·ev·er /hōōm'evər/ ▸pron. chiefly formal or poetic/lit. used instead of "whoever" as the object of a verb or preposition: *I'll sing whatever I like to whomever I like.*

whom·so·ev·er /,hōōmsō'evər/ ▸relative pron. formal used instead of "whosoever" as the object of a verb or preposition: *they supported his right to marry whomsoever he chose.*

whoop /(h)wōōp; hōōp/ ▸n. a loud cry of joy or excitement. ■ a hooting cry or sound: *the whoop of fast-approaching sirens.* ■ a long rasping indrawn breath, typically of someone with whooping cough.
▸v. [intr.] give or make a whoop: *they were **whooping with** laughter.*
▸ □ **whoop it up** inf. enjoy oneself or celebrate in a noisy way.

whoop·ee /'(h)wōōpē; '(h)wōō'pē/ inf. ▸interj. expressing wild excitement or joy.
▸n. wild revelry: *hours of parades and whoopee.* ■ dated a wild party.
▸ □ **make whoopee 1** celebrate wildly. **2** have sexual intercourse.

whoop·ee cush·ion /'wōōpē/ (also **whoop·ie cush·ion**) ▸n. a rubber cushion that makes a sound like a fart when someone sits on it.

whoop·er /'(h)wōōpər; 'hōōpər/ ▸n. **1** (also **whooper swan**) a large migratory swan (*Cygnus cygnus*) with a black and yellow bill and a loud trumpeting call, breeding in northern Eurasia and Greenland. **2** short for WHOOPING CRANE.

whoop·ing cough ▸n. a contagious bacterial disease chiefly affecting children, characterized by convulsive coughs followed by a whoop. Also called PERTUSSIS.

whoop·ing crane ▸n. a large mainly white crane (*Grus americana*) with a trumpeting call, breeding in central Canada and now endangered.

whoops /wōōps; wōōps/ ▸interj. inf. another term for OOPS.

whoosh /(h)wōōsh; (h)wōōsh/ (also **woosh**) ▸v. [intr.] move quickly or suddenly with a rushing sound: *a train whooshed by* | [as adj.] (**whooshing**) *there was a loud whooshing noise.* ■ [tr.] move (something) in such a way: *he whooshed the curtains open.*
▸n. a sudden movement accompanied by a rushing sound: *there was a big whoosh of air.*
▸interj. used to imitate such a movement and sound.

whop·per /'(h)wäpər/ ▸n. inf. a thing that is extremely or unusually large: *the novel is a 1,079 page whopper.* ■ a gross or blatant lie.

whop·ping /'(h)wäpiNG/ ▸adj. inf. very large: *a whopping $74 million loss.*

whore /hôr/ ▸n. derog. a prostitute. ■ a promiscuous woman.
▸v. [intr.] (of a woman) work as a prostitute: *she spent her life whoring for dangerous men.* ■ [often as n.] (**whoring**) (of a man) use the services of prostitutes: *he lived by night, indulging in his two hobbies, whoring and eating.* ■ debase oneself by doing something for unworthy motives, typically to make money: *he had never whored after money.*

whore·house /'hôr,hous/ ▸n. inf. a brothel.

whorl /(h)wôrl/ ▸n. a coil or ring, in particular: ■ *Zool.* each of the turns or convolutions in the shell of a gastropod or ammonoid mollusk. ■ *Bot.* a set of leaves, flowers, or branches springing from the stem at the same level and encircling it. ■ *Bot.* (in a flower) each of the sets of organs, esp. the petals and sepals, arranged concentrically around the receptacle. ■ a complete circle in a fingerprint.

whose /hōōz/ ▸interrogative possessive adj. & pron. belonging to or associated with which person: [as adj.] *whose round is it?* | [as pron.] *a minivan was parked at the curb and Juliet wondered whose it was.*
▸relative possessive adj. of whom or which (used to indicate that the following noun belongs to or is associated with the person or thing mentioned in the previous clause): *he's a man whose opinion I respect.*

whos·ev·er /,hōōz'evər/ ▸relative pron. & adj. rare belonging to or associated with whichever person; whoever's: [as pron.] *the choice, whosever it was, is interesting* | [as adj.] *she dialed whosever number she could remember.*

who·so·ev·er /,hōōsō'evər/ ▸pron. formal term for WHOEVER: *a belief that whosoever steals will be blinded.*

why /(h)wī/ ▸interrog. adv. for what reason or purpose: *why did he do it?* ■ used to make or agree to a suggestion: *why don't I give you a lift?*
▸relative adv. (with reference to a reason) on account of which; for which: **the reason why** *flu shots need repeating every year is that the virus changes.* ■ the reason for which: *each has faced similar hardships, and perhaps that is why they are friends.*
▸interj. **1** expressing surprise or indignation: *Why, that's absurd!* **2** used to add emphasis to a response: *"You think so?" "Why, yes."*
▸n. (pl. **whys**) a reason or explanation: *the **whys and wherefores** of these procedures need to be explained to students.*

Wic·ca /'wikə/ ▸n. the religious cult of modern witchcraft, esp. an initiatory tradition founded in England in the mid 20th century and claiming its origins in pre-Christian pagan religions. ▷representing Old English *wicca* 'witch.' —**Wic·can** adj. & n.

wick /wik/ ▸n. a strip of porous material up which liquid fuel is drawn by capillary action to the flame in a candle, lamp, or lighter. ■ *Med.* a gauze strip inserted in a wound to drain it.
▸v. [tr.] absorb or draw off (liquid) by capillary action: *these excellent socks will **wick away** the sweat* | [intr.] *synthetics with hollow fibers that wick well.*

wick·ed /'wikid/ ▸adj. (**-ed·er, -ed·est**) evil or morally wrong: *a wicked and unscrupulous politician.* ■ intended to or capable of harming someone or something: *he should be punished for his wicked driving.* ■ inf. extremely unpleasant: *despite the sun, the wind outside was wicked.* ■ playfully mischievous: *Ben has a wicked sense of humor.* ■ inf. excellent; wonderful: *Sophie makes wicked cakes.* ■ inf. very; extremely: *he runs wicked fast.* —**wick·ed·ly** adv. —**wick·ed·ness** n.

wick·er /'wikər/ ▸n. pliable twigs, typically of willow, plaited or woven to make items such as furniture and baskets: *a wicker chair.*

wick·er·work /'wikər,wərk/ ▸n. wicker. ■ furniture or other items made of wicker.

wick·et /'wikit/ ▸n. **1** a small door or gate, esp. one beside or in a larger one. ■ an opening in a door or wall, often fitted with glass or a grille and used for selling tickets or a similar purpose. ■ one of the wire hoops on a croquet course. **2** *Cricket* each of the sets of three stumps with two bails across the top at either end of the pitch.
▸ □ **a sticky wicket** inf. a tricky or awkward situation: *the problem of who sits where can create a sticky wicket.*

wide /wīd/ ▸adj. (**wid·er, wid·est**) **1** of great or more than average width: *a wide road.* ■ (after a measurement and in questions) from side to side: *it measures 15 feet long by 12 feet wide.* ■ open to the full extent: *wide eyes.* ■ considerable: *tax revenues have undershot Treasury projections by a wide margin.* **2** including a great variety of people or things: *a wide range of opinion.* ■ spread among a large number of people or over a large area: *the business is slowly gaining wider acceptance.* ■ [in comb.] extending over the whole of: *an industry-wide trend.* **3** at a considerable or specified distance from a point or mark: *Bodie's shot was inches wide.* ■ *Baseball* (of a pitch) outside: *the ball was **wide of** the plate.* ■ *Baseball* (of a throw) to

Pronunciation Key ə *ago*, *up*; ər *over*, *fur*; a *hat*; ā *ate*; ä *car*; CH *chin*; e *let*; ē *see*; e(ə)r *air*; i *fit*; ī *by*; i(ə)r *ear*; NG *sing*; ō *go*; ô *law, for*; oi *toy*; ōō *good*; ōō *goo*; ou *out*; SH *she*; TH *thin*; TH̲ *then*; (h)w *why*; ZH *vision*

either side of a base: *forced a wide throw to first.* ■ (in field sports) at or near the side of the field: *he played in a wide left position.*

▸*adv.* **1** to the full extent: *his eyes opened wide.* **2** far from a particular point or mark: *a shot that went wide to the right.* ■ at or near the side of the field; toward the sideline: *he will play wide on the right.* —**wide-ness** *n.*

▸ □ **wide of the mark** a long way away from an intended target. ■ inaccurate: *the accusation was a little wide of the mark.* □ **wide open 1** stretching over an outdoor expanse: *the wide open spaces of Montana.* **2** offering a great variety of opportunities: *suddenly the whole world was wide open to her.* **3** (of a contest) of which the outcome is not predictable. **4** vulnerable, esp. to attack.

wide-an-gle ▸*adj.* (of a lens) having a short focal length and hence a field covering a wide angle.

wide-a-wake ▸*n.* a soft felt hat with a low crown and wide brim.

wide-eyed ▸*adj.* having one's eyes wide open in amazement. ■ *fig.* innocent: *people think of Pinocchio as the wide-eyed, sweet-voiced puppet.*

▸*adv.* with one's eyes wide open in amazement: *we looked at each other wide-eyed.*

wide-ly /ˈwīdlē/ ▸*adv.* **1** over a wide area or at a wide interval: *he smiled widely and held out a hand.* ■ to a large degree in nature or character (used to describe considerable variation or difference): *lending policies vary widely between different banks.* **2** over a large area or range; extensively: *Deborah has traveled widely.* ■ by many people or in many places: *credit cards are widely accepted.*

wid-en /ˈwīdn/ ▸*v.* make or become wider: [*tr.*] *the incentive to dredge and widen the river* | [*intr.*] *his grin widened* | *the lane widened out into a small clearing.* —**wid-en-er** *n.*

wide-spread /ˈwīdˌspred/ ▸*adj.* found or distributed over a large area or number of people: *there was widespread support for the war.*

widg-et /ˈwijit/ ▸*n.* *inf.* a small gadget or mechanical device, esp. one whose name is unknown or unspecified. ■ *Comput.* a component of a user interface that operates in a particular way.

wid-ow /ˈwidō/ ▸*n.* **1** a woman who has lost her husband by death and has not remarried. ■ *humorous* a woman whose husband is often away participating in a specified sport or activity: *a golf widow.* **2** *Printing* a last word or short last line of a paragraph falling at the top of a page or column and considered undesirable.

▸*v.* [*tr.*] [usu. as *adj.*] (**widowed**) make into a widow or widower: *she had to care for her widowed mother.* ▷Old English *widewe,* from an Indo-European root meaning 'be empty'; compare with Sanskrit *vidh* 'be destitute,' Latin *viduus* 'bereft, widowed,' and Greek *ēitheos* 'unmarried man.' —**wid-ow-hood** *n.*

wid-ow-er /ˈwidō-ər/ ▸*n.* a man who has lost his wife by death and has not remarried.

wid-ow's peak ▸*n.* a V-shaped growth of hair toward the center of the forehead, esp. one left by a receding hairline in a man.

width /widTH; witTH/ ▸*n.* the measurement or extent of something from side to side: *the yard was about seven feet in width.* ■ a piece of something at its full extent from side to side: *a single width of plywood.* ■ the sideways extent of a swimming pool as a measure of the distance swum. ■ the quality of covering or accepting a broad range of things; scope: *the width of experience required for these positions.* —**width-wise** *adj.*

wield /wēld/ ▸*v.* [*tr.*] hold and use (a weapon or tool): *a masked raider wielding a handgun.* ■ have and be able to use (power or influence): *faction leaders wielded enormous influence within the party.* —**wield-er** *n.*

wie-ner /ˈwēnər/ (also *inf.* **wee-nie, wie-nie** /-nē/) ▸*n.* a frankfurter or similar sausage.

wife /wīf/ ▸*n.* (*pl.* **wives** /wīvz/) a married woman considered in relation to her husband. ■ the wife of a man with a specified occupation: *a faculty wife.* ■ *archaic* or *dial.* a woman, esp. an old or uneducated one. —**wife-li-ness** /ˈwīflēnis/ *n.* —**wife-ly** *adj.*

wig[1] /wig/ ▸*n.* a covering for the head made of real or artificial hair, typically worn by people to conceal their baldness or in England by judges and barristers in courts of law. —**wigged** *adj.*

wig[2] ▸*v.* (**wigged, wig-ging**) [*tr.*] *Brit., inf., dated* rebuke (someone) severely.

▸*phrasal v.* □ **wig out** *inf.* become deliriously excited; go completely wild.

wig-gle /ˈwigəl/ ▸*v.* move or cause to move up and down or from side to side with small rapid movements: [*tr.*] *Stacy wiggled her toes* | [*intr.*] *my tooth was wiggling around.* ■ (**wiggle out of**) avoid (something), esp. by devious means: *they're trying to wiggle out of their agreement.*

▸*n.* a wiggling movement: *a slight wiggle of the hips.* ■ a deviation in a line: *a wiggle on a chart.* —**wig-gler** *n.* —**wig-gly** /ˈwig(ə)lē/ *adj.* (**-gli-er, -gli-est**).

wig-wam /ˈwigˌwäm/ ▸*n.* a dome-shaped hut or tent made by fastening mats, skins, or bark over a framework of poles, used by some North American Indian peoples. ▷early 17th cent.: from Abnaki, 'their house,' from an Algonquian base meaning 'dwell.'

wi-ki /ˈwikē/ ▸*n.* a Web site that allows collaborative editing of its content and structure by its users.

wild /wīld/ ▸*adj.* **1** (of an animal or plant) living or growing in the natural environment; not domesticated or cultivated. ■ (of people) not civilized; barbarous: *the wild tribes from the north.* ■ (of scenery or a region) desolate-looking: *the wild coastline of Cape Wrath.* **2** uncontrolled or unrestrained, esp. in pursuit of pleasure: *she went through a wild phase of drunken parties and desperate affairs.* ■ haphazard, esp. rashly so: *a wild guess.* ■ extravagant or unreasonable; fanciful: *who, even in his wildest dreams, could have anticipated such a victory?* ■ stormy: *the wild sea.* ■ *inf.* very enthusiastic or excited: *I'm not wild about the music.* ■ *inf.* very angry. ■ (of looks, appearance, etc.) indicating distraction: *her wild eyes were darting back and forth.* **3** (of a playing card) deemed to have any value, suit, color, or other property in a game at the discretion of the player holding it. See also **WILD CARD**.

▸*adv.* in an uncontrolled manner: *the bad guys shoot wild.* ■ in a very excited or angry state: *the crowd went wild with enthusiasm.*

▸*n.* (**the wild**) a natural state or uncultivated or uninhabited region: *kiwis are virtually extinct in the wild.* ■ (**the wilds**) a remote uninhabited or sparsely inhabited area: *he spent a year in the wilds of Canada.* —**wild-ly** *adv.* —**wild-ness** *n.*

▸ □ **run wild** (of an animal, plant, or person) grow or develop without restraint or discipline: *fig. her imagination had run wild.* □ **wild and wool-ly** uncouth in appearance or behavior.

wild card ▸*n.* a playing card that can have any value, suit, color, or other property in a game at the discretion of the player holding it. ■ a person or thing whose influence is unpredictable or whose qualities are uncertain. ■ *Comput.* a character that will match any character or sequence of characters in a search. ■ an opportunity to enter a sports competition without having to take part in qualifying matches or be ranked at a particular level. ■ a player or team given such an opportunity.

wild-cat /ˈwīldˌkat/ ▸*n.* **1** a small native Eurasian and African cat (*Felis silvestris*) that is typically gray with black markings and a bushy tail. Its African race is believed to be the ancestor of the domestic cat. ■ any of the smaller members of the cat family, esp. the bobcat. ■ a hot-tempered or ferocious person, typically a woman. **2** an exploratory oil well.

▸*adj.* (of a strike) sudden and unofficial: *legislation to curb wildcat strikes.* ■ commercially unsound or risky.

▸*v.* [*intr.*] prospect for oil.

wil-de-beest /ˈwildəˌbēst/ ▸*n.* (*pl.* same or **-beests**) another term for **GNU**.

wil-der-ness /ˈwildərnis/ ▸*n.* an uncultivated, uninhabited, and inhospitable region. ■ a neglected or abandoned area of a garden or town. ■ a wild area purposely maintained in its natural state, usually under government protection. ■ *fig.* a position of disfavor, esp. in a political context: *the man who led the Green Party out of the wilderness* | [as *adj.*] *his wilderness years.*

▸ □ **a voice in the wilderness** an unheeded advocate of reform.

wild-fire /ˈwīldˌfīr/ ▸*n.* a large, destructive forest- or brush-fire that spreads quickly.

▸ □ **spread like wildfire** spread with great speed: *the news had spread like wildfire.*

wild-flow-er /ˈwīldˌflou(-ə)r/ (also **wild flow-er**) ▸*n.* a flower of an uncultivated variety or a flower growing freely without human intervention.

wild-fowl /ˈwīldˌfoul/ ▸*pl. n.* game birds, esp. aquatic ones; waterfowl.

wild-goose chase ▸*n.* a foolish and hopeless pursuit of something unattainable.

wild-life /ˈwīldˌlīf/ ▸*n.* wild animals collectively; the native fauna (and sometimes flora) of a region.

wild-life park ▸*n.* see **PARK** (sense 1).

wild mar-jo-ram ▸*n.* see **MARJORAM**.

wild rice ▸*n.* a tall aquatic North American grass (*Zizania aquatica*) related to rice, with edible grains. ■ the grain of this plant used as food.

Wild West ▸the western U.S. in a time of lawlessness in its early history.

wile /wīl/ ▸*n.* (**wiles**) devious or cunning stratagems employed in manipulating or persuading someone to do what one wants. ▷Middle English: perhaps from an Old Norse word related to *vél* 'craft.'

will[1] /wil/ ▸*modal verb* (*3rd sing. present* **will**; *past* **would** /wŏŏd; wəd/) **1** expressing the future tense: *you will regret it when you are older.* ■ expressing a strong intention or assertion about the future: *come what may, I* *will succeed.* **2** expressing inevitable events: *accidents will happen.* **3** expressing a request: *will you stop here, please.* ■ expressing desire, consent, or willingness: *will you have a cognac?* **4** expressing facts about ability or capacity: *a rock so light that it will float on water.* **5** expressing habitual behavior: *she will dance for hours.* ■ (pronounced stressing "will") indicating annoyance about the habitual behavior described: *he will keep intruding.* **6** expressing probability or expectation about something in the present: *they will be miles away by now.*

▶ □ **will do** *inf.* expressing willingness to carry out a request or suggestion.

will[2] ▶*n.* **1** the faculty by which a person decides on and initiates action: *she has an iron will.* ■ (also **will·pow·er**) control deliberately exerted to do something or to restrain one's own impulses: *a stupendous effort of will.* ■ a deliberate or fixed desire or intention: *Jane had not wanted them to stay against their will* | *the will to live.* ■ the thing that one desires or ordains: *the disaster was God's will.* **2** a legal document containing instructions as to what should be done with one's money and property after one's death.

▶*v.* [*tr.*] **1** *chiefly formal poetic/lit.* intend, desire, or wish (something) to happen: *he was doing what the saint willed* | *marijuana, dope, grass—call it what you will.* ■ [*tr.*] make or try to make (someone) do something or (something) happen by the exercise of mental powers: *reluctantly he willed himself to turn and go back.* **2** (**will something to**) bequeath something to (someone) by the terms of one's will. ■ leave specified instructions in one's will: *he willed that his body be given to the hospital.* —**willed** *adj.* [in *comb.*] *I'm strong-willed.*

▶ □ **at will** at whatever time or in whatever way one pleases: *it can be molded and shaped at will.* □ **if you will** said when politely inviting a listener or reader to do something or when using an unusual or fanciful term: *imagine, if you will, a typical silversmith's shop.*

will-call ▶*adj.* relating to a place (usu. a ticket window or office) where items previously purchased can be picked up: *Those picking up tickets at the will-call window must use the Trumbull entrance.*

will·ful /ˈwilfəl/ (also **wil·ful**) ▶*adj.* (of an immoral or illegal act or omission) intentional; deliberate: *willful acts of damage.* ■ having or showing a stubborn and determined intention to do as one wants, regardless of the consequences or effects: *the pettish, willful side of him.* —**will·ful·ly** *adv.* —**will·ful·ness** *n.*

wil·lies /ˈwilēz/ ▶*pl. n.* (**the willies**) *inf.* a strong feeling of nervous apprehension and discomfort: *that room gave him the willies.*

will·ing /ˈwiliNG/ ▶*adj.* ready, eager, or prepared to do something: *he was quite willing to compromise.* ■ given or done readily: *willing and prompt obedience.* —**will·ing·ly** *adv.* —**will·ing·ness** *n.*

will-o'-the-wisp /ˈwil ə THə ˈwisp/ ▶*n.* a phosphorescent light seen hovering or floating at night over marshy ground, thought to result from the combustion of natural gases. ■ *fig.* a person or thing that is difficult or impossible to find, reach, or catch.

wil·low /ˈwilō/ ▶*n.* (also **willow tree**) a tree or shrub (genus *Salix*, family Salicaceae) of temperate climates that typically has narrow leaves and pliant branches, bears catkins, and grows near water.

wil·low·y /ˈwilōē/ ▶*adj.* **1** bordered, shaded, or covered by willows: *willowy meadow land.* **2** (of a person) tall, slim, and lithe.

will·pow·er /ˈwil,pou(ə)r/ ▶*n.* see WILL[2] (sense 1).

wil·ly-nil·ly /ˈwilē ˈnilē/ ▶*adv.* **1** whether one likes it or not: *he would be forced to collaborate willy-nilly.* **2** without direction or planning; haphazardly: *politicians expanded spending programs willy-nilly.*

wilt[1] /wilt/ ▶*v.* [*intr.*] (of a plant, leaf, or flower) become limp through heat, loss of water, or disease; droop. ■ (of a person) lose one's energy or vigor.

▶*n.* any of a number of fungal or bacterial diseases of plants characterized by wilting of the foliage.

wilt[2] ▶ archaic second person singular of WILL[1].

wil·y /ˈwilē/ ▶*adj.* (**wil·i·er, wil·i·est**) skilled at gaining an advantage, esp. deceitfully: *his wily opponents.* —**wil·i·ly** /ˈwiləlē/ *adv.* —**wil·i·ness** *n.*

WIMP /wimp/ ▶*n.* [often as *adj.*] *Comput.* a graphical user interface designed to simplify or demystify computing operations.

wimp /wimp/ *inf.* ▶*n.* a weak and cowardly or unadventurous person.

▶*v.* [*intr.*] (**wimp out**) withdraw from a course of action or a stated position in a way that is seen as feeble or cowardly. —**wimp·ish** *adj.* —**wimp·ish·ly** *adv.* —**wimp·ish·ness** *n.* —**wimp·y** *adj.*

wim·ple /ˈwimpəl/ ▶*n.* a cloth headdress covering the head, the neck, and the sides of

the face, formerly worn by women and still worn by some nuns. —**wim·pled** *adj.*

win /win/ ▶*v.* (**win·ning**; *past* and *past part.* **won** /wən; wän/) [*tr.*] **1** be successful or victorious in (a contest or conflict): *the Mets have won four games in a row* | [*intr.*] *a determination to win.* **2** acquire or secure as a result of a contest, conflict, bet, or other endeavor: *there are hundreds of prizes to be won.* ■ gain (a person's attention, support, or love), typically gradually or by effort: *you will find it difficult to win back their attention.* ■ (**win someone over**) gain the support or favor of someone by action or persuasion: *her sense of humor had won him over at once.* ■ [*intr.*] (**win out**) manage to succeed or achieve something by effort: *talent won out over bureaucracy.*

▶*n.* a successful result in a contest, conflict, bet, or other endeavor; a victory: *a win against Norway.* —**win·less** *n.* —**win·na·ble** *adj.*

wince /wins/ ▶*v.* [*intr.*] give a slight involuntary grimace or shrinking movement of the body out of or in anticipation of pain or distress: *he winced at the disgust in her voice.*

▶*n.* a slight grimace or shrinking movement caused by pain or distress. —**winc·er** *n.* —**winc·ing·ly** *adv.*

winch /winCH/ ▶*n.* a hauling or lifting device consisting of a rope, cable, or chain winding around a horizontal rotating drum, turned by a crank or by motor or other power source; a windlass.

▶*v.* [*tr.*] hoist or haul with a winch. —**winch·er** *n.*

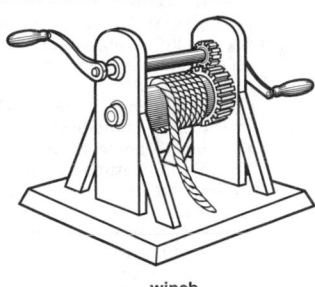

winch

wind[1] /wind/ ▶*n.* **1** the perceptible natural movement of the air, esp. in the form of a current of air blowing from a particular direction: *an easterly wind.* ■ [as *adj.*] relating to or denoting energy obtained from harnessing the wind with windmills or wind turbines. ■ used to suggest something very fast, unrestrained, or changeable: *run like the wind.* ■ used in reference to an influence or tendency that cannot be resisted: *a wind of change.* ■ used in reference to an impending situation: *he had seen which way the wind was blowing.* ■ the rush of air caused by a fast-moving body. **2** breath as needed in physical exertion or in speech. ■ the power of breathing without difficulty while running or making a similar continuous effort: *he waited while Jerry got his wind back.* See also SECOND WIND. **3** empty, pompous, or boastful talk; meaningless rhetoric. ■ air swallowed while eating or gas generated in the stomach and intestines by digestion. **4** air or breath used for sounding an organ or a wind instrument. ■ (also **winds**) [treated as *sing.* or *pl.*] wind instruments, or specifically woodwind instruments, forming a band or a section of an orchestra: *concerto for piano, violin, and thirteen winds.*

▶*v.* [*tr.*] (often **be winded**) cause (someone) to have difficulty breathing because of exertion or a blow to the stomach: *the fall nearly winded him.* —**wind·less** *adj.*

▶ □ **before the wind** *Sailing* with the wind blowing more or less from astern. □ **get wind of** *inf.* begin to suspect that (something) is happening; hear a rumor of: *Marty got wind of a plot being hatched.* □ **sail close to** (or **near**) **the wind 1** *Sailing* sail as nearly against the wind as possible while still making headway. **2** *inf.* verge on indecency, dishonesty, or disaster. □ **take the wind out of someone's sails** frustrate someone by unexpectedly anticipating an action or remark.

wind[2] /wīnd/ ▶*v.* (*past* **wound** /wound/) **1** [*intr.*] move in or take a twisting or spiral course: *the path wound among olive trees.* **2** [*tr.*] pass (something) around a thing or person so as to encircle or enfold: *he wound a towel around his midriff.* ■ repeatedly twist or coil (a length of something) around itself or a core: *Anne wound the wool into a ball.* ■ [*intr.*] be twisted or coiled in such a way: *vines wound around every tree.* ■ wrap or surround (a core) with a coiled length of something: *devices wound with*

wimple

copper wire. **3** [*tr.*] make (a clock or other device, typically one operated by clockwork) operate by turning a key or handle: *he* **wound up** *the clock every Saturday night.* ■ turn (a key or handle) repeatedly around and around: *I* **wound** *the handle as fast as I could.* ■ [*tr.*] cause (an audio or videotape or a film) to move back or forward to a desired point: *wind your tape back and listen to make sure everything is okay.*

▸*phrasal v.* □ **wind down** (of a mechanism, esp. one operated by clockwork) gradually lose power. ■ *inf.* (of a person) relax after stress or excitement. ■ (also **wind something down**) draw or bring gradually to a close: *business began to wind down as people awaited the new regime.* □ **wind up** *inf.* **1** arrive or end up in a specified state, situation, or place: *Kevin winds up in New York.* **2** another way of saying **WIND SOMETHING UP** (sense 2): *he wound up by attacking Nonconformists.* □ **wind someone up** (usu. **be wound up**) make tense or angry: *he was clearly wound up and frantic about his daughter.* □ **wind something up 1** arrange the affairs of and dissolve a company: *the company has since been wound up.* **2** gradually or finally bring an activity to a conclusion: *the experiments had to be wound up because the funding stopped.* **3** *inf.* increase the tension, intensity, or power of something: *he wound up the engine.*

▸*n.* **1** a twist or turn in a course. **2** a single turn made when winding. **—wind·er** *n.*

wind·bag /ˈwindˌbag/ ▸*n. inf., derog.* a person who talks at length but says little of value. **—wind·bag·ger·y** /-ərē/ *n.*

wind·blown /ˈwindˌblōn/ ▸*adj.* exposed to or blown around by the wind.

wind·break /ˈwindˌbrāk/ ▸*n.* a thing, such as a row of trees or a fence, wall, or screen, that provides shelter or protection from the wind.

wind·break·er /ˈwindˌbrākər/ ▸*n. trademark* a wind-resistant jacket with a close-fitting neck, waistband, and cuffs.

wind·burn /ˈwindˌbərn/ ▸*n.* reddening and soreness of the skin caused by prolonged exposure to the wind. **—wind·burned** *adj.*

wind·chill /ˈwin(d)ˌCHil/ (also **windchill fac·tor**) ▸*n.* a quantity expressing the effective lowering of the air temperature caused by the wind, esp. as affecting the rate of heat loss from an object or human body or as perceived by an exposed person.

wind·fall /ˈwindˌfôl/ ▸*n.* an apple or other fruit blown down from a tree or bush by the wind. ■ a piece of unexpected good fortune, typically one that involves receiving a large amount of money: [as *adj.*] *windfall profits.*

wind·ing sheet /ˈwīndiNG/ ▸*n.* a sheet in which a corpse is wrapped for burial; a shroud.

wind in·stru·ment /wind/ ▸*n.* a musical instrument in which sound is produced by the vibration of air, typically by the player blowing into the instrument. ■ a woodwind instrument as distinct from a brass instrument.

wind·lass /ˈwindləs/ ▸*n.* a type of winch used esp. on ships to hoist anchors and haul on mooring lines and, esp. formerly, to lower buckets into and hoist them up from wells.

windlass

wind·mill /ˈwindˌmil/ ▸*n.* a building with sails or vanes that turn in the wind and generate power to grind grain into flour. ■ a similar structure used to generate electricity or draw water.

▸*v.* [*tr.*] move (one's arms) around in a circle in a manner suggestive of the rotating sails or vanes of a windmill. ■ [*intr.*] (of one's arms) move in such a way. ■ [*intr.*] (of the propeller or rotor of an aircraft, or the aircraft itself) spin unpowered.

win·dow /ˈwindō/ ▸*n.* **1** an opening in the wall or roof of a building or vehicle that is fitted with glass or other transparent material in a frame to admit light or air and allow people to see out. ■ a pane of glass filling such an opening: *thieves smashed a window and took $600.* ■ an opening in a wall or screen through which customers are served in a bank, ticket office, or similar building. ■ a space on the inside of a store's window where goods are displayed for sale: *I prefer the red dress that's in the window.* **2** a thing resembling such an opening in form or function, in particular: ■ a transparent panel on an envelope to show an address. ■ *Comput.* a framed area on a display screen for viewing information. ■ (**window on/into/to**) a means of observing and learning about: *television is a window on the world.* ■ *Physics* a

range of electromagnetic wavelengths for which a medium (esp. the atmosphere) is transparent. **3** an interval or opportunity for action: *February 15 to March 15 should be the final window for new offers.* ■ an interval during which atmospheric and astronomical circumstances are suitable for the launch of a spacecraft. ▷Middle English: from Old Norse *vindauga,* from *vindr* 'wind' + *auga* 'eye.' **—win·dowed** *adj.*

▸ □ **go out the window** *inf.* (of a plan or pattern or behavior) no longer exist; disappear. □ **window of opportunity** a favorable opportunity for doing something that must be seized immediately if it is not to be missed.

win·dow box ▸*n.* a long narrow box in which flowers and other plants are grown, placed on an outside windowsill.

win·dow dress·ing ▸*n.* the arrangement of an attractive display in a store window. ■ an adroit but superficial or actually misleading presentation of something, designed to create a favorable impression: *the government's effort has amounted to little more than window dressing.*

win·dow·pane /ˈwindōˌpān/ ▸*n.* **1** a pane of glass in a window. **2** a broad flatfish (*Scophthalmus aquosus,* family Scophthalmidae) with numerous dark spots, found in the western Atlantic. **3** (in full **windowpane acid**) *Informal* a gelatin chip containing LSD.

win·dow-shop ▸*v.* [*intr.*] look at the goods displayed in store windows, esp. without intending to buy anything: [as *n.*] (**window-shopping**) *window-shopping is the favorite pastime of all New Yorkers.* **—win·dow-shop·per** *n.*

win·dow·sill /ˈwindōˌsil/ (also **window sill**) ▸*n.* a ledge or sill forming the bottom part of a window.

wind·pipe /ˈwindˌpīp/ ▸*n.* the air passage from the throat to the lungs; the trachea.

wind·shield /ˈwindˌSHēld/ ▸*n.* a window at the front of the passenger compartment of a motor vehicle.

wind·shield wip·er ▸*n.* a motor-driven device for keeping a windshield clear of rain, typically one with a rubber blade on an arm that moves in an arc.

wind·sock /ˈwindˌsäk/ ▸*n.* a light, flexible cylinder or cone mounted on a mast to show the direction and strength of the wind, esp. at an airfield.

wind·surf·ing /ˈwindˌsərfiNG/ ▸*n.* the sport or pastime of riding on water on a sailboard. **—wind·surf** *v.* **—wind·surf·er** *n.*

wind·swept /ˈwindˌswept/ ▸*adj.* **1** (of a place) exposed to strong winds: *the windswept moors.* **2** (of a person or their appearance) affected, shaped, or mussed by exposure to the wind: *his windswept hair.*

wind tun·nel /wind/ ▸*n.* a tunnel-like apparatus for producing an airstream of known velocity past models of aircraft, buildings, etc., in order to investigate flow or the effect of wind on the full-size object. ■ an open space through which strong winds are channeled by surrounding tall buildings.

wind·up /ˈwīndˌəp/ ▸*n.* **1** an act of concluding or finishing something: *the windup of the convention.* **2** *Baseball* the motions of a pitcher immediately before delivering the ball, in which they take a step back, lift the hands over the head, and step forward.

▸*adj.* (of a toy or other device) functioning by means of winding a key or handle: *a windup clock.*

wind·ward /ˈwindwərd/ ▸*adj. & adv.* facing the wind or on the side facing the wind: [as *adj.*] *the windward side of the boat.* Contrasted with **LEE·WARD.**

▸*n.* the side or direction from which the wind is blowing: *the ships drifted west, leaving the island quite a distance* **to windward.**

wind·y[1] /ˈwindē/ ▸*adj.* (**wind·i·er, wind·i·est**) **1** (of weather, a period of time, or a place) marked by or exposed to strong winds: *a very windy day.* ■ resembling the wind in sound or force: *Pratt's sigh was windy.* **2** *inf.* using or expressed in many words that sound impressive but mean little: *windy speeches.* **—wind·i·ly** /-əlē/ *adv.* **—wind·i·ness** *n.*

wind·y[2] /ˈwīndē/ ▸*adj.* (of a road or river) following a curving or twisting course.

wine /wīn/ ▸*n.* an alcoholic drink made from fermented grape juice. ■ an alcoholic drink made from the fermented juice of specified other fruits or plants: *a glass of dandelion wine.* ■ (also **wine red**) a dark red color like that of red wine.

▸*v.* [*tr.*] (**wine and dine someone**) entertain someone by offering them drinks or a meal: *members of Congress have been lavishly wined and dined by lobbyists for years.* ■ [*intr.*] (of a person) take part in such entertainment. **—wine·y** (also **win·y**) *adj.*

wine cel·lar ▸*n.* a cellar in which wine is stored. ■ a stock of wine.

wine·glass /ˈwīnˌglas/ ▸*n.* a glass with a stem and foot, used for drinking wine. **—wine·glass·ful** /ˈwīnglas ˌfo͝ol/ *n.* (*pl.* **-fuls**).

wine·grow·er /'wīn,grōər/ ▶n. a cultivator of grapes for wine.

wine·press /'wīn,pres/ ▶n. a press in which grapes are squeezed in making wine.

win·er·y /'wīnərē/ ▶n. (pl. **-er·ies**) an establishment where wine is made.

wine tast·ing ▶n. an event at which people taste and compare a number of wines. ■ the action of judging the quality of wine by tasting it. **—wine tast·er** n.

wing /wiNG/ ▶n. **1** any of a number of specialized paired appendages that enable some animals to fly, in particular: ■ (in a bird) a modified forelimb that bears large feathers. ■ (in a bat or pterosaur) a modified forelimb with skin stretched between or behind the fingers. ■ (in most insects) each of two or four flat extensions of the thoracic cuticle, either transparent or covered in scales. ■ the meat on the wing bone of a bird used as food. ■ (usu. **wings**) fig. power or means of flight or rapid motion: time flies by **on wings**. **2** a rigid horizontal structure that projects from both sides of an aircraft and supports it in the air. ■ (in a plane) a pilot's certificate of ability to fly a plane, indicated by a badge representing a pair of wings: Michael earned his wings as a commercial pilot. **3** a part that projects, in particular: ■ a part of a large building, esp. one that projects from the main part: the maternity wing at South Cleveland Hospital. ■ either end (port or starboard) of a ship's navigational bridge. ■ Anat. a lateral part or projection of an organ or structure. ■ Bot. a thin membranous appendage of a fruit or seed that is dispersed by the wind. **4** a group within a political party or other organization that holds particular views or has a particular function: Sinn Fein, the political wing of the IRA. **5** a side area, or a person or activity associated with that area, in particular: ■ (**the wings**) the sides of a theater stage out of view of the audience. ■ (in soccer, rugby, and other games) the part of the field close to the sidelines. ■ (in soccer, ice hockey, and other games) an attacking player who plays mostly forward close to one side of the field or rink. ■ a flank of a battle array. **6** an air force unit of several squadrons or groups.
▶v. **1** [intr.] travel on wings or by aircraft; fly: a bird came winging around the corner. ■ move, travel, or be sent quickly, as if flying: the prize will be **winging** its way to you soon. ■ [tr.] throw with the arm: he scooped up the ball and winged it toward Freddie. ■ [tr.] send or convey (something) quickly, as if by air: just jot down the title on a postcard and wing it to us. **2** [tr.] shoot (a bird) in the wing, so as to prevent flight without causing death: one bird was winged for every bird killed. ■ wound (someone) superficially, esp. in the arm or shoulder. **3** (**wing it**) inf. speak or act without preparation; improvise: a little boning up puts you ahead of the job seekers who try to wing it. ▷Middle English (originally in the plural): from Old Norse vængr, plural of vængr. **—winged** adj. **—wing·less** adj. **—wing·like** /-,līk/ adj.
▶ □ **in the wings** ready to do something or to be used at the appropriate time: there are no obvious successors waiting **in the wings**. □ **under one's wing** in or into one's protective care.

wing chair ▶n. a high-backed armchair with side pieces projecting from the back, originally in order to protect the sitter from drafts.

wing·er /'wiNGər/ ▶n. **1** an attacking player on the wing in soccer, hockey, and other sports. **2** [in comb.] a member of a specified political wing: a left-winger.

wing nut (also **wing·nut**) ▶n. a nut with a pair of projections for the fingers to turn it on a screw.

wing chair

wing·span /'wiNG,span/ (also **wing·spread** /-,spred/) ▶n. the maximum extent from wingtip to wingtip of an aircraft, bird, or other flying animal. ■ the distance between opposite fingertips of the outstretched arms of an athlete, especially a basketball player: Warrick's massive wingspan got in the way of Kansas's national championship hopes.

wing tip (also **wing·tip**) ▶n. **1** the tip of the wing of an aircraft, bird, or other animal. **2** a shoe with a toe cap having a backward extending point and curving sides, resembling the shape of a wing.

wink /wiNGk/ ▶v. [intr.] close and open one eye quickly, typically to indicate that something is a joke or a secret or as a signal of affection or greeting: he winked at Nicole as he passed. ■ (**wink at**) pretend not to notice (something bad or illegal): the authorities winked at their illegal trade. ■ (of a bright object or a light) shine or flash intermittently.
▶n. an act of closing and opening one eye quickly, typically as a signal.
▶ □ **in the wink of an eye** (or **in a wink**) very quickly. □ **not sleep** (or **get**) **a wink** (or **not get a wink of sleep**) not sleep at all.

win·kle /'wiNGkəl/ ▶n. a small herbivorous shore-dwelling mollusk with a spiral shell. Also called PERIWINKLE.

win·ner /'winər/ ▶n. a person or thing that wins something: a Nobel Prize winner. ■ a goal or shot that wins a winner or point. ■ Bridge a card that can be relied on to win a trick. ■ inf. a thing that is a success or is likely to be successful: the changes failed to make the soap opera a winner.

win·ning /'winiNG/ ▶adj. **1** gaining, resulting in, or relating to victory in a contest or competition: a winning streak. **2** attractive; endearing: a winning smile.
▶n. (**winnings**) money won, esp. by gambling: he went to collect his winnings. **—win·ning·ly** adv.

win·now /'winō/ ▶v. [tr.] blow a current of air through (grain) in order to remove the chaff. ■ remove (chaff) from grain. ■ reduce the number in a set of (people or things) gradually until only the best ones are left: the contenders had been winnowed to five. ■ find or identify (a valuable or useful part of something): in this welter of confusing signals, it's difficult to **winnow out** the truth. ■ identify and remove (the least valuable or useful people or things): guidelines that would help **winnow out** those not fit to be soldiers. **—win·now·er** n.

win·o /'wīnō/ ▶n. (pl. **-os**) inf. a person who drinks excessive amounts of cheap wine or other alcohol, esp. one who is homeless.

win·some /'winsəm/ ▶adj. attractive or appealing in appearance or character: a winsome smile. **—win·some·ly** adv. **—win·some·ness** n.

win·ter /'wintər/ ▶n. the coldest season of the year, in the northern hemisphere from December to February and in the southern hemisphere from June to August: [as adj.] the winter months. ■ Astron. the period from the winter solstice to the vernal equinox. ■ (**winters**) poetic/lit. years: a hundred winters old.
▶adj. (of fruit and vegetables) ripening late in the growing season and suitable for storage over the winter: a winter apple. ■ (of wheat or other crops) sown in autumn for harvesting the following year.
▶v. [intr.] (esp. of a bird) spend the winter in a particular place: birds wintering in the Channel. ■ [tr.] keep or feed (plants or cattle) during winter. **—win·ter·er** n. **—win·ter·less** adj. **—win·ter·ly** adj.

win·ter·green /'wintər,grēn/ ▶n. **1** a North American plant from which a pungent oil is obtained. ■ (also **oil of wintergreen**) a pungent oil containing methyl salicylate, now obtained chiefly from the sweet birch or made synthetically, used medicinally and as a flavoring. **2** a low-growing plant (Chimaphila, Pyrola and other genera, family Pyrolaceae) of acid soils in north temperate regions, with spikes of white bell-shaped flowers.

win·ter·ize /'wintə,rīz/ ▶v. [tr.] (usu. **be winterized**) adapt or prepare (something, esp. a house or an automobile) for use in cold weather: a winterized waterfront cottage. **—win·ter·i·za·tion** /,wintəri'zāSHən/ n.

win·ter sol·stice ▶n. the solstice that marks the onset of winter, at the time of the shortest day, about December 22 in the northern hemisphere and June 21 in the southern hemisphere. ■ Astron. the solstice in December.

win·try /'wintrē/ (also **win·ter·y** /'wint(ə)rē/) ▶adj. (**-tri·er**, **-tri·est**) characteristic of winter, esp. in feeling or looking very cold and bleak: a wintry landscape | fig. his eyes were decidedly wintry. **—win·tri·ly** /-trəlē/ adv. **—win·tri·ness** n.

win·try mix ▶n. variable precipitation consisting of rain, freezing rain, sleet, or snow: the wintry mix slowed down drivers.

wipe /wīp/ ▶v. [tr.] clean or dry (something) by rubbing its surface with a cloth, a piece of paper, or one's hand: Paul wiped his face with a handkerchief. ■ [tr.] remove (dirt or moisture) from something by rubbing its surface with a cloth, a piece of paper, or one's hand: she wiped away a tear. ■ clean (something) by rubbing it against a surface: the man wiped his hands on his hips. ■ [tr.] spread (a liquid) over a surface by rubbing: gently wipe the lotion over the eyelids. ■ [tr.] fig. remove or eliminate (something) completely: things have happened to wipe the smile off Kate's face. ■ erase (data) from a magnetic medium.

Pronunciation Key ə ago, up; ər over, fur; a hat; ā ate; ä car; CH chin; e let; ē see; e(ə)r air; i fit; ī by; i(ə)r ear; NG sing; ō go; ô law, for; oi toy; o͝o good; o͞o goo; ou out; SH she; TH thin; T͟H then; (h)w why; ZH vision

▶*phrasal v.* □ **wipe out** *inf.* fall over or off a vehicle. ■ be capsized by a wave while surfing. □ **wipe someone out 1** kill a large number of people: *the plague had wiped out whole villages.* **2** (usu. **be wiped out**) ruin someone financially. **3** *inf.* exhaust or intoxicate someone. □ **wipe something out** eliminate something completely: *their life savings were wiped out.*

▶*n.* **1** an act of wiping. **2** a piece of disposable absorbent cloth or paper, esp. one treated with a cleansing agent, for wiping something clean. **3** a cinematographic effect in which an existing picture seems to be wiped out by a new one as the boundary between them moves across the screen. —**wipe·a·ble** *adj.*

wipe·out /ˈwīpˌout/ ▶*n. inf.* an instance of complete destruction: *a nuclear wipeout.* ■ a complete failure. ■ a fall from a surfboard.

wire /wī(ə)r/ ▶*n.* **1** metal drawn out into the form of a thin flexible thread or rod. ■ a piece of such metal. ■ a length or quantity of wire used, for example, for fencing or to carry an electric current. ■ *Horse Racing* a wire stretched across and above the track at the finish line of a racetrack. ■ an electronic listening device that can be concealed on a person. **2** *inf.* a telegram or cablegram.

▶*v.* [*tr.*] **1** install electric circuits or wires in: *wiring a plug.* ■ connect (someone or something) to a piece of electronic equipment: *a microphone wired to a loudspeaker.* **2** provide, fasten, or reinforce with wires: *they wired his jaw.* **3** *inf.* send a telegram or cablegram to: *she wired her friend for advice.* ■ send (money) to (someone) by means of a telegram or cablegram: *he was expecting his brother to wire him $1,500.* ▷Old English *wīr*, of Germanic origin, probably from the base of Latin *viere* 'plait, weave.' —**wir·er** *n.*

▶ □ **down to the wire** *inf.* used to denote a situation whose outcome is not decided until the very last minute: *it was probable that the test of nerves would go down to the wire.* □ **under the wire** *inf.* at the last possible opportunity; just in time.

wire-draw ▶*v.* (*past* **-drew**; *past part.* **-drawn**) [*tr.*] (often as *n.*) (**wire-drawing**) draw out (metal) into wire by passing it through a series of holes of diminishing diameter in a steel plate. —**wire-draw·er** *n.*

wire gauze ▶*n.* see GAUZE.

wire-haired ▶*adj.* (esp. of a dog breed) having stiff or wiry hair: *a wire-haired terrier.*

wire·less /ˈwīrlis/ ▶*n. dated, chiefly Brit.* **1** (also **wire·less set**) a radio receiving set. **2** computer networking, broadcasting, telephony, or telegraphy using radio signals.

▶*adj.* lacking or not requiring wires.

wire·less hot spot (also **wire·less hot·spot**) ▶*n.* an area with a usable signal to allow wireless connection to the Internet or some other computer network.

wire·less·ly /ˈwī(ə)rlislē/ ▶*adv.* without a wire connection; using a wireless technology: *a patented FM technology that broadcasts music wirelessly.*

wire serv·ice ▶*n.* a news agency that supplies syndicated news by wire to newspapers, radio, and television stations.

wire·tap·ping /ˈwī(ə)rˌtapiNG/ ▶*n.* the practice of connecting a listening device to a telephone line to secretly monitor a conversation. —**wire·tap** *n. & v.* —**wire·tap·per** /-ˌtapər/ *n.*

wir·ing /ˈwī(ə)riNG/ ▶*n.* a system of wires providing electric circuits for a device or building. ■ the installation of this. ■ *inf.* the structure of the nervous system or brain perceived as determining a basic or innate pattern of behavior.

wir·y /ˈwī(ə)rē/ ▶*adj.* (**wir·i·er**, **wir·i·est**) resembling wire in form and texture: *his wiry black hair.* ■ (of a person) lean, tough, and sinewy: *a small, wiry woman.* —**wir·i·ly** /ˈwī(ə)rəlē/ *adv.* —**wir·i·ness** *n.*

wis·dom /ˈwizdəm/ ▶*n.* the quality of having experience, knowledge, and good judgment; the quality of being wise. ■ the soundness of an action or decision with regard to the application of such experience, knowledge, and good judgment: *some questioned the wisdom of building the dam so close to an active volcano.* ■ the body of knowledge and principles that develops within a specified society or period: *Buddhist wisdom.*

wis·dom tooth ▶*n.* each of the four rearmost molars in humans, which usually appear at about the age of twenty.

wise[1] /wīz/ ▶*adj.* having or showing experience, knowledge, and good judgment: *she seems kind and wise.* ■ responding sensibly or shrewdly to a particular situation: *it would be wise to discuss the matter with the chairman.* ■ having knowledge in a specified subject: *families wise in the way of hurricane survival.* ■ (**wise to**) *inf.* alert to or aware of: *at seven she was already wise to the police.* —**wise·ly** *adv.*

▶*phrasal v.* **wise off** *Informal* make wisecracks: *Jake and I would wise off to him.* □ **wise up** [often in *imper.*] *inf.* become alert to or aware of something: *wise up and sort yourselves out before it's too late.*

wise[2] ▶*n. archaic* the manner or extent of something.

▶ □ **in no wise** not at all.

wise·a·cre /ˈwīzˌākər/ ▶*n.* a person with an affectation of wisdom or knowledge, regarded with scorn or irritation by others; a know-it-all.

wise·crack /ˈwīzˌkrak/ *inf.* ▶*n.* a clever and pithy spoken witticism.

▶*v.* [*intr.*] make a wisecrack: [as *n.*] (**wisecracking**) *his warmth, boisterousness, and constant wisecracking.* —**wise·crack·er** *n.*

wise guy *inf.* ▶*n.* **1** a person who speaks and behaves as if they know more than others. **2** a member of the Mafia.

wish /wiSH/ ▶*v.* [*intr.*] feel or express a strong desire or hope for something that is not easily attainable; want something that cannot or probably will not happen: *we wished for peace.* ■ silently invoke such a hope or desire, esp. in a ritualized way: *I closed my eyes and wished.* ■ feel or express a desire to do something: *they wish to become involved.* ■ [*tr.*] ask (someone) to do something or that (something) be done: *I wish it to be clearly understood.* ■ express a desire for (the success or good fortune) of (someone): *they wish her every success.* ■ [*tr.*] (**wish something on**) hope that something unpleasant will happen to: *I would not wish it on the vilest soul.*

▶*n.* a desire or hope for something to happen: *the union has reiterated its wish for an agreement.* ■ (usu. **wishes**) an expression of such a desire, typically in the form of a request or instruction: *she must carry out her late father's wishes.* ■ an invocation or recitation of a hope or desire: *he makes a wish.* ■ (usu. **wishes**) an expression of a desire for someone's success or good fortune: *they had received kindness and good wishes from total strangers.* ■ a thing or event that is or has been desired; an object of desire: *the petitioners eventually got their wish.* —**wish·er** *n.* [in *comb.*] an ill-wisher.

wish·bone /ˈwiSHˌbōn/ ▶*n.* **1** a forked bone between the neck and breast of a bird. According to a popular custom, this bone from a cooked bird is broken by two people, with the holder of the longer portion being granted a wish. **2** an object of similar shape, in particular: ■ *Football* an offensive formation in which the fullback lines up immediately behind the quarterback with the two halfbacks behind and on either side of the fullback. ■ a forked element in the suspension of a motor vehicle or aircraft, typically attached to a wheel at one end with the two arms hinged to the chassis.

wish·ful /ˈwiSHfəl/ ▶*adj.* having or expressing a desire or hope for something to happen. ■ expressing or containing a desire or hope for something impractical or unfeasible: *without resources the proposed measures were merely wishful thinking.* —**wish·ful·ly** *adv.* —**wish·ful·ness** *n.*

wish·y-wash·y /ˈwiSHē ˈwäSHē; -ˈwôSHē/ ▶*adj.* (of drink or liquid food such as soup) weak; watery. ■ feeble or insipid in quality or character; lacking strength or boldness: *wishy-washy liberalism.*

wisp /wisp/ ▶*n.* a small thin or twisted bunch, piece, or amount of something: *wisps of smoke rose into the air.* ■ a small bunch of hay or straw used for drying or grooming a horse. ■ a small thin person, typically a child: *a fourteen-year-old wisp of a girl.* —**wisp·i·ly** /ˈwispilē/ *adv.* —**wisp·i·ness** /ˈwispēnis/ *n.* —**wisp·y** *adj.* (**wisp·i·er**, **wisp·i·est**) .

wis·te·ri·a /wiˈsti(ə)rēə/ (also **wis·ta·ri·a** /-ˈste(ə)r-/) ▶*n.* a climbing shrub (genus *Wisteria*) of the pea family, with hanging clusters of pale bluish-lilac flowers.

wist·ful /ˈwistfəl/ ▶*adj.* having or showing a feeling of vague or regretful longing: *a wistful smile.* —**wist·ful·ly** *adv.* —**wist·ful·ness** *n.*

wit[1] /wit/ ▶*n.* **1** mental sharpness and inventiveness; keen intelligence: *he does not lack perception or native wit.* ■ (**wits**) the intelligence required for normal activity; basic human intelligence: *he needed all his wits to figure out the way back.* **2** a natural aptitude for using words and ideas in a quick and inventive way to create humor: *a player with a sharp tongue and a quick wit.* ■ a person who has such an aptitude: *she is such a wit.* —**wit·ted** *adj.* [in *comb.*] *slow-witted.*

▶ □ **be at one's wits' end** be overwhelmed with difficulties and at a loss as to what to do next. □ **be frightened** (or **scared**) **out of one's wits** be extremely frightened; be immobilized by fear. □ **have** (or **keep**) **one's wits about one** be constantly alert and vigilant.

wit[2] ▶*v.* (**wot** /wät/, **wit·ting**; *past* and *past part.* **wist** /wist/) [*intr.*] (**to wit**) that is to say (used to make clearer or more specific something already said or referred to): *the textbooks show an irritating parochialism, to wit an almost total exclusion of papers not in English.*

witch /wiCH/ ▶*n.* **1** a woman thought to have evil magic powers. Witches are popularly depicted as wearing a black cloak and pointed hat, and flying on a broomstick. ■ a follower or practitioner of modern witchcraft; a Wiccan priest or priestess. ■ *inf.* an ugly or unpleasant old woman; a hag. ■ a girl or woman capable of enchanting or bewitching a man. **2** an edible North Atlantic flatfish (*Glyptocephalus cynoglossus*, family Pleuronectidae) that is of some commercial value. —**witch·like** /-,līk/ *adj.* —**witch·y** *adj.*

witch·craft /'wicH,kraft/ ▶*n.* the practice of magic, esp. black magic; the use of spells and the invocation of spirits. See also WICCA.

witch doc·tor ▶*n.* (among tribal peoples) a magician credited with powers of healing, divination, and protection against the magic of others.

witch·er·y /'wicHərē/ ▶*n.* the practice of magic: *warding off evil spirits and acts of witchery.* ■ compelling power exercised by beauty, eloquence, or other attractive or fascinating qualities.

witch·es' sab·bath ▶*n.* see SABBATH (sense 2).

witch ha·zel ▶*n.* a shrub (genus *Hamamelis,* family Hamamelidaceae) with fragrant yellow flowers that is widely grown as an ornamental. ■ an astringent lotion made from the bark and leaves of this plant, esp. *H. virginiana.*

witch-hunt ▶*n. hist.* a search for and subsequent persecution of a supposed witch. ■ *inf.* a campaign directed against a person or group holding unorthodox or unpopular views. —**witch-hunt·ing** *n.*

with /wiTH; wiTH/ ▶*prep.* **1** accompanied by (another person or thing): *a nice steak with a bottle of red wine.* ■ in the same direction as: *marine mammals generally swim with the current.* ■ along with (with reference to time): *wisdom comes with age.* ■ in proportion to: *the form of the light curve changes with period in a systematic way.* **2** possessing (something) as a feature or accompaniment: *a flower-sprigged blouse with a white collar.* ■ marked by or wearing: *a tall dark man with a scar on one cheek.* **3** indicating the instrument used to perform an action: *cut it with a knife.* ■ indicating the material used for some purpose: *fill the bowl with water.* **4** in opposition to: *we started fighting with each other.* **5** indicating the manner or attitude of the person doing something: *with great reluctance.* **6** indicating responsibility: *leave it with me.* **7** in relation to: *my father will be angry with me.* **8** employed by: *she's with IBM now.* ■ as a member or employee of: *he plays with the Cincinnati Cyclones.* ■ using the services of: *I bank with the TSB.* **9** affected by (a particular fact or condition): *with no hope.* ■ indicating the cause of an action or condition: *trembling with fear.* **10** indicating separation or removal from something: *their jobs could be dispensed with.*

▶ □ **be with someone 1** agree with or support someone: *we're all with you on this one.* **2** *inf.* follow someone's meaning: *I'm not with you.* □ **with it 1** knowledgeable about and following modern ideas and fashions: *a young, with-it film buyer.* **2** alert and comprehending: *I'm not really with it this morning.*

with·draw /wiTH'drô; wiTH-/ ▶*v.* (past **-drew**; past part. **-drawn**) **1** [*tr.*] remove or take away (something) from a particular place or position: *slowly Ruth withdrew her hand from his.* ■ take (money) out of an account: *normally you can withdraw up to $50 in cash.* ■ take back or away (something bestowed, proposed, or used): *withdrew its support for the government.* ■ (in parliamentary procedure) remove or recall a motion, amendment, etc., from consideration. ■ say that (a statement one has made) is untrue or unjustified: *he failed to withdraw his remarks and apologize.* ■ [*intr.*] (of a man) practice coitus interruptus. **2** [*intr.*] leave or come back from a place, esp. a war zone: *Iraqi forces withdrew from Kuwait.* ■ [*tr.*] cause (someone) to leave or come back from a place, esp. a war zone: *agreed to withdraw their troops.* ■ no longer participate in an activity or be a member of a team or organization: *his rival withdrew from the race on the second lap.* ■ depart to another room or place, esp. in search of quiet or privacy. ■ retreat from contact or communication with other people: *he went silent and withdrew into himself.* **3** [*intr.*] cease to take an addictive drug: *withdraw from cocaine without medication.*

with·draw·al /wiTH'drôl; wiTH-/ ▶*n.* the action of withdrawing something: *the withdrawal of legal aid.* ■ an act of taking money out of an account. ■ a sum of money withdrawn from an account: *a cash withdrawal.* ■ the action of ceasing to participate in an activity. ■ the process of ceasing to take an addictive drug. ■ coitus interruptus.

▶ □ **withdrawal symptoms** the unpleasant physical reaction that accompanies the process of ceasing to take an addictive drug.

with·er /'wiTHər/ ▶*v.* **1** [*intr.*] (of a plant) become dry and shriveled: [as *adj.*] (**withered**) *withered leaves.* ■ (of a person, limb, or the skin) become shrunken or wrinkled from age or disease: [as *adj.*] (**withered**) *a girl with a withered arm.* ■ cease to flourish; fall into decay or decline: *programs would wither away if they did not command local support.* ■ [*tr.*] cause harm or damage to: *a business that can wither the hardiest ego.* ■ mortify (someone) with a scornful look or manner: *she withered me with a look.*

with·ers /'wiTHərz/ ▶*pl. n.* the highest part of a horse's back, lying at the base of the neck above the shoulders.

with·hold /wiTH'hōld; wiTH-/ ▶*v.* (past and past part. **-held**) [*tr.*] refuse to give (something that is due to or is desired by another): *the name of the dead man is being withheld* | [as *n.*] (**withholding**) *the withholding of consent to treatment.* ■ suppress or hold back (an emotion or reaction). ■ (of an employer) deduct (tax) from an employee's paycheck and send it directly to the government. —**with·hold·er** *n.*

with·in /wiTH'in; wi'TH-/ ▶*prep.* inside (something): *the spread of fire within the building.* ■ inside the range of (an area or boundary): *a field located within the city.* ■ inside the range of (a specified action or perception): *within reach.* ■ not further off than (used with distances): *lives within a few miles of Honesdale.* ■ occurring inside (a particular period of time): *sold out within two hours.* ■ inside the bounds set by (a concept, argument, etc.): *full cooperation within the terms of the treaty.*

▶*adv.* inside; indoors: *inquire within.* ■ internally or inwardly: *beauty coming from within.*

with·out /wiTH'out; wiTH-/ ▶*prep.* in the absence of: *he went to Sweden without her.* ■ not having the care or benefit of: *the first person to make the ascent without oxygen.* ■ in circumstances in which the action mentioned does not happen: *they sat looking at each other without speaking.*

▶*adv. archaic* or *poetic/lit.* outside: *the enemy without.*

with·stand /wiTH'stand; wiTH-/ ▶*v.* (past and past part. **-stood**) [*tr.*] remain undamaged or unaffected by; resist: *the structure had been designed to withstand winds of more than 100 mph.* ■ offer strong resistance or opposition to (someone or something). —**with·stand·er** *n.*

wit·less /'witlis/ ▶*adj.* foolish; stupid: *a witless retort.* ■ to such an extent that one cannot think clearly or rationally: *I was scared witless.* —**wit·less·ly** *adv.* —**wit·less·ness** *n.*

wit·ness /'witnis/ ▶*n.* **1** a person who sees an event, typically a crime or accident, take place: *police are appealing for witnesses to the accident.* ■ a person giving sworn testimony to a court of law or the police. ■ a person who is present at the signing of a document and signs it themselves to confirm this. **2** evidence; proof: *the memorial service was witness to the wide circle of his interest.* ■ used to refer to confirmation or evidence given by signature, under oath, or otherwise: *in witness thereof, the parties sign this document.* ■ open profession of one's religious faith through words or actions: *faithful Christian witness.* **3** a member of the Jehovah's Witnesses.

▶*v.* **1** [*tr.*] see (an event, typically a crime or accident) take place: *a bartender who witnessed the murder.* ■ have knowledge of (an event or change) from personal observation or experience: *what we are witnessing is the birth of a dangerously liberal orthodoxy.* ■ (of a time, place, or other context) be the setting in which (a particular event) takes place: *the 1980s witnessed an unprecedented increase in the scope of the electronic media.* ■ be present as someone signs (a document) or gives (their signature) to a document and sign it oneself to confirm this: *the clerk witnessed her signature.* ■ [in *imper.*] look at (used to introduce a fact illustrating a preceding statement): *the nuclear family is a vulnerable institution—witness the rates of marital breakdown.* **2** [*intr.*] (**witness to**) give or serve as evidence of; testify to: *his writings witness to an inner toughness.* ■ (of a person) openly profess one's religious faith in: *witness to Jesus.*

wit·ness stand (*Brit.* **witness box**) ▶*n.* Law the place in a court where a witness stands to give evidence.

wit·ti·cism /'witi,sizəm/ ▶*n.* a witty remark.

wit·ting /'witiNG/ ▶*adj.* done in full awareness or consciousness; deliberate: *the witting and unwitting complicity of the institutions.* ■ (of a person) conscious or aware of the full facts of a situation: *there is no proof that the Chinese were witting accomplices.* —**wit·ting·ly** *adv.*

wit·ty /'witē/ ▶*adj.* (**-ti·er, -ti·est**) showing or characterized by quick and inventive verbal humor: *a witty remark* | *Marlowe was charming and witty.* —**wit·ti·ly** /'witəlē/ *adv.* —**wit·ti·ness** *n.*

wives /wīvz/ ▶ plural form of WIFE.

wiz /wiz/ ▶*n.* variant spelling of WHIZ (noun sense 2).

wiz·ard /'wizərd/ ▶*n.* **1** a man who has magical powers, esp. in legends and fairy tales. ■ a person who is very skilled in a particular field or activity: *a financial wizard.* **2** Comput. a help feature of a software package that automates complex tasks.

▶*adj. inf.,* dated, chiefly Brit. wonderful; excellent. —**wiz·ard·ly** *adj.* —**wiz·ard·ry** *n.*

wiz·ened /'wizənd; 'wē-/ ▶*adj.* shriveled or wrinkled with age: *a wizened, stooped old man.*

wk. ▶*abbr.* week: *75 mg per day for 3 wks.*

Pronunciation Key ə *ago, up;* ər *over, fur;* a *hat;* ā *ate;* ä *car;* cH *chin;* e *let;* ē *see;* e(ə)r *air;* i *fit;* ī *by;* i(ə)r *ear;* NG *sing;* ō *go;* ô *law, for;* oi *toy;* o͝o *good;* o͞o *goo;* ou *out;* sH *she;* TH *thin;* ŧH *then;* (h)w *why;* zH *vision*

WLAN /ˈdəbəlyo͞o ˌlan/ ▶*abbr. Comput.* wireless local area network.

WNW ▶*abbr.* west-northwest.

WO ▶*abbr.* Warrant Officer.

wob·ble /ˈwäbəl/ ▶*v.* [*intr.*] move unsteadily from side to side: *the table wobbles where the leg is too short.* ■ [*tr.*] cause to move in such a way. ■ move in such a way in a particular direction: *they wobble around on their bikes.* ■ (of the voice) tremble; quaver: *her voice wobbled dangerously.* ■ *fig.* hesitate or waver between different courses of action; vacillate: *the president wobbled on Bosnia.*

▶*n.* an unsteady movement from side to side. ■ a tremble or quaver in the voice. ■ a moment of hesitation or vacillation. —**wob·bler** *n.*

wob·bly /ˈwäb(ə)lē/ ▶*adj.* (**-bli·er, -bli·est**) tending to move unsteadily from side to side: *the car had a wobbly wheel.* ■ (of a person or their legs) weak and unsteady from illness, tiredness, or anxiety. ■ (of a person, action or state) uncertain, wavering, or insecure: *the evening gets off to a wobbly start.* ■ (of a speaker, singer, or voice) having a tendency to move out of tone or slightly vary in pitch. ■ (of a line or handwriting) not straight or regular; shaky. —**wob·bli·ness** *n.*

woe /wō/ ▶*n. often humorous* great sorrow or distress: *they had a complicated tale of woe.* ■ (**woes**) things that cause sorrow or distress; troubles.

woe·be·gone /ˈwōbiˌgôn; -ˌgän/ ▶*adj.* sad or miserable in appearance.

woe·ful /ˈwōfəl/ ▶*adj.* characterized by, expressive of, or causing sorrow or misery: *her face was woeful.* ■ very bad; deplorable: *the remark was enough to establish his woeful ignorance about the theater.* —**woe·ful·ly** *adv.* —**woe·ful·ness** *n.*

wok /wäk/ ▶*n.* a bowl-shaped pan used in Chinese cooking.

wok

woke /wōk/ ▶ past of WAKE¹.

wok·en /ˈwōkən/ ▶ past participle of WAKE¹.

wolf /wo͝olf/ ▶*n.* (*pl.* **wolves** /wo͝olvz/) **1** a wild carnivorous mammal (*Corvus frugilegus*) that is the largest member of the dog family, living and hunting in packs. It is native to both Eurasia and North America, but has been widely exterminated. ■ used in names of similar or related mammals, e.g., **maned wolf, Tasmanian wolf. 2** used in similes and metaphors to refer to a rapacious, ferocious, or voracious person or thing. ■ *inf.* a man who habitually seduces women. **3** a harsh or out-of-tune effect produced when playing particular notes or intervals on a musical instrument.

▶*v.* [*tr.*] devour (food) greedily: *he wolfed down his breakfast.* ▷Old English *wulf*, of Germanic origin; related to Dutch *wolf* and German *Wolf*, from an Indo-European root shared by Latin *lupus* and Greek *lukos*. The verb dates from the mid 19th cent. —**wolf·ish** *adj.* —**wolf·ish·ly** *adv.* —**wolf·like** /-ˌlīk/ *adj.*

▶ □ **cry wolf** call for help when it is not needed, with the effect that one is not believed when one really does need help. □ **throw someone to the wolves** leave someone to be roughly treated or criticized without trying to help or defend them. □ **a wolf in sheep's clothing** a person or thing that appears friendly or harmless but is really hostile.

wolf·hound /ˈwo͝olfˌhound/ ▶*n.* a dog of a large breed originally used to hunt wolves.

wol·ver·ine /ˌwo͝olvəˈrēn/ ▶*n.* a heavily built short-legged carnivorous mammal (genus *Gulo*) of the weasel family, with a shaggy dark coat and a bushy tail, native to the tundra and forests of arctic and subarctic regions.

wolves /wo͝olvz/ ▶ plural form of WOLF.

wom·an /ˈwo͝omən/ ▶*n.* (*pl.* **wom·en** /ˈwimin/) an adult human female. ■ a female worker or employee. ■ a wife, girlfriend, or lover: *Billy had his woman with him.* ■ a female person associated with a particular place, activity, or occupation: *a young American woman.* ■ female adults in general: *woman is intuitive.* ■ a female paid to clean someone's house and carry out general domestic duties. ■ a peremptory form of address to a woman: *don't be silly, woman.*

wom·an·hood /ˈwo͝omənˌho͝od/ ▶*n.* the state or condition of being a woman: *she was on the very brink of womanhood.* ■ the qualities

considered to be natural to or characteristic of a woman: *an ideal of womanhood.* ■ women considered collectively.

wom·an·ish /ˈwo͝omənisH/ ▶*adj. derog.* suitable to or characteristic of a woman: *he confused introspection with womanish indecision.* ■ (of a man) effeminate; unmanly. —**wom·an·ish·ly** *adv.* —**wom·an·ish·ness** *n.*

wom·an·ize /ˈwo͝oməˌnīz/ ▶*v.* [*intr.*] (of a man) engage in numerous casual sexual affairs with women: [as *n.*] (**womanizing**) *there were rumors that his womanizing had now become intolerable.* —**wom·an·iz·er** *n.*

wom·an·kind /ˈwo͝omənˌkīnd/ ▶*n.* women considered collectively.

wom·an·ly /ˈwo͝omənlē/ ▶*adj.* relating to or having the characteristics of a woman or women: *her smooth, womanly skin.* ■ (of a girl's or woman's body) fully developed and curvaceous: *I've got a womanly figure.* —**wom·an·li·ness** *n.*

womb /wo͞om/ ▶*n.* the uterus. ■ a place of origination and development: *the womb of evil.* —**womb·like** /-ˌlīk/ *adj.*

wom·bat /ˈwämˌbat/ ▶*n.* a burrowing plant-eating Australian marsupial (family Vombatidae) that resembles a small bear with short legs.

wom·en /ˈwimin/ ▶ plural form of WOMAN.

wom·en·folk /ˈwiminˌfōk/ ▶*pl. n.* the women of a particular family or community considered collectively.

wom·en's lib·er·a·tion (also **wom·en's lib**) ▶*n.* the advocacy of the liberation of women from inequalities and subservient status in relation to men, and from attitudes causing these (now generally replaced by the term *feminism*).

won¹ /wən/ ▶ past and past participle of WIN.

won² /wän/ ▶*n.* (*pl.* same) the basic monetary unit of North and South Korea, equal to 100 jun in North Korea and 100 jeon in South Korea.

won·der /ˈwəndər/ ▶*n.* a feeling of surprise mingled with admiration, caused by something beautiful, unexpected, unfamiliar, or inexplicable: *he had stood in front of it, observing the intricacy of the ironwork with the wonder of a child.* ■ the quality of a person or thing that causes such a feeling: *Athens was a place of wonder and beauty.* ■ a strange or remarkable person, thing, or event: *the electric trolley car was looked upon as the wonder of the age.* ■ [as *adj.*] having remarkable properties or abilities: *a wonder drug.* ■ a surprising event or situation: *it is a wonder that losses are not much greater.*

▶*v.* [*intr.*] **1** desire or be curious to know something: *how many times have I written that, I wonder?* ■ used to express a polite question or request: *I wonder whether you have thought more about it?* ■ feel doubt: *I wonder about such a marriage.* **2** feel admiration and amazement; marvel: *people stood by and wondered at such bravery* | [as *adj.*] (**wondering**) *a wondering look on her face.* ■ be surprised: *not to be wondered at.* —**won·der·ing·ly** *adv.*

won·der·ful /ˈwəndərfəl/ ▶*adj.* inspiring delight, pleasure, or admiration; extremely good; marvelous: *the climate was wonderful all the year round.* —**won·der·ful·ly** /-f(ə)lē/ *adv.* —**won·der·ful·ness** *n.*

won·der·land /ˈwəndərˌland/ ▶*n.* a land or place full of wonderful things: *a wonderland of historical sites.*

won·der·ment /ˈwəndərmənt/ ▶*n.* a state of awed admiration or respect: *Corbett shook his head in silent wonderment.*

won·drous /ˈwəndrəs/ ▶*adj. poetic/lit.* inspiring a feeling of wonder or delight; marvelous: *this wondrous city.* —**won·drous·ly** *adv.* —**won·drous·ness** *n.*

wont /wônt; wänt/ ▶*adj. poetic/lit.* (of a person) in the habit of doing something; accustomed: *he was wont to arise at 5:30 every morning.*

▶*n.* (**one's wont**) *formal* or *humorous* one's customary behavior in a particular situation: *Constance, as was her wont, had paid her little attention.*

won't /wōnt/ ▶*contr.* of will not.

wont·ed /ˈwôntid; ˈwōn-/ ▶*adj. poetic/lit.* habitual; usual: *the place had sunk back into its wonted quiet.*

won·ton /ˈwänˌtän/ (also **won ton**) ▶*n.* (in Chinese cooking) a small dumpling or roll with a savory filling, often of minced pork, usually eaten boiled in soup.

woo /wo͞o/ ▶*v.* (**woos, wooed**) [*tr.*] try to gain the love of (someone, typically a woman), esp. with a view to marriage: *he wooed her with quotes from Shakespeare.* ■ seek the favor, support, or custom of: *pop stars are being wooed by film companies eager to sign them up.* —**woo·a·ble** *adj.* —**woo·er** *n.*

wood /wo͝od/ ▶*n.* **1** the hard fibrous material that forms the main substance of the trunk or branches of a tree or shrub. ■ such material when cut and used as timber or fuel: *a large table made of dark, polished wood.* ■ a golf club with a wooden or other head that is relatively broad from face to back (often with a numeral indicating the degree to which the face is angled to loft the ball). ■ a shot made with such a club. **2** (usu. **woods**) an area of land, smaller than a forest, that is covered with growing trees: *a thick hedge divided the wood from the field* | *a long walk in the woods.*

▶ □ **out of the woods** (or **wood**) out of danger or difficulty.

wood·bine /'wŏŏd,bīn/ ▶*n.* either of two climbing plants: ■ Virginia creeper. ■ *Brit.* the common honeysuckle.

wood·carv·ing /'wŏŏd,kärviNG/ ▶*n.* the action or skill of carving wood to make functional or ornamental objects. ■ an object made in this way. —**wood·carv·er** *n.*

wood·chuck /'wŏŏd,CHək/ ▶*n.* a North American marmot (*Marmota monax*) with a heavy body and short legs.

wood·cock /'wŏŏd,käk/ ▶*n.* (*pl.* same) a woodland bird (genus *Scolopax*) of the sandpiper family, with a long bill, brown camouflaged plumage, and a distinctive display flight.

wood·craft /'wŏŏd,kraft/ ▶*n.* **1** skill in woodwork. **2** knowledge of the woods, esp. with reference to camping and other outdoor pursuits.

wood·cut /'wŏŏd,kət/ ▶*n.* a print of a type made from a design cut in a block of wood, formerly widely used for illustrations in books. ■ the technique of making such prints.

wood·cut·ter /'wŏŏd,kətər/ ▶*n.* **1** a person who cuts down trees or branches, esp. for fuel. **2** a person who makes woodcuts. —**wood·cut·ting** *n.*

wood·ed /'wŏŏdid/ ▶*adj.* (of an area of land) covered with woods or many trees: *a wooded valley.*

wood·en /'wŏŏdn/ ▶*adj.* **1** made of wood: *a wooden spoon.* **2** like or characteristic of wood: *a dull wooden sound.* ■ stiff and awkward in movement or manner: *she is one of the most wooden actresses of all time.* —**wood·en·ly** *adv.* —**wood·en·ness** *n.*

wood·land /'wŏŏdlənd/ -,land/ ▶*n.* (also **woodlands**) land covered with trees: *large areas of ancient woodland.*

wood·peck·er /'wŏŏd,pekər/ ▶*n.* a strong-billed, stiff-tailed bird that climbs tree trunks to find insects and drums on dead wood to mark territory. The **woodpecker family** (Picidae) also includes the flickers and sapsuckers.

wood pulp ▶*n.* wood fiber reduced chemically or mechanically to pulp and used in the manufacture of paper.

wood·shed /'wŏŏd,SHed/ ▶*n.* a shed where wood for fuel is stored.
▶*v.* [*intr.*] practice a musical instrument: *he's off woodshedding again.*

woods·man /'wŏŏdzmən/ ▶*n.* (*pl.* -**men**) a person living or working in the woods, esp. a forester, hunter, or woodcutter.

woods·y /'wŏŏdzē/ ▶*adj.* of, relating to, or characteristic of wood or woodlands: *the woodsy smells of cedar and pine.*

wood·wind /'wŏŏd,wind/ ▶*n.* [treated as *sing.* or *pl.*] wind instruments other than brass instruments forming a section of an orchestra, including flutes, oboes, clarinets, and bassoons: *striking passages for woodwind and brass.*

wood·work /'wŏŏd,wərk/ ▶*n.* the wooden parts of a room or building, such as window frames or doors. —**wood·work·er** *n.*

▶ □ **come out of the woodwork** (of an unpleasant person or thing) emerge from obscurity; be revealed.

wood·work·ing /'wŏŏd,wərkiNG/ ▶*n.* the activity or skill of making things from wood.

wood·y /'wŏŏdē/ ▶*adj.* (**wood·i·er**, **wood·i·est**) (of an area of land) covered with trees: *a woody dale.* ■ made of, resembling, or suggestive of wood: *cut out the woody central core before boiling.* ■ *Bot.* (of a plant or its stem) of the nature of or consisting of wood. —**wood·i·ness** *n.*

woof[1] /wŏŏf/ ▶*n.* the barking sound made by a dog.
▶*v.* [*intr.*] (of a dog) bark: *the dog started to woof.* ■ *inf.* say something in an ostentatious or aggressive manner but with no intention to act: *King start woofing to keep folks off our case. Just woofing. Just talk.*

woof[2] ▶*n.* another term for WEFT.

woof·er /'wŏŏfər/ ▶*n.* a loudspeaker designed to reproduce low frequencies.

wool /wŏŏl/ ▶*n.* **1** the fine soft curly or wavy hair forming the coat of a sheep, goat, or similar animal, esp. when shorn and prepared for use in making cloth or yarn. ■ yarn or textile fiber made from such hair: *carpets made of 80 percent wool and 20 percent nylon* **2** a thing resembling such hair in form or texture, in particular: ■ the soft underfur or down of some other mammals: *beaver wool.* ■ a metal or mineral made into a mass of fine fibers: *lead wool.* ▷Old English *wull*, of Germanic origin; related to Dutch *wol* and German *Wolle*, from an Indo-European root shared by Latin *lana* 'wool,' *vellus* 'fleece.' —**wool·like** /-,līk/ *adj.*

▶ □ **pull the wool over someone's eyes** deceive someone by telling untruths.

wool·en /'wŏŏlən/ (*Brit.* **wool·len**) ▶*adj.* of or relating to the production

of wool: *the woolen industry* ■ made wholly or partly of wool: *thick woolen blankets.*
▶*n.* (usu. **woolens**) an article of clothing made of wool.

wool·ly /'wŏŏlē/ (also **wool·y**) ▶*adj.* (**-li·er**, **-li·est**) **1** made of wool: *a red woolly hat.* ■ (of an animal, plant, or part) bearing or naturally covered with wool or hair resembling wool. ■ resembling wool in texture or appearance: *woolly wisps of cloud.* **2** vague or confused in expression or character: *woolly thinking.* ■ (of a sound) indistinct or distorted: *an opaque and woolly recording.*
▶*n.* (*pl.* -**lies**) (usu. **woollies**) *inf.*, chiefly *Brit.* a garment made of wool, esp. a pullover. —**wool·li·ness** *n.*

wool·ly bear ▶*n.* a large hairy caterpillar, esp. that of a tiger moth.

wool·y ▶*adj.* variant spelling of WOOLLY.

woosh ▶*v.*, *n.*, *interj.*, & *adv.* variant spelling of WHOOSH.

wooz·y /'wŏŏzē/ ▶*adj.* (**wooz·i·er**, **wooz·i·est**) *inf.* unsteady, dizzy, or dazed: *woozy from all the pills.* —**wooz·i·ly** /-zəlē/ *adv.* —**wooz·i·ness** *n.*

wop /wäp/ ▶*n. inf.*, *offens.* a contemptuous term for an Italian or other southern European.

word /wərd/ ▶*n.* a single distinct meaningful element of speech or writing, used with others (or sometimes alone) to form a sentence and typically shown with a space on either side when written or printed. ■ a single distinct conceptual unit of language, comprising inflected and variant forms. ■ (usu. **words**) something that someone says or writes; a remark or piece of information: *a word of warning.* ■ speech as distinct from action: *he conforms in word and deed to the values of a society that he rejects.* ■ (**a word**) even the smallest amount of something spoken or written: *don't believe a word of it.* ■ (**one's word**) a person's account of the truth, esp. when it differs from that of another person: *in court it would have been his word against mine.* ■ (**one's word**) a promise or assurance: *everything will be taken care of—you have my word.* ■ (**words**) the text or spoken part of a play, opera, or other performed piece; a script: *he had to learn his words.* ■ (**words**) angry talk: *her father would have had words with her about that.* ■ a message; news: *I was afraid to leave Washington in case there was word from the office.* ■ a command, password, or motto: *someone gave me the word to start playing.* ■ a basic unit of data in a computer, typically 16 or 32 bits long.
▶*v.* [*tr.*] choose and use particular words in order to say or write (something): *he words his request in a particularly ironic way* | [as *adj.*] (**worded**) *a strongly worded letter of protest.* —**word·age** /'wərdij/ *n.* —**word·less** *adj.* —**word·less·ly** *adv.*

▶ □ **have a word** speak briefly to someone: *I'll just have a word with him.* □ **in so many words** in the way mentioned: *I haven't told him in so many words, but he'd understand.* □ **in a word** briefly. □ **keep one's word** do what one has promised. □ **take someone at their word** interpret a person's words literally or exactly, esp. by believing them or doing as they suggest. □ **word for word** in exactly the same or, when translated, exactly equivalent words. □ **word of honor** a solemn promise. □ **word of mouth** spoken language; informal or unofficial discourse.

word·ing /'wərdiNG/ ▶*n.* the words used to express something; the way in which something is expressed: *the standard form of wording for a consent letter.*

word·play /'wərd,plā/ ▶*n.* the witty exploitation of the meanings and ambiguities of words, esp. in puns.

word proc·ess·ing ▶*n.* the production, storage, and manipulation of text on a word processor or personal computer. —**word-proc·ess** *v.*

word proc·es·sor ▶*n.* a dedicated computer or program for storing, manipulating, and formatting text entered from a keyboard and providing a printout. ■ a person who uses such a program.

word·y /'wərdē/ ▶*adj.* (**word·i·er**, **word·i·est**) using or expressed in too many words: *a wordy and repetitive account.* —**word·i·ly** /-dəlē/ *adv.* —**word·i·ness** *n.*

wore /wôr/ ▶ past of WEAR.

work /wərk/ ▶*n.* **1** activity involving mental or physical effort done in order to achieve a purpose or result: *he was tired after a day's work in the fields.* ■ (**works**) [in *comb.*] a place or premises for industrial activity, typically manufacturing: *he found a job in the ironworks.* **2** such activity as a means of earning income; employment: *I'm still looking for work.* ■ the place where one engages in such activity: *I was returning home from work on a packed subway.* ■ the period of time spent during the day engaged in such activity: *he was going to the theater after work.* **3** a task or tasks to be undertaken; something a person or thing has to do: *they made sure the work was progressing smoothly.* ■ the materials for this: *she*

frequently took work home with her. ■ (**works**) *Theol.* good or moral deeds: *the Clapham sect was concerned with works rather than with faith.* **4** something done or made: *her work hangs in all the main American collections.* ■ the result of the action of a specified person or thing: *the bombing had been the work of a German-based cell.* ■ a literary or musical composition or other piece of fine art: *a work of fiction.* ■ (**works**) all such pieces by a particular author, composer, or artist, regarded collectively: *the works of Schubert fill several feet of shelf space.* ■ a piece of embroidery, sewing, or knitting, typically made using a specified stitch or method. ■ the record of the successive calculations made in solving a mathematical problem: *show your work on a separate sheet of paper.* **5** (**works**) the operative part of a clock or other machine: *she could almost hear the tick of its works.* **6** *Physics* the exertion of force overcoming resistance or producing molecular change. **7** (**the works**) *inf.* everything needed, desired, or expected: *the heavens put on a show: sheet lightning, hailstones— the works.*

▶*v.* (*past* **worked** *or archaic* **wrought**) [*intr.*] **1** be engaged in physical or mental activity in order to achieve a purpose or result, esp. in one's job; do work: *an engineer who had been **working on** a design for a more efficient wing.* ■ be employed, typically in a specified occupation or field: *Taylor has **worked in** education for 17 years.* ■ (**work in**) (of an artist) produce articles or pictures using (a particular material or medium): *he works in clay over a very strong frame.* ■ [*tr.*] produce (an article or design) using a specified material or sewing stitch: *the castle itself is **worked in** tent stitch.* ■ [*tr.*] set to or keep at work: *Jane is working you too hard.* ■ [*tr.*] cultivate (land) or extract materials from (a mine or quarry): *contracts and leases to work the mines.* ■ [*tr.*] practice one's occupation or operate in or at (a particular place): *I worked a few clubs and so forth.* ■ make efforts to achieve something; campaign: *we spend a great deal of our time **working for** the lacto-vegetarian cause.* **2** (of a machine or system) operate or function, esp. properly or effectively: *his cell phone doesn't work unless he goes to a high point.* ■ (of a machine or a part of it) run; go through regular motions: *it's designed to go into a special "rest" state when it's not working.* ■ (esp. of a person's features) move violently or convulsively: *hair wild, mouth working furiously.* ■ [*tr.*] cause (a device or machine) to operate: *teaching customers how to work a VCR.* ■ (of a plan or method) have the desired result or effect: *the desperate ploy had worked.* ■ [*tr.*] bring about; produce as a result: *with a dash of blusher here and there, you can work miracles.* ■ [*tr.*] *inf.* arrange or contrive: *the chairman was prepared to work it for Phillip if he was interested.* ■ [*tr.*] use one's persuasive power to stir the emotions of (a person or group of people): *the born politician's art of working a crowd.* **3** [*tr.*] bring (a material or mixture) to a desired shape or consistency by hammering, kneading, or some other method: *work the mixture into a paste with your hands.* ■ bring into a specified state, esp. an emotional state: *Harold had worked himself into a minor rage.* **4** move or cause to move gradually or with difficulty into another position, typically by means of constant movement or pressure: [*tr.*] *comb from tip to root, working out the knots at the end* ■ (of joints, such as those in a wooden ship) loosen and flex under repeated stress.

▶*phrasal v.* ■ **work something in** include or incorporate something, typically in something spoken or written. □ **work something off 1** discharge a debt by working. **2** reduce or get rid of something by work or activity: *one of those gimmicks for working off aggression.* □ **work out 1** (of an equation) be capable of being solved. ■ (**work out at**) be calculated at: *the losses work out at $2.94 a share.* **2** have a good or specified result: *things don't always work out that way.* **3** engage in vigorous physical exercise or training, typically at a gym. □ **work something out 1** solve a sum or determine an amount by calculation. ■ solve or find the answer to something: *I couldn't work out whether it was a band playing or a record.* **2** plan or devise something in detail: *work out a seating plan.* □ **work someone over** *inf.* treat someone with violence; beat someone severely: *the cops had worked him over a little just for the fun of it.* □ **work through** go through a process of understanding and accepting (a painful or difficult situation): *they should be allowed to feel the pain and work through their emotions.* □ **work up to** proceed gradually toward (something more advanced or intense): *the course starts with landing technique, working up to jumps from an enclosed platform.* □ **work someone up** (often **get worked up**) gradually bring someone, esp. oneself, to a state of intense excitement, anger, or anxiety: *he got all worked up and started shouting and swearing.* □ **work something up 1** bring something gradually to a more complete or satisfactory state: *painters were accustomed to working up compositions from drawings.* **2** develop or produce by activity or effort: *despite the cold, George had already worked up a fair sweat.* ▷Old English *weorc* (noun), *wyrcan* (verb), of Germanic origin; related to Dutch *werk* and German *Werk*, from an Indo-European root shared by Greek *ergon*.

▶ □ **at work** engaged in work. ■ in action: *researchers were convinced that one infectious agent was at work.* □ **have one's work cut out** be faced with a hard or lengthy task. □ **in the works** being planned, worked on, or produced.

work·a·ble /ˈwərkəbəl/ ▶*adj.* **1** able to be worked, fashioned, or manipulated: *add more flour to make a workable dough.* **2** capable of producing the desired effect or result; practicable; feasible: *a workable peace settlement.* —**work·a·bil·i·ty** /ˌwərkəˈbilitē/ *n.* —**work·a·bly** /-blē/ *adv.*

work·a·day /ˈwərkəˌdā/ ▶*adj.* of or relating to work or one's job: *the workaday world of timecards and performance reviews.* ■ not special, unusual, or interesting in any way; ordinary: *your humble workaday PC.*

work·a·hol·ic /ˌwərkəˈhôlik; -ˈhälik/ ▶*n. inf.* a person who compulsively works hard and long hours. —**work·a·hol·ism** /ˈwərkəˌhôlizəm; -ˌhäl-/ *n.*

work·bench /ˈwərkˌbenCH/ ▶*n.* a bench at which carpentry or other practical work is done.

work·day /ˈwərkˌdā/ ▶*n.* a day on which one works. ■ the part of the day devoted or allotted to work: *8-hour workdays.*

work·er /ˈwərkər/ ▶*n.* **1** a person or animal that works, in particular: ■ a person who does a specified type of work: *a farm worker | a hard worker.* ■ an employee, esp. one who does manual or nonexecutive work. ■ (**workers**) used in Marxist or leftist contexts to refer to the working class. ■ a person who works in a specified way: *she's a good worker.* ■ *inf.* a person who works hard: *I got a reputation for being a worker.* ■ (in social insects such as bees, wasps, ants, and termites) a neuter or undeveloped female that is a member of what is usually the most numerous caste and does the basic work of the colony. **2** a creator or producer of a specified thing: *a worker of precious metals.*

work force (also **work·force**) ▶*n.* [treated as *sing.* or *pl.*] the people engaged in or available for work, either in a country or area or in a particular company or industry.

work·horse /ˈwərkˌhôrs/ ▶*n.* a horse used for work on a farm. ■ a person or machine that dependably performs hard work over a long period of time: *the aircraft was the standard workhorse of Soviet medium-haul routes.*

work·house /ˈwərkˌhous/ ▶*n.* **1** *hist.* (in the UK) a public institution in which the destitute of a parish received board and lodging in return for work. **2** a prison in which petty offenders are expected to work.

work·ing /ˈwərkiNG/ ▶*adj.* **1** having paid employment: *the size of the working population.* ■ engaged in manual labor: *sufficient protection for the working man.* ■ relating to, suitable for, or for the purpose of work: *working conditions.* ■ (of a meal) during which business is discussed: *a working lunch.* ■ (of an animal) used in farming, hunting, or for guard duties; not kept as a pet or for show. ■ (of something possessed) sufficient to work with: *they have a working knowledge of contract law.* ■ (of a theory, definition, or title) used as the basis for work or argument and likely to be developed, adapted, or improved later: *the working hypothesis is tested and refined through discussion.* **2** functioning or able to function: *the mill still has a working waterwheel.* ■ (of parts of a machine) moving and causing a machine to operate: *the working parts of a digital watch.* ■ (of the face or features) moving convulsively: *working lips.*

▶*n.* **1** the action of doing work. ■ (usu. **workings**) a mine or a part of a mine from which minerals are being extracted. **2** (**workings**) the way in which a machine, organization, or system operates: *the workings of government.*

work·ing class ▶*n.* [treated as *sing.* or *pl.*] the social group consisting of people who are employed for wages, esp. in manual or industrial work: *the housing needs of the working classes.*

▶*adj.* (**working-class**) of, relating to, or characteristic of people belonging to such a group: *a working-class community.*

work·load /ˈwərkˌlōd/ ▶*n.* the amount of work to be done by someone or something: *he had been given three deputies to ease his workload.*

work·man /ˈwərkmən/ ▶*n.* (*pl.* **-men**) a man employed to do manual labor. ■ a person with specified skill in a job or craft: *you check it through, like all good workmen do.*

work·man·like /ˈwərkmənˌlīk/ ▶*adj.* showing efficient competence: *a steady, workmanlike approach.*

work·man·ship /ˈwərkmənˌSHip/ ▶*n.* the degree of skill with which a product is made or a job done: *poor workmanship.*

work of art ▶*n.* a creative product with strong imaginative or aesthetic appeal.

work·out /ˈwərkˌout/ ▶*n.* a session of vigorous physical exercise or training.

work·piece /ˈwərkˌpēs/ ▶*n.* an object being worked on with a tool or machine.

work·place /'wərk,plās/ ▸n. a place where people work, such as an office or factory.

work·sheet /'wərk,SHēt/ ▸n. **1** a paper listing questions or tasks for students. **2** a paper for recording work done or in progress. ■ Comput. a data file created and used by a spreadsheet program, which takes the form of a matrix of cells when displayed.

work·shop /'wərk,SHäp/ ▸n. **1** a room or building in which goods are manufactured or repaired. **2** a meeting at which a group of people engage in intensive discussion and activity on a particular subject or project.
▸v. [tr.] present a performance of (a dramatic work), using intensive group discussion and improvisation in order to explore aspects of the production before formal staging: the play was workshopped briefly at the Shaw Festival.

work·sta·tion /'wərk,stāSHən/ ▸n. **1** a general-purpose computer with a higher performance level than a personal computer. **2** an area where work of a particular nature is carried out, such as a specific location on a manufacturing assembly line. **3** a desk with a computer or a computer terminal and keyboard.

work-stud·y ▸adj. of or relating to a college program that enables students to work part-time while attending school.

world /wərld/ ▸n. **1** (usu. **the world**) the earth, together with all of its countries, peoples, and natural features: he was doing his bit to save the world. ■ (**the world**) all of the people, societies, and institutions on the earth: [as adj.] world affairs. ■ [as adj.] denoting one of the most important or influential people or things of its class: they had been brought up to regard France as a world power. ■ another planet like the earth: the possibility of life on other worlds. ■ the material universe or all that exists; everything. **2** a part or aspect of human life or of the natural features of the earth, in particular: ■ a region or group of countries: the English-speaking world. ■ a period of history: the ancient world. ■ a group of living things: the animal world. ■ the people, places, and activities to do with a particular thing: they were a legend in the world of British theater. ■ human and social interaction: he has almost completely withdrawn from the world. ■ (**one's world**) a person's life and activities: he felt his whole world had collapsed. ■ everything that exists outside oneself. ■ secular interests and affairs: parents are not viewed as the primary educators of their own children, either in the world or in the church.
▸ ■ **man** (or **woman**) **of the world** a person who is experienced in the ways of sophisticated society. □ **out of this world** inf. extremely enjoyable or impressive: an herb and lemon dressing that's out of this world. □ **a** (or **the**) **world of** a very great deal of: there's a world of difference between being alone and being lonely.

world-class ▸adj. (of a person, thing, or activity) of or among the best in the world.

world-fa·mous ▸adj. known throughout the world: the world-famous tenor José Carreras.

world·ly /'wərldlē/ ▸adj. (**-li·er, -li·est**) of or concerned with material values or ordinary life rather than a spiritual existence: worldly success. ■ (of a person) experienced and sophisticated. —**world·li·ness** n.
▸ □ **worldly goods** (or **possessions** or **wealth**) everything that someone owns.

World Se·ries ▸the professional championship for North American major league baseball, played at the end of the season between the champions of the American League and the National League.

world·view /'wərld,vyōō/ (also **world view**) ▸n. a particular philosophy of life or conception of the world: a Christian worldview revolves around the battle of good and evil.

World War I ▸a war (1914–18) in which the Central Powers (Germany and Austria–Hungary, joined later by Turkey and Bulgaria) were defeated by an alliance of Britain and its dominions, France, Russia, and others, joined later by Italy and the U.S.

World War II ▸a war (1939–45) in which the Axis Powers (Germany, Italy, and Japan) were defeated by an alliance eventually including the United Kingdom and its dominions, the Soviet Union, and the United States.

world-wea·ry ▸adj. feeling or indicating feelings of weariness, boredom, or cynicism as a result of long experience of life: their world-weary, cynical talk. —**world-wea·ri·ness** n.

world·wide /'wərld'wīd/ ▸adj. extending or reaching throughout the world: worldwide sales of television rights.
▸adv. throughout the world: she travels worldwide as a consultant.

World Wide Web Comput. ▸a widely used information system on the Internet that provides facilities for documents to be connected to other documents by hypertext links, enabling the user to search for information by moving from one document to another.

WORM /wərm/ ▸abbr. write-once read-many, denoting a type of computer memory device.

worm /wərm/ ▸n. **1** any of a number of creeping or burrowing invertebrate animals with long, slender, soft bodies and no limbs, including the segmented worms, the roundworms, and the flatworms. ■ short for EARTHWORM. ■ (**worms**) intestinal or other internal parasites. ■ used in names of long, slender insect larvae, esp. those in fruit or wood, e.g., **army worm, woodworm**. ■ used in names of other animals that resemble worms in some way, e.g., **slow-worm, ship-worm**. ■ a maggot supposed to eat buried corpses: food for worms. ■ Comput. a self-replicating program able to propagate itself across a network, typically having a detrimental effect. **2** inf. a weak or despicable person (used as a general term of contempt). **3** a helical device or component, in particular: ■ the threaded cylinder in a worm gear.
▸v. **1** [intr.] move with difficulty by crawling or wriggling: I wormed my way along the roadside ditch. ■ (**worm one's way into**) insinuate one's way into: the educated dealers may later worm their way into stockbroking. ■ [tr.] move (something) into a confined space by wriggling it: I wormed my right hand between my body and the earth. ■ (**worm something out of**) obtain information from (someone) by cunning persistence: I did manage to worm a few details out of him. **2** [tr.] treat (an animal) with a preparation designed to expel parasitic worms.

worm gear ▸n. a mechanical arrangement consisting of a toothed wheel worked by a short revolving cylinder (worm) bearing a screw thread.

worm gear

worm·wood /'wərm,wŏŏd/ ▸n. **1** a woody shrub (genus Artemisia) of the daisy family with a bitter aromatic taste, used, esp. formerly, as an ingredient of vermouth and absinthe and in medicine. **2** fig. a state or source of bitterness or grief.

worm·y /'wərmē/ ▸adj. (**worm·i·er, worm·i·est**) **1** (of organic tissue) infested with or eaten into by worms: the prisoners received wormy vegetables. ■ (of wood or a wooden object) full of holes made by woodworm. **2** inf. (of a person) weak, abject, or revolting. —**worm·i·ness** n.

worn /wôrn/ ▸ past participle of WEAR¹.
▸adj. damaged and shabby as a result of much use: a worn, frayed denim jacket. ■ very tired: his face looked worn and old.

worn out ▸adj. **1** (of a person or animal) extremely tired; exhausted: you look worn out. **2** damaged or shabby to the point of being no longer usable: worn-out shoes. ■ (of an idea, method, or system) used so often or existing for so long as to be considered valueless: he portrayed the Democrats as the party of worn-out ideas.

wor·ri·some /'wərē,səm/ ▸adj. causing anxiety or concern: a worrisome problem. —**wor·ri·some·ly** adv.

wor·ry /'wərē/ ▸v. (**-ries, -ried**) **1** [intr.] give way to anxiety or unease; allow one's mind to dwell on difficulty or troubles: he worried about his soldier sons in the war. ■ [tr.] cause to feel anxiety or concern: there was no need to worry her | [as adj.] (**worrying**) the level of inflation has improved but remains worrying. ■ [as adj.] (**worried**) expressing anxiety: there was a worried frown on his face. ■ [tr.] cause annoyance to: the noise never really stops, but it doesn't worry me. **2** [tr.] (of a dog or other carnivorous animal) tear at, gnaw on, or drag around with the teeth: I found my dog contentedly worrying a bone. ■ (of a dog) chase and attack (livestock, esp. sheep). ■ [intr.] (**worry at**) pull at or fiddle with repeatedly: he began to worry at the knot in the cord.
▸n. (pl. **-ries**) a state of anxiety and uncertainty over actual or potential problems: a constant source of worry. ■ a source of anxiety: the idea is to secure peace of mind for people whose greatest worry is fear of attack. —**wor·ried·ly** adv. —**wor·ri·er** n. —**wor·ry·ing·ly** adv. trade deficits are worryingly large.

wor·ry·wart /'wərē,wôrt/ ▸n. inf. a person who tends to dwell unduly on difficulty or troubles.

worse /wərs/ ▸adj. **1** comparative of BAD, ILL. **2** of poorer quality or a lower standard; less good or desirable: the accommodations were awful, and the food was worse. ■ more serious or severe: the movement made the pain worse. ■ more reprehensible or evil: it is worse to intend harm than to

be indifferent. ■ in a less satisfactory or pleasant condition; more ill or unhappy: *he felt worse, and groped his way back to bed.*
▸*adv.* **1** comparative of **BADLY**, **ILL**. **2** less well or skillfully: *the more famous I became the worse I painted.* ■ more seriously or severely: *the others had been drunk too, worse than herself.* ■ used to introduce a statement of circumstances felt by the speaker to be more serious or undesirable than others already mentioned: *The system will find it hard to sort out property disputes. Even worse, the law will discourage foreign investment.*
▸*n.* a more serious or unpleasant event or circumstance: *the small department was already stretched to the limit, but worse was to follow.* ■ (**the worse**) a less good, favorable, or pleasant condition: *the weather changed for the worse.*

wors·en /ˈwərsən/ ▸*v.* make or become worse: [*intr.*] *her condition worsened on the flight* | [*tr.*] *arguing actually worsens the problem.*

wor·ship /ˈwərSHəp/ ▸*n.* the feeling or expression of reverence and adoration for a deity: *the worship of God.* ■ the acts or rites that make up a formal expression of reverence for a deity; a religious ceremony or ceremonies: *the church was opened for public worship.* ■ adoration or devotion comparable to religious homage, shown toward a person or principle.
▸*v.* (**-shiped**, **-ship·ing**; also **-shipped**, **-ship·ping**) [*tr.*] show reverence and adoration for (a deity); honor with religious rites: *the Maya built jungle pyramids to worship their gods.* ■ treat (someone or something) with the reverence and adoration appropriate to a deity: *she adores her sons and they worship her.* ■ [*intr.*] take part in a religious ceremony: *he went to the cathedral because he chose to worship in a spiritually inspiring building.*
—**wor·ship·er** (also **wor·ship·per**) *n.*

worst /wərst/ ▸*adj.* superlative of **BAD**, **ILL**. ■ of the poorest quality or the lowest standard: *the speech was the worst he had ever made.* ■ least pleasant, desirable, or tolerable: *they were to stay in the worst conditions imaginable.* ■ most severe, serious, or dangerous: *at least 32 people died in Australia's worst bus accident.* ■ least suitable or advantageous: *the worst time to take out a bond is when rates are low but rise suddenly.*
▸*adv.* **1** superlative of **BADLY**, **ILL**. **2** most severely or seriously: *manufacturing and mining are the industries worst affected by falling employment.* ■ least well, skillfully, or pleasingly: *he was voted the worst dressed celebrity.* ■ used to introduce the fact or circumstance that the speaker considers most serious or unpleasant: *her mother had rejected her, and worst of all, her father turned out to be a cheat and a deceiver.*
▸*n.* the most serious or unpleasant thing that could happen: *when I saw the ambulance outside her front door, I began to **fear the worst**.* ■ the most serious, dangerous, or unpleasant part or stage of something: *there are signs that the recession is past its worst.*
▸*v.* [*tr.*] (usu. **be worsted**) get the better of; defeat: *this was not the time for a deep discussion—she was tired and she would be worsted.*
▸ □ **if worst comes to worst** if the most serious or difficult circumstances arise. □ **in the worst way** *inf.* very much: *he wants to win in the worst way.*

wort /wərt; wôrt/ ▸*n.* **1** [in comb.] used in names of plants and herbs, esp. those used, esp. formerly, as food or medicinally, e.g., **butterwort**, **woundwort**. **2** the sweet infusion of ground malt or other grain before fermentation, used to produce beer and distilled malt liquors.

worth /wərTH/ ▸*adj.* equivalent in value to the sum or item specified: *jewelry worth $450 was taken.* ■ sufficiently good, important, or interesting to justify a specified action; deserving to be treated or regarded in the way specified: *the museums in the district are well worth a visit.* ■ used to suggest that the specified course of action may be advisable: *a meat and potato dish that's worth checking out.* ■ having income or property amounting to a specified sum: *she is worth $10 million.*
▸*n.* the value equivalent to that of someone or something under consideration; the level at which someone or something deserves to be valued or rated: *they had to listen to every piece of gossip and judge its worth.* ■ an amount of a commodity equivalent to a specified sum of money: *he admitted stealing 10,000 dollars' worth of computer systems.* ■ the amount that could be achieved or produced in a specified time: *the companies have debts greater than two years' worth of their sales.* ■ high value or merit: *he is noble and gains his position by showing his inner worth.*

worth·less /ˈwərTHlis/ ▸*adj.* having no real value or use: *that promise is worthless.* ■ (of a person) having no good qualities; deserving contempt: *Joan had been deserted by a worthless husband.* —**worth·less·ly** *adv.* —**worth·less·ness** *n.*

worth·while /ˈwərTH(h)wīl/ ▸*adj.* worth the time, money, or effort spent; of value or importance: *extra lighting would make a worthwhile contribution to road safety.* —**worth·while·ness** *n.*

wor·thy /ˈwərTHē/ ▸*adj.* (**-thi·er**, **-thi·est**) deserving effort, attention, or respect: *generous donations to worthy causes.* ■ having or showing the

qualities or abilities that merit recognition in a specified way: *issues worthy of further consideration.* ■ good enough; suitable: *no composer was considered worthy of the name until he had written an opera.*
▸*n.* (*pl.* **-thies**) *often derog.* or *humorous* a person notable or important in a particular sphere: *schools governed by local worthies.* —**wor·thi·ly** /-THəlē/ *adv.* —**wor·thi·ness** *n.*

would /wŏŏd/ ▸*modal verb* (*3rd sing. present* **would**) **1** past of **WILL**¹, in various senses: *he said he would be away for a couple of days* | *he wanted out, but she wouldn't leave* | *the windows would not close.* **2** (expressing the conditional mood) indicating the consequence of an imagined event or situation: *he would lose his job if he were identified.* ■ (**I would**) used to give advice: *I wouldn't drink that if I were you.* **3** expressing a desire or inclination: *I would love to work in Prague.* **4** expressing a polite request: *would you pour the wine, please?* ■ expressing willingness or consent: *who would live here?* **5** expressing a conjecture, opinion, or hope: *I would imagine that they'll want to keep it.* **6** used to make a comment about behavior that is typical: *every night we would hear the boy crying.* **7** *poetic/lit.* expressing a wish or regret: *would that he had lived to finish it.*

would-be ▸*adj. often derog.* desiring or aspiring to be a specified type of person: *a would-be actress who dresses up as Marilyn Monroe.*

would·n't /ˈwŏŏdnt/ ▸*contr.* of would not.

wound¹ /wŏŏnd/ ▸*n.* an injury to living tissue caused by a cut, blow, or other impact, typically one in which the skin is cut or broken. ■ an injury to a person's feelings or reputation: *the new crisis has opened old wounds.*
▸*v.* [*tr.*] (often **be wounded**) inflict an injury on (someone): *the sergeant was seriously wounded.* ■ injure (a person's feelings): *you really wounded his pride when you turned him down.* —**wound·ing·ly** *adv.* —**wound·less** *adj.*

wound² /wound/ ▸ alternate past and past participle of **WIND**¹.

wove /wōv/ ▸ past of **WEAVE**¹.

wo·ven /ˈwōvən/ ▸ past participle of **WEAVE**¹.
▸*adj.* (of fabric) formed by interlacing long threads passing in one direction with others at a right angle to them: *women in striped, woven shawls.* ■ (of basketwork or a wreath) made by interlacing items such as cane, stems, flowers, or leaves. ■ (of a complex story or pattern) made in a specified way from a number of interconnected elements: *a neatly woven tale of intrigue in academia.*

wove pa·per ▸*n.* paper made on a wire-gauze mesh so as to have a uniform unlined surface.

wow¹ /wou/ *inf.* ▸*interj.* expressing astonishment or admiration: *"Wow!" he cried enthusiastically.*
▸*n.* a sensational success: *your play's a wow.*
▸*v.* [*tr.*] impress and excite (someone) greatly: *they wowed audiences on their recent British tour.*

wow² ▸*n.* slow pitch fluctuation in sound reproduction, perceptible in long notes. Compare with **FLUTTER** (sense 1).

WP ▸*abbr.* word processing or word processor.

wpm ▸*abbr.* words per minute (used after a number to indicate typing speed).

wrack¹ ▸*v.* variant spelling of **RACK**¹ (sense 1).

wrack² /rak/ ▸*n.* any of a number of coarse brown seaweeds of the genera *Fucus*, *Ascophyllum*, and *Pelvetia*, class Phaeophyceae, that grow on the shoreline and frequently form distinct bands that correspond to high- and low-water marks. Many have air bladders for buoyancy.

wrack³ ▸*n.* variant spelling of **RACK**⁵.

wraith /rāTH/ ▸*n.* a ghost or ghostlike image of someone, esp. one seen shortly before or after their death. ■ used in similes and metaphors to describe a pale, thin, or insubstantial person or thing: *heart attacks had reduced his mother to a wraith.* ■ *poetic/lit.* a wisp or faint trace of something: *a sea breeze was sending a gray wraith of smoke up the slopes.* —**wraith·like** /-ˌlīk/ *adj.*

wran·gle /ˈraNGgəl/ ▸*n.* a dispute or argument, typically one that is long and complicated: *an insurance wrangle is holding up compensation payments.*
▸*v.* [*intr.*] have such a dispute or argument: [as *n.*] (**wrangling**) *weeks of political wrangling.*

wran·gler /ˈraNGglər/ ▸*n.* **1** a person in charge of horses or other livestock on a ranch. ■ a person who trains and takes care of the animals used in a movie. **2** a person engaging in a lengthy and complicated quarrel or dispute.

wrap /rap/ ▸*v.* (**wrapped**, **wrap·ping**) **1** [*tr.*] cover or enclose (someone or something) in paper or soft material: *he wrapped the Christmas presents.* ■ clasp; embrace: *she wrapped him in her arms.* ■ cover (the body) with a body wrap. ■ cover (the fingernails) with a nail wrap. **2** [tr.] (**wrap something around**) arrange paper or soft material around (someone or something), typically as a covering or for warmth or protection: *wrap the bandage around the injured limb.* ■ place an arm, finger, or leg around (someone or something): *he wrapped an arm around her waist.* ■ *inf.* crash a vehicle into (a stationary object): *Richard wrapped his car around a telephone pole.* **3** [tr.] *Comput.* cause (a word or unit of text) to be carried over to a new line automatically as the margin is reached, or to fit around embedded features such as pictures. ■ [intr.] (of a word or unit or text) be carried over in such a way. **4** [intr.] *inf.* finish filming or recording: *we wrapped on schedule three days later.*

▶*phrasal v.* □ **wrap something up** complete or conclude a discussion or agreement: *they hope to wrap up negotiations within sixty days.* ■ win a game or competition: *Australia wrapped up the series 4–0.*

▶*n.* **1** a loose outer garment or piece of material. ■ [as *adj.*] denoting a garment having one part overlapping another; wraparound: *a wrap skirt.* ■ paper or soft material used for wrapping: *plastic food wrap.* ■ (usu. **wraps**) *fig.* a veil of secrecy maintained about something, esp. a new project: *details of the police operation are being kept* **under wraps**. **2** *inf.* the end of a session of filming or recording: *right, it's a wrap.* **3** a sandwich in which the filling is rolled in a soft tortilla. **4** short for BODY WRAP. ■ short for NAIL WRAP.

▶ □ **be wrapped up in** be so engrossed or absorbed in (something) that one does not notice other people or things.

wrap·a·round /ˈrapəˌround/ ▶*adj.* curving or extending around at the edges or sides: *wraparound sunglasses.* ■ (of a garment) having one part overlapping another and fastened loosely: *a wraparound skirt.*
▶*n.* **1** a wraparound garment. **2** *Comput.* a facility by which a linear sequence of memory locations or screen positions is treated as a continuous circular series.

wrap·a·round mort·gage ▶*n.* a second mortgage held by a lender who collects payments on it and the first mortgage from the borrower. The lender makes the payments to the original mortgage holder.

wrap·per /ˈrapər/ ▶*n.* a piece of paper, plastic, or foil covering and protecting something sold. ■ a cover enclosing a newspaper or magazine for mailing.

wrap·per ap·pli·ca·tion ▶*n.* a computer program that works only with another fully developed program, which it enhances in some way: *we have created a viewer that is a simple wrapper application for the underlying multimedia system.*

wrap·ping pa·per ▶*n.* strong or decorative paper for wrapping parcels or presents.

wrasse /ras/ ▶*n.* (*pl.* same or **wrass·es**) a marine fish (family Labridae) with thick lips and strong teeth, typically brightly colored with marked differences between the male and female.

wrath /raтн/ ▶*n.* extreme anger (chiefly used for humorous or rhetorical effect): *he hid his pipe for fear of incurring his father's wrath.*

wrath·ful /ˈraтнfəl/ ▶*adj.* *poetic/lit.* full of or characterized by intense anger: *natural calamities seemed to be the work of a wrathful deity.* —**wrath·ful·ly** *adv.* —**wrath·ful·ness** *n.*

wreak /rēk/ ▶*v.* [tr.] cause (a large amount of damage or harm): *torrential rainstorms* **wreaked havoc** *yesterday.* ■ inflict (vengeance): *he was determined to* **wreak** *his revenge* **on** *the girl who had rejected him.* —**wreak·er** *n.*

wreath /rēтн/ ▶*n.* (*pl.* **wreaths** /rēтнz; rēтнs/) an arrangement of flowers, leaves, or stems fastened in a ring and used for decoration or for laying on a grave. ■ a carved representation of such a wreath. ■ a similar ring made of or resembling soft, twisted material: *a gold wreath for the door.* ■ a curl or ring of smoke or cloud: *wreaths of mist swirled up into the cold air.*

wreathe /rēтн/ ▶*v.* [tr.] (usu. **be wreathed**) cover, surround, or encircle (something): *he sits wreathed in smoke.* ■ [tr.] *poetic/lit.* twist or entwine (something flexible) around or over something: *shall I once more wreathe my arms about Antonio's neck?* ■ [intr.] (esp. of smoke) move with a curling motion: *he watched the smoke wreathe into the night air.*

wreck /rek/ ▶*n.* the destruction of a ship at sea; a shipwreck: *the survivors of the wreck.* ■ a ship destroyed in such a way: *the salvaging of treasure from wrecks.* ■ something, esp. a vehicle or building, that has been badly damaged or destroyed: *the plane was reduced to a smoldering wreck.* ■ the disorganized remains of something that has suffered damage or destruction. ■ a road or rail crash: *a train wreck.* ■ a person whose physical or mental health or strength has failed: *the scandal left the family emotional wrecks.*

▶*v.* [tr.] (usu. **be wrecked**) cause the destruction of (a ship) by sinking or breaking up: *he was drowned when his ship was wrecked.* ■ involve (someone) in such a wreck: *sailors who had the misfortune to be wrecked on these coasts.* ■ destroy or severely damage (a structure or vehicle): *the blast*

wrecked more than 100 houses. ■ spoil completely: *an eye injury wrecked his chances of a professional career.* ■ [intr.] [usu. as *n.*] (**wrecking**) engage in breaking up badly damaged vehicles, demolishing old buildings, or similar activities to obtain usable spares or scrap.

wreck·age /ˈrekij/ ▶*n.* the remains of something that has been badly damaged or destroyed: *firemen had to cut him free from the wreckage of the car.*

wreck·er /ˈrekər/ ▶*n.* **1** a person or thing that wrecks, damages, or destroys something: [in *comb.*] *this bug is a game-wrecker.* ■ a person who breaks up damaged vehicles, demolishes old buildings, salvages wrecked ships, etc., to obtain usable spares or scrap. **2** a tow truck.

wren /ren/ ▶*n.* **1** a small short-winged songbird (family Troglodytidae) found chiefly in the New World. **2** any of a number of small songbirds that resemble the true wrens in size or appearance.

wrench /rencH/ ▶*n.* **1** a sudden violent twist or pull: *with a wrench Tony wriggled free.* ■ *fig.* an act of leaving someone or something that causes sadness or distress: *it will be a real wrench to leave after eight years.* **2** a tool used for gripping and turning nuts, bolts, pipes, etc. **3** *Mechanics* a combination of a couple with a force along its axis.

▶*v.* [tr.] pull or twist (someone or something) suddenly and violently: *Casey grabbed the gun and wrenched it upward from my hand* | [intr.] *fig. the betrayal wrenched at her heart.* ■ injure (a part of the body) as a result of a sudden twisting movement: *she slipped and wrenched her ankle.* ■ turn (something, esp. a nut or bolt) with a wrench.

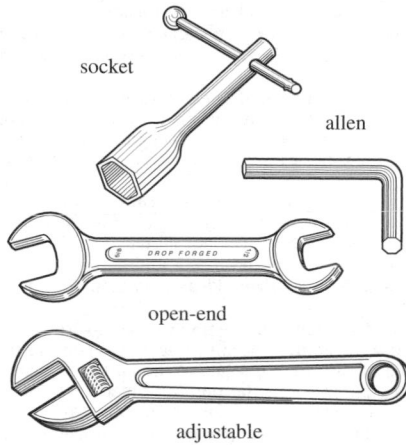

socket

allen

open-end

adjustable

wrenches

wrest /rest/ ▶*v.* [tr.] forcibly pull (something) from a person's grasp: *Leila tried to wrest her arm from his hold.* ■ take (something, esp. power or control) from someone or something else after considerable effort or difficulty: *they wanted to allow people to wrest control of their lives from impersonal bureaucracies.*

wres·tle /ˈresəl/ ▶*v.* [intr.] take part in a fight, either as a sport or in earnest, that involves grappling with one's opponent and trying to throw or force them to the ground: *as the policeman* **wrestled with** *the gunman a shot rang out.* ■ [tr.] force (someone) into a particular position or place by fighting in such a way: *the security guards wrestled them to the ground.* ■ *fig.* struggle with a difficulty or problem: *for over a year David* **wrestled with** *a guilty conscience.* ■ [tr.] move or manipulate (something) in a specified way with difficulty and some physical effort: *she wrestled the keys out of the ignition.*

▶*n.* a wrestling bout or contest. ■ a hard struggle: *a lifelong wrestle with depression.* ▷Old English, frequentative of *wrǣstan* 'wrest.' —**wres·tler** *n.* —**wres·tling** *n.*

wretch /recH/ ▶*n.* an unfortunate or unhappy person: *can the poor wretch's corpse tell us anything?* ■ *inf.* a despicable or contemptible person: *ungrateful wretches.*

wretch·ed /ˈrecHid/ ▶*adj.* (**-ed·er, -ed·est**) (of a person) in a very unhappy or unfortunate state: *I felt so wretched because I thought I might never see you again.* ■ of poor quality; very bad: *the wretched conditions of the slums.* ■ used to express anger or annoyance: *she disliked the wretched* *man intensely.* **—wretch·ed·ly** *adv. a wretchedly poor country.* **—wretch·ed·ness** *n.*

wrig·gle /'rigəl/ ▶v. [*intr.*] twist and turn with quick writhing movements. ■ [*tr.*] cause to move in such a way: *she wriggled her toes.* ■ [*intr.*] move in a particular direction with wriggling movements: *Susie wriggled out of her clothes.* ■ (**wriggle out of**) avoid (something), esp. by devious means: *don't try and wriggle out of your contract.*
▶n. a wriggling movement: *she gave an impatient little wriggle.* **—wrig·gler** *n.* **—wrig·gly** /'rig(ə)lē/ *adj.*

wright /rīt/ ▶n. *archaic* a maker or builder.

wring /riNG/ ▶v. (*past* **wrung** /rəNG/) [*tr.*] squeeze and twist (something) to force liquid from it: *she* **wrung** *the cloth* **out** *in the sink.* ■ [*tr.*] extract (liquid) by squeezing and twisting something: *I wrung out the excess water.* ■ break (an animal's neck) by twisting it forcibly. ■ squeeze (someone's hand) tightly, esp. with sincere emotion. ■ [*tr.*] obtain (something) with difficulty or effort: *few concessions were wrung from the government.* ■ cause pain or distress to: *the letter must have wrung her heart.*
▶n. an act of squeezing or twisting something.
▶ □ **wring one's hands** clasp and twist one's hands together as a gesture of great distress, esp. when one can't change the situation.

wring·er /'riNGər/ ▶n. a device for wringing water from wet clothes, mops, or other objects.
▶ □ **put someone through the wringer** *inf.* subject someone to a very stressful experience, esp. a severe interrogation.

wring·ing /'riNGiNG/ (also **wringing wet**) ▶adj. so wet that water or other liquid can be wrung out: *I was wringing in sweat* | *their clothes were wringing wet.*

wrin·kle /'riNGkəl/ ▶n. **1** a slight line or fold in something, esp. fabric or the skin of the face. ■ *inf.* a minor difficulty; a snag: *the organizers have the wrinkles pretty well ironed out.* **2** *inf.* a clever innovation, or useful piece of information or advice: *learning the wrinkles from someone more experienced saves time.*
▶v. [*tr.*] (often as *adj.*) (**wrinkled**) make or cause lines or folds in (something, esp. fabric or the skin): *Dotty's wrinkled skirt.* ■ grimace and cause wrinkles on (a part of the face): *he sniffed and wrinkled his nose.* ■ [*intr.*] form or become marked with lines or folds: *her brow wrinkled.*

wrin·kly /'riNGk(ə)lē/ ▶adj. (**-kli·er, -kli·est**) having many lines or folds: *he's old and wrinkly.*

wrist /rist/ ▶n. **1** the joint connecting the hand with the forearm. See also **CARPUS**. ■ the equivalent joint (the carpal joint) in the foreleg of a quadruped or the wing of a bird. ■ the part of a garment covering the wrist; a cuff. **2** (also **wrist pin**) (in a machine) a stud projecting from a crank as an attachment for a connecting rod.

wrist·band /'rist,band/ ▶n. a strip of material worn around the wrist, in particular: ■ a small strap or bracelet, esp. one used for identification or as a fashion item. ■ a strip of absorbent material worn during sports or strenuous exercise to soak up sweat. ■ the cuff of a shirt or blouse.

wrist·watch /'rist,wäCH/ ▶n. a watch worn on a strap around the wrist.

writ¹ /rit/ ▶n. a form of written command in the name of a court or other legal authority to act, or abstain from acting, in some way. ■ (**one's writ**) one's power to enforce compliance or submission; one's authority: *you have business here which is out of my writ and competence.*

writ² ▶v. *archaic* past participle of **WRITE**.
▶ □ **writ large** clear and obvious: *the unspoken question writ large upon Rose's face.* ■ in a stark or exaggerated form: *bribing people by way of tax allowances is the paternalistic state writ large.*

write /rīt/ ▶v. (*past* **wrote** /rōt/; *past part.* **writ·ten** /'ritn/) [*tr.*] **1** mark (letters, words, or other symbols) on a surface, typically paper, with a pen, pencil, or similar implement: *he wrote his name on the paper* | [*intr.*] *he wrote very neatly in blue ink.* ■ [*intr.*] have the ability to mark coherent letters or words in this way: *he couldn't read or write.* ■ fill out or complete (a sheet, check, or similar) in this way: *he had to write a check for $800.* ■ [*intr.*] write in a cursive hand, as opposed to printing individual letters. **2** compose, write, and send (a letter) to someone: *I wrote him a short letter* | [*intr.*] *he wrote almost every day.* ■ write and send a letter to (someone): *Mother wrote me and told me about poor Simon's death.* ■ [*tr.*] (**write in**) write to an organization, esp. a broadcasting station, with a question, suggestion, or opinion: *write in with your query.* **3** compose (a text or work) for written or printed reproduction or publication; put into literary form and set down in writing: *I didn't know you wrote poetry* | [*intr.*] *he wrote under a pseudonym: he has written a song specifically for her.* ■ (**write someone into/out of**) add or remove a character to or from (a long-running story or series). **4** [*tr.*]

Comput. enter (data) into a specified storage medium or location in store. **5** underwrite (an insurance policy).
▶*phrasal v.* □ **write something off 1** (**write someone/something off**) dismiss someone or something as insignificant: *the boy had been written off as a nonachiever.* **2** cancel the record of a bad debt; acknowledge the loss of or failure to recover an asset: *he urged the banks to write off debt owed by poorer countries.* **—writ·a·ble** *adj.*

write-back ▶n. *Finance* the process of restoring to profit a provision for bad or doubtful debts previously made against profits and no longer required.

writ·er /'rītər/ ▶n. a person who has written a particular text: *the writer of the letter.* ■ a person who writes books, stories, or articles as a job or regular occupation: *the distinguished travel writer Freya Stark.* ■ [with *adj.*] a person who writes in a specified way: *Dickens was a prolific writer.* ■ a composer of musical works: *a writer of military music.* ■ *Comput.* a device that writes data to a storage medium. ■ *Stock Market* a broker who makes an option available for purchase or sells options. ■ [with *adj.*] a person who has a specified kind of handwriting: *neat writers.* ▷Old English *wrītan* 'score, form (letters) by carving, write,' of Germanic origin.
▶ □ **writer's block** the condition of being unable to think of what to write or how to proceed with writing. □ **writer's cramp** pain or stiffness in the hand caused by excessive writing.

write-up ▶n. **1** a full written account. ■ a newspaper or magazine article giving the author's opinion of a recent event, performance, or product. **2** *Finance* an increase in the estimated or nominal value of an asset.

writhe /rīTH/ ▶v. [*intr.*] make continual twisting, squirming movements or contortions of the body: *he writhed in agony on the ground.* ■ [*tr.*] cause to move in such a way: *a snake writhing its body in a sinuous movement.* ■ (**writhe in/with/at**) respond with great emotional or physical discomfort to (a violent or unpleasant feeling or thought): *she bit her lip, writhing in suppressed fury.*

writ·ing /'rītiNG/ ▶n. **1** the activity or skill of marking coherent words on paper and composing text: *parents want schools to concentrate on reading, writing, and arithmetic.* ■ the activity or occupation of composing text for publication: *she made a decent living from writing.* **2** written work, esp. with regard to its style or quality: *the writing is straightforward and accessible.* ■ (**writings**) books, stories, articles, or other written works: *he was introduced to the writings of Gertrude Stein.* **3** a sequence of letters, words, or symbols marked on paper or some other surface: *a leather product with gold writing on it.* ■ handwriting: *his writing looked crabbed.*
▶ □ **the writing** (or **handwriting**) **is on the wall** see **HANDWRITING**.

writ·ten /'ritn/ ▶ past participle of **WRITE**.

wrong /rôNG/ ▶adj. **1** not correct or true: *that is the wrong answer.* ■ mistaken: *I was* **wrong** *about him being on the yacht that evening.* ■ unsuitable or undesirable: *they asked all the wrong questions.* ■ in a bad or abnormal condition; amiss: *something was* **wrong with** *the pump.* **2** unjust, dishonest, or immoral: *they were* **wrong to** *take the law into their own hands.*
▶*adv.* in an unsuitable or undesirable manner or direction: *what am I doing wrong?* ■ with an incorrect result: *she guessed wrong.*
▶n. an unjust, dishonest, or immoral action: *I have done you a great wrong.* ■ *Law* a breach, by commission or omission, of one's legal duty. ■ *Law* an invasion of right to the damage or prejudice of another.
▶v. [*tr.*] act unjustly or dishonestly toward (someone): *please forgive me these things and the people I have wronged.* ■ mistakenly attribute bad motives to; misrepresent: *perhaps I wrong him.* **—wrong·er** *n.* **—wrong·ly** *adv.* **—wrong·ness** *n.*

wrong·do·ing /'rôNG,dōōiNG/ ▶n. illegal or dishonest behavior: *the head of the bank has denied any wrongdoing.* **—wrong·do·er** *n.*

wrong·ful /'rôNGfəl/ ▶adj. (of an act) not fair, just, or legal: *he is suing the police for wrongful arrest.* **—wrong·ful·ly** *adv.* **—wrong·ful·ness** *n.*

wrong·ful death ▶adj. denoting a civil action in which damages are sought against a party for causing a death, typically when criminal action has failed or is not attempted: *a wrongful death lawsuit.*

wrong·head·ed /'rôNG,hedid/ ▶adj. having or showing bad judgment; misguided: *this approach is both wrongheaded and naive.* **—wrong·head·ed·ly** *adv.* **—wrong·head·ed·ness** *n.*

wrote /rōt/ ▶ past tense of **WRITE**.

wrought i·ron ▶n. a tough, malleable form of iron suitable for forging or rolling rather than casting.

wrung /rəNG/ ▶ past and past participle of **WRING**.

wry /rī/ ▶adj. (**wry·er, wry·est** or **wri·er, wri·est**) **1** using or expressing dry, esp. mocking, humor: *a wry smile* | *wry comments.* **2** (of a person's face or features) twisted into an expression of disgust, disappointment, or annoyance. ■ *archaic* (of the neck or features) distorted or turned to one side: *a remedy for wry necks.* ▷early 16th cent. (in the sense 'contorted'): from Old English *wrīgian* 'tend, incline,' in Middle English 'deviate, swerve, contort.' —**wry·ly** *adv.* —**wry·ness** *n.*

WSW ▶*abbr.* west-southwest.

wt ▶*abbr.* weight.

WTO ▶*abbr.* World Trade Organization.

WWW ▶*abbr.* World Wide Web.

Wy·an·dot /ˈwīənˌdät/ (also **Wy·an·dotte**) ▶*n.* **1** a member of an American Indian community formed by Huron-speaking peoples, originally in Ontario, now living mainly in Oklahoma and Quebec. **2** the Iroquoian language of this people. **3** (usu. **Wyandotte**) a domestic chicken of a medium-sized breed.

▶*adj.* of or relating to the Wyandot people or their language. ▷mid 18th cent.: from French *Ouendat*, from Huron *Wendat*.

wyn /win/ ▶*n.* variant spelling of WEN[2].

WYSIWYG /ˈwizēˌwig/ (also **wysiwyg**) ▶*adj.* *Comput.* denoting the display of text on screen that portrays an accurate rendition of the printed page. ▷1980s: acronym from *what you see is what you get.*

Xx

X[1] /eks/ (also **x**) ▶*n.* (*pl.* **Xs** or **X's**) **1** the twenty-fourth letter of the alphabet. ■ denoting the next after W in a set of items, categories, etc. ■ denoting an unknown or unspecified person or thing: *there is nothing in the data to tell us whether X causes Y.* ■ (**x**) (used in describing play in bridge) denoting an unspecified card other than an honor. ■ (usu. *x*) the first unknown quantity in an algebraic expression, usually the independent variable. ■ (usu. *x*) denoting the principal or horizontal axis in a system of coordinates: [in *comb.*] *the x-axis.* **2** a cross-shaped written symbol, in particular: ■ used to indicate a position on a map or diagram. ■ used to indicate a mistake or incorrect answer. ■ used in a letter or message to symbolize a kiss. ■ used to indicate one's vote on a paper ballot. ■ used in place of the signature of a person who cannot write. **3** a shape like that of a letter X: *two wires in the form of an X* | [in *comb.*] *an X-shaped cross.* **4** the Roman numeral for ten.
▶*v.* (**X's, X'd, X'ing**) [*tr.*] mark or make a sign with an X. ■ overwrite or obliterate with an X or series of X's. ■ make void or annul; invalidate: *we're all X-ing things out of our curricula.*

X[2] ▶*symb.* **1** a rating assigned to movies classified as suitable for adults only. Replaced in 1990 by **NC-17**. **2** (in systematic names of organisms) hybrid.

X chro·mo·some ▶*n. Genetics* (in humans and other mammals) a sex chromosome, two of which are normally present in female cells (designated XX) and only one in male cells (designated XY). Compare with **Y** CHROMOSOME.

Xe ▶*symb.* the chemical element xenon.

xen·o·lith /ˈzenəˌliTH; ˈzēnə-/ ▶*n. Geol.* a piece of rock within an igneous rock that is not derived from the original magma but has been introduced from elsewhere, esp. the surrounding country rock.

xe·non /ˈzēˌnän; ˈzenˌän/ ▶*n.* the chemical element of atomic number 54, a member of the noble gas series. (Symbol: **Xe**) ▷late 19th cent.: from Greek, neuter of *xenos* 'strange.'

xen·o·pho·bi·a /ˌzenəˈfōbēə; ˌzēnə-/ ▶*n.* intense or irrational dislike or fear of people from other countries: *racism and xenophobia are steadily growing in Europe.* —**xen·o·phobe** *n.* —**xen·o·pho·bic** *adj.*

X-er /ˈeksər/ ▶*n.* another term for GEN-XER.

xe·rog·ra·phy /ziˈrägrəfē/ ▶*n.* a dry copying process in which black or colored powder adheres to parts of a surface remaining electrically charged after being exposed to light from an image of the document to be copied. —**xe·ro·graph·ic** /ˌzi(ə)rəˈgrafik/ *adj.* —**xe·ro·graph·i·cal·ly** *adv.*

xe·ro·phyte /ˈzi(ə)rəˌfīt/ ▶*n. Bot.* a plant that needs very little water. —**xe·ro·phyt·ic** /ˌzi(ə)rəˈfitik/ *adj.*

Xerox /ˈzi(ə)rˌäks/ ▶*n. trademark* a xerographic copying process. ■ a copy made using such a process. ■ a machine for copying by xerography. ▶*v.* (**xerox**) [*tr.*] copy (a document) by such a process.

Xho·sa /ˈkōsə; ˈKHō-/ ▶*n.* (*pl.* same or **-sas**) **1** a member of a South African people traditionally living in the Eastern Cape Province. They form the second largest ethnic group in South Africa after the Zulus. **2** the Nguni language of this people.
▶*adj.* of or relating to this people or their language.

XHTML ▶*abbr. Comput.* Extensible Hypertext Markup Language, an HTML system for tagging text files to achieve font, color, graphic, and hyperlink effects on World Wide Web pages, incorporating user-defined elements.

xi /zī; ksī/ ▶*n.* the fourteenth letter of the Greek alphabet (Ξ, ξ), transliterated as 'x.'

Xmas /ˈkrisməs; ˈeksməs/ ▶*n.* informal term for CHRISTMAS.

X-rat·ed ▶*adj.* pornographic or indecent: *there was some X-rated humor.* ■ (of a movie) given an X classification (see **X**[2]).

X-ray /ˈeks ˌrā/ (also **x-ray** or **X ray**) ▶*n.* **1** electromagnetic radiation of high energy and very short wavelength (between ultraviolet light and gamma rays) that is able to pass through many materials opaque to light. ■ [as *adj.*] *inf.* denoting an apparent or supposed faculty for seeing beyond an outward form: *you didn't need X-ray eyes to know what was going on.* **2** a photographic or digital image of the internal composition of something, esp. a part of the body, produced by X-rays being passed through it. **3** a code word representing the letter X, used in radio communication.
▶*v.* [*tr.*] photograph or examine with X-rays: *luggage in the hold is X-rayed.*

xy·lem /ˈzīləm/ ▶*n. Bot.* the vascular tissue in plants that conducts water and dissolved nutrients upward from the root and also helps to form the woody element in the stem.

xy·lene /ˈzīˌlēn/ ▶*n. Chem.* a volatile liquid hydrocarbon, $C_6H_4(CH_3)_2$ used in fuels and solvents, and in chemical synthesis.

xy·lo·phone /ˈzīlәˌfōn/ ▶*n.* a musical instrument played by striking a row of wooden bars of graduated length with one or more wooden or plastic mallets. —**xy·lo·phon·ic** /ˌzīlәˈfänik/ *adj.* —**xy·lo·phon·ist** *n.*

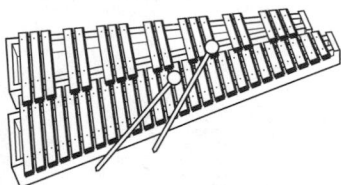

xylophone

Yy

Y[1] /wī/ (also **y**) ▶*n.* (*pl.* **Ys** or **Y's**) **1** the twenty-fifth letter of the alphabet. ■ denoting the next after X in a set of items, categories, etc. ■ denoting a second unknown or unspecified person or thing: *the claim that chemical X causes birth defect Y.* ■ (usu. **y**) the second unknown quantity in an algebraic expression, usually the dependent variable. ■ (usu. **y**) denoting the secondary or vertical axis in a system of coordinates: [in *comb.*] the *y-axis.* **2** (**Y**) a shape like that of a capital Y: [in *comb.*] *rows of tiny Y-shaped motifs.*

Y[2] ▶*abbr.* ■ yen: *Y140.* ■ *inf.* a YMCA, YWCA, YMHA, or YWHA facility: *Scott was living at the Y.*
▶*symb.* the chemical element yttrium.

y ▶*abbr.* year(s): *orbital period (Pluto): 248.5y.*

-y[1] /ē/ ▶*suffix* forming adjectives: **1** (from nouns and adjectives) full of; having the quality of: *messy | milky | mousy.* ■ with depreciatory reference: *boozy | tinny.* **2** (from verbs) inclined to; apt to: *sticky.*

-y[2] ▶*suffix* forming nouns: **1** denoting a state, condition, or quality: *glory | jealousy.* **2** denoting an action or its result: *blasphemy | victory.*

yacht /yät/ ▶*n.* a medium-sized sailboat equipped for cruising or racing. ■ a powered boat or small ship equipped for cruising, typically for private or official use: *a steam yacht.*
▶*v.* [*intr.*] race or cruise in a yacht. —**yacht·ing** *n.* —**yachts·man** *n.*

yack·e·ty-yak /'yakətē 'yak/ (also **yack·et·y-yack**) ▶*n. & v.* another term for **YAK**[2].

ya·hoo[1] /'yä,hōō; yä'hōō/ ▶*n. inf.* a rude, noisy, or violent person.

ya·hoo[2] /yä'hōō/ ▶*interj.* expressing great joy or excitement.

Yah·weh /'yä,wā; -,we; -,vä/ (also **Yah·veh** /-,vä; -,ve/) ▶*n.* a form of the Hebrew name of God used in the Bible.

yak[1] /yak/ ▶*n.* a large domesticated wild ox (genus *Bos*) with shaggy hair, humped shoulders, and large horns, used in Tibet as a pack animal and for its milk, meat, and hide.

yak[2] (also **yack** or **yack·et·y-yak**) *inf.* ▶*n.* a trivial or unduly persistent conversation.
▶*v.* (**yakked, yak·king**) [*intr.*] talk at length about trivial or boring subjects.

y'all /yôl/ ▶*contr. of* you-all.

yam /yam/ ▶*n.* **1** the edible starchy tuber of a climbing plant, widely distributed in tropical and subtropical countries. **2** the plant (genus *Dioscorea*, family Dioscoreaceae) that yields this tuber. **3** a sweet potato. ▷late 16th cent.: from Portuguese *inhame* or obsolete Spanish *iñame*, probably of West African origin.

yam·mer /'yamər/ ▶*n. inf.* or *dial.* loud and sustained or repetitive noise: *the yammer of their animated conversation | the yammer of enemy fire.*
▶*v.* [*intr.*] *inf.* or *dial.* make a loud repetitive noise. ■ talk volubly. —**yam·mer·er** *n.*

yang /yaNG; yäNG/ ▶*n.* (in Chinese philosophy) the active male principle of the universe, characterized as male and creative and associated with heaven, heat, and light. Contrasted with **YIN**.

Yank /yaNGk/ ▶*n.* another term for **YANKEE** (senses 1 and 2).

yank /yaNGk/ *inf.* ▶*v.* pull with a jerk: [*tr.*] *he yanked her to her feet* | [*intr.*] *Liz yanked at her arm.*
▶*n.* a sudden hard pull: *he gave her ponytail a yank.*

Yan·kee /'yaNGkē/ ▶*n. inf.* **1** *often derog.* a person who lives in, or is from, the U.S. **2** an inhabitant of New England or one of the northern states. ■ *hist.* a Union soldier in the Civil War. **3** a code word representing the letter Y, used in radio communication. ▷mid 18th cent.: origin uncertain; recorded in the late 17th cent. as a nickname; perhaps from Dutch *Janke*, diminutive of *Jan* 'John.'

yap /yap/ ▶*v.* (**yapped, yap·ping**) [*intr.*] give a sharp, shrill bark: *the dachshunds yapped at his heels.* ■ *inf.* talk at length in an irritating manner.
▶*n.* **1** a sharp, shrill bark. **2** *inf.* a person's mouth (used in expressions to do with speaking): *shut your yap.* —**yap·per** *n.*

yard[1] /yärd/ ▶*n.* **1** (abbr.: **yd.**) a unit of linear measure equal to 3 feet (0.9144 meter). ■ (**yards of**) *inf.* a great length: *yards and yards of fine lace.* ■ a square or cubic yard, esp. of sand or other building materials. ■ a cloth measure, of three feet in length and varying widths. **2** a cylindrical spar, tapering to each end, slung across a ship's mast for a sail to hang from. **3** *inf.* one hundred dollars; a one hundred dollar bill.

yard[2] ▶*n.* a piece of ground adjoining a building or house. ■ an area of ground surrounded by walls or buildings. ■ an area of land used for a particular purpose or business: *a storage yard.*
▶*v.* **1** [*tr.*] store or transport (timber) in or to a log yard. **2** [*intr.*] (of deer or moose) gather as a herd for the winter.
▶ □ **the Yard** *Brit.* informal term for **SCOTLAND YARD**.

yard·age /'yärdij/ ▶*n.* **1** a distance or length measured in yards. ■ *Football* the distance covered in advancing the ball. **2** *archaic* the use of a yard for storage or the keeping of animals or payment for such use.

yard·arm /'yärd,ärm/ ▶*n.* the outer extremity of a ship's yard.

yard·bird /'yärd,bərd/ ▶*n. inf.* **1** a new military recruit, esp. one assigned to menial tasks. **2** a convict.

yard·man /'yärd,man/ ▶*n.* (*pl.* **-men**) **1** a person working in a railroad or lumberyard. **2** a person who does various outdoor jobs.

yard·stick /'yärd,stik/ ▶*n.* a measuring rod a yard long, typically divided into inches. ■ a standard used for comparison: *the consumer price index, the government's yardstick for the cost of living.*

yar·mul·ke /'yämə(l)kə/ (also **yar·mul·ka**) ▶*n.* a skullcap worn in public by Orthodox Jewish men or during prayer by other Jewish men.

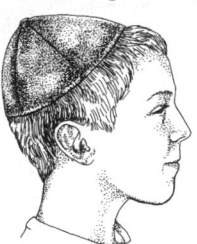

yarmulke

yarn /yärn/ ▶*n.* **1** spun thread used for knitting, weaving, or sewing. **2** *inf.* a long or rambling story, esp. one that is implausible.
▶*v.* [*intr.*] *inf.* tell a long or implausible story: *they were yarning about local legends and superstitions.*

yar·row /'yärō; 'yerō/ ▶*n.* a Eurasian plant (*Achillea millefolium*) of the daisy family, with feathery leaves and small aromatic flowers.

yash·mak /yäsH'mäk; 'yasH,mak/ ▶*n.* a veil concealing all of the face except the eyes, worn by some Muslim women in public.

yaw /yô/ ▶*v.* [*intr.*] (of a moving ship or aircraft) twist or oscillate about a vertical axis: *the jet yawed sharply to the right.*

yawl /yôl/ ▶*n.* a two-masted fore-and-aft-rigged sailboat with the mizzen boom overhanging the stern.

yawn /yôn/ ▶*v.* [*intr.*] involuntarily open one's mouth wide and inhale deeply due to tiredness or boredom. ■ [usu. as *adj.*] (**yawning**) be wide open: *a yawning chasm.*
▶*n.* a reflex act of opening one's mouth wide and inhaling deeply due to tiredness or boredom. ■ *inf.* a thing that is considered boring or tedious: *the awards show was a four-hour yawn.* —**yawn·ing·ly** *adv.*

yaws /yôz/ ▶*pl. n.* [treated as *sing.*] a contagious disease of tropical countries, caused by a bacterium that enters skin abrasions and gives rise to small crusted lesions that may develop into deep ulcers.

Yb ▶*symb.* the chemical element ytterbium.

Y chro·mo·some ▶*n. Genetics* (in humans and other mammals) a sex chromosome that is normally present only in male cells, which are designated XY. Compare with **X** CHROMOSOME.

yd. ▶*abbr.* yard (measure).

ye¹ /yē/ ▶*pron.* [second person pl.] *archaic* or *dial.* plural form of THOU¹: *gather ye rosebuds, while ye may.*

ye² /yē; T͟Hē/ ▶*adj.* pseudo-archaic term for THE: *Ye Olde Bookshoppe.*

yea /yā/ ▶*adv. archaic* or *formal* yes: *she has the right to say yea or nay.* ■ used for emphasis, esp. to introduce a stronger or more accurate word than one just used: *he was full, yea, crammed with anxieties.*
▶*n. archaic* or *formal* an affirmative answer: *the assembly would give the final yea or nay.* ■ (in the U.S. Congress) an affirmative vote.

yeah /'ye(ə); 'ya(ə)/ (also **yeh**) ▶*interj. & n.* nonstandard spelling of YES, representing informal pronunciation.

yean /yēn/ ▶*v.* [tr.] *archaic* (of a sheep or goat) give birth to (a lamb or kid).

year /yi(ə)r/ ▶*n.* **1** the time taken by a planet to make one revolution around the sun. **2** (also **calendar year**) the period of 365 days (or 366 days in leap years) starting from the first of January, used for reckoning time. ■ a period of the same length as this starting at any point. ■ a similar period used for reckoning time according to other calendars: *the Muslim year.* **3** (**one's years**) one's age or time of life: *she had a composure well beyond her years.* **4** (**years**) *inf.* a very long time; ages: *it's going to take years to put that right.*
▶ □ —— **of the year** a person or thing chosen as outstanding in a specified field or of a specified kind in a particular year: *the sports personality of the year.* □ **year in and year out** continuously or repeatedly over a period of years: *they rented the same bungalow year in and year out.*

year·book /'yi(ə)r,bo͝ok/ ▶*n.* an annual publication giving current information and listing events or aspects of the previous year, esp. in a particular field: *Yearbook of Physical Anthropology.* ■ a book containing photographs of the senior class in a school or college and details of school activities in the previous year.

year·ling /'yi(ə)rliNG/ ▶*n.* an animal a year old, or in its second year. ■ a racehorse in the calendar year after its year of foaling.
▶*adj.* having lived or existed for a year; a year old: *a yearling calf.* ■ of or relating to an something that is a year old: *the yearling market.*

year·long (also **year-long**) ▶*adj.* lasting for or throughout a year: *his yearlong battle with lung cancer.*

year·ly /'yi(ə)rlē/ ▶*adj. & adv.* happening or produced once a year or every year: [as *adj.*] *yearly visits to Africa* | [as *adv.*] *rent was paid yearly.*

yearn /yərn/ ▶*v.* [intr.] have an intense feeling of loss or lack and longing for something: *they yearned to go home* ■ *archaic* be filled with compassion or warm feeling: *no fellow spirit yearned toward her.* ▷Old English *giernan*, from a Germanic base meaning 'eager.' —**yearn·ing** *n.* —**yearn·ing·ly** *adv.*

year-round ▶*adj. & adv.* happening or continuing throughout the year: [as *adj.*] *an indoor pool for year-round use* | [as *adv.*] (also **year round**) *the center is open year-round.*

yeast /yēst/ ▶*n.* a microscopic fungus (genus *Saccharomyces*, subdivision Ascomycotina) consisting of single oval cells that reproduce by budding, and are capable of converting sugar into alcohol and carbon dioxide. ■ a grayish-yellow preparation of this obtained chiefly from fermented beer, used as a fermenting agent, to raise bread dough, and as a food supplement. ■ *Biol.* any unicellular fungus that reproduces vegetatively by budding or fission, including forms such as candida that can cause disease. ▷Old English, of Germanic origin; related to Dutch *gist* and German *Gischt* 'froth, yeast,' from an Indo-European root shared by Greek *zein* 'to boil.' —**yeast·like** /-,līk/ *adj.*

yeast·y /'yēstē/ ▶*adj.* (**yeast·i·er**, **yeast·i·est**) of, resembling, or containing yeast: *the yeasty smell of rising dough.* ■ *fig.* characterized by or producing upheaval or agitation; in a state of turbulence, typically a creative or productive one: *the yeasty days of yesterday's revolution.* —**yeast·i·ly** /'yēstlē/ *adv.* —**yeast·i·ness** *n.*

yell /yel/ ▶*n.* a loud, sharp cry, esp. of pain, surprise, or delight; a shout. ■ an organized cheer, esp. one used to support a sports team.
▶*v.* [intr.] give a loud, sharp cry: *you heard me yelling at her.*

yel·low /'yelō/ ▶*adj.* **1** of the color between green and orange in the spectrum, a primary subtractive color complementary to blue; colored like ripe lemons or egg yolks: *curly yellow hair.* ■ *offens.* having a naturally yellowish or olive skin (as used to describe Chinese or Japanese people). ■ denoting a warning of danger that is thought to be near but not actually imminent: *he put Camp Visoko on yellow alert.* **2** *inf.* cowardly: *he'd better get back there quick and prove he's not yellow.* **3** (of a book or newspaper) unscrupulously sensational.
▶*n.* **1** yellow color or pigment: *painted in vivid blues and yellows.* **2** the yolk of an egg. **3** (**yellows**) any of a number of plant diseases in which

the leaves turn yellow, typically caused by viruses and transmitted by insects.
▶*v.* [intr.] become a yellow color, esp. with age: *the cream paint was beginning to yellow* ▷Old English *geolu, geolo*; related to Dutch *geel* and German *gelb*, also to gold. —**yel·low·ish** *adj.* —**yel·low·ness** *n.* —**yel·low·y** *adj.*

yel·low-bel·ly ▶*n. inf.* **1** a coward. **2** any of various animals with yellow underparts. —**yel·low-bel·lied** *adj.*

yel·low fe·ver ▶*n.* a tropical viral disease affecting the liver and kidneys, causing fever and jaundice and often fatal. It is transmitted by mosquitoes.

yel·low·fin /'yelō,fin/ (also **yellowfin tuna**) ▶*n.* a widely distributed, commercially important tuna (*Thunnus albacares*) that has yellow anal and dorsal fins.

yel·low jack·et ▶*n. inf.* a wasp or hornet with bright yellow markings.

yel·low jour·nal·ism ▶*n.* journalism that is based upon sensationalism and crude exaggeration. —**yel·low jour·nal·ist** *n.*

Yel·low Pag·es (also **yel·low pag·es**) ▶*pl. n.* a telephone directory, or a section of one, printed on yellow paper and listing businesses and other organizations according to the goods or services they offer. ■ a similar directory available online through the Internet.

yelp /yelp/ ▶*n.* a short sharp cry, esp. of pain or alarm
▶*v.* [intr.] utter such a cry: *my dogs were yelping at Linus.* —**yelp·er** *n.*

yen¹ /yen/ ▶*n.* (pl. same) the basic monetary unit of Japan.

yen² *inf.* ▶*n.* a longing or yearning: *she always had a yen to be a writer.*
▶*v.* (**yenned**, **yen·ning**) [intr.] feel a longing or yearning: *it's no use yenning for the old simplicities.*

yeo·man /'yōmən/ ▶*n.* (pl. **-men**) **1** *hist.* a man holding and cultivating a small landed estate; a freeholder. ■ a person qualified for certain duties and rights, such as to serve on juries and vote for the knight of the shire. **2** a petty officer in the U.S. Navy or Coast Guard performing clerical duties on board ship. —**yeo·man·ly** *adj.*

Yeo·man of the Guard ▶*n.* a member of the British sovereign's bodyguard, first established by Henry VII, now having only ceremonial duties and wearing Tudor dress as uniform.

yep /yep/ (also **yup**) ▶*interj. & n.* nonstandard spelling of YES, representing informal pronunciation.

yer·ba ma·té /'ye(ə)rbə mä'tā/ ▶*n.* see MATÉ.

yes /yes/ ▶*interj.* **1** used to give an affirmative response: *"Do you understand?" "Yes."* ■ expressing agreement with a positive statement just made: *"That was a grand evening." "Yes, it was."* ■ expressing contradiction of a negative statement: *"You don't want to go." "Yes, I do."* **2** used as a response to someone addressing one: *"Oh, Mr. Lawrence." "Yes?"* **3** used to question a remark or ask for more detail about it: *"It should be easy to check." "Oh yes? How?"* **4** expressing delight: *plenty to eat, including hot roast beef sandwiches (yes!).*
▶*n.* (pl. **yes·es** or **yes·ses**) an affirmative answer or decision, esp. in voting: *answering with assured and ardent yeses.*
▶ □ **yes and no** partly and partly not: *"Did it come as a surprise to you?" "Yes and no."*

yes-man ▶*n.* (pl. **-men**) *inf.* a weak person who always agrees with their political leader or their superior at work.

yes·ter·day /'yestər,dā; -dē/ ▶*adv.* on the day before today. ■ in the recent past: *everything seems to have been built yesterday.*
▶*n.* the day before today. ■ the recent past: *yesterday's best sellers.*
▶ □ **yesterday's news** a person or thing that is no longer of interest.

yes·ter·year /'yestər,yir/ ▶*n. poetic/lit.* last year or the recent past, esp. as nostalgically recalled: *those thrilling days of yesteryear.*

yet /yet/ ▶*adv.* **1** up until the present or an unspecified or implied time; by now or then: *I haven't told anyone else yet* | *I have yet to be convinced* ■ as soon as the present or a specified or implied time: *wait, don't go yet.* ■ from now into the future for a specified length of time: *I hope to continue for some time yet.* ■ referring to something that will or may happen in the future: *further research may yet explain the enigma.* ■ up to and including the present or time mentioned; still: *is it raining yet?* **2** still; even (used to emphasize increase or repetition): *snow, snow, and yet more snow* | *yet another diet book* | *the rations were reduced yet again.* **3** nevertheless; in spite of that: *every week she gets worse, and yet it could go on for years.*
▶*conj.* but at the same time; but nevertheless: *the path was dark, yet I slowly found my way.*

yet·i /'yetē; 'yātē/ ▶*n.* a large hairy creature resembling a human or bear, said to live in the highest part of the Himalayas.

yew /yo͞o/ ▶*n.* (also **yew tree**) a coniferous tree (genus *Taxus*, family

Taxaceae) that has red berrylike fruits, and most parts of which are highly poisonous.

Yid·dish /'yidiSH/ ▶*n.* a language used by Jews in central and eastern Europe before the Holocaust. It was originally a German dialect with words from Hebrew and several modern languages and is today spoken mainly in the U.S., Israel, and Russia.
▶*adj.* of or relating to this language.

yield /yēld/ ▶*v.* **1** [*tr.*] produce or provide (a natural, agricultural, or industrial product): *the land yields grapes and tobacco.* ■ (of an action or process) produce or deliver (a result or gain): *this method yields the same results.* ■ (of a financial or commercial process or transaction) generate (a specified financial return): *such investments yield direct cash returns.* **2** [*intr.*] give way to arguments, demands, or pressure: *he yielded to the demands of his partners.* ■ [*tr.*] relinquish possession of (something); give (something) up: *they had to yield up their secrets | they are forced to yield ground.* ■ [*tr.*] cease to argue about: *I yielded the point.* ■ (esp. in a legislature) allow another the right to speak in a debate: *I yield to the gentleman from Kentucky.* ■ give right of way to other traffic. ■ (of a mass or structure) give way under force or pressure: *he reeled into the house as the door yielded.*
▶*n.* the full amount of an agricultural or industrial product: *the milk yield was poor.* ■ *Finance* the amount of money brought in, e.g., interest from an investment or revenue from a tax; return: *an annual dividend yield of 20 percent.* ■ *Chem.* the amount obtained from a process or reaction relative to the theoretical maximum amount obtainable. ■ (of a nuclear weapon) the force in tons or kilotons of TNT required to produce an equivalent explosion: *yields ranging from five kilotons to 100 tons.*

yield·ing /'yēldiNG/ ▶*adj.* **1** (of a substance or object) giving way under pressure; not hard or rigid: *yielding cushions.* ■ (of a person) complying with the requests or desires of others. **2** [in *comb.*] giving a product or generating a financial return of a specified amount: *higher-yielding wheat.*

yin /yin/ ▶*n.* (in Chinese philosophy) the passive female principle of the universe, characterized as female and sustaining and associated with earth, dark, and cold. Contrasted with YANG.

yip·pee /'yipē; ,yip'ē/ ▶*interj.* expressing wild excitement or delight.

yip·pie /'yipē/ ▶*n.* (*pl.* **-pies**) a member of a group of politically active hippies, originally in the U.S.

yin and yang

YMCA ▶*n.* a welfare movement that began in London in 1844 and now has branches all over the world. ■ a hostel or recreational facility run by this association.

yo[1] /yō/ ▶*interj. inf.* used to greet someone, attract their attention, or express excitement.

yo[2] ▶*pron.* nonstandard spelling of YOU, used to represent black English.
▶*adj.* nonstandard spelling of YOUR, used to represent black English.

yo·del /'yōdl/ ▶*v.* (**-deled, -del·ing;** *Brit.* **-delled, -del·ling**) [*intr.*] practice a form of singing or calling marked by rapid alternation between the normal voice and falsetto.
▶*n.* a song, melody, or call delivered in such a way. —**yo·del·er** *n.*

yo·ga /'yōgə/ ▶*n.* a Hindu spiritual and ascetic discipline, a part of which, including breath control, simple meditation, and the adoption of specific bodily postures, is widely practiced for health and relaxation. —**yo·gic** /-gik/ *adj.*

yo·gi /'yōgē/ ▶*n.* (*pl.* **-gis**) a person who is proficient in yoga.

yo·gurt /'yōgərt/ (also **yo·ghurt**) ▶*n.* a semisolid sourish food prepared from fermented milk, often sweetened and flavored.

yoke /yōk/ ▶*n.* **1** a wooden crosspiece that is fastened over the necks of two animals and attached to the plow or cart that they are to pull. ■ (*pl.* same or **yokes**) a pair of animals coupled together in such a way: *a yoke of oxen.* ■ a frame fitting over the neck and shoulders of a person, used for carrying pails or baskets. ■ used of something that is regarded as oppressive or burdensome: *the yoke of imperialism.* ■ used of something that represents a bond between two parties: *the yoke of marriage.* **2** something resembling or likened to such a crosspiece, in particular: ■ a part of a garment that fits over the shoulders and to which the main part of the garment is attached. ■ a control lever in an aircraft.
▶*v.* [*tr.*] put a yoke on (a pair of animals); couple or attach with or to a yoke: *a camel and donkey yoked together | fig. Hong Kong's dollar has been yoked to America's. inf.* rob; mug: *two crackheads yoked this girl.*

yo·kel /'yōkəl/ ▶*n. inf., often derog.* an uneducated and unsophisticated person from the countryside.

yolk /yōk/ ▶*n.* the yellow internal part of a bird's egg, which is surrounded by the white, is rich in protein and fat, and nourishes the developing embryo. ■ *Zool.* the corresponding part in the ovum or larva of all egg-laying vertebrates and many invertebrates. ▷Old English *geol(o)ca,* from *geolu* 'yellow.'

Yom Kip·pur /'yōm ki'pŏŏr; 'yōm; 'yäm; 'kipər/ ▶*n.* the most solemn religious fast of the Jewish year, the last of the ten days of penitence that begin with Rosh Hashanah.

yon /yän/ ▶*adj. & adv. poetic/lit.* or *dial.* yonder; that: [as *adj.*] *you'll find some big ranches yon side of the Sierra.*
▶*pron. poetic/lit.* or *dial.* yonder person or thing: *what do you make of yon?*

yon·der /'yändər/ ▶*adv. archaic* or *dial.* at some distance in the direction indicated; over there: *there's a ford south of here, about nine miles yonder.*
▶*adj. archaic* or *dial.* that or those (used to refer to something situated at a distance): *what light through yonder window breaks?*
▶*n.* (**the yonder**) the far distance: *flying off into the wild blue yonder.*

yoo-hoo /'yŏŏ ,hŏŏ/ ▶*interj.* a call used to attract attention to one's arrival or presence: *Yoo-hoo!—Is anyone there?*
▶*v.* [*intr.*] (of a person) make such a call.

yore /yôr/ ▶*n.* (in phrase **of yore**) *poetic/lit.* of long ago or former times: *a great empire in days of yore.*

York·shire pud·ding ▶*n.* a side dish made of unsweetened egg batter, typically baked in roast beef drippings.

York·shire ter·ri·er ▶*n.* a dog of a small, long-haired blue-gray and tan breed of terrier.

Yo·ru·ba /'yôrəbə/ ▶*n.* (*pl.* same or **-bas**) **1** a member of a people of southwestern Nigeria and Benin. **2** the Kwa language of this people and an official language of Nigeria.
▶*adj.* of or relating to the Yoruba or their language.

you /yŏŏ/ ▶*pron.* [second person sing. or pl.] **1** used to refer to the person or people that the speaker is addressing: *are you listening? | I love you.* ■ used to refer to the person being addressed together with other people regarded in the same class: *you Australians.* ■ used in exclamations to address one or more people: *you fools | hey, you!* **2** used to refer to any person in general: *after a while, you get used to it.*
▶ □ **you and yours** you together with your family and close friends. □ **you-know-who** (or **you-know-what**) used to refer to someone (or something) known to the hearer without specifying their identity.

you-all /'yŏŏ ,ôl; yôl/ (also **y'all**) ▶*pron. dial.* (in the southern U.S.) you (used to refer to more than one person): *how are you-all?*

you'd /yŏŏd/ ▶*contr. of* ■ you had: *you'd better remember it.* ■ you would: *I was afraid you'd ask me that.*

you'll /yŏŏl/ ▶*contr. of* you will; you shall: *you'll find many exciting features.*

young /yəNG/ ▶*adj.* (**young·er, young·est**) having lived or existed for only a short time: *a young girl* | [as *pl. n.*] (**the young**) *the young are amazingly resilient.* ■ not as old as the norm or as would be expected: *more people were dying young.* ■ relating to, characteristic of, or consisting of young people: *young love | the Young Communist League.* ■ immature or inexperienced: *she's very young for her age.* ■ having the qualities popularly associated with young people, such as enthusiasm and optimism: *all those who are young at heart.* ■ (**the Younger**) used to denote the younger of two people of the same name: *Pitt the Younger.* ■ (**younger**) *Scot.* denoting the heir of a landed commoner: *Hugh Magnus Macleod, younger of Macleod.*
▶*n.* [treated as *pl.*] offspring, esp. of an animal before or soon after birth: *this species carries its young.* —**young·ish** /'yəNGiSH/ *adj.*
▶ □ **with young** (of an animal) pregnant.

young·ster /'yəNGstər/ ▶*n.* a child, young person, or young animal.

Young Turk ▶*n.* a member of a revolutionary party in the Ottoman Empire who carried out the revolution of 1908. ■ a young person eager for radical change to the established order.

young 'un ▶*n. inf.* a youngster.

your /yôr; yŏŏr/ ▶*adj.* **1** belonging to or associated with the person or people that the speaker is addressing: *what is your name?* **2** belonging to or associated with any person in general: *the sight is enough to break your heart.* ■ *inf.* used to denote someone or something that is familiar or typical of its kind: *I'm just your average Joe | she is one of your chatty types.* **3** (**Your**) used when addressing the holder of certain titles: *Your Majesty | Your Eminence.*

Pronunciation Key ə *ago,* up; ər *over, fur;* a *hat;* ā *ate;* ä *car;* CH *chin;* e *let;* ē *see;* e(ə)r *air;* i *fit;* ī *by;* i(ə)r *ear;* NG *sing;* ō *go;* ô *law, for;* oi *toy;* ŏŏ *good;* ŏŏ *goo;* ou *out;* SH *she;* TH *thin;* TH *then;* (h)w *why;* ZH *vision*

you're /yŏŏr; yôr/ ▶*contr. of* you are: *you're an angel, Deb!*

yours /yŏrz; yŏŏrz/ ▶*possessive pron.* **1** used to refer to a thing or things belonging to or associated with the person or people that the speaker is addressing: *the choice is yours* | *it's no business of yours.* ■ *dated* (chiefly in commercial use) your letter: *Mr. Smythe has sent me yours of the 15th inst. regarding the vacancy.* **2** used in formulas ending a letter: *Yours sincerely, John Watson* | *Yours, Jim Lindsay.*

your·self /yər'self; yôr-; yŏŏr-/ ▶*pron.* [*second person sing.*] (*pl.* **-selves**) **1** [*reflexive*] used to refer to the person being addressed as the object of a verb or preposition when they are also the subject of the clause: *help yourselves, boys* | *see for yourself.* **2** you personally (used to emphasize the person being addressed): *you're going to have to do it yourself.*

youth /yŏŏтн/ ▶*n.* (*pl.* **youths** /yŏŏтнs; yŏŏтнz/) **1** the period between childhood and adult age: *he had been a keen sportsman in his youth.* ■ the state or quality of being young, esp. as associated with vigor, freshness, or immaturity: *she imagined her youth and beauty fading.* ■ an early stage in the development of something: *this publishing sector is no longer in its youth.* **2** [treated as *sing.* or *pl.*] young people considered as a group: *middle-class youth have romanticized poverty* | [as *adj.*] *youth culture.* ■ a young man: *he was attacked by a gang of youths.*

youth·ful /'yŏŏтнfəl/ ▶*adj.* young or seeming young: *people aspiring to remain youthful.* ■ typical or characteristic of young people: *youthful enthusiasm.* —**youth·ful·ly** *adv.* —**youth·ful·ness** *n.*

youth hos·tel ▶*n.* a place providing cheap accommodations aimed mainly at young people on hiking or cycling tours.

you've /yŏŏv/ ▶*contr. of* you have: *you've changed.*

yowl /youl/ ▶*n.* a loud wailing cry, esp. one of pain or distress.
▶*v.* [*intr.*] make such a cry: *he yowled as he touched one of the hot plates.*

yo-yo /'yō ‚yō/ ▶*n.* (*pl.* **-yos**) a toy consisting of a pair of joined discs with a deep groove between them in which string is attached and wound, which can be spun alternately downward and upward by its weight and momentum.. ■ [often as *adj.*] a thing that repeatedly falls and rises again: *the yo-yo syndrome of repeatedly losing weight and gaining it again.* ■ *inf.* a stupid, insane, or unpredictable person.
▶*v.* (**-yoes, -yoed**) [*intr.*] move up and down; fluctuate: *popularity polls yo-yo up and down with the flow of events.* ■ [*tr.*] manipulate or maneuver (someone or something): *don't yo-yo me around.*

yr. ▶*abbr.* ■ year or years. ■ younger. ■ your.

yrs. ▶*abbr.* ■ years. ■ yours (as a formula ending a letter).

yt·ter·bi·um /i'tərbēəm/ ▶*n.* the chemical element of atomic number 70, a silvery-white metal of the lanthanide series. (Symbol: **Yb**)

yt·tri·um /'itrēəm/ ▶*n.* the chemical element of atomic number 39, a grayish-white metal generally included among the rare-earth elements. (Symbol: **Y**)

Yu·an /yŏŏ'än/ ▶a dynasty that ruled China AD 1259–1368, established by the Mongols under Kublai Khan. It preceded the Ming dynasty.

yu·an /yŏŏ'än/ ▶*n.* (*pl.* same) the basic monetary unit of China, equal to 10 jiao or 100 fen.

yuc·ca /'yəkə/ ▶*n.* a plant (genus *Yucca*) of the agave family with stiff swordlike leaves and spikes of white bell-shaped flowers, found esp. in warm regions of North America and Mexico.

yuck /yək/ *inf.* ▶*interj.* (also **yuk**) used to express strong distaste or disgust: *"Raw herrings! Yuck!"*
▶*n.* something messy or disgusting: *I can't bear the sight of blood and yuck.*
—**yuck·y** *adj.*

Yu·go·slav /'yŏŏgō‚släv; ‚yŏŏgō'släv; -gə-/ ▶*n.* a native or national of Yugoslavia or its former constituent republics, or a person of Yugoslav descent.
▶*adj.* of or relating to Yugoslavia, its former constituent republics, or its people.

Yule /yŏŏl/ ▶*n.* archaic term for **Christmas.** ▷Old English *gēol(a)* 'Christmas Day'; compare with Old Norse *jól*, originally applied to a heathen festival lasting twelve days, later to Christmas.

yule log ▶*n.* a large log traditionally burned in the fireplace on Christmas Eve. ■ a log-shaped chocolate cake eaten at Christmas.

yum /yəm/ (also **yum-yum**) *inf.* ▶*interj.* used to express pleasure at eating, or at the prospect of eating, a particular food.
▶*adj.* (of food) delicious.

Yu·ma /'yŏŏmə/ ▶*n.* **1** (*pl.* same or **-mas**) a member of an American Indian people living mainly in southwestern Arizona. **2** the Yuman language of this people.
▶*adj.* of or relating to this people.

yum·my /'yəmē/ ▶*adj.* (**-mi·er, -mi·est**) *inf.* (of food) delicious: *yummy pumpkin cakes.* ■ highly attractive and desirable: *this yummy young man.*

yup¹ /yəp/ ▶*interj. & n.* variant spelling of **YEP.**

yup² ▶*n.* short for **YUPPIE.**

Yu·pik /'yŏŏpik/ ▶*n.* (*pl.* same or **-piks**) **1** a member of an Eskimo people of Siberia, the Aleutian Islands, and southwestern Alaska. **2** any of the Eskimo languages of this people.
▶*adj.* of or relating to this people or their languages.

yup·pie /'yəpē/ (also **yup·py**) ▶*n.* (*pl.* **-pies**) *inf., derog.* a well-paid young middle-class professional who works in a city job and has a luxurious lifestyle. ▷1980s: elaboration of the acronym from *young urban professional.* —**yup·pie·dom** *n.*

yurt /yŏŏrt; yərt/ ▶*n.* a circular tent of felt or skins on a collapsible framework, used by nomads in Mongolia, Siberia, and Turkey.

YWCA ▶*n.* a welfare movement with branches in many countries that began in Britain in 1855. ■ a hostel or recreational facility run by this association.

Zz

Z¹ /zē/ (also **z**) ▶ *n.* (*pl.* **Zs** or **Z's**) **1** the twenty-sixth letter of the alphabet. ■ denoting the next after Y in a set of items, categories, etc. ■ denoting a third unknown or unspecified person or thing: *X sold a car to Y (a car dealer) who in turn sold it to Z (a finance company).* ■ (usu. **z**) the third unknown quantity in an algebraic expression. ■ (usu. **z**) denoting the third axis in a three-dimensional system of coordinates: [in comb.] the z-*axis.* **2** a shape like that of a capital Z: [in comb.] a *Z-shaped crack in the paving stone.* **3** used in repeated form to represent the sound of buzzing or snoring.
▶ □ **catch some** (or **a few**) **Zs** *inf.* get some sleep: *I'll go back to the hotel and catch some Zs.*

Z² ▶ *symb. Chem.* atomic number.

zag /zag/ ▶ *n.* a sharp change of direction in a zigzag course: *we traveled in a series of zigs and zags.*
▶ *v.* (**zagged**, **zag·ging**) [*intr.*] make a sharp change of direction: *a long path zigged and zagged through the woods.*

za·ny /'zānē/ ▶ *adj.* (**-ni·er**, **-ni·est**) amusingly unconventional and idiosyncratic: *zany humor.*
▶ *n.* an erratic or eccentric person. ■ *hist.* a comic performer partnering a clown, whom he imitated in an amusing way. —**za·ni·ly** /-nəlē/ *adv.* —**za·ni·ness** *n.*

zap /zap/ *inf.* ▶ *v.* (**zapped**, **zap·ping**) **1** [*tr.*] destroy or obliterate: *zap the enemy's artillery before it can damage your core units.* **2** [*tr.*] cause to move suddenly and rapidly in a specified direction: *the boat zapped us up river.* ■ [*intr.*] move suddenly and rapidly, esp. between television channels or sections of videotape by use of a remote control: *video recorders mean the audience will zap through the ads.* **3** [*tr.*] cook or warm (food or a hot drink) in a microwave oven.
▶ *n.* a sudden effect or event that makes a dramatic impact, esp. a sudden burst of energy or sound: *the eggs get an extra zap of UV light.*

zap·per /'zapər/ ▶ *n. inf.* **1** a remote control for a television, video, or other piece of electronic equipment. **2** an electronic device used for killing insects: *a bug zapper.*

zeal /zēl/ ▶ *n.* great energy or enthusiasm in pursuit of a cause or an objective: *his zeal for privatization.*

zeal·ot /'zelət/ ▶ *n.* a person who is fanatical and uncompromising in pursuit of their religious, political, or other ideals. —**zeal·ot·ry** /-ətrē/ *n.*

zeal·ous /'zeləs/ ▶ *adj.* having or showing zeal: *the council was extremely zealous in the application of the regulations.* —**zeal·ous·ly** *adv.* —**zeal·ous·ness** *n.*

ze·bra /'zēbrə/ ▶ *n.* **1** an African wild horse (genus *Equus*) with black and white stripes and an erect mane. **2** a large butterfly with pale bold stripes on a dark background, in particular: a yellow and black American butterfly (*Heliconius charitonius*, family Nymphalidae). **3** (also **zebra fish**) a silvery-gold sea bream (*Diplodus cervinus*) with vertical black stripes. ▶ early 17th cent.: from Italian, Spanish, or Portuguese, originally in the sense 'wild ass,' perhaps ultimately from Latin *equiferus*, from *equus* 'horse' + *ferus* 'wild.'

ze·bu /'zē,b(y)ōō/ ▶ *n.* another term for **BRAHMAN** (sense 3).

zed /zed/ ▶ *n. Brit.* the letter Z.

zee /zē/ ▶ *n.* the letter Z.

Zen /zen/ (also **Zen Buddhism**) ▶ *n.* a Japanese school of Buddhism emphasizing the value of meditation and intuition. —**Zen Bud·dhist** *n.*

ze·nith /'zēniTH/ ▶ *n.* the highest point reached by a celestial or other object: *the missile reached its zenith and fell.* ■ the point in the sky or celestial sphere directly above an observer. The opposite of **NADIR.** ■ the

time at which something is most powerful or successful: *under Justinian, the Byzantine Empire reached its zenith of influence.* —**ze·nith·al** /-nəTHəl/ *adj.*

ze·o·lite /'zēə,līt/ ▶ *n.* any of a large group of minerals consisting of hydrated aluminosilicates of sodium, potassium, calcium, and barium. They are used as cation exchangers and molecular sieves. —**ze·o·lit·ic** /,zēə'litik/ *adj.*

zeph·yr /'zefər/ ▶ *n.* **1** *poetic/lit.* a soft gentle breeze. **2** *hist.* a fine cotton gingham. ■ a very light article of clothing.

ze·ro /'zi(ə)rō/ ▶ *cardinal number* (*pl.* **-ros**) no quantity or number; the figure 0: *figures from zero to nine.* ■ a point on a scale or instrument from which a positive or negative quantity is reckoned. ■ the temperature corresponding to 0° on the Celsius scale (32° Fahrenheit), marking the freezing point of water: *the temperature was below zero.* ■ the temperature corresponding to 0° on the Fahrenheit scale (approx. minus 18° Celsius), considered a very cold temperature, esp. for outdoor activities. See also **SUBZERO.** ■ [usu. as *adj.*] *Linguistics* the absence of an actual word or morpheme to realize a syntactic or morphological phenomenon: *the zero plural in "three sheep."* ■ the lowest possible amount or level; nothing at all: *I rated my chances as zero.* ■ *inf.* a worthless or contemptibly undistinguished person: *her husband is an absolute zero.*
▶ *v.* (**-roes**, **-roed**) [*tr.*] adjust (an instrument) to zero: *zero the counter when the tape has rewound.* **2** set the sights of (a gun) for firing.
▶ *phrasal v.* □ **zero in** take aim with a gun or missile: *jet fighters zeroed in on the rebel positions.* ■ focus one's attention: *they zeroed in on the clues he gave away about.* □ **zero out** phase out or reduce to zero: *the bill would zero out capital gains taxes.*

ze·ro-sum ▶ *adj.* (of a game or situation) in which whatever is gained by one side is lost by the other: *altruism is not a zero-sum game.*

zest /zest/ ▶ *n.* **1** great enthusiasm and energy: *they campaigned with zest and intelligence.* ■ a quality of excitement and piquancy: *I used to try to beat past records to add zest to my monotonous job.* **2** the outer colored part of the peel of citrus fruit, used as flavoring. —**zest·ful** /-fəl/ *adj.* —**zest·ful·ly** *adv.* —**zest·ful·ness** *n.* —**zest·y** *adj.*

ze·ta /'zātə/ ▶ *n.* the sixth letter of the Greek alphabet (Z, ζ), transliterated as 'z.'

zeug·ma /'zōōgmə/ ▶ *n.* a figure of speech in which a word applies to two others in different senses (e.g., *John and his license expired last week*) or to two others of which it semantically suits only one (e.g., *with weeping eyes and hearts*). —**zeug·mat·ic** /zōōg'matik/ *adj.*

Zeus /zōōs/ *Greek Mythol.* ▶ the supreme god who was the protector and ruler of humankind, the dispenser of good and evil, and the god of weather and atmospheric phenomena (such as rain and thunder). Roman equivalent **JUPITER.**

zi·do·vu·dine /zī'dävyə,dēn; zə-; -'dō-/ ▶ *n. Med.* an antiviral drug, $C_{10}H_{13}N_5O_4$, used in the treatment of AIDS. It slows the growth of HIV infection in the body, but is not curative.

zig /zig/ ▶ *n.* a sharp change of direction in a zigzag course: *he went round and round in zigs and zags.*
▶ *v.* (**zigged**, **zig·ging**) [*intr.*] make a sharp change of direction: *we zigged to the right.*

zig·gu·rat /'zigə,rat/ ▶ *n.* (in ancient Mesopotamia) a rectangular stepped tower, sometimes surmounted by a temple. Ziggurats are first attested in the late 3rd millennium BC and probably inspired the biblical story of the Tower of Babel.

zig·zag /'zig,zag/ ▶ *n.* a line or course having abrupt alternate right and left turns. ■ a turn on such a course: *a series of sharp zigzags.*

▸*adj.* having the form of a zigzag; veering to right and left alternately: *when chased by a predator, some animals take a zigzag course.*

▸*adv.* so as to move right and left alternately: *she drives zigzag across the city.*

▸*v.* (**-zagged, -zag·ging**) [*intr.*] have or move along in a zigzag course: *the path zigzagged between the trees.* —**zig·zag·ged·ly** /-ˌzaɡədlē/ *adv.* ▷early 18th cent.: from French, from German *Zickzack*, symbolic of alternation of direction, first applied to fortifications.

zilch /zilCH/ *inf.* ▸*pron.* nothing: *I did absolutely zilch.*

▸*adj.* not any; no: *the character has zilch class.*

zil·lion /ˈzilyən/ ▸*cardinal number inf.* an extremely large number of people or things: *we had zillions of customers.* —**zil·lionth** /-yənTH/ *adj.*

zinc /ziNGk/ ▸*n.* the chemical element of atomic number 30, a silvery-white metal that is a constituent of brass and is used for coating (galvanizing) iron and steel to protect against corrosion. (Symbol: **Zn**) ■ [usu. as *adj.*] galvanized iron or steel, esp. as the material of domestic utensils or corrugated roofs: *a zinc roof.*

zinc ox·ide ▸*n.* an insoluble white solid used as a pigment and in medicinal ointments.

zing /ziNG/ *inf.* ▸*n.* energy, enthusiasm, or liveliness: *he was expected to add some zing to the lackluster team.* ■ strong or piquant flavor: *sprinkle the seasoning on fish to give it zing.*

▸*v.* [*intr.*] move swiftly: *he could send an arrow zinging through the air.* ■ [*tr.*] attack or criticize sharply: *he zinged the budget deal.* —**zing·y** *adj.*

zing·er /ˈziNGər/ ▸*n. inf.* a striking or amusing remark: *open a speech with a zinger.* ■ an outstanding person or thing: *a zinger of a shot.*

zin·ni·a /ˈzinēə/ ▸*n.* an American plant (genus *Zinnia*) of the daisy family, widely cultivated for its bright showy flowers.

Zi·on /ˈzīən/ (also **Si·on**) ▸*n.* the Jewish people or religion. ■ (in Christian thought) the heavenly city or kingdom of heaven.

Zi·on·ism /ˈzīəˌnizəm/ ▸*n.* a movement for (originally) the reestablishment and (now) the development and protection of a Jewish nation in what is now Israel. —**Zi·on·ist** *n. & adj.*

zip /zip/ ▸*v.* (**zipped, zip·ping**) **1** [*tr.*] fasten with a zipper: *I zipped up my sweater.* ■ (**zip someone up**) fasten the zipper of a garment that someone is wearing: *he zipped himself up.* ■ *Comput.* compress (a file) so that it takes less space in storage. **2** [*intr.*] *inf.* move at high speed: *swallows zipped back and forth across the lake.* ■ [*tr.*] cause to move or be delivered or dealt with rapidly: *he zipped a pass out to his receiver.*

▸*n.* **1** (also **zip fastener**) *chiefly Brit.* a zipper. ■ [as *adj.*] denoting something fastened by a zipper: *a zip pocket.* **2** short for ZIP CODE.

▸*pron.* (also **zip·po** /ˈzipō/) *inf.* nothing at all: *you got zip to do with me and my kind, buddy.*

zip code (also **ZIP code**) ▸*n.* a group of five or nine numbers that are added to a postal address to assist the sorting of mail.

Zip drive ▸*n. trademark Comput.* a disk drive that stores data on high-capacity removable magnetic disks, often used for data backup.

zip file (also **ZIP file, zipped file**) ▸*n.* a computer file whose contents of one or more files are compressed for storage or transmission, often carrying the extension .ZIP: *a self-extracting zip file.*

zip·per /ˈzipər/ ▸*n.* **1** a device consisting of two flexible strips with metal or plastic interlocking projections closed or opened by pulling a slide along them, used to fasten garments, bags, and other items. **2** a display of news or advertisements that scrolls across an illuminated screen fixed to the upper part of a building.

▸*v.* [*tr.*] fasten or provide (something) with a zipper: *he wore a running suit zippered up tight.*

zip·py /ˈzipē/ ▸*adj.* (**-pi·er, -pi·est**) *inf.* bright, fresh, or lively: *a zippy, zingy, almost citrusy tang.* ■ fast or speedy: *zippy new sedans.* —**zip·pi·ly** *adv.* —**zip·pi·ness** *n.*

zir·con /ˈzərˌkän/ ▸*n.* a mineral occurring as prismatic crystals, typically brown but sometimes in translucent varieties of gem quality. It consists of zirconium silicate and is the chief ore of zirconium.

zir·co·ni·um /ˌzərˈkōnēəm/ ▸*n.* the chemical element of atomic number 40, a hard silver-gray metal of the transition series. (Symbol: **Zr**)

zit /zit/ ▸*n. inf.* a pimple on the skin.

zith·er /ˈziTHər; ˈziTH-/ ▸*n.* a musical instrument consisting of a flat wooden sound box with numerous strings stretched across it, placed horizontally and played with the fingers and a plectrum. It is used esp. in central European folk music. —**zith·er·ist** *n.*

zlo·ty /ˈzlôtē; ˈzlä-/ ▸*n.* (*pl.* same, **-tys**) the basic monetary unit of Poland, equal to 100 groszy.

Zn ▸*symb.* the chemical element zinc.

zo·di·ac /ˈzōdēˌak/ ▸*n. Astrol.* a belt of the heavens within about 8° either side of the ecliptic, including all apparent positions of the sun, moon, and most familiar planets. It is divided into twelve equal divisions or signs (Aries, Taurus, Gemini, Cancer, Leo, Virgo, Libra, Scorpio, Sagittarius, Capricorn, Aquarius, Pisces). ■ a representation of the signs of the zodiac or of a similar astrological system. —**zo·di·a·cal** /zōˈdīəkəl/ *adj.*

zo·di·a·cal sign ▸*n.* see SIGN (sense 3).

zom·bie /ˈzämbē/ ▸*n.* **1** originally, a snake-deity of or deriving from West Africa and Haiti. **2** a soulless corpse said to be revived by witchcraft, esp. in certain African and Caribbean religions. ■ *inf.* a person who is or appears lifeless, apathetic, or completely unresponsive to their surroundings. **3** a tall mixed drink consisting of several kinds of rum, liqueur, and fruit juice. —**zom·bie-like** /-ˌlīk/ *adj.*

zone /zōn/ ▸*n.* **1** an area or stretch of land having a particular characteristic, purpose, or use, or subject to particular restrictions: *a pedestrian zone.* ■ *Geog.* a well-defined region extending around the earth between definite limits, esp. between two parallels of latitude. ■ (also **time zone**) a range of longitudes where a common standard time is used. ■ *Sports* in basketball, football, and hockey, a specific area of the court, field, or rink, esp. one to be defended by a particular player, or the mode of defensive play using this system. See ZONE DEFENSE below. ■ a specific region or area within which uniform rates are charged for transportation, parcel post delivery, or other service. ■ formerly, any of the numbered areas into which a large city or metropolitan area was divided for facilitating mail delivery. **2** *Math.* an area between two exact or approximate concentric circles. ■ a part of the surface of a sphere enclosed between two parallel planes, or of a cone or cylinder, etc., between such planes cutting it perpendicularly to the axis. **3** *Geol., Paleontol.* a range between specified limits of depth, height, etc., esp. a section of strata distinguished by characteristic fossils.

▸*v.* [*tr.*] **1** divide into or assign to zones, in particular: ■ [often as *n.*] (**zoning**) divide (a town or stretch of land) into areas subject to particular planning restrictions: *an experimental system of zoning.* ■ designate (a specific area) for use or development in such a manner: *the land is zoned for housing.* **2** *archaic* encircle as or with a band or stripe.

▸*phrasal v.* □ **zone out** *inf.* fall asleep or lose concentration or consciousness: *I just zoned out for a moment.* ▷late Middle English: from French, or from Latin *zona* 'girdle,' from Greek *zōnē*. —**zon·al** /ˈzōnl/ *adj.* —**zon·al·ly** /ˈzōnl-ē/ *adv.*

zonked /zäNGkt; zôNGkt/ ▸*adj. inf.* under the influence of drugs or alcohol: *the others got zonked on acid* | *a zonked-out beach bum.* ■ exhausted; tired out: *we hit the sack, zonked out.*

zoo /zoo/ ▸*n.* an establishment that maintains a collection of wild animals, typically in a park or gardens, for study, conservation, or display to the public. ■ *inf.* a situation characterized by confusion and disorder: *it's a zoo in the lobby.* —**zoo·ey** *adj. inf.* .

zoo·ge·og·ra·phy /ˌzōəjēˈäɡrəfē/ ▸*n.* the branch of zoology that deals with the geographical distribution of animals. —**zo·o·ge·og·ra·pher** /-fər/ *n.* —**zo·o·ge·o·graph·ic** /-ˌjēəˈɡrafik/ *adj.* —**zo·o·ge·o·graph·i·cal** /-ˌjēəˈɡrafikəl/ *adj.* —**zo·o·ge·o·graph·i·cal·ly** /-ˌjēəˈɡrafik(ə)lē/ *adv.*

zo·oid /ˈzōˌoid/ ▸*n. Zool.* an animal arising from another by budding or division, esp. each of the individuals that make up a colonial organism and typically have different forms and functions.

zool. ▸*abbr.* ■ zoological. ■ zoologist. ■ zoology.

zo·o·log·i·cal /ˌzōəˈläjikəl; ˌzōōə-/ ▸*adj.* of or relating to zoology: *zoological classification.* ■ of or relating to animals: *eighty zoological woodcuts.* —**zo·o·log·i·cal·ly** /-ik(ə)lē/ *adv.*

zo·ol·o·gy /zōˈäləjē; zōō-/ ▸*n.* the scientific study of the behavior, structure, physiology, classification, and distribution of animals. ■ the animal life of a particular area or time: *the zoology of Russia's vast interior.* —**zo·ol·o·gist** /-jist/ *n.*

zoom /zoom/ ▸*v.* [*intr.*] **1** (esp. of a car or aircraft) move or travel very quickly: *he jumped into his car and zoomed off.* ■ [*intr.*] (of prices) rise sharply: *the share index zoomed by about 136 points.* **2** (of a camera) change

zither

smoothly from a long shot to a close-up or vice versa: *the camera zoomed in for a close-up of his face.* ■ [*tr.*] cause (a lens or camera) to do this.
▶*n.* a camera shot that changes smoothly from a long shot to a close-up or vice versa: [as *adj.*] *the zoom button.* ■ short for ZOOM LENS.
▶*interj.* used to express sudden fast movement: *zoom!, he's off.*
zoom lens ▶*n.* a lens allowing a camera to change smoothly from a long shot to a close-up or vice versa by varying the focal length.
zo·o·mor·phic /ˌzōəˈmôrfik/ ▶*adj.* having or representing animal forms or gods of animal form: *pottery decorated with anthropomorphic and zoomorphic designs.* —**zo·o·mor·phism** *n.*
zo·o·phyte /ˈzōəˌfīt/ ▶*n. dated Zool.* a plantlike animal, esp. a coral, sea anemone, sponge, or sea lily.
zo·o·plank·ton /ˈzōəˌplaNGktən/ ▶*n. Biol.* plankton consisting of small animals and the immature stages of larger animals.
ZPG ▶*abbr.* zero population growth.
Zr ▶*symb.* the chemical element zirconium.

zuc·chi·ni /zo͞oˈkēnē/ ▶*n.* (*pl.* same or **-nis**) a green variety of smooth-skinned summer squash.
Zu·lu /ˈzo͞olo͞o/ ▶*n.* **1** a member of a South African people living mainly in KwaZulu-Natal province. ■ the Nguni language of this people. **2** a code word representing the letter Z, used in radio communication.
▶*adj.* of or relating to the Zulu people or language.
Zu·ni /ˈzo͞onē/ (also **Zu·ñi** /ˈzo͞onyē/) ▶*n.* (*pl.* same or **Zu·nis**) **1** a member of a Pueblo Indian people of western New Mexico. **2** the language of this people.
▶*adj.* of or relating to this people or their language.
zwie·back /ˈswēˌbak; ˈzwē-; ˈswī-; ˈzwī-/ ▶*n.* a rusk or cracker made by baking a small loaf and then toasting slices until they are crisp.
zy·go·mat·ic bone ▶*n. Anat.* the bone that forms the prominent part of the cheek and the outer side of the eye socket.
zy·gote /ˈzīˌgōt/ ▶*n. Biol.* a diploid cell resulting from the fusion of two haploid gametes; a fertilized ovum. —**zy·got·ic** /zīˈgätik/ *adj.*

Ready Reference

Commonly Misspelled Words

absence
absolutely
acceptance
accessible
accidentally
accommodate
accompany
accuracy
ache
achieve
achievement
acquaintance
acquire
acre
across
actually
administration
admittance
adolescent
advantageous
advertisement
advisable
affectionate
affidavit
aficionado
afraid
again aisle
aggravate
aghast
allege
allotment
allotment
ally
amateur
analysis
analyze
anesthetic
angel

angle
annually
answer
anticipate
anxiety
apartheid
aperitif
apology
apparatus
apparent
appearance
appetite
appreciate
approach
appropriate
approximately
argue
argument
arrangement
ascend
ascertain
assistant
athletic
attendance
authority
auxiliary
available
awkward
bachelor
because
beggar
beginning
behavior
believe
benefit
benefited
bicycle
bouillon

boundary
bulletin
bureau
buried
business
cafeteria
calendar
campaign
cancellation
captain
carburetor
career
ceiling
cemetery
census
certificate
chamois
changeable
character
characteristic
chauffeur
chic
chief
chocolate
choice
choose
chose
Christian
clothes
collateral
colonel
color
column
commercial
commission
committee
community
compel

competitor
completely
conceivable
concentrate
condemn
confidence
confidential
confusion
connoisseur
conscience
conscious
continuous
controlled
controversial
convertible
cooperate
copyright
corps
correspondence
counterfeit
courageous
courteous
criticism
criticize
cruelly
curiosity
curious
cylinder
dealt
debtor
deceive
decision
definite
dependent
describe
despair
desperate
despise

develop	experiment	hanger	knowledge
difference	extraordinary	happened	laboratory
dilemma	extremely	happiness	laborer
disappearance	facsimile	harass	laid
disappoint	familiar	Hawaii	legitimate
disastrous	fantasy	heavily	leisure
discipline	fascinate	height	liaison
discrepancy	fashionable	heinous	library
disease	fasten	heroine	license
doctor	fatal	hors d'oeuvre	lieutenant
duplicate	favorite	hospital	lightning
easily	February	humor	likely
ecclesiastical	field	humorous	liquefy
ecstasy	fiery	hungrily	liquidate
effect	finally	hygiene	listener
efficient	financial	hypocrisy	literature
eighth	forehead	hypocrite	livelihood
elementary	foreign	ignorance	lively
eligible	forfeit	illiterate	loneliness
embarrass	fortunately	imagine	luxury
eminent	forty	immediately	magazine
emphasize	forward	impossible	magnificent
encouragement	fourth	incidentally	maintenance
encumbrances	freight	increase	maneuver
enforceable	friend	indefinite	manufacturer
entirely	fulfill	independent	marriage
entourage	further	indictment	marvelous
envelope	gauge	indispensable	mathematics
environment	genius	individually	meant
equipped	gourmet	inevitable	mechanic
escape	government	influence	medical
especially	governor	ingredient	medicine
essential	gracious	innocence	melancholy
exaggerate	grammar	inoculate	merchandise
excellent	guarantee	insurance	millionaire
exciting	guerrilla	intelligence	miniature
exercise	guess	interference	minimum
exhilarating	guidance	interrupt	minuscule
exhort	gymnasium	iridescent	minute
existence	gypsy	irrelevant	miscellaneous
expense	handsome	itinerary	mischief
experience	hangar	jealous	mischievous

misspell	peculiar	quite	semester
mortgage	performance	realize	separate
muscle	permanent	really	sergeant
mysterious	perseverance	realtor	shepherd
narrative	personality	realty	siege
naturally	personnel	receipt	similar
necessary	perspiration	recognize	sincerely
nickel	persuade	recommend	skein
niece	pessimistic	referred	skiing
niece	phenomenal	reign	skillful
ninety	Philippines	relevant	sophomore
noisily	philosophy	relieve	soufflé
non sequitur	physical	religious	source
noticeable	picnicking	removal	souvenir
obstacle	pleasant	rendezvous	specifically
occasionally	politician	repertoire	specimen
occurrence	Portuguese	repetition	sponsor
offensive	possession	rescind	statistics
official	possibility	reservoir	straight
often	practically	resistance	strength
omission	practice	resource	stretch
omit	prairie	responsibility	strictly
omitted	preferred	restaurant	stubborn
once	prejudice	rheumatism	substitute
operate	preparation	rhythm	subtle
opponent	presence	ridiculous	succeed
opportunity	pressure	roommate	successful
optimistic	pretension	sachet	suede
orchestra	privilege	sacrifice	sufficient
ordinarily	probably	sacrilegious	summary
organization	procedure	safety	superintendent
originally	proceed	satisfied	supersede
outrageous	procure	scarcely	surgeon
pageant	professor	scarcity	surprise
paid	proffered	scene	susceptible
parallel	promissory	schedule	suspense
paralleled	pronunciation	scholar	swimming
paralyze	propaganda	scissors	sympathetic
parliament	psychology	scurrilous	synonym
particular	pursuit	seance	temperamental
pastime	questionnaire	secretary	temperature
peaceful	quiet	seize	tendency

therefore	twelfth	vague	weather
thorough	typical	valuable	Wednesday
though	unanimous	variety	weird
thoughtful	unnecessary	various	whether
tomorrow	useful	vegetable	whole
tragedy	useless	vengeance	yacht
transferred	usually	vilify	yield
tremendous	vacillate	villain	
truly	vacuum	warrant	

Guide to Punctuation

Punctuation is an essential element of good writing because it makes the author's meaning clear to the reader. Although precise punctuation styles may vary somewhat among published sources, there are a number of fundamental principles worthy of consideration. Discussed below are these punctuation marks used in English:

comma	apostrophe
semicolon	quotation marks
colon	parentheses
period	dash
question mark	hyphen
exclamation point	

Comma

The **comma** is the most used mark of punctuation in the English language. It signals to the reader a pause, which generally clarifies the author's meaning and establishes a sensible order to the elements of written language. Among the most typical functions of the comma are the following:

1. It can separate the clauses of a compound sentence when there are two independent clauses joined by a conjunction, especially when the clauses are not very short:

    It never occurred to me to look in the attic, and I'm sure it didn't occur to Rachel either.

    The Nelsons wanted to see the canyon at sunrise, but they overslept that morning.

2. It can separate the clauses of a compound sentence when there is a series of independent clauses, the last two of which are joined by a conjunction:

    The bus ride to the campsite was very uncomfortable, the cabins were not ready for us when we got there, the cook had forgotten to start dinner, and the rain was torrential.

3. It is used to precede or set off, and therefore indicate, a nonrestrictive dependent clause (a clause that could be omitted without changing the meaning of the main clause):

    I read her autobiography, which was published last July.

    They showed up at midnight, after most of the guests had gone home.

    The coffee, which is freshly brewed, is in the kitchen.

4. It can follow an introductory phrase:

    Having enjoyed the movie so much, he agreed to see it again.

    Born and raised in Paris, she had never lost her French accent.

    In the beginning, they had very little money to invest.

5. It can set off words used in direct address:

   Listen, people, you have no choice in the matter.

   Yes, Mrs. Greene, I will be happy to feed your cat.

   Do you really believe, Eliza, that he will return the fifty dollars?

6. It can separate two or more coordinate adjectives (adjectives that could otherwise be joined with *and*) that modify one noun:

   The cruise turned out to be the most entertaining, fun, and relaxing vacation I've ever had.

   The horse was tall, lean, and sleek.

   Note that cumulative adjectives (those not able to be joined with and) are not separated by a comma:

   She wore bright yellow rubber boots.

7. It is used to separate three or more items in a series or list:

   Charlie, Melissa, Stan, and Mark will be this year's soloists in the spring concert.

   We need furniture, toys, clothes, books, tools, housewares, and other useful merchandise for the benefit auction.

   Note that the comma between the last two items in a series is sometimes omitted in less precise style:

   The most popular foods served in the cafeteria are pizza, hamburgers and nachos.

8. It is used to separate and set off the elements in an address or other geographical designation:

   My new house is at 1657 Nighthawk Circle, South Kingsbury, Michigan.

   We arrived in Pamplona, Spain, on Thursday.

9. It is used to set off direct quotations (note the placement or absence of commas with other punctuation):

   "Kim forgot her gloves," he said, "but we have a pair she can borrow."

   There was a long silence before Jack blurted out, "This must be the world's ugliest painting."

   "What are you talking about?" she asked in a puzzled manner.

   "Happy New Year!" everyone shouted.

10. It is used to set off titles after a person's name:

    Katherine Bentley, M.D.

    Martin Luther King, Jr., delivered the sermon.

Semicolon

The **semicolon** has two basic functions:

1. It can separate two main clauses, particularly when these clauses are of equal importance:

   The crowds gathered outside the museum hours before the doors were opened; this was one exhibit no one wanted to miss.

   She always complained when her relatives stayed for the weekend; even so, she usually was a little sad when they left.

2. It can be used as a comma is used to separate such elements as clauses or items in a series or list, particularly when one or more of the elements already includes a comma:

   The path took us through the deep, dark woods; across a small meadow into a cold, wet cave; and up a hillside overlooking the lake.

   Listed for sale in the ad were two bicycles; a battery-powered, leaf-mulching lawn mower; and a maple bookcase.

Colon

The **colon** has five basic functions:

1. It can introduce something, especially a list of items:

   In the basket were three pieces of mail: a postcard, a catalog, and a wedding invitation.

   Students should have the following items: backpack, loose-leaf notebook, pens and pencils, pencil sharpener, and ruler.

2. It can separate two clauses in a sentence when the second clause is being used to explain or illustrate the first clause:

   We finally understood why she would never go sailing with us: she had a deep fear of the water.

   Most of the dogs in our neighborhood are quite large: two of them are St. Bernards.

3. It can introduce a statement or a quotation:

   His parents say the most important rule is this: Always tell the truth.

   We repeated the final words of his poem: "And such is the plight of fools like me."

4. It can be used to follow the greeting in a formal or business letter:

   Dear Ms. Daniels:

   Dear Sir or Madam:

5. It is used in the United States to separate minutes from hours, and seconds from minutes, in showing time of day and measured length of time:

   Please be at the restaurant before 6:45.

   Her best running time so far has been 00:12:35.

Period

The period has two basic functions:

1. It is used to mark the end of a sentence:

    It was reported that there is a shortage of nurses at the hospital. Several of the patients have expressed concern about this problem.

2. It is often used at the end of an abbreviation:

    On Fri., Sept. 12, Dr. Brophy noted that the patient's weight was 168 lb. and that his height was 6 ft. 2 in.

    (Note that another period is not added to the end of the sentence when the last word is an abbreviation.)

Question Mark and Exclamation Point

The only sentences that do not end in a period are those that end in either a question mark or an exclamation point.

Question marks are used to mark the end of a sentence that asks a direct question (generally, a question that expects an answer):

Is there any reason for us to bring more than a few dollars?

Who is your science teacher?

Exclamation points are used to mark the end of a sentence that expresses a strong feeling, typically surprise, joy, or anger:

I want you to leave and never come back!

What a beautiful view this is!

Apostrophe

The apostrophe has two basic functions:

1. It is used to show where a letter or letters are missing in a contraction.

    The directions are cont'd [continued] *on the next page.*

    We've [we have] *decided that if she can't* [cannot] *go, then we aren't* [are not] *going either.*

2. It can be used to show possession:

    The possessive of a singular noun or an irregular plural noun is created by adding an apostrophe and an *s*:

    the pilot's uniform
    Mrs. Mendoza's house
    a tomato's bright red color
    the oxen's yoke

The possessive of a regular plural noun is created by adding just an apostrophe:

the pilots' uniforms [referring to more than one pilot]

the Mendozas' house [referring to the Mendoza family]

the tomatoes' bright red color [referring to more than one tomato]

Quotation Marks

Quotation marks have two basic functions:

1. They are used to set off direct quotations (an exact rendering of someone's spoken or written words):

    "I think the new library is wonderful," she remarked to David.

    We were somewhat lost, so we asked, "Are we anywhere near the gallery?"

    "In his letter he had written, "The nights here are quiet and starry. It seems like a hundred years since I've been wakened by the noise of city traffic and squabbling neighbors."

    Note that indirect quotes (which often are preceded by *that*, *if*, and *whether*) are not set off by quotation marks:

    He told me that he went to school in Boston.

    We asked if we could still get tickets to the game.

2. They can be used to set off words or phrases that have specific technical usage, or to set off meanings of words, or to indicate words that are being used in a special way in a sentence:

    The part of the flower that bears the pollen is the "stamen."

    When I said "plain," I meant "flat land," not "ordinary."

    Oddly enough, in the theater, the statement "break a leg" is meant as an expression of good luck.

    What you call "hoagies," we call "grinders" or "submarine sandwiches."

    He will never be a responsible adult until he outgrows his "Peter Pan" behavior.

    Note that sometimes single quotation marks, rather than double quotation marks, may be used to set off words or phrases:

    The part of the flower that bears the pollen is the 'stamen.'

    What is most important is to be consistent in such usage. Single quotation marks are also used to set off words or phrases within material already in double quotation marks, as:

    "I want the sign to say 'Ellen's Bed and Breakfast' in large gold letters," she explained.

Parentheses

Parentheses are used, in pairs, to enclose information that gives extra detail or explanation to the regular text. Parentheses are used in two basic ways:

1. They can separate a word or words in a sentence from the rest of the sentence:

    On our way to school, we walk past the Turner Farm (the oldest dairy farm in town) and watch the cows being fed.

    The stores were filled with holiday shoppers (even more so than last year).

    Note that the period goes outside the parentheses, because the words in the parentheses are only part of the sentence.

2. They can form a separate complete sentence:

    Please bring a dessert to the dinner party. (It can be something very simple.) I look forward to seeing you there.

    Note that the period goes inside the parentheses, because the words in the parentheses are a complete and independent sentence.

Dash

A **dash** is used most commonly to replace the usage of parentheses within sentences. If the information being set off is in the middle of the sentence, a pair of long (or "em") dashes is used; if it is at the end of the sentence, just one long dash is used:

On our way to school, we walk past the Turner Farm—the oldest dairy farm in town—and watch the cows being fed.

The stores were filled with holiday shoppers—even more so than last year.

Hyphen

A **hyphen** has three basic functions:

1. It can join two or more words to make a compound, especially when doing so makes the meaning more clear to the reader:

    We met to discuss long-range planning.

    There were six four-month-old piglets at the fair.

    That old stove was quite a coal-burner.

2. It can replace the word "to" when a span or range of data is given. This kind of hyphen is sometimes keyed as a short (or "en") dash:

    John Adams was president of the United States 1797–1801.

    Today we will look for proper nouns in the L–N section of the dictionary.

    The ideal weight for that breed of dog would be 75–85 pounds.

3. It can indicate a word break at the end of a line. The break must always be between syllables:

> *It is important for any writer to know that there are numerous punctuation principles that are considered standard and proper, but there is also flexibility regarding acceptable punctuation. Having learned the basic "rules" of good punctuation, the writer will be able to adopt a specific and consistent style of punctuation that best suits the material he or she is writing.*

COMMON CLICHÉS TO AVOID

A **cliché** is a worn-out expression. It was once fresh and meaningful, but it has lost its original impact through overuse. Numerous clichés have become so familiar that it would be virtually impossible to eradicate them from one's vocabulary. However, writers and speakers should make the effort to avoid using them, especially in formal material.

above and beyond the call of duty
accident waiting to happen
acid test
add insult to injury
after all is said and done
all hands on deck
all in all
all wet
all's well that ends well
almighty dollar
along the same lines
A-OK
as luck would have it
at a loss for words
at arm's length
avoid like the plague
back in the saddle
back on track
backseat driver
ball is in your court
barking up the wrong tree
be your own worst enemy
beat a dead horse
beat around the bush
been there, done that

beggars can't be choosers
be an open book
believe me
better late than never
between a rock and a hard place
between you, me, and the lamppost
big picture
big spender
bigger fish to fry
bird's-eye view
bitter end
bone of contention
born and bred
both sides of the coin
brain trust
bring home the bacon
broad spectrum
broaden one's horizons
bundle of nerves
bury the hatchet
busy as a bee
buy into
by leaps and bounds
by the skin of one's teeth
call her bluff

Common clichés to avoid (*continued*)

can't judge a book by its cover
can't take a joke
cast the net
catbird seat
catch as catch can
center of attention
cheat death
chew the fat
clear as a bell
clear as mud
cloak and dagger
coast is clear
cold as ice
cold shoulder
come full circle
come to no good
come up for air
conspicuous by their absence
cool it
cop out
could eat a horse
counting on you
count your blessings
cover all the bases
crazy like a fox
cream of the crop
creature of habit
crossing the line
cut me some slack
cut to the chase
dead in the water
dead wrong
dog-eat-dog
done deal
done to death
don't know him from Adam
down and dirty
down and out
down in the dumps
down in the mouth
dressed to the nines

due in large measure to
duly noted
dumb luck
easier said than done
easy come, easy go
easy mark
easy target
eat crow
end of discussion
every fiber of my being
face the music
fair and square
fall from grace
fall through the cracks
far and away
feast or famine
few and far between
fighting the tide
fill the bill
find it in your heart
fit as a fiddle
fit to be tied
fits like an old shoe
flat as a pancake
fly in the ointment
fly off the handle
for all intents and purposes
for love or money
for your information
fork it over
free as a bird
from the frying pan into the fire
from time immemorial
game plan
get behind the eight ball
get down to brass tacks
get off scot-free
get our ducks in a row
get the lead out
get the show on the road
get to the bottom of it

give a damn

give rise to

go for the kill

go it alone

go the distance

go the extra mile

go to pieces

go with the flow

goes without saying

good for nothing

goodly number

grass is always greener

green with envy

grist for the mill

hammer out the details

handwriting on the wall

hang in there

has a screw loose

have your heart in your mouth

head over heels

heated argument

his bark is worse than his bite

hit or miss

hit the ceiling

hit the ground running

hit the nail on the head

hold that thought

holding back the tide

hook, line, and sinker

hour of need

I wasn't born yesterday

icing on the cake

if looks could kill

if the price is right

I'm all over it

I'm speechless

in a nutshell

in due course

in hot water

in layman's terms

in one fell swoop

in over their heads

in seventh heaven

in the bag

in the ballpark

in the driver's seat

in the event that

in the final analysis

in the groove

in the near future

in the neighborhood of

in the nick of time

in the same boat

in the zone

in this day and age

irons in the fire

it could be worse

it stands to reason

it takes all kinds

it takes guts

it's your baby

join the club

keep your fingers crossed

keep the home fires burning

keeping score

kill the fatted calf

kiss of death

knock on wood

knock the socks off of

know the ropes

last but not least

last straw

lay an egg

learning curve

leave no stone unturned

left to his own devices

lend me an ear

let the cat out of the bag

let your hair down

letter perfect

lie low

light of day

like a bull in a china shop

like a bump on a log

Common clichés to avoid (*continued*)

like greased lightning	on cloud nine
like rolling off a log	on the one hand/on the other hand
little does he know	on the road
live it up	on the same page
lock, stock, and barrel	on the same track
look like a million bucks	on the wagon
low man on the totem pole	on top of the world
make ends meet	out of my league
make tracks	out of the woods
makes her blood boil	over a barrel
method in (*or* to) my madness	pan out
millstone around your neck	par for the course
mince words	pass the buck
misery loves company	pay the piper
moment of truth	perish the thought
Monday-morning quarterback	piece of cake
monkey on your back	playing for keeps
more money than God	powers that be
more than meets the eye	practice makes perfect
more than you could shake a stick at	proud as a peacock
nail to the wall	pulling my leg
naked truth	pulling no punches
nearing the finish line	put faces to names
needle in a haystack	put on hold
needs no introduction	put the bite on
never a dull moment	put words in one's mouth
nip and tuck	put your money where your mouth is
nip in the bud	quick and dirty
no harm, no foul	rags to riches
no skin off my nose	rant and rave
no strings attached	reading me like a book
no-brainer	real McCoy
none the worse for wear	red as a beet
nose to the grindstone	regret to inform you
not one red cent	reign supreme
nothing new under the sun	rings a bell
off the cuff	ripe old age
old as the hills	rise and shine
old hat	rolling over in his grave
old soldiers never die	rub elbows
older than dirt	rule the roost

run circles around

run it up the flagpole

run off at the mouth

sadder but wiser

safe to say

salt of the earth

scarce as hen's teeth

sea of faces

see the forest for the trees

sell like hotcakes

set in stone

shake a leg

sharp as a tack

ships that pass in the night

shoot the breeze

shooting himself in the foot

shot in the arm

shot to hell

sight for sore eyes

sitting duck

skeleton in the closet

skin alive

sleep on it

smells fishy

smooth sailing

snake in the grass

spill the beans

stay in the loop

steal the limelight

stem the tide

stick to your guns

stick your neck out

straight from the horse's mouth

strange bedfellows

strike a balance

strong as an ox

stubborn as a mule

sturdy as an oak

suffice it to say

sweating bullets

take a breather

take into consideration

take on board

take one's word for

take pleasure in

take the bitter with the sweet

take the easy way out

take the liberty of

talk shop

talk the talk

talk through your hat

talk your ear off

that's all she wrote

the die is cast

they'll be sorry

thick as thieves

thin as a rail

think outside the box

think tank

those are the breaks

through thick and thin

throw caution to the wind

thrown to the wolves

tighten our belts

time is money

time marches on

time waits for no man

to each his own

to your heart's content

too funny for words

took the words right out of my mouth

touch base

turn the other cheek

turn up your nose

two peas in a pod

ugly as sin

under the wire

up a creek

upset the applecart

venture a guess

vicious circle

waiting for the other shoe to drop

walk the walk

walking encyclopedia

Common clichés to avoid (*continued*)

walking on air	with bated breath
welcome with open arms	without further ado
when the cows come home	without further delay
where angels fear to tread	wonders never cease
where there's smoke, there's fire	words fail me
whole nine yards	wreak havoc
wild-goose chase	yada, yada, yada
wipe the slate clean	you said a mouthful
wishful thinking	you'll never know if you don't try

REDUNDANT EXPRESSIONS

A **redundant expression** is a group of words (usually a pair) in which at least one word is superfluous—that is, unnecessary. The superfluous element can be removed without affecting the meaning of the expression. In formal speech or writing, redundant expressions should be strictly avoided.

In the following list of common redundant expressions, the superfluous elements have been crossed out.

~~absolute~~ guarantee	~~brief~~ moment
~~absolutely~~ certain	~~but~~ however
~~absolutely~~ essential	~~but~~ nevertheless
~~absolutely~~ necessary	came ~~at a time~~ when
AC ~~current~~	cancel ~~out~~
~~actual~~ fact	~~chief~~ protagonist
~~actual~~ truth	~~clearly~~ obvious
add ~~an additional~~	climb ~~up~~
adding ~~together~~	~~close~~ proximity
~~advance~~ reservations	~~close~~ scrutiny
~~advance~~ warning	collaborate ~~together~~
after ~~the end of~~	combine ~~into one~~
all meet ~~together~~	commute ~~back and forth~~
alongside ~~of~~	~~complete~~ monopoly
~~already~~ existing	~~completely~~ destroyed
~~and~~ moreover	~~completely~~ eliminated
~~annoying~~ pest	~~completely~~ empty
ATM ~~machine~~	~~completely~~ filled
~~awkward~~ predicament	~~completely~~ random
bald-~~headed~~	consensus ~~of opinion~~
~~basic~~ essentials	continue ~~on~~
~~basic~~ fundamentals	~~continue to~~ remain
blend ~~together~~	cooperate ~~together~~

currently ~~today~~

DC ~~current~~

~~decorative~~ garnish

~~deep~~ chasm

~~definitely~~ decided

descend ~~down~~

~~different~~ varieties

~~difficult~~ dilemma

~~direct~~ confrontation

drop ~~down~~

during ~~the course of~~

dwindled ~~down~~

each ~~and every~~

earlier ~~in time~~

~~empty~~ space

~~end~~ result

enter ~~in~~

equal ~~to one another~~

~~established~~ fact

estimated at ~~about~~

estimated ~~roughly~~ at

~~every~~ now and then

~~evil~~ fiend

~~exact~~ duplicate

~~exact~~ opposites

~~fake~~ copy

~~false~~ pretenses

~~fellow~~ classmates

~~fellow~~ teammates

few ~~in number~~

filled ~~to capacity~~

~~final~~ conclusion

~~final~~ outcome

first ~~and foremost~~

~~first~~ began

~~first~~ introduction

first ~~of all~~

~~first~~ started

follow ~~after~~

for ~~a period of~~ six months

for ~~the purpose of~~

~~foreign~~ exports

~~foreign~~ imports

forever ~~and ever~~

foundered ~~and sank~~

~~free~~ gift

~~free~~ pass

~~future~~ prospects

gather ~~together~~

gave birth to a ~~baby~~ girl/boy

~~glowing~~ ember

~~good~~ bargain

~~good~~ benefits

had done ~~previously~~

~~harmful~~ injury

HIV ~~virus~~

~~honest~~ truth

~~hopeful~~ optimism

~~hot~~ water heater

I ~~myself personally~~

if ~~and when~~

~~important~~ breakthrough

in ~~close~~ proximity

~~intense~~ fury

introduced ~~for the first time~~

~~invited~~ guests

ISBN ~~number~~

joined ~~together~~

~~just~~ recently

kneel ~~down~~

last ~~of all~~

lift ~~up~~

look back ~~in retrospect~~

~~major~~ breakthrough

may ~~possibly~~

~~mental~~ telepathy

merged ~~together~~

meshed ~~together~~

~~midway~~ between

might ~~possibly~~

mix ~~together~~

~~mutual~~ cooperation

~~natural~~ instinct

never ~~at any time~~

Redundant expressions to avoid (continued)

~~new~~ beginning

~~new~~ bride

~~new~~ innovation

~~new~~ recruit

nine A.M. ~~in the morning~~

no trespassing ~~allowed~~

none ~~at all~~

~~now~~ pending

null ~~and void~~

~~old~~ cliché

~~old~~ proverb

~~opening~~ introduction

~~originally~~ created

over ~~and done with~~

~~over~~exaggerate

~~pair of~~ twins

parched ~~dry~~

~~passing~~ fad

~~past~~ experiences

~~past~~ history

~~past~~ memories

~~past~~ records

penetrate ~~into~~

~~perfect~~ ideal

permeate ~~throughout~~

~~personal~~ friend

~~personal~~ opinion

~~personally~~ believes

PIN ~~number~~

plan ~~in advance~~

~~poisonous~~ venom

~~positively~~ true

~~possibly~~ might

postponed ~~until a later time~~

~~pre~~recorded

~~present~~ incumbent

probed ~~into~~

proceed ~~ahead~~

protest ~~against~~

protrude ~~out~~

~~proven~~ facts

raise ~~up~~

reason ~~why~~

refer ~~back~~

reflect ~~back~~

repeat ~~again~~

reply ~~back~~

revert ~~back~~

Rio Grande ~~River~~

~~sad~~ tragedy

same ~~identical~~

seemed ~~to be~~

share ~~together~~

short ~~in length~~

since ~~the time when~~

~~sincerely~~ mean it

skipped ~~over~~

~~solemn~~ vow

spelled out ~~in detail~~

stacked ~~on top of each other~~

~~still~~ continues

~~still~~ persists

~~still~~ remains

strangled ~~to death~~

~~stupid~~ fool

~~suddenly~~ exploded

sufficient ~~enough~~

~~sum~~ total

summer ~~season~~

~~sworn~~ affidavit

~~temporary~~ recess

~~temporary~~ reprieve

~~terrible~~ tragedy

~~thoughtful~~ contemplation

~~thoughtful~~ deliberation

~~totally~~ eliminated

~~true~~ fact

~~twelve~~ midnight

~~twelve~~ noon

~~two~~ twins

~~ultimate~~ conclusion

~~unexpected~~ surprise

~~unintentional~~ mistake

~~uninvited~~ party crashers

UPC ~~code~~

~~usual~~ custom

~~utter~~ annihilation

~~very~~ unique

ways ~~and means~~

~~well-known old~~ adage

when ~~and if~~

whether ~~or not~~

widow ~~woman~~

written ~~down~~

Proofreader's Marks

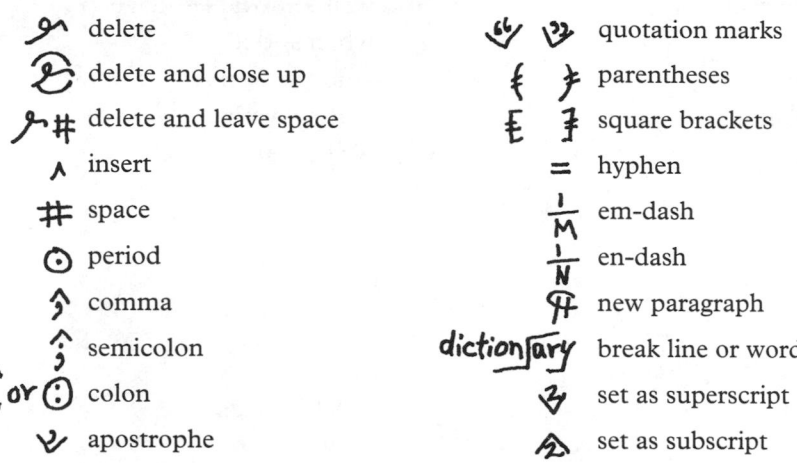

ๆ	delete
⟶	delete and close up
ๆ#	delete and leave space
∧	insert
#	space
⊙	period
⸲	comma
⸔	semicolon
∴ or ⊙	colon
⸕	apostrophe

⸜⸝	quotation marks
{ }	parentheses
⟦ ⟧	square brackets
=	hyphen
⊢M⊣	em-dash
⊢N⊣	en-dash
¶	new paragraph
diction⌐ary	break line or word
⸿	set as superscript
⸿	set as subscript

diction⸢ra⸣y	transpose
(tr)	transpose (note in margin)
③	spell out
(sp)	spell out (note in margin)
d̲i̲c̲tionary	capitalize
(cap)	set as capitals (note in margin)
Ðictionary	make lower case
(lc)	set in lower case (note in margin)
dictionary	make boldface
(bf)	set in boldface (note in margin)
dictionary	make italic
(ital)	set in italic (note in margin)
dictionary	small caps
(sc)	set in small caps (note in margin)
(lf)	lightface (note in margin)
(rom)	set in roman (note in margin)

Usage Notes

aggravate

Aggravate in the sense 'annoy or exasperate' dates back to the 17th century and has been so used by respected writers ever since. This use is still regarded as incorrect by some traditionalists on the grounds that it is too radical a departure from the etymological meaning of 'make heavy.' It is, however, comparable to meaning changes in hundreds of other words that have long been accepted without comment.

alternate, alternative

Alternate can be a verb, noun, or adjective, while **alternative** can be a noun or adjective. In both American and British English, the adjective **alternate** means 'every other' (*there will be a dance on **alternate** Saturdays*) and the adjective **alternative** means 'available as another choice' (*an **alternative** route*; ***alternative** medicine*; ***alternative** energy sources*). In American usage, however, **alternate** can also be used to mean 'available as another choice': *an **alternate** plan called for construction to begin immediately rather than waiting for spring.* Likewise, a book club may offer an 'alternate selection' as an alternative to the main selection.

Some traditionalists maintain, from an etymological standpoint, that you can have only two alternatives (from the Latin *alter* 'other (of two); the other') and that uses of more than two alternatives are erroneous. Such uses are, however, normal in modern standard English.

altogether, all together

Note that **altogether** and **all together** do not mean the same thing. **Altogether** means 'in total, totally' as in *there are six bedrooms **altogether***, or *that is a different matter **altogether***, whereas **all together** means 'all in one place' or 'all at once,' as in *it was good to have a group of friends **all together***, or *they came in **all together***.

anticipate

Anticipate in the sense 'expect, foresee' is well established in informal use (*he **anticipated** a restless night*), but this sense is regarded as a weakening of the meaning by many traditionalists. The formal sense is more specific in its meaning, 'be aware of and deal with beforehand' (*the doctor **anticipated** the possibility of a relapse by prescribing new medications*).

anyone, any one

Any one is not the same as **anyone**, and the two forms should not be used interchangeably. **Any one**, meaning 'any single (person or thing),' is written as two words to emphasize singularity: ***any one** of us could do the job*; *not more than ten new members are chosen in **any one** year*. Otherwise it is written as one word: ***anyone** who wants to come is welcome*.

Asian, Asiatic

The standard and accepted term when referring to individual people is **Asian** rather than **Asiatic**, which can be offensive. However, **Asiatic** is standard in scientific and technical use, for example in biological and anthropological classifications. See note for **Oriental**.

author, coauthor

In the sense 'be the author of,' the verb **author** is objected to by some traditionalists who regard it as an awkward or pretentious substitute for *write* or *compose*. This usage is widespread and well established though, and has been in use since the end of the 16th century. The verb **coauthor**, for which there is no common synonym, is useful and unobjectionable.

bad, badly

Confusion in the use of **bad** versus **badly** usually has to do with verbs called copulas, such as *feel* or *seem*. Thus, standard usage calls for *I feel **bad***, not *I feel **badly***. As a precise speaker or writer would explain, *I feel **badly*** means 'I do not have a good sense of touch.'

beg the question

The original meaning of the phrase **beg the question** belongs to the field of logic. It is a translation of the Latin rhetorical term *petitio principii*, literally meaning 'laying claim to a principle,' that is, assuming something that ought to be proved first, as in the following sentence: *dogs should be locked up, otherwise attacks by wild dogs on children will continue to increase*. This **begs the question** (among other questions) whether, in fact, such attacks are increasing. Usually such a statement will give the impression that the problem of proving the argument has been sidestepped. From this impression of sidestepping, a new meaning has developed: 'avoid the question, evade the issue,' as in *they said he **begged the question** by criticizing his opponent's program*. Also, over the last 100 years or so, another, more general use has arisen: 'invite an obvious question,' as in *some definitions of mental illness **beg the question** of what constitutes normal behavior*. Both of these newer meanings are widely accepted in modern standard English, although they have been criticized as being misunderstandings of the Latin rhetorical term. To some traditionalists, the sense of 'assume the truth of an argument to be proved' is still the only correct meaning of **beg the question**. Both of the newer meanings of **beg** are used not only with *question*, but with other words as well: *beg the point, beg the issue, beg the difficulties*.

between, among

Between is used in speaking of only two things, people, etc.: *we must choose **between** two equally unattractive alternatives*. **Among** is used for collective and undefined relations of usually three or more: *agreement on landscaping was reached **among** all the neighbors*. But where there are more than two parties involved, **between** may be used to express one-to-one relationships of pairs within the group or the sense 'shared by': *there is close friendship **between** the members of the club*; *diplomatic relations **between** the U.S., Canada, and Mexico*.

between you and me

Between you and I, between you and he, etc., are incorrect; **between** should be followed only by the objective case: *between you and me, between you and him,* etc.

bimonthly

The meaning of **bimonthly** (and other similar words such as **biweekly** and **biyearly**) is ambiguous. The only way to avoid this ambiguity is to use alternative expressions like *every two months* and *twice a month.* In the publishing world, the meaning of **bimonthly** is more fixed and is invariably used to mean 'every two months.'

black

Black, designating Americans of African heritage, became the most widely used and accepted term in the 1960s and 1970s, replacing **Negro**. It is not usually capitalized: *black Americans.*

Through the 1980s, the more formal *African American* replaced **black** in much usage, but both are now generally acceptable. *Afro-American*, first recorded in the 19th century and popular in the 1960s and 1970s, is now heard mostly in anthropological and cultural contexts. See note for **colored.**

blonde, blond

The spellings **blonde** and **blond** correspond to the feminine and masculine forms in French. Although the distinction is usually retained in Britain, American usage since the 1970s has generally preferred the gender-neutral **blond**. The adjective **blonde** may still refer to a woman's (but not a man's) hair color, though use of the noun risks offense (*See that **blonde** over there?*): the offense arises from the fact that the color of hair is not the person. The adjective applied to inanimate objects (such as *wood* or *beer*) is typically spelled **blond**.

both and

When **both** is used in constructions with **and**, the structures following 'both' and 'and' should be symmetrical in well-formed English. Thus, *studies of zebra finches, **both** in the wild **and** in captivity* is stronger and clearer than *studies of zebra finches, **both** in the wild **and** captivity*. In the second example, the symmetry or parallelism of 'in the wild' and 'in captivity' has been lost.

Caribbean

There are two possible pronunciations of the word **Caribbean**, and both are used widely and acceptably in the U.S. In the Caribbean itself, the preferred pronunciation puts the stress on the **-rib-**. In Britain, speakers more often put the stress on the **-be-**, although in recent years, the other pronunciation has gained ground in Britain as the more 'up-to-date' and, to some, the more 'correct' pronunciation.

co-

In modern American English, the tendency increasingly is to write compound words beginning with **co-** without hyphenation, as in *costar, cosignatory,* and *coproduce*. British

usage generally tends more often to show a preference for the older, hyphenated, spelling, but even in Britain the trend seems to be in favor of less hyphenation than in the past. In both the U.S. and the UK, for example, the spellings of *coordinate* and *coed* are encountered with or without hyphenation, but the more common choice for either word in either country is without the hyphen.

Co- with the hyphen is often used in compounds that are not yet standard (*co-golfer*), or to prevent ambiguity (*co-driver*—because *codriver* could be mistaken for *cod river*), or simply to avoid an awkward spelling (*co-own* is clearly preferable to *coown*). There are also some relatively less common terms, such as *co-respondent* (in a divorce suit), where the hyphenated spelling distinguishes the word's meaning and pronunciation from that of the more common *correspondent*.

colored

Colored referring to skin color is first recorded in the early 17th century and was adopted in the U.S. by emancipated slaves as a term of racial pride after the end of the Civil War. The word is still used in the National Association for the Advancement of Colored People (NAACP), but otherwise **colored** sounds old-fashioned at best, and is usually offensive.

People of color, has gained some favor, but is also used in reference to other nonwhite ethnic groups: *a gathering spot for African Americans and other **people of color** interested in reading about their cultures.*

In South Africa, the term **colored** (normally written **Coloured**) has a different history. It is used to refer to people of mixed-race parentage rather than, as elsewhere, to refer to African peoples and their descendants, i.e., as a synonym for *black*. In modern use in this context, the term is not considered offensive or derogatory. See note for **black.**

compare to, compare with

Traditionally, **compare to** is used when similarities are noted in dissimilar things: *shall I **compare** thee **to** a summer's day?* To **compare with** is to look for either differences or similarities, usually in similar things: ***compare** the candidate's claims **with** his actual performance.* In practice, however, this distinction is rarely maintained.

comprise

According to traditional usage, **comprise** means 'consist of,' as in *the country **comprises** twenty states*, and should not be used to mean 'constitute or make up (a whole),' as in *this single breed **comprises** 50 percent of the Swiss cattle population*. But confusion has arisen because of uses in the passive, which have been formed by analogy with words like *compose*: when **comprise** is used in the active (as in *the country **comprises** twenty states*) it is, oddly, more or less synonymous with the passive use of the second sense (as in *the country is comprised of twenty states*). Such passive uses of **comprise** are common and are fast becoming part of standard English.

continual, continuous

In precise usage, **continual** means 'frequent, repeating at intervals' and **continuous** means 'going on without pause or interruption': *we suffered from the **continual** attacks of* *mosquitoes; the waterfall's* **continuous** *flow creates an endless roar.* The most common error is the use of **continuous** where **continual** is meant: *continual* (that is, 'intermittent') *rain or tantrums can be tolerated;* **continuous** (that is, 'uninterrupted') *rain or tantrums cannot be tolerated.* To prevent misunderstanding, some careful writers use *intermittent* instead of **continual**, and *uninterrupted* in place of **continuous**. **Continuous** is the word to use in describing spatial relationships, as in *a* **continuous** *series of rooms* or *a* **continuous** *plain of arable land.* Avoid using **continuous** (or *continuously*) as a way of describing something that occurs at regular or seasonal intervals: in the sentence *our synagogue's Hanukkah candle-lighting ceremony has been held continuously since 1925,* the word *continuously* should be replaced with *annually.*

data

Data was originally the plural of the Latin word *datum,* 'something (e.g., a piece of information) given.' **Data** is now used as a singular where it means 'information': *this* **data** *was prepared for the conference.* It is used as a plural in technical contexts and when the collection of bits of information is stressed: *all recent* **data** *on hurricanes are being compared.* Avoid *datas* and *datae,* which are false plurals, neither English nor Latin.

deaf-mute

In modern use, **deaf-mute** has acquired offensive connotations (implying, wrongly, that such people are without the capacity for communication). It should be avoided in favor of other terms such as *profoundly deaf.*

decimate

Historically, the meaning of the word **decimate** is 'kill one in every ten of (a group of people).' This sense has been superseded by the later, more general sense 'kill or destroy a large percentage or part of,' as in *the virus has* **decimated** *the population.* Some traditionalists argue that this and other later senses are incorrect, but it is clear that these extended senses are now part of standard English. It is sometimes also argued that **decimate** should refer to people and not to things or animals such as weeds or insects. It is generally agreed that **decimate** should not be used to mean 'defeat utterly.'

due to

The use of **due to** as a prepositional phrase meaning 'because of,' as in *he had to retire* **due to** *an injury* first appeared in print in 1897, and traditional grammarians have opposed this prepositional usage for more than a century on the grounds that it is a misuse of the adjectival phrase **due to** in the sense of 'attributable to, likely or expected to' (*the train is* **due to** *arrive at 11:15*), or 'payable or owed to' (*render unto Caesar what is* **due to** *Caesar*). Nevertheless, this prepositional usage is now widespread and common in all types of literature and must be regarded as standard English.

The phrase *due to the fact that* is very common in speech, but it is wordy, and, especially in writing, one should use the simple word 'because.'

dumb

Although **dumb** meaning 'not able to speak' is the older sense, it has been overwhelmed by the newer sense (meaning 'stupid') to such an extent that the use of the first sense is now almost certain to cause offense. Alternatives such as *speech-impaired* should be used instead.

dwarf

In the sense 'an abnormally small person,' **dwarf** is normally considered offensive. However, there are no accepted alternatives in the general language, since terms such as *person of restricted growth* have gained little currency.

either . . . or

In good English writing style, it is important that **either** and **or** are correctly placed so that the structures following each word balance and mirror each other. Thus, sentences such as *either I accompany you or I wait here* and *I'm going to buy either a new camera or a new video* are correct, whereas sentences such as *either I accompany you or John* and *I'm either going to buy a new camera or a video* are not well-balanced sentences and should not be used in written English.

enormity

This word is imprecisely used to mean 'great size,' as in *it is difficult to comprehend the enormity of the continent,* but the original and preferred meaning is 'extreme wickedness,' as in *the enormity of the mass murders.* To indicate enormous size, the words *enormousness*, *immensity*, *vastness*, *hugeness*, etc., are preferable.

enthuse

The verb **enthuse** is formed as a back-formation from the noun *enthusiasm* and, like many verbs formed from nouns in this way, it is regarded by traditionalists as unacceptable. It is difficult to see why: back-formation is a perfectly established means for creating new words in the language (verbs like *classify*, *commentate*, and *edit* were also formed as back-formations from nouns, for example). **Enthuse** itself has been in the language for more than 150 years.

equal, unique

It is widely held that adjectives such as **equal** and **unique** have absolute meanings and therefore can have no degrees of comparison. Hence they should not be modified, and it is incorrect to say *more equal* or *very unique* on the grounds that these are adjectives that refer to a logical or mathematical absolute.

equally, equally as

The construction **equally as**—as in *follow-up discussion is equally as important*—is relatively common but is sometimes criticized on the grounds of redundancy. **Equally** used alone is adequate: *follow-up discussion is equally important.*

Eskimo

In recent years, **Eskimo** has come to be regarded as offensive because of one of its possible etymologies (Abnaki *askimo* 'eater of raw meat'), but this descriptive name is accurate since Eskimos traditionally derived their vitamins from eating raw meat. Another etymology (Montagnais *ayaškimew* 'netter of snowshoes') is possible, but the etymological problem is still unresolved.

The peoples inhabiting the regions from northwestern Canada to western Greenland call themselves *Inuit*. Since there are no Inuit living in the U.S., **Eskimo** is the only term that can be properly applied to all of the peoples as a whole, and it is still widely used in anthropological and archaeological contexts. The broader term *Native American* is sometimes used to refer to Eskimo and Aleut peoples. See note for **Inuit.**

espresso

The often-occurring variant spelling *expresso*—and its pronunciation /ik'spresō/—is incorrect and was probably formed by analogy with *express*.

everyday, every day

The adjective **everyday**, 'pertaining to every day, ordinary,' is correctly spelled as one word (*carrying out their everyday activities*), but the adverbial phrase **every day**, meaning 'each day,' is always spelled as two words (*it rained every day*).

everyone, every one

The pronoun **everyone,** meaning 'every person,' is correctly spelled as one word: *everyone had a great time at the party*. The pronoun **every one**, meaning 'each one,' is spelled as two words: *every one of the employees got a bonus at the end of the year*. The word *everybody* is substitutable in the first example but not in the second example.

exceptionable, exceptional

Exceptionable means 'open to objection' and is usually found in negative contexts: *there was nothing exceptionable in the evidence*. It is sometimes confused with the much more common **exceptional**, meaning 'unusual, outstanding.' Their opposites, *unexceptionable* ('unobjectionable, beyond criticism') and *unexceptional* ('ordinary'), are also sometimes confused.

feasible

The primary meaning of **feasible** is 'capable of being done or effected.' There is rarely a need to use **feasible** to mean 'likely' or 'probable' when those words can do the job. There are cases, however, in which a careful writer finds that the sense of likelihood or probability (as with an explanation or theory) is more naturally or idiomatically expressed with **feasible** than with *possible* or *probable*.

first, second, third

First, **second**, **third**, etc., are adverbs as well as adjectives: *first, dice three potatoes; second, add the bouillon*. *Firstly, secondly*, etc., are also correct, but make sure not to mix the two groups: *first, second, third* or *firstly, secondly, thirdly*; not *first, secondly, thirdly*.

fortuitous

The traditional, etymological meaning of **fortuitous** is 'happening by chance': a *fortuitous meeting* is a chance meeting, which might turn out to be either a good thing or a bad thing. In modern uses, however, **fortuitous** tends more often to be used to refer to fortunate outcomes, and the word has become more or less a synonym for 'lucky' or 'fortunate.' This use is frowned upon as being not etymologically correct and is best avoided except in informal contexts.

go and

The use of **go** followed by **and**, as in *I must go and change* (rather than *I must go to change*), is extremely common but is regarded by some grammarians as an oddity. *Go* used in the sense of *say* (*She goes, "No way!"*) is informal, on a par with *I'm like, "No way!"*

good, well

The adverb corresponding to the adjective **good** is **well**: *she is a good swimmer who performs well in meets.* Confusion sometimes arises because **well** is also an adjective meaning 'in good health, healthy,' for which **good** is widely used informally as a substitute: *I feel well*, meaning 'I feel healthy'—versus the informal *I feel good*, meaning either 'I feel healthy' or 'I am in a good mood.'

graduate, graduate from

The traditional use is 'be graduated from': *she will be graduated from medical school in June.* However, it is now more common to say **graduate from**: *she will graduate from medical school in June.* The use of **graduate** as a transitive verb, as in *he graduated high school last week*, is increasingly common, especially in speech, but is considered incorrect by most traditionalists.

grow

Although **grow** is typically intransitive, as in *he grew two inches taller over the summer*, its use as a transitive verb has long been standard in such phrases as *grow crops* and *grow a beard.*

Recently, however, **grow** has extended its transitive sense and has become trendy in business, economics, and government contexts: *growing the industry, growing your business, growing your investment*, and so on. Many people stumble over this extended sense and label it 'jargon.'

handicapped, disabled

Handicapped in the sense referring to a person's mental or physical disabilities is first recorded in the early 20th century. For a brief period in the second half of the 20th century, it looked as if **handicapped** would be replaced by **disabled**, but both words are now acceptable and interchangeable in standard American English, and neither word has been overtaken by newer coinages such as *differently abled* or *physically challenged.*

harass

Traditionally, the word **harass** has been pronounced with stress on the first syllable **har-**. But the newer pronunciation that puts the stress on the second syllable **-ass** is increasingly more widespread and is considered standard. This pronunciation fact is also true for *harassment*.

he

Until recently, **he** was used uncontroversially to refer to a person of unspecified sex, as in *every child needs to know that he is loved*. This use has become problematic and is a hallmark of old-fashionedness and sexism in language. Use of **they** as an alternative to **he** in this sense *(everyone needs to feel that they matter)* has been in use since the 16th century in contexts where it occurs after an indefinite pronoun such as *everyone* or *someone*. It is becoming more and more accepted both in speech and in writing. Another acceptable alternative is *he or she*, although this can become tiresomely long-winded when used frequently. See note for **they**.

hopefully

The traditional sense of **hopefully**, 'in a hopeful manner' (*he stared hopefully at the trophy*), has been used since 1593. The first recorded use of **hopefully** as a sentence adverb, meaning 'it is to be hoped that' (*hopefully, we'll see you tomorrow*), appears in 1702 in the *Magnalia Christi Americana*, written by Massachusetts theologian and writer Cotton Mather. This use of **hopefully** is now the most common one. Sentence adverbs in general (*frankly, honestly, regrettably, seriously*) are found in English since at least the 1600s, and their use has become common in recent decades. However, most traditionalists take the view that all sentence adverbs are inherently suspect. Although they concede that the battle over **hopefully** is lost on the popular front, they continue to withhold approval of its use as a sentence adverb. Attentive ears are particularly bothered when the sentence that follows does not match the promise of the introductory adverb, as when *frankly* is followed not by an expression of honesty but by a self-serving proclamation (*frankly, I don't care if you go or not*). See note for **thankfully**.

however, how ever

When **ever** is used as an intensifier after *how, what, when, where,* or *why*, it should be separated by a space. Thus, *how ever did you find her?* could be rephrased, with no change of meaning, *how did you ever find her?* This rule tends to be more often followed—or more widely understood—in Britain than in the U.S.

However in the sense of 'no matter how' (*however gently you correct him, Peter always takes offense*) should be spelled as one word.

humanitarian

Humanitarian is not synonymous with *human*, but usage often belies this fact, as evident in this sentence: *Red Cross volunteers rushed to the scene of what may be the the worst humanitarian disaster this country has seen*. This use of **humanitarian** to mean 'human' is quite common, esp. in 'live reports' on television, but is not generally considered good English style. Strictly speaking, it could be argued that *a **humanitarian disaster*** would more accurately refer to "a catastrophe to which no relief agencies responded."

Indian, Native American

Indian, meaning 'native of America before the arrival of Europeans,' is objected to by many who now favor **Native American**. There are others (including many members of these ethnic groups), however, who see nothing wrong with **Indian** or *American Indian*, which are long-established terms, although the preference where possible is to refer to specific peoples, as *Apache, Delaware*, and so on.

The terms *Amerind* and *Amerindian*, once proposed as alternatives to **Indian**, are used in linguistics and anthropology, but have never gained widespread use. Newer alternatives, not widely used or established, include *First Nation* (esp. in Canada) and the more generic *aboriginal peoples*.

It should be noted that **Indian** is held by many not to include some American groups, for example, Aleuts and Eskimos. A further consideration is that **Indian** also (and in some contexts primarily) refers to inhabitants of India or their descendants, who may be referred to as *Asian Indians* to prevent misunderstanding.

innocent, not guilty

Innocent properly means 'harmless,' but it has long been extended in general language to mean 'not guilty.' The jury (or judge) in a criminal trial does not, strictly speaking, find a defendant **innocent**. Rather, a defendant may be *guilty* or *not guilty* of the charges brought. In common use, however, owing perhaps to the concept of the *presumption of innocence*, which instructs a jury to consider a defendant free of wrongdoing until proven guilty on the basis of evidence, **not guilty** and **innocent** have come to be thought of as synonymous.

interface

The word **interface** is a relatively new word, having been in the language (as a noun) since the 1880s. However, in the 1960s it became widespread in computer use and, by analogy, began to enjoy a vogue as both a noun and a verb in many other spheres. Traditionalists object to it on the grounds that there are plenty of other words that are more exact and sound less like trendy jargon.

Inuit

The peoples inhabiting the regions from northwestern Canada to western Greenland speak **Inuit** languages and call themselves **Inuit** (not *Eskimo*), and **Inuit** now has official status in Canada. By analogy, **Inuit** is also used in the U.S., usually in an attempt to be politically correct, as a general synonym for *Eskimo*. This, however, is inaccurate because there are no **Inuit** in Alaska and **Inuit** therefore cannot include people from Alaska. Only *Eskimo* includes all of these peoples. See note for **Eskimo**.

last, latest

In precise usage, **latest** means 'most recent' (*my **latest** project is wallpapering my dining room*), and **last** means 'final' (*the **last** day of the school year will be June 18*). But **last** is often used in place of **latest**, esp. in informal contexts: *I read his **last** novel.*

latter

Latter means 'the second-mentioned of two.' Its use to mean 'the last-mentioned of three or more' is common, but is considered incorrect by some because **latter** means 'later' rather than 'latest.' *Last* or *last-mentioned* is preferred where three or more things are involved.

less, fewer

In standard English, **less** should be used only with uncountable things (***less** money*; ***less** time*). With countable things, it is incorrect to use **less**: thus, ***less** people* and ***less** words* should be corrected to ***fewer** people* and ***fewer** words*.

literally

In its standard use, **literally** means 'in a literal sense, as opposed to a nonliteral or exaggerated sense,': *I told him I never wanted to see him again, but I didn't expect him to take it **literally***. In recent years, an extended use of **literally** (and also *literal*) has become very common, where **literally** (or *literal*) is used deliberately in nonliteral contexts, for added effect: *they bought the car and **literally** ran it into the ground*. This use can lead to unintentional humorous effects (*we were **literally** killing ourselves laughing*) and is not acceptable in formal English.

locate

In formal English, one should avoid using **locate** to mean 'find (a missing object)': *he can't seem to **locate** his keys*. In precise usage, **locate** means 'discover the exact place or position of' or 'fix the position of, put in place': *the doctors hope to **locate** the source of the bleeding*; *the studio should be **located** on a north-facing slope.*

a lot of, lots of

A lot of and **lots of** are very common in speech and writing, but they still have a distinctly informal feel and are generally not considered acceptable for formal English, where alternatives such as *many* or *a large number* are used instead.

Written as one word, *alot* is incorrect, although not uncommon.

man

Traditionally, the word **man** has been used to refer not only to adult males but also to human beings in general, regardless of sex. There is a historical explanation for this: in Old English, the principal sense of **man** was 'a human being,' and the words *wer* and *wif* were used to refer specifically to 'a male person' and 'a female person,' respectively. Subsequently, **man** replaced *wer* as the normal term for 'a male person,' but at the same time the older sense 'a human being' remained in use.

In the second half of the 20th century, the generic use of **man** to refer to 'human beings in general' (*reptiles were here long before **man** appeared on the earth*) became problematic; the use is now often regarded as sexist or old-fashioned. In some contexts, terms such as *the human race* or *humankind* may be used instead of **man** or *mankind*. However, in other cases, particularly in compound forms, alternatives have not yet become established: there are no standard accepted alternatives for *manpower* or the verb **man**, for example.

-man

Traditionally, the form **-man** was combined with other words to create a term denoting an occupation or role, as in *fireman, layman, chairman,* and *mailman*. As the role of women in society has changed, with the result that women are now more likely to be in roles previously held exclusively by men, many of these terms ending in **-man** have been challenged as sexist and out of date. As a result, there has been a gradual shift away from **-man** compounds except where referring to a specific male person. Gender-neutral terms such as *firefighter* and *mail carrier* are widely accepted alternatives. And new terms such as *chairperson, layperson,* and *spokesperson*, which only a few decades ago seemed odd or awkward, are common today.

may, might

Traditionalists insist that one should distinguish between **may** (present tense) and **might** (past tense) in expressing possibility: *I **may** have some dessert after dinner if I'm still hungry; I **might** have known that the highway would be closed because of the storm.* In casual use, though, **may** and **might** are generally interchangeable: *they **might** take a vacation next month; he **may** have called earlier, but the answering machine was broken.*

Myriad

Myriad is derived from a Greek noun and adjective meaning 'ten thousand.' It was first used in English as a noun in reference to a great but indefinite number. The adjectival sense of 'countless, innumerable' appeared much later. In modern English, use of **myriad** as a noun and adjective are equally standard and correct, despite the fact that some traditionalists consider the adjective as the only acceptable use of the word.

native

In contexts such as *a **native** of Boston*, the use of the noun **native** is quite acceptable. But when used as a noun without qualification, as in *this dance is a favorite with the **natives**,* it is more problematic. In modern use, it is used humorously to refer to the local inhabitants of a particular place: *that bar is no longer popular with the **natives**.* In other contexts, it has an old-fashioned feel and, because of being closely associated with a colonial European outlook on nonwhite peoples living in remote places, it may cause offense.

neither . . . nor

When **neither** is followed by **nor**, it is important in good English style that the two halves of the structure mirror each other: *she saw herself as **neither** wife **nor** mother* rather than *she **neither** saw herself as wife **nor** mother.*

normalcy

Normalcy has been criticized as an uneducated alternative to *normality*, but actually is a common American usage and can be taken as standard: *we are anticipating a return to* **normalcy**.

octopus, octopuses, octopodes

The standard English plural of **octopus** is **octopuses**. However, the word **octopus** comes from Greek, and the Greek plural form is **octopodes** (/äk'täpə,dēz/). Modern usage of **octopodes** is so infrequent that many people mistakenly create the erroneous plural form *octopi*, formed according to rules for Latin plurals.

older, oldest; younger, youngest

Where two, and no more, are involved, they may be **older** and **younger**: *the **older** of the twins, by ten minutes, is Sam; the **younger** is Pamela.* Where there are more than two, one may be the **oldest** or **youngest**: *I have four siblings, of whom Jane is the **oldest**.*

Oriental

The term **Oriental**, denoting a person from the Far East, is regarded as offensive by many Asians, esp. Asian Americans. It has many associations with European imperialism in Asia. Therefore, it has an out-of-date feel and tends to be associated with a rather offensive stereotype of the people and their customs as inscrutable and exotic. *Asian* and more specific terms such as *East Asian*, *Chinese*, and *Japanese* are preferred. See note for **Asian**.

ought, ought not

The verb **ought** is a modal verb, which means that, grammatically, it does not behave like ordinary verbs. In particular, the negative is formed with the word **not** by itself, without auxiliary verbs such as *do* or *have*. Thus the standard construction for the negative is *he **ought not** to go*. Note that the preposition *to* is required in both negative and positive statements: *we **ought to** accept her offer*, or *we **ought not to** accept her offer* (not *we **ought** accept* or *we **ought not** accept*). The alternative forms *he **didn't ought** to have gone* and *he **hadn't ought** to have gone*, formed as if **ought** were an ordinary verb rather than a modal verb, are not acceptable in formal English.

Reserve **ought** for expressing obligation, duty, or necessity, and use *should* for expressing suitability or appropriateness.

plus

The use of **plus** as a conjunction meaning 'furthermore' (***plus**, we will be pleased to give you personal financial advice*) is considered informal and should be avoided in formal writing.

prove

For complex historical reasons, **prove** developed two past participles: **proved** and **proven**. Both are correct and can be used more or less interchangeably: *this hasn't been* *proved yet*; *this hasn't been **proven** yet*. **Proven** is the more common form when used as an adjective before the noun it modifies: *a **proven** talent* (not *a **proved** talent*). Otherwise, the choice between **proved** and **proven** is not a matter of correctness, but usually of sound and rhythm—and often, consequently, a matter of familiarity, as in the legal idiom *innocent until **proven** guilty*.

rob

In law, to **rob** is to take something from someone by causing fear of harm, whether or not actual harm occurs. The term is widely, but incorrectly, used to refer to *theft*: *our house was **robbed** while we were away*. Technically, the more correct statement would be *our house was burglarized while we were away*.

Scottish, Scot, Scots, Scotch

The terms **Scottish**, **Scot**, **Scots**, and **Scotch** are all variants of the same word. They have had different histories, however, and in modern English they have developed different uses and connotations.

The normal everyday word used to mean 'of or relating to Scotland or its people' is **Scottish**: ***Scottish** people*; ***Scottish** hills*; ***Scottish** Gaelic*; *she's English, not **Scottish***.

The normal, neutral word for 'a person from Scotland' is **Scot**, along with *Scotsman*, *Scotswoman*, and the plural form **the Scots** (or, less commonly, **the Scottish**).

Scots is also used, like **Scottish**, as an adjective meaning 'of or relating to Scotland.' However, it tends to be used in a narrower sense to refer specifically to the form of English used in Scotland: ***Scots** accent*; *the **Scots** word for 'night.'*

The word **Scotch**, meaning either 'of or relating to Scotland' or 'a person/the people from Scotland,' was widely used in the past by Scottish writers such as Robert Burns and Sir Walter Scott. In the 20th century, it became less common. It is disliked by many Scottish people (as being an 'English' invention) and is now regarded as old-fashioned in most contexts. It survives in certain fixed phrases, as, for example, ***Scotch** broth* and ***Scotch** whiskey*.

sink

In modern English, the past tense of **sink** is generally **sank** (less commonly **sunk**), and the past participle is always **sunk**. The form **sunken** now survives only as an adjective: *a **sunken** garden*; ***sunken** cheeks*.

spastic

Spastic, usually used as an adjective, has been used in medical senses since the 18th century and is still a neutral term for conditions like ***spastic** colon* or ***spastic** paraplegia*. In the 1970s and 1980s, **spastic**, usually used as a noun, became a term of abuse and was directed toward anyone regarded as incompetent or physically uncoordinated. Nowadays, this latter use of **spastic**, whether as a noun or as an adjective, is likely to cause offense, and even in medical use it is preferable to use phrasing such as *person with cerebral palsy* instead of the noun **spastic**.

spinster

The development of the word **spinster** is a good example of the way in which a word acquires strong connotations to the extent that it can no longer be used in a neutral sense. From the 17th century, the word was appended to names as the official legal description of an unmarried woman: *Elizabeth Harris of Boston, Spinster*. This type of use survives today in some legal and religious contexts. In modern everyday English, however, **spinster** cannot be used to mean simply 'unmarried woman'; it is now always a derogatory term, referring or alluding to a stereotype of an older woman who is unmarried, childless, prissy, and repressed.

split infinitive

Is it wrong to use a **split infinitive**, separating the infinitive marker *to* from the verb? If so, then these statements are grammatically incorrect: *you have to really watch him*; *to boldly go where no one has gone before*. Writers who long ago insisted that English could be modeled on Latin created the "rule" that the English infinitive must not be split: *to clearly state* violates this rule; one must say *to state clearly*. But the Latin infinitive is one word (e.g., *amare*, 'to love') and cannot be split, so the rule is not firmly grounded, and treating two English words as one can lead to awkward, stilted sentences. In particular, the placing of an adverb in English is extremely important in giving the appropriate emphasis. Consider, for example, the "corrected" forms of the previous examples: *you really have to watch him*; *to go boldly where no one has gone before*. The original, intended emphasis of each statement has been changed, and for no other reason than to satisfy an essentially unreasonable rule. Some traditionalists may continue to hold up the split infinitive as an error, but in standard English, the principle of allowing split infinitives is broadly accepted as both normal and useful.

thankfully

Thankfully has been used for centuries to mean 'in a thankful manner,' as in *she accepted the offer thankfully*. Since the 1960s, it has also been used as a sentence adverb to mean 'fortunately,' as in *thankfully, we didn't have to wait*. Although this use has not attracted the same amount of attention as *hopefully*, it has been criticized for the same reasons. It is, however, far more common now than is the traditional use. See note for **hopefully.**

that, who, which

The word **that** can be omitted in standard English where it introduces a *subordinate* clause, as in *she said (that) she was satisfied*. **That** can also be dropped in a *relative* clause where it is the *object* of the clause, as in *the book (that) I've just written*. **That**, however, is obligatory when it is the *subject* of the relative clause, as in *the company that employs Jack*.

It is sometimes argued that, in relative clauses, **that** should be used for *nonhuman* references and **who** should be used for *human* references: *a house that overlooks the park*, but *the woman who lives next door*. In practice, while it is true to say that **who** is restricted to human references, the function of **that** is flexible. It has been used for both human and nonhuman references since at least the 11th century. In standard English, it is interchangeable with **who** in this context.

Is there any difference between the use of **that** and **which** in sentences such as *any book* ***that*** *gets children reading is worth having*, and *any book* ***which*** *gets children reading is worth having*? The general rule is that, in *restrictive* relative clauses, where the relative clause serves to define or restrict the reference to the particular one described, **that** is the preferred relative pronoun. However, in *nonrestrictive* relative clauses, where the relative clause serves only to give additional information, **which** must be used: *this book,* ***which*** *is set in the last century, is very popular with teenagers*, but not *this book,* ***that*** *is set in the last century, is very popular with teenagers.*

they

The word **they** (with its counterparts *them*, *their*, and *themselves*) as a singular pronoun to refer to a person of unspecified sex has been used since at least the 16th century. In the late 20th century, as the traditional use of **he** to refer to a person of either sex came under scrutiny on the grounds of sexism, this use of **they** has become more common. It is now generally accepted in contexts where it follows an indefinite pronoun such as *anyone*, *no one*, *someone*, or *a person*: ***anyone*** *can join if* ***they*** *are a resident*; ***each*** *to* ***their*** *own*. In other contexts, coming after singular nouns, the use of **they** is now common, although less widely accepted, esp. in formal contexts. Sentences such as *ask* ***a friend*** *if* ***they*** *could help* are still criticized for being ungrammatical. Nevertheless, in view of the growing acceptance of **they** and its obvious practical advantages, **they** is used in many cases where **he** would have been used formerly. See note for **he**.

thus, thusly

The expansion of the adverb **thus** to **thusly** is usually considered unnecessary, but it can serve a distinct function, as in introducing a direct quotation: *He answered her* ***thusly***: *"your evidence is lacking and your conclusions are just plain wrong!"*

transpire

The common use of **transpire** to mean 'occur, happen' (*I'm going to find out exactly what* ***transpired***) is a loose extension of an earlier meaning, 'come to be known' (*it* ***transpired*** *that Mark had been baptized a Catholic*). This loose sense of 'happen,' which is now more common in American usage than the sense of 'come to be known,' was first recorded in U.S. English toward the end of the 18th century and has been listed in U.S. dictionaries from the 19th century. Careful writers should note, however, that in cases where *occur* or *happen* would do just as well, the use of **transpire** may strike readers as an affectation or as jargon.

utilize

Utilize, borrowed in the 19th century from the French *utiliser*, means 'make practical or effective use of.' Because it is a more formal word than *use* and is often used in contexts (as in business writing) where the ordinary verb *use* would be simpler and more direct, **utilize** may strike readers as pretentious jargon and should therefore be used sparingly.

various, various of

In standard English, the word **various** is normally used as an adjective. It is best reserved for contexts indicating variety, and should not be used as a synonym for *several*. In colloquial American speech, **various** is sometimes also used (as though it were a pronoun) followed by *of*, as in ***various of*** *her friends had called*—another way of saying *some of* or *several of.* This use is discouraged by some traditionalists, however, because **various** is properly an adjective, not a pronoun, and **various of** erodes the sense of variety, diversity, and distinctness. This erosion or blurring of meaning is further evident in the use of *various different*, as in ***various different*** *kinds of oak*, a redundant wording that should be avoided.

vis-à-vis

The expression **vis-à-vis** literally means 'face to face.' Avoid using it to mean 'about, concerning,' as in *he wanted to talk to me* ***vis-à-vis*** *next weekend.* In the sense 'in contrast, comparison, or relation to,' however, **vis-à-vis** is generally acceptable: *let us consider government regulations* ***vis-à-vis*** *employment rates.*

well

The adverb **well** is often used in combination with past participles to form compound adjectives: *well-adjusted, well-intentioned, well-known*, and so on. As far as hyphenation is concerned, there are three general rules: (1) if the compound adjective is placed before the noun (i.e., in the attributive position), it should be hyphenated (*a* ***well-intentioned remark***); (2) if the compound adjective is preceded by an adverb (*much, very, surprisingly*, etc.), the compound adjective is open (*a* ***thoroughly well prepared*** *student*); (3) if the compound adjective is placed after the noun or verb (i.e., in the predicate position), it may, but need not, be hyphenated (*her remark was* ***well-intentioned*** or *her remark was* ***well intentioned***). Likewise, other, similar compounds with *better, best, ill, little, lesser, least*, etc., are hyphenated before the noun (*a* ***little-known*** *author*), often open after a noun or verb (*the author was* ***little known***), and open if modified by an adverb (*a* ***very little known*** *author*).

whatever, what ever

In the sentence *I will do* ***whatever*** *you ask of me* (in which **whatever** means 'anything'), **whatever** is correctly spelled as one word. But in the interrogative sense (***what ever*** *was Mary thinking?*), the emphasis is on *ever*, and it should be spelled as the two words **what ever** because *ever* is serving as an intensifier to the pronoun *what*.

while, whereas

While is sometimes used, without causing any misunderstandings, in the sense of **whereas** ('although,' 'by contrast,' 'in comparison with the fact that'). This usage is frowned on by some traditionalists, but **while** is sometimes preferable, as in contexts in which **whereas** might sound inappropriately formal: ***while*** *you say you like her, you've never stood up for her*). **Whereas** is preferable, however, for preventing ambiguity in contexts in which **while** might be read as referring to time, or might falsely suggest simultaneity: *whereas Burton promised to begin at once, he was delayed nine months for lack of funding*; *whereas Jonas was an excellent planter and cultivator, Julius was a master harvester.*

worthwhile

The adjective **worthwhile** is used both attributively (that is, before the noun) and predicatively (that is, when it stands alone and comes after the verb). In both positions, it is almost always written as one word: *a worthwhile book, the book was worthwhile.* But it is occasionally hyphenated (*a worth-while book*) or written as two words (*the book was worth while*).

wrought havoc

The phrase **wrought havoc**, as in *they wrought havoc on the countryside*, is an acceptable variant of *wreaked havoc.* Here, **wrought** is an archaic past tense of *work.* It is not, as is sometimes assumed, a past tense of *wreak.*

How Words Are Built:
Prefixes, Suffixes, and Combining Forms

Combining Form	Meaning	Example(s)
a-	not; without; to; toward	*atheistic, atypical*
-a	of; have; to	*coupla, mighta*
ab-	away; from	*abaxial, abominate*
-ability	forming nouns of quality corresponding to adjectives ending in *-able*	*suitability*
-able	able to be; due to be; subject to; relevant to; having the quality to	*calculable; payable; taxable; fashionable; suitable*
-ably	forming adverbs corresponding to adjectives ending in *-able*	*suitably*
ac-	variant spelling of *ad-* assimilated before *c* and *q*	*accept, acquit, acquiesce*
-ac	forming adjectives that are also often (or only) used as nouns	*maniac*
ad-	denoting motion or direction to; reduction or change into; addition or intensification	*advance; adapt; adhere*
-ad	forming nouns: in collective numerals; in groups, periods, or aggregates; in names of females in classical mythology; in names of districts; in names of poems and similar compositions; forming names of members of some taxonomic groupings	*pentad, triad; Olympiad; Dryad, Naiad; Troad; Iliad, jeremiad; bromeliad*
-ade	forming nouns: denoting an action that is completed; denoting the body concerned in an action or process; denoting the product or result of an action or process	*barricade, blockade; brigade, cavalcade; arcade, lemonade, marmalade*
adeno-	relating to a gland or glands	*adenocarcinoma*
-aemia	see *-emia*	
-age	forming nouns: denoting an action; the product of an action; a function; a sphere of action; denoting an aggregate or number of; fees payable for; the cost of using; denoting a place or abode	*leverage, voyage; spillage, wreckage; homage, peerage; mileage, percentage, signage; postage; tonnage; vicarage, village*
agro-, agri-	of or involving agriculture	*agrobiology, agribusiness*
-al	(forming adjectives) relating to; of the kind of: from Latin words; from Greek words; from English nouns; forming nouns chiefly denoting verbal action	*annual, infernal; historical, comical; tidal; arrival, transmittal*
-algia	of or involving pain	*neuralgia*
allo-	other; different	*allotrope*

Combining Form	Meaning	Example(s)
-ally	forming adverbs from adjectives ending in –*al*	*radically*
amphi-	both; around	*amphibian, amphitheater*
an-	variant spelling of *a*- before a vowel; variant spelling of *ad*- assimilated before *n*; variant spelling of *ana*- shortened before a vowel	*anemia, anechoic; annihilate, annotate; aneurysm*
-an	forming adjectives and nouns esp. from: names of places; names of systems; names of zoological classes or orders; names of founders or leaders when referring to them as sources; forming names of organic compounds, chiefly polysaccharides	*Ohioan, Russian; Anglican, Presbyterian; crustacean; Chomskyan, Lutheran; dextran*
ana-	up; back; again	*anabasis; anamnesis; anabiosis*
-ana	(forming plural nouns) denoting things associated with a person, place, or field of interest	*Americana; Victoriana*
-ance	forming nouns: denoting a quality or state or an instance of one; denoting an action	*allegiance, extravagance, perseverance; appearance, utterance*
-ancy	(forming nouns) denoting a quality or state	*buoyancy, expectancy*
-androus	having male parts	*monandrous*
angio-	of blood or seed vessels	*angiography, angiosperm*
ante-	before; in front	*antecedent*
antho-, -anth	of or relating to flowers	*anthophilous*
anthropo-, -anthropic	of humans	*anthropology*
anti-	opposed to; against; preventing; reversing or undoing; the opposite of; (Physics) the opposite state of matter or of a specified particle; acting as a rival; unlike the conventional form	*antiaircraft; antibacterial; anticoagulant, antigravity, antipruritic; antimatter, antiproton; antipope; anti-hero*
aqua-	of or relating to water	*aquaculture*
arch-	chief; principal	*archbishop*
archaeo-, archeo-	ancient; prehistoric	*archaeomagnetism*
arterio-	of or relating to the arteries	*arteriosclerosis*
arthro-, arthr-	of or relating to joints	*arthroscope*
-ary	forming adjectives; forming nouns	*budgetary, capillary; dictionary, granary*
-ase	(Biochemistry) forming names of enzymes	*amylase*
astro-	of stars or space	*astrophysics*
-ate	forming nouns: denoting status or office; a state or function; denoting a group; (Chemistry) denoting a salt or ester, esp. of an acid with a corresponding name ending in –*ic*; denoting a product (of a chemical process); forming adjectives and nouns; forming adjectives from Latin; forming verbs	*doctorate, episcopate; curate, mandate; electorate; chlorate, nitrate; condensate, filtrate; associate, duplicate, separate; caudate; fascinate, hyphenate*

Combining Form	Meaning	Example(s)
audio-, audi-	of or relating to hearing or sound	*audiometer*
auto-, aut-	self; spontaneous	*autoxidation*
baro-, bar-, -baric	of or relating to pressure	*baroreceptor*
bathy-, batho-	of or relating to depth	*bathysphere*
be-	forming verbs: all over; all around; thoroughly; excessively; (added to intransitive verbs) expressing transitive action; (added to adjectives and nouns) expressing transitive action; (added to nouns) affect with; (added to adjectives) cause to be; (forming adjectives ending in *-ed*) having; covered with	*bespatter; bewilder; bemoan; befool, befriend; befog; befoul; bejeweled*
bi-	two; twice; every two; lasting two	*biathlon, biannual, biennial*
biblio-	of or relating to books	*bibliomania*
bin-	variant spelling of bi- before a vowel	*binaural*
bio-	of or relating to life	*biosynthesis*
-biosis, -biotic	denoting or relating to a mode of life	*symbiosis*
brachy-, -brach	short	*brachycephalic*
broncho-, bronch-	of or relating to air passages	*bronchopneumonia*
by-	subordinate; incidental; secondary	*by-form, byproduct*
caco-, cac-, kak-	bad or worst	*cacology*
calli-, cal-	good, beautiful	*calligraphy*
carcino-	of or relating to cancer	*carcinoma*
cardio-, cardi-, -cardia	of or relating to the heart	*cardiology*
cata-, cat-, kata-	down(ward); wrongly or badly; completely; against	*cataract, catastrophe*
-cele, -coele	swelling; hernia	*meningocele*
centi-	one hundredth; hundred	*centiliter*
-cephalic, -cephalous, cephalo-	of or relating to the head; -headed	*macrocephalous, cephalometry*
cerato-, cerat-	see *kerato-*	
cerebro-, cerebr-	of or relating to the brain	*cerebrospinal*
cheiro-	see *chiro*	
chemi-, chemico-, chemo-	of or relating to drugs or chemicals	*chemotherapy*
chiro-, cheiro-	of the hand or hands	*chiromancy*
chlor-, chloro-	green; of or relating to chlorine	*chlorophyll, chloracne*
chromato-, chromat-, chromo	color; of colors	*chromotopsia*
chrono-, chron-	of or relating to time	*chronometry*
chrys-, chryso-	of or relating to gold	*chrysalis*
-cide, -cidal	of killing or a killer	*insecticide*

Combining Form	Meaning	Example(s)
cine-	of or relating to film	*cinematography*
circum-	about; around	*circumambulate, circumpolar*
clado-, clad-	of or relating to a branch or branching	*cladogram*
-cle	forming nouns which were originally diminutives	*article, particle*
clin-, -clinal, -cline, -clinic	of, denoting, or relating to a slope	*clinometer*
co-	(forming nouns) joint; mutual; common; (forming adjectives) jointly; mutually; (forming verbs) together with another or others; (Mathematics) of the complement of an angle; the complement of	*coeducation; coeducation; coproduce, co-own; cosine; colatitude, coset*
-coele	see *-cele*	
con-	variant spelling of *com-* assimilated before *c, d, f, g, j, n, q, s, t, v,* and sometimes before vowels	*concord, condescend, confide*
contra-	against or opposite; below or beyond	*contradict, contralto*
copro-	of or relating to dung or feces	*coprophilic*
cortico-, cortic-	of or relating to a cortex	*conticosterone*
cosmo-, cosm-	of or relating to the world or universe	*cosmography*
counter-	denoting opposition, retaliation, or rivalry; denoting movement or effect in the opposite direction; denoting correspondence, duplication, or substitution	*counterattack, counterespionage; counterbalance, counterpoise; counterpart, counterpoint*
-cracy	denoting a form of government or rule	*democracy*
cranio-, crani-	of or relating to the skull	*craniotomy*
-crat	denoting a member or supporter of a form of government or rule	*plutocrat*
-cratic	of or relating to a form of government or rule	*bureaucratic*
cryo-	of or involving cold	*cryostat*
crypto-, crypt-	concealed; secret	*cryptogram*
-cule	forming nouns which were originally diminutives	*molecule, reticule*
cupr-, cupro-	of or relating to copper	*cuprammonium*
-cy	denoting state or condition; denoting rank or status	*bankruptcy; baronetcy*
cyano-, cyan-	of or relating to blue or dark blue	*cyanosis*
cyber-	of or relating to electronic communications	*cyberspace*
cyno-	of or relating to dogs	*cynodont*
cysto-, cyst-	of or relating to the bladder	*cystotomy*
-cyte, cyt-	denoting a mature cell	*leukocyte*

Combining Form	Meaning	Example(s)
cyto-	of a cell or cells	*cytoplasm*
de-	forming verbs and their derivatives) down; away; completely; (added to verbs and their derivatives) denoting removal or reversal; denoting formation from	*descend, deduct; denude, derelict, deaerate, de-ice; deverbal*
deca-, dec-	ten	*decahedron*
deci-	tenth	*deciliter*
demi-	half; inferior or partial	*demitasse*
demi-	half; half-size; partially; in an inferior degree	*demisemiquaver, demitasse; demigod, demimonde*
dendro-, dendron	denoting or relating to a tree	*dendrology*
dermato, dermat-	of or relating to the skin	*dermatologist*
dextro-	on or to the right	*dextrorotatory*
di-	twice; two; double; (Chemistry) containing two atoms, molecules, or groups of a speci-fied kind; variant spelling of *dis-* before *l, m, n, r, s* (followed by a consonant), and *v*; also often before *g*, and sometimes before *j*	*dichromatic; dioxide diameter, diaphanous, diuretic;*
dia-, di-	through; across; apart	*diakinesis*
dis-	expressing negation; denoting reversal or absence of an action or state; denoting sepa-ration; denoting expulsion; denoting removal of the thing specified; expressing complete-ness or intensification of an unpleasant or unattractive action	*dislike, disquiet; dishonor, disinte-grate; discharge, disengage; disbar, disinherit; disbud, dismember; dis-combobulate, disgruntled*
-dom	forming nouns: denoting a state or condi-tion; denoting rank or status; denoting a domain; denoting a class of people or the attitudes associated with them, regarded col-lectively	*freedom; earldom; fiefdom; official-dom*
dorsi-, dorso-	of, to, or on the back	*dorsiventral*
-drome	denoting a place for running or racing; run-ning or proceeding a certain way	*velodrome, palindrome*
dys-	bad; difficult	*dyspepsia*
e-	variant spelling of *ex-*; denoting anything in an electronic state, esp. the use of electronic data transfer in cyberspace for information exchange and financial transactions, esp. through the Internet	*elect, emit; e-business, e-cash, e-world, e-zine*
eco-	relating to ecology	*ecowarrior*
ecto-	outer; external	*ectoderm*
-ectomy	denoting removal of a part	*appendectomy*

Combining Form	Meaning	Example(s)
-ed	forming adjectives: (added to nouns) having; possessing; affected by; (added to nouns) characteristic of; used in phrases consisting of adjective and noun	*talented, diseased; ragged; bad-tempered, three-sided*
-een	(Irish) forming diminutive nouns	*colleen*
-eer	(forming nouns) denoting a person concerned with or engaged in an activity; (forming verbs) denoting concern or involvement with an activity	*auctioneer, puppeteer; electioneer, profiteer*
ef-	variant spelling of *ex-* assimilated before *f*	*efface, effloresce*
-el	variant spelling of *-le*	
em-	variant spelling of *en-* assimilated before *b, p*	*emblazon, emplacement*
-eme	(Linguistics) forming nouns denoting linguistic units that are in systemic contrast with one other	*grapheme, phoneme*
-emia, -hemia, -aemia	denoting presence of a substance	*septicemia, leukemia*
en-	forming verbs (added to nouns) expressing entry into the specified state or location; forming verbs (added to nouns and adjectives) expressing conversion into the specified state; often forming verbs having the suffix *-en*; (added to verbs) in; into; on; as an intensifier; within; inside	*engulf, embed; encrust, ennoble; embolden, enliven; ensnare; entangle; encyst, endemic, embolism, empyema*
-en	forming verbs: (from adjectives) denoting the development, creation, or intensification of a state; from nouns; forming adjectives from nouns: made or consisting of, resembling; forming past participles of strong verbs: as a regular inflection; as an adjective; forming the plural of a few nouns; forming diminutives of nouns; forming feminine nouns; forming abstract nouns	*widen, deepen, loosen; strengthen; earthen, woolen; golden, silvern; spoken; mistaken, torn; children, oxen; chicken, maiden; vixen; burden*
-ence	forming nouns: denoting a quality or an instance of it; denoting an action or its result	*impertinence; reference, reminiscence*
encephalo-, encephal-	of or relating to the brain	*encephalopathy*
-ency	forming nouns: denoting a quality; denoting a state	*efficiency; presidency*
endo-, end-	internal; within	*endoderm*
-ene	denoting an inhabitant; (Chemistry) forming names of unsaturated hydrocarbons containing a double bond	*Nazarene; benzene, ethylene*
-ent	(forming adjectives) denoting an occurrence of action; denoting a state; (forming nouns) denoting an agent	*refluent; convenient; coefficient*
entero-, enter-	of or relating to the intestine	*enterovirus*

Combining Form	Meaning	Example(s)
-eous	(forming adjectives) resembling; displaying the nature of	*aqueous, erroneous*
epi-, ep-	upon; above; in addition	*epicycle; epicontinental; epiphenomenon*
-er	denoting a person, animal, or thing that performs a specified action or activity; denoting a person or thing that has a specified attribute or form; denoting a person concerned with a specified thing or subject; denoting a person belonging to a specified place or group; forming the comparative of adjectives and adverbs; (forming nouns) denoting verbal action or a document effecting such action	*farmer, sprinkler; foreigner, two-wheeler; milliner, philosopher; city-dweller, New Yorker; bigger, faster; disclaimer, misnomer*
-ery	forming nouns: denoting a class or kind; denoting an occupation, a state, a condition, or behavior; denoting a place set aside for an activity or a grouping of things, animals, etc.	*confectionery, greenery; archery, bravery, slavery; knavery, tomfoolery; orangery, rookery*
erythro-, erythr-	red	*erythrocyte*
-es	forming plurals of nouns ending in sibilant sounds; forming plurals of certain nouns ending in –o; forming the third person singular of the present tense: in verbs ending in sibilant sounds; in verbs ending in -o (but not -oo):	*boxes, kisses; potatoes, heroes; pushes; goes*
-esce	forming verbs, often denoting the initiation of action	*coalesce, effervesce*
-ese	forming adjectives and nouns: denoting an inhabitant or language of a country or city; often derogatory (esp. with reference to language) denoting character or style	*Taiwanese, Viennese; journalese, officialese*
-esque	(forming adjectives) in the style of; resembling	*carnivalesque, Reaganesque, Houdini-esque*
-ess	forming nouns denoting female gender; forming abstract nouns from adjectives	*abbess, adulteress, tigress; largess*
-est	forming the superlative of adjectives and of adverbs; (archaic) forming the second person singular of verbs	*shortest, widest; soonest; canst, goest*
-et	forming nouns which were originally diminutives; forming nouns such as comet, and often denoting people	*baronet, hatchet, tablet; comet, poet*
-ete	variant spelling of -*et*	*athlete*
-eth	variant spelling of –*th*; (archaic) forming the third person singular of the present tense of verbs	*fiftieth; doeth, saith*
ethno-	of or relating to a people or nation	*ethnographer*

Combining Form	Meaning	Example(s)
-ette	forming nouns: denoting relatively small size; denoting an imitation or substitute; denoting female gender	*kitchenette; flannelette; suffragette*
eu-	good; well; easily	*euphony*
eury-	denoting a wide variety or range	*eurytopic*
ex-	out; outside of; up and away; upward; thoroughly; removal or release; forming verbs expressing inducement of a state; forming nouns (from titles of office, status, etc.) expressing a former state; out	*expand, express; excel, extol; exacerbate, excruciate; excommunicate, exculpate, expel; exasperate, excite; ex-husband, ex-convict*
exo-	external; from outside	*exodermis*
extra-	outside; beyond; beyond the scope of	*extracellular, extraterritorial; extracurricular*
-ey	variant spelling of *-y*	*Charley, Limey*
-facient	producing a specified action or state	*abortifacient*
-faction	denoting a specified action or state	*satisfaction*
-ferous	having, bearing, or containing (a specified thing)	*Carboniferous, pestiferous*
-ferous, -iferous	having, bearing, or containing	*pestiferous*
ferro-, ferr-	containing iron	*ferroconcrete*
-fic, -fication	making	*prolific*
fluvio-	of or relating to a river or rivers	*fluvioglacial*
-fold	forming adjectives and adverbs from cardinal numbers: in an amount multiplied by; consisting of so many parts or facets	*threefold; twofold*
for-	denoting prohibition; denoting abstention, neglect, or renunciation; denoting extremity of negative state expressed	*forbid; forgive, forget, forgo; forlorn, forsake*
-fuge	expelling or dispelling	*vermifuge*
-ful	(forming adjectives from nouns) full of; having the qualities of; forming adjectives from adjectives or from Latin stems with little change of sense; (forming adjectives from verbs) apt to; able to; accustomed to (pl. *-fuls*) forming nouns denoting the amount needed to fill the specified container, holder, etc.	*sorrowful; masterful; grateful; forgetful, watchful; bucketful, handful*
-fully	forming adverbs corresponding to adjectives ending in *-ful*	*sorrowfully,*
-fy	(added to nouns) forming verbs denoting making or producing; denoting transformation or the process of making into; forming verbs denoting the making of a state defined by an adjective; forming verbs expressing a causative sense	*speechify; deify, petrify; amplify, falsify; horrify*

Combining Form	Meaning	Example(s)
Gallo-	French	*Gallo-German*
-gamous, -gamy	of or relating to marriage or reproduction	*monogamous, polygamy*
gastr-, gastro-	of or relating to the stomach	*gastrectomy, gastroenteritis*
-gate	denoting an actual or alleged scandal	*Watergate, Irangate*
-gen	denoting a substance producing or produced	*allergen*
-genic	producing, produced, or suited to	*carcinogenic*
-genous	producing; inducing; originating in	*endogenous*
-geny	denoting a mode of production	*orogeny*
geo-, ge-	of or relating to the earth	*geocentric*
geront-, geronto-, gero-, ger-	of or relating to old age	*gerontology*
glyco-, glyc-	of, relating to, or producing sugar	*glycogenesis*
-gon	having a certain number of angles	*pentagon*
-gram	denoting something written or recorded	*telegram*
-graph	denoting something written or drawn; denoting a recording instrument	*autograph; phonograph*
-grapher	denoting a person concerned with a subject	*biographer*
-graphic	of a subject or study	*demographic*
-graphy	denoting a science or technique, a style, or a kind of writing	*geography, hagiography, calligraphy*
gymno-, gymn-	naked	*gymnosophist*
gyneco-	of or relating to women	*gynecology*
-gynous, -gyne	having female organs	*epigynous*
gyro-	of or relating to rotation	*gyromagnetic*
haemato-, haemo-	see *hemo-*	
-haemia	see *-emia*	
hagio-, hagi-	of or relating to saints or saintliness	*hagiography*
halo-, hal-	of or relating to salinity or halogens	*halophile*
helio-	of or relating to the sun	*heliostat*
hemato-, haemato-, hemo	of or relating to blood	*hematoma*
hemi-	half	*hemicylindrical, hemiplegia*
-hemia	see *–emia*	
hemo-	see *hemato-*	
hepato-, hepat-	of or relating to the liver	*hepatitis*
hepta-	seven	*heptathlon*
hetero-, heter-	different; diverse	*heterosexual*
hexa-, hex-	six	*hexagon*
hiero-, hier-	sacred; holy	*hierophant*

Combining Form	Meaning	Example(s)
histo-, hist-	of or relating to organic tissue	*histocompatibility*
holo-, hol-	whole; complete	*holocaust*
homeo-	similar	*homeopathy*
homo-, hom-	same; relating to homosexual love	*homogametic; homoerotic*
-hood	forming nouns: denoting a condition or quality; denoting a collection or group	*falsehood, womanhood; brotherhood*
hydr-, hydro-	of or relating to water; of accumulation of fluid	*hydraulic; hydrocephalous*
hyper-	over or beyond; exceeding; excessively	*hypernym; hypersonic; hyperthyroidism*
hypno-, hypn-	relating to sleep or hypnosis	*hypnotherapy*
hypo-, hyp-	below or lower	*hypothermia*
-ia	forming nouns adopted unchanged from Latin or Greek and modern Latin or Greek terms; forming names of: (Medicine) states and disorders; (Botany & Zoology) genera and higher groups; forming names of countries	*mania, militia, utopia; anemia, diphtheria; dahlia, Latimeria; India*
-ial	forming adjectives	*celestial, primordial*
-ian	forming adjectives and nouns	*antediluvian, Christian*
iatro-, -iatry, -iatric	of or relating to doctors or medical treatment	*iatrogenic*
-ic	forming adjectives; forming nouns; denoting a particular form or instance of a noun ending in -*ics*; (Chemistry) denoting an element in a higher valence	*Islamic, terrific; lyric, mechanic, aesthetic, dietetic, tactic; ferric, sulfuric*
-ical	forming adjectives: corresponding to nouns or adjectives usually ending in –*ic*; corresponding to nouns ending in -*y*	*comical; pathological*
ichthyo-, ichthy-	of or relating to fish	*ichthyology*
icono-, icon-	of or relating to images or icons	*iconography*
-id	forming adjectives;forming nouns: (Biology) forming names of structural constituents; (Botany) forming names of plants belonging to a family with a name ending in –*idaceae*; (Zoology) denoting an animal belonging to a family with a name ending in -*idae* or to a class with a name ending in –*ida*; denoting a member of a specified dynasty or family; (Astronomy) denoting a meteor in a shower radiating from a specified constellation; denoting a star of a class like one in a specified constellation	*putrid, torrid; chrysalid, pyramid; plastid; orchid; carabid, arachnid; Achaemenid, Sassanid; Geminids; cepheid*

Combining Form	Meaning	Example(s)
-ide	(Chemistry) forming nouns: denoting binary compounds of a nonmetallic or more electronegative element or group; denoting various other compounds; denoting elements of a series in the periodic table	*cyanide, sodium, chloride; peptide, saccharide; lanthanide*
ideo-	of or relating to an idea or form	*ideology*
idio-	distinct; private; personal	*idiotype*
il-	variant spelling of *in-* assimilated before *l*	*illustrate, illogical*
-il	forming adjectives and nouns	*civil, fossil*
-ile	forming adjectives and nouns; (Statistics) forming nouns denoting a value of a variate that divides a population into the indicated number of equal-sized groups, or one of the groups itself	*agile, juvenile; decile, percentile*
im-	variant spelling of *in-* assimilated before *b, m, p*	*imbibe, immure, impart*
in-	(added to adjectives) not; (added to nouns) without; lacking; in; into; toward; within	*inanimate, intolerant; inadvertence, inappreciation; induce, influx, inborn*
-in	(Chemistry) forming names of organic compounds, pharmaceutical products, proteins, etc.; denoting a gathering of people having a common purpose, typically as a form of protest	*insulin, penicillin, dioxin; sit-in, sleep-in, love-in*
-ine	(forming adjectives) belonging to; resembling in nature; forming adjectives from taxonomic names; forming adjectives from the names of minerals, plants, etc.; forming feminine common nouns and proper names; forming chiefly abstract nouns and diminutives; (Chemistry) forming names of alkaloids, halogens, amines, amino acids, and other substances	*Alpine, canine; bovine; crystalline, hyacinthine; heroine, Josephine; doctrine, medicine, chlorine, thymine*
infra-	below or under	*infrared, infrasonic*

Combining Form	Meaning	Example(s)
-ing	denoting a verbal action, an instance of this, or its result; denoting a verbal action relating to an occupation, skill, etc.; denoting material used for or associated with a process, etc.; denoting something involved in an action or process but with no corresponding verb; forming the gerund of verbs; forming the present participle of verbs; forming present participles used as adjectives; forming adjectives from nouns; (used esp. in names of coins and fractional parts) a thing belonging to or having the quality of	*fighting, outing, building; banking, ice, skating, welding; cladding, piping; scaffolding; painting; doing, calling; charming; hulking; farthing, riding*
inter-	between or among; mutually	*interagency*
intra-	on the inside or within	*intramural*
intro-	into or inwards	*introvert*
-ion	forming nouns denoting verbal action; denoting an instance of this; denoting a resulting state or product	*communion; a rebellion; oblivion, opinion*
-ique	archaic spelling of *-ic*	
ir-	variant spelling of *in-* assimilated before *r*	*irrelevant, irradiate*
-ise	variant spelling of *-ize*; forming nouns of quality, state, or function	*expertise, franchise, merchandise*
-ish	forming adjectives: (from nouns) having the qualities or characteristics of; of nationality or religious or ethnic group; (from adjectives) somewhat; informal denoting an approximate age or time of day; forming verbs	*apish, girlish; Swedish, Amish, Flemish; yellowish; sixish; abolish, establish*
-ism	denoting an action, result, or quality; denoting a system or principle; denoting a peculiarity in language; denoting a condition	*baptism; barbarism; feminism; Canadianism; alcoholism*
iso-	equal	*isoceles*
-ist	forming personal nouns and some related adjectives: denoting an adherent of a system of beliefs, principles, etc., expressed by nouns ending in *-ism*; denoting a person who subscribes to a prejudice or practices discrimination; denoting a member of a profession or business activity; denoting a person who uses a thing; a person who does something expressed by a verb ending in *-ize*	*hedonist, Marxist; sexist; dentist, dramatist, florist; flutist, motorist; plagiarist*

Combining Form	Meaning	Example(s)
-ite	forming names denoting natives of a country; often derogatory denoting followers of a movement, doctrine, etc.; used in scientific and technical terms: forming names of fossil organisms; forming names of minerals; forming names of constituent parts of a body or organ; forming names of explosives and other commercial products; (Chemistry) forming names of salts or esters of acids ending in –*ous*; forming adjectives; forming nouns; forming verbs	*Israelite, Samnite; Luddite, Trotskyite; ammonite; graphite; somite; dynamite, vulcanite; sulfite; composite, erudite; appetite; unite*
-itic	forming adjectives and nouns corresponding to nouns ending in -*ite*	*Semitic*
-itis	forming names of inflammatory diseases; informal used with reference to a tendency or state of mind that is compared to a disease	*cystitis, hepatitis; creditcarditis*
-ity	forming nouns denoting quality or condition; denoting an instance or degree of this	*humility, probity; a profanity*
-ium, -um	forming nouns adopted unchanged from Latin or based on Latin or Greek words; forming names of metallic elements; denoting a region of the body; denoting a biological structure	*alluvium, euphonium; cadmium, magnesium; pericardium; mycelium*
-ive	(forming adjectives, also nouns derived from them) tending to; having the nature of	*active, corrosive, palliative*
-ize	forming verbs meaning: make or become; cause to resemble; treat in a specified way; treat or cause to combine with a specified substance; follow a specified practice; subject to a practice	*fossilize, privatize; Americanize; pasteurize; carbonize, oxidize; agonize, theorize; hospitalize*
-izer	forming agent nouns corresponding to adjectives ending in -*ize*	*theorizer*
kak-	see *caco-*	
kerato-, kerat-, cerato-, cerat-	of or relating to horny tissue or the cornea	*keratotomy*
kilo-	one thousand	*kilogram*
kineto-, kinet-, -kinesis	of or relating to movement	*telekinesis*
labio-	of or relating to the lips	*labiodental*

Combining Form	Meaning	Example(s)
lacto-, lact-	of or relating to milk, lactic acid, or lactose	*lactobacillus*
-later	denoting a worshiper	*idolater*
-latry	denoting a kind of worship	*idolatry*
-le	forming names of appliances or instruments; forming names of animals and plants; forming nouns having or originally having a diminutive sense; forming adjectives (from an original verb)	*bridle, thimble; beetle; mantle, battle, castle; brittle, nimble*
lepto-, lept-	small; narrow	*babble, dazzle, nestle*
-less	forming verbs, chiefly those expressing repeated action or movement, or having diminutive sense	
-let	(forming nouns) denoting a smaller or lesser kind; denoting articles of ornament or dress	*booklet, starlet; anklet, bracelet*
leuko-, leuk-, leuco-	white	*leukoma*
ligni-, ligno-, lign-	of or relating to wood	*lignify*
-ling	forming nouns from nouns, adjectives, and verbs	*hireling, youngling*
lipo-, lip-	relating to fat or lipids	*liposuction*
-lite	a kidney stone, or a mineral	*zeolite*
litho-, lith-, -lith, -lithic,	denoting or relating to stone,	*lithotomy*
-log, -logue	denoting a discourse or compilation	*dialog, catalogue*
-logist, -loger	denoting a person skilled or involved in a branch of study or art	*biologist*
logo-	of or relating to words	*logorrhea*
-logy, -ology, -logical, -logic	denoting or relating to a subject of study or type of speech or language	*psychology, eulogy*
-ly	forming adjectives meaning: having the qualities of; recurring at intervals of; forming adverbs from adjectives, chiefly denoting manner or degree	*brotherly, rascally; hourly, quarterly; greatly, happily, pointedly*
-lysis, lyso-, lys-	denoting disintegration or decomposition	*autolysis*
-lytic, -lyte	corresponding to nouns ending in -*lysis*	*autolytic*
macro-, macr-	long; large	*macroscale; macronutrient*
mal-	unpleasantly; badly; improperly; not	*malodorous; malfunction; malpractice; maladroit*
-mancy, -mantic	denoting or relating to divination by a specified means	*geomancy*
-manship	(forming nouns) denoting skill in a subject or activity	*marksmanship*
mega-	very large; by a factor of one million	*megalith; megahertz*
megalo-, megal-	abnormally large or great	*megalopolis*

Combining Form	Meaning	Example(s)
-meister	skilled or prominent in a specified activity	*spinmeister*
melano-, melan-	black or dark	*melanosis*
-ment	forming nouns expressing the means or result of an action; forming nouns from adjectives	*curtailment, excitement, treatment; merriment*
mero-	partly; partial	*meronym*
-merous	having a specified number of (biological) parts	*pentamerous*
meso-, mes-	middle; intermediate	*mesothelia*
meta-, met-	denoting a change; denoting position behind, after, or beyond; denoting something of a higher or second order	*metamorphosis; metacarpus; metalanguage*
-meter, -metric, -metrical	measuring; having a particular measure	*thermometer, hexameter*
-metry	denoting procedures and systems involving measurement	*calorimetry*
micro-, micr-	small; reduced; one millionth	*microcar; microdot; microfarad*
milli-	a thousand (chiefly denoting a factor of one thousandth)	*milliliter*
mis-	wrongly; badly; unsuitably	*misapply; mismanage; misname*
mis-	(added to verbs and their derivatives) wrongly; badly; unsuitably; occurring in a few words adopted from French expressing a sense with negative force	*misapply; mismanage; misname; misadventure, mischief*
-monger	dealer or trader; promoter of some activity or feeling	*cheesemonger*
-morph, -morphic, -morphism, morpho-	having, denoting, or relating to a specified form or character	*polymorph*
-most	forming superlative adjectives and adverbs from prepositions and other words indicating relative position	*innermost, uppermost*
-mycin	in names of antibiotics derived from fungi	*streptomycin*
myco-	relating to fungi	*mycoprotein*
myo-, my-	of or relating to muscles	*myocardium*
nano-	very small; denoting a factor of 10^{-9}	*nanometer*
narco-	of a state of insensibility; of narcotic drugs or drug traffic	*narcoleptic; narcoterrorism*
naso-	of or relating to the nose	*nasolabial*
necro-	relating to a corpse or death	*necropolis*
neo-	new; a new or revived form	*neonate; neoconservative*

Combining Form	Meaning	Example(s)
-ness	forming nouns chiefly from adjectives: denoting a state or condition; an instance of this; something in a certain state	*liveliness, sadness; a kindness; wilderness*
neuro-, neur-	relating to nerves or the nervous system	*neuroscience*
-nik	(forming nouns) denoting a person associated with a specified thing or quality	*beatnik, refusenik*
-nomy	an area of knowledge or the laws governing it	*astronomy*
non-	not doing; not involved with; not of the kind or class described; also forming nouns used attributively; not of the importance implied; a lack of; (added to adverbs) not in the way described; (added to verbs to form adjectives) not causing or requiring; expressing a neutral negative sense when a corresponding form beginning with *in-* or *un-* has a special connotation	*nonaggression, nonrecognition; nonbeliever, nonconformist; nonunion; nonissue; nonsense; nonuniformly; nonskid, noniron; nonhuman*
nor-	(Chemistry) denoting an organic compound derived from another, in particular by the shortening of a chain or ring by the removal of one methylene group or by the replacement of one or more methyl side chains by hydrogen atoms	*norepinephrine*
ob-	denoting exposure or openness; expressing meeting or facing; denoting opposition, hostility, or resistance; denoting hindrance, blocking, or concealment; denoting extensiveness, finality, or completeness; (in modern technical words) inversely; in a direction or manner contrary to the usual	*obverse; observe; obstacle; obliterate, obviate; obdurate, obsolete; obconical*
odonto-, -odon, -odont	relating to a tooth or teeth; having teeth of a particular type	*odontology*
of-	variant spelling of *ob-* assimilated before *f*	*offend*
-oid	denoting resemblance	*spheroid*
-ol	(Chemistry) forming names of organic compounds: denoting alcohols and phenols; denoting oils and oil-derived compounds	*glycerol, retinol; benzol*
oleo-, ole-	relating to or containing oil	*oleomargarine*
oligo-, olig-	having or involving few	*oligopoly*
-ology	see *-logy*	
-oma	denoting tumors or growths	*carcinoma*
-ome	(chiefly Biology) forming nouns denoting objects or parts having a specified nature	*rhizome, trichome*
-on	(Physics, Biochemistry, & Chemistry) forming nouns: denoting subatomic particles or quanta; denoting molecular units; denoting substances	*neutron, photon; codon; interferon*

Combining Form	Meaning	Example(s)
onco-	of or relating to tumors or cancer	*oncology*
-one	(Chemistry) forming nouns denoting various compounds, esp. ketones	*quinone*
-ont, ont-	denoting or relating to an individual or cell of a specified type	*schizont*
onto-, ont-	of or relating to existence	*ontology*
-onym, -onymous, -onymic	denoting or relating to names	*patronymic*
oo-	of or denoting an egg or ovum	*oocyte*
-oon	forming nouns, originally from French words having the final stressed syllable *-on*	*balloon, buffoon*
op-	variant spelling of *ob-*; assimilated before *p*	*oppress, oppugn*
-opia	denoting a visual disorder	*myopia*
-opsy	denoting an examination	*biopsy*
-or	(forming nouns) denoting a person or thing performing the action of a verb, or denoting another agent; forming nouns denoting a state or condition; forming adjectives expressing a comparative sense	*escalator, governor, resistor; error, pallor, terror; minor, major*
ornitho-, ornith-	relating to or like a bird or birds	*ornithologist*
oro-	of or relating to mountains	*orogeny*
ortho-, orth-	straight; correct	*orthodontist*
-ory	(forming nouns) denoting a place for a particular function; forming adjectives (and occasionally nouns) relating to or involving a verbal action	*dormitory, repository; compulsory, directory, mandatory*
-ose	(forming adjectives) having a specified quality; (Chemistry) forming names of sugars and other carbohydrates	*bellicose, comatose, verbose; cellulose, glucose*
-osis	denoting a process or condition; denoting a pathological state	*metamorphosis; neurosis, thrombosis*
-osity	forming nouns from adjectives ending in *-ose* and from adjectives ending in *-ous*	*verbosity, pomposity,*
osteo-, oste-	of or relating to the bones	*osteopath*
-ot	forming nouns that were originally diminutives; forming nouns) denoting a person of a particular type; denoting a native of a place	*ballot, parrot; harlot, idiot; Cypriot*
-otic	forming adjectives and nouns corresponding to nouns ending in *-osis*	*neurotic*
oto-, ot-	of or relating to the ears	*otoscope*
-our	(chiefly Brit.) variant spelling of *-or*	*saviour, ardour, colour*

Combining Form	Meaning	Example(s)
-ous	forming adjectives: characterized by; of the nature of; (Chemistry) denoting an element in a lower valence	*dangerous, mountainous; ferrous, sulfurous*
out-	to the point of surpassing or exceeding; external; separate; from outside; away from; outward	*outfight, outperform; outbuildings, outpatient; outbound, outpost*
over-	excessively; to an unwanted degree; completely; utterly; upper; outer; extra; overhead; above	*overambitious, overcareful; overawe, overjoyed; overcoat, overtime; overcast, overhang*
ovi-, ovo-	of or relating to eggs or ova	*oviparous*
oxy-, ox-	denoting sharpness; having oxygen	*oxytone*
paedo-	see *pedo-*	
paleo-, palaeo-	older or ancient	*paleography*
pan-	all-inclusive	*pansexual*
panto-	all; universal	*pantomime*
para-	protecting or warding off	*parachute, parasol*
para-, par-	beside or adjacent to; analogous to	*parameter; paramilitary*
-parous	bearing offspring or reproducing in a specified manner	*viviparous*
-path	practitioner of curative treatment; sufferer from a disease	*homeopath; psychopath*
patho-	relating to disease	*pathology*
-pathy	denoting feelings; denoting disorder; relating to curative treatment	*homeopathy*
-pede, -pedal	denoting or relating to feet	*centipede, bipedal*
pedo-, ped-, paedo-	of or relating to a child or children	*pedophile*
penta-	five; having five	*pentagram*
per-	through or all over; completely; to destruction or ill effect	*perforation; perturb; pervert*
peri-	round or about; nearest	*pericardium*
-petal	seeking or moving toward	*centripetal*
petro-, petr-	of or relating to rock; relating to petroleum	*petrochemical*
-phagous, -phage	feeding on a particular food	*coprophagous*
-phagy	denoting eating of a particular food	*anthropophagy*
pheno-, phen-, -phane	derived from benzene; showing	*phenobarbital; phenotype*
-phil	having a chemical affinity	*neutrophil*
-philia, -phily	denoting (esp. abnormal) fondness or inclination	*pedophilia*
philo-, phil-, -phile	denoting a liking for a specific thing	*cinephile*
-phobe	having a fear or dislike of something	*xenophobe*
-phobia	extreme or irrational fear or dislike	*arachnophobia*

Combining Form	Meaning	Example(s)
-phone	denoting a sound instrument; denoting a speaker of a specific language	*Francophone*
phono-, phon-, -phony	relating to sound	*phonograph*
-phore	denoting an agent or bearer	*semaphore*
photo-, phot-	relating to light; relating to photography	*photochemical; photocomposition*
phren-, -phrenia, -phrenic	of or relating to the mind	*phrenology; schizophrenia*
phyllo-, phyll-, -phyllous	of or relating to a leaf or leaves	*phyllotaxis*
phylo-	of or relating to a race, tribe, or species	*phylogenesis*
physio-, phys-	relating to nature; relating to physiology	*physiography*
-phyte	denoting a plant or plantlike organism	*epiphyte*
phyto-	of or relating to plants	*phytogeography*
pisci-, pisc-	of or relating to fish	*piscivorous*
-plasty, -plast, -plastic	molding, grafting, or formation	*rhinoplasty*
pleo-, pleio-, plio-	more	*pleonasm*
pneumato-	of or containing air; relating to the spirit	*pneumatophore; pneumatology*
pneumo-, pneum-	of or relating to the lungs or to the presence of air or gas	*pneumogastric; pneumothorax*
-pod, -pode, -podous, pod-	of or like a foot	*tripod, cephalopod*
poly-	many, much	*polyandry; polychrome*
post-	after in time or order	*postdate, postoperative*
pre-, prae-	before	*preadolescent*
pro-	favoring; supporting; acting as a substitute or deputy for; on behalf of; for; denoting motion forward, out, or away; before in time, place, order, etc.	*pro-choice, pro-life; proconsul, procure; proceed, propel, prostrate; proactive, prognosis, program*
proto-, prot-	original; primitive; first or anterior	*prototype; protozoan*
pseudo-, pseud-	purported or false; resembling or imitating	*pseudonym; pseudohallucination*
psycho-	relating to the mind or psychology	*psychopath*
ptero-, -pter	relating to or having wings	*pterodactyl*
pyro-, pyr-	of or relating to fire; denoting a mineral or compound formed or affected by heat or having a fiery color	*pyromaniac; pyrope*
quasi-	apparently but not really; partly or almost	*quasi-scientific; quasicrystalline*
radio-, radi-	denoting radio waves or broadcasting; connected with radioactivity; belonging to the radius	*radiogram; radiograph; radio-carpal*

Combining Form	Meaning	Example(s)
re-	once more; afresh; anew; with return to a previous state; in return; mutually; in opposition; behind or after; in a withdrawn state; back and away; down; with frequentative or intensive force; with negative force	*reaccustom, reactivate; restore, revert; react, resemble; repel, resistance; relic, remain; recluse, reticent; recede, relegation; redouble, resound; rebuff, recant*
retro-	denoting backward or reciprocal action; denoting location behind	*retroject; retrosternal*
rhino-	of or relating to the nose	*rhinoplasty*
rhodo-, rhod-	roselike, rosy	*rhodochrosite*
-rrhea, -rrhoea, rheo-	discharge, flow	*diarrhea*
-ry	a shortened form of –*ery*	*devilry, rivalry*
sapro-, sapr-	relating to putrefaction or decay	*saprogenic*
sarco-, sarc-	of or relating to flesh	*sarcophagus*
schizo-, schiz-	divided or split; relating to schizophrenia	*schizocarp; schizotype*
sclero-, scler-	hard, hardened, or hardening	*sclerotherapy*
-sect, -section	of cutting or dividing	*dissect*
semi-	half; twice; partly	*semicircular; semiannual; semi-sweet*
sero-	relating to serum; involving a serous membrane	*serotype; serositis*
sesqui-	denoting one and a half	*sesquicentennial*
-ship	forming nouns: denoting a quality or condition; denoting status, office, or honor; denoting a tenure of office; denoting a skill in a certain capacity; denoting the collective individuals of a group	*companionship, friendship; ambassadorship, citizenship; chairmanship; entrepreneurship; membership*
Sino-	Chinese, Chinese and	*Sino-American*
-sion	forming nouns	*mansion, persuasion*
socio-	relating to society; relating to sociology	*socioeconomic*
somato-	of or relating to the human body	*somatotype*
-some	denoting a part of the body or of a cell	*chromosome*
somn-	of or relating to sleep	*somnolent*
sono-	of or relating to sound	*sonometer*
spiro-	spiral or in a spiral	*spirochete*
spiro-	relating to breathing	*spirometer*
-stasis, -static	slowing down or stopping	*hemostasis*
-stat	denoting instruments, etc., maintaining a controlled state	*thermostat*
steno-	narrow	*stenography*
-ster	denoting a person engaged in or associated with a particular activity or thing; denoting a person having a particular quality	*gangster, songster; youngster*

Combining Form	Meaning	Example(s)
stereo-	of solid forms with three dimensions; of three-dimensional effect	*stereophonic*
strati-, strat-	of or relating to layers or strata	*stratiform*
-style	(forming adjectives and adverbs) in a manner characteristic of	*family-style, church-style*
sub-, suc-, suf-, sur-	lower; somewhat; secondary; supporting	*subalpine; subdivision; subvention*
super-, sur-	above or beyond; to a great degree; extra large; of a higher kind	*superstructure; superabundant; supercontinent; superfamily*
supra-	above; beyond	*supranational*
sur-	variant spelling of *sub-* assimilated before *r*	*surrogate*
-sy	forming diminutive nouns and adjectives, also nicknames or hypocoristics	*folksy, mopsy, Patsy*
syl-	variant spelling of *syn-* assimilated before *l*	*syllogism*
sym-	variant spelling of *syn-* assimilated before *b, m, p*	*symbiosis, symmetry, symphysis*
syn-	united; acting or considered together	*synchrony, syncarpous*
tacho-, tachy-	relating to speed; rapid	*tachometer*
tauto-	same	*tautology*
taxo-, taxi-, tax-	of or relating to grouping or arranging	*taxonomy*
-teen	forming the names of numerals from 13 to 19	*fourteen, eighteen*
tele-, tel-	of or at a distance; operating over a distance; relating to television; done over the telephone	*telekinesis, telemedicine; telemarketing*
-teria	denoting self-service establishments	*washeteria*
tetra-	four, having four	*tetragram*
theo-, the-	relating to God or to deities	*theocracy*
thermo-, -therm, -thermy	relating to heat	*thermoplastic*
-tion	forming nouns of action, condition, etc.	*completion, relation*
-tome	denoting an instrument for cutting; denoting a section or fragment	*microtome; myotome*
-tomy, -otomy	cutting	*episiotomy*
topo-, top-	of or relating to places or forms	*topography*
toxi-, toxico-, toxo-, -toxic	of or relating to poisons	*toxicology*
trans-	across or beyond; on or to the other side; through; going beyond	*transcontinental; transalpine; transonic; transhuman*
-trix	denoting a woman (where a man would be denoted *-tor*)	*executrix*
-tron	denoting a subatomic particle; denoting a particle accelerator; denoting a vacuum tube	*positron; cyclotron; ignitron*

Combining Form	Meaning	Example(s)
-trophic	relating to nutrition; relating to maintenance or regulation	*phototrophic*
-tropic, trop-	turning toward; affecting; maintaining or regulating	*heliotropic; psychotropic*
-tude	forming abstract nouns	*beatitude, solitude*
-ty	forming nouns denoting quality or condition; denoting specified groups of ten	*beauty, royalty; forty, ninety*
-type	(forming adjectives) resembling or having the characteristics of a specified thing	*dish-type, champagne-type*
uber-	denoting an outstanding or supreme example of a particular kind of person or thing	*uberbabe, uberregulator*
-ule	forming diminutive nouns	*capsule, pustule*
ultra-	beyond; extreme	*ultramontane; ultraradical*
-um	variant spelling of *-ium*	
un-	(added to adjectives, participles, and their derivatives) denoting the absence of a quality or state; not; the reverse of (usually with an implication of approval or disapproval, or with another special connotation); (added to nouns) a lack of; added to verbs: denoting the reversal or cancellation of an action or state; denoting deprivation, separation, or reduction to a lesser state; denoting release	*unabashed, unacademic, unrepeatable; unselfish, unprepossessing, unworldly; unrest, untruth; untie, unsettle; unmask, unman; unburden, unhand*
under-	below; beneath; lower in status; subordinate; insufficiently; incompletely	*underclothes, undercover; undersecretary; undernourished*
up-	(added to verbs and their derivatives) upward; to a more recent time; to a newer or better state; (added to nouns) denoting (direction of) motion up; added to nouns) higher; increased	*upturned, upthrow; upbeat, update, upgrade, upscale; upriver, uphill, upwind; upland, upstroke; up-tempo*
ur-	primitive, original, or earliest	*urtext*
urano-, uran-	relating to the heavens; relating to uranium	*uranography*
-ure	forming nouns: denoting an action, process, or result; denoting an office or function; denoting a collective	*censure, closure, scripture; judicature; legislature*
-urgy, -urge	of work; one who works	*dramaturge*
-uria	designating that a substance is present in the urine, esp. in excess	*glycosuria*
uro-	of or relating to urine or the urinary organs	*urogenical*
vaso-, vas-	of or relating to vessels, esp. blood vessels	*vasodilator*
vermi-	relating to or like a worm	*vermiform*
-vorous, -vore	feeding on	*carnivorous*

Combining Form	Meaning	Example(s)
-ward, -wards	added to nouns of place or destination and to adverbs of direction: (forming adverbs) toward the specified place or direction; (forming adjectives) turned or tending toward	*eastward, homewards; onward, upward*
-ways, -way	forming adjectives and adverbs of direction or manner	*edgeways, lengthways*
-wise	forming adjectives and adverbs of manner or respect; informal with respect to; concerning	*clockwise, otherwise; security-wise*
xeno-, xen-	relating to foreigners; other or different	*xenophobia*
xero-, xer-	dry	*xeroscape*
-xion	forming nouns	*fluxion*
xylo-, xyl-	of or relating to wood	*xylophone*
-y	forming adjectives: (from nouns and adjectives) full of; having the quality; with depreciatory reference; (from verbs) inclined to; apt to; forming diminutive nouns and adjectives, nicknames, etc.; forming verbs; forming nouns: denoting a state, condition, or quality; denoting an action or its result	*messy, milky, mousy; boozy, tinny; sticky; aunty, Tommy, nightie; shinny; glory, jealousy, orthodoxy; blasphemy, victory*
-yl	(Chemistry) forming names of radicals	*hydroxyl, phenyl*
-yne	(Chemistry) forming names of unsaturated organic compounds containing a triple bond	*ethyne*
-zoic	forming adjectives relating to a particular manner of animal existence; of or relating to a particular geologic era	*cryptozoic; Paleozoic*
zoo-	of animals; relating to animal life	*zoogeography*
zygo-	relating to joining or pairing	*zygodactyl*

States of the United States of America

State	Traditional & Postal Abbreviations	Capital	State	Traditional & Postal Abbreviations	Capital
Alabama	Ala.; AL	Montgomery	Montana	Mont.; MT	Helena
Alaska	Alas.; AK	Juneau	Nebraska	Nebr.; NE	Lincoln
Arizona	Ariz.; AZ	Phoenix	Nevada	Nev.; NV	Carson City
Arkansas	Ark.; AR	Little Rock	New Hampshire	N.H.; NH	Concord
California	Calif.; CA	Sacramento	New Jersey	N.J.; NJ	Trenton
Colorado	Col.; CO	Denver	New Mexico	N. Mex.; NM	Santa Fe
Connecticut	Conn.; CT	Hartford	New York	N.Y.; NY	Albany
Delaware	Del.; DE	Dover	North Carolina	N.C.; NC	Raleigh
Florida	Fla.; FL	Tallahassee	North Dakota	N. Dak.; ND	Bismarck
Georgia	Ga.; GA	Atlanta	Ohio	O.; OH	Columbus
Hawaii	Haw.; HI	Honolulu	Oklahoma	Okla.; OK	Oklahoma City
Idaho	Ida.; ID	Boise	Oregon	Ore.; OR	Salem
Illinois	Ill.; IL	Springfield	Pennsylvania	Pa.; PA	Harrisburg
Indiana	Ind.; IN	Indianapolis	Rhode Island	R.I.; RI	Providence
Iowa	Ia.; IA	Des Moines	South Carolina	S.C.; SC	Columbia
Kansas	Kan.; KS	Topeka	South Dakota	S. Dak.; SD	Pierre
Kentucky	Ky.; KY	Frankfort	Tennessee	Tenn.; TN	Nashville
Louisiana	La.; LA	Baton Rouge	Texas	Tex.; TX	Austin
Maine	Me.; ME	Augusta	Utah	Ut.; UT	Salt Lake City
Maryland	Md.; MD	Annapolis	Vermont	Vt.; VT	Montpelier
Massachusetts	Mass.; MA	Boston	Virginia	Va.; VA	Richmond
Michigan	Mich.; MI	Lansing	Washington	Wash.; WA	Olympia
Minnesota	Minn.; MN	St. Paul	West Virginia	W. Va.; WV	Charleston
Mississippi	Miss.; MS	Jackson	Wisconsin	Wis.; WI	Madison
Missouri	Mo.; MO	Jefferson City	Wyoming	Wyo.; WY	Cheyenne

Presidents of the United States of America

Name and life dates	Party (term in office)
1. George Washington 1732–99	Federalist (1789–97)
2. John Adams 1735–1826	Federalist (1797–1801)
3. Thomas Jefferson 1743–1826	Democratic-Republican (1801–09)
4. James Madison 1751–1836	Democratic-Republican (1809–17)
5. James Monroe 1758–1831	Democratic-Republican (1817–25)
6. John Quincy Adams 1767–1848	Democratic-Republican (1825–29)
7. Andrew Jackson 1767–1845	Democrat (1829–37)
8. Martin Van Buren 1782–1862	Democrat (1837–41)
9. William Henry Harrison 1773–1841	Whig (1841)
10. John Tyler 1790–1862	Whig (1841–45)
11. James Knox Polk 1795–1849	Democrat (1845–49)
12. Zachary Taylor 1784–1850	Whig (1849–50)
13. Millard Fillmore 1800–74	Whig (1850–53)
14. Franklin Pierce 1804–69	Democrat (1853–57)
15. James Buchanan 1791–1868	Democrat (1857–61)
16. Abraham Lincoln 1809–65	Republican (1861–65)
17. Andrew Johnson 1808–75	Democrat (1865–69)
18. Ulysses Simpson Grant 1822–85	Republican (1869–77)
19. Rutherford Birchard Hayes 1822–93	Republican (1877–81)
20. James Abram Garfield 1831–81	Republican (1881)
21. Chester Alan Arthur 1830–86	Republican (1881–85)
22. (Stephen) Grover Cleveland 1837–1908	Democrat (1885–89)
23. Benjamin Harrison 1833–1901	Republican (1889–93)
24. (Stephen) Grover Cleveland 1837–1908	Democrat (1893–97)
25. William McKinley 1843–1901	Republican (1897–1901)
26. Theodore Roosevelt 1858–1919	Republican (1901–09)
27. William Howard Taft 1857–1930	Republican (1909–13)
28. (Thomas) Woodrow Wilson 1856–1924	Democrat (1913–21)
29. Warren Gamaliel Harding 1865–1923	Republican (1921–23)
30. Calvin Coolidge 1872–1933	Republican (1923–29)
31. Herbert Clark Hoover 1874–1964	Republican (1929–33)
32. Franklin Delano Roosevelt 1882–1945	Democrat (1933–45)
33. Harry S Truman 1884–1972	Democrat (1945–53)
34. Dwight David Eisenhower 1890–1969	Republican (1953–61)
35. John Fitzgerald Kennedy 1917–63	Democrat (1961–63)
36. Lyndon Baines Johnson 1908–73	Democrat (1963–69)
37. Richard Milhous Nixon 1913–94	Republican (1969–74)
38. Gerald Rudolph Ford 1913–	Republican (1974–77)
39. James Earl Carter, Jr. 1924–	Democrat (1977–81)
40. Ronald Wilson Reagan 1911– 2004	Republican (1981–89)
41. George Herbert Walker Bush 1924–	Republican (1989–93)
42. William Jefferson Clinton 1946–	Democrat (1993–2001)
43. George Walker Bush 1946–	Republican (2001–)

Countries of the World

Country	Capital	Continent/Area	Nationality
Afghanistan	Kabul	Asia	Afghan
Albania	Tirana (Tiranë)	Europe	Albanian
Algeria	Algiers	Africa	Algerian
Andorra	Andorra la Vella	Europe	Andorran
Angola	Luanda	Africa	Angolan
Antigua and Barbuda	Saint John's	North America	Antiguan, Barbudan
Argentina	Buenos Aires	South America	Argentinian
Armenia	Yerevan	Europe	Armenian
Australia	Canberra	Australia	Australian
Austria	Vienna	Europe	Austrian
Azerbaijan	Baku	Europe	Azerbaijani
Bahamas, The	Nassau	North America	Bahamian
Bahrain	Manama	Asia	Bahraini
Bangladesh	Dhaka	Asia	Bangladeshi
Barbados	Bridgetown	North America	Barbadian
Belarus	Minsk	Europe	Belorussian, Belarussian, *or* Belarusian
Belgium	Brussels	Europe	Belgian
Belize	Belmopan	North America	Belizean
Benin	Porto Novo	Africa	Beninese
Bhutan	Thimphu	Asia	Bhutanese
Bolivia	La Paz; Sucre	South America	Bolivian
Bosnia and Herzegovina	Sarajevo	Europe	Bosnian, Herzegovinian
Botswana	Gaborone	Africa	Motswana, *sing.*, Batswana, *pl.*
Brazil	Brasilia	South America	Brazilian
Brunei	Bandar Seri Begawan	Asia	Bruneian
Bulgaria	Sofia	Europe	Bulgarian
Burkina Faso	Ouagadougou	Africa	Burkinese
Burma *(see* Myanmar)			
Burundi	Bujumbura	Africa	Burundian, *n.*; Burundi, *adj.*
Cambodia	Phnom Penh	Asia	Cambodian
Cameroon	Yaoundé	Africa	Cameroonian
Canada	Ottawa	North America	Canadian
Cape Verde	Praia	Africa	Cape Verdean
Central African Republic	Bangui	Africa	Central African
Chad	N'Djamena	Africa	Chadian
Chile	Santiago	South America	Chilean
China	Beijing	Asia	Chinese
Colombia	Bogotá	South America	Colombian
Comoros	Moroni	Africa	Comoran
Congo, Democratic Republic of the (*formerly* Zaire)	Kinshasa	Africa	Congolese
Congo, Republic of the	Brazzaville	Africa	Congolese, *n.*; Congolese *or* Congo, *adj.*
Costa Rica	San José	North America	Costa Rican

Country	Capital	Continent/Area	Nationality
Côte d'Ivoire	Yamoussoukro	Africa	Ivorian
Croatia	Zagreb	Europe	Croat, *n.*; Croatian, *adj.*
Cuba	Havana	North America	Cuban
Cyprus	Nicosia	Europe	Cypriot
Czech Republic	Prague	Europe	Czech
Denmark	Copenhagen	Europe	Dane, *n.*; Danish, *adj.*
Djibouti	Djibouti	Africa	Djiboutian
Dominica	Roseau	North America	Dominican
Dominican Republic	Santo Domingo	North America	Dominican
East Timor	Dili	Asia	East Timoran
Ecuador	Quito	South America	Ecuadorean
Egypt	Cairo	Africa	Egyptian
El Salvador	San Salvador	North America	Salvadoran
Equatorial Guinea	Malabo	Africa	Equatorial Guinean *or* Equatoguinean
Eritrea	Asmara	Africa	Eritrean
Estonia	Tallinn	Europe	Estonian
Ethiopia	Addis Ababa	Africa	Ethiopian
Fiji	Suva	Oceania	Fijian
Finland	Helsinki	Europe	Finn, *n.*; Finnish, *adj.*
France	Paris	Europe	French
Gabon	Libreville	Africa	Gabonese
Gambia, The	Banjul	Africa	`Gambian
Georgia	Tbilisi	Europe	Georgian
Germany	Berlin	Europe	German
Ghana	Accra	Africa	Ghanaian
Greece	Athens	Europe	Greek
Grenada	Saint George's	North America	Grenadian
Guatemala	Guatemala City	North America	Guatemalan
Guinea	Conakry	Africa	Guinean
Guinea-Bissau	Bissau	Africa	Guinea-Bissauan
Guyana	Georgetown	South America	Guyanese
Haiti	Port-au-Prince	North America	Haitian
Holy See	Vatican City	Europe	
Honduras	Tegucigalpa	North America	Honduran
Hungary	Budapest	Europe	Hungarian
Iceland	Reykjavik	Europe	Icelander, *n.*; Icelandic, *adj.*
India	New Delhi	Asia	Indian
Indonesia	Djakarta	Asia	Indonesian
Iran	Tehran	Asia	Iranian
Iraq	Baghdad	Asia	Iraqi
Ireland, Republic of	Dublin	Europe	Irish
Israel	Jerusalem	Asia	Israeli
Italy	Rome	Europe	Italian
Jamaica	Kingston	North America	Jamaican
Japan	Tokyo	Asia	Japanese
Jordan	Amman	Asia	Jordanian
Kazakhstan	Astana	Asia	Kazakhstani
Kenya	Nairobi	Africa	Kenyan
Kiribati	Bairiki (on Tarawa)	Oceania	I-Kiribati

Country	Capital	Continent/Area	Nationality
Korea, North (*see* North Korea)			
Korea, South (*see* South Korea)			
Kuwait	Kuwait City	Asia	Kuwaiti
Kyrgyzstan	Bishkek	Asia	Kyrgyz
Laos	Vientiane	Asia	Lao *or* Laotian
Latvia	Riga	Europe	Latvian
Lebanon	Beirut	Asia	Lebanese
Lesotho	Maseru	Africa	Mosotho, *sing.*; Basotho, *pl.*; Basotho, *adj.*
Liberia	Monrovia	Africa	Liberian
Libya	Tripoli	Africa	Libyan
Liechtenstein	Vaduz	Europe	Liechtensteiner, *n.*; Liechtenstein, *adj.*
Lithuania	Vilnius	Europe	Lithuanian
Luxembourg	Luxembourg	Europe	Luxembourger, *n.*; Luxembourg, *adj.*
Macedonia	Skopje	Europe	Macedonian
Madagascar	Antananarivo	Africa	Malagasy
Malawi	Lilongwe	Africa	Malawian
Malaysia	Kuala Lumpur	Asia	Malaysian
Maldives	Male	Asia	Maldivian
Mali	Bamako	Africa	Malian
Malta	Valletta	Europe	Maltese
Marshall Islands	Majuro	Oceania	Marshallese
Mauritania	Nouakchott	Africa	Mauritanian
Mauritius	Port Louis	Africa	Mauritian
Mexico	Mexico City	North America	Mexican
Micronesia	Kolonia	Oceania	Micronesian
Moldova	Chiṣinǎu	Europe	Moldovan
Monaco	Monaco	Europe	Monacan *or* Monegasque
Mongolia	Ulaanbaatar	Asia	Mongolian
Morocco	Rabat	Africa	Moroccan
Mozambique	Maputo	Africa	Mozambican
Myanmar (Burma)	Yangoon	Asia	Burmese
Namibia	Windhoek	Africa	Namibian
Nauru	Yaren District	Oceania	Nauruan
Nepal	Kathmandu	Asia	Nepalese
Netherlands	Amsterdam; The Hague	Europe	Dutchman *or* Dutchwoman, *n.*; Dutch, *adj.*
New Zealand	Wellington	Oceania	New Zealander, *n.*; New Zealand, *adj.*
Nicaragua	Managua	North America	Nicaraguan
Niger	Niamey	Africa	Nigerien
Nigeria	Abuja	Africa	Nigerian
North Korea	P'yongyang	Asia	North Korean
Norway	Oslo	Europe	Norwegian
Oman	Muscat	Asia	Omani
Pakistan	Islamabad	Asia	Pakistani
Palau	Koror	Oceania	Palauan
Panama	Panama City	North America	Panamanian

Country	Capital	Continent/Area	Nationality
Papua New Guinea	Port Moresby	Oceania	Papua New Guinean
Paraguay	Asunción	South America	Paraguayan
Peru	Lima	South America	Peruvian
Philippines	Manila	Asia	Filipino, *n.*; Philippine, *adj.*
Poland	Warsaw	Europe	Pole, *n.*; Polish, *adj.*
Portugal	Lisbon	Europe	Portuguese
Qatar	Doha	Asia	Quatari
Romania	Bucharest	Europe	Romanian
Russia	Moscow	Europe & Asia	Russian
Rwanda	Kigali	Africa	Rwandan, Rwandese
Saint Kitts and Nevis	Basseterre	North America	Kittsian; Nevisian
Saint Lucia	Castries	North America	St. Lucian
Saint Vincent and the Grenadines	Kingstown	North America	St. Vincentian *or* Vincentian
Samoa (*formerly* Western Samoa)	Apia	Oceania	Samoan
San Marino	San Marino	Europe	Sammarinese
São Tomé and Príncipe	São Tomé	Africa	Sao Tomean
Saudi Arabia	Riyadh	Asia	Saudi *or* Saudi Arabian
Scotland	Edinburgh	Europe	Scot, *n.*; Scots *or* Scottish, *adj.*
Senegal	Dakar	Africa	Senegalese
Serbia and Montenegro	Belgrade	Europe	Serbian; Montenegram
Seychelles	Victoria	Indian Ocean	Seychellois, *n.*; Seychelles, *adj.*
Sierra Leone	Freetown	Africa	Sierra Leonean
Singapore	Singapore	Asia	Singaporean, *n.*; Singapore, *adj.*
Slovakia	Bratislava	Europe	Slovak
Slovenia	Ljubljana	Europe	Slovene, *n.*; Slovenian, *adj.*
Solomon Islands	Honiara	Oceania	Solomon Islander
Somalia	Mogadishu	Africa	Somali
South Africa	Pretoria; Cape Town; Bloemfontein	Africa	South African
South Korea	Seoul	Asia	South Korean
Spain	Madrid	Europe	Spanish
Sri Lanka	Colombo	Asia	Sri Lankan
Sudan	Khartoum	Africa	Sudanese
Suriname	Paramaribo	South America	Surinamer, *n.*; Surinamese, *adj.*
Swaziland	Mbabane	Africa	Swazi
Sweden	Stockholm	Europe	Swede, *n.*; Swedish, *adj.*
Switzerland	Bern	Europe	Swiss
Syria	Damascus	Asia	Syrian
Taiwan	Taipei	Asia	Taiwanese
Tajikistan	Dushanbe	Asia	Tajik
Tanzania	Dar es Salaam	Africa	Tanzanian
Thailand	Bangkok	Asia	Thai
Togo	Lomé	Africa	Togolese
Tonga	Nuku'alofa	Oceania	Tongan

Country	Capital	Continent/Area	Nationality
Trinidad and Tobago	Port-of-Spain	South America	Trinidadian; Tobagonian
Tunisia	Tunis	Africa	Tunisian
Turkey	Ankara	Asia & Europe	Turk, *n.*; Turkish, *adj.*
Turkmenistan	Ashgabat	Asia	Turkmen
Tuvalu	Funafuti	Oceania	Tuvaluan
Uganda	Kampala	Africa	Ugandan
Ukraine	Kiev	Europe	Ukrainian
United Arab Emirates	Abu Dhabi	Africa	Emirian
United Kingdom	London	Europe	Briton, n.; British, *collective pl. & adj.*
United States of America	Washington, DC	North America	American
Uruguay	Montevideo	South America	Uruguayan
Uzbekistan	Tashkent	Asia	Uzbek
Vanuatu	Vila	Oceania	Ni-Vanuatu
Venezuela	Caracas	South America	Venezuelan
Vietnam	Hanoi	Asia	Vietnamese
Western Samoa (*see* Samoa)			
Yemen	Sana'a	Asia	Yemeni
Yugoslavia (*see* Serbia and Montenegro)			
Zaire (*see* Congo)			
Zambia	Lusaka	Africa	Zambian
Zimbabwe	Harare	Africa	Zimbabwean

Chemical Elements

Element	Symbol	Atomic Number	Element	Symbol	Atomic Number
actinium	Ac	89	mendelevium	Md	101
aluminum	Al	13	mercury	Hg	80
americium	Am	95	molybdenum	Mo	42
antimony	Sb	51	neodymium	Nd	60
argon	Ar	18	neon	Ne	10
arsenic	As	33	neptunium	Np	93
astatine	At	85	nickel	Ni	28
barium	Ba	56	niobium	Nb	41
berkelium	Bk	97	nitrogen	N	7
beryllium	Be	4	nobelium	No	102
bismuth	Bi	83	osmium	Os	76
bohrium*	Ns	107	oxygen	O	8
boron	B	5	palladium	Pd	46
bromine	Br	35	phosphorus	P	15
cadmium	Cd	48	platinum	Pt	78
calcium	Ca	20	plutonium	Pu	94
californium	Cf	98	polonium	Po	84
carbon	C	6	potassium	K	19
cerium	Ce	58	praseodymium	Pr	59
cesium	Cs	55	promethium	Pm	61
chlorine	Cl	17	protactinium	Pa	91
chromium	Cr	24	radium	Ra	88
cobalt	Co	27	radon	Rn	86
copper	Cu	29	rhenium	Re	75
curium	Cm	96	rhodium	Rh	45
dubnium*	Db	105	rubidium	Rb	37
dysprosium	Dy	66	ruthenium	Ru	44
einsteinium	Es	99	rutherfordium*	Rf	104
erbium	Er	68	samarium	Sm	62
europium	Eu	63	scandium	Sc	21
fermium	Fm	100	seaborgium*	Sg	106
fluorine	F	9	selenium	Se	34
francium	Fr	87	silicon	Si	14
gadolinium	Gd	64	silver	Ag	47
gallium	Ga	31	sodium	Na	11
germanium	Ge	32	strontium	Sr	38
gold	Au	79	sulfur	S	16
hafnium	Hf	72	tantalum	Ta	73
hassium*	Hs	108	technetium	Tc	43
helium	He	2	tellurium	Te	52
holmium	Ho	67	terbium	Tb	65
hydrogen	H	1	thallium	Tl	81
indium	In	49	thorium	Th	90
iodine	I	53	thulium	Tm	69
iridium	Ir	77	tin	Sn	50
iron	Fe	26	titanium	Ti	22
krypton	Kr	36	tungsten (wolfram)	W	74
lanthanum	La	57	uranium	U	92
lawrencium	Lr	103	vanadium	V	23
lead	Pb	82	xenon	Xe	54
lithium	Li	3	ytterbium	Yb	70
lutetium	Lu	71	yttrium	Y	39
magnesium	Mg	12	zinc	Zn	30
manganese	Mn	25	zirconium	Zr	40
meitnerium*	Mt	109			

* Names formed systematically based on atomic numbers are preferred by the International Union of Pure and Applied Chemistry (IUPAC) for numbers from 104 onward. These names are formed on the numerical roots nil (= 0), un (= 1), bi (= 2), etc. (e.g., unnilquadium = 104, unnilpentium = 105, unnilhexium = 106, unnilseptium = 107, unniloctium = 108, unnilnovium = 109, etc.).

Standard Weights and Measures
with Metric Equivalents and Conversions

Equivalents

1 inch = 2.54 centimeters
1 foot = 12 inches   = 0.3048 meter
1 yard = 3 feet   = 0.9144 meter
  = 36 inches
1 (statute) mile = 1,760 yards = 1.609 kilometers
   = 5,280 feet

Square Measure
1 sq. inch   = 6.45 sq. centimeters
1 sq. foot = 144 sq. inches = 9.29 sq. decimeters
1 sq. yard = 9 sq. feet = 0.836 sq. meter
1 acre = 4,840 sq. yards = 0.405 hectare
1 sq. mile = 640 acres = 259 hectares

Cubic Measure
1 cu. inch   = 16.4 cu. centimeters
1 cu. foot = 1,728 cu. inches = 0.0283 cu. meter
1 cu. yard = 27 cu. feet = 0.765 cu. meter

Capacity Measure
DRY MEASURE
1 pint = 33.60 cu. inches = 0.550 liter
1 quart = 2 pints   = 1.101 liters
1 peck = 8 quarts   = 8.81 liters
1 bushel = 4 pecks = 35.3 liters
LIQUID MEASURE
1 fluid ounce   = 29.573 milliliters
1 gill = 4 fluid ounces = 118.294 milliliters
1 pint = 16 fluid ounces = 0.473 liter
  = 28.88 cu. inches
1 quart = 2 pints   = 0.946 liter
1 gallon = 4 quarts = 3.785 liters

Avoirdupois Weight
1 grain   = 0.065 gram
1 dram   = 1.772 grams
1 ounce = 16 drams = 28.35 grams
1 pound = 16 ounces = 0.4536 kilograms
  = 7,000 grains (0.45359237 exactly)
1 stone (British) = 14 pounds = 6.35 kilograms
1 ton = 2,000 pounds
1 hundredweight (US) = 100 pounds
20 hundredweight (US) = 2,000 pounds

Conversions

Standard	Multiply By	To Get Metric
Length		
inches	2.5	centimeters
feet	30	centimeters
yards	0.9	meters
miles	1.6	kilometers
Area		
square inches	6.5	square centimeters
square feet	0.09	square meters
square yards	0.8	square meters
square miles	2.6	square kilometers
acres	0.4	hectares
Weight		
ounces	28	grams
pounds	0.45	kilograms
short tons	0.9	metric tons
Volume		
teaspoons	5	milliliters
tablespoons	15	milliliters
cubic inches	16	milliliters
fluid ounces	30	milliliters
cups	0.24	liters
pints	0.47	liters
quarts	0.95	liters
gallons	3.8	liters
cubic feet	0.03	cubic meters
cubic yards	0.76	cubic meters

Temperature
degrees Fahrenheit subtract 32, then degrees Celsius
      multiply by 5/9

Metric Weights and Measures
with Standard Equivalents and Conversions

Equivalents

Linear Measure

1 millimeter (mm)	= 0.039 inch
1 centimeter (cm) = 10 millimeters	= 0.394 inch
1 decimeter (dm) = 10 centimeters	= 3.94 inches
1 meter (m) = 10 decimeters	= 1.094 yards
1 decameter = 10 meters	= 10.94 yards
1 hectometer = 100 meters	= 109.4 yards
1 kilometer (km) = 1,000 meters	= 0.6214 mile

Square Measure

1 sq. centimeter	= 0.155 sq. inch
1 sq. meter	= 1.196 sq. yards
= 10,000 sq. centimeters	
1 are = 100 sq. meters	= 119.6 sq. yards
1 hectare = 100 ares	= 2.471 acres
1 sq. kilometer = 100 hectares	= 0.386 sq. mile

Cubic Measure

1 cu. centimeter	= 0.061 cu. inch
1 cu. meter	= 1.308 cu. yards
= 1,000,000 cu. centimeters	

Capacity Measure

1 milliliter (ml)	= 0.034 fluid ounce
1 centiliter (cl) = 10 milliliters	= 0.34 fluid ounce
1 deciliter (dl) = 10 centiliters	= 3.38 fluid ounces
1 liter (l) = 10 deciliters	= 1.06 quarts
1 decaliter = 10 liters	= 2.64 gallons
1 hectoliter = 100 liters	= 2.75 bushels

Weight

1 milligram (mg)	= 0.015 grain
1 centigram = 10 milligrams	= 0.154 grain
1 decigram (dg) = 10 centigrams	= 1.543 grains
1 gram (g) = 10 decigrams	= 15.43 grains
1 decagram = 10 grams	= 5.64 drams
1 hectogram = 100 grams	= 3.527 ounces
1 kilogram (kg) = 1,000 grams	= 2.205 pounds
1 ton (metric ton)	= 0.984 (long) ton
= 1,000 kilograms	

Conversions

Metric	Multiply By	To Get Standard
Length		
millimeters	0.04	inches
centimeters	0.4	inches
meters	3.3	feet
meters	1.1	yards
kilometers	0.6	miles
Area		
square centimeters	0.16	square inches
square meters	1.2	square yards
square kilometers	0.4	square miles
hectares	2.5	acres
Weight		
grams	0.035	ounces
kilograms	2.2	pounds
metric tons	1.1	short tons
Volume		
milliliters	0.03	fluid ounces
milliliters	0.06	cubic inches
liters	2.1	pints
liters	1.06	quarts
liters	0.26	gallons
cubic meters	35	cubic feet
cubic meters	1.3	cubic yards
Temperatures		
degrees Celsius	9/5, then add 32	degress Fahrenheit

Metric Weights and Measures
with Standard Equivalents and Conversions

Equivalents

Linear Measure
1 millimeter (mm)	= 0.039 inch
1 centimeter (cm) = 10 millimeters	= 0.394 inch
1 decimeter (dm) = 10 centimeters	= 3.94 inches
1 meter (m) = 10 decimeters	= 1.094 yards
1 decameter = 10 meters	= 10.94 yards
1 hectometer = 100 meters	= 109.4 yards
1 kilometer (km) = 1,000 meters	= 0.6214 mile

Square Measure
1 sq. centimeter	= 0.155 sq. inch
1 sq. meter	= 1.196 sq. yards
= 10,000 sq. centimeters	
1 are = 100 sq. meters	= 119.6 sq. yards
1 hectare = 100 ares	= 2.471 acres
1 sq. kilometer = 100 hectares	= 0.386 sq. mile

Cubic Measure
1 cu. centimeter	= 0.061 cu. inch
1 cu. meter	= 1.308 cu. yards
= 1,000,000 cu. centimeters	

Capacity Measure
1 milliliter (ml)	= 0.034 fluid ounce
1 centiliter (cl) = 10 milliliters	= 0.34 fluid ounce
1 deciliter (dl) = 10 centiliters	= 3.38 fluid ounces
1 liter (l) = 10 deciliters	= 1.06 quarts
1 decaliter = 10 liters	= 2.64 gallons
1 hectoliter = 100 liters	= 2.75 bushels

Weight
1 milligram (mg)	= 0.015 grain
1 centigram = 10 milligrams	= 0.154 grain
1 decigram (dg) = 10 centigrams	= 1.543 grains
1 gram (g) = 10 decigrams	= 15.43 grains
1 decagram = 10 grams	= 5.64 drams
1 hectogram = 100 grams	= 3.527 ounces
1 kilogram (kg) = 1,000 grams	= 2.205 pounds
1 ton (metric ton)	= 0.984 (long) ton
= 1,000 kilograms	

Conversions

Metric	Multiply By	To Get Standard
Length		
millimeters	0.04	inches
centimeters	0.4	inches
meters	3.3	feet
meters	1.1	yards
kilometers	0.6	miles
Area		
square centimeters	0.16	square inches
square meters	1.2	square yards
square kilometers	0.4	square miles
hectares	2.5	acres
Weight		
grams	0.035	ounces
kilograms	2.2	pounds
metric tons	1.1	short tons
Volume		
milliliters	0.03	fluid ounces
milliliters	0.06	cubic inches
liters	2.1	pints
liters	1.06	quarts
liters	0.26	gallons
cubic meters	35	cubic feet
cubic meters	1.3	cubic yards
Temperatures		
degrees Celsius	9/5, then add 32	degress Fahrenheit

CONCISE Oxford AMERICAN Thesaurus

- 15,000 entries and over 350,000 synonyms
- Unique "Synonym Studies" guide you to the exact word
- The ideal resource for home, school, or office

THE WORLD'S MOST TRUSTED DICTIONARIES

Based on the acclaimed *Oxford American Writer's Thesaurus,* this concise edition includes more than 15,000 main entries and over 350,000 synonyms, with sample sentences for virtually every sense.

0-19-530485-3